The MILLION WORD Crossword Dictionary

Second Edition

Books by Daniel Stark (Author/Editor)

The Crossword Answer Book (with Stanley Newman)
Square One Crossword Dictionary (with Stanley Newman)
Random House Mega Crossword Omnibus
Crosswords Challenge (with Roslyn Stark)
Large-Print Crosswords Challenge (with Roslyn Stark)
The Ultimate Crosswords Omnibus (with Roslyn Stark)
The Ultimate Large-Print Crosswords Omnibus (with Roslyn Stark)
Cross Codes (with Helene Hovanec)

Books by Stanley Newman (Author/Editor)

The Million Word Crossword Answer Book (with Daniel Stark)
15,003 Answers: The Ultimate Trivia Encyclopedia (with Hal Fittipaldi)
Stanley Newman's Crossword Shortcuts
Cruciverbalism: A Crossword Fanatic's Guide to Life in the Grid (with Mark Lasswell)
Crossword Superstars series
Superhard Crosswords
Ultrahard Crosswords
Movie Mania Crosswords
Trivia Crosswords series
Comedy Crosswords
Literary Crosswords
Reader's Digest Mind Stretchers series
Par 3 Golf Crosswords
Silver Screen Crosswords
Random House Winter Treat Crosswords
Random House Harvest Moon Crosswords
Random House Summer Nights Crosswords
Random House Year Round Crossword Omnibus
Random House All-Weather Crossword Omnibus
Random House Springtime Crosswords
Random House Endless Summer Crosswords
Stanley Newman's Sunday Crosswords series
Random House Sunday Crossword MegaMonster
Stanley Newman's Sitcom Crosswords
Random House Cabin Fever Crosswords
Random House Back to the Beach Crosswords
Random House Cozy Crosswords
Random House More Vacation Crosswords
Random House By the Fireside Crosswords
Random House Monster Crossword Puzzle Omnibus
Random House Monster Sunday Crossword Omnibus
Sport Magazine Crosswords
Random House Cryptic Crosswords series
Random House Sunday Crosswords series
The Expert's Book of Crosswords series
The Crossworder's Own Puzzle Book series
Bull's Eye Crosswords series
The Ultimate Crossword Book

The MILLION WORD Crossword Dictionary

Second Edition

Stanley Newman and Daniel Stark

HarperCollins books may be purchased for educational, business, or sales promotional use. For information please write: Special Markets Department, HarperCollins Publishers Inc., 10 East 53rd Street, New York, NY 10022.

Text design and typography by Daniel Stark

The Library of Congress has cataloged a previous edition as follows:

Newman, Stanley
The million word crossword dictionary/Stanley Newman and Daniel Stark.
p. cm.
ISBN 0-06-051756-5
1. Crossword puzzles—Glossaries, vocabularies, etc. I. Stark, Daniel. II. Title.

GV1507.C7N45 2005
793.73'2'03—dc22 2003056769

ISBN 978-0-06-168901-7

14 15 ❖/RRD 10 9 8 7

INTRODUCTION

For almost as long as there have been crossword puzzles, there have been crossword dictionaries. Within just a few months of the fad for crosswords starting in 1924, books appeared to help solvers with their emus, okapis, esnes, and other strange but common denizens of Crosswordland.

No matter how carefully crosswords are constructed, some words do show up in them much more frequently than in everyday speech and writing. In fact, many crosswords contain words that even a well-rounded person may never encounter outside a puzzle context.

If you run into a puzzle that has too many answers you don't know, or if the answers to two unknowable clues cross, you may need help to finish.

The Million Word Crossword Dictionary, compiled by my colleagues Stanley Newman and Daniel Stark, has been created to break solving impasses. Two years in the making, and designed from the ground up, it contains more than 250,000 clues and 1,000,000+ words, specifically chosen to help with crosswords of the kind found in newspapers, books, and magazines today.

All the classic clues are here: "Celebes ox" (ANOA), "Arrow poison" (INEE), "Sea eagle" (ERN or ERNE), "Eskimo knife" (ULU), and other obscurities from the depths of the unabridged dictionary.

The volume also contains tens of thousands of names from modern culture that frequently crop up in puzzles now: "Singer DiFranco" (ANI), "Golfer Ernie" (ELS), "Sarah McLachlan hit" (ADIA), "Peter Fonda title role" (ULEE), and so on.

Of special help are lists of Oscar winners, Nobelists, Wimbledon champions, popes, makes of autos, dogs in TV shows, and dozens of other fact-based categories useful to puzzlers.

The book even contains tens of thousands of fill-in-the-blank clues like "__ minute" (IN A) and "__ point" (TO THE), based on phrases you know but may not be able to complete on the spot.

This new edition has been thoroughly updated, to incorporate the latest factual information, slang terms, celebrity names and other recent arrivals on the crossword scene.

The result is the largest, most up-to-date, and most useful crossword dictionary available.

Is it cheating to use a book like this?

Well, say you're stuck in the middle of a puzzle. You can give up . . . or you can get an answer or two, allowing you to proceed and finish the puzzle on your own. In a situation like this, it makes sense to get help. Using a reference book is educational besides.

Whatever "rules" you follow, it's ultimately your puzzle. Solve it any way you like!

Will Shortz
Crossword Editor
The *New York Times*

How to Use *The Million Word Crossword Dictionary*

Generally speaking, you'll find the clue you're looking for under the clue's most important word. For example, "Artist's need" would be under "artist." Clues are indexed under multiple words if they have more than one "important" word.

Thumb Indexes

Use the "thumb index" black rectangles at the edge of each page to quickly find your clue. The thumb index on left-hand pages has the first two letters of the first entry on the page; the thumb index on right-hand pages has the first two letters of the last entry on the page (very much like the thumb index of a regular dictionary).

Headwords

"Headwords" are the main boldface clues that introduce each set of answers. Answers that follow headwords are generally listed alphabetically by word length. Sub-headwords, those indented in boldface under a headword, should be read with the headword preceding it. For example, the headword "circle" has the sub-headword "portion," which should be read "circle portion" (answer ARC). In sub-headwords that contain a tilde (~), the tilde takes the place of the headword in the reading. For example: the sub-headword "flattened ~" under "circle" should be read "flattened circle" (answers OVAL and ELLIPSE).

Alphabetization of Headwords

Headwords are alphabetized on a letter-by-letter basis. Solid words precede hyphenated words or words with spaces, and lowercase letters precede capital letters. Headwords followed by a "fill-in-the-blank" follow the same stand-alone headword.

Leading articles (A, The, An) in titles are ignored in alphabetization.

Multiword personal names are listed "last name first."

Fill-in-the-blank clues that start with the fill-in are alphabetized in full. Alphabetization for other fill-in-the-blank clues ends at the fill-in, so "Fort __, IN" precedes "Fort Apache."

To make clues that start with numbers easy to find, they are sorted numerically at the beginning of the initial letter, considering how the number is spoken. So "400" is at the beginning of F, and "2001" is at the beginning of T.

Inflected Forms

Most clues that are nouns are listed in the singular form. Most clues that are verbs are listed in the infinitive form. There are exceptions for inflected answers that don't follow normal American spelling rules.

Clues that involve a country or nationality are listed under the name of the country ("Denmark" or "Mexico") rather than the nationality ("Danish" or "Mexican").

Foreign Words

Clues for common foreign words are listed under both the language and the English meaning. Crossword clues for foreign words often use references to foreign places and names, such as "Here, to Henri," so hundreds of names and places with language cross-references are listed herein. For example, you will find "*see also* French" under "Henri."

Clues by Example

Clues like "Man, for one" (ISLE) and "Sycamore, e.g." (TREE) are crossword staples. So, unlike other crossword dictionaries, you will not only find the "specific" listed under the "generic" (SYCAMORE under "tree") but also the other way around (TREE under "sycamore").

"Starters" and "Enders"

Clues like "Back starter" (HORSE), "Novel ender" (ETTE), and "Type of dance" (BARN) require another word or prefix/suffix to be added to a clue word. When the answer forms a solid word with the clue, it is indexed as a "starter" if added at the beginning, and "ender" if added at the end. If the answer is hyphenated or has more than one word, it is indexed as a fill-in-the-blank. Thus, HORSE will be found under "Back starter." And BARN will be found under "__ dance."

Abbreviations and Acronyms

The many common crossword abbreviations and acronyms in this book can be readily identified as such, either by a period at the end or their rendering in all uppercase letters. When looking up clues that contain abbreviations, be sure to check both the abbreviated word ("dr.") and its unabbreviated form ("doctor").

Answer Words

For the sake of clarity and accuracy, answer words (as well as clue words) are given with the appropriate capitalization, diacritical marks, and spacing for multiple words.

Other Things to Keep in Mind

A word in parentheses at the end of a clue, such as "File (by)" (MARCH), is added to the answer word to give the indicated meaning—"File by" means "march by."

The clue you're looking for will often be found under a related nearby entry, so be sure to look nearby if necessary.

Miscellaneous Conventions

Some longer titles have been truncated, indicated by an ellipsis (…).

A country's monetary units may be current or previous.

The listings of celebrity marriages represent both current and previous relationships.

Lists of a person's works (films, books, songs, etc.) give the best-known works and are generally not exhaustive. Similarly, listings for films include the top-billed cast only, and exclude a director credit if not well-known. These listings are presented alphabetically and omit letter counts.

Word lengths are often omitted from "credit" answers, such as the singer of a song or author of a book.

Within film credits, "AA" after the year indicates the actor or director received an Academy Award for that film.

Within song credits, both the composer and lyricist are called "composer."

Titles can be inferred as such from their capitalization and/or context, and lack the usual italics or quotation marks.

Headwords that are the full name of a person often include as answers the person's occupation and nationality, if not American.

Frequently Asked Questions

Q: Why will this book be so much more useful to me than any other crossword dictionary?
A:
- It is the only crossword dictionary based on the actual clues and answers in today's puzzles.
- It has more than twice as many answers as any other crossword dictionary.
- It is the only crossword dictionary compiled entirely by crossword professionals.
- It will have the answer you're looking for more than twice as often as any other crossword dictionary.

Q: Where did the material in this book come from?
A: The heart of *The Million Word Crossword Dictionary* is hundreds of thousands of clues and answers from actual crosswords. They were selected by the authors one by one, from an archive of more than 2,000,000 clues that have appeared in America's most popular crosswords over the past 10 years. These entries were then supplemented by clues and answers that, based on the authors' extensive experience in the crossword field, are most likely to be needed by puzzlers.

Q: What are these additional clues and answers, and where did they come from?
A: Additional synonym-type clues were gleaned from dozens of current dictionaries and thesauruses. Factual clues were obtained from hundreds of authoritative reference books and Web sites. Every factual subject area that appears in today's crosswords is comprehensively covered. These include academic subjects such as science, literature, and geography; popular culture including films, music, and celebrities; and contemporary life such as slang, politics, and brand names. Thus, *The Million Word Crossword Dictionary* is the only book that fully reflects the diversity of contemporary crosswords. No other reference book of any kind includes all of these: members of the British Commonwealth, songs of George Gershwin, characters in *Aïda*, films of Brad Pitt, colors of Crayola crayons, and the names of Santa's reindeer.

Q: Why are there so few answer words more than 10 letters long?
A: With only occasional exceptions, "synonym" answers of 11 letters or more have been omitted because more than 95 percent of all "synonym" crossword answers are 10 letters or less. This has made possible the inclusion of many more shorter synonyms that are far more likely to be answers to puzzle clues.

Q: Are there really more than 1,000,000 words in this book?
A: Yes, there are exactly 1,355,276 words in this book, as counted by our computer. You're welcome to check our count, if you'd like.

Free Yearly Updates!

With this edition, *Million Word* becomes the first crossword dictionary to provide its users with free annual updates, to keep your book current. To take advantage of this free service, e-mail us at MillionXword@aol.com, with "Free Annual Update" in the subject line. Please include your full name and hometown in the body of the e-mail.

Once a year, we will e-mail back to you an electronic file (in PDF format) with all the new clues and answers we have compiled since this edition was published, in the same alphabetical format as the book, ready for you to print out. For maximum usefulness, the second annual update will have all the new clues and answers from the previous two years, so you'll be able to discard the previous update.

Annual updates are also available to *Million Word* users without e-mail access. To receive a paper copy, send $3.00 in U.S. stamps to: Stanley Newman and Daniel Stark, P.O. Box 69, Massapequa Park, NY 11762.

These annual updates will continue until the next edition of *Million Word* is published.

What's New in This Edition

New Entries

Many thousands of entries are new to this edition, including:

- Clues from recent nationally published crosswords
- Slang terms and brand names
- The latest films, novelists' works, sports Hall of Famers, models of automobiles, etc.
- Celebrities from all walks of life, from Pope Benedict XVI and Barack Obama, to TV host Ryan Seacrest and supermodel Elsa Benitez

Plus, **all chronological lists have been updated**, from Nobel Prizes to Academy Awards.

Special thanks to the hundreds of Puzzle Patrollers, who took us up on our 1st-edition request to send us **suggestions for new entries** to include. As promised, we are sending a complimentary copy of the Second Edition to the 25 Patrollers who sent us the most new entries that we used here. They are:

Brian Agan, Nick and Claire De Pilla, Richard Dibon-Smith, Earl Freise, Fred Hinker, Mary Husa, John M. Jones, Ruth Leitner, Nicholas Liatsos, Elizabeth Merz, Paul & Esther Migacz, Linda Morey, Norbert Newfield, Raymond Ortsey, Judy Perillo, Annabelle Robson, Frank Romagnolo, Carolyn Scott, John L. Spooner, Chuck Taft, Cheryl Tyson, Elaine Ven Rooy, Duane Wilkins, Eric Zanto and Terry Zboril. Thanks also to John Jarvis, who would have been on this list, but graciously declined a book.

We are continuing the Puzzle Patrol for this edition. See page xi for the details.

Thumb Indexes

(See "How to Use" on page vi for more info.)

Larger Type Size

Owners of the 1st edition of *Million Word* will notice the easier-to-read type right away. If this Second Edition is your first *Million Word*, compare the "before" and "after" actual-size excerpts below.

Before

calamity: **3** ill, woe **4** bane, blow, doom, loss, ruin **5** curse, event, havoc, shame **6** blight, misery, mishap, ordeal, plague **7** scourge, tragedy, undoing **8** accident, casualty, disaster, distress, hard luck, hardship **9** adversity, cataclysm, detriment, nightmare, ruination **10** affliction, misfortune
Calamity Jane (1953 film)
cast: Doris Day, Howard Keel
calamus: **5** quill
calando: **6** slower, softer
Calaveras County jumper: **4** frog
calaverite: **3** ore
calc-__: **4** spar, tufa, tuff **6** sinter
Calchas: **4** seer
daughter of ~: **8** Cressida
calcify: **6** harden **8** indurate
calcite to Mohs: **5** three
calcium: **7** element
hydroxide: **6** alkali
like ~ oxide: **4** limy
oxide: **4** lime
source: **4** milk
calcium __: **5** light, oxide **7** blocker, carbide, hydrate, nitrate, oxalate, sulfide
calculable: **9** countable, estimable
caldarium: **5** sauna
Caldecott __: **5** medal
Calder: **9** Alexander **10** Willingham
Calder, Alexander: **6** artist **8** sculptor
work: **6** mobile
Calderón, Pedro: **6** author **7** Spanish **10** playwright
Caldwell: **3** Zoe **4** city, town **5** Bobby, Sarah **6** Taylor **7** Erskine
locale: **5** Idaho
Caldwell, Erskine: **6** author, writer
spouse: Margaret Bourke-White
work: Annette
Close to Home
Georgia Boy
God's Little Acre
Tobacco Road
Trouble in July
Caldwell, Sarah: **9** conductor
Cale: **10** Yarborough
Caleb: **4** Carr
son of ~: **4** Elah
Caledonia: **4** city, town **8** Scotland
locale: **9** Wisconsin
calefaction: **4** heat
calendar: **4** card, list **6** agenda, docket **7** daybook, Filofax, program **8** schedule **10** chronology

After

calamity: **3** ill, woe **4** bane, blow, doom, loss, ruin **5** curse, event, havoc, shame **6** blight, misery, mishap, ordeal, plague **7** scourge, tragedy, undoing **8** accident, casualty, disaster, distress, hard luck, hardship **9** adversity, cataclysm, detriment, nightmare, ruination **10** affliction, misfortune
Calamity Jane (1953 film)
cast: Doris Day, Howard Keel
calamus: **5** quill
calando: **6** slower, softer
Calaveras County jumper: **4** frog
calaverite: **3** ore
Calchas: **4** seer
daughter of ~: **8** Cressida
calcify: **6** harden **8** indurate
calcite to Mohs: **5** three
calcium: **7** element
hydroxide: **6** alkali
like ~ oxide: **4** limy
oxide: **4** lime
source: **4** milk
calculable: **9** countable, estimable **10** computable, imaginable, meas-
caldarium: **5** sauna
Caldecott __: **5** medal
Calder: **9** Alexander **10** Willingham
Calder, Alexander: **6** artist **8** sculptor
work: **6** mobile **7** stabile
Calderón, Pedro: **6** author, writer **7** Spanish **10** playwright
Caldwell: **3** Zoe **5** Bobby, Sarah **6** Taylor **7** Erskine
Caldwell, Erskine: **6** author, writer
spouse: Margaret Bourke-White
work: Annette
Close to Home
Georgia Boy
God's Little Acre
Tobacco Road
Trouble in July
Caldwell, Sarah: **9** conductor
Cale: **10** Yarborough
Caleb: **4** Carr
son of ~: **4** Elah
Caledonia: **8** Scotland
calefaction: **4** heat
calendar: **4** card, list **6** agenda, docket **7** daybook, Filofax, program **8** schedule **10** chronology

Write to Us!

In our ongoing effort to keep this book the most useful and up-to-date crossword dictionary, we hope to hear from you. Please write us if you have questions, comments, quibbles, or suggestions for new material to include. We would especially appreciate your sending along any "new" clues and/or answers you encounter in your crossword solving, so we can consider including them in future editions. (See below for more info on that.) Writing to us constitutes consent to publish your material without compensation.

Concerning quibbles: Thousands of person-hours have gone into the preparation, proofreading, and fact-checking of the material in this book, but it is possible that a few errors have gotten through. If you think you have found one, please let us know. But, before you write, we ask that you check standard reference sources (such as unabridged dictionaries, almanacs, etc.) to be as sure as you can be that what you have found actually is an error. Since we will need verification in order to make any correction, we ask that you include with your correspondence the source(s) you consulted.

Wanted—Puzzle Patrollers. Reward!

Professional lexicographers, whose job it is to compile "real" dictionaries, depend on contributors to send them examples of how words are used in contemporary writing. For this reason, we established the first-ever such system for crossword dictionaries with the first edition of *Million Word*: "Stan and Dan's Puzzle Patrol," which we are pleased to continue for this new edition.

Please send us any "new" answer words, clues, celebrity names, fill-in-the-blanks, etc. that you encounter in your crossword-solving, so we can consider using them in future editions. (Factual clues only, please. Wordplay clues are beyond the scope of this book.) Each submission should include the puzzle's source (newspaper, magazine, or Web site address) and date, along with your name, street address, and e-mail address (if any).

We will thank our 25 most prolific Puzzle Patrollers (the first senders of 50 or more original entries that we will print in subsequent editions of the book) with a free copy of the next edition of *The Million Word Crossword Dictionary*.

See "What's New in This Edition" (page x) for the names of the Puzzle Patrol free-book winners of this new edition.

How to Contact Us

We can be reached in both low-tech and high-tech fashion.

Regular mail: Stanley Newman and Daniel Stark, P.O. Box 69, Massapequa Park, NY 11762. Please enclose a self-addressed, stamped envelope if you'd like a reply.

E-mail: MillionXword@aol.com

Acknowledgments

The assistance of many people have made this book possible. The authors would especially like to thank:

- Joseph Vallely, our literary agent, who edited our proposal and skillfully guided it to the right publisher
- Our HarperCollins editors Toni Sciarra and Stephanie Meyers
- John Chaneski, Jon Delfin and Nancy Schuster, who proofread the manuscript
- Adam Cohen and Lisa Marie Marselle, who assisted in the gathering of entries
- Our puzzle colleagues Emily Cox and Henry Rathvon, Rich Norris, Fred Piscop, Merl Reagle, Mike Shenk, and Wayne Robert Williams, for their kind comments, which are excerpted on the back cover
- Will Shortz, for his many helpful suggestions and thoughtful Introduction
- Roslyn Stark, for her invaluable assistance in many areas

and...

- Our battalion of Puzzle Patrollers, owners of the first edition of *Million Word*, who sent us new entries, many of which have been incorporated into this second edition.

A

a: 3 one
in code: 4 able, alfa
in French: 2 un 3 une
in German: 3 ein 4 eine
in Italian: 2 un 3 una, uno
in Spanish: 3 una, uno
a __: 3 bit, to z 5 leg up, tempo, tergo 6 little, priori, trifle
a __ a dozen: 4 dime
a __ and a day: 4 year
a __'clock scholar: 4 ten o
a __ cry: 3 far
a __ dozen: 5 dime a
a __ for one's money: 3 run
a __ for sore eyes: 5 sight
a __ in one's bonnet: 3 bee
a __ in one's ear: 4 flea
a __ in the bucket: 4 drop
a __ lease on life: 3 new
a __ nut to crack: 4 hard 5 tough
a __ of: 6 couple
a __ of another color: 5 horse
a __ of fate: 5 twist
a __ of one's mind: 5 piece
a __ of the action: 5 piece
a __ one's bonnet: 5 bee in
a __ on one's escutcheon: 4 blot
a __ order: 4 tall
a __ pass: 6 pretty
a __ row to hoe: 5 tough
a __ situation: 5 no-win 6 win-win
a __ unto itself: 3 law
a __ up: 3 leg
A: 4 mark, type 5 grade, vowel, width 6 letter 8 Martinez 9 blood type
in communications: 4 alfa
in phonetic alphabet: 5 Alpha
list: 5 elite
major: 3 key
minor: 3 key
A __: 3 one 4 list, star, Team 5 level 6 supply 7 battery, horizon
A __ apple: 4 as in
A __ of Honey: 5 Taste
A, __ adorable...: 5 you're
A-__: 4 axes, axis, bomb, line 5 frame
A-__, A-Tasket: 6 Tisket
__ A: 4 Q and, Type 6 Cygnus, Linear, radium 7 Project, vitamin
'A' __ Alibi: 5 Is for
__-A: 5 Retin
A6
manufacturer: 4 Audi
AA: 5 width 7 battery
candidate: 5 toper
like ~ shoes: 3 nar.
part of ~: 4 Anon.
A.A.: 4 Fair 5 Milne
affiliate: 6 Al-Anon
AAA: 5 width 7 battery 8 top-rated 9 top-drawer, topflight
class ~ baseball: 6 minors
giveaway: 3 map 7 road map
job: 3 tow
opposite: 3 EEE
suggestion: 3 hwy., rte. 5 route 7 highway
Aachen: 4 city, town
locale: 7 Germany
Aage: 4 Bohr
aah
partner: 3 ooh
Aaker: 3 Lee
Aaliyah
last name: Haughton
song: At Your Best (1994)
Back & Forth (1994)
The One I Gave My Heart To (1997)
Try Again (2000)
Aalto: 5 Alvar
AAM
firer: 3 MiG
Aames: 6 Willie
A and E
alternative: *see* cable channel
__ A and M: 5 Texas
Aar: 5 river
city on the ~: 5 Berne
aardvark: 6 animal, mammal
feature: 5 snout
food: 3 ant
home: 6 Africa
young: 3 pup
Aare: 5 river
city on the ~: 4 Bern
Aaron: 4 Burr, Hank, Klug 5 Tommy 6 Sorkin, Tommie 7 Copland, Eckhart, Neville 8 Caroline, Lipstadt, Spelling
brother: 5 Moses
daughter: 4 Tori
idol: 4 calf
parent: 5 Amram 8 Jochebed
sister: 6 Miriam
son: 3 Eli 5 Abihu, Amram, Nadab 7 Eleazar, Ithamar
wife: 8 Elisheba
Aaron, Hank: 5 Brave 6 hitter 7 slugger 10 outfielder
weapon: 3 bat
AARP
concern: 5 aging 6 ageism
member: 2 sr. 3 snr.
part of ~: 3 Ret. 4 Amer. 5 Assoc. 7 Persons, Retired 8 American
__ A. Arthur: 7 Chester
ab: 6 muscle
neighbor: 3 pec
ab __: 3 ovo 4 esse 5 extra, intra 6 initio 7 aeterno, origine
Ab: 5 month 6 Hebrew
month after: 4 Elul
AB: 4 type 9 blood type
A.B.: 4 Dick 7 Guthrie
aba: 4 robe 6 fabric 7 garment
Aba __ Honeymoon, The: 4 Daba
ABA
member: 3 att. 4 atty. 6 lawyer
part of ~: 3 Bar 4 Amer., Assn. 8 American
title: 3 esq.
__ Ababa: 5 Addis
abaca: 4 hemp, rope 5 fiber
aback: 8 confused, off-guard, unawares 9 surprised, thrown off 10 by surprise
take ~: 4 faze, stun 5 shake 7 astound, nonplus, stagger, startle 8 astonish, bowl over, surprise 9 discomfit, dumbfound, give a turn 10 disconcert
taken ~: 7 fuddled
abacus: 10 calculator
unit: 4 bead
use an ~: 3 add
user: 5 adder
__ a bad example: 3 set
__ a bad moon rising: 4 I see
abaft: 4 back 6 astern 8 backward 9 to the rear
not ~: 7 forward
__ a ball: 4 have
abalone: 5 shell 7 mollusk 8 seashell
eater: 5 otter 8 sea otter
product: 5 nacre
shell: 5 ormer
abandon: 4 cede, drop, duck, dump, élan, fail, jilt, kick, quit, sell, shed 5 break, chuck, ditch, forgo, leave, let go, scrap, scrub, sever, verve, waive, yield 6 betray, bow out, cop out, desert, disown, forego, give up, maroon, opt out, reject, resign, strand, vacate 7 bail out, discard, forfeit, forsake, freedom, impulse, let down, let go of, license, pull out, scuttle, ship out 8 abdicate, cut loose, forswear, get rid of, give up on, hand over, jettison, lay aside, lewdness, part with, renounce, run out on, throw out, wildness, withdraw 9 back out of, cast aside, dispose of, disregard, foreswear, frivolity, looseness, lubricity, repudiate, skip out on, surrender, take a walk, throw away, throw over, walk out on 10 chicken out, exuberance, fly the coop, go away from, relinquish, storm out of, wantonness
Abandon (2002 film)
cast: Benjamin Bratt, Zooey Deschanel, Katie Holmes
Abandon __!: 4 ship
abandoned: 4 left, lone, lorn, lost 5 alone, empty, loose, stray 6 lonely, rakish, vacant, wicked 7 lustful, outcast, run-down, shunned 8 cast away, derelict, deserted, desolate, forsaken, helpless, isolated, passed up, stranded, untended 9 cast aside, corrupted, debauched, discarded, dissolute, forgotten, left alone, neglected, ownerless, shameless, sidelined 10 dissipated, eliminated, friendless, high and dry, licentious, profligate, unattended, unoccupied
infant: 4 waif
abandonment: 6 waiver 8 apostasy 10 abdication
__ a bang out of: 3 get
__ a barrel: 4 over
abase: 5 lower, shame 6 demean, humble, insult, reduce 7 corrupt, cut down, deflate, degrade, depress, put down, run down, vitiate 8 belittle, bring low, cast down, dishonor, take down 9 bring down, devaluate, disparage, downgrade, humiliate 10 put to shame
oneself: 5 crawl 6 grovel
abased: 4 vile
abasement: 8 dishonor 10 degeneracy, depression
abash: 4 faze 5 shame, shock 6 dismay, humble, rattle, ruffle 7 chagrin, fluster, mortify 8 confound 9 discomfit, embarrass, humiliate 10 demoralize, discompose, disconcert, disgruntle, dishearten
abashed: 5 fazed 6 afraid, bugged, shamed 7 anxious, ashamed, crushed, fuddled, humbled, nervous, panicky, rattled 8 confused, hesitant, in a tizzy, sheepish, timorous 9 awestruck, chagrined, diffident, flinching, ill at ease, mortified 10 bewildered, confounded, humiliated, taken aback
abashment: 3 awe 5 shame 6 dismay 7 chagrin, shyness 8 vexation 9 confusion
abate: 3 die, ebb 4 cool, ease, fade, fall, flag, lull, sink, slow, wane 5 allay, drain, let up, lower, quash, quell, relax, remit, slack, taper 6 dampen, deaden, ease up, go down, lessen, modify, recede, reduce, slow up, soften, subdue, weaken 7 abolish, cut down, decline, die down, drop off, dwindle, ease off, mollify, relieve, slacken, subside, tail off 8 abrogate, blow over, decrease, diminish, fade away, head away, level off, mitigate, moderate, palliate, peter out, slack off, taper off 9 attenuate, quiet down 10 invalidate, slacken off
abatement: 3 ebb 4 curb, fall 5 check, letup 6 easing, fading, relief, waning 7 anodyne, control, cutback, decline, falloff 8 decrease, discount, markdown, quashing, quelling, stoppage, write-off 9 abolition, allowance, annulment, deduction, lessening, reduction, remission, restraint, softening, tempering, weakening 10 arrestment, diminution, limitation, mitigation, moderation, palliation, prevention, repression, subsidence
__ a bath: 4 draw, take
__ a Battlefield: 6 Love Is
Abba: 4 Eban
ABBA (pop group)
homeland: Sweden
song: Chiquitita (1979)
Dancing Queen (1977)
Fernando (1976)
I Do, I Do, I Do, I Do, I Do (1976)
Knowing Me, Knowing You (1977)
Mamma Mia (1976)
SOS (1975)
Take a Chance on Me (1978)
Waterloo (1974)
The Winner Takes It All (1980)
abbé: 4 monk 5 friar, padre, prior, title 6 cleric, curate, divine, pastor, priest 7 Prévost 8 celibate, minister, monastic 9 clergyman 10 monastical
Abbe: 4 Lane 9 Cleveland
abbess: 3 nun 4 rank 5 title 7 Héloïse 9 religious
Abbess, The
author: Athol Fugard
abbey: 6 church, friary, priory, temple 7 convent, nunnery 8 cloister, ministry 9 monastery 10 tabernacle
dweller: 3 nun 4 monk 5 friar, prior
Abbey: 5 Edwin 6 Edward
Abbey __: 4 Road 7 Theatre
__ Abbey: 7 Tintern
Abbey Road Studios
owner: 3 EMI

A B

Abbie: **7** Hoffman
Abbie an' __: **5** Slats
abbot: **3** Dom **4** abbé, monk, rank **5** title **6** cleric **8** minister **9** churchman, religious
charge: **4** monk
headwear: **5** miter
subordinate: **5** prior
Abbott: **3** Bud **6** George, Philip **7** Gregory **8** Berenice
Abbott and Costello: **3** duo **4** pair, team
Abbott, Berenice: **12** photographer
abbreviate: **4** clip, pare, trim **5** prune, slash **6** cut off, cut out, digest, narrow, recede, reduce, shrink **7** abridge, compact, curtail, cut back, cut down, shorten **8** abstract, boil down, compress, condense, contract, diminish, minimize, restrict, truncate **9** capsulize, stop short, summarize, telescope
abbreviated: **3** cut **5** short **7** partial, sketchy **9** condensed **10** compressed, unfinished
version: **4** mini
abbreviation: **3** cut **6** digest, sketch **7** outline, summary **8** abstract, clipping, synopsis
Abby: **6** Dalton **8** Van Buren
sister: **3** Ann
__ Abby: **4** Dear
ABC: **3** net **7** network
a.m. show: **3** GMA
follower: **3** DEF **4** DEFG **5** DEFGH
HQ: **3** NYC
part of ~: **4** Amer.
rival: **3** CBS, Fox, NBC, PBS **5** The CW
telephone ~: **3** two
watchdog: **3** FCC
ABC (1970 song)
artist: Jackson 5
__ ABC: **6** easy as
ABCs: **6** basics, letter **8** alphabet **9** rudiments **10** essentials, foundation
ABC's __ World of Sports: **4** Wide
__ Abdel Nasser: **5** Gamal
abdicate: **4** cede, drop, quit **5** bag it, demit, forgo, leave, yield **6** abjure, depart, forego, give up, opt out, resign, retire, secede, vacate **7** abandon, bail out **8** abnegate, renounce, step down, withdraw **9** go to sleep, quitclaim, surrender **10** relinquish
abdication: **6** ceding, waiver **7** cession **8** retiring, transfer, yielding **9** demission, deserting, desertion, disowning, rejection, resigning, surrender **10** abnegation, renouncing, retirement, transferal
abdomen: **3** gut, pot **5** belly, tummy **6** middle, paunch **7** midriff, stomach **10** midsection
combining form: **4** celi- **5** celio-, coeli-, ventr- **6** coelio-, ventri-, ventro-
crustacean ~: **5** pleon
muscle: **6** rectus
muscles: **5** recti
of the ~: **6** celiac **7** coeliac
terminus: **5** groin
abdominal
exercise: **5** sit-up
abdominous: **3** fat **5** obese, plump, pudgy, round, tubby **6** chubby, portly, rotund **7** paunchy **9** corpulent **10** big-bellied, overweight, potbellied, well-padded
abduct: **4** take **5** seize, steal **6** collar, kidnap, ravish, snatch **7** capture **8** carry off, grab away, shanghai, take away **9** carry away **10** run off with, spirit away
combining form: **3** -nap
abduction: **7** seizure
abductor: **9** kidnapper
Abdul Abulbul __: **4** Amir
Abdul-Jabbar, Kareem
alma mater: **4** UCLA
milieu: **5** court
org.: **3** NBA
sport: **10** basketball
Abdul, Paula
song: Blowing Kisses in the Wind (1991)
Cold Hearted (1989)
Forever Your Girl (1989)
Opposites Attract (1990)
The Promise of a New Day (1991)
Rush, Rush (1991)
Straight Up (1988)
The Way That You Love Me (1989)
spouse: Emilio Estevez
Abe: **4** Kobo **5** Beame **6** Attell, Fortas, Pollin, Vigoda **7** Burrows, Lincoln, Simpson **10** Saperstein
boy: **3** Tad
grandson: **4** Bart
like ~: **6** honest
Mary, to ~: **4** wife
parent: **3** Tom **5** Nancy
son: **5** Homer
wife: **4** Mary
__ a bead on: **3** get **4** draw
Abebe: **6** Bikila
abecedarian: **4** tiro, tyro **6** novice **7** learner **8** beginner, neophyte **10** tenderfoot
phrase: **4** as in
abecedary: **7** primary **10** elementary
__ à Becket: **6** Thomas
abed: **5** not up **6** laid up **7** retired **8** sleeping, snoozing, tucked in **9** in the sack, sacked out **10** sawing logs, slumbering
maybe: **3** ill
not ~: **5** astir
__-abed: **3** lie
__-A-Bed: **4** Hide
__ a bee: **6** busy as
a bee in one's __: **6** bonnet
__ a beet: **5** red as
Abel: **3** Bob **4** Alan, Elie **5** Gance **6** Jeanne, Rudolf, Tasman, Walter **7** Ferrara **8** Magwitch
brother: **4** Cain, Seth
composer: Thomas Arne
father: **4** Adam
love: **4** Rima
mother: **3** Eve
nephew: **4** Enos
abele: **4** tree **6** poplar
Abe Lincoln in Illinois: **4** film, play
author: Robert E. Sherwood
character: **3** Ann **4** Gale, Seth
studio: **3** RKO
Abe Lincoln in Illinois (1940 film)
cast: Ruth Gordon, Gene Lockhart, Raymond Massey
__ a bell: **4** ring
Abel, Rudolf: **3** spy
Aberdeen: **4** city, port, town
locale: **8** Maryland, Scotland
river: **3** Dee
Aberdeen __: **5** Angus **7** terrier
Aberdeen __ Ground: **7** Proving
aberrance: **5** quirk
aberrant: **3** odd **4** eery **5** eerie, flaky, weird **6** atypic, flakey, freaky, morbid, quirky, way-out **7** bizarre, deviant, off-base, offbeat, strange, unalike, unusual **8** abnormal, atypical, freakish, peculiar, uncommon **9** anomalous, different, divergent, eccentric, fantastic, grotesque, irregular, monstrous, not normal, out of line, unnatural **10** nonuniform, unorthodox
aberrate: **7** deviate
aberration: **3** pip **4** blip, warp **5** freak, lapse, mania, quirk **6** oddity **7** anomaly, mistake, veering **8** delusion **9** deformity, departure, deviation, diversion, variation, wandering, weirdness **10** difference, distortion, divergence
abet: **3** aid **4** back, help **5** egg on **6** assist, excite, foment, foster, incite, lead on, spur on, urge on **7** advance, collude, forward, support **8** embolden, imbolden **9** encourage, instigate, lend a hand, stimulate, subsidize
__ a bet: **5** place
__ a bet!: **5** Not on
abetment: **3** aid **4** help **6** assist **10** assistance
abettor: **4** ally **5** agent **6** helper **8** henchman **9** accessory, assistant **10** accomplice
abeyance: **4** lull **5** pause **6** recess **7** latency, waiting **8** deferral, dormancy, reprieve, stoppage **9** remission **10** inactivity, quiescence, suspension
be in ~: **4** pend **5** await
hold in ~: **8** postpone
in ~: **5** on ice **6** latent **10** unrealized
abeyant: **6** latent, put off, tabled **7** dormant, resting, shelved, waiting **8** deferred, inactive, set aside **9** postponed, quiescent, suspended
abhor: **4** hate **5** scorn **6** detest, loathe **7** deplore, despise, disdain, dislike, hold low **8** execrate **9** abominate, can't stand **10** look down on, recoil from
old-style: **5** spise
abhorrence: **4** hate **5** odium **6** enmity, hatred, horror, malice **7** disgust **8** aversion, distaste, loathing **9** antipathy, hostility, repulsion, revulsion **10** execration, ill feeling, repellence
abhorrent: **4** base, foul, grim, poor **5** awful, lousy, nasty, woful **6** crumby, crummy, dismal, horrid, odious, rotten, woeful **7** accurst, baleful, baneful, beastly, doleful, ghastly, hateful, heinous, satanic, vicious **8** accursed, dreadful, Godawful, grievous, horrible, shameful, stinking, terrible, wretched **9** appalling, atrocious, defective, execrable, frightful, insidious, loathsome, miserable, offensive, repellant, repellent, repugnant, repulsive, revolting, satanical **10** abominable, despicable, detestable, disastrous, forbidding, horrendous, petrifying
Abib
follower: **4** Iyar
preceder: **4** Adar
abide: **2** go **4** bear, last, live, lump, stay, take, wait **5** brook, dwell, exist, lodge, sit by, stand, stick, tarry **6** accept, endure, hang in, hold on, inhere, keep on, linger, remain, reside, settle, suffer, take it **7** consent, persist, sojourn, stomach, sustain, swallow, undergo **8** continue, kill time, stand for, tolerate **9** persevere, put up with, withstand **10** hang around, stay a while, wait around
apt rhyme for ~: **6** reside
by: **4** heed, mind, obey **5** bow to **6** accept, adhere, bend to, follow, fulfil, hold to, redeem **7** agree to, conform, consent, defer to, fulfill, observe, respect, stand by, stick to **8** adhere to, carry out, listen to, submit to **9** conform to, discharge, persist in, stick with **10** comply with, keep in step, toe the line
abiding: **4** fast, firm **5** fixed **6** stable, steady **7** chronic, durable, endless, eternal, lasting, undying **8** constant, enduring, timeless, unending **9** ceaseless, chronical, perennial, permanent, perpetual, steadfast, unabating, unceasing **10** changeless, continuing, habituated, inveterate, persistent, unchanging, unwavering
__-abiding: **3** law
Abidjan: **4** city, port, town **7** capital
capital east of ~: **5** Accra, Akkra
locale: **10** Ivory Coast
Abie's Irish Rose (1946 film)
cast: Joanne Dru
Abigail: **5** Adams **7** Breslin **8** Fillmore, Van Buren
sib: **3** Ann
Abigail Adams, __ Smith: **3** née
Abilene: **4** city, town
locale: **5** Texas **6** Kansas
ability: **4** bent, gift, head **5** craft, flair, knack, might, power, reach, savvy, sense, skill, touch **6** talent **7** command, faculty, finesse, freedom, know-how, mastery, prowess, stature **8** aptitude, artistry, capacity, deftness, facility, hang of it, strength **9** adeptness, dexterity, endowment, expertise, handiness, ingenuity, intellect, knowledge, potential **10** adroitness, competence, efficiency, expertness, green thumb, right stuff
has no ~ to: **6** cannot
having the ~ for: **9** capable of
natural ~: **5** knack **6** genius **8** instinct **9** endowment
__ a bill of goods: **4** sell
__-A-Billy: **4** Rock
__ a bird,...: **3** It's
__ a bite: **4** grab
abject: **3** low **4** base **5** sorry **6** broody,

humble, menial, sordid **7** fawning, forlorn, hangdog, ignoble, outcast, pitiful, servile **8** degraded, dejected, hopeless, penitent, pitiable, wretched **9** groveling, miserable, prostrate, worthless **10** deplorable, despicable, humiliated, submissive
abjectly
act ~: **6** cringe
abjectness: **3** woe **10** depression, woefulness
abjuration: **8** apostasy
abjure: **3** ban, bar, nix **4** veto **5** debar, forgo **6** disown, eschew, forbid, forego, recall, recant, reject **7** abstain, disavow, forsake, retract **8** abdicate, disallow, disclaim, forswear, keep from, prohibit, renounce, swear off, withdraw **9** foreswear, proscribe, repudiate **10** contravene
ablactate: **4** wean
__ a blank: **4** draw
__ a blanket: **5** pig in
ablare: **4** loud **10** trumpeting
ablate: **4** melt **5** erode **8** vaporize **9** dissipate
ablative: **4** case
ablaze: **3** lit **5** afire, aglow, angry, fiery, light, shiny **6** aflame, alight, bright, flashy, fuming, heated, on fire, raging **7** aroused, beaming, blazing, burning, fervent, flaming, flaring, fulgent, furious, glowing, ignited, lambent, lighted, radiant, shining, zealous **8** dazzling, flashing, frenzied, gleaming, incensed, in flames, luminous, lustrous, vehement **9** brilliant, refulgent, sparkling
be ~: **4** burn
set ~: **3** lit **5** light **6** ignite
able: **3** apt, fit **4** deft, good, keen **5** adept, can-do, handy, hardy, quick, savvy, sharp, smart **6** adroit, artful, clever, expert, facile, gifted, strong, up to it **7** knowing, skilled, trained **8** adequate, dextrous, equipped, powerful, prepared, skillful **9** competent, dexterous, effective, efficient, empowered, masterful, permitted, practiced, promising, qualified, versatile **10** proficient
become ~: **5** learn
be ~ to: **3** can **6** afford
facetiously: **3** ept
follower: **5** baker
isn't ~ to: **4** can't
is ~ to: **3** can
able-__ seaman: **6** bodied
Able __ ere...: **4** was I
Able, Baker, __: **7** Charlie
able-bodied: **3** fit **4** hale, iron, well, wiry **5** beefy, burly, hardy, hefty, hunky, husky, lusty, stout, tough, whole **6** brawny, hearty, mighty, potent, robust, rugged, sinewy, steely, stocky, strong, sturdy, virile **7** doughty, healthy **8** athletic, forceful, indurate, muscular, powerful, puissant, stalwart, vigorous **9** Atlantean, Herculean, strapping, well-built **10** red-blooded
Able to __ tall buildings...: **4** leap
Able was I __...: **3** ere **4** ere I
__ a blind eye: **4** turn
__-a-block: **5** chock
abloom: **8** in flower **9** flowering **10** blossoming
ablush: **3** red **4** pink **8** reddened
ablution: **4** bath, wash **6** shower **7** washing **8** lavation **9** cleansing, showering
Islamic ~: **4** wudu
ably: **4** well **6** deftly **7** capably, rightly **8** adroitly, laudably, worthily **10** skillfully
ABM: **6** weapon
part of ~: **4** Anti **7** Missile **9** Ballistic
user: **4** USAF
abnegate: **4** deny **6** disown, give up, recant, refuse, refute, reject **7** abstain **8** abdicate, disclaim, keep from, renounce **10** relinquish
abnegating: **5** sober
abnegation: **6** denial **7** refusal **8** eschewal **9** rejection, sacrifice, surrender **10** abdication, abstinence, self-denial, temperance
Abner: **5** Yokum **9** Doubleday
creator: **6** Al Capp
father: **3** Ner
friend: **3** Lum
__ Abner: **3** Li'l
abnormal: **3** odd **5** gross, queer, weird **6** atypic, morbid, off-key, screwy, way-out **7** bizarre, curious, deviant, oddball, off-base, strange, unusual **8** aberrant, atypical, freakish, isolated, peculiar, uncommon **9** anomalous, deviating, divergent, eccentric, fantastic, heterodox, irregular, malformed, out of line, shapeless, unnatural **10** unexpected, unorthodox
combining form: **4** anom- **5** anomo-
prefix: **3** mal- **4** para-
abnormality: **4** flaw **6** oddity **7** anomaly **8** deviance **9** variation
abnormally: **5** oddly **10** especially
aboard: **6** loaded, on base, on deck **7** en route, on a ship **8** embarked **9** consigned, in transit, traveling
climb ~: **5** get in, get on **7** enplane, entrain
come ~: **4** join **6** embark, jump on **9** affiliate
go ~: **6** embark **7** emplane, entrain, set sail, ship out **9** leave port
put ~: **4** lade, load
ship: **4** asea **5** at sea
__ aboard!: **3** All
__ a board: **6** flat as
abode: **3** pad **4** base, co-op, digs, farm, flat, home, iglu, nest, seat, tipi **5** cabin, condo, house, igloo, lodge, manor, place, shack, tepee **6** teepee **7** address, château, domicil, habitat, housing, lodging, mansion **8** domicile, dwelling, fireside, log cabin, quarters **9** apartment, motor home, residence
animal ~: **3** den **4** lair
bird ~: **4** aery, eyry, nest **5** aerie, eyrie
fowl ~: **4** coop **5** roost
humble ~: **3** hut **5** hovel, shack **6** shanty
Indian ~: **4** tent, tipi **5** hogan, tepee **6** teepee, wigwam
see also home, house
aboil: **7** cooking **8** seething, steaming **9** simmering
abolish: **3** end, nix, rid, zap **4** kill, undo, void **5** abate, annul, erase, quash, scrub **6** cancel, finish, negate, repeal, revoke, vacate **7** call off, destroy, expunge, inhibit, nullify, rescind, root out, squelch, subvert, vitiate, wipe out **8** abrogate, dissolve, overturn, prohibit, set aside, stamp out, suppress **9** eradicate, extirpate, liquidate, overthrow, repudiate, supersede, terminate **10** annihilate, do away with, extinguish, invalidate, obliterate, put an end to
abolition: **9** abatement, annulment, overthrow **10** abrogation, rescinding, rescission, revocation, subversion, withdrawal
A-bomb
scientist: **4** Urey **5** Fermi
target: **8** Nagasaki **9** Hiroshima
test site: **6** Bikini **8** Eniwetok **10** Alamogordo
abominable: **3** bad **4** base, foul, grim, poor, vile **5** awful, curst, gross, hairy, lousy, seamy, woful **6** crumby, crummy, cursed, dismal, grisly, horrid, odious, rotten, wicked, woeful **7** accurst, baleful, baneful, beastly, doleful, ghastly, hateful, heinous, hellish, hideous, satanic, squalid **8** accursed, dreadful, God-awful, grievous, gruesome, horrible, inferior, shameful, shocking, stinking, terrible, wretched **9** abhorrent, appalling, atrocious, defective, execrable, frightful, insidious, invidious, loathsome, miserable, nefarious, obnoxious, offensive, repellant, repellent, repugnant, repulsive, revolting, satanical **10** despicable, detestable, disastrous, disgusting, horrendous, petrifying
snowman: **4** yeti
Abominable __: **7** Snowman
abominate: **4** hate **5** abhor **6** detest, loathe **7** despise, disgust, dislike, hold low **8** execrate **10** recoil from
abomination: **4** hate **5** crime, odium, wrong **6** hatred **7** disgust, offense **8** enormity, iniquity **9** revulsion
__ a bone: **5** dry as
__ a bone to pick: **4** have
__ a book: **4** like **5** crack
__-a-Boom: **5** Chick
aboriginal: **3** old **5** early, first **6** native **7** ancient, endemic, primary **8** primeval **9** endemical, primaeval, primitive, unevolved **10** indigenous, primordial
aborigine: **6** native **7** bushman **8** indigene, original **10** inhabitant
Antilles: **5** Carib
Australia: **4** Mara
call: **5** cooee
hatchet: **4** mogo
India: **4** Gond
Japan: **4** Ainu
New Zealand: **5** Maori
Panama: **4** Cuna
Sri Lanka: **5** Vedda **6** Veddah
weapon: **5** spear, waddy **6** waddie
abort: **3** end **5** cease, check, scrub **6** arrest, cancel **8** cut short **9** terminate **10** contravene
abortive: **4** vain **7** useless **9** premature
Abou Ben Adhem: **4** poem
author: Leigh Hunt
abound: **4** flow, teem **5** crawl, crowd, swarm, swell **6** infest, rich in, thrive **7** prevail, run riot **8** flourish, overflow **9** luxuriate
abounding: **4** full, rich, rife **5** alive, flush, leafy, thick **6** filled, heaped, plenty **7** copious, profuse, replete **8** infested, prodigal, prolific **9** plentiful
about: **3** say **4** as to, back, in re **5** anent, circa **6** active, almost, around, moving, nearby, nearly, toward **7** apropos, close to, roughly, towards **8** backward, in motion, relative, stirring, well-nigh **9** apropos of, as regards, generally, regarding, somewhere **10** as concerns, concerning, give or take, relating to
prefix: **4** peri-
starter: **3** gad, lay, run **4** here, turn, walk **5** knock, round, roust, there
suffix: **3** -ish
about-__: **4** face
__ about: **3** gad, get, put, see, set **4** cast, come, just, kick, muck, nose, on or **5** knock, noise, up and
About __: **4** a Boy, Adam **5** a Girl
About __ Night ...: **4** Last
About a Boy (2002 film)
cast: Toni Collette, Hugh Grant, Rachel Weisz
About a Girl (1994 song)
artist: Nirvana
About a Quarter to Nine
composer: Al Dubin, Harry Warren
__ About Bob?: **4** What
__ About Eve: **3** All
about-face: **4** turn **5** shift, U-turn **6** change, switch **7** reverse, setback **8** apostasy, flip-flop, reversal, variance **9** inversion, one-eighty, vice versa **10** alteration, conversion
do an ~: **9** back-pedal
About Last Night... (1986 film)
cast: James Belushi, Rob Lowe, Demi Moore, Elizabeth Perkins
director: Edward Zwick
__ about that: **3** how
__ about the bush: **4** beat
__ about the gills: **5** green
__ about time!: **3** It's
__ about town: **3** man **5** woman
__ About You: **3** How, Mad
above: **3** o'er **4** atop, high, over **5** aloft, on top, upper **6** beyond, on high, upward **7** aloft of, north of, on top of, skyward, topping **8** hovering, in heaven, more than, overhead, superior, upraised, upstairs **9** aforesaid, exceeding, foregoing, upwards of **10** better than, heavenward, larger than, superior to, surpassing, up in the sky
ender: **5** board **6** ground
in German: **4** über
prefix: **3** epi-, sur- **5** hyper-, super-, supra-
above __: **3** all **5** it all, water **6** stairs
above __ beyond: **3** and
__ above: **4** a cut
aboveboard: **4** fair, just, open, true **5** frank, legal, legit, licit, moral,

overt, right 6 candid, honest, lawful, openly, square 7 sincere, up-front, upright 8 straight, truthful 9 guileless, high-toned, sincerely, veracious 10 believable, forthright, from the hip, virtuously

above it __: 3 all

above-mentioned: 5 prior

above the __: 3 law 4 line

Above the Law (1988 film)

cast: Pam Grier, Steven Seagal, Sharon Stone

ab ovo: 3 new

__ a bow: 4 take

__ a boy!: 3 It's

__-a-brac: 4 bric

abracadabra: 5 magic, spell 7 sorcery

see also baloney

abrade: 3 bug, irk, rub 4 file, gall, rasp, sand, skin, wear 5 annoy, chafe, erode, grate, graze, grind, scour, scrub, scuff 6 scrape 7 flatten, roughen, rub down, wear off 8 irritate, wear away, wear down 9 excoriate, sandpaper, scrape off, stone-wash

abraded: 3 raw

Abraham: 6 Cowley 7 F. Murray, Lincoln

brother: 5 Haran, Nahor

father: 5 Terah

grandfather: 5 Nahor

grandson: 4 Esau 5 Jacob

half-sister: 5 Sarah

nephew: 3 Lot 4 Hazo 5 Gaham, Tebah 6 Kemuel, Maacah, Tahash 7 Pildash

partner: 6 Straus

son: 5 Isaac, Medan, Shuah 6 Midian, Zimrah 7 Ishmael

wife: 5 Sarah, Sarai 7 Keturah

Abraham, F. Murray: 5 actor

film: Amadeus (1984, AA)
Finding Forrester (2000)
Last Action Hero (1993)
Mighty Aphrodite (1995)
The Name of the Rose (1986)

Abraham, Martin and John (1968 song)

artist: Dion

Abrahams: 3 Jim 5 Peter

Abraham's __: 5 bosom

abrasion: 4 sore, wear 5 chafe, scuff, wound 6 injury, lesion, scrape 7 erosion, grating, rubbing, scratch 8 friction

abrasive: 4 grit, sand 5 emery, harsh, nasty, rough, sharp, spiky 6 biting, gritty 7 caustic, cutting, erosive, galling, hateful, hurtful 8 annoying, cleanser, grinding, scratchy, scuffing 9 polishing, smoothing 10 hard to take, irritating, scratching, sharpening, unpleasant

mineral: 5 emery 6 garnet

use an ~: 5 scour

__ a Break!: 5 Gimme

abreast: 4 near 5 equal, level 6 au fait, beside, in line, versed 7 in touch 8 familiar, informed, opposite, up-to-date 9 au courant, laterally 10 acquainted, side by side

keep ~ of: 6 follow 7 monitor

of: 2 by 6 beside

of things: 6 versed 8 up-to-date

abridge: 3 cut 4 chop, clip, pare, snip, trim 5 elide, limit, prune, slash 6 censor, digest, lessen, narrow, recede, reduce, shrink 7 compact, curtail, scissor, shorten 8 abstract, boil down, compress, condense, contract, cut short, decrease, diminish, downsize, restrict, simplify, truncate 9 capsulize, summarize, telescope 10 abbreviate, blue-pencil

perhaps: 4 edit

abridged: 3 cut 5 short 7 capsule, concise, partial, reduced, sketchy 9 condensed 10 compressed, synopsized, unfinished

not ~: 5 uncut

abridgment: 4 lack 5 brief 6 digest, précis 7 epitome, pandect, summary 8 synopsis 10 compendium

abroad: 4 away 7 oversea, touring 8 in Europe, overseas 9 elsewhere, not at home, traveling

bring from ~: 6 import

go ~: 4 tour 6 travel 8 sightsee, vacation

move ~: 8 emigrate

sell ~: 6 export

abrogate: 3 end, nix 4 do in, undo, void 5 abate, annul, quash, scrub 6 cancel, negate, recant, reject, renege, repeal, revoke, vacate 7 abolish, nullify, rescind, retract, torpedo, vitiate 8 dissolve, knock out 9 discharge, finish off 10 invalidate, neutralize, put an end to

abrogation: 9 abolition, annulment, desertion

abrupt: 4 curt, rude 5 bluff, blunt, brief, brusk, crude, frank, gruff, hasty, jerky, quick, rough, sharp, short, steep, swift, terse 6 candid, crusty, direct, snappy, snippy, sudden 7 brusque, hurried, offhand, rushing, uncivil 8 headlong, impolite, pell-mell, snippety, tactless 9 impatient, impetuous, impulsive, outspoken 10 indelicate, surprising, unexpected, unforeseen, ungracious

abruptly: 4 bang, wham 5 sharp 8 pell-mell, suddenly, unawares

Abruzzi

commune: 4 Atri

Absalom

father: 5 David

sister: 5 Tamar

Absalom, Absalom!

author: William Faulkner

Absalom and Achitophel: 4 poem

author: John Dryden

Absalom My __: 3 Son

abscond: 2 go 3 fly, get, run 4 bolt, flee, jump, quit, slip 5 break, eloin, elope, leave, scram, split 6 beat it, decamp, defect, depart, desert, eloign, escape, go AWOL, run off, vanish 7 duck out, go south, make off, pull out, ride off, run away, skip out, take off, vamoose 8 clear out, fugitate, hightail, light out, run for it 9 cut and run, disappear, skedaddle, sneak away, steal away 10 fly the coop, hightail it, make a break

absconder: 4 AWOL 6 coward, dodger 7 escapee, runaway 8 defector, deserter, recreant, renegade, swindler

absence: 4 lack, need, void, want 5 hooky 6 dearth, drouth, hookey, no-show 7 drought, paucity, truancy, vacancy, vacuity 8 exiguity, omission, sparsity, truantry 9 privation 10 deficiency, inadequacy

leave of ~: 3 R 'n' R 4 rest 5 break, leave, R and R 7 holiday, respite, time off 8 furlough, vacation 10 sabbatical

of order: 4 mess, riot 5 havoc, snarl 6 bedlam, mayhem, tumult, uproar 7 anarchy, clutter, discord, turmoil 8 disarray, shambles 9 confusion 10 unruliness

prefix: 3 dis-, non-

Absence of Malice (1981 film)

cast: Bob Balaban, Sally Field, Paul Newman

director: Sydney Pollack

absent: 3 off, out 4 away, AWOL, bare, gone 5 blank, empty, minus 6 astray, devoid, hollow, no-show, vacant 7 lacking, missing, not here, omitted, vacuous, wanting, without 8 listless, not there, vanished 9 elsewhere, not around 10 not in class, on vacation, part of AWOL

be ~ from: 4 skip

in Latin: 6 ab esse

not ~: 4 here

oneself: 5 leave 6 retire 8 withdraw

absent __ leave: 7 without

absent-__: 6 minded

absente __: 3 reo

absentee: 6 truant

absentee __: 4 vote 5 voter 6 ballot

absently: 8 dreamily, musingly, sloppily 10 carelessly, heedlessly

absent-minded: 4 lost 5 moony 6 dreamy, remote, spacey, vacant 7 bemused, faraway, mooning 8 careless, distrait, dreaming, heedless 9 forgetful

Absent-Minded Professor, The (1961 film)

cast: Fred MacMurray, Nancy Olson, Keenan Wynn

dog: 7 Charlie

absent without __: 5 leave

absinthe: 5 drink 8 beverage

relative: 6 pastis

Absinthe Drinker

artist: Édouard Manet

Absolut: 5 vodka

competitor: 4 Skyy 5 Popov, Stoli 6 Rodnik, Starka 8 Smirnoff 9 Grey Goose

absolute: 4 flat, free, full, pure, rank, sure 5 clean, exact, final, fixed, ideal, plumb, rigid, sheer, stark, total, utter, whole 6 actual, all-out, direct, entire, simple, strict, utmost 7 certain, decided, factual, flat-out, genuine, perfect, plenary, precise, supreme 8 accurate, almighty, complete, decisive, definite, despotic, emphatic, explicit, flawless, implicit, inerrant, infinite, outright, positive, profound, thorough, ultimate, unflawed 9 arbitrary, axiomatic, downright, faultless, out-and-out, sovereign, unfailing, unlimited 10 autocratic, autonomous, conclusive, consummate, definitive, despotical, impeccable, inarguable, infallible, monocratic, peremptory, preeminent, tyrannical, unabridged, unarguable, undeniable

not ~ in law: 4 nisi

ruler: 4 tsar 6 despot, tyrant

absolute __: 4 zero 5 music, pitch, scale, space, value 7 alcohol, ceiling, maximum, minimum, monarch

absolutely: 2 da, ja, sí 3 oui 4 amen, flat, just, sí sí, very 5 good-o, plumb, quite, right, roger, stark, truly, uh-huh 6 agreed, and how, gladly, good-oh, I agree, indeed, just so, purely, rather, really, righto, simply, wholly, yowzah 7 exactly, go ahead, indeedy, mais oui, quite so, ten-four, totally, utterly 8 all right, as you say, entirely, for a fact, thumbs up, very well 9 be my guest, darn right, decidedly, expressly, hands down, no mistake, on the nose, perfectly, precisely, sure thing, you said it 10 altogether, completely, decisively, definitely, far and away, on the money, sure as heck, sure as hell, sure enough, that's right, thoroughly, to the limit

see also of course

Absolutely Fabulous

character: 5 Edina, Patsy

Absolute Power (1997 film)

cast: Clint Eastwood, Gene Hackman, Ed Harris, Laura Linney

director: Clint Eastwood

absolution: 6 pardon 7 amnesty, release 9 acquittal, exemption

absolutism: 7 tyranny 9 autocracy

absolve: 4 free 5 clear, remit, spare 6 acquit, bleach, excuse, exempt, let off, pardon, purify, redeem, spring, wink at 7 blink at, forgive, release, relieve, set free 8 go easy on, liberate, sanctify, sanitize 9 discharge, exculpate, exonerate, vindicate, whitewash

absolved: 6 exempt

absorb: 3 eat, get, sop 4 blot, hold, soak 5 co-opt, drink, grasp, learn, mop up, rivet, sense, sopup 6 arrest, devour, digest, engage, engulf, follow, imbibe, ingest, ingulf, obsess, occupy, osmose, retain, soak in, soak up, suck in, suck up, take in 7 concern, consume, drink in, engross, enthral, get into, immerse, inthral, involve, swallow 8 enthrall, interest, inthrall, sponge up 9 apprehend, captivate, entertain, fascinate, latch onto, preoccupy, swallow up 10 assimilate, comprehend, monopolize, understand

facts: 4 cram 6 soak up, take in 7 drink in 8 memorize

absorbed: 4 deep, lost, rapt 5 fixed 6 enrapt, intent 7 focused, pensive 8 held fast 9 undivided, wrapped up 10 thoughtful

by: 4 into

__-absorbed: 4 self

absorbent: 6 porous, spongy 7 thirsty 8 bibulous 9 permeable, pregnable,

retentive **10** penetrable
cloth: **5** terry, towel **6** diaper
absorbent __: **6** cotton
__ **absorber:** **5** shock
absorbing: **8** readable **9** arresting, consuming **10** engrossing, impressive, intriguing
absorption: **6** intake **8** interest **9** attention, digestion, immersion, ingestion, reception, retention **10** engagement, exhaustion, intentness, saturation
absquatulate: **3** run **4** flee
abstain: **4** curb, fast, shun **5** avoid, cease, evade, forgo, spurn **6** abjure, desist, eschew, forego, pass up, refuse, resist, sit out **7** decline, forbear, refrain **8** abnegate, fence-sit, keep from, leave off, renounce, withhold **9** constrain, do without
from: **4** duck, omit, shun **5** avoid, dodge, forgo, shirk **6** bypass, eschew, forego **7** forbear **8** renounce **10** circumvent
abstainer: **10** nondrinker, teetotaler
abstaining: **5** sober **6** frugal **7** ascetic, austere, sparing **8** moderate **9** continent, temperate **10** moderating, restrained
abstemious: **5** sober **6** frugal **7** ascetic, austere, sparing **8** moderate, ungiving **9** continent, temperate **10** moderating, restrained
abstinence: **8** chastity, eschewal, sobriety **9** austerity, avoidance, frugality, restraint, soberness **10** abnegation, asceticism, continence, moderation, refraining, self-denial, temperance
org.: **4** WCTU
abstinent: **5** sober **6** frugal **7** ascetic, austere, sparing **8** moderate **9** continent, temperate **10** moderating, restrained
abstract: **4** deep, lift, pure **5** brief, ideal **6** digest, précis, résumé, review, unreal **7** abridge, complex, epitome, outline, shorten, summary **8** abstruse, academic, compress, condense, synopsis **9** capsulize, difficult, imaginary, recondite, summarize, synopsize, telescope **10** abbreviate, compendium, conspectus, impersonal, indefinite, intangible, literature
of only ~ interest: **4** moot
painter: **4** Klee **7** Picasso **8** Mondrian, Paul Klee **9** Kandinsky
abstract __: **3** art **4** noun **5** music, space **6** number **7** algebra
abstracted: **4** lost **6** remote, vacant **7** pensive **8** listless **9** condensed, forgetful **10** compressed, synopsized
abstraction: **3** art **4** idea **7** concept
abstract of __: **5** title
abstruse: **4** dark, deep **5** heavy, muddy, vague **6** arcane, hidden, mystic, occult, opaque, subtle **7** complex, cryptic, learned, obscure, unclear **8** abstract, esoteric, involved, mystical, nebulous, pedantic, profound, puzzling **9** confusing, cryptical, enigmatic, intricate, recondite, technical **10** indistinct, intangible, mysterious, pedantical, perplexing
absurd
see foolish
absurdity: **4** joke **5** farce, folly **6** bêtise, lunacy **7** baloney, boloney, fatuity, inanity **8** nonsense **9** craziness, goofiness, silliness, stupidity **10** applesauce, flapdoodle
seeming ~: **7** paradox
Abt __: **6** Vogler
ABT
locale: **3** NYC
Abt Vogler
author: Robert Browning
Abu __: **5** Dhabi **6** Simbel
Abu-__: **4** Bakr
Abu Dhabi: **4** city, town **7** capital
denizen: **4** Arab
leader: **4** amir, emir **5** ameer, emeer
locale: **3** UAE **4** Asia **7** Mideast **10** Middle East
__ **a bug...:** **6** Snug as
__ **a bug in one's ear:** **3** put
A Bug's Life
bugs: **4** ants
Abuja: **4** city, town **7** capital
locale: **7** Nigeria
predecessor: **5** Lagos
Abukir: **3** bay
__ **Abulbul Amir:** **5** Abdul
abundance: **3** lot, sea **4** heap, many, mine, much **5** flood, hoard, ocean, store **6** argosy, bounty, myriad, plenty, riches, wealth **7** fortune **8** lushness, mountain, opulence, opulency, plethora, quantity **9** affluence, ampleness, amplitude, fecundity, fertility, frequency, greatness, plenitude, profusion **10** efficiency, exuberance, prosperity
in ~: **6** galore
Abundance
author: Beth Henley
abundant: **4** full, lush, many, much, rich, rife **5** ample, flush, great, heavy, large, leafy, thick **6** a lot of, divers, enough, filled, gobs of, heaped, lavish, lots of, myriad, plenty, umteen, untold **7** a host of, a slew of, copious, eco-rich, fertile, heaps of, liberal, no end of, piles of, profuse, replete, scads of, teeming, umpteen **8** a bunch of, affluent, an army of, fruitful, generous, handsome, infested, manifold, numerous, oodles of, princely, prodigal, prolific, scores of, umpsteen **9** a passel of, bounteous, bountiful, capacious, countless, exuberant, luxuriant, plenteous, plentiful, quite a few, unsparing **10** voluminous, zillions of
be ~: **4** teem
not ~: **4** rare
source: **10** cornucopia
with: **9** rolling in
(with): **5** lousy
abundantly: **4** much, well **6** enough, vastly **7** greatly, largely **10** adequately, handsomely, incredibly
aburst: **8** erupting
abuse: **3** dig, hit, mar, rag **4** barb, bash, beat, flak, gibe, harm, hurt, jeer, jibe, lash, mall, maul, mock, ride, slam, slap, slur, snub, zing **5** decry, flack, knock, libel, roast, scold, scorn, smear, spurn, taint, taunt, trash, wrong **6** assail, attack, bang up, berate, damage, defame, defile, deride, dump on, heckle, hosing, impugn, injure, injury, insult, malign, misuse, molest, offend, play on, punish, rebuff, revile, slight, tirade, vilify **7** affront, asperse, assault, beating, calumny, catcall, chew out, corrupt, degrade, disdain, exploit, lambast, mauling, mockery, obloquy, offense, oppress, outrage, overtax, profane, put down, railing, rank out, rip into, rough up, run down, slander, torment, torture, traduce, upbraid, violate **8** aggrieve, backbite, badmouth, belittle, berating, breakage, contempt, denounce, derision, derogate, diatribe, ill-treat, inequity, keep down, lambaste, maltreat, misapply, mistreat, play upon, reproach, ridicule, sail into, scolding, vilipend **9** aspersion, blaspheme, castigate, cheap shot, contumely, denigrate, deprecate, desecrate, discredit, disparage, dissipate, excoriate, humiliate, injustice, insolence, invective, lash out at, maligning, manhandle, misemploy, mishandle, mismanage, persecute, profanity, victimize, violation **10** assailment, backbiting, calumniate, debasement, defamation, defilement, disrespect, excruciate, impairment, impugnment, imputation, kick around, knock about, oppression, opprobrium, overburden, punishment, revilement, roughhouse, tormenting, upbraiding, vituperate, wrongdoing
verbal ~: **3** rap **6** outcry **9** criticism
abuser: **5** bully **6** sadist
abusive: **4** foul, rude **5** harsh, nasty **7** profane **8** insolent, libelous **9** injurious, insulting, offensive, sarcastic, truculent **10** defamatory, scurrilous
abut: **4** join, meet **5** end at, touch, verge **6** adjoin, border, lean on **7** bolster, touch on **8** border on, finish at, neighbor **9** juxtapose, touch upon
abutment: **5** joint **7** support **8** end piece **10** contiguity
abutting: **4** near, next **6** beside **8** adjacent **10** contiguity, contiguous, juxtaposed
__ **a button:** **6** cute as
abuzz: **4** busy **6** active **7** humming
__**-a-bye:** **4** rock
abysmal: **3** bad **4** base, deep **5** awful **7** yawning **8** profound, terrible, unending **9** boundless, cavernous, plumbless **10** bottomless, fathomless, unknowable
abyss: **3** pit **4** gulf, hell, hole, rift, void, well **5** chasm, depth, gorge **6** cavity, depths, ravine **7** crevice, vacuity **8** low point, nihility **9** black hole **10** underworld
the ~: **5** Hades
abyssal: **4** deep **10** bottomless
Abyssinia: **8** Ethiopia, farewell
city: **5** Harar
cry: **5** miaou
monkey: **6** grivet
peak: **5** Amara
prince: **3** ras
Abyssinian: **3** cat **5** felid **6** feline
word from an ~: **3** mew **4** meow **5** miaou, miaow, miaul
Abyssinian __: **3** cat **4** gold, well **6** banana, Church
Abyss, The (1989 film)
cast: Michael Biehn, Ed Harris, Mary Elizabeth Mastrantonio
director: James Cameron
Abzug: **5** Bella
Ac: **4** elem. **7** element **8** actinium
89 for ~: **4** at. no.
AC: **6** cooler **9** appliance
part of ~: **3** air
place: **2** rm.
power: **4** elec.
time: **3** Aug., Jul.
unit: **3** BTU
see also air conditioner
acacia: **4** tree **5** plant, shrub **6** flower, locust **7** shittah **9** gum arabic
Hawaiian ~: **3** koa
relative: **6** mimosa
tree: **3** koa **5** babul
acad.: **3** sch. **4** coll., inst.
award: **3** deg.
academe: **6** lector **8** lecturer
academes: **8** literati **9** longhairs
academese: **6** patois
academic: **4** moot **5** pupil, tutor **6** formal, lector **7** bookish, erudite, learned, scholar, student **8** abstract, highbrow, lecturer, notional, pedantic, studious, unproved **9** pedagogic, professor, recondite, scholarly **10** collegiate, pedantical, scholastic
climber: **3** ivy
locale: **6** school **7** college **10** university
rookie: **5** frosh **8** freshman
specialty: **5** major
stat: **3** GPA
work: **5** study
year part: **3** sem. **4** term **8** semester
see also college, school
academic __: **4** gown, rank, year **5** dress **7** costume, freedom
__ **academic:** **3** it's
academician: **6** artist, fellow, savant **7** scholar **9** scientist
academics: **7** faculty **9** lecturers
academy: **3** sch. **5** lycée **6** circle, league, lyceum, school **7** council **8** alliance, brainery, seminary **9** institute **10** federation, foundation, fraternity, halls of ivy, prep school
freshman: **4** pleb **5** plebe
in French: **5** école, lycée
member: **6** fellow
student: **5** cadet
__ **academy:** **5** naval
Academy
founder: Plato
Academy Awards
see Oscar
Acadia: **4** park
locale: **5** Maine
__**-a-cake:** **3** pat
__ **a Camera:** **3** I Am
__ **a candle to:** **4** hold
Acapulco: **4** city, port, town
locale: **6** Mexico **8** Guerrero
see also Spanish

__ Acapulco: 5 Fun in
__-a-car: 4 rent
acarid: 3 bug 4 mite, tick
acarus: 3 bug 4 mite, tick
__ a case for: 4 make
__-a-cat: 3 one, two 4 four 5 three
ACC
school: 3 FSU, U. Va. 4 Duke 7 Clemson 8 Maryland, Virginia 10 Wake Forest 11 Georgia Tech
accede: 2 OK 3 let 4 okay 5 admit, agree, allow, grant, yield 6 accept, accord, assent, cave in, comply, concur, fess up, give in, permit, say yes 7 approve, concede, consent, go along, succeed 8 cry uncle 9 acquiesce, cooperate 10 come around, get crowned
to: 3 let 5 brook 6 accept, permit 8 assent to, sanction, tolerate 9 approve of, authorize, put up with
accelerando: 6 faster
undoer: 6 a tempo
accelerate: 3 gun, rev 4 rush 5 build, drive, hurry, impel, raise, rev up, speed, spirt, spurt 6 fire up, hasten, jack up, open up, step up 7 advance, forward, further, quicken, speed up 8 expedite 9 fast-track, stimulate 10 burn rubber, make tracks, peel rubber
accelerated: 4 fast 5 quick, rapid 6 speedy
acceleration: 5 speed, spirt, spurt, surge 8 rapidity, velocity
unit of ~: 3 gal
accelerator: 3 gas 5 pedal
item: 4 atom
opposite: 5 brake
accent: 4 beat, burr, tone 5 acute, drawl, grave, twang 6 brogue, play up, rhythm, speech, stress, timbre, weight 7 cadence, cadency, point up 8 contrast, emphasis, language, localism, locution, tonality 9 emphasize, highlight, intensify, punctuate, spotlight, underline 10 decoration, inflection, intonation, modulation, underscore
kind of ~: 4 burr 5 acute, drawl, grave 6 brogue
lacking ~: 6 atonic
lack of ~: 5 atony 6 atonia
accent __: 4 mark
__ accent: 4 word 5 acute, tonic 6 agogic 7 graphic, primary
Accent: 3 car 4 auto 7 Hyundai 10 automobile
Ac-cent-__-ate the Positive: 4 tchu
accented: 8 emphatic
in music: 3 sfz. 8 marcando 9 sforzando
Ac-cent-tchu-ate the Positive
composer: Harold Arlen, Johnny Mercer
accentuate: 6 play up, stress 7 feature, point up 8 heighten, overplay, reassert 9 emphasize, highlight, intensify, italicize, punctuate, spotlight, underline 10 strengthen, underscore
accentuation: 8 emphasis
accept: 2 OK 3 buy, get, let, use 4 avow, bear, gain, heed, hold, like, mind, obey, okay, pass, pick, take 5 abide, admit, adopt, agree, allow, bow to, brook, defer, elect, enrol, favor, go for, grant, let in, say OK, serve, stand, trust, yield 6 accede, affirm, assent, assume, bank on, bend to, comply, credit, endure, enroll, fess up, follow, fulfil, grow on, join in, listen, look to, obtain, pardon, permit, ratify, relish, rely on, say yes, secure, suffer, tackle, take on 7 abide by, acquire, agree to, approve, believe, concede, conform, consent, count on, defer to, embrace, fulfill, observe, receive, respect, sign for, stomach, swallow, welcome, yield to 8 accede to, adhere to, assent to, carry out, deal with, depend on, grow upon, hold with, live with, sanction, shoulder, stand for, submit to, take part, tolerate 9 acquiesce, approbate, approve of, authorize, believe in, count upon, partake of, put up with, recognize, reconcile, sign off on 10 capitulate, concur with, give the nod, set store by, toe the line, understand
don't ~: 8 turn down 9 challenge 10 disbelieve
eagerly: 5 eat up, lap up 6 jump at, leap at
acceptable: 2 OK 3 A-OK 4 fair, fine, good, nice, okay, okeh, okey, so-so, tidy 5 great, legit, licit, moral, noble, valid 6 decent, enough, kasher, kosher, likely, proper 7 correct, ethical, livable, right on, up to par 8 adequate, all right, eligible, laudable, liveable, passable, pleasant, pleasing, splendid, standard, suitable, superior 9 admirable, agreeable, allowable, copacetic, desirable, excellent, hunky-dory, in the swim, on the ball, on the beam, palatable, reputable, tolerable, up to grade, up to snuff, wonderful 10 admissible, believable, beneficial, convenient, convincing, creditable, delightful, fairly good, infallible, in the rules, peachy keen, reasonable, sufficient
be ~: 4 suit 5 serve
is ~: 4 goes
least ~: 5 worst
Acceptable Risk
author: Robin Cook
acceptably: 4 well 6 enough
acceptance: 2 OK 3 nod 4 okay, okeh, okey 5 usage, vogue 6 assent, belief 7 passage, receipt 8 adoption 9 accedence, accession, acquiring, admission, agreement, belonging, enrolment, fosterage, reception 10 assumption, compliance, concession, enrollment, green light, permission
exclamation: 3 def, rad 4 cool, fine, good, neat, nice, phat 5 dandy, ducky, neato, super 6 dreamy, far-out, gnarly, groovy, peachy, terrif, wicked 7 amazing, awesome, stellar 8 terrific 9 bodacious, fantastic, hunky-dory, marvelous 10 out of sight, peachy-keen, super-duper
propose for ~: 5 offer
accepted: 3 OK'd, rcd. 4 OK'ed, recd. 5 known, legit, let in, liked, sound, usual 6 chosen, common, kasher, kosher, normal, okayed, proper 7 current, general, in vogue, popular, regular, welcome 8 habitual, orthodox, standard 9 canonical, customary, unanimous, universal, unwritten 10 accustomed, legitimate, understood
be ~: 4 rate 5 fit in, get in
by: 6 in with
accepting: 9 credulous 10 falling for
callers: 2 in 6 at home
access: 2 in 3 get, tap, way 4 door, gate, path, ramp, road 5 enter, entry, get at, get to, route, spirt, spurt 6 avenue, course, entrée, obtain 7 get into, ingress, passage 8 approach, entrance, entryway, outburst 9 admission, gangplank, influence, penetrate 10 admittance, connection, passageway
ending: 3 ory
gain ~: 5 get in
garden ~: 7 postern
give ~ to: 5 admit
means of ~: 4 door, ramp 6 avenue, entrée
provide ~ to: 5 let at, let in
right of ~: 7 ingress 10 admittance
access __: 4 code, road, time 5 point 6 charge, method
__-access: 6 direct, random, serial
accessible: 4 easy, near, open 5 handy, ready 6 at hand, public, usable 7 exposed, getable, obvious, popular, useable 8 exoteric, passable, possible, sociable 9 available, easy to use, operative, reachable, receptive, unblocked, unguarded 10 attainable, convenient, employable, hospitable, obtainable, up for grabs
accession: 6 assent 7 arrival, receipt 8 addition, kingship 9 accedence, accretion, admission, agreement, enrolment, extension, increment, induction, reception 10 acceptance, assumption, attainment, enrollment, investment, succession, taking over
accessories: 3 rig 4 gear 5 stuff
accessory: 3 aid 4 aide, tool 5 add-on, extra, minor, plant, shill, stall 6 device, helper, ringer 7 abetter, abettor, adjunct, fitting, fixture, insider, partner 8 henchman, ornament 9 adornment, ancillary, appendage, appliance, assistant, associate, attendant, auxiliary, colleague, component, conducive, extension 10 accomplice, attachment, collateral, decoration, supplement
auto ~: 5 alarm
accessory __ the fact: 5 after 6 before
accident: 3 hap 4 blow, loss, luck 5 crash, event, fluke, smash, wreck 6 chance, hazard, mishap, pileup 7 crack-up, setback, smashup, stack-up, tragedy, wrack-up 8 calamity, casualty, disaster, fortuity 9 collision, happening, rear-ender 10 misfortune, occurrence
investigation agcy.: 4 NTSB
like some ~s: 5 freak
opposite: 6 design
sound: 5 splat
accident-__: 5 prone
Accident
author: Danielle Steel
accidental: 5 happy 6 casual, chance, random 9 haphazard, unplanned, unwitting 10 contingent, extraneous, fortuitous, incidental, unexpected, unforeseen, unintended
accidentally: 8 by chance, unawares
Accidental Man, An
author: Iris Murdoch
Accidental Tourist, The: 4 film 5 novel
author: Anne Tyler
dog: 6 Edward
Accidental Tourist, The (1988 film)
cast: Geena Davis, William Hurt, Kathleen Turner
composer: John Williams
director: Lawrence Kasdan
Accident, The
author: Elie Wiesel
acclaim: 4 clap, fame, hail, laud, rave, tout 5 cheer, éclat, exalt, extol, honor, kudos 6 credit, eulogy, extoll, homage, honors, praise, renown, salute 7 applaud, approve, commend, flatter, glorify, laurels, lionize, ovation, plaudit, tribute 8 accolade, applause, approval, cheering, clapping, encomium, eulogize, flattery, good word, plaudits 9 celebrate, laudation, panegyric, recommend 10 compliment, exaltation, panegyrize, popularity
attain ~: 7 succeed
acclaimed: 5 noted 6 famous 8 laureate, renowned 9 well-known 10 celebrated
acclamation: 5 cheer, éclat, honor 6 eulogy, praise 7 big hand, ovation, tribute 8 applause, encomium, plaudits 9 standing O
exclamation: 4 hail 5 hallo 6 hurrah, huzzah
acclamatory: 9 laudatory
acclimate: 5 adapt, enure, inure 6 harden, season 7 conform, toughen 8 accustom, indurate 9 get used to, habituate
acclimated: 5 hardy 8 seasoned
get ~: 6 attune
acclimatize: 5 adapt, enure, inure 6 adjust, harden, orient 8 accustom
acclivitous: 5 steep 6 uphill
acclivity: 4 bank, hill, rise 5 grade 6 ascent, glacis 7 hillock, incline, upgrade 8 gradient, hillside 9 elevation 10 high ground
accolade: 4 kudo 5 award, brava, bravo, honor, huzza, kudos, prize 6 eulogy, homage, huzzah, praise, reward, salute 7 acclaim, big hand, laurels, plaudit, tribute 8 approval, encomium, flattery, good word 9 extolment, laudation, panegyric 10 decoration, exaltation
accommodate: 3 aid, fit 4 help, hold, lend, loan, rent, seat, suit, take 5 adapt, board, defer, favor, fit in, house, humor, lodge, put up, serve, shape, stoop 6 adjust, assist, attune, comply, harbor, oblige,

pamper, please, settle, supply, tailor, take in 7 conform, contain, embrace, furnish, gratify, harbour, include, indulge, provide, quarter, receive, shelter, support, sustain, welcome 8 accustom
accommodating: 4 easy, kind 5 civil, handy 6 aidful, decent, polite 7 helpful, patient, willing 8 flexible, friendly, generous, gracious, obliging, yielding 9 compliant
one: 5 sport
accommodation: 3 inn 4 room 5 berth, favor 7 fitting, lodging 8 courtesy, kindness, quarters
accommodation ___: 4 bill, line 5 paper, train 6 collar, ladder
accommodations: 3 inn, pad 4 digs, roof 5 board, hotel, house, motel, rooms, suite 6 billet 7 housing, lodging, shelter 8 quarters
deluxe ~: 5 suite
accompanied by: 4 with
accompaniment: 7 adjunct
accompanist: 6 escort
accompany: 3 see, tag 4 join, show, take 5 bring, guard, guide, usher 6 attend, convoy, escort, follow, go with, shadow, squire 7 coexist, conduct, consort, go along, stick to 8 chaperon, join with 9 associate, chaperone, come along, look after, occur with 10 appear with, go together, happen with, show around, supplement
to a seat: 3 ush
accompanying: 4 with 7 related
accompli
fait ~: 4 fact 5 given 7 reality 9 actuality, certainty
accomplice: 3 aid 4 aide, ally, tool 5 crony, plant, shill, stall 6 cohort, helper, jackal 7 abetter, abettor, insider, partner 8 henchman 9 accessory, assistant, associate, auxiliary, colleague, companion
be an ~: 4 abet
unwitting ~: 4 pawn
accomplish: 2 do 3 get, win 4 gain, work 5 carry, reach, sew up 6 attain, commit, effect, finish, fulfil, manage, obtain 7 achieve, execute, fulfill, perfect, perform, produce, pull off, realize, satisfy, succeed, work out 8 bring off, carry out, complete, conclude, generate, make good, progress 9 discharge, go forward, hammer out 10 bring about, complement, consummate, do the trick, effectuate, get through, make good on, put through, take care of
fail to ~: 4 miss
old-style: 5 doeth
perfectly: 3 ace 4 nail
accomplished: 4 able, deft, done, good, over 5 adept, savvy, sharp, slick 6 adroit, au fait, brainy, expert, gifted, learnt, nimble, versed 7 capable, learned, skilled, trained 8 dextrous, graceful, lettered, masterly, polished, seasoned, skillful, talented 9 competent, dexterous, efficient, masterful, practiced, qualified, versatile, virtuosic 10 proficient
accomplishment: 3 act 4 coup, deed, feat, gain, work 5 doing, skill 6 action, effort, record, stroke 7 ability, exploit, success, triumph 8 fruition
cry: 4 ta-da 5 ta-dah 6 I did it
accord: 4 deal, give, pact 5 admit, agree, amity, endow, grant, peace, truce, union, unity 6 accede, affirm, assent, concur, confer, impart, render, square, tender, treaty, unison 7 comport, concede, concert, concord, entente, harmony, keeping, present, rapport 8 alliance, decision, sympathy 9 acquiesce, agreement, communion, concordat, congruity, consensus, good vibes, harmonize, reconcile, unanimity, vouchsafe 10 compromise, congruence, friendship, settlement, solidarity
be in ~: 4 jibe
bring into ~: 6 attune
in ~: 5 as one, at one 6 united 8 together 9 agreeable, unanimous 10 harmonious, like-minded
of one's own ~: 6 at will, freely, gladly 7 happily, readily 8 by choice 9 agreeably, voluntary, willingly
one in ~: 6 agreer
Accord: 3 car 4 auto 5 Honda 10 automobile
accordance: 9 agreement, congruity, propriety
in ~ (with): 5 along
accordant: 7 regular 8 amicable 9 congruous, consonant, unanimous 10 compatible, consistent, harmonious, true to type
according: 4 akin 7 regular, similar, uniform 8 relevant 9 accordant, agreeable, analogous, congenial, congruous, consonant, unanimous 10 coincident, comparable, compatible, concordant, consistent, harmonious
to: 3 à la, per 5 as per
to Hoyle: 5 legal, legit, licit, valid 6 kosher 8 bona fide, orthodox 9 allowable 10 admissible, authorized, meticulous, on the level, scrupulous
accordingly: 4 duly, ergo, then, thus 5 fitly, hence 7 equally 8 suitably 9 therefore
according to ___: 5 Hoyle
accordion ___: 5 pleat
accordion-___: 4 fold
accost: 4 face, hail, meet, talk 5 annoy, greet 6 bother, harass, waylay 7 address, run into 8 approach, confront 9 challenge 10 buttonhole
account: 3 log, rpt., tab 4 bill, book, news, tale, word 5 annal, books, diary, score, story, tally, worth 6 behalf, client, detail, ledger, legend, litany, memoir, notice, reason, reckon, regard, report, sketch 7 adjudge, history, journal, lowdown, reading, recital, rundown, version 8 keep tabs, portrait, register 9 chronicle, inventory, liability, narration, narrative, rationale, reckoning, statement 10 play-by-play
abbr.: 3 bal., int., NSF
bank ~: 6 escrow 7 savings
book: 6 ledger
call to ~: 3 rag 5 blame, scold 6 rebuke 7 reprove 9 reprehend, reprimand 10 take to task
entry: 4 item 5 debit 6 credit
exec: 3 rep 8 salesman
fictional ~: 5 novel
for: 5 solve 6 recite 7 explain 9 attribute, elucidate 10 illuminate
give an ~ of: 4 tell 6 relate 7 narrate, recount
keep ~: 3 log 4 file, list 5 tally 6 report 7 archive, catalog, itemize, jot down, journal, monitor, put down, set down 8 mark down, register, tabulate 9 chronicle, inventory, write down
long ~: 4 saga 6 litany
of no ~: 7 trivial
on ~ of: 5 due to 7 because 9 therefore
on that ~: 4 thus
put on ~: 6 charge
receivable: 3 IOU
take into ~: 4 heed, note 5 cover 7 respect 8 allow for, consider
take no ~ of: 8 override, overrule
take ~ of: 6 reckon
taking that into ~: 6 even so
third-party ~: 6 escrow
total: 7 balance
turn to ~: 3 use 7 utilize
account ___: 3 for 4 book 7 current, payable
___ account: 3 NOW 4 bank, cash, long, on no, open, wrap 5 joint, Keogh, share, short, sweep, trust 6 charge, income, margin 7 banking, capital, control, current, drawing, expense, savings, trustee
accountability: 5 blame 9 liability
accountable: 6 liable 7 at fault, obliged, subject 8 culpable, indebted 10 chargeable
hold ~: 5 blame 6 accuse
accountant: 3 CPA 7 actuary, analyst, auditor 8 examiner 10 bookkeeper, calculator
at times: 5 adder
concern: 3 net 4 item 5 audit, books, costs, debit, taxes 6 credit, income, ledger, return 9 deduction, exemption
___ accountant: 4 cost 6 public
accounted for: 4 here 5 there 6 on hand 7 present
accounting: 8 auditing
abbr.: 3 ROA, YTD 4 FIFO, LIFO
period: 2 yr. 3 qtr. 4 year 7 quarter
accounting ___: 5 clerk 6 period 7 machine
___ accounting: 4 cost
accounts
check the ~: 5 audit
falsify ~: 3 pad
settle ~: 3 pay 5 pay up, repay 6 avenge
accounts ___: 7 current, payable 10 receivable
___ accounts: 5 at all
accouter: 3 arm, fit, rig 4 deck, garb, gear, trap 5 adorn, dress, equip, fit up, habit, rig up 6 attire, bedeck, clothe, fit out, gear up, invest, outfit, rig out, supply 7 apparel, bedrape, deck out, furnish, provide, turn out 8 decorate, munition, ornament 9 caparison, provision
anew: 5 refit
accouterment: 4 garb 5 dress 7 apparel, clothes, fitting 8 trapping
accouterments: 3 kit, rig 4 garb, gear, tack 5 dress, stuff 6 attire, livery, outfit, tackle 7 apparel, baggage, clothes, effects, fixings, harness, rigging, vesture 8 equipage, fittings, fixtures 9 caparison, trappings, trimmings
Accra: 4 city, port, town 7 capital
locale: 5 Ghana
accredit: 2 OK 4 okay 5 refer 6 assign, charge, enable, impute, ratify 7 appoint, approve, ascribe, certify, empower, endorse, entrust, indorse, intrust, license 8 delegate, relegate, sanction, vouch for 9 attribute, authorize, chalk up to, recognize 10 commission
accredited: 5 valid 8 official
accrete: 4 grow
accretion: 4 gain 7 buildup 8 addition, increase 9 accession, increment
accrual: 4 gain 6 growth, return 7 buildup 8 addition, amassing, increase 9 increment
accrue: 3 add 4 grow 5 add up, amass, build, yield 6 gather, result 7 build up, collect, enlarge, mount up 8 hold on to, increase 10 accumulate
accrued ___: 6 income 7 expense, revenue 8 interest
acct.: 3 CPA
bank ~ datum: 3 SSN
entry: 2 cr. 3 int.
insurer: 4 FDIC 5 FSLIC
kind of ~: 2 CD 3 IRA, sav.
see also account, accountant, accounting
acct. ___: 4 exec.
___ acct.: 4 svgs.
acctg.
see accounting
accumulate: 4 cull, gain, grow, heap, hold, keep, mass, pile, save 5 add to, amass, cache, glean, hoard, lay by, lay up, mount, put by, run up, stack, store, swell 6 accrue, bundle, garner, gather, heap up, pile up, rack up, retain, roll up, save up 7 acquire, collect, compile, harvest, procure, put away, round up, scare up, stack up, store up 8 assemble, gather up, hang onto, hold onto, increase, load up on, maintain, multiply, put aside, salt away 9 aggregate, collocate, stockpile 10 amalgamate, centralize
slowly: 5 glean
accumulation: 3 set 4 gain, heap, help, hunk, mass, pile 5 batch, cache, chunk, drift, group, hoard, stack, stock, store, trove 6 bundle, growth, pileup, supply 7 backlog, buildup, deposit 8 addition, assembly, increase, lodgment, quantity 9 congeries, reservoir
accumulator: 5 piler 7 pack rat
accuracy: 5 right, truth 6 verity 7 clarity 8 fidelity, sureness, verac-

ity **9** certainty, closeness, exactness, precision **10** exactitude, factuality, perfection

accurate: 2 OK, so **4** good, just, okay, okeh, okey, true **5** exact, right, solid, sound, valid **6** deadly, direct, trusty **7** careful, certain, correct, factual, genuine, literal, perfect, pointed, precise **8** absolute, concrete, definite, detailed, faithful, flawless, inerrant, on the dot, rigorous, straight, truthful, unerring, verified **9** authentic, errorless, faultless, on the nose, veracious **10** conclusive, definitive, impeccable, infallible, methodical, meticulous, on the money, particular, scrupulous, systematic, unarguable, undeniable, undoubtful, unmistaken
prefix: 4 docu-

accurately: 4 to a T, well **5** right, sharp, smack **6** aright, to a tee **7** rightly **8** verbatim **9** correctly, just right, precisely

accursed: 4 base, foul, grim, poor, vile **5** awful, hexed, lousy, woful **6** crumby, crummy, dismal, doomed, horrid, odious, rotten, woeful **7** baleful, baneful, beastly, doleful, done for, ghastly, hateful, heinous, hellish **8** devilish, dreadful, God-awful, grievous, horrible, ill-fated, inferior, infernal, luckless, shameful, stinking, terrible, wretched **9** abhorrent, appalling, atrocious, bedeviled, condemned, defective, execrable, frightful, insidious, loathsome, miserable, offensive, revolting **10** abominable, despicable, detestable, disastrous, horrendous

accusation: 4 slur **5** blame **6** charge **7** lawsuit **9** complaint, invective **10** allegation, imputation, indictment
false ~: 4 slur **5** smear **6** bad rap, bum rap **7** calumny
response: 6 denial

accusatory: 10 censorious

accuse: 3 sue, tax **4** book, cite **5** blame, brand, fault **6** allege, attack, charge, delate, impute, indict, malign **7** arraign, asperse, censure, charges, impeach, slander **8** confront, denounce **9** attribute, implicate, inculpate, prosecute **10** villainize, vituperate
falsely: 6 defame **7** asperse **8** backbite **10** calumniate

accused: 8 litigant
need: 4 bail

Accused, The (1988 film)
cast: Jodie Foster, Kelly McGillis
director: Jonathan Kaplan

accuser: 8 informer, litigant **9** informant

accustom: 5 adapt, enure, inure, train **6** adjust, harden, orient, season **7** break in **8** acquaint, indurate **9** acclimate, condition, get used to, habituate, reconcile

accustomed: 4 wont **5** prone, typic, usual **6** common, normal **7** grooved, regular, routine, trained, typical **8** accepted, everyday, familiar, habitual, ordinary, orthodox, prepared **9** confirmed, customary, prevalent, settled in **10** acquainted, habituated, in the habit, inveterate, prevailing
get ~: 5 adapt
get ~ to: 6 grow on **8** grow upon
grow ~: 5 inure **6** adjust, harden, orient **7** conform **9** acclimate, reconcile **10** assimilate, come around
(to): 4 used **5** given

ace: 3 one, pro, top **4** A-one, best, card, deft, good, sole, star, whiz **5** adept, brain, crack, excel, flier, flyer, great, pilot, super **6** au fait, bullet, dollar, expert, facile, fly boy, genius, master, superb, talent, tiptop, wizard **7** aviator, egghead, hotshot, old hand, one-spot, prodigy, skilled, thinker, war hero **8** dextrous, Einstein, highbrow, masterly, peerless, polished, skillful, superior, talented, virtuoso **9** brilliant, dexterous, excellent, first-rate, hole in one, honor card, marvelous, masterful, matchless, practiced, top-drawer, topflight, wonderful **10** A number one, mastermind, proficient, remarkable, specialist, super-duper
emulate an ~: 3 fly **6** aviate
plus one: 5 deuce

ace ___ hole: 5 in the

ace-___: 4 high

Ace: 3 car **4** auto, Jane **6** Parker, Willys **7** bandage, Frehley, Goodman, Ventura **8** Drummond **10** automobile
alternative: 5 Curad **7** Band-Aid

acedia: 5 sloth **6** apathy, torpor **7** inertia, languor **8** idleness, laziness, otiosity **9** faineance, indolence, torpidity **10** difference, stagnation

ace in the ___: 4 hole

Acela Express
offerer: 6 Amtrak

Ace of Base
homeland: Sweden
song: All That She Wants (1993)
Cruel Summer (1998)
Don't Turn Around (1994)
The Sign (1994)

acerb: 4 sour, tart **5** harsh **6** biting, bitter **7** caustic, mordant **8** incisive, vinegary **9** acidulous, corrosive, sarcastic

acerbate: 3 bug, get, ire, irk, nag, try, vex **4** faze, fret, gall, hurt, miff, pain, ride, rile, roil, tire, wear **5** anger, annoy, chafe, chivy, eat at, grate, harry, haunt, hound, peeve, pique, press, spite, stump, taunt, tease, upset, weary, worry **6** badger, bother, chivvy, fester, harass, hassle, hector, madden, needle, nettle, noodge, offend, pester, plague, pother, put out, rankle, ruffle **7** afflict, agitate, bedevil, disturb, enflame, grate on, inflame, perturb, provoke, tick off, torment, trouble, turn off **8** aggrieve, confound, disquiet, distress, embitter, exercise, imbitter, irritate **9** aggravate, displease, embarrass **10** antagonize, discompose, exasperate

acerbic: 3 dry **4** acid, sour, tart **5** acrid, harsh, sharp, spiky **6** acidic, biting, bitter **7** caustic, cutting **8** incisive **9** acidulous, corrosive, sarcastic, trenchant

acerbity: 6 rancor **7** acidity, sarcasm **8** acrimony, asperity, mordancy, rudeness, sourness, tartness **9** ill temper **10** bitterness, irritation, unkindness

acerola: 4 tree **5** fruit

aces
see wonderful

___ Aces: 4 Easy

acetal: 7 solvent **8** vinegary

acetaminophen: 5 amide **9** analgesic

acetate: 4 salt **5** ester

___ acetate: 4 amyl, lead **5** butyl, ethyl, vinyl **6** anisyl, benzyl, bornyl, methyl, nickel, phenyl **7** chromic, isoamyl, linalyl

acetic: 4 acid, sour **5** tangy **8** vinegary **10** astringent

acetic ___: 4 acid **5** ether

acetol: 6 ketone

acetous: 4 acid, sour **5** tangy **8** vinegary **10** astringent

acetum: 7 vinegar

acetylene
starter: 3 oxy
use an ~ torch: 4 weld

acetylsalicylic ___: 4 acid

Ace Ventura: Pet Detective (1994 film)
cast: Jim Carrey, Courteney Cox, Tone Loc, Sean Young
director: Tom Shadyac

acey-___: 5 deucy

___ a chance: 5 stand

___ a chance!: 3 Not

Ach du ___!: 6 lieber

ache: 3 ail, yen **4** hurt, long, lust, mope, pain, pang, pine, sigh, stab, want **5** angst, cramp, crick, dolor, grief, mourn, smart, spasm, throb, throe, yearn **6** desire, grieve, misery, sorrow, strain, suffer, twinge **7** anguish, anxiety, craving, feel bad, lumbago **8** distress, migraine, pounding, smarting, soreness, yearning **9** complaint, hankering, suffering, throbbing **10** discomfort
for: 4 pity, want **5** covet, crave **6** desire
(for): 4 feel, long, pant, pine **5** yearn **6** hanker, starve
starter: 3 ear **4** back, head **5** belly, heart, tooth **7** stomach

aches
and pains: 3 woe

Acheson: 4 Dean

Achetes
friend: 5 Eneas **6** Aeneas

achievable: 6 doable, likely, viable **8** credible, feasible, possible, workable **9** available, plausible, potential, practical **10** attainable, imaginable

achieve: 2 do **3** get, win **4** earn, find, gain, make, work **5** close, enact, reach, score, solve **6** attain, commit, effect, finish, fulfil, manage, obtain, rack up, secure, settle, wind up **7** acquire, compass, deliver, execute, fulfill, get done, make out, perfect, perform, pull off, realize, resolve, succeed, triumph, work out **8** bring off, carry out, complete, conclude, generate, progress **9** actualize, discharge, go forward, negotiate **10** accomplish, bring about, consummate, put through, see through

achieved: 4 done **8** complete

achievement: 3 act **4** coup, deed, feat, gain **5** doing, level, stunt **6** action, effort, output, record **7** exploit, success, triumph, victory **8** conquest, progress **9** milestone
cry: 4 ta-da **5** ta-dah **6** presto
heroic ~: 4 coup, deed **7** exploit, triumph, victory **8** conquest
symbol of ~: 5 award

achiever: 4 doer **6** dynamo

Achille ___: 5 Lauro

Achilles: 4 hero **5** Greek
epic: 5 Iliad
friend: 4 Aias, Ajax
heel: 8 exposure, weakness **10** deficiency **12** vulnerablity
horse: 7 Xanthus
parent: 6 Peleus, Thetis
slayer of ~: 5 Paris
weak spot: 4 heel
wife: 8 Deidamia

Achilles ___: 4 heel, jerk **6** reflex, tendon

aching: 4 hurt, pain, sore **6** in pain, tender **7** hurtful, painful **10** in distress

___ aching back!: 4 Oh my

achoo
cause: 4 cold **7** allergy **8** hay fever

___ à chou: 4 pâte

achromatic: 5 white **7** neutral **9** colorless

achromatic ___: 4 lens **5** prism

achromatize: 4 fade **6** bleach

acht: 5 eight **6** German
a quarter of ~: 4 zwei
follower: 4 neun
preceder: 6 sieben

Achtung Baby
producer: Brian Eno

achy: 4 sore **7** bruised, hurting, painful **9** throbbing

achy-breaky: 5 dance

Achy Breaky Heart
artist: Billy Ray Cyrus

acid: 3 HCl **4** sour, tart **5** folic, harsh, low-pH, sharp, spiky **6** acetic, biting, bitter, formic, lemony, oxalic **7** acerbic, caustic, cutting, mordant, nucleic, prussic, pungent, sarcasm, vinegar, vitriol **8** incisive, stinging, vinegary, vitamin C **9** sarcastic, splenetic, trenchant, vitriolic **10** aqua fortis
amino ~: 3 leu. **4** dopa **6** lysine
antiseptic ~: 5 boric **7** boracic
combining form: 3 oxy-
derivative: 6 acetyl
dye: 5 eosin **6** eosine
essential ~: 5 amino
fatty ~: 3 DHA **5** oleic
house: 5 dance
nutritive ~: 5 folic **8** Vitamin C
opposite: 4 base **6** alkali
plus alcohol product: 5 ester
salt: 5 ester
solution: 4 bath
suffix: 3 -oic **4** -olic, -onic
test: 5 proof, trial

work with ~: **4** etch
acid __: **3** dye **4** bath, cell, drop, dust, rain, rock, salt, soil, test **5** house, value **6** number, rocker, tongue **7** radical
acid-__: **4** fast **6** loving, washed **7** forming, tongued
__ acid: **4** bile, thio **5** amino, boric, Caro's, fatty, folic, humic, iodic, Lewis, malic, mixed, mucic, oleic, usnic, xenic, xylic **6** acetic, adipic, agaric, bromic, capric, chinic, cholic, citric, cyanic, decoic, erucic, formic, gallic, kainic, lactic, lauric, maleic, niobic, nitric, oxalic, oxygen, pectic, phytic, picric, quinic, sorbic, sylvic, tannic, tiglic, toluic **7** abietic, acrylic, alginic, arsenic, behenic, benzoic, boletic, butyric, caproic, cerinic, cerotic, cetylic, chloric, chromic, decylic, ellagic, ferulic, folinic, fumaric, hydroxy, linolic, malonic, nitrous, nucleic, pimelic, pyruvic, racemic, sebacic, selenic, silicic, stannic, stearic, suberic, terebic, thionic, titanic, valeric, vanadic, xanthic
__ Acidalium: **4** Mare
acidic: **4** sour, tart **5** low pH, sharp **7** acerbic **8** vinegary
acidify: **4** clot, sour, turn **5** spoil **6** curdle, go sour **7** thicken
acidity: **8** acerbity, pungency, sourness, tartness **9** acridness **10** bitterness, causticity
measure: **2** pH
acid rain
watchdog org.: **3** EPA
acid-tongued: **5** acerb
acidulate: **8** embitter, imbitter
acidulous: **4** sour, tart **5** acerb, sharp **6** bitter **7** acerbic, sourish **9** sarcastic
acid-washed
fabric: **5** denim
ack-ack: **3** gun **9** artillery
Ackerman: **6** Bettye
acknowledge: **3** nod, own **4** avow, hail, sign **5** abide, admit, agree, allow, grant, greet, let on, nod to, react, thank, yield **6** accede, accept, answer, avouch, credit, fess up, notice, ratify, salute, uphold **7** abide by, approve, certify, concede, confess, declare, defer to, endorse, indorse, mention, own up to, profess, respond, support **8** attest to, face up to **9** recognize
refuse to ~: **6** disown
acknowledged: **5** known **8** orthodox
universally ~: **5** given **7** evident, granted, obvious **8** manifest **9** axiomatic **10** understood
acknowledgment: **3** nod **4** hail **5** reply, toast **6** answer, assent, avowal, credit, letter, notice, salute, thanks **7** apology, receipt, tribute **8** applause, greeting, reaction, response **9** reception, statement
acle: **4** tree, wood
__ a clean breast of: **4** make
__ à clef: **5** roman
ACLU
concern: **3** rts. **6** rights
part of ~: **3** Civ. **4** Amer. **5** Civil, Union **8** American **9** Liberties
__ a clue: **4** nary
acme: **3** cap, top **4** apex, head, peak, pink **5** crest, crown, spire **6** climax, height, heyday, heydey, summit, tiptop, vertex, zenith **8** capstone, high spot, meridian, pinnacle **9** high point
at the ~ of: **4** atop
__ a cog: **4** slip
__ a coin: **4** flip
__ a cold...: **4** Feed
acolyte: **4** aide **6** helper **8** altar boy, disciple, follower **9** assistant, attendant
spot: **5** altar
acomia: **8** baldness
Aconcagua: **4** peak **5** mount **8** mountain
locale: **5** Andes **9** Argentina
aconite: **5** plant **6** flower
__ a consummation devoutly...: **3** 'tis
acorn: **3** nut **4** seed **5** hazel
cap: **6** cupule
coating: **5** testa
producer: **3** oak **6** bur oak
acorn __: **4** tube, worm **5** chair, clock, spoon, sugar **6** squash
__ a corner: **4** turn
__ a course: **3** lay
acoustic: **5** audio, aural, music **6** audile, phonic **7** sensory **8** auditory **9** sensorial
insulation: **5** kapok
organ: **3** ear
pro: **5** tuner
unit: **3** bel **4** sone **5** sabin
see also sound
acoustic __: **3** ohm **4** mass, mine **5** nerve **6** guitar **7** coupler, feature, torpedo
acoustical __: **4** tile **5** cloud
acoustics: **7** science
study: **5** sound
ACP
member: **2** dr., MD
acquaint: **4** post, tell, warn **6** advise, ground, inform **7** mention, present **8** accustom, instruct **9** enlighten **10** put on guard
with: **8** advise of
acquaintance: **3** ken **4** mate **5** grasp **6** friend **7** contact **8** intimacy, neighbor
acquaintances: **4** kith
acquainted: **5** aware, privy **6** wise to **7** abreast, advised, clued in **8** familiar **9** cognizant, conscious **10** accustomed, conversant
be ~ with: **4** know
get ~ with: **4** meet
with: **6** used to **8** versed in
acquiesce: **3** bow, nod **4** obey **5** adapt, agree, allow, bow to, yield **6** accede, accept, accord, adjust, assent, cave in, comply, concur, give in, permit, relent, say yes, submit, suffer **7** approve, conform, consent, go along **8** cut a deal, play ball, say uncle **9** reconcile, subscribe **10** come across, come around, condescend
acquiescence: **6** assent **7** consent **8** approval **9** surrender
acquiescent: **4** meek **6** docile **7** passive **8** amenable, lamblike, resigned, yielding **9** compliant, tractable
acquire: **3** bag, buy, cop, get, win **4** earn, find, gain, grab, have, land, snag, take **5** amass, annex, catch, incur **6** accept, assume, attain, come by, corral, gather, line up, lock up, obtain, pick up, rack up, secure, take on, wangle **7** achieve, bring in, capture, collect, garners, inherit, possess, preempt, procure, realize, receive, scare up, succeed **8** come into, invest in, purchase, scrape up **9** get hold of, latch onto **10** accumulate, fall heir to, get hands on, monopolize
again: **5** rebuy, reget, rewin
information: **4** read **5** study **6** absorb, pick up **7** find out
acquired
not ~: **6** inbred
acquisition: **3** buy **4** gain, gift **5** award, bonus, grant, prize **6** income, profit, return, reward, wealth **7** benefit, receipt **8** addition, dividend, donation, earnings, learning, proceeds, purchase, recovery, winnings **9** reception
acquisitive: **4** avid **6** grabby, greedy **7** hoggish, lustful **8** covetous, desirous, grasping **9** mercenary
acquisitiveness: **4** lust **5** greed **6** hunger **7** avarice, avidity, craving **8** cupidity, rapacity, voracity
acquit: **3** act **4** free **5** clear, let go **6** behave, deport, excuse, let off, pardon, redeem, unhand **7** absolve, comport, conduct, deliver, forgive, perform, release **8** liberate **9** discharge, exculpate, exonerate, vindicate **10** disculpate
oneself: **6** behave
acquittal: **6** pardon **7** release **9** clearance, discharge, dismissal, exemption, releasing **10** absolution, liberation, observance
acquittance: **6** refund **7** release
acquitted: **10** off the hook, vindicated
__ a crab: **5** catch
__ a crack at it: **4** take
acre: **4** unit **7** measure
anagram: **4** care, race
ender: **3** age
one-quarter ~: **4** rood
starter: **4** wise
acre-__: **4** foot, inch
Acre: **4** city, port, town
locale: **6** Israel
acreage: **3** lot **4** area, land, plot **5** field, ranch **6** estate, parcel **7** expanse, grounds **8** property **9** farmstead **10** real estate
acres: **4** land, lots **5** scads, tract **6** estate **8** plottage, property
__ Acres: **5** Green
acrid: **4** rank, sour, tart **5** harsh, sharp **6** bitter **7** acerbic, caustic, pungent **8** alkaline **9** corrosive **10** astringent
acridity: **10** bitterness
acrimonious: **3** ill **4** acid, sour **5** angry, cross, irate, nasty, sharp, testy **6** biting, bitter, heated, ireful, morose **7** acerbic, caustic, cutting, mordant, peevish, pungent **8** captious, churlish, petulant, scathing, spiteful, virulent, wrathful **9** sarcastic, splenetic, stringent
acrimony: **4** bile, fury **5** anger, odium, spite, venom, wrath **6** enmity, hatred, malice, rancor, spleen **7** ill will, sarcasm **8** acerbity, asperity, mordancy, rudeness, tartness **9** animosity, antipathy, harshness, nastiness, virulence **10** bitterness, grumpiness, irritation, resentment, unkindness
acrobat: **7** gymnast, tumbler, vaulter **9** aerialist, trapezist
feat: **5** nip-up, split, stunt
security: **3** net
wear: **6** tights **7** leotard, unitard
workplace: **4** ring **6** circus
__ Acrobat: **5** Adobe
acrobatics: **5** sport
acrophobe
fear: **7** heights
acropolis: **4** fort **7** citadel **8** fortress
Acropolis
goddess: **6** Athena, Athene
locale: **6** Athens, Greece
__ a cropper: **4** come
across: **4** over, thru **6** beyond, facing **7** athwart, through **8** spanning **9** astraddle **10** side to side, straddling, traversing
an ocean: **6** abroad **7** far away, foreign
come ~: **4** find, meet **5** dig up, spend **6** locate, strike **7** stumble **8** chance on **9** acquiesce, encounter, light upon **10** capitulate, chance upon, happen upon
come ~ with: **3** pay
cut ~: **8** go beyond, traverse **9** intersect, rise above, transcend
distance ~: **5** width **7** breadth
get ~: **5** speak **6** convey, effect **7** explain **8** convince, spell out **9** bring home, elucidate, make clear **10** illustrate
go ~: **4** ford, span **5** reach **6** bridge **7** connect, stretch **8** pass over, traverse **10** extend over
nautically: **5** abeam **7** athwart
old-style: **4** thro
prefix: **3** dia- **5** trans-
reach ~: **4** span **5** cover **6** bridge **8** traverse
run ~: **4** find, meet **5** hit on **7** hit upon **8** bump into, chance on, come upon **9** encounter, stumble on **10** chance upon
stumble ~: **5** hit on **6** strike
the way from: **3** opp. **8** opposite
__ across: **3** cut, get, put, run **4** come
across-the-board: **5** total **7** blanket, general **8** complete, sweeping
__ Across the Sea: **5** Hands
__ Across the Table: **5** Hands
__ a crowd: **6** three's
acrylic: **5** Orlon, paint
acrylic __: **4** acid **5** ester, fiber, resin
act: **2** do **3** job, law **4** deed, feat, move, play, pose, sham, show, step **5** bylaw, doing, edict, emote, feign, front, labor, put on, serve, shtik, stunt **6** acquit, affect, appear, assume, behave, facade, fake it, shtick **7** charade, conduct, display, exploit, get busy, ham it up, hop to it, measure, perform, portray, posture, pretend, respond, routine, show off, statute **8** function, judgment, maneuver, pretense, rehearse, simulate **9** dramatize,

make a move, ordinance, play a part, take steps 10 false front, make a scene, masquerade, perpetrate, put on a show, resolution, simulation
catch in the ~: 8 surprise
clean up one's ~: 6 reform 7 rectify
ender: 3 ion, ive 4 gong
failure to ~ in law: 6 laches
for: 2 do 5 serve, speak 6 fill in 8 pinch-hit 9 represent 10 substitute
formal ~: 4 rite 6 ritual 8 ceremony
get in the ~: 7 partake
hypocritical: 7 deceive, mislead 8 simulate 9 dissemble, misinform
injurious ~: 4 tort 9 violation
in the ~: 9 red-handed
introducer: 2 MC 5 emcee
junta ~: 4 fiat 5 order 6 decree, dictum 7 command, dictate, mandate 9 directive, manifesto 10 injunction
last ~: 3 end 6 climax, ending, finale, finish, windup 10 conclusion, denouement
like: 3 ape 4 copy 5 mimic 6 mirror 7 imitate 8 simulate
on: 4 head, obey 5 alter 6 affect, change, follow, modify 7 respond, yield to 9 conform to, influence, transform 10 comply with, take care of
out: 7 express 9 dramatize, pantomime
portion: 5 scene
properly: 6 behave
put on an ~: 4 fake 6 fake it 7 pretend 8 simulate 9 dissemble, misinform
quickly: 4 leap
read the riot ~ to: 3 hit 4 flay, flog, slam 5 blast, chide, scold 6 berate, rebuke 7 bawl out, censure, chasten, chew out, condemn, lecture, reprove, upbraid 8 admonish, chastise, denounce, lambaste, reproach, sail into, tear into, threaten 9 castigate, criticize, dress down, excoriate, reprehend, reprimand 10 come down on, discipline, take to task, vituperate
starter: 5 inter, trans 7 counter
suffix: 3 -ure
together: 6 club up
toward: 5 treat
unlawful ~: 4 tort 5 crime, heist, theft, wrong 6 felony, holdup, murder 7 larceny, misdeed, offense, treason 8 atrocity, burglary, delictum, thievery 9 violation 10 infraction
unwise ~: 5 taboo
up: 7 carry on 8 be bratty, be unruly 9 misbehave 10 make a scene
upon: 4 head, obey 5 alter 6 affect, change, follow, modify 7 yield to 9 conform to, influence, transform 10 comply with
vainly: 5 groom, preen 7 deck out, dress up, spiff up
act ___: 3 out 4 call, drop 5 a part, of God, of war 7 curtain, warning
act ___ hunch: 3 on a
___ act: 4 riot, test 5 class 6 circus, public, reflex, ripper, speech 7 novelty, special
___-act: 4 play
Act: 9 mouthwash
alternative: 4 Plax 5 Scope 6 Signal 7 Lavoris 9 Listerine 10 Fluorigard
Act ___: 3 One
___ Act: 3 Tea 4 Riot 5 Hatch, Stamp, Sugar 6 Canada, Reform, Sister, Wagner 7 Kinkaid, Morrill
acta: 4 proc. 5 deeds
Actaeon: 6 hunter
___'acte: 4 entr
Acte
author: Lawrence Durrell
___-acter: 3 one
ACTH
part: 6 adreno, tropic 7 cortico, hormone
Actifed
alternative: *see* cold remedy
acting: 4 mime 6 deputy, pro tem 7 interim, mimicry 8 pretense 9 depiction, dramatics, imitation, portrayal, surrogate, temporary, tentative 10 pro tempore, stagecraft
as one: 6 allied
award: 4 Emmy, Obie, Tony 5 Oscar
for: 10 in behalf of, on behalf of
group: 4 cast 6 troupe 8 ensemble
job: 4 role
up: 3 bad 6 errant
___-acting: 4 long 6 direct, double, single
actinium: 7 element
action: 3 job, vim 4 case, deed, feat, fray, move, plot, rush, step, stir, suit 5 claim, doing, fight, sport, trial, vigor 6 battle, bustle, combat, effect, effort, energy, flurry, hoopla, motion, spirit 7 agility, exploit, gesture, lawsuit, measure, process, service, turmoil 8 activity, alacrity, conflict, exercise, exertion, goings-on, industry, maneuver, measures, movement, practice, response, skirmish, vitality, vivacity 9 animation, commotion, execution, happening, operation, procedure, shootouts 10 engagement, enterprise, excitement, initiative, litigation, liveliness, locomotion, proceeding
combining form: 3 cin-, kin- 4 cino-, kine-, kino-
starter: 5 inter, trans
suffix: 3 -ism 4 -ence
action ___: 4 line 5 grant 6 replay 7 painter
___ action: 3 job 4 knee 5 class, lever 6 covert, direct, police, reflex, rising, social 7 falling
___-action: 4 bolt, live, pump 5 after, cross, slide 6 double, single 7 delayed
actionable: 7 illegal 8 unlawful
wrong: 4 tort
___ Action Hero: 4 Last
Action Man
British ~: 5 GI Joe
___-action photography: 4 stop
actions: 8 behavior 10 deportment
___-action suit: 5 class
Actium: 6 battle
activate: 3 jog 4 stir 5 begin, impel, liven, pep up, put on, rouse, spark, start 6 awaken, call up, enable, engage, kindle, prompt, propel, pump up, turn on, vivify 7 animate, enliven, juice up, liven up, quicken, trigger 8 energize, initiate, mobilize, switch on, vitalize 9 intermesh, stimulate 10 predispose
activated ___: 4 mine 6 carbon, sludge 7 alumina
___-activated: 5 voice
activated by
combining form: 5 -ergic
activation: 4 spur 9 awakening
active: 4 bold, busy, go-go, live, spry 5 about, agile, alert, alive, astir, brisk, fresh, jazzy, peppy, perky, quick, ready, voice 6 at work, daring, feisty, frisky, in play, lively, living, moving, nimble, on duty, speedy, strong 7 animate, dynamic, engaged, flowing, healthy, in force, on the go, pushing, roaring, rocking, rolling, running, serving, working, zealous 8 animated, bustling, diligent, employed, forceful, in effect, involved, occupied, spirited, swarming, tireless, vigorous, youthful 9 assiduous, effective, energetic, enlivened, laborious, on the move, operating, sprightly, streaming, strenuous, vivacious 10 aggressive, unflagging, up and about
become ~: 4 stir
combining form: 7 -kinetic
not ~: 4 idle, retd. 5 inert 7 retired
one: 4 doer
starter: 4 over 5 radio, retro
active ___: 3 sun 4 duty, mass, site, wear 5 layer 6 reason 7 service
activist: 4 doer 7 fanatic 8 militant
concern: 5 cause
activity: 3 ado, job 4 life, task, to-do, work 5 doing, hobby, labor, stunt 6 action, bustle, energy, hoopla, hustle, motion 7 pastime, project, pursuit, venture 8 endeavor, exercise, exertion, function, industry, interest, movement 9 animation, avocation, operation 10 discipline, enterprise, excitement, liveliness, occupation
combining form: 7 -kinesis
___ activity: 5 solar 7 optical
act of ___: 3 God, war 5 faith
act on a ___: 5 hunch
Act One
author: Moss Hart
actor: 3 ham 4 fake, lead, star 5 mimic, party 6 artist, emoter, mummer, player 7 trouper 8 imposter, impostor, thespian 9 performer 10 leading man, understudy
blunder: 5 fluff
concern: 5 lines 6 script 7 billing
direction: 4 exit 5 enter
goal: 4 part, role
workplace: 3 set 5 stage
actors: 4 cast 6 troupe 7 company
org.: 3 AEA, SAG 5 AFTRA
Actors' ___: 6 Equity
___ Actors Guild: 6 Screen
actress: 3 ham 4 diva, lead, star 5 actor 6 artist, emoter, player 7 ingénue, starlet, trouper 8 thespian, virtuoso 9 performer 10 prima donna
actresses: 4 cast 6 troupe 7 company
acts: 4 does 9 res gestae
group of ~: 5 revue 6 review
Acts: 4 book
follower: 6 Romans
preceder: 4 John
Acts ___ Apostles: 5 of the
Acts of Faith
author: Erich Segal
act the ___: 4 fool
actual: 2 so 4 just, live, real, true, very 5 exact, right 6 living 7 certain, correct, de facto, genuine, literal, sincere 8 absolute, bona fide, concrete, definite, existent, existing, explicit, material, physical, positive, tangible, truthful, verified 9 authentic, confirmed, happening, veritable 10 definitive, historical, true-to-life, undeniable, unimagined, unmistaken
not ~: 9 imaginary
actuality: 4 fact 5 being, right, truth 6 entity, gospel, verity 7 de facto, reality 9 existence, real world, substance 10 attainment, brass tacks, experience, phenomenon
in ~: 5 truly 6 really 7 de facto
actualization: 8 fruition
actualize: 5 begin 6 create, effect 7 achieve, develop, realize 9 implement
actualized: 9 fulfilled
not ~: 6 latent
actually: 4 just 5 quite, truly 6 indeed, in fact, really 7 de facto, in truth 8 in effect 9 in reality, literally
in Latin: 6 in esse 7 ex facto
actuary: 10 accountant
concern: 3 age 4 rate
actuate: 4 move, spur 5 cause, drive, egg on, impel, key up, rouse 6 arouse, bestir, effect, fire up, incite, induce, kindle, propel, turn on 7 animate, inspire, quicken 8 energize, mobilize, motivate, touch off 9 instigate, stimulate
actuation: 4 spur 7 impulse
Act your ___!: 3 age
acuate: 5 sharp 7 pointed 9 sharpened
___ a cucumber: 6 cool as
Acuff: 3 Roy
acuity: 3 wit 5 depth, sense 8 eagle eye, keenness 9 intellect, sharpness, vigilance
mental ~: 6 brains
___ acuity: 6 visual
acumen: 3 wit 4 wits 5 depth, grasp, guile 6 brains, genius, reason, sanity, smarts, wisdom 7 cunning, finesse, insight 8 judgment, keenness, sagacity 9 awareness, ingenuity, intellect, intuition, mentality, reasoning, sharpness, smartness 10 astuteness, brilliance, cleverness, horse sense, perception, shrewdness
acuminate: 4 hone, whet 5 sharp 7 sharpen

acuminous: **5** sharp
Acura: **3** car **4** auto **5** Honda **10** automobile
model: **3** CSX, MDX, NSX, RDX, RSX, SLX, TSX **5** Vigor **6** Legend **7** Integra
__ a customer: **5** one to
acute: **4** dire, fine, keen, sore **5** canny, grave, quick, ready, sharp, smart, vital **6** accent, astute, clever, severe, shrewd, shrill, strong, sudden, urgent **7** crucial, cutting, exigent, intense, pungent, racking, raucous, serious, violent **8** critical, decisive, deep-felt, exigeant, incisive, keen-eyed, lynx-eyed, piercing, pressing, profound, vigilant **9** astucious, desperate, exquisite, important, intuitive, sagacious **10** discerning, imperative, insightful, perceptive, pronounced
combining form: **3** oxy-
make ~: **7** sharpen
acute __: **5** angle **6** accent
acute-__: **4** care
acutely: **4** very **5** sharp **6** keenly, vastly **8** severely **9** extremely
acuteness: **3** wit **4** wits **7** gravity **9** extremity, intensity
ACV: **10** hovercraft
ad: **4** bill, plug **5** blurb, flier, flyer, pitch, promo **6** come-on **7** leaflet **8** circular **9** billboard, publicity
agency account: **6** client
answer an: **5** apply
award: **4** Clio
business: **6** agency
classified ~ abbr.: **3** EEO, EOE
directive: **3** buy **6** act now
free media ~: **3** PSA
infinitum: **4** ever **5** no end **7** forever
Internet ~: **6** banner
lib: **6** freely **7** offhand **9** improvise **10** off the cuff
name: **5** brand
personal ~ abbr.: **3** SWF, SWM
place the same ~: **5** rerun
publisher ~: **5** blurb
realty ~ abbr.: **3** EIK, fpl., rms. **4** bdrm., bsmt.
rem: **7** germane **8** directly, material, relevant **9** pertinent **10** to the point
sign: **4** neon
space: **6** linage **7** lineage
spiel: **4** hype
target: **5** buyer
teaser ~: **5** promo
two-page ~: **6** spread
word: **3** new **4** free, sale
ad __: **3** fin, hoc, inf., int., loc., rem, val. **4** init., quem **5** infin., litem, vitam, vivum **6** damnum, hocery, patres, verbum **7** feminam, gloriam, hockery, hominem, initium, interim, libitum, nauseam, valorem
ad __ per aspera: **5** astra
ad-__: **3** lib **6** libbed, libber
ad-__ committee: **3** hoc
__ ad: **4** want **7** display
A.D.: **4** Hope
coiner: **4** Bede **5** Baeda
part: **4** Anno **6** Domini
Ada: **4** city, town **5** Maris, Rehan **8** Comstock, Huxtable, language, Lovelace
alternative: ***see*** computer language
author: Vladimir Nabokov
locale: **4** Okla. **8** Oklahoma
ADA
member: **3** DDS, DMD
adage: **3** saw **5** axiom, maxim, moral, motto **6** byword, dictum, saying, truism **7** bromide, precept, proverb **8** aphorism, apothegm **10** apophthegm
like an ~: **5** pithy
start: **4** if at **6** no news
adages: **4** lore
adagio: **4** slow **5** music, tempo **6** slowly
faster than ~: **7** andante
slower than ~: **5** largo, lento
Adagio for Strings
composer: Samuel Barber
adagio non __: **6** troppo
Adah
father: **4** Elon
husband: **4** Esau
son: **7** Eliphaz
Adair: **3** Red **7** Deborah
__-a-Dale: **4** Alan **5** Allan
Adam: **3** Ant **4** Bede, Rich, Wade, West **5** Arkin, Smith **6** Powell, Robert **7** Adolphe, Baldwin, Sandler **9** Dalgliesh **10** Cartwright, Mickiewicz
brother: **3** Joe **4** Hoss **9** Little Joe
first wife: **6** Lilith
grandson: **4** Enos **5** Enoch
habitation: **4** Eden
mate: **3** Eve
son: **4** Abel, Cain, Seth
to Ben: **3** son
Adam __: **4** Bede
Adam 12 (NBC drama)
cast: Kent McCord (Jim Reed) Martin Milner (Pete Malloy)
org.: LAPD
producer: Jack Webb
Adam, Adolphe
ballet: Giselle
Adam and Eve
painter: Albrecht Dürer
Adam and Eve __ raft!: **3** on a
adamant: **4** firm, iron **5** fixed, flint, rigid, stony, tough **6** steely, stoney, wilful **7** hard-set, piggish, willful **8** obdurate, resolute, stubborn **9** hard-nosed, immovable, implicable, insistent, obstinate, pigheaded, steadfast, tenacious, unbending **10** determined, hardbitten, headstrong, inexorable, inflexible, relentless, set in stone, unshakable, unswayable, unyielding
be ~: **6** insist
adamantine: **4** firm, hard **5** stern **6** steely **7** lithoid **8** indurate **9** lithoidal **10** inexorable, inflexible
Adam Bede
author: George Eliot
character: **4** Rann, Seth **5** Burge, Dinah, Hetty **6** Arthur, Bartle, Hester, Irwine, Joshua, Martin, Massey, Morris, Poyser, Rachel, Sorrel **7** Lisbeth, Mattias **8** Jonathan
Adam Clayton __: **6** Powell
Adam had 'em
poet: Ogden Nash
Adams: **3** Amy, Doc, Don, Sam **4** Edie, Joey, John, Maud, Nick, peak **5** Ansel, Bryan, Cindy, Gerry, Henry, Julie, Mason, mount, Oleta **6** Brooke, Hannah, Samuel **7** Abigail, Richard **8** mountain
locale: **8** Cascades **10** Washington
Adam's __: **3** ale, cup, Rib **5** apple **6** Bridge
__ Adams: **5** Alice, Patch, Sarah
Adam's ale: **5** water
Adams, Ansel: **12** photographer
milieu: **8** Yosemite **10** California
Adams, Edie: **6** singer **7** actress
spouse: Ernie Kovacs
Adams, Gerry
land: **4** Eire
org.: **3** IRA
Adams, John: **9** president
alma mater: **7** Harvard
excellent instrument: **3** pen
former occupation: **6** lawyer
home: **6** Quincy
opponent: **9** Jefferson
V.P.: **9** Jefferson
wife: **7** Abigail
Adams, John Quincy: **9** president
alma mater: **7** Harvard
former occupation: **6** lawyer
mother: **7** Abigail
opponent: **4** Clay **7** Jackson **8** Crawford
V.P.: **7** Calhoun
wife: **6** Louisa
Adam's-needle: **5** yucca
Adamson: **3** Joy
pet: **4** Elsa **7** lioness
Adam's Rib (1949 film)
cast: Tom Ewell, Katharine Hepburn, Judy Holliday, Spencer Tracy, David Wayne
director: George Cukor
adapt: **2** do **3** fit **4** edit, gear, suit, tune **5** alter, enure, inure, shape **6** adjust, attune, change, harden, make do, modify, orient, revise, square, tailor **7** conform, convert, fashion, make fit, prepare, qualify, remodel, restyle **8** accustom, go native, regulate **9** acclimate, acquiesce, condition, get used to, reconcile **10** assimilate, come around
(to): **7** get used
adaptable: **5** fluid **6** docile, lissom, mobile, supple, usable **7** lissome, pliable, useable **8** flexible, obedient **9** all-around, alterable, compliant, easygoing, malleable, resilient, revocable, tractable, versatile **10** adjustable, changeable, compatible, convenient, modifiable
adaptation: **7** version **9** agreement, allowance, refitting, reworking, variation **10** adjustment, alteration, compliance, conversion, remodeling
Adaptation (2002 film)
cast: Nicolas Cage, Meryl Streep, Tilda Swinton
director: Spike Jonze
Adar: **5** month **6** Hebrew
holiday: **5** Purim
predecessor: **6** Shebat, Shevat
successor: **5** Nisan
__ a dare!: **5** Not on
__ a dark and stormy...: **5** It was
__ a darn: **4** give
__ a date: **3** set
__ a date!: **3** It's
...a date which will live in __: **6** infamy
__-A-Day: **3** One
__ a day..., An: **5** apple
...__ a day in June?: **6** rare as
__ a day's work: **5** all in
ADC: **4** asst.
part of ~: **4** aide, camp
Adcock: **3** Joe **5** Fleur
add: **3** say, sum, tag, tot **4** go on, lace, tack **5** affix, annex, count, dub in, put in, put on, sum up, tag on, tally, total, tot up **6** accrue, adjoin, append, appose, chip in, edge in, extend, figure, fold in, foot up, hook on, insert, number, reckon, slap on, stir in, suffix, tack on, take on, toss in, tote up **7** amplify, augment, bring to, compute, count up, enlarge, include, overdub, stick on, subjoin, thicken, throw in **8** figure in, increase, multiply, tabulate **9** calculate, enumerate, interject, introduce, keep score **10** complement, contribute, count heads, supplement
a lane to: **7** broaden
fuel to fire: **4** spur **5** rouse **6** whip up, work up **7** agitate **9** stimulate
liquor to: **5** spike **7** fortify
on: **5** affix, annex **6** append, attach, expand
(on): **3** tag **5** build
to: **4** grow, hike, rise **5** boost, build, raise, swell, widen **6** append, enrich, expand, extend, step up **7** amplify, augment, broaden, build up, enhance, enlarge, magnify, spice up **8** compound, escalate, expand on, heighten, increase, lengthen **9** aggravate, branch out, increment, intensify, reinforce, spread out **10** accumulate, aggrandize, complement, exacerbate, exaggerate, expand upon, strengthen, supplement
to the payroll: **4** hire **6** employ, engage, sign on, take on **7** bring on
up: **3** sum **4** tote **5** count, prove, tally, total **6** accrue, amount, figure, reckon **9** aggregate, enumerate, keep score, make sense **10** count heads
up again: **5** retot
up to: **4** make, mean **5** equal, spell **6** number, reveal **7** contain, express, signify **8** comprise, indicate **9** aggregate
up (to): **6** amount
value to: **6** better **7** build up, elevate, enhance, fortify **8** decorate **9** embellish **10** supplement
water to: **4** thin **6** weaken
zest to: **5** pep up **6** excite, perk up, spur on, stir up, vivify **7** animate **8** energize, vitalize **10** exhilarate, invigorate
zing to: **5** spice **6** pepper
add __: **4** up to
Addams: **4** Chas, Jane **5** Gomez **7** Charles, Pugsley **8** Morticia **9** Wednesday
__ Addams: **4** Chas.

Addams Family, The (1991 film)
cast: Anjelica Huston, Raul Julia, Christopher Lloyd, Christina Ricci
director: Barry Sonnenfeld
Addams Family, The (ABC sitcom)
cast: John Astin (Gomez Addams)
Ted Cassidy (Lurch/Thing)
Jackie Coogan (Uncle Fester)
Carolyn Jones (Morticia Addams)
Lisa Loring (Wednesday Addams)
Blossom Rock (Grandmama)
Felix Silla (Cousin Itt)
Ken Weatherwax (Pugsley Addams)
dance: 5 tango
lion: 8 Kitty Kat
nickname: 4 Tish
addax: 8 antelope
relative: *see* antelope
added: 3 new 5 extra, fresh, other, ran up 7 another, further, updated 9 aggregate 10 additional
something ~: 6 augend
to: 4 plus
added ___: 4 line 5 entry, value
___-added: 5 value
___ added attraction: 5 extra
___-added tax: 5 value
addendum: 2 PS 4 supp. 5 annex, extra, rider 7 adjunct, codicil 8 appendix 9 appendage, extension 10 attachment, postscript, supplement
insurance ~: 9 amendment
second: 3 pps
third: 4 ppps
adder: 5 snake 6 animal, summer 7 reptile, serpent 9 milk snake
relative: *see* snake
___ adder: 4 milk, puff 7 chicken, spotted
Adderley, Cannonball
genre: 4 jazz
instrument: 3 sax 7 alto sax
real first name: Julian
Adderley, Nat
genre: 4 jazz
instrument: 6 cornet 7 trumpet
addict: 3 fan, nut 4 buff 5 fiend, freak, hound 6 zealot 7 devotee, fanatic, habitué 8 follower 10 aficionado, chocoholic, enthusiast
combining form: 5 -holic 6 -aholic
addiction: 5 habit 9 obsession 10 dependance, dependence, sweet tooth
Addie: 4 Joss
adding
device: 6 abacus 10 calculator
adding ___: 7 machine
Adding Machine, The
author: Elmer Rice
Addis Ababa: 4 city, town 7 capital
locale: 3 Eth. 8 Ethiopia
Addison
partner: 6 Steele
addition: 3 ell 4 gain, hike, plus, wing 5 annex, bonus, boost, extra, raise, rider 6 lean-to 7 accrual, adjunct, codicil, summing 8 appendix, counting, dividend, figuring, increase, totaling 9 accession, accretion, appendage, expansion, extension, increment, reckoning, summation 10 arithmetic, attachment, elongation, postscript, supplement, tabulating
column: 4 ones, tens 8 hundreds
house ~: 3 ell 5 annex
in ~: 3 and, too, yet 4 also, else, more, over, plus 5 again 6 as well, at that 7 besides 8 likewise, moreover
injury ~: 6 insult
in ~ (prefix): 3 sur-
in ~ to: 3 and 6 beyond 9 apart from, aside from
problem: 3 sum
additional: 3 aux., new 4 else, more, plus, supp. 5 extra, fresh, other, spare 6 longer, second 7 affixed, further 8 appended, optional 9 ancillary, auxiliary, increased 10 extraneous
in ads: 4 xtra
ones: 6 others
prefix: 3 sur-
additionally: 3 and, too, yet 4 also, else, over, then 5 again 6 to boot 7 besides, further 8 likewise, moreover 9 on the side
addle: 5 cloud, floor, mix up, spoil, throw 6 baffle, bemuse, go sour, muddle, puzzle, rattle 7 confuse, flummox, fluster, nonplus, perplex, shake up, stupefy, unhinge 8 befuddle, bewilder, confound, scramble 9 disorient, inebriate, unbalance 10 discompose, disconcert, intoxicate
ender: 5 pated
addled: 4 asea, hazy 5 at sea, dizzy, tipsy 6 punchy, shaken 7 fuddled, mixed up, out of it, rattled, unglued 9 befuddled, slaphappy 10 bewildered
addlepate
see ninny
addlepated
see foolish
add-on: 4 plus 5 rider 8 appendix 9 accessory, extension, surcharge 10 peripheral, supplement
address: 3 aim, woo 4 call, home, talk 5 abode, hallo, hillo, house, hullo, label, level, orate, route, see to, speak, spiel, title 6 accost, direct, halloa, halloo, hallow, have at, hilloa, hulloo, preach, recite, salute, sermon, speech, take up 7 bespeak, consign, discuss, domicil, focus on, lecture, lodging, monolog, oration, pep talk 8 attend to, domicile, dwelling, engage in, inscribe, location, rhetoric 9 chalk talk, discourse, have a go at, honorific, monologue, readiness, residence, sermonize, touch base, undertake 10 apostrophe, plug away at, recitation, salutation, take care of
abbr.: 2 rd., st. 3 ave., hts., rte. 4 blvd.
change one's ~: 4 move
courteous ~: 3 sir 4 ma'am 5 madam
familiar ~: 3 bub, mac 5 deary, kiddo 6 dearie
location: 3 env. 8 envelope
make an ~: 5 orate
nonspecific ~: 3 GPO
palindromic ~: 3 bub 4 ma'am 5 madam
part: 3 zip 4 city 5 PO box, state 7 zip code
phrase: 6 care of
preceder: 4 name
addressee: 6 tenant 8 occupant 10 inhabitant
adduce: 4 cite, show 5 quote 6 affirm, impute, reason 7 mention 8 point out 10 illustrate
ade: 5 drink 6 cooler 8 beverage 9 soft drink
starter: 4 lime 5 block, lemon, stock 6 cannon, orange
___ a deaf ear: 4 turn
___ a deal: 3 cut
___ a deal!: 3 It's
___-a-Dee-Doo-Dah: 3 Zip
___, a deer: 3 doe
Ade, George: 6 writer
nickname: Aesop of Indiana
work: Artie
The College Widow
The County Chairman
Doc Horne
Fables in Slang
Forty Modern Fables
Hand-Made Fables
Modern Fables
The Old Time Saloon
Peggy from Paris
Pink Marsh
The Sultan of Sulu
Adela: 5 Turin 7 St. Johns 8 Nicolson
Adelaide: 4 city, port, town 7 Manning
locale: 9 Australia
river: 7 Torrens
Adelaide's Lament
composer: Frank Loesser
Adele: 4 Mara 7 Astaire, Jergens, Simpson, Wiseman
to Fred: 3 sis
Adélie ___: 4 Land 5 Coast 7 penguin
Adelina: 5 Patti
___ Adeline: 5 Sweet
Adelle: 5 Davis
Aden: 4 city, port, town
locale: 5 Yemen
Adenauer: 6 Konrad 7 Der Alte
see also German
adenoidal: 5 nasal
adept: 3 ace, apt 4 able, deft, good, whiz 5 crack, great, handy, quick, ready, savvy, sharp, slick, smart 6 adroit, artful, au fait, clever, expert, facile, habile, master, nimble, smooth, wizard 7 capable, hotshot, maestro, old hand, skilled, veteran 8 delicate, dextrous, masterly, skillful, talented, topnotch, virtuoso 9 dexterous, efficient, masterful, on the ball, on the beam, practiced, qualified, top-drawer, top-flight 10 past master, proficient, specialist, well-versed
adeptly: 4 neat, well 7 rightly 8 laudably
adeptness: 5 craft, skill 7 ability, finesse, mastery, sleight 9 dexterity 10 efficiency, expertness, nimbleness
adequacy: 7 fitness, utility 8 capacity 10 capability, competence, efficiency
words of ~: 6 it'll do
adequate: 2 OK 3 fit 4 able, fair, good, okay, okeh, okey, so-so, tidy 6 decent, enough, up to it 7 capable, livable 8 all right, liveable, middling, passable, suitable 9 competent, effective, efficient, qualified, requisite, tolerable, unnotable, up to grade 10 acceptable, fairly good, sufficient
be ~: 2 do 5 serve 7 satisfy, suffice
informally: 4 enuf
more than ~: 5 ample
not ~: 4 puny 5 scant
adequately: 4 so-so, well 7 rightly 9 copiously, fittingly, tolerably 10 abundantly, acceptably, fairly well, well enough
Adeste ___: 7 Fideles
adhere: 4 bond, glue, hold, join 5 cling, paste, stick 6 attach, be true, cement, cleave, fasten, hang on 7 abide by, be loyal, conform 8 hold fast 9 stick fast 10 toe the line
to: 4 heed, keep, meet, mind, obey 6 accept, follow, fulfil, redeem 7 abide by, fulfill, observe, respect 8 belong to, carry out 9 agree with 10 comply with
adherence: 7 loyalty 8 cohesion, devotion, sticking, traction 9 coherence, constancy, fixedness, stability 10 allegiance, dedication, observance
adherent: 3 fan, nut 5 pupil 6 backer, helper 7 devotee, sponsor 8 advocate, believer, disciple, follower, henchman, loyalist, partisan 9 sectarian, supporter, worshiper 10 aficionado, enthusiast
suffix: 3 -ist, -ite 5 -arian
adherents: 6 school 9 following
adhesive: 3 gum 4 glue 5 epoxy, gluey, gooey, gummy, paste, putty, tacky 6 cement, clingy, sticky 7 stickum, viscose, viscous 8 clinging, fixative, mucilage
pane ~: 5 putty
philatelist's ~: 5 hinge
adhesive ___: 4 tape 6 factor 7 bandage, binding, plaster
ad-hoc: 9 impromptu, temporary 10 improvised, pro tempore
coalition: 4 bloc
Adidas: 6 sneaks 8 sneakers
rival: 3 Ked 4 Avia, Nike 6 Reebok 8 Converse
___ a diet: 4 go on
adieu: 3 bye 4 exit, ta-ta 5 leave 6 bye-bye, so long 7 goodbye, parting 8 farewell, Godspeed, sayonara 9 departure
bid ~: 6 depart
in Hawaiian: 5 aloha
in Italian: 4 ciao
in Latin: 3 ave 4 vale
in Spanish: 5 adios
Adige: 5 river
city on the ~: 5 Trent 6 Trento, Verona
locale: 5 Italy
a dime a ___: 5 dozen
___ a dim view: 4 take
adios: 3 bye 4 ta-ta 6 bye-bye, so long 7 goodbye 8 au revoir, farewell, Godspeed, sayonara
in French: 5 adieu

in Hawaiian: 5 aloha
in Italian: 4 ciao
in Latin: 3 ave 4 vale
adipose: 4 oily 5 beefy, fatty, fubsy, obese, plump, pudgy, pursy, stout 6 chubby, fleshy, portly, pyknic, rotund, stocky, zaftig, zoftig 7 paunchy 8 roly-poly 9 corpulent 10 overweight
___-à-dire: 4 c'est
Adirondack ___: 5 chair
Adirondacks: 3 mts. 4 mtns. 5 range 9 mountains
locale: 7 New York
mountain: 5 Marcy
___ a disadvantage: 5 put at
___ a distance: 4 from
adit: 4 ramp 5 entry 6 portal, tunnel 7 ingress 8 entrance
adjacency: 8 nearness 10 contiguity
adjacent: 4 near, next, nigh 5 close, handy 6 at hand, beside, nearby 7 close by 8 abutting, imminent, next-door, touching 9 alongside, bordering, immediate, impending, proximate 10 contiguous, convenient, juxtaposed
lie ~ to: 4 abut, join, meet 5 touch, verge 6 adjoin 8 border on, neighbor
to: 4 near 6 beside
(to): 4 next
adjective: 4 word 8 modifier 9 attribute, qualifier 10 identifier
modifier: 3 adv. 6 adverb
suffix: 3 -ant, -ary, -ate, -ent, -ern, -ese, -est, -eth, -ful, -ial, -ian, -ier, -ile, -ine, -ior, -ish, -ive, -oid, -ory, -ose, -ous, -tic, -ule 4 -able, -eous, -etic, -fold, -free, -ible, -ical, -ious, -less, -like, -long, -most, -otic, -some, -tory, -ward 5 -ative, -atory, -esque, -istic, -itive, -orial, -proof, -tious, -ulent, -ulous, -urous, -wards 6 -aceous, -escent, -itious, -worthy
adjoin: 3 add 4 abut, link, meet 5 affix, annex, touch, unite, verge 6 append, attach, border, couple 7 connect 8 border on, neighbor 9 juxtapose
adjoining: 4 near, next 6 beside, nearby 8 next-door 9 impinging 10 approximal, connecting, contiguous, convenient, juxtaposed
adjourn: 3 end 4 halt, quit, stay, stop 5 cease, close, delay 6 finish, put off, recess, shelve, wind up, wrap up 7 break up, hold off, suspend 8 conclude, dissolve, pack it in, postpone 9 terminate 10 call it a day
adjournment: 3 end 5 close, delay 7 respite
adjt.: 4 asst.
see also adjutant
adjudge: 3 try 4 rate 6 decide, regard 7 account, referee 8 appraise, sentence 9 arbitrate
___ adjudicata: 3 res
adjudicate: 3 try 4 hear, rule 6 decide, settle, umpire 7 mediate, referee 9 arbitrate, determine, negotiate
adjudication: 6 ruling 7 verdict 8 decision
adjudicator: 6 umpire 7 arbiter, referee 10 peacemaker
adjunct: 5 extra 6 helper 7 fitting 8 addendum, addition, appendix, henchman, offshoot 9 accessory, appendage, assistant, associate, auxiliary, extension 10 attachment, elongation, supplement
adjuration: 4 oath
adjure: 3 beg 4 pray, urge 5 order 6 attest, enjoin 7 beseech, command, entreat, implore, require, swear in 8 obligate 10 supplicate
adjust: 3 fit, fix, pay, set 4 gear, suit, true, tune 5 adapt, align, aline, alter, fix up, focus, reset, scale, tweak 6 attune, change, doctor, harden, modify, orient, refund, repair, settle, square, tailor, tune up 7 arrange, balance, conform, correct, fashion, improve, prepare, realign, rectify, redress, restyle, sharpen 8 accustom, fine-tune, modulate, regulate, set right 9 acquiesce, calibrate, get over it, habituate, negotiate, reconcile 10 assimilate, coordinate, fiddle with, straighten, tinker with
adjustable: 7 movable, pliable 8 flexible, moveable 9 adaptable, versatile
adjustable-___ mortgage: 4 rate
adjusted: 5 ready 8 prepared
adjusted ___ income: 5 gross
___-adjusting: 4 self
adjustment: 5 tweak 6 change, fixing, payoff, repair 7 fitting, revisal, setting, shaping 8 revision 9 agreement, allotment, allowance, balancing, refitting, reshaping 10 adaptation, alteration, compromise, concession, correction, regulation, settlement
adjustments
make ~: 5 adapt
adjutant: 4 aide, asst. 6 helper 9 auxiliary
adjutant ___: 4 bird 5 stork 7 general
Adlai: 9 Stevenson
opponent: 3 Ike
running mate: 5 Estes
Adlai ___ Stevenson: 5 Ewing
Adler: 3 Lou 4 Kurt 5 Irene, Larry, Peter, Polly 6 Alfred, Luther, Stella 8 Mortimer
Adler, Larry
forte: 9 harmonica
ad lib: 4 quip 6 devise, fake it, make up, whip up, wing it 9 improvise, play by ear
ad lib.: 6 freely
ad-lib: 7 offhand 8 informal 9 extempore, impromptu, unplanned 10 improvised, off-the-cuff, unprepared
comedy: 6 improv
Adlon: 5 Percy 6 Pamela
adm.
employer: 3 USN
see also admiral
___ Adm.: 4 Rear
admeasure: 9 apportion
admin.: 3 mgr., mgt. 4 mgmt.
admin. ___: 4 asst.
administer: 3 run, use 4 boss, deal, give, head, keep, rule, tend 5 apply, issue, offer, serve 6 direct, govern, handle, impose, manage, supply, tender 7 conduct, control, deliver, dole out, execute, furnish, inflict, mete out, oversee, preside, proffer, provide 8 carry out, disburse, dispense 9 apportion, authorize, supervise 10 contribute, distribute, measure out, ride herd on, run the show
administration: 3 ins 4 rule, term 5 board, power, reign 6 agency, bureau, policy, record, regime, tenure 7 cabinet, command, conduct, control, running 8 advisors, handling, top brass
___ administration: 6 public
administrative ___: 3 law 5 leave 6 county 9 assistant
administrator: 3 CEO 4 boss, dean, exec, head, prin. 5 chair, chief 6 honcho, leader, tycoon, warden 7 curator, manager, officer 8 director, executor, governor, official, overseer 9 principal
admirable: 4 fine, good, keen, neat, nice, okay 5 grand, great, legit, moral, noble, super 6 lovely, peachy, proper, superb, worthy 7 ethical 8 all right, laudable, pleasant, pleasing, splendid, superior 9 agreeable, beautiful, copacetic, deserving, estimable, excellent, exemplary, exquisite, hunky-dory, praisable, reputable, wonderful 10 acceptable, attractive, beneficial, creditable, out of sight, super-duper
act: 4 feat
name meaning ~: 7 Miranda
Admirable Crichton, The
author: James M. Barrie
admirably: 4 well 7 rightly 8 laudably, worthily
admiral: 4 rank
answer to an ~: 3 aye 6 aye aye 9 aye aye sir
org.: 3 USN
subordinate: 4 capt. 7 captain
white ~: 3 bug 6 insect
WWI German ~: 4 Spee
WWII: 6 Halsey, Nimitz
see also navy
___ admiral: 3 red 4 rear 5 fleet, white
___-admiral: 4 vice
Admiral
alternative: appliance brand
Admiral ___ Fleet: 5 of the
Admiral Benbow ___: 3 Inn
admiration: 4 love 5 favor, honor 6 esteem, homage, praise, regard, wonder 7 respect, valuing, worship 8 approval, idolatry 9 adoration, affection, amazement, deference, marveling, obeisance, reverence 10 compliment, estimation, popularity, veneration, wonderment
exclamation: 6 good-oh, touché
___ Admiration Society: 6 Mutual
admire: 4 laud, like, look, love, ogle 5 adore, go for, honor 6 esteem, praise, regard, revere 7 adulate, cherish, glorify, idolize, respect, worship 8 hand it to, look up to, venerate 9 care about 10 appreciate
oneself: 5 preen
admired: 7 beloved
one: 4 hero, idol
admirer: 3 fan, nut 4 beau, buff 5 freak, hound, liker, lover, swain, wooer 6 patron, rooter, suitor 7 booster, devotee, fancier, groupie 8 disciple, follower, partisan 9 boyfriend, inamorato, supporter 10 enthusiast, girlfriend, sweetheart
group: 4 cult
admiring: 6 loving 7 valuing 10 respectful
greatly ~: 5 in awe
admissibility: 7 fitness
admissible: 2 OK 4 good, okay 5 jural, legal, licit, right 6 lawful 7 allowed 8 passable 9 allowable, permitted, pertinent, tolerable, tolerated, warranted 10 acceptable, applicable, concedable, in the rules, legitimate, reasonable
admission: 4 pass 5 entry 6 access, assent, avowal, entrée, ticket 7 ingress, receipt 8 entrance 9 accession, affidavit, allowance, assertion, enrolment, reception, statement, testimony 10 acceptance, concession, confession, deposition, disclosure, divulgence, enrollment, initiation, permission, profession, revelation, unbosoming
gain ~: 5 get in
price of ~: 4 fare
refuse ~: 5 block 6 forbid 7 exclude, keep out 9 freeze out
requirement: 6 ticket
select for ~: 3 tap
admit: 2 OK 3 own 4 avow, fess, okay, take 5 adopt, agree, allow, enrol, go for, grant, house, let in, let on, own up, see in 6 accede, accept, accord, affirm, assent, avouch, comply, enroll, expose, fess up, induct, listen, open up, reveal, take in 7 concede, confess, confide, confirm, declare, divulge, embrace, include, lay bare, own up to, profess, receive, shelter, welcome 8 disclose, face up to, initiate, proclaim, stand for 9 come clean, make known, put up with, recognize, sign off on 10 concur with, give the nod
defeat: 4 quit 5 yield
guilt: 9 apologize, beg pardon 10 make amends
to: 5 let on
admit ___: 3 one
admittance: 5 entry 6 access, entrée 7 ingress, passage 8 entrance 9 inclusion
refuse ~ to: 7 exclude
admitted: 5 known, let in 10 undisputed
be ~: 5 get in
admittedly: 6 indeed, really
admix: 5 alloy, blend 6 mingle 7 blend in, combine 8 compound 9 commingle, interlard 10 amalgamate
admixed: 6 impure
admixture: 5 blend 6 fusion 7 mélange 8 blending 10 sprinkling
admonish: 3 rag, rap 4 urge, warn 5 chide, scold 6 advise, berate, exhort, preach, punish, rebuke 7 caution, censure, counsel,

lecture, reprove, tell off, upbraid **8** forewarn, threaten **9** criticize, reprimand
admonisher
comment: **3** shh, tsk **6** tsk tsk
admonition: **5** alert **6** caveat, homily, lesson, notice, rebuke **7** caution, censure, warning **8** berating, reminder, reproval **10** correction, injunction, upbraiding
mom's ~: **4** don't **6** be good, be nice
theater ~: **3** shh **4** hush
Adnan: **4** Etel **9** Khashoggi
ado: **4** flap, fuss, spat, stir, tiff **5** furor, hoo-ha, melee, scene, stink **6** bother, bustle, clamor, dustup, flurry, fracas, hoopla, hubbub, racket, ruckus, rumpus, tumult, uproar **7** big deal, blether, clutter, fanfare, travail, trouble, turmoil **8** activity, brouhaha, busyness, foofaraw, rowdydow, squabble **9** commotion, confusion, hue and cry, whoop-de-do **10** difficulty, excitement, hullabaloo, hurly-burly
without further ~: **3** now, PDQ **6** at once **8** promptly, right now **9** forthwith, right away
Ado ___: **5** Annie
___ Ado About Nothing: **4** Much
Ado Annie
what ~ couldn't do: **5** say no
adobe: **4** clay **5** brick
ingredient: **5** straw
___: a Dog: **3** Lad
adolescence: **5** teens, youth **7** boyhood, puberty **8** girlhood **10** immaturity
adolescent: **3** kid **4** girl, teen **5** child, minor, young, youth **6** boyish **7** girlish, puerile, teenage **8** immature, juvenile, teenager, youthful **9** beardless, half-grown, pubescent, stripling, youngster
affliction: **4** acne
mustache: **4** wisp
no longer ~: **5** adult, of age **6** mature **7** grown up
Adolf: **7** Windaus **9** Butenandt, von Baeyer
___, a dollar..., A: **6** dillar
Adolph: **4** Ochs, Rupp **5** Green, Zukor **6** Caesar
Adolphe: **3** Sax **4** Adam **6** Menjou
Adonai: **3** God **4** Lord **5** Jahve, Jahwe, Yahve, Yahwe **6** Jahveh, Jahweh, Yahveh, Yahweh **8** Almighty
Adonais: **4** poem **5** elegy
author: Percy Bysshe Shelley
honoree: **5** Keats
last word of ~: **3** are
Adonis: **6** beauty
daughter: **5** Beroe
lover: **9** Aphrodite
parent: **6** Myrrha **7** Cinyras
slayer of ~: **4** boar
son: **6** Golgos
___-a-doodle-doo!: **4** Cock
___-a-dope: **4** rope
adopt: **3** use **4** okay, pass, pick, take **5** admit, allow, co-opt, go for **6** accept, assent, assume, borrow, choose, comply, follow, listen, prefer, take in, take on, take up **7** approve, embrace, espouse, include, observe, welcome **8** stand for, take over **9** put up with, recognize, sign off on **10** concur with, give the nod, legitimize, settle upon
adoptee: **4** ward
shelter ~: **3** cat, dog **5** stray
adoption: **8** approval, espousal **9** fosterage, selection **10** acceptance, assumption, employment
org.: **4** SPCA
adorable: **4** cute, dear **6** comely, dreamy, lovely, pretty **7** angelic, darling, lovable, winning, winsome **8** alluring, charming, fetching, gorgeous, handsome, heavenly, loveable, pleasing, precious, stunning **9** angelical, appealing, covetable, delicious, desirable, endearing **10** attractive, delectable, delightful
___ adorable..., A: **5** you're
adoration: **4** love **5** ardor, honor **6** esteem, homage, praise, prayer **7** passion, worship **8** devotion, idolatry **9** extolment, hankering, puppy love, reverence **10** admiration, attachment, estimation, exaltation, veneration
adore: **3** dig **4** laud, like, love **5** deify, eat up, enjoy, exalt, fancy, go for, honor, prize, swain **6** admire, dote on, praise, revere **7** adulate, care for, cherish, glorify, idolize, worship **8** dote upon, enshrine, fawn over, flip over, hold dear, inshrine, look up to, sanctify, treasure, venerate **9** care about, delight in
nonstandardly: **3** luv
adored: **3** pet **7** beloved **8** precious
one: **4** idol
Adorée: **5** Renee
adorer: **3** fan **5** swain **9** inamorata, inamorato
poem: **3** ode
adoring: **4** fond **6** devout, loving **7** valuing **8** enamored
one: **5** doter
adorn: **4** deck, gild, trim **5** array, color, grace **6** bedeck, doll up, emboss, enrich, purfle **7** bedizen, bejewel, deck out, dress up, encrust, enhance, festoon, flatter, furbish, garnish, gussy up, incrust, varnish **8** accouter, accoutre, beautify, decorate, emblazon, ornament, prettify, spruce up **9** bespangle, caparison, embellish, glamorize
adorned: **5** fancy **6** frilly **9** gussied up
culinarily: **5** garni
not ~: **5** plain, stark
adornment: **4** trim **5** dodad, floss, frill **6** choker, doodad, finery, geegaw, gewgaw **7** dingbat, garnish, gilding, jewelry **8** fretwork, frippery, froufrou, ornament, trimming **9** accessory, fandangle **10** decoration, embroidery
helmet ~: **7** feather
lobe ~: **4** hoop **7** earring
adornments: **9** trappings
___ a doubt: **6** beyond **7** without
___ a dozen: **5** a dime
Adrastos
domain: **5** Argos
adread: **7** terrify
___ a dream: **5** I have
adrenal ___: **5** gland **6** cortex **7** medulla
adrenaline: **7** hormone **9** energizer, stimulant **11** epinephrine
catalyst: **4** fear **5** panic **6** danger, phobia, terror
Adrian: **4** city, Lyne, Paul, pope, town, Zmed **5** Boult, Edgar **6** Balboa, Pasdar **7** Dantley, pontiff
locale: **8** Michigan
Adriatic: **3** sea
country: **3** Alb. **5** Italy **6** Bosnia **7** Albania, Croatia
gulf: **6** Venice **7** Trieste **8** Quarnero
locale: **5** Italy
peninsula: **6** Istria
river to the ~: **4** Drin **5** Adige, Piave **7** Livenza, Rubicon
town: **4** Bari, Fano **5** Zadar **6** Ancona
wind: **4** bora
Adrien: **5** Arpel, Brody
Adrienne: **4** Rich **7** Barbeau
adrift: **4** lost **5** amiss, at sea, loose, wrong **6** astray, erring **7** aimless **8** becalmed, castaway, floating, goalless, unmoored **10** unanchored, unattached
go ~: **3** err
adroit: **3** apt **4** able, deft, foxy, good, neat, spry **5** adept, canny, crack, great, handy, nifty, quick, ready, savvy, sharp, slick **6** artful, astute, au fait, clever, expert, facile, gifted, habile, nimble **7** capable, cunning, politic, skilled, trained **8** dextrous, graceful, masterly, seasoned, skillful, talented **9** astucious, competent, dexterous, efficient, ingenious, inventive, masterful, versatile **10** proficient
starter: **3** mal
adroitly: **4** ably, neat **7** handily **10** swimmingly
adroitness: **3** art **4** ease **5** craft, knack **7** ability, faculty, finesse, know-how, mastery, sleight **8** facility **9** dexterity, handiness, readiness, smartness **10** cleverness, nimbleness
adroop: **7** sagging
___ ads: **4** want
adsuki: **4** bean **6** legume
Adu: **6** Freddy
___-a-dub: **3** rub
adulate: **5** adore, honor **6** praise **7** flatter, lionize, worship **8** fawn over, gush over, kowtow to
adulated
one: **4** hero, icon, idol
adulation: **5** honor **6** homage, praise **7** worship **8** flattery **10** compliment, sycophancy
adulator: **5** toady **6** fawner, flunky, yes man **7** flunkey **8** bootlick, courtier, truckler **9** flatterer, sycophant, toadeater
adulatory: **4** oily **6** honied **7** buttery, candied, fawning, glowing, honeyed, servile, slavish **8** obeisant, toadyish, unctuous **9** laudatory **10** obsequious
adult: **3** big, man **4** ripe **5** grown, imago, of age, woman **6** mature, X-rated **7** grownup, naughty, ripened **8** full-size **9** developed, full-grown **10** fully grown
education subj.: **3** ESL
to be: **3** kid **4** teen
adulterate: **3** cut, mar, mix **4** thin **5** alloy, alter, blend, spike, sully, taint **6** debase, defile, dilute, doctor, impair, poison, weaken **7** cheapen, corrupt, degrade, devalue, pollute, vitiate **8** denature, intermix **9** attenuate, commingle, devaluate, transfuse, water down **10** amalgamate, depreciate, infiltrate
adulterated: **4** sham **6** impure, watery **7** corrupt **8** maculate
adulteration: **3** mix **7** mixture **8** impurity
adulthood: **8** majority, maturity **9** voting age
reach ~: **6** grow up, mature
adumbrate: **3** dim **4** blur, hide, hint, mark, mean, veil, warn **5** bedim, chart, cloud, cover, draft, gloom, image, paint, shade, trace **6** darken, denote, emblem, muddle, opaque, shadow, sketch, typify **7** becloud, conceal, confuse, diagram, eclipse, explain, obscure, outline, portend, portray, predict, presage, suggest **8** describe, forecast, foreshow, foretell, indicate, overcast, prophesy, rough out **9** cloud over, delineate, obfuscate, prefigure, represent, symbolize, tell about **10** allegorize, foreshadow, overshadow, silhouette
adumbration: **6** sketch
advance: **2** go **3** put **4** abet, bump, come, gain, grow, hype, lead, leap, lend, lift, loan, make, move, near, pass, plug, pose, push, rise, send, step, walk **5** boost, drive, early, exalt, go far, lobby, march, prior, raise, speed, trust **6** better, bump up, course, credit, evolve, feeler, foster, growth, hasten, inroad, look up, mature, motion, move up, propel, push on, submit, thrive, uplift **7** assault, deposit, develop, earlier, elevate, enlarge, forward, furnish, further, go ahead, go forth, headway, impetus, improve, magnify, make for, nurture, press on, proceed, produce, proffer, promote, propose, prosper, provide, suggest, support, upgrade **8** advocate, approach, ballyhoo, escalate, get ahead, go places, go toward, increase, leapfrog, movement, overture, progress, retainer, threaten **9** allowance, cultivate, encourage, go forward, hold forth, promotion, push ahead, recommend, volunteer **10** accelerate, beforehand, betterment, forge ahead, front money, gain ground, lay forward, move onward, prepayment, put forward
after a catch: **5** tag up
cash ~: **4** loan
get an ~: **3** owe
go in ~: **5** usher **6** herald **7** precede, presage **8** antecede, run ahead **10** anticipate, come before
in ~: **3** ere **5** ahead, early, first, prior **6** before **7** betimes, forward **9** preceding **10** beforehand, previously
info: **3** tip **4** omen

in ~ of: 5 until
oneself: 5 climb
person: 5 scout
rudely: 5 elbow
showing: 6 prevue 7 preview
advance __: 3 fee, man 5 guard 6 notice, person
advanced: 3 new 4 late 5 ahead, front 7 extreme, forward, liberal, radical 8 up-to-date 10 avant-garde, precocious
degree: 3 Ed.D., Ed.M., MBA, Ph.D. 4 D.Lit.
in age: 7 elderly
it may be ~: 5 money
more ~: 6 senior 7 ahead of 8 superior
advancement: 3 aid 4 gain, rise, step 8 progress 9 promotion
advances
make ~: 3 woo
advancing: 7 en route, forward, ongoing 8 oncoming, thriving, underway 9 on the move 10 aggressive, cumulative, on the march
not ~: 5 mired, stuck 8 moribund
advantage: 3 aid, use 4 boon, edge, good, jump, lead, luck, odds, plus, sake 5 asset, avail, break, leg up, merit, start 6 beauty, behoof, profit, virtue 7 benefit, vantage 8 blessing, handicap, interest, leverage, purchase 9 allowance, dominance, influence, landslide, privilege, seniority, supremacy, upper hand 10 ascendance, ascendancy, ascendence, ascendency, expediency, percentage, precedence, preference
at an ~: 5 ahead, one up
show to ~: 7 flatter
take ~: 5 avail
take ~ of: 3 use 4 gull, milk 5 abuse, cozen, wrong 6 impose, play on, prey on 7 deceive, exploit, put upon, utilize 8 hoodwink, play upon 9 victimize
take ~ of again: 5 reuse
without ~: 7 useless
advantageous: 4 good 5 handy, happy, lucky, utile 6 aidful, benign, usable, useful 7 gainful, healthy, helpful, hopeful, useable 8 enviable, fruitful, positive, remedial, salutary, valuable 9 effectual, favorable, lucrative, opportune, rewarding 10 productive, profitable, propitious, worthwhile
most ~: 7 optimum
advantageously: 4 well
more ~: 6 better
advantageousness: 7 utility
advent: 4 dawn 5 onset, start 6 coming, outset 7 arrival, kickoff, leadoff 8 entrance, exordium 9 beginning, inception 10 appearance
adventitious: 5 lucky 6 random
adventure: 4 dare, deed, feat, lark, risk, saga, yarn 5 geste, jaunt, novel, peril, quest, story 6 hazard, thrill, travel 7 episode, exploit, journey, romance, venture 8 incident, long shot 9 happening 10 enterprise, excitement, experience, occurrence
ender: 4 some
grand ~: 4 epic, saga, tale, yarn 5 story 6 legend 9 chronicle
in search of ~: 6 errant
story: 4 epic, gest, saga, tale 5 conte, geste
adventurer: 5 rover, scout 6 risker 7 gambler, voyager 8 explorer, traveler, wanderer, wayfarer 9 charlatan, daredevil, journeyer, mercenary 10 speculator
Adventurers, The
author: Harold Robbins
Adventures __ Juan: 5 of Don
Adventures __ Tin Tin, The: 5 of Rin
__ Adventures in Wonderland: 6 Alice's
Adventures of Augie March, The
author: Saul Bellow
Adventures of Ford Fairlane, The (1990 film)
cast: Andrew Dice Clay
Adventures of Ozzie and Harriet, The (ABC sitcom)
cast: Don DeFore (Thorny Thornberry)
David Nelson
Harriet Nelson
Kris Nelson
Ozzie Nelson
Ricky Nelson
Adventures of Rin Tin Tin, The (ABC western)
cast: Lee Aaker (Rusty)
Adventures of Robin Hood, The (1938 film)
cast: Olivia de Havilland, Errol Flynn, Claude Rains, Basil Rathbone
director: Michael Curtiz
Adventures of Rocky and Bullwinkle, The (2000 film)
cast: Jason Alexander, Robert De Niro, Rene Russo
Adventures of Sherlock Holmes, The (1939 film)
cast: Nigel Bruce, Ida Lupino, Basil Rathbone
Adventures of Superman, The (TV sci-fi)
cast: Phyllis Coates (Lois Lane)
John Hamilton (Perry White)
Jack Larson (Jimmy Olsen)
Noel Neill (Lois Lane)
George Reeves (Superman/Clark Kent)
Robert Shayne (Inspector Henderson)
Adventures of Wild Bill Hickok, The (TV western)
cast: Andy Devine (Jingles)
Guy Madison (Wild Bill Hickok)
adventuresome: 6 daring 8 reckless
adventuring
go ~: 5 sally
adventurous: 4 bold, game, rash 5 brace, brave, gutsy, nervy, risky 6 awless, daring, gritty, heroic, plucky, spunky 7 aweless, dashing, defiant, doughty, gallant, staunch, valiant 8 fearless, heroical, intrepid, reckless, resolute, romantic, stalwart, unafraid, valorous 9 audacious, daredevil, dauntless, dreadless, undaunted, unfearful 10 courageous
be ~: 4 dare
not ~: 5 staid
one: 5 darer
adverb: 3 too 4 very, word 6 hardly, likely, poorly, rudely, softly 7 quickly 8 modifier, politely, probably 9 qualifier
archaic ~: 4 erst
poetic ~: 3 e'en, e'er, o'er, oft, yon 4 enow, ne'er 5 anear
suffix: 4 -ably, -ally, -ibly, -ward, -ways, -wise 5 -fully, -wards 6 -ically
adversary: 3 foe, opp. 5 enemy, rival 6 foeman 7 opposer 8 attacked, opponent 9 ill-wisher 10 antagonist, competitor, contestant, opposition
adverse: 3 bad, ill 5 toxic 6 malign, ornery, tragic 7 baleful, baneful, counter, harmful, hostile, opposed, ruinous 8 contrary, damaging, inimical, negative, opposite, tragical, untoward 9 dangerous, injurious, reluctant, resistive 10 calamitous, disastrous
prefix: 7 counter-
to: 7 athwart
__ Adverse: 7 Anthony
adversely: 3 ill
affect ~: 4 hurt
adversity: 3 woe 4 harm 5 trial 6 crunch, misery, mishap 7 bad luck, reverse, tragedy, travail, trouble, undoing 8 bad break, calamity, disaster, distress, hard luck, hardship, pressure 9 deep water, extremity, hard times, mischance, situation, suffering, tough luck 10 affliction, can of worms, difficulty, hard knocks, misfortune
overcome ~: 3 win 4 beat 6 attain, manage 7 achieve, conquer, make out, prevail, pull off, realize, succeed, triumph 8 struggle 9 withstand 10 accomplish
advert: 3 see 4 heed, mark, mind, view 5 imply, refer, see to, watch 6 hint at, look at, notice, regard, remark 7 mention, observe, refer to, suggest 8 allude to, attend to, glance at, indicate, intimate, listen to 9 insinuate, look after, touch upon 10 commercial, take care of, take heed of, take note of
advertent: 7 heedful 9 attentive
advertise: 4 hawk, hype, plug, puff, push, tout 5 boost, pitch 6 flaunt, herald, market, regard, spread 7 display, exhibit, promote, show off 8 announce, ballyhoo, proclaim 9 broadcast, make known, publicize 10 promulgate
advertisement: 4 bill, plug 5 blurb, flyer 6 poster 7 display, leaflet 8 handbill 9 publicity
Advertiser: 5 paper 9 newspaper
locale: 8 Honolulu
advertising: 4 hype 5 promo 6 hoopla 8 ballyhoo, hard sell 9 publicity
arrangement: 5 tie-in
award: 4 Clio
circular: 6 insert
lure: 6 coupon
pitch: 5 try it
selling point: 6 status 7 benefit, feature
sign: 4 neon
trademark: 4 logo
watchdog: 3 FTC
advice: 3 aid, tip 4 help, info, word 5 input, steer 6 caveat, earful, sermon, tipoff 7 caution, counsel, pointer, tidings, warning 8 guidance 10 directions, dissuasion, persuasion, suggestion
bad ~: 8 bum steer
doctor ~: 4 rest
follow, as ~: 4 heed, obey
give unwanted ~: 6 kibitz, meddle
in Britain: 4 rede
name: 3 Ann 4 Abby 7 Landers 8 Van Buren
piece of ~: 3 tip 4 don't, MYOB
seek the ~ of: 6 look to 7 consult
take ~: 4 heed 5 act on 6 listen
advice and __: 7 consent
Advil: 9 analgesic 10 painkiller
alternative: *see* pain reliever brand
target: 4 ache, pain
advisable: 3 apt, fit 4 well, wise 5 sound 6 seemly 7 fitting, politic, prudent 8 sensible, suitable 9 desirable, expedient, judicious, suggested 10 reasonable
advise: 3 tip 4 post, tell, tout, urge, warn 5 alert, brief, coach, guide, teach 6 clue in, direct, exhort, fill in, inform, notify, preach, report, tip off 7 apprise, apprize, caution, commend, counsel, let in on, preside, propose, put on to, suggest 8 acquaint, admonish, advocate, dissuade, forewarn, instruct, persuade, point out 9 encourage, make known, prescribe, recommend 10 keep posted
against: 8 dissuade
in Britain: 4 rede
of: 6 impart, inform, notify, relate, report 7 apprise, apprize, let in on 9 enlighten, make known
Advise and Consent
author: Allen Drury
Advise and Consent (1962 film)
cast: Henry Fonda, Charles Laughton, Don Murray
director: Otto Preminger
advised: 10 acquainted, considered
be ~: 4 hear
__-advised: 3 ill 4 well
advisedly: 9 carefully, prudently 10 cautiously, discreetly
advisement: 9 direction
take under ~: 8 consider
advisor: 4 aide 5 coach, guide, tutor 6 expert, helped, lawyer, mentor, oracle, priest 7 counsel, teacher 8 attorney 9 authority, confidant, counselor 10 consultant, Dutch uncle, instructor
chief ~: 5 elder
female ~: 6 egeria
financial ~: 3 CPA 10 accountant
legal ~: 3 att. 4 atty. 6 lawyer 8 attorney
personal ~: 4 guru 5 rabbi, rebbe
advisory: 5 alert 6 notice
group: 5 board, panel 7 cabinet
advocacy: 3 aid 6 urging 7 backing, defense, support 8 espousal 9 promotion 10 assistance

advocate: **4** back, plug, tout, urge **5** agent, boost, favor, urger **6** advise, backer, defend, friend, lawyer, praise, uphold, votary **7** advance, apostle, bolster, booster, counsel, espouse, further, nurture, paladin, pleader, promote, push for, root for, sponsor, suggest, support **8** adherent, argue for, attorney, champion, crusader, defender, endorser, exponent, plead for, press for, promoter, proposer, propound, reformer, speak for, stand for, stump for **9** barrister, counselor, encourage, expounder, paraclete, proponent, recommend, subscribe, supporter **10** campaigner, go to bat for
combining form: **4** -crat **5** -arian, -ocrat
org.: **3** ABA
suffix: **3** -ist, -ite **5** -arian
__ advocate: **5** judge **6** devil's
__ advocate general: **5** judge
adz: **4** tool **8** smoother
relative: **2** ax **3** axe
adze: **4** tool **8** smoother
Adzharistan
capital: **6** Batumi
adzuki: **4** bean **6** legume
A&E
part of ~: **4** arts
A.E.: **7** Housman, van Vogt **8** Hotchner
AEC
part of ~: **4** Comm. **6** Atomic, Energy
successor: **3** NRC
aedes
kin: **5** culex
aedile: **5** Roman
garb: **4** toga
Aeetes
daughter: **5** Medea
sister: **5** Aeaea, Circe, Kirke
A.E.F.
author: Carl Sandburg
conflict: **3** WWI
Aegean: **3** sea **7** islands
ancient ~ region: **5** Ionia
gulf: **5** Izmir, Saros **7** Argolis, Saronic **8** Salonika
island: **3** Cos, Ios, Kea, Kos, Zea **4** Keos, Milo **5** Chios, Crete, Delos, Khios, Leros, Melos, Milos, Naxos, Paros, Samos, Thera **6** Candia, Euboea, Icaria, Lemnos, Lesbos, Patmos, Rhodes, Rhodos, Skiros, Skyros, Thasos **7** Mykonos, Syphnos, Tenedos **8** Cyclades
locale: **6** Greece
river to the ~: **6** Struma **7** Maritsa
Aegeus
son: **7** Theseus
wife: **5** Medea
aegis: **3** aid **4** care **5** favor, guard **6** escrow, shield **7** backing, custody, keeping, support **8** auspices, security, umbrella **9** oversight, patronage, safeguard **10** protection
aeiou: **6** vowels
Aeneas: **4** hero
brother: **4** Eryx **5** Lyrus
companion: **7** Achates
daughter: **7** Aemilia
friend: **7** Achates
home: **4** Troy
mother-in-law: **5** Amata
parent: **5** Venus **8** Anchises **9** Aphrodite
son: **5** Etias **7** Silvius **8** Ascanius
wife: **4** Dido **6** Creusa
Aeneid, The: **4** epic, epos, poem **8** epic poem
author: Vergil, Virgil
character: **4** Anna, Dido, Opis **5** Amata, Anius, Aruns, Eneas, Nisus **6** Aeneas, Creusa, Nautes, Pallas, Turnus **7** Acestes, Camilla, Celaeno, Evander, Latinus, Lavinia
site: **4** Troy **5** Egean **6** Aegean
starter: **4** Arma
Aeolian __: **4** harp, lyre, mode **7** Islands
Aeon: **4** __ Flux
aer-: **4** atmo-
Aer __: **6** Lingus
aerate: **4** foam **5** froth **6** bubble, purify, refine **7** freshen, inflate **9** oxygenate, oxygenize, ventilate
aerator
soil ~: **4** root, worm **6** tiller
aerial: **4** high, pass **5** aloft, lofty **6** flying, volant **7** antenna **8** elevated, ethereal, in the sky, overhead **9** dreamlike, from above, TV antenna **10** rabbit ears
maneuver: **4** loop, spin
support: **4** mast
view provider: **5** blimp **7** airship, balloon **8** aircraft, zeppelin **9** dirigible
aerialist: **7** acrobat, gymnast, vaulter
like an ~: **5** agile
safeguard: **3** net
aerie: **4** nest **5** perch **6** refuge **7** retreat **8** fortress, hideaway **9** sanctuary
resident: **4** hawk **5** eagle **6** condor, eaglet
Aer Lingus: **7** airline
land: **4** Eire, Erin **7** Ireland
aero-: **4** atmo-
aerobatic
maneuver: **4** loop, spin
aerobe: **4** germ **9** bacterium
aerobicize: **7** work out
aerobics: **5** drill, sport **7** workout **8** exercise
aftereffect: **4** ache
center: **3** gym, spa
command: **6** exhale
measure: **5** pulse
outpouring: **5** sweat
prefix: **3** oxy-
__ aerobics: **4** step
aerodynamic: **5** sleek
aerodynamics: **8** aviation
aeronaut: **5** flier, flyer, pilot **6** fly boy **7** aviator
aeronautics: **7** science **8** aviation
org.: **3** NAA
study: **6** flight
__ Aeronautics Board: **5** Civil
aerophobe
fear: **6** drafts
Aerosmith
leader: Steven Tyler
song: Angel (1988)
Dream On (1976)
I Don't Want to Miss a Thing (1998)
Janie's Got a Gun (1989)
Love in an Elevator (1989)
Walk This Way (1976)
What It Takes (1990)
aerosol: **9** vaporizer
aerosol __: **3** can **4** bomb **5** spray
Aerospatiale
product: **3** jet, SST **5** plane
Aerostar: **3** van **4** Ford
aerostat: **5** blimp **7** balloon **8** zeppelin **9** dirigible
aery: **9** pneumatic
see also aerie
AES
opponent: **3** DDE
Aeschylus: **4** poet **5** Greek **10** playwright
work: Agamemnon
Eumenides
Libation Bearers
Oresteia
The Persians
Prometheus Bound
Seven Against Thebes
The Suppliant Women
Aesir: **4** gods **5** Norse
VIP: **4** Odin **5** Othin
Aesop: **8** fabulist
character: **3** ant, cat, dog, fox **4** bear, crow, dove, fawn, frog, hare, lamb, lion, mole, mule, swan, wolf **5** crane, eagle, mouse, raven, snake, stork **6** pigeon **8** Hercules, tortoise
lesson: **5** moral
like ~'s grapes: **4** sour
aesthete: **8** longhair
passion: **4** arts
aesthetes: **8** literati **9** longhairs **10** illuminati
aesthetic: **7** refined **8** artistic, creative, graceful, tasteful **10** artistical
putting on ~ airs: **4** arty **5** artsy
aestheticism: **5** taste **7** culture
Aetna: **5** nymph
competitor: ***see*** insurance company
parent: **4** Gaea **6** Uranus
A.F. __: **3** of L.
__ a face: **4** make
__ à fait: **4** tout
__ a Falling Star: **5** Catch
afar: **3** off **6** way off, yonder **7** distant **8** outlying
not ~: **4** near
a far __: **3** cry
__ a fashion: **5** after
__ a fast one: **4** pull
... __ a fat pig: **5** to buy
AFB
nautical counterpart: **3** NAS
see also Air Force Base
AFC
division: **4** East, West
part: **4** Amer., Conf. **8** American, Football **10** Conference
team: **4** Jets **5** Bills, Colts **6** Browns, Chiefs, Ravens, Texans, Titans **7** Bengals, Broncos, Jaguars, Raiders **8** Chargers, Dolphins, Patriots, Steelers
afeard: **6** scared, trepid **10** frightened
a feather in one's __: **3** cap
__ a Feeling: **4** What
__ a Few Dollars More: **3** For
affability: **4** ease **7** amenity **9** geniality **10** cordiality, fellowship, good nature
affable: **4** easy, kind, nice, warm **5** bland, close, suave **6** benign, breezy, chummy, clubby, genial, gentle, hearty, jovial, kindly, polite, urbane **7** amiable, cordial **8** amicable, familiar, friendly, gracious, intimate, likeable, obliging, outgoing, pleasant, sociable **9** congenial, convivial, courteous, expansive **10** benevolent, buddy-buddy, gregarious, neighborly, personable, solicitous
affair: **2** do **4** duty, fest, fete, gala **5** event, party, thing, topic **6** dinner, formal, matter, soiree **7** benefit, concern, episode, mission, project, romance, shindig **8** business, function, incident, intrigue, luncheon, occasion **9** festivity, gathering, happening, operation, reception **10** assignment, enterprise, occurrence, proceeding
fancy ~: **2** do **4** ball, bash, gala **7** banquet, shindig **8** function, wingding
of honor: **4** duel
__ Affair: **3** XYZ **4** Love **6** Family **7** Holiday
__ Affair, A: **6** Family **7** Foreign
affaire d'honneur: **4** duel
affaires __: **5** d'état
affairs: **7** matters **8** dealings
foreign ~: **9** diplomacy **10** statecraft
state of ~: **9** situation
Affair to Remember, An (1957 film)
cast: Cary Grant, Deborah Kerr
director: Leo McCarey
affect: **3** act, get **4** fake, move, pose, stir, sway, tint **5** act on, alter, feign, get to, lobby, put on, reach, set on, touch, upset **6** assume, bear on, change, fake it, grow on, impact, matter, modify, sicken, take on **7** act upon, disturb, impinge, impress, inspire, involve, pertain, perturb, pretend **8** bear upon, come over, contrive, distress, grow upon, impact on, interest, persuade, simulate **9** determine, influence, penetrate, transform **10** predispose
adversely: **4** hurt
personally: **7** concern
strongly: **4** stir
affectation: **3** act, air **4** airs, mask, pomp, pose, sham **5** front, put-on, quirk **6** facade, vanity **7** display **8** pretense **9** mannerism **10** pretension
exclamation: **6** la-de-da, la-di-da **8** lah-di-dah
affected: **3** coy **4** arty, camp, fake **5** apish, artsy, campy, false, hammy, phony, stagy **6** chichi, coyish, cutesy, demure, forced, formal, la-de-da, la-di-da, phoney, stagey **7** assumed, awkward, cutesie, feigned, labored, mincing, pompous, prudish, stilted, studied, touched **8** lah-di-dah, mannered, overcome, overdone, pedantic, schmalzy, shmaltzy, spurious **9** conceited, contrived, grandiose, high-toned, impressed, insincere,

pretended, schmaltzy, unnatural **10** artificial, factitious, pedantical, theatrical
be ~ by: 4 feel
easily ~: 9 sensitive
manner: 4 airs
not ~: 6 immune
affectedness: 4 camp
affecting: 4 near **7** pitiful **8** dramatic, pathetic, poignant, touching **9** emotional, sorrowful **10** impressive, pathetical
affection: 4 care, love **5** amore, ardor, crush **6** desire, liking, regard, warmth **7** feeling, passion **8** devotion, fondness, interest, intimacy, kindness **9** appetence, closeness, hankering, puppy love, sentiment **10** admiration, attachment, endearment, friendship, propensity, solicitude, tenderness
evoke ~: 6 endear
have ~ for: 4 love
lavish ~: 4 dote
show of ~: 3 hug **4** kiss **6** caress **7** embrace
term of ~: 3 luv, pet **4** baby, dear, love **5** angel, chéri, cooky, cutey, cutie, deary, ducky, honey, lovey, sugar, sweet **6** chérie, cookie, dearie, sweets **7** beloved, dearest, sweetie, tootsie **8** chou-chou, cutie pie, precious, snookums, sugar pie, sweetums **10** honeybunch, sweetheart, sweetie pie, turtledove
affectionate: 4 dear, fond, kind, soft, warm **5** close, kissy, mushy, sweet **6** caring, chummy, clubby, doting, filial, genial, kindly, loving, tender **7** affable, amatory, amiable, amorous, cordial, devoted, gushing **8** amicable, friendly, intimate, outgoing, parental, sociable **9** amatorial, convivial, fraternal **10** benevolent, buddy-buddy, neighborly, solicitous
sound: 3 coo
affective: 7 piteous **9** emotional, intuitive **10** perceptual
affiance: 3 vow **6** engage **7** betroth, promise
affiancing: 9 betrothal
affidavit: 5 paper, proof **8** evidence **9** admission, agreement, statement, testimony **10** deposition
give an ~: 5 swear, vouch **6** attest
affiliate: 3 arm **4** ally, band, join **5** align, aline, unite **6** branch, hook up, member, team up **7** chapter, combine, connect, partner **8** division, offshoot, unionize **9** associate **10** amalgamate, come aboard, go partners
affiliated: 4 akin **6** allied, joined, united **7** cognate, related **8** familial, hooked up, in league **9** ancestral, bracketed, connected
be ~: 6 belong
affiliation: 3 tie **4** bond **5** union **6** hookup, league **7** cahoots, merging **8** alliance, relation
affinity: 6 liking **7** analogy, empathy, kinship, rapport **8** fondness, intimacy, likeness, penchant, relation, sympathy, velleity **9** appetence, belonging, closeness, communion, community, good vibes **10** attachment, attraction, connection, friendship, partiality, proclivity, propensity, similarity
affinity __: 4 card **5** group
affirm: 3 say, vow **4** aver, avow, hold **5** admit, posit, prove, state, swear, utter, vouch **6** accept, accord, adduce, allege, assert, assure, attest, avouch, depone, insist, ratify, uphold **7** believe, certify, confess, confirm, contend, declare, endorse, indorse, profess, protest, ratifie, testify **8** attest to, maintain, make sure, proclaim, validate, vouch for **9** enunciate, guarantee, predicate, pronounce **10** asseverate
affirmation: 2 OK **3** vow **4** oath, okay, okeh, okey **5** claim **6** assent, avowal **8** averment, evidence **9** statement, testimony
terse ~: 3 I do
affirmative: 2 da, ja, sí **3** nod, oui **4** sí sí **5** good-o, quite, right, roger, uh-huh **6** agreed, gladly, good-oh, indeed, just so, rather, righto, yowzah **7** exactly, go ahead, indeedy, mais oui, quite so, ten-four **8** all right, as you say, positive, thumbs up, very well **9** be my guest, certainly, darn right, precisely, sure thing, you said it **10** by all means, definitely, sure enough, that's right
astronaut ~: 3 A-OK
beatnik ~: 4 I dig
emphatic ~: 6 yes yes
gesture: 3 nod
oater ~: 3 yep, yup **10** darn tootin'
pilot ~: 5 roger
sailor ~: 3 aye
see also of course, yes
Affirmed
rival: 6 Alydar
affix: 3 add, pin, set, tag **4** bind, glue, join, tack **5** add on, annex, paste, put on, rivet, sew on, stick, tag on, tie on **6** adjoin, append, attach, fasten, glue on, hook on, iron on, slap on, staple, tack on **7** appends, stick on, subjoin **9** thumbtack
one's name: 4 sign
Affleck, Ben: 5 actor
colleague: Matt Damon
film: Armageddon (1998)
The Boiler Room (2000)
Bounce (2000)
Changing Lanes (2002)
Dogma (1999)
Gigli (2003)
Gone Baby Gone (2007)
Good Will Hunting (1997)
Hollywoodland (2005)
Jersey Girl (2004)
Pearl Harbor (2001)
The Sum of All Fears (2002)
spouse: Jennifer Garner
afflict: 3 ail, irk, try, vex **4** hurt, rack, rend **5** annoy, beset, harry, visit, worry **6** bother, burden, grieve, harass, pester, plague, sicken **7** agonize, disturb, oppress, scourge, torment, torture, trouble **8** aggrieve, distress, keep down **9** force upon, persecute
suddenly: 5 seize
afflicted: 3 ill **4** sick, sore **5** ailed, woful **6** ailing, infirm, laid up, sickly, unwell, woeful **7** unhappy, unsound **8** diseased, dolorous, wretched **9** aggrieved, bedridden, miserable, sorrowful **10** distressed, indisposed
be ~ with: 3 get **4** have **8** contract
affliction: 3 ill, woe **4** bane, care, hurt, load **5** curse, grief, trial **6** blight, burden, injury, malady, misery, ordeal, plague, rebuke, regret, sorrow **7** disease, illness, scourge, torment, trouble, undoing **8** calamity, disorder, distress, hardship, sickness **9** adversity, annoyance, complaint, grievance, ill health, infirmity, suffering **10** difficulty, heartbreak, misfortune, unwellness, woefulness
Affliction (1998 film)
cast: James Coburn, Willem Dafoe, Nick Nolte, Sissy Spacek
director: Paul Schrader
afflictive: 7 hurtful **10** calamitous, deplorable, lamentable
affluence: 4 ease **5** funds, means, money, purse **6** luxury, plenty, riches, wealth **7** fortune **8** good life, opulence, opulency **9** abundance, substance, well-being **10** exuberance, prosperity
affluent: 4 full, rich **5** flush **6** loaded, monied **7** copious, moneyed, opulent, upscale, wealthy, well-off **8** abundant, in clover, thriving, well-to-do **9** bountiful, doing well, fortunate, luxurious, plenteous, well-fixed **10** in the dough, in the money, privileged, propertied, prosperous, upper-class, well-heeled
the ~: 5 haves
afflux: 6 inflow
afford: 4 bear, give, lend **5** allow, grant, incur, offer, spare, yield **6** bestow, impart, manage, pay for, render, supply **7** furnish, produce, provide, radiate, sustain
affordable: 7 low-cost **10** reasonable
not: 4 dear, high **5** steep **6** costly
affray: 3 row **5** brawl, clash, fight, melee **6** barney, combat, fracas, rumpus, strife, tumult **7** contest, quarrel, scuffle **10** donnybrook, free-for-all
affright: 5 dread **6** dismay **7** horrify, startle **9** give a turn
affront: 3 dig, dis **4** barb, gibe, jeer, jibe, mock, slam, slap, slur, snub **5** abuse, anger, annoy, decry, libel, pique, scorn, sneer, spurn, taunt, wrong **6** defame, deride, dump on, heckle, impugn, injury, insult, malign, offend, rebuff, slight, vilify **7** aggress, asperse, calumny, catcall, degrade, disdain, mockery, obloquy, offense, outrage, provoke, put-down, rank out, slander, traduce **8** belittle, brickbat, contempt, defiance, denounce, derision, irritate, ridicule, vexation, vilipend **9** aspersion, cheap shot, contumely, criticize, denigrate, discredit, disparage, grievance, humiliate, indignity **10** calumniate, defamation, disrespect, impugnment, opprobrium
affronted: 4 hurt, sore
be ~: 4 mind
afghan: 5 shawl, throw **7** blanket **8** coverlet, coverlid
material: 4 wool
Afghan: 3 dog **5** canid, Kafir **6** canine **7** Turkmen **8** language
neighbor: 5 Irani
Afghanistan: 6 nation **7** country
airline: 6 Ariana
capital: 5 Kabul
city: 5 Herat, Kabul **8** Kandahar
continent: 4 Asia
goat: 7 markhor **8** markhoor
language: 6 Pashto, Pushto, Pushtu
money: 3 pul **7** afghani
mountain: 9 Hindu Kush
neighbor: 4 Iran **5** China **8** Pakistan **10** Tajikistan, Uzbekistan
river: 5 Farah
aficionado: 3 fan, nut **4** buff **5** fiend, freak, lover **6** addict, rooter **7** devotee, fanatic, groupie **8** adherent, follower **10** enthusiast
__ a fiddle: 5 fit as
afield: 4 away, awry **5** amiss, wrong **6** astray **7** off base **8** straying **9** off course **10** far and wide, off the mark, ungrounded
__ afield: 3 far
__ a finger: 4 lift
afire: 3 lit **4** avid **5** fiery, het up **6** ablaze, ardent, flambé, red-hot **7** blazing, burning, excited, flaming, flaring, zealous **8** in flames **9** combusted
like a house ~: 6 wildly **8** fiercely **9** furiously **10** vigorously
set ~: 6 ignite, kindle
__ a fire under: 5 build, light, start
__ a fit: 5 throw
AFL: 5 union
chapter: 3 lcl. **5** local
members: 5 labor
partner: 3 CIO
part of ~: 3 Fed. **4** Amer. **5** Labor **8** American **10** Federation
aflame: 3 lit **5** eager, fiery, wired **6** ablaze, on fire, red-hot **7** blazing, burning, excited, fired up, flaring, lighted **8** juiced up **9** burning up
set ~: 6 ignite, kindle
AFL-CIO: 5 union
constituent: 3 UAW
afloat: 4 asea **5** at sea, awash **7** buoyant, solvent **8** swimming **9** out of debt **10** on the water, waterborne
keep ~: 4 swim **7** survive
set ~: 6 launch
aflutter: 4 agog
AFM
member: 6 oboist **7** cellist, flutist, violist **8** flautist, musician **9** violinist **10** bassoonist
afoot: 5 astir **7** going on, walking **8** in motion, stirring, underway **9** happening, in process, on the move **10** in progress, in the works
it may be ~: 4 game
set ~: 8 motivate
afore: 3 ere **6** erenow **7** earlier, in front
ender: 4 said, time **7** thought **9** mentioned
__ a for effort: 5 get an

aforementioned: **4** prec., prev., said, same, such **5** above, prior **8** previous **9** foregoing, preceding
aforesaid: **4** prec., prev., said, same, such **5** above, prior **8** previous **9** foregoing, preceding
__ aforethought: **6** malice
afoul: **5** amiss **7** tangled
run ~ of: **3** irk **4** rile
__ afoul of: **3** run **4** fall
__ a fox: **5** sly as
__ A. Fox: **6** Vivica
Afr.: **4** cont.
former ~ nation: **4** Rhod.
nation: **3** Ang., Eth., Mor.
neighbor: **3** Eur.
see also Africa
afraid: **4** loth **5** cowed, funky, loath, pavid, timid **6** gun-shy, scared, trepid, uneasy, yellow **7** abashed, alarmed, anxious, chicken, daunted, fearful, nervous, panicky, spooked, uneager, worried **8** cowardly, hesitant, recreant, startled, timorous **9** nerveless, petrified, regretful, reluctant, terrified, tremulous, unwilling **10** distressed, frightened, indisposed
be ~ of: **4** fear
__ Afraid of Virginia Woolf?: **4** Who's
A-frame: **4** roof **6** chalet **8** ski lodge
feature: **4** eave
site: **3** lot
afresh: **3** new **4** anew, over **5** again, newly **6** de novo, lately, of late **8** once more, recently, repeated **9** once again, over again **10** from the top
Africa: **9** continent
ancient ~ land: **5** Nubia
ancient ~ town: **4** Zama
antelope: **3** gnu, kob **4** kudu, oryx, pala, puku, topi, tora **5** ariel, bongo, eland, nyala, oribi **6** dik-dik, duiker, impala, koodoo **7** gazelle
assn.: **3** OAU
beast: **3** ape, asp, gnu, kob **4** croc, ibex, kudu, lion, oryx, pala, puku, topi, tora **5** ariel, bongo, camel, civet, cobra, eland, hyena, hyrax, mamba, nyala, okapi, oribi, rhino, xerus, zoril **6** aoudad, dassie, dik-dik, duiker, fennec, hyaena, impala, jackal, koodoo, quagga, serval **7** caracal, cheetah, gazelle, gorilla, leopard, zorilla, zorille **9** crocodile
bird: **4** coly **6** bishop, drongo, lanner, turaco, whidah, whydah **7** courser, finfoot, marabou, ostrich **8** marabout, oxpecker, whinchat, woodchat **9** francolin, hammerkop **10** hammerhead
board game: **3** bao
bovine: **4** Kuri, Tuli **5** Barka, N'dama, Nguni **6** Ankole **7** Mashona
canine: **6** fennec, jackal
cape: **5** Verde
capital: **4** Lomé **5** Abuja, Accra, Akkra, Cairo, Dakar, Rabat, Tunis **6** Asmara, Bamako, Bangui, Bissau, Dodoma, Harare, Kigali, Luanda, Lusaka, Malabo, Maputo, Maseru, Niamey **7** Abidjan, Algiers, Conakry, Kampala, Mbabane, Nairobi, Tripoli, Yaoundé **8** Cape Town, Djibouti, Freetown, Gaborone, Khartoum, Kinshasa, Lilongwe, Monrovia, Pretoria, Windhoek **9** Bujumbura, Mogadishu, Porto-Novo **10** Addis Ababa, Libreville, Nouakchott **11** Brazzaville, Ouagadougou
cattle enclosure: **5** craal, kraal
council: **6** indaba
country: **4** Chad, Mali, Togo **5** Benin, Congo, Egypt, Gabon, Ghana, Kenya, Libya, Niger, Sudan **6** Angola, Gambia, Malawi, Uganda, Zambia **7** Algeria, Eritrea, Lesotho, Morocco, Namibia, Nigeria, Senegal, Somalia, Tunisia **8** Botswana, Cameroon, Ethiopia, Tanzania, Zimbabwe **9** Swaziland **10** Ivory Coast, Madagascar, Mauritania, Mozambique **11** Burkina Faso, Côte d'Ivoire, Sierra Leone, South Africa **12** Guinea-Bissau
country former: **5** Zaire
dance: **4** juba
delta: **4** Nile
desert: **5** Namib **6** Libyan, Nubian, Sahara **7** Arabian **8** Kalahari
easternmost point of ~: **5** Hafun
equine: **5** zebra **6** quagga
evergreen: **4** akee
explorer: **4** Park **7** Johnson, Stanley **11** Livingstone
feline: **4** lion **5** civet **6** serval **7** caracal, cheetah, leopard
fish: **5** bolti **6** anabas, bichir **7** tilapia **8** characin **10** coelacanth
fly: **6** tsetse, tzetze **8** glossina
fox: **4** asse **6** fennec
game warden: **6** askari
garment: **4** bubu, izar **5** kanzu, pagne **6** boubou, kaross **7** dashiki **9** djellabah
goat: **4** ibex
grass: **4** teff **6** kikuyu, napier **7** esparto
grassland: **4** veld **5** veldt
gulf: **6** Guinea
Iron Age pottery: **5** Urewe
it's n. of ~: **5** Medit.
knife: **5** panga
lake: **4** Chad, Tana **5** Mweru, Ngami, Nyasa, Tsana
language: **3** Ebo, Ibo, Kwa, Tiv **4** Eboe, Igbo, Lozi, Zulu **5** Bantu **7** Kirundi
largest city: **5** Cairo
lily: **4** aloe **5** plant **6** flower
menace: **4** croc **6** tsetse, tzetze **8** glossina
mountain: **4** Batu, Guna, Meru **5** Elgon, Gughe, Kenya **7** Toubkal **9** Ras Dashan **11** Kilimanjaro
music: **3** rai
musical instrument: **5** mbira
people: **3** Ebo, Edo, Ewe, Fan, Fon, Ibo, Ijo, Luo, Tiv, Yao **4** Afar, Akan, Beja, Cewa, Eboe, Efik, Fang, Fula, Hutu, Igbo, Ijaw, Lozi, Luba, Nama, Nuer, Riff, Tusi, Xosa, Yedo **5** Bantu, Bemba, Chaga, Chewa, Dinka, Dogon, Fante, Galla, Gbari, Gwari, Hausa, Kamba, Lunda, Makua, Masai, Mende, Mongo, Mossi, Nandi, Ngoni, Nguni, Oromo, Rundi, Shilh, Shona, Sotho, Swazi, Temne, Tigré, Tussi, Tutsi, Wolof, Xhosa, Yeddo, Zande **6** Amhara, Asante, Azande, Basuto, Chagga, Dorobo, Fulani, Haussa, Herero, Ibibio, Kanuri, Kikuyu, Kpelle, Maasai, Mbundu, Nubian, Nyanja, Pangwe, Senufo, Sidamo, Somali, Sukuma, Tswana, Tuareg, Watusi, Yoruba **7** Ashanti, Bambara, Danakil, Makonde, Malinka, Malinke, Mashona, Ndebele, Pahouin, Shilluk, Songhai, Turkana, Watutsi **8** Khoekhoe, Khoikhoi, Mandingo, Mandinka, Matabele, Nyamwezi **9** Ovimbundu, Wandorobo
plain: **4** veld **5** veldt
primate: **5** chimp, drill, potto **6** baboon, chacma, galago, guenon, vervet **7** colobus, gorilla, guereza **8** bush baby, mandrill, mangabey, talapoin **10** Barbary ape, chimpanzee
rebel org.: **5** SWAPO
region: **5** Sahel **6** Gezira
river: **4** Bomu, Geba, Juba, Nile, Tana, Uele, Vaal **5** Benin, Benue, Chari, Congo, Kafue, Kasai, Mbomu, Niger, Shari, Tsana, Volta, Zaire **6** Atbara, Kagera, Molopo, Orange, Rovuma, Ruvuma, Shashi, Ubangi **7** Aruwimi, Calabar, Limpopo, Lualaba, Luapula, Mangoky, Senegal, Zambezi **8** Blue Nile, Okavango
rodent: **4** jird **5** gundi, xerus **6** gerbil, jerboa **7** mole rat
rope material: **4** riem
sanctuary: **6** casbah
sea: **3** Red
sheep: **6** aoudad
shrub: **4** aloe **5** aalii, buchu
skunk: **5** zoril **7** zorilla, zorille
snake: **3** asp **5** cobra, mamba **8** ringhals **9** boomslang
spiritual power: **4** ngai
squirrel: **5** xerus
tableland: **5** karoo
tree: **4** kola, shea **5** babul, limba **6** baobab, gaboon, obeche, sapele **7** almique, assagai, assegai, avodire, yohimbe **8** alamiqui, sandarac **9** bloodwood
village: **4** stad
volcano: **3** Oku **4** Fogo **7** Erta-Ale **8** Karthala **10** Nyiragongo
waterfall: **8** Victoria
weapon: **5** panga
weasel: **5** ratel
wind: **6** samiel
Africa (1982 song)
artist: Toto
__ Africa: **4** West **5** North, Out of **6** German, Inside
African Queen, The: **4** film **5** novel
author: C.S. Forester
African Queen, The (1951 film)
cast: Humphrey Bogart, Katharine Hepburn, Robert Morley
director: John Huston
screenwriter: James Agee
Afrikaans: **4** Taal **8** language
Afrikaner: **4** Boer
Afrin
alternative: ***see*** cold remedy
Afrique
part of ~: **5** Tchad
Afrique du __: **3** Sud
Afro: **2** do **4** coif **6** hairdo **8** coiffure **9** hairstyle
like an ~: **5** bushy
Afro-__: **3** pop **5** Asian, Cuban **7** Asiatic
aft: **4** back, rear **5** arear, stern **6** astern, behind **8** backward, rearward, tailward **9** at the back, backwards, in the rear, sternward, to the rear
aft.: **2** p.m.
AFT: **5** union
part of ~: **3** Fed. **4** Amer. **8** American, Teachers **10** Federation
rival: **3** NEA
after: **4** anon, back, post, soon, then **5** later **6** behind, in a bit, in time **7** by and by, chasing, ensuing, later on, seeking, someday **8** in a while, pursuing, rearmost, sometime **9** following, hereafter, in honor of, in quest of **10** before long, eventually, gunning for, in search of, subsequent, succeeding
ender: **4** care, clap, damp, deck, glow, life, math, most, noon, time, word, work **5** image, piece, shock, taste, world **6** burner, effect **7** thought
in French: **5** après
prefix: **3** epi- **4** meta-, post- **5** infra-
starter: **4** here **5** there **6** herein **7** therein
after __: **3** all **4** mast **5** a sort
after-__: **3** run, tax **5** hours, shave **6** action, dinner, market
__ after: **3** get, run, see **4** look, take **7** inquire
__-after: **6** sought
After __ Gone: **5** You've
after a __: **4** sort **7** fashion
After All (1989 song)
artist: Cher, Peter Cetera
after-bath
wear: **4** robe
after-dinner
drink: **4** port **6** brandy, cognac
after-dinner __: **4** mint
aftereffect: **4** scar **6** result, upshot **7** fallout, outcome **9** outgrowth
afterglow: **6** luster **8** twilight
After Henry
author: Joan Didion
after-hours
joint: **9** nightclub, nightspot **10** supper club
aftermath: **4** wake **5** rowen **6** effect, impact, result, sequel, upshot **7** fallout, outcome, product **8** backwash, residual **9** remainder
workout ~: **4** ache **5** cramp **8** soreness
__ After Midnight: **6** Walkin'

aftermost: 4 hind, last
afternoon: 2 p.m.
early ~: 3 one, two 5 one p.m., two p.m.
gathering: 3 tea
late ~: 4 five, four 6 five p.m., four p.m. 8 twilight
meal: 5 lunch
prayers: 5 nones
ritual: 3 nap 6 siesta
Afternoon of __, The: 5 a Faun
after-school
org.: 3 PTA
treat: 4 Oreo 5 cooky 6 cookie
aftershave: 6 bay rum, lotion
name: 4 Afta, Brut 8 Gillette, Old Spice 9 Aqua Velva 10 Skin Bracer
powder: 4 talc
aftershock: 5 quake 6 tremor
after the __: 4 fact
After the __: 4 Fall 5 Lovin'
After the Bath
artist: Edgar Degas, Raphaelle Peale
After the Fall: 4 play 5 drama
author: Arthur Miller
character: 3 Dan, Lou 5 Elsie, Holga, Lucas 6 Felice, Louise, Maggie 7 Quentin
After the Last Race
author: Dean Koontz
After the Rehearsal (1984 film)
cast: Lena Olin
...after they've seen __: 5 Paree
afterward: 4 anon, next, soon, then 5 later 6 in a bit, in time, not now 7 by and by, later on, someday 8 in a while, sometime 9 following, hereafter, thereupon 10 before long, eventually
immediately ~: 6 hereon
in Latin: 7 post hoc
afterword: 6 epilog 8 epilogue 10 postscript
After You've __: 4 Gone
__ Afton: 5 Sweet
Afton Water
author: Robert Burns
AFTRA
cousin: 3 SAG
aftward: 4 back 5 arear 6 astern, behind 9 at the back, in the rear, to the rear
afuché: 6 shaker 10 percussion
__ a Fugitive From a Chain Gang: 3 I Am
__ a fuse: 4 blow
Ag: 4 elem. 6 silver 7 element
47 for ~: 4 at. no.
A.G.
part of ~: 3 Att., Gen. 4 Atty. 7 General 8 Attorney
Aga __: 4 Khan
Agadir: 4 city, port, town
locale: 7 Morocco
again: 3 bis 4 also, anew, over, then 5 ditto, twice 6 afresh, de novo, encore 7 besides, further 8 moreover, once more 9 thereupon 10 from the top, in addition, repeatedly
come ~: 7 revisit
do ~: 6 repeat 7 iterate, run over 8 practice 9 reiterate
happen ~: 6 repeat, return
make usable ~: 5 renew 9 refurbish
now and ~: 7 at times 9 sometimes
obtain ~: 4 find 6 ransom, recoup, redeem, regain, retake 7 get back, reclaim, win back 8 reoccupy, retrieve, take back 9 bring back, reacquire, recapture, repossess
prefix: 3 ana-
time and ~: 4 a lot, much 5 often 9 quite a bit, regularly
working ~: 7 rebuilt
__ again: 4 come, over, then
__ again!: 5 Guess
__-again: 4 born
Again!: 6 encore
__ Again: 3 Try 4 Dead, Do It 5 Hello, Never 7 Breathe, Goodbye
__ Again, Sam: 6 Play It
against: 3 con 4 anti, loth 5 in rem, loath 6 contra, facing, versus 7 athwart, counter, opposed, vis-à-vis 8 opposing, opposite 9 counter to, opposed to 10 regardless, unfriendly
prefix: 3 cat- 4 anti-, cata-, cath- 6 contra-
__ against: 3 run
...against __ of troubles: 4 a sea
Against All Odds (1984 song)
artist: Phil Collins
__ Against Thebes: 5 Seven
__ Against the Machine: 4 Rage
__ against the tide: 4 swim
Against the Wind (1980 song)
artist: Bob Seger
__ against time: 4 race 5 a race
Aga Khan
son: 3 Aly
agama: 6 animal 7 reptile
Agamemnon: 8 asteroid
author: Aeschylus
brother: 8 Menelaus
daughter: 7 Electra 9 Iphigenia
lover: 9 Cassandra
parent: 6 Aerope, Atreus
sister: 8 Anaxibia
sister-in-law: 5 Helen
son: 6 Pelops 7 Orestes 9 Teledamus
wife: 12 Clytemnestra
agamid: 6 animal 7 reptile
Agana: 4 city, town
locale: 4 Guam
agape: 4 open 5 in awe 6 aghast, amazed, jolted 7 staring, yawning 8 wide-eyed, wide open 9 astounded, awestruck, stupefied, surprised 10 astonished, bewildered, dumbstruck, slack-jawed, spellbound
Agar: 4 John 7 Herbert
agaric: 6 fungus 8 mushroom
Agar, John: 5 actor
spouse: Shirley Temple
__ a gasket: 4 blow
agasp: 6 bushed 7 shocked, stunned 8 startled 10 breathless
Agassi, Andre: 7 netster 9 tennis pro
milieu: 5 court
rival: 5 Chang, Stich
spouse: Steffi Graf, Brooke Shields
Agassiz: 4 lake 5 Louis
agate: 4 type 6 marble 7 mineral 10 chalcedony
alternative: *see* point size
origin: 4 lava
Agatha: 5 saint 8 Christie
colleague: 3 Rex 4 Erle 6 Ellery 8 Dashiell
Agatha (1979 film)
cast: Timothy Dalton, Dustin Hoffman, Vanessa Redgrave
director: Michael Apted
agave: 5 plant, sisal, yucca 6 flower 9 amaryllis, succulent
fiber: 5 istle, ixtle, sisal
root: 5 amole
agaze: 7 staring
agcy.: 3 org.
age: 3 eon, era 4 aeon, gray, grey, grow, span, time 5 cycle, epoch, get on, ripen, years 6 mature, mellow, period, season 7 develop 8 long time 9 antiquate, fossilize, grow older, obsolesce 10 generation
a coon's ~: 5 years
act one's ~: 6 behave
awkward ~: 5 teens, youth
come of ~: 6 grow up, mature
counter: 6 candle
ender: 4 less
group: 10 generation
important ~: 3 era 5 epoch
in a way: 4 rust
in this day and ~: 3 now 5 today
of ~: 5 adult 6 mature 7 grown-up 9 full-grown
of an ~: 4 eral
of the same ~: 6 coeval
one under legal ~: 5 minor 6 infant
proof of ~: 2 ID
starter: 3 dam, man, out, pot, tow 4 acre, band, bond, cart, coin, cord, cork, dock, flow, foot, garb, haul, herb, leaf, leak, line, link, mess, mile, mill, mint, moor, over, pack, pass, peer, pill, port, post, root, seep, sign, sink, soil, stow, teen, till, vent, volt, watt, word, yard 5 baron, block, break, cover, drain, dress, drift, equip, float, floor, front, fruit, graft, grill, layer, lever, pilot, pound, rough, sabot, short, spill, spoil, steer, under, vicar, wharf, wreck 6 anchor, append, broker, cellar, cooper, hermit, orphan, parent, parson, patron, person, pilfer, porter, report, shrink, vassal 7 baronet, brigand, percent, pilgrim
tender ~: 5 teens, youth 6 cradle 7 infancy, puberty 8 minority 9 childhood, juniority 10 immaturity, juvenility, schooldays
this day and ~: 3 now 4 here
under legal ~: 8 juvenile 10 adolescent
voting ~: 8 majority 9 adulthood
age __ beauty: 6 before
age-__: 3 old
__ age: 3 ice 4 dog's 5 coon's, legal 6 golden, heroic, mental, middle, school, silver 7 awkward, nuclear
__ Age: 3 Ice, New 4 Iron, Jazz 5 Space, Stone 6 Atomic, Bronze, Copper, Gilded 9 Victorian
aged: 4 ripe 6 mature, mellow 7 ancient, antique, elderly, wizened 8 grizzled 9 geriatric, getting on, up in years, venerable 10 antiquated, gray-haired
__-aged: 6 middle
agee: 4 awry 7 crooked 8 cockeyed
Agee: 3 Jon 5 James 6 Tommie
Agee, James: 6 writer
work: A Death in the Family
Letters to Father Flye
Let Us Now Praise Famous Men
The Morning Watch
Agee, Tommie
sport: 8 baseball
ageless: 6 eterne 7 eternal 10 immemorial
agency: 4 firm 5 means, organ, power 6 bureau, factor, medium, office 7 channel, company, machine, vehicle 8 auspices 9 expedient, franchise, implement, influence, machinery, mechanism 10 commission, department, expediency, instrument
worker: 4 temp 5 clerk 6 typist
__ agency: 4 news, wire 6 credit, Indian, ticket, travel 9 insurance
agenda: 4 card, list, plan, sked 5 slate, table 6 docket, lineup, roster 7 listing, program 8 calendar, schedule, time line, to-do list 9 ax to grind, checklist, procedure, timetable
component: 4 item
guide's ~: 4 tour
__ agenda: 6 hidden
Agendas
author: George Sand
__ Agenda, The: 6 Icarus
agendum: 4 item
agent: 3 Fed, rep, spy 4 G-man, mole, narc, nark, pawn, T-man, tool 5 cause, envoy, fixer, force, means, organ, party, proxy, spook 6 broker, deputy, factor, jobber, lawyer, legate, medium, origin, seller, shamus 7 abetter, abettor, channel, employe, handler, officer, stand-in, steward, vehicle 8 advocate, assignee, attorney, catalyst, delegate, emissary, employee, executor, factotum, minister, official, promoter 9 appointee, deal maker, detective, go-between, implement, messenger, middleman, negotiant, operative, surrogate 10 ambassador, connection, instrument, interceder, mouthpiece, negotiator, substitute
appoint an ~: 6 depute
be an ~ of: 6 act for 9 represent
client: 5 actor 6 artist, author, singer, writer
cut: 5 tenth 7 percent 10 percentage
double ~: 3 spy 4 mole 8 turncoat
org.: 3 CIA, FBI, KGB
press ~: 5 flack 8 promoter
quest: 4 role
__ agent: 3 FBI, IRS 4 free, land, play, road 5 house, press 6 county, double, estate, fiscal, Indian, secret, ticket, travel 7 booking, freight, revenue, special, station, wetting
Agent 86: Maxwell Smart
Age of Anxiety, The
author: W.H. Auden
composer: Leonard Bernstein

Age of Aquarius
show: 4 Hair
Age of Innocence, The: 4 film 5 novel
author: Edith Wharton
character: 3 Ned 5 Ellen
director: Martin Scorsese
Age of Innocence, The (1993 film)
cast: Daniel Day Lewis, Michelle Pfeiffer, Winona Ryder
Age of Napoleon, The
author: Will Durant
Age of Reason, The
author: Thomas Paine
Age of Scandal, The
author: T.H. White
age-old: 7 ancient, antique 9 venerable
ager: 3 sun 7 ripener
starter: 4 teen
Ager: 6 Milton
ages: 3 eon 4 aeon 7 forever 8 eternity, long time 9 millennia
ago: 4 once, yore
from ~ past: 3 old 7 ancient
__ Ages: 4 Dark 5 Three 6 Middle
Agfa
rival: 4 Fuji 5 Kodak
aggie: 3 mib, taw 6 marble
Aggies: 9 Utah State
agglomerate: 4 clot 8 assemble
agglomeration: 4 heap, load, lump, mass, pile 5 bunch, hoard, stack 6 jumble 7 cluster 9 congeries
agglutinant: 8 adhesive
agglutinate: 4 clot 5 clump
aggrandize: 5 add to, boast, boost, build, ensky, exalt 6 beef up, enrich, expand, extend, jack up, praise 7 augment, enlarge, ennoble, glorify, inflate, lionize, magnify, promote 8 heighten, increase, multiply 9 embroider, intensify
aggrandizement: 6 growth 8 increase
aggravate: 3 bug, get, irk, nag, vex 4 gall, rile, roil, sink, slip 5 add to, anger, annoy, decay, get to, grate, peeve, pique, slide, tease, upset 6 bother, deepen, needle, nettle, pester, pick on, put out, rankle, worsen 7 enflame, inflame, magnify, provoke 8 compound, distress, embitter, imbitter, irritate 9 displease, infuriate, intensify 10 complicate, degenerate, exacerbate, exaggerate, exasperate, retrogress
aggravated: 5 angry 6 ireful
aggravating: 5 pesky, pesty 6 trying 7 irksome 9 vexatious
aggravation: 4 bane, care, pain 5 anger, worry 6 bother, hassle, tsuris 7 tsouris 8 distress, headache, pet peeve, vexation 9 annoyance
aggregate: 3 all, lot, mix, sum 4 bulk, heap, lump, mass, mixt, pile 5 added, add up, amass, gross, group, mixed, total, whole 6 amount, entire, gather, heaped, number 7 add up to, amassed, collect, combine 8 assemble, compound, ensemble, entirety, hold on to, integral, quantity, totality 9 assembled, collected, composite, corporate, gathering 10 accumulate, assemblage, collection, collective, complement, constitute, cumulation, cumulative, everything
aggregation: 4 band, heap, mass 5 array, batch, group, hoard, stack, swarm 7 company 8 assembly 9 congeries, multitude
aggress: 5 begin, start 6 attack, foment, incite 7 affront, assault, besiege, provoke 8 commence, initiate
aggression: 5 fight, onset 6 attack 7 offense 9 hostility, incursion, offensive, onslaught, pugnacity 10 antagonism, assailment, blitzkrieg
aggressive: 4 go-go 5 macho, pushy, type A 6 active, strong 7 defiant, dynamic, forward, hawkish, martial, rampant, warlike 8 fighting, militant, military, ravaging, ructious 9 advancing, ambitious, assertive, assertory, attacking, bellicose, bumptious, combative, imperious, intruding, intrusive, masterful, offensive, predatory, rapacious, strenuous, truculent 10 disruptive, disturbing, jingoistic, peremptory, pugnacious
not ~: 5 timid, type B
one: 5 Rambo, tiger
aggressiveness: 5 moxie 8 gumption
aggressor: 3 foe 5 enemy 6 raider 7 fighter, invader 8 attacker, intruder, provoker 9 assailant
aggrieve: 3 vex 4 harm, hurt, miff, pain, rack 5 abuse, harry, worry, wrong 6 bruise, damage, harass, ill-use, injure, misuse, offend, plague 7 afflict, agonize, oppress, outrage, torment, torture, trouble 8 bullyrag, distress, ill-treat, keep down, maltreat, mistreat 9 mishandle, persecute
aggrieved: 4 hurt, sore 5 woful 6 harmed, pained, peeved, woeful 7 injured, unhappy, wronged 9 afflicted, depressed, disturbed, oppressed 10 persecuted
aghast: 4 agog 5 agape 6 amazed, scared 7 alarmed, shocked, shook up, stunned 8 appalled, dismayed, frighted 9 astounded, awestruck, horrified, mortified, terrified 10 astonished, frightened, speechless
leave ~: 8 surprise
agile: 3 fit, yar 4 deft, spry, wiry, yare 5 brisk, fleet, light, lithe, quick, smart 6 active, dapper, limber, lissom, lively, nimble, speedy, supple 7 catlike, lambent, lissome, springy 8 athletic, dextrous, graceful 9 dexterous, lightsome, lithesome, sprightly 10 surefooted
not ~: 6 clumsy
agility: 5 speed 6 action 8 legerity 9 dexterity, lightness 10 liveliness, nimbleness
agin: 7 opposed
not ~: 3 fer
Agincourt: 6 battle
aging: 7 ancient, elderly, wizened 8 grizzled 9 geriatric, getting on, senescent, up in years
__ a girl!: 3 It's
__ a girl, just...: 5 I want
A Girl Like I
author: Anita Loos
agita: 9 heartburn
agitate: 3 bug, get, jar, jog, vex 4 beat, flap, move, rile, rock, roil, stir, toss 5 alarm, anger, annoy, churn, egg on, get to, psych, rouse, shake, shock, swirl, upset 6 arouse, bother, dismay, excite, foment, incite, jiggle, kindle, ruffle, whip up, work up 7 concuss, disrupt, disturb, enflame, fluster, inflame, perturb, shake up, startle, trouble, unhinge, unnerve 8 convulse, disquiet, distress, exercise, unsettle, unstring 9 impassion 10 cause a riot, discompose, disconcert, exasperate
agitated: 3 hot, mad 5 antsy, fazed, het up, irate, itchy, jumpy, manic, tense, upset 6 hectic, jangly, uneasy, yeasty 7 anxious, foaming, frantic, jittery, keyed up, nervous, restive, uptight 8 feverish, fluttery, frenetic, frenzied, in a state, restless, skittish, troubled, unstrung 9 concerned, excitable, ill at ease, turbulent, unsettled 10 high-strung, infuriated
be ~: 4 stew 6 simmer
state: 4 snit, stew
agitation: 4 flap, fuss, to-do 5 anger, furor, tizzy, upset 6 clamor, dismay, frenzy, lather, motion, racket, tumult, unrest 7 emotion, ferment, turmoil 8 movement, upheaval 9 commotion, confusion, sensation 10 combustion, convulsion, ebullience, excitement, impatience
agitator: 5 rebel, riler 7 hellion, heretic, inciter 8 fomenter, frondeur, inflamer 9 anarchist, demagogue, disrupter, dissident, extremist, firebrand, insurgent 10 instigator, malcontent
Aglaia: 5 Grace
colleague: 6 Thalia 10 Euphrosyne
aglare: 7 blazing, shining, staring 8 blinding
agleam: 3 lit 5 shiny 6 bright 7 radiant, shining 9 sparkling
aglet
target: 6 eyelet
agley: 4 awry
aglow: 3 lit, red 4 warm 5 happy, light, lit up, shiny 6 ablaze, bright, flashy 7 beaming, blazing, burning, fulgent, lambent, radiant, shining 8 dazzling, gleaming, luminous, lustrous 9 brilliant, exuberant, refulgent, sparkling 10 shimmering
agnate: 7 kindred, kinsman, related 8 paternal, relative 10 equivalent
Agnes: 5 saint 7 de Mille 9 Moorehead
in Spanish: 4 Ines, Inez
to Cecil B.: 5 niece
Agnes __: 4 Grey 5 of God
Agnes Grey
author: Anne Brontë
Agnes of God (1985 film)
cast: Anne Bancroft, Jane Fonda, Meg Tilly
director: Norman Jewison
Agnew: 5 Spiro
plea, for short: 4 nolo
agnolotti: 5 pasta
alternative: *see* pasta
agnomen: 4 name 9 sobriquet
Agnon, Shmuel: 6 Hebrew, writer 8 Nobelist
agnostic: 6 unsure 8 nescient
Agnus __: 3 Dei
__ Agnus Dei: 4 Ecce
ago: 3 ere 4 back, past 5 since 6 before, gone by, lapsed 7 earlier, history 8 formerly, long gone, until now 9 before now, in the past 10 back in time, heretofore
a while ~: 4 once 6 before 7 earlier 9 at one time, in the past 10 beforehand
in German: 3 vor
in Scottish: 4 syne
long ~: 4 once, past, then, yore 5 of old 6 erenow 8 formerly 9 in the past 10 previously
not long ~: 5 newly 6 lately, of late 8 latterly, recently 9 yesterday
__ ago: 4 long
__ Ago and Far Away: 4 Long
__ a go at: 4 have
agog: 4 awed, keen 5 eager, het up, in awe 6 aghast, amazed, ardent 7 anxious, bug-eyed, excited, in shock, psyched, shook up, stunned 8 atwitter, in a tizzy, thrilled, wide-eyed, worked up 9 awestruck, ebullient, expectant, stirred up 10 astonished, bewildered, breathless, enthralled, fascinated, slack-jawed
Agon: 6 ballet
composer: Igor Stravinsky
__ Agonistes: 6 Samson
agonize: 4 fret, stew 5 brood, mourn, sweat, worry 6 grieve, harrow, sorrow, squirm, suffer, writhe 7 afflict, bedevil, torment 8 aggrieve, distress 10 excruciate
agonizing: 5 sharp, woful 6 fierce, woeful 7 intense, painful 8 grievous, piercing 9 harrowing, torturing 10 disturbing, tormenting
agony: 3 woe 4 pain 5 dolor, grief 6 misery, ordeal, sorrow, throes, trauma 7 anguish, torment, torture, travail 8 distress 9 heartache, martyrdom, suffering 10 bitterness, heartbreak
Agony and the Ecstasy, The
author: Irving Stone
__ a Good Day: 3 It's
__ a good example: 3 set
__ a good mind to: 4 have
...__ a good night!: 5 to all
__ a good word: 5 put in
__ a go of it: 4 make
agora: 5 money
modern ~: 4 mall
site: 6 Athens, Greece
agoraphobe
fear: 6 crowds
agosto: 3 mes 6 August 7 Spanish
agouti: 6 animal, mammal, rodent
relative: *see* rodent
Agra: 4 city, town
attire: 4 sari 5 saree
locale: 5 India
river: 5 Jumna 6 Yamuna
__ a grain of salt: 4 with
__ a Grand Night for Singing: 3 It's

— **a Grand Old Flag:** **5** You're
— **a Grand Old Name:** **5** Mary's
agrarian: **5** rural **6** rustic **7** bucolic, country **8** pastoral **9** bucolical
— **a Grecian Urn:** **5** Ode on
agree: **2** go **3** fit, nod **4** gibe, gybe, heed, jibe, mesh, mind **5** admit, allow, chime, defer, get on, match, say OK, tally, yield **6** accede, accept, accord, adhere, assent, belong, cohere, comply, concur, decide, follow, fulfil, listen, permit, say yes, settle, square **7** approve, chime in, comport, concede, conform, consent, fulfill, go along, observe, promise, resolve, respect **8** coincide, cut a deal, get along, hit it off, parallel, play ball **9** acquiesce, cooperate, harmonize, negotiate, recognize, shake on it, stipulate, subscribe **10** condescend, coordinate, correspond, go together, sympathize, toe the line
don't ~: **4** balk **5** demur **6** resist
don't ~ to: **3** nix **4** veto
silently: **3** nod
to: **2** OK **4** obey, okay, okeh, okey **5** allow, grant **6** accept **7** abide by **8** carry out **10** keep in step
(to): **3** bow **4** bend
to do: **6** take on **9** undertake
with: **4** suit **7** support
(with): **4** side **6** square
agreeable: **4** fine, good, nice, okay, open **5** dandy, great, legit, moral, nifty, noble, ready, suave, sweet, swell **6** genial, gentle, lovely, peachy, proper, smooth **7** amiable, cordial, dutiful, easeful, ethical, fitting, likable, lovable, lyrical, melodic, musical, welcome, willing **8** all right, amenable, becoming, gracious, in accord, laudable, likeable, loveable, obedient, pleasant, pleasing, resigned, splendid, superior, yielding **9** according, admirable, approving, befitting, compliant, complying, congenial, congruent, congruous, consonant, delicious, desirable, enjoyable, excellent, favorable, hunky-dory, in keeping, palatable, reputable, temperate, tractable, unextreme, wonderful **10** acceptable, attractive, beneficial, compatible, concurring, consenting, consistent, convenient, creditable, delectable, delightful, gratifying, harmonious, infallible, permissive, personable, responsive, satisfying, submissive
to: **5** up for
agreeably: **7** happily **9** favorably, in keeping, willingly **10** charmingly, cheerfully, graciously, obligingly, peacefully, pleasantly, pleasingly
agreed
not ~ to, as demands: **5** unmet
to: **3** OK'd **4** OK'ed **6** okayed
upon: **5** given, joint **6** mutual, united **9** concerted, unanimous, undivided **10** collective, concurrent
see also of course
agreeing: **5** as one, at one **9** accordant, according, unanimous **10** like-minded
agreement: **2** OK **4** bond, deal, mise, okay, pact, sync **5** amity, lease, peace, terms, truce, unity **6** accord, assent, avowal, pledge, treaty, unison **7** bargain, charter, compact, concert, concord, entente, harmony, promise, proviso, rapport **8** alliance, approval, contract, covenant, decision, likeness, protocol, symmetry, sympathy **9** accession, affidavit, assenting, coherence, communion, community, congruity, endorsing, good vibes, guarantee, indenture, mediation, orthodoxy, provision, ratifying, unanimity, verifying **10** acceptance, accordance, adaptation, adjustment, bargaining, compliance, complicity, compromise, concession, conclusion, concurring, conditions, conformity, congruence, consonance, friendship, permission, proportion, settlement, similarity
bring into ~: **5** align, aline **6** attune
bring to ~: **7** mediate
come to an ~: **6** settle
component: **4** term
cowboy ~: **3** yep, yup
emphatic ~: **6** yes yes
formal ~: **4** pact **6** accord, treaty **7** charter, compact, concord **8** contract, protocol **9** concordat **10** convention
ham's ~: **5** roger, wilco
in ~: **3** one **5** as one, at one **6** jibing, united **9** unanimous **10** like-minded
nonverbal ~: **3** nod
not in ~: **6** at odds
slangy ~: **3** yep, yup **4** yeah **5** uh-huh
word of ~: **2** ay **3** aye, yes **4** amen
words of ~: **4** I too **5** as am I, me too, so am I, so do I
agricultural: **5** rural **6** rustic **7** bucolic **9** bucolical
business: **4** farm
club: **5** Four-H
agriculturalist: **6** farmer **7** granger
agriculture: **7** farming, science, tillage
association: **6** grange
goddess: **5** Ceres **7** Demeter
study: **7** farming
Agri Dagi: **5** mount **6** Ararat **8** mountain
Agrippa: **5** Roman
son: **4** Nero
wife: **5** Julia
see also Latin
— **Agrippa:** **5** Herod
agronomic: **5** rural
agronomist: **6** farmer, grower
agronomy: **7** farming
Agronsky: **6** Martin
aground: **7** beached **8** marooned, stranded **9** foundered **10** high and dry
run ~: **4** fail **5** wreck **8** stranded
where ships run ~: **4** reef
agt.: **3** rep **4** G-man, T-man
agua: **5** water **7** Spanish
desire for: **3** sed
ague: **5** chill, fever
cousin: **3** flu
Aguilera, Christina
song: Come On Over (2000)
Genie in a Bottle (1999)
I Turn to You (2000)
Lady Marmalade (2000)
What a Girl Wants (1999)
Agulhas: **4** cape
locale: South Africa
— **a gun:** **5** son of
agush: **8** spouting
Ah —: **3** Sin
Ah!: **3** oho **4** I see, sigh **5** got it **6** I get it
Aha!: **4** I see **5** got it **6** I get it
A-HA
homeland: Norway
song: Take On Me (1985)
Ahab
father: **4** Omri
foe: **5** whale
god: **4** Baal
wife: **7** Jezebel
— **a hair:** **4** turn
— **a hand:** **4** lend
— **a hand in:** **4** have
— **a handle on:** **3** get **4** have
— **a hang:** **4** care, give
— **a Hap-Hap-Happy Day:** **3** It's
— **a Happy Face:** **5** Put On
— **a happy note:** **5** end on
— **a hasty retreat:** **4** beat
Ahasuerus
wife: **6** Esther
— **a hatter:** **5** mad as
ahead: **3** ldg. **5** early, first, forth, on top, prior **6** before, onward **7** already, earlier, forward, in front, leading, onwards, winning **8** advanced, in the van, oncoming **9** at the fore, in advance, in the lead **10** beforehand, out in front, previously
barely ~: **5** one up, up one
be ~: **4** lead
forge ~: **4** lead **5** march **7** advance, recover **8** continue, progress **9** go forward
get ~: **3** win **4** grow **5** go far **6** make it, pan out, thrive **7** advance, luck out, make out, prevail, prosper, triumph, work out **8** flourish, go places, grow rich, hit it big, make good, progress **9** go forward **10** gain ground
get ~ of: **4** lead **5** one-up **9** forestall
go ~ of: **4** lead **7** precede, presage **8** antecede **9** introduce
go ~ with: **5** act on **6** follow
keep a step ~ of: **5** outdo
look ~: **4** plan **7** prepare
of: **3** ere **4** up on **6** before, beyond **7** beating, prior to **9** in advance, preceding **10** outranking, superior to, surpassing
of its time: **3** new
of time: **5** early **7** betimes **9** in advance **10** beforehand
one who's ~: **3** ldr. **6** leader
plunge ~: **3** ram **4** race
run ~: **4** lead **5** scout **7** precede **8** antecede, go before **10** show the way, trail-blaze
shoot ~: **4** pass **5** outdo **8** progress **9** go forward
— **ahead:** **3** get **4** plan
ahead of —: **4** time
— **a heart:** **4** have
— **A. Heinlein:** **6** Robert
Ahem!: **3** pst **4** psst **8** excuse me
Ahern: **6** Bertie
Aherne, Brian: **5** actor
— **a high note:** **5** end on
— **a high standard:** **3** set
— **a hike:** **4** take
Ahmad: **6** Rashad
Ah, me!: **4** alas **5** alack
Ahmet: **7** Ertegun
Ahn: **6** Philip
Ahna: **5** Capri
ahold: **4** grip **5** grasp
— **ahold of:** **3** get
— **a hole in one's pocket:** **4** burn
— **a hoot:** **4** care, give
— **a hornet:** **5** mad as
ahorse: **6** riding
— **a Hot Tin Roof:** **5** Cat on
— **a house:** **5** big as
ahoy: **8** greeting
Ah Sin
author: Bret Harte
Ahura —: **5** Mazda
Ah, Wilderness!: **4** film, play
author: Eugene O'Neill
character: **3** Nat, Sid **4** Lily **5** Belle, Essie, Norah **6** Muriel
Ah, Wilderness! (1935 film)
cast: Lionel Barrymore, Wallace Beery, Aline MacMahon
Ah, Wilderness were Paradise —!: **4** Enow
Ah, yes!: **4** I see **6** so I see
ai: **5** sloth **6** mammal
AI: Artificial Intelligence (2001 film)
cast: Jude Law, Frances O'Connor, Haley Joel Osment
director: Steven Spielberg
aid: **4** abet, back, boon, egis, help, lift **5** aegis, a hand, boost, favor, guide, serve, speed **6** advice, assist, buck up, prop up, relief, remedy, rescue, succor, uphold **7** backing, bailout, benefit, bolster, charity, comfort, forward, further, help out, largess, pitch in, promote, redress, relieve, service, stand by, stick by, subsidy, support, sustain, welfare **8** advocacy, altruism, donation, guidance, kindness, largesse, recourse, sympathy, tide over **9** accessory, advantage, auxiliary, cooperate, encourage, intercede, lend a hand, patronage, subsidize **10** accomplice, ameliorate, assistance, facilitate, go to bat for, stick up for, sustenance
driver ~: **6** mirror
financial ~: **5** grant **6** credit **7** alimony, backing, pension, subsidy, support **8** donation **9** allowance, endowment, patronage **10** assistance, fellowship, honorarium
first ~ job: **4** gash **6** lesion **8** fracture
in wrongdoing: **7** collude
visual ~: **3** map **4** grid, plan, plot **5** chart, graph, table **6** sketch **7** diagram **9** blueprint, floor plan
— **aid:** **5** first, legal, state **6** mutual, visual **7** foreign, hearing
— **Aid:** **4** Rite **6** Ladies
—**-Aid:** **4** Band, Kool
Aida: **8** Turturro
Aïda: **5** opera, slave
character: **6** Ramfis **7** Amneris, Radames **8** Amonasro

composer: Giuseppi Verdi
goddess: 4 Isis
opener: 4 Act I
piece: 4 aria
setting: 4 tomb 5 Egypt 6 Thebes 7 Memphis
where ~ premiered: 5 Cairo
Aidan: 5 Quinn, saint
aid and ___: 4 abet
aide: 3 ADC 4 asst., hand, page, secy. 5 gofer 6 cohort, deputy, flunky, gopher, helper, second 7 acolyte, adviser, advisor, attaché, flunkey, orderly, staffer 8 adjutant, factotum, henchman, minister, sidekick 9 accessory, assistant, attendant, companion, gal Friday, man Friday, secretary, underling 10 accomplice, apprentice, girl Friday, lieutenant
in baseball: 6 batboy
aide-___: 7 mémoire
___ aide: 6 nurse's 8 teacher's
aide-de-camp: 4 adjt., asst. 8 adjutant 9 assistant
British ~: 6 batman
aides: 4 help 5 staff
aidful: 6 benign, useful 7 helpful 8 flexible, obliging, positive, remedial, salutary 9 effectual, favorable, of service 10 productive, worthwhile
___-aid kit: 5 first
aidman: 5 medic
Aiea: 4 city, town
locale: 4 Oahu 6 Hawaii
Aiello, Danny: 5 actor
AIG
competitor: see insurance company
aigret: 5 plume
aiguille: 4 peak
Aiken: 4 city, town 6 Conrad
locale: 4 S. Car.
Aiken, Conrad: 4 poet 6 writer
work: Blue Voyage
Brownstone Eclogues
The Charnel Rose
Great Circle
House of Dust
The Jig of Forslin
The Kid
aikido: 5 sport
Aikman, Troy: 2 QB
sport: 8 football
ail: 4 ache, hurt, pain 5 annoy, upset, worry 6 bother, sicken, suffer 7 afflict, disturb, feel bad, perturb, trouble 8 distress, languish
aileron: 4 flap, wing
Ailes: 5 Roger
Ailey: 5 Alvin
ailing: 3 bad, ill, low 4 sick, weak 6 infirm, laid up, poorly, sickly, unwell 7 invalid, not well, run-down, unsound 8 below par, diseased, under par 9 afflicted, bedridden, miserable, unhealthy 10 indisposed, out of sorts
perhaps: 4 abed
ailment: 3 bug, flu 6 malady 7 disease, illness 8 disorder, sickness, syndrome 9 complaint, condition, ill health, infirmity 10 unwellness
modern ~: 6 stress
suffix: 4 -itis
ailurophobe
fear: 4 cats
aim: 3 end, set, try 4 goal, mean, plan, sake, seek, want, will, wish 5 angle, drift, essay, level, point, sight 6 aspire, design, desire, direct, intend, intent, motive, object, reason, scheme, strive, target 7 address, attempt, meaning, mission, propose, purport, purpose, thought 8 ambition, bearings, endeavor, zero in on 9 draw a bead, intention, objective 10 aspiration
at: 5 shoot, train 6 gun for, target 8 aspire to, shoot for 9 strive for
for: 6 pursue
(for): 3 try 4 head 5 angle, labor, steer 6 strive
high: 5 dream 6 aspire
improver: 5 scope, sight
(to): 4 mean 6 aspire, intend, strive
Aim: 10 toothpaste
alternative: see toothpaste
aimara: 4 fish
Aimee: 4 Mann 9 McPherson
Aimee ___ McPherson: 6 Semple
Aimée, Anouk: 7 actress
aimless: 4 idle 5 unled 6 adrift, casual, chance, errant, random 7 erratic, flighty, wayward 8 drifting, feckless, headless, unguided, vagabond 9 desultory, excursive, haphazard, hit-or-miss, irregular, pointless, unplanned, wandering 10 capricious, disjointed, incohesive, indecisive, undirected, unintended, willy-nilly
Ain: 4 star
Ainge: 5 Danny
ain't: 6 are not
Ain't ___ a Shame: 4 That
Ain't ___ Fun: 5 We Got
Ain't ___ Sweet?: 3 She
Ain't ___ truth?: 5 it the
Ain't!
response: 5 Am too, Are so
Ain't 2 Proud 2 Beg (1992 song)
artist: TLC
___ ain't broke...: 4 If it
Ain't it the truth!: 4 amen
Ain't No Mountain High Enough (song)
artist: Diana Ross, Tammi Terrell
Ain't No Sunshine (1971 song)
artist: Bill Withers
Ain't Nothing Like the Real Thing (1968 song)
artist: Marvin Gaye, Tammi Terrell
Ain't No Way to Treat a Lady (1975 song)
artist: Helen Reddy
Ain't No Woman (1973 song)
artist: Four Tops
Ain't She Sweet?
composer: Milton Ager
___ ain't so!: 5 Say it
Ain't That a Shame (1955 song)
artist: Fats Domino, Pat Boone
Ain't That Peculiar (1965 song)
artist: Marvin Gaye
Ain't Too Proud to Beg (song)
artist: Rolling Stones, Temptations
Ain't We ___ Fun?: 3 Got
air: 3 gas 4 aria, aura, cast, face, feel, look, mask, mien, mood, odor, pose, puff, show, song, tell, tone, tune, vent, wind 5 carol, carry, ditty, draft, music, ozone, speak, state, style, utter, voice, whiff 6 aspect, breeze, chanty, expose, flavor, manner, melody, oxygen, parade, report, reveal, shanty, spirit, strain 7 bearing, chantey, declare, display, divulge, exhibit, express, feeling, freshen, lay bare, publish, quality, refresh, shantey 8 ambiance, ambience, attitude, carriage, demeanor, disclose, presence, proclaim, telecast, televise 9 broadcast, character, circulate, leitmotif, make known, mannerism, oxygenate, publicize, put on view, semblance, talk about, ventilate 10 appearance, atmosphere, deportment, exhalation, impression, make public
anew: 5 rerun
arrive by ~: 5 fly in
be in the ~: 8 threaten
be up in the ~: 4 pend
breath of ~: 4 wind
bubble: 4 bleb
build castles in the ~: 9 speculate
castle in the ~: 5 dream 6 revery 7 fantasy, reverie 8 daydream 9 pipe dream
chambers: 5 plena
combining form: 3 atm- 4 atmo- 6 pneumo- 7 pneumat- 8 pneumato-
come up for ~: 4 vent 6 emerge
component: 5 argon, xenon 6 oxygen 8 nitrogen
current: 4 wind 5 draft 6 stream
dead ~: 5 quiet 7 silence
duct: 4 flue, vent
ender: 3 man, men, way 4 boat, crew, date, drop, fare, flow, foil, glow, head, lift, line, mail, park, play, port, ship, sick, time 5 borne, brush, burst, craft, field, frame, liner, plane, power, screw, space, strip, tight, waves 6 mobile, worthy 7 freight
fight for ~: 4 gasp
fill with ~: 4 pump
float through the ~: 4 blow, waft
force: 8 military, soldiers
fresh ~: 5 ozone 7 outside 8 outdoors
full of hot ~: 5 gassy, windy, wrong 7 verbose 9 talkative
get some ~: 6 inhale
go by ~: 3 fly 6 fly out
go on the ~: 6 report 7 network 8 announce, televise, transmit 9 advertise, broadcast, publicize 10 make public
hero: 3 ace 5 pilot 7 aviator
homophone: 3 ere
hot ~: see baloney
in the ~: 5 aloft 6 flying, volant 8 imminent
like morning ~: 5 brisk
mass: 5 front
monitoring org.: 3 EPA
move on a puff of ~: 4 waft
navigate in ~: 6 aviate
navigation system: 5 loran
nip in the ~: 4 bite, cold 5 chill
open ~: 6 nature 7 outside 8 outdoors
organ: 4 gill, lung
out: 4 vent 7 freshen 8 talk over 9 ventilate
passage: 4 flue 5 naris 6 intake 7 nostril
pollution: 4 haze, smog 5 smaze
resistance: 4 drag
rifle: 5 BB gun
route: 4 lane
sac: 8 alveolus
sign: 5 Libra 6 Gemini 8 Aquarius
something in the ~: 4 odor
starter: 3 mid
stir the ~: 3 fan
strike: 4 raid
take ~: 6 inhale 7 breathe
take off the ~: 6 cancel
test the ~: 5 smell, sniff
to a poet: 5 ether 6 aether
traffic controller's place: 5 tower
traveler's bane: 4 wait
unlike desert ~: 5 humid
up in the ~: 4 high, iffy, open 5 aloft, angry, shaky, unset, vexed 6 chancy, unsure 7 pending 9 ambiguous, perturbed, suspended, uncertain, undecided, unsettled 10 indefinite, undecided, unresolved
walking on ~: 4 glad, high 5 happy, merry 6 blithe, cheery, elated, jovial, joyful, joyous, upbeat 7 gleeful, pleased, tickled 8 blissful, cheerful, ecstatic, euphoric, exultant, jubilant, mirthful, thrilled 9 delighted, overjoyed, rapturous, rejoicing, rhapsodic
walk on ~: 5 exult
air ___: 3 arm, bag, bed, bus, dam, gap, gas, gun, log, map, sac, tee, war 4 ball, base, bell, cell, cock, crew, door, duct, fare, hole, horn, kiss, lane, lift, lock, mail, mass, mile, plot, plug, pump, raid, shed, sign, sock, taxi, time, trap, well, wood 5 alert, blast, brake, brick, cargo, coach, cover, drill, fleet, force, gauge, hoist, lance, layer, meter, plant, power, rifle, route, scoop, shaft, space, speed, stack, train, twist, valve, varié
air-___: 3 dry 4 cool, core, ship 5 bound, dried, lance, slake, spray 6 logged, minded 7 breathe, twisted
___ air: 3 hot 4 dead, free, open 5 fresh, in the, light, plein, tidal, upper 6 liquid
___-air: 3 off 4 open
Air ___: 5 Corps, Force, India, Medal 6 France, Jordan, Police, Supply 7 America
Air ___ Breathe, The: 5 That I
Air ___ One: 5 Force
___ Air: 3 Bel, Con
Air America (1990 film)
cast: Robert Downey Jr., Mel Gibson, Nancy Travis
Air and Angels
author: John Donne
___-air balloon: 3 hot
airborne: 6 eolian, flying, volant
Airbus: 3 jet 5 plane
air-condition: 4 cool 5 chill
air-conditioned: 4 cool
Air-Conditioned Nightmare, The
author: Henry Miller

air conditioner: **5** Rheem, Trane **6** Lennox **7** Carrier, Fedders **9** Friedrich
feature: **3** fan
measure: **3** BTU
outlet: **4** vent
aircraft: **3** jet, SST, UFO **4** giro, STOL, VTOL **5** blimp, liner, plane **6** copter, glider **7** balloon, chopper **8** autogiro, autogyro, zeppelin **9** dirigible **10** helicopter
carrier: **4** ship **7** warship **8** man-of-war
company: **4** Lear **5** Piper **6** Airbus, Boeing, Cessna **10** Beechcraft, Gulfstream
detecting grp.: **5** NORAD
door: **5** hatch
Russian ~: **3** MiG
safety device: **6** deicer
US detection ~: **5** AWACS
walkway: **5** aisle
see also airplane
aircraft-accident
investigator: **4** NTSB
Aire: **5** river
city on the ~: **5** Leeds
locale: **7** England
Airedale: **3** dog **5** pooch **6** canine **7** terrier
__ Aires: **6** Buenos
airflow: **6** breeze
airfoil: **3** fin **4** wing
Air Force
arm: **3** SAC **5** NORAD
join the ~: **6** enlist
member: **5** pilot **6** fly boy
missile: **4** Thor
NCO: **4** TSgt.
officer: **2** lt. **3** col., gen., maj. **4** capt. **5** lieut., major **7** captain, colonel, general
refusal: **5** no sir
unit: **4** wing
woman: **3** WAF
Air Force __: **3** One **5** Cross
Air Force Academy
athletes: **7** Falcons
freshman: **6** doolie
locale: **8** Colorado
Air Force Base: **5** Altus, Beale, Dover, Dyess, Minot, Moody, Vance **6** Arnold, Brooks, Cannon, Hickam, Nellis, Offutt, Robins, Travis **7** Andrews, Bolling, Buckley, Edwards, Keesler, Kessler, Langley, Maxwell, Patrick **8** Columbus, Holloman, Kirtland, Lackland, Laughlin, Peterson, Sheppard **9** Barksdale, Ellsworth, Fairchild **10** Charleston, Goodfellow, Vandenberg
Air Force One: **3** jet **5** plane
Air Force One (1997 film)
cast: Glenn Close, Harrison Ford, Gary Oldman, Dean Stockwell
director: Wolfgang Petersen
Airframe
author: Michael Crichton
Air France
alternative: ***see*** airline
destination: **4** Orly **5** Paris **8** de Gaulle
former plane: **3** SST
air freshener: **5** Glade **6** Wizard **7** Airwick, Renuzit **8** Stick-Ups
asset: **5** scent
form: **5** spray
scent: **4** pine **5** lilac
target: **4** odor
air-gun
ammo: **3** BBs
airhead: **3** nit **4** ditz, dodo, dolt, simp **5** dummy, dunce **7** dullard **8** dumbbell
airiness: **8** delicacy **9** joviality, lightness **10** liveliness
airing: **4** on TV, ride **6** junket, stroll **7** saunter **8** exposure, telecast **9** broadcast **10** discussion, exhibition
Air Jordans
maker: **4** Nike
airless: **5** fuggy, musty **6** stuffy **10** oppressive, sweltering
airline: **3** ANA, JAL, KLM, LAN, SAS, TWA **4** El Al **5** Aloha, Delta, MALEV, Pan Am, US Air, Varig **6** Ariana, Iberia, QANTAS, Sabena, United **7** Jet Blue, Olympic **8** Aeroflot, Alitalia, American **9** Lufthansa, Southwest, US Airways **11** America West, Continental
Afghanistan: **6** Ariana
Australia: **6** QANTAS
Belgium: **6** Sabena
Brazil: **5** Varig
bygone ~: **3** TWA **4** BOAC **5** Ozark, Pan Am **7** Braniff, Eastern **8** National
Chile: **3** LAN
employee: **5** agent, pilot **7** steward **8** mechanic
European ~: **3** KLM, SAS **5** MALEV **6** Iberia, Sabena **7** Olympic **8** Aeroflot, Alitalia **9** Lufthansa
former name: **5** USAir
Germany: **9** Lufthansa
Greece: **7** Olympic
Holland: **3** KLM
Hungary: **5** MALEV
Israel: **4** El Al
Italy: **8** Alitalia
Japan: **3** ANA
patron: **5** flier, flyer
regulating org.: **3** FAA
Russia: **8** Aeroflot
transfer point: **3** hub
U.S.: **5** Delta **6** United **7** Jet Blue **8** American **9** Southwest, US Airways **11** Continental
airliner: **3** jet **5** plane
airman: **2** GI **4** rank **5** flier, flyer, pilot **6** fly boy, Yeager **7** aviator, recruit **9** Lindbergh
Air Music
composer: Ned Rorem
__ Air Patrol: **5** Civil
airplane: **3** jet **5** craft, liner
'60s spy ~: **4** U two
access: **4** ramp
engine: **5** turbo **6** fanjet
flap: **6** elevon
fuel: **5** avgas
maker: **4** Lear **5** Piper **6** Airbus, Boeing, Cessna **10** Beechcraft, Gulfstream
maneuver: **4** loop
model ~: **3** toy
needing little runway: **4** STOL
part: **4** flap, nose, wing **5** aisle, strut **7** aileron, cockpit **9** propeller
ride: **6** flight
speed indicator: **4** Mach
tracker: **5** radar
WWI ~: **4** Spad
see also aircraft
Airplane! (1980 film)
cast: Lloyd Bridges, Peter Graves, Julie Hagerty, Robert Hays, Leslie Nielsen, Robert Stack
director: Jim Abrahams, David Zucker, Jerry Zucker
dog: **6** Scraps
air-pollution
measure: **3** ppm
airport
annoyance: **5** delay
area: **4** gate **5** apron **6** lounge, runway **7** Customs
Atlanta: **10** Hartsfield
booth lessee: **4** Avis **5** Alamo, Hertz **6** Budget, Dollar
Boston: **5** Logan
Calcutta: **6** Dum Dum
California: **3** LAX, SFO
Caracas: **7** Bolívár
Chicago: **3** ORD **5** O'Hare **6** Midway
closer: **3** fog
control center: **5** tower
corridor: **4** ramp
do winter ~ work: **5** deice
event: **7** takeoff
Florence: **8** Vespucci
fluid: **6** deicer
Genoa: **8** Columbus
Havana: **5** Martí
Houston: **5** Hobby **10** George Bush
info: **3** arr., ETA, ETD **5** delay **7** arrival **9** departure
Israel: **3** Lod
Istanbul: **7** Ataturk
Las Vegas: **8** McCarran
major ~: **3** hub
Mexico City: **6** Juárez
monitor: **3** FAA
Montreal: **7** Mirabel
Nairobi: **8** Kenyatta
Nebraska ~ code: **3** OMA
Newfoundland: **6** Gander
New York: **7** Kennedy **9** La Guardia
NYC: **3** JFK, LGA
Oklahoma City: **10** Will Rogers
Paris: **4** Orly **8** de Gaulle
Phoenix: **9** Sky Harbor
Pisa: **7** Galileo
Rio de Janeiro: **5** Galea
Rome: **7** da Vinci
San Diego: **9** Lindbergh
service: **3** ATC
St. Louis: **7** Lambert
strand at an ~: **5** ice in
Tel Aviv: **9** Ben-Gurion
Tokyo: **6** Narita
Toronto: **7** Pearson
vehicle: **3** bus, cab **4** limo **6** jitney **7** shuttle
Venice: **9** Marco Polo
Washington: **6** Dulles, Reagan **8** National
Airport (1970 film)
cast: Jacqueline Bisset, Helen Hayes, Van Heflin, George Kennedy, Burt Lancaster, Dean Martin, Jean Seberg
director: George Seaton
Airport '77 (1977 film)
cast: Lee Grant, George Kennedy, Jack Lemmon, James Stewart, Brenda Vaccaro
air pressure
measure: **6** atm. PSI
air-race
marker: **5** pylon
air-raid __: **5** siren **6** warden **7** shelter, warning
airs: **5** pride **6** vanity **7** hauteur **8** pretense, snobbery **9** arrogance, pomposity **10** false front, pretension, snootiness
one with ~: **4** snob
put on ~: **4** pose **5** mince, strut **6** fake it **7** swagger
putting on ~: **8** snobbish
airship: **5** blimp, craft **7** balloon **8** zeppelin **9** dirigible
like a ~: **5** rigid
airshow
maneuver: **4** loop **5** flyby
airspeed
unit: **4** Mach
airstrip: **6** runway
Air Supply
homeland: Australia
song: All Out of Love (1980)
Even the Nights Are Better (1982)
Every Woman in the World (1980)
Here I Am (1981)
Lost in Love (1980)
Making Love Out of Nothing at All (1983)
The One That You Love (1981)
Sweet Dreams (1982)
Air Tahiti __: **3** Nui
Air That I Breathe, The (1974 song)
artist: Hollies
airtight: **4** shut **5** tight **6** closed, sealed **9** leakproof
it may be ~: **4** case **5** alibi
make ~: **4** calk, seal **5** caulk **6** enseal
airway: **4** flue, lane, vent **5** route **7** sky path **8** corridor, windpipe
Airwick
alternative: **5** Glade **6** Wizard **7** Renuzit **8** Stick-Ups
Airwolf dog: **3** Tet
airy: **4** open **5** fresh, light, lofty, sheer, windy **6** breezy, fluffy, jaunty, jovial, rakish **7** buoyant, utopian **8** carefree, ethereal, gossamer, graceful, spacious **9** lightsome, spiritual, sprightly **10** diaphanous, immaterial, nonchalant, unbothered, unfeasible, unphysical, ventilated
airy-__: **5** fairy
__ Airy: **5** Mount
'A' Is for Alibi
author: Sue Grafton
Aishwarya: **3** Rai
aisle: **3** row **4** lane, path, walk **5** alley **7** gangway, hallway, passage, walkway **8** corridor **10** passageway
lead down the ~: **3** ush **4** seat **5** guide, usher **6** escort, show in **7** conduct **9** accompany
walk down the ~: **3** wed **5** marry **10** get hitched, tie the knot
aisle __: **4** seat **6** sitter
__ aisle: **6** cereal

A I

aisles
roll in the ~: **4** howl, roar **5** laugh **6** guffaw **7** break up, crack up **8** convulse
Aisne: **5** river **10** department
capital of ~: **4** Laon
River locale: **6** France
tributary: **4** Aire
ait: **4** eyot, isle **5** islet
in French: **3** île
aitch
preceder: **3** gee
Aix-en-Provence: **3** spa **4** city, town
locale: **6** France
Aix-les-Bains: **3** spa **6** resort
A.J.: **4** Foyt **6** Cronin, Langer
ajar: **4** open **10** discordant
not ~: **4** shut **6** closed
Ajax: **4** city, hero, town **8** cleanser **9** detergent
alternative: **3** Joy **4** Bab-O, Dawn **5** Comet **6** Bon Ami **7** Cascade **8** Sunlight **9** Palmolive, Soft Scrub **10** Electrasol
author: Sophocles
father: **7** Telamon
foe: **4** dirt **5** grime
friend: **8** Achilles
locale: **6** Canada **7** Ontario
parent: **7** Telamon **8** Periboea
son: **8** Philaeus **9** Eurysaces
wife: **8** Tecmessa
Ajijic: **4** city, town
locale: **6** Mexico **7** Jalisco
Ajman
locale: **3** UAE
___ a jolly good fellow: **3** he's
AK
native: **3** Esk.
once: **3** ter. **4** terr.
see also Alaska
AK-47
kin: **3** Uzi
AKA: **5** alias
business ~: **3** DBA
indicator: **9** pseudonym
part of ~: **4** also **5** known
__ akbar: **5** Allah
AKC
part of ~: **4** Amer., Club **6** Kennel
reject: **3** mut **4** mutt
akee: **4** tree **5** fruit
relative: **5** genip **6** lichee, litchi, longan, lungan **7** genipap, leechee **9** soapberry
Akeelah and the Bee (2006 film)
cast: Angela Bassett, Laurence Fishburne, Keke Palmer
Akeem: **8** Olajuwon
Akela
org.: **3** BSA
__ à Kempis: **6** Thomas
Akers: **5** Karen
Akhmadulina, Bella: **4** poet **7** Russian
Akhmatova, Anna: **4** poet **7** Russian
__ a Kick Out of You: **4** I Get
__-a-Kid: **5** Ident
Akihito
son: **3** Aya
Akim: **8** Tamiroff
akimbo: **4** bent **7** angular **8** angulose, angulous
akin: **4** like, near, such **5** alike, level **6** allied, on a par **7** cognate, kindred, related, similar **8** parallel **9** analogous, bracketed, connected, consonant **10** affiliated, comparable, equivalent, resembling
__ a kind: **5** one of, two of
__ a Kind of Hush: **6** There's
Akins: **3** Zoë **6** Claude
Akins, Claude
TV role: **4** Lobo
Akio: **6** Morita
Akira: **8** Kurosawa
Akita: **3** dog, pet **4** city, port, town **5** canid, pooch **6** canine
locale: **5** Hondo, Japan **6** Honshu
__ a kite: **5** go fly
__ A. Knopf: **6** Alfred
Akron: **4** city, town
athlete: **3** Zip
conference: **3** MAC
county: **6** Summit
locale: **4** Ohio
product: **4** tire
Ak-Sar-Ben Coliseum
site: **5** Omaha
al __: **4** fine **5** dente **6** fresco
Al: **4** Capp, elem., Gore, Hirt **5** Green, Hodge, Lewis, Lopez, Purdy, Roker, Unser **6** Capone, D'Amato, Jolson, Kaline, Oerter, Pacino, Wilson **7** element, Franken, Hibbler, Jardine, Jarreau, Martino, McGuire, Schacht, Simmons, Stewart **8** aluminum, Molinaro, Neuharth, Sharpton **9** aluminium, Geiberger **10** Hirschfeld
13 for ~: **4** at. no.
veep before ~: **3** Dan
Al-__: **4** Anon
AL
award: **3** MVP
cap letters: **3** SOX
team: **5** A's, The, Bosox, Twins, Yanks **6** Angels, Chisox, Red Sox, Royals, Tigers **7** Indians, Orioles, Rangers, Yankees **8** Blue Jays, Mariners, White Sox **9** Athletics **10** Buccaneers
see also Alabama, baseball
see also baseball, American League
ala: **4** wing
à la __: **4** king, mode **5** carte **6** broche, maison, vapeur **7** rigueur
Ala.
neighbor: **3** Fla. **4** Miss., Tenn.
see also Alabama
Al Aaraaf
author: Edgar Allan Poe
Alabama: **4** band **5** river, state
bay: **6** Mobile
city: **5** Selma **6** Auburn, Dothan, Emelle, Hoover, Mobile, Smiths **7** Cullman, Decatur, Gadsden, Madison, Opelika **8** Anniston, Bessemer, Florence, Homewood, Prichard **9** Alabaster **10** Birmingham, Enterprise, Huntsville, Montgomery, Phenix City, Prattville, Tuscaloosa
city on the ~: **10** Montgomery
conference: **3** SEC
Indian: **5** Creek
neighbor: **7** Florida, Georgia **9** Tennessee **11** Mississippi
rival: **6** Auburn
school: **6** Auburn **9** Troy State
state flower: **8** camellia
state game bird: **10** wild turkey
state mineral: **8** hematite
state nut: **5** pecan
state rock: **6** marble
state saltwater fish: **6** tarpon
alabaster: **5** milky, white **7** mineral, niveous **9** yellowish
alack
partner: **4** alas
alacrity: **4** zeal **5** haste, hurry, speed **6** action, fervor **8** celerity, dispatch, rapidity, velocity **9** briskness, eagerness, fleetness, quickness, readiness, swiftness **10** enthusiasm, expedition, liveliness, promptness
Aladdin: **4** Arab, hero
discovery: **4** lamp
topper: **3** fez
Aladdin (1992 film)
role: **3** Abu, Ali **4** Iago **5** genie, Jafar, Rajah **7** Jasmine
voice cast: Gilbert Gottfried, Robin Williams
__ a Lady: **4** She's
alae: **5** wings
__ alai: **3** jai
Alai: **5** range
locale: **4** Asia **10** Kyrgyzstan
Alain: **5** Delon, Locke, Prost **6** Lesage **7** Lombard, Resnais **8** Chartier **9** Grandbois
in English: **4** Alan
Alain __-Grillet: **5** Robbe
Alaina: **4** Reed **8** Reed-Hall
Alain und __: **5** Elise
Alamance County
college: **4** Elon
__ a lamb: **6** meek as
Alameda: **4** city, town
locale: **10** California
__ Alamitos, CA: **3** Los
alamo: **4** tree **6** poplar **10** cottonwood
Alamo: **4** city, town **6** battle **7** mission **9** car rental **10** auto rental
alternative: **4** Avis **5** Hertz **6** Budget, Dollar **7** Thrifty **8** National **10** Enterprise
defender: **5** Bowie, Texan **6** Travis **8** Crockett
locale: **3** Tex. **5** Texas **6** Mexico **8** Veracruz **10** San Antonio
à la mode: **3** new
__ à la mode: **3** pie
Alamogordo: **4** city, town
county: **5** Otero
detonation: **5** A-bomb, A-test
locale: **9** New Mexico
__ Alamos, NM: **3** Los
Alamo, The (1960 film): **5** oater
cast: Laurence Harvey, John Wayne, Richard Widmark
composer: Dimitri Tiomkin
director: John Wayne
Alan: **4** Abel, Alda, Bean, Dale, Hale, King, Ladd, O'Day, Opie, Page, Raph, Reed, Ruck, Sues **5** Arkin, Ashby, Bates, Freed, Keyes, Paton, Young **6** Ameche, Clarke, Heeger, Metter, Napier, Osmond, Pakula, Parker, Seeger, Thicke, Turing **7** Bergman, Bridges, Cumming, Hodgkin, Jackson, Marshal, Mowbray, Myerson, Parsons, Rachins, Rickman, Rudolph, Seymour, Shepard, Simpson **8** Cranston, Crosland, Osbiston, Sillitoe, Trammell **9** Ayckbourn, Greenspan, Hovhaness, Moorehead, Rosenberg **10** Dershowitz, MacDiarmid
in French: **5** Alain
Alan __ Foster: **4** Dean
Alan __ Lerner: **3** Jay
Alan __ Project: **7** Parsons
Alan-__: **5** a-dale
Alan Alexander __: **5** Milne
Alan Dean __: **6** Foster
Alanis: **10** Morissette
Alan J. __: **6** Pakula
Alan Jay __: **6** Lerner
Alannah: **5** Myles
alar: **6** winged **8** axillary, winglike **10** wing-shaped
__-Al-Arab: **5** Shatt
Alarcón, Pedro de: **6** writer **7** Spanish
A la recherche du temps __: **5** perdu
alarm: **4** bell, call, care, fear **5** alert, chill, clock, daunt, dread, pager, panic, scare, shake, siren, spook, upset **6** arouse, beeper, buzzer, caveat, dismay, fright, horror, Mayday, signal, terror, tocsin, unease, war cry **7** agitate, anxiety, concern, disturb, horrify, perturb, petrify, red flag, shake up, startle, terrify, unnerve, warning **8** cold feet, disquiet, distress, frighten, high sign, surprise, unstring **9** give a turn, give pause, hue and cry, terrorize, trepidity **10** discomfort, intimidate, scare stiff, waker-upper
activate the ~: **3** set
button: **5** reset **6** snooze
cause for ~: **5** alert, peril **6** danger
cry of ~: **2** oy **3** eek **4** yipe **5** yikes, yipes
ender: **3** ist
heed the ~: **4** rise, stir **5** arise, awake, get up **6** awaken, bestir, wake up
show ~: **5** cower
sound the ~: **4** warn **6** arouse
time, perhaps: **3** six **5** seven, six a.m. **7** seven a.m.
view with ~: **4** fear **5** dread, panic **6** dismay
alarm __: **4** bell **5** clock
__ alarm: **4** fire **5** false, smoke, still **6** silent **7** burglar
alarmable: **8** skittish **9** excitable
alarmed: **5** jumpy, timid **6** afraid, aghast, scared, trepid, uneasy **7** anxious, chicken, daunted, fearful, nervous, panicky **8** cowardly, fearsome, hesitant, timorous
be ~ about: **4** fear
easily ~: **5** timid
alarming: **4** dire **5** awful, dread, scary **6** unsafe **7** dreaded **8** dreadful, menacing **9** dangerous, frightful, harrowing, ill-omened
Alarms and Diversions
author: James Thurber
alarum: **7** warning **10** call to arms
alas: **3** tsk, woe **4** ah me, oh no **5** alack, sadly **6** dear me, lament, tsk tsk
in German: **3** ach
partner: **5** alack
Alas! __ Yorick...: **4** poor
Alaska: **4** gulf, peak **5** mount, state **8** mountain

art form: 5 totem
bay: 7 Prudhoe
cape: 4 Nome
city: 4 Nome 5 Homer, Kenai, Sitka 6 Barrow, Bethel, Haines, Juneau, Kodiak, Seward, Valdez 7 Skagway, Wasilla 9 Anchorage, Fairbanks, Ketchikan
craft: 5 kayak, umiak
first governor: 4 Egan
glacier: 4 Muir
Indian: 3 Han 4 Eyak 5 Ahtna, Haida 6 Ahtena, Tanana 7 Chilcat, Chilkat, Koyukon, Kutchin, Tanaina, Tlingit
island: 3 Rat 4 Adak, Atka, Attu 6 Kodiak 8 Unalaska 9 Aleutians
jacket: 5 parka
mountain: 5 Baird 6 Brooks 8 McKinley 9 Aleutians
national park: 6 Denali, Katmai 9 Lake Clark 10 Glacier Bay
native: 3 Esk. 5 Aleut, Inuit 6 Eskimo, Innuit, Inupik 8 Aleutian
native language: 5 Aleut, Haida 7 Tlingit 8 Aleutian
neighbor: 5 Yukon 6 Canada, Russia 7 Siberia
peninsula: 5 Kenai
port: 4 Nome 9 Ketchikan
river: 5 Yukon
sea: 6 Bering 8 Beaufort
state fish: 10 king salmon
state gem: 4 jade
state land mammal: 5 moose
state mineral: 4 gold
state sport: 10 dog mushing
vehicle: 4 sled
volcano: 6 Katmai, Pavlof 7 Gareloi, Iliamna, Redoubt 8 Wrangell
Alaska __: 3 cod 4 crab, time 5 cedar, Range 7 Current, Highway, pollock
__ Alaska: 5 baked
Alaska king __: 4 crab
Alaskan: 5 Aleut 6 Eskimo 8 Aleutian
Alaskan __ crab: 4 king
Alaskan Highway
river near the ~: 5 Liard
Alaskan Malamute: 3 dog 5 canid 6 canine
__-Alaska Pipeline: 5 Trans
Alas! poor __: 6 Yorick
Al-Assad: 5 Hafez
Alastair: 3 Sim
Alastor
author: Percy Bysshe Shelley
a law __ oneself: 4 unto
alb: 7 garment 8 vestment
coverer: 5 orale
partner: 5 amice, orale
Al B. __: 4 Sure
Alba: 7 Jessica
to Goya: 5 model
albacore: 4 fish, tuna 5 tunny
kin: 6 bonito
Alban: 4 Berg 5 saint
Albanese, Licia: 6 singer 7 soprano
specialty: 5 opera
Albania: 6 nation 7 country
bay: 6 Valona
capital: 6 Tirana, Tiranë
former president: 4 Alia
from ~: 6 Balkan
guerrilla: 6 klepht
lake: 7 Scutari
money: 3 lek 6 qindar, qintar
mountain: 5 Korab
neighbor: 6 Greece 9 Macedonia 10 Yugoslavia
Nobelist in Peace: 6 Teresa
port: 5 Vlore 6 Durres
river: 4 Drin
Albany: 4 city, town
canal: 4 Erie
college near ~: 5 Siena
father-in-law: 4 Lear
locale: 6 Oregon 7 Georgia, New York
river: 6 Hudson
albatross: 4 bird, load 5 goony 6 burden, gooney 9 hindrance, mallemuck, millstone, mollymawk, mollymoke
abode: 4 nest
Albee, Edward: 6 writer 9 dramatist 10 playwright
work: All Over
The American Dream
At Home at the Zoo
The Ballad of the Sad Cafe
Box
Breakfast at Tiffany's
Counting the Ways
The Death of Bessie Smith
A Delicate Balance
Everything in the Garden
Fam and Yam
Finding the Sun
Fragments
The Goat: or, Who Is Sylvia?
Knock! Knock! Who's There?
The Lady From Dubuque
Listening
Lolita
The Lorca Play
Malcolm
The Man Who Had Three Arms
Marriage Play
Me, Myself and I
Occupant
Peter & Jerry
The Play About the Baby
The Sandbox
Seascape
Three Tall Women
Tiny Alice
Who's Afraid of Virginia Woolf?
The Zoo Story
albeit: 3 tho 5 altho 6 even if, though 7 thought 8 although 10 even though
Alben: 7 Barkley
Albéniz: 5 Isaac 8 composer
piano opus: 6 Iberia
Albert: 3 Lee 4 band, Carl, Kahn, King, lake, Marv, pope 5 Belle, Camus, Eddie, Sabin, Salmi 6 Brooks, Claude, Dekker, Edward, Finney, Lasker, Lutuli, Morris, Pujols 7 Hackett, Hammond, Luthuli, Moravia, Paulsen, pontiff, Terhune 8 Einstein 9 Michelson 10 Schweitzer
locale: 5 Congo 6 Uganda
Victoria, to ~: 4 wife 6 cousin 8 relative
__ Albert: 3 Fat
Alberta: 6 Hunter 8 province
city: 4 Olds 5 Banff, Hanna, Leduc, Taber 6 Onoway 7 Calgary, Red Deer 8 Edmonton, St. Albert 10 Lethbridge, Strathcona
hockey player: 5 Oiler
lake: 6 Louise 9 Athabasca
locale: 6 Canada
mountain: 8 Columbia
native: 4 Cree
waterfall: 7 Panther
Albert, Eddie: 5 actor
spouse: Margo
TV: Green Acres, Switch
Albert Herring
composer: Benjamin Britten
Alberti: 4 Leon 6 Rafael
Alberti __: 4 bass
Albert, Morris
song: Feelings (1975)
Alberto: 5 Tomba 6 Vitale 10 Giacometti
Alberto-__: 6 Culver
Alberto VO5
rival: 5 Prell
Albertson, Jack: 5 actor
Albertville
gear: 3 ski 4 skee
locale: 4 Alps 6 France
albescent: 3 wan 4 pale 5 ashen, milky, white 6 chalky, pallid, sallow 8 blanched, bleached 9 bloodless
Albine
author: Émile Zola
Albion: 7 Britain, England
neighbor: 4 Eire, Erin 7 Ireland
Albom: 5 Mitch
Ålborg: 4 city, port, town
locale: 7 Denmark
Albrecht: 5 Dürer 6 Kossel
Albright: 4 Lola 6 Tenley 9 Madeleine
album: 2 LP 4 book 6 volume 9 anthology, blank book, portfolio, scrapbook 10 collection, memory book
cover: 5 liner
item: 5 photo
like some ~s: 4 mono 6 stereo
place in a stamp ~: 5 mount
selection: 5 track
__ album: 5 stamp 6 record
albumen: 5 white 8 egg white
Albuquerque: 4 city, town
athletes: 5 Lobos
locale: 9 New Mexico
newspaper: 7 Journal, Tribune
river: 9 Rio Grande
school: 3 UNM
alc.: 3 liq.
ALC: 8 division
team: 5 Twins 6 Chisox, Royals, Tigers 7 Indians 8 White Sox
Alcan Highway
site: 5 Yukon 6 Alaska
Alcatraz: 6 island
Birdman of ~: 5 lifer 6 Stroud
Alcestis
author: Euripides
alchemist
element: 3 air 4 fire 5 earth, water
liquid: 6 elixir
mercury: 5 azoth
Alchemist, The
author: Ben Jonson
alcohol: 4 grog, kava 5 booze, drink, hooch, sauce 6 hootch, liquor, redeye, rotgut, whisky 7 liqueur, spirits, whiskey 8 vermouth 9 aqua vitae, firewater, hard stuff, inebriant, moonshine 10 intoxicant
acid + ~ product: 5 ester
awareness org.: 4 MADD
burner: 4 etna
ender: 5 meter
high in ~: 4 hard
not partaking of ~: 5 sober
rose-scented ~: 5 nerol
solution: 5 tinct. 8 tincture
solvent: 6 acetal
__ alcohol: 4 amyl, wood 5 allyl, butyl, cetyl, decyl, ethyl, grain, nonyl, octyl, oleyl, vinyl 6 anisic, anisyl, benzyl, bornyl, lauryl, methyl, propyl 7 caustic, cetylic, decatyl, rubbing
alcoholic: 4 hard 9 distilled, fermented, inebriant, sprituous
beverage: 3 ale, gin, rum, rye 4 beer, grog, mead, ouzo, port, sake, saki, wine 5 booze, hooch, lager, stout, toddy, vodka 6 brandy, bubbly, cassis, hootch, liquor, redeye, scotch, whisky 7 bourbon, liqueur, sloe gin, tequila, whiskey 8 aperitif, cocktail, Drambuie, Galliano, highball, nightcap, potation 9 applejack, champagne, firewater, hard cider, moonshine
Alcor: 4 star
Alcott: 3 Amy 7 Bronson
Alcott, Amy: 6 golfer
Alcott, Louisa May: 6 writer
character: 2 Jo 3 Amy, Meg 4 Beth 5 March
work: Eight Cousins
Flower Fables
Hospital Sketches
The Inheritance
Jo's Boys
Little Men
Little Women
alcove: 3 bay 4 apse, cell, nook, room 5 arbor, booth, bower, inlet, niche 6 carrel, corner, cranny, grotto, recess 7 carrell, chamber, cubicle 8 anteroom 9 cubbyhole
ald.: 3 pol.
Alda: 4 Alan 6 Robert 7 Frances
Alda, Alan: 5 actor 8 director
colleague: Harry Morgan, Jamie Farr, Larry Linvile, Loretta Swit, McLean Stevenson, Mike Farrell, Wayne Rogers
father: 6 Robert
film: The Aviator (2004)
Betsy's Wedding (1990)
California Suite (1978)
Canadian Bacon (1995)
Crimes and Misdemeanors (1989)
Everyone Says I Love You (1996)
The Four Seasons (1981)
Manhattan Murder Mystery (1993)
The Mephisto Waltz (1971)
Murder at 1600 (1997)
A New Life (1988)
The Object of My Affection (1998)
Paper Lion (1968)
Same Time, Next Year (1978)
The Seduction of Joe Tynan (1979)
Sweet Liberty (1986)
TV: MASH, The West Wing

Aldebaran: 4 star 5 K star
Alden: 4 John 6 Nowlan
al dente: 4 firm
alder: 4 tree 5 birch, shrub
  ender: 3 man, men
  in Scottish: 3 arn
  relative: 5 birch, hazel 8 hornbeam
Alder, Kurt: 7 chemist 8 Nobelist
Aldine: 4 font 8 typeface
Aldiss, Brian: 6 writer 7 British
Aldo: 3 Ray 4 Moro 5 Gucci, Rossi 7 Fabrizi, Leopold 8 Mannucci
  in English: 6 Donald
Aldous: 6 Huxley
Aldrich: 4 Ames 6 Robert
Aldrich Family, The: 9 radio show
Aldrich, Robert: 8 director
  film: The Dirty Dozen (1967)
    Hush ... Hush, Sweet Charlotte (1965)
    The Longest Yard (1974)
    What Ever Happened to Baby Jane? (1962)
Aldridge: 3 Ira
Aldrin, Buzz: 5 Edwin 8 explorer 9 astronaut
  alma mater: 3 MIT
  craft: 5 Eagle
Aldus: 4 font 8 Manutius, typeface
ale: 3 nog 4 brew, grog, suds 5 draft, drink, quaff 6 bitter, porter 7 draught 8 beverage, Guinness 10 malt liquor
  Adam's ~: 5 water
  cousin: 4 beer 5 lager, stout
  ender: 4 wife 5 house
  ginger ~: 4 soda 5 mixer 9 soft drink
  head: 4 foam
  holder: 3 mug 4 toby 5 stein 7 growler
  how ~ may be offered: 5 on tap
  ingredient: 4 hops, malt
  measure: 2 pt. 4 pint
  source: 3 pub 7 brewery
  tasting of ~: 5 malty
___ ale: 4 pale 5 Adam's, draft 6 ginger
___ Ale: 4 Bass
ALE: 8 division
  team: 4 Rays 6 Red Sox 7 Orioles, Yankees 8 Blue Jays
___ alea est: 5 lacta, Jacta
Alec: 5 Waugh 6 Wilder 7 Baldwin, McCowen 8 Guinness 9 Templeton
Alec Douglas-___: 4 Home
aleck
  smart: 8 quipster, wiseacre
Alecto: 4 Fury 6 Erinys
  colleague: 7 Megaera 9 Tisiphone
alee: 8 downwind 9 protected
Alef
  alternative: *see* computer language
___ a left: 4 hang
___ a leg: 5 break, shake
___ Alegre, Brazil: 5 Porto
Alegría, Ciro: 6 writer 8 Peruvian
___ a leg up: 3 get 4 give
alehouse: 3 bar, pub 6 bistro, saloon, tavern 7 barroom, ginmill, rummery, taproom 8 grogshop 9 speakeasy 10 beer parlor
  fixture: 3 tap
  order: 5 draft
___ aleichem: 6 shalom
Aleichem, Shalom: 6 writer 7 Yiddish 8 humorist
Alejandro: 3 Rey 4 Peña
Alekhine, Alexander
  forte: 5 chess
Aleksandr: 4 Blok, Grin 6 Kuprin 7 Borodin, Fadayev, Pushkin 8 Glazunov 9 Prokhorov
Aleksei: 7 Kosygin
Alemán, Mateo: 6 writer 7 Spanish
alembic: 5 cruet, still 6 beaker, carafe, retort 7 arcanum, refiner 8 crucible, purifier 9 converter, distiller
  locale: 3 lab
Alençon: 4 city, lace, town
  department: 4 Orne
  locale: 6 France
...___ a lender be: 3 nor
aleph: 6 Hebrew, letter
  successor: 3 bes, bet 4 beth
aleph-___: 4 null, zero
Aleppo: 4 city, town
  archeological site near ~: 4 Ebla
Alero: 3 car 4 auto, Olds 10 automobile, Oldsmobile
alert: 3 APB 4 flag, live, spry, warn, wary, wise 5 alarm, alive, awake, aware, fresh, peppy, perky, quick, ready, scare, sharp, siren, smart 6 active, advise, arouse, awaken, bright, inform, intent, lively, living, nimble, notify, prompt, signal, tip off, tocsin, with it 7 all ears, careful, caution, heads-up, heedful, mindful, on guard, wakeful, warning 8 advisory, cautious, forewarn, high sign, keen-eyed, spirited, vigilant, watchful, wide-eyed 9 Argus-eyed, attentive, conscious, expectant, observant, on the ball, receptive, sharp-eyed, sprightly, vivacious, wide awake 10 admonition, call to arms, insightful, keen-witted, on one's toes, on the stick, perceptive, put on guard
  became ~: 5 sat up
  be ~ to: 4 heed
  keep ~: 6 beware 7 look out
  military ~ status: 6 DEFCON
  on the ~: 7 wakeful 8 vigilant
  ozone ~ prompter: 3 fog 4 murk, smog 5 brume, vapor 9 fogginess
___ alert: 3 air, red 4 blue 5 on the, white 6 ground, yellow
___ Alert: 5 First
alertness: 4 care, heed 7 caution 9 assiduity, awareness, diligence, vigilance 10 enterprise, weather eye
Alessandro: 5 Volta 7 Manzoni
  see also Italian
Aleta
  son: 3 Arn
___ a Letter to My Love: 5 I Sent
Aleut: 6 Eskimo 7 Alaskan
  abode: 4 iglu 5 igloo
  carving: 5 totem
  craft: 5 kayak, umiak
  language: 5 Inuit 6 Innuit, Inupik
  outerwear: 5 parka
Aleutians: 4 isle 5 range 6 island
  island: 3 Rat 4 Adak, Atka, Attu 8 Unalaska
  locale: 6 Alaska
  volcano: 6 Katmai
  wind: 8 williwaw
Aleve: 9 analgesic 10 painkiller
  alternative: *see* pain reliever brand
alewife: 4 fish
Alex: 3 Cox 4 Cord 5 Haley, March, Rocco, Segal 6 Désert, Karras, Proyas, Rieger, Trebek, Winter 7 Comfort, English, Raymond 8 Van Halen 10 Delvecchio
alexander: 5 drink 8 beverage, cocktail
___ alexander: 6 brandy
Alexander: 3 Ben 4 Haig, Hall, Jane, Knox, pope, Todd, tsar 5 Jason, Korda, Lebed, Shana 6 Calder, Müller, Nevski, Nevsky, Parkes, Siddig 7 Fleming, Godunov, pontiff, Scourby 8 Alekhine, Glazunov, Hamilton, Smallens 9 Mackenzie, Woollcott 10 Cartwright
  group: 4 band
  in Russian: 5 Sacha
  in Spanish: 9 Alejandro
Alexander (2004 film)
  cast: Rosario Dawson, Colin Farrell, Angelina Jolie, Val Kilmer, Jared Leto
  director: Oliver Stone
Alexander ___: 6 Nevski, Nevsky 7 Severus
Alexander Graham ___: 4 Bell
Alexander, Grover Cleveland: 6 hurler 7 pitcher
Alexander, Jason: 5 actor
  film: The Adventures of Rocky and Bullwinkle (2000)
    White Palace (1990)
  TV: Seinfeld
Alexander Nevsky
  composer: Sergei Prokofiev
Alexander Nevsky (1938 film)
  director: Sergei Eisenstein
Alexander's Bridge
  author: Willa Cather
Alexander's Ragtime Band
  composer: Irving Berlin
Alexander the Great
  horse: 10 Bucephalus
Alexandra: 4 Paul 7 czarina, tsarina 8 Danilova 9 David-Neel
Alexandre: 3 Aja 5 Dumas, Hardy 6 Eiffel
  see also French
Alexandria: 4 city, port, town
  ancient ~ lighthouse: 6 Pharos
  locale: 5 Egypt 8 Virginia 9 Louisiana
  river: 4 Nile
Alexandria Quartet
  author: Lawrence Durrell
  book: 4 Clea 7 Justine 9 Balthazar 10 Mountolive
Alexei: 7 Kosygin
  see also Russian
Alex & Emma (2003 film)
  cast: Kate Hudson, Sophie Marceau, Luke Wilson
  director: Rob Reiner
Alexis: 3 Kim 4 czar, tsar 5 Smith 6 Bledel, Carrel 8 Arquette
  see also Russian
Aléxis: 5 Léger
Alexsandr: 6 Yashin 8 Scriabin
Alf: 6 Landon 7 Kjellin
ALF: 2 ET 5 alien
ALF (NBC sitcom)
  cast: Paul Fusco (ALF/Gordon Shumway)
  cat: 5 Lucky
  food: cats
  home planet: Melmac
alfalfa: 3 hay 6 clover, lucern 7 fodders, lucerne
Alfalfa
  friend: 5 Darla, Porky 6 Spanky 9 Buckwheat
Alfa Romeo: 3 car 4 auto 10 automobile
  model: 3 GTV 4 MiTo 5 Brera 6 Milano, Spider
Alfie (1966 film)
  cast: Michael Caine, Millicent Martin, Shelley Winters
  character: 3 Flo 4 Perc, Ruby 5 Carla, Gilda, Lacey, Lofty 6 Siddie
  director: Lewis Gilbert
Alfie (1967 song)
  artist: Dionne Warwick
al fine: 8 to the end
Alfonse: 6 Capone, D'Amato
Alfonso: 3 rey 4 king 7 Spanish
  queen: 3 Ena
Alfre: 7 Woodard
Alfred: 4 king, Lunt 5 Adler, Binet, Drake, Fried, Green, Jarry, Kazin, Knopf, Krupp, Mahan, Nobel, Noyes, Ryder, Sloan 6 Austin, Bester, Cortot, Döblin, Fuller, Gilman, Kinsey, Molina, Neuman, Newman, Piscop, Werker, Werner 7 Brendel, Dreyfus, Hershey, Kastler, Wegener 8 de Musset, Tennyson 9 Hitchcock, Stieglitz, Whitehead
  composer: Thomas Arne
  poet: Henry James Pye
Alfred ___ Birney: 5 Earle
Alfredo: 5 sauce 6 Oriani 7 Casella
  alternative: 5 pesto 8 marinara
Alfred the ___: 5 Great
alfresco: 7 outdoor, outside
  dining ~: 6 picnic
  locale: 5 patio
  not ~: 6 indoor, inside 7 indoors
alga: 4 kelp 5 plant 6 diatom, nostoc 7 seaweed 9 spirogyra, stonewort
  and fungus: 6 lichen
algae: 4 kelp, scum 5 dulse, sloke 6 diatom 7 seaweed 9 spirogyra
  combining form: 4 phyc- 5 phyco-
  genus: 6 chorda
  Japanese ~: 4 nori
___ algae: 3 red 5 green
algebra: 4 math
Algeciras: 4 city, port, town
  locale: 5 Spain
Alger: 4 Hiss 7 Horatio
Alger, Horatio: 6 writer
  work: Frank's Campaign
    Luck and Pluck
    Ragged Dick
    Tattered Tom
    The Young Miner
Algeria: 6 nation 7 country
  capital: 7 Algiers
  cavalryman: 5 spahi 6 spahee
  city: 4 Oran 5 Batna, Blida, Saida, Setif 6 Annaba 7 Algiers
  desert: 6 Sahara
  governor: 3 dey
  group: 4 OPEC 10 Arab League
  it's n. of ~: 5 Medit.

money: **5** dinar
mountains: **5** Atlas
music: **3** rai
neighbor: **4** Mali **5** Libya, Niger **7** Morocco, Tunisia **10** Mauritania
people: **6** Tuareg
port: **4** Oran **6** Skikda **7** Algiers
writer: **6** Djebar
Algerian: **5** Orani
Algernon: **9** Blackwood, Swinburne
algid: **3** icy **4** cold, cool **6** chilly **7** ice-cold
Algiers: **4** city, port, town **7** capital
area: **6** Casbah, Kasbah
locale: **7** Algeria
Algiers (1938 film)
cast: Charles Boyer, Hedy Lamarr
Algol: **4** star **8** language
alternative: ***see*** computer language
Algonquian: **4** Cree **8** language
Indian: **5** Miami **6** Ottawa **7** Arapaho **8** Arapahoe, Illinois **9** Blackfoot
Algonquin: **4** city, town **6** Indian
locale: **8** Illinois
transport: **5** canoe
tribe: **5** Unami
Algonquin Round Table
member: **3** wit **5** Broun **6** Parker **8** Benchley, Woolcott
algophobe
fear: **4** pain
Algorab: **4** star
Algren, Nelson: **6** writer
work: The Last Carousel
The Man With the Golden Arm
The Neon Wilderness
Never Come Morning
Notes From a Sea Diary
Somebody in Boots
A Walk on the Wild Side
Who Lost an American?
Ali: **5** Ahmed, Laila **6** Landry, Larter **7** MacGraw, Mahomet, Tatyana **8** Mohammed, Muhammad
carried one in '96: **5** torch
defeat, à la ~: **4** whup
faith: **5** Islam
formerly: **4** Clay
stat: **3** KOs
stung like one: **3** bee
see also boxing
Ali (2001 film)
cast: Jamie Foxx, Will Smith, Mario Van Peebles, Jon Voight
director: Michael Mann
Ali ___: **4** Baba **5** Pasha
Ali ___ and the Forty Thieves: **4** Baba
alia
et ~: **9** and others
___ alia: **5** inter
alias: **3** aka, nom **4** name **5** pseud. **6** anonym, handle **7** moniker, pen name **8** monicker, nickname **9** false name, pseudonym, stage name **10** nom de plume
common ~: **5** Jones, Smith
Ali Baba: **4** Arab, hero
brother: **6** Cassim
command: **10** open sesame
locale: **4** cave
alibi: **4** plea, yarn **5** cover, story **6** excuse **7** defense, pretext, voucher
Alibi ___: **3** Ike
___ Alibi: **3** Her
Alicante: **4** city, port, town
locale: **5** Spain
Alice: **4** blue, city, Faye, town **5** Brady, Braga, Krige, Munro **6** Cooper, Marble, Toklas, Walker, Waters **7** grayish, Kramden **8** Ghostley **9** Childress, Longworth, Roosevelt
chronicler: **4** Arlo
husband: **5** Ralph
locale: **5** Texas
relative: ***see*** blue color
Alice (1990 film)
cast: Alec Baldwin, Blythe Danner, Judy Davis, Mia Farrow
director: Woody Allen
Alice (CBS sitcom)
cast: Polly Holliday (Flo Castleberry)
Beth Howland (Vera Gorman)
Linda Lavin (Alice Hyatt)
Philip McKeon (Tommy Hyatt)
Martha Raye (Carrie Sharples)
Vic Tayback (Mel Sharples)
Celia Weston (Jolene Hunnicutt)
setting: **4** Mel's **5** diner **7** Arizona, Phoenix
spinoff: **3** Flo
Alice ___: **4** blue **5** Adams **7** Springs
Alice ___ Gown: **4** Blue
Alice ___ Miller: **4** Duer
___ Alice: **4** Tiny
Alice Adams: **4** film **5** novel
author: Booth Tarkington
cast: Katharine Hepburn, Fred MacMurray, Fred Stone
director: George Stevens
Alice Doesn't Live Here Anymore (1974 film)
cast: Ellen Burstyn, Kris Kristofferson
director: Martin Scorsese
Alice in Wonderland cat: **5** Dinah
Alice's Adventures in Wonderland
author: Lewis Carroll
character: **3** Two **4** Bill, Cook, Crab, Dodo, Duck, Five, King **5** Dinah, Elsie, Knave, Lacie, Lorry, Puppy, Queen, Seven **6** Eaglet, Lizard, Pigeon, Rabbit, Tillie **7** Duchess, Gryphon, William **8** Baby Crab, Dormouse, Flamingo, Hedgehog **9** Mad Hatter, March Hare **10** Mock Turtle **11** Caterpillar, Cheshire Cat, Fish Footman, Frog Footman
Alice's Restaurant: **4** film, song
artist: Arlo Guthrie
cast: James Broderick, Arlo Guthrie, Pat Quinn
director: Arthur Penn
Alicia: **3** Ana **4** Keys, Witt **6** Alonso **7** Bridges, Markova **10** de Larrocha
Alida: **5** Valli
___ a lid on it!: **3** Put
alien: **3** ALF, odd **4** Mork, Yoda **5** outer, Sarek, Spock **6** exotic, Klaatu, remote **7** foreign, invader, Klingon, Martian, offbeat, outside, oversea, refugee, Romulan, Starman, strange, unknown, unusual **8** contrary, emigrant, intruder, newcomer, offshore, outsider, overseas, stranger, uncommon, Venusian **9** auslander, different, extrinsic, foreigner, immigrant, nonnative, outlander, peregrine, unheard-of **10** noncitizen, outlandish, unfamiliar
combining form: **3** xen- **4** xeno-
investigation: **5** X file
search org.: **4** SETI
spacecraft: **3** UFO **6** saucer
subj.: **3** ESL
Alien (1979 film)
cast: John Hurt, Tom Skerritt, Sigourney Weaver
cat: **6** Jonesy
character: **5** Brett **6** Dallas, Ripley **7** Lambert
director: Ridley Scott
Alien and ___ Acts: **8** Sedition
alienate: **4** sour **6** divide, offend, sicken **7** disgust, fend off, hold off, repulse, turn off **8** disunite, drive off, embitter, estrange, imbitter, separate, turn away **9** disaffect **10** antagonize, set against
alienated: **6** bitter **8** factious **10** antisocial, friendless, rebellious, unfriendly
alienation: **4** rift **5** anomy, break, split **6** anomie, breach, enmity **9** defection, sundering **10** remoteness, separation, withdrawal
Alienist, The
author: Caleb Carr
Aliens (1986 film)
cast: Michael Biehn, Carrie Henn, Sigourney Weaver
character: **4** Newt **5** Ellen, Hicks **6** Dwayne, Ripley
director: James Cameron
___-a-lievio: **4** ring
___ a life!: **3** Get
Ali-Foreman fight site: **5** Zaire
Alighieri: **5** Dante
alight: **4** land **5** light, perch, roost **6** ablaze, arrive, debark, get off, hop off, settle **7** descend, flaming, get down, jump off, step off **8** come down, dismount **9** disembark, touch down
set ~: **6** ignite, kindle
upon: **9** encounter
align: **3** fix, set **4** ally, even, join, rank, true **5** array, level, order, range, reset **6** adjust, even up, line up, orient, square, true up **7** arrange, marshal **8** regulate **9** affiliate, associate, calibrate, collimate, cooperate **10** coordinate, join up with, straighten
the crosshairs: **3** aim **5** aim at
(with): **4** side
aligned: **4** true **5** level **6** in a row **7** abreast **8** parallel, straight
___ alignment: **5** wheel
alii: **6** others
et ~ cousin: **3** etc.
___ alii: **5** inter
alike: **4** akin, both, same, such **5** equal, level **6** allied, evenly, on a par **7** cognate, equally, kindred, related, similar, the same, uniform **8** in common, parallel **9** analogous, identical, similarly, uniformly **10** comparable, comparably, equivalent, synonymous, the same way
look ~: **5** match
make ~: **6** equate
not ~: **9** different **10** dissimilar
think ~: **5** agree
___-alike: **4** look
alikeness: **10** similarity
___ a limb: **5** out on
aliment: **4** chow, diet, eats, fare, feed, food, grub, keep, meal, meat **5** board, bread, manna **6** fodder, forage, living, repast, viands **7** commons, edibles, nurture, rations, victual, vittles **8** eatables, victuals **9** foodstuff, nutriment, provender, refection **10** livelihood, provisions, sustenance
alimentary: **7** dietary **9** digestive, nutritive **10** comestible, digestible, nourishing, nutritious, sustaining
canal part: **5** ileum
alimentary ___: **5** canal
alimony: **7** payment, subsidy, support
recipients: **4** exes
Ali, Muhammad: **3** pug **5** boxer
daughter: **5** Laila
milieu: **4** ring
aline
see align
___ a line: **4** drop
Aline: **8** MacMahon, Saarinen
A-line: **5** dress, skirt **7** skimmer
creator: **4** Dior
alined: **6** in a row
___ a lineman for the county: **3** I Am
___-a-liner: **5** penny
___-a-ling: **4** ding, ting
___ alios: **5** inter
Alioto: **6** Joseph
aliped: **3** bat
Alison: **5** Doody, Lurie, Moyet **6** Krauss **7** Arngrim, La Placa **8** Steadman **9** Skipworth
Alison's House
author: Susan Glaspell
alist: **6** tilted **7** heeling, leaning, listing, tilting **8** inclined **9** careening
Alistair: **5** Cooke **7** MacLean
alit: **6** got off, landed **7** set down, settled **8** debussed, deplaned **9** descended **10** came to rest, dismounted
Alito: **6** Samuel
___ a little: **3** not **4** just
___ a Little Bit of Luck: **4** With
___ a Little Help...: **4** With
___ a Little Prayer: **4** I Say
___ a Little Tenderness: **3** Try
alive: **4** rife, spry **5** alert, awake, brisk, quick, vital **6** active, extant, feisty, mortal, upbeat, viable, with us **7** animate, dynamic, growing, replete, running, teeming, vibrant, wakeful, working, zestful **8** animated, bustling, existent, existing, spirited, stirring, swarming, vigorous **9** abounding, breathing, cognizant, conscious, energetic, observant, operative, sprightly, vivacious **10** responsive, subsisting
act ~: **6** perk up
and kicking: **4** well **5** sound
combining form: **4** vivi-
keep ~: **7** sustain
remain ~: **5** exist **6** manage **7** subsist, survive
skin ~: **4** flay **6** review, vilify **9** criticize
to: **7** aware of **9** mindful of

(with): 4 rife 7 profuse, replete, teeming 8 thronged 9 abounding
__ alive!: 3 It's 4 Look 5 Sakes
Alive: 4 book, film
author: Piers Paul Read
cast: Ethan Hawke, Vincent Spano
director: Frank Marshall
setting: 5 Andes
Alive!
band: Kiss
__ Alive: 6 Stayin'
alive and __: 4 well 7 kicking
__ a living!: 3 It's
Alka-__: 7 Seltzer
alkali: 3 KOH, lye 4 base, lime, NaOH 6 potash 7 antacid 9 hydroxide
measure: 2 pH
opposite: 4 acid
alkali __: 4 blue, flat, rock, soil 5 grass, metal
alkaline: 5 acrid, basic, salty 6 bitter 7 caustic
not ~: 6 acidic
Alka-Seltzer: 7 antacid
alternative: *see* antacid
sound: 4 fizz, plop
all: 3 sum 4 full, just, only 5 every, fully, gross, quite, total, whole 6 entire, in toto, purely, solely, wholly 7 bar none, pronoun, totally, utterly 8 complete, entirely, entirety, everyone, the works 9 aggregate, everybody 10 completely, everything, lion's share, nothing but
combining form: 3 omn-, pan- 4 omni-, pano-, pant- 5 panta-, panto-
ender: 4 heal, over, seed 5 spice
in music: 5 tutti
in Spanish: 4 toda, todo
name meaning ~: 4 Ella
starter: 4 hold 5 carry, catch
the time, to a poet: 3 e'er
together: 6 at once 7 en masse
wound up: 5 tense
all __: 3 but, set, wet 4 ears, eyes, gone, hail, over, told 5 along, clear, fours, in all, right, there 6 thumbs
all __ and a yard wide: 4 wool
all __ and bothered: 3 hot
all __ day's work: 3 in a
all __ good: 5 to the
all __ out: 3 get
all __ sudden: 3 of a
all __ up: 3 het
all-__: 3 day, out 4 heal, pass, star, time, year 5 clear, fired, in-one, night, right, round, State 6 around 7 nighter, purpose, weather
__ all: 4 bare 5 above, after, not at
__-all: 3 end, you 4 cure, heal, know
All: 9 detergent
alternative: *see* detergent
All __: 4 of Me, Over, Star 5 Alone, at Sea, I Know, I Need, of You 6 My Sons, Saints
All __!: 4 rise, stop 6 aboard
All __ Airways: 6 Nippon
All __ and Heaven Too: 4 This
All __ are off!: 4 bets
All __ Day: 5 Fools', Souls' 6 Saints'
All __ day's work: 3 in a
All __ down: 4 fall
All __ Eve: 5 About 7 Hallows'
All __ Family: 5 in the
All __ for Christmas...: 5 I Want
All __ Glitters: 4 That
All __ is a tall ship...: 4 I ask
All __ Is Dream of You: 3 I Do
All __ Jazz: 4 That
All __ Long: 5 Night 6 Summer
All __ Need Is Love: 3 You
All __ Need Is You: 5 I Ever
All __ on the Western Front: 5 Quiet
All __ that's going...: 6 ashore
All __ the Watchtower: 5 Along
All __ to Do Is Dream: 5 I Have
All __ Up: 5 Shook
All __ were the borogoves: 5 mimsy
All __ Years Ago: 5 Those
All-__: 3 Pro 4 Bran
All-__ Game: 4 Star
__ All: 5 After, Armor
alla __: 5 breve, prima 6 marcia
Alla: 8 Nazimova
All About __: 3 Eve 4 Soul
All About Eve (1950 film)
cast: Anne Baxter, Bette Davis, Celeste Holm, George Sanders
character: 4 Bill 5 Karen, Margo 6 DeWitt 7 Addison, Sampson 8 Channing, Richards 10 Harrington
director: Joseph L. Mankiewicz
alla breve: 7 cut time
...__ all a good night: 5 and to
Allah: 3 God 4 Lord
worship of ~: 5 Islam
Allahabad river: 6 Ganges
All Alone
composer: Irving Berlin
All Alone Am I (1962 song)
artist: Brenda Lee
all along the __: 4 line
Allan: 4 Dwan 5 Arbus, Jones 6 Nevins 7 Cormack, Sherman 8 Gurganus 9 Pinkerton
Allan-__: 5 a-Dale
__ Allan Poe: 5 Edgar
Allan Quatermain
author: H. Rider Haggard
Allante: 3 car 4 auto 8 Cadillac 10 automobile
all-around: 6 global 7 general 8 sweeping 9 adaptable, inclusive, versatile
All Around the Town
author: Mary Higgins Clark
All Around the World (1990 song)
artist: Lisa Stansfield
__ alla Scala: 6 Teatro
all at __: 3 sea 4 once
allay: 4 calm, cool, ease, lull 5 abate, blunt, quell, quiet, slake 6 dampen, lessen, pacify, quench, reduce, settle, smooth, soften, solace, soothe, temper 7 appease, assuage, compose, lighten, mollify, relieve 8 decrease, mitigate, moderate, palliate 9 alleviate, put to rest, untrouble 10 propitiate
one's fears: 6 assure
All bets __ off: 3 are
__-all book: 4 tell
All-Bran: 6 cereal
alternative: *see* cereal
Allbritton: 6 Louise
All by Myself
composer: Irving Berlin
All by Myself (song)
artist: Celine Dion, Eric Carmen
all-consuming: 7 intense
All Creatures __ and Small: 5 Great
all-day __: 6 sucker
All Dogs Go to Heaven
dog: 3 Flo 5 Itchy 6 Killer 7 Carface, Charlie
__ allé: 3 pas
allegation: 5 claim, story 6 charge 9 assertion, statement 10 accusation, contention, deposition, indictment, profession
allege: 3 say 4 aver, hold 5 claim, state 6 accuse, affirm, assert, attest, avouch, charge 7 charges, contend, declare, pretend, profess, purport, testify 8 maintain 10 asseverate
alleged: 7 nominal, reputed 8 putative, reported, so-called 9 pretended 10 ostensible
reason: 5 alibi, bluff, cover, guise 6 excuse 7 cover-up 8 pretense 10 cover story
allegedly: 8 so-called 10 apparently
Alleghenies: 5 range 9 mountains
Allegheny: 5 river
city on the ~: 5 Olean 10 Pittsburgh
ex-name: 5 USAir
locale: 4 Penn. 7 New York
Allegheny Moon (1956 song)
artist: Patti Page
allegiance: 3 tie 4 love 5 faith 6 fealty, homage 7 loyalty 8 devotion, fidelity 9 adherence, constancy, deference, fixedness, obedience 10 conformity, dedication, obligation
owe ~: 6 adhere, belong
allegiant: 4 true 5 loyal 6 ardent, steady 7 devoted, dutiful, staunch 8 constant, faithful, true-blue, yeomanly 9 dedicated, steadfast
allegorical: 8 mythical, symbolic 9 legendary
allegorize: 9 adumbrate 10 illustrate
allegory: 4 myth 5 fable, story 7 parable 8 metaphor 10 fairy story
relative: 6 apolog 8 apologue
Allegory of Love, The
author: C.S. Lewis
Allegret: 4 Marc
allegro: 4 fast 5 tempo
faster than ~: 6 presto
slower than ~: 8 moderato
allegro __: 5 assai
__ allegro: 5 molto
Allegro: 7 musical
composer: Oscar Hammerstein, Richard Rodgers
allegro con __: 4 brio
allele: 4 gene
alleluia: 4 pean 5 paean 10 hallelujah
allemande: 5 dance, sauce
ingredient: 4 yolk
all-embracing: 3 big 4 vast 6 cosmic 7 general, overall 8 catholic, cosmical, sweeping, thorough 9 universal
Allen: 3 Ira, Mel, Rex, Tim 4 Fred, Funt, Joan, Lane, Tate 5 Byron, Drury, Ethan, Irwin, Karen, Lewis, Nancy, Peter, Steve, Woody 6 Curnow, Debbie, Du Mont, George, Gracie, Hervey, Ludden, Marcus 7 Barbara, Iverson, Jenkins 8 Garfield, Ginsberg 9 Elizabeth, Steverino
Keaton, to ~: 6 costar
partner: 5 Burns, Rossi
successor: 4 Paar
to Burns: 4 foil, wife
Allen __: 5 screw 6 wrench
__ Allen belt: 3 Van
Allenby: 6 Edmund
conquest of 1918: 6 Beirut 8 Beyrouth
all-encompassing: 6 global 7 generic 8 sweeping 9 generical, unlimited
Allende, Isabel: 6 writer 7 Chilean
work: City of the Beasts
Daughter of Fortune
Eva Luna
The House of the Spirits
The Infinite Plan
Mothers and Sons
Of Love and Shadows
Paula
Portrait in Sepia
Allen, Ethan brother: 3 Ira
Allen, Fred: 3 wit 8 comedian
feuder with ~: Jack Benny
milieu: 5 radio
spouse: Portland Hoffa
Allen, George: 5 coach
sport: 8 football
Allen, Gracie: 5 comic 7 actress 10 comedienne
milieu: 5 radio
spouse: George Burns
Allen, Nancy: 7 actress
spouse: Brian De Palma
Allen, Peter
spouse: Liza Minnelli
Allen, Steve
spouse: Jayne Meadows
Allen, Tim: 5 actor
film: Big Trouble (2002)
Galaxy Quest (1999)
Joe Somebody (2001)
The Santa Clause (1994)
film (voice): Toy Story (1995)
movie character: 5 Santa
TV: Home Improvement
Allentown: 4 city
city near ~: 6 Easton 9 Bethlehem
locale: 4 Penn.
river: 6 Lehigh
Allentown (1982 song)
artist: Billy Joel
Allen, Woody: 5 actor 8 director
film: Alice (1990)
Annie Hall (1977, AA)
Another Woman (1988)
Anything Else (2003)
Bananas (1971)
Broadway Danny Rose (1984)
Bullets Over Broadway (1994)
Casino Royale (1967)
Cassandra's Dream (2007)
Celebrity (1998)
Crimes and Misdemeanors (1989)
The Curse of the Jade Scorpion (2001)
Everyone Says I Love You (1996)
The Front (1976)
Hannah and Her Sisters (1986)
Hollywood Ending (2002)
Husbands and Wives (1992)
Interiors (1978)
Love and Death (1975)
Manhattan (1979)
Manhattan Murder Mystery (1993)

Match Point (2005)
Melinda and Melinda (2005)
A Midsummer Night's Sex Comedy (1982)
Mighty Aphrodite (1995)
Play It Again, Sam (1972)
The Purple Rose of Cairo (1985)
Radio Days (1987)
Scoop (2006)
Shadows and Fog (1992)
Sleeper (1973)
Small Time Crooks (2000)
Stardust Memories (1980)
Sweet and Lowdown (1999)
Take the Money and Run (1969)
Vicky Cristina Barcelona (2008)
Whatever Works (2009)
What's Up, Tiger Lily? (1966)
Zelig (1983)
film (voice): Antz (1998)
spouse: Louise Lasser
allergen
dispenser: 6 anther
__-allergenic: 4 hypo
allergic: 6 averse
reaction: 4 itch, rash 6 asthma
allergy: 8 aversion, hay fever 9 antipathy
medication: 5 Afrin 6 Contac, Nyquil, Tavist 7 Actifed, Comtrex, Dayquil, Dristan, Sinutab, Sudafed 8 Benadryl, Dimetapp, Drixoral, TheraFlu 9 Coricidin, Triaminic 10 Robitussin
sound: 5 achoo 6 ahchoo, hachoo 7 kerchoo
alleviate: 4 calm, cure, ease, help 5 allay, loose, quell, salve 6 deaden, defuse, defuze, lessen, loosen, pacify, quench, remedy, smooth, soften, solace, soothe 7 appease, assuage, lighten, mollify, relieve, sweeten 8 mitigate, moderate, palliate 9 soft-pedal, untrouble 10 ameliorate
alleviation: 6 relief, solace 7 anodyne 9 abatement
alleviative: 8 curative
all-expenses-__: 4 paid
alley: 4 mews, path, road, walk 5 aisle, track 6 street 7 back way, passage, pathway 8 corridor, cul-de-sac 10 back street, passageway
blind ~: 7 dead end, impasse 8 cul-de-sac
bowling ~: 4 lane
button: 5 reset
challenge: 5 split
ender: 3 way
haunt an ~: 5 prowl
org.: 3 PBA
player: 6 bowler, kegler 7 kegeler
score: 5 spare 6 strike
target: 3 pin
see also bowling
alley __: 3 cat 5 light
alley-__: 3 oop
__ alley: 5 blind, shaft 7 bowling
__-alley: 4 back
Alley: 5 Mills 7 Kirstie
Alley __: 3 Cat, Oop
__ Alley: 6 Tin Pan
Alley Cat (1962 song)
artist: Bent Fabric
Alley, Kirstie: 7 actress
film: Drop Dead Gorgeous (1999)
Look Who's Talking (1989)
role: 4 Howe
spouse: Parker Stevenson
TV: Cheers
Alley Oop
creator: V.T. Hamlin
dinosaur: 5 Dinny
friend: 5 Foozy
girlfriend: 5 Ooola
king: 4 Tunk 6 Guzzle
kingdom: 3 Lem, Moo
lab assistant: 3 Ava
queen: 10 Umpateedle
scientist: 6 Wonmug
All Fall Down: 4 film 5 novel
author: James Leo Herlihy
subject: 4 Iran
__ All Fears, The: 5 Sum of
__ All Flesh, The: 5 Way of
__ all, folks!: 5 That's
All Fools' __: 3 Day
All for Love
poet: John Dryden
All for Love (1993 song)
artist: Bryan Adams, Rod Stewart, Sting
All for one and one for all: 5 motto
all fours: 4 game 8 card game
variety: 5 cinch
all get __: 3 out
All gone!: 4 poof
Allgood: 4 Sara
Allhallows __: 3 Eve
__ all hang out: 5 let it
alliance: 3 tie 4 bloc, bond, club, pact, ring 5 guild, junto, trust, union, unity 6 accord, league, treaty 7 academy, compact, entente, society 8 marriage, relation 9 agreement, anschluss, coalition, matrimony 10 federation, fellowship, friendship
former ~: 3 PAU, UAR 5 SEATO
global ~: 3 OAS 4 NATO
political ~: 4 bloc 5 junta
WWII ~: 4 Axis
Alliance: 4 city, town
locale: 4 Ohio
Alliance __ Progress: 3 for
__ Alliance: 4 Dual, Holy 6 Little, Triple
All I ask is __ ship: 5 a tall
Allie: 5 Light 7 Sherman 8 Reynolds
friend: 4 Kate
__ & Allie: 4 Kate
allied: 3 wed 4 akin 5 alike 6 joined, linked, united 7 cognate, kindred, related, similar, unified 8 combined, friendly, hooked up, in league, parallel, relative 9 analogous, bracketed, connected, corporate, in cahoots 10 affiliated, associated, comparable, equivalent
Allied: 5 mover
rival: 6 Global, United
Allier: 5 river
city on the ~: 5 Vichy
locale: 6 France
Allies
opponent: 4 Axis
All I Ever Need Is You (1971 song)
artist: Sonny and Cher
alligator: 5 dance 6 animal, lizard 7 leather, reptile
female: 3 cow
home: 5 swamp
label: 4 Izod
male: 4 bull
on a shirt: 4 logo
relative: 4 croc 6 caiman, cayman 9 crocodile
young: 9 hatchling
alligator __: 3 gar 4 clip, pear, weed 5 clamp, shear 6 lizard, wrench 7 snapper
Alligator __: 5 Alley
alligator pear: 5 fruit 7 avocado
All I gotta do __ naturally: 5 is act
All I Have to Do Is Dream (1958 song)
artist: Everly Brothers
all-important: 5 vital 8 critical 9 necessary 10 portentous
all in __ time: 4 good
all in __ work: 5 a day's
all-in-__: 3 one
all-inclusive: 3 big 4 a to z, full, vast, wide 5 broad, roomy, total, uncut, whole 6 entire, global 7 blanket, general, plenary 8 catholic, complete, detailed, far-flung, finished, spacious, sweeping, thorough, umbrella 9 capacious, expansive, extensive, universal, unreduced, wholesale 10 exhaustive, unabridged, widespread
category: 4 misc.
all in good __: 4 time
all-in-one: 6 entire
All in the Family (CBS sitcom)
cast: Carroll O'Connor (Archie Bunker)
Rob Reiner (Mike 'Meathead' Stivic)
Jean Stapleton (Edith 'Dingbat' Bunker)
Sally Struthers (Gloria Bunker Stivic)
producer: Lear
setting: Queens, New York
spinoff: The Jeffersons, Maude
__ all in this together!: 4 We're
Allison: 3 Roe 4 Fran, Mose 5 Bobby 6 Anders
on Peyton Place: 3 Mia
Allison, Bobby: 9 auto racer
milieu: 5 track
Allison, Mose: 7 pianist
genre: 4 jazz
Alliss: 5 Peter
allium: 4 leek 5 bulbs, chive, onion 6 garlic 7 shallot
All I Wanna Do (1994 song)
artist: Sheryl Crow
all kidding __: 5 aside
all-knowing: 4 wise 10 omniscient
__ All Laughed: 4 They
Allman: 5 Duane, Gregg
Allman Brothers Band
song: Midnight Rider (1975)
Ramblin Man (1973)
Allman, Gregg: 8 musician
spouse: Cher
All My __: 4 Sons 8 Children
All My __ Live in Texas: 3 Ex's
All My Children (ABC): 4 soap 9 soap opera
cast: Kelly Ripa
Susan Lucci
role: 4 Kane, Opal 5 Erica
All My Sons: 4 film, play
author: Arthur Miller
cast: Burt Lancaster, Edward G. Robinson
character: 3 Joe, Sue 4 Anne, Bert, Kate 5 Lydia
director: Irving Reis
all-nighter: 5 binge, event
pull an ~: 4 cram
All Night Long (1981 film)
cast: Gene Hackman, Diane Ladd, Barbra Streisand
All Night Long (song)
artist: Faith Evans, Joe Walsh, Lionel Richie, Puff Daddy
allocate: 3 set 4 mete 5 allot, allow, divvy, grant, spend, split 6 assign, assort, budget, devote, divide, parcel, ration 7 divvy up, earmark, mete out, portion 8 dispense, regulate, set aside 9 apportion, designate 10 distribute, measure out
allocation: 4 dole 5 grant, quota, share 6 budget, ration 7 portion 9 allotment, allowance 10 assignment
allocution: 6 speech 7 lecture
all of a __: 6 sudden
All of Me (1984 film)
cast: Steve Martin, Lily Tomlin
director: Carl Reiner
dog: 3 Bix
All of You (1984 song)
artist: Diana Ross
all-or-__: 4 none 7 nothing
allosaur: 5 biped 7 reptile
allot: 3 set 4 deal, dole, mete 5 allow, divvy, grant, leave, share, split 6 assign, bestow, devote, divide, parcel, ration, render 7 carve up, dole out, give out, hand out, mete out, portion, prorate, station 8 allocate, dedicate, dispense, divide up, set aside 9 apportion, parcel out 10 distribute, measure out, proportion
allotment: 3 cut, lot 4 dole, part, time 5 grant, piece, quota, share, slice 6 ration 7 measure, portion 8 dividend, quantity 9 allowance 10 adjustment, allocation, assignment
all-out: 4 firm, full 5 total, utter 6 utmost 7 maximum, optimum, supreme 8 absolute, complete, emphatic, forceful, full-bore, resolute, sweeping, thorough, to the max, whole-hog 9 full-blown, full-dress, full-scale, intensive, last-ditch, unlimited 10 conclusive, exhaustive, soup to nuts, unswerving, unwavering
All Out of Love (1980 song)
artist: Air Supply
all-over: 9 universal 10 ubiquitous
__ all over: 4 fall
All Over
author: Edward Albee
__ All Over: 4 Glad
allow: 2 OK 3 let, own 4 avow, bear, give, lend, loan, mete, okay 5 admit, adopt, agree, allot, brook, go for, grant, leave, let on, spare, spell, stand, yield 6 accede, afford, assent, comply, deduct, enable, fess up, impart, permit, suffer 7 agree to, approve, concede, confess, empower, entitle, include, intitle, let pass, license, provide, support, welcome 8 allocate, assent to, legalize, sanction, set

aside, stand for, submit to, tolerate **9** acquiesce, apportion, approve of, authorize, be game for, give leave, put up with, recognize, sign off on **10** concur with, give the nod
for: 6 offset **7** forgive, include **8** consider
(for): 4 plan
to enter: 5 admit, greet, let in **6** accept **7** embrace, receive, welcome
to go: 4 free **5** loose **6** acquit, let off, pardon, parole **7** cashier, dismiss, release, set free **8** liberate **9** exonerate, muster out, terminate
to pass: 5 let by
to use: 4 lend
allowable: 2 OK **3** apt **4** good, okay **5** jural, legal, legit, licit **6** kasher, kosher, lawful, proper, venial **8** all right, optional, suitable **9** excusable, legalized **10** acceptable, admissible, approvable, forgivable, in the rules, legitimate
allowance: 3 cut, pay **4** dole, gift, odds, room **5** grant, leave, quota, share, slice, start **6** margin, ration, rebate, refund **7** advance, pension, percent, stipend, subsidy, support **8** headroom **9** abatement, admission, advantage, allotment, clearance, deduction, endowment, endurance, exception, insurance, reduction **10** adaptation, adjustment, allocation, commission, concession, confession, fellowship, honorarium, indulgence, percentage, recompense, remittance, sufferance, toleration, unbosoming
make ~ for: 7 include **8** overlook
scale ~: 4 tare, tret
time ~: 5 grace
allowed: 5 legal, legit, licit **6** kasher, kosher, lawful, proper **8** rightful **9** by the book, permitted **10** admissible, sanctioned
is not ~ to: 5 mayn't
allowing: 6 though **7** lenient
alloy: 3 mix **5** admix, blend, brass, Invar, metal, Monel, steel **6** alnico, bronze, latten, mingle, oreide, ormolu, oroide, pewter, solder, tambac, tombac **7** amalgam, combine, Elinvar, Everdur, Inconel, mixture, Mumetal, nitinol, platina, pollute, tinfoil **8** bismanol, calamine, cast iron, electrum, gunmetal, intermix, kamacite, Manganin, Nichrome, pot metal **9** barberite, bell metal, composite, duralumin, Dutch foil, Dutch gold, Dutch leaf, magnalium, pinchbeck, Platinite, platinoid, type metal, Vitallium, white gold **10** adulterate, amalgamate, constantan, Dutch metal, gold bronze, misch metal, mosaic gold, soft solder, superalloy, terne metal, Wood's metal
aluminum ~: 6 alnico **9** duralumin, magnalium
antimony ~: 9 type metal
bismuth ~: 8 bismanol **10** Wood's metal
brasslike ~: 6 latten
cadmium ~: 10 Wood's metal
carbon ~: 5 steel **8** cast iron
cerium ~: 10 misch metal
chromium ~: 7 Elinvar, Inconel **8** Nichrome **9** Vitallium
cobalt ~: 6 alnico **9** Vitallium **10** superalloy
component: 5 metal
copper ~: 5 brass, Monel **6** bronze, latten, oreide, ormolu, oroide, tambac, tombac **7** Everdur, Mumetal **8** gunmetal, Manganin, pot metal **9** barberite, bell metal, duralumin, Dutch foil, Dutch gold, Dutch leaf, pinchbeck, platinoid **10** constantan, Dutch metal, gold bronze, mosaic gold
gold ~: 8 electrum
heat-resistant ~: 6 cermet **7** ceramal
iridium ~: 7 platina
iron ~: 5 Invar, Monel, steel **7** Elinvar, Inconel, Mumetal **8** kamacite, Nichrome **9** Platinite **10** superalloy
lanthanum ~: 10 misch metal
lead ~: 5 terne **6** pewter **7** tinfoil **8** calamine, pot metal **9** type metal **10** gold bronze, soft solder, terne metal, Wood's metal
magnesium ~: 9 magnalium
magnetic ~: 6 alnico
manganese ~: 5 Monel **7** Everdur **8** bismanol, Manganin
mercury ~: 7 amalgam
molybdenum ~: 9 Vitallium
nickel ~: 5 Invar, Monel **6** alnico **7** Elinvar, Inconel, Mumetal, nitinol **8** electrum, kamacite, Manganin, Nichrome **9** barberite, Platinite, platinoid, white gold **10** constantan, superalloy
osmium ~: 7 platina
palladium ~: 7 platina **9** white gold
platinum ~: 7 platina **9** white gold
silicon ~: 7 Everdur **9** barberite
silver ~: 7 amalgam **8** electrum
tin ~: 5 terne **6** bronze, oreide, oroide, pewter **8** calamine, gunmetal **9** barberite, bell metal, type metal **10** gold bronze, soft solder, terne metal, Wood's metal
titanium ~: 7 nitinol
zinc ~: 5 brass **6** latten, oreide, ormolu, oroide, tambac, tombac **8** calamine, gunmetal **9** Dutch foil, Dutch gold, Dutch leaf, pinchbeck, platinoid, white gold **10** Dutch metal, gold bronze, mosaic gold
alloyed: 4 mixt **5** mixed **6** impure
alloys
science of ~: 10 metallurgy
all-points bulletin: 7 dragnet
__ all possible: 4 if at
all-powerful: 6 divine **10** omnipotent
All praise to __: 5 Allah
All-Pro: 4 star **10** footballer
all-purpose: 6 useful **9** versatile
All Quiet on the Western Front: 4 film **5** novel
author: Erich Maria Remarque
cast: Lew Ayres, Louis Wolheim, John Wray
character: 3 Kat **4** Erna, Leer **6** Müller
director: Lewis Milestone
all right: 4 okay **5** roger
All Said and Done
author: Simone de Beauvoir
All Saints' __: 3 Day
All sales __: 5 final
all-seeing: 8 lynx-eyed **10** omniscient
__ all she wrote: 5 That's
All Shook Up (1957 song)
artist: Elvis Presley
All Souls' __: 3 Day
allspice: 4 tree **7** pimento
all-sports
channel: 4 ESPN
first ~ radio station: 4 WFAN
All-Star Games
like ~: 6 annual
Allstate
competitor: *see* insurance company
owner: 5 Sears
All's Well That Ends Well
author: William Shakespeare
character: 5 Lafeu **6** Helena **7** Bertram, Lavache, Rinaldo **8** Marianna, Parolles, Violenta
All systems go: 3 A-OK
all-terrain __: 4 bike **7** vehicle
all-terrain vehicle: 3 SUV **4** jeep
__ All That: 4 She's
All that glitters __ gold: 5 is not
All That Glitters
author: Thomas Tryon
All That Jazz (1979 film)
cast: Jessica Lange, Ann Reinking, Roy Scheider
director: Bob Fosse
All That She Wants (1993 song)
artist: Ace of Base
all the __: 4 rage, same
All the Best People
author: Sloan Wilson
All the King's Men: 4 film **5** novel
author: Robert Penn Warren
cast: Broderick Crawford, Joanne Dru, John Ireland, Mercedes McCambridge
director: Robert Rossen
All the Man That I Need (1991 song)
artist: Whitney Houston
All the news that's fit to print
coiner: 4 Ochs
All the perfumes of __: 6 Arabia
All the President's Men (1976 film)
cast: Martin Balsam, Dustin Hoffman, Hal Holbrook, Robert Redford, Jason Robards, Jack Warden
director: Alan J. Pakula
All the Pretty Horses (2000 film)
cast: Penélope Cruz, Matt Damon, Henry Thomas
director: Billy Bob Thornton
All the Right Moves (1983 film)
cast: Tom Cruise, Craig T. Nelson, Lea Thompson
All the Things You Are
composer: Jerome Kern, Oscar Hammerstein
All the Way (1957 song)
artist: Frank Sinatra
composer: Jimmy Van Heusen, Sammy Cahn
__ All the Way Home: 4 I Ran
All the world's __: 6 a stage
All Things Considered (NPR news)
host: Linda Wertheimer, Melissa Block, Michelle Norris, Noah Adams, Robert Siegel
All This and Heaven Too (1940 film)
cast: Charles Boyer, Bette Davis
director: Anatole Litvak
All This Time (song)
artist: Sting, Tiffany
All Those Years Ago (1981 song)
artist: George Harrison
All Through the Night (1942 film)
cast: Humphrey Bogart, Conrad Veidt
dog: 6 Hansel
All Through the Night (1984 song)
artist: Cyndi Lauper
__ all together: 5 get it, put it
all to the __: 4 good
__ All True: 3 It's
allude: 5 refer, touch
to: 4 cite, hint, mean **5** imply, quote **6** advert, hint at, impute **7** mention, purport, suggest, touch on **8** intimate **9** insinuate, touch upon
alluded
to: 5 tacit **7** implied **9** intimated
allure: 4 bait, coax, draw, hook, lure, pull **5** charm, decoy, grace, shill, spell, tempt **6** appeal, beauty, beckon, engage, entice, entrap, glamor, lead on, pull in **7** attract, beguile, bewitch, charism, enchant, glamour, win over **8** appeal to, charisma, entrance, interest, inveigle **9** captivate, enrapture, fascinate, infatuate, magnetism **10** attraction, come hither, enticement, loveliness, sultriness, temptation
Allure
competitor: 4 Elle **5** Vogue
allurement: 4 bait, lure **5** charm, decoy, snare **6** appeal, come-on **7** baiting, teasing **9** appetence, incentive **10** attraction, enticement, invitation
alluring: 4 cute, foxy, glam, sexy **5** bonny, siren **6** bonnie, comely, lovely, pretty **7** darling, lovable, winning, winsome **8** adorable, charming, enticing, fetching, gorgeous, handsome, heavenly, inviting, loveable, magnetic, pleasing, striking, stunning, tempting **9** beautiful, beguiling, glamorous, ravishing **10** attractive, bewitching, magnetical, persuasive
woman: 5 houri, siren
allusion: 4 hint **7** mention **8** innuendo **9** inference, reference **10** imputation, intimation, suggestion
alluvial: 5 silty
alluvial __: 3 fan **4** cone **5** plain
alluvium: 4 ooze, silt **5** drift, earth **7** deposit
__ All We Know: 3 For
all-wise: 10 omniscient
all wool __ yard wide: 4 and a
ally: 3 pal **4** chum, mate **5** align, aline, amigo, buddy, crony, unite **6** backer, cohort, friend, helper, league **7** abetter, abettor, comrade, conjoin, connect, partner **8** co-worker, henchman, partisan, sidekick, unionize **9** affiliate, associate, auxiliary, bedfellow, colleague, companion, confidant, supporter **10** accomplice, close ranks, compatriot, well-wisher

opposite: 3 foe 5 enemy
Ally: 6 McBeal, Sheedy, Walker
Allyce: 7 Beasley
__, All Ye Faithful: 5 O Come
Ally McBeal (Fox drama)
cast: Lisa Nicole Carson (Renee Raddick)
Calista Flockhart (Ally McBeal)
Greg Germann (Richard Fish)
Jane Krakowski (Elaine Bassell)
Peter MacNicol (John Cage)
Courtney Thorne-Smith (Georgia Thomas)
all-you-can-eat
place: 6 buffet
All You Need Is Love (1967 song)
artist: Beatles
Allyson, June: 7 actress
spouse: Dick Powell
Alma: 5 Gluck 6 Kruger, Mahler
Alma-Ata: 4 city, town
locale: 10 Kazakhstan
alma mater: 6 school 7 college 9 old school 10 university
souvenir: 2 yb. 8 yearbook
visitor: 4 alum, grad 6 alumna 7 alumnus 8 graduate
almanac: 4 book 6 record
feature: 5 atlas, facts, index
almandine: 3 gem 8 gemstone
Almay: 6 makeup
alternative: *see* cosmetic brand
almighty: 5 maker 6 deific, divine 7 eternal, godlike, supreme 8 absolute, heavenly, immortal, infinite, puissant 10 invincible, omnipotent, omniscient
almighty __: 6 dollar
Almighty: 3 God 7 Creator
__ Almighty: 4 Evan 5 Bruce
Almodóvar: 5 Pedro
almond: 3 nut, tan 4 tree 5 beige, brown, color
combining form: 7 amygdal- 8 amygdalo-
relative: *see* apple, brown color
almond __: 3 oil 4 bark, cake, meal, milk 5 paste
almond-__: 4 eyed 6 shaped
__ almond: 5 burnt, earth, sweet 6 bitter, Indian, Jordan
Almond Joy: 3 bar 5 candy 8 candy bar 9 chocolate
alternative: *see* candy brand
almost: 4 most, near, nigh 5 about, close, quasi 6 barely, nearly, nigh on, toward 7 close to, halfway, short of, towards 8 as good as, in effect, narrowly, not quite, well-nigh 9 just about, virtually
combining form: 3 pen- 4 pene-
never: 6 rarely, seldom 8 not often 10 hardly ever, now and then
prefix: 4 para-
there: 4 near 6 nearby
up: 4 next
Almost Famous (2000 film)
cast: Billy Crudup, Kate Hudson, Jason Lee, Frances McDormand
director: Cameron Crowe
Almost Like Being in Love
composer: Alan Jay Lerner, Frederick Loewe
Almqvist, Carl: 6 writer 7 Swedish
alms: 4 dole, gift 5 grant 6 income 7 charity, handout, largess 8 donation, largesse, offering 9 baksheesh 10 liberality
ask ~: 3 beg
dispense ~: 4 dole
seeker: 6 beggar
__ a load of: 3 get
__ a loaf...: 4 Half
aloe: 4 lily 5 plant, shrub 9 emollient, succulent
aloe __: 4 vera
__ aloe: 5 false 6 golden
__ aloes: 6 bitter
aloft: 4 atop, high, over 5 above, risen 6 aerial, flying, high up, on high, upward 7 sky-high, skyward, soaring 8 at the top, in flight, in heaven, in the air, overhead, skywards, to heaven 9 on the wing 10 up in the air, up in the sky
bear ~: 4 lift 5 hoist 7 upheave
combining form: 4 hyps- 5 hypsi-, hypso-
gone ~: 6 arisen
of: 5 above
aloha: 5 hello 7 goodbye 8 Hawaiian
gift: 3 lei
in French: 5 adieu
in Hebrew: 6 shalom
in Italian: 4 ciao
in Latin: 3 ave 4 vale
in Spanish: 5 adios
aloha __: 5 shirt
Aloha
State: 6 Hawaii
Aloha __: 4 Bowl
Aloha 'Oe
instrument: 3 uke 7 ukelele, ukulele
Alomar: 5 Sandy 6 Carlos 7 Roberto
alone: 4 sole, solo, stag 5 apart, aside, per se, solus, unled, unwed 6 remote, single, singly, solely, unique 7 forlorn, unaided 8 by itself, dateless, desolate, detached, eremitic, forsaken, hermitic, isolated, marooned, peerless, secluded, separate, set apart, singular, solitary, unhelped 9 abandoned, by oneself, matchless, on one's own, privately, separated, unequaled, unmatched, unrivaled 10 friendless, individual, personally, separately, solitarily, unassisted, unattached, unattended, unequalled, unescorted, unexcelled, unrivalled
combining form: 3 mon- 4 mono-, soli-
in Latin: 5 solus
leave ~: 5 let be 6 lay off, resist 7 neglect
left ~: 9 abandoned
living ~: 5 unwed 6 single 8 isolated, solitary 9 by oneself, on one's own, separated, unmarried 10 spouseless, unattached
on stage: 4 sola 5 solus
prefix: 7 mono- mon-
that ~: 5 per se 6 itself
__ alone: 3 let 4 go it 5 leave
__-alone: 5 stand
Alone (1987 song)
artist: Heart
__ Alone: 3 All, One 4 Home
__ a Lonely Number: 5 One Is
aloneness: 7 privacy 8 solitude 9 seclusion
Aloneness
author: Gwendolyn Brooks
along: 3 too, via, yet 4 also 5 forth 6 as well, beside, onward 7 besides, forward, onwards 8 likewise 10 lengthways, lengthwise
ender: 4 side 5 shore
starter: 3 tag
along __ the ride: 3 for
__ along: 3 all, get, run, tag 4 come, inch, pass, play 6 follow, string
__-along: 4 sing, take
Along __ a spider...: 4 came
Along Came Polly (2004 film)
cast: Jennifer Aniston, Debra Messing, Ben Stiller
Along Comes Mary (1966 song)
artist: Association, The
along for the __: 4 ride
along in __: 5 years
__ Along Little Dogie: 3 Git
__ a long shot: 5 not by
alongside: 4 near, next, with 6 next to 7 close by, equal to 8 adjacent, parallel 10 parallel to
lie ~: 5 skirt
place ~: 6 appose
prefix: 4 para-
__ along the line: 3 all
__ Along the Mohawk: 5 Drums
__ Along the Watchtower: 3 All
__ a Long Way to Tipperary: 3 It's
__ along with: 3 tag
__ Along With Mitch: 4 Sing
Alonso, Alicia: 6 dancer 8 danseuse 9 ballerina
specialty: 5 dance 6 ballet
Alonzo: 3 cat 8 Mourning
__ Alonzo Stagg: 4 Amos
aloof: 3 icy, shy 4 cold, cool 5 stiff, stoic 6 chilly, formal, frigid, modest, offish, remote, snooty 7 bashful, distant, glacial, haughty, ice-cold, neutral, offhand, removed, stoical, stuck up 8 contrary, detached, reserved, reticent, retiring, snobbish, solitary, taciturn, unbiased 9 apathetic, diffident, impassive, incurious, reclusive, unbending, unstirred, withdrawn 10 above it all, antisocial, insociable, nonchalant, phlegmatic, unaffected, unagitated, unamicable, unfriendly, unsociable
stand ~ from: 4 shun
aloofness: 5 chill 6 apathy 7 reserve 9 arrogance 10 detachment, neutrality
with ~: 5 icily
alop: 4 awry 5 askew 6 droopy, tilted, uneven 7 crooked 10 unbalanced
__ à l'orange: 4 duck
__ alors!: 3 Zut
Alou: 5 Jesús, Matty 6 Felipe, Moises
sport: 8 baseball
aloud: 6 orally, spoken, voiced 7 audible, audibly, noisily, vocally 8 hearable, verbally, viva voce
wonder ~: 7 request
Alouette
word: 4 tête
__ a Lovely Day Today: 3 It's
Alp: 3 mtn. 4 peak, Zupo 5 Eiger 6 Arslan, Castor, Ecrins 7 Bernina, Pilatus 8 Jungfrau, mountain 9 Mont Blanc, Monte Rosa, Taschhorn, Weisshorn 10 Matterhorn, Piz Bernina
ender: 3 ine
alpaca: 4 wool 6 animal, fabric, mammal 8 ruminant
habitat: 4 Peru 5 Andes
herder, once: 5 Incan
relative: 5 camel, llama 6 vicuña 7 guanaco 8 Bactrian 9 dromedary
alpe: 4 mont
alpenhorn: 4 wind 10 instrument
alpenstock: 5 staff
Alpert and the Tijuana Brass, Herb
song: Casino Royale (1967)
The Lonely Bull (1962)
Mame (1966)
Spanish Flea (1966)
A Taste of Honey (1965)
Tijuana Taxi (1966)
Alpert, Herb: 9 trumpeter
instrument: 4 horn
song: Diamonds (1987)
Rise (1979)
This Guy's in Love With You (1968)
__-Alpes: 6 Basses, Hautes
alpha: 5 Greek 6 letter
ender: 7 numeric
follower: 4 beta
opposite: 5 omega
alpha __: 3 ray 4 iron, male, test 5 brass, decay, helix 6 rhythm 7 blocker
Alpha __: 4 Bits 6 Crucis
Alpha __ Majoris: 5 Ursae
Alpha __ Minoris: 5 Ursae
alpha and __: 5 omega
alphabet: 4 ABCs, soup 7 letters
beginning: 3 ABC 4 ABCD 5 ABCDE
British ~ ender: 3 zed
ender: 3 zee
Koran: 5 Kufic
Korean: 6 Hangul
old Irish ~: 4 ogam 5 ogham
phonetic: 3 IPA
quartet: 4 ABCD, BCDE, CDEF, DEFG, EFGH, FGHI, GHIJ, HIJK, IJKL, JKLM, KLMN, LMNO, MNOP, NOPQ, OPQR, PQRS, QRST, RSTU, STUV, TUVW, UVWX, VWXY, WXYZ
quintet: 5 ABCDE, BCDEF, CDEFG, DEFGH, EFGHI, FGHIJ, GHIJK, HIJKL, IJKLM, JKLMN, KLMNO, LMNOP, MNOPQ, NOPQR, OPQRS, PQRST, QRSTU, RSTUV, STUVW, TUVWX, UVWXY, VWXYZ 6 vowels
soup letter: 6 noodle
trio: 3 ABC, BCD, CDE, DEF, EFG, FGH, GHI, HIJ, IJK, JKL, KLM, LMN, MNO, NOP, OPQ, PQR, QRS, RST, STU, TUV, UVW, VWX, WXY, XYZ
unit: 6 letter
written right-to-left: 6 Arabic, Hebrew
alphabet (phonetic):
A - Alpha
B - Bravo
C - Charlie
D - Delta
E - Echo
F - Foxtrot
G - Golf
H - Hotel
I - India

J - Juliet
K - Kilo
L - Lima
M - Mike
N - November
O - Oscar
P - Papa
Q - Quebec
R - Romeo
S - Sierra
T - Tango
U - Uniform
V - Victor
W - Whiskey
X - X-ray
Y - Yankee
Z - Zulu

alphabet __: 4 code, soup
__ alphabet: 5 Latin, Morse, Roman 6 manual
alphabetical: 4 A to Z 7 indexed, ordered
guide: 5 index
alphabetical __: 5 order
Alphabetical Order
author: Michael Frayn
alphabetize: 4 file, sort 5 index, order 6 assort 8 classify, tabulate 10 pigeonhole
alphabetizers
word ~ ignore: 3 the
alphabets: 5 pasta
Alphabet Song
start: 3 ABC 4 ABCD 5 ABCDE
Alphabet St. (1988 song)
artist: Prince
Alphabet, The
artist: Erté
Alpha Bits: 6 cereal
competitor: *see* cereal
Alpha Centauri: 4 star
Alphonse: 6 Daudet
friend: 6 Gaston
alpine: 4 high, tall 5 Swiss 8 elevated, towering
alpine __: 3 fir 6 garden, tundra 7 bistort
Alpine
abode: 6 chalet
archer: 4 Tell
capital: 4 Bern 5 Berne 6 Vienna
comeback: 4 echo
enthusiast: 5 skier
feature: 5 arête
gear: 3 ski 4 skee
locale: 5 Tirol, Tyrol 6 Europe, France 7 Austria
music: 5 yodel, yodle
outfit: 6 dirndl
resort: 6 Gstaad
river: 3 Aar 4 Aare 5 Isère
snowfield: 4 firn
surface: 4 snow
tool: 5 ice ax, piton
wind: 4 bise, bora, fohn 5 foehn
Alpine __: 4 ibex 6 azalea, skiing 7 currant
Alpo: 7 dog food
alternative: *see* pet food brand
Alps: 3 mts. 5 range 8 Pennines
locale: 6 Europe, France 7 Austria 9 Australia
mountain: 4 Zupo 5 Eiger 6 Arslan, Castor, Ecrins 7 Bernina, Pilatus 8 Jungfrau 9 Mont Blanc, Monte Rosa, Taschhorn, Weisshorn 10 Matterhorn, Piz Bernina
river: 5 Rhone
__ Alps: 5 Savoy, Swiss 6 Carnic, French, Julian 7 Bernese, Bernina, Cottian, Dinaric, Italian, Pennine 8 Maritime
already: 4 once 5 by now 6 by then 8 formerly 9 at present, before now 10 beforehand, by that time, heretofore, previously
enough ~: 4 OK OK
Already?: 6 so soon
Alsatian: 3 dog 5 canid, pooch 6 canine
__ al-Sheikh: 5 Sharm
also: 3 and, too, yet 4 more, plus 5 again, along, ditto 6 as well, either, to boot 7 besides, further 8 likewise, moreover 9 along with, including, similarly, what's more 10 conjointly, in addition
called: 5 alias
not: 3 nor
also-__: 3 ran
Alsop: 6 Joseph 7 Stewart
also-ran: 5 loser 7 failure 9 nonwinner
__ Also Rises, The: 3 Sun
__ also serve...: 4 They
Also Sprach Zarathustra
composer: Richard Strauss
Also Sprach Zarathustra (1973 song)
artist: Deodato
Alston: 6 Dodger, Walter 7 manager
alt: 4 high
alt.: 3 hgt. 4 elev. 6 height
Alt: 5 Carol
emulate ~: 4 pose 5 model
ALT: 3 key
Alta: 4 city, town 6 resort 9 ski resort
locale: 4 Utah 7 Rockies
Alta.: 4 prov.
neighbor: 3 NWT 4 Mont., Sask.
Altadena: 4 city, town
locale: 10 California
__-Altaic: 4 Ural
Altair: 4 star
constellation: 6 Aquila
altar: 6 shrine 9 sanctuary
act: 3 vow
activity: 4 rite 7 wedding
area: 4 bema
cloth: 6 dossal, dossel
compartment: 7 loculus
constellation: 3 Ara
exchange: 3 I do
item: 4 icon, ikon 5 eikon 6 ancona 7 reredos
leave at the ~: 4 jilt
locale: 6 church
neighbor: 4 apse
path to the ~: 5 aisle
plate: 5 paten
robe: 3 alb
stone: 5 mensa
altar __: 3 boy 4 call, card, girl, rail, slab, wine 5 board, bread, cloth, stand, stone
Alt, Carol
spouse: Ron Greschner
__-ALT-DEL: 4 CTRL
Altdorf canton: 3 Uri
alte
opposite: 4 neue
__ Alte: 3 Der
__-Altenburg: 4 Saxe
alter: 3 fit 4 edit, hoke, spay, turn, vary 5 act on, adapt, amend, color, let in, lobby, morph, resew, shift, tweak 6 adjust, affect, change, divert, doctor, juggle, modify, mutate, neuter, recast, reform, remold, revamp, revise, tailor, take up, tamper 7 act upon, convert, correct, distort, inflect, permute, qualify, remodel, replace, reshape, restyle 8 disguise, fine-tune, impact on, innovate, make over, override, overrule, redirect, renovate 9 diversify, influence, rearrange, refashion, sterilize, transform, translate, transmute, transpose 10 adulterate, blue-pencil, fiddle with, reposition
again: 5 refit, rehem
ego: 3 pal 4 ally, chum, mate 5 buddy, crony 6 backer, cohort, friend 7 comrade, consort, partner 8 intimate, playmate, sidekick, soulmate 9 associate, companion, confidant 10 bosom buddy, compatriot
alter __: 3 ego 4 idem
alteration: 4 flux 5 shift 6 change, switch 7 revisal, veering 8 mutation, revision, variance 9 about-face, amendment, deviation, diversion, refitting, reshaping, variation 10 adaptation, adjustment, conversion, correction, difference, divergence, emendation, innovation, remodeling, switchover
__ alteration: 7 author's
altercate: 3 row 4 spat, tiff 5 brawl, fight 6 bicker 7 quarrel, quibble 9 have words
altercation: 3 row 4 feud, flap, fuss, spat, tiff 5 brawl, clash, fight, melee, run-in, scene, set-to 6 barney, blowup, fracas, hassle, rumble, rumpus, strife 7 contest, dispute, quarrel, wrangle 8 argument, skirmish, squabble
altered: 3 new 5 let in 7 unalike 9 different
altered __: 5 chord, state
Altered __: 6 States
Altered States
author: Paddy Chayefsky
Altered States (1980 film)
cast: Bob Balaban, Blair Brown, William Hurt
director: Ken Russell
alter ego
fictional: 4 Hyde, Kent
alternate: 3 sub, var. 4 turn, vary 5 other, proxy 6 backup, change, double, fill-in, rotate, seesaw 7 librate, stagger, stand-in, variant 8 periodic 9 change off, come and go, different, fill in for, fluctuate, oscillate, recurrent, secondary, surrogate, take turns, temporary, vacillate 10 equivalent, every other, reciprocal, substitute, understudy
route: 6 bypass, detour
alternately: 6 rather 7 by turns, instead
alternating __: 5 group, light 6 series 7 current, voltage
alternating current
pioneer: 5 Tesla
alternative: 3 way 4 pick 5 other, plan B 6 acting, choice, option, second 7 variant 8 loophole, recourse 9 variation
combining form: 6 allelo-
word: 3 syn. 7 synonym
alternative __: 6 energy, school 7 society
alternatively: 4 else 5 if not 6 rather 7 instead 9 otherwise
alternatives: 6 others
Althea: 6 Gibson
Althing locale: 4 Icel. 7 Iceland
although: 2 if 3 yet 5 while 6 albeit, even if, though, whilst 7 despite 9 in spite of 10 regardless
alti-: 4 high
Altima: 3 car 4 auto 6 Nissan 10 automobile
Altiplano: 7 plateau
beast: 5 llama
locale: 4 Peru 5 Andes 7 Bolivia 9 Argentina
altitude: 2 ht. 3 hgt. 4 elev. 5 level 6 height 8 eminence 9 elevation, loftiness
combining form: 4 hyps- 5 hypsi-, hypso-
gain ~: 4 rise, soar 5 climb 6 ascend
lose ~: 4 drop, fall 7 descend
sickness: 4 puna
altitudinous: 4 high, tall 5 lofty 7 soaring 8 elevated, towering, uplifted
Altman: 6 Robert, Sidney
Altman, Robert: 8 director
film: 3 Women (1977)
Brewster McCloud (1970)
Cookie's Fortune (1999)
Countdown (1968)
Gosford Park (2001)
Images (1972)
MASH (1970)
McCabe & Mrs. Miller (1971)
Nashville (1975)
A Perfect Couple (1979)
The Player (1992)
Popeye (1980)
A Prairie Home Companion (2006)
Secret Honor (1984)
Short Cuts (1993)
Streamers (1983)
Thieves Like Us (1974)
Vincent & Theo (1990)
alto: 5 range, voice 6 singer 7 caroler 8 vocalist 9 chorister
instrument: 5 viola
alto __: 3 sax 4 clef, horn 5 flute
__ Alto, CA: 4 Palo
altocumulus: 5 cloud
altogether: 5 fully, in sum, quite, sheer, stark 6 bodily, in toto, purely, wholly 7 en masse, totally, utterly 8 as a whole, entirely 9 generally, perfectly 10 absolutely, by and large, completely, conjointly, on the whole, thoroughly
in the ~: 4 bare, nude 5 naked
altohorn: 4 wind 10 instrument
Altoids
alternative: 5 Certs 6 Binaca, Mentos, Tic Tac 7 Clorets, Dentyne
Alton: 4 city, town
locale: 8 Illinois
Altoona: 4 city, town

locale: 4 Penn.
— Altos, CA: 3 Los
altostratus: 5 cloud
altruism: 3 aid 7 charity 8 goodwill, kindness 9 tolerance 10 knighthood
altruist: 5 donor 7 grantor 10 benefactor
altruistic: 3 big 4 good, kind 5 human 6 decent, gentle, humane, kindly, tender 7 clement, largess, lenient, liberal, sparing 8 all heart, generous, gracious, largesse, merciful, princely 9 brotherly, good scout, unselfish, unsparing 10 benevolent, bighearted, charitable, munificent, openhanded, unstinting
—-a-luck: 5 chuck
aludel: 6 bottle, vessel
—-A-Lula: 5 Be-Bop
alum: 4 grad 6 emetic, reuner 7 styptic 8 graduate 10 astringent
aluminum: 5 metal 7 element
alloy: 6 alnico 9 duralumin, magnalium
boat: 5 canoe
company: 5 Alcoa 8 Reynolds
foil alternative: 5 Saran
sheet: 4 foil
source: 3 ore 7 bauxite
yarn: 5 lurex
alumna: 4 grad 6 female, reuner 8 graduate
bio word: 3 née
alumni do
what ~: 5 reune
alumnus: 4 grad, male 6 reuner 8 graduate
next year's ~: 2 sr. 3 snr. 6 senior
Alva: 5 Luigi 6 Myrdal
Alvar: 5 Aalto
Alvarado, Trini: 7 actress
alveolus: 6 air sac
Alvin: 3 Lee 4 city, town, York 5 Ailey 7 Toffler 8 chipmunk
brother: 5 Simon 8 Theodore
locale: 5 Texas
Alvino: 3 Rey
ALW: 8 division
team: 6 Angels 7 Rangers 8 Mariners 9 Athletics
alway: 2 ay 3 aye, e'er
opposite: 4 ne'er
always: 3 e'er 4 ever 7 forever 8 evermore, for keeps 9 eternally 10 constantly, enduringly, inevitably, invariably, unendingly
in music: 6 sempre
not ~: 7 at times
there: 6 trusty 9 unfailing
Always: 4 song 5 waltz
composer: Irving Berlin
Always (1989 film)
cast: Richard Dreyfuss, John Goodman, Holly Hunter
director: Steven Spielberg
Always (song)
artist: Atlantic Starr, Bon Jovi
Always a Reckoning
author: Jimmy Carter
— Always a Woman: 4 She's 6 There's
Always Be My Baby (1996 song)
artist: Mariah Carey
— always liked you best!: 3 Mom
— Always Love You: 3 I'll 5 I Will
Always on My Mind (song)
artist: Pet Shop Boys, Willie Nelson
— always say...: 3 As I
— Always Something: 3 It's
Alworth, Lance
sport: 8 football
Aly: 4 Khan
dad: 3 Aga
— Al Yankovic: 5 Weird
Alysheba: 5 horse
Alyson: 8 Hannigan
Alyssa: 6 Milano
Alzado: 4 Lyle
Alzira
composer: Giuseppe Verdi
a.m.: 4 morn 7 morning 8 forenoon
broadcaster: 3 sta., stn. 7 station
early ~: 3 one, two 4 four 5 three 7 wee hour
part: 4 ante 8 meridiam
when ~ meets p.m.: 4 noon 6 midday
—-am: 3 pro
Am: 4 elem. 7 element 9 americium
95 for ~: 4 at. no.
Am —: 5 I Blue?
Am — believe...: 3 I to
Am — brother's keeper?: 3 I my
Am — to see you!: 5 I glad
Am — understand...: 3 I to
AM: 4 band 5 radio
part: 9 amplitude 10 modulation
AMA: 3 org.
member: 2 dr., GP, MD 3 doc 6 doctor
part: 3 Med. 4 Amer., Assn. 5 Assoc. 7 Medical 8 American
Amadeus: 4 film, play
author: Peter Shaffer
cast: F. Murray Abraham, Elizabeth Berridge, Tom Hulce
choreographer: Twyla Tharp
director: Milos Forman
— Amadeus Mozart: 8 Wolfgang
— a Mad Mad Mad Mad World: 3 It's
Amado, Jorge: 6 writer 9 Brazilian
work: Dona Flor and Her Two Husbands
The Golden Harvest
Sea of Death
Showdown
The War of the Saints
Amahl and the Night Visitors: 5 opera
composer: Gian Carlo Menotti
— a Male War Bride: 4 I Was
amalgam: 3 mix 5 alloy, blend, union 6 hybrid 7 filling, mixture 8 compound 9 coalition, composite, immixture, synthesis
component: 6 silver 7 mercury
amalgamate: 3 mix 4 fuse, join, meld, pool 5 admix, alloy, blend, merge, unify, unite 6 commix, embody, harden, hook up, imbody, league, team up 7 combine 8 coalesce 9 affiliate, associate, commingle, integrate 10 accumulate, adulterate, centralize, synthesize
amalgamated: 4 mixt 5 mixed 6 united
amalgamation: 3 mix 5 union 6 merger 8 compound
Amalthea: 4 moon 5 nymph, sibyl
planet: 7 Jupiter
...a man — mouse?: 3 or a
Amana: 4 city, town 7 commune 9 appliance
alternative: *see* appliance brand
locale: 4 Iowa
Amanda: 4 Pays, Peet 5 Blake, Bynes, Cross 6 Bearse 7 Coetzer, Donohoe, Plummer 8 Seyfried
son: 5 Spock
Amanda (1986 song)
artist: Boston
— amandine: 4 sole 5 trout
— à manger: 5 salle
— a Man Loves a Woman: 4 When
— a man's heart..., The: 5 way to
Amantium —: 4 Irae
amanuensis: 5 clerk 6 copier, scribe 7 copyist 9 scrivener, secretary
...— a man with...: 4 I met
amaranth: 3 azo, dye, red 5 plant 6 flower, purply 8 purplish
relative: *see* purple color, red color
amaranthine: 6 purple 7 endless, undying 8 unending 11 everlasting
— a March hare: 5 mad as
— a march on: 5 steal
Amarcord (1974 film)
director: Federico Fellini
amaretto
flavor: 6 almond
Amarillo: 4 city, town
locale: 5 Texas
— Amarna: 3 Tel 5 Tel el
amaryllis: 5 agave, plant 6 flower
family plant: 4 aloe
—, amas, amat: 3 amo
—, amas, I love a lass: 3 amo
amass: 4 cull, heap, hold, keep, lump, pile, save 5 cache, glean, hoard, lay by, lay up, put by, run up, stack, stock, store 6 accrue, corral, garner, gather, heap up, load up, pile up, rake in, retain, roll up, save up 7 acquire, build up, collect, compile, deposit, harvest, lay away, put away, round up, scare up, store up 8 assemble, gather up, hang onto, hold onto, maintain, put aside, salt away, scrape up, set aside, stow away 9 aggregate, stockpile 10 accumulate
amassment: 4 heap 5 array, hoard 6 pileup 7 accrual 10 collection, cumulation
amateur: 3 lay 4 tiro, tyro 5 unfit 6 layman, novice, simple 7 dabbler 8 beginner, putterer 9 greenhorn, layperson, untrained 10 apprentice, dilettante, uninitiate
lose ~ status: 5 go pro
mag: 4 zine
opposite: 3 pro
radio operator: 3 ham
sports org.: 3 AAU 4 NCAA
amateur —: 4 hour 5 night 6 status
amateurish: 4 bush 5 crude, inept, rough 6 coarse 7 awkward 8 fumbling, homemade, inexpert 9 inelegant, makeshift, primitive, unrefined 10 bush league, dilettante, unpolished, unskillful
Amateurs, The
author: David Halberstam
Amati: 6 Nicolò, violin
kin: 5 Strad
amatol: 9 explosive
ingredient: 3 TNT
— Amatoria: 3 Ars
amatory: 4 fond 6 ardent, doting, erotic, loving, tender 7 fervent 8 romantic 10 passionate
writing: 3 ode
amaze: 3 awe, wow 4 jolt, stun 5 floor, shock 6 baffle, boggle, dazzle 7 astound, impress, perplex, petrify, stagger, startle, stupefy 8 astonish, bewilder, blow away, bowl over, confound, surprise 9 dumbfound, overwhelm
amazed: 4 agog 5 agape, in awe 6 aghast, jolted 8 wide-eyed 9 awestruck 10 dumbstruck, speechless, spellbound
amazement: 3 awe 6 marvel, wonder 8 surprise 9 confusion 10 admiration, perplexity, wonderment
show ~: 4 gape
word of ~: 3 gee
Amazin' —: 4 Mets
amazing: 3 def, ooh, rad, wow 4 aces, A-one, boss, braw, cool, dece, fine, gear, keen, neat, nice, phat, tuff 5 dandy, ducky, grand, great, marvy, neato, nobby, prime, slick, super, swell 6 bang on, bang-up, bonzer, bosker, choice, divine, dreamy, far-out, gnarly, groovy, lovely, peachy, slap-up, spot on, superb, terrif, tiptop, unreal, whizzo, wicked 7 awesome, capital, corking, perfect, ripping, skookum, stellar, sublime, unusual 8 dazzling, especial, eximious, fabulous, five-star, four-star, frabjous, glorious, heavenly, jim-dandy, slam-bang, smashing, splendid, standout, sterling, stickout, stunning, superior, terrific, top-level, topnotch, very good, wondrous 9 bodacious, Endsville, excellent, exemplary, exquisite, first-rate, high-grade, hunky-dory, marvelous, sollicker, top-flight, unrivaled, wonderful 10 first-class, hotsy-totsy, incredible, jack-a-dandy, miraculous, out of sight, peachy-keen, phenomenal, prodigious, remarkable, stupendous, super-duper, tremendous, unexpected, unrivalled
Amazing —, The: 5 Randi 7 Kreskin
Amazing!: 3 ooh, wow
Amazing Grace: 4 hymn
ending: 4 I see
Amazing Race, The (CBS reality)
host: Phil Keoghan
Amazon: 5 giant, river, woman 6 female 10 bookseller
estuary: 4 Pará
father: 4 Ares
feeder: 3 Içá 4 Napo 5 Juruá, Negro, Purús, Xingú 6 Japurá, Javari, Javary 7 Madeira, Marañón, Tapajós, Ucayali 8 Putumayo
how the ~ flows: 4 east
language: 4 Tupi
locale: 4 Peru 6 Brazil
monkey: 4 titi 6 uakari
origin: 4 Peru
people: 4 Tupi
port: 4 Pará 5 Belém 6 Manaus
rodent: 6 agouti
Amazon.com
offering: 4 book 5 e-book, novel

ambassador: **5** agent, envoy **6** consul, deputy, legate **8** delegate, diplomat, emissary, minister **9** messenger **10** peacemaker
address: **3** exc. **10** excellency
asset: **4** tact
place: **3** emb. **7** embassy **9** consulate
ambassadorship
often: **4** plum
Ambassadors, The
author: Henry James
amber: **5** brown, color, resin **6** fossil, yellow **7** old gold **9** yellowish
combining form: **6** succin- **7** succino-
ender: **4** jack
nectar: **4** beer, brew, suds **5** lager **7** brewski
relative: ***see*** brown color, yellow color
Amber: **7** Tamblyn **8** Valletta
__ Amber: **7** Forever
ambergris
source: **5** whale
ambience: **3** air **4** aura, feel, mood, tone **6** medium, milieu **7** setting **10** atmosphere, local color
ambient: **9** embracing, enclosing **10** encircling, enveloping
ambient __: **5** noise
ambiguity: **5** doubt **9** obscurity, vagueness **10** equivocacy
ambiguous: **4** iffy, open **5** mirky, murky, vague **6** chancy, unsure **7** Delphic, dubious, evasive **8** doubtful, nebulous, oracular, puzzling, tortuous **9** deceptive, enigmatic, equivocal, imprecise, tenebrous, uncertain, unsettled **10** borderline, indefinite, indistinct, inexplicit, misleading, unexplicit, unresolved, unspecific, up for grabs, up in the air
thing: **6** enigma
ambit: **5** orbit, range, reach, scope, sweep **6** bounds, extent, radius, sphere **7** circuit, compass **8** boundary **9** dimension, perimeter
ambition: **3** aim **4** goal, hope, plan, push, will, wish **5** dream, drive, quest, vigor **6** desire, intent, target **7** avidity, craving, longing, passion, purpose **8** initiate, yearning **9** eagerness, objective **10** aspiration, enterprise, enthusiasm, get up and go, initiative, pretension
devoid of ~: **4** lazy
excessive ~: **5** greed
have ~: **6** aspire
lack of ~: **5** sloth
one without ~: **5** idler
ambitious: **4** avid, bold, hard **5** eager, grand, lofty, pushy **6** ardent, hungry, intent **7** arduous, wishful, zealous **8** aspiring, desirous **9** demanding, designing, difficult, elaborate, energetic, grandiose, strenuous, visionary **10** aggressive, determined, formidable, impressive, purposeful
ambivalence: **7** dubiety **9** dubiosity
ambivalent: **5** mixed, timid **6** fickle **8** hesitant, wavering **9** debatable, equivocal, faltering, uncertain, undecided **10** borderline, irresolute, of two minds, unexplicit, unresolved, weak-willed, wishy-washy
amble: **3** lag **4** gait, idle, laze, loaf, poke, roam, rove, walk **5** dally, drift, mosey, stall, tarry **6** canter, dawdle, linger, loiter, ramble, sashay, stroll, wander **7** meander, saunter **8** lollygag, straggle **9** promenade **10** dilly-dally
ambler: **10** pedestrian
Ambler, Eric: **6** writer **7** British
work: The Care of Time
Epitaph for a Spy
Journey Into Fear
The Mask of Dimitrios
A Passage of Arms
Ambling Alp, The: Primo Carnera
__ Amboy, NJ: **5** Perth
Ambrose: **5** saint **6** Bierce **7** Stephen
ambrosia: **7** dessert **8** delicacy
ambrosial: **5** balmy, godly, sweet, tasty **6** divine, savory, toothy **7** elysian, scented **8** aromatic, empyreal, empyrean, ethereal, fragrant, heavenly, luscious, perfumed, supernal, tasteful **9** celestial, delicious, flavorful, nectarous, palatable, toothsome **10** delectable, delightful
ambulance: **7** vehicle **9** transport
destination: **2** ER
driver: **3** EMS, EMT **5** medic
equipment: **6** litter
sound: **5** siren
ambulate: **4** foot, hoof, pace, roam, rove, step, trek, walk **5** range, tread **6** ramble, stroll, travel **7** saunter **8** gad about **9** gallivant, promenade
ambulatory: **5** astir **7** walking
ambuscade: **4** trap
ambush: **3** mug **4** jump, trap **5** seize, sneak, stalk, trick **6** assail, attack, entrap, lay for, pounce, recess, refuge, waylay **7** assault **8** surprise **9** blindside, bushwhack, intercept
lie in ~: **4** lurk, wait **5** sculk, skulk
AMC: **3** car **4** auto **7** channel **10** automobile
alternative: ***see*** cable channel
car: **5** Eagle, Pacer, Rebel **6** Hornet, Marlin, Spirit **7** Concord, Gremlin, Javelin, Matador, Rambler **10** Ambassador
offering: **4** film **5** movie
series radio station: **4** WENN
AMD rival: **5** Intel
__-a-Me: **5** Botch
ameba
see amoeba
Ameche: **3** Don **4** Alan
Amédée
author: Eugène Ionesco
Amedeo: **8** Avogadro **10** Modigliani
see also Italian
Amelia: **7** Bloomer, Earhart, Peabody
author: Henry Fielding
emulate ~: **3** fly **6** aviate
ameliorate: **3** aid **4** ease, help, lift **5** amend, fix up, quiet **6** better, enrich, look up, pacify, polish, reform, remedy **7** correct, enhance, improve, lighten, mollify, relieve, shape up, sharpen, upgrade **8** mitigate, spruce up **9** alleviate **10** recuperate
amelioration: **6** relief
amen: **3** yea, yep, yes **5** truly **6** be it so, I agree, I'll say, indeed, it is so, so be it, so true, verily **7** right on **8** for a fact **9** you said it **10** absolutely, positively
amen __: **6** corner
Amen (NBC sitcom)
cast: Clifton Davis (Reverend Reuben Gregory)
Jester Hairston (Rolly Forbes)
Sherman Hemsley (Deacon Ernest Frye)
Anna Maria Horsford (Thelma Frye)
Roz Ryan (Amelia Hetebrink)
amenability: **9** liability
amenable: **4** easy, game, open, tame **6** docile, liable, polite **7** dutiful, pliable, willing **8** gracious, resigned, yielding **9** agreeable, compliant, receptive, tractable **10** hospitable, open-minded, submissive
Amen Corner, The
author: James Baldwin
amend: **3** fix **4** edit **5** alter **6** better, change, modify, reform, repair, revise, update **7** correct, enhance, improve, rectify, redress, touch up **8** rephrase **10** ameliorate
amendment: **5** rider **6** change, clause, reform **7** codicil, redress, revisal **8** revision **10** alteration, attachment, betterment, correction, suggestion, supplement
letters: **3** ERA
subject: **5** right
amends: **7** payment, redress **8** requital **9** atonement, expiation **10** recompense, reparation
make ~: **3** pay **5** atone, repay **6** redeem, reform, refund **7** appease, expiate, redress, requite **8** atone for **9** apologize, indemnify **10** compensate, recompense
Amenhotep: **7** pharaoh **8** Egyptian
god: **4** Aten, Aton
amenities: **8** protocol **9** etiquette, propriety
amenity: **5** charm, frill **6** luxury **7** comfort **8** courtesy, facility, kindness **9** geniality, gentility **10** affability, amiability, cordiality, politeness, refinement
Amen-Ra
wife: **3** Mut
ament: **6** catkin
Amer.
Central ~ country: **3** Nic., Pan. **4** Guat.
counterpart: **4** Natl.
Hist. subj.: **3** WWI **4** WWII
news org.: **4** USIA
northern ~: **3** Esk.
propaganda source: **4** USIA
S. ~ country: **3** Arg., Col., Uru. **4** Ecua. **5** Venez.
Amerada __: **4** Hess
amerce: **4** fine **5** mulct **6** punish **8** penalize
amercement: **4** fine **5** mulct
America: **4** song **5** The US **6** anthem **7** Ferrera
song: A Horse With No Name (1972)
I Need You (1972)
Lonely People (1975)
Sister Golden Hair (1975)
Tin Man (1974)
Ventura Highway (1972)
You Can Do Magic (1982)
word: **3** 'tis **4** thee
America (1981 song)
artist: Neil Diamond
America __: **6** Online **7** Firster
__ America: **3** Air **4** Miss **5** Latin, Men of, North, South **6** Little, Middle **7** British, Central, Spanish
America, America (1963 film)
director: Elia Kazan
__ America Line: **7** Holland
American: **3** car **4** auto, Yank **6** cheese **7** airline, Rambler **10** automobile
alternative: ***see*** airline, U.S.
early ~: **8** colonial
flag color: **3** red **4** blue **5** white
former rival: **3** TWA **5** Pan Am **7** Eastern
former ~ territory: **4** Utah **5** Idaho **6** Dakota, Hawaii, Oregon **7** Arizona, Montana, Wyoming **8** Colorado **9** New Mexico **10** Washington
majority: **5** women
American __: **3** elk, elm, ivy, Pie, rig **4** aloe, bond, plan, star **5** bison, Breed, chair, cloth, dream, eagle, Falls, Heart, holly, lotus, Movie, Music, Notes, organ, party, sable, Samoa, senna, Storm, twist, Woman **6** Beauty, blight, cheese, copper, cotton, Empire, Flyers, Gothic, Indian, ipecac, League, Legion, linden, marten **7** bittern, buffalo, cowslip, English, Express, kestrel, Madness, Spanish
American __, An: **5** Dream **7** Tragedy
American __ Award: **4** Book
American __ Exchange: **5** Stock
American __ Language: **4** Sign
__ American: **3** Pan **5** Asian, Early, Latin, South **6** native **7** Central, General, Spanish
__-American: **3** all **4** Afro, Arab, Euro **5** Anglo, Italo **6** Franco, Middle **7** African, Mexican
Americana
author: Don DeLillo
set: **3** enc. **4** ency. **5** encyc.
American Appetites
author: Joyce Carol Oates
American Bandstand (ABC music)
fan: **4** teen
host: Dick Clark
American Beauty: **4** rose **5** plant **6** flower
American Beauty (1999 film)
cast: Annette Bening, Thora Birch, Kevin Spacey, Mena Suvari
director: Sam Mendes
American Bobtail: **3** cat **5** felid **6** feline
American Buffalo: **4** film, play
author: David Mamet
cast: Dennis Franz, Dustin Hoffman, Sean Nelson
American Century, The
author: Harold Evans
__ American Cousin: **3** Our
American Crisis, The
author: Thomas Paine
American Dream, An
author: Norman Mailer

American Dream, The
author: Edward Albee
American Dynasty, An
subject: 5 Fords
American Express
use: 3 owe 6 charge
American Flyer
rival: 6 Lionel
American Flyers (1985 film)
cast: Rae Dawn Chong, Kevin Costner, David Grant
director: John Badham
dog: 5 Eddie
__ American Games: 3 Pan
American Gangster (2007 film)
cast: Russell Crowe, Denzel Washington
American Gigolo (1980 film)
cast: Richard Gere
American Gothic: 8 painting
artist: Grant Wood
American Graffiti (1973 film)
cast: Richard Dreyfuss, Ron Howard, Paul LeMat, Cindy Williams
director: George Lucas
drive-in: 4 Mel's
__-American Highway: 3 Pan
American Hot Wax (1978 film)
cast: Fran Drescher, Jay Leno, Tim McIntire
American Idol (Fox reality)
host: Ryan Seacrest
judge: Ellen DeGeneres, Kara DioGuardi, Paula Abdul, Randy Jackson, Simon Cowell
American in Paris, An
composer: George Gershwin
American in Paris, An (1951 film)
cast: Leslie Caron, Gene Kelly, Oscar Levant
director: Vincente Minnelli
Americanization of Emily, The (1964 film)
cast: Julie Andrews, James Coburn, James Garner
director: Arthur Hiller
American Kennel Club
reject: 3 mut 4 mutt
American League
division: 4 East, West 7 Central
team: 5 A's, The, Bosox, Twins, Yanks 6 Angels, Chisox, Red Sox, Royals, Tigers 7 Indians, Orioles, Rangers, Yankees 8 Blue Jays, Mariners, White Sox 9 Athletics 10 Buccaneers
three-time ~ batting champ: Tony Oliva
American Legion
member: 3 vet 7 veteran
relative: 3 VFW
American Masters
genre: biography
network: PBS
American Pie (1971 song)
artist: Don McLean
car: 5 Chevy
place: 5 levee
American Pie (1999 film)
cast: Jason Biggs, Shannon Elizabeth, Alyson Hannigan, Chris Klein
director: Paul Weitz
American Popular Songs
author: David Ewen
American President, The (1995 film)
cast: Annette Bening, Michael Douglas, Richard Dreyfuss, Michael J. Fox, Martin Sheen
director: Rob Reiner
American Psycho: 4 film 5 novel
author: Bret Easton Ellis
American Psycho (2000 film)
cast: Christian Bale, Willem Dafoe, Jared Leto, Reese Witherspoon
director: Mary Harron
American Revolution: 3 war
supporter: 4 Tory, Whig
American Samoa capital: 8 Pago Pago
American Scoundrel
author: Thomas Keneally
American Shorthair: 3 cat 5 felid 6 feline
American Storm (1986 song)
artist: Bob Seger
__-American Symphony: 4 Afro
American Tail, An
character: 5 mouse 6 Fievel
American, The
author: Henry James
__ American, The: 4 Ugly
American Tragedy, An
author: Theodore Dreiser
character: 3 Asa 4 Esta, Myra 5 Alden, Bella, Titus 6 Elvira, Hester
__ American Union: 3 Pan
American University
locale: 6 Beirut 7 Lebanon 8 Beyrouth
__-American War: 7 Spanish
American Wirehair: 3 cat 5 felid 6 feline
American Woman (1970 song)
artist: Guess Who
America's Cup: 6 trophy
contender: 5 sloop, yacht
__ America Singing: 5 I Hear
America's longest-lasting car: 3 Reo
America's Most Wanted (Fox)
host: John Walsh
info: 5 alias
America's Sweethearts (2001 film)
cast: Billy Crystal, John Cusack, Julia Roberts, Catherine Zeta-Jones
director: Joe Roth
__ America, The: 5 Other
America the Beautiful
composer: Katharine Lee Bates, Samuel Ward
ender: 3 sea
pronoun: 4 thee
America West: 7 airline
alternative: *see* airline, U.S.
americium: 7 element
Amerigo: 4 font 8 typeface, Vespucci
Amerika
author: Franz Kafka
Amerind
see Indian
Ames: 2 Ed 3 Joe, Vic 4 city, Gene, Leon, town 5 Nancy 6 Jessie 7 Aldrich
athletes: 8 Cyclones
locale: 4 Iowa
river: 5 Skunk
school: 3 ISU
Ames, Aldrich
ex-employer: 3 CIA
Ames Brothers: 2 Ed 3 Joe, Vic 4 Gene
real last name: Urick
song: It Only Hurts for a Little While (1956)
Melodie d'Amour (1957)
My Bonnie Lassie (1955)
The Naughty Lady of Shady Lane (1954)
Rag Mop (1950)
Tammy (1957)
You You You (1953)
Ames, Ed
song: My Cup Runneth Over (1967)
amethyst: 3 gem 5 color 6 purple 8 gemstone
month: 8 February
relative: *see* purple color
Amethyst Ring, The
author: Scott O'Dell
AMEX: 3 mkt.
alternative: 3 OTC 4 NYSE 6 NASDAQ
buy: 5 stock
number: 5 quote
overseer: 3 SEC
unit: 3 shr., stk. 5 share
AMF
competitor: 4 Voit 6 Wilson 8 Rawlings, Spalding 9 Brunswick
AM/FM regulator: 3 FCC
Amherst: 4 city, town
athletes: 9 Minutemen
school: 4 Mass. 5 U Mass.
__ ami: 3 bon, mon
Ami: 6 Dolenz
Am I __?: 4 Blue
amiability: 7 amenity 8 kindness 9 geniality 10 cordiality, friendship, good nature
amiable: 4 calm, cool, easy, kind, mild, nice, soft, warm 5 close, quiet, sweet, type B 6 benign, chummy, clubby, genial, gentle, jovial, kindly, lovely, loving, low-key, mellow, placid, polite, sedate, serene 7 affable, cordial, equable, lenient, likable, lovable, pacific, relaxed 8 charming, composed, engaging, fireside, friendly, gracious, intimate, laid-back, likeable, loveable, obliging, outgoing, peaceful, pleasant, pleasing, sociable, tranquil 9 agreeable, collected, convivial, easy-going, peaceable, quiescent, temperate, unexcited, unruffled 10 benevolent, buddy-buddy, neighborly, personable, solicitous, unagitated, untroubled
look: 4 grin 5 smile
not ~: 5 type A
amiably
act ~: 6 be nice
Am I Blue author: Beth Henley
Amica
competitor: *see* insurance company
composer: Pietro Mascagni
amicable: 4 calm, cool, kind 5 close, quiet, sweet 6 chummy, clubby, genial, kindly, low-key, mellow, placid, polite, sedate, serene 7 affable, cordial, equable, pacific, relaxed, stoical 8 composed, familiar, friendly, gracious, intimate, laid-back, likeable, outgoing, peaceful, sociable, tranquil 9 accordant, collected, congenial, convivial, courteous, easy-going, favorable, peaceable, quiescent, temperate, unexcited, unruffled 10 benevolent, buddy-buddy, harmonious, hospitable, neighborly, personable, solicitous, unagitated, untroubled
amice: 4 cape
__ A. Michener: 5 James
amici __: 6 curiae
Amick: 7 Mädchen
amicus __: 6 curiae
amid: 5 among, 'twixt 6 during, in with, mongst 7 amongst, between, betwixt 9 in-between
...__ a Midnight Clear: 4 Upon
amidst: 2 in 5 among, 'twixt 6 during, mongst 7 amongst, between 10 in the hub of
Amiens: 4 city, town
locale: 6 France
river: 5 Somme
amigo: 3 pal 4 ally, chum 5 buddy, crony 6 cohort, friend 7 comrade 8 compadre, sidekick 9 associate, colleague, compañero, confidant 10 compatriot, well-wisher
Amigo: 3 SUV 5 Isuzu
__, amigos!: 5 Adios
__ Amigos!: 5 Three
Amilcare: 10 Ponchielli
__ a Mile in My Shoes: 4 Walk
__ a million: 5 one in 6 thanks
__ a million years!: 5 Not in
Am I my brother's __?: 6 keeper
Amin: 3 Idi 5 exile 7 Gemayel
__ Amin Dada: 3 Idi
amino acid: 3 leu. 4 dopa 6 lysine, serine, valine 7 alanine, cystine, glycine, leucine, praline 8 arginine, creatine, cysteine, tyrosine 9 histidine, ornithine, threonine 10 asparagine, citrulline, isoleucine, tryptophan
suffix: 3 ine
__-aminobenzoic acid: 4 para
Aminta
author: Torquato Tasso
__ a minute: 4 wait 5 a mile
amir: 5 Osman 6 Othman 9 potentate
__ a Miracle: 3 It's
__ Amiri Baraka: 5 Imamu
__ amis: 3 mes
Amis: 4 Suzy 6 Martin 8 Kingsley
Amish: 4 sect
Amis, Kingsley: 6 writer 7 British
work: Ending Up
The Folks That Live on the Hill
Girl, 20
The Green Man
How's Your Glass?
I Like It Here
I Want It Now
Jake's Thing
Lucky Jim
The Old Devils
The Russian Girl
Stanley and the Women
Take a Girl Like You
That Uncertain Feeling
Amis, Martin: 6 writer 7 British
work: London Fields
Money
The Rachel Papers
Success
Time's Arrow

amiss: 3 bad 4 awry 5 afoul, badly, wrong 6 adrift, astray, faulty, flooey, flooie, rotten 7 off base, wrongly 8 cockeyed, erringly, faultily, not right 9 defective, deficient, foolishly, imperfect 10 improperly, mistakenly, off the mark, out of joint, out of order, out of place, out of whack, unsuitably
go ~: 3 err
Amis, Suzy: 7 actress
spouse: James Cameron
Amistad (1997 film)
cast: Morgan Freeman, Nigel Hawthorne, Anthony Hopkins, Matthew McConaughey
composer: John Williams
director: Steven Spielberg
role: 5 Adams, slave 6 Cinque
Amittai
son: 5 Jonah
amity: 4 love 5 peace, unity 6 accord, comity 7 concord, harmony 8 goodwill 10 cordiality, fellowship, friendship
Amityville Horror, The: 4 book, film
author: Jay Anson
cast: James Brolin, Margot Kidder, Rod Steiger
dog: 5 Harry
Amman: 4 city, town 7 capital
locale: 6 Jordan
ammo
see ammunition
ammonia
compound: 5 amide, imide, imine
derivative: 5 amine
__ ammoniac: 3 gum, sal
ammonite: 5 shell 6 fossil 8 seashell
ammunition: 3 BBs 4 fuel, shot 5 bombs, shots, slugs 6 beebee, bullet, rounds, shells 7 bullets, missile 8 grenades, materiel, missiles, ordnance 9 armaments, cartridge, explosive, gunpowder, munitions, torpedoes 10 cannonball, cartridges, explosives
air-gun ~: 3 BBs 6 beebee
blowgun ~: 4 dart
holder: 4 clip 7 arsenal 8 magazine
kiddie ~: 3 cap, pea
material: 5 niter
military: 4 ordn. 8 ordnance
oater ~: 5 blank
prankster's ~: 3 egg 6 tomato
provide ~: 3 arm
put ~ in: 4 load
round of ~: 5 salvo
slanderer's ~: 3 mud
starter pistol's ~: 5 blank
unit: 3 rnd. 5 round
Amne Machin: 4 peak 5 mount 8 mountain
locale: 4 Asia 5 China
amnemonic: 9 forgetful
Amneris
slave of ~: 4 Aïda
amnesty: 5 truce 6 pardon 9 remission 10 absolution
Amnesty Intl.
concern: 3 MIA
Am not
answer: 5 are so 6 are too
amo, __, amat: 4 amas
Amo, __, I love a lass: 4 amas
Amoco: 3 gas 8 gasoline
rival: 4 Gulf, Hess 5 Exxon, Getty, Shell 7 Chevron
amoeba: 4 cell 5 monad 6 animal 7 microbe 9 protozoan 10 animalcule
emulate an ~: 6 divide
amok: 4 loco 6 crazed, wildly 7 berserk, flipped, haywire 8 frenzied 9 rampaging 10 on a rampage
__ amok: 3 run
amole: 4 root 8 manfreda 9 soap plant
source: 5 yucca
Amonasro
daughter: 4 Aïda
among: 3 mid 4 amid, with 5 'twixt 6 amidst, in with 7 between, betwixt 9 in-between
in French: 5 entre
in Spanish: 5 entre
prefix: 5 inter-
Among My Souvenirs (1959 song)
artist: Connie Francis
among other persons: 10 inter alios
among other things: 9 inter alia
amongst: 4 amid 5 'tween 6 amidst
Among the Cannibals
author: Jules Verne
__ Among the Ruins: 4 Love
__ a monkey's uncle!: 5 I'll be
Amon-Ra
wife: 3 Mut
__ a Moon Out Tonight: 6 There's
amoral: 3 bad 5 wrong 6 wicked 9 libertine, qualmless, unethical 10 licentious, nonethical
amore: 4 love 9 affection
__ amore: 3 con
Amore: 7 cat food
alternative: *see* pet food brand
__ Amore: 5 That's
Amores
poet: Ovid
amoretto: 4 Eros 6 cherub
amorous: 4 fond, warm 6 doting, in love, loving, tender 7 hugging, kissing 8 romantic 10 lovey-dovey, passionate
amorousness: 4 love
amorphous: 5 baggy, vague 6 blobby 8 formless, inchoate, nebulous, unformed, unshaped 9 irregular, shapeless
mass: 4 blob, glob
Amory, Cleveland: 6 critic, writer
Amos: 2 Oz 4 city, John, Otis, Tori, town 5 Jones, McCoy, Rusie, Stagg, Wally 6 Alcott, Tupper
book after: 4 Obad. 7 Obadiah
book before ~: 4 Joel
locale: 6 Canada, Québec
partner: 4 Andy
Amos __: 5 'n' Andy
Amos __ Stagg: 6 Alonzo
__ Amos: 6 Famous
Amos & Andrew (1993 film)
cast: Nicholas Cage
Amos Bronson __: 6 Alcott
Amos, John: 5 actor
TV: Good Times, Roots
Amos 'n' Andy: 9 radio show
Amos, Tori
real first names: Mary Ellen
__ a Most Unusual Day: 3 It's
amount: 3 qty., sum, tab 4 cost, deal, size, span 5 add up, batch, order, price, reach, shade, total, value 6 charge, degree, extent, number, outlay, output, supply, volume 7 add up to, expense, measure, quantum 8 price tag, quantity 9 aggregate, magnitude 10 complement
determine the ~ of: 6 assess
end ~: 3 net
excessive ~: 5 spate
full ~: 3 all 4 body 5 total, whole 8 entirety, the works, totality 9 aggregate
greatest ~: 7 maximum
indefinite ~: 3 any 4 some
large ~: 3 sea 4 lots, mint, much, scad, slew, tons 5 ocean 6 bagful, oodles, plenty
least ~: 3 jot 4 iota, whit 7 minimum 9 scintilla
measured ~: 4 dose
necessary ~: 5 quota
outstanding ~: 4 debt, levy 6 arrear 7 arrears
prescribed ~: 4 dose
red-ink ~: 4 debt 5 debit 7 deficit
small ~: 3 bit, dot, fig, tad 4 atom, dash, drab, dram, drib, drop, hoot, iota, lick, mite, song, whit 5 grain, minim, pinch, skosh, speck, touch, trace 6 little, trifle 7 modicum 8 pittance
smaller ~: 4 less
small in ~: 5 light 6 little
taken in: 4 gate
to: 4 cost, make 5 equal, reach, spell, total
(to): 4 come
vague ~: 3 any
vitamin ~: 4 pill 6 tablet
worthless ~: 3 fig, sou 6 diddly
amour
see sweetheart
amour-propre: 3 ego 5 pride 7 conceit 10 self-esteem
__, a mouse!: 3 Eek
__ a move on: 3 get 4 make
amp
attachment: 4 mike
AMPAS trophy: 5 Oscar
ampere: 4 unit 7 measure
Ampère, André: 9 physicist, scientist
ampersand: 3 and, sym. 6 symbol
amphibian: 3 eft, olm 4 frog, hyla, newt, toad 5 ranid 6 anuran, mud eel, peeper 7 axolotl, crapaud, tadpole 8 mudpuppy 10 salamander
order: 5 anura
utterance: 5 croak
amphibious
fish: 6 anabas
vehicle: 6 amtrac 7 amtrack
Amphion: 7 centaur 8 Argonaut
father: 4 Zeus
instrument: 4 lyre
wife: 5 Niobe
amphitheater: 4 bowl, hall, oval, ring 5 arena, field 6 lyceum 7 stadium, theater, theatre 8 coliseum 9 colosseum
natural ~: 3 cwm
section: 4 tier
amphitheaters
Roman ~: 6 arenae
amphora: 3 jar, pot, urn 5 crock 6 flagon, vessel 9 container 10 jardiniere
handle: 4 ansa
ample: 3 big 4 full, much, tidy, vast, wide 5 broad, great, heavy, hefty, large, roomy, stout 6 decent, enough, goodly, lavish, plenty, portly 7 copious, liberal, profuse, sizable 8 abundant, generous, handsome, prodigal, sizeable, spacious 9 bounteous, bountiful, capacious, expansive, extensive, good-sized, luxuriant, plenteous, plentiful, unsparing 10 commodious, munificent, overweight, sufficient, voluminous
amount: 8 plethora
amplified
beam: 5 laser
amplifier
wave ~: 5 maser
amplify: 3 add, pad, wax 4 grow 5 add to, boost, swell 6 beef up, expand, hike up, overdo, ramble 7 augment, build up, develop, enhance, enlarge, inflate, magnify 8 escalate, heighten, increase, lengthen 9 elaborate, expatiate 10 exaggerate, make much of
amplitude: 4 mass, size 5 scope, width 6 extent, volume 7 bigness, breadth, fulness 8 capacity, hugeness, loudness, vastness, wideness 9 abundance, broadness, greatness, immensity, largeness, magnitude, plenitude, roominess 10 dimensions
amply: 4 very, well 6 enough, galore, vastly
ampule: 4 bulb, hypo, vial 5 phial
Amram
daughter: 6 Miriam
son: 5 Aaron, Moses
Amrita
author: Ruth Prawer Jhabvala
Amscray!: 3 git 4 scat, shoo 5 scoot, scram 6 beat it, begone, get out
Amstel: 4 Beck, beer 5 Dutch
alternative: *see* beer
city on the ~: 9 Amsterdam
Amsterdam: 4 city, port, town 5 Morey 7 capital
locale: 7 Holland, New York 11 Netherlands
neighbor: 3 Ede
river: 6 Amstel
see also Dutch
__ Amsterdam: 3 New 5 Nieuw
amt.: 3 num., qty.
comparable ~: 5 equiv.
largest ~: 3 max.
least ~: 3 min.
see also amount
Am too!
response: 5 are so 6 are not
Amtrak: 2 RR 3 rwy. 7 railway 8 railroad
advisory: 3 ETD
bullet train: 5 Acela
car: 5 diner 7 sleeper
overseer: 4 NTSB
stop: 3 sta., stn. 7 station
track: 4 rail
worker: 4 engr. 8 engineer 9 conductor
see also train
amuck: 6 crazed
run ~: 4 rage, riot 7 rampage 8 have a fit

Amu Darya: 4 Oxus 5 river
origin: 6 Pamirs
outlet: 7 Aral Sea
amulet: 4 ankh, juju, mojo 5 charm, jewel, spell 6 fetich, fetish, grigri, scarab 7 periapt 8 greegree, grisgris, talisman 9 horseshoe
word: 7 abraxas
Amundsen: 3 sea 4 gulf 5 Norse, Roald
locale: 10 Antarctica
Amundsen, Roald: 8 explorer 9 Norwegian
contemporary: 5 Peary
quest: 4 Pole 9 South Pole
Amur: 5 river
locale: 6 Russia 9 Manchuria
river to the ~: 6 Ussuri 7 Songhua
amuse: 3 get 5 cheer 6 divert, occupy, please, regale, tickle 7 beguile, crack up, delight, disport, satisfy 8 interest 9 entertain, knock dead, make merry, titillate 10 tickle pink
oneself: 4 play
to the max: 4 slay
amused
look: 4 grin 5 smile
amusement: 3 fun, rec 4 game, play 5 cheer, humor, mirth, party, sport, treat 6 frolic, laughs 7 delight, disport, jollies, pastime 8 laughter, pleasure 9 avocation, diversion, enjoyment, festivity, funniness, merriment 10 recreation, regalement, relaxation, risibility
center: 6 arcade
exclamation: 4 ha-ha 5 te-hee 6 haw-haw, tee-hee
expression of ~: 5 laugh 8 laughter
amusement __: 3 tax 4 park
amusement park
feature: 4 maze, ride, whip 5 flume, slide 6 Dodgem 8 carousel 10 water slide
shout: 4 whee
amusing: 3 fun 4 nice, rich 5 comic, droll, funny, kicky, light, merry, silly, witty 6 har-har, jocose 7 comical, jocular, waggish 8 farcical, humorous, pleasant, readable 9 facetious, laughable, priceless, quizzical, whimsical 10 delightful
sort: 3 wag, wit 5 comic 6 gagman 7 gagster 8 comedian
Amy: 3 Ray, Tan 5 Adams, Grant, March, Smart 6 Alcott, Carter, Irving, Locane, Lowell, Wright 7 Madigan, Poehler, Yasbeck 8 Clampitt, Van Dyken 9 Brenneman 10 Heckerling, Vanderbilt
sister: 4 Beth
amyl __: 7 acetate, alcohol, nitrite, sulfide
An: 4 Wang
ana: 10 compendium, miscellany
ANA: 3 org. 7 airline
member: 2 RN 3 LPN
Anabaptist sect: 5 Amish
Anabasis
author: Xenophon
anabolic __: 7 steroid
__ Ana, CA: 5 Santa
anachronistic: 8 obsolete, outdated, outmoded 9 out-of-date
Anacin: 7 aspirin 9 analgesic 10 painkiller
alternative: *see* pain reliever brand
anaconda: 3 boa 4 game 5 snake 6 animal 7 reptile 8 card game
relative: *see* snake
Anacostia: 5 river
city on the ~: 10 Washington
anadem: 6 wreath 7 coronet 9 headpiece
anaglyph: 5 cameo
anago: 3 eel
anagogic: 6 mystic 8 mystical
anagrams: 4 game 8 word game
Anaheim: 4 city, town
county: 6 Orange
locale: 10 California
team: 6 Angels
town near ~: 4 Brea
Anaheim __ and Cucamonga: 5 Azusa
Anaïs: 3 Nin
see also French
Anakin
child: 4 Leia, Luke
analects: 6 pieces 7 sayings 8 excerpts, extracts, passages 9 anthology, citations 10 quotations, selections
analeptic: 9 stimulant 10 comforting
analgesic: 3 APF 4 balm, Cope 5 Advil, Aleve, Bayer 6 Anacin, Datril, Motrin 7 anodyne, aspirin, Ecotrin, soother, Tylenol 8 Bufferin, Excedrin, St. Joseph, Vanquish 9 Ascriptin 10 anesthetic, painkiller
need an ~: 4 ache
target: 4 pain
analog: 8 parallel
not ~: 7 digital
analog __: 5 clock, watch
analogize: 6 relate
analogous: 4 akin, like, same, such 5 alike 6 allied, on a par 7 cognate, kindred, related, similar, uniform 8 matching, parallel, relative 9 consonant 10 comparable, equivalent, homogenous, homologous, resembling
analogy: 8 affinity, likeness, likening, metaphor, parallel, sameness 9 semblance 10 comparison, similarity
make an ~: 5 liken
phrase: 4 is to
analysis: 4 test, view 5 assay, audit, check, study, trial 6 review, survey 7 opinion, profile, remarks, summary, therapy 8 critique, exegesis, judgment, research, scrutiny 9 breakdown, criticism, reasoning, treatment, voice-over 10 commentary, dissection, evaluation, inspection
financial ~ tool: 5 chart
kind of ~: 4 qual.
mental ~: 6 reason
analyst: 6 critic, shrink 8 examiner 9 columnist, evaluator, therapist 10 accountant
concern: 2 id 3 ego
__ analyst: 3 lay 4 news 7 systems
analytical: 5 sound 6 cogent 7 logical, tenable 8 cerebral, coherent, methodic, rational, sensible, thinking 9 heuristic, inquiring, pragmatic 10 consistent, reasonable
analyze: 4 sift, test, x-ray 5 assay, audit, check, prove, study, think, weigh 6 decode, detail, digest, peruse, review 7 compare, dissect, examine, explain 8 construe, decipher, evaluate, factor in, identify 9 criticize, enter into, figure out, interpret, pick apart 10 brainstorm
grammatically: 5 parse
mentally: 6 reason
verse: 4 scan
Analyze __: 4 That, This
Analyze That (2002 film)
cast: Billy Crystal, Robert De Niro, Lisa Kudrow
director: Harold Ramis
Analyze This (1999 film)
cast: Billy Crystal, Robert De Niro, Lisa Kudrow
director: Harold Ramis
__ a Name: 4 I Got
Ananias
emulate ~: 3 lie
Ananke: 4 moon
planet: 7 Jupiter
anapest: 4 foot
relative: 4 iamb 6 dactyl 7 pyrrhic, spondee, trochee
anarchic: 7 chaotic, lawless, radical, riotous 8 confused 9 insurgent 10 disorderly, tumultuous, ungoverned
anarchist: 5 rebel, Sacco 7 leftist, radical 8 agitator, ultraist, Vanzetti 9 insurgent, terrorist 10 malcontent
anarchy: 4 mess 5 chaos 6 bedlam, mayhem, tumult, unrest, uproar 7 ferment, license, mob rule, turmoil 8 civil war, disarray, disorder, nihilism, shambles, upheaval 9 confusion, mobocracy 10 revolution, turbulence
__ an arrow...: 5 I shot
Anastasia
father: 4 czar, tsar, tzar
see also Russian
Anastasia (1956 film)
cast: Ingrid Bergman, Yul Brynner, Helen Hayes, Akim Tamiroff
director: Anatole Litvak
anat.: 3 sci.
anathema: 4 bane, tabu 5 taboo 6 pariah 7 bugbear 10 not allowed
anathematize: 5 blast 7 condemn 8 denounce 9 imprecate
Anatole: 6 France, Litvak
Anatolian: 4 Turk
Anatoly: 6 Karpov 8 Dobrynin
anatomical: 7 organic 8 corporal 9 corporeal
canal: 4 iter 5 lumen
cavities: 4 vasa 5 antra
cavity: 5 lumen, sinus 6 antrum
dividers: 5 septa
fold: 5 plica
foot: 3 pes
hinge: 4 knee
hooked ~ part: 5 uncus
loop: 4 ansa
pouch: 3 sac
ring: 6 areola, areole
sac: 5 bursa
tissue: 4 tela
tissues: 5 telae
vessel: 3 vas
wrinkle: 4 ruga
anatomist: 4 Gray 5 Galen
anatomize: 7 dissect
anatomy: 4 body, form 5 build, frame 6 figure, makeup 7 science 9 structure
back, in ~: 6 dorsum
branch of ~: 7 myology
external, in ~: 5 ectal
inner, in ~: 5 ental
knee, in ~: 4 genu
of the back, in ~: 5 notal
study: 9 structure
__ anatomy: 5 gross
__ Anatomy: 5 Gray's, Grey's
Anatomy Lesson, The
author: Philip Roth
Anatomy of a Murder (1959 film)
cast: Eve Arden, Ben Gazzara, Arthur O'Connell, Lee Remick, James Stewart
director: Otto Preminger
dog: 5 Muffy
__ Ana winds: 5 Santa
Anaxagoras: 5 Greek 11 philosopher
Anaximander: 5 Greek 11 philosopher
ANC
part of ~: 3 Afr., Nat. 4 Cong., Natl. 7 African 8 Congress, National
ancestor: 4 sire 6 father, mother, origin, parent 9 precursor, prototype 10 forefather, forerunner, progenitor
ancestors: 5 roots 7 kinfolk 8 kinfolks, kinsfolk 9 forebears
ancestral: 6 lineal, racial 7 genetic 8 familial, primeval 9 genetical, inherited, primaeval 10 affiliated, congenital, connatural, derivative, hereditary
image: 5 totem
ancestry: 4 line 5 birth, blood, class, roots, stock 6 origin, strain 7 descent, kinfolk, lineage 8 heredity, heritage, kinfolks, kinsfolk, pedigree 9 etymology, forebears, genealogy 10 derivation, extraction
Anchises
son: 5 Eneas 6 Aeneas
anchor: 3 fix, set, tie 4 dock, host, moor 5 bower, imbed, kedge, plant, rivet 6 Brokaw, fasten, Lehrer, Rather, secure 7 Huntley, lookout, MacNeil 8 Brinkley, Cronkite, entrench, foothold, hold down, Jennings, mainstay, reporter 9 stabilize 10 newscaster
a ship: 5 lay to
botanical ~: 4 root
domain: 3 sea 4 news
drop ~: 4 land 6 arrive 8 get there
ender: 3 age, man, men 5 woman, women 6 person
hole for an ~ cable: 5 hawse
lift ~: 4 sail 7 set sail 8 shove off
mountain-climber's ~: 5 belay
overseer: 4 bo's'n 5 bosun
position: 4 desk 5 apeak, apeek, atrip 6 aweigh
race: 5 relay
remain at ~: 4 ride 5 lie to
rope: 6 hawser
sound: 5 clank
anchorage: 3 bay 4 dock, pier, port, quay 5 basin, berth, haven, jetty, wharf 6 asylum, harbor, refuge 7 harbour, landing, mooring, shelter 9 harborage, sanctuary

Anchorage: 4 city, town
  locale: 6 Alaska
  newspaper: 4 News
anchored: 4 firm 6 secure, stable 8 embedded, immobile 10 stationary
anchoress: 3 nun 7 eremite, recluse
anchoret
  see anchorite
anchorite: 4 monk 5 loner 6 hermit 7 eremite, isolato, recluse 8 solitary 9 religious 10 troglodyte
  abode: 4 cell
  like an ~: 4 lone
Anchors Aweigh: 4 song
  group: 3 USN 4 Navy
Anchors Aweigh (1945 film)
  cast: Kathryn Grayson, Gene Kelly, Frank Sinatra
  director: George Sidney
anchovies: 4 fish
  how ~ are packed: 5 in oil
  like ~: 5 salty
  sauce: 4 alec
Anchurus
  father: 5 Midas
ancien ___: 6 régime
ancient: 3 old 4 aged 5 aging, early, hoary, of old, olden, passé 6 ageing, age-old, bygone, creaky, former, native 7 antique, archaic, elderly, wizened 8 grizzled, Noachian, obsolete, primeval 9 geriatric, getting on, primaeval, primitive, senescent, unevolved, up in years, venerable, vestigial 10 aboriginal, antiquated, immemorial, primordial
  combining form: 4 pale- 5 palae-, paleo- 6 archeo-, palaeo-, palaio- 7 archaeo-
ancient ___: 6 regime 7 history
Ancient Evenings: 5 novel
  author: Norman Mailer
  setting: 5 Egypt
Ancient Mariner's
  cry: 5 asail
Ancient Wonders
  one of the ~: 6 Pharos 7 pyramid 8 Colossus
ancillary: 4 side 5 extra, minor 9 accessory, appendage, attendant, attending, auxiliary, dependant, dependent, satellite, secondary 10 additional, coincident, collateral, incidental, subsidiary
  combining form: 3 par- 4 para-
and: 3 too 4 also, more, plus 6 bridge, joiner, linker 7 besides, further 8 as well as, moreover 9 along with, ampersand, connector, including, what's more 10 connective, in addition
and ___: 3 how 4 so on
and ___ some: 4 then
...and ___ far: 5 yet so
...and ___ grow on!: 5 one to
...and ___ in the morning: 5 see me
...and ___ my cap: 3 I in
...and ___ need to know: 5 all ye
...and ___ the child: 5 spoil
...and ___ well: 4 all's 5 all is
And ___ bed: 4 so to
And ___ goes: 4 so it
And ___ grow on: 5 one to
And ___ Her: 5 I Love
And ___ I wrote...: 4 then
And ___ off!: 6 they're
And ___ the opposite shore...: 3 I on
And ___ There Were None: 4 Then
And ___ to every purpose...: 5 a time
And ___ word from...: 4 now a
And ___ wrote...: 5 then I
___ and aah: 3 ooh
___ and Abélard: 7 Héloise
___ and abet: 3 aid
___ and abetting: 6 aiding
___ and Abner: 3 Lum
___ and a bone...: 4 a rag
...and a bottle of ___: 3 rum
___ and above: 4 over
___ and Accepted Masons: 4 Free
___ and a day: 5 a year 7 forever
___ and Aeneas: 4 Dido
___ and aft: 4 fore
___ and after: 6 before
___ and again: 3 now 4 ever, time
___ and age: 3 day
___ and a half: 4 time
___ and alack: 4 alas
___ and Ale: 5 Cakes
___ and a leg: 5 an arm
___ and Alexander: 5 Fanny
___ and all: 3 one 5 still, warts
___ and Allen: 5 Burns
And all ye ___ to know: 4 need
Andaman: 3 sea
  locale: 8 Malaysia, Thailand 9 Indonesia
___ and anon: 4 ever
andante: 5 music, tempo 6 slowly
  faster than ~: 8 moderato
  slower than ~: 5 largo, lento 6 adagio
...and a partridge in a ___ tree: 4 pear
___ and a Peck, A: 6 Bushel
___ and a Prayer: 4 Wing
___ and a promise: 4 lick
___ and asked: 3 bid
___ and assigns: 5 heirs
...and a time to ___: 3 sew 4 heal, lose
___ and away: 3 far, out
___ and Away: 3 Far 4 Up Up
And away ___!: 4 we go
___ and a Woman: 4 A Man
___ and axle: 5 wheel
___ and balances: 6 checks
___-and-ball foot: 4 claw
___ and Barbuda: 7 Antigua
___ and Bars: 5 Stars
___ and battery: 7 assault
___ and bear it: 4 grin
___ and bees: 5 birds
___ and bells: 3 cap
...and bells on her ___: 4 toes
___ and Bess: 5 Porgy
___ and between: 7 betwixt
___ and beyond: 5 above
___ and Bill: 3 Min
___ and bit: 5 brace
___ and blood: 5 flesh
___-and-blue: 5 black
___ and blues: 6 rhythm
___ and board: 3 bed 4 room
___ and bobtail: 6 ragtag, tagrag
___ and bolts: 4 nuts
___ and bones: 4 skin
___ and Bones: 5 Skull 6 Sticks
___ and bothered: 3 hot
___ and bounds: 5 butts, leaps, metes
___ and Bows: 7 Buttons
___ and Bradstreet: 3 Dun
___-and-break: 4 make
___ and breakfast: 3 bed
___ and bred: 4 born
___-and-brimstone: 4 fire
___-and-buggy: 5 horse
___ and bugle corps: 4 drum
___-and-bull story: 4 cock
___ and burn: 5 crash, slash
___-and-bust: 4 boom
___ and butter: 5 bread
___ and caboodle: 3 kit
___ and Caicos Islands: 5 Turks
___ and call: 4 beck
___ and carry: 4 cash
___ and center: 5 front
___-and-cents: 7 dollars
___ and chain: 4 ball
___ and cheese: 3 ham
___ and Cher: 5 Sonny
___ and Child: 7 Madonna
...and children of all ___!: 4 ages
___ and Child Reunion: 6 Mother
___ and chips: 4 fish
___ and Chloe: 7 Daphnis
___ and Chocolate: 5 Bread
___ and Chong: 6 Cheech
___ and choose: 4 pick
___ and Circumstance: 4 Pomp
___ and circuses: 5 bread
___ and Civilization: 4 Eros
___ and Clark: 4 Lois 5 Lewis
___-and-claw foot: 4 ball
___ and clear: 4 free, loud
___ and Cleopatra: 6 Antony, Caesar
___ and Clover: 7 Crimson
___ and Clyde: 6 Bonnie
___ and Coca-Cola: 3 Rum
___ and Coke: 3 rum
___ and con: 3 pro
___ and Confused: 5 Dazed
___ and conquer: 6 divide
___ and cons: 4 pros
___ and Consent: 6 Advise
___ and coo: 4 bill
___ and Costello: 6 Abbott
___-and-cover: 3 cut
___ and crafts: 4 arts
___ and cranny: 4 nook
___ and cream: 7 peaches
___ and Cressida: 7 Troilus
___ and Crofts: 5 Seals
___ and crossbones: 5 skull
___-and-crosses: 7 noughts
___ and cry: 3 hue
___-and-dagger: 5 cloak
___ and dance: 4 song
___ and dandy: 4 fine
___ and dangerous: 5 armed
___ and Daniel Webster, The: 5 Devil
___ and dart: 3 egg
___ and Dave: 3 Sam
___ and Day: 5 Night
___ and deal: 5 wheel
___ and Death: 4 Love
___ and Decker: 5 Black
___ and Delilah: 6 Samson
___ and Deliver: 5 Stand
___ and desist: 5 cease
___ and die: 4 tool
___-and-dime: 4 five 6 nickel
___ and dine: 4 wine
___ and dip: 4 chip
___-and-dirty: 4 down 5 quick
___ and Dolls: 4 Guys
___ and don'ts: 3 do's
___ and doom: 5 gloom
___ and downs: 3 ups
___ and drabs: 5 dribs
___ and drakes: 5 ducks
___-and-dried: 3 cut
___ and Driver: 3 Car
___ and Drug Administration: 4 Food
___ and dry: 4 high
Andean: 4 Inca 5 lofty 7 Chilean 8 Peruvian
  see also Andes
___ and early: 6 bright
___ and easy: 4 free
...and eat ___: 5 it too
___ and effect: 5 cause
___-and-egg: 7 chicken
___-and-egg man: 6 butter
___ and eggs: 3 ham 5 bacon, steak
___ and ends: 4 odds
___ and error: 5 trial
Anders: 5 Luana 7 Allison, Celsius 8 Ångström
Andersen, Hans Christian: 4 Dane 6 Danish, writer
  work: The Little Mermaid
    The Princess and the Pea
    The Snow Queen
    The Tinderbox
    The Ugly Duckling
Anderson: 3 Ian, Wes 4 Bill, Brad, Carl, city, Ivie, Jack, Loni, Lynn, town 5 Daryl, Eddie, Harry, Leroy, Louie 6 Judith, Marian, Melody, Pamela, Philip, Robert, Sparky 7 Barbara, Gillian, Herbert, Lindsay, Maxwell, Michael, Richard 8 Sherwood
  locale: 7 Indiana
Anderson, Carl: 8 Nobelist 9 physicist
Anderson, Judith: 4 Dame 7 actress
Anderson, Leroy: 8 composer
  work: Belle of the Ball
    Blue Tango
    Bugler's Holiday
    Fiddle-Faddle
    Jazz Pizzicato
    The Phantom Regiment
    Plink, Plank, Plunk!
    Sandpaper Ballet
    Sleigh Ride
    The Syncopated Clock
    A Trumpeter's Lullaby
    The Typewriter
    The Waltzing Cat
Anderson, Loni
  spouse: Burt Reynolds
Anderson, Lynn
  song: Rose Garden (1970)
Anderson, Marian: 4 alto 6 singer 9 contralto
  specialty: 5 opera
Anderson, Maxwell: 6 writer
  work: Anne of the Thousand Days
    The Bad Seed
    Barefoot in Athens
    The Buccaneer
    Candle in the Wind
    Elizabeth the Queen
    The Eve of St. Mark
    First Flight
    Gods of the Lightning
    Joan of Lorraine
    Key Largo
    Knickerbocker Holiday
    Lost in the Stars
    Mary of Scotland
    Night Over Taos
    Storm Operation

Valley Forge
What Price Glory?
Winterset
Anderson, Pamela
spouse: Tommy Lee
Anderson, Robert: 6 writer **10** playwright
work: Absolute Strangers
After
All Summer Long
Getting Up and Going Home
I Never Sang for My Father
The Last Act Is a Solo
Tea and Sympathy
A Wreath and a Curse
You Know I Can't Hear You When the Water's Running
Anderson, Sherwood: 6 writer
work: Horses and Men
Marching Man
The Triumph of the Egg
Winesburg, Ohio
Anderson Tapes, The: 4 film **5** novel
author: Lawrence Sanders
cast: Martin Balsam, Dyan Cannon, Sean Connery
director: Sidney Lumet
Andersson: 4 Arne, Bibi
Andes: 3 mts. **4** mtns. **5** range **9** mountains
ancient ~ dweller: 4 Inca **5** Incan
animal: 4 pudu **5** llama **6** alpaca, vicuña
capital: 4 Lima **5** Quito **6** Bogotá **8** Santiago
city: 4 Cali **5** Cusco, Cuzco
country: 4 Ecua., Peru **5** Chile **8** Colombia
explorer: 4 Peck
flyer: 6 condor
Indian: 6 Aymara
mountain: 4 Ruiz, Solo, Toro **5** Cachi, Chani, Cusco, Cuzco, Galan, Laudo, Negro, Pular, Quela **6** Ampato, Bonete, Juncal, Pissis, Sajama **7** Huandoy, Illampu, Palermo, San Juan **8** Ancohuma, Coropuna, El Condor, El Muerto, Famatina, Illimani, Polleras, Solimana, Tortolas, Yerupaja **9** Aconcagua, Antofalla, Condoriri, Huascarán, Incahuasi, Marmolejo, Pumasillo, Salcantay, Tupungato **10** Chimborazo, Mercedario, Nacimiento, Parinacota, Tres Cruces
native language: 6 Kechua **7** Kechuan, Quechua, Quichua **8** Quechuan
shrub: 4 coca **8** cinchona
tuber: 3 oca, oka
__ and Eve: 4 Adam
__ and every: 4 each
__ and Ewell: 5 Epsom
__ and excursions: 7 alarums
__ and eye: 4 hook
__ and fall: 4 rise **7** decline
__ and famous: 4 rich
__ and far: 4 near
__ and far between: 3 few
__ and farewell: 4 Hail
__ and fast: 4 hard
__ and fauna: 5 flora
__ and feather: 3 tar
__ and feathers: 4 fuss, plug
__ and feel: 4 look
__ and female: 4 male
__ and field: 5 track
__ and file: 4 rank
__ and fill: 3 cut **4** back
__ and flowers: 6 hearts
__ and Fog: 7 Shadows
__ and foot: 4 hand
__ and for all: 4 once
__ and foremost: 5 first
__ and Forever: 3 Now
__ and forth: 4 back
__ and fortune: 4 fame
__ and found: 4 lost
__-and-four: 5 coach
__ and Fruity: 4 Good
__ and Futuna Islands: 6 Wallis
__ and Future King, The: 4 Once
__ and Galatea: 4 Acis
__ and games: 3 fun
__ and Garfunkel: 5 Simon
__ and Get It: 4 Come
...__ and gimble...: 4 gyre
And giving __, up...: 4 a nod
__ and Glory: 4 Hope **5** Power
__ and glove: 4 hand
__ and go: 4 come **5** touch
__-and-go: 4 stop **5** get-up
__-and-go-seek: 4 hide
__ and gown: 3 cap
__ and grill: 3 bar
__ and groan: 4 moan
__-and-groove joint: 6 tongue
__ and Gus: 6 Tillie
__-and-guts: 5 blood
__ and Hammer: 3 Arm
__ and Hardy: 6 Laurel
__ and Harriet: 5 Ozzie
And hast thou __ the Jabberwock?: 5 slain
__ and haw: 3 hem
__ and hearty: 4 hale
__ and Herb: 7 Peaches
__ and hers: 3 his
__ and Her Sisters: 6 Hannah
__ and Herzegovina: 6 Bosnia
__ and His Brothers: 6 Joseph
__ and his money...: 5 A fool
__ and hiss: 3 boo
__ and Hobbes: 6 Calvin
__ and holler: 4 hoot
__ and Honey: 4 Milk
__ and Hopin': 6 Wishin'
__ and hounds: 4 hare
And how!: 6 I'll say, you bet
__ and Howard: 6 Melvin
__ and Howell: 4 Bell
...__ and hungry look: 5 a lean
__ and Hyde: 6 Jekyll
__ and I: 3 You
...and I __: 5 quote
__ and Ice: 4 Fire
Andie: 9 MacDowell
And I Love Her (1964 song)
artist: Beatles
And I Love You So (1973 song)
artist: Perry Como
__ and improved: 3 new
__ and Indians: 7 cowboys
__ and Indian War: 6 French
__ and Innocent: 5 Sweet, Young
...and into __ martini: 4 a dry
andiron: 7 firedog
__ and Isolde: 7 Tristan
__ and Issas: 5 Afars
__ and I, The: 3 Egg **4** King **5** Klone
__ and Ives: 7 Currier
__ and Ivory: 5 Ebony
__ and Janis: 4 Arlo
__ and Jeff: 4 Mutt
__ and Jeremy: 4 Chad
__ and jerk: 5 clean
__ and Jerry: 3 Tom
__ and jetsam: 7 flotsam
__ and Jill: 4 Jack
And Jill came tumbling __: 5 after
__ and Jim: 5 Jules
__ and Joan: 5 Darby **6** Bobbin
__ and Johnny: 5 Santo **7** Frankie
__ and joy: 5 pride **7** comfort
__ and Judy: 5 Punch
__ and Juliet: 5 Romeo
... And Justice for All (1979 film)
cast: John Forsythe, Al Pacino, Lee Strasberg, Jack Warden
director: Norman Jewison
__ and kicking: 5 alive
__ and kin: 4 kith
__ and labor: 5 parts
__ and ladder: 4 hook
__ and Ladders: 6 Chutes
__-and-ladies: 5 lords
__ and last: 5 first
...__ and lasting peace: 5 a just
__ and Leander: 4 Hero
__ and learn: 4 live
__ and left: 5 right
__ and Let Die: 4 Live
__ and letters: 4 arts
__ and Lisa: 5 David
__ and Livingstone: 7 Stanley
__ and loan: 7 savings
__ and Lomb: 6 Bausch
__ and loss: 6 profit
__ and Lovers: 4 Sons **7** Friends
__ and low: 4 high
__ and Lowdown: 5 Sweet
__ and Ludmilla: 7 Russlan
__ and Mabel: 4 Cain, Mack
__ and Magog: 3 Gog
__ and main: 5 might
And make it snappy!: 3 PDQ **6** pronto
__ and Mammon: 3 God
__ and Marge: 4 Myrt
__ and Marian: 5 Robin
__ and Marie: 5 Donny
__ and Marriage: 4 Love
__ and Martin: 5 Rowan
__ and Mary: 7 William
__-and-match: 3 mix
__ and Maude: 6 Harold
__ and Me: 3 You **5** Molly, Roger
__ and mean: 4 lean
__ and means: 4 ways
__ and Meek: 3 Eek
__ and mehitabel: 5 archy
__ and mighty: 4 high
__ and Mike: 3 Pat
__ and mild: 4 meek
And miles to go before I __: 5 sleep
__ and minds: 6 hearts
__ and mirrors: 5 smoke
__ and Misdemeanors: 6 Crimes
__-and-miss: 3 hit
__ and Models: 7 Artists
__ and Moe: 4 Izzy
and more: 3 etc.
__ and mortar: 6 bricks, clicks
__ and motion study: 4 time
__ and mouse: 3 cat
__ and Mrs. Muir, The: 5 Ghost
__ and My Gal: 5 For Me
__ and nail: 5 tooth
__ and Nancy: 3 Sid
__ and near: 3 far
__ and needles: 4 pins
__ and Nevis: 7 St. Kitts
__ and Noble: 6 Barnes
...and not __ to drink: 5 a drop
...__ and not heard: 4 seen
__ and Nothingness: 5 Being
__ and now: 4 here
__ and Old Lace: 7 Arsenic
__ and Oman: 6 Muscat
__ and omega: 5 alpha
__ and on: 3 off
__ and onions: 5 liver
__ and only: 3 one
__ and Only: 5 My One
__ and order: 3 law
Andorra: 4 city, town **6** nation **7** capital, country
locale: 6 Europe
neighbor: 5 Spain **6** France
and others: 4 et al. **6** et alia, et alii
__ and Other Strangers: 6 Lovers
__ and Our Gang: 6 Spanky
__ and out: 4 down, over
__-and-outer: 4 down
__ and outs: 3 ins
Andover: 4 city, town **6** school **10** prep school
address: 3 sir
attendee: 5 pupil
locale: 4 Mass. **9** Minnesota
__ and pains: 5 aches
__ and papa: 4 mama
__ and parcel: 4 part
__ and paste: 3 cut
__ and Peace: 3 War
__ and peck: 4 hunt
__ and penates: 5 lares
__ and pepper: 4 salt
__ and Perrins: 3 Lea
__ and pieces: 4 bits
__-and-pinion: 4 rack
__ and Pins: 7 Needles
__ and play: 4 plug
__ and Plenty: 4 Good
__ and Pluck: 4 Luck
__ and polish: 4 spit
__ and Pollux: 6 Castor
__ and pony show: 3 dog
__-and-pop: 3 mom
__ and potatoes: 4 meat
__ and pray: 4 hope
__ and Prejudice: 5 Pride
__ and Present Danger: 5 Clear
And pretty maids all in __: 4 a row
__ and proper: 3 due **4** prim
__ and puff: 4 huff
__ and Punishment: 5 Crime
__-and-putt: 5 pitch
__ and Pythias: 5 Damon
__ and quarter: 4 draw
__ and quiet: 5 peace
__ and rabbet: 6 square
Andrade, Mario: 4 poet **9** Brazilian
__ and Rain: 4 Fire
__ and rat: 3 cat
__ and rave: 4 rant
Andre: 4 seal **6** Agassi, Dawson, de Toth **8** Braugher
André: 4 Gide **5** Lwoff, Watts **6** Ampère, Breton, Derain, Norton, Previn **7** Citroën, Maginot, Malraux, Maurois **8** Cournand, Eglevsky **9** de Chénier
ex: 3 Mia
in English: 6 Andrew
see also French

Andrea: 5 Doria, Leeds 7 Bocelli, McArdle 8 del Sarto, Mantegna, Mitchell, Palladio 10 Marcovicci
Andrea __: 5 Doria
Andrea __ Robbia: 5 Della
Andrea del Sarto: 4 poem
author: Robert Browning
Andrea Doria: 4 boat, ship 5 liner
__ and ready: 4 good
__-and-ready: 5 rough
Andreanof
island: 4 Atka
Andreas: 8 Gryphius, Marggraf, Vesalius
in English: 6 Andrew
__ Andreas Fault: 3 San
Andre de __: 4 Toth
__ and reel: 3 rod 4 bead
Andrei: 4 Bely 7 Amalrik, Gromyko 8 Sakharov
see also Russian
Andres: 9 Galarraga
Andrés: 5 Bello 7 Segovia
Andress, Ursula: 7 actress
spouse: John Derek
Andre the __: 5 Giant
Andretti, Mario: 9 auto racer
milieu: 5 track
__-andrew: 5 merry
Andrew: 3 Ure 4 Gold, Lang, Shue 5 Cuomo, Davis, saint, Wyeth, Young 6 Huxley, Marton, Mellon, Motion, Tobias 7 Bergman, Fleming, Greeley, Jackson, Johnson, Marvell, Schally, Stevens, Windsor 8 Burnside, Carnegie, McCarthy, McLaglen 10 Duke of York
brother: 6 Edward 7 Charles
ex: 5 Sarah 6 Fergie
in French: 5 André
in German: 7 Andreas
in Italian: 6 Andrea
sister: 4 Anne
Andrew __ Clay: 4 Dice
Andrew __ Webber: 5 Lloyd
Andrew Lloyd __: 6 Webber
Andrews: 3 AFB 4 Dana, Tige 5 Julie, Patty 6 Maxene 7 LaVerne
Andrews, Julie: 4 Dame 6 singer 7 actress
film: 10 (1979)
The Americanization of Emily (1964)
Darling Lili (1970)
Hawaii (1966)
Mary Poppins (1964, AA)
The Princess Diaries (2001)
S.O.B. (1981)
The Sound of Music (1965)
Star! (1968)
The Tamarind Seed (1974)
That's Life! (1986)
Thoroughly Modern Millie (1967)
Torn Curtain (1966)
Victor/Victoria (1982)
spouse: Blake Edwards
Andrews Sisters: 4 trio
members: Patty, Maxene, LaVerne
song: Bei Mir Bist du Schoen (1938)
Boogie Woogie Bugle Boy (1941)
Rum and Coca-Cola (1945)
Andric, Ivo: 6 writer 7 Bosnian 8 Nobelist
__-and-ride: 4 kiss, park
__ and robbers: 4 cops
Androcles: 5 Roman, slave
friend: 4 lion
Androcles and the Lion: 4 film, play
author: George Bernard Shaw
cast: Jean Simmons, Alan Young
director: Chester Erskine
locale: 5 arena
android
model: 5 human
relative: 5 robot
Star Trek ~: 4 Data
__ and roll: 4 rock
Andromache
author: Euripides
husband: 6 Hector
Andromaque
author: Jean Racine
Andromeda: 6 galaxy
daughter: 10 Gorgophone
husband: 7 Perseus
parent: 7 Cepheus 10 Cassiopeia
son: 6 Heleus, Mestor, Perses 7 Alcaeus, Cynurus 9 Electyron, Sthenelus
Andromeda Strain, The
author: Michael Crichton
__ Andronicus: 5 Titus
androphobe fear: 3 men
Andropov: 4 Yuri
Andros
locale: 7 Bahamas
__ and Roses: 5 Bread, Tears
__ and ruin: 4 rack 5 wrack
__ and run: 3 cut, eat, hit
__-and-run: 5 pitch
__ and running: 3 off
Andrzej: 5 Wajda
ands
no ifs ~ or buts: 7 exactly 10 absolutely, definitely, positively
__ and saddles: 5 boots
__ and Sade: 3 Vic
__-and-salt: 6 pepper
__ and Sand: 5 Blood
...__ and sane Fourth: 5 a safe
__ and Satires: 4 Odes
__ and saucer: 3 cup
__ and sciences: 4 arts
__ and scrape: 3 bow
__ and Sedition Acts: 5 Alien
__ and see: 4 wait
__-and-seek: 4 hide
__ and Sensibility: 5 Sense
__-and-serve: 5 brown
__ and shaker: 5 mover
__ and Sheba: 7 Solomon
__ and shine: 4 rise
__-and-shoot: 5 point
__ and shoulders: 4 head
__ and Shout: 5 Twist
__ and shovel: 4 pick
__-and-shut: 4 open
__ and sickle: 6 hammer
__ and sign in please: 5 Enter
__ and Sing!: 5 Awake
__ and Sixpence, The: 4 Moon
__ and skittles: 4 beer
__ and Smell the Roses: 4 Stop
__ and Smoke: 6 Summer
and so __: 5 forth, to bed 6 it goes
__ and soda: 6 scotch
and so forth: 3 etc.
__ and Son: 6 Dombey 7 Sanford
__, ands, or buts: 5 no ifs
And so to bed
author: Samuel Pepys
__ and soul: 4 body 5 heart
__ and sound: 4 safe
__-and-sour: 5 sweet
__-and-span: 4 spic 5 spick
__-and-spoke: 3 hub
__ and spoon race: 3 egg
__ and square: 4 fair
__ and squeak: 6 bubble
__ and Stacey: 3 Ned
__-and-stick: 4 peel 6 carrot
And Still __: 5 I Rise
__ and Stimpy: 3 Ren
__ and Stream: 5 Field
__ and Stress: 5 Storm
__ and Stripes: 5 Stars
__ and substance: 3 sum
__-and-suiter: 5 cloak
__ and sway: 5 swing
__ and sweet: 5 short
__ and switch: 4 bait
__ and Sympathy: 3 Tea
__ and Taboo: 5 Totem
__ and tackle: 5 block
__ and take: 3 put 4 give
__ and take notice: 5 sit up
__ and tan: 5 black
__ and tear: 4 wear
__ and tell: 4 kiss, show
__-and-ten: 4 five
__ and tenon: 7 mortise
__ and terminer: 4 oyer
__ and that: 4 this
And that __ hay!: 4 ain't
And that's the way __: 4 it is
And the __ Sing: 6 Angels
__ and the Americans: 3 Jay
__ and the Arrow, The: 5 Flame
__ and the Art of Motorcycle Maintenance: 3 Zen
__ and the Bandit: 6 Smokey
And the Band Played On (1993 film)
cast: Alan Alda, Matthew Modine, Richard Gere
__ and the Beast: 6 Beauty
__ and the Beautiful, The: 3 Bad 4 Bold
__ and the Bees, The: 5 Birds
__ and the Belmonts: 4 Dion
__ and the Black, The: 3 Red
__ and the Blowfish: 6 Hootie
__ and the Brightest, The: 4 Best
__ and the Canary, The: 3 Cat
__ and the Cruisers: 5 Eddie
__ and the Dead, The: 5 Naked, Quick
__ and the Detectives: 4 Emil
__ and the Dominos: 5 Derek
__ and the Dragon: 3 Bel
__ and the Dreamers: 7 Freddie
__ and the Ecstasy, The: 5 Agony
__ and the Family Stone: 3 Sly
__ and the Fatman: 4 Jake
__ and the Fiddle, The: 3 Cat
__ and the Furious, The: 4 Fast
__ and the Fury, The: 5 Sound
__ and the Gang: 4 Kool
__ and the Giant Peach: 5 James
__ and the Glory, The: 5 Power
__ and the Hound, The: 3 Fox
__ and the Id, The: 3 Ego
__ and the Jets: 6 Bennie
__ and the Juniors: 5 Danny
__ and the King of Siam: 4 Anna
__ and the Limelites: 4 Shep
And the Lord set __ upon Cain...: 5 a mark
__ and the Man: 4 Arms 5 Chico
__ and the Mighty, The: 4 High
__ and the Minor, The: 5 Major
and then __: 4 some 6 I wrote
__ and then: 3 now 5 there
__ and the Night Visitors: 5 Amahl
And Then There Were None: 4 film 5 novel
cast: Barry Fitzgerald, Louis Hayward, Walter Huston
director: René Clair
writer: Agatha Christie
__ and the Pacemakers: 5 Gerry
__ and the Papas, The: 5 Mamas
__ and the Pauper, The: 6 Prince
__ and the Paycock: 4 Juno
__ and the Pebble, The: 4 Clod
__ and the Pendulum, The: 3 Pit
__ and the Pirates: 5 Terry
__ and the Pussycats: 5 Josie
__ and the Pussycat, The: 3 Owl
__ and there: 4 here, then
And thereby __ a tale: 5 hangs
And thereby hangs __: 5 a tale
__ and the Restless, The: 5 Young
__ and the Romantics: 4 Ruby
__ and the Rose, The: 4 Ring 5 Sword 7 Slipper
__ and the Seven Hoods: 5 Robin
__ and the short of it, the: 4 long
__ and the Single Girl: 3 Sex
__ and the Swan: 4 Leda
__ and the Tramp: 4 Lady
__ and the Wolf: 5 Peter
__ and thin: 5 thick
__ and think: 4 stop
And This __ Beloved: 4 Is My
__ and Thisbe: 7 Pyramus
__ and thither: 6 hither
__ and thread: 6 needle
__ and Thummim: 4 Urim
__ and tide: 4 time
__ and tie: 4 suit
__ and Tina Turner: 3 Ike
__ and tired: 4 sick
__ and tittle: 3 jot
...and to __ good night!: 4 all a
__-and-toe: 4 heel
__ and tongs: 6 hammer
__ and tonic: 3 gin
__ and Tonto: 5 Harry
__ and trouble: 4 toil
__ and true: 5 tried
__ and tuck: 3 nip
__ and tucker: 3 bib
__-and-tumble: 5 rough
__ and turf: 4 surf
__ and turn: 4 toss
__ and Turnin': 6 Tossin'
__-and-turn indicator: 4 bank
__ and verse: 7 chapter
__ and vigor: 3 vim
__ and vinegar: 3 oil
__ and void: 4 null
__-and-wear: 4 wash
__ and weave: 3 bob
__ and weep: 6 read 'em
__ and well: 5 alive
And we'll have __ good time: 5 a real
__ and Wesson: 5 Smith
__ and western: 7 country
And When I Die (1969 song)
artist: Blood, Sweat & Tears
composer: Laura Nyro
__ and wherefores: 4 whys

__ and whey: 5 curds
__ and whistles: 5 bells
__ and white: 5 black
__ and wide: 3 far
__ and wife: 3 man
__ and Winding Road, The: 4 Long
__ and Wine: 5 Bread
__ and wing: 4 buck
__ and wiser: 5 older
__ and woof: 4 warp
__-and-woolly: 4 wild
Andy: 3 Kim 4 Bean, Capp, Dick, doll, Gibb, Gump 5 Clyde, Hardy 6 Devine, Garcia, Rooney, Warhol 7 Kaufman, rag doll, Russell, Tennant 8 Bathgate, Griffith, Pettitte, Van Slyke, Williams 10 Granatelli, Robustelli
aunt: 3 Bee
partner: 4 Amos
__ Andy: 5 Amos 'n', Handy 7 Raggedy
__ and yang: 3 yin
__, and ye shall...: 3 Ask
...and yet so __: 3 far
Andy Griffith Show, The (CBS sitcom)
cast: Frances Bavier (Aunt Bee Taylor)
Elinor Donahue (Ellie Walker)
Andy Griffith (Andy Taylor)
Ronny Howard (Opie Taylor)
Don Knotts (Barney Fife)
George Lindsey (Goober Pyle)
Hal Smith (Otis Campbell)
dog: 8 Gulliver
setting: Mayberry, N. Car.
__ and yon: 6 hither 7 thither
__ and Zooey: 6 Franny
anear: 4 nigh 5 close
__ an ear: 4 bend, give, lend
__ an ear to the ground: 4 have, keep
anecdotal
knowledge: 3 ana 4 lore 5 myths, tales 6 fables 7 legends, sayings 10 traditions
anecdote: 4 tale, yarn 5 story 9 narration, narrative
anecdotist: 8 narrator 9 raconteur
__ a neck: 5 win by
__ an egg: 3 lay
anemia: 6 pallor 7 fatigue, frailty, wanness 8 debility, paleness, puniness, weakness 9 fragility, tiredness 10 enervation, exhaustion, feebleness, insipidity, pallidness
anemic: 3 wan 4 pale, puny, weak 5 frail, pasty, wimpy 6 atonic, effete, feeble, flimsy, infirm, sallow 7 fragile, wimpish 8 delicate, helpless, listless, pithless 9 faltering, powerless 10 exsanguine, vulnerable
anemometer: 5 gauge
reading: 3 vel. 8 velocity
spinner: 4 gust, wind
anemone: 5 plant 6 flower
sea ~: 5 polyp 6 animal
__ anemone: 3 rue, sea 4 wood 5 clown, poppy
anent: 2 re 4 as to, in re 5 about 9 as regards, regarding 10 concerning
__ an era, the: 5 end of
anesthetic: 3 gas 4 drug, numb 5 ether 6 ethane, opiate 7 anodyne, dulling, numbing 8 deadened, hypnotic, narcotic, sedative 9 analgesic, deadening, soporific 10 painkiller
__ anesthetic: 5 local
anesthetize: 4 numb 6 benumb, deaden
anesthetized: 4 numb 5 under 9 unfeeling
anew: 4 over 5 again, fresh, newly 6 afresh, de novo, lately 7 freshly 8 once more, recently 9 once again, over again 10 from the top
in Latin: 6 de nova
__ an eye on: 4 keep
anfractuous: 4 mazy 5 curvy, snaky 6 coiled, curved, curvey, volute 7 crooked, sinuous, turning, twisted, winding 8 flexuous, tortuous 10 convoluted, meandering, serpentine
Ang: 3 Lee
ange feature: 4 aile
angel: 3 gem 5 donor, jewel, saint, Uriel 6 Azrael, backer, Moroni, patron, seraph, vision 7 Gabriel, grantor, Israfil, Lucifer, Michael, paragon, Raphael, sponsor 8 guardian, treasure 9 valentine 10 benefactor, underwrite
accessory: 4 halo, harp
be an ~: 4 give
ender: 4 fish
fallen ~: 5 devil, Satan 6 Belial, diablo 7 evil one, Lucifer 9 Beelzebub
guardian ~: 6 savior 7 saviour
hair: 5 pasta
in Persian mythology: 3 mah
little ~: 4 baby 5 child
nightmare: 4 flop 6 turkey
place: 6 heaven
theater ~: 6 backer, patron
see also sweetheart
angel __: 3 bed 4 cake, hair 5 light, shark
angel __ cake: 4 food
Angel: 5 Criss, falls 7 Cordero, Vanessa 9 waterfall
Angel (song)
artist: Aerosmith, Madonna, Sarah McLachlan
Angel __: 4 Baby, Eyes 5 Falls
Angel __ Shoulder: 4 on My
__ Angel: 4 Blue, I'm No, Teen 5 Black, Earth, Hell's 6 Fallen, Johnny, Street
Angela: 5 Davis 6 Merici, Merkel 7 Bassett 8 Baddeley, Lansbury 10 Cartwright
Broadway role for ~: 4 Mame
Angela's Ashes: 4 book, film
author: Frank McCourt
cast: Joe Breen, Robert Carlyle, Ciaran Owens, Emily Watson
director: Alan Parker
sequel: 3 'Tis
__ Angeles, CA: 3 Los
Angeles, Victoria de los: 6 singer 7 soprano
specialty: 5 opera
Angel Eyes (2001 film)
cast: Sonia Braga, Jim Caviezel, Terrence Howard, Jennifer Lopez
director: Luis Mandoki
angel food __: 4 cake
angelhair: 5 pasta
alternative: *see* pasta
angelic: 4 holy 5 godly, pious, sweet 6 devout, divine 7 lovable, saintly 8 adorable, beatific, cherubic, ethereal, heavenly, innocent, loveable, seraphic, supernal 9 beautiful, celestial, righteous 10 seraphical
glow: 4 aura
provide an ~ aura: 6 enhalo
Angelico, Fra: 6 artist 7 painter
homeland: 5 Italy
Angelina: 5 Jolie
father: 3 Jon
Angeli, Pier: 7 actress
spouse: Vic Damone
Angélique
composer: Jacques Ibert
Angell: 5 Roger 6 Norman
Angelo: 6 Dundee, Maggio
Angel of Light
author: Joyce Carol Oates
Angel of the Battlefield: 6 Barton
Angel of the Morning (song)
artist: Juice Newton, Merrilee Rush and the Turnabouts
Angel of the Odd, The
author: Edgar Allan Poe
Angelo, My Love (1983 film)
director: Robert Duvall
__ Angelo, TX: 3 San
Angelou, Maya: 4 poet
work: Gather Together in My Name
The Heart of a Woman
How Sheba Sings the Song
I Know Why the Caged Bird Sings
I Shall Not Be Moved
Lessons in Living
Life Doesn't Frighten Me
Shaker, Why Don't You Sing
A Song Flung up to Heaven
Still I Rise
Wouldn't Take Nothing for My Journey Now
Angels: 3 ten 4 team
home: 7 Anaheim 10 California
org.: 3 ALW, MLB
rival: *see* baseball team
sport: 8 baseball
__ Angels: 5 Hell's
Angels & Demons (2009 film)
cast: Tom Hanks, Ewan McGregor, Ayelet Zurer
director: Ron Howard
Angels With Dirty Faces (1938 film)
cast: Humphrey Bogart, James Cagney, Pat O'Brien
director: Michael Curtiz
Angel, The
artist: Erté
__ Angel, The: 4 Blue, Dark, Lost
angelus: 4 bell 10 church bell
pair on an ~: 4 alae
anger: 3 get, ire, sin, vex 4 bait, boil, burn, fury, gall, heat, miff, rage, rile, roil 5 annoy, get to, peeve, pique, shock, steam, venom, wrath 6 arouse, burn up, choler, dander, enmity, enrage, fire up, get mad, madden, nettle, offend, rankle, ruffle, spleen, stir up, tee off, temper, tirade 7 affront, agitate, dudgeon, emotion, enflame, hackles, incense, inflame, offense, outrage, passion, perturb, provoke, steam up, tick off, umbrage 8 acrimony, embitter, imbitter, irritate, rankling, vexation 9 aggravate, agitation, animosity, displease, distemper, hostility, infuriate, petulance, surliness 10 antagonism, antagonize, conniption, exasperate, irritation, resentment, run afoul of, unkindness
display of ~: 5 scene
express, as ~: 4 vent
inclination to ~: 4 bile
internalize ~: 4 fret, fume, stew 5 chafe 6 seethe
symbol of ~: 4 fist
unleash one's ~: 4 rail, rant, rave, yell 5 erupt, freak, storm 6 blow up, scream 7 bluster, bristle, explode, rampage 8 boil over, have a fit, run amuck 9 blow a fuse, fulminate, go berserk 10 hit the roof, kick up a row
angered
easily ~: 5 testy
see also angry
Anger Management (2003 film)
cast: Jack Nicholson, Adam Sandler, Marisa Tomei
Angie: 6 Harmon 8 Everhart 9 Dickinson
Angie (1973 song)
artist: Rolling Stones
Angie (1994 film)
cast: Geena Davis, James Gandolfini, Stephen Rea
director: Martha Coolidge
Angie Baby (1974 song)
artist: Helen Reddy
angioplasty target: 6 artery
Angkor __: 3 Vat, Wat 4 Thom
__ anglais: 3 cor 6 jardin
__ anglaise: 5 crème
angle: 3 aim, bow 4 bend, bias, fish, hook, ruse, side, tilt 5 crook, light, phase, pitch, slant, slope, stand, troll 6 corner, dogleg, recess, scheme 7 flexure, outlook, purpose 8 flection, maneuver, position, strategy 9 intention, viewpoint 10 motivation, standpoint
at an ~: 5 atilt, bevel 6 aslant 9 crossways, crosswise, on the bias, slantways, slantwise 10 diagonally
be at an ~: 4 lean, tilt
botanist's ~: 4 axil
brace: 4 L bar
carpenter's ~: 5 bevel
combining form: 4 goni- 5 gonio-
ender: 4 worm
(for): 3 aim, try
kind of ~: 5 acute, right 6 obtuse, reflex
leaf ~: 4 axil
off: 4 skew, veer 5 slant
on an ~: 6 aslant, aslope
projecting ~: 4 cant
reporter ~: 5 focus 9 viewpoint 10 standpoint
right ~: 3 ell
sharp ~: 3 zag, zig
starter: 3 tri 4 pent, rect
writer's ~: 5 focus, slant
__ angle: 4 face, hour, seat 5 acute, Bragg, drift, glide, phase, plane, polar, right, round, shelf, solid 6 danger, facial, obtuse, reflex 7 central, oblique

Angle
  counterpart: 5 Saxon
angled: 4 bent 5 bevel 6 skewed 7 crooked 8 diagonal
__-angle lens: 4 wide
angler: 5 eeler 6 fisher 7 trawler, troller 8 piscator 9 fisherman
  see also fisherman
angles
  at right ~: 4 orth., perp. 5 plumb 10 orthogonal
  at right ~ to the keel: 5 abeam
  without ~: 6 agonic
Anglican
  clergyman: 5 vicar
  headdress: 5 mitre
angling
  see fishing
Anglo-__: 5 Irish, Latin, Saxon 6 French, Gallic, Indian, Norman
Anglo-__ War: 4 Boer
Anglophobe fear: 7 England
Anglo-Saxon
  bailiff: 5 reeve
  council: 5 witan
  freeman: 5 ceorl
  kingdom: 5 Essex
  letter: 3 edh 4 wynn, yogh
  lord: 5 thane, thegn
  money: 3 ora 5 sceat 7 sceatta
  tax: 4 geld
  worker: 4 esne
Angola: 6 nation 7 country
  capital: 6 Luanda
  desert: 5 Namib
  language: 6 Mbundu
  money: 4 lwei 6 kwanza
  neighbor: 5 Congo 6 Zambia 7 Namibia
  people: 5 Lunda 6 Herero, Mbundu 9 Ovimbundu
  rebel org.: 5 UNITA
Angora: 3 cat 4 goat, wool 5 felid 6 fabric, feline, rabbit
  relative: ***see*** feline, goat, rabbit
  today: 6 Ankara
angry: 3 hot, mad 4 ired, sore, ugly, warm 5 cross, het up, huffy, irate, livid, moody, riled, sharp, upset, vexed, wroth 6 ablaze, fierce, fuming, galled, heated, ireful, miffed, peeved, piqued, raging, red-hot, stormy 7 boiling, burnt up, enraged, furious, hostile, steamed, teed off 8 choleric, fighting, frowning, hopped up, incensed, inflamed, lowering, maddened, outraged, reddened, spiteful, up in arms, vehement, volcanic, white-hot, worked up, wrathful 9 indignant, irascible, irritated, resentful, seeing red, splenetic, ticked off, wrought up 10 hopping mad, infuriated, up in the air
  be ~: 4 burn 6 seethe, simmer 7 bristle
  be ~ about: 6 resent
  become ~: 6 get mad
  be quietly ~: 4 fume
  get ~: 4 fume, snap 6 rear up, see red
  look: 5 frown, glare, scowl
  looking ~: 6 aglare
  make ~: 3 ire 4 rile 5 frost, peeve 6 burn up, enrage, fire up, madden 9 infuriate
  mood: 4 huff, snit
  one: 5 rager
  reaction: 4 rise
  retort: 5 my eye
  with: 5 mad at 6 down on
angry __ man: 5 young
__ Angry Man, The: 4 Last
__ Angry Men: 5 Seven 6 Twelve
Angry Young Men, The
  author: Kingsley Amis
angst: 3 woe 4 ache, fear 5 blues, dread, worry 7 anxiety, malaise 8 disquiet 10 inquietude, uneasiness
angstrom __: 4 unit
Ångström, Anders: 7 Swedish 9 physicist 10 astronomer
anguilliform creature: 3 eel
anguish: 3 woe 4 ache, care, fret, hell, pain 5 agony, dolor, gloom, grief, worry, wound 6 harrow, misery, ordeal, regret, sorrow, trauma 7 despair, remorse, sadness, torment, torture, travail 8 distress, hangover, the blues 9 dejection, heartache, suffering 10 bitterness, depression, desolation, heartbreak, heavy heart, loneliness, melancholy
  cry of ~: 4 oh no
anguished: 5 woful 6 tragic, woeful 8 dolorous, tragical
  be ~: 4 ache
angular: 4 bent, lean 5 bowed, gaunt, lanky 6 akimbo, meager, skewed, zigzag 7 crooked, scrawny, v-shaped, winding 8 cockeyed
  combining form: 3 -gon
  cut: 5 notch
  lead-in: 3 tri 4 equi, rect
  letter: 3 ell
Angus: 3 cow 4 bull, Scot 5 steer, Young 6 bovine, cattle, Wilson
__ Angus: 3 Red 5 Black
Anheuser Busch
  rival: 5 Coors, Pabst, Stroh 8 Heineken
anhydrate: 3 dry 5 parch 9 dehydrate, desiccate, evaporate, exsiccate 10 devitalize
anhydrous: 3 dry 4 arid 5 unwet
ani: 6 cuckoo 8 tickbird 9 blackbird
Ani: 8 DiFranco, Kavafian
__ a nice day!: 4 Have
anigh, not: 4 afar
__ a Nightingale: 5 Ode to
Anil: 6 Kapoor
aniline source: 6 indigo
anima: 4 soul 6 psyche
__ anima: 3 con
animadversion: 4 flak, slam 5 flack, knock, swipe 6 rebuke 7 censure 8 reproach 9 criticism, invective, stricture
animal: 2 ox 3 ant, ape, asp, ass, auk, ayu, bat, bee, bot, bug, cat, cod, cow, dab, dog, dor, eel, elk, emu, ern, ewe, fly, fox, fry, gar, ged, gnu, hen, ide, ihi, jay, kea, koi, man, mew, moa, nit, orf, owl, pie, pig, ram, rat, ray, roc, sey, sow, tai, tit, tui, yak 4 anoa, barb, bass, bear, bird, blay, boar, boce, boga, bret, brit, buck, bull, calf, carp, cero, char, chat, chub, chum, coho, colt, coot, crab, crow, cusk, dace, deer, dodo, dory, dove, drum, duck, dupe, emeu, erne, fawn, flea, foal, frog, fugu, game, gnat, goat, goby, grub, guan, gull, hake, hare, hart, hawk, hiku, huia, huss, ibis, jack, jocu, kagu, kaka, kite, kiwi, knot, kudu, lamb, lark, lice, lija, ling, lion, loon, loro, lory, lynx, mado, mapo, mare, masu, mean, meat, merl, mero, mina, mink, mite, mola, mole, moth, mule, myna, nene, opah, orfe, oryx, parr, pega, pest, peto, pike, pogy, pony, pout, puma, pupa, quab, raad, rail, rhea, rook, rudd, ruff, sama, scad, seal, sesi, shad, shag, skil, skua, slug, smew, sole, sora, spet, stag, swan, teal, tern, tick, tine, toad, tody, tope, tuna, ulua, unau, wasp, wild, wolf, wren, zebu 5 akule, aphid, aphis, beast, being, betta, biped, bison, bleak, bolti, booby, borer, brant, bream, brill, bruin, brute, burro, buteo, camel, chimp, chiro, chopa, cimex, cisco, civet, coati, cobia, colin, coney, cooty, crake, crane, dance, danio, dingo, drone, eagle, egret, eider, eland, elver, emmet, feral, filly, finch, galah, goony, goose, grebe, grope, grunt, guasa, guppy, harsh, heron, hilsa, horse, hound, hyena, imago, jager, junco, jurel, koala, koloa, krill, larva, lemur, llama, loach, lotte, louse, macaw, manta, mavis, merle, midge, minah, moose, moray, mouse, murre, mynah, nasty, noddy, okapi, otter, ousel, ouzel, oxeye, panda, pargo, perch, pewee, pewit, pipit, pitta, plane, porgy, potoo, prawn, quail, raven, roach, robin, sable, saker, sargo, saury, scaup, scrod, serin, shama, shark, sheep, skate, skunk, sloth, smelt, smolt, snake, snipe, snook, solan, sprat, steed, steer, stilt, stint, stoat, stork, swift, swine, tapir, tench, tetra, tiger, torsk, trout, tunny, twite, vireo, vixen, wahoo, whale, yager, zebra 6 agouti, aimara, alpaca, anabas, avocet, baboon, badger, barbel, barbet, beaver, becard, bedbug, beetle, beluga, beshow, bichir, bigeye, bishop, blenny, bonaci, bonito, bonxie, botfly, bowfin, brolga, brutal, bulbul, burbot, canary, caplin, caribe, chafer, chebec, chigoe, chinch, chough, chukar, cicada, cocoon, condor, congér, conure, cootie, cougar, coyote, cuchia, cuckoo, cunner, curlew, darter, dayfly, dipper, donkey, drongo, dunlin, earthy, earwig, equine, ermine, falcon, feline, ferret, fierce, fulmar, gadfly, gander, gannet, gerbil, godwit, gooney, gopher, grilse, groper, grouse, gunnel, hapuku, heifer, hilsah, hoopoe, hornet, iguana, impala, inanga, insect, Io moth, isopod, jabiru, jacana, jackal, jaeger, jaguar, kakapo, kitten, koodoo, lanner, larvae, linnet, lizard, locust, looper, louvar, maggot, magpie, maigre, mammal, mantid, mantis, marlin, marmot, marten, martin, mayfly, medaka, merlin, minnow, monkey, motmot, mud hen, mullet, musk ox, mussel, nonnat, ocelot, onager, oriole, osprey, parrot, parula, peewit, petrel, phoebe, pigeon, piraña, plaice, plakat, plover, pollan, possum, pouter, puffer, puffin, puneca, python, quezal, rabbit, remora, rodent, roller, roughy, saithe, salele, salema, salmon, saurel, savage, savola, scarab, schrod, scoter, sea mew, sennet, shiner, shrike, shrimp, simian, siskin, sucker, suslik, takahe, tandan, tarpon, tautog, testar, tetard, thrips, thrush, tiñosa, tityra, tomcod, tomtit, toucan, towhee, trogon, turaco, turbot, turkey, tussah, unkind, verdin, vermin, vicuña, walrus, wanton, wapiti, weasel, weever, weevil, whidah, whydah, wigeon, willet, wombat, wrasse, zander 7 alewife, alfiona, anchovy, anhinga, ant lion, axolotl, babbler, bacalao, barbudo, barn owl, beastly, beefalo, billbug, bittern, bloater, blowfly, bluefin, bluejay, brutish, buffalo, bunting, bustard, buzzard, cabezon, callous, capelin, cariama, caribou, catbird, catfish, cavalla, cheetah, chicken, chigger, codfish, corbina, corvina, cotinga, courser, crappie, creeper, cricket, critter, crittur, croaker, decapod, dogfish, dottrel, dovekey, dovekie, echidna, eelpout, elaenia, elepaio, escolar, fantail, finfoot, finspot, firefly, flycast, gadwall, garlopa, garpike, gazelle, gemsbok, giraffe, gorilla, goshawk, gourami, grackle, gray jay, graylag, graysby, greylag, gribble, grindle, grouper, grunion, guanaco, gudgeon, gurnard, gwyniad, haddock, halcyon, halibut, hamster, harrier, helleri, hen hawk, herring, hexapod, hoatzin, hurtful, inconnu, jacamar, jackass, jackdaw, katydid, kestrel, kinglet, ladybug, lamprey, lapwing, leopard, limpkin, lingcod, lobster, mallard, manakin, marabou, margate, meerkat, mojarra, mollusc, mollusk, mooneye, mudlark, mustang, nibbler, no-see-um, oldwife, opaleye, opossum, ortolan, ostrich, panther, peacock, peafowl, pelican, penguin, phoenix, pigfoot, piranha, pismire, pochard, polecat, pollack, pollock, pomfret, pompano, quetzal, redpoll, redwing, reptile, ronquil, sandbug, sand dab, sardine, sawfish, scalare, scooter, sculpin, sea bass, seagull, seriema, serpent, skimmer, skylark, snapper, sockeye, souslik, sparrow, sterlet, swallow, sweeper, tanager, tattler, termite, tilapia, tinamou, titlark, torpedo, touraco, unicorn, untamed, varment, varmint, viceroy, vicious, vulture, wagtail, walleye, waxbill, waxwing, whapuku, whiting, widgeon, wolf-eel, wryneck 8 aardvark, albacore, amadavat, amphipod, anableps, anaconda, antelope, arapaima, armyworm, avadavat, barbaric, barnacle, baysmelt, bee-eater, bell-

bird, bigmouth, blackcap, bloodfin, blowfish, bluebill, bluebird, bluefish, bluegill, bluehead, boatbill, bobolink, bobwhite, brisling, bullhead, bullneck, cabrilla, caracara, cardinal, characin, chimaera, chipmunk, cirriped, cockatoo, conenose, coturnix, crawfish, crayfish, creature, crevalle, curassow, dabchick, didapper, dormouse, dotterel, dragonet, eagle owl, elephant, fiendish, firebrat, fish hawk, flamingo, flathead, flounder, fruit fly, gambusia, garganey, gilthead, glowworm, goldfish, grayback, grayling, grosbeak, guacharo, halfbeak, halfmoon, hawfinch, hedgehog, hemipode, hiwi hiwi, hoactzin, honeybee, hornbill, housefly, inhumane, John Dory, kangaroo, killdeer, kinkajou, kiskadee, lacewing, landrail, longspur, lorikeet, lungfish, mackerel, macruran, manacode, mandrill, manta ray, marabout, marmoset, mealybug, medregal, megapode, menhaden, mole crab, mongoose, moorfowl, mosquito, muckworm, mulloway, murrelet, nannygai, nightjar, notornis, nuthatch, organism, oxpecker, palometa, parakeet, paraquet, paroquet, parroket, pearleye, peetweet, pheasant, pilchard, pitiless, platypus, porpoise, redshank, redstart, reduviid, reindeer, ringdove, ruthless, sadistic, scorpion, screamer, sea bream, sea eagle, sea horse, sea otter, sea raven, shelduck, shoebill, shoveler, silkworm, skipjack, snowbird, squirrel, stallion, starling, stingray, stinkbug, sturgeon, terrapin, thrasher, titmouse, tommycod, topsmelt, tortoise, tragopan, trembler, tremblor, trevally, troupial, tubenose, vengeful, water hen, wheatear, whimbrel, whinchat, whistler, white ant, white-eye, woodchat, woodcock, woodlark, woodworm, wrymouth **9** albatross, alligator, amberjack, amphibian, angelfish, argentine, arthropod, bandicoot, barbarian, barracuda, barreleye, beach flea, beastlike, blackbird, blue shark, broadbill, bullfinch, bumblebee, butterfly, cassowary, chaffinch, chameleon, chickadee, cockateel, cockatiel, cockroach, cormorant, corn borer, crocodile, crossbill, currawong, cutthroat, damselfly, dobsonfly, doodlebug, dorbeetle, Dover sole, dowitcher, dragonfly, dromedary, earthworm, eelblenny, feel about, ferocious, fieldfare, flinthead, francolin, frogmouth, gallinule, gerfalcon, goldeneye, goldfinch, grassquit, greenling, grenadier, groundhog, guillemot, guinea pig, gyrfalcon, hammerkop, jellyfish, kittiwake, lake trout, mallemuck, marsupial, martinico, merciless, merganser, millipede, mollymawk, mollymoke, monstrous, mudminnow, neon tetra, nighthawk, orangutan, ossifrage, pachyderm, pardalote, parrakeet, parroquet, partridge, peregrine, phalarope, pikeperch, porcupine, primitive, ptarmigan, quadruped, razorbill, redbreast, red mullet, sand lance, sandpiper, saturniid, schnapper, sea urchin, seedeater, sharpbill, sheep tick, sheldrake, shellfish, spikedace, spoonbill, sprigtail, stonechat, surfperch, swordfish, swordtail, tarantula, thickhead, threadfin, topminnow, truculent, trumpeter, tubesnout, turnstone, whitebait, whitefish, wolverine, woodborer, woodchuck, wood louse, yellowfin, zebrafish **10** Beanie Baby, bitterling, blanquillo, bluebottle, brook trout, brown trout, budgerigar, budgerygah, calicoback, chiffchaff, chimpanzee, chinchilla, coelacanth, crustacean, deathwatch, demoiselle, dickcissel, digger wasp, flycatcher, froghopper, goatsucker, greenfinch, greenshank, hammerhead, honeyeater, kingfisher, kookaburra, licentious, nutcracker, pear thrips, pikeblenny, prairie dog, pratincole, red snapper, rhinoceros, rose chafer, salamander, sanderling, sandroller, sea anemone, shearwater, sheathbill, sicklebill, silverside, spittlebug, squaretail, tiger shark, treehopper, troutperch, turtledove, vindictive, whale shark, white cloud, white shark, woodpecker, woolly bear, yellow jack, yellowlegs, yellowtail, zoological

category: **4** bird, fish **5** breed **6** insect, mammal **7** reptile **9** amphibian, marsupial
combining form: **2** zo- **3** zoo- **4** -zoon
doc: **3** DVM, vet
feed: **4** bran **6** fodder, forage
prehistoric ~: **4** T-rex **7** aurochs, mammoth **8** allosaur, dinosaur, dire wolf, eohippus, sauropod, smilodon, stegodon, theropod **9** dinothere, iguanodon, pterosaur, stegosaur, supersaur **10** brontosaur, diplodocus, megalosaur, titanosaur **11** brachiosaur, ichthyosaur, pterodactyl, titanothere, triceratops, tyrannosaur
protection org.: **4** PETA, SPCA **5** ASPCA
sound: **4** bark, roar **5** bleat, chirp, growl **6** squawk
see also beast

animal __: **4** park, pole **5** black, faith **6** rights, starch, warden **7** cracker, kingdom, shelter, spirits
__ animal: **4** moss, pack **5** draft, party
Animal __: **4** Farm **7** Factory
Animal Crackers: **4** film, play
alternative: ***see*** cookie brand
author: George S. Kaufman
cast: Margaret Dumont, Chico Marx, Groucho Marx, Harpo Marx, Zeppo Marx
animalcule: **5** ameba **6** amoeba
animal descriptions, science of: **9** zoography
Animal Farm: **5** fable, novel
author: George Orwell
beast: **3** dog, pig **5** horse, raven **6** donkey
dog: **6** Jessie **7** Pincher **8** Bluebell
donkey: **8** Benjamin
horse: **5** Boxer
pig: **8** Napoleon, Old Major, Snowball, Squealer
raven: **5** Moses
Animal House
see National Lampoon's Animal House
Animal Planet: **7** channel
alternative: ***see*** cable channel
animals: **5** fauna, stock **9** livestock
combining form: **3** -zoa
science of ~: **7** zoology
Animals
leader: Eric Burdon
__ Animal, The: **4** Male
Animaniacs
character: **3** Dot **4** Rita, Runt **5** Bobby, Mindy, Pesto, Pinky, Squit, Wakko, Yakko **7** Buttons **8** the Brain **11** Minerva Mink **14** Slappy Squirrel
__ Animas, CO: **3** Las
animate: **4** fire, live, spur **5** drive, flush, light, liven, pep up, rouse, spark **6** active, arouse, awaken, excite, incite, infuse, kindle, lively, living, mortal, pump up, thrill, turn on, vivify **7** actuate, dynamic, enliven, inspire, juice up, liven up, organic, quicken **8** activate, energize, enspirit, inspirit, spirited, vitalize **9** breathing, encourage, energetic, galvanize, impassion, inebriate, sprightly, stimulate, vivacious **10** exhilarate, intoxicate, strengthen
animated: **3** gay **4** busy, keen, live, pert, spry, warm **5** alive, astir, brisk, eager, jazzy, light, peppy, perky, vivid, zingy, zippy **6** active, at work, fervid, hearty, hectic, jaunty, lively, living, yeasty **7** buoyant, dashing, dynamic, excited, fervent, hyped-up, rocking, rousing, vibrant, working, zestful, zinging **8** bustling, grooving, inspired, spirited **9** assiduous, ebullient, energetic, exuberant, sprightly, vivacious **10** keen-witted
character: **4** toon
animated __: **3** oat **7** cartoon
animater: **5** alive
animation: **3** pep, vim, zip **4** brio, dash, élan, fire, life, snap, soul, zeal, zest, zing **5** oomph, spark, verve, vigor **6** action, bounce, energy, esprit, fervor, gaiety, gayety, spirit **7** cartoon, sparkle **8** activity, buoyance, buoyancy, movement, vitality, vivacity **9** briskness, élan vital, existence, life force **10** ebullience, enthusiasm, exaltation, excitement, exuberance, liveliness
collectible: **3** cel **4** cell
animato: **5** tempo **6** lively
animosity: **4** hate **5** anger, odium, spite, venom **6** enmity, grudge, hatred, malice, rancor, strife **7** discord, dislike, ill will **8** acrimony, aversion, bad blood, conflict, friction **9** antipathy, hostility, malignity, nastiness, prejudice, virulence **10** antagonism, bitterness, ill feeling, resentment, unkindness
animus: **4** hate, mind, will **5** odium **6** enmity, grudge, hatred, malice, rancor, spirit, temper **7** dislike, ill will, purpose **8** bad blood **9** antipathy, hostility, intention, malignity, surliness **10** antagonism, ill feeling, resentment
anise: **4** herb, seed **5** drink, spice **8** beverage
flavored drink: **4** ouzo **6** pastis
anise __: **3** oil **4** seed **6** hyssop **7** camphor
anisette: **5** drink **8** beverage
Anissa: **5** Jones
Aniston, Jennifer: **7** actress
film: The Object of My Affection (1998)
Rock Star (2001)
spouse: Brad Pitt
TV: Friends
Anita: **4** Hill, Kerr, Loos, O'Day, Ward **5** Baker, Desai **6** Bryant, Ekberg, Louise, Morris **8** Brookner, Gillette
__ Anita: **5** Santa
Anitra: **4** Ford
Anitra's Dance
composer: Edvard Grieg
Anjanette: **5** Comer
Anjelica: **6** Huston
Anjou: **4** city, pear, town
kin: **4** Bosc **6** Comice, Seckel **8** Bartlett
locale: **6** Canada, Québec
Anka, Paul
homeland: Canada
song: Dance on Little Girl (1961)
Diana (1957)
Eso Beso (1962)
Having My Baby (1974)
I Don't Like to Sleep Alone (1975)
It's Time to Cry (1959)
Lonely Boy (1959)
My Home Town (1960)
One Man Woman/One Woman Man (1974)
Puppy Love (1960)
Put Your Head on My Shoulder (1959)
Times of Your Life (1975)
You Are My Destiny (1958)
Ankara: **4** city, town **6** Angora **7** capital
locale: **6** Turkey
Ankers: **6** Evelyn
ankh
shape: **3** tau **5** cross
ankle: **4** hock **5** joint, talus **6** tarsus **10** astragalus
animal ~: **4** hock
bones: **4** tali **5** tarsi
combining form: **4** tali- **5** tarso-
counterpart: **5** wrist
cover: **4** spat
ender: **4** bone
hurt an ~: **5** twist
sore ~ treatment: **6** ice bag **7** ice pack
anklet: **4** hose, sock **6** bangle **7** hosiery, jewelry **8** ornament
alternative: **6** argyle
feature: **3** toe **4** heel **5** clasp **7** elastic
ankylosaur feature: **5** armor
Ann: **3** Lee **4** cape, Rule, Todd **5** Blyth, Curry, Doran **6** Darrow, Dvorak, Meyers, Miller, Petrie,

Turkel, Wilson 7 Beattie, Compton, Harding, Jillian, Landers, rag doll, Sothern 8 Jellicoe, Magnuson, Reinking, Richards, Rutledge, Sheridan 9 Radcliffe 10 Dusenberry, Rutherford, Wedgeworth
in Russian: 4 Nina
to Abby: 4 twin
Ann __: 5 Arbor, Marie 7 Vickers
Ann-__: 7 Margret
__ Ann: 4 Cape 5 Edith 7 Barbara
Anna: 3 Lee, Sui 4 Held, Sten 5 Faris, Freud, Moffo 6 Neagle, Paquin, Sewell 7 Comnena, Magnani, Pavlova 8 Chlumsky, Christie, Ivanovna, Quindlen 9 Akhmatova, Leonowens 10 Kournikova
author: Robert Burns
Anna __: 6 Bolena
Anna __ Alberghetti: 5 Maria
Anna __ Horsford: 5 Maria
Anna __ Wong: 3 May
__ Anna: 5 Santa
Anna and the King of Siam (1946 film)
cast: Lee J. Cobb, Linda Darnell, Irene Dunne, Rex Harrison, Gale Sondergaard
director: John Cromwell
Annabel __: 3 Lee
Annabella: 7 Sciorra
Annabel Lee: 4 poem
author: Edgar Allan Poe
Annabeth: 4 Gish
Anna Bolena
composer: Gaetano Donizetti
Anna Christie (1930 film)
cast: Charles Bickford, Marie Dressler, Greta Garbo
character: 3 Mat 4 Owen 5 Burke, Chris 6 Marthy
Anna Karenina: 4 film 5 novel
author: Leo Tolstoy
cast: Freddie Bartholomew, Greta Garbo, Fredric March
character: 5 Darya, Levin, Tanya 6 Alexei, Alexey, Grisha, Stepan
director: Clarence Brown
Annakin, Ken: 8 director
annal: 7 account
Annales
author: Tacitus
annalist: 6 scribe 9 historian 10 chronicler
annals: 5 files 6 record 7 archive, history 8 register 9 chronicle, recountal
Anna Maria __: 8 Horsford
Anna May __: 4 Wong
Annamese land measure: 3 mau
Annan, Kofi: 8 diplomat, Nobelist
Annapolis: 4 city, town
freshman: 4 pleb 5 plebe
grad: 6 ensign
locale: 8 Maryland
org.: 3 USN 4 Navy, USNA
river: 6 Severn
student: 3 mid 5 middy 10 midshipman
Annapurna: 4 peak 5 mount 8 mountain
locale: 4 Asia 5 Nepal
Ann Arbor: 4 city, town
athletes: 10 Wolverines
locale: 4 Mich. 8 Michigan

Ann B. __: 5 Davis
Anne: 4 peak, Rice 5 Frank, Heche, Klein, Meara, mount, saint, Tyler 6 Archer, Baxter, Boleyn, Brontë, Geddes, Hébert, Murray, Ramsey, Revere, Sexton 7 Francis, Jackson, Nichols, Seymour, Shirley, Wheeler 8 Bancroft, Collette, Hathaway, Jeffreys, mountain, Sullivan 9 Lindbergh, McCaffrey, Parillaud 10 Bradstreet
locale: 10 Antarctica
sister: 5 Emily 9 Charlotte
to Margaret: 5 niece
Anne-__ Mutter: 6 Sophie
anneal: 4 gird, tone 5 build, shore, steel 6 beef up, firm up, harden, prop up, temper, tone up 7 bolster, brace up, build up, burgeon, develop, empower, enhance, fortify, shore up, stiffen, toughen 8 bourgeon, buttress, energize, indurate, vitalize 9 intensify, reinforce 10 invigorate, strengthen
annealing oven: 4 lehr
Anne de Beaupré: 3 Ste.
__-Anne Down: 6 Lesley
annelid: 4 worm
Annenberg: 6 Walter
Anne of __: 6 Cleves, France 7 Austria, Bohemia, Denmark
Anne of Green Gables
author: Lucy Maud Montgomery
character: 3 Ira, Pye 5 Allan, Diana, Josie, Lynde, Moody 6 Minnie, Rachel, Stearn 7 Marilla
loc.: 3 PEI 6 Canada
Anne of the Thousand Days: 4 film, play
author: Maxwell Anderson
cast: Genevieve Bujold, Richard Burton, Irene Papas
__ Anne Porter: 9 Katherine
__ Anne's lace: 5 Queen
Anne-Sophie: 6 Mutter
Annette: 6 Bening, O'Toole 9 Funicello
author: Erskine Caldwell
annex: 3 add, arm, ell, get 4 gain, link, tack, wing 5 add on, affix, seize, usurp 6 adjoin, append, assume, attach, branch, fasten, hook up, lean-to, obtain, secure, tack on, take on 7 acquire, connect, hitch on, procure 8 addendum, addition, appendix 9 appendage, extension 10 attachment, commandeer, elongation, supplement
annexation: 4 gain 7 seizure 9 increment 10 attachment
Annie: 5 Potts 6 Lennox, Oakley 7 Dillard, musical 9 Leibovitz
to Warbucks: 4 ward
Annie (1982 film): 7 musical
cast: Carol Burnett, Tim Curry, Albert Finney, Edward Herrmann, Geoffrey Holder, Bernadette Peters, Aileen Quinn, Ann Reinking
composer: Charles Strouse, Martin Charnin
role: 3 FDR 4 Lily 5 Grace, Healy, Sandy 6 Oliver, Pepper, Punjab 7 Farrell, Rooster 8 Hannigan, Warbucks 9 Roosevelt

Annie __: 4 Hall 5 Allen 6 Laurie
__ Annie: 3 Ado, For 5 Apple 7 Six-Pack
Annie Allen
author: Gwendolyn Brooks
Annie Get Your Gun: 7 musical
composer: Irving Berlin
Annie Hall (1977 film)
cast: Woody Allen, Diane Keaton, Tony Roberts
director: Woody Allen
Annie Oakley: 7 freebee, freebie 8 marksman
like an ~: 4 free
Annie's Song (1974 song)
artist: John Denver
annihilate: 4 do in, ruin, slay 5 blast, crush, erase, quash, smash 6 defeat, devour, negate, ravage, rub out, squash, uproot 7 abolish, blot out, destroy, expunge, wipe out 8 decimate, demolish, massacre, suppress 9 dismantle, eliminate, eradicate, extirpate, finish off, liquidate 10 extinguish, invalidate, obliterate
annihilation: 4 doom 5 waste 6 defeat, finish
Annika: 9 Sorenstam
anniversaries:
1st - Paper
2nd - Cotton
3rd - Leather
4th - Linen, Silk
5th - Wood
6th - Iron
7th - Wool, Copper
8th - Bronze
9th - Pottery, China
10th - Tin, Aluminum
11th - Steel
12th - Silk
13th - Lace
14th - Ivory
15th - Crystal
20th - China
25th - Silver
30th - Pearl
35th - Coral, Jade
40th - Ruby
45th - Sapphire
50th - Gold
55th - Emerald
60th - Diamond
anniversary: 4 date 5 event 7 holiday
item: 4 cake
Ann-Margret: 7 actress, Swedish
film: Bye Bye Birdie (1963)
Carnal Knowledge (1971)
The Cheap Detective (1978)
The Cincinnati Kid (1965)
Grumpier Old Men (1995)
Grumpy Old Men (1993)
Murderers' Row (1966)
A New Life (1988)
The Outside Man (1973)
State Fair (1962)
Tommy (1975)
Twice in a Lifetime (1985)
Viva Las Vegas (1964)
spouse: Roger Smith
__ Ann Miller: 8 Penelope
anno __: 5 mundi, regni 6 Domini 7 Hejirae
annotate: 4 edit, mark, note 5 gloss 7 explain 8 footnote 9 interpret
annotation: 4 note 5 gloss 7 comment 8 footnote 10 commentary, definition, exposition

announce: 3 say 4 call, page, tell 5 break, state, utter, voice 6 herald, impart, report, reveal, unfold 7 declare, deliver, divulge, precede, signify, trumpet 8 antecede, disclose, indicate, proclaim 9 advertise, broadcast, make known, pronounce, publicize 10 make public, promulgate
announced: 6 spoken
announcement: 2 ad 3 cry 4 call, memo, news, word 6 notice, report 7 message, release 8 bulletin, handbill 9 publicity, statement, utterance 10 communiqué
announcer: 2 DJ, VJ 5 crier, sayer 6 deejay, herald 8 reporter 10 disc jockey, disk jockey, forerunner, journalist, newscaster, proclaimer, telecaster 11 video jockey
in horse racing: 6 caller
annoy: 3 ail, bug, eat, get, ire, irk, nag, rag, try, vex 4 bait, fret, gall, goad, miff, poke, ride, rile, roil, tire 5 anger, beset, chafe, eat at, egg on, get at, get to, grate, grind, harry, hound, peeve, pique, spite, tease, tweak, upset, weary, worry 6 abrade, accost, badger, bother, burn up, harass, hassle, heckle, hector, madden, needle, nettle, noodge, offend, pester, plague, pother, put out, rankle, ruffle, tee off, wear on 7 afflict, affront, agitate, bedevil, disturb, enflame, henpeck, inflame, perturb, provoke, tick off, torment, trouble 8 disquiet, exercise, irritate 9 aggravate, beleaguer, displease 10 antagonize, discompose, disconcert, disgruntle, exasperate
annoyance: 3 bur, rub 4 drag, pain, pest 5 gripe, peeve, pique, thorn, worry 6 bother, burden, gadfly, hassle, regret, riding, vexing 7 bugging, chagrin, dogging, nagging, offense, problem, teasing, trouble, umbrage 8 bullying, headache, hounding, irritant, nettling, nuisance, ruffling, taunting, vexation 9 bothering, commotion, complaint, grievance, harassing, pestering 10 affliction, difficulty, discomfort, discontent, disturbing, harassment, impatience, incitement, irritating, irritation, resentment
exclamation: 3 bah, duh, fie, tsk 4 heck, rats, umph 6 tsk tsk
neck ~: 4 kink, pain 5 spasm 6 twinge
annoyed: 4 ired, sore 5 cross, huffy, irate, testy, tired, upset 6 galled, ireful 9 indignant, irritable, irritated, resentful
state: 4 snit 5 pique
with: 5 mad at
annoying: 4 sore 5 nasty, pesky, pesty 6 odious, trying 7 grating, hateful, irksome, naughty, prickly, tedious 8 a bit much, abrasive, tiresome, worrying 9 invidious, obnoxious, offensive, troubling, vexatious, worrisome 10 bothersome, in one's hair, irritating, nettlesome, unpleasant
one: 3 nag 4 pain, pest 5 vexer

6 **gadfly**
succeed in ~: 5 get to
__ Ann Seton: 9 Elizabeth
annual: 4 corn **5** beans, plant **6** flower, yearly, zinnia **8** larkspur, marigold, periodic, yearbook **9** once-a-year
division: 5 month
visitor: 5 Santa
annual __: 4 ring, wage **6** report
annually: 4 yrly. **5** a year **6** yearly **7** per year **8** per annum
annual-ring tissue: 6 cambia
annuit __: 7 coeptis
annuity: 6 income **7** payment, pension, revenue
alternative: 3 IRA **5** Keogh
annul: 3 nix **4** kill, lift, undo, void **5** erase, quash **6** cancel, delete, negate, recall, recant, repeal, revoke, vacate **7** abolish, disavow, redress, rescind, reverse, scratch **8** abrogate, dissolve, override, overrule, overturn, renounce, set aside **9** discharge, liquidate, repudiate, supersede, terminate **10** contravene, counteract, invalidate, neutralize
annular __: 4 gear, ring **5** clock **7** eclipse
annulet: 4 ring
annulment: 6 recall, repeal **7** undoing **9** abatement, abolition, discharge, vitiation **10** abrogation, rescinding, rescission, retraction, revocation
annum, per: 6 yearly
annunciate: 9 broadcast
Annunzio: 9 Mantovani
__ Annus: 6 Magnus
Ann Vickers
author: Sinclair Lewis
__ Ann Warren: 6 Lesley
__ Ann Womack: 3 Lee
año: 4 year **7** Spanish
starter: 5 enero
año __: 5 nuevo
anoa: 5 bovid **6** animal, bovine, mammal
home: 3 zoo **7** Celebes **8** Sulawesi
relative: *see* bovine
anode: 8 terminal **9** electrode
like some ~s: 3 neg., pos. **8** negative, positive
anodize: 4 coat **5** plate
anodyne: 4 balm **5** letup, opium, poppy, salve **6** easing, opiate **7** comfort, relieve, respite **8** easement, laudanum, lenitive, mandrake, morphine, narcotic, nepenthe, sedative, soothing **9** abatement, analgesic, assuasive, calmative, demulcent, relieving, remission, softening **10** anesthetic, mitigation, painkiller, palliation, palliative
target: 4 pain
anoint: 3 oil **4** name **5** anele, apply, bless **6** choose, hallow, ordain **7** promote **8** coronate, dedicate, sanctify **9** designate, embrocate, lubricate **10** consecrate
anointed: 6 divine
anomalous: 3 odd **4** eery **5** eerie, queer, weird **6** atypic, freaky, offkey, quirky, unique **7** bizarre, deviant, offbeat, strange, unusual **8** aberrant, abnormal, atypical, freakish, isolated, peculiar, uncommon **9** dissonant, divergent, eccentric, fantastic, irregular, shapeless, unnatural, untypical **10** prodigious, unfamiliar, unorthodox
anomaly: 3 dev. **5** freak, quirk **6** oddity **7** paradox **8** mutation, original **9** curiosity, deviation, exception **10** aberration, difference, phenomenon
anon: 3 now **4** soon, then **5** after, later **6** at once, in a bit, in time, not now, pronto **7** betimes, by and by, erelong, in a wink, later on, shortly, someday **8** directly, hereupon, in a jiffy, in a while, in no time, promptly, right now, right off, sometime **9** afterward, any day now, any minute, any second, forthwith, hereafter, in a moment, instantly, presently, right away, thereupon **10** afterwards, any time now, before long, eventually, in good time, this moment
companion: 4 ever
ever and ~: 3 oft
__ año nuevo!: 5 Feliz
anonym: 5 alias **7** pen name **9** pseudonym **10** nom de plume
anonymity opposite: 4 fame
anonymous: 7 Jane Doe, John Doe, unfamed, unknown **8** nameless **9** incognito, unclaimed **10** innominate, Richard Roe, unattested, uncredited
no longer ~: 5 named
one, maybe: 6 author, writer
anorak: 4 coat **5** parka **6** jacket **7** cover-up **9** ski jacket **10** winter coat
__ a nose: 5 win by
another: 4 more **5** added, other **6** second **7** one more **10** substitute
at ~ time: 4 anon **5** later
from ~ country: 5 alien **7** foreign, oversea **8** offshore, overseas
have ~ opinion: 4 vary **7** deviate, dissent, diverge **8** disagree
in Spanish: 4 otra, otro
one after ~: 7 by turns
one time or ~: 7 someday
one way or ~: 7 somehow
send to ~: 4 pass **5** refer
take ~ look: 5 audit, check, weigh **6** assess, go over, rehash, survey **7** analyze, examine, inspect, revisit **8** appraise, critique, evaluate, reassess **9** reexamine, think over **10** reconsider, reevaluate, run through, scrutinize
time: 4 anew, anon, soon, then **5** after, again **6** in a bit, in time **7** by and by, later on, someday **8** in a while, sometime **9** afterward, hereafter **10** before long, eventually
to ~ place: 4 away
Another __: 3 Day, You **4** Time **5** Night, Woman, World **7** Country
Another card!: 5 hit me
Another Country
author: James Baldwin
Another Day (1971 song)
artist: Paul McCartney
__ Another Day: 3 Die **4** Just
Another Day in Paradise (1989 song)
artist: Phil Collins
Another Green World
composer: Brian Eno
Another One Bites the Dust (1980 song)
artist: Queen
Another Op'nin', Another Show
composer: Cole Porter
Another Sad Love Song (1993 song)
artist: Toni Braxton
Another Saturday Night (song)
artist: Cat Stevens, Sam Cooke
Another Somebody Done... (1975 song)
artist: B.J. Thomas
Another Time
author: W.H. Auden
Another Woman (1988 film)
cast: Mia Farrow, Ian Holm, Gena Rowlands
director: Woody Allen
Another World (NBC): 4 soap **9** soap opera
Another year __...: 5 older
Another You
author: Ann Beattie
Anouilh, Jean: 6 French **10** playwright
work: Antigone
The Ermine
The Lark
Ring Around the Moon
Thieves' Carnival
Anouk: 5 Aimée
ans.: 4 resp., soln. **5** reply **6** retort
evoker: 4 ques.
see also answer
Ansara, Michael: 5 actor
spouse: Barbara Eden
TV: Broken Arrow
ansate __: 5 cross
anschluss: 4 bloc **6** league **7** combine **8** alliance **9** coalition **10** federation
Ansel: 5 Adams
Anselm: 5 saint **11** philosopher
anserine: 5 silly
bird: 5 goose
Ansermet, Ernest: 9 conductor
Anson: 3 Cap **8** Williams
Anspach, Susan: 7 actress
answer: 3 key, pay, say **4** echo, meet, resp., RSVP, suit **5** field, rebut, reply, serve, solve **6** letter, oracle, recite, refute, rejoin, result, retort, ripost **7** clarify, counter, defense, dispute, explain, hit back, resolve, respond, riposte, satisfy, suffice, verdict **8** comeback, disprove, feedback, reaction, rebuttal, response, solution, talk back **9** deduction, rejoinder, respond to, retaliate, write back **10** refutation
a charge: 5 plead, rebut
affirmative ~: 3 yes
again: 5 resay
back: 4 sass **5** react **8** get fresh
don't take no for an ~: 6 be firm, insist **7** persist, protest **8** speak out **9** stand firm
evasive ~: 5 parry
find the ~: 5 solve
for: 7 sponsor **9** guarantee, undertake
(for): 3 pay
get the same ~: 5 agree
indefinite ~: 5 maybe **7** perhaps **8** possibly, probably **9** it could be, it might be, perchance **10** imaginably
kind of ~: 5 yes/no
negative ~: 3 nay
quiz ~: 4 true **5** false
answer __: 3 key **4** back **5** print, sheet
answerability: 5 blame, guilt **9** liability
answerable: 6 liable **7** subject **8** blamable, governed, indebted **9** blameable, obligated **10** chargeable
Answered Prayers
author: Danielle Steel
answering machine
option: 5 erase
sound: 4 beep, tone
unit: 3 msg. **7** message
answers, try to get: 3 ask **4** pump, quiz **5** grill, query **7** canvass, consult, inquire, request
ant: 3 bug **4** army, pest **5** emmet, kelep, queen **6** insect, worker **7** pismire **8** micraner **9** carpenter
combining form: 6 myrmec- **7** myrmeco-
cow: 5 aphid, aphis
ender: 4 hill **5** eater
group: 6 colony
home: 4 hill
morsel: 5 crumb
of an ~: 6 formic
white ~ genus: 6 termes
worker ~: 6 ergate
ant __: 3 cow, egg **4** bear, farm, hill, lion
ant.: 3 opp.
opposite: 3 syn.
__ ant: 3 red **4** army, bull, fire **5** honey, slave, thief, white **6** Amazon, driver, jumper, velvet, worker **7** bulldog, parasol, Pharaoh
Ant: 4 Adam
antacid: 4 Tums **6** alkali, bicarb, Maalox, Pepcid, Riopan, Zantac **7** Gelusil, Lactaid, Mylanta, Rolaids **8** Gaviscon, magnesia **9** limewater **10** baking soda **11** Alka-Seltzer, Pepto-Bismol
target: 5 agita
Ant, Adam real name: Stuart Goddard
antagonism: 4 feud, hate **5** anger **6** animus, enmity, hatred, rancor **7** discord, dislike, ill will **8** aversion, conflict, friction **9** animosity, antipathy, hostility **10** aggression, antithesis, contention, difference, dissension, dissonance, opposition, oppugnancy, resistance
antagonist: 3 foe **4** part **5** enemy, rival **7** fighter, opposer **8** opponent **9** adversary, assailant, contender, disputant, ill-wisher, oppugnant **10** competitor, contestant
prefix: 4 anti-
antagonistic: 3 ill **4** cold, cool, mean **5** aloof, nasty, rival, surly **6** at odds, averse, bitter, chilly, down on, ornery **7** adverse, counter, glacial, hateful, hostile, opposed, warlike **8** clashing, contrary, inimical, negative, opposing, opposite, rivaling,

spiteful, venomous, virulent **9** bellicose, competing, malicious, truculent **10** antithetic, malevolent, pugnacious, unfriendly
antagonize: 3 vex **5** anger, annoy, repel, shock **6** insult, offend, oppose, resist **8** alienate, estrange, irritate **9** disaffect, displease **10** counteract, neutralize
antagonized: 3 hot, mad **4** ired, sore **5** angry, cross, huffy, irate, livid, riled, wroth **6** fuming, ireful, raging, raving, red-hot **7** furious, ranting **8** choleric, wrathful **9** indignant, resentful, splenetic
Antal: 6 Dorati
Antananarivo: 4 city, town **7** capital
locale: 10 Madagascar
Antarctic __: 4 Zone **5** Ocean, Plate **6** Circle
Antarctica: 9 continent
bay: 6 Whales
bird: 4 skua **7** penguin
cape: 5 Adare
coast: 6 Adelie
covering: 6 icecap
explorer: 4 Byrd, Ross **6** Mawson **8** Amundsen **10** Shackleton
ice shelf: 5 Amery
like ~: 6 frigid
mountain: 4 Anne, Mohl, Wade **5** Astor, Coman, Falla, Minto, Press, Shear, Shinn, Tyree **6** Erebus, Kaplan, Lister, Sabine, Sidley, Wexler **7** Epperly, Gardner, Lysaght, Markham, Odishaw, Ostenso, Sellery
of ~: 5 polar
sea: 4 Ross **7** Weddell **8** Amundsen
volcano: 6 Erebus
Antares: 4 star **5** M star **8** red giant
ante: 3 bet, fee **5** pay up, put in, put up, stake, wager **6** chip in, kick in, pony up **7** cough up **8** entry fee, shell out
again: 5 rebet
destination: 3 pot
follower: 4 deal
lowest ~: 4 cent, chip **5** penny
meridiem: 7 morning
penny ~: 5 minor
relative: 3 pre-
up: 3 pay **4** give **5** pay in, spend **6** chip in, kick in **8** disburse, shell out **9** subscribe **10** contribute, recompense, remunerate
up the ~: 5 raise, rebid
__ ante: 4 vide **5** penny
anteater: 6 animal, mammal **7** echidna **8** aardvark, pangolin
feature: 5 snout
__ anteater: 5 giant, scaly, silky, spiny **6** banded **7** two-toed
antebellum: 6 prewar
antecede: 4 head, lead **6** head up, herald **7** outrank, predate, presage, usher in **8** announce, foreshow, go before, outstrip, proclaim **9** come first, go ahead of, introduce **10** anticipate, come before
antecedence: 8 priority
antecedent: 4 root **5** basis, cause, prior **6** origin, reason, source **8** occasion, previous **9** beginning, foregoing, precedent, preceding, precursor, prototype **10** forebearer, forefather, forerunner, hypothesis, precursory, progenitor
antecessor: 10 forerunner
antechamber: 5 foyer, lobby **9** vestibule
antedate: 7 precede
antediluvian: 3 old **4** aged **5** hoary **7** ancient, antique **8** medieval, obsolete, outmoded, primeval **9** mediaeval, primaeval **10** antiquated
antelope: 3 gnu, goa, kob **4** guib, kudu, oryx, puku, topi **5** addax, bongo, bovid, chiru, eland, goral, korin, nyala, oribi, saiga, sasin, serow **6** animal, chammy, dik-dik, duiker, impala, koodoo, lechwe, mammal, nilgai, rhebok, shammy, shamoy **7** blaubok, blesbok, chamois, defassa, gazelle, gemsbok, gerenuk, grysbok, nylghai, nylghau, sassaby **8** blesbuck, bontebok, bushbuck, gemsbuck, reedbuck, steenbok, steinbok **9** blackbuck, pronghorn, sitatunga, springbok, waterbuck **10** hartebeest, wildebeest
Asian goat ~: 5 serow
female: 3 cow, doe, ewe
foot: 4 hoof
gait: 4 stot
male: 4 bull
playmate: 4 deer
young: 3 kid **4** calf
antenna: 4 ears **5** organ **6** aerial, feeler **10** rabbit ears
alternative: 4 dish **5** cable **7** cable TV
owner: 6 insect
pole: 4 mast
range: 3 UHF, VHF
tip: 6 arista
anterior: 3 bow **4** past **5** front, prior **6** former **7** forward **8** forepart, previous **9** foregoing, preceding
prefix: 3 pro-
anteroom: 4 hall **5** foyer, lobby **6** alcove, parlor **7** ingress, narthex **8** entrance **9** vestibule
anthem: 4 hymn, pean, song **5** music, paean **8** canticle
author: Francis Scott Key
Civil War: 5 Dixie
ender: 5 brave
preposition: 3 o'er
start: 4 o say **5** oh say
anthill: 4 nest **5** mound
anthologize: 4 cull **5** amass **6** garner, gather, muster **7** arrange, collect, compile, marshal **8** assemble, organize **10** accumulate
anthology: 5 album **7** omnibus **8** analecta, analects, treasury **9** selection **10** collection, compendium, cumulation, miscellany
Anthony: 3 Ray **4** Earl, Eden, Hope, Mann, Marc, Page, West **5** Clark, Geary, Heald, Price, Quinn, Zerbe **6** Eisley, Fokker, Harvey, Joseph, Newley, Powell, Quayle **7** Asquith, Burgess, Edwards, Hopkins, Kennedy, Perkins, Shaffer, van Dyck **8** LaPaglia, Trollope **9** Franciosa, Minghella **10** Montgomery
in German: 5 Anton
in Spanish: 7 Antonio
Anthony Adverse: 5 novel
author: Hervey Allen
Anthony, Earl: 6 bowler
milieu: 5 alley
org: 3 PBA
__ Anthony Hopkins: 3 Sir
Anthony Michael __: 4 Hall
Anthony of Padua: 5 saint
__ Anthony Ray: 4 Gene
Anthony, Saint cross: 3 tau
Anthony, Susan B.: 6 dollar **8** feminist **10** suffragist
anthracite: 4 coal
deposit: 4 seam
kin: 7 lignite **10** bituminous
anthropoid: 3 ape **6** monkey
anthropologist: 4 Mead **6** Frazer, Leakey **10** Malinowski
prefix: 5 paleo-
anthropology: 7 science
branch of ~: 9 ethnology
prefix with ~: 5 paleo
study: 6 humans
anti: 3 con, foe, opp. **7** against, opposed, opposer **8** naysayer, negative, opponent, opposing **9** counter to
opposite: 3 pro
vote: 2 no **3** nay
anti-: 6 contra-
anti-__ bar: 4 roll, sway
Anti-__ League: 6 Saloon
antiaircraft fire: 4 flak **5** flack **6** ack ack
anti-apartheid org.: 3 ANC
antiar: 4 tree, upas
relative: 3 fig **4** upas **5** ficus, ramon **6** fustic **8** mulberry **10** breadfruit
antiballistic __: 7 missile
Antibes neighbor: 4 Nice
antibiotic: 4 drug **5** sulfa **8** medicine **9** antitoxin **10** antiseptic, medication
combining form: 5 -mycin
predecessor: 5 sulfa
source: 4 mold
antibody: 6 ligand
in tears: 3 IGA
target: 5 toxin
antic: 4 dido, jape, joke, lark, romp **5** caper, funny, prank, trick **6** frolic **7** foolery, hotfoot **8** clowning, escapade, mischief, sporting, sportive **9** grotesque, ludicrous **10** buffoonery, frolicsome, hanky-panky, ridiculous, shenanigan, tomfoolery
Antic Hay
author: Aldous Huxley
anticipate: 3 see **4** hope, look, mean, wait **5** await, parry, sense **6** expect, plan on **7** count on, foresee, hope for, look for, obviate, precede, predict, preempt, prepare, prevent, wait for **8** antecede, envisage, envision, forecast, foretell, theorize, watch for **9** apprehend, calculate, count upon, entertain, forestall, foretaste, intercept, prevision, see coming, visualize **10** bargain for, conjecture, have a hunch, jump the gun, prepare for
anticipating: 5 ready **7** hopeful
anticipation: 4 hope **7** inkling, thought **8** optimism, prospect, suspense **9** foretaste **10** precaution
Anticipation (1972 song)
artist: Carly Simon
anticipatory: 5 early
shout: 4 TGIF
anticlimax: 6 bathos **7** decline, letdown **8** comedown
anticrime acronym: 4 RICO
antics: 5 sport **7** foolery **8** jocosity **9** horseplay **10** tomfoolery
anti-discrimination org.: 4 EEOC **5** NAACP
antidotal: 8 curative **10** corrective
antidote: 4 cure **6** remedy **8** medicine **10** medication
target: 5 toxin
antidrug
advice: 5 say no
cop: 4 narc, nark **5** narco
org.: 3 DEA
anti-DWI org.: 4 MADD, SADD
Antietam: 6 battle
general: 3 Lee
locale: 8 Maryland
antifreeze: 6 glycol
use ~: 5 deice
anti-fur org.: 4 PETA
Antigone
author: Jean Anouilh, Sophocles
brother: 8 Eteocles **9** Polynices
husband: 6 Haemon
parent: 7 Jocasta, Oedipus
sister: 6 Ismene
son: 5 Maeon
uncle: 5 Creon
Antigua: 4 isle **6** island
Antigua and Barbuda: 6 nation **7** country
capital: 7 St. John's
org.: 3 OAS
antiknock
fluid: 5 ethyl
number: 6 octane
Antilles: 4 isls. **5** isles **7** islands
Indian: 5 Carib **6** Arawak
island: 4 Cuba, Saba **5** Aruba **7** St. Croix **8** Dominica, St. Thomas **10** Hispaniola, Martinique
jaunt: 6 cruise
language: 5 Carib
__ Antilles: 6 Lesser **7** Greater
antilock __: 5 brake
antimacassar: 4 tidy **5** doily **6** doyley
make an ~: 3 tat
antimonopoly org.: 3 FTC
antimony: 5 metal **7** element
combining form: 4 stib- **5** stibi-, stibo- **6** stibio-
ore: 8 stibnite
anti-narcotics org.: 3 DEA
anti-nuke org.: 4 SANE
__ Antipas: 5 Herod
antipasto: 9 appetizer **10** finger food
ingredient: 5 olive
antipathetic: 6 averse, down on **7** opposed **8** clashing, opposing
be ~ toward: 6 detest
antipathy: 4 hate **5** odium, spite **6** animus, enmity, grudge, hatred, malice, rancor **7** allergy, discord, disdain, disgust, dislike, ill will **8** acrimony, aversion, bad blood, contempt, distaste, loathing **9** animosity, avoidance, hostility, prejudice, repulsion, revulsion **10** abhorrence, antagonism, opposition, repellence, repellency, repugnance, unkindness
antiphon: 5 reply **8** response
Antiphus
brother: 5 Paris **6** Hector

parent: 5 Priam 6 Hecuba 7 Priamus
sister: 9 Cassandra
antipodal: 4 last 5 polar 7 counter 8 converse, opposite
antipode: 7 reverse 8 converse, opposite
antipodean: 5 polar 8 opposite 10 antithetic
antipole: 8 converse
antipollution org.: 3 EPA
anti-prohibitionist: 3 Wet
__ Antiqua: 3 Ars
antiquark + quark: 5 meson
Antiquary, The author: Walter Scott
antiquate: 3 age 6 retire 7 outdate, outmode, replace 8 archaize 9 supersede
antiquated: 3 obs., old, out 4 aged 5 dated, dowdy, fusty, hoary, moldy, mossy, musty, olden, passé, stale 6 old hat, quaint 7 ancient, archaic, fogyish 8 decrepit, medieval, obsolete, outdated, outmoded, out of use, timeworn, unusable 9 hackneyed, mediaeval, out-of-date 10 old-fangled, out of style
term: 8 archaism 10 archaicism
antique: 3 old 4 aged 5 curio, hoary, passé, relic 6 quaint 7 ancient 8 heirloom, obsolete, outdated, outmoded, valuable 9 out-of-date
store adjective: 4 olde
__ antique: 4 verd
antiques
love of ~: 5 vertu, virtu
work with ~: 7 restore
Antiques Roadshow (PBS)
host (U.K.): Fiona Bruce, Hugh Scully, Michael Aspel
host (U.S.): Lara Spencer, Mark L. Walberg
antiquing medium: 4 ager
antiquity: 3 eld 4 past, yore 5 relic 9 days of old, hoariness, olden days 10 archaicism, days of yore
anti-racketeering org.: 3 FBI
antiseptic: 4 pure 5 clean, iodin, iodol 6 iodine 7 sterile 8 cleanser, fumigant, germfree, hygienic, pristine, purifier, sanitary 9 boric acid, germicide, medicated, purifying 10 antibiotic, germicidal, immaculate, preventive, sterilized, sterilizer, unpolluted
pioneer: 6 Lister
antisocial: 5 aloof 6 remote 7 ascetic, recluse 8 eremitic, hermitic, reserved, solitary, taciturn 9 alienated, reclusive, withdrawn 10 hermitlike, unfriendly, unsociable
one: 4 nerd 5 loner
antisubmarine weapon: 4 Y gun
antithesis: 4 foil 7 inverse, reverse 8 converse, flip side, negation, opposite 9 inversion, other side 10 antagonism, difference, opposition
antithetic: 7 counter, inverse, opposed, reverse, unalike 8 contrary, converse, opposite 9 different 10 antipodean, contrasted, poles apart
antithetical: 5 polar 7 counter, opposed, reverse 8 contrary, converse, opposing, opposite
antitoxin: 5 serum 7 vaccine 8 medicine 9 antiserum, antivenin 10 antibiotic, medication, preventive
like an ~: 6 serous
antitoxins: 4 sera
__ Antitrust Act: 7 Clayton, Sherman
antitrust org.: 3 FTC
antivenins: 4 sera
antler: 4 horn 7 hatrack
budding ~: 4 knob
part: 4 tine 5 prong
wearer: 3 elk 4 deer, hart, stag 5 moose 8 reindeer
__ antler: 3 bay, bes, bez 4 brow 5 crown, royal 6 rusine
antlers: 4 rack
remove ~: 6 dehorn
Antoine: 6 Le Nain 7 Watteau 9 Becquerel, Lavoisier
see also French
Antoinette: 5 Bower, Marie, Perry
see also French
Anton: 5 Dolin, Karas, Susan 6 Cermak, Webern 7 Arensky, Chekhov 8 Bruckner, Walbrook 10 Rubinstein
Antonia: 4 Bird 6 Fraser
Antonin: 6 Scalia
Antonín: 6 Dvorák
Antonio: 3 Lou 5 Gaudí, Moniz 6 Sabáto, Scotti 7 Salieri, Vivaldi 8 Banderas 9 Correggio 10 Stradivari
in Evita: 3 Che
Antonio __ Jobim: 6 Carlos
__ Antonio, TX: 3 San
__ Antonius: 6 Marcus
Antony: 4 Marc, Mark, Sher 5 Roman, saint 6 Hewish
attendant: 4 Eros
foe: 6 Brutus
friend: 4 Cleo 6 Caesar 9 Cleopatra
see also Latin
__ Antony: 4 Marc, Mark
Antony and Cleopatra
author: William Shakespeare
character: 4 Eros, Iras 5 Menas, Philo 6 Alexas, Gallus, Pompey, Scarus, Silius, Taurus 7 Agrippa, Mardian, Octavia, Thyreus 8 Canidius, Charmian, Dercetas, Octavius 9 Cleopatra 10 Marc Antony
antonym: 3 opp. 8 opposite
antonymous: 7 opposed 8 opposing 10 dissimilar
antre: 4 cave 6 cavern, grotto
Antron: 5 fiber, nylon 8 material
antrum: 6 cavity
ants in one's __: 5 pants
ant-sized: 3 wee 4 tiny 5 small, teeny
ants, of: 6 formic
antsy: 4 edgy 5 eager, itchy, jumpy, tense 6 on edge, uneasy 7 anxious, fidgety, jittery, keyed up, nervous, restive, uptight, zealous 8 agitated, restless, skittish, troubled 9 concerned, excitable, ill at ease, impatient, overeager, unsettled 10 high-strung
be ~: 6 fidget
Antwerp: 4 city, port, town
locale: 7 Belgium
river: 7 Schelde, Scheldt
Antz (1998 film)
director: Eric Darnell
voice cast: Woody Allen, Gene Hackman, Sylvester Stallone, Sharon Stone
Anubis father: 6 Osiris
A number __: 3 one
anvil: 4 bone 5 incus
site: 3 ear
sound: 5 clang
user: 5 smith
anvil __: 3 top 5 cloud
Anvil __: 6 Chorus
Anwar: 5 Sadat 9 Gabrielle
anxiety: 3 woe 4 ache, care, fear, pain 5 agita, alarm, angst, qualm, worry 6 dismay, misery, nerves, phobia, strain, stress, terror, unease, unrest 7 concern, fidgets, jitters, malaise, scruple, tension, turmoil, willies 8 disquiet, distress, suspense 9 misgiving, tightness, trepidity, worriment 10 difficulty, foreboding, impatience, inquietude, insecurity, solicitude
__ Anxiety: 4 High
__ Anxiety, The: 5 Age of
anxious: 4 agog, avid, edgy, keen 5 antsy, eager, hyper, itchy, jumpy, nervy, tense, wired, worry 6 afraid, gung-ho, loving, on edge, pacing, queasy, queazy, scared, uneasy 7 abashed, alarmed, fearful, gulping, jittery, keyed up, longing, nervous, panicky, restive, uptight, worried 8 agitated, desirous, fluttery, hesitant, hopped up, in a state, in a tizzy, restless, skittish, troubled 9 concerned, excitable, expectant, ill at ease, impatient, unsettled 10 breathless, disquieted, distressed, frightened, high-strung, inspirited, solicitous
be ~: 5 sweat, worry
make ~: 3 nag 5 alarm
any: 4 a bit, part, some 5 at all, aught, ought 7 a little, even one, pronoun 8 whatever 9 whichever
and every: 3 all
at ~ cost: 10 regardless
at ~ point: 8 even once
at ~ rate: 3 yet 5 still 6 anyhow, anyway 7 at least 10 all the same, regardless
at ~ time: 4 ever 8 even once
day: 4 anon, soon 7 shortly 8 sometime 10 imminently
ender: 3 how, one, way 4 body, more, time, ways, wise 5 place, thing, where
hardly ~: 3 few 5 light, scant 6 little, meager, paltry 7 limited 8 one or two
in ~ way: 5 at all
not ~: 4 nary, none, null, zero
not at ~ time: 5 never
not ~, in law: 3 nul
not in ~ way: 5 no how
old way: 5 about 6 remiss 8 reckless 9 haphazard 10 incautious
on ~ occasion: 6 always 10 at all times, invariably
to ~ extent: 3 any 4 ever
any __ can play: 6 number
any __ in a storm: 4 port
any __ now: 3 day
any __ you slice it: 3 way
Any __?: 5 ideas 6 takers
Any __ Way You Can: 5 Which
Anya: 5 Seton
anybody: 5 whoso
not ~: 5 no one
anybody's game: 5 close 10 nip and tuck, up for grabs
any day __: 3 now
...__ any drop to drink: 3 nor
Any Given Sunday (1999 film)
cast: Cameron Diaz, Al Pacino, Dennis Quaid, James Woods
director: Oliver Stone
anyhow: 10 all the same, carelessly, in any event, regardless
Anyidoho, Kofi: 4 poet 8 Ghanaian
any number can __: 4 play
Any Old Iron
author: Anthony Burgess
anyone: 5 whoso 7 whoever 8 somebody 9 whosoever
but us: 6 others
not ~: 4 none 5 no one
not with ~: 5 alone
__, anyone?: 6 Tennis
Anyone home?: 6 yoo-hoo
Anyone Who Had a Heart (1964 song)
artist: Dionne Warwick
any port __ storm: 3 in a
anything: 8 whatever
before ~ else: 5 first 6 maiden, mainly, virgin 7 chiefly, initial, leading, lead-off, opening, pioneer, premier, to start 8 above all, earliest, foremost, original, virginal 9 in advance, inaugural, initially, primarily, primitive, prototype 10 originally
like ~: 4 a lot 7 acutely, awfully 8 terribly, very much
not ~: 4 none
anything __: 3 but
__ anything!: 5 Ask me
Anything __?: 4 else
__ Anything: 4 I'd Do
Anything Else (2003 film)
cast: Woody Allen, Jason Biggs, Christina Ricci
director: Woody Allen
Anything for Billy
author: Larry McMurtry
Anything for You (1988 song)
artist: Gloria Estefan
Anything Goes: 7 musical
character: 4 Hope, Ling, Reno 5 Ching 6 Elisha 7 Sweeney
composer: Cole Porter
Anything You Can Do...: 4 duet, song
composer: Irving Berlin
anytime: 6 at will 7 someday
any time __: 5 at all
anyway: 5 at all 7 somehow 8 after all 10 all the same, in any event, regardless
any way you __ it: 5 slice
Any Wednesday (1966 film)
cast: Jane Fonda, Jason Robards
anywhere: 7 all over
__ anywhere for your smile...: 4 I'd go
Any Which Way You Can (1980 film)
beast: 5 Clyde, orang
cast: Clint Eastwood, Geoffrey Lewis, Sondra Locke

Any Woman's Blues
author: Erica Jong
Anzac: 6 Aussie 7 soldier
Anzio: 4 city, town 6 battle
locale: 5 Italy
Aoide: 4 Muse
A-OK: 4 fine 5 dandy 7 perfect 9 copacetic, excellent, hunky-dory 10 acceptable, impeccable
Aoki, Isao: 6 golfer
AOL: 3 ISP
access ~: 5 log in 6 dial up
competitor: 3 MSN 4 Juno 5 Gmail, Web TV, Yahoo! 7 Comcast, Hotmail, NetZero 9 EarthLink
customer: 4 user
exchange: 2 IM 3 AIM 5 e-mail
Aon
competitor: *see* insurance company
__ a one: 3 not 4 nary
A-one
see wonderful
aorta: 5 trunk 6 artery
aortic __: 4 arch 5 valve
aoudad: 5 sheep 6 animal
relative: *see* sheep
août: 4 mois 5 month 6 August, French
follower: 9 septembre
preceder: 7 juillet
AP
archive item: 5 photo
former ~ equipment: 3 TTY
part: 5 Assoc., Press 10 Associated
rival: 3 UPI 7 Reuters
A.P.: 8 Giannini
apace: 3 PDQ 4 ASAP, fast 5 swift 6 presto 7 fleetly, hastily, quickly, rapidly, swiftly 8 in a flash, in a jiffy, in no time, pell mell, speedily 9 forthwith, hurriedly, instantly, like a shot, posthaste 10 in high gear
with: 9 alongside
Apache: 5 tribe 6 archer, Indian 7 Amerind, Cochise 8 Geronimo
__ Apache: 4 Fort
__ a Parade: 5 I Love
Aparajito (1956 film)
director: Satyajit Ray
Aparicio, Luis: 9 shortstop
apart: 3 off, sep. 4 away 5 alone, aside, in two, loose, per se, split 6 cut off, lonely, remote, singly 7 asunder, distant, divided, split up, strange 8 broken up, by itself, detached, discrete, distinct, divorced, excluded, in pieces, isolated, separate, sundered, unjoined 9 by oneself, different, in reserve, separated 10 disjointed, disjointly, out of touch, segregated, separately
combining form: 4 dich- 5 dicho-
come ~: 4 open, snap, tear 5 burst, panic, ravel, split 7 unweave 8 fragment, separate 9 break down
cut ~: 5 sever 8 separate
drive ~: 8 alienate, separate 9 disaffect
fall ~: 3 rot 6 go awry 8 collapse, disunite 9 break down, decompose
falling ~: 5 shaky 7 rickety, rundown 8 decrepit 9 crumbling 10 ramshackle, tumbledown
far ~: 3 few 4 rare 6 meager, scarce, seldom, sparse 7 limited, unusual 8 isolated, sporadic, uncommon 9 irregular, scattered, spasmodic, uncrowded 10 infrequent, occasional, sporadical, unfrequent
from: 3 bar 6 beyond, except 7 besides, outside 9 except for, excluding, other than 10 beyond that, leaving out
(from): 5 aside
keep ~: 6 enisle 7 isolate, seclude 8 separate
pick ~: 3 pan 5 probe, roast, study, trash 6 assess, review 7 analyze, examine, run down 8 evaluate 9 criticize, cut to bits, find fault 10 scrutinize
poles ~: 5 split 6 at odds, unlike 7 unalike, unequal 9 different, disparate, divergent 10 antithetic, dissimilar
prefix: 3 dis-
pull ~: 4 rend, tear, undo 5 split 7 split up 9 find fault
set ~: 4 part, save 5 alone, lay by, lay up, sever, split, store 6 cut off, detach, devote, divide, enisle, unlink 7 disjoin, earmark, isolate, lay away, put away, reserve, rope off, split up, store up 8 break off, dedicate, disunite, reserved, sanctify, separate, uncouple 9 preferred, segregate, sequester 10 disconnect, pigeonhole
stand ~: 6 differ
take ~: 4 ruin, undo 5 level, spoil, unrig, unrip, wreck 6 detach, tinker 7 destroy, dissect 8 demolish, tear down 9 devastate, dismantle, knock down 10 demoralize, disconnect
tear ~: 4 rive 5 rip up 6 avulse, rebuke
torn ~ old-style: 4 reft
__ apart: 3 set 4 fall, pick, pull, take 5 poles 6 worlds
apartment: 3 eff., pad 4 co-op, flat, home, loft, room, unit 5 abode, condo, house, place, suite 6 duplex, walk-up 7 domicil, habitat, housing, lodging, shelter, vacancy 8 domicile, lodgment, quarters 9 penthouse, residence 10 efficiency
converted ~: 4 loft
dweller: 3 res. 6 lessee, renter, tenant 8 occupant, resident
feature: 2 AC, rm. 3 EIK 4 bdrm., room 6 closet 7 bedroom, kitchen 8 bathroom 10 dining room, living room
get an ~: 4 rent
heater: 5 steam
in England: 4 flat
invite to one's ~: 5 ask in, ask up
like some ~s: 5 unlet
location, maybe: 4 bsmt.
manager: 4 supt. 5 super
number: 4 one A, one B, one C, one D, one E, one F, one G, six A, six B, six C, six D, six E, six F, six G, two A, two B, two C, two D, two E, two F, two G 5 five A, five B, five C, five D, five E, five F, five G, four A, four B, four C, four D, four E, four F, four G 6 three A, three B, three C, three D, three E, three F, three G
owned ~: 4 co-op 5 condo
owner: 6 lessor 8 landlord
pest: 3 ant 5 roach
prohibition: 6 no pets
sign: 5 to let
apartment __: 5 hotel, house
__ apartment: 4 co-op 5 condo 6 duplex, garden, studio, walk-in, walk-up
apartments
like some ~: 5 relet
Apartment, The (1960 film)
cast: Jack Lemmon, Shirley MacLaine, Fred MacMurray
director: Billy Wilder
apathetic: 4 blah, cool, lazy, logy, numb 5 aloof, blasé, musty, stoic, tepid 6 otiose, stolid, torpid, unawed 7 languid, passive, stoical, unmoved, warmish 8 dallying, detached, indolent, listless, lukewarm, slothful, sluggish, uncaring 9 impassive, lethargic, negligent, shiftless, unfeeling, untouched 10 insensible, neglectful, nonchalant, phlegmatic, spiritless, unagitated, world-weary
be ~: 4 mope
one: 5 moper
apathy: 5 ennui 6 acedia, stupor, torpor 7 boredom, inertia, languor, laxness 8 coolness, doldrums, dullness, laziness, lethargy, loginess 9 aloofness, disregard, indolence, inertness, lassitude
apatite to Mohs: 4 five
APB: 5 alert 7 dragnet
broadcaster: 2 PD
datum: 3 AKA
part of ~: 3 all 6 points 8 bulletin
APC riders: 5 troop
ape: 2 do 3 lug 4 boor, copy, echo, goon, hood, lout, luny, mime, mock, sham 5 biped, Bonzo, brute, chimp, jocko, loony, mimer, mimic, Muggs, orang 6 baboon, galoot, gibbon, looney, lummox, mammal, mirror, parody, parrot, pongid, simian 7 act like, bananas, bruiser, Cheetah, copycat, emulate, galloot, gorilla, hoodlum, imitate, primate, siamang 8 imitator, King Kong, lunkhead, make like, simulate, talk like 9 orangutan, pantomime 10 caricature, chimpanzee, follow suit, orangutang
big ~: 6 galoot, lummox 7 galloot 8 lumberer
combining form: 6 pithec- 7 pitheco-
dog ~: 6 baboon
go ~: 4 flip, rage, rave 5 crack, freak 6 lose it 8 freak out
naked ~: 3 man 5 being, human
relative: *see* primate
__ ape: 3 dog 5 great 6 lesser 7 Barbary
Ape in Me, The
author: Cornelia Otis Skinner
apeman: 6 Tarzan
Apennines: 5 peaks, range 9 mountains
locale: 5 Italy 6 Europe
peak: 5 Amaro 9 Monte Como
religious center: 6 Assisi
__ a penny...: 5 In for
aper: 4 mime 5 mimer, mimic 6 copier, Little, parrot 7 copycat 8 emulator, imitator 10 Rich Little
aperçu: 5 sight 6 digest, glance, précis 7 glimpse, outline, summary
__ a perfumed sea...: 3 o'er
apéritif: 3 kir 4 ouzo 5 drink 7 liqueur 8 beverage, libation 9 appetizer
flavoring: 5 anise
aperitive: 10 appetizing
aperture: 3 gap 4 hole, leak, pore, rift, slit, slot, vent 5 crack, mouth, space 6 louver, outlet 7 ingress, keyhole, opening, pinhole 10 interspace, interstice
camera lens ~: 5 f-stop, t-stop
leaf ~: 5 stoma
violin ~: 5 f hole
apery: 7 mimicry 9 imitation
__ Ape, The: 5 Naked
apex: 3 tip, top 4 acme, cusp, head, noon, peak 5 crest, crown, point, ridge, spire 6 apogee, climax, height, summit, tipoff, tiptop, vertex, zenith 7 maximum 8 high spot, meridian, pinnacle 9 crescendo, high point
at the ~ of: 4 atop
APF: 9 analgesic 10 painkiller
alternative: *see* pain reliever brand
Apgar: 8 Virginia
aphid: 3 bug 4 pest 5 louse 6 ant cow, insect
milker: 3 ant
aphis
see aphid
aphonic: 3 mum 4 mute 6 silent 8 nonvocal 9 soundless 10 speechless
aphorism: 3 saw 4 rule 5 adage, axiom, gnome, maxim, moral, motto, truth 6 byword, dictum, phrase, saying, truism 7 epigram, precept, proverb 8 apothegm, laconism 10 apophthegm
Hindu ~: 5 sutra
mysterious ~: 4 rune
aphoristic: 5 terse 6 gnomic 9 axiomatic 10 of few words
Aphrodite
animal sacred to ~: 3 ram 4 dove, goat, hare, swan 7 sparrow, swallow
daughter: 5 Beroe 8 Harmonia
equivalent: 5 Venus
girdle of ~: 6 cestus
lover: 4 Ares 5 Butes 6 Adonis, Hermes 8 Anchises, Dionysus, Phaethon 10 Hephaestus
parent: 4 Zeus 5 Dione
plant sacred to ~: 4 rose 5 apple, poppy 6 myrtle
sculptor: Erté
son: 4 Eros, Eryx 5 Eneas, Lyrus 6 Aeneas, Deimos, Phobus 8 Astynous
__ Aphrodite: 6 Mighty
Aphrodite in Aulis
author: George Moore
Apia: 4 city, town 7 capital
locale: 5 Samoa, Upolu

apian defense: **5** sting
__ a Piano: **5** I Love
apiarist: **9** beekeeper
apiary: **4** hive **7** beehive
resident: **3** bee
apical: **5** sharp **8** loftiest **9** uppermost
apiculture concern: **4** bees, hive **5** honey
__-à-pie: **3** cap
apiece: **3** per **4** a pop, each **6** for one, singly **7** per unit **8** one by one **9** per capita, per person **10** separately
a piece of one's __: **4** mind
a piece of the __: **6** action
à pied: **6** on foot
__ a pin: **6** neat as
apiphobe fear: **4** bees
apis: **3** bee
apish: **5** silly **9** emulative, imitative
APL: **8** language
alternative: *see* computer language
__ a Place: **5** I Know
__, a plan..., A: **3** man
__ a play for: **4** make
__ a plea: **3** cop
aplenty: **4** enow, lots, much **6** galore **7** liberal, profuse
aplite: **7** granite
aplomb: **4** cool, ease **5** poise, style **7** balance **8** calmness **9** assurance, composure, sang-froid, stability **10** confidence, equanimity, sedateness, steadiness
APO
addressee: **2** GI **3** PFC, pvt., sgt.
apocalypse: **4** doom
Apocalypse __: **3** Now
Apocalypse, Horseman of the: **3** War **5** Death **6** Famine **10** Pestilence
Apocalypse Now (1979 film)
cast: Marlon Brando, Robert Duvall, Martin Sheen
director: Francis Ford Coppola
role: **5** Hicks, Kurtz **7** Kilgore, Willard
setting: **3** Nam **7** Vietnam
Apocalypse Postponed
author: Umberto Eco
Apocalypse Watch, The
author: Robert Ludlum
apocalyptic: **5** vatic **7** fatidic, ominous, vatical **8** oracular **9** prophetic **10** predictive, revelatory
Apocalypto (2006 film)
director: Mel Gibson
Apocrypha book: **3** Esd., Tob. **4** Macc. **5** Tobit **6** Baruch, Esdras, Judith, Sirach **7** Azariah, Susanna **8** Manasseh **9** Maccabees
apocryphal: **6** untrue **8** spurious **9** equivocal, imaginary, legendary, ungenuine **10** fictitious, inaccurate, unverified
apod: **3** eel **4** worm **5** ameba, snail, snake **6** amoeba
lack: **4** foot
apodal: **8** footless
Apodes member: **3** eel
apodictic: **9** axiomatic **10** infallible
apogee: **3** top **4** apex, head, peak **5** bound, crest, limit, spire **6** climax, height, summit, tip-top, vertex, zenith **7** maximum **8** meridian, pinnacle **9** extremity **10** outer limit
__ a poke: **5** pig in
Apollo: **3** car, god **4** auto, font, hunk, seer **5** Buick, Creed **6** beauty **8** asteroid, Olympian, typeface **10** automobile
animal sacred to ~: **4** hawk, swan, wolf **5** mouse, raven, snake
astronaut: **4** Bean, Duke **5** Evans, Haise, Irwin, Roosa, Scott, Young **6** Aldrin, Anders, Borman, Cernan, Conrad, Eisele, Gordon, Lovell, Worden **7** Collins, Schirra, Schmitt, Shepard, Swigert **8** McDivitt, Mitchell, Stafford **9** Armstrong, Mattingly **10** Cunningham **11** Schweickart
attendant: **5** Erato
birthplace: **5** Delos
daughter: **6** Phoebe, Scylla **7** Eriopis, Hilaira **9** Parthenos
destination: **4** moon
instrument: **4** lyre
opponent: **5** Rocky
org.: **4** NASA
parent: **4** Leto, Zeus **7** Jupiter
shrine: **6** Delphi, oracle
son: **3** Ion **4** Apis **7** Troilus
twin: **5** Diana **7** Artemis
vehicle: **3** LEM
victim of ~: **6** Tityus
Apollo 13 (1995 film)
cast: Kevin Bacon, Tom Hanks, Ed Harris, Bill Paxton, Kathleen Quinlan, Gary Sinise
director: Ron Howard
role: **5** Haise **6** Lovell **7** Swigert **9** Mattingly
subject: **4** NASA
__ Apollo Forte: **4** Nick
Apollo in Masagète: **6** ballet
composer: Igor Stravinsky
Apollonian: **6** serene
Apollo Theater site: **3** NYC **6** Harlem **7** New York **9** Manhattan
Apolo: **4** Ohno
apolog: **5** fable
apologetic: **5** sorry **6** rueful **8** contrite, penitent **9** expiatory, regretful, repentant **10** remorseful
apologia: **6** reason
Apologia pro vita __: **3** sua
Apologies!: **5** sorry **7** I'm sorry **8** mea culpa
apologist: **5** urger **6** arguer **7** pleader **8** champion, defender, seconder **9** justifier, proponent, supporter
apologize: **6** regret **9** beg pardon, make up for **10** make amends
for: **6** defend
to: **10** make up with
apologue: **5** fable
apology: **4** plea **5** sorry **6** reason, regret **7** defense **8** mea culpa **10** reparation
accept one's ~: **7** forgive
in Italian: **5** scusa
response: **5** it's OK
Apology
author: Plato
Apopka: **4** city, town
locale: **7** Florida
aport: **9** to the left
__-à-porter: **4** prêt
__ a positive note: **5** end on
apostasy: **8** flip-flop, reversal **9** about-face, defection, desertion, forsaking, one-eighty, rebellion, sundering, turnabout **10** abjuration, changeover, copping out, recidivism, switcheroo, switchover, withdrawal
apostate: **3** rat **7** impious, sceptic, skeptic, traitor **8** betrayer, defector, deserter, disloyal, forsaker, recreant, renegade, turncoat
apostatize: **5** lapse **6** recant
apostle: **4** John, Paul **5** envoy, James, Judas, Peter, Simon, urger **6** Andrew, Philip, Thomas **7** Matthew **8** advocate, believer, champion, disciple, follower, preacher **9** expounder, proponent, supporter, Thaddaeus **10** missionary, Simon Peter
Apostle of California: **5** Serra
Apostle of the Slavs: **5** Cyril **9** Methodius
Apostles' __: **5** Creed
Apostles, The
composer: Edward Elgar
Apostle, The
author: Sholem Asch
Apostle, The (1997 film)
cast: Robert Duvall, Farrah Fawcett, Miranda Richardson, Billy Bob Thornton
director: Robert Duvall
apostolic: **8** clerical
apostolic __: **3** age **5** vicar
__ apostolic: **5** vicar **7** prefect
apostrophe: **4** mark **6** speech **7** address, oration **10** digression, discursion, salutation
apothecary: **4** phar. **5** pharm. **8** druggist, pharmacy **9** drugstore **10** pharmacist
measure: **3** scr. **4** dram **7** scruple
apothecary __: **3** jar
apothegm: **3** saw **5** adage, axiom, motto **6** dictum **7** proverb **8** aphorism, laconism
apothegmatic: **9** axiomatic
apotheosis: **5** ideal **7** epitome, paragon **8** cynosure **9** elevation, extolment **10** embodiment, exaltation
apotheosize: **8** enshrine, inshrine
...__ a pound: **5** in for
__ a powder: **4** take
__ app: **6** killer
appal: **4** faze, stun **5** daunt, shock **6** dismay, revolt **7** disgust, horrify, mortify, outrage, petrify, terrify, unnerve **8** frighten, gross out **9** terrorize **10** disconcert, dishearten, scandalize, scare stiff
Appalachia
composer: Frederick Delius
Appalachian __: **3** tea **5** Trail **6** Spring
Appalachians: **5** range **9** mountains
locale: **3** Ala. **4** N. Car., Penn., S. Car., Tenn. **5** Maine **6** Canada **7** Alabama, Georgia, New York, Vermont **8** Virginia **9** Tennessee
peak: **6** Rogers **8** Katahdin, Mitchell
Appalachian Spring: **6** ballet
composer: Aaron Copland
Appalachian Trail start: **5** Maine
appall: **4** faze, stun **5** daunt, shock **6** dismay, revolt **7** disgust, horrify, mortify, outrage, petrify, terrify, unnerve **8** frighten, gross out **9** terrorize **10** disconcert, dishearten, scandalize, scare stiff
appalled: **6** aghast **9** awestruck
appalling
see awful
Appaloosa: **5** horse **6** equine
apparatus: **3** kit, rig **4** gear, tool **5** gizmo, means, thing **6** device, engine, gadget, outfit, tackle **7** machine **8** workings **9** appliance, doohickey, equipment, hierarchy, implement, invention, machinery, mechanism, structure **10** instrument
provide with ~: **5** equip
apparel: **4** duds, garb, gear, togs, vest, wear **5** array, dress, getup, habit, robes **6** attire, livery, outfit, things **7** clothes, costume, garment, raiment, threads **8** accouter, accoutre, clothing, garments, wardrobe **9** trappings **10** habiliment, Sunday best
put on ~: **3** don **6** clothe
see also clothing
apparent: **4** easy, open, over **5** clear, gross, overt, plain, quasi, vivid **6** cogent, in view, likely, marked, patent, public **7** evident, exposed, express, glaring, nominal, obvious, outward, seeming, surface, visible **8** clear-cut, distinct, explicit, illusive, illusory, manifest, palpable, possible, probable, supposed, unhidden, unveiled **9** barefaced, big as life, graspable, plausible, prominent **10** noticeable, observable, ostensible, pronounced, spelled out, unshrouded
become ~: **4** dawn
__ apparent: **4** heir
apparently: **8** probably **9** allegedly, at a glance, doubtless, evidently, expressly, obviously, outwardly, plausibly, reputably, seemingly **10** manifestly, most likely, officially, ostensibly, reasonably, speciously, supposedly
__ apparent reason: **5** for no
apparition: **5** ghost, shade **6** fantom, spirit, wraith **7** eidolon, fantasy, phantom, specter **8** bogeyman, delusion, illusion, presence, revenant
apparitional: **7** ghostly
A&P part: **3** Atl., Pac. **7** Pacific **8** Atlantic
Appassionata Sonata
composer: Ludwig van Beethoven
appeal: **3** ask, beg, sue **4** call, plea, pray, pull, suit **5** apply, argue, charm, drive, plead, savor, tempt **6** allure, beauty, demand, desire, engage, entice, glamor, please, prayer, speech **7** attract, beseech, charism, enchant, entreat, glamour, implore, request, solicit **8** charisma, entreaty, litigate, petition, proposal, recourse, telethon **9** captivate, fascinate, go to court, impetrate, importune, magnetism **10** allurement, attraction, fund-raiser, invitation, invocation, recitation, supplicate
lose ~: **4** pall
make an ~: **3** ask **4** pray
to: **3** sue **4** draw, hook, lure, urge

5 plead, press, tempt 6 allure, entice, invoke, pull in 7 attract, entreat 8 interest
urgent ~: 4 suit 6 orison, prayer 8 entreaty, petition
___ appeal: 3 eye, sex 4 curb, mass, snob
appealing: 4 cute, nice 5 sweet 6 pretty 7 likable, lovable 8 adorable, charming, inviting, loveable, readable 9 beautiful 10 appetizing, attractive, enchanting
find ~: 4 like
make more ~: 5 sugar
appeals-court ruling: 6 denial
appear: 3 act, pop 4 come, form, look, loom, peep, peer, rise, seem, show 5 arise, begin, break, occur, pop in, pop up 6 arrive, attend, blow in, come up, crop up, drop in, emerge, fade in, grow up, happen, loom up, result, roll in, show up, spring, turn up 7 check in, clock in, punch in, surface, turn out 8 breeze in, look as if, look like, spring up 10 burst forth
again: 5 recur
as: 7 perform 9 represent
gradually: 5 set in 6 fade in
imminent: 4 loom
like: 8 resemble
suddenly: 5 bob up, pop up
to be: 4 seem 5 sound
with: 9 accompany
appearance: 3 air 4 aura, cast, face, form, look, mask, mien, rise, role, show, side, view 5 debut, dress, front, guise, image, phase, shape, sight 6 advent, aspect, coming, facade, facies, format, manner, veneer, vision 7 arrival, bearing, outside 8 attitude, carriage, demeanor, entrance, epiphany, features, likeness, presence, pretense 9 character, condition, emergence, semblance, showing up, turning up, unveiling 10 attendance, complexion, deportment, exhibition, impression, phenomenon, reflection
assumed ~: 5 guise
brief ~: 5 cameo
combining form: 5 -phany
enhance one's ~: 5 primp
external ~: 4 look, mask, mien, pose, role 5 cover, front, guise 6 aspect, facade, outfit 7 posture 8 demeanor, likeness 9 semblance
false ~: 4 sham 5 guise 10 camouflage
first ~: 4 rise 5 debut 7 baptism, kickoff 8 premiere 9 coming out 10 initiation
in ~: 9 outwardly
make an ~: 4 come, show 5 arise, enter, visit 6 attend, show up, turn up 7 turn out
outward ~: 3 air 4 face, look, mask, mien, pose 5 cloak, cover, front, guise, shape 6 aspect, facade, manner, veneer 7 bearing 8 demeanor, disguise, exterior 9 semblance 10 camouflage, false front, impression, masquerade
appearing combining form: 4 phen- 5 pheno-
appease: 3 lay 4 calm, sate 5 allay, quell, quiet, slake 6 pacify, smooth, soften, soothe, subdue 7 assuage, compose, content, gratify, mollify, placate, relieve, satisfy, sweeten 8 mitigate, moderate 9 alleviate, reconcile, untrouble 10 conciliate, make amends
Appelfeld, Aharon: 6 writer 7 Israeli
appellant: 8 litigant 9 applicant
appellation: 4 name, term 5 label, title 6 handle 7 epithet, moniker 8 monicker, nickname
appellative: 5 title
append: 3 add, tag 4 join, tack 5 add on, add to, affix, annex, tag on 6 adjoin, attach, fasten, tack on 7 conjoin, include 10 supplement
appendage: 3 arm, tab, toe 4 limb, tail, wing 5 annex, digit 6 finger, member 7 adjunct 8 addendum, addition, offshoot 9 accessory, ancillary, auxiliary, extension, extremity 10 attachment, elongation, projection, supplement
legislative ~: 7 proviso 9 amendment
appendix: 5 annex, table 7 adjunct, codicil 8 addendum, addition 9 extension 10 attachment, elongation, postscript, supplement, tabulation
neighbor: 5 index
appertain: 5 apply, refer 6 belong, relate 8 belong to 9 touch upon
to: 7 concern
appetence: 4 bias, lure, lust, need, want, wish 5 drive 6 desire, hunger, liking, thirst 7 craving, leaning, longing, passion 8 affinity, instinct, penchant, tendency, yearning 9 affection, magnetism 10 allurement, attraction, partiality, propensity
___ appétit!: 3 Bon
appetite: 3 yen 4 itch, lust, urge, will, zest 5 gusto, taste 6 desire, hunger, liking, relish, thirst 7 craving, longing, passion, stomach 8 fondness, penchant, voracity, weakness, yearning 9 esurience, hankering 10 love of life, proclivity
arouser: 5 aroma
build an ~: 4 whet
combining form: 6 -orexia
in French: 4 faim
in psychology: 6 orexis
voracious ~: 3 maw
whet the ~: 5 tempt
appetizer: 3 lox 4 Brie, Edam, food, pâté, pupu, whet 5 tapas 6 canapé, celery, course, dim sum, fondue, nachos, radish, rumaki 7 bean dip, ceviche, egg roll, fajitas, gravlax, saltine 8 caponata, cocktail, crabcake, crab puff, crudités, drumette, empanada, escargot, fruit cup, party mix 9 antipasto, guacamole, macédoine 10 black olive, breadstick, deviled egg, finger food, green olive, potato skin
avocado ~: 9 guacamole
bar mitzvah ~: 5 knish
chicken ~: 8 drumette
Chinese ~: 4 pupu 6 dim sum
eggplant ~: 8 caponata
fish ~: 3 lox 7 ceviche, gravlax
follower: 6 entrée
French ~: 9 macédoine
Japanese ~: 6 rumaki
liver ~: 4 pâté 6 rumaki
Mexican ~: 6 nachos 7 fajitas
Spanish ~: 5 tapas
appetizing: 5 sapid, spicy, tasty, yummy 6 delish, divine, savory, spicey, toothy 8 luscious, tempting 9 aperitive, appealing, delicious, flavorful, nectarous, palatable, succulent, sweetened, toothsome 10 delectable, flavorsome
___ Appia: 3 Via
Appian Way terminus: 4 Rome 5 Capua
applaud: 4 clap, hail, laud 5 cheer, exalt, extol, honor 6 extoll, praise, salute 7 acclaim, clap for, commend, flatter, glorify, root for 8 eulogize, hand it to 9 approve of, encourage, recommend 10 compliment, panegyrize
applauder: 5 toady 6 claque
applause: 4 hand 5 éclat, kudos 6 praise 7 acclaim, big hand, ovation, tribute 8 plaudits 9 standing O
acknowledge ~: 3 bow
burst of ~: 4 hand 5 round
response: 6 encore
Applause: 4 book 7 musical
character: 3 Eve 4 Bert, Buzz 5 Duane, Karen, Margo
composer: Charles Strouse, Lee Adams
writer: Adolph Green, Betty Comden
apple: 3 pie 4 crab, Gala, Lodi, pome, Rome, tree 5 fruit, Mutsu 6 Empire, Ida Red, medlar, pippin, russet, sphere 7 Baldwin, Bramley, costard, Freedom, Liberty, Spartan, Wealthy, Winesap 8 Cortland, Jonathan, McIntosh 9 Delicious 10 Rome Beauty
acid: 5 malic
center: 4 core
cider girl: 3 Ida
color: 3 red 5 green 6 yellow
combining form: 4 pomi-
custard ~: 5 papaw 6 pawpaw
drink: 5 cider, juice 9 hard cider
eater: 3 Eve 4 Adam
ender: 4 jack 5 sauce
European ~ tree: 4 sorb
family: 4 rose
gadget: 5 corer, parer
in ~ pie order: 4 neat, tidy
invader: 4 worm
juice brand: 5 Mott's
like an ~: 5 round 6 crispy 7 crunchy 8 spheroid 9 spherical
of discord contender: 4 Hera
of one's eye: 3 pet 5 pearl 7 darling 8 favorite
quantity: 4 peck 6 bushel
relative: 4 pear, plum 5 peach 6 almond, cherry, medlar, quince 7 apricot 8 hawthorn, oiticica 10 blackthorn
search for ~s: 3 bob
seed: 3 pip
skin: 4 peel
spray: 4 Alar
spread: 3 jam 5 jelly
starter: 4 crab, pine
targeter: 4 Tell
tosser of myth: 4 Eris
apple ___: 3 bee, pie 5 dowdy, green, grunt 6 brandy, butter, sucker 7 blossom
apple ___..., An: 4 a day
apple ___ la mode: 4 pie à
apple-___: 6 polish
apple-___ order: 3 pie
___ apple: 3 bad, may, oak 4 crab, lady, love, rose, snow, sorb, star 5 Adam's, baked, blade, candy, cedar, hedge, sugar, taffy, thorn 6 balsam, bitter, cashew, mammee, potato 7 custard, Mexican
___-apple: 3 kei 4 cran, pond
Apple: 5 Fiona 8 computer
alternative: 2 PC 3 IBM
device: 3 Mac 4 iMac, iPad, iPod 5 eMate, iBook 6 iPhone, laptop 7 desktop, MacBook, netbook 8 computer
founder: Steve Jobs, Steven 'Woz' Wozniak
Apple ___: 4 Isle 5 Jacks
___ Apple: 3 Big
Applebee's
rival: *see* restaurant chain
apple brown ___: 5 Betty
___ apple every day...: 5 Eat an
Apple, Fiona
real last name: Maggart
Applegate, Christina: 7 actress
TV: Jesse, Married...With Children
applejack: 5 drink 8 beverage
ingredient: 5 cider 6 brandy
Apple Jacks: 6 cereal
competitor: *see* cereal
apple of ___: 4 Peru 7 discord
apple of one's ___: 3 eye
apple-pie ___: 5 order 7 à la mode
apple-polish: 4 fawn 5 toady 6 cajole, grovel 7 adulate, flatter 8 fawn over, play up to
apple-polisher: 5 toady 6 fawner, flunky 7 flunkey 8 adulator, kowtower
apples and oranges: 6 unlike
applesauce
brand: 5 Mott's
see also baloney
Appleseed: 6 Johnny
apple strudel: 6 pastry 7 dessert
applet: 7 program 8 software
Appleton: 4 city, town 6 Edward
locale: 4 Wisc. 9 Wisconsin
Apple Valley: 4 city, town
locale: 9 Minnesota 10 California
Apple Zaps: 6 cereal
competitor: *see* cereal
appliance: 4 tool, unit 6 device, gadget 7 fixture, machine 9 accessory, apparatus, furniture, implement, mechanism 10 employment, instrument
brand: 5 Amana, Norge, Oster 6 Bendix, Maytag, Tappan 7 Admiral, Jenn-Air, Kenmore 8 Hotpoint 9 Magic Chef, Whirlpool 10 Frigidaire, Kelvinator, KitchenAid
button: 5 reset
household ~: 2 TV 3 fan, vac, VCR 4 iron, oven 5 drier, dryer,

grill, mixer, radio, range, stove, TV set **6** fridge, icebox, juicer, vacuum, washer **7** blender, freezer, grinder, hot comb, toaster **8** barbecue, hot plate, icemaker **9** blow-dryer, can opener, compactor, DVD player, microwave, top loader **10** clock radio, dehydrator, dishwasher, television **11** front loader, toaster oven, water heater **12** dehumidifier, refrigerator
ID: 2 SN
letters: 4 ACDC
part: 4 cord, plug
applicability: 7 fitness, service, utility
applicable: 3 apt, fit **4** meet **5** utile, valid **6** proper, usable, useful, viable **7** apropos, fitting, germane, helpful, on point, useable **8** apposite, material, on target, relative, relevant, suitable, workable **9** available, befitting, connected, on the nose, pertinent **10** admissible, associable, felicitous, to the point
be ~ to: 7 concern
applicant: 6 seeker **7** entrant, hopeful **8** aspirant, claimant **9** appellant, candidate, job-hunter, postulant, suppliant **10** petitioner
accept an ~: 4 hire
application: 3 use **4** form, suit **5** claim, usage, value **6** appeal, demand, effort, praxis **7** purpose, request **8** entreaty, exercise, function, hard work, petition, practice
abbr.: 3 NMI
find a new ~ for: 5 reuse
job ~ entry: 3 sex **4** name **7** address, hobbies **9** reference **10** experience
lack of ~: 6 disuse
submitter: 5 filer
wrong ~: 6 misuse
applicator: 4 swab, swob, wand
Appling, Luke: 8 White Sox **9** shortstop
appliqué: 4 lace **5** patch **6** iron-on **10** decoration
apply: 3 fit, rub, set, use **4** give, hold **5** exert, lay on, put on, refer, rub on, smear, spend, wield **6** anoint, appeal, belong, devote, direct, employ, engage, invoke, relate, resort **7** enforce, enquire, execute, exploit, harness, inflict, inquire, pertain, request, smear on, utilize **8** dedicate, dispense, exercise, petition, practice, put in for, put to use, spread on **9** appertain, embrocate, implement, put to work **10** administer, be relevant
again: 5 reuse
as lotion: 5 smear
(for): 3 sue, try **5** put in
gently: 3 dab
lace: 4 edge **5** adorn **6** bedeck **7** dress up **8** decorate, ornament, pretty up **9** embellish
lipstick: 4 tint **5** color, paint
logic: 3 see **4** muse **5** guess, infer, judge, study, weigh **6** assume, deduce, gather, ideate, ponder, reason, reckon **7** analyze, examine, presume, reflect, sort out, surmise, suspect **8** appraise, cogitate, conceive, conclude, consider, estimate, evaluate, mull over, perceive, ruminate, theorize **9** cerebrate, determine, figure out, speculate **10** conjecture, deliberate
oneself: 4 work **5** labor, lay to, study **6** hustle, pursue
oneself to: 7 address
to: 7 concern
(to): 6 matter, relate
unguent: 3 oil **5** bless **6** ordain **8** sanctify **9** lubricate **10** consecrate
wrongly: 6 misuse
apply for __: 5 a loan
appoggiatura: 4 note
appoint: 3 rig, tap **4** make, name **5** equip, place **6** assign, choose, engage, enlist, instal, outfit, select, settle, supply **7** furnish, install, provide, station, turn out **8** accredit, delegate, deputize, nominate, schedule **9** designate, prescribe **10** commission, constitute, settle upon
appointed: 3 set
finely ~: 4 posh
time: 4 D-day, hour **5** H-hour **8** zero hour
__-appointed: 4 self, well
appointee: 5 agent, envoy, proxy **6** deputy, factor, legate **7** nominee, officer **8** delegate, emissary, mediator, selectee **9** assistant, candidate, go-between, middleman, surrogate **10** commissary
appointment: 3 gig **4** date, gear, post **5** berth, tryst, visit **6** billet, choice, naming, office, outfit **7** fixture, meeting, session **8** election, position, trapping **9** situation
book slot: 4 date, hour
make an ~: 4 name **6** select
Appointment in Samarra
author: John O'Hara
appointments: 3 rig **4** gear, tack **5** decor, stuff **6** outfit, tackle **7** harness, rigging, turnout **8** fittings, fixtures, schedule **9** apparatus, caparison, equipment, trappings **10** habilments, outfitting
Appomattox: 4 city, town **5** river
figure: 3 Lee **5** Grant
locale: 8 Virginia
monogram: 3 REL, USG
part of an ~ signature: 4 E. Lee
apportion: 4 deal, mete **5** allot, allow, cut up, divvy, share, split **6** assign, bestow, budget, devote, divide, ration **7** divvy up, dole out, give out, mete out, portion, prorate, split up **8** allocate, dedicate, dispense, divide up **9** admeasure, designate, parcel out, partition **10** administer, distribute, measure out
apportioned: 8 separate
apportionment: 4 dole **5** quota, share **6** ration
apportune: 8 apposite
apposite: 3 apt, fit, pat **4** meet **6** cogent, proper, seemly, suited, timely **7** apropos, fitting, germane, well put **8** becoming, material, relative, relevant, suitable **9** apportune, befitting, pertinent **10** applicable, convenient, felicitous, seasonable, to the point, well-suited
not ~: 5 unapt
appositeness: 7 fitness
appraisal: 5 price, value **6** rating, review **8** estimate, judgment **9** criticism, reckoning, valuation **10** assessment, estimation, evaluation
appraise: 3 eye, see **4** rate **5** assay, audit, gauge, judge, price, set at, think, value, weigh **6** assess, figure, reckon, review, size up, survey **7** adjudge, examine, inspect, measure, valuate **8** check out, estimate, evaluate, factor in, keep tabs, look over
the situation: 6 ponder
appraiser: 5 rater **6** lister
appreciable: 3 any **5** large **6** goodly, marked **7** evident, healthy, obvious, sizable **8** clear-cut, definite, manifest, material, sizeable, tangible
amount: 4 much
effect: 4 dent, mark **10** impression
appreciate: 3 dig, get, see **4** boom, gain, grok, grow, know, like, rise **5** enjoy, grasp, prize, savor, savvy, sense **6** admire, esteem, fathom, follow, praise, relish **7** cherish, realize, respect, welcome **8** conceive, flip over, increase, perceive, relate to, treasure **9** apprehend, care about, delight in, get high on, recognize **10** comprehend, freak out on, give thanks, understand
I ~ it: 5 danke, merci **6** grazie, thanks **7** gracias **8** thank you
appreciated: 7 welcome **8** valuable
appreciation: 3 ear **4** gain, love, rise **5** grasp, sense, taste **6** growth, liking, praise, regard, thanks **7** empathy, premium, thought, tribute
exclamation: 2 ah **3** gee, ooh, wow **5** great, huzza **6** hoorah, hooray, hurrah, hurray, huzzah, thanks
informal ~: 5 thanx
show ~: 4 clap **5** thank
token of ~: 4 gift
appreciative: 5 proud **6** loving **7** mindful, obliged, pleased **8** admiring, grateful, indebted, thankful
like ~ fans: 5 aroar
apprehend: 3 bag, get, nab **4** bust, grab, hear, know, nail, take **5** catch, grasp, pinch, run in, seize, sense **6** absorb, arrest, collar, detain, fathom, follow, intuit, pick up, pull in, take in **7** capture, cognize, discern, realize, receive **8** perceive **9** extradite, recognize, track down **10** anticipate, appreciate, comprehend, understand
apprehended: 6 in jail **10** behind bars
apprehensible: 5 lucid **8** knowable, luminous
apprehension: 3 ken **4** care, fear **5** alarm, doubt, dread, grasp, qualm, worry **6** arrest, dismay, fright, phobia, reason **7** anxiety, booking, capture, concern, seizure, tension **8** disquiet, suspense **9** collaring, detention, misgiving **10** foreboding, misgivings, perception, uneasiness
expression: 4 oh-oh, uh-oh, yipe **5** yikes, yipes **7** omigosh
apprehensive: 3 shy **4** wary **5** chary, jumpy, leery, tense, timid **6** afraid, on edge, scared, trepid, uneasy, unsure **7** abashed, alarmed, anxious, chicken, daunted, dubious, fearful, guarded, jittery, nervous, spooked, uptight, worried **8** cautious, cowardly, doubtful, doubting, fearsome, hesitant, timorous **9** skeptical, uncertain **10** frightened, suspicious
be ~: 5 worry **8** mistrust
be ~ about: 4 fear
apprehensively: 6 in fear
apprehensiveness: 4 fear **5** qualm **9** misgiving
apprentice: 3 cub **4** aide, hand, tiro, tyro **5** labor, learn, newie, pupil **6** greeny, helper, intern, novice, rookie **7** amateur, employe, interne, learner, recruit, student, trainee **8** beginner, employee, henchman, neophyte, newcomer **9** assistant, fledgling, greenhorn, novitiate **10** tenderfoot
apprenticed: 5 bound
Apprentice, The (NBC reality)
host: Donald Trump
apprise: 4 tell, warn **5** brief **6** advise, fill in, inform, notify, tip off **8** advise of, forewarn, instruct **9** enlighten **10** put on guard
apprised: 3 hep, hip **4** wise **5** aware, privy, savvy **6** versed, with it **7** knowing, mindful **9** cognizant, in the know
be ~ of: 3 see **5** learn
of: 4 in on **7** privy to
approach: 3 way **4** come, meet, mode, near, path, plan, tack **5** light, means, reach, rival, slant, stalk, start, style, verge **6** access, accost, avenue, come at, course, embark, gain on, go near, go up to, loom up, manner, method, policy, talk to **7** advance, apply to, contact, ingress, solicit, speak to, tactics **8** attitude, commence, draw near, go toward, overture, set about, sound out, strategy, threaten **9** belly up to, catch up to, close in on, creep up on, procedure, technique, treatment, undertake, verge upon **10** converge on, draw near to, get a hold of, move toward
a deadline: 5 laten
eagerly: 5 run to
furtively: 5 sidle
intrusively: 6 accost
journalist ~: 5 angle, pitch, slant, twist **7** opinion **9** viewpoint
quickly: 5 run to
way of ~: 6 access, avenue
approachable: 4 open **7** affable **8** gracious, outgoing, sociable **9** receptive
approaching: 4 near, nigh **5** close **6** almost, at hand, coming, in view, nearly, toward **7** brewing, in store, looming, pending, towards **8** imminent, in the air, oncoming, on the way **9** impending, in the wind
the hour: 5 ten of, ten to
approbate: 5 favor **6** accept
approbation: 5 favor **6** praise, regard **7** acclaim, respect

approbative: 9 laudatory
appropriate: 3 apt, cop, due, fit, nip, rob 4 good, grab, just, lift, loot, meet, take 5 allot, annex, co-opt, filch, right, seize, steal, swipe, usurp 6 assign, assume, borrow, budget, decent, devote, fitted, pilfer, pocket, proper, rip off, seemly, snatch, timely, useful 7 condign, correct, earmark, fitting, germane, in order, preempt, procure, ransack, receive, require, reserve, utilize 8 allocate, apposite, becoming, decorous, dedicate, deserved, disburse, eligible, glom on to, relative, relevant, rightful, set apart, set aside, suitable 9 allowable, opportune 10 commandeer
be ~: 4 suit 5 apply, befit 6 beseem
more ~: 6 better
not ~: 5 inapt, unapt
to: 3 for
appropriately: 4 well 5 right 6 aright
appropriateness: 7 fitness 9 congruity, propriety
appropriation: 4 grab 5 grant, theft 6 taking 7 funding, seizure, stipend, subsidy 8 adoption, stealing
approval: 2 OK 4 okay 5 favor, leave 6 assent, credit, esteem, praise, regard, the nod 7 acclaim, consent, go-ahead, license, support 8 accolade, adoption, blessing, plaudits, sanction 9 agreement, clearance 10 admiration, green light, permission, popularity
enthusiastic ~: 6 yes yes
exclamation: 2 ah, ay 3 aah, aye, boy, olé, rah, yay, yea, yes 4 amen, good, yeah 5 brava, bravo, goody, great, zowie 6 by Jove, encore, goodie, good-oh, hoorah, hooray, hurrah, hurray, rather, whizzo 7 attaboy, by jingo 8 all right, attagirl
gesture of ~: 3 nod 5 V sign
give a stamp of ~: 2 OK 4 pass 5 bless 7 approve, certify, confirm, consent, endorse, license 8 sanction, validate 9 authorize, sign off on
legal ~: 3 lic. 7 license
seal of ~: 6 cachet 8 sanction
show ~: 4 buoy, clap, yell 5 cheer, elate, huzza, liven, pep up, shout, whoop 6 buck up, hoorah, hooray, hurrah, hurray, huzzah, perk up, praise, revive, scream, uplift 7 acclaim, applaud, elevate, enliven, gladden, hearten, root for, support 8 enspirit, inspirit, reassure 9 encourage 10 brighten up, exhilarate, strengthen
silent ~: 3 nod
approve: 2 OK 3 let, nod 4 back, hail, laud, like, okay, pass 5 adopt, agree, allow, bless, favor, stamp 6 accede, accept, assent, comply, concur, permit, praise, ratify, second, uphold 7 acclaim, certify, commend, confirm, consent, endorse, go along, indorse, support, sustain 8 accede to, accredit, legalize, sanction, validate 9 acquiesce, authorize, get behind, give leave, recognize, recommend, sign off on, subscribe 10 underwrite
don't ~: 3 nix 4 veto
of: 3 let 5 allow, brook, favor 6 accept, permit 7 applaud 8 accede to, assent to, sanction, stand for, tolerate 9 authorize, put up with
approved: 2 OK 3 OK'd 4 okay, OK'ed 5 liked, tried 6 okayed 7 popular, regular 8 official, orthodox, standard 9 canonical, preferred
approving: 5 OK'ing 7 okaying 9 agreeable, favorable, laudatory 10 permissive
approx.: 3 abt., est.
approximal: 9 adjoining 10 contiguous
approximate: 4 near, rude 5 alike, close, loose, rival, rough, round 6 nearby, reckon 7 general, inexact, similar, verge on 8 adjacent, approach, border on, come near, relative, resemble 9 adumbrate, imprecise, uncertain
approximately: 3 say 4 or so 5 about, circa 6 almost, around, nearly 7 close to, loosely, roughly 9 somewhere 10 more or less
suffix: 3 -ish
approximation: 5 guess 8 estimate 9 guesswork 10 conjecture, estimation
appt.: 3 mtg.
appurtenance: 5 annex, extra 7 adjunct, ancilla, apanage 8 appanage 9 accessory, appendage, auxiliary 10 subsidiary
appurtenances: 3 rig 5 stuff
appurtenant: 7 adjunct 8 relative 9 accessory, auxiliary, belonging 10 subsidiary
to: 6 part of
Apr.: 2 mo.
agency: 3 IRS
busy ~ worker: 3 CPA
predecessor: 3 Mar.
APR
part: 4 rate 6 annual 10 percentage
__ a Prayer: 4 Like
__-a Preacher Man: 5 Son-of
__ a precedent: 3 set
après __ le déluge: 3 moi
après-__: 3 ski 4 midi
après-midi: 6 French 9 afternoon
follower: 4 nuit, soir
après-ski beverage: 5 cocoa, toddy
Après un __: 4 rêve
apricot: 4 pink, tree 5 color, drupe, fruit 6 orange, yellow 7 pinkish 9 yellowish
family: 4 rose
Japanese ~: 3 ume
Korean ~: 4 ansu
relative: *see* fruit, yellow color
spread: 6 lekvar
April: 5 month 7 Stevens
birthstone: 7 diamond
concern: 3 tax 5 taxes 9 tax return
fifth: 5 nones
follower: 3 May
fool: 3 gag 5 prank
forecast: 4 rain
preceder: 5 March
sign: 3 Ram 4 Bull 5 Aries 6 Taurus
victim: 4 fool
April __: 4 fool, Love 7 Morning, Showers
April __ Day: 5 Fools'
April 13: 4 ides
April 5: 5 nones
April is the cruellest month
poet: T.S. Eliot
April Love (1957 song)
artist: Pat Boone
composer: Paul Francis Webster, Sammy Fain
April Morning
author: Howard Fast
April Showers (1922 song)
artist: Al Jolson
a priori: 9 deductive
__ a profit: 4 turn
apron: 5 smock 7 garment 8 pinafore 9 forestage 10 proscenium, protection
part: 3 bib 7 strings
wearer: 4 chef, cook, maid
apron __: 5 piece 6 string
apropos: 3 apt, fit, pat 5 about 6 proper, timely, toward 7 fitting, germane, on point, towards, well-put 8 apposite, material, relative, relevant, suitable 9 opportune, pertinent, well-timed 10 applicable, felicitous, to the point
of: 4 as to, in re
apse: 6 chevet, concha, recess
path to an ~: 5 aisle
table: 5 altar
__ apso: 5 Lhasa
apt: 3 fit, pat 4 able, deft, good, just, meet 5 adept, given, happy, prone, quick, ready, right, savvy, sharp, smart 6 adroit, astute, bright, clever, cogent, decent, expert, gifted, liable, likely, proper, seemly, timely 7 apropos, capable, fitting, germane, skilled, subject, tending, well-put 8 apposite, dextrous, disposed, inclined, on target, probable, relevant, rightful, skillful, suitable 9 advisable, allowable, astucious, befitting, dexterous, efficient, ingenious, on the mark, opportune, pertinent, promising, qualified, sagacious 10 applicable, felicitous, precocious, proficient, to the point
be ~ (to): 4 tend
(to): 5 prone 7 of a mind, tending 8 disposed, inclined
apt.
see apartment
Apted, Michael: 8 director
apterous, not: 5 alary 6 winged
apteryx: 3 moa 4 kiwi
aptitude: 4 bent, gift, head, turn 5 craft, flair, knack, sense, skill 6 smarts, talent 7 ability, faculty, fitness, know-how, leaning, promise 8 capacity, facility, instinct 9 endowment, intellect, potential, smartness 10 capability, cleverness, competence, proclivity, proficient, propensity, right stuff
aptitude __: 4 test
Aptiva maker: 3 IBM
aptly: 5 right 6 aright
aptness: 4 gift, tact 5 flair, knack 7 faculty, fitness 9 dexterity, expertise, readiness
__ a puddy tat!: 4 I taw
Aqaba: 4 city, gulf, port, town
Gulf of ~ port: 4 Elat 5 Eilat, Elath
Gulf of ~ strait: 5 Tiran
aqua: 5 water 6 liquid 8 greenish, sea green 9 blue-green, Nile green, turquoise
vitae: 3 rye 5 booze, drink, sauce, vodka 6 brandy, liquor, scotch, whisky 7 alcohol, bourbon, liqueur, potable, spirits, whiskey 8 beverage 9 firewater, inebriant, moonshine 10 intoxicant
aqua __: 4 pura 5 regia, vitae 6 fortis 7 ammonia
Aqua __: 5 Velva
Aqua-__: 4 Lung
aquaculture: 7 science
Aquafina: 5 water
alternative: 4 Naya 5 Evian 7 Perrier 9 Arrowhead
aqua fortis: 4 acid
Aquafresh: 10 toothpaste
alternative: *see* toothpaste
aquake: 5 shaky
Aqua-Lung device: 5 scuba
aquamarine: 3 gem 4 blue 5 beryl, color, green 7 sea blue 8 gemstone, greenish
mineral: 5 beryl
month: 5 March
relative: *see* blue color, green color
aquanaut: 5 diver
gear: 5 scuba
Aquarian __: 3 Age
__ Aquarids: 3 Eta 5 Delta
aquarium: 4 tank
accessory: 6 filter
dweller: 3 eel, orf 4 barb, orfe 5 danio, guppy, platy, skate, tetra 6 medaka 7 gourami, helleri, scalare 8 bloodfin, goldfish 9 neon tetra, swordtail
freshen a ~: 6 aerate
Aquarium
artist: Erté
Aquarius: 4 sign
month: 3 Feb., Jan. 7 January 8 February
predecessor: 9 Capricorn
show: 4 Hair
successor: 6 Pisces
tote: 4 ewer 5 water
__ Aquarius: 5 Age of
Aquarius/Let the Sunshine In (1969 song)
artist: Fifth Dimension
__ a Quarter to Nine: 5 About
aquatic: 5 naval 6 marine 7 oceanic 8 maritime, natatory, nautical
bird: 4 gull, swan, tern 5 grebe 6 jaçana
mammal: 4 seal 5 hippo, otary, otter 6 desman, dugong
nymph: 5 naiad
organism: 4 alga
plant: 5 lotus 6 elodea 8 duckweed 9 arrowhead, water lily
rodent: 5 coypu 7 muskrat
worm: 5 leech
Aqua Velva: 6 lotion 10 aftershave
competitor: 4 Brut 8 Gillette, Old Spice 10 Skin Bracer
aquavit: 5 drink 6 liquor 7 alcohol 8 beverage
aqueduct: 4 pipe 5 canal 6 course

7 channel, conduit 8 pipeline
contents: 5 water
Aqueduct transaction: 3 bet 5 wager
aqueous: 3 wet 5 fluid 6 liquid, serous, watery 7 hydrous 9 water-like
material: 6 liquid
aqueous __: 5 humor 7 ammonia
aquifer feature: 4 pore
Aquila: 5 Eagle
aquiline: 5 Roman 6 beaked, curved, hooked 9 eagle-like, prominent 10 protruding
Aquinas, Thomas: 5 saint 7 Italian 11 philosopher
Aquino: 4 Cory 5 Ninoy 7 Benigno, Corazon
predecessor: 6 Marcos
Aquitaine: 5 duchy
locale: 6 France
noble: 7 Eleanor
Aquitaine Progression, The
author: Robert Ludlum
aquiver: 5 shaky 7 vibrant 9 jellylike
Ar: 4 elem. 5 argon 7 element
18 for ~: 4 at. no.
AR
see Arkansas
ara: 4 bird 5 macaw
Ara: 9 Berberian 10 Parseghian
Ara __: 5 Pacis
Arab: 4 amir, emir 5 ameer, emeer, horse, Iraki, Iraqi, Omani, Saudi, sheik, steed 6 Beduin, equine, Qatari, Semite, shaikh, sheikh, Syrian, Yemeni 7 Bedouin, Kuwaiti, Saracen 8 Egyptian, Lebanese 9 Damascene, Jordanian
animal: 5 camel 9 dromedary
bazaar: 3 suk, suq 4 souk
boat: 3 dau, dow 4 dhow
demon: 5 afrit 6 afreet
garment: 3 aba 4 abba, haik 5 haick 7 burnous 8 burnoose
grp.: 3 PLO
headband cord: 4 agal
lute: 3 oud
name part: 3 ibn
noble: 3 aga 4 agha, amir, emir 5 ameer, emeer, sheik 6 shaikh, sheikh
of song: 4 Ahab
prename: 3 Ali
street ~: 4 waif 6 urchin
tea: 3 qat
Arab __: 6 League, Legion
Arabella: 5 opera
composer: Richard Strauss
arabesque: 5 motif 6 linear, spiral 8 position 9 anthemion, sinuosity 10 decoration, embroidery, undulation
Arabesque (1966 film)
cast: Sophia Loren, Gregory Peck
director: Stanley Donen
Arabia: 9 peninsula
coffee: 5 mocha
desert: 5 Nafud, Nefud
gazelle: 5 ariel
gulf: 4 Aden
nation: 4 Oman 5 Dubai, Katar, Qatar, Yemen 6 Koweit, Kuwait 8 Abu Dhabi
old ~ sultanate: 4 Nejd
peninsula: 4 Aden
port: 4 Aden
primate: 6 baboon
sea: 3 Red 7 Arabian
shrub: 3 kat, qat 4 khat 5 retem
stopover: 5 serai
__ Arabia: 5 Saudi, South
Arabian: 5 horse, steed 6 equine
Arabian __: 3 Sea 4 Gulf 5 camel 6 coffee, Desert 7 jasmine
Arabian Nights
bird: 3 roc
character: 3 Ali 5 Ahmed, genie 7 Ali Baba
locale: 7 Baghdad
ruler: 5 calif, kalif 6 caliph, kaliph, khalif
Arabian Sea
gulf: 4 Oman
river to the ~: 5 Indus 7 Narbada 8 Nerbudda
territory: 3 Goa
__ arabic: 3 gum
Arabic: 3 Sem. 7 Semitic 8 language
father, in ~: 3 abu
first ~ letter: 4 alif
glottal stop: 5 hamza
letter: 2 ba, fa, ha, ra, ta, ya, za 3 ain, dad, dal, jim, kaf, kha, lam, mim, qaf, sad, sin, tha, waw 4 alif, dhal, shin 5 qhain
master, in ~: 5 saheb, sahib
name of Egypt: 4 Misr
wise men: 5 ulama, ulema
Arabic __: 7 numeral
arabica: 6 coffee
arable: 5 loamy 7 fertile 8 farmable, plowable, tillable 10 cultivable, productive
area: 5 field
Arab League: 8 alliance
headquarters: 5 Cairo, Tunis
member: 3 UAE 4 Irak, Iraq, Oman 5 Egypt, Katar, Libya, Qatar, Sudan, Syria, Yemen 6 Jibuti, Jordan, Koweit, Kuwait 7 Algeria, Bahrain, Bahrein, Comoros, Lebanon, Morocco, Somalia, Tunisia 8 Djibouti 9 Palestine 10 Mauritania
__ Arab Republic: 6 Syrian, United
Arab Republic of __: 5 Egypt
Arab Song
artist: Paul Klee
Arachne home: 5 Lydia
arachnid: 4 mite, tick 6 spider 8 scorpion 10 harvestman
creation: 3 web 6 cobweb
arachnophobe fear: 7 spiders
Arachnophobia (1990 film)
cast: Jeff Daniels, John Goodman
Arafat: 4 Arab 5 Yasir 6 Yasser 8 Nobelist
birthplace: 5 Cairo, Egypt
grp.: 3 PLO
Arafura: 3 sea
locale: 9 Australia, New Guinea
strait off the ~: 6 Torres
Aragón: 5 river 7 kingdom
locale: 5 Spain
river through ~: 4 Ebro
__ a Rag Picker: 3 He's
__ a rail: 6 thin as
Araldo
composer: Giuseppe Verdi
Aral Sea: 4 lake
river to the ~: 8 Amu Darya, Syr Darya
Aram: 7 Avakian, Saroyan
father: 4 Shem
grandfather: 4 Noah
Aramaic: 8 language
Aramis
colleague: 5 Athos 7 Porthos 9 d'Artagnan
Aran: 4 isls. 5 isles 7 islands
locale: 7 Ireland
Aran Islands, The
author: John Millington Synge
Arapaho: 5 tribe 6 Indian 7 Amerind 8 language
abode: 4 tipi 5 tepee 6 teepee
enemy: 3 Ute
Ararat: 4 peak 5 mount 8 Agri Dagi, mountain
locale: 4 Asia 6 Turkey
visitor: 3 ark, Ham 4 Noah, Shem 7 Japheth
__ a rat: 5 smell
Araucanian: 6 Indian 7 Amerind
Arawak: 5 Taino 6 Indian 7 Amerind 8 language
arbiter: 3 ref, ump 5 judge 6 critic, umpire 7 referee 8 mediator 9 authority, evaluator, go-between 10 interceder
arbitrageur concern: 3 stk. 4 risk 5 hedge, stock
arbitrarily: 8 at random
arbitrary: 5 bossy 6 biased, chance, fickle, lordly, random, unfair, unjust, wilful 7 erratic, offhand, partial, willful 8 absolute, despotic, dogmatic, one-sided, partisan 9 downright, frivolous, haphazard, imperious, tyrannous, vagarious, whimsical 10 autocratic, capricious, despotical, dogmatical, fortuitous, high-handed, irrational, monocratic, peremptory, prejudiced, subjective, tyrannical, unbalanced, undisputed
arbitrate: 5 judge 6 decide, settle, strike 7 adjudge, mediate, referee 9 determine, intercede, interpose, intervene, make a deal, negotiate, reconcile 10 adjudicate, compromise, conciliate
arbitration: 7 verdict 8 judgment 9 mediation
arbitrator: 3 ref, ump 5 judge 6 umpire 7 referee 8 mediator 9 go-between 10 interceder, peacemaker
agcy.: 4 NLRB
arbor: 5 bower 6 ramada, recess 7 pergola, trellis
arbor __: 5 vitae
Arbor Day month: 5 April
arboreal: 5 shady 6 ramose, silvan, sylvan, wooded 8 branched, dendroid, forested, ramiform, treelike 9 dendritic 10 branchlike, dendriform, tree-shaped
fluid: 3 sap
home: 4 nest
lizard: 5 anole 6 iguana
mammal: 5 koala, lemur, sloth
rodent: 8 squirrel
arboretum specimen: 4 tree
__ Arbor, MI: 3 Ann
arborvitae: 4 tree 5 thuja, thuya 9 evergreen
relative: 7 cypress, juniper 8 sandarac
Arbuckle: 3 Jon 5 Fatty 6 Roscoe
Arbuckle, Jon pet: 4 Odie 8 Garfield
Arbus: 5 Allan, Diane
Arbus, Diane: 12 photographer
arbutus: 4 tree 5 plant, shrub 6 flower 9 evergreen
relative: 5 erica, heath, salal 6 azalea, kalmia, sorrel 7 madrone, rhodora 8 cassiope, cowberry 9 blueberry, deerberry
Arby's rival: *see* restaurant chain
arc: 3 bow, lob 4 bend, loop, turn, weld 5 curve, spark, sweep, twist 7 azimuth, flexure, rainbow 8 crescent, half-moon, parabola 9 curvature, hyperbola, sinuosity 10 semicircle
arc __: 3 cos, cot, csc, sec, sin, tan 4 lamp, sine 5 light 6 cosine, secant, second 7 furnace, tangent, welding
__ Arc: 6 Joan of
arcade: 4 mall, stoa 6 loggia 7 gallery, ingress, portico 8 cloister 9 colonnade, peristyle 10 passageway
habitué: 4 teen 5 gamer
infraction: 4 tilt
like ~ games: 6 coin-op
pioneering ~ game: 4 Pong
price, once: 5 penny
arcade __: 4 game
__ arcade: 5 penny, video
Arcadia: 4 city, Eden, town 6 heaven, utopia 8 paradise
author: Philip Sidney
locale: 10 California
Arcadian: 5 rural 6 rustic 7 bucolic, country 8 pastoral 9 bucolical
ancient ~ city: 4 Alea
arcana: 5 tarot 7 secrets 9 mysteries
arcane: 4 dark, deep 5 vague 6 exotic, hidden, mystic, occult, secret 7 cryptic, obscure, unclear 8 abstruse, esoteric, mystical, nebulous, oracular, puzzling, uncommon 9 confusing, cryptical, enigmatic, recherché, recondite 10 cabalistic, indistinct, mysterious, perplexing, unknowable
arcanum: 6 cabala, elixir, engima, kabala, secret 7 alembic, cabbala, kabbala, mystery, nostrum, panacea 9 conundrum
Arcaro, Eddie: 6 jockey
milieu: 5 track
prop: 4 crop
arced: 5 curvy 6 curvey 9 bow-shaped
arch: 3 bow, coy, sly 4 bend, cagy, camp, flex, foxy, hump, loop, main, ogee, span, wily 5 cagey, canny, chief, curve, embow, hunch, major, vault 6 artful, bridge, crafty, instep, ironic, portal 7 cunning, knowing, leading, primary, roguish, waggish 8 foremost, greatest 9 curvature, principal, quizzical, sinuosity 10 consummate, preeminent, serpentine
architectural ~: 4 ogee 5 ogive
end: 8 abutment
over: 4 span 6 bridge
(over): 4 hang
site: 3 St. L. 4 foot 5 Paris 7 St. Louis
slightly: 6 camber
support: 4 pier 6 insole
type of ~: 6 lancet

arch __: 3 dam 4 beam, head 5 board, brace 7 support
__ arch: 3 pot 4 bell, drop, flat, gill, jack, ogee, rood, skew 5 Roman, round, Tudor 6 aortic, braced, corbel, French, Gothic, lancet 7 Moorish, pointed, trefoil, trimmer
Arch: 6 Oboler
__ Arch: 7 Gateway
archaeologist: 5 Evans 6 Carter, digger, Petrie 7 Woolley 8 Breasted 10 Schliemann
British ~: 5 Evans 6 Petrie 7 Woolley
datum: 3 age
Egyptian ~ site: 5 Luxor 6 Amarna, Karnak
find: 4 abri, ansa, bone, idol, ruin 5 mound, relic, ruins, shard, sherd, stela, stele 6 fossil 8 artifact
German ~: 10 Schliemann
Hindu ~ site: 6 Ellora
Kenya ~ site: 7 Olduvai
Maya ~ site: 5 Copan
prefix: 5 paleo-
site: 3 dig
Switzerland ~ site: 4 Biel
Syria ~ site: 4 Ebla
archaeology: 7 science
archaic: 3 obs., old, out 5 dated, fusty, olden, passé 6 bygone, old hat 7 ancient, extinct, fogyish 8 obsolete, outdated, outmoded, out of use, timeworn 9 out of date, primitive 10 antiquated, out of style
archaism: 5 relic 9 throwback
archaize: 9 antiquate
archangel: 5 Uriel 7 Gabriel, Lucifer, Michael, Raphael
Archangel: 4 port
locale: 6 Russia
archbishop: 4 rank 6 cleric, priest 7 prelate 8 minister
archdeacon: 6 cleric
archduchess: 4 lady 5 noble
archduke: 5 noble
arched: 5 round 6 convex
ceiling: 5 vault
combining form: 3 tox- 4 toxi-, toxo-
recess: 4 apse
archeologist
see archaeologist
archer: 4 Amor, Eros, Tell 5 Cupid 6 Apache, bowman, Indian 9 Robin Hood 10 longbowman
mythical ~: 4 Amor, Eros 5 Cupid
need: 3 bow 5 arrow 6 quiver
shield: 5 pavis 6 pavise
skill: 3 aim
supplier: 6 bowyer
Archer: 3 Lew 4 Anne, sign 5 Miles 6 George, Martin 7 Jeffrey
month: 3 Dec., Nov. 8 December, November
predecessor: 8 Scorpion
successor: 4 Goat
Archer, Anne: 7 actress
film: The Art of War (2000)
Clear and Present Danger (1994)
Fatal Attraction (1987)
Patriot Games (1992)
mother: Marjorie Lord
Archerd, Army: 6 writer 9 columnist
periodical: 7 Variety
Archer, George: 6 golfer
Archer, Miles
partner: 8 Sam Spade
Archers of St. George
artist: Frans Hals
archery: 5 sport
sound: 5 twang
wood: 3 yew
Arches National Park
city near ~: 4 Moab
locale: 4 Utah
archetypal: 5 ideal, model 8 original 9 inceptive
archetype: 5 ideal, model 6 avatar 7 epitome, example, paragon, pattern 8 exemplar, original, paradigm, standard 9 criterion, prototype 10 embodiment, progenitor, touchstone
archfiend: 4 ogre 5 beast, brute, demon, devil, ghoul, Satan 6 bad guy, daemon, daimon, diablo 7 evil one, incubus, monster, villain
Archibald: 3 Cox 4 Hill, Nate, Tiny 8 MacLeish
Archibald, Nate
milieu: 5 court
org.: 3 NBA
sport: 10 basketball
Archie: 4 Bell, Mayo, teen 5 Moore, strip 6 Bunker 7 Andrews, Griffin, Manning
daughter: 6 Gloria
friend: 5 Betty, Moose 7 Jughead 8 Veronica
to Mike: 5 in-law
wife: 5 Edith
Archie Bunker's Place (CBS sitcom)
cast: Martin Balsam (Murray Klein)
Danielle Brisebois (Teresa Betancourt)
Anne Meara (Veronica Rooney)
Carroll O'Connor (Archie Bunker)
Archies
song: Jingle Jangle (1969)
Sugar, Sugar (1969)
Archimedes: 5 Greek 9 physicist
forte: 4 math
shout: 6 Eureka
tool for ~: 5 lever
archipelago: 4 isls. 5 isles 6 islets 7 islands
Asian: 5 Malay
Baltic: 5 Aland
Indian Ocean ~: 7 Comoros
Pacific: 4 Fiji
__ Archipelago, The: 5 Gulag
architect: 3 Lin, Pei 4 Adam, Nash, Wren 5 Bacon, Hoban, I.M. Pei, maker, Pelli, White 6 artist, Morris, parent, Scopas, Wright 7 builder, creator, founder, Gilbert, Gropius, Johnson, Latrobe, Maya Lin, Olmsted, planner 8 Bulfinch, designer, Saarinen 9 fashioner 10 mastermind, originator, prime mover
British ~: 4 Nash, Wren 6 Morris
Civil Rights Memorial ~: 3 Lin
detail: 4 spec
Finland ~: 5 Aalto
glass pyramid ~: 3 Pei 5 I.M. Pei
Greek ~: 6 Scopas
John Hancock Building ~: 3 Pei 5 I.M. Pei
Kennedy Library: 3 Pei 5 I.M. Pei
measure: 4 sq. ft. 10 square feet
Mile High Center ~: 3 Pei 5 I.M. Pei
neoclassical ~: 4 Adam
org.: 3 AIA
architectural
addition: 3 ell
adornments: 5 putti
arch: 5 ogive
brace: 5 strut
convexity: 7 entasis
crossbeam: 5 trave
decoration: 6 frieze
deg.: 3 MFA
detail: 4 dado, ogee
do ~ work: 6 design
drawing: 4 plan 5 epure
drop: 5 gutta
Gothic ~ feature: 5 gable
moldings: 4 tori
order: 5 Doric, Ionic 10 Corinthian
pier: 4 anta
rib: 6 lierne
school: 7 Bauhaus
style: 5 Tudor 6 Gothic
support: 5 ancon 6 lintel
vault feature: 5 groin
architecture: 5 shape 6 design, make-up 7 science 8 building 9 structure
first name in ~: 4 Eero, Ieoh 5 Eliel
archival: 10 historical
archive: 4 list 5 files 6 annals, museum, record 7 catalog, dossier, records 8 treasury 9 catalogue 10 chronicles, depository
archives: 6 record 8 register 9 reference
archivist: 6 keeper 9 historian
Arch of __: 5 Titus 7 Triumph
archon: 5 ruler
Archway
competitor: *see* cookie manufacturer
Archy
friend: 9 Mehitabel
arc-lamp
gas: 5 xenon
arco: 3 bow 5 bowed
arc-shaped
mark: 5 paren.
arctic: 3 icy 4 cold, cool, wind 5 chill, gelid, nippy, north, polar 6 biting, chilly, frigid, frosty, frozen, wintry 7 glacial, ice-cold, numbing, shivery, wintery 8 freezing
bird: 4 skua, tern 5 brant 6 fulmar 9 gerfalcon, gyrfalcon
bovine: 6 muskox
coat: 5 parka 6 anorak
dweller: 3 Esk. 4 Lapp 5 Inuit 6 Eskimo, Innuit, Inupik
dwelling: 4 iglu 5 igloo
explorer: 3 Rae 4 Ross 5 Davys 7 Barents
explorer's base: 4 Etah
finger: 5 fiord
hazard: 4 berg, cold, floe
hill: 5 pingo
island: 6 Baffin
leave stranded in the ~: 5 ice in
mammal: 6 walrus 9 polar bear
of the ~: 5 polar
position: 4 N. Lat.
sea: 4 Kara 7 Barents
sight: 6 aurora, icecap
surface: 3 ice
trout: 4 char
vehicle: 4 sled 5 kayak, umiak
Arctic __: 3 fox 4 char, seal, tern, Zone 5 daisy, Ocean 6 Circle 7 Current
Arctic Ocean
bay: 6 Baffin
island: 7 Wrangel
river to the ~: 6 Kolyma 7 Pechora 9 Mackenzie 10 Coppermine
Arcturus: 4 star 5 K star
constellation: 6 Boötes
Arden: 3 Eve 4 Dale, John 5 Enoch 6 forest 9 Elizabeth
rival: *see* cosmetic brand
ardency: 4 zeal 6 fervor 10 enthusiasm
Arden, Eve: 7 actress
TV: Our Miss Brooks
Arden, John: 7 British 10 playwright
Ardennes waterway: 4 Oise
ardent: 3 hot 4 agog, avid, fast, keen, true, warm 5 afire, eager, fiery, loyal, ready 6 devout, fervid, fierce, gung-ho, hearty, loving, rah-rah, red-hot, steady, torrid 7 amatory, burning, devoted, earnest, fervent, flaming, glowing, intense, longing, staunch, zealous 8 constant, desirous, faithful, resolute, romantic, spirited, vehement, vigorous 9 allegiant, amatorial, ambitious, emotional, exuberant, heartfelt, steadfast, strenuous 10 hot-blooded, passionate, solicitous
ardently: 4 hard 5 madly 6 keenly 8 heartily 9 fervently, like crazy
Ardmore: 4 city, town
locale: 8 Oklahoma
Ardolino, Emile: 8 director
film: Chances Are (1989)
Dirty Dancing (1987)
Sister Act (1992)
ardor: 4 élan, fire, heat, love, soul, zeal, zest, zing 5 flame, gusto, oomph, verve 6 desire, energy, fervor, spirit 7 avidity, emotion, loyalty, passion 8 devotion, fervency, keenness, lyricism, vitality 9 adoration, affection, eagerness, inner fire, intensity, puppy love 10 enthusiasm, exuberance, fierceness, liveliness
in Tin Pan Alley: 4 pash
arduous: 4 hard 5 harsh, heavy, rocky, rough, steep, stiff, tight, tough 6 rugged, severe, taxing, thorny, trying, uphill 7 hard-won, labored, onerous, operose, painful, serious 8 grueling, tiresome, toilsome 9 ambitious, demanding, difficult, herculean, laborious, murderous, punishing, strenuous 10 burdensome, enervating, exhausting, formidable, oppressive
arduously: 4 hard 8 mightily
are: 5 equal, exist 7 breathe
in French: 4 êtes
in Spanish: 3 son 5 están
not: 4 ain't
Are __ Bromide?: 4 You a
Are __ Lonesome Tonight?: 3 You
Are __ pair?: 3 we a
__ Are: 3 You 7 Chances
area: 3 lot 4 beat, belt, 'hood, land, site, size, turf, ward, zone 5 field,

patch, place, range, scope, sheet, space, sweep, tract **6** domain, extent, locale, métier, milieu, parcel, region, sector, sphere, square **7** acreage, breadth, compass, environ, expanse, grounds, purlieu, purview, quarter, section, stretch, surface, terrain **8** confines, district, dominion, environs, locality, location, plottage, precinct, province, purlieus, vicinage, vicinity **9** bailiwick, enclosure, incidence, largeness, specialty, territory **10** department, discipline, floor space
ender: **3** way
in French: **4** aire
unit: **4** acre, sq. ft., sq. in., sq. mi. **7** hectare **10** square foot, square inch, square mile, square yard
area __: **3** rug **4** code **5** study **7** bombing
__ area: **4** fire, gray, rest **5** focal, relic **6** acting, Broca's, dollar, fringe, graded **7** culture, penalty, special, staging
__ are a few of my favorite...: **5** these
__ a real nowhere man: **3** He's
__ area network: **4** wide **5** local
arear: **3** aft **6** astern
areas: **4** loca, loci
__ a Rebel: **3** He's
areca: **4** palm, tree
__ are called...: **4** Many
__ are for kids!: **4** Trix
__ Are Funny: **6** People
...__ are getting fat, the: **5** geese
__ are Heard, The: **5** Muses
__ Are Love: **3** You
__ are lovely..., The: **5** woods
__ Are My Destiny: **3** You
__ Are My Lucky Star: **3** You
__ Are My Sunshine: **3** You
arena: **3** gym **4** bowl, dome, rink **5** field, realm, scene, space, stage **6** domain, region, sector, sphere **7** ice rink, stadium, theater, theatre **8** bullring, coliseum, province **9** colosseum, palaestra, territory **10** hippodrome
accommodation: **4** seat
section: **4** loge, tier **5** level **10** grandstand
arena __: **7** theater, theatre **8** football
__ Arenas, Chile: **5** Punta
Arendt: **6** Hannah
arenose: **5** sandy
__ Are Not Alone: **3** You
Are not! response: **4** am so **5** am too
Arens: **5** Moshe
Aren't __?: **5** We All
Areopagitica
author: John Milton
__ are red...: **5** Roses
__ Are Ringing: **5** Bells
Ares: **3** god **6** war god
animal sacred to ~: **3** dog **4** boar **7** vulture
daughter: **4** Nike **6** Amazon, Phoebe **9** Hippolyte
equivalent: **4** Mars
parent: **4** Enyo, Hera, Zeus
sister: **4** Eris, Hebe
son: **5** Remus **6** Deimos, Phobus **7** Romulus **8** Diomedes
twin: **4** Eris
__ Are So Beautiful: **3** You
arête: **4** crag **5** ledge, ridge
Aretha: **8** Franklin
music: **4** soul
__ Are There: **3** You
__ Are the Sunshine of My Life: **3** You
__ are the times...: **5** These
Arethusa: **5** nymph **6** Nereid
father: **5** Atlas
Aretino, Pietro: **6** writer **7** Italian
__ a retreat: **4** beat
Are we __?: **5** a pair
Are we having fun __?: **3** yet
Are we there __?: **3** yet
Are We There Yet? (2005 film)
cast: Ice Cube, Nia Long
Are You a Bromide?
author: Gelett Burgess
Are you a man __ mouse?: **3** or a
Are you calling me __?: **5** a liar
Are you for __?: **4** real
Are You Lonesome Tonight? (song)
artist: Donny Osmond, Elvis Presley
Are you sure?: **6** really
arf: **4** bark, woof **6** bowwow
sayer: **5** Sandy
ar follower: **3** ess
Arg.
locale: **5** S. Amer.
neighbor: **3** Bol., Uru.
see also Argentina
argent: **5** metal, white **6** silver **7** silvery
relative: ***see*** white color
Argent
author: Émile Zola
Argentina: **6** nation **7** country
bird: **7** cariama, seriema
city: **5** Jujuy, Lanus, Moron, Salta, Tigre **6** Paraná **7** Córdoba, La Plata, Quilmes, Rosario **9** La Matanza, San Isidro **10** Avellaneda, Corrientes
dance: **5** tango
desert: **10** Patagonian
dictator: **5** Perón
gulf: **8** San Jorge **9** San Matias
Indian: **9** Tehuelche
money: **4** peso **7** austral
mountain: **4** Solo, Toro **5** Cachi, Chani, Galan, Laudo, Negro, Quela **6** Bonete, Juncal, Pissis **7** Palermo, San Juan **8** El Condor, El Muerto, Famatina, Polleras, Tortolas **9** Aconcagua, Antofalla, Incahuasi, Marmolejo, Tupungato **10** Mercedario, Nacimiento, Tres Cruces
musical set in ~: **5** Evita
neighbor: **5** Chile **6** Brazil **7** Bolivia, Uruguay **8** Paraguay
Nobelist in Chemistry: **6** Leloir
Nobelist in Medicine: **7** Houssay
Nobelist in Peace: **5** Lamas **8** Esquivel
org.: **3** OAS
plain: **5** campo, pampa
poet: **6** Storni
port: **7** La Plata
river: **5** Negro
stateman: **9** Sarmiento
tennis pro: **5** Vilas
waterfall: **6** Iguaçu **7** Iguassú
wind: **7** pampero
writer: **6** Borges, Gálvez, Sábato **8** Cortázar **9** Güiraldes, Sarmiento
see also Spanish
argentite: **3** ore **7** mineral **9** silver ore
Argo: **4** boat, ship
captain: **5** Jason
Argolis: **4** gulf
ancient city near ~: **4** Alea
argon: **3** gas **7** element **8** noble gas
like ~: **5** inert
argonaut: **5** shell **8** seashell
Argonaut: **4** Idas **5** Argus, Jason **6** Augeas, Castor **7** Laocoon, Orpheus **8** Heracles
patron: **4** Hera
Argonautica: **4** epic
character: **5** Medea
Argonne Forest river: **5** Aisne
Argos, king of: **8** Adrastos
argosy: **4** boat, brig **5** fleet **6** armada, carack, trader **7** carrack, galleon **8** flotilla, schooner **9** abundance, plenitude **10** brigantine
argot: **4** cant, talk **5** idiom, lingo, slang **6** jargon, patois, patter, tongue **7** dialect **8** language, parlance, shoptalk **10** vernacular
arguable: **4** moot **7** dubious, tenable **9** debatable **10** disputable, reasonable
argue: **4** spat, talk, tiff **5** brawl, claim, clash, fight, plead, scrap **6** appeal, assert, attest, bicker, debate, dicker, differ, evince, haggle, niggle, oppose, reason **7** contend, contest, dispute, dissent, explain, face off, mix it up, protest, quarrel, quibble, suggest, testify, wrangle **8** conflict, disagree, hash over, have at it, indicate, maintain, squabble, vocalize **9** establish, fight over, have words, lock horns, take issue, thrash out **10** controvert, deliberate
against: **5** rebut **6** refute
back: **5** rebut
for: **4** urge **7** justify **8** advocate
into: **7** win over **8** persuade **9** influence, prevail on
arguer: **6** lawyer **8** attorney, polemist **9** apologist, disputant
argument: **3** row **4** beef, feud, flap, fuss, plea, spat, text, tiff **5** brawl, claim, clash, fight, issue, point, proof, run-in, scrap, set-to, theme, topic **6** barney, blowup, breach, debate, hassle, jangle, matter, reason, ruckus, rumpus, strife, theory, thesis **7** discord, dispute, dissent, lawsuit, polemic, premise, quarrel, rhubarb, wrangle **8** conflict, disunity, polemics, question, skirmish, squabble, variance **9** assertion, bickering, encounter, imbroglio, reasoning **10** bone to pick, contention, difference, war of words
closer: **3** QED
side: **3** con, for, pro **7** against
starter: **7** counter
argumentation: **5** logic **6** reason
argumentative: **6** ornery **7** hostile **8** fighting, forensic **9** bellicose, litigious **10** pugnacious
arguments
hear ~: **5** judge
like some ~: **5** sound **6** heated
Argus: **3** dog **5** giant
Argus-eyed: **5** alert
argyle: **4** hose, sock **7** hosiery
Ari: **6** Meyers **7** Onassis
Jackie, to ~: **4** wife
aria: **3** air **4** solo, song, tune **5** music **6** melody
ace: **4** diva
aria da __: **4** capo
Ariadne
father: **5** Minos
lover: **7** Theseus **8** Dionysus
Ariadne __ Naxos: **3** auf
Arial: **4** font **8** typeface
-arian cousin: **3** -ist, -ite, -nik **4** -ster
Arias: **5** Jimmy, Oscar
__ Arias Sanchez: **5** Oscar
arid: **3** dry **4** bare, drab, dull, flat, sere **5** baked, dusty, stale, unwet, vapid **6** barren, boring, desert, dreary, jejune, torrid **7** bone-dry, dried up, humdrum, insipid, parched, parches, Saharan, sapless, tedious, thirsty **8** dried out, droughty, lifeless, pedantic, rainless **9** anhydrous, colorless, juiceless, ponderous, unfertile, waterless, wearisome **10** dehydrated, desertlike, lackluster, pedantical, spiritless, unanimated, uninspired
area: **6** desert
combining form: **3** xer- **4** xero-
plateau: **4** puna
__ a ride: **3** bum **5** thumb
aridity: **5** waste **6** desert **7** dryness **8** jejunity **9** sterility **10** insipidity
Arie: **8** Luyendyk
ariel: **7** gazelle **8** antelope
relative: ***see*** antelope
Ariel: **4** moon **6** Durant, Sharon **7** Dorfman
author: André Maurois, Sylvia Plath
planet: **6** Uranus
Aries: **3** car, ram **4** auto, sign **5** Dodge **7** sky sign **8** fire sign **10** automobile
month: **3** Apr., Mar. **5** April, March
predecessor: **6** Pisces
successor: **6** Taurus
arietta: **4** solo **5** music
arigato: **6** thanks **8** Japanese
__ arigato: **4** domo
aright: **2** OK **4** duly, okay, okeh, okey, well **5** aptly, fitly, truly **6** justly **7** exactly, in order **8** properly, suitably, worthily **9** correctly **10** accurately
__ a right: **4** hang
Arikara: **3** Ree **5** tribe **6** Indian **7** Amerind
aril: **4** husk **8** pericarp **10** integument
Arion: **5** horse
father: **8** Poseidon
lifesaver: **4** lyre
mother: **4** Gaea **7** Demeter
ariose: **7** melodic, musical, tuneful **8** songlike
Ariosto, Lodovico: **4** poet **7** Italian
patron: **4** Este
work: Orlando Furioso
arise: **4** dawn, go up, leap, lift, rise, soar, stem, wake **5** awake, begin, bob up, climb, ensue, get up, occur, pop up, rebel, stand, start,

surge, waken 6 appear, ascend, awaken, come up, crop up, emerge, grow up, happen, loom up, move up, result, spring, wake up 7 develop, emanate, proceed, roll out, stand up, surface, turn out 8 commence, escalate, flow from, spring up 9 come about, grow out of, originate, transpire 10 come to mind, hit the deck
(from): 4 flow, stem 5 ensue, issue 6 derive, follow, result 7 emanate, proceed
unexpectedly: 5 bob up, pop up
arisen: 2 up 6 sprung 8 out of bed 10 on one's feet
not ~: 4 abed
arista: 3 awn 5 beard 7 bristle
Aristarchus: 5 Greek 10 astronomer
home: 5 Samos
Aristide: 6 Briand 7 Maillol 9 Boucicaut
realm: 5 Haiti
see also French
aristo: 3 nob 5 elite 9 patrician 10 upper class, upper crust
aristocracy: 5 elite 6 gentry 7 peerage, society 8 nobility
aristocrat: 4 dame, lord, peer 5 baron, noble 8 nobleman 9 authority, blueblood, patrician 10 noblewoman
aristocratic: 5 aloof, elite, noble, royal 7 courtly, elegant, haughty, refined 8 highborn, ladylike, snobbish, well-born, well-bred 9 patrician 10 upper-class
Ariston
son: 5 Plato
Aristophanes: 5 Greek 10 playwright
work: The Birds
The Clouds
The Frogs
The Knights
Plutus
Aristos, The
author: John Fowles
Aristotelian __: 5 logic
Aristotle: 5 Greek 7 Onassis 11 philosopher
teacher: 5 Plato
arithmetic: 4 math 8 addition, figuring 9 reckoning 10 estimation
device: 6 abacus 10 calculator
do ~: 3 add, sum 6 cipher, divide, figure 8 multiply, subtract
figure: 3 sum 6 addend 7 divisor, minuend, product 8 dividend, quotient 10 difference, subtrahend
sign: 4 plus 5 minus
term: 3 LCD
arithmetic __: 4 mean 6 series
__ a River: 5 Cry Me
Arizona: 5 state
city: 4 Mesa, Yuma 5 Tempe, Tubac 6 Bisbee, Peoria, Sedona, Tucson 7 Gilbert, Kingman, Nogales, Phoenix, Sun City, Winslow 8 Avondale, Carefree, Chandler, Glendale, Goodyear, Prescott, Surprise 9 Flagstaff, Oro Valley 10 Casa Grande, Scottsdale
conference: 6 Pac-Ten
county: 4 Yuma
desert: 7 Sonoran 10 Chihuahuan
elevation: 4 mesa
fish: 9 spikedace
Indian: 4 Hopi, Pima, Tewa, Yuma 5 Piute 6 Mohave, Mojave, Navaho, Navajo, Paiute, Papago, Pueblo 7 Yavapai 8 Maricopa 9 Havasupai
much of ~: 6 desert
national park: 7 Saguaro
neighbor: 3 Cal., Nev. 4 Colo., N. Mex., Utah 5 Calif. 6 Mexico, Nevada 8 Colorado 9 New Mexico 10 California
observatory: 6 Lowell
once: 3 ter. 4 terr. 9 territory
pro team: 6 D-Backs 9 Cardinals
river: 4 Gila, Salt
state amphibian: 8 tree frog
state bird: 10 cactus wren
state fish: 5 trout
state gemstone: 9 turquoise
state mammal: 8 ringtail
state neckwear: 7 bola tie
state tree: 9 palo verde
Arizona Ames
author: Zane Grey
Arizona Clan
author: Zane Grey
Arizona Republic: 5 paper 9 newspaper
locale: 7 Phoenix
Arizona State
athletes: 9 Sun Devils
conference: 6 Pac-Ten
locale: 5 Tempe
ark: 4 boat 5 barge 6 asylum 8 flatboat
builder: 4 Noah
group: 3 duo, two 4 pair
landing site: 6 Ararat
passenger: 3 Ham 4 Shem 7 Japheth
scroll in an ~: 4 Tora 5 Torah
Ark __ Covenant: 5 of the
Ark.
see Arkansas
__ Ark: 4 Holy 5 Noah's 7 Joan Van
Arkansas: 5 river, state
city: 4 Mena 6 Benton, Conway, Rogers 8 El Dorado, Sherwood 9 Fort Smith, Jonesboro, Paragould, Pine Bluff, Texarkana 10 Hot Springs, Little Rock, Springdale
city on the ~: 4 Mena 5 Tulsa 10 Little Rock
conference: 3 SEC
mountains: 6 Ozarks
national forest: 5 Ozark
national park: 10 Hot Springs
neighbor: 5 Texas 8 Missouri, Oklahoma 9 Louisiana, Tennessee
River locale: 6 Kansas 8 Colorado, Oklahoma
river to the ~: 8 Canadian, Cimarron
state beverage: 4 milk
state gem: 7 diamond
state insect: 8 honeybee
state instrument: 6 fiddle
state mineral: 7 bauxite
state tree: 4 pine
Arkansas State athletes: 7 Indians
Arkin, Adam: 5 actor
father: 4 Alan
TV: Chicago Hope
Arkin, Alan: 5 actor
film: Catch-22 (1970)
Get Smart (2008)
Glengarry Glen Ross (1992)
Grosse Pointe Blank (1997)
Havana (1990)
Indian Summer (1993)
The In-Laws (1979)
Jakob the Liar (1999)
Last of the Red Hot Lovers (1972)
Little Miss Sunshine (2006, AA)
Little Murders (1971)
Marley & Me (2008)
Popi (1969)
The Rocketeer (1991)
The Seven-Per-Cent Solution (1976)
Slums of Beverly Hills (1998)
Thirteen Conversations About One Thing (2001)
Wait Until Dark (1967)
Ark. neighbor: 3 Tex. 4 Miss, Okla., Tenn.
Arky: 7 Vaughan
Arledge: 5 Roone
Arleen: 6 Sorkin
Arlen: 6 Harold 7 Michael, Richard, Specter
Arlene: 4 Dahl 7 Francis, Golonka
Arlen, Harold: 8 composer
collaborator: 7 Harburg, Koehler
song: Ac-cent-tchu-ate the Positive
Any Place I Hang My Hat Is Home
Between the Devil and the Deep Blue Sea
Blues in the Night
Come Rain or Come Shine
Get Happy
If I Only Had a Brain
I Gotta Right to Sing the Blues
I Love a Parade
It's Only a Paper Moon
I've Got the World on a String
Let's Fall in Love
Lydia, the Tattooed Lady
The Man That Got Away
One for My Baby
Over the Rainbow
Stormy Weather
That Old Black Magic
This Time the Dream's on Me
We're Off to See the Wizard
Arlen, Michael: 6 writer 7 British
work: The Green Hat
Arles: 4 city, town
locale: 6 France
neighbor: 5 Nîmes
river: 5 Rhone
Arli$$ (HBO sitcom)
cast: Robert Wuhl (Arliss Michaels)
Arlington: 4 city, town
locale: 5 Texas 8 Virginia
Arlington __, IL: 3 Hts.
Arlington Heights: 4 city, town
locale: 8 Illinois
__ Arlington Robinson: 5 Edwin
Arliss: 6 George, Howard
Arliss, George: 5 actor
film: Disraeli (1929, AA)
House of Rothschild (1934)
Arlo: 7 Guthrie
to Woody: 3 son
arm: 3 bay, fit, rig 4 cove, limb, load, unit, wing 5 annex, bough, crank, equip, power, rifle 6 branch, cannon, member, musket, outfit, supply, weapon 7 estuary, fortify, officer, prepare, shotgun 8 accouter, accoutre, division, embattle, howitzer, offshoot, revolver, tentacle 9 affiliate, appendage, extension, extremity, flintlock 10 department, militarize, six-shooter
an ~ and a leg: 4 dear, high 5 pricy, steep 6 costly, pricey 7 ruinous 9 expensive 10 exorbitant
band: 8 bracelet
bone: 4 ulna 6 radius 7 humerus
bones: 5 radii
builder: 6 chin-up
combining form: 6 brachi- 7 brachio-
ender: 3 ory, pit 4 hole, load, rest 5 chair
good right ~: 8 backbone, linchpin, mainstay
in French: 4 bras
joint: 5 elbow, wrist
muscle: 6 biceps 7 triceps
of an ~ bone: 5 ulnar
opposite: 3 leg
put the ~ on: 5 run in 9 shake down
shot in the ~: 4 lift 5 boost, tonic 8 pick-me-up, stimulus 9 stimulant
starter: 4 fire, fore, side, tone, yard
strong ~: 5 might 9 authority
twist one's ~: 4 make 5 force 6 coerce, compel, lean on 8 browbeat, bulldoze, pressure 10 bear down on
__ arm: 3 air 4 side, tone 5 small, upper 6 pickup, rocker, spiral
Arm & __: 6 Hammer
armada: 4 navy 5 boats, fleet, ships 6 argosy 8 flotilla, sea power, warships
__ Armada: 7 Spanish
armadas, of: 5 naval
armadillo: 4 apar, peba, tatu 5 apara, tatou 6 animal, mammal, peludo 7 tatuasu
like an ~: 5 scaly
plate: 5 scute
plates: 5 scuta
protection: 5 armor
Armageddon
author: Leon Uris
Armageddon (1998 film)
cast: Ben Affleck, Billy Bob Thornton, Liv Tyler, Bruce Willis
director: Michael Bay
Armageddon It (1988 song)
artist: Def Leppard
Armageddon nation: 3 Gog 5 Magog
Armah, Ayi Kwei: 6 writer 8 Ghanaian
armament: 6 shield 8 ordnance
armaments: 8 materiel, ordnance 9 munitions 10 ammunition, protection
Armand: 6 Hammer 7 Assante 8 Salacrou
__ Armand, The: 7 Vampire
Armani: 7 Giorgio 8 designer
rival: 5 Blass, Klein 6 Lauren 7 Versace

Armatrading: 4 Joan
Arma virumque ___: 4 cano
armed: 6 girded, loaded 7 packing 8 carrying, equipped, supplied 9 fitted out, fortified, outfitted 10 accoutered
  conflict: 6 battle, hot war
  service: 3 USA, USN 4 army, navy, USAF, USMC 7 marines 8 air force, military
armed ___: 6 forces 7 robbery
___-armed bandit: 3 one
armed to the ___: 5 teeth
Armen: 3 Kay
Armendariz, Pedro: 5 actor
Armenia: 6 nation 7 country
  capital: 7 Yerevan
  city: 6 Erevan, Erivan, Gyumri 7 Yerevan 8 Vanadzor
  mountain: 7 Aragats
  neighbor: 4 Iran 6 Turkey 7 Georgia 10 Azerbaijan
  once: 3 SSR
Armenian: 8 language
Armey: 4 Dick
armful: 3 lot 4 load 6 plenty
Arm & Hammer: 9 detergent 10 baking soda, toothpaste
  detergent alternative: *see* detergent
  toothpaste alternative: *see* toothpaste
Armies of the Night, The
  author: Norman Mailer
armistice: 5 peace, truce 6 treaty 9 ceasefire, white flag 10 suspension
Armistice ___: 3 Day
armless
  combining form: 5 anopi- 6 anoplo-
  couch: 5 divan
  garment: 4 vest
  statue: 5 Venus
armlet: 4 cove 6 bangle 7 jewelry 8 bracelet
___ arm of the law: 4 long
armoire
  alternative: 6 closet
armor: 5 guard 6 shield, tuille 7 panoply 8 chamfron, plastron 9 brassardo, nosepiece, safeguard 10 protection
  breaker: 4 mace
  chink in one's ~: 8 weakness
  cover with ~: 5 plate
  defect: 5 chink
  elbow ~: 6 couter
  equine ~: 4 bard 5 barde
  leather ~: 6 lorica
  leg ~: 6 greave
  part: 5 fauld, visor, vizor
  piece: 5 culet 6 helmet
  plate: 4 tace 5 tasse
  shin ~: 6 greave
  shirt: 7 hauberk
  thigh ~: 5 cuish 6 cuisse
  throat ~: 6 gorget
  wearer: 6 knight
armor ___: 5 plate 7 plating
armor-___: 4 clad 6 plated
___ armor: 4 soft 5 plate 6 Gothic, parade
Armor ___: 3 All
armored ___: 3 car 4 rope 5 cable, scale
armored-car job: 5 heist
armory: 5 depot 7 arsenal, gun room 8 magazine
  supply: 4 ammo
Armour: 5 Tommy 6 hot dog 7 Richard
  alternative: 5 Kahn's 8 Ball Park 10 Oscar Mayer
Armour, Tommy: 6 golfer
armpit: 6 axilla
arms: 4 guns, ordn. 6 rifles, sabers, swords 7 pistols, weapons 8 bayonets, materiel, ordnance, shotguns, weaponry 9 artillery, firepower, munitions
  call to ~: 5 alert, rally 6 alarum 7 recruit 8 mobilize
  clash of ~: 3 war 7 warfare
  coat of ~: 4 seal 6 emblem 7 insigne 8 insignia
  hold in one's ~: 6 cradle
  lay down ~: 5 yield 6 submit
  position: 6 akimbo
  take in one's ~: 3 hug
  take up ~: 3 war 4 rise 5 arise, rebel 6 revolt
  up in ~: 4 ired 5 angry, irate 6 roused 7 excited, furious, keyed-up 8 incensed, militant 9 indignant, wrought up
  with ~ held low, in ballet: 5 en bas
  with open ~: 6 warmly 8 friendly 9 cordially 10 graciously
arms ___: 4 race 6 akimbo 7 control
arm's
  at ~ length: 5 aloof
  keep at ~ length: 6 rebuff 7 neglect, ward off
arm's-___: 6 length
___ arms: 4 port, up in 5 order 7 present
___-arms: 5 man-at
Arms and the man ___: 5 I sing
Arms and the Man: 4 play
  author: George Bernard Shaw
armstand: 4 dive
Armstrong: 2 R.G. 4 Bess, Neil, Otis 5 Edwin, Henry, Lance, Louis 6 Robert
___ Armstrong Custer: 6 George
Armstrong, Louis: 9 trumpeter
  genre: 4 jazz
  nickname: 4 Pops 7 Satchmo
  song: Hello, Dolly! (1964)
    What a Wonderful World (1988)
Armstrong, Neil: 9 astronaut
  program: 6 Apollo
  transport: 3 LEM 5 Eagle
Armstrong, Robert: 5 actor
  film: King Kong (1933)
    Mighty Joe Young (1949)
    The Son of Kong (1933)
arm-twist: 4 coax 6 coerce
arm-twisting: 6 duress
army: 3 ant, mob 4 host 5 array, corps, crowd, flock, force, horde, squad, swarm, troop 6 cohort, detail, legion, myriad, scores, throng, troops 7 brigade, cavalry, legions, platoon 8 division, infantry, military, regiment, soldiers 9 battalion, multitude 10 detachment
  address: 3 sir
  an ~ of: 6 divers, myriad, umteen, untold 7 copious, profuse, umpteen 8 abundant, manifold, numerous, umpsteen 9 bountiful, countless, quite a few
  bed: 3 cot
  British ~ orderly: 6 batman
  coll. ~ program: 4 ROTC
  command: 5 march 6 at ease 8 left face 9 about face, attention, right face
  cops: 3 MPs
  doc: 5 medic
  E-2: 3 pvt.
  E-6: 4 SSgt.
  E-7: 3 SFC
  food: 3 MRE 4 chow, mess
  glitch: 5 snafu
  group: 3 rgt., trp. 4 regt., unit 5 troop 7 brigade 8 infantry, regiment 12 division unit
  helicopter: 6 Apache
  housing for singles: 3 BOQ
  instructional facility (abbr.): 3 OTC, OTS
  job: 5 recon
  join the ~: 5 serve 6 enlist
  leaders: 5 brass
  magazine: 4 Yank
  mail addr.: 3 APO, FPO
  medal: 3 DSC
  member: 3 ant 7 soldier
  moving ~: 6 convoy
  need: 4 ammo
  officer: 3 col., gen., maj. 4 capt. 5 lieut., major 7 captain, colonel, general
  post: 4 base, fort
  rank: 3 Col., gen., maj., NCO, PFC, SFC, sgt. 4 SSgt. 5 lieut., lt. col. 7 private 8 corporal, sergeant
  refusal: 5 no sir
  Roman ~: 6 legion
  rookie: 3 rct. 7 recruit
  shelter: 8 barracks
  stay in the ~: 4 reup
  training site: 3 OCS, OTS
  truant: 4 AWOL
  vehicle: 4 jeep, tank 6 amtrac 7 amtrack
  wear: 3 ODs 5 khaki 6 khakis
  woman: 3 WAC 4 WAAC
  WWI ~: 3 AEF
  see also G.I., military
army ___: 3 ant 4 brat 5 corps
army-___ store: 4 navy
Army: 7 Archerd
  academy: 4 USMA 9 West Point
  athletes: 6 Cadets
  competitor: 4 Navy
___ Army: 3 Red 4 Blue 5 Bonus 6 Arnie's 7 Regular
army battle, name meaning: 6 Harvey
___ army knife: 5 Swiss
army-navy ___: 5 store
___ Army of the Republic: 5 Grand
___ Army Plaza: 5 Grand
Arn
  domain: 3 Orr
  father: Prince Valiant
  mother: Aleta
Arna: 8 Bontemps
Arnaz: 4 Desi 5 Lucie
Arnaz, Desi
  spouse: Lucille Ball
Arnaz, Lucie
  spouse: Laurence Luckinbill
Arndt, Felix
  tune: 4 Nola
Arne: 5 nymph 6 Thomas 7 Carlson 8 Nordheim, Tiselius 9 Andersson
  parent: 4 Thea 6 Aeolus
Arness: 5 James
  brother: Peter Graves
  costar: 5 Blake, Stone 6 Weaver
Arne, Thomas: 7 British 8 composer
  alma mater: 4 Eton
  work: Abel
    Alfred
    Artaxerxes
    Britannia
    Caractacus
    Comus
    Dido and Aeneas
    Eliza
    The Judgment of Paris
    Judith
    Olimpiade
    Opera of Operas
    Rosamond
    Rule Britannia
    Zara
Arngrim: 6 Alison
Arnhem: 4 city, town
  locale: 7 Holland
  neighbor: 3 Ede
Arnie: 6 Herber, Morton, Palmer
Arnie's ___: 4 Army
Arno: 3 Sig 4 Holz 5 Peter, river 7 Penzias
  city on the ~: 4 Pisa 8 Florence
  River locale: 5 Italy
Arnold: 3 Bax, Hap, Tom 4 city, Eddy, Jack, Moss, town 5 Stang, Zweig 6 Edward, Palmer, Wesker 7 Bennett, Matthew, Toynbee 8 Benedict 9 Rothstein 10 Schoenberg
  locale: 8 Maryland, Missouri
  mother-in-law: 6 Eunice
Arnold ___ Schwarzenegger: 5 Alois
Arnold, Benedict: 7 traitor 8 recreant, turncoat
Arnold, Matthew: 4 poet 7 British
  work: Dover Beach
    Empedocles on Etna
    The Scholar-Gipsy
    Thyrsis
Arnold, Tom
  spouse: Roseanne
aroar: 4 loud 5 noisy 8 shouting 9 bellowing, clamorous 10 boisterous, thundering, tumultuous
___ a Rock: 3 I Am 4 Like
___ a Rolling Stone: 4 Like
aroma: 4 nose, odor, tang, waft 5 scent, smell, spice, whiff 6 breath 7 bouquet, incense, perfume 9 emanation, fragrance, redolence 10 atmosphere
  faint ~: 5 sniff, whiff
  in Britain: 5 odour
aromatic: 5 balmy, spicy, sweet 6 spicey 7 odorous, pungent, scented 8 fragrant, perfumed, redolent 9 ambrosial
  compound: 5 ester
  flavoring: 5 anise
  herb: 4 mint, nard, sage 5 myrrh, tansy, thyme 6 fennel, hyssop
  hydrocarbon: 5 arene
  oil: 6 bay rum
  ointment: 4 balm 6 balsam
  radical: 4 aryl
  root: 5 orris
  seed: 5 cumin

tree: 4 pine 5 cedar 8 bayberry, rosewood
___-A-Roni: 4 Rice
Aron's love: 4 Abra
Aroostook: 5 river
locale: 5 Maine
arose: 5 got up 6 went up 7 stood up 9 levitated
around: 4 near 5 about, circa, round 6 in town, living, nearby 7 all over, close by, roughly 9 in the area, somewhere 10 more or less
combining form: 4 peri- 6 circum-
prefix: 3 epi-
starter: 3 run 4 turn, wrap
___ around: 3 bat, bum, end, get, pal, sit 4 been, come, fool, hang, kick, loaf, mess, muck, nose, push, shop, talk, toss 5 bring, crowd, horse, knock, stick, up and
___-around: 3 all 4 roll
___ Around: 4 I Get, Jump, Shop 5 I'll Be
around the ___: 4 bend 5 clock
___ Around the Clock: 4 Rock
___ around the collar: 4 ring
___ Around the Corner, The: 4 Shop
Around the Fish
painter: Paul Klee
.... ___ around the neck: 4 a hug
___-around-the-rosey: 4 ring
Around the Way Girl (1991 song)
artist: LL Cool J
Around the World in 72 Days
author: Nellie Bly
Around the World in Eighty Days: 4 film 5 novel
author: Jules Verne
cast: Cantinflas, Shirley MacLaine, Robert Morley, David Niven
director: Michael Anderson
hero: 4 Fogg 7 Phileas
___ around to: 3 get
___ Around Us, The: 3 Sea
arouse: 3 get, jog 4 fire, goad, poke, spur, stir, wake, whet 5 alarm, alert, anger, awake, drive, evoke, flush, hop up, impel, liven, pique, rally, rouse, spark, start, waken 6 awaken, bestir, buck up, elicit, entice, excite, fillip, fire up, foment, foster, heat up, hype up, incite, kindle, recall, rile up, stir up, thrill, turn on, wake up, whip up, work up 7 actuate, agitate, animate, disturb, enflame, enliven, fortify, hearten, impress, inflame, inspire, provoke, quicken 8 embolden, engender, enkindle, enspirit, imbolden, inspirit, interest, motivate, psyche up, summon up, vitalize 9 electrify, enhearten, galvanize, impassion, instigate, recollect, stimulate, titillate 10 get excited, intoxicate
aroused: 6 ablaze 7 violent 8 inspired 10 passionate
arow: 7 in a line, lined up 8 queued up
Arp: 4 Hans, Jean
contemporary: 6 Calder
genre: 4 Dada
Arpel: 6 Adrien
Arp, Hans: 6 artist 7 painter 8 sculptor
homeland: 6 France
Arp, Jean: 6 artist 7 painter 8 sculptor
homeland: 6 France
Arquette: 5 Cliff, David 6 Alexis 7 Rosanna 8 Patricia
Arquette, David
spouse: Courteney Cox
Arquette, Patricia
spouse: Nicolas Cage, Jane, Thomas
arr.
opposite: 3 dep.
arraign: 3 tax 6 accuse, charge, indict 9 inculpate, prosecute
arraignment: 5 trial 7 lawsuit
offering: 4 bail, plea
Arraignment of Paris, The
author: George Peele
Arran: 4 isle 6 island
locale: 8 Scotland
arrange: 2 do 3 fix, lay, set 4 do up, edit, file, form, pose, rank, sort 5 align, aline, drape, fix up, frame, group, index, order, place, ready, set up, stack, stage 6 adjust, assort, codify, deploy, design, devise, direct, divide, format, get set, lay out, line up, settle, spread, tailor, tidy up, wangle 7 compile, display, dispose, iron out, marshal, prepare, work out 8 classify, contrive, engineer, graduate, organize, position, regulate, schedule, spruce up, tabulate 9 establish, make plans, make ready, methodize, negotiate, reconcile 10 pigeonhole
for: 4 book
arranged: 3 set 5 ready 6 packed 7 regular 8 prepared
carefully ~: 4 neat, tidy
arrangement: 3 set, sys. 4 deal, form, syst. 5 array, order, setup 6 design, format, layout, lineup, scheme, series, system 7 display, pattern 8 contract, covenant, grouping, ordering, sequence 9 provision, rendition, structure
combining form: 3 tax- 4 -nomy, taxi-, taxo-, -taxy 5 -taxis
flower ~: 4 posy 5 spray 7 nosegay
arrangements: 5 plans 10 groundwork, provisions
make ~: 4 plan
arrant: 4 rank 5 sheer, utter 6 brazen 7 blatant, extreme, glaring 8 flagrant, impudent, outright, thorough 9 barefaced, downright, itinerant, notorious, out-and-out, shameless
arras: 7 drapery 8 tapestry
spot: 4 wall
Arras: 4 city, town
locale: 6 France
Arrau, Claudio: 7 Chilean, pianist
array: 3 lot, rig, set 4 army, deck, duds, garb, gear, host, rank, show, sort, trim, vest 5 adorn, align, aline, batch, bunch, crowd, drape, dress, equip, field, getup, order, range, stock 6 attire, bedeck, bundle, clothe, dude up, finery, fit out, format, lineup, matrix, muster, outfit, parade, series, spread, suit up, tog out 7 apparel, battery, bedrape, clothes, cluster, deck out, display, dispose, dress up, exhibit, furnish, marshal, panoply, pattern, threads, variety 8 beautify, clothing, decorate, ensemble, garments, glad rags, organize, ornament, sequence, showcase 9 amassment, cavalcade, embellish, glamorize, methodize 10 assortment, collection, cumulation, exhibition, procession, Sunday best
arrayed: 4 clad
arrears: 4 debt 6 red ink 7 deficit 8 lateness 9 liability, shortfall 10 obligation
be in ~: 3 owe
in ~: 3 due 6 behind, unpaid 9 unsettled
arrest: 3 bag, fix, get, nab, nip 4 book, bust, cuff, grab, grip, halt, hold, hook, jail, nail, raid, slow, snag, stay, stem, stop, take 5 abate, abort, block, catch, check, pinch, rivet, run in, seize, snare, stall 6 absorb, collar, detain, engage, freeze, haul in, hinder, pick up, pull in, retard, stanch 7 capture, control, custody, engross, inhibit, jailing, prevent, refrain, round up, staunch, suspend 8 blockage, hold back, imprison, interest, intermit, obstruct, paralyse, paralyze, restrain, restrict, shut down, slowdown, stalling, stoppage, suppress, transfix 9 apprehend, cessation, detention, extradite, fascinate, frustrate, intercept, interrupt, restraint, stalemate 10 constraint, internment, prevention, put a stop to, suspension
don't ~: 5 let go
under ~: 6 in jail
___ arrest: 5 false, house
arrested: 5 ran in 6 in jail
Arrested Development offering: 3 rap
arresting: 5 lofty 6 marked 7 salient, unusual 8 dazzling, exciting, magnetic, striking, stunning 9 absorbing, prominent 10 commanding, impressive, magnetical, noteworthy, noticeable, remarkable
Arrid: 9 deodorant
alternative: *see* deodorant
___ 'Arris Goes to Paris: 3 Mrs.
arrival: 4 mail 6 advent, coming, influx, parcel 7 package, receipt 8 delivery, entrance, shipment 9 accession, passenger 10 appearance, homecoming
recent ~: 6 infant 8 newcomer
arrive: 4 come, go in, land, show 5 debut, enter, get in, light, pop in, reach, set in, visit 6 alight, appear, blow in, drop in, edge in, fall in, happen, make it, mature, pull in, pull up, roll in, roll up, show up, sign in, spring, thrive, turn up, walk in 7 barge in, check in, clock in, deplane, fetch up, hit town, prosper, punch in, succeed, turn out, weigh in 8 breeze in, dismount, get there, go ashore, hit it big, make good 9 disembark, make it big, touch down 10 drop anchor
at: 3 fix, hit 4 find 5 get to, infer, reach 6 attain, derive
at, as a solution: 5 hit on
back: 6 return
by air: 5 fly in
unexpectedly: 5 pop in
arrivederci: 3 bye 4 ciao, ta-ta 5 aloha 6 bye-bye, so long 7 goodbye, Italian 8 farewell
Arrivederci, ___: 4 Roma
arrived, recently: 3 new 6 just in
arriving: 3 due
arriviste: 5 yahoo 7 parvenu, upstart, wannabe 9 vulgarian
arrogance: 3 ego 4 airs, gall 5 brass, cheek, crust, nerve, pride, scorn 6 hubris, hutzpa, hybris, vanity 7 bluster, chutzpa, conceit, disdain, egotism, hauteur, hutzpah, license, swagger 8 audacity, chutzpah 9 aloofness, assurance, insolence, loftiness, pomposity 10 assumption, effrontery, pretension
arrogant: 3 big 4 smug, vain 5 bossy, cocky, lofty, proud 6 cheeky, lordly, snooty 7 fustian, haughty, pompous, stuck-up 8 assuming, boastful, cavalier, cocksure, dogmatic, gloating, snobbish, superior 9 audacious, big-headed, conceited, egotistic, hubristic, imperious, sarcastic 10 autocratic, big-talking, disdainful, dogmatical, hoity-toity, swaggering
one: 6 egoist
arrogate: 4 take 5 claim, seize, usurp 6 assume 7 preempt, receive 10 commandeer, confiscate, plagiarize
arrogation: 10 usurpation
arrow: 4 bolt 6 cursor, marker, weapon 7 missile, pointer, Sagitta 10 projectile, street sign
combining form: 3 tox- 4 toxi-, toxo-
crossbow ~: 4 bolt
desktop ~: 6 cursor
ender: 4 head, root
group: 5 sheaf
launcher: 3 bow
like an ~: 6 linear, unbent 7 unbowed 8 straight 10 unswerving
maker: 5 brave 6 Indian 8 fletcher
notch: 4 nock
part: 5 notch, shaft
poison: 4 inee, upas 5 urare 6 antiar, curara, curare
straight as an ~: 8 orthodox
Arrow: 5 shirt
competitor: 4 Izod 8 Hathaway 9 Van Heusen
___ Arrow: 5 Time's 6 Broken, Pierce
arrowhead: 5 plant 6 flower
makings: 5 flint
part: 4 barb
shape an ~: 4 knap
Arrowhead: 5 water
alternative: 4 Naya 5 Evian 7 Perrier 8 Aquafina
Arrowrock Dam
locale: 5 Idaho
river: 5 Boise
arrows'
partner: 6 slings
___ arrows: 4 love 6 Cupid's
Arrowsmith
author: Sinclair Lewis
character: 3 Fox 5 Leora, Tozer 6 Martin 8 Madeline
arrowsmith, name meaning: 8 Fletcher
arroyo: 4 wadi, wady 5 cañon, gorge, gulch, gully 6 canyon, coulee, gulley, ravine, valley 7 channel
arroz con ___: 5 pollo

ars __ artis: 6 gratia
ars __, vita brevis: 5 longa
Ars __: 4 Nova 7 Antiqua, Poetica
Ars Amatoria
poet: 4 Ovid
arsenal: 5 store 6 armory 8 magazine 9 stockpile 10 depository, repository, storehouse
stock: 4 ammo, arms, guns 8 ordnance
arsenic: 5 metal 7 element
ore: 7 realgar
Arsenic and Old Lace (1944 film)
cast: Cary Grant, Priscilla Lane, Raymond Massey
director: Frank Capra
role: 4 Abby 5 Gibbs, O'Hara, Teddy 6 Elaine, Martha, Rooney 8 Brewster, Mortimer
Arsenio: 4 Hall
buddy: 5 Eddie
ars gratia __: 5 artis
arsis: 6 upbeat
ars longa, __ brevis: 4 vita
arson: 5 crime 6 felony 8 torching, torch job 9 pyromania
arsonist: 4 pyro 5 felon, match, torch 6 burner 7 firebug 10 incendiary, pyromaniac
Ars Poetica
author: Horace
art: 3 oil 4 oils, wile 5 busts, craft, dance, guile, knack, mural, skill, trick, wiles 6 ballet, canvas, deceit, medium, mobile, murals, poetry, sketch 7 carving, collage, cunning, etching, finesse, gouache, ikebana, know-how, mastery, picture, pottery, science, slyness, theater, theatre 8 canvases, facility, juggling, ornament, painting, pictures, portrait, trickery, wiliness 9 canniness, composing, dexterity, duplicity, expertise, ingenuity, landscape, paintings, sculpture, showpiece, technique 10 adroitness, astuteness, caricature, cleverness, craftiness, creativity, livelihood, profession, sculptures, virtuosity, watercolor
black ~: 5 magic 7 sorcery 10 necromancy, witchcraft
combining form: 4 -urgy 6 techno-
deg.: 3 BFA, MFA
ender: 3 ist 4 work
figure: 4 nude
gallery: 5 salon
gum: 6 eraser
hardly fine ~: 6 kitsch
in Italian: 4 arte
in Latin: 3 ars
love of fine ~: 5 vertu, virtu
martial ~: 4 judo 5 kendo, taebo, wushu 6 aikido, karate, kung fu, t'ai chi 7 jujitsu 9 tae kwon do
medium: 3 ink 4 oils 10 watercolor
movement prefix: 3 neo
pens: 5 styli
performance ~: 4 mime
print: 4 lith. 5 litho 10 lithograph
stand: 5 easel
state of the ~: 6 latest
studio: 4 loft 7 atelier
style: 4 Dada, Deco 5 genre 6 Ashcan, Cubism 7 Nouveau
suffix: 4 -ship
work of ~: 5 litho, mural, print 6 fresco 7 drawing, etching 8 painting, pastiche 10 lithograph
work with ~: 6 curate 7 restore
art __: 4 deco, film, form, rock, song 5 glass, house, salon, union 6 editor, lining, runner 7 nouveau, theater, theatre
__ art: 3 pop 4 body, cave, clip, fine, folk, junk, land, line 5 black, earth, found, tramp, video 6 gentle 7 concept, kinetic, minimal, optical, plastic
Art: 4 Wall 5 Shell, Tatum, Ulene 6 Blakey, Carney, Pepper, Rooney, Sansom 7 Donovan, Fleming, Shamsky, Stevens 8 Buchwald 9 Garfunkel 10 Linkletter
Art __: 4 Deco 7 Nouveau
Art __, The: 5 of War
Art __ Trophy: 4 Ross
Artaxerxes
composer: Thomas Arne
foe: 5 Cyrus
art-class wear: 5 smock
Art Deco
artist: Erté
Arte: 7 Johnson
Artemis
animal sacred to ~: 3 dog 4 bear, boar, hind
birthplace: 5 Delos
companion: 4 Aura 5 Maera
equivalent: 5 Diana
parent: 4 Leto, Zeus
temple of ~ site: 5 Ionia
tree sacred to ~: 3 fir 6 laurel
twin: 6 Apollo
victim: 5 Orion
Artemus: 4 Ward
arterial, not: 6 venous
artery: 3 hwy., way 4 duct, line, road 5 aorta, canal, route, track 6 avenue, course, street 7 channel, conduit, freeway, highway, passage, pathway 8 corridor 9 auto route, boulevard, heart line
clogger: 3 fat
major ~: 3 hwy. 5 aorta 7 highway
of a major ~: 6 aortal, aortic
opposite: 4 vein
__ artery: 5 iliac, renal, ulnar 7 carotid, femoral
artesian __: 4 well
art for art's __: 4 sake
artful: 3 coy, sly 4 able, arch, deft, foxy, glib, wily 5 adept, canny, sharp, slick 6 adroit, clever, crafty, shrewd, smooth, subtle, tricky 7 cunning, devious, furtive, knavish, politic 8 dextrous, guileful, masterly, scheming, skillful 9 deceitful, designing, dexterous, ingenious, insidious 10 diplomatic, serpentine
deception: 4 ploy 5 guile
artfulness: 5 guile, wiles 7 finesse, knavery 9 diplomacy
arthropod: 6 insect, spider 10 crustacean
Arthur: 3 Bea 4 Agee, Ashe, Hill, Jean, king, Lake, Penn, Zura 5 Brown, Evans, Franz, Freed, Kopit, Krock, Lewis, Lubin, Lyman 6 Conley, Hailey, Hallam, Harden, Hiller, Miller, Murray 7 Balfour, Compton, Fiedler, Godfrey, Kennedy, Nielsen, Rimbaud 8 Ferrante, Goldberg, Honegger, Koestler, Kornberg, Laurents, Mitchell, O'Connell, Schawlow, Sullivan, Treacher 9 Eddington, Henderson 10 Rubinstein, Schnitzler
Arthur (1981 film)
cast: Sir John Gielgud, Liza Minnelli, Dudley Moore
Arthur __ Doyle: 5 Conan
Arthur __ Sulzberger: 4 Hays, Ochs
Arthur Ashe Stadium inits.: 4 USTA
Arthur, Bea: 7 actress
TV: The Golden Girls, Maude
__ Arthur Blair: 4 Eric
Arthur C. __: 6 Clarke
Arthur, Chester A.: 9 president
alma mater: 5 Union
former occupation: 6 lawyer
home: 7 New York, Vermont
middle name: 4 Alan
wife: 5 Ellen
Arthur Conan __: 5 Doyle
Arthur, King
father: 5 Uther
foster brother: 3 Kay
knight: 3 Kay, Tor 4 Bors, Eric 5 Ector 6 Gareth, Gawain, Hector 7 Galahad, Mordred, Tristan 8 Lancelot, Percival, Tristram
lady: 4 Enid 6 Elaine 9 Guinevere
locale: 7 Camelot
nephew: 6 Gareth, Gawain
paradise: 6 Avalon
sister: 4 Anne
sword holder: 5 stone
time of ~: 4 yore
__ Arthur, TX: 4 Port
artichoke: 5 plant, tuber 6 flower, veggie 9 vegetable
morsel: 5 heart
article: 3 the 4 item, unit, ware, word 5 essay, piece, prose, story, thing 6 clause, column, entity, object, report, review 7 feature, write-up, writing 8 doctrine 9 commodity, editorial, narrative, provision, something 10 commentary, literature
legal ~: 7 codicil, proviso 9 amendment
length: 6 linage 7 lineage
newspaper ~: 4 item, Op-Ed 5 piece 6 column 9 editorial
topper: 6 byline
unusual ~: 5 relic 7 bibelot, whatnot 9 objet d'art 10 knickknack
article of __: 5 faith 6 belief
articles: 5 wares
of faith: 5 canon, creed, dogma 6 belief, tenets 8 doctrine, ideology, religion 9 teachings 10 persuasion, principles
touch up ~: 4 edit
articulate: 3 say 4 glib, oral, talk 5 clear, lucid, speak, state, utter, vocal, voice 6 fluent, intone, spoken 7 breathe, express 8 coherent, distinct, eloquent, set forth 9 emphasize, enunciate, pronounce, talkative, verbalize 10 coherently, expressive, well-spoken
articulated: 5 vocal
articulateness: 8 literacy
articulation: 4 form, link 6 accent, speech 7 clarity, diction 8 language, locution 9 statement, utterance
Artie: 4 Shaw 7 Shapiro 8 Auerbach
author: George Ade
ex: 3 Ava 4 Lana
artifact: 5 relic 6 eolith
place: 6 museum
to an archaeologist: 4 find
artifice: 3 con 4 hoax, ploy, ruse, scam, sham, trap, wile 5 craft, dodge, feint, fraud, guile, shift, trick 6 deceit, device, dupery, gambit, humbug, racket, tactic 7 finesse, gimmick, sleight, snow job, swindle 8 intrigue, maneuver, pretense, strategy, trickery 9 chicanery, deception, duplicity, expedient, imposture, stratagem 10 craftiness, imposition, subterfuge
artificer: 5 maker 7 artisan, builder, creator, deviser 8 designer, inventer, inventor 9 contriver, craftsman 10 originator
artificial: 4 camp, fake, faux, mock, sham 5 bogus, campy, faked, false, phony, put-on, stiff 6 ersatz, forced, forged, hollow, la-de-da, la-di-da, phoney, pseudo, unreal 7 assumed, feigned, labored, mincing, plastic, stilted 8 affected, lah-di-dah, mannered, specious, spurious 9 contrived, fantastic, imitation, insincere, pretended, simulated, synthetic, unnatural 10 fabricated, factitious, fictitious, fraudulent, substitute, theatrical
artificial __: 3 aid 4 gene, life, turf 5 blood, heart 6 person 7 gravity, horizon, reality
artificial intelligence: 7 science
study: 8 learning 9 computers
artificiality: 4 camp
artillery: 4 arms 7 battery, big guns, cannons, weapons 8 bazookas, materiel, ordnance, weaponry 9 munitions
burst: 5 salvo 9 cannonade
need: 4 ammo
__ artillery: 5 coast, field, heavy, light 6 medium
artiodactyl: 4 deer
Artis: 7 Gilmore
artisan: 4 hand 6 joiner, master, worker 9 artificer, carpenter, craftsman 10 journeyman
league: 4 gild 5 guild
name meaning ~: 5 Faber
artist: 3 Arp 4 Dali, diva, Dufy, Goya, Gris, Hals, Kent, Klee, Lely, Miró, Reni, Sert, whiz, Wood 5 actor, Bosch, Corot, Degas, Dürer, Ensor, Ernst, Homer, Johns, Kahlo, Klimt, Léger, Manet, Monet, Moore, Moses, Munch, Peale, Rodin, Shahn, Sloan, Steen, Wyeth 6 Benton, Braque, Calder, Copley, drawer, Eakins, etcher, expert, French, Giotto, Hassam, Hopper, imager, Ingres, Inness, Leutze, Man Ray, master, player, Renoir, Rivera, Rothko, Rubens, Seurat, singer, Stuart, Tanguy, Tissot, Titian, Warhol 7 actress, Bonheur, Borglum, Bruegel, Cassatt, Cellini, Cezanne, Chagall, creator, da Vinci, Duchamp, El Greco, Gauguin, Hans Arp, Hogarth, Holbein, Indiana, Jean Arp,

jeweler, Matisse, N.C. Wyeth, Noguchi, O'Keeffe, painter, Picasso, Pisarro, Pollock, Raphael, Sargent, Tiepolo, Utrillo, van Dyck, van Eyck, van Gogh, Vermeer **8** Angelico, Ben Shahn, composer, del Sarto, Dubuffet, Jan Steen, Joan Miró, José Sert, Juan Gris, Magritte, Max Ernst, Mondrian, musician, Paul Klee, Reynolds, Rockwell, sculptor, Ter Borch, virtuoso, Whistler **9** architect, Constable, de Kooning, Delacroix, Donatello, Frans Hals, Grant Wood, Guido Reni, John Sloan, Kandinsky, performer, Peter Lely, Raoul Dufy, Rembrandt, Remington, Velázquez **10** Botticelli, Edgar Degas, Frida Kahlo, Henry Moore, James Ensor, Jamie Wyeth, Jan van Eyck, Jan Vermeer, Jean Ingres, Modigliani, prima donna, Tintoretto, Yves Tanguy **11** Rosa Bonheur **12** Camille Corot, Gainsborough, Michelangelo
abstract ~: **3** Arp **4** Klee **7** Picasso **8** Mondrian, Paul Klee **9** Kandinsky **10** Botticelli
Austrian: **5** Klimt
Baroque: **6** Rubens **9** Velázquez
Belgian: **8** Magritte
British: **5** Moore **7** Hogarth **8** Reynolds **9** Constable **10** Henry Moore **12** Gainsborough
bunco ~: **4** liar **5** cheat, quack, rogue, shark, sneak, taker **6** bad guy, bilker, conman, robber **7** grifter, hustler, scammer **8** swindler **9** defrauder, hypocrite
cel ~: **5** inker
Cubist: **6** Braque **7** Picasso
Dada: **3** Arp, Ray **6** Man Ray **7** Duchamp, Hans Arp, Jean Arp
Dutch: **4** Hals, Lely **5** Steen **7** van Gogh, Vermeer **8** Jan Steen, Mondrian, Ter Borch **9** de Kooning, Frans Hals, Peter Lely, Rembrandt **10** Jan Vermeer
escape ~: **8** magician
Fauvist: **4** Dufy **7** Matisse **9** Raoul Dufy
Flemish: **5** Bosch **6** Rubens **7** Bruegel, van Eyck **10** Jan van Eyck
French: **3** Arp **4** Dufy **5** Corot, Léger, Manet, Monet, Rodin **6** Braque, Ingres, Renoir, Seurat, Tanguy, Tissot **7** Bonheur, Cézanne, Duchamp, Gauguin, Hans Arp, Jean Arp, Matisse, Utrillo **8** Dubuffet **9** Delacroix, Raoul Dufy **10** Jean Ingres, Yves Tanguy **12** Camille Corot
German: **5** Dürer **7** Holbein
gum: **6** eraser
headgear: **5** beret
Impressionist: **5** Monet **6** Renoir **7** Cassatt, Utrillo
Italian: **4** Reni **6** Giotto, Titian **7** Cellini, da Vinci, Mexican, Raphael, Tiepolo **8** Angelico, del Sarto **9** Donatello, Guido Reni **10** Botticelli, Modigliani, Tintoretto **12** Michelangelo
like a con ~: **5** shady
like some ~ models: **4** nude **5** naked
Mexican: **5** Kahlo **6** Rivera **10** Frida Kahlo
mobile ~: **6** Calder
need: **5** chalk, light, paint, smock **6** canvas, eraser **7** palette
Norwegian: **5** Munch
paste: **5** gesso
performance ~: **4** mime
place: **4** loft **6** colony, garret
pop ~: **6** Warhol **7** Indiana **10** Andy Warhol
prefix: **3** neo-
Renaissance: **5** Dürer **6** TItian **7** Raphael **8** Angelico, del Sarto **9** Donatello **10** Botticelli
rep: **5** agent
Russian: **7** Chagall **9** Kandinsky
Spanish: **4** Dalí, Gris, Miró, Sert **7** El Greco, Picasso, Pisarro **8** Joan Miró, José Sert, Juan Gris **9** Velázquez
subject: **4** anat. **7** anatomy
Surrealist: **4** Dalí **6** Tanguy **10** Yves Tanguy
Swiss: **4** Klee **8** Paul Klee
__ artist: **3** con **4** body, junk **6** escape **7** trapeze
artiste: **6** master, singer **8** musician, virtuoso
artistic: **7** elegant, stylish **8** creative, cultural, esthetic, graceful, talented, tasteful **9** aesthetic, ingenious, inventive, uplifting **10** expressive
be ~: **6** create
expression: **5** style
judgment: **5** taste
merit: **5** vertu, virtu
skill: **5** craft
style: **5** genre, idiom
theme: **5** motif
work: **4** opus
artistry: **5** craft, flair, skill, style, touch **6** beauty, genius, talent **7** ability, finesse, mastery **9** dexterity, technique **10** brilliance, creativity, expertness, virtuosity
Artists in Crime
author: Ngaio Marsh
artless: **4** naif, open **5** frank, fresh, inept, naive **6** honest, simple **7** genuine, natural, sincere **8** innocent, lamblike **9** childlike, guileless, ingenuous, outspoken, primitive, unguarded, unworldly **10** unaffected
one: **4** lamb, naif
artlessness: **7** naiveté
Art of Love, The
author: Ovid
Art of Loving, The
author: Erich Fromm
Art of the Deal, The
author: Donald Trump
Art of the Fugue
composer: J.S. Bach
Artoo __: **5** Detoo
Art Ross Trophy
org.: **3** NHL
arts: **10** humanities
fed. ~ sponsor: **3** NEA
one of the ~: **5** dance, drama
__ arts: **4** fine **5** beaux **6** visual **7** graphic, liberal, martial
arts and __: **6** crafts **7** letters
artsy: **5** showy **6** too-too **8** affected, bohemian, mannered
artsy-__: **7** craftsy
Artur: **8** Schnabel **9** Rodzinski **10** Rubinstein
Arturo: **9** de Cordova, Toscanini
arty: **5** showy **6** chichi **8** affected, bohemian, overdone **10** avant-garde
arty-__: **6** crafty
ARU
part of ~: **4** unit **5** audio **8** response
Aruba: **4** isle **6** island, resort
capital: **10** Oranjestad
__ a rug: **3** cut
arugula: **6** veggie **9** vegetable
family: **7** mustard
arum: **5** calla **9** calla lily **10** cuckoopint
Arum: **3** Bob
Arundel
author: Kenneth Roberts
a run for one's __: **5** money
Arvada: **4** city, town
locale: **8** Colorado
Aryan: **6** Nordic **9** Caucasian
__-Aryan: **4** Indo
Arye: **5** Gross
as: **3** qua
as __: **3** for, one, yet **4** such, well **5** a rule, far as, of now, usual **6** though **7** regards
as __ as: **3** far **4** good, long, much, well
as __ as ABC: **4** easy **6** simple
as __ as a fiddle: **3** fit
as __ as life: **3** big
as __ as one's word: **4** good
as __ as rain: **5** right
as __ get-out: **3** all
as __ man: **3** one
as __ possible: **6** soon as
as __ resort: **5** a last
as __ to: **4** told
__ as: **4** such **5** as far, so far
As: **4** elem. **7** arsenic, element
33 for ~: **4** at. no.
As __ and breathe!: **5** I live
As __ as It Gets: **4** Good
As __ care!: **3** if I
As __ didn't know!: **3** If I
As __ Dying: **4** I Lay
As __ Goes By: **4** Time
As __ going to St. Ives: **4** I was
As __ It: **4** I See
As __ Like It: **3** You
As __ my witness: **5** God is
As __ Never Said Goodbye: **4** If We
As __ on TV: **4** seen
As __ saying...: **4** I was
As __, so shall...: **5** ye sow
A's
get straight ~: **5** excel
see also Athletics
A.S.: **5** Byatt
__ as 1,2,3: **4** easy
as a __: **4** rule **5** whole
as a __ of fact: **6** matter
Asa: **4** Gray **7** Candler
ASA
cousin: **3** ISO
__ as a bat: **5** blind
__ as ABC: **4** easy **6** simple
__ as a bear: **6** hungry
__ as a beaver: **4** busy
__ as a bee: **4** busy
__ as a beet: **3** red
__ as a bell: **5** clear, sound
__ as a bird: **4** free
__ as a board: **4** flat **5** stiff
__ as a bone: **3** dry
__ as a brick: **5** thick
__ as a button: **4** cute
__ as a church mouse: **4** poor
__ as a clam: **5** happy
__ as a cucumber: **4** cool
__ as a daisy: **5** fresh
...as a day in __: **4** June
__ as a dog: **4** sick
__ as a dollar: **5** sound
__ as a doornail: **4** dead
__ as a drum: **5** tight
__ as a feather: **5** light
__ as a fiddle: **3** fit
__ as a fox: **3** sly
__ as a fruitcake: **5** nutty
__ as a ghost: **4** pale **5** white
__ as a goose: **5** loose, silly
__ as a hatter: **3** mad
__ as a hornet: **3** mad
__ as a horse: **7** healthy
__ as a house: **3** big **5** as big
__ as a jaybird: **5** naked
__ as a judge: **5** sober
__ as a kite: **4** high
__ as a lamb: **6** gentle
__ as a lark: **5** happy
__ as a loon: **5** crazy
__ as a March hare: **3** mad
as a matter of __: **4** fact
__ as a mouse: **5** quiet
asana
practicer: **4** yogi **5** yogin
__ as an oak: **6** mighty
__ as an owl: **4** wise
__ as an ox: **4** dumb **6** strong
à __ santé: **5** votre
ASAP: **3** now, PDQ **4** stat **5** apace, quick **6** pronto **7** quickly, soonest **8** chop-chop, directly, right now, right off **9** forthwith, posthaste, right away
part of ~: **6** as soon, soon as **8** possible
__ as a pancake: **4** flat
__ as a peacock: **5** proud
__ as a picture: **6** pretty
__ as a pin: **4** neat
__ as a pistol: **3** hot
__ as a rail: **4** thin
__ as a reed: **4** thin
__ as a rock: **4** hard **5** solid
__ as a seal upon thine heart: **5** Set me
__ as a sheet: **5** white
__ as a skunk: **5** drunk
__ as a Stranger: **3** Not
__ as a tack: **5** sharp
__ as a team: **4** work
__ as a three-dollar bill: **5** phony
__ as a wet hen: **3** mad
__ as a whip: **5** smart
__ as a whistle: **5** clean
...as a wild bull in __: **4** a net
__ as a wink: **5** quick
as big as __: **4** life
ASCAP
alternative: **3** BMI
part of ~: **3** Soc. **4** Amer. **7** Authors, Society **8** American **9** Composers **10** Publishers
ascend: **3** fly **4** go up, leap, lift, rise, soar, upgo **5** arise, climb, mount, scale, slope **6** move up, shinny **7** clamber, lift off, shinney, take off **8** escalate **9** succeed to

ascendancy: **4** rise, rule **5** power, reign **7** command, control, mastery, primacy, success, triumph, victory **8** dominion, kingship, leverage **9** advantage, authority, dominance, influence, supremacy **10** domination
ascendant: **9** sovereign **10** forebearer
ascendency: **8** priority
Ascender: **3** SUV **5** Isuzu
ascending: **6** uphill **9** acclivous
ascension: **10** incipience
Ascension: **4** isle **6** island
Ascension __: **3** Day
Ascension Oratorio
composer: J.S. Bach
ascent: **4** rise, upgo **5** climb, slope, way up **6** glacis **7** incline, liftoff, takeoff, upgrade **9** acclivity, elevation **10** flight path
Ascent __, The: **5** of Man
Ascent of F6, The
author: W.H. Auden
ascertain: **3** see **4** find, hear, tell **5** check, gauge, glean, infer, judge, learn, prove **6** define, detect, verify **7** certify, confirm, discern, find out, unearth **8** discover, smell out **9** check up on, determine, establish, ferret out, get hold of, get to know, get word of **10** get down pat
ascertainable: **8** knowable **9** definable
ascetic: **4** monk **5** faker, fakir, faqir, sober, stern **6** faquir, hermit, severe **7** austere, recluse, Spartan **9** abstinent, reclusive, religious **10** abstaining, abstemious, antisocial
ancient ~: **6** Essene
Asian ~: **4** Sufi, yogi **5** faker, fakir, faqir, sadhu, yogin **6** faquir
asceticism: **9** austerity **10** abstinence
Asch, Sholem: **6** writer
work: The Apostle
East River
Mary
Moses
The Nazarene
The Prophet
ascorbic acid: **7** vitamin **8** vitamin C
ascot: **3** tie **5** scarf **6** cravat **7** necktie **8** neckwear **10** four-in-hand
ascribe: **3** lay **4** name **6** credit, impute, relate **7** project, qualify **8** accredit **9** attribute, chalk up to, insinuate
Ascriptin: **9** analgesic **10** painkiller
alternative: ***see*** pain reliever brand
__ as day: **5** plain
__ as directed: **3** use
__ as dust: **3** dry
asea: **4** lost **6** addled, afloat, in a fog, unsure **7** at a loss, baffled, bemused, in a daze, muddled, puzzled, sailing, stumped **8** clueless, confused, cruising, drifting, floating, offshore, voyaging, yachting **9** befuddled, flummoxed, perplexed, uncertain, under sail **10** bewildered, nonplussed
not ~: **6** ashore
ASEAN
kin: **5** SEATO
__ a seat: **4** have, take
__ a secret: **4** in on
aseptic: **5** clean **7** sterile **8** germ-free, hygienic, pristine, sanitary **10** immaculate
__ A session: **4** Q and
as fit __ fiddle: **3** as a
Asgard
dweller: **4** Odin, Thin, Thor **5** Aesir
__ as gold: **4** good
...as good as __: **5** a mile
As Good as It Gets (1997 film)
cast: Cuba Gooding Jr., Helen Hunt, Greg Kinnear, Jack Nicholson
director: James L. Brooks
dog: **7** Verdell
as good as one's __: **4** word
ash: **4** gray, grey, tree **5** ember, rowan **6** blonde, cinder, dottel, dottle **7** cinders **8** hardwood **9** shade tree **10** incinerate, silver-gray
ender: **3** can **4** cake, tray
family: **5** olive
holder: **4** dump, tray **8** landfill
relative: ***see*** gray color
volcanic ~ formation: **4** maar
ash __: **3** can **4** fall, flow, gray, grey, heap **5** blond, color **6** blonde
Ash: **7** Mary Kay
ashake: **9** trembling, tremulous
ashamed: **5** sorry **7** abashed, bashful, debased, humbled **8** blushing, penitent, sheepish **9** regretful **10** remorseful
be ~: **3** rue **6** repent
make ~: **5** abash
Ashanti: **8** language
capital of ~: **6** Kumasi
home: **5** Ghana **6** Africa
A-sharp
equivalent: **5** B-flat
Ashburn, Richie: **7** Phillie **10** outfielder
__-Ashbury: **6** Haight
Ashby: **3** Hal **4** Alan
ashcan: **4** dump **6** barrel **7** dustbin **8** wastebin
target: **3** sub
Ashcan __: **6** school
Ashcroft, Peggy: **4** Dame **7** actress
Oscar: A Passage to India
Ashdod: **4** city, town
locale: **6** Israel
Ashe, Arthur: **7** netster **9** tennis pro
milieu: **5** court
Asheboro: **4** city, town
locale: **4** N. Car.
ashen: **3** wan **4** gray, grey, pale **5** livid, lurid, pasty, white **6** chalky, pallid, peaked, sallow **7** ghastly, greyish, whitish **8** blanched **9** albescent, bloodless, cinereous, colorless, gray-faced, terrified, whey-faced **10** cinderlike, pasty-faced
__ as hen's teeth: **4** rare **6** scarce
Asher
brother: **3** Dan, Gad **4** Levi **5** Judah **6** Joseph, Reuben, Simeon **7** Zebulun **8** Benjamin, Issachar, Naphtali
parent: **5** Jacob **6** Zilpah
sister: **5** Dinah
son: **5** Imnah, Ishvi **6** Beriah, Ishvah
ashes: **5** ruins **6** relics **7** remains **8** leavings, vestiges
reduce to ~: **4** burn
sackcloth and ~: **7** penance
__ Ashes: **7** Angela's
Ashe Stadium
area: **5** court
need: **3** net
Ashes to Ashes
author: Harold Pinter, Tami Hoag
Asheville: **4** city, town
locale: **4** N. Car.
sch.: **3** UNC
Ashford: **4** Nick **6** Evelyn **8** Nickolas
Ashford, Evelyn: **6** runner **8** sprinter
Ashford, Nickolas: **6** singer **8** composer
spouse: Valerie Simpson
ashine: **7** glowing **8** gleaming **10** glimmering, glistening
__ a shine to: **4** take
Ashkenazy, Vladimir: **7** pianist, Russian
Ashkhabad: **4** city, town **7** capital
locale: Turkmenistan
Ashland: **4** city, town
locale: **4** Ohio **6** Oregon **8** Kentucky **10** California
Ashlee: **7** Simpson
Ashley: **4** Judd **5** Laura, Olsen **7** Montagu **9** Elizabeth
rival: **5** Rhett
Ashley, Elizabeth
spouse: James Farentino, George Peppard
Ashman: **6** Howard
ashore: **6** in port, landed, on land **7** on leave **8** grounded, stranded **9** on liberty
cast ~: **6** maroon
go ~: **4** land **6** arrive, debark **9** disembark
not ~: **4** asea **5** at sea
ashram: **6** temple
Ashtabula: **4** city, town
lake: **4** Erie
locale: **4** Ohio
Ashton: **7** Kutcher
Ashton-under-__: **4** Lyne
Ashton-Warner, Sylvia: **6** writer
Ash Wednesday: **4** poem
author: T.S. Eliot
preceder: **9** Mardi Gras
season: **4** Lent
ashy: **3** wan **4** gray, grey, pale **5** livid, pasty **6** pallid **7** cindery, ghastly, grayish, greyish, whitish **9** cinderous, colorless, pale-faced, whey-faced **10** pasty-faced
residue: **4** calx
As I ___: **5** see it
As I __ saying...: **3** was
Asia: **4** cont. **6** Orient **9** continent
antelope: **3** goa **5** saiga
archipelago: **5** Malay
bean: **3** soy, urd
bird: **4** lory, ruff, smew **5** shama **6** argala, chukar, drongo, lanner **7** courser, dottrel, finfoot, marabou, ostrich **8** amadavat, avadavat, dotterel, eagle owl, leafbird, lorikeet, marabout, megapode, tragopan **9** cormorant, francolin, friarbird, frogmouth, ossifrage **10** greenfinch, honeyeater, weaverbird
border part: **5** Urals
bovine: **3** yak **4** anoa, zebu
buy from ~: **6** import
canine: **5** dhole **6** corsac, jackal
capital: **4** Baku, Dili, Doha, Malé, Sana **5** Amman, Dacca, Dhaka, Hanoi, Kabul, Sanaa, Seoul, Tokyo **6** Ankara, Bagdad, Beirut, Manama, Muscat, Riyadh, Taipei, Tehran, Yangon **7** Baghdad, Bangkok, Beijing, Bishkek, Colombo, Jakarta, Rangoon, Teheran, Thimphu **8** Abu Dhabi, Beyrouth, Damascus, Djakarta, Dushanbe, Katmandu, New Delhi, Tashkent **9** Islamabad, Jerusalem, Phnom Penh, Pyongyang, Ulan Bator, Vientiane **10** Kuwait City **11** Kuala Lumpur, Ulaanbaatar
cereal grass: **4** ragi **5** raggy **6** raggee
country: **3** Isr., Leb., Nam, Pak., Syr. **4** Irak, Iran, Iraq, Laos, Oman **5** China, India, Japan, Korea, Nepal, Qatar, Syria, Tibet, Yemen **6** Brunei, Israel, Taiwan, Turkey, Xizang **7** Lebanon, Myanmar, Sitsang, Vietnam **8** Cambodia, Malaysia, Maldives, Mongolia, Pakistan, Sri Lanka, Thailand **9** Indonesia, Kirghizia, New Guinea **10** Kazakhstan, North Korea, South Korea, Uzbekistan **11** Philippines
country of old: **4** Siam **5** Burma
cuisine: **3** Tai **4** Thai **5** Hunan **7** Chinese **8** Szechuan
deer: **4** sika **6** thamin **7** muntjac, muntjak
desert: **4** Gobi, Tahr, Thar, Tuhr **6** Syrian **7** Arabian, Kara Kum **8** Kyzyl Kum **9** Dasht-e Lut, Great Salt
divided ~ nation: **5** Korea
equine: **6** onager
feline: **4** lion **5** civet, ounce, tiger **7** cheetah, leopard
fish: **5** betta, loach, tench **6** anabas **7** gourami, sterlet
fruit: **6** durian, loquat **7** bilimbi **8** tamarind
goat: **4** ibex
goat antelope: **5** goral, serow
herb: **5** orach **6** orache
island: **4** Java **5** Macao, Macau
island chain: **6** Kurile
kingdom: **6** Bhutan
language: **3** Lao, Tai **4** Shan, Thai **5** Malay **7** Kirghiz **8** Scythian
language group: **5** Indic
mountain: **3** Api **4** Alai, Jaja, Mana **5** Altai, Horeb, Kabru, Kamet, Sinai **6** Ararat, Cho Oyu, Gilead, Hermon, Kangto, Kungur, Lhotse, Makalu, Nunkun, Nuptse, Pisgah, Trisul **7** Everest, Manaslu, Pyramid, Trikora, Trisuli **8** Anapurna, Baruntse, Chamlang, Changtzu, Dunagiri, Pauhunri, Stanovoi, Tent Peak **9** Ama Dablam, Annapurna, Badrinath, Broad Peak, Istoro Nal, Kanjut Sar, Lenin Peak, Nanda Devi, Nepal Peak, Rakaposhi, Sia Kangri, Tirich Mir
onetime ~ kingdom: **4** Anam **5** Annam

palm: 4 nipa 5 areca, betel
peninsula: 5 Malay 6 Arabia
people: 4 Kurd 5 Tajik 6 Tadjik 7 Tadzhik
place-name suffix: 4 -stan
primate: 6 gibbon, langur 7 macaque
river: 3 Fly, Han, Qom, Qum, Red 4 Amur, Kura, Lena, Liao, Oxus, Yalu, Yüen 5 Argun, Atrak, Atrek, Indus, Jumna, Kabul, Karun, Murat, Ouémé, Tarim, Tobol, Tumen 6 Angara, Chenab, Cydnus, Gambia, Ganges, Irtish, Irtysh, Jhelum, Jordan, Khabur, Kolyma, Mekong, Orkhon, Seyhan, Sutlej, Tigris, Ussuri, Yamuna, Yarmuk, Yellow 7 Cauvery, Helmand, Hooghly, Huang He, Karkheh, Krishna, Narbada, Orontes, Salween, Selenga, Songhua, Xi Jiang, Yangtze, Yenisei 8 Amu Darya, Chindwin, Godavari, Granicus, Menderes, Nerbudda, Syr Darya 9 Euphrates, Irrawaddy 10 Chao Phraya
rodent: 4 jird 6 gerbil, jerboa, suslik 7 hamster, souslik
sea: 4 Aral 7 Caspian
sheep: 5 argal, shapu, urial 6 argali 7 Karakul
shrub: 4 gumi 5 henna, ramee, ramie 6 aucuba, kerria 7 skimmia 8 camellia, caragana 9 firethorn
snake: 5 krait 6 dhaman
tree: 4 toon 5 henna 6 cassia, durian, lichee, litchi, padauk, padouk 7 champac, leechee, zelkova 8 caragana, champaca 9 candlenut
volcano: 3 Aso, Usu 4 Akan, Fuji, Gaua, Nasu, Taal 5 Alaid, Asama, Azuma, Kelut, Manam, Mayon, Raung, Unzen, Yasur 6 Ambrym, Bagana, Bandai, Chokai, Dukono, Lopevi, Merapi, Ontake, Oshima, Rabaul, Semeru, Slamet, Tiatia, Ulawun 7 Adatara, Bulusan, Canlaon, Kerinci, Langila 8 Gamalama, Karymsky, Pinatubo 9 Tolbachik
weasel: 8 kolinsky
weight: 4 tael 5 picul
weights: 5 artal

Asia Minor
ancient city: 4 Myra, Teos 5 Iasus, Lydia, Troia 6 Cnidus, Sardis
ancient country: 5 Lycia 6 Pontus
ancient district: 5 Caria
ancient language: 8 Phrygian
ancient region: 5 Troad, Troas 6 Aeolia, Aeolis
capital: 6 Angora, Ankara
peak: 5 Mt. Ida
region: 5 Ionia

Asian: 3 Tai 4 Kurd, Sikh, Thai, Turk 5 Iraki, Iraqi, Tamil 6 Indian, Korean, Mongol 7 Bornean, Burmese, Chinese, Laotian, Tibetan 8 Balinese, Japanese, Lebanese 9 Bhutanese, Cambodian, Dravidian, Pakistani, Taiwanese 10 Vietnamese
ancient ~: 4 Mede, Pers. 7 Persian

Asian __: 3 flu 4 pear

Asian Princess
sculptor: Erté

__ as I can tell: 5 As far

__ as ice: 4 cold

aside: 2 by 3 off 4 away, near 5 alone, apart 6 nearby 9 by oneself, in private, in reserve, privately 10 digression, discursion, separately
all joking ~: 9 seriously, sincerely
brush ~: 7 neglect 9 disregard
cast ~: 4 cede, drop, dump, jilt, sell, shed, shun, veto 5 chuck, ditch, forgo, spurn, yield 6 bounce, forego, give up, pass on, rebuff, reject 7 abandon, discard, disdain, dismiss, exclude, forfeit, forsake 8 disallow, forswear, get rid of, hand over, jettison, leave out, part with, throw out, turn down 9 abandoned, blackball, dispose of, foreswear, repudiate, surrender, throw away 10 relinquish
from: 6 except 7 besides 9 except for, excluding, other than 10 beyond that, leaving out, regardless
held ~: 9 in reserve
leap ~: 4 duck 5 avoid
push ~: 5 elbow, shunt 8 shoulder
put ~: 4 drop, hold, keep, save 5 allow, amass, annul, cache, defer, delay, lay by, lay in, lay up, on ice, quash, shunt, store, table, waive 6 cancel, devote, ignore, refuse, reject, repeal, revoke, shelve 7 abandon, abeyant, abolish, deposit, discard, earmark, lay away, rescind, reserve, rope off, store up, suspend 8 allocate, file away, hold on to, laid away, override, overrule, overturn, postpone, renounce, reserved, salt away, stow away 9 designate, disregard, in reserve, pay no mind, stockpile, supersede 10 pigeonhole, relinquish
step ~: 6 resign 9 stand down
turn ~: 4 skew, veer 5 avert, avoid, parry, shunt 6 divert, swerve 7 deflect, prevent, ward off 10 discourage

__ aside: 3 lay, put, set 4 cast, step

As if!: 3 hah 7 get real

a sight for __ eyes: 4 sore

__ as I know: 5 as far

As I Lay Dying
author: William Faulkner
character: 4 Anse, Cora, Darl, Lafe, Tull 5 Addie

__ a silly question...: 3 Ask

Asimov, Isaac: 6 writer
genre: sci-fi
work: The Caves of Steel
The Currents of Space
Foundation
In Joy Still Felt
In Memory Yet Green
Inside the Atom
I, Robot
The Naked Sun
The Stars Like Dust

__ a Simple Melody: 4 Play

asinine: 4 daft, dumb 5 goosy, inane, silly 6 absurd, goosey, simple 7 fatuous, foolish, idiotic 8 mindless 9 fatuitous, idiotical, laughable, senseless 10 ridiculous, sophomoric, weak-minded

asininity: 6 lunacy 7 fatuity

__ asinorum: 4 pons

__ a Sin to Tell a Lie: 3 It's

as it __: 4 were 6 stands 7 happens

__ as it is: 4 such

__ as it seems: 7 strange

As I was going to St. __...: 4 Ives

ask: 3 beg, bid, inq. 4 pose, pray, pump, quiz, seek, urge 5 grill, plead, probe, put to, query 6 appeal, call on, charge, invite, summon 7 beseech, canvass, consult, enquire, entreat, implore, inquire, propose, put it to, request, require, solicit 8 call upon, petition, question 9 catechize, impetrate, interview
a toughie: 5 stump 6 baffle, puzzle, stymie 7 confuse, mystify, nonplus, perplex 8 bewilder, confound 9 dumbfound
desperately: 3 beg 5 plead
for: 3 bid 6 desire, incite, induce 7 bespeak, bring on, inspire, provoke, request, solicit 9 encourage, instigate 10 bring about
(for): 4 call 6 clamor
forgiveness: 5 atone
out: 4 date
pardon: 9 apologize
too much: 5 snoop 6 impose

ask __: 3 for, out 5 for it

ask __ trouble: 3 for

Ask __ what your country...: 3 not

askance: 6 canted 7 asquint, charily 8 cockeyed
look ~: 6 squint

askant: 7 athwart 9 obliquely

asked for
not ~: 5 unbid

__ Asked for It: 3 You

__ asked you?: 3 Who

asker: 9 requester, solicitor 10 supplicant

__ A Sketch: 4 Etch

askew: 3 off, wry 4 alop, awry, bent 5 atilt, bandy, wrong 6 aslant, canted, flooey, zigzag 7 athwart, crooked, oblique, slanted, twisted 8 cockeyed, diagonal, lopsided 9 off-center, out of line, to one side 10 diagonally, topsy-turvy
in Scottish: 4 agee

Ask for it __: 6 by name

asking: 7 enquiry, inquiry 10 invitation
for the ~: 4 free 6 gratis 7 as a gift 8 costless 9 on the cuff 10 on the house

asking __: 3 bid 5 price

Ask me if __!: 5 I care

__ Ask of You: 4 All I

Ask Your Mama
author: Langston Hughes

ASL
part of ~: 4 Amer., Lang., Sign 8 American, Language

aslant: 3 wry 5 askew 6 tilted 7 crooked, leaning, oblique, sideway, sloping 8 cockeyed, inclined, sideways, sidewise 9 at an angle, crossways, crosswise, obliquely, on an angle, on the bias 10 diagonally

asleep: 3 lax, out 4 abed, idle, lazy, numb 5 inert, tired, under 6 dozing, draggy, torpid 7 dormant, napping, nodding, passive, resting 8 dreaming, inactive, indolent, lifeless, slothful, sluggish, snoozing 9 gone to bed, lethargic, sacked out, sedentary, somnolent, zonked out 10 disengaged, in la-la land, sawing logs, slumbering
at the switch: 6 remiss 9 negligent
fall ~: 3 nap, nod 4 doze, rest 5 droop 6 catnap, drowse, snooze 7 drop off 8 drift off
half ~: 6 drowsy

__-asleep: 4 half

Asleep __ Deep: 5 in the

asleep at the __: 6 switch

__ as life: 3 big

As Long __ Needs Me: 4 As He

As Long as the Grass Shall Grow
author: Oliver La Farge

aslope: 6 tilted 7 sideway, slanted 8 inclined, sideways, sidewise 9 on an angle 10 diagonally

__ a Small Hotel: 6 There's

__ a Small World: 3 It's

Asmara: 4 city, town 7 capital
locale: 7 Eritrea

__ as Methuselah: 3 old

__ a smile: 5 crack

Asmodée
author: François Mauriac

__ as molasses: 4 slow

__ as mud: 5 clear

__ a snag: 3 hit

__ as nails: 4 hard 5 tough

__-a-snee: 5 snick

Asner: 2 Ed 5 Jules 6 Edward

Asner, Edward: 5 actor
film: Daniel (1983)
Fort Apache, The Bronx (1981)
Gus (1976)
JFK (1991)
film (voice): Up (2009)
TV: Lou Grant, The Mary Tyler Moore Show, Roots

Asnières-__-Seine: 3 sur

asocial one: 5 loner

as of __: 3 now

as one __: 3 man 6 person

__ a song: 3 for

__ a Song: 4 Sing 7 Without

__ a Song Comin' On: 5 I Feel

__ a Song Go...: 4 I Let

__ a Song in My Heart: 4 With

__ à son goût: 6 chacun

asonia: 6 tin ear

asor: 4 lyre

__ a soul: 4 nary

__ a sour note: 5 end on

asp: 5 snake, viper 6 animal, uraeus 7 reptile, serpent 8 ophidian
home: 4 Nile
relative: see snake
victim: 4 Cleo 9 Cleopatra
weapon: 4 fang 5 venom

__ a spade a spade: 4 call

asparagus: 4 fern 6 veggie 9 vegetable
shoot: 5 spear

asparagus-like
plant: 3 udo

ASPCA: 3 org.
cousin: 4 PETA
document: 3 lic. 7 license
offering: 7 shelter
part of ~: 3 Soc. 4 Amer. 7 Animals, Cruelty, Society 8 American 10 Prevention
aspect: 3 air 4 aura, face, item, look, mask, mien, part, role, side, view 5 facet, guise, light, phase, slant, thing 6 detail, manner, nature, regard, visage 7 bearing, element, feature, outlook, quality 8 attitude, demeanor, position, qualitie 9 attribute, character, dimension, semblance, viewpoint 10 appearance, complexion, deportment
aspect __: 5 ratio
Aspects of Love: 7 musical
composer: Andrew Lloyd Webber
aspen: 4 tree
emulate an ~: 5 quake
Aspen: 3 car 4 auto, city, town 5 Dodge 6 resort 9 ski resort 10 automobile
enjoy ~: 3 ski 4 skee
feature: 4 J-bar, snow, T-bar 5 slope 6 ski tow
locale: 8 Colorado
visitor: 5 skier
asperity: 4 fury 5 rigor, wrath 6 temper 8 acerbity, acrimony, meanness 9 crossness, harshness 10 crabbiness, unkindness
Aspern Papers, The
author: Henry James
asperse: 4 gibe, jeer, jibe, mock, slam, slur, snub 5 abuse, decry, libel, scorn, smear, spurn, sully, taint, taunt 6 accuse, attack, defame, deride, dump on, heckle, impugn, malign, offend, rebuff, slight, vilify 7 affront, blacken, censure, degrade, disdain, put down, rank out, run down, slander, spatter, traduce 8 backbite, badmouth, belittle, denounce, derogate, reproach, ridicule, sprinkle, vilipend 9 denigrate, deprecate, discredit, disparage, fling dirt, humiliate 10 besprinkle, calumniate, depreciate, disrespect, speak ill of, stigmatize, throw mud on
asperser: 8 vilifier 9 detractor
aspersion: 3 dig, lie 4 barb, gibe, jibe, slam, slap, slur, snub 5 abuse, libel, scorn, smear, taunt 6 insult, rebuff, slight 7 affront, calumny, catcall, disdain, mockery, obloquy, offense, put-down, sarcasm, slander 8 contempt, derision, innuendo, ridicule 9 cheap shot, contumely, criticism, invective 10 backbiting, defamation, detraction, disrespect, impugnment, imputation, muckraking, opprobrium, reflection
aspersive: 8 libelous 10 detractive
asphalt: 3 tar 5 pitch
lay ~: 4 pave
asphalt __: 4 rock 5 paper 6 jungle
Asphalt Jungle, The (1950 film)
cast: Louis Calhern, Jean Hagen, Sterling Hayden, Marilyn Monroe
director: John Huston
asphodel: 5 plant 6 flower
aspic: 5 gelée, jelly
shaper: 4 mold
aspidistra: 5 plant 6 flower
__ as pie: 4 easy, nice
aspin: 8 whirling
Aspin: 3 Les
aspirant: 7 entrant 9 applicant, candidate, job-hunter
aspirate: 4 sigh
aspiration: 3 aim, end 4 goal, hope, plan, wish 5 dream 6 desire 7 longing, purpose, thought 8 ambition, yearning 9 direction, eagerness, hankering, objective 10 inhalation, right stuff
aspire: 3 aim, try 4 hope, lift, long, mean, seek, soar, want, wish 5 dream 6 hope to, intend, long to, pursue, seek to, strive, wish to 7 aim high, dream to, propose, yearn to 8 desire to 10 have in view
to: 5 aim at, covet 6 desire, try for 7 hope for 8 shoot for
(to): 3 aim 4 long
aspirin: 9 analgesic 10 painkiller
brand: 5 Bayer 6 Anacin 8 Bufferin, St. Joseph
like ~: 3 OTC
open, as an ~ bottle: 5 uncap
target: 4 ache, pain
unit: 4 pill
aspiring: 5 eager 7 hopeful, wishful, would-be 8 desirous 9 ambitious
aspish: 5 snaky 8 venomous, viperous
__ as pitch: 5 black
__ as Punch: 7 pleased
asquint: 4 awry 5 askey, slyly 6 askant 7 askance, sideway 8 sidelong, sideways, sidewise 9 furtively, obliquely
Asquith: 7 Anthony, Herbert
as right as __: 4 rain
ass: 5 burro, genet, jenny, kiang 6 brayer, donkey, equine, jennet, onager
emulate an ~: 4 bray
relative: *see* equine
starter: 4 jack
see also ninny
Assad
nation: 5 Syria
assai: 4 palm, very 9 extremely
assail: 3 ply 4 bash, go at, pelt 5 abuse, beset, blast, fly at, sally, set at, set on, storm 6 ambush, attach, attack, berate, engage, fall on, have at, hit out, impugn, invade, malign, oppose, oppugn, rail at, resist, revile, strike, vilify, waylay 7 assault, besiege, bombard, censure, falls on, go after, lambast, lay into, rip into, set upon, slander 8 fall upon, lace into, lambaste, pounce on, strike at, tear into 9 beleaguer, criticize, descend on, excoriate, haul off on, intrude on, lash out at, light into 10 villainize
the ramparts: 6 attack, charge
assailable: 6 liable 8 vincible
assailant: 3 foe, for 5 enemy 6 mugger 7 fighter, invader 8 attacker, opponent 9 aggressor, ill-wisher 10 antagonist
assailment: 5 abuse 6 attack 10 aggression, impugnment
Assam
product: 3 tea
silkworm: 3 eri 4 eria
Assante: 6 Armand
assassin: 6 killer
Assassins (1995 film)
cast: Antonio Banderas, Julianne Moore, Sylvester Stallone
director: Richard Donner
Assateague: 4 isle 6 island
locale: 8 Maryland, Virginia
assault: 3 mug 4 bash, raid, rush 5 abuse, blast, blitz, fight, fly at, foray, force, onset, sally, set on, storm 6 ambush, assail, attack, batter, battle, change, charge, engage, fall on, felony, invade, oppose, sortie, strike 7 advance, aggress, barrage, bombard, lay into, offense, set upon, violate 8 fall upon, gang up on, invasion, lace into, violence 9 broadside, bushwhack, cannonade, haul off on, incursion, intrude on, light into, offensive, onslaught, violation 10 ambushment, impugnment
blunt an ~: 4 stem
the ear: 6 deafen
the nostrils: 4 reek
verbal ~: 5 salvo, shout 7 barrage, ovation 8 outburst 9 explosion
assault __: 4 boat 5 rifle 6 jacket
assault and __: 7 battery
assay: 4 test 5 prove, study, trial 6 assess, regard, size up, survey, try out 7 analyze, examine, explore, venture 8 analysis, appraise, check out, endeavor, estimate, evaluate 10 scrutinize
assay __: 3 cup, ton 6 groove, office
assayer: 6 tester
concern: 3 ore
cup: 5 cupel
As seen __!: 4 on TV
assemblage: 3 mob, set 4 band, gang, herd, pile, unit 5 batch, bunch, crowd, group, rally 6 huddle, throng 7 cluster, company 8 audience, ensemble, junction, juncture 9 aggregate, concourse, congeries, gathering, listeners 10 attendance, collection, concursion, confluence, convention, cumulation
assemble: 3 sit 4 band, call, form, herd, join, leap, make, mass, meet, mold 5 amass, build, bunch, erect, flock, focus, forge, frame, group, merge, model, piece, put up, rally, set up, shape, troop, unite 6 corral, create, gang up, garner, gather, hook up, huddle, muster, summon 7 collate, collect, compile, convene, convoke, fashion, marshal, prepare, produce, reunite, round up, scare up, turn out 8 contrive, converge, hold on to, mobilize, scrape up 9 aggregate, construct, establish, fabricate, forgather 10 accumulate, close ranks, congregate
again: 5 resit
something to ~: 3 kit
assembled: 6 united 7 grouped 9 aggregate 10 collective
assembler: 6 framer 10 fabricator
assemblies
full ~: 5 plena
assembly: 3 set 4 band, bevy, body, unit 5 bunch, crowd, flock, forum, group, rally, salon, synod, troop, union, whole 6 caucus, confab, hookup, huddle, muster, throng 7 chamber, cluster, company, council, joining, meeting, reunion, session, turnout, viewers 8 audience, building, conclave, congress, ecclesia, visitors 9 concourse, gathering, listeners, multitude, symposium, witnesses 10 collection, conference, convention
combining form: 4 -fest
instruction: 4 step
room: 3 aud. 10 auditorium
assembly __: 4 line
assembly-line
innovator: 4 Ford
worker: 5 robot
assent: 2 OK 3 nod, yes 4 okay, okeh, okey 5 admit, adopt, agree, allow, go for, leave, say OK, yield 6 accede, accept, accord, comply, concur, give in, say yes 7 approve, consent, go-ahead, go along, include, welcome 8 approval, sanction, stand for, thumbs-up, very well 9 accession, acquiesce, admission, agreement, recognize, sign off on 10 acceptance, compliance, concession, concur with, green light, permission, submission
nautical ~: 3 aye 6 aye aye 9 aye aye sir
silent ~: 3 nod
slangy ~: 3 yeh, yep, yup 4 yeah 5 uh-huh 6 righto
to: 3 let 5 allow, brook 6 accept, permit 8 sanction, tolerate 9 approve of, authorize, put up with
word of ~: 3 yea, yes 4 amen 5 right 6 rather
assenter: 5 sheep, toady 6 yes man 7 Babbitt
assert: 3 own, say, vow 4 aver, avow, cite, hold, show 5 argue, claim, posit, press, speak, state, swear, utter, voice, vouch 6 affirm, allege, attest, avouch, depone, insist, submit 7 comment, confess, contend, declare, express, profess, protest, purport, speak up, testify, warrant 8 insist on, maintain, point out, proclaim, propound, put forth, speak out 9 emphasize, postulate, predicate, pronounce 10 asseverate, put forward
assertion: 4 oath 5 claim, posit, say-so 6 avowal, remark 7 premise 8 argument 9 admission, assurance, statement, stressing, utterance 10 allegation, confession, contention, expression, insistence, profession
without proof (Lat.): 9 ipse dixit
assertive: 4 firm, sure 5 bossy, macho, pushy 7 assured, certain, decided, forward 8 decisive, emphatic, forceful, militant 9 confident, demanding, insistent, presuming 10 aggressive, commanding, peremptory
not ~: 5 timid
too ~: 5 bossy, pushy
assertory: 10 aggressive

A S

assess: 3 fix, peg, set, tax 4 levy, rate, test 5 assay, check, gauge, guess, judge, value, weigh 6 figure, impose, reckon, regard, review, size up, survey 7 compute, eyeball, measure, valuate 8 appraise, check out, estimate, evaluate, factor in, judgment, keep tabs 9 criticize, determine, pick apart
too highly: 8 overrate
assessed __: 5 value
assessment: 3 fee, tax 4 dues, duty, fine, levy, toll, view 5 price, value 6 charge, rating, tariff, towage 7 opinion 8 estimate, exaction, judgment, usage fee 9 appraisal, criticism, reckoning, valuation 10 estimation, evaluation
amount: 5 ratal
assessor: 5 rater 6 lister 9 inspector
asset: 4 bond, boon, cash, help, plus, tact 5 charm, poise, stock, value 6 beauty, brains, credit, virtue, wealth 7 benefit, capital, holding, service 8 blessing, deftness, good name, good will, resource, strength, valuable 9 advantage, commodity, integrity, inventory 10 investment
financial ~: 2 CD 4 bond, cash 5 money, stock 7 capital, savings 10 investment, real estate
in Italian: 4 bene
negotiator ~: 8 delicacy 9 diplomacy
personal ~: 4 pull 5 charm, magic 6 allure, appeal, glamor 7 charism, glamour 8 charisma, mystique, presence 9 magnetism
__ asset: 5 fixed 6 liquid 7 capital, working
assets: 4 cash 5 funds, goods, means, money, stock, worth 6 equity, estate, riches, wealth 7 capital, chattel, effects, reserve, savings 8 bankroll, holdings, property, reserves 9 principal, resources 10 belongings
aplenty: 6 riches
__ assets: 3 net 5 quick 6 frozen 7 current
__ asset value: 3 net
asseverate: 3 say, vow 4 aver, avow 5 swear, utter, vouch 6 affirm, allege, assert, assure, attest, avouch 7 certify, protest 8 attest to, maintain
asseveration: 3 vow 4 oath 5 claim 6 avowal, pledge 8 averment 9 assurance, utterance
__ as she goes!: 6 Steady
__ as shootin': 4 sure
assibilate: 4 lisp
assiduity: 4 care, zeal 8 industry, keenness, tenacity 9 alertness, attention, briskness, diligence 10 intentness
assiduous: 4 busy, spry 5 astir, fussy, perky 6 active, at work, lively 7 careful, dynamic, finicky, prudent, working 8 animated, bustling, cautious, diligent, exacting, finiking, finnicky, rigorous, sedulous, studious, thorough 9 attentive, energetic, engrossed, judicious, laborious, motivated, observant, sprightly, unfailing 10 fastidious, meticulous, particular, persistent, scrupulous, unflagging
assiduously: 4 hard
assign: 3 put, set, tap 4 cede, deal, give, mete, name, post, rank, send 5 allot, elect, order, place, share 6 assort, choose, commit, devote, enlist, heap on, impute, ration, select 7 appoint, dole out, earmark, empower, entrust, give out, hand out, intrust, mete out, pass out, qualify, specify, station 8 accredit, allocate, dedicate, delegate, deputize, dispense, instruct, nominate, relegate, separate, transfer, turn over 9 apportion, authorize, designate, prescribe 10 commission, distribute, settle upon
assignation: 4 date 5 tryst 7 meeting 10 rendezvous
Assignation, The
author: Edgar Allan Poe
assigned __: 4 risk 7 counsel
assignee: 5 agent
assignment: 3 job 4 duty, post, task, text, work 5 chore, drill, paper, quota, stint 6 affair, charge, errand, lesson, ration 7 mission, project 8 homework, transfer 9 allotment, selection 10 allocation, ascription, commission, delegation, department, employment, hypothesis, nomination, transferal
enviable ~: 4 plum
on ~: 4 busy
work ~: 5 chore, stint 6 errand 7 project 8 activity
__ as silk: 6 smooth
assimilate: 5 adapt, co-opt, sop up 6 absorb, adjust, digest, draw in, embody, gather, imbody, ingest, mingle, osmose, soak up, suck up, take in 7 blend in, conform, drink in, swallow 8 go native, intermix 9 integrate, swallow up 10 comprehend, correspond, homogenize, homologize, understand
as simple as __: 3 ABC
Assisi: 4 city, town 10 embroidery
locale: 5 Italy
assist: 3 aid 4 abet, back, hand, help, lift, tide 5 boost, favor, leg up, serve 6 back up, chip in, second, squire, succor, uphold, wait on 7 backing, bail out, benefit, bolster, further, help out, pitch in, promote, relieve, support, sustain, work for 8 abetment, expedite, stump for, tide over, wait upon 9 be good for, cooperate, court stat, encourage, give a hand, lend a hand 10 facilitate, give a boost, give a leg up, go to bat for, rally round
to a Cockney: 3 'elp
with: 2 go 4 join 5 coact 6 team up 7 connive, go along 8 conspire, take part 9 cooperate, synergize 10 join forces
assistance: 3 aid 4 hand, help, lift, serv. 5 boost, leg up 6 relief, succor 7 backing, comfort, offices, redress, service, subsidy, support 8 abetment, advocacy, donation, guidance, kindness 9 patronage 10 sustenance
Cockney ~: 3 'elp
deserving ~: 5 needy
exclamation: 4 help
of ~: 6 aidful, useful
without ~: 4 solo 5 alone
assistant: 4 aide, mate, temp 5 gofer 6 backup, cohort, deputy, flunky, gopher, helper, second 7 abetter, abettor, acolyte, adjunct, employe, flunkey, partner, teacher 8 employee, henchman, minister 9 accessory, appointee, associate, attendant, auxiliary, coadjutor, colleague, companion, gal Friday, man Friday, secretary, supporter 10 accomplice, aide-de-camp, apprentice, benefactor, coadjutant, cooperator, girl Friday, substitute
Cockney ~: 5 'elper
graduate ~: 7 teacher 10 instructor
legal ~: 10 amanuensis
remedial ~: 5 coach 7 trainer
assistants: 4 help 5 staff
Assistant, The
author: Bernard Malamud
assists: 4 stat
assn.: 2 gp. 3 grp., org., soc.
assoc.: 2 gp. 3 grp., org., soc.
associate: 3 bro, mix, pal 4 ally, chum, link, mate, peer, yoke 5 align, aline, amigo, buddy, crony, group, unite 6 cohort, couple, degree, equate, fellow, friend, hobnob, league, member, mingle, relate 7 adjunct, comrade, conjoin, consort, partner 8 co-worker, intimate, roommate, sidekick, workmate 9 accessory, accompany, affiliate, assistant, attribute, auxiliary, colleague, companion, confidant, correlate, implicate, integrate, pal around, socialize, truck with 10 accomplice, amalgamate, compatriot, connection, cooperator, fraternize, go partners, hang around, join up with, well-wisher
with: 3 mix, see 4 know 5 tie to 6 hobnob, mingle 8 befriend 9 accompany, socialize 10 fraternize
(with): 5 get in, swing 6 attach, line up, take up
with riffraff: 4 slum
associated: 6 allied, joined, mutual, united 7 cognate, related 8 in league, relative 9 attendant, bracketed, connected
be ~ with: 8 belong to
one ~ with (suffix): 3 -eer
Associated __: 5 Press
Associate of __: 4 Arts 7 Science
associates: 6 cohort 9 entourage, personnel
associate's __: 6 degree
association: 3 set, tie 4 band, bond, clan, club, crew, gild, link, ring 5 bunch, crowd, group, guild, order, troop, union 6 circle, clique, league, outfit 7 company, contact, linkage, pairing, society 8 alliance, assembly, congress, marriage, relation 9 syndicate
in close ~: 10 hand in hand
__ association: 4 free, word 5 block, press, trade 6 alumni 7 benefit, stellar
Association, The
song: Along Comes Mary (1966)
Cherish (1966)
Everything That Touches You (1968)
Never My Love (1967)
Windy (1967)
__ as Solomon: 4 wise
Assommoir
author: Émile Zola
assort: 4 cull, rank, rate, sift, sort, type, vary 5 class, grade, group, order, range 6 assign, divide, lay out 7 arrange, catalog, collate 8 allocate, classify, separate, tabulate 9 catalogue, match with 10 categorize, distribute, pigeonhole
assorted: 3 var. 4 misc., mixt 5 mixed 6 divers, hybrid, motley, sundry, varied 7 diverse, several, unalike, various 8 manifold, multiple 9 different
assortment: 3 lot, mix, set 4 hash, olio, pile 5 array, batch, bunch, group, range 6 bundle, choice, jumble, medley 7 mélange, mixture, package, variety 8 mishmash, mixed bag, pastiche 9 diversity, potpourri, selection 10 collection, cumulation, hodgepodge, miscellany
asst.: 3 ADC, dep. 4 adjt., secy.
asst. __: 4 prof.
__ asst.: 5 admin.
assuage: 4 calm, cool, ease 5 allay, quell, quiet, quite, salve, slake, still 6 lessen, pacify, quench, remedy, smooth, soften, solace, soothe, temper 7 appease, comfort, compose, console, lighten, mollify, placate, qualify, relieve, satisfy, sweeten 8 mitigate, moderate, palliate 9 alleviate, reconcile, untrouble 10 conciliate, propitiate
assuagement: 4 balm 7 anodyne
assuasive: 3 lax 4 easy, kind, mild, soft 5 loose 6 easing, gentle, kindly 7 anodyne, clement, lenient, ruthful, sparing 8 flexible, laid-back, merciful, placable, tolerant 9 compliant, easygoing, forgiving, indulgent 10 forbearing, permissive, unexacting
assumably: 6 likely 8 probably
assume: 3 act 4 deem, fake, hold, seem, take 5 adopt, annex, begin, bluff, endue, feign, grant, indue, infer, mimic, posit, put on, seize, swipe, think, trust, usurp 6 accept, affect, bank on, borrow, deduce, gather, look to, reckon, rely on, snatch, take on, take up 7 acquire, believe, count on, imagine, imitate, preempt, presume, pretend, receive, succeed, suppose, surmise, suspect 8 arrogate, conclude, depend on, shoulder, simulate, take over, theorize 9 calculate, count upon, enter upon, postulate, speculate, undertake 10 commandeer, confiscate, conjecture, embark upon, presuppose, set about to, understand
one can ~: 8 probably
the form of: 6 become 8 turn into
assumed: 4 fake, sham 5 bogus, false, given, phony, put-on, tacit 6 ersatz, forged, made-up, phoney, pseudo, unreal 7 feigned, reputed 8 affected, putative, spurious,

unproved, unspoken, unvoiced **9** axiomatic, imaginary, imitation, pretended, synthetic, unnatural **10** artificial, fictitious, fraudulent, understood
appearance: 5 guise
as fact: 5 given **9** axiomatic **10** postulated, understood
identity: 5 cover
name: 5 alias **6** anonym
assuming: 4 bold, rude **5** given, pushy **7** forward, haughty **8** arrogant **9** conceited, egotistic, given that, imperious, providing
that: 4 if so **8** as long as
assumption: 5 basis, guess, hunch, posit **6** belief, taking, theory **7** opinion, premise, seizure, surmise, theorem, thought **8** adoption, takeover **9** accepting, accession, arrogance, cockiness, deduction, embracing, inference, insolence, postulate, suspicion **10** acceptance, arrogation, conjecture, expectancy, hypothesis, usurpation
logical ~: 5 axiom, given, lemma
assurance: 3 vow **4** oath, pawn, seal, sign, word **5** nerve, poise **6** aplomb, pledge, safety **7** bravery, courage, promise **8** audacity, boldness, chutzpah, coolness, firmness, optimism, reliance, security, warranty **9** arrogance, assertion, certainty, certitude, composure, guarantee, impudence, insurance, stability, statement, sure thing **10** collateral, commitment, confidence, conviction, effrontery, engagement, equanimity, expectancy, profession, protection, sedateness
assure: 3 vow **4** aver, avow, seal **5** cinch, sew up, swear, vouch **6** affirm, attest, avouch, clinch, lock up, pledge, secure, settle **7** certify, comfort, confirm, hearten, promise, protect, satisfy, warrant **8** attest to, convince, keep safe, nail down, persuade, put on ice, vouch for **9** guarantee **10** asseverate, underwrite
assured: 3 set **4** bold, cool **5** gutsy, on ice, solid **6** brazen, poised, sealed **7** certain, decided, settled **8** clear-cut, composed, decisive, definite, fearless, in the bag, positive, sanguine **9** assertive, audacious, automatic, confident, presuming **10** conclusive, courageous, inevitable, unagitated, undisputed
__ assured: 4 rest
__-assured: 4 self
assuredly: 5 truly **6** really **8** for a fact
see also of course
Assyria
city: 6 Arbela, Kalakh **7** Nineveh
foe: 4 Mede
language: 8 Accadian, Akkadian
Asta: 3 dog **5** pooch **6** canine **7** terrier
owner: Nick Charles, Nora Charles
Astaire: 4 Fred **5** Adele
and Rogers: 3 duo **4** pair, team
Astaire, Fred: 5 actor **6** dancer
film: The Band Wagon (1953)
The Barkleys of Broadway (1949)
Blue Skies (1946)
Broadway Melody of 1940 (1940)
Carefree (1938)
Daddy Long Legs (1955)
A Damsel in Distress (1937)
Easter Parade (1948)
Finian's Rainbow (1968)
Flying Down to Rio (1933)
Follow the Fleet (1936)
Funny Face (1957)
The Gay Divorcee (1934)
Ghost Story (1981)
Holiday Inn (1942)
On the Beach (1959)
The Pleasure of His Company (1961)
Roberta (1935)
Royal Wedding (1951)
Shall We Dance (1937)
Silk Stockings (1957)
The Sky's the Limit (1943)
The Story of Vernon & Irene Castle (1939)
Swing Time (1936)
Three Little Words (1950)
Top Hat (1935)
The Towering Inferno (1974)
You'll Never Get Rich (1941)
You Were Never Lovelier (1942)
Ziegfeld Follies (1946)
hometown: 5 Omaha
like ~: 5 suave
partner: Ginger Rogers
prop: 4 cane **6** top hat
sister: 5 Adele
spouse: Robyn Smith
__ a stand: 4 take
astare: 6 gaping, gazing **7** gawking, glaring **8** goggling, open-eyed **10** goggle-eyed
astart: 8 suddenly
astatine: 7 element, halogen
compound: 6 halide
asteam: 7 boiling **8** vaporous
aster: 5 plant **6** flower **8** starwort
ending: 3 oid
__ aster: 4 tree **5** beach, China **6** golden **7** Italian
asterisk: 4 star
neighbor: 3 PRS **4** OPER **9** ampersand **10** paren. eight
Asterius
wife: 6 Europa
astern: 3 aft **4** back, rear **5** abaft **6** behind **7** aftward **8** backward, rearward **9** backwards, to the rear
asteroid: 3 Ida **4** Eros, Hebe, Iris, Juno **5** Aegle, Ceres, Doris, Elpis, Freia, Hilda, Irene, Palma, Vesta **6** Alauda, Apollo, Aurora, Bertha, Chiron, Cybebe, Cybele, Daphne, Davida, Egeria, Europa, Gaspra, Hygiea, Icarus, Nereus, Pallas, Prokne, Psyche, Rodari, Shipka, Sylvia **7** Camilla, Diotima, Elektra, Eugenia, Eunomia, Nemesis, Siegena **8** Aletheia, Bamberga, Hermione, Kalliope, Lachesis, Mathilde, Pretoria **9** Agamemnon, Herculina, Patientia **10** Amphitrite, Euphrosyne, Geographos, Interamnia, Winchester
fourth-largest ~: 4 Juno
largest ~: 5 Ceres
region: 4 belt
second-largest ~: 6 Pallas
third-largest ~: 5 Vesta
as the __ flies: 4 crow
__ as the driven snow: 4 pure
__ as the eye can see: 5 as far
__ as the hills: 3 old
Asther: 4 Nils
As the World Turns: 4 soap **9** soap opera
As Thousands Cheer: 7 musical
composer: Irving Berlin
Asti: 4 city, town
locale: 5 Italy **8** Piedmont
product: 4 vino
river: 6 Tanaro
__ a stick at: 5 shake
__ a stiff upper lip: 4 keep
As Time Goes By: 4 song
requester: 4 Ilsa
singer: 3 Sam
Astin: 4 John, Sean **9** Mackenzie
Astin, John
spouse: Patty Duke
__ a stink: 4 make **5** raise
__ a stinker?: 5 Ain't I
astir: 2 up **4** busy, spry **5** afoot, perky **6** active, at work, lively, moving, roused **7** abroach, buzzing, dynamic, excited, wakeful, walking, working **8** animated, bustling, in motion, out of bed, stirring, underway, waking up **9** assiduous, energetic, on the move, sprightly **10** ambulatory, busy as a bee, up and about
set ~: 8 motivate
Astley: 4 Rick
Astolat
lily maid of ~: 6 Elaine
astonish: 3 awe **4** daze, jolt, stun **5** amaze, floor, shock, throw **6** boggle, dazzle **7** astound, nonplus, perplex, petrify, stagger, startle, stupefy **8** bewilder, blow away, bowl over, confound, surprise **9** dumbfound, knock over, overwhelm, take aback
astonished: 4 agog **5** agape **6** aghast **10** bewildered
astonishing: 7 awesome, strange, uncanny, unusual **8** striking **9** marvelous, wonderful **10** prodigious, stupendous
astonishingly: 4 very
astonishment: 3 awe **5** shock **6** wonder **8** surprise
exclamation: 3 wow **4** jeez, whew **5** zowie **6** by Jove, crikey, cripes **7** by jingo, caramba, holy cow **8** holy moly
show ~: 4 gape, gasp
astoop: 4 bent **8** bent over
Astor: 4 Mary, peak **5** mount, Nancy **6** Brooke **8** mountain **9** John Jacob, Piazzolla
concern: 3 fur **4** pelt
locale: 10 Antarctica
Astoria
author: Edgar Allan Poe
locale: 3 Ore. **6** Oregon
__ Astoria: 7 Waldorf
astound: 3 wow **4** daze, jolt, stun **5** amaze, floor, shock **6** baffle, boggle **7** nonplus, perplex, petrify, stagger, startle, stupefy **8** astonish, bewilder, blow away, bowl over, surprise **9** dumbfound, knock over, overwhelm, take aback
astounded: 5 agape **6** aghast **9** awestruck **10** bewildered, breathless, speechless
astounding: 7 strange, uncanny **8** fabulous **9** appalling, marvelous, wonderful **10** incredible, prodigious
astraddle: 2 on **6** across **7** astride **9** pickaback, piggyback **10** indecisive
astragalus: 4 bone **5** ankle
__ a straight face: 4 keep
astrakhan: 3 fur **5** cloth **6** fabric
astral: 6 sphery, starry **7** stellar **8** heavenly, sidereal, starlike **9** celestial, unworldly **10** of the stars, star-shaped
__ a Stranger: 5 Not as
astraphobe
fear: 7 thunder **9** lightning
astray: 3 off **4** awry, lost, wide **5** amiss, wrong **6** absent, adrift, afield, erring **7** in error, missing, roaming **8** errantly **9** far afield, off course, wandering **10** off the beam, off the mark, off the path
go ~: 3 err, sin **4** fail **6** derail, ramble, wander **9** backslide, misbehave
gone ~: 4 lost **7** mislaid, missing **9** misplaced
lead ~: 4 ruin **5** tempt **6** outwit **7** deprave, mislead **8** outsmart **9** misinform
Astre: 3 car **4** auto **7** Pontiac **10** automobile
astride: 4 atop **7** athwart **9** astraddle
get ~: 5 mount
astringency: 7 acidity
astringent: 4 alum, sour, tart **5** acrid, harsh, sharp, stern **6** acetic, biting, bitter, severe **7** cutting, pungent
astro-: 4 star
Astro: 3 dog, van **4** NLer **5** Chevy **9** Chevrolet
astrobiology: 7 science
Astro Boy: 5 anime
astrochemistry: 7 science
astrogeology: 7 science
astrologer: 5 magus **7** diviner, prophet
concern: 3 zod. **4** cusp, moon, sign **6** zodiac **9** horoscope
astrologers: 4 magi
astrological sign: 3 Leo, Ram **4** Bull, Crab, Goat, Lion **5** Aries, Libra, Twins, Virgo **6** Archer, Cancer, Fishes, Gemini, Maiden, Pisces, Scales, Taurus **7** Balance, Scorpio **8** Aquarius, Scorpion **9** Capricorn **11** Sagittarius, Water Bearer
astron.: 3 sci.
astronaut: 8 spaceman **9** cosmonaut, rocketeer **10** moonwalker
affirmative: 3 A-OK
Apollo ~: 4 Bean, Duke, Ride **5** Evans, Haise, Irwin, Roosa, Scott, Young **6** Aldrin, Anders, Borman, Cernan, Conrad, Eisele, Gordon, Lovell, Worden **7** Collins, Schirra, Schmitt, Shepard, Swigert **8** McDivitt, Mitchell, Stafford **9** Armstrong, Mattingly **10** Cunningham **11** Schweickart
concern: 6 G force **7** reentry
drink: 4 Tang
excursion: 3 EVA

Gemini ~: 5 Scott, White, Young 6 Aldrin, Borman, Cernan, Conrad, Cooper, Gordon, Lovell 7 Collins, Grissom, Schirra 8 McDivitt, Stafford 9 Armstrong
Mercury ~: 5 Glenn 6 Cooper 7 Grissom, Schirra, Shepard, Slayton 9 Carpenter
milieu: 4 moon 5 ether, space 6 aether 10 outer space
org.: 4 NASA
rotate, to an ~: 3 yaw
vehicle: 3 LEM
wear: 5 G-suit 6 helmet
astronautics: 7 science
astronomer: 4 Ryle 5 Brahe, Sagan 6 Draper, Halley, Hubble, Kepler, Piazzi, Sitter 7 Celsius, Galilei, Huggins, Huygens, Laplace, Ptolemy 8 Ångström, Herschel, Lagrange, Tombaugh 9 Eddington 10 Copernicus, Hipparchus 11 Aristarchus, Omar Khayyám 12 Eratosthenes, Schiaparelli
British ~: 4 Ryle 6 Halley 7 Huggins 8 Herschel 9 Eddington
Danish ~: 5 Brahe 10 Tycho Brahe
Dutch ~: 6 Sitter 7 Huygens
Egyptian ~: 7 Ptolemy
French ~: 7 Laplace 8 Lagrange
German ~: 6 Kepler
Greek ~: 10 Hipparchus 11 Aristarchus 12 Eratosthenes
Italian ~: 6 Piazzi 7 Galilei 12 Schiaparelli
Persian ~: 4 Omar
Polish ~: 10 Copernicus
Swedish ~: 7 Celsius 8 Ångström
astronomical: 4 vast 8 enormous
adjective: 5 lunar, solar
difference: 5 epact
instrument: 6 gnomon 9 telescope
shadow: 5 umbra
unit: 4 year
astronomical ___: 4 unit, year 5 clock
astronomy: 7 science 9 uranology 10 astrometry, selenology, stargazing
high point in ~: 6 apogee
study: 5 stars
Astrophel
author: Algernon Swinburne, Edmund Spenser
Astrophel and Stella: 4 poem
author: Philip Sidney
astrophysics: 7 science
study: 5 stars 9 radiation
Astros: 4 nine, team
home: 5 Texas 7 Houston
org.: 3 MLB, NLC
rival: *see* baseball team
sport: 8 baseball
Astroturf
alternative: 3 sod 5 grass
component: 5 nylon, vinyl
Astrud: 8 Gilberto
Asturias, Miguel: 6 writer 8 Nobelist 10 Guatemalan
astute: 3 apt, hip, sly 4 foxy, keen, sage, wily, wise 5 acute, canny, quick, ready, savvy, sharp, smart 6 adroit, brainy, bright, clever, crafty, shrewd, subtle 7 cunning, knowing 8 sensible 9 brilliant, farseeing, ingenious, in the know, inventive, judicious, on the ball, realistic, sagacious 10 discerning, insightful, longheaded, perceptive, thoughtful
astuteness: 3 art, wit 4 wits 5 depth 6 acumen, genius, vision, wisdom 8 judgment, keenness 9 smartness 10 cleverness, horse sense
ASU
conference: 6 Pac-Ten
___ a sudden: 5 all of
Asunción: 4 city, port, town 7 capital
locale: 8 Paraguay
see also Spanish
asunder: 4 torn 5 apart, in two, loose, riven, split 6 ripped 7 divided 8 separate 9 disjoined, separated 10 into pieces
prefix: 3 dis-
put ~: 3 cut, hew, rip 4 chop, part, rend 5 sever, slash, split 6 cleave, divide 7 disjoin 8 dissever, disunite, separate
Aswan: 3 dam 4 city, town
locale: 5 Egypt
river: 4 Nile
Aswan High ___: 3 Dam
aswarm: 7 buzzing, teeming
___ a swath: 3 cut
___ as we speak: 4 even
aswim: 5 dizzy 8 floating
aswirl: 7 eddying, turning 8 twisting
aswoon: 8 fainting 10 blacked out
asylum: 3 ark 4 nest 5 cover, haven, oasis 6 harbor, refuge, safety 7 harbour, retreat, shelter 8 hideaway 9 anchorage, safe house, sanctuary 10 ivory tower
seeker: 5 alien 6 émigré
asymmetric: 6 skewed, uneven 7 crooked, unequal 8 cockeyed, lopsided
asymmetry: 9 deformity 10 contortion, difference, distortion
___ a Symphony: 5 I Hear
as you ___: 4 were
___ as you are: 4 come
___-as-you-go: 3 pay
As You Like It
author: William Shakespeare
character: 4 Adam 5 Celia, Corin, Phebe 6 Amiens, Audrey, Jaques, Le Beau, Oliver 7 Charles, Orlando, Silvius, William 8 Rosalind 9 Frederick 10 Duke Senior, Touchstone
setting: 5 Arden
As you wish: 6 so be it
at: 2 by, on 4 when
at ___: 3 all, bat, one, sea, war 4 best, cost, ease, hand, heel, home, last, most, odds, once, rest, risk, that, will, work 5 a blow, a clip, a loss, an end, a word, fault, heart, issue, large, least, peace, sight, stake, times, worst 6 bottom, length, random 7 liberty, present
at ___ and sevens: 5 sixes
at ___ cost: 3 any
at ___ ebb: 3 low
at ___ end: 4 wit's
at ___ ends: 5 loose
at ___ for words: 5 a loss
at ___ glance: 5 first
at ___ juncture: 4 this
at ___ last: 4 long
at ___ length: 4 arm's
at ___-purposes: 5 cross
at ___ rate: 3 any
at ___ sight: 5 first
at ___ tilt: 4 full
at ___ time: 3 one 4 this
at ___ turn: 5 every
___ at: 3 aim, eat, fly, get, has, set 4 come, gnaw, have, hint, keep, pick, play, rail, tear, wink 5 drive, laugh, scoff, snipe, swear 6 arrive, nibble, sneeze
'at
where to 'ang one's ~: 3 'ome
___ a T: 4 do to 5 fit to
At: 4 elem. 7 element 8 astatine
85 for ~: 4 at. no.
At ___!: 4 ease
At ___ end: 4 wit's
At ___ Last Love: 4 Long
AT: 2 PC 3 IBM
at a ___: 4 blow, clip, loss, word 5 price 6 gallop, glance 7 premium, venture
at a ___ date: 5 later
at a ___ for words: 4 loss
at a ___ notice: 7 moment's
at a ___ pace: 6 snail's
___-Ata: 4 Alma
Atacama Desert
locale: 5 Chile
___ a tad: 4 just
___ at a disadvantage: 3 put
___ at a glance: 4 tell
___ at a gnat: 6 strain
Atahualpa: 4 Inca
Atalanta: 6 hunter
composer: George Frideric Handel
fruit: 5 apple
like ~: 5 fleet
lover: 4 Ares
Atalanta in Calydon: 4 poem
author: Algernon Swinburne
at a later ___: 4 date
___ a tale told by an idiot: 4 It is
at a moment's ___: 6 notice
___ a tangent: 5 off on
at any ___: 4 cost, rate
___ at Any Speed: 6 Unsafe
atap: 4 nipa, palm 6 thatch
ataraxy: 10 equanimity
Atari
early ~ game: 4 Pong
rival: 6 Coleco
at arm's ___: 6 length
___-at-arms: 3 man 6 master
at a snail's ___: 4 pace
___-a-tat: 3 rat
___ at a time: 3 one, two
Atatürk: 5 Kemal
Atatürk, Kemal
colleague: Ismet Inonu
atavism: 9 reversion, throwback 10 recurrence
atavistic: 9 primitive
at bat: 4 stat
has an ~: 4 is up
successful ~: 3 hit
___ at Bay: 4 Bech
___ at Campobello: 7 Sunrise
___ at Diablo: 4 Duel
ate: 5 dined 6 eroded, noshed, supped 7 snacked
ate ___: 4 crow
Ate
parent: 4 Eris, Zeus
A-team: 7 varsity
A-Team, The (NBC adventure)
cast: Dirk Benedict (Templeton 'Face' Peck) Mr. T (B.A. 'Bad Attitude' Baracus) George Peppard (John 'Hannibal' Smith) Dwight Schultz (H.M. 'Howling Mad' Murdock)
___ at ease: 3 ill
___ a Teen-age Werewolf: 4 I Was
___ at Eight: 6 Dinner
atelier: 3 den 4 loft 6 garret, studio 8 workroom, workshop
item: 5 easel 7 palette
occupant: 6 artist
___ at 'em!: 5 Up and
a tergo: 9 in the back
___ à terre: 6 ventre
___-à-terre: 4 pied
Ates: 6 Roscoe
at every ___: 4 turn
ATF
department: 8 Treasury
part: 7 Alcohol, Tobacco 8 Firearms
at first ___: 5 sight 6 glance
___ at First Bite: 4 Love
___ at first sight: 4 love
at full ___: 4 tilt
Athabasca: 4 lake
locale: 6 Canada 7 Alberta
Athamas
brother: 8 Sisyphus
wife: 3 Ino
at hand
not: 4 afar
___ at hand: 4 near 5 close
___ at Heart: 5 Young
At Heaven's Gate
author: Robert Penn Warren
___-at-heel: 4 down
atheism: 8 nihilism 9 disbelief, nonbelief
atheist: 5 pagan 6 denier 7 infidel, sceptic, skeptic
noted: Madalyn Murray O'Hair
atheistic: 7 godless, impious, profane 9 heretical
athel: 4 tree 9 evergreen
Athena: 7 goddess 8 Olympian
animal sacred to ~: 7 rooster, serpent 8 sea eagle
artist: Erté
epithet of ~: 4 Alea, Nike**equivalent:** 7 Minerva
lover: 10 Hephaestus
parent: 4 Zeus 5 Metis 8 Poseidon
shield: 4 egis 5 aegis
symbol: 3 owl
___ Athena: 6 Pallas
athenaeum: 7 library
Athenian: 5 Attic
see also Greek
Athens: 4 city, town 5 polis 7 capital
athletes: 7 Bobcats 8 Bulldogs
locale: 4 Ohio 6 Greece 7 Georgia
of America: 6 Boston
region: 6 Attica
rival: 5 Argos 6 Sparta, Thebes
school: 3 U. Ga. 5 Ohio U. 7 Georgia
see also Greek
Atherton: 7 William
athirst: 3 dry 4 avid, keen 5 eager 7 craving, longing, orectic, parched, wishful 8 desirous, yearning

athlete: **3** end **4** jock **5** boxer, guard **6** bowler, goalie, golfer, jockey, player, runner, tackle **7** catcher, forward, gymnast, hurdler, pitcher **8** fullback, halfback **9** shortstop, sportsman **10** competitor, marathoner, outfielder
assignment: **6** locker
contract clause: **5** no-cut
energy source: **4** carb
__ Athlete Dying Young: **4** To an
athlete's foot: **5** tinea
like ~ foot: **5** itchy
athletic: **3** fit **4** hale, iron, team, wiry **5** agile, beefy, burly, hardy, hefty, hunky, husky, lusty, stout, tough **6** brawny, hearty, mighty, potent, robust, rugged, sinewy, steely, stocky, strong, sturdy, virile **7** doughty, healthy **8** forceful, indurate, muscular, powerful, puissant, sporting, stalwart, vigorous **9** Atlantean, Herculean, strapping, well-built **10** able-bodied, red-blooded
activity: **5** sport
award: **6** letter
club: **3** gym
event: **4** bout, game, meet **5** match
field: **5** arena **7** stadium
group: **3** sqd. **4** team **5** squad
old ~ contest: **4** agon
shirt: **6** jersey
trial: **4** heat
athletic __: **4** shoe
Athletic Hall-of-Famer: **6** Bender
athletics: **5** games, races, sport **6** sports **7** contest **9** exercises **10** recreation
Athletics: **3** ten **4** team
home: **7** Oakland **10** California
org.: **3** ALW, MLB
rival: *see* baseball team
sport: **8** baseball
Athol: **6** Fugard
at-home: **5** party
__-at-home: **4** stay
Athos
companion: **6** Aramis **7** Porthos **9** d'Artagnan
...a thousand __ no!: **5** times
__ a Thousand Faces: **5** Man of
__, a thousand times...: **4** No no
athrob: **7** beating, pulsing **8** pounding **9** pulsating
athwart: **4** awry **5** askew **6** across, askant, versus **7** against, astride, sideway **8** sidelong, sideways, sidewise **9** adverse to, counter to, crossways, crosswise, obliquely, on the bias, opposed to **10** contrary to, contrawise, crisscross, perversely
__ a tie: **5** end in
__ a Tightrope: **5** Man on
atilt: **5** askew **6** canted **7** leaning, listing **8** cockeyed, inclined, jousting, lopsided, off plumb, slanting **9** at an angle, off-center **10** out of whack
__ a time: **4** many **5** one at, two at
atip: **9** expectant
A-Tisket, A-Tasket
artist: Ella Fitzgerald
__ at it: **4** keep
__ at Joe's: **3** Eat
Atkins
diet no-no: **5** bread, carbs, sugar
__ Atkins: **5** Tommy
Atkins, Chet: **9** guitarist
Atkinson: **5** Rowan **6** Brooks
Atlanta: **4** city, town
city near ~: **5** Macon
county: **6** Fulton
for Delta Airlines: **3** hub
former ~ arena: **4** Omni
health agcy.: **3** CDC
locale: **7** Georgia
network: **3** CNN
pro team: **5** Hawks **6** Braves **7** Falcons **9** Thrashers
school: **3** GIT **5** Emory **6** Emory U.
transit system: **5** MARTA
zone: **3** EDT, EST
Atlantean
see brawny
Atlantic: **5** ocean **6** avenue
bay: **4** Faxa, Vigo **5** Fundy **6** Biscay, Walvis **7** Setúbal, Walfish **8** Biscayne, Delaware **9** Frobisher, Penobscot **10** Chesapeake
cape: **3** Cod
desert on the ~: **6** Sahara
fish: **3** cod, sey **4** cero, cusk, hake, jack, mapo **5** lotte, porgy, saury, snook **6** gunnel, saithe, tarpon, tautog, tomcod **7** cavalla, croaker, graysby, haddock, halibut, herring, margate, pollack, pollock, pomfret, torpedo, whiting **8** mackerel, sea raven, wrymouth **9** amberjack
flier: **3** ern **4** erne **5** Lindy **9** Lindbergh
gulf: **6** Guinea, Mexico **8** San Jorge **9** San Matias
island: **4** Icel. **7** Bermuda, Iceland
on the ~: **4** asea **5** at sea
river to the ~: **4** Miño **5** Congo, Douro, Loire, Minho, Tagus, Zaire **6** Amazon, Gambia, Orange, Pee Dee, Santee, Thjórs **7** Orinoco, Shannon **8** Demerara, Hamilton, Kennebec, Parnaiba, Savannah **9** Merrimack
state: **3** Del., Fla. **4** Mass., N. Car., S. Car. **5** Maine **7** Florida, Georgia, New York **8** Delaware, Maryland, Virginia **9** New Jersey **11** Rhode Island
Atlantic City: **4** town
attraction: **4** surf **5** beach **6** casino, dealer **7** pit boss **8** croupier, employee **9** boardwalk
game: **4** faro, keno **5** craps, poker **8** baccarat, roulette
locale: **9** New Jersey
treat: **5** taffy
Atlantic City (1981 film)
cast: Burt Lancaster, Kate Reid, Susan Sarandon
director: Louis Malle
Atlantic Coast Conference
school: **3** FSU **4** Duke **7** Clemson **8** Maryland, Virginia **10** Wake Forest **11** Georgia Tech
__-Atlantique: **5** Loire
Atlantis: **4** isle **6** island **7** shuttle
org.: **4** NASA
Atlantis (1969 song)
artist: Donovan
atlas: **3** map **4** book **7** telamon
abbr.: **3** Atl., isl., lat., mtn., mts., Pac., riv., str., ter., tpk. **4** isth., terr.
alternative: **5** globe
amend an ~: **5** remap
blowup: **5** inset
datum: **4** area
dot: **3** isl. **4** isle, town **5** islet **6** island
line: **4** road **5** route
section: **4** Asia
unit: **3** map **4** sq. mi. **10** square mile
__ atlas: **4** road
Atlas: **4** ICBM, moon, star **5** giant, he-man, range, Titan **7** Charles, missile
brother: **10** Prometheus
daughter: **4** Maia **7** Alcyone, Calypso, Electra **8** Ambrosia, Arethusa, Hesperia
mountains locale: **3** Afr. **6** Africa, Sahara **7** Algeria, Morocco, Tunisia
parent: **7** Clymene, Iapetus
planet: **6** Saturn
rocket: **5** Agena
son: **4** Hyas
Atlas Shrugged
author: Ayn Rand
character: **3** Ben, Dan **4** Dick, Galt, Hank, Mort, Owen, Paul **5** Balph, Boyle, Dagny, Eddie, Ellis, Liddy, Mouch, Mowen, Nealy, Orren, Simon, Wyatt **6** Conway, Eubank, Halley, Larkin, Ragnar, Robert, Wesley **7** Bertram, Kellogg, Lillian, Reardon, Richard, Scudder, Stadler, Taggart, Willers **8** d'Anconia, McNamara **9** Francisco, Pritchett
Atli: **3** Hun
at long __: **4** last
At Long Last Love
composer: Cole Porter
at loose __: **4** ends
at low __: **3** ebb
ATM
action: **5** swipe
button: **5** enter **6** cancel
code: **3** PIN
device: **3** CRT
maker: **3** NCR
part: **6** keypad, teller **7** machine **9** automatic
ATM __: **3** fee
atmo-
kin: **3** aer- **4** aero-
Atmos: **5** clock
atmosphere: **3** air, sky **4** aura, feel, mood **5** aroma, clime, sense **6** milieu, spirit **7** climate, heavens **8** ambiance, ambience, empyrean, envelope **9** character, semblance, undertone **10** background, impression, local color
combining form: **3** aer- **4** aeri-, aero-
part of the ~: **4** neon **5** argon, ozone **6** oxygen **8** nitrogen
unhealthful ~: **9** pollution
upper ~: **3** sky **5** ether **6** aether
atmospheric: **4** airy **5** light **6** aerial
__ at Nite: **4** Nick
at no __: **4** cost, time
at no extra __: **4** cost **6** charge
__ at nothing: **4** stop
a to __: **3** zed
atoll: **4** reef, Wake **6** Bikini, island **8** Eniwetok
feature: **5** coral **6** lagoon
like an ~: **5** reefy
__ a toll on: **4** take
atom: **3** bit, dot, jot **4** iota, mite, mote, whit **5** crumb, grain, scrap, shred, speck, trace **6** morsel **7** modicum, smidgen, smidgin **8** particle, smidgeon **9** scintilla
charged ~: **3** ion **5** anion **6** cation
ender: **3** ism
exciter: **5** maser
group of ~s: **3** mol. **8** molecule
ID: **4** at. no.
smashing: **7** fission
with a valence of one: **5** monad
atom __: **4** bomb **7** smasher
atomic: **3** wee **4** puny, tiny **5** bitty, least, small, teeny **6** little, minute, peewee, petite, teensy **7** nuclear, trivial **9** itsy-bitsy, itty-bitty, miniature, pint-sized **10** diminutive, teeny-weeny, vest-pocket
clock device: **5** maser
energy org.: **3** NRC
experiment: **5** A-test, N-test
reaction: **6** fusion **7** fission
atomic __: **4** bomb, mass, pile **5** clock, power **6** energy, number, theory, volume, weight **7** orbital, reactor
Atomic __: **3** Age
Atomic __ Commission: **6** Energy
__ Atomic Dustbin: **4** Ned's
Atomic Leda
artist: Salvador Dalí
atomize: **5** grind, spray **9** granulate, pulverize
atomizer: **9** vaporizer
output: **4** mist **5** scent, spray **7** perfume
atomlike: **3** wee **4** puny, tiny **5** small
Atoms for __: **5** Peace
atonal: **7** keyless, raucous, unkeyed **9** dissonant, unmelodic **10** discordant
__ at once: **3** all
atone: **3** pay **5** purge **6** make up, purify, repent **7** satisfy **9** indemnify, make right, reconcile **10** compensate, make amends
for: **6** redeem **7** expiate **8** make good, outweigh, set right **9** make right **10** recompense
at one __: **4** time
at one __ swoop: **4** fell
atonement: **6** amends **7** penance, redress **8** offering **9** expiation **10** recompense, redemption, reparation
Atonement (2007 film)
cast: Keira Knightley, James McAvoy
__ Atonement: **5** Day of
atoner: **4** ruer
at one's __: **5** elbow, mercy **7** leisure
at one's __ and call: **4** beck
at one's __ end: **4** wit's
__ at one's door: **3** lay
__ at one's word: **4** take
atonic: **4** puny, weak **5** frail, wimpy **6** anemic, effete, feeble, flabby, flimsy **7** anaemic, fragile, wimpish

8 delicate, helpless, pithless 9 faltering, out of tune, powerless 10 unaccented, unstressed, vulnerable
atop: 3 o'er 4 over, upon 5 above, aloft 6 upward 7 astride 8 overhead 9 resting on, sitting on 10 straddling
rest ~: 5 lie on
__ a torch: 5 carry
__ at Oxford: 5 A Yank
atoxic: 6 benign
__ A to Z: 4 from
__ at Pooh Corner, The: 5 House
__ atque vale: 3 ave
__ a trail: 5 blaze
__ a trap: 3 set
atremble: 5 jumpy
atrip: 6 aweigh 7 hoisted
atrium: 5 court, lobby 9 courtyard
atrocious *see* awful
atrocity: 3 sin 4 evil 5 crime 6 infamy 7 outrage 8 enormity 10 corruption, inhumanity, wickedness
atrophy: 5 decay, waste 6 wither 7 decline 8 decrease, emaciate
Atropos: 4 Fate
colleague: 6 Clotho 8 Lachesis
mother: 6 Themis
__ at Sea: 3 All 4 Saps 5 Dames, Souls 7 Pilgrim
At Seventeen (1975 song)
artist: Janis Ian
AT&SF: 2 RR 8 railroad
stop: 3 sta., stn. 7 station
at sixes and __: 6 sevens
__ at straws: 5 grasp
att.: 3 LL.B., LL.D., rep. 4 lwyr.
Att. __: 3 Gen.
AT&T
competitor: 3 GTE, MCI 6 Nextel 7 T-Mobile, Verizon
employee: 4 oper. 8 operator
part of ~: 3 Tel. 4 Amer., Tele. 8 American 9 Telegraph, Telephone
spin-off: 5 NYNEX
__ Atta Annan: 4 Kofi
attach: 3 fix, pin, tie 4 bind, glue, join, lace, link, nail, tack, weld, yoke 5 add on, affix, annex, cling, hitch, pin on, river, rivet, sew on, stick, tie on, unite 6 adhere, adjoin, append, assail, cement, cleave, clip on, cohere, couple, enroot, fasten, hook on, hook up, impute, iron on, secure, slap on, staple, tack on, take on 7 combine, conjoin, connect, garnish, hitch on, latch on, stick on 8 hook onto 9 thumbtack
weight to: 6 accept 7 presume
attaché: 3 bag 4 aide 5 envoy 6 consul, legate 8 diplomat 9 briefcase
case: 3 bag 9 portfolio
attaché __: 4 case
attached: 4 fast 5 loyal 6 adnate, loving
be ~ to: 4 love
no strings ~: 8 optional
attachment: 3 tie 4 bond, lien, link, love 5 annex, extra, rider 6 liking, regard, Velcro 7 adapter, adaptor, adjunct, fitting, loyalty, passion, romance 8 addendum, addition, affinity, appendix, coupling, devotion, fastener, fondness, junction, juncture, vinculum 9 accessory, adoration, affection, amendment, appendage, auxiliary, belonging, coherence, connector, constancy, extension, fastening, fixedness, hankering, puppy love 10 annexation, attraction, connection, elongation, endearment, friendship, high regard, partiality, supplement, tenderness
attack: 3 fit, mob, mug, ply, rip, sic, war 4 bash, bomb, bout, claw, fire, flay, go at, lash, raid, rush, slam, tilt, turn 5 abuse, beset, blast, blitz, blows, fight, fly at, foray, go for, lay to, libel, onset, run at, sally, salvo, set at, set on, siege, spasm, spell, stone, storm, swoop 6 accuse, ambush, assail, battle, charge, claw at, combat, dump on, engage, fall on, have at, hit out, impugn, invade, jump on, larrup, oppose, oppugn, pounce, prey on, rail at, sortie, strafe, strike, tackle, take up, vilify, volley, wallop, waylay 7 aggress, asperse, assault, barrage, battery, besiege, bombard, calumny, charges, contest, descent, go after, lambast, lash out, lay into, mugging, offense, rip into, set upon, slander 8 backbite, campaign, deal with, denounce, dive into, fall upon, fire upon, gang up on, invasion, lambaste, outbreak, outburst, skirmish, tear into, violence 9 broadside, criticism, criticize, encounter, excoriate, fustigate, haul off on, incursion, intrude on, intrusion, irruption, lash out at, light into, offensive, onslaught, pitch into, start in on 10 aggression, ambushment, assailment, impugnment, lay siege to, plunge into, pounce upon
like a hawk: 7 descend, plummet 9 sweep down
open to ~: 9 unguarded 10 vulnerable
starter: 7 counter
succumb to ~: 4 fall
surprise ~: 4 raid 5 foray 6 ambush 10 ambushment
time: 4 D-Day 5 H-Hour
unfair ~: 9 cheap shot
unlikely to ~: 4 tame
verbally: 4 bash, belt, damn, slur 5 abuse, smear 6 defame, deride, impugn, insult, malign, scathe, vilify 7 potshot, run down, slander 8 badmouth, belittle, lace into, lambaste, reproach, throw mud 9 castigate, criticize, disparage, shoot down
word: 3 sic
attack __: 3 dog
__ attack: 4 Shaq 5 panic, sneak
Attack!: 5 sic 'em
attacker: 3 foe 5 enemy 6 critic, mugger, raider 7 invader 8 vilifier 9 aggressor, assailant, assaulter, combatant, ill-wisher
__ Attacks!: 4 Mars
attain: 3 get, hit, win 4 earn, find, gain 5 get to, grasp, learn, reach 6 come by, come to, fulfil, obtain, rack up, secure 7 achieve, acquire, compass, fulfill, procure, realize 8 arrive at, bring off, glom onto 10 accomplish
fail to ~: 4 miss
attainable: 6 doable, likely, viable 7 in reach 8 credible, feasible, possible, workable 9 available, no problem, plausible, potential, practical, reachable, securable 10 accessible, achievable, imaginable, obtainable, procurable, realizable
attainment: 4 feat, gain 7 mastery, success, triumph 8 fruition 9 accession, actuality, obtaining 10 background, completion, succeeding
attaint: 8 disgrace, dishonor
attar: 7 essence, perfume 9 fragrance
Atta Troll: 4 poem
author: Heinrich Heine
Attell: 3 Abe 4 Dave
attempt: 2 go 3 aim, bid, try 4 seek, shot, stab 5 crack, essay, fling, trial, whack, whirl 6 chance, effort, header, intend, pursue, strive, tackle, take on, tryout 7 pursuit, venture 8 endeavor, struggle 9 give it a go, undertake 10 enterprise, experiment, make a run at
again: 5 retry
boldly ~: 4 dare
brief ~: 4 stab 5 whirl
failed ~: 4 miss
Attenborough, Richard: 3 Sir 5 actor 8 director
film: Chaplin (1992)
A Chorus Line (1985)
Doctor Dolittle (1967)
Flight of the Phoenix (1966)
Gandhi (1982, AA)
The Great Escape (1963)
Jurassic Park (1993)
The Sand Pebbles (1966)
attend: 3 see, tag 4 be at, go to, hark, heed, look, mark, mind, show, tend 5 guard, guide, nurse, pop up, see to, serve, sit in, visit, watch 6 appear, come to, drop in, escort, listen, look to, make it, notice, occupy, regard, show up, squire, take in, turn up, wait on 7 care for, cater to, check in, clock in, go to see, hearken, hear out, pay heed, punch in, sit with, turn out, witness 8 chaperon, don't skip, get there, listen to, wait upon 9 accompany, be present, chaperone, give ear to, look after 10 minister to, result from, take care of
again: 5 resee
don't ~: 6 ignore 8 stay away 9 play hooky
to: 4 mind 5 nurse, serve 6 advert, wait on 7 address 8 see about, wait upon 10 take care of
attendance: 4 draw, gate 5 crowd 7 turnout 8 audience, presence 9 attending, box office, gathering, observers, onlookers, witnesses 10 appearance, assemblage, spectators
book notation: 6 absent 7 absence
in ~: 4 here 5 there 6 on hand 7 present
attendant: 4 aide, hand, page 5 guide, usher, valet 6 coeval, convoy, escort, helper, keeper, lackey, server 7 acolyte, janitor, lacquey, orderly, servant 8 chaperon, courtier, follower, guardian, henchman, incident, retainer, servitor, watchdog 9 accessory, ancillary, assistant, attending, auxiliary, chaperone, companion, custodian, following, secretary 10 associated, baby sitter, coincident, collateral, consequent, incidental, understudy, waitperson
__ attendant: 5 cabin 6 flight
attendants: 4 help 5 court, suite 7 retinue 9 entourage, hangers-on, retainers
attended: 5 was at
attendee: 4 goer 6 viewer 9 spectator
attendees: 5 crowd 7 turnout 8 audience 9 listeners
attending: 4 here 6 with us 7 present 9 ancillary, attendant 10 attendance, coincident
attention: 3 ear, TLC 4 care, heed, look, mind 5 study 6 notice, regard 7 caution, concern, thought 8 emphasis, scrutiny 9 assiduity, awareness, deference, diligence, immersion, precision, publicity, spotlight, treatment, vigilance 10 absorption, discretion, importance, indulgence, intentness, solicitude
at ~: 5 erect
attract ~: 8 stand out
attracting ~: 5 showy
call ~ to: 4 note 6 accent, advert, play up, stress 7 feature, mention, point up 8 point out 9 highlight, punctuate, spotlight, underline 10 underscore
center of ~: 5 focus 8 cynosure
direct one's ~: 3 fix
don't pay ~: 3 nap
exclamation: 3 hey, say 4 ahem, ahoy, ecce, help, yo-ho 5 hello 6 behold, yoo-hoo
hold one's ~: 5 rivet 6 absorb, arrest, engage 7 bewitch, engross 8 enthrall, transfix 9 captivate, enrapture, fascinate, preoccupy
hold the ~ of: 4 grab, grip, lure 5 catch, rivet, tempt 6 absorb, divert, engage, entice, occupy 7 attract, engross, impress, involve 8 enthrall 9 entertain, fascinate, tantalize, titillate
lavisher of ~: 5 doter
needing immediate ~: 4 dire 5 acute 6 urgent 7 crucial, exigent, serious 8 critical, pressing 9 desperate, important 10 compelling, imperative
one paying ~: 5 noter
opposite: 6 at ease
pay ~: 4 hark, heed, mark 5 sit up, watch 6 harken, listen, regard 7 hearken, look out, observe, respect
paying ~: 5 alert
pay no ~ to: 4 snub 6 ignore 7 disobey, neglect, tune out 8 overlook, sneeze at
pay ~ to: 4 hear, heed, mind, note 5 court, study 6 advert, attend, notice
public ~: 9 spotlight
shower ~: 4 dote

snap to ~: 6 salute
stop paying ~: 5 drift
to detail: 4 care 9 diligence
watchful ~: 5 vigil
attention __: 4 line, span
__ attention: 3 pay 5 pay no
attention-getter: 2 yo 3 hey, pst 4 ahem, psst, yo-ho 5 gavel 6 halloo, hey you
attention-getting: 5 lurid 6 catchy
attentions: 9 deference, gallantry 10 compliment, politeness
attentive: 4 kind, rapt, wary 5 alert, awake, aware, fussy, glued 6 enrapt, intent, loving, polite 7 all ears, all eyes, careful, devoted, finicky, focused, gallant, heedful, mindful, prudent, wakeful 8 cautious, diligent, exacting, finiking, finnicky, friendly, gracious, obliging, on the job, rigorous, sensible, studious, thorough, vigilant, watchful 9 assiduous, concerned, conscious, courteous, judicious, listening, observant, on the ball, regardful, wide-awake 10 enthralled, fascinated, fastidious, interested, meticulous, on one's toes, particular, respectful, scrupulous, solicitous, thoughtful
be ~: 5 watch 6 listen
one: 6 heeder
attentiveness: 4 heed 7 thought 9 vigilance
attenuate: 3 sag, sap 4 fade, flag, slim, thin, tire, wane 5 abate, blunt 6 dilute, impair, lessen, reduce, shrink, slight, soften, weaken 7 deplete, exhaust, fatigue, lighten, vitiate 8 contract, enervate, enfeeble, minimize, mitigate, undercut 9 constrict, dissipate, extenuate, undermine 10 adulterate, debilitate, devitalize
attenuated: 4 thin 5 lanky 6 narrow 7 tenuous 9 emaciated
attenuation: 9 abatement
attest: 4 aver, avow, mean, seal 5 argue, prove, quote, swear, vouch 6 adjure, affirm, allege, assert, assure, avouch, depone, depose, ratify, uphold, verify 7 bear out, certify, confess, confirm, declare, protest, stand by, testify, warrant, witness 8 indicate, maintain, manifest, validate, vouch for 9 guarantee 10 asseverate
to: 4 aver 5 vouch 6 affirm, assure, avouch, back up, depose, ensure, insure 7 endorse, indorse, stand by, swear to, testify, warrant, witness 8 vouch for 9 guarantee 10 asseverate
attestation: 3 vow 4 oath 5 proof 8 evidence
at the __: 5 ready, wheel 6 latest
at the __ minute: 4 last
at the __ of: 4 hand
at the __ of a hat: 4 drop
at the __ of one's lungs: 3 top
at the __ of one's rope: 3 end
at the __ time: 4 same
At the __: 3 Hop 4 Copa
At the Ball
artist: Erté
__ at the Bat: 5 Casey
__ at the bit: 5 champ
At the Circus (1939 film)
cast: Margaret Dumont, Chico Marx, Groucho Marx, Harpo Marx
At the Copa
girl: 4 Lola
at the drop of __: 4 a hat
__ at the elbows: 3 out
at the end of one's __: 4 rope
__ at the Gates: 5 Enemy
__ at the heels: 3 out 4 down
at the last __: 6 minute
__ at the mouth: 4 down
__ at the office!: 5 I gave
__ at the Opera, A: 5 Night
__ at the Races: 4 A Day
at the same __: 4 time
__ at the Savoy: 7 Stompin'
At the sound of the __...: 4 tone
__ at the Stars: 4 I Aim
__ at the switch: 6 asleep
__ at the Top: 4 Room
at the top of one's __: 5 lungs
__ at the Wheel: 6 Asleep
at this __: 4 time 6 moment 8 juncture
at this __ in time: 5 point
At This Moment (1986 song)
artist: Billy Vera
attic: 4 loft 6 garret 7 mansard 9 storeroom
end: 5 gable
like some ~s: 5 dusty, musty
view: 4 eave
window: 6 dormer
attic __: 3 wit 4 salt
Attic: 5 Greek 8 Athenian 9 classical
dialect: 5 Ionic
Attica
district: 4 deme
locale: 6 Greece
Atticism: 3 saw
Attila: 3 Hun 6 József
composer: Giuseppe Verdi
Attila the __: 3 Hun
attire: 3 rig, tux 4 deck, duds, garb, gear, rags, suit, togs, tuck, wear 5 array, drape, dress, getup, guise, habit, robes 6 clothe, doll up, dude up, enrobe, finery, fit out, invest, livery, outfit, rig out, suit up, things, tog out 7 apparel, bedrape, clothes, costume, deck out, dress up, garment, raiment, regalia, threads, toggery, uniform 8 accouter, accoutre, clothing, ensemble, garments, vestment, wardrobe 9 trappings 10 canonicals, Sunday best
don ~: 5 dress
formal ~: 3 tux 4 gown, tuck 5 tails 6 finery 8 black tie, white tie
night ~: 3 PJs 6 kimono, nighty 7 jammies, nightie, pajamas 8 negligee
see also clothes, clothing
attired: 4 clad
well ~: 6 dapper
attitude: 3 air 4 bent, bias, mien, mood, pose, side, tone, vein, view 5 light, slant, stand, state, thing 6 aspect, belief, esprit, manner, morale, spirit, stance 7 bearing, conduct, feeling, leaning, mindset, opinion, outlook, posture 8 approach, carriage, demeanor, position, reaction 9 character, mentality, sentiment, viewpoint 10 appearance, proclivity, standpoint
strike an ~: 4 pose
attitudes
group ~: 5 ethos, mores
attitudinize: 4 camp, pose 7 show off 8 camp it up 9 put on airs 10 put on an act
Attleboro: 4 city, town
locale: 4 Mass.
Attlee, Clement: 2 P.M. 7 British
predecessor: 9 Churchill
successor: 9 Churchill
attorney: 5 agent 6 arguer, jurist, lawyer, legist 7 adviser, advisor, counsel 8 advocate 9 barrister, counselor, go-between 10 legal eagle, mouthpiece
be ~ for: 9 represent
concern: 3 law
degree: 2 J.D. 3 LL.B., LL.D., LL.M., S.J.D.
hire an ~: 6 retain
income: 3 fee 8 retainer
org.: 3 ABA
title: 3 esq. 7 esquire
to-be exam: 4 LSAT
see also lawyer, legal
attorney __: 5 at law 7 general
attorney general
first female ~: 4 Reno
Reagan ~: 5 Meese
attract: 3 wow 4 bait, draw, hook, lure, pull 5 charm, tempt 6 allure, appeal, beckon, center, draw in, endear, engage, entice, invite, pull in, rope in 7 beguile, bewitch, enchant, enthral, inthral 8 appeal to, enthrall, entrance, interest, inthrall, intrigue 9 captivate, enrapture, fascinate, magnetize
attention: 8 stand out
attractant: 4 lure
attracted: 10 fascinated, interested
be ~ to: 4 like
attracting
attention: 5 showy
attraction: 4 bait, draw, lure, pull 5 charm, savor 6 allure, appeal, beauty, come-on, glamor, liking 7 glamour 8 affinity, interest, velleity 9 appetence, chemistry, magnetism, obsession 10 allurement, attachment, come hither, endearment, enticement, friendship, inducement, invitation, temptation
center of ~: 5 focus, Mecca
kitchen ~: 4 odor 5 scent, smell, whiff 9 fragrance, redolence
Milan ~: 7 La Scala
__ attraction: 5 added
__ Attraction: 5 Fatal
attractive: 4 cute, fair, foxy, nice, sexy 5 bonny, sweet 6 bonnie, comely, dainty, lovely, pretty 7 likable, lovable, popular, winning, winsome 8 adorable, alluring, engaging, enticing, fetching, gorgeous, handsome, inviting, likeable, loveable, magnetic, pleasing, striking, stunning 9 admirable, agreeable, appealing, beautiful, beckoning, covetable, desirable, excellent, exquisite, glamorous, palatable, ravishing 10 bewitching, delightful, enchanting, magnetical, well-formed
find ~: 4 like
one: 4 hunk 6 looker
attractively
more ~: 6 better
attractiveness: 5 charm, grace 6 appeal, beauty
attributable: 5 owing
attribute: 3 lay, owe 5 blame, facet, quirk, trace, trait 6 accuse, aspect, credit, impute, symbol 7 ascribe, connect, earmark, feature, qualify, quality 8 accredit, property 9 adjective, associate, chalk up to, character, endowment, reference 10 account for, indication, speciality
to: 4 cite 5 pin on
(to): 6 credit
attribution: 5 blame 6 credit
attrit: 5 erode 6 weaken 8 wear down
attrition: 4 wear 7 erosion 9 penitence, weakening 10 contrition, repentance
attritive: 7 erosive
Attu: 4 isle 6 island
52° 56', for ~: 4 N. Lat.
island group: 4 Near
resident: 5 Aleut 8 Aleutian
Attucks: 7 Crispus
attune: 5 adapt 6 adjust, tailor 7 balance, blend in 9 get used to, harmonize, reconcile 10 coordinate
attuned
perfectly ~: 5 at one
__ at twice the price: 5 cheap
atty. __: 3 gen.
__ atty.: 4 dist., pros.
... __ a tuffet: 5 sat on
ATV: 3 ute 9 dune buggy
part of ~: 3 all 7 terrain, vehicle
__ at will: 4 fire
Atwill, Lionel: 5 actor
__ at windmills: 4 tilt
atwist: 9 contorted
At Wit's End
author: Erma Bombeck
atwitter: 4 agog, gaga
Atwood, Margaret: 6 writer 8 Canadian
work: Bodily Harm
Cat's Eye
The Circle Game
The Handmaid's Tale
Lady Oracle
Life Before Man
Power Politics
The Robber Bride
__ at Work: 3 Men
At Your Best (1994 song)
artist: Aaliyah
atypical: 3 odd 4 eery 5 eerie, queer, weird 6 freaky, quirky 7 bizarre, deviant, oddball, offbeat, strange, unalike, unusual 8 aberrant, abnormal, freakish, isolated, peculiar, singular, uncommon 9 anomalous, different, divergent, eccentric, fantastic, irregular, unnatural 10 unorthodox
of: 6 unlike
au __: 3 jus, vol 4 fait, fond, lait, pair 6 gratin, poivre, revoir 7 courant, naturel

A
U

Au: **4** elem., gold **7** element
79 for ~: **4** at. no.
auberge: **3** inn **5** hotel, lodge **8** rest stop **10** guesthouse
aubergine: **6** veggie **8** eggplant **9** vegetable
Auberjonois, René: **5** actor
Auberon: **5** Waugh
Aubrey: **5** Menen **9** Beardsley
auburn: **4** rust **5** brown, color **7** reddish **9** hair color, yellowish
relative: ***see*** brown color, yellow color
Auburn: **4** city, town
athletes: **6** Tigers
conference: **3** SEC
locale: **5** Maine **6** Auburn **7** Alabama, New York **10** Washington
Auburn Hills: **4** city, town
locale: **8** Michigan
auburn locks
one with ~: **5** Annie
Auchincloss, Louis: **6** writer
work: Diary of a Yuppie
The House of Five Talents
I Come as a Thief
Portrait in Brownstone
The Rector of Justin
Auckland: **4** city, port, town
locale: **10** New Zealand
au contraire: **2** no **3** nah, naw, nay, nix, non **4** nein, nope, nyet, uh-uh **5** I won't, ixnay, never, no how, not so, no way **6** no deal, noways, nowise **7** I refuse **8** forget it, I will not, negative, negatory **9** by no means, fat chance, I think not **10** count me out, not a chance, thumbs down
au courant: **3** hot, new **5** aware, newsy **6** posted, versed, wise to **7** abreast, updated **8** familiar, informed, up-to-date **9** cognizant, conscious, in fashion, observant **10** conversant
not ~: **5** passé
auction: **4** sale, sell **5** put up **7** sell-off **9** vendition
action: **3** bid **5** offer, rebid
caveat: **4** as is
ender: **3** eer **4** sold
hammer: **5** gavel
ID: **5** lot no.
Internet ~ site: **4** eBay
off: **4** sell, vend **6** peddle, unload **9** dispose of, liquidate
signal: **3** bid, nod
try to buy at ~: **5** bid on
unit: **3** lot
victor: **5** buyer
word: **4** gone, once **5** going, twice
auction __: **5** block, pitch **6** bridge **8** pinochle
__ auction: **5** Dutch **6** silent
auctioneer: **2** MC **5** emcee **6** seller
audacious: **4** bold, game, pert, rash, rude **5** brash, brave, gutsy, nervy, saucy **6** awless, brassy, brazen, cheeky, daring, gritty, heroic, plucky, spunky **7** assured, aweless, defiant, doughty, forward, gallant, glaring, staunch, valiant **8** arrogant, fearless, heroical, impudent, insolent, intrepid, reckless, resolute, spirited, stalwart, unafraid, valorous **9** barefaced, daredevil, dauntless, desperate, dreadless, foolhardy, shameless, uncareful, undaunted, unfearful, unfearing **10** courageous, undismayed, ungoverned
be ~: **4** dare
audacity: **4** gall, guts, sass **5** brass, cheek, crust, moxie, nerve, sauce, spunk, valor **6** daring, hubris, hybris, mettle **7** bravery, courage, hauteur, license **8** boldness, chutzpah, defiance, rashness, rudeness, temerity **9** arrogance, assurance, cockiness, gallantry, hardiness, impudence, insolence **10** effrontery, enterprise, feistiness
have the ~: **7** presume
Audacity of Hope, The
author: Barack Obama
Auden, W.H.: **4** poet **6** writer **7** British
work: The Age of Anxiety
Another Time
The Ascent of F6
City Without Walls
The Double Man
Homage to Clio
Musée des Beaux Arts
Night Mail
On the Frontier
The Orators
Audi: **3** car **4** auto **7** Quattro **10** automobile
rival: ***see*** automobile (German)
audial: **4** otic
audible: **5** aloud, clear, plain **7** sensory **8** definite, distinct **9** sensorial **10** detectable
barely ~: **5** faint **7** muffled
something ~: **5** sound
audibly: **5** aloud
overwhelm ~: **5** drown **8** drown out
Audie: **6** Murphy
audience: **3** ear **5** crowd, house **6** public **7** gallery, hearers, hearing, meeting, turnout, viewers **8** assembly **9** attendees, gathering, listeners, observers, onlookers, playgoers, showgoers, witnesses **10** assemblage, attendance, moviegoers, spectators
before an ~: **4** live
be in the ~: **6** attend
give ~ to: **4** hear **6** listen
praise: **5** brava, bravo **6** cheers, encore **7** ovation **8** applause **9** standing O
reading to an ~: **10** recitation
audience __: **4** room **5** share
audile: **8** acoustic **10** acoustical
audio: **5** sound **8** acoustic **10** acoustical
add in ~: **3** dub, mix
alter the ~: **5** remix
component: **5** tuner **8** CD player **9** turntable
ender: **4** gram, tape **5** meter, phile **6** metric, typist, visual **8** cassette
partner: **5** video
problem: **4** echo
receiver: **3** ear **4** hi-fi **6** stereo **7** boombox
audio __: **4** book, disk
audio-__: **6** visual **7** lingual
__ audiodisk: **7** digital
audiotape
name: **3** TDK **4** Sony **6** Maxell **7** Memorex
__ audiotape: **7** digital
audiovisual: **7** sensory **9** sensorial
audiovisual __: **3** aid
audit: **4** view **5** check **6** go over, listen, review, survey, verify **7** analyze, enquiry, examine, inquiry, inspect, monitor, sit in on **8** analysis, appraise, checking, listen in, look into, scrutiny **9** go through **10** inspection, scrutinize
ace: **3** CPA **4** acct. **10** accountant
a course: **5** sit in
ending: **3** ory
org.: **3** IRS
audit __: **5** trail
__ audit: **4** cash **6** energy
auditing: **10** accounting
audition: **4** read, test **5** trial **6** tryout **7** hearing, reading
attendee: **5** actor
objective: **4** part, role
tape: **4** demo
auditor: **3** CPA **7** monitor **8** examiner **9** inspector **10** accountant, bookkeeper
concern: **3** acc. **4** acct. **7** account
federal: **3** GAO
auditorium: **4** hall, room **5** odeon, odeum **6** lyceum **7** theater, theatre **9** music hall, playhouse **10** movie house, opera house
sign: **4** Exit
auditory: **4** otic **7** sensory **8** acoustic **9** sensorial **10** acoustical
auditory __: **5** canal, nerve **7** aphasia, vesicle
Audra: **7** Lindley
Audrey: **6** Tautou, Totter **7** Hepburn, Landers, Meadows
to Jayne: **3** sis
Audubon
of interest to ~: **5** avian
Audubon Society
member: **6** birder
Auel, Jean: **6** writer
work: The Clan of the Cave Bear
The Mammoth Hunters
The Plains of Passage
The Shelters of Stone
The Valley of Horses
Auer: **6** Mischa **7** Leopold
Auerbach: **3** Red **5** Artie
Auerbach, Red: **5** coach
milieu: **5** court
org.: **3** NBA
sport: **10** basketball
Auer, Leopold: **9** Hungarian, violinist
Auer, Mischa: **5** actor
au fait: **3** ace **4** able, deft **5** adept, slick, smart **6** adroit, expert, nimble, posted, proper, versed **7** abreast, capable, skilled, trained **8** decorous, dextrous, graceful, informed, masterly, seasoned, skillful **9** competent, dexterous, efficient, masterful, qualified **10** conversant, proficient, well-versed
__-au-feu: **3** pot
au fond: **6** wholly **7** in depth, totally **8** from A to Z, in detail, whole hog **9** to the full **10** completely, thoroughly, to the limit
auf Wiedersehen: **3** bye **4** ciao, ta-ta, vale **5** adieu, adios, aloha, later, peace, see ya **6** bye-bye, shalom, sholom, so long **7** cheerio, goodbye **8** au revoir, farewell, sayonara, toodle-oo
Aug.: **2** mo.
follower: **3** Sep. **4** Sept.
hrs.: **3** DST
preceder: **3** Jul.
see also August
Augean __: **7** stables
Augean stables
cleaner: **8** Heracles, Hercules
auger: **3** bit **4** tool **5** borer, drill **10** jackhammer
combining form: **6** trypan- **7** trypano-
product: **4** hole
auger __: **3** bit
Auger: **8** Claudine
aught: **3** any, nil **4** none, zero **6** cipher **7** nothing
augment: **3** add, eke, pad, wax **4** feed, grow, hike, incr., rise **5** add to, bloat, boost, build, mount, raise, swell, widen **6** beef up, dilate, expand, extend, jack up, step up **7** amplify, broaden, build up, burgeon, develop, enhance, enlarge, improve, inflate, magnify, recruit, scale up **8** bourgeon, escalate, heighten, increase, lengthen, multiply **9** increment, intensify, reinforce, spread out **10** aggrandize, strengthen, supplement
augmentation: **4** gain, hike, rise **5** boost, raise **6** growth, upping **7** buildup **8** addendum, addition, increase
augmented: **6** bigger, longer
Augsburg: **4** city, town
locale: **7** Germany
river: **4** Lech
augur: **4** bode, mean, omen, seer, sign **5** sibyl **6** auspex, herald, oracle **7** aruspex, betoken, diviner, portend, predict, presage, promise, prophet **8** forecast, foreshow, foretell, haruspex, indicate, prophesy, threaten **9** foretoken, harbinger, predictor **10** forecaster, foreshadow, soothsayer
augury: **4** omen, sign **5** hunch **6** oracle **7** portent, warning **8** forecast, prophecy **9** foretoken, harbinger **10** divination, foreboding, forerunner, indication, prediction
august: **5** grand, great, lofty, noble, proud, regal, royal **6** lordly, proper, solemn **7** awesome, courtly, elegant, eminent, exalted, stately **8** baronial, decorous, glorious, highbred, highbrow, imposing, kinglike, majestic **9** dignified, grandiose, honorable, venerable **10** ceremonial, impressive, majestical
August: **5** month **6** Möbius, Wilson **8** Weismann **10** Strindberg
birthstone: **7** peridot
like Kansas in ~: **5** corny
period: **7** dog days
sign: **3** Leo **4** Lion **5** Virgo **6** Virgin
August 13: **4** ides
August 15, 1945: **5** V-J Day
August 5: **5** nones
Augusta: **4** city, peak, town **5** mount **8** mountain

county: 8 Kennebec
locale: 5 Maine 7 Georgia
river: 8 Kennebec
Auguste: 5 Comte, Rodin 7 Piccard 9 Beernaert, Escoffier
see also French
__-Auguste Renoir: 6 Pierre
Augustine: 5 saint 11 philosopher
augustness: 8 grandeur
Augusto: 8 Pinochet
Augustus: 5 Roman 6 Caesar
wife: 5 Livia
see also Latin
Augustus Saint-__: 7 Gaudens
aujourd'hui: 5 today 6 French
auk: 4 bird 5 murre 6 puffin 7 dovekey, dovekie 9 razorbill
__ au lait: 4 café
Aulby, Mike: 6 bowler
milieu: 5 alley
org.: 3 PBA
auld lang syne: 4 past, yore 9 yesterday
Auld Lang Syne: 4 poem
author: Robert Burns
auld sod, the: 4 Eire, Erin 7 Ireland
Auletta: 3 Ken
aulos: 4 wind
origin: 6 Greece
Aumont, Jean-Pierre: 5 actor
au naturel: 3 raw 4 bare, nude 5 naked 9 unattired
aunt: 3 kin, rel. 5 woman 6 female 7 kinsman 8 relative 9 kinswoman
fictional: 2 Em 3 Bee 4 Mame 5 Polly
in French: 5 tante
in Spanish: 3 tía
kid: 3 coz 6 cousin
of song: 5 Rhody
's husband: 3 unc, unk 5 uncle
sis: 3 Mom
__-aunt: 5 great
Aunt __ Cope Book: 5 Erma's
Aunt Helen
author: T.S. Eliot
Auntie Em's home: 3 Kan. 6 Kansas
Auntie Mame: 4 film 5 novel
author: Patrick Dennis
cast: Peggy Cass, Fred Clark, Rosalind Russell, Forrest Tucker
character: 3 Ito 4 Vera 5 Agnes, Gooch, Norah 6 Osbert, Pegeen
director: Morton Da Costa
Aunt March
creator: Louisa May Alcott
Aunt Millie's: 10 pasta sauce
alternative: 4 Ragú 5 Prego 6 Prince 8 Classico 10 Newman's Own
Aunt Polly
creator: Mark Twain
au pair: 4 maid 5 nanny 6 nannie 8 domestic 9 launderer, nursemaid
__-au-Prince: 4 Port
aura: 3 air 4 feel, halo, mien, mood, tone, vibe 5 scent, sense, vibes 6 aspect, nimbus 7 charism, essence, feeling, quality 8 ambiance, ambience, charisma, gloriole, mystique, presence 9 character, emanation, radiation, semblance 10 appearance, atmosphere, suggestion
Aura
author: Carlos Fuentes
Aura __: 3 Lee
aural: 4 otic 7 sensory 8 acoustic 9 sensorial 10 acoustical
auras: 5 nimbi
aureate: 4 gild 5 flaxy 6 flaxen, golden, ornate
__ Aurelius: 6 Marcus
aureole: 4 halo 6 circle, corona, nimbus 8 gloriole, radiance, radiancy 10 effulgence
au revoir: 3 bye 4 ciao, ta-ta 5 adieu, adios, aloha, later, see ya 6 byebye, so long 7 goodbye 8 farewell, sayonara
in Hawaiian: 5 aloha
in Italian: 4 ciao
in Latin: 3 ave 4 vale
in Spanish: 5 adios
Au Revoir, Les Enfants (1987 film)
director: Louis Malle
__ au rhum: 4 baba
auric: 6 golden
Auric: 10 Goldfinger
auricle: 3 ear 5 pinna
auricular: 4 otic
problem: 6 earwax 7 cerumen
auriculate: 5 eared
aurify: 4 gild
Auriga: 10 Charioteer
aurophobe
fear: 4 gold
aurora: 4 dawn 5 light 7 morning, sky show, sunrise 8 daybreak, daylight
locale: 3 sky
aurora __: 7 polaris 8 borealis 9 australis
Aurora: 3 car 4 auto, city, Olds, town 8 asteroid, Greenway 10 automobile, Oldsmobile
artist: Guido Reni
brother: 3 Sol
equivalent: 3 Eos
locale: 6 Canada 7 Ontario 8 Colorado, Illinois
realm: 4 dawn
auroral: 4 eoan
Aurora Leigh
author: Elizabeth Barrett Browning
aurous: 6 golden
Aus.
locale: 3 Eur.
neighbor: 3 Ger. 5 Switz.
see also Austria
auslander: 5 alien
auspex: 4 seer 5 augur, sibyl 6 herald, oracle 7 diviner, prophet 9 predictor 10 soothsayer
auspice: 4 omen, sign 7 presage 8 foreshow 10 indication
auspices: 4 care, egis 5 aegis 6 agency, charge 7 backing, custody, keeping, support 8 wardship 9 authority, patronage 10 protection
auspicious: 4 good, ripe, rosy 5 blest, lucky 6 bright, golden, timely 7 blessed, charmed, favored, hopeful, on a roll 8 oracular 9 favorable, fortunate, on a streak, opportune, promising, welltimed 10 felicitous, fortuitous, indicative, propitious, prosperous
auspiciously: 4 well
Aussie: 3 emu 4 emeu 5 dingo, koala 6 sheila 7 swagman 8 jackeroo 9 Paul Hogan
see also Australia
Aust.
see Australia, Austria
__ Austen: 6 Godwin
Austen, Jane: 6 writer 7 British
work: Emma
Mansfield Park
Northanger Abbey
Persuasion
Pride and Prejudice
Sense and Sensibility
austere: 4 bare, firm, grim, hard 5 bleak, bossy, cruel, harsh, picky, plain, rigid, rough, sharp, sober, stark, stern, stiff, stoic, tough 6 barren, Lenten, rustic, severe, simple, solemn, strict 7 ascetic, Spartan 8 despotic, exacting, hardline, pitiless, rigorous 9 barebones, cheerless, demanding, draconian, primitive, stringent, unadorned, unbending, unsparing 10 abstemious, despotical, inflexible, iron-fisted, no-nonsense, oppressive, tenebrific, tyrannical
austerely: 4 hard
austerity: 5 rigor 6 thrift 8 bareness, chastity, dourness, eschewal, hardship, iron hand, stoicism 9 exactness, formality, harshness, plainness, rusticism, solemnity, spareness, starkness, sternness, stiffness 10 abstinence, asceticism, barrenness, chasteness, continence, inclemency, puritanism, refraining, self-denial, simplicity, Spartanism, strictness, stringency, temperance
Austerlitz: 6 battle
Austin: 4 city, Teri, town 5 Patti, Steve, Tracy 6 Alfred, Powers 7 Roberts, Stephen 9 Pendleton
county: 6 Travis
locale: 3 Tex. 4 Minn. 5 Texas 9 Minnesota
river: 8 Colorado
Austin Powers
cat: Mr. Bigglesworth
Austin Powers in Goldmember (2002 film)
cast: Michael Caine, Seth Green, Beyoncé Knowles, Mike Myers, Verne Troyer, Robert Wagner, Michael York
director: Jay Roach
Austin Powers:International Man of Mystery (1997 film)
cast: Verne Troyer
Austin Powers: International Man of Mystery (1997 film)
cast: Elizabeth Hurley, Mike Myers, Mimi Rogers, Robert Wagner, Michael York
director: Jay Roach
Austin Powers: The Spy Who Shagged Me (1999 film)
cast: Heather Graham, Elizabeth Hurley, Rob Lowe, Mike Myers, Verne Troyer, Robert Wagner, Michael York
director: Jay Roach
Austin, Tracy: 7 netster 9 tennis pro
milieu: 5 court
austral: 4 wind 5 money 8 southern
__ Australe: 4 Mare
Australia: 4 cont., isle 6 island, nation 7 country 9 continent
airline: 6 QANTAS
bay: 6 Botany 10 Port Philip
bird: 3 emu, iao 4 emeu, koel, lory 5 galah 6 brolga, drongo 7 mudlark 8 cockatoo, lorikeet, lyrebird, megapode 9 bowerbird, cassowary, cockateel, cockatiel, currawong, friarbird, frogmouth, pardalote, riflebird 10 budgerigar, budgerygah, honeyeater, kookaburra
buddy: 4 mate
canine: 5 dingo
capital: 8 Canberra
city: 5 Perth 6 Cairns, Darwin, Hobart, Sydney 7 Geelong 8 Adelaide, Brisbane, Canberra 9 Melbourne, Newcastle 10 Townsville, Wollongong
college: 3 uni
desert: 6 Gibson 7 Simpson 10 Great Sandy, Sturt Stony
egg: 4 goog
explorer: 6 Mawson 8 Flinders 9 Vancouver
fish: 4 mado 6 groper, roughy, tandan 8 mulloway, nannygai, trevally 9 schnapper
golfer: 6 Norman 9 Stevenson 10 Baker-Finch
hello: 4 g'day
horse: 4 moke 5 neddy, waler
island: 4 Tasm. 5 Adele 8 Tasmania
island near ~: 7 Norfolk
journalist: 7 Slessor
jumper: 3 'roo 4 euro 7 wallaby 8 kangaroo, wallaroo
lake: 4 Eyre 7 Torrens
marsupial: 4 euro, tait 5 bilby, koala 6 jerboa, numbat, wombat 7 opossum, wallaby 8 kangaroo, wallaroo 9 bandicoot, phalanger
mineral: 4 opal
money: 4 cent 5 penny 6 dollar
moth: 6 bogong
mountain: 9 Kosciusko
national blossom: 6 acacia
native: 3 abo 4 Mara 5 Maori 9 aborigine
Nobelist in Chemistry: 9 Cornforth
Nobelist in Literature: 5 White
Nobelist in Medicine: 6 Burnet, Eccles 7 Doherty
pilots: 4 RAAF
playwright: 6 Palmer, Porter 7 Seymour, Stewart
poet: 4 Hope, Stow 6 Palmer, Porter, Wright 7 Brennan, Slessor, Stewart
port: 6 Darwin, Sydney 7 Geelong 8 Adelaide, Brisbane 9 Melbourne, Newcastle
reptile: 6 goanna, moloch, taipan
river: 5 Tamar 6 Murray 7 Darling, Durwent 9 Macquarie
rock: 5 Ayers
rock band: 4 ACDC, INXS
sea: 5 Coral, Timor 6 Tasman 7 Arafura
shout: 5 cooee
shrub: 5 aalii, hakea, mulga 6 pituri 7 banksia, geebung, logania 8 myoporum
soldier: 5 Anzac
soprano: 5 Melba 10 Sutherland
state: 3 NSW, Tas. 4 Tasm. 8 Tasmania, Victoria 10 Queensland 13 New South Wales

A U

strait off ~: **6** Torres
swag: **5** bluey
swamp monster: **6** bunyip
swimmer: **5** Gould **6** Fraser
tennis pro: **4** Hoad **5** Court, Laver **6** Fraser, Rafter, Stolle **7** Emerson **8** Newcombe, Rosewall **9** Goolagong
tree: **5** bunya, hakea, karri, mulga **6** jarrah, pituri, wandoo **7** banksia, cajeput, geebung **8** beefwood, coolabah **10** eucalyptus
tree-dweller: **5** koala
waterfall: **5** Tully
writer: **4** Stow, West **5** Stead, White **6** Furphy, Jolley, Palmer, Porter **7** Herbert, Manning, Travers **8** Franklin, Keneally **9** Moorehead **10** McCullough
Australian __: **4** Alps, pine **5** crawl **6** ballot, kelpie **7** doubles, terrier
Australian Open
game: **6** tennis
locale: **9** Melbourne
__ australis: **6** aurora
Australopithecas
descendant: **5** human
fossil: **4** Lucy
Austria: **6** nation **7** country
ancient ~ town: **4** Enns
botanist: **6** Mendel
capital: **4** Wien **6** Vienna
city: **4** Graz, Linz, Wien **6** Vienna **8** Salzburg **9** Innsbruck
composer: **4** Berg, Wolf **6** Mozart
conductor: **4** Böhm, Graf **5** Adler, Krips, Rudel **6** Krauss, Mahler **7** Karajan, Kleiber **9** Leinsdorf
dance: **5** waltz **7** ländler
horse: **10** Lippizaner
language: **6** German
legislature: **9** Bundesrat
money: **5** krone **8** groschen, kreutzer **9** schilling
mountains: **4** Alps **5** Alpen **10** Carnic Alps
neighbor: **5** Italy **7** Germany, Hungary **8** Slovakia, Slovenia
Nobelist in Chemistry: **5** Pregl
Nobelist in Economics: **8** von Hayek
Nobelist in Medicine: **6** Bárány, Kandel **13** Wagner-Jauregg
Nobelist in Peace: **5** Fried **10** von Suttner
Nobelist in Physics: **4** Hess **11** Schrödinger
painter: **5** Klimt **7** Schiele
physicist: **5** Pauli **7** Doppler, Meitner
pianist: **7** Brendel **8** Schnabel
playwright: **10** Schnitzler **11** Grillparzer
poet: **7** Bachman
psychiatrist: **5** Adler, Freud
region: **5** Tirol, Tyrol
river: **3** Mur **4** Enns, Raab, Raba
scientist: **5** Pauli **6** Mendel **7** Doppler, Meitner
sharpshooter: **5** yager
skier: **7** Klammer
soprano: **4** Popp
violinist: **8** Kreisler
waterfall: **7** Gastein **8** Krimmler
western boundary: **5** Rhine
wine: **7** heurige
writer: **5** Broch, Freud, Kafka, Kraus, Musil, Zweig **6** Handke, Lorenz, Werfel **7** Stifter **8** Bernhard **9** Aichinger **10** Wassermann
see also German
Austria-__: **7** Hungary
Austrian __, The: **3** Oak
Austronesian
language: **5** Malay, Maori
autarch: **6** despot
autarchy: **7** freedom, liberty
aut Caesar, aut __: **5** nihil
auteur: **8** director **9** filmmaker
authentic: **4** good, just, real, true **5** legit, pucka, pukka, right, valid **6** actual, dinkum, kasher, kosher, trusty **7** certain, factual, genuine, literal **8** accurate, bona fide, credible, faithful, original, straight, verified **9** realistic, veritable **10** believable, convincing, creditable, dependable, historical, legitimate, true-to-life, undoubtful, unimagined
authenticate: **5** prove **6** attest, ratify, verify **7** bear out, certify, confirm, witness **8** validate, vouch for
authenticated: **4** real **5** valid **7** genuine **8** official
authentication: **4** seal **5** proof **8** hallmark
authenticity: **4** fact **5** right, truth **7** reality
author: **3** pen **4** poet **5** ghost, write **6** byline, create, origin, parent, scribe, source, writer **7** compose, creator, produce **8** composer, essayist, inventer, inventor, novelist, reporter **9** columnist, wordsmith **10** biographer, journalist, librettist, playwright
concern: **4** plot
correspondent: **6** editor
submission: **2** ms. **10** manuscript
unknown: **4** anon. **9** anonymous
work: **4** book, play **5** novel **6** column **7** article
Author! Author! (1982 film)
cast: Dyan Cannon, Al Pacino, Tuesday Weld
director: Arthur Hiller
authoritarian: **4** firm, hard, tsar **5** bossy, cruel, harsh, picky, rigid, stern, tough **6** despot, severe, strict, tyrant **7** austere, Spartan **8** absolute, autocrat, despotic, dictator, dogmatic, exacting, hard-line, rigorous **9** demanding, draconian, stringent, unbending, unsparing **10** despotical, dogmatical, inflexible, iron-fisted, no-nonsense, oppressive, tyrannical
authoritarianism: **7** tyranny
authoritative: **4** true **5** legal, legit, sound, valid **6** lawful, proven **7** certain, factual **8** accurate, approved, decisive, imperial, masterly, official, oracular, orthodox, powerful, reliable, verified **9** canonical **10** peremptory
order: **4** fiat **5** edict, ukase **6** decree
source: **5** bible
authority: **3** law **4** boss, czar, dean, exec, guru, rank, rule, sage, sway, tsar, tzar **5** basis, bible, clout, force, judge, maven, mavin, might, power, right, say-so, title **6** bigwig, credit, critic, domain, expert, master, pundit, savant, source, top dog, weight, wizard **7** adviser, advisor, arbiter, big shot, captain, command, control, kingpin, license, potence, potency, regency, scholar **8** auspices, dominion, eminence, higher-up, kingship, leverage, prestige, validity **9** big cheese, dominance, evaluator, executive, franchise, influence, precedent, privilege, professor, strong arm, supremacy, upper hand **10** aristocrat, ascendance, ascendancy, ascendence, ascendency, commission, domination, executives, foundation, government, leadership, legitimacy, management, permission, power elite, powerhouse, specialist
be in ~: **4** rule **5** reign **6** direct, govern, manage **7** command, control, preside
challenge ~: **5** rebel
give ~ to: **4** name **6** assign, charge, commit, depute, invest, ordain **7** appoint, consign, empower, entrust, intrust, license **8** accredit, delegate, deputize, hand over, relegate, turn over **9** authorize, designate **10** commission
state with ~: **4** aver **6** attest
symbol of ~: **4** mace **5** staff
to act for another: **5** proxy
authority __: **4** file **6** figure **7** control
__ authority: **4** port
__ Authority: **6** Sports
authorization: **2** OK **4** okay, seal **5** leave, order **6** assent, permit, signal, ticket **7** go-ahead, liberty, license, mandate, warrant **8** approval, passport, sanction **9** privilege
authorize: **2** OK **3** let **4** okay, sign, tell, vest **5** allow, brook, grant, order **6** accept, assign, commit, enable, invest, permit, ratify **7** approve, certify, empower, endorse, entitle, indorse, intitle, license, qualify, warrant **8** accede to, accredit, assent to, delegate, deputize, legalize, sanction, tolerate, validate **9** approve of, designate, establish, give leave, put up with **10** administer, commission, constitute, say the word
authorized: **3** OK'd **4** OK'ed **5** jural, legal, legit, licit **6** kasher, kosher, lawful, okayed, proper, vested **7** allowed **8** official, rightful **9** by the book, canonical, permitted **10** legitimate, sanctioned
Authors: **4** game **8** card game
authorship: **6** source
auto
racing: **5** sport
see also automobile, car
auto __: **4** lift **5** court **6** racing
auto-: **4** self
auto-__: **4** da-fé, dial **5** focus **6** dialer
autobahn: **4** pike **7** highway
auto: **3** BMW **4** Audi, Opel
unit: **2** km. **9** kilometer
autobiography: **4** life **5** story **6** memoir **7** memoirs
Autobiography of Alice B. Toklas, The
author: Gertrude Stein
Autobiography of Malcolm X, The
author: Alex Haley
autocade: **6** parade
autochthon: **6** native **10** inhabitant
autochthonous: **6** native **8** original **10** aboriginal, indigenous
auto-club
service: **3** tow
autocracy: **7** fascism, tyranny **8** iron hand **9** despotism, monocracy **10** absolutism, oppression
autocrat: **4** czar, tsar, tzar **6** Caesar, despot, tyrant **7** monarch **8** dictator, overlord **9** sovereign
autocratic: **5** royal, stern **6** kingly **8** absolute, arrogant, despotic, imperial, kinglike **9** arbitrary, imperious, tyrannous **10** commanding, despotical, imperative, iron-willed, monocratic, peremptory, tyrannical
Autocrat of the Breakfast-Table, The
author: Oliver Wendell Holmes
autogiro: **8** aircraft
capability: **4** STOL
autograph: **3** pen, sig **4** name, sign **5** write **7** endorse, indorse, writing **8** inscribe, longhand **9** handwrite, signature, subscribe
hound target: **4** star **5** celeb **9** celebrity
site: **4** cast **5** album
autographed: **3** sgd. **6** signed
autoharp: **6** string, zither **10** instrument
automaker
see automobile
automated: **9** automatic, motorized **10** electrical, electronic, industrial, mechanical, mechanized, programmed
automated __ machine: **6** teller
automatic: **3** gun, Uzi **4** mech. **5** Luger **6** reflex, weapon **7** assured, certain, firearm, regular, robotic **8** electric, habitual, knee-jerk, mindless **9** automated, impulsive, intuitive, motorized **10** electrical, electronic, inevitable, mechanical, mechanized, self-moving, unthinking
automatic __: **5** drive, pilot, rifle **6** dialer, pistol, redial, teller **7** writing
automatic __ processing: **4** data
automaton: **5** droid, golem, robot **7** android, machine
automobile: **3** AMC, Bug, car, Fox, FTO, Geo, GTO, GTX, Kia, LTD, Reo, XJS, XKE, XKR **4** Audi, Colt, Dart, Echo, Ford, Fury, Golf, heap, Lada, Lynx, Nash, Neon, Nova, Olds, Omni, Opel, Vega, Vibe **5** Acura, Aerio, Alero, Aries, Aspen, Astre, buggy, Buick, Caddy, Camry, Capri, Chevy, Ciera, Civic, Cobra, Comet, coupe, crate, Delta, Dodge, Eagle, Edsel, Essex, Excel, Fiero, Focus, Honda, Isuzu, Jetta, Laser, Le Car, Magna, Mazda, Metro, Miata, Monza, Omega, Pacer, Paseo, Pinto, Prizm, Probe, Ranch, Rebel, Regal, Rolls, Royal,

Sable, sedan, Sigma, Storm, Supra, Targa, T-Bird, Tempo, Topaz, Viper **6** Accent, Accord, Altima, Apollo, Aspire, Aurora, Avalon, Beetle, Bel Air, Bobcat, Breeze, Bronco, Cabrio, Calais, Camaro, Catera, Celica, Cirrus, Cordia, Cougar, Custom, Daewoo, Del Sol, DeLuxe, DeSoto, Duster, Escort, Esteem, Falcon, Fiesta, Futura, Galant, Hornet, hot rod, Hudson, Impala, Jaguar, jalopy, Kadett, Kaiser, Kissel, Laguna, Lancer, landau, Legend, LeMans, Lumina, Malibu, Marlin, Matrix, Maxima, Meteor, Mirada, Mirage, Model A, Model B, Model T, Monaco, Nissan, Passat, Pierce, Polara, Precis, Pulsar, Rabbit, Reatta, Royale, Safari, Saturn, Scoupe, Seneca, Sentra, Shadow, Sierra, Solara, Sonata, Spirit, Spyder, Stanza, Subaru, Suzuki, Taurus, Tercel, Torino, Toyota, Tracer, Tredia, Volare, wheels, Willys, Zephyr **7** Acclaim, Achieva, Allante, Avenger, Bentley, Beretta, Boxster, Caprice, Carrera, Century, Charger, Checker, Citroen, clunker, compact, Concord, Contour, Cordoba, Corolla, Coronet, Corsica, Corvair, Cutlass, DeVille, Dynasty, Eclipse, Elantra, Electra, Ferrari, Festiva, Firenza, flivver, Galaxie, Grabber, Granada, Gremlin, hardtop, Horizon, Hyundai, Integra, Javelin, La Salle, LeBaron, LeSabre, Lincoln, machine, Marquis, Matador, Maxwell, Mercury, Monarch, Montego, Mustang, Newport, Packard, phaeton, Phantom, Phoenix, Pioneer, Pontiac, Porsche, Prelude, Protege, Prowler, Quattro, Rambler, Reliant, Renault, Riviera, Sebring, Seville, Skyhawk, Skylark, Starion, Stealth, Stratus, St. Regis, Sunbird, Sunfire, Swinger, Tempest, Tiburon, Torpedo, Town Car, Trans Am, Valiant, vehicle, Ventura, Voyager, Wildcat **8** Biscayne, Cadillac, Camargue, Catalina, Cavalier, Chevelle, Chrysler, Cimarron, Citation, Concorde, Concours, Conquest, Corniche, Corvette, Cressida, Daihatsu, Dauphine, Diamante, Diplomat, dragster, Eldorado, Fairlane, Fairmont, Firebird, Gran Fury, Imperial, Intrepid, Intrigue, Marauder, Maverick, Medalist, Millenia, Monterey, motor car, Mystique, Parklane, Plymouth, roadster, runabout, Starfire, Sting Ray, Suburban, Sundance, Toronado **9** Alfa Romeo, Barracuda, Belvedere, cabriolet, Celebrity, Chevrolet, Evolution, Fleetwood, Grand Prix, hatchback, Hupmobile, limousine, Medallion, Montclair, New Yorker, PT Cruiser, Satellite, sports car, tin lizzie, transport, two-seater **10** Ambassador, Bonneville, Challenger, Duesenberg, gas guzzler, Mitsubishi, Monte Carlo, Oldsmobile, Park Avenue, rattletrap, Road Runner, Rolls Royce, Silver Dawn, Silver Spur, Studebaker, subcompact, Volkswagen **11** Eighty-Eight, Fifth Avenue, Lamborghini, Ninety-Eight, Silver Cloud, Silver Ghost, Thunderbird **12** Coupe de Ville, Sedan de Ville, Silver Seraph, Silver Shadow, Silver Spirit, Silver Wraith
ad stat: 3 mpg
antique ~: 3 Reo **4** Aero, Cord, Nash **5** Edsel, Essex, Stutz
body: 7 chassis
brand: 4 make
British ~: 2 MG **5** Rolls **6** Austin, Jaguar **10** Rolls-Royce
British ~ part: 4 boot, tyre **6** bonnet
certain ~ worker: 5 robot
club: 3 AAA
defective ~: 4 heap **5** crate, lemon
document: 5 title
emporium: 6 car lot
family ~: 5 sedan
fancy ~: 3 BMW **4** limo **5** Caddy, Lexus, Rolls **7** Bentley, Ferrari, Lincoln, Porsche, Town Car **8** Cadillac, Maserati, Mercedes **10** Rolls-Royce
fast ~: 5 racer **6** hot rod
financing letters: 3 APR **4** GMAC
fuel: 3 gas **8** gasoline
gauge: 3 odo **4** tach **8** odometer **10** tachometer
German ~: 3 BMW **4** Audi, Opel **7** Porsche **10** Volkswagen
grille protector: 3 bra
ID: 3 VIN **5** plate
inspection evidence: 5 decal
Japanese ~: 6 Accord, Datsun, Nissan, Subaru, Toyota
job: 3 LOG, lub **4** lube
mishap: 4 dent, ding
motor: 4 V-six **5** V-four **6** V-eight
option: 2 AC **3** air, bra **5** alarm, lease, phone **7** nose bra, ski rack
part: 3 cam **4** axle, carb, horn, tire **5** brake, grill, strut, wheel, wiper **6** aerial, engine, fender, filter, gas cap, grille, heater, hubcap **7** nose bra **10** carburetor
parts brand: 4 Fram, Napa
problem: 5 no oil
race: 4 Indy **5** rally **6** enduro, Le Mans
race area: 3 pit
racer: 4 Foyt **5** Jones, Mears, Petty, Rahal, Sneva, Unser **6** A.J. Foyt **7** Allison, Al Unser, Garlits, Jarrett **8** Andretti, Luyendyk, Oldfield, Tom Sneva **9** Breedlove, Earnhardt, Muldowney, Rick Mears **10** Bobby Rahal, Don Garlits, Fittipaldi, Yarborough
racing org.: 4 NHRA
renter: 4 Avis **5** Alamo, Hertz **6** Budget, Dollar **7** Thrifty **8** National **10** Enterprise
route: 6 artery
Russian ~: 3 Zil **4** Lada
safety advocate: 5 Nader
safety device: 6 airbag
shelter: 6 garage
sound: 4 beep, honk, toot
South Korean ~: 3 Kia **7** Hyundai
supercharger: 5 turbo
Swedish ~: 4 Saab **5** Volvo
testing org.: 3 EPA
theft deterrent: 4 club
track: 3 rut
trim: 6 chrome
see also car
autonomous: 4 free **8** absolute, separate **9** sovereign, voluntary **10** democratic, self-ruling
autonomy: 7 freedom, liberty
autostrada: 7 highway, Italian
autosuggestion
popularizer: 4 Coué
Autry: 4 Gene
film: 5 oater
autumn: 4 fall **6** season
beverage: 5 cider
bloom: 3 mum **5** aster
fruit: 4 pear
like ~ leaves: 3 dry **4** sere **7** parched **9** shriveled
like ~ weather: 5 crisp
month: 3 Dec., Nov., Oct., Sep. **4** Sept. **7** October **8** December, November **9** September
sign: 5 Libra **7** Scorpio **11** Sagittarius
toiler: 5 raker
tool: 4 rake
Autumn __: 4 Tale **6** Leaves, Sequel, Sonata
Autumn __ York: 5 in New
__ Autumn: 3 'Tis **5** Ode to
autumnal __: 5 point **7** equinox
Autumn Leaves (1955 song)
artist: Roger Williams
Autumn Poem
author: Rubén Dario
Autumn Sequel
author: Louis MacNeice
Autumn Sonata (1978 film)
cast: Ingrid Bergman, Lena Nyman, Liv Ullmann
director: Ingmar Bergman
setting: 6 Sweden
__ au vin: 3 coq
aux.: 4 add'l.
auxiliary: 3 aid **4** ally, side **5** extra, other **6** helper **7** adjunct **8** adjutant **9** accessory, ancillary, appendage, assistant, associate, attendant, colleague, companion, secondary, supporter **10** accomplice, attachment, collateral, subsidiary, substitute, supporting
verb: 3 are **4** been **5** would
auxiliary __: 4 note, tone, verb **6** memory, rafter **7** storage
__ Auxiliary: 6 Ladies
Av: 5 month **6** Hebrew
predecessor: 6 Tammuz
successor: 4 Elul
AV
part: 5 audio **6** visual
Ava: 7 Gardner
ex: 5 Artie, Frank **6** Mickey
__ a vacation!: 5 I need
avail: 2 do **3** use **4** gain, good **5** serve, worth **6** look to, profit **7** benefit, promote, purpose, satisfy, service, succeed, suffice, utility **8** efficacy, put to use **9** advantage, make use of **10** usefulness
of some ~: 5 utile
oneself of: 3 use **6** resort **7** consume, embrace, exploit, utilize
to no ~: 4 vain **6** futile, in vain, otiose, vainly **8** bootless **9** fruitless, uselessly **10** for nothing
__ avail: 4 to no
availability: 7 opening
available: 4 free, open **5** handy, on tap, ready, to let **6** at hand, at home, on hand, usable, vacant **7** for hire, for rent, for sale, untaken, useable **8** optional, possible, prepared **9** derivable, getatable, reachable, ready to go, securable **10** accessible, achievable, applicable, attainable, convenient, disposable, obtainable, procurable, realizable, unoccupied, up for grabs
make ~: 4 rent **5** offer **6** afford, free up, render **7** provide
no longer ~: 5 taken
not generally ~: 4 rare
availing: 5 utile
Avakian, Aram: 8 director
avalanche: 4 rush **5** flood, spate **6** deluge, onrush **7** barrage, cascade, torrent **9** earthfall, landslide, snowslide **10** inundation
research center site: 5 Davos
Avalanche: 3 six, van **4** team **5** Chevy **9** Chevrolet
home: 8 Colorado
milieu: 3 ice **4** rink
org.: 3 NHL
rival: *see* hockey team
Avalon: 3 car **4** auto, isle **6** Toyota **7** Frankie **10** automobile
rival: *see* car
Avalon (1990 film)
cast: Armin Mueller-Stahl, Elizabeth Perkins, Aidan Quinn
director: Barry Levinson
dog: 4 Nemo
Avalon, Frankie: 5 actor **6** singer
film: Back to the Beach (1987)
Beach Blanket Bingo (1965)
Beach Party (1963)
Bikini Beach (1964)
Muscle Beach Party (1964)
film partner: Annette Funicello
song: Bobby Sox to Stockings (1959)
A Boy Without a Girl (1959)
DeDe Dinah (1958)
Ginger Bread (1958)
Just Ask Your Heart (1959)
Venus (1959)
Why (1959)
avant-garde: 3 odd **4** arty **5** artsy, novel **6** exotic, far-out, modern **7** liberal, new wave, oddball, pioneer, radical **8** advanced, original, up-to-date, vanguard **9** inventive **10** innovative, pioneering
Avant Garde: 4 font **8** typeface
Avanti: 3 car **4** auto **10** automobile, Studebaker
Avanti! (1972 film)
cast: Jack Lemmon, Juliet Mills, Clive Revill
director: Billy Wilder
avarice: 3 sin **5** greed **8** cupidity, rapacity **9** esurience, gold fever **10** grabbiness
avaricious: 5 tight **6** grabby, greedy, sordid, stingy **7** hoggish, lustful, miserly, selfish, sparing **8** covetous, grasping, ravenous, ungiv-

ing **9** mercenary, penurious, rapacious **10** economical, skinflinty
one: **5** miser
avast: **4** halt, stop **5** cease
avatar: **7** Krishna **9** archetype **10** embodiment
Avatar (2009 film)
cast: Stephen Lang, Zoe Saldana, Sigourney Weaver, Sam Worthington
character: **4** Jake, Mo'at **5** Grace, Miles, Sully, Trudy **7** Eytucan, Neytiri **8** Quaritch **9** Jake Sully
director: James Cameron
goddess: **4** Eywa
material: **10** unobtanium
Na'vi abode: **8** Hometree
Na'vi skin color: **4** blue
planet: **7** Pandora
princess: **7** Neytiri
species: **4** Na'vi
Avaunt!: **4** away **5** hence **6** begone
avdp.: **2** wt.
ave: **4** hail **5** Latin **7** welcome
ave.: **2** st. **3** rte. **4** blvd.
Ave ___: **5** Maria
___ Ave.: **3** Lex., Mad. **4** Park, Penn. **5** Fifth **7** Madison
ave atque ___: **4** vale
avec: **4** with **6** French
opposite: **4** sans
avec ___: **7** plaisir
avec ___ permission: **5** votre
Avedon, Richard: **12** photographer
Aveeno: **6** lotion
alternative: **4** Keri **5** Curel, Nivea **7** Eucerin, Jergens, Pacquin **9** Lubriderm
avena: **3** oat
avenaceous: **4** oaty **5** oaten
avenge: **5** repay, right **6** punish **7** get even, pay back, redress, requite, revenge **9** pay in kind, retaliate, retribute, vindicate **10** get back for, get even for
___ a vengeance: **4** with
avenged
be ~: **9** get back at
avenger
of unrequited love: **7** Anteros, Anterus
Avenger: **3** car **4** auto **5** Dodge **10** automobile
Avengers, The (1998 film)
cast: Jim Broadbent, Sean Connery, Ralph Fiennes, Uma Thurman
Avengers, The (ABC drama)
cast: Patrick Macnee (John Steed) Diana Rigg (Emma Peel) Linda Thorson (Tara King)
avenging: **10** vindictive
avenue: **3** way **4** path, road **5** byway, drive, means, paseo, route **6** access, artery, course, medium, outlet, street **7** channel, ingress, passage, pathway **8** approach **9** boulevard, concourse
___ Avenue: **4** Park **5** Fifth, On the **6** Acacia, Wabash **7** Madison, Seventh **8** Atlantic, Michigan **9** Lexington
aver: **4** avow, hold **5** claim, opine, swear **6** affirm, allege, assert, assure, attest, avouch, insist **7** certify, confess, confirm, contend, declare, express, profess, swear to **8** attest to, maintain, proclaim **9** guarantee, predicate **10** asseverate, insist upon
average: **3** par **4** fair, mean, norm, so-so **5** lowly, typic, usual **6** common, median, medium, middle, modest, normal **7** typical **8** everyday, mediocre, middling, moderate, ordinary, passable, standard **9** customary, tolerable, unnotable **10** fairly good, mainstream, reasonable, stereotype
below ~: **4** poor
better than ~: **5** C plus
financial ~: **3** Dow
grade: **3** cee
guy: **3** Joe **7** Joe Blow **9** Joe Doakes
on ~: **7** usually **9** generally, typically
(out): **4** even **7** balance
___ average: **4** on an **6** moving **7** batting, general
___ averages: **5** law of
___ averaging: **6** dollar
Averell: **8** Harriman
Averill, Earl: **6** Pirate **10** outfielder
averment: **4** oath **5** claim
Averno: **4** lake
locale: **5** Italy
Avernus: **5** Hades
averse: **3** shy **4** loth **5** balky, loath **7** hostile, opposed, uneager **8** allergic, contrary, hesitant, inimical, opposing **9** reluctant, shrinking, unwilling **10** indisposed, uninclined
be ~ to: **6** loathe **7** dislike
to: **3** con **6** down on **8** opposing **10** at odds with
to work: **4** idle **6** otiose, torpid **7** laggard, languid, passive **8** indolent, slothful **9** do-nothing, lethargic, sedentary, shiftless **10** languorous
aversion: **4** hate **5** dread, odium **6** enmity, hatred, horror, phobia, rancor **7** allergy, disdain, disgust, dislike, ill will **8** contempt, disfavor, distaste, loathing **9** animosity, antipathy, hostility, prejudice, repulsion, revulsion **10** abhorrence, antagonism, opposition, reluctance, repellence, repugnance
exclamation: **3** ack, ick, ugh **4** yuck **5** yecch
avert: **4** foil, veer **5** shunt **6** escape, thwart **7** deflect, fend off, head off, inhibit, obviate, prevent, rule out, ward off **8** forefend, preclude, sidestep, stave off, turn away **9** forestall, frustrate, sidetrack, turn aside **10** circumvent
Avery: **3** Tex, Val **5** James **6** Brooks **8** Brundage **9** Schreiber
to Murphy: **3** son
___ a Very Good Year: **5** It Was
aves
have them: **4** alae
___ aves: **5** rarae
avg.: **3** std.
bigger than ~: **3** lge.
size: **3** med.
Avia
rival: **4** Nike **6** Etonic, Reebok
avian: **8** birdlike
aviary: **4** cage **6** volary **7** dovecot **8** birdcage, dovecote **9** birdhouse, enclosure
sound: **5** cheep, chirp, tweet
aviate: **3** fly **4** go up, soar **5** pilot **7** take off **8** navigate, take wing **9** barnstorm, hit the sky
aviation: **6** flight, flying **8** piloting **10** volitation
combining form: **3** aer- **4** aero-
concern: **3** fog **4** fuel, wind **7** weather **8** airspeed, headwind, tailwind
marker: **5** pylon
science of ~: **8** avionics
watchdog agcy.: **3** CAB
aviator: **3** ace **5** flier, flyer, pilot **6** airman, fly boy **7** war hero **8** aeronaut
Aviator: **3** SUV **4** Linc **7** Lincoln
Aviator, The (2004 film)
cast: Alan Alda, Alec Baldwin, Kate Beckinsale, Cate Blanchett, Leonardo DiCaprio
director: Martin Scorsese
aviatrix: **3** ace **5** flier, flyer, pilot, woman **8** aeronaut
for short: **3** WAF
avid: **3** mad **4** keen, wild **5** afire, eager, itchy **6** ardent, fervid, greedy, gung-ho, hearty, on edge, red-hot **7** anxious, athirst, earnest, emotive, fired up, glowing, intense, longing, lustful, thirsty, wishful, zealous **8** desirous, effusive, grasping, inspired, spirited, wild-eyed **9** ambitious, dedicated, fanatical, voracious **10** all fired up, cupidinous, insatiable, inspirited, inveterate, passionate, raring to go, solicitous
avidity: **4** lust, zeal **5** ardor, greed **6** desire **8** ambition, cupidity, yearning **9** eagerness **10** enthusiasm
avidly: **4** hard **6** keenly **8** heartily
avifauna: **5** birds, ornis
Avignon: **4** city, town
locale: **6** France
river: **5** Rhone
Avila: **4** city, town
locale: **5** Spain
saint: **6** Teresa
Avildsen, John G.: **8** director
film: The Karate Kid (1984) Lean on Me (1989) Neighbors (1981) Rocky (1976, AA) Save the Tiger (1973)
___ avion: **3** par
avionics: **7** science
study: **8** aviation
aviophobe
fear: **6** flying
___ a Virgin: **4** Like
avis: **4** bird **5** Latin
pair: **4** alae
rara ~: **3** gem **6** oddity, wonder **7** oddball
___ avis: **4** rara
Avis: **9** car rental **10** auto rental
alternative: **5** Alamo, Hertz **6** Budget, Dollar **7** Thrifty **8** National **10** Enterprise
Avison, Margaret: **4** poet **8** Canadian
___ Aviv: **3** Tel
Avnet, Jon: **8** director
avocado: **4** tree **5** color, fruit, green **6** veggie **9** vegetable
appetizer: **9** guacamole
color relative: *see* green color
family: **6** laurel
avocation: **5** field, hobby **7** pastime, pursuit **8** activity, interest, sideline **9** amusement, diversion **10** employment, occupation, recreation
avocet: **4** bird **5** wader **9** shorebird
avodire: **4** tree
relative: **4** neem **6** acajou, carapa, sapele **8** andiroba, crabwood, mahogany
Avogadro, Amedeo: **7** chemist, Italian **9** physicist
Avogadro's ___: **3** law **6** number
avoid: **4** duck, fear, jump, lose, omit, shun, skip **5** dodge, elude, evade, hedge, parry, shake, shirk, skirt, spare **6** beware, bypass, escape, eschew, ignore **7** abstain, boycott, dislike, fend off, forbear, prevent, quibble, refrain, shy from, ward off **8** flee from, get out of, hide from, keep from, shake off, sidestep **9** get around, go without, leap aside, ostracize, pussyfoot, turn aside **10** circumvent, escape from, get clear of, recoil from, shrink from, work around
thing to ~: **4** no-no, tabu **5** taboo
work: **4** idle, laze, loaf **5** dog it, shirk, slack **6** dawdle **7** goof off **8** lollygag, malinger, slack off **9** bum around, pussyfoot **10** featherbed, mess around
avoidance: **6** escape **7** evasion, veering **9** absention, antipathy, departure, desertion, restraint, runaround **10** abstinence, prevention
avoiding
others: **3** shy **5** timid
avoirdupois: **4** heft **6** weight
à ___ voix: **5** haute
Avon: **5** river **6** makeup
alternative: *see* cosmetic
city on the ~: **4** Bath
Earl of ~: **4** Eden
feeder: **4** Leam **5** Leame
River locale: **7** England
à votre santé: **5** toast **6** French
avouch: **4** aver, avow **5** admit **6** affirm, allege, assert, assure, attest, depone, depose **7** certify, confess, declare, profess, protest, testify **8** attest to **9** guarantee **10** asseverate
avouchment: **4** oath
___ à vous: **4** tout
avow: **3** own **4** aver, hold **5** admit, allow, claim, grant, let on, state, swear, vouch **6** accept, affirm, allege, assert, attest, avouch, fess up, insist, pledge **7** certify, concede, confess, confirm, contend, declare, own up to, profess, promise, protest, swear to **8** maintain, proclaim, speak out **9** recognize **10** asseverate
avowal: **4** oath **5** claim **6** pledge **7** promise **9** admission, agreement, assertion, statement, testimony **10** confession, profession, unbosoming
avowed: **5** known, sworn **10** ostensible
avower: **8** deponent

avril: 4 mois 5 April, month 6 French
  follower: 3 mai
  preceder: 4 mars
a vuestra __: 5 salud
avulse: 7 extract
avulsion: 10 extraction
avuncular: 4 kind 10 protective
aw-__: 6 shucks
A&W: 3 pop 4 soda 8 root beer 9 soft drink
  alternative: *see* soft drink
AWACS: 5 plane 8 airplane
  device: 5 radar
  mission: 5 recon
await: 4 bide, look, pend, wait 6 expect, impend 7 expects, look for, stand by, stay for 8 sit up for, watch for 10 anticipate, hang out for
  judgment: 6 dangle 8 hang fire
awake: 4 rise, stir 5 alert, alive, arise, aware, get up, risen, rouse 6 arouse, come to, living, revive, roused 7 enliven, heedful, on guard 8 stirring, vigilant, watchful 9 attentive, cognizant, conscious, impassion, observant, on the ball, up and at 'em 10 come around, on the stick, responsive, up and about
__-awake: 4 wide
Awake and Sing!
  author: Clifford Odets
awaken: 4 rise, spur, stir, whet 5 alert, arise, get up, rally, rouse, roust 6 arouse, bestir, come to, excite, kindle, recall, revive, stir up 7 animate, enliven, quicken, realize, roll out 8 activate, summon up 9 galvanize, impassion, recollect
awakening: 5 birth 7 arousal, revival 8 kindling 9 animating, evocative 10 activation, enlivening, incitement, stirring up
  time: 2 a.m. 4 morn 7 morning
__ awakening: 4 rude
Awakenings (1990 film)
  cast: Robert De Niro, Julie Kavner, Robin Williams
  director: Penny Marshall
Awakening, The
  character: 4 Edna
__ a walk: 4 take
award: 3 MVP 4 Clio, Emmy, gift, give, Hugo, Obie, Tony 5 Edgar, endow, grant, honor, medal, Oscar, prize, purse, stake 6 bestow, confer, donate, extend, Grammy, plaque, reward, trophy 7 hand out, jackpot, laurels, present, tribute 8 accolade, bestowal, citation, gold star 9 conferral, endowment 10 confer upon, decoration
  advertising ~: 4 Clio
  British ~: 3 MBE, OBE
  British military ~: 3 DFM, DSO
  Cannes ~: 9 Grand Prix
  computer-game ~: 5 Arkie
  dance ~: 6 Bessie
  film ~: 5 Oscar
  French film ~: 5 César
  jury ~: 5 costs 7 damages, penalty 9 indemnity 10 reparation
  military ~: 3 DFC, DSM
  music ~: 6 Grammy
  mystery writers' ~: 5 Edgar
  rock-video ~: 3 Ava
  science-fiction ~: 4 Hugo
  sports ~: 3 MVP 6 letter
  theater ~: 4 Obie, Tony
  TV ~: 4 Emmy
  university ~: 7 diploma, master's 9 doctorate, sheepskin
__ Award: 7 Academy, Newbery
awarded
  be ~: 3 win
award-winning: 5 prize
aware: 3 hep, hip 4 onto, wise 5 alert, awake, privy, savvy 6 posted, wise to, with it 7 heads-up, heedful, knowing, mindful, tactful, tuned in 8 apprised, familiar, informed, lynx-eyed, sensible, sentient, vigilant, watchful 9 attentive, au courant, cognizant, conscious, in the know, observant, on the ball, on the beam, plugged in, regardful, wide-awake 10 acquainted, conversant, on the stick, perceptive, responsive, thoughtful
  be ~ of: 3 see 4 know 5 sense 6 intuit 7 cognize, realize 8 perceive 9 recognize 10 appreciate, understand
  make ~: 4 warn 5 alert, cue in 9 enlighten
  of: 4 in on, onto 5 hep to, hip to 7 alive to, privy to
__-aware: 4 well
awareness: 3 ken, wit 4 wits 5 grasp, light, sense 6 acumen, memory 7 feeling, insight 8 judgment, keenness 9 alertness, aliveness, attention, knowledge, sensation, sentience 10 cognizance, experience, observance, perception, weather eye
__-awareness: 4 self
awash: 3 big 4 full, rife 6 afloat, imbued, packed 7 brimful, crowded, flooded, replete, swamped 8 brimfull, brimming, floating
away: 3 fro, off, out 4 gone 5 apart, aside, forth, hence 6 abroad, absent, avaunt, far-off, loiter, remote, yonder 7 distant, missing, outside 8 departed, vanished 9 elsewhere, far afield, on the road 10 on vacation, out of range
  combining form: 3 apo-
  in Italian: 3 via
  starter: 3 cut, far, fly, get, lay, run 4 cast, fade, give, hide, roll, stow, take, that, this, walk, well 5 break, throw 8 straight
__ away: 3 eat, get, lay, put, run 4 back, blow, draw, fall, fire, fool, give, hide, pack, pull, salt, slip, sock, stow, tear, tuck, turn 5 carry, clear, laugh, right, swept, throw 6 fiddle, square 7 explain
__ away!: 5 Bombs
Away __ Manger: 3 in a
__ Away: 3 Run 4 Cast, Fade, Look, Move, Slip 5 Drift, So Far, Steal, Swept 7 Walking
__-away camp: 5 sleep
__ away from: 3 shy 4 take, walk
Away in a Manger: 4 noel 5 carol
__-Away Places: 3 Far
__ Away Renee: 4 Walk
__ away with: 3 get, run 4 make
__ a way with: 4 have
__-away zone: 3 tow
Aw, c'mon!: 6 please
awe: 3 cow, wow 4 stun 5 amaze, dread, floor, scare, shock 6 dazzle, marvel, terror, wonder 7 impress, respect, startle, terrify, worship 8 astonish, blow away, bowl over, frighten, knock out, overcome, surprise, transfix 9 abashment, amazement, disbelief, dumbfound, overpower, overwhelm, reverence, terrorize 10 intimidate, scare stiff, veneration, wonderment
  ender: 4 some 6 struck 8 stricken
  exclamation: 3 boy, gee, ooh 4 gosh 5 golly, hello 6 jiminy 7 jeepers
  hold in ~: 6 revere
  in ~: 4 agog, rapt 5 agape 6 amazed 7 stunned 9 bedazzled, blown away 10 bowled over, dumbstruck, spellbound
  stand in ~: 6 marvel
aweary: 5 all in, tired, wiped 6 bushed, pooped 9 exhausted
aweather
  opposite: 4 alee
awed: 4 agog, rapt 10 speechless
aweigh: 5 atrip
__ Aweigh: 7 Anchors
awe-inspiring: 5 grand, weird 6 solemn 7 unusual 8 terrible 9 wonderful 10 impressive
aweless: 4 bold, flip, game, pert, rude 5 fresh, gutsy, nervy, sassy, saucy 6 brazen, cheeky, daring, gritty, heroic, plucky, snippy, spunky 7 defiant, doughty, gallant, staunch, uncivil, valiant 8 fearless, flippant, heroical, impolite, impudent, insolent, intrepid, resolute, snippety, stalwart, unafraid, valorous 9 audacious, dauntless, dreadless, out of line, undaunted, unfearful, unfearing 10 courageous, irreverent
awesome
  see wonderful
Awesome!: 3 ooh, rad, wow
awesomeness: 8 grandeur
awestruck: 4 agog, rapt 5 agape, blank, cowed 6 aghast, amazed, solemn 7 abashed, daunted, humbled, stunned 8 appalled, dismayed, reverent 9 astounded 10 bewildered
  be ~: 6 wonder
  look ~: 4 gape, gawk, gaze 5 stare 6 goggle, marvel
__ a wet hen: 5 mad as
awful: 3 bad 4 dire, foul, grim, poor, ugly 5 dread, gross, lousy, nasty, weird, woful 6 crumby, crummy, dismal, grisly, horrid, no-good, odious, putrid, rotten, tragic, unholy, wicked, woeful 7 accurst, baleful, baneful, beastly, doleful, fearful, ghastly, hateful, heinous, hideous, ill-done, the pits, ungodly 8 accursed, alarming, dreadful, flagrant, grievous, gruesome, horrible, horrific, inferior, shameful, shocking, stinking, terrible, terrific, tragical, wretched 9 abhorrent, appalling, atrocious, defective, execrable, fifth-rate, frightful, insidious, loathsome, miserable, monstrous, offensive, repellant, revolting, third-rate, unsightly 10 abominable, deplorable, despicable, detestable, disastrous, disgusting, formidable, fourth-rate, horrendous, lamentable, petrifying, second-rate, tremendous, unpleasant
  be ~: 5 stink
  feel ~: 3 ail
  feel ~ about: 3 rue 6 regret
  feeling ~: 3 ill
  find ~: 4 hate 5 abhor 6 detest, loathe
  most ~: 5 worst
  something ~: 5 loser
awfully: 3 too 4 much, very 6 hugely 8 terribly 9 extremely, immensely, unusually
__ a whack at: 4 have, take
awhile: 7 shortly 8 for a time 9 for a spell
awhirl: 5 giddy 8 rotating, spinning
__ a wide swath: 3 cut
awkward: 5 bulky, gawky, inapt, inept, messy, unapt, wrong 6 clumsy, gangly, gauche, klutzy, oafish, sloppy, sticky, thorny, trying, uneasy, wooden 7 boorish, gawkish, halting, labored, lumpish, strange, unadept, uncouth 8 affected, bumbling, bungling, cloddish, delicate, fumbling, gangling, improper, inexpert, lubberly, strained, tactless, ticklish, ungainly, unpoised, unsubtle, untimely, unwieldy 9 all thumbs, graceless, ill at ease, inelegant, lumbering, maladroit, ponderous, stumbling, unskilled, unwieldly 10 amateurish, blundering, cumbersome, galumphing, leadfooted, left-handed, outlandish, unbecoming, unpolished, unskillful
  age: 5 teens, youth
  one: 5 klutz 6 galoot, lubber
  situation: 6 plight
awkward __: 3 age
Awkward Age, The
  author: Henry James
awl: 4 tool 5 punch 6 gimlet
awn: 5 beard 6 arista 7 bristle
awning: 5 cover, shade 6 canopy, screen 7 marquee, shelter 8 covering, sunshade
AWOL: 4 gone 6 absent, no show 7 missing 8 deserter
  go ~: 4 flee 7 abscond
  part of ~: 3 out 4 with 5 leave 6 absent 7 without
  pursuer: 2 MP, SP
__ a Woman: 4 Born, I Got, She's
__ a Wonderful Life: 3 It's
__ a Wonderful World: 3 It's 4 Wh
Awoonor, Kofi: 6 writer 8 Ghana
awry: 3 off 4 agee, agly, ajee, a 5 agley, amiss, askew, bad bandy, wrong 6 afield, a canted, faulty, flooey skewed, zigzag 7 a crooked, twisted sided 9 off-cen the mark, ou
  go ~: 3 er
  someth
Aw, sh
ax: 3 ca drop, du

sack, tool **5** hewer, let go, slash **6** bounce, cancel, cleave, hack up, lay off **7** cashier, chopper, cleaver, cut down, destroy, dismiss, drum out, hack off, hatchet, kick out, release, scissor, turn out **8** chop down, furlough, get rid of, hack down, pink-slip, throw out, tomahawk **9** discharge, eliminate, get rid off, terminate
grind an ~: **4** edge, file, hone **5** strop **7** sharpen
handle: **4** haft **5** helve
prehistoric ~ head: **4** Celt
relative: **3** adz **4** adze **5** vouge
starter: **4** pick, pole **5** broad
to grind: **9** grievance
use an ~: **3** hew **4** chop, fell **7** cut down
Ax: **7** Emanuel
AXA
competitor: ***see*** insurance company
axatse: **6** rattle **10** percussion
origin: **6** Africa
axe
see ax
Axe-Helve, The
author: Robert Frost
axel: **4** jump, leap
do an ~: **5** skate
where to do an ~: **3** ice **4** rink
__ axel: **6** double, triple
Axel: **5** Foley **6** Schulz **7** Paulsen **8** Stordahl, Theorell
__ Axel Karlfeldt: **4** Erik
Axelrod: **6** George, Julius
Axel's Castle
author: Edmund Wilson
axeman: **5** hewer **10** lumberjack
Ax, Emanuel: **7** pianist
axenic: **7** sterile **8** germfree
axes
standard ~: **5** X and Y
where ~ cross: **5** graph **6** origin
axilla: **6** armpit
axillary: **4** alar **5** alary
axiom: **3** law, saw **4** rule **5** adage, given, maxim, moral, motto, truth **6** byword, dictum, saying, truism **7** precept, proverb, theorem **8** aphorism, apothegm, doctrine, standard **9** postulate, principle **10** apophthegm, principium
ender: **4** atic
Axiom: **3** SUV **5** Isuzu
axiomatic: **5** given, pithy, terse **6** gnomic **7** assumed, certain, evident, granted, obvious **8** absolute, gnomical, manifest **9** apodictic **10** aphoristic, proverbial, understood, undoubtful
axis: **4** deer, line, stem **5** pivot, shaft, stalk **7** fulcrum, spindle
central ~: **5** spine
combining form: **3** axi-, axo-
extremity: **4** pole
having no ~ extremities: **6** apolar
relative: ***see*** deer
__ axis: **4** real **5** major, minor, optic, polar, screw **7** neutral, radical
Axis __: **5** Sally
Axl: **4** Rose
axle: **3** rod **4** pole **5** pivot, shaft **7** spindle **8** auto part
cover: **6** hubcap
end: **3** hub
holder: **5** U-bolt
axle __: **6** grease
axolotl: **4** newt **7** Mexican **9** amphibian **10** salamander
axon
site: **5** nerve
Axton: **4** Hoyt
Axxess: **3** van **6** Nissan
Ay, __ the rub: **6** there's
ayah: **4** maid **5** nurse **9** governess
Ayako: **7** Okamoto
Ayatollah: **5** title **6** cleric
land: **4** Iran
language: **5** Farsi
preceder: **4** shah
subject: **5** Irani
title: **4** imam **5** imaum
Ayckbourn, Alan: **7** British **10** playwright
work: Absurd Person Singular
Bedroom Farce
By Jeeves
A Chorus of Disapproval
House & Garden
How the Other Half Loves
Intimate Exchanges
Invisible Friends
Just Between Ourselves
Making Tracks
Man of the Moment
The Norman Conquests
Private Fears in Public Places
Relatively Speaking
A Small Family Business
Standing Room Only
Taking Steps
Time and Time Again
Time of My Life
Way Upstream
Woman in Mind
aye: **2** da, ja, sí **3** e'er, for, oui, pro, yea, yep, yes, yup **4** fine, okay, sure, vote, yeah **6** backer **7** in favor, vote for, yes vote **8** thumbs up **9** proponent, supporter
opposite: **3** nay
voting ~: **3** for
see also of course, yes
__-a-year man: **6** dollar
aye-aye: **5** lemur **6** mammal **7** primate
relative: ***see*** primate
Ayelet: **5** Zurer
__ a Yellow Ribbon...: **3** Tie
ayem: **4** morn **7** morning
Ayers __: **4** Rock
Ayesha
author: H. Rider Haggard
Haggard's ~: **3** She
ayin: **6** Hebrew, letter
predecessor: **6** samech, samekh
successor: **2** pe **3** peh
Aykroyd, Dan: **5** actor **8** comedian
film: 1941 (1979)
The Blues Brothers (1980)
Chaplin (1992)
Coneheads (1993)
The Curse of the Jade Scorpion (2001)
Diamonds (1999)
Doctor Detroit (1983)
Dragnet (1987)
Driving Miss Daisy (1989)
Ghostbusters (1984)
Ghostbusters II (1989)
The Great Outdoors (1988)
Grosse Pointe Blank (1997)
My Fellow Americans (1996)
My Girl (1991)
My Stepmother Is an Alien (1988)
Neighbors (1981)
Sgt. Bilko (1996)
Sneakers (1992)
Spies Like Us (1985)
Trading Places (1983)
spouse: Donna Dixon
TV: Saturday Night Live
Ayla
creator: Jean Auel
portrayer: **5** Daryl
Ayn: **4** Rand
Ayr: **4** city, port, town
locale: **8** Scotland
Ayres: **3** Lew **8** Mitchell
Ayres, Lew: **5** actor
spouse: Ginger Rogers
Ayrshire: **3** cow **4** bull **6** bovine, cattle
Ay, there's the __: **3** rub
AZ
see Arizona
azalea: **5** plant, shrub **6** flower **10** ornamental
relative: **5** heath, salal **6** kalmia **7** arbutus, rhodora **8** cassiope, cowberry **9** blueberry, deerberry
Azaria, Hank: **5** actor
spouse: Helen Hunt
TV: The Simpsons
Azerbaijan: **6** nation **7** country
bovine: **5** Kurdi **6** Sarabi
capital: **4** Baku
location: **4** Asia
mountains: **8** Caucasus
neighbor: **4** Iran **6** Russia, Turkey **7** Armenia, Georgia
once: **3** SSR
azimuth: **3** arc
Azinger, Paul: **6** golfer
Aziyad
author: Pierre Loti
Aznavour: **7** Charles
azo: **3** dye **8** amaranth
Azores: **4** isls. **5** isles **7** islands
essentially: **4** lava
island: **4** Pico **5** Corvo, Faial, Fayal **6** Flores **8** Graciosa, Sao Jorge, Terceira **9** Sao Miguel **10** Santa Maria
loc.: **3** Atl. **8** Atlantic
Azov: **3** sea
feeder: **5** Kuban
locale: **6** Russia
Azrael: **5** angel
author: Henry Wadsworth Longfellow
Aztec: **5** Nahua **8** language
foe: **6** Cortés
ruler: **9** Montezuma
spear-thrower: **6** atlatl
__-Aztecan: **3** Uto
__ azure: **3** sky **4** blue **5** color, lapis, skyey **6** cobalt, heaven, purply **7** sky blue **8** cerulean, deep-blue, empyrean, purplish **9** firmament **10** cobalt blue
relative: ***see*** blue color
azurite: **3** gem, ore **7** mineral **8** gemstone
Azusa: **4** city, town
locale: **10** California

B

B: 4 elem., mark, type 5 boron, grade, width 6 letter 7 element
5 for ~: 4 at. no.
and B: 3 inn 7 lodging
in phonetic alphabet: 5 Bravo
plus: 5 grade
team: 6 scrubs
type ~: 7 amiable, patient 8 laid-back 9 easygoing
vitamin: 6 biotin, folate, niacin
B __: 4 and B, and O, cell, star 5 meson, movie 6 school 7 battery, complex, horizon, picture, vitamin
B __ boy: 4 as in
B-__: 4 axes, axis, girl, Rock
__ B: 3 Jon, Mel 4 B and, R and, Type 6 Linear, radium, Stevie 7 vitamin
'B' __ Burglar: 5 Is for
__-B: 4 Oral
B-1: 6 bomber
B12: 7 vitamin
B-29: 6 bomber
B-52: 6 bomber
B6: 7 vitamin
Ba: 4 elem. 6 barium 7 element
56 for ~: 4 at. no.
B.A.: 6 degree
institute: 7 college 10 university
part of ~: 4 arts 8 bachelor
baa: 4 blat, bray 5 bleat
relative: 3 moo 4 oink 5 quack
Baa Baa Black Sheep
dog: 8 Meatball
__ b-a-a-d boy!: 3 I'm a
baal: 4 idol 8 false god
Baal
author: Bertolt Brecht
baba: 4 cake 6 pastry 7 rum cake
Baba __: 4 Wawa
__ Baba and the 40 Thieves: 3 Ali
baba au rhum: 4 cake 6 pastry
Babaloo
singer: Desi Arnaz
Babbage: 7 Charles
Babbitt: 5 Bruce, sheep, toady 6 yes man 8 assenter, emulator, orthodox 10 conformist
author: Sinclair Lewis
character: 3 Ted 4 Myra 5 Doane, Tanis, Zilla 6 Eunice, Seneca, Verona
babble: 3 jaw, yak, yap 4 chat, gush, rave, talk 5 bleat, noise, prate, run on, sound 6 cackle, drivel, footle, gabble, gibber, gossip, gurgle, humbug, jabber, jargon, mumble, murmur, patter, ramble, rattle, tattle, uproar, wander 7 blather, blether, chatter, maunder, prattle 8 nonsense, rattle on 9 gibberish, go on and on, jabbering, loquacity
starter: 6 psycho
babbler: 4 bird 6 gossip, magpie
babbling: 3 gab 4 blab 5 noise, noisy, prate, wordy 6 drivel, hot air 7 blather, blether, chatter, gabbing, palaver, prating, prattle, unterse 8 chit-chat, nonsense 9 garrulity, garrulous, gibberish, jabbering, prattling, small talk 10 chattering, loquacious
babbling __: 5 brook
Babcock: 7 Barbara
babe: 3 hon, tot 4 naif 5 bairn, child 6 infant, rug rat 7 neonate, newborn 8 innocent 9 greenhorn, little one
in the woods: 4 fawn, lamb, naif 6 victim
like a ~ in the woods: 4 naif 5 naïve 9 unworldly
babe __ woods: 5 in the
Babe: 3 pig 4 Ruth 6 Herman, Phelps 8 Zaharias 9 Didrikson
Babe (1979 song)
artist: Styx
Babe (1995 film)
character: 4 Esme
director: Chris Noonan
dog: 3 Fly, Rex
babel: 3 din 6 hubbub, jangle, racket, tumult, uproar 8 shambles 9 cacophony, gibberish 10 hullabaloo
Babel: 5 Isaak, tower
Babel (2006 film)
cast: Cate Blanchett, Brad Pitt
Babel, Isaak: 6 writer 7 Russian
Babel Tower
author: A.S. Byatt
Babenco, Hector: 8 director
Babes in Arms: 7 musical
composer: Lorenz Hart, Richard Rodgers
Babes in Toyland (1934 film)
cast: Oliver Hardy, Stan Laurel
Babette: 7 Deutsch
babiche: 5 thong
babies: 5 young
kiss ~: 3 run 4 gush 5 stump 6 hustle 8 campaign, politick
__ Babies: 6 Beanie
Babilonia, Tai: 6 skater
babka: 4 cake 6 Slavic
Bab-O: 8 cleanser
alternative: 4 Ajax 5 Comet 6 Bon Ami 9 Soft Scrub
baboon: 3 ape 4 boor 5 jocko 6 animal, dimwit, dog ape, gelada, monkey, simian 7 primate 8 mandrill
relative: *see* primate
babu: 3 sir
babushka: 4 nana 5 scarf 8 kerchief
baby: 3 kid, pet, tot, wee 4 dear, dote, puny, tiny 5 bairn, bitty, child, nurse, small, spoil, teeny, young 6 bantam, bon ami, chérie, cherub, coddle, cosset, coward, dote on, infant, little, midget, minute, nipper, pamper, peewee, petite, rug rat, teensy 7 bambino, cater to, crawler, indulge, newborn, papoose, preemie, project, toddler 8 dote upon, dumpling, immature, juvenile, nonvoter, weakling 9 itsy-bitsy, itty-bitty, little one, miniature, offspring, pint-sized, spoon-feed, undersize, youngster 10 diminutive, girlfriend, humorminor, teeny-weeny, vest-pocket
act like a ~: 3 cry 4 bawl, pule
admonition: 4 no no
bed: 4 crib 6 cradle
boomer offspring: 4 Gen-X
bouncer: 4 knee
boy's clothes color: 4 blue
bringer: 5 stork
caretaker: 4 nana
carriage: 4 pram 5 buggy
comfort for ~: 6 bottle
cover: 3 bib
cry: 3 goo, wah 4 dada, mama 5 daddy, mamma, mommy
digestion aid: 4 burp
ender: 3 ish, sit
girl's clothes color: 4 pink
grand: 5 piano
in French: 4 bébé
in Italian: 5 bimbo
in Spanish: 4 bebé, nena
kisser: 3 pol
like ~ food: 5 bland
like ~ hair: 5 silky
meal: 3 pap 6 din-din
mind the ~: 3 sit
often: 5 crier
outfit: 7 layette
seat: 3 lap
shoe: 6 bootee, bootie
sitter: 5 nanny 8 watchdog 9 attendant, caregiver, caretaker
soothe a ~: 4 rock
soother: 4 talc 7 lullaby
sound: 3 coo 4 mewl
starter: 3 cry 5 grand
start on ~ food: 4 wean
talk: 4 lisp 6 goo-goo
wear: 6 bonnet, diaper
see also sweetheart
baby __: 4 beef, blue, bond, book, boom, bust, doll, face, food, spot, step, talk 5 blues, buggy, coach, grand, split, teeth, tooth 6 boomer, buster, sitter
baby __ ribs: 4 back
baby-__: 3 sat, sit 5 faced, proof, tears 7 sitting
baby-__-eyes: 4 blue
__ baby: 3 tar 4 bush 5 bonus, notch 6 bottle
__-baby: 3 cry
Baby (song)
artist: Brook Benton, Brandy
Baby __: 4 Baby, Bell, Boom, Doll, Face, Jane, Love, Ruth, Talk 5 LeRoy 7 Workout
Baby __ Back: 3 Got 4 Come
Baby __ Nelson: 4 Face
__ Baby: 3 Cry, Tar 4 Abie, Baby, Be My, Do It, Ruby 5 Angel, Angie, Beach, Be-Bop, Dream 6 Pretty 7 Goodbye
Baby and Child Care
author: Benjamin Spock
Baby Baby (1991 song)
artist: Amy Grant
Baby-Baby-Baby (1992 song)
artist: TLC
Baby, Baby Don't Cry (1969 song)
artist: Miracles
Baby Bell, former: 5 NYNEX
baby-blue-eyes: 5 plant 6 flower
Baby Boom (1987 film)
cast: Diane Keaton, Harold Ramis, Sam Shepard
Baby Boomer kid: 3 X-er
Baby, Come to Me (1982 song)
artist: Patti Austin, James Ingram
Baby Doc country: 5 Haiti
babydoll
see sweetheart
Baby Doll (1956 film)
cast: Carroll Baker, Karl Malden, Eli Wallach
director: Elia Kazan
Baby Don't Get Hooked on Me (1972 song)
artist: Mac Davis
baby-faced: 4 cute
baby-food name: 6 Gerber
Baby Got Back (1992 song)
artist: Sir Mix-a-Lot
Baby Hold On (1978 song)
artist: Eddie Money
babyhood: 6 cradle 7 infancy
Baby I Love You (song)
artist: Aretha Franklin, Andy Kim
Baby I'm-a Want You (song)
artist: Bread
Baby I'm Yours (song)
artist: Barbara Lewis, Shai
Baby I Need Your Loving (song)
artist: Four Tops, Johnny Rivers
babying: 10 indulgence
babyish: 6 infant, little 7 kiddish, puerile 8 immature, juvenile 9 infantile
Baby, It's Cold Outside
artist: Ella Fitzgerald
Baby It's You (song)
artist: Shirelles, Smith
Baby Jane (1983 song)
artist: Rod Stewart
Babylonia
battle site: 6 Cunaxa
city of ancient ~: 5 Accad, Akkad
goddess: 6 Ishtar
language: 8 Accadian, Akkadian
neighbor: 4 Elam
region: 5 Sumer
sun god: 3 Utu
today: 4 Irak, Iraq
underworld: 5 Aralu 6 Arallu
Baby Love (song)
artist: Regina, Supremes
Baby Mama (2008 film)
cast: Tina Fey, Greg Kinnear, Amy Poehler
...Baby One More Time (1998 song)
artist: Britney Spears
Baby Ruth: 3 bar 5 candy 8 candy bar 9 chocolate
alternative: *see* candy brand
baby's __: 5 tears 6 breath
baby-sit: 4 mind, tend 5 guard, watch 7 oversee 9 look after 10 take care of
Baby, Take __: 4 a Bow
Baby Talk (1959 song)
artist: Jan & Dean
__-Baby, The: 3 Tar
Baby The Rain Must Fall (1965 film)
cast: Steve McQueen, Lee Remick
Baby, What a Big Surprise (1977 song)
artist: Chicago
Baby You're a Rich Man (1967 song)
artist: Beatles
Baby (You've Got What It Takes) (1960 song)
artist: Dinah Washington
Bacall, Lauren: 7 actress
film: The Big Sleep (1946)
Confidential Agent (1945)
Dark Passage (1947)
Designing Woman (1957)

Diamonds (1999)
Flame Over India (1959)
Harper (1966)
How to Marry a Millionaire (1953)
Key Largo (1948)
The Mirror Has Two Faces (1996)
Murder on the Orient Express (1974)
My Fellow Americans (1996)
Sex and the Single Girl (1964)
The Shootist (1976)
To Have and Have Not (1944)
The Walker (2007)
Written on the Wind (1956)
Young Man With a Horn (1950)
spouse: Humphrey Bogart, Jason Robards
Bacardi: **3** rum **5** drink **8** beverage
baccalaureate: **6** degree **8** graduate
baccanal: **5** menad **6** maenad **7** reveler **8** bacchant, carouser **9** bacchante, frolicker, party-goer, wassailer **10** merrymaker
baccarat: **4** game **8** card game
cry: **5** banco
play ~: **3** bet
table item: **4** shoe
Bacchae
author: Euripides
bacchanalia: **4** bash **5** binge, feast, party, revel, spree **6** frolic, revels **7** revelry **8** carnival, carousal, Dionysia, festival, partying, reveling **10** saturnalia
bacchanalian: **3** gay, mad **4** wild **5** merry **6** jocund, wanton **7** bacchic, festive, riotous **8** frenetic, frenzied, sportive **9** abandoned, Dionysian, dissolute **10** dissipated, licentious
cry: **4** evoe
bacchante: **5** menad **8** baccanal
Bacchus: **3** god **5** Roman
attendant: **5** satyr
equivalent: **8** Dionysus
parent: **4** Zeus **6** Semele
Bach: **3** P.D.Q. **4** Jean **7** Barbara, Richard **9** Catherine
Bacharach, Burt: **8** composer
collaborator: **5** David, Sager
song: Alfie
Anyone Who Had a Heart
Baby, It's You
Blue on Blue
Close to You
Don't Make Me Over
Do You Know the Way to San Jose?
A House Is Not a Home
I'll Never Fall in Love Again
I Say a Little Prayer
The Look of Love
Make It Easy on Yourself
Message to Michael
One Less Bell to Answer
Raindrops Keep Fallin' on My Head
This Guy's in Love With You
Walk on By
Wishin' and Hopin'
spouse: Angie Dickinson, Carole Bayer Sager
Bach, Barbara: **7** actress
spouse: Ringo Starr
bachelor: **4** male **5** unwed **6** single **8** graduate **9** unmarried
home: **3** pad
lack: **4** wife **6** spouse
last words of a ~: **3** I do
party: **4** stag
bachelor __: **4** girl **5** chest, party **6** of arts
Bachelor __: **5** Party **6** Father, Mother
Bachelor and the Bobby-Soxer, The (1947 film)
cast: Cary Grant, Myrna Loy, Shirley Temple
director: Irving Reis
bachelor-at-__: **4** arms
Bachelor Father (CBS/NBC/ABC sitcom)
cast: Noreen Corcoran (Kelly Gregg)
John Forsythe (Bentley Gregg)
Sammee Tong (Peter Tong)
dog: Jasper
Bachelor of __: **4** Arts **7** Science
bachelor's __: **6** button, degree
bachelor's-button: **5** plant **6** flower
Bachelor, The (ABC reality)
host: Chris Harrison
Bach, Johann Sebastian: **6** German **8** composer
contemporary: **6** Handel
instrument: **5** organ
work: The Art of Fugue
Ascension Oratorio
Brandenburg Concertos
Christmas Oratorio
Easter Oratorio
English Suites
French Suites
Passion According to St. John
Passion According to St. Matthew
Twelve Little Preludes
The Well-Tempered Clavier
Bachman-Turner Overdrive
song: You Ain't Seen Nothing Yet (1974)
Bach's Mass __ Minor: **3** in B
Bach's Partita __ Minor: **3** in E
bacillus: **3** bug **4** germ **7** microbe **9** bacterium
shape: **3** rod
back: **3** aft, ago, aid, end, fro **4** abet, fund, hind, rear **5** abaft, about, after, bet on, boost, favor, set up, spine, stake, stern, vouch **6** assist, astern, dorsal, dorsum, foster, recede, second, uphold **7** approve, confirm, endorse, espouse, finance, forward, indorse, nurture, promote, reverse, sponsor, support, sustain, tail end, warrant **8** advocate, bankroll, champion, hindmost, returned, sanction, side with, stand for, vouch for **9** encourage, get behind, patronize, recommend, subscribe, subsidize, to the rear **10** go to bat for, rally round, stand up for, stick up for, strengthen, underwrite
a borrower: **6** cosign
and forth: **6** fickle **7** by turns **8** to and fro, wavering **9** tentative, uncertain, undecided **10** indecisive
answer ~: **4** sass **5** react, rebut
at the ~: **3** aft **6** astern
a while ~: **4** once
bat ~ and forth: **4** mull **6** debate
beat ~: **5** repel
behind one's ~: **5** slyly **7** falsely **8** secretly, sneakily **9** deviously, furtively **10** disloyally
be on the ~ burner: **4** pend
biter: **4** flea
bone: **6** sacrum
bounce ~: **4** echo **5** carom, rally, react **6** carrom, return, revive **7** rebound, recover **8** ricochet **9** boomerang **10** recuperate
bring ~: **6** revive **7** recover, restore **9** reinstate
bring ~ to snuff: **5** rehab
bug ~: **5** notum
buy ~: **6** redeem, unpawn **10** repurchase
call ~: **6** recall, recant
chair ~: **5** splat
change ~: **6** revert
choke ~: **6** stifle
combining form: **3** not- **4** dors-, noto- **5** dorsi-, dorso- **7** opistho-
come ~: **5** reply **6** return **7** revisit
come ~ to mind: **5** recur
come ~ to school: **5** reune
country: **4** wild **5** wilds
cut ~: **4** clip, pare, slow, snip, thin, trim **5** limit, lower, prune, shave, shear, skimp, slash **6** lessen, reduce **7** curtail, shorten **8** conserve, downsize, lessened **9** condensed **10** abbreviate, compressed, synopsized
door: **7** postern
double ~: **4** turn **6** return **7** reverse
down: **5** blink, yield **6** recant
draw ~: **3** shy **5** quail, start, wince **6** cringe, flinch, recede, recoil, retire, shrink **7** retreat **8** withdraw **9** sequester
drop ~: **7** retreat
ender: **3** bit, hoe, lit, log, saw, set **4** ache, beat, bite, bone, date, door, drop, fire, hand, lash, list, pack, rest, room, rush, side, slap, slid, spin, stab, stay, stop, ward, wash, yard **5** bench, biter, board, cloth, court, cross, field, light, pedal, shore, slide, space, stage, stair, swept, sword, track, water, woods **6** ground, handed, logged, packer, stairs, stitch, stroke **7** breaker, country, scatter, stabber, stretch, swimmer **8** breaking, pressure, woodsman
fall ~: **3** ebb **5** lapse, trail **6** recede, retire **7** regress, relapse, retreat **8** withdraw **9** retrocede **10** lose ground, recidivate
fall ~ on: **3** use **6** employ, look to, resort, take to **7** count on **8** call upon, resort to, retire to **9** count upon, make use of, retreat to **10** withdraw to
fight ~: **5** react, rebel, reply **6** mutiny, resist **7** respond
financially: **4** fund **5** stake
fire ~: **5** rebut, reply **6** answer, retort **7** counter, respond **9** rejoinder
flat on one's ~: **6** beaten, laid up **7** forlorn **8** helpless **9** abandoned, destitute, powerless **10** friendless
flow ~: **3** ebb **4** fade, wane **5** abate **6** recede **7** dwindle, subside **8** slack off **9** retrocede
force ~: **5** repel **6** defeat, put off, rebuff **7** fend off, repulse, ward off **8** drive off, turn back **9** drive away
from way ~: **5** of old **6** age-old **7** veteran
from work: **4** home
get ~: **6** recoup, redeem, regain **7** reclaim, recover, salvage **8** retrieve **9** reacquire, recapture
get ~ at: **5** react, repay **6** avenge **7** revenge **9** pay in kind, retaliate
get ~ in shape: **5** rally
get one's ~ up: **3** irk **4** rile **5** peeve, upset
get ~ on one's feet: **7** rebound, recover
get ~ to: **5** reply **7** respond
get ~ together: **9** reconcile **10** conciliate
give ~: **5** repay **6** refund, return **7** reflect, replace, restore
go ~: **3** ebb **4** turn **6** recede, return, revert **7** regress, retreat, revisit **9** retrocede, weasel out
go ~ and forth: **3** wag **4** jolt, pace, reel, rock, roll, sway, toss, yo-yo **5** hedge, hover, lurch, pitch, shake, shift, swing, waver **6** careen, dither, jiggle, jounce, seesaw, teeter, waffle, wobble **7** vibrate **8** fence-sit, hesitate, straddle **9** alternate, fluctuate, hem and haw, oscillate, pussyfoot, vacillate
go ~ on: **3** lie **4** deny **5** belie, renig **6** betray, cop out, recant, renege **7** disavow, forsake, retract **9** play false, repudiate
go ~ on one's word: **5** unsay **6** renege **7** back off, retract **8** back down, take back **9** backpedal, weasel out, worm out of
hang ~: **3** lag **4** poke **5** trail **6** boggle, falter, loiter, shrink **8** hesitate
hanging ~: **3** shy **5** balky, chary **7** fearful **8** wavering **9** reluctant, skeptical, tentative **10** wishy-washy
hark ~: **6** recall **8** look back **9** recollect, reminisce
held ~: **6** pent-up **8** reined in **9** in reserve
hit ~: **5** react, reply **6** answer, resist **7** counter, revenge **9** retaliate
hold ~: **3** dam **4** curb, halt, hide, save, slow, stay, stem, stop **5** check, demur, deter, leash, sit on, stint, tarry **6** arrest, bridle, detain, hinder, impede, refuse, rein in, slow up **7** confine, contain, control, inhibit, prevent, prolong, repulse, reserve, trammel **8** handicap, hesitate, restrain, slow down, stave off, suppress, withhold **9** constrain, keep at bay **10** discourage, keep a lid on, keep in line
in ~: **7** lagging **8** trailing
in anatomy: **6** dorsum
in French: **3** dos
in ~ of: **6** behind **7** ensuing **9** following **10** succeeding
in time: **3** ago **4** once, then

keep ~: **5** check, dam up, delay, flunk **6** detain **7** forbear, reserve **8** withhold
keep nothing ~: **5** level **9** come clean
kept ~: **9** in reserve
kick ~: **3** pay **5** relax **7** rebound
kicking ~: **6** at ease **7** content, relaxed **8** carefree
knock ~: **4** gulp **5** drink **6** guzzle
laid ~: **4** calm **5** Type B **6** serene **10** unbothered
lay ~: **4** lull **5** relax, slack **6** relent **7** slacken **9** lighten up
look ~: **4** muse **5** brood **6** ponder, recall, regret, review **7** reflect **8** dredge up, mull over, remember, ruminate **9** recollect, reminisce
lower ~: **6** lumbar
money ~: **6** rebate, refund
muscle, in the gym: **3** lat
number: **7** vintage **8** obsolete, outdated, outmoded **9** out-of-date **10** antiquated
of a 45: **5** B-side
of a book: **5** spine
off: **4** stop **5** cease, let up, wince **6** ease up, recant, relent **7** forbear, refrain, retreat **8** keep from, withdraw **9** lighten up
of the ~ in anatomy: **5** notal
of the neck: **4** nape **5** nucha, nuque
one of the ~ forty: **4** acre
out: **5** leave **6** recant, renege **8** withdraw
out of: **7** abandon, scuttle **8** give up on
part: **5** small, stern
pat oneself on the ~: **4** brag, crow
pat on the ~: **4** hail, kudo, laud **5** exalt, extol, honor, kudos **6** credit, extoll, homage, praise, salute **7** acclaim, applaud, commend, flatter, glorify, plaudit, tribute **8** accolade, approval, encomium, flattery, good word **9** laudation, panegyric, patronize **10** compliment, exaltation, panegyrize
pay ~: **3** fix **6** avenge, punish, refund, render, return **7** get even, revenge **8** make good, square up **9** indemnify, reimburse, retaliate **10** recompense
play ~: **6** repeat **7** recount **9** reiterate
pull ~: **5** quail **6** recoil, retire **7** retract, retreat **8** hesitate, withdraw
pulling ~: **10** evacuation
put ~: **6** return **7** replace, restore **8** postpone
put on a ~ burner: **5** table **6** shelve **7** suspend **8** postpone
put ~ on one's feet: **4** heal, mend **5** treat
put ~ to zero: **5** reset
read ~: **6** repeat
roll ~: **5** lower, skimp **6** deduct, lessen, reduce, return **7** regress, tail off **8** decrease, downsize **10** underspend
rub: **7** massage
scrubber: **5** loofa, luffa **6** loofah
send ~: **6** remand, return
set ~: **4** mire, slow **5** delay **6** detain, hang up, hinder, hold up, impede, retard, slow up **7** bog down, reverse **8** slow down **9** depressed
settle ~: **5** relax **9** lose speed
shift ~ and forth: **5** waver
sit ~: **4** rest **5** relax **6** unwind **9** lose speed
slip ~: **7** relapse **10** recidivate
snap ~: **6** bounce, recoil, resile **7** rebound, recover
stab in the ~: **4** sell **5** cross **6** betray **7** sell out **9** duplicity, treachery
starter: **3** cut, die, fat, fin, hog, net, out, pay, run, set, tie **4** bare, blow, call, come, draw, fall, fast, feed, full, give, half, hard, hump, kick, moss, play, plow, pull, push, roll, seat, sell, skew, sway, tail, wing **5** camel, crook, flare, flash, green, hatch, horse, hunch, lease, notch, paper, piggy, quill, razor, ridge, rough, shell, spill, sweep, thorn, throw, touch, whale **6** calico, canvas, corner, hackle, narrow, piggie, saddle, silver, switch, turtle **7** flanker, leather, quarter, stickle
street: **5** alley
strike ~: **6** resist **9** retaliate
take ~: **5** rewin, unsay **6** recall, recant, regain, return, revoke **7** disavow, forgive, reclaim, recover, retract **8** disclaim, exchange, withdraw **9** backpedal, recapture, repossess, repudiate
take a ~ seat (to): **5** defer
talk: **3** jaw, lip **4** echo, guff, sass **5** cheek, mouth, reply, sauce **8** defiance, reaction, response **9** impudence, insolence, wisemouth **10** smartmouth
talk ~: **4** sass **5** react **6** answer **7** respond **8** mouth off
the wrong horse: **4** fail, lose
think ~: **6** recall, relive **8** remember **9** reminisce
throw ~: **6** revert **7** reflect, regress
throw ~ and forth: **5** bandy
tooth: **5** molar
toss ~: **5** drink **6** imbibe
toward the ~: **3** aft **6** astern
turn ~: **5** repel, spurn **6** rebuff, thwart **7** regress, relapse, repulse **8** stave off
turn one's ~ on: **4** shun **5** scorn **6** desert, disown, ignore, refuse, reject **7** abandon, forsake, neglect **8** overlook, renounce **9** disregard, repudiate **10** apostatize, leave alone
up: **5** prone, prove **6** assist, defend, second, uphold **7** further, support **8** attest to **9** reinforce
when: **4** once, past, yore **8** formerly **9** at one time **10** previously
win ~: **6** recoup, redeem, regain **7** recover, restore **8** retrieve **9** reacquire
with one's ~ to the wall: **4** dire **5** grave **6** hard up **7** drastic, frantic **8** frenzied, hopeless **9** desperate, in the soup **10** despairing, up the creek
write ~: **5** reply **6** answer **9** respond to
back __: **3** hoe, lot, off, out, run **4** away, dive, door, down, gear, nine, road, room, seat, talk, vent, yard **5** and to, bacon, bench, float, focus, forty, order, score, shaft, staff **6** anchor, burner, matter, number, office, stairs, street **7** channel, country, molding
back-__: **4** load **5** alley, check, cloth, pedal, story, trail **6** mutate, paddle **7** patting
back-__ driver: **4** seat
__ back: **3** bow, cut, get, jig, lay, set **4** call, come, fall, flat, give, hang, hark, hold, hoop, keep, kick, loop, lyre, plow, pull, roll, seat, snap, take, talk, turn **5** choke, heart, knock, roach, shell, throw, water **6** answer, center, corner, hollow, shield, window **7** channel, flanker, gondola, running, Watteau
__-back: **3** arc **4** laid **6** bounce
Back __: **3** Bay **5** at One **6** Street
Back __!: **4** at ya
Back __ USSR: **5** in the
__ Back: **3** Get **5** Stand **7** Looking, Welcome
backache pill maker: **4** Doan
back and __: **4** fill **5** forth
back-and-forth: **6** banter
__ back at: **3** get
Back Bay
locale: **6** Boston
backbeat, provide the: **4** drum
back-bending dance: **5** limbo
backbite: **4** slur **5** abuse, belie, decry, libel, smear, sully **6** attack, defame, engage, impugn, malign, revile, smirch, vilify **7** asperse, cry down, run down, slander, traduce **8** badmouth, belittle, besmirch, mistreat, throw mud **9** criticize, denigrate, deprecate, disparage, fling dirt, fustigate **10** calumniate
backbiting: **5** abuse, catty **6** gossip, malice **7** calumny, obloquy, slander, vicious **8** libelous **9** aspersion, cattiness, dishonest, invective **10** defamation, detraction, impugnment, muckraking
backboard: **4** goal
attachment: **4** hoop
shot off the ~: **5** lay up
backbone: **4** base, grit, guts, will **5** basis, chine, heart, nerve, pluck, ridge, spine, spunk, valor **6** mettle, spirit **7** bravery, courage, essence, reserve, stamina **8** decision, firmness, mainstay, tenacity **9** fortitude, stability, toughness, vertebrae, willpower **10** confidence, foundation, moral fiber, resolution
boat ~: **4** keel
lacking ~: **5** timid
backbreaking: **4** hard **5** heavy, tough **6** taxing **7** arduous, onerous, weighty **8** grueling, toilsome **9** herculean, laborious **10** exhausting
__-back chair: **4** slat **5** press, spoon, wheel **6** barrel, ladder
backcomb: **5** tease
backcountry: **4** bush **8** frontier
Back Country, The
author: Gary Snyder
backdoor: **6** secret, sneaky **7** furtive, illicit **8** indirect
Backdraft (1991 film)
cast: William Baldwin, Robert De Niro, Rebecca De Mornay, Kurt Russell, Donald Sutherland
crime: **5** arson
director: Ron Howard
gear: **5** hoses
special effect: **4** fire
backdrop: **5** scene, scrim **7** scenery, setting
in westerns: **4** mesa **5** cañon **6** canyon
__-backed: **3** hog **5** razor **6** saddle
backer: **3** aye **4** ally **5** angel, donor, giver **6** friend, helper, patron, votary **7** grantor, sponsor **8** adherent, advocate, champion, defender, endorser, exponent, financer, investor, partisan **9** financier, guarantor, proponent, supporter **10** benefactor, well-wisher
favorite sign: **3** SRO
play ~: **5** angel
starter: **4** line
backfire: **4** bomb, fail, flop **5** react **6** recoil **7** explode, go kaput, rebound, wash out **8** reaction **9** boomerang, explosion
sound: **4** bang
backflow: **3** ebb **4** eddy
Back & Forth (1994 song)
artist: Aaliyah
backgammon: **4** game **8** card game
cube: **3** die
impossibility: **3** tie
piece: **5** stone
background: **5** scene, stock **6** milieu, record **7** history, setting **8** literacy, training **9** education, framework, grounding, seasoning, tradition **10** atmosphere, attainment, experience, groundwork, local color, upbringing
in heraldry: **5** field
in the ~: **6** unseen **8** offstage, retiring **9** backstage, unnoticed **10** out of sight
backhanded: **9** insincere, sarcastic
compliment: **5** taunt **7** affront
backhoe: **6** digger **9** excavator
__ Back in Anger: **4** Look
Back in Black
artist: AC/DC
backing: **3** aid, for **4** egis, help **5** aegis, favor, funds, grant, means **6** assist, behind, lining **7** subsidy, support **8** advocacy, auspices, blessing, sanction **9** insurance, patronage, resources **10** assistance, investment
mirror ~: **4** foil, tain
picture ~: **3** mat
screw ~: **6** cap nut
stamp ~: **3** gum **4** glue
stop ~: **6** defund
stucco ~: **4** lath
Back in Love Again (1977 song)
artist: L.T.D.
Back in My Arms Again (1965 song)
artist: Supremes
Back in the High Life Again (1987 song)
artist: Steve Winwood

Back in the Saddle: 5 oater
Back In The Saddle Again (1939 song)
artist: Gene Autry
__ Back in Town: 5 Lulu's
backlash: 4 kick 8 reaction
backless
seat: 5 stool
slipper: 4 mule
sofa: 5 divan
__ Back, Little Sheba: 4 Come
backlog: 5 stock, store 6 excess, supply 8 reserves 9 inventory, reservoir, stockpile
back-number: 6 bygone, former 7 onetime, vintage 8 obsolete, outdated 9 out-of-date
Back Off Boogaloo (1972 song)
artist: Ringo Starr
__ back on: 3 cut 4 fall
backpack: 3 bag 4 hike 6 kitbag 7 holdall, tote bag 8 knapsack, rucksack
contents: 4 gear
backpacker: 5 hiker, toter
accessory: 4 tent
snack: 4 gorp
stuff: 4 gear
backpacking: 5 sport
back-pedal: 5 unsay 6 cop out, recant, renege 7 disavow, rescind, retract, retreat, reverse 8 flip-flop, withdraw
back-pedaler's words: 5 I mean
__-back position: 4 fall
__ back ribs: 4 baby
backroom denizen: 3 pol
backrub, need a: 4 ache
backscratcher: 9 sycophant
target: 4 itch
backseat driver: 3 nag 6 critic 7 adviser, advisor 8 busybody
backslapper: 5 toady 6 yes man 8 adulator 9 sycophant
backslide: 3 sin 4 fail, fall, sink, slip, turn 5 lapse 6 revert 7 decline, regress, relapse 8 go astray 10 apostatize, degenerate
backsliding: 5 lapse 7 decline 8 apostasy, reaction
backspace: 5 erase
backspace __: 3 key
backspin a tennis ball: 5 slice
backstabber: 5 Judas, viper 7 traitor
Back Stabbers (1972 song)
artist: O'Jays
backstage section: 4 wing
backstop: 4 cage
Back Street
author: Fannie Hurst
backstroke: 4 swim
back talk: 3 jaw, lip 4 echo, guff, sass 5 cheek 7 comment
prone to ~: 5 fresh
back the wrong __: 5 horse
back-to-__: 6 basics
back-to-back: 10 successive
Back to Methuselah
author: George Bernard Shaw
character: 3 Eve, Lua, Zoo 4 Acis, Adam, Cain 5 Chloe, Enoch, Zozim 7 Ecrasia
back-to-school
month: 3 Sep. 4 Sept. 9 September
Back to School (1986 film)
cast: Rodney Dangerfield, Sally Kellerman, Burt Young
name: 5 Melon
Back to the Beach (1987 film)
cast: Frankie Avalon, Annette Funicello, Lori Loughlin
Back to the Future (1985 film)
cast: Michael J. Fox, Christopher Lloyd, Lea Thompson
character: 4 Biff
director: Robert Zemeckis
dog: 8 Einstein 10 Copernicus
event: 5 dance
medium: 4 time
backtrack: 6 recant 7 retreat
backtracking: 9 turnabout
backup: 3 sub 4 copy 5 extra, plan B, spare 6 deputy, helper, logjam 7 stand-in 8 henchman 9 alternate, assistant, secondary, surrogate 10 subsidiary, substitute, understudy
make a ~: 4 save
performer, perhaps: 5 sysop
prez ~: 2 VP 4 veep 6 veepee
strategy: 5 plan B
Backus, Jim: 5 actor
TV: Gilligan's Island
voice: Mr. Magoo
backward: 3 aft, fro, shy 4 slow 5 abaft, about 6 astern, behind, simple 7 lumpish 8 inverted 9 inside out, reluctant 10 retrograde, upside-down
bend over ~: 6 strive 8 struggle
go ~: 7 reverse 8 flip-flop
lean ~: 4 arch, flex
prefix: 3 ana- 5 retro-
Backward Glance, A
author: Edith Wharton
backwash: 4 wake 6 result 9 aftermath
backwater: 3 bog 4 bush, hick, naif, pond, rude, slow, snye 5 bayou, marsh, naive, swamp, wilds, woods 6 simple 7 boorish, outback, uncouth 8 ignorant, salt pond 9 backwoods, boondocks, unlearned, unrefined 10 uncultured, unpolished
in Canada: 4 snye
Louisiana ~: 5 bayou
Back When We Were Grownups
author: Anne Tyler
backwoods: 4 bush 5 rural 6 forest, inland, Podunk, rustic, sticks 7 boonies, country 8 frontier, outlying 9 backwater, boondocks, isolation 10 hinterland, provincial, timberland
person: 5 yokel
turndown: 3 naw
backyard: 4 lawn
deck: 5 patio
device: 6 hot tub
planting: 5 shrub
seat: 5 swing
structure: 4 shed 6 feeder
swing part: 4 tire
Backyards
artist: John Sloan
Baclanova, Olga: 6 dancer 7 Russian
bacon: 3 pay 4 meat, wage 5 wages 6 salary 10 sustenance
bring home the ~: 4 earn
cook ~: 3 fry
cut of ~: 4 slab
ingredient: 4 pork
like ~: 6 crispy
on the hoof: 3 pig 5 swine
partner: 5 liver
portion: 5 slice, strip 6 rasher
save one's ~: 5 spare
__ bacon: 4 back 5 white
Bacon: 5 Henry, Kevin, Lloyd, Roger 7 Francis
product: 5 essay
Bacon, Francis: 7 British 11 philosopher
Bacon, Henry: 9 architect
Bacon, Kevin: 5 actor
film: Apollo 13 (1995)
Diner (1982)
A Few Good Men (1992)
Flatliners (1990)
Footloose (1984)
Friday the 13th (1980)
He Said, She Said (1991)
JFK (1991)
My Dog Skip (2000)
Mystic River (2003)
The River Wild (1994)
She's Having a Baby (1988)
Sleepers (1996)
Stir of Echoes (1999)
Wild Things (1998)
spouse: Kyra Sedgwick
bacteria: 4 bugs 5 cocci, germs, staph, strep 7 bacilli 8 microbes 9 pathogens
destroyer: 5 phage
fighter: 5 sulfa
remover: 5 lymph
spherical ~: 5 cocci, staph
bacteriologist: 4 Koch 7 Fleming
medium: 4 agar 8 agar-agar
wire: 4 oese
bacterium: 3 bug 4 germ 6 aerobe 7 microbe 8 bacillus, pathogen
Bactria: 6 nation 7 country
today: 4 Iran
Bactrian: 5 camel
feature: 4 hump
relative: 5 llama 6 alpaca, vicuña 7 guanaco 9 dromedary
bad: 3 ill, low, off, sad 4 base, evil, fake, icky, mean, poor, rank, sick, sour, vile 5 amiss, cruel, error, grave, harsh, junky, moldy, sorry, wrong 6 ailing, amoral, cheesy, faulty, grungy, rancid, severe, sinful, sordid, spoilt, unruly, unwell, vulgar 7 adverse, brutish, corrupt, decayed, demonic, harmful, hurtful, immoral, invalid, lawless, naughty, noisome, painful, ruinous, serious, spoiled, unsound, vicious 8 acting up, criminal, daemonic, damaging, demoniac, depraved, diabolic, disloyal, dreadful, indocile, inedible, infamous, inhumane, overripe, sinister, slipshod 9 corrupted, dangerous, deficient, demonical, erroneous, falsified, imperfect, inclement, incorrect, injurious, nefarious, troubling, unhealthy 10 delinquent, diabolical, disastrous, fallacious, ill-behaved, inadequate, inexpiable, iniquitous, malodorous, pernicious, treasonous, unpleasant, unreliable, villainous, virtueless
see also awful, gloomy
as ~ as it gets: 5 worst
as weather: 5 nasty
be ~: 5 act up 9 misbehave
blood: *see* animosity
boy: 3 imp 4 brat 10 holy terror
break: 8 hard luck 10 ill fortune, rotten luck
bringer of ~ luck: 4 jinx
bring ~ luck: 4 jinx 5 curse
combining form: 3 cac-, dys-, mal- 4 caco-
deed: 3 sin 5 crime, wrong
don't be ~: 6 behave
dream: 9 nightmare
end: 7 undoing 8 calamity, disaster, downfall 9 cataclysm, ruination 10 extinction
ender: 5 lands, mouth
experience: 6 bummer 9 nightmare
faith: 5 fraud 6 deceit, dupery 8 betrayal, quackery 9 deception, duplicity, treachery 10 dishonesty, disloyalty
feel ~: 3 ail 4 ache
form: 8 improper, unseemly 9 graceless 10 indecorous, indelicacy, indelicate, out of order, unsuitable
get the ~ guy: 3 nab
give a ~ name: 7 asperse, slander 8 backbite
give a ~ time to: 3 vex 6 harass
go ~: 3 rot 4 sour, turn 5 decay, spoil
gone ~: 3 off 4 rank 6 rancid, rotten, turned 7 curdled 8 vinegary
guy: 3 cad, dog, rat 4 heel, toad 5 brute, churl, creep, crook, enemy, fraud, heavy, knave, louse, nasty, phony, rogue, snake 6 con man, outlaw, rascal, rotter, wretch 7 bounder, brigand, caitiff, dastard, lowlife, monster, ruffian, sharpie, shyster, stinker, villain, wastrel 8 blighter, chiseler, criminal, evildoer, hooligan, offender, spalpeen, swindler 9 archfiend, con artist, desperado, libertine, reprobate, scoundrel 10 blackguard, black sheep, malefactor, mountebank, profligate, scapegrace
habit: 4 vice 6 foible
hat: 3 cad 5 knave, scamp, skunk 6 rascal 8 picaroon, recreant, scalawag 9 reprobate, scoundrel 10 blackguard, ne'er-do-well, scapegrace
have a ~ time: 6 suffer
having a ~ odor: 4 foul, rank 5 fetid, musty, reeky 6 putrid, rancid, rotten, stinky, strong 7 noisome, reeking 8 mephitic, stinking 10 malodorous
health: 7 illness
in ~: 9 on the outs 10 out of favor
in a ~ mood: 4 mean, sour, ugly 5 cross, gruff, huffy, nasty, short, surly, testy 6 crabby, grouty, grumpy, ireful, morose, ornery, touchy 7 bearish, bristly, peevish, prickly, waspish 8 choleric, grumpish, petulant 9 crotchety, truculent
in a ~ way: 3 ill 4 illy, sick
in ~ shape: 5 ratty 6 shoddy

7 pitiful, run-down **8** untended
in ~ taste: 4 lewd **8** unseemly
judge as ~: 3 pan, rap **4** bash, damn, flay, slam **5** blame, blast, decry, knock, roast, trash **6** assail, berate, impugn, oppugn, rail at **7** censure, condemn, run down **8** belittle, denounce, talk down **9** cut to bits, disparage, excoriate, find fault, frown upon, skin alive **10** come down on, disapprove
like ~ news: *see* gloomy **7** ghastly, serious **10** lamentable
lot: 7 rotters **8** stinkers, villains **10** no-goodniks, scoundrels **11** ne'er-do-wells
luck: 4 blow, jinx, loss, pity **6** downer, hoodoo **7** reverse, setback, tragedy, undoing **8** distress **9** adversity, mischance **10** hard knocks, infelicity, misfortune
luck, old-style: 5 unhap
mark: 2 ef **5** stain
mood: 4 funk, huff, sulk, tiff **6** temper **8** ill humor **9** surliness **10** grumpiness
move: 5 error, folly **7** misstep **9** indecorum
news: 5 rogue, worry **6** downer, misery, sorrow **7** problem, trouble **9** liability, reckoning, scoundrel **10** misfortune, unpleasant
not ~: 2 OK **4** fair, okay, okeh, okey, so-so **9** tolerable, unnotable **10** fairly good
not so ~: 6 better
not too ~: 8 passable **9** excusable
off: 4 poor **5** broke, needy **6** hard up, in need, in want **7** pinched **8** bankrupt, beggarly, indigent, strapped **9** destitute, insolvent, moneyless, penniless, penurious **10** down and out, pauperized, straitened
period: 5 slump
prefix: 3 dys-, mal-, mis-
react to a ~ joke: 4 moan **6** flinch **7** grimace **9** make a face
regardless: 5 no-win
review: 3 pan
scene: 4 mess **6** downer **10** unpleasant
service result: 5 no tip
sign: 4 omen
smell: 4 reek **5** stink
taste: 9 indecorum **10** indelicacy
temper: 4 bile, snit **8** asperity
thing: 4 bane **6** bummer
times: 5 slump **9** recession **10** depression
treatment: 5 abuse
very ~: 5 awful, lousy **8** wretched **10** outrageous, unbearable
vibes: 5 doubt, qualm, smell **6** augury, signal, threat **7** warning **8** distrust, mistrust, wariness **9** chariness, harbinger, misgiving **10** foreboding, indication, prediction
write a ~ check: 6 bounce
bad __: 3 egg, hop, man, off, rap, rep **4** news **5** actor, apple, blood, faith, paper, vibes **6** breath
bad __ day: 4 hair
bad-__: 5 mouth
__ bad: 3 not **5** not so
__ bad!: 3 Too
Bad (1987 song)
artist: Michael Jackson
Bad __: 3 Axe, Boy, Ems **4** Boys, Girl, Love, Luck, Time, to Me
Bad __, The: 4 Seed **5** Place
Bad!: 3 tsk **6** tsk tsk
Bad and the Beautiful, The (1952 film)
cast: Kirk Douglas, Dick Powell, Lana Turner
director: Vincente Minnelli
__ Bad Apple: 3 One
Bad, Bad Leroy Brown (1973 song)
artist: Jim Croce
Bad Behaviour
cast: Stephen Rea
Bad Blood (1975 song)
artist: Neil Sedaka
__ bad boy!: 3 I'm a
Bad Boy (1986 song)
artist: Gloria Estefan
__ Bad Boy: 5 Peck's
Bad Boys (1983 film)
cast: Esai Morales, Sean Penn, Reni Santoni
Bad Case of Loving You (1979 song)
artist: Robert Palmer
bad-check
letters: 3 NSF
writer: 5 kiter
Bad Day at Black Rock (1955 film)
cast: Walter Brennan, Anne Francis, Dean Jagger, Robert Ryan, Spencer Tracy
Baddeley: 6 Angela **8** Hermione
baddie: 7 villain **8** evil sort **9** no-goodnik
fairy-tale ~: 4 ogre **5** giant
bade: 7 offered, ordered **8** beckoned, directed **9** commanded
Bad Ems: 3 spa **4** city, town
locale: 7 Germany
Baden: 3 spa **4** city, town
locale: 7 Germany
Badenov: 5 Boris
Baden-Powell: 6 Robert
Bader: 8 Diedrich
__ Bader Ginsburg: 4 Ruth
__ bad example: 4 set a
badge: 2 ID **3** pin, tag **4** mark, pass, sign **5** award, brand, ID tag, medal, token **6** cordon, device, emblem, ensign, riband, shield, symbol, ticket **7** insigne, laurels, officer **8** hallmark, heraldry, insignia **9** medallion **10** decoration
employee ~: 6 ID card
material: 3 tin
merit ~ org.: 3 BSA
of authority: 6 ensign
wearer: 6 deputy **7** marshal, sheriff
__ badge: 4 film **5** merit **6** rating
Badge 714 holder: 6 Friday
__ Badge of Courage, The: 3 Red
badger: 3 bug, nag, ply, rag, vex **4** bait, goad, haze, ride, roil **5** annoy, beset, bully, harry, hound, nudge, tease **6** animal, bother, harass, hassle, heckle, hector, needle, noodge, pester, pick at, pick on, plague, pursue, put out, weasel **7** bedevil, disturb, henpeck, torment **8** browbeat, insist on **9** importune, persecute
female: 3 sow
group: 4 cete
male: 4 boar
name meaning ~: 5 Brock
relative: *see* weasel
young: 3 cub, kit
Badger State: 3 Wis. **4** Wisc. **9** Wisconsin
Bad Girls (1979 song)
artist: Donna Summer
bad hair __: 3 day
Badham, John: 8 director
Bad Henry: 5 Aaron
badinage: 3 rag, wit **4** jest, quip, talk **5** humor, roast **6** banter, joking **7** jesting, joshing, kidding, ribbing, teasing **8** quiddity, raillery, repartee, wordplay **10** jocoseness, persiflage
__ Bad John: 3 Big
badlands: 5 waste, wilds **10** wilderness
Badlands: 4 park
locale: 11 South Dakota
sight: 5 bison
__ bad light: 3 in a
Bad Love
author: Jonathan Kellerman
bad-luck bringer: 4 jinx **5** Jonah
badly: 3 ill **4** awry **5** amiss, wrong **6** poorly, ragged **8** severely, terribly, very much **9** seriously **10** malapropos
in French: 3 mal
prefix: 3 mal-
bad-mannered: 4 rude **5** rough **7** boorish, loutish **8** impolite, inurbane **10** ungracious
Bad Medicine (1988 song)
artist: Bon Jovi
badminton: 4 game **5** sport
call: 3 let
former name for ~: 5 poona
need: 3 net
stroke: 3 lob
target: 6 birdie
Bad Moon Rising (1969 song)
artist: Creedence Clearwater Revival
start: 4 I see
badmouth: 3 dis, pan, rap, rip **4** slam **5** abuse, decry, knock, libel, rip on, roast, smear **6** defame, demean, dump on, malign, vilify **7** asperse, blacken, put down, run down, slander, traduce **8** backbite, belittle, tear down, throw mud **9** blaspheme, criticize, denigrate, deprecate, disparage, fustigate **10** calumniate, villainize
bad-natured: 9 malicious **10** evil-minded
badness: 3 ill **4** evil
Bad News Bears, The (1976 film)
cast: Walter Matthau, Vic Morrow, Tatum O'Neal
Bad Place, The
author: Dean Koontz
Bad Seed, The
author: Maxwell Anderson
bad-smelling: 4 foul **6** rotten
bad-tasting: 4 sour **8** unsavory
bad-tempered: 4 mean, ugly **5** gruff, nasty, short, surly, testy **6** crabby, grouty, grumpy, ireful, ornery, touchy **7** bearish, bristly, peevish, prickly, waspish **8** choleric, grumpish, petulant **9** crotchety, truculent
Bad Time (1975 song)
artist: Grand Funk
Badu, Erykah: 6 singer
Baedeker: 4 Karl **8** handbook
alternative: 5 Fodor
Baekeland: 3 Leo
Baer: 3 Max **4** Bugs **5** Buddy **6** Parley
Baer, Max: 5 boxer
milieu: 4 ring
Baeza, Braulio: 6 jockey
milieu: 5 track
Baez, Joan: 6 singer **9** protester
Baffin: 3 bay **4** isle **6** island **7** William
Baffin Bay sight: 4 berg
Baffin Island
locale: 6 Canada
baffle: 4 daze, foil, lose, stun **5** addle, amaze, elude, floor, stick, stimy, stump, stymy, throw **6** hamper, muddle, outwit, puzzle, rattle, retard, stymie, thwart **7** astound, buffalo, confuse, mystify, nonplus, perplex, prevent **8** befuddle, bewilder, confound, outsmart **9** discomfit, dumbfound **10** disconcert
ender: 3 gab
baffled: 4 asea **5** at sea, stuck **7** at a loss, puzzled **9** flummoxed
bafflement: 10 difficulty
baffler: 6 enigma
baffling: 4 dark **5** tough **6** knotty, thorny **7** elusive, elusory **8** puzzling **9** difficult, insoluble **10** mysterious
question: 5 poser
bag: 3 get, job, nab, net, sag, win **4** base, case, gain, haul, hook, land, nail, poke, sack, take, tote, trap **5** catch, hobby, pouch, purse, score, seize, shoot, snare, thing **6** arrest, collar, duffel, duffle, entrap, pocket, secure, valise **7** acquire, attaché, bladder, capture, carry-on, ensnare, holdall, insnare, luggage, satchel **8** backpack, carryall, knapsack, reticule, rucksack, suitcase **9** apprehend, briefcase, container, extradite, gunnysack, haversack, intumesce, portfolio, specialty **10** pocketbook
baseball ~: 4 base **5** rosin
brand: 4 Glad
carrier: 5 caddy, toter **6** caddie
ender: 3 man, men, wig **4** pipe, worm **5** piper
half in the ~: 5 tipsy
in the ~: 4 sure **5** on ice **6** secure **7** assured, certain, decided, settled **8** definite, positive, resolved **10** conclusive, determined, guaranteed, inevitable
it: 4 quit **5** leave **8** abdicate
job: 7 break-in
let the cat out of the ~: 3 air **4** bare, blab, leak, tell **5** admit, blurt, spill **6** betray, expose, gossip, reveal, squeal, tattle **7** divulge, let slip **8** disclose, give away **9** make known
material: 6 burlap
mixed ~: 3 mix **4** olio, stew **6** medley **7** mélange, mixture, variety **9** diversity, potpourri **10** assortment, hodgepodge, miscellany, salmagundi
of bones: 3 nag

old-fashioned ~: 4 grip
one left holding the ~: 4 dupe, goat 5 chump, patsy 6 sucker, victim 7 cat's-paw, fall guy 9 scapegoat
shoulder ~: 5 purse 9 haversack
small ~: 4 poke
starter: 3 gas, rag 4 bean, feed, flea, hand, mail, nose, sand, wind 5 money 6 carpet, litter, saddle, school
traveling ~: 3 kit 4 grip
bag __: 3 job 5 table
__ bag: 3 air, ice, kit, sea, tea 4 belt, book, bota, burn, club, feed, golf, grab, nose, poly, roll, tote, wine 5 brown, dilly, ditty, doggy, green, in the, mixed, mummy, paper, rosin 6 Boston, bowser, clutch, crocus, croker, doggie, duffel, duffle, flight, Lister, pounce, sponge, string, vanity, Ziploc 7 bowling, Douglas, evening, garment, musette, weekend
__-bag: 5 brown, gunny 6 tucker
bagatelle: 3 toy 4 game, gaud 5 dodad 6 bauble, doodad, geegaw, gewgaw, trifle 7 fribble, trinket 8 gimcrack, kickshaw, nick-nack 9 brummagem 10 knickknack
__ bagatelle!: 5 A mere
Bagdad: 4 city, town
locale: 4 Irak, Iraq
Bagdad Cafe (1988 film)
cast: Jack Palance, CCH Pounder, Marianne Sägebrecht
director: Percy Adlon
Bagdasarian: 4 Ross
bagel: 4 roll 5 bread 8 hard roll
alternative: 5 bialy
companion: 3 lox
feature: 4 hole
ingredient: 6 gluten
look-alike: 5 donut
shape: 5 torus
shop: 4 deli
topping: 4 salt 5 onion, poppy 6 sesame
bagful: 4 haul, heap
baggage: 4 case, gear 5 cargo, trunk 6 things 7 luggage 8 carry-ons, equipage 9 equipment, hindrance, liability, suitcases
excess ~: 4 load 6 weight 9 unwelcome
handler: 4 cart 5 toter 6 porter, redcap
baggage __: 3 car 7 handler
__ baggage: 6 excess 7 carry-on
bagged out: 10 disheveled
__-bagger: 3 one, two 4 four 5 brown, three
bagger starter: 4 sand 6 carpet
Baggie: 7 plastic
Baggins: 5 Bilbo, Frodo
baggy: 4 limp, wide 5 loose, slack 6 droopy, flabby, floppy 7 flaccid, hanging, sagging 8 dangling, drooping 9 amorphous, oversized, shapeless 10 ill-fitting
Baghdad: 4 city, town 7 capital
bigwig: 5 calif, kalif 6 caliph, kaliph, khalif
locale: 4 Irak, Iraq
river: 6 Tigris
baglike structure: 3 sac
bagnio: 9 bathhouse
Bagnold: 4 Enid
bag of __: 4 wind 5 bones 6 tricks
Bag of Bones author: Stephen King
bagpipe: 4 wind 6 biniou 7 musette
key: 5 B-flat
origin: 8 Scotland
play the ~: 5 skirl
sound: 5 drone
bagpiper garment: 4 kilt
Bagpipers, The
author: George Sand
bags'
three ~ contents, in rhyme: 4 wool
baguette: 3 gem 5 bread, jewel
like a ~: 6 crusty
surface: 5 facet
Bagwell, Jeff
sport: 8 baseball
Bah!: 3 fie 4 pfui, pooh 5 pshaw
in German: 3 ach
__-Bah: 4 Pooh
Baha'i
origin: 4 Iran
preceder: 4 Babi
__ Bahama: 5 Grand
Bahamas: 4 isls. 5 isles 6 nation 7 country, islands
group: 6 Indies
island: 3 Cat 4 Long 5 Abaco, Exuma 6 Andros, Bimini, Inagua 7 Acklins, Crooked 9 Eleuthera, Mayaguana
locale: 3 BWI 10 West Indies
money: 4 cent 6 dollar
org.: 3 OAS
Bahia: 5 grass
Bahrain: 4 isle 6 island, nation 7 country
capital: 6 Manama
group: 10 Arab League
money: 4 fils 5 dinar
native: 4 Arab
VIP: 4 amir, emir 5 ameer, emeer, sheik 6 shaikh, sheikh
Bai: 4 Ling
Baikal: 4 lake
locale: 6 Russia 7 Siberia
bail: 4 bond, flee 5 chuck, scoop 6 dipper, pledge, surety 7 draw off, warrant 8 drain off, fugitate, security, warranty 10 break loose, collateral
jump ~: 3 fly 6 run out 7 skip out 10 fly the coop
out: 3 aid 4 bolt, free, help, jump, quit, save 5 eject, leave, spare 6 assist, desert, escape, get out, give up, rescue, resign 7 abandon, make off, release, relieve 8 abdicate, liberate, run for it, withdraw 9 extricate, give a hand, parachute
bail __: 3 out 4 bond
__ bail: 4 jump, skip
Bailamos (1999 song)
artist: Enrique Iglesias
bailer: 4 pail 5 scoop 6 dipper, trough
bailey: 4 wall
Bailey: 3 Lee 4 F. Lee, Jack 5 Pearl 6 Philip 7 Mildred, Raymond
partner: 6 Barnum
__ Bailey: 3 Old 6 Beetle
Bailey, Beetle: 2 GI 4 toon 7 private, soldier
barracks-mate: 4 Zero
superior: 5 sarge
Bailey, F. Lee: 6 lawyer 8 attorney
org.: 3 ABA
Bailey, Pearl: 6 singer
middle name: 3 Mae
spouse: Louis Bellson
bailiff: 5 jurat 6 deputy 7 marshal, sheriff 9 constable 10 magistrate
Anglo-Saxon ~: 5 reeve
cry: 4 oyes, oyez 6 hear ye
obey the ~: 4 rise
bailing, in need of: 5 leaky
bailiwick: 3 job 4 area, turf 5 field, place 6 domain, locale, region, sphere 7 purview 8 dominion, locality, province 10 department
bailout: 3 aid 6 escape, rescue
PC ~: 3 ESC
Bain: 6 Conrad 7 Barbara
Bain, Barbara: 7 actress
spouse: Martin Landau
Bainbridge: 5 Beryl 6 Merril
Bain de __: 6 Soleil
Baines, Harold
sport: 8 baseball
__ Baines Johnson: 4 Luci
Bainter, Fay: 7 actress
Baio: 5 Jimmy, Scott
Baird: 3 Bil 4 Cora
bairn: 3 lad 4 babe, baby 5 child, kiddy 6 infant, lassie
like a ~: 3 sma, wee
bait: 3 irk, nag, rag 4 chum, draw, gall, lure, mock, ride, roil, trap, twit, worm 5 anger, annoy, beset, decoy, get on, hound, shill, snare, tease, tempt, worms, worry 6 allure, badger, bother, chivvy, come-on, entice, harass, heckle, incite, lead on, minnow, needle, pick on 7 attract, bedevil, beguile, enflame, minnows, mislead, provoke, torment 8 inveigle, irritate, ridicule 9 beleaguer, fascinate, incentive, make fun of, persecute, tantalize 10 allurement, attraction, enticement, inducement, temptation
and switch: 8 trickery
dangle ~: 3 dap
fish ~: 4 chub, dace, lure, worm 6 minnow
mousetrap ~: 6 cheese
take the ~: 4 bite 5 react
bait and __: 6 switch
Bait, The
author: John Donne
Baiul, Oksana: 6 skater
baiza: 5 money
locale: 4 Oman
baize: 6 fabric
Baja: 6 desert
creature: 6 iguana
locale: 6 Mexico
neighbor: 3 USA
Baja California
city: 6 La Joya, Tecate 7 Tijuana 8 Ensenada, Mexicali, Rosarito
bake: 4 burn, cook, heat, warm 5 roast, shirr 6 scorch 7 swelter 8 barbecue, escallop
ender: 4 shop, ware
pottery: 4 fire
sale: 7 benefit 10 fund-raiser
starter: 4 clam
bake __: 4 sale 5 apple
Bake-__: 3 Off
baked: 3 dry 4 arid
dessert: 5 crisp
goody: 5 knish
ham insert: 5 clove
starter: 3 sun
baked __: 3 ham 4 meat, ziti 5 apple, beans, goods 6 Alaska, potato
__-baked: 4 half 5 slack
...baked __ pie: 3 in a
baked Alaska: 7 dessert
alternative: 5 bombe 6 frappe 9 milk shake 10 peach Melba
ingredient: 8 ice cream
__ baked beans: 6 Boston
baked-potato garnish: 5 chive
baker: 4 chef, cook
creation: 3 bun, pie 4 cake, loaf, roll 5 bread, cooky, donut, scone 6 cookie, éclair, muffin, pastry 8 doughnut
device: 4 oven
ingredient: 3 egg 5 flour, spice, sugar, yeast
like a ~ hands: 6 floury
measure: 5 dozen
name meaning ~: 4 Beck 6 Baxter, Becker
product: 4 cake, roll 5 bread
tool: 4 peel 5 sieve
Baker: 4 Chet, diva, Ward 5 Anita, Diane, Dusty, Dylan, Frank, James, Kathy, Kenny 6 George, LaVern, Samuel 7 Carroll, Russell, Stanley 9 Josephine
word before ~: 4 Able
__ Baker: 6 Joe Don 7 Home Run
Baker, Anita
song: Giving You the Best That I Got (1988)
Sweet Love (1986)
__, Baker, Charlie: 4 Able
__ Baker Eddy: 4 Mary
Baker-Finch, Ian: 6 golfer
Baker, Janet: 4 Dame
Baker, Kathy: 7 actress
TV: Boston Public, Picket Fences
Baker, LaVern
song: I Cried a Tear (1958)
Tweedlee Dee (1955)
Baker, Russell specialty: 5 essay
baker's __: 5 dozen, yeast
Baker, Samuel: 3 Sir 8 explorer
Bakersfield: 4 city, town
city near ~: 6 Delano
locale: 10 California
Baker Street (1978 song)
artist: Gerry Rafferty
baker's yeast: 6 fungus
bakery: 4 shop 5 store 9 sweet shop 10 patisserie
call: 4 next
fixture: 4 oven
item: 3 bun, pie, rye 4 loaf, roll, tart 5 bread, cooky, donut, scone 6 cookie, éclair, pastry
lure: 4 odor 5 aroma
machine: 6 glazer
worker: 4 icer
bake sale sponsor: 3 PTA
baking: 3 hot 6 sultry 8 in the sun 10 sweltering
ingredient: 3 egg 5 flour, spice, sugar, yeast
pan: 3 tin 5 sheet
baking __: 4 soda 5 sheet 6 powder
baking-dish name: 5 Pyrex
baking powder: 6 leaven
ingredient: 4 alum

Bakker
org.: 3 PTL
Bakker, Jim: 10 evangelist
Bakker, Tammy Faye: 10 evangelist
baklava: 6 pastry
__-Bakr: 3 Abu
baksheesh: 4 alms
Bakshi: 5 Ralph
Bakst: 4 Leon
Baku: 4 city, port, town 7 capital
locale: 10 Azerbaijan
Bakula: 5 Scott
Bakunin: 7 Mikhail
bal __: 6 masqué
Bal __: 7 Harbour
Balaam: 7 diviner
beast: 3 ass
father: 4 Beor
Balaban, Bob: 5 actor
balaclava: 3 cap, hat
Balaklava: 6 battle
locale: 6 Crimea 7 Ukraine
balalaika: 4 lute 6 string
origin: 6 Russia
play the ~: 5 strum
balance: 3 par, tie 4 even, mean, rest, wits 5 level, perch, poise, reset, scale, weigh 6 adjust, aplomb, attune, equate, even up, offset, parity, redeem, refund, sanity, square, stasis, steady, teeter, wisdom 7 compare, isonomy, nullify, recover, redress, remnant, residue, surplus 8 consider, equality, equalize, evaluate, evenness, modulate, outweigh, regulate, residual, symmetry 9 composure, equipoise, liability, make up for, reimburse, remainder, stability, stabilize 10 compensate, counteract, equanimity, moderation, neutralize, proportion, recompense, sedateness
beam: 5 event
center: 3 ear
combining form: 5 stato-
due: 7 arrears
heavenly ~: 5 Libra
in the ~: 6 at risk 7 pending
lose ~: 4 fall, reel, slip, trip 5 lurch, slide 6 sprawl, teeter, topple, totter, tumble, wobble 7 stagger, stumble
out: 6 cancel 7 average
starter: 7 counter
throw off ~: 5 upset 7 fluster, stagger
balance __: 3 lug 4 beam 5 shaft, sheet, staff, wheel 6 spring 7 control
__ balance: 4 bank, head, hull 5 Jolly, trade, trial 6 occult 7 current, torsion
Balance: 4 sign 5 Libra
month: 3 Oct., Sep. 4 Sept. 7 October 9 September
predecessor: 6 Virgin
successor: 8 Scorpion
balanced: 4 even, fair, just, sane 5 equal, level 6 square, stable 7 regular, uniform 8 moderate, rational, unbiased 9 equitable, impartial, objective, uncolored 10 evenhanded, harmonious
precariously ~: 5 tippy
balanced __: 4 diet, fund, line, step 5 valve 6 rudder, ticket
__-balanced diet: 4 well
balance of __: 5 power, trade 6 nature, terror
balance sheet
check: 5 audit
guru: 3 CPA
item: 4 debt 5 asset
word: 4 loss
Balanchine, George: 6 dancer 7 danseur
specialty: 6 ballet
balancing: 7 redress 9 measuring 10 adjustment, comparison
balas: 3 gem 4 ruby 8 gemstone
balata: 4 tree
family: 9 sapodilla
relative: 4 shea 7 almique 8 alamiqui
Balaton: 4 lake
locale: 7 Hungary
Balbo: 5 Italo, pilot 7 aviator
balboa: 5 money
Balboa, Vasco Núñez de: 7 Spanish 8 explorer
Balch, Emily: 8 Nobelist, pacifist
balcony: 5 porch 6 loggia, piazza 7 gallery, portico, terrace, veranda 8 platform, verandah 10 balustrade
area: 4 loge
church ~: 4 loft
Balcony, The: 4 play 8 painting
author: Jean Genet
painter: Édouard Manet
bald: 5 naked, stark 6 barren 8 glabrate, glabrous, hairless 9 treadless, unadorned, uncovered
baby: 6 eaglet
ender: 4 head, pate
head: 4 dome
name meaning ~: 6 Calvin
starter: 3 pie 4 skew
bald __: 5 eagle 7 cypress
bald-__ lie: 5 faced
baldachin: 6 canopy
bald cypress: 4 tree 7 redwood, sequoia
bald eagle: 4 bird 6 raptor
look-alike: 3 ern 4 erne
Balder: 3 god 5 Norse
brother: 4 Thor
parent: 4 Odin 5 Othin 6 Frigga
balderdash
see baloney
Balderdash!: 5 pshaw
bald-faced: 4 bare, bold, dare, flip, loud, pert, rude 5 brash, cocky, fresh, gutsy, nervy, sassy, saucy, smart 6 arrant, awless, brassy, brazen, cheeky, daring, flashy, snippy, tawdry 7 assured, aweless, blatant, defiant, forward, glaring, lowbred, uncivil 8 flagrant, flippant, immodest, impolite, impudent, insolent, overbold, snippety 9 audacious, barefaced, out of line, shameless, unabashed, unashamed 10 outrageous, unblushing, ungracious
bald-faced __: 3 lie
baldness: 6 acomia 8 alopecia
Baldr
see Balder
Baldridge: 7 Letitia, Malcolm
Bald Soprano, The
author: Eugène Ionesco
Baldwin: 4 Adam, Alec, city, town 5 apple, Billy, Faith, James, piano 6 Daniel 7 Stanley, Stephen, William
locale: 7 New York
relative: ***see*** apple
Baldwin, Alec: 5 actor
film: Alice (1990)
The Aviator (2004)
Beetlejuice (1988)
Ghosts of Mississippi (1996)
Glengarry Glen Ross (1992)
The Hunt for Red October (1990)
The Juror (1996)
Malice (1993)
Married to the Mob (1988)
The Marrying Man (1991)
Mercury Rising (1998)
Outside Providence (1999)
Prelude to a Kiss (1992)
The Shadow (1994)
She's Having a Baby (1988)
State and Main (2000)
Talk Radio (1988)
Working Girl (1988)
spouse: Kim Basinger
TV: 30 Rock
Baldwin, James: 6 writer
work: The Amen Corner
Another Country
Blues for Mister Charlie
The Fire Next Time
Giovanni's Room
Go Tell It on the Mountain
If Beale Street Could Talk
Just Above My Head
Nobody Knows My Name
Notes of a Native Son
Tell Me How Long the Train's Been Gone
Baldwin, Stanley successor: 11 Chamberlain
Baldwin, William: 5 actor
spouse: Chynna Phillips
bale: 4 bind, pack 5 bunch 6 bundle, parcel 7 package
binder: 5 twine
contents: 3 hay
Bale: 9 Christian
Balearic Islands
city: 5 Mahon, Palma
island: 5 Ibiza, Iviza 7 Majorca, Minorca
Baled Hay
author: Bill Nye
baleen: 9 whalebone
baleen __: 5 whale
baleful: 5 fatal, toxic 6 lethal, malign, nocent 7 adverse, harmful, ominous, ruinous 8 damaging, God-awful, menacing, negative, sinister, venomous 9 dangerous, ill-omened, injurious, malicious, poisonous 10 calamitous, malevolent, pernicious
see also awful
baler: 7 machine 8 farmhand
material: 3 hay
Balfour, Arthur: 2 P.M. 7 British
Bali: 4 isle 6 island
island near ~: 6 Lombok
Bali Ha'i: 4 isle
composer: Oscar Hammerstein, Richard Rodgers
Balin: 3 Ina 5 Marty
Balinese: 3 cat 5 Asian, felid 6 feline 8 language
dance: 7 djanger
Balint: 6 Eszter
balk: 4 flub 5 check, demur, stimy, stymy 6 flinch, recoil, refuse, resist, retard, stymie, thwart, timber 7 decline, dissent, letdown, nonplus, perplex, prevent, scruple 8 hesitate 9 frustrate, stop short 10 put up a fuss
as a horse: 5 reest
caller: 3 ump 6 umpire
ender: 4 line
Balkan: 5 range 9 peninsula
capital: 5 Sofia 6 Athens, Skopje, Sofiya, Tirana, Zagreb 8 Belgrade, Sarajevo 9 Bucharest
locale: 6 Europe
nation: 6 Bosnia, Greece, Serbia 7 Albania, Croatia, Romania 8 Bulgaria, Roumania 9 Macedonia 10 Montenegro
native: 4 Slav 5 Greek 7 Bosnian, Serbian 8 Albanian, Croatian, Romanian 9 Bulgarian 10 Macedonian
river: 4 Drin 6 Danube
skirt: 10 fustanella
Balkan __: 3 War 5 frame 6 States
Balk, Fairuza: 7 actress
balky: 5 rigid 6 averse, gun-shy, mulish, ornery, unruly 7 piggish, restive 8 contrary, hesitant, negative, obdurate, perverse, stubborn 9 obstinate, pigheaded, reluctant, resistive, unbending 10 hard-bitten, inflexible, refractory
beast: 3 ass 4 mule 5 burro
ball: 2 do 3 orb, wad 4 fest, fete, gala, lump, prom, shot 5 blast, dance, globe, party, spree 6 formal, sphere 7 globule, pigskin, shindig 9 festivity, great time, horsehide, reception 10 recreation
AAA ~: 6 minors
advance on a fly ~: 5 tag up
and chain: 6 burden
attendee: 3 deb 5 belle
attire: 4 gown
balancer: 4 seal
behind the eight ~: 6 in a fix, in a jam 7 trapped
black billiard ~: 5 eight
caller: 3 ump 6 umpire
carrier: 4 back
celestial ice ~: 5 comet
club: 4 team
club VIP: 2 GM 3 mgr. 5 owner 7 manager
combining form: 5 spher- 6 sphaer-, sphero- 7 sphaero-
cricket ~: 6 googly
drop the ~: 3 err 4 miss, slip 6 bumble, bungle, falter, fumble 7 blunder 8 misjudge
ender: 4 game, park, room 6 flower 7 carrier
fast ~: 4 heat 5 smoke
follower: 3 oon
game: 5 bocce, bocci, lotto, rugby 6 squash 7 jai alai 9 situation
get the ~ rolling: 4 open 5 begin, cause, start 6 launch, tackle 8 commence, initiate 10 lead the way
give up the ~: 4 punt
have a ~: 4 play 5 caper, enjoy, party, revel 6 cavort, frolic,

gambol, prance **7** carouse, roister, rollick **9** celebrate, make merry
high ~: 3 lob **5** pop up
hit the ~ hard: 5 drive
indoor ~: 4 Nerf
jai alai ~: 6 pelota
kind of ~ game: 5 no-hit, no-run **7** perfect, shutout
make into a ~: 5 wad up
mirrored ~ locale: 5 disco
musket ~: 4 slug
of cotton: 3 wad
of fire: 3 sun **6** dynamo **7** hustler **8** tireless **9** ambitious, energetic
of yarn: 4 clew **5** skein
on the ~: 5 adept, alert, awake, aware, quick, ready, sharp, smart **6** astute, prompt, up to it **7** capable, mindful **8** vigilant, watchful **9** astucious, attentive, competent, effective, observant, wide-awake **10** acceptable
play ~: 5 agree **6** comply **9** acquiesce, cooperate
rubber ~: 3 toy
run with the ~: 7 perform
simple ~ game: 5 catch
starter: 3 air, cue, eye, gum, low, odd, pin **4** base, bean, corn, fast, fire, foot, fork, goof, hair, hand, hard, heel, high, meat, moth, puff, push, snow, soft, sour, spit **5** black, broom, curve, screw, stick, stink, stoop **6** basket, butter, button, cannon, ground, paddle, sinker, tether, volley **7** knuckle, racquet
use a crystal ~: 4 gaze
well-hit ~: 5 drive, liner
whole ~ of wax: 3 all **5** total **8** entirety, sum total **9** aggregate **10** everything
ball __: 3 boy, cap, ice **4** clay, club, cock, fern, foot, game, girl, hawk, mill, park **5** joint, of wax, valve **7** bearing, carrier, control, turning **8** handling
ball-__ hammer: 4 peen
__ ball: 3 air, cue, fly, ink, tar, tea **4** bean, coal, curb, dust, fair, foul, golf, jump, mast, Nerf, nine, play **5** beach, carom, curve, dodge, have a, matzo, on the, stoop, witch **6** anchor, cannon, gopher, ground, masked, matzah, matzoh, object, passed, rabbit, rubber, tennis **7** bowling, camphor, crystal, knuckle **8** medicine
__ ball!: 4 Play
__-ball: 3 low **4** best
Ball: 4 Hugo **5** Kenny **6** Ernest **7** Lucille
__ Ball: 6 Rubber, Wiffle
__-Ball: 4 Skee
ballad: 3 lay **4** poem, song **5** carol, ditty, music, verse **8** love song, serenade
ender: 3 eer
German ~: 4 lied
subject: 4 love
ballade: 4 poem, song
ending: 5 envoi
balladist: 4 poet
balladmonger: 4 bard
Ballad of __ Hayes, The: 3 Ira
Ballad of Davy Crockett (1955 song)
artist: Bill Hayes, Fess Parker, Tennessee Ernie Ford
Ballad of East and West, The: 4 poem
author: Rudyard Kipling
Ballad of John and Yoko, The (1969 song)
artist: Beatles
Ballad of Reading Gaol, The
author: Oscar Wilde
Ballad of the Green Berets, The (1966 song)
artist: Barry Sadler
Ballad of the Sad Cafe, The
author: Carson McCullers
__ Ballads: 3 Bab **7** Lyrical
ball and __: 4 ring **5** chain
ball-and-__ foot: 4 claw
ball-and-__ joint: 6 socket
Ballantine: 3 ale, Ian **4** beer, Carl
alternative: *see* beer
Ballard: 4 Hank, Kaye **8** Florence
ballast: 6 weight **10** stabilizer
ballerina: 6 dancer, étoile **8** danseuse
asset: 3 toe
costume: 4 tutu
painter: Edgar Degas
prop: 3 bar **5** barre
step: 3 pas
__ ballerina: 5 prima
Ballerina Girl (1987 song)
artist: Lionel Richie
Ballesteros, Seve: 6 golfer
ballet: 3 art **5** dance **8** Swan Lake
barre: 4 rail
bend: 4 plie
darting ~ movement: 6 élancé
duet: 6 adagio
glide: 6 chassé
held, in ~: 5 tendu
move: 3 pas **4** jete, leap, lift **5** fondu
movement: 6 frappé
pivot: 3 toe
pose: 9 arabesque
position: 6 à terre, écarté, en haut
rail: 3 bar **5** barre
Russian ~: 5 Kirov
step: 5 coupe, pique, tombé
turn: 6 chaine
wear: 4 tutu **6** tights
with arms held low, in ~: 5 en bas
ballet __: 5 blanc, suite **6** master **7** slipper
__ ballet: 5 water
Ballet __: 5 Russe
__ Ballet: 5 At the **7** Bolshoi, Spandau
Ballet Class, The
painter: Edgar Degas
ballet dancer
American ~: 5 Tharp **6** Duncan **7** Bujones, Farrell **8** d'Amboise, Eglevsky, Mitchell, Villella **9** Tallchief **10** Balanchine
British ~: 5 Dolin **7** Fonteyn, Markova
Cuban ~: 6 Alonso
Danish ~: 5 Bruhn **7** Martins
French ~: 6 Béjart
German ~: 5 Jooss
Irish ~: 8 De Valois
Russian ~: 5 Lifar **7** Massine, Nureyev, Pavlova, Ulanova **8** Danilova, Nijinsky **11** Baryshnikov, Youskevitch
Scottish ~: 7 Shearer
Ballet Rehearsal
artist: Edgar Degas
ballfield protector: 4 tarp
__-ball foursome: 4 best
ballgame
anybody's ~: 10 up for grabs
arbiter: 3 ump **6** umpire
division: 6 inning
fare: 6 hot dog
opener: 6 anthem
stat: 2 AB, BA, BB, HR, SB **3** ERA
see also ballpark, baseball
Ball, Hugo movement: 4 Dada
ballistic
go ~: 4 rant, vent **5** freak **6** lose it
missile: 4 ICBM, MIRV, Thor
ballistic __: 4 wind **6** camera **7** missile
Ball, Lucille: 7 actress **10** comedienne
film: Easy to Wed (1946)
Room Service (1938)
Too Many Girls (1940)
Without Love (1945)
Yours, Mine and Ours (1968)
spouse: Desi Arnaz
TV: Here's Lucy, I Love Lucy, The Lucy Show
ball of __: 3 wax **4** fire
Ball of Confusion (1970 song)
artist: Temptations
ballon: 5 grace **9** lightness
balloon: 3 toy **4** blot, grow, rise **5** blimp, bloat, bulge, swell **6** billow, blow up, dilate, expand, puff up, pump up **7** airship, distend, enlarge, inflate, mount up **8** aircraft, zeppelin **9** billow out, dirigible
atmospheric ~: 5 sonde
filler: 3 air, gas **6** helium, hot air
go by ~: 6 aviate
lead ~: 3 dud **4** flop **6** fiasco **7** failure
material: 5 Mylar
sound: 3 pop
trial ~: 4 poll, test **6** feeler **7** enquiry, inquiry
trip: 6 ascent
balloon __: 4 sail, seat, tire, vine **5** chuck, clock, frame, shade **6** flower **7** barrage, payment
__ balloon: 4 fire, free, lead **5** pilot, trial **7** barrage, weather
Balloon Hoax, The
author: Edgar Allan Poe
ballooning: 5 sport
go ~: 4 rise, soar **7** lift off
balloonist: 8 aeronaut
balloonlike: 5 round
balloons, like some: 3 LTA
ballot: 4 poll, vote **6** voting **9** franchise **10** plebiscite, referendum
cast a ~: 3 x'ed **4** vote **6** choose
month: 3 Nov. **8** November
ballot __: 3 box
__ ballot: 5 short **6** secret **7** Indiana
balloting: 6 voting **8** election
__ Ballou: 3 Cat
ballpark: 8 vicinity
aide: 6 bat boy
antic: 4 wave
area: 5 seats **6** dugout, stands **7** bullpen, infield **8** outfield **9** bleachers **10** scoreboard
display: 6 banner
entertainment: 5 organ
fare: 5 frank, weeny **6** hot dog
figure: 8 estimate **9** appraisal **10** assessment
in the ~: 4 near **5** close **6** almost, around, nearby, nearly **13** approximately
level: 4 tier
official: 3 ump **5** usher **6** umpire
see also ballgame, baseball
Ball Park: 6 hot dog
alternative: 5 Kahn's **6** Armour **10** Oscar Mayer
ball-peen __: 6 hammer
ballplayer: 6 hitter **7** athlete, catcher, pitcher
ballpoint: 3 pen
ancestor: 5 quill
maker: 3 Bic **6** Parker **9** Paper-Mate
point: 3 nib
use a ~: 5 write
ballroom: 4 hall
dance: 5 conga, mambo, rumba, samba, tango, waltz **6** cha-cha, rhumba **7** beguine, fox trot, lambada, one-step, peabody, two-step **8** habanera **9** bossa nova, polonaise **10** Charleston
glide: 6 chassé
balls
base on ~: 4 walk
four ~: 4 walk
ball-shaped: 5 round **8** globular
__ Balls of Fire: 5 Great
Ball State: 6 school **10** university
athletes: 9 Cardinals
conference: 3 MAC
locale: 6 Muncie **7** Indiana
Ballston __, NY: 3 Spa
Balluet, Paul: 6 French **8** Nobelist
ballyhoo: 3 row **4** hype, tout **6** herald, hoopla, hype up, talk up **7** advance, clatter, fanfare, promote, puffery **9** advertise, commotion, promotion, publicity
balm: 4 aloe, calm, herb, lull, save **5** cream, salve **6** arnica, lotion, potion, relief, remedy, solace, soothe **7** anodyne, comfort, perfume, soother, unction, unguent **8** easement, lenitive, liniment, medicine, ointment, poultice **9** analgesic, demulcent, emollient, fragrance **10** medication, mitigation, palliative
of Gilead: 5 resin **6** balsam
__ balm: 3 bee **5** horse, lemon
balmacaan: 4 coat **6** jacket **8** overcoat
balminess: 8 calmness **9** fragrancy, redolence
balm of __: 6 Gilead
balmoral: 3 cap, hat, tam **4** shoe **8** footwear
Balmoral: 6 estate
Balmoral Castle
locale: 8 Scotland
purchaser: Prince Albert
river: 3 Dee
balmy: 4 fair, mild, warm **5** bland, dotty, inane, sweet **6** gentle, whacky **7** clement, scented, summery **8** aromatic, fragrant, perfumed, pleasant, soothing, tropical **9** ambrosial, eccentric, soporific, temperate, unextreme **10** refresh-

ing
see also foolish
balon: 5 grace 9 lightness
baloney: 3 gas, rot 4 blah, bosh, bull, bunk, guff, jazz, jive, pooh, tosh, wind 5 bilge, fudge, hokum, hooey, prate, story, stuff, trash, tripe 6 bunkum, bushwa, drivel, footle, gabble, gammon, gibber, havers, hot air, humbug, jabber, jargon, kibosh, piffle 7 blarney, blather, blether, bushwah, eyewash, flannel, flubdub, fustian, garbage, hogwash, inanity, malarky, rubbish, twaddle 8 buncombe, claptrap, falderal, falderol, fast talk, flimflam, flummery, folderal, folderol, malarkey, nonsense, slipslop, tommyrot, trumpery 9 absurdity, banana oil, gibberish, goofiness, kidstakes, moonshine, poppycock, rigmarole 10 applesauce, balderdash, bilge water, codswallop, double-talk, flapdoodle, galimatias, Jabberwock, mumbo jumbo, rigamarole, taradiddle
full of ~: 6 all wet
___-baloney: 5 phony
Baloney!: 3 hah 5 my eye, nerts, nertz, pshaw
balsa: 4 tree, wood 8 corkwood
balsam: 3 fir 4 tolu, tree 9 evergreen
ender: 4 root
balsam ___: 3 fir 4 pear 5 apple, of fir 6 capivi, family, poplar
___ balsam: 4 Peru 5 black, Mecca 6 Canada, Indian
balsamic: 9 emollient
balsamic ___: 7 vinegar
Balsam, Martin: 5 actor
Balt: 7 Latvian 8 Estonian 10 Lithuanian
Balthazar: 5 Getty
and others: 4 Magi
author: Lawrence Durrell
colleague: 6 Caspar 8 Melchior
like ~: 4 wise
Baltic: 3 sea
capital: 4 Riga 5 Vilna 7 Tallinn, Vilnius
country: 6 Latvia 7 Estonia 9 Lithuania
feeder: 4 Oder, Odra 5 Memel, Neman, Peene 6 Niemen 7 Vistula
gulf: 4 Riga 6 Danzig 7 Bothnia, Finland
island: 4 Aero 5 Oland
locale: 6 Europe
port: 4 Kiel 6 Gdansk
Baltic ___: 3 Sea 6 States
Baltic Sea
archipelago: 5 Aland
feeder: 5 Dvina
Baltimore: 4 city, port, town 5 David
locale: 8 Maryland
newspaper: 3 Sun
pro team: 6 Ravens 7 Orioles
river: 8 Patapsco
Baltimore ___: 4 chop 6 Canyon, heater, oriole 7 clipper
___ Baltimore cake: 4 Lady, Lord
Baltimore, David: 8 Nobelist
___ Baltimore, The: 4 Hot l
Balto (1995 film)
director: Simon Wells
Balto-___: 6 Slavic
Baltoro Kangri: 2 mt. 3 mtn. 4 peak 5 mount 8 mountain
locale: 4 Asia 7 Kashmir 8 Cashmere 9 Himalayas
Baluchistan: 6 desert
baluster: 3 leg, rod 4 pole, post 5 spoke 7 spindle, upright 8 vertical
balustrade: 4 rail 6 wallop 7 balcony, railing
Balzac, Honoré de: 6 French, writer
work: The Black Sheep
The Country Doctor
Cousin Bette
Cousin Pons
The Human Comedy
Le Père Goriot
A Shady Business
Bam!: 3 pow
Bama group: 3 SEC
Bamako: 4 city, town 7 capital
locale: 4 Mali
Bambara home: 4 Mali 6 Africa
Bambara, Toni: 6 writer
Bambi: 4 deer 5 novel
aunt: 3 Ena
author: Felix Salten
Bambi (1942 film)
character: 3 Ena 4 Gobo 5 Bambi, Karus, Ronno 6 Faline, Flower, Marena, Nettla
director: David Hand
bambino: 4 baby 5 child, kiddy 6 infant 9 offspring
watcher: 5 mamma
Bambino, The: Babe Ruth
bamboo: 4 cane, reed 5 grass
eater: 5 panda
shoot: 6 veggie 9 vegetable
swordplay: 5 kendo
bamboo ___: 4 ware 5 shoot 6 shoots 7 turning
Bamboo
artist: Erté
Bamboo ___: 7 Curtain
bamboozle: 3 con 4 bilk, dupe, fool, gull, have, hoax, nick, snow, take 5 cheat, cozen, trick 6 delude, fleece, outwit, puzzle, suck in, take in 7 deceive, defraud, mystify, swindle, two-time 8 flimflam, hoodwink, outsmart, pettifog 9 disinform, four-flush, victimize 10 run a game on
bamboozlement: 3 con 5 fraud 6 fakery
bamboozler: 6 conman
Bamm Bamm: 6 Rubble
father: 6 Barney
mother: 5 Betty
ban: 3 bar, nix 4 tabu, veto 5 debar, estop, expel, money 6 abjure, censor, enjoin, except, forbid, ice out, outlaw, reject 7 boycott, embargo, exclude, keep out, refusal, rule out, shut out 8 disallow, outlawry, prohibit, restrict, sanction, throw out 9 blackball, exclusion, interdict, ostracize, proscribe, restraint 10 censorship, do away with, injunction
___ ban: 4 test
Ban: 9 deodorant
alternative: *see* deodorant
Ban-___: 3 Lon
Bana: 4 Eric
banal: 4 blah, flat 5 bland, campy, corny, hokey, musty, stale, stock, trite 6 common, jejune 7 humdrum, insipid, mundane, prosaic, tedious 8 ordinary, plebeian, trifling 9 hackneyed, innocuous, played out, prosaical 10 pedestrian, threadbare, uninspired, warmed-over
banality: 6 tedium 8 flatness 10 insipidity
banana: 4 tree 5 fruit 8 ice cream 9 Cavendish 10 Martinique
alternative: *see* fruit, ice cream flavor
bunch: 4 hand
buy: 5 bunch
covering: 4 peel
family plant: 5 abaca
oil: 5 ester 8 fast talk
peel mishap: 4 slip
top ~: 5 comic 8 comedian 9 commander
banana ___: 3 oil 4 seat 5 shrub, split 6 spider
___ banana: 3 top 5 dwarf 6 second 7 Chinese
Banana ___ Song, The: 4 Boat
___ Banana: 3 Top
Banana Boat Song, The: 4 Day-o
banana cream ___: 3 pie
bananahead
see ninny
bananas: 3 ape, mad 4 bats, gaga, loco 5 batty 7 bonkers, tetched 8 nonsense 10 freaked out, moonstruck
drive ~: 3 irk 4 rile 5 annoy, upset 6 harass 7 torment
go ~: 4 rave 6 lose it
go ~ over: 5 eat up
Bananas (1971 film)
cast: Woody Allen, Louise Lasser, Carlos Montalban
director: Woody Allen
banana split: 7 dessert
alternative: 5 bombe 6 frappe 9 milk shake 10 peach Melba
holder: 4 boat
ingredient: 6 cherry 8 ice cream
Banbury ___: 3 bun 4 cake, tart
banc: 4 seat
___-banc: 5 char-à
Bancroft: 4 Anne 6 George
Bancroft, Anne: 7 actress
film: 84 Charing Cross Road (1987)
Agnes of God (1985)
The Elephant Man (1980)
Garbo Talks (1984)
G.I. Jane (1997)
The Graduate (1967)
Great Expectations (1998)
How to Make an American Quilt (1995)
Keeping the Faith (2000)
The Miracle Worker (1962, AA)
The Prisoner of Second Avenue (1975)
The Pumpkin Eater (1964)
The Raid (1954)
The Turning Point (1977)
Young Winston (1972)
spouse: Mel Brooks
band: 3 set, tie 4 belt, bevy, body, clan, club, crew, gang, gird, girt, hoop, join, lace, line, pack, ring, tape, team, zone 5 bunch, chain, combo, corps, covey, girth, group, junto, layer, merge, party, range, squad, strap, strip, troop, unite 6 circle, clique, fasten, gather, girdle, league, outfit, ribbon, streak, stripe, troupe 7 binding, brigade, caravan, cluster, combine, company, coterie, faction, jewelry, shackle 8 assemble, assembly, cincture, encircle, ensemble, federate, ligature 9 affiliate, gathering, orchestra, shortwave 10 assemblage, collection
acknowledge the ~: 4 clap
alternative: 2 DJ 6 deejay
arm ~: 8 bracelet
bartender's ~: 6 garter
be in a ~: 4 play
biceps ~: 6 armlet
booster: 3 amp
combining form: 3 zon- 4 zono-
dance ~: 5 combo
ender: 3 age, box 5 shell, stand, wagon, width 6 leader, master
engagement: 3 gig
grouping: 3 set
hair ~: 6 fascia
heraldic ~: 4 orle 5 fesse
hillbilly ~ instrument: 3 jug
horizontal ~: 6 fascia
instrument: 3 sax 4 drum, horn, oboe, tuba 5 brass, bugle 8 clarinet
marching ~ hat: 5 shako
marching ~ need: 4 drum
mourning ~: 5 crape, crepe
narrow ~: 4 rein 5 leash
number: 4 song, tune
of a sort: 4 trio 5 nonet, octet 6 septet, sestet 7 octette, quartet, quintet
of color: 7 rainbow
of color, in zoology: 5 vitta
one-man ~: 4 solo
ornamental ~: 4 sash 5 patte 6 armlet, frieze 8 bracelet
radio ~: 2 AM, FM
sheriff's ~: 5 posse
spectrum ~: 3 red 4 blue 5 green 6 indigo, orange, violet, yellow
starter: 3 hat 4 head, neck, nose, side, wave 5 belly, broad, sweat, train, waist, watch, wrist
to beat the ~: 7 like mad
together: 5 group, merge, troop, unite
TV ~: 3 UHF, VHF
waist ~: 3 obi 4 sash
wedding ~: 4 ring
band ___: 3 saw 4 mill 5 brake, razor, shell
___ band: 3 big, ear, gum, jug 4 bird, file, jazz, mast, side, wave 5 brake, brass, dance, guard, spasm, steel 6 dentil, energy, garage, guttae, Möbius, one-man, rhythm, rubber, spider 7 falling, futtock, wedding
Band ___ On, The: 6 Played
Band-___: 3 Aid
Banda: 3 sea
locale: 7 Celebes 8 Sulawesi
bandage: 3 Ace, tie 4 tape, wrap 5 Curad, dress, spica, truss 6 swathe 8 dressing, ligature
applier: 5 medic
material: 5 gauze
nature's ~: 4 scab
Band-Aid: 7 stopgap 8 dressing, solution 9 makeshift, temporary
alternative: 3 Ace 5 Curad

bandanna: **5** do-rag, scarf **8** kerchief, neckwear
bandeau: **3** bra
Bandeira, Manuel: **4** poet **9** Brazilian
bandelet: **4** ring
__ Band Era: **3** Big
Banderas, Antonio: **5** actor
film: The 13th Warrior (1999)
Assassins (1995)
Crazy in Alabama (1999)
Evita (1996)
Frida (2002)
Interview With the Vampire: The Vampire Chronicles (1994)
The Mask of Zorro (1998)
My Mom's New Boyfriend (2008)
Original Sin (2001)
Play It to the Bone (1999)
Spy Kids (2001)
role: **3** Che
spouse: Melanie Griffith
banderillero adversary: **6** el toro
banderole: **4** flag **6** ensign **7** pennant **8** standard
bandicoot: **6** animal, mammal **9** marsupial
relative: ***see*** marsupial
banding: **4** lace
bandit: **4** thug **5** crook, thief **6** outlaw, pirate, raider, robber **7** brigand, ravager, rustler **8** criminal, gangster, hijacker, hooligan, marauder, opponent, pillager **9** buccaneer, desperado, masked man, plunderer, purloiner, Robin Hood **10** highwayman
Asian ~: **6** dacoit, dakoit
casino ~ feature: **3** arm
furry ~: **4** coon **7** raccoon
Bandit Queen, The: Belle Starr
banditry: **5** theft **8** thievery
Bandits (2001 film)
cast: Cate Blanchett, Billy Bob Thornton, Bruce Willis
director: Barry Levinson
__ Bandits: **4** Time
bandleader's cue: **5** hit it
__ Band music: **3** Big
Band of __: **6** Renown
Band of Gold (song)
artist: Don Cherry, Freda Payne
bandoleer: **4** belt
Bandolero! (1968 film)
cast: George Kennedy, Dean Martin, James Stewart, Raquel Welch
Band on the Run (1974 song)
artist: Paul McCartney
Bando, Sal
sport: **8** baseball
bandshell: **8** pavilion
bandstand: **5** kiosk
equipment: **3** amp
bandwagon
get on the ~: **4** back **5** boost **7** espouse, promote, sponsor, support **8** advocate, champion
jumper's phrase: **5** me too
Band Wagon, The (1953 film)
cast: Fred Astaire, Jack Buchanan, Cyd Charisse, Nanette Fabray, Oscar Levant
director: Vincente Minnelli
studio: **3** MGM
bandy: **4** awry, bent, game, pass, swap, swop, toss **5** askew, bowed, rally, throw, trade **6** barter, curved **7** crooked, shuffle, twisted **8** exchange **9** bowlegged, toss about
words: **3** rap **4** spar **5** argue
bandy-__: **6** legged
Bandy: **3** Moe
bane: **4** pest, ruin **5** curse, trial **6** blight, misery, plague, poison **7** bugaboo, bugbear, nemesis, scourge, undoing **8** anathema, calamity, disaster, distress, downfall, headache, nuisance **9** bête noire, detriment, nightmare, ruination **10** affliction
ender: **5** berry
starter: **3** bug, cow, dog, hen **4** flea, rats **5** wolfs
baneful: **4** evil **5** fatal, toxic **6** malign, nocent, odious **7** adverse, harmful, hurtful, malefic, nocuous, noisome, noxious, ominous, ruinous **8** damaging, negative, sinister, venomous, virulent **9** dangerous, injurious, pestilent, poisonous, unhealthy **10** calamitous, pernicious
see also awful
Banff: **4** city, lake, town **6** resort
lake: **6** Louise
locale: **4** Alta. **6** Canada **7** Alberta
bang: **3** hit, jar, pop, tip **4** beat, blow, boom, jolt, kick, shot, slam, slap, sock, thud, wham **5** blast, burst, crack, crash, knock, noise, pound, salvo, smack, smash, sound, thump, whack **6** hammer, impact, pummel, rattle, report, strike, thrill, tipoff, wallop **7** clatter **8** abruptly, bludgeon, suddenly **9** discharge, explosion, fisticuff, violently **10** detonation
big ~ creator: **5** nitro
ender: **4** tail
into: **3** hit, ram **4** jolt **5** knock **6** impact, jostle, justle
out: **5** write
up: **3** bar, mar **4** dent, mall, maul **5** abuse, wreck **6** bruise, damage **7** lay into **8** work over **9** manhandle **10** knock about
see also wonderful
__-bang: **4** slam, slap, whiz **5** whizz
Bang a Gong (1972 song)
artist: T. Rex
Bangalore: **4** city, town
locale: **5** India
Bang and Blame (1995 song)
artist: R.E.M.
Bang Bang (1966 song)
artist: Cher
banger: **7** sausage
bangers
partner: **4** mash
Banger Sisters, The (2002 film)
cast: Goldie Hawn, Geoffrey Rush, Susan Sarandon
Bangkok: **4** city, port, town **7** capital
locale: **8** Thailand
Bangladesh: **6** nation **7** country
bay: **6** Bengal
capital: **5** Dacca, Dhaka
city: **5** Tongi **6** Khulna **7** Saidpur **8** Rajshahi
continent: **4** Asia
language: **7** Bengali
money: **4** pice, taka **5** paisa **6** poisha
neighbor: **5** Burma, India
bangle: **5** charm, jewel **6** anklet, armlet, geegaw, gewgaw **7** circlet, jewelry, trinket **8** bracelet, ornament, wristlet
Bangor: **4** city, town
college: **4** Beal
locale: **5** Maine
neighbor: **5** Orono
__ bang out of: **4** get a
bangs: **4** coif **6** hairdo **8** coiffure
bangtail: **5** horse, mount
Bang the Drum Slowly (1973 film)
cast: Robert De Niro, Vincent Gardenia, Michael Moriarty
__ Bang Theory: **3** Big
Bangui: **4** city, port, town **7** capital
locale: **22** Central African Republic
river: **6** Ubangi
bang-up
do a ~ job: **5** excel
see also wonderful
bani
100 ~: **3** leu, ley
Bani-Sadr: **5** Irani
banish: **4** oust **5** eject, evict, exile, expel, purge **6** deport, dispel, outlaw, remove **7** cast out, discard, dismiss, isolate, kick out **8** displace, get rid of, relegate, send away **9** drive away, eradicate, ostracize, proscribe, transport **10** expatriate
from a flat: **5** evict
banishment: **5** exile **9** dismissal, expulsion
banister: **4** post, rail **7** railing, support **8** handrail
go down the ~: **5** slide
post: **5** newel
banjo
ancestor: **4** lute
cousin: **3** uke **6** guitar **7** ukelele
key changer: **4** capo
perch: **4** knee
play the ~: **4** pick **5** plunk, strum, twang
banjo __: **5** clock
Banjo Eyes: Eddie Cantor
banjoist: **6** Seeger **7** Scruggs
__ Banjos: **7** Dueling
Banjul: **4** city, town **7** capital
locale: **6** Gambia
bank: **3** dam, pot **4** dike, pile, pool, reef, save, tier **5** carom, coast, drift, mound, shelf, shore, slope, stack, store **6** branch, carrom, depend, glacis, lender, lienor, pile up **7** jackpot **8** salt away, treasury **9** acclivity **10** depository
account: **6** escrow **7** savings
acct. datum: **3** SSN
breaker: **3** run
canal ~: **4** berm **5** berme
claim: **4** lien **8** mortgage
contents: **3** fog **4** cash **5** money
customer: **5** saver **6** lienee **9** depositor
deal: **4** loan, mtge. **8** mortgage
deposit: **5** pay-in
deposit abuser: **5** kiter
employee: **5** guard **6** teller **7** cashier
ender: **4** book, card, note, roll
feature: **4** safe **5** vault
figure: **3** int., IRT
job: **5** heist **7** robbery
like some ~ checking: **5** no-fee
modern ~ teller: **3** ATM
money in the ~: **5** asset **7** deposit, savings
offering: **2** CD **3** IRA **4** loan **6** credit
officer: **5** treas. **9** treasurer
on: **4** lean, rely **5** count, trust **6** accept, assume, credit, depend, expect, look to, reckon **7** believe, presume, swear by **8** be sure of, gamble on **9** calculate **10** set store by
org.: **3** FRS, IMF **4** SBLI **5** FSLIC
patron: **3** acc. **4** acct. **7** account
posting: **4** rate **6** CD rate
river ~: **5** shore
robber's nemesis: **5** alarm **6** camera
sight: **4** line **5** queue
stack: **4** ones, tens **5** fives **8** hundreds, twenties
stamp: **3** NSF
starter: **4** data, sand, snow **5** piggy, river
statement entry: **3** bal., dep., int. **5** debit **7** balance, deposit **8** interest
statement period: **5** month
takeback: **4** repo
teller's call: **4** next
total: **7** balance
up: **5** stack
visit a blood ~: **6** donate
bank __: **3** box **4** barn, bill, card, loan, note, rate, shot **5** check, clerk, draft, heist, money, night, paper **7** account, annuity, balance, deposit, holiday, swallow
__ bank: **3** fog, job **4** data, food, land, soil **5** blood, piggy, spoil, state **6** memory **7** central, reserve, savings, wildcat
Bank: **5** Frank
Bank __: **3** One **4** Shot **5** Leumi
Bank __, The: **4** Dick
__ Bank: **4** Left, West **5** Grand, Right, World **6** Dogger **7** Georges, Jodrell
bankable: **10** marketable
Bank Dick, The (1940 film)
cast: W.C. Fields, Una Merkel, Cora Witherspoon
banker: **6** dealer, lender **8** croupier, investor **9** financier, treasurer
byword: **4** save
Banker
author: Dick Francis
bankers' __: **5** hours
Bankhead, Tallulah: **7** actress
Ban Ki-moon
predecessor: **5** Annan
banking: **7** finance **9** economics
see also bank
banknote: **4** bill, buck **5** money **6** dollar, tenner **7** sawbuck, smacker **8** currency, frogskin, simoleon **9** greenback
banknotes
see moolah
__ Bank Observatory: **7** Jodrell
bankroll: **3** wad **4** back, fund **5** funds, means, money, purse, stake **6** assets, invest **7** finance, sponsor, support, sustain **8** hard cash **9** resources, subsidize **10** underwrite

bankroller: **6** backer, patron **9** financier
bankrupt: **4** poor, ruin, sink **5** break, broke, drain, needy **6** bad off, busted, hard up, ill off, in need, in want, pauper, reduce, ruined **7** belly-up, deplete, pinched **8** badly off, beggarly, depleted, deprived, indigent, straiten, strapped **9** destitute, insolvent, moneyless, penniless, penurious, tapped out **10** down and out, impoverish, pauperized, straitened
go ~: **4** bust, fail, fold, sink
bankruptcy: **4** ruin **7** default, failure, poverty **8** collapse **9** indigence, overdraft, pauperism, privation, recession, ruination **10** depression, exhaustion, insolvency, nonpayment
Banks: **4** Tyra **5** Ernie **6** Joseph
__ Banks: **5** Grand, Outer
Banks, Ernie: **3** Cub **9** shortstop
Banks, Joseph: **7** British **8** botanist
__ Banks, NC: **5** Outer
Banks o'Doon, The
author: Robert Burns
bank statement entry: **5** debit
period: **5** month
Banks, Tyra: **5** model
Banky: **5** Vilma
banned: **4** tabu **5** taboo **7** illegal, illicit **8** criminal, improper, outlawed, unlawful, verboten, wrongful **9** felonious, forbidden **10** not allowed, prohibited
act: **4** no-no, tabu **5** taboo
chemical: **3** PCB
fruit spray: **4** Alar
pesticide: **3** DDT
Banneker, Benjamin: **10** astronomer
Bannen: **3** Ian
banner: **4** flag, sign **5** title, Web ad **6** burgee, emblem, ensign, poster **7** pennant, stellar **8** gonfalon, headline, standard, streamer **9** red-letter **10** successful
church ~: **7** labarum
puller: **5** blimp **9** dirigible
roll up a ~: **4** furl
banner __: **3** day **4** line **5** cloud
Banner: **4** John
Star-Spangled ~: **4** flag
Bannister: **5** miler, Roger
distance for ~: **4** mile
emulate ~: **3** run **4** race
Bannock: **6** Indian **7** Amerind
Bannockburn: **6** battle
locale: **8** Scotland
__ Banos, CA: **3** Los
banque payment: **5** rente
banquet: **3** sup **4** dine, fete, meal **5** feast, party **6** dinner, repast, spread **9** festivity, reception
attend a ~: **3** eat **4** dine **5** feast
course: **4** fish, meat, soup **5** salad **6** entrée **7** dessert **9** appetizer
delicacy: **4** paté **6** caviar **7** caviare
give a ~ for: **4** fete **5** honor
need: **2** MC **5** china, emcee
platform: **4** dais
provide a ~: **5** cater
banshee: **5** ghost
lament: **4** wail
like a ~: **6** Gaelic
bant: **4** diet **6** reduce
bantam: **3** hen, wee **4** baby, fowl, puny, tiny **5** bitty, saucy, small, teeny **6** little, midget, minute, peewee, petite, teensy **7** chicken, rooster, stunted **9** itsy-bitsy, itty-bitty, miniature, pint-sized, undersize **10** diminutive, teeny-weeny, vest-pocket
ender: **6** weight
bantamweight, like a: **4** wiry
banter: **3** kid, rib, wit **4** jeer, jest, jive, joke, josh, mock, quip, razz, talk **5** chaff, humor, taunt, tease **6** deride, joking **7** jesting, joshing, kidding, ribbing, sarcasm, teasing **8** badinage, chitchat, fast talk, raillery, repartee, ridicule, wordplay **9** make fun of, small talk, table talk, witty talk **10** jocoseness, joke around, persiflage
banterer: **3** wag, wit
bantering: **9** quizzical
__ B. Anthony: **5** Susan
Banting, Frederick: **3** Sir **8** Canadian, Nobelist
__-ban treaty: **4** test
Bantu: **4** Zulu **5** tribe **7** Swahili **8** language, Matabele
home: **6** Africa
language: **3** Yao **4** Lozi, Luba, Xosa, Zulu **5** Bemba, Chaga, Kongo, Makua, Mongo, Ngoni, Rundi, Shona, Sotho, Swazi, Xhosa **6** Kikuyu, Ruanda
people: **4** Goma, L'uba, Zulu
territory: **5** Venda **6** Ciskei
banyan: **3** fig **4** coat, tree **5** ficus, shirt **6** jacket **8** mulberry
banzai: **5** huzza **6** hoorah, hooray, hurrah, hurray, huzzah
Bao __: **3** Dai
baobab: **4** tree
family: **6** bombax
relative: **6** durian
baptism: **4** rite **5** debut **6** ritual **9** launching, sacrament **10** initiation
area: **4** font **5** laver
baptism of __: **4** fire
Baptist: **4** sect **8** religion **10** Protestant
baptize: **3** dub **4** call, name, term **5** bless, title **7** convert, entitle, immerse, intitle **8** christen, sprinkle
bar: **3** ban, but, dam, nix, pub, rod **4** bolt, boom, cake, deny, dike, dive, halt, line, lock, pole, rail, reef, rung, save, seal, shut, slab, snag, stop, tabu, veto **5** block, close, court, crank, debar, estop, expel, haunt, ingot, latch, ledge, lever, limit, shaft, spoke, stick, strip, table **6** abjure, bang up, bistro, cookie, enjoin, except, forbid, hinder, hurdle, impede, lounge, oppose, outlaw, reject, saloon, secure, streak, stripe, tavern **7** besides, boycott, embargo, exclude, hangout, inhibit, keep out, lock out, measure, prevent, railing, rule out, shut off, shut out, suspend, taproom, without **8** alehouse, blockade, blockage, disallow, estoppel, gin joint, leave out, obstacle, obstruct, omitting, preclude, prohibit, restrain, taphouse **9** apart from, constrain, deterrent, except for, excluding, exclusion, foreclose, freeze out, hindrance, honky-tonk, interdict, judiciary, nightclub, ostracize, other than, outside of, proscribe, restraint, roadblock **10** constraint, crosspiece, disqualify, impediment, limitation, restaurant
bill: **3** tab
candy ~: **5** snack
car ~: **4** axle **5** strut
car with a ~: **4** limo
chart: **5** graph
chaser: **4** soda
cheap ~: **4** dive **5** joint
code: **3** UPC
companion: **5** grill
container: **3** mug **5** glass, stein **8** schooner
dance under a ~: **5** limbo
ender: **3** fly, hop, man, men **4** bell, girl, keep, king, maid, room, ware **5** berry, guest, stool **6** keeper, tender
for draft animals: **4** yoke
horizontal ~: **5** event **7** railing
hostess: **5** B-girl
ice: **5** rocks
j ~: **6** ski tow **7** ski lift
legally: **5** estop
member: **3** att. **4** atty. **6** lawyer **8** attorney **9** barrister
member's abbr.: **3** esq., LL.B.
metal ~: **5** ingot
millstone ~: **4** rynd
mixer: **4** soda **5** water **7** bitters
mouthful: **3** sip **4** swig
none: **3** all
of gold: **5** ingot
of soap: **4** cake
order: **3** ale, rum, rye **4** beer, flip, neat, pint, shot, sour **5** Bronx, draft, drink, lager, round, sling, usual, vodka **6** bishop, brandy, chaser, Cognac, double, eggnog, Gibson, gimlet, mai tai, mimosa, posset, rickey, rob roy, scotch, whisky, zombie **7** Collins, martini, negroni, sidecar, stinger, whiskey **8** cocktail, coco loco, daiquiri, highball, Jack Rose, pink lady, salty dog, vermouth **9** alexander, Manhattan, margarita, moosemilk **10** Bloody Mary, golden fizz, horse's neck, Moscow mule, piña colada, rock and rye, silver fizz
pivoted ~: **4** pawl
pry ~: **5** jimmy, lever **7** crowbar
pull: **3** tap
read ~ codes: **4** scan
rectangular ~: **6** billet
request: **5** glass
rocks: **3** ice
sand ~: **4** reef **5** shoal
seat: **5** stool
selection: **5** salad
shot: **3** tot **5** snort
sign: **5** on tap
snack: **4** nuts **5** sushi **7** peanuts, popcorn
sound: **3** hic
starter: **4** crow, draw, sand, side **5** cross **6** handle
supply: **3** ale, ice **4** beer **6** liquor
toothed ~: **5** ratch
wheel ~: **4** axle
work at the ~: **3** mix **4** tend **5** serve
bar __: **3** car, pin, pit **4** cart, code, exam, foot, girl, line, none, tack **5** chart, clamp, ditch, gemel, graph, joist, syrup **6** magnet, mizvah **7** mitsvah, mitzvah
bar-__: **4** b-que **5** le-duc
__ bar: **3** bus, pry, tie, tow, wet **4** cash, claw, fern, gill, grab, high, Mars, milk, muck, open, roll, sand, sash, sway, toll, wine, wing **5** angle, inner, joint, outer, panic, piano, pinch, salad, sissy, slice, snack, space, sushi, utter **6** boring, cutter, dating, double, public, sickle, sports **7** azimuth, bay-head, capstan, quarter, reverse, ripping, singles, torsion
Bar __: **6** Harbor
__ Bar: **4** Dove
Barabbas
author: Pär Lagerkvist
Barack: **5** Obama
Baracus, B.A.
group: **5** A-Team
portrayer: **3** Mr. T
Barada: **5** river
city on the: **8** Damascus
locale: **5** Syria
__ barada nikto: **6** Klaatu
Baraka, Imamu Amiri: **6** writer
real name: **10** LeRoi Jones
Barak, Ehud: **2** P.M. **7** Israeli
predecessor: **9** Netanyahu
successor: **6** Sharon
bar and __: **5** grill
Baranof Island city: **5** Sitka
Baranski: **9** Christine
Bara, Theda: **5** siren **7** actress
contemporary: **5** Negri
Bar at the Folies-Bergère, A
painter: Édouard Manet
barb: **3** cut, dig **4** fish, gibe, hook, jibe, quip, slam, slap, slur, snub, spur **5** abuse, horse, libel, point, scorn, spike, taunt, thorn **6** equine, insult, needle, rebuff, ripost, slight, zinger **7** affront, calumny, catcall, disdain, mockery, obloquy, offense, potshot, prickle, put-down, riposte, slander, stinger **8** contempt, critique, derision, ridicule **9** aspersion, cheap shot, contumely **10** defamation, disrespect, opprobrium
combining form: **3** onc- **4** onch-, onci-, onco- **5** oncho-
feather ~: **4** herl
bar-b-__: **3** que
Barbados: **4** isle **6** island, nation **7** country
capital: **10** Bridgetown
export: **4** aloe
locale: **3** BWI **10** West Indies
money: **4** cent **6** dollar
org.: **3** OAS
Barbara: **3** Pym **4** Bach, Bain, Bush, Eden, Hale, Heck, Luna, Lynn, Rush **5** Allen, Boxer, Lewis, major, Mason, saint, Trent **6** Barrie, Bosson, Feldon, George, Harris, Hutton, Jordan, McNair **7** Babcock, Britton, Carrera, Hershey, Parkins, Tuchman, Walters **8** Anderson, Cartland, Hepworth, Mandrell, Michaels, Stanwyck **9** Bel Geddes **10** Kingsolver, McClintock
Barbara __ Bradford: **6** Taylor

__ Barbara: **5** Major, Santa
Barbara Ann (song)
artist: Beach Boys, Regents
Barbara Bush, __ Pierce: **3** née
Barbara Frietchie: **4** poem
author: John Greenleaf Whittier
Barbara Mc__: **4** Nair
Barbara Taylor __: **8** Bradford
Barbarella (1968 film)
cast: Jane Fonda, Milo O'Shea
director: Roger Vadim
barbarian: **3** hun, pig **4** boor, Goth, ogre, wild **5** beast, brute, crude, cruel, fiend **6** animal, brutal, coarse, savage, vandal, vulgar **7** bestial, boorish, heathen, inhuman, lowbrow, monster, uncivil, vicious **8** inhumane, ruthless **9** graceless, hellhound, ignoramus, merciless, primitive **10** philistine, troglodyte, uncultured
6th-century ~: **4** Avar
behave like a ~: **4** sack **6** invade **7** overrun, plunder
barbaric: **4** mean, wild **5** crude, cruel, feral, harsh, nasty **6** animal, brutal, coarse, fierce, Gothic, savage, unholy, unkind, vulgar, wanton **7** beastly, bestial, boorish, callous, hellish, hurtful, inhuman, lawless, loutish, lowbrow, uncivil, uncouth, ungodly, vicious **8** fiendish, inhumane, pitiless, ruthless, sadistic, vengeful **9** atrocious, cutthroat, ferocious, graceless, heartless, merciless, monstrous, primitive, truculent, unpitying **10** outlandish, outrageous, uncultured, vindictive
barbarism: **7** cruelty, outrage **8** ferocity **9** brutality, crudeness, vulgarity **10** coarseness, corruption, inhumanity, savageness
Barbary
beast: **3** ape
pirate's vessel: **5** zebec **6** zebeck **7** chebeck
sheep: **6** aoudad
Barbary __: **3** ape, fig **5** Coast, sheep **6** States
Barbary ape: **5** magot **7** primate
relative: *see* primate
Barbary Coast city: **5** Tunis
Barbary State
former ~: **5** Tunis **7** Algiers
barbate: **7** bearded
barbe: **5** scarf
Barbeau: **8** Adrienne
barbecue: **4** bake, cook, meal, meat, sear **5** broil, grill, party, roast **6** picnic **7** broiler, cookout, roaster **10** rotisserie
fare: **4** brat, ribs, slaw **5** kabab, kabob, kebab, kebob, patty, salad, steak **6** hot dog, pattie **7** chicken **8** coleslaw **9** bratwurst, hamburger
garb: **5** apron
leftover: **3** ash **5** ember
like ~ sauce: **5** tangy, zesty
need: **4** coal **5** ember **6** butane **8** charcoal
part: **5** grill **6** ashpit, grille
rocks: **4** lava
rod: **4** spit
southwestern ~: **5** asado
spot: **4** deck, yard **5** patio **8** backyard
barbecue __: **5** sauce
barbed: **5** sharp, spiny **6** thorny **7** cutting, pointed, prickly **8** spiteful
barbed __: **4** wire
barbed-wire
barricade: **6** abatis
item: **5** fence
barbell: **6** weight
material: **4** iron
unit: **2** lb. **5** pound
use a ~: **4** jerk, lift
barbeque
need: **6** Sterno
barber: **4** trim **5** shave **6** Figaro, shaver **7** stylist **10** hair cutter
belt: **5** strop
call: **4** next
challenge: **3** mop
ender: **4** shop
job: **3** cut **4** snip, trim **5** shave
mishap: **4** nick
name meaning ~: **7** Scherer
pole color: **3** red **5** white
shout: **4** next
sign: **4** pole
sound: **4** snip
sweepings: **4** hair
symbol: **4** pole
tool: **5** razor **6** shears **8** scissors
barber __: **4** pole **5** chair **7** college
Barber: **3** Red **4** Tiki **5** Chris **6** Samuel
Barbera: **3** red **4** wine **6** Joseph
origin: **5** Italy
__-Barbera: **5** Hanna
barberite: **5** alloy
component: **3** tin **6** copper, nickel **7** silicon
Barber of Seville, The: **5** opera
composer: Gioacchino Rossini
role: **5** Berta **6** Figaro, Rosina **7** Bartolo, Basilio **8** Almaviva, Fiorello **10** Don Basilio
setting: **5** Spain
barberry: **5** fruit, shrub
family shrub: **7** agarita, mahonia **8** algerita
barber's __: **4** itch **5** chair
Barber, Samuel
work: Adagio for Strings
Capricorn Concerto
A Hand of Bridge
Toccata Festiva
Vanessa
barbershop quartet member: **4** bari, bass **5** tenor **8** baritone
Barber, Tiki
sport: **8** football
Barbet: **9** Schroeder
Barbi: **6** Benton
Barbie: **4** doll
boyfriend: **3** Ken
dog: **4** Wags **6** Beauty, Ginger
friend: **5** Midge
rival: **3** Jem
Barbie __: **4** doll, Girl
Barbie Girl (1997 song)
artist: Aqua
Barbirolli, John: **3** Sir **7** British **9** conductor
Barbizon __: **6** School
Barbra: **9** Streisand
barbs
throw ~ at: **3** dis **4** zing **6** insult, offend
barbule: **5** thorn
barcarole: **4** song
Barcelona: **4** city, port, town
city near ~: **6** Lérida
locale: **5** Spain **6** España
Barchester Towers
author: Anthony Trollope
bard: **4** poet, scop **5** odist, rimer **6** rhymer **8** minstrel, poetizer **9** poetaster, rhymester, sonneteer, versifier
ametrical ~: **4** Nash
old-style: **4** scop
Scandinavian ~: **5** scald, skald
work: **4** epic, poem, rime, tale **5** rhyme, verse **6** ballad
see also poet
Bard
see William Shakespeare
Bardeen, John: **8** Nobelist **9** physicist
Bardem, Javier: **5** actor
film: Before Night Falls (2000)
No Country for Old Men (2007, AA)
Vicky Cristina Barcelona (2008)
homeland: **5** Spain
bardic: **7** of poets
Bard of __: **4** Avon
Bardolino: **3** red **4** wine **7** red wine
origin: **5** Italy
Bardot, Brigitte: **6** French **7** actress
spouse: Roger Vadim
bare: **4** arid, nude, open, poor, show, skin, void **5** basic, blank, bleak, clear, empty, naked, plain, scant, shorn, spare, stark, strip **6** absent, barren, denude, desert, devoid, divest, expose, meager, modest, peeled, reveal, scanty, scarce, shabby, simple, unclad, unmask, unveil, used up, vacant **7** austere, denuded, display, divulge, drained, exhibit, exposed, publish, slender, sold out, sterile, tell all, uncover, unrobed, vacated, vacuous **8** depleted, deserted, desolate, disclose, disrobed, divested, in the raw, knowable, leafless, lifeless, stripped, unclothe, undraped **9** au naturel, baldfaced, come clean, evacuated, exhausted, in the buff, make known, publicize, put on view, unadorned, unattired, unclothed, uncovered, undressed **10** make public, unshielded
combining form: **4** gymn-, nudi-, psil- **5** gymno-, psilo-
ender: **4** back, foot **5** faced **6** footed, handed, headed, legged
facts: **7** outline
fix some ~ spots: **5** resod
lay ~: **3** air **4** blab, leak, skin, tell **5** admit, strip **6** denude, expose, relate, reveal, show up, unfold, unmask, unveil **7** breathe, confess, divulge, exhibit, let slip, publish, uncloak, uncover **8** blurt out, disclose, unburden **9** broadcast, make known **10** make public
on top: **4** bald
peak: **3** tor **4** crag **5** spire **6** needle
rocky slope: **4** scar
starter: **6** thread
the teeth: **4** gnar **5** gnarl, growl, snarl
bare __: **5** bones
bare-__: **4** root **5** bones **7** knuckle
Bare: **5** Bobby
bare-bones: **5** stark **6** barren, severe **7** austere, Spartan **9** unadorned
bare-faced: **4** bold, open **5** brash **6** arrant, brassy, brazen **7** blatant, forward, glaring, obvious **8** apparent, flagrant, immodest, impudent, insolent, manifest, palpable, unsubtle **9** audacious, shameless, unabashed
barefoot: **6** unshod **8** shoeless
go ~: **3** pad
not ~: **4** shod
Barefoot Boy, The: **4** poem
author: John Greenleaf Whittier
Barefoot Contessa, The (1954 film)
cast: Humphrey Bogart, Ava Gardner, Edmond O'Brien
Barefoot in Athens
author: Maxwell Anderson
Barefoot in the Park: **4** film, play
author: Neil Simon
cast: Charles Boyer, Jane Fonda, Robert Redford
director: Gene Saks
barege: **6** fabric **8** material
barehanded: **7** unarmed **8** ungloved **10** vulnerable, weaponless
bareheaded: **7** hatless
barely: **4** just, only **6** almost, hardly, little, simply **7** by a hair, by a nose **8** narrowly, scarcely **10** by a whisker
Barenaked Ladies
song: It's All Been Done (1999)
One Week (1998)
Pinch Me (2000)
Barenboim, Daniel: **9** conductor
bareness: **9** austerity **10** desolation
Barents: **3** sea **6** Willem
locale: **6** Arctic
Barents, Willem: **5** Dutch **8** explorer
bare one's __: **4** soul **5** teeth
barest: **5** least **7** minimal, minimum
Baretta (ABC drama)
cast: Robert Blake (Tony Baretta)
cockatoo: Fred
barfly: **3** sot **4** lush **5** toper **7** tippler
bargain: **3** buy, low **4** deal, find, pact, sale, swap, swop **5** cheap, steal, value **6** dicker, haggle, higgle, pledge **7** cut-rate, good buy, low-cost, promise, traffic **8** closeout, contract, discount, good deal, markdown, moderate, purchase **9** agreement, low-priced, negotiate, reduction, stipulate **10** compromise, do business, economical, reasonable
at a ~: **5** cheap **6** on sale **7** reduced
caveat: **3** irr. **5** irreg.
for: **4** plan **5** incur **6** reckon **9** undertake **10** anticipate
hunter delight: **4** sale **7** auction **8** yard sale **9** clearance **10** garage sale
in the ~: **3** too **4** also **5** extra
terrific ~: **3** buy **4** deal **5** steal
with: **6** haggle **9** negotiate
bargain __: **3** for **7** counter
__-bargain: **4** plea
bargain-basement: **4** poor **5** cheap, tatty **6** budget, cheesy, shlock **7** schlock **8** inferior **9** low-priced, third-rate **10** reasonable, second-rate

bargain-hunt: **4** shop
bargaining chip: **8** leverage
barge: **3** ark, hoy **4** boat, dory, scow, ship **5** craft **6** lumber, vessel **7** intrude, lighter **8** flatboat **9** interrupt
  canal of song: **4** Erie
  helper: **3** tug **7** tugboat
  in: **5** burst, enter **6** arrive, meddle, muscle **7** intrude, obtrude **9** intercede, interfere, interpose, interrupt, intervene, push aside
  into: **3** ram **7** collide, rear-end
  like a ~: **5** in tow
  locale: **4** lake, Nile **5** canal, river **6** harbor
Barge Canal alias: **4** Erie
barger: **8** deckhand
__-bargle: **5** argle
__-bargy: **4** argy
Bar Harbor: **4** city, town **6** resort
  locale: **5** Maine
  park near: **6** Acadia
barhop: **8** pub-crawl **9** do the town
Bari: **4** city, Lynn, port, town
  locale: **5** Italy **6** Apulia
Baring: **4** Earl **7** Francis
barite: **3** ore **4** spar
baritone: **4** deep, male **5** range, voice **6** Duncan, Milnes, Warren **7** Merrill, Tibbett **8** vocalist
  aria: **5** eri tu
  fiddle: **5** cello
  in Marouf: **3** Ali
  voice above ~: **5** tenor
  voice under ~: **4** bass
barium: **5** metal **7** element
bark: **3** arf, bay, cry, rap, rub, yap, yip **4** bawl, boat, case, coat, howl, husk, peel, rind, roar, skin, snap, woof, yell, yelp **5** candy, craft, crust, growl, shell, shout, snarl, sound, speak **6** bellow, bowwow, casing, cortex, mutter, scrape, vessel **7** grumble, kyoodle **10** integument
  boat: **5** canoe
  combining form: **6** phello-
  comic-strip ~: **3** arf **4** woof
  for tanning: **5** sumac **6** sumach
  high-pitched ~: **3** yap, yip **4** yelp
  mulberry ~: **4** tapa
  place: **4** bole, tree **5** trunk
  starter: **3** tan **4** nine, shag, soap **5** shell
  up the wrong tree: **3** err **7** blunder **8** misjudge
barkentine: **4** boat
barker: **3** dog **4** seal **5** carny **6** carney **8** huckster, pitchman
  baby ~: **3** pup **5** puppy
  come-on: **5** spiel
  partner: **5** shill
Barker: **2** Ma, MC **3** Bob, Lex **5** Clive, emcee
Barker, Lex
  spouse: Arlene Dahl, Lana Turner
Barkin, Ellen: **7** actress
  film: The Big Easy (1987)
    Daniel (1983)
    Desert Bloom (1986)
    Diner (1982)
    Drop Dead Gorgeous (1999)
    The Fan (1996)
    Sea of Love (1989)
    This Boy's Life (1993)
  spouse: Gabriel Byrne
barking __: **4** deer, frog
barking up the wrong tree: **6** all wet **8** mistaken
Barkley: **4** Iran **5** Alben **7** Charles
Barkleys of Broadway, The (1949 film)
  cast: Fred Astaire, Ginger Rogers
barks
  animal that ~: **3** dog **4** deer, seal
  like some tree ~: **5** mossy, rough **6** smooth
Bark Tree, The
  author: Raymond Queneau
barley: **4** feed **5** grain
  bristle: **3** awn
  ender: **4** corn
  product: **4** beer, malt
barley __: **4** coal, corn, sack **5** candy, sugar, water **6** stripe
__ barley: **5** pearl **6** winter
__ Barleycorn: **4** John
Barlow: **5** Kevan
Barlow, Joel: **4** poet
bar mitzvah: **4** rite
  appetizer: **5** knish
  dance: **4** hora
  official: **5** rabbi, rebbe
  reading: **4** Tora **5** Torah
barmy: **4** luny **5** foamy, loony, spumy **6** frothy, looney, yeasty **10** fermenting
barn: **7** theater, theatre
  area: **4** loft **5** stall **6** haymow
  baby: **3** kid **4** calf, colt, foal, lamb **5** owlet
  bellow: **3** low, moo
  cow ~: **5** dairy
  dance: **4** reel
  dweller: **3** cow, ewe, owl, ram **4** goat **5** horse
  ender: **4** yard **5** storm **6** burner
  handful: **3** hay **5** straw, udder
  locale: **4** farm
  loft: **6** haymow
  neighbor: **4** silo
  storage unit: **4** bale
  symbol: **7** hex sign
  topper: **4** vane
barn __: **3** owl **5** dance, grass **7** raising, swallow
Barnabas: **5** saint
Barnaby __: **5** Jones, Rudge
Barnaby Jones (CBS drama)
  cast: Buddy Ebsen (Barnaby Jones)
    Lee Meriwether (Betty Jones)
    Mark Shera (J.R. Jones)
Barnaby Rudge
  author: Charles Dickens
  character: **3** Ned **4** Emma
barnacle: **10** crustacean
Barnard: **4** coll. **6** Hughes **7** college **10** Christiaan
  grad: **5** woman **6** alumna
  locale: **7** New York
barnburner: **5** event **7** success
Barnes: **5** Clive, Djuna **6** Binnie, Joanna, Julian, Norman **9** Priscilla
  & Noble competitor: **6** Amazon **7** Borders
Barnet: **6** Miguel **7** Charlie
Barnet, Charlie: **11** saxophonist
  genre: **4** jazz
Barnet, Miguel: **5** Cuban **6** writer
barney: **3** row **4** fray, spat, tiff **5** brawl, error, fight, melee, scrap **6** affray, dustup, engine, tussle **7** blunder, dispute, mistake, quarrel, rhubarb, scuffle, wrangle **8** argument, squabble **9** brannigan **10** donnybrook, free-for-all, locomotive, prizefight
Barney: **3** Lem, Rex **4** Fife **6** Kessel, Miller, Rubble **8** Oldfield
  buddy: **4** Fred
  partner: **6** Snuffy
Barney Google kid: **5** Tater
Barney Miller (ABC sitcom)
  cast: Max Gail (Det. Stanley Wojo Wojohowicz)
    Ron Glass (Det. Ron Harris)
    Hal Linden (Capt. Barney Miller)
    Gregory Sierra (Det. Sgt. Chano Amenguale)
    Jack Soo (Det. Nick Yemana)
    Abe Vigoda (Det. Sgt. Phil Fish)
Barnstable: **4** city, town
  locale: **4** Mass.
barnstorm: **3** fly **4** tour **6** aviate, travel **8** campaign
barnstormer: **5** flier, flyer **7** aviator **8** traveler
  feat: **4** dive, loop **8** nosedive
Barnum: **2** P.T. **7** Phineas
  attraction: **3** Eng **4** Lind **5** Chang, Thumb **6** circus **8** Tom Thumb **9** Jenny Lind
Barnum of Wall Street, The: **4** Fisk
barnyard: **4** farm
  animal: **3** cow, ewe, hen, hog, pig, ram, sow **4** duck, goat **5** goose, horse, sheep **6** rabbit
  baby: **3** kid, pig **4** calf, colt, foal, lamb **5** chick **6** piglet **7** gosling **8** duckling
  bird: **3** hen **4** duck, fowl **5** drake, goose, layer **6** gander **7** chicken, rooster
  cry: **3** baa, low, maa, moo **4** bray, honk, oink **5** bleat, neigh, quack **6** squawk, whinny **7** whinney
  enclosure: **3** pen, sty **6** corral
  female: **3** cow, ewe, hen, sow **4** duck **5** goose, nanny
  grub: **3** hay **4** corn, feed, oats, slop **5** swill
  grunter: **3** hog, pig, sow **4** boar **5** shoat
  swinger: **4** vane
Barolo: **3** red **4** wine **7** red wine
  origin: **5** Italy
barometer: **4** norm **5** gauge, scale **8** standard
__ barometer: **6** marine **7** aneroid, mercury
barometric
  line: **6** isobar
  unit of ~ pressure: **4** torr
baron: **4** lord, peer, rank **5** mogul, nawab, noble, title **6** tycoon **7** big boss, magnate **8** nobleman **9** blue-blood, financier, patrician **10** aristocrat
  certain oil ~: **5** sheik **6** shaikh, sheikh
  ender: **3** age, ess
  superior: **8** viscount
__ baron: **5** press **6** cattle, robber
baroness: **4** dame, lady, peer **5** noble, title **10** noblewoman
baronet: **5** noble **8** nobleman
  title: **3** Sir
  wife: **4** dame, Lady
baronial: **5** noble **6** august, lordly
baron of __: **4** beef
__ Baron, The: **3** Red
Baron, The Red: **3** ace **5** pilot
baroque: **5** style **6** florid, ornate, quaint **10** decorative, ornamented
Baroque: **3** Era
  composer: **4** Bach **6** Handel
  instrument: **4** lute, viol
  painter: **6** Rubens **9** Velázquez
barque: **4** boat
Barr: **7** Douglas **8** Roseanne
Barrack-Room Ballads
  author: Rudyard Kipling
  part: **5** Tommy
barracks: **3** bed **4** camp, tent **6** billet, casern **7** bivouac, caserne **8** garrison, quarters **10** encampment, Quonset hut
  assignment: **6** billet
  officer: **3** NCO, sgt. **8** sergeant
  picture: **5** pin-up
barracuda: **4** fish, spet **6** sennet
  habitat: **3** sea **5** ocean
Barracuda: **3** car **4** auto **8** Plymouth
barrage: **4** boom, fire, hail, pelt **5** blast, blitz, burst, salvo, shoot, storm, surge **6** attack, battle, deluge, launch, shower, volley **7** assault, battery, bombard, gunfire **8** enfilade, fire upon, plethora, shelling **9** avalanche, broadside, cannonade, crossfire, discharge, fusillade, onslaught, profusion **10** cannonfire
  media ~: **4** hype **5** blitz
  naval ~: **5** salvo **6** volley **7** barrage **9** broadside, cannonade, fusillade
Barranquilla: **4** city, port, town
  locale: **8** Colombia
barre: **4** tail **8** handrail
  bend at the ~: **4** plie
Barre: **4** city, town
  locale: **7** Vermont
barred: **8** excluded **9** unwelcome
barrel: **3** fly, hie, keg, rip, run, tub, vat, zip **4** cask, dart, dash, drum, flit, race, rush, tear, zoom **5** hurry, scoot, speed **6** ashcan, firkin, gallop, hasten, hustle, move it, rocket, scurry **7** floor it, hop to it, oil unit, quicken, scamper **8** hogshead, OPEC unit, step on it **9** hotfoot it, shake a leg, skedaddle **10** burn rubber, get a move on, hightail it
  beer ~: **3** keg
  bottom contents: **4** lees **5** dregs **8** sediment
  bottom of the ~: **5** worst
  component: **4** hoop **5** stave
  diameter: **4** bore
  ender: **4** head **5** house
  filler: **4** beer, pork, wine
  fraction: **6** gallon
  groove: **5** croze
  herring ~: **4** cade
  hoop wood: **3** elm
  into: **3** ram **7** collide, rear-end
  lock, stock and ~: **6** in toto, wholly
  maker: **6** cooper
  of laughs: **4** card, riot
  oil ~: **4** drum
  open a ~: **3** tap
  over a ~: **5** broke **7** trapped **8** helpless **9** penniless
  pork ~: **9** patronage

stopper: 4 bung
barrel __: 4 bolt, cuff, knot, race, roll, roof 5 chair, chest, organ 6 cactus, engine, racing
barrel-__: 5 racer 7 chested, vaulted
__ barrel: 4 pork 5 over a
__-barrel: 6 single 7 cracker
__ Barrel: 7 Cracker
__-barreled: 6 double
barreleye: 4 fish
__ barrelhead: 5 on the
barrelhouse: 3 bar
barrelmaker, name meaning: 6 Cooper
barrel of __: 6 laughs 7 monkeys
Barrel-Organ, The
author: Alfred Noyes
__ Barrel Polka: 4 Beer
barrels: 4 a lot, lots, tons 5 heaps, scads
barrel-shaped obj.: 3 cyl. 8 cylinder
barren: 3 dry 4 arid, bald, bare, dull, poor, vain, void 5 blank, bleak, empty, stark, vapid, waste 6 desert, devoid, effete, fallow, severe, used up, vacant 7 austere, drained, parched, Spartan, sterile, useless, vacated 8 depleted, deserted, desolate, infecund, lifeless 9 bare-bones, evacuated, exhausted, fruitless, infertile, unadorned 10 lackluster, profitless, unprolific
area: 6 desert, Sahara
barrenness: 9 austerity 10 desolation
barrens: 5 wilds 10 wilderness
__ barrens: 4 pine
Barrès, Maurice: 6 French, writer
Barrett: 3 Syd 4 Rona, Tina 5 Majel 7 Jacinda
__ Barrett Browning: 9 Elizabeth
barrette: 4 clip 5 clasp
Barretts of Wimpole Street, The (1934 film)
cast: Charles Laughton, Fredric March, Norma Shearer
barricade: 3 bar, dam 4 dike, jump, stop, wall, weir 5 block, fence 6 hurdle, shut in 7 bulwark, defense, rampart 8 obstruct, palisade 9 roadblock 10 difficulty, impediment
barbed-wire ~: 6 abatis
Barrie: 4 Mona 5 Chase, Wendy 7 Barbara 10 Pan creator
character: 4 Smee 5 Wendy 8 Peter Pan
Barrie, Barbara: 7 actress
Barrie, James M.: 6 writer 8 Scottish 10 playwright
dog: 4 Nana
work: The Admirable Crichton
Dear Brutus
Peter Pan
Quality Street
What Every Woman Knows
The Will
barrier: 3 bar, dam 4 dike, gate, moat, rail, reef, snag, wall, weir 5 block, fence, hedge, limit, minus 6 hurdle 7 embargo, railing, rampart 8 blockade, boundary, drawback, handicap, obstacle, weakness 9 detriment, hindrance, liability, partition, restraint 10 bottleneck, impediment, protection
build a better ~: 5 redam
court ~: 3 net
farm ~: 4 rail 5 fence
island: 3 cay, key
mosquito ~: 3 net
movable ~: 4 gate
openwork ~: 5 grill 6 grille
race-winner's ~: 4 tape
river ~: 4 dike 5 levee 10 embankment
room ~: 4 wall
water ~: 3 dam 4 dike, mole, weir 5 jetty, levee, wharf 7 sea wall 10 breakwater, embankment
zoo ~: 4 moat
barrier __: 4 reef 5 beach 6 island
__ barrier: 4 heat 5 sonic, sound, trade, vapor 7 thermal
__ Barrier Reef: 5 Great
barring: 3 but 4 save 6 except, unless 7 besides 9 exception 10 leaving out
this: 4 else 9 otherwise
barrio: 4 slum 6 ghetto 7 quarter
city: 6 East L.A.
kid: 4 niña, niño 8 muchacha, muchacho
store: 6 bodega
Barrios, Eduardo: 6 writer 7 Chilean
Barris, Chuck: 2 MC 4 host 5 emcee
barrister: 3 att. 4 atty. 6 jurist, lawyer, legist 7 counsel 8 advocate, attorney 9 counselor, solicitor
org.: 3 ABA
wear: 3 wig
Barron: 5 Steve
Barron's
reader: 4 exec, lion, suit 6 broker, tycoon 7 magnate 8 investor
rival: 6 Forbes 7 Fortune
subject.: 2 co. 4 corp., firm 5 stock 7 company 8 business
barroom: 3 pub 4 dive 5 local 6 lounge, saloon, tavern 7 gin mill, taproom 8 alehouse, groggery, grog shop, taphouse 9 speakeasy
see also bar
barroom __: 5 brawl
barrow: 3 hog 4 cart, hill 5 dolly, mound, swine 7 tumulus 8 handcart, pushcart 9 hand truck
in America: 8 pushcart
starter: 4 hand 5 wheel
Barrow: 4 city, town 5 Clyde
locale: 6 Alaska
resident: 6 Eskimo
__ Barrow: 5 Point
Barry: 3 Len 4 Dave, Gene, Gibb, Jeff, Mann, Rick 5 Bonds, Morse, White, Young 6 Diller, Gordon, Kelley, Marion, Nelson, Newman, Philip, Sadler 7 Manilow, McGuire 8 Bostwick, DeVorzon, Levinson, Sullivan, Williams 9 Goldwater, Sharpless 10 Fitzgerald, Livingston, Sonnenfeld
Barry, Gene: 5 actor
TV: Bat Masterson, Burke's Law, The Name of the Game
Barry Lyndon (1975 film)
cast: Marisa Berenson, Patrick Magee, Ryan O'Neal
director: Stanley Kubrick
Barrymore: 4 Drew, John 5 Ethel 6 Lionel
Barrymore, Diana to Ethel: 5 niece
Barrymore, Drew: 7 actress
film: 50 First Dates (2004)
Boys on the Side (1995)
Charlie's Angels (2000)
E.T. The Extra-Terrestrial (1982)
Ever After (1998)
Firestarter (1984)
Guncrazy (1992)
He's Just Not That Into You (2009)
Irreconcilable Differences (1984)
Music and Lyrics (2007)
Never Been Kissed (1999)
Scream (1996)
The Wedding Singer (1998)
Whip It (2009)
Barry, Philip: 6 writer
work: The Philadelphia Story
Barry, Rick: 5 cager
milieu: 5 court
org.: 3 NBA
sport: 10 basketball
bars: 4 jail 6 prison
final ~: 4 coda
frequent ~: 4 tope 8 pub-crawl
game square with ~: 4 jail
mdse. ~: 3 UPC
one behind ~: 6 inmate 7 convict 8 prisoner
__ bars: 6 behind, killer, monkey
Barstow: 4 city, Stan, town
locale: 10 California
Bart: 5 Starr 6 Lionel 7 Simpson 8 Maverick 9 Braverman
grandpa: 3 Abe
sister: 4 Lisa
to Homer: 3 son
to Lisa: 3 bro 7 brother
bartender: 10 mixologist
band: 6 garter
request: 2 ID
see also bar
barter: 4 deal, sell, swap, swop 5 bandy, trade 6 change, dicker, haggle 7 traffic 8 exchange 10 quid pro quo
Bartered Bride, The: 5 opera
composer: Bedrich Smetana
barterer, birthright: 4 Esau
Barth: 4 John, Karl
Barthelme, Donald: 6 writer
Barthelmess, Richard: 5 actor
Barth, John: 6 writer
work: Chimera
Coming Soon!!!
Giles Goat-Boy
Lost in the Funhouse
Sabbatical
The Sot-Weed Factor
The Tidewater Tales
Bartholdi: 8 Frédéric
contemporary: 5 Rodin
Bartholomew: 5 saint 7 Freddie
Bartholomew, Freddie: 5 actor
Bartles partner: 6 Jaymes
Bartlesville: 4 city, town
locale: 4 Okla. 8 Oklahoma
Bartlet: 3 Jed
Bartlett: 4 city, Hall, John, pear, town 6 Bonnie 8 Jennifer
locale: 8 Illinois 9 Tennessee
relative: 4 Bosc 5 Anjou 6 Comice, Seckel
Bartlett, John: 6 writer 8 compiler
work: Familiar Quotations
Bartlett's entry: 4 anon., quot. 5 quote 9 anonymous
Bartok: 3 Eva
Bartók, Béla: 8 composer 9 Hungarian
work: Bluebeard's Castle
Concerto for Orchestra
Mikrokosmos
The Miraculous Mandarin
Petite Suite
Bartolomeo: 10 Cristofori
see also Italian
Bartolomeu: 4 Dias
Barton: 4 Enos, Fink 5 Clara, Derek 7 Charles, MacLane
Barton, Clara: 5 nurse
Barton Fink (1991 film)
cast: Judy Davis, John Goodman, John Turturro
director: Joel Coen
Barty: 5 Billy
Baruch: 7 Bernard, Spinoza 8 Blumberg
baryon: 8 particle
container: 4 atom
Baryshnikov, Mikhail: 6 dancer 7 danseur, Latvian, Russian
birthplace: 4 Riga 6 Latvia
specialty: 6 ballet
baryton: 6 string 8 bass viol
Barzun, Jacques: 6 writer
bas __: 4 bleu 6 mizvah 7 mitsvah, mitzvah
Bas-__: 4 Rhin
basal: 5 basic, least 6 bottom, lowest 7 minimum, organic, primary, radical 10 elementary, underlying
basalt: 4 lava, rock 7 mineral
base: 3 bad, bag, bed, KOH, low 4 butt, camp, evil, foot, foul, home, lewd, mean, NaOH, post, root, sack, seat, site, ugly, vile 5 abode, cheap, crude, depot, first, found, hinge, lousy, lowly, model, seamy, small, snide, sorry, stand, third, wrong 6 abject, alkali, bottom, center, coarse, common, depend, derive, dismal, ground, humble, little, locate, menial, odious, origin, second, shoddy, sleazy, sneaky, sordid, trashy, unholy, vulgar, wicked 7 abysmal, accurst, beastly, bedrock, bestial, caddish, corrupt, footing, heinous, ignoble, immoral, knavish, lowdown, roguish, servile, squalid, station, support 8 accursed, backbone, beggarly, cowardly, degraded, depraved, dreadful, foothold, garrison, home port, indecent, plebeian, shameful, sinister, stinking, terminal, terrible, unworthy, wretched 9 abhorrent, construct, dastardly, establish, home plate, hydroxide, invidious, loathsome, nefarious, offensive, predicate, repugnant, revolting, underside 10 abominable, despicable, foundation, groundwork, indecorous, indelicate, iniquitous, lower-class, maleficent, settlement, substratum, traitorous, villainous
baseball ~: 3 bag 4 home 5 first, third 6 second
be off ~: 3 err
clearer: 5 homer
computer ~: 6 binary
ender: 3 man 4 ball, born, less, line 5 board 6 burner
formula: 3 KOH 4 NaOH
kind of ~ hit: 5 bloop 6 looper

9 line drive
neutralizer: 4 acid
numerical ~: 5 radix
off ~: 4 AWOL 5 amiss, wrong 6 afield 8 mistaken 10 inaccurate, inapposite
of operations: 7 station
reach ~ headfirst: 5 slide
set up ~: 4 camp 6 encamp 7 bivouac
starter: 4 data, fire 5 wheel
touch ~: 4 talk 5 phone, tag up 7 contact 9 telephone
see also army, military
base __: 3 box, hit, map, pay 4 camp, line, load, pair, path, rate, unit, wage 5 house, level, metal, price 6 burner, estate, period, runner, salary, tenant 7 bullion, running, station
__ base: 3 air 4 data, home, rate 5 Attic, cloud, first, Lewis, power, third, touch 6 kettle, second
__-base: 3 off 4 zero
__ Base: 5 Ace of
baseball: 4 game 5 sport 6 sphere 8 card game
area: 5 mound 6 dugout 7 bullpen, infield 8 backstop, outfield 10 scoreboard
assistant: 6 bat boy
award: 3 MVP
base: 3 bag 4 home 5 first, third 6 second
bat first in ~: 7 lead off
bat wood: 3 ash
boss: 2 GM 3 mgr. 5 owner 7 manager
broadcaster: 4 Buck 5 Allen, Canel, Caray, Gowdy, Wolff 6 Barber, Hodges, Murphy, Nelson, Prince, Scully, Uecker 7 Harwell 8 Bob Wolff, Hamilton, Jack Buck, McCarver, Mel Allen 9 Bob Murphy, Bob Prince, Bob Uecker, Buck Canel, Curt Gowdy, Garagiola, Red Barber, Vin Scully 10 Brickhouse, Harry Caray, Russ Hodges
cap feature: 5 visor, vizor
card company: 5 Fleer, Topps
class AAA ~: 6 minors
climax, usually: 5 ninth
club: 3 bat
contents of a ~ bag: 5 rosin
division: 6 inning
event: 3 fly, hit, out 4 foul, walk 5 bloop, drive, homer, pop-up, steal 6 looper, series 9 line drive
family name: 4 Alou
fare: 6 hot dog
feature: 4 seam
fourth hitter: 7 clean-up
fumble: 5 error 6 bobble
gear: 4 mitt 5 glove 6 helmet
Hall of Fame executive: 4 Kuhn 5 Frick, Giles, Veeck 6 Barrow, Landis, Manley, Rickey, Yawkey 7 Johnson, O'Malley 8 Chandler, Ed Barrow, Griffith, MacPhail, Spalding 9 Bill Veeck, Bowie Kuhn, Ford Frick, Tom Yawkey 10 Ban Johnson, Effa Manley
Hall of Fame manager: 4 Mack 5 Lopez, Selee 6 Alston, Hanlon, Harris, McGraw, Weaver 7 Al Lopez, Huggins, Lasorda, Stengel 8 Anderson, Durocher, McCarthy, Williams 9 McKechnie, Ned Hanlon 10 Connie Mack, Earl Weaver, Frank Selee, John McGraw, Southworth
Hall of Fame player: 3 Day, Fox, Ott 4 Babe, Bell, Cobb, Dean, Doby, Fisk, Ford, Foxx, Hoyt, Mays, Mize, Rice, Ruth, Ryan, Wynn, Yogi 5 Aaron, Anson, Banks, Bench, Boggs, Brett, Brock, Carew, Combs, Doerr, Evers, Flick, Gomez, Grove, Gwynn, Irvin, Kiner, Klein, Lemon, Paige, Perez, Reese, Rixey, Roush, Rusie, Smith, Spahn, Terry, Vance, Waner, Wheat, Young, Yount 6 Bender, Carter, Cepeda, Cronin, Cuyler, Dihigo, Feller, Foster, Frisch, Gehrig, Gibson, Gordon, Goslin, Hunter, Kaline, Koufax, Lajoie, Mantle, Mel Ott, Morgan, Murray, Musial, Niekro, Palmer, Ripken, Seaver, Sisler, Snider, Sutter, Sutton, Ty Cobb, Wagner, Wilson 7 Appling, Ashburn, Averill, Bunning, Carlton, Collins, Cy Young, Fingers, Gossage, Hornsby, Hubbell, Jackson, Jenkins, Jim Rice, Johnson, Lazzeri, Leon Day, Mathews, McCovey, Medwick, Molitor, Puckett, Rizzuto, Roberts, Ruffing, Sam Rice, Schmidt, Speaker, Stearns, Traynor, Vaughan, Waddell, Wilhelm 8 Al Kaline, Aparicio, Babe Ruth, Bob Lemon, Boudreau, Cap Anson, Clemente, Cochrane, DiMaggio, Drysdale, Edd Roush, Lou Brock, Marichal, Marquard, Robinson, Rod Carew, Sandberg, Stargell, Williams, Winfield 9 Alexander, Amos Rusie, Bill Terry, Bob Feller, Bob Gibson, Cal Ripken, Dandridge, Dizzy Dean, Don Sutton, Early Wynn, Eckersley, Eppa Rixey, Greenberg, Hank Aaron, Henderson, Jim Palmer, Joe Cronin, Joe Gordon, Joe Morgan, Killebrew, Larry Doby, Lou Gehrig, Mathewson, Mazeroski, Nap Lajoie, Nellie Fox, Newhouser, Nolan Ryan, Paul Waner, Radbourne, Slaughter, Tom Seaver, Tony Gwynn, Tony Perez, Wade Boggs, Waite Hoyt, Yogi Berra, Zack Wheat 10 Bobby Doerr, Campanella, Charleston, Chuck Klein, Dazzy Vance, Duke Snider, Earle Combs, Elmer Flick, Ernie Banks, Gary Carter, Hack Wilson, Jim Bunning, Jimmie Foxx, Joe Medwick, Josh Gibson, Kiki Cuyler, Lefty Gomez, Lefty Grove, Lloyd Waner, Monte Irvin, Ozzie Smith, Phil Niekro, Pie Traynor, Ralph Kiner, Red Ruffing, Robin Yount, Rube Foster, Stan Musial, Whitey Ford, Willie Mays 11 Yastrzemski
Hall of Fame umpire: 4 Klem 6 Chylak, Conlan 7 Barlick, Hubbard 8 Bill Klem 9 Al Barlick
hit: 4 bunt 5 drive, homer 6 double, single, triple 7 home run 9 line drive
home run in ~: 6 dinger
hot corner: 5 third
infraction: 4 balk
inning: 5 frame
kind of ~ game: 5 no-run 8 no-hitter
league: 4 Amer., Natl. 8 American, National
list: 6 lineup, roster
miscue: 5 error
next in ~: 6 on deck
nickname: 3 Yaz
not fair in ~: 4 foul
not foul in ~: 4 fair
not out in ~: 4 safe
objective: 3 win 7 pennant
official in ~: 3 ump 6 umpire
pass: 4 walk
pitch: 6 sinker, slider 8 change-up, forkball, splitter
pitcher and catcher in ~: 7 battery
ploy: 4 bunt 5 slide, steal 7 squeeze 8 pitchout 9 sacrifice
pop fly: 5 bloop 6 looper
position: 2 CF, LF, RF, SS 7 baseman, catcher, pitcher 9 shortstop
rare ~ game: 5 no-hit 8 no-hitter
score: 3 run
scoreboard heading: 3 RHE
shoe piece: 5 cleat
situation: 5 one on, two on
solid hit, in ~: 5 liner 9 line drive
star: 3 Cey, Nen 4 Agee, Alou, Blue, Gant, Kaat, Mota, Nomo, Otis, Rose, Sosa, Valo, Yost 5 Bando, Belle, Boggs, Bonds, Brown, Burks, Davis, Evans, Grace, Jeter, Lopes, Maris, Oliva, Reese, Staub, Tatis, Tiant, Torre 6 Alomar, Baines, Baylor, Dawson, Franco, Garvey, Harrah, Hodges, Maddux, Maglie, Newsom, Olerud, Orosco, Pappas, Piazza, Pinson, Pujols, Raines, Ron Cey, Suzuki, Tanana, Thomas, Walker 7 Bagwell, Canseco, Clemens, Glavine, Griffey, Jim Kaat, Johnson, McGriff, McGwire, Nettles, Ramirez, Robb Nen, Ron Gant, Ventura 8 Amos Otis, Blyleven, Joe Torre, Martinez, Palmeiro, Pete Rose, Sal Bando, Trammell, Vida Blue, Williams 9 Eddie Yost, Elmer Valo, Galarraga, Gil Hodges, Hershiser, Hideo Nomo, Luis Tiant, Manny Mota, Mark Grace, Sal Maglie, Sammy Sosa, Schilling, Tim Raines, Tony Oliva, Wade Boggs 10 Barry Bonds, Bobby Bonds, Bobo Newsom, Davey Lopes, Derek Jeter, Greg Maddux, John Franco, Ken Griffey, Mike Piazza, Milt Pappas, Moises Alou, Roger Maris, Rusty Staub, Toby Harrah, Tommie Agee, Vada Pinson
stat in ~: 2 AB, HR, SB 3 ERA, RBI 4 save 5 at bat, ribby 6 assist, put-out 7 shutout
strikeout: 5 whiff
tag: 3 out
team: 4 Cubs, Mets, Nats, Rays, Reds 5 Twins 6 Angels, Astros, Braves, Giants, Padres, Red Sox, Royals, Tigers 7 Brewers, Dodgers, Indians, Marlins, Orioles, Pirates, Rangers, Rockies, Yankees 8 Blue Jays, Mariners, Phillies, White Sox 9 Athletics, Cardinals, Nationals
term: 3 bag, bat, fly, hit, out, RBI, run, tag, ump 4 balk, bunt, fair, foul, home, safe, save, walk 5 at bat, bloop, error, fungo, homer, mound, no-hit, pitch, plate, slump, steal, swing, tag up, whiff 6 assist, batboy, bobble, clutch, dinger, double, inning, lineup, on base, on deck, pop fly, put-out, rubber, single, sinker, slider, strike, triple, umpire, windup 7 battery, bullpen, catcher, clean-up, fielder, home run, infield, lead off, pennant, pick off, pitcher, rundown, sandlot, shutout, slugger, squeeze 8 backstop, box score, change-up, farm team, forkball, grounder, no-hitter, outfield, pitchout, southpaw, splitter
throw: 3 peg
up, in ~: 5 at bat
VIP: 3 mgr, ump 5 coach 6 umpire 7 manager
woe: 4 loss 5 slump
baseball __: 3 bat, cap 5 glove
baseball-card flaw: 6 crease
__ Baseball Confederacy, The: 4 Iowa
baseballer: 4 ALer, NLer
California ~: 5 Angel
Chicago ~: 3 Cub
Cincinnati ~: 3 Red
Detroit ~: 5 Tiger
Kansas City ~: 5 Royal
Minnesota ~: 4 Twin
New York ~: 3 Met 4 Yank 6 Yankee
San Diego ~: 5 Padre
San Francisco ~: 5 Giant
Texas ~: 5 Astro
Washington ~: 3 Nat
Baseball is __ of inches: 5 a game
Baseball Tonight network: 4 ESPN
baseborn: 3 low 5 lowly 6 common, vulgar 7 ignoble 8 plebeian, ungentle, untitled 10 lower-class
__-base budgeting: 4 zero
based: 7 located
be ~ on: 4 rest 6 depend
__-based: 5 broad 7 reality
based on __ story: 5 a true
Basehart, Richard: 5 actor
__-base hit: 3 one, two 5 extra, three
Basel: 4 city, font, town 8 typeface
locale: Switzerland
river: 5 Rhine
Basel-__: 4 Land 5 Stadt
baseless: 4 idle 6 flimsy, untrue 7 invalid 8 fanciful, spurious 9 erroneous, unfounded, untenable 10 bottomless, fallacious, gratuitous, groundless, ill-founded

baseline
beyond the ~: 4 foul
in geometry: 5 x-axis
material: 4 lime
__ baseman: 5 first, third 6 second
Basemath
husband: 4 Esau
basement: 5 floor 6 cellar
bargain ~ caveat: 3 irr. 4 as is 5 irreg.
fixture: 5 drier, dryer 6 boiler, washer 7 furnace
in the ~: 4 last 5 below
like a wet ~: 4 dank 5 moldy, musty 6 smelly 8 mildewed
opposite: 4 loft 5 attic
reading: 5 meter
seating: 5 stool
__ basement: 7 bargain
baseness: 4 evil 8 iniquity, venality 9 depravity 10 corruption
Basenji: 3 dog 5 canid, hound 6 canine
baby ~: 3 pup 5 puppy
base on __: 5 balls
__-base paint: 3 oil 5 water 6 rubber
baserunner ploy: 4 lead 5 steal
bases
all ~ covered: 5 ready 8 prepared
column ~: 4 tori
__ base with: 5 touch
bash: 2 do 3 bit, dis, hit 4 beat, belt, blow, club, fest, fete, gala, mall, maul, orgy, slam, slap, slug 5 abuse, blast, flail, knock, party, paste, pound, punch, smash, smite, spree, swipe, thump, whack, whang, wreck 6 assail, attack, batter, fiesta, strike, thwack, wallop 7 assault, blowout, clobber, rough up, shindig, trounce 8 jamboree, mistreat, uppercut, wingding 9 criticize, festivity
celebrity ~: 5 roast
old-style: 5 smite
throw a ~: 4 host
see also party
Bash: 4 Dana
basher: 6 critic
__ Bashevis Singer: 5 Isaac
bashful: 3 coy, shy 5 aloof, chary, mousy, timid 6 demure, humble, modest, mousey, silent 7 ashamed, distant 8 blushing, reserved, reticent, retiring, sheepish, timorous 9 diffident, flinching, reclusive, shrinking, withdrawn 10 unassuming, uneffusive
Bashful: 5 dwarf
colleague: see dwarf
bashfulness: 7 modesty
Bashkir: 8 republic
capital: 3 Ufa
Basho, Matsuo: 4 poet 8 Japanese
verse: 5 haiku
basic: 3 key, raw 4 bare, easy, elem., main, real 5 basal, plain, stock, vital 6 bottom, earthy, innate, simple, staple 7 central, initial, minimal, organic, primary, radical, unfussy 8 alkaline, cardinal, inherent, integral, standard, ultimate 9 elemental, essential, innermost, intrinsic, necessary, primitive, principal, right-hand, uncomplex, vestigial 10 elementary, primordial, underlying
assumption: 5 axiom, given 9 principle
beliefs: 5 ethos
idea: 4 core, gist, pith 5 drift, heart 7 essence, keynote
not ~: 6 acidic
skills: 3 RRR 4 ABCs
solution: 6 alkali
unit: 4 atom 8 molecule
Basic (2003 film)
cast: Samuel L. Jackson, John Travolta
BASIC: 8 language
alternative: *see* computer language
term: 3 rem 4 go to
Basic 4: 6 cereal
competitor: *see* cereal
basically: 7 at heart 8 in effect 9 in essence, primarily, radically, virtually 10 implicitly, inherently, originally, ultimately
Basic Instinct (1992 film)
cast: Michael Douglas, George Dzundza, Sharon Stone
director: Paul Verhoeven
basics: 4 ABCs 5 needs 8 training 9 resources, rudiments
get down to ~: 6 lay out 7 explain 8 simplify, spell out
Basic Training of Pavlo Hummel, The
author: David Rabe
Basie, Count: 7 pianist, William 10 bandleader
genre: 4 jazz
basil: 4 herb
sauce: 5 pesto
__ basil: 4 bush 5 sweet
Basil: 4 Toni 5 saint 7 Dearden, Radford 8 Rathbone
costar: 5 Nigel
in Russian: 6 Vasily
successor: 4 Ivan
basilica: 6 church, temple 9 cathedral 10 tabernacle
feature: 3 pew 4 apse, nave
treasure: 4 icon, ikon 5 eikon
Basilio, Carmen: 5 boxer
milieu: 4 ring
Basil, Toni
song: Mickey (1982)
basin: 3 bay, pot, tub 4 bowl, ewer, font, lake, pond, pool, sink 5 fiord, fjord, inlet, lough 6 harbor, hollow, valley, vessel 7 harbour 8 boatyard, washbowl 9 container, reservoir, watershed 10 depression
catch ~: 4 sump
cirque ~: 4 tarn
companion: 4 ewer 7 pitcher
geological ~: 4 tala
holy-water ~: 4 font 5 stoup
mountain ~: 3 cwm 6 cirque
parker: 5 yacht
starter: 4 wash
stone ~: 6 lavabo
__ basin: 4 slop 5 catch, river, sugar, tidal
Basin __: 6 Street
__ Basin: 4 Saar 5 Great, Minas, Tarim 6 Donets
Basinger, Kim: 7 actress
film: Batman (1989)
Cool World (1992)
Final Analysis (1992)
The Informers (2009)
L.A. Confidential (1997, AA)
The Marrying Man (1991)
My Stepmother Is an Alien (1988)
Nadine (1987)
The Natural (1984)
Never Say Never Again (1983)
spouse: Alec Baldwin
basis: 3 bed, eat 4 core, crux, root 5 cause, gauge 6 ground, motive, origin, reason, source, theory 7 essence, footing, grounds, keynote, nucleus, premise, pretext, warrant 8 backbone, evidence, keystone, occasion, rudiment 9 authority, criterion, principle 10 antecedent, assumption, derivation, foundation, groundwork
movie ~ often: 4 book, play 5 novel
of comparison: 6 analog
of life: 6 carbon
tax ~: 5 ratal 10 assessment
without ~: 9 unfounded
basis __: 5 point 6 weight
__ basis: 4 cash, gold 7 accrual
bask: 3 sun, tan 4 laze, loll 5 relax 6 lounge, wallow 8 sunbathe 9 luxuriate
in: 5 revel, savor 7 delight
basker acquisition: 3 tan
Baskerville: 4 font 8 typeface
Baskervilles beast: 5 hound
basket: 4 hoop 5 score 6 dosser, hamper 10 two-pointer
capacity: 4 peck 6 bushel
easy ~: 5 lay up, tap in
ender: 4 ball
farm ~: 4 peck, skep 6 bushel
filler: 4 eggs 5 fruit 6 apples 7 produce
for dried fruit: 5 frail
jai alai ~: 5 cesta
like a ~: 5 woven
made a ~: 4 sank, wove
make a ~: 4 sink 5 plait, score, weave
making: 5 craft
Mexican ~ grass: 5 otate
picnic ~: 6 hamper
starter: 5 bread, waste
weaver's twig: 5 osier, withe 6 willow
wicker ~: 5 creel
basket __: 4 fern, fish, hilt, star 5 chair, weave 6 dinner, flower
__ basket: 3 tea 5 salad 6 market, picnic, pollen
basketball: 3 orb 4 game 5 hoops, sport 6 sphere
1997 ~ film: 6 Air Bud
announcer's cry: 5 swish
area in ~: 5 court 8 foul line
brand: 4 Voit
call: 4 foul
center's position: 5 pivot
coach: 3 Iba, Yow 4 Daly, Rupp 5 Brown, Olson 6 Knight, Wooden 7 Holzman 8 Auerbach 10 Carnesecca
defunct ~ org.: 3 ABA
filler: 3 air
Hall-of-Famer: 3 Iba, Yow 4 Bing, Bird, Daly, Gola, Reed, Rupp, West 5 Barry, Brown, Cousy, Ewing, Greer, Hayes, Issel, Jones, Lucas, Mikan, Olson 6 Baylor, Cowens, Dumars, Erving, Gervin, Holman, Jordan, Kay Yow, Knight, Lanier, Malone, McAdoo, Meyers, Monroe, Parish, Pettit, Stokes, Thomas, Twyman, Unseld, Walton, Wooden, Worthy 7 Barkley, Bellamy, Bradley, Dantley, Drexler, Frazier, Holzman, Johnson, K.C. Jones, Russell, Schayes, Tom Gola, Wilkens, Wilkins 8 Auerbach, Bob Cousy, Dan Issel, Dave Bing, Goodrich, Hal Greer, Havlicek, Heinsohn, Maravich, Olajuwon, Petrovic, Robinson, Sam Jones, Stockton, Thurmond 9 Ann Meyers, Archibald, Bob Lanier, Bob McAdoo, Bob Pettit, Jerry West, Larry Bird, Nat Holman, Robertson, Wes Unseld 10 Bill Walton, Carnesecca, Dave Cowens, Earl Monroe, Elvin Hayes, Jerry Lucas, John Wooden 11 Abdul-Jabbar, Chamberlain, DeBusschere
hoop site: 5 court 6 garage
infraction: 4 foul 7 palming
like many ~ pros: 4 tall 5 rangy
maneuver: 4 dunk, pass, pick, shot 5 block, press, steal 7 dribble, rebound
org.: 3 NBA
path: 3 arc 5 curve
player: 5 cager 8 hoopster
position: 3 ctr. 5 guard 6 center 7 forward
shot: 4 dunk, trey 5 deuce, lay up, tip-in 6 jumper 8 slam dunk 9 free throw
star: 3 Bol 4 Kidd 5 O'Neal 6 Bryant, Jordan, Pippen, Rodman 7 Gilmore, Iverson 8 Mourning, Olajuwon 9 Manute Bol
starter in ~: 6 tip-off
stat: 5 point 6 assist
substitute in ~: 8 sixth man
target: 3 net, rim 4 hoop
team: 4 Cavs, five, Heat, Jazz, Mavs, Nets, Suns 5 Bucks, Bulls, Hawks, Kings, Magic, Spurs 6 Knicks, Lakers, Pacers, Sixers 7 Celtics, Hornets, Nuggets, Pistons, Raptors, Rockets, Wizards 8 Clippers, Warriors 9 Cavaliers, Grizzlies, Mavericks
term: 3 rim 4 dunk, foul, hoop, pass 5 block, court, guard, lay up, press, shoot, steal, swish 6 center, period, tip-off 7 dribble, forward, palming, rebound, set shot, time-out 8 foul line, foul shot, hook shot, jump ball, jump shot, overtime, sixth man, slam dunk
tiebreaker: 2 OT 8 overtime
tourney: 3 NIT 4 NCAA
venue: 3 gym 5 arena, court
where ~ was first played: 4 YMCA
basketballer
Boston ~: 4 Celt 6 Celtic
Indiana ~: 5 Pacer
Los Angeles ~: 5 Laker
Miami ~: 4 Heat

New Jersey ~: 3 Net
Oklahoma City ~: 7 Thunder
Phoenix ~: 3 Sun
Sacramento ~: 4 King
San Antonio ~: 4 Spur
basketry palm: 4 nipa
Baskett: 5 James
basketwork material: 5 osier 6 willow
bit of: 4 twig 5 withe
Baskin-Robbins: 8 ice cream
order: 4 cone
see also ice cream
basmati: 4 rice 5 grain
Basov, Nicolay: 7 Russian 8 Nobelist 9 physicist
basque: 6 bodice
pas de ~: 4 step
saut de ~: 4 leap
Basque: 8 language
bonnet: 5 beret
port: 6 Bilbao
Basra: 4 city, port, town
locale: 4 Irak, Iraq
bass: 3 low 4 clef, deep, fish, male 5 Pinza, Ramey, range, voice 6 singer 7 caroler 8 game fish, low-toned, vocalist 9 Chaliapin, chorister, deep-toned, sport fish 10 low-pitched
booster: 3 amp
ender: 3 oon 4 wood
higher than ~: 5 tenor
instrument: 3 sax 4 viol 6 fiddle 9 saxophone
Italian ~: 5 Pinza
notation: 5 F clef
Russian ~: 9 Chaliapin
bass __: 3 sax 4 clef, drum, horn, viol 5 staff 6 fiddle, reflex
__ bass: 3 sea 4 kelp, rock 5 black, green, stone, white 6 calico, double, ground, silver, string
Bass: 3 Sam 8 Fontella
Bass __: 3 Ale 6 Strait
Bassani, Giorgio: 6 writer 7 Italian
bass drum: 4 drum 8 gran casa
Basse-__: 5 Terre
Basses-__: 5 Alpes
basset __: 4 horn 5 hound, table
Basset: 3 dog 5 canid, hound 6 canine
comic-strip ~: 4 Fred
features: 4 ears
like ~ hounds' ears: 5 loppy 6 floppy
__ Basset: 4 Fred
Basse-Terre: 4 city, town 7 capital
locale: 10 Guadeloupe
Bassett, Angela: 7 actress
film: How Stella Got Her Groove Back (1998)
Malcolm X (1992)
Music of the Heart (1999)
The Score (2001)
Waiting to Exhale (1995)
What's Love Got to Do With It (1993)
Bassey, Shirley: 6 singer
song: Goldfinger (1965)
Bass, Fontella
song: Rescue Me (1965)
bassinet: 3 bed 4 crib 6 cradle
bassist, jazz: 6 Mingus 7 Blanton 9 Pettiford
basslike fish: 5 snook
basso: 6 singer 9 chorister
bassoon: 4 reed, wind
cousin: 4 oboe
essentially: 4 tube
bass viol: 6 string 7 baryton
basswood: 4 tree 6 linden
bast: 4 hemp, jute, rope 5 fiber
fiber shrub: 5 urena
baste: 3 sew 4 beat, club, drub, lash, tack 5 pound, scold, whomp 6 batter, pummel, revile, stitch, thrash, wallop 7 clobber, moisten, trounce 9 castigate
basted: 5 moist
baster, turkey: 5 pipet 7 pipette
bastille: 4 gaol, jail 6 prison
Bastille
locale: 5 Paris 6 France
Bastille __: 3 Day
bastinado: 6 cudgel 9 truncheon
basting, rip out: 5 unsew
__-basting turkey: 4 self
bastion: 4 rock, wall 7 bulwark, citadel, defense, parapet, rampart 8 fastness, fortress, mainstay 10 breastwork, stronghold
bat: 4 cane, club, flap, slam, slug, wink 5 blink, stick, whack 6 animal, cudgel, mammal 7 clobber, flutter, missile 8 bludgeon, rapidity 9 truncheon 10 fledermaus
again: 5 rehit
an eye: 4 wink 5 blink
around: 4 roam 5 drift, prowl 6 confer, debate, ramble, wander 7 discuss, meander 8 talk over
at ~: 4 turn 7 hitting
back and forth: 6 debate 7 discuss, hash out
baseball ~ wood: 3 ash
ender: 3 boy, man, men 4 fish, fowl, girl
eyelashes: 5 flirt
go to ~ for: 3 aid 4 back, help 6 assist, defend 7 endorse, indorse, stick by, support 8 advocate, champion 10 rally round, speak up for
haven: 4 cave 5 antre, attic 6 belfry
like a ~: 6 aliped
maker: 5 lathe
move like a ~: 4 flit
navigational aid: 4 echo 5 sonar
not ~ an eye: 8 keep cool 9 stay loose
of an eye: 4 jiff 5 jiffy 6 minute, second
right off the ~: 6 at once, pronto 7 quickly, rapidly, swiftly 8 in a flash, in no time, on the fly 9 instantly, like a shot
starter: 4 bull, ding 5 brick
swinger: 6 hitter
turns at ~: 6 inning
wield a ~: 5 swing
bat __: 3 boy, ray 4 girl, turn 6 mizvah 7 mitsvah, mitzvah
__ bat: 5 brown, fruit, fungo 7 mastiff, vampire
Bat: 9 Masterson
Bat*21 (1988 film)
cast: Danny Glover, Gene Hackman, Jerry Reed
Bataan: 6 battle 9 peninsula
Bataille, Georges: 6 French, writer
Batang: 4 font 8 typeface
Batavia: 4 city, town
locale: 8 Illinois
batch: 3 lot, set 4 hunk, lump, mass, pack, pile, sort 5 array, bunch, clump, group, sheaf 6 amount, bundle 7 cluster, mixture 8 quantity, shipment 9 aggregate 10 assemblage, assortment, collection, cumulation
color ~: 6 dye lot
miller's ~: 5 grist
Batdance (1989 song)
artist: Prince
bate: 3 ebb 6 lessen, reduce, subdue 7 flutter 8 diminish, moderate, restrain
bateau: 4 boat 6 vessel
bated: 3 low 5 faint, piano, quiet
Bateman: 5 Jason 7 Justine
Bates: 2 H.E. 4 Alan 5 Kathy 6 Norman
establishment: 5 motel
Bates, Alan: 5 actor
Bates, H.E.: 6 writer 7 British
Bates, Kathy: 7 actress
film: Cheri (2009)
Dolores Claiborne (1995)
Dragonfly (2002)
Failure to Launch (2006)
Fried Green Tomatoes (1991)
Misery (1990, AA)
Prelude to a Kiss (1992)
Primary Colors (1998)
Shadows and Fog (1992)
Titanic (1997)
The Waterboy (1998)
__ bat for: 4 go to
bath: 2 WC 3 dip, loo, spa 4 pool, wash 6 laving, sponge 7 dunking, reverse, soaking 8 ablution, infusion, lavation, lavatory, restroom, washroom 9 cleansing, scrubbing 10 powder room
aftermath: 4 ring
combining form: 5 balne- 6 balneo-
decor: 4 tile
ender: 3 mat, tub 4 robe, room 5 house
item: 4 soap 5 towel 9 facecloth, washcloth
kind of ~: 3 dye
like a Turkish ~: 6 steamy
long ~: 4 soak
need a ~: 4 reek 5 smell, stink
powder: 4 talc 6 talcum
sponge: 5 loofa, luffa 6 loofah
starter: 3 sun 4 bird, foot
steam ~: 5 sauna
take a ~: 4 lose, wash 6 shower
bath __: 3 mat 5 salts, sheet, towel, water 6 sponge 7 mitsvah, mitzvah
__ bath: 3 dye, eye, mud 4 half, sitz, stop 5 blood, draw a, steam, take a, water 6 bubble, master, sponge 7 Turkish
Bath: 3 spa 4 city, town
brew: 3 tea
county: 4 Avon
locale: 5 Maine 7 England
river: 4 Avon
Bath __: 3 bun 5 chair
__ Bath and Beyond: 3 Bed
__ Bath Book: 6 Ernie's
bathe: 3 dip, lap, wet 4 lave, soak, swim, wade, wash 5 clean, cover, imbue, rinse, scrub, steep 6 splash 7 deterge, immerse, launder, moisten 8 saturate, submerse, surround 9 disinfect
starter: 3 sun
bathed: 5 clean 6 washed
bathetic: 5 mushy, trite 7 maudlin, mawkish 10 threadbare
__ Bathgate: 5 Billy
Bathgate, Andy: 6 skater 8 puckster
org.: 3 NHL
bathhouse: 6 bagnio, cabana
bathing: 9 immersion
go ~: 4 swim
starter: 3 sun
suit: 5 thong 6 bikini 7 maillot 8 one-piece, two-piece
suit top: 3 bra
bathing __: 3 cap 4 suit 6 beauty
Bathing Beauty (1944 film)
cast: Basil Rathbone, Red Skelton, Esther Williams
bathos: 5 nadir 7 schmalz, shmaltz 8 schmaltz 10 anticlimax
bathrobe: 6 kimono 7 cover-up
material: 4 wool 5 terry 6 fleece 8 chenille
bathroom: 2 WC 3 lav 4 john 7 latrine 8 lavatory
accessory: 5 towel 6 tissue
bottle: 5 iodin 6 iodine 8 peroxide
cabinet item: 4 Q-tip 5 floss 6 lotion 9 ChapStick, hand cream 10 toothbrush, toothpaste
cleaner: 5 Comet, Tilex 7 Mr. Clean
device: 5 scale
feature: 4 tile
fixture: 3 tub 6 shower
tissue: 5 Scott 6 Marcal 7 Charmin 8 Northern, Soft Weve 10 Cottonelle, White Cloud
worker: 5 tiler
baths: 4 spas 7 thermae 10 hot springs
Bathsheba
father: 5 Eliam
husband: 5 David, Uriah
son: 7 Solomon
bathtub
ancient Roman ~: 6 labrum
feature: 4 plug 5 drain
gin: 5 hooch 6 hootch
toy: 4 boat, duck
bathtub __: 3 gin
bathwater
like ~: 5 soapy
tester: 6 big toe
bathyscaphe operator: 5 diver
batik: 6 fabric 8 material
need: 3 dye
Batista, Fulgencio: 5 Cuban 8 dictator
batiste: 6 fabric
Batman: 4 hero 9 superhero 10 Bruce Wayne, comic strip
butler: 6 Alfred
creator: Bob Kane
dog: 3 Ace
foe: 5 Joker 7 Penguin, Riddler, Two-Face
headquarters: 4 cave
like TV's ~: 4 camp
partner: 5 Robin
portrayer: Christian Bale, George Clooney, Michael Keaton, Val Kilmer, Adam West
wear: 4 cape, mask

Batman (1989 film)
cast: Kim Basinger, Michael Keaton, Jack Nicholson
director: Tim Burton
Batman (ABC adventure)
cast: Madge Blake (Aunt Harriet)
Victor Buono (King Tut)
Yvonne Craig (Barbara Gordon/Batgirl)
Frank Gorshin (The Riddler)
Neil Hamilton (Commissioner Gordon)
Eartha Kitt (Catwoman)
Burgess Meredith (The Penguin)
Alan Napier (Alfred)
Julie Newmar (Catwoman)
Stafford Repp (Chief O'Hara)
Cesar Romero (The Joker)
Burt Ward (Dick Grayson/Robin)
Adam West (Bruce Wayne/Batman)
Batman __: 7 Forever, Returns
Batman and Robin: 3 duo **4** pair, team
Batman Begins (2005 film)
cast: Christian Bale, Michael Caine, Morgan Freeman, Katie Holmes, Liam Neeson, Gary Oldman
director: Christopher Nolan
Batman Forever (1995 film)
cast: Jim Carrey, Tommy Lee Jones, Nicole Kidman, Val Kilmer, Chris O'Donnell
director: Joel Schumacher
Batman Returns (1992 film)
cast: Danny DeVito, Michael Keaton, Michelle Pfeiffer, Christopher Walken
director: Tim Burton
Batman & Robin (1997 film)
cast: George Clooney, Chris O'Donnell, Arnold Schwarzenegger, Alicia Silverstone, Uma Thurman
director: Joel Schumacher
Bat Masterson (NBC western)
cast: Gene Barry (Bat Masterson)
baton: 3 rod **4** club, mace, wand **5** staff, stick **6** cudgel **9** billy club, truncheon **10** nightstick
magician's ~: 4 wand
passer's race: 5 relay
perform with a ~: 5 twirl **7** conduct
Baton Rouge: 4 city, port, town
locale: 9 Louisiana
river: 11 Mississippi
school: 3 LSU
__ Bator: 4 Ulan
bats in the __: 6 belfry
battalion: 4 army, unit **5** corps, force, squad **6** legion **7** legions, phalanx **9** multitude **10** contingent
group: 3 rgt. **4** regt. **8** regiment
batted
object: 6 eyelid **7** eyelash
run ~ in: 5 ribby
strike: 4 foul
__ batted in: 3 run
batten: 3 tie **4** slat **6** fasten, secure, thrive **7** board up, bolster, cover up, tighten **8** grow rich, nail down **9** clamp down
battened down: 4 fast, shut **6** secure
batter: 3 hit, mix, ram **4** bash, beat, drub, hurt, lash, maim, mall, maul, mush, pelt, slam **5** baste, dough, flail, knock, paste, pound, punch, smash, smite, thump, wreck **6** beetle, bruise, buffet, damage, hammer, injure, pommel, pummel, strike, thrash, thwack, wallop **7** assault, bombard, cake mix, clobber, lambast, mixture, rough up **8** lambaste
bane: 3 out **4** foul **5** slump **6** strike
challenge: 5 curve **8** forkball, splitter
ender: 4 cake
face the first ~: 5 start
goal: 3 hit **4** bunt **5** homer
hit the ~: 4 bean
ingredient: 3 egg **4** yolk **5** yeast
mix ~: 4 beat, stir
place: 3 box **4** home **5** plate
stat: 3 avg., RBI **7** average
to the pitcher: 3 foe
batter-__: 3 fry
battercake: 7 pancake **8** flapjack
battering ram: 6 engine
battery: 3 set **4** guns **5** array, group, suite **6** attack, felony, mayhem, series, volley **7** barrage, beating, offense, weapons **8** cannonry, violence **9** artillery, cannonade, onslaught
brand: 5 Delco
charge: 5 boost
chemical: 4 acid
part: 4 cell **5** anode **7** cathode
size: 2 AA **3** AAA **5** C cell, D cell
start a dead ~: 4 jump
terminal: 3 neg., pos. **5** anode **7** cathode **8** negative, positive
type: 5 D cell, NiCad, solar **7** dry cell, storage, Voltaic
word on a ~: 4 volt
__ battery: 3 AAA, air, dry **4** NiCd **5** nicad, solar **7** storage, Voltaic
Battery __: 4 Park
batting: 7 filling
order: 6 line-up
practice area: 4 cage
batting __: 3 eye **5** order **7** average
battle: 3 war **4** bout, feud, fray, to-do **5** brawl, clash, fight, mix-up, run-in, set-to, siege **6** action, affray, attack, combat, dustup, engage, fracas, go at it, have at, oppose, racket, resist, ruckus, rumpus, sortie, strife, tangle, tussle **7** assault, barrage, bombing, compete, contend, contest, crusade, dispute, grapple, mix it up, quarrel, rhubarb, ruction, warfare, wrangle, wrestle **8** brouhaha, campaign, conflict, fighting, long haul, skirmish, struggle **9** encounter, hostility, imbroglio, onslaught, scrimmage **10** blitzkrieg, contention, donnybrook, engagement, free-for-all, resistance
1798 ~: 4 Nile
1806 ~: 4 Jena
1813 ~: 4 Erie
1836 ~: 5 Alamo
1914 ~: 4 Yser **5** Marne, Ypres
1916 ~: 5 Somme
1918 ~: 5 Marne
1944 ~: 4 Truk **5** Bulge, Leyte
begin a ~: 6 attack, engage, invade
boldness in ~: 4 guts **5** valor **7** courage
conditioned by ~: 10 hard-bitten
cry: 5 motto, whoop **6** byword, charge, slogan, war cry **8** Geronimo, war whoop **9** catchword
doing ~: 5 at war
ender: 4 ship **5** field, front, truce, wagon **6** ground
equip for ~: 3 arm **5** rearm
lineup: 5 array
name meaning ~: 5 Boris
of honor: 4 duel
prepare for ~ old-style: 5 enarm
ready for ~: 5 armed **7** psyched
remove from a ~ zone: 7 retreat **8** evacuate, withdraw
site: 5 arena
WWI ~: 5 Aisne, Marne, Somme, Ypres
WWII ~: 6 Bataan
battle __: 3 cry **4** line, plan, star **5** clasp, dress, group, royal, wagon **6** jacket **7** cruiser, fatigue, lantern, station
battle-__: 3 axe **7** scarred
__ battle: 5 proxy **7** pitched
Battle: 8 Kathleen
Battle __: 3 Cry **4** Hymn
Battle __ Bulge: 5 of the
Battle __ of Freedom, The: 3 Cry
Battle __ of the Republic, The: 4 Hymn
__ Battle Book, The: 6 Butter
Battle Creek: 4 city, town
locale: 8 Michigan
Battle Cry
author: Leon Uris
battlefield: 5 arena, front
healer: 5 medic
battleground: 5 arena **8** landmark
1950s ~: 5 Korea
1960s ~: 3 Nam
Santa Anna ~: 5 Alamo
vehicle: 4 tank
Battle Hymn of the Republic, The
author: Julia Ward Howe
starter: 4 mine
word: 5 glory, sword, wrath
Battle, Kathleen: 4 diva **6** singer **7** soprano
specialty: 4 aria **5** opera
battlement: 4 wall **5** redan **7** parapet, rampart
opening: 6 crenel **8** crenelle
Battle of Alcazar, The
author: George Peele
Battle of Angels
author: Tennessee Williams
Battle of Blenheim, The
author: Robert Southey
battle of the __: 5 bands, sexes
Battle of the __: 5 Bulge
battler: 8 crusader **9** combatant **10** contestant
battleship: 4 boat, game **7** carrier, cruiser, flattop, frigate, gunboat **8** corvette, man-of-war **9** destroyer
blast: 5 salvo
letters: 3 USS
of 1898: 5 Maine
battleship __: 4 gray, grey
Battleship Potemkin, The
locale: 6 Odessa
__ Battle's Opinions of Whist: 3 Mrs.
battle station, take a: 3 man
battling: 4 at it **5** at war
batty: 3 mad **4** zany **5** flaky, inane **6** absurd, cuckoo, flakey **7** bananas, bonkers, touched **8** crackers **9** eccentric, half-baked, senseless **10** off-the-wall
Bat Yam: 4 city, town
locale: 6 Israel
bauble: 3 gem, toy **5** curio, dodad, jewel **6** doodad, geegaw, gewgaw, locket, tinsel, trifle **7** jewelry, spangle, trinket **8** gimcrack, nick-nack, ornament **9** bagatelle **10** decoration, knickknack
Baucus: 3 Max
Baudelaire, Charles: 4 poet **6** French
work: The Flowers of Evil
Baudolino
author: Umberto Eco
Baudrons: 3 cat **5** felid **6** feline
Bauer: 4 Hank **5** Eddie **6** Steven
Bauer, Steven: 5 actor
spouse: Melanie Griffith
Baugh: 5 Laura, Sammy
Baugh, Laura: 6 golfer
Baugh, Sammy: 2 QB
sport: 8 football
Bauhaus: 4 font **8** typeface
name: 4 Klee, Rohe
baum: 4 tree **6** German
Baum: 5 Vicki **6** L. Frank
Bauman: 3 Jon
Baum, L. Frank: 6 writer
beast: 4 lion
dog: 4 Toto
first name: 5 Lyman
work: Father Goose
The Wonderful Wizard of Oz
Bausch and __: 4 Lomb
bauxite: 3 ore **7** mineral
giant: 5 Alcoa
__ b'Av: 5 Tisha **6** Tishah
Bavaria
mountain range: 4 Harz, Rhon
peak: 3 Alp
river: 4 Isar **8** Naab. Eger
Bavarian cream __: 3 pie
Bavier: 7 Frances
bawdy: 4 blue, lewd, racy, rude **5** dirty, salty **6** coarse, ribald, risqué, unmeet, vulgar **7** naughty, obscene **8** off-color **9** low-minded **10** indecorous, indelicate
bawl: 3 cry, sob **4** bark, howl, mewl, pule, roar, wail, weep, yaup, yawp, yell, yowl **5** shout **6** bellow, boohoo, clamor, holler, lament, scream, shriek, snivel **7** blubber, bluster, screech, ululate, whimper **9** caterwaul, shed a tear **10** take it hard, vociferate
out: 4 lash, whip **5** scold **6** berate, rebuke **7** upbraid **8** reproval **9** castigate, reprehend **10** upbraiding, vituperate
bawl __: 3 out
bawler: 7 crybaby
bawling: 5 noisy **7** in tears, tearful **9** sniveling
out: 6 earful, rebuke **8** scolding **9** reprimand
sound: 3 wah
Bax: 6 Arnold
Baxter: 3 Les, Ted **4** Anne **5** James **6** Warner **8** Meredith
Baxter, Anne: 7 actress
film: All About Eve (1950)

The Ten Commandments (1956)
Baxter, Meredith: 7 actress
spouse: David Birney
bay: 3 arm, cry 4 bark, Coos, cove, Faxa, gulf, howl, Huna, nook, roar, tree, Vigo, wail, yowl 5 basin, bayou, bight, brown, Casco, color, Dvina, fiord, firth, fjord, frith, Fundy, Green, horse, inlet, James, Manta, niche, Onega, shout, shrub, Tampa 6 Abukir, alcove, Baffin, bellow, Bengal, Biscay, Botany, Brunei, cranny, Dublin, equine, harbor, Hudson, lagoon, laguna, laurel, Manila, Mobile, Naples, Newark, recess, Sagami, Sarera, Suruga, Ungava, Valona, Walvis, Whales 7 Delagoa, estuary, Glacier, harbour, Prudhoe, reddish, Saginaw, Setúbal, Thunder, ululate, Walfish 8 Biscayne, Buzzards, Cardigan, chestnut, Delaware, Georgian, Hangchow, Hangzhou, Humboldt, Jiaozhou, Kiaochow, Monterey, San Pablo 9 anchorage, Apalachee, caterwaul, Frobisher, Galveston, Guanabara, Magdalena, Penobscot, Pensacola, ululation 10 Chesapeake, Guantánamo, Port Philip
Alabama ~: 6 Mobile
Alaska ~: 7 Prudhoe
Albania ~: 6 Valona
Antarctica ~: 6 Whales
Arctic ~: 6 Baffin
at ~: 5 treed 6 caught, frozen 7 held off, in check, trapped 8 cornered, helpless 9 paralysed, powerless 10 motionless
Atlantic ~: 4 Faxa, Vigo 5 Fundy 6 Biscay, Walvis 7 Setúbal, Walfish 8 Biscayne, Delaware 9 Frobisher, Penobscot 10 Chesapeake
Australia ~: 6 Botany 10 Port Philip
away from the ~: 6 inland
Bangladesh ~: 6 Bengal
Beaufort Sea ~: 7 Prudhoe
bring to ~: 3 nab 4 trap, tree 5 catch 6 collar, corner 7 capture
California ~: 8 Monterey, San Pablo
Canada ~: 5 Fundy, James 6 Baffin, Hudson, Ungava 8 Georgian 9 Frobisher
China ~: 8 Hangchow, Hangzhou, Jiaozhou, Kiaochow
color kin: *see* brown color
Cuba ~: 10 Guantánamo
Ecuador ~: 5 Manta
Egypt ~: 6 Abukir
ender: 4 side 5 berry
Florida ~: 5 Tampa 8 Biscayne 9 Apalachee, Pensacola
France ~: 6 Biscay
Greenland ~: 6 Baffin
Gulf of Mexico ~: 5 Tampa 6 Mobile 9 Galveston, Pensacola
hold at ~: 5 parry, repel 6 rebuff 7 fend off, repulse, ward off 8 stave off
Iceland ~: 4 Faxa, Huna
Indian Ocean ~: 6 Bengal 7 Delagoa
Indonesia ~: 6 Sarera
Ireland ~: 6 Dublin
Irish ~: 5 Sligo
Italy ~: 6 Naples
Japan ~: 6 Sagami, Suruga
Lake Huron ~: 7 Saginaw
Maine ~: 5 Casco 9 Penobscot
Malaysia ~: 6 Brunei
Maryland ~: 10 Chesapeake
Massachusetts ~: 8 Buzzard's
Mexico ~: 9 Magdalena
Michigan ~: 7 Saginaw
Mideast ~: 6 Abukir
Mozambique ~: 7 Delagoa
Myanmar ~: 6 Bengal
Namibia ~: 6 Walvis 7 Walfish
New Guinea ~: 6 Sarera
New Jersey ~: 6 Newark 8 Delaware
Norwegian ~: 5 fiord, fjord
Nova Scotia ~: 5 Fundy
Pacific ~: 5 Manta 8 Monterey
Philippines ~: 5 Subic 6 Manila
Portland's ~: 5 Casco
Portugal ~: 7 Setúbal
Ross Sea ~: 6 Whales
rum: 10 aftershave
Russia ~: 5 Dvina, Onega
sick ~: 8 hospital 9 infirmary
South China Sea ~: 6 Brunei
Spain ~: 4 Vigo 6 Biscay
starter: 4 rose, sick
Texas ~: 9 Galveston
transport: 5 ferry 9 hydrofoil
tree: 6 laurel
Virginia ~: 10 Chesapeake
Wales ~: 8 Cardigan
White Sea ~: 5 Dvina, Onega
window: 5 belly, oriel 6 paunch
Wisconsin ~: 5 Green
bay ___: 3 ice, oil, rum 4 leaf, lynx, salt, tree 6 antler, laurel, poplar, window 7 scallop
___ bay: 3 red 4 bomb, bull, case, lock, sick 5 cargo, drive, sweet 7 payload
___ Bay: 3 Emu, Ise 4 Back, Coos, Faxa, Hilo 5 Casco, Dvina, Goose, Green, James, Manta, Onega, Subic, Tampa, Tiger, Tokyo 6 Baffin, Botany, Hudson, Manila, Mobile, Newark, Oyster, Sarera, Ungava, Walvis 7 Chaleur, Delagoa, Glacier, Montego, Prudhoe, Saginaw, Thunder
___-Bay: 5 Put-in
___ Ba Yah: 3 Kum
Bay Area county: 4 Napa 5 Marin
bayberry: 4 tree 5 fruit, shrub 6 candle
___ Bay Buccaneers: 5 Tampa
Bay City: 4 town
locale: 8 Michigan
Bay City Rollers
homeland: Scotland
song: Money Honey (1976) Saturday Night (1975)
___ Bay Company: 7 Hudson's
bayer: 3 dog 4 wolf 5 husky 6 coyote
Bayer: 7 aspirin 9 analgesic 10 painkiller
competitor: *see* pain reliever brand 5 Aleve
___ Bayer Sager: 6 Carole
Bayes: 4 Nora
Bayeux neighbor: 4 St. Lô
Bayh: 4 Evan 5 Birch
bay leaf: 4 herb
Baylor: 3 Don 4 univ. 5 Elgin 6 school 10 university
athletes: 5 Bears
conference: 9 Big Twelve
locale: 4 Waco 5 Texas
Baylor, Don
sport: 8 baseball
Baylor, Elgin: 5 cager
milieu: 5 court
org.: 3 NBA
sport: 10 basketball
bayman: 7 clammer
Bay of ___: 3 Uri 4 Acre, Pigs 6 Biscay
Bay of Bengal
city: 6 Madras
island: 7 Nicobar 8 Andamans
river to the ~: 6 Ganges 7 Cauvery, Hooghly, Krishna, Salween 8 Godavari 9 Irrawaddy
Bay of Biscay
ocean: 3 Atl. 8 Atlantic
peninsula: 6 Iberia
port: 5 Gijón 6 Bilbao
Bay of Fundy
feature: 4 tide
river to the ~: 6 St. John
Bay of Naples
island: 5 Capri
Bay of Pigs
locale: 4 Cuba
bayonet: 4 stab 5 knife 6 weapon
Bayonne: 4 city, port, town
locale: 6 France 9 New Jersey
bayou: 3 arm, bay 4 gulf 5 inlet, swamp 6 lagoon
boat: 6 bateau
dweller: 5 Cajan, Cajun 6 Creole
feature: 5 marsh
___ Bayou: 4 Blue
___ Bay Packers: 5 Green
Bayreuth: 4 city, town
locale: 7 Germany
Bay State
see Massachusetts
Baywatch (NBC adventure)
cast: Traci Bingham (Jordan Tate)
Yasmine Bleeth (Caroline Holden)
Donna D'Errico (Donna Marco)
Nicole Eggert (Summer Quinn)
Carmen Electra (Lani McKenzie)
Erika Eleniak (Shauni McLain)
David Hasselhoff (Mitch Bucannon)
Pamela Anderson Lee (C.J. Parker)
Gena Lee Nolin (Neely Kapshaw)
Alexandra Paul (Stephanie Holden)
Parker Stevenson (Craig Pomeroy)
setting: 5 beach 6 Malibu
bazaar: 4 fair, fete, mart 6 market 7 benefit 8 emporium 10 flea market, fund-raiser
ancient ~: 5 agora
Arab ~: 3 suk, suq 4 souk
indoor ~: 4 mall
___ Bazaar: 7 Harper's
bazoo: 3 yap 4 nose, puss, trap 5 mouth, snoot 6 honker, kisser
bazooka: 9 artillery
essentially: 4 tube
target: 4 tank
Bazooka: 3 gum 9 bubble gum
bazookas: 8 weaponry
BB: 4 ammo, shot 6 pellet
gun: 8 air rifle
gun sound: 4 ping
propellant: 3 air
BB ___: 3 gun 4 shot
B&B: 3 inn
alternative: 5 motel
part of ~: 3 bed 9 breakfast
B.B.: 4 King
b-ball: 5 hoops
BBC
competitor: 3 ITV
home: 6 London
meridian: 3 GMT
nickname: 4 Beeb
receiver: 4 tele 5 telly
series: 5 Dr. Who
bbl.: 4 meas.
bigger than a ~: 3 hhd.
see also barrel
B.C.: 4 prov. 5 comic 8 province
cartoonist: 4 Hart
character: 4 Grog, Thor
currency: 4 clam
home: 4 cave
insect: 3 ant
neighbor: 3 Alb., Ida. 4 Alta.
sound: 3 zot
see also British Columbia
BCE, part of: 3 Era 6 Before, Common 7 Current
B-complex: 7 vitamin
acid: 5 folic
component: 4 PABA 6 biotin, niacin 7 choline 8 inositol, Vitamin H
B.D.: 4 Wong
___ B. Davis: 3 Ann
___ B. DeMille: 5 Cecil
bdl.: 3 pkg.
see also bundle
Bd. of Ed. concern: 3 sch.
___ B. Driftwood: 4 Otis
be: 4 live, verb 5 exist, occur 6 happen, remain 7 breathe, subsist, survive 9 come about, take place, transpire 10 come to pass
at: 6 attend, show up
in French: 4 être
in Italian: 3 ser
in Latin: 4 esse
in Spanish: 3 ser
be ___ as it may: 4 that
be-___: 3 bop, ins
___ be!: 5 Glory
___-be: 5 would
Be: 4 elem. 7 element 9 beryllium
4 for ~: 4 at. no.
Be ___, It's My Heart: 7 Careful
Be ___ to Your School: 4 True
___ Be: 3 I'll 5 Let It
be a ___: 3 pal 5 sport
Bea: 6 Arthur, Lillie 9 Benaderet
beach: 4 land 5 coast, plage, shore, wreck 6 maroon, strand 8 littoral, seacoast, seashore 10 oceanfront, waterfront
acquisition: 3 tan
bird: 3 ern 4 erne, gull 7 seagull
building: 3 hut 6 cabana
cause of ~ erosion: 4 tide
creation: 6 castle
ender: 4 head, side, wear 5 front, scape 6 comber
enjoy the ~: 5 bathe
find: 5 shell
impostor: 5 ho-dad

item: 5 radio, towel 6 cooler, lotion
like a ~ day: 5 sunny
like the ~: 5 sandy
location: 5 coast
on the ~: 6 ashore
patron: 6 basker
prohibition: 6 no pets
relax at the ~: 3 sun 4 bask 5 float
residue: 4 grit
surface: 4 sand
terrace: 4 berm 5 berme
toy: 4 ball, pail
water: 4 surf
wear: 5 thong 6 bikini, caftan, kaftan, sandal, shorts, trunks 7 cover-up, maillot 8 one-piece, swimsuit, two-piece
woe: 4 burn 7 sunburn
beach __: 3 bum, pea 4 ball, berm, crab, face, flea, plum 5 aster, buggy, drift, grass, ridge, scarp
__ beach: 4 free 6 muscle 7 barrier
Beach __: 3 Red 4 Baby, Boys 5 Party
__ Beach: 4 Long, Palm, Vero 5 China, Cocoa, Dover, Miami, Omaha, On the, Pismo 6 Bikini, Delray, Laguna, Myrtle, Pebble 7 Daytona, Newport, Pompano
Beacham: 9 Stephanie
beach ball filler: 3 air
Beach Blanket Bingo (1965 film)
cast: Frankie Avalon, Annette Funicello, Paul Lynde
director: William Asher
Beach Boys
members: Wilson, Love, Jardine
song: Barbara Ann (1966)
Be True to Your School (1963)
California Girls (1965)
Dance, Dance, Dance (1964)
Don't Worry Baby (1964)
Fun, Fun, Fun (1964)
Good Vibrations (1966)
Help Me, Rhonda (1965)
I Get Around (1964)
In My Room (1963)
Kokomo (1988)
Rock and Roll Music (1976)
Sloop John B (1966)
Surfer Girl (1963)
Surfin' Safari (1962)
Surfin' U.S.A. (1963)
When I Grow Up (1964)
Wouldn't It Be Nice (1966)
beachcomber: 6 loafer 7 forager 8 gadabout, scrounge, wanderer 9 scavenger
find: 5 conch, shell
tool: 4 pail 5 sieve 6 bucket
beached: 6 ashore 7 aground 8 stranded
Beaches (1988 film)
cast: John Heard, Barbara Hershey, Bette Midler
director: Garry Marshall
beachhead: 8 foothold, lodgment
Beach Party (1963 film)
cast: Frankie Avalon, Bob Cummings, Annette Funicello, Dorothy Malone
director: William Asher
__ Beach Party: 6 Muscle
Beach, The (2000 film)
cast: Leonardo DiCaprio, Tilda Swinton
director: Danny Boyle
Be a Clown
composer: Cole Porter
__ be a cold day...: 4 It'll
beacon: 4 beam, lamp, sign 5 flare, guide, light 6 Pharos, signal 7 lantern, lookout, warning 8 lodestar 9 indicator 10 lighthouse, watchtower
radar ~: 5 racon
__ beacon: 5 radar, radio
Beacon __: 4 Hill
bead: 4 blob, drop, glob 6 bubble 7 driblet, droplet, globule, granule, trinket 8 spherule
draw another ~ on: 5 reaim
draw a ~ on: 3 aim 5 aim at, train
ender: 4 work
material: 5 coral, nacre 9 turquoise
rosary ~: 3 ave 4 gaud
tube-shaped ~: 5 bugle
bead __: 4 fern, test, tree 5 plane, plant 7 molding
__ bead: 4 rail, stop 5 borax, bugle, weave 7 glazing
beadle: 6 sexton
Beadle, George: 8 Nobelist 10 geneticist
__ bead on: 4 get a 5 draw a
beads: 4 peag 5 sewan 6 choker, rosary, seawan, wampum 7 jewelry 8 necklace, ornament
certain ~: 5 sweat
Indian ~: 4 peag 5 sewan 6 wampum
item with ~: 6 abacus
mantra ~: 4 mala 6 rosary
__ beads: 4 love 5 worry 6 Baily's, prayer
beady: 10 glittering
beady-__: 4 eyed
beagle: 3 dog 4 boat, ship 5 canid, hound, pooch 6 canine, Snoopy
feature: 3 ear
beak: 3 neb, nib 4 bill, nose 5 mouth, snoot, snout 6 schnoz 7 schnozz 9 proboscis, schnozzle 10 schnozzola
base: 4 cere
bird ~: 3 neb, nib
combining form: 5 rostr- 6 rhamph-, rostri-, rostro- 7 rhampho-
beaked: 8 aquiline
vessel: 5 cruet 6 beaker, carafe 7 alembic
beaker: 3 cup 5 flask, glass, stein 7 alembic 9 container, glassware, lab vessel
cousin: 4 vial 5 flask, phial
material: 5 glass, Pyrex
Beale __ Blues: 6 Street
Beale Street
locale: 7 Memphis
be-all and __-all: 3 end
Beals: 8 Jennifer
beam: 3 ray 4 boom, emit, grin, jamb, lath, pole, post, prop, rump, shed, slow, spar, stud 5 brace, flash, gleam, jambe, joist, level, shaft, shine, slant, smile, spark, stare, strut, train 6 beacon, column, girder, lintel, member, piling, pillar, rafter, regard, streak, timber 7 give off, glitter, radiate, send off, sparkle, trestle 8 crossbar, throw off, transmit 9 broadcast, emanation, irradiate, stanchion, two-by-four 10 cantilever, crosspiece
balance ~: 5 event
boat's ~: 5 width
bright ~: 3 ray 5 laser 9 spotlight
combining form: 5 actin- 6 actino-
emit an intense ~: 4 lase
ender: 3 ish
fastener: 5 rivet
floor ~: 6 header
generator: 5 laser, maser
make ~: 4 send 5 cheer, elate, liven 6 buoy up, lift up, perk up, please, puff up, thrill, tickle, turn on 7 delight, elevate, gladden, happify, hearten, lighten, overjoy, satisfy 9 enrapture, inebriate, make happy 10 exhilarate, intoxicate
nautical: 7 carling, cathead
off the ~: 4 loco, lost 6 astray 9 wandering
on the ~: 5 adept, aware, right 6 posted, wise to 7 correct 9 cognizant 10 acceptable, conversant, proficient, unmistaken
penetrating ~: 4 X-ray 5 laser
railroad ~: 3 tie
roof ~: 6 header
ship ~: 4 keel
splitter: 5 prism
starter: 3 sun 4 horn, moon 5 cross
steel ~: 4 I-bar, L bar 5 I-beam 6 girder
supporting ~: 5 truss
beam __: 3 sea 4 fill, mill, wind 5 brick, light, reach, trawl 6 weapon 7 antenna, compass
__ beam: 3 box, low, tie 4 arch, grub, high, warp 5 cloth, laser, on the, radio
Beam __, Scotty!: 4 me up
Beame: 3 Abe
beaming: 3 lit 5 aglow, happy, lit up, lucid, shiny, sunny 6 ablaze, bright, elated, flashy, joyful, lucent 7 blazing, fulgent, glowing, lambent, radiant, shining 8 cheerful, dazzling, euphoric, gleaming, luminous, lustrous, splendid 9 beautiful, brilliant, effulgent, refulgent, sparkling 10 flying high
Beamon, Bob: 10 long jumper
beams
high ~: 7 brights
low ~: 6 dimmer
beamy: 4 wide 5 broad
bean: 3 nob, nut, pea 4 conk, fava, lima, mung, navy, pole, snap, soya 5 green, pinto, tonka 6 adzuki, castor, coffee, cowpea, frijol, kidney, legume, lentil, noggin, noodle, string 7 frijole, haricot, refried, vanilla 8 garbanzo 9 vegetable
Asian ~: 3 soy, urd
chili ~: 5 pinto 6 kidney
chocolate ~: 5 cacao
cluster ~: 4 guar
curd: 4 tofu
ender: 3 bag 4 pole 5 stalk
horse ~: 4 fava
hull: 3 pod
Japanese ~: 6 adzuki
locust ~: 5 carob
Mexican ~: 6 frijol 7 frijole
paste: 4 miso
pole: 5 stalk
soup ~: 4 lima
starter: 3 soy 4 buck, snap 5 broad, jelly
use one's ~: 5 think
vine of the ~ family: 5 vetch
bean __: 3 pod, pot 4 ball, curd, shot, tree 5 aphid, caper 6 beetle, weevil 7 counter, sprouts
__ bean: 3 pea, wax 4 bayo, buck, bush, ceci, fava, jack, lima, Lyon, moth, mung, navy, pole, rice, snap, soya, wild 5 azuki, black, broad, cacao, chile, chili, cocoa, green, horse, pinto, screw, shell, sieva, sword, tonka 6 adsuki, adzuki, butter, castor, chilli, French, Indian, kidney, locust, mescal, ordeal, poison, potato, runner, string, tepary, velvet, winged 7 Calabar, cluster, jumping, vanilla
Bean: 2 L.L. 3 Roy 4 Alan, Andy, Sean 5 Orson
Bean __, The: 5 Trees 6 Eaters
beanbag: 3 toy 6 pillow 7 cushion
beanbag __: 5 chair
beanball: 5 pitch
bean counter: 3 CPA 4 acct. 10 accountant
top ~: 3 CFO
Bean Eaters, The
author: Gwendolyn Brooks
beanery: 5 diner 6 eatery 10 restaurant
__ Beanfield War, The: 7 Milagro
beanie: 3 cap, hat 8 skullcap
Beanie Babies: 3 fad 5 craze
beanpole: 4 slim 5 lanky, scrag, stick 7 slender
beans: 5 dough 6 annual
full of ~: 5 wrong 8 mistaken
partner: 4 pork
prepare coffee ~: 5 grind
prepare Mexican ~: 5 refry
spill the ~: 3 rat 4 blab, blat, leak, sing, talk, tell 5 blurt, let on 6 tattle 7 confess
__ beans: 5 baked, jelly 7 refried
beanstalk: 4 slim 5 lanky 7 slender
owner: 5 giant
Bean Town: 6 Boston
Bean Trees, The
author: Barbara Kingsolver
Beany
pal: 5 Cecil
bear: 2 go 3 lug 4 cart, have, hold, lump, Pooh, take, tend, tote 5 abide, allow, beget, breed, bring, brook, carry, ferry, grump, sloth, stand, stick, teddy, ursid, yield 6 accept, afford, animal, Boo-Boo, convey, endure, Fozzie, harbor, Kodiak, mammal, permit, Smokey, suffer, uphold 7 deliver, exhibit, grizzly, harbour, include, possess, produce, receive, ride out, signify, stomach, support, survive, sustain, undergo 8 cinnamon, engender, fructify, grumbler, maintain, omnivore, shoulder, tolerate, transfer 9 entertain, Gentle Ben, propagate, put up with, reproduce, send forth, silvertip, transport, withstand 10 bring forth, Paddington
advice: 4 sell
baby ~: 3 cub

bring to ~: 3 use 5 apply, exert 6 employ 8 exercise
cartoon ~: 4 Yogi 6 Boo Boo
CBer's ~: 3 cop
combining form: 4 arct- 5 arcto-
constellation: 4 Ursa
counterpart: 4 bull
cross to ~: 4 onus 5 trial
down: 3 try 5 labor, press 6 reduce, strain, strive 9 overpower
down on: 6 burden, coerce, compel, strain 7 focus on 8 draw near, get after
ender: 3 cat, ish 4 skin 5 berry
female: 3 sow
food: 5 honey 7 berries
foot: 3 paw
grin and ~ it: 4 take 5 stick 6 adjust, submit 7 stomach 8 overlook, tolerate
hair: 3 fur
home: 3 den, zoo 4 lair 5 woods 6 forest
hug: 6 clench
in Latin: 4 Ursa
in mind: 4 heed 6 recall 7 bethink 8 remember 9 recognize, recollect 10 reckon with
in Spanish: 3 oso
Kipling, Rudyard ~: 5 Baloo
male: 4 boar
name meaning ~: 5 Bjorn 6 Ursula
of very little brain: 4 Pooh
on: 3 sit 4 lean 6 affect 7 concern, pertain 9 pertain to
out: 5 prove 6 attest, ratify, verify 7 certify, confirm, justify, reflect, warrant, witness 8 validate 10 strengthen
starter: 3 bug
stuffed ~: 5 Teddy
trap: 5 snare
up: 5 shore 6 endure, manage, resist 7 bolster, weather
upon: 5 touch 6 regard, relate
(upon): 5 weigh
up under: 5 stick 7 sustain
utterance: 3 grr 5 growl, grunt
with: 4 take 5 abide, stand 6 excuse, suffer 7 forgive, stomach, sustain 8 overlook, tolerate
woolly ~: 3 bug 6 insect
bear __: 3 hug, out 4 claw, down 5 fruit, grass 6 garden, leader
__ bear: 3 ant, sun 4 cave 5 black, brown, honey, Malay, panda, polar, sloth, teddy, water, white 6 Kodiak, woolly 7 grizzly
Bear: 4 peak 5 mount, river 6 Bryant 8 mountain
author: Marian Engel
River locale: 4 Utah 5 Idaho 7 Wyoming
Bear __: 7 Stearns
__ Bear: 4 Br'er, Papa, Yogi 5 Great 6 Edward, Lesser, Little, Smokey 7 Running
bearable: 7 livable 8 liveable, moderate 9 tolerable
bearably: 8 somewhat
bearcat: 5 panda
beard: 4 defy, fuzz, hair, mask 6 goatee 7 stubble, Vandyke 8 disguise, imperial, whiskers
combining form: 5 pogon- 6 pogono-
cut the ~ off: 5 shave
ender: 6 tongue
grain ~: 3 awn 6 arista
locale: 4 chin
pluck by the ~: 4 twit
remover: 5 razor
site: 3 jaw
starter: 4 Blue, gray, grey 5 Black, goats, white
the lion: 4 face 5 brave 8 confront
Beard: 5 Frank, James 7 Charles
bearded: 5 hairy 7 barbate, bristly, goateed, hirsute, unshorn 8 unshaven 9 incognito, whiskered
animal: 3 gnu 4 goat 6 aoudad
as grain: 5 awned
brothers' surname: 5 Smith
flower: 4 iris
Beard, James: 4 chef
beardless: 5 green 6 callow 8 immature 10 adolescent
Beardsley: 6 Aubrey
beard the __: 4 lion
bearer: 5 envoy, payee, toter 6 herald, porter, runner 7 carrier, courier 8 conveyer, emissary 9 consignee, messenger
combining form: 4 -pher, -phor 5 -phore
starter: 3 cup, fur 4 live, mace, tale 5 torch, train
bearer __: 4 bond
__ Bearer: 5 Water 7 Serpent
bear in __: 4 mind
bearing: 3 air, way 4 look, mien, pose, west 5 front, poise, style 6 aspect, import, manner, regard, stance 7 conduct, heading, kinship, meaning, posture, purport 8 attitude, behavior, carriage, demeanor, presence, relation, tendency 9 direction, relevance, semblance 10 appearance, connection, deportment, generation, pertinence
combining form: 6 -gerous, -parous, -phoria 7 -phorous
have a ~ on: 6 regard 7 concern
in heraldry: 6 charge 8 ordinary
on: 8 relevant
starter: 3 fur 4 ever, tale 5 child
bearing __: 4 rail, rein, wall 5 plate, sword
__ bearing: 4 ball 5 plain 6 roller, thrust
bearings: 3 aim 5 track 8 location, position 9 direction, situation
get one's ~: 6 orient
bearish: 5 crass, cross, crude, gruff, rough, surly, testy 6 coarse, cranky, crusty, grumpy, ireful, lumpen, oafish, ornery, touchy, vulgar 7 bilious, boorish, doltish, grouchy, ill-bred, loutish, peevish, uncivil, uncouth 8 choleric, churlish, cloddish, growling, grumpish, snappish, snarling 9 crotchety, difficult, dyspeptic, irascible, irritable, querulous, splenetic 10 ill-natured, out of sorts, ungracious
bearlike: 6 ursine
mammal: 5 koala, panda
name meaning ~: 5 Orson
béarnaise: 5 sauce
__ Be Around: 3 I'll
bear paw: 6 pastry
Bears: 6 eleven
home: 7 Chicago
org.: 3 NFC
rival: *see* NFL team
see also Baylor, Brown
__ Bears: 5 Gummi, Teddy 6 Silver
Bearse: 6 Amanda
bearskin: 3 fur, rug
Béart: 10 Emmanuelle
Bear, The
author: William Faulkner
bear: 4 Bart
Beasley: 6 Allyce
beast: 5 brute, churl, demon, devil, fiend, swine 6 animal, daemon, daimon, lummox, savage 7 critter, crittur, Lucifer, monster, varment, varmint, wild man 8 creature 9 archfiend, barbarian, hellhound 10 blackguard
combining form: 4 ther- 5 -there, thero- 6 therio-
of burden: 2 ox 3 ass, yak 4 mule 5 burro, camel, horse, llama 6 donkey
Beast
author: Peter Benchley
beastly: 3 low 4 base, evil, grim, mean, vile 5 brute, cruel, feral, harsh, rabid 6 animal, brutal, coarse, ferine, fierce, ogrish, savage, unkind, vulgar, wanton 7 bestial, boorish, brutish, callous, hurtful, inhuman, untamed, vicious 8 barbaric, depraved, fiendish, inhumane, pitiless, ruthless, sadistic, unbroken, vengeful 9 barbarous, cutthroat, ferocious, malicious, merciless, truculent, unbridled 10 outrageous, vindictive
place: 3 zoo 9 menagerie
see also awful
Beastmaster, The (1982 film)
role: 3 Dar 4 Kiri, Maax
beast of __: 4 prey 6 burden
beasts: 5 fauna, stock 6 cattle
king of ~: 4 lion
Beasts and Super Beasts
author: Saki
Beast's companion: 5 Belle 6 Beauty
beat: 3 cap, hit, mix, ram, rap, top, win, zap 4 area, bang, bash, belt, best, cane, club, cuff, drop, drub, drum, flap, flog, foil, harm, lash, lick, mall, mash, maul, pelt, post, rime, rout, slam, slap, slug, sock, stir, swat, take, tick, trim, whip, whup, worn 5 abuse, all in, baste, blend, break, crush, flail, kaput, knock, meter, outdo, parry, pound, pulse, punch, rhyme, route, scoop, smack, spank, stamp, swing, tempo, throb, thump, tired, trump, upset, weary, whack, worst 6 accent, batter, beetle, better, bruise, buffet, bushed, cudgel, defeat, dished, exceed, gammon, hammer, injure, larrup, lather, outrun, outwit, patrol, patter, pommel, pooped, pummel, punish, puzzle, quiver, rebuff, resist, rhythm, ripple, rounds, stress, strike, subdue, switch, thrash, thwack, wallop 7 agitate, at a loss, cadence, cadency, circuit, clobber, conquer, drained, flutter, get past, hold off, lambast, measure, mystify, nose out, outplay, overrun, pulsate, repulse, scourge, surpass, trounce, vibrate, wearied, worn out 8 bludgeon, defeated, dog-tired, dragging, fatigued, give it to, knock out, lambaste, maltreat, outclass, out of gas, outrival, outscore, outshine, outsmart, outstrip, overcome, overtake, push back, turn back, undulate, vanquish 9 castigate, checkmate, exhausted, force back, itinerary, oscillate, overpower, overwhelm, palpitate, played out, pulsation, throbbing, vibration, withstand 10 knocked out, outperform, put to shame, undulation
around the bush: 5 fence, hedge, skirt, stall, waver 6 ramble, waffle 9 pussyfoot
as wings: 4 flap
at bridge: 3 set
back: 4 rout 5 repel 6 rebuff
badly: 4 rout 5 cream, skunk, stomp, thump, whomp
barely ~: 3 nip 4 clip, edge, nose 7 nose out 8 slip past
down: 5 quell 6 reduce 7 flatten, oppress 8 suppress 9 overpower
fast: 9 palpitate
for a poet: 5 meter
get ~: 4 lose
it: 2 go 3 git, lam, rip, run 4 exit, flee, scat, shoo 5 hurry, leave, scram, split 6 begone, decamp, depart, get out, go away 7 abscond, dash off, get lost, go south, make off, pull out, push off, retreat, ride off, take off 8 hightail, shove off, withdraw 9 skedaddle 10 go fly a kite, hightail it, hit the road
musical ~: 6 rhythm, stress 7 battuta
one's gums: 3 yak, yap 7 chatter
starter: 3 off 4 back, brow, dead, down, drum, fare 5 heart
the bushes: 4 hunt, seek 7 rummage 9 track down
the drums: 6 talk up 7 advance, promote 9 publicize
the rap: 4 walk 6 get off, go free
up: 3 mug 4 mall, maul 5 knock, seedy, thump 6 pommel, pummel, thrash 10 threadbare
walker: 3 cop 9 policeman
walk the ~: 5 guard 6 patrol
beat __: 3 man, out 4 poet 6 hollow
beat __ to one's door: 5 a path
__ beat: 3 big 5 world 6 Mersey
__ Beat: 4 Teen 7 Foolish
beatable: 8 vincible
beat around the __: 4 bush
beaten: 6 broken, frothy, undone 8 overcome
get ~ by: 4 lose 6 lose to
go off the ~ path: 4 veer 5 stray 7 deviate
it may be ~: 3 egg, rap, rug 4 path
off the ~ path: 6 afield, lonely, remote 8 isolated, secluded
path: 5 trace, track, trail
starter: 4 brow
beaten __: 4 path
beater: 5 mixer, whisk
__-beater: 4 fare

Beat Goes On, The (1967 song)
artist: Sonny and Cher
beatific: **6** divine **7** angelic, elysian, radiant, saintly **8** blissful, ecstatic, heavenly **9** angelical, celestial, rapturous
vision: **8** afflatus
beatify: **4** laud **5** bless **6** revere **7** enthral, inthral, rejoice **8** canonize, enravish, enthrall, inthrall, venerate **9** enrapture, transport **10** consecrate
beating: **4** rout **5** abuse **6** athrob, defeat, hiding **7** ahead of, battery, licking **8** conquest, flitting **9** trouncing **10** punishment
it takes a ~: **4** drum
take a ~: **4** lose
__-beating: **6** breast
beat it: **4** away, scat, shoo **5** scram
Beat It (1983 song)
artist: Michael Jackson
Beatles
award: **3** MBE
film: **4** Help
hairstyle: **3** mop **6** mop-top
manager: Brian Epstein
members: McCartney, Lennon, Harrison, Starr, Best, Sutcliffe
record label: Apple
song: All You Need Is Love (1967)
And I Love Her (1964)
Baby You're a Rich Man (1967)
The Ballad of John and Yoko (1969)
Can't Buy Me Love (1964)
Come Together (1969)
Day Tripper (1965)
Do You Want to Know a Secret (1964)
Eight Days a Week (1965)
Eleanor Rigby (1966)
Free as a Bird (1995)
Get Back (1969)
Got to Get You Into My Life (1976)
A Hard Day's Night (1964)
Hello Goodbye (1967)
Help! (1965)
Hey Jude (1968)
I Feel Fine (1964)
I Saw Her Standing There (1964)
I Want to Hold Your Hand (1964)
Lady Madonna (1968)
Let It Be (1970)
The Long and Winding Road (1970)
Love Me Do (1964)
Nowhere Man (1966)
Paperback Writer (1966)
Please Please Me (1964)
P.S. I Love You (1964)
Revolution (1968)
She Loves You (1964)
She's a Woman (1964)
Something (1969)
Strawberry Fields Forever (1967)
Ticket to Ride (1965)
Twist and Shout (1964)
We Can Work It Out (1965)
Yellow Submarine (1966)
Yesterday (1965)
beatnik: **8** bohemian, longhair **10** unorthodox
affirmative: **4** I dig **5** I'm hip
buddy: **6** daddy-o
cousin: **5** hippy **6** hippie
drum: **5** bongo
exclamation: **3** man
home: **3** pad
topper: **5** beret
Beaton: **5** Cecil
beat one's __: **4** gums
Beatrice: **4** Webb **6** Lillie **8** Straight
beau: **5** Dante
mother: **5** Sarah
to Charles: **5** niece
to Leonato: **5** niece
Beatrix: **6** Potter
beats me: **5** dunno **6** I dunno, no idea **8** who knows
beat the __: **3** rap **4** drum **6** bushes
Beat the Clock: **8** game show
activity: **5** stunt
host: Bud Collyer
Beat the Devil (1954 film)
cast: Humphrey Bogart, Jennifer Jones, Gina Lollobrigida
director: John Huston
Beattie: **3** Ann **5** James
Beattie, Ann: **6** writer
work: Another You
Chilly Scenes of Winter
The Doctor's House
Falling in Place
Park City
Perfect Recall
Picturing Will
Beattie, James: **8** Scottish **11** philosopher
beat to the __: **4** draw **5** punch
Beatty: **3** Ned **6** Warren
Beatty, Ned: **5** actor
Superman role: **4** Otis
Beatty, Warren: **5** actor
film: All Fall Down (1962)
Bonnie and Clyde (1967)
Bugsy (1991)
Bulworth (1998)
Dick Tracy (1990)
$ (Dollars) (1971)
Heaven Can Wait (1978)
Ishtar (1987)
Love Affair (1994)
McCabe & Mrs. Miller (1971)
The Only Game in Town (1970)
The Parallax View (1974)
Reds (1981, AA)
Shampoo (1975)
Splendor in the Grass (1961)
spouse: Annette Bening
TV: The Many Loves of Dobie Gillis
beat-up: **4** worn **6** ragged, shabby **7** run-down **9** rusted-out **10** threadbare
beau: **4** date **5** dandy, fella, wooer **6** fellow, fiancé, squire **7** sweetie
ideal: **5** model **7** paragon **8** paradigm
monde: **5** elite **6** jet set **7** society
see also sweetheart
beau __: **5** geste, ideal, monde **6** dollar
Beau: **7** Bridges **8** Brummell
Beau __: **4** Père **5** Geste, James **7** Brummel
Beau Brummell: **3** fop **4** dude **5** dandy, swell **8** popinjay
Beauchamp: **6** Pierre
Beauchampe
author: William Simms
beaucoup: **4** a lot, much **9** in a big way
__ beaucoup: **5** merci
Beaufort: **3** sea **7** Francis
locale: **6** Alaska
Beaufort Scale measure: **4** wind
Beaufort Sea bay: **7** Prudhoe
Beau Geste
author: P.C. Wren
Beau Geste (1939 film)
cast: Gary Cooper, Brian Donlevy, Ray Milland, Robert Preston
Beau Ideal, The
composer: John Philip Sousa
Beaujolais: **3** red, vin **4** wine
color: **3** red
grape: **5** gamay
origin: **6** France
Beaumont: **3** Ned **4** city, Hugh, town **5** Harry
locale: **5** Texas
Beauregard: **3** gen. **6** Pierre **7** general
boss: **3** Lee
org.: **3** CSA
beaut: **3** gem, pip **4** lulu, oner **5** dandy, dilly, doozy, peach **6** doozie **9** humdinger
beauteous: **6** lovely, pretty **8** gorgeous, stunning
beautician, often: **4** dyer
beauties, group of: **4** bevy
beautiful: **4** cute, fair, sexy, trim **5** grand, ideal, sweet **6** comely, dainty, divine, lovely, pretty, scenic, superb **7** angelic, beaming, elegant, radiant, sublime, winsome **8** alluring, becoming, enticing, esthetic, glorious, gorgeous, handsome, heavenly, pleasing, scenical, splendid, striking, stunning, tasteful **9** angelical, appealing, covetable, desirable, excellent, exquisite, marvelous, ravishing **10** attractive, bewitching, delightful, ornamental, statuesque, well-formed
combining form: **4** call-, calo- **5** calli-, callo-
make more ~: **5** adorn **7** dress up, enhance **8** decorate
name meaning ~: **5** Shana **7** Belinda
people: **5** elite **6** jet set
person: **6** vision **7** stunner **8** knockout
see also wonderful
beautiful __: **6** people
Beautiful __: **5** Girls **7** Dreamer
Beautiful __, A: **4** Mind **7** Morning
__ Beautiful: **5** House
__ Beautiful Doll: **5** Oh You
Beautiful Dreamer
composer: Stephen Foster
Beautiful Girls (1996 film)
cast: Matt Dillon, Noah Emmerich, Annabeth Gish, Lauren Holly, Timothy Hutton
director: Ted Demme
__ Beautiful Girl, The: **4** Most
Beautiful Mind, A (2001 film)
cast: Jennifer Connelly, Russell Crowe, Ed Harris
director: Ron Howard
Beautiful Morning, A (1968 song)
artist: Rascals
__ beautiful pea-green boat: **3** in a
__ Beautiful Sea: **5** By the
Beautiful Stranger (1999 song)
artist: Madonna
beautify: **4** deck, gild, trim **5** adorn, array, grace, primp **6** bedeck, make up **7** develop, dress up, enhance, flatter, garnish, improve **8** decorate, emblazon, ornament, prettify **9** embellish, embroider, glamorize, smarten up
beauty: **3** pip **4** doll **5** asset, charm, class, dandy, doozy, grace, merit, style, value, Venus, worth **6** Adonis, allure, Apollo, appeal, eyeful, glamor, looker, vision **7** benefit, charmer, glamour, Miss U.S.A., stunner **8** artistry, elegance, radiance, radiancy **9** advantage, dreamboat, good looks, humdinger **10** attraction, loveliness, refinement
add ~ to: **5** adorn **7** dress up, enhance **8** decorate
aid: **4** kohl **5** gloss, liner, rouge **6** powder **7** blusher, mascara **8** cosmetic, lipstick, war paint **9** cosmetics **10** face powder
ender: **4** bush **5** berry
goddess of ~: **5** Venus **6** Hathor **9** Aphrodite
magazine: **4** Elle **5** Vogue **6** Allure
name meaning ~: **5** Jamal **6** Jamaal
parlor: **5** salon
preceder: **3** age
realm of ~: **3** art
beauty __: **4** mark, shop, spot **5** quark, salon, sleep **6** parlor **7** contest
Beauty __ the eye...: **4** is in
__ Beauty: **4** Rome **5** Black, She's a **7** Bathing
Beauty and the Beast (1946 film)
director: Jean Cocteau
Beauty and the Beast (1992 song)
artist: Peabo Bryson, Celine Dion
Beauty and the Beast (CBS drama)
cast: Linda Hamilton (Catherine Chandler)
Ron Perlman (Vincent)
Vincent's home, in ~: **5** sewer
__ Beauty apple: **4** Rome
beauty cream additive: **4** aloe
...beauty is __ forever: **4** a joy
Beauty is only skin-deep: **3** saw **5** adage **6** saying
beauty pageant
accessory: **4** sash
award: **5** tiara, title **7** bouquet
title: **4** Miss
VIP: **5** judge
beauty parlor: **5** salon
application: **3** dye **4** tint **5** henna, rinse **6** bleach, mousse **7** mud pack
item: **3** dye, net **4** comb, tint **5** drier, dryer, rinse **6** curler, mousse, roller **7** hairpin, shampoo **9** blow dryer, hair spray
treatment: **3** set **4** perm, trim **5** rinse **6** dye job, facial **7** shampoo, touch-up **8** manicure
Beauty's beloved: **5** Beast
Beauty's Punishment
author: Anne Rice

Beauty's Release
author: Anne Rice
Beauvoir, Simone de: 6 French, writer
friend: Sartre
work: All Said and Done
The Mandarins
The Prime of Life
The Second Sex
She Came to Stay
beaux __: 4 arts **5** ideal **6** gestes, mondes **7** esprits
beaver: 3 fur, hat **6** animal, mammal, rodent
construction: 3 dam **5** lodge
eager ~: 6 dynamo
emulate a ~: 4 gnaw
ender: 5 board
female: 3 sow
like a ~: 5 eager
male: 4 boar
pelt: 3 plu **4** plew
relative: ***see*** rodent
young: 3 kit
__ beaver: 5 eager
Beaver: 7 Cleaver
parent: 4 June, Ward
show: Leave It to Beaver
State: 3 Ore. **6** Oregon
Beaver __: 3 Dam
Beavers: 6 Louise
Beaverton: 4 city, town
locale: 6 Oregon
Beavis: 4 teen, toon
Bebe: 6 Rebozo **7** Daniels **8** Neuwirth
bebop: 4 jazz **5** dance, music
Be-Bop-A-Lula (1956 song)
artist: Gene Vincent
Be-Bop Baby (1957 song)
artist: Ricky Nelson
be-bopper: 3 cat
becalm: 4 halt, lull, stop **5** quell, quiet, stall **6** soothe **7** compose
becalmed: 5 still **8** windless **10** motionless
becard: 4 bird
Be Careful, It's My Heart
composer: Irving Berlin
because: 3 for **5** due to, since **6** in that **7** owing to, whereas **8** as long as, by reason, by virtue, in view of **10** inasmuch as, seeing that
of: 5 due to **7** owing to, through **8** thanks to
of this: 6 hereat
Because (1964 song)
artist: Dave Clark Five
Because __ so: 5 I said
Because I __ so!: 4 said
Because I Love You (1990 song)
artist: Stevie B
Because of Love (1994 song)
artist: Janet Jackson
Because of You (1951 song)
artist: Tony Bennett
Because They're Young (1960 song)
artist: Duane Eddy
Because You Loved Me (1996 song)
artist: Celine Dion
béchamel __: 5 sauce
__-bêche: 4 tête
bêche-de-__: 3 mer
Bechet, Sidney: 11 clarinetist, saxophonist
genre: 4 jazz
Bech is Back
author: John Updike
Bechke: 5 Elena
beck: 3 nod **6** signal **7** gesture, summons
at one's ~ and call: 5 ready
Beck: 4 Jeff, John **6** Martin **8** Kimberly
beck and __: 4 call
Becker: 4 Gary **5** Boris, Sandy **6** Harold
Becker (CBS sitcom)
cast: Ted Danson (Dr. John Becker)
Terry Farrell (Reggie Costa)
Becker, Boris: 7 netster **9** tennis pro
rival: Ivan Lendl
Becker, Gary: 8 Nobelist **9** economist
Becket (1964 film)
cast: Richard Burton, Sir John Gielgud, Peter O'Toole
__ Becket: 7 Thomas à
Beckett: 6 Samuel, Scotty
Beckett, Samuel: 5 Irish **6** writer **8** Nobelist **9** dramatist **10** playwright
friend: James Joyce
work: Echo's Bones
Endgame
Malone Dies
Molloy
Murphy
The Unnamable
Waiting for Godot
Watt
Beckham: 5 David **8** Victoria
Beckinsale, Kate: 7 actress
film: The Aviator (2004)
Click (2006)
Cold Comfort Farm (1995)
The Golden Bowl (2001)
The Last Days of Disco (1998)
Laurel Canyon (2002)
Pearl Harbor (2001)
Serendipity (2001)
Vacancy (2007)
Van Helsing (2004)
Whiteout (2009)
Beckmann: 3 Max
beckon: 3 nod **4** call, coax, draw, lure, wave **5** tempt **6** allure, entice, invite, motion, signal, summon **7** attract, gesture
beckoned: 4 bade
beckoning: 10 attractive
Becks: 4 beer
competitor: ***see*** beer
becloud: 3 dim, fog **4** blur, fade, hide, roil, veil **5** bedim, befog, shade **6** darken, puzzle, shadow **7** confuse, eclipse, mystify, obscure **8** bewilder, confound **9** adumbrate, obfuscate **10** overshadow
become: 3 fit, get **4** suit, turn **5** end up **6** beseem, modify **7** enhance, flatter **8** emerge as, turn into **9** morph into **10** change into, evolve into, look good on, look well on, mature into
__ Becomes Her: 5 Death
becoming: 4 cute, fine, good, nice **6** comely, decent, pretty, proper, seemly **7** fitting **8** apposite, decorous, handsome, suitable **9** agreeable, beautiful, enhancing
becomingly: 4 well
becomingness: 9 propriety
Be Cool (2005 film)
cast: Uma Thurman, John Travolta, Vince Vaughn
Becquerel, Antoine: 6 French **8** Nobelist **9** physicist
__ Be Cruel: 4 Don't
bed: 3 cot **4** base, bunk, crib, doss, king, plot, sack, twin **5** basis, berth, futon, layer, patch **6** bottom, cradle, garden, ground **7** stratum, trundle **8** barracks, bassinet, mattress **9** furniture, underside **10** foundation, groundwork, substratum
and breakfast: 3 inn **7** lodging
baby ~: 4 crib **6** cradle **8** bassinet
board: 4 slat
camp ~: 3 cot **4** bunk
care for a ~: 3 hoe **4** make, weed
coal ~: 4 seam **7** stratum
combining form: 4 clin- **5** clino-
covering: 5 duvet, eider, quilt **6** canopy, spread **9** comforter
day ~: 4 sofa **5** divan
ender: 3 bug, rid **4** fast, mate, post, rock, roll, room, side, time **5** plate, stead, straw **6** fellow, ridden, spread, spring **7** chamber, clothes
fabric: 5 linen, sheet **10** pillowcase
flower ~: 4 plot **6** garden
frame: 5 stead
go to ~: 3 lie **5** sleep **6** retire, turn in **7** sack out **10** hit the sack
hop out of ~: 4 rise, wake **5** arise, awake, get up, rouse, waken **6** awaken, wake up
in ~: 5 not up **6** asleep, laid up **7** resting, retired **8** sleeping **9** sacked out
in England: 3 kip **4** doss
it can hide a ~: 4 sofa
Japanese ~: 3 mat **5** futon
material: 5 brass
Murphy ~ place: 6 closet
occupant: 4 seed **5** plant **6** flower **7** sleeper
of roses: 4 ease **6** luxury **7** comfort **8** good life, opulence
out of ~: 5 astir **6** arisen
portable ~: 3 cot **5** futon
put to ~: 5 close, print **6** finish **7** let roll **8** complete **10** consummate
roll out of ~: 4 rise, wake **5** awake, get up, rouse, waken **6** awaken, bestir, wake up
ship's ~: 4 bunk **5** berth
size: 4 king, twin **5** queen **6** double
starter: 3 day, hot, sea **4** flat, lake, road, seed, sick, snub **5** child, river, water **6** stream **7** feather
bed __: 3 bug **4** bolt, load, rest, tray **5** board, chair, check, linen, place, stone, table **6** jacket **7** molding
bed-__: 3 sit **6** sitter
__ bed: 3 air, box, car, day, hot, pie, pig **4** boat, bunk, camp, loft, mast, sofa, tent, twin **5** angel, chair, field, press, put to, stump **6** anchor, double, filter, French, Murphy, oyster, parade, sleigh **7** feather, tanning, truckle, trundle
__-bed: 4 flat
__-Bed: 5 Hide-A
bed and __: 5 board
bed-and-breakfast: 3 inn
visitor: 5 guest
__ be darned!: 3 I'll
bedaub: 4 blot, soil **5** smear, stain, touch **6** bedeck, blotch, doll up, dude up, smirch, smudge **7** bedizen, begrime, deck out, plaster **8** ornament **9** bespatter, overdress
bedaze: 4 stun **7** confuse
bedazzle: 4 stun **5** shine **7** enchant **9** captivate, overwhelm
bedazzled: 5 in awe
Bedazzled (1967 film)
cast: Eleanor Bron, Peter Cook, Dudley Moore
director: Stanley Donen
Bedazzled (2000 film)
cast: Brendan Fraser, Elizabeth Hurley
director: Harold Ramis
Bed Bath and __: 6 Beyond
bedbug: 5 cimex **6** chinch, insect
bedclothes: 3 PJs **4** gown **6** nighty **7** nightie, pajamas **9** nightgown **10** sleep shirt
bedcover: 5 duvet, eider, quilt **6** canopy, spread **9** comforter
bedding: 5 cover, eider, linen, quilt, sheet **6** linens, pillow **7** blanket **9** comforter, down quilt, eiderdown **10** pillowcase
Beddoe: 5 Philo
beddy-__: 3 bye
Bede: 4 Adam **5** saint
bedeck: 4 gild, trim **5** adorn, array, grace **6** bedaub **7** bedizen, dress up, enhance, festoon, garnish **8** accouter, accoutre, beautify, decorate, ornament **9** caparison, embellish, embroider, glamorize
bedecked: 4 clad
Bedelia
home in a folk song: 4 Erin
Bedelia, Bonnie: 7 actress
bedevil: 3 bug, vex **4** bait, gall, jinx, roil **5** annoy, chaff, harry, haunt, tease, worry **6** badger, bother, harass, muddle, needle, noodge, obsess, pester **7** agonize, confuse, provoke, torment **8** befuddle, confound, distress, irritate
bedeviled: 7 accurst **8** accursed, obsessed **9** possessed
bedew: 3 wet **6** dampen **7** moisten **8** sprinkle
bedewed: 3 wet **4** damp **5** moist **10** glistening
bedfellow: 4 ally
Bedfordshire: 6 county
city: 5 Luton
locale: 7 England
river: 4 Ouse
bedim: 4 blur **5** cloud, shade **6** darken, shadow **7** becloud, obscure **9** adumbrate **10** overshadow
bedizen: 5 adorn **6** bedaub, bedeck **8** decorate, ornament
bedlam: 3 din **4** mess, riot **5** chaos, noise **6** hubbub, mayhem, tumult, unrest, uproar **7** anarchy, ferment, turmoil **8** disarray, madhouse, shambles, upheaval **9** commotion, confusion, mobocracy **10** hullabaloo, hurly-burly, turbulence
Bednarik: 5 Chuck
Bednorz, Georg: 8 Nobelist **9** physicist
Bedny, Demyan: 4 poet **7** Russian
bed of __: 5 nails, roses

Bed of Flowers, A
author: Auberon Waugh
bed of nails
user: **5** faker, fakir, faqir **6** faquir
Bed of Roses (1993 song)
artist: Bon Jovi
bedog: **5** hound **6** harass
Bedouin: **4** Arab **5** tribe
headcord: **4** agal
language: **6** Arabic
leader: **5** sheik **6** shaikh, sheikh
mount: **5** camel
robe: **3** aba **4** abba
bedraggle: **4** muss, soil **6** rumple
bedraggled: **5** dowdy, grimy, seedy, soggy, soppy **6** blowsy, blowzy, filthy, frowsy, frowzy, frumpy, shabby, sloppy, sodden, soiled, unneat, untidy **7** blowsed, blowzed, dirtied, muddied, scruffy, sullied, unclean, unkempt **8** decrepit, drenched, dripping, slipshod, slovenly **9** ungroomed **10** besmirched, disheveled, disordered, threadbare
bedrape: **3** rig **4** deck, garb **5** array, cover, dress **6** attire, clothe, fit out, outfit, tog out **7** costume **8** accouter, accoutre **9** caparison
Bedrich: **7** Smetana
Bed Riddance
author: Ogden Nash
bedridden: **3** ill **4** sick **6** ailing, infirm, laid up, sickly, unwell **7** unsound **8** confined **9** afflicted **10** indisposed
bedrock: **4** base **5** dance **10** foundation
deposit: **3** oil, ore **9** gemstones, petroleum **10** natural gas
Bedrock
see Flintstones
bedroll
alternative: **3** cot **4** bunk **5** futon **6** pallet
bedroom: **5** berth, bower **7** boudoir, chamber
adjunct: **6** closet
community: **4** burb **5** exurb **6** suburb **9** outskirts
furniture: **4** lamp **5** suite **6** bureau, vanity **7** dresser **8** wardrobe
__ bedroom: **6** master
Bedroom at __: **5** Arles
Bedroom Farce
author: Alan Ayckbourn
Bedrosian: **5** Steve
bedsheets: **5** linen
bedside
book: **5** diary
companion: **5** nurse
furnishing: **4** lamp **5** table **8** end table
item: **5** clock
bedside __: **6** manner
__ Beds National Monument: **4** Lava
bedspread: **5** cover **7** blanket **8** coverlet, coverlid
fabric: **8** chenille **10** marseilles
bedstead
light ~: **3** cot **4** bunk
part: **3** leg **4** slat **5** frame
bedtime: **5** night, sleep **6** curfew
approach ~: **5** laten
beverage: **4** milk **5** cocoa, toddy
in ads: **4** nite
late ~: **2** a.m. **3** two **4** four **5** one a.m., three, two a.m. **6** four a.m. **7** three a.m. **8** midnight, wee hours
reading: **5** novel, story
sound: **5** snore
bedtime __: **5** story
Bedtime for Bonzo (1951 film)
cast: Ronald Reagan
bee: **3** bug **5** drone, grade, party **6** insect, social, worker **7** stinger **9** carpenter, gathering, spelldown **10** pollinator
busy ~: **7** hustler **8** live wire
compete in a ~: **5** spell
defense: **5** sting **7** stinger
ender: **4** hive, line **5** bread **6** keeper
follower: **3** cee
genus: **4** apis
home: **4** hive **6** apiary
like a ~: **5** apian
male ~: **5** drone
name meaning ~: **5** Debra **7** Deborah
participant: **6** husker **7** quilter, speller
product: **3** wax **4** comb **5** honey, quilt
starter: **5** honey **6** bumble, humble
stingless ~: **5** drone
target: **6** flower
bee __: **3** fly, gum **4** balm, bird, glue, moth, tree **5** block, plant **6** beetle, martin
bee-__: **5** eater, stung
__ bee: **4** king **5** apple, honey, mason, queen, sweat **6** bumble, killer, social, worker **7** husking
Bee: **4** aunt **5** paper **9** newspaper
locale: **6** Fresno **10** Sacramento
to Andy: **4** aunt
Bee __: **4** Gees
Beebe, William: **8** explorer
milieu: **3** sea **4** deep **5** ocean
beech: **3** nut **4** fern, tree **9** shade tree
tree: **8** chestnut
Beech-__: **3** Nut
competitor: **6** Gerber
Beecham, Thomas: **3** Sir **7** British **9** conductor
Beecher, Henry Ward: **6** writer
daughter: Harriet
Beecher, Lyman: **8** preacher
__ Beecher Stowe: **7** Harriet
Beechwood 4-5789 (1962 song)
artist: Marvelettes
bee-eater: **4** bird
beef: **4** kick, meat, moan **5** brawn, cavil, chuck, gripe, might, power, sinew, whine **6** cattle, charge, grouse, muscle, plaint, repine, squawk, yammer **7** dispute, grumble, protest, quarrel, red meat **8** argument, complain, strength **9** bellyache, complaint, criticism, grievance, make a fuss, objection
cut: **3** eye **4** chop, loin, rump **5** chuck, filet, patty, roast, round, shank, steak, T-bone **6** pattie **7** sirloin **9** club steak, cube steak **11** filet migñon, porterhouse
designation: **5** prime **6** grade A
dish: **4** stew **6** fajita
dried ~: **5** jerky
ender: **4** wood **5** eater, steak
eschewer: **5** vegan **10** vegetarian
full of ~ fat: **5** suety
half a ~: **4** side
in French: **5** boeuf
large joint of ~: **5** baron
like some ~: **4** lean
product: **5** jerky
rating org.: **4** USDA
so to speak: **4** turf
up: **4** gird, grow, tone **5** bloat, boost, build, shore, steel, swell, widen **6** anneal, dilate, expand, fatten, harden, temper **7** amplify, augment, bolster, broaden, burgeon, develop, empower, enhance, enlarge, fortify, inflate, stiffen, toughen **8** bourgeon, buttress, energize, heighten, indurate, lengthen, vitalize **9** intensify, reinforce **10** aggrandize, invigorate, strengthen, supplement
young ~: **4** veal
beef __: **3** tea **4** stew **6** cattle **7** extract
__ beef: **4** baby, corn, Kobe **5** bully **6** corned **7** chipped, corn-fed
beefalo: **5** bovid **6** animal, bovine, hybrid
relative: *see* bovine
beefcake: **4** hunk, stud
beefiness: **3** vim **4** dint, thew **5** brawn, force, might, power, thews, vigor **6** energy, muscle **7** fitness, muscles, potence, potency, stamina **8** vitality **9** endurance, fortitude, puissance, toughness **10** brute force
beefsteak: **4** meat **6** tomato
relative: **4** Roma **6** Big Boy **9** Better Boy, Early Girl, Quick Pick
beefsteak __: **3** rye **6** tomato
beefwood: **4** tree
beefy: **5** bulky, hardy, hulky, meaty, solid **6** chunky **7** filling, hulking, massive **9** filled-out
see also brawny, obese
Bee Gees: **4** trio
member: Barry, Maurice, Robin, Gibb
song: How Can You Mend a Broken Heart (1971)
How Deep Is Your Love (1977)
I Started a Joke (1969)
I've Got to Get a Message to You (1968)
Jive Talkin' (1975)
Lonely Days (1970)
Love So Right (1976)
Love You Inside Out (1979)
Night Fever (1978)
Nights on Broadway (1975)
One (1989)
Stayin' Alive (1977)
Too Much Heaven (1978)
Tragedy (1979)
You Should Be Dancing (1976)
beehive: **4** coif, nest, skep **6** apiary, hairdo **7** upsweep **8** coiffure **9** hairstyle
boss: **5** queen
cousin: **4** Afro
like a ~: **4** ahum, busy
sound: **4** buzz
straw ~: **4** skep
Beehive State
see Utah
beekeeper: **8** apiarist
beeline: **5** route
in a ~: **8** directly, straight
make a ~: **5** hurry **6** hasten
Beelzebub: **5** demon, devil, Satan **6** daemon, daimon **7** Lucifer
forte: **4** evil
Bee Movie (2007 film)
voice cast: Matthew Broderick, John Goodman, Jerry Seinfeld, Renée Zellweger
been: **5** lived **6** stayed **7** existed
had ~: **3** was **4** were
__-been: **3** has
__ Been a Long, Long Time: **3** It's
Been Around the World (1998 song)
artist: Mase, Notorious B.I.G., Puff Daddy
Beene: **8** Geoffrey
__ been had!: **3** I've
__ Been Kissed: **5** Never
__ Been Lonely Too Long: **3** I've
__ been robbed!: **3** I've
__ been sleeping in my bed?: **4** Who's
been there, __ that: **4** done
__ been thinking...: **3** I've
__ Been Working on the Railroad: **3** I've
beep: **4** call, honk, page, tone, toot **6** signal, summon
beeper: **4** horn **5** alarm, pager
beer: **3** Bud **4** brew, suds **5** Becks, Coors, drink, Kirin, lager, Pabst, quaff **6** Amstel, chaser, Corona, Labatt, liquor, Miller, Molson, stingo, Stroh's **7** brewski, cold one, pilsner, Schlitz **8** beverage, Dos Equis, Heineken, Michelob **9** Budweiser, inebriant, Lowenbrau, Moosehead **10** Ballantine
agave ~: **6** pulque
barrel: **3** keg
category: **4** lite **5** draft
characteristic: **4** body, foam, head **5** froth
corn ~: **6** chicha
dark ~: **4** bock
Dutch ~: **6** Amstel **8** Heineken
holder: **3** keg, mug **5** glass, stein **6** barrel, bottle, cooler, fridge **8** schooner
ingredient: **4** hops, malt, wort **5** grain, yeast **6** barley
Japanese ~: **5** Kirin
joint: **3** bar, pub **6** saloon, tavern **8** alehouse **9** bierstube, roadhouse
keg adjunct: **3** tap
light ~: **5** lager
like bock ~: **4** aged
like some ~: **5** on tap
low-calorie ~: **4** lite
make ~: **4** brew
Mexican ~: **6** Corona **8** Dos Equis
nickname: **3** Oly
nonalcoholic ~: **6** Odoul's
old ~ brand: **5** Piels
Polynesian ~: **4** kava
quantity: **3** keg **4** case **6** barrel **7** six-pack
relative: **3** ale **5** stout
reminiscent of ~: **5** malty
Russian ~: **5** kvass, quass
spring ~: **4** bock
beer __: **4** bust, hall, pump **5** on tap **6** engine, garden

— **beer:** 3 ice, rye 4 bock, near, root 5 birch, draft, lager, small, steam, weiss 6 ginger, spruce
Beer Barrel —: 5 Polka
Beerbohm, Max: 6 writer 7 British
beer on —: 3 tap
Beersheba: 4 city, town
locale: 6 Israel
region: 5 Negeb
Beery: 4 Noah 7 Wallace
Beery, Wallace: 5 actor
film: Ah, Wilderness! (1935)
The Bowery (1933)
The Champ (1931, AA)
China Seas (1935)
Dinner at Eight (1933)
Flesh (1932)
Grand Hotel (1932)
Min and Bill (1930)
Old Ironsides (1926)
Slave Ship (1937)
Treasure Island (1934)
Viva Villa! (1934)
spouse: Gloria Swanson
bees
do it: 5 sting
ender: 3 wax
group of ~: 5 swarm
of ~: 5 apian
bee's —: 5 knees
bee-sting result: 4 itch, welt
beet: 4 root 5 chard 6 veggie 9 vegetable
ender: 4 root
product: 5 sugar 6 borsch 7 borscht
beet —: 5 sugar
— **beet:** 4 leaf 5 sugar
beet-faced: 3 red 5 ruddy 6 florid
Beethoven, Ludwig van: 6 German 8 composer
birthplace: 4 Bonn
piece: 4 opus 5 opera, rondo 6 sonata 8 concerto, symphony
work: Appassionata Sonata
Choral Symphony
Coriolanus Overture
Emperor Concerto
Eroica Symphony
Fidelio
Für Elise
Kreutzer Sonata
Leonore Overture
Missa Solemnis
Moonlight Sonata
Pastoral Symphony
Pathétique Sonata
Spring Sonata
Waldstein Sonata
Wellington's Victory
beetle: 3 bug, dor, ram 4 beat, dorr, form, mold, pelt, uang 5 crush, forge, lay on, pound, shape 6 batter, chafer, hammer, insect, pummel, scarab 7 firefly, ladybug, project 8 overhang, protrude, stand out 10 projecting, protruding
click ~: 6 elater
eater: 6 mantid, mantis
ender: 4 weed
larva: 4 grub
rhinoceros ~: 4 uang
starter: 4 lady
Beetle: 2 VW 3 car 4 auto 6 German 10 automobile, Volkswagen
Beetle Bailey: 5 comic 10 comic strip
artist: Mort Walker
dog: 4 Otto
organization: 4 army
soldier: 4 Zero 5 Plato, Sarge 7 Snorkel
Beetlejuice (1988 film)
cast: Alec Baldwin, Geena Davis, Michael Keaton
director: Tim Burton
beetleweed: 5 galax
— **beets:** 7 Harvard, pickled
beeves: 6 cattle
beezer: 5 snoot 6 schnoz 7 schnozz 9 schnozzle 10 schnozzola
bef.: 4 prev.
befall: 4 pass 5 occur, visit 6 happen 7 occur to 8 happen to, overtake 9 come about, take place, transpire 10 come to pass
cause to ~: 5 incur
befit: 4 suit 6 beseem
befitting: 3 apt, fit 4 just, nice 5 right 6 beseem, kasher, kosher, proper, seemly 7 fitting 8 apposite, decorous, rightful, suitable 9 agreeable, behooving, beseeming, on the nose 10 applicable, conforming, felicitous
befog: 3 dim 4 blur, mist 5 cloud 6 darken, muddle 7 becloud, confuse, mystify, obscure, steam up 8 confound 9 obfuscate
befool: 5 trick 8 hoodwink
be for: 4 back 5 favor 7 support
before: 2 by 3 ago, ere 4 once, till 5 ahead, prior, until 6 erenow, gone by, hereto 7 ahead of, earlier, prior to, up to now 8 formerly, hitherto 9 a while ago, in advance, in front of, in the past, preceding 10 previously, previous to
combining form: 4 fore- 6 proter- 7 protero-
ender: 4 hand, time
in German: 3 von
old-style: 4 erst
prefix: 3 pre-, pro- 4 ante-, fore-
the present: 3 ago 4 past
the rest: 5 first 9 preceding
to a poet: 3 ere
before —: 4 long
Before and After (1996 film)
cast: Edward Furlong, Liam Neeson, Meryl Streep
director: Barbet Schroeder
— **before beauty:** 3 age
— **Before Dying:** 5 A Kiss
beforehand: 5 ahead, early, first, prior 6 sooner 7 advance, already, betimes, earlier 9 a while ago, in advance 10 in good time, precocious, previously
Before I Say Good-Bye
author: Mary Higgins Clark
— **before swine:** 6 pearls
Before the Next Teardrop Falls (1975 song)
artist: Freddy Fender
— **before the storm:** 4 calm
beforetime: 8 formerly 10 previously
— **Before Time, The:** 4 Land
— **before you leap:** 4 look
Before You Walk out of My Life (1995 song) artist: Monica
befoul: 3 mar 4 soil 5 dirty, smear, spoil, stain, sully, taint 6 defile, malign, smudge 7 begrime, blacken, pollute, profane, tarnish 8 besmirch 9 desecrate
befouled: 5 grimy, sooty 6 filthy, grubby, grungy 7 unclean 8 maculate, slovenly 10 unsanitary
befriend: 7 promote, sustain, welcome 8 cotton to 9 buddy up to 10 take up with
— **be friends!:** 4 Let's
befuddle: 4 daze 5 addle, mix up, throw 6 baffle, muddle, puzzle 7 bedevil, confuse, fluster, perplex 8 bewilder, confound, unsettle 9 disorient, dumbfound, inebriate 10 intoxicate
befuddled: 4 asea, dopy, hazy 5 at sea, dizzy, loopy 6 addled, in a fog 7 reeling 9 slaphappy 10 bewildered
beg: 3 ask, sue, woo 4 pray, seek, urge 5 cadge, hit up, mooch, plead, press 6 adjure, appeal, grovel 7 beseech, entreat, implore, request, solicit 8 freeload, petition, scrounge, sponge on 9 impetrate, importune, mendicate, panhandle 10 pass the hat, supplicate
off: 5 demur 6 bow out, refuse 7 decline
pardon: 5 sorry 8 excuse me 9 apologize
beg —: 3 off
Bega: 3 Lou
beget: 4 bear, have, sire 5 breed, cause, spawn 6 create, father 7 produce 8 engender, result in 9 procreate, propagate, reproduce 10 bring about, give rise to
beggar: 4 hobo, ruin 5 faker, fakir, faqir, tramp 6 faquir, pauper, rascal 7 have-not, vagrant 8 deadbeat, indigent, vagabond 9 mendicant, scrounger 10 impoverish, panhandler, ragamuffin, supplicant
request: 4 alms
beggarly: 4 base, mean, poor 5 broke, needy, sorry 6 bad off, hard up, ill off, in need, in want, meager, measly, paltry, shabby 7 pinched, pitiful, servile 8 badly off, bankrupt, indigent, piddling, strapped, wretched 9 destitute, insolvent, miserable, moneyless, penniless, penurious 10 down and out, inadequate, pauperized, straitened
Beggar Maid, The: 4 poem
author: Alfred Tennyson
Beggar on Horseback
author: George S. Kaufman
beggars can't be choosers: 3 saw 5 adage 6 saying
Beggar's Opera, The
composer: John Gay
beggary: 4 need 6 penury, rabble 7 poverty 8 riffraff 9 indigence, neediness, pauperism 10 insolvency
begin: 4 dawn, open, rise 5 arise, enter, found, set in, set to, set up, start 6 appear, assume, crop up, emerge, fall to, go to it, launch, let rip, set off, set out, spring, tackle, wade in 7 aggress, develop, go ahead, jump off, kick off, lead off, preface, take off, usher in 8 activate, commence, embark on, get going, initiate, set about, set forth, touch off 9 actualize, come forth, enter into, establish, eventuate, germinate, get to work, institute, introduce, originate, strike out, undertake 10 inaugurate, plunge into
again: 5 renew 6 resume
a journey: 2 go 4 pack, sail 5 board, leave, start 6 embark, set off, set out 7 emplane, entrain, jump off, set sail, ship out 8 go aboard, set forth 9 leave port, undertake
a paragraph: 6 indent
business: 4 open
hostilities: 5 set on, storm 6 attack, engage, invade, strike 7 set upon
to develop: 3 bud 6 sprout 9 germinate
to like: 6 grow on
to ~ with: 5 first
Begin, Menachem: 2 P.M. 7 Israeli 8 Nobelist
Nobelist Peace partner: 5 Sadat
predecessor: 5 Rabin
successor: 6 Shamir
beginner: 3 cub 4 tiro, tyro 5 newie, pupil 6 greeny, newbie, novice 7 amateur, dabbler, entrant, learner, new hand, recruit, trainee 8 freshman, initiate, neophyte, newcomer, putterer 9 fledgling, greenhorn, novitiate 10 apprentice, dilettante, first-timer, tenderfoot
beginner's —: 4 luck
beginning: 3 top 4 as of, dawn, germ, rise, seed 5 birth, early, first, front, get-go, git-go, intro, onset, start 6 advent, day one, origin, outset, source, spring 7 genesis, infancy, initial, kickoff, leadoff, nascent, opening, preface, prelude, premier, primary 8 creation, entrance, original, preamble, premiere 9 emanation, etymology, inception, inceptive, incipient, induction, principle, square one, threshold 10 antecedent, conception, derivation, elementary, envisaging, generation, incipience, initiation
beginnings: 4 root 6 origin 7 infancy
Beginnings (1971 song)
artist: Chicago
— **Beginning to Look a Lot...:** 3 It's
— **Begins at Forty:** 4 Life
— **Begins for Andy Hardy:** 4 Life
Begin the Beguine
bandleader: 4 Shaw
composer: Cole Porter
begird: 3 tie 4 belt, bind 5 bound, box in, hem in, truss 6 buckle, circle, fasten, shut in 7 confine, contain, enclose, inclose 8 cincture, encircle, surround 9 encompass
be glad to: 6 no prob 8 you got it 9 no problem
see also of course
Begley, Ed: 5 actor
Begley Jr., Ed: 5 actor
TV: St. Elsewhere
begone: 4 away, scat, shoo 5 scram 6 avaunt, beat it, get out 7 amscray, buzz off, get lost, push off, vamoose 9 take a hike 10 go fly a kite
starter: 3 woe

begonia: **5** plant **6** flower
__, Be Good!: **4** Lady
Beg pardon!: **4** ahem **5** sorry **8** excuse me
begrime: **4** foul, soil **5** dirty, stain, sully, taint **6** bedaub, befoul, smirch, smudge **7** besmear, blacken, pollute, tarnish **8** besmirch
begrimed: **5** dirty, grimy, smoky, sooty **6** filthy, grubby, grungy **7** unswept **8** maculate, polluted, slovenly, unwashed **10** unsanitary
begrudge: **4** envy **5** covet, spite, stint
begrudging: **7** envious, jealous **9** unwilling
beg to __: **6** differ
beguile: **3** con, lie, wow **4** bait, coax, dupe, fool, lure, rook, scam, sell, snow, trap, vamp, wile **5** amuse, charm, cheat, tempt, trick **6** allure, cajole, delude, divert, entice, entrap, lead on, rope in, take in, tickle **7** attract, bewitch, deceive, defraud, delight, enchant, enthral, finagle, finesse, inthral, mislead, pretend, two-time **8** enthrall, entrance, flimflam, hoodwink, inthrall, inveigle **9** captivate, disinform, enrapture, entertain, fascinate, infatuate
beguiled: **4** rapt **5** led on **7** far gone **8** held fast, ravished **10** infatuated
beguiler: **4** vamp **5** siren **6** gigolo **7** charmer **9** inveigler, temptress **10** gold digger
beguiling: **5** siren **8** alluring, delusive, inviting, specious **9** deceitful, deceptive **10** enchanting, fallacious, misleading
beguine: **5** dance
  relative: **5** rumba **6** rhumba
begum
  spouse: **3** aga **4** agha
begun: **8** underway **9** happening **10** in progress
behalf: **4** part, sake, side **7** account, benefit **8** interest
  on ~: **6** in lieu
  on ~ of: **3** for **7** instead **9** acting for, in place of
Behan, Brendan: **5** Irish **6** writer
  work: Borstal Boy
    The Hostage
    The Quare Fellow
Behar: **3** Joy
behave: **2** do **3** act **4** mind, work **5** react **6** acquit, deport **7** act well, comport, conduct, conform, go along, operate, perform, respond **8** function **10** act one's age, stay in line, toe the line
  toward: **5** treat **6** handle
__-behaved: **4** well
behaved, badly: **7** naughty
__ Behaving Badly: **3** Men
behavior: **3** way **4** form, mien **6** habits, manner, morals, policy **7** actions, bearing, conduct, manners **8** carriage, demeanor, protocol **9** treatment **10** deportment
  brave ~: **5** valor **7** courage
  code of ~: **5** ethic **6** ethics **8** morality, protocol
  past ~: **6** record
  pattern: **5** habit, type A, Type B **8** syndrome
  well-mannered ~: **4** tact **7** decorum **8** breeding, civility, courtesy, protocol, urbanity **9** etiquette, gallantry, gentility **10** politeness, refinement
__ behavior: **4** good **6** animal
behavioral science: **10** psychology
behemoth: **5** giant **7** mammoth, monster **8** colossus **9** leviathan
behest: **4** word **5** order **6** charge, urging **7** bidding, command, dictate, mandate, precept, request **9** direction, directive, prompting
behind: **3** aft, for, off, pro **4** last, late, next, slow **5** after, tardy **6** astern, in back, in debt, latish, losing **7** backing, belated, causing, delayed, ensuing, lagging, overdue, past due **8** backward, in back of, trailing **9** following, in arrears, later than **10** delinquent, succeeding, supporting
  combining form: **7** opistho-
  prefix: **4** meta-, post- **5** retro-
behind __: **4** bars
__ behind: **3** lag **4** drop, fall
Behind Closed Doors (1973 song)
  artist: Charlie Rich
behindhand: **3** lax **4** late **5** tardy **7** belated, overdue **9** negligent, unheedful
Behind That Curtain hero: **4** Chan
behind the __: **5** times, wheel **6** scenes
behind the __ ball: **5** eight
__ behind the ears: **3** wet
behind-the-scenes: **6** covert, secret
behold: **3** see **4** ecce, espy, look, tada, view **5** sight, ta-dah, voilà **6** look at, notice, peek at, regard, remark **7** discern, observe, witness **8** gaze upon, perceive **10** get a load of
  in Latin: **4** ecce
  something to ~: **6** eyeful
  the man, in Latin: **8** ecce homo
__ behold: **5** lo and
Behold: **6** polish
  competitor: **6** Endust, Pledge **10** Liquid Gold, Old English
beholden: **4** into **5** owing **6** in hock **7** obliged **8** grateful, indebted, thankful **9** obligated **10** honorbound
  be ~: **3** owe
beholder: **6** viewer **7** watcher, witness **8** observer, onlooker **9** spectator **10** eyewitness
__ Be Home For Christmas: **3** I'll
behoof: **3** use **7** benefit **9** advantage
behoove: **5** befit **6** beseem
Behrman, S.N.: **6** writer
Beiderbecke: **3** Bix
  first name: Leon
  genre: **4** jazz
  instrument: **5** piano **6** cornet
beige: **4** gray, grey **5** brown, color **6** almond, suntan **7** neutral **8** brownish **9** earth tone
  relative: *see* brown color
beignet: **6** pastry
Beijing: **4** city, town **7** capital
  locale: **3** PRC **5** China
Beijing __: **4** duck
Bei Mir Bist du Schoen (1938 song)
  artist: Andrews Sisters
__ be in England...: **4** Oh to
being: **4** body, esse, life, self, soul **5** human **6** animal, entity, matter, mortal, nature, person **7** essence, reality **8** creature, life form, organism **9** actuality, existence, something **10** individual, living soul
  artificial ~: **5** droid, robot **9** automaton
  big ~: **5** giant, titan **7** Cyclops, mammoth **9** leviathan
  bring into ~: **4** make **5** breed **6** create
  combining form: **3** ont- **4** onto-
  come into ~: **5** arise, start **6** grow up, spring **7** develop
  divine ~: **3** god **4** daka **5** deity **6** dakini **7** goddess
  enjoy ~ alive: **4** live **5** party **7** have fun **9** delight in, whoop it up
  for the time ~: **3** now **9** meanwhile, temporary
  have ~: **3** are **5** exist
  human ~: **3** man **4** life, soul **6** person **10** individual, living soul
  in Latin: **4** esse
  mode of ~: **5** state
  strike one as ~: **4** seem **6** appear
  supernatural ~: **3** imp
  that ~ the case: **2** so **4** ergo, if so, then, thus **5** hence
  time ~: **5** nonce **7** present
__ being: **5** human
__-being: **3** ill **4** well
Being and Having
  author: Gabriel Marcel
Being and Nothingness
  author: Jean-Paul Sartre
Being John Malkovich (1999 film)
  cast: John Cusack, Cameron Diaz, Catherine Keener, John Malkovich
  director: Spike Jonze
Being There: **4** film **5** novel
  author: Jerzy Kosinski
  cast: Melvyn Douglas, Shirley MacLaine, Peter Sellers, Jack Warden
  director: Hal Ashby
Beirut: **4** city, port, town **7** capital
  locale: **7** Lebanon
Be it __ so humble...: **4** ever
__ be it from me: **3** far
bejewel: **5** adorn
bejeweled: **6** ornate **10** glittering
Be kind to your web-__ friends: **6** footed
bel __: **5** canto
Bel: **7** Kaufman
Bel __: **3** Air **5** Paese
Bela: **3** Kun **5** Fleck **6** Bartók, Lugosi, Schick **7** Karolyi
  father: **8** Benjamin
  son: **3** Iri
Béla: **6** Bartók
belabor: **4** lash **6** overdo, rehash, stress **7** dwell on **8** go too far, overwork **9** dwell upon, go on about **10** hammer home
Belafonte: **5** Harry, Shari
Belafonte, Harry: **5** actor **6** singer
  daughter: Shari
  song: Day-O (1957)
Bel Air: **3** car **4** auto, city, town **5** Chevy **9** Chevrolet **10** automobile
  locale: **8** Maryland **10** California
Belarus: **6** nation **7** country
  capital: **5** Minsk
  city: **5** Brest, Gomel, Orsha, Pinsk
  neighbor: **6** Latvia, Poland, Russia **7** Ukraine **9** Lithuania
Belasco: **5** David
belated: **4** slow **5** tardy **6** behind, remiss **7** delayed, overdue **8** detained **10** behindhand, last-minute, unpunctual
belay: **4** stop **6** fasten
belch: **4** burp, spew, spue **5** eruct **9** discharge
Belch, Toby: **3** sot
beldam: **3** hag **5** crone, shrew, witch **6** virago **8** harridan **9** henpecker
Beldar Conehead's daughter: **6** Connie
beleaguer: **4** bait **5** annoy, harry, tease, worry **6** assail, harass, noodge, plague **7** shut off, shut out **8** surround **9** persecute
beleaguerment: **5** siege
Belém: **4** city, port, town
  locale: **6** Brazil
  once: **4** Pará
belemnite: **5** shell **6** fossil **8** seashell
Belfast: **4** city, port, town
  locale: **7** Ireland
  org.: **3** IRA
  town near ~: **6** Antrim
belfry: **5** spire, tower **6** cupola **7** steeple **8** pinnacle **9** bell tower
  dweller: **3** bat
  sound: **4** bong, peal, ring, toll
Belg.
  see Belgium
belga: **5** money
Bel Geddes: **6** Norman **7** Barbara
Bel Geddes, Barbara: **7** actress
  TV: Dallas
Belgian __: **4** hare **5** Congo **6** endive **7** griffon
Belgium: **6** nation **7** country
  ancient ~: **4** Gaul
  capital: **8** Brussels
  chemist: **6** Solvay
  city: **4** Mons **5** Aalst, Alost, Ghent, Liege, Ypres **6** Bruges, Ostend **7** Antwerp **9** Zeebrugge
  marble: **5** rance
  money: **5** belga, franc **7** centime
  neighbor: **6** France **7** Germany, Holland **10** Luxembourg **11** Netherlands
  Nobelist in Chemistry: **9** Prigogine
  Nobelist in Literature: **11** Maeterlinck
  Nobelist in Medicine: **6** Bordet, de Duve **7** Heymans
  Nobelist in Peace: **4** Pire **9** Beernaert **10** La Fontaine
  org.: **4** Leie, NATO
  painter: **5** Ensor **8** Magritte
  port: **5** Ghent **6** Ostend **7** Antwerp **9** Zeebrugge
  province: **5** Namur
  resort: **3** Spa
  river: **3** Lys **4** Oise, Yser **5** Meuse, Senne
  stew: **10** carbonnade
  violinist: **5** Ysaye
Belgrade: **4** city, town **7** capital
  city near ~: **5** Vrsac
  locale: **10** Yugoslavia
  native: **4** Slav
  river: **4** Sava **6** Danube
Belial: **5** devil, Satan

belie: 4 mock 5 rebut 6 negate, refute 7 explode, gainsay, slander 8 backbite, disprove 10 calumniate, contradict, controvert
belief: 3 ism 4 idea, side, view 5 cause, credo, creed, dogma, faith, guess, logic, maxim, stand, tenet, trust 6 ethics, notion, school, theory, thesis 7 feeling, mindset, opinion, precept, thought 8 attitude, credence, doctrine, ideology, judgment, position, reliance, religion, standard 9 principle, rationale, sentiment, suspicion, teachings, tradition 10 acceptance, assumption, conclusion, confidence, conjecture, contention, conviction, dependance, dependence, estimation, hypothesis, impression, persuasion
prefix: 4 ideo-
beliefs: 4 lore 5 ethos 8 ideology 10 philosophy
set of ~: 5 crédo, creed, dogma 6 mythos
believable: 6 honest, likely 7 tenable 8 credible, possible, probable, rational 9 authentic, fiduciary, plausible, thinkable 10 aboveboard, acceptable, convincing, creditable, imaginable, impressive, persuasive, presumable, reasonable, satisfying, supposable
believe: 3 buy 4 deem, feel, hold, hope, view 5 fancy, judge, sense, think, trust 6 accept, affirm, assume, bank on, credit, expect, gather, hold to, look to, reckon, regard, rely on 7 count on, imagine, presume, suppose, suspect, swallow, swear by 8 conceive, consider, depend on, gamble on, hold with, maintain, theorize 9 count upon, postulate 10 conjecture, presuppose, understand
hard to ~: 4 tall 10 incredible
in: 4 rely 5 trust 6 accept 7 swear by 10 put faith in
lead to ~: 4 hint 5 imply, infer, let on 6 tip off 7 suggest 8 indicate, intimate, persuade 9 brainwash, catechize, insinuate
make ~: 3 lie 4 fool, play, pose 5 dream, enact, feign 7 act as if, act like, imagine, playact, pretend 8 simulate 9 fantasize
old-style: 4 trow
__-believe: 4 make
...believe __ the whole thing!: 4 I ate
Believe (1999 song)
artist: Cher
believed: 7 reputed 8 reported
__ Believe in Magic: 5 Do You
__ believe in yesterday: 3 Oh I
Believe It or Not!
creator: Robert Ripley
entry: 6 oddity
believer: 5 deist 7 apostle 8 adherent, canonist, disciple, follower, upholder 9 dogmatist, layperson, supporter
suffix: 3 -ist, -ite 5 -arian
__ believer: 4 true
__ Believer: 3 I'm a, Old 4 True
__ Believes in Me: 3 She
believing: 4 sure 5 loyal 7 certain 8 positive, sanguine 9 convinced, credulous, satisfied 10 falling for, optimistic
Belinda: 4 moon 8 Carlisle
author: Anne Rice
planet: 6 Uranus
belittle: 3 dis, pan, rip 4 gibe, jeer, jibe, mock, slam, slur, snub 5 abase, abuse, cavil, decry, knock, libel, lower, roast, scoff, scorn, smear, sneer, spurn, taunt 6 defame, demean, deride, dump on, heckle, impugn, jibe at, malign, offend, rebuff, show up, slight, vilify 7 affront, asperse, blister, cry down, degrade, detract, disdain, laugh at, mortify, put down, rank out, run down, scoff at, slander, sneer at, traduce 8 backbite, badmouth, denounce, derogate, diminish, discount, downplay, minimize, play down, ridicule, take down, talk down, tear down, vilipend 9 blaspheme, criticize, denigrate, deprecate, discredit, disparage, frown upon, humiliate, shoot down, underrate 10 calumniate, disrespect, undervalue
belittlement: 5 abuse 7 slander
belittler: 6 critic 8 vilifier 9 detractor
belittling: 8 critical 10 derogatory, detractive, minimizing
Beliveau: 4 Jean
Belize: 4 city, port, town 6 nation 7 country
capital: 8 Belmopan
money: 4 cent 6 dollar
neighbor: 6 Mexico 9 Guatemala
org.: 3 OAS
bell: 4 gong, sign 5 alarm, chime 6 curfew, densho, dinger, kenong, ringer, signal, tocsin 8 angklung, carillon 10 percussion
alternative: 4 gong
church ~: 7 angelus
ender: 3 boy, hop 4 bird, wort 6 flower
literary ~ town: 4 Atri 5 Adano
Longfellow, Henry Wadsworth ~ town: 4 Atri
ring a ~: 6 recall 8 remember 9 recognize
ringer: 3 cow, ewe 4 lama 6 caller, priest 7 visitor
sound: 4 bong, ding, dong, peal, ring, ting, toll 5 clang, knell 6 jingle, tinkle
starter: 3 bar, cow 4 blue, door, dumb, hare, snow
tongue of a ~: 7 clapper
tower: 6 belfry 7 steeple
what a ~ ends: 5 round
bell __: 3 cow, jar, lap 4 arch, bird, book, buoy, frog, pull, push, seat, toad 5 crank, curve, glass, metal 6 beaker, pepper 7 captain, heather, housing
bell-__: 3 hop 6 bottom 7 cranked
__ bell: 3 air, tap 5 ring a 6 anchor, dinner, diving, jingle, Lutine, silver, vesper 7 Angelus, Sanctus
Bell: 2 Ma 3 Tom 4 city, town 5 Acton, Ellis 6 Archie, Currer
locale: 10 California
partner: 6 Howell
Watson to ~: 4 asst. 9 assistant
Bell __: 4 Labs
__ Bell: 4 Baby, Taco 5 Ellis, Glass 7 Liberty, Mission, Packard
Bella: 5 Abzug
belladonna: 5 toxin 6 poison 10 nightshade
belladonna __: 4 lily
Bellamy: 4 Walt 5 Madge, Ralph
Bellamy, Walt: 5 cager
milieu: 5 court
org.: 3 NBA
sport: 10 basketball
Bell and __: 6 Howell
Bell, Book and Candle (1958 film)
cast: Jack Lemmon, Kim Novak, Janice Rule, James Stewart
cat: 9 Pyewacket
director: Richard Quine
bell-bottoms: 5 jeans, pants 8 trousers
like ~: 3 mod 6 flared
Bellboy, The (1960 film)
cast: Jerry Lewis
director: Jerry Lewis
Bell, Cool Papa: 10 outfielder
belle: 6 looker 8 ballgoer 9 debutante
admirer: 4 beau
époque: 3 era
of the ball: 3 deb 9 debutante
belle __: 6 époque
Belle: 4 Lulu 5 Starr 6 Albert
Belle, Albert
sport: 8 baseball
Belleau Wood: 6 battle
Bellefleur
author: Joyce Carol Oates
Belle of the Ball
composer: Leroy Anderson
Bellerophon: 5 horse
owner: 7 Pegasus
belles-lettres: 7 writing 10 literature
belletristic: 8 literary
Bellevue: 4 city, town
locale: 8 Nebraska 10 Washington
Bell for Adano, A
author: John Hersey
bellhop: 4 page 5 toter 6 porter 7 carrier
call for a ~: 5 front
Belli: 6 Melvin 8 Giuseppe
bellicose: 4 cold, cool, mean, ugly 5 nasty, surly, upset 6 chilly, ornery 7 glacial, hateful, hawkish, hostile, martial, warlike, warring 8 contrary, factious, fighting, inimical, militant, ructious, spiteful 9 combative, litigious, malicious, wrangling 10 aggressive, jingoistic, malevolent, pugnacious, rebellious
god: 4 Ares, Mars
__-bellied sapsucker: 6 yellow
belligerence: 5 fight 8 acrimony 9 hostility
belligerent: 4 cold, mean 5 nasty, surly, upset 6 fierce, ornery 7 fighter, glacial, hateful, hostile, martial, warlike, warring 8 battling, contrary, fighting, inimical, militant, spiteful 9 bellicose, combative, litigious, malicious, offensive, truculent, wrangling 10 aggressive, jingoistic, malevolent, pugnacious
stance: 6 akimbo
Belli, Melvin: 3 att. 4 atty. 6 lawyer 8 attorney
org.: 3 ABA
Bellingham: 4 city, town
locale: 10 Washington
Belling the Cat
source: 4 Esop 5 Aesop
Bellini: 8 Giovanni, Vincenzo
Bellini, Vincenzo work: Norma
Bell Jar, The
author: Sylvia Plath
Bell Labs creation: 4 Unix
bell metal: 5 alloy
component: 3 tin 6 copper
Bello, Andrés: 4 poet 10 Venezuelan
Belloc, Hilaire: 6 writer 7 British
work: Cautionary Tales
Mr. Burden
On Everything
On Nothing
The Path to Rome
Bell of __, The: 4 Atri
Bellona brother: 4 Mars
bellow: 3 bay, cry 4 bark, bawl, bray, call, howl, rant, roar, wail, yaup, yawp, yell, yelp, yowl 5 growl, noise, shout, whoop 6 clamor, holler, scream, shriek 7 bluster, exclaim, resound, sing out, thunder 8 let loose 10 vociferate
bellowing: 4 loud 5 aroar, noisy
Bellows: 3 Gil
Bellow, Saul: 6 writer 8 Nobelist
work: The Adventures of Augie March
Dangling Man
The Dean's December
Henderson the Rain King
Herzog
Him With His Foot in His Mouth
Humboldt's Gift
It All Adds Up
More Die of Heartbreak
Mr. Sammler's Planet
Ravelstein
Seize the Day
A Theft
To Jerusalem and Back
The Victim
bell pepper: 6 veggie 9 vegetable
__ Bell Rock: 6 Jingle
bells: 8 carillon, gankogui
Canterbury ~: 5 plant 6 flower
eight ~: 6 midday
sound of ~: 4 bong, ding, dong, peal, ring, ting, toll 5 chime, clang 6 jingle, tinkle
with all the ~ and whistles: 6 deluxe 8 complete
__ bells: 5 coral, hell's 6 sleigh
__ Bells: 3 Bow 6 Jingle, Silver 7 Tubular
Bells Are Ringing (1956 musical)
choreographer: Bob Fosse
composer: Betty Comden, Adolph Green, Jule Styne
Bells Are Ringing (1960 film)
cast: Fred Clark, Judy Holliday, Dean Martin
character: 3 Sue 4 Ella, Jeff 6 Sandor
director: Vincente Minnelli
bell-shaped __: 5 curve
bell-shaped flower: 5 tulip
Bells of St. Mary's, The (1945 film)
cast: Ingrid Bergman, Bing Crosby, Henry Travers
director: Leo McCarey
Bell Song, The opera: 5 Lakme
bells on her __: 4 toes
Bellson, Louis: 7 drummer
genre: 4 jazz
spouse: Pearl Bailey

Bells, The: **4** poem
author: Edgar Allan Poe
bell the ___: **3** cat
Bell, The
author: Iris Murdoch
___ Bell, The: **7** Liberty
bellum opposite: **3** pax
starter: **4** ante
bellwether mate: **3** ewe
belly: **3** gut, pot, tum **4** craw **5** swell, tummy **6** inside, paunch **7** abdomen, gizzard, stomach **9** bay window, intumesce, spare tire **10** midsection
button: **5** navel **9** umbilicus
dancer accessory: **4** veil **5** zills **6** armlet
ender: **4** ache, band **6** button
fire in the ~: **5** drive **7** longing **8** ambition
flop: **4** dive
go on one's ~: **5** crawl
go ~ up: **4** fail, fold **6** topple
laugh: **4** boff, roar **6** guffaw
muscles: **3** abs
starter: **3** pot, sow
up to: **4** near **8** approach
yellow ~: **4** wimp **5** sissy **6** coward, craven **7** chicken, dastard **8** weakling **9** fraidy cat, jellyfish
belly ___: **3** pan **4** bust, flop, girt, slam **5** dance, girth, laugh **6** buster, button, dancer **7** landing
___ belly: **4** pork
bellyache: **4** beef, carp, crab, fuss, moan **5** gripe, groan, whine **6** grouch, grouse, kvetch, repine, squawk, yammer **7** grumble, protest **8** complain **9** grievance, make a fuss
bellyacher: **5** grump **6** grouch, moaner **7** crybaby **8** grumbler
bellyband: **4** belt
belly-button variety: **5** innie, outie
bellyful: **6** enough **7** surfeit **8** up to here
Belly of Pairs
author: Émile Zola
Belmondo, Jean-Paul: **5** actor
film: Breathless (1959)
Cartouche (1964)
Two Women (1961)
Belmont: **5** track **9** racetrack
racer: **6** equine
transaction: **3** bet **5** wager
Belmonts
leader: **4** Dion
Belmont Stakes: **4** race **9** horse race
Belmopan: **4** city, town **7** capital
locale: **6** Belize
Belo, Carlos: **8** Nobelist, Timorese
Belo Horizonte: **4** city, town
locale: **6** Brazil
Beloit: **4** city, town
locale: **9** Wisconsin
belong: **2** go **3** fit **4** bide, jibe, live, mesh, rank, suit, vest **5** agree, apply, fit in, lodge, relax, tie in **6** go with, inhere, reside, settle **7** blend in, connect, pertain, qualify **9** appertain, chime with, correlate, harmonize **10** feel at home, go together
to: **6** relate **7** pertain **8** adhere to **9** appertain
belonging: **6** native **7** kinship, loyalty, rapport **8** affinity **9** commodity, inclusion **10** acceptance, attachment
cost of ~: **4** dues
to: **5** under
to thee: **5** thine
belongings: **4** gear **5** goods, stuff **6** assets, estate, things, wealth **7** effects **8** chattels, holdings, property **9** equipment
belote: **4** game **8** card game
beloved: **6** adored, prized **7** admired, doted on, revered **8** cared for, endeared, esteemed, hallowed, idolized **9** cherished, treasured, venerated, worshiped
by: **6** dear to
make ~: **6** endear
name meaning ~: **3** Amy **4** Cara **5** Aimee, David **6** Amanda **7** Erasmus
see also sweetheart
___ beloved...: **6** Dearly
Beloved
author: Toni Morrison
below: **4** down **5** infra, neath, under **7** beneath, south of **8** inferior, less than **9** downwards **10** inferior to, too good for, underneath, unworthy of
combining form: **6** infero-
ender: **6** ground
in French: **4** à bas
prefix: **3** sub- **5** infra-, under- **6** contra-
belowdecks, put: **4** lade, load, stow
below the ___: **4** belt, line
below the belt: **4** foul **5** dirty, nasty **6** unfair, unjust **8** cowardly **9** dishonest
Bel Paese: **6** cheese
Belson: **5** Jerry
belt: **3** bop, hit, obi **4** area, band, bash, beat, biff, blow, cuff, flog, gird, hurt, ring, road, sash, slam, slug, sock, swat, swig, whip, zone **5** blast, cinch, paste, punch, smack, smash, smite, snort, spank, speed, strap, strip, swath, tract, whack, whang **6** begird, cestus, circle, fascia, fasten, girdle, hamaki, imbibe, locale, pommel, pummel, region, ribbon, swathe, thrash, thwack, wallop **7** baldric, clobber, expanse, scourge, section, swallow **8** baldrick, ceinture, cincture, conveyer, conveyor, district, locality, uppercut **9** bandoleer, bandolier, bellyband, haul off on, surcingle, territory, waistband **10** cummerbund, expressway
barber ~: **5** strop
below the ~: **4** foul **6** unfair, unjust
black ~: **4** rank **6** expert
clip-on: **4** mike **5** pager **6** beeper **8** tie clasp **10** microphone
combining form: **3** zon- **4** zono-
decorative ~: **3** obi **4** sash **5** patte
don a ~: **4** gird
ender: **3** way **4** line
holder: **4** loop
Japanese ~: **3** obi **6** hamaki
makeshift ~: **4** rope
out: **4** sing, yell **5** shout **8** vocalize
part: **6** buckle
quick ~: **3** tot **5** snort **6** jigger
seat ~: **5** strap
tightening: **6** layoff **7** cutback **8** decrease **9** lessening, reduction **10** diminution
tighten one's ~: **3** eke **4** save **5** skimp, stint **6** reduce **7** cut back **9** economize
belt ___: **3** bag **4** line **6** course, sander **7** highway
___ belt: **3** fan, lap **4** farm, life, rust, seat **5** black, brown, chain, cinch, money, sword, white **6** marine, Orion's, safety, timing, weight **7** borscht, tornado
___ Belt: **3** Sun **4** Corn, Rust, Snow **5** Bible, Frost **6** Cotton
belt, black
see karate
belted: **4** girt **7** cinched
constellation: **5** Orion
belted ___: **4** tire
___-belted tire: **4** bias
beltless dress: **4** sack, tent **6** muumuu, sheath
beltline: **5** waist
beltmaker tool: **3** awl
Beltran, Robert: **5** actor
TV: Star Trek: Voyager
beluga: **4** fish **5** whale **6** caviar **7** caviare **8** cetacean, sturgeon **9** leviathan
product: **3** roe
relative: ***see*** cetacean
Belushi: **3** Jim **4** John **5** James
Belushi, James: **5** actor
film: About Last Night... (1986)
Diary of a Hitman (1992)
K-9 (1989)
Once Upon a Crime (1992)
Only the Lonely (1991)
The Principal (1987)
Red Heat (1988)
TV: According to Jim
Belushi, John: **5** actor **8** comedian
film: The Blues Brothers (1980)
Continental Divide (1981)
National Lampoon's Animal House (1978)
Neighbors (1981)
TV: Saturday Night Live
Belva: **5** Plain
belvedere: **6** cupola, gazebo **7** lookout
Belvedere: **3** car **4** auto **8** Plymouth
Belvidere: **4** city, town
locale: **8** Illinois
___ Belvoir: **4** Fort
Belzer: **7** Richard
bema: **9** sanctuary
neighbor: **4** apse, nave
Beman, Deane: **6** golfer
___ Be Me: **5** Let It
bemean: **5** lower
Bemelmans, Ludwig: **6** writer
work: Madeleine
bemire: **4** soil **5** dirty, muddy
bemoan: **3** rue **4** wail, weep **5** mourn **6** bewail, grieve, lament, regret, sorrow **7** cry over, deplore, weep for **9** grieve for **10** take it hard
bemuse: **4** daze, stun **5** addle **6** puzzle **7** confuse, mystify, nonplus, perplex, stupefy **8** bewilder, confound, distract, paralyse, paralyze **9** give pause, preoccupy
bemused: **4** asea, lost, rapt **5** at sea **10** spellbound
Be My Baby (1963 song)
artist: Ronettes
___ Be My Girl: **5** Use Ta
be my guest
see of course
Be My Guest (1959 song)
artist: Fats Domino
Ben: **4** Blue, Bova, Gunn, Lyon **5** Casey, Cross, Hecht, Hogan, Shahn, Stein, uncle **6** Bernie, Jonson, Maddow, Murphy, Piazza, Savage, Turpin, Vereen **7** Affleck, Bradlee, Gazzara, Johnson, Matlock, Stiller, Stoloff **8** Crenshaw, Franklin, Kingsley **9** Alexander, Mottelson **10** Cartwright, Sharpsteen
of films: **3** rat
Ben (1972 song)
artist: Michael Jackson
Ben-___: **3** Hur **4** Ammi
___ Ben: **3** Big
Benaderet: **3** Bea
___ Ben Adhem: **4** Abou
Benadryl
competitor: ***see*** cold remedy
Ben-Ammi father: **3** Lot
Benatar, Pat
song: Hit Me With Your Best Shot (1980)
Invincible (1985)
Love Is a Battlefield (1983)
We Belong (1984)
Benavente, Jacinto: **6** writer **7** Spanish **8** Nobelist **10** playwright
Benazir: **6** Bhutto
father: **3** Ali
Benben, Brian: **5** actor
spouse: Madeleine Stowe
Ben Casey (ABC drama)
cast: Vince Edwards (Dr. Ben Casey)
Sam Jaffe (Dr. David Zorba)
bench: **3** pew **4** seat **5** chair, court, judge, ledge, table **6** exedra, settee **7** exhedra **9** courtroom, furniture, judiciary, worktable
ender: **4** mark **6** warmer
judge's ~: **4** banc
locale: **6** church, dugout **9** courtroom
rapper: **5** gavel
ride the ~: **3** sit
starter: **4** work
warmer: **3** sub **5** scrub **9** alternate **10** substitute
wear: **4** robe **7** uniform
bench ___: **3** dog **4** hook, mark, show, stop, test, work **5** check, press, screw, table **6** jockey, warmer **7** warrant
___ bench: **4** back, milk **5** front, piano, water
___ Bench: **5** King's **6** Queen's
bench-clearer: **5** brawl, fight, melee **10** free-for-all
benching, reason for a: **5** slump
Bench, Johnny: **3** Red **7** catcher
Benchley: **5** Peter **6** Robert
Benchley, Peter: **6** writer
work: Beast
The Deep
The Island
Jaws
Rummies
Shark Trouble
Benchley, Robert: **3** wit **6** writer
benchmark: **3** par **4** norm **5** gauge, index **7** measure **8** landmark, stan-

dard **9** criterion, yardstick **10** touchstone
bench-press target: 3 pec **4** pecs
bend: 3 arc, bow, jog, mar, nod, sag, tip, yaw **4** arch, curl, flex, fold, hook, kink, lean, loop, mold, sway, tack, tilt, turn, veer, warp **5** angle, budge, crook, curve, droop, elbow, hunch, shape, sinus, slant, slope, slump, stoop, sweep, twine, twist, yield **6** buckle, camber, crease, crouch, dog-ear, dogleg, hunker, slouch, soften, submit, swerve **7** contort, deflect, diverge, flexure, incline **8** flection, flecture, landmark, lean over, persuade **9** curvature, deviation, genuflect, influence, sinuosity **10** compromise, divergence, lumber flaw, predispose
an elbow: 3 sip **4** swig, tope **5** drink, snort **6** imbibe, tipple
ballet ~: 4 plié **5** fondu
down: 5 hunch, kneel, stoop **6** crouch **8** lean over
fairway ~: 6 dogleg
fisherman's ~: 4 knot
hawser ~: 4 knot
one's ear: 3 gab, yak **4** talk **5** run on
out of shape: 4 warp
over backward: 4 arch **6** strive
plumbing ~: 3 ell, ess **5** elbow
river ~: 5 bight, elbow, oxbow
the head: 3 nap, nod **4** doze **6** drowse
the knee: 3 bow **7** bow down **9** genuflect
to: 4 heed, mind, obey **5** agree **6** accept, follow, fulfil **7** abide by, fulfill, observe, respect, truckle **8** carry out
to one's will: 4 boss **5** bully, force **8** arm-twist, dominate, domineer, override, overrule **10** boss around, intimidate
U-shaped ~: 5 oxbow
bend __: 5 an ear **6** dexter
bend __ backward: 4 over
__ bend: 4 knee
__ Bend: 4 Gila
bendable: 4 soft **6** lissom **7** lissome, pliable **8** flexible
bended knee, go on: 3 ask, beg, sue **4** urge **5** crawl, plead **7** beseech, declare, entreat, implore, propose **8** petition **9** importune **10** supplicate
bender: 3 jag **4** tear, toot **5** binge, spree
elbow ~: 3 sot **4** lush
eyeball ~: 5 op art
fender ~: 4 dent **5** crash
metal ~: 5 swage
of a sort: 4 knee **5** elbow
wire ~: 6 pliers
__ bender: 3 on a **4** mind **6** fender, gender
Bender, Chief: 7 pitcher **8** Athletic
Bend It Like Beckham (2003 film)
cast: Keira Knightley, Parminder Nagra
Bendix
competitor: *see* appliance brand
Bendix, William: 5 actor
TV: The Life of Riley
Bend Me, Shape Me (1967 song)
artist: American Breed
__ Bend National Park: 3 Big
__ bene: 4 nota
Ben E. __: 4 King
Be Near Me (1985 song)
artist: ABC
beneath: 3 low **5** below, infra, lower, under **8** less than **10** inferior to, unworthy of
prefix: 4 hypo- **5** under-
__ Beneath My Wings: 4 Wind
Benedetto: 5 Croce
benedict: 5 groom **7** husband **10** bridegroom
Benedict: 4 Dirk, Paul, pope **5** saint **6** Arnold **7** pontiff
__ Benedict: 4 eggs
Benedictine: 4 monk **5** drink **8** beverage **9** religious
address: 6 frater **7** brother
title: 3 Dom
benediction: 2 OK **4** okay **5** grace **6** orison, prayer, thanks **8** blessing
give a ~: 5 bless
windup: 4 amen
Benedict XVI: 4 pope **7** pontiff
benefaction: 4 boon, gift **5** favor, grant **7** largess, present, service **8** blessing, courtesy, donation, good deed, good turn, kindness, largesse, offering **9** patronage
benefactor: 5 angel, donor, giver **6** backer, friend, patron **7** founder, grantor, sponsor **8** altruist, financer **9** assistant, protector, supporter **10** grubstaker, Santa Claus, subscriber, subsidizer, well-wisher
Benefactor, The
author: Susan Sontag
benefice: 6 office **7** prebend, revenue, stipend **8** sinecure **9** emolument **10** preferment
ecclesiastical ~: 5 glebe
beneficence: 4 alms, boon, gift **5** heart **6** relief, succor **7** benefit, charity, present **8** altruism, blessing, donation, goodness, kindness, largesse, offering **10** generosity
beneficent: 4 good, kind **5** noble **6** kindly **7** liberal **8** generous, gracious, merciful, princely **10** benevolent, charitable
one: 5 donor, giver
beneficial: 4 fine, good, nice, okay **5** great, handy, legit, lucky, moral, noble, of use, utile **6** proper, useful **7** ethical, gainful, healthy, helpful, hopeful **8** all right, friendly, fruitful, laudable, pleasant, pleasing, positive, remedial, salutary, splendid, superior, valuable **9** admirable, agreeable, covetable, desirable, excellent, expedient, favorable, healthful, reputable, rewarding, wholesome **10** acceptable, convenient, creditable, profitable, propitious, salubrious, worthwhile
least ~: 5 worst
see also wonderful
beneficiary: 4 heir **5** donee, payee **6** bearer, coheir **7** grantee, heiress, legatee **8** assignee, receiver
benefit: 3 aid, use **4** boon, gain, gala, gift, good, help, perk, plus, sake **5** asset, avail, bazar, edify, event, favor, fruit, merit, serve, value, worth **6** assist, bazaar, beauty, behalf, behoof, pay off, profit, raffle, return, upside, virtue **7** behoove, enhance, further, godsend, improve, promote, service, utility, welfare, work for **8** bake sale, blessing, interest **9** advantage, privilege, well-being **10** betterment, expediency, fundraiser, percentage
added ~: 4 perk **5** bonus
fringe ~: 4 boon, ESOP, perk, plus **5** bonus **6** reward
from: 5 enjoy, learn **6** profit
have the ~ of: 3 use **5** enjoy **6** access
reap the ~: 6 profit
unexpected ~: 4 boon **5** gravy
__ benefit: 6 fringe, strike
__-benefit: 4 cost, risk
benefit of the __: 5 doubt
Beneke, Tex: 11 saxophonist
genre: 4 jazz
Benelux
locale: 6 Europe **7** Belgium, Holland **10** Luxembourg **11** Netherlands
Benes: 6 Eduard, Elaine
Benet, Stephen Vincent: 4 poet **6** writer
work: The Devil and Daniel Webster
John Brown's Body
Benét, William Rose: 4 poet
benevolence: 4 help, pity **5** amity, mercy **6** comity, lenity **7** charity **8** altruism, goodness, goodwill, humanity, kindness, lenience, sympathy **9** tolerance
benevolent: 3 big **4** good, kind **5** close, lofty, noble **6** benign, caring, chummy, clubby, decent, genial, gentle, humane, kindly, loving, tender **7** affable, amiable, clement, cordial, helpful, largess, lenient, liberal, saintly, sparing **8** all heart, amicable, friendly, generous, gracious, intimate, largesse, merciful, outgoing, parental, princely, sociable, tolerant **9** bounteous, bountiful, brotherly, convivial, favorable, unselfish **10** altruistic, beneficent, bighearted, buddy-buddy, charitable, chivalrous, freehanded, humanistic, neighborly, solicitous
order: 4 Elks
__ Ben Ezra: 5 Rabbi
Bengal: 3 bay **6** fabric **10** footballer
Bay of ~ city: 6 Madras
country: 5 India
Bengal __: 5 tiger **6** lancer
Bengali: 5 Indic **8** language
wrap: 4 sari **5** saree
Bengals: 6 eleven
home: 10 Cincinnati
org.: 3 AFC
rival: *see* NFL team
Ben-Gay
rival: 4 Heet
Benghazi: 4 city, port, town
locale: 5 Libya
Ben-Gurion Airport
client: 4 El Al
locale: 3 Lod **6** Israel
Ben-Gurion, David: 9 Israeli. P.M.
contemporary: 4 Meir
predecessor: 7 Sharett
successor: 6 Eshkol **7** Sharett
Ben-Hur: 4 epic **5** Judah, novel, slave
author: Lew Wallace
character: 4 Iras **5** Jesus **6** Ben Hur, Esther, Pilate, Tirzah **7** Messala, Quintus **9** Balthasar, Simonides
Ben-Hur (1959 film)
cast: Stephen Boyd, Hugh Griffith, Jack Hawkins, Charlton Heston, Sam Jaffe, Martha Scott
costume designer: Erté
director: William Wyler
garb: 4 toga
studio: 3 MGM
Benicia: 4 city, town
locale: 10 California
Benicio: 7 Del Toro
benighted: 8 ignorant **9** in the dark **10** illiterate, uneducated
benign: 4 easy, good, kind, mild, soft **5** lucky, noble **6** aidful, genial, gentle, humane, kindly, useful **7** affable, amiable, healthy, helpful, lenient **8** friendly, gracious, harmless, merciful, obliging, parental, positive, remedial, salutary **9** congenial, effectual, favorable, healthful, temperate **10** benevolent, productive, propitious, worthwhile
Benigni, Roberto: 5 actor
Oscar: Life Is Beautiful
benignity: 5 favor
Benin: 5 river **6** nation **7** country
capital: 9 Porto-Novo
city on the Bight of ~: 5 Lagos
former name: 7 Dahomey
language: 3 Fon, Gbe **6** French
money: 5 franc
neighbor: 4 Togo **5** Niger **7** Nigeria
people: 3 Fon **6** Yoruba
port: 7 Cotonou
River locale: 7 Nigeria
ruler: 3 oba
Benin City: 4 town
locale: 7 Nigeria
Bening, Annette: 7 actress
film: American Beauty (1999)
The American President (1995)
Being Julia (2004)
Bugsy (1991)
The Great Outdoors (1988)
The Grifters (1990)
Guilty by Suspicion (1991)
Love Affair (1994)
Mars Attacks! (1996)
Regarding Henry (1991)
Richard III (1995)
The Siege (1998)
The Women (2008)
spouse: Warren Beatty
benison: 8 blessing **10** good wishes
Benitez: 4 Elsa
Benito: 6 Juárez **9** Mussolini
Benito Cereno
author: Herman Melville
benjamin: 4 coat **6** jacket **8** overcoat
Benjamin: 3 Orr **4** West **5** Bratt, Spock **7** Britten, Cardozo, Latrobe, Richard **8** Banneker, Disraeli, Franklin, Harrison **9** Netanyahu
brother: 3 Dan, Gad **4** Levi **5** Asher, Judah **6** Joseph, Reuben, Simeon **7** Zebulun **8** Issachar, Naphtali

father: 5 Jacob
mother: 6 Rachel
sister: 5 Dinah
son: 3 Ard, Ehi 4 Bela, Gera, Rosh 5 Nohah, Rapha 6 Ashbel, Becher, Huppim, Muppim, Naaman 7 Jediael
__ Benjamin: 7 Private
Benjamin Moore: 5 paint
Benjamin, Richard: 5 actor 8 director
film: Catch-22 (1970)
City Heat (1984)
Diary of a Mad Housewife (1970)
Goodbye, Columbus (1969)
House Calls (1978)
Love at First Bite (1979)
Mermaids (1990)
The Money Pit (1986)
Mrs. Winterbourne (1996)
My Favorite Year (1982)
My Stepmother Is an Alien (1988)
Racing With the Moon (1984)
The Sunshine Boys (1975)
Westworld (1973)
spouse: Paula Prentiss
Ben Jelloun, Tahar: 6 writer 8 Moroccan
Ben & Jerry's: 8 ice cream
competitor: *see* ice cream
Benji: 3 dog, pet 4 mutt 5 stray 6 canine
__ Ben Jonson!: 5 O rare
Bennett: 4 Boyd, Cerf, Joan, Tony 5 Bruce, Hywel 6 Arnold 9 Constance, Gwendolyn
Bennett, Arnold: 6 writer 7 British
Bennett, Gwendolyn: 6 writer
Bennett, Tony
song: Because of You (1951)
Cold, Cold Heart (1951)
The Good Life (1963)
If I Ruled the World (1965)
I Left My Heart in San Francisco (1962)
In the Middle of an Island (1957)
I Wanna Be Around (1963)
Rags to Riches (1953)
Who Can I Turn To (1964)
Ben Nevis: 4 peak 5 mount 8 mountain
locale: 6 Europe 8 Scotland
Bennie and the Jets (1974 song)
artist: Elton John
__ Benning: 4 Fort
Benny: 4 Hill, Jack 6 Carter 7 Goodman 8 Mardones
Benny, Jack: 8 comedian
spouse: Mary Livingstone
to Rochester: 4 boss
Benny & Joon (1993 film)
cast: Johnny Depp, Mary Stuart Masterson, Aidan Quinn
Benoit, Joan: 6 runner 10 marathoner
__ Be Not Proud: 5 Death
__ Ben's: 5 Uncle
Benson: 4 Ezra 5 Robby 6 George
Benson (ABC sitcom)
cast: Missy Gold (Katie Gatling)
Robert Guillaume (Benson DuBois)
James Noble (Governor James Gatling)
Inga Swenson (Gretchen Kraus)
Benson, George
song: Give Me The Night (1980)
On Broadway (1978)
This Masquerade (1976)
Turn Your Love Around (1981)
__ Ben Stein's Money: 3 Win
bent: 3 set 4 bias, firm, gift, head, turn, vein 5 askew, bandy, bound, bowed, flair, habit, knack, leant, slant, trait, trend 6 akimbo, angled, curved, gnarly, intent, liking, skewed, talent, warped, zigzag 7 ability, angular, crooked, faculty, impulse, leaning, sinuous, slouchy, stooped, twisted, winding 8 angulose, angulous, aptitude, attitude, cockeyed, facility, inclined, penchant, resolute, spurious, tendency, tortuous, velleity 9 insistent 10 determined, out of shape, preference, proclivity, propensity
be ~ upon: 4 want 6 desire 7 hope for
combining form: 4 cyrt- 5 curvi-, cyrto- 6 campto-
easily ~: 5 lithe 6 supple 7 elastic, plastic 8 flexible 9 lithesome
from the waist (ballet): 8 renverse
it may be ~: 3 ear 5 elbow
out of shape: *see* angry
over: 6 astoop 7 hunched
__-bent: 4 hell
Bentham, Jeremy: 7 British 11 philosopher
Bentley: 2 E.C. 3 car, Wes 4 auto 10 automobile
model: 5 Azure, Turbo 6 Arnage 8 Mulsanne
Bentley, E.C.: 6 writer 7 British
creation: clerihew
sleuth: 5 Trent
work: Trent's Last Case
Benton: 4 city, town 5 Barbi, Brook 6 Robert
locale: 8 Arkansas
Benton, Brook
song: Baby (1960)
The Boll Weevil Song (1961)
Hotel Happiness (1962)
It's Just a Matter of Time (1959)
Kiddio (1960)
Rainy Night in Georgia (1970)
A Rockin' Good Way (1960)
So Many Ways (1959)
Benton, Robert: 8 director
film: Bad Company (1972)
Billy Bathgate (1991)
Kramer vs. Kramer (1979, AA)
The Late Show (1977)
Nadine (1987)
Nobody's Fool (1994)
Places in the Heart (1984)
Twilight (1998)
Benton, Thomas Hart: 6 artist 7 painter
Bentonville: 4 city, town
locale: 8 Arkansas
Bentsen: 5 Lloyd
benumb: 4 dull, stun 5 blunt 6 deaden, freeze 7 petrify, stupefy 8 paralyse, paralyze
benumbed: 6 frozen, torpid 9 unfeeling
Benvenuti, Nino: 5 boxer
milieu: 4 ring
Benvenuto Cellini: 5 opera
composer: Hector Berlioz
Benz: 4 Karl
benzene base: 3 tar
benzoate: 4 salt
benzocaine: 5 ester
benzoic __: 4 acid
benzoyl peroxide target: 3 zit 4 acne
Beowulf: 4 epic, hero, saga
beverage: 4 mead
character: 7 Grendel 8 Hrothgar
Beowulf (2007 film)
cast: Anthony Hopkins, Angelina Jolie, Ray Winstone
director: Robert Zemeckis
BEP
department: 5 Treas. 8 Treasury
part: 6 Bureau 8 Printing 9 Engraving
Beppo
author: Lord Byron
Be prepared: 5 motto
org.: 3 BSA
bequeath: 4 give, will 5 endow, leave 6 bestow, donate, legate 8 hand down, transmit 10 contribute
bequeathed: 10 handed down, hereditary
be ~: 7 inherit
__ be Queen o' the May: 4 I'm to
bequest: 4 gift, will 5 grant, leave 6 legacy 7 subsidy 8 donation, heirloom 9 endowment, patrimony
document: 4 will
testator's ~: 6 estate
Be quiet!: 3 shh 4 hush 5 can it, shush 6 shut up 8 pipe down
berate: 3 hit, jaw, nag, rag 4 drub, flay, lash, rail, ride, twit, whip 5 abuse, chide, scold 6 assail, rail at, rebuke, vilify 7 bawl out, censure, chew out, henpeck, lambast, lecture, put down, reprove, tell off, upbraid 8 admonish, chastise, harangue, lambaste, reproach 9 castigate, criticize, dress down, excoriate, exprobate, fulminate, fustigate, lash out at, light into, reprehend, reprimand 10 take to task, tongue-lash, vituperate
Berber: 4 Moor, Riff 6 Hamite 8 language
people: 5 Riffi
region: 3 Rif
Berberian: 3 Ara
Berbick, Trevor: 5 boxer
milieu: 4 ring
berceuse: 7 lullaby
bereave: 3 rob 5 strip 7 deprive, despoil 10 dispossess
bereaved: 3 sad 4 lorn 6 devoid 7 forlorn, missing 8 grieving, mourning
bereavement: 4 loss 5 grief 6 sorrow 8 distress, mourning
bereft: 4 lorn 6 devoid, robbed 7 forlorn, lacking, missing 8 deprived, divested 9 destitute
of: 7 needing
Berenger, Tom: 5 actor
Berenice: 6 Abbott
author: Edgar Allan Poe
composer: George Frideric Handel
__ Berenices: 4 Coma
Berenson: 6 Marisa 7 Bernard
Berenson, Bernard: 6 writer
Berenstain: 3 Jan 4 Stan
Beresford, Bruce: 8 director
beret: 3 cap, hat, tam
site: 4 tête
__ Beret: 5 Green
berg: 4 floe 7 growler
feature: 3 tip
source: 7 glacier, ice pack 8 ice sheet
Berg: 3 Moe 4 Paul 5 Alban, Molly, Patty 8 Gertrude
Berg, Alban: 8 Austrain, composer
like ~'s music: 6 atonal
work: Lulu
Wozzeck
bergamot: 4 pear, tree 5 fruit 6 citrus
relative: *see* citrus
Bergen: 4 city, port, town 5 Edgar, Polly 7 Candice
dummy: 5 Snerd 7 Klinker 8 McCarthy
locale: 6 Norway
prop: 5 dummy
Bergen, Candice: 7 actress
film: 11 Harrowhouse (1974)
Bite the Bullet (1975)
Bride Wars (2009)
Carnal Knowledge (1971)
Gandhi (1982)
The Group (1966)
Rich and Famous (1981)
The Sand Pebbles (1966)
Starting Over (1979)
Sweet Home Alabama (2002)
spouse: Louis Malle
TV: Boston Legal, Murphy Brown
Bergenfield: 4 city, town
locale: 9 New Jersey
Berger: 4 Erna 5 Senta 6 Helmut, Thomas
Bergerac: 7 Jacques
__ Bergère: 6 Folies
Berger, Erna: 6 singer 7 soprano
specialty: 5 opera
Bergeron: 3 Tom
Berger, Thomas: 6 writer
work: Arthur Rex
Crazy in Berlin
Killing Time
Little Big Man
Neighbors
Nowhere
Orrie's Story
Reinhart in Love
Vital Parts
Bergius, Friedrich: 7 chemist 8 Nobelist
Bergman: 4 Alan 6 Andrew, Ingmar, Ingrid 7 Hjalmar, Marilyn, Sandahl
Bergman, Hjalmar: 6 writer 7 Swedish
Bergman, Ingmar: 7 Swedish 8 director
film: Autumn Sonata (1978)
Cries and Whispers (1972)
Fanny and Alexander (1983)
The Passion of Anna (1969)
Persona (1966)
Sawdust and Tinsel (1953)
Scenes From a Marriage (1973)
The Seventh Seal (1957)
Shame (1968)
The Silence (1963)
Smiles of a Summer Night (1955)
Through a Glass, Darkly (1962)
Wild Strawberries (1957)
Bergman, Ingrid: 7 actress, Swedish
film: Anastasia (1956, AA)

Arch of Triumph (1948)
Autumn Sonata (1978)
The Bells of St. Mary's (1945)
Cactus Flower (1969)
Casablanca (1942)
Dr. Jekyll and Mr. Hyde (1941)
For Whom the Bell Tolls (1943)
Gaslight (1944, AA)
Goodbye Again (1961)
Indiscreet (1958)
The Inn of the Sixth Happiness (1958)
Intermezzo (1939)
Murder on the Orient Express (1974, AA)
Notorious (1946)
Spellbound (1945)
The Yellow Rolls-Royce (1964)
role: 4 Ilsa, Meir 5 Golda
spouse: Roberto Rossellini
Berg, Moe: 3 spy 7 catcher
Berg, Patty: 6 golfer
Bergström, Sune: 8 Nobelist
Beriah father: 5 Asher
beribbon: 4 trim 5 adorn 8 decorate
Berigan: 5 Bunny
Be right with you!: 6 coming 7 in a jiff 8 just a sec 9 in a minute
Bering: 3 sea 5 Vitus 6 strait 8 explorer
locale: 6 Alaska
Bering __: 3 Sea 4 Time 6 Strait
Bering Sea
island: 4 Attu 8 Pribilof
river to the ~: 5 Yukon
sighting: 4 floe
swimmer: 4 seal
Bering, Vitus: 6 Danish 8 explorer
Berke: 8 Breathed
Berkeley: 4 city, town 5 Busby 6 George, Xander
county north of ~: 4 Napa
locale: 10 California
berkelium: 7 element
Berkley: 9 Elizabeth
Berkow: 3 Ira
Berks: 6 county
locale: 7 England
Berkshire: 3 pig 5 swine 6 county
city: 5 Ascot 6 Slough 7 Reading
locale: 7 England
school: 4 Eton
Berkshire Music Festival site: 5 Lenox
Berle, Milton: 5 actor, comic 8 comedian
contemporary: 6 Caesar
Berlin: 4 city, town 6 Irving, Isaiah 7 capital, Jeannie
composition: 4 song, tune 5 score
E. ~ locale, once: 3 GDR
had one: 4 wall
locale: 7 Germany
river: 5 Havel, Spree
Berlin __: 4 Wall, wool 7 Express
__ Berlin: 4 East, Judy, West
Berliner: 5 Emile 6 German
Berlin, Irving: 8 composer
musical: Annie Get Your Gun
As Thousands Cheer
Call Me Madam
The Cocoanuts
Face the Music
Louisiana Purchase
Miss Liberty
Mr. President
Music Box Revue
This Is the Army
org.: 5 ASCAP
score: Blue Skies
Carefree
Easter Parade
Follow the Fleet
Holiday Inn
Top Hat
White Christmas
song: Alexander's Ragtime Band
All Alone
All by Myself
Always
Anything You Can Do
Be Careful, It's My Heart
Blue Skies
Change Partners
Cheek to Cheek
Count Your Blessings Instead of Sheep
A Couple of Swells
Doin' What Comes Natur'lly
Easter Parade
The Girl That I Marry
God Bless America
Heat Wave
How Deep Is the Ocean
I Got the Sun in the Morning
I Love a Piano
It's a Lovely Day Today
Lazy
Let Me Sing and I'm Happy
Let's Face the Music and Dance
Let's Have Another Cup of Coffee
Let's Take an Old-Fashioned Walk
Let Yourself Go
Mandy
Oh, How I Hate to Get Up in the Morning
Play a Simple Melody
A Pretty Girl Is Like a Melody
Puttin' on the Ritz
Say It With Music
The Song Is Ended
Steppin' Out With My Baby
There's No Business Like Show Business
They Say It's Wonderful
This Is the Army, Mr. Jones
This Year's Kisses
Top Hat, White Tie and Tails
What'll I Do
When I Lost You
White Christmas
You Can't Get a Man With a Gun
You'd Be Surprised
Berlin Stories, The
author: Christopher Isherwood
Berlin-to-Cologne dir.: 3 WSW
Berlioz, Hector: 6 French 8 composer
work: Benvenuto Cellini
The Damnation of Faust
Harold in Italy
Symphonie Fantastique
The Trojans
Berlitz, Charles: 8 linguist
berm: 4 bank, path 5 ledge, shelf
Berman: 3 Len, Ted 5 Chris 7 Shelley
Bermuda: 3 car 4 auto, isle 5 Edsel, grass 6 island, Willys 10 automobile
capital: 8 Hamilton
city: 8 Hamilton, St. George
hrs.: 3 AST
ocean: 3 Atl. 8 Atlantic
petrel: 5 cahow
vehicle: 5 moped
wear: 6 shorts
Bermuda __: 3 rig 4 high, lily 5 grass, onion 6 cutter, petrel, shorts
Bermudas: 5 pants 6 shorts
Bern: 4 city, town 6 canton 7 capital
city near ~: 4 Sion 6 Gstaad
lake: 6 Brienz
locale: Switzerland
river: 3 Aar 4 Aare
Bernadette: 3 Ste. 5 saint 6 Peters
Bernard: 3 Lee 4 Kalb, Katz, Rose, Shaw 5 saint 6 Baruch, De Voto, Kliban 7 Crystal, Malamud 8 Berenson, Cornfeld, Herrmann 10 Mandeville
Saint ~ burden: 3 keg 6 brandy
Saint ~ home: 4 Alps
Saint ~ sound: 3 arf, grr 4 bark, woof 5 growl
Bernardi: 8 Herschel
__ Bernardino: 3 San
Bernardo: 7 Houssay 8 O'Higgins 10 Bertolucci
__ Bernard Shaw: 6 George
Bernays: 6 Edward
Berne: 4 Eric
see also Bern
Bernese Alps: 5 range
locale: 6 Europe 11 Switzerland
peak: 5 Eiger
river: 3 Aar 4 Aare
Bernhard: 6 Langer, Sandra, Thomas
Bernhardt: 5 Sarah 6 Curtis
Bernhard, Thomas: 6 writer 8 Austrian
Bernhardt, Sarah: 6 French 7 actress
birthplace: 5 Paris
contemporary: 4 Duse
Bernie: 3 Ben, Mac 5 Casey, Kosar 6 Kopell, Parent, Taupin 7 Federko 8 Williams
Bernina: 4 peak 5 mount 8 mountain
locale: 4 Alps 5 Italy 6 Europe 11 Switzerland
Bernsen, Corbin: 5 actor
role: 5 Arnie
spouse: Amanda Pays
TV: L.A. Law
Bernstein: 4 Carl 5 Elmer 6 Eduard 7 Leonard
Bernstein, Carl: 10 journalist
spouse: Nora Ephron
Bernstein, Leonard: 8 composer 9 conductor
work: The Age of Anxiety
Chichester Psalms
Fancy Free
Jeremiah Symphony
Kaddish Symphony
Mass
Beroea today: 6 Aleppo
Berra, Yogi: 4 Yank 6 Yankee 7 catcher
gear for ~: 4 mitt 5 glove
Berriozabal: 4 city, town
locale: 6 Mexico 7 Chiapas
berry: 5 drupe, fruit, maqui, salal, toyon 6 acinus 7 currant 8 sea grape
Christmas ~: 5 toyon
combining form: 4 cocc- 5 bacci-, cocci-, cocco-
patch hazard: 5 briar, brier, thorn 7 prickle
purple ~: 5 maqui, salal 8 sea grape
red ~: 8 barberry 9 bearberry, raspberry 10 strawberry
starter: 3 bar, bay, cow, dew, dog, ink, tea, wax 4 bane, bear, blue, crow, hack, ling, poke, rasp, shad, snow, soap, twin, wolf 5 black, bunch, china, choke, cloud, coral, elder, goose, honey, nanny, sheep, spice, straw, sugar, young
tree: 5 elder
__ berry: 5 wheat 7 buffalo, juniper, miracle
Berry: 3 Jan, Ken 5 Chuck, Gordy, Halle 7 Wendell
Berry, Chuck
song: Johnny B. Goode (1958)
Maybellene (1955)
My Ding-a-Ling (1972)
No Particular Place to Go (1964)
Rock & Roll Music (1957)
Roll Over Beethoven (1956)
School Day (1957)
Sweet Little Sixteen (1958)
__ Berry Farm: 6 Knott's
Berry, Halle: 7 actress
film: Bulworth (1998)
Catwoman (2004)
Die Another Day (2002)
Executive Decision (1996)
Gothika (2003)
Losing Isaiah (1995)
Monster's Ball (2001, AA)
Swordfish (2001)
Things We Lost in the Fire (2007)
Berryman, John: 4 poet
work: The Dream Songs
Homage to Mistress Bradstree
Love & Fame
Berry, Wendell: 6 writer
berserk: 3 mad 4 amok, wild 5 amuck, manic, rabid 7 flipped, haywire, hog-wild, violent 8 demented, frenzied, in a furor, maniacal 9 possessed 10 hysterical
go ~: 4 rage, riot, snap 5 freak 6 lose it 7 rampage, run wild 8 have a fit
Bert: 4 Lahr 5 Convy, Jones, Parks 6 Kalmar 7 Bobbsey, Sakmann, Wheeler 8 Blyleven 9 Kaempfert
friend: 5 Ernie 6 Kermit
sister: 3 Nan
berth: 3 bed, cot, job 4 bunk, dock, land, moor, pier, quay, slip, spot 5 cabin, jetty, lower, place, upper, wharf 6 billet, harbor 7 bedroom, bunk bed, harbour 8 position 9 anchorage
come to ~: 4 dock, land
give a wide ~ to: 4 shun 5 avoid, elude, evade, scorn, skirt 6 eschew 8 flee from, sidestep 10 circumvent, recoil from, shrink from
place: 4 dock, pier, port, quay 5 wharf
wide ~: 6 leeway 7 license
__ berth: 3 mud 5 lower, upper

bertha: 6 collar
cousin: 5 fichu
like a ~: 4 lacy
Bertha: 3 gun 5 saint 6 cannon 8 asteroid
__ Bertha: 3 Big
Berthe: 6 Sister 7 Morisot
Berthold: 8 Schwartz
Bertie: 7 Higgins
Bertil: 5 Ohlin
Bertinelli, Valerie: 7 actress
spouse: Eddie Van Halen
Bertolt: 6 Brecht
Bertolucci, Bernardo: 8 director
film: The Conformist (1971)
The Last Emperor (1987, AA)
Last Tango in Paris (1973)
Luna (1979)
Stealing Beauty (1996)
Bertram: 10 Brockhouse
Bertrand: 7 Russell 9 Tavernier
Bertrille: 3 nun 6 sister 9 Flying Nun
Berwick-upon-__: 5 Tweed
Berwyn: 4 city, town
locale: 8 Illinois
beryl: 4 blue 5 green 6 bluish 7 blueish, emerald, mineral 8 gemstone 9 morganite 10 aquamarine
color kin: *see* green color
Beryl: 7 Markham 10 Bainbridge
beryllium: 5 metal 7 element
Berzelius, Jöns: 7 chemist, Swedish
bes: 6 Hebrew, letter
predecessor: 5 aleph
successor: 5 gimel
__ Be Sad Songs: 7 There'll
Bésame __: 5 Mucho
Besant, Annie Wood: 6 orator, writer 8 activist 11 philosopher
beseech: 3 ask, beg, bid, sue 4 pray, urge 5 plead, press 6 adjure, appeal, exhort 7 entreat, implore, request, solicit 8 petition 9 impetrate, importune 10 supplicate
beseechment: 4 plea 6 prayer
__ Be Seeing You: 3 I'll
beseem: 4 suit 5 befit, match 6 become 7 behoove 9 befitting 10 accord with
beset: 3 dun, ply, rag 4 bait 5 annoy, haunt, hem in, hound, press, spite, storm, swamp, worry 6 assail, attack, harass, in a box, noodge 7 afflict, bombard, overrun, plagued, studded, trouble 8 embattle, fire upon, obsessed, surround, troubled 9 importune
besetting: 8 habitual 10 compulsive
beside: 4 near, next 5 along 6 next to 7 abreast, close to, lateral 8 abutting, adjacent 9 abreast of, adjoining 10 adjacent to, juxtaposed
combining form: 3 par- 4 para-
besides: 3 and, bar, too, yet 4 also, else, more, plus 5 again, along 6 as well, at that, beyond, except, to boot 7 barring, further, on top of 8 likewise, moreover, more than 9 apart from, aside from, excepting, excluding, other than, otherwise, outside of, what's more 10 in addition, in excess of, leaving out
prefix: 3 epi-
beside the __: 4 mark 5 point
besiege: 3 ply 4 rush 5 haunt, press, storm, swamp 6 assail, attack, harass 7 aggress, bombard, envelop, rip into 8 encircle, fire upon, surround 9 close in on, importune
besieged: 6 in a fix, in a jam 7 up a tree 10 in hot water, up the creek
one's remark: 5 why me 8 not again
besmear: 3 dab 4 blur, foul, soil 5 stain, sully 6 blotch, smirch, smudge 7 begrime, draggle 8 discolor
besmirch: 3 mar, tar 4 foul, slur, soil, spot 5 dirty, muddy, smear, stain, sully, taint 6 befoul, blotch, crud up, defame, defile, malign, smudge 7 begrime, blacken, draggle, pollute, slander, tarnish 8 backbite, discolor, disgrace, throw mud 9 denigrate 10 villainize
besmirched: 5 grimy, sooty 6 filthy, fouled, grubby, grungy 7 unclean 8 maculate, slovenly 10 bedraggled, unsanitary
__ Beso: 3 Eso
besom: 5 broom
material: 4 twig
use a ~: 5 sweep
__ Be So Nice...: 4 You'd
__ be sorry!: 5 You'll
besot: 7 stupefy 9 inebriate, infatuate 10 intoxicate
besotted: 5 tipsy 6 blotto 7 far gone 9 irrigated 10 infatuated
bespangle: 5 adorn
bespatter: 4 blot, spot 6 bedaub, malign
bespattered: 5 muddy
bespeak: 4 bode, show 6 ask for, bid for, reveal, secure, tell of 7 address, betoken, display, exhibit, portend, promise, reflect, request, reserve, signify, testify 8 indicate, register 9 predicate
bespeckle: 3 dot
besprinkle: 3 wet 6 dampen 7 asperse, scatter
__ Be Square: 5 Hip to
Bess: 6 Truman 7 Myerson 9 Armstrong
to Harry: 4 wife
Bessell: 3 Ted
Bessemer: 4 city, town 5 Henry
locale: 7 Alabama
Bessemer __: 5 steel 7 process
Bessemer, Henry: 3 Sir 7 British 8 inventor
product: 5 steel
Bessie: 4 Head, Love 5 Smith
Besson, Luc: 8 director
Bess Truman, __ Wallace: 3 née
Bess, You Is My Woman Now: 4 duet
composer: George Gershwin
best: 3 ace, cap, top 4 A-one, beat, lick, most, peak, pick, rout, tops, whip 5 cream, crown, elite, ideal, one up, outdo, prime, primo, trump, worst 6 defeat, exceed, finest, finish, grade A, select, superb, tiptop, unique, wallop 7 capital, conquer, highest, in front, leading, optimal, optimum, outplay, perfect, special, supreme, surpass, triumph, vintage 8 champion, choicest, foremost, four-star, greatest, outscore, overcome, peerless, surmount, top-grade, topnotch, top-rated, ultimate, vanquish 9 first-rate, high-class, matchless, nonpareil, number one, paramount, sovereign, strongest, top drawer, topflight, unequaled, unrivaled, virtuosic, worthiest 10 consummate, first-class, inimitable, preeminent, put to shame, unrivalled, world-class
at ~: 6 partly 7 ideally 9 maximally, optimally
barely ~: 4 clip, edge 7 nose out
combining form: 6 aristo-
come out second ~: 4 lose, show
condition: 4 pink
days: 5 prime
do one's ~: 3 try
ender: 6 seller
get the ~ of: 3 win 5 unarm 6 defeat, master, subdue 7 conquer 9 overpower
had ~: 5 ought 6 should 7 ought to
in one's ~ interests: 7 politic
in the ring: 2 KO
make the ~ of: 5 get by 6 make do, manage 8 tolerate 9 put up with, reconcile
man's ~ friend: 3 dog
of seven: 6 series
part: 4 lead, most 5 cream 6 flower 8 majority 9 highlight
roster of the ~: 5 A-list
select the ~: 4 cull, sift 6 screen 9 high-grade
Sunday ~: 4 duds, garb, gear, rags, togs, wear 5 array, dress, frock, getup, mufti 6 attire, civies, finery, livery, outfit, things 7 apparel, civvies, clothes, costume, raiment, regalia, threads 8 ensemble, frippery, garments, wardrobe 9 trappings 10 habiliment
wishes: 7 regards 8 respects
wish the ~ for: 5 bless
best __: 3 boy, man 5 of all
best __ and tucker: 3 bib
best __ possible worlds: 5 of all
best __ to be, the: 5 is yet
best-__ plans: 4 laid
best-__ scenario: 4 case
__ best: 6 second, Sunday
Best: 4 Edna, Pete 5 James 7 Charles
Best and the Brightest, The
author: David Halberstam
Best Boy (1979 film)
director: Ira Wohl
__ best friend: 4 man's
bestial: 3 low 4 base, mean, vile 5 cruel, feral 6 brutal, coarse, oafish, savage, sordid 7 brutish, debased, inhuman, loutish 8 barbaric, inhumane 9 barbarian, barbarous, primitive, unpitying 10 unmerciful
Be still!: 3 shh 4 hush 5 quiet
best in __: 4 show
Best in Show (2000 film)
cast: Christopher Guest, Eugene Levy, Michael McKean, Catherine O'Hara
director: Christopher Guest
bestir: 4 move, wake 5 rally, rouse, waken 6 arouse, awaken, kindle, vivify, wake up 7 actuate, inspire 8 motivate 9 get moving, impassion, stimulate
best is __ be, the: 5 yet to
Best Is __ Come, The: 5 Yet to
Best Laid Plans, The
author: Sidney Sheldon
best-loved: 3 pet 8 favorite 9 preferred
one: 4 fave
best man's offering: 5 toast
Best Man, The (1964 film)
cast: Edie Adams, Henry Fonda, Cliff Robertson
Best Man, The (1999 film)
cast: Morris Chestnut, Taye Diggs, Nia Long, Harold Perrineau
director: Malcolm D. Lee
Best of My Love (song)
artist: Eagles, Emotions
Best of Times, The (1981 song)
artist: Styx
Best of Times, The (1986 film)
cast: Holly Palance, Pamela Reed, Kurt Russell, Robin Williams
bestow: 4 deal, give, vest 5 allot, award, endow, endue, grant, indue, lodge, share, spare, spend 6 afford, confer, devote, donate, extend, heap on, impart, lavish, return 7 furnish, hand out, present, provide 8 bequeath 9 apportion, vouchsafe 10 contribute, distribute
bestowal: 4 gift, will 5 award, grant 8 largesse 9 endowment
bestower: 5 donor 7 grantor
best-quality: 5 prime 6 choice, select
bestrew: 3 sow 6 spread 7 diffuse, radiate, scatter 8 disperse, sprinkle 9 broadcast, cast about
bestride: 4 span 7 overtop 8 dominate, step over, straddle 9 cross over, stand over, tower over
bestseller: 3 hit 4 book 5 novel
Best That You Can Do (1981 song)
artist: Christopher Cross
Best Things in Life Are Free, The (1992 song)
artist: Janet Jackson, Ralph Tresvant, Luther Vandross
Best Thing That Ever Happened to Me (1974 song)
artist: Gladys Knight and the Pips
__ Best Thing, The: 4 Next
Best Western: 5 motel
competitor: *see* motel
Best Years of Our Lives, The (1946 film)
cast: Dana Andrews, Hoagy Carmichael, Myrna Loy, Fredric March, Virginia Mayo, Harold Russell, Teresa Wright
director: William Wyler
studio: 3 RKO
__ be surprised!: 4 You'd
bet: 3 lay 4 ante, noir, play, risk 5 put up, rouge, stake, wager 6 chance, exacta, gamble, Hebrew, letter, parlay 7 lay odds, venture 8 chance it, long shot, make book, perfecta, trifecta 9 speculate
accepter: 5 taker
amount: 5 stake
collect a ~: 3 win
first: 4 open
meet a poker ~: 3 see
offset a ~: 5 hedge
on: 4 back 5 trust 6 chance 8 put money

BE

one's bottom dollar: **4** rely **5** trust **6** depend **7** believe
predecessor: **5** aleph
roulette ~: **3** odd, red **4** even, noir **5** black, rouge
successor: **5** gimel
taker: **6** bookie
track ~: **4** show **5** place **6** exacta, parlay **8** perfecta, quinella, trifecta
you ~: ***see*** of course **2** da, ja, sí **3** oui **4** amen, okay, sure, true **5** good-o, quite, right, roger, uh-huh **6** agreed, and how, gladly, good-oh, indeed, just so, rather, righto, yowzah **7** exactly, go ahead, granted, indeedy, mais oui, quite so, right on, ten-four **8** all right, for a fact, thumbs up, very well **9** be my guest, darn right, precisely, sure thing **10** absolutely, definitely, sure enough, that's right
___ bet: **3** you **4** side **6** if-come **7** pyramid
___ bet?: **5** Wanna
BET: **7** channel
alternative: ***see*** cable channel
beta: **5** Greek **6** letter **10** prerelease
preceder: **5** alpha
successor: **5** gamma
beta ___: **3** ray **4** cell, iron, line, test, wave **5** brass, decay **6** rhythm **7** blocker
___ Beta Kappa: **3** Phi
betake: **4** move **6** repair **9** cause to go
Betamax: **3** VCR
creator: **4** Sony
Betcha By Golly, Wow (1972 song)
artist: Stylistics
bête
noire: **8** anathema
betel: **3** nut **4** palm **5** areca
Betelgeuse: **4** star **5** M star
constellation: **5** Orion
bête noire: **4** bane, fear **7** bugbear **8** pet peeve
beth: **6** Hebrew, letter
preceder: **4** alef **5** aleph
successor: **5** gimel
Beth: **6** Daniel, Henley **7** Howland **9** Broderick
sister: **2** Jo **3** Amy, Meg
Beth (1976 song)
artist: Kiss
Beth ___: **3** Din **6** Hillel **7** Midrash, Shammai
be that ___ may: **4** as it
___ Be the Day: **6** That'll
bethel: **6** chapel, hostel **9** sanctuary
Bethel: **4** city, town **6** Leslie
locale: **6** Alaska
___ Be the One: **5** Let Me
___ Be There: **3** I'll **5** Got to, Let Me
Bethesda: **4** city, town
locale: **8** Maryland
___ be the tie that binds: **5** blest
___ Beth Hurt: **4** Mary
bethink: **6** recall, remind **8** remember **9** recognize, recollect **10** bear in mind, keep in mind
Bethlehem: **4** city, town
athletes: **9** Engineers
city near ~: **6** Easton
gift: **4** gold **5** myrrh **12** frankincense
locale: **4** Penn. **6** Jordan
school: **6** Lehigh
trio: **4** Magi
Bethlehem ___: **4** sage **5** Steel
___ Bethlehem: **6** Star of
Bethlehem Steel for short: **6** Bessie
Bethune, Zina: **7** actress
betide: **5** occur **6** happen **7** turn out **8** happen to **9** take place, transpire **10** come to pass
___ be tied: **5** fit to
betimes: **4** anon, soon **5** early **9** in advance **10** beforehand
bêtise: **6** trifle **7** faux pas **9** absurdity
Betjeman, John: **4** poet **7** British
betoken: **4** bode, mark, mean, show **5** augur, imply **6** denote **7** bespeak, connote, portend, predict, presage, promise, signify **8** forebode, forecast, foreshow, foretell, indicate, prophesy, stand for **9** represent, symbolize **10** foreshadow
betray: **4** sell, sing **5** cross, rat on, spill **6** delude, desert, expose, fink on, reveal, squeal, take in, turn in **7** abandon, deceive, divulge, forsake, let slip, mislead, sell out **8** blurt out, disclose, give away, go back on, inform on, register **9** break with, disinform
a confidence: **4** blab, tell **6** gossip
betrayal: **6** dupery **7** perfidy, treason **8** exposure, giveaway **9** deception, treachery
betrayer: **5** enemy, Judas, knave, snake, viper **6** ratter **7** ratfink, traitor **8** apostate, forsaker, informer, recreant, renegade, turncoat **9** ill-wisher, informant
betroth: **6** engage **7** promise
betrothal: **6** plight **7** promise **8** espousal **10** affiancing, engagement
announcement: **4** bans **5** banns
betrothed: **4** love **6** fiancé **7** fiancée **8** intended, wife-to-be
Be True to Your School (1963 song)
artist: Beach Boys
bets
hedging one's ~: **4** sage, wary, wise **5** chary, leery **7** careful, guarded, politic, prudent **8** cautious **9** judicious, provident, sagacious, tentative
take ~: **8** give odds, make book
Betsey: **7** Johnson
Betsy: **4** Ross **5** Blair, Drake, Rawls **6** Palmer
Betsy's Wedding (1990 film)
cast: Alan Alda, Joey Bishop, Catherine O'Hara, Joe Pesci, Molly Ringwald, Ally Sheedy
director: Alan Alda
Betsy, The: **4** film **5** novel
author: Harold Robbins
cast: Robert Duvall, Tommy Lee Jones, Laurence Olivier, Katharine Ross
director: Daniel Petrie
Bette: **5** Davis **6** Midler
nickname: **5** Miss M
Bette Davis Eyes (1981 song)
artist: Kim Carnes
Bettelheim, Bruno: psychologist
Bettendorf: **4** city, town
locale: **4** Iowa
better: **3** cap, top, win **4** beat, help, more **5** amend, cured, emend, finer, fix up, outdo, raise, trump **6** enrich, exceed, fitter, polish, refine, reform **7** advance, correct, enhance, forward, further, greater, improve, promote, recover, recruit, shape up, sharpen, surpass, touch up, upgrade **8** improved, not so bad, outshine, outstrip, souped up, spruce up, stronger, superior, surmount, worthier **9** cultivate, healthier, improving, meliorate, on the mend, sharpened, transcend **10** ameliorate, preferable, preferably, recovering
get ~: **4** heal, mend **5** rally **6** look up, pick up **7** rebound, recover **10** recuperate
get ~ in the bottle: **3** age **6** mellow
get into ~ condition: **7** restore, work out **8** exercise
get the ~ of: **5** one up, trump, upset, worst **6** defeat, outwit **7** conquer **8** outsmart, overcome
go one ~: **3** top **5** outdo **7** surpass
had ~: **5** ought **6** should **7** ought to
half: **4** mate, wife **6** spouse **7** husband
like ~: **6** prefer
make ~: **7** improve **10** ameliorate
none ~: **4** best, tops
old enough to know ~: **5** adult, grown, of age **6** mature **7** grown-up
part: **4** bulk, most **8** majority **10** lion's share
than: **5** above
than nothing: **4** fair, so-so **6** decent **8** adequate, bearable, mediocre, passable **9** something, tolerable **10** acceptable
think ~ of: **3** rue **6** regret
turn for the ~: **5** rally
better ___: **3** off **4** half
better ___ than never: **4** late
better ___ than sorry: **4** safe
___ better: **5** go one
Better ___ and Gardens: **5** Homes
___ better believe it!: **4** You'd
Better Boy: **6** tomato
relative: **4** Roma **6** Big Boy **9** beefsteak, Early Girl, Quick Pick
Better Business ___: **6** Bureau
Better Days (1992 song)
artist: Bruce Springsteen
Better Man (1994 song)
artist: Pearl Jam
betterment: **7** advance, benefit **8** progress **9** amendment, promotion, upgrading **10** prosperity
___ better or for worse: **3** for
___ Betters: **3** Our
___ better to have loved...: **3** 'Tis
___ Better Watch Out: **3** You
Bettger: **4** Lyle
bet the ___: **5** ranch
betting
game: **4** faro **5** craps, poker **8** baccarat, roulette **9** blackjack, twenty-one
parameters: **4** odds
quit ~: **6** cash in
setting: **3** OTB **4** Reno **5** track, Vegas **6** casino **8** Las Vegas **9** racetrack
Betti, Ugo: **7** Italian **10** playwright
bettong: **9** marsupial
relative: ***see*** marsupial
bettor: **5** taker **6** player, punter **7** gambler, plunger, wagerer **8** gamester **9** risk taker
concern: **3** nag **4** ante, pony **6** action
declaration: **5** banco
mecca: **3** OTB **4** Reno **5** track, Vegas **6** casino **8** Las Vegas **9** racetrack
note: **3** IOU
___ betty: **5** brown
Betty: **4** Ford **5** Field, Smith, White **6** Comden, Grable, Hutton, Rollin, Rubble, Thomas, Wright **7** Buckley, Everett, Friedan, Furness, Garrett, Johnson **8** Williams
Betty ___: **4** Boop, Coed, lamp **7** Crocker
___ Betty: **5** Nurse
Betty Crocker product: **3** mix **7** cake mix
Bettye: **8** Ackerman
Betty Ford Center purpose: **5** rehab
between: **4** amid **5** among, 'twixt **6** amidst, middle, midway, mongst, within **7** amongst, through **9** bounded by **10** enclosed by, separating
in French: **5** entre
in Spanish: **5** entre
prefix: **5** inter-
us: **9** entre nous
between ___ and a hard place: **5** a rock
between ___ and me: **3** you
between-meal food: **4** nosh **5** snack
between-rounds area: **6** corner
Between Tears and Laughter
author: Alden Nowlan
Between the Acts
author: Virginia Woolf
___ between the cracks: **4** slip
Between the Devil and the Deep Blue Sea
composer: Harold Arlen, Ted Koehler
___ between the lines: **4** read
___ Between the States: **3** War
___ Between the Tates, The: **3** War
Between Walls
author: William Carlos Williams
between you ___: **5** and me
betwixt: **4** amid **5** among **6** amidst, mongst **7** amongst
betwixt and ___: **7** between
___ Bet Your Life: **3** You
Betz: **4** Carl
Beulah: **5** Bondi
Beulah, peel ___ grape: **3** me a
beurre ___: **4** noir **5** blanc, fondu, manié
___ beurre: **5** petit
Bevans: **4** Clem
bevel: **4** cant, tilt **5** miter, slant, slope **6** angled, canted, tilted **7** chamfer, mitered, oblique, slanted, sloping **8** diagonal, inclined **9** at an angle
beveled: **6** skewed **8** diagonal
beverage: **3** ade, ale, gin, Joe, nog, pop, rum, rye, tea **4** beer, bock, brew, cola, fizz, flip, grog, kava, marc, maté, mead, milk, ouzo, port, raki, sake, saki, wine **5** anise, Bronx, cider, cocoa, decaf, drink, float, juice, julep, kvass, lager,

mocha, negus, pekoe, perry, punch, shrub, sling, stout, toddy, vodka, water **6** bishop, brandy, cassis, coffee, Cognac, eggnog, gimlet, kirsch, kumiss, kummel, mai tai, malted, mescal, Mickey, mimosa, nectar, oolong, Pernod, porter, posset, pulque, rickey, rob roy, Scotch, shandy, tisane, whisky, zombie **7** aquavit, Bacardi, bourbon, Campari, collins, cordial, curaçao, herb tea, iced tea, limeade, liqueur, martini, mint tea, negroni, oenomel, pale ale, potable, ratafia, sangría, seltzer, sidecar, sloe gin, soda pop, stinger, tequila, whiskey **8** absinthe, anisette, apéritif, black tea, bouillon, calvados, club soda, coco loco, daiquiri, Drambuie, eau de vie, espresso, green tea, Guinness, highball, Jack Rose, lemonade, libation, pilsener, pink lady, potation, salty dog, schnapps, skim milk, souchong, spritzer, Tia Maria, vermouth **9** alexander, applejack, aqua vitae, Cointreau, cream soda, drinkable, ginger ale, hard cider, Manhattan, margarita, milk shake, mint julep, moonshine, moosemilk, orangeade, slivovitz, soda water, soft drink, ward eight, yerba maté **10** apple juice, Bloody Mary, buttermilk, café au lait, caffé latte, cappuccino, chartreuse, fruit juice, ginger beer, golden fizz, grape juice, horse's neck, Jamaica rum, malted milk, Mickey Finn, Moscow mule, piña colada, rock and rye, shandygaff, silver fizz, tonic water, Vichy water
alcoholic ~: **3** ale, gin, rum, rye **4** beer, bock, grog, mead, ouzo, port, sake, saki, wine **5** booze, hooch, julep, kvass, lager, sling, stout, toddy, vodka **6** bishop, brandy, bubbly, cassis, chicha, Cognac, gimlet, hootch, liquor, mai tai, mescal, mimosa, porter, pulque, redeye, rob roy, scotch, whisky, zombie **7** aquavit, Bacardi, bourbon, Campari, Collins, cordial, curaçao, liqueur, martini, negroni, pale ale, ratafia, sangria, sidecar, sloe gin, spirits, stinger, tequila, whiskey **8** absinthe, anisette, aperitif, calvados, cocktail, coco loco, daiquiri, Drambuie, eau de vie, Galliano, Guinness, highball, Jack Rose, libation, nightcap, pilsener, pink lady, potation, salty dog, schnapps, Tia Maria, vermouth **9** alexander, applejack, aqua vitae, champagne, Cointreau, firewater, hard cider, Manhattan, margarita, mint julep, moonshine, moosemilk, slivovitz **10** Bloody Mary, Jamaica rum, Moscow mule, piña colada, rock and rye
après-ski ~: **5** cocoa, toddy
autumn ~: **5** cider
bedtime ~: **4** milk **5** cocoa
Beowulf ~: **4** mead
brewed ~: **3** ale, tea **4** beer **5** lager, stout
British ~: **3** ale, tea
carbonated ~: **3** pop **4** cola, soda **8** root beer **9** ginger ale
chest: **6** cooler
diner ~: **3** joe **4** java **6** coffee
dinner ~: **4** wine
eggy ~: **3** nog
fermented ~: **3** ale **4** beer, mead, wine **5** cider, lager, stout **6** chicha, pulque
fruit ~: **3** ade **5** cider
green ~: **3** tea
herbal ~: **3** tea
holder: **3** cup, pot, urn **5** flute, glass **6** carafe
hot ~: **3** tea **5** cocoa, toddy **6** coffee
iced ~: **3** tea
in French: **3** thé, vin
Japanese ~: **4** sake, saki
malt ~: **3** ale **4** beer **7** brewage
Middle East ~: **4** arak **6** arrack
morning ~: **3** tea **4** milk **6** coffee
suffix: **3** -ade
Yuletide ~: **3** nog **6** eggnog
see also drink

Beverly: **4** city, town **5** Sills **6** Cleary **7** D'Angelo, Garland, Johnson
locale: **4** Mass.
Beverly Hillbillies, The (1993 film)
cast: Dabney Coleman, Erika Eleniak, Cloris Leachman, Lily Tomlin, Jim Varney
Beverly Hillbillies, The (CBS sitcom)
cast: Max Baer Jr. (Jethro Bodine) Raymond Bailey (Milburn Drysdale)
Donna Douglas (Elly May Clampett)
Buddy Ebsen (Jed Clampett)
Nancy Kulp (Jane Hathaway)
Irene Ryan (Granny)
dog: Duke
Beverly Hills: **4** city, town
Drive in ~: **5** Rodeo
home: **6** estate
locale: **10** California
Beverly Hills 90210 (Fox drama)
cast: Shannen Doherty (Brenda Walsh)
Jennie Garth (Kelly Taylor)
Luke Perry (Dylan McKay)
Jason Priestley (Brendon Walsh)
Tori Spelling (Donna Martin)
Ian Ziering (Steve Sanders)
Beverly Hills Cop (1984 film)
cast: Eddie Murphy, Judge Reinhold
director: Martin Brest
role: **4** Axel **5** Foley
bevy: **4** band, herd, pack **5** bunch, covey, crowd, flock, group, horde, swarm **6** muster, throng, troupe **7** cluster **8** assembly **9** gathering **10** collection, whole bunch
member: **5** quail **6** beauty
bewail: **3** rue **4** moan, weep **5** mourn **6** bemoan, grieve, lament, regret, repent, sorrow **7** cry over, deplore **8** bawl over, weep over **9** grieve for, moan about **10** groan about, show sorrow, take it hard
beware: **4** look, mind, shun **5** avoid **6** caveat, danger **7** look out, pay heed, warning **8** mistrust, take care, take heed, watch out **9** keep alert **10** look out for
beware of the dog in Latin: **9** cave canem
beware the __ of March: **4** ides
bewhiskered: **5** hairy **7** bearded
animal: **3** cat **4** seal **5** otter **6** walrus
bewilder: **4** daze, snow, stun **5** addle, amaze, floor, mixup, stump, throw **6** baffle, bemuse, boggle, flurry, fuddle, muddle, outwit, puzzle, rattle **7** astound, becloud, confuse, fluster, mystify, nonplus, perplex, perturb, shake up, stupefy, unnerve **8** astonish, befuddle, confound, entangle, outsmart **9** give pause, overwhelm **10** disconcert
bewildered: **4** agog, asea, hazy, lost **5** agape, at sea, blank, dizzy **6** addled, in a fog, punchy **7** abashed, at a loss, fuddled, puzzled, reeling **9** astounded, awestruck, befuddled, delirious, flummoxed, flustered, in a dither, mystified, perplexed, staggered, stupefied, surprised, uncertain **10** astonished, bowled over, dumbstruck, flipped out, speechless, taken aback
response: **3** huh
bewildering: **7** complex **8** puzzling
system: **4** maze
bewilderment: **3** fog **4** haze **6** enigma, stupor
bewitch: **3** hex **4** draw, jinx, lure, take **5** charm, tempt **6** allure, dazzle, disarm, enamor, ravish **7** attract, beguile, conjure, enchant, engross, enthral, inthral **8** enthrall, entrance, inthrall, transfix **9** captivate, enrapture, fascinate, hypnotize, inebriate, infatuate, spellbind, transport **10** intoxicate
bewitched: **4** gaga **5** magic **7** far gone **8** obsessed **9** enchanted, entranced, fallen for, possessed **10** captivated, enraptured, fascinated, infatuated, mesmerized, spellbound
Bewitched (2005 film)
cast: Michael Caine, Will Ferrell, Nicole Kidman, Shirley MacLaine
director: Nora Ephron
Bewitched (ABC sitcom)
cast: Marion Lorne (Aunt Clara)
Elizabeth Montgomery (Samantha Stevens)
Agnes Moorehead (Endora)
Dick Sargent (Darrin Stephens)
David White (Larry Tate)
Dick York (Darrin Stephens)
producer: **5** Asher
twitcher: **4** nose
Bewitched, Bothered and Bewildered
composer: Lorenz Hart, Richard Rodgers
bewitching: **5** magic, siren, spell **6** lovely **7** lovable, magical, winning, winsome **8** alluring, inviting, loveable, magnetic **9** beautiful, disarming, glamorous **10** attractive, enchanting, magnetical
bey: **5** ruler, title **8** governor
locale: **5** Tunis **6** Turkey
robe: **3** aba **4** abba
Bey: **6** Turhan
Beymer: **7** Richard
Beyoncé: **7** Knowles
beyond: **3** too **4** more, over, past **5** above, outer **6** across, free of, onward, yonder **7** ahead of, besides, clear of, further, onwards, outside, without **8** as well as **9** apart from **10** superior to, surpassing
combining form: **3** par- **4** para- **6** preter- **7** praeter-
in German: **4** über
prefix: **3** out- **4** meta-, para- **5** extra-, hyper-, trans-, ultra- **6** preter-
the horizon: **4** afar
beyond __: **5** price **6** number **7** compare, measure
beyond a __: **5** doubt
Beyond Good and Evil
author: Friedrich Nietzsche
Beyond Peace
author: Richard Nixon
Beyond Rangoon
setting: **5** Burma
beyond the __: **4** pale
Beyond the Sea (1960 song)
artist: Bobby Darin
bezel: **3** rim **6** flange
contents: **5** jewel
bezillions: **4** lots, many, tons **5** heaps, scads
bezique: **4** game **8** card game
variety: **7** binocle
B.F.: **7** Skinner **8** Goodrich
BFA
part of ~: **4** arts, fine **8** bachelor
BFG, The
author: Roald Dahl
B-flat: **3** key
equivalent: **6** A-sharp
__ B. Goode: **6** Johnny
__ B'Gosh: **7** OshKosh
Bhagalpur: **4** city, town
locale: **5** India
river: **6** Ganges
Bhagavad-__: **4** Gita
Bhagavad-Gita: **4** epic, poem
characters: **6** Arjuna **7** Krishna
original language: **8** Sanskrit
setting: **3** war **5** India
vehicle: **7** chariot
__ B. Hayes: **10** Rutherford
Bhopal: **4** city, town
locale: **5** India
Bhutan: **6** nation **7** country
bovine: **4** Siri
capital: **6** Thimbu **7** Thimphu
locale: **4** Asia
mountain: **10** Chomo Lhari, Kula Kangri
neighbor: **5** Assam, China, India
people: **6** Lepcha
Bhutto, Benazir: **2** P.M. **9** Pakistani
bi-
predecessor: **3** uni-
successor: **3** tri-
Bi: **4** elem. **7** bismuth, element
83 for ~: **4** at. no.
Bialik: **5** Chaim, Mayim
bialy: **4** roll **5** bread
flavoring: **5** onion
Bialystock: **3** Max
Bianca: **4** moon **6** Jagger
planet: **6** Uranus
Bianchi: **7** Daniela

bianci
opposite: 4 neri
___ Bianco: 6 Tony Lo
Biarritz: 3 car 4 auto, city, town 8 Cadillac 10 automobile
locale: 6 France
bias: 4 bent, skew, sway, tilt, warp 5 angle, slant, slope, trend, twist 6 liking, racism 7 bigotry, distort, incline, leaning 8 attitude, diagonal, jaundice, penchant, tendency 9 appetence, influence, injustice, prejudice, sentiment 10 chauvinism, favoritism, narrowness, partiality, predispose, preference, proclivity, propensity, unfairness
on the ~: 6 aslant 7 athwart 8 diagonal 9 at an angle, crossways, crosswise, slantways, slantwise 10 diagonally
without ~: 4 fair, just 9 objective
bias-___ tire: 3 ply 6 belted
biased: 6 myopic, narrow, skewed, unfair, unjust 7 bigoted, leaning, not fair, oblique, partial 8 diagonal, disposed, on a slant, one-sided, partisan 9 arbitrary, parochial 10 intolerant, prejudiced, subjective, unbalanced
be ~: 4 tend 6 prefer
one: 5 bigot
bias-ply: 4 tire
biathlon: 5 event
equipment: 5 rifle
take part in a ~: 3 ski 5 shoot
bib: 6 napkin
and tucker: 6 attire, finery
ender: 4 cock
require a ~: 5 drool
wearer: 3 tot 7 toddler
bib and ___: 6 tucker
bibb: 6 faucet, timber 7 bracket
Bibb: 6 county 7 lettuce
county seat: 5 Macon
bibber: 3 sot 4 lush 5 toper 7 tippler
starter: 4 wine
Bibbidi ___ Boo: 7 Bobbidi
bibble: 4 tope
bibcock: 3 tap
bibelot: 5 curio 6 trifle 7 trinket 8 nicknack 10 knickknack
Bibi: 9 Andersson, Osterwald
bible: 4 book 5 guide 6 manual 8 handbook 9 authority, guidebook, vade mecum
Bible: 7 the Word 8 holy book 9 scripture 10 scriptures
book: 3 Eph., Isa., Job, Lev., Mic., Neh., Num., Psa., Rev., Rom. 4 Acts, Amos, Exod., Ezra, Joel, John, Jude, Luke, Macc., Mark, Obad., Prov., Ruth, Thes. 5 Chron., Hosea, James, Jonah, Kings, Levit., Micah, Nahum, Peter, Thess., Titus, Tobit 6 Baruch, Daniel, Esdras, Esther, Exodus, Haggai, Isaiah, Joshua, Judges, Judith, Psalms, Romans, Samuel, Sirach 7 Azariah, Ezekiel, Genesis, Hebrews, Malachi, Matthew, Numbers, Obadiah, Susanna, Timothy 8 Habakkuk, Jeremiah, Manasseh, Nehemiah, Philemon, Proverbs 9 Ephesians, Galatians, Leviticus, Maccabees, Zechariah, Zephaniah 10 Chronicles, Colossians, Revelation
distributor: 7 Gideons
edition: 3 RSV 5 Douay 7 Vulgate
last word of the ~: 4 amen
line: 3 ver. 5 verse
Bible ___: 4 Belt 6 school 7 Society
Biblical
beast: 3 ass
boat: 3 ark
brother: 4 Abel, Cain, Esau, Seth, Shem 5 Aaron
city: 4 Zoar 5 Sodom 6 Bethel
comforter: 5 staff
food: 5 manna
garden: 4 Eden
gift: 4 gold 5 myrrh 12 frankincense
hunter: 4 Cain, Esau
idol: 4 Baal
juniper: 5 retem
king: 3 Asa 4 Saul 5 David, Herod 7 Solomon
kingdom: 4 Elam, Moab 5 Ophir, Sheba
land: 6 Goshen
language: 5 Greek 6 Hebrew 7 Aramaic
matriarch: 4 Leah 5 Sarah
measure: 4 omer
mountain: 4 Nebo 5 Horeb, Sinai 6 Ararat, Carmel, Pisgah
name for Israel: 6 Beulah
nation: 5 Magog
ointment: 4 nard
Palestine: 6 Canaan
patriarch: 4 Enos 5 Isaac 7 Abraham
pause: 5 selah
preposition: 4 unto
priest: 3 Eli
prison escapee: 5 Peter
pronoun: 3 thy 4 thee, thou 5 thine
prophet: 4 Amos, Joel 5 Hosea, Jonah, Micah, Moses, Nahum 6 Elijah, Elisha, Nathan, Samuel 7 Ezekiel, Malachi, Obadiah 9 Zechariah, Zephaniah
scribe: 4 Ezra
shepherd: 4 Abel
spy: 5 Caleb
stargazers: 4 Magi
subject of a ~ miracle: 4 wine 6 loaves
tax: 5 tithe
topic: 3 sin
tree: 5 algum, almug
twin: 4 Esau 5 Jacob
underworld: 5 Sheol
verb: 4 hast, hath, wast, wert 5 didst, seest, shalt
verb ender: 3 est, eth
wall word: 4 mene 5 tekel
wedding site: 4 Cana
weed: 4 tare
bibliographic
suffix: 3 ana 4 iana
bibliography: 4 list 6 record 7 catalog 9 catalogue
abbr.: 4 auth., et al., ibid. 5 et seq., op. cit.
phrase: 6 et alii
word: 4 idem
bibliophile: 8 bookworm 9 booklover
purchase: 4 book, tome 6 volume
bibliophobe fear: 5 books
bibliotheque item: 5 livre
bibulous: 6 spongy 7 soaking 9 absorbent, permeable
one: 3 sot 4 wino 7 tippler
Bic: 3 pen 5 razor
alternative: 5 Pilot 6 Parker, Schick 7 Uni-Ball 8 Gillette 9 PaperMate
filler: 3 ink
bicarb: 7 antacid
___ bicarbonate: 6 sodium
bicarbonate of ___: 4 soda
bice: 4 blue 5 color, green
Bicentennial Man (1999 film)
cast: Wendy Crewson, Sam Neill, Robin Williams
character: 5 robot
director: Chris Columbus
dog: 5 Woofy
biceps: 6 flexor, muscle
band: 6 armlet
exercise: 4 curl 6 chin-up
show off the ~: 4 flex
Bichette: 5 Dante
Bichon Frise: 3 dog 5 canid 6 canine
bicker: 4 deal, feud, spar, tiff 5 argue, brawl, cavil, fight, scrap 6 haggle, hassle, niggle, rattle 7 dispute, quarrel, quibble, wrangle 8 disagree, pettifog, squabble 9 altercate, have words
bickering: 4 at it, feud, fuss, spat, tiff 6 fracas, strife 7 dispute, quarrel 8 argument, friction, polemics, squabble 9 imbroglio 10 difficulty, dissension
Bickford, Charles: 5 actor
Bickle, Travis drove one: 4 taxi
bicorne: 3 hat
bicuspid neighbor: 5 molar
bicycle: 4 ride 5 wheel 7 vehicle
area: 4 lane, path
kind of ~ seat: 6 banana
part: 4 bell, gear, seat, tire 5 brake, pedal, spoke, wheel 9 handlebar
power ~: 5 moped
ride a ~: 5 pedal
ten-speed ~: 5 racer
bicycle ___: 4 kick, path, race, seat
___ bicycle: 4 push 6 tandem 8 ten-speed
Bicycle ___ for Two: 5 Built
Bicycle Rider in Beverly Hills, The
author: William Saroyan
Bicycle Thief, The (1947 film)
director: Vittorio De Sica
bicycling: 5 sport
bicyclist: 5 rider
bid: 3 ask, say, try 4 tell, wish 5 crack, essay, offer, order, quote 6 ask for, demand, direct, effort, enjoin, exhort, invite, render, submit, summon, tender 7 attempt, beseech, command, invited, proffer, propose, request, require, venture 8 endeavor, offering, overture, proposal 9 make a play, quotation 10 invitation, make a pitch, submission
bridge ~: 5 one no
farewell: 4 wave 5 leave 6 depart
first: 4 open
make a ~: 3 try 5 offer
proposal: 5 offer, quote
silent ~: 3 nod
to take no tricks: 5 nullo
___ bid: 3 cue 4 dumb, free, jump 5 shift 6 asking, demand, sealed
bid and ___: 5 asked
Bidart, Frank: 4 poet
biddable: 4 tame 8 resigned, yielding 9 tractable
Biddeford: 4 city, town
locale: 5 Maine
bidder: 8 opponent
after East: 5 South
amount: 5 offer
bidding: 4 word 5 order 6 behest 7 command, dictate, mandate, precept 9 direction
do one's ~: 4 obey
old-style: 4 hest
Biddle: 8 Nicholas
biddy: 3 hen 4 fowl 6 pullet 7 cackler, chicken 10 fussbudget
young ~: 5 chick
bide: 4 live, stay, wait 5 await, dwell, tarry 6 belong, endure, hold on, linger, remain, reside 7 sojourn 8 tolerate 10 hang around
one's time: 4 wait 5 await, delay, tarry 6 lie low 7 stand by
Bide-___: 4 a-Wee
Biden: 3 Joe 4 Beau, Jill, veep 6 Joseph
bide one's ___: 4 time
Bidin' My Time
composer: George Gershwin
Biehn, Michael: 5 actor
Biel: 7 Jessica
___ bien: 3 est, muy 4 está, très
Bien Hoa: 4 city, town
locale: 7 Vietnam
biennial: 5 event, plant
___ Bien Phu: 4 Dien
Bierce, Ambrose: 6 writer 8 satirist 10 journalist
employer: Hearst
friend: Harte, Twain
work: The Devil's Dictionary
biff: 4 belt, blow, swat 5 punch, whack 8 uppercut
bifid: 5 cleft, in two
bifocals: 5 specs 7 glasses 10 eyeglasses
bifold: 6 double
biform: 4 dual 6 Sphinx 7 mermaid
bifurcate: 4 fork, part 5 forky, split 6 branch, forked, spread 7 deviate, diverge, radiate 8 separate
bifurcation: 4 fork 5 split
big: 4 free, full, high, huge, kind, tall, vast, wide 5 adult, ample, awash, broad, bulky, burly, giant, great, gross, grown, heavy, hefty, hippy, husky, jumbo, large, lofty, mondo, noble, proud, roomy, stout, super 6 goodly, kindly, mature, mickle, mighty, rugged, strong 7 bloated, copious, eminent, endless, haughty, hulking, immense, leading, liberal, mammoth, man-size, massive, monster, pompous, popular, selfish, serious, sizable, titanic, weighty 8 arrogant, boastful, bragging, brimming, colossal, enormous, far-flung, generous, gigantic, gracious, heavyset, imposing, infinite, inflated, king-size, outsized, oversize, powerful, selfless, sizeable, spacious, stalwart, sweeping, thumping, tolerant, whapping, whopping 9 boundless, capacious, conceited, cyclopean, excessive, expansive, extensive, front-page, full-grown, heavy-duty,

herculean, humongous, imperious, important, leviathan, limitless, momentous, outspread, overblown, panoramic, paramount, ponderous, prominent, strapping, unbounded, universal, unlimited, walloping, well-built, well-known, whalelike, worldwide **10** altruistic, benevolent, commodious, embonpoint, exhaustive, family-size, flamboyant, gargantuan, meaningful, monumental, munificent, prodigious, staggering, stupendous, thundering, tremendous, voluminous, widespread
and strong: 5 burly **9** strapping
ape: 5 orang **6** galoot, lummox **7** galloot, gorilla
as life: 5 plain **7** visible **8** apparent, manifest
be ~: 3 let **4** give **5** allow
break: 4 luck **7** opening
deal: 3 ado **4** flap, stir, to-do **6** uproar
do: 4 fete, gala **5** event
ender: 3 eye, wig **4** head, horn, shot, time **5** mouth
eyes: 6 hunger **8** ambition
game: 4 lion **5** rhino, tiger **8** elephant
go over ~: 3 wow **5** score **6** please, thrill, turn on **7** impress, succeed **8** blow away **9** electrify
hand: 5 kudos **6** praise **7** ovation, plaudit **8** accolade, applause, cheering **9** standing O
hit: 3 win **5** smash **6** winner **7** success, triumph, victory
hit it ~: 6 arrive, do well, thrive **7** make out, prosper, succeed, triumph **8** fare well, flourish, get ahead, get lucky, go places, make good
house: 3 jug, pen **4** gaol, jail **5** clink, manor, villa **6** castle, cooler, estate, lockup, palace, prison **7** palazzo **10** plantation
house resident: 3 con **5** crook, felon, lifer **7** convict **8** criminal, jailbird, prisoner, yardbird **10** lawbreaker
in a ~ way: 4 a lot, lots, much, tons **5** loads, no end **6** galore, highly, hugely, oodles, vastly **7** aplenty, grandly, greatly, largely **8** beaucoup, lavishly, terribly **9** copiously, extremely, immensely, liberally, profusely **10** abundantly, a great deal, enormously, prodigally
make a ~ thing about: 4 carp, fuss **7** quibble
name: 5 celeb **7** notable **8** luminary **9** celebrity
on: 4 into
picture: 4 plan **5** mural, whole **6** blowup, fresco **8** time line
piece: 5 chunk
shot: 3 VIP **4** head, king, lion, name **5** baron, chief, mogul, nabob, nawab, wheel **6** fat cat, kahuna, top dog, tycoon **7** magnate, notable **8** higher-up, kingfish, official **9** authority, celebrity, commander, dignitary, executive, key player, personage
stink: 5 fetor **6** foetor **9** grievance
talk ~: 4 brag, crow **5** boast, vaunt **6** overdo **7** bluster, lay it on **9** gasconade

big __: 3 end, gun, lie, one, toe, top **4** band, beat, deal, game, hair, hook, idea, mama, name, road, shot, talk, time, tree **5** bucks, daddy, house, labor, money, skate, stick, wheel **6** casino, cheese, kahuna, laurel, league, sister **7** brother, leaguer, picture, science
big __ elephant: 4 as an
big __ outdoors: 5 as all
big __ theory: 4 bang
big-__: 4 name **5** boned, timer **6** ticket **7** hearted
big-__ item: 6 ticket
__ big: 4 talk **5** hit it
Big (1988 film)
cast: Tom Hanks, John Heard, Robert Loggia, Elizabeth Perkins
director: Penny Marshall
Big __: 3 Ben, Mac, Man, Red, Sur, Ten **4** Bird, Blue, East, Five, Foot, Gulp, Love, Nate, Shot, Time **5** Apple, Board, Daddy, Muddy, Poppa, Steal **6** Bertha, Bopper, Dipper **7** Brother, Trouble
Big __!: 4 deal
Big __ Conference: 3 Ten **4** East
Big __ Don't Cry: 5 Girls
Big __ Era: 4 Band
Big __ for the Little Lady, A: 4 Hand
Big __ Island: 7 Diomede
Big __ John: 3 Bad
Big __ Love, A: 5 Hunk O'
Big __ National Park: 4 Bend
Big __ One, The: 3 Red
Big __ Taxi: 6 Yellow
Big __, The: 3 Fix, Hit, Sea, Sky **4** Easy, Heat, Hurt, Town, Unit **5** Chill, Clock, Combo, House, Knife, Money, Sleep, Store, Tease, Trail **6** Kahuna, Parade, Valley **7** Country
Big __ Turner: 3 Joe
Big 10
see Big Ten
Big 12
see Big Twelve
Big Apple: 3 NYC **6** Gotham **7** New York **9** Manhattan
airport: 3 JFK, LGA
ave.: 3 Lex.
commuter rte.: 4 LIRR
cultural center: 4 MOMA
force: 4 NYPD
hotel: 5 Plaza
initials: 3 NYC
neighborhood: 4 Soho **6** Bowery, Harlem **7** Tribeca
newspaper: 3 NYT **4** News, Post **5** Times
parade sponsor: 5 Macy's
player: 3 Met **4** Yank **7** Yankees
restaurant: 6 Lutèce, Sardi's **7** Elaine's
retailer: 4 Saks **5** Macy's
school: 3 NYU
stadium: 4 Shea
subway agency: 3 MTA
theater: 6 Apollo
transport: 6 A Train
big as __: 4 life
big as a __: 5 house

Big as Life
author: E.L. Doctorow
Big Bad __: 4 John, Mama
Big Bad John (1961 song)
artist: Jimmy Dean
Big Bad John (1990 film)
cast: Jack Elam, Jimmy Dean
Big Bad Love (2002 film)
cast: Rosanna Arquette, Arliss Howard, Paul LeMat, Debra Winger
Big Bad Wolf, emulate the: 4 blow, huff, puff
Big Band music: 4 jazz, jive **5** swing
Big Ben
home: 6 London
numeral: 3 III, VII, XII **4** VIII
sound: 4 bong
Big Bend: 4 park
locale: 5 Texas
Big Bertha: 3 gun **6** cannon
birthplace: 5 Essen **7** Germany
milieu: 3 WWI
Big Bird
colleague: 4 Bert **5** Ernie, Piggy **6** Kermit **9** Miss Piggy
network: 3 PBS
street: 6 Sesame
Big Blue: 3 IBM
home: 6 Armonk **7** New York
product: 2 PC **4** chip **6** server **8** computer
Big Board: 4 NYSE
alternative: 4 AMEX
initials: 3 IBM
street: 4 Wall
Big Boned Gal (1989 song)
artist: k.d. lang
Big Bopper
song: Chantilly Lace (1958)
Big Boy: 3 car **4** auto **6** Hudson, tomato
relative: 4 Roma **9** beefsteak, Better Boy, Early Girl, Quick Pick
rival: *see* restaurant chain
__ Big Boy: 4 Bob's
Big Broadcast of 1938, The (1938 film)
cast: W.C. Fields, Bob Hope, Dorothy Lamour, Martha Raye
Big Broadcast, The (1932 film)
cast: Gracie Allen, George Burns, Bing Crosby, Kate Smith
Big Brother
creator: George Orwell
Big Brother (CBS reality)
host: Julie Chen
Big Business (1988 film)
cast: Edward Herrmann, Bette Midler, Lily Tomlin
big-cat hybrid: 5 liger **6** tiglon
Big Chill, The (1983 film)
cast: Tom Berenger, Glenn Close, Jeff Goldblum, William Hurt, Kevin Kline, Mary Kay Place, Meg Tilly, JoBeth Williams
director: Lawrence Kasdan
Big Combo, The (1955 film)
cast: Cornel Wilde
director: Joseph H. Lewis
Big Country, The (1958 film)
cast: Burl Ives, Gregory Peck
director: William Wyler
Big D: 6 Dallas
Big Daddy
portrayer: Burl Ives
Big Daddy (1999 film)
cast: Joey Lauren Adams, Adam Sandler, Rob Schneider, Jon Stewart

Big Dance, The: 4 NCAA
Big deal!: 6 so what **8** who cares
Big Dipper: 5 ladle **9** Ursa Major
constellation near the ~: 5 Draco
star: 5 Alcor
unit: 4 star
big-eared animal: 3 ass **5** bunny, burro, hound **6** basset, rabbit
Big East: 10 conference
school: 3 NDU **5** Miami, UConn **7** Rutgers, St. John's **8** Syracuse **9** Notre Dame, Seton Hall, Villanova **10** Georgetown, Pittsburgh, Providence **11** Connecticut
Big Easy: 8 Ernie Els **10** New Orleans
Big Easy, The (1987 film)
cast: Ellen Barkin, Ned Beatty, Dennis Quaid
role: 4 Remy
Bigelow: 3 tea **7** Kathryn
competitor: 6 Lipton, Nestea, Salada, Tetley **7** Red Rose **8** Twinings
Bigelow, Kathryn: 8 director
film: The Hurt Locker (2009, AA)
spouse: James Cameron
bigeye: 4 fish
big-eyed: 4 owly
Bigfoot
cousin: 4 Yeti **9** Sasquatch
__ big for one's britches: 3 too
bigger
get ~: 3 wax **4** grow **6** expand, mature **7** enlarge, fill out
than life: 4 epic **6** heroic
__ bigger and better things!: 4 On to
Biggers, Earl Derr: 6 writer
creation: Charlie Chan
work: Seven Keys to Baldpate
__ bigger than a breadbox?: 4 Is it
biggest: 7 maximum
share: 4 bulk, most **8** majority
Biggest Little City, The: 4 Reno
Biggest Part of Me (1980 song)
artist: Ambrosia
biggie: 3 VIP **5** mogul, mover **6** fat cat, shaker, tycoon **7** hotshot, magnate
biggin: 3 cap
Biggio: 5 Craig
Big Girls Don't Cry (1962 song)
artist: Four Seasons
Big Green: 9 Dartmouth
Biggs: 5 Jason
Biggs-Dawson: 6 Roxann
Biggs, E. Power: 8 organist
Big Hand for the Little Lady, A (1966 film)
cast: Henry Fonda, Joanne Woodward
big-headed: 4 smug, vain **5** cocky **7** fustian, haughty, pompous, stuck-up **8** arrogant, boastful, snobbish **9** conceited
big-headedness: 5 pride **6** vanity **7** conceit **9** arrogance
big-hearted: 4 free, kind **5** noble **7** liberal **8** generous, gracious, princely, selfless **10** altruistic, benevolent, charitable, humanistic
one: 5 softy **6** softie
bighorn: 5 sheep **6** animal, mammal
covering: 4 wool
relative: *see* sheep

Bighorn: 5 range, river
locale: 7 Montana, Wyoming
river to the ~: 8 Shoshone
__ Bighorn: 6 Little
Bighorns: 3 mts. 5 range 9 mountains
big house: 3 jug, pen 4 jail, stir 5 clink 6 cooler, prison
resident: 3 con 5 lifer 6 inmate 7 convict 8 prisoner
bight: 3 bay 4 bend, gulf, loop 5 fiord, fjord, inlet
West African ~: 6 Biafra
Bight of Benin
city on the ~: 5 Lagos
Big Hunk O' Love, A (1959 song)
artist: Elvis Presley
Big Joe: 6 Turner
Big Kahuna, The (2000 film)
cast: Danny DeVito, Kevin Spacey
Big Knife, The
author: Clifford Odets
big-league: 3 pro 5 major 7 eminent, serious 9 high-level, important, prominent
Big Lebowski, The (1998 film)
cast: Jeff Bridges, Steve Buscemi, John Goodman, Julianne Moore
director: Joel Coen
Big Love (1987 song)
artist: Fleetwood Mac
Biglow Papers, The
author: James Russell Lowell
Big Mac: 6 burger 9 hamburger
ingredient: 4 beef, meat 5 patty 6 cheese, pattie, tomato 7 lettuce
__ Big Man: 6 Little
Big Money, The
author: John Dos Passos
trilogy: 3 USA
bigmouth: 4 fish 7 tattler 10 taleteller, tattletale
bigmouthed: 4 long 5 gabby, gassy, tumid, windy, wordy 6 prolix 7 diffuse, fustian, hyped up, lengthy, orotund, pompous, ranting, stilted, unterse, verbose, voluble 8 boastful, inflated, rambling 9 bombastic, garrulous, grandiose, high-flown, overblown, redundant, rhapsodic, talkative 10 big-talking, discursive, euphuistic, flamboyant, histrionic, long-winded, loquacious, palaverous, rhetorical
Big, Mr.: 3 VIP 4 boss, king 6 honcho, top dog 7 kingpin
Big Muddy: 5 river 11 Mississippi
locale: 4 Iowa 8 Illinois, Missouri 9 Louisiana, Tennessee
big-name: 5 noted 7 eminent 8 renowned 9 prominent 10 celebrated
bigness: 4 bulk, size 8 enormity, free hand 9 amplitude, immensity, largeness, magnitude 10 dimensions, liberality
bigot: 5 hater, jingo 6 zealot 7 diehard, fanatic 9 sectarian 10 chauvinist, monomaniac
bigoted: 5 rabid 6 biased, little, narrow, unfair 7 insular, partial 9 parochial, sectarian 10 intolerant, prejudiced
bigotry: 4 bias, hate 6 racism 9 prejudice 10 unfairness
Big Poison: 5 Waner
Big Poppa (1995 song)
artist: Notorious B.I.G.
Big Red: 7 Cornell
home: 6 Ithaca
Big Red Dog, The dog: 8 Clifford
Big Red One, The (1980 film)
cast: Robert Carradine, Mark Hamill, Lee Marvin
Big Sea, The
author: Langston Hughes
Big Shot (1979 song)
artist: Billy Joel
Big Sky state: 4 Mont. 7 Montana
Big Sleep, The: 4 film 5 novel
author: Raymond Chandler
cast: Lauren Bacall, Humphrey Bogart, Martha Vickers
composer: Max Steiner
director: Howard Hawks
Big Store, The (1941 film)
cast: Margaret Dumont, Tony Martin, Chico Marx, Groucho Marx, Harpo Marx
Big Sur: 4 city, town
attraction: 4 surf, view 5 ocean
author: Jack Kerouac
locale: 10 California
big-talking: 4 smug, vain 5 cocky, proud 6 la-de-da, la-di-da, stuffy 7 fustian, haughty, pompous, stuck-up 8 affected, arrogant, assuming, boastful, cocksure, immodest, lah-di-dah, puffed up, snobbish 9 bigheaded, bombastic, conceited, know-it-all, loudmouth 10 complacent, egocentric, hoity-toity
Big Ten school: 3 Ill., MSU, OSU, PSU 4 Iowa, Mich., Minn., Wisc. 6 Purdue 7 Indiana 8 Illinois, Michigan 9 Minnesota, Ohio State, Penn State, Wisconsin
Big Three site of 1945: 5 Yalta
big-ticket: 6 costly 9 expensive
big-ticket __: 4 item
big-time: 5 noted 7 eminent
operator: 4 doer 5 mover, wheel 6 shaker
Big Time (1987 song)
artist: Peter Gabriel
big top: 6 circus
regular: 5 clown, tamer 7 acrobat 9 aerialist, lion tamer 10 ringmaster
Big Top Pee-wee (1988 film)
cast: Valeria Golino, Pee-wee Herman, Kris Kristofferson, Penelope Ann Miller
Big Town, The (1987 film)
cast: Matt Dillon, Tommy Lee Jones, Diane Lane, Tom Skerritt
director: Ben Bolt
Big Trouble (2002 film)
cast: Tim Allen, Rene Russo, Tom Sizemore, Stanley Tucci
director: Barry Sonnenfeld
Big Twelve school: 3 ISU, Kan., KSU, Neb., OSU, Tex., TTU 4 Colo., Nebr., Okla., TAMU 5 Texas 6 Baylor, Kansas 7 Texas A&M 8 Colorado, Missouri, Nebraska, Oklahoma 9 Iowa State, Texas Tech 11 Kansas State
Big Valley, The (ABC drama)
cast: Peter Breck (Nick Barkley) Linda Evans (Audra Barkley) Richard Long (Jarrod Barkley) Lee Majors (Heath Barkley) Barbara Stanwyck (Victoria Barkley)
big-voiced: 5 forte, noisy 7 blaring, booming, jarring, pealing, rackety, raucous, reboant, roaring 8 crashing, piercing, plangent, rumbling, sonorous, strident, turned up 9 clamorous, deafening 10 boisterous, resounding, stentorian, strepitous, thundering, uproarious, vociferous
Big West school: 4 UNLV
bigwig: 3 VIP 4 exec, head, lion, name, star 5 brass, chief, mogul, nabob 6 honcho, top dog 7 headman, hotshot, magnate, notable 9 authority, celebrity, dignitary, personage
Big Yellow Taxi (1975 song)
artist: Joni Mitchell
Bihar capital: 5 Patna
bijou: 3 gem 5 jewel 6 locket 7 trinket
bike: 5 cycle, pedal, wheel 6 tandem 7 vehicle 8 ten-speed 10 go for a ride, two-wheeler
ender: 3 way
ride a ~: 5 cycle, pedal
starter: 4 mini 5 motor
see also bicycle
bike __: 4 lane 5 trail
__ bike: 4 dirt 5 trail
Bikel, Theodore: 5 actor
biker: 7 cyclist 10 Hell's Angel
aid: 4 clip
gear: 6 helmet
ride: 3 hog
roar: 5 vroom
selection: 5 speed
stop: 6 hostel
bikeway: 4 lane, path
Bikila, Abebe: 6 runner 10 marathoner
bikini: 8 swimsuit
part: 3 bra
Bikini: 4 isle 5 atoll 6 island
event: 4 test 5 A-test, N-test
Bikini Beach (1964 film)
cast: Frankie Avalon, Annette Funicello, Martha Hyer, Keenan Wynn
Biko: 5 Steve
Bil: 5 Baird, Keane
bilateral: 6 mutual 8 two-sided 10 reciprocal, respective
Bilbao: 4 city, port, town
locale: 5 Spain
bile: 4 gall 5 venom, wrath 6 choler, malice, rancor, temper 10 irritation
carrier: 4 duct
combining form: 4 chol- 5 chole-, cholo-
source: 5 liver
Biletnikoff, Fred: 10 footballer
bilge
see baloney
bilingual
book: 6 diglot
bilious: 3 wan 5 surly 6 ornery, peaked, queasy, queazy, sallow 7 bearish 8 liverish, snappish 9 splenetic 10 ill-humored, out of sorts
biliousness: 6 spleen
bilk: 2 do 3 con 4 burn, gull, hose, nick, rook, shun, snow, take 5 cheat, cozen, gouge, pluck, screw, sting, trick 6 fleece, take in 7 deceive, defraud, mislead, swindle 8 flimflam, hoodwink 9 bamboozle, four-flush, shake down 10 overcharge, run a game on
Bilko: 3 NCO, Sgt. 5 Ernie, sarge 8 sergeant
bill: 2 ad 3 dun, fin, neb, nib, tab 4 beak, brim, chit, debt, list 5 bylaw, check, C-note, fiver, flyer, lobby, money, price, score, visor, vizor 6 dollar, poster, roster, tenner 7 account, invoice, lawsuit, leaflet, measure, placard, program, sawbuck, smacker, statute 8 banknote, circular, currency, frogskin, proposal, schedule, simoleon 9 broadside, greenback, liability, publicize, reckoning, statement 10 paper money
abbr.: 3 amt., inv. 4 stmt.
addition: 3 tax
and coo: 3 woo 4 neck 5 spoon 6 cuddle
attachment: 5 rider
bar ~: 3 tab
bird's ~: 3 neb, nib
blocker: 3 nay 4 veto
dollar ~: 3 one 6 single
enclosure: 3 SAE
ender: 3 bug 4 fish, fold, head, hook 5 board 6 poster
fill the ~: 4 suit 5 cater, serve 6 please 7 qualify, satisfy
five-dollar ~: 3 fin
foot the ~: 3 pay 5 spend, treat 6 defray
Franklin's ~: 5 C-note 7 hundred
Grant's ~: 5 fifty
Hamilton's ~: 3 ten 7 sawbuck
Jackson's ~: 6 twenty
Lincoln's ~: 3 fin 4 five
lowest ~: 3 one
monthly ~: 3 gas, tel. 4 util. 5 phone 8 electric, mortgage 9 utilities
of fare: 4 menu 5 carte, table
on a cap: 5 visor, vizor
pass a ~: 5 adopt, enact
restaurant ~: 5 check
sell a ~ of goods: 2 do 3 con, rob 4 bilk, burn, clip, dupe, fool, gull, have, hoax, nick, rook, scam, take, trim 5 cheat, cozen, fraud, gouge, mulct, pluck, set up, shaft, stiff, sting, trick 6 diddle, extort, fleece, hustle, outwit, rip off, sucker 7 deceive, defraud, finagle, sandbag, swindle 8 flimflam, hoodwink, outsmart 9 bamboozle, four-flush, shake down, victimize 10 run a game on
send a ~ collector: 3 dun
settler: 5 payer
starter: 3 wax, way 4 blue, boat, duck, hand, horn, play, shoe 5 cross, hawks, ivory, razor, spoon, sword 6 cranes, sheath, sickle, storks
thousand-dollar ~: 5 G-note
three-dollar ~: 4 fake, sham 5 phony 6 phoney
unpaid ~: 4 debt 6 arrear, red ink 7 arrears, deficit 9 liability, shortfall 10 obligation

utility ~ abbr.: 3 kwh
Washington's ~: 3 one
__ bill: 3 due 4 bank, show, time, true, twin 6 bottle, demand, dollar, double, inland, public, ripper 7 banker's, finance, foreign, private
Bill: 3 cat, Day, Nye 4 Dana, Klem, Macy, Tony 5 Bixby, Black, Blass, Conti, Cosby, Daily, Gates, Haley, Hayes, Krohn, Maher, Terry, Veeck, Walsh, Wyman 6 Cullen, Dickey, Gaines, Graham, Hunter, Justis, Medley, Monroe, Moyers, Murray, Paxton, Persky, Rigney, Tilden, Toomey, Walton, Willis, Wilson 7 Bradley, Buffalo, Clinton, Doggett, Forsyth, Hartack, Madlock, Mauldin, Pullman, Rodgers, Russell, Sharman, Travers, Withers 8 Anderson, Buchanan, Melendez, Parcells, Plympton, Robinson 9 Mazeroski, McKechnie, Shoemaker, Watterson 10 footballer, Smitrovich
Bill & __ Bogus Journey: 4 Ted's
Bill & __ Excellent Adventure: 4 Ted's
Bill __ and His Comets: 5 Haley
Bill __, the Science Guy: 3 Nye
__ Bill: 5 Pecos 6 Reform 7 Buffalo
bill and __: 3 coo
billboard: 2 ad 4 sign 5 lobby 6 poster 9 publicity, publicize
in Britain: 8 hoarding
Billboard: 3 mag 8 magazine
category: 3 rap 4 rock, soul 7 country
entry: 3 hit 4 song
list: 5 chart
__-billed auk: 5 razor
billed item: 3 cap
__-billed platypus: 4 duck
billet: 3 hut, job 4 bunk, live, post, slab, spot 5 berth, house, lodge, put up, rooms, stick 6 letter, living, reside, take in 7 housing, lodging, quarter, shelter 8 barracks, lodgings, lodgment, position, quarters 9 situation 10 employment
billet doux: 10 love letter
word in a: 4 cher 6 cherie
billfish: 3 gar
billfold: 6 wallet
filler: 3 fin, one, ten 4 cash 5 bucks, fiver, money 7 dollars
__ Bill Hickok: 4 Wild
billiard __: 4 ball, room 5 table 6 parlor
billiards: 4 game, pool 5 sport
black ball: 5 eight
cushion: 4 bank
glancing contact in ~: 4 kiss
need: 3 cue 4 rack 5 chalk 6 bridge
shot: 5 carom, massé 6 carrom
table cloth: 5 baize
__ billiards: 6 pocket
Billie: 4 Dove 5 Burke 7 Holiday
spouse: 3 Flo
Billie, __, Lena, Sarah: 4 Ella
Billie Jean (1983 song)
artist: Michael Jackson
Billie Jean King: 7 netster 9 tennis pro
opponent: 5 Riggs 6 Evonne
Billie Jean King, __ Moffitt: 3 née
billing: 9 publicity
cycle: 5 month
get top ~: 4 star
share ~: 6 costar
Billings: 4 city, Josh, town
locale: 7 Montana
school: 3 MSU
Billings, Josh: 6 writer 8 humorist
Billingsley: 4 John 5 Peter 7 Barbara
billion
about 6 ~ miles: 4 lt. yr. 9 light year
ender: 4 aire
prefix: 4 giga-
years, in geology: 3 eon 4 aeon
billionaire: 6 fat cat 9 moneybags, plutocrat
billions: 4 mint, tons 5 loads, scads 6 hoards, scores 7 legions 11 lots and lots
Billions and billions... guy: 5 Sagan
billionth prefix: 4 nano-
Bill, Mr. cry: 4 oh no
bill of __: 4 fare, sale 5 entry, goods 6 health, lading
Bill of Divorcement, A (1932 film)
cast: John Barrymore, Billie Burke, Katharine Hepburn
director: George Cukor
__ bill of goods: 5 sell a
__ bill of health: 5 clean
bill-of-lading abbr.: 4 recd.
Bill of Rights advocacy grp.: 4 ACLU
billow: 4 flap, rise, roll, tide, wave 5 crest, heave, pitch, surge, swell 6 puff up, ripple, well up 7 balloon, breaker 8 undulate, whitecap 10 ebb and flow
out: 5 swell 7 balloon
billowing: 10 voluminous
garment: 4 cape 5 cloak
billowy: 5 puffy
bills
behind on ~: 5 owing 6 in debt 9 in arrears
fat roll of ~: 3 wad
have ~: 3 owe
like new ~: 5 crisp
run up ~: 3 buy 5 spend 6 charge
see also moolah
Bills: 6 eleven
home: 7 Buffalo
org.: 3 AFC
rival: *see* NFL team
bill-signing souvenir: 3 pen
Bill & Ted's Excellent Adventure (1989 film)
cast: George Carlin, Bernie Casey, Keanu Reeves, Alex Winter
Bill the Cat comment: 3 ack
billy: 4 club, cosh, goat 5 baton, stick 6 cudgel 8 bludgeon 9 truncheon
billy __: 4 club, goat
__ billy: 5 silly
Billy: 4 Conn, Gray, Idol, Joel, Mumy, Paul, Rose, Swan, Vera, Welu, Zane 5 Barty, Bland, Hayes, Mauch, Ocean 6 Carter, Casper, Crudup, Curtis, Graham, Herman, Martin, Squier, Sunday, Vaughn, Wilder 7 Baldwin, Collins, Crystal, DeWolfe, Grammer, Preston, Vaughan 8 Eckstine, Williams 9 Strayhorn
Billy & __: 6 Lillie
Billy __: 4 Budd, Liar 6 Elliot, the Kid
Billy __ Cyrus: 3 Ray
Billy __ Williams: 3 Dee
__ Billy: 6 Bronco
__-Billy: 5 Rock-A
Billy Bathgate: 4 film 5 novel
author: E.L. Doctorow
cast: Dustin Hoffman, Nicole Kidman, Bruce Willis
director: Robert Benton
Billy Bob: 8 Thornton
Billy Budd: 5 novel, opera
author: Herman Melville
captain: 4 Vere
composer: Benjamin Britten
Billy, Don't Be a Hero (1974 song)
artist: Bo Donaldson and the Heywoods
billy goat: 4 male
feature: 5 beard
mate: 5 nanny 6 nannie
offspring: 3 kid
Billy Goats Gruff adversary: 5 troll
Billy Rose's Jumbo (1962 film)
cast: Stephen Boyd, Doris Day, Jimmy Durante, Martha Raye
Billy Straight
author: Jonathan Kellerman
Billy the Kid: 6 ballet, outlaw
composer: Aaron Copland
__ biloba: 6 gingko, ginkgo
Biloxi: 4 city, port, town
state: 4 Miss.
Biloxi Blues: 4 film, play
author: Neil Simon
cast: Matthew Broderick, Matt Mulhern, Christopher Walken
director: Mike Nichols
bimonthly: 3 mag 8 magazine
bin: 3 box 4 case, crib 5 hutch 6 bunker, coffer, hamper, hopper, manger 7 coal box 8 corn crib, Dumpster 9 container 10 receptacle
__ bin: 5 trash
Binaca
competitor: 5 Certs 6 Mentos, Tic Tac 7 Altoids, Clorets, Dentyne
binal: 6 double 7 twofold
binary: 4 dual 6 double 7 twofold, two-part
digit: 3 one 4 zero
star: 6 Sirius
binary __: 4 cell, code, form, star 5 color, digit 7 fission
binate: 4 dual 6 double 7 in pairs, two-fold
binaural: 6 stereo
Binchy, Maeve: 5 Irish 6 writer
work: Aches and Pains
Circle of Friends
The Copper Beech
Echoes
Evening Class
Firefly Summer
The Glass Lake
Heart and Soul
Light a Penny Candle
The Lilac Bus
Nights of Rain and Stars
Quentins
Scarlet Feather
Silver Wedding
Tara Road
A Time to Dance
Whitethorn Woods
bind: 3 fix, jam, pin, sew, tie, wed 4 bale, bond, know, lace, lash, link, rope, tape, weld, wrap, yoke 5 affix, cinch, clamp, force, hitch, leash, stick, tie up, truss 6 attach, begird, bundle, cement, compel, crunch, enlace, fasten, fetter, hamper, hobble, hogtie, hook up, inlace, lace up, ligate, lock up, oblige, pickle, pinion, ratify, secure, strait, tether 7 confine, conjoin, connect, dilemma, enchain, manacle, pin down, promise, require, shackle, tighten 8 enfetter, handcuff, hot water, make fast, obligate, quandary, restrain, restrict 9 constrain, constrict, deep water, indenture, interlace, prescribe, tight spot 10 difficulty
ender: 4 weed
in a ~: 5 stuck 7 up a tree 10 up the creek
nautically: 4 frap
starter: 5 spell
__ bind: 3 in a 6 double
binder: 8 notebook 9 loose-leaf
package ~: 4 cord, tape 5 twine
starter: 4 book 5 spell
__ binder: 4 ring
Binder: 5 Steve
binding: 4 band 5 cover, strap, valid 8 dressing, ligature, limiting, required 9 incumbent, mandatory, necessary, requisite, stringent 10 compulsory, imperative, obligatory, peremptory
legally ~: 5 valid
make ~: 4 pass, sign 6 decree 8 validate
material: 4 cord, rope 5 twine
molecule: 6 ligand
name meaning ~: 7 Rebecca, Rebekah
not ~: 4 null 5 loose 7 invalid
part: 5 cover, npard, spine
starter: 4 book 5 spell
type of book ~: 4 yapp
__ binding: 4 full, half, seam, yapp 6 spiral 7 circuit, edition, library, perfect, quarter
bindlestiff: 3 bum 4 hobo 5 tramp
binds, tie that: 7 wedlock 8 marriage
bine: 4 stem
starter: 4 wood
__ bin ein Berliner: 3 Ich
Binet: 6 Alfred
Binet-Simon __: 4 test 5 scale
Bing: 4 Dave 6 cherry, Crosby, Rudolf
cherry relative: 7 marasca, morello, oxheart
film buddy: 3 Bob
Bing, Dave: 5 cager
milieu: 5 court
org.: 3 NBA
sport: 10 basketball
binge: 3 jag 4 tear, toot 5 fling, gorge, revel, spree 6 bender, pig out 7 blowout, rampage, splurge 8 carousal 10 all-nighter, gormandize
__ binge: 3 on a
Bingham: 5 Traci
Binghamton: 4 city, town
city near ~: 6 Elmira
locale: 7 New York
__ Bingle: 3 Der
bingo: 3 aha 4 game 5 right 8 you got it
call: 4 B one, B six, B ten, B two 5 B five, B four, B nine 6 B eight,

B seven, B three **7** B eleven, B twelve
official: **6** caller
relative: **4** keno **5** beano, lotto
bingo __: **4** card, hall
Bingo Eli Yale
composer: Cole Porter
Bingo Long..., The (1976 film)
cast: James Earl Jones, Richard Pryor, Billy Dee Williams
director: John Badham
Binh Dinh: **4** city, town
locale: **7** Vietnam
today: **6** An Nhon
biniou: **4** wind **7** bagpipe
Binnie: **6** Barnes
Binnig, Gerd: **8** Nobelist **9** physicist
Binoche, Juliette: **7** actress
Oscar: The English Patient
binocle: **4** game **8** card game
binocular
component: **5** prism
lens: **5** optic
bio: **4** life **5** story **6** memoir, résumé **7** memoirs, profile **9** life story
datum: **3** age, née
ender: **4** tech **7** science
final ~: **4** obit
job-seeker's ~: **4** vita **6** résumé
Bio-Bio: **5** river
locale: **5** Chile
biochemical
catalyst: **6** enzyme
compound: **5** lipid **6** lipide
energy source: **3** ATP
biodegradable: **5** green
biodynamics: **7** science
bioflavonoid: **5** rutin **6** citrin
biographer: **6** author, writer
Biographer's Tale, The
author: A.S. Byatt
biography: **4** life, vita **5** genre, story **6** memoir **7** memoirs, profile **9** life story **10** adventures, literature
biol.: **3** sci.
branch: **4** anat.
course: **3** bot.
biological: **7** organic
breakdown: **5** lysis
class: **5** taxon
classes: **4** taxa
duct: **3** vas
grouping: **7** kingdom
map: **5** genom **6** genome
partition: **6** septum
partitions: **5** septa
process: **6** ecesis **7** osmosis
subdivision: **5** class, genus, order **6** phylum **7** species
biological __: **5** child, clock **6** parent
biology: **7** science
branch of ~: **5** space **6** botany, marine, osmics **7** anatomy, bionics, ecology, zoology **8** genetics, mycology **9** molecular **10** biophysics, exobiology, morphology **11** biodynamics
lab stain: **5** eosin
prefix with ~: **5** macro, micro, neuro
strand: **3** DNA
study: **4** life
__ biology: **4** cell **5** space **6** marine **9** molecular
biome: **6** desert **10** rain forest
biomedical research agcy.: **3** NIH
Biondi, Matt: **7** swimmer
bionic, human: **6** cyborg
Bionic Woman, The (ABC/NBC adventure)
cast: Lindsay Wagner (Jaime Sommers)
dog: **3** Max
org.: **3** OSI
role: **6** cyborg
bionomics: **7** ecology **8** oecology
biopic: **4** film
biosphere: **5** earth, world **7** habitat
biota component: **5** fauna, flora
biotic: **7** organic
biotin: **8** B vitamin
biotite: **4** mica **7** mineral
biped: **3** ape, emu, man **4** bird, duck, emeu, T-rex, yeti **5** chimp, goose, human, orang **7** chicken, gorilla, ostrich, primate **8** allosaur, theropod **9** orangutan **10** orangutang
biplane
support: **5** strut
WWI ~: **4** Spad
birch: **3** rod **4** beer, tree, whip, wood **5** alder, shrub **6** cudgel, thrash **10** flagellate
family shrub: **5** alder, hazel **8** hornbeam
product: **5** canoe
spike: **5** ament **6** catkin
tree: **5** alder, hazel **8** hornbeam
birch __: **4** beer
__ birch: **3** red **4** gray, grey **5** black, canoe, paper, river, sweet, white **6** cherry, yellow
Birch: **4** Bayh **5** Thora
__ Birch: **5** Simon
birchbark: **5** canoe
Birches: **4** poem
author: Robert Frost
Birch, Thora: **7** actress
film: American Beauty (1999)
Ghost World (2001)
Monkey Trouble (1994)
Paradise (1991)
bird: **3** auk, daw, emu, ern, hen, jay, kea, mew, moa, owl, pie, roc, tit, tui **4** chat, coot, crow, dodo, dove, duck, emeu, erne, guan, gull, hawk, huia, ibis, kagu, kaka, kite, kiwi, knot, lark, loon, lory, merl, mina, myna, nene, rail, rhea, rook, ruff, shag, skua, smew, sora, swan, teal, tern, tody, wren **5** biped, booby, brant, buteo, colin, crake, crane, dance, eagle, egret, eider, finch, galah, goony, goose, grebe, heron, jager, junco, koloa, macaw, mavis, merle, minah, murre, mynah, noddy, ousel, ouzel, oxeye, pewee, pewit, pipit, pitta, plane, potoo, quail, raven, robin, saker, scaup, serin, shama, snipe, solan, stilt, stint, stork, swift, twite, vireo, yager **6** avocet, barbet, becard, bishop, bonxie, brolga, bulbul, canary, chebec, chough, chukar, condor, conure, cuckoo, curlew, darter, dipper, drongo, dunlin, falcon, fulmar, gander, gannet, godwit, gooney, grouse, hoopoe, jabiru, jacana, jaeger, kakapo, lanner, linnet, magpie, martin, merlin, motmot, mud hen, oriole, osprey, parrot, parula, peewit, petrel, phoebe, pigeon, plover, pouter, puffin, quezal, roller, scoter, sea mew, shrike, siskin, takahe, thrush, tityra, tomtit, toucan, towhee, trogon, turaco, turkey, verdin, whidah, whydah, wigeon, willet **7** anhinga, babbler, barn owl, bittern, bluejay, bunting, bustard, buzzard, cariama, chicken, cotinga, courser, creeper, dottrel, dovekey, dovekie, elaenia, elepaio, fantail, finfoot, gadwall, goshawk, grackle, gray jay, graylag, greylag, halcyon, harrier, hen hawk, hoatzin, jacamar, jackdaw, kestrel, kinglet, lapwing, limpkin, mallard, manakin, marabou, mudlark, ortolan, ostrich, peacock, peafowl, pelican, penguin, phoenix, pochard, quetzal, redpoll, redwing, scooter, seagull, seriema, skimmer, skylark, sparrow, swallow, tanager, tattler, tinamou, titlark, touraco, vulture, wagtail, waxbill, waxwing, widgeon, wryneck **8** amadavat, avadavat, bee-eater, bellbird, blackcap, bluebill, boatbill, bobolink, bobwhite, bullneck, caracara, cardinal, cockatoo, coturnix, curassow, dabchick, didapper, dotterel, eagle owl, fish hawk, flamingo, garganey, grayback, grosbeak, guacharo, hawfinch, hemipode, hoactzin, hornbill, killdeer, kiskadee, landrail, longspur, lorikeet, manacode, marabout, megapode, moorfowl, murrelet, nightjar, notornis, nuthatch, oxpecker, parakeet, paraquet, paroquet, parroket, peetweet, pheasant, redshank, redstart, ringdove, screamer, sea eagle, shelduck, shoebill, shoveler, starling, thrasher, titmouse, tragopan, trembler, tremblor, troupial, water hen, wheatear, whimbrel, whinchat, whistler, white-eye, woodchat, woodcock, woodlark **9** albatross, broadbill, bullfinch, cassowary, chaffinch, chickadee, cockateel, cockatiel, cormorant, crossbill, currawong, dowitcher, fieldfare, flinthead, francolin, frogmouth, gallinule, gerfalcon, goldeneye, goldfinch, grassquit, guillemot, gyrfalcon, hammerkop, kittiwake, mallemuck, merganser, mollymawk, mollymoke, nighthawk, ossifrage, pardalote, parrakeet, parroquet, partridge, peregrine, phalarope, ptarmigan, razorbill, redbreast, sandpiper, seedeater, sharpbill, sheldrake, spoonbill, sprigtail, stonechat, thickhead, trumpeter, turnstone **10** budgerigar, budgerygah, chiffchaff, clay pigeon, demoiselle, dickcissel, flycatcher, goatsucker, greenfinch, greenshank, hammerhead, honeyeater, kingfisher, kookaburra, nutcracker, pratincole, sanderling, shearwater, sheathbill, sicklebill, turtledove, woodpecker, yellowlegs
aerie ~: **4** hawk **5** eagle **6** falcon
African ~: **4** coly **6** bishop, drongo, lanner, turaco, whidah, whydah **7** courser, finfoot, marabou, ostrich **8** lovebird, oxpecker, whinchat, woodchat **9** francolin, hammerkop **10** hammerhead, weaverbird
almost any ~: **5** flier, flyer
anserine ~: **5** goose
Antarctic ~: **6** adelie **7** emperor, penguin
aquatic ~: **4** coot, duck, gull, ibis, loon, swan, teal, tern **5** crane, egret, goose, grebe, heron **6** jaçana **7** finfoot, mallard, penguin **8** flamingo **9** gallinule, phalarope
Arabian Nights ~: **3** roc
Arctic ~: **4** skua **5** brant **6** fulmar **9** gerfalcon, gyrfalcon
Argentine ~: **7** cariama, seriema
artificial ~: **5** decoy
Asian ~: **4** lory, ruff, smew **5** shama **6** bulbul, chukar, drongo, lanner **7** courser, finfoot, marabou, ostrich **8** amadavat, avadavat, dotterel, eagle owl, leafbird, lorikeet, megapode **9** cormorant, francolin, friarbird, frogmouth, ossifrage **10** greenfinch, honeyeater, weaverbird
attractor: **4** suet **6** feeder
Australian ~: **3** emu, iao **4** emeu, lory **5** galah **6** brolga, drongo **7** mudlark **8** cockatoo, lorikeet, lyrebird, megapode **9** bowerbird, cassowary, cockateel, cockatiel, currawong, friarbird, frogmouth, pardalote, riflebird **10** budgerigar, budgerygah, honeyeater, kookaburra
baby ~: **5** chick, owlet **6** eaglet **7** gosling **8** duckling, nestling **9** fledgling, hatchling
bald ~: **5** eagle
beak: **3** neb, nib
big ~: **3** emu **4** emeu, rhea **7** ostrich
black ~: **3** daw **4** crow, merl **5** raven **7** jackdaw **8** starling
black-and-orange ~: **6** oriole
blue ~: **3** jay **5** heron **7** bunting **8** bluebird
Brazilian ~: **7** cariama, seriema
brilliantly colored ~: **3** kea **5** macaw **6** parrot **8** parakeet
call: **3** caw **4** peep, pipe, twee **5** cheep, chirp, tweet **6** cuckoo **7** chirrup, twitter
cattle ~: **5** egret
Central American ~: **4** guan **5** potoo **7** quetzal, tinamou **8** caracara, curassow
Christmas ~: **5** goose
claw: **5** talon
coastal ~: **3** ern **4** erne, gull, tern **7** pelican
colonel's ~: **5** eagle
combining form: **3** avi- **5** -ornis **6** ornith- **7** ornitho-
crested ~: **3** jay **6** hoopoe **10** woodpecker
crop: **4** craw
crowlike ~: **4** huia **6** chough
diving ~: **3** auk **4** coot, loon **5** booby, grebe, murre, ousel, ouzel, solan **6** auklet, dipper **8** murrelet **10** kingfisher
dog: **5** hound **7** pointer **9** retriever
domestic ~: **3** hen **4** duck, fowl **5** drake, goose **6** gander **7** chicken, rooster

early ~ prize: 4 worm
eat like a ~: 4 peck, pick
Egyptian sacred ~: 4 ibis
ender: 3 dog, man, men 4 bath, cage, call, feed, lime, seed, shot 5 brain, house 6 feeder 7 watcher
European ~: 4 chat, lark, rook, ruff, shag, smew 5 ousel, ouzel, saker, twite 6 chough, cuckoo, hoopoe, lanner, linnet, siskin 7 babbler, graylag, greylag, jackdaw, lapwing, pochard, redwing, skylark, sunbird, wagtail, waxbill 8 coturnix, dotterel, eagle owl, garganey, hawfinch, ringdove, starling, whinchat, woodchat, woodlark 9 bullfinch, cormorant, fieldfare, francolin, goldfinch, ossifrage, stonechat 10 greenfinch, turtledove
extinct ~: 3 moa 4 dodo, huia
feature: 4 beak, wing 6 air sac 7 feather 8 feathers
fish-eating ~: 3 ern 4 erne, gull, tern 5 heron 7 pelican
flight feather: 5 remex
flightless ~: 3 emu, moa 4 dodo, emeu, kiwi, rhea 6 takahe 7 ostrich, penguin 8 notornis 9 cassowary
food: 4 seed, suet
fork-tailed ~: 4 tern
game ~: 5 quail 6 grouse 8 pheasant 10 wild turkey
gull-like ~: 6 bonxie, fulmar 7 skimmer
hangar ~: 5 plane
harsh-voiced ~: 3 jay, kea, pie 4 crow 5 macaw 6 parrot
Hawaiian ~: 2 oo 4 nene, omao 5 koloa, shama 7 elepaio
hieroglyphics ~: 4 ibis
home: 4 cage, nest, tree 5 aerie 6 aviary, hangar, jungle
honey-eating ~: 3 iao
house: 6 aviary 9 enclosure
hunter: 6 fowler
imitate a ~: 4 sing
in Latin: 4 avis
keelbone: 6 carina
larklike ~: 5 pipit
long-legged ~: 4 ibis 5 crane, egret, heron
long-necked ~: 4 swan
long-plumed ~: 5 egret 7 ostrich, peacock
marsh ~: 4 rail, sora, teal 5 crake, egret, snipe 6 mud hen 7 bittern 9 gallinule
Mexican ~: 5 potoo 7 quetzal
move like a ~: 3 fly, hop 4 dart, flit
name meaning ~: 5 Vogel
New Guinean ~: 7 mudlark 8 manacode 9 bowerbird, cassowary
New Zealand ~: 3 kea, moa, oii, tui 4 huia, kaka, kiwi, weka 6 kakapo, takahe 8 notornis
nocturnal ~: 3 owl
of peace: 4 dove
of prey: 4 hawk, kite 5 eagle, glede 6 elanet, falcon, lanner 7 kestrel
ostrichlike ~: 3 moa 4 rhea
Pacific ~: 4 kagu 5 goony 6 gooney
palindromic ~: 3 tit
pampas ~: 4 rhea
parson ~: 3 tui
passerine ~: 5 vireo
ploverlike ~: 6 jacana 7 courser
pouched ~: 7 pelican 9 cormorant
preacher ~: 5 vireo
quail-like ~: 8 hemipode
rare ~: 4 oner 7 prodigy
ratite ~: 3 emu 4 emeu
razor-billed ~: 3 auk
red-breasted ~: 5 robin
roost: 5 perch
sanctuary: 6 aviary
sandpiper-like ~: 9 phalarope
shelter: 4 cote, nest
small ~: 3 tit 4 wren 5 dicky, pewit 6 dickey, dickie, peewit
snipelike ~: 9 dowitcher
snowy ~: 3 owl 5 egret
South American ~: 4 guan, rhea, yeni 5 potoo 7 finfoot, hoatzin, quetzal, tinamou 8 caracara, curassow, guacharo, hoactzin, ovenbird, screamer, troupial
starter: 3 cat, cow, jay, oil, red, sun 4 bell, blue, fire, jail, king, lady, love, lyre, oven, rail, reed, rice, snow, song, surf, tick 5 black, bower, cedar, friar, moose, mound, rifle, shore, snake, sugar 6 tailor, tropic, wattle, weaver, yellow 7 butcher, humming, mocking, thunder
stomach: 4 craw
storklike ~: 8 shoebill
strigiform ~: 3 owl
swallowlike ~: 5 swift
swimming ~: 4 duck, loon, swan 5 goose 7 anhinga 9 snakebird
talking ~: 4 mina, myna 5 macaw, minah, mynah 6 parrot
that has red meat: 3 emu 4 emeu
that lays green eggs: 3 emu 4 emeu
throat: 6 gorget
thrushlike ~: 8 thrasher
thumb: 5 alula
titmouse-like ~: 6 verdin
top of a ~ head: 6 pileus
tropical ~: 4 guan, mina, myna 5 macaw, minah, mynah, pitta 6 barbet, becard, bulbul, motmot, parrot, tityra, toucan, trogon, turaco 7 antbird, elaenia, jacamar, manakin, oilbird, touraco 8 bee-eater, boatbill, hornbill, parakeet, puffbird, white-eye 9 broadbill, grassquit, seedeater, sharpbill 10 tailorbird
turkeylike ~: 4 guan
wading ~: 4 ibis, rail 5 crane, egret, heron, snipe, stilt, stork 6 avocet, jaçana 7 bittern, limpkin 8 boatbill, flamingo, shoebill 9 hammerkop, spoonbill 10 demoiselle, hammerhead
watcher's aid: 6 feeder 8 spyglass 10 binoculars
web-footed ~: 3 auk 4 duck, loon, swan 5 goose, solan
West Indies ~: 4 tody
white ~: 4 swan 5 egret
whose male hatches the eggs: 4 kiwi
wise ~: 3 owl
yellow-breasted ~: 4 chat

bird __: 3 dog, flu 4 band, call, farm, feed, ring, shot, walk 5 grass, louse 6 cherry, feeder, pepper, plague, ringer 7 banding, colonel, watcher
bird-__: 7 brained, watcher
__ bird: 3 bee 4 bell, cage, dodo, game, tick 5 bosun, dough, early, goony, rifle, shore, state, water, widow 6 bishop, gooney, indigo, meadow, mutton, parson, regent, tropic, wading 7 apostle, buffalo, diamond, frigate, man-o'-war, peabody, teacher
__ bird..: 4 It's a
Bird: 4 Brad 5 Lance, Larry 7 Antonia
milieu: 3 NBA
of Paradise constellation: 4 Apus
played it: 3 sax 4 alto
Bird (1988 film)
cast: Diane Venora, Forest Whitaker
director: Clint Eastwood
subject: Charlie Parker
Bird __ Gilded Cage, A: 3 in a
__ Bird: 3 Big 4 Free 5 Do the 6 Silver, Yellow
birdbath organism: 4 alga
birdbrain: 4 dodo, twit 5 looby *see also* ninny
birdbrained: 3 mad 4 daft, luny 5 loony, silly 6 looney 7 fatuous, vacuous
birdcage: 6 aviary, volary
device: 6 feeder
swing: 5 perch
birdcage __: 5 clock
Birdcage, The
artist: Erté
Birdcage, The (1995 film)
cast: Gene Hackman, Nathan Lane, Dianne Wiest, Robin Williams
director: Mike Nichols
birdcall: 4 song 5 cheep, chirp, tweet 7 twitter
bird-dog: 4 seek 5 stalk 6 pursue 9 track down
Bird Dog (1958 song)
artist: Everly Brothers
Bird Falls Down, The
author: Rebecca West
bird feeder staple: 4 suet 5 seeds
birdhouse: 4 cote 6 aviary, volary
birdie
beater: 5 eagle
plus one: 3 par
bird in __: 4 hand
__ Bird Johnson: 4 Lady 5 Lynda
birdland: 5 dance
Bird, Larry: 5 cager
milieu: 5 court
org.: 3 NBA
sport: 10 basketball
birdman: 5 pilot
Birdman of Alcatraz: 5 lifer 6 Stroud
Birdman of Alcatraz (1962 film)
cast: Burt Lancaster, Karl Malden, Thelma Ritter
director: John Frankenheimer
bird of __: 4 prey 7 passage
bird-of-paradise: 5 plant 6 flower
__ Bird of Youth: 5 Sweet
Bird on a Wire (1990 film)
cast: David Carradine, Mel Gibson, Goldie Hawn
director: John Badham

birds: 4 aves, fowl
do it: 3 fly 4 peck, sing, soar 5 chirp, glide, perch, roost, tweet 7 twitter
for the ~: 5 inane, silly 6 absurd 9 worthless 10 ridiculous
like ~: 5 alate, avian 6 alated
of a feather: 7 cohorts, cronies 10 colleagues
of a region: 5 ornis
partner: 4 bees
science: 11 ornithology
thumbs: 6 alulae
tops of ~' heads: 5 pilea
where ~ fly in the fall: 5 south
Birds __, bees...: 4 do it
birds and __: 4 bees
Birds, Beasts, and Flowers
author: D.H. Lawrence
Birds Do It (1966 film)
cast: Soupy Sales
bird's-eye __: 4 view
Birdseye: 8 Clarence
rival: 5 Libby 6 Libby's
bird's-eye view: 8 panorama
bird's-nest __: 4 soup
birds of a __: 7 feather
Birdsong: 4 Otis 5 Cindy
__ bird special: 5 early
Birds, The
author: Aristophanes
character: 4 Iris 5 Epops
Birds, The (1963 film)
cast: Tippi Hedren, Suzanne Pleshette, Jessica Tandy, Rod Taylor
director: Alfred Hitchcock
__ Birds, The: 5 Thorn
Bird thou never __: 4 wert
Birdy (1984 film)
cast: Nicolas Cage, Matthew Modine
bireme: 4 boat 6 galley
equipment: 3 oar
projection: 3 ram
biretta: 3 cap, hat
Birgit: 7 Nilsson
birler need: 3 log
birling: 5 sport
competitor: 10 lumberjack
match: 5 roleo
Birmingham: 4 city, town
athletes: 7 Blazers 11 Crimson Tide
locale: 7 Alabama, England
school: 3 UAB
Birnbach: 4 Lisa
Birney, David: 5 actor
spouse: Meredith Baxter
birth: 4 dawn, rank 5 class, onset, start 6 origin, outset, source, spring 7 descent, genesis, infancy, lineage 8 ancestry, creation, delivery, heritage, nascency, natality, nativity, pedigree 9 awakening, beginning, emergence, inception 10 extraction
bird: 5 stork
by ~: 3 née 9 naturally 10 originally
ender: 3 day 4 mark, root, wort 5 place, right, stone
from ~: 6 innate
give ~: 4 yean 5 calve
give ~ to: 4 bear, have 5 begin, breed, spawn 6 create, parent 7 deliver 8 engender, generate, initiate 9 originate 10 bring forth
high ~: 8 nobility 9 blue blood,

gentility **10** upper class, upper crust
name meaning ~: 4 Edna
of ~: 5 natal
birth __: 4 name, rate **6** family, father, mother, parent
birthday: 5 event **7** jubilee
celebration: 5 party
count: 5 years
expression: 4 wish
figure: 3 age
in one's ~ suit: 4 bare, nude **5** naked **8** starkers
mail: 4 card
name meaning ~: 7 Natalie
party item: 4 cake, gift **5** favor **6** candle, piñata **7** present
birthday __: 4 cake, suit **5** party
Birthday Party, The: 4 film, play
author: Harold Pinter
cast: Patrick Magee, Robert Shaw
director: William Friedkin
__ Birthday to You: 5 Happy
birthing __: 4 room **6** center
training: 6 Lamaze
birthmark: 4 mole **5** nevus **7** blemish
Birth of a Nation, The (1915 film)
cast: Lillian Gish, Mae Marsh, Henry B. Walthall
director: D.W. Griffith
birthplace: 4 home **6** cradle, source
birthright: 5 claim **6** legacy **7** liberty **8** heritage **9** privilege
barterer: 4 Esau
birthstone: 3 gem **5** jewel
April ~: 7 diamond
August ~: 7 peridot
December ~: 9 turquoise
February ~: 8 amethyst
January ~: 6 garnet
July ~: 4 ruby
June ~: 5 pearl
March ~: 10 aquamarine
May ~: 5 agate **7** emerald
November ~: 5 topaz
October ~: 4 opal
September ~: 8 sapphire
bis: 5 twice **6** encore
Bisbee: 4 city, town
locale: 7 Arizona
Biscay, Bay of
feeder: 5 Loire
peninsula: 6 Iberia
port: 5 Gijón **6** Bilbao
Biscayne: 3 bay, car **4** auto, park **5** Chevy **9** Chevrolet **10** automobile
Biscayne Bay
county on ~: 4 Dade
locale: 5 Miami **7** Florida
Bischoff: 3 Sam
biscotto: 6 cookie
flavoring: 5 anise
biscuit: 3 bun, tan **5** bread, brown, cooky, scone, wafer **6** cookie, suntan **7** cracker
color kin: ***see*** brown color
crisp ~: 4 rusk
Londoner's ~: 5 scone
saltless ~: 4 tack
thin ~: 5 wafer
__ biscuit: 3 dog, sea, tea **4** drop, ship, soda **5** pilot, water
bise: 4 wind
bisect: 3 cut, saw **4** fork **5** halve, in two, sever, split **6** cleave, divide **7** split up **8** separate **9** branch off, intersect
bisected: 5 split **6** in half
bisection: 4 half **8** division
'B' Is for Burglar
author: Sue Grafton
Bishkek: 4 city, town **7** capital
locale: 10 Kyrgyzstan
bishop: 3 man **4** bird, pope, rank **5** drink, piece **6** cleric, eparch, exarch, priest **7** pontiff, prelate, primate **8** beverage, cocktail, diocesan, minister, overseer **9** patriarch **10** archpriest, chess-piece
crosier: 5 crook
decree: 5 canon
domain: 3 see **7** diocese, prelacy
Eastern ~: 4 abba **6** exarch
ingredient: 4 port **6** cloves, orange
neighbor: 6 knight
of a ~: 9 episcopal
of Rome: 4 pope **7** pontiff
onetime TV ~: 5 Sheen
protector, maybe: 4 pawn
seat: 9 cathedral
South African ~: 4 Tutu
starter: 4 arch
topper: 5 miter, mitre
Bishop: 3 Jim **4** Joey **5** Elvin, Julie **7** Michael, Stephen
Bishop at Sea, The
author: Andrew Greeley
Bishop Orders His Tomb, The: 4 poem
author: Robert Browning
bishopric: 3 see **7** diocese, prelacy
bishops: 6 clergy
body of ~: 10 episcopacy
council: 5 synod
Bishop, Stephen
song: It Might Be You (1983)
On and On (1977)
Bishop's University
locale: 6 Canada, Quebec
Bishop's Wife, The (1947 film)
cast: Cary Grant, David Niven, Loretta Young
dog: 7 Queenie
Bismarck: 3 sea **4** boat, city, ship, town
city near ~: 5 Minot
county: 8 Burleigh
locale: 4 N. Dak. **9** New Guinea
river: 8 Missouri
Bismarck __: 3 Sea
__ Bismarck: 7 Otto von
__-Bismol: 5 Pepto
bismuth: 5 metal **7** element
Bisoglio: 3 Val
bison: 5 bovid **6** animal, bovine, cattle, wisent
feature: 4 hump
relative: ***see*** bovine
Bison: 6 Howard **8** Bucknell
bisque: 4 soup **5** color, gumbo **6** yellow
__ bisque: 7 lobster
Bissau: 4 city, town **7** capital
Bissell: 3 vac **4** Whit **6** vacuum
competitor: 5 Kirby, Oreck **6** Hoover **10** Electrolux
Bisset, Jacqueline: 7 actress
film: Airport (1970)
Bullitt (1968)
Dangerous Beauty (1998)
Day for Night (1973)
The Deep (1977)
The Grasshopper (1970)
Let the Devil Wear Black (2000)
The Mephisto Waltz (1971)
Murder on the Orient Express (1974)
Rich and Famous (1981)
Under the Volcano (1984)
Bissett: 5 Josie
bistro: 3 bar **4** cafe **5** diner **6** eatery, lounge, tavern **7** cabaret **8** taphouse **9** brasserie, nightclub, nightspot **10** restaurant
menu: 5 carte
name word: 4 chez
patron: 5 diner, eater
patronize a ~: 3 eat, sup **4** dine
bit: 3 dab, dot, job, jot, tad **4** atom, bash, dash, iota, jiff, lick, lump, mite, mote, part, role, slab, snip, time, tool, whit, wisp **5** auger, crumb, drill, flake, fleck, grain, jiffy, money, piece, pinch, scrap, shard, sherd, shred, skosh, space, speck, spell, stint, taste, tinge, touch, trace **6** dollop, gobbet, little, moment, morsel, ration, sample, sliver, snatch, tidbit, trifle **7** driblet, droplet, granule, instant, modicum, oddment, portion, remnant, segment, shaving, smidgen, smidgin, snippet, trickle, went for **8** fraction, fragment, molecule, particle, pittance, smidgeon, specimen, spoonful **9** cameo role, scintilla, short time **10** jackhammer, sprinkling
attachment: 4 rein
part: 5 cameo
partner: 5 brace
starter: 3 hen, tid **4** back, rare **5** frost
bit __: 3 key, map **4** part, stop **5** gauge **6** player
__ bit: 3 in a **4** a wee, not a, wing **5** auger, bergy, check, drill, every
__-bit: 3 two **5** frog's, wait-a **6** devil's
bit-by-bit: 7 gradual **9** gradually
get ~: 5 amass, glean **6** gather **7** collect
bite: 3 fee, nip, tax, zip **4** burn, gnaw, kick, nosh, snap, tang, zest **5** champ, chill, chomp, lunch, munch, piece, punch, scrap, share, slice, snack, spice, sting, taste **6** charge, crunch, gnaw at, gnaw on, incise, injury, morsel, nibble, outlay, sample, tidbit **7** section **8** fraction, fragment, mouthful, piquancy, pungency, spoonful **9** crispness, liability, light meal, masticate, volunteer **10** percentage
bug ~: 4 welt
government's ~: 3 tax
grab a ~: 3 eat, sup **4** dine, nosh **5** lunch, snack **6** gobble, nibble **7** munch on, put away **8** chow down, wolf down **9** have a meal, scarf down
just a ~: 3 bit **5** taste **6** morsel, nibble, sample, tidbit, trifle **7** forkful, soupçon **8** mouthful, spoonful
like a mosquito ~: 5 itchy
not apt to ~: 4 tame
off too much: 6 overdo
one's lip: 7 forbear, refrain, repress
one's nails: 5 worry **7** agonize
process a ~: 4 chew
react to a ~: 4 itch **5** sting, swell
sound ~: 4 clip **5** blurb, piece **6** slogan **7** excerpt, snippet **8** buzzword, one-liner, spot news **9** newsbreak
starter: 4 back, flea **5** frost, snake
take the ~ out of: 5 allay **6** lessen
the dust: 3 bow **4** bomb, bust, fail, flop, lose, slip, trip **5** flunk **6** blow it, falter **7** blunder, founder, go under, go wrong, misstep, stumble, wash out **8** fall flat, flounder, lay an egg **9** strike out
bite-__: 4 size **5** sized
__ bite: 5 grab a, sound
bite one's __: 3 lip **6** tongue
biter: 3 dog **4** flea, gnat **5** midge **6** insect **7** incisor **8** mosquito
dog ~: 4 flea
night ~: 6 bedbug
target: 3 lip **4** nail **10** fingernail
tiny ~: 4 flea, gnat **5** midge
__ Bites: 4 Love **7** Reality
bite the __: 4 dust **6** bullet
Bite the Bullet (1975 film)
cast: Candice Bergen, James Coburn, Gene Hackman
biting: 3 dry, icy, raw **4** acid, cold, cool, sour, tart **5** acerb, brisk, chill, harsh, nippy, polar, rough, sharp, tangy **6** arctic, bitter, chilly, frigid, frosty, frozen, severe, strong, wintry **7** acerbic, caustic, cutting, glacial, intense, mordant, numbing, piquant, pungent, satiric, shivery, wintery **8** abrasive, freezing, incisive, piercing, poignant, scathing, stinging **9** corrosive, insulting, offensive, sarcastic, satirical, trenchant, withering **10** astringent
nail ~: 4 vice
pest: 4 flea, gnat **8** mosquito
Bit-o-__: 5 Honey
bit of talcum..., A
author: Ogden Nash
bit-part performer: 5 extra
__ bits: 3 two **4** four
__ Bits: 5 Alpha
Bits and Pieces (1964 song)
artist: Dave Clark Five
bits partner: 6 pieces
bitsy: 3 wee **4** tiny **5** teeny **6** teensy
__-bitsy: 4 itsy
bitt: 4 post
__ bitten...: 4 Once
__-bitten: 4 flea, hard
bitter: 3 ale, icy, raw **4** acid, cold, dire, hard, sore, sour, tart **5** acerb, acrid, cruel, gelid, harsh, nasty, rough, sharp, stern, taste, woful **6** biting, crabby, fierce, frigid, frosty, frozen, heated, savage, severe, sullen, woeful **7** acerbic, caustic, cutting, cynical, galling, glacial, hateful, hostile, hurtful, ice-cold, intense, painful, pungent, satiric **8** alkaline, brackish, freezing, grievous, liverish, piercing, rigorous, ruthless, sardonic, scathing, stinging, vinegary, virulent **9** acidulous, alienated, corrosive, estranged, inclement, malicious, rancorous, resentful, sarcastic, satirical, vitriolic **10** astringent, calamitous, disturbing, unpleasant, vindictive

alternative: 5 stout
combining form: 4 picr- 5 picro-
dispute: 4 feud 7 quarrel
feel ~: 6 resent
it may be ~: 3 end
pill: 6 misery 7 letdown
plant: 5 vetch
purgative: 5 aloin
vetch: 3 ers

bitter __: 3 ale, end, rot 4 dock, herb, lake, pill, root 5 aloes, apple, cress, gourd, vetch 6 almond, orange 7 cassava
bitterling: 4 fish
bitterly: 6 keenly 9 viciously
bittern: 4 bird
milieu: 5 marsh
relative: 5 egret, heron
bitterness: 5 agony 7 acidity, anguish 8 acerbity, acridity, acrimony
see also animosity
bitters: 7 quinine
bittersweet: 6 ironic, orange
Bittersweet
author: Danielle Steel
Bitter Sweet (1940 film)
cast: Nelson Eddy, Jeanette MacDonald
Bitter Sweet Symphony (1998 song) artist: Verve
bitty: 3 wee 4 baby, puny, tiny 5 small, teeny 6 atomic, bantam, little, minute, peewee, petite, teensy 8 atomical, atomlike 9 miniature, pint-sized 10 diminutive, teeny-weeny, vest-pocket
__-bitty: 4 itty 6 little
__ Bitty Pretty One: 6 Little
__ Bitty Tear, A: 6 Little
bitumen: 3 tar
bituminous deposit: 4 coal, seam
bivalve: 4 clam, pipi 5 capiz, shell 6 cockle, macoma, mussel, oyster, pectin, quahog 7 paddock, quahaug, scallop, telling 8 seashell, shipworm
bivouac: 4 camp 5 étape 6 casern, encamp 7 caserne 8 barracks, lodgment 10 encampment
quarters: 4 tent
biwa: 4 lute 6 string
origin: 5 Japan
Biwa: 4 lake
locale: 5 Japan
biweekly: 8 magazine 9 newspaper
Bixby, Bill: 5 actor
TV: The Courtship of Eddie's Father, The Incredible Hulk, My Favorite Martian
biz: 7 pursuit 10 profession
show ~: 2 TV 5 stage 6 movies 10 television
__ biz: 4 show
Biz: 9 detergent
rival: *see* detergent
Biz __: 6 Markie
bizarre: 3 odd 4 camp, eery, wild 5 crazy, eerie, funny, gonzo, kooky, outré, queer, weird 6 atypic, far out, freaky, kookie, quaint, quirky, way out 7 curious, deviant, erratic, oddball, offbeat, strange, surreal, unusual 8 aberrant, abnormal, atypical, freakish, peculiar, striking, uncommon 9 anomalous, divergent, eccentric, fantastic, grotesque, irregular, laughable, ludicrous, unnatural 10 off-the-wall, outlandish, ridiculous, unfamiliar, unorthodox
in a ~ way: 5 oddly
Bizet, Georges: 6 French 8 composer
work: Carmen
The Fair Maid of Perth
Ivan IV
L'Arlésienne
Le Docteur miracle
Les pêcheurs de perles
Marche Funèbre
The Pearl Fishers
Roma
Biz Markie
song: Just a Friend (1990)
B.J.: 6 Thomas
__ B. Johnson: 6 Lyndon
Bjorn: 4 Borg
bk.: 3 vol.
addendum: 3 app.
after Amos: 4 Obad.
after Exodus: 3 Lev. 5 Levit.
after Ezra: 3 Neh.
after Proverbs: 4 Eccl
Apocrypha ~: 4 Macc.
before Daniel: 4 Ezek.
before Job: 4 Esth.
before Jonah: 4 Obad.
before Numbers: 3 Lev. 5 Levit.
category: 3 ref. 4 biog., fict., hist. 5 sci fi
drug-reference ~: 3 PDR
large-size ~: 3 fol.
New Testament ~: 3 Eph 4 Thes.
old ~ collector: 5 antiq.
place: 3 lib.
writer: 4 auth.
see also book
Bk: 4 elem. 7 element 9 berkelium
97 for ~: 4 at. no.
bks.-to-be: 3 mss.
blab: 3 gab, yak 4 chat, leak, sing, tell 5 bleat, blurt, prate, run on, speak, spill 6 gossip, jabber, let out, patter, reveal, snitch, squeal, tattle, yammer 7 chatter, divulge, lay bare, let slip, prattle, tell all 8 babbling, disclose, give away, let it out, ramble on, rattle on 9 name names 10 chew the rag, yackety-yak
blabbermouth: 5 sieve 6 gabber, gasbag, gossip, magpie, tattle, yapper 7 tattler, windbag 8 blowhard, gossiper, informer, jabberer 10 tattletale
black: 3 jet, tea 4 bear, ebon, inky, onyx, ugly 5 dirty, ebony, raven, sable, smoky, sooty 6 dismal, filthy, swarth 7 swarthy, unclean, unlucky 8 charcoal, darkness, starless 9 lightless, pitch-dark 10 inexpiable, villainous
art: 10 necromancy
bird: 3 daw 4 crow, merl 5 raven 7 jackdaw 8 starling
box: 9 mechanism
brown and ~ butterfly: 5 comma
card: 4 club 5 spade
cat: 4 omen
cloud: 4 pall
color: 3 jet 4 inky, onyx 5 ebony, raven, sable, sooty 7 aniline, channel
combining form: 3 mel- 4 atro-, mela-, melo- 5 melan- 6 melano-
deep ~: 3 jet 4 ebon, inky, onyx 5 ebony, raven 9 pitch-dark
ender: 3 cap, leg, out, top 4 ball, bird, body, buck, cock, damp, face, fish, head, jack, legs, list, mail, ness, poll, wash 5 berry, board, guard, smith, snake, strap, thorn
eye: 4 blot, slur 5 mouse, odium, stain 6 bruise, insult, shiner 7 slander
fuel: 3 oil 4 coal
gem: 4 opal
give a ~ eye: 3 hit 4 slur, sock 5 libel, shame, smear 6 defame, vilify 8 mistreat
gold: 3 oil
goo: 3 tar
hat wearer: 6 bad guy 7 villain
hole, once: 4 star
in ~ and white: 5 clear, plain 8 explicit
in French: 4 noir 5 noire
in heraldry: 5 sable
in the ~: 7 solvent 9 lucrative
lacquer: 5 japan
look: 5 frown, glare, scowl
magic: 5 magic 6 voodoo 7 sorcery 9 diabolism 10 necromancy, witchcraft
make ~ and blue: 4 hurt 6 bruise, injure 7 contuse 8 discolor
mark: 4 slur, smut 6 stigma
name meaning ~: 7 Melanie 8 Schwartz
out: 5 faint, swoon 6 censor, delete, go limp, stifle
piano key: 5 A-flat, B-flat, D-flat, E-flat, G-flat 6 A-sharp, C-sharp, D-sharp, F-sharp, G-sharp
pitch ~: 4 dark 5 unlit 8 moonless
plus white: 4 gray, grey
sheep: 5 rogue 6 bad guy, rascal 9 miscreant, scoundrel 10 delinquent
starter: 4 bone, boot, lamp
tea: 5 bohea, congo, oopak 6 congou, oopack
tie: 6 tuxedo
to a poet: 4 ebon
use ~ magic: 3 hex 5 curse 7 bewitch
wear ~: 5 mourn
wood: 5 ebony
see also gloomy
black __: 3 art, box, cod, cow, dog, eye, fly, fog, fox, gum, hat, haw, ice, oak, out, rat, rot, tea, tie 4 bass, bean, bear, belt, bile, book, buck, duck, flag, flux, gang, gnat, gold, gram, hole, kite, knot, land, lead, mark, mold, opal, ring, ruff, rust, sage, spot, stem 5 alder, birch, bread, chaff, cumin, dwarf, frost, humor, light, magic, maple, molly, money, olive, perch, racer, shank, sheep, snake, whale, witch 6 acacia, balsam, bottom, bryony, butter, cherry, cohosh, comedy, copper, cosmos, grouse, letter, liquor, locust, market, pepper, pewter, poplar, powder, scoter, spruce, sucker, velvet, walnut, wattle
black __ spider: 5 widow
__ black: 3 gas 4 bone, drop 5 in the, ivory, pitch 6 animal, carbon 7 aniline, channel
__-black: 3 jet 4 blue 5 pitch
Black: 3 sea 4 Bill, Hawk, Hugo, Jack, Noel 5 Cilla, Clint, James, Karen, range 6 Jeanne, Joseph
Sea locale: 7 Eurasia
Black __: 3 Box, Cat, Rod, Sea 4 Flag, Fury, Girl, Hand, Hawk, Mesa, Monk, Oxen, Pope, Rain 5 Angel, Angus, Friar, Hills, Maria, Shirt, Stump, Volta, Watch, Water, Widow 6 Armour, Beauty, Canyon, Comedy, Forest, Legion, Muslim, Plague, Prince, Stream, Sunday, Velvet 7 Orpheus, Panther, Rainbow, Russian, Tuesday
Black __ cake: 6 Forest
Black __ of Calcutta: 4 Hole
Black __, The: 3 Cat 4 City, Room, Rose, Swan 5 Arrow, Sheep, Tulip 6 Knight, Marble, Pirate, Riders
Black __ War: 4 Hawk
__ Black: 5 Men in
black-and-blue: 5 livid 7 bruised
mark: 4 hurt 5 mouse 6 boo-boo, bruise
black and tan: 5 drink 8 beverage, cocktail
ingredient: 3 ale 5 stout 6 porter
black-and-white: 5 print
animal: 3 auk 5 panda, skunk, zebra
snack: 4 Oreo
Black Angus: 3 cow
Black Armour
author: Elinor Wylie
black as __: 4 coal 5 night, pitch
Black as He's Painted
author: Ngaio Marsh
blackball: 3 ban 4 oust, shun, snub, tabu, veto 5 debar, expel, spurn 6 bounce, pass on, rebuff, reject 7 disdain, dismiss, exclude 8 disallow, turn down 9 cast aside, exclusion, ostracize, repudiate
blackballed: 9 unwelcome
Black Bears
home of the ~: 5 Maine, Orono
Black Beauty: 5 horse 6 equine
author: Anna Sewell
black belt: 4 rank, sash 6 expert
gym: 4 dojo
move: 4 chop
sport: 4 judo 6 karate
blackberry: 5 fruit 8 ice cream
alternative: *see* fruit, ice cream flavor
BlackBerry: 3 PDA
Blackberry Winter
author: Margaret Mead
blackbird: 3 ani 4 merl, rook 5 merle 7 grackle
comment: 3 caw
European ~: 5 ousel, ouzel
...blackbirds baked in __: 4 a pie
Blackbirds' school: 3 LIU
blackboard: 5 slate
accessory: 6 eraser
erase the ~: 4 wash, wipe 5 clean
like a ~ eraser: 5 dirty, dusty 7 powdery, unclean 8 unwashed
marker: 5 chalk
Blackboard Jungle: 4 film 5 novel
author: Evan Hunter
cast: Glenn Ford, Anne Francis, Vic Morrow
blackbuck: 5 sasin 8 antelope
relative: *see* antelope

Black Camel, The
hero: **4** Chan
blackcap: **4** bird
Black Cat, The
author: Edgar Allan Poe
cat: **5** Pluto
Black Cat, The (1934 film)
cast: Boris Karloff, Bela Lugosi
Black City, The
author: George Sand
Black, Clint: **6** singer
spouse: Lisa Hartman
Black Comedy
author: Peter Shaffer
black-currant cordial: **6** cassis
Black & Decker
rival: **4** Skil
blacked out: **4** dark **5** unlit **6** aswoon **7** fainted, swooned
blacken: **3** rip **4** char, foul, sear, slur, soil, soul **5** dirty, libel, shade, singe, smear, stain, sully, taint **6** befoul, crud up, darken, defame, defile, malign, scorch, smudge, vilify **7** asperse, begrime, contuse, ebonize, grow dim, pollute, slander, tarnish, traduce **8** badmouth, besmirch, dishonor, grow dark, throw mud **9** denigrate **10** calumniate
blackened: **4** inky **5** grimy, sooty **6** filthy, fouled, grubby, grungy **7** injured **8** maculate, slovenly **10** unsanitary
__ blackest dye: **5** of the
Blackett, Patrick: **8** Nobelist **9** physicist, scientist
black-eyed __: **3** pea **5** Susan
black-eyed pea: **6** legume
black-eyed Susan: **5** plant **6** flower
Black Flag: **11** insecticide
rival: **4** Raid
target: **3** ant, bug **6** insect
Blackfoot: **5** tribe **6** Indian **7** Amerind **8** language
Black Forest
city: **5** Baden
locale: **7** Germany
tree: **5** larch
Black Forest __: **4** cake
blackguard: **3** cad, cur **4** heel, toad, worm **5** beast, churl, knave, louse, rogue, scamp, viper **6** bad guy, bad hat, defame, malign, rascal, revile, rotter, vilify, wretch **7** bounder, run down, villain **8** blighter, picaroon, rakehell, scalawag **9** miscreant, reprobate, scallawag, scallywag, scoundrel, vulgarian **10** delinquent, ne'er-do-well, scapegrace, vituperate
Black Hawk: **3** Sac, war **4** Sauk
foe: **6** Keokuk
Black Hawk Down (2001 film)
cast: Josh Hartnett, Ewan McGregor, Tom Sizemore
director: Ridley Scott
Blackhawks: **3** six **4** team
home: **7** Chicago
milieu: **3** ice **4** rink
org.: **3** NHL
rival: ***see*** hockey team
black-hearted: **4** evil **5** cruel **8** ruthless, sinister **9** malicious, merciless
Black Hills
locale: **4** S. Dak.
mountain: **6** Harney

Black Horse Troop, The
composer: John Philip Sousa
black-ink
item: **5** asset
Black is Black (1966 song)
artist: Los Bravos
blackjack: **4** club, cosh, game **6** cudgel **8** bludgeon, card game **9** truncheon, vingt-et-un
alias: **7** pontoon **9** twenty-one, vingt-et-un
card: **3** ace, six, ten, two **4** five, four, jack, king, nine **5** deuce, eight, queen, seven, three
dealer: **4** bank **5** house
dealer's device: **4** shoe
dealer's headwear: **5** visor, vizor
option: **3** hit **4** stay
place: **4** Reno **5** Vegas **6** casino
play ~: **3** bet
request: **5** hit me
tie: **4** push
work at the ~ table: **4** deal
Black Jack: **7** general **8** Pershing
command: **3** AEF
Black Knight, The
composer: William Elgar
blacklist: **6** punish **7** exclude **9** ostracize, proscribe, repudiate **10** thumbs down
Black Magic Woman (1970 song)
artist: Santana
blackmail: **5** bleed, force **6** coerce, compel, extort, prey on, threat **8** coercion, threaten **9** extortion, hush money, shakedown **10** protection
Blackman: **4** Joan **5** Honor
black-market: **7** illegal, illicit, traffic
Black Mesa
author: Zane Grey
Black Mischief
author: Evelyn Waugh
Black Monday event: **5** crash, panic
Blackmore
character: Lorna Doone
Blackmun: **5** Harry
Black Narcissus
author: Rumer Godden
Black Orpheus: **4** film
setting: **3** Rio **6** barrio **8** Carnival
Black or White (1991 song)
artist: Michael Jackson
blackout: **4** skit
Black Panthers
founder: Bobby Seale, Huey P. Newton
Black Pearl, The: **4** Pelé
author: Scott O'Dell
black-pudding ingredient: **4** pork
Black Rain (1989 film)
cast: Kate Capshaw, Michael Douglas, Andy Garcia
director: Ridley Scott
Black Riders, The
author: Stephen Crane
Black Rose, The
author: Thomas Costain
Black Russian: **5** drink **8** cocktail
ingredient: **5** vodka **6** Kahlúa
Blacksburg: **4** city, town
athletes: **6** Hokies **8** Gobblers
locale: **8** Virginia
school: **3** VPI
Black Sea
arm of the ~: **4** Azov
feeder: **4** Rion **5** Rioni
locale: **6** Crimea

port: **5** Odesa, Varna **6** Odessa
resort: **5** Sochi, Yalta
river to the ~: **5** Dnepr **6** Dnestr **7** Dnieper **8** Dniester
villa: **5** dacha
Black Sheep, The
author: Honoré de Balzac
blacksmith: **7** farrier
at times: **5** shoer
furnace: **5** forge
need: **4** rasp **5** anvil
target: **4** hoof
__ Blacksmith, The: **7** Village
Black Stallion, The (1979 film)
boy: **4** Alec
cast: Teri Garr, Kelly Reno, Mickey Rooney
Black Star, Bright Dawn
author: Scott O'Dell
Blackstone: **5** Harry **7** William
Black Sunday (1977 film)
cast: Bruce Dern, Marthe Keller, Robert Shaw
blackthorn: **4** sloe, tree **5** shrub
family: **4** rose
relative: ***see*** rose family plant
black-tie: **6** dressy
affair: **4** ball, gala **6** formal **7** banquet
not ~: **6** casual
blacktop: **4** pave
Black Tulip, The
author: Alexandre Dumas
black velvet: **5** drink **8** beverage, cocktail
ingredient: **5** stout **9** champagne
Black Velvet (1980 song)
artist: Alannah Myles
Black Watch: **5** plaid
wear: **4** kilt
Black Water (1975 song)
artist: Doobie Brothers
Blackwell: **4** Earl **9** Elizabeth
Black & White (1972 song)
artist: Three Dog Night
black widow __: **6** spider
Black Widow (1987 film)
cast: Dennis Hopper, Theresa Russell, Nicol Williamson, Debra Winger
Blackwood, Algernon: **6** writer **7** British
Blackwood Farm
author: Anne Rice
bladder: **3** sac
blade: **3** fop, oar **4** edge, epee, foil, leaf, shiv **5** frond, kilij, knife, saber, straw, sword **6** cutlas, dagger, lancet, rapier **7** coxcomb, cutlass, scapula, sidearm **8** scimitar, scimiter **9** dapper Dan, pretty boy, swordsman **10** jack-a-dandy
British ~: **5** sabre
copter ~: **5** rotor
fencing ~: **4** épée
gay ~: **3** fop **4** dude **5** dandy, swell **10** jack-a-dandy
harrow ~: **4** disc, disk
holder: **5** razor **6** knight **9** Musketeer, swordsman
hood's ~: **4** shiv
hussar's ~: **5** saber
Malay ~: **4** kris **6** crease, creese
medieval ~: **4** snee **5** sword
mixer ~: **6** beater
nautical: **6** rudder

of yore: **4** snee **5** estoc
plow ~: **6** colter **7** coulter
rub a ~ on stone: **4** whet
sharpener: **5** strop
starter: **5** razor **6** switch
three-sided ~: **4** épée
turbine ~: **4** vane
windmill ~: **4** vane
__ blade: **5** razor, rotor
Blade: **5** paper **9** newspaper
locale: **6** Toledo
Blade (1998 film)
cast: Stephen Dorff, Kris Kristofferson, Wesley Snipes
Blade Runner (1982 film)
cast: Harrison Ford, Rutger Hauer, Edward James Olmos, Sean Young
director: Ridley Scott
Blades of Glory (2007 film)
cast: Will Ferrell, Jon Heder
Blades, Ruben: **5** actor **10** Panamanian
blaff: **4** stew
blah: **4** drab, dull, flat, mild, pooh, punk, so-so **5** banal, bland, ho-hum, unfun, vapid **6** boring, jargon, jejune, stuffy **7** insipid, languid, prosaic **8** lifeless, listless, mediocre, sluggish, unsalted **9** apathetic, dry-as-dust, lethargic, prosaical, tasteless, wearisome **10** dullsville, flavorless, lackluster, monotonous, pedestrian, spiritless, unexciting
see also baloney
blahs: **4** woes **5** blues **7** languor, sadness **8** doldrums **10** depression, melancholy, woefulness
having the ~: **3** sad **4** blue **6** morose **8** dejected
Blaine: **4** Rick **6** Vivian
Blaine, Rick love: **4** Ilsa
Blair: **4** Tony **5** Betsy, Brown, Janet, Linda, Selma **6** Bonnie **9** Underwood
Blair, Bonnie: **6** skater
Blair, Tony: **2** P.M. **7** British
predecessor: **5** Major
wife: **6** Cherie
Blair Witch Project (1999 film)
cast: Heather Donahue, Joshua Leonard, Michael Williams
Blaise: **5** saint **6** Pascal **7** Modesty **8** Cendrars
Blake: **5** Eubie, Madge **6** Amanda, Lively, Robert **7** Edwards, Whitney, William
Blake, Colonel aide: **5** Radar
Blake, Eubie: **7** pianist **8** composer
collaborator: Noble Sissle
genre: **4** jazz
Blakely: **5** Colin, Susan
Blake, Robert: **5** actor
TV: Baretta
Blake, William: **4** poet **7** British
homeland: England
work: The Book of Los
The Book of Thel
The Clod and the Pebble
The Four Zoas
The Sick Rose
The Song of Los
The Tyger
Blakey, Art: **7** drummer
genre: **4** jazz

Blakley: 5 Ronee
Blalock: 6 Jolene
blamable: 5 wrong 6 guilty, liable 7 at fault 8 culpable 9 imputable 10 answerable, chargeable, delinquent, in the wrong
blame: 3 rag, rap, tax 4 onus 5 blast, chide, decry, fault, guilt, odium, scold, thank 6 accuse, burden, charge, finger, impute, indict, pick on, rebuke, saddle, stigma 7 censure, condemn, obloquy, reproof, reprove, upbraid 8 credit to, denounce, disfavor, reproach, sentence 9 attribute, criticism, criticize, discredit, implicate, liability, reprimand, stick it to 10 accusation, credit with, denunciate, imputation, indictment, reflection, take to task, vituperate
  assign ~ to: 5 pin on 6 accuse, charge
  deflector: 5 alibi
  ender: 6 worthy
  free from ~: 5 clear 9 vindicate
  her: 4 Mame
  taker: 4 goat 5 patsy 9 scapegoat
  take the ~: 5 admit, own up
  to ~: 5 wrong 6 guilty, liable 7 at fault 8 culpable 10 in the wrong
Blame ___ the Bossa Nova: 4 it on
Blame It on Rio (1984 film)
  cast: Joseph Bologna, Michael Caine, Valerie Harper, Michelle Johnson, Demi Moore
  director: Stanley Donen
Blame It on the Bossa Nova (1963 song)
  artist: Eydie Gorme
Blame It on the Rain (1989 song)
  artist: Milli Vanilli
blameless: 4 good, pure 5 clean, clear, moral 6 worthy 7 upright 8 innocent, spotless, unsoiled, virtuous 9 crimeless, exemplary, faultless, guilt-free, guiltless, not guilty, righteous, stainless, unspotted, unsullied 10 immaculate, impeccable, inculpable, in the clear
___ Blame Me: 4 Don't
blamer: 5 shrew 6 critic
___ blanc: 3 vin 6 ballet, beurre, boudin
Blanc: 3 alp, Mel 4 Mont
___ Blanc: 4 Mont 5 Pinot 6 Chenin
blanch: 3 wan 4 fade, pale 5 chalk, quail, start, steam, wince 6 flinch, recoil, shrink, whiten 7 parboil 8 etiolate
___ blanche: 5 carte, pomme
Blanche: 5 Sweet
blanched: 4 pale 5 ashen, livid, white 6 chalky 7 whitish 9 albescent, colorless
Blanchett, Cate: 7 actress
  film: The Aviator (2004, AA)
    Bandits (2001)
    The Curious Case of Benjamin Button (2008)
    The Gift (2000)
    I'm Not There (2007)
    Notes on a Scandal (2006)
    Pushing Tin (1999)
    The Shipping News (2001)
    The Talented Mr. Ripley (1999)
blanco: 4 vino
___ blanco: 3 oso
___ Blanco: 3 Rio
bland: 3 dry 4 blah, dull, flat, mild, soft, tame 5 balmy, banal, ho-hum, suave, vapid 6 boring, polite, smooth, stuffy, urbane 7 affable, humdrum, insipid, tedious 8 pleasant, soothing, unsalted, unsavory 9 calmative, innocuous, tasteless, wearisome 10 flavorless, monotonous, unexciting
  fare: 3 pap
  not ~: 3 hot 5 spicy, tangy 6 spicey
Blanda, George: 2 QB
  sport: 8 football
blandish: 4 coax 5 press 6 cajole 7 flatter, wheedle 8 butter up, inveigle, persuade, play up to, soft-soap 9 sweet-talk
blandishment: 7 blarney, coaxing 8 cajolery, flattery 9 adulation
Blane: 5 Ralph 6 Marcie
Blane, Marcie
  song: Bobby's Girl (1962)
blank: 4 bare, form, null, void, zero 5 clean, clear, dazed, empty, space, stony 6 absent, barren, bullet, cipher, glassy, lacuna, stoney, unused, vacant 7 deadpan, shut out, vacuous 8 masklike, omission, spotless, unfilled, unmarked 9 awestruck, impassive, untouched 10 bewildered, confounded, nonplussed, poker-faced, speechless
  book: 5 album, diary 7 journal
  contest entry ~: 4 name
  document: 4 form
  draw a ~: 6 forget
  look: 5 stare
blank ___: 4 book, tape, wall 5 check, shell, stare, verse
___ blank: 5 draw a, entry
___-blank: 5 point
blanked out: 9 forgotten, repressed 10 suppressed
blanket: 4 veil, wrap 5 cover, layer, quilt, sheet, throw 6 afghan, spread 7 bedding, coating, conceal, envelop, general, generic, overall, overlay, overlie 8 covering, sweeping 9 bedspread, comforter, extensive, generical, inclusive 10 spread over
  adjustment: 4 tuck
  hobo ~: 6 bindle
  horse ~: 5 manta
  light ~: 5 throw 6 afghan
  material: 4 wool 6 fleece
  Mexican ~: 6 sarape, serape
  wet ~: 4 bore, drag, drip 7 killjoy 9 pessimist, worrywart
blanket ___: 4 roll, toss 5 chest, sheet 6 stitch
___ blanket: 3 wet 6 saddle 7 quarter
___ Blanket Bingo: 5 Beach
blankness: 4 void 7 vacuity 9 emptiness
Blanton, Jimmy: 7 bassist
  genre: 4 jazz
blare: 4 bray, honk 5 noise, sound 6 clamor, cry out, racket, scream, shriek 7 clangor, fanfare, tantara 9 broadcast
blaring: 4 loud 5 forte, noisy 6 brassy, shrill 7 booming, clarion, jarring, pealing, rackety, raucous, reboant, roaring 8 crashing, piercing, plangent, rumbling, sonorous, strident, turned up 9 big-voiced, clamorous, deafening 10 boisterous, resounding, stentorian, strepitous, thundering, uproarious, vociferant, vociferous
blarney
  see baloney
Blarney Stone
  city near the ~: 4 Cork
  site: 4 Eire, Erin 7 Ireland
___ Blas: 3 Gil, San
blasé: 5 bored, jaded, sated, weary 6 casual, cloyed 7 glutted, unmoved, worldly 8 satiated 9 apathetic, surfeited, unexcited 10 nonchalant, world-weary
  hardly ~: 3 hot 4 awed 5 eager 6 gung-ho 7 excited
___ Blas Overture: 3 Ruy
blaspheme: 4 cuss 5 abuse, curse, swear 6 deride, impugn, oppugn, revile, vilify 7 profane, put down, run down, slander, traduce 8 badmouth, belittle, execrate 9 desecrate 10 vituperate
blasphemous: 4 vile 7 impious, profane, ungodly
blasphemy: 3 sin 6 heresy 7 impiety 8 swearing 9 indignity, invective, profanity, sacrilege, violation 10 execration, scurrility
Blass, Bill: 8 designer
  rival: 5 Klein 6 Armani, Lauren 7 Versace
blast: 3 din 4 ball, bang, bash, belt, blow, bomb, boom, bray, damn, drub, fest, flay, gala, gale, gust, honk, nuke, peal, puff, rail, riot, roar, ruin, shot, slam, toot, wham, wind 5 blame, burst, crack, crash, draft, noise, party, roast, salvo, shoot, smash, storm, wreck 6 assail, attack, blow-up, deafen, hit out, impugn, kaboom, oppugn, rail at, report, squall, thrill, volley, wallop 7 assault, barrage, blowout, bombard, clobber, condemn, destroy, explode, fun time, lambast, scourge, shatter, tempest, thunder, torpedo, whistle 8 big party, demolish, denounce, dynamite, eruption, fire upon, good time, great fun, lambaste, open fire, outbreak, outburst, shivaree 9 castigate, criticism, criticize, discharge, explosion, festivity, great time, lash out at 10 annihilate, detonation, saturnalia
  cannon ~: 5 salvo
  from the past: 4 oldy 5 oldie
  full ~: 6 in toto, wholly 7 flat out, totally, utterly 8 entirely 9 to the hilt 10 completely, thoroughly, to the limit
  have a ~: 5 enjoy, party, revel
  material: 3 TNT 5 nitro
  sound: 3 pow 4 roar 6 kaboom 7 thunder 9 explosion
  starter: 4 ecto, endo, sand
  wind ~: 4 gust
blast ___: 3 off 4 cell, lamp, wave 7 furnace
blast ___ the past: 4 from
___ blast: 3 air 4 full, rice
blasted: 6 damned 7 hateful 8 infernal
___-blasted: 3 dad
Blast From the Past (1999 film)
  cast: Brendan Fraser, Alicia Silverstone, Sissy Spacek, Christopher Walken
blast-furnace fuel: 4 coke
blasting: 5 noisy
  cap: 4 fuse, fuze 7 lighter
  compound: 3 TNT 5 nitro 6 amatol
  starter: 4 sand
blast it: 4 damn, darn, drat, durn
blastoff: 5 start 9 departure
  org.: 4 NASA
blat: 3 baa, cry 4 bray 8 blurt out
blatant: 4 loud, open, rank 5 campy, gross, naked, overt 6 arrant, brassy, brazen, flashy, garish, patent, shrill, tawdry 7 glaring, obvious, raucous 8 flagrant, impudent, overbold, palpable, piercing, strident, unsubtle 9 barefaced, deafening, downright, flaunting, obtrusive, screaming, shameless, unabashed 10 unblushing
  mistake: 5 gaffe 6 bêtise 7 faux pas
blather: 3 gab, yak, yap 4 talk 5 bleat, prate 6 babble, bunkum, gossip, hot air, jabber, ramble 7 chatter, palaver, prattle 8 babbling, fast talk, ramble on, rattle on 9 loquacity 10 chew the rag, double-talk
  see also baloney
blathering: 4 long 5 gabby, gassy, tumid, windy, wordy 6 prolix 7 diffuse, fustian, hyped up, lengthy, orotund, pompous, ranting, stilted, unterse, verbose, voluble 8 boastful, inflated, rambling 9 bombastic, garrulous, grandiose, high-flown, overblown, redundant, rhapsodic, talkative 10 big-talking, discursive, euphuistic, flamboyant, histrionic, long-winded, loquacious, palaverous, rhetorical
blaze: 4 burn, fire, lick, mark 5 burst, flame, flare, flash, glare, light, shine 6 flames 7 bonfire, burning, flare up, torrent 8 landmark, outburst, radiance, radiancy, wildfire 10 brilliance, combustion, effulgence, incandesce
  a trail: 4 lead 5 guide 7 pioneer
  remnant: 3 ash 4 coal 5 ember 6 cinder
  up: 5 flare 6 ignite
Blaze (1989 film)
  cast: Lolita Davidovich, Paul Newman
blaze a ___: 5 trail
Blaze of Glory (1990 song)
  artist: Bon Jovi
blazer: 4 coat 6 jacket
  detail: 4 vent
  starter: 5 trail
Blazer: 3 SUV 5 cager, Chevy 9 Chevrolet
Blazers: 4 five
  home: 8 Portland
  org.: 3 NBA
  rival: *see* NBA team
blazing: 3 hot, lit 5 afire, aglow, fiery, shiny 6 ablaze, aflame, aglare, bright, flashy, red-hot, torrid 7 flaring, fulgent, glaring, lambent, radiant 8 luminous, lustrous 9 bril-

liant **10** passionate
star: 5 plant **6** flower
Blazing Saddles (1974 film)
cast: Madeline Kahn, Harvey Korman, Cleavon Little, Gene Wilder
director: Mel Brooks
role: 4 Bart
singer: Frankie Laine
blazon: 7 display **8** proclaim **9** embellish
blazonry: 8 heraldry
bldg. unit: 3 apt.
see also building
bldr.: 3 mfr.
see also builder
bleach: 4 fade **5** chalk, Purex, Snowy, Vivid **6** bluing, Clorox, whiten **7** absolve, blueing, decolor, lighten, wash out **8** Borateem, etiolate **10** decolorize
bottle: 3 jug
needing ~: 4 gray **5** dingy **7** stained
target: 5 stain
bleached: 3 wan **4** pale **5** light, white **6** chalky **9** albescent, colorless, washed-out
bleachers: 5 seats **6** stands **7** benches, seating **9** Ruthville **10** grandstand
activity: 6 booing, waving **8** cheering, clapping
bum: 3 fan
feature: 3 row **4** tier
sound from the ~: 3 boo, rah, yea **4** yell **5** chant **6** go team
bleaching
agent: 5 lemon, ozone **8** peroxide
vat: 4 keir, kier
bleak: 3 raw **4** bare, fish **5** gaunt, no-win, stark **6** barren, lonely, severe, wintry **7** austere, drizzly, sterile, wintery **8** blighted, mournful **9** bulldozed **10** deforested
see also gloomy
Bleak House
author: Charles Dickens
cat: 8 Lady Jane
character: 3 Ada **4** Rosa **6** Esther
bleakness: 3 woe **5** gloom **7** sadness **10** depression, desolation, loneliness, woefulness
blear: 3 dim **4** blur, mist **5** cloud, fuzzy **6** blurry, dimmed, smudge **7** blurred, clouded, dimness, obscure, unclear **9** teary-eyed **10** cloudiness
bleared: 10 indistinct
bleary: 3 dim **4** dark, hazy **5** dusky, faded, fuzzy, mirky, misty, murky, muted, spent, tired, vague **6** blurry **7** blurred, joyless, shadowy, unclear **9** unfocused **10** indistinct, out of focus
bleary-___: 4 eyed
bleat: 3 baa, cry, maa **4** blab, call **5** whine **7** blather
bleater: 3 ewe, ram **4** lamb **5** sheep
blecch: 3 ugh, yek **4** yuck
Bledel: 6 Alexis
Bledsoe: 8 Tempestt
bleed: 3 run, sap **4** milk, mope, ooze **5** drain, exude, mourn, screw **6** extort, fleece, grieve, lament, prey on, suffer **7** deplete, exhaust, flow out, squeeze **9** blackmail, empathize, percolate, shake down, strong-arm **10** extort from, overcharge, sympathize
dry: 5 drain **7** exhaust
for: 4 pity **10** sympathize
starter: 4 nose
bleeding heart: 5 plant **6** flower
bleep: 5 erase **6** censor, delete, signal **7** edit out **9** expurgate
Bleeth: 7 Yasmine
blemish: 3 mar, zit **4** blot, flaw, mark, scar, slur, spot, wart **5** fault, speck, spoil, stain, sully, taint **6** blotch, damage, defect, smudge, stigma **7** eyesore, scratch, tarnish **8** weakness **9** birthmark **10** beauty spot, imputation
fender ~: 4 dent, ding
skin ~: 3 wen, zit **4** wart
wood ~: 4 knar, knot
blemished: 9 defective
blench: 4 fade **5** cower, quail, start, wince **6** flinch, recoil, whiten **7** shy away **10** shrink from
blend: 2 go **3** mix, wed **4** beat, brew, fuse, join, meld, olio, stir, tone, whip **5** admix, alloy, cross, elide, fit in, immix, marry, merge, unify, union, unite, weave **6** commix, fusion, make up, mingle **7** amalgam, combine, harmony, mixture **8** coalesce, compound, intermix, solution **9** admixture, commingle, composite, harmonize, immixture, integrate, potpourri, synthesis **10** adulterate, amalgamate, concoction, homogenize, interbreed, interweave, synthesize
in: 6 belong **8** go native
into: 4 melt **8** dissolve
not ~ well: 5 clash
with: 10 complement
blende: 3 ore
starter: 4 horn **5** pitch
blended: 5 mixed **6** melded **7** kneaded **9** composite
blender: 5 mixer **9** appliance
alternative: 5 whisk **9** eggbeater
brand: 5 Oster
setting: 3 mix **4** chop **5** purée, speed
sound: 4 whir **5** whirr
use the ~: 3 mix **4** chop, whip **5** purée
blending: 6 in tune
Blenheim: 6 battle
blesbok: 8 antelope
relative: *see* antelope
bless: 4 laud **5** endow, ensky, exalt, extol, honor, thank **6** anoint, devote, extoll, hallow, ordain, permit, praise, ratify **7** approve, baptize, beatify, commend, glorify, magnify, smile on **8** canonize, dedicate, enshrine, eulogize, inshrine, sanctify, sanction **9** smile upon, subscribe **10** consecrate, panegyrize
old-style: 4 sain
opposite: 4 damn **5** curse
blessed: 4 holy **5** happy, lucky **6** divine, joyful, joyous, sacred **7** saintly **8** blissful **9** celestial, fortunate, inviolate **10** auspicious, felicitous, fortuitous, inviolable
abode of the ~: 7 Elysium
be ~ with: 4 have **5** enjoy
declare ~: 7 beatify
event: 5 birth
name meaning ~: 5 Zelig **8** Benedict
blessed ___: 5 event
Blessed ___: 6 Virgin
Blessed Damozel, The
author: Dante Gabriel Rossetti
Blessed, Land of the: 6 Avalon
blessing: 2 OK **4** boon, luck, okay **5** asset, grace, mercy **6** thanks **7** backing, benefit, benison, consent, godsend, support **8** approval, sanction, windfall **9** advantage, hallowing **10** dedication, good wishes, invocation, lucky break, permission
give one's ~: 6 concur, permit **7** approve, consent **9** acquiesce **10** condescend
preceder: 5 achoo **6** ahchoo, sneeze **7** kerchoo
___ blessing: 5 mixed
Blessing, The
author: Nancy Mitford
blest: 4 holy **5** happy **6** gifted **7** favored **8** hallowed **10** sanctified
bleu ___: 6 cheese
___ bleu: 5 Sacré **6** cordon
bleu cheese: 8 dressing
blewit: 6 fungus **7** blue-leg **8** mushroom
Blige, Mary J.
song: I'll Be There for You (1995) Not Gon' Cry (1996) Real Love (1992)
Bligh: 7 captain, William
blight: 3 mar, rot, woe **4** bane, dash, ruin, rust **5** decay, taint, wreck **6** foul up, infect, mess up, mildew, plague, wither **7** corrupt, destroy, eyesore, scourge **8** calamity, disaster **9** detriment, frustrate, nightmare, pollution, ruination **10** affliction
urban ~: 4 slum, smog **6** litter, sprawl
blighted: 5 bleak **8** ill-fated
tree: 3 elm
blighter: 3 cad **5** knave, rogue, scamp, swine **6** bad guy **8** scalawag **9** scallawag, scallywag **10** blackguard, scapegrace
blimp: 5 craft **7** airship, balloon **8** aircraft, zeppelin **9** dirigible
home: 6 hangar
like a ~: 3 LTA **5** rigid
part: 3 pod **4** hull
___ Blimp: 7 Colonel
blind: 4 mask, rash, ruse **5** front, hasty, shade, tight, trick **6** dazzle, hidden, screen **7** covered, dead end, deceive, knavery, unaware **8** covering, heedless, mindless, obscured, partisan, reckless **9** concealed, impetuous, oblivious, senseless, unknowing, unmindful **10** camouflage, obstructed, regardless, subterfuge
alley: 7 dead end, impasse **8** cul-de-sac
cheat at ~ man's buff: 4 peek
ender: 4 fold, side, worm
name meaning ~: 5 Cecil **6** Cicely **7** Cecilia
spot: 7 failing **8** weakness
turn a ~ eye to: 8 overlook
unit: 4 slat **6** louvre
blind ___: 3 pig **4** copy, date, door, hole, seed, side, spot **5** alley, faith, floor, snake, tiger, trust **6** casing, flange, roller
blind ___ bat: 3 as a
___ blind: 3 rob **4** duck **6** window **8** Venetian
___-blind: 5 color **6** double, single
Blind Ambition
author: John Dean
Blind Date
author: Jerzy Kosinski
Blinded by the Light (1976 song)
artist: Manfred Mann
___ blind eye: 5 turn a
Blind Fireworks
author: Louis MacNeice
blindfold: 7 obscure **9** obfuscate
get past the ~: 4 peek
blinding: 6 aglare **7** glaring **8** dazzling
light: 6 dazzle
blindingly bright: 4 neon **10** florescent
blindly: 8 at random, pell-mell
search ~: 5 grope
blindman's buff: 4 game
___ Blind Mice: 5 Three
___ Blindness: 5 On His
blindside: 6 ambush
Blind Side, The (2009 film)
cast: Sandra Bullock
blini: 7 pancake
kin: 5 crêpe
partner: 3 lox **6** butter, caviar **9** sour cream
blink: 3 bat **4** wink **5** flash **6** recoil, twitch **7** flicker, flutter, glimmer, glitter, nictate, shimmer, sparkle, twinkle **8** back down, bat an eye **9** nictitate
at: 6 ignore **7** absolve **8** overlook, tolerate **9** disregard
on the ~: 5 kaput **6** broken **7** damaged **9** defective, disrepair **10** broken-down
starter: 3 ice **4** snow
___ blink: 5 on the
blinker: 6 eyelid, signal
screen ~: 6 cursor
blintz: 7 pancake
partner: 9 sour cream
blip: 6 signal **7** anomaly **10** aberration
on a polygraph: 3 lie
radar ~: 4 ping
sonar ~: 4 echo
Blish, James: 6 writer
genre: 5 sci-fi
bliss: 3 joy **6** heaven, utopia **7** delight, ecstasy, elation, nirvana, rapture **8** euphoria, felicity, gladness, paradise, pleasure **9** happiness **10** ebullience
bliss ___: 3 out
Bliss: 4 Fort **6** Carman
author: Katherine Mansfield
blissed out: 4 rapt **8** ecstatic
blissful: 4 glad **5** blest, happy, merry **6** blithe, cheery, divine, edenic, elated, golden, jovial, joyful, joyous, upbeat **7** blessed, gleeful, pleased, radiant, tickled **8** beatific, cheerful, ecstatic, euphoric, exultant, heavenly, jubilant, mirthful, thrilled **9** delighted, gladdened, in

ecstasy, overjoyed, rapturous, rejoicing, rhapsodic 10 enraptured, flying high
  place: 4 Eden 6 Avalon, heaven, utopia 7 Elysium, nirvana
blister: 3 sac, wen 4 bleb, cyst, lash, slur, sore 5 blain, smear 6 bubble, insult, scorch, vilify 7 lambast, vesicle 8 belittle, lambaste, swelling 9 castigate, denigrate
  cause a ~: 3 rub
blistered: 3 raw 4 sore
blistering: 3 hot 6 red-hot, torrid 8 white-hot
B.Lit.: 3 deg.
blithe: 3 gay 4 glad 5 happy, jolly, light, merry, sunny 6 breezy, cheery, chirpy, genial, jaunty, jocund, jovial, joyful, joyous, lively, upbeat 7 buoyant, gleeful, jocular, pleased, tickled 8 blissful, carefree, cheerful, ecstatic, euphoric, exultant, gladsome, heedless, jubilant, mirthful, thrilled 9 delighted, lightsome, overjoyed, rejoicing, sprightly 10 flying high, unbothered, unthinking, untroubled
Blithedale Romance, The
  author: Nathaniel Hawthorne
Blithe Spirit
  author: Noël Coward
Blithe Spirit (1945 film)
  cast: Constance Cummings, Kay Hammond, Rex Harrison
  director: David Lean
  scene: 6 seance
blitz: 4 raid, rush 5 storm 6 attack, charge, invade, red dog, strike, thrust 7 assault, barrage, bombard, bombing, offense 8 fire upon, gang up on, shelling 9 offensive, onslaught
blitz ___: 3 can 5 chess
___ blitz: 5 media
Blitzen: 8 reindeer
  colleague: *see* reindeer
Blitzer: 4 Wolf
blitzkrieg: 6 battle 7 offense 10 aggression
Blitzstein: 4 Marc
Blixen: 5 Karen 7 Dinesen 11 Isak Dinesen
Blix, Hans: 7 Swedish 8 diplomat
blizzard: 4 snow 5 storm 9 snowstorm
  configuration: 5 swirl
  pileup: 4 bank 5 drift
bloat: 4 grow, puff 5 bulge, swell, widen 6 beef up, dilate, expand, fatten, puff up, pump up, spread 7 augment, balloon, broaden, burgeon, distend, enlarge, inflate, swell up 8 bourgeon, heighten, lengthen, swell out 9 intumesce
bloated: 3 big 5 gassy, puffy, tumid 7 swollen
blob: 3 dab 4 bead, daub, drop, glob, lump, mark, mass, spot 5 clump, patch, smear 6 bubble, dollop, smudge, splash 7 droplet, globule, splotch 8 spherule
blobby: 9 amorphous
Blob, move like the: 4 ooze
bloc: 4 bund, ring, sect 5 group, junta, party, union 6 cartel, clique, league, muster 7 combine, council, entente, faction 8 alliance 9 anschluss, coalition, syndicate 10 federation
  en ~: 6 in full 8 as a whole 10 altogether
  political ~: 5 labor
Bloch: 3 Ray 5 Felix 6 Ernest, Konrad
block: 3 bar, dam, jam, lot, toy 4 bolt, cake, clog, cork, cube, halt, hunk, loaf, lock, lump, mass, plug, seal, shut, slab, snag, stem, stop, unit 5 brick, check, chock, choke, chunk, close, cross, dam up, delay, deter, embar, estop, hitch, ingot, jam up, latch, parry, solid, stall, stimy, stymy, wedge 6 arrest, clog up, cut off, defeat, forbid, hamper, hang up, hinder, hold up, impede, lock up, plug up, region, retard, seal up, secure, square, stop up, stymie, tackle, thwart 7 barrier, congest, exclude, obviate, occlude, prevent, seal off, section, segment, shut off, shutter, stopper, ward off 8 button up, close off, encumber, handicap, obstacle, obstruct, prohibit, sabotage, stoppage 9 barricade, foreclose, frustrate, hamstring, hindrance, intercept, stonewall, territory 10 bottleneck, impediment, limitation
  a broadcast: 3 jam
  and tackle: 5 hoist 6 lifter
  builder's ~: 3 lot
  building ~: 4 atom, unit
  chip off the old ~: 3 lad, son 5 image, scion 9 offspring
  down the ~: 4 near 5 close
  ender: 3 ade, age 4 head 5 house 6 buster
  hardwood ~: 5 rabot
  illegally: 4 clip
  make ~ letters: 5 print
  marble ~: 4 slab
  material: 6 cement 8 concrete
  new kid on the ~: 3 cub 4 tiro, tyro 5 pupil 6 greeny, novice 7 amateur, dabbler, entrant, learner, recruit, trainee 8 beginner, freshman, initiate, neophyte, newcomer, putterer 9 fledgling, greenhorn, novitiate 10 apprentice, dilettante, first-timer, tenderfoot
  off: 7 enclose, isolate
  of ice: 4 berg, cube, floe
  out: 4 form, plan 5 frame, shape 6 design, screen, sketch 7 shut off
  patio ~: 5 paver
  paving ~: 4 sett
  plastic building ~: 4 Lego
  road ~: 7 barrier
  seller of old: 6 iceman
  starter: 4 cell, road, wood 6 breech, cinder
  stumbling ~: 3 bar, rub 4 snag 5 catch, hitch 6 hurdle, kicker 7 barrier, pitfall, problem, setback 8 drawback, handicap, obstacle 9 hindrance 10 impediment
  sun ~: 3 oil 5 cloud, shade 6 lotion
  unit: 4 cell
  up: 3 dam 4 plug
block ___: 3 out, tin 4 coal, lava, line, mast 5 chord, front, grant, house, party, plane, print, trade 6 caving, heater, letter, signal, system
___ block: 3 sun 5 plate, sound 6 breeze, cinder, engine 7 auction, butcher, writer's
Block ___: 6 Island
blockade: 3 bar, dam 4 bolt, clog, cork, lock, plug, seal, shut, snag, stop 5 dam up, latch, siege 6 clog up, hold up, lock up, picket, plug up, seal up, secure, stop up 7 barrier, closure, enclose, inclose, seal off, shut off, shut out, shutter 8 button up, obstacle, obstruct, stoppage, surround 9 foreclose 10 impediment
___blockade: 5 naval
blockade-___: 6 runner
Blockade Runners, The
  author: Jules Verne
blockage: 3 bar 4 clog, stop 5 tie-up 6 arrest, hurdle, logjam 7 embargo 8 gridlock, stoppage 9 impedance 10 congestion, impediment, traffic jam
  reliever: 5 stent
  remove a ~: 5 unjam 6 unclog
block and ___: 6 tackle
Blockbuster
  rental: 5 movie, video
  section: 3 DVD 5 sci-fi 6 action, comedy, horror 7 romance
blocked: 5 tight 6 stuffy 10 impassable
  it may be ~: 5 sinus
  it's ~ by sunblock: 5 UV ray
blocker
  bill ~: 3 nay 4 veto
  channel ~: 5 V-chip
  river ~: 3 dam
  sun ~: 3 fog, oil 4 tree 5 cloud, shade, smaze 6 awning, lotion
  UV ~: 5 ozone
  x-ray ~: 4 lead
___ blocker: 4 beta 5 alpha 7 calcium
Blocker, Dan: 5 actor
  role: Hoss Cartwright
blockhead
  see ninny
blockheaded: 5 dense, silly, thick, unapt 6 cloddy
Block, Lawrence: 6 writer
block-shaped: 5 cubic 6 chunky
___-blo fuse: 3 slo
Blois: 4 city, town
  locale: 6 France
  river: 5 Loire
bloke: 2 he 3 guy, sir 4 chap, gent, male 5 fella 6 feller, fellow, mister
  British ~: 3 guv 4 chap, mate
  friendly ~: 5 matey
  that ~: 3 him
blond: 4 fair 5 flaxy, light, sandy 6 blonde, flaxen, yellow 7 towhead 9 towheaded 10 auricomous, fair-haired
  go ~: 6 bleach
  kin: *see* yellow color
___ blonde: 3 ash 8 platinum
___ Blonde: 7 Legally, Suicide
Blondell, Joan: 7 actress
  spouse: Dick Powell, Mike Todd
blondie: 4 cake 7 dessert
Blondie (1938 film)
  cast: Arthur Lake, Penny Singleton
Blondie (comic strip)
  character: 4 Cora, Elmo, Herb 6 Cookie 7 Dagwood, Dithers 9 Alexander
  dog: 5 Daisy
  surname: 8 Bumstead
  work like ~: 5 cater
Blondie (rock group)
  leader: Debbie Harry
  song: Call Me (1980)
    Heart of Glass (1979)
    Rapture (1981)
    The Tide Is High (1980)
blondish: 4 fair 5 light, sandy
Blonsky: 5 Nikki
blood: 3 kin 4 race 6 origin, strain 7 descent, kinfolk, kinship, lineage 8 ancestry, pedigree, relative
  bad ~: *see* animosity
  be out for ~: 6 avenge 7 pay back, revenge
  blue ~: 5 count, noble 8 nobleman 9 gentility, patrician 10 aristocrat
  British blue ~: 6 aristo
  carrier of white ~ cells: 5 lymph
  classification: 3 ABO 4 O neg 5 type A, type B, type O
  combining form: 3 hem- 4 -emia, hema-, hemo- 5 -aemia, hemat-, -hemia 6 -haemia, hemato-, sangui- 8 sanguine-
  component: 5 serum 6 plasma 10 hemoglobin
  ender: 4 bath, line, root, shed, shot, worm 5 guilt, hound, stain, stone 6 mobile, stream, sucker 7 letting, thirsty 8 curdling
  flesh and ~: 3 kin 4 aunt, soul 5 being, uncle 6 cousin, family, sister 7 brother, kinfolk, sibling 8 relation, relative
  fluids: 4 sera
  in cold ~: 9 knowingly, on purpose, willfully
  in the ~: 6 innate 9 ingrained
  like ~: 5 thick
  make one's ~ boil: 3 irk, vex 4 rile 5 anger, peeve, upset 6 insult, offend 9 infuriate
  obstruction: 4 clot
  of ~ fluid: 6 serous
  of the gods: 5 ichor
  vessel: 4 vein 5 aorta 6 artery 9 capillary
  visit a ~ bank: 6 donate
blood ___: 3 red 4 bank, bath, cell, clot, feud, heat, knot, lily, meal, test, type 5 count, donor, fluke, group, level, money, royal, serum, sport, sugar 6 orange, plasma, vessel 7 brother, pudding, sausage
___ blood: 3 bad, new 4 blue, full, half 5 whole, young 6 pigeon 7 dragon's
Blood ___: 4 Test 5 Money, Sport 6 Simple
___ Blood: 3 Bad 4 Wise 5 First, Young 7 Captain
blood-and-___: 4 guts
Blood and Gold
  author: Anne Rice
___ Blood and Guts: 3 Old
blood bank
  depositor: 5 donor
  quantity: 4 pint, unit
  worker: 5 typer
___ blood cell: 3 red 5 white
blood-chilling: 4 gory 5 eerie, lurid,

scary **6** creepy **8** horrible **10** terrifying
bloodcurdling: 4 gory **5** eerie, lurid, scary **6** creepy **8** horrible **10** terrifying
Blood Diamond (2006 film)
cast: Jennifer Connelly, Leonardo DiCaprio
__-blooded: 3 hot, red **4** blue, cold, full, warm
bloodhound: 3 dog **6** canine, shamus **9** detective
emulate a ~: 5 sniff, trace, track **6** follow
feature: 4 jowl **6** dewlap
like a ~: 5 jowly
lips: 5 flews
trail: 4 odor **5** scent, smell, spoor
Blood Knot, The
author: Athol Fugard
bloodless: 3 wan **4** cold, pale **5** ashen, livid, pasty, white **6** chalky, pallid, sallow, unkind **8** unlively **9** albescent, colorless, impassive, unfeeling **10** insensible, spiritless
bloodline: 5 roots **9** forebears, genealogy
Bloodline
author: Sidney Sheldon
Blood of Abraham, The
author: Jimmy Carter
Blood of a Poet, The (1930 film)
director: Jean Cocteau
blood-red: 7 crimson
Blood Red, Sister Rose
author: Thomas Keneally
bloodroot: 5 plant **6** flower
bloodshot: 3 red
Blood Simple (1984 film)
cast: John Getz, Dan Hedaya, Frances McDormand
director: Joel Coen
dog: 4 Opal
Blood Sport
author: Dick Francis
bloodsucker: 4 tick **5** leech **6** bedbug **8** parasite
Blood, Sweat & Tears
leader: David Clayton-Thomas
song: And When I Die (1969) Spinning Wheel (1969) You've Made Me So Very Happy (1969)
Blood Test
author: Jonathan Kellerman
bloodthirsty: 4 mean **5** cruel, harsh, nasty **6** animal, brutal, fierce, lupine, savage, unkind, wanton **7** beastly, callous, hurtful, inhuman, vicious, violent, warlike **8** barbaric, fiendish, inhumane, pitiless, ruthless, sadistic, vengeful **9** cutthroat, ferocious, merciless, monstrous, predatory, truculent **10** vindictive
blood-tingling: 9 thrilling
blood-typing system: 3 ABO
Blood Work (2002 film)
cast: Jeff Daniels, Clint Eastwood, Anjelica Huston
director: Clint Eastwood
bloody: 3 raw, red **4** gory **5** lurid
Bloody Mary: 5 drink, Tudor **8** cocktail
daughter: 4 Liat
ingredient: 5 vodka **11** tomato juice
blooey: 10 on the fritz, out of order
bloom: 3 bud **4** boom, grow, pink, posy **5** prime, ripen, youth **6** floret, flower, mature, open up, sprout, thrive **7** blossom, burgeon, develop, prosper, succeed **8** bourgeon, flourish, fructify, vegetate **9** bear fruit, freshness, germinate, luxuriate **10** effloresce, nasturtium
full ~: 8 maturity
see also flower
Bloom: 5 Bobby, Verna **6** Claire, Harold **7** Orlando
Bloom, Bobby
song: Montego Bay (1970)
Bloom, Claire: 7 actress
spouse: Philip Roth, Rod Steiger
Bloom County: 5 strip **10** comic strip
cat: 4 Bill
penguin: 4 Opus
__ bloomer: 4 late
Bloomer: 6 Amelia
Bloomfield: 4 city, town
locale: 8 Michigan **9** New Jersey
Bloom, Harold: 6 writer
blooming: 4 ripe, rosy, well **5** ruddy, young **6** waxing **7** glowing, growing, healthy, radiant, verdant **8** fruitful, thriving **9** flowering **10** blossoming, prospering, prosperous, successful
early: 4 rath **5** rathe
starter: 4 ever
Bloomingdale's
rival: 4 Saks
Bloomington: 4 city, town
athletes: 8 Hoosiers
locale: 7 Indiana **8** Illinois **9** Minnesota **10** California
...bloom in the spring, __: 5 tra la
Bloom, Molly last word: 3 yes
Bloom of Life, The
author: Anatole France
bloop: 3 fly **6** looper, pop fly
blooper: 4 goof, slip **5** boner, error, fluff, gaffe, lapse **6** boo-boo, bungle **7** blunder, faux pas, mistake
Blore: 4 Eric
blossom: 3 bud **4** posy **5** bloom, ripen, yield **6** floret, flower, mature, thrive, unfold **7** burgeon, develop, produce, prosper, succeed **8** bourgeon, flourish, fructify, progress, vegetate **9** germinate **10** effloresce
see also flower
__ blossom: 5 apple, peach **6** double, orange
Blossom: 4 Rock **6** Dearie
Blossom (NBC sitcom)
cast: Mayim Bialik (Blossom Russo)
Blossom Fell, A (1955 song)
artist: Nat King Cole
blossoming: 5 happy, young **6** abloom **9** fulfilled
blossoms, of: 6 floral
blot: 3 dry, mar, sop **4** blur, flaw, mark, slur, soil, spot **5** dirty, fault, odium, patch, shame, smear, speck, spoil, stain, sully, taint **6** absorb, bedaub, defect, pat dry, smirch, smudge, stigma **7** balloon, blemish, calumny, slander, tarnish **8** black eye, disgrace **9** bespatter **10** imputation
out: 4 hide **5** erase **6** delete, efface, excise, rub off **7** destroy, eclipse, expunge **9** eliminate, eradicate **10** annihilate, extinguish
blotch: 4 mark, spot **5** blain, stain **6** bedaub, measle, smudge, stigma **7** besmear, blemish, ink spot **8** besmirch, mottling **9** gravy spot
combining form: 5 macul- **6** maculi-, maculo-
blotchy: 6 spotty **7** mottled
blotted out: 9 forgotten, repressed **10** suppressed
blotter
name on a police ~: 3 Doe, Roe **4** Jane, John
place for a ~: 4 desk
police ~ entry: 2 MO **3** AKA **5** alias
spot: 3 ink
subject: 4 perp **7** suspect
blotto: 3 lit **5** drunk, oiled **6** stewed, tanked **8** squiffed **10** inebriated
blouse: 3 top **5** middy, shirt, V-neck, waist **6** bodice, halter, huipil, T-shirt **7** garment, puff out **8** pullover, separate **10** turtleneck
adornment: 3 pin **5** cameo **7** corsage
fabric: 4 poly, silk **5** linen, nylon **6** cotton, eyelet
long ~: 5 tunic
loose ~: 5 middy
make a ~: 3 sew
part: 4 neck, yoke **8** neckline
sleeveless ~: 5 shell
trim: 5 jabot **6** ruffle
__ blouse: 5 middy
blouson: 5 shirt
bloviate: 4 rail, rant, rave **5** decry, orate, spout **7** declaim, thunder **8** denounce, harangue, perorate **9** fulminate, hold forth
blow: 3 bop, hit, jab, rap **4** bang, bash, belt, biff, flee, flub, gale, gust, honk, hurt, jolt, kick, muff, pant, puff, sigh, slam, slap, slug, sock, stab, swat, tick, toot, waft, wind **5** blast, botch, clout, draft, go off, knock, punch, shock, smack, sound, spend, spill, split, storm, swipe, thump, treat, use up, waste, whack, whomp **6** breeze, buffet, bungle, exhale, flurry, impact, mishap, strike, stroke, thwack, trauma, wallop **7** bad luck, debacle, explode, reverse, screw up, setback, take off, tempest, tragedy, typhoon, undoing, whistle **8** accident, calamity, disaster, hightail, run for it, squander, uppercut **9** bombshell, buffeting, collision, dissipate, fisticuff, hurricane, mishandle, take a hike, throw away **10** concussion, gamble away, hit the road, misfortune, run through
a fuse: 4 flip, rage, rant, rave **5** erupt, freak, go ape, storm **6** lose it, see red, seethe **7** explode, flare up, flip out **10** hit the roof
as the wind: 4 gust, howl, waft **5** sough
away: 3 awe **4** stun **5** amaze, crush, floor **6** delete, thrill **7** astound, impress, stupefy, triumph **8** astonish, surprise **9** dumbfound, go over big, overpower
deal a ~: 6 strike
ender: 3 fly, gun, off, out **4** fish, hard, hole, pipe **5** torch
glancing ~: 5 swipe
glancing ~ in cricket: 5 snick
hard ~: 4 gale, gust **5** blast, storm **6** squall **7** cyclone, tempest **9** windstorm
hot and cold: 4 sway, vary **5** hedge, shift, waver **6** falter **9** fluctuate, vacillate
in: 4 come, show **5** enter, pop up **6** appear, arrive, show up, turn up **7** turn out **8** get there
it: 3 err **4** bomb, bust, fail, flop, flub, goof, lose, miss, slip, trip **5** flunk, misdo **6** falter, foul up, goof up, mess up **7** blunder, founder, go under, go wrong, lose out, misstep, screw up, stumble, wash out **8** fall flat, flounder, lay an egg **9** mishandle, mismanage, strike out
karate ~: 4 chop
loud ~: 4 thud, wham, whap **5** thump, whang
low ~: 4 foul **6** insult **9** cheap shot
mark from a ~: 4 weal, welt **6** bruise
off: 5 spurn **6** reject
off steam: 4 rant, rave, vent, yell **6** holler, scream
one's horn: 4 toot
one's own horn: 4 brag, crow **5** boast
open-handed ~: 4 slap
out: 5 douse, dowse, quash **6** exhale, quench **7** smother **9** extirpate **10** extinguish
out of proportion: 7 magnify **8** overplay **10** exaggerate
out of the water: 4 beat, best, rout, stun **5** cream, crush **6** dazzle, defeat, thrash **7** astound, conquer, overrun, stagger, stupefy, trounce **8** astonish, bowl over, vanquish **9** devastate, dumbfound, overpower, overwhelm
over: 3 end **4** pass, wane **5** abate **7** subside **8** decrease, diminish **10** settle down
powerful ~: 4 kayo, swat **5** whomp
sky high: 5 rebut **6** refute **8** disprove, puncture **9** discredit, shoot down **10** invalidate
the joint: 2 go **4** exit **5** leave **6** bow out, cut out, decamp, depart, get out **7** abscond, bail out, pull out, push off **8** check out, hang it up, knock off, light out, pack it in, run out on, shove off, skip town **9** take a hike, walk out on **10** call it a day
the lid off: 4 leak, tell **6** reveal
the whistle: 3 rat **4** blab, halt, sing, tell **5** blame **6** accuse, betray, charge, expose, inform, squeal, turn in
up: 4 boil, bomb, fume, rage, rant, ruin **5** crack, erupt, swell **6** expand, get mad **7** balloon, bristle, enlarge, explode, fill out, inflate, magnify, stretch **8** detonate, dynamite, have a fit, mushroom **9** embroider, intumesce, overstate **10** exaggerate, hit the roof

blow __: 3 fly, off, out 4 away, over 5 a fuse, drier, dryer
blow __ steam: 3 off
blow-__: 3 dry 4 comb, hard 5 drier, dryer
__ blow: 3 at a, low 4 body
Blow: 3 Joe
blow a __: 4 fuse 6 gasket
blow-by-blow: 4 full 8 detailed, thorough 10 disclosure
blower: 3 fan 5 phone 9 hair dryer, telephone 10 ventilator
use the ~: 3 dry
__ blower: 4 snow 5 glass
__-blower: 7 whistle
blowfish: 4 fugu 6 puffer
blowfly: 3 bug 6 insect
Blow, Gabriel, Blow
composer: Cole Porter
blowgun ammo: 4 dart
blowhard: 5 raver 6 gasbag, gascon 8 fanfaron 9 loud-mouth, swaggerer
blowhole: 4 vent
emanation: 5 spout
blow hot and __: 4 cold
blow-in: 8 newcomer, stranger
blowing: 5 windy 6 breezy
hot and cold: 6 fickle 7 erratic, flighty, mutable 8 hesitant, variable, volatile, wavering 9 impulsive, mercurial, undecided 10 capricious, changeable, inconstant, on the fence
__-blowing: 4 mind
Blowing Kisses in the Wind (1991 song)
artist: Paula Abdul
Blowin' in the Wind (song)
artist: Bob Dylan, Peter Paul and Mary, Stevie Wonder
composer: Bob Dylan
blown: 5 spent 8 misspent 10 dissipated
away: 5 in awe 8 overcome
it may be ~: 5 glass
it may be ~ off: 5 steam
over: 9 forgotten
blow off __: 5 steam
blow one's __: 3 top 4 cool, mind 5 stack
blow one's own __: 4 horn
blowout: 4 bash, fete, flat, gala, luau, orgy 5 binge, blast, feast, party, revel, spree 6 spread 7 jubilee, shindig 8 jamboree 9 explosion, festivity 10 detonation
Blow Out (1981 film)
cast: Nancy Allen, John Lithgow, John Travolta
director: Brian De Palma
blowpipe emission: 6 gas jet
blows: 8 fighting
exchange ~: 3 box, row 4 duel, spar, swat 5 argue, brawl, brush, fight, punch, run-in, scrap, whack 6 attack, battle, bicker, combat, go at it, oppose, rumble, take on, tussle 7 assault, contend, contest, grapple, mix it up, quarrel, scuffle, vie with, wage war, wrangle, wrestle 8 do battle 9 altercate, slug it out, square off 10 fisticuffs, tangle with
blowsy: 5 dowdy, ruddy 6 frumpy
blow the __: 4 coop 7 whistle
blow the __ off: 3 lid
blowtorch, use a: 4 fuse, melt, weld
blowup: 3 enl., row 5 blast, burst, photo 6 strife 7 rampage, tantrum 8 argument, eruption, outbreak, upheaval 9 explosion 10 detonation, photograph
cause of a ~: 3 TNT 5 nitro 8 dynamite 9 explosive
Blowup (1966 film)
cast: David Hemmings, Sarah Miles, Vanessa Redgrave
__ Blow Your Horn: 4 Come
blowzy: 3 red 5 messy, ruddy 6 florid, sloppy, unneat, untidy 7 tousled, unkempt 8 red-faced, rubicund, sanguine, slovenly, uncombed 10 bedraggled, disheveled
B.L.S.: 3 deg.
holder: 9 librarian
part: 5 Labor 6 Bureau 10 Statistics
BLT: 8 sandwich
locale: 5 diner 6 eatery 10 restaurant
part of ~: 5 bacon 6 tomato 7 lettuce
spread: 4 mayo
blubber: 3 cry, sob 4 bawl, howl, mewl, pule, wail, weep 6 boohoo, snivel 7 whimper 9 caterwaul, shed tears
remove ~: 6 flench, flense
Blubber
author: Judy Blume
bludgeon: 3 bat, hit, sap 4 bang, beat, club, cosh, mall, maul, whip 5 bully, clout, smite, stick 6 beat on, coerce, cudgel, hector, strike 7 clobber, lambast 8 browbeat, lambaste 9 billy club, blackjack, terrorize, truncheon 10 intimidate, nightstick
__ Blu Dipinto Di Blu: 3 Nel
blue: 3 sad 4 cyan, foul, lewd, mopy, navy, racy, teal 5 azure, bawdy, beryl, color, dirty, mopey, ocean, royal, salty, skyey, spicy 6 cheese, cobalt, cyanic, erotic, ribald, risqué, spicey, vulgar, wicked 7 crushed, naughty, obscene 8 cerulean, indecent, off-color, sapphire 9 saturnine, turquoise 10 chapfallen, indelicate, lascivious, spiritless, suggestive
and yellow: 5 green
baby ~: 3 eye
baby in ~: 3 boy
big ~ marble: 5 Earth
bird: 3 jay 5 heron 7 bunting 8 bluebird
blood: 4 duke, earl, peer 5 count, noble 8 nobleman 9 patrician 10 aristocrat
bloods: 5 elite, lords 8 nobility
British ~ blood: 6 aristo
chips: 5 stock
collar: 5 labor 6 worker
color: 4 anil, aqua, cyan, navy, Nile, teal 5 Alice, azure, perse, slate 6 cobalt, indigo, raisin, violet 7 peacock 8 cerulean, sapphire 9 turquoise 10 aquamarine, periwinkle
combining form: 4 cyan- 5 cyano-
dark ~: 4 navy 5 perse
dye: 4 anil, woad 6 indigo
earn a ~ ribbon: 3 win 7 succeed, triumph
ender: 4 bell, bill, bird, book, coat, fish, gill, nose, stem, weed 5 beard, berry, blood, curls, grass, jeans, point, print, stone 6 bonnet, bottle, jacket, tongue 8 stocking
flag: 5 plant 6 flower
flower: 4 flag, flax, iris 5 bluet, camas 6 camass, indigo, lupine, violet 7 aconite, gentian 8 aconitum, ageratum, boltonia, harebell, larkspur, veronica 9 columbine, ground ivy, hydrangea 10 cornflower, delphinium, periwinkle
greenish ~: 4 aqua, cyan, Nile, teal 7 peacock 9 robin's-egg, turquoise 10 aquamarine
in a ~ funk: 6 morose 7 unhappy 8 dejected 9 depressed 10 melancholy
in heraldry: 5 azure
it turns litmus ~: 6 alkali
jeans: 5 pants 6 denims 9 dungarees
language: 9 profanity
make black and ~: 4 hurt 6 bruise, injure 7 contuse 8 discolor
men in ~: 6 police
mineral: 5 beryl 6 iolite 9 turquoise 10 peacock ore
once in a ~ moon: 6 rarely, seldom 9 sometimes
out of the ~: 6 sudden 8 abruptly, suddenly 10 unexpected
ox: 4 Babe
pigment: 4 bice
plate: 8 luncheon
plate special: 4 meal
plate special spot: 4 café 5 diner 6 eatery
point: 3 cat 7 Siamese
reddish ~: 6 violet
ribbon: 5 prize 6 trophy 7 laurels
slightly ~: 4 racy 6 risqué 10 suggestive
spot on a map: 3 bay, sea 4 lake 5 ocean
sun: 5 O star
talk a ~ streak: 3 yak 5 prate, run on 7 chatter, prattle
the ~: 3 sky
toon: 5 Smurf
true ~: 4 fast 5 loyal
wildflower: 4 flax 5 bluet
wild ~ yonder: 3 sky 5 ether 6 aether
see also gloomy
blue __: 3 cat, flu, fox, gas, gum, ice, jay, law, mud, tit 4 book, bull, chip, crab, flag, funk, jack, line, lips, mass, mold, moon, note, onyx, pike, stem 5 alert, blood, coral, crane, curls, daisy, dicks, flash, giant, goose, grama, heron, jeans, lotus, peter, phlox, point, racer, shark, sheep, shift, state, wavey, whale 6 cheese, marlin, Monday, myrtle, ribbon, spruce, streak
blue __ face: 5 in the
blue __ special: 5 plate
blue-__: 3 leg, red, sky 4 eyed 5 black, green, rinse, water 6 collar, pencil 7 blooded
blue-__ law: 3 sky
__ blue: 3 ice, sky 4 baby, bice, code, cyan, iron, navy, Nile, teal, true 5 Alice, beryl, cadet, china, copen, king's, pearl, royal, slate, steel 6 alkali, cobalt, indigo, powder 7 Antwerp, peacock
__-blue: 4 true
Blue: 3 Ben 4 Vida 5 range 6 iceman
artist: LeAnn Rimes
river: 4 Nile
Blue __: 3 Sky 4 Army, Jean, Moon, Nile, Nose 5 Angel, Bayou, Cross, Denim, Flame, Magic, Money, skies, Swede, Tango 6 Collar, Demons, Grotto, Hawaii, Monday, Shield, Velvet, Voyage 7 Prelude
Blue __ Mountains: 5 Ridge
Blue __, The: 4 Lamp, Veil 5 Angel 6 Dahlia, Hammer, Lagoon 7 Lantern
Blue __ Waltz: 6 Danube
__ Blue: 3 Am I, Big 4 Deep, Navy, N.Y.P.D., True 5 Misty 6 Desert, Jackie
Blue Angel (1960 song)
artist: Roy Orbison
Blue Angels
org.: 3 USN
Blue Angel, The (1930 film)
cast: Marlene Dietrich, Emil Jannings
role: 4 Lola
Blue Bayou (song)
artist: Roy Orbison, Linda Ronstadt
Bluebeard
wife: 6 Fatima
Bluebeard's Castle
composer: Béla Bartók
blueberry: 5 fruit, shrub 8 bilberry
family: 5 heath
relative: *see* heath family shrub
Blueberry Hill (1956 song)
artist: Fats Domino
opener: 6 I found
bluebird residence: 4 nest
blue blood: 4 dame, duke, earl, lady, lord, peer 5 baron, elite 7 marquis 10 aristocrat, noblewoman
org.: 3 DAR
blue-blooded: 5 noble 8 highborn, well-born, well-bred 9 patrician 10 upper-class
blue bloods: 5 elite 8 nobility
bluebonnet: 3 cap, hat 5 plant 6 flower, lupine
bluebottle: 3 bug, fly 5 plant 6 flower, insect
Blue Carbuncle, Sherlock's: 3 gem
Blue Chips (1994 film)
cast: Nick Nolte, Shaquille O'Neal
BlueChoice: 3 HMO
bluecoat: 3 cop 9 policeman 11 policewoman
blue-collar worker: 7 laborer
Blue Cross
alternative: *see* insurance company
offering: 3 HMO
Blue Dahlia, The (1946 film)
cast: William Bendix, Alan Ladd, Veronica Lake
Blue Danube Waltz
composer: Johann Strauss
Blue Demons: 6 DePaul
Blue Devils: 4 Duke
Blue Eagle org.: 3 NRA

Blue Estuaries
poet: Louise Bogan
Blue Eyes Crying in the Rain (1975 song)
artist: Willie Nelson
bluefin: 4 fish, tuna **5** tunny
blue-flowered ground cover: 5 ajuga
blue-glazed pottery: 4 delf **5** delft
__ Blue Gown: 5 Alice
bluegrass: 5 music
genus: 3 poa
instrument: 5 banjo **6** fiddle
Bluegrass State: 3 Ken. **8** Kentucky
blue-gray: 6 steely
blue-green: 4 aqua, cyan **9** turquoise
organism: 4 alga
Blue Grotto
locale: 5 Capri
Blue Hammer, The
author: Ross Macdonald
Blue Hawaii (1961 film)
cast: Joan Blackman, Angela Lansbury, Elvis Presley
bluehead: 4 fish
Blue Hen State: 3 Del. **8** Delaware
__ blue heron: 5 great **6** little
Blue II
painter: Joan Miró
blue in the __: 4 face
bluejacket: 3 gob, tar **4** salt **6** seaman **7** jack-tar, mariner
Blue Jackets: 3 six **4** team
home: 8 Columbus
org.: 3 NHL
rival: *see* hockey team
blue jay: 4 bird
topper: 5 crest
Bluejays: 9 Creighton
Blue Jays: 3 ten **4** team
home: 7 Ontario, Toronto
org.: 3 ALE, MLB
rival: *see* baseball team
Blue Jean (1984 song)
artist: David Bowie
Blue Knight, The dog: 3 Leo
Blue Lagoon, The (1980 film)
cast: Christopher Atkins, William Daniels, Leo McKern, Brooke Shields
Blue Lantern, The
author: Colette
__ Blue Line, The: 4 Thin
Blue Meridian
author: Peter Matthiessen
blue mold: 6 fungus
Blue Monday (1957 song)
artist: Fats Domino
Blue Money (1971 song)
artist: Van Morrison
Blue Monster, The: 5 Doral
Blue Moon: 4 Odom, song
composer: Lorenz Hart, Richard Rodgers
blue moon, like a: 4 rare
Blue Nile: 5 river
explorer: 5 Baker
locale: 5 Sudan **8** Ethiopia
source: 4 Tana **5** Tsana
bluenose: 4 prig **5** priss, prude **6** censor **7** Puritan **9** formalist, nice Nelly
blue-nose: 4 prim **6** prissy **7** prudish **8** priggish **10** censorious
Blue on Blue (1963 song)
artist: Bobby Vinton
blue-pencil: 4 edit **5** alter, amend, emend **6** censor, delete, excise, redact, revise **7** expunge **9** expurgate
notation: 4 dele, stet **5** caret
wielder: 6 editor
Blue Plate Special
author: Damon Runyon
blue point: 3 cat **5** felid **6** feline **7** Siamese
blueprint: 4 plan **5** chart, draft, model **6** design, layout, scheme, sketch **7** diagram, formula, outline, picture, specify **8** game plan, strategy, time line **9** floor plan, visual aid
detail: 4 door, spec **5** stair **6** closet, window
blue-ribbon: 4 A-one **9** first-rate
...blue ribbon __: 4 on it
__ Blue Ribbon: 5 Pabst
blue-ribbon awarder: 4 fair
blues: 3 woe **4** funk, jazz, mood **5** angst, dolor, dumps, genre, gloom, mopes, music **6** misery, sorrow **7** anguish, despair, sadness **8** doldrums, glumness **9** dejection, heartache, moodiness **10** depression, heavy heart, melancholy, woefulness
baby ~: 4 eyes, orbs
guitarist: 4 King **6** B.B. King **7** Diddley **9** Bo Diddley
have the ~: 4 mope **5** brood
rhythm and ~: 5 music
singing the ~: 3 low **4** down **6** morose **8** downcast **9** sorrowful
street: 5 Basin, Beale
__ blues: 4 baby
Blues: 3 six **4** team
home: 7 St. Louis
milieu: 3 ice **4** rink
org.: 3 NHL
rival: *see* hockey team
sport: 6 hockey
Blues __ Night: 5 in the
__ Blues: 3 Yer **4** Navy **5** Miami, Moody, Paris, Po' Boy, Sugar **6** Biloxi, Outlaw, Wabash
Blues Brothers, The (1980 film)
cast: Dan Aykroyd, John Belushi, Cab Calloway
director: John Landis
__ Blue Sea: 4 Deep
Blues for Mister Charlie
author: James Baldwin
blue shark: 4 fish
Blues in the Night
composer: Harold Arlen, Johnny Mercer
second word of ~: 4 mama
Blue Skies
composer: Irving Berlin
Blue Skies (1946 film)
cast: Fred Astaire, Joan Caulfield, Bing Crosby
blue-sky __: 3 law
Blue Sky (1994 film)
cast: Powers Boothe, Tommy Lee Jones, Jessica Lange
bluesman's lick: 4 riff
Blues Suite
choreographer: Alvin Ailey
Bluest Eye, The
author: Toni Morrison
bluestocking: 7 egghead
__ blue streak: 5 talk a
Blue Suede Shoes (1956 song)
artist: Carl Perkins, Elvis Presley
bluet: 5 plant **6** flower
Blue Tail Fly
artist: Burl Ives
Blue Tango
composer: Leroy Anderson, Mitchell Parish
__ blue terrier: 5 Kerry
Blue Triangle org.: 4 YWCA
Blue Velvet (1963 song)
artist: Bobby Vinton
Blue Velvet (1986 film)
cast: Laura Dern, Dennis Hopper, Kyle MacLachlan, Isabella Rossellini
director: David Lynch
Blue, Vida
sport: 8 baseball
Blue Voyage
author: Conrad Aiken
bluff: 3 lie **4** fake, fool, hill, jive, ruse, sham, snow **5** blunt, cliff, feign, feint, frank, put on, ridge, spoof, trick **6** abrupt, assume, candid, deceit, delude, direct, humbug, take in, threat **7** bluster, deceive, fake out, finesse, mislead, pretend, pretext **8** headland, mountain, pretense, psych out, simulate **9** deception, disinform, four-flush, outspoken, precipice **10** false front, forthright, from the hip, prominence, promontory, subterfuge, unreticent
__ Bluff: 4 Pine **7** Coogan's
bluffer: 4 fake **5** fraud **8** imposter, impostor **9** hypocrite
bluing: 6 bleach
Blume in Love (1973 film)
cast: Susan Anspach, Kris Kristofferson, George Segal
director: Paul Mazursky
Blume, Judy: 6 writer
work: Blubber
Deenie
Double Fudge
Forever
Freckle Juice
Fudge-a-mania
Iggie's House
The Pain and the Great One
Smart Women
Summer Sisters
Superfudge
Then Again, Maybe I Won't
Tiger Eyes
Wifey
blunder: 3 dud, err **4** bomb, bust, flop, flub, goof, lose, loss, miss, muff, slip, trip **5** boner, botch, error, fault, fluff, flunk, gaffe, lapse, lurch, wrong **6** barney, blow it, boo-boo, bungle, defeat, falter, fiasco, foozle, foul up, fumble, goof up, howler, mishap, muddle, slip-up, totter, turkey **7** blooper, debacle, faux pas, founder, go under, go wrong, misstep, mistake, screwup, stumble, washout **8** downfall, fall flat, flounder, lay an egg **9** gaucherie, indecorum, mishandle, mismanage, oversight, strike out **10** inaccuracy
social ~: 5 gaffe **6** bêtise **7** faux pas
blunderbore: 4 ogre
blunderbuss: 3 oaf **4** boor **5** rifle **6** musket
blunderer: 2 ox **3** oaf **4** lout **5** klutz, looby **6** lummox
blundering: 6 clumsy **7** awkward, unadept **8** bungling, cloddish, inexpert, lubberly, tactless, unsubtle **9** maladroit
blunt: 3 sag, sap **4** curt, dull, flag, rude, tire, wane **5** allay, bluff, brusk, frank, gruff, plain, short, stark, terse, vocal **6** abrupt, benumb, candid, dampen, deaden, direct, honest, impair, obtund, obtuse, reduce, shrink, soften, weaken **7** brusque, deplete, exhaust, fatigue, mollify, rounded, uncivil **8** edgeless, enervate, enfeeble, impolite, mitigate, outfront, straight, succinct, tactless, undercut, unsubtle **9** attenuate, downright, outspoken, pointless, trenchant, undermine, water down **10** debilitate, devitalize, forthright, free-spoken, from the hip, point-blank, to the point, ungracious, unmediated, unpolished, unreserved, unreticent
combining form: 5 ambly- **6** amblyo-
end: 4 stub
Blunt: 5 Emily
blunted: 4 dull
bluntly: 7 up front **10** point-blank
bluntness: 7 honesty
Blunt, Wilfrid: 6 writer **7** British
blur: 3 dim, fog **4** blot, daze, fade, mist, spot **5** bedim, befog, blear, cloud, fog up, muddy, smear, stain, sully, taint **6** darken, fuzz up, smudge **7** becloud, besmear, dimness, obscure **8** discolor, haziness **9** adumbrate
blurb: 2 ad **4** puff **5** promo **6** review **9** promotion, publicity, puff piece, sound bite
blurred: 3 dim **4** hazy **5** blear, foggy, fuzzy, misty, muzzy, vague **6** bleary, cloudy **9** unfocused **10** indistinct
blurry: 4 dark, hazy **5** blear, dusky, faded, fuzzy, mirky, murky, muted **6** bleary, fogged **7** shadowy **9** unfocused **10** indistinct, out of focus
blurt out: 4 blab, blat **5** utter **6** betray **7** exclaim, lay bare, let slip
blush: 4 pink, wine **5** color, flush, rouge **6** makeup, redden **8** cosmetic, rosiness **9** reddening, ruddiness
first ~: 7 morning
make ~: 5 abash, shame **6** praise **9** embarrass **10** compliment
blush __: 4 wine
blusher: 5 paint, rouge **8** cosmetic
blushing: 3 coy, red **4** pink, rosy **5** ruddy, timid **6** demure, modest **7** ashamed, bashful, flushed
bluster: 3 cow, gas **4** bawl, brag, crow, flap, rage, rant, rave, roar **5** bluff, storm, swash **6** bellow, hector, hot air **7** bombast, bravado, clatter, show off, swagger, talk big, tempest **8** browbeat **9** arrogance, gasconade **10** intimidate
blusterer: 6 gasbag **7** windbag
blustering: 4 loud, wild **5** windy **6** raging **7** huffish, rampant **9** turbulent

blustery: **3** raw **4** wild **5** windy **6** breezy, raging, stormy **7** furious **9** turbulent
Bluth: **3** Don
Bluto: **3** gob, tar **4** salt **6** sailor
 to Popeye: **5** rival
blvd.: **2** st. **3** ave. **4** pkwy.
__ Blvd.: **6** Sunset
Bly: **6** Nellie, Robert
Blyden: **5** Larry
Blyleven, Bert
 sport: **8** baseball
Blynken shipmate: **3** Nod **6** Wynken
Bly, Robert: **6** writer
Blyth: **3** Ann **4** city, town
 locale: **7** England
Blythe: **6** Danner
 daughter: **7** Gwyneth
Blyton: **4** Enid
__ B. Mayer: **5** Louis
BME awarder: **3** MIT
BMI
 rival: **5** ASCAP
BMOC: **3** VIP **5** celeb
 house: **4** frat
 part: **3** Big, Man **6** Campus
BMT
 kin: **3** IRT
 locale: **3** NYC
BMW: **3** car **4** auto **6** German, import **10** automobile
 alternative: **2** MG **3** Jag **4** Audi **5** Lexus
 part: **5** Motor, Works **8** Bavarian
B'nai B'rith
 org.: **3** ADL
bn.com
 rival: **6** Amazon
__-bo: **3** tae
Bo: **5** Derek, Gritz **7** Diddley, Hopkins, Jackson, Svenson
B&O: **2** RR
 employee: **4** engr.
 part of ~: **4** Ohio **9** Baltimore
 stop: **3** sta., stn.
B.O.: **9** box office
 buy: **3** tkt. **6** ticket
 sign: **3** SRO
boa: **4** wrap **5** scarf, snake, stole, throw **6** animal **7** reptile **9** neckpiece
 relative: *see* snake
boar: **3** hog, pig **5** swine **6** animal, tusker **9** razorback
 ender: **4** fish **5** hound
 mate: **3** sow
 tooth: **4** tusk
__ boar: **4** wild
board: **4** eats, food, jury, lath, meal, sign, slab, slat **5** catch, get on, hop on, lodge, meals, panel, plank, put up, strip, table **6** bureau, harbor, take in, ticket, timber **7** aliment, cabinet, care for, climb on, council, emplane, enplane, entrain, harbour, quarter **8** trustees, victuals **9** committee, directors, syndicate **10** commission, department, executives, management, provisions
 African ~ game: **3** bao
 amateur on a ~: **5** ho-dad
 bed ~: **4** slat
 bring on ~: **4** hire **6** employ, engage
 bulletin ~ material: **4** cork, felt
 by the ~: **4** gone
 cleaner: **6** eraser
 clean the ~: **4** wash, wipe **5** erase
 clear the cribbage ~: **5** unpeg
 covering: **5** emery, paint, stain **6** enamel **7** shellac, varnish
 drawing ~ original: **5** plan A **9** blueprint
 emery ~: **4** file
 ender: **4** room, walk **7** sailing
 fasten to a ~: **4** tack **6** staple
 flight ~: **4** sked **5** sched. **8** schedule
 flight ~ datum: **3** ETA, ETD
 game: **4** Clue, Risk **5** chess, pente, shogi, Sorry **7** Careers, pachisi, Reversi **8** checkers, Monopoly, Scrabble **10** backgammon
 game need: **3** man **4** dice **5** piece
 get on ~: **6** embark **7** enplane, entrain
 holder: **4** nail, vise **5** screw **8** sawhorse
 imperfection: **4** hole, knot **5** crack
 informally: **5** hop on
 insert: **3** peg
 Japanese ~ game: **5** shogi
 lodging on ~: **5** cabin **9** stateroom
 material: **4** pine, wood **5** emery **6** timber
 member: **3** CEO, dir. **4** exec, pres., suit **6** regent **7** trustee **9** executive
 membership: **4** seat
 narrow ~: **4** lath, slat
 not on ~: **6** ashore
 on ~: **4** here **6** with us **7** present
 put on ~: **4** lade, load, ship, stow
 review ~: **5** panel **7** inquest **9** committee
 room and ~: **4** keep **7** lodging, pension
 spiritualist's ~: **5** Ouija
 starter: **3** box, cup, key, lap, lee, mop, out, peg, sea **4** back, base, bill, buck, call, card, clap, clip, cork, dart, dash, duck, fall, fire, foot, free, hard, head, knee, mill, mold, over, sail, ship, side, sign, snow, star, surf, tail, wall, wash **5** above, barge, black, bread, chalk, chess, fiber, flash, floor, liner, match, paper, paste, press, punch, scale, score, skate, sound, story, straw **6** beaver, bridge, center, cradle, finger, mother, paddle, splash, spring, string, switch, teeter **7** checker, plaster, scraper, scratch, shuffle, weather **8** particle **9** container
 trim a ~: **5** resaw
 up: **5** cover **6** batten
 went off the ~: **4** dove
 work: **6** agenda
board __: **4** feet, foot, game, room, rule, side **5** check **7** measure
__ board: **3** bed, low **4** arch, hack, half, high, hunt, jute, lear, lens, snow, tilt, tote **5** altar, angle, bilge, broom, draft, emery, facia, idiot, layer, otter, Ouija, slant, table **6** batter, comber, county, cradle, diving, fascia, gypsum, leader, ledger, louver, Malibu, preset, school, scrive, signal, window **7** Bristol, circuit, control, cutting, drawing, ironing, molding, running, tilting, warping
__-board: **3** off **4** call
__ Board: **3** Big **6** Boogie
__-Board: **3** Peg
boarder: **5** guest, liver **6** lessee, lodger, tenant
 starter: **4** sail, snow, surf **5** skate
boarding
 device: **4** ramp **9** gangplank
 house: **5** B and B **7** lodging **8** lodgment
 house rental: **4** room
 place: **4** dock, pier, stop **5** wharf **7** airport, station **8** terminal
 school: **4** acad., prep **7** academy
 starter: **4** sail, snow, surf **5** skate
boarding __: **4** pass, ramp **5** house, party **6** school
boarding house __: **5** reach
boardlike: **5** rigid, stiff **6** wooden
Board of Elections concern: **6** ballot
__ Board of Trade: **7** Chicago
boardroom display: **5** graph
boards: **5** stage **6** lumber **7** theater, theatre
 gone by the ~: **3** out **5** dated, fusty, hoary, passé, stale **6** démodé, old hat **7** archaic, outworn **8** obsolete, outdated, outmoded **9** forgotten, moss-grown, out-of-date **10** antiquated, superseded
 tread the ~: **3** act **4** play **7** perform
boardwalk: **9** promenade
 section: **5** plank
 structure: **4** pier
Boardwalk buy: **5** hotel, house
Boas: **5** Franz
boast: **3** own **4** brag, crow, tout **5** claim, enjoy, gloat, pride, spout, swash, vaunt **6** flaunt, parade **7** bravado, lay it on, possess, show off, swagger, talk big, trumpet **9** gasconade **10** aggrandize, exaggerate, grandstand
boastful: **3** big **4** smug, vain **5** cocky, gassy, proud, windy **6** snooty **7** crowing, fustian, haughty, pompous, stuck-up **8** arrogant, bragging, snobbish, vaunting **9** bigheaded, bombastic, conceited, egotistic, strutting **10** big-talking, swaggering, triumphant
 one: **6** crower, gasbag, gascon **7** showoff **8** braggart, fanfaron **9** loudmouth
 what the ~ blow: **5** smoke
boastfulness: **3** ego **4** wind **6** vanity **7** bravado, conceit, ego trip **9** arrogance, gasconade
boat: **3** ark, dau, dow, gig, hoy, tub, tug **4** Argo, bark, brig, dhow, dory, hulk, junk, prao, prau, proa, punt, raft, scow, ship, yawl **5** barge, canoe, craft, ferry, float, kayak, ketch, liner, oiler, scull, shell, skiff, sloop, smack, umiak, xebec, yacht, zebec **6** argosy, barque, bateau, bireme, caique, carack, carvel, cutter, dinghy, drakar, dugout, galley, launch, lugger, packet, sampan, tanker, tender, trader, vessel, whaler, wherry, zebeck **7** caravel, carrack, chebeck, clipper, coaster, collier, coracle, corsair, cruiser, dredger, felucca, frigate, galleon, gondola, lighter, monitor, pinnace, pontoon, steamer, trawler, trireme, vehicle **8** car ferry, corvette, dahabeah, fireship, flagship, ironclad, man-of-war, runabout, schooner, trimaran **9** catamaran, destroyer, freighter, hydrofoil, minelayer, oil tanker, outrigger, privateer, steamship, submarine, troopship **10** barkentine, battleship, brigantine, Hovercraft, hydroplane, icebreaker, ocean liner, quadrireme, supply ship, tea clipper, watercraft, windjammer
 aluminum ~: **5** canoe
 animal ~: **3** ark
 any ~: **3** her, she
 Arab ~: **4** dhow **7** felucca **8** dahabeah
 backbone: **4** keel
 bark ~: **5** canoe
 bayou ~: **6** bateau
 big ~: **4** ship **5** liner, yacht **7** steamer **9** freighter, steamship
 canal ~: **5** barge **7** gondola
 Chinese ~: **4** junk **6** sampan
 clumsy ~: **3** ark, tub **4** hulk, scow
 coal carrier ~: **7** collier
 combining form: **5** scaph- **6** scapho-
 cruise ~: **5** liner **7** steamer **9** steamship
 dip out a ~: **4** bail
 dispatch ~: **5** aviso
 don't rock the ~: **3** bow **4** mind **5** agree, yield **6** accede, accept, assent, comply, give in, relent, submit **7** go along, respect **8** play ball **9** acquiesce, cooperate **10** come around
 Dutch fishing ~: **6** dogger
 East Indies freight ~: **5** oolak
 ender: **3** man, men **4** bill, lift, load **5** house, swain
 end of a ~: **3** aft **5** stern **6** astern
 Eskimo ~: **5** kayak, umiak
 fast ~: **6** cutter **9** hydrofoil, speedboat **10** Hovercraft, hydroplane
 fishing ~: **4** dory **5** smack **6** lugger, whaler **7** coaster, trawler
 flat-bottomed ~: **4** dory, junk, punt, raft, scow **5** barge, float **7** lighter, pontoon
 follower: **4** wake
 for cars: **5** ferry
 front of a ~: **3** bow **4** prow **7** forward
 Greek ~: **6** galley
 harbor ~: **3** tug
 hazard: **3** fog, ice **4** berg, floe, gale, reef, snag **5** shoal **7** typhoon **9** hurricane
 hold a ~ steady: **4** dock **5** lie to **6** anchor
 Indian ~: **5** canoe **9** birchbark
 Indonesian ~: **4** prao, prau, proa
 jolly ~: **4** yawl
 kitchen: **6** galley
 lateen-rigged ~: **4** dhow **6** carvel **7** caravel, felucca
 merchant ~: **6** argosy, carack, trader **7** carrack, clipper, galleon **8** schooner **9** freighter **10** brigantine, tea clipper
 miss the ~: **3** err **4** fail **7** mistake **8** go astray
 motor ~: **6** launch
 narrow ~: **5** canoe, kayak, skiff

9 outrigger
oared ~: 3 gig 4 dory 5 scull, shell, skiff 6 caique, dinghy, dugout, sampan, wherry 9 outrigger
on a slow ~ to China: 4 asea 5 at sea
paddled ~: 5 canoe, kayak, umiak
pantry: 5 cuddy
part: 4 deck, helm, hold, hull, prow 5 cabin, hatch, stern 6 gunnel, tiller 7 gunwale 10 figurehead
patrol ~: 5 aviso
pea-green ~ passenger: 3 owl 8 pussycat
person: 7 refugee
pirate ~: 7 corsair 9 privateer 10 Jolly Roger
pleasure ~: 5 yacht 7 cruiser 8 trimaran 9 catamaran
poled ~: 4 punt, raft 5 float 7 gondola
portable ~: 5 canoe, kayak, umiak
propeller: 3 oar 4 sail 5 motor 6 engine, paddle
PT ~: 7 warship
racing ~: 5 scull, shell, yacht
Red Sea ~: 4 dhow
ritzy ~: 5 yacht
river ~: 4 raft 5 barge, canoe, ferry 8 car ferry
rock the ~: 5 rebel, upset 6 revolt
Roman ~: 6 bireme, galley 7 trireme 10 quadrireme
round ~: 7 coracle
runway: 4 ramp
sailing ~: 5 yacht 7 clipper 10 barkentine, tea clipper, windjammer
Scottish fishing ~: 6 baldie
secure a ~: 4 dock, moor 6 anchor
silt clearer ~: 7 dredger
single-masted ~: 5 sloop 6 cutter 8 dahabeah
small ~: 4 dory, yawl 5 canoe, skiff 7 coracle, rowboat 8 sailboat 9 outrigger
South Seas ~: 4 prao, prau, proa 9 outrigger
square-ended ~: 4 pram
square-rigged ~: 4 bark, brig 6 barque
starter: 3 air, cat, fly, gun, ice, pig, row, tow, tug 4 bull, cock, fire, flat, fold, john, keel, life, long, sail, show, surf, work 5 ferry, house, jolly, motor, power, river, sauce, speed, steam, whale 6 cockle, paddle
that ~: 3 her, she
three-masted ~: 5 xebec, zebec 6 zebeck 7 clipper 10 tea clipper
trip: 4 sail 6 cruise, voyage
two-masted ~: 4 yawl 5 ketch
underwater ~: 3 sub 9 submarine
wake: 4 wash
with square sails: 4 junk 8 dahabeah
see also ship
boat __: 3 bed, bug 4 deck, hook, lily, nail, neck, ramp, tail 5 patch, spike, train 6 people
__ boat: 3 jet 5 gravy 6 flying 7 torpedo
__ Boat: 4 Show
boater: 3 hat, lid 7 yachter, yachtie 8 straw hat 9 yachtsman 11 yachtswoman
boathouse gear: 3 oar 6 paddle
Boating
painter: Édouard Manet
boatman: 3 gob 6 sailor, sea dog 7 jack tar
river: 5 Volga
water ~: 3 bug 6 insect
__ Boat Song, The: 6 Banana
__ Boat, The: 4 Love, Open 6 Golden
__ boat to China: 4 slow
boatyard: 5 basin
Boaz
father: 6 Salmon
son: 4 Obed
wife: 4 Ruth
bob: 3 jig, wag 4 clip, coif, duck, jerk, jump, skip, toss, trim 5 float, money 6 bounce, curtsy, hairdo, jiggle, joggle, jounce, lollop, wabble, wobble 7 curtsey, pendant, shorten 8 coiffure, cut short, shilling 9 hairstyle, oscillate
ender: 3 cat 4 sled, stay, tail 5 white
fishing bait: 3 dap, dib
no siree ~: 3 nay
plumb ~: 6 weight
starter: 3 ear, ski 4 skee
up: 4 rise 6 appear, emerge
__ bob: 5 Dutch, plumb
Bob: 3 Rae 4 Abel, arum, Dole, Goen, Hope, Kane, Lind, Tway, Vila, Weir, Wynn 5 Clark, Cousy, Crane, Dishy, Dylan, Estes, Fosse, Hayes, Lemon, Lilly, Luman, Saget, Seger, Smith, Welch, Wills 6 Barker, Beamon, Brenly, Costas, Crosby, Dahlin, Denver, Eberly, Feller, Geldof, Gibson, Goalby, Greene, Griese, Gunton, Kerrey, Knight, Lanier, Mackie, Marley, McAdoo, Newman, Pettit, Uecker, Watson 7 Balaban, Elliott, Eubanks, Hartley, Hoskins, Keeshan, Kelljan, Mathias, Montana, Newhart, Seagren 8 Carlisle, Cummings, Rafelson, Richards, Woodward
bob and __: 5 weave
Bob and __: 3 Ray
Bobbettes
song: Mr. Lee (1957)
__ Bobbidi Boo: 7 Bibbidi
Bobbie: 6 Gentry
bobbin: 5 spool
in Britain: 4 pirn
lace: 5 Cluny
bobble: 3 err 4 flub, muff 5 botch, fluff 6 fumble, jiggle, joggle, jounce, mess up 7 mistake, screw up
Bobbsey twin: 3 Nan 4 Bert 7 Flossie, Freddie
bobby: 3 cop 6 copper, lawman 9 policeman
follower: 5 soxer
stick: 4 cosh
bobby __: 3 pin, sox 4 calf 5 socks, soxer 7 dazzler
Bobby: 3 Day, Orr, Van, Vee 4 Bare, Flay, Hart, Hebb, Hull 5 Bloom, Breen, Brown, Darin, Doerr, Ewing, Helms, Jones, Layne, Lewis, Mauch, Rahal, Riggs, Seale, Short, Troup, Unser 6 Fuller, Knight, Rydell, Vinton, Womack 7 Allison, Bonilla, Fischer, Freeman, Hackett, Pickett, Russell, Sherman, Thomson 8 Caldwell, Driscoll, Farrelly, McFerrin, Mitchell 9 Goldsboro
__ Bobby McGee: 5 Me and
Bobby's Girl (1962 song)
artist: Marcie Blane
Bobby Shaftoe's gone __: 5 to sea
bobby-sock
relative: 6 anklet
bobby-soxer: 4 girl, miss, teen
dance: 3 hop
wow a ~: 5 croon
Bob & Carol & Ted & Alice (1969 film)
cast: Dyan Cannon, Robert Culp, Elliott Gould, Natalie Wood
bobcat: 4 lynx 5 felid 6 animal, feline 8 toboggan
relative: ***see*** feline
Bobcat: 3 car 4 auto 7 Mercury 10 automobile, Goldthwait
Bob Newhart Show, The (CBS sitcom)
cast: Peter Bonerz (Jerry Robinson)
Bill Daily (Howard Borden)
Bob Newhart (Bob Hartley)
Suzanne Pleshette (Emily Hartley)
Marcia Wallace (Carol Kester)
producer: MTM
setting: Chicago, Illinois
trains: 3 els
Bobo: 6 Newsom
bobolink: 4 bird 7 ortolan
relative: 6 oriole
Bob Roberts (1992 film)
cast: Tim Robbins
Bob's __ Boy: 3 Big
bobsledding: 5 sport
track: 5 chute
bobstay: 3 rod 4 rope 5 chain
bobtail: 5 horse 6 equine
__ Bob Thornton: 5 Billy
bobwhite: 4 bird 5 colin, quail
family: 5 covey
bocane: 5 dance
Boca Raton: 4 city, town
locale: 7 Florida
Boccaccio, Giovanni: 4 poet 7 Italian
work: Decameron
boccie: 4 game
boce: 4 fish
Bocelli: 6 Andrea
Bochco: 6 Steven
Bochner: 4 Hart 5 Lloyd
bock: 4 beer 5 drink 8 beverage
alternative: 3 ale 5 lager, stout
Bock: 5 Jerry
Bock's __: 3 Car
bod: 4 form 5 build 6 figure 8 physique
bodacious
see wonderful
bode: 5 augur 6 waited 7 bespeak, betoken, point to, portend, presage, promise, signify 8 foreshow, foretell 9 foretoken 10 foreshadow
bodega: 7 grocery 8 wine shop 9 warehouse
locale: 6 barrio
owner: 6 grocer
patron: 5 señor 6 Latina, Latino, señora
bodement: 4 omen 8 prophecy
Bodenheim, Maxwell: 4 poet
bodice: 3 top 6 basque, blouse 9 dress part
ripper: 7 romance
short-sleeved ~: 6 angiya
__-bodied: 4 able, full
__-bodied seaman: 4 able
bodies: 6 people, somata
bodiless: 9 lightsome, spiritual 10 discarnate, immaterial, impalpable, intangible, unphysical
bodily: 4 real 5 fully 6 wholly 7 en masse, organic, sensual, somatic, totally 8 as a group, corporal, entirely, personal, physical 9 corporeal 10 altogether, completely, in the flesh
bodily __: 4 harm
Bodily Harm
author: Margaret Atwood
__-boding: 3 ill
bodkin: 3 awl 4 pick 6 dagger, needle 7 hairpin 8 stiletto
__ bodkins: 3 ods
Bodoni: 4 font 8 typeface
body: 3 mob, set, sum 4 band, bulk, crux, form, gist, mass, soma, sort, soul, team, zest 5 being, build, corps, frame, group, human, party, shape, suite, torso, total, troop, trunk 6 corpus, entity, figure, legion, makeup, matter, mortal, person 7 anatomy, chassis, company, essence 8 assembly, fuselage, majority, organism, physique 9 gathering, substance 10 contingent, individual, membership, opera omnia
auto ~: 7 chassis
build: 5 frame 8 physique
celestial ~: 3 orb 4 moon, star 5 comet 6 planet, sphere
check: 5 frisk
combining form: 4 -soma, -some 5 somat- 6 somato-
ender: 4 sera, surf, work 5 guard 6 fluids 7 builder
fluid: 5 blood, lymph, serum 6 saliva
governing ~: 5 board, House, panel 6 Senate 7 council 8 Congress, trustees 9 directors 10 commission, executives, management, parliament
heat: 5 fever 7 pyrexia
language: 4 pose 5 shrug 7 gesture, posture
main ~: 4 text
of an organism: 4 soma
of knowledge: 4 lore 6 mythos 7 science 9 tradition
of laws: 4 code 5 canon
of principles: 5 ethic, ethos
of soldiers: 4 army, unit 5 troop 6 cohort, legion 9 battalion
of water: 3 bay, sea 4 cove, lake, loch, pond, pool, tarn 5 inlet, ocean, sound 6 harbor, lagoon
of work: 6 oeuvre
part: 3 arm, ear, eye, hip, jaw, leg, lip, rib, toe 4 back, bone, brow, calf, chin, face, foot, gums, hair, hand, head, heel, iris, knee, lens, limb, lung, nape, neck, nose, pate, shin, skin, ulna, vein 5 ankle, aorta, belly, blood,

brain, cheek, chest, colon, digit, elbow, femur, flesh, gland, heart, ileum, ilium, liver, lymph, molar, mouth, nares, navel, organ, pupil, scalp, shank, skull, spine, thigh, thumb, tibia, tooth, torso, trunk, uvula, velum, wrist **6** armpit, artery, biceps, canine, carpus, coccyx, cornea, eyelid, fibula, finger, gullet, instep, kidney, larynx, marrow, muscle, neuron, palate, pelvis, pinkie, retina, sacrum, septum, spleen, tarsus, temple, tendon, thorax, throat, thymus, tongue **7** abdomen, adenoid, adrenal, cranium, cuticle, deltoid, eardrum, eyeball, eyebrow, forearm, hipbone, ischium, knuckle, medulla, midriff, nostril, pharynx, scapula, sternum, stomach, synapse, thyroid, trachea, triceps **8** appendix, backbone, cerebrum, clavicle, forehead, ganglion, inner ear, ligament, mandible, pancreas, shinbone, shoulder, skeleton, voice box, windpipe **9** capillary, cartilage, cheekbone, corpuscle, diaphragm, esophagus, extremity, funny bone, hamstring, intestine, lymph node, middle ear, pituitary, thighbone, umbilicus, vocal cord **10** Adam's apple, breastbone, cerebellum, collarbone, epiglottis, optic nerve, quadriceps, spinal cord
politic: **4** weal **5** state **6** nation, people **10** population
political ~: **4** pact **5** union **8** alliance
rhythm: **5** pulse
shop: **3** gym **6** garage
starter: **3** any **4** anti, busy, home, some **5** black, every
body __: **3** art, rub **4** blow, drop, mike, plan, post, shop, slam, suit, type, wave **5** check, clock, image, press, shirt, track **6** artist, double, rhythm **7** bolster, English, politic
body-__: **4** surf **7** builder
__ body: **4** Barr, cell, gray, grey, main **5** basal, Golgi, polar, stake **6** astral **7** student
...body __ body...: **5** meet a
Body __: **4** Heat **6** Double
Body Artist, The
author: Don DeLillo
bodybuilder: **5** he-man
bane: **4** flab
exercise: **4** curl **5** shrug, squat
goal: **5** brawn **8** strength
iteration: **3** rep
material: **4** iron
need: **7** trainer **8** barbells, Nautilus **9** dumbbells
pride: **3** abs **4** pecs, quad, tone **5** delts **6** biceps, muscle **7** triceps **8** physique
Body Count (1987 film)
cast: Ice-T
Body Double (1984 film)
cast: Melanie Griffith, Craig Wasson
director: Brian De Palma
bodyguard: **6** escort **8** defender, henchman, watchdog, watchman **9** custodian, protector
Body Heat (1981 film)
cast: Richard Crenna, William Hurt, Kathleen Turner
character: **3** Ned
director: Lawrence Kasdan
Body Language (1982 song)
artist: Queen
__ body meet...: **3** If a
Body of Lies (2008 film)
cast: Russell Crowe, Leonardo DiCaprio
__-body plane: **4** wide
body-shop
job: **4** dent **6** repair
offering: **6** loaner
body-slamming gp.: **3** WWF
Body Snatcher, The
author: Robert Louis Stevenson
Boeing: **7** William
product: **3** jet **5** plane
rival: **6** Airbus **8** Lockheed
Boeing Boeing (1965 film)
cast: Tony Curtis, Jerry Lewis
Boeotia neighbor: **6** Attica
seaport: **6** Delium
Boer: **9** Afrikaner
Boer __: **3** War
Boesky: **4** Ivan
Boesman and Lena
author: Athol Fugard
Boetticher: **4** Budd
boff: **6** strike, wallop **10** belly laugh
boffo: **5** socko **8** smashing **9** first-rate
review: **4** rave
show: **3** hit **5** smash
Bofors guns: **3** AAs
bog: **3** fen **4** mire, quag, sink **5** marsh, swamp **6** morass, slough **7** lowland, wetland **8** quagmire, wetlands **9** backwater, marshland
combining form: **4** helo-
down: **4** mire, slow **6** detain, hold up, slow up **7** set back **8** slow down
fruit: **9** cranberry
fuel: **4** peat
bog __: **3** oak, ore **4** hole, moss **6** myrtle, turtle
__ bog: **4** peat
boga: **4** fish
Bogan, Louise: **4** poet **6** writer
Bogarde, Dirk: **5** actor
Bogart: **4** Paul **8** Humphrey
Bogart, Humphrey: **5** actor
film: Action in the North Atlantic (1943)
The African Queen (1951, AA)
All Through the Night (1942)
Angels With Dirty Faces (1938)
The Barefoot Contessa (1954)
Beat the Devil (1954)
The Big Sleep (1946)
Black Legion (1936)
Brother Orchid (1940)
Bullets or Ballots (1936)
The Caine Mutiny (1954)
Casablanca (1942)
Dark Passage (1947)
Dark Victory (1939)
Dead End (1937)
Deadline U.S.A. (1952)
Dead Reckoning (1947)
The Desperate Hours (1955)
The Enforcer (1951)
The Harder They Fall (1956)
High Sierra (1941)
In a Lonely Place (1950)
Key Largo (1948)
Kid Galahad (1937)
The Left Hand of God (1955)
The Maltese Falcon (1941)
Marked Woman (1937)
The Oklahoma Kid (1939)
The Roaring Twenties (1939)
Sabrina (1954)
Sahara (1943)
Stand-In (1937)
They Drive by Night (1940)
To Have and Have Not (1944)
The Treasure of the Sierra Madre (1948)
spouse: Lauren Bacall
Bogdanovich, Peter: **8** director
film: The Last Picture Show (1971)
Mask (1985)
Nickelodeon (1976)
Noises Off (1992)
Paper Moon (1973)
Saint Jack (1979)
Targets (1968)
Texasville (1990)
They All Laughed (1981)
What's Up, Doc? (1972)
bogey: **3** UFO **4** ogre **5** ghoul **7** monster **9** hobgoblin **10** apparition
minus one: **3** par
bogeyman: **4** ogre **5** ghoul **6** scarer **7** monster **10** apparition
boggle: **4** flub, muff **5** amaze, botch, demur, pause, waver **6** bungle, falter, foul up, fumble, goof up, mess up, wonder **7** astound, confuse, louse up, mystify, nonplus, perplex, screw up, stagger, stupefy **8** astonish, bewilder, bowl over, hang back, hesitate **9** dumbfound, overwhelm
Boggle: **8** word game
boggler: **2** ox **3** oaf **4** lout **6** enigma
__-boggling: **4** mind
Bogg, Phineas time travel device: **4** Omni
Boggs, Wade
sport: **8** baseball
bogie: **5** ghost, shade **9** hobgoblin
Bogie costar: **6** Bacall
Bogosian: **4** Eric
Bogotá: **4** city, town
city near ~: **4** Cali
locale: **8** Colombia
see also Spanish
bogus: **4** fake, mock, sham **5** false, phony, put-on **6** ersatz, forged, phoney, pseudo, unreal **7** assumed, feigned **8** spurious **9** imitation, pretended, simulated, synthetic **10** artificial, fabricated, factitious, fictitious, fraudulent
not ~: **4** real **5** legit **7** genuine
bogyman
see bogeyman
Bohai: **4** gulf
locale: **5** China
sea: **6** Yellow
Bohay: **5** Heidi
bohea: **3** tea **8** black tea
bohemian: **4** arty **5** artsy, gypsy, hippy **6** hippie **7** beatnik, offbeat, raffish **8** left-bank **10** free spirit, iconoclast, unorthodox
Bohemian: **5** Czech
city: **5** Plzen
dance: **5** polka
saint: **10** Wenceslaus
Bohemian Rhapsody (1976 song)
artist: Queen
Böhm, Karl: **9** conductor
Bohr: **4** Aage **5** Niels
concern: **4** atom
Bohrer: **7** Corinne
boil: **4** brew, burn, cook, fume, heat, rage, rave, stew **5** anger, flare, froth, poach, steam, steep, storm, swirl **6** blow up, bubble, coddle, decoct, fire up, see red, seethe, simmer **7** bristle, flare up, smolder, swelter **8** smoulder **9** evaporate, fulminate
almost ~: **5** scald **6** simmer
down: **4** trim **6** decoct, digest **7** abridge, distill, shorten **8** compress, condense, simplify **9** capsulize, summarize, synopsize, telescope **10** abbreviate
in oil: **3** fry **5** sauté **7** deep-fry
make one's blood ~: **3** irk, vex **4** rile **5** anger, peeve, upset **6** offend
over: **4** rage, rant, rave **5** erupt **8** have a fit
boiled: **10** a l'anglaise
combining form: **5** cocto-
down: **5** brief, short, terse **6** gnomic **7** compact, concise, refined **8** succinct
boiled __: **3** oil **5** shirt, sweet **6** dinner
__-boiled: **4** hard, soft
boiler: **3** pan **6** kettle **7** caldron, furnace **8** cauldron, saucepan
ender: **5** maker, plate
starter: **3** pot
tend the ~: **5** stoke
boiler __: **4** room, suit **5** plate
__ boiler: **5** steam **6** double
boilermaker
component: **4** beer **6** chaser, whisky **7** whiskey
Boilermakers: **6** Purdue
boilerplate: **8** standard
Boiler Room, The (2000 film)
cast: Ben Affleck, Vin Diesel, Nia Long
boil-in-__: **3** bag
boiling: see angry
at the ~ point: **3** hot **5** angry **6** raging **7** furious, steamed **8** bubbling, scalding **9** simmering **10** infuriated
boiling __: **5** point
Bois de Boulogne: **4** parc
artist: Raoul Dufy
Boise: **4** city, town
athletes: **7** Broncos
conference: **3** WAC
county: **3** Ada
locale: **5** Idaho
school: **3** BSU
Boise __: **7** Cascade
__ Boise: **4** Fort
boisterous: **4** loud, wild **5** aroar, forte, noisy, rowdy **6** bouncy, hectic, hoiden, hoyden, robust, unruly **7** blaring, booming, jarring, lowbred, pealing, rackety, rampant, raucous, reboant, riotous, roaring **8** brawling, crashing, piercing, plangent, rumbling, sonorous, strident, turned up **9** big-voiced, clamorous, deafening, impetuous,

turbulent **10** disorderly, in an uproar, resounding, rollicking, stentorian, strepitous, thundering, tumultuous, uproarious, vociferant, vociferous
boisterousness: 5 noise **8** hilarity
Boitano, Brian: 6 skater
boîte: 4 café **7** cabaret **9** nightclub, night spot
boîte de __: 4 nuit
Boito opera: 4 Nero
Bojangles'
rival: ***see*** restaurant chain
Bojer, Johan: 6 writer **9** Norwegian
bok __: 4 choy
Bok: 5 Derek
bok choy: 6 veggie **7** cabbage **9** vegetable
Bokhara __: 3 rug **6** clover
Bol.
see Bolivia
__-Bol: 3 Ty-D
bola
alternative: 5 lasso, reata, riata **6** lariat
Boland: 4 Mary **5** Eavan
Bolcom, William: 7 pianist
bold: 4 game, pert, rude **5** brash, brave, fresh, gutsy, manly, nervy, pushy, risky, sassy, saucy, showy, smart, stout, vivid **6** active, awless, brassy, brazen, cheeky, daring, flashy, gritty, heroic, hoiden, hoyden, jaunty, plucky, spunky, strong, virile **7** assured, aweless, dashing, defiant, doughty, forward, gallant, impavid, staunch, uncivil, valiant, visible **8** assuming, fearless, forceful, heroical, immodest, impudent, insolent, intrepid, manifest, resolute, spirited, stalwart, unafraid, valorous **9** ambitious, audacious, barefaced, confident, daredevil, dauntless, desperate, dreadless, foolhardy, outspoken, presuming, shameless, undaunted, unfearful, unfearing **10** chivalrous, courageous, forthright, incautious, mettlesome, pronounced, undismayed, ungracious, unreserved
be ~: 4 dare **7** venture **8** confront **9** challenge
be so ~: 7 presume, venture
ender: 4 face **5** faced
look: 4 leer
not ~: 3 shy **5** timid **7** bashful
woman: 4 vamp **5** hussy, siren **9** temptress
bold-__: 5 faced
Bold: 9 detergent
competitor: ***see*** detergent
Bold and the Beautiful, The (CBS): 4 soap **9** soap opera
boldface
alternative: 6 italic **7** italics
bold-faced: 6 brazen **8** impudent
boldness: 4 face, gall, guts, sass **5** cheek, heart, moxie, nerve, pluck, sauce, valor **6** daring, mettle, spirit, starch **7** bravery, courage, heroism, license, prowess **8** audacity, defiance, temerity **9** assurance, fortitude, gallantry, hardiness, impudence, insolence **10** confidence, effrontery, enterprise, knighthood
bole: 3 log **4** clay **5** trunk **7** reddish **8** brownish **9** tree trunk
color kin: ***see*** brown color
__ Bolena: 4 Anna
bolero: 4 coat **5** dance, music **6** jacket
Bolero
composer: Maurice Ravel
instrument in ~: 4 oboe
Bolero (1984 film)
cast: Bo Derek
director: John Derek
Boleyn, Anne: 5 queen **7** British
Bolger, Ray: 5 actor **6** dancer
costar: 4 Lahr **5** Haley **7** Garland
film: The Harvey Girls (1946)
Where's Charley? (1952)
The Wizard of Oz (1939)
bolide: 6 meteor **8** fireball
bolivar: 5 money
Bolívar, Simón: 9 liberator, statesman **10** Venezuelan
birthplace: 7 Caracas
Bolivia: 6 nation **7** country
beast: 5 llama **6** alpaca
capital: 5 La Paz, Sucre
city: 5 Oruro **6** El Alto, Potosí, Tarija **9** Santa Cruz **10** Cochabamba
export: 3 tin
Indian: 4 Moxo **6** Aymara **7** Quechua
lake: 8 Titicaca
language: 6 Aymara **7** Quechua, Spanish
mining town: 5 Oruro
money: 4 peso **7** bolivar **9** boliviano
mountain: 6 Sajama **7** Illampu **8** Ancohuma, Illimani **9** Condoriri **10** Parinacota
neighbor: 4 Peru **5** Chile **6** Brazil **8** Paraguay **9** Argentina
org.: 3 OAS
range: 5 Andes
river: 4 Beni
tanager: 4 yeni
see also Spanish
boll: 3 pod **7** seed pod
cleaner: 3 gin
boll __: 6 weevil
Böll, Heinrich: 6 German, writer **8** Nobelist
Bolling: 7 Tiffany
bollix: 4 foil **5** botch, snafu **6** bungle, foul up, fumble, mess up **7** disrupt
bollixed: 7 puzzled, stumped
Boll Weevil Song, The (1961 song)
artist: Brook Benton
Bol, Manute: 5 cager
milieu: 5 court
org.: 3 NBA
sport: 10 basketball
bolo: 3 tie **5** knife **8** neckwear **9** string tie
kin: 7 machete
bolo __: 3 tie **5** knife
bologna: 4 meat **7** sausage
unit: 5 slice
Bologna: 4 city, town **6** Joseph
locale: 5 Italy **6** Italia
Bologna, Joseph: 5 actor
film: Blame It on Rio (1984)
Cops and Robbers (1973)
Made for Each Other (1971)
My Favorite Year (1982)
spouse: Renee Taylor
Bolshevik: 3 Red **9** Communist
leader: 5 Lenin
victim: 4 czar, tsar
Bolshevism: 9 Communism, socialism
Bolshevist: 7 leftist
Bolshoi __: 6 Ballet
rival: 5 Kirov
bolster: 3 aid, pad **4** abut, buoy, feed, gird, help, hold, prop, tone **5** boost, brace, build, shore, steel **6** anneal, assist, batten, bear up, beef up, buck up, expand, harden, hold up, prop up, temper, tone up, uphold **7** brace up, build up, bulwark, burgeon, develop, empower, enhance, fortify, promote, shore up, stiffen, support, sustain, toughen **8** advocate, bourgeon, buttress, energize, indurate, reassure, vitalize **9** cultivate, encourage, intensify, reinforce **10** invigorate, rally round, strengthen
bolt: 3 bar, dam, eat, fly, rod, run **4** clog, cork, dart, dash, flee, gulp, lock, plug, race, rush, seal, shut, skip, stud, T-bar, tear, wolf **5** arrow, block, close, dam up, elope, flash, gorge, latch, rivet, scoot, shoot, split, start **6** clog up, cut out, decamp, desert, devour, escape, fasten, gallop, gobble, guzzle, hasten, hurtle, inhale, lock up, plug up, run off, seal up, secure, spring, stop up **7** abscond, bail out, closure, consume, dart off, dash off, engorge, go south, javelin, make off, missile, run away, scamper, seal off, shutter, startle, swallow, take off **8** blockade, button up, fastener, fugitate, gulp down, hightail, material, obstruct, run for it, step on it, turn tail, wolf down **9** go swiftly, hotfoot it, lightning, scarf down, skedaddle, stabilize **10** burn rubber, hightail it, make tracks, projectile, take flight
contents: 5 cloth **6** fabric **8** material
cover: 6 cap nut
down: 3 eat **4** wolf **5** rivet
ender: 4 hole, rope
holder: 3 lug, nut **4** T-nut
lightning ~: 5 flash
location: 6 breech
part: 4 yard **5** shank
starter: 3 eye **4** dead, king, ring **7** thunder
upright: 5 rigid **8** vertical
__ bolt: 3 bed, box, fox, lag, rag, rod, tap **4** barb, dead **6** anchor, barrel, bottom, toggle
Bolt: 5 Tommy, Usain **6** Robert
author: Dick Francis
Bolt (2008 film)
voice cast: Miley Cyrus, John Travolta
bolted: 4 firm, shut **5** tight
bolt from the __: 4 blue
Bolton, Michael
real last name: Bolotin
song: How Am I Supposed to Live Without You (1989)
How Can We Be Lovers (1990)
Love Is a Wonderful Thing (1991)
Said I Loved You...But I Lied (1994)
Time, Love and Tenderness (1991)
When a Man Loves a Woman (1991)
When I'm Back on My Feet Again (1990)
bolts
bucket of ~: 3 car **4** auto, heap **5** crate, lemon **6** jalopy
nuts and ~: 3 nub **4** knub, pith **6** detail **7** reality
bolus: 4 pill
bomb: 3 dud **4** ammo, bust, fail, flop, lose, loss, mine, rase, raze, slip, trip **5** blast, flunk, shell, speed **6** attack, blow it, blow up, defeat, falter, fiasco, mishap, rocket, turkey **7** blunder, clunker, debacle, failure, fizzler, founder, go under, go wrong, grenade, lose out, missile, misstep, stumble, torpedo, wash out, wipe out **8** backfire, downfall, fall flat, flounder, lay an egg, munition **9** explosive, strike out **10** ammunition, nonsuccess
A ~: 6 Fat Man **9** Little Boy
defective ~: 3 dud
do ~ squad work: 6 defuse, defuze
ender: 5 proof, shell, sight
sound: 5 blast **6** kaboom **9** explosion
starter: 4 fire
trial: 10 N-test A-test
bomb __: 3 bay, run **4** rack **5** ketch, lance, squad **7** shelter
__ bomb: 4 atom, buzz, tear, time **5** depth, dirty, robot, smart, smoke, stink, water **6** atomic, cherry, flying, fusion, rocket, stench **7** aerosol, cluster, fission
__-bomb: 4 dive
bombard: 3 zap **4** pelt **5** beset, blast, blitz, hound, shell, shoot, storm, throw **6** assail, attack, batter, harass, launch, pester, strike **7** assault, barrage, besiege, rip into **8** fire upon, open fire **9** cannonade, haul off on
in Britain: 5 prang
bombardment: 4 fire **5** blitz, burst **6** volley **7** barrage **9** broadside, cannonade
bombast: 3 gas **4** rant, talk **6** hot air, speech **7** bluster, bravado, padding **8** claptrap, nonsense, rhetoric **9** gasconade, pomposity **10** empty words, pretension, vocalizing
bombastic: 4 long **5** gabby, gassy, tumid, windy, wordy **6** prolix **7** diffuse, fustian, hyped up, lengthy, orotund, pompous, ranting, stilted, unterse, verbose, voluble **8** boastful, inflated, rambling **9** garrulous, grandiose, high-flown, overblown, redundant, rhapsodic, talkative **10** big-talking, discursive, euphuistic, flamboyant, histrionic, long-winded, loquacious, palaverous, rhetorical
Bombay: 3 cat **4** city, port, town **5** felid **6** feline
city near ~: 4 Puna **5** Poona, Thana **6** Indore
locale: 5 India
bombe: 7 dessert

alternative: 6 frappe, sundae 10 peach Melba
ingredient: 8 ice cream
Bombeck, Erma: 3 wit 6 writer 8 humorist
bomber: 4 coat 5 plane 6 jacket 8 airplane, warplane
crew: 6 airmen
dive ~ descent: 5 swoop
org.: 3 SAC
WWII ~: 5 Stuka 8 Bock's Car, Enola Gay
__ bomber: 4 dive 5 heavy, light 6 medium
bombinate: 3 hum
...bombs bursting __: 5 in air
bombshell: 4 blow, jolt 5 shock 8 surprise 9 sensation 10 revelation
__ bombshell: 6 blonde
Bombshell (1933 film)
cast: Jean Harlow
bomb squad
do ~ work: 6 defuse, disarm
worker: 5 robot
bombycid: 4 moth
__ b'Omer: 3 Lag
bon __: 3 ami, mot, ton 4 soir 6 marché, vivant, voyage 7 appétit
Bon __: 3 Ami 4 Jovi
Bonaduce: 5 Danny
bona fide: 4 good, just, real, safe, true 5 legit, right, solid, valid 6 actual, honest, kasher, kosher, lawful 7 genuine, literal, regular, sincere 8 official, rightful, verified 9 authentic, heartfelt, veritable
Bon Ami: 8 cleanser
alternative: 4 Ajax, Bab-O 5 Comet 9 Soft Scrub
bonanza: 3 ore 4 lode, mine, vein 7 cash cow 8 gold mine, windfall
Bonanza (NBC western)
cast: Dan Blocker (Hoss Cartwright)
David Canary (Candy)
Lorne Greene (Ben Cartwright)
Michael Landon (Little Joe Cartwright)
Pernell Roberts (Adam Cartwright)
Victor Sen Yung (Hop Sing)
setting: 5 ranch 6 Nevada 9 Ponderosa
Bonaparte: 8 Napoleon
fate: 5 exile
island: 4 Elba 8 St. Helena
symphony first called ~: 6 Eroica
Bonar: 3 Law
Bonaventure: 5 saint
St. ~ locale: 5 Olean 7 New York
bonbon: 5 candy, sweet 6 nougat 7 dessert, fondant 9 chocolate, sweetmeat 10 confection
Bon-Bon
author: Edgar Allan Poe
bond: 3 fix, gum, tie, wed 4 bail, bind, fuse, gage, glue, link, lock, pact, pawn, rope, tape, weld, yoke 5 asset, chain, marry, paper, paste, stick, union, unite 6 adhere, cement, fasten, fetter, hookup, pledge, treaty 7 combine, compact, connect, loyalty, manacle, network, promise, rapport, shackle, stickum 8 alliance, contract, covenant, fastener, fixative, handcuff, junction, juncture, ligature, marriage, relation, security, vinculum, warranty 9 agreement, debenture, guarantee, indenture 10 attachment, collateral, connection, friendship, obligation
alternative: 5 stock
attachment: 6 coupon
combining form: 4 desm- 5 desmo-
emotional ~: 3 tie 4 love 9 affection
ender: 3 age, man, men 4 maid 5 woman, women 6 holder 7 servant
kind of ~: 3 deb. 4 Euro, muni 5 no par 9 debenture, municipal
rating: 3 AAA, BAA, BBB, CCC
return: 5 yield
short-term ~: 3 deb. 9 debenture
__ bond: 4 baby, bail, clip, flat, gold, junk, muni, pair 5 Dutch, ionic, strip 6 bearer, common, coupon 7 Liberty, peptide, revenue, running, savings
Bond: 4 Ward 5 James 6 Julian
bondage: 4 yoke 6 chains 7 fetters, slavery 8 trammels 9 captivity, restraint, servitude 10 internment
place into ~: 6 enserf 7 capture, enslave
bonded __: 6 whisky 7 whiskey
Bondi, Beulah: 7 actress
__ bonding: 4 male, pair
bonding agent: 4 glue 5 epoxy
bond-issuing org.: 4 GNMA
Bond, James: 3 spy 4 hero 5 agent 7 British
portrayer: Pierce Brosnan, Sean Connery, Daniel Craig, Timothy Dalton, George Lazenby, Roger Moore
school: 4 Eton
bondman: 5 helot
bonds: 5 irons 6 chains 7 fetters 8 shackles, trammels 9 servitude
buy ~: 6 invest
how some ~ sell: 5 at par
like some ~: 5 risky
seller: 6 broker
stocks and ~: 6 assets, wealth
Bonds: 5 Barry, Bobby
Bonds, Barry
sport: 8 baseball
bondservant: 4 serf 5 slave 6 thrall 7 chattel
bond-service employee: 5 rater
Bonds, Gary U.S.
song: Dear Lady Twist (1962)
New Orleans (1960)
Quarter to Three (1961)
School Is Out (1961)
Twist, Twist Senora (1962)
bondsman, ancient: 4 esne, serf 5 helot
__ Bonds Today?: 3 Any
Bond, Ward: 5 actor
TV: Wagon Train
bone: 3 jaw, rib 4 coxa, ulna 5 china, femur, filet, hyoid, ilium, incus, inion, jugal, malar, skull, talus, tibia, vomer, white 6 carpal, carpus, coccyx, concha, cuboid, fibula, fillet, hammer, pelvis, radius, sacrum, stapes, tarsal, tarsus, zygoma 7 carpale, cranium, ethmoid, humerus, ischium, malleus, maxilla, patella, phalanx, scapula, sternum, stirrup 8 clavicle, cuboidal, glabella, mandible, off-white, palatine, parietal, skeleton, sphenoid, vertebra 9 braincase, occipital, olecranon, trapezium, trapezoid, yellowish, zygomatic 10 astragalus, metacarpus, metatarsus, premaxilla
ankle ~: 5 talus 6 tarsus 10 astragalus, metatarsus
arm ~: 4 ulna 6 radius 7 humerus 9 olecranon
breast ~: 7 sternum
cavity: 5 fossa 6 antrum
cheek ~: 5 jugal, malar
color kin: *see* white color
combining form: 3 -ost 4 ossi-, oste- 5 osteo-
cranial ~: 5 vomer 6 zygoma 7 ethmoid 8 parietal, sphenoid 9 zygomatic
depression: 5 fovea
dinosaur ~: 6 fossil
ear ~: 5 anvil, incus 6 hammer, stapes 7 malleus, stirrup
ender: 3 set 4 fish, head 5 black
facial ~: 8 glabella
fide: 5 legit 6 lawful 7 genuine
fish: 5 filet
foot ~: 5 talus 6 cuboid, tarsal, tarsus 8 cuboidal
forearm ~: 4 ulna 6 radius 9 olecranon
head ~: 3 jaw 7 maxilla 8 mandible
hip ~: 5 ilium 6 pelvis
horn-shaped ~: 5 cornu
innominate ~: 4 coxa
jaw ~: 7 maxilla 8 mandible 10 premaxilla
knee ~: 7 patella
leg ~: 4 shin 5 femur, tibia 6 fibula
longest ~: 5 femur
middle-ear ~: 5 anvil, incus
mouth ~: 8 palatine
nasal ~: 5 vomer 6 concha 7 ethmoid
of contention: 5 issue 8 argument
of the hip ~: 5 iliac
opening: 6 meatus
pelvic ~: 4 coxa 7 ischium
postaxial ~: 4 ulna
shoulder ~: 7 scapula 8 clavicle
skull ~: 5 vomer 6 zygoma 7 cranium, ethmoid 8 parietal, sphenoid 9 braincase, occipital, zygomatic
spinal ~: 6 coccyx
starter: 3 hip, jaw 4 back, ring, shin, tail, wish 5 aitch, ankle, cheek, thigh, whale 6 breast, collar, marrow 7 feather, herring, knuckle
structure: 8 skeleton
tongue ~: 5 hyoid
to pick: 4 feud, spat, tiff 5 gripe 7 dispute, quarrel 8 argument, conflict, squabble 9 exception 10 contention, difference
turn to ~: 6 ossify
up on: 4 cram, read 5 study 6 master
vertebral ~: 3 rib 6 sacrum
work one's fingers to the ~: 4 toil 5 slave 6 drudge
wrist ~: 6 carpal, carpus, hamate 7 carpale 9 trapezium 10 metacarpus
zygomatic ~: 5 malar
bone __: 3 ash, oil 4 cell, meal, up on 5 black, china, felon 6 marrow, shaker
bone-__: 3 dry
__ bone: 4 heel, keel, long 5 crazy, funny, jugal, malar 6 cannon, coffin, fetter, haunch, pulley, splint 7 frontal, mastoid, stirrup
...bone, __ of hair: 5 a hank
__-Bone: 4 Milk
Bone Collector, The (1999 film)
cast: Angelina Jolie, Queen Latifah, Michael Rooker, Denzel Washington
director: Phillip Noyce
Bonecrack
author: Dick Francis
__-boned: 3 big, raw
bone-dry: 4 arid, sere 7 parched, thirsty 9 juiceless
bonehead
see ninny
boneheaded
see foolish
boneless cut: 5 filet
boner: 4 flub, goof, muff 5 error, gaffe, snafu 6 boo-boo, bungle, foulup, miscue, muddle, slipup 7 blooper, blunder, faux pas, misstep, mistake 8 dumb move 9 false move, indecorum
Boner's __: 3 Ark
Boner's Ark dog: 4 Spot
Bonerz, Peter: 5 actor
TV: The Bob Newhart Show
bones: 4 dice 6 doctor 8 skeleton 9 physician
ankle ~: 4 tali 5 tarsi
arm ~: 5 radii
back ~: 5 sacra
bare ~: 9 framework
foot ~: 4 tali 5 tarsi
in Latin: 4 ossa
leg ~: 6 femora
pelvic ~: 4 ilia 5 sacra
remove ~: 5 filet 6 fillet
skin and ~: 4 lean, thin 5 rangy, spare 9 emaciated
starter: 3 saw 4 lazy 5 cross
__ bones: 4 bare 7 Napier's
__ Bones: 4 Brom, Lazy 5 Bag of, Echo's
Bones, Brom prey: 5 Crane
Bonesetter's Daughter, The
author: Amy Tan
bone-tired: 5 all in, weary, wiped 6 bushed 7 drained 9 exhausted 10 knocked out
Bonet, Lisa: 7 actress
spouse: Lenny Kravitz
TV: The Cosby Show, A Different World
bone to __: 4 pick
bonfire: 5 blaze
fuel: 4 wood 6 sticks
residue: 3 ash 4 coal 5 ember 6 cinder
started a ~: 3 lit
Bonfire of the Vanities, The: 4 film 5 novel
author: Tom Wolfe
cast: Kim Cattrall, Morgan Freeman, Melanie Griffith, Tom Hanks, Bruce Willis
director: Brian De Palma

bong: 4 peal, ring, toll 5 chime
bongo: 4 drum 8 antelope
relative: see antelope
Bonham Carter, Helena: 7 actress
film: Getting It Right (1989)
Hamlet (1990)
Howards End (1992)
Lady Jane (1985)
Mighty Aphrodite (1995)
Novocaine (2001)
Planet of the Apes (2001)
A Room With a View (1986)
Bonheur, Rosa: 6 artist 7 painter
homeland: 6 France
Bonhomme __: 7 Richard
boniface: 9 innkeeper
place: 3 inn
Boniface: 4 pope 5 saint 7 pontiff
Bonilla: 5 Bobby
Bonita: 9 Granville
Bonita Springs: 4 city, town
locale: 7 Florida
bonito: 4 fish, tuna
bon jour: 5 hello 7 welcome
Bonjour Tristesse
author: Françoise Sagan
Bon Jovi: 3 Jon
members: Bon Jovi, Sambora
song: Always (1994)
Bad Medicine (1988)
Bed of Roses (1993)
Blaze of Glory (1990)
Born to Be My Baby (1988)
I'll Be There for You (1989)
Lay Your Hands on Me (1989)
Living in Sin (1989)
Livin' on a Prayer (1987)
Wanted Dead or Alive (1987)
You Give Love a Bad Name (1986)
bonk: 6 strike
bonkers: 4 bats, daft, gaga, loco 5 batty, dotty, kooky, nutty 6 kookie 7 bananas, flipped, haywire, touched 10 over the top
drive ~: 3 irk 5 annoy 6 bother, pester 8 irritate
go ~: 5 crack, freak 6 lose it
bon mot: 4 jest, joke, quip 6 remark 7 epigram 8 repartee, wordplay 9 witticism 10 pleasantry
Bonn: 4 city, town
city near ~: 5 Essen
locale: 7 Germany
river: 5 Rhine
bonne: 4 maid
amie: see sweetheart
bonne __: 3 foi 4 amie, idée, nuit 5 femme 6 bouche, chance
Bonne __!: 4 nuit 6 chance
bonne chance: 8 good luck
__ bonne heure: 3 à la
Bonner: 5 Elena, Frank 6 Junior
bonnet: 3 hat, lid 4 poke 8 covering 9 headdress
Brit's ~: 4 hood
bug: 3 bee
Easter ~: 6 finery
holder: 6 hatbox
starter: 3 sun 4 blue
bonnet __: 3 top 5 glass, rouge, shark 6 monkey 7 macaque
__ bonnet: 3 war 4 poke 6 Easter
Bonneville: 3 car, dam 4 auto 7 Pontiac
Bonneville Salt Flats site: 4 Utah
bonnie: 4 cute, fair 6 comely, dainty, pretty 7 winsome 9 appealing 10 attractive
girl: 4 lass
Bonnie: 4 Hunt 5 Blair, Raitt, Tyler 6 Guitar, Parker 7 Bedelia 8 Bartlett, Franklin
Bonnie and Clyde (1967 film)
cast: Warren Beatty, Faye Dunaway, Gene Hackman, Estelle Parsons, Michael J. Pollard
director: Arthur Penn
Bonnies
where the ~ play: 3 SBU
bonny: 4 cute, fair 6 comely, dainty, pretty 7 winsome 10 attractive
one: 4 lass
__ bono: 3 cui, pro
Bono: 5 Sonny 6 singer 8 Chastity
Bono, Chastity
mother: 4 Cher
Bonoff: 5 Karla
Bono, Sonny
spouse: Cher
__ bono work: 3 pro
bonsai: 3 art 4 tree 5 dwarf, plant 9 miniature
locale: 5 Japan
__ Bont: 5 Jan De
Bontemps, Arna: 6 writer
bonus: 3 tip 4 gift, perk, plum, plus 5 award, extra, goody, gravy 6 bounty, goodie, rebate, reward 7 premium, subsidy 8 addition, dividend, gratuity, largesse 9 lagniappe 10 percentage
buyer's ~: 6 coupon, rebate
concert ~: 6 encore
Cracker Jack ~: 5 prize
bon vivant: 7 epicure, gourmet 8 hedonist, sybarite 9 epicurean 10 voluptuary
quality: 6 esprit
bon voyage site: 4 deck, dock, pier, ship 5 berth, liner, wharf 7 steamer 10 cruise ship, waterfront
bony: 4 lank, lean, thin 5 gaunt, lanky, spare 6 ill-fed, knobby, meager, osteal, skinny 7 osseous, scrawny 8 indurate 9 emaciated 10 unfilleted
structure: 3 jaw 8 skeleton
Bonzo: 5 chimp 10 chimpanzee
nosh: 6 banana
boo: 4 jeer 5 scoff, scorn, whoop 6 heckle, hiss at 7 catcall 9 raspberry
not saying ~: 5 quiet 6 silent
say ~: 5 scare 8 frighten
Boo __: 3 Hoo
boo and __: 4 hiss
boob
like a ~: 5 inept
tube: 2 TV 5 TV set 8 idiot box 10 television
tube, in Britain: 5 telly
see also ninny
boob __: 4 tube
Boo Berry: 6 cereal
competitor: see cereal
boo-boo: 3 cut, err 4 goof, hurt, slip 5 boner, error, gaffe, lapse, wound 6 bruise, injury, scrape, slipup 7 blooper, blunder, faux pas, misstep, mistake, scratch 9 oversight
make a ~: 3 err 4 flub, goof
publishing ~: 4 typo 7 erratum
remover: 6 eraser
Boo-Boo: 4 bear
buddy: 4 Yogi
booby: 3 oaf 4 bird, fool 5 dunce, prize 6 gannet 7 seabird
deserving the ~ prize: 5 worst
trap: 4 mine, ruse, trap 5 snare 7 pitfall 8 obstacle 9 explosive
booby __: 4 trap 5 hatch, prize
boodle: 3 lot, wad 4 loot, mint, pile, swag 5 booty, bribe, bunch, graft, money 7 jobbery 8 kickback
Boog: 6 Powell
boogaloo: 5 dance
boogie: 4 jazz 5 dance 7 get down
Boogie __: 4 Down 5 Board, Fever 6 Nights
Boogie Nights (1997 film)
cast: Heather Graham, Julianne Moore, Burt Reynolds, Mark Wahlberg
Boogie On Reggae Woman (1974 song)
artist: Stevie Wonder
Boogie Wonderland (1979 song)
artist: Earth, Wind & Fire, Emotions
boogie-woogie: 4 jazz 5 music
Boogie Woogie Bugle Boy (1973 song)
artist: Bette Midler
boo-hoo: 3 cry, sob 4 bawl, mewl, pule, wail, weep 6 snivel 7 blubber, whimper 9 shed tears
boojum: 4 tree
Boojum: 5 Snark
book: 3 log 4 hire, take, text, tome, work 5 album, atlas, bible, codex, diary, enter, novel, order, print, prose, set up, story 6 accuse, arrest, charge, engage, line up, manual, pick up, primer, reader, record, script, volume 7 account, charter, edition, lexicon, omnibus, procure, program, reserve, romance, speller, writing 8 hardback, libretto, register, schedule, textbook, thriller, whodunit 9 directory, hardcover, narrative, paperback, preengage, softcover, thesaurus 10 arrange for, bestseller, compendium, cyclopedia, dictionary, regulation, roman à clef
absorb a ~: 4 cram, read 5 study 6 peruse
accountant's ~: 6 ledger
art ~ publisher: 6 Abrams
autograph hound's ~: 5 album
bedside ~: 5 diary
bestselling ~: 5 Bible
bilingual ~: 6 diglot
binding: 5 cover, paper 7 leather
blank ~: 5 album
Buddhist sacred ~: 5 sutra 6 tantra
buyer: 6 editor, reader, school 7 library
by the ~: 5 legit, licit, stern 6 kasher, kosher, lawful, proper 7 allowed 8 methodic, orthodox, rightful 9 permitted, stringent 10 authorized, methodical, sanctioned
captain's ~: 3 log
cartographer's ~: 5 atlas
Chinese ~ of divination: 6 I Ching
closed ~: 6 enigma, riddle 7 mystery
combining form: 6 biblio-
corrections: 6 errata
cover: 6 jacket
crack a ~: 4 cram, read 5 study 6 peruse
ender: 3 end, let 4 case, lore, mark, rack, shop, worm 5 louse, maker, plate, shelf, stall, stand, store 6 binder, keeper, making, mobile, seller 7 bindery, binding, keeping
extra: 6 insert
feature: 5 index 6 dog-ear
genre: 4 play 5 drama, how-to, novel, sci-fi 6 horror, poetry 7 fiction, romance 10 non-fiction, short-story
heavy ~: 4 tome
Hindu sacred ~: 4 Gita, Veda
holder: 5 shelf
ID: 4 ISBN
illustration: 5 plate
item in a ~: 5 match
jacket feature: 3 bio 4 ISBN 5 blurb, price, title 6 author, review, writer 7 bar code
large ~ size: 5 folio
like a ~: 6 wholly 8 entirely, from A to Z 10 completely, thoroughly
make ~: 3 bet 4 punt 5 stake, wager 6 gamble 8 give odds, take bets 9 speculate
map ~: 5 atlas
of photos: 5 album
of public records: 5 liber
page: 5 recto, verso
part: 4 flap 5 cover, pages, spine 6 jacket 7 binding
pew ~: 6 hymnal
pocket ~: 9 paperback
reference ~: 3 gaz., OED 4 dict., ency., text, tome 5 atlas, encyc. 6 encycl., manual 9 gazetteer, thesaurus 10 dictionary
repository: 7 library
reviewer: 5 rater 6 critic
sacred ~: 5 Bible, Koran, Quran
scholarly ~: 4 text, tome
school ~: 4 text
section: 4 chap., leaf, page, part 5 part I 6 part II 7 chapter, part III
starter: 3 day, log 4 bank, blue, case, cash, chap, code, cook, copy, flip, hand, horn, hymn, note, over, pass, play, stud, text, word, work, year 5 check, guide, match, scrap, story, style 6 pocket, prompt, school, sketch
throw the ~ at: 6 punish 7 condemn, convict 8 sentence
type of ~ binding: 4 yapp
book __: 3 bag 4 club, gill, list, lore, lung, tile 5 louse, match, share, value 6 jacket, review 7 burning, society
book-__: 4 work 8 learning
__ book: 3 fly 4 baby, bell, blue, code, fake, gill, make, Mass, open, rare, roll 5 audio, black, blank, comic, dream, funny, how-to, like a, phone, stock, trade, white 6 church, closed, phrase, pocket, prayer, sealed, sketch, source 7 account, cookery, picture, service, statute, talking, tell-all

__ **Book:** 4 Good 6 Jungle
__, **Book and Candle:** 4 Bell
bookbinder
material: 4 glue, roan 5 cloth 7 buckram, leather
bookcase: 9 furniture
part: 5 shelf
place: 4 wall 5 study 6 alcove
__ **Book Club:** 6 Oprah's
__ **Book Confidential:** 5 Comic
Booke: 7 Sorrell
booked: 7 engaged 8 reserved
Book 'em, __!: 4 Dano 5 Danno
Booker T. and the MGs
song: Green Onions (1962)
Hang 'Em High (1968)
Time Is Tight (1969)
bookie
alternative: 3 OTB
concern: 3 bet
protection: 5 hedge
quote: 4 odds
booking: 3 gig, job 5 order 10 engagement
booking __: 5 agent, clerk 6 office
bookish: 3 dry 5 fussy, stiff 6 brainy, formal, stuffy 7 donnish, erudite, learned, precise, stilted 8 academic, cerebral, highbrow, literary, longhair, pedantic, studious 9 pedagogic, scholarly 10 fastidious, pedantical, scholastic
type: 4 nerd 7 egghead
bookkeeper: 3 CPA 4 acct. 5 clerk 7 auditor 8 recorder 9 registrar 10 accountant, controller
abbreviation: 3 ROA
book: 6 ledger 7 journal
term: 3 net 5 asset, debit 6 credit, income, profit 7 expense 9 liability
booklet: 5 tract 8 brochure, pamphlet
book-lined room: 3 den 5 study 7 library
Bookman: 4 font 8 typeface
bookmark: 3 tab 6 dog-ear
bookmarked item: 3 URL
Book of __: 4 Odes 5 Books, Hours, Kells 6 Mormon 7 Changes
Book of __ Prayer: 6 Common
Book of Burlesques, A
author: H.L. Mencken
Book of Changes: 6 I Ching
Book of Daniel, The
author: E.L. Doctorow
Book of Hours, The
poet: Rainier Rilke
Book of Lights, The
author: Chaim Potok
Book of Los, The author: William Blake
Book of Love (1958 song)
artist: Monotones
Book of Merlyn, The
author: T.H. White
Book of Nonsense, A
author: Edward Lear
Book of Snobs, The
author: William Makepeace Thackeray
Book of Songs, The
author: Heinrich Heine
Book of Thel, The
author: William Blake
bookplate
phrase: 5 ex lib. 8 ex libris
books: 6 ledger 7 account 10 literature
check the ~: 5 audit
concerning ~: 8 literary
five ~ of Moses: 4 Tora 5 Torah
hit the ~: 4 cram, read 5 study 6 master
it's on the ~: 3 law 7 statute
like some kids' ~: 5 pop-up
manipulate the ~: 4 cook 6 tamper
one for the ~: 3 gem 5 doozy 6 marvel
wipe off the ~: 5 erase 6 cancel 7 rescind, scratch 8 dissolve 10 invalidate
bookseller, online: 4 eBay 6 Amazon
bookstore
category: 4 diet 5 how-to, humor, sci-fi 6 horror 7 fiction, history 9 biography
enjoy a ~: 6 browse
bookworm: 4 nerd, wonk 6 reader 7 learner, scholar
what a ~ does: 4 pore, read 5 study
boola boola: 5 huzza 6 hoorah, hooray, hurrah, hurray, huzzah
singer: 3 Eli 5 Yalie 7 Bulldog
Boole, George: 7 British 8 logician
boom: 3 bar 4 bang, beam, mast, pole, roar, roll, slam, spar, wham 5 blast, bloom, burst, crack, crane, crash, noise, smash, sound, spirt, spurt 6 expand, flower, growth, report, rumble, thrive, timber, upturn 7 barrage, develop, explode, prosper, resound, succeed, thunder, upsurge, upswing 8 drumfire, flourish, increase, mushroom 9 barricade, cannonade, explosion, intensify 10 appreciate, detonation, prosperity
alternative: 4 bust
cannon ~: 5 salvo
go ~: 5 erupt 7 explode, thunder 8 detonate 9 discharge
lower the ~: 5 scold 6 berate 9 reprimand
nautical ~: 4 gaff, spar 5 sprit
support: 4 mast
time: 2 up 6 uptick 7 upswing
boom __: 3 box 4 shot, town
__ **boom:** 3 jib 4 baby 5 sonic 7 whisker
boom-and-__: 4 bust
__ **boom bah!:** 3 Sis
boombox: 5 radio 6 stereo 8 CD player 10 tape player
button: 4 stop 5 pause 6 record, rewind
letters: 4 AMFM
sound: 5 blare, noise
boomer: 8 kangaroo
baby ~ offsprings: 4 Gen-X
__ **boomer:** 4 baby
Boomer: 7 Esiason
boomerang: 5 react 7 rebound 8 backfire 10 bounce back
like a ~: 6 curved
booming: 4 loud 5 forte, large, noisy, palmy 7 blaring, orotund, rackety, raucous, reboant, roaring, wealthy 8 piercing, plangent, resonant, sonorous, strident, thriving, turned up 9 big-voiced, clamorous, deafening, doing well 10 boisterous, prosperous, stentorian, strepitous, successful, uproarious, vociferant, vociferous
boom-or-__: 4 bust
boomslang: 5 snake 6 animal 7 reptile
relative: see snake
boon: 3 aid 4 gift, help, plus 5 asset, favor, jolly 6 virtue 7 benefit, gleeful, godsend 8 blessing, largesse, windfall 9 advantage, convivial, endowment, privilege 10 lucky break
companion: 3 pal 5 buddy 6 friend 8 alter ego
boondocks: 4 town 5 wilds 6 Podunk, sticks 7 country 8 frontier 9 backwater, backwoods 10 wilderness
in the ~: 6 remote
Boone: 3 Pat 4 Bret 5 Debby 6 Daniel 7 Richard
Boone, Daniel: 4 hero 7 pioneer 8 explorer
Boone, Debby
song: You Light Up My Life (1977)
Boone, Pat
real first name: Charles
song: Ain't That a Shame (1955)
April Love (1957)
At My Front Door (1955)
Chains of Love (1956)
Don't Forbid Me (1956)
Friendly Persuasion (1956)
I Almost Lost My Mind (1956)
If Dreams Came True (1958)
I'll Be Home (1956)
It's Too Soon to Know (1958)
Long Tall Sally (1956)
Love Letters in the Sand (1957)
Moody River (1961)
Remember You're Mine (1957)
Speedy Gonzales (1962)
Sugar Moon (1958)
Why Baby Why (1957)
A Wonderful Time Up There (1958)
Boone, Richard: 5 actor
TV: Have Gun Will Travel, Hec Ramsey, Medic
Boone's Lick
author: Larry McMurtry
boonies
see boondocks
Boop, Betty: 4 toon 7 flapper
dog: 5 Pudgy
voice: 4 Kane
boor: 3 ape, cad, oaf 4 boob, clod, goon, hick, jerk, lout 5 brute, churl, clown, looby, swine, yahoo, yokel 6 baboon, lummox, rustic 7 buffoon, hayseed, peasant 9 barbarian, vulgarian 10 philistine
boorish: 3 dim 4 loud, rude 5 brash, crass, crude, dense, gross, gruff, nervy 6 clumsy, coarse, obtuse, rustic, vulgar 7 awkward, bearish, beastly, ill-bred, loutish, lowbred, raffish, selfish, unadept, uncouth 8 barbaric, churlish, heedless, impolite, inurbane, tactless, unpoised 9 backwater, barbarian, barbarous, difficult, graceless, ungallant, unrefined 10 indecorous, outlandish, uncultured, ungracious, unpolished, unthinking
Boorman, John: 8 director
Boorstin: 6 Daniel
Boosler: 6 Elayne
boost: 3 aid 4 back, buoy, gain, hand, help, hike, jump, laud, lift, loot, plug, puff, push, rise, tout 5 add to, build, exalt, heave, hoist, impel, leg up, lobby, raise, shove, speed, steal 6 assist, beef up, expand, extend, foster, growth, haul up, jack up, jerk up, mark up, pilfer, praise, rip off, step up, thieve, thrust, uphold, upturn 7 advance, amplify, augment, bolster, buildup, elevate, endorse, enhance, enlarge, further, improve, indorse, inflate, inspire, magnify, nurture, promote, raise up, scale up, support, upgrade, upraise, upswing 8 addition, advocate, embolden, heighten, imbolden, increase, multiply, pick-me-up, shoplift 9 advertise, elevation, encourage, expansion, increment, intensify, promotion, publicity, publicize, reinforce, subscribe 10 aggrandize, assistance, exaggerate, exhilarate, rally round
give a ~ to: 3 aid 4 back, help 6 assist 7 bail out, further, promote, support
morale: 7 enthuse, hearten, support 9 encourage
booster: 5 urger 6 jaycee, patron, rooter, votary 7 admirer, devotee 8 advocate, exponent, partisan 9 flatterer, proponent
amount: 4 dose
club member: 4 alum, grad 6 alumna
rocket: 5 Agena
seat user: 3 kid, tot 5 child 7 toddler
shot: 4 hypo
booster __: 4 dose, seat, shot 5 cable
boot: 2 ax 3 axe, can, pac 4 drop, fire, kick, muff, oust, sack, shoe 5 botch, eject, evict, expel, let go, match, wader 6 bounce, buskin, depose, galosh, golosh, lay off, mucluc, mukluk, ouster, patten, slip-up 7 cashier, dismiss, drum out, galoshe, heave-ho, kick out, release 8 chase out, drive out, footgear, footwear, furlough, get rid of, muckluck, overshoe, pink-slip, snow shoe, throw out 9 discharge, eighty-six, terminate 10 Wellington
attachment: 4 spur
ender: 3 leg 4 jack, lace, lick 5 black, strap
Europe's ~: 5 Italy
fisherman's ~: 5 wader
fix a ~: 4 sole 6 resole
hip ~: 5 wader
in America: 5 trunk
out: 3 axe, can 4 fire, oust, sack 5 evict, exile, expel 6 bounce, depose 9 discharge
part: 3 lug, toe 4 lace, sole, vamp 6 insole
snow ~ brand: 5 Sorel
starter: 4 free, jack
the ball: 3 err
to ~: 3 too, yet 4 also 6 as well 7 besides, further 8 moreover
wearer: 4 puss

boot __: **4** camp, hook, tree
__ boot: **3** hip, ski, top **4** half, jump **6** chukka, combat, cowboy, Denver, Desert, riding **7** Hessian, jodhpur
Boot __: **4** Hill
__ Boot: **3** Das
boot camp
command: **6** at ease, fall in
figure: **3** sgt. **6** gyrene, Marine **8** sergeant
reply: **3** sir **5** no sir **6** yes sir
routine: **5** drill
booted: **4** shod
bootee: **4** shoe **8** baby shoe, footgear, footwear
booth: **4** cell, coop, mart, seat **5** kiosk, stall, stand **6** alcove, carrel, market **7** carrell, cubicle **8** boutique **9** cubbyhole, enclosure **10** repository
Brit's phone ~: **5** kiosk
mall ~: **5** kiosk
occupant: **5** voter **6** caller
offering: **4** info
__ booth: **4** toll **5** phone **7** polling
Booth: **5** Edwin **6** Hubert **7** Shirley **10** Tarkington
__ Boothe Luce: **5** Clare
Boothe, Powers: **5** actor
Booth, Shirley: **7** actress
film: Come Back, Little Sheba (1952, AA)
TV: Hazel
bootie: **4** shoe **8** baby shoe
booties, make: **4** knit **7** crochet
bootleg: **5** hooch **6** hootch **7** illegal, illicit, smuggle, traffic **8** unlawful **9** moonshine **10** contraband
bootlegger: **5** felon **8** criminal **9** miscreant
material: **4** mash **5** hooch **6** hootch **9** moonshine
nemesis: **3** Fed **4** Ness
bootless: **4** vain **6** unshod **7** inutile, useless **8** unusable **9** for naught, pointless, to no avail, worthless **10** profitless, unavailing
bootlick: **4** fawn **5** toady **6** grovel **7** adulate, flatter **8** kowtow to
bootlicker: **5** toady **6** fawner, flunky, lackey, yes man **7** flunkey **8** courtier, kowtower **9** sycophant
bootlicking: **7** servile **8** flattery
Bootnose: **3** Sid **4** Abel
boots
shake in one's ~: **5** cower **6** cringe
Boots: **8** Randolph
__ Boots: **5** Puss 'N
boots and __: **7** saddles
__ Boots Are Made...: **5** These
boot-shaped country: **5** Italy
booty: **4** haul, loot, pelf, swag, take **5** goods, trove **6** boodle, spoils, trophy **7** jobbery, pillage, plunder, takings
Bootylicious (2001 song)
artist: Destiny's Child
booze: **5** drink, hooch, sauce **6** hootch, liquor, rotgut, whisky **7** alcohol, spirits, whiskey **9** inebriant, moonshine **10** hard liquor, intoxicant
bop: **3** pow **4** belt, blow, conk, jazz, sock **5** dance, music, punch **6** wallop **7** clobber
Bop __ You Drop: **3** 'Til
__ Bop: **3** She
Bo-Peep
call to ~: **3** baa **5** bleat
charge: **5** sheep
Bopha! (1993 film)
cast: Danny Glover, Malcolm McDowell, Alfre Woodard
director: Morgan Freeman
__-Bopp comet: **4** Hale
__-bopper: **5** teeny
__, Bopper: **3** Big
Bora Bora: **4** isle **6** island
locale: **9** Polynesia, South Seas
borage: **4** herb
Borah: **4** peak **5** mount **8** mountain
locale: **5** Idaho
Borat (2006 film)
cast: Sacha Baron Cohen
borate: **4** salt
Borateem: **6** bleach
competitor: **5** Purex, Snowy, Vivid **6** Clorox
borax: **3** ore
Boraxo: **4** soap
rival: ***see*** soap
__ Borch: **3** Ter
Bordeaux: **3** vin **4** city, port, town, wine **6** claret
locale: **6** France
river: **7** Garonne
wine: **5** Médoc
Bordelaise __: **5** sauce
Borden: **4** Gail **6** Lizzie
competitor: **5** Kraft
cow: **5** Elmer, Elsie
product: **4** glue, milk
weapon: **3** axe
border: **3** hem, lip, rim **4** abut, brim, edge, join, lace, line, meet, side, trim **5** brink, frame, front, limit, shore, skirt, touch, verge **6** adjoin, edging, fringe, limbus, margin, stripe **8** boundary, division, frontier, land's end, lie along, neighbor, surround **9** extremity, outskirts, perimeter, periphery, state line, threshold
circular ~: **4** band, belt, ring **6** collar, girdle **8** cincture
ender: **4** line
fabric ~: **3** hem **4** seam **6** edging, fringe
on: **4** abut, join **5** touch **6** adjoin **9** juxtapose
ornamental ~: **4** dado
road ~: **4** curb **5** verge **8** shoulder
water ~: **4** bank **5** beach, coast, shore **7** seaside **8** littoral, seaboard, seashore **9** shoreline
border __: **3** tax **4** line
Border __: **6** collie, States **7** terrier
bordering: **4** near, nigh **6** at hand, nearby **8** adjacent, imminent, nextdoor **9** impending, proximate **10** contiguous, convenient, juxtaposed
on: **4** near **6** beside **8** touching
borderline: **3** end **4** iffy **6** fringe, limbic **8** doubtful, marginal, unstable **9** ambiguous, debatable, dubitable, equivocal, on the edge, uncertain, undecided, unsettled **10** ambivalent, indecisive, indefinite
Borderline (1984 song)
artist: Madonna
borders: **5** limbi **8** confines
Borders: **9** bookstore **10** bookseller
Border, The (1982 film)
cast: Harvey Keitel, Jack Nicholson, Warren Oates, Valerie Perrine
Bordet, Jules: **7** Belgian **8** Nobelist
Bordoni, Irene: **6** singer
bore: **3** dig **4** cloy, drag, drip, jade, mine, pain, pall, pest, pill, ream, tire, well **5** creep, drill, gouge, prick, stare, weary **6** burrow, gasbag, pierce, tunnel, yawner **7** dullard, fatigue, turn off, wear out, windbag **8** gouge out, irritant, nuisance, puncture **9** penetrate, perforate, tidal wave **10** discomfort, jackhammer, put to sleep, wet blanket
broaden a ~: **4** ream
tidal ~: **5** eager, eagre
__ bore: **5** snail, tidal
__-bore: **4** full **5** small
boreal: **4** wind **5** north **8** northern
__ borealis: **6** aurora, corona
boreas: **4** wind
Boreas: **3** god
parent: **3** Eos **6** Aeolus
bored: **5** blasé, jaded, tired, weary **6** in a rut **7** worn out **8** listless **9** incurious **10** world-weary
feeling: **4** blah
get ~: **4** tire
like ~ kids: **5** antsy, itchy **7** fidgety **8** restless **9** unsettled
(of): **4** sick
reaction: **4** yawn
boredom: **5** ennui **6** apathy, tedium **7** fatigue **8** flatness, lethargy, monotony **9** jadedness, lassitude, weariness **10** melancholy
express ~: **4** sigh, yawn **5** ho-hum
borer: **3** bug **4** pest, worm **5** auger, drill, larva, tirer **6** insect **7** termite **8** white ant
combining form: **6** trypan- **7** trypano-
product: **4** hole
starter: **4** wood
__ borer: **4** corn, twig **7** currant
bore to __: **5** tears
Borg, Bjorn: **5** Swede **7** netster **9** tennis pro
milieu: **5** court
Borges, Jorge Luis: **6** writer **9** Argentine
Borge, Victor: **6** Danish **7** pianist
Borgia: **6** Cesare **8** Lucrezia
in-law: **4** Este
see also Italian
Borglum, Gutzon: **6** artist **8** sculptor
Borgnine, Ernest: **5** actor
film: The Dirty Dozen (1967)
Emperor of the North (1973)
Escape From New York (1981)
Ice Station Zebra (1968)
Jubal (1956)
Marty (1955, AA)
The Poseidon Adventure (1972)
The Wild Bunch (1969)
spouse: Katy Jurado, Ethel Merman
TV: McHale's Navy
Bori, Lucrezia: **6** singer **7** soprano
specialty: **5** opera
boring: **3** dry **4** arid, blah, drab, dull, flat, tame **5** bland, heavy, ho-hum, unfun, vapid, yawny **6** draggy, dreary, jejune, stodgy, stuffy **7** humdrum, insipid, nowhere, operose, prosaic, routine, tedious **8** dragging, tiresome **9** ponderous, prosaical, tasteless, wearisome **10** dullsville, enervating, lackluster, monotonous, pedestrian, uneventful **11** mind-numbing
experience: **4** drag, yawn
get ~: **4** pale, pall
person: **4** drag, pill
tool: **3** awl, bit **5** auger, drill **10** jackhammer
Boris: **4** czar, tsar **6** Becker **7** Badenov, Godunov, Karloff, Spassky, Yeltsin **9** Goldovsky, Pasternak
wife: **5** Naina
Boris Godunov: **5** opera
composer: Modest Mussorgsky
role: **5** Pimen, Xenia **6** Dmitri, Feodor **7** Gregory, Shuisky, Varlaam
setting: **6** Poland, Russia
Bork: **6** Robert
Borman, Frank: **9** astronaut
born: **3** née **6** innate, living **7** hatched **8** destined, inherent **9** delivered, intrinsic **10** congenital
be ~: **9** originate
first: **5** elder, older **6** eldest
loser: **4** dupe **5** patsy
loser's question: **5** why me
not ~ yesterday: **5** sharp, smart **6** astute
starter: **3** low, new **4** base, free, high, last, true, twin, well **5** earth
to the manner ~: **5** noble **7** genteel **9** patrician
yesterday: **3** raw **4** naif **5** naive
born __: **5** loser
born-__: **5** again
__-born: **3** sea **4** city, last **5** first, twice **6** heaven, middle, native **7** foreign, natural
Born __: **4** Free **5** to Run
__ Born, A: **6** Star Is
born-again: **5** pious **9** religious
born and __: **4** bred
borne: **5** toted **6** wafted **7** carried, endured
starter: **3** air, sea **4** ship **5** space, water
Borneo: **4** isle **6** island
archipelago: **5** Malay
country on ~: **6** Brunei
island near ~: **4** Bali, Java, Laut **7** Celebes **8** Sulawesi
language: **5** Dayak
port: **10** Balikpapan
primate: **5** orang **9** orangutan **10** orangutang
region: **5** Sabah
sea: **4** Sulu
__ Bornes: **5** Mille
Born Free: **4** film, song
artist: Roger Williams
author: Joy Adamson
cast: Virginia McKenna, Bill Travers
lioness: **4** Elsa
Born in the U.S.A. (1984 song)
artist: Bruce Springsteen
bornite: **3** ore

Born Loser, The: 7 cartoon
dog: 6 Kewpie
Born, Max: 7 British **8** Nobelist **9** physicist
Born on the Fourth of July (1989 film)
cast: Tom Cruise, Willem Dafoe
director: Oliver Stone
setting: 3 Nam **7** Vietnam
Born to Be My Baby (1988 song)
artist: Bon Jovi
Born to Be Wild (1968 song)
artist: Steppenwolf
Born to Be With You (1956 song)
artist: Chordettes
Born to Dance (1936 film)
cast: Eleanor Powell, James Stewart
composer: Cole Porter
Born to Run (1975 song)
artist: Bruce Springsteen
born to the __: 6 purple
Born Yesterday: 4 film **5** novel
author: Garson Kanin
cast: Broderick Crawford, William Holden, Judy Holliday
director: George Cukor
Borodin, Aleksandr: 7 Russian **8** composer
work: Prince Igor
boron: 7 element
ore: 7 kernite
Boros, Julius: 6 golfer
borough: 4 town
boss: 5 mayor
London ~: 6 Barnet, Ealing
New York ~: 5 Bronx **6** Queens **8** Brooklyn **9** Manhattan
borrow: 3 bum, owe **4** copy, rent, take **5** adopt, mooch, usurp **6** assume, pirate **7** imitate **8** simulate **10** plagiarize
a phrase: 4 cite **5** quote
from: 5 hit up, mooch **7** imitate
on: 4 hock, pawn **8** mortgage
opposite: 4 lend
trouble: 5 worry
borrowed: 10 derivative
amount ~: 4 loan
car: 6 loaner
borrowed __: 4 time
borrower
back a ~: 6 cosign
figure: 3 APR **8** interest
funds: 4 loan
borscht: 4 soup
base: 4 beet
borscht __: 4 belt **7** circuit
Borstal Boy
author: Brendan Behan
Boru, Brian land: 4 Erin
Borzage, Frank: 8 director
borzoi: 3 dog **5** canid **6** canine
BOS
see Boston
Bosc: 4 pear
relative: 5 Anjou **6** Comice, Seckel **8** Bartlett
boscage: 5 copse **7** coppice
Bosch: 4 Carl **10** Hieronymus
Bosch, Carl: 6 German **7** chemist **8** Nobelist
Bosch, Hieronymus: 6 artist **7** Flemish, painter
Bosco: 4 John **6** Philip
Bosco, John: 5 saint
Bose
rival: 4 TEAC
bosh
see baloney
bosket: 5 grove **7** thicket
bosky: 6 silvan, sylvan, woodsy
Bosley: 3 Tom **8** Crowther
Bosley, Tom: 5 actor
TV: Happy Days, Murder She Wrote
bo's'n: 3 off. **5** bosun **6** sailor **7** jack tar, officer
boss: 4 cap'n, capt. **7** captain
Bosnia and Herzegovina
capital: 8 Sarajevo
city: 5 Doboj, Tuzla **6** Mostar, Zenica **8** Prijedor, Sarajevo **9** Banja Luka
neighbor: 7 Croatia **10** Yugoslavia
peacekeeping org.: 4 NATO
writer: 6 Andric
bosom: 4 soul **5** chest **8** intimate
buddy: 3 pal **4** chum **5** buddy, crony **6** friend **7** adviser, advisor, comrade **8** alter ego, intimate **9** companion, confidant
Bosom Buddies (ABC sitcom)
cast: Tom Hanks (Kip Wilson)
Peter Scolari (Henry Desmond)
boson: 4 pion **5** meson **6** photon **7** pi meson **8** particle
Bosox
see Red Sox
boss: 3 run, top **4** exec, head, king, lord, stud, supt., tuff **5** chief, hirer, Mr. Big, ruler **6** cheese, direct, gerent, honcho, leader, manage, top dog, tycoon **7** captain, control, foreman, headman, manager, oversee, skipper **8** dominate, employer, especial, governor, higher-up, kingfish, official, overseer, superior **9** authority, commander, executive, officiate, organizer, supervise **10** administer, head honcho, politician, supervisor, taskmaster **16** brass hatdirector
around: 5 order **6** demand **8** domineer **9** trample on, tyrannize
baseball ~: 3 mgr. **7** manager
be the ~: 4 rule **6** govern **7** control **8** hold sway
company ~: 3 CEO **4** exec, suit **9** executive
echo: 5 toady **6** flunky, yes man **7** flunkey
in Spanish: 3 amo **4** jefe
mean ~: 4 ogre
mob ~: 3 don **4** capo
note from the ~: 5 see me
often: 5 firer, hirer, owner
shield ~: 4 umbo
straw ~: 6 gerent **7** manager **8** overseer **10** figurehead, supervisor
workers: 5 staff
see also wonderful
__ boss: 3 pit **4** fire **5** straw, trail, wagon **7** section
Boss: 4 Hugo
Boss __: 5 Tweed
bossa nova: 5 dance, music
cousin: 5 samba
Bossa Nova Baby (1963 song)
artist: Elvis Presley
bosses: 10 management
Boss Lady (1952 film)
cast: Lynn Bari
Bosson, Barbara: 7 actress
Boss's Son, The (1978 film)
director: Bobby Roth
bossy: 4 firm, hard **5** cruel, picky, pushy, rigid, stern, tough **6** severe **7** austere, Spartan **8** arrogant, despotic, exacting, hard-line, rigorous, superior **9** arbitrary, demanding, draconian, imperious, officious, stringent, unbending, unsparing **10** commanding, despotical, inflexible, iron-fisted, ironhanded, no-nonsense, oppressive, peremptory, tyrannical
Bossy: 3 cow **4** Mike
Bossy, Mike: 8 puckster
milieu: 3 ice **4** rink **5** arena
org.: 3 NHL
Bostic: 4 Earl
Boston: 4 city, fern, game, port, town **5** dance, novel **8** Beantown, card game
airport: 5 Logan
athletes: 7 Huskies
author: Upton Sinclair
campus: 5 Tufts, U Mass
county: 7 Suffolk
entrée: 3 cod **5** scrod **7** chowder
locale: 4 Mass.
monkey: 5 dance
newspaper: 5 Globe **6** Herald
nickname: 3 Hub
pro team: 3 Sox **5** Celts **6** Bruins, Red Sox **7** Celtics
river: 6 Mystic **7** Charles
skyscraper, for short: 3 Pru
song: Amanda (1986)
Don't Look Back (1978)
More Than a Feeling (1976)
We're Ready (1986)
suburb: 4 Lynn **6** Lowell
zone: 3 EDT, EST
Boston __: 3 bag, ivy **4** bull, fern, Pops **5** Globe **6** Common, Market, Public, rocker, states **7** Brahmin, lettuce, terrier
Boston baked __: 5 beans
Boston College
athletes: 6 Eagles
conference: 7 Big East
Boston Common: 4 park
Boston cream __: 3 pie
Boston Garden: 5 arena
player: 4 Celt **6** Celtic
Boston Harbor
feature: 4 quay
jetsam: 3 tea
Bostonians, The
author: Henry James
Boston Legal (ABC drama/comedy)
cast: Candice Bergen (Shirley Schmidt)
John Larroquette (Carl Sack)
William Shatner (Denny Crane)
James Spader (Alan Shore)
Tara Summers (Katie Lloyd)
Boston Public (Fox drama)
cast: Kathy Baker (Meredith Peters)
Loretta Devine (Marla Hendricks)
Fyvush Finkel (Harvey Lipschultz)
Jessalyn Gilsig (Lauren Davis)
Anthony Heald (Scott Guber)
Rashida Jones (Louisa Fenn)
Nicky Katt (Harry Senate)
Sharon Leal (Marilyn Sudor)
Chi McBride (Steven Harper)
Jeri Ryan (Ronnie Cooke)
extra: 4 teen
Boston Tea __: 5 Party
Bostridge: 3 Ian
Bostwick: 5 Barry
bosun: 6 sailor **7** jack tar **9** boatswain
boss: 4 cap'n, capt. **7** captain
Boswell: 5 James **6** Connee
Boswell, James: 6 writer **7** diarist **8** Scottish
Boswell, James subject: Johnson
Bosworth: 4 Kate **5** Brian
Bosworth Field: 6 battle
locale: 7 England
loser: 10 Richard III
winner: 8 Henry VII
bot.: 3 sci.
botanical __: 6 garden
botanist: 4 Cohn, Gray **5** Banks, Vries **6** Carver, Mendel, Torrey **8** Linnaeus
angle: 4 axil
Austrian ~: 6 Mendel
bract: 5 palea
British ~: 5 Banks
bud: 5 gemma
capsule: 5 theca
creation: 6 hybrid
Dutch ~: 5 Vries
filament: 6 elater
German ~: 4 Cohn
opening: 5 stoma
openings: 7 stomata
ridge: 6 carina
sac: 5 ascus
scion: 5 graft
space: 6 areola, areole
study: 5 flora **6** plants
suffix: 3 -ody **5** -aceae
Swedish ~: 8 Linnaeus
botany: 7 science
branch of ~: 8 bryology, pomology **9** phytology **10** dendrology, floristics
Botany __: 3 Bay **4** wool
Botany Bay, like: 5 penal
botch: 3 err, mar **4** blow, boot, flub, goof, mess, miss, muff, ruin **5** gum up, misdo, mix up, snafu, spoil, wreck **6** blow it, bobble, boggle, bollix, bumble, bungle, foozle, foul up, fumble, goof up, mess up, muck up, muddle, slip-up **7** blunder, louse up, mistake, screw up **8** flounder, shambles **9** mishandle, mismanage
Botch-a-Me (1952 song)
artist: Rosemary Clooney
botched: 6 faulty, sloppy **8** slipshod, slovenly **10** unthorough
effort: 4 goof **5** error **6** slip-up **7** mistake
botcher: 2 ox **3** oaf **4** lout **5** klutz
botfly: 3 bug **6** insect
both: 3 duo **5** alike, twain **6** either, the two **7** equally, pronoun
combining form: 3 bis- **4** ambi- **5** amphi-, ampho-
for ~ sexes: 4 coed **6** unisex
Botha, P.W.: 9 statesman **12** South African
bother: 3 ado, ail, bug, dog, eat, get, irk, kid, nag, rag, vex **4** bait, care,

carp, drag, faze, fret, fuss, gall, goad, miff, pain, pest, ride, rile, to-do **5** annoy, chafe, eat at, get to, harry, hound, nag at, nudge, peeve, shake, taunt, tease, upset, worry **6** accost, badger, dismay, gnaw at, harass, hassle, heckle, impede, madden, molest, needle, nettle, noodge, obsess, pester, pick on, plague, pother, put out, rankle, rattle, ruffle **7** afflict, agitate, bedevil, concern, disturb, fluster, grate on, henpeck, perturb, problem, provoke, torment, trouble **8** browbeat, disquiet, distress, exercise, headache, irritant, irritate, nuisance, unsettle, vexation **9** aggravate, annoyance, discomfit, displease, give a darn, incommode, interrupt, take pains **10** difficulty, discompose, disconcert, exasperate, irritation
don't ~: **9** never mind
ender: **4** some
botheration: **3** ado **4** pest **6** hassle **7** anxiety, problem
bothered: **5** upset **6** uneasy **7** in a snit, in a stir, put upon, worried
be ~ by: **4** mind
no longer ~ by: **5** rid of
bothersome: **5** messy, pesky, pesty **6** thorny, trying, vexing **8** annoying, worrying **9** demanding, difficult, troubling, vexatious **10** disturbing, in one's hair, irritating
Bothe, Walther: **6** German **8** Nobelist **9** physicist
Bothnia: **4** gulf
locale: **6** Sweden **7** Finland
sea: **6** Baltic
Both Sides Now (1968 song)
artist: Judy Collins
___ both ways: **3** cut
Bothwell: **4** Scot
Botkin: **5** Perry
Botswana: **6** nation **7** country
bovine: **6** Tswana
capital: **8** Gaborone
coin: **5** Thebe
desert: **8** Kalahari
lake: **5** Ngami
money: **4** pula **5** thebe
neighbor: **7** Namibia **8** Zimbabwe
people: **5** Sotho **6** Basuto, Herero, Tswana
Botticelli, Sandro: **6** artist **7** Italian, painter
work: **4** nude **5** Venus
bottle: **3** jar, jug **4** tree, vial **5** cruet, flask, glass, phial **6** carafe, carboy, flacon, flagon **7** canteen, repress **8** decanter, preserve, suppress **9** container
British ~ size: **5** litre
capacity: **4** pint **5** liter, quart
dweller: **5** genie
edge: **3** lip
ender: **4** neck **5** brush
get better in the ~: **3** age **6** mellow
hit the ~: **4** tope **5** booze, drink
lab ~: **5** flask **6** aludel
material: **5** glass
medicine-chest ~: **6** iodine **7** alcohol **8** peroxide
open a ~: **5** uncap **7** unscrew
perfume ~: **4** vial **5** phial **6** flacon
returnable ~: **5** empty
spin the ~: **4** game
starter: **4** blue
stopper: **3** cap, lid, top **4** cork
top: **3** cap, lid **4** neck
up: **4** hold **5** cramp, quash **6** corner, hold in **7** confine, contain, repress **8** suppress **9** constrain
use a ~ opener: **5** uncap
whiskey ~: **5** fifth
wine ~: **6** carafe, flagon
withdraw from a ~: **4** wean
bottle ___: **3** cap, imp **4** baby, bill, club, fern, shop, tree **5** glass, gourd, green, party **7** gentian, turning
bottle-___: **3** fed **4** feed **6** washer
bottle-___ dolphin: **5** nosed
___ bottle: **5** gemel, Klein **6** Nansen, siphon, vacuum **7** pilgrim, squeeze, thermos
bottled ___: **3** gas **5** water **6** in bond
___-bottled: **6** estate
bottled-up: **4** pent **9** inhibited, repressed
bottleneck: **3** jam **4** snag **5** block, jam-up, tie-up **6** hangup, hinder, holdup, logjam **7** barrier **8** cul-de-sac, gridlock, obstacle **10** congestion, impediment, traffic jam
cause a ~: **3** jam **5** block **6** impede
bottle-nosed ___: **5** whale **7** dolphin
bottom: **3** bed, end **4** base, foot, root, side, soul **5** basal, basic, floor, least, nadir **6** depths, ground, lesser, lowest, valley **7** minimum, radical, support **8** low point **9** lowermost, underside **10** foundation, underlying
at ~: **6** au fond
at the ~ of: **6** behind
bet one's ~ dollar: **4** rely **6** depend
deal from the ~: **5** cheat
dress ~: **3** hem
ender: **4** land, most
feeder: **4** carp
floor: **6** cellar
food-chain ~: **4** alga **5** algae
from the ~ of one's heart: **9** sincerely
get to the ~ of: **5** plumb, solve **6** fathom
hit ~: **4** fell, sink **6** go down, plunge **7** founder, go under **8** flounder, submerge
lake ~: **3** bed **7** benthos
line: **3** net, sum **4** cost, crux **5** limit, point, tally, total **6** outlay, payoff, profit **7** essence, meaning, reality, revenue **8** key point, receipts **9** essential, main point **10** conclusion
of the barrel: **5** worst
on the ~: **7** aground **10** underneath
river ~: **3** bed
rock ~: **4** zero **5** nadir, worst
sea ~: **3** bed **7** benthos
send to the ~: **4** sink
ship ~: **4** hull, keel
top to ~: **6** wholly **7** totally
touch ~: **4** sink
bottom ___: **3** dog, ice, out **4** bolt, fish, gear, heat, land, line, time **5** grass, quark, round, yeast **6** drawer, feeder
___ bottom: **4** rock **5** false, top to
___-bottom: **4** bell **6** sulfur
___ Bottom: **5** Foggy
___ Bottom Boat, The: **5** Glass
bottomless: **4** deep **7** abysmal, abyssal, yawning **8** baseless, profound **9** cavernous, limitless, unfailing, unfounded, unsounded **10** fathomless, groundless, unfathomed, unmeasured
pit: **5** abysm, abyss
bottomless ___: **3** pit
bottom-line: **5** vital **8** critical **9** essential
figure: **3** net, sum **5** count, score, tally, total **6** amount **9** aggregate, reckoning
bottom-of-the-___: **4** line
bottom-out: **7** decline **9** downswing, recession
bottoms: **5** swamp **6** meadow
like some ~: **5** false
Bottoms: **3** Sam **6** Joseph **7** Timothy
bottoms up: **5** salud, skoal, toast **6** cheers, kampai, prosit
Bottrop: **4** city, town
locale: **7** Germany
Botts ___: **4** dots
botulin: **5** toxin
Botvinnik, Mikhail forte: **5** chess
boudoir: **4** room **5** bower **7** bedroom
Boudreau, Lou: **6** Indian **9** shortstop
bouffant: **4** coif **6** hairdo **8** coiffure **9** hairstyle
___ bouffe: **5** opera
bougainvillea: **5** plant **6** flower
Bougainville, Louis Antoine de: **6** French **8** explorer
bough: **3** arm **4** limb **6** branch
place: **4** tree **5** trunk
stunted ~: **4** spur
take a ~: **3** lop **5** prune
boughpot: **4** vase
___-bought: **5** store
bought, just: **3** new **6** cherry **8** brand-new **9** never used
bouillabaisse: **4** soup, stew
base: **4** fish
bouillon: **4** soup **5** broth, stock **8** beverage, julienne
bouillon ___: **3** cup **4** cube **5** spoon
___ bouillon: **4** beef **7** chicken
Boulanger: **5** Nadia
boulder: **4** rock, slab **5** stone
breaker: **3** TNT **5** nitro **8** dynamite
Boulder: **4** city, town
athletes: **9** Buffaloes
locale: **8** Colorado
newspaper: **6** Camera
sports org.: **4** USOC
Boulder ___: **3** Dam **6** Canyon
Boulder Dam: **6** Hoover
lake: **4** Mead
boulevard: **3** way **4** mall, road **5** paseo, route **6** artery, avenue, street **7** ingress **9** concourse
divider: **6** island
liner: **4** tree
Los Angeles ~: **4** Pico **6** Sunset
boulevardier: **3** fop **5** dandy
Boulevard of Broken Dreams
composer: Al Dubin, Harry Warren
Boulez, Pierre: **6** French **9** conductor
Boulle, Pierre: **6** French, writer
work: The Bridge Over the River Kwai Planet of the Apes
Boulogne: **4** city, port, town
Bois de ~: **4** parc, park
see also French
Boulogne-sur-___: **3** Mer
Boult, Adrian: **3** Sir **7** British **9** conductor
Boulting: **3** Roy **4** John
bounce: **2** ax **3** axe, bob, can, hop, jar, jog, pep, vim, zip **4** boot, bump, drop, echo, flop, jerk, jump, leap, life, oust, sack, shun, skip, veto, zest **5** carom, eject, evict, frisk, let go, spurn, start, vault, verve, vigor **6** carrom, depose, energy, glance, jiggle, joggle, jounce, lay off, pass on, rattle, rebuff, recoil, reject, remove, spring **7** boot out, cashier, disdain, dismiss, dribble, drum out, exclude, kick out, rebound, release, say no to **8** buoyance, buoyancy, disallow, dynamism, furlough, get rid of, pink-slip, ricochet, snap back, turn down, vitality, vivacity **9** animation, blackball, cast aside, discharge, eighty-six, élan vital, rejection, repudiate, terminate **10** elasticity, exuberance, friskiness, get up and go, liveliness, resilience, spring back
back: **4** echo **5** carom, rally, react **6** carrom, return, revive **7** rebound, recover **8** backfire, ricochet **9** boomerang **10** recuperate
checks: **4** kite
infield ~: **3** hop
off: **6** glance **7** deflect
on water: **3** dap **4** skip
sound ~: **4** echo
Bounce
competitor: **5** Downy **7** Snuggle **9** Cling Free **10** Final Touch
Bounce (2000 film)
cast: Ben Affleck, Natasha Henstridge, Gwyneth Paltrow
director: Don Roos
___ Bounce: **6** Jersey
bounced-check letters: **3** NSF
bouncer: **5** guard
baby ~: **4** knee
demand: **2** ID **3** out
like a ~: **5** burly **6** strong
bounciness: **6** spring **10** elasticity
bouncing: **8** vigorous
off the walls: **4** edgy **5** antsy, hyper
bouncy: **3** gay **5** fresh, jolly, perky **6** frisky, jovial, lively, yeasty **7** buoyant, rocking, romping, rubbery, springy **8** cheerful, spirited **9** ebullient, energetic, exuberant, resilient, sprightly, vivacious **10** boisterous
gait: **3** jog **4** lope, skip, trot
melody: **4** lilt
bound: **3** end, hop, run **4** bent, edge, jump, leap, line, skip, sure **5** bourn, fated, fence, hem in, limit, lunge, start, tight, vault **6** apogee, begird, doomed, driven, forced, hasten, hurdle, intent, liable, margin, pounce, prance, secure, spring **7** captive, confine, hop over, limited, obliged, pledged **8** con-

fined, destined, hemmed in, impelled, indebted, required, restrict, stalwart, surround **9** compelled, obligated **10** contracted, purposeful, relentless
and determined: 7 decided **8** resolute, stubborn
by: 9 subject to
by oath: 5 sworn
for: 5 off to
not ~ by: 6 exempt
starter: 3 fog, ice, pot **4** east, hard, hide, home, hoof, iron, snow, soft, west **5** brass, cloth, house, north, paper, south **6** strike
to happen: 4 sure **7** certain, cinched **8** definite, in the bag, positive **10** guaranteed, inevitable
up: 8 absorbed, immersed, obsessed
__ bound: 5 lower, upper
__-bound: 3 air **4** rock, tide **5** earth, honor **6** muscle, spiral **7** outward, weather
__ Bound: 7 Alabamy, Outward
boundaries: 4 area, term **5** limit, orbit, range, scope, sweep **6** bounds, region **7** borders, compass, purview, terrain **8** confines, environs **9** perimeter, periphery, territory
locate ~: 6 demark, survey
push back the ~: 5 widen
set ~: 6 define
boundary: 3 end, rim **4** edge, line, mete, side **5** ambit, brink, hedge, limit, verge **6** border, limbus, limits, margin, radius **7** barrier, compass **8** division, frontier **9** extremity, outskirts, perimeter, periphery, territory **10** outer limit
marker: 4 rail **5** fence, stake
boundary __: 4 line **5** layer, rider
Boundary Peak: 5 mount **8** mountain
locale: 3 Nev. **6** Nevada
bounded: 7 limited **9** qualified **10** measurable, terminable
by: 6 amidst **7** between
bounder: 3 cad **4** roué **5** knave, rogue, scamp, swine, yahoo **6** bad guy **8** scalawag **9** scallawag, scallywag, scoundrel **10** blackguard, scapegrace
Bound for Glory (1976 film)
cast: David Carradine, Ronny Cox, Melinda Dillon
director: Hal Ashby
bounding main: 3 sea **5** ocean
on the ~: 4 asea **5** at sea
ride the ~: 4 sail **6** cruise, voyage
boundless: 3 big **4** vast, wide **6** eonian, untold **7** abysmal, endless, immense **8** infinite, spacious, unending **9** countless, excessive, extensive, limitless, no-strings, unbounded, unfailing, unlimited **10** indefinite, tremendous, unconfined, unnumbered, widespread
bounds: 4 pale **5** ambit, limit, orbit, range, verge **6** extent, limits, reason **7** measure **8** confines, premises **9** perimeter
keep within ~: 4 curb **5** check, limit **6** temper **7** confine, contain **8** moderate, regulate, restrain, restrict **9** constrict
out of ~: 4 tabu **5** shady, taboo, ultra **6** banned, errant **7** illegal, illicit, naughty **8** outlawed, straying, unlawful, verboten **9** forbidden, frowned on, off-limits **10** closed-down, not allowed, prohibited, proscribed, unorthodox
within ~: 6 in line **9** allowable
__ bounds: 5 out of
bounteous: 4 full, rich **5** ample, noble, palmy **6** enough, plenty **7** copious, liberal, profuse **8** abundant, generous, handsome, prodigal **9** bountiful, plentiful **10** benevolent, munificent
bountiful: 4 many, rich **5** ample **6** divers, enough, gobs of, lavish, lots of, myriad, plenty, umteen, untold **7** copious, fertile, heaps of, liberal, no end of, piles of, profuse, scads of, umpteen **8** abundant, affluent, generous, handsome, manifold, numerous, oodles of, princely, prodigal, prolific, scores of, umpsteen **9** bounteous, countless, exuberant, luxuriant, plenteous, plentiful, quite a few, unsparing **10** benevolent, charitable, dime a dozen, hospitable, munificent, zillions of
name meaning ~: 5 Doris
Bountiful: 4 city, town
locale: 4 Utah
__ Bountiful: 4 Lady
bounty: 4 gift, loot **5** bonus, flood, grant, price **6** reward, wealth **7** premium, subsidy, tribute **8** largesse **9** abundance, endowment, plenitude, profusion **10** lavishness, liberality, prosperity
bounty __: 6 hunter
__ bounty: 5 king's **6** queen's
Bounty: 4 boat, ship **10** paper towel
competitor: 4 Viva **5** Scott **6** Brawny
event: 6 mutiny
port of call: 6 Tahiti
Bounty, The (1984 film)
cast: Mel Gibson, Anthony Hopkins, Laurence Olivier
bouquet: 4 nose, odor, posy **5** aroma, odour, scent, smell, spray **7** incense, nosegay, perfume **9** fragrance, redolence
element: 4 posy **6** flower
holder: 4 frog, vase
maker: 7 florist
wine ~: 4 nose **5** aroma, scent **9** fragrance
bouquet-by-phone: 3 FTD
bourbon: 6 whisky **7** whiskey
drink: 5 julep **9** mint julep
bourbon __: 4 rose **6** whisky **7** whiskey
Bourbon: 5 royal **6** street
see also French
bourgeois: 4 non-U **6** common, people **8** plebeian **9** hidebound, illiberal, landowner, Victorian **10** capitalist, philistine
alternative: *see* point size
__ bourgeois: 5 petit
__ bourgeoise: 6 petite
__ bourgeoisie: 5 haute, petty
Bourgeois, Léon: 8 Nobelist
__ bourguignon: 4 beef **5** boeuf
Bourke-White, Margaret: 12 photographer
spouse: Erskine Caldwell
Bourne Identity, The: 4 film **5** novel
author: Robert Ludlum
cast: Chris Cooper, Matt Damon, Clive Owen
character: 5 Jason
Bournemouth: 4 city, town
locale: 6 Dorset **7** England
Bourne Supremacy, The
author: Robert Ludlum
Bourne Supremacy, The (2004 film)
cast: Matt Damon, Julia Stiles
Bourne Ultimatum, The
author: Robert Ludlum
Bourne Ultimatum, The (2007 film)
cast: Matt Damon, Julia Stiles
bourrée: 5 dance
pas de ~: 4 step
bourse: 6 market
Wall Street ~: 4 AMEX, NYSE
bout: 4 duel, tilt, time **5** event, fight, match, round, scrap, set-to, shift, spell **6** attack, battle, tussle **7** contest, scuffle **8** conflict, struggle **9** encounter, fistfight, main event **10** engagement, fisticuffs
division: 5 round
ender: 2 KO **3** TKO **4** kayo
have a ~ with: 3 box **4** spar
locale: 4 ring **5** arena
long ~: 5 siege
wild ~: 5 binge, spree
see also boxing
__ bout: 5 title
boutique: 4 mart, shop **5** booth, salon, store **8** emporium **9** gift store
employee: 6 fitter
Bouton, Jim: 6 hurler, writer **7** pitcher
work: Ball Four
boutonniere site: 5 lapel
Boutros-__: 5 Ghali
Bouvier des Flandres: 3 dog **5** canid **6** canine
Bouvier, Jacqueline in 1947: 3 deb **9** debutante
bouzouki: 4 lute **6** string
origin: 6 Greece
Bova, Ben: 6 writer
genre: 5 sci-fi
bovarism: 3 ego
Bovary: 4 Emma
title: 3 Mme. **6** Madame
bovine: 2 ox **3** cow, yak **4** anoa, arna, dull, gaur, urus, zebu **5** bison, dense, gayal, steer, takin **6** heifer, mithan, muskox, obtuse, oxlike, stolid **7** aurochs, banteng, banting, beefalo, buffalo, carabao, cattalo, cowlike, kouprey, lumpish, tamarao, tamarau, timarau **8** sluggish **9** impassive **10** cattlelike, phlegmatic
Africa ~: 4 Glan, Kuri, Tuli **5** Barka, Boran, Horro, Maure, N'dama, Nguni **6** Angeln, Ankole, Ovambo, Tswana **7** Mashona **8** Bonsmara, Gelbvieh
Arctic ~: 6 muskox
Australia ~: 10 Murray Grey
Azerbaijan ~: 5 Kurdi **6** Sarabi
Bhutan ~: 4 Siri
Bosnia ~: 4 Busa
Brazil ~: 6 Nelore **7** Canchim
breed: 3 Gir **4** Busa, Glan, Kuri, Rath, Siri, Tuli **5** Angus, Barka, Boran, Dajal, Dangi, Deoni, Devon, Fjall, Horro, Kerry, Kurdi, Luing, Malvi, Maure, N'dama, Nguni, Oropa, Rathi, Sanhe, Wagyu **6** Angeln, Ankole, Aubrac, Baladi, Channi, Dexter, Dhanni, Dulong, Gaolao, Herens, Jaulan, Jersey, Lohani, Mewati, Nagori, Nelore, Nimari, Ongole, Ovambo, Ponwar, Rojhan, Salers, Sarabi, Sussex, Tswana, Vosges **7** Alberes, Bachaur, Barzona, Brahman, Brahmin, Cachena, Canchim, Istoben, Mashona, Red Poll, Retinta, Sahiwal, Yanbian **8** Ayrshire, Bonsmara, Charbray, Chianina, Galloway, Gelbvieh, Guernsey, Hereford, Holstein, Limousin **9** Charolais, Shorthorn, Simmental **10** Lincoln Red, Murray Grey, Welsh Black
Cambodia ~: 7 kouprey
chew: 3 cud
China ~: 5 takin **6** Dulong **7** Yanbian
Croatia ~: 4 Busa
England ~: 5 Devon **6** Jersey, Sussex **7** Red Poll **8** Guernsey, Hereford **10** Lincoln Red
Eritrea ~: 5 Barka
extinct ~: 4 urus **7** aurochs
foot: 4 hoof
France ~: 6 Aubrac, Herens, Salers, Vosges **7** Alberes **8** Limousin **9** Charolais
gland: 5 udder
group: 4 herd
Himalayas ~: 3 yak **5** takin
humped ~: 4 zebu **5** bison **7** buffalo
hybrid: 6 catalo **7** beefalo, cattalo
India ~: 3 Gir **4** arna, Rath, Siri, zebu **5** Dajal, Dangi, Deoni, Malvi, Rathi **6** Channi, Gaolao, Mewati, Nagori, Nimari, Ongole, Ponwar, Rojhan **7** Bachaur, Brahman, Brahmin, Sahiwal
Indonesia ~: 4 anoa
Iran ~: 5 Kurdi **6** Sarabi
Ireland ~: 5 Kerry **6** Dexter
Israel ~: 6 Baladi
Italy ~: 5 Oropa **8** Chianina
Japan ~: 5 Wagyu
Jordan ~: 6 Baladi
Laos ~: 7 kouprey
Lebanon ~: 6 Baladi
Macedonia ~: 4 Busa
Malay ~: 4 gaur **5** gayal **6** mithan **7** banteng, banting
Mideast ~: 6 Baladi, Jaulan
Mongolia ~: 5 Sanhe
Myanmar ~: 5 takin
name: 5 Bossy
Netherlands ~: 8 Holstein
of ads: 5 Elsie
Pakistan ~: 6 Channi, Dhanni, Lohani **7** Sahiwal
Philippines ~: 7 carabao, tamarao, tamarau, timarau
Pyrenees ~: 7 Alberes
Russia ~: 7 Istoben
Scotland ~: 5 Angus, Luing **8** Ayrshire, Galloway
Serbia ~: 4 Busa

- **shaggy ~:** 3 yak 5 bison 7 buffalo
- **Sikkim ~:** 4 Siri
- **sound:** 3 low, moo
- **Spain ~:** 7 Alberes, Cachena, Retinta
- **stomach:** 6 omasum
- **stomachs:** 5 omasa
- **Sweden ~:** 5 Fjall
- **Switzerland ~:** 6 Herens 9 Simmental
- **Syria ~:** 6 Baladi, Jaulan
- **Tibet ~:** 3 yak
- **Turkey ~:** 5 Kurdi
- **young ~:** 4 calf
- **Yugoslavia ~:** 4 Busa

bovines: 4 kine

bow: 3 arc, nod, sag 4 arch, bend, cave, flex, fore, loop, prow, stem 5 angle, curve, debut, front, greet, kotow, yield 6 accede, cave in, comply, crouch, curtsy, give in, kowtow, launch, relent, salaam, salute, slouch, submit, suffer, weapon 7 concede, flexure, gesture, rainbow, succumb 8 anterior, crescent, flection, forepart 9 acquiesce, curvature, reverence, sinuosity, surrender 10 capitulate, salutation, semicircle
- **and scrape:** 4 fawn 5 court, kneel, toady 6 grovel, kowtow 8 bootlick, fawn upon, suck up to 10 curry favor, pay court to
- **application:** 5 rosin
- **bearer:** 4 Amor, Eros 5 Cupid 6 hunter 7 warrior
- **boat with a high ~:** 4 dory
- **component:** 4 loop
- **down to:** 5 kneel, thank 6 praise 9 genuflect, prostrate
- **ender:** 3 fin, leg, man, men, wow 4 head, knot, line, shot 5 front, sprit 6 string
- **in music:** 4 arco
- **lady's ~:** 6 curtsy
- **make a ~:** 3 tie
- **missile:** 5 arrow
- **notch:** 4 nock
- **opposite:** 5 stern
- **out:** 4 quit 5 leave 6 beg off, resign 7 abandon 8 withdraw
- **part of the ~:** 5 hawse 10 figurehead
- **sound:** 5 twang
- **starter:** 3 fog, sun 4 down, long, rain, wing 5 cross 6 saddle
- **structure:** 6 fo'c's'le
- **to:** 4 heed, mind, obey 5 defer 6 accept, follow, fulfil, listen 7 abide by, conform, consent, fulfill, observe, respect, succumb 8 carry out 9 acquiesce
- **toward the ~:** 4 fore
- **violin ~ part:** 4 frog
- **with the ~:** 4 arco
- **wood:** 3 yew

bow ___: 3 net, oar, out, saw, tie 5 front, shock 6 rudder, window 7 compass

bow-___: 3 wow 4 iron

___ bow: 4 face, wing 5 sound, spoon 6 Cupid's, fiddle

Bow: 5 Clara
- **nickname:** 9 The It Girl

Bowa: 5 Larry

bow and ___: 6 scrape

bowdlerize: 4 edit 6 censor 8 mutilate 9 expurgate, red-pencil

Bowdoin: 6 school 7 college
- **locale:** 5 Maine

bowed: 4 bent 5 bandy, round 6 zigzag 7 angular, crooked, winding 8 angulose, angulous, cockeyed
- **combining form:** 3 tox- 4 toxi-, toxo-

Bo Weevil (1956 song)
- **artist:** Teresa Brewer

bower: 3 cot, hut 4 nook 5 arbor, cabin, house, lodge, shack 6 alcove, anchor, chalet, grotto, recess 7 bedroom, boudoir, close in, cottage, enclose, inclose, pergola 8 bungalow, encircle, surround
- **ender:** 4 bird

Bower: 10 Antoinette

Bowe, Riddick: 5 boxer
- **milieu:** 4 ring

Bowery Boys film: 5 Mr. Hex

Bowery denizen: 4 wino

Bowery, The (1933 film)
- **cast:** Wallace Beery, Jackie Cooper, George Raft
- **director:** Raoul Walsh

___ Bowes: 6 Pitney

Bowes, Major medium: 5 radio

bowfin: 4 amia, fish 7 dogfish, grindle, mudfish

Bowfinger (1999 film)
- **cast:** Christine Baranski, Heather Graham, Steve Martin, Eddie Murphy
- **dog:** 5 Betsy

bowie ___: 5 knife

Bowie: 3 Jim 4 city, Kuhn, town 5 David
- **locale:** 8 Maryland

Bowie, David
- **producer for ~:** 3 Eno
- **real last name:** Jones
- **song:** Blue Jean (1984)
  China Girl (1983)
  Dancing in the Street (1985)
  Fame (1975)
  Golden Years (1976)
  Let's Dance (1983)
- **spouse:** Iman

Bowie, Jim last stand: 5 Alamo

bowl: 4 roll 5 arena, basin, crock 6 saucer, tureen, vessel 7 stadium 8 coliseum 9 colosseum, container 10 receptacle
- **drinking ~:** 5 mazer
- **dust ~:** 9 wasteland
- **filler:** 4 soup, stew 5 chili 6 cereal
- **game prelude:** 6 parade
- **large ~:** 5 jorum
- **mixing ~:** 6 krater
- **of cherries, maybe:** 4 life
- **ornamental ~:** 5 tazza
- **over:** 3 awe, wow 4 jolt, slay, stun 5 amaze, floor, shock, upset 6 boggle, dazzle 7 astound, stagger, stupefy, unnerve 8 astonish, overcome, surprise 9 dumbfound, overwhelm, take aback
- **pedestal ~:** 5 tazza
- **starter:** 4 fish, wash

bowl ___: 4 game, over

___ bowl: 4 fish, slop 5 float, punch, salad, sugar 6 bubble, finger, mixing

___ Bowl: 3 Pro 4 Dust, Hula, Rose, Yale 5 Alamo, Aloha, Gator, Sugar, Super 6 Fiesta, Orange

bowlegged: 5 bandy

bowler: 3 hat 4 Roth, Welu 5 Aulby, derby, Weber 6 Burton, Carter, kegler 7 Anthony, athlete, kegeler 9 Don Carter 10 cricketeer
- **strikes, to a ~:** 3 xes

Bowles: 4 Jane, Paul 5 Sally

bowline: 4 knot, rope

bowling: 5 sport
- **alley button:** 5 reset
- **alley part:** 4 lane 6 gutter 7 channel 8 foul line
- **division:** 5 frame
- **goal:** 6 pocket
- **group:** 6 league
- **lawn ~:** 5 bocce, bocci 6 boccia, boccie
- **milieu:** 4 lane 5 alley
- **pin:** 5 maple
- **score:** 4 mark 5 spare 6 strike
- **term:** 3 tap 4 foul, hook, mark 5 alley, frame, spare, split 6 bucket, double, gutter, kegler, pocket, strike, triple, turkey 7 channel, headpin, kingpin 8 foul line, pushaway
- **three straight strikes in ~:** 6 triple, turkey
- **two straight strikes in ~:** 6 double
- **woe in ~:** 3 tap 5 split

bowling ___: 3 bag 4 ball 5 alley, green 6 center, crease

Bowling for Columbine (2002 film)
- **director:** Michael Moore

Bowling Green: 4 city, town
- **athletes:** 7 Falcons
- **conference:** 3 MAC
- **locale:** 4 Ohio 8 Kentucky

___ Bowl of Tea: 4 Eat a

bowman: 6 archer 9 Robin Hood

Bowman: 3 Lee

bownet: 4 trap

bowpot: 4 vase

bowser ___: 3 bag

Bowser's pal: 4 Fido, Spot 5 Rover

bow-shaped: 5 arced

bowsprit: 4 spar
- **place:** 4 prow
- **support:** 3 fid

bowstring
- **groove:** 4 nock
- **like a ~:** 4 taut
- **protection:** 3 wax
- **pull a ~:** 4 draw

bowtie: 5 pasta 8 neckwear
- **style:** 6 clip-on

bowwow: 3 arf, dog 4 bark, woof 5 pooch 6 canine

___ Bow Wow: 3 Lil'

box: 3 bin, jam, pen 4 cage, case, cuff, duke, pack, slap, spar, swat, till 5 chest, crate, fight, hutch, punch, shrub, smack, spank, trunk, TV set, whack 6 bunker, carton, coffer, encage, encase, incase, packet, strike 7 confine, humidor, package 9 container, slug it out 10 receptacle, television
- **black ~:** 9 mechanism
- **boom ~:** 5 radio 6 stereo
- **boom ~ letters:** 4 AMFM
- **buyer:** 3 fan
- **carpenter's ~:** 5 miter
- **cash ~:** 4 till
- **contents:** 5 lunch
- **corrugated ~:** 6 carton
- **cylindrical ~:** 5 pyxis
- **end:** 4 flap
- **ender:** 3 car 4 fish, haul, wood 5 board, thorn
- **food in a ~:** 6 cereal
- **geisha's ~:** 4 inro
- **goggle ~:** 2 TV 4 tube 5 TV set 8 boob tube 10 television
- **grocery ~ letters:** 3 RDA 5 net wt.
- **idiot ~:** 2 TV 4 tube 5 TV set 8 boob tube 10 television
- **in:** 4 trap 5 siege 6 begird, encase, entrap, hinder, shut up 7 confine 8 surround
- **jewelry ~:** 6 casket
- **music ~:** 5 phono 10 phonograph
- **office:** 4 gate 10 attendance
- **office disaster:** 4 bomb, flop
- **on a string:** 4 kite
- **one in a ~:** 5 juror
- **opera ~:** 4 loge
- **picnic ~:** 6 cooler
- **safe-deposit ~:** 5 vault
- **social:** 5 event 10 fundraiser
- **starter:** 3 hat, hot, ice, sky 4 band, fire, gear, hell, juke, mail, pill, post, salt, sand, shoe, soap, tool 5 bread, match, sauce, snuff, sweat 6 letter, pepper, rattle, shadow, strong, tinder 7 chatter, squeeze
- **still in the ~:** 3 new 6 unused
- **storage ~:** 5 trunk
- **top:** 3 lid
- **up:** 4 wrap 5 crate 6 incase 7 enclose, package
- **voice ~:** 6 larynx
- **warehouse ~:** 5 crate 6 carton

box ___: 3 bed, set, top 4 beam, bolt, calf, coat, iron, keel, kite, loom, nail, plot, room, seat, sill 5 elder, frame, lunch, plait, pleat, score, stall, stoop, store 6 camera, canyon, column, girder, gutter, office, social, spring, staple, turtle, wrench 7 cornice

___ box: 3 toe 4 bank, base, boom, call, coin, damp, drop, fuse, gear, jury, poor 5 black, glove, idiot, jewel, light, miter, money, music, press, voice 6 ballot, dialog, flower, letter, pencil, puzzle, sentry, signal, sluice, squawk, switch, vanity, window 7 batter's, dealing, packing, penalty, pouncet

___-box: 3 out 4 salt 6 goggle, tucker 7 witness

Box: 4 play 5 drama
- **author:** Edward Albee

boxcar: 5 train
- **contents:** 7 freight
- **rider:** 4 hobo

boxcars: 6 twelve

___ Box Derby: 4 Soap

boxed in: 4 pent

box elder genus: 4 acer

boxer: 3 Ali, dog, Pep, pet, pug 4 Baer, Bowe, Conn, Zale 5 Lewis, Louis, Moore, Tyson 6 canine, Hagler, Holmes, Liston, Norton, Spinks, Tunney 7 athlete, Basilio, Berbick, Charles, Corbett, Dempsey, fighter, Foreman, Frazier, Johnson, La Motta, Leonard, Max Baer, Walcott,

BO

Willard **8** Braddock, Graziano, Griffith, Joe Louis, Marciano, pugilist, Robinson, Tony Zale **9** Benvenuti, Billy Conn, gladiator, Holyfield, Ken Norton, Mike Tyson, Patterson, Schmeling, Willie Pep **10** Gene Tunney, Joe Frazier, Joe Walcott, Leon Spinks
attire: 4 robe **6** trunks
baby ~: 3 pup **5** puppy, whelp
countenance: 5 scowl
cue: 4 bell
gear: 5 glove
glove of ancient Rome: 6 cestus
handicap: 8 glass jaw
injury: 3 cut **4** welt
match: 4 bout **10** fisticuffs
move: 3 bob **4** chop, kayo **5** feint, lunge, punch, weave **6** clinch
nickname: 5 Champ
official: 3 ref **7** referee
org.: 3 WBA, WBC
punch: 3 jab **4** hook, left **5** cross, right **8** haymaker, uppercut
quest: 5 title
ritual: 7 weigh-in
starter: 4 kick
stat: 2 KO **3** TKO **4** kayo **5** reach
target: 3 jaw
three minutes: 5 round
training: 8 roadwork
venue: 4 ring **5** arena
warning: 3 grr
weapon: 4 fist
boxer __: 6 shorts
Boxer: 7 Barbara
boxers: 6 shorts **7** jockeys **9** underwear
Boxers: 4 cult
home: 5 China
Boxer, The (1969 song)
artist: Simon and Garfunkel
Boxiana
author: Pierce Egan
boxing: 4 ring **5** sport **8** pugilism, slugfest **10** fisticuffs
area: 4 ring **5** apron, ropes **8** ringside
term: 2 KO **3** bob, jab, pug, TKO **4** bell, bout, gate, hook, kayo, ring, spar **5** apron, count, cross, feint, ropes, round, weave **6** canvas, clinch, prelim **7** handler, weigh-in **8** glass jaw, haymaker, knockout, ringside, roadwork, uppercut
see also boxer
boxing __: 4 ring **5** glove
__ boxing: 4 kick
Boxing Day mo.: 3 Dec.
Boxleitner, Bruce: 5 actor
spouse: Melissa Gilbert
box office
adjective: 5 socko
buy: 3 tix, tkt. **5** ducat **6** ticket
disaster: 3 dud **4** bomb, flop **6** turkey
figure: 4 gate, take **10** attendance
hit: 4 boff **5** boffo, smash **7** boffola
letters: 3 SRO
box score entry: 2 HR **3** hit, RBI, run **5** at bat, error
Box Socials
author: W.P. Kinsella
Boxster: 3 car **4** auto **7** Porsche
boxtop piece: 3 tab
boxwood: 4 tree **5** shrub
boxy: 5 squat **6** square **8** thickset
boy: 3 cub, kid, lad, son, tad **4** male **5** cadet, child, minor, sonny, sprig, youth **6** fellow, junior, laddie, shaver, sprout, squirt **7** brother, sapling **8** half-pint, juvenile, small fry, young man **9** stripling, youngster
ender: 3 ish **6** friend
starter: 3 bat, bus, cow, fly, low, pot, tom **4** atta, bell, call, copy, foot, high, home, news, page, play, plow, tall **5** bully, choir, dough, house, paper **6** school
__ boy: 3 bat, bus, day, old, pin **4** atta, ball, best, copy, it's a, poor **5** altar, cabin, cover, mama's, ship's, stock, Teddy, water **6** chorus, office, powder, wonder **7** glamour
Boy __ Dolphin: 3 on a
__ Boy: 3 Bad **4** Best, It's a **5** Bugle, Danny, Rover, Sonny **6** Golden, Lonely, Nature **7** Borstal, Georgia, Soldier
__-Boy: 3 La-Z
__ Boy-Ar-Dee: 4 Chef
Boyce: 5 Tommy
boycott: 3 ban, bar **4** snub **5** avoid, rebel, spurn **6** eschew, ice out, picket, strike **7** embargo, protest, shut out **8** sanction **9** exclusion, ostracize, proscribe
Boyd: 7 Bennett, Stephen, William
__ Boyd: 6 Oil Can
__ Boyd Orr: 4 John
Boyd, Stephen: 5 actor
Boyer: 3 Ken **4** Paul **5** Clete **7** Charles
Boyer, Charles: 5 actor
film: Algiers (1938)
Fanny (1961)
Gaslight (1944)
Tovarich (1937)
__ Boy Floyd: 6 Pretty
boyfriend
in French: 3 ami
in Spanish: 5 amigo
see also sweetheart
Boy Friend, The (1971 film)
cast: Twiggy
director: Ken Russell
Boy From New York City, The (1965 song)
artist: Ad Libs
boyhood: 5 youth
Boy in __ Vest: 4 a Red
Boyington: 5 Pappy
boyish: 5 green, young **6** callow **8** childish, immature, innocent, juvenile, youthful **10** adolescent
Boy Is Mine, The (1998 song)
artist: Brandy, Monica
Boy King, The: 3 Tut
Boyle: 3 Kay **5** Danny, Peter **6** Robert **9** Lara Flynn
Boyle, Danny: 8 director
film: A Life Less Ordinary (1997)
Slumdog Millionaire (2008, AA)
Trainspotting (1996)
Boyle, Kay: 6 writer
Boyle, Lara Flynn: 7 actress
film: The Temp (1993)
Wayne's World (1992)
TV: The Practice
Boyle, Peter: 5 actor
TV: Everybody Loves Raymond
Boyle, Robert: 7 British, chemist **9** physicist
Boyle's __: 3 law
__ Boy Lost: 6 Little
boy-meets-girl event: 5 mixer
Boy Named Sue, A (1969 song)
artist: Johnny Cash
__-boy network: 3 old
boy next __: 4 door
Boynton Beach: 4 city, town
locale: 7 Florida
boys: 3 he's
club: 4 YMCA, YMHA
rural ~ org.: 3 FFA
Boys __: 4 Club, Town
__ Boys: 3 Bad, Jo's, Pep **5** Beach **6** Wonder **7** Beastie
Boy Scout
act: 4 deed
founder: Daniel Beard
group: 3 den **6** patrol
like a ~: 4 kind, true **5** brave, clean, loyal **7** helpful, thrifty **8** cheerful, friendly, obedient, reverent **9** courteous
rank: 3 Cub **4** Life, Star **5** Eagle
wear: 4 sash
__ Boy Scout, The: 4 Last
Boys Don't Cry (1999 film)
cast: Peter Sarsgaard, Chloë Sevigny, Hilary Swank
boysenberry: 5 fruit
Boys for Pele
artist: Tori Amos
Boys From Brazil, The: 4 film **5** novel
author: Ira Levin
boys: 6 clones
cast: James Mason, Laurence Olivier, Gregory Peck
Boys From Syracuse, The: 7 musical
composer: Lorenz Hart, Richard Rodgers
Boys of Summer, The
author: Roger Kahn
name: 3 Gil, Roy **4** Carl **6** Jackie, Pee Wee **8** Preacher
subject: 3 Cox, Roe **5** Black, Reese **6** Hodges, Labine, Snider **7** Erskine, Furillo **8** Billy Cox, Joe Black, Newcombe, Robinson **9** Gil Hodges **10** Campanella, Clem Labine, Duke Snider
Boys of Summer, The (1984 song)
artist: Don Henley
Boys on the Side (1995 film)
cast: Drew Barrymore, Whoopi Goldberg, Matthew McConaughey, Mary-Louise Parker
director: Herbert Ross
Boys Town (1938 film)
cast: Mickey Rooney, Spencer Tracy
director: Norman Taurog
locale: 4 Nebr. **5** Omaha **8** Nebraska
Boy's Will, A: 4 poem
author: Robert Frost
__ Boy, The: 5 Stone **6** Errand **7** Persian, Winslow
Boy Who Cried Wolf, The
source: 4 Esop **5** Aesop
Boy Without a Girl, A (1959 song)
artist: Frankie Avalon
Boyz II Men
members: Morris, McCary, Stockman
song: 4 Seasons of Loneliness (1997)
End of the Road (1992)
I'll Make Love to You (1994)
In the Still of the Nite (1992)
It's So Hard to Say Goodbye to Yesterday (1991)
Motownphilly (1991)
On Bended Knee (1994)
One Sweet Day (1995)
A Song for Mama (1997)
Water Runs Dry (1995)
Boyz N the Hood (1991 film)
cast: Laurence Fishburne, Cuba Gooding Jr., Ice Cube, Nia Long
director: John Singleton
Boz: 6 Scaggs **7** Dickens
boy: 3 Pip, Tim **7** Tiny Tim
Bozeman: 4 city, town
locale: 7 Montana
school: 3 MSU
bozo: 5 clown
see also ninny
BP
acquisition: 5 Amoco
BPOE: 4 Elks
cousin: 4 IOOF
meeting site: 5 lodge
__-B-Q: 3 Bar
__-b-que: 3 bar
Br: 4 elem. **7** bromine, element
35 for ~: 4 at. no.
bra: 7 bandeau **8** lingerie
__-brac: 5 bric-a
Bracco, Lorraine: 7 actress
film: GoodFellas (1990)
Medicine Man (1992)
Radio Flyer (1992)
spouse: Harvey Keitel, Edward James Olmos
TV: The Sopranos
brace: 3 duo, leg, tie, two **4** beam, gird, grip, hold, pair, prop, stay **5** clamp, ready, shore, steel **6** couple, fasten, girder, hold up, prop up, rafter, steady, timber, uphold **7** bolster, fortify, prepare, refresh, shore up, stiffen, support, sustain, twosome **8** buttress, mainstay, reassure **9** reinforce, stabilize, stanchion, undergird, withstand **10** invigorate, strengthen
angle ~: 4 L bar
architectural ~: 5 strut
oneself: 4 gird **5** steel **6** hang on
relative: 5 paren
up: 4 gird, tone **5** build, rally, shore, steel **6** anneal, harden, temper **7** bolster, burgeon, develop, empower, enhance, enliven, fortify, stiffen, toughen **8** bourgeon, buttress, energize, indurate, vitalize **9** intensify, reinforce **10** invigorate
__ brace: 4 arch, knee, main **5** stage **6** batter
braced: 3 set **4** firm **5** ready
bracelet: 5 chain **6** armlet, bangle **7** arm band, jewelry, manacle, trinket **8** ornament
dangler: 5 charm
site: 3 arm **5** ankle, wrist
__ bracelet: 5 charm, slave **6** tennis
bracelets: 5 cuffs, irons **8** manacles, shackles **9** handcuffs

snap the ~ on: 5 pinch, run in 6 arrest
bracer: 5 drink, tonic 8 libation, pick-me-up, stimulus 9 stimulant 10 invigorant
__ Bracer: 4 Skin
braces: 10 suspenders
Brach's: 5 candy
bracing: 4 cool 5 brisk, crisp, fresh 7 healthy, rousing 8 vigorous 10 energizing, fortifying, refreshing
braciola: 4 meat
bracken: 4 fern
Bracken: 3 Peg 5 Eddie
bracket: 3 tie 4 clip, hasp, join, kind, link, prop, sort, yoke 5 clamp, clasp, class, joint, ledge, range, stand 6 corbel, couple, holder, staple 7 concole, connect, section, support 8 buttress, category, classify, division, fastener, grouping 9 underline 10 cantilever
cornice ~: 5 ancon
fixer: 5 screw
mast ~: 4 bibb
relative: 5 brace, paren
bracket __: 3 saw 4 foot 5 clock, creep
__ bracket: 3 tax 5 angle 6 square
_-bracket creep: 3 tax
bracketed: 4 akin 6 allied, joined 7 related 8 coherent, relative 9 connected, continual, pertinent, undivided 10 affiliated, applicable, associated, continuous
brackish: 5 briny, salty 6 bitter, saline 7 saltish 8 stagnant 10 unpleasant
bract: 4 leaf 5 frond, palea 6 spathe
brad: 4 tack 8 fastener
Brad: 4 Bird, Hall, Park, Pitt 5 Davis 6 Dexter, Dourif, Renfro 7 Garrett, Johnson 8 Anderson
Bradbury: 3 Ray 7 Malcolm
Bradbury, Malcolm: 6 writer
Bradbury, Ray: 6 writer
genre: sci-fi
work: Dandelion Wine
Fahrenheit 451
The Golden Apples of the Sun
The Illustrated Man
I Sing the Body Electric!
The Martian Chronicles
Something Wicked This Way Comes
Urban Horrors
Braddock, Jim: 5 boxer
dethroned him: 4 Baer
milieu: 4 ring
Bradenton: 4 city, town
locale: 7 Florida
Bradford: 5 Jesse 7 Dillman, William
Bradlee, Ben: 6 editor
Bradley: 2 Ed 3 Tom 4 Bill, Omar
athletes: 6 Braves
locale: 6 Peoria 8 Illinois
rank: 3 gen. 7 general
Bradley, Bill: 5 cager
milieu: 5 court
org.: 3 NBA
sport: 10 basketball
Bradley Center: 5 arena
Bradley, Ed
colleague: Steve Kroft,, Morley Safer, Lesley Stahl, Mike Wallace
Bradshaw, Terry: 2 QB 7 Steeler
sport: 8 football
Bradstreet partner: 3 Dun
Bradstreet, Anne: 4 poet 6 writer
Brady: 5 Alice, James, Scott 6 Mathew 8 Nicholas
Brady Bill opponent: 3 NRA
Brady Bunch Movie, The (1995 film)
cast: Gary Cole, Shelley Long, Michael McKean
Brady Bunch, The (ABC sitcom)
cast: Ann B. Davis (Alice Nelson)
Florence Henderson (Carol Brady)
Christopher Knight (Peter Brady)
Mike Lookinland (Bobby Brady)
Maureen McCormick (Marcia Brady)
Susan Olsen (Cindy Brady)
Eve Plumb (Jan Brady)
Robert Reed (Mike Brady)
Barry Williams (Greg Brady)
dog: 5 Tiger
threesome: 4 sons 9 daughters
Brady, Mathew: 12 photographer
Braeden: 4 Eric
Braff: 4 Zach
brag: 4 crow, game, tout 5 boast, extol, exult, gloat, pride, spout, vaunt 6 extoll, flaunt, hotdog, parade 7 bluster, show off, swagger, talk big 8 card game, showboat 9 gasconade, loudmouth 10 grandstand
nothing to ~ about: 4 so-so 7 average 8 mediocre
Braga: 5 Alice
Braga, Sonia: 7 actress
film: Angel Eyes (2001)
Kiss of the Spider Woman (1985)
The Milagro Beanfield War (1988)
Moon Over Parador (1988)
Bragg: 4 Fort 7 Braxton, William
braggadocio: 3 gas 4 wind 5 boast 7 bravado, showoff
braggart: 4 snob 6 crower, egoist, gascon 7 showoff 8 fanfaron 9 know-it-all, loud-mouth, swaggerer
Bragg, William: 3 Sir 7 British 8 Nobelist 9 physicist
__ bragh: 6 Erin go
Brahe, Tycho: 6 Danish 10 astronomer
Brahma: 3 cow 4 bull, fowl, poem 5 steer 6 bovine, cattle 7 chicken
bovine feature: 4 hump 6 dewlap
chicken relative: *see* chicken
Brahman: 3 god 5 Atman, caste, Hindu
co-equal: 5 Shiva 6 Vishnu
Brahmin: 4 snob 5 caste, elite
__ Brahmin: 6 Boston
Brahms, Johannes: 6 German 8 composer
work: Academic Festival Overture
German Requiem
Lullaby
Tragic Overture
braid: 4 coil 5 plait, queue, tress, twist, weave 6 cordon, enlace, inlace, splice 7 cornrow, entwine, intwine, pigtail 8 ponytail 9 hairstyle, interlace 10 decoration, intertwine, interweave
burning ~: 4 wick
crochet ~: 5 lacet
gold ~: 5 orris
ornamental ~: 4 gimp
braided
bread: 6 hallah
cord: 4 rope
locks: 6 dreads 8 pigtails
braids: 4 coif 6 hairdo 8 coiffure
Braille: 5 Louis
mark: 3 dot
use ~: 4 read
writing need: 6 stylus
brain: 3 ace, hit 4 conk, head, mind, sage, whiz, wonk 5 organ 6 genius, reason 7 clobber, creator, egghead, prodigy, scholar, thinker, whiz kid 8 cerebrum, Einstein, highbrow, longhair, virtuoso 9 intellect, mentality, professor 10 cerebellum, gray matter, mastermind
combining form: 6 cerebr- 7 cerebro- 8 encephal- 9 encephalo-
computer's ~: 3 CPU
convolution: 5 gyrus
ender: 3 pan 4 case, stem, wash, work 5 child, power, storm 6 teaser
medical prefix: 5 neuro-
membrane: 4 dura
messenger: 5 nerve 6 neuron
opening: 4 pyla
part: 4 lobe 6 cortex
passage: 4 iter
protector: 5 skull 7 cranium
starter: 3 end 4 bird, fore, hind, lame 5 crack 6 rattle 7 between, feather, scatter
tissue: 4 tela 5 telae
trust: 7 cabinet, council
use one's ~: 5 think 8 cogitate
brain __: 4 case, cell, gain, scan, stem, wash, wave 5 child, coral, drain, trust
Brain: 5 novel
author: Robin Cook
__ Brain: 6 Broca's
Brainard: 3 Ned
braincase: 6 sconce 7 cranium
brainchild: 4 idea 6 scheme 7 concept, thought 8 creation, proposal 9 invention
brained starter: 4 bird, hare, lame 5 crack 7 scatter
brainless: 4 dull 5 giddy 8 headless *see also* foolish
brainpower: 2 IQ 3 wit 4 mind, wits 6 smarts 9 mentality
measure: 6 IQ test
brains: 3 wit 4 mind, wits 5 asset, sense 6 acumen, reason, wisdom 9 erudition, ingenuity, intellect, mentality, smartness 10 cleverness, horse sense, mastermind
cudgel one's ~: 4 mull 5 think 6 figure, puzzle 7 work out 8 ruminate 10 deliberate
opposite: 5 brawn
pick the ~ of: 7 consult 8 question
rack one's ~: 4 mull 5 think 6 figure, puzzle 7 work out 8 ruminate 10 deliberate
brainstorm: 4 idea 5 hatch 6 confer, ideate, ponder 7 analyze, consult, imagine, thought 8 cogitate, conceive 9 fabricate, improvise, speculate
in French: 4 idée
Brainstorm (1983 film)
cast: Louise Fletcher, Christopher Walken, Natalie Wood
brainteaser: 5 poser 6 enigma, riddle 7 problem, stumper 9 conundrum
Braintree: 4 city, town
locale: 4 Mass.
brain-twister: 5 poser 6 enigma, riddle 7 problem, stumper
brainwash: 4 sway 5 teach, train 8 persuade 9 catechize, condition, inculcate, influence, pound into
brain wave chart: 3 EEG
brainwork: 7 thought 10 cogitation, reflection
brainy: 5 sharp, smart 6 astute, bright, clever, gifted, mental, shrewd 7 bookish, erudite, knowing, learned, sapient 8 cerebral, highbrow, skillful 9 astucious, brilliant, ingenious, inventive 10 insightful, thoughtful
bunch: 5 Mensa
not ~: 4 slow 5 dense, thick
one, maybe: 4 nerd
braise: 4 cook, sear, stew 5 brown, sauté 6 simmer
brake: 4 curb, fern, halt, slow, snag, stop 5 check, delay, pedal, stall 6 dampen, damper, hamper, hinder, impede, pull up, retard, slow up 7 control, fetch up, inhibit 8 slow down 9 deterrent, hindrance, restraint 10 constraint, decelerate
device: 4 shoe
jockey's ~: 4 rein
neighbor: 3 gas
problem: 4 skid
wagon ~: 5 sprag
brake __: 3 pad 4 band, drum, fade, shoe 5 fluid, light, pedal, wheel 6 lining
__ brake: 3 air 4 band, disc, disk, dive, drum, foot, hand 5 cliff, power, press, prony, speed, track 7 coaster, parking
brakes: 3 ABS 4 disc, disk
fix the ~: 5 repad
hit the ~: 4 slow, stop 6 ease up, hold up, rein in, slow up 7 ease off 8 hold back, moderate, slow down 10 decelerate
__ brakes: 5 power
Bram: 6 Stoker
bramble: 4 burr, bush 5 briar, brier, furze, gorse, shrub, spine, thorn 6 nettle 7 thistle
family: 4 rose
fruit: 9 raspberry 10 blackberry
relative: rose family plant
brambly: 6 thorny 7 prickly
Brampton: 4 city, town
locale: 6 Canada 7 Ontario
Bram Stoker's Dracula (1992 film)
cast: Anthony Hopkins, Gary Oldman, Keanu Reeves, Winona Ryder
director: Francis Ford Coppola
bran: 5 grain 6 cereal 8 roughage 10 health food
content: 5 fiber
source: 3 oat, rye 4 corn 5 wheat
bran __: 6 muffin
__ bran: 3 oat 6 raisin

__-Bran: 3 All
Branagh, Kenneth: 5 actor 8 director
film: Celebrity (1998)
Dead Again (1991)
Henry V (1989)
Much Ado About Nothing (1993)
Othello (1995)
Peter's Friends (1992)
Wild Wild West (1999)
spouse: Emma Thompson
Branca: 5 Ralph
branch: 3 arm 4 bank, cion, fork, limb, part, stem, wing 5 annex, bough, creek, perch, prong, ramus, scion, split, sprig, stick 6 bureau, member, office, ramify, spread, stream 7 chapter, deviate, diverge, outpost, radiate, section 8 category, division, offshoot, position, separate 9 affiliate, bifurcate, confluent, extension, outgrowth, tributary 10 department, subsection, subsidiary
combining form: 4 clad- 5 clado-
dove ~: 5 olive
graft a tree ~: 6 inarch
hanger: 5 sloth
off: 4 fork 6 bisect, ramble, spread
olive ~: 5 peace, truce 7 amnesty 9 armistice, ceasefire 10 moratorium
out: 4 grow 5 add to, widen 6 expand, extend 7 broaden, develop, enlarge, radiate 8 increase 9 diversify
railroad ~: 4 spur 6 feeder
river ~: 4 trib. 9 tributary
small ~: 4 twig 5 shoot
structure: 4 nest
tree ~: 4 limb, rame 5 bough
branch __: 3 cut, out 4 line, wilt 5 point, water
__ branch: 5 olive
Branch: 6 Rickey
branched: 6 ramous 8 arboreal
branches: 4 rami
decorative ~: 6 bocage
remove ~: 3 lop 5 prune
tree ~: 6 canopy
branchlike: 6 ramose
brand: 3 ilk 4 kind, logo, mark, name, scar, sear, slur, sort, stab, type 5 badge, class, genre, genus, label, odium, stain, stamp, taint, title 6 accuse, kidney, manner, stigma 7 product, variety 8 flambeau, hallmark 9 trademark 10 impression, imputation, stigmatize
name: 4 make, mark 5 label 9 trademark
__ brand: 4 name 5 house, store 7 private
Brand: 3 Max 7 Neville
author: Henrik Ibsen
branded beasts: 6 cattle
Brandeis, Louis: 5 judge 6 jurist 7 justice
Brandenburg Concertos
composer: J.S. Bach
Brandenburg Gate
site: 6 Berlin
branding iron, use a: 4 mark, sear
brandish: 4 show, wave 5 shake, wield 6 dangle, flaunt, parade 7 display, show off, swagger, trot out 8 flourish 10 wave around
brand-new: 3 new 4 mint 5 fresh, novel 6 cherry, red-hot, virgin 7 updated 8 up-to-date, virginal
Brand New Key (1971 song)
artist: Melanie
Brando, Marlon: 5 actor
adopted home: 5 Samoa
birthplace: 3 Neb. 4 Nebr. 5 Omaha 8 Nebraska
film: Apocalypse Now (1979)
A Countess From Hong Kong (1967)
Don Juan DeMarco (1995)
The Freshman (1990)
The Godfather (1972, AA)
Guys and Dolls (1955)
Julius Caesar (1953)
Last Tango in Paris (1973)
The Men (1950)
One-Eyed Jacks (1961)
On the Waterfront (1954, AA)
Sayonara (1957)
The Score (2001)
A Streetcar Named Desire (1951)
Superman (1978)
The Teahouse of the August Moon (1956)
Viva Zapata! (1952)
The Wild One (1954)
The Young Lions (1958)
Brandon: 3 Lee 4 Cruz 5 Routh 7 de Wilde
Brandt, Willy: 6 German 8 Nobelist
brandy: 4 marc, raki 5 drink 6 cognac, grappa, liquor 8 beverage, eau de vie
apple ~: 8 calvados
cherry ~: 6 kirsch
flavoring: 4 plum 5 apple, peach 6 cherry 10 blackberry
French ~: 4 marc
glass: 7 snifter
Italian ~: 6 grappa
letters: 3 VSO 4 VSOP
Peruvian ~: 5 pisco
plum ~: 9 slivovitz
ready to sell, as ~: 4 aged 8 mellowed
South American ~: 5 pisco
store ~: 3 age
brandy __: 4 mint 7 snifter
Brandy
last name: Norwood
song: Baby (1995)
The Boy Is Mine (1998)
Brokenhearted (1995)
Have You Ever? (1998)
I Wanna Be Down (1994)
Sittin' Up in My Room (1996)
What About Us? (2002)
Bran Flakes: 6 cereal
competitor: *see* cereal
Branford: 8 Marsalis
Branigan, Laura
song: Gloria (1982)
Self Control (1984)
Solitaire (1983)
brannigan: 4 riot 5 melee 6 barney 7 quarrel, wrangle 10 difference
Branson: 4 city, town 7 Richard
locale: 8 Missouri
brant: 4 bird, fowl 5 goose
relative: 4 nene 7 graylag
Branwell: 6 Brontë
Braque, Georges: 6 artist 7 painter
homeland: 6 France
style: 6 Cubism
__ Brasco: 6 Donnie
brash: 4 bold, loud, pert, rash, rude 5 cocky, hasty, nervy, pushy, rough, sassy, saucy, unshy 6 brassy, brazen, cheeky, jaunty, madcap, unwary 7 boorish, forward, selfish, uncivil 8 cocksure, headlong, heedless, impolite, impudent, insolent, reckless, tactless, unsubtle 9 audacious, barefaced, foolhardy, hotheaded, impetuous, impolitic, imprudent, impulsive, shameless, unadvised, uncareful, untactful, vivacious 10 headstrong, ill-advised, incautious, indiscreet, sophomoric, ungracious, unthinking, vociferant
brashness: 4 gall, sass 5 cheek, nerve, sauce 10 confidence, effrontery
Brasilia: 4 city, town 7 capital
locale: 6 Brazil
Brasov: 4 city, town
locale: 7 Romania, Rumania 8 Roumania
brass: 4 gall, mgmt., tuba 5 alloy, cheek, metal, moxie, nerve, sauce 6 cornet, hubris, hybris, yellow 7 reddish, trumpet 8 audacity, chutzpah, official, rudeness, superior, temerity, trombone 9 arrogance, executive, impudence, insolence, personage 10 effrontery, executives, management, sousaphone
color kin: *see* yellow color
combining form: 5 chalc-, chalk- 6 chalco-, chalko-
component: 4 zinc 6 copper
ender: 4 ware 5 bound
fanfare: 5 tusch
get down to ~ tacks: 6 detail 7 account, itemize, specify 9 make clear, stipulate
hat: 4 boss 6 top dog 7 manager 8 employer, superior 9 executive
instrument: 4 horn, tuba 5 bugle 6 cornet 7 trumpet 8 trombone 10 sousaphone
source of future ~: 3 OCS, OTC, OTS
tacks: 5 facts 7 reality 9 actuality, essential 10 foundation
top ~: 4 mgmt. 5 chief 7 officer 8 kingfish 9 commander, key player 10 management
brass __: 3 hat 4 band, ring 5 tacks 8 knuckles
__ brass: 3 low, red, top 4 beta 5 alpha, horse
brass-colored: 7 aeneous
Brasselle: 5 Keefe
brasserie: 6 bistro, eatery 10 restaurant
brassie: 4 club, wood 8 golf club
brasslike alloy: 6 latten
Brass Monkey: 5 drink
brassy: 4 bold, loud, rude 5 brash, nervy, saucy, unshy 6 brazen, cheeky, daring, not shy, shrill, vulgar 7 blaring, blatant, forward, lowbred 8 fearless, flippant, impudent, insolent, overbold, strident 9 audacious, barefaced, clamorous, outspoken, shameless, unabashed 10 unblushing, vociferant
brat: 3 imp 4 punk, snip 5 child, kiddy 6 bad boy, urchin 7 hellion 9 prankster, rotten kid, youngster 10 holy terror
be a ~: 4 sass 5 act up 7 disobey 9 misbehave
Christmas present for a ~: 4 coal
ender: 5 wurst
smile: 5 smirk
__ brat: 4 army
Brat __: 4 Pack
Brat Farrar author: Josephine Tey
Bratislava: 4 city, town 7 capital
locale: 8 Slovakia
river: 6 Danube
Bratt, Benjamin: 5 actor
spouse: Talisa Soto
bratty: 5 nasty 6 impish, spoilt, unruly 7 spoiled 8 impudent 10 ill-behaved
bratwurst: 4 meat 7 sausage
unit: 4 link
Braugher: 5 Andre
bräuhaus order: 4 bier
Braulio: 5 Baeza
Braun: 5 razor 6 shaver
alternative: 7 Norelco 9 Remington
Braun, Carl: 6 German 8 Nobelist 9 physicist
Braunschweiger: 4 meat 7 sausage
brava: 5 cheer
__ Brava: 5 Costa
Bravada: 3 SUV 4 Olds 10 Oldsmobile
bravado: 5 boast, pluck, spunk, swash 7 bluster, bombast 8 bragging, defiance 9 gasconade, pomposity 10 feistiness, pretension, swaggering
brave: 4 bold, dare, defy, face, game, risk 5 gutsy, manly, nervy, stout 6 daring, endure, gritty, heroic, plucky, strong, suffer 7 dashing, defiant, doughty, gallant, impavid, ride out, valiant, venture, warrior, weather 8 confront, fearless, heroical, intrepid, resolute, spirited, stalwart, unafraid, valorous 9 audacious, challenge, confident, daredevil, dauntless, go through, herculean, stand up to, undaunted, unfearful, unfearing, withstand 10 chivalrous, courageous, mettlesome, undismayed
abode: 4 tipi 5 lodge, tepee 6 teepee
be ~: 4 dare, defy 5 fight 6 oppose 7 venture 9 challenge
deed: 4 coup
it out: 4 last, stay 6 endure, hang in 8 stand pat
name meaning ~: 5 Casey
one: 4 hero 7 heroine 8 explorer 10 adventurer
Brave
Hall-of-Famer: 5 Aaron, Spahn 7 Mathews 9 Ed Mathews, Hank Aaron 10 Henry Aaron
Brave __, The: 3 One 5 Bulls
Braveheart (1995 film)
cast: Mel Gibson, Sophie Marceau, Patrick McGoohan
director: Mel Gibson
garb: 4 kilt
group: 4 clan

Brave Little Toaster, The (1987 film)
director: Jerry Rees
Brave Men
author: Ernie Pyle
Brave New World
author: Aldous Huxley
character: **4** Marx, Mond **5** Linda **6** Lenina **7** Bernard
drug: **4** soma
Braverman: **4** Bart
bravery: **4** dash, grit, guts **5** heart, nerve, pluck, spunk, valor **6** daring, mettle, spirit, starch **7** courage, heroism, prowess **8** audacity, backbone, boldness, gumption, strength **9** assurance, endurance, fortitude, gallantry, hardiness **10** confidence, knighthood, moral fiber
Braves: **4** nine, team **7** Bradley
home: **7** Atlanta
org.: **3** MLB, NLE
rival: *see* baseball team
sport: **8** baseball
bravo: **3** rah **5** cheer, huzza **6** hoorah, hooray, hurrah, hurray, huzzah
in Spanish: **3** olé
preceder: **4** alfa
Bravo: **7** channel
alternative: *see* movie channel
offering: **4** film **5** movie
__ Bravo: **3** Rio
bravos: **7** ovation
bravura: **5** éclat
brawl: **3** row **4** feud, fray, riot **5** argue, clash, fight, melee, mix-up, scrap, set-to **6** affray, barney, battle, bicker, fracas, go at it, racket, ruckus, rumble, rumpus, strife, tumult, tussle, uproar **7** contest, dispute, quarrel, rhubarb, rioting, scuffle, wrangle **8** argument, brouhaha, disorder, outbreak, squabble, struggle **9** altercate, brannigan, duke it out, imbroglio, raise Cain **10** donnybrook, free-for-all, roughhouse
weapon: **4** fist
brawling: **4** wild **5** rowdy **10** boisterous, disorderly
brawn: **3** vim **4** beef, dint, meat, thew **5** force, might, power, sinew, thews, vigor **6** energy, muscle **7** fitness, muscles, potence, potency, stamina **8** strength, vitality **9** beefiness, endurance, fortitude, hardiness, huskiness, puissance, stoutness, toughness **10** brute force, mightiness, robustness, ruggedness, sturdiness
brawny: **3** fit **4** hale, iron, wiry **5** beefy, burly, hardy, hefty, hunky, husky, lusty, macho, nervy, stout, tough **6** hearty, mighty, potent, robust, rugged, sinewy, steely, stocky, strong, sturdy, virile **7** doughty **8** athletic, forceful, indurate, muscular, powerful, puissant, Stallone, stalwart, thickset, vigorous **9** Atlantean, herculean, strapping, well-built **10** able-bodied, red-blooded
guy: **5** he-man
Brawny: **10** paper towel
competitor: **4** Viva **5** Scott **6** Bounty
Braxton: **4** Toni **5** Bragg
Braxton, Toni
song: Another Sad Love Song (1993)
Breathe Again (1993)
Un-Break My Heart (1996)
You Mean the World to Me (1994)
You're Makin' Me High (1996)
bray: **3** baa, cry **4** blat, honk, hoot, rasp, wail **5** blare, blast, bleat, crush, neigh **6** bellow, heehaw, whinny
half a ~: **3** haw, hee
brayer: **3** ass **4** mule **5** burro **6** donkey
Braz.
neighbor: **3** Arg., Bol., Uru., Ven.
see also Brazil
braze: **4** weld **6** solder
brazen: **4** bold, dare, flip, loud, pert, rude **5** brash, cocky, fresh, gutsy, nervy, sassy, saucy, smart **6** arrant, awless, brassy, cheeky, daring, flashy, snippy, tawdry **7** assured, aweless, blatant, defiant, forward, glaring, lowbred, uncivil **8** flagrant, flippant, immodest, impolite, impudent, insolent, overbold, snippety **9** audacious, barefaced, out of line, shameless, unabashed, unashamed **10** outrageous, unblushing, ungracious
female: **4** minx **5** hussy **7** Jezebel
brazenness: **4** gall, sass **5** cheek, nerve, sauce **8** defiance **9** insolence **10** effrontery
brazier: **5** grill
residue: **4** coal **5** ember **6** cinder
Brazil: **6** nation **7** country
airline: **5** Varig
bandleader: **5** Cugat
bird: **7** cariama, seriema
capital: **8** Brasilia
Christmas in ~: **5** Natal
city: **4** Mauá, Pará **5** Bauru, Belém, Natal, Serra **6** Aruana, Canoas, Cuiabá, Franca, Goiâna, Ilhéus, Lorena, Maceió, Manaos, Manaus, Olinda, Osasco, Recife, Santos **7** Aracaju, Caruaru, Diadema, Guarujá, Jundiaí, Limeira, Maringá, Niterói, Pelotas, Taubaté, Uberaba, Vitoria **8** Anápolis, Blumenau, Campinas, Contagem, Curitiba, Londrina, Paulista, Salvador, Santarém, Sao Paulo, Sorocaba, Teresina **9** Fortaleza, Guarulhos, Joinville, Vila Velha **10** Imperatriz, Juiz de Fora, Nova Iguaçu, Pórto Velho, Santo André **11** Pórto Alegre
dance: **5** samba **6** maxixe **7** batuque, lambada **9** bossa nova
diamond-mining region: **5** Goias
emperor: **5** Pedro
explorer: **6** Cabral
fish: **5** piaba **8** arapaima
language: **4** Tupi **10** Portuguese
macaw: **3** ara
money: **3** rei **5** conto **7** milreis, moidore **8** cruzeiro
mountain: **9** Sugar Loaf **10** Serra do Mar
neighbor: **4** Peru **6** Guyana **7** Bolivia, Uruguay **8** Colombia, Paraguay, Suriname **9** Argentina, Venezuela
org.: **3** OAS
palm: **5** assai
people: **3** Oti **4** Tupi **8** Caingang
poet: **7** Andrade **8** Bandeira
port: **3** Rio **4** Pará **5** Bahia, Belem, Ceara, natal **6** Cuiabá, Ilhéus, Recife, Santos **9** Fortaleza
river: **4** Acre **5** Negro, Purus, Xingu **6** Amazon, Javari
soccer star: **4** Pelé
state: **4** Acre, Pará **5** Amapa, Bahia, Ceara, Goias, Piaui **6** Parana **7** Alagoas, Paraiba, Roraima, Sergipe **8** Amazonas, Maranhao, Rondonia, Sao Paulo **9** Tocantins **10** Mato Grosso
tennis pro: **5** Bueno
title: **3** dom **6** senhor **7** senhora
tree: **7** araroba, seringa **8** carnauba, oiticica
waterfall: **6** Iguaçu **7** Iguassú
writer: **5** Amado, Ramos **7** Alencar, Queiròs
Brazil (1985 film)
cast: Robert De Niro, Kim Greist, Jonathan Pryce
director: Terry Gilliam
Brazil __: **3** nut **7** Current
Brazilian __: **4** ruby **5** guava, plume **7** emerald, peridot, rhatany
Brazos: **5** river
city on the ~: **4** Waco
locale: **5** Texas
Brazzaville: **4** city, port, town **7** capital
locale: **5** Congo
Brazzi, Rossano: **5** actor
breach: **3** gap **4** foul, gulf, hole, rent, rift, tear **5** break, chasm, clash, cleft, crack, lapse, split **6** cranny, hiatus, invade, schism, sunder **7** discord, dispute, dissent, fissure, infract, interim, offense, opening, quarrel, rupture, violate **8** argument, conflict, disunity, fracture, interval, invasion, trespass, variance **9** deviation, violation **10** alienation, contravene, disharmony, dissension, encroach on, falling-out, infraction
of contract: **4** tort **9** improbity
of judgment: **5** error, lapse
of law: **5** crime, wrong **6** felony **7** misdeed, offense **9** violation **10** misconduct, wrongdoing
of secrecy: **4** leak
Breach (2007 film)
cast: Chris Cooper, Laura Linney, Ryan Phillippe
breach of __: **5** faith, trust **7** promise
Breach of Faith
author: Theodore H. White
bread: **3** bun, nan, rye **4** carb, food, loaf, pita, pone, roll, rusk **5** bagel, bialy, matzo, poori, toast, white **6** muffin **7** aliment, anadama, bannock, biscuit, brioche, challah, chapati, crouton, crumpet, oatcake, popover, pretzel, saltine **8** baguette, cracknel, hardtack, zwieback **9** croissant, sourdough, sweet roll **10** johnnycake, melba toast, sustenance, whole-grain, whole-wheat
and butter: **6** living **7** aliment **10** livelihood
base: **5** flour
braided ~: **6** hallah
break ~: **3** eat, sup **4** dine
brown ~: **5** toast
chamber: **4** oven
choice: **3** rye **5** white **10** whole-grain, whole-wheat
combining form: **4** arto-
daily ~: **4** diet, food **10** sustenance
dry ~: **4** rusk
emanation: **5** aroma
end: **4** heel **5** crust
ender: **3** box, nut **4** root **5** board, fruit **6** basket, winner
Eucharist ~: **5** wafer
India ~: **3** nan
in French: **4** pain
in Italian: **4** pane
in Japanese: **3** pan
in Spanish: **3** pan
like old ~: **5** moldy, stale
make ~: **4** bake, earn **5** knead
mold: **6** fungus
morsel: **5** crumb
need: **5** yeast **6** gluten
pocket ~: **4** pita
pudding: **7** dessert
Southern ~: **4** pone
spread: **3** jam **4** mayo, oleo **5** honey, jelly **9** margarine, marmalade
starter: **3** bee **4** corn, flat **5** short, sweet **6** ginger
store: **6** bakery **10** patisserie
unbaked ~: **5** dough
unit: **4** loaf **5** slice
unleavened ~: **5** matzo **6** matzah, matzoh
see also moolah
bread __: **4** line, mold **5** flour, knife **7** pudding
__ bread: **3** rye, sea **4** corn, holy, loaf, pita, pone, ship, soda **5** altar, black, break, brown, light, pilot, quick, spoon, wheat, white **6** batter, French, garlic, gluten, Indian, monkey **7** anadama, Italian
Bread
song: Baby I'm-a Want You (1971)
Everything I Own (1972)
If (1971)
It Don't Matter to Me (1970)
Lost Without Your Love (1976)
Make It With You (1970)
bread-and-breakfast: **3** inn **7** lodging
bread-and-butter: **8** economic
Bread and Wine
author: Ignazio Silone
breadbasket: **3** gut, tum **5** belly, tummy **7** abdomen, stomach
province: **3** Alt., Man. **4** Alta. **7** Alberta **8** Manitoba
state: **3** Ill., Kan., Neb. **4** Iowa, N. Dak., Nebr., S. Dak. **6** Kansas **8** Illinois, Nebraska
breadfruit: **4** tree
family: **8** mulberry
relative: **3** fig **4** upas **5** ficus, ramon **6** antiar, fustic
breadth: **4** area, size, span **5** gamut, range, reach, scale, scope, space, sweep, width **6** extent, length, spread **7** compass, expanse

8 diameter, distance, fullness, latitude, vastness, wideness 9 amplitude, broadness, dimension, full range, immensity, largeness, magnitude, ranginess, roominess 10 liberality
add ~ to: 5 widen 6 expand 7 broaden, educate
of view: 6 vision
__-breadth: 5 hand's
Bread, Wine, and Salt
author: Alden Nowlan
breadwinner: 5 labor 6 earner, worker 8 employee
break: 2 go 3 fly, gap, mar, top 4 beat, bust, chip, flee, halt, harm, hole, hurt, luck, lull, rend, rent, rest, rift, rive, ruin, shot, snap, stay, stop, tame, tear, tilt, time, verb 5 burst, cleft, crack, crash, crush, letup, occur, outdo, pause, smash, snack, split, start, wreck, yield 6 appear, breach, breath, catnap, cesura, chance, change, convey, cut out, damage, decamp, decode, demote, emerge, escape, exceed, get out, happen, hiatus, impair, impart, inform, injure, injury, lacuna, lessen, let out, ravine, recess, reduce, refute, relief, reveal, schism, soften, subdue, sunder, unglue, weaken 7 abandon, abscond, caesura, crumble, cushion, destroy, disable, disjoin, disobey, divulge, fissure, getaway, holiday, implode, infract, interim, lighten, opening, respite, run away, rupture, shatter, split up, surpass, suspend, take ten, time out, violate 8 announce, bankrupt, breather, clear out, cleavage, decipher, demolish, diminish, disclose, dispirit, disprove, division, downtime, fracture, fragment, go beyond, infringe, intermit, interval, leverage, moderate, omission, outstrip, proclaim, puncture, separate, straiten, take five, vacation 9 advantage, cessation, come forth, cut and run, disregard, downgrade, hesitancy, humiliate, interlude, interrupt, pauperize, punctuate, transpire, violation 10 alienation, come to pass, come undone, contravene, controvert, demoralize, disconfirm, disruption, divergence, impoverish, make public, separation, suspension, transgress
a bronc: 4 tame
abruptly: 4 snap 5 crack 7 shatter
a fast: 3 eat
afternoon ~: 3 nap 6 siesta, snooze
a habit: 4 kick, wean
a law: 3 sin 6 breach, offend 7 disobey, do wrong, infract, violate 8 encroach, infringe 9 disregard 10 transgress
a promise: 3 lie 6 renege 7 violate
a record: 5 excel 6 exceed
away: 5 leave, rebel 6 escape, revolt, secede
bad ~: 6 mishap 8 hard luck 9 adversity 10 misfortune
big ~: 4 luck 7 opening
bread: 3 eat, sup 4 dine
camp: 5 leave 6 depart, pack up
coffee ~: 4 lull, rest 5 pause
down: 3 cry, rot, sob 4 fail, weep, wilt 5 decay, erode, spoil 6 die out, fall in, go awry 7 conk out, crumple, dissect, founder, go kaput, succumb 8 collapse, dissolve, simplify 9 come apart, decompose, dismantle, fall apart, inculcate 10 go to pieces
ender: 4 away, down, fast, neck 5 front, point, water 7 dancing, through
even: 3 tie 10 keep up with
faith: 6 betray, renege 7 sell out 8 go back on
forth: 4 spew, spue 5 erupt, spout
ground: 4 plow 5 begin 7 advance, kick off, pioneer
in: 3 rob, use 4 open, raid 5 barge, enter, enure, inure, steal, teach, train 6 burgle, irrupt, meddle, school 7 educate, obtrude, prepare 8 accustom, instruct, trespass 9 condition, get used to, habituate, interrupt, penetrate 10 burglarize, inaugurate
in hostilities: 5 truce 9 ceasefire
in relations: 4 rift 6 breach, schism 7 quarrel 10 falling-out
in the action: 4 lull 5 lapse 6 recess
into pieces: 5 smash 6 shiver 7 shatter 8 fragment, splinter
in two: 5 halve 6 bisect
loose: 4 bail, flee 6 escape, run off 7 get away
lucky ~: 4 boon 5 fluke, mercy 6 chance 7 godsend 8 blessing, fortuity, windfall
make a ~: 2 go 3 run 4 bolt 6 escape 7 abscond, so south 8 skip town 10 fly the coop, go on the lam
of day: 4 dawn, morn 5 sunup 7 morning, sunrise
off: 3 end 4 halt, part, quit, snap, stop, wean 5 cease, sever, spall, split 6 cancel, desist, detach, divide, recess, unlink 7 disjoin, split up 8 disunite, separate, set apart, surcease, uncouple 9 close down 10 call it a day, disconnect
one's heart: 4 dump, jilt 6 bum out, sadden 7 abandon, depress, let down 8 dispirit, distress 9 throw over 10 disappoint, dishearten
one's neck: 4 toil 5 slave, sweat 6 hustle, strain, strive 8 bear down, struggle
open: 5 burst, crack, force
out: 4 flee 5 arise, erupt, occur, set in, start 6 appear, emerge, escape, happen 7 abscond, explode 8 commence, separate, spring up 10 burst forth
point: 5 ad out
price ~: 4 sale 6 rebate 9 reduction
sentence ~: 4 dash 5 colon, comma 6 hyphen 9 semi-colon
silence: 3 say 5 speak
soldier's ~: 5 leave 8 furlough
starter: 3 day 4 fire, jail, news, wind 5 heart, house
stride: 6 falter
take a ~: 4 rest 5 pause, relax 6 lay off, recess, rest up, unwind 8 loosen up
the ice: 5 begin, start 6 embark, launch 8 commence
the news: 3 air 4 leak, tell 6 advise, clue in, inform, report, reveal, tip off 7 let slip 8 announce, disclose 9 make known 10 make public
the peace: 4 riot
the record of: 3 top 4 beat, best, pass 5 outdo 6 better 7 eclipse, surpass 8 outshine, outstrip, surmount
the rules: 4 defy 5 cheat, flout 7 disobey 9 disregard
through: 4 loom 6 appear, pierce
up: 3 end 4 ha-ha, halt, part, quit, rend, ruin 5 cease, close, end it, laugh, loose, smash, split 6 cackle, divide, finish, giggle, guffaw, harrow, loosen, ravage, recess, titter, weaken 7 adjourn, chortle, chuckle, disband, suspend 8 conclude, convulse, disperse, levigate, pack it in, separate 9 decompose, dismantle, knock down, pulverize, terminate 10 call it a day
up with: 4 dump 7 divorce 8 separate 9 throw over
with: 5 rebel 7 quarrel 9 repudiate
break __: 3 off, out 4 a leg, camp, down, even, into, rank 5 bread, cover, dance, loose, of day, point 6 ground 7 dancing, through
break __ ground: 3 new
__ break: 3 tea 4 fast 5 take a, tough 6 coffee, spring, winter 7 service, station
breakable: 5 frail 6 flimsy 7 brittle, fragile, rickety, unsound 8 delicate 9 frangible, splintery
breakage: 4 harm, loss 5 abuse, crack 6 damage, injury 9 liability 10 impairment
breakaway group: 4 cult, sect
Breakdance (1984 song)
artist: Irene Cara
breakdown: 6 fiasco 7 debacle, failure 8 analysis, collapse 9 diagnosis 10 disruption
beacon: 5 flare
combining form: 4 -lyze
diplomacy ~: 4 rift
of cells: 5 lysis
societal ~: 5 anomy 6 anomie
breaker: 4 surf, wave 5 surge 6 billow
circuit ~: 4 fuse
combining form: 5 -clast
ground ~: 3 hoe 5 spade 6 shovel 7 pioneer 8 inventor
ice ~: 4 pick
sound-barrier ~: 3 SST
starter: 3 ice, jaw, law, tie 4 back 5 trail 6 ground, strike
Breaker Morant (1979 film)
cast: Bryan Brown, Jack Thompson, John Waters, Edward Woodward
director: Bruce Beresford
break-even amount: 4 cost
breakfast: 3 eat 4 meal
bed and ~: 3 inn 7 lodging
beverage: 2 OJ 3 tea 4 milk 5 cocoa, juice 6 coffee
British ~ item: 6 kipper
Brooklyn ~: 5 bagel
choice: 3 ham 4 eggs 5 bacon, juice, links, toast 6 cereal, Danish, omelet, waffle 7 hotcake, pancake, sausage 9 sweet roll
continental ~ item: 3 tea 4 milk 5 donut, fruit 6 coffee, Danish, muffin 8 doughnut
device: 3 urn 6 brewer, juicer 7 toaster
fish: 3 lox
fruit: 5 melon 6 orange 9 cantaloup 10 grapefruit
grain: 3 oat, rye 5 wheat 6 cereal
holder: 4 bowl, tray 6 eggcup
late ~ hour: 3 ten 5 ten a.m.
nook: 6 alcove
pancake ~: 7 benefit 10 fundraiser
pastry: 5 donut 6 Danish 8 doughnut 9 sweet roll
roll: 5 bagel 9 croissant
spread: 3 jam 4 oleo 5 honey, jelly 6 butter 9 margarine, marmalade
time: 7 morning
__ breakfast: 4 dog's 7 English
Breakfast at Tiffany's: 4 book, film
author: Truman Capote
cast: Buddy Ebsen, Audrey Hepburn, Patricia Neal, George Peppard
composer: Henry Mancini
director: Blake Edwards
Breakfast Club, The (1985 film)
cast: Emilio Estevez, Anthony Michael Hall, Judd Nelson, Molly Ringwald, Ally Sheedy
director: John Hughes
break-in: 3 job 5 heist, theft 6 bag job 7 robbery 8 burglary, thievery
Break In
author: Dick Francis
breaking: 3 hot
and entering: 5 crime 6 felony
combining form: 6 -clasis 7 -clastic
new ground: 5 fresh, novel 6 clever 7 unusual 8 creative, inspired, original, singular 9 ingenious, inventive 10 innovative
point: 5 limit 8 showdown
starter: 5 heart 6 ground
__-breaking: 4 back
Breaking Away (1979 film)
cast: Barbara Barrie, Dennis Christopher, Paul Dooley, Dennis Quaid, Daniel Stern
cat: 7 Fellini
director: Peter Yates
vehicle: 4 bike 7 bicycle
Breaking Up Is Hard to Do (1962 song)
artist: Neil Sedaka
Break It to Me Gently (song)
artist: Brenda Lee, Juice Newton
breakneck: 4 fast 5 brisk, fleet, hasty, quick, rapid, steep, swift 6 flying, racing, snappy, speedy 7 express, hurried, instant 8 headlong, reckless 9 dangerous, foolhardy, rapid-fire, uncareful, whirlwind 10 double-time, hypersonic, supersonic
break new __: 6 ground
break of __: 3 day 4 dawn

Break of Day
author: John Donne
break one's __: **4** neck **5** heart
Breaks of the Game, The
author: David Halberstam
break the __: **3** ice
breakthrough: **5** boost **7** advance **8** advanced, progress **9** milestone
break-up: **5** split **7** divorce, parting **10** separation
Break-Up, The (2006 film)
cast: Jennifer Aniston, Vince Vaughn
Break Up to Make Up (1973 song)
artist: Stylistics
breakwater: **4** mole, pier **5** jetty, levee, wharf **7** sea wall **10** embankment
__ Breaky Heart: **4** Achy
bream: **4** fish **5** porgy **7** sunfish **8** bluegill
relative: **4** dace **6** minnow
Bream: **3** Sid
breast: **5** chest
beat one's ~: **6** lament
ender: **4** bone, work **5** plate **6** stroke
make a clean ~ of: **5** admit **7** own up to
starter: **3** red
breastbone combining form: **5** stern- **6** sterno-
__-breasted: **6** double, single
Breasted: **5** James
breastwork: **7** bastion, rampart
breath: **4** gasp, gulp, hint, jiff, life, odor, pant, puff, rest, wind **5** aroma, break, jiffy, pause, shade, smell, touch, trace, vapor, whiff **6** eupnea, minute, murmur, wheeze **7** respite, soupçon, whisper **10** exhalation, inhalation, suggestion
baby's ~: **5** plant **6** flower
brief ~: **4** gasp, huff, pant, puff
catch one's ~: **4** rest **5** pause
combining form: **4** -pnea **5** -pnoea **6** pneumo- **7** pneumat- **8** pneumato-
deep ~: **4** sigh
draw ~: **4** live
ender: **6** taking
freshener: **4** mint **6** cachou
holder: **4** lung
mint: **4** Cert
of air: **4** wind **6** breeze
of life: **5** anima **6** spirit
out of ~: **5** puffy **7** gasping, panting **8** wheezing
take one's ~ away: **3** awe, wow **4** stun **5** amaze **6** boggle, excite, thrill **7** astound, stagger, stupefy **8** astonish **9** take aback
breath __: **4** test
__ breath: **3** bad **5** baby's, bated, in one, out of
breathe: **3** are, say **4** gasp, gulp, live, pant, puff, tell **5** exist, imbue, utter **6** draw in, exhale, impart, infuse, inhale, inject, instil, wheeze **7** confide, express, instill, respire, subsist, whisper **10** articulate
a word: **4** tell
easy: **5** relax
fire: **4** boil, fume, rage, stew **5** storm **6** see red, seethe **7** smolder **10** hit the roof
hard: **4** gasp, huff, pant, puff **5** heave
in: **5** sniff **6** inhale
live and ~: **3** are **5** exist
new life into: **6** revive **7** refresh **10** regenerate
out: **4** sigh **6** exhale
roughly: **6** wheeze
breathe __ of relief: **5** a sigh
Breathe (1999 song)
artist: Faith Hill
Breathe Again (1993 song)
artist: Toni Braxton
Breathed, Berke: **10** cartoonist
breathe down one's __: **4** neck
breather: **4** lull, lung, rest **5** break, pause, truce **6** recess, relief **7** respite **8** reprieve **10** suspension
take a ~: **4** rest, stop **5** pause, relax **6** recess
breath freshener: **5** Certs **6** Binaca, Mentos, Tic Tac **7** Altoids, Clorets, Dentyne
breathing: **4** live **5** alive **6** eupnea, living **7** animate **10** inhalation
combining form: **4** spir- **5** spiri-, spiro-
disorder: **5** apnea **6** apnoea, asthma
fire: *see* angry **7** angered
organ: **4** gill, lung
passage: **5** naris **6** airway
passages: **5** nares
sound: **4** rale, sigh **6** wheeze
spell: **4** lull, rest **5** pause **6** recess **7** respite **8** reprieve
underwater ~ apparatus: **4** gill **5** scuba **7** snorkel
breathing __: **4** room **5** space, spell
Breathing Lessons
author: Anne Tyler
breathless: **4** agog **5** agasp **6** winded **7** anxious, excited, gasping, gulping, panting **9** astounded, exhausted, expectant, impatient **10** incoherent, stertorous
Breathless (1958 song)
artist: Jerry Lee Lewis
Breathless (1959 film)
cast: Jean-Paul Belmondo, Jean Seberg
director: Jean-Luc Godard
breathtaking: **3** def, rad **4** aces, A-one, boss, braw, cool, dece, fine, gear, keen, neat, nice, phat, tuff **5** dandy, ducky, grand, great, marvy, neató, nobby, prime, slick, super, swell **6** bang on, bang-up, bonzer, bosker, choice, divine, dreamy, far-out, gnarly, groovy, lovely, peachy, scenic, slap-up, spot on, superb, terrif, tiptop, unreal, whizzo, wicked **7** amazing, awesome, capital, corking, perfect, ripping, skookum, stellar, sublime **8** dazzling, dramatic, especial, exciting, eximious, fabulous, five-star, four-star, frabjous, glorious, heavenly, jim-dandy, scenical, slam-bang, smashing, splendid, standout, sterling, stickout, superior, terrific, top-level, topnotch, very good, wondrous **9** bodacious, Endsville, excellent, exemplary, exquisite, first-rate, high-grade, hunky-dory, marvelous, sollicker, thrilling, top-flight **10** first-class, hotsy-totsy, jack-a-dandy, out of sight, peachy-keen, phenomenal, remarkable, stupendous, super-duper
see also wonderful
__ Breath You Take: **5** Every
breccia: **4** rock **5** stone
Brecht, Bertolt: **4** poet **6** German **10** playwright
collaborator: **5** Weill
work: Baal
The Life of Galileo
Mother Courage and Her Children
The Threepenny Opera
Breck: **5** Peter **7** shampoo
competitor: **5** Prell
__ Breckinridge: **4** Myra
__-bred: **3** ill **4** city, well **7** country
bred-in-the-__: **4** bone
bred starter: **3** low **4** high, home, pure **5** color, cross **8** standard
breech ender: **5** block, cloth, clout **6** loader
breeches: **5** jeans, pants **6** Capris, shorts, slacks **8** Bermudas, jodhpurs, knickers, trousers **9** plus fours
__ breeches: **4** knee **6** riding
breechloader: **3** gun **5** rifle **6** musket
breed: **4** bear, kind, line, race, rear, sire, sort, type **5** beget, cause, class, raise, spawn, stock **6** create, foster, kidney, manner, strain **7** bring up, develop, lineage, nourish, nurture, produce, species, variety **8** engender, generate, multiply, pedigree **9** cultivate, procreate, propagate, reproduce **10** give rise to
mixed ~: **3** cur, mut **4** mule, mutt **7** mongrel **8** alley cat
breeder __: **7** reactor
Breeder's Cup event: **4** race
breeding: **5** grace **6** polish **7** culture, lineage, manners **8** civility, courtesy, elegance, noblesse, prolific, urbanity **9** gentility, propriety **10** generation, refinement
good ~: **6** polish **7** conduct, culture, decorum, p's and q's **8** behavior, courtesy, urbanity **9** etiquette, politesse **10** deportment, politeness, refinement
ground: **6** hotbed
place: **4** nest
Breedlove, Craig: **5** racer **9** auto racer
Breed's __: **4** Hill
breeks: **5** pants
Breen: **5** Bobby
breeze: **3** air **4** blow, gust, puff, snap, wind **5** cinch, cushy, draft, speed **6** flurry, picnic, simple, zephyr **7** airflow, current **8** duck soup, kid stuff, painless, pushover, workable **9** no problem **10** child's play, effortless
ender: **3** way
faint ~: **4** waft **6** breath
float on the ~: **4** waft
hang in the ~: **3** dry **6** air-dry
in: **4** come **5** enter, pop up **6** appear, arrive, show up, turn up **8** get there
like a tropical ~: **5** balmy
make a ~: **3** fan
shoot the ~: **3** gab, jaw, rap **4** blab, chat **5** prate, speak **6** gossip, jabber **7** blather, blether, chatter **8** chitchat, talk idly **10** chew the fat, chew the rag
sudden ~: **4** gust
through: **3** ace, zip
__ breeze: **3** sea **4** lake, land **5** fresh, light **6** gentle, strong
Breeze: **3** car **4** auto **8** Plymouth
Breeze __, The: **4** and I
breezeway terminus: **5** house **6** garage
breezy: **3** raw **4** airy, mild, pert **5** fresh, gusty, light, windy **6** blithe, casual, drafty, jaunty, lively, rakish **7** affable, blowing, buoyant, dashing, offhand **8** blustery, carefree, cheerful, debonair, informal **9** debonaire, easygoing, lightsome, sprightly, vivacious **10** debonnaire, unbothered, ventilated
__ brei: **5** matzo **6** matzah, matzoh
Brel: **7** Jacques
Bremen: **4** city, port, town
locale: **7** Germany
port near ~: **5** Emden
river: **5** Weser
Bremer: **7** Lucille **8** Fredrika
Bremerhaven: **4** city, port, town
locale: **7** Germany
Bremerton: **4** city, town
locale: **10** Washington
Bremner: **4** Ewen
Bren: **3** gun **7** British **10** machine gun
Brenda: **3** Lee **5** Starr **7** Fricker, Russell, Vaccaro **8** Marshall
Brendan: **4** Gill **5** Behan **6** Fraser, Sexton
Brenda Starr (1989 film)
cast: Timothy Dalton, Diana Scarwid, Brooke Shields
Brendel, Alfred: **7** pianist **8** Austrian
Brendon: **8** Nicholas
Brenly: **3** Bob
Brennan: **6** Eileen, Walter **7** William
Brennan, Christopher: **4** poet **10** Australian
Brennan, Walter: **5** actor
film: Bad Day at Black Rock (1955)
Come and Get It (1936, AA)
Kentucky (1938, AA)
My Darling Clementine (1946)
Northwest Passage (1940)
The Pride of the Yankees (1942)
Red River (1948)
Sergeant York (1941)
Support Your Local Sheriff (1969)
To Have and Have Not (1944)
The Westerner (1940, AA)
song: Old Rivers (1962)
TV: The Real McCoys
Brenneman: **3** Amy
Brenner: **5** David **6** Sydney
Brenner Pass region: **5** Tirol, Tyrol
Brent: **6** George, Spiner **9** Geiberger, Musberger
Brentano, Clemens: **4** poet **6** German
Brent, George: **5** actor
spouse: Ann Sheridan

Brenton: 4 Wood
Br'er: 3 Fox 4 Bear 6 Rabbit
Brescia: 4 city, town
  locale: 5 Italy
Breslau: 4 city, town
  river: 4 Oder, Odra
Breslin: 5 Jimmy 7 Abigail
Breslow: 3 Lou
Bresnahan: 5 Roger
Brest: 4 city, port, town 6 Martin
  locale: 6 France 7 Belarus 8 Brittany
  native: 6 Breton
Brest ___: 7 Litovsk
Brest, Martin: 8 director
  film: Beverly Hills Cop (1984)
    Going in Style (1979)
    Meet Joe Black (1998)
    Midnight Run (1988)
    Scent of a Woman (1992)
bret: 4 fish
Bret: 5 Harte 8 Maverick, Michaels 10 Saberhagen
brethren: 3 kin 6 parish 7 kinfolk 8 kinfolks, kinsfolk
Breton: 3 hat 4 cape, Celt 5 André
___ Breton Island: 4 Cape
Brett: 5 Favre 6 Butler, George, Jeremy, Ratner, Somers
Brett, George: 5 Royal 10 baseballer
Bretton ___ Conference: 5 Woods
breve: 4 mark, note 9 whole note
___ breve: 4 alla
brevier
  alternative: *see* point size
breviloquent: 4 curt 5 brief, terse 7 concise, laconic
brevity: 8 laconism 9 briefness, shortness
brew: 3 ale, tea 4 beer, boil, cook, form, make, perk, plan, plot, stew, suds 5 blend, drink, hatch, lager, mocha, steep, stout 6 coffee, devise, foment, infuse, medley, porter, potion, scheme, stir up, whip up 7 concoct, develop, distill, ferment, Pilsner 8 beverage, contrive, infusion, Pilsener 10 concoction
  breakfast ~: 3 joe, tea 4 java 6 coffee
  ender: 3 pub 5 house 6 master
  ingredient: 6 barley
  milieu: 3 bar, pub 6 saloon, tavern 8 alehouse
  sour ~: 6 alegar
  witches' ~ need: 4 newt
  see also beer
___ brew: 4 home 7 witches
brewed beverage: 3 ale, tea 4 beer 5 lager, stout 6 coffee
brewer: 3 urn 7 samovar
  café ~: 4 urne
  concern: 4 wort
  need: 3 tun, vat 4 barm, malt, oast, wort 5 yeast 6 barley
  product: 3 ale 4 beer 5 lager, stout
Brewer: 3 Gay 4 Mike 6 Teresa
  Brewers: 4 nine, team
  Hall-of-Famer: 5 Yount 10 Robin Yount
  home: 9 Milwaukee, Wisconsin
  org.: 3 MLB, NLC
  sport: 8 baseball
Brewers
  rival: *see* baseball team
Brewer, Teresa
  song: Bo Weevil (1956)
    Let Me Go, Lover (1954)
    A Sweet Old Fashioned Girl (1956)
    A Tear Fell (1956)
    You Send Me (1957)
brewery starter: 5 micro
brewing: 8 imminent 9 in the wind
  be ~: 4 loom 6 impend 8 threaten
  leaf for ~: 3 tea 5 pekoe
brewpub
  offering: 3 ale 4 beer
brewski: 4 beer, suds 7 cold one
Brewster: 7 Jordana, William
Brewster ___: 5 chair 7 McCloud
___ Brewster: 5 Punky
Brewster McCloud (1970 film)
  cast: Bud Cort, Shelley Duvall, Sally Kellerman
  director: Robert Altman
Brewster's Millions (1945 film)
  cast: June Havoc
Breyer: 7 Stephen
Breyer's: 8 ice cream
  competitor: *see* ice cream
Brezhnev, Leonid: 7 Russian 9 statesman
  domain: 4 USSR 7 Kremlin
Brian: 3 Eno, May 4 Boru, Mary 5 Friel, Jones, Keith, Kelly, Moore, Orser 6 Aherne, Aldiss, Benben, Hyland, Kerwin, Setzer, Wilson, Wimmer 7 Boitano, Dennehy, De Palma, Donlevy, Epstein, Holland, Piccolo 8 Bosworth, McKnight, Mitchell, Mulroney, Williams 9 Gottfried, Josephson
Briand, Aristide: 6 French 8 Nobelist 9 statesman
___-Briand Pact: 7 Kellogg
Brian's Song (1971 film)
  cast: Billy Dee Williams, James Caan
briar: 4 bush 5 shrub, spine, thorn 7 bramble, prickle
  ender: 4 root, wood
  starter: 5 sweet
briard: 3 dog 5 canid 6 canine
bribable: 5 venal 7 corrupt 9 mercenary
bribe: 3 buy, fix, sop 4 lure 5 get at, get to, graft, smear 6 boodle, buy off, grease, payoff, payola, ransom, square, suborn, tamper 7 corrupt, rake-off, schmear 8 kickback 9 hush money, influence, lubricate 10 inducement
bribery: 5 graft 8 venality 10 corruption
bric-a-brac: 5 curio 6 trifle 7 memento, whatnot 8 nicknack, souvenir 10 knickknack
  place: 5 shelf
Brice: 5 Fanny 6 Marden
Brice, Fanny: 6 singer 7 actress
  character: Baby Snooks
  movie based on ~: Funny Girl, Funny Lady
  musical based on ~: Funny Girl
  spouse: Billy Rose
brick: 4 cake, pave 5 adobe, block, color 6 cheese, fellow
  alternative: *see* brown color, red color
  carrier: 3 hod
  ender: 3 bat 4 kiln, work, yard 5 layer
  food in a ~: 6 cheese
  material: 4 clay 5 straw
  Southwestern ~: 5 adobe
  starter: 4 fire, gold
  worker: 5 layer, mason
brick ___: 3 red 6 cheese
___ brick: 3 air 4 beam, iron 5 glass, Roman 6 salmon 7 pressed
brickbat: 4 gibe, jibe, twit 7 affront 8 derision 9 criticism 10 imputation
Brickell, Edie
  spouse: Paul Simon
Brick House (1977 song)
  artist: Commodores
bricklayer: 5 mason
  implement: 3 hod
bricklaying: 5 craft, skill
___ brickle: 6 butter
Brickman: 4 Paul
___ Brick Road: 6 Yellow
bricks
  hit like a ton of ~: 3 jar 4 daze, jolt, kayo, stun 5 shock 6 bedaze 7 astound, flummox, horrify, nonplus, outrage, stagger, stupefy, terrify 8 astonish, bewilder, blow away, bowl over, knock out, unsettle 9 dumbfound, overpower, overwhelm, take aback 10 discompose
  hit the ~: 2 go 4 exit, move 5 leave 6 beat it, depart, go away, move on 7 make off, pull out, push off, take off, vamoose 8 shove off, slip away 10 shuffle off
  partner: 6 mortar
Brickyard event: 4 race
bridal: 7 marital, nuptial, spousal, wedding 8 conjugal 9 connubial
  accessory: 4 veil 6 garter, wreath 7 bouquet
  gown feature: 5 train
  month: 4 June
  notice word: 3 née
  wear: 4 lace 5 satin, tulle, white
bridal ___: 4 gown, veil 5 party, suite 6 shower, wreath
Bridal Ballad
  author: Edgar Allan Poe
Bridal Veil ___: 5 Falls
bride: 4 mate, wife 5 woman 6 missis, missus, spouse 8 helpmate, newlywed
  acquisition: 4 band, ring 5 in-law
  attendant: 10 flowergirl 11 maid of honor
  bestowal: 5 dowry 6 dowery
  companion: 5 groom
  destination: 5 altar
  ender: 5 groom
  future ~: 7 fiancée
  new title: 3 Mrs.
  response: 3 I do
  ride: 4 limo
  walkway: 5 aisle
___ bride: 3 war 5 child
___ Bride: 4 June 7 Runaway
Bride Came ___, The: 3 C.O.D.
Bride Elect, The
  composer: John Philip Sousa
bridegroom: 4 mate 6 spouse 7 husband 8 benedict, newlywed
  acquisition: 4 band, ring 5 in-law
  attendant: 5 usher 7 best man 10 ring bearer
  future ~: 6 fiancé
Bride of Frankenstein (1935 film)
  cast: Colin Clive, Valerie Hobson, Boris Karloff, Elsa Lanchester, Una O'Connor
  director: James Whale
Bride of Lammermoor, The
  author: Walter Scott
  character: 4 Lucy 5 Edgar
Brideshead: 6 estate
Brideshead Revisited
  author: Evelyn Waugh
  character: 3 Rex 4 Cara 5 Beryl, Celia, Ryder
Bride Wars (2009 film)
  cast: Candice Bergen, Anne Hathaway, Kate Hudson
bridge: 4 arch, game, join, link, span 5 cross 7 catwalk, connect, stretch, subtend, trestle, viaduct 8 arch over, card game, crossing, go across, overpass, traverse, vinculum 9 cross over, overpasse 10 connection, dental work
  beat, at ~: 3 set
  builder: 4 engr. 8 engineer
  builder's concern: 6 stress
  builder's deg.: 3 BCE
  call: 3 bid 5 I pass, one no, rebid
  coup: 4 slam
  declaration: 5 trump
  electric ~: 3 arc
  end: 8 abutment
  ender: 4 head, work
  expert: 5 Goren 6 Sharif
  fare: 4 toll
  forerunner: 5 whist
  group: 4 club
  guard of folklore: 5 troll
  holding: 4 hand
  honor: 3 ace, ten 4 jack, king 5 queen
  in French: 4 pont
  in Italian: 5 ponte
  land ~: 7 isthmus
  move: 5 raise
  musical ~: 5 segue
  need: 4 deck 5 cards
  opening: 3 bid
  pontoon: 6 bateau
  position: 4 East, West 5 North, South
  quorum: 4 four
  response: 4 pass
  ruff, in ~: 5 trump
  site: 4 nose
  starter: 4 draw, foot
  support: 4 I-bar, pier 5 cable, pylon 6 girder 7 trestle
  team: 3 duo 4 pair
  term: 5 trick
  the gap: 3 aid 6 assist 8 tide over 9 help along 10 see through
  toll ~ unit: 4 axle
bridge ___: 4 club, deck, lamp, loan 5 chair, cloth, house, table
___ bridge: 3 ore 4 land, lift, rope, toll 5 ferry, float, Irish, light, paint, truss 6 Bailey, bateau, flying, monkey, rubber 7 auction, covered, docking, kissing, pontoon
Bridge ___ Far, A: 3 Too
___ Bridge: 3 Mrs. 4 Eads 5 Adam's 6 London 7 Natural, Rainbow
Bridge at ___: 5 Arles
Bridge for Passing, A
  author: Pearl S. Buck
bridgehead: 8 foothold
Bridge of ___: 5 Asses, Sighs

Bridge of Narni
artist: Camille Corot
Bridge of San Luis Rey, The
author: Thornton Wilder
character: **3** Pio **5** Clara, Jaime **6** Pepita
Bridge on the Drina, The
author: Ivo Andric
Bridge on the River Kwai, The (1957 film)
cast: Sir Alec Guinness, Jack Hawkins, Sessue Hayakawa, William Holden
director: David Lean
setting: **4** Siam
Bridge Over the River Kwai, The
author: Pierre Boulle
Bridge Over Troubled Water (song)
artist: Aretha Franklin, Simon and Garfunkel
Bridgeport: **4** city, port, town
locale: **4** Conn.
town near ~: **6** Easton
Bridges: **4** Alan, Beau, Jeff, Todd **5** James, Lloyd **6** Alicia, Robert
__ Bridges: **4** Nash **7** Burning, Natural
Bridges at Toko-Ri, The (1955 film)
cast: William Holden, Grace Kelly, Fredric March
director: Mark Robson
Bridges, Beau: **5** actor
film: The Fabulous Baker Boys (1989)
The Hotel New Hampshire (1984)
The Incident (1967)
The Landlord (1970)
Norma Rae (1979)
Bridges, Jeff: **5** actor
film: American Heart (1993)
Bad Company (1972)
The Big Lebowski (1998)
Crazy Heart (2009, AA)
The Fabulous Baker Boys (1989)
Fat City (1972)
Fearless (1993)
The Fisher King (1991)
Hearts of the West (1975)
Iron Man (2008)
Jagged Edge (1985)
King Kong (1976)
The Last American Hero (1973)
The Last Picture Show (1971)
The Mirror Has Two Faces (1996)
The Muse (1999)
Nadine (1987)
Rancho Deluxe (1975)
Seabiscuit (2003)
Stay Hungry (1976)
Texasville (1990)
Thunderbolt and Lightfoot (1974)
Tucker: The Man and His Dream (1988)
White Squall (1996)
Bridges, Lloyd: **5** actor
film: Airplane! (1980)
son: **4** Beau, Jeff
TV: Sea Hunt
Bridges of Madison County, The (1995 film)
cast: Clint Eastwood, Meryl Streep
director: Clint Eastwood
setting: **4** Iowa
Bridget: **5** Fonda, Riley
Bridge, The: **4** poem
author: Hart Crane
Bridget Jones's Diary (2001 film)
cast: Colin Firth, Hugh Grant, Gemma Jones, Renée Zellweger
Bridge Too Far, A
author: Cornelius Ryan
river: **5** Rhine
Bridge Too Far, A (1977 film)
cast: Dirk Bogarde, James Caan, Michael Caine
Bridgetown: **4** city **7** capital
locale: **8** Barbados
bridle: **4** curb, rein, tame **5** check, leash **6** halter, muzzle, pull in, rear up, rein in, subdue **7** control, inhibit, repress **8** hold back, restrain, suppress, withhold **9** deterrent, restraint **10** keep in line
part: **3** bit **4** curb, rein
path: **5** trail
Brie: **6** cheese, French
alternative: *see* cheese
covering: **4** rind
brief: **4** curt, memo, post **5** brusk, crisp, edify, hasty, pithy, prime, quick, ready, short, swift, teach, terse **6** abrupt, advise, digest, fill in, gnomic, inform, little, précis, report, sketch, skimpy, update **7** apprise, apprize, brusque, compact, concise, cursory, explain, hurried, laconic, limited, outline, pandect, passing, summary **8** abstract, fleeting, flitting, instruct, meteoric, succinct, synopsis **9** curtailed, enlighten, ephemeral, momentary, short-term, summarize, temporary, thumbnail, transient **10** abridgment, boiled down, compendium, compressed, evanescent, pro tempore, short-lived, to the point, transitory, unenduring
appearance: **5** cameo
attempt: **4** stab **5** whirl
but meaningful: **5** pithy
contact: **5** brush, graze
ender: **4** case
hold a ~ for: **6** defend, second **7** approve, endorse, indorse, support **8** champion, sanction, side with
look: **4** peek **5** recon **6** glance
statement: **5** flash, squib **9** news flash, sound bite
stay: **8** stopover
stop: **4** lull **5** pause
summary: **5** recap
time: **3** sec **4** jiff **5** jiffy, spell, trice **6** minute, moment, second
trip: **4** tour **5** drive **6** errand, outing **7** sojourn **9** excursion
__ brief: **4** news
briefcase: **3** bag **6** valise **7** attaché **9** portfolio
closer: **4** hasp
Brief Encounter (1945 film)
cast: Stanley Holloway, Trevor Howard, Celia Johnson
director: David Lean
doctor: **4** Alec
Brief History of Time, A
author: Stephen Hawking
briefing: **6** fill-in **7** rundown
briefly: **7** briskly, hastily, in short, quickly, shortly, swiftly **8** suddenly **9** cursorily, hurriedly
briefs: **4** BVDs **5** pants **6** shorts, undies **7** jockeys **8** skivvies **9** underwear
__ Brief, The: **7** Pelican
Brienz: **4** lake
locale: **4** Bern **5** Berne **11** Switzerland
brier: **5** shrub, spine, thorn **7** bramble, prickle
starter: **3** cat **5** green, sweet
brig: **3** jug **4** boat, jail, ship **5** craft **6** argosy, cooler, lockup, prison **10** guardhouse
ender: **3** ade
brigade: **4** army, band, crew, unit **5** corps, fleet, force, group, squad, troop **6** legion, outfit **7** company, phalanx **10** contingent, detachment
__ brigade: **4** fire **5** light **6** bucket
brigadier: **4** rank **7** general
Brigadoon
composer: Alan Jay Lerner, Frederick Loewe
Brigadoon (1954 film): **7** musical
cast: Cyd Charisse, Van Johnson, Gene Kelly
character: **3** Meg **5** Angus, Fiona, Tommy
director: Vincente Minnelli
brigand: **4** hood, thug **5** rogue, thief **6** bad guy, bandit, looter, mugger, outlaw, pirate, raider, robber, sacker, sea dog, vandal, viking **7** corsair, footpad, hoodlum, ruffian, sea wolf **8** criminal, gangster, marauder, picaroon, pillager, predator, rapparee, tough guy **9** buccaneer, desperado, plunderer, privateer **10** freebooter, highwayman
brigantine: **4** boat, ship **6** argosy
Brigati: **5** Eddie
Briggs: **5** Clare
Brigham City: **4** town
locale: **4** Utah
Brigham Young: **6** school **10** university
athletes: **7** Cougars
letters: **3** BYU
locale: **4** Utah **5** Provo
bright: **3** apt, gay, lit **4** fair, keen, pert, rich, rosy **5** aglow, alert, clean, clear, fresh, happy, jolly, light, lucid, merry, nitid, peppy, perky, quick, ready, sharp, shiny, smart, sunny, vivid, witty **6** ablaze, agleam, astute, brainy, clever, flashy, glossy, golden, joyful, joyous, limpid, lively, silver, strong, sunlit **7** beaming, blazing, burning, clement, fulgent, glowing, hopeful, knowing, lambent, moonlit, obvious, radiant, shining, well-lit **8** cheerful, colorful, dazzling, flashing, gleaming, incisive, keen-eyed, luminous, lustrous, polished, sanguine, spirited, splendid **9** astucious, brilliant, cloudless, effulgent, eggheaded, favorable, ingenious, inventive, lightsome, observant, promising, receptive, refulgent, sparkling, sprightly, unclouded, vivacious **10** auspicious, discerning, glittering, keen-witted, optimistic, precocious, shimmering
beam: **3** ray **5** laser **9** spotlight
blindingly ~: **4** loud, neon **5** gaudy **7** glaring **8** dazzling
group: **5** Mensa
looking on the ~ side: **7** hopeful **8** optimism **10** optimistic
make less ~: **3** dim **5** bedim, shade **6** soften
name meaning ~: **5** Clara, Clare **6** Bertha, Claire, Xavier
not ~: **4** dark, drab, dumb, gray, grey, slow **5** dense, dingy, thick
bright-__: **4** eyed
bright and __: **5** early
brighten: **4** gild **5** cheer, light, liven, scrub, shine **6** buff up, buoy up, illume, kindle, perk up, polish, revive **7** burnish, cheer up, enliven, furbish, gladden, hearten, lighten, light up, relieve, spiff up **8** emblazon, illumine, ornament **9** embellish, intensify, irradiate, take heart **10** illuminate
bright-eyed: **4** pert **5** alert, eager, fresh, sunny **7** healthy **8** youthful
Bright Lights, Big City (1988 film)
cast: Phoebe Cates, Michael J. Fox, Swoosie Kurtz, Kiefer Sutherland
brightness: **4** glow **5** gleam, gloss, light, sheen, shine **6** gaiety, gayety, luster **7** glitter **8** optimism, radiance, radiancy, splendor **9** freshness, smartness **10** cleverness, effulgence
lose ~: **3** dim **4** fade
unit: **5** lumen **7** lambert
Brighton: **4** city, town
locale: **6** Sussex **7** England, New York **8** Colorado
town opposite ~: **6** Dieppe
Brighton Beach Memoirs: **4** film, play
author: Neil Simon
cast: Blythe Danner, Bob Dishy, Jonathan Silverman
character: **4** Kate, Nora **6** Eugene
director: Gene Saks
Brighton Rock
author: Graham Greene
brights: **9** high beams
bright sword, name meaning: **6** Egbert
Brigid: **5** saint **6** Brophy
Brigitte: **6** Bardot **7** Nielsen
see also French
brilliance: **3** wit **4** glow **5** blaze, éclat, glare, gleam, gloss, light, shine **6** acumen, genius, luster, polish **7** glitter, sparkle **8** artistry, grandeur, radiance, radiancy, splendor **10** effulgence, virtuosity
brilliant: **3** ace, lit **4** star **5** aglow, light, lucid, noble, ready, sharp, shiny, slick, smart, sunny, vivid, witty **6** ablaze, astute, brainy, bright, clever, flashy, gifted, glossy, golden, lucent, ornate, strong, superb **7** beaming, blazing, flaming, fulgent, glowing, knowing, lambent, radiant, shining, vibrant **8** dazzling, gleaming, glorious, luminous, lustrous, masterly, readable, splendid, stunning **9** astu-

cious, effulgent, eggheaded, excellent, ingenious, inventive, prominent, refulgent, sparkling **10** celebrated, discerning, expressive, flamboyant, glittering, precocious
alternative: *see* point size
be ~: **4** glow, star **5** shine
not exactly ~: **4** slow **5** dense, thick
see also wonderful
Brilliant Disguise (1987 song)
artist: Bruce Springsteen
___ brillig...: **4** 'Twas
Brillo: **3** pad **7** soap pad
rival: **3** SOS
use ~: **5** scour, scrub
brim: **3** lip, rim **4** bill, edge, teem **5** brink, chime, limit, shore, skirt, verge, visor, vizor **6** border, flange, fringe, margin **7** run over **8** flow over, overflow, well over **9** periphery, spill over
ender: **5** stone
over: **4** fill **5** flood
Brim: **6** coffee
competitor: **5** Sanka
brimful: **4** full **5** awash **6** packed **7** teeming
___-brim hat: **4** snap
brimless hat: **5** toque **7** pillbox
Brimley: **7** Wilford
brimming: **3** big **4** full, rife **5** awash, laden **6** filled, imbued, jammed, loaded, packed **7** crammed, crowded, flooded, fraught, replete, stuffed **8** overfull
over: **4** full **5** awash **6** packed
Brindisi: **4** city, port, town
locale: **5** Italy
town near ~: **4** Oria
brindle: **3** cat **5** felid, tabby **6** feline
brindled: **4** pied **5** tawny **7** dappled, mottled, spotted, striped **8** speckled, streaked
brine: **8** sea water **9** salt water
steep in ~: **5** souse **6** pickle **8** preserve
brine-cured delicacy: **3** lox
Brinegar: **4** Paul
bring: **3** lug **4** bear, cart, draw, earn, haul, lead, take, tote **5** carry, cause, fetch, go get, guide, offer, truck, usher, yield **6** convey, escort, gather, induce, reduce, return, supply **7** conduct, deliver, drop off, provide, sell for **8** chaperon, engender, motivate, result in, transfer **9** accompany, chaperone, take along, transport
about: **4** form, make **5** beget, cause, spark, wreak **6** ask for, create, effect, induce, lead to **7** achieve, compass, produce, realize, trigger **8** conclude, engender, engineer, generate, occasion **9** hammer out, implement, instigate, originate **10** accomplish, effectuate, give rise to, make happen, put through
action: **3** sue **9** prosecute
along: **3** lug **4** tote **5** carry
around: **6** reason, revive **7** refresh, restore, win over **8** persuade **9** prevail on
a smile to: **5** amuse, cheer, elate
back: **5** rehab **6** revive **7** recover, restore **9** reinstate
bad luck: **3** hex **4** jinx **5** curse
before a judge: **3** try **5** retry
charges: **4** book **6** accuse, allege
down: **4** fell, land, ruin, sink, undo **5** abase, level, lower, shoot **6** bum out, deject, demean, dismay, humble, sadden, tackle, topple **8** dispirit, overturn, undercut **9** humiliate, overthrow, prostrate, undermine **10** dishearten
down the curtain on: **3** end **8** conclude
down the house: **3** wow **4** rase, raze **5** level **6** topple **7** delight, flatten **8** bulldoze, demolish, entrance
force to bear: **5** impel **6** compel **8** arm-twist, pressure **9** strongarm
forth: **4** bear, make **5** evoke, hatch, spawn, yield **6** derive, elicit **7** produce **10** come up with
forward: **3** lay **6** adduce **7** advance, produce
home: **3** net **4** earn **7** clarify, clear up **8** manifest **9** elucidate, explicate, get across, make clear, make plain **10** illuminate, illustrate
home the bacon: **4** earn, work
in: **3** get, net, pay **4** earn, gain, land, make, pipe, reap **5** co-opt, fetch, gross, usher, yield **6** garner, return **7** acquire, realize, receive
into court: **4** haul
into existence: **4** cast, form, make, rear **5** beget, breed, hatch, order, set up, shape, spawn, train **6** cook up, create, effect, father, invent, mature **7** arrange, compose, concoct, develop, outline, pioneer, produce, think up, turn out **8** assemble, conceive, engineer, generate, initiate **9** actualize, construct, establish, fabricate, hammer out, originate, take shape **10** give life to, mastermind
into play: **3** use **5** apply, exert **6** entail, resort
into the open: **3** air **4** leak, tell, vent **6** reveal, unveil **7** display, exhibit, freshen, publish **8** disclose **9** broadcast, make known, talk about
into the world: **4** bear **5** beget
low: **4** bust, ruin **5** abase, crush, lower **6** defeat, demean, demote, humble, reduce, weaken **7** conquer, deflate, degrade **8** bankrupt, pull down, vanquish **9** humiliate, knock down, overpower, pauperize, subjugate **10** impoverish
off: **6** attain, effect, manage, wangle **7** achieve, execute, perform, realize, work out **10** accomplish, put through
on: **5** cause, incur **6** ask for, induce
on board: **4** hire **6** employ, engage
out: **3** say **4** show **5** educe, evoke, issue, stage, state, utter **6** elicit, expose, stress **7** comment, extract **9** circulate, introduce **10** accentuate
pressure to bear: **5** lobby **7** squeeze **8** arm-twist **9** strongarm
to a close: **3** end **4** halt **6** finish, wrap up **9** terminate
to a screeching halt: **6** arrest, forbid, stifle **8** suppress
to a standstill: **4** stem **5** tie up **6** arrest, becalm, hinder **7** prevent **8** obstruct
to bay: **3** nab **4** trap, tree **5** catch **6** collar, corner **7** capture
to bear: **3** use **5** apply, exert **6** employ **8** exercise
to fruition: **7** realize **8** complete
together: **3** wed **4** join, weld **5** amass, group, rally, shape, unify, unite **6** adduct, center, gather, muster **7** compile, convene, convoke **8** assemble
to heel: **4** tame **6** subdue
to justice: **3** try **4** hear **9** prosecute **10** adjudicate
to light: **3** air **4** bare, find, show **5** admit, dig up **6** elicit, evince, expose, reveal, turn up, unmask, unveil **7** lay bare, uncover, unearth **8** disclose, discover **9** track down
to mind: **5** evoke **6** recall **7** suggest **9** visualize
to naught: **4** do in, raze, ruin, undo **5** annul **6** cancel, negate **7** abolish, destroy, nullify, reverse, wipe out **8** abrogate, bulldoze, demolish, sabotage **9** devastate **10** annihilate, invalidate, neutralize, obliterate
to pass: **5** cause **6** ask for **7** achieve **10** effectuate
to terms: **7** mediate **9** negotiate, reconcile
to the surface: **4** mine **5** dig up **6** dredge, exhume, uproot **7** uncover, unearth **8** excavate
to trial: **6** charge, indict **9** prosecute
up: **3** say **4** form, lift, rear, spew, spue, tell **5** breed, nurse, raise **6** broach, prompt **7** mention, nourish, nurture, refer to **8** throw out **9** introduce
upon oneself: **5** cause, incur **6** invite
up the rear: **3** lag **5** trail **6** follow
up to date: **5** refit **6** revise, update **7** remodel **9** modernize
bring ___: **3** off, out **4** down, home **5** forth, round **6** around **7** forward
bring ___ end: **4** to an
bring ___ rear: **5** up the
bring down the ___: **5** house
...bring forth ___: **4** a son
bring home the ___: **5** bacon
Bringing Down the House (2003 film)
cast: Steve Martin, Queen Latifah
Bringing Up Baby (1938 film)
cast: Cary Grant, Katharine Hepburn, May Robson, Charlie Ruggles
director: Howard Hawks
leopard: **4** Baby
studio: **3** RKO
Bringing Up Buddy aunt: **4** Iris
Bringing Up Father: **5** strip **10** comic strip
character: **4** Nora **5** Jiggs **6** Maggie
dog: **4** Fifi **7** Pretzel
bring into ___: **4** line, play
Bring Larks and Heroes
author: Thomas Keneally
___ Bring Me Down: **4** Don't
Bring On the Night (1985 film)
cast: Omar Hakim, Sting
director: Michael Apted
Bring the Boys Home (1971 song)
artist: Freda Payne
bring to ___: **4** bear, life, mind, pass, task **5** a boil, a halt, an end, light, terms
bring to a ___: **4** halt
bring to one's ___: **5** knees
bring up the ___: **4** rear
brink: **3** eve, lip, rim **4** brim, edge **5** limit, shore, skirt, verge **6** border, fringe, margin **7** extreme **8** boundary, frontier **9** extremity, precipice, threshold
be on the ~: **6** teeter
on the ~: **5** ready
Brinker, Hans: **6** skater
Brinkley: **5** David **8** Christie
Brinkley, Christie
emulate ~: **4** pose **5** model
spouse: Billy Joel
Brinkley, David: **10** newscaster
partner: Chet Huntley
Brink's Job, The (1978 film)
cast: Peter Boyle, Peter Falk, Warren Oates
director: William Friedkin
Brinks truck protection: **5** armor
briny: **3** sea **4** deep, main **5** ocean, salty **6** saline **8** brackish
drop: **4** tear
on the ~: **4** asea **5** at sea **8** cruising, off-shore
septet: **4** seas
brio: **3** vim, zip **4** dash, élan, fire, life, zest, zing **5** gusto, punch, verve, vigor **6** energy, esprit, pizazz, spirit **7** panache **8** fervency, lyricism, vivacity **9** animation, élan vital **10** liveliness
___ brio: **3** con
brioche: **4** roll **5** bread
briolette: **3** gem
briquets: **8** charcoal
use ~: **5** grill
Brisbane: **4** city, port, town
locale: **9** Australia
brisé: **4** leap
Brisebois: **8** Danielle
brisk: **4** busy, cool, fast, keen, pert, spry **5** agile, alive, crisp, fleet, fresh, hasty, nippy, peart, peppy, perky, quick, rapid, sharp, smart, stiff, swift, windy, zippy **6** active, biting, chilly, dapper, flying, lively, living, nimble, prompt, racing, snappy, speedy **7** bracing, express, hurried, instant, roaring, rocking, rousing **8** animated, bustling, vigorous **9** breakneck, efficient, energetic, sprightly, vivacious **10** double-time, fortifying, hypersonic, refreshing, supersonic
in music: **5** mosso
brisket: **4** meat, ribs **5** chest
briskly: **7** briefly, rapidly

briskness: **3** nip **4** snap **5** haste, speed, vigor **8** alacrity, celerity, rapidity **9** animation, diligence, quickness
brisling: **4** fish
bristle: **3** awn **4** boil, fume, hair, rage, seta, teem **5** thorn **6** arista, blow up, rear up, see red, seethe **7** flare up, prickle, stubble, whisker
combining form: **4** seti- **5** chaet- **6** chaeto-
ender: **4** tail
grain ~: **3** awn
bristlecone: **4** pine
bristles
having ~: **5** awned
tool with ~: **5** brush
bristling: **5** thick **7** fraught, teeming **8** swarming, thronged
bristly: **4** wiry **5** hairy, rough, setal, spiny **6** crabby, cranky, hispid, setose, spined, thorny, touchy **7** bearded, prickly, stubbly, unshorn **8** prickled **9** irascible, irritable, whiskered
Bristol: **4** city, port, town **6** Johnny **7** channel
city near ~: **4** Bath
dance: **5** Stomp
fashion: **4** neat
locale: **7** England **9** Tennessee
partner: **5** Myers
river at ~: **4** Avon
see also British
see also English
Bristol __: **5** board, Stomp **7** Channel, fashion
Bristol-__: **5** Myers
Bristol Channel
island: **5** Lundy
brit: **4** fish **5** sprat **7** herring **8** plankton
Brit: **4** Hume
Brit.
corp: **3** ltd.
legislators: **3** MPs
lexicon: **3** OED
military branch: **3** RAF
money: **3** LSD
pilots: **3** RAF
pound: **4** ster.
__ Britain: **5** Great
Brit ally: **4** Yank
__ Britannia: **4** Rule
Britannia metal: **5** alloy
component: **3** tin **6** copper **8** antimony
Britannica: **3** enc. **4** ency. **5** encyc.
__ Britannica: **3** Pax
Britannicus
author: Jean Racine
britches: **5** pants **8** trousers
Brite: **7** cleaner
competitor: **5** Lysol **6** Top Job **7** Lestoil, Mr. Clean, Pine Sol **9** Fantastik, Step Saver
__ B'rith: **4** B'nai
British
Airways former plane: **3** SST
ancient monument: **5** henge **10** Stonehenge
anthropologist: **6** Frazer, Leakey **10** Malinowski
archeologist: **7** Woolley
architect: **4** Nash, Wren
astronomer: **4** Ryle **6** Halley **7** Huggins
auto: **2** MG **3** MGB **5** Rolls, Rover **6** Austin, Jaguar **9** Land Rover **10** Rolls- Royce
ballet dancer: **5** Dolin **7** Fonteyn, Markova
beverage: **3** tea **6** hot tea
breakfast item: **6** kipper
brew: **3** ale **5** stout **6** porter
carbine: **4** sten
card game: **5** gleek **7** primero
cathedral town: **3** Ely **6** Exeter
cellist: **5** du Pré
charity: **5** Oxfam
cheese: **9** Leicester, Wiltshire
china: **5** Spode
cleric: **5** vicar
coat: **5** jemmy, tunic
composer: **4** Arne **5** Holst
conductor: **5** Boult **7** Beecham, Sargent **8** Goossens, Marriner **10** Barbirolli
conservative: **4** Tory
court of old: **4** leet
explorer: **3** Rae **5** Baker, Parry, Scott, Speke **6** Burton, Mawson **7** Markham, Stanley **8** Flinders, Franklin **9** Frobisher, Vancouver **10** Shackleton
FBI: **3** CID
figure skater: **7** Cousins
golfer: **5** Faldo
historian: **6** Gibbon
Honduras today: **6** Belize
honorary initials: **3** MBE
island: **3** Man **5** Lundy **6** Jersey
jacket: **5** jemmy, tunic **9** greatcoat
journalist: **6** Morris
legal society: **3** inn
medal: **3** DCM, DSO
medical journal: **6** Lancet
medical org.: **3** NHS
mil. branch: **3** RNR
money: **5** groat, pence, pound **6** guinea **7** coppers **8** shilling
Museum's marbles: **5** Elgin
Nobelist in Chemistry: **4** Todd **5** Aston, Kroto, Pople, Smith, Soddy, Synge **6** Barton, Harden, Martin, Porter, Ramsay, Sanger **7** Haworth, Hodgkin, Norrish **8** Mitchell, Robinson **9** Wilkinson **10** Rutherford **11** Hinshelwood
Nobelist in Economics: **5** Coase, Hicks, Lewis, Meade, Stone **8** Mirrlees
Nobelist in Literature: **5** Eliot **7** Golding, Kipling, Naipaul, Russell **9** Churchill **10** Galsworthy
Nobelist in Medicine: **4** Dale, Hill, Katz, Ross, Vane **5** Black, Chain, Jerne, Krebs, Nurse **6** Adrian, Florey, Huxley, Porter **7** Brenner, Fleming, Hodgkin, Hopkins, Medawar, Roberts, Sulston, Wilkins **8** Milstein **9** Tinbergen **10** Hounsfield **11** Sherrington
Nobelist in Peace: **3** Orr **5** Cecil **6** Angell, Cremer **9** Henderson, Noel-Baker **11** Chamberlain
Nobelist in Physics: **4** Born, Mott, Ryle **5** Bragg, Dirac, Gabor **6** Barkla, Hewish, Powell, Strutt, Wilson **7** Thomson **8** Appleton, Blackett, Chadwick **9** Cockcroft, Josephson **10** Richardson
noble: **4** dame, duke, earl, lady, lord, peer **6** knight **7** marquis
North America: **6** Canada
Order: **6** Garter
painter: **7** Hogarth **8** Reynolds **9** Constable **12** Gainsborough
Petroleum acquisition: **5** Amoco
philosopher: **6** Popper
physicist: **5** Dirac **6** Stokes
pianist: **4** Hess **8** Helfgott
playwright: **3** Fry, Gay, Kyd **4** Bolt, Gray, Shaw **5** Arden, Brome, Frayn **6** Cibber, Coward, Dekker, Dryden, Henley, Jonson **7** Barstow, Delaney, Heywood **8** Congreve, Farquhar, Fielding **9** Ayckbourn **10** Galsworthy
poet: **3** Gay, Pye **4** Gray, Gunn, Hood, Hunt, Rowe, Tate **5** Blake, Byron, Carew, Clare, Davie, Gower, Hardy, Keats **6** Arnold, Austin, Brontë, Brooke, Bryher, Cibber, Cotton, Cowley, Cowper, Crabbe, Daniel, Dryden, Empson, Eusden, Fuller, Henley, Hughes, Jonson, Motion, Warton **7** Bridges, Campion, Chaucer, Collins, Crashaw, Drayton, Herrick, Heywood, Hopkins, Housman, Johnson, Southey **8** Betjeman, Browning, Day Lewis, de la Mare, Shadwell, Tennyson **9** Cleveland, Coleridge, Masefield, Whitehead **10** Chatterton, FitzGerald, Wordsworth **12** Bulwer-Lytton
political party: **6** Labour
porcelain: **5** Spode
prep school: **4** Eton
racecourse: **5** Ascot, Epsom
record label: **3** EMI
resort: **4** Bath
rock group: **3** Who, XTC **6** Stones **7** Beatles **10** Spice Girls
royal house: **4** York **5** Tudor **6** Stuart **7** Hanover, Windsor **9** Lancaster
rule in India: **3** raj
runner: **3** Coe **5** Ovett
scientist: **4** Ryle **5** Dirac **6** Leakey, Stokes **7** Huggins, Woolley **10** Malinowski **11** Sherrington
sculptor: **5** Moore
sheep breed: **5** Devon **6** Oxford, Romney **7** Cheviot, Lincoln, Ryeland, Suffolk **8** Cotswold, Dartmoor **9** Hampshire, Leicester, Southdown, Wiltshire **10** Dorset Horn, Shropshire
soprano: **6** Garden
sport: **4** polo **5** rugby **7** cricket
tenor: **5** Pears
title: **3** sir **4** dame, lady, lord
West Point: **3** RMA
writer: **4** Amis, Cary, Dahl, Ford, Glyn, Hall **5** Arlen, Auden, Bates, Blunt, Bowen, Byatt, Defoe, Doyle, Eliot, Frayn, Green, Hardy, James, Milne, Noyes, Powys, Wells **6** Aldiss, Ambler, Austen, Barnes, Binyon, Braine, Brontë, Brophy, Bryher, Bunyan, Butler, Evelyn, Fowles, Fraser, Gibbon, Graves, Greene, Hallam, Hilton, Hudson, Huxley, Morris, Popper **7** Bennett, Bentley, Blunden, Burgess, Carroll, Chatwin, Collins, Corelli, Douglas, Drabble, Durrell, Firbank, Fleming, Forster, Francis, Gissing, Golding, Grahame, Haggard, Hartley, Hazlitt, Johnson, Kipling, Ustinov **8** Beerbohm, Brookner, Connelly, Fielding, Forester, Jhabvala **9** Blackwood, Churchill, Goldsmith, Isherwood **10** Bainbridge, Chesterton, Galsworthy
see also England, Great Britain
British __: **3** gum **4** Open, warm **5** India, Isles **6** dollar, Empire, gallon, Guiana, Legion, Malaya, Museum **7** America, English, Library
British __ Indies: **4** West
British __ unit: **7** thermal
British Columbia: **8** province
city: **5** Delta, Kaslo, Lumby, Sooke **6** Fernie, Surrey, Vernon **7** Burnaby, Kelowna, Langley, Mission, Nanaimo, Osoyoos, Saanich **8** Kamloops, Richmond, Victoria **9** Coquitlam, Penticton, Port Moody, Vancouver **10** Abbotsford, Chilliwack, Maple Ridge
Indian: **5** Haida, Kaska **6** Nootka **7** Kutenai, Tlingit **8** Kwakiutl, Squamish **9** Tsimshian **10** Bellabella, Bellacoola
locale: **6** Canada
mountain: **6** Robson
river: **5** Liard **6** Fraser
school: **3** SFU, TWU **11** Simon Fraser
tribe: **5** Haida
waterfall: **5** Della
British Commonwealth
member: **4** Fiji **5** Ghana, India, Kenya, Malta, Nauru, Samoa, Tonga **6** Belize, Brunei, Canada, Cyprus, Gambia, Guyana, Malawi, Tuvalu, Uganda, Zambia **7** Bahamas, England, Grenada, Jamaica, Lesotho, Namibia, Nigeria, St. Lucia, Vanuatu **8** Barbados, Botswana, Cameroon, Dominica, Kiribati, Malaysia, Maldives, Sri Lanka, Tanzania **9** Australia, Mauritius, Singapore, Swaziland **10** Bangladesh, Mozambique, New Zealand, Saint Lucia, Seychelles **11** Sierra Leone, South Africa
British English words
aide-de-camp: **6** batman
apartment: **4** flat
auto accessory: **4** tyre
bed: **3** kip
bigwig: **3** nob
bloke: **3** guv **4** chap
blue blood: **6** aristo
bobbin: **4** pirn
boob tube: **5** telly
bottle size: **5** litre
bouquet: **5** odour
broke: **5** skint
buddy: **4** mate **5** matey
butter substitute: **5** marge
candy: **5** lolly
car hood: **6** bonnet
car trunk: **4** boot

cat: 3 mog 5 moggy
cavalry weapon: 5 sabre
chap: 4 mate 5 bloke, matey
chunk: 5 wodge
collide with: 5 prang
counsel: 4 rede
cow: 5 stirk
crankcase: 4 sump
crowded area: 3 wen
daft: 5 potty
dairy merchant: 6 eggler
ditch: 4 sike, syke
dog it: 5 skulk
drop feathers: 5 moult
eccentric: 5 potty
elevator: 4 lift
exam: 6 A level
exasperation: 5 aggro
exclamation: 4 I say 5 blimy 6 blimey, good-oh, rather, righto, whizzo 7 cheerio
expletive: 3 gor 5 blimy 6 blimey, bloody
farewell: 4 ta ta
fashion plate: 4 toff
fertilizer: 5 nitre
filament: 5 fibre
fishing reel: 4 pirn
flashlight: 5 torch
floor covering: 4 lino
French fries: 5 chips
fungus: 5 mould
glamorous: 5 dishy
goof off: 5 skulk
greeting: 5 hullo
gully: 4 sike, syke
hooligan: 3 yob
ice-cream cone: 6 cornet
inc.: 3 ltd.
inferior wine: 5 plonk
informer: 4 nark
irritable: 5 tilty
lavatory: 3 loo
length measure: 5 metre
letter: 3 zed
lockup: 4 gaol, quod
loose: 5 lowse
lout: 3 yob
maid: 4 char
male sheep: 3 tup
meddlesome: 5 nebby
metal: 9 aluminium
mime show: 5 panto
mother: 3 mum
neat: 4 trig
nightshirt: 4 sark
oath: 3 gor
pants: 6 breeks
parent: 3 mum 5 mater, pater
petty criminal: 4 spiv
phone booth: 5 kiosk
plan: 4 rede
potato chip: 5 crisp
pound: 4 quid
prison: 4 gaol
quaint: 4 twee
quart: 5 litre
raincoat: 3 mac
recall: 5 rub up
recon: 5 recce, recco
road edge: 4 kerb
room: 6 bed-sit
rooming house: 3 kip
sausage: 6 banger
scent: 5 odour
school test: 6 A level
shed feathers: 5 moult
sift: 3 lue
spool: 4 pirn
stench: 5 odour
stew: 6 hot pot
stoolie: 4 nark
street: 4 mews
streetcar: 4 tram
stroller: 4 pram
subway: 4 tube
sulk: 4 mump
sword: 5 sabre
tale: 4 rede
term of endearment: 3 luv
thanks: 2 ta
thread: 5 fibre
tout: 4 spiv
tree trunk: 4 stam
truck: 5 lorry
undergraduate: 5 sizar, sizer
verb ender: 3 ise
weight unit: 3 tod 5 stone

British Honduras: 6 Belize
British Petroleum
buy: 5 Amoco
British Virgin Islands capital: 8 Road Town
Britney: 6 Spears
Briton: 7 Cockney, Oxonion 8 Londoner 9 mac wearer, Tony Blair 10 Englishman
ancient ~: 4 Celt, Gael, Jute, Pict 5 Angle, Iceni, Saxon
Britt: 3 May 4 Reid 6 Ekland
Brittain: 4 Vera
Brittany: 3 dog 5 canid, duchy 6 canine, Morgan, Murphy, region 8 province
city: 6 Rennes
locale: 6 France
native: 6 Breton
neighbor: 5 Anjou
Brittany ___: 7 spaniel
Britten, Benjamin: 8 composer
collaborator: 5 Auden
work: Albert Herring
Billy Budd
Paul Bunyan
Peter Grimes
Simple Symphony
Spring Symphony
War Requiem
Welcome Ode
brittle: 5 crisp, frail, stiff 6 crispy, crusty 7 crumbly, crunchy, fragile, friable 9 breakable, frangible, unpliable 10 nondurable
ender: 4 bush
peanut ~: 5 candy 10 confection
resin: 5 copal
brittleness: 9 fragility
Britton: 6 Connie, Pamela 7 Barbara
Britz: 7 Jerilyn
Brno: 4 city, town
from ~: 5 Czech
bro: 3 pal, rel., sib 4 chum, dude, mate 5 buddy, crony, kiddo 6 frater, friend 7 compeer, comrade, partner, sibling 8 intimate, relative 9 associate, colleague, good buddy
parent's ~: 3 unc, unk
unc's ~: 3 pop
broach: 3 tap 4 open, talk 5 raise 6 hint at, open up, pierce, uncork 7 bring up, mention, propose, suggest 8 puncture 9 introduce
broad: 3 big, lax 4 deep, full, vast, wide 5 ample, large, money, roomy, squat, thick 6 gaping, portly 7 copious, general, immense, liberal 8 extended, far-flung, spacious, sweeping, tolerant, unstrict 9 capacious, cavernous, expansive, extensive, inclusive, open-ended, outspread, universal, wholesale 10 indefinite, large-scale, ubiquitous, unspecific, voluminous, widespread
combining form: 4 eury-, plat- 5 platy-
ender: 3 axe 4 band, bean, cast, leaf, loom, side, tail 5 cloth, sheet, sword 6 caster 7 casting
foot: 3 EEE
in ~ daylight: 6 openly
not ~: 6 subtle
street: 3 ave. 4 blvd. 6 avenue 9 boulevard
valley: 4 dale, glen, lawn, park 5 field, green, plaza 6 common, meadow
broad ___: 4 bean, gage, jump, seal 5 arrow, gauge, glass, reach 6 jumper 7 hatchet
broad-___: 5 based, brush 6 leafed, leaved, minded
Broad: 3 Eli
Broadbent, Jim: 5 actor
film: The Avengers (1998)
Iris (2001, AA)
Moulin Rouge (2001)
Princess Caraboo (1994)
Richard III (1995)
Topsy-Turvy (2000)
broadcast: 3 air, sow 4 beam, emit, news, on TV, seed, send, sown 5 blare, carry, cover, relay, strew 6 airing, flaunt, get out, herald, report, splash, spread 7 bestrew, divulge, lay bare, network, program, radiate, scatter, spatter 8 announce, disperse, proclaim, televise, transmit 9 advertise, circulate, propagate, publicize, telephone, ventilate 10 annunciate, disclosure, distribute, make public, promulgate, radiograph
again: 5 reair
agency: 3 FCC
bands: 4 AMFM
block a ~: 3 jam
component: 5 audio, video
initials: 3 ABC, CBS, NBC, PBS
instructional ~: 3 ETV, PBS
medium: 2 CB 5 radio 10 television
need: 4 mike 10 microphone
broadcaster: 4 DJ. VJ 6 anchor, deejay, veejay 7 station 9 announcer
baseball ~: 4 Buck 5 Allen, Canel, Caray, Gowdy, Wolff 6 Barber, Hodges, Murphy, Nelson, Prince, Scully 7 Harwell 8 Bob Wolff, Hamilton, Jack Buck, McCarver, Mel Allen 9 Bob Murphy, Bob Prince, Buck Canel, Curt Gowdy, Garagiola, Vin Scully 10 Brickhouse, Harry Caray, Russ Hodges
on wheels: 4 CBer
Broadcast News (1987 film)
cast: Albert Brooks, Holly Hunter, William Hurt
director: James L. Brooks
___ Broadcast, The: 3 Big
broadcloth: 6 fabric 8 material
broaden: 3 wax 4 grow 5 add to, bloat, flare, swell, widen 6 beef up, dilate, expand, extend, fatten, open up, spread 7 augment, burgeon, develop, enlarge, inflate, stretch 8 bourgeon, escalate, heighten, increase, lengthen 9 branch out, spread out 10 liberalize, supplement
broadening: 8 cultural, increase 9 expansion, extension, uplifting
broad-jump: 5 event, sport
broadloom: 3 rug 6 carpet 9 carpeting
broad-minded: 4 open 7 liberal 8 catholic, flexible, tolerant, unbiased
broad-mindedness: 9 tolerance
broadness: 5 width 7 breadth 9 amplitude
broadside: 3 ram 4 bill 5 flyer, salvo, storm 6 attack, poster, volley 7 assault, barrage, censure, handout, placard 8 brochure, circular, fire upon, handbill, pamphlet 9 cannonade, criticism, onslaught
broad side of ___: 5 a barn
broad-topped hill: 4 loma
Broadway: 4 font 5 stage 8 typeface
angel's delight: 3 hit, SRO 4 boff 5 boffo, smash
award: 4 Tony
backer: 5 angel
brightener: 4 neon
eatery: 6 Sardi's
figure: 5 actor, angel 7 actress 8 director, producer
musical: 3 Big 4 Cats, Coco, Hair, Mame, Nine, Rent 5 Annie, Dolly!, Evita, Gypsy, Hello, Zorba 6 Barnum, Can-Can, Grease, I Do! I Do!, Kismet, Les Miz, Oliver!, Pippin, Purlie, Wiz, The 7 Allegro, Cabaret, Camelot, Chicago, Company, Follies, Pal Joey, Passion, Ragtime, Titanic, Whoopee 8 Applause, Big River, Carousel, Fiorello!, Godspell, Oklahoma!, Peter Pan, Show Boat, Two by Two 9 Brigadoon, Funny Girl, Girl Crazy, No Strings, On the Town, Pipe Dream 10 Dreamgirls, Kiss Me Kate, Lady Be Good!, Miss Saigon, My Fair Lady, Shenandoah 11 Chorus Line, A, Crazy For You, Damn Yankees, King and I, The, Leave It to Me, Lion King, The, Me and Juliet, Music Man, The, No No Nanette, Of Thee I Sing, Sweeney Todd
offering: 4 show 5 drama, revue 6 review 7 musical
opener: 6 act one
see also theater
Broadway ___: 3 Joe 4 Bill 5 Bound 6 Melody
Broadway Bound
author: Neil Simon
Broadway Danny Rose (1984 film)
cast: Woody Allen, Mia Farrow, Nick Apollo Forte
director: Woody Allen
Broadway Limited: 5 train

Broadway Melody of 1940 (1940 film)
cast: Fred Astaire, George Murphy, Eleanor Powell
composer: Cole Porter
__-Broadway show: 3 off
Broadway's in Fashion
artist: Erté
broast: 4 cook
Brobdingnagian: 3 big **4** huge **5** giant **7** immense, titanic **8** gigantic
brocade: 6 fabric **8** material
Broca's Brain
author: Carl Sagan
broccoli: 6 veggie **9** vegetable
bit: 6 floret
variety: 4 rabe
broccoli __: 3 rab **4** raab, rabe
__ broche: 3 à la
brochette: 4 spit **5** kabab, kabob, kebab, kebob
brochure: 5 flyer, tract **7** booklet, handout, leaflet **8** circular, handbill, pamphlet **9** broadside **10** literature, prospectus
Brock: 3 Lou **6** Peters
Brock, Lou: 10 outfielder
theft: 4 base
Brockovich: 4 Erin
Brockton: 4 city, town
city near ~: 6 Boston
locale: 4 Mass.
Brockville: 4 city, town
locale: 6 Canada **7** Ontario
Brodber, Erna: 6 writer **8** Jamaican
Broderick: 4 Beth **5** Helen, James **7** Matthew **8** Crawford
Broderick, Matthew: 5 actor
film: Biloxi Blues (1988)
The Cable Guy (1996)
Election (1999)
Family Business (1989)
Ferris Bueller's Day Off (1986)
The Freshman (1990)
Glory (1989)
Godzilla (1998)
Ladyhawke (1985)
The Producers (2005)
The Road to Wellville (1994)
WarGames (1983)
You Can Count on Me (2000)
spouse: Sarah Jessica Parker
Brodie: 5 Steve
Brodkey, Harold: 6 writer
Brody: 4 Jane **6** Adrien
Brody, Adrien: 5 actor
film: Bread and Roses (2001)
The Brothers Bloom (2008)
Cadillac Records (2008)
The Darjeeling Limited (2007)
King Kong (2005)
Liberty Heights (1999)
Manolete (2007)
The Pianist (2002, AA)
The Thin Red Line (1998)
brogan: 4 shoe **8** footgear, footwear
brogue: 4 shoe **6** accent, oxford **7** dialect **8** footwear
broil: 4 burn, cook, heat **5** grill, melee, roast **6** scorch, sizzle, tumult **7** quarrel, swelter **8** barbecue, brouhaha, struggle
starter: 4 char
__ broil: 6 London
__-broil: 3 pan
broiler: 4 oven **7** chicken
broiling: 3 hot **6** red-hot, sultry, toasty, torrid **7** boiling, summery **8** ovenlike, tropical **10** sweltering
Brokaw, Tom: 6 anchor **9** anchorman **10** newscaster
beat: 4 news
employer: 3 NBC
broke: 4 poor **5** kaput, needy **6** bad off, busted, hard up, ill off, in need, in want, ruined **7** cracked, pinched **8** badly off, bankrupt, beggarly, deprived, indigent, strapped **9** destitute, insolvent, moneyless, penniless, penurious, tapped out **10** cleaned out, down and out, pauperized, straitened
go ~: 4 bust, fail, fold, sink
go for ~: 4 dare, risk **6** gamble, hazard, strain, strive **9** persevere
in Britain: 5 skint
starter: 5 house
__-broke: 5 stone
Brokeback Mountain (2005 film)
cast: Jake Gyllenhaal, Anne Hathaway, Heath Ledger
director: Ang Lee
broken: 4 dead, tame, torn **5** cleft, kaput, rough, split, tamed **6** beaten, busted, docile, faulty, flawed, jagged, marred, pliant, ragged, undone, uneven **7** cracked, crushed, damaged, haywire, injured, smashed, subdued, trained, unsound **8** crumbled, fallible, impaired, in pieces, lamblike, obedient, sporadic, sundered **9** collapsed, compliant, defective, destroyed, fractured, imperfect, in the shop, irregular, shattered, tractable **10** disjointed, fragmented, incomplete, inoperable, manageable, on the blink, on the fritz, out of order, out of whack, spiritless, sporadical, submissive, vanquished
combining form: 6 fracto-
easily ~: 6 flimsy **7** rickety
ender: 7 hearted
glass: 6 cullet
isn't ~: 4 runs **5** works
it may be ~ at parties: 3 ice
not ~: 5 whole **6** entire, intact
starter: 5 heart, house
up: 3 sad **5** apart **7** in tears
broken __: 3 lot **5** chord, heart
broken-__: 4 down
Broken __: 5 Arrow, Lance, Wings **7** Lullaby, Rainbow
broken-arm holder: 5 sling
Broken Arrow: 4 city, town
locale: 8 Oklahoma
tribe: 6 Apache
Broken Arrow (1996 film)
cast: Delroy Lindo, Samantha Mathis, Christian Slater, John Travolta
director: John Woo
Broken Arrow (ABC western)
cast: Michael Ansara (Cochise) John Lupton (Tom Jeffords)
broken-down: 5 tired **6** shoddy, sleazy **7** rickety, squalid **8** decrepit, timeworn **10** ramshackle
horse: 3 nag **4** jade
brokenhearted: 5 upset **7** crushed *see also* gloomy
Brokenhearted (1995 song)
artist: Brandy
Broken Hearted Me (1979 song)
artist: Anne Murray
Broken-Hearted Melody (1959 song)
artist: Sarah Vaughan
Broken Wings (1985 song)
artist: Mr. Mister
broker: 5 agent, fixer **6** dealer, jobber **7** Realtor **8** mediator, merchant **9** financier, go-between, middleman, negotiant **10** negotiator
concern: 3 Dow, mkt. **4** bond, DJIA **5** stock **6** assets, market, return **7** economy **8** dividend **9** portfolio
money ~: 4 bank **5** S and L **6** banker, lender, usurer
second mortgage, to a ~: 4 refi
starter: 4 pawn **5** power, stock
stat: 5 quote
suggestion: 3 buy **4** fund, muni, sell **6** invest
work with a ~: 4 hock, pawn, sell
__ broker: 4 bill, note **5** floor, power, stock **7** customs
brokerage: 7 percent **10** commission
Internet ~: 6 E-Trade
starter: 5 stock
term: 3 buy, put **4** bear, bull, call, muni, sell **5** share **6** invest, return **8** dividend **9** portfolio
brolga: 4 bird
Brolin: 4 Josh **5** James
Brolin, James: 5 actor
film: Capricorn One (1978)
Westworld (1973)
spouse: Barbra Streisand
TV: Hotel, Marcus Welby M.D.
brolly: 4 gamp **8** umbrella
Bromfield, Louis: 6 writer
bromide: 3 saw **5** adage **6** cliché, saying **9** platitude
bromidic: 4 dull **5** corny, hokey, passé, stale, trite, vapid **6** common, jejune, old hat **7** clichéd, fatuous, humdrum, prosaic **8** outdated, outmoded **9** hackneyed, prosaical **10** uninspired, unoriginal
bromine: 7 element, halogen
combining form: 4 brom- **5** bromo-
compound: 6 halide
Bromo Seltzer: 7 antacid
competitor: *see* antacid
Bron: 7 Eleanor
bronc: 4 pony **5** horse, mount, steed **6** animal, equine
see also bronco
bronchial __: 4 tube
bronchiole
locale: 4 lung
bronco: 4 pony **5** horse, mount, steed **6** animal, equine
break a ~: 4 ride, tame
buster: 5 tamer **6** cowboy
catcher: 5 lasso, noose
emulate a ~: 4 buck, rear **5** throw
Bronco: 3 car, SUV **4** auto, Ford **5** oater **10** footballer
Bronco Billy (1980 film)
cast: Clint Eastwood, Geoffrey Lewis, Sondra Locke
director: Clint Eastwood
broncobuster: 6 cowboy
meet: 5 rodeo
Broncos: 6 eleven **10** Boise State
home: 6 Denver **8** Colorado
org.: 3 AFC
rival: *see* NFL team
Bronfman: 5 Edgar **7** Charles
Bronko: 8 Nagurski
Bronowski: 5 Jacob
Bronson: 6 Alcott **7** Charles, Pinchot
__ Bronson Alcott: 4 Amos
Bronson, Charles: 5 actor
film: Breakheart Pass (1976)
Breakout (1975)
Death Wish (1974)
The Dirty Dozen (1967)
The Great Escape (1963)
Hard Times (1975)
The Magnificent Seven (1960)
Master of the World (1961)
The Sandpiper (1965)
Telefon (1977)
spouse: Jill Ireland
Bronstein: 3 Ena
Brontë: 4 Anne **5** Emily **8** Branwell **9** Charlotte
Brontë, Anne: 4 poet **7** British
pseudonym: Acton Bell
work: Agnes Grey
The Tenant of Wildfell Hall
Brontë, Charlotte: 6 writer **7** British
pseudonym: Currer Bell
work: Jane Eyre
The Professor
Shirley
Villette
Brontë, Emily: 6 writer **7** British
hero: 10 Heathcliff
pseudonym: Ellis Bell
work: Wuthering Heights
Bronx: 5 drink **7** borough **8** cocktail
athletes: 4 Rams
attraction: 3 zoo
Bomber: 4 Yank **6** Yankee
cheer: 4 jeer, razz **8** derision **9** raspberry
give a ~ cheer: 4 jeer, mock **5** taunt
ingredient: 3 gin **8** vermouth
locale: 3 NYC **7** New York
school: 7 Fordham
Bronx __: 5 cheer
Bronx __..., The: 4 is up
Bronx? No, thonx!, The
author: Ogden Nash
Bronx Tale, A (1993 film)
cast: Robert De Niro, Chazz Palminteri
director: Robert De Niro
Bronx Zoo, The
author: Sparky Lyle
Bronx Zoo, The (NBC drama)
cast: Ed Asner
bronze: 3 tan **5** alloy, brown, color, medal, metal **6** statue, suntan **8** brownish, preserve
coating: 6 patina
coin: 4 cent
color kin: *see* brown color
combining form: 5 chalc-, chalk- **6** chalco-, chalko-
component: 3 tin **6** copper
disk: 4 gong
medal: 3 DSC **5** third
Roman ~ coin: 3 aes **5** uncia
Bronze __: 3 Age **4** Star **5** Medal
bronzed: 3 tan **9** suntanned
Bronze Horseman, The
author: Aleksandr Pushkin

Bronze Star: **5** medal
reason: **5** valor **7** bravery
brooch: **3** pin **5** cameo, clasp **7** jewelry
remove a ~: **5** unpin
brood: **3** sit **4** fret, mope, pine, pout, stew, sulk **5** covey, flock, hatch, spawn, think, worry, young **6** chicks, clutch, family, grieve, lament, litter, ponder **7** agonize **8** children, incubate, languish, look back, ruminate **9** nestlings, offspring, posterity **10** hatchlings, introspect, take it hard
over: **4** mull, muse, stew **5** study, worry **6** ponder **8** remember
brooder: **3** hen **9** introvert
brooding: **4** blue, down, glum **5** moody **6** morbid, solemn, sullen **8** downcast, lowering, taciturn **10** unsociable
broodmare: **3** dam **5** horse
broody: **4** mopy **5** mopey **6** abject **7** sagging, subdued **8** drooping, shot down **9** in the pits, prostrate **10** meditative
see also gloomy
brook: **2** go **3** let **4** bear, lump, race, rill, take **5** abide, allow, bourn, creek, rille, stand **6** accept, endure, permit, runlet, stream **7** rivulet, stomach, sustain **8** accede to, assent to, live with, sanction, stand for, tolerate **9** approve of, authorize, put up with, streamlet, withstand
sound: **4** purl **6** babble, burble, gurgle, murmur
brook ___: **5** trout
Brook: **5** Clive, Peter **6** Benton
Brooke: **5** Adams, Astor, Smith **6** Rupert **7** Hillary, Shields
groom: **5** André
Brooke, Rupert: **4** poet **7** British
Brookhaven Laboratory site: **5** Upton
Brookline: **4** city, town
locale: **4** Mass.
Brooklyn: **7** borough
athletes: **10** Blackbirds
breakfast: **5** bagel
ender: **3** ese, ite
locale: **3** NYC **7** New York
pronoun: **5** youse
school: **3** LIU
what grows in ~: **5** a tree
Brooklyn Bridge
artist: John Marin
Brooklyn Center: **4** city, town
locale: **9** Minnesota
Brooklyn Park: **4** city, town
locale: **9** Minnesota
Brookner, Anita: **6** writer **7** British
Brook Park: **4** city, town
locale: **4** Ohio
Brooks: **3** Kix, Mel **5** Avery, Garth, range **6** Albert, Donnie, Foster, Louise **7** Cleanth, Richard, Van Wyck **8** Atkinson, Robinson **9** Geraldine, Gwendolyn
peak: **4** Isto **6** Mt. Isto
range locale: **5** Yukon **6** Alaska, Canada **7** Rockies
Brooks, Albert: **5** actor
film: Broadcast News (1987)
Defending Your Life (1991)
Lost in America (1985)
The Muse (1999)
My First Mister (2001)
Brooks, Avery: **5** actor
TV: Spenser: For Hire, Star Trek: Deep Space Nine
Brooks Brothers buy: **3** tie **4** suit **5** shirt
Brooks, Cleanth: **6** writer
Brooks, Garth: **6** singer
birthplace: **5** Tulsa
song: Lost in You (1999)
Brooks, Gwendolyn: **4** poet
work: Aloneness
Annie Allen
The Bean Eaters
In the Mecca
Maud Martha
Brooks, Mel: **5** actor **8** comedian, director
film: Blazing Saddles (1974)
High Anxiety (1977)
The Producers (1968)
Robin Hood: Men in Tights (1993)
Silent Movie (1976)
Spaceballs (1987)
The Twelve Chairs (1970)
Young Frankenstein (1974)
spouse: Anne Bancroft
Brooks, Van Wyck: **6** writer
Brookville campus: **6** C.W. Post
Brookwood: **3** car **4** auto **5** Chevy **9** Chevrolet **10** automobile
broom: **5** besom, plant, sweep, whisk **6** flower **7** sweeper
ender: **4** ball, corn **5** stick
material: **5** straw
partner: **3** mop **7** dustpan
rider: **5** witch
starter: **5** whisk
use a ~: **5** sweep
___ broom: **4** bush, corn, push **5** brush, dyer's, whisk **6** Scotch **7** Spanish
Broom-Hilda: **5** comic, witch **10** comic strip
creator: Russell Myers
Brophy, Brigid: **6** writer **7** British
Brosnan, Pierce: **5** actor
film: Die Another Day (2002)
GoldenEye (1995)
The Lawnmower Man (1992)
Mars Attacks! (1996)
Mrs. Doubtfire (1993)
The Tailor of Panama (2001)
The Thomas Crown Affair (1999)
Tomorrow Never Dies (1997)
The World Is Not Enough (1999)
role: **4** Bond **6** Steele **9** James Bond
TV: Remington Steele
broth: **4** soup **5** stock **6** liquid, liquor **8** bouillon, consommé, julienne
clarify ~: **5** defat
brother: **3** boy, guy, kin, pal, sib **4** male, monk, twin **5** friar, padre, prior **6** feller **7** kinsman **8** relative
address: **3** fra
combining form: **7** adelpho-
starter: **4** step
___ brother: **3** big, lay **4** half, soul **5** blood, whole **6** foster
Brother ___: **3** Rat **4** John **5** Louis **6** Orchid
___ Brother: **3** Big
Brother, Can You Spare ___?: **5** a Dime
Brother From Another Planet, The (1984 film)
director: John Sayles
brotherhood: **4** gild **5** guild, order, union, unity **6** league **7** coterie, society **8** alliance
brotherly: **4** kind **9** comradely, forgiving, fraternal **10** altruistic, benevolent, charitable, solicitous
___ Brothers: **3** Ice **4** Ames, Marx, Ritz **5** Isley, Joyce, Lever, Mills **6** Doobie, Everly **7** Statler
___ Brothers Band: **6** Allman
Brothers Karamazov, The: **5** novel
author: Fyodor Dostoyevsky
character: **4** Ivan **5** Mitya **6** Dmitri
___ Brothers, The: **5** Blues
brouhaha: **3** ado, din, row **4** flap, fray, spat, stir, to-do **5** brawl, broil, furor, melee, scene, set-to, stink **6** clamor, flurry, fracas, hoopla, hubbub, pother, ruckus, rumpus, uproar **7** dispute, ferment, scuffle, wrangle **9** commotion, imbroglio **10** free-for-all, hullabaloo, hurly-burly
Broun: **7** Heywood
Brouthers: **3** Dan
brow: **3** rim **4** edge, peak **8** forehead
ender: **4** beat **6** beaten
starter: **3** eye, low **4** high
browbeat: **3** cow, nag **4** carp **5** bully **6** badger, bother, coerce, harass, hector, lean on, menace **7** bluster, oppress **8** bludgeon, bulldoze, domineer, keep down, threaten **9** castigate, terrorize, trample on, tyrannize **10** intimidate
browbeaten: **5** timid **7** fearful
browbeater: **3** nag **5** bully **6** tyrant
browbeating: **6** duress **8** coercion
___-browed: **6** beetle
brown: **3** bay, fry, tan **4** cook, ecru, puce, rust, sear **5** amber, beige, brick, cocoa, hazel, khaki, mocha, ocher, ochre, sauté, sepia, tawny, toast, umber **6** auburn, braise, bronze, coffee, copper, ginger, russet, sorrel, tanned **8** chestnut, cinnamon, mahogany **9** chocolate, earth tone
be in a ~ study: **4** mull, muse **6** ponder **7** reflect
color: **3** bay, dun, tan **4** bole, ecru, fawn, foxy, nude, seal **5** amber, beige, camel, cocoa, hazel, khaki, mocha, sepia, tawny, umber **6** auburn, bister, bistre, bronze, coffee, copper, ginger, russet, sienna, sorrel, suntan, walnut **7** biscuit, caramel, dogwood **8** chestnut, cinnamon, mahogany **9** butternut, chocolate
do up ~: **3** ace
ender: **3** out **5** shirt, stone
flower: **7** bulrush, cattail **8** reed mace **10** aspidistra
get ~: **3** tan **6** bronze **8** sunbathe
light ~: **3** tan **4** ecru **5** beige **6** suntan
name meaning ~: **5** Bruno
pigment: **5** umber **6** bister, bistre
purplish ~: **4** puce
reddish ~: **3** bay **4** bole, foxy, rust **5** cocoa, henna, rusty, umber **6** auburn, copper, ginger, russet, sorrel, titian, walnut **8** chestnut, cinnamon, mahogany
study: **6** revery, trance **7** reverie
brown ___: **3** bag, bat, off, rat, rot **4** alga, bear, belt, bent, coat, rice, spot **5** bag it, betty, bread, dwarf, goods, heart, hyena, sauce, soils, study, sugar, trout **6** butter, hackle, thrush **7** creeper, mustard
brown-___: **3** bag **6** bagger
___ brown: **4** Mars, seal **6** Cassel **7** Cologne, Vandyke
Brown: **3** Dee, Jim, Les, Ron, Tom **4** Foxy, H. Rap, John, Paul, Tina **5** Blair, Bobby, Bruce, Bryan, James, Jerry, Kevin, Kwame, Larry, Peter **6** Arthur, Claude, Louise, Murphy **7** Charlie, Herbert, Michael, Rita Mae **8** Clarence, Sterling **10** footballer, university
athletes: **5** Bears
league: **3** Ivy
locale: **10** Providence
___ Brown: **5** Cluny **6** Father, Jackie, Murphy **7** Charlie
Brown Adam: **5** horse
brown-and-___: **5** serve
brown-bag contents: **4** meal **5** apple, candy, fruit, lunch **6** banana, cookie **8** sandwich
brown betty: **7** dessert
ingredient: **5** apple
Brown, Bobby
song: Don't Be Cruel (1988)
Every Little Step (1989)
Good Enough (1992)
My Prerogative (1988)
On Our Own (1989)
Rock Wit'cha (1989)
Roni (1988)
She Ain't Worth It (1990)
spouse: Whitney Houston
___ brown bread: **6** Boston
Brown, Charlie
exclamation: **4** rats
friend: **4** Lucy **5** Linus
strip: **7** Peanuts
toy: **4** kite
___ Brown collar: **6** Buster
Browne: **3** Dik **6** Thomas **7** Jackson
___ Browne belt: **3** Sam
Browne, Jackson
song: Doctor My Eyes (1972)
Somebody's Baby (1982)
Browne, Thomas: **6** writer **7** English
Brown Eyed Girl (1967 song)
artist: Van Morrison
brown-eyed Susan: **5** plant **6** flower
Brown, Father house: **5** manse
Brown, Foxy
song: I'll Be (1997)
Brown, Georg Stanford
spouse: Tyne Daly
brown-haired: **6** brunet **8** brunette
Brown, Herbert: **7** chemist **8** Nobelist
Brownian ___: **6** motion
brownie: **3** elf **4** cake **5** dwarf, fairy, nisse **6** cookie, sprite **7** dessert **10** confection, leprechaun
like a fresh ~: **5** moist
Brownie: **5** scout **6** camera **9** Girl Scout
cap: **6** beanie
creator: **5** Kodak
points: **6** credit
Browning: **3** Tod **6** Robert

Browning, Elizabeth Barrett: **4** poet **7** British
husband: Robert
work: Aurora Leigh
Grief
The Lady's Yes
My Heart and I
Only a Curl
Sonnets From the Portuguese
Browning, Robert: **4** poet **7** British
work: Abt Vogler
Andrea del Sarto
Cleon
Fra Lippo Lippi
Give a Rouse
In a Gondola
The Inn Album
Love in a Life
My Last Duchess
Paracelsus
Pauline
The Pied Piper of Hamelin
Pippa Passes
Rabbi Ben Ezra
The Ring and the Book
Saul
Sordello
brownish
color: **3** tan **4** buff, drab, nude, puce, sand **5** beige, olive, putty, taupe **6** bronze **7** nankeen **10** terra cotta
Brown, James
nickname: Godfather of Soul
song: Cold Sweat (1967)
I Got the Feelin' (1968)
I Got You (1965)
It's a Man's Man's Man's World (1966)
Living in America (1986)
Papa's Got a Brand New Bag (1965)
Say It Loud - I'm Black and I'm Proud (1968)
Brown, Jim
sport: **8** football
__ Brown Jug: **6** Little
Brown, Kevin
sport: **8** baseball
Brown, Larry: **5** coach
milieu: **5** court
org.: **3** NBA
sport: **10** basketball
Brown, Murphy
portrayer: Candice Bergen
show: **3** FYI
Brown, Paul: **5** coach
sport: **8** football
Brown, Rita Mae: **6** writer
__ browns: **4** hash
Browns: **6** eleven
home: **4** Ohio **9** Cleveland
org.: **3** AFC
rival: *see* NFL team
Brownstone Eclogues
author: Conrad Aiken
brownstone feature: **5** stoop
Brownsville: **4** city, port, town
locale: **5** Texas
Brown, Tina: **6** editor
brown-winged butterfly: **5** satyr
browse: **4** leaf, look, read, scan, skim **5** graze **6** forage, peruse **7** examine, meander **8** glance at **9** check over **10** look around, window-shop
online without posting: **4** lurk
the Internet: **4** surf
through: **4** leaf, page, scan **5** thumb
browser: **6** reader **8** Explorer, Netscape
address for a: **3** URL
button: **4** home **7** refresh
spot: **3** Web **6** stacks **7** library **8** Internet
Broz, Josip: **4** Slav, Tito
Brubaker (1980 film)
cast: Jane Alexander, Yaphet Kotto, Robert Redford
Brubeck, Dave: **7** pianist
genre: **4** jazz
song: Take Five (1961)
Bruce: **3** Lee **4** Dern **5** Brown, Cabot, Lenny, Nigel, Wayne **6** Catton, Geller, Jenner, Morton, Willis **7** Babbitt, Bennett, Channel, Chatwin, Davison, Hornsby **8** Virginia **9** Beresford **10** Boxleitner
Robert the ~: **4** Scot
Bruce __ Friedman: **3** Jay
Bruce Almighty (2003 film)
cast: Jennifer Aniston, Jim Carrey, Morgan Freeman
Bruch: **3** Max
Bruckheimer: **5** Jerry
Bruckner, Anton: **8** Austrian, composer
Bruegel, Pieter: **6** artist **7** Flemish, painter
Bruhn, Erik: **6** dancer **7** danseur
specialty: **6** ballet
Bruin: **5** UCLAn **6** iceman
Bruins: **3** six **4** team, UCLA
hockey great: **3** Orr
home: **6** Boston
milieu: **3** ice **4** rink
org.: **3** NHL
rival: *see* hockey team
bruise: **3** mar **4** beat, harm, hurt, mall, mark, mash, maul, welt **5** knock, wound **6** bang up, batter, boo-boo, damage, injure, injury, lesion, scrape, shiner, squash **7** contuse **8** aggrieve, black eye, discolor, swelling **9** contusion **10** knock about
one's shins: **4** bark
treatment: **3** ice **6** arnica
bruised: **3** raw **4** achy, hurt, lame, sore **5** livid **6** rotten, tender **8** reddened
easily ~ item: **3** ego
bruiser: **3** ape **4** goon **5** boxer, he-man **6** lummox **7** fighter **8** tough guy
bruit: **5** rumor
__ brûlé: **4** bois
Brulé: **6** Indian **7** Amerind
__ brulée: **5** creme
__ brûlée: **5** crème
__ brûlot: **4** café
brumal: **4** cold **6** wintry **7** ice-cold, wintery **8** freezing
brume: **3** fog **4** haze, mist
Brumel, Valery: **10** high jumper
brummagem: **6** geegaw, gewgaw **9** bagatelle
Brummell, Beau: **4** dude **5** dandy
brumous: **5** foggy
brunch: **3** eat **4** meal
choice: **3** lox **4** eggs **5** bagel, crape, crêpe **6** Danish, omelet, pastry, quiche, waffle **8** hot-cakes, omelette, pancakes **9** sweet roll
Brundage: **5** Avery
Brunei: **3** bay **6** nation **7** country
locale: **4** Asia **6** Borneo
money: **3** sen **4** cent **6** dollar
neighbor: **8** Malaysia
brunette: **4** dark **5** brown
Bruni: **5** Carla
Brunner: **4** Emil, John
Brünnhilde
husband: **7** Gunther
mother: **4** Erda
Bruno: **5** Kirby, saint **6** Walter **8** Giordano **10** Bettelheim
__ Bruno: **3** San
Bruno, Giordano: **7** Italian **11** philosopher
Brunswick: **4** city, stew, town
competitor: **3** AMF **4** Voit **6** Wilson **8** Rawlings, Spalding
locale: **4** Ohio **5** Maine
brunt: **5** force **6** impact, strain
brush: **3** rub **4** lick, wipe **5** clash, clean, copse, fight, gorse, graze, groom, melee, nudge, run-in, scour, scrap, scrub, sedge, set-to, shave, shine, sweep, touch, whisk **6** bushes, fracas, stroke, tickle, tussle **7** coppice, fox tail, thicket **8** conflict, kindling, skirmish, spruce up, struggle **9** chaparral, close call, encounter, shrubbery **10** engagement
aside: **6** ignore **7** neglect **8** overlook **9** disregard
broom: **5** besom
carelessly: **4** daub **5** smear
combining form: **5** scopi-
cut: **9** hairstyle
ender: **3** off **4** fire, wood, work
off: **4** snub **5** spurn, whisk **6** ignore, pass up, rebuff, refuse, reject, slight **7** dismiss, neglect **8** discount, sneeze at **9** disregard
past: **4** skim **5** graze
starter: **3** air **4** hair, nail, sage, snow **5** paint, tooth, under **6** bottle
up: **7** retouch
up on: **5** learn **6** polish, review **7** refresh, relearn
wield a ~: **5** paint
with liquid: **5** baste **7** moisten
with the law: **4** bust **5** pinch **6** arrest, collar
brush __: **3** cut, off **4** fire, up on **5** broom
__ brush: **3** end, fox **4** wire **5** dandy, scrub **6** pastry, pollen **7** shaving
__ Brush: **6** Fuller
brushed hide: **5** suede
brushing sound: **5** swish
brush-off: **4** snub **6** rebuff, slight **9** dismissal, rejection
Brush Up Your Shakespeare
composer: Cole Porter
brusque: **4** curt, rude **5** blunt, brief, frank, gruff, rough, short, surly, terse **6** abrupt, candid, crusty, ireful, morose, snippy **7** laconic, offhand, raucous **8** impolite, snippety, succinct, tactless **9** impatient, outspoken **10** indelicate, ungracious, unmannerly
Brussels: **4** city, town **7** capital
city near ~: **5** Ghent
locale: **7** Belgium
org.: **3** EEC **4** NATO
river: **5** Senne
Brussels __: **4** lace **6** carpet **7** griffon, sprouts
Brussels Griffon: **3** dog **5** canid **6** canine
brussels sprouts: **6** veggie **9** vegetable
brut: **3** dry
relative: **3** sec
brutal: **4** hard, mean, ugly **5** cruel, feral, harsh, nasty, rough **6** animal, fierce, savage, severe, unkind, wanton **7** beastly, bestial, callous, hurtful, inhuman, vicious, violent **8** barbaric, fiendish, grueling, inhumane, pitiless, ruthless, sadistic, vengeful **9** barbarian, barbarous, cutthroat, draconian, ferocious, heartless, merciless, monstrous, murderous, truculent, unfeeling, unpitying **10** oppressive, unmerciful, vindictive
brutality: **7** cruelty **8** ferocity, iron hand, violence **9** barbarism, barbarity, grossness **10** fierceness, inhumanity, oppression, savageness
brutalize: **4** warp **6** ill-use, misuse **8** mistreat **10** demoralize
brute: **3** ape, lug **4** boor, jerk, lout, ogre **5** beast, bully, demon, devil, fiend, knave, rowdy, swine, yahoo **6** animal, bad guy, daemon, daimon, lummox, savage, strong **7** beastly, monster, ruffian, villain **8** lifeless **9** archfiend, barbarian, hellhound, vulgarian
force: **3** vim **4** dint, thew **5** brawn, might, power, thews, vigor **6** energy, muscle **7** fitness, muscles, potence, potency, stamina **8** strength, violence, vitality **9** beefiness, endurance, fortitude, hardiness, huskiness, puissance, stoutness, toughness **10** browniness, mightiness, robustness, sturdiness
__, Brute: **4** et tu
brutish: **3** bad **4** wild **5** cruel, nasty, rough, rowdy **6** animal, fierce **7** beastly, bestial **8** devilish, fiendish **9** ferocious
one: **4** ogre **5** bully, fiend, yahoo **6** tyrant
Brutus: **5** Roman
foe: **6** Antony
like ~: **5** noble
question to ~: **4** et tu
see also Latin
Bryan: **5** Adams, Brown **6** Forbes, Singer **8** Trottier **9** Greenberg
Bryant: **4** Bear, Kobe **5** Anita **6** Gumbel
__ Bryant Ford: **5** Edsel
Bryant, Kobe: **5** cager
milieu: **5** court
org.: **3** NBA
sport: **10** basketball
Bryant, Paul nickname: **4** Bear
Bryant, William Cullen: **4** poet
newspaper: Post
work: The Embargo
Thanatopsis
To a Waterfowl
Bryan, William Jennings: **6** orator

Bryce Canyon: 4 park
locale: 4 Utah
Brynhild
brother: 4 Atli
husband: 6 Gunnar
Bryn Mawr: 4 coll. 7 college
grad: 5 woman 6 alumna
locale: 4 Penn.
Brynner, Yul: 5 actor
film: Anastasia (1956)
The Brothers Karamazov (1958)
The Buccaneer (1958)
Futureworld (1976)
The Journey (1959)
The King and I (1956, AA)
The Magnificent Seven (1960)
Solomon and Sheba (1959)
The Ten Commandments (1956)
Westworld (1973)
kingdom: 4 Siam
bryology: 7 science
study: 4 moss
bryophyte: 4 moss
Bryson, Peabo
song: Beauty and the Beast (1992)
If Ever You're in My Arms Again (1984)
Tonight, I Celebrate My Love (1983)
A Whole New World (1993)
Bryusov, Valery: 6 writer 7 Russian
Brzezinski: 8 Zbigniew
B.S.: 3 deg
BSA: 3 org.
part: 3 Boy 5 Scout 7 America
unit: 3 den 5 troop
B-sharp
equivalent: 5 C-flat
BSN holder: 5 nurse
B's, one of the musical: 4 Bach 6 Brahms 9 Beethoven
BSU
see Ball State, Boise State
__ B. Taney: 5 Roger
BTU
100,000 ~s: 5 therm 6 therme
part: 4 unit 7 British, thermal
relative: 3 cal., erg 7 calorie
user: 2 AC
bub: 3 bud, mac 6 buster
Bubba: 5 Smith
__ Bubba: 5 Hubba
bubble: 4 bead, bleb, blob, boil, drop, fizz, foam, rave 5 froth 6 aerate, gurgle, seethe, simmer 7 blister, droplet, froth up, smolder, sparkle 8 smoulder 9 percolate 10 effervesce
air ~: 4 bleb
ender: 3 gum, top 4 head
enjoy ~ gum: 4 blow, chew
maker: 3 gum 4 pipe, soap 7 aerator 8 fountain 9 detergent
over: 4 boil, gush 7 enthuse 8 overflow
tool with a ~: 5 level
wrap: 7 padding
bubble __: 3 gum, top 4 bath, pack, wrap 6 memory 7 chamber
__ bubble: 4 soap
__-bubble: 6 hubble
Bubble __: 3 Yum
bubble and __: 6 squeak
bubble-bath feature: 4 foam, suds 5 froth
bubblegum: 8 ice cream
alternative: ***see*** ice cream flavor
bubblehead
see ninny
bubble-headed: 5 ditsy, ditzy, giddy 9 mercurial
bubbles: 4 fizz, foam, soap, suds 5 froth 6 lather
fill with ~: 6 aerate
make ~: 4 blow
minus ~: 4 flat
Bubbles
author: Beverly Sills
__ Bubbles: 4 Tiny
Bubbles in the Wine bandleader: 4 Welk
Bubbles, John: 6 dancer
bubble wrap, play with: 3 pop
bubbling: 5 fizzy
over: 4 avid, keen 5 aboil, eager, perky 6 elated 8 enthused 9 vivacious
quality: 3 zip 4 zest 5 oomph 9 happiness
bubbly: 4 fizz, soda 5 fizzy, jolly, peppy, perky 6 feisty, frothy 7 foaming, lathery 9 champagne
name: 4 Moet
Buber, Martin: 8 Austrian 11 philosopher
Bubka, Sergey: 11 pole vaulter
bubkes: 3 nil 4 nada 6 naught, nought 7 nothing
Buc
see Buccaneer, Pirate
bucatini: 5 pasta
alternative: ***see*** pasta
buccal: 4 oral
buccaneer: 6 bandit, outlaw, pirate, robber, sea dog, viking 7 brigand, corsair, sea wolf 8 marauder, picaroon, rapparee, sea rover 9 privateer 10 freebooter
Buccaneers: 6 eleven
home: 5 Tampa 7 Florida 8 Tampa Bay
org.: 3 NFC
rival: ***see*** NFL team
Buccaneer, The
author: Maxwell Anderson
Bucephalus: 5 horse, steed 6 equine
Buchanan: 3 Pat 4 Bill, Edna, Jack 5 Edgar, James
Buchanan, James: 8 Nobelist 9 economist, president
alma mater: 9 Dickinson
former occupation: 6 lawyer
home: 9 Lancaster, Wheatland
opponent: 7 Frémont 8 Fillmore
veep: 12 Breckinridge
Buchan, John: 6 writer 8 Scottish
Bucharest: 4 city, town 7 capital
locale: 7 Romania, Rumania 8 Roumania
river: 9 Dambovita, Dimbovita
Buch der Lieder
poet: Heinrich Heine
Buchholz, Horst: 5 actor
Buchwald, Art: 3 wit 6 writer 8 humorist
buck: 3 dol., one, roe 4 bill, deer, defy, jerk, jump, kick, male, stag 5 fight, money, pitch, reach, repel, start, throw 6 animal, dollar, oppose, resist, spring, unseat 7 contest, coxcomb, dispute, protest, smacker 8 banknote, dislodge, frogskin, simoleon, struggle 9 greenback, withstand 10 jack-a-dandy
baby ~: 4 fawn
cry: 5 troat
ender: 3 eye, saw 4 aroo, bean, eroo, horn, jump, shot, skin 5 board, hound, teeth, thorn, tooth, wheat
feature: 6 antler
fraction: 2 ct. 4 cent, dime 6 nickel 7 quarter
make a ~: 4 earn, work
mate: 3 doe 4 hind
pass the ~: 5 blame, refer
starter: 3 roe, saw 4 bush, reed 5 black, water 6 spring
the system: 4 defy 5 rebel 6 oppose, resist 7 protest
up: 3 aid 4 help, stir 5 cheer, liven, rouse, steel 6 arouse 7 bolster, console, enliven, hearten, inspire 8 embolden, enspirit, imbolden, inspirit, motivate 9 encourage, enhearten 10 invigorate
buck __: 4 bean, moth, slip 5 fever, sheet 6 passer
buck __ here, the: 5 stops
buck-__: 5 naked
__ buck: 4 door, fast, half 5 black, cross 6 golden
Buck: 5 cager, Henry, NBAer, Owens, Pearl 6 Rogers 7 Leonard 8 hoopster
partner: 3 Roy
buck and __: 4 wing
buckaroo: 6 cowboy 7 cowpoke 8 horseman, wrangler
buckboard: 3 rig
bucket: 4 pail 5 scoop 6 vessel 9 container
brigade member: 7 fireman
champagne ~: 4 icer 6 cooler
defect: 4 hole
drop in the ~: 8 pittance
easy ~: 4 dunk
handle: 4 bail
like a certain ~: 5 oaken
locale: 4 barn, well
of bolts: 3 car 4 auto, heap 5 crate, lemon 6 jalopy 7 flivver
Sandburg's ~ of ashes: 4 past
starter: 3 gut
use a ~: 4 bail, fill 6 convey
wood: 3 oak
bucket __: 4 seat 5 bench 7 brigade
__ bucket: 3 ice 4 slop
Bucket List, The (2007 film)
cast: Morgan Freeman, Jack Nicholson
director: Rob Reiner
bucket of ashes, a: 4 past
Bucket of Blood, A (1959 film)
director: Roger Corman
buckets: 4 a lot, much
come down in ~: 4 pour, rain 6 deluge
buckeye: 3 nut 4 tree 5 shrub
Buckeyes: 3 OSU 9 Ohio State
Buckeye State: 4 Ohio
Buckingham: 7 Lindsey
Buckingham Palace
dweller: 4 king 5 queen, royal 6 prince 8 princess
inits.: 3 HRH
locale: 6 London 7 England
bucking the tiger: 4 faro
Buck in the Snow, The
author: Edna St. Vincent Millay
buckle: 4 bend, clip, warp 5 catch, clasp, yield 6 begird, cave in, fasten, submit 7 contort, crumple, distort, give way, succumb 8 collapse, fastener
down: 4 work 5 fight 6 wade in 7 get busy, get to it, pitch in 10 launch into
holder: 4 belt, shoe 5 strap
starter: 4 turn 5 swash
Buckley: 5 Betty 7 William
Bucknell: 6 school 10 university
athletes: 5 Bison
locale: 4 Penn. 9 Lewisburg
Buckner: 4 Noel 5 Jerry
bucko: 3 bub, kid, lad, mac 4 chap
Buck, Pearl S.: 6 writer 8 Nobelist
heroine: 4 O-Lan
milieu: China
pseudonym: Sedges
work: A Bridge for Passing
Dragon Seed
The Exile
Far and Near
Fighting Angel
The Good Deed
The Good Earth
A House Divided
Imperial Woman
The Living Reed
Mandala
My Several Worlds
Sons
The Spirit and the Flesh
Buck Privates (1941 film)
cast: Bud Abbott, Lou Costello
buckram: 6 fabric 8 material 9 formality, stiffness
Buck Rogers... (NBC sci-fi)
cast: Gil Gerard (Buck Rogers)
Erin Gray (Wilma Deering)
Felix Silla (Twiki)
bucks
starter: 4 mega
see also moolah
__ bucks: 3 big 5 white
Bucks: 4 five 6 county
home: 9 Milwaukee, Wisconsin
locale: 7 England
org.: 3 NBA
rival: ***see*** NBA team
buckskin: 5 cloth 7 leather
buck stops here, The
monogram: 3 HST
buckthorn: 4 tree 6 jujube 7 cascara
buckwheat: 5 grain 6 cereal
dish: 5 kasha 8 hotcakes, pancakes 9 flapjacks
nutrient in ~: 5 rutin
buckwheat __: 4 coal, note 5 flour 8 pancakes
Buckwheat
assent: 4 otay
dog: 4 Pete 5 Petey
friend: 5 Darla, Porky 6 Spanky 7 Alfalfa
Bucky: 4 Dent 6 Harris, Lasek 7 Walters
__ buco: 4 osso
bucolic: 4 calm, idyl 5 idyll, rural 6 rustic 7 country 8 agrarian, Arcadian, farmlike, pastoral 10 provincial
plot: 4 acre
poem: 4 idyl 5 idyll

surroundings: 7 country 8 outdoors
Bucs
see Buccaneers, Pirates
bud: 3 guy, mac, pal 4 germ, node 5 bloom, graft, shoot 6 feller, floret, friend, nodule, sprout 7 blossom, burgeon, compeer 8 bourgeon, vegetate 9 germinate, pullulate 10 burst forth, effloresce
combining form: 5 -blast 6 blasto-
eventually: 4 leaf 5 bloom 6 flower 7 blossom
holder: 4 limb, stem, twig, vase 5 bough, stalk
in botany: 5 gemma
in the ~: 5 early
nip in the ~: 4 foil, halt, stem, stop 5 avert, quash 6 arrest, put out, scotch 7 obviate, prevent, put down, squelch 8 preclude, stamp out 9 forestall 10 extinguish, put an end to
pickled flower ~: 5 caper
spicy flower ~: 5 clove
starter: 3 red 4 rose
__ bud: 4 leaf 5 brood, mixed, taste 6 flower 7 lateral
Bud: 4 beer, Cort 5 Grant, Selig 6 Abbott, Fisher, Yorkin 7 Collyer
partner: 3 Lou
see also Budweiser
Budapest: 4 city, port, town 7 capital
airline to ~: 5 MALEV
locale: 7 Hungary
river: 6 Danube
Budd: 5 Billy 9 Schulberg 10 Boetticher
Budd, Billy: 3 gob, tar 6 sailor
creator: Herman Melville
Buddenbrooks
author: Thomas Mann
Buddha: 6 Gotama 7 Gautama 10 Siddhartha
attribute: 4 calm 10 compassion
contemporary: 6 Lao-tse, Lao-tze, Lao-tzu
cousin: 6 Ananda
discourse: 5 sutra
enemy: 4 Mara
meditation spot: 6 bo tree
mother: 4 Maya
of the future: 8 Maitreya
title: 6 prince
Buddhism: 3 Zen 4 ch'an 6 tantra 8 Mahayana, religion 9 Theravada, Vajrayana
awakening to reality in ~: 5 bliss 7 nirvana
canon: 5 agama
chant: 2 om 6 mantra
community: 6 sangha
delusion about reality: 7 samsara
doctrine: 6 anatta, anicca, dharma, dukkha
drum: 6 damaru 7 mokugyo
energy: 5 prana
energy center: 6 chakra
energy channels: 4 nadi
eon: 5 kalpa
flower: 5 lotus
furnishing: 3 mat 5 tanka 6 candle 7 cushion, incense, thangka 10 butter lamp
gesture: 5 mudra
homage word: 4 namu
language of ~ scriptures: 4 Pali 8 Sanskrit
meditation cushion: 4 zafu 7 zabuton
meditative state: 5 rigpa, zhiné 6 satori 10 shikantaza
meditative technique: 7 samadhi 8 dzogchen 9 mahamudra
monk: 4 lama 5 bonze 7 bhikshu 9 bhikshuni
monument: 4 tope 5 stupa
musical instrument: 4 bell, drum, gong 5 conch 6 drilbu 7 cymbals, trumpet
ritual: 4 puja 7 sadhana
ritual object: 4 bell 5 dorje, torma, vajra 6 bhumpo, phurba 7 mandala
sacred city: 4 Lasa 5 Lassa, Lhasa 8 Bodh-gaya
sacred mountain: 4 Meru, Omei
sacred syllable: 2 ah, om 3 aum, dza, hri, hum 4 hung
shrine: 5 stupa 6 Ajanta
sitting mat: 7 zabuton
symbol of the indestructible: 5 lotus, vajra
symbol of the universe: 7 mandala
symbol of Ultimate Reality: 5 lotus, vajra
teachings: 5 sutra 6 dharma, tantra
temple: 3 wat 5 zendo 8 lamasery
Tibetan ~ icon: 5 tanka 7 thangka
Tibetan school of ~: 4 Rimé 5 Bon Po, Kagyu, Sakya 7 Gelugpa, Nyingma
title: 4 guru, lama 5 geshe, Roshi 6 khenpo, sensei 7 Karmapa 8 Rinpoche 9 Dalai Lama
Ultimate Reality: 7 sunyata
virtue: 3 joy 4 love 8 paramita, patience 10 bodhicitta, compassion, equanimity, generosity
vow: 6 samaya
wisdom: 5 jñana 6 prajna
__ Buddies: 5 Bosom
budding: 5 early, young 6 spring 7 nascent 8 juvenile, youthful 9 fledgling, incipient, potential, promising 10 developing, unrealized
buddy: 3 bro, bub, guy, lad, mac, pal 4 ally, chum, dude, mate 5 amigo, crony, kiddo, pally 6 cohort, feller, frater, friend 7 compeer, comrade, partner 8 alter ego, intimate, roommate, sidekick 9 associate, colleague, companion, confidant 10 compatriot, well-wisher
beatnik ~: 6 daddy-o
cowboy's ~: 4 pard 7 pardner
good ~: 3 bro, pal 4 CBer
in Australian English: 4 mate
in British English: 4 mate
in French: 3 ami 4 amie
in Spanish: 5 amiga, amigo
buddy __: 4 seat 6 system
__ buddy: 4 good 5 bosom
Buddy: 3 Guy 4 Baer, Rich 5 Ebsen, Greco, Holly, Miles 6 Rogers 7 DeSylva, Hackett
to Bill: 3 dog, pet
buddy-buddy: 4 kind 5 close, thick 6 chummy, clubby, genial, kindly 7 affable, amiable, cordial 8 amicable, familiar, friendly, intimate, outgoing, sociable 9 convivial 10 benevolent, neighborly, solicitous
Buddy Holly Story, The (1978 film)
cast: Gary Busey
budge: 4 bend, move, stir, sway 5 shift, yield 6 change 7 give way 8 convince, dislodge, persuade 9 influence 10 knock loose
don't ~: 4 stay 6 insist, refuse
Budge, Don: 7 netster 9 tennis pro
milieu: 5 court
budgerigar: 3 pet 4 bird 8 parakeet
budget: 5 funds, means, total 6 ration, upkeep 7 plan for, program 8 allocate 9 apportion, resources, statement 10 allocation
concern: 5 outgo
DC ~ watchdog: 3 GAO
item: 3 gas 4 elec., rent, util. 8 electric 9 utilities 10 car payment
limit: 3 cap 7 ceiling
starter: 4 fuss
stretch the ~: 3 eke 5 skimp, stint 6 eke out 9 economize
__ budget: 5 water 7 capital
__-budget: 3 low, off
Budget: 9 car rental 10 auto rental
competitor: *see* car rental
budgetary: 6 fiscal 8 economic, monetary
budgeting: 7 finance 9 financial
abbr.: 3 YTD
budgie: 8 parakeet, paraquet, paroquet, parroket 9 parrakeet, parroquet
__ Bud Melman: 5 Larry
buds combining form: 7 -blastic
Budweiser: 4 beer
competitor: *see* beer
dog: 5 Spuds
__ Bueller's Day Off: 6 Ferris
__ Buena: 5 Yerba
Buena Park: 4 city, town
locale: 10 California
buenas __: 6 noches, tardes
__ Buenaventura: 3 San
Buena Vista: 4 city, town 6 battle
locale: 6 Mexico
Bueno, Maria: 7 netster 9 tennis pro
milieu: 5 court
buenos __: 4 días
Buenos Aires: 4 city, port, town 7 capital
city near ~: 5 Salto, Tigre
locale: 3 Arg. 9 Argentina
musical set in ~: 5 Evita
river: 5 Plata
see also Spanish
buff: 3 fan, nut, rub, tan 4 wipe 5 color, flaxy, freak, gloss, lover, maven, mavin, scour, scrub, shine 6 addict, flaxen, polish, rooter, suntan, yellow 7 admirer, burnish, devotee, furbish, groupie 8 brownish, follower, muscular 9 sandpaper 10 aficionado, enthusiast
cheat at blind man's ~: 4 peek
color kin: *see* brown color, yellow color
in the ~: 4 nude 5 naked 9 unattired
up: 3 wax 5 shine 6 polish 8 brighten
buffa: 5 comic 8 humorous
opposite: 5 seria
__ buffa: 5 opera
buffalo: 4 dupe, foil 5 addle, bovid, bully, stump 6 animal, baffle, bovine, puzzle 7 deceive, mystify, nonplus, perplex, unnerve 8 hoodwink 9 bamboozle 10 intimidate
Cape ~ home: 6 Africa
feature: 4 hump
female: 3 cow
group: 4 herd
male: 4 bull
relative: *see* bovine
young: 4 calf 8 buffalo's
buffalo __: 3 bug 4 bird, fish, gnat, robe 5 berry, cloth, grass, plaid, wings 7 currant, soldier
__ buffalo: 4 Cape 5 black, dwarf, water
Buffalo: 4 city, port, town
canal to ~: 4 Erie
conference: 3 MAC
county: 4 Erie
lake: 4 Erie
like ~ winters: 5 snowy
locale: 7 New York
newspaper: 4 News
pro team: 5 Bills 6 Sabres
suburb: 5 Depew
Buffalo __: 4 Bill, Gals 5 Girls
Buffalo Bill: 4 Cody
buffaloed: 4 asea 5 stuck 7 stumped
buffaloes, water: 4 oxen
Buffalo Girls
author: Larry McMurtry
buffer: 5 guard 6 shield 7 bulwark, cushion, defense, padding 9 safeguard 10 protection
buffer __: 4 zone 5 state
Bufferin: 7 aspirin 9 analgesic 10 painkiller
alternative: *see* pain reliever brand
buffet: 3 hit, jar 4 beat, blow, cuff, lash, meal, sock, swat, toss 5 crack, knock, pound, punch, smack, smite, spank, table, thump, whack, whang 6 batter, dinner, pommel, pummel, strike, supper, thrash, thwack, wallop 7 clobber 9 furniture, reception
choice: 3 ham 4 fish, food, soup 5 fruit, salad 6 entrée, shrimp, turkey 7 chicken, dessert 9 roast beef
enjoy the ~: 3 eat 5 gorge, stuff
patron: 5 diner, eater 8 gourmand
buffeting: 3 jar 4 blow 5 shock 6 impact 9 collision, explosion 10 concussion
Buffett: 5 Jimmy 6 Warren
Buffett, Jimmy: 6 singer
song: Margaritaville (1977)
Buffett, Warren
HQ: 3 Neb. 4 Nebr. 5 Omaha 8 Nebraska
buffo: 5 comic 8 humorous
buffoon: 3 wag 4 geek, joke, zany 5 chump, comic, joker, sport 6 jester, sucker, turkey 7 pierrot 8 comedian, funnyman, meathead 9 harlequin, leg-puller
see also ninny
buffoonery: 3 fun 5 antic, farce, humor 7 fooling 8 zaniness 9 funniness, merriment 10 jocoseness
bit of ~: 4 joke 5 antic, prank
Buffy __-Marie: 6 Sainte

Buffy the Vampire Slayer (1992 film)
cast: Paul Reubens, Donald Sutherland, Kristy Swanson
director: Fran Rubel Kuzui
Buffy the Vampire Slayer (WB sci-fi)
cast: Nicholas Brendon (Xander Harris)
Sarah Michelle Gellar (Buffy Summers)
bug: 3 ant, bee, bot, dor, dun, fad, flu, fly, get, irk, nag, nit, tap, tip, vex **4** flaw, flea, gall, germ, gnat, grub, lice, mite, moth, pest, pupa, rage, ride, rile, snag, tick, tine, wasp, wire **5** annoy, aphid, aphis, borer, chafe, cimex, cooty, craze, drone, eat at, emmet, error, freak, get on, hound, imago, larva, louse, mania, midge, peeve, spy on, upset, virus, worry **6** abrade, acarid, badger, beetle, botfly, bother, chafer, chigoe, chinch, cicada, cocoon, cootie, defect, earwig, gadfly, glitch, grippe, harass, hassle, hornet, insect, larvae, locust, looper, maggot, malady, mantis, mayfly, needle, nettle, noodge, pester, plague, pother, punkie, pursue, put out, scarab, thrips, tipoff, tussah, vermin, weevil, work on **7** agitate, ailment, ant lion, bedevil, blowfly, chigger, cricket, disease, disturb, fanatic, firefly, hexapod, illness, katydid, microbe, no-see-um, perturb, pismire, provoke, termite, trouble, viceroy, wiretap **8** armyworm, bacillus, conenose, distress, firebrat, glowworm, honeybee, housefly, irritate, lacewing, listen to, mosquito, muckworm, reduviid, sickness, silkworm, woodworm **9** aggravate, bacterium, bumblebee, butterfly, chrysalis, cockroach, corn borer, damselfly, dobsonfly, dorbeetle, dragonfly, earthworm, eavesdrop, infection, influenza, obsession, saturniid, sheep tick, tarantula, woodborer **10** bluebottle, calicoback, deathwatch, deficiency, digger wasp, disconcert, froghopper, pear thrips, rose chafer, woolly bear
baby ~: 5 larva
back: 5 notum
bite: 4 welt **5** sting
bonnet ~: 3 bee
busy ~: 3 ant, bee
catch a ~: 3 ail
chest: 6 thorax
ender: 4 bane, bear **5** house
June ~: 3 dor **4** dorr **6** beetle
like a cold ~: 5 viral
like a ~ in a rug: 4 snug
mouth parts: 5 labra
off: 5 scram **7** get lost
out: 2 go **5** leave, scram **6** decamp **7** vamoose **8** fugitate, run for it **10** make tracks
pesky ~: 3 fly **4** gnat **5** midge **6** punkie **7** no-see-um **8** mosquito
phone ~: 3 tap **4** mike
pill ~: 6 isopod
repellent: 4 Deet
science: 5 entom. **10** entomology
starter: 3 bed, hum, mud, red **4** bill, fire, lady **5** mealy, stink **6** doodle, jitter, litter, tumble **7** shutter
stinging ~: 3 bee **4** wasp **6** hornet
tiny ~: 4 gnat, mite **5** midge **6** punkie **7** no-see-um
user: 3 spy
see also insect
bug __: 3 off, out **6** zapper
bug-__: 4 eyed
__ bug: 3 bed, mud, sow, tow **4** boat, flat, June, lace, leaf, love, pill, toad, true **5** cinch, grass, lygus, plant, shore, stilt, stink, water, wheel **6** ambush, calico, carpet, chinch, coreid, Croton, damsel, flower, fungus, potato, spider, squash **7** buffalo, cabbage, lygaeid
Bug: 2 VW **3** car **4** auto **5** river **10** automobile, Volkswagen
River locale: 6 Poland **7** Ukraine
river to the ~: 5 Narew
bugaboo: 4 bane, fear, jinx **7** problem
Bugatti: 3 car **4** auto **6** Ettore **7** Italian **10** automobile
bugbear: 4 bane, bogy, ogre **6** fantom, goblin **7** bogyman, phantom, spectre **8** anathema, pet peeve **9** bête noire, hobgoblin, nightmare
bug-eyed: 4 agog, gaga
monster: 2 ET
Buggles
song: Video Killed the Radio Star (1979)
buggy: 4 auto, loco, pram **5** wagon **7** vehicle **8** carriage
drivers: 5 Amish
dune ~: 3 ATV
venue: 4 dune
__ buggy: 4 baby, dune **5** beach, marsh, swamp **6** bundle
...bug in __: 4 a rug
__ bug in one's ear: 4 put a
bugle: 4 horn, wind **7** trumpet
call: 4 Taps
ender: 4 weed
play a ~: 4 blow
signal: 4 taps **6** charge **8** reveille
Bugle __: 3 Boy
Bugler's Holiday
composer: Leroy Anderson
bugles, animal that: 3 elk
bugleweed: 5 ajuga
Bugliosi: 7 Vincent
Bugs: 4 Baer **5** Moran
Bugs Bunny: 4 hare **7** cartoon **9** comic book
adversary: 3 Taz **4** Fudd **9** Elmer Fudd
like ~: 5 eared
voice: Mel Blanc
Bug's Life, A
bug: 3 ant
role: 3 Dot **4** Atta, Flik **6** Hopper
Bug's Life, A (1998 film)
voice cast: Phyllis Diller, Julia Louis-Dreyfus, Kevin Spacey
Bugsy: 6 Siegel
wife: 4 Esta
Bugsy (1991 film)
cast: Warren Beatty, Annette Bening, Elliott Gould, Harvey Keitel, Ben Kingsley
director: Barry Levinson
__ Bug, The: 4 Gold, Love **5** Satan
Buick: 3 car **4** auto **10** automobile
endorser: 5 Woods
model: 5 Regal **6** Apollo, Reatta **7** Century, Electra, Enclave, Invicta, LeSabre, Limited, Lucerne, Rainier, Riviera, Skyhawk, Skylark, Special, Wildcat **8** Somerset **9** Centurion, Gran Sport **10** Park Avenue, Roadmaster, Sportwagon
build: 3 wax **4** body, form, gird, grow, make, mold, rear, rise, tone **5** add to, boost, erect, forge, found, frame, mount, put up, raise, set up, shape, shore, steel **6** accrue, anneal, beef up, create, enrich, expand, extend, figure, gather, harden, prop up, step up, temper, tone up **7** anatomy, augment, bolster, brace up, burgeon, compile, compose, develop, empower, enhance, enlarge, fashion, fortify, improve, produce, shore up, stiffen, throw up, toughen **8** assemble, bourgeon, buttress, energize, engineer, escalate, heighten, increase, indurate, initiate, multiply, physique, vitalize **9** construct, establish, fabricate, formulate, increment, institute, intensify, originate, reinforce, structure **10** accelerate, aggrandize, inaugurate, invigorate, strengthen, supplement
a wing: 3 add **5** add on, annex **6** adjoin, append, tack on
body ~: 5 frame **8** physique
castles in the air: 5 dream **7** imagine **9** fantasize
on: 3 add **4** rely **5** trust **6** depend
something to ~ on: 3 lot **4** spec **10** foundation
up: 3 get, wax **4** gird, grow, laud, lift, rise, tone **5** add to, amass, boost, build, exalt, lay by, lay up, lobby, shore, steel **6** accrue, anneal, enrich, expand, fatten, harden, praise, temper **7** amplify, augment, bolster, burgeon, develop, empower, enhance, fortify, improve, inflate, magnify, prepare, promote, recruit, stiffen, toughen **8** bourgeon, buttress, energize, escalate, heighten, increase, indurate, multiply, overrate, progress, vitalize **9** condition, increment, intensify, publicize, reinforce **10** exaggerate, invigorate, strengthen, supplement
build __ egg: 5 a nest
__-build: 5 jerry **6** custom
build a __ under: 4 fire
builder: 5 mason **6** framer **7** erector **8** engineer, inventer, inventor **9** architect, artificer, carpenter, developer **10** contractor, fabricator, mastermind
choice: 4 site
detail: 4 spec
empire ~: 5 baron, mogul, mover **6** bigwig, shaker, tycoon **7** magnate **9** financier, plutocrat **10** capitalist
starter: 4 home, ship
__ builder: 6 empire, master
__-builder: 4 body
__ Builder, The: 6 Master
building: 4 barn, home **5** cabin, condo, house, shack **6** duplex, garage, lean-to, museum, palace **7** cottage, edifice, mansion, stadium **8** assembly, dwelling, high-rise **9** structure **10** skyscraper
block: 4 unit **5** brick
brace: 5 strut
circular ~: 4 dome **6** tholos
component: 4 beam, stud **5** I-beam, joist, truss **6** girder, rafter
crude ~: 4 shed **5** cabin, shack **6** lean-to
designers' org.: 3 AIA
detail: 4 spec
extension: 3 ell **4** wing **5** add-on, annex
feature: 4 deck **5** porch, spire, tower **6** column, cupola **7** balcony, steeple, veranda **9** bay window, bow window
govt. ~ agency: 3 HUD
level: 5 attic, story **6** cellar **8** basement
manager: 4 supe **5** super
material: 4 wood **5** adobe, brick, steel, stone **6** cement, thatch **8** concrete
nature's ~ block: 3 DNA, RNA **4** atom, cell, gene **10** chromosome
occupy an abandoned ~: 5 squat
office ~ area: 5 court, lobby **6** atrium **9** courtyard
plastic ~ block: 4 Lego
regulations: 4 code
religious ~: 5 zendo **6** chapel, church, pagoda, shrine, temple **8** lamasery **9** cathedral
site: 3 lot
site sight: 5 crane
starter: 4 body, ship
support: 4 beam **5** I-beam **6** girder
tall ~: 5 tower **10** skyscraper
tumbledown ~: 4 ruin
utility ~: 4 shed **6** garage, lean-to
building __: 4 code, line **5** block, paper **6** permit, trades **7** society
__ building: 4 body, loft **6** sliver
Building a Mystery (1997 song)
artist: Sarah McLachlan
building-block material: 6 cement, cinder **8** concrete
buildings: 8 property
grounds and ~: 8 premises
build on __: 4 spec
build-up: 4 gain, heap, hype **5** boost **6** growth, hoopla **7** accrual **8** increase, training **9** accretion, expansion, inflation, publicity, stockpile **10** escalation
household ~: 4 junk **5** trash **7** garbage
built: 5 put up
for speed: 5 sleek **8** souped-up
powerfully ~: 5 stout **8** muscular
to last: 5 solid, sound **6** rugged, strong, sturdy **8** well-made
built __: 6 to last
__-built: 3 cat **4** well **5** jerry, stick **6** carvel, custom **7** clinker, clipper
__ built a railroad...: 5 Once I
built-in: 6 innate, native **9** ingrained, intrinsic **10** deep-seated
built-up: 5 urban

area: 4 city, town 5 exurb 6 suburb 7 village 10 metropolis, settlement
Buisson, Ferdinand: 6 French 8 Nobelist
Bujold, Genevieve: 7 actress
Bujones, Fernando: 6 dancer 7 danseur
milieu: 6 ballet
Bujumbura: 4 city, town 7 capital
locale: 7 Burundi
Bukowski, Charles: 6 writer
bulb
crocus ~: 4 corm
edible ~: 4 leek 5 camas, onion 6 camass, garlic
garden ~: 4 glad, iris 5 tulip 6 allium, scilla 8 daffodil, gladiola, hyacinth, snowdrop 9 Dutch iris, gladiolus, narcissus
hypo ~: 5 ampul 6 ampule 7 ampoule
light ~ filler: 4 neon 5 argon
light ~, in the comics: 4 idea
like a low-watt ~: 3 dim
place: 4 lamp 7 fixture 10 chandelier
planter: 5 spade 6 dibble
pungent ~: 5 onion 6 garlic
starter: 5 flash
within a bulb: 5 clove
__ bulb: 3 dim 5 flash, light
__ Bulba: 5 Taras
bulb-like stem: 4 corm
bulbous: 5 round, thick 7 rounded 8 globular
__-bulb thermometer: 3 dry, wet
bulbul: 4 bird 8 songbird
Bulfinch: 6 Thomas 7 Charles
Bulfinch, Charles: 9 architect
Bulgaria: 6 nation 7 country
capital: 5 Sofia 6 Sofiya
city: 4 Ruse 5 Varna 6 Burgas, Dobric, Pleven, Sliven 7 Plovdiv
king: 5 Boris
money: 3 lev 4 leva 8 stotinka
mountain: 6 Musala 7 Rhodope
neighbor: 6 Greece, Turkey 7 Romania 9 Macedonia 10 Yugoslavia
Nobelist in Literature: 7 Canetti
port: 5 Varna
weight: 3 oke
Bulgarian: 4 Slav 6 Balkan 8 language
neighbor: 4 Turk 5 Greek
bulge: 3 jut, sag 4 bump, hump, knob, lump, node 5 bloat, heave, start, swell 6 dilate, expand, nodule, paunch 7 balloon, distend, enlarge, project, puff out, swell up 8 dilation, overhang, protrude, stand out, stick out, swelling, swell out 9 intumesce, outgrowth 10 distension, projection, prominence, protrusion
battle the ~: 4 diet, lose 6 reduce 7 work out 8 exercise
bulging: 5 puffy 6 convex 9 distended, obtrusive, prominent 10 lenticular
bulgur: 5 grain, wheat
bulk: 3 sum 4 body, girt, heft, lump, mass, most, size 5 girth, total, whole 6 extent, volume, weight 7 bigness 8 enormity, majority, quantity 9 aggregate, dimension, immensity, largeness, magnitude, plurality 10 dimensions, lion's share
buy in ~: 4 save
ender: 4 head
in ~: 9 wholesale
up: 3 pad 6 expand
bulk __: 4 mail
bulkhead: 4 wall 5 panel 9 partition
locale: 3 jet 4 ship 5 plane 8 airplane
bulkiness: 4 heft, mass 9 immensity 10 fleshiness
bulky: 3 big 4 huge 5 beefy, burly, great, gross, hefty, large, plump, stout, thick 6 portly 7 awkward, hulking, immense, mammoth, massive, unhandy, weighty 8 colossal, enormous, unwieldy 9 corpulent, ponderous 10 cumbersome, overweight, voluminous, well-padded
bull: 4 male, toro 6 animal, Brahma 8 investor, optimist
advice: 3 buy
at times: 5 gorer
combining form: 4 taur- 5 tauri-, tauro-
constellation: 6 Taurus
delight: 5 rally 6 uptick 7 upswing
disarm a ~: 6 dehorn
ender: 3 bat, dog, ish, ock, pen 4 boat, doze, frog, head, horn, ring, whip 5 dozer, fight, finch 6 necked, roarer 7 fighter, mastiff
holder: 4 gate 6 corral 7 pasture
in a china shop: 3 oaf 5 klutz
in Britain: 5 stirk
in Spanish: 4 toro
market: 4 rise 5 rally 6 uptick 7 upswing
mate: 3 cow 6 heifer
meal: 5 grass
papal ~: 5 edict 6 decree
riding event: 5 rodeo
session: 3 gab, jaw, rap, yak 4 chat, talk 7 palaver 10 conference, discussion
session site: 4 dorm
shoot the ~: 3 gab, jaw, rap, yak 4 talk
sound: 5 snort 6 bellow
weapon: 4 horn
young ~: 4 calf
see also baloney
bull __: 3 ant, bay, gun, pen 4 gear, horn, rope 5 block, chain, float, shark, snake, trout, wheel 6 fiddle, header, riding, tongue 7 mastiff, session, terrier, thistle
bull-__: 3 bar 4 whip 6 necked, roarer
__ bull: 3 pit 4 blue 5 Irish, papal 6 Boston, Cretan
Bull: 3 May, Ole 4 Olaf, sign 5 April 6 Halsey, Taurus
follower ~: 5 Twins
preceder ~: 3 Ram
Bull __: 3 Run 5 Moose 6 Durham
__ Bull: 4 John 6 Golden, Raging 7 Sitting
bulla: 4 seal
bulldog
its logo is a ~: 4 Mack
like a ~: 6 jowled 9 tenacious 10 pugnacious
relative: 3 pug
Bulldog: 3 Eli 5 Yalie
school: 4 Yale 5 Drake 7 Citadel, Gonzaga
bulldoze: 3 cow, dig 4 dupe, rase, raze, ruin 5 bully, level, outdo, press, shove, wreck 6 coerce, compel, hector, topple 7 destroy, dragoon, flatten, unbuild 8 browbeat, demolish, domineer, pull down, take down, tear down 9 devastate, dismantle, knock down, overpower, take apart, terrorize 10 intimidate
bulldozing: 8 leveling 10 demolition
Bull Durham (1988 film)
cast: Kevin Costner, Tim Robbins, Susan Sarandon
bullet: 3 ace 4 ammo, shot, slug 6 dum-dum 7 missile 9 cartridge 10 ammunition, projectile
ender: 5 proof
fake ~: 5 blank
poker ~: 3 ace
sound: 4 ping, zing 5 whine
bullet __: 4 tree, wood 5 train
__ bullet: 5 magic 6 silver, tracer
Bullet for Joey, A (1955 film)
cast: George Raft
bulletin: 4 news, word 6 notice 7 handout, message, program, tidings 8 dispatch, pamphlet 9 news flash 10 communiqué
all points ~: 7 dragnet
board material: 4 cork
like a news ~: 6 just in
police ~: 3 APB 5 alert
bulletin __: 5 board
__ bulletin: 4 news
bulletin-board
computer ~ manager: 5 sysop
fastener: 4 tack 7 pushpin 9 thumbtack
Bullet in the Head, A (1990 film)
director: John Woo
Bullet Park
author: John Cheever
bulletproof vest material: 6 Kevlar
__ bullets: 5 sweat
Bullets Over Broadway (1994 film)
cast: John Cusack, Jennifer Tilly, Dianne Wiest
director: Woody Allen
bullfight: 7 corrida
bullfighter: 7 matador 8 toreador
cloak: 4 capa
maneuver: 4 pase
bullfighting: 5 sport
site: 5 arena
bullfinch: 4 bird
bullfrog genus: 4 rana
bullhead: 4 fish
bullheaded: 5 rigid, stern 6 wilful 7 hard-set, willful 8 dogmatic, stubborn 9 tenacious 10 hard-bitten, iron-willed, refractory
bullion: 4 gold
shape: 3 bar 5 ingot
site: 6 Ft. Knox
bullish: 10 optimistic
advice: 3 buy 6 invest
Bullitt (1968 film)
cast: Jacqueline Bisset, Steve McQueen, Robert Vaughn
director: Peter Yates
bullmastiff: 3 dog 5 canid 6 canine
see also dog
Bull Moose: 5 party
name: 5 Teddy
Bullock, Sandra: 7 actress
film: 28 Days (2000)
The Blind Side (2009, AA)
Crash (2005)
Demolition Man (1993)
Divine Secrets of the Ya-Ya Sisterhood (2002)
Gun Shy (2000)
Hope Floats (1998)
Miss Congeniality (2000)
Murder by Numbers (2002)
The Net (1995)
Practical Magic (1998)
Premonition (2007)
The Proposal (2009)
Speed (1994)
A Time to Kill (1996)
While You Were Sleeping (1995)
film (voice): The Prince of Egypt (1998)
bullock's heart: 5 fruit
Bull, Olaf: 4 poet 9 Norwegian
Bull, Ole: 9 Norwegian, violinist
bullpen fixture: 3 ace 5 phone 6 closer, hurler 7 pitcher 8 reliever
bullring: 5 arena
figure: 4 toro 7 matador 8 toreador
Bull Run: 6 battle, stream 8 Manassas
boomer: 6 cannon
soldier: 3 Reb
victor: 3 Lee
bulls: 3 he's 6 cattle
Bulls: 4 five
home: 7 Chicago
rival: *see* NBA team
bull's-eye: 5 candy 6 center, target 10 ground zero
eye the ~: 3 aim 5 point 6 target
hitter: 4 dart 5 arrow 6 bullet
Bullwinkle: 5 moose
foe: 5 Boris 7 Natasha
to Rocky: 3 pal
bully: 3 cow 4 goad, good, haze 5 brute, daunt, rowdy, snarl, tough 6 abaser, abuser, badger, coerce, extort, harass, hector, lean on, meanie, menace, pick on, prey on, rascal, tyrant 7 buffalo, coercer, control, dragoon, harrier, henpeck, oppress, ruffian, swagger, torment 8 bludgeon, browbeat, bulldoze, domineer, keep down, overbear, prey upon, threaten 9 despotize, miscreant, oppressor, persecute, shake down, strong-arm, swaggerer, terrorize, tormentor, trample on, tyrannize 10 browbeater, intimidate, persecutor, push around
ender: 3 boy
offering: 5 mouse 6 fat lip, shiner 8 black eye
bully __: 4 beef, tree 6 pulpit
__ Bully: 5 Wooly
bullyboy: 4 goon, thug 5 tough
bullyrag: 3 cow 5 tease 7 torment 8 aggrieve 10 intimidate
Bulova: 5 watch 10 wristwatch
alternative: *see* wristwatch
Bülow, Hans von: 6 German 7 pianist
Bulow, Sunny von
portrayer: 5 Close
bulrush: 4 reed, tule 5 sedge
bulwark: 4 wall 5 guard, shore 6 buffer, secure, shield 7 bastion,

bolster, defense, fortify, protect, railing, rampart **8** buttress, fastness, mainstay **9** barricade, safeguard **10** protection, stronghold

BU

Bulwark, The
author: Theodore Dreiser
Bulwer-Lytton, Edward: 4 poet **6** writer **7** British
heroine: 4 Ione
work: Eugene Aram
Harold
The Last Days of Pompeii
Leila
Pelham
Rienzi
Zanoni
Bulworth (1998 film)
cast: Warren Beatty, Halle Berry, Don Cheadle, Oliver Platt, Paul Sorvino, Jack Warden
director: Warren Beatty
bum: 3 veg **4** hobo **5** cadge, idler, leech, louse, mooch, scamp, tramp **6** borrow, loafer, lounge, rascal, rotten **7** drifter, failure, lowlife, outcast, solicit, sponger, vagrant **8** deadbeat, derelict, freeload, scrounge, spurious, vagabond, wanderer **9** do-nothing, no-goodnik **10** ne'er-do-well, panhandler, ragamuffin
around: 4 laze, loaf, roam, rove **7** goof off **10** knock about
bleacher ~: 3 fan
give a ~ steer: 8 misguide **9** misinform
out: 5 peeve **6** deject, dismay, sadden **7** depress, incense **8** dispirit **9** bring down **10** dishearten
rap: 5 frame **7** raw deal
starter: 7 stumble
bum __: 3 rap **5** steer
__ bum: 3 ski **5** beach
bumbershoot: 4 gamp **6** brolly **8** umbrella
bumble: 4 muff **5** botch, lurch **6** falter, fumble, muddle **7** stumble
ender: 3 bee
bumblebee: 3 bug **6** insect
Bumble Bee: 4 tuna
rival: 8 Star Kist
bumbler: 2 ox **3** ass, oaf **4** boob, clod, jerk, lout **5** klutz, looby **6** lubber
cry: 4 oops
bumbling: 5 gawky, inept **6** clumsy, gauche, klutzy, oafish, wooden **7** awkward, gawkish, halting, unadept **8** bungling, fumbling, inexpert, ungainly **9** all thumbs, graceless, lumbering, maladroit, stumbling, unskilled **10** unskillful
Bumbry, Grace: 6 singer **12** mezzo-soprano
bummed out: 5 upset **7** furious **9** exanimate **10** distressed
see also gloomy
bummer: 4 drag **6** downer **7** raw deal
Bummer!: 4 alas **6** too bad
bump: 3 hit, jar, jog **4** dent, jerk, jolt, lump, node, push **5** bulge, carom, dance, eject, elbow, gnarl, nudge, raise, shake, shock, wound **6** bounce, carrom, jostle, jounce, justle, move up, nodule, pimple, reduce, step up **7** advance, elevate, jostles, preempt, promote, upgrade **8** dislodge, displace, increase, obstacle, swelling **9** contusion, increment, smash into **10** knock loose, projection, prominence
down: 6 demote
heads: 5 argue **6** debate **7** wrangle **8** disagree
into: 4 find, jolt, meet **6** strike **8** chance on, happen on **9** encounter, run across **10** chance upon **11** collide with
into, in Britain: 5 prang
result: 6 bruise
skin ~: 3 wen, zit
sound: 4 thud **5** thump
up against: 4 abut **5** touch **6** adjoin
__ bump: 5 speed
bumper: 6 fender, shield **8** auto part **9** plentiful
adjunct: 6 air dam
coating: 6 chrome
flaw: 4 dent, ding
sticker words: 4 honk **5** I love **9** honk if you
bumper __: 3 car **4** crop, jack, pool **5** guard **7** sticker
bumper-car ride: 6 Dodgem
Bumpers: 4 Dale
bumper-to-bumper: 6 jammed **10** gridlocked
bumpkin: 3 oaf **4** clod, hick, lout, rube **5** looby, yokel **6** galoot, lummox, rustic **7** galloot, hayseed, peasant, plowboy, redneck **9** hillbilly **10** clodhopper, provincial
Bump 'n Grind (1994 song)
artist: R. Kelly
bump on a log, like a: 5 inert
Bumppo, Natty
quarry: 4 deer
__ bumps: 5 chill, goose
bumps, have goose: 6 shiver, tingle
bumptious: 5 cocky, nervy, pushy **6** cheeky **7** forward **8** impudent **9** obtrusive **10** aggressive
bumpy: 5 jerky, lumpy, nubby, rough, warty **6** choppy, jouncy, knobby, rugged, rutted, uneven **7** jarring, knurled, nodular **8** potholed **9** irregular, turbulent **10** nonuniform
__ Bums: 3 Dem.
bum's rush, give the: 4 boot, oust **6** bounce **7** boot out, cast out, kick out, turn out **8** throw out **9** chase away
Bumstead: 6 Cookie **7** Blondie, Dagwood **9** Alexander
boss: 7 Dithers
boss's wife: 4 Cora
dog: 5 Daisy
neighbor: 4 Elmo, Herb
nickname: 3 Dag
__ Bums, The: 6 Dharma
bun: 4 coif, hair, loaf, roll **5** bread **6** Danish, hairdo **7** chignon, upsweep **8** coiffure **9** hairstyle, sweet roll
locale: 4 head, nape **5** diner **6** bakery
__ bun: 4 Bath **5** honey **6** sticky **7** Banbury **8** cinnamon
bunch: 3 gob, lot, set, ton, wad **4** bale, band, bevy, clan, gang, heap, herd, host, lump, mass, pack, pile, raft, ring, slew, team, unit **5** array, batch, clock, covey, crowd, flock, group, press, sheaf, stack, swarm, troop **6** boodle, bundle, gather, huddle, league, muster, passel, pileup, throng **7** cluster, numbers **8** assemble, assembly, quantity **9** gathering, multitude **10** assemblage, assortment, collection, congregate
ender: 5 berry, grass **6** flower
of: 6 divers, myriad, umteen, untold **7** copious, profuse, umpteen **8** abundant, manifold, numerous, umpsteen **9** bountiful, countless, quite a few
up: 4 heap, herd **5** crowd, group **6** gather, huddle **7** combine **9** squeeze in **10** congregate
wild ~: 3 mob **4** gang, pack **5** tribe
bunch __: 4 pink **5** grass, light
Bunche, Ralph: 8 diplomat, Nobelist
bunches: 5 reams
__ Bunch, The: 4 Wild **5** Brady
bunco: 3 con **4** scam **5** cheat **7** con game, swindle **8** flimflam
artist: 6 con man
buncombe
see baloney
bund: 4 bloc
Bündchen: 6 Gisele
Bundesrat
locale: 7 Austria, Germany
Bundestag
locale: 7 Germany
bundle: 3 lot, pkg., set, tie, wad **4** bale, bind, heap, load, loot, mint, pack, pile, stow, wisp, wrap **5** array, batch, bunch, clump, group, means, money, sheaf, stack **6** fardel, packet, parcel **7** cluster, package, snuggle **10** accumulate, assortment, collection, cumulation
binder: 4 cord, rope **5** twine **6** string
drop a ~: 4 lose
hay ~: 4 bale **5** stack
of energy: 6 dynamo
off: 4 oust, rush, send, ship **5** split **6** decamp, depart, hustle, kidnap **7** vamoose
of joy: 3 tot **4** baby **6** infant **7** bambino, newborn, toddler **9** little one
of nerves: 5 antsy, itchy, jumpy, tense **6** uneasy **7** anxious, jittery, keyed up, nervous, restive, uptight **8** agitated, restless, skittish, troubled **9** concerned, excitable, ill at ease **10** high-strung
up: 4 wrap **6** enwrap, muffle, swathe **9** dress warm
wheat ~: 5 sheaf
bundled software: 5 suite
bundle-of-joy bringer: 5 stork
bundler, hay: 5 baler
Bundt __: 3 pan **4** cake
Bundy: 2 Al **3** Peg **8** McGeorge
bung: 4 cork, dent, plug
up: 3 mar **4** dent, hurt **6** damage, injure
bungalow: 3 hut **4** home **5** bower, house **6** cabana, casita **7** cottage
language: 5 Hindi
__-Bungay: 4 Tono
bungee __: 4 cord **7** jumping
bungle: 3 err **4** blow, flub, goof, muff, slip, trip **5** boner, botch, gumup, lapse, misdo, shank **6** boggle, bollix, foozle, foul up, fumble, goof up, mess up, muddle, slip-up **7** blooper, blunder, failure, louse up, misstep, mistake, screw up **9** mishandle, mismanage
bungler: 2 ox **3** oaf **4** clod, dolt, fool, lout **5** dunce, idiot, klutz, looby **7** jackass **8** bonehead, cloddish, goofball **9** blockhead, harebrain **10** addlebrain
bungling: 5 gawky, inept **6** clumsy, klutzy, oafish **7** awkward, gawkish, loutish, unadept **8** botching, bumbling, fumbling, inexpert, lubberly, tactless, ungainly **9** all thumbs, graceless, lumbering, maladroit, stumbling, unskilled **10** blundering, ungraceful, unskillful
Bunin, Ivan: 4 poet **7** Russian **8** Nobelist
bunk: 3 bed, cot **4** stay **5** berth, lodge, put up **6** billet **7** quarter
bed: 5 berth
ender: 4 mate, room **5** house
position: 3 top **5** on top **6** bottom
see also baloney
bunk __: 3 bed
bunker: 3 bin, box **4** trap **5** chest **6** coffer, hazard **8** sand trap **10** receptacle
club: 5 wedge
filler: 4 sand
machine-gun ~: 4 nest
Bunker: 3 Eng **5** Chang
Bunker, Archie: 5 bigot
wife: 5 Edith
Bunker Hill: 6 battle
locale: 4 Mass.
bunkhouse item: 3 bed, cot
bunko squad concern: 5 fraud
bunkum
see baloney
Bunning, Jim: 3 sen. **6** hurler **7** pitcher, senator
bunny: 3 pet **6** rabbit **10** cottontail
dumb ~: 3 ass, nit, oaf, sap, wag **4** boob, boor, bozo, clod, dolt, fool, geek **5** chump, clown, cluck, dunce, joker, ninny, patsy **6** dimwit, lummox, nitwit, sucker, turkey **7** buffoon, dingbat, dullard, fathead, half-wit, jackass, pierrot, pinhead, saphead **8** bonehead, meathead, numskull **9** birdbrain, blockhead, lamebrain, numbskull, simpleton **10** dunderhead
emulate a ~: 3 hop
feature: 3 ear **4** ears
hop: 5 dance
hug: 5 dance
like a ~: 5 furry
tail: 4 scut
bunny __: 3 hop, hug
__ bunny: 4 dust **6** Easter
Bunny: 7 Berigan
Bunny __: 5 O'Hare
__ Bunny: 4 Bugs
bunny hop: 5 dance
bunny hug: 5 dance
bunnylike: 5 eared

Bunsen __: 6 burner
nozzle: 6 gas jet
bunt: 3 hit
ender: 4 line
situation, perhaps: 5 one on
bunt __: 6 single
__ bunt: 3 lag 4 drag
bunting: 4 bird, pape 5 cloth, finch, flags 6 fabric 7 ortolan, pennant 10 dickcissel
buntline: 4 rope
Buntline, Ned: 5 alias 6 writer
real name: Judson
subject: Cody, Buffalo Bill
Bunton: 4 Emma
Bunts
author: George Will
Buñuel, Luis: 8 director
Bunyan, John: 6 writer 7 British
work: Grace Abounding
The Holy War
Pilgrim's Progress
Bunyan, Paul: 4 hero 5 giant, opera 10 lumberjack
blue ox: 4 Babe
composer: Benjamin Britten
cook: 3 Ole
dog: 4 Fido 5 Elmer
tool: 3 axe
buon __: 6 fresco, giorno
buona __: 4 sera 5 notte
Buoniconti, Nick
sport: 8 football
Buono, Victor: 5 actor
buoy: 5 float 6 marker
place: 3 sea 5 ocean
sitter: 4 gull
unlit ~: 3 nun
up: 4 lift, prop 5 boost, cheer, elate, raise 6 uphold, uplift 7 bolster, cheer up, elevate, enliven, hearten, lighten, support, sustain 8 brighten, embolden, imbolden, reassure 9 encourage 10 exhilarate
buoyancy: 3 pep 4 élan 6 bounce, gaiety, gayety, levity, spring 7 jollity, rapture 8 optimism 9 animation, jocundity, lightness 10 ebullience, exuberance, friskiness, liveliness
buoyant: 4 airy 5 happy, jolly, light, perky, sunny 6 afloat, blithe, bouncy, breezy, cheery, floaty, jaunty, jovial, lively, upbeat, yeasty 7 springy 8 animated, carefree, cheerful, floating, mirthful, sanguine, youthful 9 exuberant, lightsome, resilient 10 flying high, optimistic, unbothered
be ~: 5 float
Buoyant Billions
author: George Bernard Shaw
bupkes: 3 nil 4 nada 6 naught, nought 7 nothing
bur: 7 sticker 8 irritant 9 annoyance
starter: 4 sand 6 butter, cockle
Burbank: 3 cat 4 city, town 6 Luther
locale: 10 California
burberry: 6 fabric 8 material
burble: 3 lap 4 foam, purl 5 froth 6 murmur
burbling: 5 foamy
burbot: 3 cod 4 fish, ling
'burbs, The (1989 film)
cast: Bruce Dern, Carrie Fisher, Tom Hanks
director: Joe Dante

burden: 3 lay, tax 4 care, drag, duty, lade, levy, load, onus, task, yoke 5 blame, chore, point, tenor, trial, weary, weigh 6 charge, fardel, hassle, hinder, lading, lumber, misery, saddle, strain, stress, upshot, weight 7 afflict, concern, oppress, overtax, purport, refrain, trouble 8 encumber, entangle, handicap, hardship, irritant, overhead, overload, pressure 9 adversity, albatross, annoyance, hindrance, incommode, liability, millstone, substance, weigh down 10 affliction, bear down on, difficulty, impediment, imposition, infliction
beast of ~: 3 ass, yak 4 mule 5 burro, camel, horse, llama 6 donkey
beasts of ~: 4 oxen
name meaning ~: 4 Amos
burdened: 5 laden 10 encumbered
combining form: 6 -ridden
burden of __: 5 proof
Burden of Proof, The
author: Scott Turow
burdensome: 4 hard 5 heavy, hefty 6 leaden, taxing 7 arduous, onerous, weighty 8 exacting, tiresome, unwieldy 9 demanding, difficult, laborious, ponderous, unwieldly 10 cumbersome, disturbing, enervating, oppressive
Burdette, Lew: 6 hurler 7 pitcher
Burdick: 6 Eugene
Burdon, Eric group: 7 Animals
bureau: 5 board, chest 6 agency, branch, lowboy, office 7 dresser 8 division 9 committee, furniture, suite part 10 chiffonier, commission, department, news center
part: 4 knob 6 drawer
__ bureau: 5 press 6 credit, travel
__ Bureau: 4 Farm 7 Weather
bureaucracy: 4 maze 7 red tape 8 city hall
bureaucrat: 7 officer 8 official
paper: 4 form 10 triplicate
Bureau of __: 5 Mines 7 Customs
Bureau of __ Affairs: 6 Indian
Bureau of __ Management: 4 Land
Bureau of __ Statistics: 5 Labor
Bureau of the __: 6 Budget, Census
burg: 4 city, town 6 hamlet 7 village 10 metropolis
burgee: 4 flag 6 banner 7 pennant
burgeon: 3 bud 4 gird, grow, rise, tone 5 bloat, bloom, build, shore, steel, swell, widen 6 anneal, beef up, dilate, expand, flower, harden, prop up, spread, spring, sprout, temper, thrive, tone up 7 augment, blossom, bolster, brace up, broaden, build up, develop, empower, enhance, enlarge, fortify, inflate, leaf out, shoot up, shore up, stiffen, toughen 8 buttress, energize, flourish, heighten, increase, indurate, lengthen, multiply, mushroom, put forth, shoot out, snowball, vegetate, vitalize 9 germinate, intensify, luxuriate, pullulate, reinforce 10 effloresce, invigorate, strengthen
burger: 4 meat 6 Big Mac 7 Whopper 8 fast food
partner: 3 pop 4 Coke 5 fries, Pepsi, shake 7 soda pop 9 milkshake
starter: 3 ham 5 chili 6 cheese
topper: 5 bacon, onion, Swiss 6 catsup, cheese, pickle, tomato 7 ketchup, lettuce, mustard 8 mushroom
Burger: 6 Warren 8 Hamilton
Burger, Hamilton: 2 DA
nemesis: 5 Mason
Burger King
rival: *see* restaurant chain
burgers, prepare: 5 grill
Burger, Warren: 5 judge 6 jurist 7 justice
Burgess: 6 Gelett 7 Anthony 8 Meredith
Burgess, Anthony: 6 writer 7 British
pseudonym: Kell
work: Any Old Iron
A Clockwork Orange
The Long Day Wanes
Burgess, Gelett: 6 writer
subject: Goops, Purple Cow
work: Are You a Bromide?
Burghoff, Gary: 5 actor
costar: 4 Alda, Farr
role: 5 Radar
show: 4 MASH
burglar: 4 yegg 5 crook, felon, thief 6 outlaw, robber 7 filcher, prowler, stealer 8 intruder, pilferer 9 purloiner
deterrent: 3 dog, grr 4 lock, safe 5 alarm, guard, vault 8 deadbolt, watchman
diamonds, to a ~: 3 ice
ender: 5 proof
need: 5 fence 7 lookout
potential ~: 5 caser
target: 4 loot, safe 7 jewelry 9 valuables
burglar __: 5 alarm
__ burglar: 3 cat
burglarize: 3 rob 4 loot 5 rifle, steal 6 invade, thieve 7 break in
burglary: 3 job 5 caper, crime, heist, theft 6 felony, holdup 7 break-in, larceny, robbery 8 filching, stealing, thievery 9 pilferage
burgle: 3 rob 5 rifle, steal 6 thieve 7 break in 9 knock over
burgoo: 4 stew
Burgoyne, John: 7 British, general
burgundy: 3 red 4 wine 5 color
color kin: *see* purple color
Burgundy: 3 vin 4 wine 5 pinot 6 region 8 province
kingdom: 5 Arles
locale: 6 France
region: 6 Bresse
river: 5 Saône
type of ~: 5 Mâcon 7 chablis
vessel: 3 vat 4 cask 5 cruet 6 carafe 7 pitcher 8 decanter
buried: 4 deep 6 hidden 8 immersed, overcome, ulterior 9 forgotten, unexposed 10 undivulged
burin: 4 tool 5 flint
Burke: 4 Jack, Paul 5 Delta 6 Billie, Edmund, Johnny
__ Burke: 6 Stoney
Burke, Billie: 7 actress
spouse: Flo Ziegfeld
Burke, Delta: 7 actress
spouse: Gerald McRaney

Burke, Jack: 6 golfer
Burke's Law (ABC drama)
cast: Gene Barry (Amos Burke)
Burkina Faso: 6 nation 7 country
money: 5 franc
neighbor: 4 Mali, Togo 5 Benin, Ghana, Niger 10 Ivory Coast
people: 5 Mossi 6 Senufo, Tuareg 7 Songhai
Burks, Ellis
sport: 8 baseball
burl: 4 knar, knot, node, slub 6 nodule
Burl: 4 Ives
burlap: 6 fabric 8 material
carrier: 4 sack
fiber: 4 hemp, jute
Burleigh: 6 Grimes
Burleson: 4 city, town
locale: 5 Texas
burlesque: 4 show, twit 5 farce, mimic, sneer, spoof 6 comedy, parody, satire 7 imitate, lampoon, mockery, satiric, takeoff 8 ridicule, satirize, travesty 9 dramatize, ludicrous, satirical 10 caricature, lampoonery, vaudeville
bit: 3 act 4 skit, turn
show: 5 revue 6 review
burley: 7 tobacco
Burlingame: 4 city, town
locale: 10 California
Burlington: 4 city, town
athletes: 10 Catamounts
locale: 7 Vermont
Burlington Zephyr: 5 train
burly: 3 big 5 bulky, plump, thick, tough 6 portly 7 hulking, sizable 8 bruising, sizeable 9 corpulent, filled-out 10 well-padded
see also brawny
__-burly: 5 hurly
Burma: 6 nation 7 country, Myanmar
bandit: 6 dacoit, dakoit
capital: 6 Yangon 7 Rangoon
export: 4 teak
former capital: 3 Ava
leader: 3 U Nu
measure: 3 lan
money: 3 pya 4 kyat
neighbor: 4 Laos 5 Assam, China, India 8 Thailand 10 Bangladesh
neighbor, once: 4 Siam
org.: 5 ASEAN
ox: 5 gayal
people: 4 Nosu
port: 6 Sittwe, Yangon 7 Rangoon
Burma __: 4 Road 5 Shave
Burma Road terminus: 6 Lashio
Burma Shave creation: 5 verse
Burmese: 3 cat 5 Asian, felid 6 feline
Burmese __: 3 cat 4 jade 5 glass
burn: 3 get 4 bake, bilk, bite, boil, char, cook, fume, gall, hurt, lick, pain, sear 5 anger, blaze, broil, cheat, flame, flare, light, parch, peeve, roast, scald, singe, smart, sting, toast, torch, use up, wound 6 chisel, fleece, ignite, injury, kindle, refute, reject, scorch, seethe, simmer 7 combust, deceive, defraud, smolder, swindle, two-time 8 enkindle, flimflam, hoodwink, irritate, overcook, smoulder, squander 9 carbonize, catch fire, cauterize, victimize

B U

10 incandesce, incinerate, run a game on
cause: 3 lye, sun 4 fire 5 stove 9 hot coffee
do a slow ~: 4 fume 6 seethe 7 smolder
for: 4 want 6 desire
(for): 4 long, pant 5 yearn
out: 4 jade, tire
partner: 5 crash, slash
rubber: 3 hie, rev, zip 4 bolt, dash, race, rush, zoom 5 hurry, speed 6 barrel, career, hasten, hustle, scurry 8 step on it 9 hotfoot it, make haste, shake a leg 10 accelerate
slightly: 4 char, sear 5 singe
slow ~: 5 anger, pique 6 temper 9 surliness 10 irritation
soother: 3 ice 4 aloe, balm 5 salve 8 vitamin E
starter: 3 sun 4 wind 5 heart
the midnight oil: 4 cram, pore 5 learn, study
treatment: 3 ice 4 aloe, balm 5 salve, sulfa 8 vitamin E
up: 3 ire, sap 5 anger, annoy, drain, trash, waste 6 nettle 7 deplete, incense, outrage 8 fool away, squander 9 dissipate
up the road: 4 race, rush, zoom 5 speed
with liquid: 5 scald
burn __: 3 bag, out 6 rubber
burn __ in one's pocket: 5 a hole
__ burn: 4 slow 5 flash 7 freezer
burnable: 9 flammable
Burn After Reading (2008 film)
cast: George Clooney, John Malkovich, Frances McDormand, Brad Pitt, Tilda Swinton
burned: 4 hurt 5 stung, taken 6 flambé, rooked 7 cheated, fleeced, injured, taken in, wounded 8 swindled 9 disabused
out: 4 worn 5 jaded, tired, weary 7 drained 9 exhausted
starter: 3 sun 4 wind
up: *see* angry
burned __ crisp: 3 to a
__-burned: 3 dad
burned-out shell: 4 hulk
burner: 6 gas log 7 furnace
Bunsen ~ nozzle: 6 gas jet
lab ~: 4 etna 6 Bunsen
on the back ~: 7 pending
place: 5 range, stove
put on the back ~: 5 table 6 shelve 7 suspend 8 postpone
starter: 4 barn, base 5 after
__ burner: 3 gas, oat, oil 4 back, base, lime, weed 5 front, Meker, pilot 6 Argand, Bunsen
Burnett: 7 Frances
Burnett, Carol: 10 comedienne
alma mater: 4 UCLA
Burnette: 5 Rocky 6 Johnny
Burney, Fanny: 6 writer 7 English
work: Evelina
__ Burnie: 4 Glen
burning: 3 hot, lit 4 dire, fire, live, sore 5 afire, aglow, blaze, eager, fiery, irate, itchy, smoky 6 ablaze, aflame, ardent, bright, fervid, heated, on fire, red-hot, torrid, urgent 7 caustic, crucial, excited, exigent, fervent, flaring, frantic, hurry-up, instant, intense, painful, zealous 8 critical, exigeant, feverish, frenzied, hopped up, in flames, kindling, pressing, sizzling, spirited, vehement, white-hot 9 fanatical, important, insistent, irritated, scorching 10 compelling, imperative, irritating, passionate, sweltering
braid: 4 wick
bush: 5 wahoo
combining form: 4 igni-
desire: 5 ardor
evidence of ~: 3 ash 5 coals, smoke 6 embers 7 cinders
malicious ~: 5 arson
start ~: 6 ignite
burning __: 4 bush, ghat 5 glass
Burning __: 4 Bush, Love 5 Heart 7 Bridges
Burning Bush
author: Louis Untermeyer
Burning Down the House (1983 song)
artist: Talking Heads
Burning Giraffe, The
artist: Salvador Dali
Burning Heart (1985 song)
artist: Survivor
Burning Love (1972 song)
artist: Elvis Presley
burnish: 3 rub 4 buff 5 gloss, scour, sheen, shine 6 luster, polish, smooth 7 furbish 8 brighten
burnished: 5 light, shiny 6 glassy, glossy 8 lustrous
burn one's __: 7 bridges
burnoose: 5 cloak
wearer: 4 Arab 7 Bedouin
burnout: 7 fatigue 10 exhaustion
cause of ~: 6 stress 8 overwork
Burns: 3 Ken 6 George, Robert
see also Scottish
Burns and Allen: 3 duo 4 pair, team
Burns, Frank: 5 major
series: 4 MASH
Burns, George: 5 actor 8 comedian
cigar: 4 prop
film: A Damsel in Distress (1937)
Going in Style (1979)
Oh, God! (1977)
The Sunshine Boys (1975, AA)
role: 3 God
spouse: Gracie Allen
Burnside: 6 Andrew
Burns, Robert: 4 poet 8 Scottish
work: Afton Water
Anna
Auld Lang Syne
The Banks o'Doon
Comin' Thro' the Rye
Duncan Gray
For A' That
The Holy Fair
John Anderson My Jo
A Red, Red Rose
Sweet Afton
Tam Glen
Tam o'Shanter
To a Louse
To a Mountain Daisy
To a Mouse
burnt
color: 5 umber 6 sienna
in cookery: 5 brulé 6 brulée
starter: 3 sun
up: *see* angry
burnt __: 4 lime 5 umber 6 almond, sienna
burnt __ crisp: 3 to a
burnt almond: 8 ice cream
alternative flavor: *see* ice cream flavor
burn the __ at both ends: 6 candle
burn the midnight __: 3 oil
Burnt Norton
poet: T.S. Eliot
burnt-offering spot: 5 altar
burnt-out: 5 jaded, spent, tired, weary 9 exhausted
Burnt Ship, A
author: John Donne
burn up the __: 4 road
burp: 5 belch, eruct 10 eructation
burp __: 3 gun
Burpee offering: 4 bulb, flat, root, seed, tree 5 plant 6 hybrid
burr: 4 husk 6 accent 7 seed pod, sticker
burr __: 3 cut 7 haircut
Burr: 5 Aaron 7 Raymond 9 Tillstrom
author: Gore Vidal
to Hamilton: 3 foe
burrito: 8 tortilla
cousin: 4 taco
filler: 4 beef 5 beans 6 cheese
burro: 3 ass 6 animal, brayer, donkey, equine 7 jackass
comment: 4 bray
go by ~: 4 ride
relative: *see* equine
Burroughs: 4 John 5 Edgar
successor: 6 Unisys
Burroughs, Edgar Rice: 6 writer
character: 3 ape 4 Jane 6 Tarzan
creation: Tarzan
Burroughs, John: 6 writer
friend: Whitman, Edison
work: Riverby
Burroughs, William S.: 6 writer
pseudonym: Lee
work: Naked Lunch
Nova Express
burrow: 3 den, dig 4 bore, grub, hole, lair, mine, root 5 delve, gouge, lodge, scoop 6 kennel, nestle, tunnel 7 snuggle 8 excavate, hideaway, scoop out 9 hollow out 10 excavation
burrowing rodent: 4 degu, jird 6 gerbil, gopher, rabbit 7 hamster, mole rat, visacha 8 tuco-tuco 9 groundhog, woodchuck 10 prairie dog
Burrows, Abe: 6 writer
Burr, Raymond: 5 actor
film: Godzilla... (1954)
Pitfall (1948)
Rear Window (1954)
TV: Ironside, Perry Mason
bursa: 3 sac 7 vesicle
bursar: 6 purser 7 cashier 9 treasurer 10 controller
boss: 4 prex, prez 5 prexy
burst: 3 pop, rip 4 bang, boom, gush, gust, open, shot, slam, torn 5 blast, blaze, crack, erupt, flash, go off, laugh, lunge, sally, salvo, smash, sound, spasm, spate, spirt, split, spurt, storm 6 blow up, shiver, splash, volley 7 barrage, explode, fly open, give way, implode, rupture, shatter, torrent 8 break out, detonate, eruption, fracture, fragment, mushroom, outbreak, outburst, puncture, splinter 9 break open, cannonade, come apart, discharge, explosion, fusillade, gush forth
artillery ~: 5 round, salvo
at the seams: 4 teem
forth: 3 bud 4 gush 5 erupt, issue 6 appear, emerge, sprout 7 leaf out 9 germinate
in: 5 barge, enter 9 interrupt
in on: 7 startle 8 surprise
of laughter: 4 gale, roar
of speed: 4 dash 5 spurt
of wind: 4 gust
out: 3 cry 7 exclaim
starter: 3 air, sun 4 down, star 5 cloud
with pride: 5 gloat, kvell, preen
bursting: 4 full, rife 7 teeming 8 thronged 9 chock-full
Burstyn, Ellen: 7 actress
Burt: 4 Ward 5 Young 7 Kennedy 8 Reynolds 9 Bacharach, Lancaster
Burton: 3 Tim 4 city, Lane, town 5 Edith, LeVar 6 Nelson 7 Richard, Richter 8 Cummings
locale: 8 Michigan
Burton, LeVar: 5 actor
TV: Roots, Star Trek: The Next Generation
Burton, Nelson: 6 bowler
milieu: 5 alley
org: 3 PBA
Burton, Richard: 3 Sir 7 British 8 explorer
Burton, Richard (actor): 5 Welsh
film: Alexander the Great (1956)
Anne of the Thousand Days (1969)
Becket (1964)
Cleopatra (1963)
The Desert Rats (1953)
The Longest Day (1962)
Look Back in Anger (1958)
My Cousin Rachel (1952)
The Night of the Iguana (1964)
Nineteen Eighty-Four (1984)
The Sandpiper (1965)
The Spy Who Came in From the Cold (1965)
The Taming of the Shrew (1967)
The V.I.P.s (1963)
Where Eagles Dare (1969)
Who's Afraid of Virginia Woolf? (1966)
spouse: Elizabeth Taylor
Burton, Tim: 8 director
film: Batman (1989)
Batman Returns (1992)
Beetlejuice (1988)
Charlie and the Chocolate Factory (2005)
Corpse Bride (2005)
Edward Scissorhands (1990)
Ed Wood (1994)
Mars Attacks! (1996)
Planet of the Apes (2001)
Sleepy Hollow (1999)
Sweeney Todd (2007)
Burton-upon-__: 5 Trent
Burundi: 6 nation 7 country
capital: 9 Bujumbura
it begins in ~: 4 Nile
language: 7 Kirundi

money: 5 franc
neighbor: 5 Congo 6 Rwanda 8 Tanzania
people: 4 Tusi 5 Rundi, Tussi, Tutsi 6 Watusi 7 Watutsi
bury: 4 hide, rout 5 cache, cover, embed, imbed, inter, outdo, plant, stash 6 engulf, ingulf, inhume, thrash 7 conceal, cover up, implant, repress, secrete, trounce 8 ensconce, enshroud, stow away, suppress 9 overpower, overwhelm
the hatchet: 6 make up, pardon 7 forgive 9 negotiate, reconcile
Bury my heart at Wounded Knee
originator: 5 Benét
Bury the Dead
author: Irwin Shaw
bus: 5 coach 6 jitney 7 vehicle 9 Greyhound, transport
alternative: 3 cab, car, jet 4 auto 5 plane, train 8 airplane
depot: 3 sta. 7 station 8 terminal
ender: 3 boy 4 load
garage: 4 barn
route: 4 line, loop
shuttle ~: 6 jitney
sign: 5 local 7 express
starter: 4 auto, mini, omni 5 motor
station info: 3 arr., ETA 5 sched. 8 schedule
take the ~: 4 ride 7 commute
ticket price: 4 fare
unit: 4 seat
bus ___: 3 bar, boy 4 girl, line 6 driver 7 station
___ bus: 6 school
Bus ___: 4 Stop
___ Bus: 5 Magic
Busa: 3 cow 4 bull 6 bovine, cattle
busboy burden: 4 tray
Busby: 8 Berkeley
Buscaglia, Leo: 5 Dr. Hug 6 writer
Buscemi, Steve: 5 actor
Busch: 3 Mae 5 Fritz, Niven 7 Charles
Busch, Charles: 6 writer
Busch, Fritz: 9 conductor
Busch Gardens city: 5 Tampa
Busch Stadium team: 3 St. L. 4 Rams 7 St. Louis
Busey, Gary: 5 actor
Busfield: 7 Timothy
bush: 4 tire 5 briar, hedge, plant, shrub, wilds 6 jungle 7 bramble, fatigue, guayule, logania, outback, thicket 8 justicia, woodland 9 backwater, backwoods 10 hinterland, wilderness
beat around the ~: 5 fence, hedge, skirt, stall, waver 6 ramble, waffle 9 hem and haw, pussyfoot
burning ~: 5 wahoo
combining form: 5 thamn- 6 thamno-
decorative ~: 4 rose 6 azalea 7 jasmine 8 camellia, gardenia
dweller: 6 Aussie 9 aborigine
ender: 4 buck 5 whack 6 master, ranger
protector: 3 bur 4 burr 5 briar, brier, spine, thorn 7 prickle
starter: 4 rose, salt, shad, snow 6 beauty, button, fetter, hobble, pepper 7 brittle, stagger, steeple
thorny ~: 7 bramble
bush ___: 3 hog, lot, pig, tit 4 baby, bean, coat 5 broom, pilot, poppy 6 clover, hammer, jacket, league, parole
___ bush: 5 sugar 6 calico 7 burning, flannel
Bush: 4 Kate 5 Laura 6 George 7 Barbara
bush baby: 7 primate
relative: *see* primate
bushbuck: 8 antelope
relative: *see* antelope
bushed: 4 beat, worn 5 all in, spent, tired, weary 6 dished, pooped 7 worn-out 8 dog-tired, tired out 9 bone-tired, exhausted 10 knocked out
bushel
Egyptian ~: 5 ardeb
fraction: 4 peck
Hebrew ~: 4 epha, omer 5 ephah
Bushel ___ Peck, A: 4 and a
bushels: 4 lots, many, tons 5 scads 6 hoards
bushes: 5 brush 9 shrubbery
beat the ~: 4 hunt, seek 6 search 7 rummage 9 track down
row of ~: 5 hedge
Bush, George: 3 Eli 9 president
adviser: 6 Sununu
alma mater: 4 Yale 7 Andover
birthplace: 4 Mass. 6 Milton
cabinet member: 4 Barr, Card, Dole, Kemp 5 Baker, Brady, Lujan 6 Cheney, Martin 7 Cavazos, Madigan, Skinner, Watkins, Yeutter 8 Sullivan
child: 3 Jeb 4 Doro, Neil 6 Marvin
former org.: 3 CIA
home: 5 Texas
middle name: 6 Walker 7 Herbert
opponent: 7 Clinton, Dukakis
parent: 7 Dorothy 8 Prescott
previous occupation: 6 oilman
veep: 6 Quayle
wife: 7 Barbara
word in a ~ quote: 4 lips, read
Bush, George W.: 3 Eli 5 Dubya 9 president
advisor: 4 Rice
alma mater: 4 Yale 7 Andover, Harvard
birthplace: 8 New Haven
cabinet member: 4 Chao, Rice, Snow 5 Evans, Gates, Paige, Peake, Ridge 6 Bodman, Mineta, Norton, O'Neill, Peters, Powell 7 Abraham, Jackson, Johanns, Leavitt, Mukasey, Paulson, Preston, Schafer, Veneman 8 Ashcroft, Chertoff, Gonzalez, Martinez, Principi, Rumsfeld, Thompson 9 Gutierrez, Nicholson, Spellings 10 Kempthorne
child: 5 Jenna 7 Barbara
degree: 3 MBA
home: 5 Texas 8 Crawford
middle name: 6 Walker
mother: 7 Barbara
opponent: 4 Gore 5 Kerry, Nader
veep: 6 Cheney
wife: 5 Laura
bushido: 4 code 8 Japanese
follower: 7 samurai
virtue: 5 honor 7 bravery 10 simplicity
Bush, Laura
maiden name: 5 Welch
bush-league: 5 dinky, lower, minor, small 6 lesser 10 inadequate, low-ranking
bushman: 9 aborigine
bushmaster: 5 snake 6 animal 7 reptile
relative: *see* snake
Bushmiller, Ernie: 10 cartoonist
creation: 5 Nancy
Bushnell: 5 David, Nolan
bushranger: 7 rustler
bushwa
see baloney
bushwhack: 4 trap 6 ambush, waylay 7 assault 8 surprise
bushy: 5 hairy, thick 6 shaggy 7 unshorn
hair: 3 mop 4 mane
mass: 3 tod
bushy-tailed: 5 furry
animal: 3 fox
bright-eyed and ~: 5 alert, fresh, perky, sunny 7 healthy 9 vivacious
business: 3 job 4 duty, firm, line, mart, role, shop, task, work 5 field, house, store, thing, topic, trade 6 affair, career, cartel, market, matter, métier, office, outfit 7 calling, company, concern, factory, mission, project, pursuit, service, traffic 8 commerce, dealings, function, goings-on, industry, lifework, monopoly, practice, province, vocation 9 patronage 10 employment, enterprise, happenings, livelihood, occupation, profession, walk of life
aka: 3 DBA
arrangement: 4 deal 8 contract
attire: 3 tie 4 suit
bloc: 6 cartel
card symbol: 4 logo
channel: 4 CNBC
collapse: 5 crash
concern: 4 cost, loss 6 profit, red ink 7 economy 8 expenses, overhead 9 operation
confab: 3 mtg. 4 conf., conv. 7 meeting 10 conference, convention
consideration: 4 cost 7 expense 8 overhead
degree: 3 BBA, MBA
division: 4 dept. 10 department
do ~: 3 buy 4 deal, fire, hire, sell, ship 5 trade, truck 6 employ, export, import 7 bargain, deliver, traffic 8 transact
document: 4 memo 6 report
do ~ for: 9 represent
doing ~: 4 open
do ~ with: 9 patronize
drum up ~: 4 hype 6 hustle 7 promote 9 advertise
execs: 3 mgt. 4 mgmt. 10 management
expansion: 4 boom
for short: 3 inc., ltd., org. 4 assn. 5 estab.
funny ~: 5 antic, caper, humor, trick 6 deceit, levity 7 hijinks 8 mischief, trickery
get down to ~: 5 begin, start 7 shape up
give the ~ to: 3 bug, nag, rag 4 haze, ride 5 harry, hound, scold 6 berate, harass, hassle, heckle, needle, plague 7 chew out, upbraid 8 browbeat 14 put on the carpet
go out of ~: 4 fail, fold 6 fold up
letter notation: 3 enc. 4 attn., SASE
loss: 4 bath 7 reverse 8 reversal
magazine: 3 Inc. 6 Forbes 7 Barron's, Fortune
meaning ~: 7 serious 8 resolute 10 determined
minding other's ~: 4 nosy 5 nosey 6 prying, snoopy 7 curious, gossipy
misbehavior: 5 fraud
monkey ~: 6 antics
officer: 6 bursar 7 trustee 9 president
order of ~: 6 agenda 7 program 8 schedule
out of ~: 5 kaput 6 closed 8 bankrupt
partner, often: 3 son
phone: 3 ext. 9 extension
place of ~: 4 mall, mill, shop 5 kiosk, stall, store 6 office 7 factory 8 boutique
record: 5 check 7 receipt
records check: 5 audit
reduction of ~ activity: 9 downswing, recession 10 depression
risky ~: 4 dare, spec 5 wager 6 hazard
school: 4 GMAT
starter: 4 agri
subject: 4 econ. 7 finance 9 economics
subordinate: 3 sec. 4 asst., sec'y 9 assistant, secretary
suit shade: 4 blue, gray, grey, navy
takeover: 3 LBO 6 buyout
VIP: 3 CEO, CFO, mgr. 4 exec 5 owner
business ___: 3 end 4 card, case, park, suit 5 agent, class, cycle, reply 7 affairs, college, English, machine
___ business: 3 big, rag 4 mean, show 5 funny, stage 6 monkey
___ business!: 5 I mean
___ Business: 3 Big 5 Risky 6 Family, Monkey
business as ___: 5 usual
___ Business Bureau: 6 Better
business letter
abbr.: 3 att., enc. 4 attn.
encl.: 4 SASE
word: 3 sir 4 sirs 6 madame 9 gentlemen
businesslike: 4 tidy 5 sober, staid 6 solemn, somber 7 deadpan, orderly, serious 8 methodic 9 humorless, practical, pragmatic, realistic, unamusing 10 no-nonsense, unhumorous
Business Man, The
author: Edgar Allan Poe
business-related: 8 economic
Business Week: 3 mag 8 magazine
rival: 6 Forbes 7 Barron's, Fortune
buskin: 4 boot, shoe 5 drama 6 acting 7 tragedy 8 footwear
busman's ___: 7 holiday

Busman's Honeymoon
  author: Dorothy Sayers
Buson: 4 poet 8 Japanese
  genre: 5 haiku
Busoni: 9 Ferruccio
buss: 4 kiss 5 smack 6 smooch 8 osculate 10 osculation
Bus Stop: 4 film, play
  author: William Inge
  cast: Marilyn Monroe, Don Murray, Arthur O'Connell
  director: Joshua Logan
Bus Stop (1966 song)
  artist: Hollies
bust: 3 dud, nab 4 bomb, fail, flop, fold, lose, loss, raid, ruin, slap, slip, tame, tear, trip 5 break, catch, flunk, pinch, run in, seize, spree 6 arrest, blow it, collar, defeat, demote, detain, falter, fiasco, fold up, mishap, pick up, pull in, reduce, statue, turkey 7 blunder, capture, debacle, failure, fizzler, founder, go under, go wrong, jailing, misstep, seizure, stumble, washout 8 bring low, disaster, downfall, fall flat, flounder, fracture, lay an egg 9 apprehend, downgrade, recession, sculpture, strike out 10 depression, impoverish, nonsuccess
  go ~: 4 fail, fold
  in: 5 barge, enter 9 interrupt
  locale: 5 niche 6 alcove 8 pedestal
  material: 6 marble
  open: 3 pry 5 force, jimmy 7 break in
  opposite: 4 boom
  out: 6 escape
  participant: 4 narc, nark 5 narco
  Roman ~: 4 herm
__ bust: 4 baby, beer
Busta: 6 Rhymes
Bust a Move (1989 song)
  artist: Young MC
bustard: 4 bird
Busta Rhymes
  song: Dangerous (1998)
    Turn It Up (1998)
    What's It Gonna Be?! (1999)
    Woo-Hah!! Got You All in Check (1996)
busted: 4 tame 5 broke, kaput, ran in, skint 6 broken 8 bankrupt, deprived, finished, indigent 9 destitute, insolvent, penniless 10 out of order
  party: 4 perp
  up: 4 hurt 7 damaged, injured
Busted (1963 song)
  artist: Ray Charles
buster: 3 bud, mac 5 kiddo
  bronco ~: 6 cowboy 7 cowpoke 8 wrangler
  clod ~: 3 hoe
  starter: 3 sod 4 gang 5 block, crime, trust 6 bronco
__ buster: 5 union
Buster: 6 Crabbe, Keaton
Buster Brown: 3 boy 4 toon 6 collar
  dog: 4 Tige
__ Bus, The: 4 Last 5 Lilac 7 Wayward
bustier: 3 top 5 shirt
Bustin' Loose (1981 film)
  cast: Richard Pryor, Cicely Tyson
bustle: 3 ado, hum, run, zip 4 dash, fuss, move, rush, stir, teem, to-do, whir 5 furor, haste, hoo-ha, hurry, press, swirl, whirr 6 action, clamor, flurry, hasten, hoopla, hubbub, hustle, lather, scurry, tumult, uproar 7 clutter, ferment, mad rush, scamper, turmoil 8 activity, brouhaha, disorder, foofaraw, scramble 9 commotion, confusion 10 excitement, get hopping, hullabaloo
bustling: 4 busy, spry 5 alive, astir, brisk, perky 6 active, at work, lively 7 dynamic, working 8 animated 9 assiduous, energetic, sprightly
busts: 3 art 9 sculpture
busy: 4 at it, nosy, spry 5 abuzz, astir, brisk, in use, nosey, perky 6 active, at work, engage, hectic, lively, on duty, ornate, prying, snoopy, snowed, tied up 7 crowded, dynamic, engaged, humming, immerse, on the go, popping, swamped, working 8 animated, bustling, employed, immersed, laboring, occupied, studious 9 assiduous, energetic, engrossed, officious, on the move, sprightly 10 in a meeting, in an uproar, meddlesome, overloaded
  act ~: 4 toil, work 5 hurry, slave 6 bustle, hustle, scurry
  as a phone: 5 in use
  bee: 7 hustler 8 live wire
  ender: 4 body, work
  extremely ~: 4 ahum, at it 7 humming 8 occupied 10 overworked
  get ~: 4 move 5 begin, start 6 fall to, jump in, tackle 7 hop to it, pitch in 8 get going 9 take steps 10 buckle down
  insect: 3 ant, bee
  keep ~: 5 tie up 6 employ, engage, occupy
  not ~: 4 free, idle, slow 5 slack
  period: 4 rush
  place: 3 zoo 4 hive 6 hotbed
  very ~ schedule: 5 whirl
busy __: 3 bee 6 signal
busy as a __: 3 bee 6 beaver
busybody: 3 hen 5 snoop 6 gossip 7 meddler, snooper, tattler 8 fat mouth, quidnunc 9 buttinsky 10 meddlesome, Nosy Parker, rubberneck, taleteller, tattletale, yenta. prier
  be a ~: 3 pry 6 meddle
  like a ~: 4 nosy 5 nosey 6 snoopy 7 curious 8 meddling
busy old fool, Donne's: 3 sun
but: 3 bar, yet 4 just, only, save 5 if not 6 and yet, except, merely, singly, solely, though, unless 7 barring, however, save for 9 other than 10 except that, leaving out, regardless
  in Spanish: 3 más
but __: 3 yet
__ but: 3 all
...but __ has her way: 5 woman
...but __ itself: 4 fear
But __ art?: 4 is it
But __ buts: 4 me no
But __ for Me: 3 Not
But __ me, give me liberty...: 5 as for
But __ on forever: 3 I go
butane: 3 gas 4 fuel
  form of ~: 3 LPG 5 LP gas
butch: 4 coif 6 hairdo 7 haircut
Butch: 7 Cassidy, Patrick
Butch Cassidy and the Sundance Kid (1969 film)
  cast: Paul Newman, Robert Redford, Katharine Ross
  director: George Roy Hill
butcher: 4 ruin 5 wreck 7 louse up 8 bollix up
  ender: 4 bird
  implement: 3 saw
  offering: 4 beef, chop, lamb, meat, pork, veal 5 joint, links, roast, shank, steak, T-bone, tripe 6 cutlet, mutton, rib eye 7 sausage, sirloin
  scraps: 5 offal
  shop fixture: 5 scale 6 cooler
  unit: 2 lb. 5 pound
butcher __: 4 shop 5 block, knife, linen, paper, rayon
Butcher Boy, The (1999 film)
  cast: Stephen Rea
butcher, the __, the: 5 baker
Butch Van __ Kolff: 5 Breda
Butenandt, Adolf: 7 chemist 8 Nobelist
buteo: 4 bird
But Gentlemen Marry Brunettes
  author: Anita Loos
__ but goodies: 6 oldies
...but I know what __: 5 I like
__ but known!: 4 Had I
Butkus, Dick: 7 analyst 10 linebacker
  sport: 8 football
butler: 3 man 4 male 5 Lurch, valet 6 Alfred, flunky, Jeeves 7 flunkey 9 major-domo 10 manservant
  Batman ~: 6 Alfred
  sitcom ~: 5 Lurch
  teammate: 4 chef, cook, maid 7 footman
butler __, The: 5 did it
__ butler: 6 silent
Butler: 4 Daws 5 Brett, David, Jerry 6 Gerard, Murray, Samuel 7 Octavia 9 Gable role
Butler, Octavia: 6 writer
Butler, Rhett
  love: Scarlett O'Hara
butler's __: 4 tray 5 table 6 pantry
Butler, Samuel: 4 poet 6 writer 7 British
  work: Erewhon
    Hudibras
    The Way of All Flesh
__ Butler Yeats: 7 William
__, but no cigar: 5 Close
But Not for Me
  composer: George Gershwin
__ but not heard: 4 seen
__ but not least: 4 last
but only God can __ tree: 5 make a
buts: 10 objections
  no ifs, ands or ~: 6 really 7 exactly 9 precisely 10 absolutely, definitely, positively
butt: 3 end, hit, ram, sap, tip 4 base, cask, dupe, poke, rear, stub 5 chump, patsy, sport, stump 6 pigeon, sucker, target, thrust, victim 7 fall guy, project, remnant, run into 8 easy mark 9 extremity, posterior, scapegoat
  against: 5 touch 6 adjoin 8 neighbor
  in: 3 pry 4 nose 6 jump in, kibitz, meddle, tamper 7 intrude, obtrude 8 trespass 9 intercede, interfere, interpose, interrupt, intervene
  out: 7 project 8 protrude
butt __: 3 end 4 weld 5 hinge, joint, plate, shaft 6 chisel, stroke
butte
  form a ~: 5 erode
  kin: 4 mesa 7 plateau
Butte: 4 city, town
  city near ~: 6 Helena
  locale: 7 Montana
butter: 3 jam, ram 4 goat 6 spread 9 preserves
  bread and ~: 6 living 7 aliment 10 livelihood
  container: 3 tub 5 crock
  ender: 3 bur, cup, fat, fly, nut 4 ball, fish, milk, weed, wort 6 scotch 7 fingers
  holder: 3 tub 6 firkin
  Indian ~: 4 ghee
  like ~: 6 creamy, smooth
  maker: 5 churn, dairy
  rating: 6 grade A
  spreader: 5 knife
  substitute: 4 oleo 9 margarine
  substitute, in Britain: 5 marge
  unit: 3 pat 5 pound
  up: 3 woo 4 coax 6 cajole 7 flatter, lay it on, wheedle 8 blandish, fawn over, kowtow to 9 get next to, shine up to 10 compliment
butter __: 4 bean, clam, tree 5 knife, sauce 6 cookie, muslin 7 brickle
__ butter: 4 shea 5 apple, black, brown, cacao, cocoa, drawn, peach 6 mowrah, peanut 7 coconut, kneaded
__ Butter: 3 Hot
butter-and-__ man: 3 egg
Butter and Egg Man, The
  author: George S. Kaufman
Butter Battle Book, The
  author: Dr. Seuss
butter bean: 4 lima
buttercup: 5 akene, plant 6 achene, flower
buttercup __: 6 squash
__ buttercup: 4 tall 7 Bermuda, bulbous
__ buttered rum: 3 hot
Butterfield 8: 4 film 5 novel
  author: John O'Hara
  cast: Eddie Fisher, Laurence Harvey, Elizabeth Taylor
  director: Daniel Mann
Butterfinger: 3 bar 5 candy 8 candy bar 9 chocolate
  alternative: *see* candy brand
butterfingered: 5 inept, unapt 6 clumsy 8 lubberly 10 unskillful
butterfingers: 2 ox 3 oaf 4 clod, dolt, lout 5 klutz 6 lubber, lummox 7 bungler
  cry: 4 oops
Butterflies Are Free (1972 film)
  cast: Edward Albert, Goldie Hawn, Eileen Heckart
butterflies in the stomach: 6 nerves
butterfly: 3 bug 5 satyr 6 insect, stroke 7 monarch

catcher: 3 net
cousin: 4 moth
do the ~: 4 swim
emulate a ~: 4 flit
kin: 5 crawl 9 dog paddle 10 backstroke, sidestroke 12 breaststroke
social ~: 5 mixer
stage: 4 pupa 5 larva, pupae 6 cocoon
valve: 6 damper
butterfly __: 3 net, nut, pea 4 bomb, bush, roof, weed 5 chair, table, valve, wedge 6 damper, effect, flower, orchid 7 closure
__ butterfly: 3 owl, sea 4 leaf 5 satyr, zebra 6 sulfur 7 alfalfa, cabbage, emperor, monarch, thistle, troilus
Butterfly: 7 McQueen
__ Butterfly: 4 Iron 6 Madama, Madame 7 Elusive
butterfly-bee
analogist: 3 Ali
buttermilk: 8 beverage
make ~: 5 churn
Buttermilk: 5 horse 6 equine
rider: Dale Evans
__ Buttermilk Sky: 3 Ole
butternut: 4 tree 5 brown 6 squash
color kin: *see* brown color
butter pecan: 8 ice cream
alternative: *see* ice cream flavor
butterscotch: 5 candy 8 ice cream 9 sweetmeat
alternative: *see* ice cream flavor
Butterworth: 3 Mrs. 7 Charles
Butterworth's, Mrs.: 5 syrup
rival: 4 Karo 8 Log Cabin
buttery: 4 oily 6 creamy, smooth 9 adulatory 10 lubricious
__ but the Best: 7 Nothing
__ but the brave...: 4 None
__ But the Lonely Heart: 4 None
But there is __ in Mudville: 5 no joy
But thy __ summer shall not fade: 7 eternal
buttinsky: 4 pest 5 snoop 7 meddler 8 busybody 10 Nosy Parker
__ but to do...: 6 theirs
button: 4 stud 5 close 6 fasten, switch 8 fastener, mushroom
alternative: 4 snap 6 Velcro, zipper
belly ~: 5 navel 9 umbilicus
down: 6 secure 7 specify 8 identify 9 designate 10 categorize, consummate
ender: 4 ball, bush, hole, hook, mold, wood
material: 4 bone 5 nacre 7 plastic
neat as a ~: 4 tidy 7 orderly
one's lip: 5 quiet 6 clam up, shut up
panic ~: 5 alarm
remote ~: 5 reset
replace a ~: 3 sew 5 sew on
ridge: 4 nurl 5 knurl
right on the ~: 5 exact, right, sharp 7 correct 8 accurate
starter: 4 push 5 belly
up: 4 bolt, lock, seal, shut 5 close, latch 6 fasten, secure 7 seal off
word: 4 push 5 press
button __: 3 ear, man 5 quail
button-__ shirt: 4 down
__ button: 3 hot 4 cuff, hold, hunt, push, turn 5 belly, egads, on the, panic 6 collar 7 Spanish
Button: 4 Dick 8 Gwinnett
buttonbush: 5 plant 6 flower
Button, Dick: 6 skater 7 analyst
button-down: 5 shirt, yuppy 6 square, yuppie
buttoned up: 4 done 5 quiet 6 silent 9 secretive 10 unspeaking
buttonhole: 4 slit 5 delay, press 6 accost, detain, hold up
button one's __: 3 lip
buttons
popping one's ~: 5 proud
push the ~: 7 control
__ Button Shoes: 4 High
Buttons, Red: 5 actor 8 comedian
film: Sayonara (1957, AA)
buttonwood: 4 tree 8 sycamore
Buttram: 3 Pat
buttress: 4 gird, hold, pier, prop, stay, tone 5 brace, build, shore, steel 6 anneal, beef up, column, harden, prop up, temper, tone up, uphold 7 bolster, bulwark, burgeon, defense, develop, empower, enhance, fortify, shore up, stiffen, support, sustain, thicken, toughen 8 bourgeon, energize, indurate, mainstay, vitalize 9 intensify, reinforce, stabilize, stanchion, undergird 10 invigorate, strengthen, supplement
__ buttress: 6 flying
__ but wiser: 5 older
__ but world enough...: 5 Had we
Butz: 4 Earl
buxom: 5 plump, pudgy 6 zaftig, zoftig 9 filled-out 10 Rubenesque
buy: 3 get, own 4 deal, shop, take 5 bribe, order, spend, steal, value, yield 6 accept, deal in, obtain, pay for, pick up, secure 7 acquire, bargain, believe, corrupt, fall for, procure, shop for, swallow 8 closeout, invest in, purchase, transact 9 subscribe 10 investment
alternative: 4 rent 5 lease 6 borrow 7 charter
opposite: 4 sell
time: 5 delay, stall, table 6 put off 8 postpone
buy __: 3 off, out 4 boat, into, time
buy __ in a poke: 4 a pig
__ Buy: 4 Best
buyback: 6 assent, patent 8 discount, giveback, rollback, yielding 9 admission, agreement, allowance, privilege, surrender 10 acceptance, adjustment, compliance, compromise, concession, confession, indulgence, permission
buyer: 5 owner, payer, taker 6 client, emptor, patron, vendee 7 end user 8 consumer, customer
bonanza: 4 sale 7 auction 9 clearance
bonus: 5 no tax 6 coupon, rebate
caution: 4 as is 6 beware
concern: 5 price 8 warranty 9 guarantee
find a ~: 4 push, sell 5 foist 7 promote 9 advertise
proposal: 3 bid 5 offer
request: 8 charge it
round ~ phrase: 4 on me
buyers: 6 public 9 clientele, consumers
buyer's __: 6 market
buying: 9 ownership, patronage
and selling: 5 trade 7 traffic 8 business, commerce, dealings, exchange, industry 9 patronage
shop without ~: 6 browse
buying __: 5 power
buy low, sell __: 4 high
__ Buy Me Love: 4 Can't
buy on __: 4 spec
buyout: 4 deal 8 takeover
Buz: 6 Sawyer
buzz: 3 hum, tip, yak 4 coif, kick, ring, talk, whir, whiz, zoom 5 drone, noise, phone, rumor, sound, whirr 6 clamor, gossip, hoopla, murmur, report, tipoff 7 chatter, hearsay, whisper 8 pleasure 9 grapevine, telephone 10 excitement
ender: 4 word
off: 4 scat, shoo 5 scram 6 begone, get out 10 go fly a kite
buzz __: 3 off, saw, wig 4 bomb
Buzz: 5 Kulik 6 Aldrin 8 Clifford
capsule-mate: 4 Neil
buzzard: 4 bird 5 buteo
honey ~: 4 pern
__ buzzard: 5 honey 6 turkey
Buzzard's __: 3 Bay
buzz-cut opposite: 4 Afro
buzzed: 4 high 5 tight, tipsy
buzzer: 3 bee, fly 5 alarm 6 cicada 8 doorbell
__ buzzer: 3 joy
Buzzi: 4 Ruth
buzzing: 4 ahum, go-go, talk 5 astir, noise 6 aswarm, lively, murmur
about: 4 stir, to-do
sound: 3 hum 4 zoom 5 drone
__ B. Vance: 8 Courtney
BVDs: 6 briefs, shorts 7 jockeys 9 underwear
rival: 5 Hanes 6 Jockey
B-vitamin source: 4 meat 5 yeast
__ B. Wallis: 3 Hal
bwana: 3 sir 4 boss 6 hunter, master
expedition: 6 safari
helper: 6 bearer
B'way
see Broadway
B.W.I. part: 4 West 6 Indies 7 British
by: 3 per, via 4 as of, away, near, over, past 5 along, aside 6 at hand, before, beside, beyond, nearby, next to 7 close to, through 9 abreast of, alongside, to one side
any chance: 4 ever
itself: 4 lone, solo 5 alone, per se 6 singly 8 solitary
prefix: 4 para-
by __: 3 far, gum 4 half, hand, Jove, rote 5 a hair, a mile, and by, golly, heart, the by, turns, way of 6 chance, cracky, rights 7 degrees, request
by __ and bounds: 5 leaps
by __ and starts: 4 fits
by __ means: 3 all, any
by __ of: 3 way 4 dint 5 means 6 reason, virtue
by __ or by crook: 4 hook
by __ shot: 5 a long
by-__: 4 blow, line, name, pass, path, play, plot, road, talk, work 6 bidder, street 7 product
by-__-leave: 4 your
__ by: 3 get, lay, lie, put, set 4 come, drop, stop 5 abide, by and, by the, stand, swear, swing 6 squeak 7 squeeze
__-by: 4 blow 5 close
By __: 4 Jove 7 Jupiter
by a __: 4 hair
by a __ shot: 4 long
by all means: 4 sure 9 no problem
see also of course
__ by an Angel: 7 Touched
by and __: 5 large
by any __: 5 means
__ by any other name...: 5 a rose
Byatt, A.S.: 6 writer 7 British
sister: Drabble
work: Babel Tower
The Biographer's Tale
The Game
Possession
The Shadow of a Sun
Still Life
bye: 4 pass, ta-ta 5 aloha, later, see ya 6 see you, so long 7 goodbye 8 au revoir, farewell, sayonara
__-bye: 4 good 5 beddy, rock-a
__ by ear: 4 play
__ by east: 5 north, south
bye-bye: 4 ta-ta 5 adieu, aloha, later, see ya 6 so long 8 farewell
in French: 5 adieu 8 au revoir
in Hawaiian: 5 aloha
in Italian: 4 ciao
in Japanese: 8 sayonara
in Latin: 3 ave 4 vale
in Portuguese: 5 adeus
in Spanish: 5 adios
make ~: 4 wave
Bye Bye Birdie (1960 musical)
composer: Lee Adams, Charles Strouse
Bye Bye Birdie (1963 film)
cast: Ann-Margret, Janet Leigh, Paul Lynde, Maureen Stapleton, Dick Van Dyke
director: George Sidney
role: 3 Kim 5 Rosie
song: 4 Kids
Bye Bye Bye
artist: 'Nsync
Bye Bye Love (1957 song)
artist: Everly Brothers
Bye Bye, Love (1995 film)
cast: Janeane Garofalo, Matthew Modine, Randy Quaid, Paul Reiser
Byelorussia once: 3 SSR
__ by fire: 5 trial
byform: 7 variant
__-by-four: 3 two
__ By Golly, Wow: 6 Betcha
bygone: 3 old 4 late, lost, once, over, past 5 dated, of old, olden, passé 6 former, of yore 7 ancient, archaic, defunct, extinct, old-time, one-time, quondam 8 obsolete, outmoded, out of use, previous, vanished 9 erstwhile, forgotten, grievance, out-of-date 10 back-number
bygones
let ~ be bygones: 5 let go 6 excuse, forget, pardon 7 forgive 8 overlook, play past
By gosh!: 3 wow 4 egad 5 egads
Byington, Spring: 7 actress
TV: December Bride
By Jove!: 4 egad, I say 5 egads
__ by jowl: 5 cheek

B Y

By Jupiter: 7 musical
composer: Lorenz Hart, Richard Rodgers
__ by jury: 5 trial
by land __: 5 or sea
__ by land...: 5 One if
bylaw: 3 act **4** bill, code, fiat, rule **5** canon, edict, tenet **7** mandate, measure, precept, statute **9** enactment, guideline, ordinance **10** observance, regulation
by leaps and __: 6 bounds
byline: 6 credit
name: 6 author, editor, writer
By Love Possessed
author: James Gould Cozzens
__ by Me: 5 Stand
__ by Myself: 3 All
byname: 6 handle **8** cognomen
Byner: 4 John
Bynes: 6 Amanda
__-by-night: 3 fly
by no __: 5 means
__ by north: 4 east, west
__ by Northwest: 5 North
BYOB part: 3 own **4** beer, your **5** booze, bring **6** bottle
__ by one's guns: 5 stand, stick
__ by one's wits: 4 live
bypass: 4 duck, jump, omit, shun, skip **5** avoid, dodge, evade, shirk, shunt, skirt **6** detour, eschew, ignore **7** abstain, neglect, rule out, shy from **8** flee from, go around, sidestep **9** get around, runaround **10** circumvent, work around
bypath: 4 lane, road, walk **6** detour
byproduct: 6 result **7** product, spinoff **8** offshoot **9** outgrowth **10** derivative
Byrd: 6 Donald, Robert **7** Charlie, Richard
Byrd, Charlie: 9 guitarist
genre: 4 jazz
__ Byrd Land: 5 Marie
Byrd, Richard: 8 explorer
fox terrier: 5 Igloo
work: Alone
Byrds
song: Mr. Tambourine Man (1965) Turn! Turn! Turn! (1965)
byre: 4 shed **7** cowshed
Byrne: 4 Rose
Byrne, Gabriel: 5 actor
spouse: Ellen Barkin
Byrnes, Edd: 5 actor
TV role: 6 Kookie
byroad: 4 lane **8** short cut
Byron: 5 Allen, White **6** Haskin, Nelson **7** British **9** MacGregor
Byron, Lord: 4 poet **7** British
contemporary: 5 Keats **7** Shelley
daughter: 3 Ada
homeland: England
work: Beppo
Cain
Childe Harold's Pilgrimage
Don Juan
Hours of Idleness
Lara
Manfred
Parisina
The Prisoner of Chillon
She Walks in Beauty
__ by south: 4 east, west
__ Bysshe Shelley: 5 Percy
bystander: 7 witness **8** onlooker **9** spectator **10** eyewitness
__ by Starlight: 6 Stella
__ by storm: 4 take
bytalk: 8 chitchat
byte
part: 3 bit
starter: 4 giga, mega, tera
transmitter: 5 modem
__ by Temptation: 3 Def
bytes
1024 ~: 4 one K
what ~ measure: 6 memory
by that fact in Latin: 6 eo ipso
by the __: 3 way **7** numbers
by the __ of one's pants: 4 seat
by the __ of one's teeth: 4 skin
by the __ token: 4 same
__ by the bell: 5 saved
by-the-book: 5 rigid, stern **8** exacting
__ by the Dozen: 7 Cheaper
by the grace of God in Latin: 9 Dei gratia
By the Light of the Silvery __: **4** Moon
__ by the nose: 4 lead
By the Rivers of Babylon
author: Nelson DeMille
by the same __: 5 token
__-by-the-Sea: 6 Carmel
By the Time I Get to Phoenix (1967 song)
artist: Glen Campbell
composer: Jimmy Webb
By the Waters of Babylon
author: Emma Lazarus
by the way in French: 9 en passant
__ by the wayside: 4 fall
BYU
church: 3 LDS
conference: 3 WAC
locale: 4 Utah **5** Provo
rival: 4 UTEP
byway: 4 lane, path, road, walk **5** route, trail **6** avenue, street **8** side road
__ by west: 5 north, south
__-by-wire: 3 fly
byword: 3 saw **5** adage, axiom, gnome, maxim, motto **6** dictum, phrase, saying, slogan **7** precept, proverb **8** aphorism **9** battle cry
by-your-__: 5 leave
__ By Your Man: 5 Stand
Byzantine: 7 complex **8** involved **9** entangled, intricate
coin: 6 besant, bezant **7** bezzant
division: 5 thema
empress: 3 Zoe **5** Irene **8** Theodora
image: 4 icon, ikon **5** eikon
ruler: 6 exarch **7** emperor, empress
Byzantine __: 4 rite **5** chant **6** Church, Empire
Byzantium
author: William Butler Yeats

C: 3 key, pos., vit. 4 clef, elem., mark, note 5 grade, width 6 carbon, letter 7 vitamin
6 for ~: 4 at. no.
almost ~: 5 D plus
and W: 5 music
equivalent: 6 B-sharp
get a ~: 4 pass
in phonetic alphabet: 7 Charlie
major relative: 6 A minor
measure: 3 deg. 6 degree
vitamin ~: 4 acid
vitamin ~ source: 6 citrus
C __: 3 in C 4 and W, clef, star 6 ration, supply 7 battery, horizon
C __ cat: 4 as in
C'__ la vie!: 3 est
C-__: 4 axes, axis, bias, note, SPAN 5 clamp 6 scroll
C. __ Koop: 7 Everett
__ C: 3 C in, Mel 6 middle 7 vitamin
__ C.: 3 K. of
'C' __ Corpse: 5 Is for
C2H4: 6 ethene
C2H5OH: 3 alc. 7 alcohol
C2H6: 6 ethane 8 dimethyl
C3H5N3O9: 5 nitro
C-3P0: 5 droid, robot
C4H8: 6 alkene
Ca: 4 elem. 7 calcium, element
20 for ~: 4 at. no.
CA
clock setting: 3 PDT, PST
see also California
C.A.
country: 4 Guat., Hond.
see also Central America
Caan: 5 James, Scott
Caan, James: 5 actor
film: Cinderella Liberty (1973)
Countdown (1968)
El Dorado (1967)
Eraser (1996)
For the Boys (1991)
Gardens of Stone (1987)
The Godfather (1972)
Hide in Plain Sight (1980)
Honeymoon in Vegas (1992)
Misery (1990)
Rollerball (1975)
Slither (1973)
Thief (1981)
TV: Las Vegas
cab: 4 hack, taxi 6 hansom, jitney 7 taxicab, vehicle 9 transport 10 conveyance
alternative: 2 el 3 bus 5 train
clock: 5 meter
cost: 4 fare
ender: 3 man, men 5 stand 6 driver
go by ~: 4 ride
horse-drawn ~: 6 hansom
illicit ~: 5 gypsy
of Asia: 6 gharri, gharry
signal a ~: 4 hail
starter: 4 pedi, taxi
cab __: 6 driver
__ cab: 5 gypsy 6 hansom, livery
Cab: 8 Calloway
cabal: 3 mob 4 ring 5 junta, junto, party 6 clique, scheme 7 collude, coterie, faction, in-group 8 intrigue, plotters, schemers 10 conspiracy
cabala: 6 secret 7 arcanum 9 esoterics, mysticism, occultism
Jewish ~ work: 5 zohar
cabalistic: 6 arcane, occult 8 oracular
caballero: 6 Latino 9 gentleman
cabana: 3 hut 5 house 7 cottage 8 bungalow 9 bathhouse
boy offering: 5 towel
cabaret: 5 boîte 6 bistro, eatery 9 nightclub, nightspot 10 supper club
group: 4 band 5 combo
number: 4 song, tune
cabaret __: 3 tax
Cabaret (1972 film)
cast: Joel Grey, Liza Minnelli, Michael York
composer: Fred Ebb, John Kander
director: Bob Fosse
role: 5 emcee
setting: 6 Berlin, Kit-Kat 7 Germany
cabasa: 6 shaker 10 percussion
origin: 6 Brazil
cabbage: 4 kale 6 veggie 9 vegetable
color: 5 green
cousin: 4 kail, kale 5 cress
dish: 4 slaw
field: 5 patch
in French: 4 chou
skunk ~ family: 4 arum
unit: 4 head
see also moolah
__ cabbage: 3 red, sea 4 palm, stem 5 Savoy, skunk, swamp 6 celery, turnip 7 Chinese, stuffed
cabbagehead
see ninny
Cabbage Patch Kids: 5 craze, dolls
company: 6 Coleco
cabbie: 4 hack 6 driver 9 chauffeur 10 taxi driver
credential: 3 lic. 7 license
income: 3 tip 4 fare
invite: 5 hop in
Cabell: 4 Enos
Cabernet: 3 red 4 wine 5 grape
origin: 6 France
relative: ***see*** wine
caber tosser: 4 Scot
cabin: 3 hut 4 home, room 5 abode, berth, bower, house, hutch, lodge, shack 6 chalet, shanty 7 cottage, lodging, retreat 8 dwelling, lodgment, log house, quarters 9 stateroom
cruiser: 4 boat 5 yacht
material: 3 log
wood: 4 pine
cabin __: 3 boy 4 deck, hook 5 class, court, fever 7 cruiser
__ cabin: 3 log
Cabin __ Sky: 5 in the
cabinet: 4 wine 5 board, chest, hutch, white 6 closet, locker 7 council, dresser 8 advisors, cupboard 9 committee, furniture 10 brain trust, counselors, executives
department: 3 Agr., DoD, HUD, Int. 4 Educ. 5 Labor, State, Treas. 6 Energy 7 Defense, Justice 8 Interior, Treasury 9 Education
division: 4 dept. 10 department
ender: 4 work 5 maker 6 making
finish: 5 stain
former dept.: 3 HEW
former post: 3 PMG
medicine ~ item: 5 floss 6 iodine 7 aspirin 10 toothpaste
member: 4 secy. 8 minister 9 secretary
part: 4 door 5 hinge
wood: 5 alder, ebony
__ cabinet: 4 file 5 china 6 corner, liquor, shadow 7 Hoosier, kitchen
cabinetmaker: 6 joiner 10 woodworker
Cabin in the Sky (1943 film)
cast: Lena Horne, Ethel Waters
cable: 4 line, news, rope, wire 5 media, pay TV, telex 6 report, stitch, strand 8 telegram 9 radiogram
anchor ~ hole: 5 hawse
car: 4 tram
channel: 3 AMC, BET, CMT, CNN, HBO, HSN, IFC, ION, MTV, QVC, SHO, TBS, TLC, TMC, TNT, USA 4 CNBC, ESPN, Flix, HGTV 5 A and E, Bravo, C-SPAN, MSNBC, Spike, Starz, Style, truTV 6 Encore, Noggin, Tech TV, TV Land 7 Cinemax, Ovation, ShopNBC, SoapNet 8 Lifetime, Showtime, Sundance
ender: 3 way 4 cast, gram 6 vision
former ~ channel: 3 PAX, TNN 7 Court TV
hub: 5 spool
install ~: 3 lay
like some ~: 4 co-ax
nautical: 6 hawser
outlet: 2 TV 5 TV set
overseer: 3 FCC
post for a ship's ~: 4 bitt 7 bollard
power ~: 4 line
predecessor: 6 aerial
runway: 4 duct
service: 4 CATV
support: 5 pylon
TV worker: 5 wirer
cable __: 3 car 4 bend, buoy 5 crane 6 length, stitch
cable-__: 5 ready
__ cable: 3 pay 5 power 6 ground, jumper, leader 7 armored, booster, coaxial
cablegram: 4 wire 5 telex
Cable Guy, The (1996 film)
cast: Matthew Broderick, Jim Carrey, George Segal
director: Ben Stiller
cable stitch, make a: 4 knit
cabman: 4 hack 6 driver
Cabo __ Lucas: 3 San
caboodle
kit and ~: 3 all 6 entire
caboose: 3 car
neighbor: 6 boxcar
position: 4 rear
Cabo San Lucas: 4 city, town
locale: 6 Mexico
Cabot: 3 str. 4 John 5 Bruce 6 strait 9 Sebastian
Cabot __: 4 Cove 6 Strait
Cabot Cove doc: 4 Seth
Cabot, John: 7 Italian 8 explorer
__ Cabot Lodge: 5 Henry
Cabot, Sebastian: 5 actor 8 explorer
Cabral, Pedro Alvarez: 8 explorer
Cabrillo: 4 Juan
Cabrini, Mother: 3 nun 7 Frances
cabriole: 4 leap
Cabriolet: 3 car 4 Audi, auto 10 automobile
cacao: 4 tree 5 fruit 9 evergreen
exporter: 5 Ghana
cacao __: 4 bean 6 butter
__ cacciatore: 4 alla
cache: 4 bury, hide, hold, keep, mask, mine, save, stow, veil 5 amass, cloak, couch, cover, hoard, kitty, put by, stash, stock, store, trove 6 garner, load up, retain, save up, supply 7 conceal, harvest, lay away, nest egg, obscure, put away, reserve, savings, secrete 8 disguise, ensconce, gold mine, hang onto, hold onto, magazine, maintain, put aside, salt away, stow away, treasure 9 hidey-hole, stockpile 10 accumulate, camouflage, depository, storehouse
like a ~: 6 hidden
cache __: 6 memory 7 storage
cachet: 5 state 6 status 7 stature 8 position, prestige, standing
cachinnate: 5 laugh
cachinnation: 8 laughter
cackle: 3 cry 4 crow, ha-ha 5 clack, cluck, laugh, sound 6 babble, gabble, giggle, guffaw, rattle, squawk, titter 7 break up, chortle, chuckle, crack up 8 laughter
cackleberry: 3 egg
cackler: 3 hen 5 biddy
cackling: 8 giggling
cacophonic: 8 jangling 9 unmusical
cacophonous: 4 loud 5 aroar, harsh, noisy 6 ablare, shrill 7 raucous 9 dissonant
cacophony: 3 din 5 Babel, noise 6 clamor, jangle 7 discord, grating 9 stridency 10 dissonance
cactus: 4 tuna 5 agave, nopal, plant 6 cereus, cholla, flower, maguey, mescal, peyote 7 opuntia, saguaro 9 succulent
bud: 6 areola, areole
defense: 5 spine
fruit: 5 nopal 7 saguaro 8 pitahaya
kin: 5 yucca
like ~: 5 spiny, xeric
milieu: 6 desert, Mexico 7 Arizona
suitable for: 3 dry 4 arid
__ cactus: 4 chin, crab, star, vine 6 barrel, Easter, old-man, orchid 7 rainbow, rat-tail
Cactus Flower (1969 film)
cast: Ingrid Bergman, Goldie Hawn, Walter Matthau
director: Gene Saks
cad: 3 cur 4 boor, heel, jerk, lout, rake, roué, toad 5 crumb, knave, louse, rogue, scamp, swine 6 bad guy, bad hat, rascal, rotter, varlet 7 bounder, dirtbag, lowlife, villain 8 blighter, rakehell, two-timer

9 miscreant, no-goodnik, scoundrel, vulgarian 10 blackguard, ne'er-do-well
rebuke: 4 slap
Cadbury: 5 candy 9 chocolate
caddie: 5 gofer, toter 7 carrier
burden: 3 bag 5 irons, woods
hire a ~: 4 golf
offering: 3 tee 4 club, iron, wood 6 driver, mashie, putter 7 niblick
caddish: 4 base 5 crude 7 ignoble, ill-bred, uncivil, uncouth 9 ungallant 10 unmannerly
caddy
see caddie
__ caddy: 3 tea
Caddy: 3 car 4 auto 10 automobile
competitor: 4 Linc
Caddyshack (1980 film)
cast: Chevy Chase, Rodney Dangerfield, Ted Knight, Bill Murray, Michael O'Keefe
director: Harold Ramis
cadence: 4 beat, lilt, rime, tone 5 meter, pulse, rhyme, swing, tempo 6 accent, rhythm 7 measure 10 intonation, modulation
word: 3 hup
cadent: 8 rhythmic
cadet: 3 boy 4 pleb 5 plebe 7 soldier 9 legionary
Colorado: 6 airman
freshman ~: 4 pleb 5 plebe
meal: 4 mess
naval ~: 3 mid 5 middy
response: 5 no sir 6 yes sir
school: 3 VMI 9 West Point
__ cadet: 5 space
Cadets: 4 Army, USMA
Cadette: 5 scout 9 Girl Scout
cadge: 3 beg, bum 5 mooch 6 sponge 8 freeload, scrounge 9 impetrate, panhandle
cadger: 6 sponge 7 sponger 8 parasite 10 freeloader
Cadillac: 3 car 4 auto 10 automobile
model: 3 BLS, CTS, DTS, ESV, SRX, STS 6 Calais, Catera 7 Allante, DeVille, Seville 8 Biarritz, Cimarron, Eldorado, Escalade 9 Fleetwood
Cadillac __: 3 Man 4 Jack
like a ~ interior: 5 roomy
__ Cadillac: 4 Pink
Cadillac Jack
author: Larry McMurtry
Cadillac Man (1990 film)
cast: Fran Drescher, Pamela Reed, Tim Robbins, Robin Williams
Cádiz: 4 city, gulf, port, town
city on the Gulf of ~: 6 Huelva
locale: 5 Spain
cadmium: 5 metal 7 element
__-cadmium battery: 6 nickel
Cadmus
daughter: 3 Ino 5 Agave 6 Semele
sister: 6 Europa
wife: 8 Harmonia
cadre: 4 cell, core 5 force, staff 6 scheme 7 nucleus 9 framework, personnel
caduceus: 4 wand 5 staff
org. with a ~: 3 AMA
caducity: 7 frailty 8 weakness
Cady: 5 Frank
__ Cady Stanton: 9 Elizabeth
Caen: 4 city, Herb, town
locale: 6 France
neighbor: 4 St. Lô
river: 4 Orne
caesar: 5 ruler, salad, title
Caesar: 3 Sid 4 Nero 5 Galba, Roman, ruler, salad, title, Titus 6 Adolph, Julius, Trajan 7 Hadrian 8 Augustus, Aurelian, Caligula, Tiberius 9 Vespasian 10 Diocletian
contemporary: 5 Berle
in Italian: 6 Cesare
month named for a ~: 3 Aug., Jul. 4 July 6 August
partner: 4 Coca
Caesar __: 5 salad
__ Caesar: 6 Julius, Little
__, Caesar!: 4 Hail
Caesar and Cleopatra
author: George Bernard Shaw
__ Caesar, aut nihil: 3 aut
Caesar Cascabel
author: Jules Verne
Caesar, Julius: 5 Roman
city: 4 Rome
duds: 4 toga
early post of ~: 5 edile
foe: 4 Cato, Gaul 5 Casca 6 Brutus 7 Cassius
part of a ~ boast: 4 I saw, veni, vici, vidi 5 I came
question: 4 et tu
tongue: 3 Lat. 5 Latin
unlucky day for ~: 4 ides
__ Caesar's ghost!: 5 Great
Caesar, Sid: 8 comedian
TV: Your Show of Shows
Caesar's Palace site: Las Vegas
caesura: 3 gap 4 halt, rest 5 break, pause 6 lacuna
café: 5 boîte, diner 6 bistro, coffee, eatery, French 7 cabaret 9 lunchroom, nightclub, nightspot 10 restaurant
addition: 4 lait
alternative: 3 thé
attraction: 5 aroma
container: 4 urne 5 tasse
customer: 5 diner, eater
feature: 4 menu 6 awning
royale ingredient: 6 cognac
waiter: 6 garçon
café __: 3 car 4 noir 5 crème 6 au lait, brûlot, filtre, royale 7 curtain, society
café __ leche: 3 con
__-café: 6 pousse
__ Cafe: 6 Bagdad
café au __: 4 lait
cafeteria: 6 eatery 9 lunchroom 10 dining room, restaurant
item: 4 tray
patron: 5 eater
selection: 4 food
worker: 4 cook
__ Cafe, The: 6 Atomic
caffè __: 5 latte
caffeine source: 4 cola, kola 5 cacao
caftan: 4 mumu, robe 5 dress 6 muumuu 7 cover-up, garment 9 beachwear 10 loungewear
cage: 3 box, pen 4 cell, coop, jail, shut 5 frame, hutch 6 aviary, intern, lock up, shut in, shut up 7 capture, confine, enclose, impound, inclose, interne 8 backstop, imprison 9 enclosure, structure
dweller: 4 bird, myna 5 mynah 6 canary, parrot 8 parakeet
protector: 6 goalie
starter: 4 bird
__ cage: 3 rib 4 roll 6 gilded 7 Faraday
Cage: 4 John 7 Nicolas
caged: 4 pent 7 captive
Cage, Nicolas: 5 actor
aunt: Talia Shire
film: Adaptation (2002)
Bangkok Dangerous (2008)
Birdy (1984)
Bringing Out the Dead (1999)
Captain Corelli's Mandolin (2001)
City of Angels (1998)
Con Air (1997)
Face/Off (1997)
The Family Man (2000)
Guarding Tess (1994)
Honeymoon in Vegas (1992)
It Could Happen to You (1994)
Knowing (2009)
Leaving Las Vegas (1995, AA)
Lord of War (2005)
Matchstick Men (2003)
Moonstruck (1987)
National Treasure (2004)
Peggy Sue Got Married (1986)
Racing With the Moon (1984)
Raising Arizona (1987)
Red Rock West (1993)
The Rock (1996)
Valley Girl (1983)
World Trade Center (2006)
spouse: Patricia Arquette, Lisa Marie Presley
uncle: Francis Ford Coppola
cager: 5 NBAer 8 hoopster
former ~ org.: 3 ABA
like many ~s: 4 tall 5 rangy
pro ~: 3 Cav, Mav, Net, Sun 4 Buck, Bull, Hawk, Heat, Jazz, King, Spur 5 Knick, Laker, Magic, Pacer, Sixer 6 Celtic, Hornet, Nugget, Piston, Raptor, Rocket, Wizard 7 Clipper, Grizzly, Thunder, Warrior 8 Cavalier, Maverick 10 Timberwolf
see also basketball
cagey: 3 sly 4 arch, wary, wily 5 canny, chary, leery, slick 6 clever, crafty, shifty, shrewd, tricky 7 careful, cunning, elusive, elusory, evasive, guarded, mindful 8 cautious, guileful, slippery 9 sagacious, secretive 10 suspicious
cageyness: 5 craft
Cagney: 3 cop 5 Chris, James
Cagney, James: 5 actor
film: Angels With Dirty Faces (1938)
Blood on the Sun (1945)
Boy Meets Girl (1938)
Captains of the Clouds (1942)
Ceiling Zero (1935)
City for Conquest (1940)
Each Dawn I Die (1939)
Footlight Parade (1933)
The Gallant Hours (1960)
'G' Men (1935)
Lady Killer (1933)
Love Me or Leave Me (1955)
Man of a Thousand Faces (1957)
The Mayor of Hell (1933)
A Midsummer Night's Dream (1935)
Mister Roberts (1955)
The Oklahoma Kid (1939)
One, Two, Three (1961)
Picture Snatcher (1933)
The Public Enemy (1931)
Ragtime (1981)
The Roaring Twenties (1939)
Shake Hands With the Devil (1959)
The Strawberry Blonde (1941)
Torrid Zone (1940)
Tribute to a Bad Man (1956)
White Heat (1949)
Yankee Doodle Dandy (1942, AA)
imitator word: 3 rat 5 dirty
role: 5 Cohan
Cagney & Lacey (CBS drama)
cast: Tyne Daly (Det. Mary Beth Lacey)
Sharon Gless (Det. Chris Cagney)
Caguas: 4 city, town
locale: 10 Puerto Rico
Cahn, Sammy: 8 composer
collaborator: Jimmy Van Heusen, Jule Styne
cahoots: 10 conspiracy
be in ~: 4 plan, plot 6 scheme, wangle 7 collude, connive 8 conspire, intrigue, maneuver 9 machinate
in ~: 6 allied, united 8 hooked up, in league
Cahuilla: 5 tribe 6 Indian 7 Amerind
Caicos: 4 isls. 5 isles 7 islands
locale: 7 Bahamas 10 West Indies
caiman: 4 croc 6 animal 7 reptile 9 crocodile
Cain: 4 Dean 6 eldest
author: Lord Byron
brother: 4 Abel, Seth
dwelling place: 3 Nod
grandson: 4 Irad
nephew: 4 Enos
parent: 3 Eve 4 Adam
query start: 3 am I
raise ~: 4 rage, rave, riot 5 brawl, clash 6 clamor, squawk 7 carouse
raising ~: 5 noisy
son: 5 Enoch
victim: 4 Abel
__ Cain: 5 raise
Caine, Michael: 3 Sir 5 actor
film: Alfie (1966)
Batman Begins (2005)
Billion Dollar Brain (1967)
Blame It on Rio (1984)
California Suite (1978)
The Cider House Rules (1999, AA)
The Dark Knight (2008)
Deathtrap (1982)
The Destructors (1974)
Dirty Rotten Scoundrels (1988)
Dressed to Kill (1980)
The Eagle Has Landed (1977)
Educating Rita (1983)
Gambit (1966)
Hannah and Her Sisters (1986, AA)

The Man Who Would Be King (1975)
Miss Congeniality (2000)
The Muppet Christmas Carol (1992)
Noises Off (1992)
The Prestige (2006)
Pulp (1972)
Quills (2000)
The Romantic Englishwoman (1975)
Silver Bears (1978)
Sleuth (1972)
Surrender (1987)
Sweet Liberty (1986)
Too Late the Hero (1970)
The Whistle Blower (1986)
The Wilby Conspiracy (1975)
The Wrong Box (1966)
Zulu (1964)
Caine Mutiny Court-Martial, The
author: Herman Wouk
Caine Mutiny, The (1954 film)
cast: Humphrey Bogart, José Ferrer, Van Johnson, Fred MacMurray
composer: Max Steiner
director: Edward Dmytryk
Cain, James M.: 6 writer
work: Double Indemnity
Mildred Pierce
The Moth
The Postman Always Rings Twice
Rainbow's End
Serenade
Three of a Kind
Cairn __: 7 terrier
Cairo: 4 city, port, town **7** capital
city near ~: 5 Tanta
it ends at ~: 4 Ohio
language: 6 Arabic
locale: 5 Egypt **7** Mideast
opera that premiered in ~: 4 Aïda
river: 4 Nile
caisson: 5 chest, float **9** container
load: 4 ammo
cajole: 4 coax, lure, urge, wile **5** tempt **6** entice, induce, pander, praise, work on **7** beguile, flatter, lay it on, wheedle **8** blandish, butter up, inveigle, persuade, play up to, soft-soap, suck up to **9** sweet-talk **10** compliment
cajolery: 7 blarney, coaxing, palaver **8** flattery, hard sell, humoring, jollying, soft soap, stroking **9** sweet talk, wheedling **10** compliment, enticement, persuasion
Cajun: 7 Acadian
cousin: 6 Creole
craft: 6 bateau
dish: 4 okra **5** gumbo
home: 5 bayou
like ~ cooking: 5 spicy **6** spicey
music: 6 zydeco
seasoning: 4 file
stew: 8 étouffée
__ Cajuns: 5 Ragin'
cake: 3 bar **4** baba, loaf, lump, mass, slab, soap, tart **5** babka, blini, block, brick, Bundt, crêpe, latke, pound, torte **6** blintz, danish, gâteau, harden, kuchen, marble, sponge, trifle, waffle **7** brownie, congeal, dessert, encrust, genoise, savarin, stollen, tartlet, thicken **8** flapjack, solidify **9** angel food, chocolate, dacquoise, jelly roll, madeleine, sally lunn **10** confection, devil's food, ladyfinger, upside-down
cousin: 3 pie **4** tart
decorate a ~: 3 ice **5** frost
decoration: 5 icing **6** dragée
decorator: 4 icer
ender: 4 walk
first name in ~: 4 Sara
fried ~: 5 donut **8** doughnut
frosting on the ~: 5 bonus
in French: 6 gateau
ingredient: 5 flour, mocha, sugar, yeast **6** batter **9** chocolate
like some ~: 4 iced, oaty, rich **5** moist, oaten
make a ~: 4 bake
makings: 3 mix
no piece of ~: 4 hard **5** tough
part: 5 layer
piece of ~: 4 easy, snap **5** cinch, crumb, cushy, slice, wedge **6** breeze, picnic, simple **8** duck soup, painless, pushover **10** child's play, effortless, unexacting
pro: 5 baker **10** pastry chef
rum ~: 4 baba
sale: 10 fundraiser
serving: 5 piece, slice
starter: 3 ash, cup, hoe, hot, oat, pan, tea **4** corn **5** fruit, short **6** batter, cheese, coffee, johnny, yellow **7** griddle
take the ~: 3 win **7** triumph
topper: 5 icing **6** candle
wedding ~ doll: 4 wife **5** bride, groom
cake __: 3 mix, pan **5** eater, flour **6** makeup
__ cake: 3 hot, oil **4** corn, fish, rice, salt, soul **5** angel, Bundt, layer, pound, wheat, yeast **6** almond, cheese, coffee, cotton, funnel, groom's, icebox, marble, simnel, sponge **7** Banbury, flannel, linseed, wedding
__-cake: 4 pat-a **5** patty
caked: 5 muddy, thick
__-Cake makeup: 3 Pan
Cakes and Ale
author: W. Somerset Maugham
character: 3 Amy **4** Kear, Kemp **5** Alroy, Rosie
cakewalk: 4 romp, snap **5** cinch **6** breeze, picnic **8** pushover
in a ~: 6 easily
cal.
column: 3 Fri., Mon., Sat., Sun., Thu., Tue., Wed. **4** Thur., Tues. **5** Thurs.
notation: 4 appt.
page: 2 mo. 3 Apr., Aug., Dec., Feb., Jan., Jul., Jun., Mar., May, Nov., Oct., Sep.
unit: 2 mo., wk.
see also calendar
__-cal: 3 low
Cal: 5 Trask **6** Ripken, Thomas **7** Hubbard
rival: 3 USC
twin: 4 Aron
Cal __: 4 Poly
Cal.
neighbor: 3 Nev., Ore., Pac. **4** Ariz.
see also California
Calabar __: 4 bean
Calabasas: 4 city, town
locale: 10 California
calabash: 4 tree **5** gourd
see also gourd
__ Calabash: 3 Mrs.
calaboose: 4 jail, poky, stir **5** joint, pokey **6** lockup, prison
Calais: 3 car **4** auto, city, Olds, port, town **8** Cadillac **10** Oldsmobile
city near ~: 5 Lille
locale: 6 France
__ Calais: 5 Pas de
Calama: 4 city, town
locale: 5 Chile
calamari: 5 squid
calamine: 5 alloy
component: 3 tin **4** lead, zinc
lotion: 4 balm
target: 4 bite, itch
calamine __: 5 brass **6** lotion
calamitous: 4 dire **5** toxic, woful **6** bitter, malign, tragic, woeful **7** adverse, baleful, baneful, fateful, harmful, ruinous, unlucky **8** damaging, grievous, negative, tragical **9** blighting, dangerous, ill-omened, injurious **10** afflictive, deplorable, disastrous, lamentable, pernicious
calamity: 3 ill, woe **4** bane, blow, doom, loss, ruin **5** curse, event, havoc, shame **6** blight, misery, mishap, ordeal, plague **7** scourge, tragedy, undoing **8** accident, casualty, disaster, distress, hard luck, hardship **9** adversity, cataclysm, detriment, nightmare, ruination **10** affliction, misfortune
Calamity Jane (1953 film)
cast: Doris Day, Howard Keel
calamus: 5 quill
calando: 6 slower, softer
Calaveras County jumper: 4 frog
calaverite: 3 ore
Calchas: 4 seer
daughter: 8 Cressida
calcify: 6 harden **8** indurate
calcite to Mohs: 5 three
calcium: 7 element
hydroxide: 6 alkali
like ~ oxide: 4 limy
oxide: 4 lime
source: 4 milk
calculable: 9 countable, estimable **10** computable, imaginable, measurable, reckonable
calculate: 3 add, sum **4** find, make, plan, plot, tell **5** count, gauge, sum up, tally, total **6** assume, bank on, cipher, divide, figure, number, plan on, reckon, rely on **7** compute, count on, measure, project, work out **8** depend on, estimate, keep tabs, multiply, subtract **9** count upon, determine, enumerate, keep score **10** anticipate
roughly: 8 estimate
calculated: 7 studied **9** conscious, strategic **10** deliberate
calculated __: 4 risk
calculating: 3 sly **4** keen, wary, wily **5** canny, chary **6** artful, crafty, shrewd **7** careful, cunning, devious, furtive, politic **8** cautious, discreet, guileful, scheming **9** observant
calculation: 3 age **4** area **5** count, ratio, yield **6** adding **7** caution, thought **8** dividing, estimate, figuring, forecast, planning, prudence **9** reckoning
calculator: 6 abacus **10** accountant
feature: 3 key, LCD, LED **6** keypad, memory **7** display
figure: 3 sum **5** total **6** addend **7** divisor **8** dividend
key: 3 CLR, cos, dot, sin, tan **4** plus, sine **5** clear, minus, times **6** cosine, equals **7** percent
use a ~: 3 add **6** divide **8** multiply, subtract
work: 4 math **10** arithmetic
__ calculator: 5 solar **6** pocket
calculus: 4 math
calculation: 3 lim., vol. **4** area **5** limit **6** volume **8** integral
pioneer: 5 Euler
Calcutta: 4 city, port, town
city near ~: 6 Howrah
clothing: 4 sari **5** saree
locale: 5 India **6** Bengal
mother: 6 Teresa
river: 5 Hugli
see also India
caldarium: 5 sauna
Caldecott __: 5 medal
Calder: 9 Alexander **10** Willingham
Calder, Alexander: 6 artist **8** sculptor
work: 6 mobile **7** stabile
Calderón, Pedro: 6 writer **7** Spanish **10** playwright
Caldwell: 3 Zoe **5** Bobby, Sarah **6** Taylor **7** Erskine
Caldwell, Erskine: 6 writer
spouse: Margaret Bourke-White
work: Annette
Close to Home
Georgia Boy
God's Little Acre
Tobacco Road
Trouble in July
Caldwell, Sarah: 9 conductor
Cale: 10 Yarborough
Caleb: 4 Carr
son: 4 Elah
Caledonia: 8 Scotland
calefaction: 4 heat
calendar: 4 card, list **6** agenda, docket **7** daybook, Filofax, program **8** schedule **10** chronology
Chinese ~ year: 2 ox **3** dog, rat **4** boar **5** horse, sheep, snake, tiger **6** dragon, monkey, rabbit **7** rooster
church ~: 4 ordo
column: 3 Fri., Mon., Sat., Sun., Thu., Tue., Wed. **4** Thur., Tues. **5** Thurs. **6** Friday, Monday, Sunday **7** Tuesday **8** Saturday, Thursday **9** Wednesday
court ~: 6 docket
division: 2 mo., wk., yr. **3** day **4** date, week, year **5** month
for short: 4 sked
French Revolution ~ month: 6 Nivôse **7** Floréal, Ventôse **8** Brumaire, Frimaire, Germinal, Messidor, Pluviôse, Prairial **9** Fructidor, Thermidor **11** Vendémiaire
Hebrew ~ month: 2 Av **4** Adar,

Elul, Iyar **5** Nisan, Sivan, Tevet **6** Kislev, Shevat, Tammuz, Tishri **7** Heshvan
Islamic ~ month: 4 Rabi **5** Rajab, Safar **6** Jumada, Shaban **7** Ramadan, Shawwal **8** Muharram **9** Dhu al-Qa'da **10** Dhu al-Hijja
model: 5 pin-up
page: 3 Apr., Aug., Dec., Feb., Jan., Jul., Jun., Mar., May, Nov., Oct., Sep. **4** July, June **5** April, March, month **6** August **7** January, October **8** December, February, November **9** September
Roman ~ day: 4 ides **5** nones **7** calends, kalends
run: 5 MTWTF
stone ~ user: 5 Aztec
calendar __: 3 art, day **4** year **5** clock, month, watch
__ calendar: 4 desk **5** Hindu, Roman **6** church, Hebrew, Jewish, Julian, Moslem, Muslim **7** Chinese, Islamic
Calendar Girl (1960 song)
artist: Neil Sedaka
calendario
page: 4 mayo **5** abril, enero, julio, junio, marzo **6** agosto **7** febrero, octubre **9** diciembre, noviembre **10** septiembre
calendario page: 3 mes
calends follower: 4 ides
calescent: 3 hot
calf: 4 dogy, shin, veal **5** dogey, dogie **6** animal, heifer **7** foreleg **8** maverick
catcher: 5 reata, riata, roper **6** cowboy, lariat
cry: 5 bleat
ender: 4 skin
food source: 5 udder
front of the ~: 4 shin
golden ~: 4 idol
locale: 3 leg
lone ~: 4 dogy, waif **5** dogey, dogie, leppy, stray **6** doggie **8** maverick
look at with ~ eyes: 4 ogle
meat: 4 veal
muscle: 6 soleus
muscles: 5 solei
on the range: 4 dogy **5** dogey, dogie
starter: 4 moon
calf __: 4 love **6** roping
__ calf: 3 box, sea **5** bobby **6** fatted, golden
calf-length: 4 midi
calf-roping event: 5 rodeo
Calgary: 4 city, town
hockey player: 5 Flame
locale: 3 Alb. **4** Alta. **6** Canada **7** Alberta
newspaper: 3 Sun **6** Herald
Stampede: 5 rodeo
Stampeders' org.: 3 CFL
Calgon
alternative: ***see*** detergent
Calhern, Louis: 5 actor
spouse: Ilka Chase
Calhoun, Rory: 5 actor
Cali: 4 city, town
locale: 8 Colombia
Caliban: 4 moon
planet: 6 Uranus
tormentor: 5 Ariel
caliber: 4 bore, size **5** value, worth **6** degree, status **7** quality, stature **8** diameter **9** character, largeness
calibrate: 5 align, aline, gauge, reset, scale **6** adjust **7** measure **8** fine-tune, graduate
anew: 5 reset
calico: 3 cat **5** cloth, felid **6** feline **7** spotted **9** patchwork
calico __: 3 bug, cat **4** bass, bush, clam, crab **6** flower
calicoback: 3 bug **6** insect
Calico Pie
author: Edward Lear
calidity: 4 heat
caliente: 3 hot
__ caliente: 3 ojo
__ Caliente: 4 Agua
Calif.
campus: 3 USC
clock setting: 3 PDT, PST
neighbor: 3 Nev., Ore. **4** Ariz., Oreg.
school: 3 USC **4** UCLA
-to-Fla. route: 4 I-Ten
see also California
Califano: 6 Joseph
California: 4 gulf **5** state
airport: 3 LAX, SFO
animal on ~ flag: 4 bear
bay: 8 Monterey, San Pablo
city: 4 Bell, Brea, Galt, Lodi, Napa, Ojai **5** Arden, Azusa, Ceres, Chico, Chino, Davis, Hemet, Indio, Norco, Poway, Selma, Tracy, Vista, Wasco, Yreka **6** Arcade, Big Sur, Carmel, Carson, Clovis, Colton, Corona, Covina, Cudahy, Delano, Downey, Duarte, Dublin, East L.A., El Toro, Eureka, Florin, Folsom, Fresno, Frisco, Gilroy, Goleta, Graham, Irvine, Laguna, La Mesa, Lennox, Lomita, Lompoc, Madera, Marina, Merced, Newark, Novato, Oakley, Orange, Orcutt, Orinda, Oxnard, Perris, Pomona, Rialto, Santee, Sonoma, Sonora, Tulare, Tustin, Upland, Walnut **7** Alameda, Anaheim, Antioch, Arcadia, Ashland, Atwater, Banning, Barstow, Belmont, Benicia, Brawley, Burbank, Compton, Concord, Cypress, El Cajon, El Monte, Fontana, Fremont, Gardena, Hanford, Hayward, La Habra, La Presa, La Verne, Lemoore, Lynwood, Manteca, Maywood, Modesto, Norwalk, Oakland, Oildale, Ontario, Parkway, Redding, Reedley, Rocklin, Salinas, San Jose, Seaside, Stanton, Tarzana, Turlock, Valinda, Vallejo, Visalia, Windsor, Yucaipa **8** Alhambra, Altadena, Bay Point, Berkeley, Calexico, Campbell, Carlsbad, Cerritos, Coronado, Daly City, Danville, El Centro, Elk Grove, Fair Oaks, Florence, Glendale, Glendora, Hercules, Hesperia, Highland, Lakeside, Lakewood, La Mirada, La Puente, La Quinta, Lawndale, Los Altos, Los Banos, Los Gatos, Martinez, Millbrae, Milpitas, Monrovia, Monterey, Moorpark, Morro Bay, Murrieta, Pacifica, Palmdale, Palo Alto, Paradise, Pasadena, Petaluma, Redlands, Richmond, Rosemead, Rosemont, Rubidoux, San Bruno, San Diego, San Dimas, San Mateo, San Pablo, San Ramon, Santa Ana, Saratoga, Stockton, Temecula, Torrance, Westmont, Whittier, Woodland, Yuba City **9** Brentwood, Buena Park, Calabasas, Camarillo, Casa de Oro, Claremont, Coachella, Costa Mesa, Cupertino, Dana Point, El Cerrito, Encinitas, Escondido, Fairfield, Fallbrook, Fullerton, Hawthorne, Hollister, Inglewood, Isla Vista, Lafayette, Lancaster, Livermore, Long Beach, Los Nietos, Menlo Park, Montclair, Oceanside, Paramount, Pittsburg, Placentia, Riverside, Roseville, San Carlos, San Marcos, San Rafael, Santa Cruz, Santa Rosa, Seal Beach, South Gate, Sunnyvale, Union City, Vacaville **10** Aliso Viejo, Atascadero, Bellflower, Burlingame, Carmichael, Chino Hills, Chula Vista, Culver City, Diamond Bar, Foster City, Lake Forest, Lemon Grove, Los Angeles, Montebello, Morgan Hill, Mount Helix, Orangevale, Palm Desert, Pico Rivera, Pismo Beach, Pleasanton, Ridgecrest, Sacramento, San Gabriel, San Jacinto, San Leandro, San Lorenzo, Santa Clara, Santa Maria, Santa Paula, Simi Valley, Suisun City, Temple City, West Carson, West Covina, Yorba Linda
clock setting: 3 PDT, PST
cop grp.: 4 LAPD
county: 4 Inyo, Lake, Napa **5** Marin **6** Orange **7** Ventura
desert: 6 Mohave **7** Sonoran **11** Death Valley
fish: 7 alfiona, finspot, grunion, sculpin **8** halfmoon **10** yellowtail
former ~ congressman: 4 Bono
fort: 3 Ord
garlic center: 6 Gilroy
Indian: 4 Pomo, Yahi, Yana **5** Maidu, Miwok, Modoc, Piute, Washo, Wintu, Yurok **6** Mohave, Mojave, Paiute, Patwin, Wintun, Yokuts **7** Chumash **8** Cahuilla
industry: 4 film **6** cinema, movies
lake: 4 Mono **5** Tahoe **8** Lahontan **9** Salton Sea
mountain: 4 Muir, Sill **5** Lyell **6** Lassen, Shasta, Wilson **7** Granite, Langley, Palomar, Russell, Tyndall, Whitney **8** Panamint **9** El Capitan **10** Williamson
national park: 7 Redwood, Sequoia **8** Yosemite **10** Joshua Tree
neighbor: 6 Mexico, Nevada, Oregon **7** Arizona
newspaper: 7 L.A. Times
peninsula: 4 Baja **8** Monterey
port: 7 Oakland **8** San Diego **10** Los Angeles
pro team: 5 Kings, the A's **6** Angels, Giants, Lakers, Niners, Padres, Sharks **7** Dodgers, Raiders **8** Chargers, Clippers, Warriors **9** Athletics **11** Mighty Ducks
racetrack: 6 Del Mar **10** Santa Anita
river: 3 Eel
school: 3 USC **4** UCLA **5** Menlo **6** Eureka **8** Stanford, Whittier **10** Pepperdine
seaside rte.: 3 PCH
state flower: 5 poppy
state gem: 9 benitoite
state marine fish: 9 garibaldi
state marine mammal: 9 gray whale
state mineral: 4 gold
state motto: 6 Eureka
state rock: 10 serpentine
state tree: 7 redwood
student: 5 UCLAn
tree: 5 toyon **7** redwood, sequoia
tribe: 4 Hupa **5** Wintu **6** Wintun
University of ~ campus: 5 Davis
volcano: 6 Lassen
waterfall: 7 Feather
wind: 8 Santa Ana
winery: 5 Gallo
wine valley: 4 Napa
California __: 3 Sun **4** gull, Love, mink, roll, rose **5** Girls, poppy, quail, Suite **6** condor, laurel, nutmeg, privet
__ California: 4 Alta, Baja **5** Hotel, Lower, Upper
California Dreamin' (1966 song)
artist: Mamas & the Papas
California Girls (song)
artist: Beach Boys, David Lee Roth
California, Here I Come! (1924 song)
artist: Al Jolson
composer: Joseph Meyer
California Love (1996 song)
artist: Dr. Dre, Roger, Tupac
California Suite (1978 film)
cast: Alan Alda, Michael Caine, Bill Cosby, Jane Fonda, Walter Matthau, Elaine May, Richard Pryor, Maggie Smith
director: Herbert Ross
writer: Neil Simon
californium: 7 element
caliginous: 5 mirky, murky
Caligula: 5 Roman **6** Caesar
author: Albert Camus
horse: 9 Incitatus
nephew: 4 Nero
caliph: 3 Ali **4** imam, male **5** imaum, ruler **6** gerent
Calisher, Hortense: 6 writer
Calista: 9 Flockhart
calisthenics: 7 workout **8** aerobics, exercise **9** athletics **10** daily dozen, gymnastics, isometrics
calix: 3 cup **7** chalice
Calixtus: 4 pope **7** pontiff
call: 3 cry, dub, tag **4** beep, dial, levy, name, need, page, peep, plea, ring, roar, term, wake, yell **5** alarm,

bleat, cheep, chirp, guess, hallo, hillo, hullo, judge, label, phone, pop by, pop in, rally, rouse, run in, shout, style, title, tweet, visit, voice, waken **6** appeal, beckon, bellow, come by, cry out, demand, dial up, drop by, drop in, excuse, gather, halloa, halloo, hallow, hilloa, holler, hulloo, notice, notify, option, outcry, pursue, reason, reckon, ring up, signal, stop by, stop in, summon, warble **7** address, baptize, command, contact, convene, convoke, entitle, exclaim, grounds, intitle, predict, request, sing out, solicit, summons, swing by **8** announce, assemble, christen, come over, consider, estimate, nominate, occasion, proclaim, proposal, subpoena **9** designate, necessity, rehearsal, telephone, touch base **10** denominate, get a hold of, incitement, invitation, obligation, vociferate
a bet: **3** see
again, in poker: **5** resee
a halt to: **3** end **6** finish
a meeting: **6** gather, muster, summon **7** convene, convoke, marshal **8** assemble
at one's beck and ~: **5** ready
attention-getting ~: **2** yo **3** hey
attention to: **4** note **6** accent, advert, play up, stress **7** feature, mention, point up **8** point out **9** highlight, punctuate, spotlight, underline **10** underscore
back: **6** recant
bird ~: **3** caw **4** peep, pipe, twee **5** cheep, chirp, tweet **6** cuckoo **7** chirrup, twitter
bugle ~: **4** taps **8** reveille
cat ~: **3** mew **4** meow, yowl **5** miaou, miaow, miaul
cattle ~: **3** moo **7** meeting **9** interview
close ~: **5** brush **8** near miss
coin-toss ~: **5** heads, tails
director's ~: **3** cut **5** print **6** action
end a ~: **6** hang up
ender: **3** boy **4** back **5** board
for: **4** hail, need, page, take, want **5** claim, exact **6** demand, entail, invoke, pick up **7** request, warrant
(for): **3** ask
forth: **5** evoke **6** elicit, invoke **7** provoke **8** summon up
in: **6** recall, redeem **7** consult, convene
into question: **5** doubt **6** impugn, oppose **7** dispute **9** challenge
it a day: **3** end **4** halt, quit, stop **5** cease, close **6** finish, retire, turn in, wind up, wrap up **7** adjourn, break up **8** break off, conclude, finish up, knock off, pack it in **9** terminate
it quits: **4** stop **5** cease
make the ~: **6** decide
off: **3** end **4** drop **5** abort, scrub **6** cancel **7** abolish, retract
on: **3** ask **5** visit **6** drop by, invite, invoke **7** go to see **10** pay court to
on ~: **5** ready
one's own: **4** have **5** adopt
on the carpet: **5** chide **6** rebuke **8** admonish **9** reprimand
opposite: **3** put
out: **3** cry **5** shout **7** exclaim
partner: **4** beck
perhaps: **4** wake **5** waken **6** awaken
starter: **3** cat **4** bird
the shots: **4** boss, lead, rule **5** order **6** direct, govern, manage, settle **7** control, dictate, oversee **8** dominate **9** supervise
time: **5** pause **6** recess
to: **4** hail **6** summon **7** shout at **8** holler at, wave down
to account: **3** rag **5** blame, scold **6** rebuke **7** reprove **9** reprehend, reprimand **10** take to task
to arms: **5** alert, rally **6** alarum **7** recruit **8** mobilize
together: **6** muster **7** convoke **8** assemble
to mind: **5** think **6** recall, review **8** remember **9** recollect, visualize
trumpet ~: **7** fanfare, tantara **8** flourish
umpire: **3** out **4** balk, ball, foul, safe **6** strike
up: **4** dial, levy, ring **5** draft, evoke, phone, raise **6** access, enlist, muster, recall **7** convoke, recruit **8** activate, mobilize, remember **9** visualize
upon: **3** ask, use **4** pray, tell **5** visit **6** enjoin, exhort, invoke **7** require **10** fall back on
call ___: **3** box, for, off, out **4** back, down, loan, rate, sign, slip, upon **5** forth, money, names **6** market, number, option **7** letters, waiting
call ___ day: **3** it a
call ___ question: **4** into
call ___ to: **5** a halt
___ call: **3** act **4** bird, cold, junk, mail, mess, open, roll, sick, toll, wolf **5** altar, close, crank, house, phone, trunk **6** cattle, margin, wake-up **7** collect, curtain
___-call: **4** will
Call ___ cab!: **3** me a
Call ___ Wild, The: **5** of the
Callaghan, James: **2** P.M. **7** British
predecessor: **6** Wilson
successor: **8** Thatcher
Callaghan, Morley: **6** writer **8** Canadian
calla lily: **5** aroid, plant **6** flower
family: **4** arum
like a ~: **5** showy
milieu: **5** marsh
callaloo: **4** soup
ingredient: **4** crab **6** greens
Callan, Michael: **5** actor
Callao: **4** city, port, town
site: **4** Peru
Callas: **5** Maria **7** Charlie
Callas, Maria: **4** diva **6** singer **7** soprano
specialty: **4** aria **5** opera
called
also ~: **5** alias
for: **8** required **9** necessary
old-style: **6** yclept
once ~: **3** née **4** born **8** formerly
...called for his fiddlers ___: **5** three
___ Called Horse: **4** A Man
___ Called To Say I Love You: **5** I Just
___ Called Wanda: **5** A Fish
___ Callender's: **5** Marie
caller: **5** guest **7** visitor **10** bell ringer
gentleman ~: **4** beau
identify a ~: **5** trace
play ~: **2** QB **11** quarterback
sports ~: **3** ref, ump **6** umpire **7** referee
___-caller: **4** name
callers: **7** company
accepting ~: **6** at home
calligrapher: **6** scribe
need: **3** ink, nib, pen **6** inkpot
calligraphy: **5** print **6** script **7** writing
line: **5** serif
calling: **3** gig, job **4** line, walk, work **5** craft, niche, trade **6** career, day job, métier, racket **7** mission, pursuit **8** business, lifework, vocation **9** life's work **10** occupation, profession, walk of life
a spade a spade: **6** candid
calling ___: **4** card
___ calling: **4** Avon, cold
___-calling: **4** name
Calling all ___: **4** cars
Calling all cars...: **3** APB
Calling America
artist: ELO
calliope: **8** keyboard **10** instrument
power: **5** steam
relative: **5** organ, piano
Calliope: **4** Muse
colleague: *see* Muse
lover: **6** Apollo
parent: **4** Zeus **9** Mnemosyne
son: **5** Linus **7** Orpheus
Callisto: **4** bear, moon
planet: **7** Jupiter
call it ___: **4** a day **5** quits
Call It Love (1989 song)
artist: Poco
Call It Sleep
author: Henry Roth
Call Me (song)
artist: Blondie, Al Green, Johnny Mathis
Call Me ___: **4** Anna **5** Bwana, Madam
Call Me Irresponsible
composer: Sammy Cahn, Jimmy Van Heusen
Call Me Ishmael
author: Charles Olson
Call Me Madam: **7** musical
cast: Ethel Merman
composer: Irving Berlin
inspiration: Perle Mesta
___ Call Me MISTER Tibbs: **4** They
Call of the Canyon
author: Zane Grey
Call of the Toad, The
author: Günter Grass
Call of the Wild, The: **5** novel
author: Jack London
dog: **4** Buck, Dave **5** Spitz **7** Solleks
setting: **5** Yukon **6** Alaska
___ call on: **4** pay a
call one's ___: **5** bluff
Call on Me (1974 song)
artist: Chicago
callous: **4** hard, mean **5** cruel, harsh, nasty, stony, tough **6** animal, brutal, fierce, flinty, savage, stoney, unkind, wanton **7** beastly, coarsen, hurtful, roughen, vicious **8** barbaric, fiendish, hardened, indurate, inhumane, pitiless, ruthless, sadistic, uncaring, vengeful **9** cutthroat, ferocious, heartless, impassive, inclement, insensate, merciless, monstrous, truculent, unfeeling, unpitying, unstirred **10** hard-boiled, unaffected, vindictive
callow: **3** raw **4** naif **5** fresh, green, naive, young **6** boyish, jejune, tender **7** puerile **8** immature, juvenile, underage, untested, youthful **9** beardless, guileless, half-grown, untrained **10** sophomoric
one: **3** boy, cub, lad, pup **4** tiro, tyro **5** puppy, youth **6** novice **8** beginner **9** youngster **10** apprentice
Calloway: **3** Cab
callowness: **9** freshness, greenness, ignorance
call the ___: **4** tune **5** shots
___ Call the Whole Thing Off: **4** Let's
___ Call the Wind Maria: **4** They
call to ___: **4** arms, task **5** order **7** account
call-up: **5** draft, order **6** muster
org.: **3** SSS
status: **4** one A
___ call us...: **4** Don't
callused
become ~: **6** harden
___ Call You Sweetheart: **5** Let Me
calm: **4** cool, ease, easy, even, hush, lick, lull, mild, rest **5** allay, level, order, peace, poise, quell, quiet, relax, rural, sober, staid, still, stoic **6** defuse, defuze, docile, gentle, hushed, low-key, mellow, pacify, placid, poised, repose, sedate, serene, settle, smooth, soften, soothe, stable, steady, temper **7** amiable, appease, assuage, at peace, bucolic, clement, compose, console, cool out, easeful, equable, halcyon, harmony, mollify, orderly, pacific, patient, placate, relaxed, relieve, restful, silence, stoical, unfazed **8** amicable, carefree, composed, coolness, inactive, in repose, laid-back, mitigate, moderate, pastoral, peaceful, quietude, rational, reassure, resigned, serenity, soothing, together, tranquil, waveless, windless **9** alleviate, bucolical, collected, composure, easygoing, impassive, nerveless, peaceable, placidity, quiescent, quiet down, quietness, reposeful, soft-pedal, soundless, stillness, stormless, temperate, unexcited, unextreme, unruffled, unstirred, unworried **10** cool-headed, dispassion, equanimity, harmonious, motionless, nonchalant, phlegmatic, placidness, propitiate, restrained, rippleless, sedateness, simmer down, stress-free, unaffected, unagitated, unbothered, untroubled
be ~: **5** relax
down: **4** lull, rest **5** quiet, relax **6** cool it, soothe, unwind **7** cool off **8** loosen up
in music: **7** placido

...calm, __ bright: 5 all is
__ **Calm:** 3 Sea 4 Dead
calmative: 5 bland 6 easing 7 anodyne 8 sedative
Calm down!: 4 easy 5 chill, relax 6 cool it 8 chill out
calming: 6 dreamy 8 narcotic 9 soporific
calmness: 4 ease, lull, rest 5 peace, poise, quiet, still 6 aplomb, repose, temper 7 concord, reserve 8 coolness, optimism, patience, presence, serenity 9 balminess, composure, placidity, quietness, sang-froid, stillness 10 dispassion, equanimity, moderation, steadiness
caloric in ads, less: 4 lite
caloricity: 4 heat 8 warmness
calorie: 4 unit
  counters' retreat: 3 spa
  cousin: 3 BTU
__ **calorie:** 4 gram 5 empty, large, small
calories
  count ~: 4 diet
  loaded with ~: 4 rich
  needing ~: 6 hungry
calorify: 4 heat 6 heat up
Calpurnia
  husband: 6 Caesar
Calrissian: 5 Lando
Caltech
  grad: 2 EE 3 Eng. 4 engr.
  rival: 3 MIT
caltrop: 3 nut
calumet: 9 peace pipe
Calumet City: 4 town
  locale: 8 Illinois
calumniate: 3 hit 4 gibe, jeer, jibe, mock, slam, slur, snub 5 abuse, belie, decry, libel, scorn, smear, spurn, sully, taunt 6 defame, deride, dump on, heckle, impugn, malign, offend, rebuff, revile, slight, smirch, vilify 7 affront, asperse, blacken, degrade, disdain, put down, rank out, rip into, run down, slander, spatter, traduce 8 backbite, badmouth, belittle, denounce, ridicule, tear down, throw mud, vilipend 9 denigrate, discredit, disparage, humiliate 10 depreciate, disrespect, stigmatize
calumnious: 8 critical, libelous 9 invidious 10 defamatory, derogatory
calumny: 3 dig, lie 4 barb, blot, gibe, jibe, slam, slap, slur, snub 5 abuse, libel, scorn, taunt 6 attack, rebuff, slight, smrich 7 affront, catcall, disdain, mockery, obloquy, offense, put-down, slander, untruth 8 contempt, derision, reproach, ridicule 9 aspersion, cheap shot, contumely 10 backbiting, defamation, derogation, devalution, disrespect, impugnment, imputation, opprobrium, revilement
calvados: 5 drink 8 beverage
Calvados
  capital: 4 Caen
Calvary __: 5 cross
Calvé, Emma: 6 singer 7 soprano
  specialty: 5 opera
Calvert: 8 DeForest
calves: 5 young 6 cattle
  bearer of ~: 3 cow 5 whale
calves' __: 5 liver
Calvet, Corinne: 7 actress
Calvin: 4 John 5 Klein, Peete 6 Melvin, Murphy 7 Trillin 8 Coolidge
Calvin and Hobbes: 5 comic, strip 7 cartoon 10 comic strip
  character: 3 Moe 5 Susie
  tiger: 6 Hobbes
Calvin Klein
  competitor: 4 DKNY, Polo 5 Guess, Karan 6 Armani, Lauren
Calvino, Italo: 6 writer 7 Italian
  work: Cosmicomics
    Invisible Cities
    Mr. Palomar
calx: 5 oxide 9 quicklime
Calydon, king of: 6 Oeneus
calypso: 5 music, plant 6 flower
  kin: 3 ska 4 soca
  standard: 4 Dayo
Calypso: 4 moon 5 nymph
  father: 5 Atlas
  planet: 6 Saturn
Calypso (1975 song)
  artist: John Denver
calyx leaf: 5 sepal
cam: 3 cog 7 trippet 8 auto part
  ender: 5 shaft 6 corder
__-cam: 3 sky
Camacho: 5 Avila 6 Hector
Camagüey: 4 city, town
  locale: 4 Cuba
camaraderie: 5 amity, cheer 7 jollity, rapport, society 8 intimacy
Camarillo: 4 city, town
  locale: 10 California
Camaro: 3 car 4 auto, IROC 5 Chevy 9 Chevrolet 10 automobile
camass: 4 bulb 5 plant 6 flower
Camay
  alternative: ***see*** soap
camber: 4 bend, flex 5 curve, slant, toe-in 9 sinuosity
Cambodia: 6 nation 7 country
  capital: 9 Phnom Penh
  continent: 4 Asia
  lake: 8 Tonle Sap
  language: 5 Khmer
  money: 3 sen 4 riel
  neighbor: 4 Laos 7 Vietnam 8 Thailand
  temple: 3 wat
Cambodian: 5 Asian, Khmer
  neighbor: 3 Lao, Tai 4 Thai
Cambrian: 3 Era
Cambrian Mountains site: 5 Wales
cambric: 3 tea 5 linen 6 fabric
Cambridge: 3 car 4 auto, city, town 7 Godfrey 8 Plymouth 10 automobile
  academic: 3 don 5 tutor
  athletes: 7 Crimson
  exam: 6 tripos
  grad: 2 EE 3 eng. 4 engr.
  locale: 4 Mass. 6 Canada 7 England, Ontario
  school: 3 MIT 7 Harvard
  student: 6 Cantab
Cambridgeshire: 6 county
  locale: 7 England
Cambs: 6 county
  locale: 7 England
camcorder
  attachment: 3 VCR
  button: 3 rec 5 focus 6 record
  format: 3 VHS 4 Beta
  maker: 4 Sony
  use a ~: 4 tape
Camden: 4 city, town
  locale: 9 New Jersey
Camden Yards: 5 arena 7 stadium 8 ballpark
  player: 6 Oriole
  see also baseball
came
  I ~: 4 veni
  to rest: 3 lit 4 alit
__ **came a spider...:** 5 Along
__ **Came Bronson:** 4 Then
__ **Came C.O.D., The:** 5 Bride
camel: 3 tan 5 brown, mount 6 animal, mammal 8 Bactrian 9 dromedary, yellowish
  backbreaker: 5 straw
  cousin: 5 llama 6 alpaca, vicuña 7 guanaco
  driver's command: 5 kneel
  ender: 4 back
  execute a ~: 5 skate
  feature: 4 hoof, hump
  female: 3 cow
  fermented ~ milk: 6 kumiss
  go by ~: 4 ride
  in India: 4 oont
  male: 4 bull
  metaphorically: 4 ship
  milieu: 3 ice 4 rink 5 oasis 6 desert, Sahara 7 caravan
  relative: ***see*** brown color
  young: 4 calf
__ **Camel:** 7 Sopwith
camelhair fabric: 3 aba 4 abba
camellia: 5 plant, shrub 6 flower
Camellia State: 3 Ala. 7 Alabama
Camelot: 7 musical
  actor: 4 Nero 6 Harris 8 Redgrave
  composer: Alan Jay Lerner, Frederick Loewe
camel's __ coat: 4 hair
Camembert: 6 French
  alternative: ***see*** cheese
cameo: 3 bit 4 part, role 6 walk-on 7 bit part, jewelry 8 anaglyph
  do a ~: 3 act 7 perform
  make a ~: 6 emboss 7 engrave
  shape: 4 oval
  stone: 4 onyx
cameo __: 4 role
camera: 3 SLR 4 Fuji 5 Canon, Kodak, Leica, Nikon, Ricoh 6 Konica, Pentax, Rollei 7 Brownie, Minolta, Olympus, Vivitar, Yashica 8 Polaroid
  activate a ~: 6 expose
  adjust a ~: 5 focus
  ender: 3 man, men 5 woman, women 6 person 7 persons
  filler: 4 film
  follower: 6 action
  lens scope: 5 field
  lens shield: 4 gobo
  part: 4 iris, lens, zoom 5 flash
  prepare for the ~: 3 mug 4 pose
  setting: 5 f-stop, speed, t-stop
  shot: 6 fade-in 7 closeup
  wheels: 5 dolly
camera __: 4 tube 6 lucida 7 obscura
camera-__: 3 shy 5 ready
__ **camera:** 3 box, gun 4 disc, disk, view 5 gamma, Kodak, sound, video 6 candid, reflex 7 instant, pinhole
__-camera: 3 off
__ **Camera:** 4 I Am a 6 Candid
Cameron: 4 Diaz, Kirk 5 Crowe, James 8 Mitchell
Cameron, James: 8 director
  film: The Abyss (1989)
    Aliens (1986)
    Avatar (2009)
    The Terminator (1984)
    Titanic (1997, AA)
    True Lies (1994)
  spouse: Suzy Amis, Kathryn Bigelow, Linda Hamilton
__ **Cameron Swayze:** 4 John
Cameroon: 6 nation 7 country
  capital: 7 Yaoundé
  city: 5 Duala, Kaélé, Kumba 6 Douala, Garoua, Maroua 7 Bamenda, Yaoundé 9 Bafoussam
  lake: 4 Chad, Nios, Nyos
  locale: 3 Afr. 6 Africa
  money: 5 franc
  neighbor: 4 Chad 5 Congo, Gabon, Gabun 7 Nigeria
  people: 3 Fan 4 Fang, Fula 6 Fulani, Kanuri, Pangwe 7 Pahouin
  port: 5 Duala 6 Douala
  river: 5 Benue
  volcano: 3 Oku
  writer: 4 Beti
__ **Came Running:** 4 Some
__ **Came, The:** 5 Rains
__ **Came You:** 4 Then
Camiletti: 3 Rob
Camilla: 5 Sparv
Camilla Parker-__: 6 Bowles
Camille: 5 Corot, novel 7 Pisarro 8 Pissarro 10 Saint-Saëns
  author: Alexandre Dumas
  love: 6 Armand
  see also French
Camillo: 5 Golgi
Camino __: 4 Real
Camino Real
  author: Tennessee Williams
camise: 5 shirt, smock
camisole: 5 shift 8 lingerie
camomile: 3 tea 4 herb 5 plant 6 flower
camouflage: 4 hide, lure, mask, veil 5 blind, cache, cloak, couch, cover, guise, shade 6 screen, shroud 7 conceal, obscure, secrete 8 disguise 9 dissemble, obfuscate 10 keep secret, masquerade, red herring
  color: 5 green
  one in ~: 5 hider
  wearer: 6 hunter 7 soldier 8 commando
camouflaged: 6 covert, hidden, secret, unseen 7 furtive, private 8 hush-hush 10 undercover, under wraps
camp: 3 set 4 arch, base, sect, side, tent, wild 5 droll, étape, farce, lodge, weird 6 far-out, resort 7 bivouac, bizarre, comical, faction, jocular, Lejeune, lodging, rough it 8 affected, barracks, garrison, humorous 9 laughable, Pendleton 10 artificial, pitch a tent, theatrical

berth: 3 cot
boss: 2 CO
break ~: 5 leave 6 depart
cousin: 6 kitsch
craft: 5 canoe
employee: 4 cook
ender: 4 fire, oree, site 5 stool 6 ground
fixture: 4 tent
meal: 4 mess
opposite ~: 3 foe 5 enemy
order: 4 halt 5 march 6 at ease
prison ~: 5 gulag
routine: 5 drill
set up ~: 4 tent 5 pitch, roost
camp __: 3 bed, car, out 4 it up 5 chair, shirt, stove 6 robber 7 meeting
__ camp: 3 day 4 base, boot, work 5 break, honor, sugar 6 strike, summer 7 trailer
__-camp: 6 aide-de
Camp: 3 Joe 6 Walter 7 Colleen
Camp __: 5 David 6 Swampy 7 Lejeune
Camp __ Accords: 5 David
Camp __ Girl: 4 Fire
__ Camp: 5 Space
Campagna di __: 4 Roma
campaign: 3 bid 4 push, race 5 drive, fight, lobby, quest, stump 6 attack, battle 7 canvass, crusade, promote, tactics, warfare 8 movement, politick 9 barnstorm, offensive, operation 10 enterprise, expedition
button word: 4 vote 5 elect 7 reelect
donor: 3 PAC 6 fat cat
for: 7 support 8 advocate
(for): 3 run 5 lobby, stump 7 contend
political ~: 3 bid 4 race
pro: 3 pol 10 politician
promises: 8 platform
staffer: 4 aide
tactic: 3 mud 5 smear 6 attack, debate 7 slander
topic: 5 crime, issue 7 defense, economy
campaign __: 3 hat 4 fund 5 chest, medal 6 button, ribbon
__ campaign: 5 smear
campaigner: 7 warrior 8 advocate, crusader, reformer 10 politician
corporate ~: 5 adman
campaign name
of 1936: 3 Alf
of 1952/1956: 3 Ike 5 Adlai
of 1992: 4 Bill, Ross
of 1996: 3 Bob 4 Bill, Dole, Ross
of 2000: 5 Ralph 6 George
of 2004: 4 John 6 George
of 2008: 4 John 6 Barack
Campanella: 3 Joe, Roy
Campanella, Roy: 6 Dodger 7 catcher, slugger
teammate: 5 Reese 6 Hodges, Snider 8 Newcombe, Robinson
Campania
city: 4 Nola 6 Amalfi, Naples, Napoli 7 Salerno
locale: 5 Italy 6 Italia
stream: 4 Sele
campanile: 5 tower 7 steeple 8 pinnacle
feature: 4 bell
Campari: 5 drink 8 beverage
Campbell: 3 Kim 4 Earl, Glen, Neve, town 5 Naomi, Scott, Tevin, Tisha 6 Luther, Thomas
Campbell, Earl
sport: 8 football
Campbell, Glen
song: By the Time I Get to Phoenix (1967)
Galveston (1969)
Gentle on My Mind (1968)
It's Only Make Believe (1970)
Rhinestone Cowboy (1975)
Southern Nights (1977)
Wichita Lineman (1968)
Campbell, Kim: 2 P.M. 8 Canadian
predecessor: 8 Mulroney
successor: 8 Chrétien
__ Campbell, KY: 4 Fort
Campbell, Neve: 7 actress
film: Drowning Mona (2000)
Panic (2000)
Scream (1996)
Wild Things (1998)
TV: Party of Five
__ Campbell Scott: 6 Duncan
Campbell Soup: 7 company
competitor: 5 Knorr 9 Progresso
headquarters: 6 Camden
Camp David Accords: 4 pact 6 treaty
conferee: 5 Begin, Sadat 6 Carter
nation: 5 Egypt 6 Israel
camper: 2 RV 9 Winnebago 10 mobile home
driver: 4 RVer
fuel: 3 LPG
relative: 3 van
__ camper: 5 happy, truck 6 pickup
campfire
remains: 5 ashes
starter: 5 spark
treat: 5 frank, s'more 6 hot dog, wiener
Camp Fire __: 4 Girl
campground: 4 site
convenience: 6 hookup
initials: 3 KOA
camphor: 4 tree
relative: 6 laurel 7 avocado 8 cinnamon 9 sassafras
camphor __: 3 ice, oil 4 ball, tree
Campion: 4 Jane 6 Thomas
Campion, Jane
film: The Piano (1993)
Camp Meeting, The
composer: Charles Ives
campo: 3 lea, ley 5 veldt 7 lowland, prairie 9 grassland
Campobello: 4 isle 6 island
locale: 6 Canada
monogram: 3 FDR
camporee
attendee: 5 Scout 8 Boy Scout
unit: 4 tent
Camptown Races
composer: Stephen Foster
campus: 4 quad 7 grounds 10 university
cheer: 3 rah
disruption: 5 sit-in
facility: 3 gym, lab 4 dorm, hall, quad
like ~ walls: 5 ivied
misfit: 4 nerd
organization: 3 sor. 4 frat 6 Hillel 8 sorority 10 fraternity
outcast: 4 nerd
person: 4 dean, prof 6 bursar
sports org.: 4 NCAA
starter: 5 hippo
student: 4 BMOC, coed 5 frosh 6 junior, senior 8 freshman 9 sophomore
see also college
__-campus: 3 off
campy: 4 zany 5 banal, droll, funky, witty 6 absurd 7 blatant 8 affected, humorous, mannered, overdone 9 laughable 10 artificial, outlandish, theatrical
exclamation: 3 oof, pow 5 zowie
perhaps: 5 retro
Camry: 3 car 4 auto 6 Toyota
Camryn: 7 Manheim
Camus, Albert: 6 French, writer 8 Nobelist 10 playwright
birthplace: Algeria
work: Caligula
Cross Purpose
The Fall
L'Étranger
The Myth of Sisyphus
No Exit
The Plague
The Rebel
State of Siege
The Stranger
can: 2 ax 3 axe, tin 4 boot, drop, fire, jail, john, oust, poky, sack 5 expel, let go, pokey, put up, store 6 bounce, lay off, lockup, pickle, prison, record, vessel 7 cashier, deep-six, dismiss, drum out, hoosgow, kick out, latrine, package, process, release, slammer, turn out 8 furlough, get rid of, hoosegow, pink-slip, preserve 9 container, discharge, terminate
combining form: 5 scyph- 6 scyphi-, scypho-
covering: 5 label
do what one ~: 3 try 6 strive 7 attempt, have a go, venture 9 have a go at, have a shot, have a stab 10 have a whack
it: 5 quiet 6 shut up
of worms: 7 problem 9 adversity
opener: 3 tab 6 gadget
opener target: 3 lid
producer: 5 Alcoa
can __: 4 buoy 6 opener
__ can: 3 ash, oil, tin 5 blitz, jerry, spray, trash 6 squirt 7 aerosol, garbage
Can __ Top This?: 3 You
Can __ you?: 5 I help
Can.
currency: 3 dol.
neighbor: 3 Ida., USA 4 Alas., Mich., Minn., Mont., N. Dak., Wash.
police force: 4 RCMP
province: 3 Alb., Man., Nfd., Ont., PEI, Que. 4 Alba., Alta., Newf., Nfld., Sask.
region: 3 NWT
see also Canada
__ Can: 4 Yes I
Canaan
deity: 4 Baal
father: 3 Ham
grandfather: 4 Noah
land of ~: 6 Israel
Canada: 3 Lee 6 nation 7 country
agreement with ~: 5 NAFTA
alphabet ender: 3 zed
Arctic explorer: 3 Rae
baseballer: 4 Expo 7 Blue Jay
bay: 5 Fundy, James 6 Baffin, Hudson, Ungava 8 Georgian 9 Frobisher
bird: 4 loon 5 goose
bird on a ~ $1 coin: 4 loon
capital: 6 Ottawa
city: 4 Ajax, Alma, Amos, Baie, Faro, Hull, Mayo, Olds 5 Anjou, Craik, Delta, Elgin, Hanna, Kaslo, Laval, Leduc, Lévis, Lumby, Rouyn, Sooke, Sorel, St. Luc, Taber, Truro, Unity 6 Argyle, Aurora, Aylmer, Barrie, Birtle, Brigus, Comeau, Dundas, Fernie, Granby, Guelph, Inuvik, Kanata, La Baie, London, Milton, Nepean, Onoway, Oshawa, Ottawa, Pictou, Québec, Regina, Sarnia, Scugog, Souris, Ste.-Foy, St. John, Surrey, The Pas, Val-d'Or, Verdun, Vernon, Whitby 7 Avonlea, Baddeck, Botwood, Brandon, Burnaby, Caledon, Calgary, Cap-Pele, Chambly, Chatham, Eastend, Grimsby, Halifax, Iqaluit, Kelowna, Lachine, Langley, La Salle, Lincoln, Markham, Melfort, Mirabel, Mission, Moncton, Nanaimo, Nipawin, Noranda, Old Crow, Orillia, Osoyoos, Red Deer, Saanich, St. John's, Sudbury, Timmins, Tisdale, Toronto, Vaughan, Welland, Weyburn, Windsor, Wynyard, Yorkton 8 Alberton, Ancaster, Beauport, Bradford, Brampton, Brossard, Carcross, Cornwall, Edmonton, Flin Flon, Fort Erie, Gatineau, Georgina, Hamilton, Hay River, Kamloops, Keno City, Kingston, Montréal, Moose Jaw, New Minas, North Bay, Oakville, Richmond, Rimouski, Sept-Iles, St. Albert, Ste.-Julie, St.-Hubert, St.-Jérôme, St. Thomas, Victoria, Waterloo, Winnipeg 9 Brantford, Cambridge, Coquitlam, Côte-St.-Luc, Dartmouth, Haldimand, Innisfail, Jonquière, Kitchener, Longueuil, Mascouche, Miramichi, Nanticoke, Newmarket, Outremont, Owen Sound, Penticton, Pickering, Port Elgin, Port Moody, Sackville, Saskatoon, St.-Georges, St.-Lambert, St.-Laurent, St.-Léonard, Stratford, Val-Belair, Vancouver, Westmount, Woodstock 10 Abbotsford, Belleville, Blainville, Boisbriand, Brockville, Burlington, Cape Breton, Chicoutimi, Chilliwack, Clarington, Cumberland, Dawson City, Gloucester, Lethbridge, Maple Ridge, Mount Lorne, Mount Pearl, New Glasgow, Repentigny, Sherbrooke, St.-Constant, Ste.-Thérèse, St.-Eustache,

Strathcona, Terrebonne, Thunder Bay, Whitchurch, Whitehorse
coat: **7** kuletuk
conductor: **9** Pelletier
critic: **7** McLuhan
explorer: **9** Champlain
flag feature: **4** leaf **9** maple leaf
fliers: **4** RCAF
footballer: **6** Eskimo
gulf: **7** Boothia **10** St. Lawrence
Indian: **3** Han **4** Cree **5** Haida, Kaska **6** Abnaki, Micmac, Nootka, Ottawa **7** Abenaki, Kutchin, Kutenai, Naskapi, Tlingit **8** Kwakiutl, Malecite, Wabanaki **9** Saulteaux, Tsimshian **10** Assiniboin, Bellabella, Bellacoola
island: **6** Baffin **8** Victoria **9** Ellesmere, Vancouver
lake: **4** Erie **5** Huron, Rainy **6** Louise, Simcoe **7** Nipigon, Ontario **8** Manitoba, Michigan, Superior, Winnipeg **9** Athabasca, Great Bear **10** Great Slave
language: **6** French **7** English
leader: **2** p.m.
legislature: **6** Senate
money: **4** cent, dime **5** penny **6** dollar, loonie, toonie **7** quarter
mountain: **4** King **5** Logan, Walsh **6** Robson, Steele **7** Lucania, Rockies, St. Elias **8** Caubvick, Columbia
native: **5** Inuit **6** Innuit, Inupik
neighbor: **3** Ida., USA **4** Alas., Mich., Minn., Mont., N. Dak., Wash., Wisc.. **5** Idaho, Maine **6** Alaska **7** Montana, New York, Vermont **8** Michigan **9** Wisconsin **10** Washington **11** North Dakota **12** New Hampshire
Nobelist in Chemistry: **5** Taube **6** Marcus **7** Polanyi **8** Herzberg
Nobelist in Economics: **7** Mundell, Scholes, Vickrey
Nobelist in Medicine: **7** Banting
Nobelist in Peace: **7** Pearson
Nobelist in Physics: **6** Taylor **10** Brockhouse
org.: **3** OAS **4** NATO
peninsula: **5** Gaspé **6** Avalon, Ungava **7** Boothia **8** Labrador **10** Nova Scotia
physician: **5** Osler
pianist: **5** Gould **8** Peterson
pie: **5** rappe **6** rappie
poet: **4** Page **5** Blais, Dudek, Klein, Pratt, Purdy, Scott, Smith **6** Avison, Carman, Hébert **7** Garneau, Newlove, Service, Souster **8** Sangster **9** Choquette, Fréchette, Grandbois, Gustafson
police force: **4** RCMP
political party: **3** Lib. **7** Liberal
port: **7** Halifax, Toronto **8** Montreal **9** Churchill, Vancouver **10** Thunder Bay
province: **3** Alb., Man., Nfd., Ont., PEI, Que. **4** Alba., Alta., Newf., Nfld., Sask. **6** Quebec **7** Alberta, Nunavut, Ontario **8** Manitoba **10** Nova Scotia **12** New Brunswick, Newfoundland, Saskatchewan **15** British Columbia
region: **5** Gaspé, Yukon **6** Acadia
river: **4** Nass **5** Liard, Peace, Slave, Yukon **6** Fraser, Nelson, Ottawa, St. John, Thelon **7** Niagara, St. Clair **8** Columbia, Hamilton, Klondike, Kootenay, Saguenay **9** Churchill, Mackenzie, Richelieu **10** Coppermine, St. Lawrence
Rockies park: **5** Banff
school: **3** TWU **4** York **5** Brock, Laval, Trent **6** Acadia, McGill, Queen's **7** Bishop's, Brandon, Ryerson **8** Carleton, Lakehead, McMaster, Memorial **9** Concordia, Dalhousie **11** Simon Fraser
sea: **8** Labrador **9** Hudson Bay
town official: **5** reeve
tree: **5** maple
valley: **5** droke
waterfall: **5** Della **7** Niagara, Panther
wildcat: **4** lynx
writer: **3** Roy **5** Blais, Engel, Moore, Mowat, Munro, Wiebe **6** Atwood, Davies, Moodie, Nowlan, Parker, Wilson **7** Findley, Gallant, McLuhan, Richter **9** Callaghan **10** Haliburton, Montgomery
Canada __: **3** Act, Day, Dry, jay **5** goose
__ Canada: **3** Air **5** Lower, Upper
Canada Day month: **4** July
Canada Dry: **3** pop **4** soda **9** soft drink
alternative: ***see*** soft drink
Canada prime ministers:
2006- Stephen Harper
2003-2006 Paul Martin
1993-2003 Jean Chrétien
1993 Kim Campbell
1984-1993 Brian Mulroney
1984 John Turner
1980-1984 Pierre Trudeau
1979-1980 Joe Clark
1968-1979 Pierre Trudeau
1963-1968 Lester Pearson
1957-1963 John Diefenbaker
1948-1957 Louis St. Laurent
1935-1948 W.L. Mackenzie King
1930-1935 Richard Bennett
1926-1930 W.L. Mackenzie King
1926 Arthur Meighen
1921-1926 W.L. Mackenzie King
1920-1921 Arthur Meighen
1911-1920 Sir Robert Laird Borden
1896-1911 Sir Wilfrid Laurier
1896 Sir Charles Tupper
1894-1896 Sir Mackenzie Bowell
1892-1894 Sir John Thompson
1891-1892 Sir John Abbott
1878-1891 Sir John MacDonald
1873-1878 Alexander Mackenzie
1867-1873 Sir John MacDonald
Canadian: **5** river
locale: **8** Oklahoma **9** New Mexico
Canadian __: **5** bacon, Falls, goose **6** whisky
Canadian Bacon (1995 film)
cast: Alan Alda, John Candy, Rhea Perlman
director: Michael Moore
Canadien: **6** iceman
Canadiens: **3** six **4** team
home: **8** Montreal
milieu: **3** ice **4** rink
org.: **3** NHL
rival: ***see*** hockey team
canaille: **3** mob **6** rabble
canal: **4** duct, Erie, Göta, Kiel, Suez **5** Grand **6** artery, course, groove, Panama, Rideau, trench, trough **7** channel, conduit, passage, Welland **8** aqueduct, waterway **10** passageway
anatomical ~: **4** iter **5** lumen
bank: **4** berm **5** berme
feature: **4** lock
sight: **5** barge **7** gondola
site: **3** ear **4** root **5** tooth **7** isthmus
__ canal: **3** ear **4** root
Canal __: **4** Zone
__ Canal: **4** Erie, Kiel, Suez **5** Grand **6** Panama
__ Canals: **3** Soo
canapé: **4** nosh, sofa **5** snack, taste **7** munchie **9** appetizer **10** finger food
topping: **3** lox, roe **4** pâté **6** caviar, cheese, salmon **7** caviare
canard: **4** hoax, tale **5** rumor, story **6** report **7** falsity, untruth, whapper, whopper **9** falsehood
__ Canaria Island: **4** Gran
canary: **3** pet **4** bird, fink, nark, wine **5** color, dance, finch **6** singer, yellow **7** stoolie, tattler **8** informer, songbird **9** informant **10** taleteller, tattletale
bill: **3** nib
home: **4** cage **6** aviary
imitate a ~: **4** sing **6** warble
relative: ***see*** yellow color
seat: **5** perch
sound: **5** tweet
canary __: **4** seed **5** grass **6** yellow
Canary: **4** isls. **5** David, isles **7** islands
Canary Islands
island: **5** Palma **6** Hierro **7** La Palma **8** Tenerife **9** Teneriffe
owner: **5** Spain
port: **9** Las Palmas
canasta: **4** game **8** card game
cousin: **3** gin
holding: **4** meld, trey
Canaveral: **4** cape
org.: **4** NASA
Canberra: **4** city, town **7** capital
locale: **9** Australia
river: **8** Molonglo
__ can be told!: **5** Now it
__ Can Boyd: **3** Oil
Canby: **7** Vincent
cancan: **5** dance
do the ~: **4** kick
like ~ dancers: **5** leggy
Can-Can (1960 film): **7** musical
cast: Maurice Chevalier, Louis Jourdan, Shirley MacLaine, Frank Sinatra
composer: Cole Porter
director: Walter Lang
setting: **5** Paris **6** France
__ Can Can: **5** Yes We
cancel: **2** ax **3** axe, nix, zap **4** drop, kill, lift, null, undo, void, X out **5** abort, annul, erase, quash, remit, scrap, scrub **6** delete, efface, negate, offset, recall, recant, refute, repeal, revoke **7** abolish, call off, expunge, nullify, redress, rescind, retract, reverse, scratch, torpedo, wipe out **8** abrogate, break off, close out, cross out, disallow, dissolve, override, overrule, set aside, write off **9** discharge, eliminate, liquidate, repudiate, strike out, terminate **10** balance out, counteract, invalidate, neutralize, scratch out
a launch: **5** scrub
out: **6** negate, offset, refute **8** outweigh **10** compensate, counteract
(out): **5** equal
canceled: **3** off **4** no-go, void
canceled check notation: **3** NSF **4** paid
cancellation: **6** recall **7** receipt
avoid ~: **5** renew
Cancer: **4** crab, sign
month: **3** Jul., Jun. **4** July, June
predecessor: **6** Gemini
successor: **3** Leo
Cancer Ward
author: Aleksandr Solzhenitsyn
__ Can Cook: **3** Yan
Cancún: **4** city, town
locale: **6** Mexico
see also Spanish
candescence: **6** luster
Candice: **6** Bergen
father: **5** Edgar
candid: **4** naif, open **5** bluff, blunt, brusk, frank, naive, photo, plain **6** abrupt, direct, honest **7** brusque, genuine, natural, sincere, up-front, upright **8** impolite, out-front, snapshot, straight, tactless, truthful, unartful **9** downright, guileless, impartial, ingenuous, outspoken, unfeigned, unguarded, unslanted **10** aboveboard, flat-footed, forthright, foursquare, free-spoken, from the hip, indelicate, pointblank, unaffected, unmediated, unreserved, unreticent
be ~: **5** level
don't be ~: **3** haw, hem **10** equivocate
Candid __: **6** Camera
Candida
author: George Bernard Shaw
Candida (1970 song)
artist: Tony Orlando & Dawn
candidate: **6** runner, seeker **7** entrant, hopeful, nominee **8** aspirant, opponent, prospect **9** applicant, appointee, contender, dark horse, job-hunter, pothunter, successor **10** competitor, contestant, handshaker, petitioner, solicitant
be a ~: **3** run
concern: **5** issue, slate, voter **6** ballot, debate
successful ~: **2** in
candidates: **5** field
Candid Camera (ABC/NBC/CBS comedy)
host: Allen Funt, Peter Funt
plant: **4** mike
request: **5** smile
Candide
author: Voltaire
candidly: **4** true **5** truly **6** as it is, openly, simply **8** directly, straight **9** naturally, sincerely **10** pointblank

candied: 5 glacé, sweet 6 honied, sugary 7 honeyed, sugared 8 cajoling 9 adulatory 10 flattering, saccharine
candied ___: 3 yam
candle: 5 light, taper 6 bougie, shames 7 shammes 8 bayberry 9 luminaria
circler: 4 moth
count: 3 age
ender: 3 nut, pin 4 fish, wick, wood 5 berry, light, power, stick 6 holder 7 snuffer
holder: 4 cake 6 sconce
ingredient: 3 wax 4 suet, wick 7 beeswax 8 paraffin
make a ~: 3 dip
poetically: 4 glim
use a ~: 5 light 6 censed
candle ___: 5 power
___ candle: 5 Roman
___-candle: 4 foot 5 meter
Candle in the Wind
author: Maxwell Anderson
Candle in the Wind (1987 song)
artist: Elton John
Candle in the Wind, The
author: T.H. White
candlelight: 5 flame
candlelit: 3 dim
candlenut: 4 tree 5 Asian
family: 6 spurge
tree: 5 kukui
candlepower: 5 light
unit: 5 lumen
Candler: 3 Asa
___ Candles: 7 Sixteen
candlestick: 7 pricket 8 flambeau 9 girandole
maker's partner: 5 baker 7 butcher
Candlestick ___: 4 Park
___ candle to: 5 hold a
can-do: 4 able 9 efficient
Can do!: 4 easy
candor: 5 truth 7 honesty, naiveté 8 openness, veracity 9 frankness, good faith, sincerity 10 simplicity
___ Can Dream: 3 If I
candy: 3 bar 4 bark, kiss, mint 5 crème, fudge, goody, snack, sweet, taffy 6 bonbon, comfit, dragée, goodie, halvah, jujube, nougat, red-hot, sucker, toffee 7 caramel, fondant, gumdrop, penuche, praline, process 8 bull's-eye, divinity, licorice, lollipop, marzipan, sourball 9 chocolate, jellybean, lemon drop, marchpane, nonpareil, sugarplum, sweetmeat 10 almond bark, confection, jawbreaker, peppermint
after-dinner ~: 4 mint
brand: 3 PEZ 4 Mars, Rolo, Twix 5 Clark, Heath, Lindt, Necco, Reese 6 Brach's, Charms, Godiva, Kit Kat, M and M's, Mounds, Nestle, PayDay, Reese's, Zagnut 7 Cadbury, Goobers, Hershey, Krackel, Oh Henry, Sno-Caps 8 Baby Ruth, Chuckles, Milk Duds, Milky Way, Perugina, Skittles, Snickers 9 Almond Joy, Mr. Goodbar, Raisinets, Starburst, Toblerone, Twizzlers 10 Jelly Belly, Lifesavers, NutRageous, SweetTarts
British ~: 5 lolly
chewy ~: 5 taffy, toffy 6 toffee
chocolate ~: 3 bar 4 kiss
cost, once: 5 penny
ender: 4 tuft
hard ~: 4 drop 5 charm, lolly
ingredient: 5 anise, cocoa, sugar
like ~: 5 sweet
nut: 6 almond
pecan ~: 7 praline
peppermint ~: 5 patty 6 pattie
pillow ~: 4 mint
shape: 3 bar 4 drop
Turkish ~: 5 halva 6 halvah 7 halavah
candy ___: 3 bar 4 cane, corn, dish, pull 5 apple, floss 6 stripe 7 striper
___ candy: 3 ear, eye 4 hard, rock 5 sugar 6 barley, cotton
Candy: 4 Etta, John 5 Clark 8 Cummings
Candy (1991 song)
artist: Iggy Pop
Candy ___: 4 Girl, Land, Rain
Candy ___, The: 3 Man
candy-apple color: 3 red 6 cerise
candy-coated: 5 sweet
Candy Girl (1963 song)
artist: Four Seasons
Candy is dandy...
poet: Ogden Nash
Candy, John: 5 actor
film: Canadian Bacon (1995)
Cool Runnings (1993)
The Great Outdoors (1988)
Once Upon a Crime (1992)
Only the Lonely (1991)
Spaceballs (1987)
Splash (1984)
Stripes (1981)
Uncle Buck (1989)
Volunteers (1985)
Candy Man, The (1972 song)
artist: Sammy Davis Jr.
Candy-O band: 4 Cars
candy striper: 4 aide
candytuft: 5 plant 6 flower
cane: 3 bat, hit, rap, rod 4 beat, drub, flog, pole, prop, whip 5 grass, plant, ratan, spank, staff, stave, stick 6 bamboo, cudgel, Melaka, rattan, strike, thrash, thwack 7 Malacca, scourge 9 truncheon
for Chaplin: 4 prop
material: 6 bamboo
product: 3 rum 5 berry, chair, sugar
cane ___: 5 chair, sugar
___ cane: 5 candy, sugar
ça ne ___ rien: 4 fait
___ Cane: 5 Mondo
Canea: 4 port
locale: 5 Crete 6 Candia
native: 6 Cretan
___ canem: 4 cave
Canetti, Elias: 6 writer 8 Nobelist 9 Bulgarian 10 playwright
canfield: 4 game 8 card game
canful: 3 tin
Can I ___ Witness?: 4 Get a
___ Can I Be Sure: 3 How
Caniff: 4 Milt 6 Milton
Canin: 5 Ethan
canine: 3 dog, fox, pet, pom, pug 4 Asta, fang, Odie, wolf 5 boxer, dhole, dingo, hound, husky, pooch, tooth 6 Bullet, corsac, coydog, coyote, cuspid, fennec, jackal, Lassie 8 Alsatian, Checkers, eyetooth, shepherd 9 Rin Tin Tin 10 snarleyyow
Africa: 6 fennec, jackal
Asia: 5 dhole 6 corsac, jackal
Australia: 5 dingo
bane: 4 flea 5 mange
cartilage: 5 lytta
category: 3 toy
cinema ~: 4 Asta, Toto 5 Balto 6 Lassie 9 Rin Tin Tin
comics ~: 4 Fuzz, Odie, Otto, Ruff 5 Barfy, Bitsy, Daisy, Snert 6 Grimmy 7 Dogbert 9 Marmaduke
command: 3 beg, sit 4 come, heel, stay 5 fetch, shake, sit up, speak 6 drop it 8 roll over
core of a ~: 4 pulp
cousin: 5 molar
covering: 3 cap, fur 6 enamel
cross: 3 mut 4 mutt
drink like a ~: 5 lap up
holder: 3 gum
hotel: 5 pound 6 kennel 7 shelter 8 doghouse
offspring: 3 pup 5 puppy, whelp
registry org.: 3 AKC
related: 6 dental
restraint: 5 leash
retrieval: 5 stick
small ~: 3 pom, pug 4 peke 5 corgi 6 lap dog
snatch a ~: 6 dognap
sound: 3 arf, grr 4 bark, howl, woof 5 gnarl, growl, snarl, whine 6 bowwow
tooth: 4 fang
wild ~: 3 fox 4 wolf 5 dingo 6 coyote, jackal
see also dog
Canine Cantata
composer: PDQ Bach
Canio: 5 tenor
opera: 9 Pagliacci
wife: 5 Nedda
canis: 3 dog
Canis ___: 5 Major, Minor 7 Majoris, Minoris
Canis Major
author: Robert Frost
neighbor: 4 Argo
owner: 5 Orion
star in ~: 6 Sirius
canister: 4 case 9 container
Can it!: 3 shh 5 quiet 6 shut up
___ Can I Turn To: 3 Who
canned: 5 let go, put up
food: 4 corn, peas, Spam, tuna 5 beans
not ~: 5 fresh
Canned ___: 4 Heat
cannel: 4 coal
cannelloni: 7 noodles
alternative: *see* pasta
Cannery Row: 4 film 5 novel
author: John Steinbeck
cast: Nick Nolte, Debra Winger
Cannes: 4 city, port, town
award: 9 Grand Prix
group: 6 jet set
locale: 6 France
neighbor: 4 Nice
topic: 6 cinema
Cannibals and Missionaries
author: Mary McCarthy
canniness: 3 art 5 craft 7 caution 8 keenness 9 foresight, smartness 10 cleverness, discretion, precaution
canning item: 3 jar 5 sieve
cannoli: 6 pastry 7 dessert, Italian
make ~: 5 stuff
cannon: 3 arm, gun 4 arty. 6 big gun, mortar 8 howitzer, ordnance 9 artillery
command: 4 fire
ender: 3 ade, eer 4 ball
fodder: 8 infantry
loose ~: 5 rogue
nickname: 6 Bertha 9 Big Bertha
part: 6 breech
roar: 4 boom 5 salvo
water ~ target, perhaps: 5 crowd
cannon ___: 4 ball, bone 6 fodder
___ cannon: 5 loose, water
Cannon: 2 J.D. 4 Dyan 5 towel 6 Freddy
Cannon (CBS drama)
cast: William Conrad (Frank Cannon)
cannonade: 4 boom, fire, pelt, roll 5 burst, salvo, shell, storm 6 volley 7 assault, barrage, battery, bombard, thunder 8 fire upon, shelling 9 broadside
cannonball: 4 ammo 10 ammunition
human ~ terminus: 3 net
Cannonball: 5 train 8 Adderley
___ Cannonball: 6 Wabash
Cannonball Run, The (1981 film)
cast: Dom DeLuise, Jack Elam, Farrah Fawcett, Roger Moore, Burt Reynolds
director: Hal Needham
Cannon, Dyan: 7 actress
spouse: Cary Grant
cannoneer often: 5 firer
cannonfire: 4 boom, fire, roll 5 burst, salvo, shell, storm 6 volley 7 assault, barrage, battery, bombard, thunder 8 fire upon, shelling 9 broadside
cannonry: 7 battery
cannons: 4 arty. 8 materiel, weaponry 9 artillery, munitions
___ cannot wither her: 3 Age
canny: 3 sly 4 arch, cagy, foxy, wary, wily, wise 5 acute, cagey, quick, slick, smart 6 adroit, artful, astute, clever, crafty, shrewd 7 careful, cunning, guarded, heedful, knowing, politic, prudent, sunning, thrifty 8 cautious, dextrous, discreet, guileful, skillful, watchful 9 astucious, dexterous, ingenious, judicious, provident, sagacious 10 thoughtful
canoe: 4 boat 5 craft, kayak, skiff 6 dugout, paddle, vessel 7 pirogue, vehicle 9 birchbark, outrigger 10 watercraft
anagram: 5 ocean
Eskimo ~: 5 kayak, umiak
paddle: 3 oar
spot: 4 lake 5 river 6 rapids
wood: 5 birch
canoeing: 5 sport
can of ___: 5 worms
___ can of worms: 5 open a
canola: 3 oil
canon: 3 law 4 code, rule 5 bylaw, creed, dogma, edict, tenet 6 cleric,

decree, oeuvre 7 dictate, precept, statute 8 doctrine, standard 9 criterion, ordinance, principle 10 convention, regulation
Buddhist: 5 agama
composer: 4 Bach
marking: 5 presa
markings: 5 prese
Canon: 3 SLR 6 camera, copier
alternative: *see* camera
Canon City: 4 city, town
locale: 8 Colorado
cañon feature: 5 tilde
canonical: 5 jural, legal, sound 6 lawful 8 accepted, approved, clerical, dogmatic, official, orthodox, rightful, standard 9 classical, episcopal, religious, statutory 10 authorized, dogmatical, legitimate, recognized, sanctioned
hour: 4 sext 5 matin, nones, terce 7 worship
canonical ___: 3 age 4 hour
canonicals: 3 alb 4 cope, garb 5 habit, stole 6 attire 7 cassock, maniple, vesture 8 surplice
canonist: 8 believer
canonize: 5 bless 7 beatify, glorify, idolize, worship 8 dedicate, sanctify 10 consecrate
canonized one: 2 st. 3 ste. 5 saint 6 sainte
canonry: 6 clergy
canoodle: 4 neck 6 caress, fondle
Canopus: 4 star
canopy: 3 sky 5 cover, shade 6 awning, screen 7 marquee 8 covering, overhang, pavilion, sunshade 9 baldachin
it has a ~: 6 forest
Canova: 4 Judy 5 Diana
___ Can Say Goodbye: 5 Never
___ can say that again!: 3 You
Canseco, José
sport: 8 baseball
...can Spring be ___ behind?: 3 far
canst
relative: 6 mayest
cant: 3 sag, tip 4 keel, lean, sham, talk, tilt 5 argot, bevel, idiom, lingo, lurch, pitch, slang, slant, slope 6 deceit, humbug, jargon, patois, patter 7 dialect, incline, recline, tip over 8 language, parlance, pretense, shoptalk 9 hypocrisy 10 dishonesty, lip service, vernacular, vocabulary
can't
help but: 4 must 6 have to, should 7 ought to
live without: 5 crave 7 hurt for, require
stand: 4 hate 5 abhor 6 detest, loathe
Can't ___: 4 Stop 5 Let Go, We Try
Can't ___ Friends?: 4 We Be
Can't ___ Love: 5 Buy Me
Can't ___ Lovin' Dat Man: 4 Help
Cantab
rival: 3 Eli 5 Yalie 7 Bulldog
___ cantabile: 4 aria
Cantabrian river: 4 Ebro
Cantabrigian: 4 Brit 6 Briton
river: 3 Cam
cantaloupe: 4 pepo 5 melon 6 orange
kin: *see* melon
cantankerous: 4 dour, mean, sour, ugly 5 cross, huffy, moody, surly, testy 6 crabby, cranky, crusty, grumpy, morose, ornery, stuffy, touchy 7 bearish, bristly, grouchy, loutish, peevish, prickly, waspish 8 captious, choleric, churlish, contrary, grumpish, petulant, snappish, stubborn 9 crotchety, difficult, irascible, irritable, obstinate, querulous, splenetic 10 ill-humored, out of sorts
one: 4 crab 5 grump 6 grouch
cantankerousness: 6 spleen, temper
Cantar de Rodrigo hero: 5 El Cid
cantata: 5 music
like a ~: 6 choral
maestro: 4 Bach
singers: 5 choir
tune: 4 aria
___ can't be!: 4 This
___ Can't Be Love: 4 This
Can't Buy Me Love (1964 song)
artist: Beatles
___ Can't Cheat an Honest Man: 3 You
canted: 4 awry 5 askew, atilt, bevel, leant 6 askant 7 askance, crooked 8 cockeyed, lopsided
canteen: 5 flask 6 bottle 7 kitchen, thermos 9 container, lunchroom 10 chuck wagon, restaurant
initials: 3 USO
canter: 3 jog, run 4 gait, lope, pace, skip, step, trip, trot, walk 5 amble 6 gallop 7 dogtrot, saunter 9 gallopade
Canterbury: 4 city, town
locale: 4 Kent 7 England
Canterbury ___: 5 bells, Tales
Canterbury Tales, The: 4 poem
author: Geoffrey Chaucer
character: 4 Cook, Dyer, Monk 5 Canon, Clerk, Friar, Harry, Reeve 6 Bailey, Doctor, Knight, Miller, Parson, Squire, Weaver, Yeoman 7 Chaucer, Plowman, Shipman 8 Franklin, Geoffrey, Manciple, Merchant, Pardoner, Prioress, Sergeant, Summoner 9 Carpenter, Second Nun 10 Nun's Priest, Wife of Bath 11 Haberdasher
drink: 4 mead
inn: 6 Tabard
Canterbury topper, Archbishop of: 5 mitre
Can't Fight This Feeling (1985 song)
artist: REO Speedwagon
___ Can't Get a Man With a Gun: 3 You
Can't Get Enough of Your Love, Babe (1974 song)
artist: Barry White
Can't Get It Out of My Head (1975 song)
artist: ELO
___ Can't Go Home Again: 3 You
___ Can't Have Everything: 3 You
___ Can't Have You: 3 If I
Can't Help Falling in Love (1961 song)
artist: Elvis Presley
___ Can't Help It, The: 4 Girl
Can't Help Lovin' Dat Man
composer: Oscar Hammerstein, Jerome Kern
Canth, Minna: 6 writer 7 Finnish
___ Can't Hurry Love: 3 You
canticle: 3 ode 4 hymn, song 5 music, psalm 6 anthem
cantilever: 4 beam 5 truss 7 bracket
cantilever ___: 6 bridge
cantillate: 4 sing
cantina: 3 bar 6 saloon
shout: 5 salud
snack: 4 taco, tapa
Cantique de Noël
composer: Adolphe Adam
Can't Let Go (1991 song)
artist: Mariah Carey
Can't Nobody Hold Me Down (1997 song)
artist: Mase, Puff Daddy
canto: 3 air 4 song 5 verse 6 melody
___ canto: 3 bel
canton: 4 ward 5 lodge, state 7 quarter 8 province
Swiss ~: 3 Uri, Zug 4 Bern, Vaud 5 Berne 6 Aargau, Valais
Canton: 4 city, town
attraction: 3 HoF 10 Hall of Fame
ender: 3 -ese
locale: 4 Ohio 5 China 8 Michigan
river: 3 Hsi
cantor: 5 hazan 6 hazzan 7 chazzan
place: 4 shul 5 schul 9 synagogue
Cantor: 3 Ida 5 Eddie
Cantor, Eddie: 5 actor 8 comedian
film: Whoopee! (1930)
Cantos
author: Ezra Pound
Cantrell: 4 Lana
cantrip: 3 hex 5 spell
Can't Smile Without You (1978 song)
artist: Barry Manilow
Can't Stay Away From You (1988 song)
artist: Gloria Estefan
Can't Stop This Thing We Started (1991 song)
artist: Bryan Adams
___ Can't Take It With You: 3 You
Can't Take My Eyes Off You (1967 song)
artist: Frankie Valli
___ can't take that away...: 4 They
___ Can't We Be Friends?: 3 Why
Can't We Try (1987 song)
artist: Dan Hill, Vonda Shepard
Can't You Hear My Heartbeat (1965 song)
artist: Herman's Hermits
Can't You See (1995 song)
artist: Notorious B.I.G., Total
Can't You See That She's Mine (1964 song)
artist: Dave Clark Five
Can't you take ___?: 5 a hint, a joke
Canucks: 3 six
home: 9 Vancouver
milieu: 3 ice 4 rink
org.: 3 NHL
rival: *see* hockey team
Canute: 4 king 6 Danish
foe: 4 Olaf, Olav
canvas: 3 art, oil 4 sail, tarp 6 fabric 7 picture, tenting 8 painting, portrait 9 sailcloth, still life, tarpaulin 10 watercolor
ender: 4 back
product: 4 tarp, tent 6 awning 9 sailcloth
support: 4 mast 5 easel
user: 6 artist 7 painter
canvasback: 4 duck, fowl
relative: *see* duck
canvaslike
fabric: 5 wigan
canvass: 3 ask 4 case, poll, talk 5 study 6 review, survey, voting 7 examine, inspect, solicit 8 campaign
___ Can Wait: 6 Heaven
Can we talk? lady: 6 Rivers
___ Can Whistle: 4 Some 6 Anyone
canyon: 4 gulf 5 Bryce, chasm, gorge, gulch, gully 6 arroyo, canada, coulee, gulley, ravine, valley
edge: 3 lip, rim
form a ~: 5 erode
mouth: 4 abra
phenomenon: 4 echo
___ canyon: 3 box
___ Canyon: 5 Black, Bryce, Grand, Steve 6 Laurel 7 Boulder
___ Canyon Dam: 4 Glen
Canyonlands: 4 park
city near: 4 Moab
locale: 4 Utah
___ Canyon Suite: 5 Grand
Can you ___?: 5 dig it
Can You Feel the Love Tonight (1994 song)
artist: Elton John
___, Can You Hear Me?: 4 Papa
___ can you see: 4 O say 5 Oh say
canzone: 3 ode
CaO
containing: 4 limy
Ca(OH)2: 6 alkali
cap: 3 fez, hat, lid, taj, tam, tip, top 4 acme, beat, best, cork, kepi, seal, slur 5 beret, crest, crown, excel, limit, outdo 6 beanie, better, biggin, exceed, finial, letter, outwit, pileus, summit, tipoff, top off, topper, vertex, wrap up, zenith 7 biretta, ceiling, eclipse, maximum, surpass 8 balmoral, berretta, birretta, coonskin, covering, outshine, outsmart, outstrip, round off, round out, surmount, yarmelke, yarmulka, yarmulke 9 balaclava, bottle top, cockscomb, culminate, Glengarry, headdress, high point, transcend, zucchetto 10 bluebonnet, complement, consummate, crownpiece, upper limit
AL ~ letters: 3 SOX
and gown wearer: 4 grad
combining form: 8 calyptri-, calyptro-
conical ~ wearer: 5 dunce
doff the ~ to: 5 greet
ender: 5 stone
feather in one's ~: 4 fame 5 award, badge, glory, honor, kudos, medal, prize 6 credit, honors, praise, renown, reward, trophy 7 acclaim, laurels, triumph, victory 8 accolade, citation, gold star, prestige 10 decoration
French ~: 5 beret, shako
part: 4 bill 5 visor, vizor 6 earlap
plumed ~: 5 shako

polar ~: 3 ice
put on one's thinking ~: 8 meditate
set one's ~ for: 3 woo 4 date 5 court 6 pursue 7 take out 9 cultivate
sheepskin ~: 6 calpac 7 calpack
starter: 3 hub, ice, mad, mob, red, sky, toe 4 knee, snow 5 black, fools, night, skull, white
stocking ~: 5 toque, tuque
tasseled ~: 3 fez, tam
visored ~: 4 kepi
visorless ~: 3 tam 5 beret
cap __: 3 gun 6 pistol
cap-__: 4 a-pie
__ cap: 3 ice 5 cloud, dunce, fool's, polar 6 bottle, dunce's, salary 7 bathing, bishop's, chimney
Cap: 5 Anson
capa: 5 cloak
Capa: 6 Robert
capabilities: 5 gifts 6 powers, skills 7 talents 9 aptitudes, faculties, potential
capability: 5 means, might, power, skill 6 talent 7 faculty, know-how, potence, potency, promise 8 adequacy, aptitude, efficacy, facility, resource 9 endowment, potential 10 competence, efficiency, right stuff
lessen the ~ of: 6 derate
Capablanca, José forte: 5 chess
capable: 3 apt, fit 4 deft, good 5 adept, handy, hardy, quick, slick 6 adroit, au fait, expert, nimble, strong, suited, up to it 7 skilled, trained 8 adequate, dextrous, graceful, masterly, powerful, seasoned, skillful, talented 9 competent, dexterous, effective, efficient, masterful, on the ball, practiced, qualified, up to snuff, up to speed 10 proficient
humorously: 3 ept
isn't ~ of: 4 can't
make ~: 10 capacitate
more ~: 5 abler
not ~: 5 unfit
of: 4 up to 6 open to 8 liable to, likely to
suffix: 3 -ile 4 -able, -ible
Capable of Honor
author: Allen Drury
capably: 4 ably, well 5 aptly, great 6 deftly, nimbly 7 handily, rightly 8 laudably, worthily
capacious: 3 big 4 vast, wide 5 ample, broad, large, roomy 7 liberal, sizable 8 abundant, extended, far-flung, generous, sizeable, spacious, sweeping 9 dilatable, expansive, extensive, plentiful 10 commodious, expandable, voluminous, widespread
capaciousness: 4 room, size 5 space, sweep 9 amplitude
capacitance unit: 5 farad
capacitate: 6 enable 7 empower, qualify
__ capacitor: 4 flux
capacity: 4 fill, gift, head, role, room, size 5 knack, limit, might, power, reach, scope, sense, skill, space, state 6 office, sphere, status, talent, volume 7 ability, faculty, makings, potence, potency, stature 8 adequacy, aptitude, facility, function, judgment, province, quantity, standing 9 amplitude, dimension, endowment, endurance, largeness, magnitude, potential, readiness 10 competence, leadership, propensity, right stuff
at ~: 4 full 9 chock-full
have a ~ for: 4 hold
in the ~ of: 3 qua
of large ~: 5 ample, roomy
suffix: 7 -ability, -ibility
unit of ~: 5 liter, litre, quart 6 gallon
__ Capades: 3 Ice
cap and __: 4 gown 5 bells
cap-a-pie: 6 wholly
caparison: 3 rig 4 deck, gear 5 adorn, rig up 6 bedeck, clothe, dude up, finery, fit out, outfit, rig out 7 bedrape, clothes, deck out, dress up, full fig, rigging, turn out 8 accouter, accoutre, glad rags, housings 9 trappings
Capa, Robert: 12 photographer
cape: 3 Ann, Bon, Cod, May, ras 4 Horn, ness, Race, Roca, Skaw, wrap, York 5 Alava, amice, capot, cloak, Coral, fichu, Hafun, point, Sable, Wrath 6 almuce, Breton, capote, dolman, Helles, mantle, muleta, tabard, tippet 7 Agulhas, Comorin, Dezhnev, Froward, garment, Gris-Nez, La Hague, Lookout, manteau, mantlet, Matapan, mozetta, Nordkyn, Ortegal, paletot, pelisse 8 Columbia, Farewell, Flattery, foreland, Gallinas, Good Hope, Hatteras, headland, Land's End, mantilla, mozzetta, palatine, pelerine, San Lucas 9 Canaveral, Mendocino, Trafalgar 10 Chelyuskin, Finisterre, Lizard Head, promontory
Africa: 5 Verde
Alaska: 4 Nome
Antarctica: 5 Adare
Carolina: 4 Fear
church: 5 amice, fanon, orale 6 almuce 7 mozetta 8 mozzetta
Dakar: 5 Verde
ender: 4 skin
Gallipoli: 6 Helles
Hebrides: 5 Sleat
Japan: 3 Oma 4 mino
Lisbon: 4 Roca
Massachusetts: 3 Ann, Cod
matador's ~ color: 4 rojo
New Jersey: 3 May
Nova Scotia: 5 Canso
Portugal: 4 Roca
South America: 4 Horn
Spanish: 8 mantilla
Washington: 5 Alava
Cape __: 3 Ann, Cod, fox, May 4 Fear, Horn, Roca, Town 5 Alava, Dutch, Verde 6 Colony 7 Agulhas, buffalo, Gris-Nez, jasmine, Kennedy
Cape __, AK: 4 Nome
Cape __ cottage: 3 Cod
Cape __ Island: 6 Breton
Cape __, Liberia: 6 Palmas
Cape __, MA: 3 Ann, Cod
Cape __, NC: 4 Fear
Cape __-Nez: 4 Gris
Cape __, NJ: 3 May
Cape __, Portugal: 4 Roca
Cape __, Senegal: 5 Verde
Cape Breton: 4 city, isle, town 6 island
locale: 6 Canada 10 Nova Scotia
Cape Canaveral
beach near ~: 5 Cocoa
locale: 3 Fla. 7 Florida
org.: 4 NASA
Cape Cod
cottage feature: 5 gable
island off ~: 9 Nantucket
sight: 4 dune
town: 5 Truro 7 Hyannis
__ Cape Cod: 3 Old
Cape Codder
ingredient: 5 vodka
Cape Cod Lighter, The
author: John O'Hara
Cape Coral: 4 city, town
locale: 7 Florida
Cape Farewell
author: Harry Matinson
Cape Fear (1991 film)
cast: Robert De Niro, Jessica Lange, Juliette Lewis, Nick Nolte
De Niro in ~: 5 ex-con
director: Martin Scorsese
Cape Fear's loc.: 4 N. Car.
Cape Girardeau: 4 city, town
locale: 8 Missouri
Cape Gris-__: 3 Nez
Capek, Karel: 5 Czech 6 writer 10 playwright
work: The Insect Play
The Life of the Insects
Meteor
An Ordinary Life
Power and Glory
R.U.R.
The War With the Newts
Capeman, The
composer: Paul Simon
Cape May: 4 city, town
locale: 9 New Jersey
Cape of Good Hope country: 3 RSA
caper: 3 gag 4 jape, jest, joke, lark, leap, play, romp, skip 5 antic, frisk, heist, plant, prank, shrub, spree, stunt, theft, trick 6 cavort, frolic, gambol, prance 7 foolery, garnish, hijinks, robbery, rollick 8 burglary, escapade, mischief, thievery 9 condiment, have a ball, high jinks, horseplay, whoop it up 10 shenanigan, tomfoolery
Caper
author: Lawrence Sanders
Cape Roca
locale: 6 Iberia, Lisbon 8 Portugal
Capet: 4 Hugh
Cape Town: 4 city, port
locale: 3 RSA
Cape Verde: 6 nation 7 country
capital: 5 Praia
city: 5 Dakar, Praia
Cape Verde Islands
volcano: 4 Fogo
Cape Wrangell
locale: 4 Attu 6 Alaska
capgun: 3 toy
capillary: 4 vein
capillary __: 4 tube 6 action
cap in __: 4 hand
capital: 4 city, main, seat 5 asset, funds, means, prime, rhino 6 assets, letter 7 dollars, funding, optimum 9 resources 10 investment, metropolis
African: 4 Lomé 5 Abuja, Accra, Akkra, Cairo, Dakar, Rabat, Tunis 6 Asmara, Bamako, Bangui, Bissau, Dodoma, Harare, Kigali, Luanda, Lusaka, Malabo, Maputo, Maseru, Niamey 7 Abidjan, Algiers, Conakry, Kampala, Mbabane, Nairobi, Tripoli, Yaoundé 8 Cape Town, Djibouti, Freetown, Gaborone, Khartoum, Kinshasa, Lilongwe, Monrovia, Pretoria, Windhoek 9 Bujumbura, Mogadishu, Porto-Novo 10 Addis Ababa, Libreville, Nouakchott 11 Brazzaville, Ouagadougou
Alpine: 4 Bern 5 Berne 6 Vienna
Andean: 4 Lima 5 La Paz, Quito, Sucre 6 Bogotá 8 Santiago
Asia Minor: 6 Angora, Ankara
Asian: 4 Baku, Dili, Doha, Malé, Sana 5 Amman, Dacca, Dhaka, Hanoi, Kabul, Sanaa, Seoul, Tokyo 6 Ankara, Bagdad, Beirut, Manama, Muscat, Riyadh, Taipei, Tehran, Yangon 7 Baghdad, Bangkok, Beijing, Bishkek, Colombo, Jakarta, Rangoon, Teheran, Thimphu 8 Abu Dhabi, Beyrouth, Damascus, Djakarta, Dushanbe, Katmandu, New Delhi, Tashkent 9 Islamabad, Jerusalem, Phnom Penh, Pyongyang, Ulan Bator, Vientiane 10 Kuwait City 11 Kuala Lumpur, Ulaanbaatar
Baltic: 4 Riga 5 Vilna 7 Tallinn, Vilnius
Caribbean: 6 Havana, Nassau 7 St. John's 8 Castries, Kingston, Road Town 9 Kingstown, St. George's 10 Basseterre, Bridgetown, George Town, Oranjestad 11 Port of Spain 12 Fort-de-France, Port-au-Prince
Central American: 7 Managua, San José 8 Belmopan 10 Panama City 11 San Salvador, Tegucigalpa
European: 4 Bern, Kiev, Oslo, Riga, Roma, Rome, Wien 5 Berne, Minsk, Paris, Praha, Sofia, Vaduz, Vilna 6 Athens, Berlin, Dublin, Lisboa, Lisbon, London, Madrid, Moscow, Prague, Skopje, Sofiya, Tirana, Tiranë, Vienna, Warsaw, Zagreb 7 Belfast, Cardiff, Den Haag, Nicosia, Tallinn 8 Belgrade, Brussels, Chisinau, Helsinki, Sarajevo, The Hague, Valletta 9 Amsterdam, Bucharest, Edinburgh, Ljubljana, Stockholm 10 Bratislava, Copenhagen
like venture ~ investments: 5 dicey 6 chancy, daring, unsafe 9 uncertain 10 precarious
make ~ out of: 3 use 7 exploit
Mideast: 4 Doha, Sana 5 Amman, Sanaa 6 Bagdad, Beirut, Manama, Muscat, Riyadh,

Tehran **7** Baghdad, Teheran **8** Abu Dhabi, Beyrouth, Damascus **9** Jerusalem **10** Kuwait City
near the equator: 5 Quito
provide ~: 4 back, fund
South American: 4 Lima **5** La Paz, Quito, Sucre **6** Bogotá **7** Caracas, Cayenne **8** Asunción, Brasilia, Santiago **10** Montevideo, Paramaribo **11** Buenos Aires
South Pacific: 4 Apia, Suva **5** Agana **6** Majuro, Manila, Nouméa, Tarawa **7** Honiara, Papeete **8** Funafuti, Pago Pago, Port-Vila **9** Nuku'alofa
world's highest ~: 5 La Paz
see also moolah, wonderful

capital __: 3 sum **4** gain, levy, loss, ship, sins **5** asset, crime, goods, stock **6** budget, flight, letter, outlay **7** account, surplus
__ capital: 4 risk **5** block, fixed, small **6** equity **7** venture, working
Capital __, The: 4 Gang
Capital Crimes
author: Lawrence Sanders
capital gains __: 3 tax
Capital Gang, The (CNN talk)
topic: 8 politics
capitalism: 9 democracy **10** free market
capitalist: 6 tycoon **7** magnate **8** investor **9** bourgeois, financier, landowner, moneybags, plutocrat
capitalize: 3 use **4** fund **5** stake **7** finance **9** subsidize
on: 6 profit **7** exploit
Capitals: 3 six **4** team
home: 10 Washington
milieu: 3 ice **4** rink
org.: 3 NHL
rival: *see* hockey team
sport: 6 hockey

capitals (state) by city:
Albany - New York
Annapolis - Maryland
Atlanta - Georgia
Augusta - Maine
Austin - Texas
Baton Rouge - Louisiana
Bismarck - North Dakota
Boise - Idaho
Boston - Massachusetts
Carson City - Nevada
Charleston - West Virginia
Cheyenne - Wyoming
Columbia - South Carolina
Columbus - Ohio
Concord - New Hampshire
Denver - Colorado
Des Moines - Iowa
Dover - Delaware
Frankfort - Kentucky
Harrisburg - Pennsylvania
Hartford - Connecticut
Helena - Montana
Honolulu - Hawaii
Indianapolis - Indiana
Jackson - Mississippi
Jefferson City - Missouri
Juneau - Alaska
Lansing - Michigan
Lincoln - Nebraska
Little Rock - Arkansas
Madison - Wisconsin
Montgomery - Alabama
Montpelier - Vermont
Nashville - Tennessee
Oklahoma City - Oklahoma
Olympia - Washington
Phoenix - Arizona
Pierre - South Dakota
Providence - Rhode Island
Raleigh - North Carolina
Richmond - Virginia
Sacramento - California
Saint Paul - Minnesota
Salem - Oregon
Salt Lake City - Utah
Santa Fe - New Mexico
Springfield - Illinois
Tallahassee - Florida
Topeka - Kansas
Trenton - New Jersey

capitals (state) by state:
Alabama - Montgomery
Alaska - Juneau
Arizona - Phoenix
Arkansas - Little Rock
California - Sacramento
Colorado - Denver
Connecticut - Hartford
Delaware - Dover
Florida - Tallahassee
Georgia - Atlanta
Hawaii - Honolulu
Idaho - Boise
Illinois - Springfield
Indiana - Indianapolis
Iowa - Des Moines
Kansas - Topeka
Kentucky - Frankfort
Louisiana - Baton Rouge
Maine - Augusta
Maryland - Annapolis
Massachusetts - Boston
Michigan - Lansing
Minnesota - St. Paul
Mississippi - Jackson
Missouri - Jefferson City
Montana - Helena
Nebraska - Lincoln
Nevada - Carson City
New Hampshire - Concord
New Jersey - Trenton
New Mexico - Santa Fe
New York - Albany
North Carolina - Raleigh
North Dakota - Bismarck
Ohio - Columbus
Oklahoma - Oklahoma City
Oregon - Salem
Pennsylvania - Harrisburg
Rhode Island - Providence
South Carolina - Columbia
South Dakota - Pierre
Tennessee - Nashville
Texas - Austin
Utah - Salt Lake City
Vermont - Montpelier
Virginia - Richmond
Washington - Olympia
West Virginia - Charleston
Wisconsin - Madison
Wyoming - Cheyenne

capitals (world) by city:
Abidjan - Ivory Coast
Abu Dhabi - United Arab Emirates
Abuja - Nigeria
Accra - Ghana
Addis Ababa - Ethiopia
Agana - Guam
Algiers - Algeria
Amman - Jordan
Amsterdam - Netherlands
Andorra La Vella - Andorra
Ankara - Turkey
Antananarivo - Madagascar
Apia - Samoa
Ashkhabad - Turkmenistan
Asmara - Eritrea
Astana - Kazakhstan
Asunción - Paraguay
Athens - Greece
Bagdad - Iraq
Baku - Azerbaijan
Bamako - Mali
Bandar Seri Begawan - Brunei
Bangkok - Thailand
Bangui - Central African Republic
Banjul - Gambia
Basse-Terre - Guadeloupe
Basseterre - St. Kitts and Nevis
Beijing - China
Beirut - Lebanon
Belfast - Northern Ireland
Belgrade - Yugoslavia
Belmopan - Belize
Berlin - Germany
Bern - Switzerland
Bishkek - Kyrgyzstan
Bissau - Guinea-Bissau
Bogotá - Colombia
Brasilia - Brazil
Bratislava - Slovakia
Brazzaville - Congo (Republic)
Bridgetown - Barbados
Brussels - Belgium
Bucharest - Romania
Budapest - Hungary
Buenos Aires - Argentina
Bujumbura - Burundi
Cairo - Egypt
Canberra - Australia
Cape Town - South Africa
Caracas - Venezuela
Cardiff - Wales
Castries - St. Lucia
Cayenne - French Guiana
Chisinau - Moldova
Colombo - Sri Lanka
Conakry - Guinea
Copenhagen - Denmark
Dakar - Senegal
Damascus - Syria
Den Haag - Netherlands
Dhaka - Bangladesh
Dili - East Timor
Djakarta - Indonesia
Djibouti - Djibouti
Dodoma - Tanzania
Doha - Qatar
Dublin - Ireland
Dushanbe - Tajikistan
Edinburgh - Scotland
Fort-de-France - Martinique
Freetown - Sierra Leone
Funafuti - Tuvalu
Gaborone - Botswana
George Town - Cayman Islands
Georgetown - Guyana
Godthab - Greenland
Guatemala City - Guatemala
Hague, The - Netherlands
Hamilton - Bermuda
Hanoi - Vietnam
Harare - Zimbabwe
Havana - Cuba
Helsinki - Finland
Honiara - Solomon Islands
Islamabad - Pakistan
Jakarta - Indonesia
Jamestown - St. Helena
Jerusalem - Israel
Kabul - Afghanistan
Kampala - Uganda
Katmandu - Nepal
Khartoum - Sudan
Kiev - Ukraine
Kigali - Rwanda
Kingston - Jamaica
Kingstown - St. Vincent and the Grenadines
Kinshasa - Congo (Democratic Republic)
Koror - Palau
Kuala Lumpur - Malaysia
Kuwait City - Kuwait
La Paz - Bolivia
Libreville - Gabon
Lilongwe - Malawi
Lima - Peru
Lisbon - Portugal
Ljubljana - Slovenia
Lomé - Togo
London - United Kingdom
Luanda - Angola
Lusaka - Zambia
Luxembourg - Luxembourg
Madrid - Spain
Majuro - Marshall Islands
Malabo - Equatorial Guinea
Malé - Maldives
Managua - Nicaragua
Manama - Bahrain
Manila - Philippines
Maputo - Mozambique
Maseru - Lesotho
Mbabane - Swaziland
Minsk - Belarus
Mogadishu - Somalia
Monaco-Ville - Monaco
Monrovia - Liberia
Montevideo - Uruguay
Moroni - Comoros
Moscow - Russia
Muscat - Oman
Nairobi - Kenya
Nassau - Bahamas
N'Djamena - Chad
New Delhi - India
Niamey - Niger
Nicosia - Cyprus
Nouakchott - Mauritania
Nouméa - New Caledonia
Nuku'alofa - Tonga
Oranjestad - Aruba
Oslo - Norway
Ottawa - Canada
Ouagadougou - Burkina Faso
Pago Pago - American Samoa
Palikir - Micronesia
Panama City - Panama
Papeete - French Polynesia
Paramaribo - Suriname
Paris - France
Phnom Penh - Cambodia
Port-au-Prince - Haiti
Port Louis - Mauritius
Port Moresby - Papua New Guinea
Port of Spain - Trinidad and Tobago
Porto-Novo - Benin

Port Stanley - Falkland Islands
Port-Vila - Vanuatu
Prague, Praha - Czech Republic
Praia - Cape Verde
Pretoria - South Africa
Pyongyang - North Korea
Quito - Ecuador
Rabat - Morocco
Rangoon - Myanmar
Reykjavík - Iceland
Riga - Latvia
Riyadh - Saudi Arabia
Road Town - British Virgin Islands
Rome - Italy
Roseau - Dominica
Sanaa - Yemen
San José - Costa Rica
San Salvador - El Salvador
Santiago - Chile
Santo Domingo - Dominican Republic
Sarajevo - Bosnia and Herzegovina
Seoul - South Korea
Singapore - Singapore
Skopje - Macedonia
Sofia - Bulgaria
St. George's - Grenada
St. John's - Antigua and Barbuda
Stockholm - Sweden
Sucre - Bolivia
Suva - Fiji
Taipei - Taiwan
Tallinn - Estonia
Tarawa - Kiribati
Tashkent - Uzbekistan
Tbilisi - Georgia
Tegucigalpa - Honduras
Teheran - Iran
Tehran - Iran
Thimphu - Bhutan
Tirana - Albania
Tokyo - Japan
Tórshavn - Faeroe Islands
Tripoli - Libya
Tunis - Tunisia
Ulaanbaatar - Mongolia
Vaduz - Liechtenstein
Valletta - Malta
Victoria - Seychelles
Vienna - Austria
Vientiane - Laos
Vilnius - Lithuania
Warsaw - Poland
Wellington - New Zealand
Wien - Austria
Windhoek - Namibia
Yangon - Myanmar
Yaoundé - Cameroon
Yerevan - Armenia
Zagreb - Croatia

capitals (world) by country:
Afghanistan - Kabul
Albania - Tirana
Algeria - Algiers
American Samoa - Pago Pago
Andorra - Andorra La Vella
Angola - Luanda
Antigua and Barbuda - St. John's
Argentina - Buenos Aires
Armenia - Yerevan
Aruba - Oranjestad
Australia - Canberra
Austria - Vienna (Wien)
Azerbaijan - Baku
Bahamas - Nassau
Bahrain - Manama
Bangladesh - Dhaka
Barbados - Bridgetown
Belarus - Minsk
Belgium - Brussels
Belize - Belmopan
Benin - Porto-Novo
Bermuda - Hamilton
Bhutan - Thimphu
Bolivia - La Paz, Sucre
Bosnia and Herzegovina - Sarajevo
Botswana - Gaborone
Brazil - Brasilia
British Virgin Islands - Road Town
Brunei - Bandar Seri Begawan
Bulgaria - Sofia
Burkina Faso - Ouagadougou
Burundi - Bujumbura
Cambodia - Phnom Penh
Cameroon - Yaoundé
Canada - Ottawa
Cape Verde - Praia
Cayman Islands - George Town
Central African Republic - Bangui
Chad - N'Djamena
Chile - Santiago
China - Beijing
Colombia - Bogotá
Comoros - Moroni
Congo (Democratic Republic) - Kinshasa
Congo (Republic) - Brazzaville
Costa Rica - San José
Croatia - Zagreb
Cuba - Havana
Cyprus - Nicosia
Czech Republic - Prague (Praha)
Denmark - Copenhagen
Djibouti - Djibouti
Dominican Republic - Santo Domingo
Dominica - Roseau
East Timor - Dili
Ecuador - Quito
Egypt - Cairo
El Salvador - San Salvador
Equatorial Guinea - Malabo
Eritrea - Asmara
Estonia - Tallinn
Ethiopia - Addis Ababa
Faeroe Islands - Tórshavn
Falkland Islands - Port Stanley
Fiji - Suva
Finland - Helsinki
France - Paris
French Guiana - Cayenne
French Polynesia - Papeete
Gabon - Libreville
Gambia - Banjul
Georgia - Tbilisi
Germany - Berlin
Ghana - Accra
Greece - Athens
Greenland - Godthab
Grenada - St. George's
Guadeloupe - Basse-Terre
Guam - Agana
Guatemala - Guatemala City
Guinea-Bissau - Bissau
Guinea - Conakry
Guyana - Georgetown
Haiti - Port-au-Prince
Honduras - Tegucigalpa
Hungary - Budapest
Iceland - Reykjavík
India - New Delhi
Indonesia - Jakarta (Djakarta)
Iran - Teheran (Tehran)
Iraq - Bagdad (Baghdad)
Ireland - Dublin
Israel - Jerusalem
Italy - Rome (Roma)
Ivory Coast - Abidjan
Jamaica - Kingston
Japan - Tokyo
Jordan - Amman
Kazakhstan - Astana
Kenya - Nairobi
Kiribati - Tarawa
Kuwait - Kuwait City
Kyrgyzstan - Bishkek
Laos - Vientiane
Latvia - Riga
Lebanon - Beirut
Lesotho - Maseru
Liberia - Monrovia
Libya - Tripoli
Liechtenstein - Vaduz
Lithuania - Vilnius
Luxembourg - Luxembourg
Macedonia - Skopje
Madagascar - Antananarivo
Malawi - Lilongwe
Malaysia - Kuala Lumpur
Maldives - Malé
Mali - Bamako
Malta - Valletta
Marshall Islands - Majuro
Martinique - Fort-de-France
Mauritania - Nouakchott
Mauritius - Port Louis
Micronesia - Palikir
Moldova - Chisinau
Monaco - Monaco-Ville
Mongolia - Ulaanbaatar (Ulan Bator)
Morocco - Rabat
Mozambique - Maputo
Myanmar - Yangon (Rangoon)
Namibia - Windhoek
Nepal - Katmandu
Netherlands - Amsterdam, The Hague (Den Haag)
New Caledonia - Nouméa
New Zealand - Wellington
Nicaragua - Managua
Nigeria - Abuja
Niger - Niamey
Northern Ireland - Belfast
North Korea - Pyongyang
Norway - Oslo
Oman - Muscat
Pakistan - Islamabad
Palau - Koror
Panama - Panama City
Papua New Guinea - Port Moresby
Paraguay - Asunción
Peru - Lima
Philippines - Manila
Poland - Warsaw
Portugal - Lisbon (Lisboa)
Qatar - Doha
Romania - Bucharest
Russia - Moscow
Rwanda - Kigali
Samoa - Apia
Saudi Arabia - Riyadh
Scotland - Edinburgh
Senegal - Dakar
Seychelles - Victoria
Sierra Leone - Freetown
Singapore - Singapore
Slovakia - Bratislava
Slovenia - Ljubljana
Solomon Islands - Honiara
Somalia - Mogadishu
South Africa - Cape Town, Pretoria
South Korea - Seoul
Spain - Madrid
Sri Lanka - Colombo
St. Helena - Jamestown
St. Kitts and Nevis - Basseterre
St. Lucia - Castries
St. Vincent and the Grenadines - Kingstown
Sudan - Khartoum
Suriname - Paramaribo
Swaziland - Mbabane
Sweden - Stockholm
Switzerland - Bern (Berne)
Syria - Damascus
Taiwan - Taipei
Tajikistan - Dushanbe
Tanzania - Dodoma
Thailand - Bangkok
Togo - Lomé
Tonga - Nuku'alofa
Trinidad and Tobago - Port of Spain
Tunisia - Tunis
Turkey - Ankara
Turkmenistan - Ashkhabad
Tuvalu - Funafuti
Uganda - Kampala
Ukraine - Kiev
United Arab Emirates - Abu Dhabi
United Kingdom - London
United States - Washington
Uruguay - Montevideo
Uzbekistan - Tashkent
Vanuatu - Port-Vila
Venezuela - Caracas
Vietnam - Hanoi
Wales - Cardiff
Yemen - Sanaa
Yugoslavia - Belgrade
Zambia - Lusaka
Zimbabwe - Harare

capita, per: **4** each **6** apiece
Capitol
gofer: **4** page
group: **5** House, lobby **6** Senate
sight: **4** Mall
topper: **4** dome
VIP: **3** rep., sen. **7** senator
vote: **3** nay **7** abstain, present
Capitol __: **4** Hill
Capitol __, The: **5** Steps
Capitoline site: **4** Rome
Capitol Reef: **4** park
locale: **4** Utah
capitulate: **3** bow **4** fold, lose **5** yield **6** accept, cave in, fess up, give in, give up, relent, submit **7** concede, succumb **9** surrender **10** come across
caplet: **4** pill
Cap'n __: **3** Eri **6** Crunch
Cap'n Crunch: **6** cereal
competitor: **see** cereal
dog: **6** Seadog
capo: **3** don **9** beginning
group: **3** mob
capon: **4** bird, fowl, male, meat **7** chicken, poultry
Capone, Al: **8** gangster
colleague: Frank Nitti
nemesis: IRS, Eliot Ness
rival: Bugs Moran
Caponi, Donna: **6** golfer

capote: 4 cape, coat, wrap 5 cloak, cover 6 jacket, mantle 8 overcoat
Capote: 3 Tru 6 Truman
Capote (2005 film)
cast: Philip Seymour Hoffman, Catherine Keener
Capote, Truman: 6 writer
work: Breakfast at Tiffany's
The Grass Harp
In Cold Blood
Local Color
The Muses are Heard
Music for Chameleons
Other Voices, Other Rooms
Capp: 2 Al 4 Andy
Capp, Al
adjective: 3 Li'l
character: 5 Abner, Mammy, Pappy, Shmoo, Yokum 8 Daisy Mae
hyena: 4 Lena
Capp, Andy: 7 cartoon
wife: 3 Flo
__-capped: 4 snow 5 cloud
cappella
a ~: 5 music 6 choral
a ~ style: 6 doo-wop
cappelletti
alternative: ***see*** pasta
cappuccino: 5 drink 6 coffee 8 beverage
cousin: 5 latte
flavor: 5 mocha
place: 4 café
Capra, Frank: 8 director
film: American Madness (1932)
Arsenic and Old Lace (1944)
The Bitter Tea of General Yen (1933)
Broadway Bill (1934)
Here Comes the Groom (1951)
It Happened One Night (1934, AA)
It's a Wonderful Life (1946)
Lady for a Day (1933)
Lost Horizon (1937)
Meet John Doe (1941)
The Miracle Woman (1931)
Mr. Deeds Goes to Town (1936, AA)
Mr. Smith Goes to Washington (1939)
Platinum Blonde (1931)
Pocketful of Miracles (1961)
State of the Union (1948)
The Strong Man (1926)
You Can't Take It With You (1938, AA)
Capri: 3 car 4 Ahna, auto, isle 6 island 7 Lincoln, Mercury
attraction: 6 grotto
city near ~: 6 Naples
island near ~: 4 Elba
locale: 5 Italy
suffix: 3 -ote
Capri __: 5 pants
Capriati, Jennifer: 7 netster 9 tennis pro
foe: 4 Graf 5 Seles
milieu: 5 court
capriccio: 5 music, prank
caprice: 4 joke, whim 5 fancy, music, quirk 6 notion, vagary 7 impulse 8 crotchet
Caprice: 3 car 4 auto 5 Chevy 9 Chevrolet 10 automobile
Caprichos
artist: Francisco de Goya
capricious: 5 giddy, moody, timid 6 chancy, fickle, fitful, quirky, uneven 7 aimless, erratic, flighty, mutable, playful, unloyal, wayward 8 careless, fanciful, notional, skittish, ticklish, unstable, unsteady, variable, volatile 9 arbitrary, crotchety, eccentric, faithless, fantastic, humorsome, impulsive, irregular, mercurial, up-and-down, vagarious, whimsical 10 changeable, inconstant, lubricious, unreliable
capriciously: 7 on a whim
Capricorn: 4 goat, sign
follower: 8 Aquarius
months: 3 Dec., Jan. 7 January 8 December
preceder: 11 Sagittarius
Capricorn Concerto
composer: Samuel Barber
caprine: 7 goatish 8 goatlike
capriole: 4 jump
Capris: 5 pants
feature: 4 slit
Caps
see Capitals
__-Caps: 3 Sno
Capshaw, Kate: 7 actress
spouse: Steven Spielberg
capsize: 3 tip 4 sink, turn 5 upend, upset, wreck 6 invert, topple 7 tip over 8 keel over, overturn, turn over 9 pitchpole
Caps Lock neighbor: 3 Tab 5 Shift
capstone: 4 acme 6 climax, summit, zenith 8 high spot
capsule: 3 pod, sac 4 dose, pill 8 abridged, medicine, synopsis 9 condensed, container, shortened, synopsize 10 medication
botanical ~: 4 boll 5 theca
__ capsule: 4 time 5 space
capsulize: 5 recap 9 summarize
capt.: 4 rank
employer: 3 USN 4 USAF, USCG
heading: 3 ENE, ESE, NNE, NNW, SSE, SSW, WNW, WSW
subordinate: 2 lt. 3 cdr. 4 cmdr. 5 lieut.
superior: 3 adm., col., maj.
captain: 4 boss, exec, head, rank 5 chief, pilot, steer 6 leader, manage, master, sailor, top dog 7 jack tar, mariner, officer, oversee, skipper 8 director, helmsman, kingfish, navigate 9 authority, commander, executive
book: 3 log
destination: 4 port
fictional ~: 4 Ahab, Hook, Kirk, Nemo, Vere
insignia: 3 bar
milieu: 3 sea 4 asea, helm, main 5 at sea, ocean 6 bridge
of industry: 4 czar 5 baron, mogul 6 tycoon 7 magnate
reply to a ~: 5 no sir 6 aye aye
superior: 5 major
see also nautical
__ captain: 3 sea 4 bell, port 5 field, staff
Captain
wife: Toni Tennille
Captain __: 3 Ron 4 Fury, Hook, Kidd 5 Blood, Video 7 America
Captain Blood (1935 film)
cast: Olivia de Havilland, Errol Flynn
Captain Brassbound's Conversion
author: George Bernard Shaw
Captain Corelli's Mandolin (2001 film)
cast: Christian Bale, Nicolas Cage, Penélope Cruz, John Hurt
Captain D's
rival: ***see*** restaurant chain
Captain Kidd: 6 pirate
captain's __: 3 bed 4 mast 5 chair, table
Captains Courageous: 5 novel
author: Rudyard Kipling
character: 5 Disko, Troop 6 Harvey
Captain's Daughter, The
author: Aleksandr Pushkin
Captain's Tiger
author: Athol Fugard
Captain & Tennille
song: Do That to Me One More Time (1979)
Lonely Night (1976)
Love Will Keep Us Together (1975)
Muskrat Love (1976)
Shop Around (1976)
The Way I Want to Touch You (1975)
The Captain: Daryl Dragon
Captain Video (Dumont sci-fi)
cast: Al Hodge (Captain Video)
Captain Video (Dumont sci-fi) cast
foe: 5 Tobor
caption: 4 term 5 title 6 legend 7 heading, writing 8 headline, subtitle 9 underline
__-captioned: 6 closed
captious: 5 cross, testy 6 crabby, crusty 7 carping, finicky, fretful, nagging, peevish 8 caviling, contrary, critical, exacting, finiking, finnicky, fretsome, petulant, specious 9 demanding, fractious, irritable, querulous, sarcastic 10 censorious, nitpicking
Captiva: 4 isle 6 island
locale: 7 Florida
captivate: 4 draw, lure, take, vamp 5 charm, tempt 6 absorb, allure, appeal, dazzle, disarm, enamor, engage, ravish, rope in, turn on 7 attract, beguile, bewitch, enchain, enchant, engross, enthral, immerse, inthral 8 bedazzle, enthrall, entrance, inthrall, intrigue, transfix 9 enrapture, entertain, fascinate, hypnotize, infatuate, magnetize, mesmerize, spellbind, transport
captivated: 4 rapt 6 enrapt 7 far gone 8 held fast, obsessed, ravished 9 bewitched, delighted, engrossed, gladdened 10 fascinated, infatuated
be ~ by: 4 love 5 adore
captivating: 5 siren 6 lovely, pretty, quaint 7 darling, lovable, winning, winsome 8 adorable, alluring, loveable, magnetic, pleasing
captive: 4 held 5 bound, caged, slave 6 in jail, jailed 7 convict, hostage, subject 8 confined, detainee, ensnared, internee, locked up, prisoner 9 in custody 10 imprisoned
hold ~: 3 net 4 take 5 seize 6 immure
captivity: 4 jail 6 prison 7 bondage, fetters, slavery 8 thraldom 9 committal, detention, restraint, servitude, thralldom, vassalage 10 constraint, entombment, internment, subjection
free from ~: 5 unpen 6 let out
captor: 6 jailer 7 officer 9 conqueror, kidnapper, policeman
Hearst ~: 3 SLA
capture: 3 bag, get, nab, net, win 4 bust, cage, gain, grab, hook, land, lure, nail, rope, take, trap 5 catch, pinch, run in, seize, snare 6 abduct, arrest, collar, corner, entrap, kidnap, obtain, occupy, pick up, ravage, rope in, secure, snatch 7 acquire, ensnare, insnare, round up, seizure 8 grab away, surprise 9 apprehend, extradite, lay hold of, track down 10 bring to bay, commandeer, confiscate, kidnapping, occupation, photograph
again: 5 rewin
elude ~: 4 hide 6 escape
capuchin: 3 sai 5 cloak, jocko 6 animal, coffee, mammal, monkey 7 primate
relative: ***see*** primate
Capulet: 6 Juliet
to Montague: 3 foe
capybara: 6 animal, mammal, rodent
relative: ***see*** rodent
car: 2 MV 3 AMC, Geo, GMC, Jag, Kia, LTD, neo, Reo 4 Audi, auto, Colt, Fiat, Ford, heap, Jeep, Lada, limo, Nash, Olds, Opel, tram 5 Acura, Aries, Buick, Caddy, Chevy, Civic, coupe, diner, Dodge, Eagle, Edsel, Essex, Honda, Isuzu, Mazda, Pinto, Rolls, sedan, wagon 6 Bronco, Cougar, Daewoo, De Soto, Escort, Falcon, Fiesta, Hudson, Impala, Jaguar, jalopy, Kaiser, Kissel, Nissan, Pierce, Rabbit, Saturn, Subaru, Suzuki, Taurus, Tercel, Toyota, wheels, Willys 7 Bentley, caboose, Checker, Citroen, clunker, compact, concern, Ferrari, flivver, hardtop, Hyundai, La Salle, Lincoln, Maxwell, Mercury, Mustang, Packard, phaeton, Pontiac, Porsche, Rambler, Renault, Skylark, sleeper, vehicle 8 Cadillac, Chrysler, Daihatsu, Plymouth, roadster, wagon-lit 9 Alfa Romeo, cabriolet, Chevrolet, hatchback, Hupmobile, limousine, transport, two-seater 10 automobile, conveyance, Duesenberg, gas guzzler, Mitsubishi, Oldsmobile, rattletrap, Rolls Royce, Studebaker, Volkswagen 11 Lamborghini
1920s/1930s: 3 Reo 5 Essex
1960s: 3 GTO
ad abbr.: 3 APR, EPA, MPG

AMC: 5 Pacer 7 Gremlin
assemblers' org.: 3 UAW
bar: 4 axle 5 strut
borrowed ~: 6 loaner
British: 2 MG 3 Jag, MGB 5 Rolls, Rover 6 Jaguar 10 Rolls-Royce
British ~ part: 4 boot, tyre 6 bonnet
buyer need: 4 loan
Chrysler: 4 Neon 5 Dodge 6 De Soto
classic: 3 GTO, Reo 4 Cord, Ghia, Nash 5 Aston, Essex, Stutz, T-bird
combining form: 4 auto-
dealer sign: 4 sold, used
defective ~: 4 heap 5 crate, lemon
document: 5 lease, title
drive the getaway ~: 4 abet
electric: 5 Tesla
ender: 3 hop, top 4 fare, king, load, port, sick 5 maker, uncle
engine: 4 V-six 5 V-four 6 diesel, V-eight, Wankel
fast ~: 5 Lotus, racer 6 hot rod
feed the ~: 5 gas up
for hire: 3 cab 4 limo, taxi 9 limousine
fuel: 3 gas
General Motors: 4 Olds, Opel 5 Buick, Caddy 6 Saturn 7 Pontiac 8 Cadillac 10 Oldsmobile
German: 3 BMW 4 Audi, Opel 6 Beetle 10 Volkswagen
go by ~: 5 drive, motor
heater setting: 5 deice 7 defrost
interior material: 5 vinyl 7 leather
Italian: 4 Fiat, Ghia 7 Ferrari 8 Maserati 9 Alfa Romeo
Japanese: 5 Miata 6 Nissan, Toyota
job: 3 LOF 4 lube 6 repair, tuneup
Korean: 3 Kia
leave the ~: 4 park
lifter: 4 jack
like an old ~: 5 rusty
luxury ~: 3 BMW 4 limo, Linc 5 Lexus 7 Lincoln 8 Cadillac, Infiniti
metal: 5 steel 6 chrome 8 aluminum
necessity: 5 spare 6 engine
new ~ odometer reading: 5 OOOOO
owner's dread: 4 dent 7 scratch
parker: 5 valet
part: 4 axle, belt, carb, hood, hose, tire 5 brake, grill, motor, radio, strut, wheel, wiper 6 bumper, clutch, engine, fender, grille, heater, mirror 7 chassis, fan belt, starter 8 CD player 9 defroster 10 alternator, carburetor
part brand: 4 Fram 5 Delco
path: 4 road
problem: 4 rust 5 no oil
racing org.: 4 NHRA
radio feature: 4 scan 6 preset
registration info: 3 VIN 4 make 5 color, model, owner
repairer: 4 mech 6 garage 8 mechanic
ride: 4 lift, spin
roof: 4 T-top
Russian: 3 Zil 4 Lada
safety device: 6 airbag 8 seat belt
security device: 5 alarm
showroom ~: 4 demo
sporty ~: 3 GTO, Jag 5 coupe, T-bird, 'Vette 6 Camaro 8 Corvette
starter: 3 box 4 flat, hand, race, rail, side, tram 5 motor 6 street
Swedish: 4 Saab 5 Volvo
wax: 7 Simoniz
went by ~: 6 autoed
window: 4 vent
see also automobile

car ___: 3 bed 4 card, coat, line, park, pool, seat, wash 6 pooler
___ car: 3 bar, tow, way 4 café, camp, club, coal, dome, life, mail, pace, rack, skip, slot, tank, town, trap 5 cable, chair, funny, kiddy, larry, panda, prowl, radio, scout, sport, squad, stock, world 6 buffet, bumper, cattle, cruise, dining, estate, hopper, kiddie, lounge, luxury, muscle, outfit, parlor, patrol, police, racing, safety, saloon, sports 7 armored, baggage, command, compact, foreign, freight, gondola, mid-size, Pullman, sleeper, touring, tourist, trailer, trolley
___-car: 5 rent-a
___-Car: 5 Econo
Car 54, Where Are You? (NBC sitcom)
cast: Fred Gwynne (Francis Muldoon)
Joe E. Ross (Gunther Toody)
creator: Nat Hiken
setting: Bronx, New York
Cara: 5 Irene 8 Williams
Cara ___: 3 Mia
Caracas: 4 city, town 7 capital
locale: 9 Venezuela
see also Spanish
Caractacus
composer: Thomas Arne
carafe: 3 jug 5 cruet, flask 6 bottle, flagon 7 alembic, pitcher 8 decanter 9 container 10 wine bottle
kin: 4 ewer
Cara, Irene
song: Breakdance (1984)
Fame (1980)
Flashdance...What a Feeling (1983)
caramel: 5 candy, sweet 8 ice cream 9 sweetmeat
alternative: ***see*** ice cream flavor
candy brand: 4 Rolo
custard: 4 flan
like ~: 5 chewy, gooey
relative: ***see*** brown color, yellow color
___ caramel: 5 creme
Cara Mia (song)
artist: Jay and the Americans, Mantovani
Car and ___: 6 Driver
Carangi: 3 Gia
carapace: 4 skin 5 shell
carat: 6 weight 7 measure
24-~: 4 pure 7 sincere
fraction: 2 pt. 5 point
caravan: 4 band 5 train 6 convoy, safari 7 cortege, journey 9 cavalcade 10 expedition, procession
animal: 5 camel
stop: 5 oasis, serai
Caravan: 3 van 5 Dodge

caravansary: 3 inn 5 hotel, serai 6 hostel
caravel: 4 boat, Niña, ship 5 Pinta 10 Santa Maria
caraway: 4 herb, seed
holder: 3 rye 5 bread
Caray: 5 Harry
carb: 4 rice, spud 5 bread, pasta, tater 6 potato
carbamide: 4 urea
___ Carbide: 5 Union
carbine, British: 4 sten
carbo-___: 4 load 7 loading
carbohydrate: 3 poi, yam 4 rice, taro 5 pasta, sugar 6 manioc, potato, starch 7 cassava, dextrin, glucose, lactose, maltose, risotto, sucrose 8 couscous, dextrine, dextrose, fructose, kedgeree, semolina, wild rice 9 brown rice, home fries
plant-cell ~: 5 xylan
suffix: 3 -ose
carbolic: 4 acid
carbon: 4 copy 6 ectype 7 diamond, element, replica 8 graphite, likeness 9 lampblack, reproduce
add ~ dioxide to: 6 aerate
alloy: 5 steel 8 cast iron
coated with ~: 5 sooty
combining form: 7 anthrac- 8 anthraco-
compound: 4 enol 5 ester
compound suffix: 3 -ane, -ene
copy: 7 replica 8 likeness 9 duplicate, facsimile, identical, imitation, look-alike 10 equivalent
crystalline form of ~ gem: 7 diamond
deposit: 4 soot
form of ~: 4 coal 7 diamond 8 graphite
frozen ~ dioxide: 6 dry ice
hard crystallized ~: 7 diamond
carbon ___: 3 arc, tet 4 copy, star 5 black, cycle, fiber, paper, steel 6 dating, tissue 7 dioxide, process
carbon-___: 4 date 6 dating
carbon-14 expert: 5 dater
carbonate: 4 salt 6 alkali
form: 5 trona
carbonated: 5 fizzy, foamy
drink: 4 cola, soda
not ~: 5 still
carbonated ___: 5 water
carbonation: 3 gas 4 fizz
Carbondale: 4 city, town
locale: 8 Illinois
carbonic: 4 acid
___ Carboniferous: 5 Upper
carbonium: 3 ion
carbonize: 4 burn, char, heat, sear 5 singe 6 scorch
carbonized plants: 4 peat
carbonless paper: 3 NCR
carcajou: 6 animal, mammal, weasel
relative: ***see*** weasel
Carcassonne
department: 4 Aude
card: 3 tag, wag, wit 4 riot, zany 5 comic, cutup 6 agenda, docket, lineup, scream, ticket 7 gagster, program, punster 8 calendar, comedian, funnyman, humorist, jokester, kibitzer, quipster, schedule 9 character, leg-puller, timetable

baseball ~ company: 5 Fleer, Topps 6 Bowman 7 Donruss 9 Upper Deck
black ~: 4 club 5 spade
catalog abbr.: 5 illus.
catalogue datum: 5 title 6 author
collection: 4 deck, hand, pack
combo: 4 meld, pair
dealer's device: 4 shoe
dealer's offering: 3 cut
drawing ~: 4 lure, star 6 magnet 7 feature
ender: 5 board, sharp 6 holder 7 sharper
face ~: 4 jack, king 5 honor, queen
game stake: 4 ante
green ~ holder: 7 refugee 8 emigrant, newcomer 9 foreigner, immigrant 10 noncitizen
greeting ~ feature: 4 poem 5 rhyme 8 doggerel
greeting ~ word: 4 yule
high ~: 3 ace 4 jack, king 5 queen
honor ~: 3 ace, ten 4 king
low ~: 3 two 4 four, trey 5 deuce, three
(out): 3 log 5 punch
player's headwear: 5 visor, vizor
player's yell: 3 gin, uno
playing ~: 3 ace, six, ten, two 4 club, five, four, jack, king, nine, trey 5 deuce, eight, heart, joker, knave, queen, seven, spade, three 7 diamond
red: 5 heart 7 diamond
seer's ~: 5 tarot
select a ~: 4 draw
spot: 3 pip
starter: 4 time 5 score
top ~: 3 ace
use a credit ~: 3 owe 6 charge
used to jimmy spring locks: 4 loid
wild ~: 5 deuce, joker
card ___: 4 game 5 index, punch, shark, table, trick 7 catalog, counter 9 catalogue
___ card: 3 car, cue, key, mag, red 4 bank, case, coat, cost, down, face, file, gray, grey, hole, long, Mass, post, rate, show, side, spot, unit, wild 5 altar, balop, bingo, chase, dance, debit, donor, entry, false, flash, green, honor, idiot, index, phone, place, punch, reply, smart, store, tally, trump, union 6 bubble, charge, credit, postal, report 7 breaker, calling, compass, drawing, get-well, landing, library, picture, playing, reentry, trading
Card: 4 NLer 6 Frisch, Musial, Sisler 10 baseballer
cardamom: 4 herb 5 spice
___ card, any...: 5 Pick a
card-carrying: 5 legal 6 lawful 8 rightful
carder's request: 2 ID
card game: 3 gin, loo, nap, uno, war 4 brag, faro, fish, jass, skat, snap, stud 5 beano, cinch, gleek, monte, omber, Pedro, pitch, poker, rummy, tarok, whist 6 belote, Boston, bridge, casino, ecarte, euchre, fan-tan, go fish, hearts, hold 'em, hombre, memory, piquet, red dog 7 authors, belotte,

bezique, binocle, canasta, cooncan, high-low, lowball, old maid, pontoon, primero, seven-up **8** all fours, anaconda, baccarat, baseball, canfield, conquian, cribbage, forfeits, gin rummy, I doubt it, Michigan, napoleon, patience, pinochle, sixty-six, slapjack **9** blackjack, draw poker, freezeout, old sledge, penny ante, quadrille, solitaire, spoilfive, twenty-one, vingt-et-un **10** backgammon, klaberjass, knock rummy, panguingue **11** chemin de fer, crazy eights, high-low-jack, rouge et noir, speculation
3-handed ~: **5** omber **6** hombre
British ~: **5** gleek **7** primero
European ~: **5** tarok
French ~: **6** belote
cardiac __: **5** cycle **6** muscle, output
cardiac readout: **3** ECG, EKG
Cardiff: **4** city, Jack, port, town
Giant: **4** hoax
locale: **5** Wales
river: **4** Taff
cardigan: **6** jacket **7** sweater
craft a ~: **4** knit
Cardigan: **3** bay
locale: **5** Wales
Cardin: **6** Pierre
rival: **5** Klein **6** Armani, Lauren
cardinal: **2** no. **3** key, red **4** bird, main, male, rank **5** basic, chief, color, prime, vital **6** cleric, datary, number, ruling, utmost **7** central, leading, pivotal, prelate, primary, radical, supreme **8** headmost **9** essential, important, paramount, principal, strategic, uttermost, vermilion **10** overriding, preeminent, underlying
beak: **3** nib
color: **3** red
home: **4** nest
point: **4** east, west **5** north, south
point suffix: **3** ern
relative: *see* red color
cardinal __: **3** sin **4** sign **5** point, tetra, trait, vowel **6** flower, number, system, virtue **7** numeral
Cardinal: **4** NLer **7** Cushing, Ernesto **8** Stanford **9** Richelieu **10** baseballer, footballer
Hall-of-Famer: **4** Dean **5** Smith **6** Frisch, Gibson, Musial, Sisler **7** Medwick **12** Schoendienst
Cardinale, Claudia: **7** actress
Cardinals: **4** nine **6** eleven **9** Ball State
home: **7** Arizona, St. Louis
logo: **3** St. L.
org.: **3** MLB, NFC, NLC
rival: *see* baseball team, NFL team
Cardinal Sins, The
author: Andrew Greeley
Cardinal Virtues, The
author: Andrew Greeley
cardiogram starter: **4** echo
cardiologist concern: **5** aorta, heart
cardiology adjective: **6** aortal, aortic
cardio medication: **5** nitro
__-card monte: **5** three
Cardozo: **5** judge **7** justice **8** Benjamin
cards
be in the ~: **4** loom **7** portend
hand out ~: **4** deal
in the ~: **4** luck, near **5** fated **6** at hand, likely **7** in store **8** destined, imminent, probable **9** impending
peek at the ~: **5** cheat
put one's ~ on the table: **6** reveal
__ cards: **5** in the, Zener
Cards
see Cardinals
cardsharp: **6** rascal, robber **9** trickster
__-card stud: **4** five **5** seven
card-table project: **6** jigsaw
Carducci, Giosuè: **4** poet **7** Italian **8** Nobelist
care: **3** woe **4** duty, egis, heed, load, mind **5** aegis, alarm, pains, sweat, trial, trust, worry **6** bother, burden, charge, dismay, effort, escrow, object, regard, regret, strain, stress **7** anguish, anxiety, caution, concern, conduct, control, custody, keeping, thought, trouble **8** auspices, disquiet, distress, give a rap, hardship, industry, interest, prudence, tutelage, vexation, wardship **9** affection, alertness, assiduity, attention, diligence, exactness, give a damn, give a darn, give a hoot, hindrance, misgiving, precision, vigilance **10** affliction, discretion, foreboding, management, precaution, protection, solicitude, uneasiness, weather eye
don't ~ for: **4** hate **7** dislike
don't ~ to: **6** refuse **7** decline
ender: **4** free, worn **5** giver, taker
examine with ~: **4** sift
for: **4** keep, like, love, mind, rear, tend **5** adore, board, fancy, nurse, prize, raise, see to, serve, value, watch **6** admire, attend, dote on, esteem, manage, revere, take to, tend to, wait on **7** baby-sit, cherish, idolize, nourish, nurture, protect, support, worship **8** dote upon, enshrine, hold dear, inshrine, maintain, preserve, treasure, wait upon **9** look after, reverence **10** appreciate
freedom from ~: **4** ease **5** peace **8** calmness, serenity **9** composure
handle with ~: **6** caress
have a ~: **6** beware **7** look out
not taken ~ of: **5** unmet
prefix for ~: **4** Medi
starter: **3** day **5** after, child, elder **6** health
take ~: **6** beware
take ~ of: **3** pay **4** feed, mall, maul, tend **5** act on, nurse, see to, watch **6** advert, attend, foster, handle, reward **7** address, babysit, execute, nurture, protect, provide, shelter, sit with **8** attend to, cope with, deal with, keep safe, maintain, minister, see about, transact **9** cultivate, do justice, look after, overpower, watch over **10** accomplish, compensate, consummate
(to): **4** like **6** prefer
care __: **4** a rap **5** a hang, a hoot, label **7** package
__ care: **3** day **4** skin, take **6** foster, health **7** managed, primary
__ Care: **5** I Don't
care a __: **4** hang, hoot
__ care!, A: **4** lot I
__-care center: **3** day
cared for: **7** beloved
careen: **3** tip **4** keel, lean, list, race, reel, rock, sway, tear, tilt, veer **5** lurch, pitch, weave **6** glance, hurtle, swerve, totter, wabble, wobble **7** stagger **8** heel over, ricochet
careening: **5** alist
career: **3** job, run **4** line, race, rush, tear, walk, work **5** craft, field, speed, sweep **6** living, métier, plunge, racket, record **7** banking, calling, pursuit **8** baseball, business, lifetime, lifework, position, practice, vocation **9** specialty **10** burn rubber, livelihood, occupation, profession, walk of life
criminal: **5** felon
soldier: **5** lifer
start: **5** debut
starter: **4** grad
summary: **4** vita **6** résumé
career __: **4** goal, move **5** woman **8** diplomat, planning
Careers: **4** game **9** board game
carefree: **3** gay **4** airy, calm, cool, easy **5** happy, jolly, light, merry, staid, stoic, sunny **6** at ease, blithe, breezy, casual, cheery, jaunty, jovial, low-key, mellow, placid, secure, sedate, serene **7** at peace, buoyant, halcyon, relaxed, romping, stoical **8** cheerful, composed, feckless, grooving, laidback, reckless, tranquil, untaxing **9** collected, easygoing, footloose, impassive, lightsome, temperate, unanxious, unexcited, unruffled, unworried **10** flying high, insouciant, nonchalant, rollicking, unagitated, unbothered, unburdened, untroubled
episode: **4** idyl, lark **5** idyll
in French: **9** sans souci
Carefree: **3** gum **4** city, town
alternative: *see* chewing gum
locale: **7** Arizona
Carefree (1938 film)
cast: Fred Astaire, Ralph Bellamy, Ginger Rogers
composer: Irving Berlin
director: Mark Sandrich
Carefree Highway (1974 song)
artist: Gordon Lightfoot
careful: **4** cagy, nice, safe, wary, wise **5** alert, cagey, canny, chary, exact, fussy, leery, sober **6** choosy, frugal, minute **7** choosey, finicky, guarded, heedful, mindful, precise, prudent, sparing, thrifty, wakeful **8** accurate, cautious, delicate, diligent, discreet, exacting, finiking, finnicky, keen-eyed, methodic, reliable, rigorous, studious, thorough, vigilant, watchful **9** assiduous, attentive, defensive, judicious, observant, provident, regardful, selective **10** deliberate, fastidious, methodical, meticulous, particular, protective, scrupulous, solicitous, suspicious, thoughtful
be ~: **4** mind **6** go slow **7** heads up, look out, watch it
be ~, old-style: **4** reck
not ~: **3** lax **4** rash **10** incautious
reasoning: **5** logic
__ careful!: **4** Do be
Careful!: **4** easy
carefully: **4** well **7** charily **8** gingerly **9** advisedly, anxiously, correctly, guardedly, heedfully, honorably, inside out, precisely, prudently, tactfully, uprightly **10** cautiously, delicately, dependably, discreetly, faithfully, rigorously, thoroughly, vigilantly, watchfully
carefulness: **4** heed **6** regard, thrift **7** caution, concern **9** chariness, precision, vigilance
__ care in the world: **4** not a
careless: **3** lax **4** lazy, rash **5** hasty, loose, messy, slack **6** remiss, shoddy, sloppy, unwary, wanton **7** cursory, offhand, raffish, unaware **8** derelict, fallible, heedless, indolent, listless, mindless, off-guard, pell-mell, reckless, slapdash, slipshod, slovenly, wasteful **9** desperate, forgetful, haphazard, imprecise, imprudent, impulsive, negligent, oblivious, unadvised, uncareful, unguarded, unheedful, unmindful, vagarious **10** capricious, delinquent, incautious, indiscreet, last-minute, neglectful, nonchalant, regardless, uncritical, unthinking, unthorough
be ~: **4** lose **7** neglect
Careless Husband, The (play)
author: Colley Cibber
Careless Love
author: Alice Adams
carelessly: **6** anyhow **7** lightly **8** absently, pell-mell **10** flippantly
carelessness: **5** haste **6** laxity **7** neglect **9** oversight
Careless Whisper (1984 song)
artist: George Michael
Carell: **5** Steve
__ care of: **4** take
__ Care of Business: **5** Takin'
Care of Time, The
author: Eric Ambler
CARE package: **3** aid **10** assistance
__ cares?: **3** Who
caress: **3** hug, pat, rub, woo **4** love **5** touch **6** clinch, clutch, cuddle, stroke, tickle **7** embrace, snuggle **8** make nice
Caress
alternative: *see* soap
caretaker: **4** nana **5** super **6** keeper, sitter, warden **7** curator, janitor **8** gardener, watchdog **9** concierge, custodian, governess, nursemaid, protector **10** baby sitter, supervisor
Caretaker, The
author: Harold Pinter
caret, use a: **6** insert
Carew: **3** Rod **6** Thomas
careworn: **5** tired **7** haggard **8** footsore **9** exhausted
Carew, Rod: **4** Twin **10** baseballer
Carey: **4** Drew **5** Diane, Harry **6** Lowell, Mariah **9** Macdonald

Carey, Mariah
song: Always Be My Baby (1996)
Can't Let Go (1991)
Dreamlover (1993)
Emotions (1991)
Endless Love (1994)
Fantasy (1995)
Forever (1996)
Heartbreaker (1999)
Hero (1993)
Honey (1997)
I Don't Wanna Cry (1991)
I'll Be There (1992)
I Still Believe (1999)
Love Takes Time (1990)
Make It Happen (1992)
My All (1998)
One Sweet Day (1995)
Shake It Off (2005)
Someday (1991)
Thank God I Found You (2000)
Vision of Love (1990)
We Belong Together (2005)
Without You (1994)
cargo: 4 haul, load **5** goods **6** lading **7** baggage, exports, freight, imports, payload, tonnage, tunnage **8** contents, shipload, shipment **9** wagonload
area: 4 hold
deliver ~: 6 unload
handler: 3 van **5** lader **6** lumper **9** stevedore
ship: 5 oiler **6** argosy, tanker
take on ~: 4 lade, stow
tanker ~: 3 oil **5** crude
temporarily jettisoned ~: 5 lagan
unit: 3 ton
cargo __: 3 bay **4** cult, ship **5** liner **6** pocket
__ cargo: 3 air
carhop: 6 server, waiter **8** waitress
Carib: 6 Indian
Caribbean: 3 sea
city: 5 Ponce **6** Havana, Nassau **7** San Juan, St. John's **8** Castries, Kingston, Road Town **9** Kingstown, St. George's **10** Basseterre, Bridgetown, George Town, Oranjestad **11** Port of Spain **12** Fort-de-France, Port-au-Prince
country: 4 Cuba **5** Haiti **6** Dom. Rep. **7** Bahamas, Grenada, Jamaica, St. Lucia **8** Barbados, Dominica **10** Saint Lucia
dance: 4 soca **5** limbo, mambo **7** beguine
explorer: 8 Columbus
fish: 10 yellow jack
gear: 5 scuba
gulf: 6 Darien, Gonâve **7** San Blas **8** Gonaïves, Honduras
island: 4 Cuba, Saba **5** Aruba, Nevis **6** Tobago **7** Antigua, Barbuda, Bonaire, Curaçao, Grenada, Jamaica, St. Kitts, St. Lucia, Tortola **8** Barbados, Dominica, Trinidad **9** St. Vincent **10** Guadeloupe, Hispaniola, Martinique, Puerto Rico, Saint Lucia
islands: 3 BWI **6** Indies **7** Bahamas, Caymans **10** West Indies
liquor: 3 rum
music: 3 ska **4** zouk
native: 6 Arawak
river to the ~: 4 Coco, Ulúa **5** Hondo **6** Patuca **7** Chagres, Motagua **9** Magdalena
trip: 6 cruise
volcano: 5 Pelee
Caribbean __: 3 Sea **5** Plate, Queen **7** Current
__ Caribbean Cruises: 5 Royal
Caribbean Queen (1984 song)
artist: Billy Ocean
caribe: 4 fish **7** piranha **8** predator
caribou: 4 deer **6** animal, mammal
feature: 6 antler
hunter: 6 Eskimo
relative: ***see*** deer
Caribou: 4 city, town
locale: 5 Maine
caricature: 3 ape, art **4** draw, mock, sham **5** farce, mimic, put-on, sneer, spoof **6** parody, satire, send-up **7** burlesk, cartoon, drawing, imitate, lampoon, mockery, takeoff **8** ridicule, satirize, travesty **9** burlesque, imitation **10** distortion, exaggerate, pasquinade
feature: 4 nose
caricaturist: 4 mime **5** mimic
Carides: 3 Gia
caries: 6 cavity **10** tooth decay
carillon: 4 bell **5** bells **6** chimes **10** percussion
Carina: 4 Keel
star in ~: 7 Canopus
__ Carinae: 3 Eta
caring: 4 fond **6** humane, loving, tender **7** helpful, thought, valuing **8** maternal, parental **9** concerned, fraternal **10** benevolent, empathetic, solicitous, thoughtful
carioca: 5 dance
home: 3 Rio
relative: 5 samba
Cariou: 3 Len
carious: 7 decayed
Carl: 4 Betz, Cori, Jung, Orff **5** Bosch, Braun, Eller, Icahn, Lewis, Rowan, Sagan **6** Albert, Czerny, Dreyer, Lerner, Milles, Rakosi, Reiner, Wieman, Wilson **7** Bellman, Carlton, Douglas, Furillo, Hubbell, Laemmle, Perkins, Schultz **8** Almqvist, Anderson, Franklin, Sandburg, Weathers **9** Bernstein, Spitteler, Zuckmayer **10** Ballantine
son: 3 Rob
Carl __ Gustav: 3 XVI
Carla: 5 Bruni, Hills **6** Gugino
in Cheers: 4 Rhea
Carle: 7 Frankie
Carleton University
location: 6 Canada, Ottawa **7** Ontario
Carlin: 4 Lynn **6** George
Carlisle: 3 Bob **5** Kitty **7** Belinda
Carlisle, Belinda
song: Circle in the Sand (1988)
Heaven Is a Place on Earth (1987)
I Get Weak (1988)
Mad About You (1986)
Carlisle, Kitty
spouse: Moss Hart
Carlito's Way (1993 film)
cast: Penelope Ann Miller, Al Pacino, Sean Penn
director: Brian De Palma
Carlo: 5 Gadda, Gozzi, Ponti **6** Rubbia **7** Cassola, Collodi, Goldoni **8** Imperato
Sophia, to ~: 4 wife
__ Carlo: 5 Monte
__ Carlo Menotti: 4 Gian
Carlos: 4 Belo, Juan **5** Lamas, Wendy **6** Chávez, Reyles, Walter **7** Bousoño, Fuentes, Montoya, Santana **9** Castaneda
see also Spanish
__ Carlos: 3 Don
__ Carlos Jobim: 7 Antonio
Carlsbad: 4 city, town
locale: 9 New Mexico **10** California
Carlsbad Caverns: 4 park
locale: 9 New Mexico
Carlson: 4 Arne **7** Chester, Richard
Carlsson, Arvid: 8 Nobelist
Carlton: 4 Carl, Fisk **5** Steve
__ Carlton: 4 Ritz
Carlton, Steve: 6 hurler **7** Phillie, pitcher
Carly: 5 Simon
Carlyle: 6 Thomas
carman: 9 conductor
Carman, Bliss: 4 poet **8** Canadian
Carme: 4 moon
planet: 7 Jupiter
Carmel: 4 city, town
locale: 7 Indiana **10** California
Carmel-__-Sea: 5 by-the
Carmela: 7 Soprano
Carmelite: 3 nun **5** friar **9** religious
Carmen: 4 city, Eric, town **5** McRae, opera **6** Dragon **7** Basilio, Electra, Miranda **9** Cavallaro
author: Prosper Mérimée
composer: Georges Bizet
Don José in ~: 5 tenor
locale: 6 Mexico **8** Campeche
role: 6 Zuniga **7** Don José, Micaëla, Moralès **8** Mercédès **9** Escamillo, Frasquita
setting: 5 Spain **7** Seville
solo: 4 aria
see also Spanish
Carmen, Eric
song: All by Myself (1976)
Hungry Eyes (1987)
Make Me Lose Control (1988)
Carmen Jones (1954 film)
cast: Pearl Bailey, Harry Belafonte, Dorothy Dandridge
director: Otto Preminger
Carmen Jones (musical)
lyricist: Oscar Hammerstein
Carmen Sandiego: 9 detective
need: 3 map
Carmichael: 3 Ian **5** Hoagy **7** Stokely
Carmina Burana
composer: Carl Orff
carmine: 3 red **5** color **6** purply **7** crimson **8** purplish
relative: ***see*** red color
Carmine: 7 Coppola
Carnaby Street
locale: 4 Soho **6** London
carnage: 4 gore **5** havoc **6** murder **8** massacre **9** bloodshed, mortality, slaughter
Carnal Knowledge (1971 film)
cast: Ann-Margret, Candice Bergen, Art Garfunkel, Rita Moreno, Jack Nicholson
director: Mike Nichols
carnallite: 3 ore
carnation: 5 plant **6** flower
relative: ***see*** red color
shade: 3 red **4** pink **5** white
spot: 5 lapel
carnauba: 3 wax **4** palm, tree **6** car wax
carne: 4 meat
partner: 5 chili
Carnegie: 4 Dale **6** Andrew
Carnegie __: 4 Hall, Tech, unit **6** Mellon
carnegiea: 6 cactus
Carne, Judy: 7 actress
catchphrase: 10 Sock it to me!
spouse: Burt Reynolds
carnelian: 3 gem **4** sard **7** sardine, sardius
Carnera: 5 boxer, Primo
he KO'd ~: 4 Baer
Carner, JoAnne: 6 golfer
Carnesecca, Lou: 5 coach
milieu: 5 court
sport: 10 basketball
Carnes, Kim
song: Bette Davis Eyes (1981)
Don't Fall in Love With a Dreamer (1978)
More Love (1980)
carney: 6 barker
Carney: 3 Art **8** Lansford
Carney, Art: 5 actor
TV: The Honeymooners
carnival: 4 fair, show **5** raree **6** circus **7** jubilee **8** festival **9** Mardi Gras **10** masquerade, street fair
attraction: 4 ride **6** go-cart, go-kart
give a ~ spiel: 4 bark
prize: 4 doll **6** kewpie **8** goldfish
prop: 5 stilt
ride cry: 4 whee
setup: 4 tent **5** booth **6** midway
worker: 4 geek **6** barker
carnival __: 5 glass
Carnival
day: 5 Mardi
locale: 3 Rio **6** Brazil
offering: 6 cruise
Carnival of Harlequin
artist: Joan Miró
carnivore: 8 predator
quest: 4 meat, prey
carnotite: 3 ore
Carnovsky: 6 Morris
carny: 6 barker
carob: 3 pod **4** bean, tree **6** legume
relative: ***see*** legume tree
carol: 3 air **4** hymn, noel, sing, song, tune **5** music, troll **6** ballad, intone
start: 4 hark **5** o come **6** adeste
syllables: 4 fa la, la la **6** fa la la
word: 3 'tis
Carol: 3 Alt **4** Kane, Mann, Reed **5** Haney, Heiss **6** Leifer, Lynley, Potter **7** Burnett **8** Channing, Lawrence
Carol Burnett Show, The (CBS variety)
cast: Carol Burnett
Tim Conway
Harvey Korman
Vicki Lawrence
Lyle Waggoner
Carole: 4 King **6** Landis **7** Lombard
Carole Bayer __: 5 Sager

caroler: 4 alto, bass 5 tenor 7 soprano 8 baritone, vocalist 9 chorister
carolers: 5 choir 6 chorus
Carolina: 4 rice
alternative: 6 Minute 7 Success 9 Uncle Ben's
cape: 4 Fear
team: 8 Panthers 10 Hurricanes
Caroline: 4 Lamb, Rhea 5 Aaron 7 Kennedy
aunt: 3 Pat 5 Ethel 6 Eunice
uncle: 3 Ted
__ Caroline: 5 Sweet
Caroline in the City (NBC sitcom)
cast: Malcolm Gets (Richard Karinsky)
Eric Lutes (Del Cassidy)
Lea Thompson (Caroline Duffy)
cat: 5 Salty
Caroline Islands
part of the ~: 3 Yap 4 Truk 5 Palau
__ Carol Oates: 5 Joyce
Carol Stream: 4 city, town
locale: 8 Illinois
__ & Carol & Ted & Alice: 3 Bob
Carolus: 8 Linnaeus
Carolyn: 5 Chute, Jones, Keene 6 Forché
carom: 4 bank, bump 6 bounce, glance, recoil 7 rebound 8 ricochet 10 bounce back
light ~: 4 kiss
Caron, Leslie: 7 actress
film: An American in Paris (1951)
Daddy Long Legs (1955)
Fanny (1961)
Father Goose (1964)
Gigi (1958)
Lili (1953)
Caro nome: 4 aria
__ carotene: 4 beta
carotid __: 6 artery
carousal: 3 jag 4 riot, tear 5 binge, spree 7 revelry
carouse: 4 play, romp 5 revel 6 frolic 7 have fun, roister 9 have a ball, make merry, raise Cain, whoop it up
carousel: 4 ride
Carousel: 4 film 7 musical
Carousel (1945 musical)
composer: Oscar Hammerstein, Richard Rodgers
Carousel (1956 film)
cast: Shirley Jones, Gordon MacRae
carp: 3 koi, nag 4 dace, fish, harp, kick, moan, orfe, rail 5 cavil, gripe, groan, knock, prate, whine 6 bother, grouch, grouse, kvetch, niggle 7 censure, grumble, henpeck, nitpick, quarrel, quibble 8 browbeat, complain, goldfish 9 bellyache, criticize, find fault, make a fuss 10 tongue-lash
at: 3 nag 6 rebuke 7 censure
kin: 3 ide 4 chub, dace, rudd 6 minnow
starter: 4 endo
carpaccio base: 4 beef
carpal: 4 bone
locale: 5 wrist
starter: 4 meta
carpal __: 6 tunnel
Carpathians: 5 range 9 mountains
locale: 6 Europe 7 Romania, Rumania 8 Slovakia
mountain range: 5 Tatra
river: 4 Oder, Odra
carpe: 5 Latin, seize
carpe __: 4 diem
carpenter: 3 ant, bee 6 joiner 7 artisan, builder 10 journeyman, woodworker
angle: 5 bevel
at times: 5 sawer
companion: 6 walrus
cut: 5 miter
fastener: 4 bolt, nail, T-nut 5 screw, U-bolt
groove: 4 dado
in an 1859 novel: 4 Bede
name meaning ~: 9 Zimmerman
need: 5 apron, dowel, stain 6 ladder 7 goggles 8 miter box
strap: 3 gib
strip: 4 lath
tool: 3 adz, saw 4 adze, vise 5 clamp, drill, lathe, level, plane, plumb 6 C-clamp, chisel, hammer, pliers
wedge: 4 shim
woe: 4 knot 8 splinter
carpenter __: 3 ant, bee 4 moth 6 gothic
Carpenter: 4 John 5 Karen, Scott 7 Richard
Carpenter, John: 8 director
film: Escape From New York (1981)
The Fog (1980)
Halloween (1978)
Carpenters: 3 duo
members: Richard, Karen
song: Close to You (1970)
For All We Know (1971)
Goodbye to Love (1972)
Hurting Each Other (1972)
Only Yesterday (1975)
Please Mr. Postman (1974)
Rainy Days and Mondays (1971)
Sing (1973)
Superstar (1971)
Top of the World (1973)
We've Only Just Begun (1970)
Yesterday Once More (1973)
carpentry: 5 skill, trade
joint: 5 bevel
carper: 3 nag 4 prig 6 critic, kvetch
carpet: 3 rug, rya 4 Agra, shag 5 plush 6 Berber, rag rug, runner, Saxony, toupee 7 Persian 8 Aubusson, tapestry 9 broadloom, cover over
alternative: 4 lino 7 parquet 8 linoleum
calculation: 4 area 5 sq. yds.
call on the ~: 5 chide 6 rebuke 8 admonish 9 reprimand
cleaner: 3 vac 6 vacuum 7 sweeper
ender: 3 bag 4 weed 5 grass 6 bagger
fabric: 4 wool 5 frisé, nylon
fastener: 4 tack
feature: 3 nap 4 pile
fiber: 4 kemp 5 istle, ixtle
install: 3 lay
maker: 4 loom
old-style: 5 tapis
roll out the red ~: 5 greet, honor 7 lionize, receive, welcome
spoiler: 5 stain
carpet __: 3 bug 4 moth, tack, tile 5 grass, shark, snake 6 beetle 7 slipper, sweeper
__ carpet: 3 red 5 magic, on the 6 flying
Carpetbaggers, The
author: Harold Robbins
character: 4 Rina
__-carpet treatment: 3 red
carping: 5 picky 7 fretful, nagging, peevish 8 captious, caviling, critical, fretsome 9 criticism, grumbling, querulous
critic: 5 momus
critics: 4 momi
carpoolers, lane for: 3 HOV
carport
kin: 6 garage
carpus: 4 bone 5 wrist
neighbor: 4 ulna
starter: 4 meta
Carr: 5 Caleb, Cathy, Vikki 7 Darleen 8 Charmian
car-racing org.: 4 IROC, NHRA
Carradine: 4 John 5 David, Keith 6 Robert
Carradine, David: 5 actor
TV: Kung Fu
Carradine, Keith
song: I'm Easy
Carrara: 6 marble
Carré: 4 Otis
__ Carré: 6 John le
carrel: 4 desk 5 booth 6 alcove, recess
car rental: 4 Avis 5 Alamo, Hertz 6 Budget, Dollar 7 Thrifty 8 National 10 Enterprise
Carrera: 3 car 4 auto 7 Barbara, Porsche
Carreras, José: 5 tenor 6 singer
specialty: 5 opera
Carrere: 3 Tia
Carrey, Jim: 5 actor
film: Ace Ventura: Pet Detective (1994)
Batman Forever (1995)
The Cable Guy (1996)
Dumb & Dumber (1994)
Earth Girls Are Easy (1989)
Eternal Sunshine of the Spotless Mind (2004)
Fun With Dick and Jane (2005)
How the Grinch Stole Christmas (2000)
Lemony Snicket's A Series of Unfortunate Events (2004)
Liar Liar (1997)
Man on the Moon (1999)
The Mask (1994)
Me, Myself & Irene (2000)
The Truman Show (1998)
Yes Man (2008)
spouse: Lauren Holly
carriage: 3 air, gig, rig 4 gait, mien, pose, shay, walk 5 buggy, coach, stand, sulky, wagon 6 chaise, landau, stance, surrey, troika 7 bearing, cariole, conduct, droshky, freight, hackney, phaeton, posture, transit 8 attitude, barouche, behavior, brougham, delivery, demeanor, equipage, presence, stroller 9 cabriolet, transport 10 appearance, conveyance, deportment
baby ~: 4 pram 5 buggy 6 go-cart
Holmes ~: 4 shay
horse: 7 hackney
horse-drawn ~: 3 rig 6 calash, fiacre 7 caleche
horseless ~: 3 car 4 auto 7 vehicle 10 automobile
Javanese ~: 4 sado 5 sadoo
occupant: 4 baby, doll
of India: 6 gharri, gharry
part: 4 axle 5 while
Roman: 5 rheda
trade: 5 elite
carriage __: 3 dog 4 bolt 5 horse, house, piece, trade 6 return
__ carriage: 4 baby
carrick bend: 4 knot
Carrie: 3 Nye 4 Catt, film, Henn 5 novel 6 Fisher, Nation 9 Snodgress
author: Stephen King
cast: Amy Irving, William Katt, Piper Laurie, Sissy Spacek, John Travolta
director: Brian De Palma
Carrie-__ Moss: 4 Anne
__ Carrie: 6 Sister
Carrie-Anne: 4 Moss
Carrie-Anne (1967 song)
artist: Hollies
carried: 5 borne
away: 4 gaga, rapt
be ~: 4 ride, waft
easily ~: 8 portable
get ~ away: 8 overplay
carrier: 5 dolly, envoy, toter 6 bearer, porter, runner 7 airline, frigate, vehicle 8 conveyer, conveyor, emissary 9 messenger, transport 10 battleship, conveyance
aircraft ~: 4 ship 7 warship 8 man-of-war
bag ~: 5 caddy, toter 6 caddie, porter, skycap 7 bellhop, bellman
coal ~: 3 car 4 scow, tram 5 barge
combining form: 3 -fer 4 -pher, -phor 5 -phore
commuter ~: 3 bus, car 4 auto 5 ferry, train 7 shuttle
fare ~: 4 hack, taxi 7 taxicab
freight ~: 3 van 5 barge, truck 6 boxcar
fuel ~: 5 oiler 6 coaler, tanker
letter ~: 5 stamp 7 mailman, postman 8 envelope
ore ~: 5 barge
quiver ~: 6 archer, bowman 9 Robin Hood 10 longbowman
water ~: 3 rut 4 duct, hose, line, pail, pipe, race 5 canal, ditch, drain, flume, gulch, gully 6 arroyo, furrow, gulley, gutter, outlet, siphon, strait, syphon, trench, trough 7 channel, conduit, culvert, passage 8 aqueduct
carrier __: 4 wave 6 pigeon
__ carrier: 3 air, hod 4 ball, bulk, data, jeep, mail 5 space, spear, troop, water 6 common, letter, postal

__-carrier: 4 puck 5 spear
Carrier
rival: 5 Rheem, Trane 6 Lennox 7 Fedders 9 Friedrich
carrion: 5 offal 10 rottenness
Carroll: 3 Leo, Pat 5 Baker, David, Lewis 7 Diahann, O'Connor 9 Madeleine
Carroll, Diahann: 7 actress
spouse: Vic Damone
TV: Dynasty, Julia
Carroll, Leo G.: 5 actor
TV: The Man From U.N.C.L.E., Topper
Carroll, Lewis: 6 writer 7 British
contemporary: 4 Lear
heroine: 5 Alice
real last name: Dodgson
work: Alice's Adventures in Wonderland
The Hunting of the Snark
Sylvie and Bruno
Through the Looking-Glass
carrot: 4 lure, plum, root 6 orange, reward, veggie 7 premium 9 incentive, vegetable 10 enticement, inducement, rabbit food, temptation
dangle a ~: 5 tempt 6 entice
relative: 5 anise
source: 4 farm 6 garden
stick: 5 snack
carrot-__: 3 top
carrot-and-__: 5 stick
Carr, Vikki
song: It Must Be Him (1967)
carry: 3 air, lug, run, win 4 bear, cart, draw, haul, have, hold, keep, lift, move, pack, sell, sway, take, tote, waft 5 bring, ferry, fetch, relay, shlep, stock, truck 6 convey, convoy, deal in, handle, schlep, shlepp, uphold 7 comport, conduct, deliver, include, prevail, signify, support, sustain, win over 8 relocate, shoulder, transfer, transmit 9 broadcast, reinforce, transport 10 accomplish
a torch: 4 long, pine
a torch for: 4 love 5 adore
a tune: 4 sing
away: 4 cart 6 abduct, ablate, remove 7 enchant 8 entrance 9 discharge, transport
back: 6 return
easy to ~: 5 light
ender: 3 all, out 4 over
hard to ~: 5 heavy 10 cumbersome
off: 4 take 5 seize, steal 6 abduct, kidnap 7 succeed
on: 2 go 3 ply 4 have, hold, keep, rage, rant, rave, wage, wail, work 5 act up, emote, fight, mourn, party, serve 6 cavort, endure, extend, gambol, manage, pursue, resume, sorrow 7 conduct, persist, proceed, prolong, survive 8 continue, maintain, practice, transact 9 misbehave, persevere
out: 2 do 4 heed, meet, mind, obey 5 bow to, enact, wreak 6 accept, bend to, commit, effect, follow, fulfil, manage, redeem 7 abide by, achieve, agree to, defer to, execute, fulfill, observe, perform, realize, respect 8 adhere to, complete, conclude, dispense, listen to, transact 9 conform to, consent to, discharge, implement 10 accomplish, administer, consummate, effectuate, make good on, perpetrate
out, old-style: 5 doest
over: 4 keep 6 retain
the day: 3 win 7 succeed, triumph
through: 4 make 6 effect, finish 7 achieve, perform, persist, play out, realize
to: 5 reach
to and fro: 5 ferry
too far: 6 overdo
weight: 4 tell 5 count, weigh 6 matter
carry __: 3 off, out 4 away, over 5 a tune, light 6 permit 7 forward, through
carry __ conversation: 3 on a
carry __ of weight: 4 a lot
carry-__: 3 ons
__-carry: 4 hand
...carry __ stick: 4 a big
Carry: 6 Nation
carry a __: 5 torch
carry a __ weight: 5 lot of
carryall: 3 bag 4 tote 5 pouch, purse 7 handbag
carrying: 4 with
a grudge: 4 sore 6 bitter
a weapon: 5 armed
capacity: 6 armful
carrying __: 5 place 6 charge
__-carrying: 4 card
Carry moonbeams home __: 6 in a jar
carry-on: 3 bag 7 luggage
carryout: 4 meal
carry-over: 9 remainder
carry the __: 3 day 4 ball
Cars
leader: Ric Ocasek
song: Drive (1984)
Shake It Up (1981)
Tonight She Comes (1985)
You Might Think (1984)
Cars (1980 song)
artist: Gary Numan
Cars (2006 film)
voice cast: George Carlin, Bonnie Hunt, Paul Newman, John Ratzenberger, Tony Shalhoub, Owen Wilson
Carsey: 5 Marcy
Carson: 3 Kit 4 city, Jack, John, town 6 Johnny, Rachel 9 McCullers
locale: 3 Cal. 5 Calif. 10 California
__ Carson: 3 Kit 4 Fort
Carson City: 4 town 7 capital
lake near ~: 5 Tahoe
locale: 3 Nev. 6 Nevada
__ Carson, CO: 4 Fort
Carson, Johnny: 4 host 5 emcee
character: 6 Carnac
predecessor: 4 Paar
successor: 4 Leno
theme composer: Paul Anka
Carson, Kit: 5 scout
homesite: 4 Taos
Carson, Rachel: 6 writer
work: The Edge of the Sea
The Sea Around Us
The Sense of Wonder
Silent Spring
Under the Sea-Wind
cart: 3 lug 4 bear, dray, haul, move, take, tote, wain 5 bring, carry, dolly, ferry, shlep, sulky, wagon 6 barrow, convey, gurney, schlep, shlepp 7 deliver, ricksha, rikisha, rikshaw, tumbrel, tumbril, vehicle 8 rickshaw, tea table, transfer 9 carry away, transport
away: 4 haul, move
brake: 5 sprag
ender: 3 age 4 load 5 loads, wheel
farm ~: 4 wain
hospital ~: 6 gurney
in Britain: 6 trolly 7 trolley
lawn ~: 6 barrow
leader: 2 ox 5 horse
part: 4 axle 5 wheel
starter: 3 dog, tea, tip 4 hand, push
__ Carta: 5 Magna
cartage: 7 traffic
Cartagena: 4 city, port, town
locale: 8 Colombia
Car Talk (NPR talk)
host: Clack, Click, Ray Magliozzi, Tom Magliozzi
carte: 4 menu 8 wine list 10 bill of fare
blanche: 3 run 7 freedom, liberty, license, mandate 8 free hand
du jour: 4 list, menu 10 bill of fare
listing: 3 vin
carte __: 6 du jour 7 blanche, d'entrée
__ carte: 3 à la
cartel: 4 bloc, OPEC, ring, synd. 5 group, trust 6 treaty 7 combine 8 business, monopoly 9 syndicate 10 consortium
Carter: 3 Amy, Don, Mel 4 Chip, Gary, Jack, June, Nell, Nick 5 Benny, Billy, Deana, Dixie, Glass, Janis, Jimmy, Lynda, Terry 6 Howard 7 Hodding 8 Clarence, Maybelle, Rosalynn
Carter, Benny: 11 saxophonist
genre: 4 jazz
sax: 4 alto
__ Carter Cash: 4 June
Carter, Dixie: 7 actress
spouse: Hal Holbrook
Carter, Don: 3 PBA 6 bowler
milieu: 5 alley
Carteret: 4 city, town
locale: 9 New Jersey
Carter, Gary: 7 catcher
Carter, Howard: 12 archeologist
discovery: 3 Tut 7 King Tut
Carteris: 8 Gabriela
Carter, Jimmy: 8 Nobelist 9 president
advisor: 5 Lance 6 Jordan
alma mater: 4 USNA 9 Annapolis
cabinet member: 4 Bell 5 Adams, Brown, Kreps, Vance 6 Andrus, Harris, Muskie 8 Califano, Landrieu
child: 3 Amy 4 Chip, Jack 7 Jeffrey
home: 6 Plains 7 Georgia
middle name: 4 Earl
mother: 7 Lillian
opponent: 4 Ford 6 Reagan
previous occupation: 6 farmer
sibling: 4 Ruth 5 Billy 6 Gloria
V.P.: 7 Mondale
wife: 8 Rosalynn
work: Always a Reckoning
Everything to Gain
Faith and Freedom
The Hornet's Nest
The Hour Before Daylight
Keeping Faith
Living Faith
Our Endangered Values
Sources of Strength
Talking Peace
Turning Point
The Virtues of Aging
Why Not the Best?
Carter, Jimmy, work: The Blood of Abraham
Carter, Nick: 3 spy 5 agent
Cartesian
conclusion: 3 I am, sum
connection: 4 ergo
line: 4 axis
Carthage
ancient city near ~: 4 Zama 5 Utica
city near ~: 5 Tunis
language: 5 Punic
loc.: 3 Afr. 6 Africa
queen of ~: 4 Dido
Carthaginian: 5 Punic
Cartier-Bresson: 5 Henri
Cartier, Jacques: 6 French 8 explorer
cartilage: 6 tissue 7 gristle
canine ~: 5 lytta
carting: 8 delivery
Cartland: 4 Dame 7 Barbara
cartographer: 6 mapper 8 Mercator
abbr.: 3 alt., Atl., isl., lat., mts., Pac., str., ter. 4 terr.
product: 3 map 5 atlas, inset
speck: 3 cay, key 4 isle 6 island
unit: 6 degree, minute, second
carton: 3 box 4 case 5 crate 6 packet, parcel 7 package, six-pack, ten-pack 9 container
cartoon: 4 film 5 short 6 sketch 7 drawing, picture 9 animation 10 caricature, comic strip
credit: 5 voice 8 animator
exclamation: 3 oof 4 yeow 7 omigosh
frame: 3 cel 4 cell
Japanese ~ genre: 5 anime
sound effect: 4 bonk, wham 5 boing
TV ~: 6 kidcom
cartoonist: 4 Arno, Capp, Hart, Nast 5 Adams, Davis, Gould, Keane, Kelly, Young 6 Al Capp, artist, Browne, Caniff, drawer, Eisner, Foster, Larson, Mullin, Schulz, Searle, Soglow, Walker 7 Ketcham, Lazarus, Trudeau 8 Aragonés, Bil Keane, Goldberg, Groening, Herblock, Jim Davis, Lasswell, MacNelly, Oliphant 9 Chic Young, Dik Browne, Guisewite, Hal Foster, Peter Arno, Walt Kelly, Watterson 10 Gary Larson, Johnny Hart, Mort Walker, Scott Adams, Thomas Nast
helper: 5 inker
need: 3 ink 6 eraser
org.: 3 NCS
tool: 6 Benday
cartouche: 4 oval

cartridge: 4 ammo, case 6 bullet 7 missile 10 ammunition
cartwheel: 6 tumble
Cartwright: 3 Ben, Joe 4 Adam, Hoss 5 Nancy 6 Angela 8 Veronica 9 Alexander, Little Joe
Cartwright, Ben: 7 rancher
  child: 3 Joe 4 Adam, Hoss 9 Little Joe
  portrayer: Lorne Greene
Caruso: 5 David 6 Enrico
Caruso, Enrico: 5 tenor 6 singer
  portrayer: Mario Lanza
  specialty: 4 aria 5 opera
___ Caruso, The: 5 Great
carve: 3 cut, hew 4 etch, pare, stab 5 cut up, knife, model, sever, shape, slash, slice 6 chisel, cleave, emboss, incise, sculpt 7 engrave, whittle 9 sculpture
  out: 4 take
  up: 5 allot, split 6 parcel
  wood: 5 thurm
carved: 4 hewn 6 graven 7 incised
  combining form: 5 glypt- 6 glypto-
  Greek ~ image: 6 xoanon
  Greek ~ images: 5 xoana
carver: 7 artisan 9 craftsman
  medium: 4 jade, lava, soap, wood
Carver: 4 John 5 Steve 7 Raymond
Carver, George Washington: 8 botanist
Carvey: 4 aper, Dana
Carville, James: 6 pundit
  spouse: Mary Matalin
carving: 3 art 5 glyph, totem 8 division 9 totem pole
  mineral: 9 alabaster
carving ___: 4 fork 5 knife
car-wash
  machine: 5 waxer
  need: 3 wax 5 spray, water 6 chammy, shammy, shamoy 7 chamois
  step: 5 rinse
Car Wash (1976 song)
  artist: Rose Royce
Cary: 5 Elwes, Grant, Joyce 10 Middlecoff
  ex: 4 Dyan
casa: 8 hacienda
  grande: 5 villa
  material: 5 adobe
Casa ___ Orchestra: 4 Loma
casaba: 5 fruit, melon 9 muskmelon
Casablanca: 4 city, port, town
  city near ~: 4 Safi 5 Rabat, Saffi
  locale: 3 Mor. 7 Morocco
Casablanca (1942 film)
  cast: Ingrid Bergman, Humphrey Bogart, Sydney Greenstreet, Paul Henreid, Peter Lorre, Claude Rains, Conrad Veidt, Dooley Wilson
  composer: Max Steiner
  director: Michael Curtiz
  role: 3 Sam 4 Ilsa, Rick 6 Blaine, Laszlo, Victor 7 Renault
  screenwriter: 4 Koch
  setting: 4 café 5 Rick's 7 Morocco
Casa Loma Orchestra
  leader: Glen Gray
Casals: 5 Pablo, Rosie 8 Rosemary
Casals, Pablo: 7 cellist, Spanish
Casals, Rosemary: 7 netster
9 tennis pro
  milieu: 5 court
Casanova: 4 rake, roué 5 Romeo 7 Don Juan, Giacomo 8 lothario 9 libertine
Casbah
  locale: 4 Oran 6 Africa 7 Algeria, Algiers
  mall: 5 bazar 6 bazaar
  wear: 3 fez
cascade: 4 fall, flow, gush, pour, spew, spue 5 flood, spout 6 deluge, onrush, stream 7 descend, torrent 8 cataract, downrush, overflow 9 avalanche, waterfall 10 inundation, outpouring
Cascade
  alternative: *see* detergent
___ Cascade: 5 Boise
Cascades: 5 range 9 mountains
  locale: 6 Canada 10 Washington
  mountain: 4 Hood 5 Adams 6 Lassen, Shasta 7 Rainier 8 St. Helens
Cascades, The: 3 rag
  composer: Scott Joplin
Casco: 3 bay
  locale: 5 Maine
case: 3 bag, bin, box, pod 4 bark, grip, husk, look, suit 5 chest, claim, crate, event, frame, scout, shape, shell, sneak, spy on, state, study, topic, trial, trunk, watch 6 action, carton, coffer, dative, jacket, pack up, plight, reason, sample, survey, valise 7 baggage, canvass, check up, context, dilemma, dispute, enclose, examine, example, inclose, inspect, lawsuit, lookout, luggage, patient 8 canister, check out, incident, instance, look over, magazine, occasion, petition, position, sampling, scope out, specimen 9 cartridge, condition, container, happening, objective, obsession, portfolio, sheathing, situation 10 integument, litigation, occurrence, receptacle, scrutinize
  attaché ~: 3 bag 9 portfolio
  breaker: 4 clew, clue
  court ~: 3 res 5 trial 7 lawsuit
  do the ~ over: 5 retry
  ender: 4 book, load, mate, work 6 harden 8 hardened
  get on one's ~: 3 bug, nag 4 harp 6 badger 9 find fault, persecute
  grammatical ~: 3 abl., acc., nom., obj. 4 poss. 6 dative 8 ablative 9 objective 10 nominative, possessive
  hard ~: 4 hull, husk, thug 8 carapace 10 integument
  hear a ~: 3 try 5 judge
  history: 4 file 6 record, report 7 dossier 8 document, specimen 10 background
  hopeless ~: 5 goner
  in ~: 4 lest 6 should 9 perchance
  in any ~: 5 still 10 regardless
  in that ~: 4 if so, then
  in the ~ of: 5 as for
  legal ~ statement: 5 facta
  list: 6 docket
  lower ~: 5 small 9 minuscule
  make a federal ~ of: 6 overdo
  make one's ~: 5 prove
  needle ~: 4 etui 5 etwee
  nut ~: 3 bur 4 kook 5 crank, shell
  one bringing a ~: 4 suer
  on the ~: 4 at it 7 working
  seed ~: 3 pod
  solve a ~: 5 crack
  starter: 4 book, show, slip, suit 5 brain, brief, crank, lower, smear, stair, upper, watch
  state one's ~: 5 argue, plead
  that being the ~: 2 so 4 ergo, if so 5 hence
  upper ~: 7 capital 9 majuscule
  wind up a ~: 4 rest 6 settle
case ___: 3 bay, law 4 card, shot 5 glass, goods, knife, study 6 ending, method, system, worker 7 grammar, history
___ case: 3 egg, job, key 4 hard, in no, news, test, wing 5 brain, dairy, in any, index, jewel, spore, upper 6 pencil, vanity 7 attaché, federal
___ case for: 5 make a
casein: 4 curd
case in ___: 5 point
Casella: 7 Alfredo
casement ___: 4 door 5 cloth 6 window
Case of Identity, A
  author: Arthur Conan Doyle
Case of Lucy Bending, The
  author: Lawrence Sanders
Case of Need, A
  author: Michael Crichton
Case of Samples, A
  author: Kingsley Amis
caserne: 7 bivouac 8 barracks, garrison
___-case scenario: 4 best 5 worst
Casey: 3 Ben 4 Wian 5 Jones, Kasem 6 Bernie 7 Stengel, William
  club: 3 bat
  org.: 3 CIA
Casey at the Bat
  ender: 3 out 9 strikeout
cash
  advance: 4 loan
  alternative: 5 check 6 charge
  blow ~: 5 spend 8 squander
  bundle: 3 wad 4 pile
  cow: 7 bonanza 8 gold mine
  ender: 3 ier 4 book, less
  flow: 6 income 7 revenue 8 receipts
  get ~ for: 4 hock, pawn, sell
  holder: 3 ATM 4 safe, till 8 register
  in: 6 redeem 7 collect 8 exchange 9 liquidate
  in on: 3 use 7 exploit
  on hand: 5 asset
  partner: 5 carry
  recipient: 5 payee
  register calculation: 3 tax
  register co.: 3 IBM, NCR
  short of ~: 5 broke, needy
  stash: 3 IRA 5 Keogh 7 account, nest egg 9 piggy bank
  substitute: 3 IOU 5 scrip
  see also coin, money, moolah
cash ___: 3 bar, cow, out 4 crop, flow 5 audit, basis, money, value 6 letter 7 account, journal, machine
cash ___ barrelhead: 5 on the
___ cash: 4 cold, hard 5 petty
Cash: 3 Pat 4 Norm 6 Johnny 7 Rosanne
cash and ___: 5 carry
cash-back offer: 6 rebate
Cash Cab (Discovery game show)
  host: Ben Bailey
cashew: 3 nut 4 nosh, tree 5 snack
  relative: 5 mango, sumac 6 acajou, fustet, mastic, sumach 9 pistachio, sugarbush
cashier: 2 ax 3 axe, can 4 boot, drop, fire, oust, sack 5 clerk, expel, let go 6 bounce, bursar, depose, lay off, purser, reject, remove, teller 7 cast off, dismiss, drum out, release, turn out 8 displace, furlough, get rid of, pink-slip 9 discharge, paymaster, terminate
  cry: 4 next
cashier's ___: 5 check
Cash, Johnny
  song: A Boy Named Sue (1969) Folsom Prison Blues (1968) I Walk the Line (1956) Ring of Fire (1963)
  wife: June Carter
cashless deal: 4 swap, swop 5 trade 6 barter
cashmere: 4 goat, wool 6 fabric 7 sweater
Cashmere Bouquet
  alternative: *see* soap
casing: 4 bark, hull, rind, skin 5 frame 6 jacket, sheath 7 wrapper 8 covering 9 framework 10 integument
casino: 4 game 5 Sands 6 Sahara 7 Aladdin, Caesar's, Harrah's 8 card game, Foxwoods, MGM Grand, slot spot 9 nightclub
  action: 3 bet
  city: 4 Reno 5 Tahoe, Vegas 8 Las Vegas
  cry: 5 banco, hit me
  data: 4 odds
  employee: 6 dealer 7 pit boss 8 croupier
  furnishing: 4 deck 5 cards, table, wheel
  game: 4 faro, keno 5 craps, poker, slots 6 écarté 8 baccarat, roulette 9 blackjack, twenty-one
  implement: 4 rake, shoe
  industry: 6 gaming
  invocation: 4 luck
  locale: 3 Nev. 6 Nevada
  maximum: 5 limit
  natural: 5 seven 6 eleven
  patron: 6 better, bettor
  show: 5 revue 6 review
  sign: 4 neon
  the ~ so to speak: 5 house
  tip: 4 toke
Casino (1995 film)
  cast: Robert De Niro, Joe Pesci, Sharon Stone, James Woods
  director: Martin Scorsese
Casino ___: 6 Royale
___ Casino: 5 Clams
Casino Royale: 4 film, song 5 novel
  author: Ian Fleming
Casino Royale (1967 film)
  cast: Woody Allen, Ursula Andress, David Niven, Peter Sellers, Orson Welles
  director: John Huston
Casino Royale (1967 song)
  artist: Herb Alpert and the Tijuana Brass

Casino Royale (2006 film)
cast: Daniel Craig, Judi Dench, Eva Green
Casio: **5** watch
alternative: ***see*** wristwatch
cask: **3** bbl., keg, tub, tun, vat **4** butt **6** barrel, firkin, foudre **8** hogshead **9** container
part: **5** stave
put a hole in a ~: **3** tap
stopper: **4** bung
Cask of Amontillado, The
author: Edgar Allan Poe
casmerodius albus: **5** egret
Caspar: **5** magus **7** Van Dien **10** Weinberger **11** Milquetoast
et al.: **4** Magi
like ~: **4** wise
Caspary: **4** Vera
Casper: **4** city, Dave, town **5** Billy
locale: **3** Wyo. **7** Wyoming
the Ghost's uncle: **5** Fatso **6** Stinky **7** Stretch
Casper, Billy: **6** golfer
Casper, Dave
sport: **8** football
Caspian
locale: **7** Eurasia
Caspian Sea: **4** lake
catch: **4** carp
city near the ~: **5** Rasht, Resht
feeder: **4** Kura, Ural **5** Atrak, Atrek, Volga
land: **4** Iran
neighbor: **4** Aral
port: **4** Baku
Cass: **4** Mama **5** Peggy **6** Elliot **7** Gilbert
Cassandra: **4** seer **5** sibyl **7** prophet **10** prophetess
brother: **5** Chaon, Paris **6** Hector, Pammon **7** Polites, Troilus
parent: **5** Priam **6** Hecuba
sister: **6** Creusa, Iliona **7** Laodice **8** Polyxena
son: **6** Pelops **9** Teledamus
twin: **7** Helenus
Cassandra Compact, The
author: Robert Ludlum
Cassatt, Mary: **6** artist **7** painter
contemporary: Edgar Degas
Cassavetes: **4** John, Nick
Cassavetes, John: **8** director
spouse: Gena Rowlands
Cass County seat: **5** Fargo
casserole: **4** dish, stew **6** potpie **7** goulash **10** stroganoff
cook a ~: **4** bake
cover: **3** lid
ingredient: **4** tuna
cassette: **4** tape
alternative: **2** CD **4** disc, disk
contents: **5** movie, video
copy a ~: **3** dub
deck button: **3** REC, REW **4** stop **5** eject, pause **6** record, rewind
format: **3** DAT
half: **5** side A, side B
recorder letters: **3** mic
starter: **5** audio, video
cassette __: **4** deck, tape **6** player **8** recorder
cassia: **4** tree **5** senna, shrub, spice **6** legume **8** cinnamon
relative: ***see*** legume tree
Cassidy: **3** Ted **4** Jack **5** Butch, David, Shaun **6** Joanna **7** Patrick **8** Hopalong
Cassidy, Butch: **5** alias **6** outlaw
Cassidy, David
spouse: Kay Lenz
TV: The Partridge Family
Cassidy, Jack: **5** actor
spouse: Shirley Jones
Cassini: **4** Igor, Oleg
creation: **4** gown **5** dress
Cassini, Oleg: **8** designer
spouse: Gene Tierney
__ Cassino: **5** Monte
Cassin, René: **6** French **8** Nobelist
Cassio adversary: **4** Iago
cassiope: **5** shrub
relative: ***see*** heath family shrub
Cassiopeia
component: **4** star
daughter: **9** Andromeda
cassis: **5** drink **8** beverage
apéritif: **3** kir
cassiterite: **3** ore **6** tin ore
Cassius: **4** Clay **5** Roman
and company: **5** cabal
opponent: **5** Sonny
__ Cassius has a lean...: **4** Yond
Cass, Mama
group: Mamas & The Papas
last name: Elliot
real name: Ellen Naomi Cohen
song: Dream a Little Dream of Me (1968)
cassock: **4** coat **6** jacket **7** soutane **10** canonicals
cassoulet: **4** stew
cassowary: **4** bird **6** ratite
kin: **3** emu **4** emeu
Cass Timberlane
author: Sinclair Lewis
cast: **3** air, hue, log, peg, set **4** flip, form, hurl, lick, look, mien, mold, send, shed, tint, tone, toss, type **5** chuck, color, fling, heave, impel, level, light, model, pitch, shade, shape, sling, staff, stamp, strew, throw, tinge, trait **6** actors, kidney, launch, manner, matrix, nature, plunge, reckon, spread, troupe, visage **7** company, diffuse, plaster, players, project, radiate, reflect, scatter **8** bespread, demeanor, disperse, ejection, ensemble, throw out **9** actresses, expulsion, sculpture, semblance **10** appearance, complexion, distribute, impression
a ballot: **4** vote **6** choose
about: **4** seek **5** flail, grope, strew **6** forage, scheme, search **7** bestrew, look for **8** contrive, flounder
a fly: **4** fish **5** angle
a pall over: **6** dampen
around for: **4** hunt, seek
aside: **4** cede, drop, dump, jilt, sell, shed, shun, veto **5** chuck, ditch, forgo, spurn, yield **6** bounce, forego, give up, pass on, rebuff, reject **7** abandon, discard, disdain, dismiss, exclude, forfeit, forsake, say no to **8** disallow, forswear, get rid of, hand over, jettison, leave out, part with, throw out, turn down **9** abandoned, blackball, dispose of, foreswear, repudiate, surrender, throw away **10** relinquish
a slur on: **6** defame **7** slander
a spell: **3** hex **4** jinx
away: **4** lost **5** spend **6** maroon, strand **7** abandon **8** stranded **9** abandoned **10** high and dry
be in a ~: **3** act **7** perform
doubt on: **6** impugn **8** question
down: **4** sink **5** abase, lower, lowly **6** broody, humble **7** degrade **8** dejected, dispirit **9** humiliate **10** dishearten, spiritless
ender: **3** off **4** away
gently: **3** dap
head the ~: **4** star
join the ~ of: **5** act in
light on: **8** illumine
loose: **5** let go **7** release
member: **5** actor **7** actress
off: **4** molt, sail, shed **5** egest, eject, sluff **6** reject, slough **7** cashier, dismiss, forsake **8** derelict, forsaken, forswear, jettison, renounce **9** foreswear, ownerless, repudiate, throw away **10** repudiated
out: **4** emit, oust, spew, spue, vent **5** egest, eject, exile, expel, exude, issue **6** banish, deport, reject **7** diffuse, dismiss, emanate, give off, radiate **8** exorcise, exorcize, supplant, throw off **9** eliminate, ostracize, send forth
slot: **4** role
something to ~: **4** line, role, vote **5** spell **6** ballot
starter: **3** mis **4** down, fore, news, over, tele, type **5** broad, cable, color, rough **6** narrow, sports **7** weather
supporter: **5** sling
cast __: **3** off, out **4** iron **5** about, aside, steel, stone **6** adrift
cast __ over: **5** a pall
cast-__ stomach: **4** iron
__-cast: **3** die, fly **4** open, sand, type
Cast a Dark Shadow (1955 film)
cast: Dirk Bogarde, Margaret Lockwood
director: Lewis Gilbert
Casta diva: **4** aria
cast against __: **4** type
Castaneda: **6** Carlos
castanets: **8** clackers **10** percussion
dance: **4** jota **6** bolero **8** fandango
castaway: **6** adrift, Crusoe, reject **7** discard, outcast **8** derelict, marooned, stranded, throw-out, unmoored
call: **3** SOS
home: **3** hut **4** isle **5** atoll **6** island
transport: **4** raft
Cast Away (2000 film)
cast: Tom Hanks, Helen Hunt
director: Robert Zemeckis
Castaways of the Flag, The
author: Jules Verne
caste: **4** rank **5** class, order **6** estate, status **7** station, stratum **8** position, standing **10** immaculate
Hindu ~: **4** Ahir, Jati **5** Sudra **7** Brahman, Brahmin
member: **5** Hindu **6** Hindoo
Castel Gandolfo
lake: **6** Albano
locale: **5** Italy
resident: **4** pope **7** pontiff
Castellaneta: **3** Dan
Castellano: **7** Richard
caster: **5** cruet, wheel **6** roller
need: **3** rod **4** line, reel
starter: **4** news, surf **5** broad, rough **6** sports **7** weather
castigate: **3** hit, rag, rip **4** beat, damn, flay, flog, lash, rail, slam, whip **5** abuse, baste, blast, chide, scold **6** berate, indict, punish, rebuke, scathe, thrash **7** bawl out, blister, censure, chasten, chew out, condemn, lambast, scourge, upbraid **8** browbeat, chastise, denounce, lambaste, penalize **9** criticize, dress down, excoriate, fulminate, reprehend, reprimand **10** come down on, discipline, tongue-lash, vituperate
castigation: **5** abuse, blame **6** rebuke **7** censure, lecture **8** diatribe
castigator: **5** scold, shrew **9** henpecker
castigatory: **5** penal
Castile: **4** soap
city: **5** Avila
locale: **5** Spain
partner: **6** Aragón
Castillo: **3** Ana
casting: **5** metal
starter: **4** surf, type **5** broad, rough **6** narrow
__ casting: **3** die, fly **4** bait, plug, slip, surf **7** central
casting out __: **5** nines
cast iron: **5** alloy
component: **6** carbon
cast-iron __: **7** stomach
castle: **4** fort, home, rook **5** house, manor, tower **6** palace **7** chateau, citadel, domicil, housing, lodging, mansion **8** domicile, dwelling, fastness, fortress **10** chess piece, donjon site, stronghold
feature: **4** keep, moat **5** tower **6** donjon, turret **7** dungeon
Havana ~: **5** Morro
in chess: **4** rook
in the air: **5** dream **6** revery **7** fantasy, reverie **8** daydream **9** pipe dream
protector, maybe: **4** pawn
queenside ~ in chess notation: **3** OOO
wall: **6** bailey **7** ballium
worker: **4** serf
castle __ air: **5** in the
__ castle: **3** air **4** sand
Castle: **5** Irene **6** Vernon **7** William
Castle __: **4** walk
__ Castle: **4** Man's **5** Axel's, Morro, White **6** Maiden **7** Windsor
Castlebar's county: **4** Mayo
__ Castle, Cuba: **5** Morro
castle in __: **5** Spain
castle in the __: **3** air
Castle in the Sea, The
author: Scott O'Dell
Castle of Otranto, The
author: Horace Walpole
Castle of Saint __: **4** Elmo
Castle of the Carpathians, The
author: Jules Verne
castles
build ~ in the air: **9** speculate
Castle, The
author: Franz Kafka

character: 4 Gisa, Olga 5 Klamm, Momus 6 Amalia, Frieda 7 Sortini
castoffs: 4 junk, rags 7 rejects
cast one's __ with: 3 lot
castor: 3 oil 4 bean
bean protein: 5 ricin
castor __: 3 oil 4 bean 5 sugar
Castor: 4 star 5 Jimmy 8 Argonaut
constellation: 6 Gemini
parent: 4 Leda, Zeus
sister: 5 Helen
slayer: 4 Idas
twin: 6 Pollux
Castorini, Loretta
portrayer: 4 Cher
Castries: 4 city, town 7 capital
locale: 7 St. Lucia
Castro: 4 sofa 5 Fidel, Raoul
capital: 6 Havana
country: 4 Cuba
see also Spanish
Castrogiovanni today: 4 Enna
Castro Valley: 4 city, town
locale: 10 California
cast the __ stone: 5 first
__ cast, the: 5 die is
casual: 3 lax 4 cool, easy, homy 5 blasé, homey, light, loose 6 breezy, chance, degage, folksy, little, mellow, random 7 aimless, cursory, liberal, offhand, raffish, relaxed, tieless 8 fireside, informal, laid-back, unstrict, untaxing 9 dress code, easygoing, haphazard, hit-or-miss, impromptu, irregular, leisurely, uncertain, unplanned 10 accidental, incidental, infrequent, nonchalant, occasional, off-the-cuff, unaffected, unagitated, uncritical, unexpected, unforeseen
dress phrase: 5 no tie
not ~: 6 dressy, formal
participant: 7 amateur
wear: 3 cap, tee 5 jeans, skort 6 chinos, denims, slacks, T-shirt 10 dishabille
casual __: 6 Friday
casually: 4 idly 7 lightly 8 by chance 9 leisurely, naturally 10 flippantly
Casualties of War
locale: 3 Nam
casualty: 4 loss 6 mishap, victim 7 debacle 8 accident, calamity, disaster, sufferer 10 misfortune
casuist: 8 logician, reasoner
casuistic: 7 evasive 9 illogical
casuistry: 6 dupery 7 fallacy 9 chicanery, deception, hypocrisy, sophistry
casus __: 5 belli
cat: 3 guy, pet, tom 4 eyra, lion, lynx, Manx, puma, puss 5 civet, fossa, genet, jiver, kitty, korat, liger, ounce, tabby, tiger, tigon, zibet 6 Angora, animal, calico, cougar, feline, feller, jaguar, kitten, malkin, mammal, margay, mouser, ocelot, purrer, serval, tiglon 7 bay lynx, brindle, caracal, cheetah, hipster, leopard, Maltese, panther 8 bebopper, house pet, longhair 9 blue point, catamount, grimalkin, Himalayan, seal point, shorthair 10 colorpoint, jaguarundi, sabertooth
Africa: 4 lion 5 civet 6 serval 7 caracal, cheetah, leopard
alley ~: 5 stray
Asia: 4 lion 5 civet, ounce, tiger 7 cheetah, leopard
at times: 5 mewer, pawer 6 lapper, meower, purrer
big ~: 4 lion, puma 5 tiger 6 ocelot 7 leopard
black ~: 4 omen
breed: 3 Rex 4 Manx 5 Korat 6 Birman, Bombay, Exotic, LaPerm, Ocicat, Somali, Sphynx 7 Burmese, Persian, Ragdoll, Siamese 8 Balinese, Devon Rex, Javanese, Oriental, Siberian 9 Chartreux, Maine Coon, Singapura, Tonkinese 10 Abyssinian, Cornish Rex, Selkirk Rex, Turkish Van
British: 3 mog 5 moggy
Canada: 4 lynx
Central America: 6 margay
coat: 3 fur
combining form: 5 aelur-, ailur- 6 aeluro-, ailuro-
comment: 3 mew 4 meow, purr, yowl 5 I'm hip, miaou, miaow, miaul
cool ~: 6 daddy-o
doc: 3 DVM, vet
drink: 4 milk
drink like a ~: 5 lap up
ender: 3 gut, kin, nap, nip 4 bird, boat, call, cher, fish, head, mint, tail, walk 5 brier, fight
fat ~: 5 mogul, nabob 6 tycoon 7 big shot, Pooh-bah 9 moneybags, plutocrat 10 man of means
female: 5 queen
foot: 3 paw
fraidy ~: 4 wimp 5 sissy 7 chicken, dastard 9 jellyfish
hangout: 5 alley
hybrid: 5 liger, tigon 6 tiglon
India: 7 caracal
in French: 4 chat
in Latin: 5 felis
in Spanish: 4 gato
let the ~ out of the bag: 3 air 4 bare, leak, tell 5 admit, blurt, spill 6 betray, expose, gossip, reveal, squeal, tattle 7 divulge, let slip 8 disclose, give away 9 make known
like most ~s: 4 neat
like some ~: 3 hep 4 cool 5 feral
lives: 4 nine 6 ennead
male: 3 gib, tom
maneuver: 4 arch
Mexico: 6 ocelot
mother ~ grip: 4 nape
murmur: 3 pur 4 purr
North America: 4 lynx, puma 6 cougar 7 panther 9 catamount
of Egyptian mythology: 4 Bast
palm: 3 pad
play ~ and mouse: 7 torment
quarry: 3 rat 5 mouse
Siamese ~ marking: 5 point
South America: 4 puma 6 cougar, margay, ocelot 7 panther
spotted ~: 5 ounce 6 jaguar, ocelot, serval 7 leopard
starter: 3 bob, hep, tom 4 bear, copy, hell, pole, wild 5 stone
striped ~: 5 tiger
tailless ~: 4 Manx
Thailand: 5 korat
to a flea: 4 host
top ~: 4 boss 5 chief 7 headman
tormentor: 4 flea
toy: 4 yarn
tropical ~: 4 eyra 5 civet 10 jaguarundi
wild ~: 4 lion, puma 5 civet, tiger 6 cougar, jaguar 7 panther
young: 6 kitten
cat __: 3 rig 4 flea, suit, yawl 6 litter, tackle 7 burglar, whisker
cat-__: 4 eyed, foot
cat-__-tails: 5 o'-nine
__ cat: 3 fat, hep, mud 4 blue, coon, copy, manx, one o', palm, two o' 5 alley, civet, fossa, tiger 6 Angora, calico, fraidy, native 7 Burmese, channel, Maltese, Persian, Siamese
__-cat: 4 one-a, two-a 5 four-a 6 fraidy 7 scaredy
Cat: 7 Stevens
Cat __: 6 Ballou, People
Cat __ Hat, The: 5 in the
Cat __ Hot Tin Roof: 3 on a
__-Cat: 3 Sno
CAT __: 4 scan 7 scanner
cataclysm: 4 doom, loss, ruin 5 flood, havoc 6 mishap 7 debacle, torrent, tragedy 8 calamity, collapse, disaster, upheaval 9 tidal wave 10 convulsion, earthquake, inundation, misfortune
cataclysmic: 4 dire 6 tragic 7 fateful, harmful, ruinous 8 tragical
catacomb: 4 tomb 5 vault 6 tunnel
recess: 7 loculus
catacombs: 4 maze 9 labyrinth
catafalque: 4 bier
Catalan Landscape
artist: Joan Miró
Catalan's country: 6 España
Catalina: 3 car 4 auto, isle 6 island 7 Pontiac
__ Catalina Island: 5 Santa
catalog: 4 file, list, roll, sort 5 index, order, tally 6 assort, detail, litany, record, roster 7 archive, itemize, program 8 classify, identify, organize, register, tabulate 9 directory, inventory 10 pigeonhole, prospectus, stereotype
items: 3 ads
subject: 5 model
__ catalog: 4 card 5 title, union 6 author, online
cataloguer: 5 Sears 6 L.L. Bean
Catalonian
city: 6 Lérida
river: 4 Ebro
catalpa: 4 tree 5 plant 6 flower
relative: 8 bignonia, calabash
tree: 9 jacaranda
catalyst: 4 goad, spur 5 agent, spark 6 enzyme 7 impetus 8 reactant, stimulus 9 incentive, spark plug 10 motivation
catamaran: 4 boat 5 skiff 8 sailboat
catamount: 3 cat 4 puma 5 felid 6 animal, feline, mammal 7 panther
relative: *see* feline
cat and __: 3 dog, rat 5 mouse
Cat and Mouse
author: Günter Grass
Cat and the Curmudgeon, The
author: Cleveland Amory
Catania: 4 city, town
locale: 5 Italy
view from ~: 4 Etna 5 Aetna
catapult: 4 hurl 5 fling, heave, shoot, sling, throw 6 engine, hurler, hurtle, launch, propel, weapon
in America: 9 slingshot
missile: 5 stone
cataract: 7 cascade, torrent 8 overflow
site: 4 lens
catarrh: 5 rheum
catastrophe: 4 blow, doom, loss 5 event, havoc 6 crisis, fiasco, misery, mishap, sorrow 7 debacle, reverse, scourge, tragedy, undoing 8 calamity, casualty, disaster, hardship, upheaval
catastrophic: 4 dire 5 woful 6 costly, tragic, woeful 7 fateful, ruinous, unlucky 8 ill-fated, luckless, tragical
Catawba: 4 wine 5 grape, river, white
relative: *see* wine
Cat Ballou (1965 film)
cast: Nat King Cole, Jane Fonda, Stubby Kaye, Lee Marvin
catboat: 5 skiff
catcall: 3 boo, dig 4 barb, gibe, hiss, hoot, jeer, jibe, slam, slap, slur, snub, twit 5 abuse, libel, scorn, taunt 6 heckle, rebuff, slight 7 affront, calumny, disdain, mockery, obloquy, offense, putdown 8 contempt, derision, ridicule 9 aspersion, contumely 10 defamation, disrespect, opprobrium
catch: 3 bag, get, nab, net, nip, rub, see 4 bust, clip, game, grab, grip, hasp, hear, hook, lock, mesh, nail, pain, pawl, snag, snap, spot, take, trap 5 board, clasp, field, grasp, hitch, hop on, lasso, latch, lodge, marry, prize, seize, snare, stick, trick 6 arrest, buckle, collar, corner, corral, detect, enmesh, entrap, expose, follow, immesh, inmesh, jump at, kicker, listen, secure, snatch, take in 7 acquire, capture, climb on, discern, ensnare, find out, head off, hit upon, insnare, involve, observe, pitfall, proviso, realize, receive, reflect 8 contract, discover, drawback, entangle, fastener, glom on to, interest, lock part, obstacle, overtake, perceive, pounce on, smell out, surprise 9 apprehend, condition, get hold of, hindrance, intercept, lay hold of, provision, recognize, track down 10 bring to bay, comprehend, understand
a bug: 3 ail
advance after a ~: 5 tag up
again: 5 renab
a glimpse of: 3 see 4 espy, spot 6 descry, detect, notice 7 discern, make out
basin: 4 sump
easy ~: 5 pop up
ender: 3 all, fly 4 pole, poll, word 5 penny
fail to ~: 4 muff
fire: 4 burn 6 ignite, kindle, set off 8 enkindle 10 incinerate

flies: **4** shag, yawn
hard to ~: **4** eely **7** elusive
holder: **5** creel **6** basket
hold of: **3** nab **4** hook, land, nail, snag **5** seize **6** arrest, collar, corral, snap up, snatch **7** capture, ensnare **9** apprehend, latch onto
in a net: **6** enmesh, immesh
mechanical ~: **6** detent
off-guard: **5** shock **8** surprise
on: **3** dig, get, see **5** get it, grasp, learn, sense **6** follow **7** realize **10** understand
one's breath: **5** pause
on to: **3** get **4** know **5** learn, sense
red-handed: **3** bag, get, nab, net **4** bust, grab, nail, trap **5** catch, pinch, run in, seize **6** arrest, collar, snatch **7** capture, startle **8** surprise **9** apprehend, burst in on
sight of: **3** eye, see, spy **4** espy, find, spot **6** descry **7** discern, glimpse
some rays: **3** sun, tan **4** bask
some z's: **3** nap **4** doze, rest **5** sleep **6** turn in
the eye: **8** stand out
unprepared: **3** jar **4** numb, rock, stun **5** abash, floor **6** appall, dismay **7** astound, horrify, shake up, stagger, stupefy **8** astonish, bowl over, paralyze, surprise, unsettle **9** electrify, galvanize, overwhelm
up: **6** gain on **7** recover
up to: **5** reach **8** approach, overtake
catch __: **3** dog **4** colt, crop, fire, on to **5** a crab, basin **6** phrase, stitch
catch __ of: **4** wind **5** sight
__ catch: **4** fair **5** elbow **6** safety, spring
Catch __ You Can: **4** Me If, Us If
Catch!: **4** here
Catch-22: **4** snag, trap **5** novel **7** dilemma, paradox, proviso **8** obstacle, quandary
author: Joseph Heller
character: **3** Orr **4** Milo **5** Major **9** Yossarian
catch a __: **4** crab
Catch a falling star
author: John Donne
Catch a Falling Star (1958 song)
artist: Perry Como
catchall: **9** inclusive
abbr.: **3** etc. **4** et al., misc.
term: **4** et al. **6** et alia, et alii, others
Catch and Release (2007 film)
cast: Jennifer Garner, Timothy Olyphant
catch-as-catch-__: **3** can
catcher: **6** Piazza **7** athlete **10** baseballer
cow ~: **5** lasso, reata, riata **6** lariat
doggie ~: **5** riata
fly ~: **3** web **5** honey **6** cobweb
gear: **3** pad **4** mask, mitt **5** glove
Hall of Fame ~: **4** Fisk **5** Bench, Berra **6** Carter, Dickey, Gibson **8** Cochrane **9** Yogi Berra **10** Bill Dickey, Campanella, Gary Carter
man behind the ~: **3** ump **6** umpire
mouse ~: **3** cat **4** trap **6** feline
place: **3** rye
quotable ~: **4** Yogi **5** Berra
rat ~: **3** owl
stance: **6** crouch
starter: **3** cow, dog, fly **4** gnat **6** oyster
__ catcher: **4** dust
Catcher in the Rye, The
author: J.D. Salinger
catcher's __: **3** box **4** mitt **5** glove
catch in __: **4** a lie
catching: **5** viral **7** endemic **8** epidemic, pandemic **9** endemical, epizootic **10** contagious, epidemical, infectious, inoculable
some z's: **4** abed **6** asleep
start ~ up: **4** gain **7** close in
__-catching: **3** eye
Catch Me If You Can (2002 film)
cast: Amy Adams, Leonardo DiCaprio, Tom Hanks, Martin Sheen, Christopher Walken
director: Steven Spielberg
catch one's __: **3** eye **6** breath
__ Cat Chow: **6** Purina
catchpenny: **4** mean **5** cheap **6** stingy
catchphrase: **3** saw **5** maxim, motto **6** slogan **7** proverb **8** laconism **9** battle cry, watchword **10** shibboleth
catch some __: **4** rays
catch-up, play: **6** pursue
catchword
see catchphrase
catchy: **6** fitful, tricky **8** hummable, pleasing **9** deceptive
Catch you later!: **3** bye **4** ciao, ta ta **5** adieu, adios **6** bye-bye **7** goodbye **8** au revoir, farewell
__-Cat Club: **3** Kit
Cate: **9** Blanchett
catechism: **4** book, test **9** education
catechize: **3** ask **4** quiz **5** drill, grill, probe, query, teach, train **7** educate, enquire, examine, inquire **8** instruct, question **9** enlighten **10** evangelize
categorical: **4** firm, sure **5** plain **6** actual, all-out, direct **7** certain, express, flat-out **8** absolute, clear-cut, complete, definite, distinct, dogmatic, emphatic, explicit, forceful, positive, resolute, specific, straight, ultimate **10** conclusive, dogmatical, unswerving, unwavering
categorically: **5** truly **6** really, wholly
categories
biological ~: **4** taxa
categorize: **3** peg **4** file, rank, sort **5** group, order, place, range **6** assort, divide **8** classify, identify, tabulate, typecast **9** put down as **10** button down, distribute, pigeonhole
category: **3** ilk **4** kind, rank, sort, tier, type **5** class, genre, genus, grade, group, level, state **6** branch, league, manner, rating, sector, series **7** bracket, heading, section, species, variety **8** division, grouping **10** department, pigeonhole
biological ~: **5** taxon
catchall ~: **4** misc. **5** other
category __: **6** killer
catenate: **5** tie in
catenation: **5** chain **6** series **8** sequence
cater: **4** host **6** outfit, purvey, supply **7** furnish, provide
to: **4** baby, feed, tend **5** do for, favor, humor, spoil **6** attend, coddle, cosset, dandle, oblige, pamper, pander, please, wait on **7** gratify, indulge, work for **8** give in to, wait upon **9** spoon-feed
(to): **8** minister
Catera: **3** car **4** auto **8** Cadillac
catered event: **6** affair **7** banquet
caterpillar: **3** bug **4** grub, pest **5** bardy, egger, larva **6** grugru, insect, maggot **7** bagworm, budworm, cutworm, webworm **8** armyworm, caseworm, fireworm, glowworm, hornworm, mealworm, rootworm, silkworm **9** bloodworm
case: **6** cocoon
combining form: **5** -campa, eruci-
construction: **4** tent
like a ~: **5** hairy
__ caterpillar: **4** tent
caterwaul: **3** bay, cry **4** bawl, howl, meow, wail, yell, yowl **5** miaou, miaow, miaul **6** scream, shriek **7** blubber, screech
caterwauling: **3** din **5** noise
Cates: **6** George, Phoebe **7** Gilbert
Cates, Phoebe: **7** actress
spouse: Kevin Kline
catfight: **3** row **4** spat **5** set-to **7** quarrel
catfish: **4** raad **6** hassar, tandan **8** bullhead
catcher: **3** net
whisker: **6** barbel
Catfish: **6** Hunter
Catfish Row: **4** slum **8** tenement
locale: **10** Charleston
resident: **4** Bess **5** Porgy
cat food: **4** lams **5** Amore **6** Figaro, Purina **7** Whiskas **8** Eukanuba, Friskies **10** Chef's Blend, Fancy Feast
Cath.: **5** relig.
leader: **4** msgr.
not ~: **4** Prot.
__ Cath.: **3** Rom.
catharsis: **5** purge **9** cleansing, purgation **10** abreaction, evacuation, lustration
cathartic plant: **5** senna
Cathay: **5** China
visitor: Marco Polo
cathedral: **6** church, temple **8** basilica **9** sanctuary **10** tabernacle
British ~ town: **3** Ely **6** Exeter
clergy: **5** canon
court: **6** parvis
feature: **3** pew **4** apse, arch, icon, ikon, nave **5** eikon, spire **6** chevet
French ~ town: **5** Paris, Reims **6** Amiens, Rheims **7** Bourges **8** Chartres
head: **4** dean **6** bishop
seat: **7** diocese
Spanish ~ town: **5** Avila
style: **6** Gothic
cathedral __: **4** hull **5** glass **7** ceiling
Cathedral
author: Nelson DeMille
Cathedral City: **4** town
locale: **10** California
Catherine: **3** Ste. **4** Bach, Parr **5** Hicks, O'Hara **6** Howard, Keener **7** czarina, Deneuve, tsarina **8** de' Medici, Oxenberg **9** Zeta-Jones
the Great: **7** empress
Catherine __-Jones: **4** Zeta
Catherine of __: **5** Siena **6** Aragon **10** Alexandria
Catherines
husband of three ~: **5** Henry
Catherine the Great successor: **4** Paul **5** Paul I
Catherine Wheel, The
author: Jean Stafford
Cather, Willa: **6** writer
work: Alexander's Bridge
Death Comes for the Archbishop
A Lost Lady
Lucy Gayheart
My Antonia
My Mortal Enemy
Obscure Destinies
One of Ours
O Pioneers!
Paul's Case
Shadows on the Rock
The Song of the Lark
The Troll Garden
Cathleen: **7** Nesbitt
cathode ray tube: **8** terminal
cathodes, like some: **3** neg., pos. **8** negative, positive
catholic: **4** wide **6** cosmic, global **7** general, generic, liberal **8** cosmical, tolerant **9** generical, inclusive, receptive, unbigoted, universal, worldwide **10** ecumenical, large-scale, open-minded
__ Catholic: **5** Roman
catholicon: **7** panacea
Catholic service: **4** Mass
Cathryn: **5** Damon
Cathy: **4** Carr **5** comic, Rigby, strip **6** Dennis **8** Moriarty, O'Donnell **9** Guisewite
dog: **7** Electra
Cathy __ Crosby: **3** Lee
Cathy's Clown (1960 song)
artist: Everly Brothers
Catiline
author: Henrik Ibsen
Cat in the Hat, The
author: Dr. Seuss
catkin: **5** ament, plant
tree: **3** oak **5** alder, beech, birch, hazel **6** walnut, willow **8** bayberry, chestnut, corkwood
Catlett: **3** Sid **6** Walter
catlike: **5** agile, felid **6** feline **8** stealthy
carnivore: **5** civet
catman: **5** tamer **9** lion tamer
catnap: **4** doze **5** break, sleep **6** drowse, siesta, snooze **7** drop off, shuteye **8** downtime **10** fall asleep, forty winks
catnip: **4** herb
cat-o'-__-tails: **4** nine
Cato: **5** Roman **6** orator
garment for ~: **4** toga
see also Latin
Catoctin: **3** mts. **5** range **9** mountains
locale: **8** Maryland, Virginia

Cat on a Hot Tin Roof: 4 film, play
author: Tennessee Williams
cast: Burl Ives, Paul Newman, Elizabeth Taylor
character: 3 Mae **5** Brick, Dixie **7** Big Mama **8** Big Daddy
dog: 8 Bucky Boy
cat-o'-nine-tails: 4 whip
Catonsville: 4 city, town
locale: 8 Maryland
catorce, half of: 5 siete
Cato the __: 5 Elder **7** Younger
cats: 6 people
ender: 3 paw
fat ~: 4 rich
mice, to ~: 4 prey
rain ~ and dogs: 4 pour, teem
cats (advertising):
Leo (MGM, lion)
Morris (Nine Lives cat food)
Tony (Frosted Flakes, tiger)
cats (comic strips/comics):
Arlene (Garfield)
Attila (Mother Goose and Grimm)
Azrael (Smurfs)
Bill (Bloom County)
Bobo (The Piranha Club)
Catbert (Dilbert)
Garfield
Heathcliff
Hobbes (Calvin and Hobbes, tiger)
Hope (The Gumps)
Hot Dog (Dennis the Menace)
Kittycat (The Family Circus)
Mooch (Mutts)
Muffin (Pickles)
Sid (Ziggy)
Streaky (Supergirl)
World War II (Peanuts)
cats (films):
Am (Lady and the Tramp)
Baby (Bringing Up Baby, leopard)
Bambi (Earth Girls Are Easy)
Beeswax (Her Alibi)
Burbank (Lethal Weapon)
Cat (Breakfast at Tiffany's)
Catzilla (Mouse Hunt)
Clementine (Visit to a Small Planet)
Cosmic Creepers (Bedknobs and Broomsticks)
Elke (The Towering Inferno)
Fellini (Breaking Away)
Figaro (Pinocchio)
General Sterling Price (True Grit)
Italics (Runaway Bride)
Jacob (Dr. Dolittle, tiger)
Jake (The Cat From Outer Space)
Jarvis (The Man With Two Brains)
Jonesy (Alien)
Julius (Twins)
Leonardo (Casanova's Big Night)
Lucifer (Cinderella)
Milo (The Adventures of Milo and Otis)
Miss Kitty (Batman Returns)
Mr. Bigglesworth (Austin Powers)
Mr. Jinx (Meet the Parents)
Mufasa (The Lion King, lion)
Neutron (This Island Earth)
Oliver (Oliver & Company)
Orion (Men in Black)
Pyewacket (Bell, Book and Candle)
Rajah (Aladdin, lion)
Romeo (Romancing the Stone)
Ruby (Girl, Interrupted)
Rufus (Re-Animator)
Sassy (Homeward Bound)
Scar (The Lion King, lion)
Si (Lady and the Tramp)
Simba (The Lion King, lion)
Sweetie (The Fifth Element)
Sylvester (Warner Bros.)
Thomasina (The Three Lives of Thomasina)
Timer (The Specialist)
Tiny (Unlawful Entry)
Tom (Tom and Jerry)
Tonto (Harry and Tonto)
Whiskers (Last Action Hero)
cats (literature):
Bagheera (The Jungle Book, panther)
Bloomberg (Franny and Zooey)
Church (Pet Sematary)
Crookshanks (Harry Potter)
Dinah (Alice in Wonderland)
Grimalkin (Wuthering Heights)
Lady Jane (Bleak House)
Mehitabel (Archy and Mehitabel)
Mr. Paws (Harry Potter)
Mrs. Murphy (Rita Mae Brown)
Mrs. Norris (Harry Potter)
Pixel (The Cat Who Walks Through Walls)
Pluto (The Black Cat)
Puff (Dick and Jane)
Shere Khan (The Jungle Book, tiger)
Snowdrop (Alice in Wonderland)
Snowy (Harry Potter)
Tao (The Incredible Journey)
Tibbles (Harry Potter)
Tufty (Harry Potter)
White Nose (Happy Hollisters)
cats (TV):
Benny the Ball (Top Cat)
Bruce (Honey West, ocelot)
Choo Choo (Top Cat)
Clarence (Daktari, lion)
Elizabeth Barrett Browning (Cheers)
Felix
Henrietta (Mr. Rogers' Neighborhood)
Katnip (Herman and Katnip)
King Leonardo (lion)
Kitty Kat (The Addams Family, lion)
Kitty (South Park)
Lucky (ALF)
Minerva (Our Miss Brooks)
Nero (Remington Steele)
Rags (Crusader Rabbit, tiger)
Ruff (Ruff and Reddy)
Salem (Sabrina, the Teenage Witch)
Salty (Caroline in the City)
Scratchy (The Simpsons)
Snowball (The Simpsons)
Spartacus (Just Shoot Me)
Spot (Star Trek: The Next Generation)
Stimpy (Ren and Stimpy)
Toonces (Saturday Night Live)
Top Cat
cat's __: 4 meow **6** cradle **7** pajamas, whisker
cat's-__: 3 ear, paw **4** claw
cat's-__ marble: 3 eye
Cats: 7 musical
composer: Andrew Lloyd Webber, Trevor Nunn
inspiration: T.S. Eliot
monogram: 3 ALW, TSE
role: 3 Gus **5** Plato, Quaxo **6** Alonzo, George, Jemima, Victor **7** Admetus, Demeter, Electra, Exotica, Genghis, Gilbert **8** Etcetera, Macavity, Sillabub, Victoria **9** Asparagus, Cassandra, Coricopat, Pouncival, Tantomile **10** Grizabella, Growltiger, Jellylorum, Munkustrap **11** Bombalurina, Carbucketty, Griddlebone, Mungojerrie **12** Jennyanydots, Rumpleteazer, Rum Tum Tugger
__ cats and dogs: 4 rain
CAT scan
relative: 3 MRI
cat's cradle: 4 game
Cat's Cradle
author: Kurt Vonnegut Jr.
cat's-eye: 3 gem **6** marble **8** gemstone
relative: 5 agate, aggie
Cat's Eye
author: Margaret Atwood
Cat's in the Cradle (song)
artist: Harry Chapin, Ugly Kid Joe
Catskills: 4 mtns. **5** range **9** mountains
locale: 7 New York
cat's-paw: 4 dupe, knot, pawn, prey, tool **5** patsy **6** jackal, puppet
catsup
see ketchup
cattail: 4 reed, rush **5** plant **6** flower
site: 5 marsh
cattalo: 5 bovid **6** animal, bovine, hybrid, mammal
relative: *see* bovine
Cattaraugus County
city: 5 Olean
__ Cat, The: 5 Black
cattiness: 5 spite
cattle: 3 mob **4** beef, cows, herd, kine, oxen, yaks **5** bison, bulls, steer, stock **6** beasts, beeves, calves, dogies, masses, steers **7** bovines, Brahmas, heifers **9** livestock, longhorns **10** shorthorns
African ~ enclosure: 5 craal, kraal
ancestor: 7 aurochs
at times: 5 lower, mooer
bird: 5 egret
black ~: 5 Angus
breed: 3 Gir **4** Busa, Glan, Kuri, Rath, Siri, Tuli **5** Angus, Barka, Boran, Dajal, Dangi, Deoni, Devon, Fjall, Horro, Kerry, Kurdi, Luing, Malvi, Maure, N'dama, Nguni, Oropa, Rathi, Sanhe, Wagyu **6** Angeln, Ankole, Aubrac, Baladi, Channi, Dexter, Dhanni, Dulong, Gaolao, Herens, Jaulan, Jersey, Lohani, Mewati, Nagori, Nelore, Nimari, Ongole, Ovambo, Ponwar, Rojhan, Salers, Sarabi, Sussex, Tswana, Vosges **7** Alberes, Bachaur, Barzona, Brahman, Brahmin, Cachena, Canchim, Istoben, Mashona, Red Poll, Retinta, Sahiwal, Yanbian **8** Ayrshire, Bonsmara, Charbray, Chianina, Galloway, Gelbvieh, Guernsey, Hereford, Holstein, Limousin **9** Charolais, Shorthorn, Simmental **10** Lincoln Red, Murray Grey, Welsh Black
call: 3 low, moo **7** meeting **9** interview
catcher: 5 lasso, reata, riata
chew: 3 cud
country: 5 ranch, range
enclosure: 3 pen **4** crib, yard **6** corral
food: 6 fodder, forage
genus: 3 bos
group: 4 herd **5** drove
handler: 6 cowboy, drover **7** cowpoke
herders: 5 Masai **6** Maasai
hip joint: 5 thurl
hornless ~: 5 Angus, muley **6** mulley
mover: 4 prod
of India: 4 zebu
prod: 4 goad
raise ~: 5 ranch
South America: 4 nata
steal ~: 6 rustle
work with ~: 4 herd, rope **5** drive **6** corral, dehorn
cattle __: 3 car, run **4** call, prod
cattlelike: 6 bovine
Catton, Bruce: 6 writer **9** historian
work: The Coming Fury
Glory Road
Grant Moves South
Grant Takes Command
Mr. Lincoln's Army
Never Call Retreat
A Stillness at Appomattox
Terrible Swift Sword
Cattrall: 3 Kim
catty: 4 mean **5** nasty, snide **6** feline, unkind **7** hateful, hostile, vicious **8** spiteful, stealthy, venomous **9** malicious, rancorous **10** backbiting, evil-minded, ill-natured, malevolent
comment: 3 mew **4** meow **5** miaou, miaow, miaul, swipe
Catullus: 4 poet **5** Roman
catwalk: 6 bridge, runway
Cat Who Came for Christmas, The
author: Cleveland Amory
Cat Who Walks Through Walls, The
cat: Pixel
Catwoman
foe: 5 Robin **6** Batman
Catwoman (2004 film)
cast: Halle Berry, Benjamin Bratt, Sharon Stone
Caucasian: 5 Arian, Aryan, white
Caucasus: 3 mts. **5** range **9** mountains
extinct ~ volcano: 6 Kazbek
locale: 6 Europe, Russia **7** Georgia **10** Azerbaijan
mountain: 6 Elbrus, Elbruz
native: 5 Osset **6** Ossete
river: 4 Kurd, Rion **5** Rioni
caucho: 3 ule **6** rubber
caucus: 4 bloc, meet **6** parley, powwow **7** council, faction, meeting, session **8** assembly, conclave, congress **9** gathering **10** convention
state: 4 Iowa
caudal appendage: 4 tail
caudata member: 4 newt

caudex: **4** stem
caught: **5** at bay, stuck **10** interested
napping: **6** spacey **7** in a daze, out of it, unaware **8** heedless **9** negligent, unmindful, unwitting **10** out to lunch
up: **6** enrapt **9** engrossed
caught in __: **4** a lie
Caught you!: **3** aha **6** gotcha
cauldron: **3** pot, vat **5** crock **6** boiler, kettle **9** container
contents: **4** brew
ingredient: **4** newt
Caulfield: **4** Joan **7** Maxwell
cauliflower: **6** veggie **9** vegetable
bit: **6** floret
cauliflower __: **3** ear
caulk: **4** seal **5** close
caulking
in need of ~: **5** leaky **6** drafty
material: **5** oakum, putty
Caulkins: **5** Tracy
causation: **4** root **6** origin, reason **8** creation **9** invention
cause: **2** do **3** let **4** goal, lead, make, move, root, sake, seat, seed, side, soul, suit **5** agent, basis, beget, breed, bring, hatch, ideal, maker, raise **6** belief, compel, create, effect, elicit, entail, factor, incite, induce, kindle, lead to, motive, origin, parent, prompt, reason, source, spring **7** actuate, creator, crusade, dream up, genesis, grounds, lawsuit, produce, provoke, purpose, trigger **8** engender, generate, initiate, motivate, movement, occasion, producer, result in **9** instigate, necessity, objective, originate **10** antecedent, bring about, conviction, effectuate, enterprise, foundation, give rise to, inducement, litigation, motivation, originator, prime mover
a riot: **5** rouse **6** arouse, foment, set off, whip up, work up **7** agitate, inflame **9** instigate
combining form: **4** etio- **5** aetio-, ailio-
ender: **3** way
for alarm: **5** peril **6** danger
harm to: **3** mar **4** maim, ruin **5** abuse, spoil, stain, wound, wrong **6** batter, bruise, deface, defile, impair, injure, mangle, ravage **7** corrupt, pollute, scratch, tarnish **9** undermine
havoc: **5** wreck
help the ~: **6** chip in, donate **9** volunteer **10** contribute
horror: **5** scare **7** horrify, terrify **8** frighten **9** terrorize
irritation: **3** irk, vex **4** gall, rile **5** annoy, chafe, clash, peeve, pique **6** abrade, nettle, rankle **7** inflame, provoke **9** aggravate **10** exasperate
lost ~: **5** goner
of ruin: **6** plague **7** scourge **8** anathema, calamity, downfall
resentment: **3** vex **4** roil **5** anger, annoy, peeve, pique, upset **6** nettle, offend, put out **7** provoke **8** irritate **9** displease
to happen: **4** spur **5** incur, spark **6** incite, prompt, set off **7** produce, trigger **8** generate, motivate, touch off **9** stimulate **10** bring about
cause __: **7** célèbre
__ cause: **4** lost
cause and __: **6** effect
causeless: **8** needless **10** gratuitous, groundless, unasked-for
__ cause order: **4** show
causerie: **4** chat **9** tête-à-tête
...'cause the Bible tells __: **4** me so
causeway: **4** path, road
causing: **6** behind
combining form: **3** -fic **5** -genic **7** -facient
joy: **8** cheering, pleasant, pleasing
Causing a Commotion (1987 song)
artist: Madonna
caustic: **3** dry, lye **4** acid, sour, tart **5** acerb, acrid, harsh, sharp, snide **6** biting, bitter, ireful, severe **7** acerbic, burning, cutting, erosive, mordant, pungent, satiric **8** abrasive, alkaline, incisive, sardonic, scathing, stinging **9** corrosive, sarcastic, satirical, trenchant
solution: **3** KOH, lye **4** NaOH **6** alkali
cauterize: **4** burn, sear **5** scald **7** cleanse
Cauthen, Steve: **6** jockey
milieu: **5** track
caution: **3** tip **4** care, heed, sign, warn **5** alert **6** advice, advise, caveat, exhort, inform, notice, notify, remind, tip off **7** counsel, portent, red flag, reserve, warning **8** admonish, dissuade, forewarn, prudence, red light **9** alertness, attention, canniness, restraint, vigilance **10** admonition, discretion, precaution, providence
color of ~: **5** amber
throw ~ to the winds: **4** dare
with ~: **5** shyly **6** askant, warily **7** askance, charily, leerily, timidly **8** frugally **9** carefully, guardedly, heedfully, mindfully, sparingly, thriftily
word of ~: **4** don't **6** beware
Cautionary Tales
author: Hilaire Belloc
cautious: **3** shy **4** cagy, safe, slow, wary **5** alert, cagey, canny, chary, fussy, leery **6** unsure **7** all ears, careful, dubious, finicky, guarded, heedful, mindful, politic, prudent **8** delicate, discreet, doubtful, doubting, exacting, finiking, finnicky, hesitant, keen-eyed, moderate, reserved, rigorous, thorough, vigilant, watchful **9** assiduous, attentive, farseeing, judicious, observant, provident, skeptical, tentative, uncertain **10** deliberate, fastidious, long-headed, meticulous, on one's toes, particular, scrupulous, suspicious, uneffusive
be ~: **4** care, mind **9** have a care
one: **6** heeder
cautiously: **7** charily **8** gingerly **9** advisedly, carefully, tactfully **10** delicately
cautious seldom __, The: **3** err
__ cava: **4** vena
cavalcade: **5** array **6** parade **7** caravan **9** march-past, promenade, spectacle **10** expedition, procession
Cavalcanti, Guido: **4** poet **7** Italian
cavalier: **4** curt **5** lofty, proud **6** lordly, rakish, snooty, suitor **7** haughty, offhand **8** arrogant, horseman, insolent, scornful, superior, wasteful **10** disdainful
Cavalier: **3** car **4** auto **5** Chevy **9** Chevrolet **10** automobile
poet: **5** Carew **6** Waller **7** Herrick **8** Lovelace, Suckling
Cavaliers: **4** five
home: **3** U. Va. **9** Cleveland
org.: **4** NCAA
rival: *see* NBA team
Cavallaro: **6** Carmen
Cavalleria Rusticana: **5** opera
composer: Pietro Mascagni
cavalry: **2** tp. **4** army **5** troop **8** dragoons
command: **6** charge
headquarters: **4** fort
horse: **7** charger, trooper
sitcom: **6** F Troop
weapon: **5** lance, saber, sabre, sword
cavalryman: **6** hussar, lancer **7** soldier **10** equestrian
Algerian ~: **5** spahi **6** spahee
Prussian ~: **4** ulan **5** uhlan
cavatelli
alternative: *see* pasta
cave: **3** bow, den **4** grot, hole, lair, room **5** antre, yield **6** give in, grotto, relent, submit **7** shelter, succumb **8** hideaway **9** surrender **10** subterrane
art: **5** mural
dweller: **3** bat **5** troll **6** apeman
-dwelling combining form: **6** troglo-
ender: **3** man **4** fish
explorer: **9** spelunker
in: **3** bow, sag **4** give, sink, wilt **5** slump, yield **6** accede, buckle, fess up, relent **7** concede, crumple, give way **8** collapse **9** acquiesce **10** capitulate
(in): **5** stave
in verse: **4** grot
pigment used in ~ art: **5** ocher, ochre
sound: **4** echo
cave __: **3** art, man **4** bear **5** canem
__ Cave: **4** Niah **6** Danger, Spirit **7** Fingal's, Lascaux, Mammoth, Ventana
caveat: **5** alarm **6** notice **7** caution, red flag, warning **10** admonition
buyer ~: **4** as is
issue a ~: **4** warn
caveat __: **6** emptor
Cavell: **5** Edith
caveman
cartoon ~: **3** Oop
discovery: **4** fire
Caveman (1981 film)
cast: Barbara Bach, Ringo Starr
__ Cave National Park: **4** Wind **7** Mammoth
Cavendish: **5** Henry **6** banana
Cavendish, Henry: **7** chemist **9** physicist
birthplace: **4** Nice
cavern: **3** den **4** hole **5** antre, vault **6** grotto
see also cave
cavernous: **4** deep, huge, vast, wide **5** broad, large, roomy **6** gaping **7** abysmal, yawning **8** spacious **9** chambered **10** bottomless, commodious, fathomless, sepulchral, voluminous
opening: **3** maw
__ Caverns: **4** Howe **5** Luray
Caves of Steel, The
author: Isaac Asimov
Cavett, Dick
alma mater: **4** Yale
spouse: Carrie Nye
caviar: **3** ova, roe **4** eggs **6** canapé
companion: **5** blini, bliny
exporter: **4** Iran **6** Russia
source: **4** shad **6** beluga **7** starlet
cavil: **3** nag **4** beef, carp **5** whine **6** bicker, grouse, jibe at, pick at **7** censure, nitpick, quarrel, quibble **8** belittle, complain, pettifog **9** complaint, criticism, criticize, deprecate, disparage, find fault, make a fuss, objection **10** split hairs
caviler: **5** shrew **6** critic **9** henpecker
caviling: **5** cross **7** carping, fretful **8** captious, critical, fretsome **9** criticism, querulous
Cavill: **5** Henry
cavities, anatomical: **5** antra
cavity: **3** gap, pit **4** dent, hole, mold, nook, void **5** abysm, abyss, mouth, sinus **6** areola, areole, caries, crater, hollow, lacuna, pocket, recess, socket **7** opening, vacuity **10** depression, excavation, interspace
anatomical ~: **5** lumen, sinus **6** antrum
bone ~: **5** fossa **6** antrum
combining form: **4** -cele, coel- **5** -coele
detector: **4** X-ray
filler: **3** DDS, DMD **5** inlay **7** dentist
of a ~: **6** antral
of the nasal ~: **5** naric
oral ~: **5** mouth
plant ~: **6** locule
rock ~: **3** vug **4** vugg, vugh
volcano ~: **3** pit **6** cavity
__ cavity: **5** sinus **7** pleural
cavort: **4** lark, leap, play, romp, skip **5** caper, dance, frisk, revel **6** frolic, gambol, prance **7** carry on, rollick **9** have a ball, make merry **10** fool around
Cavs
see Cavaliers
cavy: **4** paca **6** animal, mammal, rodent
relative: *see* rodent
caw: **5** croak **6** squawk **8** birdcall
Cawdor big shot: **5** thane, thegn
Caxton: **7** William
cay: **4** eyot, isle, reef **5** islet **6** island **9** coral reef
Cayce: **5** Edgar
cayenne: **5** spice **6** pepper **9** condiment
Cayenne: **3** SUV **4** city, port, town **7** Porsche
__ Cayes, Haiti: **3** Les
cayman: **4** croc **6** animal **7** reptile **9** crocodile
__ Cayman: **5** Grand

Cayman Islands
capital: 10 George Town
money: 4 cent 6 dollar
Cayuga: 4 duck, fowl, lake 5 tribe 6 Indian 7 Amerind 8 Iroquois 10 Finger Lake
ally: 6 Mohawk, Oneida, Seneca 8 Onondaga 9 Tuscarora
locale: 7 New York
cayuse: 4 hoss, pony 5 horse, mount 6 animal, equine
catcher: 6 lariat
Cayuse: 6 Indian 7 Amerind
Cazale, John: 5 actor
CB: 5 radio
emergency ~ channel: 4 nine
knob: 3 vol. 6 volume 7 squelch
moniker: 6 handle
word: 4 over 7 ten-four
CBC: 7 network
CBer: 9 good buddy
cousin: 3 ham
CBS
HQ: 3 NYC
logo: 3 eye
part of ~: 3 Sys. 4 Syst. 8 Columbia
regulator: 3 FCC
rival: 3 ABC, Fox, NBC, PBS 5 The CW
cc.: 4 copy, meas. 7 measure
C.C. ___: 5 Rider
CCH: 7 Pounder
C-clamp: 4 vise 7 gripper
___ C. Clarke: 6 Arthur
cc, not a: 4 orig. 8 original
ccs.: 3 amt. 4 meas 6 amount, dosage 7 measure
CCU
locale: 4 hosp. 8 hospital
Cd: 4 elem. 7 cadmium, element
48 for ~: 4 at. no.
CD: 4 disc, disk 5 asset
alternative: 2 LP 3 DAT 4 tape 5 album, T-bill, T-note 8 cassette
earnings: 3 int. 8 interest
enjoy a ~: 6 listen
holder: 4 case 5 saver 9 jewel case
part of ~: 3 dep., ROM 4 Cert., disc, disk 7 compact, deposit
player: 2 DJ 6 deejay 7 boombox
player ancestor: 4 hi-fi
player maker: 3 RCA 4 Sony
player part: 5 diode, laser
put on ~: 6 encode
selection: 5 track
source: 4 bank 5 S and L
type: 2 EP 3 IRA
CD ___: 6 player, single
CD-___: 3 ROM
CDC: 4 agcy. 6 agency
department: 3 HHS
part of ~: 7 Centers, Control, Disease
CD compilation
name: 4 K-tel
cdr.: 4 rank
employer: 3 USN
CD-ROM: 4 disc, disk
Ce: 4 elem. 6 cerium 7 element
58 for ~: 4 at. no.
cease: 3 end 4 drop, halt, lull, quit, stop 5 abort, avast, can it, close, lapse, let up, pause 6 cool it, cut out, desist, expire, finish, give up, hold it, lay off, run out, stop it, wind up, wrap up 7 abstain, adjourn, back off, break up, die down, refrain, suspend 8 break off, close out, conclude, intermit, knock off, leave off, pack it in, shut down 9 close down, disappear, terminate 10 call it a day, knock it off, put an end to
starter: 3 sur
to a sailor: 5 avast
work: 4 quit 5 leave 6 bow out, retire 8 hang it up, step down 10 give notice
cease and ___: 6 desist
cease-fire: 5 truce 9 armistice, white flag
region: 3 DMZ
ceaseless: 6 eterne, steady 7 abiding, chronic, endless, eternal, nonstop, undying 8 constant, enduring, timeless, unbroken, unending, untiring, unwaning 9 chronical, continual, incessant, perennial, perpetual, unabating, unceasing, unfailing 10 continuous
ceaselessly: 5 on end 7 forever
Cebu: 4 city, port, town
city: 4 Naga
island near ~: 5 Leyte
CeCe: 8 Peniston
Cecil: 4 Earl 5 Adams, Edgar 6 Beaton, Parker, Powell, Rhodes 7 DeMille 8 Hoffmann, Kellaway, language
Agnes, to: 5 niece
alternative: *see* computer language
pal: 5 Beany
Cecil ___ Lewis: 3 Day
Cecilia: 3 ste. 5 saint 6 sainte
Cecilia (1970 song)
artist: Simon and Garfunkel
cedar: 4 tree, wood 5 savin 6 deodar, savine 7 conifer, deodara 8 hardwood
product: 4 cone
cedar ___: 5 chest
Cedar ___, IA: 5 Falls 6 Rapids
Cedar Rapids: 4 city, town
college: 3 Coe
locale: 4 Iowa
village near ~: 5 Amana
cedars of ___: 7 Lebanon
cede: 4 drop, dump, give, sell, shed 5 chuck, ditch, forgo, grant, waive, yield 6 assign, convey, forego, fork up, give up, render 7 abandon, forfeit, forsake 8 abdicate, forswear, get rid of, hand over, jettison, part with, sign away, sign over, throw out, transfer 9 cast aside, dispose of, foreswear, sacrifice, surrender, throw away 10 relinquish
starter: 4 ante 5 inter
cedilla indication: 5 soft c
ceding: 10 abdication
Cedric: 5 Errol 7 Gibbons 9 Hardwicke
cee: 5 grade
as a grade: 4 so-so
follower: 3 dee
preceder: 3 bee
starter: 3 Jay
ceiling: 3 cap, lim., top 4 dome, roof 5 limit, price, quota 6 height, record 7 maximum 8 covering
arched ~: 5 vault
device: 3 fan
domed ~: 6 cupola
hit the ~: 4 rage, rant, rave 5 freak 6 seethe
make hit the ~: 5 anger 6 madden, offend, tee off 7 incense 9 infuriate
opposite: 5 floor
price ~: 3 cap
support: 4 beam 5 joist
ceiling ___: 3 fan 4 tile, zero 5 piece
___ ceiling: 5 glass
cel: 5 frame
artist: 5 inker
subject: 4 toon
Cel.
not ~: 4 Fahr.
Celanese: 6 fabric 8 material
celeb: 3 VIP 4 name, star 6 phenom 7 big shot, notable 8 luminary 9 personage
Celebes: 3 sea 4 isle 6 island
locale: 6 Borneo
ox: 4 anoa
sea: 5 Banda
today: 8 Sulawesi
celebrant cry: 6 hoorah, hurray
celebrate: 4 fete, keep, laud, sing 5 exalt, extol, exult, feast, honor, party, revel 6 extoll, praise 7 acclaim, drink to, glorify, lionize, observe, rejoice, roister, splurge, triumph, worship 8 eulogize, live it up 9 have a ball, make merry, publicize, raise heck, raise hell, recommend, ritualize, signalize, solemnize 10 compliment, consecrate, jump for joy
Celebrate (1970 song)
artist: Three Dog Night
celebrated: 4 star 5 famed, great, known, noted 6 famous 7 big-name, eminent, notable, popular, revered, storied 8 glorious, historic, immortal, renowned, splendid 9 acclaimed, brilliant, important, legendary, memorable, prominent, topflight, well-known 10 preeminent
Celebrated Jumping Frog..., The
author: Mark Twain
celebrating: 6 joyful, joyous 8 exultant, jubilant
celebration: 4 bash, fest, fete, gala, rite 5 blast, event, feast, party, rally, revel, spree, treat 6 fiesta, hoopla 7 acclaim, blowout, holiday, jubilee, liturgy, pageant, revelry, triumph 8 birthday, carousal, ceremony, festival, function, goings-on, jamboree, occasion, wingding 9 reception
suffix: 3 -mas
Celebration (1980 song)
artist: Kool and the Gang
celebratory: 4 gala 6 festal 8 honorary
celebrities: 5 elite
celebrity: 3 VIP 4 fame, icon, idol, lion, name, star 5 éclat, glory, honor 6 bigwig, figure, renown, repute 7 big name, bigshot, hotshot, notable, stardom 8 eminence, grandeur, luminary, prestige, somebody 9 big cheese, dignitary, greatness, notoriety, personage, superstar 10 notability, popularity, prominence, reputation
bash: 5 roast
bit part: 5 cameo
Celebrity: 3 car 4 auto, Olds 5 Chevy 9 Chevrolet 10 Oldsmobile
Celebrity (1998 film)
cast: Kenneth Branagh, Judy Davis, Leonardo DiCaprio, Famke Janssen, Joe Mantegna
director: Woody Allen
celeritous: 5 hasty, quick, rapid
celerity: 4 rush 5 haste, hurry, speed 6 hustle 8 alacrity, dispatch, legerity, rapidity, velocity 9 briskness, fleetness, quickness, swiftness 10 expedition, promptness, speediness
Celeron maker: 5 Intel
celery: 6 veggie 9 appetizer, vegetable
Japanese ~: 3 udo
portion: 5 stalk
celery ___: 4 soda 5 stalk
celesta: 8 keyboard 10 instrument
Celeste: 4 Holm 5 pizza
alternative: 5 Jeno's, Tony's 6 Ellio's 7 Totino's 8 DiGiorno 9 Tombstone 10 Freschetta
Celeste Aïda: 4 aria
celestial: 4 holy 5 blest 6 astral, divine 7 angelic, blessed, elysian, godlike, sublime 8 beatific, empyreal, empyrean, ethereal, heavenly, seraphic, supernal 9 ambrosial, angelical, ineffable, spiritual, unworldly 10 immaterial, seraphical
being: 5 angel 6 cherub, seraph
body: 4 moon, star 5 comet 6 sphere
science: 6 astron. 9 astronomy
sphere: 3 sky
celestial ___: 4 pole 5 globe 6 sphere
Celestial ___: 4 City 6 Empire
celestial mechanics: 7 science
study: 6 motion 7 gravity
Celestial Navigation
author: Anne Tyler
Celestine: 4 pope 5 Peter 7 pontiff
Celia: 4 Cruz 6 Weston 7 Johnson
celibate: 4 abbé, pure 6 chaste 8 virtuous 9 continent
Celica: 3 car 4 auto 6 Toyota
Celine: 4 Dion
cell: 3 egg 4 cage, coop, germ, jail 5 booth, cadre, spore 6 alcove, amoeba, recess 7 chamber, cubicle, dungeon, faction 8 cloister 9 corpuscle, cubbyhole, enclosure
builder: 3 bee 5 drone
combining form: 3 cyt- 4 -cyte, cyto- 5 -plast
component: 4 gene 5 lipid 6 lipide 7 nucleus
dissolution: 5 lysis
ender: 4 mate, ular 5 block
feature: 3 bar
germ ~: 4 seed 5 spore 6 gamete
letters: 3 DNA, RNA
nerve ~: 5 fiber
nerve ~ part: 4 axon 5 axone

occupant: 3 con, nun 4 monk 6 inmate 7 convict
phone co.: 3 GTE, MCI 7 T-Mobile, Verizon 8 Cingular
phone kin: 5 pager
phone maker: 5 Nokia 6 Nextel 8 Ericsson, Motorola
place: 4 hive, jail 6 prison 7 beehive
retina ~: 3 rod 4 cone
cell __: 3 sap 4 body, line, pack, wall 5 cycle, phone, plate 6 fusion, theory 7 biology
__ cell: 3 air, dew, dry, egg, fat, red, wet 4 acid, beta, bone, fuel, germ, glue, hair, Kerr, mast, stem, unit 5 basal, blast, blood, brain, flame, guard, nerve, pilot, sieve, solar, swarm, white 7 storage, voltaic
cellar: 4 bsmt. 5 floor 8 basement 9 last place
contents: 4 salt, wine
ender: 3 age
in the ~: 4 last
selection: 4 port, rosé
starter: 4 salt
__ cellar: 4 cold, root, wine 5 storm 7 cyclone
Cellini, Benvenuto: 6 artist 8 sculptor
homeland: 5 Italy
patron: 4 Este
cellist: Jacquiline du Pré, János Starker, Jian Wang, Jorane, Laszlo Varga, Mstislav Rostropovich, Pablo Casals, Pierre Fournier, Terence Weil, Yo-Yo Ma
direction: 4 arco
purchase: 5 rosin
cello: 6 string 10 instrument
ending: 5 phane
feature: 5 f hole
kin: 5 viola 6 violin
part: 4 neck 6 end pin
cellophane __: 4 tape
cells
add more ~: 4 grow
breakdown of ~: 5 lysis
carrier of white blood ~: 5 lymph
combining form: 7 -blastic
destroy, as ~: 4 lyse
like some nerve ~: 6 apolar
nervous system ~: 4 glia
Cell, The
author: Athol Fugard
cellular: 7 organic
phone company: 3 ATT 7 T-Mobile, Verizon 8 MetroPCS
cellular __: 5 phone
celluloid: 4 film 6 cinema
developer: 5 Hyatt
cellulose: 4 pulp
fabric: 5 rayon
Celsius, Anders: 7 Swedish 10 astronomer
Celt: 4 Gael, Scot 5 druid 6 Breton, Briton 8 Irishman, Welshman 9 Hibernian 10 Cornishman, Highlander
Celtic: 4 Bird, Erse 5 Cousy, Irish, NBAer 8 Bob Cousy, Havlicek, language 9 Larry Bird
chariot: 5 essed
god: 3 Tiu
group: 4 clan
harvest festival: 6 lammas
instrument: 4 harp 5 rotta, rotte
language: 4 Erse, Gael, Manx 5 Welsh 6 Gaelic
Neptune: 3 Ler, Lir
paradise: 6 Avalon
poet: 4 bard
priest: 5 druid
tribe: 5 Iceni
Celtic __: 5 cross
Celtics: 4 five
home: 6 Boston
org.: 3 NBA
rival: *see* NBA team
cembalo: 8 keyboard 10 instrument
cement: 3 fix, gum 4 bind, bond, fuse, glue, join, seal, weld 5 epoxy, grout, merge, paste, putty, stick, unite 6 adhere, attach, cohere, fasten, harden, mortar, secure, solder 7 combine, connect, encrust, incrust, plaster, sealant, stickum, stiffen 8 adhesive, concrete, fixative, mucilage
brand: 4 Duco
container: 4 form
fix, as in ~: 5 embed, imbed
lay ~: 4 pave, pour
packing ~: 4 lute
sealed with ~: 5 luted
section: 4 slab 5 block
cement __: 5 mixer, steel
__ cement: 6 rubber
cemented: 3 set 4 firm 5 stiff 8 embedded
Cenci, The
author: Percy Bysshe Shelley
cen. fraction: 2 yr. 4 year
cenobite: 4 monk 7 recluse 9 religious
cenotaph: 8 monument
Cenozoic: 3 Era
epoch: 6 Eocene
cense: 7 perfume
censer: 8 thurible
censor: 3 ban, cut 4 Cato, edit 5 bleep 6 critic, delete, excise, forbid, muzzle, purify, remove 7 abridge, monitor, repress, scissor, squelch 8 black out, bluenose, disallow, examiner, naysayer, prohibit, sanitize, suppress, vilifier 9 expurgate, interdict, red-pencil, strike out 10 blue-pencil, bowdlerize, scissor out
Roman ~: 4 Cato
censored, not: 5 uncut 8 complete
censoring device, TV: 5 V-chip
censorious: 8 captious, critical 9 cavillous, culpatory, querulous 10 accusatory, condemning, denouncing, derogatory
censorship: 3 ban 7 silence 10 blue-pencil, forbidding
anti-~ org.: 4 ACLU
censurable: 5 wrong 10 delinquent
censure: 3 hit, jaw, rag, rap, tax 4 carp, damn, lash, rail, snub, twit 5 blame, cavil, chide, decry, knock, odium, scold 6 accuse, assail, berate, carp at, impugn, indict, lesson, rebuff, rebuke, tirade, vilify 7 asperse, condemn, contemn, frown on, inveigh, lambast, lecture, obloquy, reproof, reprove, squelch, tell off, upbraid 8 admonish, chastise, denounce, lambaste, reproach, reproval, scolding, sentence 9 broadside, castigate, criticism, criticize, denigrate, deprecate, discredit, disparage, excoriate, exprobate, frown upon, fulminate, invective, lash out at, ostracize, proscribe, reprehend, reprimand 10 admonition, discipline, imputation, reflection, take to task, vituperate
census: 4 list, poll, roll 5 tally 6 survey 9 head count 10 demography
Bible ~ book: 3 Num. 7 Numbers
datum: 3 age, sex
period: 6 decade
census __: 5 taker, tract
cent: 4 coin 5 money, penny 6 copper
down to one's last ~: 5 needy
mill, to a ~: 5 tenth
starter: 3 per
__ cent: 3 red 4 half
Cent
50 ~: 6 rapper
centaur: 6 Chiron, Nessus
__ Centauri: 5 Alpha 7 Proxima
centavo: 4 coin 5 money
centavos, 100: 4 peso 6 escudo
Centennial
author: James A. Michener
Centennial State: 3 Col. 4 Colo. 8 Colorado
center: 3 hub, mid, nub 4 base, core, gist, knub, pith, root, seat, Shaq 5 focus, heart, hiker, inner, midst, nexus, unify 6 inmost, inside, kernel, medial, mesial, middle, office 7 attract, collect, essence, fulcrum, keynote, lineman, nucleus, village 8 bull's-eye, converge, cynosure, focalize, interior, midpoint 9 innermost 10 crossroads, focal point, mainstream, midsection
basketball ~ position: 5 pivot
combining form: 3 mid- 4 medi- 5 medio-
ender: 4 fold, line 5 board, folds, lines, piece 6 pieces
in heraldry: 9 fess point 10 fesse point
in the ~: 4 amid 5 among 6 amidst, mongst 7 amongst
of operations: 2 HQ 4 base
point: 4 node
starter: 3 epi, sub 4 hypo, meta 5 ortho
center __: 3 bit, pin 4 back, jump, line 5 field, plate, punch, wheel 6 spread 7 fielder, forward
__ center: 3 rec 4 cost, data, dead, home, live 5 civic, guide, media, nerve, optic, storm 6 crisis, garden, profit, trauma 7 bowling, control, culture, day-care, message, optical, service
__-center: 3 off
__ Center: 3 Aon 5 Epcot 7 Garment, Medical
__-centered: 4 body, face, self
Centerfold (1981 song)
artist: J. Geils Band
centerless in heraldry: 6 voided
center of __: 4 mass 7 gravity
centerpiece: 7 epergne
center point of lower half in heraldry: 7 nombril
centers: 4 loca, loci
Centerville: 4 city, town
locale: 4 Ohio
centesimo: 4 coin 5 money
centi ender: 4 pede
centime: 4 coin 5 money
centimes, 100: 5 franc
__ centimeter: 5 cubic 6 square
centimeter-gram-second unit: 3 erg
centimo: 4 coin 5 money
centipede unit: 3 leg
central: 3 key, mid 4 main 5 basic, chief, focal, inner, polar, prime, urban, vital 6 inside, median, middle, ruling 7 crucial, nuclear, pivotal, primary, salient 8 cardinal, dominant, foremost, immanent, interior 9 essential, innermost, intrinsic, paramount, principal 10 overriding
idea: 5 motif, theme
idea, in music: 4 tema
of a ~ point: 5 nodal
part: 4 axis, body, yolk 5 spine 6 end-all
point: 5 midst, navel, nodus, pivot 6 thesis
points: 4 loca, loci, nodi
position: 5 midst, pivot
central __: 4 bank, city 5 angle 6 moment, sulcus 7 casting, heating
central __ system: 7 nervous
central __ theorem: 5 limit
Central __: 4 Park, time 6 Powers 7 America
Central African Republic: 6 nation 7 country
capital: 6 Bangui
money: 5 franc
neighbor: 4 Chad 5 Congo, Sudan 8 Cameroon
Central Amer. country: 3 Nic. 4 Guat.
Central America
bird: 4 guan 5 potoo 7 quetzal, tinamou 8 caracara, curassow
capital: 7 Managua, San José 8 Belmopan 10 Panama City 11 San Salvador, Tegucigalpa
country: 6 Belize, Panama 8 Honduras 9 Costa Rica, Guatemala, Nicaragua 10 El Salvador
feline: 6 margay
fish: 7 helleri 9 swordtail
flower: 6 dahlia
fruit: 9 sapodilla
gulf: 6 Panama 7 Fonseca 8 Honduras
Indian: 4 Cuna, Maya 5 Carib, Lenca, Mayan 7 Miskito, San Blas
palm tree: 6 cohune
primate: 7 sapajou 8 capuchin, marmoset
river: 4 Coco, Ulúa 5 Hondo, Lempa 6 Patuca 7 Chagres, Motagua
rodent: 4 paca 6 agouti 8 spiny rat
sea: 9 Caribbean
shrub: 8 cat's-claw
volcano: 4 Póas 5 Fuego, Irazú, Tacan 6 Arenal, Masaya, Pacaya 9 Momotombo
weasel: 6 grison
see also Spanish
Central Daylight __: 4 Time

CE

centralize: 5 focus, merge 9 integrate 10 accumulate, amalgamate, streamline
Central Michigan conference: 3 MAC
Central Michigan University athletes: 9 Chippewas
C E
Central Park
architect: 7 Olmsted
it's north of ~: 6 Harlem
locale: 3 NYC 9 Manhattan
sight: 6 hansom 9 reservoir
central processing __: 4 unit
Central Standard __: 4 Time
__ Centre, Toronto: 5 Eaton
centrifugal __: 5 force
centrifuge stress: 6 G force
centripetal __: 5 force
cents: 5 money
British ~: 5 pence
put one's two ~ in: 3 add 5 opine 6 meddle
cents-__ coupon: 3 off
__ Cents a Dance: 3 Ten
__-cent store: 3 ten
__ cents worth: 3 two
cents' worth, two: 3 tip 4 view 6 advice, tipoff 7 comment 9 viewpoint
centum: 7 hundred
centuries, untold: 3 eon 4 aeon, eons 5 aeons
Centurion: 3 car 4 auto 5 Buick
__ Centurions, The: 3 New
century: 3 eon 4 aeon 7 hundred 8 eternity, long time
fraction: 4 year 6 decade
plant: 4 aloe 5 agave
twenty-first ~: 6 modern
Century: 3 car 4 auto, font 5 Buick 8 typeface 10 automobile
Century Schoolbook: 4 font 8 typeface
Century's Ebb
author: John Dos Passos
CEO: 3 ldr., VIP 4 boss, exec 6 bigwig, cheese, leader 8 official, superior 9 executive
deg.: 3 MBA
métier: 4 corp. 5 board
often: 4 pres.
part of ~: 3 Off. 4 Exec. 5 Chief 7 Officer 9 Executive
cep: 6 fungus 8 mushroom
C.E., part of: 3 Era 9 Christian
__-ce pas?: 4 n'est
Cepeda, Orlando: 5 Giant
cephalalgia: 8 headache
cephalopod defense: 3 ink
Cepheus: 8 Argonaut
constellation near ~: 5 Draco
daughter: 9 Andromeda
son: 9 Narcissus
ceraceous: 4 waxy
ceramic
ancient Greek ~ piece: 6 kernos
coating: 5 glaze 6 enamel
square: 4 tile
worker: 5 tiler
ceramic __: 4 tile
ceramics: 4 ware 5 china, craft, tiles 6 crocks, jasper 7 pottery 8 clayware, crockery 9 delft ware, ironstone, porcelain, stoneware 10 dinnerware
compound: 5 ceria
tool: 6 coggle
cerastes: 5 snake, viper
cerate: 8 ointment
Cerberus: 3 dog 8 guardian
cercis: 4 tree 5 shrub
relative: *see* legume tree
cereal: 3 Kix, oat, rye 4 bran, corn, Life, oats, rice, Trix 5 grain, Kashi, Maypo, Quisp, Total, wheat 6 farina, flakes, groats, Kaboom, millet, muesli, Oreo O's, Pablum, quinoa, Smacks 7 All-Bran, Crispix, granola, Harmony, Hunny B's, Mueslix, Oat Bran, oatmeal, Pokémon 8 Boo Berry, Cheerios, Corn Chex, Corn Pops, Fiber One, porridge, Rice Chex, Special K, Uncle Sam, Wheaties 9 Alpha Bits, Apple Zaps, buckwheat, Grape-Nuts, Honey Comb, Just Right, Wheat Chex 10 Apple Jacks, bowl filler, bran flakes, Cap'n Crunch, Cocoa Puffs, corn flakes, Froot Loops, Mini-Wheats, Nutri-Grain, Puffed Rice, Quaker Oats, raisin bran, rolled oats, Smart Start 11 Cocoa Blasts, Cookie Crisp, Golden Crisp, Lucky Charms, Puffed Wheat, Sweet Crunch, Waffle Crisp
Asian ~ grass: 4 ragi 5 raggy 6 raggee
box abbr.: 3 RDA 4 nt. wt. 5 net wt.
breakfast ~: 4 bran
cooked ~: 5 gruel, kasha 6 farina 7 oatmeal 8 porridge
fungus: 5 ergot
grain: 3 oat, rye 4 corn, rice 5 wheat 6 barley
ingredient: 4 bran 5 fiber
kids' ~: 3 Kix 4 Trix
like some ~: 4 oaty 5 mushy, oaten 6 crispy
maker: 4 Post 7 Kellogg
serving: 4 bowl
sound: 3 pop 4 snap 7 crackle
spike: 3 awn, ear
tiger: 4 Tony
tool: 5 spoon
topper: 6 banana
cerebellum: 4 mind 5 brain
cerebral: 5 smart 6 brainy, mental 7 bookish, erudite 8 highbrow, longhair, rational, thinking 9 scholarly 10 analytical, reasonable
set: 5 Mensa
cerebral __: 6 cortex
cerebrate: 4 muse 5 think 6 reason 7 reflect 8 cogitate 10 deliberate
cerebrum: 4 mind 5 brain
ceremonial: 4 rite 5 state 6 august, formal, ritual, solemn 7 liturgy, stately 8 decorous 10 liturgical
ceremonious: 6 formal, ritual, solemn 7 courtly, pompous, stately 8 decorous 9 dignified
ceremony: 4 form, pomp, rite 5 state, toast 6 custom, nicety, ritual, starch 7 decorum, liturgy, service 8 courtesy, heraldry, protocol, splendor 9 etiquette, formality, propriety 10 graduation, observance, politeness
religious ~: 6 ritual 7 baptism, liturgy, service 9 communion, Eucharist, sacrament 10 observance
__ ceremony: 3 tea
Ceres: 4 city, town 8 asteroid
brother: 5 Pluto 7 Jupiter, Neptune
daughter: 10 Proserpina
equivalent: 7 Demeter
locale: 10 California
parent: 3 Ops 6 Saturn
sister: 4 Juno 5 Vesta
cereuses bloom, when: 5 night
Cerf, Bennett: 3 wit 9 publisher
specialty: 3 pun
spouse: Sylvia Sidney
cerise: 3 red 5 color
relative: *see* red color
cerium: 5 metal 7 element 9 rare earth 10 lanthanide
Cermak: 5 Anton
cero: 4 fish 8 mackerel
cert.: 4 guar.
certain: 3 set 4 firm, real, safe, sure, true 5 clear, fixed, on ice, valid 6 actual, secure, steady 7 assured, decided, ensured, express, for sure, settled, special, various 8 absolute, accurate, cocksure, decisive, definite, destined, fail-safe, implicit, inerrant, in the bag, ironclad, positive, reliable, singular, specific, unerring, verified 9 assertive, authentic, automatic, axiomatic, believing, confident, convinced, downright, foolproof, rock solid, satisfied, unfailing 10 conclusive, dependable, determined, guaranteed, inarguable, inevitable, infallible, legitimate, particular, unarguable, undeniable, undisputed, undoubtful, unimagined, verifiable
__ certain: 3 for
Certainement!: 3 oui
__ Certain Feeling: 4 That
certainly
see of course
Certain Smile, A
author: Françoise Sagan
Certain Smile, A (1958 song)
artist: Johnny Mathis
certainty: 4 fact, lock 5 cinch, truth 6 surety 7 clarity, reality, sure bet 8 accuracy, firmness, optimism, security 9 assurance, certitude, constancy, dogmatism, fixedness, guarantee, sure thing 10 confidence, conviction, positivism, steadiness
say with ~: 4 aver, avow
certificate: 3 doc. 4 deed 5 paper, scrip 6 coupon, permit, ticket 7 diploma, license, receipt, voucher 8 document, warranty
__ certificate: 3 tax 4 gift, gold 5 birth, share, stock 6 silver
certification: 5 proof 8 hallmark
certified: 4 sure 5 known, tried, valid 7 genuine 8 official 9 excellent, qualified 10 guaranteed
certified __: 4 mail, milk 5 check
certified __ accountant: 6 public
__-certified: 5 board
certify: 2 OK 3 let 4 aver, avow, okay 5 prove, swear, vouch 6 affirm, assure, attest, avouch, depone, ensure, ratify, verify 7 approve, bear out, confirm, endorse, indorse, license, qualify, testify, warrant, witness 8 accredit, sanction, validate, vouch for 9 ascertain, authorize, establish, guarantee, indemnify 10 asseverate, legitimize
certitude: 4 fact 5 trust 9 assurance, certainty 10 conviction
Certs: 4 mint 10 breath mint
alternative: 6 Binaca, Mentos, Tic Tac 7 Altoids, Clorets, Dentyne
cerulean: 4 blue 5 color 8 greenish
relative: *see* blue color
cerumen: 3 wax 6 earwax
cerussite: 7 lead ore
Cervantes, Miguel de: 6 writer 7 Spanish
work: Don Quixote
cerveza: 4 beer 7 Spanish
seller: 6 bodega
snack with ~: 4 tapa
cervid: 3 elk 4 deer 5 moose 7 caribou
__ Cervin: 4 Mont
cervine animal: 3 elk 4 deer 5 moose 7 caribou
Cesar: 4 Moro, Ritz 5 Pelli, Pugni 6 Chavez, Franck, Romero 8 Milstein
César: 3 Cui
Cesare: 5 Pugni, Siepi 6 Borgia, Danova, Pavese 8 Beccaria
cesium: 5 metal 7 element 9 rare earth
cess: 4 luck
ender: 3 pit 4 pool
cessation: 3 end 4 halt, rest, stay, stop 5 break, close, letup, pause, quiet, truce 6 arrest, cutoff, ending, finish, freeze, hiatus, layoff, period, recess 7 closure, respite, time-out 8 abeyance, curtains, stoppage 9 remission 10 conclusion, desistance, expiration, standstill, suspension
Cessna: 5 plane 8 airplane
drive a ~: 6 aviate
cesspool: 3 sty 4 sump
c'est __ chose: 5 autre
c'est-__: 5 à-dire
C'est __: 3 Moi 5 Si Bon
C'est la __!: 3 vie 6 guerre
C'est la Vie (song)
artist: Robbie Nevil, Sarah Vaughan
C'est magnifique!: 6 oo-la-la 7 ooh-la-la
C'est Magnifique
composer: Cole Porter
__ c'est moi: 5 L'état
cestus: 4 belt
cetacean: 3 orc, sei 4 susu 5 whale 6 beluga, narwal 7 cowfish, dolphin, finback, grampus, narwhal, rorqual 8 narwhale, porpoise
Cetera, Peter
song: After All (1989)
Glory of Love (1986)
Hard to Say I'm Sorry (1997)
The Next Time I Fall (1986)
One Good Woman (1988)
ceteris __: 7 paribus
Cetus, star in: 4 Mira
C. Everett __: 4 Koop
ceviche: 8 fish dish 9 appetizer
Ceylon: 8 Sri Lanka
royal capital of ~: 5 Kandy

Cey, Ron
sport: 8 baseball
Cézanne, Paul: 6 artist 7 painter
homeland: 6 France
Cf: 4 elem. 7 element 11 californium
98 for ~: 4 at. no.
CF: 3 pos. 8 position
CFC
destroyer: 5 ozone
part of ~: 6 chloro, fluoro
CFL award: 7 Grey Cup
___ C. Flippen: 3 Jay
___ C. Frémont: 4 John
cg.: 4 meas. 7 measure
Chablis: 3 vin 4 wine 5 white 9 white wine
like ~: 3 sec
origin: 6 France
Chacel, Rosa: 6 writer 7 Spanish
cha-cha: 4 step 5 dance 9 three-step
cousin: 5 mambo
Chachi's cousin: 6 Fonzie
Chacksfield: 5 Frank
___ Chaco: 4 Gran
Chacon: 4 Elio
chaconne: 5 dance
chacun ___ goût: 4 à son
Chad: 4 lake, Lowe 6 nation, Stuart 7 country, Everett
bovine: 4 Kuri
capital: 8 N'Djamena
city: 7 Moundou 8 N'Djamena
lake: 4 Chad
lake locale: 5 Niger 6 Africa 7 Nigeria 8 Cameroon
money: 5 franc
neighbor: 5 Libya, Niger, Sudan 7 Nigeria 8 Cameroon
people: 4 Fula 6 Fulani, Kanuri
chado: 8 mantilla
chador: 4 sari, veil 5 saree, shawl 6 rebozo
Chadwick: 5 James 8 Florence
chafe: 3 bug, irk, rub, vex 4 fume, gall, mope, rage, roil, stew, warm, wear 5 annoy, erode, grate, graze, sweat, worry, yearn 6 abrade, bother, fester, harass, nettle, offend, pother, rankle, ruffle, scrape 7 enflame, incense, inflame, provoke 8 abrasion, exercise, irritate 9 excoriate 10 exasperate
chafed: 3 raw 4 sore 9 irritated
chafer: 3 bug 6 beetle, insect, scarab 10 scarabaeid
rose ~: 3 bug 6 insect
chaff: 3 kid, rib 4 husk, jeer, jest, joke, josh, junk, mock, pods, razz 5 dregs, dross, husks, straw, taunt, tease, trash, waste 6 banter, debris, deride, refuse, shards, shells 7 bedevil, remains, rubbish 8 raillery, ridicule
eliminate ~: 4 sift
grain ~: 5 husks, palea
Chaffee: 4 Suzy
Chaffey: 3 Don
chaffinch: 3 pet 4 bird
chafing: 8 friction 9 impatient
chafing ___: 4 dish
Chagall, Marc: 6 artist 7 painter
homeland: 6 Russia
Museum locale: 4 Nice
chagrin: 5 abash, shame, upset 6 dismay 7 letdown, mortify, perturb, umbrage 8 disquiet 9 abashment, annoyance, discomfit, displease, embarrass 10 disappoint, disconcert, dissatisfy, infelicity
exclamation: 4 oh-oh, oops, uh-oh 6 whoops
chagrined: 6 put out 7 abashed 8 sheepish
Chagrin Falls: 4 city, town
locale: 4 Ohio
Chaim: 5 Potok, Topol 6 Bialik
chain: 3 row 4 band, bond, iron, moor, yoke 5 group, leash, queue, range, ridge, trite 6 catena, fasten, fetter, secure, sequel, series, stores, string, tether 7 confine, jewelry, manacle, pendant, shackle 8 bracelet, handcuff, restrain, sequence 9 lightning, syndicate 10 continuity, succession
ball and ~: 6 burden
gang member: 7 convict 8 prisoner
heavy ~: 4 rope
mountain ~: 5 range, ridge
nautical ~: 3 tye 7 bobstay
part: 3 mtn. 4 link 5 store 6 island 8 mountain
short ~: 3 fob
site: 4 neck 5 ankle
sound: 5 clank
chain ___: 3 saw 4 belt, fern, gang, gear, mail, pump, rule, shot, wale 5 coral, drive, plate, store 6 letter
chain-___ fence: 4 link
___ chain: 3 key 4 bull, door, drag, food, jack, open, sash, side, skid, tire 5 choke, heavy, light, pitch, power, watch
Chained ___: 4 Lady
Chain Gang (1960 song)
artist: Sam Cooke
chain-link ___: 5 fence
chain of ___: 7 command
Chain of Fools (1967 song)
artist: Aretha Franklin
chains: 5 bonds, gyves 7 bilboes, bondage, fetters, jewelry, slavery 8 manacles, shackles, trammels 9 handcuffs, restraint, servitude
Chains of Love (1956 song)
artist: Pat Boone
chair: 4 lead, seat 5 bench, sedan, stool 6 chaise, head up, leader, rocker 7 instate, preside 8 director, moderate, recliner 9 furniture, judiciary, officiate, organizer, supervise
ender: 3 man, men 5 woman, women 6 person
find another ~: 5 resit
fixer: 5 caner
grab a ~: 3 sit 4 park 5 perch
guide to a ~: 5 usher
leave the ~: 5 arise, get up, stand
like a good ~: 5 comfy
make a ~: 4 cane
mate: 5 table
offer a ~ to: 4 seat
part: 3 arm, leg 4 seat, slat, wing 5 splat 6 caster 7 cushion
starter: 3 arm 4 high, wing 5 wheel
take the ~: 7 preside 8 moderate
chair ___: 3 bed, car 4 lift, rail 5 table 6 warmer
___ chair: 4 club, deck, easy, lawn, side, wing 5 Eames 6 barber, barrel, bridge, lounge, Morris, swivel 7 folding, reading, rocking
chairman ___ board: 5 of the
___ chairman: 4 shop 5 board
___-chairman: 4 vice
Chairman ___: 3 Mao
chairperson: 4 head 6 leader 7 captain 8 director
concern: 6 agenda
need: 5 gavel
___ chairs: 7 musical
Chairs, The
author: Eugène Ionesco
chaise: 4 shay 5 coach 6 daybed 8 carriage
chaise ___: 3 d'or 6 longue, lounge
Chaka: 4 Khan
Chakiris, George
film: West Side Story (1961, AA)
chalcedony: 4 onyx, sard 5 agate, prase 7 mineral, sardine, sardius
chalet: 3 hut 5 bower, cabin, house, lodge 6 A-frame 7 cottage 8 dwelling, ski lodge
feature: 4 eave
Chaliapin: 4 bass 5 basso, Fëdor 6 Feodor, Fyodor, singer
specialty: 5 opera
chalice: 3 cup 5 calix, grail 6 goblet
partner: 5 paten
___ Chalice, The: 6 Silver
chalk: 5 score, tally 6 blanch, bleach, crayon, marker, whiten 7 mineral 9 whitewash
and clay mixture: 4 malm
ender: 5 board, stone
out: 5 trace
relative: 6 crayon
remover: 6 eraser
talk: 4 talk 6 lesson, speech 7 address, lecture, oration 8 training
target: 3 cue
up: 3 get 5 notch, score, tally 6 obtain, record, secure
up to: 3 lay 6 charge, credit, impute 7 ascribe 8 accredit 9 attribute
chalk ___: 4 line, talk 6 stripe
chalk ___ to experience: 4 it up
chalkboard: 5 slate
erase a ~: 4 wipe
chalky: 3 wan 4 pale 5 ashen, milky, white 6 pallid, sallow 7 powdery, whitish 8 blanched, bleached 9 albescent, bloodless 10 cretaceous
challah: 5 bread
make ~: 5 braid
challenge: 3 try, vie 4 dare, defy, gage, mock, test 5 brave, claim, fight, query, rally, rival, wager 6 accost, impugn, take on, threat 7 accosts, contest, dispute, protest, provoke, vie with 8 confront, defiance, denounce, face down, gauntlet, mistrust, question 9 demanding, discredit, objection, search out, stand up to, stimulate, ultimatum 10 contradict, controvert, invitation
authority: 5 rebel
medieval ~: 4 gage
meet the ~: 4 cope 7 succeed
respondent: 5 taker
___-challenge: 3 eco
___ Challenge: 5 Pepsi
challenger: 3 foe 5 darer, rival 8 opponent 9 contender 10 competitor, contestant
quest: 5 title
Challenger: 3 car 4 auto 5 Dodge 10 automobile, Studebaker
org.: 4 NASA
Challengers, The: 8 game show
host: Dick Clark
challenging: 4 bold, hard 5 brave 6 brazen, daring 7 defiant 8 insolent, mutinous, rigorous 9 obstinate, resistant, truculent 10 aggressive, pugnacious, rebellious, refractory
challis: 6 fabric 8 material
___ Chalmers: 5 Allis
Chalons: 6 battle
loser: 6 Attila
Châlons-sur-___: 5 Marne, Saône
chamber: 4 cell, hole, room 5 music 6 alcove, pocket 7 bedroom, council, cubicle, shelter 8 assembly, congress 9 container, enclosure
combining form: 4 -cele, coel- 5 -coele
ender: 4 maid
in Spanish: 4 sala
monastic ~: 4 cell
music instrument: 5 cello, viola 6 violin
piece: 4 trio 5 music, nonet, octet 7 octette, quartet
starter: 3 bed 4 ante
temple ~: 4 naos 5 cella
underground ~: 4 cave, kiva 5 crypt, vault 6 bunker, cavern, grotto
upper ~: 5 attic 6 dormer, garret
vaulted ~: 5 vault 6 recess
see also room
chamber ___: 3 mug 5 music, opera 7 concert
___ chamber: 3 air, ion 4 echo, star 5 cloud, float, lower, privy, smoke, spark, state, surge, upper 6 bubble
___ Chamber: 3 Red 4 Star 5 First 6 Second
Chambered Nautilus, The
author: Oliver Wendell Holmes
Chamberlain: 4 Owen, Wilt 6 Austen 7 Neville, Richard
Chamberlain, Austen: 8 Nobelist
Chamberlain, Neville: 2 P.M. 7 British
foreign secretary: 4 Eden
predecessor: 7 Baldwin
successor: 9 Churchill
Chamberlain, Owen: 8 Nobelist 9 physicist
Chamberlain, Richard: 5 actor
TV: Dr. Kildare, The Thorn Birds
Chamberlain, Wilt
milieu: 5 court
org.: 3 NBA
sport: 10 basketball
chamber of ___: 7 horrors
Chamber of Deputies
locale: 5 Italy
chambers: 5 suite 7 lodging 8 lodgment, quarters
in ~: 9 secretive
judge's ~: 6 camera
Chambers: 9 Whittaker
chambray: 6 fabric 8 material
chambre: 4 room 5 salle 6 French

chameleon: 5 anole 6 animal, lizard 7 reptile
kin: 5 agama 6 iguana
___ Chameleon: 5 Karma
chameleonlike: 5 fluid 7 erratic, mutable, protean 8 shifting, unstable, wavering 9 mercurial, uncertain 10 changeable
chamfer: 5 bevel
chamois: 5 cloth, color, izard 6 animal, mammal, yellow 7 grayish, leather 8 antelope
relative: *see* antelope, yellow color
use a ~: 4 wipe
chamomile: 3 tea 4 herb 5 plant 6 flower
Chamonix, sight from: 3 alp
champ: 4 bite, gnaw 5 munch 6 top dog, victor, winner 9 number one
at the bit: 5 chafe
champ ___ bit: 5 at the
champagne: 3 vin 4 fizz, wine 5 color 6 bubbly, yellow 8 greenish
blended ~: 5 cuvée
bottle: 5 split 6 magnum
bucket: 4 icer 6 cooler
category: 3 sec 4 brut, doux
glass: 5 flute
grape: 5 pinot
name: 3 Dom 4 Moet, Mumm 8 Perignon
partner: 6 caviar 7 caviare
prepare ~: 3 ice 5 chill
relative: *see* yellow color
ritual: 5 toast
stopper: 4 cork
___ champagne: 4 pink
Champagne for Caesar (1950 film)
cast: Ronald Colman, Celeste Holm, Art Linkletter, Vincent Price
Champagne music man: 4 Welk
Champagne Supernova (1996 song)
artist: Oasis
Champagne Tony: 4 Lema
Champagne wishes guy: 5 Leach
champaign: 5 plain 7 lowland
Champaign: 4 city, town
athletes: 6 Illini
locale: 8 Illinois
champ at the ___: 3 bit
champignon: 8 mushroom
champing at the bit: 4 avid 5 antsy, eager, ready 6 gung-ho, on edge
champion: 4 back, best, head, hero 5 chief, first, prime 6 backer, defend, foster, knight, master, patron, tip-top, top dog, uphold, victor, winner 7 apostle, endorse, espouse, forward, further, indorse, leading, paladin, premier, promote, protect, support 8 advocate, crusader, defender, endorser, exponent, fight for, foremost, greatest, medalist, plead for, reformer, side with, stand for, superior, thump for, top-notch 9 apologist, conqueror, nonpareil, number one, numero uno, paraclete, principal, proponent, protector, supporter, top-drawer, vindicate 10 go to bat for, rally round, speak up for, subjugator, triumphant, world-class
name meaning ~: 4 Neal, Neil
prize: 5 title
Champion: 5 Gower, horse, Marge
rider: Gene Autry
Champion, Gower: 8 director
spouse: Marge
championship: 4 egis 5 aegis, crown, prize, title 7 support, victory 8 espousal 9 patronage 10 protection
___ Championship Season: 4 That
Champlain: 4 lake
locale: 7 New York, Vermont
Champlain, Samuel de: 8 explorer
champlevé: 6 enamel, inlaid
Champs
song: Tequila (1958)
Champs ___: 7 Élysées
champs' cry: 5 we win, we won
Champ, The (1931 film)
cast: Wallace Beery, Jackie Cooper
director: King Vidor
Chan: 6 Jackie 7 Charlie
portrayer: 5 Naish, Oland, Toler 7 Ustinov, Winters
chance: 3 bet, hap, lot, odd 4 fate, luck, odds, risk, room, shot, stab, time 5 bet on, break, fluky, lucky, occur, stake, wager 6 casual, danger, flukey, gamble, hazard, random, resort 7 aimless, attempt, fortune, leisure, lottery, oddball, offhand, venture 8 accident, endanger, fortuity, long shot, occasion, prospect 9 arbitrary, fair shake, fortunate, haphazard, hit-or-miss, liability, privilege, unplanned, unwitting 10 accidental, contingent, fortuitous, incidental, jeopardize, likelihood, lucky break, unexpected, unintended
blow the ~: 4 miss
by ~: 4 idly 5 haply 7 luckily 8 at random, casually, randomly
discover by ~: 5 hit on
even ~: 6 tossup
fat ~: 4 uh-uh
found by ~: 5 lit on
game of ~: 4 keno 5 craps, lotto, poker 6 raffle 7 lottery 8 baccarat, roulette
good ~: 10 likelihood
happening: 5 fluke, quirk 8 accident, fortuity
it: 3 bet 6 gamble
not a ~: 3 nah, naw, nay, nix, non 4 nein, nope, nyet, uh-uh 5 I won't, ixnay, never, no how, no way 6 no deal, noways, nowise 7 I refuse 8 forget it, I will not, negative, negatory 9 by no means, fat chance, I think not 10 count me out, thumbs down
on: 4 find, meet 8 bump into 9 encounter, run across 10 come across
run the ~ of: 4 risk
starter: 3 per 6 happen
take a ~: 4 bite, dare, risk 5 wager 6 gamble, hazard 7 venture 9 speculate
taking, for short: 4 spec
to play: 4 turn
chance ___ lifetime: 3 of a
___ chance: 6 second
___ chance!: 3 Fat 4 Not a 5 Bonne
Chance: 5 Frank
author: Joseph Conrad
teammate: 5 Evers 6 Tinker
chancel: 6 church 9 sanctuary
hanging: 6 dossal, dossel
neighbor: 4 apse, nave
___-chancellor: 4 vice
Chancellor: 4 John
Chancellor ___ Exchequer: 5 of the
___ Chancellor: 4 Lord
Chancellorsville: 6 battle
winner at ~: 3 Lee
___ Chance on Me: 5 Take a
chances: 4 lots, odds 5 state 7 outlook 8 prospect
Chances Are (1957 song)
artist: Johnny Mathis
chancy: 4 iffy 5 dicey, hairy, risky, rocky 6 touchy, tricky, unsafe, unsure 7 dubious, erratic, parlous 8 perilous, ticklish 9 ambiguous, dangerous, debatable, hazardous, uncertain, unsettled, vagarious 10 capricious, indefinite, precarious, unresolved, up for grabs, up in the air
chandelier: 5 light 7 fixture
hanging: 5 prism
Chandler: 4 city, Gene, Jeff, Otis, town 5 Estee, Happy 7 Dorothy, Raymond
locale: 7 Arizona
Chandler, Gene
song: Duke of Earl (1962)
___ Chandler Harris: 4 Joel
Chandler, Raymond: 6 writer
sleuth: Marlowe
work: The Big Sleep
Farewell, My Lovely
The High Window
The Lady in the Lake
The Little Sister
The Long Goodbye
Playback
Chanel: 4 Coco
product: 5 scent 7 perfume
Chaney: 3 Lon
Chang: 4 twin 7 Siamese
brother: 3 Eng
Changduk Palace site: 5 Seoul
change: 3 fit 4 cash, coin, flux, move, redo, swap, swop, vary, veer, warp 5 act on, adapt, alter, amend, break, budge, coins, dimes, money, morph, shift, swing, trade, waver 6 adjust, affect, barter, evolve, juggle, modify, motion, mutate, nickel, redeem, reform, remake, revise, silver, switch, tamper 7 act upon, assault, coinage, commute, convert, diverge, inflect, lighten, meander, nickels, novelty, pennies, permute, qualify, redress, remodel, replace, reshape, restyle, reverse, revisal, shuffle, variety 8 diminish, flip-flop, innovate, make over, modulate, movement, mutation, quarters, renovate, reversal, revision, supplant, transfer, upheaval, variance 9 about-face, alternate, amendment, departure, deviation, diversify, diversion, evolution, fluctuate, oscillate, redaction, reshaping, transform, translate, transmute, transpose, vacillate, variation 10 adjustment, alteration, conversion, correction, difference, emendation, innovation, modulation, new wrinkle, refinement, regenerate, remodeling, reorganize, reposition, revolution, substitute, tamper with, transition, turnaround
apt to ~: 6 fickle 7 flighty
back: 6 revert
combining form: 4 trop- 5 tropo-
complete ~ of mind: 5 U-turn
course: 3 cut, yaw, zig 4 tack, turn, veer
ender: 4 over
get used to ~: 4 cope 5 adapt
have a ~ of heart: 6 recant 7 reverse 8 pull back, withdraw 9 back-pedal
holder: 5 purse 6 pocket 9 piggy bank
into: 6 become
likely to ~: 6 labile
make a minor ~: 6 adjust
maker: 6 editor
of direction: 5 U-turn
off: 6 rotate 9 take turns
one's address: 4 move 8 relocate
one's mind: 4 bend 6 relent 7 retract 9 vacillate
one's ways: 4 mend 6 reform 7 shape up 10 make amends
positions: 5 reset, shift
radical ~: 7 shake-up 8 upheaval 10 revolution
residence: 6 uproot 7 migrate 8 relocate
sides: 4 turn 6 defect
slowly: 6 evolve
small ~: 3 cts. 4 cent, coin, dime 5 cents, coins, dimes, penny 6 nickel 7 nickels, pennies, quarter 8 quarters
starter: 5 inter, short 7 counter
subject to ~: 9 tentative
text: 4 edit 5 emend
the order: 5 mix up 6 jumble, muddle 8 disarray, scramble 9 rearrange 10 disarrange
to suit: 5 adapt, slant
unexpected ~: 5 twist
change ___: 3 off 5 hands
___ change: 3 sea 5 chump, exact, small
___ Change: 4 Cool 5 Quick 7 Seasons
changeable: 5 fluid, moody 6 fickle, labile, mobile, uneven 7 erratic, mutable, protean, unloyal, wayward 8 shifting, slippery, ticklish, unstable, unsteady, variable, volatile, wavering 9 adaptable, faithless, impulsive, irregular, mercurial, revocable, spasmodic, temporary, transient, uncertain, unsettled, versatile, whimsical 10 capricious, inconstant, indecisive, irresolute, permutable, reciprocal, reversible, unreliable
one: 9 chameleon
___-change artist: 5 quick
changed: 7 unlike 9 different
changeless: 6 static, steady 7 abiding 8 constant, enduring, ironclad 9 immutable, permanent, steadfast 10 invariable, undecaying
Changeling (2008 film)
cast: Angelina Jolie, John Malkovich
director: Clint Eastwood

Changeling, The
author: Thomas Middleton, William Rowley
changement de pied: 4 leap
change of ___: 4 pace 5 habit, heart, venue
Change of Heart (1983 song)
artist: Tom Petty and the Heartbreakers
Change of Heart (1986 song)
artist: Cyndi Lauper
change one's ___: 4 mind, tune
changeover: 5 shift 8 apostasy 10 conversion
Change Partners
composer: Irving Berlin
___ changer: 4 coin 6 record
Changes, Book of: 6 I Ching
changes to, make: 4 redo 5 adapt, alter, amend
Change the World (1996 song)
artist: Eric Clapton
change-up: 5 pitch
changing: 7 migrant, mutable 8 variable 9 unsettled
place: 6 cabana
readily: 5 fluid
changing ___: 3 bag 4 note, room, tone 5 table
Changing Lanes (2002 film)
cast: Ben Affleck, Toni Collette, Samuel L. Jackson, Sydney Pollack
Chang Jiang, port on the: 4 Wuhu
Chang, Michael: 7 netster 9 tennis pro
rival: 6 Agassi
___ chango: 6 presto
Chan, Jackie: 5 actor
film: Police Story (1985)
Project A (1983)
Rush Hour (1998)
Shanghai Noon (2000)
channel: 3 rut, str., way 4 dike, duct, flue, line, link, neck, race, slot 5 agent, canal, ditch, drain, flume, gouge, guide, gulch, gully, means, organ, route, sound, stria, track 6 agency, arroyo, artery, avenue, convey, course, direct, funnel, furrow, groove, gullet, gulley, gutter, medium, outlet, siphon, strait, syphon, trench, trough, tunnel, valley 7 conduct, conduit, culvert, fluting, narrows, passage, pathway, vehicle 8 aqueduct, transmit 9 influence 10 instrument, passageway
anatomical ~: 4 vein 5 aorta, lumen 6 artery
blocker: 5 V-chip
British ~: 3 BBC
cable: 3 AMC, BET, CMT, CNN, HBO, HSN, IFC, ION, MTV, QVC, SHO, TBS, TLC, TMC, TNT, USA 4 CNBC, ESPN, Flix, HGTV 5 A and E, Bravo, C-SPAN, MSNBC, Spike, Starz, Style, truTV 6 Encore, Noggin, Tech TV, TV Land 7 Cinemax, Ovation, ShopNBC, SoapNet 8 Lifetime, Showtime, Sundance
clear a ~: 6 dredge
combining form: 5 solen- 6 soleno-
control: 4 dial
designation: 3 UHF, VHF
marker: 4 buoy
port: 5 Brest 6 Calais
surf: 3 zap 4 scan
surfer's need: 2 TV 5 TV set
surfers zap past them: 3 ads
TV: 3 ABC, CBS, Fox, NBC, PBS 5 The CW
water ~: 5 ditch, flume
channel ___: 4 bass, surf 5 black 6 surfer 7 surfing
___ channel: 4 back 5 clear
___ Channel: 7 English
Channel Islands
island: 4 Sark 6 Jersey 8 Guernsey
locale: 7 Britain, England
port: 8 St. Helier
Channing: 5 Carol, Margo 8 Stockard
Channing, Stockard
TV: The West Wing
chanson: 4 song 5 music
chanson ___: 6 d'amour 7 de geste
Chanson de ___: 6 Roland
chant: 2 om 4 sing, song, tune 5 drone, music, psalm, utter 6 incant, intone, litany, mantra, melody, recite 7 mantram, worship 8 vocalize 9 plainsong 10 repetition
Olympics ~: 6 USA USA
starter: 5 plain
___ chantant: 4 café
chanter: 6 singer 8 vocalist
chanterelle: 6 fungus 8 mushroom
chanteuse: 6 singer 8 vocalist
chantey: 3 air 4 song, tune
singer: 3 gob, tar 6 sailor, sea dog
chanticleer: 4 cock, fowl 7 chicken, rooster
sound: 4 crow
Chantilly ___: 4 lace 5 sauce
Chantilly Lace (1958 song)
artist: Big Bopper
chantry: 6 chapel, temple
Chanukah
see Hanukkah
Chanukah Song, The (1995 song)
artist: Adam Sandler
Chao Phraya: 5 river
locale: 8 Thailand
chaos: 4 mess, riot 5 havoc, mix-up, snafu, snarl 6 bedlam, huddle, jumble, jungle, mayhem, muddle, tumult, unrest, uproar 7 anarchy, clutter, discord, entropy, ferment, rioting, turmoil 8 disarray, disorder, madhouse, shambles, upheaval 9 confusion, mobocracy 10 hurly-burly, turbulence, unruliness
Chaos
daughter: 3 Nyx 4 Gaea
son: 4 Eros 6 Erebus
chaotic: 4 wild 5 messy, mussy, wooly 6 hectic, unneat, untidy, woolly 7 haywire, jumbled, lawless, riotous, tangled 8 anarchic, confused, pell-mell 9 turbulent 10 anarchical, disjointed, disordered, disorderly, in an uproar, incohesive, topsy-turvy, tumultuous, unpeaceful, upside-down
place: 3 zoo
chap: 2 he 3 egg, guy, man, sir 4 dude, gent, male, mate 5 bloke, bucko, crack, fella, sport 6 feller, fellow, mister, redden 7 roughen
ender: 4 book 6 fallen
young ~: 3 lad
___ chap: 3 old
Chap ___: 5 Stick
chaparajos: 8 leggings
chaparral: 5 brush
chapati: 5 bread
chapeau
see hat
chapel: 6 bethel, church, shrine, temple 7 chantry, oratory, worship 8 sacellum 9 sanctuary 10 tabernacle
___ Chapel: 5 Arena 7 Sistine
chapel de ___: 3 fer
Chapel Hill: 4 city, town
athletes: 8 Tar Heels
locale: 4 N. Car.
school: 3 UNC
___-Chapelle: 5 Aix-la
Chapel of Love (1964 song)
artist: Dixie Cups
chaperon: 4 lead 5 bring, guard, guide, watch 6 attend, convoy, duenna, escort, squire 7 conduct, oversee, protect, support 8 guardian, shepherd 9 accompany, attendant, companion, safeguard, supervise, watch over
one with a ~: 3 deb
chapfallen: 3 sad 4 blue, down, glum 5 woful 6 gloomy, morose, somber, woeful 7 doleful, hangdog, joyless, unhappy 8 dejected, downcast, lowering, troubled 9 bummed out, cheerless, heartsick, miserable, sorrowful, woebegone 10 dispirited, melancholy
Chapin: 5 Harry 6 Lauren
___ Chapin Carpenter: 4 Mary
Chapin, Harry
song: Cat's in the Cradle (1974)
Taxi (1972)
chaplain: 5 padre, rabbi, rebbe 6 cleric, parson, pastor, priest 8 minister, preacher
chaplet: 6 diadem, wreath 7 coronet, garland
Chaplin: 3 Syd 4 Oona, Saul 6 Sydney 7 Charlie 9 Geraldine
Chaplin (1992 film)
cast: Dan Aykroyd, Geraldine Chaplin, Robert Downey Jr.
director: Richard Attenborough
Chaplin, Charlie: 3 Sir 5 actor 8 director
contemporary: 5 Lloyd 6 Keaton
film: The Circus (1928)
City Lights (1931)
A Countess From Hong Kong (1967)
The Gold Rush (1925)
The Great Dictator (1940)
The Kid (1921)
A King in New York (1957)
Limelight (1952)
Modern Times (1936)
Monsieur Verdoux (1947)
A Woman of Paris (1923)
prop: 4 cane
spouse: Paulette Goddard, Oona O'Neill
Chaplin, Geraldine: 7 actress
mother: 4 Oona
Chapman: 4 John 5 Tracy 6 George, Graham
Chapman, Tracy
song: Fast Car (1988)
Give Me One Reason (1996)
chapped: 5 rough
chaps: 5 pants 8 leggings
chapter: 4 unit, wing 5 local, phase 6 branch, member 7 episode, section 8 division 9 affiliate
and verse: 6 detail
of history: 3 era
partner: 5 verse
poem ~: 5 canto
quote ~ and verse: 4 list, tell 6 relate, report 7 account, analyze, itemize, narrate, recount, specify 8 describe 9 elaborate, enumerate, expound on, make clear
start, usually: 5 recto
Chapter ___: 3 Two 6 Eleven
Chapter 11: 10 bankruptcy
go into ~: 4 bust, fail
in ~: 5 broke 8 bankrupt
chapter and ___: 5 verse
Chapter on Ears, A
author: Elia, Charles Lamb
Chapter Two: 4 film, play
author: Neil Simon
cast: James Caan, Valerie Harper, Marsha Mason
Chapultepec: 6 battle
locale: 6 Mexico
char: 4 burn, fish, heat, sear 5 singe 6 scorch 7 blacken 8 overcook 9 carbonize
ender: 4 coal 5 broil, woman
char-à-banc: 3 bus 5 coach
character: 3 air, ilk 4 aura, card, form, kind, kook, mold, mood, part, role, self, sort, soul, tone, type, vein 5 class, clown, crank, ethos, flake, genre, honor, human, state, style 6 aspect, cipher, credit, figure, flavor, kidney, letter, makeup, mettle, morale, nature, number, person, repute, scream, spirit, status, symbol, temper, virtue, weirdo 7 caliber, courage, essence, numeral, oddball, probity, quality, station, texture 8 attitude, good name, identity, ideogram, mystique, original, standing 9 attribute, eccentric, extrovert, integrity, mentality, personage, rectitude, reference 10 appearance, atmosphere, complexion, estimation, expression, hieroglyph, honestness, individual, principles, reputation
good ~ traits: 5 arete
qualities making up good ~: 5 arete
character ___: 3 set 5 actor, piece, study 6 sketch 7 builder, defense, witness
___ character: 4 flat, unit 5 out of, round, stock 7 control
character-building org.: 3 BSA
characteristic: 3 way 4 look, mark, sign 5 point, quirk, trait, typic 6 aspect, custom, innate, signal, unique 7 classic, earmark, feature, natural, quality, special, symptom, typical 8 hallmark, property, specific 9 attribute, mannerism
not ~ of: 6 unlike
of (suffix): 3 -ile, -ine, -ish
characterization: 4 role 6 acting 7 profile 8 portrait

CH

characterize: **3** peg **5** brand, label **6** define, depict, sketch, typify **7** feature, outline, portray, qualify **8** describe, identify, set apart **9** personify
characterized by: **4** with
characterless: **4** drab **8** ordinary
charade: **3** act **4** fake, pose **5** farce **6** dupery, riddle **8** disguise, pretense **9** deception, pantomime
Charade: **3** car **4** auto **8** Daihatsu
Charade (1963 film)
cast: Cary Grant, Audrey Hepburn, Walter Matthau
composer: Henry Mancini
director: Stanley Donen
charades: **4** game
play ~: **4** mime **6** act out
charcoal: **4** gray, grey **5** black, color **8** brownish
relative: ***see*** gray color
charcoal ___: **5** grill **6** burner
chard: **4** beet **6** veggie **9** vegetable
kin: **4** kail, kale
___ chard: **5** Swiss
Chardonnay: **3** vin **4** wine **5** grape, white
relative: ***see*** wine
___ Chardonnay: **5** Pinot
charge: **3** ask, fee, job, lay, owe, rap, tab, tax, zap **4** beef, bite, book, care, cost, dash, dues, duty, fare, levy, onus, push, rate, rush, task, tilt, toll, urge, ward **5** blame, blitz, claim, debit, forge, gripe, imbue, lunge, onset, order, price, quote, rally, runat, score, shoot, storm, trust **6** accuse, allege, amount, assess, attack, behest, burden, damage, direct, escrow, exhort, have at, hurtle, impose, impugn, impute, indict, invest, ionize, lading, lumber, office, onrush, outlay, plunge, sortie, tariff, thrill, towage **7** arraign, assault, command, conduct, contend, control, custody, damages, entrust, expense, impeach, intrust, keeping, mandate, mission, payment, pervade, release, tuition **8** accredit, auspices, delegate, instruct, permeate, province, purchase, relegate, reproach, stampede **9** complaint, direction, directive, electrify, explosive, implicate, inculpate, onslaught, oversight, quotation, reckoning, reprehend, statement **10** accusation, allegation, assessment, assignment, commitment, go pell-mell, imputation, indictment, management, obligation
account: **6** credit
alternative: **4** cash **5** check
answer a ~: **5** plead, rebut
be in ~: **3** run **4** head, lead, rule **5** steer **6** head up, manage **7** command, control, operate **9** supervise
cabaret ~: **5** cover
criminal ~: **3** rap
false ~: **5** frame, smear **6** bad rap, bum rap **7** frame-up
get a ~ out of: **4** like **5** enjoy
group in ~: **3** mgt. **4** mgmt. **10** management
in ~: **7** regnant **8** dominant, superior **10** commanding
it: **3** buy, owe
kind of ~: **3** neg., pos. **8** negative, positive
one in ~: **3** ldr. **4** head **5** chief, Mr. Big **6** leader, master
response: **4** plea **6** denial, guilty **9** not guilty
service ~: **3** fee
starter: **3** sur **5** turbo **7** counter
up: **5** liven **7** enliven
with: **5** blame, lay on **6** impute **8** credit to
without ~: **4** free **6** gratis, public **9** on the cuff **10** for nothing, on the house
charge ___: **4** card **5** plate **7** account, carrier
___ charge: **4** late, take **5** cover, depth, fixed **6** access, public **7** finance, service, trickle **8** carrying
chargeable: **6** liable **8** blamable **9** blameable **10** answerable, indictable
charge-card user: **4** ower
charged: **5** laden, ran at **6** loaded, went at **7** replete **8** electric **10** electrical, encumbered, portentous
electrically ~: **4** live **5** ionic
particle: **3** ion **5** anion **6** cation, kation
swimmer: **3** eel
chargé d'affaires: **5** agent, envoy **6** consul, legate **7** attaché **8** diplomat, emissary, minister **10** ambassador, negotiator, peacemaker
Charge of the Light Brigade
author: Alfred Tennyson
Charge of the Light Brigade, The (1936 film)
cast: Olivia de Havilland, Errol Flynn
charger: **5** horse, mount, steed **6** equine **7** palfrey, platter, trooper **8** destrier, war-horse
Charger: **3** car **4** auto **5** Dodge
Chargers: **6** eleven
home: **8** San Diego
org.: **3** AFC
rival: ***see*** NFL team
charges
answer ~: **5** plead
bring ~: **3** sue **4** book **6** accuse, allege **8** litigate **9** prosecute
one who ~: **4** ower **5** payer
suspend ~: **6** pardon
charily: **5** shyly **6** askant, warily **7** askance, leerily, timidly **8** frugally **9** carefully, guardedly, heedfully, mindfully, sparingly, thriftily **10** cautiously
chariness: **8** mistrust, wariness **9** leeriness, nonbelief, suspicion **10** discretion
Charing ___: **5** Cross
chariot: **5** essed **7** vehicle
builders: **6** Hyksos, Romans
Charioteer: **6** Auriga
Charioteer, The
author: Mary Renault
Chariots of Fire (1981 film)
cast: Ian Charleson, Ben Cross
highlight: **4** race
music: Vangelis
charisma: **4** aura, pull **5** charm, magic **6** allure, appeal, dazzle, glamor **7** glamour **8** mystique, presence **9** magnetism
charismatic: **7** dynamic, likable **8** magnetic **10** magnetical
Charisse, Cyd: **6** dancer **7** actress
film: The Band Wagon (1953)
Brigadoon (1954)
Silk Stockings (1957)
Singin' in the Rain (1952)
spouse: Tony Martin
charitable: **4** good, kind, nice **5** noble **6** giving, humane, kindly **7** clement, largess, lenient, liberal **8** all heart, generous, gracious, largesse, merciful, obliging, tolerant **9** bountiful, brotherly, favorable, forgiving, indulgent, righteous, unselfish, unsparing **10** altruistic, beneficent, benevolent, bighearted, forbearing, freehanded, hospitable, humanistic, thoughtful, unstinting
activity: **5** cause **6** bazaar **7** benefit **10** fundraiser
be ~: **6** donate
donation: **4** alms
one: **5** donor, giver
org.: **4** CARE **6** UNESCO, UNICEF
charity: **3** aid **4** alms, dole, gift, pity **5** grant, mercy **6** relief, virtue **7** handout, largess **8** altruism, clemency, donation, goodwill, humanity, kindness, largesse, lenience, leniency, offering **9** tolerance **10** compassion, foundation, generosity, liberality
British ~: **5** Oxfam
partner: **4** hope **5** faith
seek ~: **3** beg
___ Charity: **5** Sweet
Charity begins ___: **6** at home
charlatan: **3** con **4** fake, liar, sham **5** cheat, faker, fraud, knave, phony, quack, rogue **6** phoney, rascal **8** imposter, impostor, swindler **9** hypocrite **10** adventurer, mountebank
Charlemagne: **3** roi **4** king **7** emperor
capital: **6** Aachen
domain: **3** HRE
father: **5** Pepin
Pope who crowned ~: **3** Leo
Charlemont
author: William Simms
Charlene: **6** Tilton
Charles: **3** Ray **4** Best, Dana, Drew, Haid, Ives, lake, Lamb, Lane, Mayo, Nash, Nick, Nora **5** Atlas, Beard, Boyer, Busch, Coody, Dawes, Drake, Eames, Frend, Gobat, Goren, Jimmy, Lyell, McKim, Münch, Olson, Peale, Péguy, Reade, river, saint, Shyer, Simic, Vidor **6** Addams, Barkla, Barton, Cioffi, Coburn, Conrad, Cotton, Curtis, Darwin, Ezzard, Finley, Fuller, Gounod, Grodin, Kuralt, Martel, McGraw, Mingus, Morgan, Napier, Norton, Osgood, prince, Richet, Schulz, Schwab, Townes, Wesley, Wilson, Wright **7** Babbage, Barkley, Berlitz, Bronson, Burnett, Coulomb, Dickens, Durning, Farrell, Guiteau, Huggins, Jarrott, Laveran, Nicolle, Nordoff, Richter, Ruggles, Siebert, Strouse, Walters, Windsor, Woolley **8** Aznavour, Bickford, Bukowski, Bulfinch, Crichton, de Gaulle, Goodyear, Laughton, Nordhoff, Pedersen, Perrault, Ringling, Sangster, Scribner, Van Doren, Williams **9** Fairbanks, Guillaume, Kimbrough, Lindbergh, MacArthur, Steinmetz, Winninger **10** Baudelaire
city on the ~: **6** Boston
dog: **4** Asta
in German: **4** Karl
in Italian: **5** Carlo
in Spanish: **6** Carlos
Charles ___ Gibson: **4** Dana
Charles ___ Hughes: **5** Evans
Charles ___ Reilly: **6** Nelson
Charles, Ezzard: **5** boxer
milieu: **4** ring
Charles I
foe: **3** Pym
Charles in Charge (CBS sitcom)
cast: Scott Baio (Charles)
___ Charles, LA: **4** Lake
Charleson: **3** Ian
Charles, Prince
Beatrice, to ~: **5** niece
parent: **6** Philip **9** Elizabeth
princedom: **5** Wales
sib: **4** Anne **6** Andrew, Edward
son: **5** Harry, Henry, Wills **7** William
sport: **4** polo
Charles, Ray
portrayer: Jamie Foxx
song: Busted (1963)
Crying Time (1966)
Georgia on My Mind (1960)
Hit the Road Jack (1961)
I Can't Stop Loving You (1962)
One Mint Julep (1961)
Unchain My Heart (1961)
What'd I Say (1959)
You Don't Know Me (1962)
___ Charles spaniel: **4** King
Charles the ___: **5** Great
Charleston: **4** city, port, town **5** dance, Oscar
athletes: **8** Bulldogs
county: **7** Kanawha
dance: **8** bunny hug
locale: **3** W. Va. **4** S. Car. **8** Illinois
river: **3** Elk **7** Kanawha
school: **7** Citadel
Charles Van ___: **5** Doren
charley ___: **5** horse
Charley: **5** Pride **6** Weaver **7** Varrick
___ Charley?: **6** Where's
charley horse: **4** ache, kink **5** cramp, crick, spasm
Charley's Aunt: **4** play **5** farce
Charley Varrick (1973 film)
cast: Joe Don Baker, Felicia Farr, Walter Matthau
Charlie: **4** Byrd, Chan, Rich, Rose, tuna **5** Brown, McCoy, Pride, Sheen, Watts **6** Barnet, Callas, Finley, Gracie, Keller, Louvin, Parker **7** Chaplin, Daniels, Ruggles **8** Comiskey **9** Gehringer, Leibrandt, Schlatter
brother: **3** Syd **6** Emilio
good-time ~: **5** sport
preceder: **5** Baker
Charlie and the Chocolate Factory
author: Roald Dahl

Charlie and the Chocolate Factory (2005 film)
cast: Helena Bonham Carter, Johnny Depp
director: Tim Burton
Charlie Brown (1959 song)
artist: Coasters
opener: **3** fee **6** fee fee
Charlie Hustle: Pete Rose
Charlie's Angels: **4** trio
Charlie's Angels (2000 film)
cast: Drew Barrymore, Cameron Diaz, Lucy Liu, Bill Murray
director: McG
Charlie's Angels (ABC adventure)
cast: David Doyle (John Bosley)
Farrah Fawcett (Jill Munroe)
John Forsythe (Charlie Townsend)
Shelley Hack (Tiffany Welles)
Kate Jackson (Sabrina Duncan)
Cheryl Ladd (Kris Munroe)
Tanya Roberts (Julie Rogers)
Jaclyn Smith (Kelly Garrett)
Charlie Wilson's War (2007 film)
cast: Amy Adams, Tom Hanks, Philip Seymour Hoffman, Julia Roberts
director: Mike Nichols
Charlize: **6** Theron
charlotte: **7** dessert
Charlotte: **3** Rae **4** city, town **5** Lewis **6** Brontë, Gilman **8** Rampling
in Italian: **8** Carlotta
locale: **4** N. Car.
newspaper: **8** Observer
sister: **4** Anne **5** Emily
team: **7** Hornets
Charlotte __: **5** Russe
Charlotte __, VI: **6** Amalie
__ Charlotte Islands: **5** Queen
charlotte russe: **4** cake **7** dessert
Charlottesville: **4** city, town
athletes: **9** Cavaliers
locale: **8** Virginia
school: **3** U. Va.
Charlotte's Web
author: E.B. White
character: **3** rat **5** Avery
Charlton: **6** Heston
Charly: **7** McClain
Charly (1968 film)
cast: Claire Bloom, Cliff Robertson, Lilia Skala
charm: **3** hex, obi, woo **4** draw, juju, lure, mojo, send, take, vamp, zest **5** asset, grace, magic, obeah, spell, tempt **6** allure, amulet, appeal, bangle, beauty, disarm, enamor, endear, engage, glamor, grigri, lead on, please, ravish, scarab **7** amenity, attract, beguile, bewitch, charism, coaxing, delight, enchant, enthral, glamour, inthral, jewelry, periapt, trinket, wheedle, win over **8** charisma, elegance, enthrall, entrance, greegree, grisgris, inthrall, intrigue, inveigle, talisman, urbanity **9** captivate, enrapture, entertain, fascinate, hypnotize, inebriate, infatuate, magnetism, mesmerize, spellbind, tantalize, transport, wheedling **10** allurement, attraction, intoxicate, loveliness, tickle pink
magic ~: **4** mojo **6** amulet, fetich, fetish
charm __: **6** school **8** bracelet
Charm: **5** candy
Charmaine
composer: Erno Rapee
__ charmant!: **4** Très
charmed: **4** rapt **5** blest, lucky **7** blessed, far gone, favored, on a roll **8** held fast **9** delighted, fortunate, gladdened, on a streak, overjoyed **10** auspicious, felicitous, fortuitous, infatuated, spellbound
charmed __: **4** life **5** quark **6** circle
Charmed (WB fantasy)
cast: Holly Marie Combs (Piper Halliwell)
Shannen Doherty (Pru Halliwell)
Rose MacGowen (Paige Matthews)
Alyssa Milano (Phoebe Halliwell)
character: **5** witch
__ charmed life: **4** led a **5** lead a
Charmed Life, A
author: Mary McCarthy
Charmed Lives
author: Michael Korda
charmer: **5** cutey, cutie **6** beauty, wizard **8** beguiler, conjurer, conjuror, magician, sorcerer **9** bewitcher, enchanter
little ~: **4** pixy **5** cutey, cutie, pixie
partner: **5** cobra, snake
__ charmer: **5** snake
Charmian: **4** Carr
Charmin
alternative: **5** Scott **6** Marcal **8** Northern, Soft Weve **10** Cottonelle, White Cloud
charming: **4** cute, nice **5** suave, sweet **6** dainty, lovely, pretty, quaint, rakish **7** amiable, darling, likable, lovable, winning, winsome **8** adorable, alluring, debonair, engaging, esthetic, fetching, inviting, likeable, loveable, magnetic, mannerly, pleasant, pleasing, romantic, striking, tasteful, tempting **9** appealing, debonaire, desirable, exquisite, glamorous **10** debonnaire, delectable, delightful, magnetical, personable
__ Charming: **6** Prince
charms: **7** jewelry
Charms: **5** candy
Charm School
author: Nelson DeMille
Charnel Rose, The
author: Conrad Aiken
Charo: **7** Spanish **8** flamenco **9** guitarist
spouse: Xavier Cugat
Charon: **4** moon
circles it: **5** Pluto
father: **6** Erebus
planet: **5** Pluto
river: **4** Styx
charpoy: **3** cot **8** bedstead
charro: **6** cowboy **8** horseman
need: **5** reata, riata
chart: **3** log, map **4** plan, plot **5** graph **6** design, layout, sketch, zodiac **7** diagram, outline **8** schedule, tabulate **9** adumbrate, blueprint, delineate, floor plan, horoscope, visual aid
anew: **5** remap
indication: **5** trend
shape: **3** bar, pie
starter: **4** flow
topper: **3** hit
__ chart: **3** bar, eye, pie **4** flip, flow, star, time
__ Charta: **5** Magna
charter: **3** let **4** book, code, deed, hire, pact, rent, take **5** lease **6** employ, engage, treaty **7** license, reserve **8** contract, document **9** agreement, concordat, franchise, privilege **10** commission
charter __: **6** member
Charter __: **3** Oak
chartered: **5** legal
Charterhouse of Parma, The
author: Stendhal
Charteris: **6** Leslie
detective: **5** Saint, Simon **7** Templar
Chartier, Alain: **4** poet **6** French
Chartres: **4** city, town
feature: **9** cathedral
locale: **6** France
river: **4** Eure
chartreuse: **5** color, drink, green **8** beverage **9** yellowish
relative: ***see*** green color
Chartwell
to Churchill: **6** estate
charwoman: **4** maid **7** cleaner
chary: **3** shy **4** cagy, wary **5** cagey, leery **6** frugal, gun-shy, stingy, uneasy, unsure **7** bashful, careful, dubious, guarded, heedful, mindful, prudent, sparing, thrifty **8** cautious, discreet, doubtful, doubting, hesitant, keen-eyed, watchful **9** diffident, flinching, provident, reluctant, skeptical, uncertain **10** economical, fastidious, scrupulous, suspicious, uneffusive
Charybdis: **5** peril **9** whirlpool
parent: **4** Gaea **8** Poseidon
chase: **3** dog, tag, woo **4** hunt, race, seek, shag **5** expel, hound, quest, shoot, stalk, track, trail **6** chivvy, follow, gun for, pursue, search **7** engrave, fox hunt, go after, pursuit, run down **8** quest for, run after, stampede **9** drive away, track down
anagram for ~: **5** aches
out: **4** boot, oust, rout, shoo **5** repel **6** dispel, run off **8** drive off, send away **9** drive away
scenes: **6** action
starter: **7** steeple
__ chase: **4** give **5** paper
Chase: **3** Hal **4** Edna, Ilka **5** Chevy, David **6** Barrie, Salmon
chase-away word: **4** scat, shoo **5** scram **6** begone **8** scramola
Chase, Chevy: **5** actor **8** comedian
film: Caddyshack (1980)
Fletch (1985)
Foul Play (1978)
Modern Problems (1981)
National Lampoon's Christmas Vacation (1989)
National Lampoon's Vacation (1983)
Seems Like Old Times (1980)
Spies Like Us (1985)
Three Amigos! (1986)
TV: Community, Saturday Night Live
Chase, Ilka
spouse: Louis Calhern
__ Chase, MD: **5** Chevy
Chase of the Golden Meteor, The
author: Jules Verne
chaser: **4** beer, soda **5** drink, posse **6** whisky **7** whiskey
robber ~: **6** lawman **7** officer
without a ~: **4** neat **8** straight **10** straight up
Chase & Sanborn: **6** coffee
alternative: **5** Sanka, Yuban **7** Folgers, Melitta, Nescafé, Savarin **9** Hills Bros.
__ Chase Smith: **8** Margaret
__ Chase, The: **5** Paper
chasing: **5** after
chasm: **3** gap, maw, pit **4** gulf, hole, rift **5** abyss, cañon, gorge, gully, split **6** breach, canyon, crater, gulley, ravine, schism **7** crevice, fissure **8** cleavage, crevasse
like a ~: **6** gaping **7** yawning
chassé: **4** step **5** glide **8** movement
chassis: **4** body **5** frame, shape, shell **6** figure **8** fuselage **9** framework
Chast: **3** Roz
chaste: **4** good, pure **5** clean, moral, stark **6** decent, demure, modest, vestal **8** celibate, innocent, maidenly, spotless, unsoiled, virtuous **9** continent, incorrupt, lily-white, stainless, undefiled, unsullied, untainted, wholesome
chasten: **5** scold **6** humble, punish, thrash **7** mortify **9** castigate, humiliate
chastened: **5** sorry **7** subdued **8** contrite **10** remorseful
chastise: **3** rag **4** flay, lash, slam, whip **5** scold, spank **6** berate, lean on, punish, rebuke, strike, thrash **7** censure, chew out, lay into, upbraid **8** penalize **9** castigate, criticize, excoriate, fustigate, reprehend **10** discipline
chastity: **6** virtue **7** modesty **8** morality **9** austerity **10** abstinence, simplicity
Chastity: **4** Bono
parent: **4** Cher **5** Sonny
chasuble, garment under a: **3** alb
chat: **3** gab, jaw, rap, yak, yap **4** bird, blab, chin, talk, word **5** prate, speak, visit **6** babble, confab, dialog, gossip, jabber, natter, parley, powwow, rattle, tattle, yammer **7** discuss, palaver, prattle, schmoos **8** causerie, converse, dialogue, schmoose, schmooze, songbird **9** discourse, tête-à-tête, touch base **10** chew the fat, chew the rag, conference, yackety-yak
online ~: **2** IM
pas de ~: **4** leap
prepare to ~ perhaps: **5** log on
room chuckle: **3** LOL
starter: **4** chit, wood
striped ~: **5** tigre
chat __: **4** room
château: **4** keep **5** abode, house **6** castle, estate, palace, winery **7** mansion **8** fortress **10** manor house
château __: **4** d'eau, wine
Château __: **3** D'if **6** Lafite

CH

Château-__: 7 Thierry
Chateaubriand: 5 steak 8 François
  novel: 4 René
Château Lafite
  locale: 5 Médoc 6 France 8 Bordeaux
  product: 4 wine 6 claret
Château-Thierry: 6 battle
  locale: 6 France
  river: 5 Marne
chatroom offerer: 3 AOL
Chattanooga: 4 city, town 6 battle
  locale: 4 Tenn. 9 Tennessee
Chattanooga Choo Choo composer: Mack Gordon, Harry Warren
chattel: 4 serf 5 goods, slave 6 assets, things, thrall 7 effects, villein 8 property 9 commodity
chatter: 3 gab, gas, jaw, rap, yak, yap 4 blab, buzz, gush, talk 5 bilge, clack, noise, prate, run on, shake, sound, speak, spout 6 babble, drivel, gabble, gibber, gossip, jabber, natter, patter, pop off, ramble, rattle, tattle 7 blather, blether, maunder, palaver, prattle, twaddle, yakking 8 babbling, chitchat, rattle on 9 gibberish, loquacity, table talk 10 chew the rag
  ender: 3 box
  prone to ~: 9 talkative
__ chatter: 4 idle
chatterbox: 6 gabber, gasbag, gossip, magpie, yakker 8 prattler
chattering: 5 noisy, prate 8 babbling 9 garrulity, garrulous, talkative 10 loquacious
  quit ~: 6 shut up
__ Chatterley's Lover: 4 Lady
Chatterton: 4 Ruth 6 Thomas
chatty: 5 gabby, gassy, talky, wordy 7 gossipy, unterse 8 familiar, friendly, informal 9 garrulous, talkative 10 bigmouthed, colloquial, long-winded, loquacious
  not ~: 4 curt
Chatwin, Bruce: 6 writer 7 British
Chaucer, Geoffrey: 4 poet 7 British
  character: 4 Cook, Dyer, Monk 5 Canon, Clerk, Friar, Harry, Reeve 6 Bailey, Doctor, Knight, Miller, Parson, Squire, Weaver, Yeoman 7 Chaucer, Plowman, Shipman 8 Franklin, Geoffrey, Manciple, Merchant, Pardoner, Prioress, Sergeant, Summoner 9 Carpenter, Second Nun 10 Nun's Priest, Wife of Bath 11 Haberdasher
  work: The Canterbury Tales
chauffeur: 5 drive, ferry 6 cabbie, driver
  outfit: 6 livery 7 uniform
chauffeured car: 4 limo
Chausson: 6 Ernest
Chautauqua: 4 lake
  locale: 7 New York
chauvinism: 4 bias 8 jingoism 9 prejudice 10 fanaticism, narrowness
chauvinist: 5 bigot, jingo
__ chauvinist: 4 male
Chavez: 5 Cesar 6 Carlos
Chavez __: 6 Ravine
chaw: 3 wad 4 quid
  over: 4 mull
Chayefsky, Paddy: 6 writer
  work: Altered States
    Gideon
    Marty
    Middle of the Night
    The Tenth Man
Chazz: 10 Palminteri
Che: 7 Guevara
Che (2008 film)
  cast: Benicio del Toro
Cheadle, Don: 5 actor
  film: Bulworth (1998)
    Crash (2004)
    The Family Man (2000)
    Hotel Rwanda (2004)
    Swordfish (2001)
    Talk to Me (2007)
    Traffic (2000)
    Volcano (1997)
cheap: 3 low 4 base, mean 5 junky, lousy, petty, ratty, tacky, tatty, tight, tinny 6 cheesy, common, crumby, crummy, frugal, garish, little, low-end, modest, on sale, shabby, shoddy, sleazy, sordid, stingy, tawdry, trashy, two-bit, vulgar 7 bargain, chintzy, cut-rate, good buy, low-cost, miserly, nominal, raffish, reduced, slashed, thrifty 8 for a song, inferior, mediocre, moderate, schlocky, ungiving 9 half-price, low-priced, penurious, rinky-dink, tasteless, third-rate, worthless 10 despicable, economical, jerry-built, low-quality, marked down, reasonable, second-rate, skinflinty
  be ~: 5 skimp
  ender: 5 skate
  not ~: 4 dear 6 costly 8 generous
  sell ~: 4 dump
  shot: 3 dig 4 barb, gibe, jibe, slam, slap, slur, snub 5 abuse, libel, scorn, taunt 6 insult, rebuff, slight 7 affront, calumny, catcall, disdain, low blow, mockery, obloquy, offense, put-down, slander 8 contempt, derision, ridicule 9 aspersion, contumely 10 defamation, disrespect, opprobrium
cheap __: 4 shot
__ cheap: 5 on the
__-cheap: 3 dog 4 dirt
cheap at __ the price: 5 twice
cheapen: 6 debase, reduce 7 degrade, depress, detract, devalue 8 diminish, minimize 9 devaluate 10 adulterate
Cheaper by the Dozen (2003 film)
  cast: Hilary Duff, Bonnie Hunt, Steve Martin
cheaper than: 5 under
cheapskate: 5 miser, piker 7 miserly 8 tightwad 9 skinflint
Cheap Trick
  song: Don't Be Cruel (1988)
    The Flame (1988)
    I Want You to Want Me (1979)
cheat: 2 do 3 con, gyp, rob, sin 4 bilk, burn, clip, crib, dupe, fake, foil, fool, gull, have, hoax, hose, liar, nick, rook, scam, sham, snow, take 5 bunco, cozen, crook, dodge, fraud, fudge, gouge, knave, mulct, pluck, quack, rogue, screw, shaft, shark, shirk, spoof, steal, thief, trick, wrong 6 chisel, con man, deceit, delude, diddle, dodger, euchre, fleece, hustle, outwit, racket, rascal, ripoff, robber, rope in, sucker, take in, thwart 7 beguile, deceive, defraud, fast one, finagle, grifter, hustler, mislead, pretend, sandbag, scammer, sharper, sharpie, snow job, swindle, two-time 8 chiseler, conniver, deceiver, flimflam, hoodwink, imposter, impostor, outsmart, simulate, swindler 9 bamboozle, charlatan, con artist, deception, defrauder, disinform, four-flush, frustrate, hypocrite, imposture, scoundrel, shell game, trickster, victimize 10 dirty trick, double-deal, hanky-panky, overcharge, run a game on
  at Hide and Seek: 4 look
  on an exam: 4 copy, peek
  sheet: 4 crib, trot
cheaters: 5 specs 7 glasses 8 horn-rims 10 eyeglasses, spectacles
Cheatham, Doc: 9 trumpeter
  genre: 4 jazz
cheating: 6 deceit, racket, unfair 7 unloyal 8 disloyal, trickery 9 dishonest, faithless, two-timing, unethical 10 illegality, unfaithful
__ Cheatin' Heart: 4 Your
Chechen city: 6 Grozny
check: 3 nip, tab 4 balk, bill, curb, dike, foil, halt, page, quiz, rein, scan, slow, stay, stem, stop, tame, test, tick 5 abort, audit, baulk, block, brake, count, deter, draft, frisk, gauge, judge, leash, limit, money, proof, prove, quell, stall, trial 6 arrest, assess, bridle, dampen, damper, defeat, detain, halter, hamper, handle, hinder, impede, muzzle, oppose, pull in, rebuff, rein in, retard, review, search, slow up, stifle, thwart, ticket, verify 7 analyze, compare, confirm, control, enquiry, examine, eyeball, harness, inhibit, inquiry, inspect, measure, monitor, prevent, refrain, repress, reverse, suspend, ward off 8 analysis, evaluate, hold back, keep back, look into, look over, make sure, mitigate, moderate, obstacle, obstruct, overhaul, preclude, restrain, restrict, scrutiny, slow down, stoppage, suppress, withhold 9 abatement, ascertain, constrain, deterrent, hamstring, hindrance, intercept, interrupt, proofread, reckoning, restraint 10 comparison, constraint, counteract, discourage, effrontery, impediment, inhibition, inspection, limitation, scrutinize, standstill
  add-on: 3 tax
  blank ~: 7 mandate
  casher: 5 payee 6 drawee
  cashing need: 3 sig. 9 signature
  electronically: 4 scan 5 sweep
  ender: 3 off, out 4 book, list, mate, rein, room 5 point
  European ~: 4 giro
  for errors: 4 edit 5 proof 6 redact 9 proofread
  for fit: 5 try on
  for fraud: 6 go over 7 examine, inspect 9 go through 10 scrutinize
  give a rain ~: 5 defer, delay 6 put off 7 suspend
  hold in ~: 4 keep, rein 6 govern 7 control
  in: 4 come 5 pop up, reach 6 appear, arrive, attend, report 8 get there, register
  in ~: 5 at bay
  item to ~: 2 ID 3 hat 4 coat 6 ID card
  line: 4 date 6 amount 9 signature
  manipulator: 5 kiter
  mark: 4 tick
  of business records: 5 audit
  off: 4 mark
  one's mail, perhaps: 5 log in
  out: 3 eye, vet 4 case, ogle, quit, read, test, view 5 assay, gauge, leave, probe, prove, scout, split, spy on, study, tally, try on 6 assess, browse, peruse, size up, square, survey, verify 7 confirm, examine, glimpse, inspect, qualify 8 appraise, evaluate, follow up, look into, look over, withdraw 10 correspond
  (out): 5 scope
  pick up the ~: 3 pay 4 fund 5 spend, treat 6 defray 7 finance
  prepare to ~ out: 4 pack
  rain ~: 4 stub 10 invitation
  redeem a ~: 4 cash
  remainder: 4 stub
  send a ~: 3 pay 5 remit
  some ~ payees: 7 bearers
  stamp: 3 NSF 4 paid
  starter: 3 hat, pay 5 cross 7 counter
  the fine print: 4 pore 5 study
  up on: 4 case, quiz 6 verify 7 monitor, oversee 8 overlook 9 supervise
  word on a sample ~: 4 void
  words on a ~: 5 pay to
  write a ~: 4 draw
  write a bad ~: 4 kite 6 bounce
  writer: 5 maker, payer
check __: 3 bit, out 4 line, list, mark, over, rail, stub, up on 5 it out, valve
check __ the mail!, The: 4 is in
__ check: 3 bed, hat 4 bank, body, door, rain, spot 5 blank, sales 6 rubber 7 counter, reality
__-check: 5 cross, spell 6 double
checked: 4 safe 6 pent-up, silent 7 limited 8 reined in
checker: 3 man 5 inlay, piece 9 inspector
  ender: 5 berry, bloom, board 6 blooms
__ checker: 5 spell
Checker: 3 cab, car 4 auto, taxi 10 automobile
  model: 7 Superba 8 Marathon
  operator: 6 cabbie
checkerberry: 5 fruit
Checker, Chubby
  song: The Fly (1961)
    Let's Twist Again (1961)
    Limbo Rock (1962)
    Pony Time (1961)
    Popeye (1962)
    Slow Twistin' (1962)
    The Twist (1960)

checkered: 5 plaid 6 inlaid 9 patchwork, patterned 10 variegated
checkered __: 4 flag, lily, past 6 career
checkers: 4 game
capture, in ~: 4 jump
in Britain: 8 draughts
promote, in ~: 4 king 5 crown
side: 3 red 5 black
__ checkers: 7 Chinese
checking account
detail: 4 stmt. 9 statement
kind of: 5 no-fee
offerer: 4 bank 5 S and L
...checking it __: 5 twice
check-in place: 5 hotel, lobby, motel 7 airport
Check it out!: 4 look 6 lookee, oh look
checkless __: 7 society
checklist: 6 agenda
checkmark: 4 tick
checkmate: 3 win 4 beat, drub 6 defeat 7 conquer, triumph, trounce, victory 8 conquest, vanquish 9 discomfit
checkout
scanner ID: 3 UPC
worker: 6 bagger 7 cashier
checkout __: 7 counter
Checkpoint Charlie site: 6 Berlin
check's in the __!, The: 4 mail
checks off: 3 xes
check the __: 3 oil
checkup: 4 exam 6 review 10 inspection
command: 5 say ah
sound: 2 ah 3 aah
checkups, like some: 6 annual, dental
cheddar: 6 cheese 8 longhorn
like some ~: 4 aged 5 sharp, tangy
relative: 5 colby 7 Chester 8 American, Cheshire 9 Leicester
Cheech: 5 Marin
partner: 5 Chong
cheek: 3 lip 4 gall, jowl, sass 5 brass, mouth, nerve, sauce 6 hubris, hybris 8 audacity, back talk, boldness, chutzpah, rudeness, temerity 9 arrogance, brashness, flippancy, impudence, insolence 10 brazenness, effrontery, impishness
by jowl: 4 near 5 close, dense, thick 6 beside, packed 7 crowded 8 abutting, adjacent, touching 9 congested, jampacked 10 near-at-hand
combining form: 3 mel- 4 melo- 5 bucco-
ender: 4 bone
feature: 6 dimple
insect ~: 5 bucca
makeup: 5 blush
of the ~: 5 jugal, malar 6 buccal
place: 4 face
tongue in ~: 5 in fun 6 in jest 7 as a joke 8 jokingly 9 jestingly, kiddingly
turn the other ~: 7 forgive
with tongue in ~: 5 campy, drily
cheekbone: 5 malar
cheek by __: 4 jowl
__-cheeked: 4 rosy
cheekiness: 5 sauce 9 flippancy 10 effrontery, impishness

Cheek to Cheek: 4 song
composer: Irving Berlin
first word: 6 heaven
musical: 6 Top Hat
cheeky: 4 bold, flip, pert, rude 5 brash, fresh, nervy, sassy, saucy 6 awless, brassy, brazen, daring, snippy 7 aweless, forward, uncivil 8 arrogant, flippant, impolite, impudent, insolent, snippety 9 audacious, bumptious, out of line, shameless 10 irreverent
cheep: 4 call, peep, pipe 5 chirp, tweet 6 squeak, squeal 7 twitter 8 bird call
cheer: 3 joy, rah, yay 4 buoy, glee, hail, lift, root, yell, zest 5 amuse, bravo, elate, exult, huzza, liven, mirth, pep up, shout, whoop 6 buck up, gaiety, gayety, holler, hoorah, hooray, hurrah, hurray, huzzah, perk up, pick up, please, praise, revive, scream, solace, soothe, thrill, uplift 7 acclaim, applaud, comfort, console, delight, elevate, enliven, gladden, gratify, happify, hearten, hurrahs, lighten, rapture, refresh, root for, support, upraise 8 embolden, enspirit, gladness, hilarity, imbolden, inspirit, optimism, reassure 9 amusement, encourage, entertain, happiness, jocundity, merriment, untrouble 10 brighten up, exhilarate, joyousness, jump for joy, regalement, risibility, strengthen
Bronx ~: 4 razz 9 raspberry
ender: 6 leader 7 leading
French ~ word: 4 vive
gave a ~: 5 rahed
give a Bronx ~: 4 jeer, mock 5 sneer, taunt
good ~: 4 glee 7 jollity 8 optimism 9 geniality, happiness
holiday ~: 3 nog 6 eggnog
on: 4 root, urge 7 root for
opera ~: 5 brava, bravo
opposite: 3 boo
rousing ~: 3 yea
Spanish ~ word: 3 olé 4 viva
start: 3 hip, sis 4 viva
up: 4 buoy, perk 5 liven 6 solace 7 comfort, console, enliven, gladden, hearten, inspire, lighten, satisfy 8 brighten, reassure 9 encourage, take heart 10 exhilarate
Yale ~: 5 boola
__ cheer: 4 good 5 Bronx
Cheer
alternative: *see* detergent
cheerful: 3 gay 4 glad, high, nice, rosy, warm 5 happy, jolly, light, merry, peart, perky, riant, sunny 6 blithe, bouncy, breezy, bright, festal, genial, hearty, jaunty, jocund, jovial, joyful, joyous, lively, upbeat 7 beaming, buoyant, chipper, cordial, gleeful, jocular, pleased, radiant, romping, tickled, willing 8 blissful, carefree, ecstatic, euphoric, exultant, giggling, grooving, jubilant, laughing, likeable, mirthful, pleasant, sanguine, thrilled 9 contented, convivial, delighted, exuberant, lightsome, overjoyed, promising, rejoicing, sprightly, vivacious 10 heartening, optimistic, rollicking, unbothered
earful: 4 song, tune 5 music 6 ballad, jingle, number 7 lullaby
name meaning ~: 6 Hilary 7 Hillary
not ~: *see* gloomy
Cheerful Little Earful
composer: Ira Gershwin, Billy Rose, Harry Warren
cheerfully: 6 gladly 7 readily 9 agreeably
cheerfulness: 4 glee 5 mirth 6 gaiety, gayety 8 buoyance, buoyancy, felicity, hilarity, optimism 9 merriment
cheering: 7 acclaim, big hand, ovation 8 exultant, gladsome 9 promising 10 optimistic
loudly: 5 aroar
Cheerio!: 3 bye 4 ciao, ta-ta 5 adieu, adios, see ya, toast 6 so long 7 goodbye 8 farewell
Cheerios: 6 cereal
competitor: *see* cereal
like ~: 4 oaty 5 oaten
cheerleader: 6 rooter
feat: 4 yell 5 split
group: 3 sqd. 5 squad
like a ~: 5 peppy, perky
prop: 3 pom 5 baton 6 pompom, pompon
quality: 3 pep
shout: 3 rah 6 go team
wear: 5 skirt
cheerless: 3 sad 4 blue, dark, down, drab, dull, glum, grim, mopy 5 black, bleak, drear, mirky, mopey, murky, stark, surly, woful 6 broody, dismal, dreary, gloomy, morose, somber, sullen, woeful 7 austere, doleful, forlorn, hangdog, in a funk, joyless, unhappy 8 dejected, desolate, dolorous, downbeat, downcast, lonesome, troubled, wretched 9 bummed out, dejecting, depressed, heartsick, miserable, saddening, sorrowful, unhopeful, woebegone 10 chapfallen, depressing, despondent, dispirited, drearisome, in the dumps, lugubrious, melancholy, oppressive, out of sorts, tenebrific
cheerlessness: 4 pall 5 gloom 7 sadness
cheers
round of ~: 5 salvo
three ~: 5 huzza 6 hoorah, hooray, hurrah, hurray, huzzah
__ cheers!: 5 Three
Cheers (NBC sitcom)
cast: Kirstie Alley (Rebecca Howe)
Nicholas Colasanto (Ernie Pantusso)
Ted Danson (Sam Malone)
Kelsey Grammer (Frasier Crane)
Woody Harrelson (Woody Boyd)
Shelley Long (Diane Chambers)
Bebe Neuwirth (Lilith Sternin)
Rhea Perlman (Carla Tortelli)
John Ratzenberger (Cliff Clavin)
Roger Rees (Robin Colcord)
George Wendt (Norm Peterson)
Norm's occupation: 3 CPA
Norm's wife: 4 Vera

order: 3 ale 4 beer, brew
prop: 5 stein, stool
setting: 3 bar 6 Boston
Cheers!: 5 salud, skoal, toast 6 prosit
cheery: 3 gay 4 glad 5 happy, jolly, light, merry, perky, sunny 6 blithe, elated, genial, hearty, jocund, jovial, joyful, joyous, upbeat 7 buoyant, chipper, festive, gleeful, pleased, radiant, tickled 8 blissful, carefree, ecstatic, euphoric, exultant, jubilant, laughing, mirthful, positive, thrilled 9 delighted, lightsome, overjoyed, rejoicing, sprightly 10 delightful, heartening, unbothered
cheese: 4 bleu, blue, Brie, Edam, feta, Roka 5 banon, brick, colby, dairy, Gouda, Kraft, nacho, Swiss 6 asiago, brynza, chèvre, farmer, Leyden, mysost, Romano, Tilsit 7 cheddar, Chester, chevret, crottin, crowdie, fontina, gervais, Gjetost, Gruyère, Havarti, Limburg, ricotta, sapsago, Stilton 8 American, Beaufort, Beaumont, Bel Paese, bierkäse, Cheshire, Emmental, Liptauer, longhorn, muenster, parmesan, pecorino 9 Camembert, Emmenthal, Jarlsberg, Leicester, Limburger, Port Salut, provolone, Roquefort, Wiltshire 10 caerphilly, Emmentaler, Gorgonzola, mascarpone, mozzarella, Neufchâtel
big ~: 3 CEO, VIP 4 boss, exec, lion, name 5 celeb, chief, mogul, nabob 6 top dog 7 headman, notable 8 kingfish 9 authority, celebrity, commander
coat: 4 rind
combining form: 3 tyr- 4 tyro-
dish: 5 fondu 6 fondue
Dutch: 4 Edam 5 Gouda 6 Leyden
ender: 4 cake 5 cloth 6 burger
factory: 5 dairy
French: 4 Brie 9 Camembert
goat ~: 6 chèvre 7 chevret
improve ~: 3 age
in a mousetrap: 4 bait
it: 3 run 4 flee 5 scram
like ~: 7 caseous
like some ~: 4 aged, mild 5 moldy, sharp
like Swiss ~: 5 holey
lover: 5 mouse
prepare ~: 5 grate
product: 4 whey
Quebec Trappist: 3 oka
say ~: 4 grin, pose 5 smile
source: 4 milk
starter: 4 head
state: 3 Wis. 9 Wisconsin
unit: 4 cube, slab 5 brick, slice, wedge, wheel
cheese __: 3 pie 4 cake, tray 5 steak 6 spread
__ cheese: 3 big, pot, rat 4 bleu, blue, coon, curd, Edam, goat, hard, jack 5 brick, colby, cream, Dutch, store, Swiss 6 farmer, Romano 7 cheddar, clabber, cottage, Gruyère, pimento, process, Stilton
__ cheese!: 3 Say

cheeseburger topping: 5 bacon, onion 6 catsup, tomato 7 ketchup, lettuce
cheesecake: 8 ice cream
alternative: *see* ice cream flavor
cheesecloth: 5 gauze 6 fabric
like ~: 4 wove 5 woven
Cheese Nips
alternative: *see* cracker
cheeseparer: 5 miser 9 skinflint
cheesy: 3 bad 5 cheap 6 flimsy, shlock, shoddy 7 schlock 8 inferior 9 fifth-rate, third-rate 10 fourth-rate, second-rate
snack: 5 nacho
cheetah: 3 cat 5 felid 6 animal, feline, mammal
relative: *see* feline
Cheetah: 3 ape 5 chimp 10 chimpanzee
Cheetos: 4 nosh 5 snack
Cheever, John: 6 writer
work: Bullet Park
The Enormous Radio
Falconer
Oh What a Paradise It Seems
The Wapshot Chronicle
Cheevy, Miniver, like: 4 lean, slim
Cheez ___: 4 Whiz
Cheez-It
alternative: *see* cracker
chef: 4 cook, Kerr 5 baker, Beard, Child 9 cuisinier, Escoffier
attraction: 5 aroma
cry: 4 done
fat strip: 6 lardon 7 lardoon
gadget: 5 corer, dicer, ricer 6 baster, beater, slicer
gravy: 3 jus
herb: 4 sage 5 thyme 7 parsley 8 rosemary
measure: 3 cup, tbs., tsp. 4 tbsp. 8 teaspoon 10 tablespoon
need: 3 pan, pot 4 mitt, oven 5 apron, knife 6 kettle
offerings: 4 menu
pastry ~, at times: 4 icer
phrase: 3 à la 5 au jus
serving: 4 dish 6 entrée
The Sopranos ~: 5 Artie
chef-___: 7 d'oeuvre
___ chef: 6 pastry
Chef ___-Ar-Dee: 3 Boy
___ Chef: 5 Magic
chef de ___: 7 cuisine
chef's ___: 5 salad
Chef's Blend: 7 cat food
alternative: *see* pet food brand
Che gelida manina: 4 aria
CHEKA successor: 4 OGPU
Chekhov, Anton: 6 writer 7 Russian 10 playwright
character: 4 Olga 5 Irina, Masha
work: The Cherry Orchard
Ivanov
The Seagull
Three Sisters
Uncle Vanya
Chelsea: 4 city, town 5 Field 7 Clinton
locale: 4 Mass.
chem.: 3 sci. 4 subj.
compound: 3 alc.
reaction product: 3 ppt.
weak, in ~: 3 dil.
see also chemical, chemistry
___ chem.: 4 phys.
chemical
abbreviation: 3 alc., mol., ppt.
banned ~: 3 DDT, PCB 4 Alar
compound: 4 enol 5 amide, amine, diene, ester, imide, imine, niter, oxide 8 diolefin
concentration: 5 titer
container: 3 vat
corrosive ~: 3 lye 4 acid
dye: 3 azo 6 litmus
extract: 5 educt
prefix: 3 iso-, oxa-, oxo-, oxy- 4 nitr- 5 pheno-
radical: 4 acyl 5 allyl
reaction: 5 redox 9 oxidation, reduction
starter: 3 bio 5 petro
suffix: 3 -ane, -ase, -ate, -ene, -ide, -ine, -ite, -nol, -ose, -yne 4 -olic 5 -phane
undergo ~ change: 5 react
chemical ___: 4 bond, pulp 5 toner
___ Chemical: 3 Dow
chemin de fer: 4 game 8 card game
exclamation: 5 banco
chemise: 4 slip 5 dress, shift, shirt
British ~: 4 sark
chemist: 4 Berg, Davy, Hahn, Kuhn, Todd, Urey 5 Black, Boyle, Curie, Dewar, Libby, Nobel, Soddy 6 Bunsen, Dalton, Müller, Nernst, Perkin, Perrin, Ramsay, Remsen, Solvay 7 Crookes, Hodgkin, Pasteur, Pauling, Scheele 8 Avogadro, pharmacy, Sorensen 9 Arrhenius, Berthelot, Berzelius, Cavendish, Gay-Lussac, Lavoisier, Mendeleev, Priestley 10 pharmacist
Belgian: 6 Solvay
British: 4 Davy 5 Black, Boyle, Soddy 6 Dalton, Perkin, Ramsay 7 Crookes, Hodgkin 9 Cavendish, Priestley
Danish: 8 Sorensen
deg.: 3 BCS, Sc.B.
French: 5 Curie 6 Perrin 7 Pasteur 9 Berthelot, Gay-Lussac, Lavoisier
German: 4 Hahn, Kuhn 6 Bunsen, Müller, Nernst
in America: 10 pharmacist
Italian: 8 Avogadro
Polish: 5 Curie
Russian: 9 Mendeleev
Scottish: 4 Todd 5 Dewar
Swedish: 5 Nobel 7 Scheele 9 Arrhenius, Berzelius
vessel: 4 etna 5 flask, pipet 6 beaker, carboy 7 pipette
chemistry: 7 science 10 attraction
abbreviation: 3 mol., ppm 5 mol. wt.
class cost: 6 lab fee
room: 3 lab
starter: 3 bio 5 petro
___ chemistry: 5 laser, legal 7 colloid, organic, quantum
Chen: 4 Joan 5 Julie
Cheney: 4 Dick, veep
predecessor: 4 Gore
successor: 5 Biden
Chengchow
province: 5 Honan
chenille: 6 fabric 8 material
Chenin Blanc: 3 vin 4 wine 5 grape
relative: *see* wine
Chennault: 6 Claire
Chen Ning ___: 4 Yang
cheongsam: 5 dress
Cheops
son: 6 Khafre
___ che penso: 3 Piu
___ cher: 3 mon
Cher: 5 river 6 singer 7 actress
film: Mask (1985)
Mermaids (1990)
Moonstruck (1987, AA)
Silkwood (1983)
Suspect (1987)
The Witches of Eastwick (1987)
locale: 6 France
song: After All (1989)
Bang Bang (1966)
Believe (1999)
Dark Lady (1974)
Gypsys, Tramps & Thieves (1971)
If I Could Turn Back Time (1989)
I Found Someone (1988)
Just Like Jesse James (1989)
Take Me Home (1979)
The Way of Love (1972)
You Better Sit Down Kids (1967)
spouse: Gregg Allman, Sonny Bono
Cherbourg: 4 city, port, town
locale: 6 France
cherchez la ___: 5 femme
chéri
see sweetheart
Cheri: 5 Oteri
Chéri
author: Colette
chérie
see sweetheart
Cherie: 7 Johnson
cherish: 4 like, love 5 adore, go for, prize, savor, value 6 admire, dote on, ensoul, esteem, insoul, revere 7 care for, cling to, idolize, worship 8 dote upon, enshrine, hold dear, inshrine, treasure, venerate 9 care about, reverence 10 appreciate
Cherish (song)
artist: Association, The, David Cassidy, Kool and the Gang, Madonna
cherished: 3 pet 4 dear 5 sweet 6 sacred 7 beloved, darling, welcome 8 precious, valuable 9 priceless
make ~: 6 endear
one: 7 darling 10 sweetheart
Chernenko: 10 Konstantin
Chernobyl: 4 city
city near: 4 Kiev
locale: 3 Ukr. 7 Ukraine
Cherokee: 3 SUV 4 Jeep 5 tribe 6 Indian 7 Amerind 8 language
see also Indian
Cherokee ___: 4 rose 5 Strip
cheroot: 5 cigar, smoke 6 stogie
cherries
like ~ jubilee: 6 flambé
prepare ~: 4 stem
cherries jubilee: 7 dessert
ingredient: 8 ice cream
cherry: 3 red 4 Bing, tree, wood 5 color, drupe, fruit 7 marasca, morello, oxheart 10 maraschino
brandy: 6 kirsch
ender: 5 stone
ground ~: 9 tomatillo
leftover: 3 pit 4 stem 5 stone
picker part: 4 boom
relative: 4 pear, plum, rose, ruby, rust, sloe, wine 5 apple, brick, coral, grape, peach, poppy, rusty, sandy 6 almond, cerise, claret, damson, garnet, maroon, medlar, quince 7 apricot, carmine, crimson, fuchsia, magenta, pimento, scarlet, sultana, vermeil 8 amaranth, cardinal, dubonnet, geranium, hawthorn, oiticica, rubicund 9 carnation, cranberry, greengage, myrobalan, vermilion 10 blackthorn, strawberry
starter: 5 choke
where a ~ may go: 5 on top
cherry ___: 3 pie, red 4 bomb, coal, cola, plum, soda 6 picker, tomato
cherry-___: 3 bob 4 pick
___ cherry: 3 pin 4 Bing, bird, fire, sand, sour, wild 5 black, dwarf, heart, sweet
Cherry: 3 Don 5 Neneh 8 Eagle-Eye
Cherry Bomb (1987 song)
artist: John Cougar Mellencamp
Cherry, Cherry (1966 song)
artist: Neil Diamond
Cherry, Don
song: Band of Gold (1955)
Cherry Hill: 4 city, town
locale: 9 New Jersey
Cherry, Neneh
song: Buffalo Stance (1989)
Kisses on the Wind (1989)
Cherry Orchard, The: 4 play
author: Anton Chekhov
character: 4 Anya, Gaev 5 Boris, Fiers, Varya, Yasha 6 Leonid, Simeon 7 Ivanova
Cherry Pink and Apple Blossom White (1955 song)
artist: Perez Prado
cherrystone: 3 pit 4 clam
cherry vanilla: 8 ice cream
alternative: *see* ice cream flavor
cherub: 4 Amor, baby, Eros 5 angel, child, Cupid, putto 6 moppet 8 amoretto, innocent
Valentine's Day ~: 4 Amor, Eros 5 Cupid
cherubic: 7 angelic 9 angelical
Cherubini: 5 Luigi
chervil: 4 herb
Cheryl: 4 Ladd, Lynn 5 Hines, Tiegs 6 Miller 9 Holdridge
Chesapeake: 3 bay 4 city, town
author: James A. Michener
locale: 8 Virginia
Chesapeake and ___: 4 Ohio
Chesapeake Bay
bird: 4 tern
ketch: 6 bugeye
river to ~: 7 Potomac
Chesebrough-Pond
product: 4 Q-tip
Cheshire: 6 cheese, county
city: 5 Crewe 6 Widnes
locale: 7 Britain, England
Cheshire ___: 3 cat 6 cheese
Cheshire cat
expression: 4 grin
chess: 4 game 9 board game
action: 4 move 6 castle, gambit
call: 4 mate 5 check 9 checkmate, stalemate

choice: 5 black, white
coup: 4 fork, mate
device: 5 timer
ender: 3 man, men 5 board
Estonian ~ master: 3 Nei
Japanese ~: 5 shogi
piece: 3 man 4 king, pawn, rook 5 horse, queen 6 bishop, castle, knight
queenside castle, in ~ notation: 3 OOO
chess __: 3 set 5 clock
__ chess: 5 blitz, speed
chess champions (world):
2007- Viswanathan Anand (India)
2000-2006 Vladimir Kramnik (Russia)
1985-2000 Garry Kasparov (Russia)
1975-1985 Anatoly Karpov (Russia)
1972-1975 Bobby Fischer (USA)
1969-1972 Boris Spassky (Russia)
1963-1969 Tigran Petrosian (Russia)
1961-1963 Mikhail Botvinnik (Russia)
1960-1961 Mikhail Tal (Russia)
1958-1960 Mikhail Botvinnik (Russia)
1957-1958 Vasily Smyslov (Russia)
1948-1957 Mikhail Botvinnik (Russia)
1937-1946 Alexander Alekhine (Russia)
1935-1937 Max Euwe (Netherlands)
1927-1935 Alexander Alekhine (Russia)
1921-1927 José Capablanca (Cuba)
1894-1921 Emanuel Lasker (Germany)
1886-1894 William Steinitz (Bohemia)
chessman: 4 king, pawn, rook 5 piece, queen 6 bishop, castle
Chessman, Caryl
portrayer: Alan Alda
Chess Players, The
artist: Thomas Eakins
chest: 3 box 4 case 5 bosom, hutch, trunk 6 breast, bunker, bureau, coffer, cooler, locker, lowboy, thorax 7 cabinet, commode, dresser 8 moneybox 9 container, furniture, strongbox 10 chiffonier
combining form: 6 stetho-, thorac- 7 thoraci-, thoraco-
covering: 3 bib 4 vest 5 shirt
ender: 3 nut
get off one's ~: 3 say 4 tell 5 spill 6 relate, unload 7 confess, confide, recount, tell all, unbosom 8 unburden
material: 5 cedar
muscle: 3 pec
part: 4 knob 6 drawer
pounder: 3 ape 7 gorilla
protector: 3 bib
rattle: 4 rale
sacred ~: 3 ark 4 cist
Spanish Main ~: 4 arca
war ~: 4 fund 6 coffer 8 treasury 9 exchequer
__ chest: 3 ice, sea, war 4 hope 5 cedar
__-chested: 4 deep 6 barrel
Chester: 4 town 5 Gould, Himes 6 Arthur, cheese, Morris, Nimitz 7 Carlson, Conklin
locale: 4 Penn.
chesterfield: 4 coat, sofa 5 couch
__ Chester French: 6 Daniel
Chesterton, G.K.: 6 writer 7 British
friend: Belloc
Chester White: 3 hog, pig 5 swine
home: 3 pen, sty
chestnut: 3 bay, nut, red 4 roan, tale, tree 5 brown, color, horse 6 cliché, equine 7 reddish 9 platitude
horse ~: 6 conker
hull: 3 bur
old ~: 3 saw 5 adage
Polynesian ~: 4 rata
prepare ~s: 5 roast
relative: *see* brown color
water ~: 5 tuber
__ chestnut: 5 horse, water
Chestnut Hill athletes: 6 Eagles
Chestnuts roasting __...: 4 on an
chest of __: 7 drawers
chest protector wearer: 3 ump 6 umpire 7 catcher
chest-thumping: 5 macho
do some ~: 4 brag 5 boast, vaunt
chesty: 5 proud 9 conceited
Chet: 5 Baker 6 Atkins 7 Huntley
cheth: 6 Hebrew, letter
predecessor: 5 zayin
successor: 3 tet 4 teth
__ cheval: 5 pas de
cheval glass: 6 mirror
Chevalier, Maurice: 5 actor
film: Can-Can (1960)
Fanny (1961)
Gigi (1958)
chevet: 4 apse
Cheviot: 3 ewe, ram 4 lamb 5 sheep 6 fabric 8 material
home: 3 pen 4 cote
chèvre: 6 cheese
chevret: 6 cheese
Chevrolet: 3 car 4 auto 5 Louis 10 automobile
model: 3 Geo, HHR 4 Aveo, Nova, Vega 5 Astro, Cobra, Monza, Nomad, Tahoe, 'Vette 6 Belair, Blazer, Camaro, Cobalt, Delray, Impala, Kodiak, Laguna, Lumina, Malibu, Yeoman 7 Beretta, Caprice, Corsica, Corvair, Equinox, Express, Tracker, Venture 8 Biscayne, Cavalier, Chevelle, Citation, Colorado, Concours, Corvette, Parkwood, Sting Ray, Suburban, Townsman, Traverse 9 Avalanche, Brookwood, Celebrity, Kingswood, Silverado 10 Greenbrier, Monte Carlo 11 Trailblazer
rival: *see* automobile
chevron: 5 badge 8 insignia
shape: 3 vee
three ~ wearer: 3 NCO
Chevron: 3 gas 8 gasoline
rival: 4 Arco 5 Amoco, Exxon
Chevy
see Chevrolet
Chevy Blazer: 3 SUV
Chevy Chase: 4 city, town
locale: 8 Maryland
chew: 3 eat 4 gnaw 5 chomp, graze, grind, munch, taste 6 crunch, nibble 9 masticate
cattle ~: 3 cud
hard to ~: 5 tough
on: 3 eat 6 ponder 7 reflect 9 masticate
out: 3 rag 4 flay, lash, rail, whip 5 abuse, scold 6 berate, rebuke 7 tell off, upbraid 8 chastise, harangue 9 castigate, reprehend, reprimand 10 vituperate
over: 4 mull, muse 8 consider, ruminate 9 speculate 10 deliberate
(over): 5 think
something to ~ on: 3 gum
the fat: 3 gab, jaw, rap, yak, yap 4 chat, talk 5 prate, speak 6 gossip, jabber, parley, patter 7 blabber, blather, chatter, prattle 8 chitchat, converse, schmooze 10 yakkety-yak
the scenery: 5 emote
chew __: 3 out
__ chew: 3 dog
Chewa home: 6 Africa, Malawi, Zambia 10 Mozambique
Chewbacca: 7 Wookiee
ally: 7 Han Solo
chewer, scenery: 3 ham 6 emoter
chewing gum: 5 Extra, Orbit 7 Dentyne, Trident 8 Carefree, Chiclets, Freedent 10 Doublemint, Juicy Fruit
base: 6 chicle
like some ~ gums: 5 minty
chewing-out: 6 rebuke 8 reproval 10 upbraiding
chew the __: 3 cud, fat, rag
chewy: 5 tough 7 crunchy
candy: 4 Rolo 5 taffy, toffy 6 toffee 7 caramel
__ Chex: 3 Oat 4 Corn, Rice 5 Wheat
Cheyenne: 4 city, town 5 oater, river, tribe 6 Indian 7 Amerind 8 language
county: 7 Laramie
home: 4 tipi 5 tepee 6 teepee
locale: 3 Wyo. 7 Wyoming
show: 5 rodeo
Cheyenne (ABC western)
cast: Clint Walker (Cheyenne Bodie)
chi: 5 Greek 6 letter
follower: 3 psi
preceder: 3 phi
chi-__ test: 6 square 7 squared
__ chi: 3 tai
Chi: 7 McBride 8 Coltrane
Chi-__: 3 Rho 5 Lites
__ Chi: 5 Sigma
chia: 5 plant
Chiang: 7 Kai-shek
adversary: 3 Mao
Chianti: 3 red 4 vino, wine
container: 6 carafe
origin: 5 Italy
Chiapa: 4 city, town
locale: 6 Mexico
chic: 3 hip, mod, now 4 mode, posh 5 class, faddy, fancy, flair, haute, natty, nifty, ritzy, sharp, smart, swank, swell, vogue 6 bon ton, classy, dapper, dressy, flossy, modish, rakish, snappy, trendy, urbane, with it 7 à la mode, current, dashing, elegant, fashion, in vogue, popular, stylish, voguish 8 up-to-date 9 fanciness, gussied up, high-class, high-toned, in fashion, nattiness 10 dapperness, dressiness, modishness, refinement, swankiness
not ~: 3 out 5 dowdy, passé 6 frumpy
__ chic: 4 trés 7 radical
Chic: 5 Young 7 Johnson
Chicago: 4 city, port, town
airport: 5 O'Hare 6 Midway
area: 4 Loop
athletes: 8 Ramblers 10 Blue Demons
city near ~: 4 Gary 5 Elgin, Niles 6 Cicero, Joliet
county: 4 Cook
Cub: 4 NLer
exchange, for short: 4 Merc
Fire starter: 3 cow
hrs.: 3 CDT, CST
like ~: 5 windy
Lincoln Park: 3 zoo
lines: 3 Els
locale: 3 Ill. 8 Illinois
newspaper: 4 Trib 7 Tribune 8 Sun-Times
opera company: 5 Lyric
planetarium: 5 Adler
pro team: 3 Sox 4 Cubs 5 Bears, Bulls 8 White Sox 10 Blackhawks
school: 6 DePaul, Loyola
superstation: 3 WGN
TV show: 5 Oprah
Chicago (2002 film)
cast: Richard Gere, Queen Latifah, Renée Zellweger, Catherine Zeta-Jones
character: 4 Hart 5 Roxie, Velma
composer: Fred Ebb, John Kander
Chicago (rock group)
member: Cetera, Kath, Lamm, Loughnane, Pankow, Parazaider, Seraphine
song: Baby, What a Big Surprise (1977)
Beginnings (1971)
Call on Me (1974)
Feelin' Stronger Every Day (1973)
Hard Habit to Break (1984)
Hard to Say I'm Sorry (1982)
If You Leave Me Now (1976)
Just You 'N' Me (1973)
Look Away (1988)
Make Me Smile (1970)
Old Days (1975)
Saturday in the Park (1972)
Searchin' So Long (1974)
Wishing You Were Here (1974)
You're Not Alone (1989)
You're the Inspiration (1984)
Chicago __: 4 Fire, Hope 5 Seven
Chicago __ of Trade: 5 Board
Chicago __ Sox: 5 White
__ Chicago: 5 In Old
Chicago Hope (CBS drama)
cast: Adam Arkin (Dr. Aaron Shutt)
Peter Berg (Dr. Billy Kronk)
Hector Elizondo (Dr. Phillip Watters)

Mark Harmon (Dr. Jack McNeil)
Roxanne Hart (Camille Shutt)
Christine Lahti (Dr. Kathryn Austin)
Mandy Patinkin (Dr. Jeffrey Geiger)
extra: 2 RN 3 EMT
__ Chicago, IN: 4 East
Chicago Poems
author: Carl Sandburg
Chicana: 6 Latina
chicane: 3 con 4 dupe, fool, hoax, ruse, wile 5 fraud 9 deception
chicanery: 3 con 4 ploy, ruse, wile 5 dodge, feint, fraud, guile, wiles 6 deceit, dupery 7 knavery, quibble 8 artifice, intrigue, jugglery, trickery 9 casuistry, deception, dirty work, duplicity, fourberie, sophistry, stratagem 10 dishonesty, hanky-panky, hocus-pocus, subterfuge
Chicano neighborhood: 6 barrio
Chichén Itzá: 4 city 5 ruins
investigator: 12 archeologist
native: 4 Maya 5 Mayan
Chichester Psalms
composer: Leonard Bernstein
chichi: 2 in 3 hip, mod 4 arty, posh, tony 5 artsy, fancy, haute, ritzy, showy, swank, toney 6 dapper, frilly, modish, ornate, swanky, trendy 7 à la mode, current, elegant, in style, popular, stylish, voguish 8 affected, mannered 9 gussied up, in fashion 10 all the rage
__ chi ch'uan: 3 tai
chick: 4 bird 9 fledgling, hatchling
ender: 3 pea 4 weed
future ~: 3 egg
group: 5 brood
home: 4 coop, farm, nest 8 henhouse
like a ~: 5 downy, fuzzy
mother: 3 hen
starter: 3 dab
talk: 4 peep 5 cheep
Chick: 4 Webb 5 Corea, Hafey, Hearn
Chick-__: 5 A-Boom
chickadee: 4 bird
Chickadee, W.C. Fields': 3 Mae
Chickamauga: 6 battle
locale: 7 Georgia
chickaree: 6 animal, mammal, rodent 8 squirrel
morsel: 5 acorn
relative: *see* rodent
Chickasaw: 5 tribe 6 Indian 7 Amerind
chicken: 4 bird, cock, fowl, meat, wimp 5 biddy, biped, capon, sissy, timid 6 afraid, Ancona, bantam, Brahma, coward, craven, gun-shy, Houdan, pullet, scared, Sussex, trepid, yellow 7 alarmed, anxious, Cornish, dastard, daunted, Dorking, fearful, Leghorn, nervous, panicky, poultry, quitter, rooster, spooked, wimpish 8 Araucana, cowardly, fearsome, hesitant, Langshan, poltroon, recreant, Shanghai, timorous, weakling 9 Dominique, fraidy cat, jellyfish, Orpington, petrified, terrified, Wyandotte 10 frightened, scaredy-cat
and rice: 4 soup
appetizer: 8 drumette
Asian ~: 6 cochin
clean a ~: 5 dress
cooking ~: 5 capon, frier, fryer 7 roaster
eat like a ~: 4 peck
ender: 3 pox
feed: 4 mash 6 change 8 pittance
female: 3 hen
follower: 3 pox
group: 6 clutch
home: 4 coop, farm 8 henhouse
lack: 5 nerve 7 courage
little ~: 6 bantam
male: 7 rooster
noodle: 4 soup
out: 4 quit 5 panic, quail 7 abandon 9 run scared
(out): 4 wimp
part: 3 leg 4 neck, wing 5 thigh 6 breast
salad ingredient: 4 mayo
seat: 5 roost
spring ~: 5 youth 9 youngster
to a chicken hawk: 4 prey
wire: 4 mesh
young: 6 pullet
chicken __: 3 out, pox, run 4 coop, feed, hawk, Kiev, roll, soup, wire 5 liver 6 breast, switch, turtle 7 colonel
chicken __ king: 3 à la
chicken __ soup: 6 noodle
chicken-__: 3 fry 5 or-egg 6 and-egg 7 hearted, livered
chicken-__ steak: 5 fried
__ chicken: 4 city, mock 5 Digby 6 spring 7 prairie
Chicken __: 6 Little
Chicken __ Sea: 5 of the
chicken-and-__: 3 egg
__-chicken circuit: 6 rubber
chicken-hearted: 4 weak 5 timid 6 craven 8 cowardly
chicken in __ pot: 5 every
Chicken of the Sea: 4 tuna
alternative: 8 Star Kist 9 Bumble Bee
chicken-or-__: 3 egg
chickenpox: 9 varicella
cause: 5 virus
symptom: 4 itch 5 fever
Chick-fil-A
rival: *see* restaurant chain
chickpea: 4 gram 6 legume, veggie 9 vegetable
dip: 6 hommos, hummus
__ Chicks: 5 Dixie
chicle
product: 3 gum
source: 5 latex
Chiclets: 3 gum
alternative: *see* chewing gum
Chico: 4 city, Marx, town
brother: 5 Gummo, Harpo, Zeppo 7 Groucho
locale: 10 California
Chico and the Man (NBC sitcom)
cast: Jack Albertson (Ed Brown)
Scatman Crothers (Louie)
Freddie Prinze (Chico Rodriguez)
setting: 6 East L.A.
Chicopee: 4 city, town
locale: 4 Mass.
chicory: 4 herb
relative: 6 endive
Chicoutimi: 4 city, town
locale: 6 Canada, Québec
chide: 3 nag, rag 4 rate 5 blame, scold 6 berate, rebuff, rebuke 7 censure, condemn, lecture, reprove, tell off, upbraid 8 admonish, reproach 9 castigate, criticize, lash out at, reprehend, reprimand
chider: 5 scold, shrew 6 parent 9 henpecker, termagant
chief: 3 key, ldr., top 4 arch, boss, head, jefe, king, main, star 5 first, grand, major, nawab, prime, ruler 6 bigwig, gerent, honcho, leader, master, ruling, sachem, staple, top cat, utmost 7 captain, central, crucial, headman, highest, leading, manager, officer, premier, primary, special, supreme, viceroy 8 big wheel, cardinal, champion, deciding, director, dominant, foremost, governor, headmost, higher-up, kingfish, overseer, superior, top brass 9 big cheese, commander, essential, executive, number one, organizer, paramount, president, principal, prominent, sovereign, uppermost 10 overriding, preeminent, supervisor
crew: 5 staff 9 personnel
executive: 4 pres., prez 5 prexy 8 director 9 president
prefix: 4 arch-
suffix: 4 -arch
chief __: 4 mate 7 justice
chief __ officer: 5 petty 7 warrant
__ chief: 3 den 4 crew, fire
Chief: 6 Bender 7 gridder 10 footballer
Chief __ George: 3 Dan
chief executive __: 7 officer
chiefly: 6 mainly, mostly 7 at large, largely 8 above all 9 generally, primarily 10 especially
chief of __: 5 staff, state
Chief of __ Operations: 5 Naval
Chiefs: 6 eleven
home: 10 Kansas City
org.: 3 AFC
rival: *see* NFL team
sport: 8 football
__ Chiefs of Staff: 5 Joint
chieftain: 4 amir, emir, head 5 ameer, emeer, ruler 6 gerent, leader, master 8 superior
chiffon: 3 pie 5 filmy, gauze, ninon, sheer, voile 6 fabric, flimsy 10 diaphanous
like ~: 5 gauzy, sheer 6 clingy
chiffonier: 5 chest 6 bureau 7 dresser 8 wardrobe
Chiffons
song: He's So Fine (1963)
One Fine Day (1963)
Sweet Talkin' Guy (1966)
chigger: 3 bug 6 insect
chignon: 3 bun 4 coif, knot 6 hairdo 7 upsweep 8 coiffure
chigoe: 3 bug 4 flea 6 insect
genus: 5 tunga
Chihuahua: 3 dog 4 city, town 5 canid, pooch, state 6 canine 7 Mexican
city: 6 Juárez, Madera, Meoqui 7 Anáhuac, Camargo, Hidalgo, Jiménez, Ojinaga
like a ~: 4 tiny 5 small
toon ~: 3 Ren
see also Spanish
Chilcat: 6 Indian 7 Amerind
child: 3 boy, imp, kid, lad, son, tad, tot 4 babe, baby, brat, cion, girl, mite, teen, tike, tyke, ward 5 bairn, human, kiddy, minor, scion, youth 6 cherub, infant, kiddie, laddie, moppet, nipper, person, squirt 7 bambino, kinsman, neonate, newborn, preteen, sapling, toddler 8 daughter, half-pint, juvenile, nonvoter, small fry, teenager 9 offspring, stripling, youngster 10 adolescent, descendant, individual
adopted ~: 4 ward
annoying ~: 3 imp 4 brat
bearer: 6 mother
chant: 5 me too
combining form: 3 ped- 4 paed-, paid-, pedo- 5 paedo-, paido-, tecno-
cry: 3 mom 4 mama 5 mamma, mommy
ender: 3 bed, ish 4 care, like 5 birth, proof 7 bearing
female ~: 4 girl 8 daughter
flower ~: 5 hippy 6 hippie 8 bohemian, longhair
forsaken ~: 4 waif 6 orphan 9 foundling
foster ~: 7 adoptee
game: 3 tag, war 5 jacks, potsy 6 go fish 7 old maid 9 hopscotch
getaway: 4 camp
inner ~: 6 psyche
in Spanish: 4 niña, niño
male ~: 3 boy, son
marker: 6 crayon
not a ~: 5 adult, grown, of age
play a ~ game: 4 hide
protest: 5 not me
question: 3 why
reading program: 3 RIF
ride: 4 pony 5 trike 7 scooter 8 tricycle
sibling's ~: 5 niece 6 nephew
song finish: 3 XYZ
song starter: 3 ABC
sponsored ~: 6 godson 11 goddaughter
starter: 3 god 4 moon, step 5 brain, grand 6 school
toy: 3 top 4 ball 5 Legos 6 blocks
treat like a ~: 9 patronize
warning: 6 behave, be nice
watch a ~: 7 baby-sit
with ~: 6 gravid 8 enceinte, pregnant 9 expecting
child __: 4 wife 5 bride, labor 7 support, welfare
child-__: 4 care 5 proof
__ child: 3 lap 4 with 5 brain, inner 6 flower, foster, poster, wonder
__-child: 3 man
Child: 4 Jane 5 Julia, Lydia
__ Child: 3 O-o-h 4 Love
childbirth: 8 delivery
method: 6 Lamaze 7 natural
Childe: 6 Hassam
Childe Harold's Pilgrimage
author: Lord Byron
childhood: 4 teen 5 youth 6 cradle 7 infancy, puberty 8 minority 9 juniority 10 immaturity, juvenility, schooldays

malady: 5 colic, croup, mumps 6 otitis 7 measles 10 chickenpox
second ~: 6 dotage
__ childhood: 6 second
Childhood's End
author: Arthur C. Clarke
__ Child in the City: 3 Hot
childish: 5 silly, young 6 boyish, infant, jejune, simple, unwise 7 kiddish, peevish, puerile 8 immature, juvenile, youthful 9 frivolous, infantile
demand: 5 gimme, I want
retort: 4 am so, is so 5 am too, are so
Child, Julia: 4 chef
cuisine: 6 French
portrayer: Meryl Streep
childlike: 4 naif 5 naive, young 6 simple, tender 7 artless, kiddish, natural, puerile 8 immature, innocent, juvenile, lamblike, trustful, trusting, unartful, youthful 9 credulous, guileless, ingenuous, primitive, unfeigned 10 unaffected
Child of Fire
author: Scott O'Dell
Child of the Morning
author: Clare Boothe Luce
children: 4 kids 5 brood, heirs, issue 7 kinfolk, progeny 8 kinfolks, kinsfolk 9 offspring, posterity
combining form: 5 proli-
of ~: 6 filial
starter: 3 god 4 moon, step 6 school
what ~ should be: 4 seen
__ Children: 5 All My
Children of a Lesser God (1986 film)
cast: William Hurt, Marlee Matlin
character: 4 Edna, Orin 5 Lydia, Sarah
director: Randa Haines
Children of Paradise (1945 film)
director: Marcel Carné
Children of Sanchez
author: Oscar Lewis
Children of the Albatross
author: Anaïs Nin
Children of the Night (1990 song)
artist: Richard Marx
Children of the Poor, The
author: Jacob Riis
children's __: 4 menu
Children's Hour, The
author: Lillian Hellman, Henry Wadsworth Longfellow
character: 4 Lois 6 Amelia 7 Rosalie
Childress, Alice: 6 writer
Childress, Alvin
role: 4 Amos
Childs: 7 Lucinda, Marquis
Child's Christmas in Wales, A
poet: Dylan Thomas
Child's Garden of Verses, A
author: Robert Louis Stevenson
child's play: 4 easy, snap 5 cinch, cushy 6 facile, picnic, simple 7 no sweat 8 duck soup, painless, pushover 10 effortless, elementary, unexacting
Child's play!: 5 a snap
Child's Play (1988 film)
cast: Catherine Hicks, Chris Sarandon
chile __: 7 relleno
chile __ carne: 3 con
Chile: 6 nation 7 country
airline: 3 LAN
capital: 8 Santiago
city: 5 Arica, Talca 6 Calama, Curicó, Osorno, Temuco 7 Chillán, Iquique, Quilpué 8 Coquimbo, La Serena, Rancagua, Santiago, Valdivia 10 Concepción, Puente Alto, Talcahuano, Valparaíso, Viña del Mar
desert: 7 Atacama
export: 5 niter
from ~: 6 Andean
fruit: 5 maqui
gulf: 5 Penas
Indian: 10 Araucanian
island: 6 Easter
lake: 4 Laja
language: 7 Spanish
money: 4 peso 6 condor, escudo
mountain: 4 Toro 5 Pular 6 Bonete, Juncal 7 San Juan 8 El Muerto, Tortolas 9 Incahuasi, Marmolejo, Tupungato 10 Mercedario, Parinacota, Tres Cruces
neighbor: 4 Peru 7 Bolivia 9 Argentina
Nobelist in Literature: 6 Neruda 7 Mistral
org.: 3 OAS
pianist: 5 Arrau
poet: 5 Parra 6 Neruda 7 Mistral
port: 5 Arica 10 Valparaiso
range: 5 Andes
river: 6 Bíobío
shrub: 5 maqui
tree: 5 boldo, maqui 6 alerce, mayten
volcano: 6 Láscar
writer: 5 Rojas 6 Bombal, Donoso 7 Allende, Barrios, Dorfman, Edwards 9 Blest Gana
Chilean: 5 Latin
chile con __: 5 carne
Chiles: 4 Lois 6 Lawton
chili: 6 pepper 9 condiment
bean: 5 pinto 6 kidney
dip: 5 salsa
ender: 6 burger
ingredient: 4 bean, meat 5 carne 6 onions
pepper: 3 aji 5 spice
powder herb: 5 cumin
sauce: 5 salsa 6 relish 9 condiment
server: 5 ladle
chili __: 3 dog, oil 4 bean 5 sauce, verde 6 pepper, powder
chili __ carne: 3 con
__ chili: 7 five-way
Chili: 5 Davis
Chili's
rival: *see* restaurant chain
Chi-Lites
song: Have You Seen Her (1971) Oh Girl (1972)
Chilkat: 6 Indian 7 Amerind
chill: 3 ice, icy, nip, raw 4 ague, bite, cold, cool, idle, laze, loll 5 alarm, deter, gelid, nippy, polar, relax, stony 6 arctic, biting, dampen, dismay, freeze, frigid, frosty, frozen, murder, slight, stoney, wintry 7 glacial, horrify, hostile, ice-cold, iciness, numbing, petrify, rawness, shivery, stiffen, terrify, unnerve, wintery 8 calm down, coldness, cool down, coolness, freezing, frighten, gelidity 9 aloofness, crispness, frigidity 10 discourage, intimidate, take it easy, unfriendly
again: 5 reice
out: 5 relax 6 cool it
put the ~ on: 4 snub
Chill: 5 Wills
chilled: 4 cold, cool 5 on ice, stiff 6 frappé, frigid, frosty, frozen 7 ice-cold 8 freezing
chiller-__: 6 diller
__ chill factor: 4 wind
Chillicothe: 4 city, town
locale: 4 Ohio
chilling: 3 icy 4 eery 5 eerie, on ice, scary 9 frightful, harrowing
out: 6 at rest
chills and fever: 4 ague
__ Chill, The: 3 Big
chilly: 3 icy, raw 4 cold, cool, dank, mean 5 algid, aloof, brisk, crisp, fresh, gelid, nasty, nippy, polar, stony, surly 6 arctic, biting, drafty, frigid, frosty, frozen, ornery, remote, stoney, wintry 7 glacial, hateful, hostile, numbing, shivery, wintery 8 contrary, freezing, hibernal, inimical, lukewarm, spiteful 9 bellicose, malicious, withdrawn 10 malevolent, pugnacious, unfriendly
comment: 3 brr
in a ~ fashion: 5 icily
Chilly Scenes of Winter
author: Ann Beattie
Chimborazo: 4 peak 5 mount 8 mountain
locale: 5 Andes 7 Ecuador
chime: 4 bell, bong, brim, gong, peal, ring, toll, tone 5 agree, clang 6 tinkle 8 ding-dong, doorbell 9 harmonize
in: 4 talk 5 agree, state, utter 6 jump in, meddle 8 throw out 9 interrupt
(in): 4 join
with: 6 belong
chimera: 5 dream, fancy 6 fantom 7 fantasy, figment, monster, phantom 8 delusion, illusion 9 pipe dream
Chimera
author: John Barth
chimerical: 5 ideal 6 dreamy, irreal, unreal 7 fatuous 8 delusive, fanciful, illusive, illusory, quixotic 9 fantastic, imaginary 10 fictitious, groundless, quixotical
chimes: 7 bonnang 8 carillon 10 instrument, percussion
like some ~: 6 hourly
__ chimes: 4 wind
chimney: 3 lum 4 flue, vent 5 stack
clean a ~: 5 sweep
coating: 4 soot
emission: 5 plume
like a ~: 5 sooty
nester: 3 daw 5 stork
part: 4 flue 6 ashpit
shelf: 3 hob
chimney __: 5 sweep, swift
chimp: 3 ape 5 biped, Bonzo, jocko 6 animal, mammal 7 Cheetah, primate
food: 6 banana
home: 3 zoo 6 Africa
like a ~: 5 apish
little ~: 6 apelet
NASA ~: 4 Enos
relative: *see* primate
chin: 3 gab, jaw, rap, yak 4 chat 5 utter 6 gossip, yammer 10 yackety-yak
combining form: 5 mento-
feature: 5 cleft 6 dimple, goatee
it's tucked under the ~: 5 viola 6 violin
smoother: 5 razor
chin __: 4 rest 5 music, strap
Chin: 7 Tiffany
china: 4 bone, dish 5 Lenox, Spode 6 dishes, Mikasa, Sèvres 7 Dresden, Limoges 8 ceramics, clayware, crockery, Wedgwood 9 porcelain, Rosenthal, tableware 10 dinnerware
bull in a ~ shop: 3 oaf 5 klutz
buy: 3 set
ender: 4 ware 5 berry
flaw: 5 crack
material: 4 clay
piece: 3 cup 4 dish 5 plate
china __: 4 bark, blue, clay 6 closet 7 cabinet
__ china: 4 bone 5 set of, Spode, stone 7 Dresden, Nanking
China: 3 sea 6 Cathay, nation 7 country
ancient capital: 4 Sian, Xian 6 Singan
ancient ruler: 4 Wang
art material: 4 jade
association: 4 tong
attraction: 4 wall 9 Great Wall
bay: 8 Hangchow, Hangzhou, Jiaozhou, Kiaochow
benevolent spirit: 5 hsien
boat: 4 junk 6 sampan
book of divination: 6 I Ching
border river: 3 Ili 4 Amur, Yalu
bovine: 5 takin 6 Dulong 7 Yanbian
Buddhism of ~: 8 Mahayana
capital: 6 Peking 7 Beijing
cellist: 2 Ma 6 Yo-Yo Ma
cinnamon: 6 cassia
city: 4 Sian, Wuhu, Wuxi, Xian, Zibo 5 Jilin, Jinan, Tsuni, Tzepo, Tzupo, Wuhan, Wuhsi, Wusih, Yanan, Yenan 6 Anshan, Bengbu, Dairen, Dalian, Datong, Fushun, Harbin, Peking, Singan 7 Beijing, Chengdu, Lanzhou, Nanjing, Nanking, Qingdao, Tianjin 8 Changsha, Hangzhou, Peiching, Shanghai, Shenyang, Tientsin 9 Changchun, Chongqing, Guangzhou, Zhengzhou
combining form: 4 Sino- 6 Sinico-
council: 4 yuan
date: 6 jujube
desert: 4 Gobi
Disney film set in ~: 5 Mulan
dog: 4 chow, peke 8 chow chow 9 Pekingese
dynasty: 3 chi, Han, Jin, Qin, Wei, Xia, Yin 4 Chan, Chen, Chin,

Chou, Hsia, Ming, Tang, Tsin, Yuan **5** Liang, Shang
emperor: 4 P'u Yi, Wuti **6** Kang Xi
explorer: 4 Polo
fabric: 4 silk
farming area: 5 paddy
feminine principle: 3 yin
from ~: 5 Asian
fruit: 6 loquat
game: 5 salta **6** fan-tan **8** mah-jongg
gelatin: 4 agar **8** agar-agar
goddess: 5 Nukua
gooseberry: 4 kiwi
gulf: 5 Bohai, Pohai **8** Liaodong, Liaotung
idol: 4 joss
island off: 4 Amoy **5** Matsu **6** Quemoy, Taiwan **7** Formosa
lake: 5 Tai Hu **7** Koko Nor **9** Qinghai Hu
language: 4 Miao, Shan **5** Hmong, Kuoyu, Uigur **6** Hsiang, Kamtai, Manchu, Uighur **7** Chinese **8** Mandarin **9** Cantonese
leader: 3 Mao **4** Chou, Deng
locale: 4 Asia **6** Orient
Mahayana school in ~: 4 Chan
mammal: 5 panda
martial art: 5 wushu
masculine principle: 4 yang
measure: 4 tsun
money: 3 fen **4** tael, yuan **5** sycee
mountain: 6 Kungur, Kunlun **7** Nan Ling **8** Tian Shan, Tien Shan **9** Broad Peak **10** Amne Machin, Gasherbrum, Minya Konka, Muztagh Ata
mountain people of ~: 5 Hmong
mountain range: 5 Altai **6** Kunlun **7** Kuenlun
nanny: 4 amah
neighbor: 4 Laos **5** Burma, India, Macao, Macau, Nepal, Tibet **6** Bhutan, Russia, Xizang **7** Sitsang, Vietnam **8** Hong Kong, Mongolia, Pakistan **10** Kazakhstan, Kyrgyzstan, North Korea, Tajikistan
nut: 6 lichee, litchi **7** leechee
pagoda: 3 taa
parade feature: 6 dragon
path: 3 Tao
people: 2 Yi **4** Lolo, Miao **5** Hmong
philosopher: 4 Mo Ti **6** Lao-tzu **9** Confucius
philosophy: 3 Tao
poet: 4 Li Po, Tufu **7** Wang Wei
porcelain: 4 Ming
port: 4 Amoy, Dagu, Wuhu **5** Macao, Macau **6** Fuzhou, Weihai **7** Foochow, Tianjin, Yingkou **8** Shanghai, Tientsin
province: 5 Gansu, Henan, Honan, Hunan, Kansu **6** Fujian
rebel: 5 Boxer
river: 3 Han, Hsi **4** Liao, Yalu, Yuan, Yuen **5** Siang, Tarim
sea: 6 Yellow
shrub: 6 nardin, tobira **7** cumquat, kumquat, mahuang, nandina
sleeping platform: 4 kang
tea: 3 cha **5** bohea, congo **6** congou
tree: 5 yulan **6** gingko, ginkgo, lichee, litchi, longan, loquat, lungan **7** leechee **8** mandarin
vegetable: 3 udo
warehouse: 4 hong **6** godown
weight: 5 catty, Liang, picul
writer: 6 Lao She, Lao-tzu, Pa Chin
zodiac animal: 2 ox **3** dog, rat **4** boar **5** horse, sheep, snake, tiger **6** dragon, monkey, rabbit **7** rooster

China __: 3 oil, Sea **4** Gate, Girl, rose, Seas, silk, tree **5** aster, Beach
__ China: 3 Red **6** Poland
__-China: 4 Indo **6** Cochin
China Beach (ABC drama)
cast: Dana Delany (Colleen McMurphy)
Marg Helgenberger (K.C. Koloski)
extra: 2 RN **5** nurse
China Clipper airline: 5 Pan Am
China Girl (1983 song)
artist: David Bowie
__ China Sea: 4 East **5** South
China Syndrome, The (1979 film)
cast: Michael Douglas, Jane Fonda, Jack Lemmon
Chinatown (1974 film)
cast: Faye Dunaway, John Huston, Jack Nicholson
director: Roman Polanski
chinch: 3 bug **6** bedbug, insect
chinchilla: 3 fur **6** animal, mammal, rodent
habitat: 5 Andes
relative: *see* rodent
chine: 5 ridge, spine **8** backbone
Chinese: 5 Asian **8** language
food: 6 wonton
see also China
Chinese __: 3 ink, lug, red, tag, wax **4** Wall **7** cabbage, gelatin, juniper, lacquer, lantern, mustard, parsley, take-out
Chinese checkers: 4 game
Chinese Connection, The (1972 film)
cast: Bruce Lee
Chinese Nightingale, The
author: Vachel Lindsay
Chinese Parrot, The hero: 4 Chan
Chinese restaurant
additive: 3 MSG
condiment: 7 mustard **8** soy sauce **9** duck sauce
course: 4 pu pu **6** dim sum, lo mein, mei fun, wonton **7** chow fun, egg roll, pea pods **8** bean curd, chop suey, chow mein, dumpling, snow peas **9** fried rice, roast pork, spare ribs **10** egg foo yung, moo shu pork, Peking duck, spring roll, wonton soup
drink: 3 tea **6** hot tea
freebie: 3 tea **4** rice
menu general: 3 Tso
menu word: 3 hot **4** sour **5** spicy, sweet
menu words: 5 no MSG
pan: 3 wok
soup ingredient: 4 nest **6** wonton
style: 5 Hunan **8** Szechuan **9** Cantonese
chinfest: 6 confab, powwow
__ Ching: 5 Tao Te
chink: 4 leak, rift **5** cleft, crack, split **6** cranny, tinkle **7** fissure, opening
in one's armor: 8 weakness
chino: 5 khaki, twill **6** fabric **8** material
Chino: 4 city, town
locale: 10 California
chinook: 4 tyee, wind **6** salmon
Chinook: 5 tribe **6** Indian **7** Amerind **8** language
chinos: 5 jeans, pants **8** trousers
chintz: 6 fabric **8** material
chintzy: 4 loud **5** cheap, tacky **6** low-end, shabby, skimpy, stingy, tawdry **8** schlocky, ungiving
one: 5 miser
chin-up: 8 exercise
beneficiary: 3 arm **6** biceps
chip: 3 cut **4** clip, lump, nick, part **5** break, crack, flake, notch, piece, scrap, shard, sherd, slice **6** chisel, damage, sliver **7** crumble, shaving, whittle **8** fragment, splinter
accompaniment: 3 dip
away at: 5 erode
bargaining ~: 8 leverage
Brit's potato ~: 5 crisp
dipping ~: 5 nacho
erasable memory ~: 5 EPROM
feature: 5 ridge
in: 3 add, pay **4** ante **6** ante up, assist, donate, pay out, pony up **9** subscribe, volunteer **10** contribute
ingredient: 4 corn, salt **6** chives, potato
off the old block: 3 lad, son **4** cion **5** image, scion **7** replica **9** offspring
PC ~ maker: 5 Intel
prefix: 5 micro
starter ~: 4 ante
stone ~: 5 galet, spall **6** gallet, garret
topping: 3 dip **5** salsa **9** sour cream
toss in a ~: 3 bet **5** wager
with a ~ on one's shoulder: 5 angry, upset **6** bitter, peeved
chip __: 4 'n' dip, shot **6** and dip
chip __ the old block: 3 off
__ chip: 3 log **4** blue, corn **5** white **6** hybrid, potato
Chip __: 5 'n' Dale
chip and __: 3 dip
chipmunk: 6 animal, mammal, rodent
cartoon ~: 4 Chip, Dale **5** Alvin, Simon **8** Theodore
cheek: 5 pouch
like a ~: 5 furry
relative: *see* rodent
snack: 5 acorn
Chipmunk Song, The (1958 song)
artist: David Seville
chip 'n' __: 3 dip
Chip 'n' __: 4 Dale
Chip partner: 4 Dale
chipped __: 4 beef
Chippendale: 6 Thomas
chipper: 3 gay **4** pert, spry, tidy, well **5** fresh, happy, jolly, light, merry, perky **6** cheery, genial, jovial, lively **7** dashing, healthy **8** cheerful, mirthful **9** ebullient, exuberant, lightsome, sprightly
Chippewa: 5 tribe **6** Indian, Ojibwa **7** Amerind, Ojibway
chips: 4 nosh **5** dough, money, snack
exchange ~: 6 cash in, redeem
have ~: 3 eat **4** nosh **5** munch, snack
in the ~: 4 rich **7** wealthy
like ~: 5 salty **6** crispy
make ~: 3 fry
one in the ~: 6 fat cat
partner: 4 fish
__ chips: 4 corn, soap **5** poker **6** potato
ChiPs (NBC drama)
cast: Erik Estrada (Frank 'Ponch' Poncherello)
Randi Oakes (Bonnie Clark)
Larry Wilcox (Jon Baker)
setting: 10 California, Los Angeles
Chips Ahoy!
alternative: *see* cookie brand
chip-shot destination: 5 green
Chips, Mr.
portrayer: 5 Donat **6** O'Toole
what ~ taught: 5 Latin
Chiquita product: 6 banana
Chiquitita (1979 song)
artist: ABBA
Chirac: 7 Jacques
see also French
chirography: 7 writing **10** penmenship
chiromancer: 4 seer
chiromancy: 9 palmistry
Chiron: 7 centaur **8** asteroid
daughter: 4 Thea **8** Ocyrrhoe
father: 6 Cronos, Cronus
chiropractor concern: 4 back **5** spine
chirp: 4 call, peep, pipe, sing, twee **5** cheep, tweet **7** twitter **8** vocalize
chirping insect: 6 cicada **7** cricket
chirpy: 3 gay **5** happy, jolly, light, sunny **6** blithe, genial, jovial, lively **9** sprightly
chirr: 5 trill
chirrup: 4 peep **5** trill
chisel: 3 cut, hew **4** bilk, burn, chip, rook, tool **5** carve, cheat, edger, gouge, pluck, shape **6** incise, sculpt **7** engrave, swindle **8** flim-flam **9** victimize
ancient ~: 4 celt **5** burin
feature: 4 edge **5** bezel
relative: 3 adz **4** adze
chiseler: 5 cheat, knave, shark, thief **6** bad guy, robber **7** sharper, sharpie **8** stoneman, swindler
Chisholm: 5 trail **7** Shirley
Chisholm Trail
town: 4 Enid **7** Abilene **9** Fort Worth
users: 6 cattle
Chisinau: 4 city, town **7** capital
locale: 7 Moldova
Chisox: 3 ten **4** team
see also White Sox
chi-square __: 4 test
chit: 3 IOU, tab **4** bill **6** marker, ticket **7** receipt, voucher **9** liability
ender: 4 chat
write a ~: 3 owe
writer: 4 ower **5** maker

Chita: **6** Rivera
author: Lafcadio Hearn
chitchat: **3** gab, jaw, rap, yak **4** talk, word **5** prate **6** banter, bytalk, confab, gabble, gibber, gossip, parley **7** chatter, palaver **8** babbling, converse, idle talk, repartee **9** small talk, table talk **10** chew the rag
Chitra
author: Rabindranath Tagore
chitter: **5** tweet
Chitty Chitty Bang Bang: **4** book, film
author: Ian Fleming
cast: Sally Ann Howes, Dick Van Dyke
character: **5** Potts, Truly **11** Scrumptious
dog: **6** Edison
screenwriter: **4** Dahl
chivalrous: **4** bold, kind **5** brave, lofty **6** heroic, polite **7** courtly, gallant, genteel, valiant **8** gracious, heroical, highbred, knightly, romantic, valorous **9** courteous, honorable, unselfish **10** benevolent, courageous, high-minded, undismayed
deed: **4** gest **5** geste
chivalry: **8** courtesy **10** knighthood
participant: **6** damsel, knight
Chivas ___: **5** Regal
chive: **4** herb **6** veggie **9** vegetable
kin: **4** leek **5** onion
chivvy: **3** nag, vex **4** bait, hunt **5** chase **6** pursue
Chloe: **4** Webb
love: **7** Daphnis
Chloë: **7** Sevigny
chlorine: **3** gas **7** element, halogen
compound: **6** halide
Chloris
son: **6** Nestor
chloroform cousin: **5** ether
chlorophyll
maker: **5** plant
plant lacking ~: **6** albino, fungus
respository: **4** leaf
chlorophyta: **5** algae
Chlumsky: **4** Anna
Cho: **8** Margaret
choate: **4** full **8** integral
chock: **5** block, wedge
chockablock: **4** full, rife **5** laden, solid **6** filled, jammed, loaded, packed **7** crammed, crowded, replete, stuffed, teeming **8** brimming
chock-full: **3** SRO **4** rife **6** filled, jammed, loaded, packed **7** crammed, crowded, replete, stuffed, teeming **8** bursting, thronged **9** congested, jam-packed, plentiful, to the roof
chocoholic: **6** addict
favorite: **5** fudge
Chocolat (2000 film)
cast: Juliette Binoche, Judi Dench, Johnny Depp, Lena Olin
director: Lasse Hallström
chocolate: **4** cake **5** brown, candy, color, sweet **6** bonbon, flavor **8** ice cream **9** sweetmeat
alternative: ***see*** ice cream flavor
bar brand: **4** Mars, Twix **5** Clark, Heath, Lindt **6** Kit Kat, Mounds, Nestle, PayDay, Reese's **7** Cadbury, Hershey, Krackel, Oh Henry **8** Baby Ruth, Milky Way, Snickers **9** Almond Joy, Mr. Goodbar, Toblerone **10** NutRageous
bar ingredient: **5** sugar **6** almond
bean: **5** cacao
brand: **4** Mars **5** Lindt **6** Godiva **7** Cadbury, Hershey **8** Whitman's **9** Toblerone
candy: **3** bar **4** kiss **5** fudge
center: **5** cream, creme
dish: **5** fondu **6** fondue
hot ~: **5** cocoa
hot ~ container: **3** mug
make ~ curls: **5** shave
mark: **5** stain
marshmallow snack: **5** s'more
relative: ***see*** brown color
substitute: **5** carob
syrup brand: **4** U Bet **5** Bosco
tree: **5** cacao
chocolate ___: **3** bar, Lab **4** cake, malt, milk, tree **5** syrup **6** malted **7** soldier
___ chocolate: **3** hot **4** dark, milk **5** white
chocolate chip ___: **5** cooky **6** cookie
chocolate point: **3** cat **5** felid **6** feline
___ chocolates: **5** box of
Chocolate Soldier, The
composer: Oscar Straus
Choctaw: **5** tribe **6** Indian **7** Amerind
___ Chodesh: **4** Rosh
___-choi: **3** pak
choice: **4** aces, pick, plum, rare, vote **5** crack, elect, elite, fancy, first, prize **6** option, select **7** liberty, refusal **8** decision, election, favorite, free will, glorious, judgment, pleasure, volition **9** preferred, selection **10** assortment, discretion, hand-picked, nomination, preference
list: **4** menu
see also wonderful
___ choice: **7** dealer's, Hobson's
___ Choice: **6** O'Hara's **7** Critic's, Healthy, Sophie's, Taster's
choicest: **4** best **7** optimum **9** topflight
choices, top: **5** A-list
choir: **6** chorus **7** singers **8** ensemble **9** vocalists
area behind the ~: **4** apse
ender: **3** boy **4** girl **6** master
member: **4** alto, bass **5** basso, tenor, voice **7** soprano **8** baritone
members: **4** alti **5** bassi
place: **4** loft **5** riser
selection: **4** hymn **5** canto, motet, psalm **7** cantata
small ~: **5** nonet, octet **7** octette
tunic: **5** cotta
choir ___: **4** loft
choke: **4** clog, gulp, slow **5** block, quiet, wring **6** impede, shut up, stifle **7** congest, occlude, overrun, smother, squeeze **8** obstruct, throttle
back: **6** stifle
ender: **4** bore, damp, hold **5** berry, point **6** cherry
off: **3** dam **4** stop **7** silence
choke ___: **3** off **4** back, coil **5** chain **6** collar
choked up: **5** teary **10** tongue-tied
choker: **5** beads **7** jewelry **8** necklace **9** adornment
fastener: **5** clasp
choler: **3** ire **4** bile, rage **5** anger, wrath **6** temper **10** irritation, resentment
choleric
see angry
cholesterol
bad ~: **3** LDL
good ~: **3** HDL
part: **5** lipid **6** lipide
___ cholesterol: **5** serum
choline starter: **6** acetyl
cholla: **6** cactus
chomp: **4** bite, chew, gnaw **5** gnash, munch **6** crunch
on: **3** eat
Chomsky: **4** Noam
Chong: **5** Tommy **6** Thomas **7** Rae Dawn
partner: **5** Marin **6** Cheech
choose: **3** opt, sel., tab, tap **4** cull, like, name, pick, sort, take, vote, want, will **5** adopt, draft, elect, favor, go for, key on **6** anoint, assign, decide, desire, go into, opt for, prefer, select, settle, take up, winnow **7** appoint, embrace, excerpt, fix upon, pick out, vote for **8** bookmark, decide on, delegate, draw lots, handpick, nominate **9** designate, determine, flip a coin, preordain, single out, take sides **10** draw straws, settle upon
don't ~: **6** pass by **8** pass over
chooser choice: **4** odds **5** evens
choose up ___: **5** sides
choosy: **4** prim **5** fussy, picky **6** dainty **7** careful, finicky **8** finiking, finnicky **9** selective **10** fastidious, particular
chop: **2** ax **3** axe, cut, hew, lop **4** crop, cube, dice, fell, hack, jowl, meat, slap, slur, sock, stab **5** cut up, mince, shear, slash, slice, smack **6** cleave, divide, reduce **7** abridge, curtail, scissor, shorten **8** truncate **9** roughness
down: **2** ax **3** axe, hew **4** fell **6** hack up **7** hack off **8** hack down
ender: **5** house, logic, stick **6** fallen
finely: **4** dice **5** mince
off: **3** lop **5** sever
chop ___: **4** shop, suey
___ chop: **4** pork, veal **6** karate
chop-chop: **4** ASAP, stat
___ Chop Hill: **4** Pork
chophouse: **6** eatery **10** restaurant
order: **4** rare **8** well-done
Chopin: **4** Kate **8** Frédéric
Chopin, Frédéric: **4** Pole **8** composer
friend: George Sand
genre: **5** étude, rondo, waltz **6** sonata **7** ballade, prelude, scherzo **8** concerto, marzurka, nocturne **9** impromptu, polonaise
chopped: **4** hewn
liver: **4** pâté
chopped ___: **5** chuck, liver, steak **7** sirloin
chopper: **2** ax **3** axe **4** helo **5** tooth **6** copter **8** aircraft **10** helicopter
emulate a ~: **3** fly **4** soar **5** hover, whirr
military ~: **6** Apache
starter: **4** wood
topper: **5** rotor **6** enamel
choppers: **5** plate, teeth **8** dentures
chopping ___: **5** block
chopping firewood: **5** chore
choppy: **4** wild **5** bumpy, rough **6** jouncy **9** spasmodic, turbulent
Chopra: **6** Deepak
chops: **3** jaw, maw **4** jaws, meat **5** mouth **6** entrée
lick one's ~: **5** savor **6** relish
starter: **6** mutton
chop-shop supplier: **5** thief
choral: **4** sung **5** lyric, vocal **7** lyrical, musical **9** a cappella
ensemble: **5** octet **7** octette
member: **4** alto, bass **5** basso, tenor **7** soprano **8** baritone
members: **4** alti **5** bassi
work: **4** hymn **5** canto, motet **7** cantata
chorale: **4** hymn, song **5** music, psalm **9** vocalists
Choral Symphony: **5** ninth
composer: Ludwig van Beethoven
chord: **5** notes, triad **6** tendon **7** harmony
strike a ~: **5** touch **6** affect
chorda: **5** algae
Chordettes
song: Born to Be With You (1956)
Just Between You and Me (1957)
Lollipop (1958)
Mr. Sandman (1954)
chore: **3** job **4** duty, task, work **5** grind, labor, stint **6** burden, errand, odd job, raking, sewing **7** dusting, ironing, laundry, mopping, project, washing **8** cleaning, sweeping **9** housework, vacuuming **10** assignment
choreography: **6** ballet **7** dancing
choreophobe fear: **7** dancing
chorister: **4** alto, bass **5** basso, tenor **6** singer **7** soprano **8** baritone, vocalist
chortle: **3** heh **4** ha-ha **5** laugh **6** cackle, giggle, guffaw, titter **7** break up, chuckle, crack up, snicker, snigger **8** laughter
chorus: **4** song, tune **5** choir, music **6** melody **7** refrain **8** carolers, ensemble, glee club **9** vocalists
for full ~: **4** SATB
full ~ in music: **5** tutti
girl: **6** dancer
Greek ~ part: **5** epode
join the ~: **4** sing
member: **4** alto, bass **5** basso, tenor, voice **7** soprano **8** baritone
members: **4** alti **5** bassi
preceder: **5** verse
show: **5** revue **6** review
syllable: **3** tra
syllables: **4** la la **6** la la la **7** tra la la
___ Chorus: **5** Anvil
Chorus Line, A (1985 film): **7** musical
cast: Michael Douglas, Terrence Mann, Alyson Reed

CH

character: 2 Al 3 Don, Roy, Tom, Val 4 Bebe, Greg, Judy, Lois, Mark, Mike, Paul, Zach 5 Bobby, Butch, Diana, Frank, Larry, Vikki 6 Cassie, Connie, Maggie, Sheila, Tricia 8 Kristine
director: Richard Attenborough
original producer: 4 Papp
song: 3 One
__ chose: 5 peu de
__-chose: 7 quelque
chosen: 5 elect, elite 6 select 7 favored 8 accepted, anointed 9 preferred, spoken for, voluntary 10 fair-haired
__-chosen: 4 well
Chosen, The: 5 novel
author: Chaim Potok
__ chou: 5 pâte à
Chou: 5 En-lai
chou-chou
see sweetheart
chow: 3 dog 4 eats, food, grub, meal, meat 5 spitz 7 aliment, victual, vittles 8 K rations, victuals 9 provender
Army ~: 3 MRE 4 mess, Spam
down: 3 eat, sup 4 feed 5 dig in 6 devour, ingest 7 consume 9 grab a bite
ender: 5 hound
like a ~: 7 Chinese
chow __: 4 down, line, mein
chowder: 4 soup
like Manhattan clam ~: 5 thymy
server: 5 ladle
__ chowder: 4 clam, corn
chowderhead
see ninny
chowhound: 7 glutton
__ choy: 3 bok
Chrétien, Jean preceder: 8 Campbell
Chris: 3 Rea 4 Lowe, Noth, Penn, Pine, Rock 5 Evans, Evert, Isaak 6 Barber, Berman, Cooper, Farley, Kenner, LeDoux, Lemmon, Montez, Tucker 7 DeBurgh, Elliott 8 Columbus, O'Donnell, Robinson, Sarandon
rival: 6 Evonne
Chris-__: 5 Craft
chrism: 3 oil 7 holy oil
apply ~: 5 anele 6 anoint
Chrissie: 5 Evert, Hynde
rival: 6 Evonne
Christ: 5 Jesus 6 Savior 7 Messiah
Christa: 6 Miller 9 McAuliffe
Christabel: 4 poem
author: Samuel Taylor Coleridge
Christchurch: 4 city, town
locale: 10 New Zealand
christen: 3 dub, tag 4 call, name, term 5 title 7 baptize, entitle, intitle 8 sprinkle
christened: 3 née
christening initials: 3 USS
Christensen: 5 Erika
Christiaan: 7 Barnard, Eijkman, Huygens
Christian: 3 Era 4 Bale, Dior, Nyby 5 Lange, Linda, Roger 6 de Duve, Grabbe, Slater 7 Claudia, Doppler, Lacroix 8 Anfinsen, Fletcher
inscription: 4 INRI
symbol: 4 fish
temple: 6 church
Christian __: 3 Era 4 name, year 7 Brother, Science
__-Christian: 5 Judeo 6 Judaeo
__ Christian Andersen: 4 Hans
Christiania today: 4 Oslo
Christianity: 3 rel.
early ~ center: 6 Edessa
Christian Mysticism
author: William Ralph Inge
Christian Science
founder: Mary Baker Eddy
__, Christian Soldiers: 6 Onward
Christie: 3 Lou 4 Anna 5 Julie 6 Agatha, Hefner 8 Brinkley
concoction: 4 plot
perform a ~: 3 ski 4 skee
__ Christie: 4 Anna
Christie, Agatha: 4 Dame 6 writer 7 British
concoction: 4 plot
sleuth: Jane Marple, Hercule Poirot
work: And Then There Were None
Curtain
Death on the Nile
The Mousetrap
The Murder of Roger Ackroyd
Murder on the Orient Express
The Mysterious Affair at Styles
The Pale Horse
Witness for the Prosecution
Christie, Julie: 7 actress
film: Billy Liar (1963)
Darling (1965, AA)
Demon Seed (1977)
Doctor Zhivago (1965)
Don't Look Now (1973)
Far From the Madding Crowd (1967)
Heaven Can Wait (1978)
McCabe & Mrs. Miller (1971)
Petulia (1968)
Shampoo (1975)
role: 4 Lara
Christie's
action: 3 bid, nod 7 auction
patron: 6 bidder
Christina: 5 Ricci, saint, Stead 7 Onassis 8 Aguilera, Rossetti 9 Applegate
father: 3 Ari
Christina's World
artist: Andrew Wyeth
Christine: 5 Elise, Lahti, McVie 7 McGuire 8 Baranski
author: Stephen King
title character: 3 car 4 auto
__ Christi, TX: 6 Corpus
Christmas: 4 isle, Noel, yule 6 island
berry: 5 toyon
bird: 5 goose
carol start: 4 Hark 5 O come 6 Adeste
ender: 4 tide, time
Eve flier: 5 Comet, Cupid, Vixen 6 Dancer, Dasher, Donder 7 Blitzen, Prancer, Rudolph 8 reindeer
goodies: 4 loot 5 gifts 8 presents
greenery: 5 holly 6 wreath
in French: 4 Noël
in Portuguese: 5 Natal
in Spanish: 7 Navidad
like a ~ tree: 5 lit up 9 decorated
naughty child's ~ gift: 4 coal
pageant figures: 4 Magi
pageant prop: 4 halo
poem opener: 4 'Twas
predecessor: 3 eve
quaff: 3 nog 6 eggnog
smelling of ~: 5 piney
song: 4 Noel 5 carol
sound: 6 ho ho ho
tableau: 6 crèche
tree: 3 fir 4 pine 6 balsam
tree base: 5 stand
tree ornament: 4 ball, cane, star 6 icicle, tinsel 9 candy cane
tree topper: 4 star 5 angel
trio: 4 Magi
white ~ need: 4 snow
Christmas __: 3 Day, Eve 4 card, club, fern, rose, seal, tree 5 berry 6 cactus, factor, Island 7 Holiday, pudding
Christmas __, A: 5 Carol, Story
__ Christmas: 4 Bush 5 Merry, White 6 Father
Christmas card word: 4 Noel 5 Peace
Christmas Carol, A
author: Charles Dickens
character: 3 Bob, Tim 5 ghost, Jacob 6 Marley 7 Scrooge, Tiny Tim 8 Cratchit, Ebenezer
cry: 3 bah 6 humbug
last word of ~: 3 one
setting: 6 London 7 England
Christmas Carol, A (1951 film)
cast: Alastair Sim
Christmas Club member: 5 saver
Christmas comes but __ year: 5 once a
Christmas Oratorio
composer: J.S. Bach
Christmas Song, The
composer: Mel Tormé, Bob Wells
Christmas With the Kranks (2004 film)
cast: Tim Allen, Dan Aykroyd, Jamie Lee Curtis
Christ of St. John of the Cross
artist: Salvador Dali
Christoph: 5 Gluck, Waltz
Christopher: 3 Fry, Lee 4 Dodd, Noth, Penn, pope, Wren 5 Burke, Cross, Guest, Lloyd, Reeve, saint, Smart 6 Atkins, Dennis, George, Hewitt, Knight, Meloni, Morley, Norris, Walken, Warren 7 Brennan, Lambert, Marlowe, Plummer, pontiff 8 Columbus 9 Isherwood
friend: 4 Pooh 5 Robin
Christ Stopped at Eboli
author: Carlo Levi
__ Christ Superstar: 5 Jesus
Christy: 4 Lane 9 Mathewson
__ Christy Minstrels: 3 New
chroma: 3 hue 4 tint 5 color
chromatic: 4 hued 8 colorful
chrome: 4 trim 5 metal
chromium: 5 metal 7 element
chromium __: 5 steel
chromosome
blueprint: 6 genome
choice: 4 X or Y
component: 3 DNA, RNA
enzyme: 6 DNAase
factor: 3 sex
gene sites on a ~: 4 loca, loci
having an X ~: 6 female 8 feminine
having a Y ~: 4 male 9 masculine
locate a gene on a ~: 3 map
part: 4 gene
type of ~: 2 XX, XY
Chromosome 6
author: Robin Cook
chronic: 5 usual 6 inborn 7 abiding, lasting 8 constant, enduring, habitual, long-term, unwaning 9 ceaseless, continual, incessant, ingrained, perennial, sustained, unabating 10 deep-seated, inveterate, persistent, unyielding
become ~: 5 recur
malady (suffix): 4 -itis
not ~: 5 acute
chronicle: 4 saga, tale, tell 5 diary, enrol, story 6 annals, enroll, memoir, record, relate, report 7 account, history, journal, narrate, recount, set down, version 8 describe, register 9 expound on, narration, narrative, recountal
entry: 5 event
Chronicle: 5 paper 9 newspaper
locale: 7 Houston
chronicler: 6 scribe 8 annalist, recorder 9 historian
chronicles: 5 files 7 archive
Chronicles
follower: 4 Ezra
preceder: 5 Kings
Chronicles of Clovis, The
author: Saki
character: 4 Esme
Chronicles of Narnia, The
author: C.S. Lewis
__ Chronicles, The: 5 Heidi 6 Marlow 7 Martian, Vampire
__ Chronium: 4 Mare
chronograph: 5 clock, watch 9 timepiece
chronological: 8 temporal
adjective: 5 horal
division: 3 era
chronological __: 3 age
chronology: 4 time 7 journal 8 calendar
element: 5 event
chronometer: 5 clock, watch 9 timepiece
chrysalis: 3 bug 4 pupa 6 insect
chrysanthemum: 4 kiku 5 plant 6 flower
Chrysler: 3 car 4 auto 6 Walter 10 automobile
acquisition: 3 AMC
car: 6 De Soto
model: 4 K-car 5 Aspen, Royal 6 Cirrus 7 Cordoba, LeBaron, Newport, Sebring, Windsor 8 Concorde, Conquest, Imperial, Pacifica, Saratoga 9 Crossfire, New Yorker, PT Cruiser 11 Fifth Avenue
trademark: 4 Jeep
chrysolite: 7 mineral
chub: 4 fish 6 tautog 9 whitefish
kin: 4 carp, dace, rudd 6 barbel, minnow 7 gudgeon 8 goldfish
Chubb
competitor: *see* insurance company
chubby
see obese
Chubby: 7 Checker
chuck: 3 lob 4 bail, beef, cast, cede, drop, dump, flip, hurl, sell, shed, toss 5 ditch, fling, forgo, heave,

pitch, scrap, sling, steak, throw, yield **6** forego, give up, let fly, reject **7** abandon, discard, dismiss, forfeit, forsake **8** forswear, get rid of, hand over, jettison, part with, throw out, toss away **9** cast aside, dispose of, eighty-six, foreswear, surrender, throw away **10** relinquish
insert: **3** bit
starter: **4** wood
wagon: **7** canteen
wagon dinner: **4** chow, grub
wagon honcho: **4** cook
chuck __: **5** steak, wagon
chuck-__: **5** a-luck
Chuck: **4** Daly, Noll **5** Berry, Jones, Klein **6** Barris, Colson, Norris, Willis, Yeager **7** Connors, Woolery **8** Bednarik, Mangione **9** Fairbanks
Chuck __ Love: **4** E.'s in
chuck-a-luck: **4** game
need: **4** dice
chuckle: **3** heh, yak, yok, yuk **4** haha, yock, yuck **5** laugh **6** cackle, giggle, heehee, titter **7** snicker, snigger **8** laughter
chat room ~: **3** LOL
elicit a ~: **5** amuse
ender: **4** head
chucklehead
see ninny
Chuckles: **5** candy
chuff: **4** pant
chug
see chug-a-lug
chug-a-lug: **4** gulp, swig **5** swill **6** guzzle **7** swallow **8** gulp down
chukka: **4** boot, shoe **8** footwear
material: **5** suede
chukkers game: **4** polo
Chulalongkorn
locale: **4** Siam
Chula Vista: **4** city, town
locale: **10** California
chum: **3** bro, pal **4** ally, bait, fish, mate **5** amigo, buddy, crony, pally **6** cohort, frater, friend **7** compeer, comrade, partner **8** alter ego, intimate, playmate, sidekick **9** associate, colleague, confidant **10** bosom buddy, compatriot, well-wisher
Australian: **4** mate
British: **4** mate **5** matey
cowboy's ~: **4** pard
in French: **3** ami **4** amie
in Spanish: **5** amiga, amigo
(with): **6** hobnob, mingle **9** socialize
see also friend
Chumash: **6** Indian **7** Amerind
chummy: **4** cosy, cozy, kind **5** close, cozey, cozie, thick **6** clubby, genial, kindly **7** affable, amiable, cordial **8** amicable, familiar, friendly, intimate, outgoing, sociable **9** convivial **10** benevolent, buddy-buddy, neighborly, palsy-walsy, solicitous
get ~ with: **8** befriend
chump: **4** butt, dupe, fool, lamb, lout, tool **5** patsy **6** pigeon, sucker, turkey **7** fall guy **8** easy mark, pushover **9** schlemiel
see also ninny
chump __: **6** change
chums, meet one's old: **5** reune
__ Chung: **4** Wang
Chung, Connie: **10** journalist
spouse: Maury Povich
chunk: **3** gob, wad **4** glob, hunk, lump, mass, part, pile, slab **5** block, clump, piece, quota, scrap, share, wedge **6** morsel, nugget, parcel **7** portion, section **8** fraction, fragment **10** percentage
in Britain: **5** wodge
take a ~ out of: **3** nip **4** bite
chunk-light __: **4** tuna
chunky: **5** beefy, bulky, heavy, husky, lumpy, plump, pudgy, squat, stout, thick **6** blocky, chubby, rotund, stocky **8** heavyset, thickset **9** filled-out
alternative: **5** plain **6** smooth
church: **4** fane, sect **5** abbey **6** chapel, parish, shrine, temple **7** chancel, mission **8** basilica, ecclesia, religion **9** cathedral, sanctuary **10** house of God, persuasion, tabernacle
assistant: **6** lector
banner: **7** labarum
bell: **7** angelus
calendar: **4** ordo
cape: **5** amice **6** almuce **7** mozetta **8** mozzetta **10** cappa magna
coat: **7** cassock
combining form: **7** ecclesi- **8** ecclesio-
container: **4** font **6** censer
council: **5** curia, synod
court: **4** rota
cover-up: **4** veil **8** mantilla
desk: **4** ambo **5** ambon
donation: **5** tithe
Eastern ~ member: **5** Uniat **6** Uniate
ender: **3** man, men **4** yard **5** going, manly, woman **6** warden
exclamation ~: **4** amen **7** hosanna
fair: **5** bazar **6** bazaar
feature: **3** pew **4** apse, jube, loft, nave **5** aisle, altar, ambry, choir, organ, spire **6** atrium, belfry, chapel, pulpit, vestry **7** chancel, gallery, narthex, reredos, steeple **8** antenave, parclose, sacristy, transept, westwork
figure: **4** icon, ikon **5** cross, eikon, saint
group: **6** clergy
headdress: **5** miter, mitre
land: **5** glebe
Latin ~ service: **5** missa
law: **5** canon, dogma **7** precept **8** doctrine
medieval ~ music sign: **4** neum **5** neume
members: **5** laics, laity **6** parish
music: **4** hymn **5** motet
not of the ~: **3** lay **4** laic **6** laical
official: **3** rev. **4** msgr. **5** abbot, elder, prior, Rt. Rev., vicar **6** cleric, deacon, lector, parson, warden **8** minister, reverend **9** monsignor
offshoot: **4** sect
of the ~: **8** clerical
plate: **5** paten
portico: **6** parvis
rite: **4** Mass **7** service, worship
robe: **6** chimar, chimer **7** chimere, chrisom
Scottish ~: **4** kirk
song: **4** hymn **5** psalm
songbook: **6** hymnal
teachings: **5** dogma **6** Gospel
vestment: **3** alb **5** amice
wall recess: **5** ambry **6** aumbry **8** armarium
Church: **5** Frank **9** Frederick
churchgoing: **5** pious **9** religious
Churchill: **4** peak, port **5** mount, river, Sarah **7** Winston **8** mountain
River locale: **8** Manitoba
Churchill __: **5** Downs, Falls
Churchill Downs: **5** track
event: **4** race **5** Derby
locale: **8** Kentucky **10** Louisville
Churchill, Winston: **2** P.M. **3** Sir **7** British **8** Nobelist **9** statesman
gesture: **3** vee **5** V-sign
one of a ~ quartet: **4** toil **5** blood, sweat, tears
predecessor: **6** Attlee **11** Chamberlain
prop: **4** cane
so few, to ~: **3** RAF
successor: **4** Eden **6** Attlee
work: Closing the Ring
The Gathering Storm
The Grand Alliance
The Hinge of Fate
Their Finest Hour
Triumph and Tragedy
Church of __: **3** God **4** Rome **7** England
Churchy La __: **5** Femme
churl: **3** cad, cur, oaf **4** boor, heel, lout, worm **5** beast, clown, knave, looby, miser, rogue, scamp, yahoo **6** bad guy, grouch, rascal **7** peasant **9** miscreant, reprobate, scoundrel, vulgarian **10** blackguard, clodhopper, curmudgeon
churlish: **4** mean, rude, sour **5** crass, cross, crude, gruff, rough, surly **6** coarse, crusty, grumpy, morose, oafish, ornery, rustic, snippy, stingy, sullen, touchy **7** bearish, boorish, grouchy, loutish, lowbred, miserly, peevish, uncivil, vicious **8** cloddish, grumpish, impolite, snippety, ungiving **9** unfeeling **10** ill-natured, indecorous, uncultured, ungracious, unmannerly, unpleasant
churn: **4** mill, moil, roil **5** mix up, shake, swirl **6** seethe, simmer, stir up **7** agitate, shake up **9** container
creation: **6** butter
plunger: **6** dasher
churr: **5** trill
chute: **4** ramp **5** flume, slide, slope **6** gutter **7** incline **9** waterfall **10** water slide
alternative: **6** ladder
like a ~: **5** steep
material: **4** silk
starter: **4** para
Chutes and __: **7** Ladders
chutney: **5** sauce **6** relish **8** dressing **9** condiment
flavoring: **5** mango
chutzpah: **4** gall **5** brass, cheek, moxie, nerve, spunk **6** hubris, hybris **8** audacity, temerity, tenacity **9** arrogance, assurance, impudence, insolence **10** effrontery, feistiness
full of ~: **5** brash, nervy **6** daring
Chuvash
poet: **4** Aigi
Chuzzlewit: **6** Martin
Chynna: **8** Phillips
CIA
agent: **3** spy
counterpart: **3** KGB
forerunner: **3** OSS
nautical cousin: **3** ONI
operative: **3** agt., spy **5** agent, spook
part of ~: **4** Agcy. **6** Agency **7** Central
relative: **3** NSA
ciao: **3** bye **4** ta-ta **5** later, see ya **6** so long **7** goodbye **8** au revoir, farewell
in French: **5** adieu
in Hawaiian: **5** aloha
in Latin: **3** ave **4** vale
in Spanish: **5** adios
Ciardi, John: **4** poet **6** critic
Cibber, Colley: **4** poet **6** writer **7** British **10** playwright
cicada: **3** bug **6** buzzer, insect, locust **7** cricket
sound: **5** chirr, churr **6** chirre
cicatrix: **4** scar
Cicely: **5** Tyson
Cicero: **4** city, town **5** Roman **6** orator
emulate ~: **5** orate
locale: **8** Illinois
see also Latin
cicerone: **5** guide **6** docent
Cid, El: **4** hero **7** Spanish
cider: **5** drink **8** beverage
season: **4** fall
source: **5** apple
unit: **6** gallon
cider __: **5** press **7** vinegar
__ cider: **4** hard **5** sweet
Cider House Rules, The: **4** film **5** novel
author: John Irving
cast: Michael Caine, Delroy Lindo, Tobey Maguire, Charlize Theron
director: Lasse Hallström
Cielito __: **5** Lindo
Cielo __: **4** e mar
Ciera: **3** car **4** auto, Olds **10** Oldsmobile
cigar: **4** puro, rope **5** claro, smoke, stogy **6** corona, el ropo, Havana, stogie **7** cheroot **8** panatela, perfecto
box wood: **5** cedar
brand: **5** Te Amo
end: **3** ash **4** butt, stub
have a ~: **5** smoke
holder: **7** humidor
producer: **4** Cuba **5** Tampa
cigare filler: **5** tabac
__ cigar is a smoke: **5** a good
cilantro: **4** herb **9** coriander
Cilento, Diane
spouse: Sean Connery, Anthony Shaffer
cilia: **5** hairs, setae **6** lashes **8** filament **9** eyelashes
of ~: **5** setal
cilium: **4** hair, lash, seta **7** eyelash
Cilla: **5** Black
Cillian: **6** Murphy
Cimarron: **5** novel, river **8** Cadillac
author: Edna Ferber

Cimino, Michael
film: The Deer Hunter (1978, AA)
___ Cimmerium: 4 Mare
cinch: 3 ice, tie 4 belt, bind, easy, game, girt, grip, lock, snap 5 cushy, girth, latch 6 assure, breeze, enfold, ensure, infold, picnic, secure, simple 7 no sweat, triumph 8 cakewalk, card game, duck soup, painless, pushover, workable 9 certainty, determine, guarantee, sure thing 10 child's play, effortless, unexacting
cinch ___: 3 bug 4 belt
cinched: 4 sure 6 belted
cinchona: 4 tree 5 shrub
relative: 5 ixora 6 coffee, madder 8 gardenia 9 bouvardia
Cincinnati: 4 city, town 5 horse
athletes: 8 Bearcats 10 Musketeers
county: 8 Hamilton
fictional ~ station: 4 WKRP
locale: 4 Ohio
newspaper: 4 Post 8 Enquirer
pro team: 4 Reds 7 Bengals
rider: 5 Grant
river: 4 Ohio
school: 6 Xavier
Cinco de Mayo: 3 día 7 holiday
event: 6 fiesta
cinco minus tres: 3 dos
cincture: 4 band, belt, gird, ring 6 begird, circle, collar, girdle 8 encircle, surround 9 encompass
cinder: 3 ash 4 slag 5 ember, fleck 7 residue
collector: 6 ashman
cinder ___: 4 cone 5 block, patch, track
Cinder
ender: 4 ella
Cinderella
sibling: 10 stepsister
Cinderella (1950 film)
cat: 7 Lucifer
dog: 5 Bruno
event: 4 ball
headpiece: 5 tiara
like ~ s stepsisters: 4 ugly
mouse: 3 Gus, Jaq
setting: 4 ball
Cinderella ___: 5 story 7 Liberty
Cinderella Man (2005 film)
cast: Russell Crowe, Paul Giamatti, Renée Zellweger
character: 4 Baer
director: Ron Howard
cinderlike: 4 ashy 5 ashen 7 grayish
cinders
turn to ~: 4 char
Cinders: 4 Ella
Cindy: 5 Adams 6 Wilson 8 Crawford, Williams
cine: 4 film 5 movie
cinema: 3 pic 4 film, show 5 films, movie, odeon, odeum 6 flicks, movies 7 drive-in, theater, theatre 9 big screen, celluloid, multiplex
admonition: 3 shh
chain: 5 Loews
list: 4 cast
local ~: 4 nabe
showing: 4 film 5 short 7 cartoon
sight: 5 queue
sign: 4 Exit
snack: 5 candy 6 nachos 7 Goobers, popcorn 8 Milk Duds 9 Raisinets
suffix: 4 -plex
technique: 3 pan 4 fade, iris
unit: 5 frame
see also film, movie
cinéma ___: 6 vérité
Cinemax: 7 channel
alternative: ***see*** movie channel
offering: 4 film 5 movie
Cineplex ___: 5 Odeon
cineplex offering: 4 film 5 movie
cineraria: 5 plant 6 flower
cinereous: 4 gray, grey 5 ashen
Cinna
author: Pierre Corneille
cinnabar: 3 ore 7 mineral
cinnamon: 4 bear, fern, tree 5 brown, spice 7 reddish 8 ice cream 9 yellowish
alternative: ***see*** ice cream flavor
family: 6 laurel
relative: ***see*** brown color
tree: 6 cassia
unit: 5 stick
cinnamon ___: 3 bun 4 roll
cinque: 4 five 7 Italian
ender: 4 foil
follower: 3 sei
preceder: 7 quattro
cinquefoil feature: 3 arc
CIO: 5 union
chapter: 3 lcl. 5 local
members: 5 labor
partner: 3 AFL
Cio-Cio-San
accessory for ~: 3 obi
to Yakusidé: 5 niece
Cioffi: 7 Charles
cipher: 3 nil, zip 4 code, sign, zero 5 aught, blank, count, ought, zilch 6 figure, legend, naught, nought, number, reckon 7 compute, nothing 8 goose egg 9 calculate, character, nonentity 10 encryption
code: 3 key
expert: 5 coder
put in ~: 6 encode
solve a ~: 6 decode
ciphering: 9 reckoning 10 arithmetic
circa: 5 about 6 approx., around, nearly 7 roughly
circadian: 5 daily 7 per diem
dysrhythmia: 6 jet lag
circadian ___: 6 rhythm
Circe: 8 conjurer 9 sorceress
emulate ~: 5 tempt
lover: 8 Odysseus
parent: 5 Persa 6 Hecate, Helios
sister: 5 Medea 8 Pasiphae
son: 5 Romus 6 Agrius
circle: 3 lap, mob, set 4 band, belt, club, disc, disk, gird, gyre, halo, hoop, loop, ring, turn 5 class, crowd, curve, group, hem in, junto, orbit, pivot, shape, wheel, whirl 6 begird, clique, engird, gyrate, league, rotate, sphere 7 academy, aureola, aureole, company, coterie, enclose, envelop, environ, faction, inclose, in-group, revolve, society 8 cincture, gloriole, go around, surround 9 encompass, enwreathe, following, hangers-on, perimeter 10 revolution
back: 6 return
combining form: 3 gyr- 4 gyro-
dance: 4 hora, kolo 9 farandole
diagram developer: 4 Venn
flattened ~: 4 oval 7 ellipse
formed into a ~: 5 orbed
in a vicious ~: 4 vain 5 inane 6 absurd, futile 7 insipid 9 for naught, frivolous, pointless, worthless 10 ridiculous
inner ~: 5 cabal, elite 6 clique, jet set 7 coterie, faction 10 upper crust
lack: 3 end
line across a ~: 3 dia. 4 diam. 5 chord 8 diameter
measure: 6 radius
measures: 5 radii
numbered ~: 4 dial
of flowers: 3 lei
of light: 4 halo 6 corona 7 aureola, aureole
portion: 3 arc
ratio: 2 pi
size: 4 area
tiny ~: 3 dot
to a poet: 3 orb
traffic ~: 6 rotary
unit: 6 degree
___ circle: 4 full 5 dress, great, inner 6 family, sewing 7 traffic, vicious, winner's
___ Circle: 5 Great, Inner 6 Arctic, Family
circled: 5 orbed
Circle Game, The
author: Margaret Atwood
Circle in the Sand (1988 song)
artist: Belinda Carlisle
Circle of Friends
author: Maeve Binchy
circles
going in ~: 4 lost
run ~ around: 3 top 4 beat, best 5 outdo 6 outwit 8 outsmart 9 overwhelm
___ circles: 5 ran in, run in
circlet: 6 bangle, diadem, wreath
circle the ___: 6 wagons
Circle, The
author: Somerset Maugham
___ Circle, The: 5 First
circuit: 3 lap 4 beat, loop, ring, tour, walk, zone 5 ambit, orbit, round, route, track, wheel 6 course, hookup, league 7 compass 9 itinerary, perimeter, round trip 10 revolution
component: 4 fuse
problem: 4 leak 5 short
rubber-chicken ~: 5 stump
tend to a ~ breaker: 5 reset
three-way ~: 3 wye
unit: 3 amp, ohm 4 watt 6 ampere
circuit ___: 4 edge 5 board, court, judge, rider 7 binding, breaker
___ circuit: 4 open 5 short 6 closed
circuitous: 7 complex, devious, sinuous, winding 8 indirect, rambling, tortuous 10 collateral, meandering, roundabout
circuitry: 7 network
circular: 2 ad 3 rnd. 4 bill 5 flier, flyer, orbic, round 6 curved, insert, spiral 7 handout, leaflet 8 brochure, disklike, handbill, indirect, magazine, pamphlet, ringlike 9 broadside
border: 4 band, belt, ring 6 collar, girdle 8 cincture
follow a ~ path: 3 arc
motion: 4 gyre, spin 8 gyration
object: 4 disk
somewhat ~: 4 oval
word: 4 sale, save
circular ___: 3 saw 4 file
Circular Staircase, The
author: Mary Roberts Rinehart
circulate: 3 air, sow 4 flow, send, turn 5 issue, rumor, strew, swirl 6 mingle, report, spread, travel, wander 7 publish, radiate 8 bring out, disperse, proclaim 9 broadcast, get around, interview, make known, propagate, publicize, ventilate 10 distribute, mill around, move around, promulgate
circulating: 5 astir 7 current 8 in the air
circulation: 4 flow 5 issue 6 spread
aid: 3 fan
circulatory system part: 4 vein 5 aorta, heart 6 artery
circumambulate: 4 ring, rove 5 skirt 6 wander
circumference: 3 rim 4 edge, girt, loop 5 ambit, girth 6 border, fringe 7 compass, outline 8 boundary 9 perimeter
ratio: 2 pi
segment: 3 arc
circumlocute: 5 dodge 6 wander
circumlocutory: 5 wordy 6 prolix 7 diffuse, verbose 9 redundant 10 discursive, long-winded, pleonastic
circumnavigate: 4 ring 5 round, skirt
circumnavigator: 3 Bly 4 Fogg, Gray 5 Drake 8 Magellan 9 Nellie Bly
circumscribe: 4 ring 5 bound, fence, hem in, limit 6 define, engird 7 compass, confine, delimit, enclose, environ, inclose, mark off, outline, qualify 8 encircle, restrain, restrict, surround
circumscribed: 6 narrow 7 insular, limited 8 definite, orthodox 9 qualified
circumspect: 3 shy 4 cagy, wary 5 alert, cagey, canny, chary, fussy, leery 7 careful, finicky, guarded, heedful, politic, prudent 8 cautious, discreet, exacting, finiking, finnicky, keen-eyed, rational, rigorous, thorough, vigilant, watchful 9 assiduous, attentive, judicious, observant, provident 10 fastidious, meticulous, particular, reasonable, scrupulous
circumspection: 4 care 7 caution, finesse 9 vigilance 10 precaution
circumspectly, act: 6 beware
circumstance: 4 case 5 event, state, thing 6 action, affair 7 destiny, episode 8 accident, exigence, exigency, fortuity, grandeur, incident, occasion
partner: 4 pomp
uncontrollable ~: 4 luck 6 chance
circumstances: 3 lot 4 life 5 state, terms 6 assets 7 capital 8 position 9 situation 10 livelihood
in different ~: 9 otherwise
in reduced ~: 4 poor 5 needy
under any ~: 5 at all

…er what ~: 3 how
___ circumstances beyond...: 5 Due to
circumvent: 4 duck, foil, shun, trap 5 avert, avoid, dodge, elude, evade, parry, shirk, skirt 6 bypass, entrap, escape, eschew, outwit, thwart 7 abstain, defraud, shy from 8 flee from, outflank, outsmart, sidestep, surround 9 frustrate, get around, overreach 10 disappoint, work around
circumvention: 7 evasion
circus: 4 fair, show 6 big top 8 carnival 9 spectacle
animal: 3 dog 4 bear, flea, lion, pony, seal 5 horse, tiger 8 elephant
employee: 5 clown, tamer 6 barker 7 acrobat, juggler, spieler 9 strongman 10 ringmaster, roustabout, wire walker
need: 3 net 4 hoop, ring, tent 5 knife, stilt, sword 6 cannon
routine: 3 act 5 stunt
sound: 4 roar
wear: 6 tights
circus ___: 3 act 4 tent
___ circus: 4 flea, tent 6 flying
Circus ___: 7 Maximus
___ Circus: 5 At the
Circus Circus
locale: 8 Las Vegas
Circus Maximus: 5 arena
official: 5 edile
cirque: 3 cwm
basin: 4 tarn
Cirque du ___: 6 Soleil
cirrocumulus: 4 wisp 5 cloud
cloud: 4 wisp
cirrostratus: 5 cloud
cirrus: 4 wisp 5 cloud
like a ~: 5 wispy 7 wispish
CIS
ancestor: 4 USSR
Cisalpine ___: 4 Gaul
cisco: 4 fish 9 whitefish
Cisco ___: 3 Kid 7 Systems
Cisco Kid, The (1973 song)
artist: War
Cisco Kid, The (TV western): 5 oater
cast: Leo Carrillo (Pancho) Duncan Renaldo (The Cisco Kid)
'C' Is for Corpse
author: Sue Grafton
Cissy: 7 Houston
cistern: 3 vat 4 sump, tank 9 container, reservoir
___ cit.: 3 loc.
citadel: 4 fort, keep 5 tower 6 castle 7 bastion, defense, lookout, redoubt 8 fortress, garrison 10 stronghold
Citadel: 6 school
locale: 4 S. Car. 10 Charleston
student: 5 cadet 7 Bulldog
citation: 5 award, prize, quote 6 praise, trophy 7 example, excerpt, extract, mention, passage, summons, tribute 8 encomium 9 extolment, quotation, reference 10 decoration, imputation
abbr.: 4 et al., ibid. 5 op. cit.
invite a ~: 5 speed
Citation: 3 car 4 auto 5 Chevy, Edsel, horse 9 Chevrolet 10 automobile
rider: 6 Arcaro
citations: 8 analecta, analects
___ citato: 4 loco 5 opere
cite: 3 lay 4 name, note 5 offer, order, quote, refer 6 accuse, adduce, assert, praise, recall, summon, ticket 7 commend, excerpt, extract, itemize, mention, recount, refer to, specify 8 allude to, decorate, point out, remember, spell out, subpoena 9 enumerate, exemplify, recognize, recollect, reference, single out
cithara cousin: 4 harp
Citicorp: 4 bank
cities: 5 urbia
change ~: 4 move, relo 8 relocate
of ~: 5 civic 9 municipal
___ Cities: 4 Quad, Twin
Cities of the Interior
author: Anaïs Nin
citified: 5 urban
Citi Field: 7 stadium
player: 3 Met
citify: 8 urbanize
citizen: 5 voter 6 native 7 dweller, freeman, resider 8 indigene, national, resident, taxpayer 9 indweller 10 inhabitant
U.S. ~ ID: 3 SSN
___ citizen: 4 dual 6 senior
Citizen: 5 watch
alternative: *see* wristwatch
Citizen Kane (1941 film)
cast: Joseph Cotten, Agnes Moorehead, Everett Sloane, Orson Welles
composer: Bernard Herrmann
director: Orson Welles
prop: 4 sled 7 Rosebud 9 snow globe
studio: 3 RKO
citizen of (suffix): 3 ite
citizenry: 6 people, public 7 country 9 residents 10 population
citizens ___ radio: 4 band
citizen's ___: 6 arrest
Citizen Tom Paine
author: Howard Fast
Citizen X (1995 film)
cast: Stephen Rea
citric: 4 acid 6 fruity, lemony
Citroën: 3 car 4 auto 5 André 6 import 10 automobile
model: 4 Saxo 5 Xsara 6 Activa
citron: 4 tree 5 fruit 6 cedrat, yellow
ender: 4 ella
citronella ___: 3 oil 6 candle
citrus: 4 lime, ugli 5 fruit, lemon 6 orange, pomelo, tangor 7 cumquat, kumquat, satsuma, Seville, tangelo 8 bergamot, mandarin, shaddock, Valencia 9 tangerine 10 calamondin, grapefruit
city: 5 Ocala
colorant: 6 ethene
cover: 4 rind, skin 6 albedo
drink: 3 ade
grower bane: 5 frost 7 drought
Italian ~: 8 bergamot
peel: 4 zest
peel constituent: 5 rutin
tree: 3 bel 4 bael, lime 5 lemon 6 orange, pomelo, pumelo 7 pommelo, pummelo, tangelo 8 bergamot, mandarin, shaddock 9 tangerine 10 grapefruit
yield: 5 juice
Città ___ Vaticano: 3 del
city: 3 urb 4 burg, town 5 civic, civil, metro, place, urban 6 public 7 capital 8 downtown 9 municipal 10 metropolis
combining form: 5 metro-, -polis
ender: 4 wide 5 scape
like a ~ population: 5 dense
of a ~: 5 urban
city ___: 4 desk, hall, room 5 clerk 6 editor, father 7 council, manager, planner, slicker
city-___: 4 born, bred 5 state
___ city: 3 fat 5 inner
City ___: 4 Girl, Hall, Heat 5 of God 6 Lights 7 Streets
___ City: 3 Bay, Del, Fat, Oil, Sim, Sin, Sun 4 Daly, Dark, Holy, Iowa, Neon, Open, Park, Spin, Surf 5 Dodge, Lanai, Mason, Naked, Ocean, Ponca, Queen, Quiet, Rapid, Sioux, Windy 6 Carson, Culver, Gotham, Jersey, Kansas, Mexico, Radium 7 Circuit, Emerald, Vatican 8 Atlantic, Salt Lake, Virginia 9 Forbidden
___ City, AZ: 3 Sun
City by the Sea (2002 film)
cast: Robert De Niro, Eliza Dushku, James Franco, Frances McDormand
___ City, CA: 4 Yuba
___ City Chiefs: 6 Kansas
___ City Confidential: 6 Kansas
___ City, FL: 4 Ybor 5 Plant 6 Haines, Panama
City Hall (1996 film)
cast: Danny Aiello, John Cusack, Bridget Fonda, Martin Landau, Al Pacino
City Hall boss: 5 mayor 8 hizzoner
City Heat (1984 film)
cast: Jane Alexander, Clint Eastwood, Madeline Kahn, Burt Reynolds
___ City, HI: 5 Lanai
___ City, IA: 5 Sioux
City in the Sea, The
author: Edgar Allan Poe
City Lights (1931 film)
cast: Charles Chaplin
director: Charles Chaplin
___ City, NJ: 5 Ocean
___ City, NV: 6 Carson
City of ___: 3 God, Joy 4 Elms, Hope 5 David, Light 6 Angels, Totems
City of Angels (1998 film)
cast: Nicolas Cage, Dennis Franz, Meg Ryan
dog: 4 Earl
City of Brotherly ___: 4 Love
City of God
author: E.L. Doctorow
City of Joy setting: 5 India
City of Light, The: 5 Paree, P…
City of New Orleans: 5 tr…
City of New Orleans, T… song)
artist: Arlo Guthrie
City of Seven ___: 5 Hills
City of the Beasts
author: Isabel Allende
City of the Kings: 4 Lima
City of Trees, The: 5 Boise
___ City, OK: 3 Del
___ City, PA: 3 Oil
___ City Rollers: 3 Bay
___ City Royals: 6 Kansas
cityscape: 4 view 5 vista
___ City, SD: 5 Rapid
City Slickers (1991 film)
cast: Billy Crystal, Bruno Kirby, Jack Palance, Helen Slater, Daniel Stern
city-state, ancient: 5 Argos, polis 6 Athens, Sparta
___ City steak: 6 Kansas
___ City Sue: 5 Sioux
___ City, The: 5 Black, Naked 7 Eternal
City Without Walls
author: W.H. Auden
City Wit, The
author: Richard Brome
___ City Woman: 5 Sweet
Ciudad Juárez neighbor: 6 El Paso
civet: 3 cat 5 felid, rasse, zibet 6 animal, feline, mammal 7 wildcat
product: 4 musk
civic: 4 city 5 local, urban 6 public 8 internal 9 municipal
group: 4 Elks 7 Jaycees, Kiwanis
civic ___: 6 center, leader
civic-___: 6 minded
Civic: 3 car 4 auto 5 Honda
civics: 8 politics
civil: 4 city, kind 5 suave 6 polite, public, social, urbane 7 cordial, genteel, refined, secular, tactful 8 domestic, gracious, ladylike, mannerly, obliging, outgoing, pleasant, temporal, well-bred 9 courteous, municipal 10 diplomatic, neighborly, respectful, thoughtful
disorder: 4 riot
liberty: 2 rt. 5 right
offense: 4 tort
servant: 5 mayor 7 officer 8 official 10 bureaucrat
war: 6 revolt 7 anarchy 8 seditio… uprising 9 rebellion 10 revolu…
civil ___: 3 day, law, war 4 year 6 rights 7 defense, servant
Civil ___ Patrol: 3 Air
Civil Action, A (1998 film)
cast: Robert Duvall, W… Macy, John Travol…
Civil Aeronautics …
Civil Disobedience
author: Henry …
___ civile: 3 jus
civilian: 6 laym…
attire: 5 m…
Civilian C…
civility…

civilizing: 8 cultural 9 uplifting
Civil Rights Memorial
architect: 3 Lin
civil rights org.: 4 ACLU, CORE, EEOC, SCLC, SNCC 5 NAACP
Civil War
anthem: 5 Dixie
battle: 6 Shiloh 7 Bull Run 8 Antietam, Manassas 9 Vicksburg 10 Fort Sumter, Gettysburg, Wilderness
color: 4 blue, gray, grey
general: 3 Lee, Ord 5 Bragg, Buell, Early, Ewell, Grant, Meade 6 Custer, Hooker, Stuart 7 Forrest, Halleck, Hancock, Jackson, Pickett, Sherman, Sickles 8 Burnside, Johnston, Sheridan 9 Doubleday, McClellan 10 Beauregard, Longstreet
inits.: 3 CSA, REL, USG
nickname: 3 Abe
side: 5 North, South, union
soldier: 3 reb
veterans' org.: 3 GAR
weapon: 5 saber 6 cannon
civvies: 5 dress, mufti 7 clothes
__ C. Kenton: 4 Erle
Cl: 4 elem. 7 element, halogen 8 chlorine
17 for ~: 4 at. no.
clabber: 4 clot, curd 5 dairy 6 cheese, curdle, gelate 7 thicken
clabbered: 4 sour 5 thick
clack: 3 yak, yap 4 snap, tick 5 click, cluck, noise, sound 6 cackle, rattle 7 chatter, clatter, palaver
clacker, dancer's: 4 zill
clad: 5 robed 6 decent, garbed 7 arrayed, attired, clothed, covered, dressed, enrobed 8 bedecked 9 decked out, outfitted
in: 7 wearing
starter: 4 iron
__clad: 4 snow 5 armor
Claiborne: 3 Liz 4 Pell 5 Craig 7 Dolores
claim: 2 rt. 3 say 4 aver, avow, case, [illegible]bs, feud, hold, lien, plea 5 argue, [illegible]ast, right, share, stake, title [illegible]tion, allege, assert, avowal, [illegible]e, demand, insist, option, [illegible] 7 call for, contend, declare, [illegible], lawsuit, pretend, profess, [illegible]reserve 8 argument, arro[illegible]ment, interest, maintain, [illegible]etense, property, stake [illegible]on, challenge, owner[illegible]e, privilege 10 allega[illegible] contention,
[illegible]igate
[illegible]ion
[illegible]refund, settle
[illegible]good 9 reim[illegible]
[illegible]rtgage
[illegible]mage

claimant: 6 lienor 8 litigant 9 applicant
Claiming of Sleeping Beauty, The
author: Anne Rice
__-claims court: 5 small
__ claim to: 3 lay
Clair: 4 René 5 saint 8 Huxtable
to Cliff: 4 wife 6 spouse
Clair de Lune
composer: Claude Debussy
Claire: 3 Ina 5 Bloom, Danes 6 Trevor 7 Forlani 9 Chennault
__ Claire: 3 Eau 5 Marie
__ Claire, Que.: 6 Pointe
Clairol
competitor: 6 L'Oréal
clairvoyance: 3 ESP, psi 9 telepathy
clairvoyant: 3 fey 4 seer 5 augur, sibyl, vatic 6 medium, mental, oracle 7 aruspex, diviner, prophet, psychic, vatical 8 haruspex, oracular, telepath 9 prescient 10 predictive
need: 5 tarot 7 crystal
words: 4 I see
clam: 4 buck 5 gaper, shell 6 dollar, gweduc, quahog 7 bivalve, coquina, geoduck, mollusc, mollusk, pompano, quahaug, relaxed, seafood, smacker, steamer, toheroa 8 seashell, simoleon 9 hard-shell, shellfish, soft-shell 10 littleneck
chowder: 4 soup
ender: 4 bake, worm 5 shell 7 diggers
giant ~: 5 shell 8 seashell
like Manhattan ~ chowder: 5 thymy
part: 5 valve
sauce alternative: 5 pesto 8 marinara
up: 5 quiet 6 stifle 7 be quiet, silence 8 withhold
clam __: 5 sauce, shell 7 chowder, diggers
__ clam: 4 hard, king, long, soft, surf 5 giant, horse, pismo, razor, round 7 steamer
clamant: 5 noisy 6 urgent 8 pressing 10 compelling
clambake: 4 fete, gala, meal 5 feast, party, rally 6 picnic 9 festivity, gathering
Clambake (1967 film)
cast: Bill Bixby, Shelley Fabares, Will Hutchins, Elvis Presley
clamber: 4 shin 5 climb, crawl, mount, scale 6 ascend, ramble, shinny 7 shinney 8 scrabble, scramble
up: 5 mount
clam chowder: 4 soup
clamdiggers: 5 pants 8 knickers
clammed up: 3 mum 5 quiet 6 silent 9 secretive 10 speechless, unspeaking
clammy: 3 wet 4 cold, damp, dank 5 humid, moist, muggy, soggy, undry 6 steamy, sticky, stuffy, sultry, sweaty 7 viscose, viscous, wettish
clamor: 3 ado, cry, din, row 4 bawl, buzz, fuss, howl, peal, roar, to-do 5 blare, hoo-ha, noise, shout 6 bellow, bustle, hassle, holler, hubbub, lather, outcry, racket, ruckus, rumpus, tumult, uproar 7 clangor, cluster, ferment, protest, turmoil 8 brouhaha, disorder, hangover, proclaim 9 agitation, cacophony, commotion, hue and cry, make a fuss, raise Cain 10 clattering, hubba-hubba, hullabaloo, hurly-burly
for: 6 demand
(for): 3 ask
clamorous: 4 loud 5 aroar, forte, noisy, vocal 6 brassy 7 blaring, booming, exigent, hooting, jarring, pealing, rackety, rampant, raucous, reboant, roaring 8 crashing, exigeant, piercing, plangent, rumbling, sonorous, strident, turned up 9 big-voiced, deafening, demanding, insistent 10 boisterous, imperative, insatiable, resounding, stentorian, strepitous, thundering, tumultuous, uproarious, vociferant, vociferous
clamp: 4 bind, grip, join, lock, vise 5 brace, clasp, latch 6 clench, fasten, joiner, secure 7 bracket 8 fastener
down on: 5 quash 6 batten, stifle
clamp __: 4 down
Clampett: 3 Bob, Jed 7 Elly May
nephew: 6 Bodine, Jethro
portrayer: 5 Ebsen 7 Douglas
Clampitt, Amy: 4 poet
clams: 4 cash 5 bread, dough
prepare ~: 3 fry 5 steam
clams __: 6 casino
clamshell material: 5 nacre
clan: 3 mob, set 4 band, club, gang, race, ring, sect, sept 5 bunch, folks, group, house, stock, tribe 6 clique, family, outfit, people 7 coterie, faction, in-group, kindred, kinfolk, lineage, society 8 kinfolks, kinsfolk 10 fraternity
ancient Greek ~: 6 phyles
bigwig: 5 thane, thegn
clash: 4 feud
division: 4 sept
emblem: 5 totem
man: 4 Scot
member: 4 aunt 5 niece, uncle 6 cousin, nephew
wear: 4 kilt 5 plaid
see also family
Clancy Brothers
member: 5 Makem
Clancy, Tom: 6 writer
hero: Jack Ryan
subject: 3 CIA
work: Airborne
Armored Cav
The Cardinal of the Kremlin
Carrier
Clear and Present Danger
Debt of Honor
Executive Orders
Fighter Wing
The Hunt for Red October
Marine
Patriot Games
Rainbow Six
Red Rabbit
Red Storm Rising
SSN
Submarine
The Sum of All Fears
The Teeth of the Tiger
Without Remorse
clandestine: 3 sly 4 foxy 6 artful, closet, covert, hidden, masked, secret, sneaky, unseen, veiled 7 cloaked, furtive, illicit, on the QT, private 8 hush-hush, obscured, secluded, shrouded, sneaking, stealthy 9 concealed, disguised, underhand 10 undercover, under wraps
org.: 3 CIA, NSA, ONI
clandestinely: 7 sub rosa 8 on the sly, secretly 10 under cover
clang: 4 bong, gong, peal, ring, toll 5 chime, clink, knell, noise, sound 6 jangle, jingle 7 resound
clanger: 4 bell
clangor: 3 din 4 ring 5 blare, noise 6 clamor, hubbub, jangle, racket, tumult, uproar 7 clatter 8 clashing 10 clattering
clangorous: 4 loud 5 noisy 6 shrill 8 clashing
clank: 5 sound 6 jangle, rattle 7 clatter
clannish: 9 exclusive, sectarian
Clan of the Cave Bear, The
author: Jean Auel
character: 3 Aba, Iza, Oga, Uka 4 Ayla, Brun, Creb, Durc, Goov 5 Broud
clansperson: 4 aunt 5 uncle 6 cousin, father, mother, sister 7 brother 8 relative
Clanton: 3 Ike 5 Jimmy
foe: 4 Earp
clap: 4 peal, slam, slap 5 crack, smack, smash, sound 6 praise 7 acclaim, applaud, thunder
cuffs on: 5 run in 6 arrest
ender: 4 trap 5 board
one's hands on: 4 grab 6 snatch
starter: 4 hand 5 after 7 thunder
clapboard: 5 board 6 wooden
Clap for the Wolfman (1974 song)
artist: Guess Who
clapper: 6 tongue
place: 4 bell
clapping: 7 ovation 8 applause
Clapton, Eric: 7 British 9 guitarist
band: 5 Cream 8 Roosters 9 Yardbirds 10 Blind Faith
song: Change the World (1996)
I Can't Stand It (1981)
I Shot the Sheriff (1974)
Lay Down Sally (1978)
Layla (1972)
Promises (1978)
Tears in Heaven (1992)
claptrap
see baloney
Clap Yo Hands
composer: George Gershwin
claque: 7 fawners, rooters, toadies 9 applauder 10 applauders, flatterers, sycophants
Clara: 3 Bow 6 Barton, Spital 8 Schumann
__ Clara, CA: 5 Santa
Clare: 4 John, Luce 5 saint 6 Briggs
town in county ~: 5 Ennis
Clare __ Luce: 6 Boothe
Clare, Angel: 6 farmer
wife: 4 Tess
Clare, John: 4 poet 7 British

Clarence: 3 cat, Day 4 lion, Nash 5 Brown, Henry 6 Carter, Darrow, Thomas 7 Gilyard, Mulford 8 Birdseye, Williams
claret: 3 red, zin 4 wine 5 color, Médoc 6 purply 7 crimson 8 Bordeaux, purplish 9 table wine, zinfandel
  origin: 6 France
  relative: *see* red color
claret __: 3 cup, red
Clarice: 8 Starling
  adversary: 8 Hannibal
clarification: 8 exegesis
  words of ~: 5 I mean
clarify: 4 show, sort 5 clean, solve 6 answer, purify, refine, reword, unfold 7 explain, expound 8 illumine, simplify, spell out 9 bring home, elaborate, elucidate, interpret, make plain, translate 10 illuminate, illustrate
clarinet: 4 urua, wind 5 bumpa
  cousin: 4 oboe
  kind of ~: 4 alto
  part: 4 reed
clarinetist: 4 Shaw 6 Bechet, Herman 7 Goodman 8 Fountain
  name: 4 Pete 5 Artie, Benny, Woody 6 Sidney
clarion: 4 wind 6 shrill 7 blaring, trumpet 8 strident
Clarissa Explains It All (Nickelodeon sitcom)
  cast: Melissa Joan Hart (Clarissa Darling)
Clarissa Harlowe
  author: Samuel Richardson
clarity: 8 accuracy, lucidity 9 certainty, plainness, precision 10 directness, exactitude, legibility, simplicity
  lacking ~: 4 hazy 5 fuzzy, muzzy
Clark: 3 Bob, Dee, Joe, Roy 4 Dane, Dave, Dick, Fred, Kent 5 Candy, Gable, Susan, Terri 6 Petula, Ramsey 7 Anthony, Gillies, Kenneth, Sanford, William 8 Claudine, Griffith 9 chocolate
  colleague: 4 Lois 5 Jimmy, Lewis, Perry
__ & Clark: 4 Lois
Clark Bar: 3 bar 5 candy 8 candy bar 9 chocolate
  alternative: *see* candy brand
Clark, Dick: 2 MC 4 host 5 emcee
Clarke: 3 Mae 4 Alan
Clarke, Arthur C.: 6 writer 7 British
  home: Sri Lanka, Ceylon
  work: Childhood's End
    The Coast of Coral
    Earthlight
    A Fall of Moondust
    The Fountains of Paradise
    Rendezvous With Rama
__ Clark Five: 4 Dave
Clark Five, Dave
  song: Because (1964)
    Bits and Pieces (1964)
    Catch Us If You Can (1965)
    Glad All Over (1964)
    I Like It Like That (1965)
    Over and Over (1965)
    You Got What It Takes (1967)
Clark, Joe: 2 P.M. 8 Canadian
  predecessor: 7 Trudeau
  successor: 7 Trudeau
Clark, Kenneth: 3 Sir
Clark, Mary Higgins: 6 writer
  work: All Around the Town
    Before I Say Good-Bye
    The Cradle Will Fall
    A Cry in the Night
    Daddy's Little Girl
    Double Vision
    He Sees You When You're Sleeping
    I'll Be Seeing You
    Let Me Call You Sweetheart
    The Lost Angel
    The Lottery Winner
    Loves Music, Loves to Dance
    Lucky Day
    Moonlight Becomes You
    My Gal Sunday
    The Night Awakens
    On the Street Where You Live
    Pretend You Don't See Her
    Remember Me
    Silent Night
    Stillwatch
    A Stranger Is Watching
    Weep No More, My Lady
    We'll Meet Again
    Where Are the Children?
    While My Pretty One Sleeps
    You Belong to Me
Clark, Petula
  song: Don't Sleep in the Subway (1967)
    Downtown (1965)
    I Know a Place (1965)
    My Love (1966)
    This Is My Song (1967)
Clarkson: 8 Patricia
Clark, Susan: 7 actress
  spouse: Alex Karras
  TV: Webster
Clark, Walter van Tilburg: 6 writer
  work: The Ox-Bow Incident
Clark, William: 8 explorer
  partner: 5 Lewis
claro: 5 cigar
Clary: 6 Robert
clash: 3 jar, row 4 feud, fray, jolt, spat, tiff, tilt 5 argue, brawl, brush, fight, grate, melee, run-in, scrap, set-to, shock 6 affray, battle, breach, combat, differ, fracas, impact, jangle, racket, rumpus, strife, strike, tussle 7 collide, contend, discord, dispute, dissent, grapple, mix it up, quarrel, quibble, rupture, scuffle, wrangle 8 argument, conflict, disagree, disunity, do battle, friction, showdown, skirmish, squabble, struggle, variance 9 encounter, lock horns, raise Cain, scrimmage 10 difference, disharmony, donnybrook, engagement, falling-out
  don't ~: 2 go 5 match
  of arms: 3 war 7 warfare
  they may ~: 4 egos 5 wills
  with: 9 encounter
  (with): 7 compete
Clash by Night
  author: Clifford Odets
clashing: 5 harsh 6 at odds, unlike 7 clangor, hostile, opposed 8 contrary, jangling, opposing, rattling, strident 9 differing 10 clangorous, discordant
clasp: 3 hug, pin 4 clip, fist, grab, grip, hold, join, lock, take 5 catch, clamp, grasp, press, seize, stick 6 broach, brooch, buckle, clench, clinch, clutch, enfold, fasten, infold, snatch 7 bracket, embrace, squeeze 8 fastener 9 fastening, handshake, hold tight, keep close
  old-style: 4 ouch 5 tache
  place for a jewelry ~: 4 nape, neck
  starter: 4 hand
__ clasp: 3 tie
class: 3 ilk, set 4 chic, form, kind, luxe, mold, rank, sort, tier, type 5 birth, brand, breed, caste, genre, genus, grade, group, label, order, range, sharp, style, taxon 6 assort, beauty, bon ton, circle, clique, course, estate, family, league, lesson, manner, nobles, pizazz, polish, rating, school, sphere, status, stripe 7 bracket, coterie, culture, dashing, echelon, lineage, quality, seminar, species, station, stratum, stylish, subject, variety 8 ancestry, category, division, elective, elegance, grouping, pedigree, position, standing, urbanity 9 character, first-rate, genealogy 10 refinement
  conduct a ~: 5 teach 7 lecture
  disrupt the ~: 5 cut up
  division: 5 order
  economy ~: 5 coach
  ender: 4 bell, mate, room
  get the ~ back together: 5 reune
  head of the ~: 3 ace 4 best, tops 5 first 9 first-rate
  keep after ~: 6 detain
  leader: 4 prof 7 teacher 8 lecturer 9 professor 10 instructor
  lower ~: 4 herd, scum 5 dregs 6 masses, rabble 8 riffraff 9 commoners, hoi polloi, peasantry
  not in ~: 3 out 4 away 6 absent
  one in a ~: 5 pupil, tutee 7 student
  rank factor: 3 GPA
  ruling ~: 5 elite 7 royalty 8 nobility
  school ~: 3 art, bio., Eng., gym, soc. 4 chem.., hist., lect., math, shop, trig 6 home ec, phys ed 7 biology, English, history, lecture, physics, poli sci 8 calculus, geometry 9 chemistry, sociology 10 psychology
  simple ~: 5 easy A
  social ~: 5 caste
  unlikely ~ president: 4 nerd
  upper ~: 4 rich 5 haves, lords 6 gentry, jet set 7 society 8 nobility 9 gentility 10 haute monde
  work: 6 lesson
class __: 3 act, day, war 4 mark 5 clown 6 action 7 warfare
class-__ suit: 6 action
__ class: 4 form, word 5 Bible, cabin, first, lower, third, upper 6 best in, master, middle, second, social 7 economy, tourist, working
__-class: 4 high 5 first, third, world 6 fourth
classic: 4 oldy, tome 5 model, oldie, typic 6 simple 7 regular, typical, vintage 8 standard 9 exemplary 10 consummate, definitive, magnum opus
  starter: 3 neo
classical: 5 Attic, Doric, Greek, Ionic, model, music, Roman, style 7 elegant, Grecian, Homeric 8 Hellenic, literary 9 canonical, exemplary, Virgilian 10 harmonious, historical, humanistic, restrained, scholastic
  composer: 4 Arne, Bach, Ives, Lalo, Orff 5 d'Indy, Dukas, Elgar, Fauré, Gluck, Grieg, Haydn, Holst, Liszt, Ravel, Satie, Verdi, Weber 6 Bartók, Brahms, Chopin, Delius, Dvorák, Glinka, Gounod, Handel, Mahler, Mozart, Wagner, Webern 7 Bellini, Berlioz, Borodin, Britten, Debussy, Delibes, Milhaud, Poulenc, Puccini, Purcell, Rossini, Smetana, Strauss, Vivaldi 8 Bruckner, Clementi, Paganini, Respighi, Schubert, Schumann, Sibelius, Telemann 9 Beethoven, Buxtehude, Donizetti, Hindemith, Meyerbeer, Prokofiev, Scarlatti 10 Monteverdi, Saint-Saëns
  language: 5 Greek, Latin
  music: 4 trio 5 fugue, motet, opera, rondo, waltz 6 sonata 7 cantata, partita, quartet, toccata 8 concerto, nocturne, oratorio, serenade, symphony
  scholar: 8 humanist
  starter: 3 neo
Classical __: 3 Gas 5 Greek, Latin
Classical Gas (1968 song)
  artist: Mason Williams
classicism: 8 grandeur 9 formality, Hellenism, propriety, restraint, sublimity 10 excellence, proportion, refinement, regularity, simplicity
Classico: 5 sauce 10 pasta sauce
  alternative: 4 Ragú 5 Prego 6 Prince 10 Newman's Own 11 Aunt Millie's
classics: 7 letters 10 literature
classification: 3 ilk 4 kind 5 genre, genus, grade, group, label, niche, order 6 branch, rating, series, system 7 bracket, echelon, section, sorting 8 category, grouping, ordering, sequence
  blood ~: 5 type A, type B, type O 6 type AB
  science of ~: 8 taxonomy
classified: 2 ad 6 inside, secret, want ad 7 private, regular 8 hush-hush
  abbr.: 2 rm. 3 EEO, EIK, EOE 4 bsmt. 6 apt. gar.
  cost: 6 ad rate
  listing: 3 job 8 personal
classify: 4 file, list, name size, sort, type 5 grad index, label, order, 6 assort, divide, r bracket, catalo ate, identify, c separate, ta 10 catego hole
classma
classm
Clas
  autho

classroom: 4 hall
clanger: 4 bell
item: 3 map **4** desk **5** chalk, globe **6** eraser
jotting: 5 notes
no-no: 3 gum
sound: 3 pst, shh **4** psst
classy: 4 chic, fine, luxe, posh, rich, tony **5** haute, ritzy, sharp, swank, swell, swish, toney **6** dapper, dressy, modish, snappy, snazzy, spiffy, spruce, swanky **7** dashing, elegant, in vogue, refined, stylish, voguish **8** esthetic, tasteful **9** exclusive, first-rate, glamorous, high-toned
clatter: 3 din **4** bang, roar **5** clack, clank, noise, noisy, sound **6** clamor, hubbub, jangle, racket, rattle, rumpus, uproar **7** bluster, clangor **8** ballyhoo **9** commotion **10** hullabaloo
Claude: 4 Anet, King **5** Akins, Brown, McKay, Monet, Rains, saint, Simon **6** Albert, Harmon **7** Debussy, Lelouch, Lorrain
__-Claude Duvalier: 4 Jean
__-Claude Killy: 4 Jean
Claudel, Paul: 4 poet **6** French
Claudette: 7 Colbert
__-Claude Van Damme: 4 Jean
Claudia: 8 Schiffer **9** Cardinale, Christian
colleague: 4 Elle, Tyra **5** Cindy, Naomi
Claudine: 5 Auger, Clark **6** Longet
Claudio: 5 Arrau **6** Abbado **10** Monteverde, Monteverdi
Claudius: 5 Roman **6** Caesar
home: 4 Rome
successor: 4 Nero
see also Latin
Claus __ Bulow: 3 von
clause: 7 article, codicil, passage, proviso, section **9** amendment, paragraph, provision **10** subsection
connector: 3 and, but, nor **4** conj. **7** however **11** conjunction
escape ~: 3 out
modifier: 6 adverb
separator: 5 comma **6** em dash
__ clause: 4 main, noun, stop **6** adverb, escape **7** no-trade, reserve
__ Clause, The: 5 Santa
Clausewitz: 4 Carl
__ clausum: 4 mare
Claus von __: 5 Bulow
Clavell, James: 6 writer
work: Gai-Jin
King Rat
Noble House
Shogun
Tai-Pan
Whirlwind
verings, The
uthor: Anthony Trollope
s: 6 sticks **10** percussion
hord: 10 instrument
e: 4 bone
e: 8 shoulder
8 keyboard
ser for the ~: 4 Bach
4 mall, maul, tear **5** talon
e, pincer, scrape, ungual, unguis **7** scratch **8** lacerate **10** fingernail
at: 3 paw **6** attack
combining form: 4 chel- **5** cheli-, ungui-
crustacean ~: 5 chela
starter: 3 dew
claw __: 3 bar **4** foot **6** hammer
__ Claw, The: 7 Scarlet
claxon: 4 horn
clay: 4 loam, marl, soil **5** adobe, earth, loess **6** kaolin **7** earthen, kaoline, pottery **10** terra cotta
combining form: 3 pel- **4** pelo- **5** argil- **7** argilli-, argillo-
cooker: 4 kiln
plant that grows on ~ animals: 4 chia
product: 4 tile **5** adobe **7** ceramic, pottery **10** terra cotta
rock: 5 shale
type of ~: 4 gley, malm **5** argil **6** kaolin **7** biscuit, kaoline
work with ~: 5 knead, model, throw
clay __: 5 court **6** pigeon
Clay: 5 Aiken, Henry **7** Cassius
today: 3 Ali
claybank: 5 horse
Clayburgh, Jill: 7 actress
spouse: David Rabe
Clayderman: 7 Richard
clayey: 5 gluey, gummy, pasty **6** earthy, sticky **7** plastic **8** flexible **9** malleable
material: 4 loam, marl **5** loess
Clay, Henry: 6 orator
claymore: 5 sword
clay pigeon
launcher: 4 trap
shooting: 5 skeet
clay-rich soil, like: 5 loamy, marly
Clayson: 4 Jane
Clayton: 3 Jan **4** Jack **5** Moore
__ Clayton Powell: 4 Adam
clayware: 5 china **7** pottery **8** ceramics, crockery **9** porcelain **10** terra cotta
Clea
author: Lawrence Durrell
clean: 3 mop **4** dust, fair, lave, neat, pure, soak, soap, swab, swob, tidy, trim, wash, wipe **5** bathe, blank, brush, clear, erase, flush, fresh, groom, legal, mop up, moral, plain, rinse, scour, scrub, sharp, snowy, sop up, sweep, sweet, total, white **6** bathed, bright, chaste, decent, fairly, filter, neaten, neatly, polish, purify, refine, scrape, simple, sponge, spruce, tidy up, vacuum, washed **7** aseptic, clarify, clear up, correct, deterge, elegant, ethical, expunge, furbish, launder, legible, orderly, perfect, precise, refined, shampoo, shining, sinless, sterile, sweep up, unarmed, unfussy, upright **8** absolute, complete, decisive, definite, dirtless, distinct, drug-free, flawless, germfree, graceful, honestly, hygienic, innocent, pristine, purified, readable, sanitary, spotless, spruce up, thorough, unbribed, unfouled, unsoiled, vacuumed, virtuous, well-kept **9** blameless, deodorize, disinfect, exemplary, faultless, guilt-free, guiltless, honorable, judicious, laundered, sanitized, sparkling, stainless, sterilize, taintless, undefiled, unobscene, unsmudged, unspotted, unstained, unsullied, untainted, wholesome **10** antiseptic, conclusive, immaculate, impeccable, inculpable, in the clear, sterilized, unimpaired, uninfected, unpolluted, upstanding, weaponless
again: 5 remop
air org.: 3 EPA
come ~: 4 bare **5** admit, level, own up **6** fess up **7** confess
good ~ fun: 6 frolic
hands: 7 probity **9** innocence
house: 5 purge, sweep
keep one's nose ~: 6 behave **10** toe the line
not ~: 5 dirty, germy, grimy **6** filthy, impure, sloppy, soiled
out: 3 gut **4** ruin **5** empty, purge **7** shake up **8** evacuate
squeaky ~: 6 chaste **8** spotless **10** immaculate
sweep: 7 triumph, victory **9** landslide
thoroughly: 5 scour, scrub
up: 4 edit, lave, rake **5** sweep **6** neaten, profit, redact, reform, revise, settle **7** correct, rectify **8** legalize **9** expurgate, keep house, refurbish
up one's act: 5 atone **6** reform
wipe the slate ~: 6 pardon **7** absolve, forgive, release **8** overlook
clean __: 3 out **4** room **5** hands, house, sweep **6** energy
clean __ of health: 4 bill
clean __ whistle: 3 as a
clean-__: 3 cut **6** handed, limbed, living, shaven
__ clean: 4 come
__-clean: 3 dry **7** squeaky
clean and __: 4 jerk
clean as a __: 7 whistle
__ clean breast of: 5 make a
clean-cut: 4 neat, nice, trim **5** clear, crisp **6** proper **7** regular **8** distinct, handsome **9** wholesome
cleaned out: 5 broke **9** penniless
cleaner: 3 lye, vac **4** char, maid, soap, wipe **5** Brite, broom, Lysol, Tilex **6** Top Job, vacuum **7** Lestoil, Pine Sol **9** detergent, Fantastik, Step Saver
like some ~s: 4 piny **5** piney
partner: 4 dyer
pipe ~: 3 lye **5** Drano, snake
scent: 4 pine
target: 4 dust, spot **5** grime, stain
__ cleaner: 3 air, dry **4** pipe **6** street, vacuum
cleaning: 5 chore **7** laundry **9** housework **10** refinement
cloth: 3 rag **6** chammy, shammy, shamoy **7** chamois
device: 3 mop, vac **4** swab **5** broom, brush **6** dry mop, vacuum
needing ~: 5 dirty, dusty, messy
starter: 5 house
substance: 3 lye **4** soap
__ cleaning: 3 dry **6** spring
__-cleaning oven: 4 self
cleanliness: 7 hygiene
clean-living: 4 pure **8** virtuous
Clean, Mr.
rival: 5 Lysol **7** Lestoil, Pine Sol
clean one's __: 5 clock
cleanse: 4 swab, swob, wash **5** flush, purge, rinse, scour, scrub **6** purify, refine **7** freshen, launder **8** sanctify, sanitize **9** cauterize, disinfect, expurgate, sterilize
cleanser: 3 lye **4** Ajax, Bab-O, soap, suds **5** borax, Comet **6** Bon Ami, lather, polish **7** solvent, Woolite **8** abrasive, fumigant **9** detergent, germicide, Soft Scrub **10** antiseptic
clean-shaven: 9 beardless
cleansing: 4 bath **8** ablution, lavation **9** catharsis
cleanup: 5 purge
clean up one's __: 3 act
clear: 3 net, pay, rid **4** bare, earn, easy, fair, free, leap, make, mild, open, pure, rake, reap, safe, sure, void, wipe **5** blank, clean, empty, erase, exact, fresh, let go, light, lucid, overt, plain, sharp, shiny, stark, sunny, sweep, vault, vivid, white **6** acquit, bright, direct, excuse, exempt, glassy, hurdle, hyalin, in tune, in view, let off, limpid, lucent, marked, pardon, patent, profit, public, purify, remove, serene, settle, simple, smooth, square, unclog, unload, vacant, vacate **7** absolve, audible, certain, crystal, decided, evident, explain, exposed, express, graphic, hyaline, in focus, legible, logical, obvious, precise, realize, receive, release, relieve, set free, shining, through, unblock, unravel, vacuous, visible **8** apparent, clean-cut, coherent, definite, distinct, explicit, innocent, jump over, knowable, luculent, luminous, manifest, palpable, pass over, pellucid, pleasant, readable, resolved, shake off, simplify, surmount, take home, unburden, unhidden, unveiled, vitreous **9** blameless, cloudless, convinced, disengage, downright, eliminate, exculpate, exonerate, extricate, graphical, graspable, guilt-free, guiltless, melodious, navigable, negotiate, satisfied, trenchant, unblurred, unclouded, unimpeded, unlimited, unobscure, vindicate **10** articulate, conclusive, disculpate, easily read, observable, pronounced, see-through, spelled out, unarguable, undeniable, undoubtful, unhampered, unhindered, unshrouded, untroubled
a loan: 5 repay **7** pay back, satisfy **8** make good, settle up, square up **9** liquidate, reimburse **10** compensate
as mud: 5 mirky, murky, vague **9** equivocal **10** unexplicit
away: 5 scoop **6** remove
be ~: 5 add up **9** make sense
become ~: 3 gel **5** click **9** penetrate
crystal ~: 5 lucid **6** patent **7** obvious **8** apparent, knowable, manifest
cut: 8 apparent, knowable

fail to ~: 6 bounce
get ~ of: 4 duck, flee, lose **5** avoid, dodge, elude, evade, skirt **6** escape **7** fend off **8** sidestep **10** circumvent
in the ~: 4 safe **5** clean **8** innocent **9** blameless, guilt-free, guiltless **10** inculpable
it might be ~: 5 coast
it's not ~: 3 mud **4** blur
make ~: 4 look, show **5** state **6** decode, define, detail, evince, refine **7** exhibit, explain **8** decipher, describe, simplify **9** bring home, emphasize, explicate, expound on, get across, put across, translate **10** illuminate, illustrate
of: 4 past **6** beyond
of the bottom: 6 aweigh
out: 2 go **3** fly, run **4** flee, scat **5** break, leave, purge, scram, sweep **6** decamp, run off **7** abscond, make off, ride off, shake up, take off **8** hightail, run for it, shove off
sky: 5 ether **6** aether
steer ~ of: 4 duck, omit, shun **5** avoid, dodge, elude, evade, shirk, skirt, spurn **6** beware, bypass, eschew, lay off **7** shy from **8** flee from, sidestep **10** circumvent
the decks: 4 tidy **5** ready
the way: 3 aid **6** assist
thinking: 5 logic **6** wisdom
up: 5 clean, solve, sweep **6** settle, square, unfold **7** explain, resolve, satisfy, unravel **8** simplify, untangle **9** bring home, elucidate **10** illuminate, illustrate
clear ___: 3 ice, off, out **4** away, text **5** as mud **7** channel
clear ___ bell: 3 as a
clear-___: 3 cut, eye **4** eyed **7** coating, sighted
___ clear: 3 all **5** in the
___-clear: 7 crystal
clearance: 2 OK **4** okay, room, sale **5** leave, say-so **7** consent, go-ahead **8** approval, headroom, sanction **9** acquittal, allowance, discharge, open space, unloading **10** evacuation, green light
phrase: 4 as is
Clear and Present Danger (1994 film)
cast: Anne Archer, Willem Dafoe, Harrison Ford
hero: Jack Ryan
clear as ___: 3 mud **5** a bell
Clearasil target: 3 zit **4** acne
clear-cut: 4 open **5** exact, lucid, plain, sharp, terse, tight **6** in view, patent, public, strong **7** assured, evident, exposed, express, obvious, precise, visible **8** definite, explicit, manifest, specific, unhidden, unveiled **9** definable, trenchant **10** definitive, observable, pronounced, reasonable, unshrouded
___ Clear Day...: 3 On a
cleared: 4 open **6** exempt **8** official **10** off the hook, vindicated
out: 4 gone
clear-eyed: 5 sober
clearheaded: 4 calm, keen **5** acute, alert, lucid, sharp, smart, sober **6** astute, bright, steady, with it **7** heads-up, prudent, sapient **8** composed, rational, sensible **9** astucious, collected, judicious, on the ball, unruffled, wide-awake **10** discerning, on one's toes, on the stick, perceptive
clearheadedness: 5 sense
clearing: 4 yard **5** glade, space **6** region **7** expanse
clearly: 4 well **5** by far, plain, smack **6** easily, simply, surely **8** markedly
say ~: 10 articulate
seen: 5 plain **7** obvious
show ~: 5 prove **7** specify
clearness: 9 freshness **10** simplicity
___ clear of: 5 steer
clear-sighted: 8 keen-eyed, lynx-eyed **9** observant, sagacious
clear the ___: 3 air **4** deck
Clearwater: 4 city, town **5** range
city near ~: 5 Largo
locale: 7 Florida
Cleary: 7 Beverly
cleat: 4 calk **5** wedge
cleavage: 3 cut, gap **4** rift, slit **5** break, chasm, cleft, split **6** divide, schism **8** division, fracture **10** separation
combining form: 5 -clase
cleave: 3 axe, cut, hew, rip **4** chop, join, link, part, plow, rend, rive, stab, tear **5** carve, cling, crack, sever, slash, slice, split, stick, unite **6** adhere, attach, be true, bisect, cohere, cut off, divide, fasten, sunder **7** cling to, disjoin, scissor, stand by, stick to **8** dissever, disunite, separate
cleaver: 3 axe **4** froe, frow **5** knife
use a ~: 3 hew **4** chop
Cleaver: 4 June, Ward **5** Wally **6** Beaver **8** Eldridge
Cleaver, Beaver
word: 3 gee **5** golly
Cleaver, Wally
buddy: 5 Eddie
Cleavon: 6 Little
Cleburne: 4 city, town
locale: 5 Texas
___ Cleef: 6 Lee Van
cleek: 4 club, iron **8** golf club
Cleese: 4 John
clef: 4 bass **5** tenor **6** treble
letters: 4 FACE **5** EGBDF
locale: 5 staff
notation: 4 rest
roman à ~: 4 book **7** fiction
___ clef: 4 alto, bass **5** tenor **6** roman à, treble **7** soprano
cleft: 3 cut, gap **4** gulf, rent, rift, slit, torn **5** bifid, break, chink, crack, gorge, in two, riven, split **6** breach, broken, cranny, dimple, hollow, parted **7** cracked, crevice, fissure, incised, opening **8** cleavage, fracture, sundered **9** separated
combining form: 5 fissi-
Cleghorne: 5 Ellen
Clem: 6 Bevans, Labine
clematis: 4 vine **5** plant **6** flower
Clemenceau: 7 Georges
clemency: 4 pity **5** grace, mercy **6** lenity, pardon **7** charity, quarter, release **8** kindness, lenience, leniency **9** tolerance **10** compassion, gentleness
Clemens: 3 Sam **5** Roger, Twain **6** Krauss **8** Brentano
Clemens, Roger
sport: 8 baseball
clement: 3 lax **4** calm, easy, fair, kind, mild, soft, warm **5** balmy, loose, sunny **6** bright, decent, gentle, humane, kindly, tender **7** lenient, ruthful, sparing **8** flexible, gracious, laid-back, merciful, placable, tolerant **9** assuasive, compliant, easygoing, forgiving, indulgent, temperate, unextreme **10** altruistic, benevolent, charitable, forbearing, permissive, unexacting
Clement: 4 pope **5** Moore, saint **6** Attlee **7** pontiff
___ Clemente, CA: 3 San
Clemente, Roberto: 6 Pirate **10** outfielder
Clementine
father: 5 miner
shoe size: 4 nine
Clementi piece: 5 étude
Clements: 3 Ron
Clemson: 6 school **7** college
athlete: 5 Tiger
conference: 3 ACC
locale: 4 S. Car.
clench: 4 fist, grip, hold, lock **5** clamp, clasp, grasp, seize **6** clutch **7** bear hug, tighten **9** handshake, hold tight
clenched ___: 4 fist
Cleo: 5 Laine
Cleon
author: Robert Browning
Cleopatra: 5 queen **8** Egyptian
attendant: 4 Iras
love: 4 Marc **6** Antony, Caesar
milieu: 4 Nile **5** Egypt
serpent: 3 asp
sister: 8 Berenice
star in 1917: 4 Bara
Cleopatra (1934 film)
cast: Claudette Colbert
director: Cecil B. DeMille
Cleopatra (1963 film)
cast: Richard Burton, Rex Harrison, Elizabeth Taylor
Cleopatra's ___: 6 Needle
Cleopatre
artist: Erté
clergy: 4 nuns **6** curate, estate **7** bishops, canonry, prelacy, priests **8** deaconry, minister, ministry **9** ministers, pastorate, rabbinate **10** missionary, priesthood
deg.: 3 STB, STM
not ~: 5 laity
not of the ~: 3 lay **4** laic **6** laical
cleric: 3 rev. **4** abbé, dean, guru, imam, lama, Père, pope **5** abbot, canon, clerk, elder, imaum, padre, rabbi, rebbe, roshi, Rt. Rev., vicar **6** Becket, bishop, curate, deacon, divine, father, parson, pastor, priest, reader, rector, sensei, shaman **7** Brahman, Brother, dominie, karmapa, mahatma, pontiff, prelate, primate **8** cardinal, chaplain, minister, ordinary, preacher, reverend, rinpoche, sky pilot **9** ayatollah, churchman, Dalai Lama, deaconess, maharishi, monsignor, patriarch, precentor, religious, subdeacon, Tashi Lama **10** archbishop, archdeacon, prebendary
home: 5 manse
clerical: 5 papal, pious **7** monkish **8** churchly, hieratic, monastic, pastoral, prelatic, priestly **9** apostolic, canonical, episcopal, religious **10** monastical, parsonical, pontifical, rabbinical
court: 4 rota
garment: 3 alb **5** fanon, orale, rabat
headdress: 5 miter, mitre
subject: 3 rel. **8** religion
worker: 5 clerk **6** typist
clerical ___: 5 error **6** collar
clerihew: 4 poem **5** verse
clerk: 4 hand **5** filer, typer **6** scribe, typist **7** cashier, employe **8** employee **10** amanuensis, bookkeeper
concern: 4 file
Navy ~: 6 yeoman
spot: 4 desk
starter: 5 sales
___ clerk: 3 law, lay **4** bank, city, file, room, town **5** stock **6** county
Clermont: 4 boat, ship
power source: 5 steam
Clete: 5 Boyer
Cleveland: 4 Abbe, city, John, town **5** Amory, James **6** Grover
county: 8 Cuyahoga
lake: 4 Erie
locale: 4 Ohio **9** Tennessee
org. founded in ~: 4 WCTU
pro team: 4 Cavs **6** Browns **7** Indians **9** Cavaliers
river: 8 Cuyahoga
time zone: 3 EDT, EST
town near ~: 4 Avon **5** Berea, Parma
___ Cleveland Alexander: 6 Grover
Cleveland, Grover: 9 president
biographer: 6 Nevins
former occupation: 6 lawyer
home: 7 Buffalo, New York **9** New Jersey
opponent: 6 Blaine **8** Harrison
real first name: 7 Stephen
V.P.: 9 Hendricks, Stevenson
wife: 7 Frances
Cleveland, John: 4 poet **7** British
Cleveland Plain ___: 6 Dealer
clever: 3 apt, sly **4** able, cagy, cute, deft, foxy, good, neat, wily, wise **5** acute, adept, cagey, canny, fresh, nifty, novel, quick, ready, savvy, sharp, slick, smart, swift, witty **6** adroit, artful, astute, brainy, bright, crafty, daedal, gifted, habile, nimble, shrewd, subtle **7** cunning, knowing, unusual **8** creative, dextrous, incisive, inspired, original, readable, skillful, talented **9** astucious, brilliant, dexterous, ingenious, inventive, masterful, sprightly, strategic **10** discerning, innovative, keen-witted, proficient
comments: 6 banter
move: 4 ploy, ruse **6** device **8** artifice
person: 3 wag, wit
remark: 4 quip **5** sally **6** bon mot

__ clever by half: 3 too
cleverness: 3 art, wit 4 wits 5 craft, guile, sense, skill 6 acumen, brains, esprit 7 finesse 8 aptitude, keenness 9 canniness, dexterity, handiness, ingenuity, quickness, sharpness, smartness 10 adroitness, astuteness, brightness, shrewdness
__ Cleves: 6 Anne of
Cliburn, Van: 7 pianist
cliché: 5 stale 6 homily, phrase, saying 7 bromide 8 chestnut 9 platitude 10 stereotype
clichéd: 4 dull, worn 5 corny, hokey, musty, passé, stale, trite, vapid 6 boring, common, jejune, old hat 7 fatuous, humdrum, prosaic, worn-out 8 bromidic, outdated, outmoded 9 hackneyed, prosaical 10 threadbare, uninspired, unoriginal
click: 4 snap, tick 5 clack, snick 6 pan out 8 hit it off
Click (2006 film)
cast: Kate Beckinsale, Adam Sandler, Christopher Walken
clicker, mouse: 6 button
clickety-__: 5 clack
clicking: 4 tick
client: 3 acc. 4 acct., user 5 buyer, guest 6 patron 7 account, patient, regular, subject 8 customer
be a ~: 9 patronize
potential ~: 8 prospect
clientele: 5 trade 6 public 7 patrons 8 practice, regulars 9 clientage, following, patronage 10 dependents
Client, The (1994 film)
cast: Tommy Lee Jones, Susan Sarandon
cliff: 4 crag, scar 5 bluff, scarp 6 escarp 8 overhang, overlook 9 precipice 10 escarpment, prominence, rocky ledge
debris: 5 scree
dweller: 3 ern 4 erne 5 eagle 6 eaglet
dwelling: 4 aery, eyry 5 aerie, eyrie
feature: 3 lip 4 crag 5 shelf
Hawaiian ~: 4 pali
inlet: 5 fiord, fjord
like a ~: 5 steep
cliff-__: 6 hanger
Cliff: 5 Potts 6 Barnes, Gorman 7 Edwards, Richard 8 Arquette, Huxtable 9 Robertson
to Clair: 6 spouse 7 husband
to J.R.: 5 enemy
cliff-hanger: 5 story 6 serial 7 mystery 8 thriller 9 adventure
Clifford: 4 Buzz 5 Clark, Odets, Shull, Simak
Cliffs __: 5 Notes
Cliffside Park: 4 city, town
locale: 9 New Jersey
__ Cliffs of Dover, The: 5 White
Clift, Montgomery: 5 actor
film: Freud (1962)
From Here to Eternity (1953)
The Heiress (1949)
Judgment at Nuremberg (1961)
The Misfits (1961)
A Place in the Sun (1951)
Raintree County (1957)
Red River (1948)
The Search (1948)
Suddenly, Last Summer (1959)
Wild River (1960)
The Young Lions (1958)
Clifton: 4 Webb 5 Davis, James 7 Fadiman
Clijsters: 3 Kim
climactic: 4 last 8 crowning, dramatic
climate: 4 mood 6 milieu 7 weather 8 elements 10 atmosphere
affecter: 6 El Niño 7 current
combining form: 6 meteor-
climatize: 7 toughen
climax: 3 cap 4 acme, apex, head, peak 5 crest, crown 6 apogee, finale, height, payoff, summit, zenith 8 capstone, high spot, pinnacle, showdown 9 culminate, high point, punch line 10 denouement
starter: 4 anti
climb: 3 top 4 go up, lift, move, rise, shin, soar 5 arise, crawl, mount, reach, scale, surge 6 ascend, ascent, move up, ramble, rocket, shinny 7 clamber, takeoff 8 escalate, scramble 9 crescendo
aboard: 4 join 5 get in, get on 7 enplane, entrain
all over: 5 chide 6 berate, rebuke
on: 5 board 7 entrain
to: 5 reach
climber: 5 plant
challenge: 3 alp 5 scarp
goal: 4 acme
mountain ~: 4 lift 6 iceman
need: 4 gaff, spur 5 ice ax, piton 6 ladder
porch ~: 5 thief
rest: 5 ledge
social ~: 4 snob 7 elitist, upstart
social ~ concern: 6 status
vacation spot: 5 Nepal
__ climber: 6 social
Climb Ev'ry Mountain
composer: Oscar Hammerstein, Richard Rodgers
climbing: 6 uphill
device: 5 stair
plant: 3 ivy 4 nito, vine 5 cubeb, guaco, liana, liane, vetch 7 goldcup 8 bignonia, wistaria, wisteria
climb the __: 5 walls
clime: 5 realm 7 weather 10 atmosphere
clinch: 3 hug, ice, tie 4 grab, grip, hold, lock, nail, seal, tell 5 clasp, grasp, seize, sew up 6 assure, caress, clutch, decide, enfold, ensure, fasten, finish, infold, secure, settle 7 embrace, squeeze 8 finalize, nail down, transact 9 determine, lay hold of 10 consummate
clinched: 4 sure 8 in the bag
clincher: 5 proof 6 payoff
Cline: 5 Patsy 6 Edward
Cline, Patsy
song: Crazy (1961)
I Fall to Pieces (1961)
Walkin' After Midnight (1957)
cling: 5 peach, stick 6 adhere, attach, cleave, cohere, hang on, hold on, linger, remain 7 embrace
ender: 4 fish 5 stone
to: 3 hug 4 love 6 cleave, clutch, retain 9 hold tight
cling __: 5 peach
__ cling: 6 static
Cling Free
alternative: 5 Downy 6 Bounce 7 Snuggle 10 Final Touch
clinging: 6 sticky 8 adhesive 9 tenacious
Clingmans Dome
locale: 9 Tennessee
clingstone: 5 fruit, peach
clingy: 5 twiny 8 adhesive 9 tenacious
clothing: 4 knit
clinic: 8 hospital 9 infirmary
staffer: 2 GP, MD, RN 5 nurse 6 doctor
__ Clinic: 4 Mayo
clinical __: 5 trial
Clinic, The
author: Jonathan Kellerman
Clinique
alternative: *see* cosmetic brand
clink: 4 jail, poky, stir 5 clang, pokey, sound 6 cooler, jangle, jingle, lockup, prison, tinkle 7 hoosgow 8 hoosegow
one in the ~: 3 con 5 lifer 7 convict
clinker: 3 dud 4 goof 5 error 7 mistake
Clint: 5 Black 6 Holmes, Howard, Walker 8 Eastwood
Clinton: 4 Bill 6 De Witt, George 7 Chelsea, Hillary 8 Davisson
Clinton, Bill: 3 Eli 9 president
astrologically: 3 Leo
brother: 5 Roger
cabinet member: 4 Espy, Peña, Reno, West 5 Aspin, Brown, Cohen, Cuomo, Daley, Perry, Reich, Riley, Rubin 6 Herman, Kantor, O'Leary, Slater 7 Babbitt, Bentsen, Shalala, Summers 8 Albright, Cisneros
cat: 5 Socks
child: 7 Chelsea
home: 3 Ark. 7 New York 8 Arkansas
hometown: 4 Hope
idol: 5 Elvis
instrument: 3 sax
middle name: 9 Jefferson
mother: 8 Virginia
opponent: 4 Bush, Dole 5 Perot
original last name: 6 Blythe
party: 3 Dem. 8 Democrat
school: 4 Yale 6 Oxford 10 Georgetown
V.P.: 4 Gore
wife: 7 Hillary
Clinton, Hillary alma mater: 4 Yale
Clinton's Big Ditch: 4 Erie
Clio: 3 car 4 auto, Muse 5 award 7 Renault 10 automobile
candidate: 2 ad 5 adman 10 commercial
parent: 4 Zeus 9 Mnemosyne
see also Muse
clip: 3 bob, cut, hit, mow, nip 4 chip, crop, dock, gait, join, pare, rate, snip, sock, stab, trim 5 catch, cheat, clasp, clout, groom, knock, lower, piece, prune, punch, shave, shear, slash, smack, speed, swipe, whack, wound 6 buckle, cut out, fasten, fleece, lessen, reduce, sample, wallop 7 abridge, bracket, curtail, cut back, defraud, excerpt, extract, scissor, shorten, squeeze, swindle 8 amputate, barrette, decrease, fast pace, fragment, truncate, uppercut 9 sound bite, victimize 10 abbreviate, run a game on
at a good ~: 4 fast 5 apace, quick
ender: 5 board, sheet
news ~: 5 video
on: 6 attach
clip __: 3 art, out 5 joint
__ clip: 3 at a, tie, toe 4 film, news 5 paper
clip-on: 3 tie 8 neckwear
belt ~: 5 pager, phone 6 beeper
clipped: 5 shorn, terse 6 gnomic
clipper: 4 boat, ship 6 shears
coupon ~: 5 saver
on a ~: 4 asea 5 at sea
target: 4 nail
clippers: 4 tool 6 shears 8 scissors
use ~: 5 prune, shear
Clippers: 4 five
home: 10 Los Angeles
org.: 3 NBA
rival: *see* NBA team
clippety-__: 4 clop
clipping: 3 cut 4 foul, snip 5 piece 7 cutting, snippet 8 fragment
shopper's ~: 6 coupon
__ clipping: 4 back, fore, hind 5 press
clique: 3 mob, set 4 band, bloc, clan, club, cult, gang, pack, ring 5 cabal, class, crowd, group, junto, troop 6 circle, outfit 7 company, coterie, faction, in-crowd, in-group, society
power-seeking ~: 5 cabal
cliquish: 9 exclusive, sectarian
Clive: 4 Owen 5 Brook, Colin 6 Barker, Barnes, Donner, Revill, Robert 7 Cussler
cloak: 4 capa, cape, cowl, hide, mask, robe, veil, wrap 5 cache, capot, couch, cover, guise, manta, shawl 6 abolla, birrus, byrrus, capote, domino, enveil, facade, kaross, mantle, poncho, screen, shroud, veneer 7 burnous, conceal, cover up, envelop, garment, mandyas, manteau, mantlet, obscure, paenula, pelisse, pretext, secrete 8 burnoose, capuchin, covering, disguise, enshroud, pretense 9 dissemble, mandilion 10 camouflage, cappa magna, masquerade, roquelaure
African ~: 6 kaross
Arab ~: 7 burnous 8 burnoose
church ~: 10 cappa magna
ender: 4 room
hooded ~: 5 capot 6 capote
matador's ~: 4 capa
monk ~: 4 cowl 7 mandyas
mourning ~: 3 bug 6 insect
partner: 6 dagger
Roman ~: 6 abolla, birrus, byrrus 7 paenula
sleeveless ~: 3 aba 4 abba
Spanish ~: 5 manta
cloak-and-dagger org.: 3 CIA, KGB
cloaked: 6 covert, hidden, secret, unseen 7 furtive, private, sub rosa 8 hush-hush 9 out of view, unexposed 10 undercover, under wraps
Cloak, The: 5 opera
composer: Giacomo Puccini

clobber: **3** bat, bop, hit **4** bash, beat, belt, club, cuff, deck, drub, lick, rout, slam, slug, swat, trim, whip **5** baste, blast, brain, clout, cream, paste, pound, smack, smash, smite, spank, stomp, tromp, whack, whang, worst **6** batter, buffet, hammer, strike, thrash, wallop **7** lambast, overrun, shellac, trounce **8** bludgeon, lambaste, shellack **9** criticize, haul off on, overpower
clobbered old-style: **4** smit
cloche: **3** hat
clock: **4** time **5** alarm, meter, timer, watch **6** ticker **9** timepiece **10** timekeeper
around the ~: **7** nonstop **10** all the time, constantly
at times: **6** chimer
change the ~: **5** reset
climber of rhyme: **5** mouse
digital ~ display: **3** LCD, LED
ender: **4** wise, work
feature: **4** dial, face, gear, hand **5** alarm, chime, radio, works **6** gimmal **8** flywheel, movement
in: **4** come **5** pop up, reach **6** appear, arrive, attend, report
like ~ chimes: **5** horal
nos.: **3** hrs.
numeral: **3** III, VII, XII **4** IIII, VIII
obey the ~: **5** get up
punch a ~: **4** work
setting: **2** AM, PM **3** CDT, CST, EDT, EST, MDT, MST, PDT, PST
ship-shaped ~: **3** nef
sound: **4** tick, tock
standard setting: **3** GMT
summer ~ setting: **3** DST
watcher: **4** eyer
clock __: **5** radio **7** puncher, watcher
__ clock: **4** body, one o', shot, six o', ten o', time, two o' **5** acorn, alarm, Atmos, banjo, chess, five o', four o', nine o', quail, water **6** analog, atomic, cuckoo, eight o', lancet, pigeon, quartz, seven o', three o' **7** annular, balloon, bracket, digital, eleven o', gravity, twelve o'
Clockers (1995 film)
cast: Harvey Keitel, Delroy Lindo, John Turturro
director: Spike Lee
__ Clock Jump: **4** One o'
clock-radio switch: **4** AMFM
...__ clock scholar: **5** a ten o'
Clock Symphony
composer: Joseph Haydn
Clock Winder, The
author: Anne Tyler
clockwise: **5** right **6** deasil
combining form: **5** dextr- **6** dextro-
starter: **7** counter
Clock Without Hands
author: Carson McCullers
clockwork: **9** precision **10** regularity, smoothness
like ~: **5** paced **6** steady **7** regular, uniform **8** reliable, reliably, steadily **9** every time, regularly, uniformly **10** invariably, on schedule
__ clockwork: **4** like
Clockwork Orange, A: **4** film **5** novel
author: Anthony Burgess
character: **4** Alex
director: Stanley Kubrick
clod: **5** brute **7** bumbler, bumpkin, bungler, fumbler **9** schlemiel
ender: **6** hopper
social ~: **4** nerd
see also ninny
Clod and the Pebble, The
author: William Blake
cloddish: **4** dolt, dull **5** inept, unapt **6** clumsy, klutzy, oafish **7** awkward, bearish, bungler, doltish, loutish, unadept **8** churlish, fumbling, ungainly **9** all thumbs, maladroit **10** blundering, unskillful
clodhopper: **2** ox **3** oaf **4** hick, lout, shoe **5** churl, yokel **6** lubber, lummox, rustic **7** bumpkin, hayseed, peasant, plowboy **8** footwear **10** provincial
clodhopping: **6** rustic **7** loutish
clog: **3** dam, jam, tie **4** bolt, cork, lock, plug, seal, shoe, shut, snag, stop **5** block, choke, close, cramp, dam up, dance, delay, gum up, latch, sabot, stick, tie up **6** hamper, hang up, hinder, impede, lock up, plug up, retard, seal up, secure, stop up **7** close up, congest, occlude, seal off, shutter **8** blockade, blockage, button up, close off, encumber, footgear, footwear, obstacle, obstruct, overfill **9** hindrance, impedance, occlusion **10** congestion, impediment
Japanese ~: **4** geta
kin: **5** sabot
locale: **4** sink **5** drain
clogged: **5** stuck **6** stuffy
like a ~ dryer vent: **5** fuzzy
cloisonné: **6** enamel
cloister: **3** den **4** cell, lair, nest, walk **5** abbey **6** arcade, friary, priory, temple **7** convent, nunnery, retreat, seclude **8** lamasery **9** courtyard, hermitage, monastery, peristyle, sanctuary, sequester
courtyard: **5** garth
Cloister and the Hearth, The
author: Charles Reade
character: **4** Kate **5** Denys, Elias, Giles **6** Gerard, Pietro
cloistered: **4** pent **6** hidden **7** recluse **8** secluded, shielded, solitary **9** insulated, out of view, reclusive, seclusive, sheltered, withdrawn **10** restricted
one: **3** nun **4** monk
clomp: **5** stamp, stump, tread **6** trudge
clone: **2** PC **4** copy, dupe, same, twin **5** ditto, model, Xerox, yuppy **6** double, ectype, repeat, yuppie **7** replica **8** computer, knockoff, likeness **9** duplicate, facsimile, imitation, look-alike, photocopy, replicate, reproduce
Dolly the ~: **3** ewe **5** sheep
unit: **4** cell **5** ramet
cloned: **9** identical
clonk: **4** thud **5** thump
Clooney: **4** Nick **6** George **8** Rosemary
Clooney, George: **5** actor
film: Batman & Robin (1997)
Good Night, and Good Luck (2005)
Leatherheads (2008)
Michael Clayton (2007)
O Brother, Where Art Thou? (2000)
Ocean's Eleven (2001)
Ocean's Thirteen (2007)
Ocean's Twelve (2004)
Out of Sight (1998)
The Perfect Storm (2000)
Syriana (2005, AA)
Three Kings (1999)
Up in the Air (2009)
role: **5** Ocean
TV: ER
Clooney, Rosemary
song: Botch-a-Me (1952)
Come on-a My House (1951)
Hey There (1954)
spouse: José Ferrer
clop: **8** hoofbeat
__-clop: **4** clip
Clorets
alternative: **5** Certs **6** Binaca, Mentos, Tic Tac **7** Altoids, Dentyne
Cloris: **8** Leachman
Clorox
alternative: **5** Purex, Snowy, Vivid **8** Borateem
close: **3** bar, dam, end, zip **4** bolt, calk, clog, coda, cork, dear, fail, fast, fold, halt, kind, lace, lock, mean, near, next, nigh, plug, quit, seal, sell, shut, slam, snug, stop, warm, yard **5** anear, block, caulk, cease, dam up, dense, handy, humid, latch, muggy, quiet, sew up, sum up, terse, thick, tight, zip up **6** almost, at hand, at heel, button, chummy, clog up, clubby, desist, ending, expire, fasten, finale, finish, fold up, genial, hard by, kindly, lessen, lock up, loving, minute, narrow, nearby, packed, period, plug up, recede, run out, seal up, secret, secure, sticky, stingy, stop up, strict, stuffy, sultry, windup, wrap up **7** achieve, adjourn, affable, amiable, break up, compact, cordial, cramped, crowded, devoted, go under, literal, miserly, occlude, on the QT, play out, seal off, shut off, shut out, shutter, sparing, sweltry, thrifty, tighten, turn off **8** adjacent, amicable, button up, complete, conclude, confined, draw near, familiar, friendly, hush-hush, imminent, intimate, next-door, not quite, obstruct, outgoing, pack it in, put to bed, reserved, reticent, round off, round out, shut down, sociable, stifling, surcease, taciturn, taper off, terminus, transact, ungiving, wind down **9** cessation, confining, congested, convivial, culminate, illiberal, immediate, impending, jam-packed, make final, penurious, proximate, secretive, skintight, terminate **10** benevolent, buddy-buddy, call it a day, completion, conclusion, consummate, contiguous, convenient, denouement, desistance, expiration, juxtaposed, neighborly, nip and tuck, oppressive, palsy-walsy, resolution, solicitous, sweltering, ungenerous, unspeaking
behind: **6** at heel
be ~ to: **4** know
bring ~: **4** love **6** endear
by: **4** near, nigh **5** handy, unfar **6** around, at hand **7** locally **8** adjacent **9** alongside, proximate **10** convenient
call: **5** brush, scare
call comment: **4** phew, whew
combining form: **4** pycn-, sten- **5** plesi-, pycno-, steno- **6** plesio-
come ~ to: **8** approach, resemble
complimentary ~: **4** best, love **5** yours **6** warmly **9** sincerely **10** yours truly
down: **3** end **4** halt, shut, stop **5** cease **6** wind up **8** break off, dispatch, stamp out **9** eliminate **10** put an end to
ender: **3** out **4** down
forcefully: **4** slam
form ~ ties: **4** bond
getting ~: **4** warm
get ~ to: **6** gain on **8** approach
in: **3** pen **5** bower **6** encase, gain on, immure
in on: **4** near **7** besiege, envelop **8** approach, encircle, surround
in Scotland: **3** nar
keep ~: **3** hug **5** clasp, press, touch **6** clutch, cradle, cuddle, enfold, nestle, nuzzle **7** embrace, snuggle
not ~: **3** far
not even ~: **5** wrong **7** distant **8** mistaken **9** erroneous **10** inaccurate
of day: **6** curfew **7** bedtime **9** nightfall
off: **4** clog, seal, shut **5** block **6** impede **7** isolate, occlude **8** separate **9** segregate, sequester
out: **3** cut, end **5** cease, lower, slash **6** cancel, reduce **8** decrease, discount, mark down **9** dispose of, finish off, liquidate
ranks: **4** ally **5** merge, rally, unite **8** assemble, coalesce, converge **9** integrate
relative: **3** sib **4** twin **6** father, mother, sister **7** brother
securely: **4** seal, shut **6** batten
shave: **5** scare
starter: **4** fore
to: **2** by, on **4** like, near **5** about **6** almost, beside, hard by **7** nearing
to a poet: **4** nigh **5** anear
to (prefix): **3** epi
to the ground: **3** low **4** flat **5** short **8** knee-high, sea-level **10** unelevated
up: **3** zip **4** cork, lock, seal, shut **5** latch **6** immure **7** silence
up shop: **4** quit **10** call it a day
close __: **3** out **4** call, down, in on, shot **5** quote, ranks, reach, shave **6** helmet, quotes, stitch **7** harmony
close-__: **3** ups **4** knit **6** hauled, lipped, minded, reefed **7** cropped, fitting, grained, mouthed
close-__ drill: **5** order
Close __: **5** to You

closed: 4 dark, over, shut 6 locked, sealed 7 insular 8 airtight, shut down 9 exclusive 10 restricted
almost ~: 4 ajar
behind ~ doors: 6 inside 8 secretly 9 privately
book: 6 riddle 7 mystery 9 conundrum
combining form: 7 cleisto-
in: 4 pent 5 misty 6 pent-up
not ~: 4 open
remove the ~ sign: 6 reopen
closed ___: 3 set 4 book, shop 7 circuit
closed-___: 3 end 4 door 6 minded
Closed: 4 sign
___ closed doors: 6 behind
Close Encounters... (1977 film)
cast: Melinda Dillon, Richard Dreyfuss, Teri Garr, François Truffaut
composer: John Williams
craft: 3 UFO
director: Steven Spielberg
closefisted: 4 mean, near 5 small, tight 6 greedy, skimpy, stingy 7 miserly, selfish, thrifty 8 grasping 9 illiberal, penurious 10 avaricious, pinch-penny, skinflinty, ungenerous
one: 5 piker 9 skinflint
closefistedness: 5 greed 7 avarice
close-fitting: 4 snug 5 tight
___ close for comfort: 3 too
Close, Glenn: 7 actress
film: 101 Dalmatians (1996)
Air Force One (1997)
The Big Chill (1983)
Cookie's Fortune (1999)
Dangerous Liaisons (1988)
Fatal Attraction (1987)
Hamlet (1990)
Immediate Family (1989)
Jagged Edge (1985)
Mars Attacks! (1996)
Maxie (1985)
The Natural (1984)
The Paper (1994)
Reversal of Fortune (1990)
The Stone Boy (1984)
The World According to Garp (1982)
film (voice): Tarzan (1999)
TV: Damages
closely: 4 well 8 intently, narrowly
closemouthed: 3 mum 4 mute 5 quiet, terse 6 silent 8 hush-hush, reserved, reticent, taciturn 9 secretive, voiceless
one: 4 clam
closeness: 8 accuracy, affinity, intimacy, presence 9 affection, communion, immediacy, proximity 10 friendship, similarity
close-order ___: 5 drill
closeout: 3 buy 7 bargain, special
close-packed: 5 dense, thick, tight
closer: 6 hurler 7 pitcher 8 reliever, salesman 9 dealmaker
gate ~: 3 bar 4 bolt, hasp, hook, lock 5 catch 7 padlock
inning: 5 ninth
stat: 3 ERA 4 save
Closer (2004 film)
cast: Jude Law, Clive Owen, Natalie Portman, Julia Roberts
director: Mike Nichols
Closer I Get to You, The (1978 song)
artist: Roberta Flack, Donny Hathaway
___ close second: 4 ran a, run a
closest: 4 next 9 proximate
closet: 4 hide 6 locker, lock up, recess, secret 7 cabinet 8 cupboard, imprison, stow away, wardrobe 10 depository, repository
item: 3 tie 4 belt, shoe 5 dress, shelf, shirt 6 blouse, hanger 7 sweater
items: 4 junk 5 linen 6 attire
like some ~ doors: 6 bifold
like some ~s: 5 mothy 9 cluttered
lining: 5 cedar
pest: 4 moth
put in the ~: 4 hang 6 hang up
skeleton in the ~: 5 shame 7 scandal
utility ~ item: 3 mop 4 pail 5 broom
water ~: 2 WC 3 lav, loo 7 latrine 8 bathroom, lavatory
___ closet: 5 china, linen, water 6 walk-in 7 clothes
closeted again: 5 rehid
close the ___ on: 4 door
Close to Home
author: Erskine Caldwell
close to one's ___: 5 heart
___ close to schedule: 4 on or
Close to You (song)
artist: Carpenters, Maxi Priest
closeup: 4 view 5 photo 10 photograph
prepare for a ~: 4 zoom 5 pan in
Close-Up
alternative: *see* toothpaste
closing: 3 end 4 last 5 final 6 ending, finale, finish, latter 8 ultimate
in: 4 near
time: 6 curfew
closing ___: 4 time 5 costs
Closing the Ring
author: Winston Churchill
Closing Time
author: Joseph Heller
closure: 3 end, lid 4 bolt, bung, cork, lock, plug, seal, seam, stop 5 latch 6 ending, finish, recess, spigot 7 padlock, stopper 8 blockade, curtains, stoppage 9 cessation 10 conclusion
clot: 3 gel, set 4 curd, jell, lump, mass 5 group 6 curdle, gelate, harden 7 acidify, clabber, clobber, congeal, stiffen, thicken 8 coalesce, solidify, thrombus 9 coagulate
combining form: 6 thromb- 7 thrombo-
cloth: 3 net, rag 4 felt, silk, wool 5 baize, denim, lisse, loden, plaid, ramee, ramie, satin, serge, stuff, terry, towel 6 calico, chintz, fabric, kersey 7 bunting, flannel, gingham, worsted 8 dry goods, jacquard, material, textiles 9 grosgrain, yard goods
absorbent ~: 6 diaper
altar ~: 6 dossal, dossel
billiard table ~: 5 baize
border: 3 hem
cleaning ~: 3 rag 6 chammy, shammy, shamoy 7 chamois
cotton ~: 6 calico, chintz
dealer: 6 draper, ragman
ender: 3 ier 5 bound
fold: 5 plait, pleat
hole: 6 eyelet
India: 6 Madras
in jai alai: 5 cinta
kitchen ~: 5 towel
made ~: 4 wove
made of whole ~: 4 fake 5 bogus
make ~: 4 spin 5 weave
man of the ~: 4 abbé 5 padre 6 cleric, priest
measure: 3 ell 4 bolt, yard
metallic ~: 4 lamé
not of the ~: 3 lay 4 laic 6 laical
Polynesian ~: 4 tapa
scrap: 3 rag
starter: 3 oil 4 back, dish, face, foot, hair, loin, sack, sail, wash 5 broad, table, waist 6 breech, cheese, saddle
surface: 3 nap
those not of the ~: 5 laics, laity
use a ~: 4 dust, wipe
woolen ~: 5 loden
worker: 4 dyer
see also fabric, material
___ cloth: 4 drop, face 5 terry
clothe: 3 rig, tog 4 deck, do up, garb 5 array, cover, drape, dress, endue, indue 6 attire, enrobe, fit out, outfit, tog out 7 bedrape, costume, cover up, deck out, furnish 8 accouter, accoutre
clothed: 4 clad 6 decent, enclad
be ~ in: 4 wear 6 have on
old-style: 5 yclad
clothes: 4 duds, garb, gear, rags, togs, wear 5 array, dress, frock, getup, mufti, robes 6 attire, civies, finery, livery, outfit, things 7 apparel, civvies, costume, raiment, regalia, threads, toggery 8 covering, ensemble, frippery, garments, wardrobe 9 caparison, trappings 10 habiliment, sportswear, Sunday best
abbr.: 3 irr. 5 irreg.
dirty ~: 4 wash 7 laundry
ender: 3 pin 4 line 5 horse, press
evening ~: 4 gown 5 dress 6 tuxedo
fine ~: 5 array
fresh ~: 6 change
gym ~: 6 shorts, sweats, T-shirt
holder: 6 closet, hamper, locker
iron ~: 4 mail 5 armor, press
line: 3 hem 4 seam
nostalgic ~ style: 5 retro
old ~: 4 rags
pole: 4 tree
presser: 4 iron
riding ~: 5 habit
shop for ~: 5 try on
sister's ~: 5 habit
starter: 3 bed 5 night, small
wearing ~: 4 clad
wearing no ~: 4 bare, nude 5 naked
work ~: 5 jeans 6 denims
see also clothing
clothes ___: 4 moth, pole, rack, tree 6 closet
___ clothes: 5 plain 6 dinner, Sunday 7 evening
Clothes for a Summer Hotel
author: Tennessee Williams
clotheshorse: 3 fop 5 dandy, model, swell
clothesline: 4 rope
alternative: 5 drier, dryer
use a ~: 6 air-dry
clothespin: 3 peg
clothier: 6 fitter, tailor 9 outfitter
clothing: 3 RTW 4 garb, gear, need, suit, togs, wear 5 array, dress, getup, robes 6 attire, finery, livery, outfit, things, undies 7 apparel, costume, raiment 8 covering, ensemble, garments, wardrobe 9 trappings, underwear
category: 4 men's 6 women's
clingy ~: 4 knit
GI ~: 3 ODs 6 khakis
make ~: 3 sew 4 knit 5 weave
ordinary ~: 5 mufti
problem: 3 rip 4 fray, snag, tear 5 stain
protector: 3 bib 5 apron
specification: 2 lg., sm., XL 3 lge., med., XXL 4 long, size 5 cadet, large, short, small 6 medium, portly 10 extra large
store employee: 6 fitter
test ~: 5 try on
see also clothes
clothmaking apparatus: 4 loom
Clotho: 4 Fate
colleague: 7 Atropos 8 Lachesis
mother: 6 Themis
clotted: 5 thick
clotted ___: 5 cream
cloture ends, what: 6 debate
cloud: 3 dim, fog 4 blur, mist, roil, veil 5 addle, bedim, befog, blear 6 cirrus, dampen, darken, legion, muddle, nimbus, shadow 7 confuse, cover up, cumulus, obscure, perplex, stratus 8 confound, jaundice 9 adumbrate, disorient, mare's tail, obfuscate 10 overshadow
bit of a ~: 4 wisp
black ~: 4 pall
combining form: 4 neph- 5 nepho- 6 nephel- 7 nephelo-
contents: 4 rain 5 smoke, water
ender: 4 land 5 berry, burst, scape
fair-weather ~: 6 cirrus
formation: 4 bank
like a storm ~: 5 black
name starter: 4 alto
nine: 5 bliss 7 rapture 8 paradise
on ~ nine: 4 glad, high 5 happy, merry 6 blithe, cheery, elated, jovial, joyful, joyous, upbeat 7 gleeful, pleased, tickled 8 blissful, cheerful, ecstatic, euphoric, exultant, jubilant, mirthful, thrilled 9 delighted, overjoyed, rapturous, rejoicing, rhapsodic
over: 9 adumbrate
put on ~ nine: 5 elate, exult 6 buck up, perk up, uplift 7 delight, gladden, hearten 8 inspirit 10 exhilarate
region: 3 sky
roll ~: 5 arcus
seeding compound: 6 iodide
starter: 7 thunder
the issue: 7 confuse 8 confound 9 obfuscate

under a ~: **5** shady **7** suspect
up: **4** roil **6** darken
cloud __: **4** base, nine **5** cover
__ cloud: **3** war **4** Oort, rain
__ Cloud: **3** Red
cloudburst: **4** rain **5** storm **6** deluge **7** torrent **8** downpour **9** rainstorm
cloud chamber contents: **3** gas
clouded: **4** gray, grey, hazy **5** blear, foggy, milky, misty **6** hidden, turbid **8** overcast **9** equivocal, hard to see
Cloud Forest, The
author: Peter Matthiessen
cloudiness: **5** blear
__ cloud in the sky: **4** not a
cloudless: **4** fair **5** clear, light, sunny **6** bright **8** sunshiny
clouds: **4** rack **5** nimbi **6** scores **7** legions
in the ~: **5** aloft **7** bemused, faraway **10** abstracted, starry-eyed
like some ~: **5** puffy, wispy **6** fleecy
low-lying ~: **3** fog **4** mist
move swiftly, as ~: **4** scud
treat ~: **4** seed
Clouds, The
author: Aristophanes
Cloud, The: **4** poem
author: Percy Bysshe Shelley
cloudy: **3** dim **4** dark, gray, grey, hazy **5** mirky, misty, muddy, murky, shady, vague **6** dismal, dreary, gloomy, opaque, somber, sullen, turbid **7** blurred, obscure, sunless, unclear **8** confused, darkened, lowering, nebulous, overcast **9** imprecise, unsettled **10** indistinct
make ~: **4** roil
Clouseau: **6** Martin **7** Jacques, Sellers **9** Inspector
caper: **4** case
valet: **4** Kato
clout: **3** hit, rap **4** blow, clip, club, cuff, pull, slug, sock, swat, sway **5** crack, force, juice, knock, might, pound, power, punch, skill, smack, spank, swipe, thump, whack **6** credit, effect, muscle, strike, wallop, weight **7** clobber, control **8** bludgeon, leverage, pressure, prestige, standing, strength, uppercut **9** authority, fisticuff, influence
those with ~: **3** ins
clove: **4** bulb, tree **5** spice
clove hitch: **4** knot
cloven: **5** forky, split **6** forked **7** incised
cloven __: **4** foot, hoof
clover: **5** alyce, plant **6** fodder, riches, wealth **7** alfalfa, melilot
be in ~: **9** luxuriate
ender: **4** leaf
in ~: **4** rich **5** flush **6** loaded, monied **7** moneyed, wealthy, well-off **8** affluent, well-to-do **9** well-fixed **10** privileged, propertied, prosperous, well-heeled
like a four-leaf ~: **5** lucky
cloverleaf: **8** crossing **9** underpass
part of a ~: **4** exit, loop, ramp
cloves: **5** spice **6** garlic
__ cloves: **5** oil of
clove-scented flower: **4** pink
Clovis: **4** city, town
locale: **9** New Mexico
clown: **3** kid, wag **4** Bozo, fool, jest, joke, mime, zany **5** comic, cutup, joker, Punch **6** jester, madcap, mummer **7** buffoon, farceur, funster, gagster, pierrot **8** comedian, funnyman, humorist, kibitzer, quipster **9** character, harlequin, kid around, leg-puller, prankster
around: **3** kid **4** jest, joke
be a ~: **5** amuse
bit: **5** stunt
like a ~: **5** funny
like ~ outfits: **5** baggy
locale: **6** big top, circus
often: **4** mime **5** mimer, mimic
prop: **3** wig **5** stilt **7** red nose
see also ninny
clown __: **4** fish **5** white **6** prince
__ clown: **5** class
__ Clown: **3** Be a **6** Cathy's
clowning: **3** fun **5** antic, humor **8** jocosity, zaniness **9** funniness, horseplay **10** jocoseness
clownish: **4** zany **5** daffy, droll **6** clumsy **7** loutish, unadept, uncouth
clownishness: **7** fooling **8** jocosity
Clown Prince of Basketball, The: **5** Lemon
Clown Prince of Denmark: **5** Borge
Clowns, The (1971 film)
director: Federico Fellini
cloy: **4** bore, glut, jade, pall, sate **5** gorge, weary **7** satiate, satisfy, surfeit **8** overfill **10** gormandize
cloyed: **3** fed **4** full **5** blasé **10** world-weary
cloying: **5** sweet **6** sickly **7** maudlin, mawkish **10** saccharine
become ~: **4** pall
sweetness: **5** syrup **8** schmaltz
Clu: **7** Gulager
club: **3** bat, hit, org. **4** assn., band, bash, beat, clan, cosh, gang, gild, iron, mace, team, wood **5** assoc., baste, baton, billy, cleek, clout, disco, flail, group, guild, lodge, mashy, order, pound, spoon, staff, stick, wedge, whack **6** brassy, circle, clique, cudgel, driver, hammer, hurley, league, lounge, mallet, mashie, outfit, pommel, pummel, putter, strike, timber **7** brassey, brassie, clobber, coterie, faction, in-group, midiron, niblick, society **8** alliance, bludgeon **9** blackjack, truncheon **10** fellowship, fraternity, knobkerrie, membership, nightstick, shillelagh
aborigine war ~: **5** waddy **6** waddie
agricultural ~: **5** Four-H
ball ~: **4** team
billy ~: **4** cosh **5** baton, stick **6** cudgel **8** bludgeon
boys' ~: **4** YMCA, YMHA
carrier: **5** caddy **6** caddie
ceremonial ~: **4** mace
college ~: **3** sor. **4** frat **8** sorority **10** fraternity
combining form: **5** clavi- **6** rhopal- **7** rhopalo-
ender: **3** man, men **4** face, room **5** house, woman, women
girls' ~: **4** YWCA, YWHA
glee ~: **6** chorus **8** ensemble **9** vocalists
golf ~: **4** iron, wood **5** cleek, spoon, wedge **6** driver, mashie, putter **7** brassie, niblick **9** sand wedge
health ~: **3** gym, spa **9** gymnasium
high-IQ ~: **5** Mensa
one in a ~: **3** mem. **6** member
one ~ perhaps: **3** bid
payment: **4** dues
police ~ in India: **5** lathi **6** lathee
service ~: **4** Elks, YMCA **5** Amvet, Four-H, lodge **7** Kiwanis
soda: **4** fizz **5** mixer
starter: **5** night
supper ~: **5** boîte **6** bistro, eatery **7** cabaret **9** nightspot
swing a ~: **4** putt **5** drive, pitch
up: **5** unite **7** go along **9** cooperate **10** join forces
war ~: **4** mace **6** cudgel **9** truncheon
without ~ soda: **4** neat
club __: **3** bag, car **4** dues, foot, moss, soda, sofa **5** chair, grass, steak, wheat
__ club: **3** fan, key **4** ball, book, farm, glee, golf, men's **5** billy, yacht **6** bottle, bridge, devil's, golden, health, Indian, jockey, kennel, supper, women's **7** country, service
Club __: **3** Med **7** Nouveau
__ Club: **4** Boys, Sam's **5** Four-H, Lions, Stork **6** Kit-Cat, Kit-Kat, Rotary, Sierra **7** Culture, Horizon
clubby: **4** kind **5** close, thick **6** chummy, genial, kindly **7** affable, amiable, cordial **8** amicable, cliquish, friendly, intimate, outgoing, sociable **9** congenial, convivial, exclusive **10** benevolent, buddy-buddy, gregarious, neighborly, solicitous
clubhouse: **5** haunt
clubs: **4** suit
at times: **5** trump
five ~: **5** flush
club soda: **7** seltzer **8** beverage
__ Club, The: **6** Cotton
cluck: **6** cackle, tut-tut
see also ninny
clucker: **3** hen **7** chicken
clue: **3** key, tip **4** hint, lead, mark, sign **5** index, trace **6** tipoff **7** hot lead, inkling, pointer **8** acquaint, evidence **9** footprint, indicator, suspicion **10** indication, intimation, suggestion
crime lab ~: **3** DNA **5** print **9** tire track
drop a ~: **4** hint **8** intimate
hound's ~: **5** scent, smell
in: **4** tell, warn **6** advise, inform, relate, tip off **8** instruct
Clue: **4** game **9** board game
character: **4** Plum **5** Boddy, Green, White **7** Mustard, Peacock, Scarlet
locale: **4** hall **5** study **6** lounge **7** kitchen, library **8** ballroom **10** dining room **12** billiard room, conservatory
weapon: **4** rope **5** knife **6** wrench **8** lead pipe, revolver **11** candlestick
clueless: **4** asea, lost **5** at sea **7** puzzled **8** confused
socially ~ one: **4** nerd
Clueless (1995 film)
cast: Stacey Dash, Brittany Murphy, Alicia Silverstone
catchphrase: **4** as if
character: **4** Cher
director: Amy Heckerling
clues
like some ~: **4** down **6** across
clump: **3** gob, set, wad **4** blob, glob, hunk, lump, mass, plod, thud, tuft **5** batch, chunk, divot, group, patch, stomp, stump, thump **6** bundle, lumber, nugget, trudge **7** cluster, thicket
clumsy: **3** oxy **5** gawky, inapt, inept, unapt **6** gauche, klutzy, oafish, sloppy, unable, wooden **7** awkward, boorish, gawkish, halting, hulking, labored, loutish, lumpish, unadept, uncouth, unhandy **8** bumbling, bungling, cloddish, clownish, fumbling, helpless, inexpert, lubberly, tactless, ungainly, unpoised, unsubtle, unwieldy **9** all thumbs, graceless, ham-handed, inelegant, lumbering, maladroit, ponderous, stumbling, unskilled, untactful, unwieldly **10** blundering, cumbersome, galumphing, leadfooted, left-handed, outlandish, unbecoming, unskillful
fix: **5** kluge **6** kludge
one: **3** ape, oaf **4** clod, hulk **5** klutz **6** lubber **7** bungler
one's comment: **4** oops **6** whoops
clunk: **4** thud **5** thump **6** lumber
clunker: **3** car **4** auto, bomb, heap **5** lemon **6** jalopy **10** automobile, hunk of junk, rattletrap
feature: **4** rust
clunky: **8** unwieldy **9** graceless, unwieldly **10** cumbersome
Cluny: **4** lace
cluster: **3** set **4** band, bevy, gang, herd, knot, lump, mass, nest, pack, tuft **5** array, batch, bunch, clump, covey, crowd, drift, group, swarm **6** bundle, clamor, gather, huddle **7** collect, round up **8** assembly **9** gathering **10** assemblage, collection, cumulation
flower ~: **5** ament, umbel **6** catkin
__ cluster: **4** open, star, tone **7** oakleaf
clustered: **5** dense
clutch: **3** hug, set **4** fist, grab, grip, hold, lock, snap, sort, take **5** brood, clasp, grasp, group, pedal, pluck, purse, seize **6** caress, clench, clinch, enfold, infold, retain, snatch **7** cling to, embrace, handbag, squeeze **8** quandary, hang on to **9** keep close, spellbind **10** pocketbook
neighbor: **5** brake
clutch __: **3** bag **5** purse
__-clutch: **6** double
clutches: **4** grip **5** grasp **7** control, custody **10** possession
clutter: **4** mess, muss **5** snarl **6** bustle, jumble, jungle, litter, mess up, muddle, tangle **8** disarray, disorder, scramble, shambles **9** confusion **10** hodgepodge, untidiness
cluttered: **5** messy, mussy **6** unneat, untidy **10** disorderly, topsy-turvy

clutter-free: 4 neat, tidy 6 spruce
cluttering: 3 ado 4 daze, flap, fuss, mess, riot, stew 5 chaos, doubt, mix-up, panic, press, snarl, swirl 6 bedlam, bustle, dither, flurry, fracas, hubbub, huddle, jumble, jungle, lather, litter, mayhem, muddle, tangle, trauma, tumult, unrest, uproar 7 anarchy, clutter, mistake, turmoil 8 disarray, disorder, question, scramble, shambles 9 abashment, agitation, amazement, commotion, confusion, imbroglio, intricacy, labyrinth, patchwork 10 befuddling, bemusement, complexity, difficulty, excitement, hodgepodge, hurly-burly, perplexity, puzzlement, turbulence, untidiness, wilderness
Clyde: 4 Andy 5 river 6 Barrow, Jeremy 7 Drexler 8 Geronimi, Tombaugh 9 McPhatter
city on the ~: 7 Glasgow
Firth of ~ island: 5 Arran
Firth of ~ port: 3 Ayr
Firth of ~ tributary: 4 Doon
partner: 6 Bonnie
River locale: 8 Scotland
Clydesdale: 5 horse 6 equine
Clym: 7 teacher 8 merchant
wife: 3 Vye 9 Eustachia
Clytemnestra
brother: 6 Castor
daughter: 7 Electra, Erigone 9 Iphigenia
husband: 8 Tantalus 9 Agamemnon
mother: 4 Leda
sister: 5 Helen
son: 6 Aletes 7 Orestes
cm.: 4 meas.
Cm: 4 elem. 6 curium 7 element
96 for ~: 4 at. no.
cmdr.: 3 ldr., off.
c'mon: 6 let's go
CMT: 7 channel
alternative: ***see*** cable channel
CN __: 5 Tower
CNA
competitor: ***see*** insurance company
CNBC: 7 channel
alternative: see cable channel
CNN: 7 channel
alternative: ***see*** cable channel
anchorman: 4 Shaw 5 Dobbs 6 Cooper 7 Blitzer
home: 7 Atlanta, Georgia
host: Larry King
offering: 4 news
part of ~: 4 News 5 Cable 7 Network
piece: 4 rept. 6 report
receiver: 2 TV 5 TV set
word: 4 live
CNO: 3 VIP
grp.: 3 JCS, USN
C-note: 4 bill 7 hundred
change for a ~: 4 tens 8 twenties
ten ~s: 3 gee 5 grand
co-__: 3 eds, ops, opt, own 4 host, star 5 occur, teach 6 anchor, author, manage, parent, winner, worker 7 edition, founder, manager, ordinal, produce, publish, venture
co.: 3 mfr., org. 4 corp., firm
component: 3 div. 5 R and D
VIP: 3 CEO, mgr. 4 pres.
Co: 4 elem. 6 cobalt 7 element
27 for ~: 4 at. no.
CO
see Colorado
C&O: 2 RR 8 railroad
coach: 3 bus 5 drill, edify, prime, stage, teach, train, tutor 6 advise, chaise, ground, leader, mentor, school 7 adviser, advisor, educate, manager, phaeton, prepare, teacher, trainer, vehicle 8 carriage, educator, initiate, instruct 9 abecedary, charabanc 10 instructor
concern: 4 team
ender: 3 man, men
leave the ~: 5 debus 9 disembark
puller: 4 team 5 horse 6 engine
starter: 5 stage
coach __: 3 box, dog 5 horse, house
__ coach: 3 air, day 4 baby 5 motor, night
Coach (ABC sitcom)
cast: Shelley Fabares (Christine Fox)
Craig T. Nelson (Hayden Fox)
Jerry Van Dyke (Luther Van Dam)
dog: 6 Quincy
Coach Carter (2005 film)
cast: Samuel L. Jackson
coached, one being: 5 tutee
coaching: 6 lesson 8 training 9 education
coactively: 8 together
coadjutant: 4 aide 6 helper 8 henchman 9 assistant
coadjute: 9 cooperate
coagulate: 3 gel, set 4 clot, jell 6 curdle, gelate, harden 7 congeal, stiffen, thicken 8 coalesce, solidify 10 gelatinize, inspissate
coagulated: 5 thick 7 jellied 10 gelatinous
coagulation: 4 clot, mass
coal: 3 oil 4 coke, fuel 5 ember 6 cannel 7 lignite, mineral 8 resource 10 anthracite, bituminous, fossil fuel
add ~: 5 stoke
combining form: 7 anthrac-, carboni- 8 anthraco-
dust: 4 culm
ender: 4 fish 5 field
gem-grade ~: 3 jet
German ~ region: 4 Saar
holder: 3 bin, car, hod 4 scow, tram 5 barge 6 hopper
hot ~: 5 ember
product: 3 oil, tar 4 coke 7 diamond
residue: 6 cinder
size: 3 pea
slide: 5 chute
starter: 4 char
stratum: 4 seam, vein
tar derivative: 5 xylol 6 indene 7 creosol 8 creosote
unit: 3 ton 4 lump
user: 5 grill 7 furnace 8 barbecue
worker: 5 miner 6 stoker 7 collier
coal __: 3 car, gas, hod, oil, pit, tar 4 ball, mine, seam 5 field, miner
__ coal: 3 cob, egg, gas, nut, pea 4 hard, rice, soft, wood 5 block, steam, stove, white
Coal __ Daughter: 6 Miner's
coal-black: 4 ebon, inky 5 ebony
coaler: 4 ship
coalesce: 3 gel, mix, wed 4 clot, fuse, join 5 blend, merge, unify, unite 6 commix 7 combine, conjoin 9 coagulate, commingle, integrate 10 amalgamate
coalition: 4 bloc, ring 5 front, group, junta, junto, party, union 6 league, muster 7 amalgam, combine, faction 8 alliance 9 anschluss 10 conspiracy, federation, friendship, trade union
Coal Miner's Daughter (1980 film)
cast: Beverly D'Angelo, Tommy Lee Jones, Sissy Spacek
director: Michael Apted
coals
rake over the ~: 4 flay 5 chide, roast, scold 6 berate, rebuke 7 lambast, tell off 8 lambaste
coal tar
derivative: 7 benzene
coarse: 3 low, raw 4 base, foul, lewd, loud, rude, vile 5 bawdy, crass, crude, gross, gruff, harsh, nasty, nubby, raspy, rough, salty, seamy, tacky 6 common, earthy, gauche, grainy, hubbly, impure, ribald, rustic, smutty, unmeet, vulgar 7 bearish, beastly, bestial, boorish, ignoble, loutish, lowbred, obscene, profane, raffish, raucous, sketchy, uncivil, uncouth, unkempt 8 barbaric, churlish, degraded, immodest, impolite, impudent, indecent, off-color, plebeian, scratchy, unseemly 9 barbarian, barbarous, graceless, inelegant, low-minded, lubricous, makeshift, primitive, tasteless, unrefined 10 amateurish, indecorous, indelicate, lascivious, lower-class, regardless, scurrilous, uncultured, ungracious, unpolished
fabric: 5 chino, denim 6 burlap, linsey
fiber: 4 jute 5 istle, ixtle
file: 4 rasp
language: 9 invective, profanity
make ~: 9 granulate
one: 3 oaf 4 boor
coarse-grained: 6 gritty
coarsen: 5 enure, inure 6 harden 7 callous, roughen, toughen
coarseness: 4 woof 7 texture 8 lewdness 9 barbarism, bawdiness, crassness, harshness, indecency, roughness, vulgarity 10 disrespect, earthiness, indelicacy, smuttiness, unevenness
coast: 4 bank, skim 5 beach, glide, relax, shore, short, slide, slink 6 cruise, strand 7 goof off, seaside, slither 8 littoral, seaboard, seashore, volplane 9 freewheel, shoreline 10 take it easy
away from the ~: 6 inland
ender: 4 land, line, ward, wise 5 wards
starter: 3 sea
coast-__ cutter: 5 guard
Coast
alternative: ***see*** soap
Coast __: 5 Guard, Range
__ Coast: 4 East, Gold, Gulf, West 5 Caird, Ivory 7 Barbary, Malabar, Trucial
coastal: 6 marine 7 seaside 8 littoral, maritime
not ~: 6 inland 8 interior
phenomenon: 4 tide
recess: 4 cove 5 firth, frith
coaster: 4 boat, ride, ship, sled
see also roller coaster
coaster __: 5 brake
__ coaster: 6 roller
Coasters
song: Along Came Jones (1959)
Charlie Brown (1959)
Poison Ivy (1959)
Searchin' (1957)
Yakety Yak (1958)
Young Blood (1957)
coast-guard __: 6 cutter
Coast Guard
alert: 3 SOS
like ~ rescues: 6 air-sea
officer: 3 CPO, ens. 6 ensign
vessel: 6 cutter
woman of the ~: 4 Spar
coastline: 5 shore
calamity: 5 spill
Coast of Coral, The
author: Arthur C. Clarke
coat: 3 fur, mac, tog, tux 4 bark, pelt, rind, skin, tuck, wash, wrap 5 A-line, capot, cover, crust, frock, glaze, gloss, grego, jemmy, jibba, layer, loden, paint, parka, plate, rub on, sheet, shell, simar, smear, smock, tails, tunic, wamus 6 achkan, anorak, banian, banyan, blazer, bolero, bomber, capote, dolman, duffle, duster, ermine, finish, fleece, jacket, jerkin, lamina, raglan, reefer, spread, tabard, tuxedo, ulster, veneer, wammus, wampus 7 cagoule, cassock, cutaway, encrust, garment, incrust, kuletuk, lacquer, oilskin, overlay, paletot, plaster, slicker, spencer, surtout, varnish, zamarra 8 benjamin, chaqueta, covering, laminate, mackinaw 9 balmacaan, gloss over, Inverness, macintosh, outerwear, pea jacket, petersham, redingote, sou'wester, whitewash 10 bush jacket, fearnought, flak jacket, lamination, macfarlane, mackintosh, protection
animal ~: 3 fur 4 pelt
arctic ~: 5 parka 6 anorak
British: 5 jemmy, tunic
Canadian: 7 kuletuk
church ~: 7 cassock
close a ~: 5 zip up
cowboy ~: 8 chaqueta
ender: 4 room, tail 5 dress
expensive ~: 3 fur 4 mink 5 sable 6 ermine 10 chinchilla
fabric: 5 loden, serge 6 saxony 8 Burberry
fastener: 4 frog, snap 6 Velcro, zipper
for a house: 5 paint
formal ~: 6 tuxedo 7 cutaway
fox hunter's ~: 5 pinks
fruit ~: 4 rind
heavy ~: 5 loden, wamus 6 ulster, wammus, wampus 8 mackinaw
hooded ~: 5 grego 6 duffle

Indian: 6 achkan, banian, banyan
Japanese: 5 haori, happi
length: 4 maxi
lose one's ~: 4 shed
makeshift ~ hanger: 4 nail
military ~: 5 tunic 9 Ike jacket 10 flak jacket
Muslim: 5 jibba
of arms: 4 seal 6 emblem 7 insigne 8 insignia
of paint: 5 layer
outer ~: 4 skin
part: 3 arm 4 vent 5 lapel 6 lining, sleeve
pedicurist's ~: 6 enamel
rack: 4 tree
remove the ~: 4 pare
seed ~: 4 aril 5 testa
shaggy ~: 4 hair
shed one's ~: 4 molt
shiny ~: 6 enamel
short ~: 5 grego 6 jerkin, reefer
Spain: 7 zamarra
starter: 3 red, top 4 blue, over, rain, tail, turn 5 great, house, petti, sugar, under, waist
thin ~: 6 lamina
words on a ~ of arms: 5 motto
coat __: 4 tree 6 hanger
__ coat: 3 box, car, fur, pea 6 trench 7 cutaway, morning, scratch
__-Coat: 3 Glo
coated with ice: 5 gelid
Coates: 7 Phyllis
coati: 6 animal, mammal
coati-__: 5 mondi, mundi
coating: 4 film, peel, rind, rust, skin, wash 5 crust, glaze, layer, scale, sheet, shell 6 enamel, facing, finish, patina, patine, veneer 7 blanket, dusting, lacquer, varnish 8 covering 9 lubricant 10 integument, lamination
coat of __: 4 arms, mail
coat of arms: 5 crest 6 blazon
band: 4 orle
expert: 6 herald
figure: 5 beast
panel: 9 hatchment
coatroom accessory: 4 stub 6 hanger
Coat, The
author: Athol Fugard
coax: 3 get, nag 4 lure, urge, wile 5 egg on, tempt 6 allure, beckon, cajole, entice, incite, induce, rope in, wangle, work on 7 beguile, flatter, jawbone, wheedle 8 blandish, butter up, inveigle, persuade, soft-sell, soft-soap 9 encourage, importune, influence, sweet-talk
(into): 4 talk
coaxial __: 5 cable
coaxing: 5 charm 6 urging 7 blarney, palaver 8 cajolery, entreaty, flattery, humoring, jollying, soft soap, stroking 9 sweet talk, wheedling 10 persuasion
cob: 4 bird, male, swan 5 horse, money 6 animal, equine
attachment: 6 kernel
ender: 3 nut, web
mate: 3 pen
starter: 4 corn
young: 6 cygnet
Cobain, Kurt: 8 musician
group: 7 Nirvana
spouse: Courtney Love
cobalt: 4 blue 5 azure, metal 7 element 8 greenish
alloy: 6 alnico 9 Vitallium
ore: 8 smaltite
relative: ***see*** blue color
Cobb: 2 Ty 5 Tiger, Tyrus 10 outfielder
surpasser: 4 Rose
Cobb, Irvin S.: 6 writer
work: Exit Laughing
cobble: 4 mend, sole 5 patch 7 patch up
ender: 5 stone
Cobb, Lee J.: 5 actor
TV: The Virginian
cobbler: 3 pie 5 soler 7 dessert 9 shoemaker
concern: 4 heel, last, sole
ingredient: 4 pear 5 apple, berry, peach 6 cherry 7 rhubarb 9 cranberry, raspberry 10 blackberry, strawberry
tool: 3 awl
cobblestone: 4 road, rock
__ Cob, CT: 3 Cos
Cobh: 4 city, port, town
locale: 7 Ireland
Coblenz: 4 city, town
locale: 7 Germany
river: 5 Mosel 7 Moselle
COBOL: 8 language
alternative: ***see*** computer language
cobra: 3 asp 5 snake, viper 6 animal, elapid 7 reptile
Asian ~: 5 krait
comment: 3 sss
cousin: 5 krait, mamba
genus: 5 elaps
like a ~: 6 hooded
weapon: 4 fang 5 venom
see also snake
__ cobra: 4 king 6 Indian
Cobra: 3 car, van 4 auto, Ford 5 Chevy 9 Chevrolet 10 automobile
__-Coburg: 4 Saxe
Coburn: 5 James 7 Charles
Coburn, James: 5 actor
film: Affliction (1998, AA)
The Americanization of Emily (1964)
Bite the Bullet (1975)
The Carey Treatment (1972)
Cross of Iron (1977)
Eraser (1996)
The Great Escape (1963)
Hard Times (1975)
Harry in Your Pocket (1973)
The Last of Sheila (1973)
The Magnificent Seven (1960)
The Nutty Professor (1996)
The Our Man Flint (1966)
The President's Analyst (1967)
Sky Riders (1976)
cobweb: 3 web 4 mesh 5 snare 8 filament
site: 5 attic 8 basement
cobweblike: 4 fine 5 filmy, gauzy 6 flimsy 8 delicate, finespun, gossamer 10 diaphanous
Coca: 7 Imogene
cohort: 6 Caesar
Coca-Cola: 3 pop 4 soda 9 soft drink
alternative: ***see*** soft drink
brand: 6 Fresca
flavor: 6 cherry 7 vanilla
sometimes: 5 mixer
coccyx: 4 bone 8 tailbone
locale: 5 spine
__-cochere: 5 porte
Cochin: 4 city, port, town
locale: 5 India
Cochin China: 4 fowl 7 chicken
relative: ***see*** chicken
Cochise: 6 Apache, Indian
cochlear: 6 spiral
cochlea site: 3 ear
Cochran: 4 Thad 5 Eddie, Steve 7 Johnnie 10 Jacqueline
Cochrane: 3 Tom 6 Mickey
Cochrane, Mickey: 7 catcher
cock: 4 bird 5 valve 7 chicken, rooster
crown: 4 comb
ender: 3 ade, pit 4 boat, crow, eyed, loft, sure 5 fight, horse, roach
starter: 3 bib, hay, pea, pet, sea 4 cold, game, stop, wood 5 billy, black, pinch, poppy 7 shuttle, weather
cock __ walk: 5 of the
__ cock: 3 air 4 ball, moor, sage 5 heath 6 jungle, turkey
__-cock: 4 cold
cock-a-__: 3 poo 4 hoop 6 leekie
cock-a-doodle-doo: 4 crow 6 cackle, squawk
Cockaigne
composer: Edward Elgar
cock-a-leekie: 4 soup
cockamamie: 5 inane, silly 7 foolish 10 irrational, weak-minded
cock-and-bull story: 4 tale
cockapoo: 3 dog 5 canid 6 canine
cockatiel: 4 bird
cockatoo: 4 bird 5 galah
feature: 5 crest
kin: 5 macaw
Cockcroft, John: 8 Nobelist 9 physicist
cockcrow: 4 dawn 5 sunup 7 morning, sunrise 8 daybreak, daylight
cocked __: 3 hat
__-cocked: 4 half
Cocker: 3 Joe
cocker spaniel: 3 dog 5 canid 6 canine
cockeyed: 4 agee, ajee, awry, bent, loco 5 amiss, askew, atilt, bowed, inane, silly, wacky 6 absurd, all wet, askant, aslant, canted, screwy, skewed, whacky, zigzag 7 angular, askance, crooked, fatuous, unsound, winding 8 angulose, angulous, lopsided, specious 9 illogical, irregular, ludicrous, senseless, untenable 10 groundless, ridiculous
Cockeyed Optimist, A
composer: Oscar Hammerstein, Richard Rodgers
__ cockhorse...: 5 Ride a
cockiness: 5 pride 6 hubris, hybris 8 audacity 9 flippancy 10 assumption
cockle: 5 shell 6 mussel, pucker 8 seashell
ender: 3 bur 4 boat 5 shell
cockles of one's __: 5 heart
Cockney: 4 Brit 6 Briton
abode: 3 'ome
assistance: 3 'elp
assistant: 5 'elper
dropper: 5 aitch
endearment: 3 luv
greeting: 4 'ello
idol: 3 'ero
residence: 3 'ome
steed: 4 'orse
toast starter: 4 'ere's
see also British
cock of the __: 4 walk
cockpit: 5 arena
abbr.: 3 alt., IAS
VIP: 5 pilot 7 copilot
work in the ~: 3 fly 6 aviate
Cockpit
author: Jerzy Kosinski
cockroach: 3 bug 4 pest 6 insect
Cock Robin, like: 5 slain
cockscomb: 3 cap, hat 5 plant 6 flower
cockspur: 4 tree 8 hawthorn
cocksure: 4 smug, vain 5 brash, nervy 7 certain, hotshot 8 arrogant, impudent 9 conceited, confident, know-it-all, presuming 10 big-talking, swaggering
cocktail: 3 nog 4 flip, sour 5 Bronx, drink, sling 6 bishop, eggnog, Gibson, gimlet, mai tai, mimosa, posset, rickey, rob roy, zombie 7 Collins, martini, negroni, sidecar, stinger 8 coco loco, daiquiri, highball, Jack Rose, libation, pink lady, salty dog, vermouth 9 alexander, appetizer, Manhattan, margarita, moosemilk, Sea Breeze, ward eight 10 Bloody Mary, golden fizz, horse's neck, intoxicant, Moscow mule, piña colada, rock and rye, silver fizz
cooler: 3 ice 5 rocks
counter: 3 bar
garnish: 5 olive, twist
gin ~: 6 Gibson 7 martini
ingredient: 5 mixer 6 liquor 7 bitters
lounge: 3 bar 6 lounge, saloon
Molotov ~: 4 bomb
prepare a ~: 3 mix
cocktail __: 4 hour 5 glass, party, sauce, table 6 lounge
__ cocktail: 5 fruit 6 shrimp 7 Molotov
Cocktail (1988 film)
cast: Bryan Brown, Tom Cruise, Elisabeth Shue
locale: 3 bar
Cocktail Party, The
author: T.S. Eliot
Cocktails __ Two: 3 for
cocky: 4 smug, vain 5 brash, nervy, proud 6 brazen, daring, jaunty 7 fustian, haughty, pompous, stuck-up 8 arrogant, boastful, fearless, impudent, snobbish, superior 9 big-headed, bumptious, conceited 10 big-talking
walk: 5 strut
Coco: 5 James, river 6 Chanel
competitor: 5 Estée
concern: 5 style
River locale: 8 Honduras 9 Nicaragua
cocoa: 5 brown, drink 7 reddish 8 beverage 9 yellowish

container: 3 mug
ender: 3 nut
relative: *see* brown color
cocoa __: 4 bean 6 butter
Cocoa __: 5 Beach, Puffs
Cocoa Beach: 4 city, town
locale: 7 Florida
Cocoanuts, The: 4 film, play 7 musical
author: George S. Kaufman
cast: Margaret Dumont, Chico Marx, Groucho Marx, Harpo Marx, Zeppo Marx
composer: Irving Berlin
Cocoa Puffs
competitor: *see* cereal
coco loco: 5 drink 8 beverage, cocktail
ingredient: 3 gin
coconut: 3 oil 4 bean, head, palm 5 fruit 6 noggin 8 ice cream
alternative: *see* ice cream flavor
dried ~: 5 copra 8 copperah
exporter: 4 Fiji
fiber: 4 coir
juice: 4 milk
layer: 4 husk
prepare ~: 5 grate
coconut __: 3 oil 4 milk, palm 6 butter
coconut __ pie: 5 cream
Coconut (1972 song)
artist: Nilsson
coconut custard __: 3 pie
cocoon: 3 pod
creator: 5 larva
leave the ~: 6 emerge
made a ~: 4 wove
occupant: 4 pupa 5 pupae
product: 4 silk
Cocoon (1985 film)
cast: Don Ameche, Wilford Brimley, Hume Cronyn, Brian Dennehy, Jack Gilford, Steve Guttenberg, Maureen Stapleton, Jessica Tandy, Gwen Verdon, Tahnee Welch
craft: 3 UFO
director: Ron Howard
Cocos: 4 isls. 5 isles 7 islands
owner: 9 Australia
Cocteau, Jean: 6 artist, French, writer
friend: Picasso
cod: 4 fish 6 burbot 7 seafood 8 lutefisk
alternative: 4 sole
boiled ~: 8 lutefisk
cousin: 4 hake, ling
ender: 4 fish
starter: 3 tom 4 ling 5 pease
young: 4 parr 5 sprag
cod __ oil: 5 liver
__ Cod: 4 Cape
COD
not ~: 3 FOB, ppd. 7 prepaid
part: 4 cash 8 delivery
coda: 3 end 5 close 6 ending, epilog, finale 8 epilogue
__ Cod cottage: 4 Cape
coddle: 4 baby, boil, cook 5 humor, nurse, poach, spoil 6 cosset, dandle, dote on, pamper 7 cater to, gratify, indulge 8 dote upon 9 spoon-feed
starter: 5 molly
coddled __: 3 egg
code: 3 key, law 4 rule 5 bylaw, canon 6 cipher, cypher, ethics, legend, policy 7 charter, encrypt 8 standard 9 etiquette, ordinance, principle, semaphore 10 cryptogram, principles, regulation
breaker: 3 key
breaking org.: 3 NSA
carrier: 4 gene
ender: 4 book
in ~: 9 encrypted 10 unreadable
inventor: 5 Morse
not up to ~: 5 unfit
of conduct: 5 ethic 8 protocol
part of a ~: 3 law
word: 4 Able, Zulu 5 Baker 7 Charlie
WWII ~ machine: 6 Enigma
code __: 4 blue, book, flag, name, word
code-__: 7 sharing
__ code: 3 bar, tax, ten, zip 4 area, fire 5 color, dress, Morse, penal 6 access, binary, postal, source 7 airport, genetic
__-coded: 5 color
codeine: 6 opiate
source: 5 opium
code of __: 6 ethics
Code of the West
author: Zane Grey
Code of the Woosters, The
author: P.G. Wodehouse
__-code reader: 3 bar
codex: 4 book 5 quire 6 volume 10 manuscript
codfish: 5 gadid, scrod, torsk 6 gadoid, schrod 7 bacalao
codger: 4 coot, cuss, fogy 5 fogey 6 galoot, geezer 7 galloot 9 eccentric, graybeard
query: 2 eh
codicil: 5 rider 6 clause 8 addendum, addition, appendix 9 amendment 10 postscript, supplement
codify: 5 order 6 embody, imbody 7 arrange 8 legalize, organize, tabulate 9 formulate, legislate
cod liver __: 3 oil
__ Cod, MA: 4 Cape
codswallop
see baloney
Cody: 4 city, town
locale: 3 Wyo. 7 Wyoming
coed: 5 woman 7 scholar, student
quarters: 4 dorm
coelacanth: 4 fish
Coen: 4 Joel 5 Ethan
Coen, Joel: 8 director
film: Barton Fink (1991)
The Big Lebowski (1998)
Blood Simple (1984)
Fargo (1996)
The Hudsucker Proxy (1994)
Intolerable Cruelty (2003)
The Man Who Wasn't There (2001)
O Brother, Where Art Thou? (2000)
Raising Arizona (1987)
spouse: Frances McDormand
Coen, Joel and Ethan: 9 directors
film: Burn After Reading (2008)
The Ladykillers (2004)
No Country for Old Men (2007, AA)
A Serious Man (2009)
__ coeptis: 6 annuit
coequal: 4 mate, peer 7 compeer, matched, partner
coerce: 3 cow 4 goad, make, push 5 bully, exact, force, press, wring 6 compel, extort, lean on 7 dragoon, shotgun 8 arm-twist, bludgeon, browbeat, bulldoze, pressure, threaten 9 blackmail, constrain, shake down, strong-arm, terrorize 10 bear down on, intimidate, pressurize
coercer: 5 bully, tough 7 hoodlum
coercion: 5 force 6 duress 7 tyranny 8 bullying, iron hand, menacing, pressure, violence 9 blackmail, extortion, restraint 10 compulsion, oppression
coercive: 5 stern 6 forced 7 violent
measure: 7 embargo 8 sanction
Coe, Sebastian: 5 miler 6 runner
emulate ~: 3 run 4 race
rival: 5 Ovett
__ coeur: 5 cri de, sacre
Coeur d'Alene: 4 city, town
locale: 3 Ida. 5 Idaho
Coeur de __: 4 Lion
__ Coeur, MO: 5 Creve
coeval: 4 same 9 attendant 10 coexistent, coincident, concurrent, concurring
coexist: 9 accompany
coexistent: 6 coeval 10 concurrent, synchronal
coextensive: 4 even 8 parallel
coffee: 3 joe, mud 4 bean, brew, java, Kona, tree 5 brown, decaf, drink, fluid, latte, mocha, Sanka, shrub, Yuban 6 jamoke 7 Folgers, Melitta, mugfuls, Nescafé, Savarin 8 awakener, beverage, capuchin, espresso, ice cream 9 demitasse, eye-opener, Hills Bros., Starbuck's, stimulant 10 brown shade, café au lait, cappuccino
additive: 4 lump 5 cream, sugar
alternative: *see* ice cream flavor
brand: 5 Sanka, Yuban 7 Folgers, Melitta, Nescafé, Savarin 9 Hills Bros.
break: 4 lull, rest 5 pause 6 recess
break time: 5 ten a.m.
city: 6 Santos
companion: 3 bun 4 roll 5 bagel, donut 6 danish, éclair 7 cruller
emanation: 5 aroma
ender: 3 pot 4 cake 5 house, maker
family: 6 madder
get-together: 6 klatch
grind: 4 drip
grinder: 4 mill
grounds: 5 dregs
holder: 3 cup, mug, pot, urn 6 carafe
inferior ~: 3 mud
in French: 4 café
klatch: 5 party
liqueur: 6 Kahlúa
make ~: 4 brew, perk
makeshift ~ table: 5 spool
Mideast ~ cup: 6 finjan
order: 5 black 6 au lait
prepare ~ beans: 5 grind, roast
relative: *see* brown color
source: 4 bean
spill ~ on, perhaps: 5 scald
unit: 5 pound
coffee __: 3 urn 4 cake, hour, mill, ring, shop, tree 5 break, cream, house, maker, royal, spoon, table 6 klatch 7 klatsch
coffee-__ book: 5 table
__ coffee: 4 drip, iced, Kona, perk 5 Irish 7 Arabian, arabica, instant, robusta, Turkish
Coffee, __ Me?: 5 Tea or
Coffee, __ milk?: 5 tea or
coffeecake: 6 kuchen, pastry
Coffee Cantata
composer: J.S. Bach
coffeehouse: 4 café
music: 4 folk
order: 5 latte
staffer: 7 barista
coffeemaker need: 6 filter
Coffee or __?: 3 tea
coffeepot material: 5 Pyrex
coffee-table __: 4 book
Coffee, Tea, __?: 4 or Me
coffer: 3 bin, box 4 case, fisc 5 chest, panel, trunk 6 bunker 7 lockbox 8 treasury, war chest 9 exchequer, strongbox 10 repository
Coffin: 4 Tris 8 Tristram
cog: 3 cam 4 gear 5 tooth 8 gridlock 9 component
ender: 5 wheel
__ cog: 5 slip a
Cogburn: 6 Reuben 7 Rooster
cogency: 5 logic, punch 6 weight 8 keenness, strength, validity
cogent: 3 apt 4 just, wise 5 pithy, plain, solid, sound, valid, vivid 6 potent, strong 7 evident, express, fitting, logical, obvious, telling, tenable, weighty, well-put 8 analytic, apparent, apposite, coherent, distinct, explicit, forceful, luculent, manifest, methodic, palpable, powerful, rational, relevant, sensible, striking 9 effective, graspable, pertinent, pragmatic 10 analytical, compelling, conclusive, consistent, convincing, legitimate, meaningful, persuasive, satisfying, spelled out, unarguable
Coghlan, Eamonn: 5 miler 6 runner
cogitate: 4 mull, muse 5 think 6 devise, ponder, reason 7 reflect 8 conceive, consider, meditate, mull over, ruminate 9 cerebrate, speculate, sweat over 10 brainstorm, deliberate, kick around, think about
on: 8 mull over 9 entertain
cogitation: 7 thought 9 brainwork, deduction 10 conception, meditation, reflection, rumination
cogito: 5 Latin 6 I think
Cogito __ sum: 4 ergo
cognac: 5 drink 6 brandy, liquor 7 liqueur 8 beverage
kin: 6 kirsch
letters: 3 VSO 4 VSOP
cognate: 4 akin, like 5 alike 6 allied, on a par 7 kindred, kinsman, related, similar 8 parallel, relative, relevant 9 analogous, kinswoman

10 affiliated, associated, comparable, equivalent
cognition: 9 knowledge 10 conception
cognitive: 8 rational 10 reasonable
ability: 5 logic
cognizance: 3 ken 4 heed 5 sense 6 memory, regard 8 keenness 9 awareness 10 perception
cognizant: 3 hep, hip 4 in on, up on, wise 5 alive, awake, aware, privy, savvy 6 posted, versed, with it 7 knowing, mindful, tuned in 8 apprised, familiar, informed, sensible 9 au courant, conscious, in the know, judicious, observant, on the beam, plugged in, sensitive 10 acquainted, conversant, perceptive
be ~ of: 3 see 4 know 7 realize
of: 4 onto 5 hip to 6 wise to 7 privy to
cognize: 3 see 4 know 5 grasp 6 fathom 7 discern 8 perceive 9 apprehend 10 comprehend, understand
cognomen: 4 name 5 title 6 byname, handle 7 epithet, pen name, surname 8 last name, nickname 9 pseudonym, sobriquet 10 family name, nom de plume, patronymic
cogwheel: 4 gear
Cohan, George M.: 5 Irish 8 composer
signature part: 3 Geo.
song: Give My Regards to Broadway
Harrigan
Mary's a Grand Old Name
Over There
The Yankee Doodle Boy
You're a Grand Old Flag
coheir: 7 legatee 9 inheritor
Cohen: 3 Rob 5 Myron, Sasha 6 Morris 7 Leonard, Stanley 8 Frederic
cohere: 4 fuse, glue, jell, join, link, yoke 5 agree, cling, fit in, merge, stick, unite 6 attach, cement, cleave, couple, fasten, hook up, relate, square 7 combine, conform, conjoin, connect, hitch on 8 be united, dovetail, hold fast 9 harmonize, hold water, make sense 10 correspond
coherence: 5 logic, unity 8 lucidity 9 adherence, agreement, congruity, integrity, relations 10 attachment, conformity, connection, consonance, continuity, solidarity
coherent: 5 clear, lucid, sober, sound 6 cogent 7 legible, logical, orderly, tenable 8 analytic, methodic, rational, readable, reasoned, sensible 9 connected, organized, pragmatic 10 analytical, articulate, consistent, systematic
emit ~ light: 4 lase
cohesion: 8 sticking 9 adherence, integrity, stability 10 continuity
cohesive: 5 gluey, tough 10 integrated
become ~: 3 gel 4 jell
Cohn: 3 Roy 5 Harry, Mindy 9 Ferdinand
coho: 4 fish 6 salmon
cohort: 3 pal 4 aide, ally, army, chum, mate 5 amigo, buddy, crony 6 fellow, friend, helper 7 comrade, partner 8 alter ego, confrere, follower, henchman, roommate, sidekick 9 assistant, associate, colleague, companion, confidant, supporter 10 accomplice, compatriot, well-wisher
cohost: Dan Rowan, Dick Martin, Ed McMahon, Kathie Lee, Kelly Ripa, Pat Sajak, Vanna White
coif: 2 do 3 bob, bun, 'fro 4 Afro, buzz, conk, fade, flip, hair, pouf, punk, updo 5 bangs, butch, queue, style, twist 6 braids, hairdo, marcel, mohawk, plaits 7 beehive, chignon, crew cut, flattop, page boy, topknot, upsweep 8 bouffant, cornrows, ducktail, Dutch bob, pigtails, pin curls, ponytail, ringlets 9 hairstyle, headdress, permanent, pompadour, poodle cut, scalp lock, spit curls 10 cornbraids, dreadlocks, finger wave, Psyche knot
coign of __: 7 vantage
coil: 4 curl, hank, kink, loop, roll, wind 5 braid, crimp, curve, helix, skein, snake, swirl, twine, twirl, twist, whorl 6 enwind, inwind, scroll, Slinky, spiral, spring, tangle, volute 7 entwine, intwine, meander, sinuate, wreathe 8 curlicue, curlycue, encircle 9 convolute, corkscrew, enwreathe, labyrinth, sinuosity 10 intertwine
combining form: 4 spir- 5 spiri-, spiro-
__ coil: 5 Tesla
coiled: 5 curly, kinky, round, snaky, spiry, wound 6 looped, spiral 7 helical, looping, sinuous
coin: 4 cash, cent, dime, duro, half, mint 5 bread, dough, franc, money, penny, piece, token 6 change, copper, create, invent, make up, nickel, silver 7 quarter 8 innovate 9 neologize, originate 10 half-dollar
bird on a ~: 5 eagle
catalogue rating: 3 unc. 4 fine
collectible ~: 5 proof
collector: 4 slot
counterfeit ~: 4 slug
ender: 3 age
factory: 4 mint
finish: 3 mat 5 matte
flipper's phrase: 6 call it
former 10-cent ~: 5 disme
holder: 5 purse 6 pocket
inscription: 5 motto
Kennedy ~: 4 half
like a new ~: 5 shiny
old gold ~: 5 dobla, ducat
other side of the ~: 8 opposite
ridge: 4 nurl 5 knurl
roll: 7 rouleau
side: 3 obv. 7 obverse, reverse
sound: 5 plunk
stamp: 3 die
toss a ~: 4 flip 6 choose
toss call: 5 heads, tails
U.S. ~ word: 3 God 4 unum 5 trust 7 liberty 8 pluribus
worthless ~: 3 sou
see also money
coin __: 3 box 4 lock, toss 5 purse 6 silver 7 changer, machine
coin __ realm: 5 of the
coin-__: 3 ops
__ coin: 5 flip a
coinage: 5 money 6 change 7 neology 8 creation, original 9 invention, neologism 10 concoction, innovation
coincide: 4 gybe, jibe, meet, mesh 5 agree, match, tally 6 concur, square 8 dovetail 10 correspond
coincidence: 6 chance, hazard
coincident: 4 same 6 coeval 7 similar 8 together 9 ancillary, attendant, attending, consonant 10 collateral, concurrent, concurring, coordinate, synchronal
coincidental: 5 fluky 6 chance, flukey 7 similar
coinciding: 6 in sync 7 similar 9 congruent 10 concurrent, synchronal
coiner: 8 inventer, inventor 9 neologist
coin of the __: 5 realm
coin-op: 7 machine
feature: 4 slot
insert: 4 cash 5 money 6 change
place: 6 arcade
word: 6 insert
__ Coins in the Fountain: 5 Three
Cointreau: 5 drink 6 liquor 8 beverage
coke: 4 coal, fuel
Coke: 4 cola, soda 6 Edward 9 soft drink
see also Coca-Cola
__ Coke: 4 Diet
Cokie: 7 Roberts
col __: 5 legno
col.: 3 off. 4 rank
subordinate: 3 maj., sgt.
superior: 2 BG 3 gen.
Col.
neighbor: 3 Kan., Neb., Pan., Ven., Wyo. 4 Ariz., Ecua., Nebr.
see also Colombia, Colorado
__ Col.: 5 Lieut.
cola: 3 nut 4 Coke, Jolt, soda 5 drink, Pepsi 7 soda pop 8 beverage, Diet-Rite 9 soft drink 10 Royal Crown
buy: 3 can 5 liter
__-Cola: 4 Coca 5 Pepsi
__ colada: 4 piña
colander: 4 sift 5 sieve 8 strainer
Colasanto: 8 Nicholas
Colbert, Claudette: 7 actress
film: Cleopatra (1934)
The Egg and I (1947)
It Happened One Night (1934, AA)
Tovarich (1937)
colby: 6 cheese
Colchester: 4 city, port, town
locale: 5 Essex 7 England
Colchis-bound ship: 4 Argo
cold: 3 icy, nip, out, raw 4 arid, cool, iced, mean 5 algid, aloof, chill, crisp, frost, gelid, nasty, nippy, polar, rheum, sharp, snowy, stark, stiff, stony, surly 6 arctic, biting, bitter, chilly, clammy, drafty, frigid, frosty, frozen, glassy, hiemal, ornery, remote, stoney, stormy, winter, wintry 7 chilled, cutting, distant, glacial, hateful, hostile, iciness, joyless, numbing, rawness, shivery, wintery 8 contrary, freezing, gelidity, hardened, indurate, inimical, lifeless, loveless, lukewarm, piercing, pitiless, positive, reserved, ruthless, Siberian, sniffles, spiteful, stinging, taciturn, unbiased, unheated 9 bellicose, below zero, bloodless, frigidity, heartless, impassive, inclement, insensate, malicious, unfeeling, withdrawn 10 chilliness, frostiness, impersonal, inclemency, insociable, malevolent, mechanical, pugnacious, unagitated, unamicable, unfriendly, unsociable
be ~: 6 shiver
blow hot and ~: 4 sway, vary, yo-yo 5 hedge, shift, waver 6 dither, falter, seesaw, waffle, wobble 8 straddle 9 fluctuate, hem and haw, pussyfoot, vacillate
blowing hot and ~: 4 torn 6 fickle 7 erratic, flighty, mutable, not sure 8 hesitant, variable, volatile, waffling, wavering 9 equivocal, impulsive, mercurial, uncertain, undecided, unsettled 10 ambivalent, capricious, changeable, inconstant, indecisive, irresolute, of two minds, on the fence
catch ~: 3 ail
combining form: 4 crym-, cryo- 5 crymo-, frigo- 7 psychro-
common ~: 6 coryza
cubes: 3 ice
cut: 3 ham 4 meat 6 salami, tongue 7 bologna 8 pastrami 9 roast beef 10 corned beef
cuts store: 4 deli
drink: 3 pop 4 cola, soda 5 juice, shake
duck: 4 wine
feet: 4 fear 5 alarm, panic 8 timidity 9 cowardice
get down ~: 5 learn 6 master
go ~ turkey: 4 quit
have a ~ one: 5 drink
have ~ feet: 5 cower, quail, quake, waver 6 cringe, falter, flinch, recoil, shrink, wobble 7 tremble 8 hang back, hesitate 9 hem and haw, vacillate 10 chicken out
having ~ feet: 5 jumpy, timid 6 afraid, craven, scared, yellow 7 chicken, daunted, fearful, panicky, spooked, wimpish 8 cowardly, fearsome, recreant, sheepish, timorous 9 nerveless, spineless, terrified, tremulous 10 frightened
kin: 3 flu
leave out in the ~: 4 shun, snub 5 spurn 6 ignore, rebuff, reject, slight 7 high-hat, neglect 8 overlook 9 ostracize
like a ~ fish: 6 chilly 7 distant 8 detached 9 apathetic, impassive 10 unfriendly, unsociable
like some ~ medicines: 3 OTC
one: 4 beer, brew 7 brewski
out ~: 5 inert 7 unaware 8 lifeless
out in the ~: 5 alone 9 unwelcome
out of the ~: 6 inside
period: 6 ice age

place for a ~ one: 3 bar, pub 6 saloon
precipitation: 4 hail, snow 5 sleet 8 blizzard
protection from ~: 4 wrap 5 parka, scarf 6 anorak, gloves 7 mittens 8 earmuffs
remedy: 5 Afrin 6 Contac, Nyquil, Tavist 7 Actifed, Comtrex, Dayquil, Dristan, Sinutab, Sudafed 8 Benadryl, Dimetapp, Drixoral, TheraFlu 9 Coricidin, Triaminic 10 Robitussin
remedy name: 5 Vicks
resistant perhaps: 5 hardy
season: 6 winter
shoulder: 4 snub 6 rebuff, slight 7 refusal, repulse 9 rejection
snap: 5 frost
sound: 3 brr 5 achoo 6 ahchoo, hachoo 7 kerchoo
spell: 4 ague, snap
spot: 6 Arctic, fridge 7 Siberia 9 Antarctic, North Pole, South Pole
suffer from ~: 6 freeze
throw ~ water on: 5 deter 6 dampen, sadden 8 dispirit
weather drink: 3 tea 5 cocoa, toddy 6 eggnog, hot tea
weather need: 6 deicer 8 rock salt

cold __: 3 cut, one, war 4 call, cash, cuts, deck, duck, feet, fish, pack, pole, snap, spot, tone, type, wave 5 as ice, color, cream, drink, frame, front, light, patch, spell, steel, store, sweat, water 6 cellar, fusion, rubber, turkey 7 calling, comfort, storage, warrior
cold __ icicle: 4 as an
cold-__: 4 cock, draw, eyed, roll, weld, work 7 blooded, hearted
cold-__ flat: 5 water
__ cold: 4 down, head 5 knock 6 common
__-cold: 3 ice
cold as __: 3 ice
cold-blooded: 4 hard, mean 5 cruel, feral, harsh, nasty 6 animal, brutal, fierce, savage, steely, unkind, wanton 7 beastly, callous, hurtful, inhuman, vicious 8 barbaric, fiendish, hardened, inhumane, pitiless, ruthless, sadistic, vengeful 9 cutthroat, ferocious, merciless, monstrous, truculent, unfeeling 10 hard-bitten, vindictive
Cold Case Files (A&E documentary)
host: Bill Kurtis
Cold, Cold Heart (1951 song)
artist: Tony Bennett
cold duck: 4 pink, wine
origin: 7 Germany
Cold Fire
author: Dean Koontz
cold-hearted: 5 stony 6 frigid, stoney 8 loveless, pitiless
Cold Hearted (1989 song)
artist: Paula Abdul
Cold Mountain (2003 film)
cast: Nicole Kidman, Jude Law, Renée Zellweger
coldness: 5 chill, frost 7 cruelty, reserve 8 distance 9 frigidity 10 detachment

cold-shoulder: 4 shun, snub 5 scorn, spurn 6 ignore 9 ostracize
__ cold, starve...: 5 Feed a
Cold Sweat (1967 song)
artist: James Brown
Cold War
broadcaster: 3 VOA
capital: 4 Bonn 6 Moscow
initials: 3 KGB 4 NATO, USSR
news agcy.: 4 Tass
plane: 3 MIG 4 U-two
pres.: 3 DDE, HST, JFK, LBJ
soldier: 3 spy
threat: 5 H bomb
weapon: 2 MX 4 ICBM, MIRV
cold-water __: 4 flat
Coldwell __: 6 Banker
cole: 6 veggie 9 vegetable
cole __: 4 slaw
Cole: 3 Nat 4 Cozy, Gary, Tina 5 Paula 6 Porter, Thomas 7 Michael, Natalie, Younger
__ Cole: 7 Nat King, Old King
Coleco
rival: 5 Atari
Coleen: 4 Gray
Coleman: 2 Cy 4 Gary 6 Dabney 7 Hawkins, lantern, Ornette
Coleman, Ornette: 11 saxophonist
genre: 4 jazz
Cole, Natalie
song: I've Got Love on My Mind (1977)
Miss You Like Crazy (1989)
Our Love (1978)
Pink Cadillac (1988)
This Will Be (1975)
Unforgettable (1991)
Cole, Nat King
instrument: piano
song: A Blossom Fell (1955)
Darling Je Vous Aime Beaucoup (1955)
If I May (1955)
Looking Back (1958)
Ramblin' Rose (1962)
Send for Me (1957)
Those Lazy-Hazy-Crazy Days of Summer (1963)
Unforgettable (1961)
coleopteran: 6 beetle, insect
Cole Porter Song Book
artist: Ella Fitzgerald
Coleridge, Samuel Taylor: 4 poet 7 British
colleague: Southey
friend: 4 Elia, Lamb
work: Christabel
Dejection: An Ode
France: An Ode
Frost at Midnight
Kubla Khan
Love
The Rime of the Ancient Mariner
To Asra
Coles: 4 Honi
coleslaw: 4 side 5 salad
make ~: 5 shred
Colette: 6 French, writer
work: The Blue Lantern
Chéri
Duo
Gigi
Mitsou
Sido
colewort: 4 kail, kale

Colfax: 8 Schuyler
Colgate
alternative: *see* toothpaste
athletes: 7 Raiders
locale: 7 New York 8 Hamilton
unit: 4 tube
colic: 5 ileus
Colin: 5 Clive, Firth, Hanks 6 Friels, Powell, Wilson 7 Blakely, Farrell, Mochrie 8 MacInnes, Margaret
coliseum: 4 bowl 5 arena 7 stadium, theater, theatre 10 hippodrome
Coliseum, The
author: Edgar Allan Poe
coll.: 3 sch. 4 acad., univ.
class: 4 lect.
club: 3 sor.
course: 3 bio., Eng., sem., soc. 4 geol., hist., stat. 10 chem.. phys. ed.
deg.: 3 BCE, BCS
senior's exam: 4 LSAT
student: 2 jr., sr. 3 jnr., snr. 4 soph.
see also college
collaborate (with): 4 join, work 6 assist, hook up, team up 8 interact
collaboration: 4 team 8 alliance
collaborative: 5 joint
group: 4 team
collaboratively: 8 mutually 9 in concert
collaborator: 4 ally 7 partner 8 coworker, henchman, teammate
collage: 3 art 4 olio 7 mixture 8 pastiche
need: 4 glue
Collages
author: Anaïs Nin
collapse: 2 go 3 sag 4 drop, fail, fall, flop, fold, give, sink, tire, wilt 5 crash, decay, faint, plotz, shock, slump, smash, yield 6 buckle, cave in, defeat, fall in, fizzle, perish, topple, trauma 7 conk out, crumble, crumple, debacle, deflate, descend, failure, founder, give way, plummet, subside, succumb, undoing 8 downfall, fall down, fall flat, pull down 9 breakdown, cataclysm, fall apart, recession, ruination 10 bankruptcy
about to ~: 5 shaky
collapsed: 4 fell, went 6 broken, fallen
collapsing: 4 beat 5 all in, tired
collar: 3 bag, cop, get, nab, net 4 bust, find, grab, hook, nail, take, trap, yoke 5 catch, dicky, grasp, pinch, run in, seize 6 abduct, arrest, corner, detain, dickey, dickie, flange, pick up, pull in, secure, snatch 7 capture, jailing, seizure 8 cincture 9 apprehend
attachment: 5 ID tag
blue ~: 5 labor 6 worker
ender: 4 bone
extension: 5 lapel
fastener: 4 stud
hot under the ~: *see* angry
insert: 4 stay
lace: 5 ruche
lace ~: 4 ruff 6 bertha
site: 4 nape, neck
straightener: 4 iron
victim: 3 bug 4 flea, pest 6 insect
white ~: 6 worker

__ collar: 3 dog 4 Eton, flea 5 choke, horse
__-collar: 4 blue, pink 5 white
collarbone: 8 clavicle
collard __: 6 greens
collards: 7 veggies 10 vegetables
collared: 5 ran in 6 in jail
garment: 4 coat 5 shirt 6 jacket
one, for short: 4 perp
collate: 4 sort 5 group 6 assort, gather, verify 7 compare, compile, examine 8 assemble
collateral: 4 bail, bond, lien, pawn, side 5 funds 6 litter, pledge, surety 7 deposit, related 8 indirect, security 9 accessory, ancillary, assurance, attendant, auxiliary, dependant, dependent, guarantee, resources, satellite, secondary, tributary 10 adjunctive, circuitous, coincident, concurrent, coordinate, roundabout, subsidiary, supporting, synchronal
holder: 6 lienor
Collateral (2004 film)
cast: Tom Cruise, Jamie Foxx, Mark Ruffalo
collation: 4 meal, nosh 5 snack 6 dinner, repast, spread, tidbit 10 comparison, validation
serving: 3 tea
colleague: 3 bro, pal 4 ally, chum, mate 5 amigo, buddy, crony 6 cohort, friend 7 compeer, comrade, partner 8 confrere, coworker, henchman, sidekick, teammate, workmate 9 accessory, assistant, associate, auxiliary, coadjutor, companion, confidant 10 accomplice, compatriot, wellwisher
collect: 3 tap 4 cull, earn, herd, levy, mass, pile, pool, rake, reap, save, take 5 amass, claim, dig up, flock, glean, group, hoard, raise, rally 6 accrue, cash in, center, corral, garner, gather, muster, obtain, pick up, rake in, roll up, secure 7 acquire, cluster, compile, convene, convoke, deposit, harvest, marshal, receive, round up, scare up 8 assemble, hold on to, muster up, scrape up 9 aggregate, stockpile 10 accumulate, congregate, pass the hat
a bet: 3 win
ender: 3 ive
on a surface: 6 adsorb
oneself: 5 relax
collect __: 4 call
collectanea: 8 analecta, analects 9 anthology 10 miscellany
collected: 4 calm, cool 5 quiet, sober, staid, stoic 6 at ease, low-key, mellow, placid, poised, sedate, serene 7 amiable, at peace, equable, pacific, relaxed, stoical, unmoved 8 amicable, carefree, composed, laid-back, peaceful, rational, reserved, together, tranquil 9 aggregate, confident, different, easygoing, impassive, nerveless, possessed, quiescent, temperate, unexcited, unruffled 10 nonchalant, phlegmatic, unagitated, untroubled
sayings: 3 ana
works: 5 canon

collectedness: 5 poise 6 aplomb
collectible: 3 due 5 curio 8 valuable
collection: 3 lot, set 4 band, bevy, heap, herd, levy, mass, pile 5 album, array, batch, bunch, flock, group, hoard, sheaf, stack, stock, store, troop, trove 6 bundle, corpus, medley 7 cluster, company, species, variety 8 assembly, ensemble, pastiche, quantity, treasury 9 aggregate, amassment, anthology, concourse, congeries, gathering, potpourri, repertory, selection, stockpile 10 assemblage, assortment, cumulation, depository, embodiment, hodgepodge, miscellany, opera omnia
  suffix: 3 -age, -ana, -ery 4 -iana
collection __: 3 box 5 plate 6 agency
Collection, The
  author: Harold Pinter
collective: 5 joint, whole 6 mutual, shared, social, united 7 commune, general, generic, grouped, kibbutz, unified 8 combined, communal, compiled, conjoint 9 aggregate, assembled, composite, concerted, corporate, generical, undivided 10 cumulative
  Russian ~: 5 artel
collective __: 4 farm, noun
collectively: 5 as one 6 bodily, wholly 7 all told, en masse 8 together
collector: 6 editor 7 pack rat 8 gatherer
__ collector: 4 toll 5 solar
collector's item: 5 curio, vertu, virtu
Collector, The
  author: John Fowles
colleen: 4 lass, maid, miss 5 woman 6 damsel, lassie, maiden 8 fraülein
  home: 4 Eire, Erin 7 Ireland
Colleen: 4 Camp 5 Moore 8 Dewhurst 10 McCullough
college: 3 sch. 6 school 7 academy 8 univ. acad. 9 alma mater
  army prog.: 4 ROTC
  bill line: 4 room 5 board, meals 6 lab fee 7 tuition
  book: 4 text
  building: 4 dorm, hall
  choice: 5 major, minor
  club: 3 sor. 4 frat 8 sorority 10 fraternity
  conferral: 6 degree
  course: 3 art, bio., Eng., Ger., mus. 4 chem., econ., geol., math 5 drama, music, psych 6 anthro, French, German, phys. ed. 7 biology, English, geology, physics, Spanish 9 chemistry, economics, sociology 10 psychology
  courtyard: 4 quad
  cred. units: 3 hrs.
  deg.: 2 AA, AB, AS, BA, BE, MA. 3 BBA, BFA, BSC, DFA, MFA, MPA, Ph.D.
  dining room: 7 commons
  diploma word: 3 cum 5 laude, magna, summa 6 honors
  do: 5 mixer
  entrance exam: 3 SAT 4 PSAT
  exam for ~ srs.: 3 GRE 4 GMAT, LSAT
  freshman, usually: 4 teen
  grad: 4 alum 6 alumna 7 alumnus
  grounds: 6 campus
  head: 4 prex, prez 5 prexy
  keepsake: 2 yb. 4 ring 8 yearbook
  like most ~s: 4 coed
  military ~: 3 VMI 4 USMA, USNA 5 USAFA 7 Citadel 9 West Point
  offering: 6 course
  official: 4 dean 6 bursar, regent 7 provost 9 registrar
  paper: 6 thesis
  party: 5 mixer
  party site: 4 frat
  party staple: 3 keg
  protest: 5 sit-in
  sport: 4 golf 5 track 6 hockey, soccer 7 bowling 8 baseball, football, lacrosse, swimming 9 wrestling 10 basketball, volleyball
  sports org.: 3 AAU 4 NCAA
  stat: 3 GPA
  student: 4 soph 5 frosh 6 junior, senior 8 freshman 9 sophomore
  teacher: 4 prof 6 docent, lector 8 lecturer 9 professor 10 instructor
  unit: 6 credit
  website suffix: 3 edu
  woman: 4 coed
  women's ~: 5 Smith 7 Barnard 8 Bryn Mawr 9 Wellesley
  word in some ~ nicknames: 4 Tech
college __: 3 try
__ college: 3 cow 6 barber, junior
College (1927 film)
  cast: Buster Keaton
  director: James W. Horne
College __: 6 Boards
College __, The: 5 Widow
__ College: 3 Joe
__ College, NC: 4 Elon
College Park: 4 city, town
  athletes: 5 Terps 9 Terrapins
  locale: 8 Maryland
College Station: 4 city, town
  athletes: 6 Aggies
  locale: 5 Texas
  school: 4 TAMU
__ college try, the: 3 old
College Widow, The
  author: George Ade
collegian: 4 coed, soph 5 frosh 6 junior, senior 8 freshman 9 sophomore
collegiate: 8 academic
  starter: 5 inter
Collette: 4 Toni
collide: 4 meet 5 clash, crash, smash 6 hurtle, pile up, strike 7 quarrel 8 conflict, disagree
  with: 3 hit, ram 4 bump, butt, jolt 6 impact, strike
  with, in Britain: 5 prang
collie: 3 dog 5 pooch 6 canine, herder 8 sheepdog, shepherd
  charge: 5 flock, sheep
  fictional ~: 3 Lad 6 Lassie
  name for a ~: 4 Shep
__ collie: 6 Border
collier: 4 boat 5 miner
Collier: 9 Constance
Collier's
  rival: 4 Life, Look
colliery: 7 coal pit 8 coal mine
colliery exit: 4 adit
collimate: 5 align, aline 8 parallel
Collins: 4 Gary, Joan, Judy, Phil 5 Billy, drink, Eddie, Tyler 6 Eileen, Jackie, Wilkie 7 Michael, Pauline, Stephen, William 8 beverage, cocktail
  ingredient: 3 gin 4 lime, soda 9 lime juice 10 lemon juice
__ Collins: 3 Tom
__ Collins, CO: 4 Fort
Collins, Gary
  spouse: Mary Ann Mobley
collins ingredient: 4 lime
Collins, Joan: 7 actress
  spouse: Anthony Newley
  TV: Dynasty
Collins, Phil
  lead singer of: Genesis
  song: Against All Odds (1984)
    Another Day in Paradise (1989)
    Don't Lose My Number (1985)
    Do You Remember? (1990)
    Easy Lover (1984)
    Groovy Kind of Love (1988)
    I Wish It Would Rain Down (1990)
    One More Night (1985)
    Separate Lives (1985)
    Sussudio (1985)
    Take Me Home (1986)
    Two Hearts (1988)
Collins, Wilkie: 6 writer 7 British
  work: The Moonstone
    The Woman in White
collision: 3 hit, jar 4 blow, jolt, tilt 5 crash, shock, smash, wreck 6 impact, pileup 7 contact 8 accident, conflict 9 encounter, rear-ender, sideswipe 10 concussion, percussion
  avoid ~: 6 swerve
  minor ~: 4 bump
  result: 4 dent
  sound: 3 bam 4 wham
collision __: 6 course
__ collision: 6 head-on
collocate: 8 parallel 10 accumulate
Collodi, Carlo: 6 writer 7 Italian
  work: Pinocchio
colloid: 3 gel 5 algin
colloquial: 5 slang 6 chatty, common, vulgar 8 everyday, familiar, informal 9 dialectal, idiomatic 10 vernacular
colloquialism: 5 idiom, slang 8 localism
colloquy: 4 talk, word 5 forum 6 dialog, parley 8 dialogue 9 discourse 10 conference, discussion
Colloquy of Monos and Una, The
  author: Edgar Allan Poe
collude: 4 abet, plot 5 cabal 6 scheme 7 connive 8 conspire, intrigue 9 machinate
collusion: 4 plot 8 intrigue 9 shell game, whitewash 10 complicity, connivance, conspiracy, guiltiness
Collyer: 3 Bud 4 June
Colm: 6 Meaney
Colman: 6 Ronald
Colo.
  clock setting: 3 MDT, MST
  neighbor: 3 Kan., Neb., Wyo. 4 Kans., Nebr., N. Mex.
  sch.: 5 USAFA
  see also Colorado
cologne: 5 scent 7 perfume 9 fragrance
  characteristic: 4 odor
  container: 4 vial 5 phial
  ingredient: 4 musk
Cologne: 4 city, Köln, town
  city near ~: 5 Essen
  locale: 3 Ger. 7 Germany
  river: 5 Rhine
__ Cologne: 5 eau de
__ Colognie: 4 Odie
colombard: 4 wine 5 white
Colombia: 6 nation 7 country
  capital: 6 Bogotá
  city: 4 Buga, Cali 5 Neiva, Pasto, Tuluá, Tunja 6 Bogotá, Cúcuta, Ibagué, Itaguí, Soacha 7 Armenia, Cartago, Palmira, Pereira, Popayán, Soledad 8 Envigado, Medellín, Montería 9 Cartagena, Sincelejo 10 Santa Marta, Valledupar
  clothing: 5 ruana
  Indian: 4 Tama 7 Chibcha
  money: 4 peso
  neighbor: 4 Peru 6 Brazil, Panama 7 Ecuador 9 Venezuela
  Nobelist in Literature: 7 Márquez
  org.: 3 OAS
  peak: 4 Ruiz
  poet: 5 Silva 6 Rivera
  port: 9 Cartagena
  river: 4 Meta
  volcano: 4 Ruiz 5 Huila, Pasto 6 Puracé 7 Galeras
  writer: 6 Rivera 7 Márquez
  see also Spanish
Colombo: 4 city, port, town 7 capital
  locale: 8 Sri Lanka
colon: 5 money
  half a ~: 3 dot
  in analogies: 4 is to
colonel: 4 rank 5 Klink 6 Potter
  command: 3 rgt. 8 regiment
  insignia: 5 eagle
  see also Army
__ colonel: 4 bird 7 chicken
Colonel __: 5 Blimp 7 Sanders
Colonel __ Parker: 3 Tom
__ Colonel, The: 6 Little
colonial: 3 era 6 quaint
  dance: 4 reel 6 minuet 8 saraband 9 sarabande
  descendants' org.: 3 DAR, SAR
  flute: 4 fife
  loyalist: 4 Tory
  newscaster: 5 crier
  rest stop: 4 inne
  starter: 3 neo
  word in ~ place names: 3 New
colonist: 7 pioneer, settler 8 emigrant 9 immigrant 10 inhabitant
  foe: 7 redcoat
colonize: 6 settle
colonizer: 7 settler
  small ~: 3 ant, bee 5 emmet
Colonna: 5 Jerry 8 Vittoria
colonnade: 4 stoa 6 arcade 7 pergola
colonus: 4 serf
colony: 4 hive, nest 5 swarm 7 outpost 8 ant group, dominion, offshoot, province 9 community, territory 10 dependency, possession, settlement
  group: 5 swarm
  member: 3 ant

__ colony: **5** crown, penal, royal
__ Colony: **4** Cape, Lost
colophon: **4** logo **6** device, emblem, symbol
colophony: **5** rosin
color: **3** ash, bay, dun, dye, hue, jet, pea, tan **4** anil, aqua, blue, bole, bone, buff, cast, corn, cyan, dove, drab, ecru, fake, fawn, foxy, gold, inky, jade, lime, milk, navy, Nile, nude, onyx, plum, puce, race, rose, ruby, rust, sage, sand, seal, snow, teal, tint, tone, warp, wine **5** adorn, Alice, amber, azure, beige, beryl, blond, brass, breen, brick, camel, cocoa, coral, cream, dusty, ebony, flame, flaxy, fudge, glaze, gloss, grape, hazel, henna, imbue, ivory, khaki, lemon, lilac, maize, mauve, melon, merle, milky, mocha, ocher, ochre, olive, paint, peach, pearl, poppy, putty, raven, rusty, sable, sandy, sepia, shade, slant, slate, smoke, sooty, spice, stain, straw, taupe, tawny, tinct, tinge, twist, umber, virid **6** almond, argent, auburn, bister, bistre, blonde, bronze, canary, cerise, chammy, cherry, chroma, citron, claret, cobalt, coffee, copper, crocus, dahlia, damask, damson, doctor, enamel, flaxen, garble, garnet, ginger, indigo, infuse, maroon, myrtle, nature, orange, orchid, oyster, purple, raisin, redden, reseda, russet, salmon, shammy, shamoy, sienna, silver, sorrel, suntan, violet, walnut **7** apricot, avocado, biscuit, caramel, carmine, celadon, chamois, citrine, crimson, distort, dogwood, emerald, enliven, falsify, fuchsia, grizzly, heather, jasmine, magenta, magnify, mustard, nankeen, old gold, peacock, petunia, pigment, pimento, pumpkin, saffron, scarlet, sultana, verdant, vermeil, xanthic **8** amaranth, amethyst, burgundy, cardinal, cerulean, charcoal, chestnut, cinnamon, daffodil, disguise, dubonnet, eggplant, eggshell, emblazon, flamingo, flesh out, geranium, gunmetal, hyacinth, jaundice, lavender, mahogany, mulberry, platinum, primrose, rubicund, sapphire, tincture **9** alabaster, butternut, carnation, champagne, chocolate, cranberry, embellish, embroider, goldenrod, jessamine, misrender, overstate, pistachio, raspberry, robin's-egg, tangerine, turquoise, vermilion **10** aquamarine, chartreuse, complexion, exaggerate, heliotrope, illuminate, periwinkle, strawberry, terra cotta
black ~: **3** jet **4** inky, onyx **5** ebony, raven, sable, sooty
blackish ~: **8** burgundy
blue ~: **4** anil, cyan, navy, Nile, teal **5** Alice, azure, slate **6** cobalt, indigo, raisin, violet **7** peacock **8** cerulean, sapphire **9** turquoise **10** aquamarine, periwinkle
bluish ~: **4** jade, plum **5** beryl, mauve, merle, pearl, slate **6** myrtle, orchid **8** lavender, platinum **9** cranberry, turquoise
brown ~: **3** bay, dun, tan **4** bole, ecru, fawn, foxy, nude, seal **5** amber, beige, camel, cocoa, hazel, khaki, mocha, sepia, tawny, umber **6** auburn, bister, bistre, bronze, coffee, copper, ginger, russet, sienna, sorrel, suntan, walnut **7** biscuit, caramel, dogwood **8** chestnut, cinnamon, mahogany **9** butternut, chocolate
brownish ~: **4** buff, drab, nude, puce, sand **5** beige, breen, olive, putty, taupe **7** nankeen **8** charcoal **10** terra cotta
combining form: **5** chrom- **6** -chrome, chromo- **7** chromat- **8** chromato-
ender: **4** bred, cast, fast **5** blind, breed
gray ~: **3** ash **4** dove, drab **5** beige, dusty, merle, pearl, putty, slate, taupe **6** silver **7** grizzly **8** charcoal, gunmetal, platinum
grayish ~: **3** dun **4** nude, sage **5** Alice, sepia, slate **6** chammy, indigo, oyster, reseda, shammy, shamoy **7** celadon, chamois **8** mulberry
green ~: **3** pea **4** cyan, jade, sage **5** beryl, breen, olive, virid **6** myrtle, reseda **7** avocado, celadon, emerald, verdant **9** pistachio, turquoise **10** aquamarine, chartreuse
greenish ~: **4** aqua, cyan, lime, Nile, teal **6** cobalt **7** peacock **8** cerulean **9** champagne, robin's-egg, turquoise **10** aquamarine
in heraldry: **8** tincture
orange ~: **5** flame, henna **7** pumpkin, saffron **8** hyacinth **9** tangerine **10** terra cotta
orangish ~: **5** ocher, ochre, poppy **6** crocus **7** saffron
pink ~: **4** nude **5** melon **6** damask, salmon **7** apricot **8** flamingo **9** carnation
pinkish ~: **4** dove **5** coral, peach **7** apricot, heather
purple ~: **4** plum, puce **5** lilac, mauve **6** dahlia, damson, orchid **7** heather, petunia **8** amethyst, burgundy, eggplant, lavender, mulberry **9** raspberry **10** heliotrope
purplish ~: **4** dove **5** azure, grape **6** claret, raisin **7** carmine, crimson, fuchsia, magenta, sultana **8** amaranth, dubonnet
red ~: **4** rose, ruby, rust, wine **5** brick, coral, grape, poppy, rusty, sandy **6** cerise, cherry, claret, garnet, maroon **7** carmine, crimson, fuchsia, magenta, pimento, scarlet, sultana, vermeil **8** amaranth, cardinal, dubonnet, geranium, rubicund **9** carnation, cranberry, vermilion **10** strawberry
reddish ~: **3** bay **4** bole, foxy, plum, rust, sand **5** brass, cocoa, coral, flame, henna, lilac, ocher, ochre, rusty, umber **6** auburn, copper, ginger, orchid, russet, sorrel, walnut **7** petunia **8** chestnut, cinnamon, hyacinth, mahogany, rubicund **9** raspberry, tangerine **10** heliotrope
starter: **3** tri **5** water
tan ~: **4** buff **5** camel **6** almond **7** caramel
white ~: **4** bone, milk, snow **5** cream, ivory, milky **6** argent, oyster, silver **8** eggshell
whitish ~: **6** silver
yellow ~: **4** buff, corn, gold, lime, rust, sand **5** blond, brass, coral, cream, flaxy, lemon, maize, ocher, ochre, peach, rusty, straw **6** blonde, canary, chammy, citron, crocus, flaxen, shammy, shamoy **7** apricot, chamois, citrine, jasmine, mustard, nankeen, old gold, saffron, xanthic **8** daffodil, primrose **9** champagne, goldenrod, jessamine
yellowish ~: **3** tan **4** bone, drab, fawn, foxy, jade, nude, rust **5** amber, camel, cocoa, coral, cream, ivory, khaki, olive, putty, rusty, sandy, tawny **6** auburn, bister, bistre, ginger, russet, salmon, sienna, suntan **7** apricot, caramel, dogwood **8** cinnamon **9** alabaster **10** chartreuse
color __: **4** code **5** force, guard, index, phase, point, wheel **6** filter, scheme **7** printer
color-__: **3** key **4** code **5** blind, coded, field
__ color: **3** ash, oil **4** cold, corn, dove, tone **5** earth, local **7** primary
Color __, The: **6** Purple
Colorado: **5** river, state **6** desert
city: **4** Vail **5** Aspen, Ouray **6** Arvada, Aurora, Denver, Golden, Parker, Pueblo **7** Boulder, Durango, Greeley **8** Brighton, Ken Caryl, Lakewood, Longmont, Loveland, Security, Thornton **9** Canon City, Columbine, Englewood, Estes Park, Lafayette, Littleton, Telluride, Widefield **10** Broomfield, Castle Rock, Castlewood, Northglenn, Southglenn, Wheat Ridge
city on the ~: **4** Yuma **6** Austin
college: **5** Regis
conference: **9** Big Twelve
county: **4** Yuma **5** Otero
Indian: **3** Ute **4** Yuma
mountain: **4** Yale **5** Bross, Eolus, Estes, Evans **6** Antero, Elbert, Oxford, Wilson **7** Belford, Cameron, Harvard, Laramie, Lincoln, San Juan, Sawatch, Shavano, Sherman **8** Columbia, Democrat, Sneffels **9** Bierstadt, Pikes Peak, Princeton
national park: **9** Mesa Verde
neighbor: **4** Utah **6** Kansas **7** Arizona, Wyoming **8** Nebraska, Oklahoma **9** New Mexico
resort: **4** Vail **5** Aspen
river: **5** Yampa
River locale: **4** Utah **7** Arizona
river to the ~: **4** Gila **10** Pedernales
state flower: **9** columbine
state gemstone: **10** aquamarine
state grass: **9** blue grama
state tree: **10** blue spruce
team: **7** Rockies **9** Avalanche
tributary: **4** Gila **7** Dolores
Colorado Springs: **4** city, town
athletes: **7** Falcons
county: **6** El Paso
school: **5** USAFA
student: **5** cadet **6** airman
Colorado State athletes: **4** Rams
colorant: **3** dye **4** woad **5** paint, tinge **6** litmus **7** pigment
coloration: **4** tint **5** tinge **10** complexion
coloratura: **4** diva **5** lyric, voice **6** singer **7** soprano **8** vocalist
specialty: **4** aria **5** trill
colored: **5** tinct **7** partial **8** partisan
brightly ~: **4** neon **5** vivid
prefix for ~: **5** multi
__-colored glasses: **4** rose
colorfast, wasn't: **3** ran **4** bled
colorful: **4** hued **5** gaudy, juicy, vivid **6** bright, flashy, florid **7** dashing, graphic, vibrant **8** romantic **9** chromatic, graphical **10** expressive
coloring: **3** dye **4** tint, tone **5** paint, stain, tinct, tinge **8** infusion **10** complexion
agent: **4** dyer
combining form: **6** -chromy
device: **6** crayon
organic ~: **3** azo **6** azo dye
coloring __: **4** book
colorist: **4** dyer
colorless: **3** wan **4** arid, ashy, drab, dull, flat, pale, tame **5** ashen, faded, livid, mousy, vapid, waxen, white **6** common, doughy, dreary, mousey **7** grayish, hueless, insipid, prosaic **8** achromic, blanched, bleached, lifeless, mediocre, unlively **9** bloodless, prosaical, washed-out **10** achromatic, dullsville, impersonal, lackluster, monotonous
Color of Darkness
author: James Purdy
Color of Money, The (1986 film)
cast: Tom Cruise, Mary Elizabeth Mastrantonio, Paul Newman
director: Martin Scorsese
prop: **3** cue **4** rack **5** chalk
Color Purple, The: **4** film **5** novel
author: Alice Walker
cast: Margaret Avery, Danny Glover, Whoopi Goldberg, Oprah Winfrey
director: Steven Spielberg
role: **5** Celie, Sofia
colors: **4** flag **6** ensign **7** pennant
flying ~: **7** success, triumph, victory
profusion of ~: **4** riot
with flying ~: **4** fine, well **5** great **6** easily **7** handily **8** adroitly, expertly, smoothly, very well **9** hands down **10** skillfully, swimmingly
__ colors: **5** false **6** flying
Colors (1988 film)
cast: Maria Conchita Alonso, Robert Duvall, Sean Penn
director: Dennis Hopper

__ Colors: **4** True **7** Primary
Colors of the Wind (1995 song)
artist: Vanessa Williams
colossal: 3 big **4** huge, vast **5** bulky, giant, great, hefty, jumbo, large **6** mighty **7** hulking, immense, mammoth, massive, sizable, titanic **8** enormous, gigantic, king-size, oversize, sizeable, towering, whapping, whopping **9** cyclopean, herculean, humongous, monstrous, overlarge **10** formidable, gargantuan, monumental, prodigious, stupendous, tremendous
Colosseum: 5 arena
denizen: 4 lion **9** gladiator
honoree: 6 Caesar
locale: 4 Rome
colossus: 5 giant, titan, whale **7** mammoth, monster **8** behemoth **9** leviathan
Colossus of __: 6 Rhodes
Colossus of Maroussi, The
author: Henry Miller
Colossus, The
author: Sylvia Plath
__ Colossus, The: 3 New
Colour of Love, The (1988 song)
artist: Billy Ocean
Colson: 5 Chuck **7** Charles
colt: 4 foal, male **5** horse **6** animal, equine **8** newcomer
mother: 3 dam **4** mare
sibling: 5 filly
Colt: 3 car, gun, Sam **4** auto **5** Dodge **6** pistol, Samuel **10** Mitsubishi
Colter, Jessi
song: I'm Not Lisa (1975)
coltish: 4 wild **6** frisky, lively, unruly **7** playful, romping, untamed **8** playsome, spirited, sportive **9** gamboling **10** frolicsome
Colton: 4 city, town
locale: 10 California
Coltrane: 3 Chi **4** John, Ravi **5** Alice
Coltrane, John: 11 saxophonist
genre: 4 jazz
Coltrane, Roscoe deputy: 4 Enos
Colts: 6 eleven
org.: 3 AFC
rival: ***see*** NFL team
Colum: 7 Padraic
Columba, Saint
site of ~ monastery: 4 Iona
Columbia: 3 riv. **4** cape, city, peak, town **5** mount, river **6** studio **8** mountain
athletes: 5 Lions **6** Tigers **9** Gamecocks
competitor: ***see*** movie studio **6** Disney
creation: 4 film **5** movie
league: 3 Ivy
locale: 6 Canada **7** Alberta, New York, Rockies **8** Colorado, Maryland, Missouri **9** Tennessee
offering: 5 movie
org.: 4 NASA
river: 8 Congaree
River explorer: 4 Gray
River locale: 6 Oregon **10** Washington
river to the ~: 5 Snake **8** Kootenay **9** Deschutes **10** Willamette
school: 3 USC
__ Columbia: 7 British
__, Columbia: 4 Hail
__-Columbian: 3 pre
Columbia Pictures: 6 studio
owner: 4 Cohn, Sony
Columbia, the __ of the Ocean: 3 Gem
columbine: 5 plant **6** flower **8** dovelike
Columbine: 4 city, town
locale: 8 Colorado
Columbo: 3 cop, tec **4** Russ **10** lieutenant
caper: 4 case
Columbo (TV drama)
cast: Peter Falk (Lt. Columbo)
employer: LAPD
Columbus: 4 city, town **5** Chris
athletes: 8 Buckeyes
author: Joaquin Miller
county: 8 Franklin
locale: 4 Ohio **7** Georgia, Indiana **8** Nebraska
newspaper: 8 Dispatch
river: 6 Scioto
school: 3 OSU **9** Ohio State
Columbus __: 3 Day
__, Columbus: 7 Goodbye
Columbus, Christopher: 8 explorer
contemporary: 5 Cabot
discovery: 7 Bahamas
home: 5 Genoa, Italy
ship: 4 Niña **5** Pinta **10** Santa Maria
sponsor: 5 Spain **8** Isabella **9** Ferdinand
Columbus Day
event: 4 sale
month: 3 Oct. **7** October
column: 3 leg, row **4** beam, line, pier, post, rank, stay **5** piece, pylon, queue, shaft, stela, stele, totem, tower, train **6** parade, pillar, review, series **7** article, feature, obelisk, support, upright, writing **8** buttress, monolith, monument, pedestal, pilaster **9** editorial **10** procession
addition ~: 4 ones, tens **5** units **8** hundreds **9** thousands
bases: 4 tori
calendar ~: 3 Fri., Mon., Sat., Sun., Thu., Tue., Wed. **4** Thur., Tues. **5** Thurs. **6** Friday, Monday, Sunday **7** Tuesday **8** Saturday, Thursday **9** Wednesday
combining form: 4 styl- **5** -style, stylo-
credit: 6 byline
ender: 3 ist
feature: 7 entasis
formatted in a single ~: 5 one up
gossip ~ subject: 5 actor, celeb **7** actress **9** celebrity, headliner
inscribed ~: 5 stela
part: 4 dado, orlo
ridge: 5 arris
row of ~s: 6 arcade **7** pergola **9** colonnade
shaft: 5 scape
steel structural ~: 5 lally
support: 5 socle
type: 5 Doric, Ionic **6** Gothic **10** Corinthian
wall ~: 4 anta
column __: 4 inch
__ column: 5 agony, fifth **6** spinal
Column B, one from: 6 lo mein **7** chow fun **8** chow mein **9** fried rice, spare ribs **10** Peking duck
columnist: 5 press **6** author, scribe, writer **7** analyst **8** reporter **9** wordsmith **10** ink slinger, journalist
fifth ~: 5 snake **7** traitor **8** quisling, turncoat
__ columnist: 5 fifth
Colvin: 5 Shawn
__ com: 3 dot
.com
alternative: 3 .biz, .edu, .gov, .mil, .net, .org **4** .info, .movi, .name
coma: 6 torpor, trance **7** slumber **8** lethargy
Coma
author: Robin Cook
Comanche: 5 horse, tribe **6** equine, Indian **7** Amerind **8** language
language family: 5 Numic
Comaneci, Nadia: 7 gymnast **8** Romanian
comate: 5 hairy **6** tufted **7** partner **9** companion
comb: 4 rake, seek, sift, sort **5** groom, probe, scour, sweep, tease **6** dredge, forage, search **7** examine, inspect, ransack, rummage **8** untangle **10** scrutinize
combining form: 4 cten-, loph- **5** cteno-, lophi-, lopho- **6** lophio-
contents: 5 honey
impediment: 4 snag
manufacturer: 3 bee **4** hive
out: 7 unravel
part: 4 cell **5** tooth
partner: 5 brush
starter: 3 cox **5** curry, honey
with a fine tooth ~: 10 thoroughly
__ comb: 3 hot
combat: 3 war **4** buck, defy, duel, fray, tilt **5** clash, fight, jihad, joust **6** action, affray, attack, battle, oppose, resist, strife **7** contest, service, warfare **8** battling, conflict, fighting, skirmish, struggle **9** encounter, withstand **10** contention, engagement, opposition, resistance
prepare for ~: 3 arm **8** embattle
unit: 4 army **5** corps **8** division, regiment **9** battalion
vehicle: 4 tank
zone: 5 arena, front
combat __: 4 boot, team, zone **6** jacket
combat-__: 5 ready
Combat (ABC drama)
cast: Rick Jason (Lt. Gil Hanley) Vic Morrow (Sgt. Chip Saunders)
combatant: 3 foe **4** side, vier **5** enemy **6** dueler **7** battler, fighter, soldier, warrior **8** attacker **9** gladiator, ill-wisher, legionary **10** contestant
combative: 5 saucy **7** hawkish, martial, warlike **8** fighting, militant, military, ructious **9** bellicose, energetic, litigious, strenuous, truculent **10** aggressive, fire-eating, jingoistic, pugnacious, unfriendly
one: 6 bantam
comber: 4 wave
starter: 5 beach
combination: 3 mix **4** bloc, gild, stew **5** alloy, blend, group, guild, union **6** cartel, fusion, hybrid, league, medley, merger **7** amalgam, faction, mixture **8** alliance, blending, compound **9** aggregate, potpourri, synthesis **10** miscellany
combination __: 4 door, lock, shot **7** platter
combine: 3 mix, wed **4** band, bloc, bond, fuse, join, link, mesh, pool, ring, yoke **5** admix, alloy, blend, group, immix, marry, merge, party, trust, unify, unite **6** attach, cartel, cement, cohere, commix, couple, embody, hook up, imbody, league, make up, mingle, team up **7** bunch up, conjoin, connect, hitch on, mixture **8** coalesce, interact **9** affiliate, aggregate, coalition, commingle, integrate, interface, interlace, syndicate **10** amalgamate, interweave, synthesize
numbers: 3 sum, tot **5** add up, count, sum up, tally, total, tot up **6** figure **7** compute, count up **9** calculate
with: 5 add to
combined: 4 mixt **5** in all, in one, joint, mixed **6** allied, joined, united **7** grouped **8** in league, in unison, together **9** undivided **10** collective
combining __: 4 form
combining forms
abdomen: 4 celi- **5** celio-, coeli-, ventr- **6** coelio-, ventri-, ventro-
abduct: 3 -nap
abnormal: 4 anom- **5** anomo-
acid: 3 oxy-
action: 3 cin-, kin- **4** cino-, kine-, kino-
activated by: 5 -ergic
active: 7 -kinetic
activity: 7 -kinesis
acute: 3 oxy-
addict: 5 -holic **6** -aholic
advocate: 4 -crat **5** -arian, -ocrat
air: 3 atm- **4** atmo- **6** pneumo-
algae: 4 phyc- **5** phyco-
alien: 3 xen- **4** xeno-
alive: 4 vivi-
all: 3 omn-, pan- **4** omni-, pano-, pant- **5** panta-, panto-
almost: 3 pen- **4** pene-
alone: 3 mon- **4** mono-, soli-
ancient: 4 pale- **5** palae-, paleo- **6** archeo-, palaeo-, palaio- **7** archaeo-
ancillary: 3 par- **4** para-
angular: 3 -gon
animal: 2 zo- **3** zoo- **4** -zoon
animals: 3 -zoa
ankle: 4 tali-
anklebone: 5 tarso-
antibiotic: 5 -mycin
antimony: 4 stib- **5** stibi-, stibo- **6** stibio-
apart: 4 dich- **5** dicho-
appearance: 5 -phany
appearing: 4 phen- **5** pheno-
appetite: 6 -orexia
apple: 4 pomi-
arched: 3 tox- **4** toxi-, toxo-
arid: 3 xer- **4** xero-
arm: 6 brachi- **7** brachio-
armless: 5 anopi- **6** anoplo-
around: 6 circum-
arrangement: 3 tax- **4** -nomy, taxi-, taxo-, -taxy **5** -taxis
arrow: 3 tox- **4** toxi-, toxo-

arsenic: 6 arseno-
art: 4 -urgy 6 techno-
assembly: 4 -fest
atmosphere: 3 aer- 4 aeri-, aero-
back: 3 not- 4 dors-, noto- 5 dorsi-, dorso- 7 opistho-
bad: 3 cac-, dys-, mal- 4 caco-
balance: 5 stato-
ball: 5 spher- 6 sphaer-, sphero- 7 sphaero-
band: 3 zon- 4 zono-
barb: 3 onc- 4 onch-, onci-, onco- 5 oncho-
bare: 4 gymn-, nudi-, psil- 5 gymno-, psilo-
beam: 5 actin- 6 actino-
bear: 4 arct- 5 arcto-
beard: 5 pogon- 6 pogono-
bearer: 4 -pher, -phor 5 -phore
beast: 4 ther- 5 -there, thero- 6 therio-
beautiful: 4 call-, calo- 5 calli-, callo-
bed: 4 clin- 5 clino-
before: 4 fore- 6 proter- 7 protero-
behind: 7 opistho-
being: 3 ont- 4 onto-
believer: 5 -arian
below: 6 infero-
belt: 3 zon- 4 zono-
bent: 4 cyrt- 5 curvi-, cyrto- 6 campto-
berry: 4 cocc- 5 bacci-, cocci-, cocco-
beside: 3 par- 4 para-
best: 6 aristo-
beyond: 3 par- 4 para- 6 preter- 7 praeter-
bile: 4 chol- 5 chole-, cholo-
billion: 4 giga-
billionth: 3 nan- 4 nano- 5 nanno-
bird: 3 avi- 5 -ornis 6 ornith- 7 ornitho-
bitter: 4 picr- 5 picro-
black: 3 mel- 4 atro-, mela-, melo- 5 melan- 6 melano-
blood: 3 hem- 4 -emia, hema-, hemo- 5 -aemia, hemat-, -hemia 6 -haemia, hemato-, sangui-
blue: 4 cyan- 5 cyano-
boat: 5 scaph- 6 scapho-
body: 4 -soma, -some 5 somat- 6 somato-
bog: 4 helo-
boiled: 5 cocto-
bond: 4 desm- 5 desmo-
bone: 3 -ost 4 ossi-, oste- 5 osteo-
book: 6 biblio-
both: 3 bis- 5 amphi-, ampho-
bowed: 3 tox- 4 toxi-, toxo-
brain: 6 cerebr- 7 cerebro -
branch: 4 clad- 5 clado-
bread: 4 arto-
break down: 4 -lyze
breaker: 5 -clast
breaking: 6 -clasis 7 -clastic
breaking down: 5 -lysis, -lytic
breastbone: 5 stern- 6 sterno-
breath: 4 -pnea 5 -pnoea 6 pneumo-
breathing: 4 spir- 5 spiri-, spiro-
bringer: 4 -agog 6 -agogue
bristle: 4 seti- 5 chaet- 6 chaeto-
broad: 4 eury-, plat- 5 platy-
broken: 6 fracto-
bronze: 5 chalc- 6 chalco-, chalko-
brush: 5 scopi-
bud: 5 -blast 6 blasto-
bull: 4 taur- 5 tauri-, tauro-
burdened: 6 -ridden
burning: 4 igni-
can: 5 scyph- 6 scyphi-, scypho-
car: 4 auto-
carrier: 3 -fer 4 -pher, -phor 5 -phore
carved: 5 glypt- 6 glypto-
cat: 5 aelur-, ailur- 6 aeluro-, ailuro-
caterpillar: 5 -campa, eruci-
cause: 4 etio- 5 aetio-, ailio-
causing: 3 -fic 5 -genic 7 -facient
cave-dwelling: 6 troglo-
cavity: 4 -cele, coel- 5 -coele
cell: 3 cyt- 4 -cyte, cyto- 5 -plast
cells: 7 -blastic
center: 3 mid- 4 medi- 5 medio-
chamber: 4 -cele, coel- 5 -coele
change: 4 trop- 5 tropo-
channel: 5 solen- 6 soleno-
cheek: 3 mel- 4 melo- 5 bucco-
cheese: 3 tyr- 4 tyro-
chest: 6 stetho-, thorac- 7 thoraci-, thoraco-
child: 3 ped- 4 paed-, paid-, pedo- 5 paedo-, paido-, tecno-
children: 5 proli-
chin: 5 mento-
Chinese: 4 Sino- 6 Sinico-
circle: 3 gyr- 4 gyro-
city: 5 metro-, -polis
claw: 4 chel- 5 cheli-, onych-, ungui- 6 onycho-
clay: 3 pel- 4 pelo- 5 argil- 7 argilli-, argillo-
cleft: 5 fissi-
clockwise: 5 dextr- 6 dextro-
close: 4 pycn-, sten- 5 plesi-, pycno-, steno- 6 plesio-
clot: 6 thromb- 7 thrombo-
cloud: 4 neph- 5 nepho- 6 nephel- 7 nephelo-
club: 5 clavi- 6 rhopal- 7 rhopalo-
coal: 7 anthrac-, carboni-
coil: 4 spir- 5 spiri-, spiro-
cold: 4 crym-, cryo- 5 crymo-, frigo-
color: 5 chrom- 6 -chrome, chromo-
coloration: 6 -chroia
coloring: 6 -chromy
column: 4 styl- 5 -style, stylo-
comb: 4 cten-, loph- 5 cteno-, lophi-, lopho- 6 lophio-
common: 3 cen- 4 caen-, ceno-, coen- 5 caeno-, coeno-
communication: 3 -log 5 -logue
complete: 3 tel- 4 tele-, telo-
completely: 3 pan- 4 pano-, pant- 5 panta-, panto-
computer: 5 cyber-
concealed: 4 adel- 5 adelo-
constellation: 5 sider- 6 sidero-
containing: 6 -ferous
conversation: 3 -log 5 -logue
copper: 4 cupr- 5 chalc-, chalk-, cupri-, cupro 6 chalco-, chalko-
cornea: 5 cerat-, kerat- 6 cerato-, kerato-
correct: 4 orth- 5 ortho-
counterclockwise: 3 lev- 4 levo- 5 laevo-
countless: 4 myri- 5 myrio-
course: 4 drom- 5 -drome, dromo-
cover: 4 steg- 5 stego-
covering: 4 cole- 5 coleo- 7 cortico-
crest: 4 loph- 5 lophi-, lopho- 6 lophio-
crop: 4 agro-
cross: 6 stauro-
crow: 5 -corax
culture: 5 ethno-
cup: 5 cotyl-, cyath-, scyph- 6 cotyli-, cotylo-, cyatho-, scyphi-, scypho-
current: 4 rheo- 7 galvano-
custom: 4 nomo-
cut: 4 -sect, tomo- 6 -tomous
cutter: 4 -tome
cutting: 4 -tomy
dance: 5 chore- 6 choreo-, chorio-
decline: 4 clin- 5 clino-
decompose: 4 -lyze
decomposing: 5 -lytic
decomposition: 3 lys- 4 lysi-, lyso- 5 -lysis
deer: 5 cervi-
defective: 4 atel- 5 atelo-
depth: 5 batho-, bathy-
deputy: 4 vice-
desire: 6 -orexia
destroyer: 5 -clast
different: 5 heter- 6 hetero-
disease: 3 nos- 4 noso- 5 patho-, -pathy
display: 5 -orama
distant: 3 tel- 4 tele-, telo-
distinct: 5 chori-
distribution: 4 -nomy
diver: 4 -dyta 5 -dytes
diverse: 4 vari- 5 vario-
divide: 4 -sect
divided: 3 -fid 5 fissi- 6 -tomous
divination: 5 -mancy
divining: 6 -mantic
doctrine: 4 -logy
dog: 3 cyn- 4 cyno-
double: 4 dipl- 5 diplo-
doubled: 3 bis-
drawing: 4 -gram 6 -graphy
drawn: 5 -graph
dream: 4 onir- 5 oneir-, oniro- 6 oneiro-
dry: 3 xer- 4 xero-
dulled: 5 ambly- 6 amblyo-
dust: 4 coni- 5 conio-
ear: 2 ot- 3 aur-, oto- 4 auri-
earlier: 4 fore- 6 proter- 7 protero-
earliest: 4 prot- 5 proto-
earth: 3 geo-
earthquake: 5 -seism 6 seismo-
eater: 4 -phag, -vore 5 -phage
eating: 4 phag- 5 phago-, -phagy 6 -phagia, -vorous
effect: 4 -ergy
egg: 2 oo-, ov- 3 ovi-, ovo-
eight: 3 oct- 4 octa-, octo-
elderly: 6 presby- 7 presbyo-
eleven: 5 undec- 6 hendec -
embryo: 5 -blast 6 blasto-
empty: 3 ken- 4 keno-
end: 3 tel- 4 tele-, telo-
English: 5 Anglo-
enthusiasm: 5 -mania
enthusiast: 4 -phil 5 -phile
entire: 3 hol- 4 holo-, toti- 7 integri-
environment: 3 eco-
equal: 3 iso- 4 pari-
evil: 4 male-
examination: 4 -opsy
excessive: 4 macr- 5 macro-
excision: 4 -tomy 6 -ectomy
exemplary: 4 arch-
existence: 3 ont- 4 onto-
expert: 7 -meister
exposed: 4 gymn- 5 gymno-
external: 2 ex- 3 ect-, exo- 4 ecto-
extreme: 4 arch-
eye: 4 ocul-, opto- 5 oculo-
face: 6 -hedron
faced: 6 -hedral
false: 5 pseud- 6 pseudo-
far: 3 tel- 4 tele-, telo-
farming: 4 agri-
fast: 5 tachy-
fat: 3 lip- 4 adip-, lipo-, sebi-, sebo- 5 adipo-, lipar-, stear-, steat- 6 liparo-, stearo-, steato-
father: 4 patr- 5 patri-, patro-
fear: 4 phob- 5 phobo- 6 -phobia
fearer: 5 -phobe
fearing: 6 -phobic
feather: 3 pen- 4 pinn-, pter-, ptil- 5 penni-, penno-, pinni-, ptero-, ptilo- 7 pinnati-
feeding: 6 -trophy
feeling: 5 patho-, -pathy
felt: 3 pil- 4 pilo-
female: 3 gyn- 4 gyne-, gyno-, -gyny 5 gynec-, thely- 6 gyneco-, -gynous
ferment: 3 zym- 4 zymo-
fever: 5 febri-, pyret- 6 pyreto-
few: 4 olig- 5 oligo-, pauci-
field: 4 agro-
fifth: 5 quint- 6 quinti-
fighting: 5 -machy
figure: 3 eid- 4 eido-
film: 4 cine-
fine: 4 lept- 5 lepto-
finger: 6 dactyl-, digiti- 7 dactylo-
Finnish: 5 Fenno-
fire: 3 pyr- 4 igni-, pyro-
first: 4 arch-, prot- 5 arche-, archi-, proto-
fish: 5 pisci- 6 ichthy- 7 ichthyo-
fit for: 6 -worthy
five: 4 pent- 5 penta- 6 quinqu- 7 quinque-
flake: 5 lepid-, -lepis 6 lepido-
flank: 5 lapar- 6 laparo-
flat: 4 plan-, plat- 5 plani-, plano-, platy-
flesh: 3 cre- 4 creo-, kreo-, sarc- 5 creat-, sarco- 6 creato-
flow: 4 -rhea, rheo- 5 -rrhea
flower: 4 anth-, flor- 5 antho-, flori-
flowered: 7 -anthous, -florous
food: 4 sito-
foot: 3 ped-, pod- 4 -pede, pedi-, pedo-, podo-
footed: 6 -podous
footlike part: 4 -pode 6 -podium
fore: 6 antero-
foremost: 4 prot- 5 proto-
forest: 3 hyl- 4 hylo-
form: 5 -morph 6 morpho-
former: 6 proter- 7 protero-
fossil: 4 -lite, -lyte 5 oryct- 6 orycto-
four: 4 tetr- 5 quadr-, tetra- 6 quadri-, quadru-
fourth: 5 quart- 6 tetart- 7 tetarto-
freeze: 4 cryo-
French: 5 Gallo- 6 Franco-
frightful: 4 dino-
frog: 4 rani- 7 batrach- 8 batracho-
front: 4 fore- 6 antero-

frost: 4 crym- 5 crymo-
fruit: 4 -carp 5 carpo-, fruct- 6 fructi-
fruited: 7 -carpous
full of: 3 -ous
fungus: 3 myc- 4 myco- 6 -mycete
gall: 4 chol- 5 chole-, cholo-
garden: 4 -etum
gathering: 4 -fest
general: 3 cen- 4 caen-, ceno-, coen- 5 caeno-, coeno-
genetically engineered: 7 Franken-
gland: 4 aden- 5 adeno-
glass: 4 hyal-, vitr- 5 hyalo-, vitri-, vitro-
goat: 5 capri-
god: 3 the- 4 theo-
gold: 3 aur- 4 auri- 5 chrys- 6 chryso-
good: 2 eu- 4 bene- 5 agath- 6 agatho-
government: 5 -archy, -cracy
graceful: 5 habro-
grand: 3 meg- 4 mega- 5 megal- 6 megalo-
gray: 4 poli- 5 glauc-, polio- 6 glauco-
grease: 4 sebi-, sebo-
great: 3 meg- 4 macr-, magn-, mega- 5 macro-, magni-, megal- 6 megalo-
green: 4 verd- 5 chlor-, verdo- 6 chloro-
growth: 3 aux- 4 auxo- 5 -plasy
guard against: 3 par- 4 para-
guest: 3 xen- 4 xeno-
gums: 3 ulo- 6 gingiv- 7 gingivo-
hair: 3 pil- 4 pili-, pilo- 5 chaet-, crini-, trich- 6 chaeto-, -tricha, tricho-
half: 4 demi-, hemi-, semi-
hand: 5 chiro- 6 cheiro-
hard: 5 scler- 6 sclera-, sclero-
hare: 3 lag- 4 lago-
hate: 3 mis- 4 miso-
healing: 5 iatro-, -iatry 7 -iatrics
heap: 5 cumul- 6 cumuli-, cumulo-
hearing: 4 acou- 5 acouo-, audio-
heart: 5 cardi- 6 -cardia, cardio- 7 -cardium
heat: 3 pyr- 4 pyro- 5 therm- 6 calori-, thermo-, -thermy
heavens: 4 uran- 5 urano-
heavy: 4 bary- 5 gravi-
height: 3 acr- 4 acro-, hyps- 5 hypsi-, hypso-
hidden: 4 adel- 5 adelo-, crypt-, krypt- 6 crypto-, krypto-
high: 3 alt- 4 alti-
hip: 4 coxa- 5 ischi-, ischo-
hole: 5 -trema
holy: 4 hagi-, hier- 5 hagio-, hiero-
horn: 4 -corn 5 cerat-, kerat- 6 cerato-, kerato-
horse: 4 hipp- 5 hippo- 6 -hippus
human: 5 homin- 6 homini- 7 anthrop- 8 anthropo-
hundred: 4 cent-, hect-, hekt- 5 centi-, hecto-, hekto-
hundredth: 4 cent- 5 centi-
ill: 3 dys-, mal-
image: 3 eid-, typ- 4 eido-, icon-, ikon-, typo- 5 eicon-, icono-, idolo-, ikono- 6 eicono-, eidolo-
imperfect imitation: 5 -aster
implement: 4 -labe
incision: 4 -tomy
increase: 3 aux- 4 auxo-
inner: 3 eso-
insect: 6 entomo-
instrument: 4 -labe
internal: 3 end-, ent- 4 endo-, ento-
intestine: 5 enter- 6 entero-
Irish: 7 Hiberno-
iron: 5 ferri-, ferro-, sider- 6 sidero-
irregular: 4 anom- 5 anomo-
island: 4 neso-
itch: 4 psor- 5 psoro-
jaw: 5 gnath- 6 gnatho-
joining: 3 gam- 4 gamo-
joint: 5 arthr- 6 ancylo-, ankylo-, arthro-
juice: 3 opo- 4 chyl- 5 chili-, chylo-
key: 5 clavi-, clavo-
kidney: 4 reni-, reno- 5 nephr-
knee: 4 genu-
knowing: 7 -gnostic 9 -gnostical
knowledge: 5 -gnomy, -sophy 6 -gnosis
language: 4 -glot
large: 3 meg- 4 macr-, magn-, maxi-, mega- 5 macro-, magni-, megal- 6 megalo-
law: 4 nomo-
layer: 5 ptych- 6 ptycho-, strati-
lead: 5 plumb- 6 plumbo-
leader: 4 -agog 6 -agogue
leaf: 5 phyll- 6 phyllo-
leaved: 7 -folious
leaving: 4 lipo-
left: 3 lev- 4 levo- 5 laevo- 8 sinistro-
lens: 4 phac-, phak- 5 phaco-, phako-
life: 3 bio-
lifeless: 4 abio-
light: 4 luci-, phos-, phot- 5 lumin-, photo- 6 lumini-, lumino-
likeness: 4 icon-, ikon- 5 eicon-, icono-, ikono-, -opsis 6 eicono-
liking: 7 -philous
limb: 3 mel-
listening: 4 acou-
liver: 5 hepat- 6 hepato-
living: 4 vivi-
lizard: 4 saur- 5 -saura, sauro-
lonely: 4 erem- 5 eremo-
long: 3 mec- 4 macr-, meco- 5 macro- 7 dolicho-
long-running: 5 -athon
looking: 6 -scopic
lover: 4 -phil 5 -phile
loving: 4 phil- 5 philo- 6 -philic
low: 5 chame- 6 chamae-
lung: 5 pneum-, pulmo- 6 pneumo-, pulmon-
maker: 3 -fex
male: 4 andr- 5 andro-, -andry 7 -androus
man: 5 homin- 6 homini-
management: 4 -nomy
many: 4 mult-, poly- 5 multi-, pluri-
marriage: 4 -gamy 6 -gamous
marrow: 4 myel- 5 myelo-
Mars: 4 areo-
measure: 5 -meter, metro-
measured: 6 -metric
measurement: 5 -metry
measuring science: 7 -metrics
medicine: 5 iatro-, -iatry 7 -iatrics
memory: 4 mnem- 5 mnemo-
message: 4 -gram
middle: 3 mes- 4 meso- 5 centr- 6 centri-, centro-
milk: 4 lact- 5 lacti-, lacto- 6 galact- 7 galacto-
million: 3 meg- 4 mega-
mind: 3 noo- 5 menti-, phren-, psych- 6 phreni-, phreno-, psycho-
mineral: 4 -lite, -lyte 5 oryct- 6 orycto-
mite: 4 acar- 5 acari-, acaro-
model: 3 typ- 4 typo-
modified: 2 ne- 3 neo-
moist: 5 hygro-
molding: 6 -plasty
monster: 5 terat- 6 terato-
moon: 4 luni- 5 selen- 6 seleni-, seleno-
more: 4 pleo-, plio 5 pleio-
moss: 3 bry- 4 bryo-, musc- 5 musci-, -musco
mother: 4 matr- 5 matri-, matro-
motion: 3 cin-, kin- 4 cino-, kine-, kino- 6 kinesi-
mountain: 3 ore-, oro- 4 oreo-
mouse: 3 -mys
mouth: 3 ori-, oro- 5 bucco-, -stoma, -stome 6 stomat- 7 stomato-
movement: 6 kinesi- 7 -cinesia, -kinesia, kinesio-, -kinesis
movie: 4 cine-
moving: 4 plan- 5 -grade, plano- 6 kineto-
much: 4 poly-
mud: 3 pel- 4 pelo-
muscle: 2 my- 3 myo-
mushroom: 3 myc- 4 myco- 6 -mycete
naked: 4 gymn-, nudi- 5 gymno-
name: 4 -onym 7 onomato-
narrow: 4 sten- 5 steno-
nature: 3 eco- 5 physi- 6 physio-
navel: 6 omphal- 7 omphalo-
near: 5 juxta-, plesi- 6 plesio-
neck: 3 der- 4 dero- 7 trachei 8 tracheio-
needle: 3 acu-
nerve: 4 neur- 5 neuro-
net: 5 dicty- 6 dictyo-
new: 2 ne- 3 neo-, nov- 4 ceno-, novo-
night: 4 noct-, nyct- 5 nocti-, nycti-, nycto-
nine: 3 non- 4 nona- 5 ennea-
nitrogen: 3 azo-
north: 4 arct- 5 arcto-
nose: 3 nas- 4 nasi-, naso-, rhin- 5 rhino-
notion: 4 ideo-
nourishment: 5 troph- 6 tropho-
nucleus: 5 caryo-, karyo-
numerous: 4 myri- 5 myrio-
nut: 4 nuci- 5 caryo-, karyo-
oblique: 3 lox- 4 loxo- 5 plagi- 6 plagio-
odor: 3 osm- 4 osmo-
offspring: 4 toco-, toko- 5 proli-
oil: 3 ole- 4 eleo-, olei-, oleo- 5 elaeo-, elaio-
old: 4 pale- 5 palae-, paleo- 6 archeo-, palaeo-, palaio- 7 archaeo-
one: 3 mon-, uni- 4 heno-, mono-
one and a half: 6 sesqui-
order: 3 tax- 4 taxi-, taxo-, -taxy 5 -taxis
organism: 4 -zoon
organisms: 3 -zoa
origin: 4 -geny
original: 4 arch- 5 arche-, archi-
origination: 4 -gony
other: 3 all- 4 allo- 5 heter- 6 hetero-
outer: 2 ex- 3 ect-, exo- 4 ecto-
pain: 3 alg- 4 algo-, -algy, noci- 5 -algia 6 -odynia
painting: 6 -chromy
paired: 4 dipl- 5 diplo-
part: 4 -mere, -plex
partial: 3 mer- 4 mero-
past: 6 preter- 7 praeter-
peculiar: 4 idio-
people: 3 dem- 4 demo- 5 ethno-
personal: 4 idio-
perspiration: 4 hidr- 5 hidro-
pigment: 5 chrom- 6 -chrome, chromo-
pipe: 3 aul- 4 aulo- 5 solen- 6 soleno-
pit: 5 bothr- 6 bothro-
place: 3 top- 4 loco-, topo- 5 -orium
plain: 4 pedi- 5 pedio-
plant: 4 phyt- 5 -phyte, phyto-
pond: 4 limn- 5 limni-, limno-
position: 5 stasi-
possessing: 3 -ous
power: 4 dyna- 5 dynam-
practicing: 6 -pathic
pressure: 3 bar- 4 baro-, tono- 5 piezo-
prickly: 5 echin- 6 echino-
priestly: 4 hier- 5 hiero-
prior: 4 arch- 5 arche-, archi- 6 yester-
procession: 4 -cade
producer: 3 -gen 5 -arian
producing: 3 -fic 5 -genic 6 -ferous, -gerous, -parous
production: 4 -gony
prophesy: 5 -mancy
quadrillion: 4 peta-
quadrillionth: 5 femto-
quintillion: 3 exa-
quintillionth: 4 atto-
race: 4 phyl- 5 ethno-, phylo-
racecourse: 5 -drome
rain: 4 hyet- 5 hyeto-, ombro-, pluvi- 6 pluvia-, pluvio-
reaction: 4 trop- 5 tropo-
recent: 3 neo- 4 ceno-
red: 5 pyrrh-, pyrro- 6 erythr-
regulator: 4 -stat
removal: 6 -ectomy
reptile: 6 herpet- 7 herpeto-
resembling: 5 quasi-
resistant: 5 -proof
respiration: 4 -pnea 5 -pnoea
rib: 4 cost- 5 costo-, pleur- 6 pleuro-
right: 4 orth-, rect- 5 dextr-, ortho-, recti- 6 dextro-
ring: 3 gyr- 4 cycl-, gyro- 5 cyclo-
river: 5 fluvi-, potam- 6 fluvio-, potamo-
rock: 4 petr-, saxi- 5 petri-, petro-
root: 4 rhiz- 5 -rhiza, rhizo- 6 -rrhiza
rule: 5 -archy, -cracy
ruler: 4 -crat 5 -ocrat
running: 4 drom- 5 -drome, dromo- 7 -dromous
sac: 3 asc- 4 asco-

sacred: 4 hier- 5 hiero-
saint: 4 hagi- 5 hagio-
salt: 3 hal- 4 hali-, sali-
same: 3 aut-, hom- 4 auto-, equi-, homo-, taut- 5 tauto-
scandal: 4 -gate
scenery: 5 -scape
science: 4 -logy 5 -sophy
scrutiny: 5 -scopy
sea: 3 mer- 4 hali-, mari- 5 pelag- 6 pelago-
second: 4 deut- 5 deuto- 6 deuter- 7 deutero-
secret: 5 crypt-, krypt- 6 crypto-, krypto-
section: 4 tomo-
seed: 4 cocc- 5 cocci-, cocco-
self: 3 aut- 4 auto-
self-service: 5 -teria
sensitive to: 5 -ergic
separate: 4 idio-
septillion: 5 yotta-
septillionth: 5 yocto-
serpent: 4 ophi- 5 ophio-
seven: 4 hept-, sept- 5 hepta-, septi-
sextillion: 5 zetta-
sextillionth: 5 zepto-
shadow: 3 sci- 4 scia-, scio-, skia-
sharp: 3 oxy-
shield: 4 scut- 5 aspid-, scuti- 6 aspido-
shining: 4 phen- 5 pheno-
short: 5 brevi- 6 brachy-
shoulder: 3 omo-
side: 5 later-, pleur- 6 lateri-, latero-, pleuro-
sight: 4 -opia, opto- 5 -opsia
similar: 5 homeo-
single: 3 mon- 4 hapl-, mono- 5 haplo-
six: 3 hex-, sex- 4 hexa-, sexi- 5 sexti-
skill: 6 techno-
skin: 4 derm-, scyt- 5 -derma, dermo-, scyto- 6 dermat-, -dermis 7 dermato-
skull: 5 crani- 6 cranio-
sleep: 4 hypn- 5 hypno-, somni-
slime: 3 myx- 4 myxo-
slope: 4 clin- 5 -cline, clino- 6 -clinal
small: 4 micr-, mini-, parv- 5 micro-, parvi-, parvo-
smell: 3 osm-, ozo- 4 osmo-
snake: 4 ophi- 5 ophio-
sodium: 4 natr- 5 natro-
soil: 3 ped-, -sol 4 agro-, pedo-
solid: 5 stere- 6 stereo-
song: 4 melo-
soul: 4 thym- 5 psych-, thymo- 6 psycho-
sound: 3 son- 4 phon-, soni-, sono- 5 audio-, -phone, phono-, -phony
south: 5 austr- 6 austro-
space: 6 spatio-
spaceflight: 4 astr- 5 astro-
spectacle: 4 -cade 5 -orama
speech: 3 log- 4 lalo-, -laly, logo- 5 gloss-, -lalia 6 glosso-, glotto-
speed: 4 drom- 5 dromo-, tacho-
spider: 6 arachn- 7 arachno-
spinal cord: 4 myel- 5 myelo-
spindle: 4 fusi-
spine: 5 rachi- 6 acanth-, rachio-, rhachi- 7 acantho-, rhachio-, vertebr-
spiral: 3 gyr- 4 gyro- 5 helic- 6 helico-
split: 5 schiz- 6 schizo- 7 schisto-
stabilizer: 4 -stat
stalk: 4 caul- 5 cauli-, caulo-
star: 4 astr- 5 -aster, astro-, sider- 6 -astero, sidero-
starch: 4 amyl- 5 amylo-
state: 6 -phoria
stealing: 5 klept- 6 klepto-
stem: 4 caul-, corm- 5 cauli-, caulo-, cormo-, scapi-
stomach: 4 celi- 5 celio-, coeli-, gastr-, ventr- 6 coelio-, gastro-, ventri-, ventro-
stone: 4 -lith, petr- 5 litho-, petri-, petro-
straight: 4 orth-, rect- 5 ortho-, recti-
strange: 3 xen- 4 xeno-
stream: 4 rheo- 5 fluvi- 6 fluvio-
strong: 6 trachy-
structure: 5 -morph 6 morpho-
sufferer: 4 -path
suffering: 5 patho-, -pathy 6 -pathic
sugar: 4 gluc-, glyc-, sucr- 5 gluco-, glyco-, sucro- 7 sacchar- 8 sacchari-, saccharo-
sulfur: 3 thi- 4 thia-, thio- 5 thion- 6 thiono-
summit: 5 apico-
sun: 4 heli-, soli- 5 helio-
supporter: 4 -crat 5 -ocrat
surrounding: 6 circum-
swift: 5 tachy-
swimming: 4 nect- 5 necto-
swine: 3 hyo-
swordlike: 4 xiph- 5 xiphi-, xipho-
tail: 3 uro- 4 caud-, cerc- 5 caudi-, caudo-, cerco-
tears: 7 lacrimo-
technique: 4 -urgy
ten: 3 dec-, dek- 4 deca-, deka- 5 decem-
tension: 4 tono-
tenth: 4 deci-
ten thousand: 5 myria-
terrible: 3 din- 4 dein-, dino- 5 deino-
terrifying: 4 dino-
Teutonic: 7 Germano-
theft: 5 klept- 6 klepto-
theory: 4 -logy
thin: 4 lept- 5 lepto-
third: 4 trit- 5 trito-
thought: 4 -noia
thousand: 4 kilo- 5 chilo-, milli-
thousandth: 5 milli-
thread: 3 mit-, nem- 4 fili-, mito-, nema-, nemo- 5 nemat- 6 nemato-
three: 3 tri-
thrice: 3 ter-
throat: 3 der- 4 dero- 6 bronch- 7 broncho-, pharyng- 8 pharyngo-
time: 5 chron- 6 chrono-
tin: 5 stann- 6 stanno-
tissue: 4 hist- 5 histi-, histo-, -plasm 6 histio-
toe: 6 dactyl- 7 dactylo-
tongue: 4 -glot 5 gloss- 6 glosso-, glotto-
tooth: 4 dent- 5 denti-, dento-, odont- 6 odonto-
tree: 3 dry- 4 dryo- 5 dendr- 6 dendri-, dendro- 7 -dendron
tribe: 4 phyl- 5 phylo-
trillion: 4 tera-, treg- 5 trega-
trillionth: 4 pico-
tripled: 4 tris-
turn: 4 trop- 5 tropo-
twelve: 5 dodec- 6 dodeca-
twenty: 4 icos- 5 eicos-, icosa-, icosi- 6 eicosa-
two: 3 bin-, bis-, duo-, dyo-, twi-
two-part: 5 dicho-
union: 3 gam- 4 gamo-, -gamy 6 -gamous
unit: 4 -plex
universe: 4 cosm- 5 cosmo-
unpleasant: 3 cac- 4 caco-
unreal: 5 pseud- 6 pseudo-
unusual: 4 anom- 5 anomo-
urban: 5 metro-
vein: 3 ven- 4 veni-, veno- 5 phleb- 6 phlebo-
vessel: 3 vas- 4 vaso- 5 angio-
viewing: 5 -scopy 6 -scopic
vine: 4 viti-
vinegar: 4 acet- 5 aceto-
vision: 4 -opia, opto- 5 -opsia
voice: 4 phon- 5 phono-
voice box: 6 laryng- 7 laryngo-
warfare: 5 -machy
water: 4 aqua-, aqui-, hydr- 5 hydat-, hydro- 6 hydato-
wax: 3 cer- 4 cero-
wet: 5 hygro-
whale: 3 cet- 4 ceto-
white: 3 alb- 4 albo-, leuc-, leuk- 5 leuco-, leuko-
whole: 3 hol-, pan- 4 holo-, pano-, pant-, toti- 5 panta-, panto- 7 integri-
wide: 4 eury-
wind: 4 anem- 5 anemo-, venti-, vento-
wine: 2 en- 3 eno-, oen-, vin- 4 oeno-, vini-, vino-
wing: 4 pter- 5 ptero- 6 pteryg- 7 pterygo-
winged: 7 -pterous
wisdom: 5 -sophy
within: 3 end-, ent- 4 endo-, ento-
woman: 3 gyn- 4 gyne-, gyno-, -gyny
wood: 3 hyl-, xyl- 4 hylo-, lign-, xylo- 5 ligni-, ligno-
wool: 3 lan- 4 erio-, lani-, lano-
word: 4 -onym
world: 4 cosm- 5 cosmo-
worm: 5 vermi-
worship: 5 -latry
wrist: 5 carpo-
writing: 4 -gram 6 grapho-, -graphy
written: 5 -graph
wrongful: 3 mal-
yellow: 4 flav- 5 chrys-, flavo-, luteo-, xanth- 6 chryso-, xantho-

combo: 3 duo, mix 4 band, trio 5 nonet, octet 6 medley 7 mélange, mixture, octette, quartet, variety 9 potpourri 10 miscellany
Combs: 3 Ray 4 Sean 5 Earle
combust: 4 burn 10 incinerate
combusted: 5 afire 7 blazing
combustible: 4 fuel 5 fiery 8 burnable, skittish, volatile
heap: 4 pyre
substance: 3 gas, oil 4 coal
combustion: 4 fire 5 blaze 7 flaming 8 ignition, kindling 9 agitation, commotion, explosion
criminal ~: 5 arson
evidence: 5 flame, smoke
product: 3 ash 6 fly ash
Comden: 5 Betty
collaborator: 5 Green
come: 4 show 5 enter, get in, occur, pop in, pop up, reach, visit 6 appear, arrive, blow in, evolve, fall in, happen, make it, report, ring in, roll in, show up, sign in, spring, turn up 7 advance, check in, clock in, hit town, punch in, turn out 8 approach, breeze in, draw near, tag along 9 originate
aboard: 4 go in, go on 5 get in, get on 7 climb in, climb on, emplane, enplane, entrain 9 affiliate
about: 2 be 4 fall 5 arise, occur, pivot, rally 6 befall, evolve, happen, result 7 develop 9 eventuate, take place, transpire
a cropper: 4 bomb, bust, flop, lose, slip, trip 5 flunk 6 blow it, falter 7 blunder, founder, go under, go wrong, misstep, stumble, wash out 8 fall flat, flounder, lay an egg 9 strike out
across: 4 find, meet 5 dig up, spend 6 locate, strike 7 stumble 8 chance on 9 acquiesce, encounter, light upon 10 capitulate, chance upon, happen upon
across as: 4 seem
across with: 3 pay
after: 4 hunt 5 ensue, trail 6 follow, go next 7 go after, succeed
again: 5 recur 6 repeat, return 7 revisit 9 reiterate
along: 5 rally 6 look up 7 shape up 9 accompany 10 recuperate
and go: 5 recur 9 alternate, oscillate
apart: 4 open, snap, tear 5 burst, panic, ravel, split 7 unweave 8 fragment, separate 9 break down
around: 4 turn 5 adapt, awake, rally, visit, yield 6 accede, comply, mellow, relent, revive, soften, submit 7 recover 9 acquiesce, lighten up
ashore: 4 land 9 disembark
at: 5 reach 6 attack, charge 8 approach
away: 5 leave 8 separate
back: 5 reply 6 return 7 revisit
back to mind: 5 recur
back to school: 5 reune
before: 4 lead 7 precede, predate, presage 8 antecede 9 go ahead of, introduce
between: 6 divide 7 rupture 8 alienate, separate 9 disaffect
by: 3 get, win 4 call, earn 5 visit 6 attain, obtain, secure 7 acquire, procure, receive 8 purchase
clean: 3 own 4 bare 5 admit, level, own up 6 fess up 7 confess
close: 4 near 8 approach
close to: 8 resemble

down: **4** land **5** light **6** alight, fall in
down hard: **4** pour, rain, teem **5** storm
down on: **5** chide, scold **6** berate, impugn, rebuke **7** censure, condemn, reprove, tell off, upbraid **8** admonish, restrict, surprise **9** castigate, criticize, dish it out, dress down, reprimand
down quickly: **5** swoop
down with: **3** get **4** have **5** catch **7** fall ill **8** contract
down with something: **3** ail
ender: **4** back, down
first: **4** lead **7** precede **8** antecede
forth: **5** begin, break **6** emerge **7** emanate
forward: **5** offer **7** advance **9** volunteer
(from): **4** hail, stem **6** derive, emerge, follow, spring **7** proceed **9** originate
from behind: **5** rally
hard to ~ by: **4** rare
home: **5** score **6** return
in: **4** land **5** enter
in a time to ~: **7** someday
in contact with: **4** meet
in first: **3** win **7** prevail, triumph
in handy for: **3** aid **4** help
in last: **3** lag **4** lose
in second: **4** lose **5** place
into: **3** win **5** enter **6** obtain **7** acquire, inherit, receive, succeed **9** get hold of, lay hold of
into being: **5** arise, begin, start **6** grow up, spring **9** originate
into view: **4** loom, rise **5** heave **6** appear, emerge
near: **5** verge
next: **5** ensue **6** follow **7** succeed
of age: **6** grow up, mature
off: **4** work **5** occur **6** happen **7** succeed
open: **4** undo
out: **4** leak **6** emerge, spring **9** transpire
out even: **7** balance
out of hiding: **4** show **6** appear, emerge **7** surface **10** break cover
out the same: **5** agree
out with it: **3** say **5** state, utter, voice **6** reveal **7** speak up
over: **4** call **5** visit **6** affect **8** happen to
through: **5** spend **7** produce, survive, weather **8** make good, stick out
to: **4** cost, make, stir, wake **5** awake, equal, reach, total, visit, waken **6** attain, attend, awaken, return, revive **8** reawaken
(to): **6** amount
to a decision: **6** settle
to a halt: **4** stop
to a head: **5** crest **6** climax **9** culminate
to an end: **2** do **3** fix **4** draw, halt, make, quit, rule, stop **5** cease, close, glean, infer, judge, sum up, think **6** assume, decide, deduce, effect, expire, finish, fulfil, gather, reason, reckon, run out, settle, wind up, wrap up **7** achieve, fulfill, imagine, play out, presume, pull off, resolve, suppose, surmise, suspect, work out **8** carry out, complete, conclude, dispatch, finalize, round off, round out, surcease **9** culminate, determine, terminate **10** accomplish, bring about, call it a day, consummate, put through
to a point: **5** taper
to be: **3** get **6** happen
to blows: **3** row **5** brawl, fight, scrap **7** grapple, mix it up, scuffle
to fruition: **5** ripen
together: **3** gel, mix, sit **4** jell, meet, mesh **5** merge, rally, reune, touch, unite **6** concur, gather, muster **7** collect, convene **8** assemble, coalesce, converge
to grips with: **4** face **6** handle, tackle **8** cope with, deal with **9** encounter **10** meet head on
to life: **6** revive
to light: **5** arise **6** emerge **7** surface
to mind: **4** dawn **5** arise, occur **6** recall, strike
to naught: **4** bomb, bust, fail, flop, sink, wane **6** fizzle, lessen, run dry, run out **7** dwindle, founder, misfire, run down, subside, tail off, thin out **8** backfire, collapse, fall flat, flounder, peter out, taper off **9** evaporate **10** run aground
to pass: **2** be **4** fall **5** break, ensue, occur **6** befall, betide, happen, pan out, turn up **9** eventuate, intervene, take place, transpire
to rest: **4** land **5** lodge **6** settle
to see: **5** visit **6** call on
to terms: **4** jibe **5** agree, level, yield **6** accord, make up, settle **7** bargain, concede, consent, go along, resolve, work out **8** cut a deal, play ball **9** acquiesce, harmonize, negotiate **10** capitulate
to the plate: **3** bat, hit
to the rescue: **3** aid **4** help, save
(toward): **4** move
undone: **3** rip **4** fray, open, tear, wear **5** break, burst, crack, shred, split **7** frazzle, give way, rupture **8** fragment, separate **9** disengage, pull apart **10** disconnect
unglued: **4** flip, rage, rail, rant, rave, snap, yell **5** break, go ape, go mad, shout, storm **6** bellow **7** carry on, explode, flare up, give way, go crazy, lash out, thunder **8** freak out, get angry, harangue **9** come apart, go bananas, raise Cain **10** hit the roof
up: **4** lift **5** arise, occur **6** appear, happen **7** surface **9** eventuate
up against: **4** abut, cope, defy, face, meet **5** brave **6** accost, oppose, resist, tackle **8** confront, face up to **9** challenge, encounter, pitch into, stand up to, withstand
up for air: **4** vent **6** emerge
up in the world: **4** rise **7** succeed
upon: **3** hit, spy **4** find, meet **6** locate, look up **7** run into **8** discover, meet with, overtake **9** encounter, run across
up short: **3** owe **4** fail, lose
up to: **4** meet **5** reach, touch **7** satisfy
up with: **5** hatch, hit on **6** create, devise, supply **7** propose, think up **9** institute, originate, recommend **10** bring forth
what may: **6** surely **7** somehow **10** in any event
come __: **3** off, out **4** back, down, into, over, true, upon **5** about, again, along, and go, clean, in for, off it, round **6** across, around **7** between, forward, through, unglued **8** a cropper
come __ agreement: **4** to an
come __ are: **5** as you
come __ good: **4** to no
come __ head: **3** to a
come __ in the wash: **3** out
come __ line: **4** into
come __ may: **4** what
come __ of the rain: **5** in out
come __ on: **4** down
come __ one's own: **4** into
come __ or high water: **4** hell
come __ point: **3** to a
come __ the pike: **4** down
come __ the wash: **5** out in
come __ to roost: **4** home
come __ with: **3** out **4** down
come-__: **3** ons **6** hither
__ come: **3** how **7** kingdom
__-come: **5** first
Come __!: **4** on in **5** off it
Come __?: **5** again
Come __ About Me: **3** See
Come __, Come Tyre: **7** Nineveh
Come __ get it!: **3** and
Come __ it!: **3** off
Come __, Little Sheba: **4** Back
Come __ My House: **3** on-a
Come __ my parlor...: **4** into
Come __ or Come Shine: **4** Rain
Come __ to Me: **4** Back **6** Softly
Come __ With Me: **3** Fly **4** Live
Come __ Your Horn: **4** Blow
come a __: **7** cropper
Come again?: **3** huh **4** what
Come and __!: **5** get it
Come and Get It
author: Edna Ferber
Come and Get It (1970 song)
artist: Badfinger
Come and Get With Me (1998 song)
artist: Keith Sweat, Snoop Doggy Dogg
Come and Get Your Love (song)
artist: Real McCoy, Redbone
come as you __: **3** are
comeback: **4** echo **5** rally, reply **6** answer, remark, retort, return, ripost **7** rebound, revival, riposte **8** reaction, rebuttal, recovery, repartee, response **9** rejoinder **10** resurgence
like some ~s: **5** witty **6** clever, snappy
make a ~: **5** rally **6** answer **7** rebound, recover, survive
playground ~: **4** am so **5** am not, am too, are so
Comeback
author: Dick Francis
Come back, __: **5** Shane
__ Come Back: **4** Baby **5** Lover
Come Back, Little Sheba: **4** film, play
author: William Inge
cast: Shirley Booth, Burt Lancaster
character: **3** Doc **4** Lola, Turk **5** Marie
__ come back now!: **4** Y'all
Come Back to __: **4** Erin
Come Back to Me (1990 song)
artist: Janet Jackson
__, Come Back to Me: **5** Lover
Come Blow Your Horn: **4** film, play
author: Neil Simon
cast: Lee J. Cobb, Molly Picon, Frank Sinatra
Come, come!: **3** tsk **4** pooh **6** tsk tsk
Come Dancing (1983 song)
artist: Kinks
comedian: **3** wag, wit **4** card, zany **5** clown, comic, cutup, joker, mimic **6** amuser, jester, scream **7** buffoon, farceur **8** funnyman, humorist, jokester, quipster **9** leg-puller, performer, top banana
see also comic
comedienne: **3** wag, wit **4** card, zany **5** clown, comic, cutup, joker, mimic **6** amuser, jester, scream **7** buffoon, farceur **8** humorist, jokester, quipster **9** performer, top banana
comedown: **7** decline **10** anticlimax
come down the __: **4** pike
comedy: **4** play, show **5** farce, genre, humor, shtik, story **6** joking, satire, send-up, shtick **7** burlesk, jesting, takeoff **8** drollery, hilarity **9** burlesque, funniness, slapstick, spectacle
'80s ~ troupe: **4** SCTV
bit of ~: **3** gag **4** joke, quip, skit **8** one-liner
starter: **5** tragi
straight man: **4** foil **6** stooge
__ comedy: **3** low **4** high **5** black **7** musical
__ Comedy: **3** New, Old **5** Black, Love's **6** Middle
Comedy Central: **7** channel
alternative: ***see*** cable channel
comedy of __: **6** errors **7** manners
Comedy of Errors, The
author: William Shakespeare
character: **5** Pinch **6** Aegeon, Angelo, Dromio **7** Adriana, Aemilia, Luciana, Solinus **10** Antipholus
__ Comedy, The: **5** Human **6** Divine
come from __: **4** afar
Come Go With Me (song)
artist: Dell-Vikings, Exposé
come hell or __ water: **4** high
__ Come Home: **6** Lassie
__, Come Home: **6** Snoopy
come home to __: **5** roost
come into one's __: **3** own
__-come-lately: **6** Johnny
Come, let us __ Him: **5** adore
Come live with me and be my love...
author: Christopher Marlowe

comely: **4** cute, fair, trim **5** bonny **6** bonnie, dainty, lovely, pretty, proper **7** shapely, winsome **8** adorable, alluring, becoming, fetching, gorgeous, handsome, pleasing, striking, stunning **9** beautiful, ravishing **10** attractive
Come Nineveh, Come Tyre
author: Allen Drury
come on __: **4** over **6** strong
come-on: **2** ad **4** bait, line, lure, trap **5** decoy, shill, snare **9** incentive **10** allurement, attraction, enticement, inducement, loss leader, temptation
gesture: **4** wink
Come on!: **6** let's go
Come on-a My House (1951 song)
artist: Rosemary Clooney
come one's __: **3** way
Come on in!: **5** enter
Come on Over (2000 song)
artist: Christina Aguilera
come out in the __: **4** wash
comer: **7** hotshot **8** prospect **9** Young Turk **10** rising star, wunderkind
former ~: **4** goer
starter: **3** new **4** late
Comer: **9** Anjanette
Come Rain or Come Shine
composer: Harold Arlen, Johnny Mercer
Come See About Me (1964 song)
artist: Supremes
__ Comes for the Archbishop: **5** Death
__ Come She Will: **5** April
__ Comes Mary: **5** Along
__ Comes Mr. Jordan: **4** Here
__ comes on little..., The: **3** fog
__ Comes Santa Claus: **4** Here
comestible: **4** good, meat **6** edible **7** victual **9** nutritive **10** alimentary
comestibles: **4** eats, food, grub **6** viands **7** aliment **8** victuals **9** provender **10** provisions
__ Comes to Harlem: **6** Cotton
__ Comes to the Forest: **6** Tigger
comet: **6** Encke's **7** Halley's **8** Hale-Bopp, Kohoutek **9** Hyakutake
first to spot a ~ usually: **5** namer
part: **4** coma, tail
path: **3** arc
Comet: **3** car **4** auto **7** Mercury **8** cleanser, reindeer **10** automobile
alternative: **4** Ajax, Bab-O **6** Bon Ami **9** Soft Scrub
colleague: *see* reindeer
__ Cometh, The: **6** Iceman
come to __: **4** life, pass, play **5** a fork, a head, an end, blows, grief, light, terms
come to __ with: **5** grips
come to a __: **4** head
Come Together (1969 song)
artist: Beatles
Come to Grief
author: Dick Francis
Come to Me (1958 song)
artist: Johnny Mathis
come to no __: **4** good
come to think __: **4** of it
Comets' grp.: **4** WNBA
__ Come Undone: **4** She's
come up __: **4** with **5** roses, short **7** against
Come up and __: **5** see me
comeuppance: **3** due **6** rebuke, reward **7** deserts
gain ~: **6** avenge
come what __: **3** may
COMEX
rival: **4** Merc
comfit: **5** candy **10** confection
comfort: **3** aid **4** balm, ease, help, lift, pity **5** cheer, salve, style **6** assure, luxury, relief, smooth, solace, stroke, succor **7** amenity, anodyne, cheer up, console, hearten, lighten, relieve, satisfy, support, sustain **8** coziness, opulence, opulency, reassure, snugness, sympathy **9** encourage, entertain, happiness, well-being **10** assistance, bed of roses, prosperity, relaxation, sympathize
companion: **3** aid
sound of ~: **2** ah **3** aah
station: **2** WC **3** lav, loo **7** latrine **8** bathroom, washroom
words of ~: **5** it's OK
comfort __: **4** food, zone **6** letter **7** station
__ comfort: **4** cold
Comfort: **4** Alex
Comfort __: **3** Inn
comfortable: **4** cosy, cozy, easy, homy, nice, rich, snug, soft **5** cozey, cozie, cushy, flush, homey, roomy **6** at ease, at home, at rest, decent, loaded, monied, serene **7** easeful, livable, moneyed, relaxed, restful, wealthy, well-off **8** adequate, affluent, cared for, in clover, liveable, pleasant, relaxing, spacious, well-to-do **9** leisurely, luxurious, well-fixed **10** complacent, in the dough, in the money, privileged, propertied, prosperous, well-heeled
be ~: **6** nestle **7** snuggle
make ~: **5** greet **7** welcome
comforter: **4** puff **5** duvet, quilt, scarf **6** spread **7** bedding, blanket **8** coverlet, coverlid **9** eiderdown, supporter
Biblical ~: **3** rod **5** staff
Comforter (1993 song)
artist: Shai
comforting: **8** parental **9** analeptic, assuaging, consoling, relieving, remedying, restoring, softening, succoring, upholding **10** lightening, mitigating, reassuring, refreshing, sustaining
word: **5** there
words: **5** I care, I know
Comfort Inn
alternative: *see* motel
comfortless: **5** bleak, harsh **6** lonely **7** forlorn
comfrey: **5** plant **6** flower
comfy: **4** cosy, cozy, easy, homy, snug, soft **5** cozey, cozie, cushy, homey **6** at ease **8** homelike, tucked in
get ~: **6** curl up
spot: **4** nest
comic: **3** wag, wit **4** card, zany **5** clown, cutup, droll, funny, joker **6** amuser, har-har, jester, scream **7** amusing, buffoon, farceur, jesting, jocular, risible **8** comedian, funnyman, humorist, humorous, jokester, quipster **9** facetious, jokesmith, laughable, leg-puller, ludicrous, performer, top banana
beginning: **5** serio, tragi
exaggeration: **4** camp **5** farce
in music: **5** buffa, buffo
job: **3** gig
like a ~: **5** droll, funny, witty
need: **4** mike **5** stool, water **8** material
offering: **3** gag **4** joke, quip, skit **8** one-liner
reward: **4** ha-ha **5** laugh
silent ~: **4** mime **5** mimer
writer: **6** gagman **7** gagster
comic __: **4** book **5** opera, strip **6** relief
comical: **4** camp, rich, zany **5** droll, funny, goofy, silly, wacky, witty **6** absurd, har-har, whacky **7** amusing, jesting, jocular, risible, waggish **8** farcical, humorous **9** facetious, hilarious, laughable, ludicrous, quizzical, whimsical **10** gut-busting, off-the-wall, ridiculous
introduction: **5** serio, tragi
comicality: **5** humor
comic book
character: **4** toon
cry: **3** eek, ulp, wah **4** yeow
genre: **5** sci-fi
heroes: **4** X-Men
sound effect: **3** arf, bam, oof, pow **5** splat
Comic Book Confidential (1989 film)
cast: R. Crumb, Will Eisner, Jack Kirby
Comice: **4** pear, pome **5** fruit
kin: **4** Bosc **5** Anjou **6** Seckel **8** Bartlett
comics: **7** funnies
cry: **5** aargh
comic strip: **7** cartoon
artists' org.: **3** NCS
finisher: **5** inker
Comin' __!: **4** at ya
Comin' __ the Mountain: **5** Round
Comin' __ the Rye: **4** Thro'
coming: **3** due **6** advent, earned, future **7** arrival, en route, ensuing, in store **8** eventual, expected, imminent, oncoming, on the way **9** following, impending, in the wind **10** appearance, receivable, subsequent
after: **4** next **5** later
down: **5** rainy **6** stormy **9** happening
have ~: **4** earn, rate **5** merit **7** deserve
next: **3** fol. **5** after **9** following
on strong: **4** bold **7** zealous **9** undaunted
out: **4** rise **5** debut
say you're ~: **4** RSVP
see ~: **7** portend, predict **8** prophesy **10** anticipate
soon: **4** near, nigh **8** imminent
starter: **4** home **5** forth, short
up: **4** next
up short: **7** lacking
coming __: **5** of age
__-coming: **5** up-and
Coming __: **4** Home
Coming __...: **4** soon
Coming __ in Samoa: **5** of Age
__ Coming: **4** Eli's **6** Second
Coming Fury, The
author: Bruce Catton
Coming Home (1978 film)
cast: Bruce Dern, Jane Fonda, Jon Voight
director: Hal Ashby
subject: **3** Nam **7** Vietnam
Coming in __ wing...: **3** on a
Coming of Age in Samoa
author: Margaret Mead
coming-of-age period: **5** teens
coming-out: **5** debut, party
Coming Out of the Dark (1991 song)
artist: Gloria Estefan
Coming Soon!!!
author: John Barth
Coming to America (1988 film)
cast: John Amos, Arsenio Hall, James Earl Jones, Eddie Murphy
director: John Landis
role: **5** Akeem
Coming Up (1980 song)
artist: Paul McCartney
Comin' Thro' the Rye
author: Robert Burns
comique
actor: **4** Tati
__ comique: **5** opéra
Comiskey: **7** Charles, Charlie
Comiskey Park
locale: **7** Chicago
Comissiona, Sergiu: **9** conductor
comity: **4** tact **5** amity **7** harmony **8** courtesy, goodwill **10** friendship
comma: **4** lull, mark **5** pause
what a ~ signals: **5** pause
__ comma: **6** serial
command: **3** bid, law, run **4** call, fiat, grip, head, lead, rule, tell, wish, word, writ **5** edict, exact, force, grasp, might, order, pilot, power, reach, reign, skill **6** adjure, behest, biding, charge, compel, decree, dictum, direct, enjoin, firman, govern, handle, impose, insist, manage, ordain, summon **7** ability, bidding, control, dictate, enforce, know-how, mandate, mastery, oversee, potence, potency, precept, primacy, regency, require **8** dominate, dominion, hegemony, instruct, kingship, pleasure, sanction **9** authority, directive, influence, officiate, ordinance, prescribe, supervise, supremacy **10** ascendance, ascendancy, ascendence, ascendency, domination, government, injunction, leadership, management, take charge
a view: **4** face, look, view **6** survey **7** look out **8** prospect **9** look out on
be in ~: **6** direct, manage
computer ~: **3** cut **4** copy, edit, find, go to, save, sort **5** enter, erase, macro, paste, print **6** delete
ender: **3** ant, eer
high ~: **5** brass **10** management
in ~: **5** on top
oater ~: **4** whoa **7** giddyap
officer ~: **4** halt, stop **6** freeze
old-style: **4** hest

second in ~: **2** VP **4** veep **6** veepee
soldier ~: **4** fire, halt **5** march **6** at ease, fall in **8** left face **9** right face
to a dog: **3** beg, sic, sit **4** come, down, heel, mush, stay **5** fetch, sic 'em, sit up, speak **6** drop it
command __: **3** car **4** post **6** module
__ command: **3** air **4** high
__ Command: **4** Dark, Lost **6** Secret
commandeer: **4** take **5** annex, co-opt, seize, usurp **6** assume, hijack, snatch **7** capture, preempt, procure **8** arrogate, highjack, shanghai, take over **9** conscript, sequester **10** confiscate
commander: **4** amir, boss, czar, emir, exec, head, jefe, rank, tsar, tzar **5** ameer, chief, emeer, ruler **6** gerent, honcho, leader, master, top dog **7** captain, headman, kingpin, skipper **8** director, kingfish, top brass **9** big cheese, executive, key player, organizer, top banana **10** head honcho, mastermind
in Arabic: **4** amir, emir **5** ameer, emeer
__ commander: **4** wing **7** supreme
Commander: **3** car **4** auto **10** Studebaker
commander in __: **5** chief
commanding: **5** bossy, lofty **6** lordly, potent **8** decisive, dominant, forceful, imposing, in charge, kinglike, powerful, striking, superior **9** arresting, assertive, imperious, sovereign **10** autocratic, compelling, dominating, impressive, peremptory
commandment: **3** law **4** rule, word **5** canon **7** precept
break a ~: **3** sin **5** covet
number: **3** ten
starter: **4** thou
__ Commandment: **5** Fifth, First, Ninth, Sixth, Tenth, Third **6** Eighth, Fourth, Second **7** Seventh
__ Commandments: **3** Ten
commando: **7** soldier **9** legionary
action: **4** raid
weapon: **3** Uzi
comme ci, comme ça: **4** so-so
Commedia dell'__: **4** Arte
comme il faut: **5** right **6** decent, proper, seemly **7** correct, fitting **8** decorous
commemorate: **4** keep **5** honor **6** salute **7** observe **8** remember
commemoration: **5** event, medal **7** tribute **8** ceremony, monument
Commemoration __: **3** Ode
commemorative: **5** stamp **8** memorial
stone: **5** stela, stele
verse: **3** ode
commence: **4** open, rise **5** arise, begin, dig in, enter, found, set in, start **6** launch, let rip, set off, set out, spring, take up **7** aggress, develop, get to it, kick off, lead off, preface **8** approach, embark on, get going, initiate, jump into, set forth **9** enter into, enter upon, get to work, introduce, originate, undertake **10** get started, inaugurate
commencement: **4** dawn, rise **5** birth, onset, start **6** advent, origin, outset, source **7** dawning, genesis, kickoff, leadoff, opening, prelude **8** exordium **9** inception
wear: **3** cap **4** gown
commend: **4** cite, hail, laud **5** bless, exalt, extol, honor **6** advise, extoll, praise, salute, tender **7** acclaim, applaud, approve, consign, endorse, entrust, flatter, glorify, indorse, intrust, proffer, suggest **8** hand it to, hand over, relegate, turn over **9** recommend **10** compliment, panegyrize
commendable: **4** fine, good, nice, okay **5** great, legit, model, moral, noble **6** proper, worthy **7** ethical **8** all right, laudable, pleasant, pleasing, splendid, superior **9** admirable, agreeable, excellent, reputable, wonderful **10** acceptable, beneficial, creditable
commendably: **4** well
commendation: **4** puff **5** honor, kudos **6** credit, eulogy, homage, praise, salute **7** acclaim, laurels, plaudit, tribute **8** accolade, approval, citation, encomium, flattery, good word **9** laudation, panegyric **10** exaltation
commensurate: **3** due, fit **4** even, like **5** equal, level **7** fitting **8** adequate
be ~: **6** equate
comment: **3** say **4** note, word **5** gloss, input, opine **6** assert, remark **7** expound, mention, observe, opinion **8** back talk, bring out, critique, feedback, footnote, point out, throw out **9** criticism, editorial, interject, statement, wisecrack **10** annotation, discussion
biting ~: **4** barb
unprepared ~: **5** ad-lib
Comment allez-__?: **4** vous
commentary: **6** review, speech **7** article, reading, remarks **8** analysis, critique, exegesis, treatise **9** criticism, discourse, editorial, narration, voice-over **10** annotation, definition, exposition, expression
commentator: **6** critic, pundit **7** analyst **8** lecturer, reporter, reviewer
page: **4** Op-Ed
__ commentator: **5** color
comments, clever: **6** banter
commerce: **5** trade **7** traffic **8** business, dealings, exchange, industry
acronym: **4** GATT **5** NAFTA
Commerce Dept. agency: **3** SBA **4** NOAA
commercial: **2** ad **4** advt., spot **5** pitch, promo **6** advert, TV spot **7** request **8** economic, monetary **9** exploited, financial, for-profit, mercenary, pecuniary, publicity, retailing, wholesale **10** investment, marketable, mercantile, profitable
alliance: **5** trust **6** cartel
award: **4** Clio
endorsement: **4** plug
phrase: **6** act now
pro-bono: **3** PSA
promotion: **5** tie-in
skip past ~s: **3** zap
song: **6** jingle
writer: **5** adman
commercial __: **3** art, law **4** bank, code, zone **5** break, paper, pilot **6** agency, artist, credit
Commercial Appeal: **9** newspaper
locale: **7** Memphis
commingle: **3** mix, wed **4** fuse, meld **5** admix, blend, immix, merge, unify, unite **6** commix **7** combine **8** coalesce, intermix **9** integrate **10** amalgamate
commingling: **9** confluent
comminute: **5** grind **9** granulate
commiserate: **4** pity **7** condole, console
commiseration: **4** pity **5** mercy **6** lenity, pathos **7** empathy **8** sympathy **10** condolence
commissary: **9** cafeteria **10** dining room
commission: **3** cut, fee, job, let, pay **4** hire, load, name, trim, work **5** board, place, share, slice, title, trust **6** agency, assign, bureau, employ, enable, engage, enlist, errand, office, ordain, ratify **7** appoint, charter, empower, entrust, intrust, license, mandate, mission, percent, qualify, station **8** accredit, delegate, deputize, kickback, nominate, sanction **9** allowance, authority, authorize, brokerage, committee, designate, factorage, indemnity **10** assignment, constitute, delegation, department, deputation, employment, engagement, inaugurate, obligation, percentage
in ~: **7** running, working **9** operating
out of ~: **3** ill **4** idle **5** kaput **6** broken, unable **7** injured **8** disabled, inactive **9** sidelined **10** broken-down, on the bench
put out of ~: **5** smash, wreck **7** disable **8** sabotage
__ commission: **5** out of
commissioner: **6** deputy **8** official **9** appointee
__ commissioner: **4** high
commit: **3** put **4** give, send **5** trust **6** assign, decide, devote, employ, engage, pledge **7** achieve, consign, deliver, empower, entrust, intrust, perform, pull off, put away **8** carry out, dedicate, delegate, deputize, dispatch, relegate, turn over **9** authorize **10** accomplish, contribute, effectuate, perpetrate
oneself: **3** opt **6** decide
refuse to ~: **3** haw, hem **5** hedge **6** waffle **10** equivocate
commitment: **3** job, tie, vow **4** duty, must, word, work **6** charge, lock-in, pledge **7** promise, resolve **8** contract, covenant, devotion **9** assurance, guarantee, liability **10** dedication, engagement, obligation
like some ~s: **5** prior
committal: **9** captivity **10** delegation
committed: **6** intent **7** engaged **9** dedicated **10** purposeful
committee: **5** board, group, panel **6** bureau, caucus **7** cabinet, council **8** congress, legation **9** task force **10** commission, executives
ender: **3** man, men **5** woman, women
head: **5** chair
committee __: **5** of one
__ committee: **5** ad-hoc, joint, rules **6** select **7** special
committee of the __: **5** whole
commix: **5** blend, merge **7** combine **8** coalesce **9** commingle **10** amalgamate
commode: **5** chest **9** furniture
commodious: **3** big **4** wide **5** ample, large, roomy **8** spacious **9** capacious, cavernous, expansive, extensive, uncrowded **10** convenient
commodities: **5** goods, stock, wares
commodity: **4** line, ware **5** asset, thing **6** future, object **7** article, chattel, product **8** material, valuable, vendible **9** belonging, specialty **10** possession
at hand: **6** actual
exchange area: **3** pit
commodore: **4** rank
service: **4** navy
Commodores: **10** Vanderbilt
leader: Lionel Richie
song: Brick House (1977)
Easy (1977)
Just to Be Close to You (1976)
Lady (1981)
Nightshift (1985)
Oh No (1981)
Sail on (1979)
Still (1979)
Sweet Love (1976)
Three Times a Lady (1978)
common: **3** low **4** base, dull, hack, park, rife **5** banal, cheap, corny, crass, daily, green, hokey, joint, known, level, lowly, passé, plaza, prosy, stale, stock, trite, typic, usual, vapid **6** coarse, humble, jejune, mutual, normal, old hat, public, shared, shoddy, simple, sleazy, social, square, tawdry, unmeet, vulgar, wonted **7** average, clichéd, current, fatuous, general, generic, humdrum, ignoble, lowbred, popular, prosaic, regular, routine, typical **8** accepted, baseborn, bromidic, déclassé, everyday, familiar, frequent, habitual, inferior, low-grade, ordinary, orthodox, outdated, outmoded, plebeian, standard, workaday **9** bourgeois, colorless, customary, generical, hackneyed, idiomatic, pervasive, prevalent, prosaical, quotidian, unanimous, universal, well-known, worldwide **10** accustomed, colloquial, dime-a-dozen, dullsville, indecorous, lower-class, pedestrian, prevailing, provincial, reciprocal, second-rate, uninspired, unoriginal, widespread
combining form: **3** cen- **4** caen-, ceno-, coen- **5** caeno-, coeno-
ender: **3** age **4** weal **5** place **6** wealth
common __: **3** era, law **4** bond, cold, name, noun, room, weal **5** pleas, sense, stock, touch **6** factor,

ground, prayer **7** carrier, council, divisor, grackle, measure
Common __: 3 Era **5** Sense **6** Market
Common Cause: 5 lobby
founder: John W. Gardner
__ common denominator: 5 least **6** lowest
commoner: 4 pleb **7** peasant **8** plebeian
commoners: 4 raff **6** rabble **8** populace, riffraff **9** hoi polloi **10** lower class
commonly: 3 oft **6** simply **7** as a rule, usually **8** together **9** naturally, routinely **10** ordinarily
Common Market: 3 EEC
locale: 3 Eur. **6** Europe
money: 3 ecu **4** euro
prefix: 3 Eur- **4** Euro-
__ common multiple: 5 least **6** lowest
commonplace: 3 dry, ord. **4** dull **5** banal, corny, hokey, lowly, passé, prosy, stale, stock, trite, typic, usual, vapid **6** common, jejune, old hat **7** average, clichéd, fatuous, general, humdrum, mundane, prosaic, regular, trivial, typical, vanilla **8** bromidic, everyday, familiar, mediocre, ordinary, outdated, outmoded, workaday **9** hackneyed, platitude, prevalent, prosaical, quotidian **10** dullsville, uninspired, unoriginal
commons: 4 park **6** square **10** town square
common-sense: 4 sane **7** logical **9** realistic **10** reasonable
Common Sense
author: Thomas Paine
Common Sense and Nuclear Warfare
author: Bertrand Russell
commonwealth: 4 good **5** state **6** nation **7** country, kingdom, society **9** territory
Commonwealth Day month: 5 March
Commonwealth member: 4 Fiji **5** Ghana, India, Kenya, Malta, Nauru, Samoa, Tonga **6** Belize, Brunei, Canada, Cyprus, Gambia, Guyana, Malawi, Tuvalu, Uganda, Zambia **7** Bahamas, England, Grenada, Jamaica, Lesotho, Namibia, Nigeria, St. Lucia, Vanuatu **8** Barbados, Botswana, Cameroon, Dominica, Kiribati, Malaysia, Maldives, Sri Lanka, Tanzania **9** Australia, Mauritius, Singapore, Swaziland **10** Bangladesh, Mozambique, New Zealand, Saint Lucia, Seychelles **11** Sierra Leone, South Africa
Commonwealth of __: 7 England, Nations **8** Kentucky, Virginia
commotion: 3 ado, din, row **4** flap, fuss, riot, stew, stir, to-do **5** furor, hoo-ha, mania, mix-up, noise, scene, spirt, spurt, stink, storm **6** action, bedlam, bustle, clamor, dither, flurry, hassle, hoopla, hoorah, hooray, hubbub, hurrah, hurray, kickup, lather, mayhem, outcry, pother, racket, ruckus, rumpus, squall, tumult, uproar **7** clatter, clutter, dispute, ferment, quarrel, scuffle, trouble **8** ballyhoo, brouhaha, disquiet, outbreak, scramble **9** agitation, annoyance, confusion, hue and cry, rebellion, sensation **10** combustion, convulsion, excitement, hurly-burly, insurgence, turbulence
communal: 5 joint **6** mutual, public, shared, social **7** grouped **8** conjoint **9** corporate, unanimous **10** collective
word: 3 our **4** ours
commune: 4 talk **6** confer, parley **7** kibbutz **8** converse **9** discourse, touch base **10** collective
dweller: 5 hippy **6** hippie **10** kibbutznik
communicable: 8 catching **10** contagious, infectious
communicate: 3 air, say **4** call, give, send, talk, tell, wire **5** break, phone, relay, speak, utter, write **6** confer, convey, detail, impart, inform, pass on, recite, relate, report, reveal, signal **7** declare, divulge, mention, reflect, signify **8** advise of, converse, describe, disclose, hand down, interact, transmit, vocalize **9** make known, put across
silently: 3 nod **4** sign
with: 5 get to, reach **7** contact
communication: 4 info, mail, news, note, word **6** dialog, lesson, report, speech **7** contact, liaison, message, missive, tidings **8** briefing, bulletin, dialogue, dispatch, language **9** statement
combining form: 3 -log **5** -logue
device: 5 pager
facilitate ~: 6 liaise
oral ~: 4 talk **6** debate, homily, sermon **7** address, lecture, oration, oratory, pep talk **8** dialogue, rhetoric **9** chalk talk, discourse **10** discussion
system of ~: 8 language
wordless ~: 3 ESP
written ~: 4 line, memo, note **5** e-mail **6** letter **7** missive
communications: 5 media
company: 3 GTE, ITT
device: 3 TTY **5** phone
former ~ system: 5 telex
starter: 4 tele
communicative: 6 chatty, social **7** cordial **8** friendly, outgoing **9** convivial, talkative **10** gregarious
communion: 4 rite **5** unity **6** accord, prayer **7** harmony, rapport, rapture **8** affinity **9** agreement, closeness, Eucharist, good vibes, sacrament **10** fellowship
host: 5 wafer
plate: 5 paten
table: 5 altar
communion __: 3 cup **4** rail **5** cloth, plate, table
__ Communion: 4 Holy
communiqué: 4 memo, news, word **5** aviso **6** notice, report **7** message **8** bulletin, dispatch **9** statement
communism: 7 Marxism **8** Leninism **9** socialism **10** Bolshevism
Communist: 3 red **7** leftist
hero: 5 Lenin
old ~ state: 3 SSR
Communist __: 5 China, party
community: 4 town, turf **5** place, state **6** colony, hamlet, parish, public **7** kinship, society **8** affinity, locality **9** agreement, humankind, residents, territory **10** settlement, similarity
bedroom ~: 4 burb **5** exurb **6** suburb
Buddhist ~: 6 sangha
center: 4 the Y, YMCA, YMHA, YWCA, YWHA
ecological ~: 5 biome
of a ~: 5 local
community __: 5 chest **6** center, church **7** college, service
__ community: 5 gated
Community Chest
kin: 6 Chance
commutation: 6 switch, travel **8** exchange **9** shuffling
commute: 4 ride **5** drive **6** change, pardon, soften, travel **7** curtail, release, shorten **8** decrease, mitigate **9** transform, translate
starter: 4 tele
commuter: 5 rider **8** traveler **9** passenger
bane: 5 delay, tie up **6** detour
carrier: 3 bus, car **4** auto, rail **5** train **8** railroad
destination: 4 home, work **6** office
handhold: 5 strap
home: 5 burbs, exurb **6** suburb
starter: 4 tele
watering hole: 6 bar car
Como: 4 Lago, lake **5** Perry
locale: 5 Italy
¿Cómo __?: 4 está
Como, Perry
record label: 3 RCA
song: And I Love You So (1973)
Catch a Falling Star (1958)
Glendora (1956)
Home for the Holidays (1954)
Hot Diggity (1956)
It's Impossible (1970)
Juke Box Baby (1956)
Kewpie Doll (1958)
Ko Ko Mo (1955)
Magic Moments (1958)
More (1956)
Papa Loves Mambo (1954)
Round and Round (1957)
Till the End of Time (1945)
Tina Marie (1955)
Comoros: 6 nation **7** country
capital: 6 Moroni
group: 10 Arab League
money: 5 franc
volcano: 8 Karthala
__ Como Va: 3 Oye
comp: 4 pass, test **7** freebee, freebie **8** free pass, free ride **10** recompense
compact: 3 car **4** auto, bond, cram, deal, firm, snug, trim **5** brief, close, dense, pithy, short, solid, stuff, terse, thick, tight **6** league, narrow, packed, pocket, recede, reduce, shrink, treaty **7** abridge, concise, concord, crammed, crowded, curtail, entente, folding, laconic, pressed, promise, shorten, stuffed **8** alliance, compress, condense, contract, covenant, portable, protocol, succinct **9** agreement, concordat, condensed, indenture, jam-packed **10** abbreviate, automobile, boiled down, compressed, hard-packed, settlement, to the point
material: 5 rouge
reading: 5 brief **7** summary **8** abstract, synopsis
compact __: 3 car **4** disc, disk
compact __ player: 4 disc, disk
__ compact: 6 social
compacted: 4 hard **5** solid, tight **8** squeezed **9** condensed **10** compressed, synopsized
__ compactor: 5 trash
compadre: 5 amigo
compañera: 5 amiga
compañero: 5 amigo
companion: 3 pal **4** aide, ally, chum, date, mate, wife **5** buddy, crony, guide, match **6** cohort, convoy, escort, fellow, friend, spouse, squire **7** compeer, consort, partner **8** alter ego, chaperon, handbook, henchman, intimate, playmate, roommate, sidekick **9** assistant, associate, attendant, auxiliary, boyfriend, chaperone, colleague, confidant, duplicate, protector, safeguard **10** accomplice, bosom buddy, complement, girlfriend, reciprocal, sweetheart
ender: 3 way
__ companion: 4 boon
companionable: 4 kind, nice **5** close, sweet **6** chummy, clubby, genial, kindly, social **7** affable, amiable, cordial **8** amicable, friendly, intimate, outgoing, pleasant, sociable **9** convivial **10** benevolent, buddy-buddy, gregarious, neighborly, solicitous
companionless: 4 sole, solo, stag **5** alone **6** lonely, single **8** desolate, lonesome, solitary
companions: 7 retinue **9** entourage
company: 3 mob **4** band, body, cast, crew, firm, gang, pack, team **5** corps, covey, crowd, flock, group, guest, hands, house, label, party, squad, troop **6** agency, circle, clique, guests, league, legion, outfit, throng, troupe **7** brigade, callers, concern, coterie, platoon, retinue, society, visitor **8** assembly, business, employer, ensemble, presence, visitors **9** entourage, gathering, retainers, syndicate **10** assemblage, collection, enterprise, fellowship, membership
abbr.: 3 inc.
honcho: 3 CEO **4** pres. **9** president
company __: 3 man **4** town **5** store
__ company: 4 fire, road **5** ship's, stock, trust **6** engine, growth, parent, public **7** finance, holding, private
__ company...: 4 Two's
Company: 7 musical
composer: Stephen Sondheim

Company __ Keeps, The: 3 She
__ Company: 3 Bad 5 Mixed 6 London, Three's
Company She Keeps, The
author: Mary McCarthy
Company, The: 3 CIA
Compaq: 2 PC 8 computer
rival: 3 IBM, Mac 4 Dell 5 Apple 7 Gateway
comparable: 4 akin, like, same, such 5 alike, equal, level 6 allied, on a par 7 cognate, kindred, similar 8 matching, parallel 9 analogous, consonant 10 equivalent, tantamount
be ~ to: 8 approach
make ~: 6 equate
to: 4 like, near
comparably: 5 alike
comparative: 7 similar 8 relative
extent: 5 ratio
comparatively: 6 rather
compare: 5 check, liken, weigh 6 equate, oppose, size up 7 analyze, balance, collate, examine, inspect, stack up 8 contrast, parallel 9 correlate 10 correspond, scrutinize
beyond ~: 4 best 5 ideal 7 perfect 8 peerless 9 unequaled
notes: 3 gab 4 chat, meet, talk 6 confer, huddle, parley, powwow 7 consult, discuss 8 converse 9 interface, touch base 10 brainstorm, chew the fat, deliberate
to: 5 rival, touch 8 rank with
compare __: 5 notes
__ compare: 6 beyond
compared
to: 4 than 7 against, vis-à-vis 10 set against
comparison: 5 check, ratio 6 simile 7 analogy 8 contrast, likeness, likening, metaphor 9 analyzing, balancing, collating, collation, measuring, semblance 10 connection, estimation, opposition, separation, similarity
basis of ~: 6 analog
make a ~: 5 liken
numeric ~: 5 ratio
test item: 6 Brand X
word of ~: 4 best, less, than 5 worse
words: 3 as a
comparison-__: 4 shop
compartment: 3 bay 4 cell, nook, slot 5 berth, booth, cubby, niche, stall 6 alcove, carrel, corner, locker, pocket 7 carrell, chamber, cubicle, portion, section, segment 8 division 9 cubbyhole 10 pigeonhole
cover: 5 hatch
secure ~: 4 safe 5 vault
__ compartment: 5 glove
compartmentalize: 8 separate
compás point: 3 sur 4 este 5 norte, oeste
compass: 4 area, loop, ring, room 5 ambit, field, gamut, grasp, hem in, limit, orbit, range, reach, realm, scope, sweep, width 6 attain, domain, effect, extend, extent, length, obtain, radius, sphere, spread 7 achieve, breadth, circuit, enclose, fulfill, horizon, inclose, procure, purview, realize 8 boundary, confines, distance, encircle, environs, latitude, surround 9 dimension, incidence, magnitude, perimeter, ranginess 10 accomplish, boundaries, bring about, comprehend
creation: 3 arc 6 circle
direction: 3 ENE, ESE, NNE, NNW, SSE, SSW, WNW, WSW 4 east, west 5 north, point, rhumb, south 7 heading 9 northeast, northwest, southeast, southwest
holder: 6 gimbal 8 binnacle
pointer: 6 needle
Spanish ~ point: 3 sur 4 este 5 norte, oeste
use a ~: 6 orient
user: 5 hiker 9 orienteer
compass __: 3 saw 4 rose
compassion: 4 pity, ruth 5 heart, mercy 6 lenity, pathos 7 charity, empathy, quarter 8 clemency, kindness, lenience, sympathy 9 tolerance 10 condolence, humaneness, tenderness
feel ~: 4 ache, pity
lacking ~: 4 cold 8 ruthless
words of ~: 5 I care, I know
compassionate: 3 big, lax 4 easy, kind, mild, nice, soft, warm 5 loose 6 caring, decent, gentle, humane, kindly, tender 7 clement, lenient, piteous, ruthful, sparing 8 all heart, flexible, gracious, laid-back, merciful, placable, tolerant 9 assuasive, compliant, easygoing, forgiving, indulgent 10 altruistic, benevolent, bighearted, forbearing, permissive, responsive, unexacting
one: 5 carer
compatibility: 7 fitness, harmony, rapport 8 affinity
compatible: 3 fit 4 like, same 7 fitting 8 suitable 9 accordant, according, adaptable, agreeable, congenial, congruent, congruous, consonant, in harmony, in keeping, simpatico 10 concurrent, consistent, harmonious, in sync with, like-minded, synchronal
be ~: 5 agree, click
__-compatible: 3 IBM
compatriot: 3 pal 4 ally, chum 5 amigo, buddy, crony 6 cohort, friend 7 comrade 8 indigene, sidekick 9 associate, colleague, confidant 10 well-wisher
compeer: 3 bro, bud, pal 4 chum, peer 5 buddy, equal, match 6 fellow, friend 7 coequal, comrade 8 intimate, roommate, sidekick 9 colleague, companion
compel: 4 bind, make 5 cause, drive, exact, force, impel, press 6 coerce, demand, impose, oblige 7 command, dragoon, require 8 bulldoze, persuade, pressure 9 blackmail, constrain, force upon, influence, strong-arm 10 bear down on, pressurize
compelled: 5 bound 9 unwilling
be ~: 4 have, must 6 have to
compelling: 5 valid 6 cogent, potent, strong, urgent 7 burning, driving, dynamic, logical 8 luculent, powerful, pressing, striking 9 effective, mandatory, necessary, stringent 10 commanding, compulsive, conclusive, engrossing, unarguable
compendiary: 5 short 7 laconic
compendious: 5 short, terse 7 concise, laconic 9 condensed
compendium: 3 ana, set 4 book 5 brief, table 6 digest, manual, précis, sketch, survey 7 epitome, pandect, summary 8 abstract, handbook, overview, synopsis, treasury 9 anthology 10 abridgment, conspectus, tabulation
compensate: 3 pay 5 atone, cover, repay 6 make up, offset, recoup, redeem, refund, reward 7 balance, recover, redress, replace, requite, satisfy 8 outweigh 9 cancel out, indemnify, make up for, reimburse 10 counteract, invalidate, make amends, neutralize, remunerate, take care of
for: 7 expiate 10 make good on
compensation: 3 fee, pay, tip 4 wage 5 bonus, price, wages 6 amends, profit, ransom, refund, return, reward, salary 7 benefit, comfort, damages, deserts, payment, redress, stipend 8 earnings, reaction 9 emolument, expiation
__ compensation: 7 workers'
compensatory __: 7 damages
compete: 3 run, try, vie 4 play, race 5 clash, joust, rival 6 battle, strive, take on 7 contend, face off 8 scramble, struggle 9 lock horns
competely: 6 in toto
competence: 5 craft, might, power, savvy, skill 7 ability, finesse, fitness, know-how, stature 8 adequacy, aptitude, capacity 9 expertise 10 capability, efficiency, right stuff
competency: 5 skill 10 efficiency
competent: 3 fit 4 able, deft, good, sane 5 quick, savvy, slick, sound 6 adroit, au fait, expert, nimble, up to it, versed 7 capable, knowing, skilled, trained 8 adequate, dextrous, graceful, masterly, seasoned, skillful, suitable 9 all-around, dexterous, effective, efficient, masterful, on the ball, pertinent, qualified, up to snuff, up to speed 10 proficient, sufficient
humorously: 3 ept
more ~: 5 abler
not ~: 5 inept, unfit
competently: 4 ably, well 7 handily
more ~: 6 better
competition: 4 bout, duel, game, meet, race, side 5 clash, event, fight, match, sport 6 Brand X, strife 7 contest, rivalry 8 struggle, tug-of-war
component: 3 lap, leg
-free: 5 no-bid
Competition, The (1980 film)
cast: Richard Dreyfuss, Amy Irving, Lee Remick
competitive: 5 rival, type A 8 athletic
not ~: 5 type B
competitive __: 4 edge
competitor: 3 foe 4 vier 5 enemy, match, rival 6 player 7 athlete, entrant, fighter 8 opponent 9 adversary, candidate, contender, dark horse, ill-wisher, job-hunter 10 antagonist, challenger, contestant, opposition
prize: 5 medal, purse
ranked ~: 4 seed
competitors: 5 field
compilation: 3 ana 6 corpus 7 omnibus 8 analecta, analects, pastiche
compile: 4 cull 5 amass, build 6 digest, garner, gather, muster 7 arrange, collate, collect, marshal 8 assemble, hold on to, organize 9 summarize 10 accumulate, congregate
compiled: 7 grouped 10 collective
compiler: 6 editor
complacency: 7 comfort, license 8 smugness 10 confidence
complacent: 4 smug 6 placid 7 pleased 8 gloating 9 conceited, confident, contented, easygoing, egotistic, gratified, presuming, satisfied 10 obsequious
complain: 4 beef, carp, crab, fuss, harp, kick, mind, moan, rage, rail, rant, sigh, wail, weep, yell 5 cavil, demur, gripe, groan, growl, grump, mourn, whine 6 grouch, grouse, holler, kvetch, mutter, repine, squawk, squeal, yammer 7 grumble, protest, quarrel, whimper 8 sound off 9 bellyache, find fault, make a fuss
about: 6 bemoan, lament, report
constantly: 3 nag 4 carp
to: 5 nag at
complainant: 4 suer
complainer: 3 nag 4 crab 5 grump, scold, shrew 6 critic, grouch, moaner, noodge 7 crybaby, killjoy 9 henpecker, pessimist, termagant
complaining: 5 whiny 6 crabby, lament, whiney 7 fretful, peevish 8 fretsome 9 grumbling, querulous
complaint: 4 ache, beef, fuss, kick, moan 5 cavil, gripe, stink, whine 6 charge, grouse, lament, malady, outcry, squawk 7 ailment, disease, grumble, illness, protest, quarrel, quibble, trouble 8 disorder, jeremiad, sickness, syndrome 9 annoyance, condition, criticism, grievance, infirmity, objection 10 accusation, affliction, discontent
lodge a ~: 3 sue 4 cite 5 blame 6 accuse, allege, charge, impute, indict 7 arraign 8 denounce
__ complaint: 5 file a
complaints: 4 flak 5 flack
list of ~: 6 litany
complaisance: 7 amenity 8 courtesy, kindness 9 deference, gentility 10 cordiality, indulgence
complaisant: 4 easy, kind, mild 5 civil 6 benign, polite 7 amiable, lenient 8 gracious, obliging, tolerant 9 tractable
Compleat Angler, The
author: Izaak Walton
complement: 3 add, cap 4 crew, foil, mate, unit 5 add to, match, quota 6 amount, fulfil, top off 7 enhance,

flatter, fulfill, perfect **8** quantity, round off, round out **9** aggregate, companion, correlate, integrate, remainder **10** accomplish, constitute, consummate, correspond, enrichment
full ~: **4** load
complementary: **7** related, similar **10** reciprocal
complete: **2** do **3** all, end **4** done, fini, flat, form, full, rank **5** clean, close, crown, ended, gross, mop up, plumb, sew up, sheer, solid, sound, thoro, total, uncut, utter, whole **6** all-out, effect, entire, fill in, finish, fulfil, intact, make up, mature, settle, strict, wind up, wrap up **7** achieve, all over, execute, fill out, fulfill, overall, perfect, perform, play out, plenary, radical, realize, satisfy, through **8** absolute, achieved, carry out, conclude, definite, detailed, finalize, finished, implicit, integral, outright, put to bed, round off, round out, surcease, thorough, whole-hog **9** concluded, determine, full-dress, intensive, inviolate, out-and-out, plentiful, searching, terminate, undivided, unlimited, unreduced, wholesale **10** accomplish, consummate, definitive, effectuate, exhaustive, get through, integrated, put through, soup to nuts, supplement, unabridged
combining form: **3** tel- **4** tele-, telo-
easily: **3** ace
works: **6** corpus, oeuvre **10** collection, opera omnia
Complete Book of Running, The
author: Jim Fixx
completed: **4** done, over **5** ended, ready **9** fulfilled
in French: **4** fini
to a poet: **3** o'er
completely: **3** all **4** A to Z, just, well **5** fully, in all, plumb, quite, right, sheer, stark **6** bodily, in full, in toto, purely, simply, solely, wholly **7** en masse, in depth, totally, utterly **8** entirely, whole hog **9** all the way, every inch, full blast, inside out, like a book, literally, perfectly, to the hilt **10** absolutely, altogether, thoroughly, to the limit, to the teeth, ultimately
combining form: **3** pan- **4** pano-, pant- **5** panta-, panto-
in Latin: **6** in toto
completeness: **8** entirety
completion: **3** end **4** last **5** close **6** ending, finish, result, windup **8** fruition, maturity **9** execution, finishing **10** attainment, complement, conclusion, expiration, perfection
combining form: **6** teleut- **7** teleuto-
complex: **3** web **4** deep, maze **5** heavy **6** hang-up, knotty, lively, system, thorny, tricky **7** network, tangled **8** abstract, abstruse, fixation, involved, manifold, syndrome, tortuous **9** Byzantine, composite, Daedalean, difficult, elaborate, enigmatic, intricate, obsession, structure **10** circuitous, convoluted, perplexing
not ~: **4** easy **5** clear **6** simple
__ complex: **7** Electra, Oedipus
complexion: **4** cast, glow, look, tint, vein **5** color, guise, style, tinge **6** aspect, makeup, nature **8** coloring, skin tone **9** character, semblance **10** appearance, coloration
dark ~: **5** olive
kind of ~: **4** fair **5** ruddy
woe: **4** acne
complexity: **4** knot **5** snarl **6** muddle **9** confusion, imbroglio, intricacy, labyrinth
points of ~: **4** nodi
compliance: **6** assent **7** consent **9** agreement, deference, obedience, orthodoxy, passivity **10** acceptance, adaptation, concession, conformity, observance, submission
compliant: **3** lax **4** easy, kind, meek, mild, soft, tame **5** loose, mousy **6** broken, docile, gentle, kindly, mousey, pliant **7** clement, dutiful, lenient, obeying, passive, ruthful, sparing, subdued, trained, willing **8** amenable, flexible, gracious, laid-back, lamblike, merciful, obedient, obliging, placable, resigned, tolerant, yielding **9** adaptable, agreeable, assenting, assuasive, easygoing, forgiving, indulgent, malleable, tractable **10** forbearing, governable, law-abiding, manageable, permissive, submissive, unexacting
complicate: **5** mix up, snarl **6** foul up, impede, jumble, mess up, muck up, muddle **7** confuse, embroil, snarl up **8** compound, confound, entangle **9** aggravate, convolute, elaborate, interfuse, make waves **10** disarrange, interweave
complicated: **4** deep, hard, ugly **5** fancy, heavy **6** knotty, tricky **7** complex, prickly **8** abstruse, involved, tortuous **10** convoluted, perplexing
make less ~: **4** ease **8** simplify
not ~: **4** easy **6** simple
complication: **3** rub **4** kink, knot, snag **5** mix-up, nodus, snarl **6** hurdle, muddle **7** dilemma, problem **8** drawback, intrigue, obstacle **9** labyrinth
complications: **4** nodi
complicity: **4** plot **9** agreement, collusion **10** connivance, conspiracy, guiltiness
compliment: **4** hail, kudo, laud **5** exalt, extol, honor, toast **6** cajole, extoll, praise **7** acclaim, applaud, commend, flatter, glorify, tribute **8** butter up, cajolery, encomium, flattery, good word, hand it to **9** adulation, celebrate, laudation, panegyric, recommend, sentiment, warm fuzzy **10** admiration, attentions, felicitate, panegyrize
in a way: **3** ape **7** imitate
left-handed ~: **3** cut, dig **4** slam, snub **6** insult, slight, zinger **7** affront, offense, put-down
react to a ~: **4** beam **5** smile
complimentary: **4** free **6** gratis **7** as a gift, glowing **8** costless **9** laudatory, on the cuff **10** for nothing, on the house
close: **4** best, love **5** yours **6** warmly **9** sincerely **10** yours truly
word: **4** cool, fine
complimentary __: **5** close
compliments: **7** regards **8** flattery, respects
comply: **3** bow **4** heed, meet, mind, obey, okay **5** admit, adopt, agree, allow, defer, go for, yield **6** accede, accept, assent, concur, follow, fulfil, give in, give up, listen, relent, submit **7** abide by, approve, conform, consent, fulfill, go along, include, observe, perform, respect **8** adhere to, play ball **9** acquiesce, cooperate **10** come around, give the nod, keep in step, toe the line
with: **4** meet, obey **5** act on, bow to **6** bend to, follow, fulfil **7** abide by, act upon, fulfill, observe, satisfy **8** adhere to, carry out **9** cooperate, recognize, sign off on
component: **3** cog **4** item, link, part, unit **5** piece **6** detail, factor, member **7** element, feature, fitting, fixture, section, segment **9** accessory, elemental, intrinsic **10** ingredient, peripheral
components: **8** workings **9** mechanism
comport: **4** gybe, jibe **5** agree, carry **6** acquit, behave, concur, square **7** conduct **9** harmonize **10** correspond
oneself: **3** act **6** behave
comportment: **3** air **4** mien **7** bearing, conduct, manners **8** behavior, carriage, demeanor
compose: **3** pen **4** calm, draw, form, lull, make **5** allay, build, draft, frame, quell, relax, set up, write **6** author, becalm, create, indite, make up, pacify, solace, soothe **7** appease, assuage, mollify, placate, produce **8** organize **9** construct, fabricate, formulate, harmonize, originate, reconcile, untrouble **10** simmer down, straighten
for printing: **3** set **7** typeset
composed: **4** calm, cool, even, sure **5** quiet, sober, staid, stoic **6** at ease, low-key, mellow, placid, poised, sedate, serene **7** amiable, assured, at peace, equable, pacific, relaxed, stoical, unmoved **8** amicable, carefree, laid-back, peaceful, reserved, together, tranquil **9** collected, easygoing, impassive, possessed, quiescent, temperate, unexcited, unruffled, unworried **10** nonchalant, unagitated, untroubled
be ~ of: **7** contain, include
__-composed: **4** self
composer: **3** Bax, Cui **4** Arne, Bach, Berg, Cage, Foss, Ives, Kern, Lalo, Orff, Wolf **5** Arlen, Auric, Bizet, Bliss, Bloch, Bruch, Cohan, Crumb, d'Indy, Dukas, Elgar, Fauré, Glass, Gluck, Gould, Grieg, Grofé, Haydn, Holst, Ibert, Lawes, Lehár, Liszt, Loewe, Lully, Ravel, Satie, Sousa, Styne, Verdi, Weber, Weill **6** Arnold, artist, author, Barber, Bartók, Berlin, Boulez, Brahms, Busoni, Carter, Chávez, Chopin, Coates, Cowell, Delius, Dvorák, Enesco, Foster, framer, Franck, Glière, Glinka, Gounod, Handel, Hanson, Harris, Kodály, Krenek, Ligeti, lyrist, Mahler, Mennin, Mozart, Piston, Porter, Previn, Schütz, Taylor, Varèse, Wagner, Walton, Warren, Webern **7** Antheil, Babbitt, Bellini, Berlioz, Borodin, Britten, Copland, Debussy, Delibes, Diamond, Gilbert, Janácek, Menotti, Milhaud, Nielsen, Poulenc, Puccini, Purcell, Rodgers, Rossini, Schuman, Smetana, Strauss, Thomson, Tiomkin, Vivaldi **8** Anderson, Bruckner, Chabrier, Chausson, Clementi, Couperin, Gershwin, Grainger, Korngold, Mascagni, Massenet, musician, Paganini, Respighi, Schubert, Schumann, Scriabin, Sessions, Sibelius, Sondheim, Sullivan, Telemann **9** Beethoven, Bernstein, Buxtehude, Cherubini, Donizetti, Hindemith, MacDowell, Meyerbeer, Offenbach, Prokofiev, Scarlatti, Schönberg, Van Heusen **10** Blitzstein, Gottschalk, Monteverdi, Mussorgsky, Paderewski, Palestrina, Ponchielli, Rubinstein, Saint-Saëns, songwriter, Stravinsky, Villa-Lobos **11** Leoncavallo, Mendelssohn, Siegmeister, Tchaikovsky **12** Khachaturian, Rachmaninoff, Shostakovich
American: **4** Cage, Ives, Kern **5** Arlen, Bloch, Crumb, Glass, Gould, Grofé, Sousa, Styne **6** Barber, Berlin, Carter, Cowell, Foster, Hanson, Harris, Mennin, Piston, Previn, Taylor, Varèse, Warren **7** Antheil, Babbitt, Copland, Diamond, Menotti, Rodgers, Schuman, Thomson **8** Gershwin, Grainger, Korngold, Sessions, Sondheim **9** Bernstein, Hindemith, MacDowell **10** Blitzstein, Gottschalk **11** Siegmeister
Austrian: **4** Berg, Wolf **5** Haydn, Lehár **6** Krenek, Mahler, Mozart, Webern **7** Strauss **8** Bruckner, Schubert **9** Schönberg
Beggar's Opera, The ~: **3** Gay
Brazilian: **10** Villa-Lobos
British: **3** Bax **4** Arne **5** Bliss, Elgar, Holst, Lawes **6** Arnold, Coates, Handel, Walton **7** Britten, Gilbert, Purcell **8** Sullivan **15** Vaughan Williams
Czech: **6** Dvorák **7** Janácek, Smetana
Danish: **7** Nielsen **9** Buxtehude
Finnish: **8** Sibelius
French: **4** Lalo **5** Auric, Bizet, d'Indy, Dukas, Fauré, Ibert, Lully, Ravel, Satie **6** Boulez, Delius, Franck, Gounod **7** Berlioz, Debussy, Delibes, Milhaud, Poulenc **8** Chabrier, Chausson, Couperin, Massenet **9** Offenbach **10** Saint-Saëns

German: 4 Bach, Foss, Orff 5 Bruch, Gluck, Weill 6 Brahms, Schütz, Wagner 7 Strauss 8 Schumann, Telemann 9 Beethoven, Meyerbeer 11 Mendelssohn
Hungarian: 5 Liszt 6 Bartók, Kodály
Italian: 5 Verdi 6 Busoni 7 Bellini, Puccini, Rossini, Vivaldi 8 Mascagni, Paganini, Respighi 9 Cherubini, Donizetti 10 Monteverdi, Palestrina, Ponchielli 11 Leoncavallo
Mexican: 6 Chávez
Norwegian: 5 Grieg
org.: 3 BMI 5 ASCAP
output: 4 opus, trio 5 fugue, motet, nonet, opera, rondo, waltz 6 sonata 7 cantata, partita, quartet, toccata 8 concerto, nocturne, oratorio, serenade, symphony
Polish: 6 Chopin 10 Paderewski
Romanian: 6 Enesco, Ligeti
Russian: 3 Cui 6 Glière, Glinka 7 Borodin 8 Scriabin 9 Prokofiev 10 Mussorgsky, Rubinstein, Stravinsky 11 Tchaikovsky 12 Khachaturian, Rachmaninoff, Shostakovich
Scottish: 8 Hamilton
Spanish: 5 Falla 7 Albéniz
Swiss: 8 Honegger
composing: 3 art
composing __: 4 room
composite: 3 mix 5 alloy, blend, mixed, union 6 fusion, hybrid, medley, melded 7 amalgam, blended, complex, grouped, mixture 9 aggregate, immixture, synthesis 10 collective, commixture
composition: 4 opus, poem, song, tune, work 5 essay, music, paper, piece, prose, score, setup, theme 6 format, layout, makeup, melody, thesis 7 anatomy, article, content, texture 8 concerto, rhapsody, symphony, treatise 10 literature
literary ~: 4 opus 6 column, sketch 7 article, passage, writing 9 editorial
musical ~: 4 opus, song, trio 5 fugue, motet, nonet, octet, opera, rondo, waltz 6 sonata 7 cantata, octette, partita, quartet, toccata 8 concerto, nocturne, oratorio, serenade, symphony
compositor concern: 6 layout
compos mentis: 4 sane 5 lucid, right, sound
__ compos mentis: 3 non
compost: 3 rot 5 decay, humus, mulch 9 fertilize 10 fertilizer
item: 4 peel, rind
composure: 4 calm, cool, ease 5 poise 6 aplomb, temper 7 balance, dignity 8 calmness, evenness, presence, serenity 9 assurance, fortitude, placidity, sang-froid, stability 10 dispassion, equanimity, moderation, sedateness
compote: 7 dessert 9 preserves
cousin: 3 jam 5 jelly
ingredient: 4 pear 5 apple, fruit

compound: 3 mix 4 make 5 add to, admix, blend, union 6 make up, recipe, worsen 7 amalgam, mixture 8 multiply, solution 9 aggravate, aggregate, intensify, synthesis 10 exacerbate
Compound W target: 4 wart
Compoz: 8 sleep aid
alternative: 5 Nytol 6 Unisom 7 Sominex
comprehend: 3 dig, get, see 4 grok, know, tell 5 catch, get it, grasp, savvy, seize, think 6 absorb, fathom, follow, intuit, master, take in 7 cognize, compass, make out, realize 8 conceive, perceive, relate to 9 apprehend, encompass, penetrate, recognize 10 appreciate, assimilate, understand
comprehensibility: 7 clarity
comprehensible: 4 easy 5 clear, lucid, plain, vivid 6 cogent, limpid 7 evident, express, obvious 8 apparent, coherent, distinct, explicit, luculent, luminous, manifest, palpable, readable 9 graspable 10 spelled out
comprehension: 3 ken, wit 4 wits 5 grasp, light 6 acumen, reason, sanity, uptake, wisdom 7 empathy, mastery, purview 8 judgment 10 perception
words of ~: 3 ohs 4 I see
comprehensive: 3 big 4 full, incl., vast, wide 5 broad, large, roomy, total, uncut, whole 6 entire, global 7 blanket, general, generic, overall, plenary, sizable 8 catholic, complete, detailed, far-flung, finished, sizeable, spacious, sweeping, synoptic, thorough 9 capacious, expansive, extensive, generical, universal, unreduced, wholesale, worldwide 10 exhaustive, synoptical, unabridged, widespread
work: 5 summa
comprehensively: 6 wholly 7 in depth, largely, totally
comprehensiveness: 5 scope 7 breadth
Comprende?: 3 see 5 get it
compress: 3 jam, nip, wad 4 cram 5 crush, pinch, press, smush, stuff, wring 6 crunch, digest, narrow, pucker, recede, reduce, shrink, squash 7 abridge, compact, curtail, flatten, shorten, squeeze, tighten, wrinkle 8 abstract, boil down, condense, contract 9 capsulize, constrict, summarize, telescope 10 abbreviate
as a data file: 3 zip
wet ~: 5 stupe
compressed: 3 cut 4 firm, hard 5 brief, dense, scant, short, solid, thick, tight 6 cut off, narrow, packed 7 compact, concise, crammed, crowded, cutback, cut down, reduced, stuffed 8 abridged, cut short, squeezed 9 compacted, condensed, confining, curtailed, shortened 10 abstracted, hard-packed, summarized, synopsized
compressed __: 3 air
comprise: 4 form, have, make, span 5 cover, total 6 embody, imbody, make up, take in 7 add up to, contain, embrace, include, involve 9 consist of, encompass 10 constitute
comprising: 4 incl. 9 including
compromise: 4 bend, deal, pact, risk 6 accord, settle 7 bargain, imperil, work out 8 endanger, trade off 9 agreement, arbitrate, discredit, embarrass, implicate, make a deal, negotiate, prejudice 10 adjustment, concession, conciliate, jeopardize, settlement
don't ~: 6 insist
compromise __: 4 rail 5 joint 6 choice
compromising: 8 moderate
not ~: 5 rigid
Compton: 3 Ann 4 city, town 6 Arthur 9 MacKenzie
locale: 10 California
Compton-Burnett, Ivy: 6 writer 7 British
comptroller: 3 CPA 6 bursar 8 official 9 treasurer 10 accountant, bookkeeper
task: 5 audit
compulsion: 3 yen 4 need, urge 5 drive, force, mania 6 duress 8 coercion, neurosis, pressure, violence 9 emergency, extortion, liability, necessity, obsession, restraint 10 constraint, obligation
compulsive: 6 forced 7 driving 9 besetting, obsessive 10 compelling, passionate
behavior: 5 habit
compulsively, do: 6 devour
compulsory: 6 forced 7 binding 8 required 9 de rigueur, mandatory, necessary, requisite 10 imperative, inevitable, inexorable, obligatory
compunction: 5 qualm 6 regret 7 remorse, scruple 9 penitence 10 repentance
compunctions, have: 3 rue
compunctious: 5 sorry 6 humble, rueful 8 contrite, penitent 9 chastened, regretful, repentant 10 apologetic, remorseful
CompuServe
acquirer: 3 AOL
correspondence: 5 e-mail
patron: 4 user
computation: 5 count 9 reckoning
compute: 3 add, sum 4 plot, tell 5 add up, count, gauge, tally, total 6 assess, cipher, divide, figure, number, reckon 7 measure 8 keep tabs, multiply, subtract 9 calculate, keep score
computer: 2 PC 3 CPU, Mac 4 iMac, mini 5 clone, micro 6 laptop 7 machine 8 notebook 9 mainframe
abbr.: 3 RAM, ROM
access a ~ network: 5 log in
accessory: 5 mouse
acronym: 3 GUI, ram, ROM 4 gigo, RISC 5 MSDOS
aid: 5 macro
alter, as a ~ image: 5 morph
Apple ~: 3 Mac 4 iMac
attacker: 5 virus
base: 5 octal 6 binary
brain: 3 CPU
bulletin-board manager: 5 sysop
button: 5 reset
capacity: 3 meg
central ~: 4 host
chip element: 5 wafer
chip technology: 3 LSI
classification: 4 mini 5 micro
combining form: 5 cyber-
command: 3 cut 4 copy, edit, open, save, sort 5 close, enter, erase, macro, paste, print 6 delete, rename
communication device: 5 modem
component: 4 chip
correspondence: 5 e-mail
czar: 5 Gates
data: 4 file
data format: 5 ASCII
data medium: 2 CD 3 DVD 6 floppy
datum: 3 bit 4 byte
dept.: 3 EDP
device: 3 DVD 5 CD-ROM, modem, mouse 6 floppy 7 printer 8 CD burner, keyboard, touchpad 9 hard drive 10 flash drive
display: 6 bit map
dot: 5 pixel
early ~: 5 Eniac 6 abacus
early home ~: 5 Atari
early IBM ~ model: 2 AT, XT
end a ~ session: 6 log off
ender: 3 dom, ese
enthusiast: 4 geek 6 hacker
felon: 6 hacker
fictional ~: 3 Hal
fix a ~ program: 5 debug
fodder: 4 data
gain ~ access: 5 log in
game: 4 Myst 6 Tetris
game award: 5 Arkie
game brand: 3 NES, Wii 4 Sega 7 Genesis
geek: 4 guru, nerd
handheld ~ (abbr.): 3 PDA
hardware company: 5 Intel 6 Iomega
hazard: 5 surge
image file: 3 gif, tif
industry, briefly: 3 ADP
instruction: 5 macro
key: 3 Alt, Del, End, Esc, Ins, tab 4 Ctrl, Home, Pg Dn, Pg Up 5 arrow, Break, Enter, Pause, Shift 6 Delete, Escape, Insert, Page Up 7 Control, Num Lock 8 Caps Lock, Page Down, space bar 9 backslash, Backspace
kids' ~ language: 4 Logo
kind of ~ monitor: 3 LCD
kind of ~ port: 4 SCSI
knockoff: 5 clone
language: 3 Ada, APL, SQL 4 Alef, html, Icon, Java, LISP, Logo, Orca, Perl 5 Algol, Basic, Cecil, COBOL, Dylan, SISAL 6 Delphi, Eiffel, Erlang, Oberon, Pascal, Prolog, Sather, Scheme, Snobol 7 Fortran
lib.: 5 CD/ROM
like some ~ monitors: 5 hi-res 6 low-res
mag: 4 Byte
maker: 2 HP 3 IBM, NEC 4 Acer,

Cray, Dell, Sony 5 Apple 6 Compaq, Lenovo 7 Gateway, Toshiba
marker: 6 cursor
memory: 3 ram, ROM 4 core
message: 5 e-mail, error
monitor: 3 VDT, VGA
need: 3 ptr. 5 input 7 printer
network: 3 LAN
old ~ memory: 4 core
operating system: 3 DOS 4 Unix 5 MSDOS 7 Windows
options: 4 menu
owner: 4 user
perch: 3 lap
pictograph: 4 icon 8 emoticon
prefix: 5 cyber-
printer brand: 5 Epson
printer device: 5 laser
printer speed: 3 lpm
problem: 3 bug 6 glitch
program: 6 applet
program function: 6 export
programmer: 5 coder
programmer, perhaps: 4 nerd
question: 4 fail 5 abort, retry
RAM ~ program: 3 TSR
reseller: 3 OEM
save ~ files: 6 back up
screen: 3 CRT 7 monitor 8 terminal
select, on a ~: 5 click
shortcut: 5 macro
shutdown: 5 crash
sound: 4 beep
speed unit: 3 MHz 4 mips
spreadsheet company: 5 Lotus
start a ~: 4 boot 6 boot up
storage: 4 bits, disc, disk 5 bytes, cache, CD/ROM 6 buffer
terminal (abbr.): 3 VDT
text scanner (abbr.): 3 OCR
timesaver: 5 macro
typeface: 5 Arial
type of home ~: 5 tower
user's annoyance: 4 spam
view a ~ file: 6 access
virus: 4 worm
write a ~ program: 4 code 6 encode
computer __: 3 law 4 nerd 5 crime, error, virus 6 memory 7 science
__ computer: 4 home, host 6 analog, hybrid 7 digital, network, optical
__ Computer: 4 Dell 5 Apple 6 Compaq
computerese: 5 lingo 6 jargon
comrade: 3 bro, pal 4 ally, chum, mate 5 amigo, buddy, crony 6 cohort, fellow, frater, friend 7 compeer, partner 8 alter ego, coworker, intimate, sidekick 9 associate, colleague, confidant 10 bosom buddy, compatriot, well-wisher
comrade in __: 4 arms
comradeship: 5 unity 7 society
Comsat: 9 Early Bird
Comstock: 3 Ada 4 mine
deposit: 3 ore 4 lode
locale: 3 Nev. 6 Nevada
Comstock __: 4 Lode
Comte __: 3 Ory
Comte, Auguste: 6 French 11 philosopher
Comte de la Fere: 5 Athos
Comte Ory
composer: Gioacchino Rossini
Comtrex
alternative: *see* cold remedy
Comus
author: John Milton
composer: Thomas Arne
con: 2 do 3 lie, rob 4 anti, bilk, dupe, fool, gull, have, hoax, nick, rook, scam, take, with 5 bunco, cheat, cozen, felon, fraud, grift, learn, lifer, study, trick 6 delude, dupery, fleece, humbug, inmate, manage, outlaw, outwit, rip off, take in 7 against, beguile, chicane, deceive, defraud, loath to, mislead, snooker, swindle, wheedle 8 artifice, averse to, flimflam, hoodwink, internee, inveigle, jailbird, opponent, opposing, outsmart, persuade, pettifog, prisoner, talk into 9 bamboozle, charlatan, chicanery, counter to, deception, disinform, four-flush, hostile to, imposture, sweet-talk, victimize 10 at odds with, imposition, run a game on
cubicle: 4 cell
game: 4 hoax, lure, scam 5 bunco, dodge, fraud, sting 6 dupery, hosing, humbug, racket 7 knavery, swindle 8 trickery 9 deception 10 illegality
like a ~ artist: 5 shady
man: 4 liar 5 cheat, crook, knave, quack, rogue, shark, sneak, taker 6 bad guy, robber 7 grifter, hustler, sharper, sharpie 8 imposter, impostor, swindler 9 hypocrite 10 bamboozler, Harold Hill, scam artist
man's accomplice: 5 shill
opposite: 3 pro
pro and ~: 6 debate
votes: 3 nos 4 nays, noes
con __: 3 job, man, men 4 brio, game, moto 5 amore, anima, fuoco 6 artist
Con: 6 Conrad
Con __: 3 Air 6 Edison
Con Air (1997 film)
cast: Nicolas Cage, John Cusack, John Malkovich, Ving Rhames
Conakry: 4 city, town 7 capital
locale: 6 Guinea
Conan: 4 Neal 6 O'Brien
__ Conan Doyle: 6 Arthur
Conan the Barbarian (1982 film)
cast: James Earl Jones, Arnold Schwarzenegger
Conan the Destroyer character: 4 Zula
Conaway: 4 Jeff
conc.
not ~: 3 dil.
__ con carne: 5 chile, chili 6 chilli
concatenate: 4 bind, hook, join, link 5 bound, chain, unite 6 couple, joined, linked, united 7 chained, conjoin, connect 8 seriatim 9 connected, interlink, interlock
concatenation: 5 chain, nexus, queue, train 6 series 8 junction, juncture, sequence
concave: 5 round 6 curved, dented, dished, hollow, sunken 7 sagging 8 indented 9 depressed, excavated 10 scooped out
become ~: 4 sink
concavity: 4 dent, hole 5 curve 10 depression
conceal: 4 bury, hide, mask, palm, stow, veil 5 cache, cloak, couch, cover, shade, stash 6 enveil, harbor, inhume, pocket, screen, shield, shroud 7 blanket, cover up, envelop, harbour, obscure, seclude, secrete, shelter, shut off, shut out 8 disguise, ensconce, enshroud, stow away, suppress, withhold 9 adumbrate, dissemble, whitewash 10 camouflage
a message: 6 encode 7 encrypt
oneself: 4 lurk 6 hole up, lie low
concealed: 4 dark 5 blind, perdu, privy 6 covert, hidden, latent, occult, perdue, secret, unseen 7 furtive, private, unknown 8 hush-hush, ulterior 9 covered up, incognito, invisible, nonpublic, out of view, potential, recondite, underhand, unexposed 10 enshrouded, tucked away, undercover, underlying, under wraps, undetected, unviewable
again: 5 rehid
by: 5 neath, under 10 underneath
combining form: 4 adel- 5 adelo-
concealment: 4 mask, veil 5 cover, front 6 hiding 7 eclipse, privacy, secrecy 8 covering, darkness, disguise 9 seclusion 10 camouflage
in ~: 5 doggo
place of ~: 3 den 4 lair, nest, nook 5 cover 6 corner, grotto, refuge 7 hideout, shelter 9 safe house, sanctuary
concede: 3 bow, let, own 4 avow, fold, give, quit 5 admit, agree, allow, grant, let on, own up, yield 6 accede, accept, accord, cave in, fess up, give up, reveal 7 confess 8 say uncle 9 recognize, surrender 10 capitulate, understand
conceit: 3 ego 4 idea 5 pride, quirk 6 egoism, vanity 7 egotism, hauteur, swagger 8 self-love, smugness 9 arrogance, immodesty, vainglory 10 narcissism, pretension, stuffiness
conceited: 3 big 4 smug, vain 5 cocky, proud 6 chesty, la-de-da, la-di-da, stuffy 7 fustian, haughty, pompous, stuck-up 8 affected, arrogant, assuming, boastful, cocksure, immodest, lah-di-dah, puffed up, snobbish 9 bigheaded, hubristic, know-it-all, loudmouth 10 big-talking, complacent, egocentric, egoistical, hoity-toity
one: 6 egoist 7 coxcomb, egotist
smile: 5 smirk
conceitedness: 6 hubris, hybris, vanity
conceivable: 6 doable, likely, viable 7 earthly 8 credible, feasible, knowable, possible, workable 9 plausible, potential, practical, thinkable 10 achievable, attainable, imaginable
conceivably: 5 maybe 7 perhaps 8 possibly
conceive: 4 deem, form, plan 5 frame, hatch, think 6 cook up, create, design, device, devise, ideate, make up 7 believe, dream up, imagine, realize, suppose, think up, trump up 8 cogitate, engineer, envisage, envision 9 formulate, originate 10 appreciate, brainstorm, comprehend, mastermind, understand
of: 5 fancy 6 ideate, invent 7 picture 9 visualize
__-conceived: 3 ill
concentrate: 3 fix, put 4 join, mass, meet 5 amass, focus, merge, slant, spend, think, unite 6 center, fixate, gather, huddle, listen, muster, shrink, zero in 7 abridge, cluster, collect, compact 8 assemble, boil down, coalesce, compress, condense, converge
on: 7 address 8 mull over
concentrated: 4 firm 5 solid, thick 6 potent, robust, strong 7 compact, crammed, crowded, intense 8 straight 9 condensed, undivided 10 compressed
concentrating: 6 intent
concentration: 4 army, care, game, heap, mass 5 array, group, horde, swarm 7 cluster 8 card game, strength 9 specialty
alias: 6 memory
field of ~: 5 forte 9 specialty
Concentration: 8 game show
conjunction: 3 oar
genre: game show
host: Hugh Downs
objective: 5 match
puzzle: 5 rebus
Concepción: 4 Dave
concept: 4 idea, seed, view, word 5 image, thing 6 notion, theory, vision 7 thought 10 brainchild, hypothesis, impression, perception
combining form: 4 ideo-
form a ~: 5 think 6 ideate
__ concept: 4 high
conception: 4 idea, view 5 image, start 6 design, notion, origin, outset, theory, vision 7 genesis, infancy, inkling, opinion, reading, thought 8 creation, ideality 9 beginning, cognition, formation, imagining, invention, launching 10 cogitating, envisaging, exposition, impression, initiation
conceptualize: 6 ideate 7 imagine 10 brainstorm
concern: 3 car, job, TLC 4 care, fear, firm, heed, part, sake 5 alarm, house, query, refer, stake, touch, worry 6 absorb, affair, bear on, bother, burden, domain, moment, outfit, regard, regret, relate, unease 7 anxiety, apply to, company, disturb, emotion, gravity, involve, pertain, project, thought, trouble, valuing 8 bear upon, business, deal with, disquiet, distress, function, interest, province, relate to 9 attention, curiosity, pertain to, relevance 10 enterprise, importance, solicitude
exclamation: 4 alas, oh-oh, uh-oh, yipe 5 alack, yikes, yipes
__ concern: 5 going
concerned: 5 antsy, itchy, jumpy, tense, upset 6 caring, loving, pacing, polite, uneasy 7 anxious, at stake, fearful, in a stew, jittery,

keyed up, nervous, restive, uptight, worried **8** restless, skittish **9** attentive, disturbed, excitable, exercised, ill at ease, perturbed **10** distraught, distressed, high-strung, implicated, interested, solicitous, thoughtful
be ~: **4** care **9** give a darn
be ~ about: **4** fear
one: **5** carer
one ~ with (suffix): **3** -eer
response: **5** I care
with: **4** into **5** about
concerning: **4** as to, in re **5** about, anent, as for **6** toward **7** towards **8** relative, relevant **9** as regards
this: **6** hereof
concert: **3** gig **4** show **6** accord, unison **7** harmony, recital **8** musicale **9** agreement **10** jam session
act in ~: **4** join **5** unite **6** club up
bonus: **6** encore
ender: **5** going **6** finale, master **8** mistress
hall: **5** arena, odeon, odeum, venue **7** theater, theatre
hall equipment: **3** amp
halls: **4** odea
in ~: **5** as one, at one **7** jointly **8** in unison, mutually, together **10** coactively, harmonious
income: **4** gate, take
instrument: **5** grand, piano
work: **5** piece
concert ___: **5** grand
concerted: **5** as one, joint **6** mutual, united **7** grouped **9** unanimous, undivided **10** agreed upon, collective, concurrent, synchronal
concertedly: **8** together
concertina: **8** keyboard **10** instrument
concerto: **5** music, piece
conclusion: **4** coda
instrument: **4** harp, horn, oboe **5** piano, viola
movement: **5** rondo
concerto ___: **6** grosso
Concerto ___: **3** in F
___ Concerto: **7** Emperor
___ Concerto, A: **6** Lover's
Concerto for Orchestra
composer: Béla Bartók
Concerto for the Left Hand
composer: Maurice Ravel
Concerto in F
composer: George Gershwin
concession: **3** sop **4** bone **6** assent, patent **7** buyback **8** discount, give-back, rollback, yielding **9** admission, agreement, allowance, privilege, surrender **10** acceptance, adjustment, compliance, compromise, confession, indulgence, permission
ender: **4** aire
concessions for, make: **5** allow
Concetta: **5** Tomei
conch: **5** shell **8** seashell
kin: **6** limpet
liner: **5** nacre
concha: **4** apse, bone
locale: **3** ear **4** nose
Conchata: **7** Ferrell
___ Conchita Alonso: **5** Maria
concierge place: **5** hotel, lobby
conciliate: **6** pacify, soothe **7** appease, assuage, mediate, mollify, patch up, placate, reunite, satisfy, sweeten, win over **9** arbitrate, intervene, reconcile, untrouble **10** compromise
conciliation: **5** peace **6** pardon **7** redress **9** mediation
conciliator: **3** ref, ump **6** umpire **7** referee
conciliatory: **6** dovish, irenic, polite **8** irenical, yielding **9** peaceable
move: **8** overture
concise: **4** curt **5** brief, crisp, pithy, short, terse, tight **6** gnomic **7** compact, laconic **8** abridged, succinct **9** condensed **10** boiled down, compressed, synopsized, to the point
concisely: **7** in short
describe ~: **5** sum up
conciseness: **7** brevity
conclave: **5** synod **6** caucus, powwow **7** council, meeting, reunion **8** assembly, congress **9** gathering
conclude: **2** do **3** end, fix **4** draw, halt, make, quit, rule, stop **5** cease, close, end up, glean, infer, judge, sew up, sum up, think **6** assume, decide, deduce, effect, expire, finish, fulfil, gather, reason, reckon, run out, settle, wind up, wrap up **7** achieve, adjourn, break up, fulfill, imagine, play out, presume, pull off, resolve, suppose, surmise, suspect, work out **8** carry out, complete, dispatch, finalize, pack it in, round off, round out, surcease, theorize **9** culminate, determine, terminate **10** accomplish, bring about, call it a day, consummate, put through, understand
concluded: **3** o'er, set **4** done, fini, over **7** through **8** complete **9** fulfilled
concluding: **4** last **5** final **6** latter **8** eventual, terminal, ultimate **10** definitive
part: **4** coda **5** envoi **6** finale
conclusion: **3** end **4** coda, stop, tail **5** close, finis **6** belief, ending, epilog, finale, finish, payoff, period, result, sequel, upshot, windup, wrap-up **7** closure, finding, opinion, outcome, surmise, thought, verdict **8** curtains, decision, judgment, last word, surcease, terminus **9** agreement, cessation, corollary, deduction, diagnosis, discovery, induction, inference **10** bottom line, completion, conjecture, conviction, denouement, desistance, expiration, hypothesis, resolution, settlement
come to a ~: **6** decide, settle
come to a hasty ~: **4** leap **8** misjudge
draw a ~: **6** deduce, reason
in ~: **4** last, thus **6** lastly **7** finally **9** at the last **10** ultimately
preceder: **4** ergo **5** hence
ultimate ~: **6** end-all
___ conclusion...: **4** So in
conclusions, jumping to: **4** rash **5** hasty **8** careless, heedless, reckless **9** foolhardy, hotheaded, impetuous, imprudent, impulsive, overhasty **10** headstrong, incautious
conclusive: **3** net, ult. **4** firm, last, sure **5** clean, clear, final, valid **6** all-out, cogent **7** assured, certain, decided, flat-out, for sure, obvious, settled, telling **8** absolute, accurate, critical, deciding, decisive, definite, emphatic, forceful, in the bag, official, positive, resolute, resolved, ultimate, verified **9** clinching, effectual, revealing **10** compelling, convincing, definitive, determined, guaranteed, inarguable, unarguable, undeniable, undoubtful, unswerving, unwavering
conclusively: **6** surely
concoct: **3** lay, lie **4** brew, form, plan, plot **5** frame, hatch, weave **6** cook up, create, design, devise, invent, make up **7** dream up, prepare, think up, trump up **8** contrive, engineer, simulate **9** fabricate, formulate, improvise, originate
concocted: **4** fake, made **5** bogus, false **10** fictitious
concoction: **3** mix **4** brew, tale, work **5** blend **7** coinage, mixture **8** creation **9** invention
concomitant: **7** related
concord: **4** pact **5** amity, peace, union, unity **6** accord, treaty, unison **7** compact, entente, harmony, rapport **8** calmness, goodwill, protocol, serenity **9** agreement, congruity, consensus, propriety, unanimity **10** friendship, solidarity
Concord: **3** AMC, car, red **4** auto, city, town, wine **5** grape **8** Plymouth
county: **9** Merrimack
locale: **10** California
relative: *see* wine
river: **9** Merrimack
Concord ___: **6** Sonata
concordance: **6** unison **9** congruity
concordant: **6** united **9** according, congruous, consonant, unanimous **10** harmonious
concordat: **4** pact **6** accord, treaty **7** charter, compact, concord **8** contract, protocol **10** convention
Concorde: **3** car, jet, SST **4** auto, font **5** plane **8** airplane, Chrysler, typeface
home: **6** hangar
take the ~: **3** fly
Concord Hymn
author: Ralph Waldo Emerson
Concordia University
location: **6** Canada **8** Montreal
Concord Sonata
composer: Charles Ives
___ concours: **4** hors
concourse: **4** hall, path, road **5** crowd, foyer, group **6** avenue, street, throng **7** meeting, passage, session **8** assembly, junction, juncture **9** boulevard, gathering, multitude **10** assemblage, collection, concursion, confluence, passageway
concrete: **3** set **4** firm, hard, real **5** rigid, rocky, solid, stony **6** actual, cement, steely, stoney **7** factual, precise **8** accurate, definite, detailed, explicit, indurate, material, palpable, physical, positive, specific, tangible **9** touchable **10** inarguable, unimagined
foundation: **4** slab
lay ~: **4** pave
like fresh ~: **5** unset
make ~: **8** solidify
mixer: **5** paver
set in ~: **9** permanent
smoothed ~: **5** luted
strengthener: **5** rebar
concreteness: **7** reality
concretion: **4** mass
concur: **3** fit, nod **4** gybe, heed, jibe **5** agree, unite, yield **6** accede, accord, assent, comply, league **7** approve, comport, consent, go along **8** coincide **9** acquiesce, cooperate **10** give the nod
with: **4** okay **5** admit, adopt, allow, go for **6** accept, assent **7** approve, include, welcome **8** stand for **9** recognize, sign off on
concurrence: **5** unity **6** accord, assent **8** approval **9** agreement, congruity, proximity **10** solidarity
word of ~: **3** yea **4** amen **5** ditto
words of ~: **5** as am I, me too
concurrent: **6** coeval **9** concerted, confluent **10** coexistent, coexisting, coincident, coinciding, collateral, compatible, consistent, convergent, converging, harmonious, incidental, like-minded, synchronal
concurrently: **8** meantime, together **9** at one time, meanwhile **10** hand in hand
with: **6** during
concurring: **5** at one **6** coeval **9** agreeable, congruent **10** coincident
concursion: **4** hall, path, road **5** crowd, foyer, group, union **6** avenue, street, throng **7** meeting, passage, session **8** assembly, junction, juncture **9** boulevard, concourse, gathering, multitude **10** assemblage, collection, confluence, passageway
concuss: **7** agitate, shake up
concussion: **3** jar **4** blow **5** shock **6** impact **9** buffeting, collision, explosion
Condé: **4** Nast **6** Maryse
condemn: **3** hit, rap **4** damn, defy, doom, hiss **5** blame, blast, chide, curse, decry, knock, sneer **6** outlaw, rail at **7** censure, convict, deplore, dislike, reprove, upbraid **8** denounce, penalize, reproach, sentence **9** castigate, criticize, deprecate, excoriate, fulminate, fustigate, imprecate, proscribe, reprehend **10** come down on, vituperate
condemnation: **3** hit **4** slam **5** blame, knock, odium **6** rebuke, tirade **7** censure **8** sentence
condemned: **6** doomed **7** accurst **8** accursed
condensation: **3** dew **4** mist, rain **5** brief, frost, vapor **6** digest, précis **7** epitome, summary **8** abstract, synopsis

condense: 3 cut 4 edit, trim 5 press, prune, recap, sum up 6 decoct, digest, narrow, recede, reduce, shrink 7 abridge, compact, curtail, distill, shorten, stiffen, thicken, tighten 8 abstract, boil down, compress, contract, solidify 9 capsulize, summarize, synopsize, telescope 10 abbreviate
on a surface: 6 adsorb
condensed: 3 abr., cut 4 firm 5 dense, short, solid, terse, thick 6 cut off, gnomic, packed 7 capsule, compact, concise, crammed, crowded, cut back, cut down, partial, reduced, sketchy, stuffed 8 abridged, cut short, digested, squeezed, succinct 9 compacted, curtailed, shortened 10 abstracted, compressed, hard-packed, summarized, synopsized, unfinished
condensed __: 4 milk
condescend: 5 agree, deign, lower, stoop, yield 6 see fit 9 acquiesce, patronize, vouchsafe 10 talk down to
condescending: 5 lofty 6 lordly, snobby, snooty 8 arrogant, cavalier, snobbish, superior
type: 4 snob 5 snoot
condescendingly, behave: 5 deign
condescension: 5 pride 7 hauteur 9 patronage
condign: 4 fair, just, meet 5 right 6 lawful, proper 7 fitting 8 deserved, rightful, suitable
condiment: 4 NaCl, salt 5 caper, chili, gravy, onion, salsa, sauce, spice 6 catsup, garlic, pepper, relish, sambal, wasabi 7 canella, catchup, cayenne, chutney, ketchup, mustard, paprika, saffron, zedoary 8 capsicum, dressing, turmeric 9 flavoring, rocambole, seasoning
holder: 5 cruet 6 caster
__ con dios: 4 Vaya
condition: 2 if 3 and 4 case, must, term, tone, trim 5 adapt, catch, enure, equip, inure, light, phase, shape, state, train 6 fettle, health, malady, modify, plight, season, status, tone up 7 ailment, break in, build up, disease, fitness, illness, posture, prepare, proviso, qualify, quality, shape up, sharpen, specify 8 accustom, indurate, position, sickness, standing, syndrome 9 brainwash, complaint, determine, essential, exception, exemption, fine print, habituate, infirmity, necessity, provision, requisite, situation, status quo, stipulate, toughen up 10 appearance, limitation, occurrence, reputation, sine qua non, small print
best ~: 4 pink
general ~: 6 repair
get into better ~: 7 restore
good ~: 5 order 6 health, kilter 7 fitness
in good ~: 3 fit 4 hale, neat 5 hardy, right, sound 7 healthy 9 untouched
in poor ~: 5 ratty, unfit 6 beat-up 10 ramshackle
on ~: 2 if 9 providing
out of ~: 4 soft 6 flabby 7 run-down
perfect ~: 4 mint
physical ~: 6 health
suffix: 3 -dom, -ism, -ure 4 -ence, -ness, -ship
__ condition: 4 mint
conditional: 4 iffy 7 subject 8 relative 9 qualified, tentative
word: 3 may
words: 4 if so
conditioned __: 6 reflex
conditioner: 5 rinse
ingredient: 4 aloe
__ conditioner: 3 air 4 soil
conditioning: 7 workout 8 exercise
conditions: 3 ifs 5 terms 7 strings
under different ~: 9 otherwise
condo: 3 apt. 4 flat, home, unit 5 abode, house 6 duplex 7 domicil, habitat, housing, shelter 8 domicile, lodgment, quarters 9 apartment, residence
asset: 4 view
kin: 4 co-op
condole: 6 solace 7 hearten
Condoleezza: 4 Rice
condolence: 6 solace 10 compassion
condominium
see condo
Condominium
author: John D. MacDonald
Condon: 5 Eddie 7 Richard
condonable: 7 tenable 9 excusable 10 defensible, remittable, vindicable
condone: 6 excuse, wink at 7 forgive, let ride 8 overlook, stand for, tolerate 9 put up with
condor: 4 bird, coin 5 money 7 vulture
country: 4 Peru
emulate a ~: 3 fly 4 soar
home: 4 aery, eyry, nest 5 aerie, eyrie
__ condor: 6 Andean
conduce: 4 lead, tend 7 redound 9 gravitate
conducive: 9 accessory, efficient, promotive 10 convenient
be ~ (to): 4 tend
conduct: 3 act, run, way 4 care, form, head, hold, keep, lead, mien, rule, take, wage 5 bring, carry, guide, pilot, steer, usher 6 acquit, behave, charge, convey, convoy, deport, direct, escort, govern, handle, manage, manner, pursue, record, stance 7 bearing, carry on, channel, comport, control, manners, operate, oversee, posture, preside 8 attitude, behavior, carriage, chaperon, demeanor, engineer, guidance, handling, morality, organize, regulate, shepherd, transact, transmit 9 accompany, chaperone, direction, officiate, oversight, prosecute, supervise, transport, treatment 10 administer, deportment, discipline, leadership, management, principles, ride herd on
disorderly ~: 4 riot
oneself: 6 behave, deport
path of virtuous ~: 3 Tao
conductance unit: 3 mho 5 abmho
__ Conduct Medal: 4 Good
conductor: 3 Oue 4 Böhm, Foss, Graf, Muti 5 Adler, Boult, Busch, Engel, Faith, guide, Krips, Masur, Mehta, metal, Morel, Münch, Ozawa, Rudel, Solti, Szell 6 Abbado, Boulez, carman, Dorati, Hillis, Iturbi, Krauss, Kunzel, leader, Levine, Maazel, Mahler, Perlea, Previn, Reiner, Rudolf, Thomas, Walter 7 Beecham, De Waart, Fiedler, Karajan, Kleiber, Kubelik, maestro, Monteux, Ormandy, Salonen, Sargent 8 Ansermet, Caldwell, Damrosch, director, Goossens, Lockhart, Marriner, musician, Smallens, Whiteman, Williams 9 Barenboim, Bernstein, Goldovsky, Klemperer, Leibowitz, Leinsdorf, Mantovani, Markevich, Pelletier, Rodzinski, Rosenthal, Schippers, Steinberg, Stokowski, Toscanini 10 Barbirolli, Comissiona, supervisor 11 Furtwängler, Kostelanetz, Mitropoulos 12 Koussevitzky
American: 5 Engel, Faith 6 Hillis, Kunzel, Levine, Maazel, Previn, Thomas 7 Fiedler 8 Caldwell, Lockhart, Whiteman, Williams 9 Barenboim, Bernstein, Rodzinski, Schippers, Steinberg, Stokowski
Austrian: 4 Böhm, Graf 5 Adler, Krips, Rudel 6 Krauss, Mahler 7 Karajan, Kleiber 9 Leinsdorf
British: 5 Boult 7 Beecham, Sargent 8 Goossens, Marriner 10 Barbirolli
Canadian: 9 Pelletier
cheer: 5 bravo
concern: 5 tempo
cry: 6 aboard 9 all aboard
Czech: 5 Adler 7 Kubelik
Dutch: 7 De Waart
electrical ~: 4 wire 5 shunt 6 dynode
Finnish: 7 Salonen
French: 5 Morel, Münch 6 Boulez 7 Monteux 9 Leibowitz, Rosenthal
German: 4 Foss 5 Busch, Masur 6 Rudolf, Walter 8 Damrosch 9 Klemperer 11 Furtwängler
good ~: 5 metal
Greek: 11 Mitropoulos
heat ~: 4 coil
Hungarian: 5 Solti, Szell 6 Dorati, Reiner 7 Ormandy
Indian: 5 Mehta
information ~: 5 nerve
Italian: 4 Muti 6 Abbado 9 Mantovani, Toscanini
Japanese: 3 Oue 5 Ozawa
places: 5 podia
Romanian: 6 Perlea 10 Comissiona
Russian: 8 Smallens 9 Goldovsky, Markevich 11 Kostelanetz 12 Koussevitzky
Spanish: 6 Iturbi
stick: 5 baton
Swiss: 8 Ansermet
conduit: 4 duct, main, pipe, tube 5 canal, drain, flume, sewer, spout 6 artery, course, gutter 7 channel, culvert, passage 8 aqueduct, pipeline
cone: 5 shape 7 volcano 8 strobile
bearer: 3 fir 4 pine, tree 5 alder, cedar, larch
British ice-cream ~: 6 cornet
half a ~ in geometry: 5 nappe
partner: 3 rod
shape: 6 funnel
traffic ~: 5 pylon
unit: 5 scoop
__ cone: 4 nose, pine, snow
Cone: 5 David 6 hurler 7 pitcher
__ Cone: 5 Honey
__-Cone: 3 Sno
Coneheads (1993 film)
cast: Dan Aykroyd, Michelle Burke, Jane Curtin
cone of __: 7 silence
cone-shaped heater: 4 etna
Conestoga __: 5 wagon
coney: 3 fur 4 fish, pika 5 hyrax 6 dassie, rabbit
conf.: 3 mtg. 4 sess.
confab: 3 mtg. 4 chat, meet, talk, word 6 dialog, huddle, powwow 7 council, meeting 8 assembly, chinfest, chitchat, dialogue 9 tête-à-tête 10 convention, discussion
confabulate: 3 rap, yak, yap 4 chat, talk 6 huddle, parley 7 palaver 8 chitchat, converse 10 chew the fat
confection: 3 jam, mix 4 cake, kiss 5 candy, fudge, halva, lolly, sweet, torte 6 bonbon, halvah, kuchen, pastry 7 halavah, mixture 8 gumdrops 9 jelly roll, preserves, sweetmeat
confectioner: 4 chef
confectioners' __: 5 sugar
confederacy: 4 ring 5 union 6 league 8 alliance
Confederacy: 5 Dixie
opponent: 5 North, Union
Confederacy of Dunces, A
author: John Kennedy Toole
confederate: 4 ally, band 5 party, unify, unite 6 allied, league, united 7 abetter, abettor, comrade, conjoin, partner 8 combined
Confederate
general: 3 Lee 5 Early 6 Stuart 7 Forrest, Jackson 10 Beauregard, Longstreet
soldier: 3 reb 4 gray, grey
state: 3 Ala., Ark., Fla., Tex. 4 Miss., N. Car., S. Car., Tenn. 5 Texas 7 Alabama, Florida, Georgia 8 Arkansas, Virginia 9 Louisiana, Tennessee 11 Mississippi 13 North Carolina, South Carolina
confederated: 6 united
confederation: 4 bloc 5 union, unity 6 league 7 society 8 alliance 9 coalition 10 fraternity
confer: 3 gab 4 give, show, talk, vest 5 award, endow, grant, speak, spend, trust 6 accord, bestow, donate, heap on, huddle, impart, parley, powwow 7 commune, consult, discuss, palaver, present 8 converse 9 bat around, discourse, negotiate, touch base 10 brainstorm, contribute, deliberate

ender: 4 ence
upon: 4 give 5 award
with: 3 see 4 meet
conference: 4 chat 5 forum 6 Big Ten, dialog, huddle, league, Pac-Ten, parley, powwow 7 Big East, council, hearing, meeting, seminar, session 8 assembly, colloquy, congress, dialogue 9 gathering, interview, symposium 10 colloquium, convention, discussion, groupthink, round robin, round table
in ~: 4 busy
questioners: 5 media, press
record: 4 proc.
site: 5 hotel
starter: 5 video
conference __: 4 call, room
__ conference: 4 news 5 press 6 summit
conferral: 5 award
confess: 3 own 4 aver, avow, bare, sing, talk, tell 5 admit, allow, grant, let on, own up 6 affirm, assert, attest, avouch, fess up, reveal 7 concede, confirm, declare, divulge, lay bare, own up to, profess 8 disclose, unburden 9 come clean, recognize
confession: 5 story 6 avowal, exposé 7 peccavi 9 admission, allowance, assenting, assertion, narration, statement, utterance 10 concession, disclosure, divulgence, profession, recitation, revelation, unbosoming
starter: 3 mea
words of ~: 4 I did 6 I did it 7 it was me
confessional
figure: 6 priest
subject: 3 sin
visitor: 4 ruer 6 atoner 8 penitent
Confessions
author: Jean Jacques Rousseau
__ Confessions: 4 True
Confessions of Felix Krull
author: Thomas Mann
Confessions of Nat Turner, The
author: William Styron
confessor: 6 father 8 minister
father ~: 6 priest
__ confessor: 6 father
confetti, make: 5 rip up, shred
confidant: 3 pal 4 ally, chum 5 amigo, buddy, crony 6 cohort, friend 7 adviser, advisor, comrade 8 alter ego, intimate, roommate, sidekick 9 associate, boyfriend, colleague, companion 10 bosom buddy, compatriot
confidante: 10 girlfriend
see also confidant
confide: 4 talk 5 admit 6 impart, reveal 7 breathe, entrust, intrust, whisper 8 disclose, relegate, unburden
in: 5 trust
confidence: 4 cool, dash, ease, grit 5 faith, heart, nerve, pluck, poise, spunk, stock, trust 6 aplomb, belief, credit, daring, mettle, morale 7 bravery, courage, secrecy 8 backbone, boldness, credence, optimism, reliance, security, sureness, tenacity 9 assurance, brashness, certainty, fortitude, hardihood, impudence 10 conviction, dependance, dependence, equanimity, expectancy, resolution
betray a ~: 4 blab, talk, tell
game: 4 hoax, lure, scam 5 bunco, dodge, fraud, sting 6 dupery, hosing, humbug, racket 7 knavery, swindle 8 trickery 9 deception
give ~ to: 6 affirm, assure 7 hearten 8 reassure
have ~ in: 4 rely 5 trust 6 bank on 7 swear by 8 depend on
have ~ (in): 7 believe
in ~: 8 secretly
confidence __: 3 man 4 game
__-confidence: 4 self
Confidence (2003 film)
cast: Edward Burns, Andy Garcia, Paul Giamatti, Rachel Weisz
confident: 4 bold, sure 5 brave 6 secure, upbeat 7 assured, certain, hopeful, valiant 8 cocksure, fearless, intrepid, positive, sanguine, unafraid 9 assertive, collected, convinced, dauntless, expectant, expecting, presuming, satisfied, undaunted, unfearing 10 complacent, counting on, courageous, optimistic, undismayed
be ~: 6 assert
not ~: 3 shy 5 timid
overly ~: 5 cocky
__-confident: 4 self
confidential: 5 inner, privy 6 closet, inside, inward, secret 7 inwards, private 8 backdoor, esoteric, hush-hush, intimate, personal 10 privileged
confidentiality: 7 privacy, secrecy
confidentially: 7 sub rosa 9 between us, entre nous 10 off the cuff
confiding: 5 naive
configuration: 3 cut 4 form 5 setup, shape 6 design, format, sketch 7 contour, outline 9 structure
__ Configuration, The: 5 Ninth
confine: 3 box, pen, tie 4 bind, cage, hold, jail, shut 5 bound, box in, chain, cramp, fence, hedge, hem in, hutch, lay up, limit, pen up, tie up 6 begird, cage in, coop up, detain, encage, encase, fetter, ground, hamper, hinder, hogtie, immure, incase, intern, lock up, remand, shut in, shut up 7 delimit, enclose, impound, inclose, isolate, put away, repress, seclude 8 bottle up, hold back, imprison, restrain, restrict, sentence, straiten, surround 9 constrain
to home: 6 ground
confined: 4 pent, sick 5 bound, close, local, on ice, stied 6 in jail, jailed, laid up, pent-up, shut in 7 captive, limited 8 fenced in, hemmed in 9 bedridden
confinement: 4 jail 5 bonds 6 arrest, bounds, chains, prison 7 control, custody 8 solitude 9 restraint, servitude
confines: 4 area, term 5 limit, orbit, range, scope, sweep 6 bounds, region 7 borders, compass, purview, terrain 8 environs 9 perimeter, periphery, territory 10 boundaries
confining: 5 close, scant 6 narrow 7 cramped, limited 8 limiting 10 compressed, contracted, oppressive, restricted
confirm: 2 OK 4 aver, avow, back, okay, seal, sign, test 5 admit, check, prove, vouch 6 affirm, assure, attest, ensure, look up, ratify, settle, uphold, verify 7 approve, bear out, certify, confess, endorse, indorse, justify, sustain, witness 8 check out, evidence, make sure, sanction, validate, vouch for 9 ascertain, establish, guarantee, recommend, respond to, sign off on 10 strengthen
confirmation: 2 OK 3 nod 4 okay, rite, seal, test 5 check, proof 6 assent, avowal 7 consent, go-ahead 8 approval, evidence, sanction 9 collation, sacrament, testimony
exclamation: 5 uh-huh
confirmed: 3 set 4 true 5 tough, valid 6 actual 8 habitual, verified 9 customary, hard-shell, ingrained 10 accustomed, deep-rooted, deep-seated, entrenched, guaranteed, habituated, inveterate, unimagined
confiscate: 4 grab, take 5 seize 6 assume 7 capture, escheat, impound, preempt 8 arrogate 9 sequester 10 commandeer
confiscation: 7 seizure 8 takeover
confiture: 9 preserves
conflagrant: 5 fiery 6 ablaze, aflame 7 flaming
conflagrate: 4 burn
conflagration: 4 fire, pyre 5 blaze 7 bonfire, burning, flaming, inferno 8 wildfire
conflate: 4 meld 7 combine
conflict: 3 row, war 4 bout, duel, feud, flap, fray, tilt 5 argue, brush, clash, fight, jihad, run-in, scrap, set-to 6 action, battle, breach, combat, differ, fracas, hot war, ruckus, strife, tussle 7 collide, contend, contest, discord, dispute, dissent, diverge, quarrel, quibble, rivalry, warfare 8 argument, bad blood, disagree, disunity, fighting, friction, skirmish, struggle, tug-of-war, variance 9 animosity, collision, encounter, hostility, interfere, lock horns, take issue 10 antagonism, contention, difference, disharmony, dissension, dissonance, engagement, opposition
1910s ~: 3 WWI
1940s ~: 4 WWII
in armed ~: 5 at war
site: 5 arena
__ conflict: 5 armed, class
conflicting: 5 rival 6 at odds, unlike 7 adverse, counter, opposed 8 clashing, contrary, opposing, opposite 10 face-to-face
confluence: 5 union 7 meeting 8 junction, juncture 9 concourse, gathering, multitude 10 assemblage, concursion
confluent: 6 branch, feeder 7 joining, meeting 8 blending, mingling 9 tributary 10 concurrent, synchronal
conform: 2 go 3 fit 4 gybe, heed, jibe, meet, suit, tune 5 adapt, agree, defer, fit in, match, tally 6 adhere, adjust, behave, cohere, comply, listen, orient, square 7 abide by, consent, observe 8 dovetail 9 acclimate, acquiesce, harmonize, play along, reconcile 10 assimilate, correspond, toe the line
don't ~: 6 differ 7 dissent 8 disagree
to: 4 mind, obey 5 act on 6 accept, follow, fulfil 7 abide by, act upon, fulfill, respect, satisfy 9 agree with
(with): 2 go 6 square
conformable: 5 alike 6 docile, proper 7 similar 8 amenable, obedient
conformation: 5 shape 6 nature 7 outline 9 structure
conforming: 4 like 6 in step 7 correct 9 accordant, befitting, congruent
conformist: 5 sheep, toady 6 yes man 7 Babbitt 8 emulator, orthodox
starter: 3 non
conformity: 4 tune 7 harmony, keeping 8 likeness, symmetry 9 agreement, coherence, congruity, obedience, orthodoxy 10 allegiance, compliance, congruence, consonance, exactitude, observance, similarity, submission
confound: 3 vex 4 dash, daze, faze, lose, stun 5 abash, addle, amaze, befog, elude, floor, mix up, put on, rebut, stimy, stump, stymy, throw, upset 6 baffle, bemuse, defeat, foul up, jumble, muddle, puzzle, rattle, stymie 7 becloud, bedevil, confuse, flummox, fluster, mislead, mistake, mortify, mystify, nonplus, perplex, perturb, stagger, stupefy, unhinge, unnerve 8 astonish, befuddle, bewilder, disorder, surprise, throw off, unsettle 9 discomfit, disorient, overwhelm 10 complicate, disconcert
confounded: 4 damn 5 at sea, blank, fazed, sheer 6 darned 7 abashed, at a loss, fuddled, hateful 8 mistaken, unstrung 9 execrable
Confound it!: 4 dang, darn, drat
confrere: 3 pal 4 mate 5 amigo, equal 6 cohort 9 colleague
Confrey: 3 Zez
confront: 4 cope, defy, face, meet 5 brave 6 accost, accuse, breast, oppose, resist, tackle 8 face up to 9 challenge, encounter, pitch into, stand up to, withstand 10 meet head on
confrontation: 5 brush, clash, fight, mix-up, run-in, scene, set-to 6 affray, battle, crisis 7 dispute 8 conflict, defiance, one-on-one, showdown, skirmish 9 encounter
confronter: 5 facer
confronting: 6 across 7 opposed 8 opposing 10 face-to-face
Confucian principle: 3 shu, Tao
Confucius: 4 sage 11 philosopher
confuse: 3 fog 4 daze, faze, lose, stun, trip 5 addle, befog, cloud,

floor, mix up, muddy, put on, snarl, stump, throw **6** baffle, bedaze, bemuse, boggle, flurry, foul up, fuddle, garble, jumble, litter, muddle, outwit, puzzle, rattle **7** becloud, bedevil, disturb, flummox, fluster, mislead, mistake, mystify, nonplus, perplex, perturb, screw up, shuffle, snarl up, stupefy, unhinge **8** befuddle, bewilder, confound, disorder, entangle, outsmart, surprise, throw off, unsettle **9** adumbrate, discomfit, disorient, dumbfound, overwhelm **10** complicate, discompose, disconcert

confused: **4** asea, hazy, lost **5** aback, at sea, dizzy, foggy, messy, muddy, muzzy, spacy, stuck, upset, wooly **6** cloudy, hectic, in a fog, punchy, spacey, woolly **7** abashed, at a loss, chaotic, fuddled, haywire, out of it, puzzled, reeling, shook up **8** anarchic, darkened, mistaken, nebulous, pell-mell, rambling **9** flummoxed, misguided, quizzical, slaphappy, spaced out, unsettled **10** anarchical, disjointed, disorderly, in an uproar, incohesive, indefinite, in disarray, indistinct, out to lunch, topsy-turvy, upside-down
easily ~: **5** ditzy

confusing: **5** vague **6** arcane **7** cryptic, obscure, unclear **8** abstruse, involved, nebulous, puzzling **9** cryptical, difficult, enigmatic, obscuring, upsetting **10** disruptive, disturbing, embroiling, indistinct, misleading, perplexing, unsettling

confusion: **3** ado **4** daze, flap, fuss, maze, mess, riot, stew **5** Babel, chaos, doubt, havoc, mix up, panic, press, snarl, swirl **6** bedlam, bustle, dither, flurry, fracas, hubbub, huddle, jumble, jungle, lather, litter, mayhem, muddle, tangle, trauma, tumult, unrest, uproar **7** anarchy, clutter, ferment, mistake, turmoil **8** disarray, disorder, question, scramble, shambles, upheaval **9** abashment, agitation, amazement, commotion, imbroglio, intricacy, labyrinth, mobocracy, patchwork **10** bemusement, complexity, difficulty, excitement, hodgepodge, hurly-burly, perplexity, puzzlement, turbulence, untidiness, wilderness
exclamation: **3** hey, huh **4** what
state of ~: **3** fog, zoo **4** haze, mess **5** snafu **6** muddle

confute: **5** belie, parry, rebut **6** naysay, negate, oppugn, refute **7** dispute, explode **8** disagree, disprove, overturn **9** disaffirm, discredit **10** contradict, contravene, controvert, disconfirm, invalidate

__ Cong: **4** Viet

conga: **4** drum **5** dance
like a ~ line: **5** snaky
origin: **4** Cuba

conga __: **4** drum, line

Conga (1985 song)
artist: Gloria Estefan

Congaree: **5** river
city on the ~: **8** Columbia

congé: **8** farewell **9** discharge, dismissal

congeal: **3** gel, set **4** cake, clot, jell **6** curdle, freeze, gelate, harden **7** stiffen, thicken, tighten **8** solidify **9** coagulate **10** gelatinize

congealed: **5** stiff, thick **7** jellied

congenial: **4** kind, warm **6** benign, clubby, jovial, kindly, mellow, social **7** addable, affable, cordial **8** amicable, friendly, gracious, likeable, pleasant, pleasing, sociable **9** agreeable, congruous, consonant, convivial, favorable **10** compatible, consistent, delightful, harmonious, like-minded
not ~: **4** cool **5** aloof

__ Congeniality: **4** Miss

congenital: **4** born **6** inborn, innate **9** ancestral, essential, ingrained, inherited, intrinsic **10** connatural, indigenous, indwelling, inveterate, unacquired

conger: **3** eel **4** fish
hunter: **5** eeler
Old English ~: **3** ele
relative: **5** moray **7** lamprey
young ~: **5** elver

congeries: **4** heap, mass, pile **10** assemblage, collection, cumulation

congest: **3** jam **4** clog, fill, glut, pack, plug, stop **5** block, choke, crowd, flood, stuff **6** impede **7** occlude **8** obstruct, overfill, overload **9** overcrowd **10** overburden

congested: **5** close **6** packed **9** chock-full, jam-packed, stoppered, stuffed-up **10** gridlocked, obstructed, overfilled

congestion: **3** jam **4** clog **5** snarl, tie-up **6** logjam **7** squeeze **8** blockage, clogging, crowding, gridlock, overflow **9** impedance, profusion **10** bottleneck, traffic jam
spot: **5** sinus

__ congestion: **5** nasal

conglomerate: **3** mix **4** firm, pool **5** chain, merge, trust **6** cartel, empire, motley, varied **7** combine **9** syndicate

conglomeration: **3** mix **4** heap, mass, pile **5** hoard **6** medley **7** cluster, mixture, variety **8** scramble **9** congeries

Congo: **5** river
author: Michael Crichton
beast: **3** ape
city on the ~: **8** Kinshasa
language: **3** Ebo, Ibo **4** Eboe, Igbo **5** Bantu
mountain: **7** Mitumba
people: **3** Fan **4** Fang, Luba **5** Bemba, Lunda, Mongo, Rundi, Zande **6** Azande, Pangwe **7** Pahouin
region: **5** Shaba
river: **4** Uele **5** Ebola
river to the ~: **6** Ubangi
tributary: **5** Kasai **6** Ubangi
volcano: **10** Nyiragongo

Congo (Democratic Republic)
capital: **8** Kinshasa
city: **4** Boma **5** Uvira **6** Bukavu, Kikwit, Likasi, Matadi **7** Kananga, Kolwezi **8** Kinshasa **9** Kisangani **10** Lumumbashi
formerly: **5** Zaire
locale: **3** Afr. **6** Africa
money: **5** franc
neighbor: **5** Sudan **6** Angola, Rwanda, Uganda, Zambia **7** Burundi **8** Tanzania

Congo (Republic)
capital: **11** Brazzaville
city: **6** Gemena, Kamina, Likasi
locale: **3** Afr. **6** Africa
money: **5** franc
neighbor: **5** Gabon **6** Angola **8** Cameroon

Congo __: **3** dye, eel, red **5** color

Congo, The
author: Vachel Lindsay

congou: **3** tea **8** black tea

congratulate: **4** hail, laud **5** toast **6** praise, salute **7** applaud **8** hand it to

congratulations: **5** kudos **6** praise

congregate: **4** herd, meet **5** bunch, crowd, flock, group, rally, swarm **6** gather, muster **7** bunch up, collect, compile, convene, hang out, round up **8** assemble **9** forgather **10** gang around, rendezvous

congregation: **3** set **4** crew, mass **5** array, crowd, flock, group, laity, swarm **6** confab, muster, parish, throng **7** company, meeting, turnout **8** assembly, audience, ecclesia **9** multitude
home: **4** shul **5** schul **6** church **9** synagogue
leader: **5** rabbi, rebbe
member: **6** layman
response: **4** amen

congress: **4** gild **5** guild, union **6** caucus, league **7** chamber, council, meeting **8** assembly, conclave **9** committee, delegates, gathering **10** conference, convention, delegation

Congress: **5** taxer
body: **5** House **6** Senate
caucus: **4** bloc
employee: **4** aide, page
meeting: **4** sess. **7** session
member: **3** rep., sen. **4** whip **7** senator **8** lawmaker
output: **3** act, law
send back to ~: **4** veto
some ~ spending: **4** pork
vote: **3** aye, nay

Congressional __: **6** Record

Congressional __ of Honor: **5** Medal

Congress of __: **6** Vienna

Congress shall make __...: **5** no law

Congreve, William: **7** British **10** playwright
friend: Pope, Swift, Steele

congruence: **5** unity **6** accord **7** fitness **9** agreement, coherence, congruity **10** conformity, consonance, friendship

congruent: **7** logical, similar **9** agreeable, identical **10** coinciding, compatible, concurring, conforming, consistent, harmonious
be ~: **5** match

congruity: **6** accord, parity **7** concord, fitness, harmony **9** agreement, coherence **10** accordance, conformity, consonance, proportion, similarity

congruous: **4** same **7** regular, similar **8** relevant **9** accordant, according, agreeable, congenial, consonant **10** compatible, concordant, consistent, harmonious

conical: **10** strobilate
dwelling: **4** tipi **5** tepee **6** teepee

conifer: **3** fir **4** pine **5** cedar, cycad, larch **8** longleaf
covering: **4** bark
part: **4** cone **6** needle
stand: **5** taiga

coniferous: **4** piny **5** piney

conjectural: **4** iffy, moot **6** chancy, unsure **8** academic **9** ambiguous, uncertain, unsettled **10** indefinite, unresolved, up for grabs, up in the air

conjecture: **3** say **4** feel, shot, view **5** guess, hunch, infer, opine, think **6** assume, belief, reckon, theory, wonder **7** believe, imagine, opinion, predict, presume, suggest, suppose, surmise, suspect, thought **8** estimate, theorize **9** guesswork, induction, inference, postulate, speculate, suspicion, take a shot, take a stab **10** anticipate, assumption, conclusion, expectancy, hypothesis, impression

conjoin: **3** mix, tie, wed **4** ally, bind, join, link, mesh, yoke **5** hitch, unite **6** append, attach, cohere, couple, hook up, league, team up **7** combine, connect, hitch on **8** coalesce, federate **9** associate, integrate

conjoint: **6** mutual **7** grouped **8** communal **10** collective

conjointly: **4** also **5** as one **8** in unison, mutually, together **10** altogether

conjugal: **6** bridal, wedded **7** marital

conjugality: **8** marriage **9** matrimony

conjugate: **4** link **7** inflect

conjunct: **5** joint **8** combined

conjunction: **3** and, but, for, nor, tho, yet **4** lest, word **5** and/or, union **6** either, hookup, though, unless **7** meeting, neither **8** alliance, although
French: **3** que
German: **3** und
Latin: **3** sed
Spanish: **4** pero

conjuncture: **4** crux **6** crisis, crunch **9** emergency **10** crossroads

conjuration: **3** hex **5** spell

conjurer: **5** Circe, Kirke, witch **6** Hecate, Hekate, Merlin, wizard **7** charmer **8** magician, sorcerer **9** enchanter
prop: **4** wand
word: **5** hocus, pocus **6** presto

conjure up: **5** evoke, raise **6** devise, invoke **7** imagine **8** remember **9** recollect, visualize

conjuring: **5** magic **10** hocus-pocus, necromancy, witchcraft

conk: **3** bop, rap **4** bean, coif, cosh **5** brain, knock, smite **6** hairdo, strike, thwack **8** coiffure
out: **3** die **4** fail, quit **5** sleep

7 fatigue, go kaput 8 collapse, languish 9 break down
(out): 5 peter
Conklin: 6 Osgood 7 Chester
Conkling: 6 Roscoe
Conlan: 5 Jocko
__ con leche: 4 café
Conn: 4 Didi 5 Billy
foe: 5 Louis
U. ~ home: 6 Storrs
Conn.
neighbor: 4 Mass.
school: 5 USCGA, Yale U
zone: 3 EDT, EST
see also Connecticut
Connacht county: 5 Sligo
connate: 7 related 10 indigenous
connatural: 4 born 6 inborn 7 related 9 ancestral, essential, ingrained, inherited, intrinsic 10 congenital, indigenous, indwelling, inveterate, unacquired
Conn, Billy: 5 boxer
milieu: 4 ring
connect: 3 tie, wed 4 ally, bind, bond, join, link, meet, mesh, span, weld, yoke 5 annex, hitch, refer, tie in, tie on, unite 6 adjoin, attach, belong, bridge, cement, cohere, couple, dial in, enlink, fasten, hook on, hook up, plug in, relate 7 bracket, combine, conjoin, hitch on, pertain, tie into 8 go across, interact, neighbor 9 affiliate, attribute, correlate, implicate, interface, interlink
with: 5 tie to 7 contact
connected: 3 kin, one 4 akin 6 allied, joined, looped 7 related 8 coherent, in league, relative 9 bracketed, continual, pertinent, undivided 10 affiliated, applicable, associated, continuous
not ~: 5 apart
Connecticut: 5 river, state
city: 6 Darien, Haddam, Hamden, Mystic, Storrs, Wilton 7 Ansonia, Bristol, Danbury, Meriden, Milford, Norwalk, Norwich, Old Lyme, Shelton 8 East Lyme, Hartford, New Haven, Stamford, Trumbull, Westport 9 East Haven, Fairfield, Greenwich, Naugatuck, Newington, New London, Stratford, Waterbury, West Haven 10 Bridgeport, Manchester, Middletown, New Britain, North Haven, Torrington
city on the ~: 8 Hartford
collegian: 3 Eli 7 Bulldog
conference: 7 Big East
Indian: 6 Pequot
neighbor: 4 Mass. 7 New York
prep school: 6 Choate
school: 4 Yale 5 Yale U
state animal: 10 sperm whale
state bird: 5 robin
state hero: 10 Nathan Hale
state mineral: 6 garnet
state shellfish: 6 oyster
state tree: 8 white oak
Connecticut Yankee, A: 7 musical
composer: Lorenz Hart, Richard Rodgers
Connecticut Yankee..., A
author: Mark Twain
connecting: 6 hookup 9 adjoining, reference 10 juxtaposed
word: 4 conj. 11 conjunction
connection: 3 tie 4 bond, link, lock, node, seam, spot 5 agent, joint, logic, nexus, segue, tie-in, union 6 access, bridge, friend, hookup, linkup, mentor, regard, source 7 bearing, contact, kinship, liaison, sponsor 8 affinity, coupling, junction, ligature, relation, relative, sympathy, vinculum 9 associate, coherence, fastening, go-between, messenger, relevance 10 attachment, comparison, continuity
in ~ with: 4 as to
make a ~: 6 attach, liaise
make a new ~: 5 retap
__ Connection, The: 6 French
connective: 3 and, nor 4 link 8 vinculum
tissue: 6 fascia
connector: 2 or 3 and, nor 6 either 7 neither 10 attachment
connect-the-__: 4 dots
conned, easily: 5 naive
Connee: 7 Boswell
Connelly: 4 Marc 5 Cyril 8 Jennifer
Connelly, Cyril: 6 writer 7 British
Connelly, Jennifer: 7 actress
film: A Beautiful Mind (2001, AA)
Dark City (1998)
Labyrinth (1986)
Pollock (2000)
The Rocketeer (1991)
Waking the Dead (2000)
spouse: Paul Bettany
Connelly, Marc: 6 writer
collaborator: Kaufman
work: Dulcy
The Farmer Takes a Wife
The Green Pastures
Conner: 4 Bart
Connery: 4 Scot, Sean 5 Jason
Connery, Jason: 5 actor
spouse: Mia Sara
Connery, Sean: 3 Sir 5 actor
film: The Anderson Tapes (1972)
The Avengers (1998)
Cuba (1979)
Diamonds Are Forever (1971)
Dr. No (1962)
Entrapment (1999)
Family Business (1989)
Finding Forrester (2000)
A Fine Madness (1966)
First Knight (1995)
From Russia With Love (1963)
Goldfinger (1964)
The Great Train Robbery (1979)
Highlander (1986)
The Hill (1965)
The Hunt for Red October (1990)
Indiana Jones and the Last Crusade (1989)
The League of Extraordinary Gentlemen (2003)
The Longest Day (1962)
The Man Who Would Be King (1975)
Marnie (1964)
Medicine Man (1992)
The Name of the Rose (1986)
Never Say Never Again (1983)
The Next Man (1976)
Rising Sun (1993)
Robin and Marian (1976)
The Rock (1996)
The Russia House (1990)
Thunderball (1965)
Time Bandits (1981)
The Untouchables (1987, AA)
You Only Live Twice (1967)
spouse: Diane Cilento
Connick Jr., Harry: 7 pianist
spouse: Jill Goodacre
Connie: 4 Mack 5 Chung, Hines 7 Britton, Francis, Stevens 8 Corleone, Sellecca
Conniff: 3 Ray
conning __: 5 tower
Conning Tower monogram: 3 FPA
conniption: 3 fit 5 anger, pique 6 cat fit 7 tantrum 8 outburst 9 hysterics
connivance: 9 collusion 10 complicity, conspiracy
connive: 4 plot 6 scheme, wangle 7 collude, finagle, wrangle 8 conspire, intrigue 9 machinate
conniver: 5 cheat 8 swindler
quest: 5 angle
conniving: 3 sly 4 foxy 6 shifty 7 knavish 8 scheming 9 designing
connoisseur: 3 ace, fan 4 buff 5 adept, maven, mavin 6 critic, expert, master 7 devotee, epicure, esthete, gourmet 8 aesthete
Connolly: 6 Walter 7 Maureen
Connolly, Maureen: 7 netster 9 tennis pro
milieu: 5 court
Connors: 4 Mike 5 Chuck, Jimmy
Connors, Jimmy: 7 netster 9 tennis pro
colleague: 4 Ashe 5 Evert
milieu: 5 court
connotation: 4 hint 5 usage 6 nuance 7 meaning 8 overtone
connote: 4 hint, mean 5 imply, spell 6 hint at 7 betoken, purport, signify, suggest 8 indicate, intimate 9 insinuate, predicate, symbolize
Conn Smythe Trophy winner: 3 MVP
connubial: 6 bridal, wedded 7 marital, nuptial
connubiality: 8 marriage 9 matrimony
Conoco
rival: 5 Amoco, Exxon, Mobil, Shell 7 Chevron
Conon: 4 pope 7 pontiff
__ con pollo: 5 arroz
conquer: 3 win, zap 4 beat, best, drub, lick, rout, tame, whip 5 cream, crush, floor, quell, upset, worst 6 defeat, humble, master, obtain, occupy, outwit, reduce, subdue 7 prevail, subvert, succeed, triumph 8 overcome, shut down, suppress, surmount, vanquish 9 checkmate, overpower, overthrow, overwhelm, subjugate
conquerable: 4 weak
conquering __: 4 hero
conqueror: 4 hero 6 captor, master, victor, winner 8 champion 10 subjugator, vanquisher
of 1066: 6 Norman
pride: 6 empire
Conqueror Worm, The
author: Edgar Allan Poe
__ conquers all: 4 love
conquest: 3 win 4 coup, feat, rout, tour 5 score 6 defeat 7 beating, triumph, victory 9 checkmate, landslide, overthrow 10 occupation
__ Conquest: 6 Norman
conquistador
homeland: 6 España
quest: 3 oro
trait: 5 greed
Conquistador
author: Archibald MacLeish
Conrack (1974 film)
cast: Hume Cronyn, Jon Voight
director: Martin Ritt
Conrad: 3 Con 4 Bain 5 Aiken, Janis, Nagel, Veidt 6 Hilton, Joseph, Robert 7 Charles, Michael, Richter, William
Conrad, Joseph: 6 writer 7 British
birthplace: Ukraine
setting: 3 sea
work: Chance
Heart of Darkness
Lord Jim
Nostromo
The Secret Sharer
Typhoon
Under Western Eyes
Victory
Conrad, William: 5 actor
TV: Cannon, Jake and the Fatman
Conrail
colleague: 6 Amtrak
Conried: 4 Hans
Conroy, Pat: 6 writer
work: Beach Music
The Boo
The Great Santini
The Lords of Discipline
My Losing Season
The Prince of Tides
The Water Is Wide
consanguine: 7 related
consanguineous: 3 kin 4 akin
consanguinity: 8 relation
consarn it: 4 dang
conscience: 4 soul 5 qualm 6 ethics, regret 7 scruple 8 scruples, superego 10 inner voice, principles
bad ~: 5 guilt, shame 7 remorse
be stung by ~: 3 rue
in all ~: 9 seriously, sincerely
without ~: 6 amoral
Conscience, Hendrik: 6 writer 7 Belgian
conscience-stricken: 5 sorry 7 ashamed 8 contrite, penitent
conscientious: 5 fussy, moral 7 careful, dutiful, ethical, finicky, mindful, prudent, upright 8 cautious, diligent, exacting, faithful, finiking, finnicky, hustling, punctual, reliable, rigorous, sedulous, studious, thorough 9 assiduous, attentive, judicious, motivated, observant, reputable 10 fastidious, meticulous, particular, scrupulous
conscientiously: 4 hard, well
conscientiousness: 4 care 9 attention
conscious: 4 live 5 alert, alive, awake, aware 6 posted, wilful, with it 7 mindful, studied, willful 8 rational, sensible, sentient, vigilant, watchful 9 attentive, au courant, cognizant, observing, reasoning, sensitive 10 acquainted, calculated, conversant, deliberate,

discerning, perceiving, perceptive, percipient, purposeful, reasonable, reflective, responsive
become ~: 4 wake 5 waken
be ~ of: 3 see 4 know 7 realize
of: 4 on to 6 wise to
__-conscious: 4 half, self 5 class
consciousness: 3 ken 4 life, mind 5 sense 6 memory, regard 7 concern, feeling 9 sensation 10 perception
component: 2 id 3 ego 8 super-ego
lose ~: 5 faint, swoon 7 crumple, pass out 8 black out, keel over
regain ~: 4 stir, wake 5 awake, waken 6 awaken, come to, return, revive 7 recover 10 come around
suspend ~: 5 sleep
conscribe: 5 draft 6 enlist
conscript: 4 levy 5 draft, force 6 enlist, induct 7 impress, recruit, soldier, warrior 8 inductee, shanghai 10 commandeer
conscription: 5 draft
agcy.: 3 SSS
Conseco
competitor: *see* insurance company
consecrate: 4 keep 5 bless, deify, honor 6 anoint, devote, hallow, ordain 7 beatify, hallows 8 canonize, dedicate, enshrine, inshrine, sanctify 9 celebrate
consecrated: 4 holy 5 blest 6 divine, sacred 7 blessed
consecration: 8 blessing, devotion 10 commitment, dedication
consecution: 6 sequel, series, string 8 sequence
consecutive: 5 solid 6 serial 8 straight
consecutively: 6 in a row 7 running
consensus: 5 pulse, unity 6 accord 7 concord, harmony, rapport 9 agreement, unanimity
consent: 2 OK 3 bow, nod 4 bend, okay 5 abide, agree, defer, leave, say OK, yield 6 accede, assent, comply, concur, give in, permit, ratify 7 approve, conform, go-ahead, go along, license, promise 8 approval, blessing, sanction 9 acquiesce, clearance 10 compliance, give the nod, permission
age of ~: 8 majority
give ~: 2 OK 3 let 4 okay 5 agree, allow, grant, yield 6 accord, assent, cave in, comply, concur, permit 7 concede, consent 9 acquiesce, cooperate 10 come around
refuse ~: 4 deny, veto 6 forbid, reject 7 decline 8 disallow, prohibit, turn down 9 interdict, proscribe 10 disapprove
to: 2 OK 4 heed, mind, obey, okay 5 grant, say OK 6 accept, follow, fulfil, listen 7 abide by, fulfill, go along, observe, respect 8 carry out, tolerate
word of ~: 2 ay 3 aye, yes
__ consent: 5 age of 7 implied
consenting: 7 willing 9 agreeable
words: 3 I do
consequence: 4 note, rank 5 state, value, worth 6 cachet, effect, impact, import, moment, payoff, renown, repute, result, sequel, status, upshot, weight 7 fallout, gravity, outcome, product, stature 8 eminence, interest, position, prestige, reaction, standing 9 aftermath, magnitude, outgrowth
as a ~: 4 then, thus 9 therefore
be of ~: 4 rate 6 matter
of ~: 7 serious 9 important
__ consequence: 4 of no
consequences: 5 price 6 impact
alternative: 5 truth
like some ~: 4 dire
suffer ~: 3 pay
without ~: 8 scot-free
consequent: 4 next 5 sound 7 ensuing, logical 8 eventual 9 attendant, deducible, following, inferable, resultant, resulting, secondary 10 reasonable, subsequent, successive
consequential: 3 big 4 high 6 cogent 8 historic, pregnant 9 momentous 10 portentous
consequently: 4 ergo, then, thus 5 hence 9 therefore
conservation: 4 care 6 saving 7 economy 9 salvation
area: 9 sanctuary
practice ~: 5 reuse 7 recycle
__ conservation: 4 land, soil
conservation of __: 4 mass 6 energy, matter
conservative: 4 fogy, safe, Tory 5 chary, fogey, fusty, quiet, right, staid 6 narrow, square 7 diehard, prudent, thrifty 8 cautious, loyalist, moderate, old-guard, orthodox, straight, undaring 9 parochial, provident, temperate 10 economical, reasonable
British ~: 4 Tory
starter: 3 neo 5 ultra
Conservatives: 5 party
wing: 5 right
conservator: 6 keeper, savior 7 curator, saviour 8 guardian
conservatory: 7 nursery 8 hothouse 10 greenhouse
deg.: 4 B.Mus.
graduate: 6 artist 8 musician
conserve: 4 keep, save 5 hoard, lay by, lay up, skimp, stash 6 ration, scrimp 7 cut back, protect, store up 8 maintain, preserve, retrench, sock away 9 economize, safeguard 10 underspend
conserves: 3 jam 5 jelly 9 marmalade, preserves
consider: 4 call, deem, feel, heed, mull, muse, view 5 count, judge, study, think, weigh 6 credit, debate, digest, esteem, look at, look on, ponder, reckon, regard, take up 7 balance, believe, examine, inspect, presume, reflect, sleep on, suppose, surmise, suspect 8 allow for, chew over, cogitate, deal with, envisage, factor in, look upon, meditate, mull over, pore over, ruminate, see about, turn over 9 enter into, reflect on, speculate, think over 10 reckon with, toss around, understand
don't ~: 6 ignore 7 rule out
considerable: 3 big 4 good, huge, lots, much, tidy 5 ample, great, heavy, hefty, large, lotsa, major, mondo 6 divers, gobs of, goodly, lavish, lots of, marked, mighty, myriad, pretty, umteen, untold 7 copious, heaps of, no end of, piles of, profuse, scads of, sizable, umpteen, weighty 8 abundant, handsome, manifold, material, numerous, oodles of, scores of, sizeable, umpsteen 9 bountiful, countless, momentous, quite a few 10 zillions of
considerably: 3 far 4 a lot, much, well 5 extra, no end, quite 6 rather 7 greatly, largely 8 markedly, somewhat, very much 9 like crazy
considerate: 3 big 4 good, kind, nice 5 lofty, sweet 6 gentle, humane, kindly, loving, polite 7 gallant, helpful, mindful, tactful 8 discreet, generous, gracious, mannerly, moderate, obliging, sportive, well-bred 9 regardful 10 bighearted
one: 5 carer
consideration: 3 fee, pay 4 care, heed, sake, tact, wage 5 price, study 6 debate, esteem, factor, reason, regard, review, reward, salary, spring 7 concern, payment, respect, stipend, thought 8 analysis, courtesy, kindness, scrutiny, thinking 9 emolument
in ~ of: 3 for
open for ~: 4 iffy 8 doubtful 9 dependent, provisory, uncertain, undecided, unsettled 10 contingent, indefinite
considered: 6 wilful 7 advised, express, reputed, willful 8 moderate 9 designful, judicious, voluntary 10 deliberate, thought-out, well-chosen
everything ~: 5 in all
__-considered: 3 ill 4 well
considering: 5 since 7 whereas
Consider it __: 4 done
Consider it done: 6 I'm on it
Consider the Lilies
author: Auberon Waugh
Consider Yourself
musical: 6 Oliver!
Considine: 3 Bob, Tim
consign: 3 put 4 give, send, ship 5 leave, route, trust 6 commit, convey, devote 7 address, commend, deliver, entrust, forward, intrust 8 dedicate, delegate, hand over, relegate, transfer, transmit, turn over 9 surrender
consignee: 6 bearer
consignment: 3 lot 4 load 6 ration
consignor: 6 jobber 8 merchant
consist
ender: 3 ent 4 ency
of: 7 contain, include 8 comprise
consistency: 6 parity 7 harmony, texture 9 congruity
consistent: 4 even, firm, like, same 5 level, sound 6 cogent, steady 7 equable, logical, regular, tenable, uniform 8 analytic, coherent, constant, methodic, of a piece, rational, sensible 9 accordant, according, agreeable, congenial, congruent, congruous, consonant, pragmatic, rock solid, unanimous, unfailing, unvarying 10 analytical, compatible, concurrent, dependable, harmonious, homogenous, invariable, legitimate, persistent, reasonable, synchronal, true-to-type, unchanging
be ~: 5 agree 6 cohere
be ~ with: 6 follow
not ~: 6 patchy 7 erratic
consistently: 4 ever 6 always, firmly 8 steadily 9 naturally, regularly, staunchly 10 dependably, faithfully, resolutely
consolation: 4 balm, ease 5 cheer 6 refund, relief, solace, succor 7 comfort 8 sympathy
word: 5 there
words: 5 I know, it's OK
consolation __: 5 prize
Consolato __ Mare: 3 del
console: 4 calm, lift, pity 5 cheer, quiet, shelf, table 6 buck up, solace, soothe, uphold 7 assuage, cheer up, comfort, gladden, hearten, relieve, upraise 8 enspirit, inspirit, reassure 9 encourage, untrouble
console __: 5 piano, table 10 television
consoler's offering: 3 hug
consolidate: 4 band, meld, pool 5 amass, blend, merge, unify, unite 6 cement, center, embody, firm up, harden, imbody, league 7 build up, bunch up, combine, compact, compile, connect, fortify 8 coalesce, solidify 10 synthesize
consolidated: 5 joint, solid, thick 6 united
consolidation: 5 union 6 merger 8 junction, juncture
consommé: 4 soup 5 broth 8 julienne
consonance: 5 unity 7 fitness 9 agreement, coherence, congruity, orthodoxy 10 conformity, congruence, friendship
consonant: 4 akin 6 in step, in sync, in tune, on a par 7 regular, similar, uniform 8 relevant 9 accordant, according, agreeable, analogous, congenial, congruous, unanimous 10 coincident, comparable, compatible, concordant, consistent, harmonious, true to type
be ~: 3 fit
smooth ~: 4 lene
sound: 5 soft c, soft g
voiceless ~: 4 surd
with: 4 like
consonants, like some: 5 velar
consort: 3 mix 4 mate, wife 5 group 6 friend, hobnob, mingle, spouse 7 hang out, husband, partner 8 roommate 9 accompany, associate, companion, pal around, socialize 10 fraternize
with: 3 see 4 date
(with): 3 run 6 take up
__ consort: 5 queen 6 prince
consortium: 4 pool 5 union 6 cartel, league 8 monopoly
conspectus: 7 epitome 8 abstract 10 compendium
conspicuous: 4 bold, open 5 clear, famed, great, noted, plain, showy,

vivid 6 famous, flashy, garish, in view, marked, patent, public, signal 7 blatant, eminent, evident, exposed, glaring, notable, obvious, pointed, salient, splashy, unusual, visible 8 apparent, clear-cut, distinct, explicit, flagrant, manifest, palpable, renowned, singular, striking, unhidden, unveiled 9 arresting, prominent, well-known 10 noticeable, observable, remarkable, unshrouded
be ~: 5 shine 8 stand out
conspiracy: 4 plot, trap 5 cabal 6 racket, scheme 7 cahoots, frame-up 8 intrigue 9 coalition, collusion, treachery 10 complicity, connivance, disloyalty
conspiracy __: 6 theory
conspiracy of __: 7 silence
__ Conspiracy, The: 4 Open 5 Wilby
Conspiracy Theory (1997 film)
cast: Mel Gibson, Julia Roberts, Patrick Stewart
director: Richard Donner
conspiratorial: 6 secret 7 furtive
conspirators: 4 ring 5 cabal
conspire: 4 plan, plot 6 scheme, wangle 7 collude, connive 8 intrigue, maneuver 9 machinate
constable: 3 cop 6 lawman 7 officer 9 policeman
Constable, John: 6 artist 7 painter
homeland: 7 England
constabulary: 6 police
Constance: 4 lake 5 Moore 6 Towers 7 Bennett, Collier 8 Cummings
locale: 7 Austria, Germany 11 Switzerland
constancy: 6 fixity 7 loyalty 8 devotion, fidelity, firmness 9 adherence, certainty, diligence, eagerness, endurance, fixedness, fortitude, frequency, integrity, stability 10 allegiance, attachment, continuity, doggedness, permanence, perpetuity, regularity, resolution, steadiness, trustiness, uniformity
constant: 3 set 4 even, fast, firm, same, sure, true 5 fixed, level, loyal, paced, solid, usual 6 ardent, rooted, stable, static, steady, trusty 7 abiding, chronic, devoted, dutiful, endless, equable, lasting, nonstop, regular, settled, staunch, undying, uniform 8 definite, enduring, faithful, habitual, ironclad, lifelong, reliable, resolute, true-blue, unbroken, unending, untiring, unwaning 9 allegiant, ceaseless, chronical, continual, deathless, dedicated, immutable, incessant, parameter, perennial, permanent, perpetual, steadfast, sustained, unabating, unfailing, unvarying 10 changeless, consistent, continuous, dependable, invariable, inveterate, inviolable, monotonous, persistent, relentless, unchanging, unflagging, unwavering
Constant __, The: 4 Wife 5 Nymph 7 Husband
Constant Craving (1992 song)
artist: k.d. lang
Constant Gardener, The (2005 film)
cast: Ralph Fiennes, Rachel Weisz
Constantin: 8 Brancusi
Constantine: 4 city, pope, town 5 saint 6 Cavafy 7 Michael, pontiff
locale: 7 Algeria
mother: 6 Helena
wife: 6 Fausta
Constantine (2005 film)
cast: Shia LaBeouf, Keanu Reaves, Rachel Weisz
Constantinople: 4 port 8 Istanbul
locale: 6 Turkey
constantly: 3 e'er 4 ever 6 always 9 gradually 10 unendingly
Constant Wife, The
author: W. Somerset Maugham
constellation: 7 pattern
Altair's ~: 6 Aquila
altar: 3 Ara
Arcturus' ~: 6 Boötes
belted ~: 5 Orion
Betelgeuse's ~: 5 Orion
brightest star in a ~: 5 alpha 6 lucida
combining form: 5 sider- 6 sidero-
Deneb's ~: 6 Cygnus
near Cepheus: 5 Draco
near Hercules: 4 Lyra
near Hydra: 3 Leo
near Indus: 4 Grus
near Serpens: 5 Libra
near the Big Dipper: 5 Draco
near Virgo: 5 Libra 6 Corvus
Regulus' ~: 3 Leo
Rigel's ~: 5 Orion
Ring Nebula ~: 4 Lyra
second brightest star in a ~: 4 beta
Southern ~: 3 Ara 4 Argo, Grus, Vela 5 Mensa 6 Octans
Spica's ~: 5 Virgo
unit: 4 star
Vega's ~: 4 Lyra
constellations:
Andromeda (Chained Lady)
Antlia (Air Pump)
Apus (Bird of Paradise)
Aquarius (Water Bearer)
Aquila (Eagle)
Ara (Altar)
Aries (Ram)
Auriga (Charioteer)
Boötes (Herdsman)
Caelum (Chisel)
Camelopardalis (Giraffe)
Cancer (Crab)
Canes Venatici (Hunting Dogs)
Canis Major (Large Dog)
Canis Minor (Small Dog)
Capricorn (Goat)
Carina (Keel)
Cassiopeia (Seated Lady)
Centaurus (Centaur)
Cepheus (the King)
Cetus (Whale)
Chamaeleon (Chameleon)
Circinus (Pair of Compasses)
Columba (Dove)
Coma Berenices (Berenice's Hair)
Corona Australis (Southern Crown)
Corona Borealis (Northern Crown)
Corvus (Crow)
Crater (Cup)
Crux (Southern Cross)
Cygnus (Swan)
Delphinus (Dolphin)
Dorado (Swordfish)
Draco (Dragon)
Equuleus (Colt)
Eridanus (a river)
Fornax (Furnace)
Gemini (Twins)
Grus (Crane)
Hercules
Horologium (Clock)
Hydra (Water Monster)
Hydrus (Water Snake)
Indus (Indian)
Lacerta (Lizard)
Leo (Lion)
Lepus (Hare)
Libra (Balance)
Lupus (Wolf)
Lynx
Lyra (Lyre)
Mensa (Table)
Microscopium (Microscope)
Monoceros (Unicorn)
Musca (Fly)
Norma (T-square)
Octans (Octant)
Ophiuchus (Serpent Holder)
Orion (the Hunter)
Pavo (Peacock)
Pegasus (Winged Horse)
Perseus
Phoenix
Pictor (Painter's Easel)
Pisces (Fish)
Piscis Austinus (Southern Fish)
Puppis (Stern)
Pyxis (Mariner's Compass)
Reticulum (Net)
Sagitta (Arrow)
Sagittarius (Archer)
Scorpio (Scorpion)
Sculptor
Scutum (Shield)
Sextans (Sextant)
Taurus (Bull)
Telescopium (Telescope)
Triangulum Australe (Southern Triangle)
Triangulum (Triangle)
Tucana (Toucan)
Ursa Major (Large Bear)
Ursa Minor (Small Bear)
Vela (Sails)
Virgo (Virgin)
Volans (Flying Fish)
Vulpecula (Little Fox)
consternate: 5 alarm, appal, daunt 6 appall 7 stagger, startle
consternation: 4 care, fear 5 alarm, panic, shock 6 dismay, terror 8 surprise 9 abashment
cause ~: 6 appall, dismay
constituency: 4 ward 6 people, public, voters 7 faction 8 district, electors, precinct
constituent: 4 link, part, unit 5 voter 6 factor, member 7 citizen, element, feature, portion 8 fraction, material
constituents: 6 voters 8 contents 10 electorate
constitute: 4 form, make 5 draft, found, frame, set up 6 create, depute, embody, imbody, make up, ordain 7 appoint, empower, include 8 comprise, deputize, legalize, validate 9 aggregate, authorize, construct, designate, establish, integrate, legislate 10 commission, complement
constitution: 3 law 4 code, form 5 build, frame, shape 6 design, fabric, health, nature, temper 7 charter, content 8 physique, vitality
add-on: 5 bylaw 9 amendment
Constitution: 4 boat, ship 6 avenue
articles in the ~: 3 VII 5 seven
guarantee: 5 right
__ Constitution: 3 USS
constitutional: 4 hike, turn, walk 5 jaunt, legal, licit 6 innate, lawful, ramble, stroll 7 organic, radical, saunter, workout 8 exercise, inherent
constitutional __: 8 monarchy
Constitution Hall org.: 3 DAR
Constitution State: 11 Connecticut
Constitution State coll.: 5 U Conn
constitutive: 5 vital
constrain: 3 bar 4 bind, curb, make 5 check, cramp, force, hem in, impel, limit, stint 6 coerce, compel, hogtie, keep in, oblige, rein in, stifle 7 abstain, confine, control, harness, inhibit, require, trammel 8 bottle up, hold back, moderate, pressure, prohibit, restrain 9 constrict 10 intimidate, keep a lid on, keep in line, pressurize
constrained: 5 bound, sober, stiff 6 pent-up, uneasy 7 limited, stilted
constraint: 3 bar 4 curb, rein 5 brake, check, cramp, leash, stint 6 arrest, damper 7 reserve, shyness, slavery, trammel 8 timidity 9 captivity, detention, deterrent, hindrance, impulsion, necessity, restraint, timidness 10 compulsion, diffidence, imposition, inhibition, limitation, repression
constrict: 4 bind, curb 5 cramp, limit 6 corset, shrink, tauten 7 inhibit, squeeze, tighten 8 compress, restrict 9 attenuate, constrain
constricted: 5 tight 6 narrow
constriction: 7 tension
constrictor: 3 boa 5 noose, snake
construct: 4 base, form, make, mold, rear 5 build, erect, forge, frame, put up, raise, set up, shape 6 create, devise 7 compose, fashion, prepare, produce, work out 8 assemble, engineer 9 establish, fabricate, formulate, hammer out 10 constitute
in haste: 5 rig up
construction: 3 cut 4 form 5 frame, shape 7 edifice, reading 8 assembly, building
area: 3 lot 4 site
detail: 4 spec
junction: 4 weld
machine: 5 crane, dozer, hoist 6 loader 9 bulldozer
material: 4 iron, wood 5 steel 6 cement
piece: 4 H-bar, I-bar, L-bar, stud, T-bar, Z-bar 5 I-beam, joist, rebar, strut, T-beam
site tray: 3 hod
toy: 4 Lego
construction __: 4 loan, site 5 paper
constructive: 6 aidful, benign, useful 7 helpful 8 positive, remedial, salu-

tary, valuable **9** effectual, favorable, practical **10** productive, worthwhile
constructor: 5 maker **6** framer **9** artificer
construe: 4 read **5** infer, solve **6** deduce, define **7** analyze, explain **8** decipher, spell out **9** interpret, translate
Consuelo
author: George Sand
consuetude: 4 wont
consul: 5 envoy **6** legate **7** attaché **8** delegate, diplomat, emissary, minister **10** ambassador
consul __: 7 general
consulate: 7 embassy
consult: 3 ask, see **4** talk **5** refer **6** call in, confer, huddle, look to, parlay, powwow, talk to, turn to **7** speak to **9** negotiate **10** brainstorm
with: 6 advise **8** approach
consultant: 7 adviser, advisor
offering: 6 advice
consultation: 4 talk, word **6** indaba, powwow **7** hearing, meeting
consume: 3 eat, use **4** bolt, down, gulp, ruin, wolf **5** drain, drink, eat up, empty, erode, gorge, put in, scarf, spend, use up **6** absorb, devour, digest, engulf, expend, feed on, finish, guzzle, imbibe, ingest, ingulf, inhale, nosh on, obsess, prey on, ravage **7** corrode, deplete, destroy, engross, exhaust, feast on, partake, play out, put away, scarf up, smolder, snack on, swallow, utilize, wear out **8** chow down, gobble up, nibble on, smoulder, squander, toss down **9** devastate, dissipate, go through, polish off, preoccupy, scarf down **10** lay waste to, monopolize, run through
don't ~: 4 fast **6** starve
safe to ~: 6 edible
consumed: 4 lost **5** spent, tired **8** immersed, obsessed **9** possessed
was ~: 4 went
consumer: 4 user **5** buyer, eater **6** emptor, vendee **7** end user, shopper **8** customer **9** purchaser
affairs topic: 5 fraud
concern: 5 price, value
conspicuous ~: 5 yuppy **6** yuppie
crusader: 5 Nader
goods: 4 mdse.
lure: 2 ad **4** sale **6** rebate
protection org.: 3 BBB, FDA, FTC
consumer __ index: 5 price
Consumer Reports: 3 mag **8** magazine
employee: 5 rater **6** tester
lack: 3 ads
consuming: 7 erosive **9** absorbing, corrosive **10** engrossing
__-consuming: 4 time
consummate: 3 cap, end **4** arch, best, rank **5** close, crown, first, great, ideal, sew up, stark, total, utter **6** clinch, effect, finish, fulfil, superb, wind up, wrap up **7** achieve, classic, execute, fulfill, perfect, realize, supreme **8** absolute, carry out, complete, conclude, crowning, finalize, flawless, outright, peerless, profound, put to bed, thorough, ultimate **9** downright, exquisite, faultless, just right, masterful, matchless, out-and-out, perfected, polish off, practiced, terminate, unrivaled, virtuosic **10** accomplish, button down, complement, effectuate, impeccable, inimitable, preeminent, take care of, unrivalled
consummated: 4 done **8** complete
consummately: 4 to a T **9** perfectly
consummation: 3 end **4** goal **5** crest **6** ending, result, wrap-up **8** fruition
consumption: 3 use **6** eating, intake **7** burning **8** drinking
unfit for ~: 4 rank **5** moldy **6** rancid, rotten **8** inedible
cont.: 3 Afr., Eur. **4** Aust. **5** N. Amer., S. Amer.
Contac
alternative: *see* cold remedy
contact: 3 get **4** call, lens, link, meet, talk **5** get to, phone, reach, touch **6** impact, liaise, talk to **7** liaison, meeting, speak to, write to **8** approach, touching **9** check with, collision, telephone, touch base **10** connection, contiguity, get a hold of
be in ~ with: 4 abut **6** adjoin
brief ~: 5 brush
via pager: 4 beep
contact __: 4 lens, mine **5** paper, patch, print, sheet, sport **6** binary, cement, flight, flying **7** printer, process
Contact: 4 film **5** novel
author: Carl Sagan
cast: Jodie Foster, John Hurt, Matthew McConaughey, Tom Skerritt, James Woods
director: Robert Zemeckis
contacts
alternative: 5 specs **7** glasses
big name in ~: 4 Lomb **6** Bausch
brand: 4 ReNu
candidate: 5 myope
contact: 6 cornea
like some ~: 4 soft
contagion: 6 plague **7** disease **9** infection, pollution **10** corruption, pestilence
Contagion
author: Robin Cook
contagious: 5 viral **8** catching **9** epizootic, pestilent, poisonous, spreading **10** impartible, infectious, inoculable
contain: 4 curb, have, hold, take **5** cover, house **6** begird, embody, govern, hogtie, hold in, imbody, record, rein in, stifle, take in **7** add up to, control, embrace, enclose, harness, inclose, include, involve, repress, subsume **8** bottle up, comprise, hold back, restrain, restrict, suppress **9** consist of, encompass **10** keep a lid on
__-contained: 4 self
container: 3 bag, bin, box, can, cup, hod, jar, jug, keg, kit, mug, pan, pod, pot, sac, tin, tub, tun, urn, vat **4** bowl, case, cask, dish, ewer, flat, mold, pail, sack, skin, tank, tray, tube, vase, vial **5** ampul, basin, chest, churn, crate, crock, flash, flask, hutch, phial, pouch, purse, shell, stein, trunk **6** ampule, barrel, basket, beaker, bottle, bucket, carafe, carton, cradle, firkin, flacon, flagon, hamper, holder, hopper, kettle, magnum, packet, vessel **7** amphora, ampoule, caisson, caldron, canteen, capsule, chamber, cistern, humidor, package, scuttle **8** canister, cauldron, crucible, envelope **9** portfolio, reliquary, reservoir **10** receptacle, repository
flat ~: 4 tray **5** plate **7** platter
container __: 3 car **4** ship **5** board
containing: 4 with **9** including
combining form: 6 -ferous
nothing: 4 bare, void **5** empty **6** barren, hollow, vacant **7** vacated **9** evacuated
containment: 7 control
contaminant: 3 PCB **8** impurity
contaminate: 3 mar **4** foul, soil **5** dirty, spoil, stain, sully, taint **6** befoul, damage, debase, defile, infect, poison, rancid, smudge **7** begrime, blacken, corrupt, pollute, tarnish, vitiate **8** besmirch
contaminated: 4 foul **5** dirty, grimy, sooty **6** filthy, grubby, grungy, impure **7** corrupt, unclean **8** maculate, slovenly **10** unsanitary
contamination: 5 filth **6** damage **8** impurity **9** pollution **10** defilement
conte: 5 fable
Conte: 7 Richard
contemn: 4 hate, snub, twit **5** scorn, sneer, spurn **6** demean, deride, slight **7** censure, despise, disdain, dislike, sniff at **9** disregard **10** look down on, take to task
contemplate: 3 eye, see **4** mull, muse, plan, view **5** study, think, weigh **6** behold, digest, expect, gaze at, intend, look at, ponder, reason, regard, survey **7** foresee, inspect, observe, propose, reflect, stare at **8** aspire to, chew over, cogitate, consider, envisage, envision, meditate, mull over, muse over, ruminate, turn over **9** speculate **10** reckon with
contemplation: 4 look **5** study **6** musing, revery **7** reverie, thought **8** planning
object of ~: 5 navel
contemplative: 4 wise **6** intent **7** pensive, wistful **8** studious, thinking **9** religious
contempo: 6 modern, recent
contemporaneous: 6 coeval **7** present **10** coexistent
contemporary: 3 new, now **4** peer **5** in use **6** coeval, extant, living, modern, modish, recent, trendy **7** abreast, à la mode, current, in vogue, present, topical **8** up-to-date **10** coexistent
contempt: 3 dig **4** barb, gibe, jibe, sass, slam, slap, slur, snub **5** abuse, libel, odium, scorn, shame, spite, taunt **6** hatred, infamy, malice, nausea, rebuff, slight **7** affront, calumny, catcall, disdain, hauteur, mockery, obloquy, offense, put-down, sarcasm, slander **8** aversion, defiance, derision, disfavor, dishonor, distaste, ignominy, loathing, ridicule **9** antipathy, aspersion, contumely, disregard, disrepute, insolence **10** defamation, disrespect, opprobrium
exclamation: 3 aha, bah, boo, boy, huh, pah, tsk, tut, yah **4** as if, pfui, phoo, pish, pooh, posh, tush **5** faugh, ho-hum, humph, pshaw, shame **6** phooey, tsk tsk, tut-tut **8** for shame
express ~: 4 hiss, pooh **5** sniff, snort
feel ~ for: 4 hate, shun **5** abhor, scorn, spurn **6** detest, loathe, reject, revile, slight **7** despise, disdain, dislike, sneer at **8** execrate **9** abominate **10** look down on
treat with ~: 3 dis **4** jeer, mock **5** flout, scoff, spurn **6** deride, slight
contemptible: 3 bad, low **4** base, mean, vile **5** cheap, crass, dirty, lousy, mangy, nasty, seamy, slimy, sorry **6** abject, little, mangey, odious, paltry, ragged, rotten, shabby, sneaky, sordid, wicked **7** hateful, ignoble, knavish, lowdown, pitiful **8** baseborn, shameful, stinking, unworthy, wretched **9** miserable, repellant, repellent
one: 3 cad, cur **4** heel, toad, worm **5** skunk, swine, twerp, twirp **6** insect
contemptuous: 5 proud **6** cheeky **7** cynical, haughty **8** arrogant, cavalier, derisive, insolent, sardonic, scornful **9** sarcastic, vitriolic
contend: 3 run, vie, war **4** aver, avow, cope, feud, play, tilt **5** argue, claim, clash, fight, rival **6** affirm, allege, assert, battle, charge, insist, reason, refute, resist, strive, submit **7** compete, face off, grapple, purport, quarrel, vie with, wrestle **8** conflict, maintain, struggle **9** have words, lock horns, square off
(for): 2 go **5** quest **8** campaign
with: 4 face **5** rival **6** take on
contender: 4 vier **5** rival **6** player **7** fighter, nominee **9** candidate, disputant, job-hunter **10** antagonist, competitor, contestant
__ contendere: 4 nolo
content: 4 glad, size, smug, text **5** happy, value **6** at ease, matter, please, serene **7** appease, at peace, gratify, meaning, pleased, satisfy, suffice, willing **8** relieved, thankful **9** fulfilled, gratified, satisfied, substance
full of ~: 5 meaty, pithy
not ~: 5 itchy **8** restless
rich in ~: 5 meaty
starter: 3 dis, mal
substantial ~: 4 meat
contented: 4 easy, smug **5** happy, quiet **8** cheerful **9** gratified, satisfied **10** complacent
sound: 2 ah **3** aah, pur **4** purr
contention: 3 war **4** feud, view **5** claim, fight, issue, posit, set-to,

stand 6 battle, belief, combat, debate, static, strife, thesis 7 discord, dispute, dissent, feuding, opinion, quarrel, rivalry, wrangle 8 argument, conflict, disunity, friction, question, squabble, struggle 9 assertion, dialectic, discord, encounter, hostility, wrangling 10 allegation, antagonism, deposition, difference, discussion, disharmony, dissension, dissidence, dissonance, hypothesis, litigation, opposition, profession
bone of ~: 5 issue 8 argument
still in ~: 5 alive
contentious: 4 cold, cool, mean 5 aloof, nasty, surly, testy 6 chilly, ornery, remote 7 glacial, hateful, hostile, warlike 8 contrary, factious, fighting, inimical, militant, spiteful 9 bellicose, litigious, malicious, truculent, withdrawn 10 malevolent, pugnacious
be ~: 5 argue 6 bicker
one: 6 arguer
contentment: 4 ease 5 bliss, peace 7 comfort, rapture, welfare 8 felicity, gladness, pleasure, serenity
contents: 4 list, load, text 5 cargo 6 topics, volume 7 details, filling, freight, innards, insides 8 chapters, subjects 9 substance
contest: 3 row, sue, vie 4 bout, buck, duel, fray, game, meet, race, tilt 5 argue, brawl, event, fight, match, run-in, scrap, set-to, sport, trial 6 affray, attack, battle, combat, debate, defend, oppose, rumble, strife 7 dispute, lawsuit, quarrel, rivalry, wrangle 8 conflict, litigate, long jump, object to, question, skirmish, struggle, tug-of-war 9 athletics, challenge, encounter, fight over, prosecute 10 engagement, make a stand, tournament
ancient ~: 4 agon
faked ~: 5 setup
no ~: 9 hands down
orator ~: 8 polemics
qualifying ~: 4 heat
submission: 5 entry
venue: 5 arena, track
contestable: 4 moot
contestant: 4 side, vier 6 player 7 battler, entrant, fighter, hopeful, nominee, warrior 8 opponent 9 adversary, candidate, combatant, contender, contester, dark horse, disputant 10 antagonist, challenger, competitor
become a ~: 5 enter
rank a ~: 4 seed
__ contested: 5 hotly
contest, no: 4 plea
context: 4 case 5 light 7 meaning, setting
take out of ~: 8 misquote
Conti: 3 Tom 4 Bill
Conti, Bill
song: Gonna Fly Now (1977)
contiguity: 7 abuttal, contact, joining, meeting 8 abutment, abutting, touching 9 adjacence, adjacency, proximity
contiguous: 4 near 5 close 6 nearby 8 abutting, adjacent, next door, touching 9 adjoining, bordering, immediate, in contact 10 approximal, contactual, convenient, juxtaposed, near-at-hand
be ~: 4 abut 8 neighbor
to: 4 near 6 beside
continence: 9 austerity 10 abstinence
continent: 3 Afr., Eur. 4 Asia, land, pure 5 N. Amer., S. Amer., sober 6 Africa, chaste, Europe 8 celibate 9 abstinent, Antartica, Australia, inhibited, temperate, unextreme 10 abstemious, Antarctica, restrained
continental
alliance: 3 OAS, OAU
breakfast item: 3 tea 4 milk 5 bagel, donut 6 banana, coffee, danish 8 doughnut
connector: 7 isthmus
divider: 3 sea 5 ocean, Urals
drifter: 5 plate
prefix: 3 Eur- 4 Afro-, Euro- 5 trans
continental __: 5 drift, shelf 6 divide
Continental: 3 car 4 auto, Linc 7 airline, Lincoln 10 automobile
Airlines Arena team: 4 Nets
allies: 6 France, French
alternative: *see* airline, U.S.
former competitor: 5 USAir
to a Redcoat: 3 foe 5 enemy
see also U.S.
Continental __: 6 Divide
Continental Congress
meeting site: 4 York
Continental Divide (1981 film)
cast: John Belushi, Blair Brown
Continental Op, The
author: Dashiell Hammett
continental walk: 5 dance
Continent, The: 6 Europe
contingencies: 3 ifs
contingency: 4 case 5 event 6 chance 9 liability
provision: 5 plan B
contingency __: 3 fee 4 fund, plan
contingent: 4 body, team 5 corps, fluky, group, quota, troop 6 chance, flukey, likely, random 7 brigade, subject 8 not final, possible, probable, relative 9 battalion, dependant, dependent, disciples, haphazard, qualified, secondary, tentative, uncertain 10 accidental, delegation, deputation, detachment, fortuitous, incidental, unexpected, unforeseen
be ~: 4 hang, rest 5 hinge, pivot 6 depend
on: 9 providing, subject to
continual: 6 serial, steady 7 chronic, endless, eternal, lasting, regular, running 8 constant, enduring, frequent, habitual, unbroken, unending, untiring, unwaning 9 ceaseless, chronical, connected, incessant, perennial, permanent, perpetual, recurrent, unabating, unceasing, unfailing, unvarying 10 persistent, persisting, relentless, repetitive, unchanging, unflagging
continually: 4 ever 6 always 7 on and on 8 evermore
continuance: 4 life, time 6 length 8 lifetime, sequence
continuation: 6 sequel
continue: 2 go 3 run 4 go on, hold, last, live, stay 5 abide, exist, recur, renew, run on, segue, stand 6 endure, extend, hang in, hold on, keep at, keep on, keep up, linger, live on, pick up, pursue, push on, remain, reopen, resume, stream, take up 7 advance, carry on, draw out, persist, press on, proceed, prolong, restart, stick to, subsist, survive, sustain 8 go on with, lengthen, maintain, preserve, progress, protract, return to 9 go forward, persevere 10 forge ahead, perpetuate, recommence
to: 5 reach
unable to ~: 8 overcome
uninterrupted: 3 run, yak, yap 4 talk 5 run on 6 rattle 7 maunder
continued: 5 ran on, solid 6 serial 8 untiring 9 recurrent
continuing: 6 living, serial 7 abiding, lasting, ongoing, pending, undying 8 lifelong, long-term, residual, standing, untiring 9 lingering, perennial 10 inveterate
continuity: 4 flow 5 chain, train 6 course, series 7 linking, stamina 8 cohesion, duration, monotony, sequence, survival 9 coherence, constancy, endurance, extension, fixedness, stability 10 connection, durability, perpetuity, succession
continuous: 5 level, solid 6 direct, entire, looped, smooth, steady 7 endless, nonstop, ongoing, running 8 constant, straight, unbroken, unending 9 ceaseless, connected, incessant, insistent, perpetual, prolonged, unceasing, undivided, unfailing
change: 4 flux
flow: 6 stream
continuously: 5 on end 7 non-stop
continuum: 5 scale 10 perpetuity
contort: 4 bend, curl, warp 5 gnarl, screw, twist, wring 6 buckle, deform, mangle, wrench, writhe 8 misshape 9 convolute
contorted: 3 wry 4 awry 6 atwist, skewed 7 crooked 9 malformed
expression: 5 scowl, sneer
contortion: 7 grimace 9 asymmetry, deformity 10 distortion
contortionist, like a: 5 lithe 6 limber
contour: 4 edge, form, line 5 curve, shape 6 figure 7 outline, profile, terrain 8 side view 9 lineament, sculpture 10 silhouette, topography
contour __: 3 map 4 line
Contour: 3 car 4 auto, Ford
Contours
song: Do You Love Me (1962)
contra: 4 anti 6 versus 7 against, reverse 8 opposite
per ~: 7 however
Contra __, CA: 5 Costa
__-Contra: 4 Iran
contraband: 7 illegal, illicit 9 forbidden, moonshine, smuggling 10 bootlegged, prohibited, proscribed, rum-running
run ~: 7 smuggle
contrabass: 4 wind 6 string 10 instrument
contrabassoon: 4 wind 10 instrument
cousin: 4 oboe
contract: 3 ebb, get, job 4 bond, deal, pact, sell, tuck, wane, work 5 agree, catch, incur, paper 6 engage, lessen, narrow, pledge, policy, pucker, recede, reduce, shrink, take in, treaty 7 abridge, agree to, bargain, charter, compact, curtail, decline, deflate, develop, dwindle, fall off, promise, reserve, shorten, shrivel, squeeze, subside, tighten 8 compress, condense, covenant, decrease, diminish, marriage, warranty 9 agreement, attenuate, concordat, epitomize, guarantee, indenture, liability, negotiate, stipulate, undertake 10 abbreviate, commitment, engagement, obligation, settlement
add-on: 5 rider
athlete's ~ clause: 5 no cut
detail: 4 spec, term 6 clause
for: 3 buy 4 hire 5 order 6 employ 7 charter
issue: 5 hours, raise 6 rights 8 benefits
negotiator: 3 rep 5 agent
signer: 5 inker, party
term: 6 hereby, herein
try for a ~: 3 bid 5 bid on
contract __: 4 bond 5 labor 6 bridge
__ contract: 5 no-bid, no-cut 6 social 7 no-trade
contract bridge: 4 game 8 card game
contracted: 5 bound, scant, stiff, tight 6 narrow 9 confining
contraction: 3 tic 5 spasm 7 elision, falloff 8 decrease
common ~: 3 he'd, I'll, it'd, it's, I've 4 can't, don't, he'll, isn't, she'd, we'll, won't 5 aren't, didn't, hasn't, she'll, they'd, wasn't 6 doesn't, mustn't, they'll 7 couldn't, wouldn't 8 shouldn't
Dixie ~: 4 y'all
nonstandard ~: 4 ain't
old-style ~: 5 mayn't, shan't
poetic: 3 e'en, e'er, o'er, 'tis 4 ne'er, 'twas 5 neath, 'twere
contractor: 5 party 7 builder
at times: 5 paver, tiler
contractual: 5 legal
contradict: 4 defy, deny 5 belie, cross, rebut 6 impugn, naysay, negate, oppose, recant, refute 7 confute, dispute, gainsay 8 disagree, disprove 9 challenge, disaffirm, discredit, repudiate 10 contravene, counteract, prove wrong
contradiction: 6 denial 7 paradox 8 defiance, negation, variance
contradictory: 6 unlike 8 converse, opposite
contralto: 5 voice 6 singer 8 Anderson, vocalist
colleague: 4 bass 5 basso, mezzo, tenor 7 soprano 8 baritone
contraption: 3 rig 4 tool 5 gismo, gizmo 6 device, gadget, widget 7 machine 9 machinery

contrapuntal
  song: **5** canon, motet
contrariety: **7** inverse, obverse, reverse **8** converse, flip side, opposite, polarity **10** antithesis, opposition
contrariwise: **9** otherwise, vice versa
contrary: **4** cold, cool, mean **5** alien, aloof, balky, nasty, polar, rigid, surly **6** averse, chilly, feisty, gainst, mulish, ornery, remote, unlike, unruly **7** adverse, counter, defiant, glacial, hateful, hostile, naughty, opposed, piggish, restive, reverse, unalike, wayward **8** captious, clashing, factious, indocile, inimical, negative, obdurate, opposing, opposite, perverse, spiteful, stubborn, untoward **9** bellicose, crotchety, different, dissident, malicious, obstinate, pigheaded, resistive, withdrawn **10** antithetic, dissimilar, hard-bitten, headstrong, inflexible, malevolent, pugnacious, rebellious, refractory, unfriendly
  one: **4** anti
  on the ~: **2** no **3** but, nah, naw, nay, nix, non **4** nein, nope, nyet, uh-uh **5** I won't, ixnay, never, no how, noway **6** no deal, noways, nowise **7** I refuse **8** forget it, I will not, negative, negatory **9** by no means, fat chance, I think not **10** count me out, not a chance, thumbs down
  prefix: **5** retro- **7** counter-
  to: **6** versus **7** athwart
  to fact: **5** false **6** untrue **9** incorrect **10** fabricated, fallacious, fictitious, inaccurate
  vote: **3** nay
__ contrary: **5** on the
contrast: **4** foil, vary **6** accent, differ, oppose, set off **7** compare, deviate, diverge **8** mismatch, separate **9** disparity, diversity, variation **10** comparison, difference, divergence, separation
  in ~ to: **7** against, vis-à-vis
  like some ~s: **5** stark
contrasted: **6** unlike **10** antithetic
contrasting: **5** other **7** diverse **8** opposite
contravene: **4** defy, deny **5** abort, annul, break, cross, spurn **6** abjure, breach, impugn, naysay, negate, oppose, refute, reject, resist, thwart **7** confute, disobey, dispute, gainsay, infract, intrude, violate **8** disagree, disclaim, disprove **9** disaffirm, discredit, go against, interfere, interpose, repudiate **10** contradict, counteract, transgress
contretemps: **4** goof **5** gaffe, run-in **6** boo-boo, mishap, slip-up **7** blooper, blunder, faux pas
contribute: **3** add **4** give, lead, lend **5** endow, grant, pay in, put in, put up, spend **6** ante up, bestow, chip in, commit, confer, devote, donate, impart, join in, kick in, pony up, render, supply, tender **7** dole out, hand out, pitch in, present, produce, proffer, promote, provide **8** bequeath, dispense **9** cooperate, reinforce, sacrifice, subscribe, subsidize **10** administer, strengthen, supplement
  to: **4** help **6** assist **7** benefit
contribution: **4** alms, gift, help **5** grant, share, tithe **7** charity, handout, present, subsidy **8** bestowal, donation, offering
contributor: **5** donor, giver **6** backer, factor, patron, writer **8** reporter **9** columnist, supporter **10** benefactor, journalist, subscriber
  campaign ~: **3** PAC **6** fat cat
contrite: **5** sorry **6** humble **8** penitent **9** chastened, regretful, repentant **10** apologetic, remorseful
  be ~: **3** rue **6** repent
  one: **4** ruer **6** atoner
contrition: **3** rue **5** shame **6** regret **7** penance, remorse **9** attrition, hair shirt, penitence **10** repentance
contrivance: **4** plan, plot, ploy, ruse, tool **5** angle, craft, dodge, gismo, gizmo, shift, thing, trick **6** design, device, engine, gadget, scheme, widget **7** gimmick, machine **8** artifice, intrigue **9** machinery, mechanism
contrive: **3** lay, rig **4** brew, form, plan, plot **5** frame, hatch, weave **6** affect, cook up, create, design, device, devise, invent, make up, manage, whip up **7** arrange, concoct, devises, dream up, fashion, finagle, prepare, project, think up, trump up, work out **8** assemble, engineer, intrigue, maneuver **9** formulate, improvise, machinate **10** manipulate
contrived: **3** pat **4** fake, made, sham, wove **5** false, hokey, phony, stiff, woven **6** forced, phoney, stuffy, wooden **7** labored, pompous, stilted, stopgap **8** affected, overdone, spurious, strained **9** unnatural **10** artificial, factitious, jury-rigged
contriving: **4** wily **6** shifty
control: **3** own, run, say, use **4** boss, care, curb, head, helm, hold, keep, lead, rule, stem, sway, tact, work **5** brake, bully, check, clout, guide, leash, limit, might, pilot, quell, steer, wield **6** arrest, bridle, charge, direct, govern, halter, handle, head up, manage, police, ration, rein in, rudder, subdue **7** command, conduct, contain, dictate, harness, mastery, monitor, oversee, potence, potency, preside, repress, smother **8** clutches, deal with, dominate, domineer, dominion, guidance, hegemony, hold back, moderate, prestige, regulate, restrain **9** abatement, authority, constrain, direction, influence, mesmerize, occupancy, oversight, ownership, reign over, restraint, supervise, supremacy, upper hand **10** administer, ascendance, ascendancy, ascendence, ascendency, discipline, domination, government, keep in line, leadership, management, manipulate, monopolize, occupation, oppression, possession, regulation
  be in ~: **4** rule **6** govern
  device: **4** rein **5** lever, valve **6** button
  easy to ~: **4** tame **6** docile
  firm ~: **4** grip **5** grasp **6** clench, clinch **7** command, mastery
  lose ~: **4** skid, snap **5** freak, go ape, panic **6** go wild
  one out of ~: **5** rager
  out of ~: **4** amok, wild **5** amuck, loose **6** adrift, unruly **7** haywire, rampant, runaway
  under ~: **4** cool **6** in hand, in line
control __: **3** rod **4** room, unit **5** board, chart, freak, group, panel, tower **6** center
__ control: **3** gun **4** arms, ball, fire, rent, spin, tone **5** flood, price **6** cruise, damage, flight, ground, remote **7** climate, mission, portion, quality
__-control: **4** dual, self
Control (1986 song)
  artist: Janet Jackson
CONTROL
  foe: **4** KAOS
controlled: **5** sober **7** limited, orderly, subject **8** discreet, governed, moderate, obsessed **9** nerveless **10** reasonable
controller: **6** bursar, leader, master **8** director, rheostat **10** bookkeeper
controlling: **5** bossy **6** ruling **8** dominant, powerful **9** principal
control tower
  device: **5** radar
  dot: **3** pip **4** blip
controversial: **4** moot, open **7** at issue, dubious, suspect **8** arguable, disputed
controversy: **3** row **4** feud, flak, fuss, spat, tiff **5** fight, flack, issue, scrap **6** battle, debate, rumpus, strife, unrest **7** dispute, polemic, quarrel, wrangle **8** argument, question, squabble
controvert: **4** deny **5** argue, belie, break, rebut **6** debate, negate, oppose, oppugn, refute **7** confute, dispute, gainsay **8** disprove, question **9** challenge **10** disconfirm, prove wrong
contumacious: **6** wilful **7** defiant, lawless, wayward, willful **8** contrary, perverse **9** obstinate
contumacy: **8** defiance **10** fanaticism
contumely: **3** dig **4** barb, gibe, jibe, slam, slap, slur, snub **5** abuse, libel, scorn, taunt **6** insult, rebuff, slight **7** affront, calumny, catcall, disdain, mockery, obloquy, offense, put-down, slander **8** contempt, derision, ridicule **9** aspersion, cheap shot, indignity, insolence, invective **10** defamation, disrespect, opprobrium
contuse: **4** hurt **5** wound **6** bruise, injure **7** blacken **8** discolor
contused: **4** hurt **5** livid
contusion: **4** bump, hurt, welt **5** wound **6** bruise, injury **8** swelling
conundrum: **4** koan **5** poser, vexer **6** enigma, puzzle, riddle, teaser **7** arcanum, mystery, problem **10** closed book, puzzlement
conurbation: **4** city
conure: **4** bird **6** parrot
  home: **4** cage, nest
conv.: **3** mtg. **4** sess.
convalesce: **4** heal, mend **6** look up, perk up **7** rebound, recover **10** recuperate
convalescent: **6** better **7** patient
convalescing: **9** on the mend
convection __: **4** oven
convene: **3** sit **4** call, hold, meet, open **5** rally **6** call in, corral, gather, muster, summon **7** collect, convoke, round up, scare up **8** assemble **9** forgather **10** congregate
  again: **5** resit **6** remeet
convenience: **3** aid, use **4** ease, help **5** avail **6** luxury **7** amenity, benefit, comfort, leisure, liberty, service, utility **8** facility **9** handiness
  at one's ~: **7** anytime
convenience __: **4** food **5** store
convenience store
  item: **3** gum, pop **4** cola, soda **5** candy, frank **6** hot dog **8** ice cream, magazine, sandwich **9** newspaper **10** chewing gum
convenient: **3** fit **4** good, near, nigh, snug **5** close, handy, happy, of use, on tap, ready **6** at hand, nearby, timely, useful, wieldy **7** close by, helpful, hopeful, in reach **8** adjacent, apposite, imminent, next-door, portable, suitable **9** adaptable, adjoining, agreeable, all-around, available, bordering, conducive, easy to use, expedient, favorable, fortunate, immediate, impending, opportune, proximate **10** acceptable, accessible, beneficial, commodious, contiguous, seasonable, time-saving
convent: **5** abbey **7** nunnery, retreat **8** cloister **9** monastery, sanctuary
  attire: **5** habit
  dweller: **3** nun **6** abbess
  room: **4** cell
convention: **4** form, meet, mode, wont **5** canon, habit, rally, usage **6** caucus, confab, custom, powwow, praxis, treaty **7** council, fashion, meeting, precept, reunion **8** assembly, congress, jamboree, niceties, practice **9** concordat, covenance, delegates, etiquette, formality, gathering, propriety, tradition **10** assemblage, conference, delegation
  site: **4** hall **5** arena, hotel
  wear: **3** fez **5** badge, ID tag **7** name tag
__ Convention: **6** Geneva, Warsaw
conventional: **3** std. **4** dull, tame **5** corny, hokey, moral, passé, plain, rigid, sober, stale, stock, trite, typic, usual, vapid **6** common, formal, jejune, narrow, normal, old hat, proper, ritual, square, stuffy, wonted **7** clichéd, correct, current, fatuous, general, humdrum, insular, popular, prosaic, prudish, regular, routine, typical, uptight **8** accepted, bromidic, decorous,

dogmatic, everyday, expected, habitual, mediocre, ordinary, orthodox, outdated, outmoded, plebeian, standard, straight **9** customary, hackneyed, prosaical, unwritten **10** dogmatical, prevailing, uninspired, unoriginal
conventions: 5 mores **6** praxes **8** protocol **9** propriety
conventual: 3 nun
converge: 4 meet **5** flock, focus, merge, touch, unite **6** center, gather, huddle **8** assemble, focalize **9** intersect
on: 3 mob **4** near **8** approach
convergence: 8 junction, juncture
convergent: 7 joining, meeting, merging **8** blending **10** concurrent, synchronal
conversable: 8 obliging **9** agreeable **10** accessible
conversant: 3 hep, hip **5** aware **6** at home, au fait, versed, wise to **7** knowing, learned, skilled **8** familiar, informed **9** au courant, cognizant, conscious, observant, on the beam, plugged in, practiced **10** acquainted, perceptive, percipient, proficient
be ~ in: 4 know
with: 4 up on
conversation: 3 gab **4** chat, talk, word **6** confab, dialog, gossip, parley, powwow, speech **7** palaver **8** chitchat, colloquy, dialogue, exchange, language, repartee **9** tête-à-tête
center of ~: 5 topic
combining form: 3 -log **5** -logue
filler: 2 er, um **4** I see **5** I mean
make idle ~: 3 gab, rap, yak **4** chat
piece: 5 curio **6** oddity
starter: 5 hello
conversation __: 3 pit **5** chair, piece
conversational: 5 gabby, talky **6** chatty **7** gossipy **8** friendly **9** garrulous, talkative **10** big-mouthed, long-winded, loquacious
Conversation of Eiros and Chamion, The
author: Edgar Allan Poe
Conversation, The (1974 film)
cast: John Cazale, Frederic Forrest, Gene Hackman
director: Francis Ford Coppola
converse: 3 gab, rap, yak **4** chat, chin, talk **5** speak, visit **6** confer, parley **7** commune, palaver, reverse, schmoos **8** antipode, antipole, chitchat, opposite, schmoose, schmooze **9** antipodal, discourse **10** antithesis, antithetic, chew the fat
Converse
competitor: 4 Avia, Keds **6** Adidas, Reebok
conversely: 9 vice versa
conversion: 5 shift **6** change, reform **8** exchange, flip-flop **9** about-face, refitting **10** adaptation, alteration, changeover
lane ~: 5 spare, split
conversion __: 3 van
__ Convers Wyeth: 6 Newell
convert: 3 win **4** lead, sway, turn **5** adapt, alter, co-opt **6** change, decode, modify, novice, reform, switch **7** baptize, recruit, win over **8** disciple, follower, neophyte, persuade, transfer **9** liquidate, novitiate, transform, translate **10** catechumen
converted __: 4 rice
convertible: 3 car **4** auto, sofa **6** daybed, landau, liquid, mutual, ragtop **7** mutable, related **9** alterable **10** automobile, changeable, modifiable, reciprocal
convertible __: 4 bond
convertiplane acronym: 4 STOL
convex: 5 lobed **6** arched **7** bulging, rounded **9** outcurved
molding: 5 ovolo, torus
moldings: 4 tori **5** ovoli
tile: 6 imbrex
convexity, architectural: 7 entasis
convey: 3 lug, say, tow **4** bear, cart, cede, draw, give, haul, mean, move, pipe, send, take, tell, tote, waft **5** break, bring, carry, ferry, fetch, grant, shlep, speak, truck **6** funnel, impart, pass on, recite, relate, schlep, shlepp **7** channel, conduct, consign, deliver, express, forward, purport, recount, signify, sustain **8** describe, disclose, dispatch, transfer, transmit, vocalize **9** get across, make known, put across, transport **10** distribute
lightly: 4 waft
conveyance: 3 cab, car **4** deed **7** carrier, transit, vehicle **8** carriage, delivery **9** transport **10** delegation
see also vehicle
conveyor: 4 belt **6** bearer **7** carrier
convict: 5 felon, lifer **6** inmate, refute **7** captive, condemn **8** criminal, internee, jailbird, prisoner, sentence **9** miscreant
convicted: 6 guilty
conviction: 4 idea, view **5** cause, dogma, faith, prior, slant, tenet, trust **6** belief, fervor, surety **7** feeling, opinion, thought, verdict **8** credence, doctrine, firmness, reliance, sureness **9** assurance, certainty, certitude, principle, sentiment **10** conclusion, condemning, confidence, enthusiasm, impression, persuasion
erroneous ~: 5 frame **6** bad rap, bum rap **7** frame-up
lack of ~: 5 doubt
lose ~: 5 waver
state with ~: 4 aver, avow **6** assert
convince: 3 get, win **4** hook, sell **5** budge **6** assure, induce **7** satisfy, win over **8** overcome, persuade, reassure, talk into **9** prevail on, put across
convinced: 4 sold, sure **5** clear **7** certain **8** positive, sanguine **9** believing, confident, obstinate, presuming, satisfied **10** optimistic
be ~: 4 feel **5** think, trust **6** accept, assume, bank on, rely on **7** believe, count on **8** depend on **9** believe in, count upon
easily ~: 5 naive
convincing: 5 solid, sound, valid **6** cogent, moving, potent, strong **7** logical, telling **8** credible, faithful, luculent, powerful, rational **9** authentic, disarming, effective, plausible **10** acceptable, believable, conclusive, dependable, felicitous, imaginable, impressive, persuasive, presumable, reasonable, satisfying, unarguable
be ~: 4 sell, wash
convivial: 3 fun, gay **4** boon, gala, kind **5** close, happy, jolly, merry **6** chummy, clubby, festal, genial, hearty, jocund, jovial, kindly, lively, social **7** affable, amiable, cordial, festive **8** amicable, cheerful, friendly, intimate, mirthful, outgoing, pleasant, sociable **9** congenial, fun-loving, hilarious, vivacious **10** benevolent, buddy-buddy, gregarious, hospitable, neighborly, solicitous
conviviality: 6 gaiety, gayety **9** happiness, merriment
convocation: 4 diet, meet **5** rally, synod **6** confab, powwow **7** council, meeting **8** assembly, conclave, congress **9** symposium
convoke: 4 call **6** call up, gather, muster, summon **7** collect, convene, marshal, round up **8** assemble
convolute: 4 coil, curl **7** contort, sinuate **10** complicate
convoluted: 5 snaky **6** ornate **7** complex, sinuous, winding **8** flexuous, involved, tortuous **9** entangled, intricate **10** meandering
convolution: 4 coil, loop, maze **5** helix, swirl, twirl, twist **6** spiral **7** coiling, snaking **8** curlicue, curlycue **9** labyrinth
convoy: 5 carry, fleet, guard, guide, train, usher **6** escort **7** caravan, conduct, protect **8** chaperon **9** accompany, chaperone, companion, safeguard
component: 4 semi **5** truck
Convoy (1975 song)
artist: C.W. McCall
convulse: 5 shake, upset **6** quiver, tickle **7** agitate, break up, crack up, disturb, shake up, shudder **8** unsettle **10** discompose
convulsed, be: 4 roar **5** laugh **6** guffaw
convulsion: 5 quake, spasm, start, storm **6** tumult **7** seizure, tempest **8** paroxysm **9** agitation, cataclysm, commotion **10** earthquake
convulsive: 5 jerky **9** explosive, spasmodic **10** hysterical
Convy: 4 Bert
Conway: 3 Tim, Tom **4** Jack **5** Kevin **6** Twitty
Conway, Tim: 5 actor **8** comedian
character: 4 Dorf
TV: The Carol Burnett Show, McHale's Navy
cony: 3 fur **4** hare, pika **5** hyrax **6** animal, dassie, mammal, rabbit
coo: 4 peep **6** gurgle, murmur
bill and ~: 4 neck **5** spoon **6** cuddle
Cooder: 2 Ry
Coody, Charles: 6 golfer
cooer: 4 dove **6** pigeon **8** lovebird
Coogan: 5 Keith **6** Jackie
Coogan, Jackie: 5 actor
film: The Kid (1921)
spouse: Betty Grable
TV: The Addams Family
Coogan's Bluff (1968 film)
cast: Susan Clark, Lee J. Cobb, Clint Eastwood
cook: 3 fix, fry **4** bake, boil, brew, burn, chef, make, nuke, sear, stew, warm **5** baker, broil, brown, curry, devil, grill, outdo, poach, roast, sauté, scald, shirr, steam, steep, toast **6** braise, broast, coddle, decoct, doctor, heat up, panfry, scorch, simmer, sizzle, tamper **7** escalop, falsify, griddle, parboil, prepare, servant, swelter **8** barbecue, escallop, rational **9** fricassee, microwave
accessory: 4 mitt, peel **5** apron, timer **7** spatula
don't ~: 6 eat out
ender: 3 out **4** book, ware
exhortation: 5 dig in
for a crowd: 5 cater
in a microwave: 4 nuke
measure: 3 cup, tbs., tsp. **4** dash, tbsp. **5** pinch **6** cupful **8** teaspoon **10** tablespoon
need: 3 pan, pot, wok **4** oven **5** grill, stove **6** frypan, kettle, teapot, tureen, vessel **7** dishpan, roaster, skillet **8** barbecue, saucepan
one way to ~: 3 fry **4** bake, boil, sear, stew **5** broil, grill, poach, roast, sauté, scald, shirr, steam **6** braise, broast, coddle, panfry **7** parboil **8** barbecue **9** fricassee, microwave
quickly: 5 fry up
up: 4 form, make, plan, plot **5** frame, hatch **6** devise, ideate, invent **7** concoct, fashion, imagine **8** conceive, contrive, intrigue **9** fabricate, formulate
Zen ~: 5 tenzo
cook-__: 3 off, out
__ cook: 3 fry
Cook: 2 mt. **3** mtn., str. **4** Dane, isle, peak **5** James, mount, Peter, Robin **6** Elisha, island, strait **7** Fielder **8** mountain
locale: 10 New Zealand
offering: 4 tour
rival: 5 Peary
Cook __: 5 Inlet **6** Strait **7** Islands
cookbook: 6 manual
amt.: 3 tbs., tsp. **4** tbsp.
direction: 3 add, fry **4** beat, boil, chop, dice, heat, stew, stir **5** baste, purée, roast, sauté, scald, steam, toast
phrase: 3 à la **5** add in
Cooke: 3 Sam **8** Alistair
cooked: 4 done **5** ready
lightly ~: 4 pink, rare
not ~: 3 raw
cooked-up: 5 bogus, false **10** fictitious
cooker: 3 pan, pot, wok **4** oven **5** crock, grill, stove **6** frypan **8** barbecue
__ cooker: 4 slow
cookery: 4 food **7** kitchen **10** gastronomy
burnt, in ~: 5 brulé **6** brulée
stuffed, in ~: 5 farci
term: 5 au jus, garni **7** à la mode **8** au gratin

Cooke, Sam
song: Another Saturday Night (1963)
Chain Gang (1960)
Shake (1965)
Twistin' the Night Away (1962)
You Send Me (1957)
cookhouse: 7 kitchen
cookie: 3 bar 4 Oreo 5 sweet, treat, wafer 6 Droxie, fig bar, goodie 7 biscuit, brownie, oatmeal, ratafia 8 biscotto, macaroon, seed cake 9 Chips Ahoy, Fig Newton, krummkake, lebkuchen, snap goody, tollhouse 10 gingersnap, girlfriend, lady finger, Lorna Doone, shortbread, sugar wafer
box stat.: 5 net wt.
brand: 4 Lido, Oreo 5 Nilla, Pocky, Tahoe 6 Milano 7 E.L. Fudge 9 Chips Ahoy!, Sausalito 10 Fig Newtons, Lorna Doone, Mystic Mint 12 Fudge Stripes, Teddy Grahams 13 Vienna Fingers 14 Animal Crackers
cooker: 4 oven
crisp ~: 4 snap
dough container: 4 tube
holder: 3 box, jar 5 crock
ingredient: 3 fig, nut, oat 5 anise, crème, dough 6 ginger
manufacturer: 4 Dare 5 baker, McKee 6 bakery 7 Archway, Keebler, Nabisco 8 Sunshine 9 Lofthouse, Mrs. Fields 10 Famous Amos, Peak Freans 12 Little Debbie
mix: 6 batter
molasses ~: 6 hermit
nugget: 4 chip
partner: 4 milk
quantity: 5 batch 6 jarful
sheet: 3 tin
the way the ~ crumbles: 3 lot 4 fate
thin ~: 5 wafer
tidbit: 5 crumb
topping: 5 icing 9 chocolate
see also sweetheart
cookie __: 3 jar 5 press, sheet 6 cutter
__ cookie: 4 drop 6 butter 7 fortune
Cookie: 8 Bumstead 9 Lavagetto
Cookie (1989 film)
cast: Peter Falk, Emily Lloyd, Dianne Wiest
Cookie Crisp
competitor: ***see*** cereal
cookie dough
alternative: ***see*** ice cream flavor
Cookie Monster cohort: 4 Bert 5 Ernie, Piggy 6 Kermit 7 Big Bird 9 Miss Piggy
cookies and cream
alternative: ***see*** ice cream flavor
Cookie's Fortune (1999 film)
cast: Glenn Close, Julianne Moore, Chris O'Donnell, Liv Tyler
director: Robert Altman
cooking: 4 food 5 aboil 7 cuisine 8 thriving 9 housework 10 gastronomy
class: 6 home ec
direction: 3 fry 4 bake, beat, boil, heat, stew, stir 5 baste, roast, sauté, scald, steam 7 to taste 8 hard-boil, soft-boil
implement: 5 dicer, parer, ricer, sieve 6 beater 8 colander
ingredient: 3 egg, oil 4 lard, mace, sage 5 flour, spice, sugar, thyme 6 nutmeg 7 parsley, vanilla 8 cinnamon, rosemary
pot: 4 olla 6 copper
style: 5 Cajun 6 Creole
utensil: 3 pan, pot, wok 6 frypan, tureen 7 skillet
utensil coating: 6 enamel
cooking __ gas: 4 with
Cooking Egg, A: 4 poem
author: T.S. Eliot
cooking oil: 6 canola, Crisco, Mazola, Wesson 7 Puritan
source: 4 corn 5 olive 9 sunflower
Cook Islands
island: 9 Rarotonga
Cook, James: 7 British 8 explorer
cookoff
creation: 5 chili
cook one's __: 5 goose
cookout: 3 bbq, fry 4 meal 5 bar-b-q 6 picnic 8 barbecue
fare: 4 fish 5 cabob, frank, kabab, kabob, kebab, kebob, steak, wurst 6 burger, hot dog, wiener 7 chicken 9 hamburger
Hawaiian ~: 4 luau
intruder: 3 ant
need: 3 gas 4 fire 5 grill 7 propane 8 barbecue, charcoal
remnant: 3 ash 6 cinder
site: 4 deck, park, yard 5 patio
Cook, Rachael Leigh: 7 actress
film: All I Wanna Do (1998)
Antitrust (2001)
Get Carter (2000)
She's All That (1999)
Cook, Robin: 6 writer
work: Acceptable Risk
Brain
Chromosome 6
Coma
Contagion
Fatal Cure
Fever
Godplayer
Harmful Intent
Mindbend
Mortal Fear
Mutation
Outbreak
Seizure
Shock
Sphinx
Terminal
Toxin
Vector
Vital Signs
The Year of the Intern
Cook's __: 4 tour
cook the __: 5 books
cookware: 8 utensils
coating: 4 lard
name: 4 Ekco 5 Pyrex
cool: 3 def, hep, hip, icy, rad 4 aces, A-one, boss, braw, calm, cold, dece, even, fine, gear, keen, lull, mean, mild, neat, nice, phat, tuff 5 abate, algid, allay, aloof, brisk, chill, crisp, dandy, ducky, fresh, frost, gelid, grand, great, lucid, marvy, nasty, neato, nifty, nippy, nobby, poise, prime, quiet, slake, slick, sober, sound, staid, stoic, suave, super, surly, swell, tepid, zingy 6 aplomb, arctic, at ease, bang on, bang-up, biting, bonzer, bosker, casual, chilly, choice, dampen, divine, dreamy, far out, freeze, frigid, frosty, gentle, gnarly, groovy, lovely, low-key, mellow, offish, ornery, peachy, placid, poised, quench, remote, sedate, serene, slap-up, spot on, steady, stolid, superb, temper, terrif, tiptop, unreal, whizzo, wicked, wintry 7 amazing, amiable, assuage, assured, at peace, awesome, bracing, capital, chilled, corking, distant, equable, glacial, hateful, hostile, mollify, neutral, offhand, pacific, perfect, politic, rapture, refresh, relaxed, ripping, shivery, skookum, stellar, stoical, sublime, unfazed, unmoved, warmish, wintery, zinging 8 amicable, carefree, composed, contrary, dazzling, detached, especial, eximious, fabulous, five-star, four-star, frabjous, glorious, heavenly, informal, inimical, jim-dandy, laidback, loveless, lukewarm, mitigate, moderate, not so hot, peaceful, pleasant, rational, reserved, skillful, slam-bang, smashing, spiteful, splendid, standout, sterling, stickout, superior, terrific, together, toplevel, topnotch, tranquil, very good, wondrous 9 apathetic, bellicose, bodacious, collected, composure, easygoing, Endsville, excellent, exemplary, exquisite, first-rate, high-grade, hunky-dory, impassive, incurious, malicious, marvelous, nerveless, quiescent, reconcile, sollicker, temperate, topflight, unexcited, unextreme, unruffled, unstirred, unworried, withdrawn, wonderful 10 confidence, coolheaded, detachment, first-class, fortifying, hotsy-totsy, impersonal, impressive, insociable, jack-a-dandy, malevolent, nonchalant, out of sight, peachy-keen, phenomenal, phlegmatic, pugnacious, reasonable, refreshing, remarkable, restrained, sedateness, speechless, stupendous, super-duper, unaffected, unagitated, unfriendly, unsociable, untroubled
down: 3 ice 5 chill
drink: 3 ade, pop 4 beer, cola, soda
dude: 3 cat 6 daddy-o, hepcat
flavor: 4 mint
in a ~ way: 5 icily
it: 3 nix 4 halt, stop, wait 5 cease, quiet, relax 6 desist, lay off, relent 7 silence 8 calm down, chill out, loosen up 9 lighten up, seriously
lose one's ~: 4 boil, rant, rave 5 go ape 6 blow up, get mad
not ~: 5 nerdy, unhip
off: 3 fan 4 calm, lull 5 quiet, relax 6 die out, soothe, unwind 8 calm down 10 settle down, simmer down
one's heels: 4 wait 5 tarry 8 sit tight
playing it ~: 7 careful 8 cautious
spot: 5 shade
time: 4 fall
cool __: 3 out 4 jazz
cool __ cucumber: 3 as a
__ cool!: 3 Way
__-cool: 3 air 5 water
Cool __ Bell: 4 Papa
Cool __ Luke: 4 Hand
__ Cool: 3 Joe 6 Johnny, Medium
coolant: 5 Freon, sweat
cooler: 3 ade, fan, ice, pen 4 coop, icer, jail, poky, stir 5 clink, pokey, rocks 6 fridge, icebox, lockup, prison 7 freezer, hoosgow, slammer 8 hoosegow
contents: 3 ice 4 beer, cola, soda
in the ~: 5 on ice
room ~: 2 AC 3 fan
summer ~: 3 ade, ice, pop 4 cola, soda 5 slush 6 breeze 7 iced tea
__ cooler: 4 wine 5 water
Cool Hand Luke (1967 film)
cast: Lou Antonio, J.D. Cannon, George Kennedy, Strother Martin, Paul Newman
dog: 4 Blue
cool-headed: 4 calm 5 quiet, sober 10 farsighted, unagitated
Coolidge: 3 Cal 4 Rita 5 Grace 6 Calvin, Martha
Coolidge, Calvin: 9 president
alma mater: 7 Amherst
birthplace: 7 Vermont
former occupation: 6 lawyer
home: 4 Mass. 7 Vermont
like ~: 5 terse
opponent: 5 Davis 10 LaFollette
real first name: 4 John
V.P.: 5 Dawes
wife: 5 Grace
Coolidge, Rita
song: Higher and Higher (1977)
We're All Alone (1977)
spouse: Kris Kristofferson
cooling
agent: 6 dry ice
capacity unit: 3 BTU
device: 2 AC 3 fan 6 ice bag 7 ice pack
off: 5 truce 7 détente
cooling-off period: 5 delay, truce 6 autumn
Coolio: 9 Artis Ivey, rap artist
Cool it!: 4 stop 5 chill
Cool Love (1981 song)
artist: Pablo Cruise
Cool Mission, A
author: Nathanael West
Cool, Mr., no: 4 nerd 5 dweeb
coolness: 4 calm 5 chill, nerve, shade 6 apathy 7 neglect, reserve 8 calmness, distance 9 assurance, restraint, sang-froid 10 detachment, equanimity, moderation, neutrality
cool one's __: 4 jets 5 heels
Cool Papa: 4 Bell
Cool World (1992 film)
cast: Kim Basinger, Gabriel Byrne, Brad Pitt
coon dog: 5 hound 10 bloodhound
Cooney: 5 Gerry
Coon Rapids: 4 city, town
locale: 9 Minnesota
coon's __: 3 age

__ coon's age: 3 in a
coonskin: 3 cap, hat
coop: 3 pen 4 cage, cell, cote, jail, nest 5 booth, fence, house, hutch 6 cooler, lockup, prison 7 hoosgow, housing, slammer 8 henhouse, hoosegow 9 enclosure
dweller: 3 hen 5 layer
fly the ~: 2 go 4 flee, skip 6 decamp, escape 7 abandon, abscond, go south, vamoose 8 fugitate, jump bail, run for it 9 break away
group: 4 eggs, hens
sound: 3 coo 4 peep 6 cackle
starter: 3 hen
up: 3 pen 4 hold 5 cramp 6 encage 7 confine, enclose, impound, inclose
co-op: 4 flat, home, mart 5 abode, house 6 market 7 domicil, habitat, housing, shelter 8 domicile 9 residence
kin: 5 condo
cooped up: 4 pent 5 stied 8 fenced in
cooper: 7 artisan 9 craftsman
product: 4 cask 6 barrel
tool: 3 adz 4 adze
Cooper: 3 Pat 4 font, Gary, Leon 5 Alice, Chris 6 Gladys, Jackie 8 Melville, typeface
__ Cooper: 4 Mini
Cooper, Alice
song: Poison (1989)
School's Out (1972)
You and Me (1977)
cooperate: 3 aid 4 help 5 agree, align, aline, unite 6 accede, assist, club up, comply, concur, join in, league 7 go along, pitch in, promote 8 interact, play ball, take part 9 harmonize, lend a hand, play along 10 assist with, comply with, contribute, coordinate, join forces
with: 4 abet, join
(with): 4 side
cooperating: 6 united
cooperation: 3 aid 4 help 5 unity 6 assist 7 cahoots, harmony, synergy 8 teamwork
cooperative: 5 joint 6 shared, united 7 commune, helpful, unified 8 amenable, communal, obliging, synergic 9 concerted
Russia ~: 5 artel
cooperatively: 8 mutually 9 in concert
cooperator: 9 assistant, associate
Cooper, Chris: 5 actor
film: Adaptation (2002, AA)
The Bourne Identity (2002)
Great Expectations (1998)
Matewan (1987)
October Sky (1999)
The Patriot (2000)
Cooper City: 4 city, town
locale: 7 Florida
Cooper, Gary: 5 actor
deadline: 4 noon
film: Along Came Jones (1945)
Ball of Fire (1941)
Beau Geste (1939)
City Streets (1931)
Design for Living (1933)
Desire (1936)
A Farewell to Arms (1932)
For Whom the Bell Tolls (1943)
Friendly Persuasion (1956)
The Hanging Tree (1959)
High Noon (1952, AA)
If I Had a Million (1932)
Love in the Afternoon (1957)
Man of the West (1958)
Meet John Doe (1941)
Morocco (1930)
Mr. Deeds Goes to Town (1936)
One Sunday Afternoon (1933)
Peter Ibbetson (1935)
The Plainsman (1936)
The Pride of the Yankees (1942)
The Real Glory (1939)
Sergeant York (1941, AA)
Souls at Sea (1937)
Ten North Frederick (1958)
Vera Cruz (1954)
The Westerner (1940)
role: 4 York 5 Deeds, Geste 6 Gehrig
Cooper, James Fenimore: 6 writer
character: 5 Uncas 6 Bumppo
work: The Deer Slayer
The Last of the Mohicans
Leather-Stocking Tales
The Pathfinder
The Pioneers
The Prairie
The Spy
Cooperstown
locale: 7 New York
member: 3 Day, Fox, Ott 4 Babe, Bell, Cobb, Dean, Doby, Fisk, Ford, Foxx, Hoyt, Klem, Kuhn, Mack, Mays, Mize, Rice, Ruth, Ryan, Wynn, Yogi 5 Aaron, Anson, Banks, Bench, Boggs, Brett, Brock, Carew, Combs, Doerr, Evers, Flick, Frick, Giles, Gomez, Grove, Gwynn, Irvin, Kiner, Klein, Lemon, Lopez, Paige, Perez, Reese, Rixey, Roush, Rusie, Selee, Smith, Spahn, Terry, Vance, Veeck, Waner, Wheat, Young, Yount 6 Alston, Barrow, Bender, Carter, Cepeda, Chylak, Conlan, Cronin, Cuyler, Dihigo, Feller, Foster, Frisch, Gehrig, Gibson, Gordon, Goslin, Hanlon, Harris, Harvey, Herzog, Hunter, Kaline, Koufax, Lajoie, Landis, Manley, Mantle, McGraw, Mel Ott, Morgan, Murray, Musial, Niekro, Palmer, Rickey, Ripken, Seaver, Sisler, Snider, Sutter, Sutton, Ty Cobb, Wagner, Weaver, Wilson, Yawkey 7 Al Lopez, Appling, Ashburn, Averill, Barlick, Bunning, Carlton, Collins, Cy Young, Fingers, Gossage, Hornsby, Hubbard, Hubbell, Huggins, Jackson, Jenkins, Jim Rice, Johnson, Lasorda, Lazzeri, Leon Day, Mathews, McCovey, Medwick, Molitor, O'Malley, Puckett, Rizzuto, Roberts, Ruffing, Sam Rice, Schmidt, Speaker, Stearns, Stengel, Traynor, Vaughan, Waddell, Wilhelm 8 Al Kaline, Anderson, Aparicio, Babe Ruth, Bill Klem, Bob Lemon, Boudreau, Cap Anson, Chandler, Clemente, Cochrane, DiMaggio, Drysdale, Durocher, Ed Barrow, Edd Roush, Griffith, Lou Brock, MacPhail, Marichal, Marquard, McCarthy, Robinson, Rod Carew, Sandberg, Spalding, Stargell, Williams, Winfield 9 Al Barlick, Alexander, Amos Rusie, Bill Terry, Bill Veeck, Bob Feller, Bob Gibson, Bowie Kuhn, Cal Ripken, Dandridge, Dizzy Dean, Don Sutton, Early Wynn, Eckersley, Eppa Rixey, Ford Frick, Greenberg, Hank Aaron, Henderson, Jim Palmer, Joe Cronin, Joe Gordon, Joe Morgan, Killebrew, Larry Doby, Lou Gehrig, Mathewson, Mazeroski, McKechnie, Nap Lajoie, Nellie Fox, Newhouser, Nolan Ryan, Paul Waner, Radbourne, Slaughter, Tom Seaver, Tom Yawkey, Tony Gwynn, Tony Perez, Wade Boggs, Waite Hoyt, Yogi Berra, Zack Wheat 10 Ban Johnson, Bobby Doerr, Cal Hubbard, Campanella, Charleston, Chuck Klein, Connie Mack, Dazzy Vance, Duke Snider, Earle Combs, Earl Weaver, Effa Manley, Elmer Flick, Ernie Banks, Frank Selee, Gary Carter, Hack Wilson, Jim Bunning, Jimmie Foxx, Joe Medwick, John McGraw, Josh Gibson, Kiki Cuyler, Lefty Gomez, Lefty Grove, Lloyd Waner, Monte Irvin, Ozzie Smith, Phil Niekro, Pie Traynor, Ralph Kiner, Red Ruffing, Robin Yount, Rube Foster, Southworth, Stan Musial, Whitey Ford, Willie Mays 11 Carl Hubbell, Yastrzemski
site: 10 Hall of Fame
co-opt: 5 adopt, usurp 6 absorb, draw in 7 bring in, convert, include, preempt 8 take over 10 assimilate, commandeer
coordinate: 3 run 4 mate, mesh, pool 5 agree, align, aline, equal, match, synch, tie in 6 adjust, attune 7 coequal 8 mobilize, organize, parallel, regulate 9 cooperate, correlate, equalized, harmonize, integrate, reconcile 10 coincident, collateral, equivalent, proportion, reciprocal, tantamount
coordinated: 6 in sync
__-coordinated: 5 color
coordinates: 8 ensemble
use ~: 5 graph
__ coordination: 7 eye-hand, hand-eye
coordinaton loss: 5 ataxy 6 ataxia
Coors: 4 beer 6 Adolph
alternative: *see* beer
brand: 4 Zima
Coos: 3 bay 5 tribe
locale: 6 Oregon
coot: 4 bird 6 codger, geezer, mud hen 8 water hen
cooter: 6 animal, turtle 7 reptile
cootie: 3 bug 5 louse 6 insect
Cootie: 4 game
cooties: 4 lice
Coover, Robert: 6 writer
co-owned: 5 joint
cop: 3 get, nab, rob 4 lift, narc, nark 5 bobby, filch, narco, pinch, swipe 6 collar, Friday, lawman, obtain, pilfer, rip off, shamus 7 acquire, Columbo, officer, procure, receive 8 bluecoat, Drummond, flatfoot 9 detective, patrolman 10 Dirty Harry
California ~ grp.: 4 LAPD, SFPD
catch: 4 perp 5 felon 8 criminal
drug ~: 4 narc, nark 5 narco
group: 2 PD 3 FOP, PBA 5 squad 8 precinct
London ~: 5 bobby
order: 6 freeze
out: 4 quit 5 evade, shirk 6 desert, renege 7 abandon 8 go back on, slack off 9 back-pedal
Paris ~: 4 flic
route: 4 beat
TV ~: 5 Lacey 6 Cagney, Friday 7 Columbo
undercover ~: 4 narc, nark 5 agent, narco
weapon: 5 baton, taser 9 billy club
cop __: 3 out 5 a plea
__-Cop: 5 Rent-a
Copacabana: 5 beach 6 resort
locale: 3 Rio 6 Brazil
sculptor: Erté
Copacabana (1978 song)
artist: Barry Manilow
copacetic: 3 A-OK 4 jake 9 admirable 10 acceptable
copal: 5 resin 6 fossil
cope: 5 get by, stand 6 make do, manage, suffer 7 contend, grapple, make out, wrestle 8 confront, stand for, struggle 9 withstand 10 canonicals
with: 4 face, meet 6 endure, handle 8 face up to 10 meet head on, take care of
(with): 4 deal, live 6 reckon
Cope: 9 analgesic 10 painkiller
alternative: *see* pain reliever
Cope Book
name: 4 Erma
Copeland: 7 Stewart
Copeland, Stewart
band: 6 Police
band mate: 5 Sting
Copenhagen: 4 city, port, town 5 horse 6 equine 7 capital
author: Michael Frayn
locale: 7 Denmark
rider: 10 Wellington
Swedish port near ~: 5 Malmö
Copernicus: 6 crater 8 Nicolaus 10 astronomer
copier: 4 aper 6 scribe 7 epigone, machine 8 imitator 10 amanuensis
button: 5 reset
chemical: 5 toner 6 imager
company: 5 Canon, Ricoh, Xerox
for short: 5 mimeo
part: 4 drum
starter: 5 photo
coping __: 3 saw
copious: 3 big 4 full, many, much, rich, rife 5 ample, broad, large 6 bags of, divers, gobs of, lavish, lots of, myriad, plenty, umteen, untold 7 heaps of, liberal, no end

of, opulent, piles of, profuse, scads of, umpteen **8** abundant, affluent, detailed, fruitful, generous, manifold, numerous, oodles of, princely, prodigal, prolific, scores of, umpsteen **9** abounding, bounteous, bountiful, countless, extensive, exuberant, luxuriant, plenteous, plentiful, quite a few, unsparing **10** inordinate, voluminous, zillions of

copiously: 4 much **6** vastly **7** largely **10** adequately

Cop Land (1997 film)
cast: Robert De Niro, Janeane Garofalo, Harvey Keitel, Ray Liotta, Sylvester Stallone

Copland, Aaron: 8 composer
work: Appalachian Spring
Billy the Kid
El Salon Mexico
Fanfare for the Common Man
A Lincoln Portrait
Quiet City
Rodeo
Short Symphony
Symphonic Ode

Copley: 4 Teri

Copley, John Singleton: 6 artist **7** painter

cop-out: 5 alibi **6** excuse **7** evasion, pretext

copper: 4 cent, coin, fuzz **5** bobby, brown, color, metal, pence, penny **7** element, reddish **8** flatfoot
alloy: 5 brass, Monel **6** bronze, latten, oreide, ormolu, oroide, tambac, tombac **7** Everdur, Mumetal **8** gunmetal, Manganin, pot metal **9** barberite, bell metal, duralumin, Dutch foil, Dutch gold, Dutch leaf, pinchbeck, platinoid **10** constantan, Dutch metal, gold bronze, mosaic gold
coin: 4 cent
combining form: 4 cupr- **5** chalc-, chalk-, cupri-, cupro **6** chalco-, chalko-
containing ~: 6 cupric **7** cuprous
covering: 6 patina
ender: 4 head, leaf, ware **5** plate, smith
exporter: 5 Chile
ore: 7 azurite **9** malachite
relative: ***see*** brown color
source: 3 ore
tone: 3 red **6** bronze

Copper Beech, The
author: Maeve Binchy

Copperfield, David: 8 magician
first wife: 4 Dora
mother: 5 Clara
prop for ~: 4 wand

copperhead: 5 snake **6** animal **7** reptile
relative: ***see*** snake
weapon: 5 venom

Copperhead Road
artist: Steve Earle

Copper Mountain
resort near ~: 4 Vail

coppers, British: 5 pence

Copper Sun
author: Countee Cullen

Coppertone: 6 lotion
ingredient: 4 PABA
no.: 3 SPF

coppice: 4 wood **5** brush, copse, grove, woods **7** boscage, coppice, thicket

Coppola: 5 Sofia **7** Carmine

Coppola, Francis Ford: 8 director
film: Apocalypse Now (1979)
Bram Stoker's Dracula (1992)
The Conversation (1974)
The Cotton Club (1984)
Finian's Rainbow (1968)
Gardens of Stone (1987)
The Godfather (1972)
The Godfather Part II (1974, AA)
The Godfather Part III (1990)
Jack (1996)
Peggy Sue Got Married (1986)
The Rainmaker (1997)
The Rain People (1969)
Rumble Fish (1983)
Tetro (2009)
Tucker: The Man and His Dream (1988)
You're a Big Boy Now (1966)
nephew: Nicolas Cage
sister: Talia Shire

Coppola, Sofia: 8 director
spouse: Spike Jonze

coprolite: 6 fossil

cops and __: 7 robbers

copse: 4 mott, wood **5** brush, grove, motte, woods **7** boscage, coppice, thicket

copter: 4 helo **7** chopper **8** aircraft **9** eggbeater **10** whirlybird
blade: 5 rotor
forerunner: 4 giro
noise: 4 whir **5** whirr

Coptic: 6 church **8** language

copula: 4 link

copy: 2 do **3** ape, dup., fac., fax **4** draw, dupe, echo, fake, lift, mock, news, sham, stat, text, type **5** clone, ditto, image, issue, mimeo, mimic, print, repro, steal, trace, write, Xerox **6** backup, borrow, carbon, depict, double, ectype, follow, mirror, parody, parrot, pirate, record, repeat, script, sketch **7** emulate, extract, forgery, imitate, portray, reflect, replica, reprint, rewrite, set down, tracing **8** knockoff, likeness, make like, simulate, specimen **9** duplicate, facsimile, imitation, lookalike, photocopy, Photostat, replicate, reproduce **10** mimeograph, photograph, plagiarize, repetition, simulacrum, transcribe, transcript
carbon ~: 7 replica **8** likeness **9** duplicate, facsimile, identical, imitation, look-alike **10** equivalent
ender: 3 boy, cat **4** book, edit, girl **5** right **6** holder, reader, writer
not a ~: 4 orig. **8** original
starter: 5 photo

copy __: 3 boy, cat **4** desk, girl **5** paper **6** editor **7** machine

copy-__: 4 edit

__ copy: 4 fair, hard, line, soft, time **5** blind **6** carbon, ribbon **7** release

copycat: 3 ape **4** aper, mime **5** mimer, mimic **6** echoer, parrot **8** follower, imitator **9** imitative
comment: 5 ditto, me too

Copycat (1995 film)
cast: Holly Hunter, Dermot Mulroney, Sigourney Weaver
director: Jon Amiel

copyist: 6 scribe, sopher **9** scrivener, secretary **10** amanuensis

copyread: 4 edit

copyright: 6 patent **8** monopoly **10** monopolize
letter: 3 cee
relative: 2 TM **9** trademark

coq __: 5 au vin

coquette: 3 toy **4** minx, vamp **5** flirt, tease **6** trifle **10** make eyes at
act the ~: 5 flirt, tease

Coquette
sculptor: Erté

coquettish: 3 coy **6** fickle, flirty **9** frivolous, kittenish

cor __: 7 anglais

Cora: 5 Baird **6** Sandel **7** Dithers

coracle: 4 boat

coral: 3 gem, red, sea **4** pink, rosy **5** color, polyp **6** orange, sea fan, yellow **7** pinkish, reddish **9** yellowish
ender: 4 root **5** berry
formation: 3 cay, key **4** reef **5** atoll
reef denizen: 5 moray
reef pool: 6 lagoon
relative: ***see*** red color, yellow color

coral __: 4 reef **5** snake

Coral __: 3 Sea **6** Gables **7** Springs

__ Coral, FL: 4 Cape

Coral Gables: 4 city, town
athletes: 10 Hurricanes
locale: 7 Florida

Coraline (2009 film)
voice cast: Dakota Fanning, Teri Hatcher

Coral Sea: 6 battle
inlet: 5 Papua
strait off the ~: 6 Torres

Coral Springs: 4 city, town
locale: 7 Florida

cor anglais: 4 wind **10** instrument

Corazon: 6 Aquino

corbel: 7 bracket

Corbett: 5 Glenn

Corbett, James J.: 5 boxer
milieu: 4 ring

Corbin: 7 Bernsen

Corby: 5 Ellen

Corcoran: 5 Kevin **6** Noreen

cord: 3 tie **4** lace, line, rope, wick **5** twine **6** bungee, cordon, girdle, lacing, riband, string, tether **8** ligature **10** drawstring
Arab ~: 4 agal
contents: 4 wood
ender: 3 age **4** wood
fishing ~: 4 line
loom ~: 6 heddle
starter: 3 rip **4** whip

__ cord: 3 rip **6** bungee, spinal

Cord: 3 car **4** Alex, auto **10** automobile

corda: 6 string

__ corda: 3 una

cordage: 4 rope **5** twine **7** lanyard
fiber: 5 istle, ixtle, sisal
source: 4 bast **5** ramee, ramie

Corday: 4 Mara **9** Charlotte
victim: 5 Marat
see also French

corde: 7 strings

__ corde: 3 tre

corded
fabric: 3 rep **4** repp

Cordelia: 4 moon
father: 4 Lear
planet: 6 Uranus
sister: 5 Regan **7** Goneril

Cordell: 4 Hull

corder
starter: 3 cam

Cordero, Angel: 6 jockey
milieu: 5 track

Cordia: 3 car **4** auto **10** Mitsubishi

cordial: 4 kind, nice, warm **5** civil, close, drink, suave, tonic **6** cassis, chummy, clubby, genial, hearty, jovial, kindly, loving, mellow, polite, social, tender **7** affable, amiable, liqueur, sincere **8** amicable, beverage, cheerful, familiar, fireside, friendly, gracious, intimate, inviting, likeable, outgoing, pleasant, sociable **9** agreeable, congenial, convivial, courteous, welcoming **10** benevolent, buddy-buddy, gregarious, harmonious, hospitable, invigorant, neighborly, personable, solicitous
drink: 6 cassis, kummel **7** liqueur **8** anisette
flavoring: 5 anise
not ~: 4 cold **5** aloof

__ cordiale: 7 entente

cordiality: 5 amity **6** warmth **7** amenity **8** courtesy, goodwill, kindness **9** geniality, mutuality, sincerity **10** affability, amiability, good nature, heartiness

cordially: 8 heartily **9** favorably

cordite, co-inventor of: 4 Abel

cordlike: 4 ropy **5** ropey

Cordoba: 3 car **4** auto **8** Chrysler

Córdoba: 4 city, town
locale: 5 Spain

cordon: 4 cord, sash **5** badge, braid **6** riband, ribbon **7** enclose, inclose **8** surround **10** police line

cordon __: 4 bleu

Cordon Bleu
graduate: 4 chef
phrase: 3 à la

cordovan: 7 leather **8** goatskin

cords: 5 jeans, pants **8** trousers
make ~: 3 saw **5** saw up

__ cords: 5 vocal

corduroy: 6 fabric
alternative: 5 denim
feature: 3 rib **4** wale **5** ridge
like ~: 5 ridgy

corduroys: 5 jeans, pants **8** trousers

cordwood
like ~: 4 sawn
measure: 5 stere
stack: 4 rick

core: 3 hub, nub **4** crux, gist, knub, meat, pith, root, seed **5** basis, cadre, focus, heart, midst, sense **6** bowels, center, inside, kernel, marrow, middle, thrust, upshot **7** essence, keynote, nucleus, summary **8** interior, main idea **9** framework, innermost, lifeblood, main point, substance **10** foundation, midsection
to the ~: 7 utterly

__ core: 4 hard

Corea, Chick: 7 pianist
genre: 4 jazz

Corel
home of ~: 6 Ottawa
Corelli: 5 Marie 6 Franco
Corelli, Franco: 5 tenor 6 singer
specialty: 5 opera
Corelli, Marie: 6 writer 7 British
corer: 4 tool
Coretta __ King: 5 Scott
Corey: 4 Haim, Hart, Jeff 5 Elias, Irwin, Pavin 7 Feldman, Wendell
__ Corey: 7 Richard
Corey, Elias: 7 chemist 8 Nobelist
Corfu: 4 isle 6 island
island group: 6 Ionian
locale: 6 Greece
corgi: 3 dog, pet 5 pooch 6 canine
__ corgi: 5 Welsh
coriaceous: 8 leathery
coriander: 4 herb, seed 5 spice
Coricidin
alternative: *see* cold remedy
Cori, Gerty: 8 Nobelist
Corin: 5 Nemec
Corinne: 6 Bohrer, Calvet
author: Madame de Staël
Corinne Bailey __: 3 Rae
Corinth: 4 gulf 7 isthmus
ancient Gulf of ~ region: 6 Achaea
locale: 6 Greece
rival: 5 Argos
Corinthian: 5 order
alternative: 5 Doric, Ionic
Corinthians
follower: 9 Galatians
preceder: 6 Romans
Coriolanus
author: William Shakespeare
costume: 4 toga
setting: 4 Rome
Coriolanus Overture
composer: Ludwig van Beethoven
Coriolis __: 5 force 6 effect
cork: 3 cap, dam, gag, top 4 bolt, bung, clog, lock, plug, seal, shut, stop, tree 5 block, close, cover, dam up, latch, limit 6 clog up, lock up, plug up, seal up, secure, stifle, stop up 7 close up, closure, prevent, repress, seal off, shutter, stopper, stopple 8 blockade, button up, obstruct, prohibit
combining form: 6 phello-
ender: 3 age 4 wood 5 board, screw
fisherman's ~: 5 float
sound: 3 pop
source: 4 bark
up: 4 hold, seal
Cork: 4 city, port, town 6 county
locale: 3 Ire. 4 Eire, Erin 7 Ireland
port for ~: 4 Cobh
river: 3 Lee
corkboard item: 4 tack 7 pushpin
corker: 3 pip 4 joke, lulu, oner 5 beaut, dilly, doozy 6 doozie
corking
see wonderful
corkscrew: 4 coil, wind 5 curly, helix, twine, twist, whorl 6 spiral, volute 7 entwine, intwine, sinuate
corkwood: 5 balsa, shrub
Corky: 5 Nemec
Corleone: 3 Kay 4 Vito 5 Fredo, Sonny 6 Connie 7 Michael
Corleone, Sonny
portrayer: James Caan
corm: 4 bulb, taro 5 tuber
Corman, Roger: 8 director
cormorant: 4 bird, shag
corn: 3 oil 4 ears, feed 5 color, grain, maize 6 annual, cereal, fodder, veggie, yellow 7 schmalz, shmaltz 8 preserve, schmaltz, swelling 9 vegetable
amount: 4 peck, rick 6 bushel
bearing ~: 5 eared
bit of ~: 3 ear 6 kernel
borer: 3 bug 6 insect
chip flavor: 5 nacho
color: 5 maize
ender: 3 cob, fed, row 4 ball, cake, crib, husk, meal, pone 5 braid, bread, crake, stalk 6 dodger, flower, husker, starch
ground ~: 4 samp
holder: 3 bin, can, cob, ear 4 crib 5 shuck, stalk
Indian ~: 5 maize
Indian ~ genus: 3 zea
kin: 6 bunion
lily genus: 4 ixia
lover: 4 crow
Mexican ~ flour: 4 masa
pest: 5 aphid, aphis, borer
prepare ~: 4 husk 5 shuck
product: 3 oil 4 oleo, pone
protein: 4 zein
relative: *see* yellow color
rows: 8 coiffure
salad: 5 mache
starter: 3 pop, tri, uni 5 broom 6 barley, pepper
state: 3 Kan., Neb. 4 Iowa, Nebr. 6 Kansas 8 Nebraska
tassel: 4 silk 5 floss
corn __: 3 dog, oil, row 4 beef, cake, chip, lily, meal, pone, silk, smut, snow 5 borer, bread, broom, color, crake, flour, grits, plant, poppy, salad, snake, stack, stalk, sugar, syrup 6 cockle, dodger, flakes, gluten, liquor, muffin, picker, whisky 7 earworm, whiskey
corn __ cob: 5 on the
corn-__ beef: 3 fed
__ corn: 4 dent, seed 5 candy, ear of, field, flint, green, horse, sugar, sweet, table 6 barley, Guinea, hybrid, Indian, mutton
Corn __: 4 Belt, Chex
cornball: 5 hokey, trite 7 maudlin
cornbraids: 4 coif 6 hairdo 8 coiffure
Corn Chex: 6 cereal
competitor: *see* cereal
manufacturer: 12 General Mills
corn chip: 4 nosh 5 snack
name: 6 Fritos
corncob
kin: 5 briar
corncob __: 4 pipe
cornea
combining form: 5 cerat-, kerat- 6 cerato-, kerato-
cover: 3 lid 6 eyelid
corned beef: 7 cold cut
dish: 4 hash
Corneille: 6 Pierre 7 Heymans
Corneille, Pierre: 4 poet 6 French, writer 10 playwright
work: Cinna
Horace
Le Cid
Médée
cornel: 4 tree 5 shrub 7 dogwood
Cornel: 4 West 5 Wilde
Cornelia: 5 Guest, Roman
Cornelia __ Skinner: 4 Otis
Cornelius: 4 pope, Ryan 7 pontiff, Tacitus 10 Vanderbilt
Cornell: 3 Don 4 Eric, Ezra 5 Lydia 9 Katherine
athletes: 6 Big Red
lake: 6 Cayuga
league: 3 Ivy
locale: 6 Ithaca 7 New York
corner: 3 fix, jam, nab 4 nook, trap, tree 5 angle, catch, crook, hem in, joint, niche, place, stimy, stymy 6 alcove, collar, cranny, pickle, plight, recess, scrape, stymie, vertex 7 capture, dilemma, hideout, impasse, retreat 8 bottle up, hideaway, junction, monopoly, quagmire, quandary 9 tight spot 10 monopolize, standstill
around the ~: 4 near 5 close
diamond ~: 4 home 5 first, third 6 second
ender: 4 back, ways, wise 5 stone
hard to ~: 4 eely 5 cagey
just around the ~: 4 near 7 close by 8 adjacent 10 accessible, convenient
off in a ~: 5 apart
sign: 4 STOP
sitter: 5 dunce
starter: 5 cater
the market: 5 buy up, sew up 7 possess 10 monopolize
turn the ~: 5 shift
__ corner: 3 hot 4 amen 5 turn a 7 neutral
__-corner: 5 cater, catty, kitty
__ Corner: 4 Pooh 5 Poets
cornered: 5 at bay 6 in a fix, in a jam
__-cornered: 5 cater, catty, kitty
corners
cut ~: 4 save 5 skimp, stint 6 scrimp 8 retrench 9 economize 10 underspend
lacking ~: 4 oval 5 round
__ corners: 3 cut
__ Corners: 4 Five, Four
cornerstone: 4 base, rock 5 basis, coign, quoin 6 coigne 7 support 8 linchpin, lynchpin, mainstay
abbr.: 3 est. 4 estd. 5 estab.
feature: 4 date
Corner That Held Them, The
author: Sylvia Warner
__ Corner, VA: 6 Tysons
cornet: 4 horn, wind 6 pastry 7 brasses
play ~: 4 blow
corn-fed __: 4 beef
cornfield
array: 4 ears, rows 6 stalks
cry: 3 caw
Mayan ~: 5 milpa
preyer: 4 crow
Cornflake Girl (1994 song)
artist: Tori Amos
corn flakes: 6 cereal
cornhusker: 6 farmer
Cornhuskers
author: Carl Sandburg
Cornhusker State: 3 Neb. 4 Nebr. 8 Nebraska
cornice
bracket: 5 ancon
molding: 4 cyma
ornament: 6 dentil
support: 6 corbel, frieze
Corniche: 3 car 4 auto 10 Rolls-Royce
Corning
competitor: 5 Pyrex
__ Corning: 5 Owens
Corn Is Green, The
author: Emlyn Williams
Cornish: 4 fowl 7 chicken
relative: *see* chicken
__ Cornish game hen: 4 Rock
Cornishman: 4 Celt
Cornish Rex: 3 cat 5 felid 6 feline
cornmeal: 5 grain
product: 4 mush
cornmeal product: 4 mush, pone
corn on the __: 3 cob
Corn Pops
competitor: *see* cereal
cornrow: 5 braid, plait
cornrows: 4 coif 6 hairdo 8 coiffure
alternative: 4 Afro
cornstalks: 6 fodder
cornstarch name: 4 Argo
cornu: 4 horn
cornucopia: 4 horn 6 wealth 9 plenitude, profusion
item: 5 fruit
Cornwall: 4 city, town 6 county
locale: 6 Canada 7 England, Ontario
town: 5 Truro
Cornwallis alma mater: 4 Eton
Cornwell: 8 Patricia
corny: 4 dull 5 banal, hoary, hokey, inane, mushy, passé, sappy, silly, stale, tired, trite, vapid 6 common, jejune, old hat 7 clichéd, fatuous, humdrum, mawkish, prosaic 8 bromidic, overdone, outdated, outmoded, romantic, schmalzy, shmaltzy, shopworn 9 hackneyed, prosaical, schmaltzy 10 uninspired, unoriginal
__ corny as...: 4 I'm as
Corolla: 3 car 4 auto 6 Toyota
corolla part: 5 petal
corollary: 9 deduction, induction, inference 10 conclusion, end product
corona: 3 gas 4 halo, ring 5 cigar, crown 7 aureola, aureole 8 gloriole 9 flower top
part: 5 petal
Corona: 4 beer, city, font, town 8 typeface
alternative: *see* beer
locale: 10 California
Coronado: 4 city, town
locale: 10 California
Coronado, Francisco de: 8 explorer
coronary __: 4 vein 5 sinus 6 artery, bypass
coronate: 5 crown 6 anoint
Coronation Ode
composer: Edward Elgar
coronet: 5 crown, tiara 6 anadem, diadem, wreath 7 chaplet, garland 8 headband
Coronet: 3 car 4 auto 5 Dodge
Corot, Camille: 6 artist 7 painter
homeland: 6 France
corp.: 3 org.
see also corporate
__ corp.: 3 hab.

corporal: 3 NCO 4 rank 6 bodily 7 somatic 8 anatomic, physical 10 anatomical
denial: 5 no sir
___ corporal: 5 lance
___ Corporal: 6 Little
corporate: 5 joint 6 allied, shared, united 8 communal 9 aggregate 10 collective
abbr.: 3 inc., ltd.
alias: 3 DBA
concern: 4 debt 5 image
coverage: 3 HMO
cutback: 3 RIF
czar: 5 mogul
deal: 3 LBO 8 takeover
department: 5 legal, R and D, sales
employee: 2 GM 3 CEO, CFO, COO, mgr. 4 exec, pres., secy. 5 treas.
entity: 4 firm
ID: 2 TM 4 logo
illustration: 5 chart
jet: 4 Lear
section: 3 div. 4 dept.
structure: 5 rungs 6 ladder
corporate ___: 3 jet 4 park 5 image 6 ladder, raider 7 culture, welfare
corporation: 4 firm 5 house, trust 6 outfit 7 company, concern, society 8 business, employer 9 syndicate
dummy ~: 5 front
corporeal: 4 real 5 somal 6 bodily 8 anatomic, material, physical, tangible 9 earthborn, objective, touchable 10 anatomical, phenomenal
corps: 4 army, band, body, crew, team, unit 5 force, group, hands, squad, troop 6 outfit 7 brigade, company, workers 8 division, regiment, squadron 9 battalion, combatant, personnel 10 contingent, detachment
esprit de ~: 6 morale
___ corps: 4 army, drum 5 drill, press 6 signal
___ Corps: 3 Air, Job 5 Peace 6 Marine
Corpse Bride (2005 film)
voice cast: Helena Bonham Carter, Johnny Depp, Tracey Ullman, Emily Watson
corpsman: 5 medic
corpulent: 3 fat
see also obese
corpus: 4 body 5 whole 6 oeuvre 8 entirety 10 collection, cumulation, opera omnia
habeas ~: 4 writ
corpus ___: 5 juris 7 delicti
___ corpus: 6 habeas
Corpus Christi: 4 city, town
county: 6 Nueces
locale: 5 Texas
corpuscle: 4 cell
___ corpuscle: 3 red 5 blood, white
corral: 3 pen 4 find, grab, herd, trap, yard 5 amass, catch, fence, grasp, group, hedge, penin, snare 6 garner, gather, obtain 7 acquire, collect, convene, enclose, inclose, paddock, receive, round up 8 assemble 9 enclosure
part: 5 fence
put back in the ~: 5 repen
sound: 5 neigh, snort 6 whinny
corralled: 4 pent 8 fenced in
correct: 2 OK, so 3 fit, fix 4 cure, edit, good, just, mend, nice, okay, prim, true 5 alter, amend, clean, debug, emend, exact, fix up, moral, reset, right, scrub, sound, valid 6 actual, adjust, better, dead-on, decent, direct, doctor, formal, modify, polish, proper, punish, rebuke, redact, reform, remedy, repair, revise, seemly 7 clean up, factual, fitting, improve, launder, on track, perfect, precise, rectify, redress, regular, shape up, touch up, veridic 8 accurate, decorous, faithful, flawless, ladylike, make over, official, on target, orthodox, penalize, regulate, rigorous, set right, standard, straight, suitable, truthful, unerring 9 do justice, equitable, errorless, faultless, make right, on the beam, on the nose, reconcile, veracious, veridical 10 acceptable, ameliorate, conforming, diplomatic, fiddle with, impeccable, legitimate, make good on, meticulous, on the money, put in order, scrupulous, straighten, turn around, unimagined, unmistaken
a correction: 4 stet
a mistake: 5 erase
combining form: 4 orth- 5 ortho-
Correct!: 3 yes 5 bingo, right 7 exactly 8 you got it 10 that's right
correction: 6 change, rebuke 7 editing, mending, redress, revisal 8 revising, revision 9 amendment 10 adjustment, admonition, alteration, discipline, emendation, punishment, reparation
house of ~: 3 pen 4 jail, stir 6 prison 7 slammer
mid-course ~: 8 variance
correctional: 5 penal
corrections: 6 errata
officer: 6 jailer, warden 7 turnkey
corrective: 5 penal 6 curing, remedy 8 cosmetic, curative, punitive, remedial, sanative 9 antidotal 10 palliative
it may be ~: 4 lens
correctly: 4 to a T, well 5 right 6 aright, dead-on, just so, nicely 7 rightly 8 very well 9 carefully, fittingly, just right, perfectly, precisely 10 accurately, decorously, virtuously
position ~: 5 align, aline
correctness: 5 order, right, truth 6 bon ton 7 decency, decorum, fitness 8 accuracy, civility, fidelity, veracity 9 precision, propriety
Corregidor: 6 battle
correlate: 4 link 5 match, tie in 6 belong, equate 7 compare, connect 8 organize, parallel 9 associate, duplicate, harmonize 10 complement, coordinate
correlation: 4 link 5 match 6 analog 8 analogue, parallel
correlative: 3 and, nor 7 similar
Correo ___: 5 Aereo
correspond: 2 go 3 fit 4 gybe, jibe 5 agree, equal, match, tally, write 6 cohere, equate, square 7 compare, comport, conform 8 check out, coincide, dovetail, resemble 9 correlate, drop a line, drop a note, harmonize, make sense, partake of 10 assimilate, complement, epistolize
ender: 3 ent 4 ence
(to): 6 equate
correspondence: 4 mail, note 5 match, media 6 accord 7 harmony, letters, message, reports 8 likeness, symmetry, sympathy, writings 9 congruity
afterthought: 2 PS
computer ~: 5 e-mail
numerical ~: 5 ratio
correspondence ___: 6 course, school
correspondent: 5 press 6 pen pal, writer 7 related 8 epistler, reporter, stringer
corresponding: 4 akin, same, such 5 alike, equal 6 agnate, allied 7 cognate, kindred, similar 8 matching, opposite, parallel, relative 9 analogous 10 comparable, equivalent, reciprocal
to: 4 like
correspondingly: 5 alike 6 in kind 8 likewise
corrida
beast: 4 toro 6 el toro
floor: 5 arena
shout: 3 olé
corridor: 4 hall 5 aisle, alley, foyer, lobby 6 airway, artery 7 hallway, ingress, passage 10 passageway
Corridors of Power
author: C.P. Snow
Corrigan: 7 Douglas, Mairead 8 Wrong Way
Corrigan, Mairead: 8 Nobelist
corrigenda: 6 errata, errors
corrigendum: 5 error 7 erratum, mistake 8 misprint
Corrina, Corrina (1994 film)
cast: Don Ameche, Joan Cusack, Whoopi Goldberg, Ray Liotta
corroborate: 5 prove, vouch 6 attest, back up, ratify, verify 7 bear out, certify, confirm, endorse, indorse, justify, support, testify, witness 8 document, evidence, validate 9 vindicate
corroboration: 4 test 5 proof 8 evidence 9 testimony
corroborator: 7 witness 10 eyewitness
corrode: 3 eat, rot 4 rust, wear 5 decay, eat at, erode 6 damage, gnaw at 7 consume, destroy, eat away, oxidize, tarnish 8 wear away 10 degenerate
corroded: 5 rusty
corrosion: 3 rot 4 rust, wear 5 decay 6 damage 7 erosion 9 iron oxide
corrosive: 5 acerb, acrid 6 biting, bitter 7 acerbic, caustic, cutting, erosive 8 virulent 9 consuming, sarcastic, trenchant
solution: 3 HCl 5 oleum
corrugate: 4 fold 5 crimp 6 crease, ruffle 7 wrinkle
corrugated: 5 rough 6 fluted, ridged 7 creased, grooved 8 crinkled, furrowed, wrinkled 9 channeled, roughened
container: 6 carton
corrugated ___: 5 paper
corrugation: 4 fold 5 ridge 6 crease, groove 7 wrinkle
corrupt: 3 bad, buy, fix, rot 4 base, evil, foul, gamy, harm, hurt, ruin, soil, vile, warp 5 abase, abuse, bribe, dirty, false, gamey, loose, shady, spoil, stain, taint, venal 6 blight, crud up, damage, debase, defile, demean, filthy, impair, impure, infect, louche, misuse, poison, ravage, rotten, sordid, square, suborn, tamper, unholy, wicked 7 crooked, debased, defiled, degrade, deprave, despoil, ignoble, immoral, knavish, pollute, subvert, tainted, unclean, ungodly, vitiate 8 bribable, criminal, degraded, depraved, disgrace, dishonor, doctored, infamous, infected, maltreat, mistreat, perverse, polluted, shameful, sinister, suborned, two-faced, vitiated 9 dishonest, dissolute, distorted, faithless, falsified, graceless, mercenary, miscreant, nefarious, on the take, poisonous, shameless, undermine, unethical 10 adulterate, degenerate, demoralize, fraudulent, iniquitous, licentious, outrageous, perfidious, profligate, unfaithful, virtueless
corrupted: 3 bad 5 loose 6 sordid 7 immoral 8 maculate 9 abandoned, debauched, dissolute, reprobate 10 dissipated, licentious, profligate
corruptible: 5 venal
corrupting: 7 harmful 9 injurious
corruption: 4 evil, ruin, vice 5 crime, decay, filth, fraud, graft 6 damage, infamy, payoff, payola, racket 7 bribery, jobbery 8 atrocity, baseness, foulness, impurity, iniquity, nepotism, venality 9 barbarism, contagion, decadence, depravity, doctoring, extortion, fourberie, looseness, lubricity, pollution, shadiness, turpitude, vitiation, vulgarity 10 debasement, defilement, degeneracy, dishonesty, distortion, illegality, immorality, profligacy, rottenness, wickedness
Corsa: 3 car 4 auto, Opel 10 automobile
corsac: 5 canid 6 canine, mammal
relative: *see* canine
corsage: 5 spray 8 ornament
flower: 3 mum
corsair: 4 boat 6 pirate, raider, robber, viking 7 brigand 8 marauder, rapparee, sea rover 9 buccaneer, privateer 10 freebooter
quest: 5 booty 7 plunder
ship: 5 xebec, zebec 6 zebeck 7 chebeck
Corsair: 3 car 4 auto 5 Edsel
corset: 5 stays 6 enlace, girdle, inlace 8 lingerie 9 constrict, girdle kin, underwear 10 foundation
material: 6 baleen
stiffener: 4 bone, stay
tightener: 5 lacer
Corsica: 3 car 4 auto, isle 5 Chevy 6 island 9 Chevrolet 10 automobile
hero: 5 Paoli

locale: 5 Medit.
neighbor: 3 Sar. 4 Elba, Sard. 8 Sardinia
port: 6 Bastia 7 Ajaccio
sheep: 7 mouflon 8 moufflon
see also French
Corsicana: 4 city, town
locale: 5 Texas
Corso, Gregory: 6 writer
genre: Beat
Cort: 3 Bud
cortege: 5 suite, train 6 parade 7 caravan, retinue 9 entourage, following 10 procession
Cortés: 6 Hernán 8 Hernando
Cortés, Hernando: 7 Spanish 8 explorer
foe: 5 Aztec
see also Spanish
cortex: 4 bark, peel, rind 9 brain part 10 memory site, outer layer
Cortez: 4 Dave 7 Ricardo
Cortland: 5 apple
relative: *see* apple
Cortot, Alfred: 5 Swiss 7 pianist
corundum: 4 ruby 5 emery, oxide, topaz 7 mineral 8 sapphire
to Mohs: 4 nine
coruscate: 5 flame, flash, gleam, shine 7 glimmer, glisten, glitter, sparkle, twinkle 10 incandesce
coruscating: 3 lit 5 aglow, shiny 6 ablaze, bright, flashy 7 fulgent, lambent, radiant 8 luminous, lustrous 9 brilliant, sparkling
coruscation: 5 flash, gleam, light 7 glimmer, glitter, sparkle 10 brilliance
Corvair: 3 car 4 auto 5 Chevy 9 Chevrolet 10 automobile
critic: 5 Nader
Corvallis: 4 city, town
athletes: 7 Beavers
locale: 6 Oregon
school: 3 OSU
corvette: 4 boat 7 frigate, warship 10 battleship
Corvette: 3 car 4 auto 5 Chevy 9 Chevrolet 10 automobile
producer: 3 GMC
corybantic: 7 frantic 8 frenetic, frenzied 9 delirious
corydalis: 5 plant 6 flower
coryphaeus: 6 leader, singer
coryphée: 6 dancer 9 ballerina
coryza: 4 cold 10 common cold
cos: 6 veggie 7 lettuce, romaine 9 vegetable
__ cos: 3 arc
Cos __, CT: 3 Cob
Cosa __: 6 Nostra
__ Cosa: 4 Cosi
Cosby: 4 Bill, Rita
Cosby, Bill: 5 actor 8 comedian
TV: I Spy
Cosby Show, The (NBC sitcom)
cast: Tempestt Bledsoe (Vanessa Huxtable)
Lisa Bonet (Denise Huxtable)
Bill Cosby (Dr. Cliff Huxtable)
Keshia Knight Pulliam (Rudy Huxtable)
Phylicia Rashad (Clair Huxtable)
Malcolm-Jamal Warner (Theo Huxtable)
cosecant reciprocal: 4 sine
cosec. subj.: 4 trig.
Cosell: 6 Howard
Cosgrave: 4 Liam
cosh: 3 sap 4 club, conk 6 cudgel 8 bludgeon 9 billy club, blackjack, truncheon
cosher: 6 pamper
Cosi __: 4 Cosa
Così fan tutte: 5 opera
composer: Wolfgang Amadeus Mozart
role: 7 Alfonso, Despina 8 Ferrando 9 Dorabella, Guglielmo 10 Don Alfonso, Fiordiligi
setting: 5 Italy 6 Naples
cosign: 9 guarantee 10 underwrite
Cosimo: 8 de' Medici
cosine: 5 ratio
Cosmas: 5 saint
cosmetic: 4 kohl 5 blush, cream, gloss, liner, paint, rouge 6 lotion, makeup, powder 7 mascara, surface 8 lip gloss, lipstick 9 enhancing, eye shadow, improving 10 corrective, decorative, foundation
ancient ~: 4 kohl
applicator: 4 wand
brand: 4 Avon 5 Almay, Arden 6 Revlon 7 Lancome, Mary Kay 8 Clinique 9 Cover Girl, Max Factor 10 Maybelline 11 Estée Lauder, Merle Norman
ingredient: 4 aloe 6 acetal, jojoba
purchase: 3 dye 4 soap, talc, tint 5 blush, gelee, gloss, liner, rinse, toner
safety org.: 3 FDA
cosmic: 4 huge, vast 5 grand 7 immense 8 enormous, infinite 9 grandiose, limitless, universal 10 ecumenical, large-scale, stupendous
principle: 3 Tao 5 karma
ray particle: 4 muon, pion 5 meson 6 proton 7 neutron 8 electron
cosmic __: 3 ray 4 dust
Cosmicomics
author: Italo Calvino
Cosmo: 3 mag 6 Topper 7 Spacely 8 magazine
reader: 5 woman
rival: 4 Elle 5 Vogue
cosmochemistry: 7 science
Cosmological Eye, The
author: Henry Miller
cosmology: 7 science
study: 8 universe
cosmonaut: 9 rocketeer
home: 3 Mir
cosmopolitan: 5 ritzy, urban 6 global, urbane 7 worldly 8 catholic, cultured
area: 3 urb 4 city
not ~: 5 rural
Cosmopolitan
rival: 4 Elle 5 Vogue
cosmos: 5 plant, world 6 flower, galaxy, nature 8 universe
diagram: 7 mandala
Cosmos: 4 font 8 typeface
author/host: Carl Sagan
org.: 4 NASL
star: 4 Pelé
Cossack: 8 horseman 10 equestrian
chief: 6 ataman
headquarters: 4 Omsk
Cossacks, The
author: Leo Tolstoy
cosset: 3 pet 4 baby, love 6 coddle, cuddle, dandle, dote on, fondle, pamper 7 cater to, indulge 8 dote upon
cost: 3 are, fee, tab 4 bite, loss, rate, toll 5 price, quote, run to, value, worth 6 amount, charge, come to, damage, outlay, tariff 7 damages, expense, penalty, require, sell for, tuition 8 amount to, overhead 9 detriment, quotation, reckoning, sacrifice 10 bottom line, forfeiture
at ~: 9 wholesale
at any ~: 10 regardless
bear the ~: 3 pay 6 defray
effective: 10 worthwhile
of operation: 8 overhead
per unit: 4 rate
set a ~: 3 ask
cost __: 6 center 7 overrun
cost __ and a leg: 5 an arm
cost-__: 4 plus 5 share 7 benefit, cutting, justify 9 effective
__ cost: 4 at no, unit 5 at any, fixed
__-cost: 3 low
costa: 3 rib
Costa __: 4 Mesa, Rica 5 Brava, Rican 6 del Sol
Costa __, CA: 4 Mesa
Costa __ Sol: 3 del
Costa __, Spain: 5 Brava
Costa-__: 6 Gavras
__ Costa: 6 Contra
Costa del Sol attraction: 5 beach, playa
Costain, Thomas: 6 writer
work: The Black Rose
The Silver Chalice
Costa Mesa: 4 city, town
locale: 10 California
Costa, Michael oratorio: 3 Eli
cost an arm __ leg: 4 and a
costard: 5 apple
relative: *see* apple
Costa Rica: 6 nation 7 country
capital: 7 San José
city: 5 Limon 7 San José
export: 7 bananas
gulf: 8 Papagayo
leader: 5 Arias
money: 5 colon 7 centimo
neighbor: 6 Panama 9 Nicaragua
Nobelist in Peace: 7 Sanchez
org.: 3 OAS
volcano: 4 Póas 5 Irazu 6 Arenal
see also Spanish
Costa Rican: 4 Tico
Costas: 3 Bob 8 Mandylor
Costco
rival: 3 BJ's 8 Sam's Club
cost-conscious: 6 frugal 7 sparing
cost-control agcy., '40s: 3 OPA
Costello: 3 Lou 5 Elvis
part of an Abbott and ~ routine: 4 Who's
costing little: 3 low 5 cheap 6 modest, on sale 7 cut-rate, reduced, slashed 8 for a song 9 half-price 10 economical, marked down, reasonable
costless: 4 free 6 gratis 10 on the house
costly: 4 dear, high, rich 5 plush, pricy, steep 6 deluxe, lavish, pricey 7 harmful, premium, ruinous 8 damaging, precious, splendid, valuable 9 big-ticket, excessive, expensive, luxurious, priceless, sumptuous 10 disastrous, exorbitant, high-priced
Costner, Kevin: 5 actor
film: American Flyers (1985)
Bull Durham (1988)
Dances With Wolves (1990, AA)
Dragonfly (2002)
Field of Dreams (1989)
For Love of the Game (1999)
JFK (1991)
Message in a Bottle (1999)
No Way Out (1987)
Open Range (2003)
A Perfect World (1993)
Revenge (1990)
Robin Hood: Prince of Thieves (1991)
Rumor Has It (2005)
Silverado (1985)
Swing Vote (2008)
Thirteen Days (2000)
Tin Cup (1996)
The Untouchables (1987)
The Upside of Anger (2005)
Waterworld (1995)
Wyatt Earp (1994)
role: 4 Earp, Hood, Ness
TV: The Upside
cost-of-living stat: 3 CPI
costs: 6 upkeep
absorb, as ~: 3 eat
gross less ~: 3 net
including mailing ~: 3 ppd. 8 postpaid
__ costs: 5 at all 7 closing
costume: 3 rig 4 duds, garb, gear, gown, suit 5 dress, getup, guise, habit, robes, style 6 attire, clothe, livery, outfit 7 apparel, bedrape, clothes, fashion, garment, uniform 8 clothing, disguise, ensemble 9 trappings 10 masquerade, Sunday best
attend in ~: 4 go as
kind of ~: 5 clown, ghost, witch
party: 6 masque 10 masquerade
costume __: 5 party 7 jewelry
costumes: 6 guises 8 wardrobe
costume-shop item: 3 wig
cosy: 4 homy, nice, safe, snug, soft, warm 5 comfy, cushy, homey 6 chummy, folksy, secure 7 livable, nestled, restful 8 familiar, intimate, liveable, tucked in 9 cuddled up, sheltered
cot: 3 bed 4 bunk 5 bower, hutch 6 gurney 7 charpai, charpoy, trundle
on wheels: 6 gurney
__ cot: 3 arc
cote: 9 sheepfold
dweller: 3 ewe, ram 4 dove, lamb
sound: 3 baa, coo, maa 5 bleat 6 baa baa, baaing
starter: 4 dove 5 sheep
Côte __: 3 d'Or 5 d'Azur 7 d'Ivoire
Côte d'Azur resort: 4 Nice
Côte d'Ivoire: 6 nation 7 country
see also Ivory Coast
coterie: 3 mob, set 4 band, clan, club, gang, pack, ring, team 5 cabal, class, crowd, group, junto, lodge, party 6 circle, clique, outfit 7 company, faction, in-group

8 sorority 9 following, hangers-on 10 fellowship, fraternity
coterminous: 4 even
Cotillard, Márion
film: La Vie en Rose (2007, AA)
cotillion: 5 dance 9 festivity
attendee: 3 deb
Cotler: 4 Kami
Cotopaxi: 7 volcano
locale: 7 Ecuador
Cotswold: 5 sheep
cottage: 3 hut 4 home 5 bower, cabin, hovel, hutch, lodge, shack 6 cabana, chalet, lean-to, shanty 8 bungalow, lodgment, quarters
cottage __: 5 fries 6 cheese 8 industry
cottage cheese
bit: 4 curd 5 chive
relative: 7 ricotta
Cottage, The
author: Danielle Steel
Cotten: 6 Joseph
cotter: 5 wedge
cotter __: 3 pin
cotton: 4 crop, duck, lawn 6 dimity, fabric 7 padding, rapport
alternative: 5 Orlon, rayon
ball of ~: 3 wad
Egyptian ~: 3 sak
ender: 4 seed, tail, weed, wood 5 mouth
fabric: 3 rep 4 duck, lawn, leno, pima, repp 5 baize, chino, crape, crepe, denim, dhoti, dhuti, khaki, piqué, plush, scrim, terry, toile, voile 6 calico, canvas, chally, chintz, damask, dhooti, dimity, gloria, madras, moreen, muslin, oxford, pongee, poplin, sateen, wadmal 7 buckram, bunting, cambric, challie, challis, dhootie, duvetyn, etamine, flannel, foulard, fustian, galatea, gingham, jaconet, khaddar, nankeen, oilskin, organdy, percale, satinet, silesia, ticking, tiffany, Viyella 8 Burberry, chambray, corduroy, Indienne, marcella, moleskin, nainsook, oilcloth, organdie, shantung, tarlatan 9 crinoline, flannelet, gabardine, paramatta, percaline, sailcloth, satinette, silkaline, velveteen 10 balbriggan, marseilles, seersucker
fiber: 4 noil
gin name: 3 Eli 7 Whitney
knot: 3 nep
like unginned ~: 5 seedy
machine: 3 gin 5 baler
matted ~: 4 batt
mesh: 4 leno
on a stick: 4 Q-tip
pod: 4 boll
thread: 5 lisle
to: 5 enjoy 8 befriend
unit: 4 bale
cotton __: 3 gin 4 mill 5 candy
cotton-__: 7 picking
Cotton: 6 Mather 7 Charles
Land of ~: 5 Dixie
Cotton __: 4 Belt
Cotton __, The: 4 Club
__ Cotton: 4 King
Cotton Bowl site: 5 Texas 6 Dallas
Cotton-Broker's Office
artist: Edgar Degas
Cotton Candy
artist: Al Hirt
Cotton, Charles: 4 poet 7 British
Cotton Club, The (1984 film)
cast: Richard Gere, Gregory Hines, Diane Lane
director: Francis Ford Coppola
setting: 6 Harlem
Cotton Comes to Harlem
author: Chester Himes
Cottonelle
alternative: 5 Scott 6 Marcal 7 Charmin 8 Northern, Soft Weve 10 White Cloud
cottonlike fiber: 5 ramee, ramie
cottonmouth: 5 snake
cottonmouthed: 7 parched, thirsty
cotton-pickin': 6 dad-gum, darned
cottonseed __: 3 oil 4 cake, meal
cottontail: 6 mammal, rabbit, rodent
tail: 4 scut
Cottontail: 5 Peter
sibling: 5 Mopsy 6 Flopsy
cottonwood: 4 tree 5 alamo 6 poplar
cousin: 5 aspen
cottony fiber: 5 floss
Coty: 4 René
couch: 3 lie, put 4 hide, mask, seat, sofa, veil, word 5 cache, cloak, cover, divan, frame, lodge, lower, utter 6 daybed, indite, lounge, phrase, settee 7 conceal, express, obscure, seating, secrete 8 disguise, love seat 9 davenport, formulate, furniture, tête-à-tête 10 camouflage
emulate a ~ potato: 4 laze, loll
leave the ~: 4 rise 5 arise, get up
couch __: 6 potato
couch potato: 5 idler, sloth 6 loller
choice: 5 cable
like a ~: 4 lazy 5 inert
need: 2 TV 3 VCR 4 dish, tube 5 TV set 7 cable TV
spot: 3 den 4 sofa
unlike a ~: 6 active
what a ~ does: 3 veg 4 loll
cougar: 3 cat 4 puma 5 felid 6 animal, feline, mammal 7 panther, wildcat
color: 5 tawny
genus: 5 felis
relative: *see* feline
Cougar: 3 car 4 auto, Merc 7 Mercury 10 automobile
__ Cougar Mellencamp: 4 John
Cougars: 3 WSU
cough: 4 hack 6 wheeze
syrup ingredient: 4 tolu 6 ipecac
syrup measure: 4 tbsp. 10 tablespoon
up: 3 pay 4 ante 5 spend 6 pay out 8 fork over, hand over 10 recompense
cough __: 4 drop 5 syrup
cough drop: 6 troche 7 lozenge
flavoring: 4 mint 5 anise, lemon 7 menthol
like ~s: 3 OTC
name: 5 Hall's, Smith 6 Luden's
could: 3 may 5 might
it ~ be: 5 maybe
...could __ fat: 5 eat no
...could __ horse!: 4 eat a
...could __ lean: 5 eat no
Could __ Magic: 4 It Be
...could eat __: 5 no fat 6 no lean
Could I Have This Kiss Forever (2000 song)
artist: Whitney Houston
Could It Be I'm Falling in Love (1973 song)
artist: Spinners
Could It Be Magic (1975 song)
artist: Barry Manilow
couldn't __ less: 4 care
Couldn't agree more!: 6 I'll say
__ Could Read My Mind: 5 If You
__ Could Turn Back Time: 3 If I
Could You Use Me?
composer: George Gershwin, Ira Gershwin
coulee: 5 cañon, gulch 6 arroyo, canyon, ravine, valley
__ Coulee Dam: 5 Grand
coulomb per second: 3 amp
Coulter: 3 Ann
council: 4 bloc, diet 5 board, divan, house, junta, panel, synod 6 caucus, confab, jurors, powwow 7 academy, cabinet, chamber 8 assembly, conclave, congress, ecclesia 9 committee, gathering, syndicate 10 brain trust, conference, convention, executives
African ~: 6 indaba
Anglo-Saxon ~: 5 witan
chamber: 5 divan
Chinese ~: 4 yuan
church ~: 5 curia, synod
ender: 3 man, men 5 woman, women
honcho: 5 chair
member: 3 ald. 8 alderman, lawmaker
military ~: 5 junta
Muslim ~: 5 ulema
post-Reformation ~: 5 Trent
Roman ~: 6 Senate
Russian ~: 4 Duma
__ council: 4 city 5 privy
Council Bluffs: 4 city, town
locale: 4 Iowa
neighbor: 5 Omaha
council, literally,: 6 Soviet
counsel: 3 att. 4 atty., urge, warn 5 guide, steer 6 advice, advise, direct, enjoin, exhort, inform, jurist, lawyer, legist, prompt 7 adviser, advisor, caution, propose, suggest 8 admonish, advocate, attorney, guidance, instruct, persuade 9 barrister, recommend, solicitor 10 mouthpiece
in Britain: 4 rede
seek ~ from: 6 look to
counselor: 3 att. 4 atty. 5 guide 6 jurist, lawyer, leader, legist, mentor 7 adviser, advisor, teacher 8 advocate, attorney 9 abecedary, barrister, solicitor 10 instructor, legal eagle, mouthpiece
deg.: 2 J.D. 3 BSW, LL.B., LL.D., LL.M., MSW, S.J.D.
female ~: 6 egeria
counselor-__: 5 at-law
counselors: 7 cabinet 10 brain trust
Counselors-at-Law
author: Jerome Weidman
count: 3 add, sum 4 deem, poll, rank, rate 5 add up, check, gauge, judge, noble, score, stock, sum up, tally, title, total, tot up 6 cipher, figure, matter, number, reckon, regard, voting 7 compute, figures, include, itemize, tick off 8 consider, look upon, nobleman, numerate 9 blueblood, calculate, enumerate, keep score, numbering, reckoning
ender: 3 ess 4 down
in England: 4 earl
count __: 3 out 4 down, upon 5 heads, noses
__ count: 3 red 4 head 5 blood 6 pollen
Count: 5 Basie, title
Count __!: 4 me in, on me 5 me out
Count __ Blessings: 4 Your
countable: 6 finite 10 calculable, explicable
Count Chocula
competitor: *see* cereal
countdown
delay: 4 hold
discontinue the ~: 5 abort
number: 3 one, six, ten, two 4 five, four, nine, zero 5 eight, seven, three
word: 5 minus
Countdown (1968 film)
cast: James Caan, Robert Duvall
director: Robert Altman
__ Countdown, The: 5 Final
counted, first to be: 4 eeny
Countee: 6 Cullen
countenance: 3 mug 4 back, bear, cast, face, look, mien, puss, spur 5 brook, nod at, stand 6 accept, aspect, endure, handle, kisser, suffer, uphold, visage 7 applaud, approve, condone, endorse, indorse, smile on, support 8 calmness, features, hold with, live with, sanction, stand for, tolerate
don't ~: 5 scorn 6 deride
put out of ~: 6 rattle
counter: 4 desk, foil, loth 5 loath, parry, polar, react, rebut, reply, shelf, stand 6 answer, gainst, offset, oppose, refute, resist, retort, thwart 7 adverse, against, hit back, obviate, opposed, prevent, respond, reverse 8 contrary, opposing, opposite 9 antipodal, diametric, frustrate, retaliate 10 antithetic
ender: 3 act, man, men, spy, sue, top 4 blow, coup, foil, glow, mine, move, pane, part, plan, play, plea, plot, pose, sign, sink, suit 5 check, claim, force, march, offer, point, poise, punch, shaft, stain, tenor, trade, weigh, woman, women 6 attack, change, charge, person, terror 7 balance, culture, current, example, factual, measure, persons, shading 8 argument, cyclical, irritant, proposal 9 clockwise, espionage, insurgent, offensive 10 productive, revolution
go ~ to: 4 defy, vary 5 cross, flout, rebel 6 differ, ignore, oppose 7 deviate, disobey, diverge, violate 8 conflict, contrast, disagree 9 disregard 10 contravene
seat: 5 stool
to: 3 con 4 anti 6 versus 7 against,

athwart **8** opposing **10** at odds with
___ counter: 4 bean, card, dust **5** lunch **6** Geiger
counteract: 4 foil, undo **5** annul, check **6** cancel, hinder, negate, offset, oppose, thwart **7** balance, obviate, prevent, rectify, redress **9** cancel out, frustrate, go against **10** antagonize, compensate, contradict, contravene, invalidate, neutralize
counteractant: 4 cure **8** antidote
counterargue: 5 rebut
Counter-Attack and Other Poems
author: Siegfried Sassoon
counterbalance: 5 weigh **6** cancel, offset, redeem **8** outweigh, reaction **9** stabilize **10** neutralize
countercharge: 5 reply **6** answer
counterclockwise: 4 levo
counterculturist: 5 rebel
countercurrent: 4 eddy
counterevidence, offer: 5 rebut
counterfactual: 5 wrong **7** in error
counterfeit: 3 bad **4** copy, fake, imit., mock, sham **5** bogus, faked, false, forge, fraud, phony, put-on, quack, queer **6** copied, ersatz, forged, phoney, pseudo, unreal **7** assumed, feigned, forgery, pretend **8** knockoff, simulate, spurious **9** imitation, pretended, simulated, synthetic **10** artificial, fabricated, fictitious, fraudulent
counterfeiter: 5 faker **6** forger **8** swindler
nemesis: 4 T-man
Counterfeiters, The
author: André Gide
counterfoil: 4 stub **7** receipt
counterirritant: 5 salve **8** ointment
countermand: 3 nix **4** kill, lift **5** annul, quash **6** cancel, negate, recall, recant, repeal, revoke **7** rescind, retract, reverse **8** override, overrule, overturn
counterpane: 5 quilt, throw **8** coverlet, coverlid **9** bedspread, comforter, eiderdown
counterpart: 4 copy, mate, twin **5** equal, match **6** analog **7** coequal **8** analogue, likeness, opposite
counterperson: 5 clerk
counterpoint: 5 music **7** descant, discant
master: 4 Bach
counterpoise: 6 redeem, weight **8** reaction **9** stabilize
countersign: 4 word **7** endorse, indorse, witness **8** password
countersink: 4 ream **5** drill
countertenor: 4 alto **5** voice **8** vocalist
countervail: 6 redeem
counterweight: 4 tare
countess: 4 lady, peer, rank **5** noble, title, woman
husband: 4 earl
Countess Cathleen, The
author: William Butler Yeats
Countess From Hong Kong, A (1967 film)
cast: Marlon Brando, Sydney Chaplin, Tippi Hedren, Sophia Loren
director: Charles Chaplin
counting: 4 with **8** addition **9** including
aid: 6 abacus **7** fingers **9** slide rule **10** calculator
ender: 5 house
everything: 6 in toto, wholly **7** totally **10** altogether, completely
game: 3 nim
Inca ~ device: 5 quipu
not ~: 7 besides **9** apart from, aside from, other than
on: 9 confident, dependant, dependent, presuming
unit: 5 dozen, gross
counting-out word: 3 moe **4** eeny **5** meeny, miney
Counting the Ways
author: Edward Albee
countless: 4 many **6** divers, gobs of, legion, lots of, myriad, umteen, untold **7** copious, endless, heaping, heaps of, no end of, piles of, profuse, scads of, umpteen **8** abundant, infinite, manifold, numerous, oodles of, prodigal, scores of, umpsteen, unending **9** boundless, bountiful, limitless, quite a few, unlimited **10** innumerous, numberless, unnumbered, zillions of
combining form: 4 myri- **5** myrio-
Count me in!: 4 sure **6** I'm game
Count Me In (1965 song)
artist: Gary Lewis and the Playboys
Count of Monte Cristo, The: 5 novel
author: Alexandre Dumas
character: 4 Abbé **5** Julie, Louis, Luigi, Renée, Vampa **6** Dantès, Debray, Edmond, Haidée, Lucien, Morrel **7** Assunta, Eugénie, Gaspard, Herbaut, Morcerf, Peppino **8** Danglars, Mercédès **9** Villefort
director: Rowland Lee
Count on Me (song)
artist: Jefferson Starship, Whitney Houston
countrified: 4 farm, naif **5** naive, rural **6** rustic **7** bucolic **8** agrarian, down-home **9** backwoods, bucolical, parochial **10** provincial
country: 4 land, soil **5** genre, music, place, realm, rural, state **6** nation, public, region, rustic, voters **7** bucolic, grounds, kingdom, terrain **8** agrarian, Arcadian, citizens, dominion, homeland, outdoors, pastoral, populace **9** backwoods, boondocks, bucolical, citizenry, territory **10** provincial
addr.: 2 RR **3** RFD, rte.
Africa: 4 Chad, Mali, Togo **5** Benin, Congo, Egypt, Gabon, Ghana, Kenya, Libya, Niger, Sudan **6** Angola, Gambia, Malawi, Uganda, Zambia **7** Algeria, Eritrea, Lesotho, Morocco, Namibia, Nigeria, Senegal, Somalia, Tunisia **8** Botswana, Cameroon, Ethiopia, Tanzania, Zimbabwe **9** Swaziland **10** Ivory Coast, Madagascar, Mauritania, Mozambique **11** Burkina Faso, Côte d'Ivoire, Sierra Leone, South Africa **12** Guinea-Bissau
Asia: 3 Isr., Leb., Nam, Pak., Syr. **4** Irak, Iran, Iraq, Laos, Oman **5** Burma, China, India, Japan, Korea, Nepal, Qatar, Syria, Tibet, Yemen **6** Brunei, Israel, Taiwan, Turkey, Xizang **7** Lebanon, Myanmar, Sitsang, Vietnam **8** Cambodia, Malaysia, Maldives, Mongolia, Pakistan, Sri Lanka, Thailand **9** Indonesia, Kirghizia, New Guinea **10** Kazakhstan, North Korea, South Korea, Uzbekistan **11** Philippines
ender: 3 man, men **4** side, wide **5** woman, women
Europe: 3 Aus., Lux., Rus., Swe. **4** Aust., Belg., Bulg., Eire, Erin, Gr. Br., Holl., Icel., Lith., Neth., Norw., Swed. **5** Italy, Spain **6** Bosnia, España, France, Greece, Latvia, Monaco, Norway, Poland, Russia, Serbia, Sweden, Turkey **7** Albania, Andorra, Belarus, Belgium, Croatia, Denmark, England, Estonia, Finland, Germany, Holland, Hungary, Iceland, Ireland, Moldova, Romania, Ukraine **8** Bulgaria, Portugal, Slovakia, Slovenia **9** Lithuania **11** Netherlands, Switzerland, Vatican City **12** Great Britain **13** Liechtenstein
home: 5 villa **6** estate
North America: 4 Cuba **5** Haiti **6** Belize, Canada, Mexico, Panama **7** Jamaica **8** Honduras **9** Costa Rica, Guatamala, Nicaragua **10** El Salvador, The Bahamas **12** United States **17** Dominican Republic
South America: 4 Peru **5** Chile **6** Brazil, Guyana **7** Bolivia, Ecuador, Uruguay **8** Colombia, Paraguay, Suriname **9** Argentina, Venezuela
starter: 4 back
country ___: 3 ham **4** club, mile, rock **5** fries, house, music, store **6** cousin, singer **7** kitchen
country-___: 4 bred **5** dance **7** western
___ country: 3 cow, old **4** back, God's **6** mother
___-country: 3 out **5** cross
Country (1984 film)
cast: Jessica Lange, Sam Shepard
Country ___ McDonald: 3 Joe
Country ___, The: 4 Girl, Wife **6** Doctor
country club
cry: 4 fore
fee: 4 dues
instructor: 3 pro **7** golf pro
Country Doctor, The
author: Honoré de Balzac
Country Girl, The: 4 film, play
author: Clifford Odets
cast: Bing Crosby, William Holden, Grace Kelly
character: 4 Dodd **5** Elgin **6** Bennie **7** Georgie
Country Joe: 8 McDonald
countryman: 8 indigene
country music
guitar: 5 Dobro
star: 4 Cash, Ford, Gill, Hall, Hill, Lynn, Reba, Snow, Tubb **5** Acuff, Autry, Black, Cline, Fargo, Foley, Gayle, Husky, Owens, Price, Pride, Tritt, Twain, Wells, Wills, Young **6** Arnold, Brooks, McGraw, Milsap, Nelson, Parton, Ritter, Strait, Tillis, Twitty **7** Haggard, Robbins, Wagoner, Wynette, Wynonna **8** Bob Wills, Campbell, Hank Snow, Jennings, Loveless, McEntire, Ray Price, Red Foley, Roy Acuff, Tom T. Hall, Williams, Yearwood **9** Buck Owens, Ernie Ford, Faith Hill, Gene Autry, Mel Tillis, Pam Tillis, Tex Ritter, Tim McGraw, Vince Gill **10** Clint Black, Donna Fargo, Eddy Arnold, Ernest Tubb, Faron Young, Kitty Wells, Patsy Cline **11** Shania Twain
countryside: 4 land **6** nature **8** outdoors **9** landscape
of the ~: 5 rural **8** pastoral
Country Waif
author: George Sand
countrywide: 4 natl. **8** national
Country Wife, The
author: William Wycherley
___ count the ways: 5 let me
county: 5 shire **8** district, province
ender: 4 wide
England: 4 Beds, Kent, Oxon **5** Berks, Bucks, Cambs, Devon, Essex, Hants, Herts, Hunts, Lancs, Leics, Lincs, Middx, Notts, Salop, Warks, Wilts, Worcs, Yorks **6** Derbys, Dorset, Durham, Gloucs, Staffs, Surrey, Sussex **7** Norfolk, Rutland, Suffolk **8** Cheshire, Cornwall, Hereford, Somerset **9** Berkshire, Hampshire, Middlesex, Northants, Wiltshire, Yorkshire **10** Cumberland, Derbyshire, Lancashire, Shropshire
fair feature: 5 booth
Ireland: 4 Cork, Mayo **5** Cavan, Clare, Kerry, Louth, Meath, Sligo **6** Carlow, Dublin, Galway, Offaly **7** Donegal, Kildare, Leitrim, Wexford, Wicklow **8** Kilkenny, Laoighis, Limerick, Longford, Monaghan **9** Roscommon, Tipperary, Waterford, Westmeath
county ___: 4 fair, line, seat **5** clerk, court
___ County: 5 Bloom
County Cavan, river through: 4 Erne
County Chairman, The
author: George Ade
County Donegal islands: 4 Aran
Count Your Blessings...
composer: Irving Berlin
coup: 4 deed, feat **5** purge **6** revolt, stroke **7** exploit, triumph **8** conquest **10** revolution, usurpation
coup ___: 5 d'état

coup de __: 5 grâce
coup d'état: 10 revolution
pull off a ~: 5 usurp
coupe: 3 car 4 auto 7 dessert, two-door 10 automobile
cousin: 5 sedan
Coupe de Ville: 3 car 4 auto 8 Cadillac
couple: 2 pr. 3 duo, tie, two, wed 4 duad, dyad, item, join, link, pair, yoke 5 brace, deuce, hitch, match, twain, unite 6 adjoin, attach, cohere, fasten, hook on, hook up 7 bracket, combine, conjoin, connect, doublet, harness, hitch on, twosome 9 associate, newlyweds
a ~ of times: 5 twice
half of a ~: 3 one 4 wife 5 bride, groom 7 husband
new ~: 4 item
two-career ~: 4 dink
two ~s: 4 four
coupled: 4 dual 6 double
with: 3 and
(with): 5 along
Couple of Swells, A
composer: Irving Berlin
coupler: 4 link, yoke 8 vinculum
Couples, Fred: 6 golfer
couplet: 3 duo, two 4 rime 5 rhyme, verse
__ Couple, The: 3 Odd
coupling: 4 link, yoke 5 joint 6 hookup 8 junction, juncture 10 attachment, connection
coupon: 6 ticket 7 voucher 10 order blank
clipper: 5 saver
save, as a ~: 4 clip 6 cut out
site: 2 ad 5 paper 9 newspaper
use a ~: 4 save 6 redeem
coupon __: 4 bond, rate 7 clipper
__-coupon bond: 4 zero
courage: 4 dash, grit, guts, soul 5 heart, moxie, nerve, pluck, spine, spunk, valor 6 daring, mettle, spirit, starch 7 bravery, bravura, heroism, prowess, resolve 8 audacity, backbone, boldness, firmness, gumption, rashness, strength, temerity, tenacity 9 assurance, character, endurance, fortitude, gallantry, hardiness 10 confidence, enterprise, knighthood
deprive of ~: 5 unman
ending: 3 ous
lose ~: 6 falter
restore ~: 5 reman
courageous: 4 bold, game 5 brave, gutsy, hardy, manly, nervy, stout, tough 6 awless, daring, gritty, heroic, plucky, spunky, strong 7 assured, aweless, defiant, doughty, gallant, impavid, leonine, staunch, valiant 8 fearless, heroical, intrepid, resolute, spirited, stalwart, unafraid, valorous 9 audacious, confident, daredevil, dauntless, dreadless, herculean, tenacious, undaunted, unfearful, unfearing, venturous 10 chivalrous, fire-eating, mettlesome, red-blooded, undismayed
be ~: 4 dare
not ~: 3 shy 4 weak 5 faint, timid 6 afraid, craven, scared, yellow 7 fearful, gutless, panicky 8 cowardly, recreant, timorous 9 dastardly, nerveless, spineless, tremulous 10 frightened
one: 4 hero, lion 5 darer
Courage Under Fire (1996 film)
cast: Matt Damon, Meg Ryan, Denzel Washington
Courant: 5 paper 9 newspaper
locale: 8 Hartford
courant, au: 3 new 5 aware, newsy 6 posted, versed, wise to 7 abreast, updated 8 familiar, informed, up-to-date 9 cognizant, conscious, in fashion, observant 10 conversant
courante: 5 dance
Couric: 5 Katie
courier: 5 envoy 6 bearer, herald, legate, runner 8 emissary 9 messenger
Courier: 4 font 8 typeface
Courier, Jim: 7 netster 9 tennis pro
milieu: 5 court
Courier Journal: 5 paper 9 newspaper
locale: 10 Louisville
course: 3 lap, run, way 4 dish, duct, flow, mode, path, pour, race, road, rush, soup, tack, term, tide, tier, west 5 canal, class, layer, march, orbit, round, route, salad, speed, spell, steps, sweep, track, trail, train, trend 6 access, artery, avenue, entrée, length, method, period, policy, resort, scheme, series, stream 7 advance, channel, circuit, conduit, current, dessert, heading, ingress, measure, passage, process, program, regimen, seminar, subject, tactics 8 approach, aqueduct, duration, elective, lifetime, movement, progress, sequence, tendency 9 direction, golf links, itinerary, procedure, racetrack, unfolding 10 continuity, discipline, procession, succession, trajectory
audit a ~: 5 sit in
change ~: 3 yaw, zag, zig 4 tack, turn, veer 5 sheer
change of ~: 5 U-turn
college ~: 3 art, bio., bot., eco., Eng., geo., mus., sci., sem., soc. 4 chem., econ., geol., hist., math, phys, stat. 5 drama, music, psych 6 botany, Eng. Lit., French, German, phys. ed. 7 biology, English, geology, history, physics, science, seminar, Spanish 8 calculus 9 chemistry, economics, sociology 10 English Lit, literature, psychology, statistics
combining form: 4 drom- 5 -drome, dromo-
cushy ~: 5 easy A
dinner ~: 4 soup 5 salad 6 entrée 7 dessert 9 appetizer
down a ~: 3 eat
finale: 4 exam, test
first ~: 4 soup 5 salad
first ~ of action: 5 plan A
golf ~: 5 links
go off ~: 3 err, yaw, zag 4 roam, rove, skid, slue, tack, turn, veer 5 drift, lurch, range, slide, stray, swing 6 divert, ramble, swerve, wander 7 deflect, deviate, digress, diverge, maunder, meander 8 sideslip
high school ~: 3 alg., art, bio., Eng., geo., gym, lit, mus. 4 biol., chem., econ., hist., math, trig 5 music 7 algebra, biology, English, physics 8 geometry 9 chemistry 10 literature
in due ~: 3 yet 4 anon, soon 10 eventually, ultimately
in the ~ of: 4 amid 5 along, among 6 amidst, during, mongst 7 amongst
length: 4 term 8 semester
listing: 4 menu
main ~: 4 meat 6 entrée
main ~ of study: 5 major
marker: 5 pylon
math ~: 3 alg. 4 calc., geom., stat., trig 7 algebra 8 calculus, geometry 10 statistics
of ~: 2 ay, da, ja, sí 3 aye, oui, yea, yep, yes, yup 4 fine, okay, sure, yeah 5 good-o, natch, quite, right, roger, truly, uh-huh 6 agreed, and how, gladly, good-oh, indeed, just so, rather, really, righto, surely, you bet, yowzah 7 exactly, for sure, go ahead, indeedy, mais oui, no doubt, quite so, ten-four 8 all right, as you say, thumbs up, very well 9 assuredly, be my guest, certainly, darn right, naturally, obviously, precisely, sure thing, you betcha, you said it 10 absolutely, as expected, by all means, definitely, far and away, positively, sure enough, that's right
of action: 3 way 4 line, plan 6 policy 7 process 10 proceeding
of events: 4 tide
off ~: 4 awry 6 afield, astray
of thought: 5 logic, tenor
par for the ~: 4 norm 5 typic, usual 6 normal 7 typical 8 expected
plot a ~: 5 chart 8 navigate
pursue one's ~: 4 wend
reading: 4 text 8 textbook
run its ~: 3 ebb 4 ease, fade, flag, stop, wane 5 abate, let up, relax 6 ease up, lessen, recede 7 die down, dwindle, ease off, slacken, subside, tail off 8 blow over, diminish, fade away, moderate, peter out, taper off 10 slacken off
science ~: 3 bio. 4 biol., chem., geol., phys. 7 biology, geology, physics, science 9 chemistry
seafood ~: 4 bisk, sole, tuna 6 bisque, salmon, scampi, shrimp 7 lobster 8 flounder
secondary ~: 6 bypath
secondary ~ of action: 5 plan B
short ~: 6 clinic
starter: 4 race 5 water 6 string
stay the ~: 5 stand 7 persist 8 stand for, tolerate 9 persevere
take a ~: 5 enrol, learn, study 6 enroll
take a refresher ~: 6 bone up
through the ~ of: 4 amid 6 amidst
throw off ~: 6 derail
unit: 6 credit, lesson
__ course: 4 cram, golf, lay a, main 5 crash, in due
court: 3 bar, woo 4 date, love, quad, walk, yard 5 bench, forum, judge, motel, patio, plaza, spark, spoon, staff 6 atrium, call on, garden, piazza, pursue, square, street 7 retinue, take out, wheedle 8 fawn over, kowtow to, tribunal 9 cultivate, enclosure, entourage, go out with, importune, Old Bailey, shine up to 10 attendants, quadrangle
appointee: 6 elisor 7 eslisor
award: 7 damages
barrier: 3 net
bring back to ~: 5 retry
bring into ~: 4 haul
British ~ of old: 4 leet
calendar: 6 docket
call: 3 let, out 4 ad in, foul, oyes, oyez 6 hear ye
case: 3 res 5 trial 7 lawsuit
central ~s: 5 atria
church ~: 4 rota
clerical ~: 4 rota
come before the ~: 6 appear
concern: 3 law 4 case, suit 5 trial
contest: 5 match
cry: 4 oyes, oyez 6 hear ye
decision: 3 let 5 award, guilt 6 ruling 7 verdict
ender: 3 ier 4 room, ship, side, yard 5 house
entertain the ~: 4 jest
evidence: 3 DNA
expel from ~: 6 disbar
figure: 3 att. 4 atty., suer 5 juror 6 arguer, lawyer 7 jurists 8 attorney
furnishing: 5 bible
game: 6 tennis 10 basketball
go to ~: 3 sue 6 appeal 7 contest, dispute 8 file suit, litigate 9 prosecute
group: 3 ABA, NBA 4 jury, USTA 5 USLTA 9 grand jury, petit jury
hearing: 4 oyer
Indian ~ officials: 5 omlah
in jai alai: 6 cancha 7 fronton
injustice: 5 frame 6 bad rap, bum rap
introduce in ~: 5 enter
judgment: 4 fiat, writ 5 edict, order 6 decree, dictum, ruling 7 mandate, verdict 8 sanction 9 directive 10 injunction
kid at ~: 4 page
like a kangaroo ~: 4 fake, sham 5 bogus, false, hokey, phony 6 ersatz, parody, pseudo 8 so-called, spurious, travesty 9 pretended
motor ~: 8 rest stop
old Indian ~: 6 adalat
order: 4 writ 5 paper
Ottoman ~: 5 porte
personage: 2 DA 3 ADA, ref 5 clerk, judge, steno 6 umpire 7 bailiff, referee
phrase: 3 I do
Scottish ~ official: 5 macer
seat: 4 banc
session: 5 trial 6 assize
silencer: 5 gavel
starter: 4 back, down

statement: **4** oath, plea **5** alibi **9** testimony
system: **3** bar
take back to ~: **5** resue
take to a higher ~: **6** appeal
unbiased ~ advisor: **6** amicus
see also basketball, tennis
court ___: **5** of law, order **6** jester
court-___: **7** martial
___ court: **4** clay, food, hard, moot **5** day in, grass, motor, night **6** county, family **7** appeals, circuit, federal, people's, probate, tourist, traffic, trailer
___-court: **5** out-of
Court: **8** Margaret
Court ___ James's: **4** of St.
Courtenay: **3** Tom
Courteney: **3** Cox **8** Arquette
courteous: **4** kind, nice, soft **5** civil, moral, suave, sweet **6** decent, gentle, kindly, polite, proper, subtle, urbane **7** affable, cordial, gallant, genteel, politic, refined, tactful **8** amicable, debonair, discreet, gracious, ladylike, likeable, mannerly, well-bred **9** attentive, civilized, debonaire, judicious, sensitive **10** chivalrous, cultivated, debonnaire, diplomatic, hospitable, respectful, soft-spoken, thoughtful, well-spoken
be ~: **5** thank
not ~: **4** rude **7** brusque
courtesy: **4** gift, tact **5** favor **6** comity **7** amenity, manners, respect, service, suavity **8** breeding, ceremony, chivalry, civility, kindness, niceties, protocol, urbanity **9** deference, etiquette, gallantry, gentility, propriety, suaveness **10** cordiality, indulgence, knighthood, politeness, refinement
encl.: **3** SAE **4** SASE
courtesy ___: **3** car **4** call
courtier: **5** toady **6** fawner, squire, suitor **7** flunkey **8** adulator, follower, kowtower, servitor **9** attendant, flatterer, sycophant **10** bootlicker
courtiers: **9** entourage
Courting at Burnt Ranch, The
ballet: **5** Rodeo
courting one: **5** wooer
Court Jester, The (1956 film)
cast: Danny Kaye
courtliness: **8** elegance
courtly: **5** noble, regal, royal, suave **6** august, formal, polite, ritual, urbane **7** elegant, gallant, genteel, pompous, refined, stately **8** cultured, decorous, gracious, highbred, polished, well-bred **9** dignified **10** chivalrous, respectful
Court, Margaret: **7** netster **9** tennis pro
milieu: **5** court
court-martial: **3** try
Courtney: **4** Love **5** Vance
Courtney ___-Smith: **6** Thorne
court of ___: **3** law **5** honor **6** claims, equity, record **7** appeals, inquiry
court of common ___: **5** pleas
court of last ___: **6** resort
___-court press: **4** full
courtroom: **9** judiciary
see also court
courtship: **4** suit **6** dating, wooing **7** pursuit, romance **10** engagement
animal ~ site: **3** lek
Courtship of Eddie's Father, The (ABC sitcom)
cast: Bill Bixby (Tom Corbett) Brandon Cruz (Eddie Corbett) Miyoshi Umeki (Mrs. Livingston)
Courtship of Miles Standish, The
author: Henry Wadsworth Longfellow
character: **5** Alden **7** Mullins **9** Priscilla
___ Court, The: **7** People's
courtyard: **4** quad, yard **5** patio **6** atrium **8** cloister **9** enclosure, peristyle **10** quadrangle
cloister ~: **5** garth
of a ~: **6** atrial
courtyards: **5** atria
Courvoisier: **5** drink **8** beverage
couscous: **4** stew **5** grain
alternative: ***see*** pasta
cousin: **3** kin **7** kinsman **8** relative **9** kinswoman
Cousin Bette
author: Honoré de Balzac
Cousin Itt: **6** Addams
Cousin Pons
author: Honoré de Balzac
Cousins: **5** Robin **6** Norman
Cousins (1989 film)
cast: Ted Danson, Isabella Rossellini, Sean Young
Cousins, Robin: **6** skater
Cousteau, Jacques-Yves: **8** explorer
milieu: **3** mer, sea **5** ocean
Cousy, Bob: **4** Celt **6** Celtic
milieu: **5** court
org.: **3** NBA
sport: **10** basketball
couth: **7** refined **8** urbanity **9** suaveness
coutil: **6** fabric **8** material
___ couture: **5** haute
couturier: **6** fitter, tailor **8** designer **9** outfitter **10** dressmaker
French ~: **3** YSL **4** Dior
cove: **3** arm, bay **4** gulf **5** fiord, fjord, inlet **6** armlet, grotto, harbor, recess **7** harbour, shelter
shelter, as in a ~: **5** embay
___ Cove: **5** Cabot
Coveleski: **4** Stan
covenant: **3** law, vow **4** bond, deal, deed, pact **5** trust **6** pledge, treaty **7** compact, promise **8** contract, protocol, warranty **9** agreement, testament **10** commitment, settlement
Covenant, The
author: James Michener
coven member: **5** witch
Covent Garden
locale: **6** London **7** Britain, England
offering: **4** aria **5** opera
performer: **4** diva
Coventry: **4** city, town
locale: **7** England
send to ~: **4** shun **5** exile
___ Cove, NY: **4** Glen
cover: **2** do **3** lap, lee, lid, sit, top **4** bury, coat, cork, garb, hide, mask, peel, rind, skin, span, tarp, veil, wrap **5** alibi, bathe, cache, capot, cloak, couch, dress, front, glaze, guard, guise, haven, layer, liner, paint, patch, quilt, rub on, shade, smear, touch **6** asylum, awning, canopy, capote, clothe, defend, embody, encase, ensure, enveil, harbor, imbody, incase, inhume, insure, invest, mantle, offset, pepper, reason, redeem, refuge, relate, safety, screen, secure, shadow, shield, shroud, spread, survey, take in, tell of, veneer **7** bedding, bedrape, binding, blanket, board up, conceal, contain, defense, eclipse, embrace, enclose, encrust, envelop, harbour, hideout, inclose, include, incrust, involve, lodging, obscure, overlay, plaster, pretext, protect, recount, retreat, secrete, shelter, shut off, shut out, smother, stretch, suffuse, surface, touch on, varnish, write up **8** comprise, deal with, disguise, ensconce, enshroud, envelope, overflow, pinch-hit, pretense, report on, security, traverse **9** adumbrate, bedspread, broadcast, encompass, make up for, reinforce, safeguard, sanctuary, touch upon, watch over **10** camouflage, compensate, keep a lid on, keep secret, protection, provide for, spread over
bed ~: **5** duvet, quilt **6** canopy **7** blanket **9** comforter
combining form: **4** steg- **5** stego-
ender: **3** age, lid
face ~: **4** mask
(for): **6** double, fill in **7** stand in **8** pinch-hit
(for)): **10** substitute
give ~: **6** shield
ground: **3** fly, hie, run **4** rush, trot **5** speed **6** travel **8** progress
ground ~: **3** sod **4** lawn **5** grass, mulch, plant, sedum
nautically: **6** batten
neck ~: **5** dicky, scarf **6** collar, dickey, dickie **7** muffler
one under ~: **5** hider
snugly: **4** tuck **6** tuck in
starter: **4** hard, slip, soft **6** ground
story: **5** alibi **7** pretext
take ~: **4** hide **6** lie low **7** hide out
the eyes: **7** obscure **9** obfuscate
thickly: **4** slab **7** slather
under ~: **8** on the sly, secretly, ulterior **9** concealed
up: **4** bury, hide, hush, mask, veil **5** cloak, cloud, shade **6** batten, clothe, enrobe, hush up, inhume, shield, stifle **7** conceal, protect, secrete, shelter **8** suppress **9** dissemble, keep quiet, misinform, stonewall, whitewash
with veneer: **4** coat **5** layer **7** overlay
words on the ~: **5** title **6** author **9** publisher
cover ___: **3** boy **4** crop, girl, slip **5** story **6** charge, ground, letter
cover-___: **3** ups
___ cover: **3** air **4** dust, take **5** cloud, extra, under **6** ground
___-cover: **4** soft
Cover: **8** Franklin
coverage: **9** insurance
get ~ for: **6** ensure, insure **7** protect, warrant **9** indemnify
covered: **4** clad **5** blind, ready, shady **6** hidden **9** concealed, out of view, unexposed **10** enshrouded, tucked away
by: **5** neath, under **10** underneath
by, to a poet: **5** neath
not ~: **4** open **7** exposed
passage: **3** way **4** slip, stoa **5** slype **6** arcade
way: **4** stoa **7** gallery, portico **9** colonnade
with water: **5** soggy, soppy **6** soaked, sodden **7** sopping **8** drenched, dripping **9** saturated
covered ___: **5** wagon **6** bridge
cover girl: **5** model, poser
Cover Girl: **6** makeup
alternative: ***see*** cosmetic brand
covering: **2** on **3** cap, hat, lid, top **4** coat, cowl, garb, gear, hide, hull, husk, over, peel, rind, robe, roof, tarp, tent, wrap **5** blind, cloak, crust, dress, glaze, layer, scarf, shade, shawl, sheet, shell **6** awning, bonnet, canopy, canvas, casing, facing, hiding, jacket, mantle, spread, veneer **7** blanket, ceiling, clothes, coating, drapery, garment, housing, lacquer, outside, surface, wrapper **8** clothing, disguise, envelope, frosting, kerchief, mantilla, rambling **9** tarpaulin **10** integument, protection
cut the ~ off: **5** shave
floor ~: **3** mat, rug **4** lino, tile **6** carpet **8** linoleum **9** broadloom
flower-bed ~: **5** humus **7** compost
foot ~: **3** pac **4** boot, hose, shoe, sock **5** socks **9** stockings
head ~: **3** cap, hat, tam **4** cowl, hair, hood **5** beret, scarf, shawl
hot-dog ~: **4** skin **6** casing
leg ~: **4** spat **6** puttee **7** gambado
outer ~: **4** husk, rind, skin
protective ~: **4** tarp **5** armor
remove the ~: **4** peel, skin
thin ~: **4** film **5** scale
window ~: **5** drape, glass, grill, shade **6** grille, screen **7** curtain, drapery
see also cover
___ covering: **4** wall **5** floor
coverlet: **5** quilt, throw **6** afghan **9** bedspread, comforter, eiderdown
Cover Me (1984 song)
artist: Bruce Springsteen
Cover of Rolling Stone, The (1973 song)
artist: Dr. Hook
covers, under the: **4** abed **5** not up
covert: **3** sly **5** privy **6** hidden, latent, masked, refuge, secret, veiled **7** cloaked, furtive, on the QT, private, shelter **8** hideaway, hush-hush, obscured, secluded, shrouded, sneaking, stealthy, ulterior **9** concealed, disguised, invisible, nonpublic, potential, sanctuary, secretive, sheltered **10** enshrouded, undercover, under wraps, undivulged, unviewable
operative: **5** ninja
org.: **3** CIA

covertly: **7** on the QT, sub rosa **8** on the sly, secretly
covertness: **7** secrecy
cover-up: **4** sham **5** front, shirt, smock **6** anorak, caftan, kaftan **7** garment, pretext **8** disguise **10** masquerade
see also cover, covering
covet: **4** envy, long, lust, need, seek, want, wish **5** crave, fancy, yearn **6** desire **7** ache for, itch for, long for, wish for **8** aspire to, begrudge, yearn for **9** hanker for, thirst for
ending: **3** ous
covetable: **4** good **6** sultry, useful **7** helpful, lovable **8** adorable, enticing, enviable, fetching, loveable **9** beautiful, desirable, excellent **10** attractive, beneficial, gratifying, profitable, worthwhile
covetous: **5** itchy **6** greedy, hungry, sordid **7** envious, jealous, lustful, miserly, wishful **8** desirous, grasping, ravenous **9** mercenary **10** avaricious, gluttonous
covetousness: **3** sin **4** envy, lust **5** greed **6** desire **7** avarice **8** cupidity
covey: **3** set **4** band, bevy, crew, gang, herd, nest **5** brood, bunch, flock, group, swarm **7** cluster, company **10** hatchlings
member: **5** quail
Covina: **4** city, town
locale: **10** California
Covington: **3** Wes **4** city, town
locale: **3** Ken. **8** Kentucky
cow: **3** awe, she **5** bovid, bully, daunt, deter, scare **6** animal, bovine, coerce, dampen, female, hector, heifer, mammal, rattle, subdue **7** bluster, critter, crittur, overawe, unnerve **8** browbeat, bulldoze, dispirit, dissuade, frighten, threaten **9** give pause, strong-arm, terrorize **10** dishearten, intimidate
ankle: **4** hock
ant ~: **5** aphid, aphis
Asian ~: **4** zebu
bellow: **3** low, moo
breed: **3** Gir **4** Busa, Glan, Kuri, Rath, Siri, Tuli **5** Angus, Barka, Boran, Dajal, Dangi, Deoni, Devon, Fjall, Horro, Kerry, Kurdi, Luing, Malvi, Maure, N'dama, Nguni, Oropa, Rathi, Sanhe, Wagyu **6** Angeln, Ankole, Aubrac, Baladi, Channi, Dexter, Dhanni, Dulong, Gaolao, Herens, Jaulan, Jersey, Lohani, Mewati, Nagori, Nelore, Nimari, Ongole, Ovambo, Ponwar, Rojhan, Salers, Sarabi, Sussex, Tswana, Vosges **7** Alberes, Bachaur, Barzona, Brahman, Brahmin, Cachena, Canchim, Istoben, Mashona, Red Poll, Retinta, Sahiwal, Yanbian **8** Ayrshire, Bonsmara, Charbray, Chianina, Galloway, Gelbvieh, Guernsey, Hereford, Holstein, Limousin **9** Charolais, Shorthorn, Simmental **10** Lincoln Red, Murray Grey, Welsh Black
bunch: **4** herd
cash ~: **7** bonanza **8** gold mine
catcher: **5** lasso, reata, riata **6** lariat
chew: **3** cud
emulate a ~: **5** graze
ender: **3** boy, man, men, pea, pox **4** bane, bell, bird, fish, girl, hand, herb, herd, hide, lick, poke, rite, shed, slip **5** berry **7** catcher, puncher
follower: **4** town
genus: **3** bos
hip joint: **5** thurl
holy ~: **4** yipe **5** yikes, yipes
home: **4** barn **5** dairy
hornless ~: **5** muley **6** mulley
in Britain: **5** stirk
lunch: **5** grass
male: **4** bull
milking the ~: **5** chore
name: **5** Bossy **6** Bossie
offering: **4** milk
pampas ~ catcher: **4** bola
part: **4** hoof, tail **5** udder
sacred ~: **4** idol
sea ~: **6** dugong **7** manatee
shed: **4** byre
stomach: **5** rumen **6** omasum
stomachs: **5** omasa
trademark ~: **5** Elmer, Elsie
unbranded ~: **4** calf **5** stray **8** maverick
young: **4** calf **6** heifer
see also cattle
cow __: **4** pony, town **7** college, country
__ cow: **3** ant, sea **4** bell, cash, holy, milk **5** black, have a **6** sacred
__ cow!: **4** Holy
coward: **4** baby, wimp **5** mouse, sissy **6** craven **7** chicken, dastard, milksop, quitter **8** deserter, poltroon, recreant, weakling **9** fraidy-cat, jellyfish **10** scaredy-cat
lack: **4** guts **5** nerve, spine
cowardice: **4** fear **8** cold feet, timidity
cowardly: **3** shy **4** base, weak **5** faint, timid **6** afraid, craven, scared, trepid, yellow **7** alarmed, anxious, chicken, daunted, fearful, gutless, jittery, nervous, panicky, spooked, wimpish **8** fearsome, hesitant, recreant, timorous **9** dastardly, nerveless, petrified, spineless, terrified, tremulous **10** frightened
Cowardly Lion
portrayer: Bert Lahr
Coward, Noël: **3** Sir **6** writer **7** British **8** composer **10** playwright
work: Blithe Spirit
Design for Living
Future Indefinite
Not Yet the Dodo
Present Indicative
Private Lives
Coward of the County (1979 song)
artist: Kenny Rogers
cowberry: **5** fruit, shrub
relative: *see* heath family shrub
cowboy: **5** rider **6** drover, gaucho, herder **7** rancher, vaquero **8** buckaroo, herdsman, horseman, stockman, wrangler **9** ranch hand **10** equestrian
at times: **5** roper **6** herder **7** brander
be a drugstore ~: **6** loiter
bed: **4** bunk
buddy: **4** pard **7** pardner
coat: **8** chaqueta
companion: **5** horse
competition: **5** rodeo
concern: **4** dogy, herd **5** dogey, stray **6** cattle, doggie
drugstore ~: **5** ogler
exclamation: **4** heck **5** howdy, wahoo **6** giddap **7** giddyap, giddyup
flick: **5** oater **7** western **10** horse opera
food: **4** chow, grub
gear: **4** rope **5** reata, riata **6** lariat
home: **5** ranch, range
instrument: **6** guitar
Mexican ~: **6** charro
nickname: **3** Tex **5** Dusty
response: **3** yep, yup **4** nope
South American ~: **6** charro, gaucho **7** llanero, vaquero
strap: **4** rein
sweetie: **3** gal
walk like a ~: **5** mosey
wear: **3** hat **4** boot, spur
cowboy __: **3** hat **4** boot
__, cowboy!: **6** Ride 'em
__ Cowboy: **4** Neon **5** Urban **10** Rhinestone
Cowboy Bebop: **5** anime
Cowboys: **6** eleven
home: **6** Dallas
org.: **3** NFC
rival: *see* NFL team
__ Cowboys: **5** Space
cowboys and __: **7** Indians
Cowboy's Work Is Never Done, A (1972 song)
artist: Sonny and Cher
cowcatcher: **5** grill **6** grille
cowed: **5** timid **6** afraid **9** awestruck
easily ~ one: **5** softy **6** softie
Cowell: **5** Simon
Cowens, Dave
milieu: **5** court
org.: **3** NBA
sport: **10** basketball
cower: **4** fawn, hide **5** hunch, kotow, quail, quake, slink, sneak, toady, wince **6** blench, cringe, flinch, grovel, kowtow, recoil, shrink **7** slither, tremble, truckle
at: **5** dread
cowfish: **8** cetacean
relative: *see* cetacean
__ Cowgirls Get the Blues: **4** Even
cowhide: **7** leather
puncher: **3** awl
cowl: **4** hood **5** cloak **8** covering
wearer: **4** monk
cowlick: **4** hair, tuft **6** strand
cowlike: **6** bovine
cowlneck: **7** sweater
cowman: **7** rancher
coworker: **4** ally, mate **6** fellow **7** comrade, partner **9** associate, colleague
Cow Palace: **5** arena
cowpea: **4** bean **6** legume
Cowper, William: **4** poet **7** British
cowpoke: **6** drover, gaucho **7** rancher, vaquero **8** buckaroo, herdsman, wrangler
see also cowboy
cowrie: **5** shell **8** seashell
ridge: **5** varix
cows: **4** kine **5** stock **6** cattle **9** livestock
old-style: **4** kine
till the ~ come home: **7** forever
Cowsills
song: Hair (1969)
cowslip: **5** plant **6** flower
cox: **9** steersman
ender: **4** comb **5** swain
Cox: **4** Alex **5** Nikki, Ronny, Wally **7** Deborah **9** Archibald, Courteney
coxa: **4** bone
site: **3** hip **6** pelvis
coxcomb: **3** fop **4** buck, dude **5** blade, dandy, spark, swell **8** popinjay **9** pretty boy **10** jack-a-dandy
Cox, Courteney: **7** actress
film: Scream (1996)
spouse: David Arquette
TV: Cougar Town, Friends
coxswain: **5** pilot **6** sailor **7** jack tar
concern: **4** crew **5** rower
obey a ~: **3** oar
Cox, Wally
character: **7** Peepers **8** Underdog
coy: **3** shy, sly **4** arch, prim **5** timid **6** artful, cutesy, demure, modest **7** bashful, cutesie, evasive **8** affected, blushing, reserved, retiring, skittish **9** diffident, flinching, reluctant, secretive, shrinking, unwilling **10** coquettish, overmodest
act: **4** wink
__ Coy Mistress: **5** To His
coyness: **7** modesty
coyote: **3** fur **5** bayer, canid **6** animal, canine, howler, mammal
kin: *see* canine
Coyote: **5** Peter, Wile E.
city on the ~: **7** San Jose
plaint: **4** howl
Coyotes: **3** six **4** team
home: **7** Phoenix
milieu: **3** ice **4** rink
org.: **3** NHL
rival: *see* hockey team
Coyote State: **4** S. Dak.
sch.: **3** USD
Coyote Ugly (2000 film)
cast: Maria Bello, John Goodman, Piper Perabo
Coyote, Wile E. mail-order company: **4** Acme
coypu: **6** animal, mammal, nutria, rodent
relative: *see* rodent
cozen: **3** con **4** bilk, dupe, fool, gull, rook **5** cheat, trick **6** delude, fleece **7** deceive, defraud, mislead, pretend, swindle, two-time **8** hoodwink **9** bamboozle, disinform, victimize
coziness: **7** comfort **8** snugness
coz's father: **3** unc, unk **5** uncle
Cozumel: **4** city, town
locale: **6** Mexico
see also Spanish
cozy: **4** homy, nice, safe, snug, soft, warm **5** comfy, cushy, homey **6** chummy, folksy, secure **7** livable, nestled, restful **8** familiar, homelike, intimate, liveable, tucked in **9** cuddled up, sheltered
get ~: **6** curl up, nestle **7** snuggle

make ~: **4** tuck **6** tuck in
spot: **3** den **4** nest, nook **5** niche **6** hearth **9** fireplace
__ cozy: **3** tea
Cozy: **4** Cole
Cozzens, James Gould: **6** writer
work: By Love Possessed Guard of Honor
CP __: **4** Rail
C.P.: **4** Snow
CPA: **4** acct. **7** auditor **10** accountant, bookkeeper
abbr.: **3** ROA, YTD
concern: **2** bk. **3** acc., aud., irc, net **4** acct. **5** audit, books **6** ledger
employer: **3** IRS
forte: **3** nos. **7** numbers
part of ~: **4** Acct., Cert. **6** Public **9** Certified
record: **3** rct. **4** rcpt. **7** receipt
CPI
agency: **3** BLS
part of ~: **5** Index, Price **8** Consumer
cpl.: **3** NCO
like a ~: **3** enl.
subordinate: **3** PFC, pvt.
superior: **3** sgt.
see also corporal
CPO: **3** NCO
employer: **3** USN **4** Navy **6** US Navy
part of ~: **5** Chief, Petty **7** Officer
C.P.O. Sharkey (NBC sitcom)
cast: Don Rickles (Otto Sharkey)
CPR
expert: **3** EMT **9** paramedic
teacher: **4** the Y, YMCA, YMHA
CPSC part: **6** Safety **7** Product **8** Consumer **10** Commission
CPU: **2** PC **8** computer **9** mainframe
part: **4** Unit **7** Central **10** Processing
Cr: **4** elem. **7** element **8** chromium
24 for ~: **4** at. no.
crab: **4** carp **5** apple, crank, gripe, groan, grump, meany, spite, whine **6** Cancer, chider, grouch, grouse, hermit, kvetch, meanie, sidler **7** fiddler, grumble, seafood **8** complain, grumbler, sourball, sourpuss, windlass **9** bellyache, hard-shell, horseshoe, Sebastian, shellfish, soft-shell, termagant **10** complainer, curmudgeon, malcontent
claw: **5** chela
constellation: **6** Cancer
ender: **4** meat, wise **5** apple, stick
feature: **4** claw
fiddler ~: **3** uca
grass: **4** weed
larva: **4** zoea
month: **4** July
move like a ~: **5** sidle
relative: *see* apple
crab __: **3** roe **4** legs, tree **5** apple, canon, grass, louse
__ crab: **3** pea **4** blue, kelp, king, lady, land, mole, sand, snow, tree **5** stone **6** Alaska, hermit, spider **7** coconut, cracked, fiddler
Crab: **4** sign **6** Cancer
month: **3** Jul., Jun. **4** July, June
predecessor: **5** Twins
successor: **4** Lion
the ~: **4** sign
Crab __: **6** Nebula
crab apple: **4** tree
Crabbe: **6** Buster, George
Crabbe, Buster
role: **6** Gordon, Rogers, Tarzan
crabbiness: **6** spleen **8** asperity, ill humor
crabby: **4** dour, glum, mean, rude, sour, tart, ugly **5** cross, gruff, huffy, moody, nasty, sulky, surly, testy **6** bitter, crusty, fretty, gloomy, grumpy, ireful, morose, ornery, snappy, sullen, touchy **7** bristly, cynical, fretful, grouchy, huffish, peevish, prickly, waspish **8** captious, fretsome, grumpish, liverish, petulant, snappish **9** crotchety, difficult, fractious, irascible, irritable, querulous, saturnine, splenetic **10** ill-natured, out of sorts, unsociable
Crab Key
villain: **4** Dr. No
__-crab soup: **3** she
Crab, the: **4** sign
Crab, The: **5** Evers
crabwise: **8** sideways **9** laterally
crack: **2** go **3** ace, bid, cut, dig, gag, gap, hit, mot, pop, pro, rap, try **4** bang, boom, chap, chip, clap, deft, flaw, flip, good, gybe, harm, hole, hurt, jest, jibe, joke, leak, open, peal, quip, rent, rift, shot, slam, slap, slit, snap, stab, tear, tops **5** adept, blast, break, burst, chasm, chink, cleft, clout, crash, fling, go ape, noise, smack, smash, sneer, solve, split, super, taunt, whack, whirl, wreck **6** adroit, blow up, bon mot, breach, buffet, choice, cleave, damage, decode, expert, go wild, impair, injure, insult, lose it, outlet, remark, report, shiver, sunder **7** attempt, crevice, decrypt, fissure, opening, roughen, rupture, shatter, skilled, thunder, work out **8** aperture, breakage, crevasse, decipher, dextrous, discover, division, fracture, masterly, skillful, splinter, superior, talented **9** break open, dexterous, excellent, explosion, figure out, first-rate, go bonkers, penetrate, practiced, puzzle out, witticism **10** first-class, infiltrate, interspace, interstice, proficient
a book: **4** read **5** learn, study
down on: **4** halt, stop **5** quash **6** stifle **8** restrain, suppress
ender: **3** pot **4** down **5** brain
filler: **5** grout
have a ~ at: **3** try **7** attempt
jokes: **4** jest
of dawn: **5** sunup **7** morning
open: **5** force, jimmy
open a ~: **4** ajar
something to ~: **4** whip **5** smile
starter: **4** wise
take another ~ at: **5** retry
tough nut to ~: **5** poser **6** enigma **7** mystery, stumper
up: **4** ha-ha **5** amuse, laugh, wreck **6** cackle, giggle, guffaw, titter **7** chortle, chuckle **8** convulse
wise: **4** jest, joke
crack __: **4** down, wise **5** a book
crack a __: **4** book, joke **5** smile
__ crack at it: **5** take a
__ Crack'd, The: **6** Mirror
cracked: **4** torn **5** broke, cleft, split **6** broken, faulty, hoarse, rimose, rimous, solved **7** chipped, damaged, injured **8** fissured, sundered **9** fractured **10** deciphered
in a way: **4** ajar
it may be ~: **4** book, joke, safe **5** smile
cracked __: **3** ice **4** crab **5** wheat
cracked __ be: **4** up to
Cracked
rival: **3** Mad
cracked grain cereal: **6** groats
cracker: **4** Hi-Ho, Ritz, whip **5** Zesta **6** Krispy, oyster **7** biscuit, Cheez-It, saltine **8** Goldfish, Triscuit **10** Cheese Nips, Wheat Thins
box: **4** safe
ender: **4** jack
relative: **5** matzo **6** matzah, matzoh
shape: **6** animal
snack: **6** canapé
starter: **3** nut **4** fire, safe, wise
topper: **3** dip **4** Brie, Edam, pâté **6** caviar, cheese **7** caviare
vault ~: **4** yegg **5** thief **7** burglar
wanter: **5** Polly
cracker-__: **6** barrel
__ cracker: **4** soda **6** animal, graham, oyster
Cracker __: **4** Jack **6** Barrel
crackerjack: **3** ace **6** adroit, expert, master **8** masterly, skillful **9** practiced
see also wonderful
Cracker Jack: **4** nosh **5** candy, snack
dog: **5** Bingo
ingredient: **5** prize **7** peanuts, popcorn
crackers: **3** mad **4** daft, loco **5** batty, wiggy
__ Crackers: **6** Animal
cracking: **5** smart, swift
get ~: **3** hie **4** rush **5** begin, speed, start **6** go to it **7** pitch in **8** commence
needing ~: **5** coded **6** in code
starter: **4** safe, wise
__ cracking!: **3** Get
crackle: **4** snap **6** rustle, sizzle
__! Crackle! Pop!: **4** Snap
crackling: **6** crispy **7** crunchy
Cracklin' Oat Bran
competitor: *see* cereal
Cracklin' Rosie (1970 song)
artist: Neil Diamond
crack of __: **4** dawn, doom
crackpot: **4** kook, loon, wack **5** crank **6** maniac **7** lunatic
cracks
creep through the ~: **4** ooze, seep
let fall between the ~: **4** omit **5** let go **6** forget, ignore **7** let pass, neglect **8** let slide, overlook **9** disregard
crack the __: **4** whip
crackup: **5** smash, split, wreck **8** accident, collapse, laughter **9** collision
Cracow river: **7** Vistula
cradle: **3** bed, hug **4** crib, hold **6** hotbed, nestle, origin, rocker **7** infancy, nurture, protect, support **8** babyhood, bassinet **9** childhood, container **10** birthplace
ender: **4** song **5** board
holder of song: **5** bough
propel a ~: **4** rock
__ cradle: **4** cat's
Cradle of Love (song)
artist: Billy Idol, Johnny Preston
Cradle of Texas Liberty, The: **5** Alamo
cradlesong: **7** lullaby
Cradle Song
author: Gregorio Sierra
Cradle Will Fall, The
author: Mary Higgins Clark
craft: **3** art, dau, dow, hoy, job **4** bark, boat, brig, dhow, dory, line, make, raft, ruse, ship, work **5** barge, blimp, canoe, forge, guile, knack, liner, oiler, plane, razee, skill, sloop, trade, wiles, yacht **6** career, coaler, deceit, device, devise, dinghy, scheme, talent, vessel, wherry **7** ability, airship, calling, cunning, fashion, felucca, finesse, knavery, know-how, macramé, orbiter, slyness, vehicle, weaving **8** airplane, aptitude, artifice, artistry, ceramics, foxiness, runabout, strategy, subtlety, trickery, vocation, wiliness, zeppelin **9** adeptness, cageyness, canniness, dexterity, diplomacy, duplicity, expertise, hydrofoil, ingenuity, smartness, stratagem, technique **10** adroitness, cleverness, competence, embroidery, expertness, hydroplane, icebreaker, livelihood, occupation, profession, shrewdness, subterfuge, virtuosity
Alaskan ~: **5** kayak, umiak
Cajun ~: **6** bateau
Indian ~: **5** canoe
lateen-rigged ~: **3** dau, dow **4** dhow
lunar ~: **6** lander
motorless ~: **4** punt, raft **5** canoe, sloop **6** glider
partner: **3** art
racing ~: **5** scull, shell, yacht
rower's ~: **5** canoe, kayak, scull, skiff
starter: **3** air **4** hand, king, wood **5** hover, rotor, space, stage, state, trade, water, witch **6** needle **7** shuttle
suffix: **4** -ship
to pole: **4** punt
ungainly ~: **3** tub
water ~: **3** dau, dow **4** boat, dhow, punt, raft, ship **5** canoe, kayak, liner, scull, sloop, umiak
see also boat, ship
__-Craft: **5** Chris
__ craft advisory: **5** small
craftiness: **3** art **5** guile **6** deceit, dupery **7** finesse **8** artifice **9** deception **10** imposition
craftsmanship: **3** art
craftsperson: **4** hand **5** maker, smith **6** artist, worker, wright **7** artisan, builder **9** artificer
__-craftsy: **5** artsy
crafty: **3** sly **4** arch, cagy, foxy, wily **5** cagey, canny, sharp, slick,

smart, snaky **6** artful, astute, clever, shifty, shrewd, smooth, tricky **7** cunning, devious, furtive, vulpine **8** guileful, scheming, slippery, stealthy **9** astucious, deceitful, deceptive, designing, ingenious, insidious, underhand **10** serpentine, streetwise

in a ~ way: **5** slyly
one: **3** fox

C R

__-crafty: **4** arty
crag: **3** tor **4** peak, rock **5** arête, cliff, stone **8** mountain, pinnacle **9** precipice **10** escarpment, prominence
craggy: **5** harsh, ridgy, rocky, rough **6** jagged, ridged, rugged, uneven **7** unlevel
abode: **4** aery, eyry **5** aerie, eyrie
Craig: **4** Mack, Wood **5** James, Jenny **6** Daniel, Wasson, Yvonne **7** Kilborn, Sheffer, Stadler, Stevens **8** Ferguson **9** Breedlove, Claiborne
role: **4** Bond
Craig T. __: **6** Nelson
Crain: **6** Jeanne
crake: **4** bird **8** landrail
milieu: **5** marsh
cram: **3** jam, ram **4** fill, glut, load, pack, tamp, tuck, wolf **5** crowd, crush, force, jam in, learn, press, ram in, shove, study, stuff, wedge **6** bone up, gobble, master, pack in, squash **7** bunch up, compact, crowd in, engorge, force in, jampack, shove in, squeeze, stuff in, surfeit **8** compress, overfill, overpack **9** lucubrate, overcrowd, overstuff, squeeze in
cram __: **6** course
Cram, Donald: **7** chemist **8** Nobelist
Cramer, Floyd: **7** pianist
cram-full: **5** sated **6** loaded
crammed: **4** full, rife **5** dense, laden, thick **7** compact, replete, teeming **8** brimming, squeezed, thronged **9** chock-full, condensed **10** compressed, hard-packed
cramp: **4** ache, clog, hurt, kink, knot, pain, pang **5** box up, crick, limit, pinch, press, stimy, stymy **6** coop up, hamper, hinder, hobble, impede, injury, stymie, thwart, twinge **7** confine, inhibit, shackle, tighten **8** bottle up, encumber, obstruct, restrain, restrict **9** constrain, constrict, hamstring, stiffness **10** constraint, impediment, keep in line
one's style: **8** obstruct
__ cramp: **7** writer's
cramped: **4** tiny **5** close, scant, small, teeny, tight **6** little, narrow, teensy **7** crowded, limited **8** hemmed in **9** confining
quarters: **4** coop **5** booth **6** alcove, recess **7** chamber, cubicle, dungeon **8** cloister
cranberries
like ~: **4** tart
where ~ grow: **3** bog
cranberry: **3** red **5** fruit **6** bluish **7** blueish, crimson
family: **5** heath
relative: *see* red color
cranberry __: **3** bog **4** bush
Crandall: **3** Del
crane: **4** bird, boom **5** davit, hoist, wader **6** brolga, lifter **7** derrick, stretch **8** sandhill **10** demoiselle
arm: **3** jib
cousin: **4** ibis, rail **5** egret, heron **7** bustard
operator's perch: **3** cab
ship's ~: **5** davit
sound: **5** whoop
Crane: **3** Bob, Les **4** Hart **5** Denny, Niles **7** Frasier, Ichabod, Stephen
Crane, Hart: **4** poet **6** writer
work: The Bridge
Crane, Les
song: Desiderata (1971)
Crane, Niles: **6** doctor
show: **7** Frasier
wife: **5** Maris
Crane, Roy captain: **4** Easy
Crane, Stephen: **6** writer
work: The Black Riders
Maggie
The Open Boat
The Red Badge of Courage
War Is Kind
cranium: **4** bone, head **5** skull **6** noggin, noodle, sconce **9** braincase
bulge: **5** inion
cavity: **5** sinus
nerve: **5** vagus
nerves: **4** vagi
crank: **3** arm, bar, gin, nut, rev **4** crab, kook, spin, turn **5** grump, lever, start, winch **6** grouch, handle, maniac, wind up, zealot **7** capstan, fanatic, lunatic **8** crackpot, sourball, sourpuss, turn over, windlass **9** character, eccentric, intensify **10** curmudgeon
ender: **3** pin **4** case **5** shaft
up: **5** begin **8** get going **10** get started
(up): **3** rev **4** wind
crank __: **3** out, pin **4** call, down **6** letter
crankcase
contents: **3** oil
in Britain: **4** sump
problem: **5** no oil
crankiness: **6** spleen
cranky: **3** odd **5** cross, moody, surly, testy, whiny **6** crusty, grumpy, morose, ornery, touchy, whiney **7** bearish, bristly, fretful, grouchy, huffish, peevish, peppery, waspish **8** fretsome, grumpish, liverish, petulant, snappish **9** crotchety, dyspeptic, irascible, querulous, splenetic **10** out of sorts
be ~: **5** gripe, grump, whine
Cranmer: **6** Thomas
cranny: **3** bay, gap **4** hole, nook, rift **5** chink, cleft, niche **6** alcove, breach, corner, hollow, recess **7** crevice, fissure, opening **10** interspace
partner: **4** nook
Cranston: **3** sen. **4** Alan, city, town **6** Lamont **7** senator
craps: **4** game
action: **3** bet
locale: **4** Reno **5** Vegas **8** Las Vegas
natural: **5** seven **6** eleven
need: **4** dice
player: **7** gambler, shooter
crash: **3** jar, ram **4** bang, boom, drop, fall, jolt, live, peal, roar, slam, wham **5** blast, break, crack, lodge, noise, panic, shock, sleep, slump, smash, sound, total, wreck **6** fabric, hurtle, impact, invade, pileup, racket, strike, topple, tumble **7** collide, crackup, descend, descent, pancake, plummet, shatter, smashup, thunder, wrack up **8** accident, collapse, fall flat, fracture, fragment, horn in on, stampede **9** collision, hit the hay, interrupt, rear-ender, sideswipe **10** depression, percussion
into: **3** hit, ram **6** impact
(into): **4** plow **6** plunge
pad: **4** home **5** house **7** housing
place to ~: **3** bed, pad
sound: **3** bam, pow **4** thud **5** thump
the gates: **8** trespass
crash __: **3** pad **4** boat, cart, diet, dive **5** truck **6** course, helmet **7** landing
crash-__: **4** land
Crash (2005 film)
cast: Sandra Bullock, Don Cheadle, Matt Dillon
Crash __ Dummies: **4** Test
crash and __: **4** burn
__-crasher: **4** gate
crashing: **4** loud **5** forte, noisy **7** blaring, booming, jarring, rackety, raucous, reboant **8** piercing, plangent, sonorous, strident, turned up **9** big-voiced, clamorous, deafening **10** boisterous, resounding, stentorian, strepitous, uproarious, vociferous
crashing __: **4** bore
Crash Into Me (1997 song)
artist: Dave Matthews Band
crash-investigation org.: **4** NTSB
crass: **3** low, raw **4** loud, rude **5** crude, dense, gross, nervy, rough, tacky **6** coarse, common, obtuse, unmeet, vulgar **7** bearish, boorish, lowbred, lowbrow, uncouth **8** churlish, inurbane **9** inelegant, low-minded, tasteless, unfeeling, ungallant, unrefined **10** indecorous, indelicate, unmannered
one: **3** oaf **4** boor
crassness: **10** coarseness, smuttiness
Crassus: **5** Roman
Cratchit: **3** Bob, Tim
dinner: **5** goose
like young ~: **4** tiny
crate: **3** box **4** auto, case, heap **5** box up, truck, wreck **6** carton, encase, incase, jalopy, wheels **7** flivver, package, vehicle **9** container **10** automobile, rattletrap
amount: **3** doz. **5** dozen
put in a ~: **6** encase
remove from a ~: **5** unbox
still in the ~: **3** new
up again: **5** rebox
crater: **3** pit **4** hole, scar, vent **5** chasm, mouth, Tycho **6** cavity, hollow **7** lake bed **9** Haleakala **10** Copernicus, depression
contents: **4** lava
volcanic ~: **4** maar **7** caldera
Crater __: **4** Lake
__ Crater: **6** Meteor
Crater Lake: **4** park
locale: **3** Ore. **6** Oregon
cravat: **3** rep, tie **4** repp **5** ascot, scarf, stock **6** bow tie **7** foulard, necktie **8** neckwear **10** four-in-hand
fix a ~: **5** retie
crave: **4** long, lust, miss, need, pant, seek, sigh, want, will, wish **5** covet, fancy, go for, yearn **6** desire, die for, hanker **7** ache for, hope for, itch for, long for, pine for, require, sigh for, solicit **8** yearn for **9** cry out for, drool over, hunger for, thirst for
craven: **4** weak, wimp **5** sissy, timid, wimpy **6** coward, scared, yellow **7** chicken, dastard, fearful, gutless, ignoble, servile, wimpish **8** cowardly, poltroon, recreant, timorous **9** dastardly, fraidy-cat, jellyfish, tremulous, weak-kneed **10** scaredy-cat
Craven, Wes: **8** director
film: A Nightmare on Elm Street (1984)
Scream (1996)
craving: **3** yen **4** ache, itch, lust, need, urge, want, will **5** itchy, mania **6** desire, greedy, hunger, thirst **7** athirst, longing, passion, starved, thirsty **8** ambition, appetite, cupidity, munchies, starving **9** appetence, esurience, hankering
craw: **3** maw **4** crop **5** belly **6** gullet **7** gizzard, stomach
stick in one's ~: **4** rile
Crawford: **3** Sam **4** Joan, John **5** Cindy **6** Johnny **7** Michael **9** Broderick
Crawford, Cindy
emulate ~: **4** pose **5** model
spouse: Richard Gere
Crawford, Joan: **7** actress
film: Above Suspicion (1943)
The Caretakers (1963)
Dancing Lady (1933)
Flamingo Road (1949)
Grand Hotel (1932)
Harriet Craig (1950)
Humoresque (1946)
Johnny Guitar (1954)
Mildred Pierce (1945, AA)
Possessed (1931)
Possessed (1947)
Queen Bee (1955)
Rain (1932)
Sadie McKee (1934)
Strange Cargo (1940)
Sudden Fear (1952)
What Ever Happened to Baby Jane? (1962)
A Woman's Face (1941)
The Women (1939)
spouse: Douglas Fairbanks Jr., Franchot Tone
crawl: **4** drag, fawn, inch, move, plod, swim, tire, worm **5** climb, creep, plead, slink, sneak, swarm, toady **6** grovel, linger, writhe **7** clamber, truckle, wriggle
do the ~: **4** swim
ender: **5** space

make one's flesh ~: 5 chill, panic, scare, spook 6 appall, revolt 7 horrify, petrify, terrify 8 frighten 9 terrorize
(with): 4 teem 6 abound
crawl __: 5 space
__ crawl: 3 pub
crawler: 3 ant, tot 4 baby, worm 5 snake 6 infant, insect
bar ~: 5 toper
__ crawler: 5 night
Crawley: 4 city, town
locale: 6 Sussex 7 England
__-crawlies: 6 creepy
crawling: 4 poky, slow 5 itchy 6 draggy 7 gradual, impeded, languid 8 dilatory, drawn-out, hesitant, plodding, populous, slothful, sluggish, toddling 9 leisurely, lethargic, prolonged, snaillike, unhurried 10 deliberate, protracted
(with): 5 thick 7 profuse, teeming 8 abundant
crawlingly: 8 bit by bit
crawlway: 6 tunnel
crawly: 4 eery 5 eerie 6 creepy
__-crawly: 6 creepy
Cray: 7 Seymour
__ crayfish: 3 sea 4 Cape
Crayola
choice: 3 hue 5 color, shade
color: 3 red, tan 4 blue, fern, gold, gray, plum 5 black, brown, denim, green, lemon, maize, melon, peach, sepia, umber, white 6 almond, beaver, canary, carrot, cerise, copper, maroon, orange, orchid, purple, salmon, shadow, sienna, silver, violet, yellow 7 apricot, fuchsia, magenta, manatee, pig pink, sky blue, sunglow, thistle 8 blue bell, blue gray, brick red, cerulean, chestnut, eggplant, lavender, mahogany, mulberry, navy blue, raw umber, sea green, shamrock, teal blue, torch red, wisteria 9 asparagus, blue green, brink pink, cadet blue, cranberry, dandelion, goldenrod, green blue, magic mint, mauvelous, orange red, pine green, raw sienna, red orange, red violet, violet red 10 aquamarine, blue violet, cornflower, desert sand, hot magenta, laser lemon, neon carrot, olive green, outer space, periwinkle, radical red, razzmatazz, timber wolf, tumbleweed, violet blue
former ~ color: 5 flesh
crayon: 5 chalk 9 wax pencil
use a ~: 5 color
craze: 3 bug, fad 4 mode, rage 5 fever, mania, style, thing, trend, vogue 6 madden 7 derange, in thing, passion, Pokémon 8 fixation, Pet Rocks 9 Hula-Hoops, mood rings, obsession
crazed: 3 mad 4 amok, loco, wild 5 amuck, loony, manic, rabid, wacky, wiggy 6 looney, savage, whacky 7 demonic, unsound 8 daemonic, in a furor, maniacal, wild-eyed 9 demonical, fanatical, possessed, wrought-up 10 hysterical, infuriated
craziness: 5 folly, mania 6 lunacy 8 nonsense 9 absurdity
crazy: 3 mad 4 gaga, loco, wild, zany 5 dotty, gonzo, goony, inane, manic, sappy, silly, wacky, weird 6 absurd, gooney, hectic, in love, madcap, whacky 7 bananas, bizarre, fatuous, foolish, haywire, oddball, smitten, strange, touched 8 maniacal 9 fanatical, fantastic, foolhardy, half-baked, imprudent, ludicrous, senseless 10 infatuated, outrageous, ridiculous
about: 4 into 6 fond of 9 far gone on 10 infatuated
be ~ about: 4 dote, love 5 adore 6 admire
drive ~: 3 irk 5 annoy 6 pester
go ~: 4 flip, rave 5 freak 7 rampage
in a ~ way: 5 madly
like ~: 4 a lot 5 madly 6 vastly, wildly 7 greatly, rabidly 8 ardently 9 fervently, furiously, intensely 10 recklessly
like a fox: 3 sly 4 wily
plumb ~: 4 loco
quilt: 4 olio 6 jumble, medley 7 mélange 8 mishmash, mixed bag, pastiche 9 pasticcio, patchwork, potpourri 10 assortment, hodgepodge, miscellany, salmagundi
wild and ~ guy: 5 yahoo
crazy __: 5 quilt 6 eights
crazy __ loon: 3 as a
__ crazy: 4 like
__-crazy: 4 stir
Crazy (song)
artist: Patsy Cline, Seal
Crazy __: 4 Love, Mama, Moon 5 Horse, House 6 Horses
Crazy __, The: 4 Otto
Crazy __ You: 3 for
__ Crazy: 3 Get, Gun, I Go, Man 4 Girl, Stir 5 Movie
Crazy About Her (1989 song)
artist: Rod Stewart
crazy as __: 5 a loon
crazy eights: 4 game 8 card game
Crazy for You: 7 musical
composer: George Gershwin, Ira Gershwin
Crazy for You (1985 song)
artist: Madonna
CrazyGlue
competitor: 4 Duco
Crazy Heart (2009 film)
cast: Jeff Bridges
Crazy Horse
foe: 6 Custer
tribe: 5 Sioux 6 Lakota, Oglala
Crazy Horses (1972 song)
artist: Osmonds
Crazy in Berlin
author: Thomas Berger
Crazylegs: 6 Hirsch
crazy like __: 4 a fox
Crazy Love (song)
artist: Paul Anka, Poco
creak: 5 grate, groan, sound 6 squeak, squeal
creaky: 5 stiff 7 ancient 8 decrepit
cream: 3 tan, top 4 balm, best, mash, milk, pick, plum, rout, skim, soda 5 color, dairy, elite, outdo, pride, salve, white 6 choice, defeat, finest, flower, lather, lotion, marrow, ravage, yellow 7 clobber, conquer, destroy, lambast, neutral, shellac, unguent 8 cosmetic, emulsion, lambaste, liniment, ointment, shellack 9 emollient, lubricate, overpower, yellowish
add ~ to: 6 enrich
-colored: 5 flaxy 6 flaxen
get the ~: 4 skim 5 defat
of the crop: 4 A-one, best, tops 5 A-list, elect, elite
puff: 4 wimp 8 weakling
relative: *see* yellow color
serving: 4 glob 6 dollop
soothing ~: 4 balm
whipping tool: 5 whisk
without ~: 5 black
cream __: 3 ice 4 pail, puff, soda 5 sauce 6 cheese
cream __ crop: 5 of the
__ cream: 3 egg, ice 4 cold, sour 5 Devon, heavy, light 6 coffee, double, triple 7 clotted, shaving
Cream
leader: Eric Clapton
song: Sunshine of Your Love (1968)
White Room (1968)
Cream (1991 song)
artist: Prince
cream cheese
partner: 3 lox 5 bagel
creamer
relative: 4 ewer
creamery: 5 dairy
cream of __: 6 tartar 7 coconut 8 mushroom
Cream of __: 5 Wheat
cream of mushroom: 4 soup
cream of the __: 4 crop
__ cream pie: 6 Boston 7 coconut
cream puff: 3 car 4 auto, nerd, wimp 5 sissy 6 pastry 7 chicken, dessert 8 mama's boy, weakling 9 fraidy cat, jellyfish 10 automobile
kin: 6 éclair
sometimes: 3 car
cream soda: 8 beverage
creamy: 4 lush, oily, rich, soft 5 gooey, white 6 fluffy, smooth 7 buttery, velvety 8 feathery, luscious
cheese: 4 Brie 7 gervais 9 Camembert 10 mascarpone, Neufchâtel
creamy garlic: 8 dressing
creamy Italian: 8 dressing
crease: 4 bend, fold, line, ruck 5 crimp, plait, pleat, purse, ridge 6 dog-ear, furrow, groove, pucker, ruffle, rumple 7 crinkle, crumple, fluting, wrinkle 9 corrugate
create: 2 do 4 coin, form, make, work 5 beget, breed, build, cause, erect, forge, found, hatch, model, put up, set up, shape, spawn, start 6 author, design, devise, effect, father, invent, make up, whip up 7 compose, concoct, develop, dream up, fashion, imagine, pioneer, produce, think up, trump up 8 assemble, conceive, contrive, engender, engineer, generate, initiate, occasion, organize 9 actualize, construct, establish, fabricate, formulate, institute, originate 10 bring about, come up with, constitute, mastermind
creation: 4 opus, work 5 birth, world 6 making, nature, origin 7 coinage, figment, genesis, product 8 original, universe 9 beginning, causation, formation, handiwork, inception, invention 10 brainchild, conception, concoction, foundation, generation, production
cookoff ~: 5 chili
Creation of the World, The
composer: Darius Milhaud
Creation, The: 8 oratorio
basis for ~: 7 Genesis
composer: Joseph Haydn
role: 3 Eve 4 Adam
setting: 4 Eden
creative: 3 new 5 fresh, novel 6 clever, gifted 7 fertile, seminal, unusual 8 artistic, esthetic, inspired, original, prolific 9 aesthetic, ingenious, inventive, visionary 10 artistical, innovative, productive
impulse: 3 ego 4 idea 8 afflatus
start: 3 neo
type: 6 artist, author, genius, writer 8 composer, designer 9 innovator, visionary
work: 3 art 4 opus 5 music, novel 6 design 7 fiction 9 blueprint, invention
creativity: 3 art 8 artistry 9 invention
creator: 4 sire 5 brain, cause, maker 6 artist, author, framer, mother, origin 7 founder 8 begetter, designer, inventer, inventor, producer 9 architect, artificer, fashioner, initiator, innovator 10 fabricator, mastermind, originator
Creator: 3 God 5 deity, Maker 8 Almighty
Hindu ~: 6 Brahma
Muslim ~: 5 Allah
Creator (1985 film)
cast: Mariel Hemingway, Virginia Madsen, Peter O'Toole
creature: 4 pawn, soul 5 beast, being, thing 6 animal, entity, jackal, mortal, puppet 8 organism 10 individual
creature __: 7 comfort
__ Creatures: 6 Fierce
__ creature was stirring...: 4 not a
crèche trio: 4 Magi
credence: 5 faith, trust 6 belief, credit 8 reliance 10 confidence, conviction
give ~ to: 7 believe
credential: 6 ID card, ticket
credentials: 5 proof 6 papers 7 diploma 8 passport 9 reference
credenza: 6 buffet 7 cabinet 9 furniture, sideboard
credibility: 5 trust 8 solidity, validity
credibility __: 3 gap
credible: 4 sane 5 frank, legit, sound, valid 6 doable, honest, likely, square, viable 7 factual, sincere, tenable, upright 8 feasible, possible, probable, rational, reliable, straight, workable 9 authentic, plausible, potential, practical, veracious 10 achievable, attainable, believable, convincing,

dependable, forthright, imaginable, on the level, persuasive, reasonable, scrupulous
credit: **4** deem, fame, give, loan, name **5** asset, clout, faith, glory, honor, kudos, merit, thank, trust, worth **6** accept, bank on, bar tab, byline, esteem, impute, notice, praise, regard, rely on, renown, repute, status, thanks **7** acclaim, advance, ascribe, believe, laurels, plastic, voucher **8** approval, assign to, consider, credence, depend on, gamble on, good name, mortgage, prestige, relegate, reliance, standing **9** ascribe to, attribute, authority, chalk up to, character, deduction, influence **10** confidence, reputation
author ~: **6** byline
card action: **5** swipe **6** charge
ender: **6** worthy
extend ~: **4** bill, lend, loan **7** advance
give ~ for: **5** allow
letters: **3** IOU
maintain good ~: **3** pay **5** repay
opposite: **5** debit
recipient: **4** ower
source: **4** bank **6** lender
use ~: **3** owe **6** charge
with: **5** blame, lay on **6** impute **7** ascribe **9** attribute
credit __: **4** card, hour, line, memo, risk, slip **5** limit, union **6** agency, bureau, rating **7** manager, squeeze
creditable: **4** fine, good, nice, okay **5** great, legit, moral, noble **6** proper, worthy **7** ethical **8** all right, laudable, pleasant, pleasing, splendid, superior **9** admirable, agreeable, authentic, deserving, estimable, excellent, exemplary, honorable, praisable, reputable, wonderful **10** acceptable, believable, beneficial
credit card color: **4** gold **8** platinum
creditor: **5** payee **6** debtee, lender, loaner, usurer **7** Shylock
right: **4** lien
writ: **6** elegit
credo: **5** tenet **6** belief **8** doctrine, ideology **9** principle **10** philosophy
credulity: **7** naiveté **9** greenness
credulous: **4** naif **5** green, naive **6** simple, unwary **8** gullable, gullible, trusting **9** accepting, believing, childlike, fanatical **10** uncritical
Cree: **5** tribe **6** Indian **7** Amerind **8** language **10** Algonquian
creed: **3** ism **5** canon, dogma, ethic, faith, tenet **6** belief, canons **8** doctrine, ideology, religion **9** principle, teachings **10** persuasion, philosophy, principles
ender: **4** amen
Creed: **6** Apollo
__ Creed: **6** Nicene
Creedence Clearwater Revival
leader: John Fogerty
song: Bad Moon Rising (1969)
Down on the Corner (1969)
Green River (1969)
Have You Ever Seen the Rain (1971)
Lookin' Out My Back Door (1970)
Proud Mary (1969)
Sweet Hitch-Hiker (1971)
Travelin' Band (1970)
Up Around the Bend (1970)
creek: **3** ria, run **4** race, rill **5** bourn, brook, rille **6** branch, runlet, runnel, stream **7** rivulet **9** streamlet, tributary
cross a ~: **4** wade
up the ~: **6** in a fix, in a jam **8** helpless, hopeless **9** desperate
__ creek: **5** up the
Creek: **5** tribe **6** Indian **7** Amerind
__ Creek: **5** Cross **7** Coroner, Dawson's
__ Creek Pass: **4** Wolf
creel: **4** trap **6** basket
creel, one for the: **6** keeper
creep: **3** pad **4** bore, bozo, edge, inch, jerk, lurk, pest, pill **5** crawl, loser, prowl, sculk, skulk, slink, snake, sneak, steal, twerp, twirp **6** bad guy, tingle, writhe **7** lowlife, slither, villain, wriggle **9** pussyfoot, scoundrel, scuzzball
through: **4** ooze, seep **10** infiltrate
up on: **5** stalk **8** approach
Creep (1994 song)
artist: TLC
creeper: **3** ivy, tot **4** bird, vine **5** plant
starter: **5** honey
trumpet ~: **5** plant **6** flower
__ Creepers: **7** Jeepers
creepers, abounding in: **4** viny
creeping: **4** poky, slow **6** draggy **7** gradual, halting, impeded, lagging, languid **8** dilatory, drawn-out, hesitant, slothful, sluggish, toddling **9** leisurely, lethargic, prolonged, snaillike, unhurried **10** deliberate, protracted
combining form: **6** herpet- **7** herpeto-
creepingly: **8** bit by bit
creeps: **7** jimjams
give one the ~: **5** alarm, scare
Creepshow: **4** book, film
author: Stephen King
cast: Adrienne Barbeau, Ted Danson, Ed Harris, Hal Holbrook, Viveca Lindfors, E.G. Marshall, Leslie Nielsen, Carrie Nye, Fritz Weaver
director: George Romero
creepy: **4** eery **5** dread, eerie, scary, weird **6** crawly, spooky **7** dreaded, macaber, macabre, ominous, uncanny **8** dreadful, ghoulish, gruesome, peculiar, sinister **9** loathsome, repellant, repellent **10** terrifying, unsettling
creepy-crawly: **3** bug **6** insect
Creeque Alley (1967 song)
artist: Mamas & the Papas
Cregar: **5** Laird
Creighton: **10** university
athletes: **8** Bluejays
locale: **5** Omaha **8** Nebraska
creme: **5** candy, sweet
crème __: **6** brûlée **7** d'ananas, fraîche
__ crème: **4** café **6** double, triple
crème brûlée: **7** dessert
crème de __: **5** cacao **6** banane, cassis, fraise, menthe **7** bananes
crème de cacao: **5** drink **8** beverage
crème de la crème: **4** pick **5** elite, prize **6** choice, finest
crème de menthe: **5** drink **8** beverage
Cremona: **4** city, font, town **8** typeface
collectible: **5** Strad
locale: **5** Italy
violinmaker: **5** Amati **10** Stradivari
crenel: **4** slit
Crenna, Richard: **5** actor
film: Body Heat (1981)
Breakheart Pass (1976)
First Blood (1982)
The Flamingo Kid (1984)
Rambo III (1988)
Red Sky at Morning (1970)
The Sand Pebbles (1966)
Star! (1968)
Table for Five (1983)
Wait Until Dark (1967)
TV: Our Miss Brooks, The Real McCoys
Crenshaw: **3** Ben
kin: ***see*** melon
Crenshaw, Ben: **6** golfer
__ creole: **3** à la **6** shrimp
Creole: **7** cuisine **8** language
vegetable: **4** ocra, okra, okro
__ Creole: **4** King
Creon
daughter: **6** Creusa
father: **8** Heracles
sister: **7** Jocasta
creosote source: **3** tar **7** coal tar
crepe: **6** fabric **7** pancake
relative: **5** blini, bliny **6** blintz **7** blintze
crepe __: **5** paper
crêpe __: **7** suzette
crepe de __: **5** Chine
crêpe suzette: **7** dessert
crêpe suzettes
like ~: **6** flambé
crepitate: **7** crackle
crepon: **6** fabric **8** material
crepuscular: **5** dusky
crepuscule: **4** dusk **9** nightfall
crescendo: **4** apex, peak **5** climb, crest, surge, swell **6** summit, zenith **7** upsurge **8** building, increase, pinnacle
crescent: **3** arc, bow **4** lune, moon **5** lunet **6** pastry **7** falcate, rainbow **8** falcated, meniscus
fingernail ~: **6** lunula, lunule
moon end: **4** cusp, horn
-shaped: **6** bicorn, lunate
__ Crescent: **3** Red **7** Fertile
Crescent Moon, The
author: Rabindranath Tagore
Crespin, Régine: **6** singer **7** soprano
specialty: **5** opera
cress: **5** green, salad **6** veggie **7** garnish **9** vegetable
starter: **5** penny, water **6** pepper
Cressida: **3** car **4** auto, moon **6** Toyota
father: **7** Calchas
planet: **6** Uranus
to Pandarus: **5** niece
crest: **3** cap, top **4** acme, apex, head, peak, rise, sign, wave **5** crown, plume, ridge, spire, title **6** apogee, billow, climax, device, emblem, height, summit, symbol, vertex, zenith **7** hilltop, insigne, maximum, topknot **8** heraldry, high spot, insignia, meridian, pinnacle **9** crescendo, high point **10** coat of arms, prominence
combining form: **4** loph- **5** lophi-, lopho- **6** lophio-
ender: **6** fallen
inscription: **4** name **5** motto
mountain ~: **5** arête, ridge
on the ~: **4** atop
Crest
alternative: ***see*** toothpaste
unit: **4** tube
__ Crest: **6** Falcon
crested __: **4** fern, iris **5** swift **6** lizard
Crested Butte: **4** city, town **6** resort
locale: **8** Colorado
crestfallen: **3** low, sad **4** blue, down, glum **5** heavy, moody, sorry, woful **6** gloomy, morose, somber, woeful **7** doleful, in a funk, joyless, subdued, unhappy **8** dejected, downcast, lowering, troubled, wretched **9** bummed out, cheerless, heartsick, miserable, sorrowful, woebegone **10** dispirited, melancholy
Creston, Paul: **8** composer
cretaceous: **6** chalky
Cretan: **5** Minos **7** Ariadne, El Greco
Cretan __: **4** bull
Crete: **4** isle **6** island
ancient city: **7** Cnossus, Gnossus, Knossos
peak: **3** Ida **5** Mt. Ida
port: **5** Canea **6** Candia
where ~ is: **5** Medit.
cretonne: **6** fabric
Creüsa
brother: **5** Paris **6** Hector
father: **5** Creon, Priam **7** Priamus
husband: **5** Eneas **6** Aeneas
mother: **4** Gaea **6** Hecuba
sister: **9** Cassandra
son: **3** Ion
crevasse: **4** gulf, rift **5** chasm, crack, gorge, gully **6** gulley, ravine **7** fissure
crevice: **3** gap **4** hole, leak, nook, rent, rift, slit **5** abyss, chasm, cleft, crack, split **6** cranny, ravine **7** fissure, opening **10** interstice
crew: **3** mob, set **4** band, gang, pack, team **5** corps, covey, crowd, force, group, hands, party, posse, sport, squad, staff, troop **6** league, muster, outfit, troupe **7** brigade, company, faction, oarsmen, retinue, sailors, sea dogs, workers **9** deckhands, personnel, shipmates **10** complement, stagehands
cut: **6** hairdo **8** coiffure **9** hairstyle
ender: **3** cut **4** mate
hire a ~: **3** man
hire a new ~: **5** reman
implement: **3** oar
member: **3** cox, oar **4** hand **5** rower
work ~: **4** unit **5** corps
crew __: **3** cut **4** neck, sock **5** chief
__ crew: **3** air, gun **6** ground
crew cut: **4** coif **6** hairdo **8** coiffure
give a ~: **4** crop **5** shear
opposite: **4** Afro
Crew-Cuts
song: Earth Angel (1955)

Gum Drop (1955)
Ko Ko Mo (1955)
Crewe: 4 city, town
locale: 7 England 8 Cheshire
crewel: 4 yarn 5 craft 10 embroidery, needlework
create with ~: 4 knit, purl
ender: 4 work
tool: 6 needle
Crewe Train
author: Rose Macaulay
crewman: 3 gob, tar 4 hand, salt 6 sailor 7 jack tar
affirmative: 3 aye 6 aye aye
Crew, The (2000 film)
cast: Richard Dreyfuss, Dan Hedaya, Burt Reynolds
crib: 3 bed, bin 4 lift, pony, take, trot 5 cheat, filch, pinch, steal 6 cradle, manger, pilfer 8 bassinet 9 furniture 10 cheat sheet, plagiarize
cry: 3 wah 4 mama 5 mamma
datum: 6 answer
occupant: 3 tot 4 baby, corn 6 infant 7 neonate, newborn
starter: 4 corn
use a ~: 5 cheat
crib __: 5 sheet
cribbage: 4 game 8 card game
clear the ~ board: 5 unpeg
jack, in ~: 3 nob 7 his nobs
marker: 3 peg
cribbage __: 5 board
cribwear: 3 PJs 7 pajamas
Crichton: 5 James 7 Charles, Michael
Crichton, Michael: 6 writer 8 director
film: Coma (1978)
The Great Train Robbery (1979)
Westworld (1973)
work: Airframe
The Andromeda Strain
A Case of Need
Congo
Disclosure
The Great Train Robbery
Jurassic Park
The Lost World
Next
Prey
Rising Sun
Sphere
State of Fear
The Terminal Man
Timeline
crick: 3 ria 4 ache, kink, pain, rill 5 cramp, rille, spasm 6 twinge
spot: 4 neck
cricket: 3 bug, toy 4 game 5 sport 6 cicada, insect 10 percussion
ball: 6 googly
division: 6 inning
glancing blow in ~: 5 snick
jiminy ~: 4 gosh 5 golly
need: 3 bat 4 ball 6 wicket
sides: 3 ons
sound: 5 chirp, chirr, churr 6 chirre
squad: 6 eleven
term: 3 bye
wicket: 3 end
cricketeer: 6 bowler
Cricket on the Hearth
author: Charles Dickens
Crickets
song: 5 Oh Boy 6 Rave On 8 Peggy Sue 9 Maybe Baby
Crick, Francis: 8 Nobelist 10 geneticist

concern: 3 DNA
partner: 6 Watson
cri de __: 5 coeur
cri, dernier: 3 fad 4 mode, rage 5 vogue 6 latest 7 fashion 8 last word
crier: 4 baby 6 hawker, herald, pedlar, pedler, vender, vendor, weeper 7 peddler 8 huckster 9 announcer, messenger 10 proclaimer
cry: 6 hear ye
__ crier: 4 town
Cries and Whispers (1972 film)
cast: Liv Ullmann
director: Ingmar Bergman
__ C. Riley: 7 Jeannie
crime: 3 DUI, DWI, sin 4 pity, tort, vice 5 arson, bribe, graft, heist, lapse, theft, usury, wrong 6 felony, holdup, murder, racket 7 bad deed, larceny, misdeed, offense, outrage, scandal, treason 8 atrocity, burglary, delictum, iniquity, thievery, trespass 9 inside job, sacrilege, violation 10 corruption, infraction
aid in ~: 4 abet 7 collude
anti-organized ~ act: 4 RICO
lab clue: 3 DNA
lure into ~: 6 entrap
partner in ~: 4 ally 6 cohort
pin a ~ on: 5 frame
prevention dog: 7 McGruff
scene evidence: 5 print
scene of the ~: 5 venue
statistic: 6 arrest
syndicate head: 4 capo
Crime __ Punishment: 3 and
__ Crime: 4 True 5 It's No
__ Crime?: 5 Is It a
Crimean __: 3 War
Crime and Punishment: 5 novel
author: Fyodor Dostoyevsky
character: 5 Rodya, Sonia 6 Dmitri, Rodion
Crimean port: 5 Yalta
crimebuster: 3 cop 4 G-man, narc, nark, T-man
Crimes and Misdemeanors (1989 film)
cast: Alan Alda, Woody Allen, Claire Bloom, Mia Farrow
director: Woody Allen
Crimes of the Heart: 4 film, play
author: Beth Henley
cast: Diane Keaton, Jessica Lange, Sam Shepard, Sissy Spacek
character: 3 Meg 4 Babe 5 Chick, Lenny
director: Bruce Beresford
criminal: 3 bad 4 evil, perp, punk, tabu, thug, yegg 5 crook, felon, rogue, taboo, thief, wrong 6 bad guy, bandit, banned, guilty, gunsel, outlaw, sinner, unfair 7 brigand, convict, corrupt, crooked, culprit, hoodlum, illegal, illicit, lawless, mobster, villain 8 culpable, evildoer, fugitive, hooligan, improper, internee, offender, outlawed, prisoner, scofflaw, unlawful, verboten, wrongful 9 desperado, felonious, forbidden, miscreant, murderous, nefarious, purloiner, racketeer, wrongdoer 10 cat burglar, delinquent, fraudulent, indictable, lawbreaker, outrageous, pickpocket, prohibited, shoplifter, trespasser
activity: 6 racket
band: 3 mob 4 gang, ring 10 underworld
charge: 3 rap
Indian ~: 6 dacoit, dakoit
law concept: 6 intent
not ~: 5 legal, legit 6 lawful
pattern: 2 MO
petty ~ in Britain: 4 spiv
slang: 5 argot
subduer: 5 taser
criminal __: 3 law 4 code 5 court 6 lawyer 7 justice
criminality: 4 evil 5 guilt
criminate: 6 indict
criminology: 7 science
crimp: 4 coil, curl, fold, friz, kink, snag, undo, wave 5 frizz, plait, pleat, stimy, stymy, swirl 6 crease, dog-ear, groove, hamper, hinder, rumple, stymie, thwart 7 bunch up, crinkle, crumple, fluting, inhibit, sinuate, wrinkle 8 obstacle 9 corrugate
put a ~ in: 6 hinder, hobble
crimped: 5 kinky
crimson: 3 red 5 color, ruddy
relative: *see* red color
Crimson: 7 Harvard
rival: 4 Elis 6 Yalies 8 Bulldogs
Crimson __: 4 Tide
Crimson and Clover (song)
artist: Joan Jett and the Blackhearts, Tommy James and the Shondells
Crimson Tide: 4 'Bama 7 Alabama
rival: 4 Vols
Crimson Tide (1995 film)
cast: Gene Hackman, Denzel Washington
director: Tony Scott
cringe: 4 fawn 5 cower, kotow, quail, wince 6 flinch, grovel, kowtow, quiver, recoil, shrink 7 tremble 8 draw back
at: 5 dread
crinite: 6 fossil
crinkle: 4 fold, tuck 5 crimp, ridge 6 crease, furrow, pucker, ruffle, rumple, rustle 7 wrinkle 9 corrugate
crinkled fabric: 5 crape, crepe, lisse
crinkly: 5 rough
crinoid: 5 shell 8 seashell
crinoline: 5 skirt 6 fabric 8 material 9 hoop skirt, petticoat
Cripple __, CO: 5 Creek
Crisco: 3 oil 10 cooking oil
alternative: 6 Mazola, Wesson 7 Puritan 8 olive oil
crisis: 4 stew 5 panic, pinch 6 crunch, danger, plight, strait, unrest 7 dilemma, trouble, urgency 8 disaster, exigence, exigency, juncture, landmark, showdown, zero hour 9 deep water, emergency, imbroglio 10 depression, difficulty
__ Crisium: 4 Mare
crisp: 3 raw 4 cold, cool, curt, tidy 5 brief, brisk, fresh, nippy, pithy, sharp, short, smart, terse, toast 6 chilly, crusty, gnomic, snappy, spruce, wintry 7 bracing, brittle, concise, crumbly, crunchy, dessert, friable, laconic, orderly, wintery 8 clean-cut, spirited, succinct, unwilted 9 trenchant 10 fortifying, refreshing, to the point
not ~: 5 soggy, stale
Crisp: 6 Donald 7 Quentin
Crispin: 5 saint 6 Glover
product: 4 shoe
Crispix
competitor: *see* cereal
crispness: 3 nip 4 bite 5 chill, frost
lose ~: 4 wilt
Crispus: 7 Attucks
crispy: 5 chewy 6 crusty 7 brittle, crumbly, crunchy, friable 9 crackling
Criss: 5 Angel
crisscross: 5 weave 7 athwart 8 traverse 9 intersect
Criss-Cross
author: Hal Porter
Cristina: 7 Ferrare
__ Cristina Barcelona: 5 Vicky
Crist, Judith: 6 critic 8 reviewer
__ Cristo: 5 Monte
__ Cristóbal: 3 San
__-crit: 3 lit
criterion: 3 law, std. 4 norm, rule, test 5 basis, canon, gauge, model 7 measure, paragon 8 paradigm, standard 9 archetype, benchmark, parameter, precedent, principle, prototype, yardstick 10 foundation, touchstone
scholarship ~: 4 need 5 merit
critic: 3 nag 4 Reed 5 Crist, Ebert, judge, momus, rater 6 basher, blamer, carper, censor, expert, gadfly, moaner, nagger, noodge, panner, pundit, Shalit, writer 7 analyst, arbiter, caviler, crybaby, defamer, doubter, Rex Reed, scholar, scolder 8 attacker, disputer, maligner, quibbler, reviewer, Spingarn, vilifier 9 authority, belittler, detractor, evaluator, muckraker, nitpicker 10 complainer, disparager, Gene Shalit, Roger Ebert
at times: 5 raver 6 panner
unit: 4 star
critical: 3 key 4 dire, main 5 acute, fatal, fussy, grave, hairy, major, nasty, picky, sharp, tight, vital 6 minute, severe, urgent 7 burning, carping, crucial, cutting, exigent, fateful, finicky, fretful, nagging, peevish, pivotal, serious, weighty 8 captious, caviling, choleric, deciding, decisive, exacting, exigeant, finiking, finnicky, fretsome, pregnant, pressing, scathing, scolding, ticklish 9 demanding, desperate, high-level, important, memorable, momentous, querulous, sarcastic, strategic, trenchant 10 belittling, censorious, conclusive, derogatory, detracting, detractive, discerning, imperative, minimizing, nitpicking, particular, portentous, underlying
not ~: 5 minor 7 trivial
point: 5 brink
reaction: 3 pan 4 rave

regard: 8 analysis 10 inspection
remark: 4 barb 5 swipe
critical __: 4 mass
criticism: 3 rap 4 beef, flak, slam 5 abuse, blame, blast, cavil, flack, input, knock, lumps, whine 6 attack, earful, rebuke, review 7 carping, censure, comment, lecture, obloquy, opinion, panning, quibble, reproof, sarcasm 8 analysis, berating, caviling, diatribe, feedback, reproach, reproval 9 appraisal, aspersion, brickbats, broadside, complaint, objection, reprimand, sideswipe, stricture, talking-to 10 assessment, bawling-out, Bronx cheer, commentary, dissection, evaluation, exposition, impugnment, nit-picking, opprobrium, reflection, upbraiding
unjust ~: 6 bad rap
criticize: 3 hit, jaw, nag, pan, rap, rip 4 bash, carp, damn, flay, lash, rail, slam, zing 5 blame, blast, cavil, chide, cut up, decry, fault, judge, knock, probe, roast, scold, snipe, study, trash, whine 6 assail, assess, berate, impugn, jump on, lean on, oppugn, peck at, pick at, rail at, rebuke, review, scathe, vilify 7 affront, analyze, censure, clobber, condemn, examine, lambast, lay into, lecture, nitpick, quibble, reprove, run down, snipe at, upbraid 8 admonish, backbite, badmouth, belittle, chastise, denounce, evaluate, lambaste, reproach, talk down 9 castigate, cut to bits, disparage, dress down, excoriate, find fault, frown upon, fustigate, interpret, lash out at, pick apart, reprehend, reprimand, reprobate 10 come down on, denunciate, disapprove, scrutinize
Critic's Choice
author: Ira Levin
critique: 4 barb 5 essay, input 6 review, survey 7 comment 8 analysis, exegesis, judgment 9 editorial 10 commentary, exposition, literature
Critique of Judgment
author: Immanuel Kant
Critique of Pure Reason
author: Immanuel Kant
critter: 3 cow 5 beast 6 animal
Crius: 4 seer 5 giant, Titan
Cro-__: 6 Magnon
croak: 3 caw 5 grunt 6 mutter, squawk
croaker: 4 fish, frog 5 raven
croaking: 6 froggy 10 laryngitic
croaky: 5 gruff, husky 6 froggy, hoarse 8 gravelly
Croat: 4 Slav
neighbor: 4 Serb
Croatia: 6 nation 7 country
bovine: 4 Busa
capital: 6 Zagreb
city: 5 Sisak, Sisek, Split 6 Osijek, Rijeka, Zagreb
island: 3 Vis
legislature: 5 Sabor
mountain: 7 Triglov
neighbor: 7 Hungary 8 Slovenia 10 Yugoslavia
port: 4 Pulj 5 Zadar
river: 4 Sava
__-Croatian: 5 Serbo
croc: 6 animal 7 reptile
relative: 5 gator
Croce: 3 Jim 9 Benedetto
Croce, Jim
song: Bad, Bad Leroy Brown (1973)
I Got a Name (1973)
I'll Have to Say I Love You in a Song (1974)
Time in a Bottle (1973)
You Don't Mess Around With Jim (1972)
crochet: 4 knit, lace, note 6 stitch
item: 5 doily, scarf 6 afghan, bootee, bootie, doyley
need: 4 hook, wool 6 needle
crock: 3 jar, pot 4 bowl 6 cooker, flagon, vessel 7 amphora, caldron 8 cauldron 9 container, inebriate 10 intoxicate
product: 4 stew
Crock __: 3 Pot
Crocker: 5 Betty
crockery: 5 china 7 pottery 8 ceramics, clayware 9 porcelain 10 dinnerware, terra cotta
Crockett: 4 Davy 5 Sonny
beat: 5 Miami
last stand: 5 Alamo
partner: 5 Tubbs
crocodile: 6 animal, caiman, cayman, gavial, lizard 7 gharial, leather, reptile
female: 3 cow
habitat: 4 Nile
like ~ tears: 4 fake 5 false
male: 4 bull
neighbor: 5 hippo
young: 8 crocklet
crocodile __: 5 tears
Crocodile Dundee (1986 film)
cast: Paul Hogan, Linda Kozlowski
role: 3 Sue 4 Mick
Crocodile Rock (1972 song)
artist: Elton John
crocus: 5 plant 6 flower, yellow 8 orangish
bulb: 4 corm
relative: see yellow color
Croesus: 9 plutocrat
like ~: 4 rich 7 wealthy
croft: 4 farm
Crofts: 4 Dash 7 Freeman
partner: 5 Seals
__ Croft: Tomb Raider: 4 Lara
croissant: 5 bread
shape: 4 lune
croissant shape: 4 lune, moon 5 lunar
Croix de __: 6 Guerre
__ Croix, Que.: 3 Ste.
Cro-Magnon: 5 human 7 caveman
Crome Yellow
author: Aldous Huxley
Cromwell: 4 John 5 James 6 Oliver 7 Richard
nickname: 9 Ironsides
victory site: 6 Dunbar
crone: 3 hag 5 harpy, witch 6 beldam 7 beldame 8 harridan
like a ~: 5 anile
Cronin: 2 A.J. 3 Joe 5 James
Cronin, A.J.: 6 writer 8 Scottish
Cronin, James: 8 Nobelist 9 physicist
Cronin, Joe: 6 Red Sox 9 shortstop
Cronkite, Walter: 6 anchor 10 journalist, newscaster
network: 3 CBS
Cronus: 5 giant, Titan
brother: 5 Coeus, Crius 7 Iapetus, Oceanus 8 Hyperion
daughter: 4 Hera 6 Hestia 7 Demeter
equivalent: 6 Saturn
parent: 4 Gaea 6 Uranus
sister: 4 Rhea, Thia 5 Dione 6 Phoebe, Tethys, Themis 9 Mnemosyne
son: 4 Zeus 5 Hades, Pluto 6 Chiron 7 Cheiron 8 Poseidon
wife: 4 Rhea
crony: 3 bro, pal 4 ally, chum, mate 5 amigo, buddy 6 cohort, frater, friend 7 comrade, partner 8 alter ego, intimate, roommate, sidekick 9 associate, colleague, companion, confidant 10 accomplice, bosom buddy, compatriot, confidante, well-wisher
cronyism: 9 patronage
Cronyn, Hume: 5 actor
film: Brute Force (1947)
Cocoon (1985)
Conrack (1974)
The Seventh Cross (1944)
Sunrise at Campobello (1960)
spouse: Jessica Tandy
crook: 4 bend, flex, loop, wind, yegg 5 angle, cheat, curve, felon, fraud, ganef, gonef, gonif, knave, rogue, shark, staff, thief 6 bad guy, bandit, con man, corner, dogleg, goniff, outlaw, robber 7 burglar, filcher, flexure, rustler 8 criminal, gangster, pilferer, swindler 9 purloiner, racketeer, scoundrel
a finger: 6 entice, invite, signal
alternative: 4 hook
assist a ~: 4 abet
by hook or ~: 7 somehow, someway 8 someways
ender: 4 back, neck
move like a ~: 5 sculk, skulk
story: 5 alibi
crooked: 3 sly, wry 4 agee, ajee, alop, awry, bent, evil, foul, wily 5 askew, bandy, bowed, dirty, false, lying, shady, snaky, wrong 6 angled, aslant, canted, hooked, louche, rotten, shifty, skewed, tricky, unfair, warped, zigzag 7 angular, corrupt, devious, illegal, knavish, sinuous, slanted, twisted, winding 8 angulose, angulous, cockeyed, criminal, delusive, guileful, lopsided, thieving, thievish, tortuous, twisting, unlawful 9 contorted, deceitful, dishonest, distorted, falsified, insincere, irregular, larcenous, malformed, nefarious, unaligned, underhand, unethical 10 asymmetric, fraudulent, meandering, mendacious, nonuniform, serpentine, untruthful, virtueless
follow a ~ path: 3 zag, zig
not ~: 6 direct
scheme: 3 con 4 scam
crooked mouth, name meaning: 8 Campbell
crookedness: 9 improbity
Crookes, William: 7 chemist 9 physicist, scientist
Crooklyn (1994 film)
cast: Zelda Harris, Delroy Lindo, Alfre Woodard
director: Spike Lee
crookneck: 6 veggie 9 vegetable
croon: 3 hum 4 sing 6 intone, warble 8 vocalize
crooner: 4 Como 6 Crosby, singer 7 Bennett, Sinatra 8 vocalist 9 balladeer
song: 6 ballad
crop: 3 cut, hew, lop, maw, mow 4 chop, clip, corn, craw, oats, pare, rice, snip, trim, whip 5 fruit, grain, prune, shave, shear, slash, wheat, yield 6 barley, cotton, cut off, detach, forage, fruits, gullet, lessen, nibble, output, reduce 7 curtail, harvest, produce, scissor, shorten, sorghum, trim off, veggies, vintage 8 cut short, gleaning, soybeans, truncate 10 vegetables
animal's ~: 3 maw 4 craw
combining form: 4 agro-
cover ~: 6 legume
cream of the ~: 4 best 5 elite
eater: 4 crow 6 beetle, thrips
ender: 4 land
forage ~: 3 ers, urd 5 emmer, ervil, vetch 6 clover, millet 7 alfalfa
land: 5 field
plane: 6 duster
raising: 7 farming
science: 3 agr. 8 agronomy
science of ~ production: 8 agrology
second grass ~: 5 rowen
starter: 5 share, stone
unit: 3 row 4 acre
up: 4 rise 5 arise, begin, occur 6 appear, emerge, happen 7 surface
up again: 5 recur
crop-__: 4 dust 5 eared 6 duster
__ crop: 4 cash, root 5 cover, field 6 riding
__-cropped: 5 close
cropper
come a ~: 4 bomb, bust, flop, lose, slip, trip 5 flunk 6 blow it, falter 7 blunder, founder, go under, go wrong, misstep, stumble, wash out 8 fall flat, flounder, lay an egg 9 strike out
crops: 7 harvest, produce
bring in the ~: 4 reap
fit for ~: 6 arable
like some ~: 4 oaty 5 oaten
raise ~: 4 farm, till
treat ~: 4 dust
croquet: 4 game 5 sport
site: 4 lawn, yard
variation: 5 roque
wicket: 4 hoop
croquette: 4 meat 5 patty
relative: 5 latke 7 pancake
Crosby: 3 Bob 4 Bing, Mary, Norm 5 David 6 Denise
colleague: 4 Nash 5 Young 6 Stills

Crosby, Bing: 5 actor **6** singer
costar: 4 Hope **6** Lamour
film: Anything Goes (1936)
The Bells of St. Mary's (1945)
The Big Broadcast (1932)
The Birth of the Blues (1941)
Blue Skies (1946)
College Humor (1933)
The Country Girl (1954)
Dixie (1943)
Going Hollywood (1933)
Going My Way (1944, AA)
Here Comes the Groom (1951)
Here Come the Waves (1944)
High Society (1956)
Holiday Inn (1942)
Just for You (1952)
Little Boy Lost (1953)
Mississippi (1935)
Rhythm on the River (1940)
Road to Bali (1952)
The Road to Hong Kong (1962)
Road to Morocco (1942)
Road to Rio (1947)
Road to Singapore (1940)
Road to Utopia (1945)
Road to Zanzibar (1941)
Robin and the Seven Hoods (1964)
She Loves Me Not (1934)
Sing, You Sinners (1938)
Star Spangled Rhythm (1942)
Waikiki Wedding (1937)
Welcome Stranger (1947)
We're Not Dressing (1934)
White Christmas (1954)
song: Amor (1944)
Dinah (1932)
True Love (1956)
White Christmas (1955)
spouse: Kathryn Grant
Crosby, Stills & Nash
song: Just a Song Before I Go (1977)
Marrakesh Express (1969)
Our House (1970)
Suite: Judy Blue Eyes (1969)
Teach Your Children (1970)
Wasted on the Way (1982)
Woodstock (1970)
Crosetti: 5 Frank
crosier: 5 crook, staff
carrier: 5 abbot
Crosland: 4 Alan
cross: 3 hot, mad, mix **4** foil, ford, ired, rood, sell, sore, span, tick **5** angry, blend, block, huffy, irate, livid, medal, moody, punch, riled, surly, testy, upset, vexed, wroth **6** betray, bridge, crabby, cranky, crusty, divide, foul up, fretty, fuming, go over, grumpy, hinder, hybrid, impede, impugn, ireful, mingle, morose, oppose, ordeal, ornery, peeved, put out, raging, raving, red-hot, snappy, sullen, thwart, touchy **7** annoyed, bearish, enraged, fretful, furious, grouchy, huffish, in a snit, jaywalk, jewelry, louse up, mixture, mongrel, peevish, peppery, ranting, sell out, waspish **8** captious, caviling, choleric, churlish, fretsome, grumpish, incensed, inflamed, maddened, navigate, obstruct, outraged, pass over, petulant, step over, traverse, wrathful **9** crotchety, fractious, frustrate, hybridize, indignant, intersect, irascible, irritable, irritated, querulous, resentful, splenetic, truculent **10** contradict, contravene, freaked out, ill-humored, infuriated, interbreed, interweave, misfortune, out of sorts, transverse
a creek: 4 ford, wade
align the ~ hairs: 3 aim **5** sight
at ~ purposes with: 7 athwart
canine ~: 3 mut **4** mutt
combining form: 6 stauro-
Egyptian ~: 4 ankh
ender: 3 bar, bow, cut, tie, way **4** beam, bill, bred, cuts, fire, hair, head, ness, over, road, ruff, talk, town, tree, walk, wind, wise, word **5** bones, breed, check, court, hatch, patch, piece **6** bowman **7** current
one's heart: 3 vow **4** avow **5** swear **6** pledge **7** promise
one's mind: 5 occur **7** occur to
out: 4 dele, x out **6** cancel, delete, efface, excise, remove **7** mark off, redline **9** red-pencil
over: 4 span **6** bridge **8** bestride
paths with: 4 meet
section: 6 sample **8** specimen
starter: 3 out **4** auto, back, test
swords: 4 buck, defy, duel, spar, tilt **5** argue, clash, fight **6** attack, battle, bicker, combat, debate, engage, oppose, resist, tussle **7** contend, contest, dispute, quarrel, wrangle **8** conflict, disagree, do battle, struggle **9** duke it out, have it out, lock horns, slug it out, withstand
the ocean: 4 sail **5** pilot **6** cruise, voyage **7** captain, journey **8** navigate
the plate: 5 score
the threshold: 4 go in **5** enter
to bear: 4 onus **5** trial **6** burden
weapons with: 4 face **6** attack, take on
where axes ~: 5 graph **6** origin
with: 5 mad at
cross __: 3 fox, out, sea **4** buck, fire, over, talk, wind **5** hairs, ratio, wires **6** street, stroke, swords **7** product, section **8** purposes
cross __ bear: 3 as a
cross-__: 4 eyed, fade, file, link, vein, vine **5** check, match, staff, trade, train **6** action, bearer, bedded, border, cousin, garnet, legged, stitch, string **7** country, examine, grained, indexed, utilize
cross-__ tire: 3 ply
__ cross: 3 tau **4** Iona **5** Greek, Latin, Mills, papal **6** ansate, Celtic, Geneva, single **7** Calvary, Maltese, Passion
__-cross: 6 double
Cross: 3 Ben, Irv **6** Amanda, Marcia
__ Cross: 3 Red **4** Blue, Holy, Iron, Navy **5** Criss **7** Charing
cross as __: 5 a bear
crossbar: 4 beam, yoke **6** lintel
try to clear the ~: 5 vault
crossbeam: 5 trave **6** rafter
crossbill: 4 bird
genus: 5 loxia
crossbones partner: 5 skull
crossbow: 4 prod **8** arbalest
arrow: 4 bolt
ready a ~: 3 aim
user: 6 archer
cross-bred: 4 mixt **5** mixed **6** hybrid
crossbreed: 3 cur, mut **4** mule, mutt **7** mongrel
__ cross bun: 3 hot
Cross, Christopher
song: Best That You Can Do (1981)
Ride Like the Wind (1980)
Sailing (1980)
Think of Laura (1983)
cross-country, go: 4 hike, ride, tour **5** drive **6** travel
Cross Creek (1983 film)
cast: Peter Coyote, Malcolm McDowell, Mary Steenburgen, Rip Torn
director: Martin Ritt
crosscurrent: 4 eddy
crosscut: 3 saw **6** tunnel
crossed
keep one's fingers ~: 4 hope, wish **5** dream **6** aspire, expect **7** look for **10** anticipate
out: 3 x'ed
__-crossed: 4 star
cross-examine: 3 ask **4** pump, quiz **5** grill **8** question
cross-eyed, look: 6 squint
crossfire: 7 barrage
Crossfire
genre: 4 talk **6** debate
network: 3 CNN
crossing: 4 walk **6** bridge, cruise, voyage **7** meeting, opposed, passage, pathway, transit, viaduct **8** junction, juncture, opposing, overpass **9** traversal, underpass **10** cloverleaf
the ocean: 4 asea **5** at sea
crossing __: 5 guard
__ crossing: 5 grade, level, zebra
Crossing Brooklyn Ferry
author: Walt Whitman
Crossing Delancey (1988 film)
cast: Amy Irving, Peter Riegert
Crossing Guard, The
author: David Rabe
Crossing, The
author: Howard Fast
Crossing the Bar
author: Alfred Tennyson
Crossing the Border
author: Joyce Carol Oates
Cross my __ with silver: 4 palm
crossness: 8 asperity
cross of __: 7 Calvary
Cross of __: 4 Gold, Iron
Cross of Gold orator: 5 Bryan
Cross of Iron (1977 film)
cast: James Coburn, James Mason, Maximilian Schell
director: Sam Peckinpah
cross one's __: 4 mind, palm, path **5** heart **7** fingers
crossover __: 5 voter **7** network
crosspatch: 6 grouch
crosspiece: 3 bar **4** beam, rung **6** lintel
door ~: 6 lintel
cross-ply __: 4 tire
cross-pollinate: 3 mix
Cross Purpose
author: Albert Camus
cross-purposes: 4 odds
at ~: 7 opposed **8** opposing
cross-reference: 5 index
crossroads: 3 jct. **4** junc. **6** center **7** parting, village **8** junction, juncture
cross-section: 7 variety
__ Cross the Mersey: 5 Ferry
crossthreads: 4 weft
crosswalk user: 3 ped. **6** walker **10** pedestrian
crossways: 6 aslant, skewed **7** athwart **8** diagonal, opposite **9** at an angle, on the bias **10** diagonally
crosswise: 6 aslant, skewed **7** athwart **8** diagonal, opposite **9** at an angle, on the bias **10** diagonally
at sea: 5 abeam
crossword: 6 puzzle
clue abbr.: 3 var.
complete a ~: 5 solve
like ~ s in 1913: 3 new
tool: 6 eraser, pencil
where the first ~ appeared: 5 World **7** NY World
__-Crostic: 6 Double
crotchet: 4 hook, kink, whim **5** quirk **6** vagary
Crotchet Castle
author: T.L. Peacock
crotchety: 5 cross, huffy, moody, surly, testy **6** crabby, cranky, crusty, fretty, grumpy, ornery **7** bearish, fretful, grouchy, peevish, waspish **8** contrary, fretsome, grumpish, snappish, vinegary **9** difficult, eccentric, fractious, irritable, obstinate, querulous, splenetic **10** capricious, ill-natured, out of sorts
one: 4 coot **5** crank, grump
Crothers: 7 Scatman
crottin: 6 cheese
crouch: 3 bow, dip **4** bend, duck, lurk **5** hunch, squat, stoop **6** huddle, shrink, slouch **8** huddle up **10** hunker down
crouching: 3 low **5** squat
Crouching Tiger, Hidden Dragon (2000 film)
cast: Michelle Yeoh, Chow Yun-Fat, Zhang Ziyi
director: Ang Lee
croupier: 6 banker
colleague: 6 dealer
customer: 6 better, bettor
milieu: 4 Reno **5** Vegas **6** casino **8** Las Vegas
often: 5 raker
tool: 4 rake
croupy: 6 hoarse
Crouse: 6 Russel **7** Lindsay
partner: 7 Lindsay
Crouse, Lindsay: 7 actress
spouse: David Mamet
crouton: 4 cube **5** bread
crow: 3 daw **4** bird, brag, rook **5** boast, exult, gloat, laugh, pride, vaunt **6** cackle, squawk **7** bluster, rub it in, swagger, talk big, triumph **8** jubilate, laughter **9** black bird **10** jump for joy
abounding in ~s: 5 rooky
as the ~ flies: 6 direct, in a row, linear, unbent **7** unbowed **8** directly, straight **10** unswerving

combining form: 5 -corax
eat ~: 6 grovel
ender: 3 bar 4 feet, foot 5 berry
Hawaiian ~: 5 alala
home: 4 nest
relative: 3 jay 5 raven 6 magpie 7 bluejay, gray jay 10 nutcracker
sound: 3 caw
starter: 4 cock 5 scare

__ crow: 3 ate, eat
Crow: 5 tribe 6 Indian, Sheryl 7 Amerind 8 language
home: 4 tipi 5 tepee 6 teepee
crowbar: 3 pry 5 force, jimmy, lever, prier, pryer
crowd: 3 jam, mob, set 4 army, bevy, cram, crew, fill, gang, herd, host, mass, pack, pile, pour, prod, push, teem 5 array, bunch, crush, flock, flood, group, horde, press, ram in, shoal, shove, sqush, stuff, swamp, swarm, troop 6 abound, circle, clique, deluge, gather, huddle, legion, masses, muster, people, rabble, squash, squish, squush, throng 7 bunch up, cluster, company, congest, coterie, faction, hearers, in-group, jam-pack, numbers, squeeze, squoosh, turnout 8 assembly, audience 9 concourse, gathering, listeners, multitude 10 assemblage, attendance, concursion, congregate, spectators
acknowledge the ~: 3 bow 4 wave
be part of the ~: 5 fit in
disappear in the ~: 5 blend
ender: 7 pleaser 8 pleasing
in: 5 enter, troop 9 interrupt
in ~: 5 elite 6 jet set
in a ~: 4 amid 5 among 6 amidst, mongst 7 amongst
(into): 6 stream
like a stadium ~: 5 aroar
noise: 3 rah 4 roar
out: 8 displace
pleaser: 6 parade
pleasing: 7 popular
proverbially: 5 three
scene actor: 4 supe 5 extra
together: 3 mob 5 flock
together, old-style: 5 serry
work the ~: 5 stump 8 campaign 10 kiss babies
crowd __: 7 pleaser
__ **Crowd:** 5 The In
crowded: 3 SRO 4 busy, full, rife 5 awash, close, dense, laden, thick, tight 6 filled, loaded, packed 7 compact, cramped, replete, sold out, teeming 8 brimming, populous, squeezed, thronged 9 chockfull, jam-packed, to the roof 10 compressed, hard-packed, wall-to-wall
area, in Britain: 3 wen
place: 3 zoo
crowdie: 6 cheese
crowds: 4 lots 6 flocks, scores 7 legions
like some ~: 4 ugly
Crowe: 7 Cameron, Russell
Crowe, Cameron: 8 director
film: Almost Famous (2000)
Jerry Maguire (1996)
Say Anything... (1989)
Vanilla Sky (2001)
crower: 8 braggart
Crowe, Russell: 5 actor
film: 3:10 to Yuma (2007)
American Gangster (2007)
A Beautiful Mind (2001)
Body of Lies (2008)
Cinderella Man (2005)
Gladiator (2000, AA)
Good Year (2006), A
The Insider (1999)
L.A. Confidential (1997)
Proof of Life (2000)
The Quick and the Dead (1995)
__ **crow flies:** 5 as the
Crowley: 3 Pat 8 Patricia
crowlike bird: 6 chough
crown: 3 cap, tip, top 4 acme, apex, best, coin, head, pate, peak 5 crest, endow, endue, ensky, exalt, honor, indue, money, prize, ruler, spire, tiara, title 6 anadem, climax, corona, diadem, finish, fulfil, height, instal, invest, reward, summit, thwack, tipoff, top off, trophy, vertex, wreath, zenith 7 coronet, ennoble, festoon, fulfill, install, instate, jewelry, laurels, monarch, perfect, royalty 8 complete, coronate, pinnacle 9 culminate, sovereign 10 consummate
at the ~: 4 atop
combining form: 7 stephan- 8 stephano-
covering: 6 enamel
earn the ~: 3 win
material: 4 gold 6 laurel
name meaning ~: 6 Steven 7 Stephen
of light: 4 halo
wearer: 4 czar, king, tsar, tzar 5 queen, ruler 7 monarch 9 sovereign
wear the ~: 4 rule 5 reign 6 govern
crown __: 5 jewel, roast 6 colony, prince
Crown
foe: 5 Porgy
__ **Crown:** 6 Triple
Crown Colony, former: 6 Guyana
crowned, get: 4 rule 5 reign 6 accede
Crowned Heads
author: Thomas Tryon
Crowne Plaza
alternative: *see* hotel
crowning: 4 last 5 final 7 supreme 8 ultimate 9 climactic, paramount, principal, virtuosic 10 consummate
point: 4 acme 6 climax
crown of __: 6 thorns
crownpiece: 3 cap
Crown Victoria: 3 car 4 auto 7 Mercury
crow's-__: 4 feet, foot, nest
crow's-foot: 7 wrinkle
Crow, Sheryl
song: All I Wanna Do (1994)
If It Makes You Happy (1996)
Strong Enough (1995)
crow's nest: 7 lookout, station
cry: 4 ahoy, land 6 land ho
site: 4 mast
Crow, The (1994 film)
cast: Brandon Lee
Crowther: 6 Bosley
CRT: 3 VDT 8 terminal
cousin: 3 LCD
pointer: 6 cursor
__ **Cru:** 5 Grand 7 Premier
__ **Cruces, NM:** 3 Las
crucial: 3 key 4 dire, high, main 5 acute, chief, grave, major, vital 6 needed, urgent 7 burning, central, exigent, fateful, hurry-up, pivotal, primary, serious, weighty 8 critical, deciding, decisive, exigeant, pressing, required 9 desperate, essential, high-level, important, mandatory, memorable, momentous, necessary, operative, right-hand, strategic 10 imperative, portentous, underlying
not ~: 5 minor 7 trivial
point: 6 crunch
crucible: 4 test 5 trial 6 ordeal, retort, vessel 7 alembic 9 container, probation
Crucible, The: 4 play
author: Arthur Miller
event: 5 trial
setting: 4 Mass. 5 Salem
crucifix: 4 rood 5 cross
letters: 3 IHS 4 INRI
Crucifixion
artist: Salvador Dali
Crucifixion of Saint Peter
artist: Guido Reni
cruciverbalist direction: 4 down 6 across
crud: 4 dirt, gunk, muck 5 filth, grime, slime 9 sleazebag
up: 5 taint
cruddy: 6 filthy, grungy 10 disgusting
crude: 3 low, oil, raw 4 base, loud, poor, rude 5 crass, gross, harsh, nervy, rough, tacky, unref. 6 abrupt, coarse, earthy, garish, gauche, Gothic, ragged, ribald, risqué, rustic, simple, smutty, tawdry, unmeet, vulgar 7 bearish, boorish, caddish, ill-bred, loutish, lowbred, natural, profane, raffish, sketchy, uncouth, unkempt 8 barbaric, churlish, degraded, fumbling, homemade, immature, impolite, impudent, indecent, inexpert, tactless, unseemly, unsubtle, untaught 9 barbarian, barbarous, graceless, inelegant, low-minded, lubricous, makeshift, primitive, tasteless, unevolved, ungallant, unrefined, untrained, unwrought 10 amateurish, indecorous, indelicate, lascivious, regardless, uncultured, unfinished, ungracious, unpolished, unskillful
one: 3 oaf 4 boor, lout
crude __: 3 oil
crudely: 5 rawly, rough
crudeness: 8 lewdness 9 barbarity, grossness, ignorance
crude oil: 9 petroleum
component: 6 ethane 8 dimethyl
measure: 3 bbl. 6 barrel
crudités: 9 appetizer 10 vegetables
companion: 3 dip
ingredient: 6 carrot
like ~: 3 raw
crudity: 7 lowness 9 gaucherie, indecency, vulgarity 10 incivility, inelegance
with ~: 5 rawly
Crudup: 5 Billy
__ **Crüe:** 6 Motley
cruel: 3 bad 4 evil, firm, grim, hard 5 bossy, catty, harsh, nasty, picky, rigid, rough, stern, stiff, stony, tough 6 bitter, brutal, fierce, flinty, savage, severe, sinful, stoney, unfair, unkind, wanton, wicked 7 austere, beastly, bestial, brutish, callous, hateful, hellish, hurtful, inhuman, Spartan, vicious, violent 8 barbaric, demoniac, despotic, diabolic, exacting, fiendish, hardened, hard-line, horrible, inhumane, pitiless, rigorous, ruthless, sadistic, scathing, spiteful, vengeful 9 barbarian, barbarous, cutthroat, demanding, draconian, ferocious, heartless, inclement, merciless, monstrous, murderous, stringent, unbending, unfeeling, unpitying, unsparing 10 despotical, diabolical, implacable, inexorable, inflexible, iron-fisted, malevolent, no-nonsense, oppressive, relentless, tyrannical, unmerciful, vindictive, virtueless
one: 4 ogre 5 beast, brute
treatment: 6 misuse
Cruel __ Kind: 4 to Be
Cruel __, The: 3 Sea
Cruella: 5 De Vil
cruellest month: 3 Apr. 5 April
Cruel Summer (song)
artist: Ace of Base, Bananarama
cruelty: 5 spite, venom, wrong 6 malice 7 tyranny 8 coldness, ferocity, iron hand, savagery, severity, violence 9 barbarism, brutality, depravity, despotism, harshness, nastiness 10 inclemency, inhumanity, oppression
exemplar of ~: 4 Sade 6 de Sade
__ **Cruel World:** 7 Goodbye
Crüe, Mötley
members: Neil, Mars, Sixx, Lee
song: Don't Go Away Mad (1990)
Dr. Feelgood (1989)
Girls, Girls, Girls (1987)
Smokin' in the Boys Room (1985)
Without You (1990)
cruet: 6 bottle, carafe 7 alembic 8 decanter
contents: 3 oil 7 vinegar 8 dressing
cruise: 3 gad 4 ride, sail, tour, trip 5 coast, jaunt, prowl, range 6 junket, patrol, ramble, travel, voyage, wander 7 journey, meander, sailing 8 crossing, navigate, vacation 9 excursion, gallivant
accommodation: 5 cabin, suite
activity: 4 tour 6 eating
along: 5 motor
amenity: 3 gym 4 pool 5 sauna 6 buffet, casino 7 sun deck
company: 6 Cunard 8 Princess 9 Celebrity
ship: 4 QE II 5 liner 6 vessel 7 steamer
stop: 3 POC, Rio 4 isle, port 5 Aruba 6 Alaska, harbor, Mexico, Nassau 7 Bermuda, Cozumel, Curaçao, Grenada, harbour, Jamaica, San Juan, St.

Croix 8 Barbados, St. Thomas 9 Caribbean 10 port of call
taking a ~: 4 asea 5 at sea
(through): 6 breeze
cruise __: 4 ship 7 control, missile
Cruise: 3 Tom 5 Pablo
__ Cruise: 3 Sea
cruiser: 4 boat, ship 5 yacht 6 vessel 7 frigate 10 battleship
ender: 6 weight
__ cruiser: 3 day 5 cabin
Cruise, Tom: 5 actor
daughter: 4 Suri
film: All the Right Moves (1983)
Born on the Fourth of July (1989)
Cocktail (1988)
Collateral (2004)
The Color of Money (1986)
Days of Thunder (1990)
Eyes Wide Shut (1999)
Far and Away (1992)
A Few Good Men (1992)
The Firm (1993)
Interview With the Vampire (1994)
Jerry Maguire (1996)
The Last Samurai (2003)
Lions for Lambs (2007)
Magnolia (1999)
Minority Report (2002)
Mission: Impossible (1996)
Rain Man (1988)
Risky Business (1983)
Top Gun (1986)
Tropic Thunder (2008)
Valkyrie (2008)
Vanilla Sky (2001)
War of the Worlds (2005)
spouse: Katie Holmes, Nicole Kidman, Mimi Rogers
cruising: 4 asea 5 at sea
cruller: 4 cake 6 pastry
kin: 5 donut 6 churro, éclair 8 doughnut
__ cruller: 6 French
crumb: 3 bit, cad, ort 4 atom, iota, lump, mite, mote, snip, soil, whit 5 grain, pinch, scrap, shred, speck, trace 6 morsel, nibble, sliver, tidbit 7 granule, modicum, ratfink, smidgen, smidgin 8 fragment, leftover, particle, pittance
coat with ~s: 5 bread
Crumb: 6 Robert
crumble: 2 go 3 eat, rot 4 chip, fall, rust, wear 5 break, crush, decay, erode, grind, mince, spoil 6 molder, perish, powder, weaken, wither 7 break up, give way 8 collapse, dissolve, fragment 9 decompose, granulate, pulverize, triturate 10 go to pieces
crumbled: 6 broken 8 in pieces
crumbles
how the cookie ~: 3 lot 4 fate
Crumblin' Down (1983 song)
artist: John Cougar Mellencamp
crumbling: 3 old 5 musty 6 rotten 7 powdery, run-down 8 timeworn, untended 9 weathered 10 ramshackle, tumbledown
crumbly: 5 crisp, light, mealy 6 crispy 7 brittle, crunchy, fragile, friable 9 frangible 10 nondurable
crumbum: 5 louse
crumby: 3 low 6 no-good 9 worthless
crummy: 3 bad, low 4 foul, grim, poor, punk 5 awful, cheap, lousy, seedy, woful 6 dismal, filthy, horrid, no-good, odious, rotten, shabby, woeful 7 accurst, baleful, baneful, beastly, doleful, ghastly, run-down 8 accursed, dreadful, God-awful, grievous, horrible, inferior, pathetic, shameful, stinking, terrible, unusable, wretched 9 abhorrent, appalling, atrocious, defective, depressed, execrable, fifth-rate, frightful, insidious, loathsome, miserable, offensive, revolting, third-rate, worthless 10 abominable, despicable, detestable, disastrous, fourth-rate, horrendous, pathetical, second-rate
crumpet: 5 bread 6 pastry
accompaniment: 3 tea
crumple: 3 wad 4 give, muss 5 crush, grind, swoon, wad up, yield 6 buckle, cave in, crease, pucker, ruck up, rumple 7 give way, wrinkle 8 collapse 9 break down
Crumpled Papers
artist: Jean (Hans) Arp
crunch: 4 bind, bite, chew, gnaw, snag 5 chomp, crush, grind, munch 6 crisis, impact, powder, stress 7 problem, shatter, squeeze, trouble 8 pressure 9 adversity, emergency, masticate, pulverize, tight spot 10 misfortune
benefactors: 3 abs
into: 3 hit, ram
on: 4 chew 9 masticate
crunch __: 4 time
__ Crunch: 4 Cap'n 7 Nestle's
cruncher, number: 3 CPA 4 acct. 7 analyst 10 accountant
crunchy: 5 chewy, crisp 6 crispy, crusty 7 brittle, crumbly 9 crackling
food: 4 chip 6 celery, cereal 8 corn chip 10 cornflakes, potato chip
crus: 5 shank
site: 3 leg
crusade: 3 war 4 push 5 cause, drive, quest 6 battle 8 campaign, movement 10 enterprise, expedition, pilgrimage
Crusade in Europe
author: Dwight Eisenhower
crusader: 6 zealot 7 battler, fighter 8 advocate, champion, reformer 9 expounder 10 campaigner
Crusader
foe: 7 Saracen
__ Crusader: 5 Caped
Crusader Rabbit partner: 4 Rags 5 Tiger
Crusaders: 9 Holy Cross
Crusades
destination: 4 East 5 Syria
important ~ fortress: 5 Haifa
cruse: 3 jar, pot 6 bottle
crush: 3 hug, jam, mob, zap 4 beat, bray, cram, maim, mash, mill, pile, pulp, rout, ruin 5 break, crowd, grind, horde, munch, pound, press, quash, quell, smash, sqush, stamp, stave, stomp, swarm, total, tramp, tread, wad up, worst, wreck 6 beetle, crunch, defeat, grieve, impact, mangle, powder, quench, ravage, reduce, refute, rumple, scotch, squash, squish, squunsh, subdue, thrash, throng, wallop 7 conquer, crumble, crumple, destroy, embrace, flatten, oppress, passion, put down, repress, shatter, squeeze, squelch, squoosh, tighten, trample, trounce, wrinkle 8 blow away, compress, demolish, keep down, levigate, overcome, stamp out, suppress, vanquish 9 affection, granulate, multitude, obsession, overpower, overwhelm, pulverize, puppy love, subjugate 10 annihilate, dishearten, obliterate
have a ~ on: 4 love 5 adore, fancy, yearn 7 care for, idolize, worship 9 care about
underfoot: 5 stamp 7 trample
crushed: 3 low, sad 4 blue, hurt 6 broken, undone 7 abashed 8 wretched
crushing: 3 sad 5 tight 6 tragic 7 onerous, weighty 8 grueling, tragical
news: 4 blow
__-crushing: 4 bone
Crusoe: 8 castaway, Robinson
carved one: 5 canoe
Crusoe, Robinson
creator: Daniel Defoe
like ~ before Friday: 5 alone
crust: 4 bark, coat, edge, gall, hull, rind, rock, scum, skin 5 layer, nerve, shell 7 coating 8 audacity, covering 9 arrogance, impudence 10 effrontery, integument
between faults: 5 horst
earth's ~ layer: 4 moho, sial, sima 5 plate
upper ~: 4 rich 5 elite, lords 6 gentry, jet set 7 society 8 nobility 9 exclusive, gentility 10 haute monde
__ crust: 5 upper
crustacean: 4 crab 5 krill, prawn 6 isopod, mussel, shrimp 7 decapod, gribble, lobster, mollusc, mollusk, sandbug 8 amphipod, barnacle, cirriped, crayfish, macruran, mole crab 9 beach flea, shellfish, wood louse
abdomen: 5 pleon
claw: 5 chela 6 nipper
larva: 4 zoea
sense organ: 4 palp 6 palpus
sense organs: 5 palpi
crusty: 4 dour 5 brusk, crisp, cross, gruff, huffy, moody, rough, stern, surly, testy 6 abrupt, crabby, cranky, crispy, ornery, touchy 7 bearish, brittle, brusque, crunchy, friable, grouchy, peevish, waspish 8 captious, choleric, churlish, snappish, snarling, vinegary 9 crotchety, irascible, irritable, querulous, saturnine, splenetic 10 ill-humored, iron-willed, out of sorts
crutch: 4 prop 6 recess 7 support
crux: 3 nub 4 body, core, gist, knub, meat, pith 5 basis, heart, joint, point 6 enigma, kernel, thrust 7 essence, keynote 10 bottom line
Cruz: 5 Celia 7 Brandon 8 Penélope
__ Cruz: 4 Vera 5 Santa
cruzado: 4 coin 5 money
cruzeiro: 4 coin 5 money
Cruz, Penélope: 7 actress
film: All About My Mother (1999)
All the Pretty Horses (2000)
Captain Corelli's Mandolin (2001)
Elegy (2008)
Sahara (2005)
Vanilla Sky (2001)
Vicky Cristina Barcelona (2008, AA)
homeland: 5 Spain
Cruz, Sor Juana: 4 poet 7 Mexican
CRV: 3 SUV 5 Honda
crwth: 4 lyre 5 rotta, rotte 6 string
kin: 5 rebec 6 rebeck
origin: 7 Ireland
cry: 3 aha, bay, eek, hah, oho, ooh, rah, sob 4 ahoy, bark, bawl, boom, bray, call, hoot, howl, mewl, moan, roar, wail, weep, yell, yowl 5 avast, bleat, crisp, hallo, hillo, hullo, motto, mourn, shout, utter, voice, whine, whoop 6 bellow, boo-hoo, cackle, clamor, halloa, halloo, hallow, hilloa, holler, hulloo, lament, scream, shriek, snivel, squawk, squeak, uproar 7 blubber, call out, exclaim, screech, sing out, whimper 9 break down, caterwaul, shed tears 10 hullabaloo, take it hard, vociferate
barnyard ~: 3 baa, moo 4 bray, crow, oink 5 bleat
ender: 4 baby
see also exclamation
cry __: 3 off 4 down, wolf 5 havoc, uncle
cry __ spilled milk: 4 over
__ cry: 3 far, war 4 a far 6 battle
Cry (1951 song)
artist: Johnnie Ray
Cry __ River: 3 Me a
__ Cry: 4 Don't 6 Battle
crybaby: 4 wimp 5 sissy 6 bawler, critic, griper, moaner, whiner 8 grumbler, recreant, weakling 10 bellyacher, complainer, malcontent
be a ~: 4 bawl, moan, pule 5 gripe
Cryer: 3 Jon
Cry for Help (1991 song)
artist: Rick Astley
Cry Freedom (1987 film)
cast: Kevin Kline, Denzel Washington
director: Richard Attenborough
crying: 5 tears, teary, weepy 6 urgent 7 glaring, heinous, tearful 8 pressing 9 insistent, querulous, sniveling 10 lachrymose, waterworks
need: 6 hankie
noise: 3 wah
shame: 4 pity
Crying (song)
artist: Don McLean, Roy Orbison
Crying Game, The (1992 film)
cast: Jaye Davidson, Stephen Rea, Miranda Richardson, Forest Whitaker
Crying in the Chapel (1965 song)
artist: Elvis Presley
Crying in the Rain (1962 song)
artist: Everly Brothers
Crying of Lot 49, The
author: Thomas Pynchon

__ crying out loud!: 3 For
Crying Time (1966 song)
artist: Ray Charles
Cry in the Dark, A (1988 film)
cast: Bruce Myles, Sam Neill, Meryl Streep
director: Fred Schepisi
Cry in the Night, A
author: Mary Higgins Clark
Cry Like a Baby (1968 song)
artist: Box Tops
Cry Me a River (1955 song)
artist: Julie London
__ Cry of Freedom, The: 6 Battle
Cry of the Halidon, The
author: Robert Ludlum
cry one's __ out: 4 eyes 5 heart
cryonics, practice: 6 freeze
__ Cry Out Loud: 4 Don't
cry over __ milk: 5 spilt 7 spilled
crypt: 4 code, tomb 5 vault 6 recess
cryptanalyze: 6 decode 8 decipher
cryptic: 4 dark 5 mirky, murky, terse, vague 6 arcane, gnomic, hidden, secret 7 obscure, unclear 8 abstruse, esoteric, nebulous, oracular, puzzling, ulterior 9 confusing, enigmatic, recondite, secretive 10 indistinct, mysterious, perplexing
cryptogram: 4 code 6 cipher
make a ~: 6 encode
maker: 5 coder
solve a ~: 6 decode
cryptographic org.: 3 NSA
crystal: 3 gem 5 clear, glass, stone 6 glassy 8 luminous, vitreous 9 unblurred
clear: 5 lucid, plain 6 hyalin, limpid, patent 7 hyaline 8 apparent, knowable, luminous, manifest
gaze: 4 scry
gazer: 4 seer 5 sibyl 7 prophet, psychic
gazer phrase: 4 I see
gazing: 10 divination, prediction
laser ~: 4 ruby
plane: 4 face
set: 5 radio
twin ~: 5 macle
use a ~ ball: 4 gaze
crystal __: 3 set, tea 4 ball 5 gazer, radio 6 gazing
crystal-__: 5 clear
__ crystal: 4 rock, snow 6 leaded, liquid, quartz
Crystal: 5 Billy, Gayle 6 Waters 7 Bernard
Crystal __: 6 Palace
Crystal, Billy: 5 actor 8 comedian
film: America's Sweethearts (2001)
Analyze This (1999)
City Slickers (1991)
Forget Paris (1995)
Memories of Me (1988)
Mr. Saturday Night (1992)
My Giant (1998)
Throw Momma From the Train (1987)
When Harry Met Sally... (1989)
TV: Soap
Crystal Blue Persuasion (1969 song)
artist: Tommy James
Crystal Cave, The
author: Mary Stewart
__-crystal display: 6 liquid
crystal-filled rock: 5 geode
Crystal Light: 9 soft drink
crystalline: 5 lucid 6 glassy, hyalin, limpid 7 hyaline
antiseptic: 5 iodol
rock: 4 spar
crystallize: 3 gel, ppt., set 4 form, jell 5 shape 6 harden 7 stiffen 8 solidify
crystals
ice ~: 6 frazil
rock-cavity ~: 5 druse
wet ~: 4 snow
Crystals
song: Da Doo Ron Ron (1963)
He's a Rebel (1962)
Then He Kissed Me (1963)
__ Crystal, The: 4 Dark
Cry, the Beloved Country
author: Alan Paton
Cry to Heaven
author: Anne Rice
__ Cry Tomorrow: 3 I'll
Cs: 4 elem. 6 cesium 7 caesium, element
55 for ~: 4 at. no.
like some ~: 4 soft
C.S.: 5 Lewis 8 Forester
CSA: 4 Gray, Grey 5 Dixie, Grays, Greys
end of a ~ signature: 4 E. Lee
fighter: 3 reb
monogram: 3 REL
song: 5 Dixie
state: 3 Ala., Fla., Tex. 4 Miss., N. Car., S. Car. 5 Texas 7 Alabama, Ark. Tenn., Florida, Georgia 8 Arkansas, Virginia 9 Louisiana, Tennessee 11 Mississippi 13 North Carolina, South Carolina
__ csc: 3 arc
__ C. Scott: 6 George
C-sharp
equivalent: 5 D-flat
CSI (CBS drama)
cast: David Berman (David Phillips)
George Eads (Nick Stokes)
Laurence Fishburne (Ray Langston)
Jorja Fox (Sara Sidle)
Paul Guilfoyle (Jim Brass)
Robert David Hall (Al Robbins)
Marg Helgenberger (Catherine Willows)
Wallace Langham (David Hodges)
William Petersen (Gil Grissom)
Eric Szmanda (Greg Sanders)
Liz Vassey (Wendy Simms)
CSI: Miami (CBS drama)
cast: David Caruso (Horatio Caine)
Eva LaRue (Natalia Boa Vista)
Rex Linn (Frank Tripp)
Emily Procter (Calleigh Duquesne)
Adam Rodriguez (Eric Delko)
Jonathan Togo (Ryan Wolfe)
CSI: NY (CBS drama)
cast: Anna Belknap (Lindsay Messer)
Carmine Giovinazzo (Danny Messer)
Robert Joy (Sid Hammerback)
Melina Kanakaredes (Stella Bonasera)
Gary Sinise (Mac Taylor)
Csonka, Larry
sport: 8 football
C-SPAN: 7 channel
alternative: ***see*** cable channel
part of ~: 3 Net., Pub. 5 Cable 6 Public 7 Affairs, Network 9 Satellite
CST
part of ~: 3 Std. 4 Time 7 Central 8 Standard
Ct.
neighbor: 4 Mass.
region: 4 N. Eng.
see also Connecticut
CT __: 4 scan 7 scanner
C. Thomas __: 6 Howell
ctn.: 3 pkg.
handler: 3 UPS
place for ~: 4 whse.
C-to-C sequence: 5 scale
ctr.: 3 mid. 5 midpt.
community ~: 4 the Y, YMCA, YMHA, YWCA, YWHA
CTRL-__-DEL: 3 ALT
cts.
100 ~: 3 dol.
CTS: 3 car 4 auto 8 Cadillac
Cu: 4 elem. 6 copper 7 element
29 for ~: 4 at. no.
cuatro: 4 four 6 guitar 7 Spanish
follower: 5 cinco
preceder: 4 tres
twice ~: 4 ocho
cub: 3 boy, kid, lad, tot 4 lion, tiro, tyro, wolf 5 tiger, youth 6 greeny, lionet, novice 7 learner 8 beginner, reporter 9 offspring, youngster 10 apprentice
home: 3 den 4 lair
parent: 4 bear, lion
Cub: 5 scout 10 baseballer
Hall-of-Famer: 5 Banks, Evers 6 Wilson 8 Williams 10 Ernie Banks
__ Cub: 5 Piper
Cuba: 4 isle 6 island, nation 7 country, Gooding
ballet dancer: 6 Alonso
bay: 10 Guantánamo
capital: 6 Havana
castle: 5 Morro
city: 6 Bayamo, Havana 7 Holguín 8 Camaguey, Matanzas, Santiago 10 Cienfuegos, Guantánamo
dance: 5 conga, mambo, rumba 6 cha-cha, rhumba 8 habanera
island: 5 Pines
leader: 6 Castro
money: 4 peso 7 centavo
neighbor: 5 Haiti
org.: 3 OAS
poet: 5 Diego 7 Guillén
product: 5 cigar
writer: 5 Martí 6 Arenas, Barnet 10 Carpentier
see also Spanish
Cuba __: 5 libre
cubage: 6 volume
Cuban: 5 Latin
Cuban __: 4 heel
Cuban Overture
composer: George Gershwin
cubby: 4 nook 5 niche
ender: 4 hole
Cubby: 6 O' Brien
cubbyhole: 4 cell, nook, room 5 booth, niche 6 alcove 7 cubicle
place into ~s: 6 assort
cube: 3 die 4 chop, dice, loaf, lump 5 block, mince, power, solid 6 dice up 8 multiply 10 hexahedron
starter: 5 flash
cube __: 4 root 5 steak
__ cube: 3 ice 5 sugar
__ Cube: 3 Ice 6 Rubik's
cubeb: 5 fruit, shrub 6 veggie 9 vegetable
relative: 4 kava 6 pepper
cubes: 3 ice 4 dice 5 rocks
cubic: 5 solid 6 three-D
measure: 5 liter, stere 6 volume
cubicle: 4 cell, nook, room 5 booth, cubby, stall 6 alcove, recess 7 chamber 8 work area 9 cubbyhole, workplace 10 pigeonhole
library ~: 6 carrel 7 carrell
Cubism: 3 art 5 style
Cubist: 4 Gris 5 Léger 6 Braque 7 Duchamp, Picasso
cubit
relative: 4 span
cuboid: 4 bone
locale: 4 foot
cubs: 6 litter
Cubs: 4 nine, team
crosstown rivals: 3 Sox 8 White Sox
home: 3 Chi. 7 Chicago
org.: 3 BSA, MLB, NLC
rival: ***see*** baseball team
sport: 8 baseball
Cub Scout
group: 3 den 4 pack
leader: 5 Akela
__ Cucamonga, CA: 6 Rancho
cucaracha: 5 roach 9 cockroach
Cuchulainn: 4 hero 5 Irish
wife: 4 Emer
cuckoo: 3 ani, mad 4 bats, bird, daft, loco 5 batty, inane, loony, silly 6 looney 7 jackass, touched 8 bird call, rainbird 9 harebrain, simpleton
ender: 4 pint 6 flower
Malay ~: 4 koel
cuckoo __: 5 clock
__-cuckoo-land: 5 cloud
cuckoopint: 4 arum 5 aroid, plant
__ Cuckoo, The: 7 Sterile
cucullate: 6 hooded
cucumber: 4 pepo 5 gourd 6 pickle, veggie 9 vegetable
cucumberlike: 4 cool 6 as cool
cud chewers: 4 cows 6 camels, cattle, llamas
cuddle: 3 hug 4 hold, love 5 spoon, touch 6 caress, cosset, dandle, nestle, nuzzle 7 embrace, snuggle, squeeze 8 huddle up 10 bill and coo
cuddled up: 4 cosy, cozy, snug 5 cozey, cozie 8 tucked in
cuddly: 4 soft 7 lovable, snuggly 8 huggable, loveable
cuddy: 3 ass, oaf, sap 4 boob, butt, clod, dolt, dupe, fool, gull, lamb, lout, tool 5 chump, clown, cluck, dummy, dunce, joker, looby, ninny, patsy 6 dimwit, donkey, lummox, nitwit, pigeon, sucker, turkey

7 buffoon, dingbat, dullard, fall guy, fathead, half-wit, jackass, pinhead, saphead **8** bonehead, dumbbell, easy mark, meathead, numskull, pushover **9** birdbrain, blockhead, harebrain, lamebrain, numbskull, simpleton **10** dunderhead
cudgel: 3 bat, hit, rod, sap **4** beat, cane, club, cosh, flog, mace, slam **5** baton, billy, birch, pound, smite, stick **6** ferule, paddle, switch, weapon **7** lambast, war club **8** bludgeon, lambaste **9** bastinado, billy club, blackjack, truncheon **10** nightstick, shillelagh
cue: 3 tip **4** hint, prod, sign **6** prompt, signal, tipoff **7** inkling **8** mnemonic, reminder **10** indication, intimation
accessory: 5 chalk
bandleader ~: 5 hit it
fix a pool ~: 5 retip
game: 4 pool **7** snooker **9** billiards, eight ball
give a ~ to: 6 remind
on ~: 10 as expected
shot: 5 break, carom, massé
starter: 5 curly
cue __: 4 ball, card **5** sheet, stick
__ cue: 5 miss a
Cuéllar, Pérez de home: 4 Peru
Cuernavaca: 4 city, town
locale: 3 Mex. **6** Mexico **7** Morelos
cuesta: 5 ridge, slope
cuff: 3 box, hit **4** beat, belt, iron, slap, sock, swat **5** clout, knock, punch, smack, smite, spank, swipe, thump, whack **6** arrest, buffet, pummel, strike **7** clobber, manacle, scuffle **9** wristband
accessory: 4 link
off the ~: 7 offhand **9** impromptu **10** informally
on the ~: 4 free **6** gratis **10** for nothing
place: 5 shirt **6** sleeve
starter: 4 hand
cuff __: 4 link
__ cuff: 5 on the **6** barrel, French, off the **7** rotator
cuff link: 4 stud
material: 5 nacre
Cuff Links
song: Tracy (1969)
cuffs: 5 irons **8** shackles **9** bracelets
slap the ~ on: 3 nab **5** run in **6** arrest
cu. ft.: 3 vol. **4** meas.
Cugat, Xavier: 10 bandleader
Music: 5 rumba **6** rhumba
spouse: Charo, Abbe Lane
cui __: 4 bono
cuirass: 5 armor, plate **6** lorica
cuisine: 4 fare, food, menu, Thai **5** Cajun, Hunan, table **6** creole, dishes, French **7** cooking **10** gastronomy
enlivener: 5 spice
__ cuisine: 3 new **5** haute
__ Cuisine: 4 Lean
cuisinier: 4 chef
cuisse: 5 armor, plate
Cujo
author: Stephen King
Cukor, George: 8 director
film: Adam's Rib (1949)
A Bill of Divorcement (1932)
Born Yesterday (1950)
Camille (1937)
David Copperfield (1935)
Dinner at Eight (1933)
A Double Life (1947)
Gaslight (1944)
Girls About Town (1931)
Holiday (1938)
It Should Happen to You (1954)
Justine (1969)
Keeper of the Flame (1943)
Les Girls (1957)
Let's Make Love (1960)
Little Women (1933)
The Marrying Kind (1952)
My Fair Lady (1964, AA)
One Hour With You (1932)
Pat and Mike (1952)
The Philadelphia Story (1940)
Rich and Famous (1981)
Romeo and Juliet (1936)
A Star Is Born (1954)
Sylvia Scarlett (1935)
Two-Faced Woman (1941)
What Price Hollywood? (1932)
A Woman's Face (1941)
The Women (1939)
Culbertson: 3 Ely
contemporary: 5 Goren
forte: 6 bridge
cul-de-sac: 5 alley **7** dead end, impasse **10** blind alley, bottleneck
Culebra __: 3 Cut
culex
kin: 5 aedes
culinary
concoction: 4 dish, soup **5** sauce **6** entrée
directive: 3 fry **4** beat, boil, chop, cool, dice, heat, stew, stir, warm **5** baste, roast, sauté, scald, steam, toast
see also cook, cooking
Culkin: 6 Kieran **8** Macaulay
cull: 3 opt **4** pick, pull, sort, take **5** amass, glean, pluck, unmix **6** assort, choose, garner, gather, prefer, screen, select, winnow **7** collect, compile, discard, extract, harvest, pick out, round up **8** handpick, hold on to, pick over **10** accumulate, settle upon
Cullen: 4 Bill **7** Countee
__ Cullen Bryant: 7 William
Cullen, Countee: 4 poet
work: Copper Sun
The Lost Zoo
cullis: 6 gutter
neighbor: 4 eave
Cullman: 4 city, town
locale: 7 Alabama
Cullum: 4 John
culminate: 3 cap, end **4** peak **5** close, crown **6** climax, finish, mature, pan out, result, top off, wind up **8** conclude, round off, round out **9** terminate
culmination: 3 cap, end, top **4** acme, apex, peak **5** close, crest, crown **6** apogee, capper, climax, ending, finale, finish, height, payoff, summit, upshot, vertex, windup, wrap-up, zenith **8** pinnacle, showdown, terminus **10** denouement
__-culotte: 4 sans
culottes: 5 pants, skirt
kin: 5 skort
Culp: 6 Robert, Steven
culpability: 4 onus **5** blame, fault, guilt **9** liability
culpable: 5 wrong **6** guilty, liable, unholy **7** at fault, to blame **8** blamable, criminal **9** blameable, red-handed **10** delinquent, in the wrong
culpa, mea: 5 sorry **7** apology, I'm sorry
__ Culp Hobby: 5 Oveta
culprit: 5 felon **8** criminal, evildoer **9** miscreant **10** delinquent
Culp, Robert: 5 actor
TV: I Spy
cult: 4 sect **5** group **6** clique **7** faction **8** religion **10** persuasion
follower: 3 ism, ist, ure
cultivable: 6 arable
cultivar: 5 plant
cultivate: 3 hoe, woo **4** farm, plow, rear, tend, till, work **5** breed, court, labor, raise, teach, train **6** better, enrich, follow, foster, garden, harrow, pursue, refine, school **7** advance, bolster, develop, educate, further, improve, nourish, nurture, produce, promote **9** brown-nose, encourage, fertilize, get in with, get next to, patronize, propagate, shine up to **10** discipline, take care of
again: 5 rehoe **6** replow, retill
fit to ~: 6 arable
cultivated: 4 nice, tame **5** noble, suave **6** urbane **7** elegant, genteel, learned, refined **8** educated, ladylike, lettered, literate, polished, tasteful, well-bred **9** courteous
earth: 5 tilth
cultivation: 5 taste **6** growth, polish **7** farming, manners, plowing, tillage, tilling **8** agronomy, breeding, civility, delicacy, elegance, literacy
in need of ~: 5 weedy
cultivator: 3 hoe **4** plow **6** farmer, grower, harrow **8** gardener
adjunct: 4 disk
cultural: 6 ethnic **7** refined **8** artistic, refining **9** elevating, enriching, nurturing, uplifting **10** artistical, broadening, civilizing
character: 5 ethic, ethos
group: 6 ethnos
pursuit: 4 arts **5** music, opera **7** theater
Cultural Revolution leader: 3 Mao
culture: 4 race **5** class, ethos, grace, mores, taste **6** polish, values **7** customs, manners, society **8** breeding, delicacy, elegance, folklore, folkways, learning, nobility, noblesse, training, urbanity **9** education, erudition, ethnology, gentility, good taste, tradition **10** perception, refinement
combining form: 5 ethno-
medium: 4 agar **8** agar-agar
sign of ~: 5 poise, taste
starter: 3 api, avi **4** aero, agri, aqua, mari, seri, urbi, vini, viti **5** citri, flori, horti, micro, perma, pisci, silvi **7** counter
culture __: 5 shock **6** center **7** vulture
__ Culture: 7 Ethical
Culture Club
leader: Boy George
song: Church of the Poison Mind (1983)
Do You Really Want to Hurt Me (1983)
I'll Tumble 4 Ya (1983)
Karma Chameleon (1983)
Miss Me Blind (1984)
Time (1983)
cultured: 4 nice **5** suave **6** mature, polite, urbane **7** courtly, genteel, learned, refined **8** educated, esthetic, finished, highbred, highbrow, ladylike, lettered, literate, polished, tasteful, well-bred **9** scholarly
not ~: 4 non-U **6** coarse
superficially ~: 4 arty **5** artsy
cultured __: 5 pearl
cultureless environment: 5 wilds **6** desert **9** wasteland **10** wilderness
Culture of Cities, The
author: Lewis Mumford
cultures, science of: 9 ethnology
culver: 4 dove **6** pigeon
__-Culver: 7 Alberto
Culver City: 4 town
locale: 10 California
culvert: 4 duct **5** ditch, drain, gully, sewer **6** gulley, gutter **7** channel, conduit
cum __: 5 laude
cum __ salis: 5 grano
cumber: 3 tax **4** load **5** weigh **6** hinder, lumber **9** weigh down
Cumberland: 4 city, town **5** river **6** county
city on the ~: 9 Nashville
locale: 6 Canada **7** England, Ontario **8** Maryland
River locale: 8 Kentucky **9** Tennessee
river to the ~: 5 Stone
Cumberland __: 3 Gap
cumbersome: 5 bulky, heavy, hefty **6** clumsy, clunky **7** awkward, hulking, massive, onerous, unhandy, weighty **8** unwieldy **9** ponderous, unwieldly, wearisome **10** burdensome, galumphing, oppressive
cum grano __: 5 salis
cumin: 4 herb **5** spice
__ cum laude: 5 magna, summa
cum-laude stat: 3 GPA
cummerbund: 4 belt, sash
site: 5 waist
Cumming: 4 Alan
Cummings: 3 Bob **5** Candy, Quinn **6** Burton, Irving, Robert **9** Constance
cummings, e.e.: 4 poet
work: Eimi
The Enormous Room
him
ViVa
XLI Poems
cumulate: 5 lay by, lay up, merge, store **6** garner
cumulation: 4 heap, mass, pile **5** array, batch, group, hoard, stack, store **6** bundle, corpus, medley **7** cluster, variety **8** increase, pastiche, quantity, treasury **9** aggregate, amassment, anthology, congeries, gathering, potpourri,

stockpile **10** assemblage, assortment, collection, depository, hodgepodge, miscellany
cumulative: 7 grouped **9** advancing, aggregate **10** augmenting, collective, increasing, increscent
cumulonimbus: 5 cloud
cumulus: 5 cloud
starter: 4 alto
Cuna: 6 Indian **7** Amerind
fabric: 4 mola
Cunard ship: 4 QE II
cunctation: 5 delay **8** lateness
cunctatious: 4 late **5** tardy
cuneiform: 7 writing
stroke: 5 wedge
cunning: 3 art, sly **4** arch, cagy, deft, foxy, keen, wily **5** cagey, canny, craft, guile, sharp, skill, slick, smart, wiles **6** acumen, adroit, artful, astute, clever, crafty, deceit, dupery, feline, shifty, shrewd, tricky **7** devious, evasive, furtive, knavery, knavish, knowing **8** dextrous, guileful, keenness, scheming, skillful, slippery, stealthy, strategy, thievish **9** astucious, deceitful, deception, deceptive, designing, dexterous, duplicity, ingenious, insidious, masterful, strategic, underhand **10** serpentine
bit of: 4 wile
not ~: 4 naif **5** naive
one: 3 fox
with ~: 5 slyly
Cunningham: 4 Liam **5** Merce **6** Imogen
Cunning Peasant, The
composer: Antonín Dvorák
Cuomo: 5 Mario **6** Andrew
cup: 3 mug **4** zarf, zurf **5** calix, drink, glass, grail, mazer, prize **6** beaker, goblet, trophy, trough **7** chalice, tumbler **9** container, demitasse **10** receptacle
ancient Greek ~: 5 cylix, kylix
assayer ~: 5 cupel
chemist ~: 6 beaker
coffee ~: 3 mug
combining form: 5 cotyl-, cyath-, scyph- **6** cotyli-, cotylo-, cyatho-, scyphi-, scypho-
edge: 3 lip, rim
ender: 4 cake **5** board **6** bearer, flower
fraction: 5 ounce
go for the ~: 4 putt
golf ~: 4 hole **5** Ryder
handle: 3 ear
Last Supper ~: 5 Grail
Mideast coffee ~: 4 zarf, zurf **6** finjan
miss the ~: 5 spill
of tea: 3 bag **5** field, thing **7** leaning **9** specialty **10** preference
something 'twixt ~ and lip: 4 slip
starter: 3 egg, eye, tea **4** king **6** butter
tennis ~: 5 Davis
cup __: 5 of tea
__ cup: 4 dice **5** Dixie, fruit **6** loving **7** custard, Elijah's, suction
__ Cup: 3 Tin **5** Davis, Dixie, Ryder, World **6** Walker **7** Stanley
cup and __: 5 cover **6** saucer
cupboard: 5 hutch, shelf **6** closet, larder, pantry **7** cabinet **8** wardrobe **9** furniture
church ~: 5 ambry **6** aumbry **8** armarium
item: 3 can, tin
part: 4 door, knob **5** shelf
__ cupboard: 4 dole **5** court, Dutch, press **6** livery **7** tridarn
Cupertino: 4 city, town
locale: 10 California
Cupid: 4 Amor, Eros **7** love god **8** amoretto, reindeer **10** matchmaker
colleague: ***see*** reindeer
master: 5 Santa
mother: 5 Venus
target: 5 heart
weapon: 3 bow **4** dart **5** arrow
__ Cupid: 6 Stupid
cupidinous: 4 avid
cupidity: 4 lust **5** greed **6** hunger **7** avarice, avidity, craving, longing **8** rapacity, voracity **10** grabbiness
Cupid's __: 3 bow **6** arrows
__ cup of tea: 5 not my
cupola: 4 dome **6** belfry **7** furnace, lantern, lookout **9** belvedere
topper: 4 vane
cuppa: 3 tea
Cuppy: 4 Will
cuprite: 3 ore
cupronickel: 5 alloy
cups
four ~: 5 quart
in one's ~: 5 tipsy
two ~: 4 pint
cup-shaped: 6 dished, hollow
cur: 3 cad, dog, mut, rat **4** heel, mutt, toad, worm **5** canid, churl, feist, knave, rogue, scamp, skunk, snake, sneak, stray, swine **6** bad egg, canine, hybrid, rascal, wretch **7** dastard, lowlife, mongrel, stinker, villain **8** dirty dog **9** miscreant, reprobate, scoundrel, vulgarian **10** blackguard, crossbreed, ne'er-do-well, scapegrace
cur's comment: 3 grr **5** growl
curaçao: 5 drink **8** beverage
ingredient: 4 peel
Curaçao: 4 isle **6** island
neighbor: 5 Aruba **9** Venezuela
port: 10 Willemstad
Curad: 7 bandage
alternative: 3 Ace **7** Band-Aid
curare: 4 inee **5** toxin **8** alkaloid
curassow: 4 bird, fowl
relative: ***see*** fowl
curate: 4 abbé **5** padre **6** clergy, cleric, father, parson **8** minister, preacher **9** clergyman
curative: 5 tonic **6** iatric **7** healing, medical **8** remedial, salutary, sanative **9** antidotal, healthful, medicinal
curator: 6 keeper **7** manager, steward **8** director, guardian, watchdog **9** caretaker, custodian, organizer
degree: 3 MFA
curb: 3 rim, tie **4** drop, edge, rein, slow, snag, stay, stem, tame **5** brake, check, delay, leash, limit, lower, stint, tie up **6** bridle, dampen, fetter, govern, halter, hamper, hinder, hobble, impede, lessen, modify, muzzle, pull in, reduce, rein in, shrink, stifle, subdue, temper, thwart **7** abstain, contain, control, curtail, cut down, dwindle, fall off, harness, inhibit, refrain, repress, trammel **8** decrease, diminish, hold back, keep from, moderate, obstruct, peter out, preclude, restrain, restrict, straiten, suppress **9** abatement, constrain, constrict, deterrent, hindrance, intercept, restraint **10** constraint, discourage, impediment, keep a lid on, keep in line, limitation
ender: 4 side **5** stone
it: 4 park
curb __: 3 cut
curbed: 6 pent-up, silent **7** limited **8** reined in
curbside cry: 4 taxi
curch: 5 scarf **8** kerchief
curd: 4 clot **6** casein **7** clabber, clobber, thicken
bean ~: 4 tofu
__ curd: 4 bean
curdle: 4 clot, sour, turn **5** go bad, spoil **6** gelate, go sour, harden **7** acidify, clabber, clobber, congeal, stiffen, thicken **9** coagulate
curdled: 4 sour **5** thick **6** rancid
curds partner: 4 whey
cure: 3 fix **4** heal, mend, salt **5** right, smoke, treat **6** elixir, kipper, pickle, reform, remedy, repair **7** correct, nostrum, panacea, rectify, redress, relieve, restore, therapy **8** antidote, medicine, palliate, preserve **9** alleviate, treatment **10** medication
leather: 3 tan
past a ~: 8 hopeless **10** irremedial
something to ~: 3 ham **5** bacon **7** sausage
starter: 3 epi **4** mani, pedi
take the ~: 4 quit **7** refrain
cure-__: 3 all
curé: 6 father, priest
cure-all: 6 elixir, potion, remedy **7** nostrum, panacea
cured: 9 good as new
cheese: 6 brynza
meat: 5 jerky
Curel: 6 lotion
alternative: 4 Keri **5** Nivea **6** Aveeno **7** Eucerin, Jergens, Pacquin **9** Lubriderm
curer: 6 doctor, healer **9** physician
curfew: 4 bell **7** bedtime **8** deadline **9** nightfall, time limit
after ~: 4 late
maybe: 3 ten **5** ten p.m. **6** eleven **8** eleven p.m., midnight
__ curiae: 5 amici **6** amicus
Curie: 3 Eve **4** Pole **5** Marie **6** Madame, Pierre
Curie, Marie: 6 Polish **7** chemist **8** Nobelist **9** physicist
daughter: 5 Irene
discovery: 6 radium **8** polonium
spouse: 6 Pierre
title: 3 Mme. **6** Madame
Curie, Pierre: 6 French **7** chemist **8** Nobelist **9** physicist
spouse: 5 Marie
curio: 5 relic **6** bauble, geegaw, trifle **7** antique, bibelot, novelty, trinket, whatnot **8** nicknack, souvenir **9** bric-a-brac, objet d'art **10** knickknack
curios: 5 vertu, virtu
curiosity: 6 marvel, oddity, prying, rarity, regard, wonder **7** anomaly, concern **8** interest, nicknack, nosiness, snooping **9** eagerness, objet d'art, spectacle **10** knickknack, phenomenon, snoopiness
indulge one's ~: 3 ask **8** question
victim: 3 cat
__ Curiosity Shop, The: 3 Old
curious: 3 odd **4** nosy **5** funny, nosey, queer, weird **6** exotic, prying, quaint, snoopy **7** bizarre, oddball, peeping, peering, strange, unusual **8** abnormal, meddling, peculiar, puzzling, singular, uncommon **9** inquiring, quizzical, whimsical **10** interested, meddlesome, mysterious, outlandish, remarkable, unfamiliar
be ~: 3 ask **6** wonder
in a ~ way: 5 oddly
one: 5 asker
Curious Case of Benjamin Button, The (2008 film)
cast: Cate Blanchett, Brad Pitt
Curious George
author: H.A. Rey, Margret Rey
curiously: 9 unusually **10** especially
curium: 5 metal **7** element
curl: 3 set **4** bend, coil, flex, friz, kink, lock, loop, turn, wave, wind **5** crimp, curve, frizz, helix, snake, swirl, tress, twine, twirl, twist, whorl **6** spiral **7** contort, entwine, frizzle, intwine, ringlet, scallop, scollop, sinuate, wreathe **8** flourish, squiggle, undulate **9** convolute, sinuosity
a lip: 4 mock, slam **5** flout, scoff, scorn, smirk, sneer **6** slight **7** grimace, put down, sniff at, snigger **8** ridicule **9** disparage **10** look down on
around: 9 enwreathe
one's hair: 5 alarm, spook **7** horrify, terrify **8** frighten
shoot the ~: 4 surf
up: 4 furl, kink **6** nestle **7** snuggle
__ curl: 3 pin **4** spit
curled: 5 round **6** spiral **7** helical
curlew: 4 bird **8** whimbrel **9** shorebird **10** sicklebill
kin: 6 avocet
curlicue: 3 ess **4** coil **5** twist **6** spiral **8** flourish **10** decoration
curling: 4 game, wavy **5** sport **6** spiral
period: 3 end
target: 3 tee
use a ~ iron: 5 crimp
curling __: 4 iron
curl one's __: 3 lip **4** hair
curly: 4 wavy **5** kinky, nappy **6** coiled, frizzy, permed **7** frizzly, looping, twisted, winding **9** corkscrew
coiffure: 4 Afro
ender: 3 cue
Curly: 6 Howard **7** Lambeau
brother: Moe Shemp
colleague: 3 Moe **5** Larry
Curly __: 3 Sue, Top
curmudgeon: 4 crab **5** churl, crank, cynic, grump **6** grouch **8** grumbler,

sourball, sourpuss
word: **3** bah
curmudgeonly: **4** sour **5** surly **6** crusty, stingy **9** crotchety
Curnow, Allen: **4** poet
currant: **5** berry, fruit, shrub **6** raisin
currency: **3** oof **4** bill, cash, gelt, jack, kail, kale, loot, peag, pelf **5** bills, bread, bucks, dough, funds, lucre, money, moola, mopus, pesos, rhino, sewan, usage **6** dinero, do-re-mi, mammon, mazuma, moolah, seawan, silver, specie, wampum, wealth **7** cabbage, capital, dollars, lettuce, ooftish, scratch, shekels **8** banknote, bankroll, cold cash, hard cash, smackers **9** banknotes, frogskins, long green, simoleons **10** greenbacks, green stuff, popularity
convert to ~: **4** cash **6** redeem
premium: **4** agio
substitute: **5** scrip
current: **2** AC, DC **3** hep, hip, mod, new, now **4** chic, eddy, flow, live, race, tide, tony, wind **5** draft, drift, faddy, fresh, going, in use, tenor, toney, trend, usual **6** breeze, chichi, common, course, El Niño, extant, latest, living, modern, modish, recent, ruling, stream, trendy **7** à la mode, flowing, in style, in vogue, ongoing, popular, present, stylish, topical, updated, voguish **8** accepted, tendency, up-to-date **9** customary, effective, immediate, in fashion, in the news, prevalent **10** all the rage, ebb and flow, in progress, present-day, prevailing, widespread
amount: **3** bal. **7** balance
circular ~: **4** eddy
combining form: **4** rheo- **7** galvano-
discharge: **3** arc
events: **4** news
medium: **4** wire **5** cable
practice: **5** vogue
problem: **5** short, surge
producer: **6** dynamo **9** generator
South American ~: **6** El Niño
starter: **5** cross **7** counter
stay ~: **6** keep up
terminal: **5** anode **7** cathode
unit: **3** amp, ohm **4** volt **6** ampere
with: **4** up on
current __: **6** events **7** account, affairs
__ current: **3** rip **4** eddy, grid **5** field **6** direct
currently: **3** now **5** today **7** as of now **8** recently
Currents of Space, The
author: Isaac Asimov
curriculum: **7** courses, program
range: **4** elhi
section: **4** unit
vitae: **3** bio **4** vita **6** digest, précis, record, résumé **7** outline, summary **8** synopsis
curriculum __: **5** vitae
__ curriculum: **4** core
Currier: **3** Nat **9** Nathaniel
partner: **4** Ives
curry: **4** cook **5** groom, spice **9** condiment
favor: **3** woo **4** fawn **5** court **8** fawn over **9** get next to, insinuate, shine up to
loaded with ~: **3** hot
powder ingredient: **5** cumin
curry __: **5** favor **6** powder
Curry: **3** Ann, Tim
currycomb target: **4** mane
curse: **3** hex, pox **4** bane, damn, jinx, oath **5** swear **6** hoodoo, malign, misery, ordeal, plague, vilify, whammy **7** condemn, epithet, evil eye, profane, scourge, slander, torment, trouble **8** calamity **9** blaspheme, expletive, imprecate, profanity **10** affliction, imputation, infliction, vituperate
cover-up: **5** bleep
one's folly: **3** rue **6** bemoan, bewail, lament, regret, repent
cursed: **6** doomed **7** doggone, hapless, hateful, heinous, unblest, unhappy, unlucky **8** devilish, ill-fated, infernal, luckless **9** execrable, ill-omened, possessed, unblessed, unfavored **10** abominable, ill-starred
Curse of the Jade Scorpion, The (2001 film)
cast: Woody Allen, Dan Aykroyd, Helen Hunt, Charlize Theron
director: Woody Allen
Curses!: **4** oh no
Curses! __ again!: **6** Foiled
__ Curse, The: **4** Dain
cursing: **8** swearing **9** profanity
cursive: **7** running
cursor: **5** arrow, I-beam **7** flasher, pointer
mover: **5** mouse
cursory: **4** fast **5** brief, hasty, quick, rapid, short, swift **6** casual **7** hurried, offhand, passing, shallow, sketchy **8** careless, fleeting, slapdash **9** desultory, haphazard, momentary, negligent, unheedful **10** last-minute, mechanical, uncritical
curt: **4** rude **5** blunt, brief, brusk, crisp, gruff, huffy, pithy, quick, rough, sharp, short, terse **6** abrupt, snippy, unkind **7** brusque, concise, huffish, laconic, offhand, summary, uncivil **8** cavalier, snappish, snippety, succinct, taciturn **9** impatient **10** peremptory, to the point, ungracious
Curt: **5** Flood, Gowdy **7** Jurgens **9** Schilling
curtail: **3** cut **4** chop, clip, crop, curb, drop, pare, slow, stem, trim **5** elide, limit, lower, prune, slash **6** lessen, narrow, recede, reduce, shrink **7** abridge, commute, compact, cut down, dwindle, fall off, shorten, whittle **8** compress, condense, contract, cut short, decrease, diminish, downsize, minimize, pare down, peter out, restrain, truncate **10** abbreviate
curtailed: **3** cut **5** brief, lower, short **7** partial, sketchy **9** condensed **10** compressed, synopsized
curtailment: **3** cut **7** cutback **8** decrease, shortage, stoppage **9** reduction, restraint
curtain: **4** veil **5** drape, shade **6** screen **7** drapery, secrete **8** portiere
bring down the ~ on: **3** end **6** finish **8** conclude
close a ~: **4** draw
fabric: **4** iron, lace **5** ninon, scrim, voile **6** chintz, dimity, Madras, moreen **7** organdy **9** sailcloth, silkaline
holder: **3** rod
part: **6** edging
put up a ~: **4** hang
raiser: **4** Act I, play **5** event, intro **6** Act One **7** opening, prelude
stage ~: **5** scrim
curtain __: **3** rod **4** call, line, time **6** raiser
__ curtain: **4** café, drop
Curtain
author: Agatha Christie
__ Curtain: **4** Iron, Torn **6** Bamboo
curtain-call follower: **6** encore
curtained off: **6** unseen
curtainlike partitions: **4** vela
Curtain of Green, A
author: Eudora Welty
curtains: **6** the end
like some ~: **4** lacy **5** sheer
Curtin, Jane: **7** actress
film: Coneheads (1993)
role: **5** Allie
TV: 3rd Rock From the Sun, Kate & Allie, Saturday Night Live
Curtis: **3** Dan, Ken, Lee **4** Tony **5** Billy, LeMay **6** Hanson, Helene **7** Charles, Strange **8** Jamie Lee, Mayfield **9** Bernhardt
Curtis, Jamie Lee: **7** actress
film: Christmas With the Kranks (2004)
Dominick and Eugene (1988)
Drowning Mona (2000)
Fierce Creatures (1997)
A Fish Called Wanda (1988)
The Fog (1980)
Forever Young (1992)
Freaky Friday (2003)
Grandview, U.S.A. (1984)
Halloween (1978)
Love Letters (1983)
My Girl (1991)
Perfect (1985)
Prom Night (1980)
The Tailor of Panama (2001)
Terror Train (1980)
Trading Places (1983)
True Lies (1994)
parent: Janet Leigh, Tony
spouse: Christopher Guest
Curtiss: **5** Glenn
Curtis, Tony: **5** actor **8** Jamie Lee
film: Beachhead (1954)
Boeing Boeing (1965)
Captain Newman, M.D. (1963)
The Defiant Ones (1958)
Don't Make Waves (1967)
The Great Impostor (1961)
The Great Race (1965)
Houdini (1953)
Insignificance (1985)
Kings Go Forth (1958)
The Last Tycoon (1976)
Lepke (1975)
The List of Adrian Messenger (1963)
Not With My Wife You Don't! (1966)
Operation Petticoat (1959)
The Outsider (1961)
The Rat Race (1960)
Sex and the Single Girl (1964)
Some Like It Hot (1959)
Spartacus (1960)
Sweet Smell of Success (1957)
Trapeze (1956)
Who Was That Lady? (1960)
spouse: Janet Leigh
TV: Vega$
Curtiz, Michael: **8** director
film: The Adventures of Robin Hood (1938)
Angels With Dirty Faces (1938)
Black Fury (1935)
Captain Blood (1935)
Casablanca (1942, AA)
The Charge of the Light Brigade (1936)
The Comancheros (1961)
Dodge City (1939)
Female (1933)
Flamingo Road (1949)
Jim Thorpe - All-American (1951)
Kid Galahad (1937)
King Creole (1958)
Life With Father (1947)
Mildred Pierce (1945)
Night and Day (1946)
The Sea Hawk (1940)
The Sea Wolf (1941)
This Is the Army (1943)
White Christmas (1954)
Yankee Doodle Dandy (1942)
Young Man With a Horn (1950)
curtsy: **3** bob, bow, dip, nod **7** gesture **8** girl's bow, greeting, lady's bow **9** reverence
curvature: **3** arc, bow **4** arch, bend **5** shape **7** flexure **10** deflection
curve: **3** arc, bow, ess, sag **4** arch, bend, coil, curl, flex, hook, loop, ogee, turn, veer, warp, wind **5** crook, orbit, pitch, snake, sweep, swing, twist, whorl **6** camber, circle, slider, spiral **7** contour, ellipse, rainbow, scallop, scollop, sinuate **8** parabola **9** concavity, hyperbola, sinuosity **10** trajectory
double ~: **3** ess **4** ogee
ender: **4** ball
hairpin ~: **3** zag, zig
overhead ~: **4** arch
throw a ~: **4** stun **6** delude **7** stupefy **8** misquote, surprise
curve __: **4** ball
__ curve: **4** bell, sine **5** level, light, Peano **6** French, Jordan, Laffer, normal **7** caustic, derived, reverse
curveball: **4** ruse **5** pitch **8** surprise
curved: **4** bent **5** bandy, round, snaky **6** swirly **7** concave, sigmoid, sinuous, S-shaped **8** aquiline, circular, flexuous **9** sigmoidal **10** elliptical, serpentine
combining form: **4** cyrt- **5** cyrto- **6** campto- **7** -tropous
letter: **3** ess
line: **3** arc
molding: **4** ogee
not ~: **8** straight
outward: **6** convex
roof: **6** cupola
travel a ~ path: **3** arc **4** ring **5** orbit
curvet: **4** jump, leap

curving: **4** wavy **7** flexure, winding **8** tortuous
inward, as a beak: **5** adunc
curvy: **4** wavy **5** arced, round **7** sinuous, winding
Cusack: **4** Joan, John **5** Cyril
Cusack, Joan: **7** actress
film: Addams Family Values (1993)
Corrina, Corrina (1994)
Cradle Will Rock (1999)
Grosse Pointe Blank (1997)
Hero (1992)
In & Out (1997)
Married to the Mob (1988)
Men Don't Leave (1990)
Mr. Wrong (1996)
My Blue Heaven (1990)
Nine Months (1995)
Raising Helen (2004)
Runaway Bride (1999)
School of Rock (2003)
Working Girl (1988)
Cusack, John: **5** actor
film: America's Sweethearts (2001)
Being John Malkovich (1999)
Bullets Over Broadway (1994)
City Hall (1996)
Con Air (1997)
The Contract (2006)
Cradle Will Rock (1999)
Eight Men Out (1988)
Fat Man and Little Boy (1989)
Floundering (1994)
The Grifters (1990)
Grosse Pointe Blank (1997)
High Fidelity (2000)
The Journey of Natty Gann (1985)
Midnight in the Garden of Good and Evil (1997)
Must Love Dogs (2005)
Pushing Tin (1999)
The Road to Wellville (1994)
Runaway Jury (2003)
Say Anything... (1989)
Serendipity (2001)
Shadows and Fog (1992)
War, Inc. (2008)
Cush
father: **3** Ham
grandfather: **4** Noah
son: **6** Nimrod
cushaw: **6** squash **9** vegetable
Cushing: **4** font **5** Peter **8** Cardinal, typeface
cushion: **3** mat, pad **4** seat **5** break **6** buffer, deaden, muffle, pillow **7** beanbag, hassock, mollify, padding, protect **8** headrest
Buddhist meditation ~: **4** zafu **7** zabuton
fix a ~: **5** repad
starter: **3** pin
__ cushion: **3** air **7** whoopee, whoopie
__-cushioned: **3** air
cushionlike seat: **4** pouf
cushiony: **4** soft **5** downy, furry, nappy, plush **6** fleecy, fluffy, spongy **7** squishy, velvety
cushy: **4** cosy, cozy, easy, lush, plum, snug, soft **5** comfy, cozey, cozie, downy **6** simple **8** duck soup, painless **10** child's play, effortless, unexacting
job: **4** plum
cusk __: **3** eel
cusp: **3** end, eve, tip, top **4** apex, edge **5** point, wedge **6** height, tipoff
cuspid: **5** tooth **6** canine
cuspidor, sound near a: **4** ptui
cuss: **5** swear **6** geezer, vilify **7** profane **9** blaspheme, expletive
cussing: **4** vice **8** swearing **9** profanity
Cussler, Clive: **6** writer
hero: Dirk Pitt
work: Atlantis Found
Blue Gold
Cyclops
Deep Six
Dragon
Fire Ice
Flood Tide
Golden Buddha
Iceberg
Inca Gold
Mayday
The Mediterranean Caper
Night Probe
Pacific Vortex
Raise the Titanic
Sahara
The Sea Hunters
Serpent
Shockwave
Treasure
Trojan Odyssey
Valhalla Rising
White Death
cussword: **4** oath **9** profanity
custard: **4** flan **6** junket **7** dessert, pudding **8** flummery
apple: **5** papaw **6** pawpaw
ingredient: **3** egg **4** yolk
like ~: **4** eggy **5** yolky
custard __: **3** cup, pie **5** apple
Custer: **4** city, town **6** George **10** Yellowhair
colleague: **4** Reno
horse: **8** Comanche
locale: **4** S. Dak.
Custer's __ Stand: **4** Last
custodial: **10** protective
custodian: **5** super **6** keeper, warden **7** curator, janitor, manager, steward **8** executor, guardian, overseer, watchdog **9** attendant, bodyguard, caretaker, concierge, protector **10** baby sitter, doorkeeper, supervisor
of goods: **6** bailee
custody: **4** care, egis **5** aegis, trust **6** arrest, charge, escrow **7** jailing, keeping **8** auspices, clutches, wardship **9** detention, oversight **10** internment, possession, protection
give ~: **7** entrust, intrust
have ~ of: **4** keep
in ~: **6** jailed **7** captive
keep in ~: **4** hold, jail **6** arrest, detain, immure, intern, lock up, remand **7** confine, impound, put away **8** imprison, sentence
one in ~: **4** ward
release from ~: **4** bail
take into ~: **3** nab **4** book, nail **5** pinch, run in, seize **6** arrest **9** apprehend
custom: **3** rut, tax, use, way **4** form, levy, mode, rule, wont **5** habit, style, usage, vogue **6** impost, manner, method, policy, praxis, ritual, system, towage **7** fashion, pattern, routine **8** ceremony, exaction, folkways, habitude, localism, practice **9** etiquette, formality, patronage, precedent, procedure, tradition **10** convention, observance, stereotype
according to ~: **7** à la mode, usually
combining form: **4** nomo-
house: **6** douane
custom-__: **4** made, make **5** build, built, order **6** tailor
customarily: **3** usu. **6** mostly **7** as a rule, as usual, usually **9** naturally
customary: **3** set **5** stock, typic, usual **6** common, normal, proper, wonted **7** average, current, general, natural, popular, regular, routine, typical **8** accepted, everyday, familiar, frequent, habitual, ordinary, orthodox, standard **9** confirmed, household, prevalent, universal, unwritten **10** accustomed, inveterate, legitimate, prevailing, recognized, regulation, stipulated, understood
in French: **7** de règle
practice: **4** rite **5** habit
customer: **5** buyer, guest, taker **6** client, emptor, patron, person, vendee **7** account, habitué, shopper **8** consumer, purchase **10** frequenter
be a ~: **8** frequent **9** patronize
with a ~: **4** busy
__ customer: **4** cash, ugly **5** tough **6** one to a
customers, admitting: **4** open
customize: **6** modify **7** reshape
custom-made: **5** fancy **8** tailored
customs: **4** lore, ways **5** mores **6** morals, praxes **7** culture **8** folkways, protocol **9** ethnology, tradition **10** ins and outs
charge: **3** tax **4** duty **6** impost
document: **6** carnet
duty: **3** tax **6** impost
custos morum: **6** censor
cut: **2** ax **3** axe, hew, jag, lop, lot, mow, rip, saw **4** barb, chip, chop, clip, crop, dice, edit, fall, gash, hack, hurt, kerf, mown, nick, omit, pare, part, reap, rift, sawn, skip, slab, slit, slot, snip, snub, stab, take, tear, trim, verb, wage **5** carve, cleft, crack, erase, gouge, lower, lunge, mince, notch, piece, prune, quota, score, sever, share, shave, shear, shorn, shred, slash, slice, snick, spurn, stamp, style, taunt, wages, wound **6** bisect, booboo, censor, chisel, cleave, delete, digest, dilute, divide, excise, furrow, groove, gullet, hairdo, incise, injury, insult, kidney, lesion, lessen, mangle, parcel, pierce, ration, ravine, rebuff, record, reduce, revise, slight, spoils, tamper, trench, weaken **7** abridge, curtail, diluted, expunge, fashion, fissure, incised, injured, jobbery, offense, opening, partial, percent, portion, put-down, reduced, sarcasm, scissor, scratch, section, segment, sketchy **8** abridged, cleavage, clipping, close out, condense, decrease, deletion, detached, diminish, dividend, division, excision, fraction, incision, kickback, lacerate, leave out, lowering, mark down, puncture, sundered, truncate **9** allotment, allowance, broken off, capsulize, condensed, curtailed, decrement, expurgate, hairstyle, indignity, interrupt, intersect, lacerated, lessening, ostracize, perforate, reduction, sculpture, selection, shortened, telescope, water down **10** adulterate, commission, compressed, diminished, diminution, dimunition, expurgated, interspace, laceration, percentage, proportion, synopsized, unfinished
a ~ above: **4** rare **8** superior **9** unrivaled **10** unrivalled
across: **8** go beyond, traverse **9** intersect, transcend
a deal: **5** agree **9** acquiesce, negotiate
again: **5** remow, resaw
along: **5** speed
and dried: **4** dull **5** fixed, trite **6** boring **7** settled **9** hackneyed, wearisome **10** unoriginal
and paste: **4** edit
and run: **3** fly **4** flee, part **5** break **6** depart, desert, escape **7** abscond, go south, make off **8** fugitate, turn tail
apart: **5** sever **8** separate
a rug: **5** dance
back: **4** clip, pare, slow, snip, thin, trim **5** limit, lower, prune, shave, shear, skimp, slash **6** lessen, reduce **7** curtail, shorten **8** conserve, downsize, lessened **9** condensed **10** abbreviate, compressed, synopsized
barely ~: **4** nick
beef ~: **4** chop, loin, rump **5** chuck, filet, flank, roast, round, shank, steak, T-bone **6** fillet **7** sirloin **10** tenderloin
clear ~: **7** obvious **8** apparent
closely: **4** crop
cold ~: **3** ham **4** meat **6** salami **7** bologna **8** pastrami **10** corned beef
combining form: **4** -sect, tomo- **6** -tomous
corners: **4** save **5** skimp, stint **6** scrimp **8** retrench **9** economize **10** underspend
deep ~: **4** gash
down: **2** ax **3** axe, hew **4** curb, drop, fell, slow, trim **5** abase, abate, limit, lower, shave, slash **6** hack up, lessen, reduce, shrink **7** curtail, distill, dwindle, fall off, hack off, lighten, shorten **8** decrease, diminish, hack down, peter out, simplify **9** condensed, economize, summarize **10** abbreviate, compressed
down to size: **5** shame **6** demean, humble **7** deflate **8** belittle, minimize **9** humiliate
drastically: **5** slash
ender: **3** off, out **4** away, back, over, work, worm **5** grass,

purse, water 6 throat
ice: 5 count 6 matter
in: 5 share 7 intrude 9 interpose, interrupt
into: 4 etch, snip 5 notch 6 incise 7 incised
into logs: 5 saw up
into small pieces: 5 mince, shred
in two: 5 halve, sever 6 bisect 8 separate
in zigzags: 4 pink
it may be ~: 4 deck 5 price, slack
it out: 4 quit, stop 5 cease 6 desist
lesser ~ usually: 5 side B
loose: 4 free 5 let go, revel 6 escape, untied 7 abandon, run wild 9 disengage
make the ~: 6 hack it 7 qualify, survive
narrow ~: 4 slit
not ~ out for: 5 unfit 6 unable
oblique ~: 5 bevel, miter
off: 3 end, lop, top 4 crop, pare, part, skin, snip, stem, trim 5 apart, block, sever, shave, shear, split 6 cleave, detach, disown, divide, excise, hang up, impede, unlink 7 abscise, disjoin, insular, isolate, silence, split up 8 disunite, obstruct, secluded, separate, set apart, suppress, uncouple 9 condensed, intercept, interrupt, segregate, sequester, terminate 10 abbreviate, compressed, disconnect, disinherit
off (from): 4 wean
old-style: 4 snee
open: 4 slit, torn 5 lance
out: 3 end, run 4 bolt, clip, flee, omit, quit, stop, trim 5 break, cease, erase, leave, split, usurp 6 delete, depart, excide, excise, exsect, remove 7 exscind, make off 8 fugitate, run for it 9 eliminate, extirpate, skedaddle 10 abbreviate
partner: 3 run 5 paste
price ~: 6 saving 8 discount
razor ~: 2 do 4 coif 8 coiffure
roughly: 6 hackle, heckle 7 hatchel
saw ~: 4 kerf
short: 3 bob, end, nip 4 crop, ruin, stop 5 abort, elide, shave 7 curtail, silence, suspend 9 condensed, interrupt, telescope, terminate 10 compressed, synopsized, unfinished
short ~: 3 bob 5 route 6 byroad
slanting ~: 4 bias
small ~: 4 snip
some slack: 6 relent
staff ~: 3 RIF 6 layoff
starter: 4 crew, hair, wood 5 cross, short, upper
take a ~: 5 swing
the grass: 3 mow 4 trim
through: 6 pierce
timber: 3 hew, log, saw
to bits: 9 criticize, pick apart
to fit: 4 trim 5 adapt 6 tailor
too close: 5 scalp
to the quick: 4 slur 5 wound 6 insult
treatment: 6 iodine
trees: 3 hew, saw 4 chop, fell
up: 4 chop, dice, hurt, joke, romp, slur 5 carve, divvy 6 defame, divide 7 dissect, quarter 9 apportion, criticize, misbehave, partition
venison ~: 4 rump, side 5 flank, thigh
cut __: 3 off, out 4 a rug, back, down, drop, nail, rate, time 5 a deal, glass, grass, loose, no ice, short, stone 6 across, flower, square, velvet 7 corners
cut __ chase: 5 to the
cut __ for: 3 out
cut __ on: 4 back, down
cut __ quick: 5 to the
cut __ swath: 5 a wide
cut __ to size: 4 down
cut __ ways: 4 both
cut-__: 4 pile, rate
__ cut: 4 burr, cold, crew, curb, jump, line, star, step, trap 5 final, price, rough
__-cut: 4 card, fast, fine, full, open 5 clean, clear, sharp, short 6 double, French
cut a __: 3 rug
cut a __ swath: 4 wide
cut and __: 4 fill 5 paste
cut-and-__: 3 dry, try 5 cover, dried, paste
cut-and-dried: 5 usual 8 methodic
cut and paste: 4 edit
cutaneous: 6 dermal, dermic
cutaway: 4 coat 6 jacket
cutaway __: 4 coat, dive, shot
cut a wide __: 5 swath
cutback: 3 RIF 6 layoff 7 decline 8 decrease, lowering 9 abatement, decrement, lessening, reduction 10 diminution
cut both __: 4 ways
cut down to __: 4 size
cute: 4 pert 5 bonny, ducky, perky 6 bonnie, clever, comely, dainty, lovely, pretty, quaint, shrewd 7 darling, winning, winsome 8 adorable, alluring, becoming, charming, gorgeous, handsome, precious, striking, stunning 9 appealing, baby-faced, beautiful, ravishing 10 attractive
cute __ button: 3 as a
cutesy: 3 coy 8 affected, too sweet
cutesy __: 3 pie
cutesy-__: 3 poo
Cuthbert: 5 saint 6 Elisha
cutie: 7 charmer
see also sweetheart
cutie __: 3 pie
cutlass: 5 blade, knife, sword 6 dagger 7 sidearm
cousin: 4 épée 5 saber
material: 5 steel
Cutlass: 3 car 4 auto, Olds 10 automobile, Oldsmobile
cutler product: 5 knife
cutlery: 6 knives
metal: 5 steel
cutlet: 4 meat, veal
Cut me some __!: 5 slack
cut no __: 3 ice
cutoff: 4 halt, stop 6 recess 7 due date 8 deadline, stoppage 9 cessation 10 suspension
point: 5 limit, valve
cutoffs: 6 denims, shorts
cut one's __: 6 losses
cut one's __ on: 5 teeth
cutout dress
originator: Erté
cutpurse: 3 dip 5 thief 10 pickpocket
cut-rate: 3 low 5 cheap 6 on sale 7 bargain, good buy, low-cost 8 moderate, uncostly 9 half-price, low-priced 10 economical, reasonable
__ cuts: 4 cold
cutter: 3 axe, saw 4 boat 5 knife, mower, parer, razor 6 barber, shears, stylus
combining form: 4 -tome
control a ~: 5 steer
cousin: 5 sloop
starter: 4 hair, wood 5 stone
wave ~: 4 prow
__ cutter: 4 cane, coal, pipe, weed, wire 5 glass, paper 6 cookie
Cut that out!: 4 stop 6 quit it, stop it
cut the __: 7 mustard
cutthroat: 4 mean 5 cruel, harsh, nasty, trout 6 animal, brutal, fierce, killer, savage, unkind, wanton 7 beastly, callous, hurtful, vicious 8 barbaric, fiendish, inhumane, murderer, pitiless, ruthless, sadistic, vengeful 9 barbarous, desperado, dog-eat-dog, ferocious, merciless, monstrous, truculent, unpitying 10 relentless, vindictive
Cutthroat Island (1995 film)
cast: Geena Davis, Frank Langella, Matthew Modine
director: Renny Harlin
cutting: 3 dry, raw 4 acid, cold, keen, slab, snip, sour, tart 5 acute, nasty, plant, sharp, shoot, snide, sprig, tight 6 barbed, biting, bitter, severe, shrewd 7 acerbic, caustic, hateful, hurtful, ice-cold, intense, mordant, pointed, satiric 8 abrasive, clipping, critical, incisive, sardonic, scathing, stinging, virulent 9 corrosive, malicious, offensive, quotation, sarcastic, satirical, trenchant 10 astringent
affix a ~: 5 graft
combining form: 4 -tomy
edge: 3 new 4 lead 6 modern 7 current 8 advanced, up-to-date, vanguard
remark: 3 dig 4 barb 7 sarcasm
room figure: 6 editor
tool: 3 axe, die, saw 5 blade, knife 6 bowsaw, stylus
up: 8 division 10 dissection
utensil: 5 parer
cutting __: 4 edge, room 5 board
cuttlefish
cousin: 5 squid 7 octopus
defense: 3 ink
organ: 6 ink sac
pigment: 5 sepia
cut to __: 6 shreds 7 ribbons
cut to the __: 4 bone 5 chase, quick
Cutty Sark: 4 boat, ship
cutup: 3 imp, wag 4 card, zany 5 clown, comic, joker 6 fooler, jester 8 comedian, funnyman, humorist, kibitzer 9 leg-puller, prankster
Cuvier: 7 Georges
Cuxhaven: 4 port
locale: 7 Germany
river: 4 Elbe
Cuyahoga: 6 river
city on the ~: 9 Cleveland
Cuyahoga Falls: 4 city, town
locale: 4 Ohio
Cuyler, Kiki: 10 outfielder
Cuzco: 4 city, peak, town 5 mount 8 mountain
dweller: 4 Inca 5 Incan
locale: 4 Peru 5 Andes
see also Spanish
C.W.: 6 McCall
Post is part of it: 3 LIU
cwm: 5 basin 6 cirque, valley
CWO employer: 3 USN
C&W showplace: 4 Opry
Cy: 5 Young 7 Coleman 8 Endfield
cyan: 4 blue 5 green 8 greenish 9 blue-green
relative: *see* blue color, green color
Cybele: 8 asteroid
son: 5 Midas
cyber-bidders site: 4 eBay
cyber-conversation: 4 chat
cyber-crook: 6 hacker
cyber-guffaw: 3 LOL
cyberhead place: 3 net, Web 8 Internet
cyberphobe fear: 9 computers
cyber-shopping, place for: 5 e-mall
cyberspace: 3 Web 8 Internet
address: 3 URL
conversation: 4 chat
enter ~: 5 log in, log on
frequenter: 4 user
inits.: 3 AOL
junk mail: 4 spam
messages: 5 e-mail
return from ~: 6 log off
cyber-tycoon: Bill Gates
Cybill: 8 Shepherd
Cybill character: 3 Ira
cyborg: 7 RoboCop
science: 7 bionics
Cyclades: 4 isls. 5 isles 7 islands
island: 3 Ios, Kea, Zea 4 Keos, Milo 5 Delos, Melos, Milos, Naxos, Paros, Thera, Thira 8 Santorin 9 Santorini
largest of the ~: 5 Naxos
locale: 5 Egean 6 Aegean
neighbor: 5 Crete 6 Candia
cyclas: 4 robe 5 tunic 7 surcoat
cycle: 3 age, era, hog, run 4 bike, life, ring, turn 5 pedal, phase, recur, round, trike, wheel 6 Harley, period, series 7 routine 8 sequence, ten-speed 10 procession, revolution, succession, two-wheeler
billing ~: 5 month
kin: 5 moped
laundry ~: 4 soak, spin, wash 5 rinse
part: 5 phase
solar ~: 4 year
starter: 3 epi, tri, uni 4 giga, hemi, kilo, mega, mini, mono 5 motor 6 quadri
__ cycle: 4 cell, life, song 5 Krebs, lunar, rinse, solar 6 carbon 7 billing
__ Cycle: 4 Ring
cyclical: 7 regular 8 periodic 9 recurrent, recurring
in a way: 5 tidal
cycling: 5 sport

cyclist: 5 biker
  need: 4 bike 6 helmet
cycloid section: 3 arc
cyclone: 4 gale, gust, wind 5 storm 7 tempest, tornado, twister 9 hurricane, whirlwind, windstorm
  center: 3 eye
  refuge: 6 cellar

CY

cyclone __: 6 cellar 7 furnace
Cyclone __: 5 fence
Cyclones home: 4 Ames, Iowa
Cyclopean: 3 big 4 huge 5 giant, jumbo 7 immense 8 colossal, gigantic
cyclopedia: 4 book, list 7 lexicon 9 reference 10 dictionary
Cyclops: 5 Arges, giant 7 monster 10 Polyphemus
  author: Euripides
  had one: 3 eye
  parent: 4 Gaea 6 Uranus
cyclotron target: 4 atom
Cyd: 8 Charisse
  spouse: 4 Tony
cygnet: 4 bird 8 nestling 9 fledgling
  parent: 3 cob, pen 4 swan
Cygnus: 4 swan
  neighbor: 4 Lyra 6 Aquila
  star in ~: 5 Deneb
cylinder: 3 rod 4 pipe, roll, tube
  metal ~: 6 gabion
cylinder __: 3 saw 4 desk, head, seal 5 block
__ cylinders: 5 on all
cylinders, firing on all: 4 sane
cylindrical: 5 round, tubal 6 torose
  container: 4 cask 6 barrel
  fastener: 5 dowel
  instrument: 4 oboe
  structure: 4 silo
cyma __: 5 recta 7 reversa
cymbal: 3 zil 10 instrument
  finger ~: 4 zill
  relative: 4 gong
  sound: 5 clang, clash
cymbals: 5 hi-hat 6 piatti 7 crotale, high-hat 8 ceng ceng 10 percussion
  of India: 3 tal
Cymbeline
  author: William Shakespeare
  character: 6 Cloten, Imogen 7 Pisanio
  song: 5 dirge
Cymric: 5 Welsh
Cymry: 5 Welsh
Cynda: 8 Williams
Cyndi: 6 Lauper
Cynewulf: 4 poet
cynic: 7 doubter, killjoy, sceptic, scoffer, skeptic, snorter 8 naysayer 9 pessimist 10 curmudgeon, questioner
  response: 4 I bet, sure
cynical: 3 dry, wry 4 sour 6 bitter, crabby 7 mocking, satiric 8 derisive, doubtful, negative, sardonic, scoffing, scornful, sneering 9 resistive, sarcastic, satirical, skeptical 10 suspicious
  look: 5 sneer
cynicism: 7 dim view, sarcasm 8 glumness 9 nonbelief, pessimism, suspicion
cynophobe fear: 4 dogs
cynosure: 4 hero 5 focus 6 center, leader 7 paragon 8 lodestar, polestar 10 apotheosis, focal point
Cynthia: 4 Gibb, moon, poem 5 Geary, Ozick, Scott, Sikes 7 Gregory
  author: Walter Raleigh
cypress: 4 tree 7 juniper 8 sandarac 9 evergreen 10 arborvitae
  growth: 4 knee
  Japanese ~: 6 hinoki
Cypress Gardens
  locale: 3 Fla. 7 Florida
cyprinoid fish: 3 ide
Cyprus: 4 isle 6 island, nation 7 country
  capital: 7 Nicosia
  locale: 5 Medit.
  money: 4 cent
  wine: 7 retsina
Cyrano
  friend: 6 LeBret
  love: 6 Roxane
  prominent feature: 4 nose
Cyrano de Bergerac: 4 film, play
  author: Edmond Rostand
  cast: José Ferrer, Mala Powers
Cyril: 5 saint 6 Cusack 8 Connelly, Ritchard 9 Kornbluth
Cyrus: 5 Miley, Vance 9 McCormick
cyst: 3 sac, wen 4 bleb 7 blister, vesicle
Cy Young __: 5 Award
C.Z.: 5 Guest
czar: 4 king, male 5 baron, mogul, ruler 6 despot, dynast, gerent, leader, tyrant 7 emperor, magnate, monarch 8 autocrat, kingfish, overlord 9 authority, commander, potentate, sovereign
  decree: 5 ukase
  ender: 3 dom, ina, ist
  parliament: 4 Duma
  Russian ~: 4 Ivan, Paul 5 Ivan V, Paul I, Peter 6 Feodor, Ivan IV, Ivan VI, Peter I 7 Feodor I, Ivan III, Peter II, Romanov 8 Nicholas, Peter III 9 Alexander 10 Alexander I
czardas: 5 dance 9 Hungarian
czarina: 5 noble, queen, ruler 6 gerent
Czech: 4 Slav 8 Bohemian, language, Moravian, Silesian
Czech Republic: 6 nation 7 country
  capital: 5 Praha 6 Prague
  city: 4 Brno 5 Plzen, Praha, Tabor 6 Prague 7 Ostrava
  composer: 6 Dvorák 7 Smetana
  conductor: 5 Adler 7 Kubelik
  export: 5 glass 7 crystal
  leader: 5 Benes, Havel 6 Dubcek 7 Masaryk
  money: 6 korona, koruna
  mountain: 3 Erz 6 Snezka 7 Sudeten
  neighbor: 6 Poland 7 Austria, Germany 8 Slovakia
  Nobelist in Chemistry: 9 Heyrovsky
  Nobelist in Literature: 7 Seifert
  org.: 4 NATO
  playwright: 5 Capek, Havel 7 Jirásek
  play written in ~: 3 R.U.R.
  poet: 5 Havel, Holub 6 Neruda 7 Seifert
  publisher: 8 Koudelka
  river: 4 Eger, Elbe, Hron, Iser, Oder, odra, Ohre
  runner: 7 Zátopek
  tennis pro: 5 Kodes, Lendl 10 Mandlikova 11 Navratilova
  violinist: 7 Kubelik
  writer: 5 Capek, Hasek, Klíma 6 Hrabal 7 Jirásek, Kundera 9 Skvorecky
Czech Suite
  composer: Antonín Dvorák
Czerny: 4 Carl, Karl 5 Henry

D

___ d': 6 maître
D: 3 ltr., vit. 4 cell, mark 5 grade, width 6 letter 7 vitamin
get a ~: 4 pass
get below ~: 5 flunk
in code: 5 delta
D ___ day: 4 as in
___ D: 3 Big 4 Mike, R and 7 vitamin
'D' ___ Deadbeat: 5 Is for
da ___: 4 capo
___-da: 4 la-de, la-di
Da ___ Ron Ron: 3 Doo
Da ___, Vietnam: 4 Nang
DA: 6 hairdo
degree: 2 J.D. 3 LL.B., LL.D., LL.M., S.J.D.
org.: 3 ABA
part of ~: 3 att. 4 atty., dist. 8 attorney, district
quest: 5 proof
___ D.A.: 4 asst.
Daalder: 5 Renee
dab: 3 bit, pat 4 blob, drop, fish, lick, lump, spot, wipe 5 fleck, flick, rub on, smear, speck, touch, trace 6 dollop, expert, little, smudge 7 besmear, driblet, minimum, smidgen, smidgin, soupçon 8 flatfish, flounder, smidgeon
a ~ hand: 8 skillful
ender: 5 chick
preceder: 5 smack
smack ~: 8 directly
___ Daba Honeymoon, The: 3 Aba
___ dabba doo!: 5 Yabba
dabble: 5 dally 6 fiddle, loiter, paddle, play at, putter, splash, tinker, trifle 10 fool around, mess around, play around
dabbler: 4 tiro, tyro 5 toyer 6 novice 7 amateur 8 beginner, putterer, tinkerer 9 greenhorn 10 dilettante, uninitiate
Dabney: 7 Coleman
d'Abo: 6 Maryam, Olivia
d'Abruzzo, Alphonso: 4 Alda
___ da capo: 4 aria
Dacca: 4 city, town 7 capital
locale: 10 Bangladesh
dacha: 6 estate 9 residence
dachshund: 3 dog, pet 5 pooch 6 canine
like a ~: 3 low
Dacia
people of ancient ~: 4 Avar
DaCosta: 6 Morton
Dacron: 5 fiber 6 fabric 9 polyester
dactyl: 3 toe 4 foot 5 digit 6 finger
relative: 4 iamb 7 anapest, pyrrhic, spondee, trochee
starter: 5 ptero
___ da Cunha: 7 Tristan
dad: 2 pa 3 pop 4 male, papa, pops, sire 5 pappy, pater, poppa 6 father, old man, parent 8 relative
brother: 3 unc, unk 5 uncle
dad of ~: 5 gramp 6 gramps 7 grandpa
in French: 4 père
mate: 3 mom
mom of ~: 4 nana 7 grandma
related on ~'s side: 6 agnate
starter: 5 grand
dad-___: 3 gum 6 blamed, burned, gummed 7 blasted
___ Dad: 5 Major
dada: 4 papa 8 baby talk
Dada
artist: 3 Arp, Ray 4 Erté 5 Ernst 6 Man Ray 7 Duchamp, Hans Arp, Jean Arp
ender: 3 ism
___ Dada: 7 Idi Amin
da-DAH: 4 iamb
daddy: 2 pa 3 pop 4 male, papa, pops 5 poppa 6 father
longlegs: 3 bug 6 insect
mate: 5 mommy 6 mommie
sis: 5 aunty 6 auntie
starter: 5 grand
Daddy
author: Danielle Steel
Daddy ___ Legs: 4 Long
___ Daddy: 3 Big 4 Puff 5 Sugar
Daddy Don't You Walk So Fast (1972 song)
artist: Wayne Newton
Daddy Long Legs (1955 film)
cast: Fred Astaire, Leslie Caron
daddy-o: 6 hepcat 7 cool cat
Daddy's ___-hunting: 5 gone a
Daddy's Girls (MTV reality)
cast: Angela Simmons
Vanessa Simmons
Daddy's Home (song)
artist: Shep and the Limelites
Daddy's Little Girl
author: Mary Higgins Clark
dad-gum: 7 doggone
dado: 3 die 6 groove
Da Doo Ron Ron (song)
artist: Shaun Cassidy, Crystals
___ Dads: 5 My Two
daedal: 6 clever 7 complex 9 ingenious, intricate
Daedalus: 6 artist 8 Athenian, engineer, inventor
son: 5 Iapyx 6 Icarus
___ Dae Jung: 3 Kim
daemon: 3 god 5 ghoul 10 evil spirit
Daewoo: 3 car 4 auto 10 automobile
model: 5 Lanos 6 Nubira 7 Leganza
___ d'affaires: 5 homme 6 chargé
daffodil: 4 bulb 5 color, plant 6 flower, yellow
relative: see yellow color
daffy: 4 bats, loco, zany 5 dotty, goofy, goosy, inane, loony, nutty, silly, wacky 6 absurd, looney, whacky 7 foolish 8 clownish 10 off the wall, ridiculous, weak-minded
Daffy: 4 Dean, Duck
Daffy Duck, talk like: 4 lisp
Dafoe, Willem: 5 actor
film: Affliction (1998)
Animal Factory (2000)
Born on the Fourth of July (1989)
Clear and Present Danger (1994)
The English Patient (1996)
Light Sleeper (1992)
Mississippi Burning (1988)
Platoon (1986)
Shadow of the Vampire (2000)
Spider-Man (2002)
Tom & Viv (1994)
Triumph of the Spirit (1989)
White Sands (1992)
daft: 3 mad 4 gaga, loco, luny, soft 5 balmy, dingy, dotty, flaky, goosy, inane, kooky, loony, loopy, nutty, potty, silly, wacky 6 absurd, cuckoo, flakey, kookie, looney, whacky 7 asinine, bonkers, doltish, foolish, idiotic, touched, unsound, witless 9 brainless, half-baked, idiotical, senseless 10 off-the-wall, ridiculous, squirrelly, weak-minded
daftness: 5 folly
da Gama, Vasco: 8 explorer 10 Portuguese
stop for ~: 5 India
___ da gamba: 5 viola
dagger: 4 dirk, snee 5 blade, knife, knive, point 6 cutlas 7 cutlass, obelisk, poniard, sidearm 8 stiletto
Celtic ~: 5 skean, skene
handle: 4 haft, hilt
Malay ~: 4 kris 6 crease, creese
partner: 5 cloak
printer's ~: 6 obelus
Sikh ~: 6 kirpan
thrust: 4 stab
daggers at, look: 4 rage 5 glare, scowl 6 glower 8 threaten
___ Dagh: 3 Ala
Dagnabbit!: 4 darn
Daguerre: 5 Louis
daguerreotype: 5 photo 7 picture
Dagwood: 8 Bumstead
boss: 7 Dithers
boss's wife: 4 Cora
dog: 5 Daisy
frequent request: 5 raise
kid: 6 Cookie 9 Alexander
neighbor: 4 Elmo, Herb
sweetheart before Blondie: 4 Irma
wife: 7 Blondie
___-dah: 5 lah-di
dahl: 4 stew
Dahl: 4 John 5 Roald 6 Arlene
Dahl, Arlene: 7 actress
spouse: Lex Barker, Fernando Lamas
dahlia: 5 plant 6 flower, purple, violet 8 amethyst
relative: see purple color
Dahlia: 4 Lavi
___ Dahlia, The: 4 Blue
Dahl, Roald: 6 writer 7 British
birthplace: Wales
spouse: Patricia Neal
work: The BFG
Charlie and the Chocolate Factory
Going Solo
James and the Giant Peach
Matilda
The Twits
Dahomey today: 5 Benin
dah partner: 3 dit
dahs, dits and: 4 code 9 Morse code
___ Dai: 3 Bao
Daihatsu: 3 car 4 auto 10 automobile
model: 5 Cuore, Rocky 7 Charade
Dail Eireann
locale: 7 Ireland
Dailey: 3 Dan 5 Janet
daily: 5 paper 6 common 7 diurnal, journal, per diem, regular, routine 8 magazine, ordinary, periodic 9 circadian, newspaper, quotidian 10 periodical
delivery: 4 mail 5 paper 9 newspaper
dozen: 5 drill 8 exercise
drama: 4 soap
record: 5 diary
report: 4 news
routine: 3 job, rut 4 work 5 grind, habit, labor 6 groove 7 routine
daily ___: 5 dozen 6 double
Daily: 4 Bill
Daily ___: 4 News 5 Bruin 6 Planet
...___ daily bread: 3 our
Daily Bruin: 5 paper 9 newspaper
publisher: 4 UCLA
daily double: 3 bet 5 wager
Daily Planet: 5 paper 9 newspaper
reporter: 4 Kent, Lane, Lois 5 Clark, Olsen 8 Lois Lane 9 Clark Kent 10 Jimmy Olsen
Daily Show, The
host: Jon Stewart
network: Comedy Central
Daimler: 8 Gottlieb
partner: 4 Benz
Dain Curse, The
author: Dashiell Hammett
daintiness: 8 delicacy
dainty: 4 cute, fine, lacy, lank, lean, neat, nice, slim, thin, twee, wiry 5 bonny, frail, fussy, lanky, light, spare, sweet, tasty, treat, wispy 6 bonnie, choosy, comely, gangly, lovely, petite, pretty, skinny, slight, slinky, svelte, twiggy 7 choosey, darling, finicky, fragile, gracile, mincing, refined, scraggy, scrawny, slender, spidery, willowy, wispish 8 charming, delicacy, delicate, ethereal, feathery, finiking, finnicky, gangling, graceful, precious 9 beautiful, delicious, exquisite, sweetmeat, sylphlike 10 attractive, delectable, fastidious, particular, weightless
overly ~: 6 cutesy 7 cutesie
daiquiri: 5 drink 8 beverage, cocktail
ingredient: 3 rum 4 lime 9 lime juice 10 lemon juice
___ daiquiri: 6 banana, frozen
dairy: 4 farm 5 ranch 8 creamery
animal: 3 cow
British ~ merchant: 6 eggler
ender: 3 man, men 4 maid 5 woman, women
implement: 5 churn
prefix: 4 lact- 5 lacto-
product: 4 curd, eggs, milk, whey 5 cream, curds, kefir, leben 6 butter, cheese, junket, yogurt 7 clabber 8 ice cream, skim milk 9 goat's milk, sour cream 10 buttermilk, heavy cream, light cream, lowfat milk, nonfat milk
rating: 6 grade A
sound: 3 moo
starter: 3 non
unit: 3 cup 4 pint 5 quart 6 gallon
dairy ___: 4 farm 5 breed 6 cattle
Dairy ___: 5 Queen
dairy case buy: 4 milk, oleo, skim
dairymaid's seat: 5 stool
Dairy Queen: 8 ice cream 9 soft serve

alternative: *see* ice cream
order: 4 cone 5 float, shake, split
dais: 6 podium 7 rostrum 8 platform
covering: 5 drape
do ~ duty: 5 orate
VIP: 4 host 5 emcee, guest 7 speaker
daisy: 5 gowan, oxeye, plant 6 flower 7 blossom 10 marguerite, wildflower
center: 4 disk
look-alike: 5 aster
__ daisy: 5 aster, oxeye 6 Shasta 10 Michaelmas
__-daisy: 4 upsa, upsy
Daisy: 6 Miller 7 Fuentes 9 Girl Scout
__ Daisy Clover: 6 Inside
Daisy Mae
boyfriend: 5 Abner
creator: Al Capp
father-in-law: 5 Pappy
son: 3 Abe
Daisy Miller
author: Henry James
Dakar: 4 city, port, town 7 capital
cape: 5 Verde
locale: 7 Senegal
Dakota: 5 Sioux, tribe 6 Indian 7 Amerind, Fanning 8 language
abode: 4 tent, tipi 5 tepee 6 teepee
dialect: 5 Teton
Indian: 3 Ree 5 Sioux 7 Arikara
__ Dakota: 5 North, South
Daktari lion: 8 Clarence
dal __: 5 segno
DAL: 5 Delta
former rival: 3 TWA 7 Braniff, Eastern
Dalai Lama: 4 rank 6 cleric 8 Nobelist
city: 4 Lasa 5 Lassa, Lhasa
country: 5 Tibet 6 Xizang
dale: 4 glen 6 dingle, valley
companion: 4 hill
__-dale: 5 Alan-a
Dale: 3 Jim 4 Alan 5 Evans, Henry 6 Murphy 7 Bumpers, Jarrett, Messick, Midkiff 8 Carnegie 9 Earnhardt, Robertson
partner: 3 Roy 4 Chip
__ d'Alene: 5 Coeur
Dalén, Nils: 7 Swedish 8 Nobelist 9 physicist
daleth: 6 Hebrew, letter
predecessor: 5 gimel
successor: 2 he 3 heh
Daley: 5 Rosie 7 Richard
city: 3 Chi 7 Chicago
Dalgliesh: 4 Adam
dal ingredient: 6 lentil
Dali, Salvador: 6 artist 7 painter, Spanish
colleague: Frederico García Lorca, Joan Miró
feature: 8 mustache
like ~ watches: 4 limp
spouse: Gala
work: Burning Giraffe, The
Leda Atomica
Persistance of Memory, The
Tuna Fishing
Dall: 4 John
Dallas: 4 city, soap, town 6 George
athletes: 8 Mustangs
city near ~: 5 Ennis, Plano 6 Denton, De Soto, Irving
commodity: 3 oil
locale: 3 Tex. 5 Texas
pro team: 4 Mavs 5 Stars 7 Cowboys 9 Mavericks
river: 7 Trinity
school: 3 SMU
Dallas (CBS drama)
cast: Barbara Bel Geddes (Ellie Ewing)
Jim Davis (Jock Ewing)
Patrick Duffy (Bobby Ewing)
Linda Gray (Sue Ellen Ewing)
Larry Hagman (J.R. Ewing)
Ken Kercheval (Cliff Barnes)
Victoria Principal (Pam Ewing)
Charlene Tilton (Lucy Ewing)
setting: 5 ranch 9 Southfork
__ Dallas: 6 Stella
Dallas County city: 5 Selma
__ Dallas Forty: 5 North
Dallas-to-Reno dir.: 3 WNW
Dalla sua pace: 4 aria
dalliance: 9 loitering, puttering 10 carrying on, flirtation, frittering, frolicking, hanky-panky
dallier: 9 latecomer
__ Dalloway: 3 Mrs.
dally: 3 haw, lag, toy 4 drag, idle, laze, loaf, poke, stay, wait 5 amble, delay, flirt, mosey, stall, tarry, trail 6 dabble, dawdle, linger, loiter, put off, trifle 7 saunter 8 footdrag, gain time, hesitate, lollygag, lose time, slack off, straggle 9 poke along, waste time 10 boondoggle, fool around, mess around, play around
__-dally: 5 dilly
dallying: 4 lazy 6 otiose 7 unready 8 dilatory, indolent, slothful 9 apathetic, frivolity, negligent, shiftless 10 neglectful
Dalmatian: 3 dog, pet 5 canid, pooch 6 canine 7 fire dog
feature: 4 spot
seaport: 5 Zadar
Dalrymple: 3 Ian 4 Scot
Dalton: 4 Abby, city, John, town 7 Timothy
gang victim: 5 train
locale: 7 Georgia
Dalton, John: 7 British, chemist
Dalton, Timothy: 5 actor
film: Agatha (1979)
Brenda Starr (1989)
Licence to Kill (1989)
The Living Daylights (1987)
The Rocketeer (1991)
Wuthering Heights (1970)
Daltrey: 5 Roger
Daly: 4 John, Tyne 5 Chuck, James 7 Timothy
Daly, Chuck: 5 coach
sport: 10 basketball
Daly City: 4 city, town
locale: 10 California
Daly, John: 6 golfer
Daly, Tyne: 7 actress
spouse: Georg Sanford Brown
TV: Cagney & Lacey
dam: 3 bar, mom 4 bank, bolt, clog, cork, dike, lock, mama, mare, plug, seal, shut, stem, wall, weir 5 block, close, jam up, latch, levee, mamma 6 clog up, female, hinder, impede, lock up, plug up, seal up, secure, stop up 7 barrier, block up, choke up, prevent, seal off, shutter 8 blockade, button up, hold back, keep back, obstruct, restrain 9 barricade, broodmare 10 embankment
agcy.: 3 TVA
build a ~: 6 embank
builder: 6 beaver
Egyptian ~: 5 Aswan
Lake Mead ~: 6 Hoover
mate: 4 sire
Panama Canal ~: 5 Gatún
__ dam: 7 tinker's
__ Dam: 5 Aswan, Gatún 6 Beaver, Hoover, Wilson 7 Boulder
dama: 6 señora
damage: 3 mar 4 chip, cost, harm, hurt, loss, maim, nick, ruin, scar, tear, toll 5 abuse, break, crack, erode, price, split, spoil, stain, wound, wreck, wrong 6 bang up, batter, bruise, charge, deface, defile, deform, impair, injure, injury, mangle, mess up, outlay, ravage, riddle, trauma, weaken 7 blemish, corrode, corrupt, disable, expense, pollute, scratch, slander, tarnish, vitiate 8 aggrieve, breakage, mischief, mutilate, sabotage 9 corrosion, detriment, liability, pollution, prejudice, undermine, vandalism, vandalize 10 corruption, impairment, knock about, tamper with
irrevocable ~: 7 debacle 8 calamity, disaster 9 cataclysm, perdition 10 extinction
minor ~: 4 dent, ding
widespread ~: 5 havoc
damaged: 4 hurt, shot, torn, worn 5 kaput 6 broken, faulty, flawed 7 cracked, injured, unsound 8 fallible 9 defective, imperfect 10 on the blink, on the fritz, out of whack
easily ~: 5 frail 7 fragile
damages: 4 cost, fine 5 award, price 6 charge 7 expense, penalty 9 indemnity 10 punishment, reparation
damaging: 3 bad, ill 5 toxic 6 costly, malign, nocent 7 adverse, baleful, baneful, harmful, hurtful, ruinous 8 grievous, negative 9 dangerous, injurious 10 calamitous, derogatory, disastrous, pernicious
__, Daman, and Diu: 3 Goa
__ d'amandes: 4 lait
Damascene: 4 Arab
Damascus: 4 city, town 7 capital
locale: 3 Syr. 5 Syria
river: 6 Barada
VIP: 5 Assad
damask: 4 pink, rose, silk 5 linen 6 fabric
relative: 4 nude 5 melon 6 salmon 7 apricot 8 flamingo 9 carnation
damask __: 4 rose 5 steel
damask rose: 5 plant 6 flower
product: 4 atar, otto 5 athar, attar, ottar
Damasus: 4 pope 7 pontiff
D'Amato: 2 Al 7 Alfonse
d'Amboise, Jacques
specialty: 5 dance 6 ballet
Dambovita, city on the: 9 Bucharest
dame: 3 gal 4 lady 5 noble, title, woman 6 matron 7 dowager, peeress 8 baroness 9 blueblood 10 aristocrat, noblewoman
__ dame: 6 grande
__ Dame: 5 Notre
Dames (1934 film)
cast: Joan Blondell, Ruby Keeler, ZaSu Pitts, Dick Powell
Dames __: 5 at Sea
Dam, Henrik: 6 Danish 8 Nobelist 10 biochemist
Damian: 5 saint 7 Michael
daminozide: 4 Alar
Damita: 2 Jo 4 Lili
Damita, Lili
spouse: Errol Flynn
damn: 4 slam 5 blast, curse 6 outlaw, punish, vilify 7 censure, condemn 8 denounce 9 castigate, criticize, excoriate, imprecate, proscribe 10 confounded, denunciate
give a ~: 4 care, mind
not worth a ~: 5 lousy
__ damn: 7 tinker's
damnable: 4 evil 8 infernal
Damn: A Book of Calumny
author: H.L. Mencken
damnation: 4 doom 9 perdition 10 execration
Damnation of Faust, The
composer: Hector Berlioz
damn with faint __: 6 praise
Damn Yankees (1958 film)
cast: Tab Hunter, Gwen Verdon, Ray Walston
character: 3 Joe, Meg 4 Lola 5 Doris, Satan 6 Gloria 9 Applegate
composer: Richard Adler, Jerry Ross
director: George Abbott, Stanley Donen
song: 5 Heart
team: 8 Senators
Damon: 4 Mark, Matt 6 Runyon, Wayans 7 Cathryn
to Pythias: 3 pal 6 friend
Damone, Vic
spouse: Pier Angeli, Diahann Carroll
Damon, Matt: 5 actor
film: All the Pretty Horses (2000)
The Bourne Identity (2002)
The Bourne Supremacy (2004)
The Bourne Ultimatum (2007)
The Brothers Grimm (2005)
Courage Under Fire (1996)
The Departed (2006)
Dogma (1999)
The Good Shepherd (2006)
Good Will Hunting (1997)
The Legend of Bagger Vance (2000)
Ocean's Eleven (2001)
Ocean's Thirteen (2007)
Ocean's Twelve (2004)
The Rainmaker (1997)
Rounders (1998)
Saving Private Ryan (1998)
School Ties (1992)
Stuck on You (2003)
Syriana (2005)
The Talented Mr. Ripley (1999)
__ d'amore: 4 oboe 5 viola
D'amor sull'ali rosee: 4 aria
__ d'amour: 4 oboe 7 affaire, chanson
damp: 3 wet 4 dank, dewy, oozy 5 boggy, deter, humid, misty, moist, muddy, muggy, musty, soggy, steep, undry 6 clammy, deaden, drippy, hydric, liquid,

sodden, steamy, sticky, stuffy, sultry, swampy, sweaty, watery **7** depress, drizzly, mildewy, moisten, sopping, wettish **8** moisture **9** saturated **10** demoralize
habitat: 3 bog, fen **5** bayou, marsh, swamp
dampen: 3 cow, wet **4** cool, curb, dash, dull, mute, slow, soak **5** abate, allay, bedew, blunt, brake, check, chill, cloud, daunt, delay, deter, rinse, spoil, spray, water **6** deaden, deject, hamper, hinder, impede, lessen, muffle, quench, rain on, retard, sadden, slow up, stifle, temper **7** deflate, depress, humdify, inhibit, moisten, silence, slacken, wet down **8** diminish, dispirit, dissuade, humidify, irrigate, moderate, restrain, saturate, slow down, sprinkle, tone down **10** besprinkle, demoralize, discourage, dishearten, intimidate
dampened: 3 low **5** faint, moist, piano, quiet
damper: 5 brake, check, pedal **10** constraint
put a ~ on: 5 quash, slake **6** sadden
dampness: 3 dew, wet **5** vapor **7** wetness **8** humidity, moisture **9** sogginess
Damrosch, Walter: 6 German **9** conductor
damsel: 4 girl, lass, maid, miss **5** houri, woman **6** female, lassie, maiden **7** colleen **8** fraülein **9** young lady **10** demoiselle, young woman
cry: 4 help **5** never **6** my hero, save me
ender: 3 fly **4** fish
saver: 4 hero **6** knight
damselfly: 3 bug **6** insect
Damsel in Distress, A (1937 film)
cast: Gracie Allen, Fred Astaire, George Burns, Joan Fontaine
damson: 4 plum **5** color **6** purple
Dan: 4 Hill **5** Fouts, Issel, Patch, Rowan, Seals **6** Curtis, Dailey, Duryea, Frazer, Hedaya, Lauria, Marino, McGrew, O'Brien, Quayle, Rather **7** Aykroyd, Blocker, Hampton, Hartman, Majerle **8** Haggerty, Jacobson, O'Herlihy **9** Brouthers, Fogelberg
fancy ~: 4 dude **5** blade, swell **10** jack-a-dandy
parent: 5 Jacob **6** Bilhah
sibling: 3 Gad **4** Levi **5** Asher, Dinah, Judah **6** Joseph, Reuben, Simeon **7** Zebulun **8** Benjamin, Issachar, Naphtali
__ Dan: 5 fancy **6** Steely **7** England
Dana: 3 Vic **4** Bill **5** Elcar, Plato **6** Carvey, Delany, Scully, Wynter **7** Andrews, Charles
Danae
lover: 4 Zeus
son: 7 Perseus
__ Dana Gibson: 7 Charles
__ d'ananas: 5 crème
Da Nang: 4 city, town
locale: 7 Vietnam
Dana Point: 4 city, town
locale: 10 California
Dana, Richard Henry: 6 writer
work: Two Years Before the Mast
Danbury: 4 city, town
locale: 4 Conn.
dance: 2 ET **3** art, bop, dog, fly, hop, jig **4** ball, bird, bump, clog, dive, frug, gala, haka, hora, hula, jerk, jive, jota, juba, jump, khon, kolo, pogo, pony, prom, reel, rock, shag, skip, slop, step, sway, swim, walk **5** ballo, bebop, conga, disco, fling, frisk, galop, gavot, gigue, gopak, guess, hopak, horah, limbo, lindy, mambo, mixer, mouse, nasty, party, pavan, pavin, polka, rumba, salsa, samba, shake, skate, smurf, snake, stomp, strut, swing, tango, twine, twist, valse, vogue, waltz **6** ballet, bocane, bolero, boogie, Boston, bugaku, canary, cancan, cavort, cha-cha, formal, frolic, gambol, german, gyrate, hoof it, hustle, joropo, kathak, medium, minuet, monkey, morris, pavane, prance, rhumba, shimmy, stroll, trepak, Watusi **7** alegras, bedrock, beguine, bourrée, carioca, courant, csardas, cut a rug, czardas, djanger, foxtrot, freddie, gavotte, hoedown, lambada, lancers, ländler, le freak, mazurka, moshing, NY slide, one-step, peabody, perform, popcorn, shuffle, slauson, sock hop, sparkle, two-step **8** birdland, boogaloo, bunny hop, bunny hug, cachucha, cakewalk, chaconne, courante, Egyptian, fandango, flamenco, galliard, habanera, handjive, hornpipe, hula-hula, kazatsky, L.A. hustle, lindy hop, macarena, mazourka, merengue, moonwalk, rigadoon, saraband, soft-shoe, special K, tush push **9** acid house, allemande, alligator, bossa nova, breakdown, camel walk, cotillion, écossaise, farandole, festivity, hitchhike, jitterbug, malaguena, pas de deux, paso doble, passepied, Philly dog, polonaise, promenade, quadrille, sarabande, siciliano, tambourin, zapateado **10** achy-breaky, bergamasca, Charleston, corroboree, hucklebuck, hully gully, loco-motion, running man, saltarello, seguidilla, strathspey, tarantella, turkey trot, villanella
16th-century ~: 5 ballo, pavan, pavin **6** canary, pavane **8** galliard
17th-century ~: 7 courant **8** courante, galliard **9** allemande, passepied
18th-century ~: 4 juba **9** cotillion, passepied
1920s ~: 6 shimmy **10** Charleston
1930s ~: 4 shag **5** lindy
1950s ~: 4 slop **5** shake **6** stroll **8** birdland, handjive **10** hucklebuck, hully gully
1960s ~: 3 dog, fly **4** bird, frug, jerk, pony, swim **5** skate, twine, twist **6** monkey, Watusi **7** freddie, slauson **8** boogaloo **9** alligator, camel walk, hitchhike, Philly dog **10** loco-motion
1970s ~: 4 bump, sway **5** disco **6** hustle **7** popcorn, shuffle **8** L.A. hustle, special K
1980s ~: 2 ET **4** pogo, walk **5** guess, nasty, salsa, snake, vogue **7** bedrock, le freak, neutron **8** Egyptian, moonwalk **9** acid house
1990s ~: 3 hop **4** dive **5** smurf **7** moshing, NY slide **8** macarena, tush push **10** achy-breaky, running man
19th-century ~: 4 juba **5** galop
acrobatic ~: 5 limbo **9** jitterbug
African ~: 4 juba
all night: 5 revel **9** celebrate, make merry
Andalusian ~: 8 flamenco
Argentine ~: 5 tango
art form ~: 6 ballet
Austrian ~: 5 waltz **7** ländler
award: 6 Bessie
back-bending ~: 5 limbo
Balinese ~: 7 djanger
ballet ~: 7 pas seul **9** pas de deux **10** pas d'action
ballroom ~: 5 conga, mambo, rumba, samba, tango, waltz **6** cha-cha, rhumba **7** beguine, fox trot, lambada, one-step, peabody, two-step **8** habanera **9** bossa nova, polonaise **10** Charleston
band: 5 combo
bar-mitzvah ~: 4 hora
barn ~: 4 reel
bobbysoxer's ~: 3 hop
Bohemian ~: 5 polka
bolerolike ~: 8 cachucha
Brazilian ~: 5 samba **6** maxixe **7** batuque, lambada **9** bossa nova
Bristol ~: 5 stomp
British ~: 6 morris
Bucharest ~: 4 hora
Caribbean ~: 4 soca **5** limbo, mambo **7** beguine
castanet ~: 4 jota **6** bolero **8** fandango
chain ~: 5 conga
circle ~: 4 hora, kolo
colonial ~: 4 reel **6** minuet **8** saraband **9** sarabande
combining form: 5 chore- **6** choreo-, chorio-
costume ~: 6 morris
Cuban ~: 5 conga, mambo, rumba **6** rhumba **8** habanera
Dixieland ~: 5 stomp
Dominican ~: 8 merengue
ender: 4 hall, wear
flamenco ~: 7 alegras
formal ~: 4 ball, prom
French ~: 5 gavot, valse **6** branle, cancan **7** bourrée, gavotte **9** cotillion, farandole, passepied, quadrille, tambourin
genre: 3 tap
German ~: 7 ländler
grass-skirt ~: 4 hula
half a ~: 3 can, cha
hand-clapping ~: 4 juba
hand gesture, in Indian ~: 5 mudra
handkerchief ~: 9 siciliano
Hawaiian ~: 4 hula **8** hula-hula
heavily: 5 stomp
heel-stomping ~: 5 gopak, hopak
high-kicking ~: 6 cancan
highland ~: 4 reel **5** fling
hippy ~: 4 hula
Hungarian ~: 7 csardas, czardas
Indian ~: 6 kathak
in French: 3 bal
in wooden shoes: 4 clog
Irish ~: 3 jig
Israeli ~: 4 hora **5** horah
Italian ~: 5 ballo, gigue **9** siciliano **10** bergamasca, saltarello, tarantella, villanella
Japanese ~: 6 bugaku, Bukavu
jazz ~: 4 jive **5** bebop, stomp, swing **9** jitterbug
Latin ~: 5 conga, mambo, raspa, salsa, samba, tango **6** cha-cha **9** zapateado
line ~: 5 conga
lively ~: 3 jig **4** reel **5** fling, galop, polka **6** bolero, joropo **7** mazurka, peabody **8** fandango, galliard, mazourka, rigadoon **9** breakdown, cotillion, paso doble **10** bergamasca, seguidilla, tarantella
Maori war ~: 4 haka
men-only ~: 4 khon **6** bugaku, trepak **8** kazatsky
movement: 4 step **5** glide
noisy ~: 9 breakdown
no-taps tap ~: 8 soft-shoe
NYC ~ co.: 3 ABT
partner: 4 song
Peppermint Lounge ~: 5 twist
Polish ~: 7 mazurka **8** mazourka **9** polonaise
ragtime ~: 6 shimmy **10** turkey trot
recklessly: 4 mosh
Romanian ~: 4 hora **5** horah
round ~: 4 hora **5** galop
running step ~: 7 courant **8** courante
salsa club ~: 5 rumba **6** rhumba
Savoy ~: 5 stomp
school ~: 3 hop **4** prom **5** mixer
Scottish ~: 4 reel **5** fling **9** écossaise **10** strathspey
Serbian ~: 4 kolo
sing and ~: 5 party
site: 4 barn **5** disco
slangily: 4 hoof **7** cut a rug
Slavic ~: 4 kolo **8** kazatsky
slow ~: 5 pavan, pavin **6** bocane, minuet, pavane **8** chaconne, habanera **9** allemande, polonaise **10** strathspey
song and ~: 4 line, yarn **5** pitch, spiel **6** reason **9** rationale
Spanish ~: 4 jota **6** bolero **7** alegras, bourrée **8** chaconne **9** malaguena, paso doble, zapateado **10** seguidilla
starter: 4 folk
stately ~: 5 pavan, pavin **6** minuet, pavane **8** chaconne, saraband **9** sarabande
step: 6 chassé, do-si-do **7** dos-à-dos
studio rail: 3 bar **5** barre
syllable: 3 cha
Thai ~: 4 khon
Ukraine ~: 5 gopak, hopak **6** trepak
under a bar: 5 limbo
Venezuelan ~: 6 joropo
version of a song: 5 remix

Viennese ~: 5 waltz
West Indies ~: 5 limbo
with a kick: 5 conga
dance __: 4 band, card, form, hall, step 5 drama
__ dance: 3 hat, sun, tap, tea, toe, war 4 barn, clog, file, folk, line, rain, ring, slam 5 belly, break, cooch, court, ghost, round, snake, sword 6 apache, dinner, modern, morris, nautch, shadow, square, waggle 7 neutron
Dance __ Hours: 5 of the
__ Dance: 4 Last, Let's 5 I Can't, I Won't, Sabre 7 Neutron
dance-club employee: 6 deejay
Dance, Dance, Dance (song)
artist: Beach Boys, Chic
Dance of Life, The
author: Havelock Ellis
Dance of the Hours
composer: Amilcare Ponchielli
Dance of the Nymphs
artist: Camille Corot
Dance on Little Girl (1961 song)
artist: Paul Anka
dancer: 5 Bruhn, Dolin, Jooss, Kelly, Lifar, Tharp 6 Alonso, Béjart, Duncan, hoofer 7 Astaire, Bujones, Farrell, Fonteyn, Markova, Martins, Massine, Nureyev, Pavlova, Shearer, Ulanova 8 coryphée, d'Amboise, Danilova, De Valois, Eglevsky, figurant, Mitchell, Nijinsky, Rockette, Villella 9 ballerina, Gene Kelly, Tallchief 10 Balanchine, chorus girl 11 Baryshnikov, Youskevitch
ballet ~: 7 danseur 8 coryphée, danseuse, figurant
displace a ~: 5 cut in
garment: 4 tutu 6 tights
poor ~: 5 stiff
__ dancer: 3 tap 4 go-go, taxi 5 belly, gandy 6 ballet
Dancer: 8 reindeer
colleague: *see* reindeer
handler: 5 Santa
__ Dancer: 4 I Am a 7 Private
Dancer at the Bar
painter: Edgar Degas
Dancer, The
artist: Erté
Dances With Wolves (1990 film)
animal: 5 bison
cast: Kevin Costner, Graham Greene, Mary McDonnell
director: Kevin Costner
foe: 6 Pawnee
home: 4 tipi 5 tepee 6 teepee
language: 6 Lakota 7 Lakhota
Dance the Night Away (1979 song)
artist: Van Halen
Dance to Death
author: Emma Lazarus
Dance to the Music (1968 song)
artist: Sly and the Family Stone
Dance to the Music of Time, A
author: Anthony Powell
Dance With Me (song)
artist: Peter Brown, Orleans, Betty Wright
Dance With Me Henry (1955 song)
artist: Georgia Gibbs
Dance With Me Henry (1956 film)
cast: Bud Abbott, Lou Costello
__ dancing: 3 ice 4 slam 5 break 6 social, square 7 aerobic
Dancing __: 4 Lady 5 Queen 7 Machine
__ Dancing: 4 Come, Slow 5 Dirty 6 Shadow
__ Dancing!: 5 That's
Dancing Class, The
artist: Edgar Degas
Dancing Couple, The
artist: Jan Steen
Dancing in the Dark (1984 song)
artist: Bruce Springsteen
Dancing in the Street (song)
artist: Davide Bowie, Mick Jagger, Martha & the Vandellas
Dancing Machine (1974 song)
artist: Jackson 5
Dancing on the Ceiling (1986 song)
artist: Lionel Richie
Dancing Queen (1977 song)
artist: ABBA
dandelion: 4 weed, wine 5 plant 6 flower
down: 5 pappi 6 pappus
stalk: 5 scape
Dandelion (1967 song)
artist: Rolling Stones
Dandelion Wine
author: Ray Bradbury
dander: 3 ire 4 rage 5 anger, Irish, pique, wrath 6 temper 9 huffiness, surliness
get one's ~ up: 4 rile 5 anger, peeve 7 bristle
Dandie Dinmont: 3 dog, pet 5 pooch 6 canine 7 terrier
dandle: 3 pet 5 spoil 6 coddle, cosset, cuddle, pamper 7 cater to, indulge
Dandridge: 3 Ray 7 Dorothy
dandruff: 5 scall, scurf 6 flakes
dandy: 3 fop, gem, pip 4 beau, dude, prig, toff 5 beaut, natty, prize, slick, swank 6 beauty, dapper, lovely, peachy, snazzy, spiffy, spruce, swanky 7 amazing, awesome, coxcomb, foppish 8 popinjay 9 agreeable, prettyboy
British ~: 4 toff
partner: 4 fine
see also wonderful
__-dandy: 3 jim 5 handy, jack-a
Dandy (1966 song)
artist: Herman's Hermits
__ d'âne: 3 pas
Dane: 4 Cook 5 Clark 9 Zealander
ender: 3 law
__ Dane: 5 Great
Danes, Claire: 7 actress
film: The Family Stone (2005)
Les Misérables (1998)
Little Women (1994)
The Mod Squad (1999)
Polish Wedding (1998)
The Rainmaker (1997)
Romeo & Juliet (1996)
Shopgirl (2005)
Stardust (2007)
To Gillian on Her 37th Birthday (1996)
dang: 4 darn, drat, heck, oath 5 nerts, nertz 6 darn it, durn it 9 consarn it
D'Angelo: 7 Beverly
__ Dan George: 5 Chief
danger: 4 disk, risk 5 peril 6 beware, chance, crisis, hazard, menace, threat 7 pitfall, thin ice, trouble 8 exposure, jeopardy, unsafety 10 insecurity
ending: 3 ous
free from ~: 4 safe
in ~: 6 at risk, liable 7 exposed 8 vincible
in ~ of: 9 subject to
lure into ~: 6 entrap
out of ~: 4 safe 8 unharmed 9 untouched
response to ~: 4 fear
signal: 3 red 5 alert
Dangerfield, Rodney: 8 comedian
persona: 5 loser
dangerous: 3 bad 4 mean, ugly 5 hairy, nasty, risky, shaky, tight, toxic 6 chancy, lethal, malign, nocent, no joke, severe, thorny, unsafe, wicked 7 adverse, baleful, baneful, hurtful, noisome, ominous, parlous, rickety, ruinous, serious, unsound, vicious 8 alarming, damaging, headlong, menacing, negative, perilous, terrible, ticklish, unstable 9 breakneck, desperate, explosive, harrowing, hazardous, impending, injurious, insidious, malignant, murderous, pestilent, troubling, unhealthy 10 calamitous, disastrous, formidable, incendiary, jeopardous, pernicious, petrifying, portentous, precarious, serpentine, touch-and-go, vulnerable
group: 3 mob
make less ~: 6 defuse, defuze
not ~: 4 safe 8 harmless
partner: 5 armed
Dangerous (song)
artist: Busta Rhymes, Roxette
Dangerous Beauty (1998 film)
cast: Jacqueline Bisset, Catherine McCormack, Oliver Platt
Dangerous Liaisons (1988 film)
cast: Glenn Close, John Malkovich, Michelle Pfeiffer, Keanu Reeves, Uma Thurman
Dangerous When Wet (1953 film)
cast: Fernando Lamas, Esther Williams
Danger, The
author: Dick Francis
Danger Zone (1986 song)
artist: Kenny Loggins
Dang it!: 4 nuts 5 nerts, nertz
dangle: 3 sag 4 flop, hang, loll, pend, sway, wave 5 droop, sling, swing, trail 6 flaunt, follow 7 draggle, suspend 8 brandish, flourish, hang down 9 hang about, hang loose, oscillate
a carrot: 4 lure 5 tempt 6 entice
dangling: 4 limp 5 baggy, slack 6 droopy, floppy 7 flaccid, pendant, pendent 9 pendulous
Dangling Conversation, The (1966 song)
artist: Simon and Garfunkel
Dangling Man
author: Saul Bellow
Dang Me (1964 song)
artist: Roger Miller
Daniel: 4 Beth, Mann, Tsui, Yuly 5 Boone, Bovet, Craig, Defoe, Mason, Shays, Stern 6 Inouye, Petrie, Samuel, Schorr 7 Baldwin, Benzali, Deronda, Nathans, Webster 8 Boorstin, Ellsberg, Kahneman, McFadden, Travanti 9 Barenboim 10 Fahrenheit
follower: 5 Hosea
locale: 3 den
preceder: 7 Ezekiel
Daniel (1973 song)
artist: Elton John
Daniel (1983 film)
cast: Edward Asner, Ellen Barkin, Lindsay Crouse, Timothy Hutton, Mandy Patinkin
director: Sidney Lumet
Daniel __ French: 7 Chester
Daniel __ Lewis: 3 Day
Daniela: 7 Bianchi
Daniel arap __: 3 Moi
Daniel, Beth: 6 golfer
Daniel Boone
poet: Stephen Vincent Benét
Daniel Boone (NBC western)
cast: Ed Ames (Mingo)
Fess Parker (Daniel Boone)
Daniel Deronda
author: George Eliot
Daniel J. __: 8 Travanti
Danielle: 5 Steel 8 Darrieux 9 Brisebois
Daniels: 4 Bebe, Jeff 5 Faith 7 Charlie, William
Daniel, Samuel: 4 poet 7 British
Daniels, Jeff: 5 actor
film: The Answer Man (2009)
Arachnophobia (1990)
Because of Winn-Dixie (2005)
Dumb & Dumber (1994)
Gettysburg (1993)
Gods and Generals (2003)
Heartburn (1986)
Marie (1985)
Pleasantville (1998)
The Purple Rose of Cairo (1985)
Radio Days (1987)
Rain Without Thunder (1992)
Speed (1994)
Sweet Hearts Dance (1988)
Terms of Endearment (1983)
Trial and Error (1997)
Daniels, William: 5 actor
TV: St. Elsewhere
Daniel, Yuly: 6 writer 7 Russian
Danilova, Alexandra: 6 dancer 8 danseuse 9 ballerina
Dan in Real Life (2007 film)
cast: Juliette Binoche, Steve Carell, Dianne Wiest
danish: 4 cake 6 pastry 9 sweet roll
flavor: 5 prune
Danish: 5 bread 6 pastry 8 language
see also Denmark
Danish __: 3 oil 6 Modern, pastry
Danish __ Indies: 4 West
Danish __ Islands: 6 Virgin
dank: 3 raw, wet 4 damp, dewy 5 humid, moist, muggy, musty, soggy, undry 6 chilly, clammy, steamy, sticky, stuffy, sultry 7 mildewy, odorous, wettish
danke: 6 thanks 7 spasibo 8 thank you
danke __: 5 schön 6 schoen
Danke Schoen (1963 song)
artist: Wayne Newton
Dannay: 8 Frederic
Danner, Blythe daughter: Gwyneth Paltrow
Danning: 5 Sybil

D'Annunzio, Gabriele: **4** poet **7** Italian
Danny: **4** Kaye **6** Aiello, DeVito, Elfman, Glover, O'Keefe, Thomas **8** Bonaduce, Pintauro, Williams
daughter: **5** Marlo
Danny __: **3** Boy **6** Deever
Danny and the Juniors
song: At the Hop (1957)
Danny Boy (1959 song)
artist: Conway Twitty
caller: **5** pipes
locale: **4** glen **6** meadow
Danny Deever
author: Rudyard Kipling
Danny's Song (1973 song)
artist: Anne Murray
Danny Thomas Show (ABC/CBS sitcom)
cast: Angela Cartwright (Linda Williams)
Hans Conried (Uncle Tonoose)
Jean Hagen (Margaret Williams)
Rusty Hamer (Rusty Williams)
Sherry Jackson (Terry Williams)
Marjorie Lord (Kathy Williams)
Sid Melton (Charley Halper)
Danny Thomas (Danny Williams)
Dano: **5** Linda, Royal
Danova: **6** Cesare
Dan Patch: **5** horse **9** racehorse
emulate: **4** race, trot
__ dansant: **3** thé
Danse __: **7** Macabre
danse du __: **6** ventre
danseuse: **9** ballerina
support: **3** bar **5** barre
Danson, Ted: **5** actor
film: 3 Men and a Baby (1987)
Cousins (1989)
spouse: Mary Steenburgen
TV: Becker, Cheers
Dante: **3** Joe **4** font, poet **7** Italian, Lavelli **8** Bichette, Rossetti, typeface **9** Alighieri
love: Beatrice
work: The Divine Comedy
The New Life
Dante __ Rossetti: **7** Gabriel
Dantes: **6** Edmond
Dante Symphony
composer: Franz Liszt
Dantley: **6** Adrian
Danton: **3** Ray **7** Georges
Danube: **5** river
city on the ~: **3** Ulm **4** Linz **6** Braila, Galați, Vienna **8** Belgrade, Budapest **10** Bratislava
feeder: **3** Inn, Olt **4** Enns, Hron, Isar, Prut, Raab, Raba, Sava **5** Drava, Iller, Pruth, Siret, Tisza **6** Morava
in Hungary: **4** Duna
locale: **3** Aus. **7** Austria, Germany, Hungary, Romania, Rumania **8** Roumania, Slovakia
Roman province near the ~: **5** Dacia
to Czechs: **5** Dunaj
__ Danube Waltz: **4** Blue
Danza, Tony: **5** actor
TV: Taxi, Who's the Boss?
Danzig: **4** city, gulf, port **6** Gdansk
locale: **6** Poland
river: **7** Vistula
da opposite: **4** nyet
__ d'Aosta: **5** Valle

Daphne: **4** seer **5** oread **6** Zuniga **8** asteroid **9** du Maurier
lover: **6** Apollo
Daphnis: **5** nymph **7** centaur
god offended by ~: **4** Eros
lover: **5** Chloe
parent: **6** Hermes
Daphnis and Chloë: **6** ballet
composer: Maurice Ravel
dapper: **4** chic, neat, pert, spry, trim **5** agile, brisk, dandy, natty, nifty, sharp, sleek, smart, swank **6** chichi, classy, jaunty, lively, nimble, rakish, snappy, snazzy, spiffy, sporty, spruce, swanky **7** dashing, groomed, stylish, voguish **8** handsome **9** decked out, gussied up, in fashion, sprightly
fellow: **3** Dan, fop **4** dude **5** blade, swell
dapple: **3** dot **4** spot **5** fleck, horse **6** equine, mottle **9** variegate **10** variegated
dapple-__: **4** gray, grey
dappled: **4** pied **6** motley **7** brindle, flecked, mottled, piebald **8** brindled, freckled, speckled **9** multihued **10** multicolor, variegated
Darby: **3** Kim
D'Arby, Terence Trent
song: Sign Your Name (1988)
Wishing Well (1988)
__ d'arc: **4** bois
Darcel: **6** Denise
d'Arc, Jeanne: **3** Ste. **5** woman **6** leader, martyr, sainte
Dardan: **5** Priam **6** Hector, Trojan
Dardanelles end: **5** Egean **6** Aegean
Darden: **6** Severn
__-dardy: **5** lardy
dare: **4** defy, risk **5** brave, tempt **6** brazen, gamble, hazard **7** go for it, presume, venture **8** defiance **9** adventure, challenge, speculate, take a risk **10** go for broke, make a stand, take a flier
alternative: **5** truth
ender: **3** say **5** devil
__ dare: **3** on a
Dare: **8** Virginia
competitor: *see* cookie manufacturer
__ Dare: **6** Double
daredevil: **4** bold, rash **5** brave, risky **6** hotdog, madcap, risker **7** hotspur, show-off **8** headlong, heedless, overbold, reckless, stuntman **9** audacious, foolhardy, impulsive, uncareful **10** adventurer, courageous
feat: **5** stunt
lack: **3** net **5** sense
need: **5** nerve **7** courage
no ~: **5** sissy
Daredevil (2003 film)
cast: Ben Affleck, Jennifer Garner
dared old-style: **5** durst
daresay: **5** guess, think **7** presume, suppose
Dar es Salaam: **4** city, port, town
locale: **8** Tanzania
__ dare to eat a peach?: **3** Do I
d'Arezzo: **5** Guido
Darien: **4** city, town
locale: **4** Conn.
Darin, Bobby
song: Beyond the Sea (1960)
Dream Lover (1959)
If I Were a Carpenter (1966)
Mack the Knife (1959)
Queen of the Hop (1958)
Splish Splash (1958)
Things (1962)
You're the Reason I'm Living (1963)
spouse: Sandra Dee
daring: **4** bold, game, grit, guts, rash **5** brave, cocky, fresh, gutsy, moxie, nerve, nervy, pluck, risky, spunk, valor **6** active, awless, brassy, brazen, cheeky, gritty, heroic, plucky, risqué, spunky **7** aweless, bravery, courage, dashing, defiant, doughty, forward, gallant, heroism, impavid, prowess, staunch, valiant **8** audacity, boldness, fearless, headlong, heroical, impudent, intrepid, reckless, resolute, stalwart, temerity, unafraid, valorous **9** audacious, dauntless, desperate, dreadless, foolhardy, gallantry, unabashed, uncareful, undaunted, unfearful, unfearing **10** confidence, courageous, enterprise, feistiness, undismayed
act: **5** stunt
Darío, Rubén: **4** poet **10** Nicaraguan
Darius: **4** king **7** Milhaud, Persian
son: **6** Xerxes **10** Achaemenes
Darjeeling: **3** tea **4** city
locale: **5** India
Darjeeling Limited, The (2007 film)
cast: Adrien Brody, Anjelica Huston, Owen Wilson
dark: **3** dim, dun, sad **4** blue, dour, drab, dusk, ebon, evil, glum, grim, inky, mirk, murk, ugly, vile **5** black, bleak, dingy, dusky, ebony, faded, fuzzy, gloom, loury, mirky, misty, murky, muted, night, sable, shady, sober, sooty, surly, swart, unlit, vague **6** arcane, bleary, blurry, broody, closed, cloudy, dismal, dreary, gloomy, hidden, ill-lit, lowery, morbid, morose, occult, opaque, secret, shadow, sinful, somber, sullen, swarth, unseen, veiled, wicked **7** cryptic, doleful, evening, joyless, obscure, ominous, satanic, shadowy, stygian, sunless, swarthy, unknown **8** abstruse, baffling, dejected, dolorous, hopeless, horrible, ignorant, infamous, infernal, jetblack, lowering, moonless, nebulous, overcast, puzzling, sinister, ulterior **9** cheerless, concealed, cryptical, depressed, enigmatic, lightless, murkiness, nightfall, nighttime, obscurity, recondite, satanical, sorrowful, tenebrous, unlighted **10** forbidding, indistinct, lugubrious, lusterless, melancholy, mysterious, mystifying, pitch-black, tenebrific, unknowable
after ~: **5** night **7** nightly **9** nighttime, nocturnal
area: **5** umbra **8** penumbra
companion: **4** tall **8** handsome
ender: **4** ling, room
get ~: **5** bedim, laten **7** becloud, blacken
horse: **8** long shot, opponent, underdog **9** candidate **10** competitor, contestant
hunt in the ~: **6** fumble **9** feel about
in the ~: **5** unlit **6** hidden, secret **7** out of it **8** ignorant **9** benighted, secretive, unadvised, unknowing, unmindful **10** uninformed
look: **5** scowl
make ~: **6** shadow
not ~: **5** light
not in the ~: **5** aware, hep to
shadow: **4** pall
shot in the ~: **3** bet **4** risk, stab **5** flyer, guess **6** gamble **9** guesswork
side: **4** evil
to a poet: **4** ebon
dark __: **4** meat **5** horse
__ dark: **5** in the
__-dark: **5** pitch
Dark __: **4** Ages, City, Eyes, Lady, Moon
Dark __ of the Moon: **4** Side
Dark __, The: **4** Half, Past **5** Angel, Arena, Tower **6** Corner, Mirror **7** Crystal
__, dark, and handsome: **4** tall
Dark Angel (2000 film)
cast: Jessica Alba
Dark Arena, The
author: Mario Puzo
Dark at the Top of the Stairs, The: **5** novel
author: William Inge
character: **4** Cora **5** Rubin **6** Lottie, Reenie
Dark Canoe, The
author: Scott O'Dell
Dark Continent: **3** Afr. **6** Africa
Dark Crystal, The (1982 film)
director: Jim Henson, Frank Oz
darken: **3** dim, mat, tan **4** blur, dull **5** bedim, befog, black, cloud, shade **6** deaden, deject, dim out, sadden, shadow **7** becloud, blacken, cloud up, depress, obscure, tarnish **8** dispirit, tone down **9** adumbrate, obfuscate **10** overshadow
darkened: **3** dim **4** gray, grey **5** mirky, muddy, murky, shady **6** cloudy, dismal, gloomy, opaque, somber, sullen, turbid **7** obscure, sunless, unclear **8** confused, lowering, overcast **9** unsettled **10** indistinct
Dark Eye in Africa, The
author: Laurens Van der Post
Darkfall
author: Dean Koontz
Dark Half, The
author: Stephen King
Dark Horse
author: Fletcher Knebel
Dark Intruder (1965 film)
director: Harvery Hart
darkish: **3** dim
Dark Knight, The (2008 film)
cast: Christian Bale, Michael Caine, Heath Ledger
director: Christopher Nolan
Dark Lady (1974 song)
artist: Cher

Darkman (1990 film)
cast: Colin Friels, Frances McDormand, Liam Neeson
director: Sam Raimi
Dark Moon (1957 song)
artist: Bonnie Guitar, Gale Storm
darkness: 4 mirk, murk 5 black, gloom, night, shade 6 shadow 7 secrecy 8 blackout 9 ignorance, murkiness, nightfall, obscurity
Darkness at Noon
author: Arthur Koestler
character: 6 Arlova, Ivanov
Darkness, Prince of: 5 devil, Satan 7 Lucifer
Dark of the Moon
author: Sara Teasdale
Dark Passage (1947 film)
cast: Lauren Bacall, Humphrey Bogart
Dark Rivers of the Heart
author: Dean Koontz
darkroom
chemical: 6 amidol
equipment: 3 enl. 8 enlarger
image: 3 neg. 8 negative
product: 5 proof
solution: 5 fixer, toner
___ Dark Shadow: 5 Cast a
Dark Shadows (ABC): 4 soap 9 soap opera
dark-skinned: 6 swarth 7 swarthy
name meaning ~: 6 Morris 7 Maurice
Dark Tower, The
author: Stephen King
Dark Victory (1939 film)
cast: Humphrey Bogart, George Brent, Bette Davis, Geraldine Fitzgerald
composer: Max Steiner
Darla: 4 Hood
Darleen: 4 Carr
Darlene: 4 Love
___ Darlin': 3 Li'l 5 Susie 6 Little
darling: 4 cute, dear 5 jewel, loved, sweet 6 dainty, lovely, pretty, prized, valued 7 cara mia, favored, lovable, winsome 8 adorable, alluring, charming, engaging, favorite, heavenly, loveable, precious 9 cherished, treasured 10 delectable, delightful, enchanting, fair-haired
little ~: 3 tot 4 baby 5 angel 6 cherub, infant, moppet 7 neonate, newborn, toddler 8 cutie pie, dumpling, snookums 10 sweetie pie
see also sweetheart
Darling: 4 Erik 5 range, river, Wendy
dog: 4 Nana
friend: 3 Pan 5 Peter 8 Peter Pan
locale: 9 Australia
Darling (1965 film)
cast: Dirk Bogarde, Julie Christie, Laurence Harvey
Darling Be Home Soon (1967 song)
artist: Lovin' Spoonful
Darling Je Vous Aime Beaucoup (1955 song)
artist: Nat King Cole
Darling Lili (1970 film)
cast: Julie Andrews, Rock Hudson
darn: 3 sew 4 dang, drat, heck, mend 5 patch, resew 6 repair 9 doggone it 10 confound it
give a ~: 4 care, heed, mind 5 sweat, worry 6 bother, object, regret 9 make a fuss
something to ~: 4 sock
___ darn: 5 give a
Darn ___!: 5 it all
Darn!: 4 dang, drat, heck, nuts, rats 5 nerts, nertz, shoot 6 cripes
in German: 3 ach
___ Darn Cat!: 4 That
darned: 4 very 10 confounded
___ darned!: 5 I'll be
Darnell: 5 Linda 6 Martin
darner: 6 needle 9 dragonfly
___ Darn Hot: 3 Too
darning ___: 6 needle
darning, in need of: 5 holey
___ darn tootin'!: 3 Yer
Darn tootin'!: 6 I'll say
DAR part: 3 Rev. 4 Amer. 8 American 9 Daughters 10 Revolution
Darrell: 5 Evans
Darren: 5 James 7 McGavin
Darrieux: 8 Danielle
Darrow: 3 Ann 8 Clarence
client: 6 Scopes
Darryl: 6 Zanuck 7 Hickman 10 Strawberry
dart: 3 fly, hie, rip, run, zig, zip 4 bolt, dash, flap, flit, lick, race, rush, seam, shot, skim, tear, whiz, zoom 5 hurry, lunge, scoot, shoot, spank, speed, start, swoop, whisk 6 barrel, gallop, hasten, hurtle, hustle, move it, rocket, scurry, sprint, whoosh 7 floor it, hop to it, missile, quicken, scamper 8 hightail, step on it 9 fulgurate, hotfoot it, shake a leg, skedaddle 10 get a move on, hightail it
part: 5 shaft
player's drink: 3 ale 5 lager, stout
shooter: 4 Amor, Eros 5 Cupid
___ d'art: 5 objet
Dart: 3 car 4 auto 5 Dodge 10 automobile
d'Artagnan: 9 Musketeer
friend: 5 Athos 6 Aramis 7 Porthos
prop: 4 épée 5 sword
dartboard: 6 target
wood: 3 elm
darter: 4 bird, fish
___ darter: 5 snail
Dartmoor: 5 sheep
city near ~: 6 Exeter
Dartmouth: 4 city, town 7 college
athletes: 8 Big Green
league: 3 Ivy
locale: 4 Mass. 6 Canada 7 Hanover 10 Nova Scotia 12 New Hampshire
darts: 4 game 5 sport
locale: 3 pub
Darwell: 4 Jane
Darwin: 4 city, town 7 Charles
locale: 9 Australia
Darwin, Charles: 7 British 10 naturalist
ship: 6 Beagle
___ Darya: 3 Amu, Syr
Daryl: 4 Duke, Hall 6 Dragon, Hannah, Sabara 7 Dawkins 8 Anderson
Das ___: 4 Boot 7 Kapital
Das ___ von der Erde: 4 Lied
Das Boot (1981 film)
craft: 3 sub 5 U-boat
dash: 3 bit, fly, hie, nip, ram, rip, run, vim, zip 4 bolt, brio, dart, drop, élan, fire, flit, foil, lick, life, line, race, ruin, rush, slam, snap, tear, tick, tint, whit, zing, zoom 5 éclat, flair, haste, hurry, lunge, oomph, pinch, scoot, shade, shoot, spank, speed, style, taste, throw, tinge, touch, trace, verve, vigor, whiff, whisk, wreck 6 barrel, blight, bon ton, bustle, charge, dampen, dollop, energy, esprit, gallop, hasten, hustle, hyphen, little, move it, pizazz, plunge, rocket, scurry, spirit, splash, sprint, streak, thwart, trifle 7 bravery, bravura, courage, deflate, floor it, hop to it, modicum, panache, pizzazz, quicken, scamper, shatter, smidgen, smidgin, soupçon, sparkle, take off 8 confound, dispirit, flourish, smidgeon, spoonful, sprinkle, stampede, step on it, vivacity 9 animation, élan vital, frustrate, hotfoot it, shake a leg, skedaddle 10 burn rubber, confidence, disappoint, discourage, enterprise, enthusiasm, get a move on, get hopping, hightail it, liveliness, sprinkling
ender: 3 pot 5 board
hopes: 6 dismay, thwart 7 let down 10 dishearten
length: 2 em, en
Morse ~: 3 dah
off: 4 type 5 write 9 improvise
partner: 3 dot
starter: 4 slap
dash ___: 3 off 4 down 5 light
Dash: 6 Crofts, Stacey 9 detergent
alternative: *see* detergent
Dash ___!: 5 it all
___ Dashan, Ethiopia: 3 Ras
dashboard
device: 3 odo 4 dial, tach 5 gauge, radio 6 airbag, dimmer 8 CD player, odometer 10 tape player
reading: 3 mph, rpm
dashed off: 9 impromptu
Dasher: 8 reindeer
colleague: *see* reindeer
handler: 5 Santa
Dashiell: 7 Hammett
contemporary: 4 Erle 6 Agatha
dog: 4 Asta
dashiki: 7 African, garment
dashing: 4 bold, chic, fast 5 brave, class, faddy, peppy, sharp, showy, smart, swank 6 breezy, classy, dapper, daring, jaunty, lively, modish, plucky, rakish, snappy, sporty 7 chipper, elegant, gallant, raffish, rousing, stylish, voguish 8 animated, colorful, dazzling, debonair, fearless, spirited 9 debonaire, impetuous, in fashion, sprightly, vivacious 10 debonnaire, flamboyant
fellow: 4 dude 5 blade, dandy, swell
da Silva: 6 Howard
Das Kapital
author: Karl Marx
Das Lied von der Erde
composer: Gustav Mahler
Das Rheingold: 5 opera
character: 4 Erda, Froh, Loge, Mime, Norn 5 Freia, Wotan 6 Donner, Fafner, Fasolt, Fricka 8 Alberich, Woglinde 9 Wellgunde 10 Flosshilde
composer: Richard Wagner
setting: 5 Rhine 7 Germany
Dassin: 5 Jules
dastard: 3 cur 4 heel, wimp 5 devil, fiend, knave, rogue, scamp, sissy 6 bad guy, coward, craven 7 chicken 8 poltroon, recreant 9 fraidy cat, hellhound, jellyfish
dastardly: 3 low 4 base, mean, vile 5 timid 6 craven, rotten 7 ignoble, knavish, wimpish 8 recreant, shameful
dat
not ~: 3 dis
data: 4 info, news 5 facts, proof 6 notice 7 details, figures, numbers 8 evidence, material 10 statistics
computer ~ format: 5 ASCII
copy: 6 backup
disk: 5 CD/ROM 6 floppy
ender: 4 bank, base
enter ~: 4 type 5 input, key in
locate, as ~: 6 access
processing equipment: 2 PC
seek ~: 3 ask
sender: 4 ISDN 5 cable, modem
storage medium: 4 disk 5 CD/ROM 6 floppy 7 Zip disk 10 floppy disk
transfer rate: 4 baud
transmission science: 9 telemetry
unit: 3 bit 4 byte
data ___: 3 set 4 bank, base 6 center
database
function: 4 sort 6 select
Internet ~: 5 Lexis, Nexis
data-entry
area: 6 keypad
goof: 4 typo
person: 5 typer
data-sharing acronym: 3 LAN
data transmission, science of: 9 telemetry
date: 3 see, woo 4 appt., palm, time 5 court, fruit, go out, tryst 6 ask out, escort, go with, jujube, pursue, squire, suitor 7 meeting, partner, step out, take out 9 boyfriend, companion, go out with 10 engagement, girlfriend, invitation, rendezvous
at an early ~: 4 anon
bring up to ~: 6 revamp, revise, update 9 modernize
Chinese ~: 6 jujube
disappointing ~: 4 nerd
due ~: 3 end 5 limit 6 cutoff 8 deadline, zero hour
effective ~ in law: 4 nisi
ender: 4 line
entertainer's ~: 3 gig 7 booking
gal's ~: 5 fella 6 fellow
guy's ~: 3 gal 4 doll
have a ~: 5 go out
invite on a ~: 6 ask out
on a ~: 3 out
on that ~: 4 as of, then
out of ~: 5 passé 7 archaic
producer: 5 Yemen
provide a ~: 5 fix up, set up
regularly: 3 see
Roman ~: 4 ides 5 nones
starter: 3 air, pre 4 ante

to ~: 3 yet 5 as yet, so far 7 as of now 8 until now
tree: 4 palm
way to go on a ~: 5 Dutch
date __: 4 line, palm 5 stamp
__ date: 3 due, pub 4 pack, play, pull, rain, sell, set a, up to 5 blind, out of 6 cut-off, double, target 7 release
__ date!: 4 It's a
__-date: 4 up-to 5 out-of 6 carbon, double
datebook
abbr.: 3 Mon., Sat., Sun., Thu., Tue., Wed. 4 Tues. 5 Thurs.
duration: 4 year
dated: 3 obs., old, out 5 dowdy, passé, stale 6 bygone, old hat, square 7 archaic, outworn 8 obsolete, outdated, outmoded, out of use, timeworn 10 antiquated, out of style
dateless: 4 stag 5 alone
dater: 5 stamp 9 time stamp
date-setting phrase: 4 as of
dating: 4 with 9 courtship
__ **dating:** 4 code, open 6 carbon
Dating Game, The host: Jim Lange
dating-service objective: 5 match
dative: 4 case
Datril: 9 analgesic 10 painkiller
alternative: *see* pain reliever brand
datum: 4 fact, stat 9 statistic
datura: 10 jimsonweed, nightshade
daub: 3 pat 4 blob, spot 5 paint, smear, stain 6 smudge, spread, streak 7 plaster, spatter
Dauber
author: John Masefield
Daudet: 4 Léon 8 Alphonse
daughter: 3 kid, she 4 cion, girl 5 child, scion, woman 6 female 7 kinsman 9 offspring 10 descendant
starter: 3 god 4 step 5 grand
daughter-__: 5 in-law
__ **Daughter:** 5 Ryan's
daughterly: 6 filial
Daughter of Fortune
author: Isabel Allende
Daughter of the Dragon (1931 film)
cast: Warner Oland
Daughter of Time, The
author: Josephine Tey
daughters: 5 issue 7 kinfolk 8 kinfolks, kinsfolk 9 offspring
Daughters and Rebels
author: Jessica Mitford
Daughters of the Dust (1991 film)
director: Julie Dash
__ **Daughter, The:** 7 Farmer's, Ragman's
Daumier: 6 Honoré
daunt: 3 cow 4 faze 5 alarm, appal, bully, deter, scare, shake 6 appall, dampen, dismay, menace 7 depress, overawe, terrify, unnerve 8 dispirit, dissuade, frighten, paralyse, paralyze, unstring 10 demoralize, discourage, dishearten, intimidate, scare stiff
daunted: 4 down 5 timid 6 afraid, trepid 7 anxious, chicken, fearful, nervous, panicky 8 cowardly, downcast, fearsome, hesitant, timorous 9 awestruck
daunting: 5 scary 7 awesome 9 frightful 10 forbidding, formidable
dauntless: 4 bold, game 5 brave, gutsy, nervy, stout 6 awless, daring, gritty, heroic, plucky, spunky 7 aweless, defiant, doughty, gallant, impavid, staunch, valiant 8 fearless, heroical, intrepid, resolute, spirited, stalwart, unafraid, valorous 9 audacious, confident, dreadless, undaunted, unfearful, unfearing 10 courageous, invincible, mettlesome, undismayed
dauntlessness: 4 grit, guts 5 heart, nerve, valor 6 mettle, spirit 7 bravery, prowess 8 audacity
dauphin: 3 son 5 title 6 prince
Dauphine: 3 car 4 auto 7 Renault
Dausset, Jean: 6 French 8 Nobelist
Dave: 4 Bing 5 Barry, Clark, Mason 6 Casper, Cortez, Cowens, Grusin, Parker, Thomas 7 Brubeck, Edmunds, Loggins, McNally, Navarro, Stewart 8 Garroway, Matthews, Winfield 9 Letterman
singing partner: 3 Sam
TV rival: 3 Jay
Dave (1993 film)
cast: Ben Kingsley, Kevin Kline, Frank Langella, Sigourney Weaver
director: Ivan Reitman
Dave __ Five: 5 Clark
davenport: 4 desk, seat, sofa 5 couch, divan, table 6 daybed, settee 7 seating 9 furniture
Davenport: 4 city, town 5 Nigel 7 Lindsay
locale: 4 Iowa
Davenport, Lindsay: 7 netster 9 tennis pro
Daves: 6 Delmer
Dave's World (CBS sitcom)
cast: Harry Anderson (Dave Barry)
locale: 5 Miami
secretary: 3 Mia
Davey: 5 Lopes
Davi: 6 Robert
David: 3 Hal, Lee 4 camp, Cone, Frye, Groh, Hume, king, Lean, Levy, Rabe, Rose, Soul, Toms 5 Bowie, Chase, Doyle, Dukes, Duval, Ensor, Essex, Frost, Hubel, Keith, Kersh, Louis, Lynch, Mamet, Morse, Niven, saint, Selby, Spade, Swift, Wayne, White 6 Birney, Butler, Canary, Caruso, Crosby, Geddes, Geffen, Kelley, Lander, Miller, Nelson, Paymer, Rasche, Rudkin, Ruffin, Souter, Storey, Warner, Zucker 7 Beckham, Belasco, Brenner, Carroll, Cassidy, Charvet, Coulier, Diamond, Dinkins, Garrick, Hartman, Hedison, Hockney, Houston, Ignatow, Janssen, Leisure, Manners, Merrick, Packard, Ricardo, Sarnoff, Seville, Thewlis, Trimble 8 Anspaugh, Arquette, Brinkley, Bushnell, Duchovny, Farragut, Faustino, Frizzell, Helfgott, Hemmings, Johansen, McCallum, Naughton, Oistrakh, Opatoshu, Robinson, Selznick, Susskind, Thompson 9 Baltimore, Ben-Gurion, Carradine, Letterman, Rappaport, Schwimmer, Tomlinson 10 Eisenhower, Halberstam, Hasselhoff, McCullough, Strathairn
army commander: 5 Abner
co-anchor: 4 Chet
daughter: 5 Tamar
father: 5 Jesse
grandfather: 4 Obed
great-grandmother: 5 Naomi
instrument: 4 harp
king before ~: 4 Saul
nephew: 5 Amasa
sibling: 4 Ozem 5 Eliab, Ricky 6 Raddai, Shimei 7 Abigail, Shammah, Zeruiah 8 Nethanel
son: 5 Amnon, Ibhar, Nogah 6 Eliada, Nepheg 7 Absalom, Chileab, Elishua, Ithream, Shammua, Solomon 8 Adonijah, Elishama 9 Eliphilet 10 Shephatiah
song of ~: 5 psalm
to Goliath: 3 foe 5 enemy 9 adversary
warrior: 3 Ira
wife: 5 Eglah 6 Abital, Maacah, Michal 7 Abigail, Haggith 9 Bathsheba
David __ Coe: 5 Allan
David __ George: 5 Lloyd
David __-Gurion: 3 Ben
David __ Pierce: 4 Hyde
David __ Roth: 3 Lee
David __ Stiers: 5 Ogden
__ **David:** 4 Camp 5 Magen, Mogen 6 Star of
David Copperfield
author: Charles Dickens
character: 3 Ham 4 Dora, Em'ly, Emma, Heep, Jane, Mell, Rosa, Tipp 5 Agnes, Clara, Crupp, Sophy, Uriah 6 Barkis, Betsey, Daniel, Dartle, Demple, Edward, Mr. Dick, Tiffey 7 Creakle, Crewler, Francis, Jorkins, Lavinia, Markham, Quinion, Spenlow, Wilkins 8 Clarissa, Grainger, Gummidge, Littimer, Micawber, Peggotty, Traddles, Trotwood 9 Murdstone, Uriah Heep, Wickfield 10 Little Em'ly, Rosa Dartle, Steerforth
dog: 3 Jip
David E. __: 6 Kelley
David Lee __: 4 Roth
David-Neel, Alexandra: 6 French 8 explorer
David O. __: 8 Selznick
Davidovich: 6 Lolita
Davidson: 2 Jo 4 Jaye, John
partner: 6 Harley
__ **David Thoreau:** 5 Henry
Davie, Donald: 4 poet 7 British
Davies: 5 Laura 6 Marion 9 Robertson
Davies, Robertson: 6 writer 8 Canadian
work: The Deptford Trilogy
da Vinci Airport
locale: 4 Rome
Da Vinci Code, The (2006 film)
cast: Tom Hanks, Ian McKellen, Audrey Tautou
director: Ron Howard
da Vinci, Leonardo: 6 artist 7 Italian, painter
Davis: 3 Jim, Mac 4 Brad, Eric, Erin, Gail, Glen, Hope, Joan, Judy, Love, Owen, Paul, town 5 Bette, Chili, Geena, Miles, Nancy, Ossie, Patti, Peter, Sammi 6 Adelle, Andrew, Angela, Tyrone 7 Clifton, Kristin, Raymond, Skeeter 9 Jefferson
__-Davis: 4 Ziff
Davis, Bette: 7 actress
film: All About Eve (1950)
All This and Heaven Too (1940)
Bordertown (1935)
The Catered Affair (1956)
The Corn Is Green (1945)
Dangerous (1935, AA)
Dark Victory (1939)
Deception (1946)
Fashions (1934)
The Great Lie (1941)
Hush ... Hush, Sweet Charlotte (1965)
In This Our Life (1942)
It's Love I'm After (1937)
Jezebel (1938, AA)
Juarez (1939)
June Bride (1948)
Kid Galahad (1937)
The Letter (1940)
The Little Foxes (1941)
The Man Who Came to Dinner (1941)
Marked Woman (1937)
Mr. Skeffington (1944)
Now, Voyager (1942)
Of Human Bondage (1934)
Old Acquaintance (1943)
The Old Maid (1939)
Payment on Demand (1951)
The Petrified Forest (1936)
Phone Call From a Stranger (1952)
Pocketful of Miracles (1961)
The Sisters (1938)
The Star (1952)
Three on a Match (1932)
The Virgin Queen (1955)
Watch on the Rhine (1943)
The Whales of August (1987)
What Ever Happened to Baby Jane? (1962)
The Working Man (1933)
Davis, Chili
sport: 8 baseball
Davis Cup
former ~ captain: 4 Ashe
sport: 6 tennis
__ **Davis Eyes:** 5 Bette
Davis, Geena: 7 actress
film: The Accidental Tourist (1988, AA)
Angie (1994)
Beetlejuice (1988)
Cutthroat Island (1995)
Earth Girls Are Easy (1989)
The Fly (1986)
Hero (1992)
A League of Their Own (1992)
Quick Change (1990)
Speechless (1994)
Stuart Little (1999)
Thelma & Louise (1991)
Tootsie (1982)
spouse: Jeff Goldblum, Renny Harlin
Davis, Jefferson org.: 3 CSA
Davis, Jim dog: 4 Odie
__ **Davis Jr.:** 5 Billy, Sammy

DA

Davis Jr., Billy: **6** singer
spouse: Marilyn McCoo
Davis Jr., Sammy: **5** actor **6** singer
film: Johnny Cool (1963)
Ocean's Eleven (1960)
Porgy and Bess (1959)
Robin and the Seven Hoods (1964)
Tap (1989)
song: The Candy Man (1972)
I've Gotta Be Me (1969)
Something's Gotta Give (1955)
What Kind of Fool Am I (1962)
work: Yes I Can
Davis, Mac
song: Baby Don't Get Hooked on Me (1972)
Stop and Smell the Roses (1974)
Davis, Miles: **9** trumpeter
accessory: **4** mute
genre: **4** jazz
spouse: Cicely Tyson
Davison: **5** Bruce
Davis, Ossie: **5** actor
film: Black Girl (1972)
Cotton Comes to Harlem (1970)
Doctor Dolittle (1998)
Do the Right Thing (1989)
Get on the Bus (1996)
Gone Are the Days (1963)
Gordon's War (1973)
spouse: Ruby Dee
TV: Evening Shade
Davis partner: **5** Parke
Davis, Skeeter
song: The End of the World (1963)
I Can't Stay Mad at You (1963)
davit: **5** crane, hoist **7** derrick
Davos: **7** commune
enjoy ~: **3** ski
locale: **11** Switzerland
Davy: **5** Jones **7** Humphry **8** Crockett
Davy, Humphry: **3** Sir **7** British, chemist
Davy Jones' locker: **3** sea **5** ocean
daw: **6** magpie **7** grackle
kin: **3** ani **5** raven
starter: **4** jack
Dawber, Pam: **7** actress
spouse: Mark Harmon
dawdle: **3** lag **4** drag, idle, laze, loaf, loll, poke **5** amble, dally, delay, mosey, stall, tarry, trail **6** linger, loiter, lounge, put off, trifle **7** goof off, saunter **8** footdrag, lallygag, lose time, slack off, straggle **9** poke along, waste time **10** dillydally, fool around, hang around, mess around, wait around
dawdler: **4** poke **5** idler, sloth, snail **7** laggard, lie-abed, lounger, trifler **8** layabout, lingerer, loiterer, slowpoke, slugabed, sluggard **9** latecomer, lazybones
dawdling: **4** poky, slow **5** delay, tardy **6** draggy **7** gradual, impeded, languid **8** dilatory, drawn-out, hesitant, slothful, sluggish **9** leisurely, lethargic, lingering, prolonged, snaillike, unhurried **10** deliberate, protracted
Dawes, Charles: **4** veep **8** Nobelist
Dawkins, Daryl
sport: **10** basketball
dawn: **4** morn, rise **5** begin, birth, light, onset, prime, start, sunup **6** advent, aurora, emerge, origin, outset, unfold **7** genesis, infancy, morning, opening, sunrise **8** cockcrow, daybreak, daylight **9** beginning, emergence, inception, originate, threshold **10** break of day, first light, incipience
dusk to ~: **5** night
goddess: **3** Eos **4** Usha **5** Ushas **6** Aurora
meet the ~: **4** rise, wake **5** arise, awake, waken **6** awaken, wake up
music: **4** alba **6** aubade
name meaning ~: **7** Roxanne
of the ~: **4** eoan
on: **7** occur to
Dawn: **3** Lyn **5** O'Hara, Steel, Wells **6** Fraser, Upshaw
alternative: **3** Joy **4** Ajax **7** Cascade **8** Sunlight **9** Palmolive **10** Electrasol
__ Dawn: **3** Red **4** Zulu **5** Delta
__ Dawn Chong: **3** Rae
dawning: **5** onset, start **6** origin, source **7** genesis
Dawn O'Hara
author: Edna Ferber
Dawn Patrol, The (1938 film)
cast: Errol Flynn, David Niven, Basil Rathbone
dawnward: **4** east
Daws: **6** Butler
Dawson: **3** Len **5** Andre **7** Richard, Rosario
Dawson, Andre: **10** baseballer
Dawson City: **4** city, town
locale: **6** Canada
Dawson Creek: **4** city, town
locale: **6** Canada
road: **5** Alcan
Dawson, Len: **2** QB **11** quarterback
sport: **8** football
Dawson, Richard
spouse: Diana Dors
Dawson's Creek (WB drama)
cast: Katie Holmes (Joey Potter)
Joshua Jackson (Pacey Witter)
James Van Der Beek (Dawson Leery)
Michelle Williams (Jen Lindley)
day: **3** era **4** time **6** period **10** generation
a ~: **7** per diem **9** diurnally
after day: **3** oft **5** often **10** all the time
any ~: **4** anon, soon **8** sometime **10** imminently
before: **3** eve
break of ~: **4** dawn, morn **5** sunup **7** morning, sunrise
call it a ~: **3** end **4** halt, quit, stop **5** cease, close **6** finish, retire, turn in, wind up, wrap up **7** adjourn, break up **8** break off, conclude, finish up, knock off, pack it in **9** terminate
carry the ~: **3** win **7** prevail, succeed, triumph
close of ~: **5** night **6** curfew **7** bedtime **9** nightfall
ender: **3** bed, fly, hop **4** book, care, lily, long, pack, side, star, time, wear **5** break, dream, light, shift **6** flower **7** dreamer
every eighth ~: **5** octan
feast ~: **7** jubilee
field ~: **4** bash **5** binge, fling, revel, spree **6** junket
first part of the ~: **7** morning
forever and a ~: **3** eon **4** aeon, ages **8** long time
holy ~: **5** feast **6** Easter **9** Christmas
in French: **4** jour
in German: **3** tag
in Hebrew: **3** yom
in Italian: **6** giorno
in Latin: **4** diem
in Spanish: **3** día
in this ~ and age: **3** now **4** here **5** today
light: **3** sun
lily: **5** plant **6** flower
make one's ~: **5** elate **6** please
middle of the ~: **4** noon
midmonth ~: **4** ides
night and ~: **7** nonstop **9** endlessly **10** unendingly
not give the time of ~: **3** cut **4** shun, snub **5** spurn **6** ignore, rebuff, slight **8** brush off
of rest: **3** Sab., Sun. **6** Sunday **7** Sabbath **8** vacation
of the week: **3** Fri., Mon., Sat., Sun., Thu., Tue., Wed. **4** Thur., Tues. **5** Thurs.
one: **5** git-go, onset, start **6** origin **9** beginning
one ~: **4** soon **10** eventually
opposite: **5** night **7** evening
rainy ~ fund: **7** nest egg, reserve, savings
Roman calendar ~: **4** ides **5** nones **7** calends
save for rainy ~: **8** salt away
saver: **4** hero
seize the ~: **4** live
starter: **3** hey, may, mid, pay, Sun **4** holy, noon, sick, some, wash, week, work **5** birth, dooms, every
start the ~: **4** rise, wake **5** arise, awake, get up, waken
the other ~: **8** recently
time of ~: **4** dawn, dusk, hour, morn, noon **5** sunup **6** sunset **7** evening, morning, sunrise
to this ~: **5** still **8** hitherto, until now
trip: **5** jaunt **9** excursion
units: **3** hrs. **5** hours
day __: **3** bed, boy, job, man, one, spa **4** camp, care, lily, loan, name, room **5** coach, labor, shift **6** letter, school
day __ day: **5** after
day-__: **4** care, trip **5** by-day, liner, to-day **6** trader
__ day: **3** lay, tag **4** fast, fete, good, high, holy, leap, name, sick, snow, term **5** feast, field, lunar, rainy, solar **6** banner, saint's, school **7** wedding, working
__-day: **3** all, dog, man **4** long **6** degree, latter **7** present
Day: **3** Pat **4** Bill **5** Bobby, Doris **6** Dennis **7** Dorothy, Laraine **8** Clarence
Day __ Day: **5** After
Day-__: **3** Glo
__ Day: **3** Dre, May **4** Flag, Lady **5** Anzac, Arbor, Day by, Earth, Great, Green, Labor, Lucky, Rizal, Union **6** Boxing, Canada, Empire, Julian, Labour, Ladies', Lammas, Muster, School, Woman's **7** Another, Father's, Jackson, Mother's, Pioneer, Twelfth
__-Day: **3** May **4** One-A
__ Day, A: **5** Foggy
__-Day Adventist: **7** Seventh
__ Day Afternoon: **3** Dog
Day After Tomorrow, The (2004 film)
cast: Jake Gyllenhaal, Dennis Quaid, Sela Ward
Dayan: **5** Moshe
__ day and age: **4** this **6** in this
__ day at a time: **3** one
__ Day at Black Rock: **3** Bad
Da Ya Think I'm Sexy? (1978 song)
artist: Rod Stewart
Day at the Races, A (1937 film)
cast: Margaret Dumont, Allan Jones, Chico Marx, Groucho Marx, Harpo Marx
daybed: **4** sofa **5** couch, futon **6** chaise **7** seating **9** davenport
Day, Bobby
song: Rock-in Robin (1958)
daybook: **3** log **5** diary **6** ledger **7** Filofax, journal **8** calendar
daybreak: **4** dawn, morn **5** light, prime, sunup **6** aurora **7** morning, sunrise **8** cockcrow **10** first light
Day by Day
author: Robert Lowell
day-care candidate: **3** kid, tot **4** tike, tyke **5** child
Day, Clarence: **6** writer
work: Life With Father
Life With Mother
__-day cover: **5** first
Day, Dennis employer: Jack Benny
Day, Doris: **6** singer **7** actress
film: Billy Rose's Jumbo (1962)
Calamity Jane (1953)
The Glass Bottom Boat (1966)
Love Me or Leave Me (1955)
Lover Come Back (1961)
The Man Who Knew Too Much (1956)
Midnight Lace (1960)
The Pajama Game (1957)
Pillow Talk (1959)
Please Don't Eat the Daisies (1960)
Send Me No Flowers (1964)
Teacher's Pet (1958)
The Thrill of It All (1963)
The Tunnel of Love (1958)
Young at Heart (1954)
Young Man With a Horn (1950)
song: Again (1949)
Everybody Loves a Lover (1958)
Que Sera, Sera (1956)
daydream: **4** hope, moon, wish **5** fancy **6** ideate, revery, trance, vision **7** fantasy, figment, imagine, picture, reverie **8** delusion, illusion, space out **9** fantasize, imagining **10** woolgather
Daydream (1966 song)
artist: Lovin' Spoonful
Daydream Believer (song)
artist: Monkees, Anne Murray
daydreamer: **5** Mitty **8** escapist
Daydreamin' (1998 song)
artist: Tatyana Ali

Day Dreaming (1972 song)
artist: Aretha Franklin
daydreamy: 6 vacant **7** unaware, wistful **8** mindless **9** unmindful
dayfly: 3 bug **6** insect
Day for Night (1973 film)
cast: Jean-Pierre Aumont, Jacqueline Bisset
director: François Truffaut
__ Day George: 5 Lynda
day in __: 5 court
Day in the __, A: 4 Life **7** Country
Day in the Country, A (1946 film)
director: Jean Renoir
Day, Laraine: 7 actress
spouse: Leo Durocher
Day Lewis: 5 Cecil **6** Daniel
Day Lewis, Cecil: 4 poet **5** Irish **7** British **8** laureate
colleague: W.H. Auden, Stephen Spender
son: Daniel
Day Lewis, Daniel: 5 actor
film: The Age of Innocence (1993)
Gangs of New York (2002)
In the Name of the Father (1993)
The Last of the Mohicans (1992)
My Beautiful Laundrette (1985)
My Left Foot (1989, AA)
There Will Be Blood (2007, AA)
daylight: 4 dawn **5** light, sunup **6** aurora **7** morning, sunrise **8** cockcrow, sunshine
in broad ~: 6 openly
let ~ in: 6 expose, reveal **8** simplify
see ~: 7 realize
daylight-__ time: 6 saving
daylights, living: 4 wits
__ Daylights, The: 6 Living
__ Daylight Time: 7 Central, Eastern, Pacific **8** Mountain
Dayne, Taylor
song: Don't Rush Me (1988)
I'll Always Love You (1988)
I'll Be Your Shelter (1990)
Love Will Lead You Back (1990)
Prove Your Love (1988)
Tell It to My Heart (1987)
With Every Beat of My Heart (1989)
__ day now: 3 any
Day-O (1957 song)
artist: Harry Belafonte
__ Day O'Connor: 6 Sandra
day of __: 4 rest
Day of __: 6 Infamy **9** Atonement
Day of Atonement
author: Faye Kellerman
Day of Doom, The
author: Michael Wigglesworth
Day of the Locust
author: Nathanael West
Day of the Triffids, The
author: John Wyndham
Day, Pat: 6 jockey
Dayquil
alternative: ***see*** cold remedy
days: 4 life **8** lifetime
from ~ of yore: 5 olden
in olden ~: 3 ago **4** once, past, then **6** before **7** earlier, long ago, time was, way back **8** back when, formerly, years ago **9** at one time, in the past **10** heretofore, previously
off: 7 holiday **8** vacation
old ~: 3 eld **4** past, yore **7** earlier, history, long ago **8** back when **9** antiquity, yesterday **10** yesteryear
one of these ~: 4 anon, soon **9** presently
seven ~: 4 week
starter: 4 nowa
these ~: 3 now **6** lately
days __: 5 of old; on end
__ days: 3 dog **5** olden, salad
__ Days: 3 Old **4** Last **5** Ember, End of, Glory, Happy, Radio **6** School
__-day Saint: 6 Latter
__ Days and Mondays: 5 Rainy
Days and Nights of Molly __, The: 4 Dodd
__ Days Are Here Again: 5 Happy
__ Days a Week: 5 Eight
day's end: 5 night **7** evening **9** nightfall
__ Days in May: 5 Seven
Days Inn: 5 motel
alternative: ***see*** motel
__ Day's Journey into Night: 4 Long
__ Day's Night: 5 A Hard
days of __: 4 yore **5** grace
Days of Grace
author: Arthur Ashe
Days of Our Lives (NBC): 4 soap **9** soap opera
Emmy winner: 5 Carey
town: 5 Salem
__ Days of Pompeii, The: 4 Last
__ Days of the Condor: 5 Three
Days of Thunder (1990 film)
cast: Tom Cruise, Robert Duvall, Nicole Kidman, Randy Quaid
director: Tony Scott
Days of Wine and Roses: 4 film, song
artist: Henry Mancini, Andy Williams
cast: Jack Lemmon, Lee Remick
dayspring: 7 morning
__ Days Seven Nights: 3 Six
daystar: 3 sun
Days Without End
author: Eugene O'Neill
__ days' wonder: 4 nine
__ Day, The: 6 Eighth, Wicked **7** Longest
Day the Earth Stood Still, The (1951 film)
cast: Sam Jaffe, Patricia Neal, Michael Rennie
composer: Bernard Herrmann
director: Robert Wise
robot: 4 Gort
Day the Earth Stood Still, The (2008 film)
cast: Kathy Bates, Jennifer Connelly, Keanu Reeves
Day the World Went Away, The (1999 song)
artist: Nine Inch Nails
__ day this has been...: 5 What a
day-to-day: 5 usual **6** normal **7** diurnal, mundane **9** quotidian
Dayton: 4 city, town
city near ~: 4 Lima **5** Xenia
locale: 4 Ohio
Daytona Beach: 4 city, town
locale: 7 Florida
day-tripper: 7 tourist **10** vacationer
Day Tripper (1965 song)
artist: Beatles
__-Day vitamins: 4 One-a
__-Day War: 3 Six
__ Day Will Come: 3 Our
Day Without Rain, A (2000 song)
artist: Enya
__ Day Women: 5 Rainy
__-day wonder: 4 nine
Dazai Osamu: 6 writer **8** Japanese
daze: 3 fog **4** blur, jolt, stun **5** shock, whirl **6** baffle, bemuse, muddle, stupor, trance **7** astound, confuse, nonplus, stupefy **8** astonish, befuddle, bewilder, confound, surprise **9** confusion
in a ~: 4 asea **5** at sea **7** unaware **9** perplexed
__ daze: 3 in a
dazed: 4 numb **5** blank, dizzy, silly, spacy, tipsy **6** glassy, groggy, in a fog, spacey, stupid **7** fuddled, reeling **10** speechless
__-Dazs: 6 Häagen
__ d'Azur: 4 Cote
dazzle: 3 awe **4** daze **5** amaze, blind, éclat, flash, glare, shine **6** luster **7** bewitch, charism, impress, sparkle, stupefy **8** astonish, bowl over, charisma, entrance, radiance, radiancy, splendor, surprise **9** captivate, electrify, fascinate, hypnotize, overwhelm
__-dazzle: 6 razzle
Dazzle
author: Judith Krantz
dazzler: 6 eyeful, vision
dazzling: 3 lit **5** aglow, shiny **6** ablaze, bright, flashy, lovely, ornate **7** beaming, fulgent, lambent, radiant, shining **8** luminous, lustrous, meteoric **9** arresting, brilliant, ravishing, refulgent, sparkling **10** glittering
light: 5 glare
see also wonderful
Dazzy: 5 Vance
D.B.: 7 Sweeney
DBA name: 5 alias
DC
agent: 4 G-man, T-man
airport: 6 Dulles, Reagan **8** National
bank name: 5 Riggs
body: 3 Sen., USS **4** Cong. **6** Senate **8** Congress
budget watchdog: 3 GAO
campus: 3 GWU
clock setting: 3 EDT, EST
dept.: 3 Agr.
figure: 3 rep., sen. **4** pres.
group: 3 NSC
gun lobby: 3 NRA
hostess: 5 Mesta
hundred: 6 Senate
hush-hush ~ grp.: 3 NSA
initials: 3 GOP
lobby: 3 PAC
mortgage insurers: 3 FHA
network: 3 NPR
part of ~: 4 Dist. **8** Columbia, District
party: 3 Dem., Rep.
publisher: 3 GPO
record-keeping org.: 3 GSA
school: 6 Howard **10** Georgetown
stadium: 3 RFK
suburb: 5 Olney
subway: 5 Metro
tax org.: 3 IRS
type: 3 pol
see also Washington D.C.
D.C. Cab (1983 film)
cast: Adam Baldwin, Irene Cara, Mr. T
DCM: 5 medal
DD: 6 degree
institution: 3 sem. **8** seminary
D-Day
beach: 4 Gold, Juno, Utah **5** Omaha, Sword
commander: 3 DDE, Ike **10** Eisenhower
craft: 3 LCT, LST
time: 4 June **5** H Hour
town: 4 Caen, St. Lô
DDE: 3 gen., Ike **4** pres. **7** general **9** president
alma mater: 4 USMA
command: 4 NATO **5** SHAEF
milieu: 3 ETO
opponent: 3 AES
predecessor: 3 HST
successor: 3 JFK
veep: 3 RMN
see also Dwight D. Eisenhower
DDS: 6 degree **7** dentist
org.: 3 ADA
relative: 3 DMD
DDT: 9 herbicide
DDT-banning org.: 3 EPA
de __: 4 fide, jure, luxe, novo, Sade, trop **5** facto, plano, règle **6** gratia **7** rigueur
De __, IL: 4 Kalb
De __ Poetica: 4 Arte
DE
see Delaware
DEA
agent: 3 Fed **4** narc, nark **5** narco
department: 7 Justice
part of ~: 4 Drug **6** Agency
deacon: 4 rank **5** title **6** clergy, cleric, doctor, warden **7** falsify **8** minister **9** clergyman
Deacon: 5 Jones **7** Richard
deaconess: 6 cleric
deactivate: 6 defuse, defuze
__ de Açúcar: 3 Pao
dead: 3 out **5** kaput, spent, tired **7** sterile **8** lifeless, obsolete, outmoded **9** exanimate, insensate **10** broken-down, insentient, lackluster, motionless
air: 5 quiet **7** silence
end: 7 impasse **8** cul-de-sac **10** blind alley, standstill
ender: 3 eye, pan **4** beat, bolt, fall, head, line, lock, wood **5** light
heat: 3 tie **4** draw
knock ~: 5 amuse **6** divert, regale **8** enthrall **9** entertain
letter: 5 nixie
ringer: 4 twin **5** image, match **6** double **7** picture **8** likeness **9** duplicate, facsimile, identical, look-alike **10** equivalent
set: 5 rigid **8** resolute, stalwart **9** immovable, obstinate **10** inexorable, purposeful, relentless, unwavering, unyielding
stop: 10 standstill
weight: 4 load, onus **10** impediment
dead __: 3 air, end, pan, run, set **4** bolt, drop, duck, heat, lift, load,

mail, slow, spot, time 5 metal, water 6 center, letter, ringer, weight
dead __ doornail: 3 as a
Dead: 3 sea
Dead __: 4 Calm, Cert
Dead __ Kids: 3 End
Dead __ Scrolls: 3 Sea
Dead Again (1991 film)
  cast: Kenneth Branagh, Andy Garcia, Derek Jacobi
  director: Kenneth Branagh
deadbeat: 3 bum 4 ower 5 leech, loser 6 beggar, debtor, loafer, sponge 7 moocher 8 parasite 10 freeloader
deadbolt: 4 lock
  release a ~: 5 unbar
Dead Calm (1989 film)
  cast: Nicole Kidman, Sam Neill, Billy Zane
dead-center: 6 middle
  hit ~: 4 nail
Dead Cert
  author: Dick Francis
deaden: 4 damp, dull, mute, numb, stun 5 abate, blunt, quiet 6 benumb, dampen, darken, muffle, obtund, reduce, soften, stifle, subdue 7 cushion, repress, silence 8 diminish, suppress, tone down 9 alleviate 10 soundproof
dead-end: 5 blind, stimy, stymy 6 stymie
Dead End (1937 film)
  cast: Humphrey Bogart, Joel McCrea, Sylvia Sidney
  director: William Wyler
deadened: 3 low 4 numb 5 bated, faint, muted, piano, quiet 7 muffled 9 unfeeling 10 anesthetic, insentient
deadening: 8 narcotic 9 soporific 10 anesthetic
deadeye: 7 shooter 8 marksman
  prowess: 3 aim
Deadeye Dick
  author: Kurt Vonnegut Jr.
__ Dead Gorgeous: 4 Drop
deadhead: 3 oaf 4 clod 6 lummox
dead-level: 6 candid, honest 7 sincere
Deadlier Than the __: 4 Male
deadline: 3 end 5 limit 6 curfew, cutoff 7 due date 8 pressure, zero hour
  after the ~: 4 late 5 tardy
  before the ~: 5 early 6 in time, on time
deadlock: 3 jam, tie 4 halt 5 tie up 6 logjam 7 impasse 8 standoff 9 stalemate 10 difficulty, standstill
deadlocked: 4 even 6 static
__ deadly sins: 5 seven
__ Deadly Sin, The: 5 First, Third 6 Fourth, Second
Dead Man's Curve (1964 song)
  artist: Jan & Dean
dead man's hand pair: 4 aces 6 eights
Dead Man's Walk
  author: Larry McMurtry
Dead Man Walking (1995 film)
  cast: Sean Penn, Susan Sarandon
  director: Tim Robbins
  role: 3 nun
Dead Men Don't Wear Plaid (1982 film)
  cast: Steve Martin, Carl Reiner, Rachel Ward
  director: Carl Reiner
dead-on: 4 nice 5 exact, right 7 correct, exactly, perfect 8 specific 9 correctly, perfectly, precisely 10 unmistaken
__ Dead or Alive: 6 Wanted
deadpan: 5 blank, sober, staid, stony 6 solemn, somber, stoney, vacant, wooden 7 serious 9 humorless, unamusing 10 no-nonsense, unhumorous
Dead Poets Society (1989 film)
  cast: Ethan Hawke, Robin Williams
  director: Peter Weir
Dead Pool, The (1988 film)
  cast: Patricia Clarkson, Clint Eastwood, Evan C. Kim, Liam Neeson
Dead Sea: 4 lake
  feeder: 6 Jordan
  kingdom: 4 Edom, Moab
  locale: 6 Israel, Jordan
  region: 6 Canaan
Dead Sea Scrolls
  writer: 6 Essene
Dead Skunk (1973 song)
  artist: Loudon Wainwright III
Dead Souls
  author: Nikolai Gogol
dead-tired: 4 beat 5 all in 6 bushed 7 drained, worn out 8 fatigued 9 exhausted 10 knocked out
dead to __: 6 rights
Dead Toreador, The
  painter: Édouard Manet
Deadwood: 4 city, town
  locale: 4 S. Dak.
Dead Zone, The: 5 novel
  author: Stephen King
  topic: 3 ESP
deaf: 7 unaware 8 heedless 9 insensate, oblivious, unhearing, unheeding 10 regardless, unyielding
  turn a ~ ear to: 4 deny 5 scorn 6 refuse, slight
__-deaf: 4 tone
deafen: 5 blast 7 thunder 9 overwhelm
deafening: 4 loud 5 forte, noisy 6 shrill 7 blaring, blatant, booming, jarring, rackety, raucous, reboant, roaring 8 crashing, piercing, plangent, rumbling, sonorous, strident, terrific, turned up 9 big-voiced, clamorous, screaming 10 boisterous, resounding, stentorian, strepitous, thundering, thunderous, tremendous, uproarious, vociferant, vociferous
deafness, tone: 6 asonia
deal: 3 buy 4 mete, pact, sale, swap, swop 5 allot, share, trade 6 accord, amount, assign, barter, bestow, bicker, buyout, dicker, extent, merger, ration, render 7 bargain, compact, deliver, dish out, divvy up, dole out, give out, good buy, hand out, inflict, mete out, pass out, portion, project, smuggle, traffic 8 contract, covenant, disburse, dispense, disperse, exchange, fork over, quantity 9 agreement, apportion, indenture, negotiate 10 administer, buy and sell, compromise, distribute, do business, horse trade, settlement
  a blow: 5 lay to 6 damage, strike
  big ~: 3 ado 4 fuss, to-do 5 hoo-ha
  cashless ~: 4 swap, swop 5 trade
  close the ~: 3 ice 4 sell 5 shake
  cut a ~: 5 agree 9 acquiesce, negotiate
  ender: 4 fish 5 maker
  from the bottom: 5 cheat 7 swindle
  good ~: 3 lot 4 a lot, heap, lots, mass, pile 5 no end, sight, stack, steal 6 plenty 7 bargain
  in: 3 buy 4 sell 5 carry, stock, trade 6 handle 7 traffic 8 exchange, purchase 10 distribute
  make a ~: 4 sell 7 mediate 8 transact 9 arbitrate, negotiate 10 compromise
  maker: 3 rep 5 agent
  no ~: 3 nah, naw, nay, nix, non 4 nein, nope, nyet, uh-uh 5 I won't, ixnay, never 7 I refuse 8 forget it, I will not, negative, negatory 9 fat chance, I think not 10 count me out, not a chance, thumbs down
  no big ~: 6 trifle 10 immaterial
  out: 4 give, mete 5 issue 6 divide, parcel, ration 7 divvy up, inflict 8 disburse, dispense 10 distribute
  partner: 5 wheel
  preceder: 4 ante
  refuse to ~ with: 4 shun, snub 5 spurn 6 ignore, rebuff, reject 7 disavow, disdain, neglect, scoff at 8 turn down
  shady ~: 4 scam 5 cheat 6 con job, ripoff 7 swindle 9 injustice 10 corruption
  with: 4 cope, meet 5 cover, field, solve, treat 6 accept, attack, handle, join in, manage, reckon, tackle, take on 7 concern, control, embrace, grapple, process, touch on 8 consider, face up to, take part 9 get to know, partake of, patronize, touch upon 10 meet head on, speak about, take care of
deal __: 4 me in, with
__ deal: 3 big, raw 4 done 6 square 7 one-shot, package
__ deal!: 3 Big 4 It's a 5 No big
Deal __ Deal: 4 or No
Deal!: 4 fine, okay 6 agreed
__ Deal: 3 New, Raw 4 Fair
de Alarcón: 5 Pedro
dealer: 4 bank 5 owner 6 banker, broker, grocer, jobber, seller, trader, vender, vendor 8 marketer, merchant, retailer 10 franchisee, wholesaler
  concern: 4 ante, deck 5 stock
  device: 4 shoe
  directive: 6 ante up
  employer: 6 casino
  headwear: 5 visor, vizor
  illegal ~: 5 fence
  nemesis: 4 narc, nark
  offering: 3 cut 5 lease 6 rebate
  price: 3 net
  take-back: 4 repo
__-dealer: 7 wheeler
__ Dealer: 3 New 5 Plain
dealer's __: 6 choice
dealing: 8 business, exchange
  dirty ~: 5 guile 6 deceit
__ dealing: 5 plain
__-dealing: 6 double
dealings: 5 trade 6 doings 7 affairs, matters, traffic 8 business, commerce 9 relations
  have ~: 4 know 5 truck
dealmaker: 6 closer 10 negotiator
Deal or No Deal (NBC game)
  host: Howie Mandel
dealt
  hand one is ~: 3 lot 4 life
  not ~ with: 5 unmet
dean: 4 head, king 5 doyen 6 cleric, leader 8 educator, minister 9 authority, principal 10 headmaster
Dean: 4 Cain, John, Rusk 5 Daffy, Dizzy, Estus, James, Jimmy, Jones, Loren 6 Jagger, Koontz, Martin 7 Acheson, Riesner 8 Torrence 9 Stockwell
  singing partner: 3 Jan
Dean __: 6 Witter
__ Dean Anderson: 7 Richard
Dean, Dizzy: 6 hurler 7 pitcher 8 Cardinal
Deane: 5 Beman, Silas
__ Dean Foster: 4 Alan
__ Dean Howells: 7 William
Dean, James: 4 idol 5 actor
  film: East of Eden (1955)
    Giant (1956)
    Rebel Without a Cause (1955)
  persona: 5 rebel
  role: 3 Cal 4 Jett, Rink
Dean, Jimmy
  song: Big Bad John (1961)
Deanna: 4 Troi 6 Durbin
Dean's December, The
  author: Saul Bellow
dean's list fig.: 3 GPA
__ Dean Stanton: 5 Harry
dear: 4 high 5 close, loved, pricy, steep, stiff 6 costly, loving, pricey, prized 7 pet name, sincere 8 adorable, esteemed, intimate, precious, valuable 9 cherished, expensive, heartfelt, important, priceless, sumptuous, treasured 10 at a premium, exorbitant, high-priced, overpriced
  hold ~: 4 like, love 5 adore, go for, prize, value 6 esteem, revere 7 care for, cherish, idolize, worship 8 remember, treasure 9 care about
  in French: 4 cher
  in Italian: 4 cara
  in Spanish: 4 caro
  me: 4 alas, egad, gosh, my my 5 alack, egads, golly 7 heavens, my stars 10 I do declare, my goodness
  partner: 4 near
  see also sweetheart
Dear __: 3 Sir 4 Abby, Mama, Sirs
Dear __ and Gentle People: 6 Hearts
Dear __ or Madam...: 3 Sir
__, Dear: 3 Yes
Dearborn: 4 city, town
  locale: 8 Michigan
__ Dearborn: 4 Fort

Dear Brutus
author: James M. Barrie
Dearden: 5 Basil, James
__ Dearest: 6 Mommie
Dearest Enemy: 7 musical
composer: Lorenz Hart, Richard Rodgers
Dear Heart (1964 song)
artist: Andy Williams
Dearie: 7 Blossom
Dear Lady Twist (1962 song)
artist: Gary U.S. Bonds
Dear Mama (1995 song)
artist: Tupac
dear old __: 3 dad
dearth: 4 lack, need, want 6 famine 7 absence, paucity, poverty 8 exiguity, scarcity, shortage, sparsity 9 scantness 10 deficiency, inadequacy, meagerness
Death __: 4 Wish 6 Valley
__ Death: 4 Ase's
Death Becomes Her (1992 film)
cast: Goldie Hawn, Isabella Rossellini, Meryl Streep, Bruce Willis
director: Robert Zemeckis
Death be not proud
poet: John Donne
Death Be Not Proud
author: John Gunther
Death Comes for the Archbishop
author: Willa Cather
Death in the Afternoon
author: Ernest Hemingway
Death in the Family, A
author: James Agee
Death in Venice
author: Thomas Mann
Death Kit
author: Susan Sontag
Death of a Salesman: 4 play
author: Arthur Miller
character: 3 Ben 4 Biff 5 Happy, Linda, Loman, Willy 6 Howard, Wagner 7 Bernard, Charley 8 Uncle Ben
Death of Bessie Smith, The
author: Edward Albee
Death of Ivan Ilyich, The
author: Leo Tolstoy
Death of the Hired Man, The
author: Robert Frost
Death on the Nile
author: Agatha Christie
__-death overtime: 6 sudden
Death to Smoochy (2002 film)
cast: Danny DeVito, Catherine Keener, Edward Norton, Robin Williams
director: Danny DeVito
Deathtrap: 4 film, play
author: Ira Levin
cast: Michael Caine, Dyan Cannon, Christopher Reeve, Irene Worth
character: 4 Myra 5 Bruhl, Helga 6 Sidney
director: Sidney Lumet
Death Valley: 4 park 6 desert
locale: 6 Nevada 10 California
Death Valley Days (TV western)
host: Stanley Andrews, Ronald Reagan, Robert Taylor, Dale Robertson
Death Wish (1974 film)
cast: Charles Bronson, Hope Lange

__ d'eau: 4 Jeux 7 château
debacle: 3 dud 4 blow, bomb, bust, flop, loss, rout, ruin 5 havoc, smash, wreck 6 defeat, fiasco, mishap, turkey 7 blunder, failure, misstep, stumble, washout 8 casualty, collapse, disaster, downfall 9 breakdown, cataclysm, ruination, trouncing 10 misfortune
Debacle
author: Émile Zola
De Bakey: 7 Michael
__ de ballet: 5 corps 6 maître
__ de banane: 5 crème
debar: 3 ban, nix 4 veto 5 eject 6 abjure, enjoin, except, forbid, hinder, punish, reject 7 exclude, keep out, prevent, shut off, shut out, suspend 8 disallow, leave out, preclude, prohibit 9 blackball, foreclose, interdict, proscribe
debark: 4 land 6 alight, get off 8 go ashore
debarment: 9 exception, exclusion, expulsion
debase: 4 ruin, sink, soil, warp 5 dirty, lower, shame, spoil, stain, taint 6 crud up, defile, demean, humble, impair, insult, reduce, vilify, weaken 7 cheapen, corrupt, degrade, deprave, depress, devalue, pollute, profane, put down, subvert, vitiate 8 disgrace, dishonor, take down 9 devaluate, humiliate, shoot down, undermine 10 adulterate
oneself: 6 grovel
debased: 4 vile 6 impure, wicked 7 ashamed, bestial, corrupt 8 degraded, maculate
debasement: 5 abuse 8 disgrace 9 decadence, depravity, vitiation 10 corruption, defilement, degeneracy
debatable: 4 iffy, moot, open 6 chancy 7 dubious 8 arguable, doubtful, forensic 9 in dispute, uncertain, undecided, unsettled 10 ambivalent, borderline, disputable, touch and go
__ de bataille: 6 cheval
debate: 4 feud 5 argue, fight, forum, study 6 oppose, ponder, reason, refute, speech 7 contest, discuss, dispute, hash out, polemic 8 argument, consider, hash over, polemics, question 9 bat around, bump heads, lock horns, negotiate, pro and con, sweat over, thrash out 10 contention, controvert, deliberate, discussion, kick around, toss around, war of words
answer in a ~: 5 rebut
open to ~: 4 moot
side: 3 con, for, pro 4 anti
debater: 6 arguer 8 rebutter 9 disputant
Debbe: 7 Dunning
Debbi: 6 Fields, Morgan
Debbie: 5 Allen, Harry, Meyer 6 Gibson 8 Reynolds
daughter: 6 Carrie
Debby: 5 Boone
de Beauvoir: 6 Simone
de bene __: 4 esse
debenture: 3 IOU 4 bond, debt
de Bergerac: 6 Cyrano
Debi: 5 Mazar 6 Thomas

__-de-biche: 4 pied
debilitate: 3 sag, sap 4 flag, jade, tire, wane 5 blunt, drain, weary 6 impair, reduce, shrink, soften, weaken 7 deplete, exhaust, fatigue, tire out, vitiate, wear out 8 enervate, enfeeble 9 attenuate, extenuate, prostrate, undermine 10 demoralize, devitalize
debilitated: 3 low 4 puny, sick, weak 5 frail, spent, unfit, wimpy 6 anemic, atonic, effete, feeble, flabby, flimsy, infirm 7 anaemic, fragile, run-down, wimpish 8 delicate, helpless, pithless 9 faltering, lethargic, nerveless, powerless, unhealthy 10 vulnerable
debility: 6 anemia 7 anaemia, fatigue, frailty, malaise 8 puniness, weakness 9 fragility, infirmity 10 feebleness, infirmness, unwellness
debit: 4 loss 7 expense 9 liability
partner: 6 credit
debit __: 4 card
debits-and-credits book: 6 ledger
__-de-boeuf: 4 oeil
debonair: 3 gay 5 suave 6 breezy, jaunty, rakish, urbane 7 dashing, elegant, refined 8 charming, gracious, polished 9 courteous, lightsome
debone: 5 filet 6 fillet
De Bont, Jan film of 1994: 5 Speed
Deborah: 3 Cox 4 Kerr 5 Harry 6 Raffin, Walley 8 Norville
dancing partner: 3 Yul
__ de Boulogne: 4 Bois
__ de bourrée: 3 pas
Debra: 5 Paget 6 Winger 7 Messing
Debrah: 9 Farentino
Debralee: 5 Scott
debris: 4 chad, junk 5 chaff, dregs, dross, offal, ruins, scree, trash, waste, wreck 6 jetsam, jetsom, litter, refuse, rubble, shards, sherds 7 flotsam, garbage, rejects, rubbish 8 detritus, leftover, sediment, wreckage 9 driftwood
nautical ~: 6 jetsam, jetsom 7 flotsam
rocky ~: 5 scree, talus
de Broglie, Louis: 6 French 8 Nobelist 9 physicist
de Brunhoff: 4 Jean
Debs: 6 Eugene
debt: 3 IOU, tab 4 bill, hock, loan, loss, mtge. 5 score 6 arrear, bar tab, marker, red ink 7 arrears, poverty 8 mortgage 9 arrearage, debenture, liability, reckoning 10 obligation
be in ~: 3 owe
holder: 6 lienor
home buyer's ~: 4 mtge. 8 mortgage
in ~: 5 owing 6 behind 9 insolvent, mortgaged 10 straitened
marker: 3 IOU 4 chit
one in ~: 4 ower 6 lienee
recipient: 5 payee 8 creditor
satisfy a ~: 3 pay 5 pay up, repay 6 settle 9 discharge
security: 4 lien
debtee: 6 lienor 8 creditor
debt of __: 5 honor

Debt of Honor
author: Tom Clancy
debug: 3 fix 6 repair, revise 7 correct, rectify 8 overhaul
debunk: 6 expose 7 deflate, explode, flatten, lampoon 8 puncture, ridicule 9 disparage, shoot down
DeBurgh: 5 Chris
DeBusschere, Dave: 8 hoopster
Debussy, Claude: 6 French 8 composer
contemporary: 5 Faure, Satie
piece: 5 étude
work: Clair de lune
Jeux
Pelléas et Mélisande
Prelude to l'après-midi d'un faune
Vingt 5 La Mer
debut: 3 bow 4 rise 5 intro 6 arrive 7 baptism, kickoff 8 premiere 9 coming out 10 appearance, incipience, initiation
debutante: 4 girl, lass 5 belle
Debutante Ball, The
author: Beth Henley
dec-
halved: 4 pent-
Dec.: 2 mo.
day: 4 Xmas
predecessor: 3 Nov.
successor: 3 Jan.
see also December
DEC 1970s computer: 3 VAX
deca-: 3 ten
__ de cacao: 5 crème
__ de cachet: 6 lettre
decade: 3 ten 8 ten years
fraction: 3 one 4 year
__ decade: 5 mauve
decadence: 5 lapse 6 excess 7 decline 9 downgrade 10 corruption, debasement, degeneracy, devolution, regression, sensuality, sybaritism
decadent: 6 effete 11 fin de siècle
decaf: 8 beverage
brand: 5 Sanka
__ de café: 5 tasse
decal: 5 label 6 iron-on
__ de Calais: 3 Pas
Decalogue verb: 5 shalt
Decameron
author: Giovanni Boccaccio
decamp: 2 go 3 fly, run 4 bolt, exit, flee, quit 5 break, elope, leave, scram, split 6 beat it, bug out, depart, desert, escape, get out, go away, pack up, retire 7 abscond, go hurry, go south, head out, make off, pull out, retreat, ride off, run away, take off, vamoose 8 clear out, evacuate, fugitate, hightail, march off, run for it, shove off 9 bundle off, disappear, skedaddle 10 fly the coop, hightail it, hit the road
__-de-camp: 3 aid 4 aide
De Camp: 8 Rosemary
decampment: 7 getaway 9 departure, egression
De Camptown Races
composer: Stephen Foster
word: 6 doo-dah
decant: 4 pour 5 empty 7 draw off, pour out 8 rebottle

decanter: **5** cruet **6** bottle, carafe, flagon, vessel **7** pitcher
De Carlo, Yvonne: **7** actress
TV: The Munsters
__ de cassis: **5** crème
decathlete: **6** Jenner, Thorpe, Toomey **7** Johnson, Mathias
decathlon: **5** sport
event: **3** run **6** discus, hurdle, sprint **7** javelin, shot-put **8** high jump, long jump **9** pole vault
Decatur: **4** city, town
locale: **7** Alabama **8** Illinois
decay: **3** eat, ebb, rot **4** fade, fail, ruin, rust, sink, slip, turn, wane, wear **5** erode, go bad, slide, slump, spoil, taint, waste **6** blight, fading, molder, perish, weaken, wither **7** atrophy, compost, corrode, crumble, decline, dwindle, entropy, failing, go stale, putrefy, shrivel **8** collapse, decrease, downfall, go to seed, spoilage, stagnate, wear away **9** aggravate, break down, corrosion, crumbling, decompose, withering **10** corruption, degenerate, depreciate, exacerbate, impairment, retrogress, spoliation
sign of ~: **4** rust
__ decay: **5** tooth
decayed: **3** bad, old **4** worn **5** musty, rusty, seedy, stale **6** rotten, shabby **7** carious, squalid, unclean **8** overripe **10** malodorous
Deccan Plateau region: **6** Kanara
deceit: **3** art, lie **4** cant, hoax, ruse, sham, tale, wile **5** bluff, cheat, craft, feint, fraud, guile, lying, spoof, trick **6** fakery, humbug **7** cunning, fallacy, falsity, gimmick, slyness, snow job, swindle **8** artifice, bad faith, cheating, flimflam, foxiness, pretense, trickery, wiliness **9** chicanery, dirty pool, dirty work, duplicity, falsehood, falseness, fourberie, hypocrisy, imposture, invention, treachery, two-timing, whitewash **10** craftiness, defrauding, dishonesty, inveracity, subterfuge
deceitful: **3** sly **4** foxy, wily **5** dirty, false, lying, slick, snaky **6** artful, crafty, hollow, rotten, shifty, sneaky, tricky **7** crooked, cunning, devious, elusive, elusory, evasive, furtive, knavish, roguish, unloyal **8** delusive, delusory, forsworn, guileful, illusive, illusory, scheming, spurious, stealthy, two-faced **9** beguiling, designing, dishonest, faithless, insidious, insincere, underhand **10** fallacious, fraudulent, mendacious, misleading, unfaithful, unreliable, untruthful
deceivable: **4** easy, naif **5** naive
deceive: **2** do **3** con, fox, lie **4** bilk, burn, dupe, fool, gull, have, hoax, hoke, hook, jive, scam, sell, snow, take, trap **5** blind, bluff, cheat, cozen, hocus, lie to, put on, sneak, spoof, trick **6** betray, delude, entrap, fleece, lead on, outwit, suck in, take in **7** beguile, buffalo, defraud, ensnare, insnare, mislead, pretend, sell out, swindle, two-time **8** flimflam, hoodwink, outsmart, pettifog, simulate, throw off **9** bamboozle, disinform, four-flush, misinform, victimize **10** run a game on
deceived: **5** led on **9** misguided
deceiver: **4** liar **5** cheat, fraud, knave, rogue **7** traitor **9** hypocrite
decelerate: **4** slow **5** brake **6** retard, slow up **8** slow down **9** lose speed
December: **5** month
birthstone: **9** turquoise
current: **6** El Niño
day: **4** Xmas **9** Christmas
flyer: **8** reindeer
follower: **3** Jan. **7** January
January to ~: **4** year
like a ~ day: **4** cold **5** nippy **6** frosty
preceder: **3** Nov. **8** November
sign: **4** Goat **6** Archer **9** Capricorn
song: **4** Noel **5** carol
sound: **6** hohoho
temp: **5** Santa
December 13: **4** ides
December 1963 (1976 song)
artist: Four Seasons
December 5: **5** nones
December Bride (CBS sitcom)
cast: Spring Byington (Lily Ruskin)
décembre: **4** mois **5** month **6** French
janvier to ~: **5** année
preceder: **8** novembre
decency: **5** honor **6** ethics **7** dignity, modesty, probity **8** fairness, goodness, kindness, morality, niceties **9** etiquette, good faith, propriety, rectitude
decennial event: **6** census
decent: **3** apt, fit **4** clad, fair, good, just, kind, nice, okay, tidy **5** ample, clean, moral, right, solid **6** chaste, garbed, gentle, honest, kindly, polite, proper, seemly, square, tender, worthy **7** clement, clothed, correct, dressed, ethical, fitting, helpful, lenient, sizable, sparing, upright **8** adequate, all right, becoming, decorous, friendly, generous, gracious, likeable, mannerly, mediocre, merciful, middling, obliging, passable, sizeable, spotless, straight, suitable, virtuous **9** courteous, honorable, tolerable, wholesome **10** acceptable, altruistic, benevolent, immaculate, reasonable, sufficient, thoughtful, upstanding
deception: **3** con, fib, lie **4** fake, flam, hoax, jive, ruse, scam, sham, tale, trap, wile **5** bluff, cheat, decoy, dodge, feint, fraud, guile, hokum, lying, setup, shill, snare, spoof, sting, trick **6** device, dupery, hustle **7** blarney, charade, chicane, con game, cunning, fallacy, falsity, fast one, gimmick, hogwash, malarky, pretext, snow job, sophism, swindle, untruth **8** artifice, bad faith, betrayal, delusion, flimflam, illusion, jugglery, malarkey, pretense, trickery **9** casuistry, chicanery, duplicity, falsehood, fourberie, hypocrisy, imposture, mare's nest, mendacity, stratagem, treachery, whitewash **10** boondoggle, craftiness, hanky-panky, hocus-pocus, imposition, inaccuracy, masquerade, misleading, subterfuge, trickiness
free from ~: **8** disabuse
deceptive: **3** sly **4** fake, foxy, wily **5** false, lying, phony, slick **6** crafty, phoney, shifty, sneaky, tricky, untrue **7** cunning, elusive, elusory, evasive, roguish **8** deluding, delusive, delusory, guileful, illusive, illusory, scheming, slippery, specious, spurious, two-faced **9** ambiguous, beguiling, designing, dishonest, imaginary, imitative, insidious, insincere, invisible, plausible, underhand **10** fallacious, fictitious, fraudulent, inexplicit, mendacious, misleading, serpentine, unreliable
de Champlain: **6** Samuel
__ de chat: **3** pas
__ de cheval: **3** pas
__ de chine: **5** crêpe
__ de chose: **3** peu
decibels, low in: **5** quiet
decide: **3** fix, opt, say, set **4** deem, pick, rule, take, vote **5** agree, elect, judge, solve **6** choose, clinch, commit, decree, define, figure, opt for, prefer, reason, settle **7** adjudge, agree on, chooses, pick out, resolve **8** conclude, draw lots, finalize, nominate **9** arbitrate, determine, preordain, single out **10** adjudicate, settle upon, take a stand
against: **3** nix **6** pass on
unable to ~: **4** torn **8** wavering **10** of two minds, on the fence
decided: **3** set **4** firm, sure **5** clear, fixed **6** intent, marked, mulish **7** assured, certain, earnest **8** absolute, definite, emphatic, finished, in the bag, positive, resolute **9** assertive, iron-jawed, unbending **10** conclusive, deliberate, inevitable, inflexible, pronounced, purposeful, unwavering, unyielding
not ~: **4** open, tied
yet to be ~: **9** ambiguous, debatable **10** in question, unresolved, up in the air
decidedly: **3** far **4** real, very **5** quite, truly **6** easily, highly, surely, vastly **7** but good, flat out **8** for a fact, in spades, markedly, terribly **9** certainly, downright, expressly **10** absolutely, by all means, decisively, definitely, distinctly, far and away, inevitably, positively
Decider
author: Dick Francis
deciding: **3** key **5** chief, prime **7** crucial **8** critical, decisive **9** principal **10** conclusive
decile: **5** tenth
decimal
base: **3** ten
marking: **3** dot **5** point
point, in Europe: **5** comma
starter: **3** duo
decimal __: **5** place, point **6** system
__ decimal system: **5** Dewey
decimate: **3** gut **4** ruin **5** smash **6** defeat, quench **7** wipe out **8** demolish, massacre **9** slaughter **10** annihilate
decipher: **2** do **4** read **5** break, crack, solve **6** decode, deduce, reveal **7** analyze, decrypt, dope out, explain, make out, unravel **8** construe, untangle **9** figure out, interpret, make clear, penetrate, puzzle out, translate **10** understand, unscramble
decipherable: **7** legible **8** readable
decision: **4** will **5** spine, voice **6** accord, choice, result, ruling **7** finding, liberty, outcome, resolve, verdict **8** backbone, election, firmness, judgment, sentence **9** agreement, fortitude, selection, will power **10** conclusion, preference, resolution, settlement
come to a ~: **6** settle
court ~: **6** ruling **7** verdict
formal ~: **3** act
make a ~: **3** act **4** deem, rule **6** choose, direct, settle
make a judicial ~: **4** find **5** order **6** decide, decree, ordain **7** preside, resolve **8** sentence **9** prescribe, pronounce
makers: **4** jury
reverse a ~: **8** override, overrule
__ decision: **5** split **7** command
decision-making power: **5** say-so
decisive: **3** key, set **4** firm **5** acute, clean, fatal, final, vital **6** all-out, intent **7** assured, certain, crucial, fateful, flat-out, pivotal, precise, settled, telling **8** absolute, critical, definite, forceful, positive, pregnant, resolute, settling, ultimate **9** assertive, important, memorable, momentous, necessary, strategic **10** commanding, conclusive, definitive, determined, inarguable, peremptory, portentous, unarguable, undeniable
be ~: **3** act, opt **6** commit
period: **2** OT **8** overtime
De Civitate __: **3** Dei
deck: **2** KO **4** drop, gild, kayo, pack, slug, tier, trim **5** adorn, array, dress, equip, floor, grace, primp **6** attire, clothe, defeat, wallop **7** bedrape, clobber, festoon, flatten, garnish, gussy up **8** accouter, accoutre, beautify, emblazon, ornament, prettify **9** caparison, embellish, embroider, glamorize, knock down, prostrate
backyard ~: **5** patio
break the ~: **3** cut **7** shuffle
clean the ~: **3** mop **4** swab, swob
clear the ~: **4** tidy **5** ready
foreman: **4** bo's'n **5** bosun
fortuneteller's ~: **5** tarot
hands: **4** crew
hit the ~: **4** wake **5** arise, awake, get up, waken
member: **3** ace, six, ten, two **4** five, four, jack, king, nine, trey **5** deuce, eight, joker, queen, seven, three
not on ~: **5** below
on ~: **4** next, open **6** aboard **7** present **10** obtainable
opening: **5** hatch
out: **3** tog **4** garb, vest **5** adorn, array, equip, primp, prink **6** attire, bedaub, clothe, outfit **7** furnish **8** accouter, accoutre, spruce up **9** caparison
part: **4** card
protector: **5** stain
ship ~: **4** poop **5** orlop **6** fo'c's'le

stack the ~: 5 cheat 9 victimize
starter: 5 after 7 quarter
worker: 4 hand 6 sailor 7 jack tar
deck ___: 3 lid, log 4 bolt, gang, hand, hook, load 5 chair, light, plate, watch 6 tennis 7 officer, passage
___ deck: 3 gun, sun 4 boat, cold, half, laid, main, poop, rear, spar, tape 5 cabin, lower, upper 6 flight
decked out: 4 clad 5 natty 6 dapper
___-decker: 5 three 6 double, triple
Decker: 4 Mary
partner: 5 Black
decker, hall: 5 holly
deckhand: 3 ABS, gob, tar 4 mate, salt 6 barger, sailor, seaman 7 mariner
Deck of Cards (1959 song)
artist: Wink Martindale
Deck the Halls: 4 noel 5 carol
syllables: 3 fas, las 4 fa la, la la 6 fa la la, la la la
word: 3 'tis
declaim: 4 rail, rant, rave, talk 5 decry, orate, speak, spout, utter 6 recite 7 lecture, thunder 8 bloviate, denounce, harangue, perorate 9 fulminate, hold forth
rhythmically: 5 chant
declamation: 6 speech 7 oration 8 harangue 10 recitation
declamatory: 5 stagy 6 stagey 7 pompous, stilted 9 bombastic 10 oratorical, rhetorical, theatrical
declaration: 3 bid 4 oath, plea 5 claim, edict, say-so 6 avowal, dictum, notice, remark 7 receipt 8 averment, bulletin, doctrine 9 manifesto, statement, testimony, utterance
Declaration of Independence
starter: 4 When
declarative: 8 positive 9 assertive 10 expository
declare: 3 air, own, say, vow 4 aver, avow, name, tell 5 admit, claim, plead, speak, state, swear, utter, voice, vouch 6 affirm, allege, assert, attest, avouch, depone, herald, remark, reveal 7 confess, deliver, divulge, express, observe, present, profess, promise, speak up, testify, warrant 8 announce, disclose, maintain, manifest, proclaim, propound, set forth, speak out 9 enunciate, make known, predicate, pronounce 10 asseverate, promulgate, put forward
false: 5 rebut 6 impugn, negate, recant, reject 7 disavow, dispute, gainsay 8 disclaim, renounce 9 repudiate 10 contradict, controvert
I do ~: 4 my my 6 dear me 8 goodness
déclassé: 6 common 8 inferior 10 second-rate
declension: 4 tilt 5 slope 7 descent
declination: 2 no 5 slant, slope 6 denial 7 descent, refusal
decline: 3 dip, ebb, nix, rot, sag 4 balk, dive, drop, fade, fail, fall, flag, lose, pass, sink, slip, veto, wane, wilt 5 abate, baulk, decay, demur, drain, droop, lapse, lower, say no, slant, slide, slump, spurn, waive 6 beg off, ebbing, lessen, loathe, pass up, perish, rebuff, recede, refuse, reject, shrink, waning, weaken, worsen 7 abstain, cutback, descend, descent, drop off, dwindle, entropy, failing, falloff, forbear, inflect, plummet, refrain, subside, tail off 8 comedown, contract, decrease, diminish, downturn, languish, level off, lowering, moderate, nosedive, peter out, slowdown, stagnate, turn down, twilight 9 abatement, backslide, decadence, downgrade, downslide, downswing, dwindling, lessening, recession, reduction, remission, retrocede, weakening, withering, worsening 10 anticlimax, depreciate, diminution, falling off, retrograde
combining form: 4 clin- 5 clino-
economic ~: 4 bust 9 recession 10 depression
in ~: 6 sickly 9 unhealthy
period of ~: 3 ebb
Decline and Fall
author: Evelyn Waugh
Decline and Fall of the Roman Empire, The
author: Edward Gibbon
declining: 4 sick 8 downhill
declivity: 4 drop 5 scarp, slope 7 descent, incline 8 gradient 9 downgrade
___ Deco: 3 Art
decoct: 4 boil, cook 7 extract 8 boil down, condense
decoction: 6 liquor 7 extract
decode: 4 read 5 break, crack, parse, solve 6 deduce, reveal, unlock 7 analyze, convert, decrypt, dope out, explain, unravel 8 decipher, untangle 9 figure out, interpret, puzzle out, translate 10 understand, unscramble
decoders, U.S. military: 3 NSA
___ de coeur: 3 cri 7 affaire
___ de Cologne: 3 eau
decolorize: 4 fade 6 bleach, whiten
___ de combat: 4 hors
decompose: 3 eat, rot 4 turn 5 decay, spoil 6 molder 7 break up, crumble 8 dissolve 9 break down, fall apart
combining form: 4 -lyze
decomposing: 6 rancid, rotten
combining form: 5 -lytic
decomposition: 3 rot
combining form: 3 lys- 4 lysi-, lyso- 5 -lysis
DeConcini: 6 Dennis
decongestant form: 5 spray
decontainerize: 5 unbox 7 uncrate
decontaminate: 4 wash 5 bathe, clean, scrub 6 purify 7 cleanse, deterge, launder 8 fumigate, sanitize 9 disinfect, sterilize
decontaminated: 4 safe 5 clean 7 sterile
decor: 4 mode 5 style
change the ~: 4 redo
decorate: 4 cite, do up, edge, gild, trim 5 adorn, array, dress, grace, honor, paint 6 bedeck, emboss, enrich, jazz up 7 bedizen, dress up, encrust, enhance, festoon, flatter, furbish, furnish, garnish, gussy up, incrust, varnish 8 accouter, accoutre, beautify, emblazon, ornament, spruce up 9 embellish, embroider, smarten up
decorated: 5 fancy, showy 6 flashy, frilly, glitzy, lavish 7 opulent 9 elaborate, garnished, luxurious, sumptuous
decoration: 4 gilt, lace, palm, trim 5 award, badge, braid, dodad, frill, honor, inlay, medal, prize, title 6 accent, bauble, doodad, emblem, facing, geegaw, gewgaw, ribbon, sequin, stripe, tinsel, trophy 7 dingbat, festoon, garnish, gilding, insigne, laurels, pattern, pennant, spangle, tooling, trinket 8 accolade, appliqué, citation, curlicue, curlycue, filagree, filigree, flourish, fretwork, frippery, froufrou, furbelow, insignia, ornament, trapping, trimming 9 accessory, adornment, arabesque, bedecking, designing, fandangle, fillagree, garniture, gimcracks, parquetry 10 embroidery, enrichment, festooning, garnishing
object of ~: 3 fir 4 hero, tree
see also medal
decorative: 5 fancy 6 florid, frilly, ornate 7 baroque, for show 8 adorning, cosmetic 9 enhancing 10 ornamental
decorator
asset: 5 flair, style, taste
concern: 5 color, motif
de Cordova: 4 Fred 6 Arturo
decorous: 3 fit 4 nice, prim 5 moral, staid 6 au fait, august, decent, formal, proper, ritual, sedate, seemly 7 correct, courtly, elegant, fitting, orderly, pompous, refined, stately, stilted 8 becoming, highbred, highbrow, ladylike, mannerly, suitable 9 befitting, dignified 10 ceremonial
___ de corps: 6 esprit
decorticate: 4 peel, skin 5 strip
decorum: 4 form 5 taste 7 dignity, manners 8 ceremony, civility, niceties, protocol 9 etiquette, formality, gentility, propriety
___ de côté: 3 pas
de Coubertin: 6 Pierre
decoy: 4 bait, fake, lure, trap 5 shill, snare, tempt, trick 6 allure, come-on, entice, entrap, facade, lead on, rope in, suck in 8 inveigle, pretense 9 deception 10 allurement, enticement, red herring, temptation
decrease: 3 cut, dip, ebb, lag 4 clip, curb, drop, ease, fade, fall, lack, leak, loss, lull, pale, pare, sink, slow, thin, wane 5 abate, allay, decay, drain, droop, let up, lower, remit, slack, slash, slump 6 deduct, dilute, lessen, modify, muffle, narrow, rebate, recede, reduce, retard, shrink, slow up, waning, weaken, wither 7 abridge, commute, curtail, cutback, cut down, decline, deflate, deplete, die down, drop off, dwindle, erosion, falloff, lighten, mollify, plummet, shorten, shrivel, slacken, subside, tail off, take off, take out, thin out, whittle 8 blow over, close out, contract, diminish, discount, downsize, downturn, level off, mark down, minimize, moderate, peter out, roll back, slow down, subtract, take away, taper off, withhold 9 abatement, deduction, devaluate, downtrend, dwindling, evaporate, extenuate, lessening, reduction, remission, retrocede, shrinkage, withering 10 depreciate, diminution, falling off
the volume: 3 gag 4 calm, hush, lull, mute 5 quiet, shush 6 deaden, muffle, muzzle, shut up, stifle, subdue 7 be quiet 8 pipe down, suppress 9 quiet down 10 extinguish
velocity: 4 slow 5 brake 6 retard, slow up 8 slow down 10 decelerate
volume: 4 mute 7 silence 8 turn down
de-crease: 4 iron
decreased: 5 lower, short 8 lessened
by: 4 less 5 minus
decreasing: 9 on the wane
decree: 3 law, set 4 bull, fiat, rule, will, word, writ 5 canon, edict, irade, judge, order, ukase 6 decide, dictum, diktat, enjoin, firman, impose, ordain, ruling 7 adjudge, command, dictate, enforce, finding, mandate, precept, statute, verdict 8 judgment, legalize, sanction 9 directive, legislate, ordinance, papal bull, prescribe, pronounce 10 injunction, promulgate, regulation
church ~: 4 bull 5 canon
divine ~: 7 destiny
Muslim ~: 5 irade
decreed: 5 legal 6 lawful, vested 10 inevitable
decrement: 3 cut 7 cutback 9 deduction, reduction
decrepit: 4 weak, worn 5 mangy, musty, seedy, tatty, unfit 6 creaky, feeble, flimsy, mangey, shabby 7 fragile, rickety, run-down, unsound 8 timeworn, untended, well-used 10 antiquated, bedraggled, broken-down, ramshackle, threadbare, tumbledown
decrepitude: 7 malaise 8 weakness
decriminalize: 8 legalize
___ de Cristo: 6 Sangre
decry: 3 pan, rap 4 gibe, hiss, jeer, jibe, mock, slam, slur, snub 5 abuse, blame, knock, libel, lower, scorn, sneer, spurn, taunt 6 defame, deride, dump on, heckle, impugn, malign, offend, rail at, rebuff, slight, vilify 7 affront, asperse, censure, condemn, declaim, degrade, disdain, put down, rank out, run down, slander, traduce 8 backbite, badmouth, belittle, bloviate, denounce, derogate, pooh-pooh, ridicule, vilipend 9 criticize, denigrate, discredit, disparage, humiliate, reprehend 10 calumniate, disrespect, take to task, villainize
decrypt: 5 crack 6 decode 8 decipher
___ de cuisine: 4 chef
decuple: 7 tenfold
decussate: 9 intersect

DeDe Dinah (1958 song)
  artist: Frankie Avalon
___-de-dee: 6 fiddle
___ de dents: 3 mal
___ de deux: 3 pas
dedicate: 5 allot, apply, bless, put in 6 anoint, assign, commit, devote, donate, hallow, pledge 7 consign 8 canonize, give over, sanctify, set apart 9 apportion 10 consecrate, inaugurate
dedicated: 3 wed 4 avid, true 5 loyal 6 sacred, strong 7 devoted, dutiful, staunch, zealous 8 constant, faithful, true-blue, untiring, yeomanly 9 allegiant, committed, steadfast 10 purposeful, undeterred, unwavering
  to: 3 for
Dedicated to the One I Love (song)
  artist: Mamas & the Papas, Shirelles
dedication: 7 loyalty, passion 8 blessing, devotion 9 adherence, hallowing 10 allegiance, commitment, fanaticism
  stanza: 5 envoi
dedicatory: 8 memorial
  work: 3 ode
___-de-do: 4 hoop 5 whoop
___-de-Dôme: 3 Puy
deduce: 4 draw, make, tell 5 glean, guess, infer, judge, think 6 assume, decode, derive, gather, reason, take it 7 imagine, make out, surmise 8 conclude, construe, decipher, estimate, perceive 9 figure out, reason out 10 understand
deducer's need: 5 logic 6 reason
deducible: 7 logical 9 derivable, following, inferable, traceable 10 consequent, reasonable
deduct: 4 dock, take 5 allow 6 lessen, reason, rebate, reduce 7 take off, take out 8 discount, roll back, subtract, take away, withhold, write off
___-deductible: 3 tax
deduction: 5 logic 6 answer, credit, reason, rebate, saving 7 finding, surmise, theorem, thought 8 decrease, discount, judgment, write-off 9 abatement, allowance, corollary, decrement, dialectic, inference, pondering, reasoning, reduction 10 assumption, cogitation, conclusion, derivation, diminution, hypothesis, meditation, reflection, rumination, withdrawal
  game of ~: 4 Clue 5 Jotto
  make a ~: 5 add up, infer
  payroll ~: 3 tax 4 FICA 9 insurance
  weight ~: 4 tare
___ deduction: 3 tax
deductions
  after ~: 3 net
  before ~: 5 gross
deductive: 7 a priori 8 rational 10 scientific
dee: 5 grade
  ender: 3 jay
Dee: 4 Joey, Kiki, Ruby 5 Brown, Clark, river 6 Sandra, Snider 7 Frances, Wallace
  River locale: 8 Scotland
Dee and the Starliters, Joey
  song: Peppermint Twist (1961) Shout (1962)
deed: 3 act, job 4 coup, feat, gest, move, turn, work 5 doing, geste, paper, stunt, title 6 action, effort 7 charter, exploit, reality 8 covenant, document, transfer 9 adventure, indenture, occupancy, ownership, quitclaim 10 conveyance
  bad ~: 3 sin 5 crime, wrong
  brave ~: 4 coup
  chivalrous ~: 4 gest 5 geste
  do a good ~: 4 help
  good ~: 3 aid 4 help 5 favor 7 service 8 courtesy, kindness 10 kindliness
Dee Dee: 5 Myers, Sharp
Deed I Do
  artist: Lena Horne
___-Dee-Doo-Dah: 4 Zip-a
deeds: 4 acta 7 heroics 9 res gestae
Deeds: 10 Longfellow
deejay: 5 Kasem 9 announcer
  alternative: 4 band
  material: 2 CD, LP 4 demo
deem: 4 feel, hold, rate, take, view 5 count, judge, think, value 6 assume, credit, decide, look on, reckon, regard, repute 7 believe, imagine, presume, suppose, surmise 8 conceive, consider, estimate, look upon
de-emphasize: 8 play down
Deenie
  author: Judy Blume
deep: 3 low, sea 4 bass, full, loud, rapt, rich 5 briny, broad, heavy, husky, ocean, sound, thick 6 arcane, buried, hidden, occult, secret, shrewd, strong, subtle, tricky 7 abysmal, abyssal, complex, Delphic, intense, learned, low down, obscure, orotund, serious, weighty 8 absorbed, abstract, abstruse, baritone, barytone, esoteric, guttural, immersed, intimate, profound, resonant, sonorous, unbroken 9 cavernous, engrossed, heartfelt, innermost, intensely, intensive, recondite 10 bottomless, fathomless, impressive, low-pitched, meaningful, mysterious, passionate, thoughtful, unknowable
  be knee ~ in: 4 teem 5 swarm 6 infest
  down: 6 inside
  go ~ into: 5 probe 11 investigate
  in ~: 5 stuck 7 trapped 8 strapped
  off the ~ end: 9 foolhardy
  water: 3 fix, jam 4 bind, mess 5 pinch 6 crisis, pickle, plight, scrape, strait 7 dilemma, problem, trouble 8 quandary 9 adversity 10 difficulty
deep ___: 3 fat 4 down 5 floor, focus, fryer, space 6 breath, freeze 7 pockets
deep ___ bend: 4 knee
deep-___: 3 fry, sea, set, six 4 dish, draw, dyed, laid 5 fried, water 6 frozen, rooted, seated, voiced
___-deep: 4 knee, skin 5 ankle, waist
Deep ___: 4 Blue 5 South 6 Impact, Purple, Valley
Deepak: 6 Chopra
Deep Blue Good-by, The
  author: John D. MacDonald
Deep Blue Sea (1999 film)
  cast: Samuel L. Jackson, Thomas Jane
  director: Renny Harlin
Deep Cover rapper: 5 Dr. Dre
deep-dish ___: 3 pie 5 pizza
deepen: 4 grow 5 mount, shade 6 dig out, dredge, expand, extend 7 develop, magnify, thicken 8 excavate, increase, scoop out 9 aggravate, intensify 10 strengthen
Deep End of the Ocean (1999 film)
  cast: Whoopi Goldberg, Michelle Pfeiffer, Treat Williams
Deeper and Deeper (1992 song)
  artist: Madonna
___ deepest dye: 5 of the
deep-felt: 4 keen 5 acute
Deep Impact (1998 film)
  cast: Robert Duvall, Morgan Freeman, Téa Leoni, Vanessa Redgrave, Maximilian Schell, Elijah Wood
  director: Mimi Leder
___ Deep Is the Ocean: 3 How
___ Deep Is Your Love: 3 How
deep knee ___: 4 bend
deeply: 4 very 6 highly, vastly 9 sincerely 10 to the quick
Deep Purple
  song: Hush (1968) Smoke on the Water (1973)
deep-rooted: 4 firm 5 inner 6 stable 7 lasting 8 embedded, lifelong 9 confirmed, ingrained 10 habituated, inveterate
deep-sea: 5 naval 6 marine 8 maritime, nautical
  explorer: 5 diver
deep-sea diving: 5 sport
deep-seated: 3 gut 5 fixed, inner 6 inborn, inbred, rooted 7 built-in, chronic, radical 8 habitual, inherent, longtime, profound 9 chronical, confirmed, essential, ingrained, intrinsic, unabating 10 habituated, inveterate
deep-six: 3 can 4 dump, toss 5 ditch, pitch, scrap 7 discard, toss out 8 jettison, throw out
Deep South: 5 Dixie
Deep, The: 4 film 5 novel
  author: Peter Benchley
  cast: Jacqueline Bisset, Louis Gossett Jr., Nick Nolte, Robert Shaw
  director: Peter Yates
deep-toned: 4 alto, bass, rich 8 sonorous
deer: 3 doe, elk, roe 4 axis, buck, fawn, hart, hind, pudu, shou, sika, stag 5 Bambi, moose 6 animal, cervid, chital, guemal, hangul, huemul, mammal, sambar, sambur, thamin, wapiti 7 brocket, caribou, muntjac, muntjak, roebuck, sambhar, sambhur 8 reindeer, ruminant 9 barasingh, white-tail 10 chevrotain
  Asia: 4 axis, shou, sika 6 chital, hangul, sambar, sambur, thamin 7 muntjac, muntjak, sambhar, sambhur 9 barasingh
  combining form: 5 cervi-
  Disney ~: 3 Ena 5 Bambi
  ender: 3 fly 4 skin, yard 5 hound 7 stalker
  feature: 6 antler
  female: 3 doe 4 hind
  foot: 4 hoof
  genus: 4 rusa
  like a ~: 7 corvine
  male: 4 buck, hart, stag
  North America: 3 elk 6 wapiti 7 caribou
  South America: 4 pudu 6 guemal, huemul 7 brocket
  tail: 4 scut
  where ~ and antelope play: 5 range
  young: 4 fawn
Deer ___: 4 Xing
Deer ___, The: 4 Park 6 Hunter, Slayer
___ deer, a female...: 4 Doe a
deerberry: 5 shrub
  relative: *see* heath family shrub
Deere: 4 John
  product: 5 mower 7 tractor
  rival: 4 Toro
Deerfield Beach: 4 city, town
  locale: 7 Florida
Deer Hunter, The (1978 film)
  cast: John Cazale, Robert De Niro, Meryl Streep, Christopher Walken
  director: Michael Cimino
___ Dee River: 3 Pee
Deer Park, The
  author: Norman Mailer
deerskin: 7 leather
Deer Slayer, The
  author: James Fenimore Cooper
  character: 5 Hetty, Natty 6 Bumppo
deerstalker: 3 cap, hat
Dee, Ruby: 7 actress
  film: Do the Right Thing (1989) Gone Are the Days (1963) A Raisin in the Sun (1961) Up Tight (1968)
  spouse: Ossie Davis
Dees: 4 Rick
Dee, Sandra: 7 actress
  film: A Summer Place (1959)
  spouse: Bobby Darin
de-escalate: 5 lower 6 lessen 7 subside 8 level off
de-escalation: 5 truce
Dees, Rick
  song: Disco Duck (1976)
Deever: 5 Danny
___ Dee Williams: 5 Billy
def
  see wonderful
Def ___: 7 Leppard
___ Def: 3 Mos
DEF
  predecessor: 3 ABC
  successor: 3 GHI
  telephone's ~: 5 three
deface: 3 mar 4 harm, maim, ruin, scar 5 score, spoil, sully, trash 6 damage, impair, injure, mangle 7 scratch, tarnish 8 mutilate 9 vandalize
defacement: 8 graffiti
defacer: 6 vandal
de facto: 4 real 5 truly 6 actual, in fact, really 8 actually 9 actuality, in

reality **10** unimagined
defalcate: 5 steal **8** embezzle
de Falla: 6 Manuel
defamation: 3 dig, lie, mud **4** barb, dirt, gibe, jibe, slam, slap, slur, snub **5** abuse, libel, scorn, smear, taunt **6** rebuff, slight **7** affront, calumny, catcall, disdain, mockery, obloquy, offense, put-down, slander **8** contempt, derision, ridicule **9** aspersion, cheap shot, contumely **10** backbiting, detraction, disrespect, impugnment, muckraking, opprobrium
defamatory: 7 abusive, vicious **8** libelous **9** injurious, insulting, invidious, maligning, traducing, vilifying **10** calumnious, derogatory, detracting, detractive, scandalous, slanderous
defame: 3 hit, pan **4** gibe, jeer, jibe, mock, slam, slur, snub **5** abuse, cut up, decry, knock, libel, roast, scorn, smear, spurn, sully, taint, taunt, wrong **6** deride, dump on, heckle, impugn, malign, offend, rebuff, slight, vilify **7** affront, asperse, blacken, degrade, disdain, put down, rank out, run down, slander, tarnish, traduce **8** backbite, badmouth, belittle, besmirch, denounce, disgrace, dishonor, ridicule, vilipend **9** denigrate, discredit, disparage, humiliate, knock down **10** blackguard, calumniate, disrespect, scandalize, stigmatize, throw mud at, villainize, vituperate
defamer: 5 enemy **6** critic **8** vilifier **9** detractor, ill-wisher
Defarge: 3 Mme. **6** Madame
emulate ~: 4 knit
defat: 4 skim, trim
default: 4 fail, lack, lose, miss **5** lapse, shirk, stiff **7** failure, lose out, neglect **8** inaction, omission **9** oversight **10** bankruptcy, insolvency, nonpayment
on: 6 run out
result: 4 repo
security against ~: 4 lien
defaulter: 7 failure **10** delinquent
defaulting: 10 delinquent
defeat: 2 KO **3** ace, dud, get, tan, top, zap **4** beat, best, bomb, bust, deck, drub, edge, fall, flop, foil, kayo, kill, lick, loss, mate, rout, ruin, sink, skin, trim, undo, veto, whip, whup **5** block, check, cream, crush, floor, outdo, pound, quash, quell, repel, skunk, smash, stimy, stymy, swamp, trash, trump, unarm, upend, upset, whack, whomp, worst **6** fiasco, finish, hammer, lacing, master, mishap, outhit, outwit, pommel, pummel, rebuff, reduce, show up, stymie, subdue, thrash, thwart, turkey, wallop **7** beating, beat out, blunder, conquer, debacle, failure, lambast, licking, misstep, mow down, nose out, nullify, outplay, overrun, put down, repulse, scuttle, setback, shellac, stumble, trample, trounce, undoing, victory, washout, win over, wipe out **8** collapse, confound, conquest, decimate, demolish, downfall, drubbing, fight off, knock out, lambaste, outclass, outflank, outscore, outsmart, overcome, shellack, suppress, surmount, trashing, vanquish, Waterloo **9** breakdown, checkmate, discomfit, eliminate, force back, frustrate, landslide, overpower, overthrow, overwhelm, plow under, pulverize, slaughter, steamroll, subjugate, thrashing, trouncing **10** annihilate, neutralize, nonsuccess, obliterate
admit ~: 4 quit **5** yield
barely ~: 3 nip **4** edge **7** nose out
decisively: 3 wap **4** bury, drub, rout, skin, whap, whip, whop, whup **5** cream, roust, skunk, stomp, thump, tromp, whomp **7** trounce **8** vanquish
defeated: 4 beat **6** broken **8** overcome
be ~: 4 fail, fall, lose **5** yield **6** go down **7** get beat, lose out
not yet ~: 4 in it **5** alive
one's cry: 5 uncle
__-defeating: 4 self
defeatist: 7 killjoy **8** downbeat **9** pessimist, unhopeful
word: 4 can't **6** cannot
defect: 3 bug **4** blot, flaw, kink, lack, scar, turn, vice, wart **5** error, fault, leave, speck, stain, taint **6** desert, foible, glitch, run out **7** abscond, blemish, failing, forsake, go south, pull out, scratch **8** drawback, renounce, weakness **10** disability, faultiness, inaccuracy, inadequacy, inefficacy
defection: 8 apostasy **9** desertion, forsaking, rebellion, recreancy, rejection, secession, severance, sundering **10** alienation, deficiency, disloyalty, disownment, separation, withdrawal
defective: 3 bad, irr. **4** foul, grim, poor, sick **5** amiss, awful, lousy, woful **6** broken, crumby, crummy, dismal, faulty, flawed, horrid, marred, odious, rotten, woeful **7** baleful, baneful, beastly, damaged, doleful, ghastly, haywire, lacking, sketchy, unsound, wanting **8** dreadful, fallible, God-awful, grievous, horrible, impaired, inferior, shameful, stinking, terrible, wretched **9** appalling, atrocious, blemished, deficient, erroneous, execrable, frightful, imperfect, insidious, irregular, loathsome, miserable, offensive, revolting, subnormal **10** despicable, detestable, disastrous, horrendous, inaccurate, inadequate, incomplete, on the blink, on the fritz, out of order
vehicle: 3 dud **6** jalopy **7** clunker **10** hunk of junk
defector: 6 émigré **7** escapee, refugee, traitor **8** apostate, deserter, forsaker, recreant, renegade
defects and all: 4 as is
defend: 4 hold, save **5** cover, fight, guard **6** assert, back up, embank, ensure, foster, insure, patrol, screen, secure, shield, uphold **7** contest, endorse, espouse, explain, indorse, justify, protect, shelter, support, sustain, ward off **8** advocate, champion, fight for, keep safe, maintain, preserve, stave off **9** fight over, keep guard, look after, safeguard, vindicate, watch over **10** go to bat for, rally round, speak up for, stand up for, stick up for
against: 7 prevent
defendable: 5 valid **8** verified
defendant: 4 resp., reus **5** party **7** accused **8** litigant **10** respondent
answer: 4 plea **5** alibi
of 1925: 6 Scopes
option: 6 appeal
plea: 4 nolo **6** guilty **9** not guilty
defender: 5 guard **6** backer, jurist, keeper, knight, lawyer, legist, savior, votary **7** paladin, saviour **8** advocate, champion, exponent, guardian, watchman **9** apologist, bodyguard, paraclete, proponent, protector, supporter
__ defender: 6 public
Defender __ Faith: 5 of the
Defenders, The (CBS drama)
cast: E.G. Marshall (Lawrence Preston)
Robert Reed (Kenneth Preston)
Defending Your Life (1991 film)
cast: Albert Brooks, Meryl Streep, Rip Torn
defense: 4 fort, plea, wall **5** alibi, cover, fence, guard, reply **6** answer, buffer, excuse, reason, retort, shield **7** apology, bastion, bulwark, citadel, parapet, rampart, redoubt, shelter, tactics **8** advocacy, buttress, fortress, garrison, palisade, response, security **9** barricade, rejoinder, safeguard, sanctuary **10** embankment, opposition, precaution, protection, resistance, stronghold
acronym: 4 NATO **5** SEATO
advisory grp.: 3 NSC
close the ~: 4 rest
major ~ contractor: 5 Loral
mechanism: 6 denial
__ defense: 4 zone **5** civil
__-defense: 4 self
Defense Dept. org.: 3 ONI, SAC, USA, USN **4** USAF **5** NORAD
defenseless: 4 weak **5** naked **7** exposed, unarmed **8** helpless, wide open **9** powerless, unguarded
render ~: 5 unarm **6** disarm
defensible: 5 sound, valid **6** proper **7** logical, tenable **9** excusable, plausible **10** condonable, pardonable, remittable, vindicable
defensive: 4 wary **7** careful, opposed **8** opposing, watchful **9** resistive, thwarting **10** preventive, protecting, protective
on the ~: 5 at bay **7** uptight
defensive __: 3 end **4** back
defer: 4 stay **5** agree, delay, remit, table, waive, yield **6** comply, listen, put off, submit **7** conform, consent, neglect, respect, suspend **8** file away, hesitate, hold over, lay aside, postpone, put aside **10** pigeonhole, reschedule
to: 3 bow **4** heed, mind, obey **5** kotow **6** accept, follow, fulfil, kowtow, revere **7** abide by, fulfill, give way **8** carry out
__ de fer: 6 chapel, chemin
deference: 5 honor **6** homage, regard **7** regards, respect, valuing **8** courtesy **9** attention, gallantry, obedience, obeisance, reverence **10** admiration, allegiance, attentions, compliance, politeness, submission, veneration
deferential: 4 meek, mild **5** civil **6** humble, polite **7** fawning **8** gracious, obeisant **9** courteous, regardful **10** respectful
deferment: 4 stay **5** delay **7** respite **8** reprieve **10** suspension
deferments, having no: 4 one A
deferral: 4 stay **8** abeyance, lateness **9** rain check
__-deferred: 3 tax
defiance: 3 lip **4** dare, sass **5** spite **6** mutiny, revolt **7** affront, bravado, refusal **8** audacity, back talk, boldness, contempt, temerity **9** challenge, contumacy, disregard, impudence, insolence, rebellion **10** brazenness, effrontery, insurgence, opposition, resistance
exclamation of ~: 3 yah **4** nuts **5** I won't, nerts, nertz, never
in ~ of: 7 despite
defiant: 4 bold, game **5** brave, gutsy, nervy, sassy **6** awless, brazen, daring, feisty, gritty, heroic, ornery, plucky, spunky, unruly **7** aweless, doughty, gallant, naughty, staunch, valiant, wayward **8** contrary, factious, fearless, heroical, insolent, intrepid, mutinous, resolute, stalwart, stubborn, unafraid, valorous **9** audacious, dauntless, dreadless, obstinate, resistant, truculent, undaunted, unfearful **10** aggressive, courageous, pugnacious, rebellious, refractory
one: 5 darer
Defiant: 4 boat, ship
Defiant Ones, The (1958 film)
cast: Theodore Bikel, Tony Curtis, Sidney Poitier
director: Stanley Kramer
deficiency: 3 bug **4** flaw, lack, loss, need, want **5** fault, minus **6** dearth, glitch **7** absence, failing, paucity, poverty **8** drawback, exiguity, scarcity, shortage, sparsity, weakness **9** privation **10** inadequacy, meagerness, scantiness
combining form: 5 -penia
thiamine ~: 8 beriberi
deficient: 3 bad, low, shy **4** poor, slim, sort, weak **5** amiss, rusty, scant, short **6** faulty, flawed, meager, scanty, scarce, skimpy **7** failing, ill-done, lacking, slender, wanting **8** deprived, impaired, inferior **9** defective, destitute, imperfect, subnormal **10** inadequate, incomplete, unfinished
be ~: 4 lack, need
combining form: 6 -privic
prove ~: 4 fail
deficit: 4 lack, loss **5** minus **6** red ink **7** arrears **8** shortage, underage **9** shortfall **10** inadequacy
__ deficit: 5 trade

D E

defier: 5 rebel
defile: 4 foul, harm, pass, soil 5 abuse, dirty, shame, smear, spoil, stain, sully, taint, trash 6 befoul, crud up, damage, debase, embrue, imbrue, infect, malign, ravine, smudge 7 blacken, corrupt, degrade, pollute, profane, slander, tarnish, violate, vitiate 8 besmirch, disgrace, dishonor, maculate 9 desecrate 10 adulterate
defiled: 5 dirty 6 impure 7 corrupt, unclean 8 maculate
defilement: 4 harm 5 abuse, filth, taint 8 impurity, sullying 9 pollution, profaning, violation 10 corruption, debasement
definable: 5 exact, fixed 6 finite 7 fixable, precise 8 clear-cut, definite, specific
define: 3 fix 4 name 5 label, limit, shape 6 decide, demark, detail, lay out, set out, settle 7 delimit, enclose, explain, fence in, inclose, mark out, outline, specify 8 construe, describe, encircle, nail down, pinpoint, restrict, spell out 9 ascertain, delineate, demarcate, designate, determine, encompass, establish, formalize, formulate, interpret, make clear 10 stereotype
__-defined: 3 ill 4 well
definite: 3 set 4 firm, real, sure, true 5 clean, clear, exact, final, fixed, overt, plain, sharp, vivid 6 actual, limpid, marked, rooted, secure, stable, static 7 assured, audible, certain, decided, express, for sure, graphic, limited, obvious, precise, settled, special, visible 8 absolute, accurate, clear-cut, complete, concrete, constant, decisive, distinct, emphatic, explicit, implicit, incisive, in the bag, ironclad, palpable, positive, resolved, singular, specific, tangible, verified 9 definable, downright, graphical, permanent 10 conclusive, determined, forthright, guaranteed, inarguable, particular, pronounced, unarguable, unchanging, undeniable, undoubtful, unimagined, well-marked
not ~: 4 iffy 10 up in the air
definitely: 4 just 5 quite, truly 6 easily, gladly 7 exactly, for sure 8 for a fact 9 decidedly, expressly, no mistake, obviously, precisely 10 explicitly, far and away, inevitably, sure as hell, undeniably
in Spanish: 4 sí sí
see also of course
definition: 5 sense 7 meaning 9 diagnosis, outlining, rationale, rendering, rendition 10 annotation, commentary, denotation, expounding, expression
by ~: 5 per se
definitive: 4 last 5 final, fixed 6 actual 7 classic, express, flat-out, precise 8 absolute, accurate, clear-cut, complete, decisive, emphatic, explicit, reliable, specific, standard, ultimate, verified 9 downright, finishing, full-dress 10 completing, concluding, conclusive, exhaustive, nailed down, unarguable, unimagined
definitude: 8 accuracy 9 exactness, precision
Def Jam genre: 3 rap
deflate: 4 dash, void 5 abase, empty, lower 6 dampen, debunk, humble, reduce, shrink, squash 7 depress, devalue, exhaust, flatten, mortify, put down 8 collapse, contract, decrease, diminish, dispirit, puncture, ridicule, take down 9 devaluate, humiliate, shoot down 10 depreciate
deflated: 5 empty
deflating sound: 3 sss
deflator maybe: 3 pin
deflect: 4 bend, skew, veer, warp 5 avert, parry, shine 6 divert, glance, swerve 7 fend off, ward off 8 ricochet 9 bounce off, glance off, intercept, sidetrack, turn aside
deflection: 4 skew 5 shift, slant, slope 7 veering 9 curvature, departure, deviation, diversion 10 digression, divergence
combining form: 7 sphingo-
Defoe, Daniel: 6 writer 7 British
work: Journal of the Plague Year
Moll Flanders
Robinson Crusoe
__ de foie gras: 4 paté
__ de force: 4 tour
DeFore: 3 Don
deforest: 5 strip 8 clearcut
DeForest: 3 Lee 4 John 6 Kelley 7 Calvert
deform: 3 mar 4 warp 5 gnarl, twist 6 damage, mangle 7 contort, distort 8 misshape
__ de foudre: 4 coup
__ de fraise: 5 crème
__ de framboise: 5 crème
__ de France: 3 île 4 Tour 5 Marie
defraud: 2 do 3 con, gyp, rob 4 bilk, burn, clip, dupe, flay, gull, hoax, jive, milk, nick, ream, rook, scam, take 5 cheat, cozen, gouge, mulct, pluck, shaft, steal, trick 6 delude, fleece, hustle, outwit, rip off, suck in, take in 7 beguile, deceive, mislead, swindle 8 flimflam, hoodwink, outsmart 9 bamboozle, disinform, victimize 10 circumvent, run a game on
defrauder: 3 con 5 cheat, rogue 6 con man 9 charlatan, trickster
defray: 3 pay 4 fund 5 spend 6 pay for, redeem 7 finance
defrayal: 7 funding, payment
defrost: 4 thaw 7 get soft, thaw out 8 dissolve, fluidize, unfreeze
deft: 3 ace, apt 4 able, neat 5 adept, agile, crack, handy, quick, ready, slick 6 adroit, au fait, clever, expert, facile, habile, limber, nimble 7 capable, cunning, skilled, trained 8 delicate, dextrous, graceful, masterly, seasoned, skillful, talented 9 competent, dexterous, efficient, ingenious, masterful, practiced 10 proficient
deftness: 5 asset, skill, touch 7 ability, agility, mastery, sleight 8 facility, legerity 9 dexterity, expertise, lightness, readiness 10 nimbleness
__ de Fuca Strait: 4 Juan
defunct: 4 gone, late, past 5 kaput 6 bygone 7 expired, extinct
defuse: 4 calm 6 disarm, lessen, pacify, soften, soothe, weaken 7 disable, mollify 8 moderate 9 alleviate 10 deactivate, smooth over
defy: 4 buck, dare, face, foil, mock 5 brave, elude, fight, flout, rebel, repel, scorn, spurn 6 combat, deride, ignore, oppose, resist, revolt, slight, thwart 7 condemn, disobey, provoke, repulse, violate 8 confront, face down, ridicule 9 challenge, disregard, frustrate, stand up to, withstand 10 contradict
degage: 6 casual
Degas, Edgar: 6 artist, French 7 painter
contemporary: Édouard Manet
de Gaulle: 6 French 7 airport, Charles 9 statesman
alternative: 4 Orly
birthplace: 5 Lille
predecessor: 4 Coty
degauss a tape: 5 erase
degenerate: 3 rot 4 rust, sink, slip 5 decay, lapse, slide, slump 6 worsen 7 corrode, fall off, regress 8 degraded 9 aggravate, backslide 10 disimprove, exacerbate, go to pieces, retrogress
degeneration: 4 drop, fall 5 decay, lapse 7 atrophy, decline, descent 9 vitiation, worsening
DeGeneres: 5 Ellen
degerm: 5 clean 6 purify 8 sanitize 9 disinfect, sterilize
__ de geste: 7 chanson
de Givenchy: 6 Hubert
__ de grâce: 4 coup
degradable starter: 3 bio
degradation: 3 rot 5 shame 8 disgrace, dishonor, ignominy
degrade: 3 pan, rot 4 gibe, jeer, jibe, mock, ruin, sink, slam, slur, snub, soil 5 abase, abuse, decry, libel, lower, scorn, shame, spurn, taunt 6 debase, defame, defile, demean, demote, deride, dump on, heckle, humble, impugn, insult, lessen, malign, offend, rebuff, reduce, slight, vilify, weaken 7 affront, asperse, cheapen, corrupt, deprave, disdain, put down, rank out, run down, slander, traduce, vitiate 8 belittle, cast down, denounce, derogate, ridicule, take down, tear down, vilipend 9 denigrate, discredit, disparage, humiliate, shoot down 10 adulterate, calumniate, disrespect
degraded: 3 low 4 base, mean, vile 5 crude, gross, seamy 6 abject, coarse, sordid, vulgar 7 corrupt, debased, ignoble, low-down 8 depraved, shameful 9 worthless
degrading: 6 menial 8 shameful, unworthy 9 unhealthy 10 derogatory, despicable, pejorative
__ de grandeur: 5 folie
degree: 2 BA, BE, BS, MA, MD, MS 3 BBA, BCE, BCS, BFA, BPE, BSC, BSN, DDS, D.Ed., DFA, DMD, DVM, Ed.B, Ed.M., LL.D., MBA, MFA, MLS, MNA, MPA, MSE, MSN, MSW, Ph.D., Sc.D. 4 D.Lit., Lit.B, Lit.D., M.Agr., MSEd., rate, rung, step, unit 5 grade, level, limit, notch, order, phase, pitch, plane, range, scale, scope, shade, stage, title 6 amount, extent, length, rating, status, volume 7 caliber, diploma, doctor's, master's, measure 8 severity, strength 9 associate, doctorate, gradation, intensity, sheepskin 10 proportion
architectural ~: 3 MFA
art ~: 3 MFA
bridge builder ~: 3 BCE
business ~: 3 BBA, MBA
chemist ~: 3 BCS, Sc.B.
conservatory ~: 3 B.Mu.
dentist ~: 3 DDS, DMD
draftsman ~: 3 BME
English ~: 4 Lit.B., Lit.D.
entrepreneur ~: 3 MBA
extreme ~: 3 nth
farming ~: 3 MSA 4 M.Agr.
give the third ~: 4 pump, quiz 5 grill, probe 7 torture 8 question
greatest ~: 4 most
gym teacher ~: 3 BPE
holder: 4 alum, grad 6 alumna 7 alumnus 8 conferee, graduate
journalism ~: 2 MJ
law ~: 2 J.D. 3 LL.B., LL.D., LL.M., MCL, S.J.D.
librarian ~: 3 BLS, MLS
medical ~: 3 DDS 4 M.Sc.D.
MIT ~: 2 EE 3 BME
nth ~: 3 max 7 extreme 8 ultimate
nurse ~: 3 BSN, MNA, MSN
physics ~: 3 Sc.B., Sc.D.
piano instructor ~: 3 BME
religious ~: 3 SSD, STB, STM, Th.D.
requirement: 6 thesis
slight ~: 5 tinge
suffix: 4 -ness
teacher ~: 3 Ed.B., Ed.M., MSE 4 MSEd.
therapist ~: 3 MSW
to a ~: 4 a bit 5 quite 6 kind of, partly, rather, sort of 8 slightly, somewhat 10 moderately
to a high ~: 4 very 5 quite 6 deeply, rather, vastly 7 acutely, greatly 8 terribly 9 decidedly, extremely, seriously, supremely, unusually 10 enormously, especially, profoundly, remarkably, thoroughly, uncommonly
to any ~: 5 at all
to the nth ~: 6 in full, in toto, wholly 7 utterly 9 all the way, extremely 10 altogether, thoroughly
to the same ~: 5 alike
writer ~: 3 MFA 4 Lit.B., Lit.D.
zoo staffer ~: 3 VMD
degree __: 4 mill
degree-__: 3 day
__ degree: 3 nth, to a 4 pass 5 third 7 doctor's, master's 9 bachelor's
__-degree: 5 first, third 6 second
Degree: 9 deodorant
alternative: ***see*** deodorant
degrees
above the equator: 4 N. Lat.
below the equator: 4 S. Lat.

by ~: **7** gradual **8** bit by bit **9** gradually, partially, piecemeal
move by ~: **4** inch
__ Degrees of Separation: **3** Six
__ de guerre: **3** cri, nom
__ de Guerre: **5** Croix
degust: **5** savor
dehair: **5** shear
__-de-Haute Provence: **5** Alpes
De Haven, Gloria
spouse: John Payne
de Havilland, Olivia: **7** actress
film: The Adventures of Robin Hood (1938)
Alibi Ike (1935)
Anthony Adverse (1936)
Captain Blood (1935)
The Dark Mirror (1946)
Dodge City (1939)
Gone With the Wind (1939)
The Great Garrick (1937)
Hard to Get (1938)
The Heiress (1949, AA)
Hold Back the Dawn (1941)
Hush ... Hush, Sweet Charlotte (1965)
In This Our Life (1942)
It's Love I'm After (1937)
Lady in a Cage (1964)
Light in the Piazza (1962)
The Male Animal (1942)
My Cousin Rachel (1952)
Not as a Stranger (1955)
The Proud Rebel (1958)
The Snake Pit (1948)
The Strawberry Blonde (1941)
To Each His Own (1946, AA)
sister: Joan Fontaine
dehire: **2** ax **3** axe **4** fire **5** let go **6** lay off **9** discharge
dehumidify: **3** dry **9** evaporate
dehydrate: **3** dry **4** sear **5** parch **7** process, shrivel **8** preserve **9** anhydrate, desiccate, evaporate, exsiccate
dehydrated: **3** dry **4** arid, sere **5** unwet **7** parched, thirsty **8** droughty **9** juiceless, waterless
Dei __: **6** gratia
__ Dei: **5** Agnus
deice: **4** salt **7** thaw out **8** unfreeze
Deidre: **4** Hall
deific: **5** godly **6** divine **7** godlike **8** almighty
deify: **4** love **5** adore, ensky, exalt, extol **6** extoll **7** elevate, ennoble, glorify, idolize, worship **8** sanctify, venerate **10** consecrate
Deighton, Len: **6** writer
character: **3** spy
deign: **5** lower, stoop **6** see fit **8** be so kind **9** patronize, vouchsafe **10** condescend
Deimos: **4** moon
neighbor: **6** Phobos
parent: **4** Ares **9** Aphrodite
planet: **4** Mars
sibling: **6** Phobus **8** Harmonia
Deion: **7** Sanders
__ D. Eisenhower: **6** Dwight
deistic: **6** divine **9** religious
deity: **3** god **7** creator, goddess **8** divinity
see also god
__ de Janeiro: **3** Rio
déjà vu: **10** paramnesia
clothing style: **5** retro
Déjà Vu (2006 film)
cast: Val Kilmer, Denzel Washington
deject: **4** tire **6** bum out, dampen, darken, dismay, sadden **7** depress **8** dispirit **9** bring down **10** demoralize, discourage, dishearten
dejected: **3** low, sad **4** blue, dark, down, glum, mopy **5** bleak, heavy, mopey, sorry, woful **6** abject, broody, dismal, gloomy, mopish, morose, somber, woeful **7** doleful, hangdog, in a funk, joyless, sagging, subdued, unhappy **8** cast down, desolate, downbeat, downcast, drooping, shot down, wretched **9** bummed-out, cheerless, depressed, exanimate, heartsick, in the pits, miserable, prostrate, saturnine, sorrowful, unhopeful, woebegone **10** chapfallen, despondent, dispirited, melancholy, out of sorts, spiritless
be ~: **4** mope
dejection: **3** woe **5** blues, dolor, gloom, grief **6** misery, sorrow **7** anguish, despair, sadness **8** distress, doldrums, glumness, the blues **9** heartache, pessimism **10** depression, desolation, heartbreak, heavy heart, loneliness, melancholy, woefulness
Dejection: An Ode
author: Samuel Taylor Coleridge
__ déjeuner: **5** petit
déjeuner dish: **6** salade
Déjeuner sur l'herbe
painter: Édouard Manet
de jure: **7** by right
__ de justice: **3** lit
De Kalb: **4** city, town
athletes: **7** Huskies
locale: **8** Illinois
school: **3** NIU
deke: **4** fake **5** feint
victim: **6** goalie
Deke: **7** Slayton
Dekker: **6** Albert, Thomas **7** Desmond
de Klerk: **2** F.W. **4** Boer **9** president
homeland: **3** RSA **11** South Africa
predecessor: **5** Botha
de Kooning, Willem: **5** Dutch **6** artist **7** painter
Del: **5** Ennis **6** Amitri, Reeves **7** Shannon
Del __: **3** Rio **4** Taco **5** Monte, Norte
Del.
see Delaware
__ de la Cité: **3** île
Delacroix, Eugène: **6** artist, French **7** painter
__ de Lafayette: **7** Marquis
Delahanty: **2** Ed
__ de Lahore: **5** Le roi
de la Hoya: **5** Oscar
__ de la Madeleine: **4** îles
de la Mare, Walter: **4** poet **7** British
delaminate: **4** peel
__-de-lance: **3** fer
de Lancie: **4** John
DeLand: **4** city, town
athletes: **7** Hatters
locale: **7** Florida
school: **7** Stetson
Delaney: **3** Kim **7** Shelagh
Delaney, Shelagh: **7** British **10** playwright
__ Delano Roosevelt: **8** Franklin
Delany, Dana: **7** actress
TV: China Beach
__ de la Paix: **3** Rue
de Laplace: **6** Pierre
__ de la Plata: **3** Rio
de la Renta, Oscar: **8** designer
rival: **5** Blass, Klein **6** Armani, Lauren **7** Versace
__ de la Réunion: **3** île
de Larrocha: **6** Alicia
__ de la Société: **4** îles
delate: **6** accuse
De Laurentiis: **4** Dino
Delaware: **3** bay **4** city, town **5** river, state **6** Indian **7** Amerind
capital: **5** Dover
city: **5** Dover, Lewes **6** Newark **10** Wilmington
city on the ~: **6** Camden, Easton **7** Trenton
dynast: **6** DuPont
feeder: **6** Lehigh **10** Schuylkill
Indian: **5** Unami **6** Lenape **9** Nanticoke
locale: **4** Ohio
neighbor: **8** Maryland **9** New Jersey
nickname: **10** First State
River locale: **4** Penn. **7** New York **9** New Jersey
state beverage: **4** milk
state fish: **8** weakfish
state insect: **7** ladybug
state tree: **5** holly
Delaware __ Gap: **5** Water
delay: **3** gap, jam, lag, tie **4** clog, curb, drag, mire, poke, slow, stay, stop, wait **5** block, brake, dally, defer, deter, hedge, hitch, pause, remit, sit on, stall, table, tarry, tie up, trail, waive **6** dampen, dawdle, detain, hamper, hang-up, hinder, holdup, impede, linger, loiter, put off, remain, retard, shelve, slow up **7** adjourn, hold off, inhibit, lay over, neglect, problem, prolong, red tape, respite, setback, slacken, suspend, time lag **8** dawdling, demurral, downtime, encumber, file away, footdrag, hesitate, hold over, interval, keep back, lateness, lay aside, obstruct, postpone, prohibit, protract, reprieve, slowdown, stoppage, surcease, tarrying **9** deferment, detention, extension, hindrance, interlude, interrupt, lingering, runaround, stalemate **10** dillydally, filibuster, hesitation, impediment, standstill, suspension
after a ~: **5** later **6** at last
cause ~: **4** slow **6** hang up
don't ~: **6** act now
legal ~: **4** hold, stop **5** waive **8** reprieve **9** deferment, remission **10** suspension
without ~: **3** now **4** ASAP, stat **5** apace, right, short, today **6** at once **7** readily **8** directly, promptly, right now, right off **9** at present, forthwith, presently, right away, summarily **10** at this time, here and now, this minute
delayed: **4** late, slow **5** tardy **6** behind **7** belated, overdue **8** detained **9** leisurely
delaying: **4** slow **8** dilatory, hesitant **10** hesitation
Delbert: **4** Mann **9** McClinton
__ del Carmen: **5** Playa
__ del Corso: **3** Via
dele: **4** drop, edit, x off, x out **5** erase **6** excise, remove **7** edit out, expunge, take out **8** cross off, cross out **9** eliminate, expurgate, red-pencil, strike out
undo a ~: **4** stet
delectable: **5** sapid, sweet, tasty, yummy **6** dainty, divine, goodie, lovely, savory, toothy **7** darling **8** adorable, charming, enticing, fragrant, heavenly, inviting, luscious **9** agreeable, ambrosial, delicious, enjoyable, exquisite, flavorful, good to eat, nectarous, palatable, toothsome **10** appetizing, delightful, enchanting, gratifying, satisfying
delectate: **7** delight, enchant, gratify
delectation: **3** joy **4** zest **5** charm, gusto **7** delight, rapture **8** pleasure **9** enjoyment
Deledda, Grazia: **6** writer **7** Italian **8** Nobelist
delegate: **4** make, name, send **5** agent, envoy, proxy, trust, vicar **6** assign, charge, choose, commit, consul, depute, deputy, invest, nuncio, ordain, regent **7** appoint, consign, empower, entrust, intrust, license, stand-in **8** accredit, deputize, emissary, hand over, minister, nominate, relegate, settle on, transfer, turn over **9** appointee, authorize, designate, messenger, parcel out, surrogate **10** ambassador, commission, negotiator, settle upon
delegation: **8** congress **9** committal, gathering, reference, referring, submittal **10** assignment, commission, consigning, contingent, convention, conveyance, deputation, nomination, ordination, relegation
__ de León: **5** Ponce
de Lesseps: **9** Ferdinand
__ de l'est: **4** Gare
__ del Este: **5** Punta
delete: **3** cut **4** drop, omit, snip, trim, x out **5** annul, bleep, elide, erase, purge, scrub **6** cancel, censor, cut out, efface, excise, remove, rub off, rub out, strike **7** blot out, edit out, exclude, expunge, redline, scissor, scratch, take out, wipe out **8** black out, blow away, cross off, cross out, white out **9** eliminate, eradicate, expurgate, red-pencil, strike out **10** blue-pencil, obliterate
deleted: **3** x'ed
deleterious: **3** bad, ill **5** toxic **6** costly, malign, nocent **7** adverse, baleful, baneful, corrupt, harmful, hurtful, nocuous, noxious, ruinous **8** damaging, negative, sinister **9** dangerous, injurious, poisonous, unhealthy **10** calamitous, disastrous
deleteriousness: **4** harm
Delft: **4** city, port, town
locale: **7** Holland **11** Netherlands
ware: **8** ceramics
__ del Fuego: **6** Tierra

Delhi: 4 city, town
city SSE of ~: 4 Agra
locale: 5 India
river: 5 Jumna 6 Yamuna
__ Delhi: 3 New, Old
deli: 4 mart, shop 5 store 6 eatery, market 10 restaurant
item: 3 BLT, ham, lox, rye, sub 4 chub, hero, mayo, slaw, to go 5 bagel, bialy, derma, Genoa, hoagy, knish, latke, wurst 6 hoagie, kishka, Reuben, salami, tongue 7 bologna 8 pastrami 9 roast beef 10 corned beef
patron: 5 eater
scale word: 4 tare
shout: 4 next
unit: 2 lb., oz. 5 dozen, ounce, pound
Delia: 6 Ephron
Delian: 7 Artemis
League member: 5 Samos
deliberate: 3 sit 4 mull, muse, poky, slow 5 argue, meant, pause, study, sweat, think, waver, weigh 6 confer, debate, draggy, parley, ponder, reason, sedate, wanton, wilful 7 careful, decided, discuss, express, gradual, halting, impeded, lagging, languid, planned, reflect, revolve, serious, studied, willful, witting 8 cautious, chew over, cogitate, crawling, creeping, dawdling, dilatory, dragging, drawn-out, hesitant, intended, meditate, methodic, moderate, mull over, plodding, rational, resolute, ruminate, slothful, sluggish, talk over, toddling, turn over 9 cerebrate, conscious, designful, entertain, leisurely, lethargic, projected, prolonged, provident, purposive, snaillike, speculate, strategic, unhurried, voluntary 10 calculated, considered, excogitate, kick around, meticulous, protracted, purposeful, scrupulous, thoughtful, thought out, well-chosen
deliberately: 8 bit by bit, by design 9 leisurely, purposely
deliberation: 4 heed 6 debate, parley 7 caution, thought
without ~: 5 ad-lib 9 extempore 10 off-the-cuff
Delibes, Léo: 6 French 8 composer
work: 5 Lakmé
delicacy: 3 roe 4 tact 5 style, taste, treat, viand 6 caviar, dainty, luxury, morsel, nuance, tidbit 7 culture, finesse, frailty, modesty 8 airiness, ambrosia, elegance, fineness, subtlety, weakness 9 diplomacy, euphemism, fragility, frailness, lightness, propriety 10 daintiness, refinement
lacking ~: 4 rude 5 brash, crass
delicate: 4 deft, fine, lacy, nice, puny, sick, soft, thin, weak 5 adept, filmy, frail, gauzy, light, sheer, silky, wimpy, wispy 6 anemic, atonic, dainty, effete, feeble, flabby, flimsy, lovely, pastel, petite, pretty, sickly, slight, sticky, subtle, tender, tricky 7 anaemic, awkward, careful, elegant, fragile, mincing, netlike, politic, precise, refined, rickety, skilled, subdued, tactful, unsound, wimpish, wispish 8 cautious, discreet, ethereal, finespun, gossamer, graceful, helpless, masterly, perilous, pithless, skillful, ticklish, volatile 9 breakable, difficult, exquisite, faltering, frangible, powerless, sensitive, squeamish, unhealthy 10 cobweblike, diaphanous, diplomatic, ornamental, precarious, proficient, vulnerable
Delicate Balance, A
author: Edward Albee
__ Delicate Condition: 5 Papa's
delicatessen
see deli
delicious: 3 mmm, yum 4 good, nice, rich 5 apple, sapid, sweet, tasty, yummy 6 dainty, divine, lovely, savory, toothy, yum-yum 8 adorable, fragrant, heavenly, luscious, noshable 9 agreeable, ambrosial, enjoyable, exquisite, fantastic, flavorful, good to eat, nectarous, palatable, succulent, toothsome 10 appetizing, delectable, delightful, gratifying
__ delicti: 6 corpus
delicto, find in flagrante: 5 catch
delictum: 5 crime
delight: 3 joy, wow 4 glee, send, zest 5 amuse, bliss, charm, cheer, elate, exult, gusto, peach, revel 6 divert, excite, fulfil, luxury, please, ravish, regale, thrill, tickle, turn on, wallow 7 beguile, disport, ecstasy, elation, enchant, fulfill, gladden, gratify, happify, hearten, rapture, rejoice, satisfy, triumph 8 entrance, euphoria, felicity, intrigue, jubilate, knock out, pleasure, radiance, radiancy 9 amusement, delectate, enrapture, entertain, fascinate, happiness, jocundity, luxuriate, transport 10 ebullience, effervesce, exhilarate, exultation, jump for joy, regalement
cry of ~: 2 ah 3 aah, ooh 4 good, whee 5 goody, oh boy, zowie 6 goodie, hotcha, hot dog
in: 4 bask, like, love 5 adore, eat up, enjoy, revel, savor 6 relish 9 feast upon, luxuriate
show ~: 4 glow, grin 5 smile
__ delight: 6 Idiot's 7 Turkish
delighted: 4 glad, rapt 5 happy, merry 6 blithe, cheery, enrapt, jovial, joyful, joyous, upbeat 7 charmed, gleeful, pleased, radiant 8 blissful, cheerful, ecstatic, euphoric, exultant, jubilant, mirthful, ravished 9 delirious, enchanted, entranced, fulfilled, gladdened, gratified, overjoyed, rejoicing, rhapsodic 10 captivated, fascinated, flying high
be ~: 4 rave 5 exult
__ delighted!: 4 I'd be
delightful: 4 nice 5 sweet 6 cheery, clever, dreamy, golden, jovial, lovely, pretty 7 amusing, darling, lovable, sensual, winsome 8 adorable, charming, engaging, glorious, heavenly, inviting, loveable, pleasant, pleasing 9 agreeable, ambrosial, beautiful, congenial, delicious, enjoyable, ineffable, nectarous, palatable, rapturous, ravishing, thrilling 10 acceptable, attractive, delectable, enchanting, gratifying, refreshing, satisfying
place: 4 Eden
Delight in Disorder: 4 poem
author: Robert Herrick
Delilah: 5 Jones
lover: 6 Samson
Delilah (1968 song)
artist: Tom Jones
DeLillo, Don: 6 writer
work: Americana
The Body Artist
End Zone
Libra
Mao II
The Names
Running Dog
Underworld
White Noise
delimit: 6 define 7 confine 9 determine
delineate: 3 map, set 4 draw, etch, limn, mark, plot 5 chart, paint, trace 6 define, depict, design, detail, lay out, map out, recite, sketch 7 outline, picture, portray, recount 8 block out, describe 9 adumbrate, interpret 10 illustrate
delineation: 3 map 4 tale 5 chart, draft, story 6 design, report, sketch 7 account, diagram, drawing, outline, profile 8 likeness 9 depiction, narration, rendition
delinquency: 5 abuse, fault, guilt 7 neglect, offense 9 oversight
delinquent: 3 bad, lax 4 AWOL, lack, late, punk 5 felon, slack, tardy 6 behind, guilty, outlaw, rascal, remiss, unpaid 7 culprit, hoodlum, overdue, runaway, wayward 8 blamable, careless, criminal, culpable, derelict, hooligan, offender, recreant 9 blameable, defaulter, desperado, miscreant, negligent, offending, red-handed, reprobate, wrongdoer 10 blackguard, black sheep, censurable, defaultant, defaulting, lawbreaker, malefactor, neglectful
be ~: 3 owe
__ de Lion: 5 Coeur
deliquesce: 4 melt, thaw 7 liquefy, liquify 8 dissolve, fluidize
delirious: 4 wild 5 rabid 6 raving 7 excited, frantic 8 ecstatic, frenetic, frenzied, thrilled, wild-eyed 9 delighted, disturbed, gladdened, overjoyed, rapturous, unsettled, wandering 10 bewildered, corybantic, disordered, distracted, flipped out, hysterical, incoherent, irrational
be ~: 4 rave 7 carry on
Delirious (1983 song)
artist: Prince
delirium: 4 zeal 5 mania 6 fervor, frenzy 7 ecstasy, passion, rapture 8 hysteria 10 enthusiasm
__-de-lis: 5 fleur
Deli, The rapper: 4 Ice-T
Delius: 9 Frederick
deliver: 3 fax 4 bear, cart, deal, free, give, have, hurl, read, save, send, ship, take 5 bring, carry, fetch, fling, loose, pitch, relay, remit, serve, speak, throw, truck, utter 6 acquit, commit, convey, fork up, hand in, launch, loosen, ransom, recite, redeem, rescue, supply, turn in, wait on 7 achieve, consign, declare, dish out, drop off, express, forward, inflict, lecture, present, produce, provide, recruit, release 8 announce, dispatch, dispense, fork over, hand down, hand over, liberate, make good, proclaim, transfer, transmit, turn over, wait upon 9 discharge, extricate, give forth, pronounce, transport, unshackle 10 administer, distribute, emancipate
a speech: 4 rant, talk 5 orate
prepare to ~: 5 lie in
something to ~: 4 mail 5 cargo 6 letter 7 freight, package
the goods: 7 perform
up: 4 sell 5 yield 6 turn in 7 sell out 8 hand over 9 surrender
deliverance: 6 ransom, relief, rescue 7 freedom, liberty, release 9 salvation
Deliverance: 4 film 5 novel
author: James Dickey
cast: Ned Beatty, Ronny Cox, Burt Reynolds, Jon Voight
director: John Boorman
instrument: 5 banjo
delivered: 4 born
be ~ of: 4 bear
deliverer: 6 savior 7 messiah, saviour
of old: 6 iceman 7 milkman
way: 5 route
...deliver us from __: 4 evil
delivery: 3 pkg. 4 drop, mail 5 birth, issue 6 rescue 7 arrival, carting, diction, freeing, liberty, mailing, package, receipt, recital, release 8 carriage, dispatch, shipment, transfer 9 elocution, rendition, salvation, utterance 10 childbirth, conveyance, inflection, intonation, liberation, modulation, recitation, transferal
accept ~: 7 receive
acknowledgment: 4 rcpt. 7 receipt
daily ~: 4 mail 5 paper 9 newspaper
extra: 5 setup
letters: 3 COD
person: 9 messenger
service: 3 UPS 4 USPS 5 FedEx
vehicle: 3 van 5 truck
delivery __: 3 boy 4 room
dell: 4 glen 6 dingle, hollow, valley 8 clearing
dweller: 6 farmer
Dell: 2 PC 4 Gabe 7 Gabriel 8 computer
competitor: 3 IBM 7 Gateway
Della: 5 falls, Reese 6 Street 9 waterfall
creator of ~: 4 Erle
Della Robbia: 4 Luca
delle Puglie: 4 Bari
Dello Joio: 6 Norman
__ del Mar: 4 Viña
Delmer: 5 Daves

Delmonico __: **5** steak
Del Monte: **6** catsup **7** ketchup
alternative: **5** Heinz, Hunt's **6** Libby's
Delmore: **8** Schwartz
__ de l'Omelette, The: **3** Duc
Delon: **5** Alain
__ de Londres: **4** gros
DeLorean: **4** John
Delos: **4** isle **6** island
locale: **6** Greece **8** Cyclades
de los Angeles: **8** Victoria
__-de-loup: **4** trou
__ De-Lovely: **3** It's
Delphi: **4** town **8** language
alternative: ***see*** computer language
god: **6** Apollo
oracle site: **6** Phocis
priestess: **6** oracle
Delphian: **4** deep **5** vatic **7** fatidic **8** oracular **9** enigmatic, prophetic, vaticinal
Delphine
author: Madame de Staël
delphinium: **5** plant **6** flower
__ del Plata: **3** Mar
__ del Prado: **5** Museo
Delpy: **5** Julie
Delray Beach: **4** city, town
locale: **7** Florida
del Rey: **6** Lester
__ del Rey, CA: **6** Marina
Del Rio: **7** Dolores
__ del Rio, Cuba: **5** Pinar
Delroy: **5** Lindo
Del Ruth: **3** Roy
del Sarto, Andrea: **6** artist **7** Italian, painter
__ del Sol: **5** Costa
Del Sol: **3** car **4** auto **5** Honda
delt: **6** muscle
kin: **2** ab **3** pec **4** quad
delta: **5** Greek, mouth **6** letter **7** deposit
deposit: **4** silt
follower: **7** epsilon
locale: **5** mouth, river
preceder: **5** gamma
delta __: **3** ray **4** iron, team, wave, wing
Delta: **3** car **4** auto, font, Olds, town **5** Burke **7** airline **8** typeface **10** automobile, Oldsmobile
alternative: ***see*** airline, U.S.
former competitor: **3** TWA **5** Pan Am, USAir **7** Braniff, Eastern **8** National
hub: **7** Atlanta
overseer: **3** FAA
Delta __: **4** Dawn, team **6** Center **7** Wedding
Delta Dawn (1973 song)
artist: Helen Reddy
Delta Factor, The
author: Mickey Spillane
Delta of Venus, The
author: Anaïs Nin
Delta Wedding
author: Eudora Welty
deltoid: **6** muscle **10** triangular
Deltona: **4** city, town
locale: **7** Florida
Del Toro, Benicio: **5** actor
film: The Pledge (2001)
Snatch (2000)
Traffic (2000, AA)
deludable: **4** easy, naif **5** naive
delude: **3** con, lie **4** dupe, fool, hoax, jive, nick, sell, snow **5** bluff, cheat, cozen, lie to, sneak, trick **6** betray, lead on, rope in, sucker, take in **7** beguile, deceive, defraud, mislead, pretend, two-time **8** hoodwink, misguide, pettifog, throw off **9** bamboozle, disinform, four-flush
deluge: **4** gush, pour, rain, rush, teem **5** crowd, drown, flood, souse, spate, surge, swamp **6** drench, engulf, ingulf, lavish, onrush **7** barrage, cascade, overrun, torrent **8** downpour, inundate, overflow, overload, plethora, submerge **9** avalanche, overwhelm, snow under **10** cloudburst, inundation, outpouring
refuge: **3** ark
Delugg: **6** Milton
DeLuise: **3** Dom **5** Peter
DeLuise, Dom
film: Fatso (1980)
__ de Lune: **5** Clair
delusion: **4** myth **5** dream **6** dupery, fantom, mirage **7** chimera, eidolon, fallacy, fantasm, fantasy, figment, mistake, phantom **8** chimaera, daydream, phantasm **9** deception, fairy tale, mare's nest, misbelief, obsession, pipe dream **10** aberration, apparition
freedom from ~: **7** nirvana
in Buddhism: **7** samsara
delusive: **3** sly **5** false, lying **6** irreal, tricky, unreal, untrue **7** crooked, devious **8** fanciful, guileful, quixotic, specious, spurious **9** beguiling, deceitful, deceptive, dishonest, imaginary, insincere **10** chimerical, fallacious, mendacious, misleading, quixotical, unreliable, untruthful
delusory: **5** lying **9** deceitful, deceptive, visionary **10** fallacious, misleading
deluxe: **4** fine, lush, nice, posh, rich **5** fancy, grand, plush, ritzy, swank, swell **6** choice, costly, loaded, select, swanky **7** capital, elegant, opulent **8** palatial, splendid, superior, top-shelf **9** exclusive, expensive, high-class, luxuriant, luxurious, sumptuous, unrivaled **10** first-class, unrivalled
__ del Vaticano: **5** Città
delve: **3** dig **4** grub, mine, root, seek **5** plumb, probe **6** burrow, dredge **7** rummage, unearth **8** excavate, research
into: **4** look, pore, sift **5** plumb, probe **7** examine, explore **8** read up on
delve __: **4** into
Delvecchio: **4** Alex
Del Verrocchio: **6** Andrea
__-de-lys: **5** fleur
demagnetize: **5** erase
demagogue: **7** fanatic, hothead, inciter **8** agitator, fomenter, inflamer **9** firebrand **10** incendiary, instigator, politician
__ de main: **4** coup
__ de maître: **4** coup
__ de Mallorca: **5** Palma
demand: **3** bid, tax **4** call, levy, need, plea, take, urge, want, will **5** claim, exact, force, order, press, price **6** appeal, compel, enjoin, impose, insist, sue for **7** call for, enquire, enquiry, implore, inquire, inquiry, proviso, request, require, solicit **8** entreaty, insist on, occasion, petition, press for, pressure **9** clamor for, cry out for, impetrate, importune, necessity, provision, requisite, ultimatum **10** imposition, injunction, insistence, popularity, supplicate, union issue, urgent need
as a price: **3** ask
companion: **6** supply
heavy ~: **3** run
in ~: **3** hot **6** staple **7** popular **8** valuable **10** at a premium, marketable
payment: **3** dun
demand __: **3** bid **4** bill, loan, note **5** draft **7** deposit
demanding: **4** firm, hard **5** bossy, cruel, exact, fussy, picky, rigid, rough, stern, tough **6** rugged, severe, strict, taxing, thorny, trying, uphill, urgent **7** arduous, austere, exigent, finicky, nagging, onerous, Spartan **8** captious, critical, despotic, exacting, exigeant, finiking, finnicky, grueling, hardline, pressing, rigorous, tiresome, toilsome **9** ambitious, assertive, challenge, clamorous, difficult, draconian, impatient, imperious, insistent, intensive, laborious, querulous, strenuous, stringent, unbending, unsparing **10** bothersome, burdensome, despotical, enervating, exhausting, fastidious, formidable, inflexible, insatiable, iron-fisted, no-nonsense, oppressive, particular, tyrannical, unamenable
not ~: **4** easy **5** cushy, light
one: **5** taker **8** martinet **9** nit-picker
demarcate: **5** limit **6** define **7** delimit **9** determine
demarcation: **4** line **5** limit **6** margin **8** boundary, division, terminus
line of ~: **4** edge **5** verge **6** border, margin **8** frontier **9** perimeter, periphery
Demarest: **7** William
Demaret, Jimmy: **6** golfer
__-de-Marne, France: **3** Val
dematerialize: **6** vanish
de Matteo: **4** Drea
de Maupassant: **3** Guy
__ de Mayo: **5** Cinco
demean: **3** dis, pan **4** haze, sink **5** abase, lower, scorn **6** debase, dump on, humble, lessen **7** contemn, corrupt, cry down, degrade, put down **8** badmouth, belittle, bring low, derogate, diminish, play down, take down **9** bring down, disparage, humiliate, knock down
oneself: **5** stoop **6** grovel, kowtow
demeaning: **6** menial **10** derogatory, detractive, pejorative
demeanor: **3** air, set **4** cast, look, mien **5** front, guise, poise **6** aspect, manner **7** bearing, conduct, fashion **8** attitude, behavior, carriage, presence **10** appearance, deportment
de' Medici: **6** Cosimo **7** Lorenzo
in-law: **4** Este
de Médicis: **5** Marie **9** Catherine
__ de menthe: **5** crème
Dementieva: **5** Elena
Demento: **2** Dr.
__ de mer: **3** mal
__-de-mer: **4** coco **5** bêche
demesne: **6** estate, region **8** province
Demeter: **7** goddess
daughter: **4** Cora, Kore **8** Despoena **10** Persephone
epithet: **5** Chloe, Evius, Lusia, Mysia **6** Erinys, Stiria
equivalent: **5** Ceres
lover: **4** Zeus **6** Iasion **8** Poseidon
parent: **4** Rhea **6** Cronos, Cronus
sibling: **4** Hera, Zeus **5** Hades **6** Hestia **8** Poseidon
son: **5** Arion **6** Plutus **7** Eubulus **8** Dionysus
demi-: **4** half
demi-__: **3** sec **4** plié
Demi: **5** Moore
Demian
author: Hermann Hesse
demi ender: **4** urge **5** monde, tasse
__ de mieux: **5** faute
demilitarized zone: **5** limbo
de Mille: **5** Agnes
DeMille, Cecil B.: **8** director
film: The Buccaneer (1938)
The Cheat (1915)
Cleopatra (1934)
The Crusades (1935)
Dynamite (1929)
The Greatest Show on Earth (1952)
The King of Kings (1927)
Madam Satan (1930)
The Plainsman (1936)
Reap the Wild Wind (1942)
The Road to Yesterday (1925)
Samson and Delilah (1949)
The Squaw Man (1931)
The Ten Commandments (1923)
The Ten Commandments (1956)
This Day and Age (1933)
Union Pacific (1939)
genre: **4** epic
DeMille, Nelson: **6** writer
work: By the Rivers of Babylon
Cathedral
Charm School
The Gate House
The General's Daughter
The Gold Coast
The Lion's Game
Mayday
Night Fall
Plum Island
Spencerville
The Talbot Odyssey
Up Country
Wild Fire
Word of Honor
__ de Milo: **5** Venus
demise: **3** end **5** lease **8** downfall
demisemiquaver: **4** note
demit: **4** quit **5** lower **6** resign **8** abdicate, renounce
demitasse: **3** cup **6** coffee

demiurgic: 8 original 9 inventive

Demme: 3 Ted 8 Jonathan

Demme, Jonathan: 8 director
film: Cousin Bobby (1991)
Crazy Mama (1975)
Handle With Care (1977)
Last Embrace (1979)
Married to the Mob (1988)
Melvin and Howard (1980)
Philadelphia (1993)
The Silence of the Lambs (1991, AA)
Stop Making Sense (1984)

demobilize: 7 disband

democracy: 6 nation 7 freedom 8 republic 10 capitalism
participant: 5 voter
world's largest ~: 5 India

Democracy
author: Joan Didion

Democrat: 3 FDR, HST, JFK, LBJ, pol 4 peak 5 mount 8 mountain
certain ~: 7 liberal
locale: 7 Rockies 8 Colorado
opponent: 3 GOP, Ind., Rep.

__ Democrat: 6 Social

Democrat-Gazette: 5 paper 9 newspaper
locale: 8 Arkansas 10 Little Rock

democratic: 4 free 8 populist 9 socialist 10 autonomous, self-ruling

Democratic: 5 party
donkey creator: Thomas Nast
early ~ opponent: 4 Whig

Democratic-Republican: 5 party

Democritus: 5 Greek 11 philosopher

démodé: 3 old, out 5 passé 8 outdated 9 out-of-date

demographic datum: 3 age, sex 4 race 6 gender

demography: 6 census 7 science

demoiselle: 4 bird, girl 5 crane, woman 6 damsel, maiden

demolish: 4 rase, raze, ruin, sack, sink, undo 5 blast, break, crush, level, scrap, smash, spoil, total, trash, wreck 6 defeat, quench, ravage, refute, topple, uproot 7 destroy, flatten, shatter, subvert, torpedo, unbuild 8 bulldoze, decimate, dissolve, pull down, spoliate, take down, tear down 9 devastate, dismantle, eradicate, extirpate, knock down, pulverize, take apart 10 annihilate, obliterate

demolished: 4 lost 5 kaput

demolition: 5 wreck 6 razing 8 leveling, sabotage 9 explosion 10 bulldozing
material: 3 TNT 5 nitro

demolition __: 5 derby

Demolition Man (1993 film)
cast: Sandra Bullock, Wesley Snipes, Sylvester Stallone

demon: 3 imp 4 ogre 5 afrit, beast, brute, devil, fiend, ghoul, jinni, lamia, rogue 6 afreet, goblin, rascal, spirit 7 fanatic, hellion, incubus, monster, villain 8 succubus 9 archfiend, speedster 10 evil spirit
Arabian ~: 5 afrit 6 afreet
speed ~: 5 racer 6 hot rod

demon __: 3 rum

__ demon: 5 speed

Demon __: 3 Box 4 Seed, Star

Demon Box author: Ken Kesey

Demond: 6 Wilson

Demon Deacons: 10 Wake Forest

demonic: 3 bad 4 evil, vile 5 cruel, manic 6 crazed, savage, wicked 7 frantic, hellish, lunatic, satanic, violent 8 devilish, diabolic, fiendish, frenzied, infernal, maniacal 9 satanical 10 diabolical

__ Demons: 4 Blue

Demon Seed author: Dean Koontz

demonstrate: 4 cite, give, show, test 5 argue, march, prove, rally, sit in, teach 6 evince, parade, picket, reason, unfold, verify 7 bespeak, confirm, declare, display, exhibit, explain, express, produce, protest, reflect, roll out, show off, trot out 8 describe, evidence, indicate, manifest, proclaim, set forth

demonstrated, which was to be: 3 QED

demonstration: 4 show 5 flash, lie-in, march, proof, rally, sit-in, token 6 love-in, parade 7 display, protest 8 evidence 9 spectacle, testimony
sight: 6 banner, poster 10 picket line

demonstrative: 6 loving, tender 7 certain, gushing 8 decisive, definite, outgoing, specific
pronoun: 4 that, this

demonstrator: 8 militant 9 protester

demoralize: 4 damp, rout 5 abash, break, daunt, shake, stain, upset 6 dampen, deject, rattle, unglue 7 corrupt, depress, nonplus, unnerve 8 dispirit, psych out, unsettle, unstring 9 brutalize, discomfit, disparage, embarrass, give pause, overwhelm, undermine 10 debilitate, disconcert, discourage, dishearten

demoralized: 6 broken 7 crushed, daunted 8 dejected, downcast 9 depressed, dispirited 10 spiritless

DeMornay: 7 Rebecca

Demosthenes: 5 Greek 6 orator

demote: 4 bust, drop 5 break, lower 6 humble, reduce 7 degrade 8 bring low, bump down, reassign, relegate 9 downgrade, humiliate, knock down

__ de mots: 3 jeu

Dempsey: 4 Jack 7 Patrick

Dempsey, Jack: 5 boxer

demulcent: 4 balm 6 lotion 7 anodyne, unction 8 ointment, soothing 9 emollient 10 mollifying, palliative

demur: 3 haw 4 balk 5 baulk, tarry 6 beg off, boggle, object, recoil, refuse, regret, resist, shrink 7 decline, protest, scruple 8 complain, disagree, hesitate, hold back, question 9 make a fuss 10 disapprove, put up a fuss

demure: 3 coy, shy 4 meek, prim 5 sober, staid, timid 6 chaste, humble, modest, prissy, proper, sedate 7 bashful, prudish 8 affected, blushing, reserved, retiring, skittish 9 diffident 10 unassuming, uneffusive
in England: 3 mim

demureness: 7 modesty 8 humility

demurral: 5 delay 10 hesitation

demurring: 9 reluctant, unwilling

demy: 5 paper

Demy, Jacques
film: Lola (1961)

den: 4 cave, hold, lair, nest, nook, room 5 haunt, lodge, study 6 burrow, cavern, hotbed, kennel, refuge, TV room 7 atelier, hideout, library, rec room, retreat, sanctum, shelter 8 cloister, dwelling, hideaway, playroom, snuggery 9 media room, sanctuary 10 family room, rumpus room, trophy room
denizen: 3 cub 4 bear
need: 2 TV 4 sofa 5 TV set 6 settee

den __: 3 mom 5 chief 6 father, mother

Den __: 4 Haag

__ de nacre: 5 L'Etui

Denali: 3 GMC, SUV 4 park, peak 5 mount 8 McKinley, mountain
locale: 6 Alaska

denarius: 4 coin 5 money

denary: 7 tenfold

denatured __: 7 alcohol

Dench, Judi: 4 Dame 7 actress
film: Casino Royale (2005)
Chocolat (2000)
The Chronicles of Riddick (2004)
Die Another Day (2002)
GoldenEye (1995)
Iris (2001)
Mrs. Henderson Presents (2005)
Notes on a Scandal (2006)
Pride & Prejudice (2005)
Quantum of Solace (2008)
Rage (2009)
Shakespeare in Love (1998, AA)
The Shipping News (2001)
Tomorrow Never Dies (1997)
The World Is Not Enough (1999)

dendrite
counterpart: 4 axon 5 axone
locale: 5 nerve 6 neuron

dendritic: 8 arboreal

dendrology: 6 botany

dendrophobe fear: 5 trees

Deneb: 4 star
constellation: 6 Cygnus

Deneuve: 9 Catherine

Deng: 7 Chinese 8 Xiaoping
predecessor: 3 Mao

Den Haag: 4 city, town 7 capital
locale: 7 Holland 11 Netherlands

Denholm: 7 Elliott

denial: 2 no 3 nah, nay 4 nope, not I, uh-uh, veto 5 not me 6 rebuff 7 refusal 8 negation, nihilism, refusing, turndown 9 disavowal, disbelief, dismissal, rejection 10 abnegation, disclaimer, gainsaying, refutation, retraction
French ~: 3 non
German ~: 4 nein
military ~: 5 no sir
phrase: 4 not I 5 not me
Russian ~: 4 nyet
Scottish ~: 3 nae
Security Council ~: 4 veto
slangy ~: 3 nah, naw 4 nope, uh-uh 6 ain't so

Deniece: 8 Williams

denier: 7 atheist 8 Alibi Ike, naysayer

denigrate: 3 dis, hit, rip 4 gibe, jeer, jibe, mock, slam, slur, snub 5 abuse, decry, knock, libel, roast, scorn, smear, spurn, sully, taunt 6 defame, deride, dump on, heckle, humble, impugn, malign, offend, rebuff, revile, slight, vilify 7 affront, asperse, blacken, blister, censure, cry down, degrade, detract, disdain, put down, rank out, run down, slander, traduce 8 backbite, belittle, besmirch, denounce, derogate, mudsling, ridicule, tear down, throw mud, vilipend 9 discredit, disparage, downgrade, humiliate 10 calumniate, depreciate, disrespect, scandalize, villainize

denigration: 3 dig 4 barb, gibe, jibe, slam, slap, slur, snub 5 abuse, libel, scorn, taunt 6 rebuff, slight 7 affront, calumny, catcall, disdain, mockery, obloquy, offense, put-down, slander 8 contempt, ridicule 9 cheap shot, contumely 10 disrespect, opprobrium

denim: 5 cloth 6 fabric 8 material

denims: 5 jeans, pants 7 cutoffs 8 trousers 9 blue jeans, dungarees

De Niro, Robert: 5 actor
film: 15 Minutes (2001)
Analyze That (2002)
Analyze This (1999)
Awakenings (1990)
Backdraft (1991)
Bang the Drum Slowly (1973)
Brazil (1985)
A Bronx Tale (1993)
Cape Fear (1991)
Casino (1995)
Cop Land (1997)
The Deer Hunter (1978)
Falling in Love (1984)
The Fan (1996)
The Godfather Part II (1974, AA)
GoodFellas (1990)
The Good Shepherd (2005)
Greetings (1968)
Guilty by Suspicion (1991)
Heat (1995)
Hide and Seek (2005)
Hi, Mom! (1970)
Jacknife (1989)
The King of Comedy (1983)
The Last Tycoon (1976)
Mad Dog and Glory (1993)
Mean Streets (1973)
Meet the Parents (2000)
Men of Honor (2000)
Midnight Run (1988)
New York, New York (1977)
Once Upon a Time in America (1984)
Raging Bull (1980, AA)
Righteous Kill (2008)
The Score (2001)
Showtime (2002)
Sleepers (1996)
Stanley & Iris (1990)
Stardust (2007)
Taxi Driver (1976)
This Boy's Life (1993)
True Confessions (1981)
The Untouchables (1987)
Wag the Dog (1997)
What Just Happened (2008)

Denis: 5 Leary, saint 6 Potvin 7 Diderot

Denise: 3 Loo 6 Crosby, Darcel 8 Huxtable, Levertov, Nicholas, Richards
Denison: 4 city, town
locale: 5 Texas
denizen: 5 liver, voter 6 native 7 citizen, dweller, resider 8 habitant, occupant, resident 9 indweller 10 inhabitant
__ den Linden: 5 Unter
Denmark: 6 nation, strait 7 country
astronomer: 5 Brahe
ballet dancer: 5 Bruhn 7 Martins
capital: 10 Copenhagen
chemist: 8 Sorensen
city: 5 Arhus 6 Ålborg, Odense 7 Aalborg 9 Helsingör 10 Copenhagen
explorer: 6 Bering 9 Rasmussen
island off ~: 3 Fyn 4 Fano
islands: 5 Faroe
king: 4 Eric, Knut 6 Canute
legislature: 9 Folketing
money: 3 ore 4 oras 5 krone 9 rixdollar
neighbor: 7 Germany
Nobelist in Chemistry: 4 Skou
Nobelist in Literature: 6 Jensen 9 Gjellerup 11 Pontoppidan
Nobelist in Medicine: 3 Dam 5 Krogh 6 Finsen 7 Fibiger
Nobelist in Peace: 5 Bajer
Nobelist in Physics: 4 Bohr 9 Mottelson
org.: 4 NATO
physician: 6 Finsen
physicist: 4 Bohr 7 Oersted
pianist: 5 Borge
scientist: 4 Bohr 5 Brahe 6 Finsen 7 Oersted 8 Sorensen
tenor: 8 Melchior
toast: 5 skoal
toy company: 4 Lego
weight: 4 eser
writer: 4 Bang, Nexö 6 Jensen 7 Dinesen, Holberg 8 Andersen, Jacobsen 9 Gjellerup
Dennehy: 5 Brian
Denning: 7 Richard
Dennis: 3 Day 5 Cathy, Dugan, Franz, Gabor, Quaid, Sandy 6 Brutus, Coffey, Farina, Hopper, Miller, Morgan, O'Keefe, Potter, Rodman, Weaver, Wilson 7 DeYoung, Patrick, Ralston 8 Haysbert, Mitchell 9 DeConcini
Dennis, Patrick aunt: 4 Mame
Dennis the Menace: 3 imp 4 brat, pest 5 comic 10 comic strip
artist: Hank Ketcham
cat: 6 Hot Dog
character: 4 Gina, Joey 5 Alice, Henry 6 Wilson 8 Margaret
dog: 4 Ruff
like ~: 5 pesky, pesty
Dennis the Menace (CBS sitcom)
cast: Herbert Anderson (Henry Mitchell)
Gloria Henry (Alice Mitchell)
Joseph Kearns (George Wilson)
Jay North (Dennis Mitchell)
dog: 7 Fremont
Denny: 5 Crane 6 Martin, McLain 8 Reginald
Denny's
rival: ***see*** restaurant chain
denominate: 4 call, name, term 5 style, title 9 designate
denomination: 3 ilk 4 cult, kind, name, sect, sort, term, type, unit 5 brand, class, creed, faith, grade, group, label, title, value 6 belief, church 7 variety 8 category, religion
__ denominator: 6 common
denotation: 4 sign 5 sense 6 symbol 7 meaning 10 definition, importance, indication
denotative: 8 symbolic 10 figurative, indicative
denote: 4 mark, mean, name, show 5 imply, spell 6 signal 7 betoken, express, purport, signify, suggest 8 evidence, indicate, pinpoint, point out, stand for 9 adumbrate, designate, represent, symbolize
denouement: 3 end 5 close 6 climax, ending, finale, finish, result, upshot, windup, wrap-up 7 last act 8 terminus 10 conclusion, resolution
denounce: 3 hit, rap 4 damn, gibe, jeer, jibe, mock, rail, slam, slur, snub 5 abuse, blame, blast, decry, knock, libel, roast, scold, scorn, smear, spurn, taunt 6 accuse, attack, defame, deride, dump on, heckle, impugn, indict, malign, offend, rail at, rebuff, rebuke, revile, slight, vilify 7 affront, asperse, censure, condemn, declaim, degrade, deplore, disdain, impeach, lambast, put down, rank out, reprove, slander, traduce, upbraid 8 belittle, bloviate, derogate, lambaste, reproach, ridicule, vilipend 9 castigate, challenge, criticize, denigrate, discredit, disparage, dress down, excoriate, fulminate, fustigate, humiliate, proscribe, reprehend, reprimand 10 calumniate, disrespect, make a stand, stigmatize, take to task, vituperate
de novo: 3 new 4 anew 5 again 6 afresh 10 from the top
dense: 3 dim 4 dopy, dull, dumb, firm, hard, lush, rank, slow 5 close, crass, dopey, heavy, solid, thick, tight 6 bovine, jammed, oafish, obtuse, packed, simple, stolid, stupid 7 boorish, compact, crammed, crowded, doltish, fatuous, foolish, loutish, lumpish, teeming, weighty, witless 8 mindless, populous, thickset 9 close-knit, condensed, dimwitted, jam-packed, luxuriant, pigheaded 10 compressed, hard-packed, slow-witted, synopsized
one: ***see*** ninny
density: 6 weight 8 firmness, hardness
symbol: 3 rho
dent: 3 mar, pit 4 bump, bung, ding, mark, nick 5 notch 6 bang up, cavity, dimple, hollow, push in, recess 7 headway, press in 8 disallow 9 concavity 10 depression, impression
location: 6 fender
make a ~: 5 begin, solve
Dent: 5 Bucky
dental __: 4 lisp, pulp 5 floss, plate 7 hygiene
dental floss option: 3 wax
dental-rinse brand: 4 Plax
dented: 7 concave
dentist
advice: 5 brush, floss
concern: 3 gap 4 ache, chip 5 crown, decay, inlay, lower, teeth, tooth, upper 6 braces, bridge, caries, cavity, enamel 9 toothache
deg.: 3 DDS, DMD
need: 4 X-ray 5 drill 6 cement
office call: 4 next
office music: 5 Muzak
org.: 3 ADA
request: 4 bite, open 5 rinse
supply, once: 5 ether
dentistry: 7 science
Denton: 4 city, town
athletes: 9 Mean Green
locale: 5 Texas
school: 3 UNT 10 North Texas
__ d'entrée: 5 carte
__ dents: 5 mal de
Dentyne: 3 gum
alternative: ***see*** chewing gum
denude: 4 bare, peel 5 strip 6 expose, fleece 7 disrobe, lay bare, uncover, undrape, undress
__ de nuit: 5 boîte
denunciate: 4 damn 5 blame, knock, scold 6 rail at 7 upbraid 9 criticize, fulminate 10 take to task
denunciation: 4 slam 5 abuse, blame 6 attack, tirade 7 reproof 8 diatribe
Denver: 3 Bob 4 city, John, Pyle, town
college: 5 Regis
height: 4 mile
locale: 7 Rockies 8 Colorado
newspaper: 4 Post
pro team: 7 Broncos, Nuggets, Rockies
river: 11 South Platte
suburb: 6 Arvada
zone: 3 MDT, MST
Denver __: 4 boot 6 omelet 8 omelette
Denver, John
album: 5 Aerie
song: Annie's Song (1974)
Back Home Again (1974)
Calypso (1975)
I'm Sorry (1975)
Rocky Mountain High (1973)
Sunshine on My Shoulders (1974)
Take Me Home, Country Roads (1971)
Thank God I'm a Country Boy (1975)
deny: 3 bar, nix 4 veto 5 rebut 6 disown, forbid, impugn, negate, oppose, rebuff, recant, refuse, refute, reject 7 disavow, dispute, gainsay, mortify 8 abnegate, disclaim, go back on, prohibit, renounce, turn down, withhold 9 repudiate 10 contradict, controvert, cut off from
oneself: 7 abstain
use: 3 bar 5 debar, expel 6 censor, forbid, outlaw 7 boycott, exclude, rule out 8 disallow, prohibit 9 blackball, ostracize, proscribe
Denys: 5 saint
Denzel: 10 Washington
deo: 4 Mars 7 Jupiter, Mercury, Neptune
deo __: 7 gratias, volente
deodar: 4 tree 5 cedar
deodorant: 3 Ban 4 Sure 5 Arrid, Tussy 6 Degree, Secret 7 Dry Idea, Mitchum 9 fumigator 10 Right Guard, Soft and Dri, Speed Stick
form: 5 spray 6 roll-on
deodorize: 4 wash 5 clean 6 purify 7 cleanse, freshen, refresh, sweeten 8 sanitize 9 disinfect
__ de Oro: 3 Rio
deoxyribonucleic: 4 acid
De Palma, Brian: 8 director
film: Blow Out (1981)
Body Double (1984)
The Bonfire of the Vanities (1990)
Carlito's Way (1993)
Carrie (1976)
Dressed to Kill (1980)
The Fury (1978)
Greetings (1968)
Hi, Mom! (1970)
Mission: Impossible (1996)
Phantom of Paradise (1974)
Scarface (1983)
Sisters (1973)
The Untouchables (1987)
spouse: Nancy Allen
Depardieu: 6 Gérard
depart: 2 go 3 fly, run 4 exit, flee, move, quit, vary 5 go off, leave, scram, split, start, stray 6 beat it, cut out, decamp, desert, escape, get out, go away, move on, pop off, ramble, recede, retire, secede, set off, set out, vacate 7 abscond, entrain, get away, head out, make off, migrate, pull out, push off, retreat, ride off, take off 8 abdicate, bid adieu, blast off, emigrate, evacuate, hightail, light out, run along, separate, set forth, shove off, slip away, withdraw 9 break camp, bundle off, cut and run, disappear, take leave 10 hit the road, make tracks, shuffle off
ender: 3 ure
(from): 6 differ 7 deviate
departed: 4 away, gone, left, went 9 withdrawn
Departed, The (2006 film)
cast: Matt Damon, Leonardo DiCaprio, Jack Nicholson, Mark Wahlberg
director: Martin Scorsese
departing: 8 outgoing
department: 3 arm, job 4 area, duty, slot, unit, ward 5 board, field, realm 6 agency, branch, bureau, domain, office, sphere 7 section, station 8 category, division, function, precinct, province, vocation 9 bailiwick, expertise, specialty 10 assignment, commission, occupation
head: 4 prof 9 professor
heads: 5 board 7 cabinet, council 8 advisors 9 committee 10 brain trust, counselors
department __: 5 store
__ department: 4 fire 6 police

DE

Department of __: **5** Labor, State **6** Energy **7** Defense, Justice **8** Commerce **9** Education
department store: **4** mart **5** K Mart, Kohl's, Macy's, Sears **6** market, Target **7** Walmart **8** J.C. Penney, retailer
event: **4** sale **9** white sale
section: **4** boy's, men's **5** girl's **6** women's
staffer: **5** buyer, clerk **7** cashier
departure: **4** exit **5** adieu, going, leave **6** change, egress, escape, exodus, flight **7** getaway, goodbye, liftoff, novelty, parting, removal, retreat, takeoff, veering, walkout **8** blastoff, farewell, straying, variance **9** avoidance, desertion, deviation, diversion, egression, exception, going away, migration, recession, secession, taking off, variation, wandering **10** aberration, decampment, deflection, difference, digression, discursion, divergence, emigration, evacuation, expiration, innovation, new wrinkle, retirement, separation, setting out, withdrawal
from the norm: **3** pip **4** blip **8** variance **9** deviation, disparity, variation **10** aberration, divergence
hasty ~: **3** lam **6** flight
listing: **4** sked **8** schedule
point of ~: **4** gate **9** threshold
verbal ~: **10** digression
__ de Pascua: **4** Isla
__ de pasto: **4** vino
de Paul: **4** Gene **7** Vincent
DePaul
athletes: **10** Blue Demons
locale: **7** Chicago **8** Illinois
__ de pays: **3** vin
Depeche __: **4** Mode
depend: **4** bank, base, hang, rely, rest, ride **5** count, hinge, pivot
ender: **3** ent **4** ence
on: **5** trust **6** accept, assume, credit, look to, reckon **7** believe, require, swear by **9** calculate **10** set store by
(on): **3** bet **4** bank, hang, lean, rely, rest **5** count, hinge **6** gamble **8** fall back
dependability: **5** trust **7** loyalty **8** fidelity **9** stability
dependable: **4** even, good, just, sure, true **5** level, loyal, solid, sound, tried **6** honest, secure, stable, steady, trusty, worthy **7** careful, certain, durable, regular, staunch, uniform **8** constant, credible, faithful, inerrant, punctual, reliable, stalwart **9** authentic, goofproof, honorable, reputable, rock solid, steadfast, unfailing, veracious **10** consistent, convincing, infallible, true to type, unchanging
not ~: **5** shaky **7** erratic, flighty
dependence: **5** faith, stock, trust **6** belief **8** reliance **9** addiction **10** confidence
free from ~: **4** wean
dependency: **6** colony
dependent: **4** ward, weak **5** child, minor, needy **6** hooked, mutual **7** related, reliant, subject **8** helpless, immature, relative **9** ancillary, powerless, provisory, reckoning, secondary, tentative **10** collateral, contingent, counting on, reciprocal, vulnerable
be ~ (on): **4** hang
on: **7** relying **9** subject to
dependent __: **6** clause
__ Depends on You: **5** It All
depict: **4** copy, draw, limn, show, tell **5** limns, paint **6** detail, map out, relate, render, sketch **7** narrate, outline, picture, portray, recount **8** describe, rehearse **9** delineate, exemplify, interpret, represent **10** illustrate
distinctly: **4** etch
unfairly: **4** skew
depiction: **5** image **6** acting, design, sketch **7** drawing, outline, tableau **8** likeness, portrait **9** enactment, portrayal, rendering, rendition
depilatory
name: **4** Nair, Neet
target: **4** hair
deplane: **5** light **6** alight, arrive **7** descend **9** disembark
deplete: **3** dry, sag, sap, use **4** flag, milk, tire, void, wane **5** bleed, blunt, drain, dry up, eat up, empty, spend, trash, use up, waste **6** burn up, expend, finish, frivol, reduce, run out, shrink, soften, unload, weaken **7** consume, dig into, exhaust, fatigue, sell out, wear out **8** bankrupt, decrease, diminish, enervate, enfeeble, evacuate, fool away, squander **9** attenuate, dissipate, undermine **10** debilitate, devitalize, impoverish
depleted: **3** low **4** bare, gone, poor **5** all in, empty, spent **6** barren, devoid, effete, vacant **7** sold out, worn out **8** bankrupt **9** destitute
depletion: **4** lack, loss **7** using up **10** exhaustion
deplorable: **3** sad **4** dire, grim, poor **5** awful, lousy, sorry, woful **6** abject, rotten, tragic, woeful **7** piteous, pitiful **8** dolorous, dreadful, grievous, mournful, pathetic, pitiable, shameful, stinking, terrible, tragical, wretched **9** egregious, execrable, loathsome, miserable **10** afflictive, calamitous, disastrous, horrifying, lamentable, melancholy, pathetical, scandalous, unbearable
act: **3** sin
deplore: **3** rue **4** hate, moan, wail, weep **5** abhor, mourn **6** bemoan, bewail, lament, regret, repent, sorrow **7** condemn, dislike **8** denounce, object to **9** deprecate **10** recoil from
deploy: **3** put **7** arrange, marshal, station **8** maneuver
__ de plume: **3** nom
depone: **4** avow **7** testify, witness
__ de pont: **4** tête
deport: **3** out **5** exile, expel **6** acquit, banish, behave **7** cast out, conduct, kick out **8** relegate, send away **9** ostracize, transport **10** expatriate
deportee: **5** exile **7** outcast **10** expatriate
deportment: **3** air, set **4** mien **6** aspect, manner, stance **7** actions, bearing, conduct, manners, posture **8** behavior, carriage, demeanor **9** etiquette, expulsion **10** appearance
depose: **4** oust **5** eject, swear **6** attest, avouch, bounce, depone, remove, unseat **7** boot out, cashier, dismiss, drum out, kick out, subvert, testify, toss out, witness **8** attest to, dethrone, displace, throw out **9** interview, overthrow
deposit: **3** lay, put, set **4** drop, gage, keep, lees, mine, park, plop, save, seam, silt, stow **5** amass, delta, dregs, drift, embed, imbed, place, plant, put by, stash, store **6** garner, instal, locate **7** advance, collect, drop off, grounds, install, lay away, put away, savings **8** alluvium, gold mine, lodgment, put aside, retainer, salt away, sediment, sock away **9** formation, plunk down, settlings **10** collateral
deposit __: **4** slip
__ deposit: **4** bank, time **6** demand, direct
__-deposit box: **4** safe **6** safety
deposition: **5** proof **6** ouster **7** removal **8** ejection, evidence **9** admission, affidavit, discharge, dismissal, overthrow, testimony **10** allegation, contention, dethroning, unfrocking
give a ~: **4** aver, avow **6** allege, assert, attest **7** certify, declare
depositor: **5** saver
check ~: **5** payee
watchdog: **4** FDIC **5** FSLIC
depository: **4** bank, safe, slot **5** cache, depot, vault **6** closet **7** archive, arsenal **8** magazine, treasury **9** repertory, warehouse **10** collection, repository, storehouse
depot: **4** base, stop, yard **5** store **6** armory, garage **7** arsenal, station **8** landfill, magazine, terminal **9** warehouse **10** bus station, depository, repository, storehouse
abbr.: **3** arr., ETA, ETD, sta.
posting: **4** sked **8** schedule
__ Depot: **4** Home **5** Union **6** Office
Depp, Johnny: **5** actor
film: Benny & Joon (1993)
Charlie and the Chocolate Factory (2005)
Chocolat (2000)
Cry-Baby (1990)
Dead Man (1996)
Don Juan DeMarco (1995)
Donnie Brasco (1997)
Edward Scissorhands (1990)
Ed Wood (1994)
Finding Neverland (2004)
From Hell (2001)
Public Enemies (2009)
Sleepy Hollow (1999)
Sweeney Todd (2007)
role: **5** Wonka
deprave: **4** warp **5** stain **6** debase **7** corrupt, degrade, subvert, vitiate **10** lead astray
depraved: **3** bad, low **4** base, evil, ugly, vile **5** seamy **6** rakish, rotten, sinful, unholy, wanton, wicked **7** beastly, corrupt, immoral, twisted, ungodly, vicious **8** degraded, uncurbed **9** dissolute, low-minded, miscreant, nefarious, shameless **10** licentious, outrageous, profligate, villainous, virtueless
depravity: **3** ill **4** evil, vice **7** cruelty **8** baseness, enormity, iniquity **9** vitiation, ybaritism **10** corruption, debasement, degeneracy, immorality, profligacy, wickedness
deprecate: **3** rip **4** hate **5** abuse, cavil, knock, scorn **6** jibe at, malign, regret, vilify **7** asperse, censure, condemn, deplore, detract, put down, run down **8** backbite, badmouth, belittle, derogate, disfavor, minimize, play down, take down **9** disesteem, disparage, poor-mouth **10** depreciate, disapprove, discommend, discourage
deprecation: **5** abuse **7** dislike, protest
depreciate: **4** sink **5** decay, lower **6** reduce **7** asperse, decline, deflate, depress, detract, devalue, slander **8** decrease, talk down **9** denigrate, deprecate, devaluate, discredit, disparage, dispraise, downgrade, underrate **10** adulterate, calumniate, devalorize, look down on, undervalue
depreciation: **4** wear **5** decay, libel, slump **7** decline, slander **8** overhead
depredate: **3** gut, rob **4** loot, raid, sack **5** spoil, strip **6** harrow, maraud, pirate, prey on, ravage **7** despoil, pillage, plunder, ransack **8** freeboot, prey upon **9** desecrate, devastate **10** lay waste to
depress: **4** damp, faze, push, sink, tire **5** abase, daunt, drain, lower, upset, weary, worry **6** bum out, dampen, darken, debase, deject, impair, lessen, reduce, sadden, squash, unglue **7** cheapen, deflate, devalue, flatten, let down, oppress, torment **8** desolate, diminish, dispirit, distress, enervate, keep down, push down **9** devaluate, downgrade, weigh down **10** demoralize, depreciate, devitalize, discourage, dishearten
depressed: **3** low, sad **4** blue, dark, down, glum, grim, mopy **5** heavy, moody, mopey, sorry **6** broody, crumby, crummy, gloomy, hollow, morbid, morose, sunken **7** concave, doleful, forlorn, hangdog, in a funk, joyless, let down, set back, unhappy, way down **8** dejected, desolate, downcast, indented, liverish, recessed, wretched **9** aggrieved, bummed-out, cheerless, destitute, in the pits, miserable, on a downer, saturnine, sorrowful, taken down, woebegone **10** despairing, despondent, dispirited, distressed, down and out, in the dumps, lugubrious, melancholy, out of sorts, spiritless
act ~: **4** mope **5** brood

depressing: **3** sad **4** grim **5** bleak, mirky, murky, no fun, sorry, stark **6** dismal, dreary, gloomy, somber **7** joyless **8** hopeless, mournful **9** cheerless, dejecting, saddening, upsetting **10** lugubrious, melancholy, oppressive, tenebrific
event: **6** bummer, downer
depression: **3** dip, pit, sag, woe **4** bust, dent, funk, hole, mold, mood, pall, sink **5** basin, blahs, blues, chasm, crash, dolor, gloom, grief, panic, scoop, slump **6** cavity, crater, crisis, dimple, furrow, groove, hollow, misery, recess, sorrow, trench, trough, valley **7** anguish, despair, dim view, foxhole, malaise, sadness **8** bad times, distress, doldrums, glumness, sinkhole, the blues **9** abasement, abjection, bleakness, concavity, deflation, dejection, hard times, heartache, inflation, pessimism, recession **10** abjectness, affliction, bankruptcy, bear market, desolation, difficulty, discontent, dreariness, excavation, gloominess, heartbreak, heavy heart, impression, inactivity, loneliness, low spirits, melancholy, stagnation, woefulness
Depression ___: **5** glass
___ Depression: **5** Great
___ depressor: **6** tongue
deprivation: **4** lack, loss, need, want **6** denial **8** hardship
deprive: **3** rob **4** oust **5** strip, wrest **6** divest **7** bereave **10** dispossess
of (prefix): **3** dis-
of wind: **5** stall
deprived: **4** poor **5** broke, needy **6** bereft, busted **7** forlorn, lacking, wanting **8** bankrupt, indigent, strapped, wiped out **9** dead broke, deficient, destitute, flat broke, insolvent, moneyless, penniless, penurious **10** down-and-out, on the rocks, straitened
be ~: **4** need
be ~ of: **4** lose **7** forfeit
of: **7** needing
old-style: **4** reft
De profundis: **5** psalm
De Profundis
author: Oscar Wilde
dept.: **3** bur., div. **4** sect.
Deptford Trilogy, The
author: Robertson Davies
depth: **4** drop, gulf **5** abyss, nadir, scope **6** acuity, acumen, wisdom **7** insight, lowness **8** keenness, sagacity, strength **9** dimension, intellect, intensity, sharpness, thickness **10** astuteness, profundity
charge: **6** ashcan
combining form: **5** batho-, bathy-
go out of one's ~: **4** risk
having no ~: **4** one-d, two-d
in ~: **5** fully **8** from A to Z, whole hog **9** inside out **10** completely, thoroughly, to the limit
measure ~: **5** plumb, sound
out of one's ~: **4** asea **5** at sea **6** afield
sailor's ~ unit: **3** fth. **4** fath. **6** fathom
depth ___: **4** bomb **6** charge, finder
___ depth finder: **5** sonic
depthless: **4** idle **7** sketchy
depth of ___: **5** field, focus
depths: **5** abyss, midst, nadir **6** bottom, bowels, recess **9** innermost
Depths of Glory
author: Irving Stone
deputation: **8** legation **10** commission, contingent, delegation
depute: **8** delegate, transfer **9** designate **10** constitute
deputies: **4** help **5** staff
on horseback: **5** posse
deputize: **4** name **6** assign, commit **7** appoint, empower **8** delegate **9** authorize, designate **10** commission, constitute
deputy: **3** rep, sub **4** aide, help, vice **5** agent, envoy, proxy, vicar **6** acting, backup, helper, lawman, legate, regent **7** bailiff, officer, staffer **8** delegate, emissary, henchman, minister **9** appointee, assistant, go-between, man Friday, surrogate, underling **10** ambassador, legislator, lieutenant, substitute
deputy ___: **7** sheriff
Deputy ___: **4** Dawg
___ de quatre: **3** pas
de Queiroz: **3** Eca
De Quincey: **6** Thomas
Der ___: **4** Alte
deracinate: **9** eradicate, extirpate
derail: **5** wreck **6** foul up **8** go astray
Derain: **5** André
derate: **6** reduce
Der Blaue Reiter
artist: Jean (Hans) Arp
derby: **3** hat **4** race **6** bowler **9** horse race
material: **4** felt
___ derby: **6** roller
Derby: **4** city, race, town **5** shire **6** county
also-ran: **3** nag
entrant: **5** horse
ground: **4** turf
like ~ enthusiasts: **5** horsy **6** horsey
locale: **7** England
prize: **5** purse
river: **7** Derwent
track: **4** oval
winner's flower: **4** rose
Derbyshire: **5** chair **6** county
locale: **7** England
de règle: **9** customary
deregulate: **7** leave be **8** let alone **9** decontrol
Derek: **2** Bo **3** Bok **4** John **5** Jeter **6** Barton, Jacobi **7** Walcott
Derek, Bo: **7** actress
film: Bolero (1984)
Orca (1977)
spouse: John Derek
Derek, John: **5** actor
spouse: Ursula Andress, Bo Derek, Linda Evans
derelict: **3** bum, lax **4** hobo, lorn, wino **5** slack, tramp, wreck **6** remiss **7** cast off, drifter, outcast, run-down, vagrant **8** careless, castaway, deserted, desolate, forsaken, homeless, renegade, untended, vagabond **9** abandoned, discarded, neglected, negligent, ownerless, unmindful **10** delinquent, ne'er-do-well, neglectful, ragamuffin, ramshackle, regardless, unreliable
dereliction: **5** fault, guilt **6** breach, laxity **7** default, neglect **9** oversight
___ de résistance: **5** pièce
deride: **3** dis, kid, pan, rag, rib, rip **4** defy, gibe, hiss, hoot, jeer, jibe, mock, razz, slam, slur, snub, twit **5** abuse, chaff, decry, fleer, flout, knock, libel, roast, scoff, scorn, sneer, spurn, taunt **6** banter, defame, dump on, heckle, hoot at, impugn, insult, jibe at, malign, offend, parody, rebuff, slight, vilify **7** affront, asperse, contemn, degrade, disdain, laugh at, put down, rank out, scoff at, slander, traduce **8** belittle, denounce, pooh-pooh, ridicule, vilipend **9** blaspheme, denigrate, discredit, disparage, humiliate, make fun of, poke fun at **10** calumniate, disrespect
de rigueur: **10** obligatory
derision: **3** dig **4** barb, gibe, jibe, slam, slap, slur, snub **5** abuse, libel, scorn, shame, sport, taunt **6** insult, rebuff, slight **7** affront, calumny, catcall, disdain, mockery, obloquy, offense, put-down, razzing, sarcasm, slander **8** brickbat, contempt, ridicule, scoffing, sneering **9** cheap shot, contumely **10** Bronx cheer, disrespect, impugnment, opprobrium
exclamation: **3** aha, bah, fie, hah, yah **4** ha-ha, he he **5** hello, tehee **6** haw-haw, la-de-da, la-di-da, tee-hee **7** big deal **8** lah-di-dah
express ~: **4** hiss, hoot, jeer **5** snort
object of ~: **4** goat
derisive: **5** sassy, snide **6** sneery **7** jeering, mocking, mordant **8** sardonic, scoffing, scornful, taunting **9** insulting, laughable, quizzical, sarcastic, vitriolic **10** disdainful, irreverent, pejorative, ridiculing
derivable: **9** available, deducible, inferable, resultant, traceable **10** obtainable
derivation: **4** root **5** basis **6** origin, source **7** descent **8** ancestry, pedigree **9** beginning, deduction, emanation, etymology, genealogy, inception **10** extraction, foundation, hypothesis, provenance, wellspring
word ~: **9** etymology
derivative: **6** copied **7** product, spinoff **8** acquired, borrowed, inferred, offshoot, rehashed **9** ancestral, by-product, emulative, imitative, outgrowth, secondary **10** descendant, hereditary, secondhand, unoriginal
derive: **3** get **4** base, draw, earn, make, reap, rise, stem, take **5** educe, glean, hatch, infer, reach **6** deduce, elicit, gather, obtain, result, spring **7** descend, develop, emanate, extract, proceed, procure, receive **8** arrive at, come from, flow from, stem from, take from **9** arise from, determine, formulate, grow out of, originate, reason out **10** bring forth
(from): **4** come, stem **5** arise **9** originate
from reasoning: **5** infer **6** deduce, deduct, induce, induct
derived
form: **7** variant **10** inflection
derived ___: **4** form, unit **5** curve
___ de Rivoli: **3** Rue
derma: **4** skin **5** layer **6** kishka, kishke, kiskha
casing: **3** gut
dermal: **9** cutaneous
vent: **4** pore **5** stoma **10** sweat gland
dermis: **4** skin
plus epidermis: **5** cutis
starter: **3** epi
Dermot: **8** Mulroney
Dern: **5** Bruce, Laura
Dern, Bruce: **5** actor
daughter: Laura
spouse: Diane Ladd
dernier cri: **3** fad **4** mode, rage **5** vogue **6** latest **7** fashion **8** last word
Dern, Laura: **7** actress
film: Blue Velvet (1986)
Focus (2001)
Jurassic Park (1993)
Novocaine (2001)
October Sky (1999)
A Perfect World (1993)
Rambling Rose (1991)
parent: Bruce Dern, Diane Ladd
derogate: **5** abuse, decry, libel **6** demean, malign, vilify **7** asperse, degrade, detract, put down, run down, slander **8** belittle, denounce, diminish, disgrace, minimize, play down, talk down **9** denigrate, deprecate, disparage
derogation: **7** calumny **10** detraction, diminution, muckraking, reflection
derogatory: **5** snide **8** critical, damaging, decrying, libelous, scornful, spiteful **9** aspersing, degrading, demeaning, injurious, malicious, maligning, offensive, sarcastic, slighting, vilifying **10** belittling, calumnious, censorious, defamatory, detracting, detractive, disdainful, malevolent, minimizing, pejorative, slanderous
___ de Roland: **7** Chanson
Deronda: **6** Daniel
___ de rose oil: **4** bois
derrick: **5** crane, davit, hoist **6** lifter
arm: **3** jib
___ derrick: **3** oil
D'Errico: **5** Donna
Der Ring des Nibelungen: **5** cycle
composer: Richard Wagner
derring-do: **5** pluck, spunk, valor **7** heroics, prowess **9** gallantry
bit of ~: **4** feat
tale of ~: **4** gest, saga **5** geste
derringer: **6** pistol
Derringer: **5** Yancy
Der Rosenkavalier: **5** opera
Annina in ~: **4** alto
composer: Richard Strauss

role: 4 Ochs 6 Annina, Sophie 8 Marianne, Octavian
setting: 6 Vienna 7 Austria
Derry: 4 city, port, town
college: 5 Magee
locale: 7 Ireland
Dershowitz, Alan: 6 lawyer 8 attorney
Der Spiegel: 5 paper 6 German 9 newspaper
dervish: 5 faker, fakir, faqir 6 faquir 9 religious
movement: 4 spin 5 whirl
religion: 5 Islam
__ dervish: 7 howling 8 whirling
Derwent: 5 river
locale: 5 Derby 6 Hobart 7 England 8 Tasmania
Des: 7 Barlett, McAnuff, O'Connor
Des __: 6 Moines 7 Plaines
__-de-sac: 3 cul
__ de Sade: 7 Marquis
Desafinado (1962 song)
artist: Stan Getz
Desai, Anita: 6 Indian, writer
de Sales: 7 Francis
desalt: 6 purify 7 distill
DeSario: 4 Teri
__ des Beaux Arts: 5 École, Musée
__ de scandale: 6 succès
descant: 4 sing, talk 6 melody, ramble, strain 7 monolog 8 perorate 9 discourse, expatiate, monologue
Descartes, René: 6 French 8 geometer 11 philosopher
conclusion: 3 I am, sum
descend: 3 dip, set 4 dive, drop, fall, land, sink, step 5 crash, lapse, light, lower, slant, slide, slope, slump, swoop 6 alight, derive, get off, go down, hop off, plunge, settle, spring, tumble 7 cascade, decline, deplane, detrain, plummet 8 collapse, dismount, nosedive, submerge 9 disembark, originate, swoop down
ender: 3 ant, ent
on: 4 land, raid, rush 5 visit 6 assail, invade
descendant: 3 son 4 cion, heir 5 child, issue, scion 8 daughter, grandson, offshoot 9 offspring, posterity 10 derivative
suffix: 3 -ite
__ descendant: 6 lineal
descendants: 4 seed 5 issue 7 kinfolk, lineage, progeny 8 kinfolks, kinsfolk 9 posterity
colonial ~ org.: 3 DAR, SAR
line of ~: 5 stirp
descended: 4 alit
be ~ (from): 5 arise 6 spring
descending: 4 down 8 downhill, downward
__ Descending: 7 Orpheus
__ Descending a Staircase: 4 Nude
descent: 3 dip 4 dive, drop, fall, line, raid 5 birth, blood, crash, foray, lapse, roots, slide, slope, slump, stock, swoop 6 attack, origin, plunge, strain, tumble 7 decline, falling, incline, lineage, sinking 8 ancestry, downfall, downturn, heredity, invasion, lowering, nosedive, pedigree, plunging, tailspin 9 declivity, downgrade, etymology, forebears, genealogy, incursion 10 declension, derivation, extraction, plummeting
steep ~: 6 escarp
Descent from Xanadu
author: Harold Robbins
Descent into Hell
author: Charles Williams
Descent Into the Maelstrom, A
author: Edgar Allan Poe
Deschamps, Eustache: 4 poet 6 French
Deschanel: 5 Emily, Zooey
describe: 4 limn, tell, term 5 label, paint, state, sum up 6 convey, define, depict, detail, impart, recite, relate, report, set out, sketch, unfold 7 explain, express, narrate, outline, picture, portray, qualify, recount, specify, write up 8 rehearse, set forth, subtitle 9 adumbrate, chronicle, delineate, elucidate, explicate, expound on, make clear, represent 10 illustrate
briefly: 4 limn 5 sum up 6 sketch 7 outline
vividly: 5 paint 6 depict 10 illustrate
description: 3 ilk 4 kind, mold, sort, tale, type 5 class, genre, label, stamp, story, title 6 detail, nature, report, sketch, stripe 7 account, heading, profile, recital, species, variety 8 category, portrait 9 narration, narrative, rehearsal, statement
__ description: 3 job
descriptive: 5 vivid 7 graphic 9 graphical
word: 9 adjective
descry: 4 espy, hear, spot 5 sight 6 detect, notice 7 discern, glimpse, make out 8 discover, perceive 9 recognize
Desdemona: 4 moon
enemy: 4 Iago
handkerchief: 4 prop
husband: 7 Othello
planet: 6 Uranus
desecrate: 4 ruin, sack 5 abuse, spoil 6 befoul, defile, misuse, ravage 7 despoil, pillage, pollute, profane, violate 8 dishonor, spoliate 9 blaspheme, depredate, devastate
desecration: 3 sin 6 misuse 7 outrage 9 sacrilege, violation 10 defilement
desensitize: 4 dull, numb 5 blunt 6 benumb, deaden 7 coarsen
Deseret
News: 5 paper 9 newspaper
today: 4 Utah
desert: 3 dry 4 arid, bare, bolt, fail, flee, Gobi, jilt, quit, skip, Tahr, Thar, Tuhr 5 biome, ditch, leave, Namib, Negeb, Negev, split, waste, wilds 6 barren, betray, cop out, decamp, defect, depart, escape, Gibson, go AWOL, Libyan, maroon, Mohave, Mojave, Nubian, reward, Sahara, strand, Syrian 7 abandon, abscond, Arabian, aridity, Atacama, bail out, forsake, hot spot, Kara Kum, Painted, Sechura, Simpson, Sonoran, sterile, take off 8 desolate, forswear, hightail, Kalahari, Kyzyl Kum, lifeless, rainless, renounce, run out on, sneak off 9 cut and run, Dasht-e Lut, foreswear, Great Salt, infertile, leave flat, skip out on, throw over, walk out on, wasteland 10 Chihuahuan, go away from, Great Sandy, Patagonian, punishment, Sturt Stony, Taklamakan, wilderness 11 Death Valley
Africa: 5 Namib, Sahel 6 Libyan, Nubian, Sahara 7 Arabian 8 Kalahari
ancient ~ kingdom: 5 Nubia
animal: 5 camel
Arizona: 7 Sonoran 10 Chihuahuan
Asia: 4 Gobi, Tahr, Thar, Tuhr 6 Syrian 7 Arabian, Kara Kum 8 Kyzyl Kum 9 Dasht-e Lut, Great Salt
Australia: 6 Gibson 7 Simpson 10 Great Sandy, Sturt Stony
basin floor: 5 playa
California: 6 Mohave 7 Sonoran 11 Death Valley
Egypt: 6 Libyan, Sahara 7 Arabian
feature: 4 dune, reif 5 oasis
fruit: 4 date
in Arabic: 6 Sahara
India: 4 Tahr, Thar, Tuhr
inn: 5 serai
Iran: 9 Dasht-e Lut, Great Salt
lake: 6 mirage 8 illusion
largest ~: 6 Sahara
like a ~: 3 dry 4 arid, sere 6 barren
Mexico: 7 Sonoran 10 Chihuahuan
Mideast: 5 Dahna, Nafud, Nefud, Negeb, Negev, Sinai 6 Syrian
Mongolia: 4 Gobi
North America: 6 Mohave 7 Sonoran 10 Chihuahuan 11 Death Valley
Pakistan: 4 Tahr, Thar, Tuhr
plant: 5 agave, athel, retem, sotol, yucca 6 cactus, jojoba 7 saguaro
prince: 4 amir, emir 5 ameer, emeer
rodent: 5 gundi
South America: 7 Atacama, Sechura 10 Patagonian
state: 6 Nevada 7 Arizona 9 New Mexico
Sudan: 6 Libyan, Nubian 7 Arabian
surface: 4 rock, sand
desert __: 3 rat
Desert __: 3 Fox 4 Blue, boot 5 Storm 6 Shield
Desert __, The: 3 Fox 4 Rats 5 of Ice
__ Desert: 3 Lut, Red 4 Thar 5 Kavir, Namib, Nefud 6 Gibson, Indian, Libyan, Mohave, Mojave, Nubian, Syrian 7 Arabian, Atacama, Painted
Desert Bloom (1986 film)
cast: Ellen Barkin, Annabeth Gish, Jon Voight, JoBeth Williams
subject: 5 A-test
Desert Blue (1999 film)
cast: Kate Hudson, Christina Ricci
director: Morgan Freeman
deserted: 4 bare, lone, lorn, wild 5 empty 6 barren, lonely, vacant 7 forlorn 8 derelict, desolate, forsaken, isolated, lonesome, secluded, solitary, stranded 9 abandoned, neglected 10 high and dry, unoccupied
Deserted Village, The
author: Oliver Goldsmith
deserter: 4 AWOL 6 coward, dodger 7 escapee, quitter, refugee, runaway, traitor 8 apostate, defector, forsaker, recreant, renegade 9 absconder
Desert Gold
author: Zane Grey
deserting: 10 abdication
desertion: 8 apostasy 9 avoidance, defecting, defection, departure, disavowal, falseness, forsaking, marooning, recreancy, rejection, secession, treachery 10 abdication, abrogation, absconding, withdrawal
Desert of Ice, The
author: Jules Verne
Desert of Love, The
author: François Mauriac
Desert of Wheat, The
author: Zane Grey
deserts: 3 due 6 reward 10 punishment, recompense
get one's just ~: 4 earn, rate 7 deserve 10 have coming
give just ~: 5 spite 6 avenge 7 get even, hit back, pay back, requite 9 get back at, stick it to
just ~: 3 due 5 merit 7 payback 10 recompense
__ deserts: 4 just
Desert Storm: 3 war
cuisine: 3 MRE
target: 4 Irak, Iraq 5 Basra, Busra 6 Busrah
deserve: 4 earn, rate 5 claim, merit 7 warrant 10 have coming
deserved: 3 due 4 fair, just, meet 5 right 6 earned 7 condign, fitting, merited 8 rightful, suitable 9 equitable, justified 10 reasonable
__ deserved: 6 richly
deserving: 6 worthy 7 fitting 8 laudable 9 admirable, estimable, praisable, righteous 10 creditable
suffix: 6 -worthy
__ des Flandres: 7 Bouvier
__ des gens: 5 droit
DeShannon: 6 Jackie
Desi: 5 Arnaz
daughter: 5 Lucie
Lucy, to ~: 6 costar
De Sica, Vittorio: 8 director
film: The Bicycle Thief (1947)
The Earrings of Madame de ... (1953)
The Garden of the Finzi-Continis (1971)
Shoeshine (1946)
Two Women (1961)
Umberto D (1952)
Woman Times Seven (1967)
desiccate: 3 dry 4 sear 5 parch, wizen 6 wither 7 shrivel 9 anhydrate, dehydrate, evaporate 10 devitalize
desiccated: 4 arid 5 unwet 9 juiceless
Desiderata (1971 song)
artist: Les Crane

desiderate: 4 want, wish
desideratum: 3 aim 4 need, want 9 necessity, requisite
Desiderius: 7 Erasmus
__ de siècle: 3 fin
design: 3 aim, map 4 draw, form, goal, mold, plan 5 chart, décor, draft, forge, frame, hatch, label, model, motif, setup, study, style 6 create, devise, intend, invent, layout, makeup, reason, recipe, scheme, sketch, symbol 7 arrange, concoct, diagram, dope out, drawing, fashion, outline, pattern, produce, program, project, propose, purpose, think up, thought 8 block out, conceive, contrive, game plan, heraldry, maneuver, ornament, scenario, skeleton, strategy 9 blueprint, delineate, depiction, floor plan, formation, give shape, intention, invention, make plans, objective, originate, structure, treatment 10 conception, mastermind
add a ~ to: 6 emboss
by ~: 9 on purpose, purposely
criterion: 4 spec
heraldic ~: 4 ente
__ design: 7 graphic
designate: 3 dub, peg, set, tab, tag, tap 4 call, make, mark, name, pick, slot, term 5 elect, key on, label, place, point, style, title 6 anoint, assign, choose, define, denote, depute, direct, finger, record 7 appoint, earmark, entitle, intitle, qualify, specify 8 allocate, delegate, deputize, handpick, indicate, nominate, set aside 9 apportion, authorize, prescribe, single out, stipulate 10 button down, commission, constitute, denominate, put down for, settle upon
Designate a Driver sponsor: 4 MADD
designated __: 6 driver, hitter
designation: 4 mark, name, term, word 5 class, label, title 7 epithet 8 nickname
designedly: 9 knowingly, on purpose, purposely, willfully, wittingly 10 purposedly, studiously
designer: 5 maker 7 creator, deviser, founder, planner 8 engineer, inventer, inventor 9 architect, artificer, contriver, fashioner 10 mastermind, originator
collection: 4 line
deg.: 3 MFA
item: 3 tie 4 gown, suit 5 A-line, dress
label: 3 YSL 4 Dior, DKNY 5 Klein 6 Armani, Lauren 7 Versace
designer __: 4 gene 5 jeans
__ designer: 7 fashion
Design for Living
author: Noël Coward
designful: 10 considered, deliberate
designing: 3 sly 4 wily 6 artful, crafty, shrewd, subtle, tricky 7 cunning, devious, knavish 8 plotting, scheming 9 ambitious, conniving, deceitful, deceptive, dishonest, insidious, observant 10 conspiring, intriguing
Designing Woman (1957 film)
cast: Lauren Bacall, Gregory Peck
director: Vincente Minnelli
Designing Women (CBS sitcom)
cast: Delta Burke (Suzanne Sugarbaker)
Dixie Carter (Julia Sugarbaker)
Annie Potts (Mary Jo Shively)
concern: 5 decor
setting: 7 Atlanta, Georgia
designless: 6 random 9 haphazard
designs, dizzying: 5 op art
Desilu formerly: 3 RKO
desirability: 5 value, worth
desirable: 4 good 5 swell 6 sultry, useful 7 helpful, lovable, welcome 8 adorable, charming, enticing, enviable, fetching, loveable 9 advisable, agreeable, beautiful, covetable, excellent, expedient 10 acceptable, attractive, beneficial, gratifying, preferable, profitable, worthwhile
least ~: 5 worst
less ~: 5 worse
make ~: 6 endear
more ~: 6 better
most ~: 4 best, tops
thing: 4 plum
desire: 3 aim, yen 4 ache, envy, hope, itch, like, long, lust, miss, mood, need, pant, pine, seek, urge, want, whim, will, wish 5 ardor, covet, crave, fancy, go for, letch, yearn 6 appeal, ask for, choose, fervor, hunger, intent, liking, prefer, pursue, relish, thirst 7 avidity, craving, dream of, emotion, hope for, impulse, long for, longing, passion, pine for, purpose, request, require, solicit, wish for 8 ambition, appetite, aspire to, entreaty, fondness, languish, pleasure, velleity, volition, voracity, yearn for, yearning 9 affection, appetence, eagerness, esurience, hankering, intention, obsession, thirst for, will to win 10 aspiration, incitement, preference, settle upon, sweet tooth
combining form: 6 -orexia
insatiable ~: 4 urge 5 greed 6 fervor, thirst 7 avidity, craving 8 cupidity 9 appetence
personified: 4 Eros
seat of ~ to the ancients: 5 liver
show excessive ~: 5 drool
Desire (1980 song)
artist: Andy Gibb
__ Desire: 4 All I
desired: 7 welcome 8 enviable
Desirée (1977 song)
artist: Neil Diamond
Desire Under the Elms: 4 play
author: Eugene O'Neill
character: 4 Eben 5 Abbie, Cabot 6 Simeon
desirous: 4 avid, keen 5 eager, itchy 6 ardent, hungry 7 anxious, athirst, hopeful, jealous, longing, lustful, thirsty, wanting, willing, wishing, wistful 8 aspiring, covetous, grasping, ravenous, yearning 9 ambitious 10 passionate
desist: 3 end 4 halt, quit, stop 5 can it, cease, close, forgo, pause, yield 6 cool it, forego, lay off, refuse, stop it 7 abstain, forbear, refrain 8 break off, cut it out, knock off, leave off, surcease 10 knock it off
desistance: 5 close 6 ending, finish 9 cessation 10 conclusion
desk: 5 table 6 carrel 7 carrell, counter, lectern, rolltop 8 kneehole, vargueno 9 davenport, furniture, secretary, workplace 10 escritoire
church ~: 4 ambo 5 ambon
ender: 3 man, men, top
feature: 4 lamp 5 in-box 6 drawer
Italian ~: 5 stipo
item: 3 pen 4 lamp 6 eraser, pencil 8 calendar, computer
library ~: 6 carrel 7 carrell
material: 4 wood
reading ~: 7 lectern
reference: 9 thesaurus 10 dictionary
site: 3 den 5 study 6 office
desk __: 3 job, pad, set 4 work 6 copier, jockey
__ desk: 4 city, copy 5 front, Salem 7 reading, roll-top, writing
desk-bound: 9 sedentary
Desk Set (1957 film)
cast: Katharine Hepburn, Spencer Tracy
Des Moines: 4 city, town 5 river
athletes: 8 Bulldogs
city near ~: 4 Ames
county: 8 Humboldt
locale: 4 Iowa 10 Washington
newspaper: 8 Register
river: 7 Raccoon
school: 5 Drake
Desmond: 4 Paul, Tutu 5 Norma 6 Dekker, Johnny, O'Grady
Desmond, Paul: 11 saxophonist
genre: 4 jazz
instrument: 3 sax 7 alto sax
__ de société: 4 vers
__ de soie: 4 peau
__-de-soie: 5 poult
desolate: 4 bare, blue, down, lorn, ruin, sack, wild 5 alone, bleak, empty, gaunt, spoil, stark 6 barren, broody, desert, dismal, dreary, gloomy, lonely, ravage, shabby, somber, vacant 7 depress, destroy, forlorn, in a funk, joyless, pillage, private, run-down, sterile, unknown 8 dejected, derelict, deserted, dolorous, downcast, forsaken, lonesome, solitary, spoliate, wretched 9 abandoned, cheerless, depressed, devastate, miserable 10 despondent, lay waste to, melancholy, unoccupied
spot: 4 moor 6 desert
desolation: 3 woe 4 pall, ruin 5 gloom, grief, havoc 6 misery, pathos, sorrow 7 anguish, despair, sadness 8 bareness, distress, solitude 9 bleakness, dejection, emptiness, heartache, isolation, starkness 10 barrenness, depression, extinction, gloominess, heartbreak, loneliness, melancholy, woefulness
__ de Soleil: 4 Bain
DeSoto: 3 car 4 auto 10 automobile
contemporary: 4 Nash
de Soto, Hernando: 7 Spanish 8 explorer
quest: 3 oro 4 gold
despair: 3 woe 4 mope 5 dolor, gloom, grief 6 misery, sorrow 7 anguish, dim view, emotion, malaise, travail 8 glumness, the blues 9 dejection, heartache, lose faith, lose heart, pessimism 10 depression, desolation, give up hope, heartbreak, infelicity, loneliness, melancholy, woefulness
cry of ~: 4 alas, oh no
in ~: 3 low, sad 4 blue, glum, mopy 5 mopey 6 gloomy, morbid, morose 7 doleful, forlorn, unhappy 8 dejected, desolate, grieving, hopeless, wretched 9 all torn up, bummed-out, cheerless, depressed, desperate, miserable, sorrowful, woebegone 10 despondent, melancholy
despairing: 3 sad 7 forlorn 8 wretched 9 depressed, desperate, in the pits, miserable, oppressed 10 despondent, in the dumps, melancholy
desperado: 4 thug 6 bad guy, bad man, bandit, gunman, outlaw, robber 7 brigand 8 criminal, gangster 9 cutthroat 10 delinquent, gunslinger, lawbreaker
__ desperandum: 3 nil
desperate: 4 bold, dire, rash, vain 5 acute, grave, hasty, no-win, risky 6 daring, fierce, hard up, urgent 7 crucial, drastic, extreme, forlorn, frantic, intense, parlous, useless 8 careless, critical, downcast, frenzied, headlong, hopeless, reckless, shocking, terrible, vehement, wretched 9 atrocious, audacious, dangerous, foolhardy, hazardous, impetuous, in the soup, monstrous, uncareful 10 despairing, despondent, determined, headstrong, incautious, outrageous, petrifying, scandalous, up the creek
Desperate Hours, The (1955 film)
cast: Humphrey Bogart, Fredric March
director: William Wyler
Desperate Housewives (ABC comedy/drama)
cast: Marcia Cross (Bree Van de Camp)
Teri Hatcher (Susan Mayer)
Felicity Huffman (Lynette Scavo)
Eva Longoria Parker (Gabrielle Solis)
Nicollette Sheridan (Edie Britt)
Desperate Journey (1942 film)
cast: Errol Flynn, Raymond Massey
director: Raoul Walsh
desperately: 5 madly 8 terribly
Desperately Seeking Susan (1985 film)
cast: Rosanna Arquette, Madonna, Aidan Quinn
director: Susan Seidelman
Desperate People, The
author: Farley Mowat
Desperation
author: Stephen King
despicable: 3 low 4 base, foul, grim, mean, poor, ugly, vile 5 awful, cheap, dirty, lousy, nasty, seamy, slimy, sorry, woful, wrong 6 abject, crumby, crummy, dismal, filthy,

horrid, no-good, odious, rotten, shabby, sordid, woeful 7 accurst, baleful, baneful, beastly, doleful, ghastly, hateful, ignoble, pitiful, satanic, servile, squalid 8 accursed, dreadful, God-awful, grievous, horrible, inferior, shameful, stinking, terrible, wretched 9 abhorrent, appalling, atrocious, defective, degrading, execrable, frightful, insidious, loathsome, miserable, offensive, repellant, repellent, revolting, satanical, worthless 10 abominable, detestable, disastrous, horrendous
one: 3 cad, rat 4 heel, toad, worm 5 louse, skunk, slime, swine, twerp, twirp 6 wretch
Despina: 4 moon
planet: 7 Neptune
despisable: 5 sorry
despise: 4 hate, shun 5 abhor, scorn, spurn 6 detest, loathe, reject, revile, slight 7 contemn, disdain, dislike 8 execrate 9 abominate 10 look down on
despised: 7 unloved 8 loveless 9 unpopular
despite: 3 tho, yet 5 altho 6 even so, though 8 although, even with
Des Plaines: 4 city, town 5 river
locale: 8 Illinois
despoil: 3 mar, rob 4 loot, raid, ruin, sack 5 rifle, steal, strip, taint, waste, wreck 6 harrow, maraud, ravage 7 bereave, corrupt, destroy, pillage, plunder, ransack 8 freeboot 9 depredate, desecrate, devastate, vandalize
old-style: 5 reave
despoiler: 6 vandal
despondency: 3 woe 5 blues, dolor, dumps, gloom, grief, mopes 6 misery, sorrow 7 anguish, despair, emotion, sadness 8 doldrums, glumness, the blues 9 dejection, heartache, pessimism 10 depression, heartbreak, melancholy
despondent: 3 low, sad 4 blue, down, glum, mopy 5 heavy, mopey, sorry 6 broody, gloomy, morbid, morose, rueful 7 doleful, forlorn, hangdog, in a funk, unhappy 8 dejected, desolate, downcast, grieving, wretched 9 all torn up, bummed-out, cheerless, depressed, desperate, in despair, in the pits, miserable, sorrowful, woebegone 10 despairing, dispirited, melancholy
despot: 4 czar, tsar, tzar 6 satrap, tyrant 7 autarch, monarch 8 autocrat, dictator 9 oppressor
word: 3 law
despotic: 4 firm, hard 5 bossy, cruel, harsh, picky, rigid, stern, tough 6 kingly, lordly, severe, strict 7 austere, lawless, Spartan 8 absolute, dogmatic, dominant, exacting, hard-line, imperial, rigorous 9 arbitrary, demanding, draconian, imperious, stringent, tyrannous, unbending, unsparing 10 autocratic, dogmatical, high-handed, inflexible, iron-fisted, iron-handed, iron-willed, no-nonsense, oppressive, peremptory, tyrannical
despotism: 7 cruelty, fascism, tyranny 8 iron hand 9 autocracy 10 domination, oppression
despotize: 5 bully 7 oppress
__ d'esprit: 3 jeu 5 point
desquamate: 4 molt, peel 5 flake
Des'ree
song: You Gotta Be (1994)
__ d'essai: 4 coup 6 ballon
__ des Saintes: 4 îles
Dessau: 4 city, town
locale: 7 Germany
__ des Sauvages: 3 été
dessert: 3 ice, pie 4 cake, duff, flan, food, fool, meal, tart 5 bombe, coupe, crape, crepe, crisp, donut, glace, grunt, Jello, slump, sweet, torte 6 bonbon, course, éclair, frappe, gateau, gelati, gelato, junket, mousse, mud pie, pashka, sorbet, sundae, trifle 7 blondie, cobbler, compote, custard, gelatin, parfait, pudding, sherbet, soufflé, supreme, tortoni 8 ambrosia, apple pie, doughnut, dumpling, flummery, fruit cup, fruit pie, ice cream, meringue, mince pie, peach pie, pecan pie, streusel, syllabub, tiramisu 9 barquette, Chantilly, cherry pie, dacquoise, mincemeat, raisin pie 10 blancmange, brown betty, peach Melba, pumpkin pie, rhubarb pie, zabaglione 11 crème brulée
ender: 5 spoon
frozen ~ chain: 4 TCBY
like some ~s: 6 flambé
preceder: 6 entrée
to a Brit: 6 afters
to dieters: 4 no-no
topping: 5 sauce, sirup, syrup
trolley: 4 cart
dessert __: 4 cart, fork, menu, tray, wine 5 knife
__ de Staël: 6 Madame
__ d'Este: 5 Villa
__ d'estime: 6 succès
destination: 3 aim, end 4 goal, port, stop 6 target 8 ambition, terminus 9 intention, objective
reach a ~: 6 arrive 8 get there
destine: 4 doom 6 likely, ordain 9 preordain 10 foreordain
destined: 4 born 5 bound, fated, meant 6 doomed, likely, sealed 7 certain, in store 8 impelled 10 inevitable, inexorable, in the cards, undoubtful
destiny: 3 lot 4 doom, fate, luck 5 karma 6 future, kismat, kismet 7 fortune
individual ~: 5 moira
Norse goddess of ~: 3 Urd
Roman goddess of ~: 5 Parca
Destiny's Child
song: Bills, Bills, Bills (1999)
Bootylicious (2001)
Emotions (2001)
Independent Woman (2000)
Jumpin', Jumpin' (2000)
No, No, No (1997)
Say My Name (2000)
Survivor (2001)
destitute: 4 poor 5 broke, needy, sorry 6 bad off, bereft, busted, hard up, ill off, in need, in want, lonely, pauper 7 pinched, wanting 8 badly off, bankrupt, beggarly, depleted, deprived, helpless, indigent, starving, strapped, wiped out 9 dead broke, deficient, depressed, exhausted, flat broke, insolvent, miserable, moneyless, penniless, penurious, played out 10 down-and-out, on the rocks, pauperized, straitened
destitution: 4 lack, need, ruin, want 6 dearth, misery, penury 7 beggary, paucity, poverty 8 hardship 9 indigence, mendicity, neediness, pauperdom, pauperism 10 starvation
d'Estournelles de Constant, Paul: 6 French 8 Nobelist
destrier: 5 horse 6 equine 7 charger 8 war-horse
destroy: 3 axe, end, gut, sap 4 do in, nuke, rase, raze, ruin, sack, sink, slay, undo 5 blast, break, cream, crush, erase, fordo, level, quash, rip up, smash, spoil, total, trash, waste, wrack, wreck 6 blight, devour, finish, mangle, quench, ravage, topple, uproot 7 abolish, blot out, consume, corrode, despoil, expunge, nullify, pillage, scuttle, shatter, subvert, torpedo, unbuild, wipe out 8 bulldoze, demolish, desolate, dissolve, dynamite, paralyse, paralyze, pull down, sabotage, spoliate, stamp out, take down, tear down 9 devastate, dismantle, eradicate, extirpate, knock down, liquidate, overwhelm, slaughter, take apart 10 annihilate, extinguish, lay waste to
documents: 5 shred
gradually: 5 erode
destroyed: 4 gone, lost 5 kaput 6 broken, undone 7 in ruins 9 miserable
not ~: 6 extant
old-style: 4 smit
destroyer: 4 ship 6 tin can, vandal 7 frigate, warship 8 man-of-war 10 battleship
combining form: 5 -clast
letters: 3 USS
name meaning ~: 6 Gideon
Destroyer, Hindu: 5 Shiva
destroying combining form: 7 -clastic
__-destruct: 4 auto, self
destruction: 3 end 4 doom, loss, ruin 5 havoc, smash, wrack 6 damage, defeat, mayhem 7 rampage, undoing 8 downfall, sabotage
__ Destruction: 5 Eve of
destructive: 4 dire, fell 5 toxic 6 lethal, malign, savage, tragic, wicked 7 adverse, baleful, baneful, caustic, erosive, harmful, hurtful, ruinous, vicious, violent 8 damaging, negative, tragical, virulent, wasteful 9 dangerous, injurious, malignant, murderous 10 calamitous, disastrous
force: 7 scourge
one: 3 Hun 4 Goth 6 Vandal 8 Visigoth
destructiveness: 8 violence
Destry Rides Again (1939 film)
cast: Marlene Dietrich, James Stewart
__ de suite: 4 tout
desultory: 6 fitful, ragged, random, spotty 7 aimless, cursory 8 rambling 9 excursive, haphazard, irregular 10 occasional, willy-nilly
DeSylva: 2 B.G. 5 Buddy
detach: 3 lop 4 crop, part 5 loose, sever, split, unfix, unpeg, unpin 6 cut off, divide, loosen, remove, rip off, unlink 7 disjoin, divorce, isolate, pull off, split up, tear off, unhitch 8 break off, disunite, liberate, separate, set apart, uncouple, unfasten 9 disengage, take apart 10 disconnect
gradually: 4 wean
detached: 3 cut, icy 4 cool, free 5 alone, aloof, apart, loose, split, stoic 6 remote, untied 7 distant, insular, neutral, stoical 8 discrete, reserved, separate, unbiased 9 apathetic, impartial, objective, unslanted, withdrawn 10 impersonal, insociable, nonchalant, unagitated
in music: 4 stac. 5 stacc. 8 staccato
detachment: 4 army, cool, unit 5 corps, force, party, squad, troop 6 detail, patrol 7 brigade, divorce, platoon, split-up 8 coldness, coolness, disunion, division, solitude 9 aloofness, partition, task force, unconcern 10 contingent, disjoining, dreaminess, equanimity, neutrality, remoteness, separation
detail: 4 army, item, list, part, send, show, spec, tell, unit 5 force, point, squad, thing, touch, trait, troop 6 aspect, define, depict, factor, lay out, nicety, patrol, recite, regard, relate, report, reveal, set out, sketch 7 account, analyze, catalog, element, exhibit, feature, itemize, minutia, narrate, portray, recount, respect, specify 8 describe, division, instance, loose end, set forth, specific, spell out 9 catalogue, component, delineate, elaborate, embellish, enumerate, epitomize, expound on, fine point, formulate, make clear, punctilio, stipulate, task force 10 detachment, particular
attention to ~: 4 care
go into ~: 4 list 5 brief, gloss 6 lay out 7 analyze, clarify, explain, itemize, specify 8 annotate, describe, spell out 9 blueprint, elaborate, elucidate, enumerate, expound on, make clear, put across
in ~: 8 whole hog 9 inside out 10 item by item, thoroughly
product ~: 4 spec
trivial ~: 3 nit
detailed: 4 full, vast 6 minute 7 copious, graphic, precise 8 accurate, complete, concrete, seriatim, specific, thorough 9 elaborate, full-dress, graphical, technical 10 blow-by-blow, exhaustive, meticulous
details: 4 data, dope 5 facts, terms 6 trivia 7 program 8 contents,

minutiae, niceties **9** fine print **10** conditions, ins and outs
add ~: 6 fill in **7** augment **8** flesh out
handler: 4 aide
press for ~: 4 pump
tend to final ~: 5 mop up
__ Detail, The: 4 Last
detain: 3 nab **4** bust, hold, jail, keep, mire, nail, slow, stay **5** check, delay, pinch, run in, seize **6** arrest, collar, hang up, hinder, hold up, impede, intern, lock up, pick up, pull in, remand, retard **7** bog down, confine, inhibit, interne, set back **8** hold back, hold on to, hold over, imprison, keep back, make late, restrain, slow down **9** apprehend, extradite **10** buttonhole
detained: 4 slow **5** tardy
detainee: 7 captive **8** internee, prisoner
detainment: 10 internment
__ d'état: 4 coup **6** raison
detect: 3 see, spy **4** espy, find, note, spot **5** catch, dig up, hit on, learn, scent, sense, smell, sniff, trace **6** descry, expose, locate, notice, pick up, turn up, unmask **7** discern, make out, observe, uncover **8** discover, identify, pinpoint, smell out, sniff out **9** ascertain, recognize, stumble on, track down
detectable: 7 audible, visible **8** palpable, tangible
detection: 4 find **6** espial **8** exposure **9** discovery, unmasking **10** disclosure, revelation, uncovering, unearthing
device: 5 radar, sonar
detective: 2 PI **3** cop, fed, spy **4** dick, narc, nark **5** agent, narco, snoop **6** shamus, sleuth **7** gumshoe, officer **9** constable, operative **10** bloodhound, private eye, prosecutor
cry: 3 aha
discovery: 4 clew, clue
do ~ work: 5 trace
duo's dog: 4 Asta
Fed. medical ~: 3 CDC
fictional ~: 4 Chan, Fell, Rome **5** Dupin, Lupin, McGee, Queen, Small, Spade, Tibbs, Trent, Vance, Wolfe **6** Alleyn, Archer, Carter, Hammer, Holmes, Marple, Poirot, Shayne, Wimsey **7** Charles, Maigret, Marlowe, Templar **8** Drummond, Saint, The, Sam Spade, Sherlock, Tony Rome **9** Honey West, Lew Archer, Nero Wolfe **10** David Small, Mike Hammer, Nick Carter, Philo Vance
first name in ~ fiction: 4 Erle
rabbi ~: 5 Small
skill: 5 logic
story pioneer: 3 Poe
work: 4 case
__ detective: 5 house **7** private
__ Detective, The: 5 Cheap
__ detector: 3 lie **4** mine **5** metal, smoke **7** crystal
detent: 4 pawl **7** ratchet
détente: 4 thaw **5** truce **10** cooling off
detention: 5 delay **6** arrest **7** custody, jailing, keeping **9** captivity, hindrance, restraint, retention **10** constraint, detainment, immurement, impediment, indictment, internment, quarantine
place of ~: 4 jail **5** gulag **6** prison
deter: 3 cow **4** damp, turn **5** block, check, chill, daunt, delay, scare **6** dampen, hinder, impede, put off **7** fend off, inhibit, obviate, prevent, trammel, ward off **8** dispirit, dissuade, frighten, hold back, obstruct, preclude, redirect, restrain, scare off, slow down, stave off **9** foreclose, forestall, give pause, talk out of **10** discourage, dishearten, intimidate, keep in line
opposite: 4 abet
deterge: 4 lave, wash **5** bathe, clean, scrub **6** purify **7** launder **9** disinfect
detergent: 3 All, Biz, Era, Fab, Yes **4** Ajax, Bold, Dash, Gain, soap, Surf, Tide, Wisk **5** Cheer, Dreft, Ivory, Purex **6** Calgon, Dynamo, Oxydol **7** cleaner, Octagon, Woolite **8** cleanser **9** Ivory Snow
feature: 4 suds
ingredient: 5 borax **6** alkali
old ~ brand: 3 Duz **5** Rinso
target: 5 grime, stain **6** grease
deteriorate: 3 ebb, rot **4** fade, fail, flag, rust, sink, slip, wane, wear, wilt **5** decay, erode, lapse, slide, slump, spoil **6** suffer, weaken, worsen **7** corrode, crumble, decline, degrade, fall off, regress, relapse, rot away, vitiate **8** decrease, go to seed, languish, stagnate, vegetate, wear away **9** aggravate, fall apart **10** degenerate, exacerbate, go downhill, go to pieces, retrogress
deteriorated: 4 worn **6** shabby **7** worn-out **8** decrepit
deterioration: 3 ebb **4** fall, ruin, slip, wear **5** decay, lapse **6** damage **7** decline, entropy **8** downturn
determinant: 5 cause **6** factor, motive, reason, source
determinate: 4 spot **7** limited, special **8** definite
determination: 4 grit, guts, push, will, zeal **5** drive, heart, nerve, pluck, spine, spunk, stand, valor **6** choice, energy, result **7** bravery, courage, purpose, resolve, verdict **8** backbone, boldness, decision, firmness, judgment, sentence, solution, tenacity, volition **9** hardiness, stability, willpower **10** resolution
determine: 3 fix, set **4** find, mean, rate, rule, show, tell, vote **5** cinch, elect, gauge, impel, judge, learn, place, prove, solve, think **6** affect, assess, choose, clinch, decide, define, derive, figure, govern, locate, orient, settle, size up, verify **7** delimit, dictate, find out, measure, pin down, propose, resolve, specify, unearth, work out **8** complete, conclude, discover, draw lots, identify, nail down, pinpoint, regulate **9** arbitrate, ascertain, calculate, condition, establish, ferret out, figure out, get a fix on, get to know, influence, preordain **10** adjudicate, boil down to, foreordain, have a hunch, predestine, predispose, settle upon
determined: 3 set **4** bent, firm, sure **5** rigid, stout **6** dogged, driven, gritty, intent, steely, strong, sturdy, wilful **7** adamant, certain, earnest, serious, willful **8** decisive, definite, hellbent, in the bag, positive, resolute, sedulous, stalwart, stubborn, tireless, untiring **9** ambitious, desperate, obstinate, steadfast, strenuous, tenacious **10** conclusive, hardboiled, headstrong, inevitable, inflexible, persistent, purposeful, undeterred, unflagging, unwavering
be ~: 7 persist **9** persevere
determinedly: 4 hard **8** for keeps
determining: 5 chief, final **7** crucial, pivotal, supreme **8** critical, deciding, decisive **9** important **10** conclusive, definitive
__ de terre: 5 pomme
deterrent: 3 bar **4** curb, rein **5** brake, check **6** bridle, lesson **7** trammel **8** obstacle **9** hindrance, restraint **10** constraint, impediment, preventive
detest: 4 hate **5** abhor, leech **6** loathe **7** despise, dislike **8** can't take, execrate **9** abominate, can't stand **10** recoil from, shrink from
old-style: 5 spise
detestable: 3 bad **4** foul, grim, poor, vile **5** awful, lousy, seamy, sorry, woful, wrong **6** crumby, crummy, dismal, horrid, odious, rotten, woeful **7** accurst, baleful, baneful, beastly, doleful, ghastly, hateful, heinous, hideous, satanic **8** accursed, dreadful, God-awful, grievous, horrible, inferior, shameful, shocking, stinking, terrible, wretched **9** abhorrent, appalling, atrocious, defective, execrable, frightful, insidious, invidious, loathsome, miserable, monstrous, nefarious, obnoxious, offensive, repellant, repellent, repugnant, repulsive, revolting, satanical **10** abominable, despicable, disastrous, disgusting, horrendous, outrageous
detestation: 4 hate **5** odium **6** enmity, hatred **7** disgust, dislike **8** aversion, distaste, loathing **9** repulsion, revulsion
detested: 7 unloved **9** unpopular
__ de tête: 3 mal
__ de théâtre: 4 coup
dethrone: 4 oust **6** depose, remove, unseat **8** displace **9** overthrow
de Tocqueville: 6 Alexis
__ de toilette: 3 eau
detonate: 4 fire **5** burst, erupt, go off, sound **6** blow up, go boom, set off **7** explode, thunder **8** shoot off, touch off **9** discharge, fulminate
detonation: 5 blast, noise **6** blow-up, report **7** blowout **9** discharge, explosion
sound: 4 bang, boom, roar **6** kaboom
detonative: 9 explosive
detonator: 3 cap **4** fuze **7** lighter
__ de toros: 5 plaza **6** fiesta
de Toth: 5 Andre
detour: 3 err **4** turn **5** route, skirt **6** bypass, bypath **7** reroute **8** sidestep **9** deviation, diversion **10** digression, divergence
detract: 3 mar **4** slur **5** lower, sneer **6** divert, lessen, malign, reduce **7** cheapen, run down, slander **8** belittle, diminish, draw away, minimize, subtract **9** devaluate
detracting: 8 critical **9** invidious **10** defamatory, derogatory, minimizing
detraction: 7 slander **9** aspersion, disesteem, injustice, maligning, traducing **10** backbiting, defamation, derogation, muckraking, pejorative, revilement, scurrility
detractive: 8 critical, libelous **9** aspersive, demeaning, invidious **10** belittling, defamatory, derogatory
detractor: 4 hack **5** enemy **6** critic **7** defamer, reviler **8** asperser, impugner, maligner, vilifier **9** belittler, derogater, ill-wisher **10** denigrator, deprecator, disparager
detrain: 5 light **6** alight, get off **7** descend, jump off **9** disembark
where to ~: 5 depot **7** station **8** terminal
detriment: 4 bane, cost, harm, hurt, loss **5** minus **6** blight, damage, hurdle, injury, plague **7** barrier **8** calamity, disaster, drawback, handicap, obstacle, weakness **9** hindrance, liability, nightmare, prejudice, ruination **10** disservice, impairment, impediment
detrimental: 3 bad, ill **5** toxic **6** malign **7** adverse, baleful, baneful, harmful, hurtful, nocuous, ruinous **8** damaging, inimical, negative **9** dangerous, injurious, unhealthy **10** calamitous, disastrous
__ de Triomphe: 3 Arc **4** l'Arc
detritus: 5 scree **6** debris, gravel, litter **7** garbage **8** leavings
rock ~: 4 sand
__ de trois: 3 pas
Detroit: 4 city, port, town **5** river **6** Motown
arena: 4 Cobo
brew: 6 Stroh's
city near ~: 6 Ecorse
company: 3 GMC **4** Ford
county: 5 Wayne
labor group: 3 UAW
locale: 8 Michigan
newspaper: 4 News **9** Free Press
product: 3 car **4** auto **5** sedan
pro team: 5 Lions **6** Tigers **7** Pistons **8** Red Wings
River destination: 4 Erie
Detroit __ Wings: 3 Red
Detroit-to-Denver dir.: 3 WSW
de trop: 7 surplus, too much **9** redundant
detrude: 5 lower
Deucalion
author: John Ruskin
deuce: 3 tie, two **4** card **7** low card, two-spot
beater: 4 trey
point after ~: 4 ad in **5** ad out
Deuce Coupe
choreographer: 5 Tharp

DE

deuces __: 4 wild
__ Deuces, The: 6 Flying
__-deucy: 4 acey
Deuel: 5 Peter
deus ex __: 7 machina
Deus Ramos, Joao de: 4 poet
deuterium
discoverer: Harold Urey
deuteron: 8 particle
Deuteronomy
follower: 6 Joshua
peak: 4 Nebo
preceder: 7 Numbers
Deuteronomy, Old: 3 cat
Deutsch: 6 German 7 Babette
Deutsche __: 4 mark
Deutschland
see German
Deutschland __ Alles: 4 über
deux: 3 two 6 French
follower: 5 trois
preceder: 3 une
__ deux: 5 entre, pas de
Deux-Sèvres: 10 department
capital: 5 Niort
Dev: 5 Patel
__ de vache: 4 bois
De Valera, Eamon: 5 Irish 9 statesman
De Valois, Ninette: 5 Irish 6 dancer 8 danseuse 9 ballerina
devalorize: 9 downgrade 10 depreciate
devaluate: 5 abase, lower 6 debase, impair 7 detract 8 decrease
devalue: 5 lower 6 debase, impair 7 cheapen, deflate, depress 8 mark down, take down, write off 9 downgrade, underrate, write down 10 adulterate, depreciate
Devane, William: 5 actor
TV: Knots Landing
devastate: 4 raid, rase, raze, ruin, sack, sink 5 harry, level, smash, spoil, total, trash, waste, wreck 6 ravage, topple 7 consume, despoil, destroy, pillage, plunder, shatter, stagger, unbuild 8 bulldoze, demolish, desolate, freeboot, spoliate, take down, tear down 9 depredate, desecrate, dismantle, knock down, overwhelm, take apart
devastated: 4 lost 7 in a funk, in ruins 8 finished
devastating: 6 lethal 7 ruinous, telling, violent 8 stunning
devastation: 4 ruin 5 havoc, waste 7 debacle
__ de veau: 3 ris 4 tête
de Vega: 4 Lope
develop: 2 go 3 age, wax 4 boom, brew, form, gird, grow, rise, stem, tone 5 arise, begin, bloom, breed, build, educe, forge, occur, ripen, shape, shore, start, steel, train, widen 6 anneal, beef up, create, deepen, derive, emerge, enrich, enroot, evolve, expand, extend, foster, grow up, happen, harden, mature, mellow, polish, prop up, refine, result, sketch, spread, spring, sprout, temper, thrive, tone up, unfold, work up 7 advance, amplify, augment, blossom, bolster, brace up, broaden, build up, burgeon, empower, enhance, enlarge, exploit, fortify, improve, magnify, nurture, perfect, pioneer, prepare, produce, promote, prosper, realize, shape up, shore up, stiffen, toughen, work out 8 beautify, bourgeon, buttress, commence, contract, energize, engender, flourish, generate, heighten, increase, incubate, indurate, maturate, progress, take root, vitalize 9 actualize, branch out, come about, cultivate, elaborate, establish, formulate, germinate, intensify, originate, reinforce, transpire 10 invigorate, liberalize, mastermind, strengthen
begin to ~: 3 bud
gradually: 6 evolve
into: 6 become
developed: 4 ripe 5 adult 6 mature
not ~: 6 latent
developer: 7 builder, pioneer, planner
offering: 3 lot 4 land
output: 3 pix 6 photos 8 pictures
developing: 5 young 7 budding, ongoing 8 thriving 9 half-grown, incipient
development: 4 rise 5 boost, event, phase 6 course, growth, result, spread 7 advance, buildup, outcome, process, stature 8 addition, breeding, incident, increase, maturity, offshoot, progress, ripening 9 gestation, outgrowth 10 perfection
housing ~: 5 tract
unexpected ~: 5 twist
unit: 5 house
de Vere, Aubrey Thomas: 4 poet 5 Irish
Devereux: 4 Earl
__ de verre: 4 pâte
Devers, Gail: 6 runner 8 sprinter
Devi: 4 Kali 6 mother, Shakti 7 goddess, Parvati 9 Annapurna
consort: 5 Shiva
like ~: 5 Vedic
__ Devi: 5 Nanda
deviant: 3 odd 4 eery 5 eerie, weird 6 atypic, errant, freaky, off-key, quirky 7 bizarre, oddball, offbeat, strange, unusual, variant, wayward 8 aberrant, abnormal, atypical, freakish, peculiar, uncommon 9 anomalous, different, divergent, eccentric, fantastic, heretical, irregular 10 unorthodox
deviate: 3 err, sin, yaw 4 part, sway, turn, vary, veer 5 shift, slant, split, stray 6 branch, differ, spread, swerve, wander 7 digress, diverge, radiate 8 aberrate, contrast, divagate, separate 9 bifurcate, misbehave
deviating: 6 errant 7 unalike 8 abnormal 9 different, divergent
by extremes: 7 radical
deviation: 3 yaw 4 bend, flaw 5 error, shift, slope 6 breach, change, detour 7 anomaly, veering 8 mutation, neurosis, variance 9 aberrance, departure, disparity, diversion, exception, variation 10 aberration, alteration, deflection, difference, digression, divergence, innovation
standard ~ symbol: 5 sigma
device: 4 logo, plot, ploy, ruse, tool, trap, wile 5 badge, craft, crest, dodge, feint, gizmo, thing, trick 6 emblem, engine, gadget, gambit, legend, scheme, symbol, widget 7 gimmick, insigne, machine, utensil 8 artifice, colophon, conceive, contrive, heraldry, insignia, loophole, maneuver 9 accessory, apparatus, appliance, deception, expedient, flotation, implement, invention, mechanism, stratagem, strategem 10 expediency, instrument, subterfuge
__ device: 6 homing 8 mnemonic 9 flotation
deviceful: 6 clever, shrewd 9 ingenious, inventive 10 innovative
devices: 9 equipment, machinery
__ de vie: 3 eau
devil: 3 imp 4 cook, ogre 5 beast, brute, demon, fiend, rogue, Satan, tease 6 Belial, daemon, daimon, diablo, pester, rascal 7 dastard, evil one, Lucifer, monster, torment, villain 8 evildoer 9 archfiend, Beelzebub, scoundrel 10 jackanapes
between the ~ and the deep blue sea: 6 in a fix, in a jam
combining form: 6 diabol- 7 diabolo-
doll: 4 mojo
domain: 5 Hades 10 underworld
dust ~: 4 eddy
emulate the ~: 5 tempt
ender: 3 ish, try 4 fish, wood
little ~: 3 imp 4 brat 5 scamp
poor ~: 6 wretch
ray: 5 manta
starter: 4 dare
Tasmanian ~: 6 animal 8 predator 9 marsupial
devil __: 3 dog, ray
devil __, the: 5 to pay
devil-__-care: 3 may
__ devil: 3 sea 4 dust, heat, king
Devil: 5 Satan 8 puckster
__ Devil: 5 Bwana 6 Little
__-Devil: 3 She
Devil and Daniel Webster, The
author: Stephen Vincent Benet
deviled __: 3 egg
devilfish: 5 manta 8 manta ray
Devil in a Blue Dress (1995 film)
cast: Jennifer Beals, Denzel Washington
Devil in Disguise (1963 song)
artist: Elvis Presley
Devil Inside (1988 song)
artist: INXS
Devil in the Belfry, The
author: Edgar Allan Poe
devilish: 4 evil 5 curst 6 cursed, impish, wicked 7 accurst, brutish, demonic, hellish, inhuman, satanic 8 accursed, daemonic, demoniac, diabolic, fiendish, infernal, inhumane 9 demonical, execrable, nefarious, satanical 10 diabolical, villainous
devilkin: 3 imp 4 brat
DeVille: 3 car 4 auto 8 Cadillac
devil-may-care: 3 gay, lax 4 rash 5 blasé 6 jaunty, rakish, sporty 7 raffish, reckess 8 carefree, careless, heedless, rakehell, reckless, sporting, sportive 9 foolhardy, impetuous 10 rollicking, swaggering
devilment: 8 mischief 9 nastiness
__ Devil Moon: 3 Old
Devil or Angel (1960 song)
artist: Bobby Vee
devil's
paintbrush: 5 plant 6 flower
Devils: 3 six
home: 9 New Jersey
milieu: 3 ice 4 rink
org.: 3 NHL
rival: *see* hockey team
Devil's __: 6 Island
Devil's Advocate, The
author: Langlo West
Devil's Advocate, The (1997 film)
cast: Al Pacino, Keanu Reeves, Charlize Theron
Devil's Dictionary, The
author: Ambrose Bierce
Devil's Disciple, The: 4 play
author: George Bernard Shaw
character: 5 Essie
Devilseed
author: Frank Yerby
devil's food __: 4 cake
Devil's General, The
author: Carl Zuckmayer
Devil's Own, The (1997 film)
cast: Ruben Blades, Harrison Ford, Brad Pitt
director: Alan J. Pakula
Devil's Pool, The
author: George Sand
Devil's Tail
ingredient: 5 vodka
Devil's Waltz
author: Jonathan Kellerman
deviltry: 4 evil, vice 7 knavery, roguery, sorcery 8 iniquity, mischief 9 nastiness, rascality 10 friskiness, wickedness
Devil Wears Prada, The (2006 film)
cast: Emily Blunt, Anne Hathaway, Meryl Streep, Stanley Tucci
Devil With a Blue Dress On (1966 song)
artist: Mitch Ryder
Devil Woman (1976 song)
artist: Cliff Richard
Devine: 4 Andy 7 Loretta
__ de violette: 5 crème
devious: 3 sly 4 foxy, wily 5 false, shady, snaky 6 artful, crafty, louche, shifty, sneaky, subtle, tricky, zigzag 7 crooked, cunning, evasive, oblique, sinuous 8 delusive, guileful, indirect, scheming, slippery, tortuous 9 deceitful, designing, dishonest, insidious, insincere, underhand 10 circuitous, fraudulent, mendacious, misleading, roundabout, untruthful
act: 4 ploy 6 gambit
purpose: 5 angle
devise: 3 lay 4 brew, form, make, mold, plan, plot 5 ad-lib, craft, draft, forge, frame, hatch, shape 6 cook up, create, design, invent, legacy, make up, map out, whip up 7 arrange, concoct, dream up, fashion, imagine, prepare, produce, project, think up, trump up, work out 8 conceive, contrive,

engineer, intrigue **9** conjure up, construct, fabricate, formulate, improvise **10** come up with, mastermind
devisee: **4** heir **7** heiress
deviser: **6** framer **8** designer **9** artificer, fashioner **10** fabricator
devitalize: **3** sag, sap **4** flag, jade, tire, wane **5** blunt, drain, weary **6** impair, reduce, shrink, soften, weaken **7** deplete, depress, exhaust, fatigue, tire out, vitiate, wear out **8** enervate, enfeeble **9** attenuate, desiccate, undermine **10** debilitate, emasculate
DeVito: **5** Danny, Karla
DeVito, Danny: **5** actor **8** director
film: Anything Else (2003)
Batman Returns (1992)
The Big Kahuna (2000)
Death to Smoochy (2002)
Drowning Mona (2000)
Get Shorty (1995)
Heist (2001)
Hoffa (1992)
Jack the Bear (1993)
The Jewel of the Nile (1985)
Junior (1994)
Living Out Loud (1998)
Man on the Moon (1999)
Other People's Money (1991)
The Rainmaker (1997)
Renaissance Man (1994)
Romancing the Stone (1984)
Ruthless People (1986)
Terms of Endearment (1983)
Throw Momma From the Train (1987)
Tin Men (1987)
Twins (1988)
The War of the Roses (1989)
spouse: Rhea Perlman
TV: Taxi
__ de vivre: **4** joie
devoid: **5** bleak, empty, stark **6** absent, barren, bereft **7** wanting **8** depleted, desolate, lifeless
of: **7** lacking, without
(of): **4** bare, free
of interest: **4** flat **5** vapid **6** boring, jejune **7** prosaic **9** tasteless, wearisome **10** dullsville, flavorless, lackluster
devoirs: **7** regards **8** respects **10** good wishes
DeVol: **5** Frank
devolution: **5** lapse **9** decadence
Devon: **3** cow **4** bull **5** sheep, shire **6** bovine, cattle, county
city: **6** Exeter **8** Plymouth
locale: **7** England
river: **3** Exe
Devonian subdivision: **5** Erian
Devon Rex: **3** cat **5** felid **6** feline
Devonshire __: **5** cream
DeVorzon: **5** Barry
devote: **4** give **5** allot, apply, bless, put in, spend **6** assign, bestow, commit, direct, donate, hallow, pledge **7** consign, earmark, reserve **8** allocate, dedicate, sanctify, set apart, set aside **9** apportion **10** consecrate, contribute
oneself to: **2** do **6** tackle **7** address **9** undertake
devoted: **4** true **5** close, liege, loyal, pious, thick **6** ardent, doting, fervid, filial, loving **7** adoring, dutiful, earnest, staunch, valuing, zealous **8** constant, faithful, intimate, maternal, parental, reliable, trueblue, untiring, yeomanly **9** allegiant, attentive, dedicated, fraternal, steadfast, unselfish **10** solicitous, undeterred
be ~: **6** adhere, cleave
be ~ to: **5** adore **6** follow
to God, name meaning: **6** Lemuel
devotedly: **5** madly **7** rabidly
devotedness: **4** love **7** loyalty
Devoted to You (1958 song)
artist: Everly Brothers
devotee: **3** fan, nut **4** buff **5** fiend, freak, junky, lover **6** addict, rooter **7** admirer, booster, fanatic, fancier, groupie, habitué **8** adherent, disciple, follower, partisan **9** supporter, worshiper **10** aficionado, enthusiast, specialist
suffix: **3** -ist, -ite
devotion: **4** love, zeal **5** ardor, piety **6** fealty, fervor, homage, liking, prayer, regard **7** loyalty, passion, worship **8** fidelity, fondness **9** adherence, adoration, affection, constancy, fixedness, intensity, puppy love, reverence, sincerity **10** allegiance, attachment, commitment, dedication, enthusiasm, friendship
Hindu ~: **6** bhakti
letters of ~: **3** TLC
medieval ~: **7** angelus
object of ~: **4** icon, idol, ikon **5** eikon
devotional: **6** solemn **9** spiritual
De Voto: **7** Bernard
devour: **3** eat **4** bolt, gulp, read, take, wolf **5** eat up, gorge, scarf **6** absorb, engulf, feed on, finish, gobble, guzzle, ingest, ingulf, inhale, prey on, relish, take in **7** consume, destroy, engorge, feast on, partake, pillage, put away, revel in, scarf up, swallow **8** chow down, gobble up, wolf down **9** polish off, scarf down, swallow up **10** annihilate, gormandize
devout: **4** holy, pure **5** godly, pious **6** ardent, fervid, hearty **7** adoring, angelic, earnest, fervent, intense, saintly, serious, sincere, zealous **8** faithful, orthodox, reverent **9** angelical, heartfelt, religious, righteous **10** passionate, worshipful
devoutness: **5** piety **6** fervor **9** godliness, reverence
De Vries: **4** Hugo **5** Peter
De Vulgare Eloquentia
author: Dante
dew: **4** mist **5** vapor, water **8** dampness, moisture **9** sogginess
bit of ~: **4** bead, drop
ender: **3** lap **4** claw, drop, fall **5** berry, point
mountain ~: **6** whisky **7** whiskey
opposite: **5** frost
starter: **3** sun **5** honey
time: **4** morn **5** sunup **7** morning
dew __: **4** line **5** point
dew __ the thorn, The: **4** is on
DEW __: **4** line
De Waart, Edo: **5** Dutch **9** conductor
Dewar, James: **3** Sir **7** chemist **8** Scottish **9** physicist, scientist
dewdrop: **4** bead **7** globule
__ Dewdrop: **5** Daddy
Dew Drop __: **3** Inn
Dewey: **3** Tom **4** John **6** George, Melvil
brother: **4** Huey **5** Louie
uncle: **6** Donald
Dewey __ system: **7** decimal
Dewey, John: **8** educator **11** philosopher
Dewhurst, Colleen: **7** actress
spouse: George C. Scott
de Wilde: **7** Brandon
Dewitt: **7** Wallace
DeWitt: **5** Joyce
dewlap: **4** jowl **6** wattle
Dew Line acronym: **3** SAC **5** NORAD
DeWolf: **6** Hopper
DeWolfe: **5** Billy
dewy: **3** new, wet **4** damp, dank **5** fresh, humid, misty, moist, undry **7** wettish **8** unwilted
dewy-__: **4** eyed
dexter: **5** right **9** right hand
Dexter: **3** cow **4** Brad, bull **6** bovine, cattle, Gordon, Manley
Dexter, Colin inspector: **5** Morse
dexterity: **3** art **4** ease **5** craft, knack, skill **7** ability, agility, aptness, faculty, finesse, know-how, mastery, sleight **8** artistry, deftness, facility, legerity **9** adeptness, expertise, handiness, ingenuity, quickness, readiness **10** adroitness, cleverness, expertness, nimbleness, smoothness
dexterous: **3** ace, apt **4** able, deft, good, neat **5** adept, agile, canny, crack, handy, quick, ready, slick **6** adroit, artful, au fait, clever, expert, facile, habile, nimble, smooth **7** capable, cunning, skilled, trained **8** graceful, masterly, seasoned, skillful **9** competent, efficient, ingenious, inventive, masterful **10** diplomatic, effortless, proficient
dexterously: **4** neat **7** handily
dextro- opposite: **4** levo-
dextrose: **5** sugar
Dey: **5** Susan
DeYoung: **6** Dennis
DFC: **5** medal
D-flat equivalent: **6** C-sharp
DFM awarder: **3** RAF
DFW: **7** airport
locale: **3** Tex. **5** Texas
DH: **6** batter
stat: **3** RBI
D.H.: **8** Lawrence
DHA: **9** fatty acid
__ Dhabi: **3** Abu
Dhaka: **4** city, town **7** capital
locale: **10** Bangladesh
Dharma Bums, The
author: Jack Kerouac
Dharma & Greg (ABC sitcom)
cast: Jenna Elfman (Dharma Finkelstein)
Thomas Gibson (Greg Montgomery)
dog: **6** Nunzio, Stinky
Dheigh, Khigh TV series: **4** Khan
dhole: **3** dog **5** canid **6** canine
relative: *see* canine
d'honneur, affaire: **4** duel
__ d'hôte: **5** table
__ d'hôtel: **6** maitre
dhow: **4** boat, ship **5** craft **6** vessel **10** watercraft
__ diable: **3** à la
__ Diable: **5** île du
diablo: **5** demon, devil, fiend, Satan **6** daemon, daimon **7** evil one, Lucifer **9** archfiend
diabolical: **3** bad **4** evil, mean, vile **5** cruel, nasty **6** wicked **7** demonic, hellish, impious, satanic, vicious **8** daemonic, demoniac, devilish, fiendish, infernal, shameful **9** atrocious, demonical, monstrous, nefarious, satanical **10** maleficent, unhallowed, villainous
one: **5** demon, devil, fiend, Satan
diabolism: **4** evil **10** black magic
diacritical
mark: **4** shwa **5** breve, hacek, schwa, tilde **6** macron, obelus, umlaut **8** dieresis
diadem: **5** crown, tiara **6** wreath **7** chaplet, circlet, coronet, jewelry **8** headband, headgear
diag.: **5** illus.
Diaghilev: **5** Serge **6** Sergey
diagnose: **4** spot **5** place **8** identify, pinpoint **9** recognize
diagnosis: **9** breakdown, discovery, prognosis **10** conclusion, definition
Diagnosis Murder (CBS drama)
cast: Dick Van Dyke (Dr. Mark Sloan)
diagnostic: **10** indicative
test: **3** EEG, MRI **4** scan, X-ray
diagonal: **4** bias **5** askew, bevel, slant, slope **6** angled, biased, skewed, zigzag **7** beveled, oblique, on a bias, slanted **8** slanting **9** crossways, crosswise, on the bias **10** transverse
mover: **6** bishop
diagonally: **5** askew, slant **6** aslant, aslope **9** at an angle, crossways, crosswise, obliquely, on the bias, slantways, slantwise **10** cornerways, cornerwise
move ~: **3** zag, zig **6** zigzag
diagram: **3** map **4** plan **5** chart, graph, parse, table **6** design, figure, layout, scheme, sketch **7** drawing, outline, picture, profile **9** adumbrate, blueprint, floor plan, visual aid **10** tabulation
__ diagram: **4** tree, Venn
diagrammatic: **7** graphic **9** graphical
Diahann: **7** Carroll
dial: **4** call, knob, ring, tune **5** gauge, phone, tuner **6** call up, tune in **7** pointer **9** indicator, telephone, touch base
choices: **2** AM, FM
in: **5** log on **7** connect
letters: **3** ABC, DEF, GHI, JKL, MNO, PRS, TUV, WXY **4** oper.
starter: **3** sun
dial __: **4** tone
__-dial: **4** auto **6** direct
Dial: **4** soap
alternative: *see* soap
dialect: **4** cant, talk **5** argot, idiom, lingo, slang **6** brogue, jargon, patois, speech, tongue **8** language, localism, locution **10** vernacular

dialectal: **9** idiomatic **10** colloquial
dialectic: **5** logic **8** forensic **9** deduction, polemical, reasoning **10** contention, discussion, persuasion, persuasive
dialectics: **6** reason **9** reasoning
__ dialing: **4** tone **5** pulse
Dial M for Murder (1954 film)
cast: Robert Cummings, Grace Kelly, Ray Milland
character: **3** Max **4** Tony **6** Sheila
composer: Dimitri Tiomkin
director: Alfred Hitchcock
dialog: **4** chat, talk **6** confab, parley, powwow, script, speech **8** colloquy **9** discourse, tête-à-tête **10** conference, discussion
bit of ~: **4** line
Dialogues
author: Plato
dial-up device: **5** modem
diamante: **6** fabric **8** material
Diamante: **3** car **4** auto **10** Mitsubishi
diameter: **5** width **6** length **7** breadth, caliber
half: **6** radius
diametrical: **5** polar **7** counter **8** opposite
diamond: **3** gem **5** field, jewel, shape **6** carbon **7** jewelry, mineral, sandlot, stadium **8** ballpark, gemstone
alternative: *see* point size
defect: **4** flaw
dust: **4** bort **5** boart, bortz
in heraldry: **7** lozenge
jubilee number: **5** sixty
low-quality ~: **4** bort **5** boart, bortz
month: **5** April
once: **4** coal
pattern: **6** argyle
plane: **5** facet
shape: **5** rhomb
slangily: **4** rock
Smithsonian ~: **4** Hope
source: **4** mine
to Mohs: **3** ten
weight: **2** ct. **5** carat
see also baseball
diamond __: **4** ring **7** jubilee
diamond __ rough: **5** in the
__ diamond: **4** Hope
Diamond: **4** Legs, Neil **5** David, Jared, Selma
Diamond __: **3** Jim, Lil, Men **4** Girl, Head
Diamond __ Brady: **3** Jim
diamondback: **4** moth **5** snake **7** rattler **8** terrapin
danger: **4** fang **5** venom
Diamondback: **10** baseballer
Diamondbacks: **4** nine, team
home: **7** Arizona, Phoenix
org.: **3** MLB, NLW
rival: *see* baseball team
sport: **8** baseball
Diamond Girl (1973 song)
artist: Seals and Crofts
Diamond Head
locale: **4** Oahu **6** Hawaii
diamond in the __: **5** rough
Diamond, Neil
song: America (1981)
Cherry, Cherry (1966)
Cracklin' Rosie (1970)
Desirée (1977)
Girl, You'll Be a Woman Soon (1967)
Heartlight (1982)
Hello Again (1983)
Holly Holy (1969)
I Am...I Said (1971)
Kentucky Woman (1967)
Longfellow Serenade (1974)
Love on the Rocks (1980)
Play Me (1972)
September Morn (1980)
Solitary Man (1970)
Song Sung Blue (1972)
Sweet Caroline (1969)
Yesterday's Songs (1981)
You Don't Bring Me Flowers (1978)
__ Diamond Phillips: **3** Lou
Diamond Queen, The (1953 film)
cast: Arlene Dahl
__ Diamond Ring: **4** This
diamonds: **3** bid, ice **4** suit **7** jewelry
at times: **5** trump
fake ~: **5** paste
like raw ~: **5** uncut
Diamonds (1987 song)
artist: Herb Alpert
Diamonds (1999 film)
cast: Dan Aykroyd, Lauren Bacall, Kirk Douglas
Diamonds and Pearls (1991 song)
artist: Prince
Diamonds and Rust (1975 song)
artist: Joan Baez
Diamonds Are a Girl's Best Friend
composer: Jule Styne
Diamonds Are Forever: **4** film **5** novel
author: Ian Fleming
cast: Sean Connery, Charles Gray, Jill St. John
Dian: **6** Fossey **9** Parkinson
Diana: **4** Dors, Lynn, Nyad, Rigg, Ross **5** Roman, Sands **6** Canova, Hyland **7** goddess, Muldaur, Scarwid, Spencer, Wynyard
equivalent: **7** Artemis
parent: **7** Jupiter
twin: **6** Apollo
Diana (1957 song)
artist: Paul Anka
Diane: **4** Ladd, Lane **5** Arbus, Baker, Carey, Duane, Kurys, Renay, Varsi **6** Keaton, Kruger, McBain, Sawyer, Venora **7** Cilento
to Woody: **6** costar
Diane __ Fürstenberg: **3** von
Dianne: **5** Wiest **6** Lennon **9** Feinstein
dianthus: **5** plant **6** flower
diapason: **6** melody **7** harmony
diaper: **4** Luvs **5** nappy **7** Drypers, Huggies, Pampers
fix a ~: **5** repin
holder: **3** pin **9** safety pin
diaphanous: **4** airy, fine, lacy, thin **5** filmy, gauzy, lucid, sheer **6** flimsy **7** chiffon **8** delicate, finespun, gossamer, pellucid **10** cobweblike, see-through
diaphoresis: **5** sweat
diaphragm: **4** iris
diarist: **5** Frank, noter, Pepys **6** writer **7** Johnson **8** Anaïs Nin **9** Anne Frank
diarist, British: **5** Pepys
diary: **3** log **4** book **6** memoir, record **7** account, daybook, journal, writing **8** longhand, register **9** chronicle, recountal
capacity: **4** year
Internet ~: **4** blog
notation: **5** entry
online ~: **4** blog
put in one's ~: **3** log **5** enter
starter: **4** dear
__ Diary: **4** Dear, Eve's
Diary of a Genius
author: Salvador Dali
Diary of a Mad Housewife (1970 film)
cast: Richard Benjamin, Frank Langella, Carrie Snodgress
Diary of a Madman
author: Nikolai Gogol
Diary of Anne Frank, The (1959 film)
cast: Millie Perkins, Joseph Schildkraut, Shelley Winters
Diary of a Yuppie
author: Louis Auchincloss
Diary, The (1958 song)
artist: Neil Sedaka
__ días: **6** buenos
Dias: **10** Bartolomeu
diaskeuast: **6** editor
diaspora: **5** exile
Diaspora
author: Greg Egan
diatom: **4** alga **5** algae
diatomaceous earth: **7** mineral
diatribe: **4** rant **5** abuse **6** screed, speech, tirade **8** harangue, jeremiad **9** criticism, invective, philippic **10** impugnment, vocalizing
__ diavolo: **3** fra
Diaz: **7** Cameron **8** Porfirio
Diaz, Cameron: **7** actress
film: Any Given Sunday (1999)
Being John Malkovich (1999)
Charlie's Angels (2000)
Gangs of New York (2002)
The Holiday (2006)
In Her Shoes (2005)
The Mask (1994)
My Best Friend's Wedding (1997)
My Sister's Keeper (2009)
The Sweetest Thing (2002)
There's Something About Mary (1998)
Vanilla Sky (2001)
What Happens in Vegas (2008)
film (voice): Shrek (2001)
dibble: **4** tool **10** garden tool
dibs: **5** claim, title **6** rights
DiCaprio, Leonardo: **5** actor
film: The Aviator (2004)
The Beach (2000)
Blood Diamond (2004)
Body of Lies (2008)
Catch Me If You Can (2002)
Celebrity (1998)
The Departed (2006)
Gangs of New York (2002)
Man in the Iron Mask (1998)
The Quick and the Dead (1995)
Revolutionary Road (2009)
Romeo & Juliet (1996)
This Boy's Life (1993)
Titanic (1997)
nickname: **3** Leo
dice: **3** cut **4** chop, cube **5** bones, cubes, cut up, mince **6** cleave, gamble, reduce
action: **4** roll, toss **5** throw
combining form: **8** astragal- **9** astragalo-
five, in ~: **6** cinque
game: **5** craps
like ~: **7** cubical
lucky ~ throw: **5** seven **6** eleven
no ~: **8** forget it
one, in ~: **3** ace
six, in ~: **4** sise
spot: **3** pip
tamper with ~: **3** fix, rig **4** load
throw: **3** six, ten, two **4** aces, five, four, nine **5** eight, seven, three **6** eleven, twelve **7** boxcars, doubles **9** snake eyes
__ dice: **5** liars, poker
__ Dice Clay: **6** Andrew
dicey: **5** risky **6** chancy, touchy, tricky **8** perilous **9** hazardous, uncertain **10** precarious
dichotomize: **4** part **5** sever, split
dichotomy: **5** split **8** disunion, division
Dichter, Misha: **7** pianist
DiCillo: **3** Tom
Dick: **2** A.B. **4** Andy, Lane, York **5** Clark, Foran, Hyman, Motta, Shawn, Tracy, Weber **6** Butkus, Button, Cavett, Cheney, Haymes, Martin, Powell, Turpin, Vitale **7** Fosbury, Francis, Gautier, Grayson, Gregory, Sargent, Van Dyke **8** Gephardt, Smothers **9** Van Patten
Dick (1999 film)
cast: Kirsten Dunst, Dan Hedaya, Michelle Williams
__ Dick: **6** Ragged **7** Deadeye
__-Dick: **4** Moby
__, Dick and Harry: **3** Tom
Dick and Jane
cat: **4** Puff
dog: **4** Spot
verb: **3** run, see
dickens: **4** heck
little ~: **3** imp **4** brat, pest **6** urchin
Dickens: **6** Monica **7** Charles
Dickens, Charles: **6** writer **7** British
character: **3** Pip, Tim **4** Nell **5** Uriah
exclamation: **3** bah
illustrator: Phiz
pseudonym: Boz
work: American Notes
Barnaby Rudge
Bleak House
A Christmas Carol
Cricket on the Hearth
David Copperfield
Dombey and Son
Great Expectations
Hard Times
Little Dorrit
Martin Chuzzlewit
The Mystery of Edwin Drood
Nicholas Nickleby
The Old Curiosity Shop
Oliver Twist
Our Mutual Friend
Pickwick Papers
A Tale of Two Cities
dicker: **4** deal **5** argue **6** barter, haggle, higgle **7** bargain **9** negotiate
Dickerson, Eric: **10** footballer
dickey: **4** vest **6** collar **9** neck scarf, small bird
fastener: **4** stud

Dickey: 3 Lee 4 Bill 5 James
Dickey, Bill: 6 Yankee 7 catcher
Dickey, James: 6 writer
work: Deliverance
Dickie: 5 Moore
Dickinson: 5 Angie, Emily 8 Richards
Dickinson, Angie: 7 actress
spouse: Burt Bacharach
TV: Police Woman
Dickinson, Emily: 4 poet
home: Amherst
Dick, Philip K.: 6 writer
__ Dickson Carr: 4 John
__ Dick, The: 4 Bank
Dick Tracy (1990 film)
cast: Warren Beatty, Glenne Headly, Madonna, Al Pacino
director: Warren Beatty
Dick Van __: 4 Dyke 6 Patten
Dick Van Dyke Show, The (CBS sitcom)
cast: Morey Amsterdam (Buddy Sorrell)
Richard Deacon (Mel Cooley)
Larry Mathews (Ritchie Petrie)
Mary Tyler Moore (Laura Petrie)
Rose Marie (Sally Rogers)
Dick Van Dyke (Rob Petrie)
__ di Como: 4 Lago
dictate: 3 law, say, set 4 fiat, read, rule, talk, word 5 canon, edict, order, speak, utter 6 behest, decree, dictum, direct, enjoin, govern, impose, ordain 7 bidding, command, control, mandate, precept 8 dominate 9 determine, direction, preordain, prescribe, principle, ultimatum, verbalize 10 incitement, injunction, regulation
to: 9 tyrannize
dictation pro: 5 steno
dictator: 4 czar, duce, tsar, tzar 5 ruler 6 despot, gerent, satrap, tyrant 7 emperor 8 autocrat 9 oppressor
dictatorial: 4 firm, hard 5 bossy, cruel, picky, rigid, stern, tough 6 severe 7 austere, haughty, pompous, Spartan 8 absolute, arrogant, despotic, dogmatic, exacting, hard-line, imperial, rigorous 9 demanding, draconian, officious, stringent, unbending, unsparing 10 despotical, dogmatical, inflexible, iron-fisted, no-nonsense, oppressive, peremptory, tyrannical
dictatorship: 7 tyranny 9 autocracy 10 one-man rule
__ Dictator, The: 5 Great
diction: 5 style, usage 6 phrase, speech 7 oratory, wording 8 delivery, language, locution, phrasing, verbiage 9 elocution, eloquence
obsolete ~: 8 archaism 10 archaicism
dictionary: 4 book, list 5 lexis 7 lexicon 8 language 9 reference 10 cyclopedia, vocabulary
abbr.: 3 adj., adv., obs., OED, syn., var. 4 conj., etym., pron. 5 deriv.
digital ~: 5 CD/ROM
material: 10 vocabulary
range: 4 A to Z
unit: 4 word 5 entry 10 definition
use a ~: 6 look up
__ dictionary: 7 reverse 9 crossword
__ Dictionary, The: 6 Devil's
dictum: 3 saw 4 fiat, rule, word 5 adage, axiom, dogma, gnome, irade, maxim, moral, motto, order, say-so 6 byword, decree, ruling, saying, truism 7 command, decrees, mandate, precept, proverb, theorem 8 aphorism, apothegm, sentence 9 ordinance, principle, statement 10 apophthegm, principium
obiter ~: 6 remark 7 comment 9 assertion, statement, utterance
__ dictum: 6 obiter
Did __!: 3 not, too
didact: 10 instructor
didactic: 8 pedantic 9 pedagogic 10 pedantical
__-di-dah: 3 lah
didapper: 4 bird 5 grebe
didaskaleinophobe fear: 6 school
diddle: 5 cheat 6 loiter, putter 7 swindle 9 waste time
Diddley, Bo: 9 guitarist
genre: 5 blues
Diddling
author: Edgar Allan Poe
diddly: 3 nix 6 trifle
less than ~: 3 nil
diddly-__: 5 squat
__ Diddy: 5 Do Wah
Diderot, Denis: 6 French, writer 11 philosopher
__ Did For Love: 5 What I
Didi: 4 Conn
Didion, Joan: 6 writer
work: After Henry
Democracy
Miami
Play It as It Lays
Political Fictions
Run River
Salvador
Slouching Towards Bethlehem
The White Album
The Year of Magical Thinking
Did It in a Minute (1982 song)
artist: Hall and Oates
__ Didn't Believe Me: 4 They
__ Didn't Care: 3 If I
Didn't I (Blow Your Mind) (1970 song)
artist: Delfonics
Didn't I (Blow Your Mind) (1989 song)
artist: New Kids on the Block
__ Didn't Say Yes: 3 She
Didn't We Almost Have It All (1987 song)
artist: Whitney Houston
dido: 5 antic, prank
Dido: 5 queen
husband: 5 Eneas 6 Aeneas 8 Sychaeus
parent: 5 Belus
sibling: 4 Anna 9 Pygmalion
Dido and Aeneas
composer: Thomas Arne
Didrikson: 4 Babe 7 Mildred
Did you __!: 4 ever
__, Did You Evah!: 4 Well
Did you ever __ lassie...: 4 see a
Did You Ever __ Dream...: 4 See a
die: 3 ebb 4 cube, dado, fade, fail, mold, wane 5 abate, lapse, stall 6 fizzle, perish, recede, vanish 7 conk out, dwindle, ease off, fade out, slacken, subside, succumb 8 fade away, melt away, peter out
down: 3 ebb 4 lull, wane 5 abate, cease, let up 6 lessen, recede, relent 7 dwindle, subside, tail off, thin out 8 decrease, fade away, head away, level off, moderate, taper off 9 retrocede
ender: 4 back, hard 5 stock
for: 5 crave
high: 3 six
on the vine: 3 ebb, rot, sag 4 fade, wilt 5 decay, lapse 6 go soft, worsen 7 decline, dwindle 8 languish, vegetate 9 fizzle out, waste away 10 degenerate, retrogress
out: 3 ebb 4 fade 5 let up 6 vanish 7 cool off 8 decrease 9 break down
partner: 4 tool
surface: 4 face, side
die __: 4 down 7 casting
die-__: 4 cast, hard
__ die: 4 do or, open, sine, trim
Die __: 7 Walküre
Die Another Day (2002 film)
cast: Halle Berry, Pierce Brosnan, John Cleese, Judi Dench
Diedrich: 5 Bader
Diefenbaker, John: 2 P.M. 8 Canadian
successor: 7 Pearson
dieffenbachia: 5 aroid, plant
Die Fledermaus: 5 opera
composer: Johann Strauss
role: 3 Ida 5 Adele, Falke 6 Alfred 7 Gabriel 9 Rosalinde
setting: 4 jail 6 Vienna 7 Austria
Die Frau ohne Schatten: 5 opera
composer: Richard Strauss
Diego: 6 Eliseo, Rivera 9 Velázquez
in English: 5 James
__ Diego: 3 San
Diego, Eliseo: 4 poet 5 Cuban
diehard: 4 firm, fogy 5 bigot, fogey, loyal, rigid 6 zealot 7 fogyish, old-line 8 loyalist, mossback, orthodox, partisan 9 extremist, immovable 10 inflexible
cry: 5 never
Diehard: 7 battery
rival: 5 Delco
Die Hard (1988 film)
cast: Bonnie Bedelia, Alan Rickman, Bruce Willis
die is __, the: 4 cast
Diels, Otto: 6 German 7 chemist 8 Nobelist
__ diem: 3 per 5 carpe
Die Meistersinger: 5 opera
composer: Richard Wagner
role: 3 Eva 4 Hans 5 David, Sachs 6 Pogner 7 Walther 9 Magdalena
setting: 7 Germany 9 Nuremburg
__ Diemen's Land: 3 Van
__ dien: 3 Ich
Dien Bien Phu: 6 battle
Dieppe: 4 city, port, town
locale: 6 France
Dies __: 4 Irae
diesel: 3 gas 4 fuel 6 engine 8 gasoline 10 locomotive
diesel __: 3 oil 4 fuel 5 cycle 6 engine
Diesel: 3 Vin 6 Rudolf
Die Sonnette an Orpheus
poet: Rainer Maria Rilke
diet: 4 fare, food, menu 5 lo-fat 6 intake, low-cal, reduce, viands 7 aliment, council, edibles, regimen 8 slim down, victuals 9 nutriment, nutrition, treatment 10 sustenance
Atkins ~ no-no: 5 carbs, sugar
component: 3 fat 5 fiber
crash ~: 4 fast
food: 4 lite 5 no-cal, no-fat
go on a ~: 4 lose 6 reduce 8 slim down 10 lose weight
successfully: 4 lose
target: 4 flab
diet __: 4 soda 7 kitchen
__ diet: 3 fad, on a 5 crash
Diet
locale: 5 Japan
site: 5 Worms
Diet __: 4 Coke, Rite 5 Pepsi
dietary: 9 nutritive 10 alimentary
figure: 3 RDA
need: 4 iron, zinc 5 fiber
dietary __: 3 law 5 fiber
dieter
concern: 5 waist 6 figure
device: 5 scale
dread: 4 gain
fare: 5 salad 6 celery 8 skim milk
no-no: 3 fat 5 snack 7 dessert
of rhyme: 5 Sprat
resort: 3 spa
suitable for ~: 5 lo-cal, lo-fat, no-cal, no-fat
unit: 4 gram 7 calorie
Dieterle: 7 William
Diet of __: 5 Worms
Dietrich: 7 Marlene 10 Bonhoeffer
Dietrich, Marlene: 7 actress
film: Blonde Venus (1932)
The Blue Angel (1930)
Desire (1936)
Destry Rides Again (1939)
The Devil Is a Woman (1935)
The Flame of New Orleans (1941)
Follow the Boys (1944)
A Foreign Affair (1948)
Judgment at Nuremberg (1961)
The Lady Is Willing (1942)
Manpower (1941)
Morocco (1930)
No Highway in the Sky (1951)
Rancho Notorious (1952)
The Scarlet Empress (1934)
Shanghai Express (1932)
Witness for the Prosecution (1957)
Diet Rite: 3 pop 4 cola, soda 9 soft drink
alternative: *see* soft drink
Dietz: 6 Howard
__-dieu: 4 prie
Dieu __ droit: 5 et mon
__ Dieu!: 3 Mon
Die Walküre: 5 opera
composer: Richard Wagner
Die Winterreise divisions: 6 lieder
differ: 4 vary 5 argue, clash, range 6 depart 7 deviate, dissent, diverge, protest, quarrel, quibble

8 conflict, contrast, disagree
10 stand apart
ender: 3 ent 4 ence
__ differ: 5 beg to
difference: 3 gap, row 4 feud, spat, tiff 5 clash, scrap, split 6 acedia, change, strife 7 anomaly, dispute, quarrel, variety 8 argument, conflict, contrast, squabble, variance 9 asymmetry, departure, deviation, disaccord, disparity, diversity, exception, gradation, variation 10 aberration, alteration, antagonism, antithesis, contention, digression, disharmony, dissension, dissidence, dissonance, divergence, inequality, opposition, separation, unlikeness
make a ~: 5 count 6 affect, impact, matter
no ~: 4 same
of opinion: 4 rift, spat, tiff 5 break, clash 7 dispute, quarrel 8 argument, squabble, variance
slight ~: 5 shade
__ difference!: 4 Same
different: 3 new, odd 4 else 5 alien, apart, mixed, novel, other 6 atypic, sundry, unique, unlike, varied 7 altered, changed, deviant, diverse, oddball, offbeat, several, special, strange, unalike, unequal, unusual, variant, various 8 aberrant, assorted, atypical, contrary, discrete, distinct, manifold, multiple, opposite, peculiar, separate, specific, uncommon 9 alternate, collected, deviating, disparate, dissonant, divergent, fantastic, irregular, multiform, otherwise, startling, unheard-of, unrelated, unsimilar 10 antithetic, discordant, discrepant, dissimilar, individual, mismatched, poles apart, refreshing, unfamiliar, unorthodox, variegated
be ~: 4 vary
combining form: 5 heter- 6 hetero-
completely ~: 6 unlike 8 opposite
in Spanish: 4 otra, otro
make ~: 5 alter 6 change
meaning: 5 twist
one: 5 other 7 another, oddball
under ~ conditions: 9 otherwise
Different Corner, A (1986 song)
artist: George Michael
Different Drum (1967 song)
artist: Linda Ronstadt
differential part: 4 axle, gear
differentiate: 4 tell 6 winnow 8 contrast, set apart 9 tell apart
differentiation: 8 contrast
differently: 4 else 9 otherwise
__ different tune: 5 sing a
Different World, A (NBC sitcom)
cast: Lisa Bonet (Denise Huxtable)
Jasmine Guy (Whitley Gilbert)
differing: 6 at odds, uneven 7 unequal, variant 8 clashing, opposite 9 dissident, dissonant, divergent, heretical 10 discrepant
difficult: 4 hard, rude 5 fussy, hairy, heavy, messy, picky, rigid, risky, rocky, rough, stiff, tight, tough 6 Augean, crabby, feisty, knotty, oafish, opaque, rugged, severe, sticky, thorny, tricky, trying, uphill, vexing 7 arduous, bearish, boorish, complex, finicky, hard-won, obscure, onerous, operose, painful, prickly, problem, serious, tangled, unclear, weighty 8 abstract, baffling, delicate, esoteric, exacting, finiking, finnicky, grueling, involved, puzzling, strained, ticklish, tiresome, toilsome 9 ambitious, confusing, crotchety, demanding, effortful, enigmatic, entangled, fractious, hazardous, herculean, insoluble, intricate, irritable, laborious, murderous, obstinate, recondite, strenuous, wearisome 10 bothersome, burdensome, exhausting, fastidious, formidable, gargantuan, irritating, meandering, mysterious, mystifying, perplexing, refractory, unamenable, unsettling, unyielding
make less ~: 4 ease 8 simplify
make more ~: 8 encumber
not ~: 4 easy 6 simple
position: 3 fix 4 bind, spot 5 nodus
to handle: 5 bulky 7 awkward 10 cumbersome
to understand: 6 arcane 7 labored
difficulty: 3 ado, fix, jam, rub, woe 4 bind, fuss, kink, mess, need, pain, snag, spot, to-do 5 hitch, pinch, snarl, trial 6 bother, burden, crisis, hang-up, hassle, hiccup, holdup, hurdle, kicker, matter, misery, ordeal, pickle, plight, scrape, strain, strait, strife, weight 7 anxiety, dilemma, impasse, problem, quarrel, setback, trouble 8 deadlock, distress, drawback, exigence, exigency, hardness, hardship, headache, hiccough, hot water, obstacle, quagmire, quandary, question, struggle 9 adversity, annoyance, barricade, bickering, confusion, deep water, emergency, grievance, hindrance, imbroglio, millstone, suffering 10 affliction, bafflement, depression, falling-out, harassment, impediment, irritation, misfortune, oppression, perplexity
involve in ~: 4 mire 7 bog down
without ~: 6 easily 7 handily
diffidence: 7 modesty, reserve, shyness 8 meekness, timidity 9 hesitancy, mousiness, timidness 10 constraint, hesitation, insecurity, reluctance
diffident: 3 coy, shy 4 meek 5 aloof, chary, timid 6 demure, humble, modest 7 abashed, bashful, distant, fearful 8 hesitant, reserved, reticent, retiring, sheepish 9 blenching, flinching, reclusive, reluctant, shrinking, unassured, withdrawn 10 suspicious, unassuming, uneffusive
Diff'rent Strokes (NBC sitcom)
cast: Conrad Bain (Philip Drummond)
Todd Bridges (Willis Jackson)
Gary Coleman (Arnold Jackson)
Dana Plato (Kimberly Drummond)
diffuse: 4 cast, emit, long, melt, shed, soft, spew, spue, thin 5 eject, expel, exude, gabby, issue, loose, spray, strew, wordy 6 instil, prolix, spread, strewn 7 bestrew, cast out, emanate, general, give off, instill, lengthy, radiate, scatter, verbose, voluble 8 disperse, rambling, throw off, transmit 9 bombastic, dispersed, garrulous, propagate, scattered, send forth, spread out, talkative, universal 10 digressive, discursive, large-scale, long-winded, loquacious, palaverous, unspecific, widespread
diffusion: 6 spread 9 dispersal, expansion 10 dispersion, propaganda, scattering
DiFranco: 3 Ani
dig: 3 get, hoe 4 barb, bore, gibe, grok, grub, jibe, like, mine, poke, root, seek, slam, slap, slur, snub, till, work 5 abuse, adore, crack, delve, enjoy, get it, gouge, grasp, libel, probe, scorn, stick, study, taunt 6 burrow, dredge, follow, garden, insult, rebuff, relish, search, slight, tunnel 7 affront, calumny, catcall, catch on, disdain, mockery, obloquy, offense, put-down, sarcasm, slander 8 bulldoze, contempt, derision, excavate, relate to, ridicule, scoop out 9 aspersion, cheap shot, contumely, hollow out, lucubrate, undermine, wisecrack 10 appreciate, comprehend, defamation, disrespect, excavation, opprobrium, understand
discovery: 5 shard, sherd
for: 4 hunt, mine, seek
for info: 3 ask 8 research
in: 3 eat 4 wolf 5 eat up 7 scarf up 8 chow down, entrench 9 scarf down
in one's heels: 4 balk 5 baulk 6 refuse, resist
into: 4 look, pore, sift 5 plumb 6 plunge 7 deplete, examine, explore
into the past: 6 recall 8 remember
out: 5 scoop 6 deepen, elicit, hollow, remove 7 rummage 8 dislodge, excavate
starter: 4 shin
up: 4 find, mine 5 learn, raise 6 detect, dredge, exhume, locate, uproot 7 collect, rout out, uncover, unearth 8 discover, disinter, excavate, research 9 ferret out, search out 10 come across
dig __: 3 out 4 into
__ dig: 5 infra
Digby, Kenelm: 7 British 11 philosopher
digest: 3 cut, eat 4 lump, trim 5 brief, study, sum up 6 absorb, aperçu, ingest, ponder, précis, reduce, report, résumé, survey, take in 7 abridge, analyze, compile, consume, epitome, pandect, scissor, shorten, summary, swallow 8 abstract, boil down, compress, condense, consider, magazine, synopsis 9 summarize, synopsize, think over 10 abbreviate, abridgment, assimilate, compendium, paraphrase
__ Digest: 7 Reader's
digestible: 5 light 6 edible 10 alimentary
digestion: 10 absorption
aid: 4 bile 6 bicarb, enzyme
digestive: 10 alimentary
organ: 5 liver 7 stomach
digestive-tract part: 5 ileum
digger: 4 mole 5 miner 6 badger, gopher 9 groundhog, woodchuck
org.: 3 UMW
tool: 4 pick, spud 5 spade 6 shovel
wasp: 3 bug 6 insect
__ digger: 4 gold
Digger: 5 O'Dell 6 Barnes, Phelps
Diggin' on You (1995 song)
artist: TLC
__ Diggity: 3 Hot
Diggs: 4 Taye
DiGiorno: 5 pizza
alternative: 5 Jeno's, Tony's 6 Ellio's 7 Celeste, Totino's 9 Tombstone 10 Freschetta
digit: 3 one, six, toe, two 4 five, four, nine, unit 5 eight, pinky, seven, three, thumb 6 big toe, dactyl, figure, finger, member, number, pinkie 7 numeral 9 appendage
binary ~: 3 one 4 zero
double-looped ~: 5 eight
lower ~: 3 toe
opposable ~: 5 thumb
top ~: 4 nine
use a ~: 5 point
digital
adjunct: 4 nail
device: 2 PC
display: 4 time
not ~: 6 analog
watch display: 3 LCD, LED
digitize: 4 scan
dignified: 5 grand, great, lofty, noble, proud, regal, staid 6 august, formal, lordly, ritual, sedate, solemn 7 courtly, elegant, eminent, exalted, gallant, pompous, refined, stately 8 decorous, elevated, highbred, highbrow, imperial, imposing, ladylike 9 high-toned, honorable, imperious, respected, venerable
dignify: 4 lift 5 exalt, grace, honor, raise 6 praise 7 elevate, ennoble
dignitary: 3 VIP 4 lion, name, star 5 nabob 6 big gun, bigwig, figure, kahuna, leader 7 big shot, notable, officer 8 luminary, official, somebody 9 celebrity, personage
dignity: 4 rank 5 glory, honor, merit, poise, state, worth 6 regard, status, virtue 7 decency, decorum, hauteur, majesty, respect, stature 8 elegance, eminence, grandeur, nobility, prestige, standing 9 composure, etiquette, greatness, propriety, solemnity 10 kingliness, refinement, sedateness, self-esteem, worthiness
digress: 4 roam, turn, vary 5 drift, stray 6 ramble, wander 7 deviate, diverge 8 divagate
..... __ digress!: 4 But I
digression: 5 aside 6 detour 7 tangent, veering 8 drifting, straying 9 departure, deviation, diversion, excursion, variation, wandering 10 apostrophe, deflection, difference, discursion, divagation, divergence

digressive: **7** diffuse **8** episodic, rambling **9** excursive **10** discursive, episodical, tangential
digs: **3** pad **4** home **5** abode, house **7** habitat, housing **8** dwelling, lodgment, quarters **9** residence
crude ~: **3** hut **5** hovel, lodge, shack **6** lean-to
fancy ~: **5** manor, villa **6** estate **7** chateau, mansion **10** plantation
see also home
Dijon: **4** city, town **7** mustard
locale: **6** France
river: **5** Ouche
Dik: **6** Browne
dik-dik: **6** animal **8** antelope
relative: *see* antelope
dike: **3** bar, dam **4** bank, foss, wall, weir **5** check, fosse, levee **6** embank, trench **7** barrier, channel, sea wall **8** causeway, obstacle, retainer **9** barricade **10** embankment, impediment
problem: **4** leak
diktat: **7** penalty **10** punishment, settlement
__ di Lammermoor: **5** Lucia
dilapidated: **4** shot, worn **5** dingy, ratty, seedy, tacky **6** beat-up, crumby, crummy, grungy, ragged, shabby, shoddy, sleazy **7** damaged, decayed, in ruins, rickety, run-down, unkempt **8** decaying, decrepit, derelict, time-worn **10** ramshackle, tumbledown
dilapidation: **4** wear **5** decay **6** blight **7** neglect
dilate: **3** wax **4** grow **5** bloat, bulge, swell, widen **6** expand, extend, spread **7** augment, balloon, broaden, burgeon, distend, enlarge, inflate, magnify, stretch **8** bourgeon, heighten, lengthen
dilated: **4** wide
dilation: **5** bulge **6** spread **8** swelling **9** expansion
dilator's place: **3** eye **5** pupil
dilatory: **3** lax **4** late, lazy, poky, slow **5** slack, tardy **6** draggy, remiss **7** gradual, halting, impeded, laggard, lagging, languid, unready **8** crawling, creeping, dallying, dawdling, delaying, dragging, drawn-out, hesitant, plodding, slothful, sluggish, tarrying, toddling **9** leisurely, lethargic, lingering, prolonged, snaillike, unhurried **10** deliberate, last-minute, protracted
maneuver: **5** stall
Dilbert: **5** strip **10** comic strip
cartoonist: Scott Adams **5** Adams
character: **4** Asok, Tina **5** Alice, Carol, Wally **7** Catbert, Dogbert, Ratbert, The Boss
place: **4** desk **6** office
dilemma: **3** fix, jam, rub **4** bind, case, knot, mess, spot **6** corner, crisis, muddle, pickle, plight, scrape, strait **7** problem, trouble **8** exigence, exigency, juncture, quagmire, quandary **9** deep water **10** difficulty
in a ~: **4** torn
dilettante: **4** tiro, tyro **6** novice **7** amateur, dabbler **8** beginner, putterer **9** greenhorn, layperson, unskilled **10** amateurish, tenderfoot, uninitiate
dilettantish: **4** arty **5** artsy
Dili: **4** city, town **7** capital
locale: **9** East Timor
diligence: **4** care, zeal **5** labor, rigor, vigor **6** effort **8** exertion, industry, keenness, patience, tenacity **9** alertness, assiduity, attention, briskness, constancy, fixedness, intensity, quickness **10** intentness
diligent: **6** active **7** careful, earnest, intense **8** resolute, sedulous, studious, tireless **9** assiduous, attentive, laborious, unfailing **10** persistent, unflagging, unwearying
diligently: **4** hard
dill: **4** anet, herb
dill __: **6** pickle
Dillard, Annie: **6** writer
__-diller: **6** killer **7** chiller
Diller: **5** Barry **7** Phyllis
Dillinger: **4** John
foe: **3** FBI **4** G-man **6** Hoover
Dillinger (1973 film)
cast: Richard Dreyfuss, Ben Johnson, Cloris Leachman, Warren Oates, Michelle Phillips
Dillman: **8** Bradford
Dillon: **4** Matt **7** Melinda
Dillon, Matt: **5** actor
film: Beautiful Girls (1996)
The Big Town (1987)
Crash (2005)
Drugstore Cowboy (1989)
The Flamingo Kid (1984)
In & Out (1997)
One Night at McCool's (2001)
Over the Edge (1979)
Rumble Fish (1983)
Tex (1982)
There's Something About Mary (1998)
To Die For (1995)
Wild Things (1998)
You, Me and Dupree (2006)
Dill Pickle, A
author: Katherine Mansfield
dilly: **3** pip **4** lulu, oner **5** beaut, doozy, poser **6** corker, doozie **10** ripsnorter
dillydallier: **5** idler **9** lazybones
dillydally: **3** haw, lag **4** idle, laze, loaf, poke **5** amble, delay, mosey, stall, tarry, waver **6** dawdle, linger, loiter, put off, trifle **7** saunter, whiffle **8** hesitate, lollygag, straggle **9** waste time
dilute: **3** cut **4** thin, weak **5** water **6** impair, lessen, reduce, watery, weaken **7** lighten, vitiate **8** decrease, diminish **9** attenuate, water down **10** adulterate
diluted: **3** cut **4** tame, thin, weak **6** impure, watery
not ~: **4** neat, pure **5** uncut
dim: **3** fog **4** blur, dark, fade, hazy, mist, pale, slow, soft, veil, wane, weak **5** befog, blear, cloud, dense, dingy, dusky, faded, faint, fuzzy, lower, mirky, misty, muddy, murky, muted, shade, shady, thick, vague **6** bleary, cloudy, darken, gloomy, ill-lit, oafish, obtuse, opaque, shadow, somber, stupid **7** becloud, blacken, blurred, boorish, darkish, doltish, obscure, shadowy, Stygian, subdued, tarnish, unclear **8** darkened, lowering, nebulous, obscured, tone down, turn down **9** adumbrate, candlelit, lightless, obfuscate, tenebrous, toned down, uncertain, unlighted **10** ill-defined, indistinct, lackluster, lusterless, overshadow, pedestrian
ender: **3** wit
suddenly: **5** go out
take a ~ view of: **5** knock, scorn **7** censure, deplore, put down, run down **8** belittle, derogate, disfavor **9** deprecate, disesteem, disparage, poor-mouth **10** disapprove
view: **5** gloom **7** despair **8** cynicism, glumness **9** dejection, pessimism **10** depression, gloominess, melancholy
dim __: **3** sum **4** bulb
DiMaggio: **3** Dom, Joe **5** Vince
DiMaggio, Joe: **6** Yankee **10** outfielder
spouse: Marilyn Monroe
uniform number: **4** five
Dim All the Lights (1979 song)
artist: Donna Summer
dimanche: **6** French, Sunday
follower: **5** lundi
preceder: **6** samedi
__ Dimas: **3** San
Dimbovita: **5** river
city on the ~: **9** Bucharest
locale: **7** Romania
dime: **4** coin **5** money **6** change
18th-century ~: **5** disme
like a ~: **4** clad, thin
like a new ~: **5** shiny
store: **4** mart **6** market
symbol on a ~: **5** torch
without a ~: **5** broke **9** penniless
word on a ~: **3** God, one **4** unum **5** trust **6** States, United **7** America, liberty **8** pluribus
dime __: **5** novel, store
dime-a-dozen: **6** common **7** humdrum, liberal, profuse **9** bountiful
dimension: **4** bulk, size **5** ambit, depth, range, reach, realm, scale, scope, width **6** aspect, extent, format, height, length, volume **7** breadth, compass, measure **8** capacity **9** amplitude, magnitude
fourth ~: **4** time
give ~: **8** flesh out
rectangular ~: **5** width **6** length
to a builder: **4** spec
__ Dimension: **5** Fifth
Dimetapp: **10** cough syrup
alternative: *see* cold remedy
diminish: **3** cut, ebb, lag, sag **4** bate, curb, drop, fall, lull, pale, pare, sink, slow, wane **5** abate, break, drain, dwarf, let up, lower, prune, relax, slack, taper **6** change, dampen, deaden, deduct, demean, dilute, lessen, rebate, recede, reduce, shrink, soften, weaken, worsen **7** abridge, cheapen, curtail, cut down, decline, deflate, deplete, depress, detract, drop off, dwindle, fall off, mollify, put down, qualify, run down, shorten, slacken, subside, tail off, take off, take out, thin out, whittle **8** belittle, blow over, contract, decrease, derogate, discount, downsize, head away, minimize, mitigate, moderate, peter out, subtract, take away, taper off, tear down, withhold **9** extenuate, retrocede **10** abbreviate
diminished: **3** cut **4** less **5** let up, lower, short **7** limited, partial **8** lessened
by: **4** less **5** minus
diminishing: **8** decrease **9** on the wane
diminishing __: **7** returns
diminution: **3** cut, ebb **4** drop, fall, slip **7** cutback, decline **8** decrease, discount **9** abatement, deduction, lessening, reduction, remission, weakening
diminutive: **3** wee **4** baby, itsy, puny, tiny **5** bitty, dwarf, elfin, pigmy, pygmy, short, small, teeny, weeny **6** atomic, bantam, little, midget, minute, peewee, petite, pocket, slight, teensy **7** stunted, trivial **8** atomical, atomlike, nickname **9** itsy-bitsy, itty-bitty, miniature, pint-sized, undersize **10** teeny-weeny, undersized, vest-pocket
Spanish suffix: **3** -ita, -ito
suffix: **3** -cle, -ine, -kin, -let, -nik, -ock, -rel, -ula, -ule **4** -ella, -elle, -ette, -kins, -ling
Dimitri: **7** Tiomkin
__ Dimittis: **4** Nunc
dimity: **6** cotton, fabric **8** material
dimmed: **5** blear **6** bleary
dimness: **4** blur, haze, pall **5** blear, gloom, shade **6** shadow
dimple: **3** pit **4** dent **5** cleft **6** hollow **10** depression
site: **4** chin
dim sum: **9** appetizer
additive: **3** MSG
cooker: **3** wok
__ dim view: **5** take a
dimwit
see ninny
dimwitted: **4** dopy, dull, slow **5** dense, dopey, silly, thick **6** obtuse, simple **7** doltish, foolish, witless **8** mindless
din: **4** roar, stir **5** babel, blast, hoo-ha, noise, sound **6** bedlam, clamor, hubbub, jangle, racket, ruckus, rumpus, tumult, uproar **7** clangor, clatter, discord, thunder **8** brouhaha, disquiet **9** cacophony, commotion, hue and cry **10** clattering, hullabaloo
Din: **4** Beth **5** Gunga
Dina: **5** Meyer **6** Spybey **7** Merrill
Dinah: **3** cat **5** Shore **6** Manoff **10** Washington
brother: **3** Dan, Gad **4** Levi **5** Asher, Judah **6** Joseph, Reuben, Simeon **7** Zebulun **8** Benjamin, Issachar, Naphtali
parent: **4** Leah **5** Jacob
uncle: **4** Esau
__ Dinah: **4** De De
Dinah Shore Classic org.: **4** LPGA
dinar: **4** coin **5** money
country: **4** Irak, Iran, Iraq **5** Libya
Dinaric: **4** Alps

din-din: **4** meal **6** supper
d'Indy: **7** Vincent
dine: **3** eat, sup **5** feast
at home: **5** eat in
partner: **4** wine
wine and ~: **3** woo **4** feed, fete **5** treat **9** entertain
diner: **3** car **4** café **5** eater **6** bistro, eatery **8** gourmand **9** hash house, lunchroom **10** restaurant
add-on: **3** tip
ad words: **5** eat at
beverage: **3** joe, tea **4** milk, soda **6** coffee **7** iced tea
choice: **6** entrée
employee: **4** cook **6** waiter **7** cashier **8** waitress
fare: **4** eats
freebie: **4** mint, salt **5** jelly, sugar, syrup, water **6** catsup, napkin, pepper **7** ketchup, mustard
go to a ~: **6** eat out
handout: **4** menu
offering: **3** BLT, pie **5** chile, chili, lunch **6** chilli, omelet **8** omelette
order, with the: **5** usual
patron: **7** trucker
sign: **4** eats, neon
sitcom ~: **4** Mel's
tab: **5** check
see also restaurant
Diner (1982 film)
cast: Kevin Bacon, Ellen Barkin, Steve Guttenberg, Paul Reiser, Mickey Rourke, Daniel Stern
director: Barry Levinson
__ Diner: **4** Mel's, Tom's
dinero
con mucho ~: **4** rico
unit: **4** peso
where el ~ is: **5** banco
see also moolah
Diner's Club: **10** credit card
use: **3** owe **6** charge
Dinesen, Isak: **6** Danish, writer
on film: Streep
real name: Karen Blixen
work: Out of Africa
Seven Gothic Tales
Winter's Tales
dinette: **4** nook
piece: **5** chair
place: **6** alcove
dinette __: **3** set
ding: **3** mar **4** dent, nick, slam, sock, swat **5** whack **6** jingle, tinkle
ender: **3** bat
starter: **4** wing
ding-__: **4** dong **5** a-ling
__-ding: **4** wing
ding-a-ling
see ninny
dingbat
see ninny
Dingbat: **5** Edith
daughter: **6** Gloria
ding-dong: **5** chime
Ding dong __...: **4** bell
dinger: **4** bell **5** homer **7** home run
dinghy: **4** boat **5** craft, skiff **7** rowboat
need: **3** oar
propel a ~: **3** row
dingle: **4** dale, dell, glen **6** hollow, valley
Dingle Bay
locale: **7** Ireland
dingo: **3** dog **5** canid **6** animal, canine **10** Australian
relative: ***see*** canine
__ Dings: **4** Ring
dingus: **5** dodad, thing **6** doodad, widget
dingy: **3** dim **4** daft, dark, drab, gray, grey **5** dirty, grimy, mirky, murky, seedy, smoky, tacky **6** dismal, dreary, ill-lit, ragged, shabby, shoddy, somber **7** run-down, squalid **8** slovenly **10** broken-down, lusterless, threadbare
__ Dinh Diem: **3** Ngo
dining
amenity: **5** doily **6** doyley, napkin
area: **4** hall **6** alcove
car sandwich: **4** club
enticement: **5** aroma
room: **4** mess **7** commons **8** chow hall, mess hall **9** cafeteria, refectory **10** triclinium
utensil: **4** fork **5** knife, spoon
dining __: **3** car **4** hall, room **5** table
dining-room
piece: **5** hutch
staffer: **6** busboy, waiter **8** waitress
__-dink: **5** rinky
__ Dinka Doo: **4** Inka
Dinkins: **5** David
dinkum: **4** real **9** authentic
dinky: **4** punk, tiny **5** minor, small, teeny **6** lesser, little, shabby, teensy **8** picayune, trifling **9** small-time **10** bush-league, second-rate
__ Dinky Parlay Voo: **5** Hinky
__ Dinmont: **6** Dandie
dinner: **4** meal **5** feast, party **6** buffet, entrée, repast, supper **7** banquet **9** collation, reception
and a movie: **4** date
beverage: **4** port, wine
bird: **4** duck **5** capon, frier, fryer **6** turkey **7** chicken, roaster
celebrity ~: **5** roast
ceremonial ~: **5** seder
chuck wagon ~: **4** grub
course: **4** soup **5** salad **6** entrée **7** dessert **9** appetizer
ender: **4** time, ware
faux pas: **4** burp
follower: **5** movie
formal ~: **4** fete, meal **5** feast, party **6** repast, spread **7** banquet
get ready for ~: **5** dress
GI ~: **4** mess
have ~: **3** eat, sup **5** feast **10** break bread
invite to ~: **4** feed **6** ask out
jacket: **3** tux **4** tuck **6** tuxedo
make ~: **4** bake, cook **7** prepare
order for ~: **3** get **4** have **5** enjoy **7** procure
part: **6** entrée
party: **5** salon **6** soiree
preceder: **5** grace
put out ~: **5** serve
scraps: **4** orts
setting: **5** place
signal: **4** bell
stay home for ~: **5** eat in
dinner __: **4** bell, fork, ring **5** dance, dress, knife, plate, table **6** jacket **7** clothes, theater, theatre
Dinner at Antoine's
author: Frances Parkinson Keyes
Dinner at Eight: **4** play
author: Edna Ferber, George S. Kaufman
character: **3** Dan **4** Dora, Tina **5** Kitty, Paula, Ricci, Vance **6** Hattie, Oliver **7** Gustave **8** Carlotta **9** Millicent
Dinner at the Homesick Restaurant
author: Anne Tyler
__-dinner mint: **5** after
Dinner Party, The
author: Howard Fast
dinnerware: **5** china **6** dishes **8** ceramics, crockery **9** porcelain
item: **4** bowl **5** plate **6** saucer
Dinning, Mark
song: Teen Angel (1960)
Dino: **3** pet
master: **4** Fred
Dino De __: **10** Laurentiis
dino follower: **4** saur
dinornis robustus: **3** moa
dinosaur: **4** T-rex **6** animal, lizard **7** reptile **8** allosaur, obsolete, sauropod, theropod **9** iguanodon, leviathan, pterosaur, stegosaur, supersaur **10** brontosaur, diplodocus, megalosaur, titanosaur **11** brachiosaur, ichthyosaur, triceratops, tyrannosaur
bone: **6** fossil
DNA preserver: **5** amber
preserver: **3** bog, tar **6** tar pit
dinosaurian: **3** big
dinothere: **8** elephant
dinotherian: **3** big
Dinsmore: **5** Elsie
dint: **3** vim **4** thew **5** brawn, force, might, power, thews, vigor **6** effort, energy, muscle **7** fitness, muscles, potence, potency, stamina **8** exertion, strength, vitality **9** beefiness, endurance, fortitude, hardiness, huskiness, puissance, stoutness, toughness **10** brawniness, brute force, mightiness, robustness, sturdiness
Dinty: **5** Moore
diocese: **3** see **7** prelacy **9** bishopric **10** episcopacy, episcopate
Diocletian: **5** Roman **6** Caesar
Diogenes: **5** Greek **11** philosopher
specialty: **8** Cynicism
DioGuardi: **4** Kara
Diomede: **4** isls. **5** isles **7** islands
Dion
last name: Di Mucci
song: Abraham, Martin and John (1968)
Donna the Prima Donna (1963)
Drip Drop (1963)
Runaround Sue (1961)
The Wanderer (1961)
Dion and the Belmonts
song: A Teenager in Love (1959)
Dion, Celine
homeland: Canada
song: All by Myself (1997)
Beauty and the Beast (1992)
Because You Loved Me (1996)
I Drove All Night (2003)
If You Asked Me to (1992)
I'm Your Angel (1998)
It's All Coming Back to Me Now (1996)
My Heart Will Go On (1998)
A New Day Has Come (2002)
The Power of Love (1993)
That's the Way It Is (1999)
Where Does My Heart Beat Now (1991)
Dione: **4** moon **5** giant, Titan
daughter: **9** Aphrodite
parent: **4** Gaea **6** Uranus
planet: **6** Saturn
son: **6** Pelops
Dionne: **5** Marie **6** Farris, Marcel **7** Warwick
quintuplet: **5** Marie **6** Cécile, Émilie, Yvonne **7** Annette
Dionne, Marcel: **6** skater
Dionysius: **4** pope **5** saint, Thrax **7** Exiguus, pontiff
mountain where ~ was hidden: **4** Nysa
Dionysus
animal sacred to ~: **4** goat, lion, lynx **5** tiger **7** dolphin, panther
attendant: **5** satyr
equivalent: **7** Bacchus
parent: **4** Zeus **6** Semele **7** Demeter
plant sacred to ~: **3** ivy **4** rose, vine **6** laurel **8** asphodel
Dior, Christian: **6** French **8** designer
design: **5** A-line
dip: **3** nod, sag, set, wet **4** bath, dive, drop, duck, dunk, fade, fall, sink, skim, soak, swim, tilt, wash **5** bathe, droop, fondu, lower, pitch, rinse, salsa, scoop, slide, slope, slump, souse, swoop **6** crouch, drench, fondue, go down, plunge, recede, swerve, tumble **7** curtsey, decline, descend, descent, dunking, falloff, immerse, incline, moisten, plummet, soaking **8** downturn, drop down, infusion, lowering, nose-dive, submerge, submerse **9** guacamole, immersion, sour cream, worsening **10** depression, pickpocket
ender: **5** stick
ingredient: **5** chive, onion **9** sour cream
into: **4** read, scan
landscape ~: **4** glen **6** dingle, valley
out a boat: **4** bail
place for a ~: **4** pool
take a ~: **4** swim
__ dip: **4** head **5** chip 'n **6** French
__-dip: **5** sheep **6** double
__ di pesce: **5** zuppa
...Dipinto __: **5** di Blu
diploma: **5** paper **6** degree **9** sheepskin
holder: **4** grad **6** alumna **7** alumnus **8** graduate
word: **3** cum **4** arts **5** laude, magna, summa **7** science
diplomacy: **4** tact **5** craft, poise, skill **7** finesse **8** delicacy, politics, subtlety **10** artfulness, discretion, expedience, statecraft
alternative: **3** war
breakdown: **4** rift
__ diplomacy: **6** dollar **7** gunboat, shuttle
Diplomacy for the Next Century
author: Abba Eban
diplomat: **3** amb. **5** envoy, fixer **6** consul, legate **7** attaché **8** emissary, minister **10** ambassador, negotiator, peacemaker
home: **3** emb. **7** embassy

Diplomat: **3** car **4** auto **5** Dodge
diplomate: **8** graduate
diplomatic: **4** wise **5** civil, suave **6** artful, irenic, polite, subtle **7** correct, politic, prudent, tactful **8** delicate, dextrous, discreet, gracious, irenical, pleasant **9** conniving, courteous, dexterous, judicious, sensitive, strategic **10** contriving, intriguing, thoughtful
code: **8** protocol
success: **4** pact **6** accord
diplomatic __: **4** body **5** corps, pouch
dipole: **6** two-rod **7** antenna **10** rabbit ears
dipper: **4** bail, bird **5** ladle, ousel, ouzel, scoop **6** bailer, ladler
dipping: **8** downhill **9** immersion
dippy: **5** goofy, inane, silly **6** absurd **9** eccentric
dipsy-__: **6** doodle
Dipsy: **9** Teletubby
dir.: **2** NE, NW, SE, SW **3** EbN, EbS, ENE, ESE, hdg., NNE, NNW, SSE, SSW, WbN, WbS, WNW, WSW
Dirac, Paul: **7** British **8** Nobelist **9** physicist, scientist
dire: **4** grim **5** acute, awful, dread, grave, sorry, woful **6** bitter, horrid, mortal, somber, tragic, urgent, woeful **7** baleful, burning, crucial, drastic, dreaded, exigent, extreme, fearful, harmful, hurry-up, instant, ominous, painful, ruinous, serious **8** alarming, critical, dreadful, exigeant, fearsome, grievous, horrible, horrific, pressing, terrible, tragical **9** appalling, desperate, frightful, ill-boding, ill-omened, insistent **10** calamitous, deplorable, disastrous, formidable, lamentable, petrifying
in ~ straits: **5** needy **6** hard-up
straits: **6** crisis, penury **7** trouble
__ dire: **4** voir
__-dire: **3** oui **5** c'est-à
dirección: **4** este
direct: **3** aim, bid, run, set **4** boss, head, lead, mail, open, rule, send, ship, show, tell, true, turn **5** apply, bluff, blunt, clear, drive, edify, exact, focus, frank, guide, level, order, pilot, plain, point, prime, refer, right, route, short, slant, steer, swing, teach, train, tutor **6** abrupt, advise, candid, charge, devote, enjoin, govern, handle, head-on, head up, honest, inform, jockey, linear, manage, orient, simple **7** address, arrange, channel, command, conduct, control, correct, counsel, dictate, express, natural, nearest, nonstop, operate, oversee, precise, preside, produce, require, sincere **8** absolute, accurate, dominate, engineer, explicit, instruct, navigate, out-front, outright, personal, positive, regulate, shepherd, shortest, straight, unbroken **9** designate, downright, firsthand, immediate, influence, officiate, outspoken, prescribe, supervise **10** administer, continuous, face-to-face, flat-footed, forthright, foursquare, from the hip, give orders, manipulate, mastermind, point-blank, ride herd on, run the show, show the way, to the point, unaffected, unmediated, unreserved, unreticent, unswerving
elsewhere: **5** refer
ender: **3** ion, ive, ory **5** orate
in ~ opposition: **10** face-to-face, unmediated
direct __: **4** cost, mail **6** object **7** address, current, deposit
direct-__: **4** dial **6** access **7** examine
__ directed: **5** Use as
direction: **3** way **4** east, left, path, side, tack, tide, west **5** drift, north, order, route, slant, south, tenor, track, trend **6** behest, charge, course, recipe **7** bearing, bidding, conduct, control, dictate, heading, outlook, precept, purpose, quarter, running **8** bearings, guidance, tendency **9** education, guideline, influence, objective, ordinance, viewpoint **10** advisement, aspiration, government, indication, leadership, likelihood, management, proclivity, regulation, standpoint, trajectory
change ~: **3** yaw, zag **4** tack, turn, veer, wind
change of ~: **3** uey **5** U-turn **9** one-eighty
compass ~: **2** NE, NW, SE, SW **3** ENE, ESE, NNE, NNW, SSE, SSW, WNW, WSW **4** east, west **5** north, point, south
cookbook ~: **3** add, fry **4** bake, boil, chop, dice, heat, stir, warm **5** baste, chill, roast, sauté, scald, slice
finding: **5** radar
French ~: **3** est, sud **4** nord **5** ouest
German ~: **3** ost **5** osten, süden **6** norden, westen
in another ~: **4** away
it can move in any ~: **5** queen
musical ~: **5** dolce, forte, largo, secco, tacet **6** arioso, da capo
nautical ~: **3** aft, EbN, EbS, SbE **4** alee, fore **5** abeam, aport **6** astern
provide ~: **5** steer
show the ~: **5** point
sign: **5** arrow
Spanish ~: **3** sur **4** este **5** norte, oeste
stage ~: **4** exit **5** enter **6** exeunt
suffix: **3** -ern
direction __: **6** finder
directional __: **7** antenna
directionless: **5** blind **6** adrift **7** erratic
directions: **5** specs **6** advice, recipe **7** formula **10** indication
follow ~: **4** mind, obey
needing ~: **4** lost
directive: **4** memo, rule, word **5** edict, order, ukase **6** behest, charge, decree, firman, ruling **7** command, mandate, message **9** ordinance **10** injunction, memorandum, regulation
directly: **3** due, new **4** anon, ASAP, soon **5** ad rem, plumb, right, smack, spang **6** at once, openly, pronto, simply **7** exactly, frankly, quickly, shortly **8** candidly, honestly, in person, promptly, smack dab, straight, verbatim **9** forthwith, in a moment, in a second, instantly, literally, posthaste, precisely, presently, right away **10** face-to-face, forthright, personally, point-blank, unswerving
directness: **6** candor **7** clarity
director: **4** boss, exec, head **5** chair, chief, super **6** gerent, honcho, leader, master, regent, top dog, tycoon **7** captain, curator, foreman, headman, kingpin, manager, officer, skipper **8** governor, kingfish, official, overseer, superior **9** commander, conductor, executive, organizer, principal **10** controller, headmaster, mastermind, supervisor
award: **5** Oscar
shoot: **4** take **6** retake
viewing: **6** rushes **7** dailies
windup: **4** wrap
yell: **3** cut **5** print **6** action
__ director: **3** art **5** stage **6** cruise **7** casting, program **8** managing
directors: **5** board, panel **7** council **10** management
director's __: **3** cut **5** chair
directory: **4** book, list, roll **5** guide, index **6** lineup, record, roster **7** catalog, who's who **8** handbook, register **9** catalogue **10** white pages
entry: **4** name
dirge: **4** hymn, song, tune **5** elegy, music **6** lament, melody, monody **7** requiem, sad song **8** threnody
tempo: **5** lento
dirham: **5** money
country: **3** UAE **5** Libya, Qatar **6** Kuwait **7** Morocco
dirigible: **5** blimp **7** airship, balloon **8** aircraft, zeppelin
filler: **6** helium
like a ~: **3** LTA **5** rigid
Dirigo is its motto: **5** Maine
dirk: **4** shiv, snee **5** knife, skean, skene **6** dagger, weapon **7** sidearm
Dirk: **4** Pitt **7** Bogarde **8** Benedict
dirndl: **5** dress, skirt
dirt: **3** mud **4** crud, grit, guck, gunk, info, land, loam, mire, muck, scum, soil **5** earth, filth, grime, rumor **6** gossip, ground, grunge, skinny **7** earthen, lowdown, scandal, slander, topsoil **8** impurity **10** defamation
cheap: **8** a good buy **10** economical
chunk of ~: **4** clod
devoid of ~: **5** clean
dish ~: **6** gossip
do ~ to: **5** wrong
fling ~: **4** slur **5** libel, smear, sully, taint **6** defame, impugn, malign, vilify **7** asperse, slander, traduce **8** backbite, besmirch, throw mud **9** disparage **10** calumniate
get rid of ~: **4** wash **5** scour, scrub
hit pay ~: **5** score **7** prevail
hit the ~: **4** fall **5** slide **6** topple
path: **5** trail
pay ~: **3** ore **4** lode **8** solution
poor: **5** needy **8** strapped **9** penniless
remover: **4** soap
smear: **6** smudge
wet ~: **3** mud
dirt __: **4** bike, farm, road **6** farmer
dirt-__: **4** poor **5** cheap
__ dirt: **3** pay
dirtbag: **3** cad **6** bad egg
dirtied: **5** sooty **8** maculate, vitiated **10** bedraggled, insanitary
dirtiness: **4** mess **9** pollution
dirtless: **5** clean **6** washed **8** unsoiled **9** laundered
dirty: **4** blot, blue, foul, lewd, mean, soil, spot, ugly, vile **5** bawdy, black, dingy, dusty, germy, grimy, grody, lousy, mangy, messy, muddy, nasty, slimy, smear, sooty, stain, sully, taint **6** befoul, bemire, crud up, debase, defile, embrue, filthy, fouled, frowsy, frowzy, grotty, grubby, grungy, imbrue, impure, litter, mangey, mess up, ribald, rotten, sleazy, sloppy, smudge, smutty, soiled, sordid, unfair, untidy, vulgar **7** begrime, blacken, corrupt, crooked, defiled, illicit, muddied, naughty, obscene, pollute, profane, smudged, spatter, spotted, squalid, stained, sullied, tarnish, unclean, unkempt, unswept **8** begrimed, besmirch, indecent, maculate, off-color, polluted, slovenly, spiteful, stagnant, undusted, unwashed **9** deceitful, dishonest, low-minded, lubricous, tarnished, uncleaned, unethical **10** despicable, germ-ridden, insanitary, lamentable, lusterless, scurrilous, suggestive, unhygienic, unsanitary
not ~: **5** clean **8** spotless
work: **5** fraud, guile **6** deceit, dupery, racket **7** falsity, knavery, misdeed, perfidy, swindle **8** artifice **9** chicanery, deception, duplicity, hypocrisy, treachery **10** dishonesty
dirty __: **3** war **4** bomb, look, pool, rice, word, work **5** linen **6** tricks **7** laundry
Dirty __: **5** Harry
Dirty Dancing (1987 film)
cast: Jennifer Grey, Jerry Orbach, Patrick Swayze
director: Emile Ardolino
nickname: **4** Baby
dirty-dealing: **9** underhand, unethical
Dirty Dozen, The (1967 film)
cast: Ernest Borgnine, Charles Bronson, Jim Brown, John Cassavetes, Richard Jaeckel, George Kennedy, Trini Lopez, Lee Marvin, Robert Ryan, Telly Savalas, Donald Sutherland, Clint Walker
director: Robert Aldrich
Dirty Hands
author: Jean-Paul Sartre
Dirty Harry: **3** cop **8** Callahan
employer: **4** SFPD
Dirty Harry (1972 film)
cast: Clint Eastwood
director: Don Siegel
__ dirty job but...: **4** It's a
Dirty Laundry (1982 song)
artist: Don Henley

__ dirty rat!: 3 You
Dirty Rotten Scoundrels (1988 film)
cast: Michael Caine, Glenne Headly, Steve Martin
director: Frank Oz
dis: 4 gibe, jibe 5 knock, scorn 6 demean, deride, heckle, insult 7 put down 8 badmouth, belittle, mouth off 9 denigrate
not ~: 3 dat
DI
Dis: 5 Hades 10 underworld
disabuse: 3 rid 8 set right 9 enlighten, unbeguile, undeceive 10 disenchant
disaccord: 4 feud 6 refuse 8 variance 10 contention, difference, disharmony, dissension, dissidence, dissonance, heterodoxy
disaccustom: 4 wean
disadvantage: 4 flaw, harm, hurt, lack, loss, snag 5 fault, minus 6 burden, damage, defect, hamper, hurdle, injury, kicker 7 barrier, failing, problem 8 drawback, handicap, hardship, obstacle, weakness, weak spot 9 detriment, hindrance, liability 10 impediment
__ disadvantage: 3 at a
disadvantaged: 4 poor 5 broke, needy, sorry 6 bad off, hard up, ill off, in need, in want 7 pinched 8 badly off, bankrupt, beggarly, deprived, indigent, strapped 9 destitute, insolvent, moneyless, penniless, penurious 10 down and out, pauperized, straitened
disadvantageous: 7 adverse, harmful, hurtful, useless 8 contrary, damaging
disadvise: 5 deter 10 discourage
disaffect: 6 divide 8 alienate, disunite, embitter, estrange, imbitter 10 antagonize, discompose, drive apart
disaffection: 5 break 6 breach, unrest
disaffiliate: 6 detach, secede
disaffirm: 6 impugn, naysay, negate, refute 7 confute, gainsay 10 contradict, contravene
disagree: 4 spat, vary 5 argue, clash, demur 6 bicker, differ, naysay, negate, oppose, refute 7 collide, confute, dissent, diverge, protest, quarrel, quibble, wrangle 8 conflict, squabble 9 have words, square off, take issue 10 contradict, contravene
disagreeable: 3 bad 4 mean, rude, sour, ugly 5 awful, brusk, cross, nasty, seamy, surly, whiny, woful 6 bitter, feisty, ornery, rancid, rotten, snappy, unruly, whiney, woeful 7 brusque, defiant, grating, grouchy, naughty, painful, peevish, waspish, wayward 8 annoying, brackish, churlish, contrary, horrible, liverish, petulant, snappish, stubborn, unsavory 9 crotchety, offensive, repulsive, splenetic, thankless, unsightly, unwelcome 10 out of sorts, rebellious, unfriendly
disagreeing: 6 at odds 7 opposed 8 clashing, opposing
disagreement: 3 gap 4 feud, rift, spat, tiff 5 break, clash, fight, scrap 6 battle, breach, debate, hassle, strife 7 discord, dispute, dissent, faction, ill will, problem, quarrel, tension 8 argument, conflict, disunion, disunity, division, friction, squabble, variance 10 opposition
exclamation of ~: 3 nay, rot 4 bosh, uh-uh 7 baloney, rubbish
disallow: 3 ban, bar, nix 4 dent, shun, tabu, veto 5 debar, spurn 6 abjure, bounce, cancel, censor, except, forbid, negate, outlaw, pass on, rebuff, refuse, reject, revoke 7 disavow, disdain, dismiss, embargo, exclude, shut out 8 disclaim, override, overrule, prohibit, turn down 9 blackball, cast aside, interdict, proscribe, repudiate
disallowance: 4 veto 6 denial 7 refusal
__-disant: 3 soi
disappear: 2 go 3 ebb, end, fly, set 4 exit, fade, flee, lift, melt, sink, wane 5 cease, leave, scram 6 begone, decamp, depart, escape, perish, recede, vacate, vanish 7 abscond, go south, retreat, take off, vamoose 8 dissolve, evanesce, hightail, vaporize, withdraw 9 dissipate, evaporate 10 take flight
in the crowd: 5 blend
slowly: 5 erode
Disappear (1990 song)
artist: INXS
disappearance: 4 exit, loss 6 exodus, flight
exclamation: 4 poof
disappeared: 4 gone, lost 7 missing
disappearing
do a ~ act: 4 flee 5 elude
__ disappearing act: 3 do a
disappoint: 4 dash, fail, foil, mock, sell 6 bum out, dismay, sadden, thwart 7 chagrin, let down, sell out 8 embitter, fall down, imbitter 9 displease, dumbfound, frustrate 10 circumvent, disconcert, disenchant, disgruntle, dishearten, dissatisfy
disappointed: 4 down 5 burnt, upset 6 aghast, burned 7 let down, unhappy 8 downcast, shot down 9 regretful
disappointing: 3 off, sad 5 rocky
disappointment: 3 dud 4 blow, drag 6 bummer, defeat, downer, fiasco, regret 7 chagrin, failure, letdown, licking, setback, washout
exclamation of ~: 2 aw 4 darn, drat, jeez, oh no, rats, sigh 5 fudge, zooks 6 phooey, shucks, zounds 7 brother, horrors, Odzooks 8 Gadzooks
disapproval: 5 odium 6 denial, rebuke 7 censure, dislike, dissent, refusal, reproof 8 reproach
cry of ~: 3 boo, fie, och, tsk, tut 4 hiss, hoot, nuts, pooh, posh, uh-uh 5 hooey, nerts, nertz, pshaw 6 tsk tsk, tut-tut 7 big deal
show ~: 3 boo 4 hiss, hoot 5 frown
disapprove: 4 mind, veto 5 demur, spurn 6 object, oppose, refuse, regret, reject 7 frown on, quarrel 8 turn down 9 criticize, deprecate, disesteem, dispraise, reprehend, reprobate 10 discommend, look down on
of: 4 mind 5 decry 7 condemn, deplore, dislike
disapproved: 4 tabu 5 taboo
disapprover: 6 critic
disapproving: 4 cool 7 hostile, injured 8 critical
disapprovingly: 6 askant 7 askance
disarm: 3 win 4 melt 5 charm 6 defuse, defuze 7 bewitch, enchant, unnerve, win over 8 entrance 9 captivate, fascinate 10 smooth over
disarming: 7 winning, winsome 10 bewitching, convincing, inveigling, persuasive, saccharine
disarrange: 4 mess, muss 5 mix up, upset 6 jumble, litter, mess up, ruffle, tangle, tumble, untidy 7 disturb, shuffle 8 scramble, unsettle 10 complicate, disconcert
disarranged: 5 messy, mussy, upset 6 untidy 7 tousled, unkempt 8 pellmell
disarrangement: 5 mix-up 6 jumble
disarray: 4 mess, muss 5 chaos, snarl 6 bedlam, huddle, jumble, jungle, litter, mayhem, muddle, muss up, tumult, unrest, uproar 7 anarchy, clutter, derange, ferment, shuffle, turmoil 8 disorder, shambles, unsettle, upheaval 9 confusion, mobocracy 10 dishabille, turbulence, untidiness
in ~: 5 upset 6 untidy 8 confused 10 disheveled
disassemble: 4 undo 5 unrig 8 take down
disassociated: 5 apart 8 separate
disaster: 3 woe 4 bane, blow, bust, doom, flop, loss, rout, ruin 5 smash 6 blight, crisis, fiasco, misery, mishap, plague 7 debacle, tragedy, washout 8 accident, calamity, casualty, hardship, upheaval 9 adversity, cataclysm, detriment, nightmare, ruination 10 infliction, misfortune, nonsuccess
box-office ~: 4 bomb, flop
natural ~: 5 flood 8 blizzard 9 hurricane
relief org.: 4 FEMA
disaster __: 4 area
disastrous: 3 bad 4 dire, foul, grim, poor 5 awful, fatal, lousy, toxic, woful 6 costly, crumby, crummy, dismal, horrid, malign, odious, rotten, tragic, woeful 7 accurst, adverse, baleful, baneful, beastly, doleful, fateful, ghastly, harmful, ruinous, unlucky 8 accursed, damaging, dreadful, God-awful, grievous, horrible, ill-fated, inferior, luckless, negative, shameful, sinister, stinking, terrible, tragical, untoward, wretched 9 abhorrent, appalling, atrocious, dangerous, defective, execrable, frightful, ill-omened, injurious, insidious, loathsome, miserable, offensive, revolting 10 abominable, calamitous, deplorable, despicable, detestable, horrendous, ill-starred, petrifying
disavow: 4 deny 5 annul, scorn 6 abjure, impugn, recant, reject 7 forsake, gainsay, retract 8 disallow, forswear, go back on, renounce, take back, withdraw 9 back-pedal, foreswear, repudiate
disavowal: 6 denial 7 refusal 8 negation 9 desertion
words of ~: 4 not I 5 not me
disband: 4 fold 5 demob, sever, split 7 break up, scatter 10 demobilize
disbar: 5 eject 7 exclude
disbelief: 3 awe 5 doubt 6 denial 7 atheism, dubiety 8 mistrust, nihilism 9 dubiosity, rejection 10 skepticism
exclamation of ~: 2 aw 3 huh, pah 4 nuts, oh no, pooh, posh, rats, umph, what 5 hooey, humph, pshaw, zooks 6 zounds 7 baloney, Odzooks 8 Gadzooks, honestly
disbelieve: 5 doubt, query, scorn 6 be wary, reject, wonder 7 be leery, scoff at, suspect 8 discount, mistrust, question 9 discredit, repudiate, smell a rat
disbeliever: 7 sceptic, skeptic
disbelieving: 9 quizzical, skeptical
disburden: 3 rid 4 ease, free, help, shed 6 solace 7 lighten 9 discharge, exonerate, extricate
disburse: 3 pay 4 deal, fork, give, mete 5 issue, spend 6 ante up, divide, expend, lay out, pay out, ration 7 deal out, dish out, divvy up, dole out, hand out, mete out, pass out 8 dispense, shell out 10 administer, distribute
disbursement: 5 outgo, price 6 outlay 7 expense, payment 8 spending
disc: 2 CD 3 DVD 5 album, plate 6 circle 7 Frisbee, platter
jockey: 6 deejay 9 announcer
starter: 5 video
see also disk
disc __: 4 film 5 brake 6 camera, jockey, player
__ disc: 5 laser 7 compact, optical
discard: 4 cull, doff, drop, dump, jilt, junk, omit, shed, toss 5 chuck, ditch, scrap 6 banish, give up, reject 7 abandon, deep-six, forsake, let go of 8 castaway, get rid of, give up on, jettison, lay aside, part with, shake off, write off 9 cast aside, dispose of, eliminate, supersede, sweep away, throw away 10 relinquish
discarded: 8 derelict 9 ownerless
discards: 4 junk 5 trash 6 jetsam, jetsom 7 flotsam, garbage, rejects
discarnate: 8 bodiless 10 immaterial
discern: 3 see 4 espy, feel, find, know, note, spot, tell, view 5 catch, judge, learn, sense, sight 6 behold, descry, detect, fathom, notice 7 cognize, make out, observe, pick out, realize 8 perceive, smell out 9 apprehend, ascertain, figure out, penetrate, recognize 10 understand
discernible: 5 clear, plain, vivid 6 cogent, visual 7 audible, evident, express, obvious, sensory, visible

8 apparent, distinct, explicit, manifest, palpable, tangible 9 graspable, sensorial 10 spelled out
discerning: 4 keen, sage, sane, wise 5 acute, quick, sharp, smart 6 astute, bright, clever, shrewd 7 logical, prudent, refined, thought 8 critical, keen-eyed, lynx-eyed, profound, rational, sensible 9 astucious, brilliant, conscious, ingenious, judicious, observant, provident, sagacious, selective, sensitive 10 farsighted, insightful, perceptive, percipient
discernment: 3 eye, wit 4 wits 5 depth, sense, taste 6 acumen, reason, vision, wisdom 7 insight 8 elegance, judgment, keenness 10 perception
discharge: 2 ax 3 axe, can, pay 4 bang, boot, drop, emit, fire, flow, free, gush, leak, meet, ooze, oust, pour, sack, shot, spew, spit, spue, vent, void 5 annul, belch, blast, burst, congé, drain, egest, eject, empty, erupt, expel, exude, let go, loose, round, salvo, serve, shoot, spill, spirt, spout, spurt, storm, yield 6 acquit, bounce, cancel, congee, dehire, efflux, finish, firing, fulfil, go boom, launch, layoff, let off, let out, loosen, pardon, parole, pay off, recall, redeem, refund, remove, report, set off, settle, unlade, unload, vacate, volley 7 abide by, absolve, achieve, barrage, cashier, deliver, dismiss, drum out, emanate, execute, explode, freeing, fulfill, give off, heave-ho, kick out, manumit, offload, payment, perform, pouring, receipt, release, satisfy, secrete, seepage, set free, spatter, thunder 8 abrogate, carry out, detonate, disgorge, effluent, ejection, emission, emptying, eruption, furlough, get rid of, liberate, outburst, pink slip, shoot off, transact, unlading 9 acquittal, annulment, carry away, clearance, disburden, dismissal, effluence, eliminate, emanation, exclusion, exculpate, execution, exemption, exonerate, explosion, expulsion, exudation, fusillade, liquidate, muster out, pour forth, probation, secretion, send forth, supersede, terminate, unloading, unshackle 10 accomplish, deposition, detonation, disembogue, evacuation, liberation, observance, remittance, settlement
gradually: 4 leak, ooze, seep 5 exude 7 secrete
__ discharge: 9 honorable
discharged matter: 6 egesta
disciple: 3 fan 5 pupil 7 admirer, apostle, convert, devotee, learner, student 8 adherent, believer, follower 9 proselyte, supporter, worshiper
suffix: 3 -ist, -ite
__ Disciple, The: 6 Devil's
disciplinarian: 5 bully 6 tyrant 7 teacher 8 enforcer, martinet, stickler 10 taskmaster
legislative ~: 4 whip
disciplinary: 4 firm, hard 5 bossy, cruel, penal, picky, rigid, stern, tough 6 severe 7 austere, Spartan 8 despotic, exacting, hard-line, punitive, rigorous 9 demanding, draconian, stringent, unbending, unsparing 10 despotical, inflexible, iron-fisted, no-nonsense, oppressive, tyrannical
discipline: 3 job, rod 4 area, walk, whip, will 5 drill, field, order, rigor, teach, train 6 course, punish, school, sphere 7 censure, conduct, control, penalty, regimen, science, subject 8 activity, chastise, exercise, penalize, practice, punition, training 9 castigate, cultivate, education, habituate, restraint, specialty, willpower 10 correction, curriculum, limitation, punishment, regulation, strictness
__-discipline: 4 self
disciplined: 4 tame 5 sober 7 orderly 8 methodic, moderate
not ~: 3 lax 4 wild 6 unruly
disclaim: 4 deny 5 waive 6 abjure, recant, refute, reject, revoke 7 forsake, gainsay, retract 8 abdicate, abnegate, disallow, forswear, renounce, take back, withdraw 9 foreswear, repudiate 10 contravene
disclaimer: 6 denial, waiver 7 refusal 8 negation
disclose: 3 air, say 4 bare, blab, leak, open, show, tell 5 admit, break, let on, spill, unrip, utter 6 betray, convey, expose, impart, let out, relate, report, reveal, unfold, unmask, unveil 7 confess, confide, declare, divulge, exhibit, lay bare, let slip, mention, signify, uncover 8 announce, disinter, give away, proclaim, register, unburden 9 make known 10 make public
disclosed: 4 open 8 knowable, manifest
disclosure: 4 news 6 exposé 8 giveaway 9 admission, broadcast, detection, discovery, unveiling 10 blow-by-blow, confession, divulgence, revelation, unbosoming, uncovering, unveilment
Disclosure: 4 film 5 novel
author: Michael Crichton
cast: Michael Douglas, Demi Moore, Donald Sutherland
director: Barry Levinson
Discman maker: 4 Sony
disco: 3 fad 4 club 5 dance, music 9 dance hall, nightclub, nightspot
Caribbean ~: 4 zouk
dancing: 4 go-go
phrase: 5 à gogo
spinner: 2 DJ 6 deejay
Disco Duck (1976 song)
artist: Dees
Disco Lady (1976 song)
artist: Johnnie Taylor
discolor: 3 mar 4 blur, soil 5 smear, stain, sully, taint 6 bruise 7 besmear, contuse, tarnish 8 besmirch
discoloration: 4 blot, scar, spot 5 stain 6 blotch, bruise, defect 7 blemish 9 contusion
combining form: 6 -chroia
discombobulate: 3 jar 4 stun 5 abash, addle, upset 6 fuddle, muddle, puzzle, rattle 7 confuse, fluster, perplex, unnerve 8 confound
discombobulated: 4 asea 5 at sea 7 abashed, puzzled 8 unstrung
discomfit: 4 faze 5 abash, scare, shake, spite, upset 6 baffle, bother, defeat, dismay, heckle, rattle, ruffle, thwart, unglue 7 chagrin, confuse, disturb, fluster, mortify, nonplus, perplex, perturb 8 confound, unsettle, unstring 9 checkmate, embarrass, frustrate, humiliate, take aback 10 demoralize, discompose, disconcert, disgruntle
discomfiting: 5 scary
discomfiture: 7 chagrin 9 abashment
discomfort: 4 ache, bore, hurt, pain 5 alarm, upset 6 misery, regret 7 malaise, perturb, trouble 8 distress, frighten, hardship, irritate, soreness 9 annoyance, embarrass, suffering 10 discompose, inquietude, irritation, uneasiness
cause of ~: 5 thorn
exclamation: 2 ow 3 ack, ick, oof, ugh, yow 4 moan, ouch, phew, yelp, yeow, yuck 5 groan, yecch
show ~: 5 wince
discomforting: 5 hairy 6 sticky
discommend: 9 deprecate 10 disapprove
discommode: 6 put out 8 unsettle 9 disoblige, incommode, interfere
discompose: 3 irk, jar, vex 4 faze, jolt, stun 5 abash, addle, annoy, harry, shake, upset 6 bother, flurry, harass, nettle, plague, rattle, ruffle 7 agitate, confuse, disturb, fluster, perplex, perturb, shuffle, unhinge 8 convulse, irritate, psych out, unsettle, unstring 9 disaffect, discomfit, displease, embarrass 10 discomfort, disconcert
discomposed: 6 uneasy 8 unstrung
disconcert: 3 bug 4 faze, jolt, trip 5 abash, addle, annoy, appal, get to, mix up, shake, shame, throw, upset 6 appall, baffle, bother, dismay, flurry, foul up, heckle, hinder, mess up, puzzle, rattle, ruffle, unglue 7 agitate, chagrin, confuse, disturb, fluster, nonplus, perplex, perturb, shake up, trouble, unnerve 8 bewilder, confound, frighten, psych out, surprise, unsettle, unstring 9 discomfit, embarrass, frustrate, take aback, unbalance 10 demoralize, disappoint, disarrange, discompose, disgruntle
disconcerted: 5 upset 6 shaken, thrown 7 abashed, unglued 8 unstrung
disconfirm: 5 break, rebut 6 negate, refute 7 confute, gainsay 8 disprove 10 controvert
disconnect: 4 part, undo 5 loose, sever, split, unpeg, unrig, untie 6 cut off, detach, divide, hang up, loosen, unlink 7 divorce, isolate, split up, tear off 8 break off, separate, set apart, uncouple 9 break it up, disengage, dislocate, interrupt, segregate, take apart 10 break it off, come undone, dissociate
disconnected: 5 apart, loose 6 broken 7 asunder, garbled, jumbled, mixed up, muddled 8 confused, discrete, rambling, separate 9 excursive
disconnection: 3 gap 5 split 8 division
disconsolate: 3 low, sad 4 blue, down, glum, mopy 5 heavy, mopey, sorry, woful 6 abject, dreary, gloomy, lonely, morose, somber, woeful 7 crushed, doleful, forlorn, hurting, joyless, unhappy, wistful 8 dejected, desolate, downcast, troubled, wretched 9 bummed out, cheerless, heartsick, miserable, plaintive, prostrate, sorrowful, woebegone 10 chapfallen, dispirited, melancholy
disconsolateness: 5 gloom 6 sorrow
discontent: 6 unrest 8 friction 9 annoyance, complaint, displease, grumbling 10 depression, uneasiness
show ~: 4 moan 5 groan 6 kvetch 8 complain
discontented: 4 sour 5 weary 7 grouchy 9 miserable, querulous
discontinuance: 3 end 4 stop 6 disuse, ending, finish, period 7 closing 8 abeyance, stoppage
discontinue: 3 end 4 drop, halt, quit, stay, stop 5 break, cease, close, lapse, pause, scrub, sever 6 desist, finish, wind up, wrap up 7 abandon, adjourn, back off, break up, shut off, shut out, suspend 8 break off, conclude, intermit, knock off, leave off, pack it in, separate, shut down, surcease 9 close down, terminate 10 call it a day
discontinuity: 3 gap 5 break, crack 6 hiatus, lacuna 7 opening 8 cleavage, fracture 10 disruption
discontinuous: 6 broken
discord: 3 din 4 feud 5 chaos, clash, noise, split 6 breach, jangle, racket, rancor, strife, unrest 7 dissent, faction, quarrel, trouble, warfare 8 argument, conflict, disunity, friction, sour note, variance 9 animosity, antipathy, cacophony, harshness, hostility, mobocracy, wrangling 10 antagonism, contention, disharmony, dissension, dissonance, turbulence
apple of ~ contender: 4 Hera
Greek goddess of ~: 4 Eris
discordance: 9 cacophony
discordant: 4 ajar 5 harsh, noisy 6 atonal, off-key, shrill, unlike 7 grating, jarring, raucous, unalike 8 clashing, improper, jangling, strident 9 different, disparate, dissident, dissonant, divergent, unmusical 10 discrepant, incoherent, quarreling
be ~: 8 disagree
Discordia counterpart: 4 Eris
discount: 4 sale 5 lower, price, scoff, slash 6 deduct, forget, ignore, rebate, reduce, refund, reject, saving, slight 7 bargain, cut-rate,

neglect, put down, scoff at **8** belittle, brush off, close out, decrease, diminish, markdown, minimize, mistrust, overlook, pass over, rollback, subtract, take away **9** abatement, deduction, discredit, disregard, reduction, underplay **10** concession, diminution, disbelieve, percentage
store: **6** outlet
ticket: **6** coupon
discount __: **4** rate **5** house, store **6** broker, market
__ discount: **3** at a **4** deep
discounted: **4** less **6** on sale
not ~: **4** list **6** retail
discountenance: **3** irk **4** faze **5** abash, shame, upset **6** oppose, rattle, reject **7** chagrin, condemn, frown on, nonplus **8** object to
discounting: **4** save **9** except for
discount-rack abbr.: **3** irr. **5** irreg.
discourage: **4** curb, dash **5** check, chill, daunt, deter, repel, scare **6** dampen, deject, dismay, hinder, impede, rebuff, sadden, unglue **7** depress, inhibit, overawe, repress, unnerve **8** dispirit, dissuade, frighten, hold back, obstruct, restrain **9** deprecate, disadvise, disparage, frustrate, give pause, indispose, interfere, prostrate, talk out of, turn aside **10** demoralize, dishearten, disincline, intimidate, keep in line
discouraged: **3** sad **4** blue, down, glum **6** abject, broken **7** in a funk **8** dejected, downcast **9** saturnine
discouragement: **5** gloom **6** dismay, rebuff
discouraging: **3** bad, dim **5** bleak, mirky, murky, rocky **6** dismal, dreary, gloomy
discourse: **4** chat, lect., talk, word **5** orate, speak, theme **6** confer, dialog, homily, parley, reason, recite, sermon, speech, thesis **7** address, commune, lecture, monolog, oration, writing **8** colloquy, converse, dialogue, harangue, language, perorate, rhetoric, treatise **9** elaborate, expatiate, hold forth, monograph, monologue, sermonize, utterance **10** commentary, commentate, discussion, dissertate, exposition, literature, recitation, vocalizing
topic: **5** thema
Discourse on Method: **5** essay
author: René Descartes
discourteous: **4** curt, flip, pert, rude **5** brusk, fresh, gruff, harsh, nervy, rough, sassy, saucy, short, surly **6** abrupt, awless, brazen, cheeky, snippy **7** aweless, boorish, brusque, ill-bred, uncivil, uncouth **8** churlish, flippant, impolite, impudent, insolent, inurbane, snippety, tactless **9** offensive, out of line
discourtesy: **4** sass **6** insult, slight
discover: **3** see, spy **4** espy, find, hear, read, show, spot, tell **5** catch, crack, dig up, glean, hit on, learn, trace **6** descry, detect, intuit, locate, look up, notice, strike, turn up, unfold, unveil **7** find out, glimpse, hit upon, light on, nose out, observe, pioneer, realize, rout out, uncover, unearth **8** come upon, identify, perceive, smell out, surprise **9** ascertain, determine, ferret out, get to know, get wind of, light upon, originate, track down
Discover: **8** magazine **10** credit card
rival: **4** Omni, Visa
use ~: **3** owe **6** charge
discovered, just: **3** new
discovery: **4** find, news **5** trove **6** espial, strike **7** finding **9** detection, diagnosis, encounter, invention, principle **10** conclusion, disclosure, exposition, innovation, perception, revelation, uncovering, unearthing
cry of ~: **3** aha, oho **6** eureka
Discovery: **4** ship **10** spacecraft
captain: **6** Baffin, Hudson
org.: **4** NASA
passenger: **4** Garn
discredit: **4** gibe, jeer, jibe, mock, slam, slur, snub **5** abuse, blame, decry, doubt, libel, odium, rebut, scoff, scorn, shame, smear, spurn, taint, taunt, wrong **6** defame, deride, dump on, expose, heckle, humble, impugn, malign, naysay, negate, offend, rebuff, refute, reject, show up, slight, vilify **7** affront, asperse, censure, confute, degrade, explode, put down, rank out, run down, scandal, scoff at, slander, subvert, traduce **8** belittle, denounce, discount, dishonor, distrust, mistrust, reproach, ridicule, take down, tear down, throw mud, vilipend **9** challenge, denigrate, disesteem, disparage, disrepute, frown upon, humiliate, reflect on **10** calumniate, compromise, contradict, contravene, depreciate, disbelieve, invalidate, reflection, stigmatize
discreditable: **3** bad **4** poor **6** shoddy, unfair **8** unseemly
discreet: **4** safe, wary, wise **5** canny, chary, right **6** modest, polite, simple, subtle **7** careful, guarded, politic, private, prudent, tactful **8** cautious, delicate, keen-eyed, sensible **9** courteous, farseeing, judicious, provident, sensitive, temperate **10** controlled, diplomatic, longheaded, reasonable, restrained, thoughtful
Discreet Music
composer: Brian Eno
discreetness: **7** caution, modesty
discrepancy: **3** gap **5** split **8** conflict, variance **9** variation
discrepant: **7** unalike **9** different, differing, disparate, dissonant, divergent **10** at variance, discordant, inaccurate
discrete: **5** apart **6** unlike, varied **7** diverse, unalike, variant, various **8** detached, distinct, separate **9** different, unrelated **10** individual
discretion: **4** care, tact **6** choice, option **7** caution, finesse **8** judgment, prudence, volition **9** attention, canniness, chariness, diplomacy, foresight, good sense, vigilance **10** precaution, providence, shrewdness, solicitude
at one's ~: **6** freely
discretionary: **8** optional **9** voluntary
discriminate: **4** tell **6** secern **8** separate **9** segregate, victimize
discriminating: **4** fine, keen **5** acute, fussy, picky, sharp **6** astute, choose, choosy, select, shrewd, subtle **7** careful, choosey, finical, finicky, logical, refined **8** critical, eclectic, finiking, finnicky, lynx-eyed, rational, sensible, tasteful **9** astucious, observant, sagacious, selective
discrimination: **3** ear, eye, wit **4** bias, care, wits **5** sense, taste **6** acumen, wisdom **7** bigotry, culture **8** inequity, judgment, keenness **9** prejudice
discriminatory: **6** biased, unfair, unjust **7** partial **8** one-sided, partisan **9** arbitrary, selective **10** prejudiced, unbalanced
disculpate: **5** clear **6** acquit **9** vindicate
discursion: **5** aside **8** drifting, straying **9** departure, wandering **10** apostrophe, digression
discursive: **4** long **5** gabby, wordy **6** prolix **7** aimless, diffuse, erratic, lengthy, unterse, verbose, voluble **8** rambling **9** bombastic, excursive, garrulous, talkative, wandering **10** digressive, long-winded, loquacious, palaverous
discus: **5** event
competition: **4** meet
discuss: **4** chat, talk **5** touch, treat **6** confer, debate, go into, reason, rehash, review, talk of **7** address, mention, speak of **8** hash over, talk over, vocalize **9** bat around, negotiate, talk about, touch base **10** deliberate, kick around, speak about, toss around
discussing, no longer worth: **4** moot
discussion: **4** talk, word **5** input **6** airing, confab, debate, dialog, huddle, parley, powwow, review, speech **7** comment, hearing, meeting, session **8** colloquy, dialogue, question **9** dialectic, discourse, interview, symposium, tête-à-tête, wrangling **10** conference, contention, exposition, groupthink, literature, recitation
group: **5** forum, panel
matter for ~: **5** issue
up for ~: **4** open
disdain: **3** dig **4** barb, gibe, hate, jeer, jibe, mock, shun, slam, slap, slur, snub, veto **5** abhor, abuse, decry, libel, scoff, scorn, sneer, snoot, spurn, taunt **6** bounce, defame, deride, dump on, hatred, heckle, impugn, malign, offend, pass on, rebuff, reject, slight, vilify **7** affront, asperse, calumny, catcall, contemn, degrade, despise, exclude, hauteur, mockery, neglect, obloquy, offense, put down, rank out, slander, sniff at, traduce **8** aversion, belittle, contempt, denounce, derision, pooh-pooh, ridicule, sneeze at, turn down, vilipend **9** antipathy, arrogance, aspersion, blackball, cast aside, contumely, denigrate, disparage, disregard, humiliate, repudiate **10** calumniate, defamation, disrespect, ill feeling, look down on, opprobrium, recoil from
cry of ~: **3** bah, pah, tsk, tut **4** egad, pish, pooh, posh, tush **5** egads, pshaw, shame **6** tsk tsk, tut-tut **8** for shame
show ~: **4** jeer **5** shrug, sniff, snoot
with ~: **5** icily **8** snootily
disdainful: **5** lofty, proud **6** snooty **7** haughty, jeering **8** arrogant, cavalier, derisive, insolent, sardonic, superior **9** despising, egotistic, rejecting, vitriolic **10** contemning, derogatory, hoity-toity, intolerant, minimizing
disdainfulness: **5** pride **7** hauteur **9** arrogance, insolence
disease: **3** bug, ill, pox **4** rust **6** blight, malady, plague **7** ailment, illness **8** disorder, sickness **9** complaint, condition, contagion, ill health, infection, infirmity **10** affliction, unwellness
combining form: **3** nos- **4** noso- **5** patho-, -pathy
plant ~: **4** rust, wilt **5** ergot **6** blight, mildew **10** damping-off
prevent ~: **8** immunize **9** vaccinate
science of ~: **8** medicine
disease-fighting org.: **3** NIH
disease-proof: **6** immune
disembark: **4** land **5** light **6** alight, arrive, get off **7** deplane, descend, detrain, step out **8** get there, go ashore **10** come ashore
disembarkation: **7** arrival
disembarrass: **3** rid **8** liberate
disembodied: **8** bodiless, separate **9** spiritual **10** discarnate, immaterial
disenchant: **4** sour **7** let down, turn off **8** disabuse **9** undeceive **10** disappoint
disenchanted: **5** blasé, burnt, fed up **6** burned, soured **7** cynical, let down
disencumber: **3** rid **5** clear **6** unload **7** lighten, relieve **8** unburden, untangle
disengage: **3** pry **4** free, undo, wean **5** clear, let go, loose, split, unpeg, untie, unzip **6** detach, loosen, opt out, unbind **7** isolate, release, retreat **8** cut loose, separate, uncouple, unfasten, withdraw **9** dislocate, extricate, weasel out **10** come undone, disconnect, dissociate
disengaged: **3** lax **4** free, idle, lazy **5** inert **6** asleep, draggy, torpid, untied **7** dormant, neutral, passive **8** inactive, indolent, slothful, sluggish **9** lethargic, sedentary
disentangle: **4** comb, free, undo **5** clear, let go, ravel, solve, untie **6** decode, unwind **7** clear up, resolve, sort out, unravel, unsnarl, untwist, work out **8** decipher, separate, simplify, untangle **10** unscramble
disenthrall: **4** free **5** loose **6** loosen, redeem **10** emancipate
__ d'Isère: **3** Val

disestablish: **4** void **5** annul **7** abolish
disesteem: **9** deprecate, discredit, disregard, disrepute, ill repute **10** detraction, disapprove, muckraking
disfavor: **5** blame, odium, shame **7** refusal **8** aversion, contempt, mistrust **9** deprecate, ill repute
disfavorable: **8** critical, libelous **9** aspersive, demeaning, invidious **10** belittling, defamatory, derogatory, detractive
'D' Is for Deadbeat
 author: Sue Grafton
disgorge: **4** spew, spue **5** egest, eject, empty, expel, spill **6** unload **9** discharge
disgrace: **4** blot, slur, soil **5** guilt, lower, odium, shame, spoil, stain, sully, taint **6** debase, defame, defile, infamy, rascal, stigma **7** attaint, corrupt, mortify, obloquy, scandal, tarnish, undoing **8** besmirch, derogate, ignominy, take down **9** humiliate, ill repute **10** debasement, opprobrium, stigmatize
 sign of ~: **4** blot **5** stain **9** black mark
disgraced: **6** fallen
disgraceful: **3** low **4** base, foul, grim, mean, poor, vile **5** awful, lousy, nasty, shady, sorry, woful, wrong **6** crumby, crummy, dismal, horrid, odious, rotten, shabby, shoddy, woeful **7** accurst, baleful, baneful, beastly, doleful, ghastly, ignoble **8** accursed, dreadful, flagrant, God-awful, grievous, horrible, infamous, inferior, shameful, shocking, stinking, terrible, unworthy, wretched **9** abhorrent, appalling, atrocious, defective, execrable, frightful, insidious, loathsome, miserable, monstrous, offensive, revolting **10** abominable, despicable, detestable, disastrous, horrendous, scandalous
disgruntle: **5** abash, annoy, shame, upset **6** dismay, offend **7** mortify, perturb **9** discomfit, displease, embarrass **10** disappoint, disconcert
disgruntled: **5** huffy, sulky, testy, vexed **6** crabby, cranky, grumpy, peeved, put out, sullen **7** annoyed, grouchy, injured, peevish, unhappy **8** grumpish
disgruntlement: **7** chagrin
disguise: **4** fake, hide, mask, veil **5** alter, beard, cache, capot, cloak, color, couch, cover, feign, front, shade, trick **6** encode, facade, shroud **7** charade, conceal, costume, cover-up, falsify, obscure, secrete **8** covering, illusion, pretense, simulate **9** dissemble, obfuscate **10** camouflage, false front, keep secret, masquerade
 item: **3** wig **5** beard **7** glasses **8** mustache
 wear the ~ of: **4** go as **6** pass as
disguised: **5** false, incog **6** covert, hidden, masked, secret, unseen, veiled **7** furtive, private **8** hush-hush **9** incognito, invisible, out of view **10** undercover, under wraps
disgust: **4** hate, tire **5** appal, odium, repel, shock, weary **6** appall, hatred, insult, offend, revolt, sicken **7** fend off, hold off, horrify, outrage, repulse, turn off **8** alienate, aversion, drive off, gross out, loathing **9** abominate, antipathy, repulsion, revulsion **10** abhorrence, repellence, repugnance
 cry of ~: **3** ack, bah, fie, huh, ick, pah, rot, ugh, yah **4** bosh, darn, drat, heck, nuts, pfui, phew, phoo, pooh, posh, rats, yuck **5** faugh, fudge, nerts, nertz, pshaw, yecch, zooks **6** darn it, phooey, shucks, zounds **7** brother, goldarn, goldurn, Odzooks, rubbish **8** Gadzooks
disgusted: **4** sick **5** fed up, weary **7** teed off, unhappy **8** outraged **9** squeamish, turned off **10** displeased, fastidious, grossed out
 be ~ by: **6** detest
 with: **6** sick of
disgusting: **4** foul, icky, rank, ugly, vile **5** awful, gross, nasty, yucky **6** cruddy, grungy, horrid, odious, rancid, rotten, sleazy, vulgar **7** beastly, ghastly, hateful, hideous, noisome, squalid **8** gruesome, inedible, shocking, stinking **9** atrocious, execrable, frightful, loathsome, low-minded, monstrous, obnoxious, offensive, repellant, repellent, repugnant, repulsive, revolting, shameless **10** abominable, detestable, outrageous, scandalous
dish: **4** bowl, food, meal **5** china, plate, stein **6** course, entrée, gossip, recipe, saucer **7** platter **8** scoop out **9** casserole, container, tableware
 alternative: **5** cable
 ancestor: **6** aerial
 cookoff ~: **5** chili
 delectable ~: **5** viand
 dirt: **6** gossip
 dryer: **5** towel
 ender: **3** pan, rag **4** ware **5** cloth, towel, water **6** washer
 fragment: **5** shard, sherd
 holder: **4** rack, tray
 it out: **7** lambast, lay it on **8** lambaste **10** come down on
 main ~: **4** meat **6** entrée
 name words: **3** à la
 out: **3** pay **4** deal, give, mete **5** issue, ladle, serve **6** divide, ration **7** deliver, divvy up **8** disburse, dispense **10** distribute
 partner: **5** spoon
 serving ~: **4** boat **7** platter
 side ~: **4** rice, slaw **5** pasta, salad **6** potato, veggie **8** coleslaw, macaroni **9** vegetable
 up: **5** serve
dish __: **3** out, top **5** gravy, it out, night **7** antenna
__ dish: **4** side, soap **5** candy, petri **7** chafing
__-dish: **4** deep
disharmony: **4** feud **5** clash **6** breach, strife **7** discord, faction **8** conflict, friction, sour note **9** discord **10** contention, difference, dissension, dissidence, dissonance, heterodoxy, turbulence
dishcloth: **3** rag
dishearten: **3** cow **4** tire **5** abash, appal, crush, daunt, deter, unman, weary **6** appall, bum out, dampen, deject, dismay, sadden, unglue **7** depress, oppress, unnerve **8** cast down, dispirit, dissuade **9** bring down, disparage, frustrate, give pause, humiliate, indispose **10** demoralize, disappoint, discourage, disincline, intimidate
disheartened: **3** low, sad **4** blue, down, glum **5** woful **6** abject, broken, gloomy, morose, somber, woeful **7** doleful, joyless, unhappy **8** dejected, downcast, troubled **9** bummed out, cheerless, exanimate, heartsick, miserable, sorrowful, woebegone **10** chapfallen, melancholy
disheartening: **3** sad **5** bleak, mirky, murky, sorry **6** dismal, gloomy
disheartenment: **7** despair
dished: **4** beat **5** all in, spent **6** bushed, cupped, done in, pooped **7** concave, drained, wearied, worn out **8** dog-tired, tired out **9** dead tired, exhausted, played out
dishes: **4** menu **5** china **7** cuisine **10** dinnerware, gastronomy
 do the ~: **4** wash
 help with the ~: **3** dry **4** wipe
 remove ~ from the table: **3** bus
dishevel: **4** mess, muss **6** jumble, mess up, muss up, ruck up, ruffle, rumple, tangle **7** snarl up
disheveled: **4** wild **5** dowdy, messy, mussy, ratty, seedy, upset **6** blowsy, blowzy, frowsy, frowzy, grungy, sloppy, unneat, untidy **7** blowsed, blowzed, rumpled, squalid, tousled, unkempt **8** slipshod, slovenly, wrinkled **9** bagged out **10** bedraggled, disarrayed, disordered, disorderly, unbuttoned
dishonest: **3** sly **4** foul **5** dirty, false, lying, shady **6** louche, rotten, shifty, sneaky, tricky, unfair, unholy, untrue **7** corrupt, crooked, devious, immoral, knavish **8** cheating, delusive, guileful, sinister, slippery, thieving, thievish, wrongful **9** deceitful, deceiving, deceptive, designing, faithless, insidious, insincere, strategic, swindling, two-timing, underhand, unethical **10** backbiting, fictitious, fraudulent, mendacious, misleading, perfidious, traitorous, untruthful, villainous
 be ~: **3** con, lie **4** bilk, burn, dupe, fool, gull, have, hoax, hook, scam, sell, snow, take, trap **5** bluff, cheat, cozen, lie to, put on, sneak, trick **6** betray, delude, entrap, fleece, lead on, outwit, suck in, take in **7** beguile, buffalo, deceive, defraud, ensnare, insnare, mislead, pretend, sell out, swindle **8** flimflam, hoodwink, outsmart, pettifog, simulate, throw off **9** bamboozle, four-flush, misinform, victimize
 one: **4** liar **5** crook, rogue, sneak
dishonesty: **3** lie **4** cant **5** guile, lying **6** deceit, racket **7** falsity, knavery **8** bad faith, venality **9** chicanery, dirty work, duplicity, falsehood, fourberie, hypocrisy, improbity, mendacity, rascality, treachery **10** corruption, hanky-panky, hocus-pocus, illegality, infidelity, trickiness
dishonor: **5** abase, guilt, odium, shame, stain, sully, taint, wrong **6** debase, defame, defile, infamy, insult, stigma **7** attaint, blacken, corrupt, obloquy, scandal, slander **8** contempt, ignominy **9** abasement, desecrate, discredit, humiliate, ill repute, notoriety, violation **10** opprobrium
dishonorable: **3** low, sly **4** base, foul, grim, poor **5** awful, dirty, false, lousy, seamy, shady, woful **6** abject, crumby, crummy, dismal, horrid, odious, rotten, shabby, shoddy, unfair, woeful **7** accurst, baleful, baneful, beastly, corrupt, crooked, doleful, ghastly, ignoble **8** accursed, degraded, dreadful, God-awful, grievous, horrible, inferior, shameful, stinking, terrible, unworthy, wretched, wrongful **9** abhorrent, appalling, atrocious, defective, execrable, frightful, insidious, loathsome, miserable, notorious, offensive, revolting, underhand, unethical **10** abominable, despicable, detestable, disastrous, horrendous
 one: **3** cad **4** heel **5** rogue
dishonored: **6** fallen
dishpan: **4** bowl **5** basin
dishpan __: **5** hands
__-dish pie: **4** deep
dishrag
 like a ~: **4** limp
 use a ~: **4** wipe
dish the __: **4** dirt
dishwasher: **9** appliance
 cycle: **3** dry **5** rinse
 phase: **5** cycle
 sinkful: **4** suds
dishwashing detergent: **3** Joy **4** Ajax, Dawn **7** Cascade **8** Sunlight **9** Palmolive **10** Electrasol
dishwater
 like ~: **4** dull **5** soapy
 source: **6** faucet
dishy: **6** pretty **7** gossipy
Dishy: **3** Bob
disillusion: **6** dismay **7** let down **8** disabuse, embitter, imbitter **9** unbeguile, undeceive **10** disenchant
disillusioned: **4** sour **5** blasé, burnt **6** burned **7** let down
disillusionment: **6** dismay **7** letdown
disimprison: **4** free **6** let out, parole, redeem, spring
disinclination: **5** qualm **8** aversion
disincline: **10** discourage, dishearten
disinclined: **4** loth, slow **5** loath **6** afraid, averse **7** uneager **9** reluctant, unwilling
disinfect: **4** wash **5** bathe, clean, scrub **6** degerm, purify **7** cleanse, deterge, launder **8** fumigate, sanitize **9** deodorize, sterilize

disinfectant: **6** cresol **7** cleaner **8** cleanser, fumigant, purifier **9** germicide, sanitizer **10** antiseptic, sterilizer
brand: **5** Lysol
target: **4** germ **5** staph
disinfected: **4** pure **5** clean **7** sterile
disinform: **3** con, lie **4** dupe, fool, hoax, jive, sell, snow **5** bluff, cheat, cozen, trick **6** betray, delude, lead on, rope in, sucker, take in **7** beguile, deceive, defraud, mislead, pretend **8** hoodwink, misguide, pettifog, throw off **9** bamboozle, four-flush
disinformation: **3** lie **4** tale
disingenuity: **4** line, ruse, wile **5** craft, guile **6** deceit, device, scheme **7** cunning, knavery, slyness **8** artifice, foxiness, trickery, wiliness **9** cageyness, duplicity, stratagem **10** cleverness, craftiness, shrewdness, subterfuge
disingenuous: **3** sly **6** crafty, sneaky **7** unfrank **8** guileful, uncandid
exclamation: **5** who me
disinherit: **3** rob **4** lose, oust **6** cut off, disown **7** exclude **9** repudiate
disintegrate: **3** eat, rot **4** ruin, sink **5** burst, decay, erode, grind, smash, spoil **6** molder, soften **7** break up, crumble, decline, give way, rot away **8** collapse, evanesce, fragment, splinter **9** decompose
disintegrated: **4** gone
disintegration: **3** rot **4** ruin **5** decay **7** decline, erosion
disinter: **5** dig up **6** exhume **7** uncover, unearth **8** disclose
disinterest: **7** boredom **8** lethargy
show ~: **4** yawn
disinterested: **4** fair, just, open **5** aloof, tepid **6** square **7** neutral **8** balanced, detached, unbiased **9** equitable, impartial, objective, uncolored, unselfish **10** evenhanded
disjoin: **3** pry, rip **4** part, rend **5** break, loose, sever, split, untie, unzip **6** cleave, cut off, detach, divide, loosen, sunder, unlink **7** divorce, split up, tear off **8** break off, disunite, separate, set apart, uncouple **9** interrupt **10** disconnect
disjoined: **7** asunder
disjoint: **5** sever **8** disunite, separate
disjointed: **5** apart, loose **6** broken **7** aimless, chaotic, jumbled, muddled **8** confused, rambling, separate **9** displaced, disunited, separated, spaced-out, spasmodic **10** disordered, incoherent, incohesive, irrational, unattached
disjointly: **5** apart
disjunction: **4** rent **5** break, cleft, split **6** breach **8** cleavage, disunion, disunity, division, fracture **9** severance **10** separation
disk: **2** LP **5** CD/ROM, shape, wafer, wheel **6** circle, danger, floppy, harrow, medium, record, saucer **7** Frisbee, platter
1990s toy ~: **3** pog
bronze ~: **4** gong
contents: **4** data
data ~: **5** CD/ROM **6** floppy
deejay's ~: **4** demo
obsolete: **2** LP
put on ~: **3** cut
rotary ~: **3** cam
slot: **6** A drive
solar ~: **4** Aten, Aton
spinner: **2** DJ **6** deejay
starter: **5** video
disk __: **4** pack **5** brake, crank, drive, wheel **6** floret, flower, harrow, jockey, sander
__ disk: **3** sun **4** hard **5** audio, laser **6** floppy **7** compact, optical
diskette: **6** floppy
clean a ~: **6** delete
prepare a ~: **6** format **10** initialize
disk-shaped: **5** round **8** circular
dislike: **4** hate, shun **5** abhor, avoid, odium **6** animus, detest, enmity, eschew, grudge, hatred, loathe, resent **7** condemn, contemn, deplore, despise **8** aversion, execrate, loathing, object to **9** abominate, animosity, antipathy, hostility, revulsion **10** abhorrence, antagonism, execration, repellence, repugnance
disliked: **5** lousy **7** unloved **9** unpopular
dislocate: **4** pull **5** mix up, shift, upset **6** jumble, luxate, wrench **7** disrupt, shuffle, unhinge **8** dislodge, disorder **9** disengage **10** disconnect, knock loose
dislocation: **8** luxation **10** disruption
sense of ~: **5** anomy **6** anomie
dislodge: **4** buck, bump, oust **5** budge, eject, evict **6** dig out, remove, uproot **8** force out, shake off **9** dislocate, extricate **10** knock loose
disloyal: **3** bad **5** false **6** untrue **8** apostate, cheating, factious, forsworn, recreant, renegade, two-faced **9** faithless, seditious, two-timing **10** inconstant, perfidious, rebellious, subversive, traitorous, unfaithful
be ~ to: **6** betray **7** sell out
one: **3** rat **7** traitor **8** quisling
disloyalty: **7** perfidy, treason **8** bad faith **9** defection, falseness, recreancy, treachery, violation **10** conspiracy, infidelity, untrueness
dismal: **3** low, sad **4** base, blue, dark, dour, glum **5** black, bleak, dingy, drear, dusky, gaunt, heavy, lurid, mirky, moody, murky, sorry, surly **6** broody, cloudy, dreary, gloomy, leaden, somber, sullen **7** forlorn, joyless, ominous, pitiful, unhappy **8** darkened, dejected, desolate, dolorous, dreadful, God-awful, hopeless, liverish, lowering, overcast **9** cheerless, saddening, saturnine, sorrowful, tenebrous, unlighted, woebegone **10** depressing, lugubrious, melancholy, oppressive, tenebrific
see also awful
Dismal __: **5** Swamp
dismals: **7** sadness **10** melancholy
dismantle: **4** lift, part, ruin, undo **5** level, strip, unrig, wreck **6** ravage, recall, topple **7** break up, destroy, undress **8** bulldoze, demolish, pull down, take down, tear down **9** break down, devastate, knock down, take apart **10** annihilate
Dismas: **5** saint
dismay: **4** care, faze, fear **5** abash, alarm, appal, chill, daunt, dread, panic, scare, shake, shock, upset **6** appall, bother, bum out, deject, fright, put off, rattle, sadden, terror **7** agitate, anxiety, chagrin, disturb, letdown, nonplus, perturb, petrify, terrify, unnerve **8** affright, dispirit, disquiet, distress, frighten, surprise, unstring **9** abashment, agitation, bring down, discomfit, give pause, terrorize, trepidity **10** disappoint, disconcert, discourage, disgruntle, dishearten
cry of ~: **2** ow, oy **3** yow **4** alas, oh no, oh oh, oops, ouch, whew, yeow, yipe **5** alack, oyvey, yipes **6** crikey, whoops **7** caramba, horrors **8** gracious, honestly
dismayed: **5** upset **6** aghast, uneasy **9** awestruck
dismiss: **3** axe, can, cut **4** boot, drop, fire, free, omit, oust, sack, send, shoo, shun, veto **5** chuck, eject, evict, expel, let go, purge, spurn **6** banish, bounce, depose, lay off, let off, pass on, pass up, punish, rebuff, recall, reject, remove, revoke, shelve, unseat **7** cashier, cast off, cast out, disdain, drum out, exclude, kick out, neglect, put down, release, relieve, rule out, say no to, send off, turn out **8** brush off, disallow, drive out, exorcise, exorcize, force out, furlough, get rid of, laugh off, pink-slip, pooh-pooh, relegate, send away, sneeze at, turn down **9** blackball, cast aside, discharge, eliminate, freeze out, repudiate, terminate
from one's mind: **6** forget
dismissal: **4** boot **5** congé, exile, the ax **6** congee, denial, layoff, ouster, waiver **7** deposal, release, removal **8** brush-off, eviction, pink slip **9** acquittal, discharge, exclusion, expulsion, ostracism, rejection **10** banishment, deposition, liberation, old heave-ho, relegation, suspension, unfrocking
dismount: **4** land **5** light **6** alight, arrive, get off, hopoff **7** descend, get down, jump off
Disney: **3** Roy **4** Walt **6** studio
car: **6** Herbie
character: **3** Doc **4** Chip, Cleo, Dale, Huey, Nemo **5** Ariel, Bambi, Daisy, Dewey, Dopey, Dumbo, Dwarf, Goofy, Happy, Louie, Pongo, Remus **6** Donald, Faline, Figaro, Flower, Grumpy, Ludwig, McDuck, Mickey, Minnie, Oswald, Sleepy, Sneezy **7** Bashful, Cruella, Monstro, Perdita, Scrooge, Thumper **8** Geppetto, Von Drake **9** Daisy Duck, Pinocchio, Snow White **10** Cinderella, Donald Duck, Uncle Remus
competitor: ***see*** movie studio
contemporary: **5** Lantz
creation: **4** film **5** movie **7** cartoon
dog: **4** Lady **5** Pluto, Tramp
frame: **3** cel **4** cell
middle name: **5** Elias
network: **3** ABC **4** ESPN
theme park: **5** Epcot
__ Disney: **4** Euro
__ Disney World: **4** Walt
disobedience: **3** sin **6** mutiny **8** defiance **9** rebellion
__ disobedience: **5** civil
disobedient: **3** bad **4** wild **6** unruly **7** defiant, lawless, naughty, wayward **8** contrary, indocile, perverse
disobey: **4** defy **5** break, evade, flout, rebel **6** ignore, mutiny, revolt **7** infract, violate **9** disregard **10** contravene
disoblige: **6** offend, put out **9** displease, incommode **10** discommode
disobliging: **5** loath **9** unwilling
disorder: **4** fuss, mess, muss, riot, stir, to-do **5** brawl, chaos, havoc, mania, mix up, snafu, snarl, swirl, upset **6** bustle, clamor, dither, fracas, hubbub, huddle, jumble, litter, malady, mayhem, mess up, muddle, muss up, ruckus, rumple, rumpus, tumble, tumult, unrest, uproar **7** ailment, anarchy, clutter, confuse, disease, illness, license, mob rule, rioting, scatter, shuffle, snarl up, trouble, turmoil **8** confound, disarray, nihilism, outbreak, shambles, sickness, syndrome, unsettle, violence **9** complaint, confusion, dislocate, imbroglio, infirmity, looseness, mobocracy, patchwork, rebellion **10** affliction, hullabaloo, turbulence, unruliness, untidiness, unwellness
civil ~: **4** riot
disordered: **4** wild **5** messy, mussy, rough, upset **6** hectic, untidy **7** chaotic, haywire, lawless, tousled, unglued **8** pell-mell, slovenly **9** delirious, stirred up, turbulent, unsettled **10** bedraggled, disheveled, disjointed, in an uproar, incoherent, incohesive, out-of-place
disorderly: **4** wild **5** dowdy, messy, mix up, mussy, noisy, rough, rowdy **6** random, unruly, untidy **7** chaotic, jumbled, lawless, muddled, on a tear, raucous, riotous, tangled, unkempt, wayward **8** anarchic, confused, factious, pell-mell, slovenly, unlawful **9** cluttered, fractious, haphazard, irregular, out-of-line, out-of-step, scattered, scrambled, termagant, turbulent, unsettled, untrained **10** anarchical, boisterous, disheveled, disruptive, licentious, out-of-order, out-of-whack, rebellious, refractory, topsy-turvy, tumultuous, unpeaceful, upside down, vociferant
disorganization: **4** mess **5** chaos, mix-up **6** muddle **8** shambles **10** disruption, turbulence
disorganize: **5** mix up **6** jumble, ravage **7** derange, shuffle **8** unsettle
disorganized: **5** messy, upset, wooly **6** ragged, woolly **7** chaotic,

haywire, jumbled, mixed up, muddled **8** anarchic, confused, messed up, pell-mell **10** anarchical, disorderly
situation: 3 zoo
disorient: 4 lose **5** addle, cloud **6** muddle **7** confuse **8** befuddle, confound
disorientation: 3 fog
disoriented: 4 asea, lost **5** at sea, spacy **6** adrift, astray, spacey **7** mixed up **8** confused, unhinged, unstable, unstrung
disown: 4 deny **5** scorn **6** abjure, cut off, recant, reject **7** abandon, forsake **8** abdicate, abnegate, forswear, renounce **9** foreswear, repudiate **10** disinherit
disownment: 9 defection, sundering
disparage: 3 pan, rap **4** gibe, jeer, jibe, mock, slam, slur, snub **5** abase, abuse, cavil, decry, knock, libel, roast, scold, scorn, smear, sneer, spurn, taunt **6** debunk, defame, demean, deride, dump on, heckle, impugn, jibe at, malign, offend, rebuff, slight, vilify **7** affront, asperse, censure, cry down, degrade, detract, put down, rank out, run down, slander, sneer at, traduce **8** backbite, badmouth, belittle, denounce, derogate, minimize, play down, ridicule, take down, talk down, throw mud, vilipend **9** criticize, denigrate, deprecate, discredit, dispraise, disregard, downgrade, frown upon, fustigate, humiliate, shoot down, underrate **10** calumniate, demoralize, depreciate, discourage, dishearten, undervalue, villainize
disparagement: 3 dig **4** barb, gibe, jibe, slam, slap, slur, snub **5** abuse, blame, libel, scorn, taunt **6** rebuff, slight **7** affront, calumny, catcall, disdain, mockery, obloquy, offense, put-down, sarcasm, scandal, slander **8** contempt, derision, ridicule **9** aspersion, cheap shot, contumely **10** defamation, disrespect, opprobrium
disparager: 6 critic
disparaging: 5 snide **7** abusive **8** captious, critical, libelous **9** sarcastic **10** detractive, pejorative
one: 6 abaser
disparate: 5 other **6** motley, uneven, unlike, varied **7** distant, diverse, unalike, unequal, various **9** different, divergent, unsimilar **10** at variance, discordant, discrepant, dissimilar, poles apart
disparity: 3 gap **7** variety **8** contrast, mismatch **9** deviation, imbalance, otherness, variation **10** difference, dissonance, divergence, divergency, inequality, unevenness, unlikeness
dispassion: 4 calm **8** calmness **9** composure **10** sedateness
dispassionate: 4 calm, cool, fair, just, numb **5** quiet, sober, staid, stoic, stony **6** at ease, low-key, mellow, placid, sedate, serene, square, stoney **7** amiable, at peace, equable, neutral, pacific, relaxed, stoical, unmoved **8** amicable, balanced, carefree, composed, detached, laid-back, moderate, peaceful, tranquil, unbiased **9** collected, easy-going, equitable, impartial, impassive, objective, quiescent, temperate, uncolored, unexcited, unruffled **10** even-handed, nonchalant, unagitated, untroubled
dispatch: 3 eat, zap **4** ease, mail, memo, news, send, ship, slay, word, zeal **5** haste, hurry, issue, remit, route, speed **6** commit, convey, finish, hasten, hustle, launch, letter, report, settle **7** deliver, forward, message, missive, quicken, swallow **8** alacrity, bulletin, celerity, conclude, delivery, rapidity, transfer, transmit, velocity **9** close down, fleetness, news flash, order to go, polish off, quickness, readiness, swiftness **10** communiqué, expedition, memorandum, promptness
boat: 5 aviso
with ~: 3 PDQ **5** apace **6** presto **7** fleetly, hastily, quickly, rapidly, swiftly **8** in a flash, in a jiffy, in no time, pell-mell, speedily **9** forthwith, hurriedly, instantly, like a shot, posthaste
Dispatch: 5 paper **9** newspaper
locale: 4 Ohio **8** Columbus
__ Dispatch: 3 Ems
dispel: 3 rid **4** rout **6** banish **7** scatter **9** chase away, drive away
dispensable: 5 spare **8** needless
dispensary: 6 clinic **8** pharmacy
stock: 5 serum **7** vaccine **8** medicine **10** antobiotic
dispensation: 4 dole, gift **5** award, favor, leave **7** amnesty, liberty, license, portion, release, service, serving **8** bestowal, courtesy, kindness
dispense: 3 ply **4** deal, dole, dose, give, mete **5** allot, apply, issue, share, spare, spend, spray **6** assign, divide, manage, ration, render, supply **7** deal out, deliver, dish out, divvy up, dole out, execute, furnish, give out, hand out, inflict, mete out, pass out, portion, provide, release **8** allocate, carry out, disburse, shell out **9** apportion, implement **10** administer, contribute, distribute, measure out
with: 4 shed **5** scrap, spare, waive **6** refuse **7** discard **8** sign away **9** throw away
dispensed amount: 4 dose **6** dosage
dispenser: 6 jobber **7** machine **9** container
like a ~: 6 coin-op
dispersal: 6 spread **9** diffusion
disperse: 4 cast, deal, lift, melt, thin **5** strew **6** divide, fan out, spread **7** bestrew, break up, diffuse, divvy up, dole out, scatter, send off, spatter **9** broadcast, circulate, propagate **10** distribute
dispersed: 4 sown, thin **6** sparse **7** diffuse **10** fractional
dispersion: 5 issue **6** spread **9** diffusion **10** scattering
dispirit: 3 cow **4** dash, tire **5** break, daunt, deter, unman **6** bum out, dampen, darken, deject, dismay, sadden, unglue **7** deflate, depress, oppress, unnerve **8** cast down, dissuade **9** bring down, give pause **10** demoralize, discourage, dishearten, intimidate
dispirited: 3 low, sad **4** blue, down, glum, mopy **5** mopey, woful **6** broody, gloomy, morose, somber, woeful **7** doleful, hangdog, joyless, unhappy **8** dejected, downbeat, downcast **9** bummed-out, cheerless, depressed, exanimate, heartsick, miserable, saturnine, sorrowful, unhopeful, woebegone **10** chapfallen, despondent, melancholy
be ~: 4 mope
dispiritedness: 4 funk **8** the blues
dispiriting: 3 sad **5** mirky, murky **6** dismal, dreary, somber
displace: 4 bump, fire, lose, move, oust, sack, vary **5** eject, evict, exile, expel, shift, strip, usurp **6** banish, depose, follow, remove, uproot **7** cashier, replace, succeed **8** crowd out, dethrone, force out, relegate, relocate, supplant, unsettle **9** ostracize, supersede, transport **10** expatriate, infringe on, reposition, substitute, transplant
displaced person: 5 exile **6** émigré **7** outcast, refugee **8** emigrant
group: 3 IRO
displacement: 5 exile, shift
display: 3 act, air **4** bare, face, give, look, pomp, show, wear **5** array, exude, flash, front, model, scene, sight, sport, state **6** blazon, effect, evince, expose, flaunt, hold up, layout, parade, reveal, sample, set out, splash, spread, unfold, unfurl, unmask, unroll, unveil **7** arrange, bespeak, example, exhibit, feature, pageant, perform, present, produce, promote, reflect, showing, show off, trot out, uncover **8** brandish, emblazon, evidence, exposure, flourish, indicate, manifest, panorama, pretense, register, showcase, splendor, terminal **9** advertise, exemplify, make known, promenade, spectacle **10** exhibition, exposition, illustrate, pretension, promulgate, revelation
brilliant ~: 5 blaze
combining form: 5 -orama
grand ~: 4 show **5** state **7** fanfare, panoply **8** ceremony, heraldry **9** pageantry
model: 4 demo
put on ~: 4 show **5** array, shown **6** expose
wild ~: 3 mob **4** flap **5** brawl, chaos, scene **6** bedlam, fracas, mutiny, rabble, racket, ruckus, rumble, rumpus, tumult, uproar **7** rampage, turmoil **8** disorder, uprising, violence **9** commotion, imbroglio **10** donnybrook, free-for-all
display-case material: 5 glass
displease: 3 irk, vex **4** fret, gall, hurt, miff, rile, roil, tire **5** anger, annoy, peeve, pique, repel, shock, upset **6** bother, enrage, nettle, offend, put out, revolt **7** chagrin, incense, provoke, turn off **8** irritate **9** aggravate, disoblige, frustrate **10** antagonize, disappoint, discompose, discontent, disgruntle, dissatisfy, exasperate
displeased: 3 mad **4** sick **5** angry, upset **8** wrathful **9** disgusted, indignant
look ~: 4 pout **5** frown, scowl
with: 5 mad at
displeasing: 3 off **4** sour **6** bitter **8** brackish **9** offensive, unwelcome
displeasure: 3 ire **5** anger, pique, wrath **6** hatred **7** chagrin, offense, umbrage **8** vexation **9** annoyance
cry of ~: 2 ow **3** boo, boy, yow **4** hiss, moan, ouch, yeow **5** groan
show ~: 4 jeer, pout, sulk **5** frown, scoff, scowl, whoop **6** deride **7** catcall **8** ridicule
disport: 4 play, romp **5** amuse, sport **6** divert **7** delight, refresh **9** amusement, diversion, entertain **10** recreation
disposable: 9 available, throwaway **10** expendable
disposable __: 6 income
disposal: 4 sale **8** riddance
area: 8 landfill
at one's ~: 6 usable **7** useable
put at one's ~: 5 offer **9** volunteer
dispose: 3 set **4** sell, tend **5** array, order, stand **6** locate, settle **7** arrange, incline, marshal, prepare, swallow **8** motivate, organize, regulate **10** predispose
of: 3 rid **4** cede, drop, dump, junk, sell, shed, toss, vend **5** chuck, ditch, forgo, yield **6** finish, forego, give up, peddle, refute, remove, settle, unload **7** abandon, discard, forfeit, forsake **8** close out, forswear, hand over, jettison, part with, throw out, unburden **9** cast aside, eighty-six, eliminate, foreswear, liquidate, polish off, surrender, throw away **10** auction off, do the trick, relinquish, take care of
disposed: 3 apt **4** game **5** prone, ready **6** biased, liable, likely **7** of a mind, partial, tending, willing **8** inclined, prepared
be ~: 4 lean, tend **6** likely
__-disposed: 3 ill **4** well
disposition: 4 mood, side, soul, vein **5** humor **6** esprit, makeup, mettle, morale, nature, spirit, temper **7** impulse, leaning, mindset, posture, tactics **8** aptitude, attitude, decision, ordering, tendency **9** mentality, reception, sentiment **10** propensity
suffix: 3 -ive
dispositions, like some: 5 sunny
dispossess: 3 rob **4** lose, oust **5** eject, evict, expel, usurp **6** divest, put out **7** bereave, deprive **10** disinherit, infringe on
dispossessed: 6 bereft
dispossession: 4 loss
disproportional: 8 lopsided

disproportionate: **5** undue, wrong **6** uneven **7** unequal **8** lopsided **9** overblown
disproportionately: **6** unduly
disprove: **5** belie, break, rebut **6** answer, expose, naysay, negate, refute **7** confute, explode **8** puncture, tear down **9** disaffirm, vindicate **10** contradict, contravene, controvert, disconfirm, invalidate
disputable: **4** moot **7** dubious **8** arguable, doubtful **9** debatable, litigious, uncertain
disputant: **5** rival **6** arguer **7** agonist, debater, fighter **8** litigant, opponent **9** contender **10** antagonist, contestant, polemicist
disputation: **7** quarrel **8** polemics
disputatious: **6** ornery **9** bellicose
dispute: **3** row **4** beef, buck, case, deny, feud, fuss, spar, spat, tiff **5** argue, brawl, clash, fight, query, rebut, run-in, scrap **6** answer, barney, battle, bicker, breach, debate, fracas, hassle, hubbub, impugn, jangle, naysay, negate, oppose, reason, refute, resist, rumpus, strife, tirade, uproar **7** confute, contest, discord, dissent, gainsay, lawsuit, polemic, problem, quarrel, quibble, wrangle **8** argument, brouhaha, conflict, disunity, friction, litigate, mistrust, question, skirmish, squabble, variance **9** bickering, challenge, commotion, disaffirm, encounter, fireworks, go to court, imbroglio **10** contention, contradict, contravene, controvert, difference, falling-out, litigation
in ~: **4** iffy, moot, open **7** dubious **8** arguable, doubtful **9** debatable, uncertain, undecided, unsettled **10** borderline
settler: **6** umpire **7** arbiter, referee
disqualification cause: **4** foul
disqualify: **3** bar **6** recall **7** disable **9** disenable, eighty-six, eliminate **10** disentitle, invalidate
disquiet: **3** din, jar, vex **4** care, fret, jolt, roil, stir, to-do **5** alarm, angst, annoy, noise, qualm, shake, shock, upset, worry **6** bother, dismay, harass, pester, unrest **7** agitate, anxiety, chagrin, concern, ferment, fidgets, fluster, malaise, perturb, shake up, tension, trouble, turmoil, unhinge **8** distress, frighten, unsettle, unstring **9** commotion **10** foreboding, inquietude, solicitude, uneasiness
more than ~: **5** dread **6** terror
disquieted: **5** jumpy, upset **6** uneasy **7** anxious, fearful **9** ill at ease
be ~ about: **4** fear **5** dread
disquieting: **5** queer **8** grievous, sinister
disquietude: **4** fear **5** noise
disquisition: **5** essay **6** thesis **7** lecture, monolog **8** treatise **9** discourse, monologue **10** exposition, literature
Disraeli: **2** P.M. **4** earl **7** British **8** Benjamin
author: André Maurois
portrayer: **6** Arliss
to Gladstone: **5** rival
disrate: **6** reduce
disregard: **4** defy, miss, omit, skip, snub **5** break, flout, rebel, scorn, spurn, waive **6** apathy, forget, ignore, laxity, oppose, pass by, rebuff, resist, revolt, slight, wink at **7** abandon, blink at, contemn, disdain, disobey, let pass, neglect, rule out, tune out, violate **8** brush off, contempt, defiance, discount, ignoring, laugh off, lay aside, lethargy, live with, omission, overlook, override, overrule, pass over, pooh-pooh, shrug off, sneeze at, vilipend **9** brush away, disesteem, disparage, eliminate, ignorance, lassitude, oversight, pay no mind, slighting, unconcern **10** brush aside, disrespect, negligence
disregardful: **3** lax **5** slack **8** derelict, heedless **9** negligent
disregarding: **9** in spite of
disrelish: **4** hate **6** loathe
disremember: **6** forget
disrepair, in: **4** worn **6** broken **10** broken-down, on the blink, on the fritz, out of order, out of whack, tumbledown
disreputable: **3** bad, low **4** vile **5** loose, lowly, seamy, seedy, shady, slimy **6** abject, louche, no good, shabby, shoddy, sleazy, sordid **7** raffish **8** infamous, shameful, unseemly, unworthy **9** notorious, unethical **10** scandalous
disrepute: **5** odium, shame, taint **6** infamy, stigma **7** obloquy, scandal **8** contempt, ignominy **9** discredit, disesteem, notoriety **10** opprobrium
disrespect: **3** dig **4** barb, gibe, jeer, jibe, mock, sass, slam, slap, slur, snub **5** abuse, decry, libel, scorn, spurn, taunt **6** defame, deride, dump on, heckle, impugn, insult, malign, offend, rebuff, slight, vilify **7** affront, asperse, calumny, catcall, degrade, disdain, impiety, mockery, neglect, obloquy, offense, put down, rank out, slander, traduce **8** belittle, contempt, denounce, derision, ridicule, rudeness, vilipend **9** aspersion, cheap shot, contumely, denigrate, disparage, disregard, flippancy, humiliate, impudence, indignity, insolence, sacrilege **10** calumniate, coarseness, defamation, effrontery, incivility, opprobrium
disrespectful: **4** flip, pert, rude **5** fresh, nervy, rough, sassy, saucy **6** awless, cheeky, snippy **7** aweless, ill-bred, impious, uncivil **8** flippant, impolite, impudent, insolent, inurbane, snippety **9** offensive, sarcastic
be ~: **4** sass
disrobe: **4** peel **5** strip **6** denude **7** take off, undress **8** get out of, unclothe
disrobed: **4** bare, nude **5** naked **8** in the raw **9** in the buff, unattired
disrupt: **4** ruin, stop **5** cut up, mix up, smash, upset **6** bollix, heckle, impede, mess up, muck up, muddle, rattle, ravage **7** agitate, disturb, rupture, shuffle, violate **8** disunite, psych out, sabotage, unsettle **9** dislocate
disruption: **4** ruin, stop **5** break, split, upset **6** schism **7** breakup **8** division, outbreak, sabotage, upheaval **9** breakdown **10** earthquake, separation
business ~: **6** strike
disruptive: **9** confusing, out-of-line, upsetting **10** aggressive, disorderly, disturbing, unsettling
dissatisfaction: **6** regret, unrest **7** anxiety, chagrin **9** annoyance, grumbling
dissatisfied: **6** grumpy **7** unhappy **8** grumpish **9** querulous
dissatisfy: **7** chagrin, let down **9** displease **10** disappoint
dissect: **5** cut up, parse, sever, slice, study **7** analyze, examine, inspect **8** separate **9** anatomize, break down, take apart **10** scrutinize
dissection: **8** analysis **9** breakdown, criticism **10** experiment, inspection
dissemblance: **5** guile
dissemble: **3** lie **4** fake, hide, mask **5** cloak, feign **6** shroud **7** conceal, cover up, deceive, falsify, pretend, profess **8** disguise **9** four-flush, pussyfoot, stonewall, whitewash **10** camouflage, double-talk, masquerade, play possum
dissembler: **5** knave **9** hypocrite
dissembling: **5** lying **6** deceit
disseminate: **3** air, sow **4** deal **5** issue, print, spray, strew **6** effuse, spread **7** bestrew, diffuse, publish, radiate, scatter **8** disperse, proclaim, sprinkle, transmit **9** propagate
dissemination: **5** issue **6** spread
dissension: **4** feud **5** fight, split **6** breach, heresy, strife, unrest **7** discord, faction, quarrel **8** conflict, friction, variance **9** bickering, disaccord **10** antagonism, contention, difference, disharmony, dissidence, dissonance, heterodoxy
sow ~: **6** divide
dissent: **4** balk, flak, vary **5** argue, clash, flack, rebel **6** breach, differ, heresy, object, refuse, revolt, schism, strife **7** discord, dispute, diverge, protest, quarrel, refusal **8** argument, conflict, disagree, disunity, variance **9** objection, rebellion **10** contention, opposition, resistance
religious ~: **9** blasphemy, sacrilege
slangy ~: **3** nah, naw **4** nope
dissenter: **5** rebel **7** heretic, sceptic, skeptic **8** maverick, naysayer, renegade **9** dissident **10** iconoclast, malcontent
dissenting: **8** clashing, negative **9** dissident, heretical, skeptical
vote: **3** nay
dissertate: **5** speak, write **9** discourse, expatiate
dissertation: **5** essay, paper, theme, tract **6** speech, thesis **7** address, writing **8** critique, treatise **9** discourse **10** exposition
topic: **5** thema
Dissertation on Roast Pig, A
author: Charles Lamb
disserve: **4** harm
disservice: **9** detriment, injustice, prejudice **10** unkindness
dissever: **3** saw **5** split **6** cleave **8** disunite
dissidence: **6** strife **7** quarrel **8** variance **9** disaccord **10** contention, difference, disharmony, dissension, dissonance, heterodoxy
dissident: **5** rebel **7** heretic **8** agitator, contrary, factious, renegade **9** differing, dissenter, heretical, heterodox, protester, sectarian **10** discordant, dissenting, rebellious, schismatic, separatist, unorthodox
quest: **6** asylum
dissimilar: **3** new **5** other **6** motley, unlike **7** diverse, unalike, unequal, various **8** contrary, distinct, opposite **9** different, disparate, divergent, unrelated, unsimilar **10** antonymous, individual, mismatched, poles apart
be ~: **6** differ **8** disagree
dissimilarity: **8** contrast **9** variation
dissimulate: **3** lie **4** fake, hide, mask **5** beard, cloak, feign **7** conceal, pretend **8** disguise
dissimulation: **5** guile **8** disguise, pretense
dissimulator: **4** liar
dissipate: **3** eat, sap **4** blow, lift, lose **5** abuse, drain, spend, trash, use up, waste **6** burn up, expend, frivol, lavish, run out, vanish **7** ablates, consume, deplete, exhaust, play out, scatter **8** evanesce, fool away, melt away, misspend, squander **9** attenuate, disappear, drive away, evaporate, throw away **10** fail to keep, gamble away, run through, trifle away
dissipated: **4** gone, lost **5** blown, kaput, loose, spent **6** rakish **7** all gone, immoral **8** misspent **9** abandoned, corrupted, dissolute, excessive, exhausted, played out, scattered **10** gone to seed, profligate, squandered
dissipation: **4** tear, toot **5** binge, waste **6** bender, misuse **10** recreation
dissociate: **5** sever **8** distance **9** disengage, segregate **10** disconnect
dissoluble: **7** endable **9** divisible, separable, severable **10** terminable
dissolute: **3** lax **4** wild **5** loose **6** rakish, wanton, wicked **7** corrupt, immoral, lustful, raffish, wayward **8** depraved, uncurbed **9** abandoned, corrupted, indulgent, libertine, low-minded, on the take, reprobate, shameless, sybaritic **10** dissipated, lascivious, licentious, profligate
one: **4** rake, roué
dissolution: **3** end **5** decay, split **6** ending **7** divorce, parting, split-up **8** division
dissolve: **3** eat, end **4** fade, melt, ruin, thaw, void **5** annul, lysee, mix in, quash, sever **6** cancel, recess, repeal, soften, vanish **7** abolish, adjourn, crumble, defrost, destroy,

liquefy, liquify, shatter **8** abrogate, demolish, evanesce, fluidify **9** break down, decompose, disappear, evaporate, liquidate, terminate **10** deliquesce, invalidate
__ **dissolve:** **3** lap
dissolved: **4** gone **6** liquid
dissolving, remove by: **5** elute
dissonance: **5** noise **6** jangle, strife **7** discord **8** conflict **9** cacophony, disaccord, disparity, harshness **10** antagonism, contention, difference, disharmony, dissension, dissidence
dissonant: **5** harsh, noisy **6** atonal, off-key, unlike **7** grating, jarring, raucous **8** jangling, strident **9** anomalous, different, differing, divergent, irregular, out of tune, unmusical **10** cacophonic, discordant, discrepant, inharmonic
not ~: **5** tonal **7** melodic
dissuade: **3** cow **4** warn **5** daunt, deter **6** advise, dampen, reason **7** caution, prevent **8** dispirit **9** talk out of **10** discourage, dishearten, intimidate
dist. __: **4** atty.
distaff: **5** woman **6** female **8** maternal
distance: **3** gap, lap, way **4** span **5** range, reach, scope, space, width **6** extent, length, spread **7** breadth, compass, reserve, setting, stretch **8** coldness, coolness, interval **9** stiffness **10** dissociate, remoteness, separation
across: **5** width **7** breadth
around: **4** girt **5** girth
at a ~: **3** far, off **4** afar, away **5** apart **6** remote **7** far away **8** outlying
at a ~ from: **6** beyond
at a short ~: **5** anear
British ~ measure: **5** metre
close ~: **4** near
down: **5** depth
elbow-to-fingertip ~: **5** cubit
from the equator: **3** lat. **8** latitude
galactic ~: **4** lt. yr. **9** light year
go the ~: **4** last
keep one's ~: **4** shun, snub **5** evade, scorn, shirk, spurn **6** bypass, ignore, put off, rebuff, slight **7** disdain, dismiss, tune out **8** brush off, shrug off **9** disregard, pay no mind **10** disrespect, leave alone
long ~ line: **4** WATS
measure: **2** km **3** rod **4** mile, pace **5** block, meter, metre **6** fathom, league **7** furlong **9** kilometer
nautical ~: **6** fathom, league
prefix: **3** tel- **4** tele-
short ~: **3** hop **4** inch, step
__ **distance:** **3** at a **4** long **5** from a, go the
distant: **3** far, icy, shy **4** afar, away, cold, cool **5** aloof, apart, faint, other, stiff **6** far off, frigid, modest, remote, unlike, yonder **7** bashful, faraway, foreign, outside, removed, unequal, unknown **8** detached, far-flung, outlying, reserved, reticent, retiring, separate, solitary, taciturn **9** diffident, disparate, reclusive, unbending, withdrawn **10** insociable, out of range, out of reach, unagitated, unamicable, unfriendly, unsociable
combining form: **3** tel- **4** tele-, telo-
keep ~ from: **4** shun **5** avoid, skirt
least ~: **7** closest, nearest
less ~: **6** closer, nearer
more ~: **7** farther
most ~: **7** extreme **8** farthest, ultimate
distaste: **4** hate **6** hatred **8** aversion, contempt, loathing **9** antipathy, hostility, repulsion, revulsion **10** abhorrence, repellence, repugnance
cry of ~: **3** ack, ick, rot, ugh **4** bosh, yuck **5** yecch **7** rubbish
having ~ for: **8** averse to
distasteful: **4** icky, ugly, vile **5** nasty, seamy, yucky **6** bitter, odious **7** galling, hateful, insipid, painful **8** annoying, brackish, grievous, unsavory **9** offensive, repellant, repellent, repugnant, repulsive, revolting, thankless, unwelcome **10** unpleasant
distend: **4** puff **5** bloat, bulge, swell, widen **6** dilate, expand, fatten, puff up, pump up **7** balloon, enlarge, inflate **8** lengthen **9** intumesce
distended: **5** puffy, tumid **6** turgid **7** bulging, swollen
distention: **5** bulge **8** swelling **9** expansion, extension, inflation
distill: **4** brew, drip **6** desalt, filter, purify, refine **7** cut down, draw out, dribble, extract, ferment, trickle **8** boil down, condense, vaporize **9** evaporate **10** desalinate, desalinize
distillate: **7** essence, extract
distillation: **4** brew
product: **5** ester
distilled: **7** refined **9** alcoholic
distilled __: **5** water
distiller: **6** brewer **7** alembic
distinct: **4** fine **5** apart, clean, clear, exact, lucid, other, plain, sharp, vivid **6** cogent, limpid, marked, patent, single, strong, unique, unlike **7** audible, diverse, evident, express, graphic, legible, obvious, precise, several, unalike, variant, various **8** apparent, clean-cut, definite, discrete, explicit, manifest, palpable, readable, separate, specific **9** different, graphical, graspable, trenchant, unrelated **10** articulate, dissimilar, individual, noticeable, particular, pronounced, spelled out, well-marked
be ~: **8** stand out
combining form: **5** chori-
make less ~: **4** blur, fuzz
not ~: **3** dim **5** fuzzy **6** bleary
distinction: **4** fame, mark, name, note, rank **5** asset, flair, glory, honor, merit, shade, style, value, worth **6** credit, nicety, renown, repute, status **7** earmark, feature, laurels, quality **8** contrast, elegance, eminence, grandeur, prestige, subtlety **9** variation
distinctive: **4** rare **5** novel, sharp **6** proper, signal, unique **7** special **8** discrete, original, peculiar, separate, singular, uncommon
feature: **9** specialty
mark: **6** cachet
quality: **4** aura **5** aroma
distinctly: **8** markedly **9** decidedly, expressly
distinctness: **7** clarity **8** identity
distinguish: **3** see **4** know, spot, tell, view **5** judge, sight **6** define, descry, detect, notice, secern, select, set off, winnow **7** discern, make out, mark off, observe, sort out, specify **8** classify, contrast, estimate, identify, perceive, pinpoint, separate, set apart **9** recognize
between: **7** compare
oneself: **4** star **5** excel, shine
distinguishable: **5** clear, plain **7** evident, visible **8** definite, manifest **10** noticeable, well-marked
distinguished: **3** ace **4** high, star **5** famed, great, lofty, noble, noted **6** famous, signal, single **7** big-name, classic, eminent, honored, notable, special, unusual **8** esteemed, glorious, laureate, renowned, splendid, striking **9** memorable, prominent **10** celebrated, preeminent
be ~ (from): **6** differ
one: **3** VIP **5** great
Distinguished Gentleman, The (1992 film)
cast: Eddie Murphy, Sheryl Lee Ralph
distinguishing: **8** specific
feature: **5** trait **7** quality **9** specialty
distort: **3** lie **4** bias, skew, warp **5** alter, color, fudge, gnarl, screw, slant, twist, wrest **6** buckle, deform, doctor, garble, injure, mangle, squash, strain, wrench **7** falsify, phony up **8** misquote **9** prejudice
distorted: **3** wry **6** skewed, untrue **7** corrupt, crooked **9** grotesque, jaundiced, malformed
distortion: **3** lie **4** warp **5** slant **8** travesty **9** asymmetry, falsehood, hyperbole **10** aberration, caricature, contortion, corruption
distract: **5** mix up, upset **6** bemuse, divert, madden, rattle **7** unnerve **8** lead away **9** entertain, preoccupy
distracted: **4** lost, wild **7** worried **9** delirious, forgetful **10** distraught, distressed, hysterical
not ~: **6** intent **7** focused
distractedly: **5** madly **8** absently
distraction: **3** fun **5** feint, hobby **6** escape **7** pastime **10** recreation
drive to ~: **6** enrage, madden
distrait: **4** lost
distraught: **3** mad **6** pacing **7** frantic, worried **8** frenetic, frenzied **9** concerned, flustered, in a lather, perturbed, tormented, unscrewed **10** distracted, distressed, hysterical, irrational, nonplussed
distress: **3** ail, bug, irk, try, vex, woe **4** ache, bane, care, fear, fret, hurt, lack, need, pain, pang, rack, rend, rive, tire **5** agony, alarm, dolor, get to, gloom, grief, harry, hound, peeve, shake, shock, spook, tears, tense, trial, upset, worry, wound **6** affect, bother, dismay, grieve, harass, harrow, injure, injury, misery, needle, offend, ordeal, pester, pick on, plague, prey on, put out, sadden, sorrow, strain, strait **7** afflict, agitate, agonize, anguish, anxiety, bad luck, bedevil, concern, depress, malaise, oppress, sadness, shake up, tick off, torment, torture, travail, trouble, turmoil, weigh on **8** aggrieve, calamity, disquiet, exercise, exigence, exigency, hangover, hardship, hard time, irritate, unstring **9** adversity, aggravate, dejection, grievance, heartache, indigence, privation, suffering **10** affliction, bitterness, depression, desolation, difficulty, discomfort, heartbreak, heavy heart, loneliness, misfortune, woefulness
be in ~: **3** ail **4** ache **5** sweat
cause ~: **4** hurt
cause of ~: **4** bane
cry of ~: **2** oy **4** dear, help, oh no, oh oh, yowl
express ~: **4** moan, wail
one in ~: **6** damsel
signal: **3** SOS **5** flare **7** warning
distress __: **4** call **6** signal
distressed: **4** down, hurt **5** sorry, tense, tired, upset, wired, woful **6** afraid, pacing, woeful **7** anxious, doleful, frantic, in a stew, nervous, tearful, uptight, worried **8** downcast, fluttery, frenetic, frenzied, in a tizzy, wretched **9** afflicted, all torn up, bummed-out, concerned, depressed, exercised, in a lather, miserable, perturbed, sniveling, strung out, tormented, up the wall **10** distracted, distraught
distressing: **3** bad **4** hard, sore **5** sharp, sorry, tight **6** bitter, severe **7** fearful, hurtful, onerous, painful, piteous, pitiful **8** dreadful, grievous, pathetic, poignant, pressing, shocking **9** sorrowful, vexatious **10** lamentable, pathetical
distribute: **4** cast, deal, dole, give, mete, sort **5** allot, divvy, group, issue, order, serve, share, split, strew **6** assign, assort, bestow, convey, deal in, deploy, divide, parcel, ration, spread **7** deal out, deliver, dish out, divvy up, dole out, hand out, mete out, pass out, portion, publish, radiate, scatter, slice up **8** allocate, classify, disburse, dispense, disperse, separate **9** apportion, broadcast, circulate, parcel out, partition, propagate **10** administer, categorize, measure out
distribution: **4** dole **5** issue, order **6** ration **7** dealing, mailing **8** delivery, disposal, dividend, division, grouping, handling, ordering **9** allotting, publicity
agency: **3** syn. **4** synd. **9** syndicate
center: **4** whse. **9** warehouse
combining form: **4** -nomy
distributor: **6** dealer, jobber **8** auto part
part: **5** rotor
district: **4** area, belt, land, ward, zone **5** local, place, tract **6** county,

locale, parish, region, sector 7 grounds, quarter, section 8 locality, location, precinct, province, vicinity 9 territory
ecclesiastical ~: 3 see 7 prelacy 9 bishopric 10 episcopacy
of a ~: 5 zonal 6 zonary
outlying ~: 4 burb
voting ~: 4 area, zone 6 canton, parish 8 district, precinct 9 territory
___ district: 7 low-rent
Distrito Federal city: 6 México
distrust: 5 doubt, qualm, query 7 suspect 8 bad vibes, mistrust, question, wariness 9 discredit, misgiving, nonbelief, pessimism, smell a rat, suspicion 10 skepticism
distrustful: 3 shy 4 wary 5 chary, leery 6 uneasy, unsure 7 cynical, dubious, fearful, guarded, jealous 8 cautious, doubting, hesitant 9 skeptical, uncertain 10 suspicious
disturb: 3 ail, bug, irk, jar, vex 4 fret, gall, jolt, move, muss, rend, rile, rock, roil 5 alarm, annoy, harry, mix up, peeve, rouse, roust, shake, shift, shock, tease, throw, touch, upset, worry 6 affect, arouse, badger, bother, dismay, excite, flurry, foul up, harass, heckle, jumble, mess up, molest, muddle, needle, nettle, noodge, offend, pester, plague, pother, put out, rattle, ruffle, whip up 7 afflict, agitate, concern, confuse, disrupt, fluster, perturb, provoke, shake up, shuffle, trouble, unnerve 8 convulse, exercise, irritate, mess with, psych out, unsettle, unstring 9 discomfit, incommode, interrupt, overwhelm 10 disarrange, discompose, disconcert
do not ~: 5 let be 10 leave alone
___ Disturb: 5 Do Not
disturbance: 3 row 4 flap, fray, fuss, riot, stir, to-do 5 brawl, furor, scene, shock, storm, upset, worry 6 bother, clamor, flurry, fracas, hoo-hah, hubbub, racket, ruckus, rumble, rumpus, squall, tumult, unrest, uproar 7 ferment, quarrel, rampage, scuffle, trouble, turmoil 8 brouhaha, disorder, upheaval, uprising
stop a ~: 5 quell
disturbing: 5 messy, scary, tight 6 bitter 8 grievous, terrible, untoward 9 agonizing, annoyance, confusing, harrowing, vexatious 10 aggressive, bothersome, burdensome, disruptive, petrifying, unsettling
disunion: 5 split 6 schism 7 divorce, rupture 8 division 9 dichotomy 10 detachment, separation
disunite: 4 part, rend 5 sever, split, untie 6 cleave, cut off, detach, divide, unlink 7 disjoin, disrupt, divorce, scatter, split up 8 alienate, break off, disjoint, dissever, estrange, fragment, separate, set apart, uncouple 9 disaffect, dismember, fall apart, interrupt, set at odds 10 disconnect
disunited: 5 split 10 disjointed
disunity: 4 feud 5 clash 6 breach, strife 7 discord, dispute, dissent, faction 8 argument, conflict, variance 10 contention
disuse: 7 neglect
fallen into ~: 5 passé
sign of ~: 6 cobweb
disused: 5 passé 8 obsolete, outmoded
dit: 3 dot 4 code
partner: 3 dah
ditali: 5 pasta 7 noodles
ditch: 3 pit, rut 4 cede, dike, drop, dump, hide, hole, jilt, junk, moat, sell, shed, shun 5 chuck, drain, forgo, gully, leave, scrap, yield 6 desert, forego, furrow, give up, groove, gullet, gulley, gutter, ravine, reject, trench, trough 7 abandon, channel, culvert, deep-six, discard, forfeit, forsake, foxhole, let go of, scuttle 8 forswear, get rid of, give up on, hand over, jettison, part with, throw out 9 cast aside, dispose of, eighty-six, foreswear, surrender, throw away 10 excavation, relinquish
defensive ~: 5 fosse
in Britain: 4 sike, syke
make a ~: 3 dig
side of a ~: 6 escarp
___-ditch: 4 last
Dith: 4 Pran
dither: 3 fit 4 flap, halt, stew 5 shake, tizzy, waver 6 lather, shiver, tumult 7 shudder, stagger, whiffle 8 disorder, fence-sit 9 commotion, confusion, vacillate 10 excitement, mill around
get into a ~: 4 fret, fuss, stew 5 sweat, worry 7 agonize
in a ~: 4 wild 10 bewildered
___ dither: 3 in a
Dithers, Mr.: 4 boss 6 Julius
creator: Chic Young
employee: 7 Dagwood 8 Bumstead
wife: 4 Cora
Ditka: 4 Mike
dits and dahs: 4 code 9 Morse code
ditto: 4 also, copy, mock, same 5 again, clone, mimic, Xerox 6 double, ectype, repeat 7 imitate, replica, the same 8 knockoff, likeness, likewise 9 duplicate, facsimile, imitation, photocopy, reiterate
relative: 3 etc.
Ditto!: 4 also 5 me too, so am I, so do I 6 agreed, I do too 8 likewise
ditty: 3 air 4 lilt, rime, song, tune 5 music, rhyme 6 ballad, jingle, number 7 lullaby
ditty ___: 3 bag
ditz: 5 flake, ninny 7 airhead, dingbat
ditzy: 5 giddy, goofy
diurnal: 5 daily 7 per diem 8 day-to-day, everyday 9 quotidian
more than ~: 5 horal
div.: 3 seg. 4 dept.
diva: 4 Alda 5 Melba, Moffo, Sills 6 artist, Callas, Norman, Peters, singer 7 actress, Tebaldi 8 Mitchell, musician, vocalist 9 Anna Moffo 10 coloratura, prima donna, Sutherland
accolade: 5 brava 6 encore
asset: 5 voice
performance: 4 aria, song 5 opera
see also opera, singer
___ Diva: 5 Casta
divagate: 5 stray 6 ramble 7 deviate, digress
divagation: 5 slant 10 digression, divergence
divan: 4 seat, sofa 5 couch 6 day bed, lounge, settee 7 council, ottoman, seating 9 davenport
dive: 3 bar, dip, pub 4 drop, dump, fall, jump, sink, slum, swim, zoom 5 dance, haunt, joint, lunge, pitch, slide, swoop, twist 6 gainer, go down, header, lounge, plunge, pounce, saloon, tavern, tumble 7 barroom, cutaway, decline, descend, descent, hangout, plummet, taproom 8 taphouse 9 belly flop, jackknife, nightclub, worsening 10 cannonball, restaurant, submersion
in: 5 begin, start
starter: 3 sky 4 nose
take a ~: 4 lose, tank
___ dive: 4 back, nose, swan 5 crash, fancy, take a
diver: 3 auk 4 loon 5 grebe 7 frogman 8 Louganis
combining form: 4 -dyta 5 -dytes
danger: 5 moray, shark
destination: 4 reef 5 coral, wreck
gear: 3 air 4 tank 5 scuba 7 goggles
milieu: 3 sea 5 ocean
Navy ~: 4 Seal
pearl ~: 3 ama
perfect score for a ~: 3 ten
quest: 5 pearl
starter: 3 sky 4 hell
weapon: 5 spear
___ diver: 3 sky 4 skin 5 pearl, scuba
diverge: 4 bend, fork, skew, turn, vary 5 slant, split, stray 6 branch, change, differ, ramble, spread, swerve, wander 7 deviate, digress, dissent, radiate, scatter 8 conflict, contrast, disagree, separate 9 bifurcate
divergence: 3 gap 4 bend, fork, skew 5 break, slant, split 6 detour, schism 7 parting, turning, variety, veering 8 contrast, variance 9 departure, deviation, disparity, gradation, otherness, radiation, variation 10 aberration, alteration, deflection, difference, digression, divagation, separation, unlikeness
divergent: 3 odd, off 4 eery 5 eerie, other, weird 6 atypic, freaky, offkey, quirky, unlike 7 bizarre, deviant, offbeat, strange, unalike, unequal, unusual, variant, various 8 aberrant, abnormal, atypical, freakish, peculiar, separate, uncommon 9 anomalous, deviating, different, differing, disparate, dissonant, eccentric, factional, fantastic, irregular, unnatural, unsimilar, untypical 10 discordant, discrepant, dissimilar, nonuniform, poles apart, unorthodox
divers: 6 sundry, varied 7 several, various 8 assorted
diverse: 4 mixt 5 mixed, other 6 motley, sundry, unlike, varied 7 several, unalike, unequal, variant, various, varying 8 assorted, discrete, distinct, manifold, multiple, opposite, separate 9 different, disparate 10 dissimilar
combining form: 4 vari- 5 vario-
diversify: 3 mix 4 vary 5 alter 6 change, expand, modify 9 branch out, spread out, variegate
diversion: 3 fun 4 game, play 5 hobby, party, sport 6 change, detour, end run, laughs, relief 7 disport, pastime, turning, veering 8 interest, pleasure 9 amusement, avocation, departure, deviation, enjoyment, frivolity, variation 10 aberration, alteration, deflection, digression, recreation, red herring, regalement, relaxation
diversity: 5 range 6 medley 7 variety 8 contrast, mixed bag, variance 9 variation 10 assortment, difference, inequality, miscellany, unlikeness
divert: 4 turn, veer 5 alter, amuse, drain, shunt, steal 6 modify, occupy, please, regale, swerve, switch, tickle 7 beguile, deflect, delight, detract, disport, gladden, gratify, reroute, ward off 8 distract, draw away, interest, lead away, recreate, redirect 9 entertain, preoccupy, sidetrack, turn aside
diverting: 3 fun 4 rich 5 droll, funny, kicky, light, witty 9 laughable
divertissement: 10 recreation
divest: 3 rid, rob 4 bare, dump, lose, oust 5 strip 6 free of, remove, unload 7 deprive, sell off, strip of, take off 8 get rid of 9 liquidate 10 dispossess
divested: 4 bare 5 naked 6 bereft
divide: 3 cut, gap 4 chop, fork, mete, part, rend, sort, tear 5 allot, cross, cut up, grade, group, halve, order, sever, share, slice, split 6 assort, bisect, cleave, cut off, detach, parcel, ration, schism, sunder, unlink 7 arrange, break up, compute, deal out, dish out, disjoin, dole out, hand out, portion, prorate, quarrel, rope off, rupture, scatter, slice up, split up 8 alienate, allocate, break off, classify, cleavage, disburse, dispense, disperse, disunite, estrange, polarize, separate, set apart, shell out, uncouple 9 apportion, calculate, disaffect, interrupt, intersect, intervene, parcel out, partition, punctuate, segregate, set at odds 10 categorize, disconnect, distribute, measure out
in four: 7 quarter
in three: 7 trisect
in two: 4 half 5 halve 6 bisect
divided: 4 torn 5 apart, in two, split 7 asunder 8 separate 9 sectional 10 fractional
combining form: 3 -fid 5 fissi- 6 -tomous
not ~: 5 whole 6 entire
...divided against itself ___ stand: 6 cannot
Divided Self, The
author: R.D. Laing
dividend: 3 cut 4 perk, plum 5 bonus, extra, gravy, prize, share

6 income, return, reward 7 portion, premium, revenue 8 addition, interest 9 allotment
divider: 3 net 4 wall 5 fence, panel 6 screen 9 partition
nasal ~: 6 septum
divination: 4 sign 5 magic 6 augury, oracle 7 sorcery 8 prophecy 9 intuition 10 necromancy, prediction
Chinese book of ~: 6 I Ching
combining form: 5 -mancy
divinator: 6 oracle 7 prophet
divine: 4 abbé, holy, keen, look, tell 5 blest, dowse, godly, guess, sense, tasty 6 cleric, deific, dreamy, far-out, fathom, intuit, lovely, priest, sacred, scared, solemn, toothy 7 angelic, blessed, deistic, exalted, godlike, predict, saintly, supreme 8 almighty, anointed, beatific, blissful, ethereal, foretell, perceive, preacher, prophesy, theistic 9 ambrosial, angelical, beautiful, celestial, delicious, ineffable, nectarous, palatable, religious, spiritual, succulent, unearthly 10 appetizing, delectable, omnipotent, omniscient, sanctified, superhuman
one: 3 god 5 deity 7 goddess
spirit: 5 numen
will: 4 fate 7 destiny
see also wonderful
divine __: 5 right
Divine __, The: 5 Miss M 6 Comedy
Divine Comedies
author: James Merrill
Divine Comedy, The: 4 epic, epos, poem
author: Dante
character: 4 Adam, Cato, Nino 5 Aruns, Capet, Dante, Guido, Jason, Manto, Minos, Paolo, Sapia, Sinon 6 Charon, Chiron, Nessus, Nimrod, St. Lucy, Virgil 7 Cheiron 8 Beatrice
Divine Elegies
poet: Rainer Maria Rilke
Divine Milieu, The
author: Pierre Teilhard de Chardin
Divine Miss M, The: 5 Bette 6 Midler
Divine Poems
author: John Donne
diviner: 4 seer 5 augur, magus, sibyl 6 oracle, wizard 7 aruspex, prophet 8 Chaldean, haruspex, magician, sorcerer 9 predictor 10 astrologer, forecaster, soothsayer
Divine Secrets of the Ya-Ya Sisterhood (2002 film)
cast: Sandra Bullock, Ellen Burstyn, Ashley Judd
diving: 5 sport 10 water sport
area: 4 pool
bird: 3 auk 4 coot, loon 5 grebe, murre, ousel, ouzel, solan 6 auklet, dipper
duck: 5 scaup 6 scoter 7 pochard, scooter 9 goldeneye, merganser
position: 4 tuck
starter: 3 sky
diving __: 4 bell, boat, duck, suit 5 board
__ diving: 3 sky 4 skin 5 scuba
diving-bell inventor: 4 Eads
diving-suit material: 5 latex
divining: 5 vatic 8 oracular
combining form: 6 -mantic

rod: 4 twig 6 dowser
rod shape: 3 wye
use a ~ rod: 5 dowse
divinity: 3 god 5 candy, deity 7 goddess, godhood 8 holiness 9 godliness
__ divinum: 3 jus
divisible: 10 dissoluble
by two: 4 even
not ~ by two: 3 odd
division: 3 arm, cut, gap 4 army, link, part, rift, sect, side, unit, ward, wing 5 break, class, corps, crack, force, piece, round, share, slice, split, squad, stage 6 border, branch, bureau, detail, legion, member, parcel, ration, region, schism, sector 7 bracket, carving, chapter, divorce, fission, parting, phalanx, portion, rending, rupture, section, segment, species 8 boundary, breaking, category, cleavage, disunion, fraction, grouping, precinct, province, variance 9 affiliate, bisection, detaching, dichotomy, partition 10 department, detachment, disruption, disuniting, proportion, separation
word: 4 into
__ division: 4 long 5 first, short
division of __: 5 labor
__ d'Ivoire: 4 Cote
divorce: 5 sever, split 6 detach, sunder 7 breakup, disjoin, rupture 8 disunion, disunite, division, separate 10 detachment, disconnect, separation
divorced: 5 apart, split, unwed 6 single 9 unmarried
divorcée: 2 ex
__ Divorcee, The: 3 Gay
divot: 3 sod 4 turf
divulge: 3 air, say 4 bare, blab, leak, show, talk, tell 5 admit, break, let on, spill, utter, voice 6 betray, expose, impart, let out, relate, reveal, unfold, unmask, unveil 7 confess, declare, exhibit, lay bare, let slip, mention, uncover 8 announce, disclose, give away, proclaim, unburden 9 broadcast, make known 10 make public
divulgence: 6 exposé 9 admission 10 confession, disclosure, revelation, unbosoming
divulse: 4 tear
divvy up: 4 deal, give 5 allot, halve, issue, share, split 6 ration 7 deal out, dish out, dole out, hand out, mete out, pass out, portion 8 allocate, disburse, dispense, disperse 9 apportion, parcel out, partition 10 distribute, measure out
Dix: 4 Fort 7 Dorothy, Richard 8 Dorothea
Dixie: 4 toon 5 mouse, South 6 Carter 9 Deep South
ender: 4 land
fighter: 3 reb
once: 3 CSA
pronoun: 4 y'all
Dixie __: 3 Cup 4 Land 6 Chicks
__ Dixie: 7 whistle
__-Dixie: 4 Winn
Dixiebelles
song: Papa Joe's (1963)
Dixie Cups
song: Chapel of Love (1964)

Dixieland: 4 jazz 5 music
dance: 5 stomp
instrument: 5 banjo 7 trumpet
__ dixit: 4 ipse
Dixon: 4 Ivan 5 Donna, Jeane
colleague: 5 Cayce, Mason
Dixon, Donna: 7 actress
spouse: Dan Aykroyd
__-Dixon line: 5 Mason
dizain: 4 poem
dizzy: 4 gaga, hazy, zany 5 aswim, dazed, faint, flaky, giddy, inane, light, mix up, queer, rocky, shaky, silly, tipsy, woozy 6 addled, flakey, giggly, groggy, punchy, wabbly, wobbly 7 flighty, foolish, fuddled, muddled, reeling 8 confused, skittish, unstable, unsteady, whirling 9 befuddled, slaphappy, squeamish 10 bewildered, staggering, weak-minded
be ~: 4 reel, swim 5 swirl, whirl
Dizzy: 4 Dean 9 Gillespie
Dizzy (1969 song)
artist: Tommy Roe
dizzying: 5 heady, steep 10 immoderate, inordinate
designs: 5 op art
itinerary: 6 flurry
DJ: 7 spinner 10 disc jockey
need: 2 CD, LP 3 amp, mic 4 mike 5 album 10 microphone
D.J. __ Jeff: 5 Jazzy
Djakarta: 4 city, town 7 capital
locale: 9 Indonesia
Djebar, Assia: 6 writer 8 Algerian
djellabah: 4 robe
wearer: 4 Arab
Djibouti: 4 city, town 6 nation 7 capital, country
capital: 8 Djibouti
group: 10 Arab League
gulf east of ~: 4 Aden
language: 6 Somali
locale: 6 Africa
money: 5 franc
neighbor: 7 Eritrea, Somalia 8 Ethiopia
people: 4 Afar, Issa 6 Somali 7 Danakil
D.J. Jazzy Jeff: 6 rapper, singer
djun djun: 4 drum
origin: 6 Africa
DLO org.: 4 USPS
__-D.M.C.: 3 Run
Dmitri: 7 Tiomkin 9 Karamazov, Mendeleev
DMV document: 3 lic. 7 license
Dmytryk: 6 Edward
DMZ, part of: 4 zone
DNA
ender: 3 ase
part of ~: 4 acid 5 deoxy
pioneer: 5 Crick 6 Watson
segment: 3 ATP 4 exon, gene 5 helix
DNA __: 4 test
__ DNA: 4 junk
Dnepr: 5 river
city on the ~: 4 Kiev 5 Orsha
locale: 6 Russia 7 Belarus, Ukraine
river to the ~: 5 Desna 6 Pripet 8 Berezina
Dnestr
city on the ~: 5 Odesa 6 Odessa

locale: 6 Russia
Dnieper: 5 river
city on the ~: 4 Kiev 5 Orsha
locale: 6 Russia 7 Belarus, Ukraine
river to the ~: 5 Desna 6 Pripet 8 Berezina
Dniester: 5 river
city on the ~: 5 Odesa 6 Odessa
locale: 6 Russia
do: 3 act, ape, con 4 ball, bash, bilk, coif, copy, dupe, fare, fest, fete, gala, hoax, note, play, suit, tour, verb, wage, work 5 adapt, avail, cause, cheat, cover, event, get by, party, see to, serve, solve, trick, visit 6 act for, affair, behave, create, effect, finish, fleece, fulfil, look to, render, take on, wrap up 7 achieve, arrange, deceive, defraud, execute, explore, fulfill, jubilee, operate, perform, portray, prepare, produce, pull off, realize, resolve, satisfy, suffice, swindle, two-time, work out 8 attend to, carry our, carry out, coiffure, complete, conclude, decipher, flimflam, function, get along, ponytail, practice, transact, travel in 9 festivity, figure out, hairstyle, reception 10 accomplish, effectuate, feather cut, perpetrate, rejuvenate
again: 6 repeat 7 run over 8 practice 9 reiterate
agree to ~: 6 take on 9 undertake
all right: 3 win 6 hack it, make it, manage, thrive 7 make out, prevail, prosper, triumph 8 flourish, go places, make good
a number: 4 sing 5 croon 6 warble 8 vocalize
a number on: 4 bilk, dupe, gull, rook 5 cheat, shaft 6 defame, delude, take in 7 deceive, defraud, swindle 8 flimflam
away with: 3 ban, end, rid 4 kill, slay, stop 5 purge, scrap, scrub 6 efface, murder, remove, uproot 7 abolish, obviate, root out 8 demolish, dissolve, get rid of 9 eliminate, eradicate, liquidate, slaughter 10 put an end to
can't ~ without: 4 need
fail to ~: 4 miss, omit, shun, skip, snub 5 avoid, evade, scorn, shirk, spurn 6 bypass, eschew, forget, ignore, pass by 7 let pass, neglect 8 brush off, let slide, overlook, pass over 9 disregard, gloss over
for: 4 tend 5 serve 7 cater to 8 minister
have to ~ with: 6 belong, regard, relate 7 concern 9 as regards
how do you ~: 2 hi 4 ciao, hail 5 aloha, hello, howdy 7 bon jour, welcome
like: 4 echo 5 mimic 6 follow 7 imitate 8 simulate
make ~: 3 eke 4 cope 5 adapt, get by 6 eke out, manage 7 survive 8 get along, scrape by 9 just get by
make ~ with: 3 use
nothing: 3 sit, veg 4 idle, laze, loll 5 sit by, slack 6 rest up

7 slacken 8 lallygag
nothing about: 5 sit on 6 stifle 7 squelch 8 suppress, withhold
offhand: 5 ad-lib 6 wing it 7 dash off
old-style: 4 dost
one's utmost: 3 aim, try, vie 4 moil, push, toil 5 essay, fight, labor, sweat 6 strain, tackle, take on 7 attempt, compete, contend 8 bear down, endeavor, go all out, scramble, shoot for, struggle 10 go for broke, go the limit
on one's own: 5 offer 6 enlist, sign up 7 pitch in, proffer, recruit, stand up, venture 9 undertake 10 put forward
out of: 3 con, rob 5 steal
over: 6 repeat, replay 7 iterate, remodel 8 rehearse 9 replicate 10 redecorate
perfectly: 3 ace 4 nail
preceders: 4 la ti
repeatedly: 5 drill
say I ~: 5 marry 10 get hitched, tie the knot
something: 3 act
things to ~: 6 agenda
up: 3 tie 4 lace, wrap 6 clothe, fasten 8 decorate, emblazon 9 embellish, refurbish 10 rejuvenate
voraciously: 6 devour
well: 3 ace 5 excel 6 make it, thrive 7 make out, prosper 8 flourish, hit it big, make good
what one can: 3 try 6 strive 7 attempt, have a go, venture 9 have a go at, have a shot, have a stab 10 have a whack
without: 4 need 5 forgo, spare 6 forego 7 abstain, refrain 8 keep from
wrong: 3 err, sin 10 transgress
do __: 3 for 4 over, to a T, with 5 or die
do __ burn: 5 a slow
do __ on: 4 a job
do __ T: 3 to a
do __ turn: 5 a good
do __ with: 4 away
do-__: 3 all, rag 4 good, re-mi, si-do 5 or-die 6 gooder 7 nothing
__ do: 4 make
__-do: 3 can 4 do-si 7 derring
Do __: 4 Re Mi
Do __!: 4 tell
Do __ a Waltz?: 5 I Hear
Do __ Believe in Magic: 3 You
Do __ Diddy Diddy: 3 Wah
Do __ gently...: 5 not go
Do __ others...: 4 unto
Do __ say...: 3 as I
Do __ to eat a peach?: 5 I dare
__ Do: 4 But I 5 No Can
D.O.A. (1950 film)
cast: Edmond O'Brien
D.O.A. (1988 film)
cast: Randy Quaid, Meg Ryan
doable: 4 easy 6 likely, viable 8 credible, feasible, possible, workable 9 plausible, potential, practical 10 achievable, attainable, imaginable
Doak: 6 Walker
Doakes: 3 Joe
do-all: 8 factotum, handyman 9 man Friday 10 girl Friday
__ do anything better...: 4 I can
__ Doats: 6 Mairzy
DOB: 4 stat.
dobbin: 5 horse, mount 6 equine 9 farm horse
Dobbs Ferry college: 5 Mercy
Dobbs, Lou: 6 anchor 8 reporter 10 newscaster
network: 3 CNN
Doberman Pinscher: 3 dog 5 canid 6 canine
Dobie: 4 Gray 6 Gillis
Döblin, Alfred: 6 German, writer
Dobro: 6 guitar, string
dobson: 3 fly
Dobson: 5 Kevin
Doby, Larry: 6 Indian 10 outfielder
Dobyns, Stephen: 6 writer
doc
see doctor
doc.: 3 lic. 4 cert. 6 certif.
Doc: 5 Adams, dwarf 6 Savage 8 Cheatham, Holliday 10 Severinsen
colleague: ***see*** dwarf
friend: 5 Wyatt
__ Doc Duvalier: 4 Papa
docent: 5 guide 8 lecturer
Doc Hollywood (1991 film)
cast: Bridget Fonda, Michael J. Fox, Barnard Hughes, Julie Warner
Doc Horne
author: George Ade
docile: 4 easy, meek, mild, soft, tame 5 lowly, mousy, quiet 6 broken, gentle, mellow, mousey, pliant 7 dutiful, orderly, passive, pliable, subdued, trained 8 amenable, lamblike, obedient, resigned, sheepish, yielding 9 adaptable, compliant, easygoing, tractable 10 manageable, submissive
one: 5 sheep
docility: 8 humility 10 submission
dock: 3 top 4 clip, fine, land, moor, pare, pier, port, quay, slip, trim 5 berth, jetty, levee, lieup, prune, put in, tie up, wharf 6 anchor, deduct, harbor, hook up, link up, marina 7 harbour, landing, shorten 8 penalize 9 anchorage 10 waterfront
crane: 5 davit
do ~ work: 4 lade
ender: 3 age 4 hand, side, yard 6 worker
fitting: 5 cleat
leave the ~: 4 sail 8 shove off
submarine ~: 3 pen
support: 4 pile
__ dock: 3 dry 7 loading
docked, not: 4 asea 5 at sea
docket: 4 card, file, list 5 index 6 agenda, ticket 7 program 8 calendar, schedule 9 timetable
detail: 4 item 5 trial
word: 6 People, versus
Dockstader: 3 Lew
dockworker: 5 lader
org.: 3 ILA
doctor: 2 GP, MD 3 fix, rig, vet 4 cook, cure, edit, heal, mend 5 alter, amend, color, fix up, fudge, medic, taint, treat 6 adjust, deacon, garble, healer, intern, juggle, medico, modify, remedy, repair, revise, tamper 7 correct, distort, falsify, interne, patch up, rectify, retouch, surgeon, touch up 8 graduate, medicate, minister, overhaul, sawbones 9 internist, physician 10 specialist, tamper with
advice: 4 rest 5 relax
animal ~: 3 DVM, vet
assistant: 2 RN 3 LPN 5 nurse
assn.: 3 HMO
baby ~ for short: 2 OB
bk.: 3 PDR
circuit: 6 rounds
device: 5 pager 6 beeper
display: 6 degree
disreputable ~: 5 quack
ender: 3 ate
eye ~: 7 oculist
fam. ~: 2 GP
future ~ exam: 4 MCAT
GI ~: 5 medic
income: 3 fee
Islamic ~: 5 ulema
London ~ street: 6 Harley
need a ~: 3 ail
new ~: 6 intern 7 interne
office: 6 clinic
office call: 4 next
order: 2 Rx 4 dose, stat 5 say ah
org.: 3 AMA
picture: 4 X-ray
prescription: 4 drug 6 dosage
spin ~: 5 pr man
vessel: 5 ampul 6 ampule 7 ampoule
word for the ~: 3 aah
doctor __, The: 4 is in
__ doctor: 3 eye 4 foot, play, spin 5 juris, witch 6 family, script 7 medical
Doctor __: 3 Who 5 Spock 7 Detroit, Zhivago 9 Doolittle
doctoral
exam: 4 oral
presentation: 6 thesis
doctorate: 3 Ph.D. 6 degree
Doctor Detroit (1983 film)
cast: Dan Aykroyd, Donna Dixon, Howard Hesseman
Doctor! Doctor! (1984 song)
artist: Thompson Twins
Doctor Dolittle (1967 film)
cast: Richard Attenborough, Samantha Eggar, Rex Harrison, Anthony Newley
dog: 3 Jip
Doctor Dolittle (1998 film)
cast: Peter Boyle, Ossie Davis, Eddie Murphy, Oliver Platt
dog: 5 Lucky
tiger: 5 Jacob
doctored: 9 falsified
doctoring: 9 treatment 10 corruption
Doctor My Eyes (1972 song)
artist: Jackson Browne
Doctorow, E.L.: 6 writer
alma mater: Kenyon
first name: Edgar
work: Big as Life
Billy Bathgate
The Book of Daniel
City of God
Loon Lake
Ragtime
The Waterworks
Welcome to Hard Times
World's Fair
Doctor Pascal
author: Émile Zola
Doctor Sax
author: Jack Kerouac
Doctor's House, The
author: Ann Beattie
Doctor, The (1991 film)
cast: William Hurt, Christine Lahti, Elizabeth Perkins
__ Doctor, The: 4 Good 7 Country
Doctor Who
genre: sci-fi
network: BBC
Doctor Zhivago: 4 film 5 novel
author: Boris Pasternak
cast: Geraldine Chaplin, Julie Christie, Alec Guinness, Omar Sharif, Rod Steiger
character: 4 Lara, Nika, Yuri 5 Pasha, Tania, Tonia
director: David Lean
locale: 5 Urals 6 Russia
doctrinaire: 5 bigot 8 believer, pedantic 9 sectarian 10 pedantical
doctrinal: 8 dogmatic, orthodox 9 religious 10 dogmatical
doctrine: 3 ism 4 lore 5 axiom, canon, credo, creed, dogma, faith, tenet 6 belief, gospel, policy, theory 7 article, precept 8 position, religion, teaching 9 principle, teachings 10 conviction, philosophy, propaganda
combining form: 4 -logy
__ Doctrine: 4 Bush 5 Nixon 6 Monroe, Truman
document: 4 deed, form, page, show, text, writ 5 paper, prove, title 6 policy, record, report, script, ticket, verify 7 charter, itemize, license, writing 8 evidence 9 indenture 10 prospectus
addendum: 5 rider
auto ~: 5 lease, title
blank ~: 4 form
business ~: 3 rpt. 6 report
legal ~: 4 deed, will, writ 5 brief, lease 7 warrant
ownership ~: 4 deed 5 title
part: 6 clause
storage medium: 5 fiche 9 microfilm
travel ~: 4 visa 8 passport
__ Document: 4 The R
documentary: 4 film 5 drama, genre 6 report 10 production
documentation: 5 proof 6 papers, record 8 evidence
documented: 4 sure 5 valid 8 verified 10 historical
DOD
division: 3 USN 4 USAF, USMC
part of ~: 4 dept. 7 defense
place: 7 Cabinet
program: 3 SDI
VIP: 3 CNO
weapon: 3 ABM 4 ICBM
dodder: 4 limp 5 shake, weave 6 hobble, totter 7 tremble
doddering: 5 anile 6 infirm, senile 9 faltering, tottering, trembling
Dodecanese
island: 5 Leros 6 Patmos, Rhodes, Rhodos

dodeca-, one-third of: 5 tetra-
dodge: 4 duck, hoax, juke, lose, plot, ploy, ruse, scam, shun, veer, wile 5 avoid, cheat, elude, evade, feint, fence, fudge, hedge, lurch, parry, shake, shift, shirk, skirt, slack, trick, wince 6 bypass, device, dupery, escape, eschew, racket, recoil, refuse, scheme 7 abstain, con game, evasion, fend off, gimmick, quibble, slacken 8 artifice, flee from, get out of, intrigue, maneuver, shake off, sidestep, strategy, trickery 9 chicanery, deception, get around, hem and haw, pussyfoot, runaround, skip out on, stratagem 10 circumvent, equivocate, subterfuge
Dodge: 3 car 4 auto 10 automobile
model: 4 Colt, Dart, Neon, Omni 5 Aries, Aspen, Royal, Viper 6 DeLuxe, Lancer, Magnum, Mirada, Monaco, Polara, Seneca, Shadow, Sierra, Spirit 7 Avenger, Caliber, Caravan, Charger, Coronet, Durango, Dynasty, Journey, Matador, Phoenix, Pioneer, Stealth, Stratus, St. Regis, Swinger 8 Diplomat, Intrepid, Suburban, Wayfarer 9 Medallion 10 Challenger
partner: 6 Phelps
dodgeball: 4 game
Dodge City: 4 city, town
locale: 6 Kansas
marshal: 4 Earp
Dodge, Mary Mapes: 6 writer
work: Hans Brinker
dodger: 5 cheat 6 evader 7 escapee 8 deserter, swindler 9 throwaway
__ dodger: 5 draft
Dodger: 4 NLer 10 baseballer
great: 5 Reese, Vance, Wheat 6 Hodges, Koufax, Snider, Sutton 8 Drysdale, Robinson 9 Don Sutton, Gil Hodges, Zach Wheat 10 Campanella, Dazzy Vance, Duke Snider
Dodgers: 4 nine
home: 10 Los Angeles
old ~ field: 6 Ebbets
org.: 3 MLB, NLW
rival: *see* baseball team
dodging: 6 escape, shifty 7 evasion
dodgy: 7 evasive
Dodie: 5 Smith
dodo: 3 ass, nit 4 bird, dolt 5 dummy, dunce 7 airhead, dullard, old fogy 8 dumbbell, numskull 9 birdbrain, lamebrain, numbskull, simpleton 10 dunderhead, fuddy-duddy, nincompoop
Do Do Do
composer: George Gershwin, Ira Gershwin
Dodoma: 4 city, town 7 capital
locale: 8 Tanzania
Do do that ___...: 6 voodoo
Dodsworth: 5 novel
author: Sinclair Lewis
character: 3 Sam, Tub 4 Fran, Hurd, Ross 5 Brent, Emily, Matey
Dody: 7 Goodman
doe: 3 she 4 deer, hind 6 animal, female
ender: 4 skin
mate: 4 buck, hart, stag
offspring: 4 fawn
doe-__: 4 eyed
Doe: 4 Jane, John
Doe, a ___...: 4 deer
Doe, Jane: 5 woman 6 female
Doe, John: 3 man 4 male
doer: 6 dynamo, worker 7 hustler 8 achiever, activist, effector, go-getter, live wire, operator
good-deed ~: 4 hero 7 heroine
starter: 4 evil 5 wrong
suffix: 3 -ist 4 -ator
Doerr, Bobby: 6 Red Sox 10 baseballer
Does __, or doesn't...: 3 she
Does Anybody Really Know What Time It Is? (1970 song)
artist: Chicago
__ does it: 4 easy, that
__ Does It Better: 6 Nobody
doeskin: 7 leather
__ Doesn't Live Here Anymore: 5 Alice
Doesn't Really Matter (2000 song)
artist: Janet Jackson
Does the Spearmint ___...: 4 lose
Does Your Chewing Gum... (1961 song)
artist: Lonnie Donegan
__-d'oeuvre: 4 chef
do-fa filler: 4 re mi
doff: 3 tip 4 shed 5 unhat 6 remove 7 discard, take off, undress 8 get out of
opposite: 3 don
the cap to: 5 greet 6 salute
__ Do Fools Fall in Love: 3 Why
__ do for now!: 4 It'll
dog: 3 cur, Lab, mut, nag, pet, pug, pup, tag 4 chow, Fido, flop, foot, mutt, peke, puli, tail 5 boxer, canid, chase, corgi, dance, dhole, dingo, feist, haunt, hound, husky, knave, pooch, puppy, spitz, stalk, tease, track, trail, worry 6 animal, bad guy, barker, beagle, borzoi, bother, bowwow, briard, canine, collie, follow, harass, heeler, hunter, kelpie, kuvasz, mammal, Nipper, pester, plague, poodle, pursue, saluki, setter, shadow, vizsla 7 basenji, bulldog, courser, harrier, lowchen, Maltese, mastiff, mongrel, pit bull, pointer, samoyed, sheltie, shih tzu, spaniel, terrier, tootsie, whippet 8 alsatian, Brittany, chow chow, cockapoo, elkhound, foxhound, Havanese, house pet, keeshond, komondor, papillon, run after, shepherd, shiba inu, springer 9 Chihuahua, dachshund, Dalmatian, gazehound, great Dane, greyhound, Lhasa apso, Marmaduke, Pekingese, persecute, retriever, schnauzer, track down 10 bloodhound, fox terrier, otterhound, Pomeranian, rottweiler, schipperke, weimaraner, Welsh corgi 14 wolfhound akita
astronomical ~: 5 Canis
baby ~: 3 pup 5 puppy
bad ~: 5 biter
bane: 4 flea, lice 5 mange
bird ~: 5 hound, scout
black-tongued ~: 4 chow
breed: 3 Lab, pug 4 chow, peke, puli 5 akita, boxer, corgi, spitz 6 beagle, borzoi, briard, collie, kuvasz, poodle, saluki, vizsla 7 basenji, bulldog, harrier, lowchen, Maltese, mastiff, pit bull, pointer, samoyed, Shar-Pei, sheltie, shih tzu, terrier, whippet 8 Brittany, chow chow, elkhound, foxhound, Havanese, keeshond, komondor, papillon, shiba inu 9 Chihuahua, dachshund, Dalmatian, great Dane, greyhound, Lhasa apso, Pekingese, schnauzer 10 bloodhound, fox terrier, otterhound, Pomeranian, rottweiler, schipperke, weimaraner, Welsh corgi
breeder org.: 3 AKC
brush the ~: 5 groom
chain: 5 leash
combining form: 3 cyn- 4 cyno-
command: 3 beg, sic, sit 4 come, heel, mush 5 shake, sic 'em, sit up, speak 8 roll over
curly-tailed ~: 5 Akita
doc: 3 vet, VMD
document: 3 lic. 7 license
drink like a ~: 5 lap up
ender: 3 ear, leg, nap 4 bane, cart, face, fish, gone, sled, trot, wood 5 berry, fight, house, tooth, watch 7 catcher
feat: 5 trick
fennel: 4 weed
food: 6 kibble
genus: 5 canis
greet a ~: 3 pat
hot ~: 3 ham 5 frank, huzza, weeny 6 hoorah, hooray, hurrah, hurray, huzzah 10 grandstand
incite a ~: 3 sic
it: 3 lag, run 4 loaf 5 shirk 7 goof off 9 goldbrick
it, in Britain: 5 sculk, skulk
junkyard ~: 3 cur 4 mutt 5 biter 7 mongrel 10 crossbreed
lap ~: 3 pom 4 peke 6 Yorkie 7 Shih Tzu 9 Pekingese 10 Pomeranian
like a ~: 5 loyal
like a junkyard ~: 3 bad 4 ugly 5 dirty, mangy 7 lowdown, scruffy, vicious 8 churlish 9 dangerous 10 despicable, ill-natured
like a mad ~: 5 rabid
like a ~ tail: 4 awag
like some ~ ears: 5 loppy 6 droopy
name: 3 Rex 4 Fido, Shep, Spot 5 Rover
one-third of a ~ name: 3 Rin
owner shout: 4 here
paddle: 4 swim
part of a ~ tongue: 5 lytta
place: 3 lap
prairie ~: 6 animal, mammal, rodent
presidential ~: 3 Her, Him 4 Fala
put on the ~: 6 flaunt 7 show off 9 put on airs
red ~ in football: 5 blitz
relative: 6 corsac
retrieval: 5 stick
reward: 3 pat
river for which a ~ was named: 4 Aire
salty ~: 6 sailor 7 jack tar
sea ~: 3 gob, tar 4 salt 6 sailor 7 brigand, jack tar, mariner 9 buccaneer
sitter: 6 kennel
snack: 4 bone
sound: 3 arf, grr, yip 4 bark, gnar, woof 5 whine 6 bow-wow
starter: 3 fog, hot, sun 4 bird, bull, fire, hang 5 chili, sheep, under, watch
Stephen Foster ~: 4 Tray
stray ~: 3 mut 4 mutt
tag: 2 ID 7 license
tag wearer: 2 GI
top ~: 4 boss, exec, head, jefe, king, star 5 champ, first, Mr. Big, ruler 6 bigwig, gerent, honcho, leader, master, winner 7 captain, headman, manager, premier 8 big wheel, brass hat, cardinal, champion, director, foremost, governor, higher-up, kingfish, official, overseer, superior 9 authority, big cheese, commander, executive, key player, number one, personage, president, principal, sovereign 10 supervisor
walking the ~: 5 chore
walk like a ~: 3 pad
water ~: 6 sailor 7 jack tar
wild ~: 5 dhole, dingo 6 coyote, jackal
with a wavy white coat: 6 kuvasz
without papers: 3 mut 4 mutt
work like a ~: 4 toil 8 struggle
see also canine
dog __: 3 fox, tag 4 chew, days, show, sled 5 tooth 6 collar, paddle 7 biscuit
dog __ manger: 5 in the
dog-__: 3 day, ear 4 poor 5 cheap, eared, tired 6 paddle, walker
dog-__-dog: 3 eat
__ dog: 3 cur, gun, hot, lap, red, sea, top, toy 4 bird, cant, coon, corn, moon, seal, sled, wolf 5 chili, devil, guard, guide, hound, puppy, salty, stray, water 6 attack, police, yellow 7 herding, prairie
__ dog!: 3 Bad 4 Good
__ Dog: 4 Bird, Lad a 5 Great, Hound, Stray
dog-and-__ show: 4 pony
__ Dog and Glory: 3 Mad
dog ate my homework, the: 5 alibi
dogbane: 5 plant
family shrub: 7 karanda 8 oleander 10 frangipani
tree: 7 karanda
Dog Barking at the Moon
painter: Joan Miró
dogcatcher's catch: 5 stray
__ Dog Chow: 6 Purina
dog-collar attachment: 5 ID tag
__-dog contract: 6 yellow
Dog Day Afternoon (1975 film)
cast: John Cazale, Charles Durning, Al Pacino
character: 3 Sal 4 Leon
director: Sidney Lumet
dog days: 6 summer
forecast: 3 hot 5 humid
month: 3 Aug. 6 August
dog-ear: 4 bend, fold 5 crimp 6 crease 8 bookmark, fold over

dog-eared: **4** worn **5** ratty **10** threadbare
dog-eat-dog: **8** pitiless, ruthless **9** cutthroat, merciless, unpitying
dogface: **2** GI **3** pvt. **5** grunt **7** private
dogfight expert: **3** ace
dogfish: **4** huss **6** bowfin
dog food: **4** Alpo, Iams, Ken-L **5** Nutro, Rival **6** Purina **7** Kibbles **8** Eukanuba
DO
Dogg: **4** Nate **5** Snoop
genre: **3** rap
dogged: **4** grim **6** gritty, wilful **7** patient, willful **8** obsessed, perverse, resolute, stubborn, untiring **9** impliable, insistent, obstinate, tenacious, unbending **10** determined, hard-bitten, inflexible, persistent, relentless, undeterred, unflagging
doggedly: **4** hard **6** keenly
doggedness: **4** grit **5** spunk **8** tenacity **9** constancy, fixedness
__-dogger: **3** hot
doggerel: **4** rime **5** rhyme, verse **6** poetry
doggie
catcher: **5** riata
doggone: **4** dang, darn, heck, rats **5** nerts, nertz **6** dad-gum
it: **4** darn, drat, rats **5** shoot
doggy: **3** pup **5** pooch, puppy **8** woof-woof
doggy bag bits: **4** orts
__ Doggy Dogg: **5** Snoop
__ dog has his day: **5** every
doghouse: **6** kennel
dogie: **3** cow **4** calf, waif **5** stray **6** estray
call: **3** maa
catcher: **4** rope **5** lasso, noose, reata, roper **6** lariat
dog in the __: **6** manger
dogleg: **4** bend **5** angle, crook
dog-license org.: **5** ASPCA
doglike scavenger: **5** hyena **6** hyaena
dog lover, name meaning: **6** Connor
dogma: **3** ism **5** canon, creed, faith, tenet **6** belief, dictum, gospel, tenets **7** precept **8** doctrine, ideology **9** principle, teachings **10** conviction
Dogma (1999 film)
cast: Ben Affleck, Matt Damon, Linda Fiorentino, Alan Rickman
dogmatic: **6** narrow **8** arrogant, despotic, orthodox, reasoned, unerring **9** arbitrary, canonical, doctrinal, fanatical, imperious, obstinate, pigheaded, sectarian **10** bullheaded, despotical, peremptory, tyrannical
dogmatist: **8** believer **9** sectarian
__ Dog Night: **5** Three
Dog of Flanders, A
author: Ouida
Dogon home: **4** Mali **6** Africa
Dogpatch: **4** town **6** hamlet
adjective: **3** Li'l
creator: Al Capp
dad: **3** paw
expletive: **4** dang
possessive: **4** ourn
resident: **5** Abner **8** Daisy Mae
sufficient, in ~: **4** enuf, nuff
verb: **3** git
dog racing: **5** sport
dogs (advertising/products):
Beauty (Barbie)
Bingo (Cracker Jack)
Dinky (Taco Bell)
Ginger (Barbie)
McGruff (crime prevention)
Newton (Maytag)
Nipper (RCA)
Seadog (Cap'n Crunch)
Spuds MacKenzie (Budweiser)
Tige (Buster Brown)
Wags (Barbie)
dogs (comics):
Ace (Batman)
Andy (Mark Trail)
Barfy (The Family Circus)
Beauregard (Pogo)
Bitsy (Marvin)
Buck (The Gumps)
Daisy (Blondie)
Dawg (Hi and Lois)
Dogbert (Dilbert)
Dollar (Richie Rich)
Earl (Mutts)
Electra (Cathy)
Fifi (Bringing Up Father)
Fifi (Minnie Mouse)
Flip (Happy Hooligan)
Fuzz (Ziggy)
Grimmy (Mother Goose and Grimm)
Hot Dog (Jughead)
Kewpie (The Born Loser)
Killer (All Dogs Go to Heaven)
Krypto (Superman)
Marmaduke
Odie (Garfield)
Offisa Pupp (Krazy Kat)
Ol' Bullet (Snuffy Smith)
Otto (Beetle Bailey)
Poochie (Nancy)
Pretzel (Bringing Up Father)
Pudgy (Betty Boop)
Queenie (Dondi)
Roscoe (Pickles)
Rowdy (One Big Happy)
Ruff (Dennis the Menace)
Sam (The Family Circus)
Sandy (Little Orphan Annie)
Slivers (Little Nemo)
Smiley (Hazel)
Snert (Hagar the Horrible)
Spot (Boner's Ark)
Woofie (Mutts)
Zero (Little Annie Rooney)
dogs (films):
Alfie (Serpico)
Algonquin (Elvira, Mistress of the Dark)
Andromeda (The Parent Trap)
Asta (The Thin Man)
Attila (Phenomenon)
Barney (Gremlins)
Beau (WarGames)
Betsy (Bowfinger)
Bix (All of Me)
Blue (Cool Hand Luke)
Boomer (Independence Day)
Brinkley (You've Got Mail)
Bruiser (Legally Blonde)
Brutus (The Invisible Man's Revenge)
Bucky Boy (Cat on a Hot Tin Roof)
Buddy (Regarding Henry)
Buster (Nutty Professor II)
Butkus (Rocky)
Caesar (Our Man Flint)
Calico (With Six You Get Eggroll)
Carface (All Dogs Go To Heaven)
Chance (The Incredible Journey)
Charlie (All Dogs Go to Heaven)
Charlie (The Absent Minded Professor)
Charlie (The Final Countdown)
Chaucer (Foul Play)
Cheyenne (Jack the Bear)
Chiffon (The Shaggy Dog)
Chow Mein (Gypsy)
Cooper (What Lies Beneath)
Copernicus (Back to the Future)
Daphne (Look Who's Talking Now)
Dave (My Stepmother Is an Alien)
DeSoto (Oliver & Company)
Dodger (Oliver & Company)
Duke (Swiss Family Robinson)
Earl (City of Angels)
E. Buzz (Poltergeist)
Eddie (American Flyers)
Edison (Chitty Chitty Bang Bang)
Edward (The Accidental Tourist)
Einstein (Back to the Future)
Einstein (Oliver & Company)
Flo (All Dogs Go to Heaven)
Fly (Babe)
Francis (Oliver & Company)
Fred (Smokey and the Bandit)
Fritz (The Little Colonel)
Grunt (Flashdance)
Hansel (All Through the Night)
Harry (The Amityville Horror)
Harvey (E.T. the Extra Terrestrial)
Hearsay (The Firm)
Hobo (Please Don't Eat the Daisies)
Hosehead (Strange Brew)
Indiana (Indiana Jones)
Itchy (All Dogs Go to Heaven)
Jerry Lee (K-9)
Jerry (Tom and Jerry)
Kenny (Drop Dead Gorgeous)
Lafayette (The Aristocats)
Little Brother (Mulan)
Lucky (Dr. Dolittle)
Lucky (Married to the Mob)
Mandy (The Yellow Rolls Royce)
Matisse (Down and Out in Beverly Hills)
Max (Terminator 2 Judgment Day)
Max (The Little Mermaid)
Max (Volcano)
Meathead (Sudden Impact)
Merlin (Labyrinth)
Milo (The Mask)
Missy (Beethoven's 2nd)
Moose (Twister)
Muffy (Anatomy of a Murder)
Mutki (To Be or Not to Be)
Myron (Murder by Death)
Nanook (The Lost Boys)
Napoleon (The Aristocats)
Nemo (Avalon)
Opal (Blood Simple)
Pard (High Sierra)
Percy (Pocahontas)
Perdita (101 Dalmatians)
Pippet (Jaws)
Pluto (The Truman Show)
Pongo (101 Dalmatians)
Pongo (Robin Hood Men in Tights)
Puffy (There's Something About Mary)
Queenie (The Bishop's Wife)
Rags (Sleeper)
Red (Visit to a Small Planet)
Rex (Babe)
Rhett (Steel Magnolias)
Rita (Oliver & Company)
Roach (The First Wives Club)
Rocks (Look Who's Talking Now)
Romulus (Reap the Wild Wind)
Rooney (Mr. Robinson Crusoe)
Roscoe (Oliver & Company)
Rusty (Mars Attacks)
Sam (Lethal Weapon)
Scraps (Airplane!)
Scud (Toy Story)
Shadow (The Incredible Journey)
Shane (Radio Flyer)
Skipper (Runaway Bride)
Sparky (Michael)
Speck (Pee Wee's Big Adventure)
Sport (The Egg and I)
Spot (Fun With Dick and Jane)
Taffy (With Six You Get Eggroll)
Talbot (The Sword in the Stone)
Tiger (The Sword in the Stone)
Tito (Oliver & Company)
Toby (Twister)
Tom Dooley (The Misfits)
Toto (The Wizard of Oz)
Turk (Swiss Family Robinson)
Uncas (Young Sherlock Holmes)
Verdell (As Good as It Gets)
Vladimir (The Glass Bottom Boat)
Waffles (Manhattan)
Walter (To Die For)
Willie (Patton)
Woofy (Bicentennial Man)
dogs (literature):
Alec (Tortilla Flat)
Argus (Odyssey)
Asta (The Thin Man)
Athos (Ulysses)
Balthasar (The Forsyte Saga)
Bluebell (Animal Farm)
Boatswain (Omoo)
Bob (Watership Down)
Bodger (The Incredible Journey)
Bonkers (The World According to Garp)
Bruno (Cinderella)
Buck (The Call of the Wild)
Bull's-eye (Oliver Twist)
Bunchie (Portrait of a Lady)
Cerberus (Hades)
Clematis (Seventeen)
Clifford (The Big Red Dog)
Crab (Two Gentlemen of Verona)
Cujo (Stephen King)
Dave (The Call of the Wild)
Diogenes (Dombey and Son)
Dougal (Little Lord Fauntleroy)
Elmer (Paul Bunyan)
Enrique (Tortilla Flat)
Fido (Paul Bunyan)
Flopit (Seventeen)
Fluff (Tortilla Flat)
Fluffy (Harry Potter and the Sorcerer's Stone)
Gnasher (Wuthering Heights)
Hector (Natty Bumppo)
Jessie (Animal Farm)
Jip (David Copperfield)
Jip (Doctor Dolittle)
Juno (Wuthering Heights)
Kazak (The Sirens of Titan)
Knave (Lad A Dog)
Kojak (The Stand)
Luath (The Incredible Journey)

Max (How the Grinch Stole Christmas!)
Nana (Peter Pan)
Pajarito (Tortilla Flat)
Pilot (Jane Eyre)
Pincher (Animal Farm)
Rudolph (Tortilla Flat)
Skulker (Wuthering Heights)
Sol-leks (The Call of the Wild)
Spitz (The Call of the Wild)
Spot (Dick and Jane)
Toby (Sherlock Holmes)
Weenie (Eloise)
Wolf (Rip Van Winkle)
Wolf (Wuthering Heights)
Yap (The Mill on the Floss)
Zip (Happy Hollisters)

dogs (TV):
Antonio (The Drew Carey Show)
Apollo (Magnum, p.i.)
Arnold (Life Goes On)
Astro (The Jetsons)
Bandie (Life With Elizabeth)
Bandit (Jonny Quest)
Bandit (Little House on the Prairie)
Barney (Lou Grant)
Bijoux (Hooperman)
Black Tooth (Soupy Sales Show)
Boots (Emergency)
Bowser (Mr. Magoo)
Brain (Inspector Gadget)
Brandon (Punky Brewster)
Bridget (Lucas Tanner)
Buck (Married...With Children)
Buddy (Taxi)
Buddy (Veronica's Closet)
Butch (I Love Lucy)
Buttons (Animaniacs)
Chester (The Nanny)
Chipper (Land of the Giants)
Claude (The Beverly Hillbillies)
Cleo (The People's Choice)
Comet (Full House)
Cynthia (Green Acres)
Djinn Djinn (I Dream of Jeannie)
Dog (Columbo)
Dreyfuss (Empty Nest)
Duke (The Beverly Hillbillies)
Eddie (Frasier)
Flash (The Dukes of Hazzard)
Fred (I Love Lucy)
Freeway (Hart to Hart)
Fremont (Dennis the Menace)
Ginger (What Dreams May Come)
Grendel (thirtysomething)
Gulliver (The Andy Griffith Show)
Jasper (Bachelor Father)
King (Sergeant Preston of the Yukon)
Ladadog (Please Don't Eat the Daisies)
Leo (The Blue Knight)
Lord Nelson (The Doris Day Show)
Lucky (The Honeymooners)
Manfred (Tom Terrific)
Marlowe (Simon and Simon)
Max (Jake and the Fatman)
Max (The Bionic Woman)
Meatball (Baa Baa Black Sheep)
Mignon (Green Acres)
Mr. Peabody (Rocky and His Friends)
Murray (Mad About You)
Neil (Topper)
Nunzio (Dharma & Greg)
Old Blue (No Time for Sergeants)
Oliver (Family Affair)
Pax (Longstreet)
Pete/Petey (Little Rascals/Our Gang)
Porkchop (Doug)
Porthos (Enterprise)
Queequeg (The X-Files)
Quincy (Coach)
Rags (Spin City)
Reckless (The Waltons)
Reddy (Ruff and Reddy)
Ren (Ren and Stimpy)
Rex (The Life of Riley)
Rowlf (The Muppet Show)
Scruffy (The Ghost and Mrs. Muir)
Shamsky (Everybody Loves Raymond)
Simone (The Partridge Family)
Snow (The Monroes)
Snuffles (Quick Draw McGraw)
Sparky (South Park)
Speedy (The Drew Carey Show)
Sprocket (Fraggle Rock)
Spunky (Happy Days)
Stinky (Dharma & Greg)
Stormy (Life With Elizabeth)
Tet (Airwolf)
Tiger (The Brady Bunch)
Tiger (The Patty Duke Show)
Trader (Jungle Jim)
Tramp (My Three Sons)
Waldo (Nanny and the Professor)
White Fang (Soupy Sales Show)
Willie (Mama)
Wolf (Dr. Quinn, Medicine Woman)
Woofer (Winky Dink and You)
Zeus (Magnum, p.i.)

dog's __: **3** age **4** life
__ Dogs: **5** Straw
dog's age: **3** eon **4** aeon
__ Dogs and Englishmen: **3** Mad
dog-show org.: **3** AKC
dogsled pullers: **4** team
__ dog's life: **5** lead a
Dogs of War, The (1980 film)
cast: Tom Berenger, Christopher Walken
Dog star: **6** Sirius, Sothis
neighbor: **5** Orion
__-dog story: **6** shaggy
__ Dog, The: **6** Shaggy
dog-tired: **4** worn **5** spent, tired, weary, wiped **6** bushed, dished **8** fatigued **9** exhausted **10** knocked out
__ Dog Tray: **3** Old
dogtrot: **3** jog **6** canter
dogwood: **4** tree **5** brown, osier, plant, shrub **6** cornel, flower, kapuka **7** assagai, assegai **9** yellowish
relative: *see* brown color
Dog Years
author: Günter Grass
__-Doh: **4** Play
Doha: **4** city, town **7** capital
locale: **5** Katar, Qatar
Doherty: **5** Peter **7** Shannen
Doherty, Peter: **8** Nobelist **10** Australian
Doherty, Shannen: **7** actress
film: Heathers (1989)
TV: Beverly Hills 90210, Charmed
Dohnányi: **4** Erno
Do I dare to eat a peach?
poet: T.S.Eliot
Do I Do (1982 song)
artist: Stevie Wonder
Do I Hear a Waltz?: **7** musical
composer: Richard Rodgers, Stephen Sondheim
__ Do I Love You?: **3** Why
doily: **3** mat **6** napkin **8** place mat
make a ~: **3** tat
material: **4** lace
doing: **3** act **4** deed, up to **5** event **6** action **7** exploit **9** execution, handiwork, operation
keep from ~: **5** avoid **6** eschew, resist **7** back off, inhibit, refrain **8** restrain **9** interrupt
nothing: **4** idle, lazy **5** inert **6** otiose, torpid **7** dormant, jobless, loafing, resting **8** inactive, indolent, slothful, sluggish, stagnant **9** lethargic, loitering, out of work, sedentary, shiftless **10** motionless, on the shelf, stationary
nothing ~: **2** no **3** nah, naw, nay, nix, non **4** nein, nope, nyet, uh-uh **5** I won't, ixnay, never, no how, no way **6** no deal, noways, nowise, rebuff **7** I refuse **8** forget it, I will not, negative, negatory **9** by no means, fat chance, I think not, rejection **10** count me out, not a chance, thumbs down
starter: **4** evil **5** wrong
well: **4** rich **7** booming **8** affluent **10** prospering, prosperous, successful
__ doing: **7** nothing
__ Doing All Right: **4** I Was
Doing It All for My Baby (1987 song)
artist: Huey Lewis and the News
doings: **7** matters **8** dealings, goings-on **10** happenings
Doings of Raffles Haw, The
author: Arthur Conan Doyle
Doin It (1996 song)
artist: LL Cool J
Doin' What Comes Natur'lly
composer: Irving Berlin
__ Do Is Dream of You: **4** All I
__ do it: **4** Just
__ Do It: **4** Let's
Do It Again
composer: George Gershwin
Do It Again (1972 song)
artist: Steely Dan
__ Do It Again: **4** Let's
Do It Baby (1974 song)
artist: Miracles
__ do it, bees...: **5** Birds
__ Do It Every Time: **6** They'll
do-it-yourself: **8** homemade
heading: **5** how to
purchase: **3** kit
trailer: **5** U-Haul
vehicle: **3** van **5** truck
dojo activity: **4** judo **6** karate
__-doke: **4** okey
Dolby: **6** Thomas
dolce: **7** sweetly
dolce __: **4** vita
dolce __ niente: **3** far
Dolcetto: **3** red **4** wine
origin: **5** Italy
doldrums: **4** funk, mood **5** blahs, blues, dumps, ennui, gloom **6** apathy, tedium, torpor **7** inertia, malaise **8** glumness **9** dejection, lassitude **10** depression, heavy heart, stagnation
economic ~: **5** slump **8** slowdown **10** depression
in the ~: **3** low, sad **4** blue, mopy **5** moody, mopey
dole: **4** alms, gift, mete **5** allot, grant, grief **6** ration, regret, relief **7** charity, give out, handout, portion, welfare **8** donation, largesse **9** allotment, allowance **10** allocation
on the ~: **5** needy **8** leisured **9** unengaged **10** unemployed
out: **4** deal, give, mete **5** allot, divvy, issue, share **6** assign, divide, parcel, ration **7** divvy up, portion **8** disburse, dispense, disperse **9** apportion, partition **10** administer, contribute, distribute
__ dole: **5** on the
Dole: **3** Bob **5** Liddy **6** Robert **9** Elizabeth
doleful: **3** sad **4** blue, dark, down, foul, glum, grim, poor **5** awful, lousy, moody, woful **6** broody, crumby, crummy, dismal, dreary, gloomy, horrid, morose, odious, rotten, rueful, somber, tragic, woeful **7** accurst, baleful, baneful, beastly, elegiac, forlorn, ghastly, hangdog, joyless, piteous, pitiful, unhappy **8** accursed, dejected, dolorous, downcast, dreadful, God-awful, grieving, grievous, horrible, inferior, mournful, shameful, stinking, terrible, tragical, troubled, wretched **9** abhorrent, appalling, atrocious, bummed out, cheerless, defective, depressed, execrable, frightful, heartsick, insidious, loathsome, miserable, offensive, plaintive, revolting, sorrowful, woebegone **10** abominable, chapfallen, despicable, despondent, detestable, disastrous, dispirited, distressed, horrendous, lamentable, lugubrious, melancholy
sound: **5** knell
Dolenz: **3** Ami **5** Micky **6** Mickey
colleague: **4** Tork **5** Jones **7** Nesmith
Dole, Robert: **3** pol **7** senator
state: **6** Kansas
Dolin, Anton: **6** dancer **7** British, danseur
__ Dolittle: **6** Doctor
doll: **3** Ken, toy **5** cutey, cutie, GI Joe, honey **6** Barbie, beauty, figure, kewpie, looker, prince, puppet **7** darling, gussy up, kachina, katcina, sweetie **8** cutie pie, figurine, katchina **9** dreamboat, plaything **10** honeybunch, marionette, sweetheart, sweetie pie
carnival ~: **5** prize **6** kewpie
counterpart: **3** guy
ender: **4** face **5** house
fad ~: **5** troll
male ~: **3** Ken **5** GI Joe
paper ~: **6** cutout
raggedy ~: **3** Ann **4** Andy
up: **5** adorn, dress, preen, primp, prink **6** attire, bedaub
wedding cake ~: **4** wife **5** bride
word: **4** mama

__ doll: 3 rag 4 baby 5 paper 6 Barbie, kewpie 7 kachina
__ Doll: 3 Rag 4 Baby 5 Devil, Paper, Party, Satin 6 Kewpie
dollar: 3 ace, one, tip 4 bill, buck, cash, clam 5 money 6 single 7 one-spot, smacker 8 banknote, currency, frogskin, simoleon 9 greenback
  fraction: 2 ct. 3 bit 4 cent, dime 5 penny 6 nickel 7 quarter
  half ~: 4 coin
  sign, basically: 3 ess
  starter: 4 euro 5 petro
  word on a ~: 3 God, one 4 Bank, Note, ordo, Seal, unum 5 debts, Great, legal, trust 6 annuit, public, Series, States, tender, United 7 America, coeptis, Federal, private, Reserve 8 pluribus, seclorum, Treasury 9 Secretary, Treasurer 10 Washington
dollar __: 3 day, gap 4 area, bill, sign
dollar __ averaging: 4 cost
dollar-__ man: 5 a-year
__ dollar: 3 top 4 beau, fast, half, sand, yuan 5 trade 6 Levant, silver 7 Anthony, British, quarter
__-dollar: 3 rix
Dollar: 9 car rental 10 auto rental
  alternative: *see* car rental
dollars: 4 cash, gelt, jack, kail, kale, loot, peag, pelf 5 bread, dough, funds, lucre, money, moola, mopus, pesos, rhino, sewan 6 dinero, do-re-mi, mammon, mazuma, monies, moolah, seawan, silver, specie, wampum, wealth 7 cabbage, capital, lettuce, ooftish, scratch, shekels 8 bankroll, cold cash, currency, hard cash 9 long green 10 green stuff
  fistful of ~: 3 wad
  to donuts: 8 probably 9 sure thing
$ (Dollars) (1971 film)
  cast: Warren Beatty, Gert Frobe, Goldie Hawn
dollars-and-__: 5 cents
dollars to __: 6 donuts
Dolley: 7 Madison
dollface
  see sweetheart
dollop: 3 bit, dab, gob, pat 4 blob, dash, glob, glop, lump, spot 5 piece 7 portion 8 spoonful
Doll's House, A: 4 play
  author: Henrik Ibsen
  character: 4 Nils, Nora 5 Linde 6 Helmer
dolly: 4 cart 5 truck 6 barrow 7 carrier 9 hand truck
Dolly: 3 ewe 4 Levi 5 clone, sheep 6 Parton
Dolly __: 6 Varden
__, Dolly!: 5 Hello
Dolly Madison: 8 ice cream
  alternative: *see* ice cream
Dolly Sisters, The (1945 film)
  cast: Betty Grable, June Haver
Dollywood
  locale: 4 Tenn. 9 Tennessee
dolman: 4 cape, coat, robe, wrap 5 coats 6 mantle, sleeve
dolomite: 3 ore 6 marble 7 mineral
  deposit: 4 marl
Dolomites: 3 mts. 4 Alps, mtns. 5 range
  locale: 5 Italy 6 Europe
dolor: 3 woe 4 ache 5 agony, gloom, grief 6 misery, sorrow 7 anguish, despair, sadness 8 distress, the blues 9 dejection, heartache, suffering 10 depression, heartbreak, heavy heart, melancholy, woefulness
__ dolore: 3 con
Dolores: 4 Hart, Hope 6 Del Rio
Dolores Claiborne: 4 film 5 novel
  author: Stephen King
  cast: Kathy Bates, Jennifer Jason Leigh
__ dolorosa: 3 via 5 mater
dolorous: 3 sad 4 dark 5 woful 6 dismal, woeful 7 doleful, elegiac, painful, tearful 8 desolate, grievous, mournful, wretched 9 afflicted, anguished, cheerless, miserable, plaintive, sniveling, sorrowful, woebegone 10 deplorable, lamentable, lugubrious, melancholy
Dolph: 5 Sweet 7 Schayes 8 Lundgren
dolphin: 6 animal, dorado 8 cetacean
  communication: 5 sonar
  female: 3 cow
  habitat: 3 sea 5 ocean
  hazard: 3 net
  kin: *see* cetacean
  largest ~: 4 orca
  male: 4 bull
  meal: 5 squid
  relative: 6 beluga
  school: 3 pod
  young: 3 pup 4 calf
dolphin __: 4 kick
dolphinfish, half a Hawaiian: 4 mahi
dolphinlike cetacean: 4 susu
Dolphins: 4 team 6 eleven
  home: 5 Miami
  org.: 3 AFC, NFL
  rival: *see* NFL team
  sport: 8 football
dolphin-safe __: 4 tuna
Dolphin, The
  author: Robert Lowell
dolt
  old-style: 4 mome
  see also ninny
doltish: 3 dim 4 daft, dopy, dull, dumb 5 dense, dopey, silly 6 obtuse 7 bearish, foolish, loutish, witless 8 cloddish, mindless 9 dim-witted 10 weak-minded
Dom: 5 abbot, title 6 Moraes 7 DeLuise 8 DiMaggio, Pérignon
Dom. __: 3 Rep.
domain: 3 job 4 area, turf 5 arena, bourn, field, orbit, range, realm, world 6 dot-com, empire, estate, locale, nation, region, sphere 7 compass, concern, element, grounds, habitat, kingdom, quarter, terrain 8 locality, province 9 authority, bailiwick, specialty, territory 10 department
__ domain: 6 public 7 eminent
Domain of Arnheim, The
  author: Edgar Allan Poe
__ do Mar: 5 Serra
Dombey and Son
  author: Charles Dickens
  dog: 8 Diogenes
dome: 4 head, roof 5 vault 6 cupola, noggin 7 ceiling 8 mountain
  cover: 3 wig
  home: 4 iglu 5 igloo
  opening: 6 oculus
dome __: 3 car, top 5 light
__ dome: 4 salt 5 onion, smoke 6 chrome, saucer
__ Dome: 6 Teapot
domed
  projection: 4 apse
  roof: 6 cupola
Domenico: 7 Modugno 9 Scarlatti
Dome of Many-Coloured Glass, A
  author: Amy Lowell
Domesday __: 4 Book
domestic: 4 home, maid, tame 5 civil 6 au pair, native 7 servant 8 interior, internal, national 9 homegrown, household, launderer 10 indigenous
  not ~: 7 foreign
domestic __: 7 partner
domesticate: 4 tame
domesticated: 4 tame 6 broken, docile, gentle, pliant 8 lamblike, obedient 9 compliant, tractable 10 manageable, submissive
  not ~: 4 wild 5 feral
Domestic Disturbance (2001 film)
  cast: Teri Polo, John Travolta, Vince Vaughn
__ domestic product: 5 gross
domicile: 3 pad 4 co-op, crib, home, nest 5 abode, condo, house, joint, lodge, place, put up, roost 6 castle, harbor 7 address, habitat, harbour, housing, lodging, mansion, quarter 8 dwelling, fireside, lodgment, quarters 9 apartment, residence
domicilio: 4 casa
dominance: 4 rule 7 mastery 9 advantage, authority, influence, supremacy, upper hand 10 ascendance, ascendancy, ascendence, ascendency, government, prepotency
dominant: 3 top 4 main, star 5 alpha, chief, first, major, on top, prime 6 ruling 7 central, leading, primary, rampant, regnant, supreme 8 despotic, forceful, in charge, powerful, reigning, superior, unbeaten 9 imperious, paramount, prevalent, principal, sovereign, unrivaled, uppermost 10 commanding, despotical, overriding, preeminent, prevailing, triumphant, unrivalled
  feature: 5 motif
dominate: 3 hog 4 boss, head, lead, loom, rule, sway 5 reign, tower 6 direct, govern, handle, manage, obsess 7 command, control, dictate, prevail, triumph 8 bestride, loom over, outshine, override, overrule 9 reign over, subjugate, tyrannize 10 monopolize, overshadow, run the show, tower above
dominating: 5 macho
domination: 4 rule, sway 7 command, control, tyranny 8 hegemony 9 authority, despotism, influence, supremacy 10 ascendance, ascendancy, ascendence, ascendency, government, oppression, prepotency, repression, subjection
domineer: 4 rule 5 bully 6 hector, menace 7 control, henpeck, oppress, swagger 8 browbeat, bulldoze, keep down 9 trample on, tyrannize 10 boss around, intimidate
domineering: 4 firm, hard 5 bossy, cruel, macho, picky, proud, pushy, rigid, stern, tough 6 severe 7 austere, Spartan 8 arrogant, coercive, despotic, dogmatic, exacting, hard-line, imperial, rigorous 9 demanding, draconian, stringent, unbending, unsparing 10 despotical, dogmatical, inflexible, iron-fisted, no-nonsense, oppressive, peremptory, tyrannical
  one: 5 bully
Domingo: 6 Sunday 7 Plácido, Spanish 9 Sarmiento
  follower: 5 lunes
  preceder: 6 sábado
__ Domingo: 5 Santo
Domingo, Plácido: 5 tenor 6 singer
  milieu: 5 opera
  piece: 4 aria
  specialty: 5 opera
__ Domini: 4 Anno
Dominic: 5 saint 7 Keating
Dominica: 4 isle 6 island, nation 7 country
  capital: 6 Roseau
  money: 4 cent 6 dollar
  org.: 3 OAS
Dominican: 4 monk 5 friar 7 brother
  dance: 8 merengue
Dominican Republic: 6 nation 7 country
  capital: Santo Domingo
  city: 4 Moca 6 La Vega 8 Santiago
  money: 4 peso
  neighbor: 5 Haiti
  org.: 3 OAS
Dominick: 5 Dunne
Dominick and Eugene (1988 film)
  cast: Jamie Lee Curtis, Tom Hulce, Ray Liotta
dominie: 6 cleric
dominion: 4 area, hold, rule, sway 5 orbit, power, reach, realm, reign, state 6 empery, empire, nation, region, sphere 7 command, control, country, potence, potency, regency, terrain, victory 8 hegemony, kingship, province 9 authority, bailiwick, influence, ownership, supremacy, territory 10 ascendance, ascendancy, ascendence, ascendency, governance, government, possession
  hold ~: 4 rule 5 reign 6 direct 7 command, control, oversee
  in India: 3 raj
Dominion __: 3 Day
Dominique: 4 fowl 7 chicken
  relative: *see* chicken
Dominique (1963 song)
  artist: Singing Nun
domino: 4 cape, mask, tile 5 cloak 9 game piece 10 masquerade
  certain ~: 3 ace 4 trey 5 deuce
  spot: 3 pip
Domino (1970 song)
  artist: Van Morrison
dominoes: 4 game

Domino, Fats
real first name: Antoine
song: Ain't That a Shame (1955)
Be My Guest (1959)
Blueberry Hill (1956)
Blue Monday (1957)
I'm in Love Again (1956)
I'm Walkin' (1957)
It's You I Love (1957)
I Want to Walk You Home (1959)
Valley of Tears (1957)
Walking to New Orleans (1960)
Whole Lotta Loving (1958)
Domino's specialty: 5 pizza
Domitian: 6 Caesar
__ dommage!: 4 C'est, Quel
__-domo: 5 major
Dom Pedro: 4 king
wife: 4 Ines
don: 4 capo, wear **5** put on, sport **6** slip on **7** dress in, get into **8** slip into **9** godfather, professor.
apparel: 5 dress **6** clothe
the feedbag: 3 eat
Don: 2 Ho **4** Imus, King, Owen, Weis **5** Adams, Bluth, Budge, Grady, Pardo, river, Rondo, Sharp, Shula, title **6** Ameche, Baylor, Carter, Cherry, DeFore, Everly, Gibson, Henley, Hewitt, Knotts, Larsen, Martin, McLean, Murray, Porter, Siegel, Sutton, Taylor, Zimmer **7** Chaffey, Cheadle, Cornell, DeLillo, Garlits, Johnson, Marquis, Maynard, McGuire, Medford, Messick, Novello, Quixote, Rickles **8** Drysdale, Galloway, Meredith, Mitchell, Williams **9** Kirschner, Mattingly, Robertson
River locale: 6 Russia
river to the ~: 6 Donets
sea fed by the ~: 4 Azov
Don __: 4 Juan **6** Carlos **7** Quixote
Don __ de la Vega: 5 Diego
Don __ DeMarco: 4 Juan
dona: 7 senhora
dona __ pacem: 5 nobis
Doña: 5 title
Dona Flor and Her Two Husbands: 5 novel
author: Jorge Amado
Donahue: 4 Phil, Troy **6** Elinor
Donahue, Phil: 4 host
spouse: Marlo Thomas
Donahue, Troy: 5 actor
spouse: Suzanne Pleshette
Donald: 4 Byrd, Cram, Duck, Hall **5** Crisp, Davie, Trump **6** Glaser, Moffat, Petrie **7** O'Connor **8** Hamilton, McMillan **9** Barthelme, Pleasence **10** Sutherland
daughter: 6 Ivanka
in Irish: 5 Donal
in Italian: 4 Aldo
son: 6 Kiefer
spouse: 5 Ivana, Marla **7** Melania
Donald Duck
friend: 5 Daisy
nephew: 4 Huey **5** Dewey, Louie
to his nephews: 4 unca
uncle: 7 Scrooge
voice of ~: Clarence Nash, Tony Anselmo
Donaldson: 3 Sam **5** Julia, Roger
Donaldson, Sam: 8 reporter **10** newscaster
network: 3 ABC

dona nobis __: 5 pacem
donate: 4 give **5** award, endow, grant, offer, spend, tithe **6** bestow, chip in, confer, devote, kick in, pony up, render **7** hand out, present, provide, throw in **8** bequeath, dedicate **9** subscribe **10** contribute
Donatello: 6 artist **7** Italian **8** sculptor
Donath: 6 Ludwig
donation: 3 aid **4** alms, dole, gift, hand **5** grant **7** bequest, charity, largess, present, subsidy **8** gratuity, largesse, offering **9** endowment **10** assistance
make a ~: 4 give
religious ~: 5 tithe
Donat, Robert: 5 actor
film: Goodbye, Mr. Chips (1939, AA)
__ Don Baker: 3 Joe
Don Carlos: 4 play **5** opera
author: Friedrich von Schiller
composer: Giuseppe Verdi
role: 5 Eboli **7** Rodrigo **8** Theobald **9** Elizabeth
setting: 5 Spain **6** France
Doncha' Think It's Time (1958 song)
artist: Elvis Presley
Donder: 8 reindeer
colleague: ***see*** reindeer
Dondi: 6 orphan **7** cartoon **10** comic strip
dog: 7 Queenie
done: 3 old **4** fini, over, past, thru **5** ended, ready, spent, wrapt **6** cooked, finito **7** all over, through, wrapped, wrought **8** achieved, complete, executed, finished, over with, realized, rendered **9** completed, concluded, performed **10** buttoned up, terminated
by hand: 6 manual
easily ~: 6 facile, simple
for: 4 sunk **5** kaput, tired **6** doomed **7** accurst **8** accursed, obsolete, washed-up **9** vicarious
get ~: 3 end **4** cook **5** mop up **6** finish **7** achieve **10** put through
get the job ~: 4 work **6** hack it
in: 5 kaput, spent, tired, weary **6** dished **8** fatigued, finished **9** enervated, played out **10** knocked out
nicely ~: 4 neat **10** impressive
not ~: 4 no-no, rare **5** wrong
not well ~: 5 messy **6** shabby, shoddy, sloppy, untidy **7** unkempt **8** careless, fouled-up, slapdash, slipshod **9** haphazard, hit-or-miss, neglected
things to be ~: 6 agenda
to a poet: 3 o'er
with: 4 over **5** rid of **7** all over
done __ turn: 3 to a
__-done: 4 well
Done!: 5 there **6** agreed
__ Done: 5 Day Is
donee: 5 taker **8** receiver **9** recipient
Donegal: 4 port **5** tweed
locale: 7 Ireland
river: 4 Erne
Donegan: 6 Lonnie
__ Done Him Wrong: 3 She
__ Donelson: 4 Fort
Donen: 7 Stanley
Donets: 5 river

locale: 6 Russia **7** Ukraine
Donetsk: 4 city, town
locale: 7 Ukraine
__-dong: 4 ding
Don Giovanni: 5 opera
character: 4 Anna **5** Pedro **6** Elvira **7** Ottavio, Zerlina
composer: Wolfgang Amadeus Mozart
highlight: 4 duel
setting: 5 Spain **7** Seville
__ Dong School: 4 Ding
Donizetti, Gaetano
work: Anna Bolena
Don Pasquale
L'Elisir d'Amore
Lucia di Lammermoor
Lucrezia Borgia
donjon: 4 keep
site: 6 castle
Don Juan: 4 epic, poem, roué **5** opera, Romeo **6** ballet **8** lothario, tone poem **9** libertine
author: Lord Byron
composer: Christoph Gluck, Richard Strauss
mother: 4 Ines, Inez
portrayer: 5 Errol
Don Juan DeMarco (1995 film)
cast: Marlon Brando, Johnny Depp, Faye Dunaway
donkey: 3 ass **5** burro, genet, jenny, kiang, neddy **6** animal, brayer, equine, jennet, onager **7** jackass
cry: 4 bray **6** heehaw
Democratic ~ creator: Thomas Nast
dinner: 4 feed
enticement: 6 carrot
feature: 3 ear
female ~: 5 genet, jenny **6** jennet
fix a ~ tail: 5 repin
foot: 4 hoof
in French: 3 ane
in Italian: 5 asino
male ~: 7 jackass
relative: ***see*** equine
young: 4 colt, foal
Donkey __: 4 Kong
donkeys
when ~ fly: 5 never, no how, no way **8** forget it **9** fat chance **10** impossible, not a chance
donkey's __: 4 tail **5** years
Donkey Serenade
composer: Rudolf Friml
Donkey's Years
author: Michael Frayn
Donlevy: 5 Brian
__ donna: 5 prima
Donna: 4 Reed **5** Dixon, Fargo, Karan, Lewis, Loren, Mills **6** Caponi, Pescow, Summer **7** D'Errico, Douglas, Shalala
Donna (1958 song)
artist: Ritchie Valens
Donna Reed Show, The (ABC sitcom)
cast: Carl Betz (Dr. Alex Stone)
Shelley Fabares (Mary Stone)
Paul Petersen (Jeff Stone)
Donna Reed (Donna Stone)
Donna the Prima Donna (1963 song)
artist: Dion
Donne, John: 4 poet **7** British

last lamenting thing for ~: 4 kiss
start of a ~ quote: 5 no man
work: Air and Angels
The Bait
Break of Day
A Burnt Ship
Divine Poems
The Extasy
A Fever
The Flea
The Good Morrow
The Legacy
Love's Alchemy
The Message
Songs and Sonnets
The Sunne Rising
The Triple Fool
The Undertaking
A Valediction
Donner: 3 Ral **5** Clive **7** Richard
Donner __: 4 Pass
Donnie Brasco (1997 film)
cast: Johnny Depp, Bruno Kirby, Michael Madsen, Al Pacino
donnish: 7 bookish **8** pedantic **9** pedagogic **10** pedantical
Donny: 4 Most **6** Osmond **8** Hathaway
sister: 5 Marie
donnybrook: 3 row **4** fray, riot, to-do **5** brawl, clash, fight, melee, mix-up, set-to **6** affray, barney, battle, fracas, rumble, tussle, uproar **7** rhubarb, scuffle, turmoil **8** skirmish, slugfest, squabble **9** brannigan **10** free-for-all
D'Onofrio: 7 Vincent
Donohoe: 6 Amanda
donor: 5 angel, giver **6** backer, patron **7** grantor **8** altruist, bestower **10** benefactor
campaign ~: 3 PAC
no ~: 5 miser **9** skinflint
universal ~: 5 type O
Donoso, José: 6 writer **7** Chilean
Do not __: 6 pass Go **7** disturb
Do not go gentle...
author: Dylan Thomas
do-nothing: 3 bum **4** idle, lazy **5** drone, idler, slack **6** loafer, otiose, truant **7** goof-off, moocher, slacker **8** fainéant, indolent, loiterer, slothful, slugabed, sluggard **9** goldbrick, lazybones, shiftless **10** ne'er-do-well
bane: 4 work
Do not open __ Christmas!: 4 till **5** until
Donovan: 3 Art **6** Marion
daughter: Ione Skye
last name: Leitch
song: Atlantis (1969)
Hurdy Gurdy Man (1968)
Mellow Yellow (1966)
Sunshine Superman (1966)
Donovan's __: 4 Reef **5** Brain
Donovan's Reef (1963 film)
cast: Elizabeth Allen, Lee Marvin, John Wayne
director: John Ford
Donovan, Wild Bill agcy.: 3 OSS
Don Pasquale
composer: Gaetano Donizetti
setting: 4 Rome
Don Quixote: 5 novel **6** knight **9** visionary

author: Miguel de Cervantes
horse: 9 Rocinante, Rosinante
pal: Sancho Panza
don't: 4 no-no, tabu 5 taboo
Don't (1958 song)
artist: Elvis Presley
Don't __!: 3 ask
Don't __ boy to...: 5 send a
Don't __ cow, man!: 5 have a
Don't __ it!: 5 bet on
Don't __ me!: 3 ask 6 look at
Don't __ Me: 4 Rush 5 Blame
Don't __ Me in: 5 Fence
Don't __ on me: 5 tread
Don't __ on My Parade: 4 Rain
Don't __ the Small Stuff: 5 Sweat
Don't __, we'll...: 6 call us
Don't __ With Bill: 4 Mess
Don't Ask Me Why (1980 song)
artist: Billy Joel
Don't be __!: 4 late 5 silly
Don't Be Cruel (song)
artist: Bobby Brown, Cheap Trick, Elvis Presley
Don't bet __!: 4 on it
Don't bother: 6 no need, skip it
Don't Bother __ Can't Cope: 3 Me I
Don't Bring Me Down (1979 song)
artist: ELO
Don't Come Around Here... (1985 song)
artist: Tom Petty
Don't count __!: 4 on it
Don't Cry (song)
artist: Asia, Guns N' Roses
__ Don't Cry: 4 Boys
Don't Cry Daddy (1969 song)
artist: Elvis Presley
Don't Cry for Me Argentina (1997 song): 5 tango
artist: Madonna
musical: 5 Evita
Don't Cry Out Loud (1979 song)
artist: Melissa Manchester
composer: Peter Allen
Don't Do Me Like That (1979 song)
artist: Tom Petty
Don't do that!: 4 stop 6 stop it
__ Don't Eat the Daisies: 6 Please
Don't Expect Me to Be Your Friend (1973 song)
artist: Lobo
__, don't fail me now!: 4 Feet
Don't Fall in Love With a Dreamer (song)
artist: Kim Carnes, Kenny Rogers
Don't Fence Me In
composer: Cole Porter
Don't Fight It (1982 song)
artist: Kenny Loggins, Steve Perry
Don't Get Me Wrong (1986 song)
artist: Pretenders
Don't Give Up On Us (1977 song)
artist: David Soul
Don't go __!: 5 there
Don't Go __ the Water: 4 Near
__ Don't Go: 4 Baby 6 Please
Don't Go Away Mad (1990 song)
artist: Mötley Crüe
Don't Go Breaking My Heart (1976 song)
artist: Kiki Dee, Elton John
Don't Hang Up (1962 song)
artist: Orlons
Don't have __, man!: 4 a cow
dontic starter: 5 ortho
Don't It Make My Brown Eyes Blue (1977 song)
artist: Crystal Gayle
Don't It Make Ya Wanna Dance (1980 song)
artist: Bonnie Raitt
Don't Knock My Love (1971 song)
artist: Wilson Pickett
Don't Know Much (1989 song)
artist: Aaron Neville, Linda Ronstadt
Don't Leave Me This Way (1977 song)
artist: Thelma Houston
Don't let go!: 6 hang on
Don't Let Go (1996 song)
artist: En Vogue
Don't Let It End (1983 song)
artist: Styx
Don't Let the Green Grass Fool You (1971 song)
artist: Wilson Pickett
Don't Let the Stars Get in Your Eyes (1952 song)
artist: Perry Como
Don't Let the Sun Catch You Crying (1964 song)
artist: Gerry and the Pacemakers
Don't Let the Sun Go Down on Me (song)
artist: Elton John, George Michael
Don't look __!: 3 now 4 at me
Don't look __ horse...: 5 a gift
Don't Look Back (1978 song)
artist: Boston
Don't Lose My Number (1985 song)
artist: Phil Collins
Don't make __ of me!: 5 a liar
Don't Make Me Over (1963 song)
artist: Dionne Warwick
Don't Mess with Bill (1966 song)
artist: Marvelettes
Don't mind if __!: 3 I do
__ Don't Own Me: 3 You
__ Don't Preach: 4 Papa
Don't quit your __!: 6 day job
Don't Rain on My Parade
composer: Bob Merrill, Jule Styne
Don't rub __!: 4 it in
__-Don't Run: 4 Walk
Don't Rush Me (1988 song)
artist: Taylor Dayne
Don't say __!: 5 a word
__ Don't Say: 3 You
Don't Say a Word (2001 film)
cast: Michael Douglas, Famke Janssen, Brittany Murphy
Don't Sleep in the Subway (1967 song)
artist: Petula Clark
Don't Stand So Close to Me (1981 song)
artist: Police
Don't Stop (1977 song)
artist: Fleetwood Mac
Don't Stop 'Til You Get Enough (1979 song)
artist: Michael Jackson
Don't sweat it: 6 no loss 9 no big deal
Don't Talk to Strangers (1982 song) artist: Rick Springfield
Don't tell __!: 5 a soul
Don't Think Twice, It's All Right (1963 song)
artist: Peter, Paul and Mary
Don't throw bouquets __: 4 at me
Don't Throw It All Away (1978 song)
artist: Andy Gibb
Don't touch __ dial!: 4 that
Don't tread on me: 5 motto
Don't Turn Around (1994 song)
artist: Ace of Base
Don't Walk Away (1993 song)
artist: Jade
Don't Wanna Lose You (1989 song)
artist: Gloria Estefan
Don't Want to Be a Fool (1991 song) artist: Luther Vandross
Don't worry about me: 4 I'm ok
Don't Worry Baby (1964 song)
artist: Beach Boys
Don't Worry Be Happy (1988 song)
artist: Bobby McFerrin
Don't Worry Kyoko (1971 song)
artist: Yoko Ono
Don't you __!: 4 dare
Don't You Care (1967 song)
artist: Buckinghams
Don't You Know (1959 song)
artist: Della Reese
Don't You Know What the Night Can Do? (1988 song)
artist: Steve Winwood
Don't You Want Me (song)
artist: Human League, Jody Wateley
donut: 6 dunker, pastry, sinker
drown a ~: 4 dunk
feature: 4 hole 5 cream, glaze, jelly
kin: 5 bagel 7 cruller, kruller
order: 5 dozen
place: 6 bakery
shape: 5 torus
donuts
like some ~: 5 fried 6 glazed
__ Donuts: 6 Dunkin'
donut-shaped: 5 toric
doo-__: 3 wop
__-Doo: 6 Scooby
Doobie Brothers
song: Black Water (1975)
The Doctor (1980)
Listen to the Music (1972)
Long Train Runnin' (1973)
Real Love (1980)
What a Fool Believes (1970)
doodad: 5 frill, gismo, gizmo, thing 6 bauble, dingus, gadget, geegaw, gewgaw, whosis, widget 7 trinket, whatsis 8 nicknack, ornament 9 adornment, bagatelle, invention 10 decoration, instrument, knick-knack
doodle: 3 jot 4 draw 6 putter, scrawl, sketch, tinker, trifle 7 drawing 8 graffiti, scribble 10 marginalia, mess around
ender: 3 bug
starter: 4 flap
__-doodle: 5 dipsy
__ Doodle: 6 Yankee
doodlebug: 6 insect
__-doodle-doo: 5 cock-a
doodly-squat: 3 nil 5 zilch 7 nothing
Doody: 6 Alison
__ Doody: 5 Howdy
doofus
see ninny
Doogie Howser, M.D. (ABC sitcom)
cast: Neil Patrick Harris (Doogie Howser)
Doohan: 5 James
doohickey: 5 gismo, gizmo, thing 6 gadget, widget 7 whatsis 9 apparatus, mechanism
Dooley: 3 Tom 4 Paul 6 Wilson
Doolittle: 5 Eliza, Hilda
Doolittle, Eliza: 7 Cockney
Doolittle, Hilda: 4 poet
colleague: T.S. Eliot, Ezra Pound
subject: Freud
doom: 3 end, lot 4 ruin 7 condemn, destine, destiny, portion, tragedy, undoing 8 calamity, disaster, downfall 9 cataclysm, damnation, preordain, ruination 10 apocalypse, extinction, foreordain
ender: 5 sayer
partner: 5 gloom
prophet of ~: 9 Cassandra, pessimist
doomed: 4 lost, sunk 5 bound, curst, fated 6 cursed, ruined, undone 7 accurst, done for, ominous, unlucky 8 accursed, destined, ill-fated, luckless 9 condemned, ill-omened 10 inevitable
one: 5 goner
doomful: 7 fateful 8 sinister
Doomsday __: 4 Book
Doomsday Conspiracy, The
author: Sidney Sheldon
Doon: 5 river
locale: 8 Scotland
Doone: 5 Lorna
do one's __: 3 bit 4 part
do one's __ good: 5 heart
do one's __ thing: 3 own
Doonesbury: 7 cartoon 10 comic strip
artist: Garry Trudeau
character: 2 B.D. 3 Kim, Sam 4 Alex, Duke, Mark, Mike 5 Honey 6 Hedley, Roland, Zonker 7 Boopsie 8 Samantha
locale: 6 Walden
do one's heart __: 4 good
do one's own __: 5 thing
door: 4 exit, gate, trap 5 entry, hatch, storm, way in 6 access, egress, portal 7 ingress, opening, postern 8 entrance, entryway, hatchway 9 revolving, threshold 10 passageway
aircraft ~: 5 hatch
back ~: 7 postern
ender: 3 man, mat, men, way 4 bell, jamb, knob, nail, post, sill, step, stop, yard 5 woman, women 6 keeper
feature: 3 mat 4 bolt, hook, jamb, knob, lock, sill 5 hinge, jambe, latch 6 lintel
hinge site: 4 jamb 5 jambe
install a ~: 4 hang
it may be checked at the ~: 6 ID card
keep the wolf from the ~: 4 work 7 peg away 9 grind away
lay at one's ~: 3 tax 5 blame 6 accuse, charge, finger 7 censure 8 sentence 9 attribute, implicate
like a French ~: 5 paned
next ~ to: 4 near 5 close 6 at hand, nearby 8 abutting, adjacent, touching 9 adjoining, bordering, immediate 10 contiguous, convenient, jux-

taposed
open ~: 6 entrée
open a ~ illegally: 4 loid
opener: 3 key 7 key card 8 latchkey
open the ~: 4 go in 5 let in, usher
position: 4 ajar
show the ~: 4 oust
sliding ~: 6 fusuma
sliding ~ groove: 5 regle
sound: 4 slam 5 creak
starter: 3 out 4 back
sub ~: 5 hatch
take through the ~: 6 lead in
word: 3 men 4 exit, pull, push 5 enter, women
door __: 5 prize
do-or-__: 3 die
__ door: 3 air 4 back, fire, flap, open, trap 5 blind, Dutch, front, stage, storm, swing 6 French
__ Door: 5 Stage
doorbell: 5 chime 6 buzzer, ringer
eschew the ~: 5 knock
response: 6 come in
ringer: 6 caller
ring ~s: 3 run 5 stump 8 campaign
sound: 4 dong, ring
Doorbell Rang, The
author: Rex Stout
__ Door Canteen: 5 Stage
do-or-die: 6 all-out 7 crucial 9 desperate, last-ditch
doorframe: 4 jamb 5 jambe
__-door Johnny: 5 stage
doorkeeper: 5 guard, tiler, usher 6 porter, sentry, warden 7 janitor, ostiary, turnkey 8 guardian, sentinel, watchdog 9 custodian
doorman's job, do a: 5 admit, let in
doormat: 5 patsy, toady 6 jackal, lackey 7 lacquey 8 kowtower 9 sycophant
use a ~: 4 wipe
__-door neighbor: 4 next
__-door opener: 6 garage
__-door policy: 4 open
doorpost: 4 jamb 5 jambe
doors
behind closed ~: 6 inside 8 secretly 9 privately
like some ~: 5 paned 6 bifold
open ~: 3 aid 4 ease, help 6 assist 10 facilitate
path to some ~: 5 stoop
Doors
leader: Jim Morrison
song: Hello, I Love You (1968)
Light My Fire (1967)
Touch Me (1969)
door's open!, The: 5 enter 6 come in
doorstep: 9 threshold
not leave on the ~: 5 ask in
welcomer: 3 mat
Doors, The (1991 film)
cast: Kevin Dillon, Val Kilmer, Meg Ryan
director: Oliver Stone
doorstop: 5 wedge
Door, The
author: Mary Roberts Rinehart
Door to December, The
author: Dean Koontz
doorway: 4 exit, gate 5 entry, lobby 6 entrée, portal 7 ingress 8 entrance 9 threshold
accessory: 3 mat
part: 4 jamb, sill 5 jambe
do-over: 3 let 8 mulligan
doo-wop: 5 music, style
syllable: 3 dah, dum
Doo Wop (1998 song)
artist: Lauryn Hill
doozie: 3 pip 4 lulu, oner 5 beaut, dilly 6 beauty, killer 8 standout 9 humdinger 10 ripsnorter
dope: 3 tip 4 info, news 5 facts, goods 6 gossip, notice, skinny, tipoff 7 details, lowdown, pinhead 9 knowledge
out: 6 decode, design, figure, unfold 7 measure, unravel 8 decipher
see also ninny
dope __: 3 out
__-dope: 5 rope-a
dopey: 5 dense, inane, silly, thick 6 obtuse, sleepy, stupid, torpid 7 doltish, foolish, languid, lumpish, out of it, witless 8 mindless, sluggish 9 befuddled, dim-witted, lethargic, senseless, soporific 10 weak-minded
Dopey: 5 dwarf
colleague: *see* dwarf
doppelgänger: 4 twin 5 ghost, image 7 specter
Doppler __: 5 radar 6 effect
Doppler, Christian: 8 Austrian 9 physicist
dor: 3 bug 6 beetle, insect 7 June bug 8 elaterid
__ d'or: 5 louis 6 chaise, siècle
__ d'Or: 3 Val 4 Côte, L'Age 5 Le Coq, Palme
__ Dora: 4 dumb
dorado: 7 dolphin 8 mahimahi
do-rag: 5 scarf 8 kerchief
Doran: 3 Ann
Dora the Explorer (Nick children's)
voice cast: Jean Carlos Celi (Tico the Squirrel)
Regan Mizrahi (Boots the Monkey)
Caitlin Sanchez (Dora Marquez)
Lenique Vincent (Isa the Iguana)
Marc Weiner (Swiper the Fox)
Dorati, Antal: 9 conductor, Hungarian
Dorcas
emulate: 3 sew
doré: 6 gilded, golden
Doré: 7 Gustave
do-re-mi
see moolah
Do Re Mi: 7 musical
composer: Jule Styne
Do-Re-Mi
composer: Oscar Hammerstein, Richard Rodgers
Dorff: 7 Stephen
Dorfman, Ariel: 6 writer 7 Chilean
__ Doria: 6 Andrea
Dorian: 4 Gray, mode
Doric: 5 order 6 column 9 classical
alternative: 5 Ionic 10 Corinthian
column ridge: 5 arris
Do-Right, Dudley girl: 4 Nell
Doris: 3 Day 4 Duke, Hart 7 Lessing, Roberts 8 asteroid
daughter: 7 Galatea
Doritos: 5 snack 9 taco chips
__ d'Orléans: 3 Ile
dorm: 4 hall, home 5 lodge 7 bedroom, lodging 8 quarters 9 residence
drudge: 4 wonk
inhabitant: 4 coed 7 student
item: 3 bed 5 pin-up
overseer: 2 RA
sound: 5 snore
view, perhaps: 4 quad
dormancy: 5 sleep 6 torpor 7 latency, slumber 8 abeyance 10 suspension
dormant: 3 lax 4 idle, lazy, logy 5 inert, still 6 asleep, dozing, draggy, fallow, latent, torpid 7 abeyant, napping, passive 8 dreaming, inactive, indolent, in repose, listless, sleeping, slothful, sluggish, snoozing 9 lethargic, potential, quiescent, sacked out, sedentary, sidelined, somnolent, suspended 10 disengaged, on the shelf, slumbering, unrealized
lie ~: 3 sit 6 hole up 8 go unused 9 hibernate
dormer: 4 loft 6 garret, window
build a ~: 5 add on
dormouse: 4 loir 5 lerot 6 animal, mammal, rodent
relative: *see* rodent
Dormouse's Tale, The, sister in: 5 Lacie
Dorn: 4 Erik 6 Philip 7 Michael
__ d'Oro: 6 Stella
Dorobo home: 5 Kenya 6 Africa 8 Tanzania
Dorothea: 3 Dix 5 Lange
Dorothy: 3 Day, Dix 4 Gale, Gish 5 Lyman, Moore, Tutin, Uhnak 6 Fields, Fisher, Gilman, Hamill, Lamour, Loudon, Malone, Parker, Sayers 7 Hodgkin, McGuire, Provine 8 Chandler 9 Bredehorn, Dandridge, Kilgallen 10 Richardson
co-panelist of ~: 6 Arlene 7 Bennett
dog: 4 Toto
slipper material: 4 ruby
to Em: 5 niece
dorp: 6 hamlet 7 village
dorper: 5 sheep
__ Dorrit: 6 Little
dorsal: 3 fin 4 back, rear 7 fin type 9 posterior
insect's ~ surface: 5 notum
dorsal __: 3 fin
__ d'Orsay: 4 Quai
D'Orsay: 4 Fifi
Dors, Diana: 7 actress
spouse: Richard Dawson
Dorset: 6 county
city: 5 Poole 11 Bournemouth
locale: 7 England
Dorset Horn: 5 sheep
Dorsetshire: 6 county
capital: 10 Dorchester
town: 5 Poole
Dorsett, Tony: 10 footballer
Dorsey: 5 Jimmy, Tommy
Dorsey, Jimmy: 11 saxophonist
instrument: alto sax, clarinet
song: So Rare (1957)
Dorsey, Tommy: 10 trombonist
theme song: 5 Marie
tune: 3 You 4 Nola 5 Marie
dorsum: 4 back
Dortmund: 4 city, town
locale: 7 Germany
Dortmund-__ Canal: 3 Ems
dory: 4 boat, fish 5 barge, craft, skiff 6 vessel 7 rowboat 8 sailboat
move a ~: 3 oar, row
__-dory: 5 hunky
Dory: 6 Previn
dos: 3 two 6 numero 7 Spanish
follower: 4 tres
preceder: 3 uno
Dos __: 5 Equis 6 Passos
DOS
alternative: 4 Unix 5 Linux 7 Windows
command: 3 del, dir 4 copy, more, sort, type 5 erase 6 rename
part: 4 disk 6 system 9 operating
popularizer: 3 IBM
runner: 2 PC
dos-à-dos: 4 step
dosage: 6 amount
amount.: 2 cc. 3 tsp. 4 tbsp.
schedule: 3 q.i.d., t.i.d.
do's and don'ts: 4 code 5 rules 6 policy 7 customs 8 standard
dose: 4 pill 5 share, treat 6 tablet 7 capsule, measure, portion 8 dispense, medicine, quantity 10 medicament, medication
holder: 4 hypo 5 ampul 6 ampule, caplet, tablet 7 ampoule
starter: 4 mega
Doshisha University
locale: 5 Japan, Kioto, Kyoto
do-si-do: 4 step
__ Do Something to Me: 3 You
Dos Passos, John: 6 writer
work: The 42nd Parallel
The Big Money
Century's Ebb
Manhattan Transfer
Three Soldiers
U.S.A.
doss: 3 bed
dossier: 4 file 6 folder, papers, record, report 7 archive, profile 9 portfolio
Dostoyevsky, Fyodor: 6 writer 7 Russian
work: The Brothers Karamazov
Crime and Punishment
The Double
The Gambler
The House of the Dead
The Idiot
Notes From the Underground
Poor Folk
The Possessed
dot: 3 bit, jot, pip 4 atom, iota, mark, mite, mote, spot 5 dowry, fleck, grain, pixel, point, speck 6 dapple, dowery, pepper, period, tittle 7 freckle, lentigo, spatter, stipple 8 flyspeck, particle, pinpoint, sprinkle 9 bespeckle
computer ~: 3 pel 5 pixel
follower: 3 com, edu, gov, net, org
map ~: 3 cay, key 4 isle, town 5 islet 6 island
on the ~: 5 exact, right, sharp 6 prompt 7 exactly, precise 8 accurate, promptly, punctual
dot __: 6 matrix
dot-__: 3 com
__ dot: 5 on the, polka
DOT
agency: 3 FAA
part of ~: 4 Dept. 10 Department

dot-com: **7** company
auction site: **4** eBay
dream: **3** IPO
stock: **6** Amazon
dote on: **4** baby, like, love **5** adore, enjoy, spoil **6** coddle, cosset, pamper **7** cherish, idolize, indulge, worship **8** fawn over, fuss over, give in to **9** care about
Dothan: **4** city, town
locale: **7** Alabama
__ Do That: **4** I Can
Do That to Me One More Time (1979 song)
artist: Captain & Tennille
do the __: **4** math **5** trick
Do the Bird (1963 song)
artist: Dee Dee Sharp
Do the Clam (1965 song)
artist: Elvis Presley
Do the Right Thing (1989 film)
cast: Danny Aiello, Ossie Davis, Ruby Dee, Spike Lee
director: Spike Lee
pizzeria: **4** Sal's
__ doth protest..., The: **4** lady
doting: **4** fond **6** loving **7** amatory, amorous, devoted, fatuous, valuing **8** lovesick **9** amatorial, indulgent
dot-matrix __: **7** printer
Dotrice: **3** Roy **5** Karen
__ dots: **5** Botts
dotted __: **4** line
dotterel: **4** bird
Dottie: **4** West
dottle: **3** ash
dotty: **4** daft, gaga, loco **5** balmy, daffy, goofy, goosy, loopy **6** absurd **7** bonkers, foolish, touched **9** eccentric **10** off-the-wall
Douay Bible
book: **4** Osee **6** Tobias
Jacob's son in the ~: **4** Aser
Shem's father in the ~: **3** Noe
double: **3** duo, hit **4** copy, dual, fold, mate, rise, same, twin **5** binal, clone, ditto, image, match, Xerox **6** bifold, binary, binate, duplex, paired **7** coupled, replica, stand-in, twofold **8** knockoff, likeness, multiply **9** alternate, dualistic, duplicate, facsimile, imitation, look-alike, photocopy **10** dead ringer, reciprocal
agent: **3** spy **4** mole **8** turncoat
back: **4** turn **6** return **7** reverse
combining form: **4** dipl- **5** diplo-
curve: **3** ess **4** ogee
Dutch: **4** game **8** jump rope
ender: **3** ton **4** tree, wide, word **5** speak, think **6** header
entendre: **3** pun **8** wordplay
(for): **5** cover **6** fill in **10** substitute
on the ~: **3** now **4** anon, ASAP, fast, stat **5** apace, quick **6** pronto **7** hastily, quickly, rapidly, swiftly, tantivy **8** promptly **9** posthaste
over: **4** fold **5** stoop
prefix: **2** bi- **3** twi-
take: **8** reaction, response
trouble: **6** plight **8** quandary
whammy: **5** shock
Windsor: **4** knot
double __: **3** bar, bed, cup, run **4** axel, bass, bill, bind, bond, coat, date, demy, flat, ikat, jump, knit, play, reed, room, salt, star, stop, take, tape, tide, time, whip, wing **5** agent, bogey, eagle, fault, helix, steal, sugar, truck **6** boiler, dagger **7** bassoon, dribble, entente, feature
double-__: **3** cut, dip **4** bank, book, crop, date, dome, duty, knit, lock, park, reed, ring, talk, team, time, wide **5** blind, check, click, cross, digit, edged, ended, quick, sided, space **6** acting, action, bottom, clutch, decker **7** dealing, jointed
double-__ bookkeeping: **5** entry
double-__ inflation: **5** digit
double-__ sword: **5** edged
double-__ window: **4** hung
__ double: **3** RBI, see **4** body **5** daily, on the
Double __: **4** Dare **5** Dutch, Fudge
Double-__: **7** Crostic
__ Double: **4** Body **5** On the
double-blind: **4** test
double-check: **2** OK **4** back, okay, seal, sign, test **5** admit, check, prove, vouch **6** affirm, attest, ensure, look up, ratify, settle, uphold, verify **7** approve, bear out, certify, confess, confirm, endorse, indorse, justify, sustain, witness **8** check out, evidence, make sure, sanction, validate, vouch for **9** ascertain, establish, guarantee, recommend, respond to, sign off on **10** strengthen
double-cross: **3** con **4** dupe **5** cheat, guile, trick **6** betray, delude, take in **7** deceive, defraud, mislead, sell out, swindle, two-time **8** hoodwink **9** treachery
double-crosser: **3** rat **5** cheat, knave, louse, snake, sneak **7** traitor **8** turncoat
double-crossing: **5** lying **7** knavish, perfidy **8** disloyal **9** underhand, unethical
doubled: **4** dual
combining form: **3** bis-
Double Dare: **8** game show
host: Mark Summers
double-daters: **4** four
Doubleday: **5** Abner **6** Nelson
double-deal: **5** cheat **7** two-time
double-dealer: **5** cheat, fraud, snake **7** traitor **8** swindler
double-dealing: **3** sly **5** dirty, false, fraud, lying **6** artful, deceit, dupery, rotten, sneaky, tricky **7** chicane, corrupt, crooked, devious, falsity, knavish, perfidy, swindle **8** bad faith, betrayal, cheating, delusive, guileful, intrigue, pretense, recreant, trickery, two-faced **9** deceitful, deception, dishonest, duplicity, insincere, treachery **10** mendacious, traitorous, untruthful
double-decker: **3** bus
double eagle: **4** coin
double-edged: **6** ironic
Double Fantasy
artist: Yoko Ono
Double Fudge
author: Judy Blume
double-hook shape: **3** ess
double-hung: **6** window
Double Indemnity: **4** film **5** novel
author: James M. Cain
cast: Fred MacMurray, Edward G. Robinson, Barbara Stanwyck
director: Billy Wilder
Double Jeopardy (1999 film)
cast: Annabeth Gish, Tommy Lee Jones, Ashley Judd
double-jointed: **5** agile
__ double life: **4** led a
Double Lovin' (1971 song)
artist: Osmonds
Double Man, The
author: W.H. Auden
Doublemint: **10** chewing gum
alternative: *see* chewing gum
double or __: **7** nothing
Double or Nothing: **9** radio show
double-quick: **5** apace, swift **7** hastily, swiftly **9** posthaste
double-reed: **4** oboe
__ doubles: **5** mixed
doublespeak: **6** jargon **8** language **9** misinform
doublet: **3** duo, set, two **4** duad, pair **6** couple, jacket, jerkin
__ double take: **3** do a
double-talk
see baloney
Double, The
author: Fyodor Dostoyevsky
double-time: **3** hie **4** fast **5** brisk, fleet, hasty, quick, rapid, speed, swift **6** flying, racing, speedy **7** express, hurried, instant **9** breakneck, instantly
DoubleTree: **5** hotel
alternative: *see* hotel
Double Vision
author: Mary Higgins Clark
Double Vision (1978 song)
artist: Foreigner
doubloon: **4** coin, gold **5** money
doubly: **5** extra, twice **7** twofold
doubt: **5** qualm, query, worry **6** wonder **7** dubiety, problem, scruple, suspect **8** bad vibes, distrust, mistrust, quandary, question, suspense, wariness **9** ambiguity, confusion, disbelief, discredit, dubiosity, hesitancy, leeriness, misgiving, nonbelief, smell a rat, suspicion **10** disbelieve, hesitation, indecision, insecurity, skepticism
cry of ~: **2** uh, um **3** bah, hah **4** I bet **5** humph
express ~: **5** demur, query, waver **6** impugn **8** question
free from ~: **4** sure **5** prove **6** assure **7** certify, satisfy **8** convince **9** guarantee
have ~: **8** mistrust
have no ~: **4** know
no ~ should: **7** had best
without a ~: *see* of course **4** amen, true **5** by far, quite, right, truly **6** and how, indeed, rather, really, righto, verily **7** clearly, exactly, for real, quite so, readily **8** as you say, to be sure **9** darn right, decidedly, hands down, obviously, you said it **10** far and away, sure enough, undeniably
__-doubt: **4** self
Doubt (2008 film)
cast: Amy Adams, Philip Seymour Hoffman, Meryl Streep
doubter: **5** cynic **6** critic **7** sceptic, scoffer, skeptic **8** agnostic **10** questioner
__ Doubtfire: **3** Mrs.
doubtful: **4** iffy, moot, open, wary **5** chary, leery, queer, rocky, shaky, vague **6** louche, unfirm, unsure **7** cynical, dubious, guarded, puzzled, suspect, tenuous **8** agnostic, cautious, hesitant, unlikely, unstable **9** ambiguous, debatable, equivocal, skeptical, tentative, uncertain, undecided, unsettled **10** disputable, hesitating, improbable, indecisive, indefinite, infeasible, precarious, suspicious, unresolved
doubting: **4** wary **5** leery **8** hesitant **9** skeptical
Thomas: **7** sceptic, skeptic
doubtless: **4** sure **6** easily, likely, surely **8** for a fact, probably **9** assuredly, certainly, evidently, precisely, seemingly **10** absolutely, apparently, definitely, far and away, most likely, ostensibly, positively, presumably, supposedly
doubtlessly: **6** indeed
douceur: **3** tip **5** bonus **9** lagniappe
Doug: **4** Ford **6** Flutie, McKeon, Savant **7** Henning, McClure, Sanders
dough: **3** mix **4** loaf **5** bread **6** batter **7** mixture
component: **5** yeast
does it: **4** rise
ender: **3** boy, nut **4** face
lover: **5** miser **9** skinflint
Mideast ~: **4** filo
one with ~: **5** baker
prepare ~: **5** knead **6** leaven
rolling in ~: **4** rich **5** flush **6** loaded, monied **7** moneyed, wealthy, well-off **8** affluent, in clover, well-to-do **9** well-fixed **10** in the money, privileged, propertied, prosperous, well-heeled
see also moolah
doughboy: **2** GI **4** Yank
conflict: **3** WWI
group: **3** AEF
doughtiness: **4** grit **5** nerve, pluck, valor **7** bravery, heroism
doughty: **4** bold, game, hale, iron, wiry **5** beefy, brave, burly, gutsy, hardy, hefty, hunky, husky, lusty, nervy, stout, tough **6** awless, brawny, daring, gritty, hearty, heroic, mighty, plucky, potent, robust, rugged, sinewy, spunky, steely, stocky, sturdy, virile **7** aweless, defiant, gallant, impavid, staunch, valiant **8** athletic, fearless, forceful, heroical, indurate, intrepid, muscular, powerful, puissant, resolute, stalwart, unafraid, valorous, vigorous **9** Atlantean, audacious, dauntless, dreadless, Herculean, strapping, undaunted, unfearful, unfearing, well-built **10** able-bodied, courageous, red-blooded, undismayed
doughy: **3** wan **4** pale, soft **5** ashen, pasty **6** pallid
Douglas: **3** fir **4** Barr, Carl, city, Kirk, Mike, Paul, Sirk **5** Donna, Moore **6** Gordon, Hickox, Mawson, Melvyn, Norman **7** capital, Illeana, Michael, Stephen, Stewart **8** Corri-

gan, Osheroff, Trumbull 9 Fairbanks, MacArthur
locale: 9 Isle of Man
Douglas __: 3 fir
Douglas-Home, Alec: 2 P.M. 7 British
predecessor: 9 Macmillan
successor: 6 Wilson
Douglas, Kirk: 5 actor
film: The Bad and the Beautiful (1952)
The Big Carnival (1951)
The Big Sky (1952)
The Brotherhood (1968)
Champion (1949)
Detective Story (1951)
The Devil's Disciple (1959)
Diamonds (1999)
The Final Countdown (1980)
The Fury (1978)
Gunfight at the O.K. Corral (1957)
The Hook (1963)
The Indian Fighter (1955)
The Last Sunset (1961)
Last Train From Gun Hill (1959)
A Letter to Three Wives (1949)
Lonely Are the Brave (1962)
Lust for Life (1956)
The Man From Snowy River (1982)
The Man Without a Star (1955)
Out of the Past (1947)
Paths of Glory (1957)
Posse (1975)
Seven Days in May (1964)
Spartacus (1960)
The Strange Loves of Martha Ivers (1946)
There Was a Crooked Man... (1970)
Tough Guys (1986)
Town Without Pity (1961)
Two Weeks in Another Town (1962)
The War Wagon (1967)
Young Man With a Horn (1950)
Douglas, Lloyd C. novel: The Robe
Douglas, Melvyn: 5 actor
film: Annie Oakley (1935)
Being There (1979, AA)
Billy Budd (1962)
Captains Courageous (1937)
Hud (1963, AA)
I Never Sang for My Father (1970)
Ninotchka (1939)
Too Many Husbands (1940)
Two-Faced Woman (1941)
spouse: Helen Gahagan
Douglas, Michael: 5 actor
father: 4 Kirk
film: The American President (1995)
Basic Instinct (1992)
Black Rain (1989)
The China Syndrome (1979)
A Chorus Line (1985)
Coma (1978)
Disclosure (1994)
Don't Say a Word (2001)
Fatal Attraction (1987)
The Game (1997)
It Runs in the Family (2003)
It's My Turn (1980)
The Jewel of the Nile (1985)
King of California (2007)
A Perfect Murder (1998)
Romancing the Stone (1984)
The Sentinel (2006)
Shining Through (1992)
Traffic (2000)
Wall Street (1987, AA)
The War of the Roses (1989)
Wonder Boys (2000)
spouse: Catherine Zeta-Jones
TV: The Streets of San Francisco
Douglas, Norman: 6 writer 7 British
Douglass: 5 North 9 Dumbrille, Frederick 10 Montgomery
Douglas, Stephen A.: 6 orator
Do unto __: 6 others
dour: 3 sad 4 dark, glum, grim, sour, ugly 5 bleak, grave, moody, sulky, surly 6 crabby, crusty, dismal, dreary, gloomy, morose, severe, sullen 8 lowering, taciturn 9 saturnine, unsmiling 10 forbidding, ill-humored
Dourif: 4 Brad
dourness: 9 austerity
Douro: 5 river
locale: 5 Spain 8 Portugal
douse: 3 wet 4 kill, soak, wash 5 plash, snuff, souse, water 6 drench, embrue, imbrue, put out, quench, splash 7 blow out, immerse, smother, spatter, turn off 8 saturate, snuff out, submerge 10 extinguish
doused: 3 out
douser need: 4 hose 7 hydrant
__-doux: 6 billet
douze: 6 French, twelve
dove: 4 bird, gray, grey 5 cooer 6 culver, purply 7 pinkish 8 pacifist, peacenik, purplish
branch: 5 olive
ender: 3 cot 4 cote, tail
home: 4 cote
intention: 5 peace
name meaning ~: 5 Jonah, Jonas 6 Jemima
opposite: 4 hawk
relative: *see* gray color 3 ash
sound: 3 coo
starter: 4 ring 6 turtle
Dove: 4 Rita, soap 6 Billie
alternative: *see* soap
Dove __: 3 Bar
dovecote: 6 aviary, volary
dovekie: 3 auk 4 bird
dovelike: 6 gentle 8 peaceful
Dovells
song: Bristol Stomp (1961)
You Can't Sit Down (1963)
Dover: 4 city, port, town 6 strait
county: 4 Kent
fish: 4 sole
locale: 3 Del. 4 Kent 7 England 8 Delaware
sight: 5 cliff
the white cliffs of ~: 5 chalk
town opposite ~: 6 Calais
Dover __: 4 sole 5 Beach
Dover Beach
author: Matthew Arnold
Dove, Rita: 4 poet
Doves in immemorial __: 4 elms
Dove's Nest, The
author: Katherine Mansfield
dovetail: 2 go 3 fit 4 gybe, jibe, link, mesh 5 match, tenon 6 cohere 7 conform 8 coincide, junction, juncture 9 harmonize, interlink, interlock, make sense 10 correspond
__-dovey: 5 lovey
dovish: 6 irenic 8 irenical, peaceful
Dow: 4 Tony 5 index, Peggy
partner: 5 Jones
Do-Wacka-Do (1965 song)
artist: Roger Miller
dowager: 4 dame 5 woman 6 female 10 noblewoman
__ dowager: 5 queen
Do Wah Diddy Diddy (1964 song)
artist: Manfred Mann
Dowd
friend: 5 pooka 6 Harvey, rabbit
dowdy: 4 drab 5 dated, messy, passé, tacky 6 blowsy, frowsy, frowzy, frumpy, old hat, shabby, sordid, stodgy, unneat, untidy 7 unkempt 8 outdated, outmoded, slovenly 9 out-of-date, unstylish 10 antiquated, bedraggled, disheveled, disorderly
not ~: 4 neat
one: 5 frump
dowel: 3 peg, rod
__-do-well: 4 ne'er
dowel-shaping tool: 4 nogg
dowitcher: 4 bird
Dow Jones
figure: 3 low 4 high 5 close 7 average
firm: 3 IBM 5 Exxon, Kodak 7 Walmart
index: 4 rail 7 utility 10 industrial
unit: 5 point
down: 3 eat, fur, low, nap, sad 4 blue, fell, fuzz, glum, lick, moor, mopy, pile, sick, take 5 below, drink, fluff, level, lower, moody, mopey, not up, outdo, quaff, under, woful 6 broody, gloomy, imbibe, ingest, lonely, morose, sickly, somber, woeful 7 consume, daunted, doleful, falling, forlorn, hangdog, in a funk, plumage, sinking, swallow, unhappy 8 brooding, dejected, desolate, dropping, inactive, listless, overcome, sluggish, troubled 9 bummed-out, cheerless, depressed, heartsick, miserable, polish off, woebegone 10 chapfallen, descending, despondent, dispirited, distressed, in the dumps, melancholy, out of order, out of sorts, spiritless, underneath
ender: 3 bow 4 beat, cast, fall, haul, hill, link, load, play, pour, side, size, spin, tick, time, town, turn, wind, zone 5 burst, court, draft, field, grade, range, right, river, scale, shift, slide, spout, stage, state, swing, trend 6 market, rigger, stairs, stater, stream 7 hearted, trodden
not ~: 6 across
prefix: 3 cat- 4 cata-, cath-, hypo-
starter: 3 hoe, let, low, put, rub, run, sun 4 come, draw, face, look, mark, melt, push, show, shut, slow, take, tear, turn 5 break, bring, build, clamp, climb, close, count, crack, eider, knock, paste, phase, shake, shoot, spell, stand, swans, touch 6 splash, tumble 7 thistle
the road: 4 soon 5 later
down __: 4 card, cold, East 5 quark, under 7 payment
down __ mouth: 5 at the, in the
down __ wire: 5 to the
down-__: 3 bow 4 home, zone 6 easter, market
down-__-heel: 5 at-the
__ down: 3 cry, cut, die, get, lay, let, lie, mow, pat, pin, put, rub, run, set, sit, tie 4 back, bear, boil, call, chow, come, dash, deep, draw, dumb, face, fall, gear, hand, hold, keep, live, mark, nail, pare, pipe, play, pull, ride, salt, shut, slap, slim, step, take, talk, tear, tone, turn, wash, wear, wind, wolf 5 break, bring, clamp, climb, close, count, crack, crank, dress, eider, first, knock, phase, plunk, scarf, shake, shoot, shout, stand, stare, touch, track, water, weigh, write 6 buckle, powder, settle, simmer, splash, strike, thumbs, upside 7 drawing, knuckle, ratchet, talking
__ down!: 4 Pipe
__-down: 3 low, put, sit, top 4 fold 5 hands, up-and 6 broken, tumble
Down __: 3 Low 4 East 5 Under
Down __ Riverside: 5 by the
__ Down: 6 Boogie
down-and-__: 3 out 5 dirty, outer
down-and-dirty: 5 funky, nasty
down-and-out: 4 poor 5 needy 8 deprived, wretched 9 destitute, penniless
down-and-outer: 5 loser
Down and Out in Beverly Hills (1986 film)
cast: Richard Dreyfuss, Bette Midler, Nick Nolte
dog: 7 Matisse
Down and Out in Paris and London
author: George Orwell
__ down a peg: 4 take
Down at __ Joe's: 4 Papa
down at the __: 5 mouth
down-at-the-heel: 4 mean 5 seedy
downbeat: 4 glum 5 tempo 6 broody, gloomy, rhythm, solemn, thesis 7 unhappy 8 dejected, negative 9 cheerless, defeatist, unhopeful 10 dispirited
in music: 6 thesis
Down by the __: 4 Erie
Down by the Lazy River (1972 song)
artist: Osmonds
Down by the Old Mill __: 6 Stream
Down by the Salley Gardens
author: William Butler Yeats
__-down cake: 6 upside
downcast: 4 mopy 5 mopey 7 daunted, subdued 8 brooding, listless 9 desperate, exanimate 10 distressed, spiritless
one: 5 moper
see also gloomy
__-down-drag-out: 5 knock
Down East: 5 Maine
Downeaster __, The: 5 Alexa
downer: 4 drag 5 slump 6 bummer 7 bad luck, bad news, killjoy, sadness 8 bad scene, narcotic 9 pessimist, rough time
on a ~: 4 blue 9 depressed
starter: 3 sun

Downers Grove: 4 city, town
locale: 8 Illinois
Downes: 4 Olin
Downey: 4 city, Roma, town 6 Morton, Robert
locale: 10 California
Downey Jr., Robert: 5 actor
film: Air America (1990)
Black and White (2000)
Chances Are (1989)
Chaplin (1992)
Good Night, and Good Luck (2005)
Gothika (2003)
Heart and Souls (1993)
Iron Man (2008)
Only You (1994)
Restoration (1995)
Soapdish (1991)
The Soloist (2009)
Tropic Thunder (2008)
True Believer (1989)
U.S. Marshals (1998)
Wonder Boys (2000)
Zodiac (2007)
Downey, Morton: 5 tenor 6 singer
downfall: 3 dud 4 bane, bomb, bust, doom, flop, loss, ruin 5 decay, smash, wrack 6 defeat, demise, fiasco, mishap, turkey 7 blunder, debacle, descent, failure, misstep, stumble, undoing, washout 8 collapse, Waterloo 9 perdition, ruination
downgrade: 4 bust 5 abase, break, lower, slope 6 demote, reduce 7 decline, degrade, depress, descent, devalue 8 relegate, write off 9 decadence, declivity, denigrate, devaluate, disparage, overwhelm 10 degeneracy, depreciate, devalorize, undervalue
downhearted
see gloomy
downhill: 7 dipping, falling 8 dropping 9 declining 10 descending
go ~: 3 ski 4 fail, sink 5 slide, slump 6 worsen 7 decline 10 degenerate
racer: 4 luge, sled 5 skier 7 bobsled 8 skeleton
see also ski
Downhill Racer (1969 film)
cast: Gene Hackman, Robert Redford
down-home: 6 folksy
__ Down in Darkness: 3 Lie
...__ down in green pastures: 5 to lie
Downing Street
number: 3 ten
resident: 2 P.M.
Down in the Delta (1998 film)
cast: Al Freeman Jr., Wesley Snipes, Alfre Woodard
director: Maya Angelou
Down, Lesley-Anne: 7 actress
spouse: William Friedkin
downlooker: 4 snob 5 snoot
Down Low (1996 song)
artist: R. Kelly
__ down on: 3 cut 4 come, look, shut
__ down one's nose at: 4 look
__ down one's throat: 3 ram 5 shove
down on one's __: 4 luck
Down on the Corner (1969 song)
artist: Creedence Clearwater Revival
__ down on the job: 3 lie
down partner: 5 dirty
downplay: 8 belittle, minimize 9 extenuate, soft-pedal, whitewash 10 understate
downpour: 4 rain 5 flood, spate, storm 6 deluge 7 monsoon, torrent 8 drencher 9 rainstorm 10 cloudburst, inundation
downreaching: 4 deep
downright: 4 open, pure, rank, sure, very 5 blunt, clear, frank, gross, plain, plumb, sheer, stark, total, utter 6 arrant, candid, direct, honest, wholly 7 blatant, certain 8 absolute, definite, explicit, outright, specific, straight, thorough 9 arbitrary, decidedly, out-and-out 10 consummate, definitive, thoroughly, unmediated
downrush: 5 swoop 6 pounce 7 cascade
Downs: 4 Hugh
__ Downs: 5 Epsom
downscale: 6 low-end
__-down shirt: 6 button
downsize: 4 pare, trim 5 lower 6 lessen, reduce, shrink 7 abridge, curtail, cut back 8 decrease, diminish, roll back
downslide: 3 sag 4 drop 5 slump 7 decline 9 worsening
downs partner: 3 ups
downspout: 6 leader
__ Down Staircase: 5 Up the
downstairs worker: 4 maid
__-down strike: 3 sit
downswing: 5 slump 7 decline 9 worsening
down the __: 4 line, road 5 drain, hatch, tubes
__ down the curtain: 4 ring
__ down the garden path: 4 lead, take
__ down the gauntlet: 5 throw
Down the hatch!: 5 toast
__ down the hatches: 6 batten
__ down the house: 5 bring
__ down the law: 3 lay
__-down theory: 7 trickle
__ down the pike: 4 come
__ down the river: 4 sell
downtime: 4 lull, rest, wait 5 break, delay, pause 6 catnap, recess 7 interim, respite 8 interval, stoppage 9 interlude 10 suspension
down-to-__: 5 earth
__ down to: 5 speak
__ down to cases: 3 get
down-to-earth: 4 real, sane 5 sober 6 common, folksy 7 mundane 8 rational, sensible 9 practical, pragmatic, realistic
__ Down to Rio: 6 Flying
__ down to size: 3 cut
down to the __: 4 wire
downtown: 3 urb 4 city 5 urban
Downtown (1965 song)
artist: Petula Clark
Downtown Train (1989 song)
artist: Rod Stewart
downtrend: 4 drop 5 slump
downtrodden: 6 abject
downturn: 3 dip, sag 4 drip, drop, fall 5 panic, slide, slump 6 plunge 7 decline, descent, plummet, retreat 8 decrease, slowdown 9 recession, worsening
Down Under
see Australia
Down Under (1982 song)
artist: Men at Work
__ down upon: 4 look
downward: 5 under 10 descending
glide ~: 5 sweep
slope: 3 dip 4 drop 7 descent, incline 8 gradient 9 declivity
downwards: 5 below
downwind: 4 alee
__ down with: 4 come
down with in French: 4 à bas
Down With Love (2003 film)
cast: Ewan McGregor, Renée Zellweger
Down with the King (1993 song)
artist: Run-D.M.C.
downy: 4 soft 5 cushy, furry, fuzzy, light, linty, nappy, plush, wooly 6 fleecy, flossy, fluffy, napped, woolly 7 squishy, velvety 8 cushiony
duck: 5 eider
fruit: 5 peach
surface: 3 nap 4 pile
Downy: 8 softener
alternative: 6 Bounce 7 Snuggle 9 Cling Free 10 Final Touch
downy-cheeked: 5 young
dowry: 3 dot
of a ~: 5 dotal
dowse: 6 divine, put out 10 waterwitch
dowser tool: 3 rod
doxology: 6 Gloria
__ doxology: 5 great 6 lesser 7 greater
Do Ya
artist: ELO, K.T. Oslin
doyen: 4 dean, king 5 elder 6 leader
Doyle: 5 David
Doyle, Arthur Conan: 3 Sir 6 writer 7 British
work: A Case of Identity
The Doings of Raffles Haw
The Firm of Girdlestone
The Five Orange Pips
The Great Shadow
The Hound of the Baskervilles
The Land of Mist
The Lost World
The Maracot Deep
Micah Clarke
The Mystery of Cloomber
The Parasite
The Poison Belt
The Red-Headed League
The Refugees
The Ring of Thoth
A Scandal in Bohemia
The Sign of Four
Sir Nigel
A Study in Scarlet
The Tragedy of Korosko
The Valley of Fear
The White Company
Doyle, Popeye: 4 narc, nark
D'Oyly Carte: 7 Richard
Do you __?: 4 mind
Do You Believe in Love (1982 song)
artist: Huey Lewis and the News
Do You Believe in Magic (1965 song)
artist: Lovin' Spoonful
Do You Believe in Us (1992 song)
artist: Jon Secada
__ do you do: 3 how
Do You Feel Like We Do (1976 song)
artist: Peter Frampton
__ do you good!: 4 It'll
Do you have two fives for __?: 4 a ten
Do You Know the Way to San José (1968 song)
artist: Dionne Warwick
Do You Love Me (1962 song)
artist: Contours
Do you mean that?: 6 really
Do You Really Want to Hurt Me (1983 song)
artist: Culture Club
Do You Remember? (1990 song)
artist: Phil Collins
__ Do You Trust?: 3 Who
Do You Want Me (1991 song)
artist: Salt-n-Pepa
Do You Want to Dance (song)
artist: Bobby Freeman, Bette Midler
Do You Want to Know a Secret (1964 song)
artist: Beatles
doze: 3 nap, nod 4 rest, yawn 5 sleep 6 catnap, drowse, nod off, siesta, snooze 7 drop off, shuteye, slumber 8 drift off 9 get sleepy 10 fall asleep, forty winks
starter: 4 bull
doze __: 3 off
dozen: 3 qty. 6 twelve 8 quantity
courtroom ~: 4 jury
daily ~: 5 drill 8 exercise
dime a ~: 5 usual 6 common 7 humdrum, liberal, profuse 9 bountiful
moons: 4 year
one of a ~: 3 Apr., Aug., Dec., Feb., Jan., Jun., Mar., May, Nov., Oct., Sep. 4 July, Sept. 5 April, March, month 6 August 7 January, June. Jul., October 8 December, February, November 9 September
twelve ~: 5 gross
__ dozen: 4 long 5 daily 6 baker's
dozens: 4 many
__ Dozen, The: 5 Dirty
dozer: 7 machine, vehicle 10 earth mover
starter: 4 bull
Dozier: 6 Lamont
dozing: 6 asleep 7 dormant 9 sacked out, somnolent
sound: 3 zzz
dozy: 6 drowsy, sleepy 9 heavy-eyed, lethargic, somnolent, soporific 10 half-asleep
DP: 7 refugee
Dr. __: 3 Dre, Zee 4 Bull, Evil, Hook, John, Ruth 5 Quinn, Seuss 6 Jekyll, Pepper, Scholl 7 Demento, Kildare
drab: 3 tan 4 arid, blah, dark, dull, flat, gray, grey 5 dingy, dowdy, faded, ho-hum, mirky, mousy, murky, stale, vapid 6 boring, dismal, dreary, frumpy, mousey, shabby, somber 7 humdrum,

insipid, neutral, prosaic, run-down, tedious **8** brownish, lifeless **9** cheerless, colorless, prosaical, washed-out, yellowish **10** lackluster, lusterless, spiritless, tenebrific, uninspired
color: **5** khaki, olive
olive ~: **4** garb **5** dress, khaki **6** attire **7** uniform
relative: *see* gray color
Drabble, Margaret: **6** writer **7** British
sister: Byatt
drabness: **6** tedium
drabs: **8** fatigues
drachma: **4** coin **5** money
country: **6** Greece
fraction: **4** obol **6** lepton
Draco: constellation
neighbor: **4** Lyra **7** Cepheus **9** Ursa Minor
star in ~: **4** Adib
draconian: **4** firm, hard **5** bossy, cruel, harsh, picky, rigid, rough, sever, stern, tough **6** brutal, severe, strict **7** austere, drastic, extreme, Spartan **8** despotic, exacting, hard-line, rigorous **9** demanding, inclement, stringent, unbending, unsparing **10** despotical, inflexible, iron-fisted, no-nonsense, oppressive, tyrannical
Dracula: **7** vampire
airborne ~: **3** bat
author: Bram Stoker
character: **4** Lucy, Mina **6** Harker
deterrent: **6** garlic
outerwear: **4** cape
portrayer: **3** Lee **6** Lugosi
target for ~: **4** neck, vein
weapon: **4** bite
draft: **3** air, ale, map, pen, tap **4** blow, draw, eddy, gust, levy, make, plan, plot, puff, swig, wind **5** blast, check, drink, enrol, force, forge, frame, quaff, write **6** breeze, call up, cheque, choose, design, devise, draw up, enlist, enroll, indite, induct, inflow, layout, muster, sign on, sign up, sketch, summon **7** compose, current, fashion, impress, outline, prepare, project, recruit **8** nominate, potation, proposal, rough out, shanghai, skeleton **9** adumbrate, blueprint, conscribe, conscript, fabricate, formulate **10** air current, call of duty, constitute, money order, settle upon
accept a ~: **5** go pro
activity: **6** call-up
allowing a ~: **4** ajar
animal: **2** ox **5** horse
avoid the ~: **5** dodge **6** enlist
bar: **4** yoke
board initials: **3** SSS
classification: **4** one A, two A **5** four F
first ~: **5** rough
horse: **9** Percheron **10** Clydesdale
improve a ~: **4** redo **5** repen
info: **5** payee
org.: **3** NBA, NFL
starter: **2** up **4** down
draft __: **3** ale **4** beer, mark, mill, tube **5** board, chair **6** animal, dodger
__ draft: **4** bank
draftable: **4** one A
Draft Dodger Rag (1965 song)
artist: Phil Ochs
draftee: **2** GI **3** rct. **7** recruit, soldier **9** legionary
like a rejected ~: **5** unfit
draftsman's deg.: **3** BME
drafty: **4** cold **5** windy **6** breezy, chilly
drag: **3** lag, lug, tow, tug **4** bore, haul, move, pain, pest, pill, plod, puff, pull, race, road, tide, toke **5** crawl, dally, delay, force, shlep, tarry, trail, trawl, trial **6** bother, bummer, burden, dawdle, downer, inhale, loiter, ration, schlep, shlepp, street **7** shuffle **8** haul away, leverage, mark time, nuisance, stagnate, straggle, tiresome, traction **9** annoyance, hindrance, influence, liability **10** impediment, imposition, inhalation, wet blanket
a ~: **5** no fun
down: **6** burden, impede, sadden
ender: **3** net, oon **4** lift, line, ster
in: **5** foist
into court: **3** sue **8** litigate
main ~: **4** road **7** highway
off: **6** remove
on: **8** protract
oneself: **6** trudge
one's feet: **3** lag **4** idle, laze, loaf **5** amble, dally, mosey, stall, tarry **6** dawdle, linger, loiter, put off **7** saunter **8** lollygag, obstruct, straggle **9** waste time **10** dillydally
out: **5** roust **6** expand, extend **7** prolong, stretch **8** lengthen
prepare to ~: **3** rev
strip: **5** track
through the mud: **5** libel, smear, sully, taint **7** tarnish **10** calumniate
up: **5** raise
drag __: **4** bunt, hunt, link, race, rake, sail **5** chain, strip **6** racing
__ drag: **4** main
dragged, being: **5** in-tow
dragging: **4** beat, dull, long, poky **5** unfun **6** boring, sickly **7** gradual, humdrum, impeded, languid, lengthy, tedious **8** dilatory, drawn-out, hesitant, overlong, slothful, sluggish, tiresome **9** leisurely, lethargic, prolonged, snaillike, unhurried, wearisome **10** deliberate, monotonous, protracted
__-dragging: **4** foot
draggle: **5** trail **6** dangle **7** besmear **8** besmirch
draggy: **3** lax **4** dull, flat, idle, lazy, poky, slow **5** inert **6** asleep, boring, jejune, sleepy, torpid **7** dormant, gradual, halting, impeded, lagging, languid, passive **8** crawling, creeping, dawdling, dilatory, dragging, drawn-out, hesitant, inactive, indolent, lifeless, plodding, slothful, sluggish, toddling **9** leisurely, lethargic, prolonged, sedentary, snaillike, unhurried **10** deliberate, disengaged, lackluster, protracted, spiritless
dragnet: **3** APB **4** hunt, seek, trap **5** trawl **6** search **7** manhunt
get in a ~: **3** nab **4** bust, grab, nail, trap **5** catch, pinch, run in, seize **6** arrest, collar, corner, pick up, pull in, snatch **7** capture **9** apprehend
Dragnet (1987 film)
cast: Dan Aykroyd, Tom Hanks, Harry Morgan
Dragnet (NBC drama)
cast: Ben Alexander (Frank Smith) Harry Morgan (Bill Gannon) Jack Webb (Sgt. Joe Friday)
employer: LAPD
dragon: **4** Puff **5** Draco, Ladon, Ollie, Smaug **6** animal, Tiamat **7** monster, reptile
100-headed ~: **5** Ladon
constellation: **5** Draco
ender: **3** fly **4** head, root
green ~: **5** plant
in heraldry: **6** wyvern
Komodo ~: **6** animal **7** reptile
like a ~: **5** scaly
of 1950s TV: **5** Ollie
slain by Sigurd: **6** Fafnir
starter: **4** snap
dragon __: **4** lady
__ dragon: **6** Komodo
Dragon: **5** Daryl **6** Carmen
Dragon __: **4** Lady, Seed **5** Tears
__ Dragon: **3** Red **5** Pete's
Dragon Ball Z: **5** anime
company: **5** Atari
drag one's __: **4** feet **5** heels
dragonfly: **3** bug **6** darner, insect
emulate a ~: **4** dart **5** hover
young ~: **5** naiad
Dragonfly
author: Dean Koontz
Dragonfly (2002 film)
cast: Kathy Bates, Kevin Costner
Dragonheart (1996 film)
cast: Sean Connery, Dennis Quaid
Dragon in the Sea, The
author: Frank Herbert
Dragon Seed
author: Pearl S. Buck
dragon's mouth: **5** plant **6** flower
Dragons of Eden, The
author: Carl Sagan
Dragon Tears
author: Dean Koontz
Dragonwyck
author: Anya Seton
dragoon: **4** ulan **5** bully, force, uhlan **6** coerce, compel, hussar **7** oppress, trooper **8** bulldoze, horseman **9** terrorize **10** cavalryman, equestrian
dragoons: **7** cavalry
Dragoti: **4** Stan
dragster: **4** auto **5** racer **6** hot rod
org.: **4** NHRA
__ Drag, The: **7** Varsity
drain: **3** dry, eat, sap, tap **4** duct, leak, lose, milk, ooze, pipe, pour, pump, seep, sift, tire, vent, void **5** abate, bleed, ditch, empty, exude, leach, sewer, spend, trash, use up, waste, weary **6** burn up, divert, expend, filter, finish, gutter, lessen, osmose, outlet, reduce, remove, run off, siphon, syphon, unload **7** channel, conduit, consume, culvert, decline, deplete, depress, draw off, drink up, dwindle, exhaust, fatigue, flow out, pump out, suck dry, tire out **8** bankrupt, decrease, diminish, evacuate, fool away, get rid of, squander, taper off, wear down **9** discharge, dissipate, filter off, percolate, prostrate **10** debilitate, devitalize, impoverish
cleaner: **3** lye **5** Drano **11** Liquid-Plumr
down the ~: **4** gone, lost, shot **5** kaput, spent **8** misspent
ender: **3** age **4** pipe
off: **4** bail **5** bleed
pour down the ~: **5** waste **8** squander
problem: **4** clog
rain ~: **4** sump
rain ~ locale: **4** curb
storm ~: **5** sewer
__ drain: **5** brain, storm
drainage area: **4** sump **5** basin, bilge, ditch, gully **6** gulley
drained: **3** dry **4** bare, beat, void, worn **5** all in, spent, tired, trite, unwet, weary **6** barren, dished, pooped, vacant **7** far-gone, refined, run-down, vacuous, worn out **8** wiped out **9** burned out, exhausted, prostrate **10** knocked out
of color: **4** ashy, pale **5** ashen
poorly ~: **5** boggy, seepy **6** marshy, swampy
drainer: **5** sieve **8** colander
draining: **9** unstopped
drainpipe section: **4** trap
drake: **4** bird, duck, male
Drake: **3** Tom **4** Paul, Stan **5** Betsy, Edwin, Larry **6** Alfred **7** Charles, Francis
athletes: **8** Bulldogs
author: Alfred Noyes
locale: **4** Iowa **9** Des Moines
Drake, Francis: **3** Sir **7** British **8** explorer
drakes: **3** he's
dram: **3** nip, tot **4** shot, unit **8** libation
fraction: **5** minim
dram. __: **4** pers.
drama: **3** noh **4** play, show, work **5** genre, stage, story **6** hoopla, kabuki, medium, pathos **7** fiction, tension, theater, theatre, tragedy **9** soap opera, spectacle, stage play, stage show **10** grand opera, horse opera, production, tearjerker
award: **4** Obie, Tony
daily ~: **4** soap **9** soap opera
ender, maybe: **4** Act V **5** Act II, Act IV **6** Act III
Japanese ~: **3** noh **6** kabuki
musical ~: **5** opera
start: **4** Act I
starter: **4** melo **5** photo
unit: **3** act **5** scene
dramatic: **5** vivid **6** moving, scenic **8** exciting, powerful, scenical, striking **9** affecting, climactic, emotional, startling, thrilling **10** expressive, histrionic, impressive, theatrical
activity: **6** acting
be ~: **5** emote **8** overplay
conflict: **4** agon
device: **5** aside, irony
intro: **4** ta-da **5** ta-dah
overly ~: **5** lurid, stagy **6** stagey
dramatic __: **5** irony
dramatis personae: **4** cast

DR

dramatist: 6 writer **10** librettist, playwright
dramatize: 3 act **5** emote, enact **6** act out, recite **7** burlesk, perform **8** overplay **9** burlesque, embroider, emphasize, overstate **10** exaggerate, illuminate
Drambuie: 5 drink **8** beverage
Dram Shop, The
  author: Émile Zola
Drang partner: 5 Sturm
Drano
  alternative: 11 Liquid-Plumr
drape: 4 garb, hang, veil, wrap **5** array **6** attire, clothe, outfit, sprawl **7** arrange, curtain, festoon
Draper: 5 Henry, Polly, Rusty
draper measure: 3 ell **4** yard
drapery: 5 arras, scrim **7** curtain, hanging **8** covering, portiere, tapestry
  fabric: 5 ninon **6** chintz **7** tabaret **8** cretonne
  support: 3 rod
Drapier's Letters
  author: Jonathan Swift
drastic: 4 dire **5** harsh, rough, stiff, ultra **6** severe, strong **7** extreme, radical **8** forceful **9** desperate, draconian, ill-omened **10** immoderate
  change: 8 upheaval
drastically: 4 very **8** terribly
drat: 4 dang, darn, heck, nuts, oath, rats **5** fudge **9** doggone it, expletive **10** confound it
  in German: 3 ach
draught: 3 ale **4** gulp, puff, wind **5** whiff **8** libation
  deep ~: 5 swill
  place: 3 pub
draughts: 4 game
  in America: 8 checkers
Dravidian: 4 Gond **5** Asian
  language: 5 Gondi, Tamil
draw: 3 get, tap, tie, tow, tug **4** bait, copy, earn, etch, haul, hook, lead, limn, lure, plot, pull, shut, star, yank **5** bring, carry, charm, draft, evoke, fetch, graph, incur, infer, paint, pluck, poker, start, tempt, trace, trail **6** allure, beckon, convey, deduce, depict, derive, design, doodle, elicit, entice, father, gather, pull in, siphon, sketch, syphon **7** attract, bewitch, compose, enchant, extract, portray, receive, win over **8** appeal to, conclude, dead heat, deadlock, intrigue, lengthen, motivate, persuade, standoff **9** captivate, delineate, fascinate, formulate, magnetize, stalemate **10** attendance, attraction, caricature, illustrate
  a bead: 3 aim **5** aim at, train
  a blank: 6 forget
  a conclusion: 5 infer **6** deduce, reason
  a line through: 4 x-out **8** cross off, cross out
  a parallel: 6 equate
  apart: 8 separate
  a picture: 7 specify **8** simplify
  a salary: 4 earn, work
  attention to: 6 accent **7** attract **9** spotlight, underline
  away: 4 wick **6** divert **7** detract
  back: 3 shy **5** quail, start, wince **6** cringe, flinch, recede, recoil, retire, shrink **7** retreat **8** withdraw **9** sequester
  close: 4 love, near **8** approach
  ender: 3 bar **4** back, down, tube **5** knife, shave **6** bridge, string
  forth: 5 educe, evoke **7** provoke
  in: 5 co-opt, sop up **6** entice, entrap, gather, ingest, inhale, osmose, soak up, suck up **7** attract, breathe, involve, retract, swallow **9** implicate **10** assimilate
  lots: 4 pick **6** choose, decide, select **9** determine **10** settle upon
  luck of the ~: 6 chance **7** lottery
  near: 4 come **6** go up to **8** approach **9** close in on **10** bear down on
  off: 4 bail, milk, wick **5** drain **6** decant
  on: 3 tap, use **7** utilize
  on glass: 4 etch
  out: 4 milk, pump **5** educe **6** elicit, extend, retard **7** distill, extract, prolong, stretch **8** continue, elongate, lengthen, protract
  starter: 4 with
  straws: 6 choose
  the latch: 4 open
  the line: 3 bar, fix **4** halt, stop **5** check, limit **6** cut off, depart, step in **8** restrict
  to a close: 3 end **4** wane **6** finish
  together: 5 array, unite **6** adduct, center, huddle, pucker **7** compile
  top ~: 4 star
  tournament ~: 3 bye
  toward evening: 5 laten
  up: 4 lift, make, stop **5** draft, frame, raise, write **6** shrink **7** marshal, prepare **9** formulate
  water: 4 pump
draw ___: 3 out, top **4** away, down **5** a bath, poker **6** a blank, straws
draw ___ in the sand: 5 a line
draw ___ of: 5 ahead
draw ___ on: 5 a bead
draw ___ reins: 5 in the
drawback: 3 rub **4** flaw, snag **5** catch, fault, hitch, minus **6** defect, hurdle **7** barrier, failing, pitfall **8** handicap, obstacle, weakness **9** detriment, hindrance, liability **10** deficiency, difficulty, impediment, inadequacy, inefficacy, limitation
drawbacks, with no: 5 ideal **7** optimum, perfect
drawer: 4 till **6** artist **10** cartoonist
  attachment: 4 knob
  holder: 4 desk **6** bureau
  top ~: 4 A-one, best **5** A-list, elite **7** society
___-drawer: 3 top
drawing: 3 map **4** plan **6** design, doodle, raffle, scheme, sketch **7** cartoon, diagram, etching, graphic, lottery, outline, picture, profile, tracing **8** portrait **9** depiction, floor plan, graphical, work of art **10** caricature
  architectural ~: 4 plan, spec **5** epure **6** detail
  board output: 6 design
  card: 4 lure, star **6** magnet **7** feature **9** headliner
  combining form: 4 -gram **6** -graphy
  copy a ~: 5 trace
  device: 4 flue
  near: 6 at hand
  need: 6 crayon, pencil
  place: 4 well
  power: 4 pull **7** charism **8** charisma **9** magnetism
  represent by ~: 4 limn
  room: 5 salon **6** parlor
  rough ~: 6 sketch **7** croquis
  starter: 4 with
drawing ___: 3 pin **4** card, down, room **5** board, table
drawing-___ comedy: 4 room
draw in one's ___: 5 horns
draw in the ___: 5 reins
drawl: 4 talk **5** twang **6** accent, intone, speech **8** localism
___ Draw McGraw: 5 Quick
drawn: 4 taut, worn **5** gaunt, tense, tight **6** in a tie, jangly, peaked, sapped **7** haggard, starved, worn-out **8** fatigued, fluttery, starving, stressed **10** interested
  battle: 3 tie **9** stalemate
  character: 4 toon
  combining form: 5 -graph
  fine: 8 specific
  it may be ~: 4 bath
  lightly ~ line: 5 trace
  starter: 4 wire, with
  tight: 4 taut **5** tense
drawn-out: 4 long, poky **6** draggy **7** gradual, halting, impeded, lagging, languid, lengthy **8** crawling, creeping, dawdling, dilatory, dragging, extended, hesitant, plodding, slothful, sluggish, toddling **9** elongated, leisurely, lethargic, prolonged, snaillike, unhurried **10** deliberate, protracted
___-drawn-out: 4 long
drawstring: 4 cord
draw the ___: 4 line
dray: 4 cart **5** wagon **6** camion, sledge
  ender: 3 age, man, men
  place: 4 farm
Drayton, Michael: 4 poet **7** British
Drazen: 8 Petrovic
Dr. Brown's: 4 soda **9** soft drink
Dr. Dentons: 3 PJs **9** nightwear
Dr. Dre: 6 rapper
  born: Andre Young
  song: California Love (1996)
    Dre Day (1993)
    Keep Their Heads Ringin' (1995)
    No Diggity (1996)
    Nuthin' But a 'G' Thang (1993)
dread: 3 awe **4** dire, fear **5** alarm, angst, awful, panic **6** creepy, dismay, fright, horror, phobia, stress, terror **7** cower at **8** affright, alarming, aversion, cringe at, horrible, terrible **9** frightful, trepidity **10** foreboding, petrifying, recoil from, shrink from, terrifying, worry about
  ender: 5 locks **6** nought
dreaded: 4 dire **6** creepy **7** fearful **8** alarming, horrible, terrible **9** frightful **10** terrifying
dreadful: 4 base, fell **6** creepy **8** God-awful **9** nefarious
  event: 4 blow **7** tragedy **8** calamity, disaster **10** misfortune
  penny ~: 5 novel
  see also awful
Dreadful Lemon Sky, The
  author: John D. MacDonald
dreadless: 4 bold, game **5** brave, gutsy, nervy **6** daring, gritty, heroic, plucky, spunky **7** defiant, doughty, gallant, staunch, valiant **8** heroical, intrepid, resolute, stalwart, unafraid, valorous **9** audacious, undaunted, unfearful **10** courageous
dreadlocks: 2 do **4** coif **6** hairdo **8** coiffure **9** hairstyle
  wearer: 5 rasta
dreadnought: 4 ship **10** battleship
dream: 4 goal, hope, loaf, muse, sigh, wish **5** angel, fancy, ideal, quest, yearn **6** aspire, revery, trance, vision **7** aim high, chimera, fantasy, figment, imagine, reverie, utopian **8** ambition, chimaera, delusion, illusion, stargaze **9** fantasize, nightmare **10** aspiration
  acronym: 3 REM
  bad ~: 9 nightmare
  combining form: 4 onir- **5** oneir-, oniro- **6** oneiro-
  ender: 4 land **5** scape
  environment: 5 sleep
  impossible ~: 7 fantasy
  of: 5 fancy **6** desire **7** hope for, imagine, long for, pine for
  starter: 3 day
  up: 4 form, make **5** cause, fancy, frame, hatch, think **6** create, devise, ideate, invent **7** concoct, fashion, imagine **8** conceive, contrive **9** formulate, improvise, visualize **10** mastermind
dream ___: 4 team **5** world
___ dream: 4 pipe
Dream
  author: Émile Zola
Dream ___: 4 Baby, Team **5** Lover
___ Dream: 4 Pipe **5** Elsa's, Just a
Dream, A
  author: Edgar Allan Poe
Dream a Little Dream of Me (1968 song)
  artist: Mama Cass
Dream Along With Me (1956 song)
  artist: Perry Como
Dream Baby (1962 song)
  artist: Roy Orbison
dreamboat
  see sweetheart
___ Dream, Can't I?: 4 I Can
Dreamcast company: 4 Sega
Dream Catcher
  author: Stephen King
Dream Children
  author: Elia, Charles Lamb
Dream Deferred
  author: Langston Hughes
___ Dreamed: 5 I Have
dreamed-up: 9 imaginary
dreamer: 8 escapist, idealist, optimist **9** visionary
Dream Girl
  sculptor: Erté
Dreamgirls (2006 film)
  cast: Jamie Foxx, Jennifer Hudson, Beyoncé Knowles, Eddie Murphy

Dreamin' (1989 song)
artist: Vanessa Williams
dreaming: 4 lost 6 asleep, dozing, vacant 7 dormant, napping 8 snoozing 9 sacked out, somnolent 10 slumbering
__ dreaming?: 3 Am I
Dreaming (1980 song)
artist: Cliff Richard
Dream Is __ Your Heart Makes, A: 5 a Wish
Dream Is Still Alive, The (1991 song) artist: Wilson Phillips
dreamland: 3 nod 5 sleep 7 fantasy 8 illusion 9 unreality
in ~: 4 abed 6 asleep
leave ~: 5 awake 6 awaken
Dream-Land
author: Edgar Allan Poe
dreamlike: 5 vague 6 aerial, unreal 8 fanciful 9 imaginary 10 immaterial
Dreamlover (1993 song)
artist: Mariah Carey
Dream Lover (1959 song)
artist: Bobby Darin
Dream Lover, The
author: Lawrence Sanders
Dream Merchants, The
author: Harold Robbins
Dream of Gerontius, The
composer: Edward Elgar
Dream On (1976 song)
artist: Aerosmith
Dream Palace
author: James Purdy
Dreams
author: Edgar Allan Poe
Dreams (1977 song)
artist: Fleetwood Mac
__ Dreams: 4 Hoop, In My 5 Sweet
Dreams and Projects
author: Jean (Hans) Arp
Dreamscape (1984 film)
cast: Christopher Plummer, Dennis Quaid, Max von Sydow
Dreams Die First
author: Harold Robbins
__ Dreams May Come: 4 What
Dream Songs, The
author: John Berryman
Dream Team letters: 3 USA
Dream Team, The (1989 film)
cast: Peter Boyle, Stephen Furst, Michael Keaton, Christopher Lloyd
Dreamtime (1986 song)
artist: Daryl Hall
...__ Dream Walking?: 5 Seen a
Dream Weaver (1976 song)
artist: Gary Wright
Dream Within a Dream, A
author: Edgar Allan Poe
Dreamworks: 6 studio
competitor: *see* movie studio
creation: 4 film 5 movie
dreamy: 4 lost, neat, nice, rapt, slow 5 moony, vague 6 far off, irreal, unreal, vacant 7 calming, pensive, utopian, wistful 8 adorable, fanciful, illusive, illusory, listless, quixotic, relaxing, romantic, soothing 9 imaginary, unworldly, visionary, whimsical 10 chimerical, delightful, idealistic, immaterial, intangible
state: 3 kef
see also wonderful
drear: 5 bleak 6 dismal, gloomy, leaden 7 forlorn 9 cheerless 10 lugubrious
dreariness: 5 gloom 6 tedium 8 drabness, monotony 10 depression
dreary: 3 sad 4 arid, dark, dour, drab, dull, flat, glum 5 bleak, dingy, gaunt, mirky, murky, sober, stark, unfun 6 boring, cloudy, dismal, gloomy, leaden, somber 7 doleful, forlorn, humdrum, joyless, tedious, unhappy 8 desolate, downcast, lonesome, lowering, mournful, overcast, tiresome, unlively, wretched 9 cheerless, colorless, ponderous, saddening, sorrowful, unlighted, wearisome, woebegone 10 depressing, enervating, lugubrious, melancholy, monotonous, pedestrian, tenebrific, uneventful
...dreary ev'rywhere __...: 5 I roam
Dred: 5 Scott
author: Harriet Beecher Stowe
Dre Day (1993 song)
artist: Dr. Dre, Snoop Doggy Dogg
dredge: 3 dig 4 comb 5 delve, dig up, gouge, scoop 6 deepen 7 scooper, unearth 8 sprinkle 9 excavator 10 earth mover
up: 5 raise 7 unearth
dredger: 4 ship
Dreft: 9 detergent
alternative: *see* detergent
dregs: 3 end 4 lees, scum, slag 5 chaff, swill, trash, waste 6 bottom, debris, rabble, refuse 7 deposit, garbage, grounds, remnant, residue, rubbish 8 deposits, residuum, riffraff, sediment 9 leftovers, remainder, settlings 10 lower class
full of ~: 5 silty
of society: 6 proles, rabble 8 riffraff, unwashed 9 hoi polloi
drei: 4 four 6 German
dreidel: 3 top, toy
Dreiser, Theodore: 6 writer
work: An American Tragedy
The Bulwark
The Financier
The 'Genius'
Jennie Gerhardt
Sister Carrie
The Stoic
The Titan
drench: 3 dip, sog, sop, wet 4 dunk, hose, pour, soak, wash 5 douse, dowse, drown, flood, flush, imbue, souse, steep, swamp, water 6 deluge, embrue, imbrue, rain on, sodden, splash 7 immerse, moisten 8 inundate, irrigate, permeate, saturate, submerge
drenched: 3 wet 5 soggy, soppy 6 sweaty
drencher: 4 rain 5 flood 6 deluge 8 downpour 9 rainstorm 10 inundation
Drescher, Fran: 7 actress
like ~'s speech: 5 nasal
TV: The Nanny
Dresden: 4 city, town 5 china
city near ~: 5 Pirna
locale: 6 Saxony 7 Germany
river: 4 Elbe
Dresden __: 4 ware 5 china
Dresden-to-Leipzig dir.: 3 WNW
dress: 3 rig, tog 4 deck, duds, garb, gear, gown, izar, mumu, robe, sack, sari, tent, till, togs, trim 5 A-line, array, cover, frock, getup, habit, ihram, saree, shift, skirt, tog up, treat 6 attire, caftan, civies, clothe, dirndl, enrobe, fit out, kaftan, kimono, kirtle, livery, muumuu, outfit, sacque, sheath, suit up, swathe 7 apparel, bandage, bedrape, chemise, civvies, clothes, costume, garment, raiment, skimmer, threads, uniform 8 accouter, accoutre, bundle up, clothing, covering, decorate, ensemble, garments, ornament, pinafore, vestment, wardrobe 9 cheongsam, polonaise, redingote, strapless, trappings 10 appearance, habiliment, shirtwaist, Sunday best
accessory: 4 sash
African ~: 4 izar
ankle-length ~: 4 maxi
as: 7 emulate
a turkey: 5 stuff
beltless ~: 4 tent
bottom: 3 hem
calf-length ~: 4 midi
carefully: 5 primp, prink
casual ~: 6 slacks
ceremonial ~: 4 robe
change a ~ length: 5 rehem
code: 6 casual, formal
code concern: 6 attire
disorderly ~: 10 dishabille
down: 3 rag 4 whip 5 scold 6 berate, punish, rebuke, vilify 7 upbraid 8 denounce 9 castigate, criticize, reprehend, reprimand 10 come down on, tongue-lash
East Asian ~: 9 cheongsam
ender: 3 age 5 maker
evening ~: 4 gown
fabric: 5 crash, tulle, voile 6 coburg, dimity
fancy ~: 6 finery 9 caparison
fastener: 4 hook, snap 6 zipper
feature: 4 slit
Hawaiian ~: 4 mumu 6 muumuu
in: 3 don 4 wear
India ~: 4 sari 5 saree
informal ~: 3 tee 5 jeans
Japanese ~: 6 kimono
junior ~ size: 4 nine
long ~: 4 izar
loose-fitting ~: 4 tent
make a ~: 3 sew
Muslim ~: 5 ihram
old ~: 3 rag
ornament: 4 pouf
panel: 5 inset
paper-doll ~ part: 3 tab
part: 3 hem 4 yoke 5 skirt, waist 6 bodice
peasant ~: 6 dirndl
size: 2 lg. 3 lge. 6 petite
sleeveless ~: 6 jumper
starter: 3 sun 4 coat, head 5 house, night, shirt
style: 4 mini, sack, tent 5 A-line, shift 6 Empire
up: 4 doll, gild, trim 5 adorn, array, preen, primp, prink 6 attire, bedeck, tog out 8 beautify, decorate, ornament 9 caparison, embellish, glamorize, interlard
dress __: 4 coat, code, down, ship, suit 5 goods, shirt 6 circle
__ dress: 4 full, sack, tent 5 basic, court, fancy 6 battle, dinner, granny
dressage: 5 sport
factor: 4 gait
horse: 10 Lippizaner
leap: 6 curvet
dressed: 4 clad 6 decent
be ~ in: 4 wear 5 sport 6 have on
elegantly ~: 5 natty, sharp, smart 6 dapper
poorly ~: 5 dowdy 6 ragged
dressed __ nines: 5 to the
__-dressed: 4 well
Dressed to Kill (1980 film)
cast: Nancy Allen, Michael Caine, Angie Dickinson
director: Brian De Palma
dresser: 5 chest, table 6 bureau 7 cabinet, highboy 9 furniture 10 chiffonier
fancy ~: 3 fop 4 dude 5 dandy, swell
feature: 4 knob
fussy ~: 5 dandy 7 coxcomb 8 popinjay 10 jack-a-dandy
shabby ~: 5 frump
starter: 4 hair
Dresser: 4 Paul 6 Louise
dressiness: 4 chic 5 style
dressing: 3 pad 5 salve, sauce, spica 6 relish 7 bandage, binding, chutnee, chutney, plaster 8 liniment, ointment, stuffing 9 condiment, seasoning
down: 6 rebuke 7 censure, lecture 8 reproval, scolding 9 reprimand
gown: 4 robe 6 kimono
hair ~: 3 gel
leather ~: 6 dubbin 7 dubbing
place for ~: 5 salad
room: 5 bower 7 boudoir
use a ~ room: 5 try on
window ~: 4 mask 5 front 6 facade, veneer
wood ~ tool: 4 adze
dressing __: 4 gown, room 5 table
__ dressing: 5 salad 6 French, window 7 Russian
Dressler, Marie: 7 actress
role: 3 Min
dressmaker: 5 sewer 6 cutter, fitter, tailor 7 modiste 9 outfitter, tailoress 10 courturier, seamstress
cut: 4 bias
insert: 5 godet
need: 4 form 5 cloth, dummy
use ~ shears: 4 pink
dressy: 4 chic 5 fancy, natty, ritzy, sharp, smart, swank 6 classy, flossy, formal, frilly, ornate, swanky 7 elegant, for show, in style, stylish, voguish 8 black-tie 9 like gowns, not casual 10 ornamental
event: 4 gala 6 dinner 7 banquet 8 ceremony
material: 4 lamé 5 satin
not ~: 6 casual
Dress You Up (1985 song)
artist: Madonna
Drew: 4 John 5 Carey, Ellen, Nancy 7 Charles, Pearson 9 Barrymore

Drew Carey Show, The (ABC sitcom)
cast: Diedrich Bader (Oswald Harvey)
Drew Carey (Drew Carey)
Kathy Kinney (Mimi Bobeck)
Christa Miller (Kate O'Brien)
Ryan Stiles (Lewis Kinski)
dog: 6 Speedy **7** Antonio
setting: 4 Ohio **9** Cleveland
Drew co-star: 5 Rehan
Drew, Nancy: 4 teen **9** detective
boyfriend: 3 Ned
byline: 5 Keene
help for ~: 4 clue
Drexel: 10 university
athletes: 7 Dragons
locale: 4 Penn. **5** Phila.
Drexler: 5 Clyde
Dreyfus: 6 Alfred
Dreyfuss, Richard: 5 actor
film: Always (1989)
American Graffiti (1973)
The Apprenticeship of Duddy Kravitz (1974)
The Big Fix (1978)
Close Encounters of the Third Kind (1977)
The Competition (1980)
The Crew (2000)
Dillinger (1973)
Down and Out in Beverly Hills (1986)
The Goodbye Girl (1977, AA)
Jaws (1975)
Lost in Yonkers (1993)
Moon Over Parador (1988)
Mr. Holland's Opus (1995)
My Life in Ruins (2009)
Nuts (1987)
Poseidon (2006)
Postcards From the Edge (1990)
Stakeout (1987)
Tin Men (1987)
What About Bob? (1991)
Whose Life Is It Anyway? (1981)
Dr. Feelgood (1989 song)
artist: Mötley Crüe
Dr. Hook
song: The Cover of Rolling Stone (1973)
Only Sixteen (1976)
Sexy Eyes (1980)
Sharing the Night Together (1978)
Sylvia's Mother (1972)
__ Dri: 5 Wash 'n
dribble: 4 drip, drop, leak, ooze, seep, spit **5** drool, spill **6** bounce **7** distill, slobber, spatter, trickle **8** particle
driblet: 3 bit, dab **4** bead, drop **7** globule **8** pittance
dribs and __: 5 drabs
dried
cut and ~: 4 dull **5** fixed, trite **6** boring **7** settled **9** hackneyed, wearisome **10** unoriginal
up: 4 arid, gone, sere **5** stale, wrung **7** parched, wizened **9** juiceless
__-dried: 3 air, sun **6** freeze
Driesch, Hans: 6 German **11** philosopher
drift: 3 aim, gad, run, yaw **4** bank, flit, flow, gist, heap, loaf, move, pile, ride, roam, rove, sail, skid, tend, tide, tone, turn, veer, waft **5** amble, float, glide, mosey, mound, point, range, sense, shift, slide, spend, stack, stray, tenor, trend **6** effect, import, intent, linger, motion, object, ramble, stream, wander **7** cluster, current, deposit, digress, essence, flutter, leaning, meander, meaning, migrate, purport, saunter, thought **8** alluvium, snowbank, straggle, tendency **9** bat around, direction, gallivant, intention, substance **10** knock about
along: 4 waft **5** float
by: 4 slip **6** elapse
ender: 4 wood
get the ~: 3 see **5** sense
material: 4 snow
off: 3 nap, nod **4** doze **6** drowse
starter: 4 snow, spin **5** spoon
to leeward: 3 sag
drifter: 3 bum **4** hobo **5** nomad, rover, tramp **6** outlaw **7** migrant, vagrant **8** derelict, runagate, stranger, traveler, vagabond, wanderer **9** itinerant, journeyer, transient **10** hitchhiker
Drifters
members: King, Thomas, Green, Hobbs, Lewis
song: On Broadway (1963)
Save the Last Dance for Me (1960)
There Goes My Baby (1959)
Under the Boardwalk (1964)
Up on the Roof (1962)
drifting: 4 asea **5** at sea **6** afloat **7** aimless, migrant, nomadic **8** rootless, vagabond **9** migratory, wayfaring **10** digression, discursion
Drift to a Dream (1991 song)
artist: Travis Tritt
driftwood: 6 debris **8** kindling
destination: 5 beach, shore
drill: 3 bit **4** bore, sink, tool **5** auger, borer, coach, groom, march, punch, teach, train, tutor **6** lesson, pierce, review, school, season, warm-up **7** primate, riveter, routine, workout **8** aerobics, exercise, instruct, maneuver, marching, practice, puncture, rehearse, teaching, training, war games **9** catechize, implement, inculcate, maneuvers, penetrate, perforate, rehearsal, reptition **10** assignment, daily dozen, discipline, jackhammer, run-through
command: 4 halt **5** march **6** at ease, fall in **8** left face **9** right face
ender: 5 stock **6** master
grip: 5 brace
insert: 3 bit
relative: *see* primate
starter: 3 man
drill __: 3 bit **4** team **5** press
__ drill: 4 fire, hand **5** power
driller
see dentist
Drina: 5 river
locale: 6 Bosnia, Serbia
drink: 3 ade, ale, cup, gin, lap, nog, pop, rum, rye, sip, Tab, tea **4** beer, bock, brew, cola, down, fizz, flip, grog, gulp, kava, marc, mead, ouzo, port, raki, sake, saki, shot, slug, soda, spot, swig, take, Tang, wine **5** anise, booze, Bronx, cider, cocoa, draft, glass, juice, julep, kefir, kvass, lager, mocha, negus, ocean, perry, punch, quaff, sling, slurp, snort, stout, toast, toddy, tonic, touch, vodka, water **6** absorb, bishop, brandy, cassis, coffee, cognac, eggnog, gimlet, guzzle, imbibe, ingest, kirsch, kumiss, kummel, liquid, liquor, mai tai, mescal, Mickey, mimosa, nectar, Pernod, porter, posset, potion, pulque, rickey, rob roy, Scotch, shandy, soak up, tipple, whisky, zombie **7** alcohol, aquavit, Bacardi, bourbon, Campari, Collins, consume, cordial, curaçao, iced tea, limeade, liqueur, martini, negroni, oenomel, pale ale, potable, ratafia, sangría, sidecar, sloe gin, spirits, stinger, swallow, tequila, wassail, whiskey **8** absinthe, anisette, apéritif, beverage, calvados, cocktail, coco loco, daiquiri, Drambuie, eau de vie, Guinness, highball, Jack Rose, lemonade, libation, pilsener, pink lady, potation, salty dog, schnapps, spritzer, Tia Maria, vermouth **9** alexander, applejack, aqua vitae, Cointreau, hard cider, hoist a few, inebriant, jiggerful, Manhattan, margarita, mint julep, moonshine, moosemilk, slivovitz, ward eight **10** Bloody Mary, chartreuse, golden fizz, horse's neck, intoxicant, Jamaica rum, Mickey Finn, Moscow Mule, piña colada, rock and rye, shandygaff, silver fizz
after-dinner ~: 4 port **6** brandy, cognac
apple ~: 5 cider, juice **9** hard cider
Asian nomad's ~: 6 kumiss
astronaut's ~: 4 Tang
bar ~: 3 ale, rye **4** beer, shot, sour, wine **5** draft, julep, quaff, sling, snort, stout, vodka **6** brandy, cassis, chaser, cognac, gimlet, liquor, mai tai, mimosa, porter, rob roy, Scotch, whisky, zombie **7** alcohol, aquavit, Bacardi, bourbon, Collins, cordial, liqueur, martini, pale ale, sidecar, sloe gin, spirits, stinger, tequila, whiskey **8** apéritif, cocktail, daiquiri, Drambuie, Guinness, highball, pilsener, pink lady, potation, salty dog, schnapps, spritzer, Tia Maria, vermouth **9** Alexander, Cointreau, Manhattan, margarita, mint julep **10** Bloody Mary, Moscow Mule, piña colada, Tom Collins
big ~: 4 swig
breakfast ~: 2 OJ **5** cocoa, juice
British ~: 3 ale, tea
by the yard: 3 ale
carbonated ~: 3 pop **4** cola, soda **9** ginger ale
Chinese ~: 3 tea
citrus ~: 3 ade **7** limeade **8** lemonade **9** orangeade
cola ~: 4 Coke **5** Pepsi
cold ~: 3 ade **4** soda **5** juice, shake
cold-weather ~: 3 tea **4** grog **5** cocoa **6** eggnog, hot tea
container: 3 cup, mug **5** glass, stein
cooler: 3 ice
credit: 6 bar tab
curative ~: 5 tonic
extra: 5 lemon, straw, twist
fast: 4 chug, swig **5** swill **6** guzzle **8** chugalug
fermented ~: 3 ale **4** beer **5** kefir
French ~: 3 eau, thé, vin **4** lait
from a flask: 5 snort **6** guzzle, imbibe
fruit ~: 3 ade **5** juice, punch **6** frappé
fruit juice ~: 7 sangría
Greek ~: 4 ouzo
heartily: 5 quaff
honey ~: 4 mead
hot ~: 3 tea **5** cocoa, mocha, toddy **6** coffee
hot rum ~: 4 grog
in: 3 sip **5** learn, sop up **6** absorb, gather, ingest, osmose, soak up, suck up **7** swallow **10** assimilate
in a way: 3 lap
in baby-talk: 4 wawa
Japanese ~: 3 tea **4** sake, saki
knockout ~: 6 Mickey **10** Mickey Finn
like a pet: 3 lap **5** lap up
lo-cal ~: 3 Tab **4** diet, lite **6** Fresca
noisily: 5 slurp
noncarbonated ~: 3 tea **6** coffee **7** iced tea
of old: 4 mead
opener: 3 tab
order: 4 neat **5** round **10** on the rocks
Polynesian ~: 4 kava
prepare a ~: 3 mix
preprandial ~: 8 apéritif
quick ~: 3 tot **5** snort
Russian ~: 5 kvass, vodka
sailor's ~: 3 rum
sample a ~: 3 sip
slowly: 3 sip **5** nurse
small ~: 4 dram
soft ~: 3 ade, pop, Tab **4** Coke, cola, Nehi, soda **5** Moxie, Pepsi **8** Dr Pepper
stiff ~: 6 bracer
suffix: 3 ade
to: 5 toast **9** celebrate
to excess: 4 tope **6** tipple
trattoria ~: 4 vino **7** chianti
wine ~: 6 bishop **7** sangria
Yuletide ~: 3 nog **6** eggnog
see also beverage
__ drink: 4 cold, soft, tall **5** mixed
Drink __ only...: 4 to me
drinkable: 6 liquor **7** potable **8** beverage
make ~: 6 desalt, purify **10** desalinate, desalinize
drinker: 3 sot **4** lush **5** toper **7** tippler
drinkery: 6 lounge
drinking: 4 vice
age: 8 majority
aid: 5 straw
bowl: 5 mazer
cup of ancient Greece: 5 cylix, kylix
Greek ~ horn: 6 rhyton
vessel: 3 cup, mug **5** stein
drink-mix brand: 6 Wyler's **7** Kool-Aid

drinks, like some: **4** hard, soft
drip: **4** bore, jerk, leak, nerd, ooze, pest, plop, seep, slop, weep **5** exude, spill, sweat **7** distill, dribble, nebbish, slobber, trickle **8** downturn, perspire, sprinkle **9** percolate **10** wet blanket
locale: **4** eave, roof **6** faucet
drip __: **3** cap, pan **5** grind **6** coffee
Drip Drop (1963 song)
artist: Dion
drip-feed tube: **2** IV
dripping: **3** wet **5** juicy, leaky, moist, soggy, soppy, undry **6** sodden, sweaty **10** bedraggled
dripping __: **3** pan
drippings: **6** grease
drippy: **4** damp, oozy **5** moist, sappy, undry **7** mawkish, wettish **8** sluggish **10** spiritless
Dr. I.Q.: **9** radio show
Driscoll: **5** Bobby
Dristan
alternative: ***see*** cold remedy
drive: **2** go **3** pep, ram, run, zip **4** fire, gear, goad, herd, lift, make, move, prod, push, ride, road, roll, send, sink, spin, spur, stab, take, tour, trip, urge, will, zeal **5** force, hurry, impel, jaunt, labor, lunge, motor, moxie, pitch, pound, punch, rouse, spunk, stamp, steer, stick, surge, vigor **6** appeal, arouse, avenue, compel, direct, effort, energy, incite, jockey, junket, launch, motive, outing, propel, reduce, strain, street, strike, tee off, thrust, travel, urge on, whip up **7** actuate, advance, animate, commute, crusade, impetus, impulse, journey, joyride, operate, passion, roundup **8** ambition, campaign, gumption, momentum, motivate, pressure, vitality **9** appetence, chauffeur, encourage, excursion, impulsion, incentive, inner fire, stimulate, willpower **10** accelerate, compulsion, enterprise, enthusiasm, fund-raiser, get up and go, horsepower, incitement, initiative, motivation, ride herd on
apart: **9** disaffect
a semi: **4** haul
at: **4** mean
away: **4** oust, rout, shoo **5** chase, eject, repel, roust **6** banish, dispel, offend **7** disgust, repulse **8** alienate, chase out **9** dissipate, force back
bungle a ~: **4** hook **5** shank, slice
crazy: **3** bug, irk, nag **4** rile **5** annoy, peeve **6** enrage, harass, madden, pester **7** derange, torment, trouble
creative ~: **3** ego
ender: **3** way **4** line **5** shaft
fast: **4** race **6** hot rod
forward: **5** impel **6** compel, urge on
home: **7** impress **9** reiterate
in: **5** embed, enter, imbed, infix
inner ~: **4** urge
kind of ~: **3** ZIP **4** hard **5** CD/ROM **6** floppy **8** diskette
out: **4** boot, oust, pump, rout **5** exile, expel, roust **7** dismiss, exclude **8** chase off, exorcise, exorcize **9** eliminate, order to go
prepare to ~: **5** tee up
recklessly: **5** weave **6** careen
short ~: **4** spin **5** jaunt
something to ~: **4** nail
drive __: **3** bay, fit **4** time **5** shaft, train
drive __ the ground: **4** into
drive-__: **4** thru **7** through
__ drive: **4** disk, hard, line, tape, worm
__-drive: **4** test **5** front
Drive (song)
artist: Cars, R.E.M.
__ Drive: **5** Rodeo
__ Drive by Night: **4** They
drive-in: **5** movie **6** cinema **7** theater, theatre **10** restaurant
load: **6** carful
waiter: **6** carhop
drivel
see baloney
driven: **5** bound **8** hellbent, impelled, obsessed **10** determined
be ~: **4** ride
driver: **4** club, hack, wood **6** cabbie, cabman, hackie, jockey **8** golf club, motorist, operator **9** chauffeur
aid: **3** AAA, map **6** mirror
backseat ~: **3** nag **6** critic
bane: **4** flat, hook **5** slice
be in the ~'s seat: **3** run **4** lead **5** pilot, steer **6** direct **7** operate, oversee **9** supervise
camper ~: **4** RVer
goal: **5** green **7** fairway
ID: **3** lic. **7** license
license: **2** ID
license datum: **3** DOB, hgt. **4** name **5** photo **6** gender, height, weight
maneuver: **5** U-turn
org.: **3** AAA, PGA **4** USGA
peg: **3** tee
pro ~: **5** cabby, racer **6** cabbie
purchase: **3** gas **8** gasoline
shout: **4** fore
slave ~: **6** despot, master, tyrant **8** autocrat, dictator **10** taskmaster
use a ~: **4** golf
with a handle: **4** CBer
see also golf
__ driver: **3** bus, cab **4** pile, taxi **5** slave **6** Sunday
Driver, Minnie: **7** actress
film: Circle of Friends (1995)
Good Will Hunting (1997)
Grosse Pointe Blank (1997)
Hard Rain (1998)
High Heels and Low Lifes (2001)
Return to Me (2000)
film (voice): Tarzan (1999)
driver's __: **4** seat **7** license
driver's seat: **4** helm **7** command **9** supremacy
Driver, The (1978 film)
cast: Isabelle Adjani, Bruce Dern, Ryan O'Neal
driver train
element: **4** axle
drive-through order: **4** to go
driveway: **4** road **6** egress **7** ingress
do the ~: **3** tar **4** pave, seal **5** retar, retop **6** repave
ending: **6** garage
material: **3** tar **5** paver **6** gravel **8** blacktop, concrete
driving: **4** go-go **6** lively, urgent **7** dynamic, en route **8** forceful, vigorous **9** energetic, on the road, trenchant **10** compelling, compulsive, propulsive
area: **5** range
force: **4** birr **6** engine **7** impetus
hazard: **3** fog, ice **4** mist, rain, snow **5** glare, sleet **7** drizzle
driving __: **4** rain **5** range
driving-away word: **4** scat, shoo **5** scram **6** begone **8** scramola
Driving Force
author: Dick Francis
Driving Miss Daisy
author: Alfred Uhry
Driving Miss Daisy (1989 film)
cast: Dan Aykroyd, Morgan Freeman, Jessica Tandy
Drivin' My Life Away (1980 song)
artist: Eddie Rabbitt
Drixoral
alternative: ***see*** cold remedy
drizzle: **3** wet **4** mist, rain **5** spray **8** fine rain, moisture, sprinkle
drizzly: **3** wet **4** damp **5** bleak, misty, moist, rainy, undry **7** wettish **8** sprinkly
Dr. J
see Erving
Dr. Jekyll and Mr. Hyde (1932 film)
cast: Fredric March
character: **5** Carew, Poole **7** Enfield
Dr. K: **6** Gooden
Dr. Kildare (NBC drama)
cast: Richard Chamberlain (Dr. James Kildare)
Raymond Massey (Dr. Leonard Gillespie)
hospital: Blair
__ Dr. Malone: **5** Young
Dr. No: **4** film **5** novel
author: Ian Fleming
cast: Ursula Andress, Sean Connery, Joseph Wiseman
droid: **5** golem, robot **9** automaton **10** Artoo Detoo
droit: **5** claim, right
droll: **3** dry, wry **4** camp, rich **5** campy, comic, funny, queer, silly, witty **6** absurd, har-har, jocose, quaint **7** amusing, comical, jesting, jocular, risible, waggish **8** clownish, farcical, humorous **9** diverting, facetious, laughable, ludicrous, priceless, quizzical, whimsical **10** outlandish, ridiculous
drollery: **3** wit **4** jest, joke, quip **5** humor **6** comedy **7** waggery **8** jocosity, wordplay, zaniness **9** funniness, witticism **10** jocoseness, jocularity
dromedary: **5** camel **6** animal, mammal
feature: **4** hump
relative: **5** llama **6** alpaca, vicuña **7** guanaco **8** Bactrian
stop: **5** oasis
drome starter: **4** aero, velo **5** hippo
drone: **3** bee, bug, hum **4** buzz, male, slug, talk **5** chant, idler, noise, sound, thrum, whine, whirr **6** drudge, insect, jackal, loafer, murmur **7** lounger, sponger **8** parasite, sluggard **9** do-nothing, vibration **10** ne'er-do-well
home: **4** hive **6** apiary
droning: **10** monotonous
sound: **3** hum **4** buzz
Drood, Edwin
betrothed: **4** Rosa
drool: **4** gush, leak, spit **5** water **6** drivel, saliva, slaver **7** dribble, enthuse, lay it on, slobber **8** salivate **10** salivation
over: **4** want **5** crave **6** desire
droop: **3** dip, lop, nod, sag **4** bend, flag, flop, lean, loll, mope, sink, tire, wilt **5** lower, quail, slump, stoop, trail **6** dangle, go limp, settle, slouch, suffer, weaken, wither **7** decline **8** decrease, get tired, hang down, languish, peter out **9** get sleepy, hang loose **10** fall asleep
drooping: **4** alop, limp **5** baggy, saggy, tired, weary **6** broody, flabby **7** flaccid, languid **8** dejected **9** pendulous **10** knocked out
droopy: **4** alop, limp **5** baggy, loppy, saggy, slack, tired **6** flabby, floppy, wilted **7** flaccid, hanging, joyless, sagging, slouchy, stooped **8** dangling, fatigued **9** pendulous **10** melancholy, spiritless
drop: **3** axe, can, dab, dip, ebb, end, err, nip, sag, set **4** bead, beat, blob, boot, cede, curb, dash, deck, dele, dive, duck, dump, fall, fire, flop, iota, leak, loll, lose, omit, ooze, oust, quit, sack, sell, send, shed, sink, slip, spot, stop, tilt, tire, whit, wilt, x off, x out **5** cease, chuck, crash, depth, ditch, elide, forgo, grain, lapse, leave, let go, level, light, lower, reach, scrub, slash, slide, slope, slump, speck, spend, spill, spurn, swoop, taste, tinge, touch, trace, yield **6** bounce, bubble, cancel, delete, demote, forego, fumble, give up, go down, lay off, lessen, let off, morsel, plunge, recede, recess, reduce, relent, remove, shelve, shrink, supply, trifle, tumble, unload **7** abandon, call off, cashier, curtail, cut down, decline, deposit, descend, descent, discard, dismiss, dribble, driblet, drum out, dwindle, falloff, forfeit, forsake, globule, kiss off, lay down, let fall, let go of, lozenge, mark off, modicum, plummet, redline, release, scratch, smidgen, smidgin, swallow, tail off, toss out, trickle **8** abdicate, collapse, cross off, cross out, decrease, delivery, diminish, downturn, file away, forswear, furlough, get rid of, give up on, hand over, jettison, lay aside, lowering, nosedive, particle, part with, peter out, pink-slip, renounce, shake off, smidgeon, throw out, trapdoor, write off **9** cast aside, declivity, discharge, dispose of, downslide, downtrend, eighty-six, eliminate, foreswear, lessening, ostracize, parachute, plump down, precipice, reduction, repudiate, surrender, terminate, throw away, throw over **10** diminution, go away from, relinquish

about a ~: 5 minim
abruptly: 3 axe 4 dump 5 plunk
a bundle: 4 lose
a letter: 4 send, slur
a line: 4 fish 5 write 10 correspond, epistolize
anchor: 4 land 6 arrive 8 get there
architectural ~: 5 gutta
away: 5 slope
back: 3 ebb 5 trail 7 retreat
by: 3 see 4 call 5 pop in, run in, visit 6 show up 7 go to see 8 pay a call
clues: 4 hint 5 let on
cough ~: 7 lozenge
down: 3 dip 4 duck, fall
down on: 6 pounce, snatch
ender: 3 let, out 4 wort 5 forge, light
eye ~: 4 tear
feathers: 4 molt, shed 5 moult
from a list: 4 x off, x out 8 cross off, cross out
from the team: 3 cut
have a ~: 5 drink
in: 3 see 4 call 5 enter, visit 6 appear, arrive, attend, show up, stop by 7 turn out 8 pay a call
in a letter box: 4 mail
in the bucket: 8 pittance
letter ~: 7 opening 8 aperture
mail ~: 3 box, GPO 4 slot, USPS
noisily: 4 plop
off: 3 ebb, nap, nod, sag 4 doze, fall, molt, shed, sink, slip, wane 5 abate, bring, leave, slack, sleep, slide, slump 6 catnap, lessen, shrink, snooze, unload 7 decline, deliver, deposit, dwindle, present, saw logs, slacken 8 decrease, diminish, hand over 10 fall asleep, grab some z's
one's guard: 3 nap 5 relax
one's jaw: 4 gape, gawk 5 stare 6 goggle, marvel
out: 4 quit 5 leave, rebel 6 resign, secede 8 withdraw 10 apostatize
pounds: 4 slim 8 slim down
ready to ~: 4 worn 5 spent, tired, weary 9 exhausted
saline ~: 4 tear
sheer ~: 9 precipice
shot: 4 dink
starter: 3 air, dew, ear, gum 4 back, rain, snow, tear 5 eaves
target: 3 ear, eye 4 nose
the ball: 3 err 4 miss, slip 6 bumble, bungle, falter, fumble 7 blunder 8 misjudge
the curtain: 3 end 4 shut 6 finish 8 complete 9 terminate
drop __: 3 box, ell, off, out, tee 4 arch, girt, keel, kick, leaf, pass, seat, shot, zone 5 a hint, a line, cloth
drop __ to: 5 a line, a note
drop-__: 4 ship
drop-__ table: 4 leaf
__ drop: 3 act, cut, leg 4 acid, body, dead, line, mail 5 cough, lemon 6 letter, pigeon
__-drop: 4 name
Drop Dead Fred (1991 film)
director: Phoebe Cates
Drop Dead Gorgeous (1999 film)
cast: Kirstie Alley, Ellen Barkin, Kirsten Dunst, Denise Richards
dog: 5 Kenny
drop-down __: 4 menu
drop-in: 5 guest 7 visitor
__ Drop Kid, The: 5 Lemon
droplet: 3 bit 4 bead, blob, tear 6 bubble
droplets: 3 dew 4 mist 5 spray, vapor 8 dampness, moisture
drop like __: 5 a rock
drop like __ potato: 4 a hot
__ drop of a hat: 5 at the
drop-off: 8 slowdown 9 precipice
drop of golden sun, A: 3 ray
dropped jaw, with: 6 aghast, amazed 9 astounded, awestruck, stupefied, surprised 10 astonished, bewildered, dumbstruck, spellbound
dropper: 4 tube
cry: 4 oops
kin: 5 pipet 7 pipette
starter: 3 eye
__-dropper: 4 name
dropping: 4 down 8 downhill
drops: 5 spill
form ~: 4 bead 6 bead up
on the grass: 3 dew
__ drop soup: 3 egg
drop the __ shoe: 5 other
dross: 4 scum, slag 5 chaff, trash, waste 6 debris, refuse 7 garbage, remnant, residue, rubbish 8 impurity, leavings, residuum
drossy: 9 worthless
drought: 6 thirst 7 absence 8 dry spell, shortage
causer: 6 El Niño
droughty: 4 arid, sere 7 parched, thirsty 9 waterless 10 dehydrated
drove: 3 mob 4 herd, pack 5 flock, horde, press, score, swarm, troop 6 legion, rabble, throng 7 legions, numbers 9 gathering, multitude
Drove my Chevy to the __...: 5 levee
drover: 6 cowboy 7 cowpoke 8 herdsman, wrangler 9 ranch hand, trail boss
charge: 4 herd 6 cattle 9 livestock
droves: 6 flocks, hoards 7 legions
drown: 3 wet 4 dunk, sink 5 flood, souse, swamp 6 deluge, drench, embrue, engulf, imbrue, ingulf, muffle, splash 7 immerse 8 inundate, overcome, overflow, submerge 9 overpower, overwhelm
drowned __: 6 valley
Drowned and the Saved, The
author: Primo Levi
Drowning (2001 song)
artist: Backstreet Boys
Drowning Mona (2000 film)
cast: Neve Campbell, Jamie Lee Curtis, Danny DeVito, Bette Midler
drowse: 3 nap, nod 4 doze, rest, yawn 5 sleep 6 catnap, nod off, snooze 7 slumber 8 drift off 9 get sleepy 10 fall asleep, grab some z's
drowsiness: 8 laziness, lethargy
sign of ~: 4 yawn
drowsy: 4 dozy, dull, lazy, logy, slow 5 tired, weary 6 sleepy, snoozy, torpid 7 languid 8 listless, sluggish 9 heavy-eyed, lethargic, somnolent, soporific 10 half-asleep, knocked out
make ~: 9 hypnotize
Droxies: 6 cookie
alternative: *see* cookie brand
Dr Pepper: 3 pop 4 cola, soda 9 soft drink
alternative: *see* soft drink
Dr. Quinn, Medicine Woman (CBS drama)
cast: Jane Seymour (Dr. Mike Quinn)
dog: 4 Wolf
Dr. Ruth: 10 Westheimer
__ Dr. Ruth: 3 Ask
Dr. Scholl product: 6 insole
Dr. Seuss
locale: 8 Whoville
Dr. Seuss character: 3 Cat, Gox, Ned, Pam, Vug, Who, Zax 4 Gack, Grox, Jake, Mack, Rolf 5 Glunk, Lorax, Yekko 6 Grinch, Horton, Huffle, Norval, Sam I Am, Yertle 8 Thidwick 9 Sneetches
Dr. Strangelove (1964 film)
cast: Sterling Hayden, James Earl Jones, Slim Pickens, George C. Scott, Peter Sellers, Keenan Wynn
director: Stanley Kubrick
drub: 3 hit, tan, zap 4 beat, cane, flog, lick, mall, maul, rout, trim, whip 5 baste, blast, knock, paste, pound, worst 6 batter, defeat, hammer, pommel, pummel, thrash, wallop 7 clobber, conquer, overrun, shellac, trounce 8 shellack 9 checkmate, overpower, overwhelm
drubbing: 4 loss, rout 6 defeat 7 licking
Drucker: 4 Mort 5 Peter
drudge: 4 grub, hack, moil, peon, plod, toil, wade, work 5 drone, grind, labor, slave 6 jackal, menial, toiler 7 laborer, plodder, servant, slavery 8 factotum, work hard 9 grind away
ender: 4 work
Drudge: 4 Matt
drudgery: 3 job, rut 4 moil, toil, work 5 grind, labor, sweat 7 rat race, slavery, travail 8 hardship, hard work, scutwork 9 grunt work
drudging: 7 tedious 8 tiresome
drug: 5 sulfa, tonic 6 opiate, remedy, sedate 7 stupefy 8 laudanum, medicate, medicine, narcotic, sedative 9 stimulant 10 anesthetic, antibiotic, biological, depressant, medication, penicillin
amount: 4 dose
combining form: 8 pharmaco-
company: 5 Lilly, Merck 6 Pfizer
cop: 4 narc, nark 5 narco
ender: 5 store
label letters: 3 USP
science: 8 pharmacy
drug __: 4 czar
drug __ market: 5 in the, on the
__ drug: 5 sulfa 6 orphan, wonder 7 miracle
drug-bust org.: 3 ATF
drug-free: 5 clean
drugget: 6 fabric 8 material
druggist: 4 phar. 5 pharm. 10 apothecary, pharmacist, posologist
container: 4 vial 5 phial
drug-overseeing org.: 3 FDA
drug-reference bk.: 3 PDR
drugstore: 4 mart, phar. 5 pharm. 6 market 8 pharmacy 10 apothecary
be a ~ cowboy: 6 loiter 7 hang out
cowboy: 5 ogler
Drugstore Cowboy (1989 film)
cast: Matt Dillon, Kelly Lynch
director: Gus Van Sant
druid: 4 Celt 7 prophet
Dru, Joanne: 7 actress
brother: Peter Marshall
film: All the King's Men (1949)
Red River (1948)
She Wore a Yellow Ribbon (1949)
Thunder Bay (1953)
Wagon Master (1950)
Red River role: 4 Tess
spouse: Dick Haymes
drum: 3 def, rap, tap, tar, udu 4 batá, beat, ekwe, fish, krin, roar 5 bhaya, bongo, caixa, cajón, conga, cuica, dauli, davul, dhola, kakko, kundu, lobby, ngoma, okedo, pound, pulse, sabar, snare, surdo, taber, tabla, tabor, taiko, tapan, thump, tupan, wheel 6 barrel, bendir, damaru, djembé, dun dun, nakers, naqara, ntenga, odaiko, patter, poëtti, quinto, rattle, tabour, tam-tam, tom-tom 7 atumpan, batajón, bodhran, breketé, changko, dadaiko, dugdugi, ingungu, isigubu, kalungu, murumbu, pulsate, talamba, tambour, terbang, thunder, timbale, tsuzumi 8 bass drum, darabuka, djun djun, gran casa, tympanum 10 kettledrum, tambourine
accompaniment: 4 fife
Afro-Cuban ~: 5 conga
attachment: 5 snare
beatnik's ~: 5 bongo
beat the ~ for: 4 sell 6 talk up 7 advance, espouse 9 publicize
emulate a ~ major: 5 strut, twirl
ender: 4 beat, fire, head 5 stick
flourish: 5 tusch
Indian: 5 tabla
into: 5 train, tutor 6 repeat 9 inculcate
major need: 5 baton, shako
material: 5 steel
Moorish ~: 6 atabal
out: 3 axe, can 4 boot, drop, fire, oust, sack 5 expel, let go 6 bounce, depose, expell, lay off 7 cashier, dismiss, release 8 furlough, get rid of, pink-slip 9 discharge, terminate
roll exclamation: 4 ta-da 5 ta-dah
small ~: 5 bongo, taber, tabor 6 tabour
sound: 4 roll
starter: 3 ear, hum 6 kettle
twin ~: 5 bongo
up: 6 hustle, invent, obtain 7 solicit
drum __: 3 out 5 brake, corps, major
__ drum: 4 bass 5 bongo, brake, snare, steel
Drum __ Symphony: 4 Roll
drum and __ corps: 5 bugle

drumbeat: **4** roll
two-note ~: **4** flam
drumfire: **4** boom
drummer: **4** Moon, Rich, Webb **5** Krupa, Roach, Starr, Watts **6** Blakey, Puente **7** Bellson
jazz ~: **4** Rich, Webb **5** Krupa, Roach **6** Blakey, Puente **7** Bellson
rock ~: **4** Moon **5** Starr, Watts
__ Drummer Boy, The: **6** Little
__ Drummer Girl, The: **6** Little
__ drummers drumming...: **6** twelve
Drummond: **3** Ace, cop **7** Bulldog
__ Drum, NY: **4** Fort
Drum Roll Symphony
composer: Joseph Haydn
Drums (1938 film)
cast: Raymond Massey, Sabu
director: Zoltan Korda
Drums Along the Mohawk (1939 film)
cast: Claudette Colbert, Henry Fonda, Edna May Oliver
character: **3** Gil **4** Lana, Yost **5** Brant
director: John Ford
__ Drum Song: **6** Flower
drumstick: **3** leg **4** meat **10** finger food
neighbor: **5** thigh
__ Drum, The: **3** Tin
drunk: **3** lit **5** tipsy **6** bombed, loaded **10** inebriated
not ~: **5** sober
drunkard: **3** sot **5** souse, toper **6** barfly **7** tippler, tosspot
drupe: **4** kaki, plum **5** berry, fruit, mamey, peach **6** cherry **7** apricot **9** manzanita
drupelet: **6** acinus
Drury: **4** Lane **5** Allen, Janes
Drury, Allen: **6** writer
work: Advise and Consent
Capable of Honor
Come Nineveh, Come Tyre
Preserve and Protect
The Promise of Joy
Public Men
A Shade of Difference
The Throne of Saturn
Drury Lane
composer: Thomas Arne
druthers: **6** option **8** penchant **10** partiality, preference, proclivity
dry: **3** sec, wry **4** arid, blot, brut, dull, sear, sere, wipe **5** baked, bland, drain, droll, dusty, empty, mealy, parch, plain, salty, stale, toast, towel, unwet, wizen **6** barren, biting, boring, desert, harden, jejune, kipper, season, sponge, torrid, wither **7** acerbic, athirst, bookish, caustic, cutting, cynical, deplete, drained, insipid, parched, powdery, process, prosaic, raucous, Saharan, shrivel, sterile, tedious, thirsty, unmoist, weather, wizened **8** ironical, lifeless, pedantic, preserve, rainless, sardonic, scorched, shrunken, withered **9** anhydrate, anhydrous, dehydrate, desiccate, evaporate, exhausted, infertile, juiceless, ponderous, prosaical, sarcastic, shriveled, unfertile, waterless **10** dehumidify, dehydrated, desertlike, desiccated, dullsville, enervating, evaporated, lackluster, monotonous, pedantical, teetotaler, unbuttered
bleed ~: **5** drain **7** exhaust
cleaner's challenge: **5** stain
combining form: **3** xer- **4** xero-
dock: **4** port
ender: **4** wall, well
fruit: **3** nut **5** prune, regma **6** raisin
goods: **5** cloth
have a ~ run: **6** try out
having a ~ environment: **5** xeric
high and ~: **7** aground **8** cast away, deserted, marooned, stranded **9** abandoned
ink: **5** toner
in the sun: **4** bake
leave high and ~: **4** jilt **6** desert, maroon, strand **8** abdicate
not ~: **3** wet **4** damp **5** teary
off: **4** blot, wipe **5** towel
org.: **4** WCTU
out: **4** wilt **5** parch **7** sober up **9** evaporate
place: **6** desert
run: **4** test **5** trial **8** practice, rehearse **9** rehearsal
spell: **5** slump **7** drought
squeeze ~: **5** wring
up: **4** sear, wilt **5** parch, wizen **6** run out, wither **7** deplete, shrivel, silence **8** emaciate, peter out **9** evaporate
dry __: **3** fly, fog, ice, law, lot, mop, rot, run **4** bulk, cell, dock, hole, kiln, lake, milk, rent, sink, suit, wall, wash, well **5** goods, spell **6** freeze **7** cleaner
dry __ bone: **3** as a
dry-__: **4** eyed, farm, salt, shod **5** clean, gulch **7** roasted
__-dry: **3** air **4** blow, bone, damp, drip, kiln, pale, spin **5** rough, smoke **6** freeze, tumble
Dry __: **3** Ice
__ Dry: **6** Canada
dryad: **5** nymph **9** tree nymph, wood nymph
dwelling: **4** tree
dry as __: **4** dust **5** a bone
dry-as-dust: **4** blah, dull, tame
Dryden: **3** Ken **4** John
Dryden, John: **4** poet **7** British **10** playwright
work: **3** ode **5** essay
dryer
dish ~: **5** towel
hair ~: **6** blower
like a clogged ~ vent: **5** fuzzy
loss, perhaps: **4** sock
residue: **4** lint **5** fluff
tear ~: **5** hanky **6** hankie
__-dryer: **4** blow **6** washer
Dryer: **4** Fred
__ dry eye: **4** not a
dry-goods
measure: **4** yard
merchant: **6** draper
Dry Idea: **9** deodorant
alternative: *see* deodorant
drying
oven: **4** kiln, oast
spread for ~: **3** ted
dryness: **6** thirst **7** aridity **8** monotony **10** insipidity
Drypers
alternative: **4** Luvs **7** Huggies, Pampers
__, Dry Place: **5** A Cool
dry rot: **4** mold **5** decay, fungi
Drysdale, Don: **6** Dodger, hurler **7** pitcher
Dry Tortugas: **4** isle, park **6** island
locale: **7** Florida
DSC: **5** award, medal
D-sharp equivalent: **5** E-flat
DSM: **5** award, medal
DSO: **5** medal
DST end: **3** Oct. **7** October
duad: **3** two **4** pair **6** couple **7** doublet, twosome
dual: **4** twin **6** biform, binary, binate, double, paired **7** coupled, doubled, twofold, two-part **8** biformed, two-sided **9** two-person
not ~: **4** unal
Duane: **4** Eddy **5** Diane **6** Allman
Duane's Depressed
author: Larry McMurtry
Duarte: **3** Eva
dub: **3** tag **4** call, name, term **5** label, style, title **6** knight, record **7** baptize, entitle, intitle **8** christen, nickname **9** designate **10** stereotype
in: **3** add
something to ~: **4** tape
__-dub: **4** rub-a
Dubai: **4** city, town
locale: **3** UAE
native: **4** Arab
dubbed one: **3** Sir **4** Dame
dubbing need: **5** sword
Dubble Bubble: **3** gum
Dubhe: **4** star
dubiety: **5** doubt **9** disbelief **10** hesitation, indecision, skepticism
dubious: **4** iffy, moot, open, wary **5** chary, fishy, leery, queer, rocky, shady, shaky, vague **6** chancy, gun-shy, louche, unfirm, unsure **7** guarded, obscure, suspect, tenuous, unclear **8** arguable, cautious, doubtful, doubting, hesitant, unlikely, unstable **9** ambiguous, debatable, equivocal, skeptical, uncertain, undecided, unsettled **10** disputable, far-fetched, improbable, indefinite, infeasible, left-handed, precarious, suspicious, unreliable
be ~: **5** doubt **8** question
of ~ honesty: **5** shady **7** corrupt, crooked, devious **8** slippery, unsavory **9** notorious, unethical **10** fly-by-night
Dublin: **3** bay **4** city, port, town **7** capital
legislature: **4** Dail
locale: **4** Eire, Erin, Ohio **7** Ireland **10** California
river: **6** Liffey
theatre: **5** Abbey
Dubliners, The
author: James Joyce
__ du bois: **6** fraise
Du Bois: **3** WEB **5** Marta
dubonnet: **3** red **4** wine **8** purplish
Dubos: **4** René
DuBose: **7** Heyward
Dubrovnik: **4** city, port
locale: **7** Croatia
Dubuffet, Jean: **6** artist, French **7** painter **8** sculptor
Dubuque: **4** city, town
college: **5** Loras **6** Clarke
locale: **4** Iowa
ducat: **5** money **6** ticket
word: **3** row **4** seat **5** admit
ducats: **3** tix
Duc de l'Omelette, The
author: Edgar Allan Poe
Duchamp, Marcel: **6** artist, French **7** Dadaist, painter
subject: **4** nude
duchess: **4** lady, peer, rank **5** noble, title, woman
spouse: **4** duke
Duchess of __: **4** Alba, York
Duchess of Alba, The
painter: Francisco de Goya
Duchess of Malfi, The
author: John Webster
Duchin: **4** Eddy **5** Peter
Duchin, Eddy: **7** pianist **10** bandleader
son: Peter
Duchin, Peter: **7** pianist
Duchovny, David: **5** actor
film: Kalifornia (1993)
The Rapture (1991)
Return to Me (2000)
spouse: Téa Leoni
TV: The X-Files
duchy: **5** Hesse, Pinsk, Savoy **6** Saxony, Valois **7** Bavaria, Brabant, Tuscany **8** Holstein **9** Aquitaine, Franconia **10** Luxembourg, Westphalia
duck: **3** bob, dip, nod **4** bird, drop, fowl, hide, lose, meat, shun, smew, snub, teal **5** avoid, biped, dodge, eider, elude, evade, hedge, koloa, lurch, parry, pekin, Rouen, ruddy, scaup, shirk, skirt, stoop, wince **6** bypass, Cayuga, cotton, crouch, escape, eschew, fabric, hunker, plunge, scoter, swerve **7** abandon, abstain, gadwall, immerse, mallard, Muscovy, pintail, pochard, redhead, shy from, widgeon **8** bluebill, bullneck, drop down, flee from, garganey, get out of, mandarin, oldsquaw, shoveler, sidestep, submerge **9** broadbill, goldeneye, goosander, greenhead, harlequin, leap aside, merganser, sprigtail, waterfowl **10** bufflehead, canvasback, circumvent, get clear of, surf scoter
blind user: **6** hunter
cold ~: **4** wine
cousin: **5** goose
dwelling: **4** nest
ender: **3** pin **4** bill, ling, tail, weed **5** board
European ~: **4** smew **9** sheldrake
fake ~: **5** decoy
foot feature: **3** web
French ~: **6** canard
genus: **5** anser
haunt: **4** pond
Hawaiian ~: **5** koloa
hunter's boot: **5** wader
lame ~: **5** goner
male ~: **5** drake
out: **6** escape **7** abscond
Peter and the Wolf ~: **4** oboe
responsibility: **5** evade **6** cop out, renege

sea ~: 4 coot 5 eider 6 scoter
sitting ~: 4 butt, dupe, goat, prey 6 pigeon, sucker, target, victim
sound: 5 quack
soup: 4 easy, snap 5 cinch, cushy 6 picnic, simple 7 no sweat 8 easy task, painless, pushover, workable 9 uncomplex 10 child's play, effortless, elementary, unexacting
walk like a ~: 6 waddle
duck __: 4 foot, hawk, hook, soup 5 blind
duck __ rock: 3 on a 5 on the
duck-__ platypus: 6 billed
__ duck: 3 sea 4 cold, dead, fish, gray, grey, lame, musk, surf, wood 6 diving, Peking 7 Beijing, Muscovy, pressed, sitting
Duck: 5 Daffy, Daisy 6 Donald
duck à __: 7 l'orange
__ Duck Amendment: 4 Lame
Duck, Donald voice: 4 Nash
ducking __: 5 stool
ducklike bird: 4 coot
__ duckling: 4 ugly
duckpins
play: 4 bowl
ducks: 5 pants 6 slacks 8 trousers
ducks-and-drakes: 4 game
__-duck session: 4 lame
ducks in __: 4 a row
Duck Soup (1933 film)
cast: Margaret Dumont, Chico Marx, Groucho Marx, Harpo Marx, Zeppo Marx
__ Ducks, The: 6 Mighty
ducktail: 2 do 4 coif 6 hairdo 7 haircut 8 coiffure 9 hairstyle
__ Duck, The: 4 Wild
duckweed: 5 plant 6 flower
ducky
see wonderful
Ducommun, Élie: 5 Swiss 8 Nobelist
duct: 4 flue, main, pipe, tube, vein, vent 5 canal, drain, shaft 6 artery, course, gutter, outlet, trough 7 air vent, channel, conduit, culvert, passage
air ~: 4 flue, vent
anatomical ~: 3 vas 5 lumen
ender: 4 work
starter: 3 ovi, via
duct __: 4 tape
__ duct: 3 air 4 bile
ductile: 4 soft 6 supple 7 plastic 8 formable 9 malleable
material: 4 gold, iron, lead 6 copper, nickel, silver 8 aluminum, platinum
ductlike: 5 tubal
dud: 4 bomb, bust, flop, loss 5 lemon, loser 6 defeat, fiasco, mishap, turkey 7 blunder, clinker, debacle, failure, fizzler, misstep, stumble, washout 8 downfall 10 nonsuccess
__-duddy: 5 fuddy
dude: 3 bro, cat, fop, guy 4 chap, gent, toff 5 buddy, dandy, fella, kiddo 6 feller, fellow, hepcat 7 coxcomb 8 fancy Dan, gay blade, macaroni, popinjay 9 ladies' man, pretty boy 10 jack-a-dandy, tenderfoot
up: 5 array, groom, preen, primp, prink 6 attire, bedaub 9 caparison
dude __: 5 ranch
__, dude!: 5 Later
duded up: 5 natty, smart 6 dapper
Dudek, Louis: 4 poet 8 Canadian
Dude Ranger, The
author: Zane Grey
Dudevant pseudonym: 4 Sand
dudgeon: 3 ire 4 rage 5 anger, pique, wrath 6 rancor 7 umbrage 10 irritation, resentment
__ du Diable: 3 île
Dudley: 4 Earl 5 Moore
friend: 4 Nell
Dudley Do-Right (1999 film)
cast: Brendan Fraser, Eric Idle, Alfred Molina, Sarah Jessica Parker
duds: 4 garb, gear, togs 5 array, dress, robes 6 attire, things 7 apparel, clothes, costume, raiment 8 garments, wardrobe 10 Sunday best
see also clothing
__ Duds: 4 Milk
Dudweiler: 4 city
locale: 4 Saar 7 Germany
due: 3 two 4 fair, just, owed, ripe 5 jural, legal, owing, right, share, title 6 coming, earned, lawful, proper, reward, served, unpaid, vested 7 deserts, exactly, fitting, Italian, merited, overdue, payable 8 arriving, deserved, directly, expected, required, rightful, straight, suitable 9 equitable, in arrears, in line for, justified, liability, privilege, reckoning, repayment, requisite, scheduled, unsettled 10 receivable, recompense, sufficient
a ~: 8 together
balance ~: 7 arrears
date: 3 end 5 limit 6 cutoff 8 deadline, zero hour
follower: 3 tre
get one's ~: 4 earn 5 merit
in ~ time: 3 yet 4 soon 10 eventually, ultimately
past ~: 5 tardy 6 behind, unpaid
preceder: 3 uno
process: 3 law 7 justice
process championer: 4 ACLU
to: 5 since 7 because 9 because of 10 by reason of, by virtue of
to get: 5 in for
to the fact that: 7 whereas
due __: 4 bill, date 7 process
due __ of law: 7 process
__ due: 4 past 7 postage
duel: 4 bout, tilt 5 fence, fight, joust 6 combat 7 contest 8 conflict, shootout, showdown 10 engagement, sword fight
maneuver: 5 lunge
weapon: 4 épée, foil 5 saber, sabre, sword 6 pistol
with words: 4 spar 6 banter
dueler: 4 Burr 8 Hamilton 9 combatant
duenna: 6 escort 8 chaperon 9 chaperone, governess
Duenna, The
author: Richard Sheridan
due process __: 5 of law
dues: 3 fee, tax 4 rate 5 price 7 charges 10 assessment, reparation
payer: 6 member
pay one's ~: 5 atone 7 rectify, redress
Duesenberg: 3 car 4 auto 6 Samuel 10 automobile
dues-paying group: 4 club, frat
duet: 3 two 4 pair 7 twosome
__, due, tre: 3 uno
duff: 4 coal, fake, rear, rump, seat 5 cheat, fanny, slack 6 behind 7 dessert, pudding, rear end 8 backside, derrière 9 posterior
Duff: 6 Hilary, Howard 7 McKagan
duffel: 3 bag, kit 4 coat, gear 6 jacket, kitbag 7 holdall 8 knapsack 9 haversack
duffer: 2 ox 3 oaf 4 lout, tyro 5 looby 7 amateur 8 beginner
see also golf
Duff, Howard: 5 actor
spouse: Ida Lupino
Duffy: 5 Julia, Karen 7 Patrick
Duffy's Tavern: 9 radio show
__ du Flambeau, WI: 3 Lac
Dufy, Raoul: 6 artist, French 7 painter
dug
ender: 3 out
in: 9 immovable, unbending 10 entrenched
Dugan: 6 Dennis
__ Dugan Returns: 3 Max
du Gard, Roger: 6 French, writer 8 Nobelist
dugong: 6 animal, mammal, sea cow
dugout: 3 pit 4 abri, boat 5 canoe, skiff 6 trench 7 foxhole 10 excavation
see also baseball
Duh!: 7 Silly me
Duhamel, Georges: 6 French, writer
DUI fighter: 4 MADD
duiker: 8 antelope
relative: *see* antelope
Duino Elegies, The
author: Rainer Maria Rilke
Duisburg: 4 city, town
locale: 7 Germany
river: 4 Ruhr 5 Rhine
__ du jour: 4 plat, soup 5 carte
Dukakis: 5 Kitty 7 Michael, Olympia
Dukakis, Olympia: 7 actress
film: Look Who's Talking (1989) Mighty Aphrodite (1995) Moonstruck (1987, AA) Mr. Holland's Opus (1995) Steel Magnolias (1989)
Dukas, Paul: 6 French 8 composer
work: The Sorcerer's Apprentice
duke: 3 box 4 fist, hand, lord, male, peer, rank 5 noble, title 8 nobleman
daughter: 4 lady
domain: 5 duchy
ender: 3 dom
it out: 5 brawl, fight
starter: 4 arch
Duke: 5 Daryl, Doris, Patty, title 6 Snider, Vernon 9 Ellington
athletes: 10 Blue Devils
conference: 3 ACC
Indigo for ~: 4 mood
locale: 4 N. Car. 6 Durham
org.: 4 NCAA
__ Duke: 3 Sir
Duke of __: 4 Earl, York 10 Wellington
Duke of Earl (1962 song)
artist: Gene Chandler
genre: 6 doo-wop
Duke, Patty
Oscar: The Miracle Worker
real first name: Anna
spouse: John Astin
Dukes: 5 David 8 Duquesne
__ Dukes: 5 Amboy
Dukes of Hazzard, The (CBS adventure)
cast: Catherine Bach (Daisy Duke) James Best (Sheriff Roscoe P. Coltrane) Sorrell Booke (Boss Hogg) Denver Pyle (Jesse Duke) John Schneider (Bo Duke) Tom Wopat (Luke Duke)
deputy: 4 Enos
dog: 5 Flash
spinoff: Enos
Duke, The: 5 Wayne
__ Duke, The: 4 Iron 5 Grand
__ du Lac, WI: 4 Fond
Dulbecco, Renato: 7 Italian 8 Nobelist
Dulce et Decorum Est
author: Wilfred Owen
dulcet: 4 soft 5 sweet 6 in tune, liquid 7 honeyed, lilting, lyrical, melodic, musical, tuneful 8 sonorous, soothing 9 melodious 10 euphonious
dulcimer: 5 chang 6 santir, string, zither 8 cymbalom
dulcinea
see sweetheart
Dulcy
author: Marc Connelly, George S. Kaufman
__ du Lieber!: 3 Ach
dull: 3 dry 4 arid, blah, drab, flat, gray, grey, lazy, logy, mild, slow, soft, tame 5 bland, blunt, corny, dense, empty, faded, faint, hoary, ho-hum, hokey, leady, matte, mirky, mousy, muddy, murky, musty, muzzy, passé, pasty, plain, prosy, quell, slack, sober, stale, thick, tired, trite, unapt, unfun, vapid 6 barren, benumb, boring, bovine, common, dampen, darken, deaden, draggy, dreary, drowsy, glassy, hollow, jejune, leaden, mousey, muffle, obtund, obtuse, old hat, opaque, sallow, simple, sleepy, somber, stodgy, stolid, stuffy, stupid, sullen, torpid, wooden 7 blunted, clichéd, doltish, fatuous, humdrum, insipid, languid, lumpish, muffled, nowhere, prosaic, relieve, routine, shallow, silence, tarnish, tedious, unwaxed, vacuous, witless, worn-out 8 bromidic, cloddish, dragging, familiar, lifeless, listless, lubberly, mediocre, mitigate, ordinary, outdated, outmoded, overcast, pedantic, sluggish, stagnant, tiresome, unlively, unsavory 9 brainless, cheerless, colorless, dimwitted, dry-as-dust, hackneyed, lethargic, pointless, ponderous, prosaical, soporific, tasteless, unpointed, washed-out, wearisome 10 dullsville, enervating, flavorless, glassy-eyed, lackluster, lusterless,

monotonous, pedantical, pedestrian, slow-witted, spiritless, tenebrific, threadbare, uneventful, unexciting, uninspired, unoriginal
as writing: **5** prosy
become ~: **4** pale **8** languish
color: **3** dun **4** drab, gray, grey
combining form: **5** brady-
grow ~: **4** fade
not ~: **4** keen **5** sharp
one: **4** bore, nerd **5** schmo
routine: **3** rut **4** drag, rote
sound: **4** thud **5** clonk, clunk, thump, thunk
surface: **3** mat **5** matte
dull-__: **6** witted
dullard
see ninny
Dullea, Keir: **5** actor
film: 2001: A Space Odyssey (1968)
David and Lisa (1962)
The Fox (1968)
Dulles, Allen onetime org.: **3** CIA
__ dull moment!: **6** Never a
dullness: **5** sleep **6** stupor, tedium **7** languor **8** drabness, flatness, laziness, lethargy, loginess, monotony **9** heaviness, indolence, inertness, lassitude **10** inactivity, insipidity
cure: **5** strop **9** whetstone
dullsville: **3** dry **4** blah, dull, flat, tame **5** hoary, ho-hum, prosy, stale, tired, trite, unfun, vapid **6** boring, common **7** humdrum, insipid, nowhere, routine, tedious, worn-out **8** familiar, ordinary, tiresome, unlively **9** colorless, hackneyed, soporific
dull-witted: **4** slow **5** thick **6** obtuse
one: **8** see ninny
dulse: **5** algae **7** seaweed
Duluth: **4** city, port, town
locale: **9** Minnesota
duly: **6** aright **10** as expected, punctually
bound: **5** sworn
dum __, spero: **5** spiro
Duma
locale: **6** Russia
Duma __: **3** Key
Dumas __: **4** fils, père
Dumas, Alexandre: **6** French, writer
character: **5** Athos **6** Aramis **7** Porthos **9** d'Artagnan
one ~: **4** fils, père
work: The Black Tulip
Camille
The Count of Monte Cristo
La Tulipe Noire
The Three Musketeers
Twenty Years After
see also French
du Maurier: **6** Daphne, George
du Maurier, Daphne: **4** Dame **6** writer **7** British
work: Rebecca
du Maurier, George: **6** writer **7** British
work: Trilby
dumb: **4** slow **5** dense, goosy, inane, quiet, thick **6** obtuse, simple, stolid, stupid **7** asinine, doltish, foolish, vacuous **9** dimwitted, voiceless **10** speechless
ender: **4** bell **5** found **6** struck, waiter
move: **5** boner **6** booboo
one: **4** bozo **6** lummox
play ~: **3** act
strike ~: **4** stun **7** silence, stagger, stupefy **8** surprise
dumb __: **4** Dora, down, luck
dumb __ ox: **4** as an
Dumbarton: **4** city
locale: **8** Scotland
river: **5** Clyde
Dumbarton __: **4** Oaks
dumbbell
unit: **5** pound **8** kilogram
use a ~: **4** curl, lift **7** work out **8** exercise
see also ninny
dumbbells: **3** wts. **7** weights
Dumb & Dumber (1994 film): **5** farce
cast: Jim Carrey, Jeff Daniels, Teri Garr, Lauren Holly
director: Peter Farrelly
dumbfound: **3** awe, wow **4** faze, stun **5** amaze, floor, stump, throw **6** baffle, boggle, puzzle **7** astound, confuse, nonplus, perplex, petrify, shatter, stagger, stupefy **8** astonish, befuddle, blow away, bowl over, surprise **9** embarrass, overwhelm, take aback **10** disappoint
dumbfounded: **5** blank, dizzy **6** aghast
Dumbo: **8** elephant
wing: **3** ear
Dumbrille: **8** Douglass
dumbstruck: **5** agape, in awe **6** amazed, jolted **7** shocked, stunned **8** startled **10** bewildered, tongue-tied
dumbwaiter: **6** lifter **8** elevator
Dumb Waiter, The
author: Harold Pinter
dumdum: **6** bullet
Dum Dum (1961 song)
artist: Brenda Lee
Dumfries: **4** city, town
locale: **8** Scotland
notable: **5** Burns
dummy: **3** ass, nit, oaf, sap **4** boob, bozo, clod, dodo, dolt, dope, fool, gowk, jerk, mock, sham **5** chump, clown, cluck, dunce, front, joker, looby, model, ninny, patsy **6** dimwit, effigy, lummox, nitwit, sucker, turkey **7** airhead, buffoon, dingbat, dullard, fathead, halfwit, jackass, pinhead, saphead **8** bonehead, dumbbell, lunkhead, meathead, numskull, spurious **9** birdbrain, blockhead, harebrain, ignoramus, lamebrain, mannequin, numbskull, simpleton **10** dunderhead, nincompoop
corporation: **5** front
dressmaker ~: **4** form
in America: **8** pacifier
perch: **4** knee
protest ~: **6** effigy
ventriloquist ~ home: **5** trunk
__ du monde: **4** gens **5** homme
Dumont: **8** Margaret
Du Mont: **5** Allen
dump: **3** axe, hut, rid, sty, tip **4** cede, dive, drop, jilt, junk, mess, sell, shed, slum, void **5** chuck, ditch, eject, empty, expel, forgo, hovel, joint, scrap, sneer, spurn, throw, yield **6** ashcan, divest, forego, give up, pigpen, pigsty, refuse, shanty, unlade, unload **7** abandon, ash heap, deep-six, discard, forfeit, forsake, let go of, piggery **8** empty out, forswear, get rid of, hand over, jettison, junkyard, landfill, part with, renounce, throw out, unburden **9** cast aside, dispose of, foreswear, repudiate, surrender, throw away, throw over **10** relinquish
ender: **4** site **5** truck
on: **4** gibe, jeer, jibe, mock, slam, slur, snub **5** abuse, decry, libel, scorn, spurn, taunt **6** attack, defame, demean, deride, heckle, impugn, insult, malign, offend, rebuff, slight, vilify **7** affront, asperse, degrade, disdain, put down, rank out, slander, traduce **8** badmouth, belittle, denounce, mistreat, ridicule, vilipend **9** denigrate, discredit, disparage, humiliate **10** calumniate, disrespect
out: **5** spill, unbag
__ dump: **4** core **6** screen
__ dump!: **5** What a
dumping ground: **8** landfill
dumpling: **4** baby **6** dim sum **7** dessert
dumps: **4** mood **5** blues, slump **7** sadness **8** doldrums, glumness
in the ~: **3** low, sad **4** blue, down, glum **5** moody, woful **6** gloomy, morose, somber, woeful **7** doleful, forlorn, joyless, unhappy **8** dejected, troubled **9** bummed out, cheerless, depressed, exanimate, heartsick, miserable, sorrowful, woebegone **10** chapfallen, despairing, dispirited, melancholy
Dumpster: **3** bin
locale: **5** alley
material: **5** trash **7** garbage, rubbish
relative: **6** ashcan
__ Dumpty: **6** Humpty
dumpy: **5** pudgy, squat **7** rundown
dum spiro, __: **5** spero
dun: **3** bug, nag **4** bill, dark **5** beset, brown, horse, hound, press **6** equine, gloomy, mayfly, pester, plague **7** grayish **9** importune, keep after **10** lusterless
relative: *see* brown color
Dunant, Jean: **5** Swiss **8** Nobelist
Dunaway, Faye: **7** actress
film: Barfly (1987)
Bonnie and Clyde (1967)
Chinatown (1974)
Don Juan DeMarco (1995)
Eyes of Laura Mars (1978)
The First Deadly Sin (1980)
Little Big Man (1970)
Mommie Dearest (1981)
Network (1976, AA)
Oklahoma Crude (1973)
The Temp (1993)
The Thomas Crown Affair (1968)
Three Days of the Condor (1975)
The Towering Inferno (1974)
Voyage of the Damned (1976)
Dunbar: **4** Paul **7** William
Dunbar, Paul: **4** poet **6** writer
Dunbar, William: **4** poet **6** writer **8** Scottish
Duncan: **4** Arne, city, Gray, Todd, town **5** Hines, Phyfe, Sandy **6** Robert **7** Isadora, Renaldo
locale: **8** Oklahoma
Duncan Gray
author: Robert Burns
Duncan Hines product: **3** mix **7** cake mix
Duncan, Isadora: **6** dancer **8** danseuse **9** ballerina
Duncan, Robert: **4** poet
Duncan, Todd: **6** singer **8** baritone
role: **5** Porgy
specialty: **5** opera
dunce: **3** ass, nit, oaf, sap **4** boob, bozo, clod, dodo, dolt, dope, fool, gowk, jerk, simp, slow, yo-yo **5** booby, chump, clown, cluck, dummy, dunce, joker, klutz, looby, ninny, patsy **6** dimwit, lubber, lummox, nitwit, sucker, turkey **7** airhead, buffoon, bungler, dingbat, dullard, fathead, halfwit, jackass, pinhead, saphead **8** bonehead, dumbbell, lunkhead, meathead, numskull, peabrain **9** birdbrain, blockhead, harebrain, ignoramus, lamebrain, numbskull, simpleton **10** dunderhead, nincompoop
cap shape: **4** cone
seat: **5** stool
Dunciad, The
author: Alexander Pope
Dundas: **4** city, town
locale: **6** Canada **7** Ontario
Dundee: **4** city, port, town **6** Angelo **9** Crocodile
locale: **8** Scotland
Dundee, Crocodile
girl: **3** Sue
see also Australia
dunderhead
see ninny
dune: **4** hill, sand, seif **5** mound, ridge
buggy: **3** ATV
dune __: **5** buggy
__ dune: **4** sand
Dune
author: Frank Herbert
composer: Brian Eno
Dunedin: **4** city, town
locale: **7** Florida **10** New Zealand
dungarees: **5** jeans, Levi's, pants **6** denims **8** trousers
dungeon: **4** cell, hole, jail **5** vault **6** prison **9** oubliette
item: **4** rack **5** irons
like a ~: **4** dank **5** mirky, murky
place: **6** castle, cellar
Dungeons & Dragons
beast: **3** Orc **4** ogre
company: **3** TSR
fan: **5** gamer
locale: **6** castle
spellcaster: **4** mage
Dunham: **9** Katherine
Dunhill
competitor: **5** Zippo
dunk: **3** dip **4** soak **5** souse **6** drench, plunge **7** immerse **8** saturate, submerge

alternative: 5 lay up
one: 5 score
__ dunk: 4 slam
dunker: 5 donut 8 doughnut
target: 4 goal 6 basket
Dunkin' __: 6 Donuts
dunking: 3 dip 4 bath, wash 5 rinse, souse 6 plunge 7 soaking 9 immersion
Dunkirk: 4 city, port, town
locale: 6 France
dunlin: 4 bird 9 sandpiper, shorebird
Dunlop: 4 tire
Dunn: 4 Nora 5 James 7 Michael
Dunne: 5 Irene 6 Philip 7 Griffin 8 Dominick
dunned amount: 6 arrear 7 arrears
Dunne, Finley Peter: 6 writer 8 humorist
character: Dooley
Dunning: 5 Debbe
Dunninger claim: 3 ESP
Dunn, James Oscar: A Tree Grows in Brooklyn
__-du-Nord: 5 Côtes
Dunsinane: 4 fort, hill
locale: 8 Scotland
Dunstan: 5 saint
Dunst, Kirsten: 7 actress
film: All I Wanna Do (1998)
Bring It On (2000)
Dick (1999)
Drop Dead Gorgeous (1999)
Jumanji (1995)
Marie Antoinette (2006)
Mona Lisa Smile (2003)
Small Soldiers (1998)
Spider-Man (2002)
The Virgin Suicides (2000)
Wimbledon (2005)
Dunwoody: 4 city, town
locale: 7 Georgia
duo: 3 two 4 both, dyad, pair, team 5 brace, combo, twain, twins 6 couple, double 7 couplet, doublet, twosome
Duo
author: Colette
duomo: 6 temple 9 cathedral
__ du pays: 3 mal
dupe: 3 con, lie, sap 4 butt, copy, fish, fool, gull, have, hoax, jerk, lamb, mark, mock, naif, nick, pawn, prey, rook, same, scam, snow, take, tool, trap 5 cheat, chump, clone, cozen, hocus, mimeo, patsy, repro, shaft, trick 6 delude, ectype, jackal, lead on, outwit, pigeon, puppet, rip off, rope in, softie, stooge, sucker, suck in, take in, victim 7 beguile, buffalo, cat's-paw, chicane, deceive, defraud, fall guy, mislead, pretend, replica, swindle, two-time 8 bulldoze, easy mark, flimflam, hoodwink, outsmart, pushover, sucker in 9 bamboozle, disinform, four-flush, imitation, photocopy, reproduce, scapegoat, victimize 10 run a game on
not a ~: 8 original
duped: 5 taken 7 taken in 8 mistaken
easily ~: 4 naif 5 naive
__-duper: 5 super
dupery: 3 con, fib, lie 4 hoax, jive, ruse, scam, sham, trap, wile 5 dodge, feint, fraud, guile, hokum, lying, snare, sting, trick 6 hustle 7 blarney, charade, con game, cunning, falsity, fast one, gimmick, hogwash, malarky, snow job, sophism, swindle, untruth 8 artifice, bad faith, betrayal, delusion, flimflam, foul play, jugglery, malarkey, pretense, trickery 9 casuistry, chicanery, deception, dirty work, duplicity, falsehood, hypocrisy, imposture, mare's-nest, mendacity, stratagem, treachery, whitewash 10 craftiness, hanky-panky, hocus-pocus, masquerade, subterfuge
Dupin, Auguste: 9 detective
creator: Edgar Allan Poe
Dupin, Lucile pseudonym: 4 Sand
duple: 7 twofold
duplex: 4 twin 5 condo 6 double, paired 7 twofold, two-unit 8 two-sided 9 apartment
duplicate: 3 fax 4 copy, echo, mate, same, stat, twin 5 clone, ditto, equal, match, mimeo, model, trace, Xerox 6 double, ectype, repeat 7 imitate, replica, twofold 8 knockoff, likeness, matching 9 companion, correlate, facsimile, identical, imitation, lookalike, photocopy, Photostat, replicate, reproduce 10 carbon copy, dead ringer, equivalent, reciprocal, recurrence, reflection, repetition, tantamount, transcribe, transcript
duplicate bridge: 4 game 8 card game
duplicative remark: 5 ditto, me too
duplicitous: 4 wily 5 false, shady 6 crafty, sneaky 7 devious 8 cheating, guileful, two-faced 9 underhand
be ~: 3 lie
duplicity: 3 art 4 wile 5 craft, fraud, guile 6 deceit, dupery 7 cunning, falsity, perfidy, treason 8 artifice, bad faith 9 chicanery, deception, dirty pool, dirty work, falsehood, falseness, hypocrisy, Judas kiss, treachery 10 craftiness, dirty trick, dishonesty, infidelity
Duplicity (2009 film)
cast: Clive Owen, Julia Roberts
DuPont
HQ: 8 Delaware
product: 5 Lycra, Orlon 6 Kevlar, Lucite, Teflon
Duprees
song: You Belong to Me (1962)
du Pré, Jacqueline: 7 British, cellist
Duquesne: 10 university
athletes: 5 Dukes
locale: 4 Penn. 10 Pittsburgh
dura __: 5 mater
durability: 4 grit, guts 5 heart, moxie 7 stamina 8 firmness, strength 9 endurance, longevity, stability 10 continuity, permanence
durable: 5 solid, sound, tough 6 stable, steady, strong, sturdy 7 abiding, lasting 8 leathery, reliable 9 heavy-duty, long-lived, tenacious 10 dependable, reinforced
be ~: 4 last, wear
not ~: 5 tinny 6 flimsy
duralumin: 5 alloy
component: 6 copper 8 aluminum
Duran: 7 Roberto
Durand: 5 Asher
Duran Duran
song: Come Undone (1993)
Hungry Like the Wolf (1983)
I Don't Want Your Love (1988)
Is There Something I Should Know (1983)
Notorious (1986)
Ordinary World (1993)
The Reflex (1984)
Union of the Snake (1983)
A View to a Kill (1985)
The Wild Boys (1984)
Durango: 3 SUV 4 city, town 5 Dodge, state 6 estado 7 Mexican
city: 5 Lerdo 6 Poanas 8 Canatlán
locale: 6 Mexico 8 Colorado
see also Spanish
Durant: 4 Will 5 Ariel
Durant, Ariel: 6 writer 9 historian
durante __: 4 vita
Durante, Jimmy: 5 actor 8 comedian
film: Billy Rose's Jumbo (1962)
It's a Mad Mad Mad Mad World (1963)
On an Island With You (1948)
Palooka (1934)
trademark: 4 nose
Durant, Will: 6 writer 9 historian
work: The Age of Napoleon
Rousseau and Revolution
The Story of Civilization
The Story of Philosophy
Duras, Marguerite: 6 French, writer
duration: 3 run 4 life, span, term, time 5 space 6 course, extent, length, period, tenure 7 stretch 9 longevity 10 continuity, perpetuity
for the ~: 8 meantime 9 meanwhile
Durban: 4 city, port, town
locale: 3 RSA 5 Natal
Durbeyfield: 4 Tess
pursuer: 4 Alec
Durbin: 6 Deanna
Durc parent: 4 Ayla
__ dure: 4 pâte
Dürer, Albrecht: 6 artist, etcher, German 7 painter 8 engraver
duress: 5 force 8 bullying, coercion, pressure, violence 10 compulsion
Durham: 4 city, town 6 county
athletes: 8 Wildcats 10 Blue Devils
city: 6 Seaham
locale: 4 Conn., N. Car. 7 England
school: 3 UNH 4 Duke
__ Durham: 4 Bull
during: 4 amid, when 5 while 6 amidst, just as, whilst 7 through 8 all along 10 throughout
prefix: 3 dia- 5 intra-
durn: 4 dang, darn 6 shucks
Durning: 7 Charles
duro: 4 coin
Duroc: 3 hog, pig 5 swine
young ~: 5 shoat, shote, shott
Durocher, Leo: 7 manager
nickname: 3 Lip 5 Lippy 6 The Lip
spouse: Laraine Day
durra: 5 grain 7 sorghum
Durrell, Lawrence: 6 writer 7 British
work: Acte
Alexandria Quartet
Balthazar
Clea
The Ikons
Justine
Livia
Mountolive
durum: 5 flour, grain, wheat
Durward: 5 Kirby 7 Quentin
Durwent: 5 river
locale: 8 Tasmania
Duryea: 3 Dan
__ du Salut: 4 îles, Port
Duse: 8 Eleonora
__ du seigneur: 5 droit
Dusenberry: 3 Ann
Dushanbe: 4 city, town 7 capital
locale: 10 Tajikistan
Dushku: 5 Eliza
dusk: 3 e'en 4 dark 6 shadow, sunset 7 evening, sundown 8 gloaming, twilight 9 nightfall 10 crepuscule
after ~: 4 dark 5 night
of yore: 5 gloam
dusky: 3 dim 4 dark, gray, grey, soft 5 bleak, faded, fuzzy, livid, mirky, murky, muted, shady 6 bleary, blurry, dismal, gloomy, somber, swarth, twilit 7 fuscous, joyless, shadowy, swarthy 8 lowering, overcast 9 lightless, poorly lit, tenebrous, unlighted 10 indistinct
Dussault: 5 Nancy
Düsseldorf: 4 city, town
city near ~: 4 Köln 5 Essen, Neuss
locale: 7 Germany
river: 5 Rhine
dust: 3 mop 4 lint, soil, wipe 5 clean, motes, spray 6 powder, refuse, tidy up 7 trounce 8 sprinkle 9 sweepings 10 sprinkling
bit: 5 speck
bite the ~: 3 bow 4 bomb, bust, fail, flop, lose, slip, trip 5 flunk 6 blow it, falter, fizzle 7 blunder, founder, go under, go wrong, misstep, stumble, wash out 8 fall flat, flounder, lay an egg 9 strike out
collector: 3 rag
combining form: 4 coni- 5 conio-
cover item: 3 bio 5 blurb 6 review
devil: 4 eddy, wind
diamond ~: 4 bort 5 boart, bortz
ender: 3 bin, off, pan
gathering ~: 4 idle 8 inactive, not in use
leave in the ~: 6 run off 9 leap ahead
starter: 3 saw 4 star
use a ~ rag: 4 wipe
valuable ~: 4 gold
dust __: 3 gun, mop, off 4 ball, cart, shot, well 5 bunny, cover, devil, storm 6 jacket, ruffle 7 catcher
__ dust: 4 acid, gold, rock 5 dry as
__-dust: 4 crop 5 dry-as
Dust Bowl
like the ~: 3 dry 4 arid
migrant: 4 Okie
Dustbuster: 3 vac 6 vacuum
dustcloth: 3 rag
duster: 3 mop, rag 4 coat, maid 5 plane, smock 6 jacket 8 airplane, overcoat 9 housecoat
__-duster: 4 crop

Duster: 3 car 4 auto 8 Plymouth
Dustin: 6 Farnum 7 Hoffman
  role: 5 Ratso
dusting: 5 chore 7 coating 9 housework 10 sprinkling
  powder: 4 talc
___-dusting: 4 crop
Dust in the Wind (1978 song)
  artist: Kansas
Dust of Snow: 4 poem
  author: Robert Frost
___ dust shalt thou return: 4 unto
...___, dust to...: 5 ashes
Dust Tracks on a Road
  author: Zora Neale Hurston
dustup: 3 ado, row 4 spat, tiff 5 run-in, set-to 6 barney, rumpus 7 quarrel, rhubarb 8 skirmish, squabble 9 brannigan
dusty: 3 dry 4 arid, gray, grey 5 dirty, grimy 6 unused 7 powdery, tedious, unclean, unswept 8 obsolete, outdated, timeworn, unwashed 9 out-of-date, uncleaned 10 lusterless
  relative: ***see*** gray color
Dusty: 5 Baker 6 Rhodes
Dutch: 4 font 8 language, typeface
  oven: 7 stewpot
  speaking island: 5 Aruba
  uncle: 6 critic 7 adviser, advisor
  see also Netherlands
Dutch ___: 4 door, oven 5 treat, uncle 6 Guiana 7 auction
Dutch ___ disease: 3 elm
Dutch ___ Indies: 4 East, West
Dutch Courtezan, The
  author: John Marston
Dutch gold: 5 alloy
  component: 4 zinc 6 copper
Dutchman's-pipe: 5 plant 6 flower
___ Dutchman, The: 6 Flying
Dutch oven: 3 pot 6 cooker
Dutch West ___: 6 Indies
dutiful: 4 good, true 5 lowly, loyal, moral 6 docile, filial 7 devoted, staunch, willing 8 amenable, constant, faithful, gracious, obedient, true-blue, yielding 9 agreeable, allegiant, compliant, dedicated, regardful, righteous, steadfast, tractable 10 law-abiding, respectful, scrupulous, submissive
  be ~ to: 5 serve
___ du tout: 3 pas
Dutra: 4 Olin
Dutton, Charles S.: 5 actor
  TV: Roc
duty: 3 job, tax, tie 4 care, levy, must, need, onus, part, role, task, toll, work 5 chore, ought, place, stint, thing, watch 6 affair, burden, charge, excise, impost, office, tariff, towage 7 loyalty, mission, service, station 8 business, exaction, function, province 9 liability 10 assessment, assignment, commitment, department, engagement, obligation
  call of ~: 5 draft
  customs ~: 3 tax 6 impost
  do ~: 5 serve
  GI ~: 2 KP
  ignore one's ~: 5 shirk 8 slack off
  on ~: 4 busy 6 active, at work 8 employed
  roster: 4 rota
  sentry ~: 5 vigil, watch
  tour of ~: 5 hitch, spell, stint
  word of ~: 4 must 5 ought 6 should
duty-___: 4 free
___ duty: 3 sea 5 civic, guard 6 active
___-duty: 3 off 5 heavy, light 6 double
___ Duty: 5 Ode to
Duun, Olav: 6 writer 9 Norwegian
Duval, David: 6 golfer
Duvall: 6 Robert 7 Shelley
Duvall, Robert: 5 actor
  film: Angelo, My Love (1983)
    Apocalypse Now (1979)
    The Apostle (1997)
    The Betsy (1978)
    Breakout (1975)
    A Civil Action (1998)
    Colors (1988)
    Convicts (1991)
    Countdown (1968)
    Days of Thunder (1990)
    Deep Impact (1998)
    The Eagle Has Landed (1977)
    The Godfather (1972)
    Gods and Generals (2003)
    The Great Santini (1979)
    John Q (2002)
    Lawman (1971)
    MASH (1970)
    The Natural (1984)
    Network (1976)
    Open Range (2003)
    The Paper (1994)
    Phenomenon (1996)
    The Rain People (1969)
    Rambling Rose (1991)
    Secondhand Lions (2003)
    The Seven-Per-Cent Solution (1976)
    The Stone Boy (1984)
    Tender Mercies (1983, AA)
    To Kill a Mockingbird (1962)
    Tomorrow (1972)
    True Confessions (1981)
___ du Vent: 4 îles
___ du ventre: 5 danse
duvet: 5 quilt 9 comforter
du Vigneaud, Vincent: 7 chemist 8 Nobelist
Duz
  rival: 5 Rinso
DVD
  attachment: 2 TV 5 TV set
  predecessor: 3 VCR
Dvina: 3 bay 5 river
  city on the ~: 4 Riga
  locale: 6 Russia
DVM: 3 vet
Dvorak: 3 Ann
Dvorák, Antonín: 5 Czech 8 composer
  work: The Cunning Peasant
    Czech Suite
    New World Symphony
    Rhapsody for Orchestra
    Slavonic Dances
D.W.: 8 Griffith
Dwan: 5 Allan
dwarf: 3 Doc 4 runt, star, tiny 5 Dopey, gnome, Happy, stunt, teeny 6 Grumpy, petite, Sleepy, Sneezy, teensy 7 Bashful 8 diminish, minimize 9 miniature, tower over, undersize 10 diminutive, homunculus, overshadow
  tree: 6 bonsai
___ dwarf: 3 red 5 black, brown, white
dwarfs: 6 heptad
Dwarf, The
  author: Pär Lagerkvist
Dwayne: 7 Hickman
dweeb: 4 geek, jerk, nerd, wimp, wonk 5 loser, twerp, twirp
  like a ~: 6 uncool
dwell: 4 bide, harp, live, nest, stay 5 abide, exist, lodge, roost 6 inhere, linger, locate, occupy, remain, reside, settle 7 inhabit, sojourn 8 populate
  on: 5 savor 6 ponder, ramble, stress 7 belabor, iterate 8 reassert, remember 9 emphasize
dweller: 5 liver 6 tenant 7 citizen, denizen, resider 8 indigene, occupant, resident 10 inhabitant
  suffix: 3 -ian, -ite
___ dweller: 4 cave, lake 5 cliff
dwelling: 3 den, pad, res. 4 digs, home 5 abode, cabin, house, lodge, place 6 castle, chalet, palace 7 address, domicil, habitat, housing, lodging, mansion, shelter 8 building, domicile, dwelling, fireside, lodgment, quarters 9 residence
  Amerind ~: 4 tipi 5 hogan, tepee 6 teepee
  arctic ~: 4 iglu 5 igloo
  bird ~: 4 nest
  cliff ~: 4 aery, eyry 5 aerie, eyrie
  cozy ~: 4 nest
  crude ~: 3 hut 5 hovel, shack 6 lean-to
  dryad ~: 4 tree
  elevated ~: 4 aery, eyry 5 aerie, eyrie
  frontier ~: 5 cabin
  Herr ~: 4 haus
  magnificent ~: 5 manor 6 castle
  outdoor ~: 4 tent
  prehistoric ~: 4 cave
  rundown ~: 4 dive, dump, slum 5 hovel
  ski ~: 5 lodge
  Southwestern ~: 5 adobe
  urban ~: 4 co-op, flat 5 condo 6 duplex 9 apartment
  see also home, house
___ dwelling: 3 pit 4 lake 5 cliff
Dwight: 5 Evans, Moody 6 Gooden, Yoakam 7 Timothy, Twilley 10 Eisenhower
  nickname: 3 Ike
  opponent: 5 Adlai
  wife: 5 Mamie
dwindle: 3 die, ebb 4 curb, drop, fade, fall, lull, sink, wane, wilt 5 abate, decay, drain, lower, peter, slack, taper 6 lessen, recede, reduce, shrink, weaken 7 curtail, cut down, decline, die down, drop off, fall off, shrivel, slacken, subside, tail off, thin out 8 contract, decrease, diminish, head away, languish, level off, peter out, slack off, taper off 9 retrocede
dwindling: 3 ebb 4 fall 7 decline 8 decrease 9 remission
___ D. Wood Jr.: 6 Edward
Dy: 4 elem. 7 element 10 dysprosium
  66 for ~: 4 at. no.
dyad: 3 duo, two 4 pair 5 brace 6 couple 7 twosome
dyadic: 6 paired
Dyan: 6 Cannon
dye: 3 azo, hue 4 anil, tint, weld, woad 5 color, eosin, henna, paint, stain, tinct, tinge 6 anatto, eosine, indigo, kamala, litmus, madder, orchil, redden 7 alkanet, cudbear, fuchsin, gallein, genipap, logwood, pigment, recolor 8 amaranth, colorant, coloring, tincture, turmeric 9 cochineal 10 quercitron
  acid ~: 5 eosin 6 eosine
  azo ~: 8 amaranth
  bin: 3 vat 4 keir
  blue ~: 4 anil, woad 6 indigo
  brown ~: 5 henna 7 gallein, genipap
  chemical ~: 3 azo
  chemist ~: 6 litmus
  Egyptian ~: 5 henna
  ender: 4 wood 5 stuff
  green ~: 7 gallein
  hair ~: 5 henna
  ingredient: 4 alum
  lab slide ~: 5 eosin 6 eosine
  lot: 10 color batch
  name: 3 Rit
  nitrogen-based ~: 3 azo
  organic ~: 3 azo 6 kermes
  plant: 4 anil
  purple: 7 alkanet, logwood 8 amaranth
  red ~: 3 azo 5 eosin, henna 6 eosine, kermes, madder, orchil 7 alkanet, cudbear, genipap, logwood 8 amaranth 9 cochineal
  yellow ~: 4 weld 6 kamala 8 turmeric 10 quercitron
  yellow-red ~: 6 anatto
___-dyed: 3 tie
dyed-in-the-wool: 4 avid 5 loyal, stern 6 enured, inured 7 diehard 8 absolute, complete, deep-down, faithful, hard-core, hardened 9 confirmed, stringent 10 inveterate
dyeing instruction: 5 rinse
dyer: 8 colorist
Dyer: 5 Wayne
dyer's ___: 4 moss 5 broom 6 rocket
dye-with-wax technique: 5 batik 6 battik
Dying Animal, The
  author: Philip Roth
dying away in music: 7 calando
dying to know: 6 prying, snoopy 7 curious 8 meddling 9 butting in, intrusive, obtrusive 10 meddlesome
Dyken, Amy Van: 7 swimmer
Dykstra: 3 Len 5 Lenny
Dylan: 3 Bob 5 Baker, Jakob 6 Thomas 8 language 9 McDermott
  contemporary: 4 Baez
Dylan, Bob
  son: Jakob
  song: Knockin' on Heaven's Door (1973)
    Lay Lady Lay (1969)
    Like a Rolling Stone (1965)
    Positively 4th Street (1965)
    Rainy Day Women (1966)
dynamic: 4 busy, go-go, live, spry 5 alive, astir, lusty, peppy, perky, ready, vital, zippy 6 active, at work,

lively, living, moving, potent **7** animate, driving, hyped-up, intense, kinetic, vibrant, working **8** animated, bustling, electric, emphatic, forceful, powerful, vigorous **9** assiduous, energetic, masterful, sprightly, strenuous **10** aggressive, compelling, electrical, productive, unflagging
starter: 4 aero
Dynamic __: 3 Duo
dynamics: 6 motion
dynamism: 5 force, power, vigor **6** bounce **10** initiative
dynamite: 3 fab, TNT **4** rase, raze **5** blast **6** blow up **7** destroy, explode, shatter, sublime, unbuild **8** perilous, striking **9** explosive, wonderful **10** precarious, stupendous
ingredient: 5 nitro
sound: 3 pow **5** kapow **6** kaboom
dynamize: 9 galvanize
dynamo: 4 doer, Turk **5** mover **6** shaker **7** hotshot, hustler, whiz kid **8** achiever, fireball, go-getter, live wire **9** generator, spark plug **10** ball of fire
part: 5 rotor **6** stator
Dynamo: 9 detergent
alternative: ***see*** detergent
dynast: 4 czar, king, tsar, tzar **5** queen, ruler **6** gerent, prince **7** czarina, emperor, empress, tsarina, tzarina **8** princess **9** potentate
dynastic: 5 royal
Dynasts, The
author: Thomas Hardy
dynasty: 4 rule **5** house **6** empire, regime **7** kingdom
Chinese ~: 3 Chi, Jin, Qin, Wei, Xia, Yin **4** Chan, Chen, Hsia, Liao, Ming, T'ang, Tsin, Yuan **5** Liang, Shang
first Chinese ~: 4 Hsia
Dynasty (ABC drama)
cast: Diahann Carroll (Dominique Deveraux)
Joan Collins (Alexis Colby)
Sammy Jo Dean (Heather Locklear)
Linda Evans (Krystle Carrington)
John Forsythe (Blake Carrington)
Pamela Sue Martin (Fallon Colby)
Emma Samms (Fallon Colby)
setting: 6 Denver **8** Colorado
dyne-centimeter: 3 erg
Dynel: 6 fabric **8** material
Dysart: 7 Richard
dysfunctional: 7 useless
dyspeptic: 6 cranky **7** bearish **9** irritable **10** ill-natured
dysprosium: 7 element
dysrhythmia, circadian: 6 jet lag

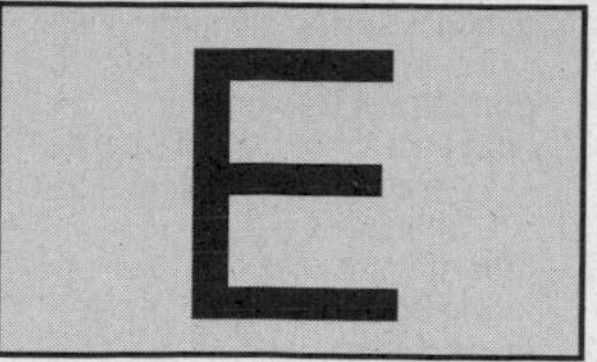

8
on a phone: 3 TUV
8 1/2 (1963 film)
cast: Anouk Aimée, Claudia Cardinale, Marcello Mastroianni
director: Federico Fellini
musical based on ~: 4 Nine
11%, about: 5 ninth
11:00 feature: 4 news
11th-grader: 6 junior
11-year-old: 5 'tween
18
holes: 5 round
play ~: 4 golf
__ 18: 4 Mila
18 Again! (1988 film)
cast: George Burns, Anita Morris, Tony Roberts, Charlie Schlatter
18 and Life (1989 song)
artist: Skid Row
18th-Amendment
subject: 6 liquor
supporter: 3 dry
18-wheeler: 4 semi 5 truck
80-day circumnavigator: 4 Fogg
84 Charing Cross Road
author: Helene Hanff
84 Charing Cross Road (1987 film)
cast: Anne Bancroft, Judi Dench, Anthony Hopkins
86: 3 nix 5 agent
87th Precinct setting: 5 Isola
88: 5 piano
88 Minutes (2008 film)
cast: Al Pacino, Alicia Witt
800 Leagues on the Amazon
author: Jules Verne
800-no.
relative: 4 WATS
808 (1999 song)
artist: Blaque
1800: 5 six p.m.
1812 Overture
composer: Peter Tchaikovsky
1857 mutineer: 5 Sepoy
1876
author: Gore Vidal
1898 rebel: 5 Boxer
e-__: 4 mail, mall, tail 7 tailing
E: 3 dir., vit. 5 vowel, width 6 letter 7 vitamin
equivalent: 5 F-flat
in phonetic alphabet: 4 Echo
part of ~ = mc2: 4 mass 6 energy
to W line: 3 hor.
E __ dell' anima: 5 il sol
E __ eagle: 4 as in
E. __ Biggs: 5 Power
E. __ Hunt: 6 Howard
E. __ Proulx: 5 Annie
__ E: 4 T and 6 Sheila
'E' __ Evidence: 5 Is for
__-E: 4 Eazy, Wall
E-2, Army: 3 pvt.
E-6, Army: 4 SSgt.
E-7, Army: 3 SFC
each: 3 per 4 a pop 5 a head, a shot, every 6 apiece, a throw, either, for one, singly 7 per head, per unit 9 per capita, per person 10 respective
one: 3 all 9 everybody
Each Dawn I Die (1939 film)
cast: James Cagney, George Raft
__ each life...: 4 Into
Each sack had __ cats...: 5 seven
eager: 3 hot 4 agog, avid, game, keen, wild 5 antsy, itchy, lanky, ready, wired 6 aflame, ardent, fervid, gung ho, hearty, hungry, intent, on edge, prompt, red-hot, strong 7 anxious, athirst, burning, earnest, excited, fervent, fired up, glowing, intense, longing, psyched, thirsty, willing, wishful, zealous, zestful 8 animated, aspiring, desirous, hopped up, juiced up, spirited, studious, tireless, vehement, yearning 9 ambitious, expectant, exuberant, hot to trot, impatient, impetuous, psyched up, strenuous, voracious 10 inspirited, passionate, raring to go, solicitous
about: 6 keen on
be ~: 4 jump
beaver: 4 doer 6 dynamo 7 busy bee, hustler 8 go-getter, live wire 10 ball of fire, hard worker
feel ~: 4 ache, long, lust, pang, pine, want 5 crave, throb, yearn 6 hanker
for company: 4 lone 5 alone 6 lonely 7 forlorn 8 desolate, forsaken, isolated, lonesome, rejected, solitary, unsocial 9 by oneself, destitute, reclusive, withdrawn 10 unattended
make ~: 4 whet
to do: 5 up for
to hear: 7 all ears 9 attentive
eager __: 6 beaver
eagerly: 4 hard 6 keenly 7 readily
eagerness: 4 fire, zeal, zest, zing 5 ardor, gusto, speed 6 desire, fervor, hunger, thirst 7 avidity, longing 8 alacrity, ambition, fervency, keenness, voracity, yearning 9 constancy, curiosity, fixedness, quickness, readiness, vehemence 10 aspiration, enterprise, enthusiasm, excitement, exuberance, greediness, heartiness, impatience, initiative, intentness, promptness, solicitude
show ~, old-style: 4 rare
eagle: 3 ern 4 bird, coin, erne 5 money 6 raptor 10 bird of prey
a par-three hole: 3 ace
attack like an ~: 5 swoop
constellation: 6 Aquila
emulate an ~: 4 soar 5 glide, swoop
eye: 5 stare, vigil, watch 6 acuity 7 lookout 8 scrutiny
feature: 4 claw 5 talon
home: 4 aery, eyry, nest 5 aerie, eyrie
legal ~: 6 lawyer 8 attorney 9 counselor
like an ~: 8 aquiline
Muppet ~: 3 Sam
plus one: 6 birdie
plus two: 3 par
sea ~: 3 ern 4 bird, erne
wearer: 3 col. 7 colonel
eagle __: 3 eye
eagle-__: 4 eyed
__ eagle: 3 sea 4 bald 5 legal 6 spread
Eagle: 3 AMC, car, LEM 4 auto 5 scout 7 Pennell 8 Boy Scout 10 automobile
where the ~ landed: 4 moon
__ Eagle: 4 Iron, Lone
Eagle and the Arrow, The
source: 4 Esop 5 Aesop
eagle-eyed: 4 wary 8 keen-eyed 9 observant
Eagle Has Landed, The (1977 film)
cast: Michael Caine, Robert Duvall, Donald Sutherland
Eagles: 4 band 6 eleven
member: Glenn Frey, Don Henley, Joe Walsh
org.: 3 BSA, NFC
rival: ***see*** NFL team
song: Best of My Love (1974)
Heartache Tonight (1979)
Hotel California (1977)
I Can't Tell You Why (1980)
Life in the Fast Lane (1977)
The Long Run (1979)
Lyin' Eyes (1975)
New Kid in Town (1976)
One of These Nights (1975)
Take It to the Limit (1976)
Witchy Woman (1972)
sport: 8 football
__ Eagles Dare: 5 Where
eagle, star whose name means: 6 Altair
eaglet: 6 raptor 8 nestling 9 fledgling
__ Eagle, The: 4 Lone
Eakins, Thomas: 6 artist 7 painter
Eames: 4 Emma 5 chair 7 Charles
Eames, Emma: 6 singer 7 soprano
specialty: 4 aria 5 opera
Eamon: 8 De Valera
E. Annie: 6 Proulx
EAP
part of ~: 3 Poe 5 Allan, Edgar
ear: 4 corn, heed 5 organ, spike 6 handle 7 auricle 8 audience, listener 9 attention 10 perception
assault the ~: 6 deafen
bend an ~: 4 hark, talk 5 lobby, run on 7 hearken 9 eavesdrop
bone: 5 anvil, incus 6 stapes 7 stirrup
cleaner: 4 Q-tip, swab, swob
collection: 3 wax 7 cerumen
combining form: 2 ot- 3 aur-, oto- 4 auri-
cover: 4 husk
ender: 3 bob, lap, wax, wig 4 ache, drop, drum, flap, lobe, mark, muff, plug, ring, shot, worm 5 phone, piece 9 splitting
feature: 5 canal
flea in one's ~: 3 tip 4 clue 6 tip-off 7 glimmer, inkling, whisper 10 glimmering, suggestion
give ~ to: 4 care, hear, heed, mind, obey 6 attend, follow, listen, notice 7 abide by, observe 8 adhere to, consider, listen to 10 bear in mind, take care of, toe the line
grain ~: 5 spica
hard on the ~: 4 loud 5 noisy 6 atonal 7 raucous
insert: 4 plug
lend an ~: 4 heed 6 listen 7 hearken, hear out
malady: 6 otitis
of an ~ part: 5 lobar
of the ~: 4 otic 5 aural 6 audial
opening: 6 meatus
outer ~: 6 concha
part: 3 cob 4 lobe 5 canal 6 hammer, kernel, tragus
play by ~: 5 ad-lib 6 invent, make up, whip up, wing it 9 improvise
pollution: 3 din 4 roar, stir 5 noise 6 bedlam, clamor, hubbub, jangle, racket, scream, shriek, tumult, uproar 7 clangor, clatter, discord 8 brouhaha, disquiet 9 commotion, hue and cry 10 hullabaloo
tin ~: 6 asonia
turn a deaf ~: 5 scorn 6 refuse, slight
winter ~ wear: 4 muff
ear __: 3 tag 4 lobe, plug 5 canal, candy, drops
__ ear: 3 tin 4 deaf 5 inner, on its, outer
__-ear: 3 dog
Earache My Eye (1974 song)
artist: Cheech and Chong
__ ear and out...: 5 in one
__-ear dog: 7 hearing
eared __: 4 seal
__-eared: 3 dog, lop
__-eared bunny: 3 lop
earful: 4 info, talk 5 rumor 6 advice, gossip, rebuke, report 7 message 8 scolding 10 bawling out, revelation, telling-off, upbraiding
cheerful ~: 4 song, tune 5 ditty, music 6 ballad, jingle, number 7 lullaby
get an ~: 4 hear, heed 6 listen, take in 7 receive 8 discover, listen in, listen to 9 eavesdrop, get wind of 10 understand
Earhart, Amelia: 5 flier, flyer 7 aviator 8 aviatrix, explorer
earing: 4 rope
earl: 4 lord, male, peer, rank 5 noble, title 8 nobleman
ender: 3 dom
equivalent: 5 count
in German: 4 graf
Earl: 4 Butz, Grey, Wild 5 Cecil, Grant, Hines, Klugh, noble, Sande, title 6 Baring, Bostic, Dudley, Monroe, Scheib, Tupper, Warren, Weaver, Wilson 7 Anthony, Averill, Scruggs 8 Campbell, Holliman 9 Blackwell 10 Sutherland
Earl __ Biggers: 4 Derr
Earl __ Hines: 5 Fatha
Earl __ tea: 4 Grey
earlap: 4 lobe 7 cap flap, hat part
Earle: 5 Combs, Hagen, Hyman, Steve
earlet: 6 tragus
Earl Grey: 3 tea
earlier: 3 ago, ere, yet 4 once, past 5 above, afore, ahead, older, prior 6 before, former 7 advance, onetime 8 foregone, formerly, previous, until now 9 a while ago, foregoing, preceding 10 beforehand, heretofore, previously
combining form: 4 fore- 6 proter- 7 protero-

prefix: 3 pre-, pro- 4 ante-
than: 3 ere 7 ahead of, prior to 10 previous to
the ~, the better: 4 ASAP, stat
earliest: 5 first, prime 6 maiden 7 initial, premier, primary 8 original, primeval 9 inceptive, primaeval, primitive, vestigial 10 primordial
combining form: 4 prot- 5 proto-
earlike projection: 5 pinna
__ Earl Jones: 5 James
Earl of __: 4 Avon 5 Essex
Earl of Avon: 4 Eden
Earl of Greystoke love: 4 Jane
early: 3 old, wee 5 ahead, young 6 prompt 7 advance, ancient, betimes, budding, forward, initial, morning, nascent, pioneer, too soon 8 germinal, immature, in the bud, original, primeval, punctual 9 beginning, embryonic, in advance, inceptive, premature, primaeval, primitive, unevolved 10 aboriginal, beforehand, in good time, precocious, primordial
early __: 4 bird 5 riser
Early: 4 Wynn 5 Jubal
Early __, early...: 5 to bed
Early Bird: 6 Comsat 9 satellite
early-blooming: 4 rath
Early Girl: 6 tomato
relative: 4 Roma 6 Big Boy 9 beefsteak, Better Boy, Quick Pick
Early in the Morning (1988 song)
artist: Robert Palmer
earmark: 3 tab, tag 4 mark, slot 5 label, stamp, trait 6 assign, devote 7 feature, insigne, quality, reserve 8 allocate, insignia, set apart, set aside 9 attribute, designate
have ~ of: 4 seem 8 resemble
earmarked: 7 special
earn: 3 get, net, win 4 draw, gain, make, rate, reap, take 5 bring, clear, fetch, gross, merit, score, yield 6 attain, come by, derive, effect, garner, gather, obtain, pick up, profit, return, secure, take in 7 achieve, acquire, bring in, collect, deserve, procure, realize, receive, support, warrant, work for, wrangle 8 pull down, take home 9 bring home, knock down, make money 10 have coming, qualify for
after taxes: 3 net 5 clear
a living: 4 live, work
homophone for ~: 3 ern, urn 4 erne
one's wings: 4 pass 5 cut it, train 6 make it 9 measure up 10 pass muster
earned: 3 due 4 owed 6 coming 7 fitting, merited 8 deserved, expected, rightful, suitable 9 justified 10 reasonable, sufficient
money ~: 8 receipts
earned __: 3 run 6 income
earned __ average: 3 run
__-earned: 4 well
earner: 6 worker 7 employe 8 employee, taxpayer
wage ~: 4 hand 5 prole 6 worker 7 employe 8 employee 9 jobholder
wage ~ cry: 4 TGIF
earnest: 4 avid, keen, pawn, warm 5 eager, staid, token 6 ardent, devout, fervid, hearty, infelt, intent, loving, pledge, urgent 7 decided, devoted, fervent, genuine, intense, promise, serious, sincere, weighty, zealous 8 diligent, resolute, security, sedulous, studious, vehement 9 heartfelt, important, strenuous, unfeigned 10 determined, meaningful, no-nonsense, passionate, purposeful, scrupulous, solicitous
begin in ~: 5 set to
in ~: 4 real 6 really
money of a sort: 4 bail
earnest __: 5 money
earnestly: 4 hard 6 keenly 8 for keeps, urgently 9 sincerely 10 thoroughly
earnestness: 4 will, zeal 5 ardor 6 fervor, spirit 7 loyalty, resolve 8 ambition, decision, devotion 9 sincerity
Earnhardt, Dale: 9 auto racer
milieu: 5 track
earnings: 3 pay 4 gain, gate, wage 5 lucre, wages, yield 6 income, payoff, profit, return, salary 7 revenue 8 proceeds, receipts 9 emolument, royalties
CD ~: 3 int. 8 interest
earnings __ share: 3 per
__-earnings ratio: 5 price
earn one's __: 5 spurs, wings
Earp: 5 Wyatt 6 Morgan, Virgil
ear-piercing: 4 loud 5 noisy 6 shrill 7 raucous
earring: 4 drop, hoop, stud 7 jewelry
kind of ~: 4 drop, loop, stud
like an ~: 6 clip-on, hooped
part: 4 wire
site: 4 lobe
ears: 4 corn 6 feeler 7 antenna
all ~: 4 rapt 5 alert 8 cautious, watchful 9 attentive, listening
animal with big ~: 4 hare 7 leveret
be all ~: 6 listen, perk up 9 eavesdrop
be up to one's: 4 teem 6 abound
easy on the ~: 4 soft 6 dulcet 7 lyrical, melodic, musical, tuneful 9 melodious
like ~: 5 lobed 6 lobate 7 lobated
like some dog ~: 4 alop 5 loppy 6 droopy
of the ~: 4 otic 5 aural 7 sensory 8 acoustic
prick up one's ~: 6 listen
rabbit ~: 6 aerial, dipole 7 antenna
spot between the ~: 4 nape
up to one's ~: 4 at it, busy 5 awash 6 hectic, tied up 7 swamped 8 bustling, immersed, occupied 9 engrossed 10 overloaded
use one's ~: 4 hear, heed, mind, obey 5 audit, catch, watch 6 attend, listen, tune in 7 hear out, monitor, observe, receive 8 hear tell, overhear, pick up on 9 eavesdrop 10 get a load of, give heed to, take advice, take notice
wet behind the ~: 4 naif 5 green, naive, young 6 callow, tender 8 immature
with eyes and ~ open: 4 wary
__ ears: 3 all 6 rabbit
__ ears!: 5 I'm all
ears, CBer's: 5 radio
earshot: 5 range 7 hearing 9 listening
within ~: 4 near 7 audible 10 detectable
earsplitting: 4 loud 5 forte, harsh, noisy 6 shrill 7 blaring, blatant, booming, jarring, pealing, rackety, raucous, reboant, roaring 8 crashing, piercing, plangent, rumbling, sonorous, strident, turned up 9 big-voiced, clamorous, deafening 10 boisterous, resounding, stentorian, strepitous, thundering, uproarious, vociferous
earsplittingly: 4 loud 5 aloud, brash, noisy, vocal 6 brassy, strong 7 blaring, booming, intense, raucous, roaring 8 crashing, piercing 9 clamorous, deafening 10 blustering, boisterous, clangorous, loud-voiced, resounding, stentorian, thundering, uproarious, vociferous
earth: 3 sod 4 clay, dirt, lair, land, loam, marl, soil, turf 6 ground, nature 7 subsoil, topsoil 8 alluvium 9 undersoil 10 terra firma
cultivated ~: 5 tilth
depression: 6 graben
ender: 3 man, men, nut 4 born, ling, rise, star, work, worm 5 bound, light, mover, quake, shine 7 shaking
fine ~: 4 dust
in French: 5 terre
in Italian: 5 terra
in Latin: 5 terra
layer of ~: 4 turf
like rich ~: 5 loamy
like the ~ in a forest: 5 rooty
mound of ~: 4 berm 5 berme
mover: 3 hoe 5 dozer 6 dredge 9 bulldozer
rare ~: 5 metal 6 cerium, cesium, erbium 7 caesium, holmium, terbium, thulium, yttrium 8 europium, lutetium, samarium, scandium 9 neodymium, ytterbium 10 dysprosium, gadolinium, promethium 12 praseodymium
science: 7 geology
tone: 5 beige, brown, ocher, ochre, umber
wet ~: 3 mud
earth __: 3 art, god 4 sign, tone 6 mother 7 goddess, science, station
__ earth: 4 rare 5 green, run to 6 mother
__-earth: 6 Middle
Earth: 3 orb 5 globe, world 6 planet, sphere 7 mankind 9 biosphere
atmosphere: 3 sky
author: Émile Zola
bowels of the ~: 5 abyss
center: 4 core
combining form: 3 geo-
conscious org.: 3 EPA
crust part: 5 plate
end of the ~: 4 pole
envelope: 3 air 5 ether 6 aether
force: 4 one G
gap in ~ surface: 5 gulch, gully 6 canyon, ravine
goddess: 4 Gaea
heaven on ~: 4 Eden 6 utopia 7 Arcadia, Elysium 8 paradise 9 Shangri-la
inheritors: 4 meek
in the bowels of the ~: 4 deep
layer: 4 moho, sial, sima 5 crust 6 mantle
model: 3 map, orb 5 globe 6 sphere
most of the ~: 3 sea 5 ocean
nearest star to ~: 3 Sol, sun
neighbor: 4 Mars 5 Venus
not of this ~: 5 alien 6 cosmic 8 cosmical
of the ~: 5 gaean
on ~: 4 here 7 present
orbiter: 3 Mir 4 moon
returned to ~: 3 lit 4 alit
return to ~: 4 land 5 light 6 alight
science: 4 ecol. 7 ecology 9 geography 10 geophysics
-sky boundary: 3 hor. 7 horizon
surface: 4 land
Teutonic ~ goddess: 4 Erda
turning point: 4 axis
walk the ~: 4 last, live, stay 5 dwell, exist 6 occupy, reside, settle, thrive 7 breathe, subsist, survive
Earth __: 3 Day 5 Angel
Earth __ Are Easy: 5 Girls
Earth, __ & Fire: 4 Wind
Eartha: 4 Kitt
Earth Angel (song)
artist: Crew-Cuts, Penguins
earthborn: 5 human 6 mortal 9 corporeal
earthen: 3 mud 4 clay, dirt
ender: 4 ware
earthenware: 5 crock 7 faience, pottery 8 ceramics, crockery, majolica 9 stoneware 10 terra cotta
Dutch ~: 4 delf 5 delft
Japanese ~: 4 raku
piece of ~: 3 jar, jug, pot 4 ewer, olla 5 crock, cruse, shard, sherd 6 bottle, carafe
__-earther: 4 flat
earthfall: 8 mudslide 9 avalanche, landslide, rockslide, snowslide
Earth Girls Are Easy (1989 film)
cast: Jim Carrey, Geena Davis, Jeff Goldblum, Damon Wayans
cat: 5 Bambi
Earth in the Balance
author: Al Gore
Earthlight
author: Arthur C. Clarke
earthling: 3 man 5 human, woman 6 mortal, person
Earthlink: 3 ISP
earthly: 6 global, likely, mortal 7 mundane, secular, terrene, worldly 8 feasible, material, possible, probable, temporal 9 potential, practical 10 imaginable
Earthly Possessions
author: Anne Tyler
earth measurement, science of: 7 geodesy
earthnut: 6 veggie 9 vegetable
earthquake: 4 jolt 5 quake, seism, shake, shock 6 tremor 7 temblor 8 upheaval 9 cataclysm 10 convulsion, disruption, macroseism,

microseism, undulation
combining form: **5** -seism **6** seismo-
tremor: **5** L wave
earthquakes, science of: **10** seismology
earth-shaking: **9** momentous
not ~: **5** minor, petty **7** trivial
Earth-shaped: **6** oblate
__ Earth, The: **4** Good
Earth, Wind & Fire
song: After the Love Has Gone (1979)
Boogie Wonderland (1979)
Got to Get You Into My Life (1978)
Let's Groove (1981)
September (1978)
Shining Star (1975)
Sing a Song (1975)
earthwork: **6** trench **7** foxhole, rampart
earthworm: **3** bug **6** insect
earthy: **3** raw **4** homy **5** basic, crude, funky, homey, lusty, salty **6** animal, clayey, coarse, folksy, ribald, robust, simple **7** clayish, natural **8** down home, indecent, off-color **9** elemental, practical, realistic, unrefined **10** indelicate, unromantic
color: **3** tan **4** ecru **5** brown **7** neutral
deposit: **4** marl, silt
pigment: **5** umber
'eart is, where the: **3** 'ome
Earvin: **5** Magic **7** Johnson
earwax: **7** cerumen
earwig: **3** bug **4** pest **6** insect
ease: **3** ebb **4** calm, fall, help, rest, snap **5** abate, allay, let up, loose, peace, poise, quell, quiet, relax, salve, skill, slack, still, style, unzip **6** aplomb, lessen, loosen, luxury, pacify, plenty, relent, relief, remedy, repose, smooth, soften, soothe, temper **7** assuage, comfort, fluency, further, leisure, lighten, mollify, redress, relieve, slacken, subside, tail off **8** calmness, decrease, dispatch, expedite, facility, fluidity, free time, good life, go slowly, humanize, idleness, mitigate, moderate, palliate, pleasure, presence, security, serenity, simplify, unburden **9** affluence, alleviate, composure, dexterity, disburden, idle hours, passivity, quietness, readiness, sugar-coat, untighten, untrouble, well-being **10** adroitness, affability, ameliorate, bed of roses, confidence, efficiency, expertness, facileness, facilitate, inactivity, legibility, liberalize, nimbleness, prosperity, quiescence, recreation, relaxation, simplicity, smoothness
at ~: **4** cool, rest **5** comfy, loose, relax, staid, stoic **6** low-key, mellow, placid, secure, sedate, serene **7** content, lolling, relaxed, resting, stoical **8** carefree, composed, laid-back, lounging, relaxing, tranquil **9** collected, impassive, temperate, unanxious, unexcited, unruffled **10** knock it off, nonchalant, unagitated, unbothered, unstressed, untroubled
away (from): **4** wean
epitome of ~: **3** ABC, pie
ill at ~: **4** edgy **5** antsy, itchy, jumpy, tense **6** on edge **7** abashed, anxious, awkward, jittery, keyed up, nervous, restive, uptight **8** agitated, restless, skittish, troubled **9** concerned, disturbed, excitable, faltering, unrelaxed, unsettled **10** disquieted, high-strung, out of place, suspicious
off: **3** die, ebb **4** lull, rest, slow, wane **5** abate, let up, loose, relax, slack **6** loosen, relent, unwind, weaken **7** slacken **8** head away, moderate
out: **4** part **8** withdraw
put at ~: **5** allay **6** assure **7** satisfy **8** reassure
up: **8** head away
ease __: **3** off, out
__ ease: **5** ill at
easeful: **4** calm **5** quiet **6** placid **7** relaxed, restful **8** peaceful, pleasant, pleasing, relaxing, tranquil **9** agreeable, unruffled **10** untroubled
easel: **5** stand **6** tripod
display: **3** art **6** canvas, sketch **7** collage, picture **8** painting
part: **3** leg
easement: **4** balm, lull **6** relief, remedy, solace **7** anodyne, comfort **9** emollient **10** mitigation, palliative
Ease On Down the __: **4** Road
easier __ than done: **4** said
Easier Said Than Done (1963 song)
artist: Essex
easily: **4** well **5** by far **6** really, simply, surely **7** clearly, handily, lightly, plainly, readily **8** for a fact, very well **9** decidedly, doubtless, going away, hands down, leisurely, naturally **10** definitely, far and away, positively, swimmingly, undeniably
easiness: **8** lenience, optimism **10** simplicity
easing: **5** letup **7** anodyne, respite **8** soothing **9** abatement, assuasive, calmative, relieving, remission, softening **10** mitigation, palliation
east: **2** pt. **5** point **8** dawnward **9** direction
ender: **3** ern **4** ward **5** bound, wards
god of the ~ wind: **5** Eurus
in French: **3** est
in Spanish: **4** este
opposite: **4** west
starter: **3** Mid **5** North, south
East: **5** river **6** Orient
bidder after ~: **5** South
much of the ~: **4** Asia
River locale: **3** NYC **7** New York
East __: **3** End **4** Asia, Goth, Side **5** Coast, Lynne, River, Timor
East __ Company: **5** India
East-__ relations: **4** West
__ East: **3** Big, Far **4** down, Near **6** Middle
East Asian
language: **3** Lao
river: **4** Amur
East Carolina
athletes: **7** Pirates
locale: **10** Greenville
East Chicago: **4** city, town
locale: **7** Indiana
East China: **3** sea
island: **4** Mazu **5** Matsu **6** Kiushu, Kyushu
locale: **5** China, Japan **6** Taiwan **10** South Korea
__-easter: **4** down
Easter: **4** isle **5** Pasch **6** island **7** holy day, Rapa Nui
dish: **3** ham **4** lamb
ender: **4** tide
event: **6** parade
island: **7** Rapa Nui
need: **3** dye **4** eggs **6** basket
preceder: **4** Lent
wear: **6** bonnet, finery
Easter __: **3** egg **4** lily **5** bunny, Seals **6** bonnet, Island, Parade, Sunday
Easter Island
explorer: **9** Heyerdahl
head: **5** stela
owner: **5** Chile
easterly
starter: **5** north, south
eastern: **8** Oriental **9** Levantine
ender: **4** most
starter: **5** north, south
Eastern Church
bishop: **6** exarch
member: **5** Uniat **6** Uniate
title: **4** abba
Eastern Daylight __: **4** Time
Eastern Michigan
athletes: **6** Eagles
conference: **3** MAC
locale: **9** Ypsilanti
Eastern title: **3** aga **4** agha, amir, emir **5** ameer, emeer
Easter Oratorio
composer: J.S. Bach
Easter Parade (1948 film)
cast: Fred Astaire, Judy Garland
composer: Irving Berlin
easter starter: **3** nor
East German secret police: **5** Stasi
East India Company
headquarters: **6** Bombay
product: **5** spice
East Indian: **5** Hindu **6** Hindoo
boat: **5** oolak
cedar: **6** deodar **7** deodara
chief: **4** raja
fruit: **5** cubeb **10** mangosteen
mast wood: **4** poon
sailor: **6** lascar **7** lashkar
shrub: **4** sunn
stew: **4** dahl
tree: **4** nipa **5** rohan
East Indies: **7** islands
East Lansing: **4** city, town
athletes: **8** Spartans
locale: **8** Michigan
school: **3** MSU
Eastman: **3** Max **6** George
Eastman __: **5** Kodak
East of Eden: **4** film **5** novel
author: John Steinbeck
cast: James Dean, Julie Harris, Burl Ives, Raymond Massey, Jo Van Fleet
character: **3** Cal, Lee **4** Abra, Adam, Ames, Aron, Faye, Liza, Will **5** Bacon, Caleb, Cathy, Trask **6** Samuel **7** Charles **8** Hamilton
director: Elia Kazan
Easton: **4** city, town **6** Sheena
athletes: **8** Leopards
locale: **4** Penn.
school: **9** Lafayette
Easton, Sheena
homeland: Scotland
real last name: Orr
song: For Your Eyes Only (1981)
The Lover in Me (1988)
Morning Train (1981)
Strut (1984)
Sugar Walls (1985)
Telefone (1983)
We've Got Tonight (1983)
East Orange: **4** city, town
locale: **9** New Jersey
East River
author: Sholem Asch
East Siberian: **3** sea
locale: **6** Russia
__ East Side: **5** Lower, Upper
East St. Louis: **4** city, town
locale: **8** Illinois
East Timor: **6** nation **7** country
capital: **4** Dili
eastward starter: **5** north, south
Eastwood, Clint: **5** actor **8** director
costar: **5** Locke
film: Absolute Power (1997)
Any Which Way You Can (1980)
The Beguiled (1970)
Bird (1988)
Blood Work (2002)
The Bridges of Madison County (1995)
Bronco Billy (1980)
Changeling (2008)
City Heat (1984)
Coogan's Bluff (1968)
The Dead Pool (1988)
Dirty Harry (1972)
The Eiger Sanction (1975)
The Enforcer (1976)
Escape From Alcatraz (1979)
Every Which Way But Loose (1978)
Fistful of Dollars (1964)
Flags of Our Fathers (2006)
For a Few Dollars More (1966)
The Gauntlet (1977)
The Good, the Bad, and the Ugly (1966)
Gran Torino (2008)
Hang 'em High (1968)
Heartbreak Ridge (1986)
High Plains Drifter (1973)
Honkytonk Man (1982)
In the Line of Fire (1993)
Kelly's Heroes (1970)
Letters From Iwo Jima (2006)
Magnum Force (1973)
Midnight in the Garden of Good and Evil (1997)
Million Dollar Baby (2004, AA)
Mystic River (2003)
The Outlaw Josey Wales (1976)
Paint Your Wagon (1969)
Pale Rider (1985)
A Perfect World (1993)
Pink Cadillac (1989)
Play Misty for Me (1971)
Space Cowboys (2000)
Sudden Impact (1983)

Thunderbolt and Lightfoot (1974)
True Crime (1999)
Two Mules for Sister Sara (1970)
Unforgiven (1992, AA)
Where Eagles Dare (1969)
White Hunter, Black Heart (1990)
TV: Rawhide
easy: **3** lax **4** calm, idly, kind, mild, naif, soft **5** a snap, basic, clear, comfy, cushy, handy, light, loose, naive, plain, quiet **6** a cinch, benign, casual, doable, docile, facile, fluent, gentle, kindly, serene, simple, smooth **7** affable, amiable, a picnic, clement, dupable, languid, lenient, natural, no sweat, obvious, relaxed, ruthful, sparing **8** amenable, apparent, carefree, duck soup, flexible, gullable, gullible, informal, laid-back, manifest, merciful, no bother, obedient, obliging, outgoing, painless, peaceful, placable, pleasant, readable, relaxing, sociable, tolerant, tranquil, trusting, unstrict, untaxing, workable, yielding **9** a pushover, assuasive, compliant, contented, deludable, forgiving, indulgent, leisurely, luxurious, no problem, no trouble, temperate, tractable, uncomplex, unextreme, unhurried, unworried **10** accessible, child's play, deceivable, effortless, elementary, forbearing, manageable, permissive, submissive, unexacting, unhardened, untroubled
breathe ~: **5** relax
ender: **5** going
free and ~: **3** lax **5** homey, loose **6** breezy, casual, folksy, mellow, simple **7** lenient, patient, relaxed **8** everyday, informal, laid back, outgoing, tolerant **9** indulgent **10** forbearing, off-the-cuff, open-minded, permissive
go ~: **5** let up, relax **10** take it slow
going ~: **3** lax **4** mild, soft **6** benign, gentle, humane **7** clement, lenient, liberal, sparing **8** allowing, excusing, merciful, obliging, tolerant, yielding **9** condoning, forgiving, indulgent, pampering, pardoning **10** charitable, permissive
go ~ on: **4** pity **5** spare **6** relent **7** absolve, release
in Portuguese: **5** facil
make ~: **8** simplify
mark: **3** sap **4** butt, dupe, goat, lamb, simp, tool **5** chump, patsy, softy **6** pigeon, softie, sucker, victim **8** pushover
on the ears: **4** soft **6** dulcet **7** lyrical, melodic, musical, tuneful **9** melodious
on the eyes: **4** fair **6** lavish, lovely **8** dazzling, gorgeous, handsome, imposing, stunning **9** beautiful, exquisite, ravishing, sumptuous **10** attractive
partner: **4** free, nice
shot: **4** dunk **5** gimme, lay up, tap in
something ~: **4** snap **5** cinch **6** picnic
starter: **5** speak
take it ~: **3** sit **4** idle, laze, loaf, lull, rest **5** coast, relax, slide, unlax **6** lounge, repose, rest up, unwind **9** luxuriate
taking it ~: **5** still **6** at rest **8** inactive, unmoving **10** motionless
task: **4** plum, snap **5** cinch **6** breeze, picnic **8** cakewalk, duck soup, sinecure **10** child's play
to steer: **3** yar **4** yare
to teach: **3** apt **5** quick, sharp
to understand: **5** clear, exact, lucid, overt, sharp, stark, vivid **6** direct, marked, simple, square **7** audible, crystal, evident, graphic, legible, logical, precise, visible **8** apparent, coherent, distinct, explicit, knowable, manifest, palpable, readable **9** graspable, unclouded, unimpeded **10** observable, pronounced, spelled out, unarguable, unhampered, unhindered
to use: **6** nearby, wieldy **7** close by **8** portable **10** accessible, convenient, time-saving
undertaking: **4** snap **5** cinch **6** breeze **8** duck soup, kid stuff **9** no trouble **10** child's play
win: **4** romp, rout **5** waltz
easy __: **5** as ABC, as pie, chair, money
easy __, easy go: **4** come
easy-__: **4** care **5** going
__ easy: **4** over **7** breathe
Easy: **6** Street **7** Rollins
Easy (1977 song)
artist: Commodores
Easy __: **4** Aces **5** Rider, to Wed **6** Street
Easy __ Hard: **4** to Be
Easy __ it!: **4** does
Easy-__: **3** Off
__ Easy: **5** It's So, Nice 'N'
Easy Aces: **9** radio show
easy as __: **3** ABC, pie
Easy Come, Easy Go (1970 song)
artist: Bobby Sherman
easygoing: **3** lax **4** calm, cool, kind, mild, soft **5** light, loose, slack, type B **6** breezy, casual, docile, genial, gentle, kindly, low-key, placid, serene **7** clement, equable, lenient, offhand, patient, relaxed, ruthful, sparing **8** carefree, composed, familiar, fireside, flexible, informal, laid-back, listless, merciful, placable, tolerant, unstrict **9** adaptable, assuasive, collected, compliant, congenial, forgiving, hang-loose, indulgent, unhurried **10** complacent, forbearing, insouciant, nonchalant, permissive, personable, unaffected, unagitated, unbothered, uncritical, unexacting, unhardened
not ~: **5** type A
easygoingness: **5** mercy **6** lenity **8** clemency, lenience, mildness, softness, sympathy **9** tolerance **10** compassion, gentleness, indulgence, moderation, tenderness, toleration
Easy Lover (1984 song)
artist: Philip Bailey, Phil Collins
easy on the __: **4** eyes
__ Easy Pieces: **4** Five
Easy Rider (1969 film)
cast: Karen Black, Peter Fonda, Dennis Hopper, Jack Nicholson
director: Dennis Hopper
Easy Street
on ~: **4** rich **5** flush **6** loaded, monied **7** moneyed, wealthy, well-off **8** affluent, in clover, well-to-do **9** well-fixed **10** in the chips, in the dough, in the money, privileged, propertied, prosperous, well-heeled
Easy Street (NBC sitcom)
cast: Dana Ivey (Eleanor Standard), Jack Elam (Uncle Bully), Loni Anderson (L.K. McGuire)
__ Easy, The: **3** Big
Easy to Be Hard (1969 song)
artist: Three Dog Night
Easy to Be Hard musical: **4** Hair
eat: **3** irk, rot, sup **4** bolt, chew, dine, down, gnaw, gulp, have, nosh, rust, take, wolf **5** annoy, basis, decay, dig in, drain, erode, feast, gorge, graze, lunch, munch, scarf, snack, taste, touch, use up, waste, worry **6** absorb, bother, brunch, chew on, devour, digest, dine on, feed on, gobble, guzzle, incept, ingest, inhale, live on, nibble, nosh on, picnic, pig out, prey on, sample, take in, tuck in **7** chomp on, consume, corrode, crumble, do lunch, exhaust, feast on, munch on, partake, put away, scarf up, snack on, swallow **8** bolt down, chow down, dispatch, dissolve, fill up on, gobble up, nibble on, pack away, pack it in, shovel in, squander, take food, tuck away, wear away, wolf down **9** breakfast, decompose, dissipate, feast upon, finish off, have a bite, have a meal, masticate, partake of, polish off, scarf down **10** break bread, gormandize, have dinner, take tiffin
at: **3** bug **4** gnaw, rust **5** annoy, erode, get to, worry **6** bother, gnaw on, nibble **7** corrode
away: **4** gnaw, rust **5** erode, waste **7** corrode **9** undermine
bite to ~: **4** nosh **5** snack
don't ~: **4** fast **7** abstain **8** go hungry
fit to ~: **4** good **5** tasty **6** edible
get ready to ~: **4** wash
good to ~: **4** rich **5** spicy, yummy **6** delish, savory, toothy **8** heavenly, luscious **9** delicious, flavorful, palatable, succulent, toothsome **10** appetizing, delectable
grass: **4** feed **5** graze
hungrily: **4** wolf
in German: **5** essen
like a bird: **4** peck, pick
like a horse: **5** chomp, gorge **10** gormandize
more sensibly: **4** diet
noisily: **4** gnaw **5** chomp, munch, slurp **6** crunch
not fit to ~: **3** bad **4** sour **5** fetid, yucky, yukky **6** putrid, rotten, turned **7** spoiled, tainted **8** inedible **10** disgusting
one's heart out: **4** fret, mope **5** mourn **6** grieve, lament, sorrow
one's words: **6** grovel, recant **7** retract **9** back-pedal
quickly: **4** bolt **5** scarf **6** devour, inhale **7** scarf up **8** wolf down **9** scarf down
ready to ~: **4** done **6** cooked
something to ~: **4** meal **5** lunch
through: **9** penetrate
too much: **5** stuff
up: **3** use **5** dig in, enjoy **6** devour, gobble, relish **7** consume, deplete, exhaust, feast on, revel in **9** delight in, finish off, luxuriate, polish off, scarf down
up the road: **4** zoom
well: **4** dine **5** feast
what you ~: **4** diet, fare, food **6** intake **7** aliment, edibles, regimen **8** victuals **9** nutriment **10** sustenance
eat __: **4** away, crow, into
eat __ eaten: **4** or be
eat __ house and home: **5** out of
eat __ off the hog: **4** high
eat __ pie: **6** humble
eatables: **4** fare **6** viands **7** aliment **8** victuals **9** provender **10** provisions, sustenance
eat-all: **8** omnivore
eat and __: **3** run
Eat at __: **4** Joe's
__ Eat Cake: **5** Let 'em
Eat, drink __ merry...: **5** and be
__-eaten: **4** moth, worm
eater: **5** diner **6** nosher **7** epicure, glutton, gobbler, luncher, nibbler, snacker **8** consumer, devourer, gourmand, predator
combining form: **4** -phag, -vore **5** -phage
selective ~: **3** cat **5** vegan **6** dieter
starter: **3** ant **4** beef, seed, toad **5** honey
__-eater: **3** bee **4** fire **5** lotus
__ Eaters: **4** Odor
eatery: **4** café **5** diner **6** bistro **7** cabaret **9** brasserie, cafeteria, hash house, lunchroom, trattoria **10** restaurant
chain ~: **3** KFC **4** HoJo, IHOP **5** Arby's **6** Subway **8** Pizza Hut **9** Applebee's, McDonald's, Roy Rogers **10** Burger King, TGI Friday's
listing: **4** menu
lure: **5** aroma
NYC ~: **4** deli **6** Lutèce, Sardi's **7** Elaine's
order: **3** BLT
eating: **10** at the table
away: **7** erosion, wearing **8** decrease **9** attrition, corrosion
combining form: **4** phag- **5** phago-, -phagy **6** -phagia, -vorous **7** -phagous
good ~: **7** cuisine **10** gastronomy
place: **5** table
utensil: **4** fork **5** spoon, spork
__ Eating Gilbert Grape?: **5** What's
Eating Raoul (1982 film)
cast: Paul Bartel, Robert Beltran, Mary Woronov

Eat It (1984 song)
artist: Weird Al Yankovic
eat like ___: **5** a bird
Eaton: **7** Shirley
eat one's ___: **4** fill **5** words
eat one's ___ out: **5** heart
eat out of ___ and home: **5** house
eat out of one's ___: **4** hand
eats: **4** chow, fare, food, grub, meal **5** board, snack **7** aliment, goodies **8** victuals **9** provender **10** provisions
Eat your broccoli ___ dessert!: **4** or no
eau ___: **5** de vie
Eau Claire: **4** city, town
locale: **9** Wisconsin
eau de ___: **3** vie **7** Cologne
eau de Cologne: **5** scent **7** perfume
eau de vie: **5** drink **6** brandy **8** beverage
eave: **8** overhang **10** projection
adornment: **6** icicle
locale: **4** roof
eavesdrop: **3** bug, pry, spy, tap **4** hear **5** snoop **6** listen **7** monitor, wiretap **8** listen in, overhear **9** bend an ear
eavesdropper: **5** snoop, yenta **6** gossip **7** meddler **8** busybody, quidnunc **9** buttinsky **10** Nosy Parker
what an ~ gets: **6** earful
eavesdropping: **4** nosy **5** nosey
eaves ender: **4** drop **7** dropper
eaves-trough: **4** duct **5** chute, drain **6** groove, gutter, sluice, trough
Eb
wife: **3** Flo
E.B.: **5** White
Eban: **4** Abba
ebb: **3** die, lag **4** bate, drop, ease, fade, fall, flag, lull, sink, tide, wane, wilt **5** abate, decay, go out, let up, relax **6** die out, ease up, go down, lessen, recede, reflux, relent, shrink, waning **7** decline, die down, drop off, dwindle, ease off, fall off, low tide, outflow, outflux, regress, retreat, slacken, subside, tail off **8** backflow, contract, decrease, diminish, drop back, fade away, fall away, fall back, flagging, flow away, flow back, languish, low water, moderate, peter out, slack off, twilight, withdraw **9** abatement, disappear, dwindling, lessening, recession, refluence, remission, retrocede **10** diminution, fading away, regression, slackening, withdrawal
and flow: **4** flux, tide, wash **5** swing **6** billow **7** current **9** fluctuate, oscillate
lowest ~: **5** nadir
opposite: **4** flow
ebb ___: **4** tide
___ ebb: **5** at low
Ebb: **4** Fred
Ebbets Field great: **5** Reese **6** Hodges **7** Furillo **8** Newcombe, Robinson **10** Campanella
ebbing: **7** decline **9** on the wane, remission
Ebel: **5** watch
alternative: *see* wristwatch
Ebenezer: **7** Scrooge
exclamation: **3** bah **6** humbug
partner: **5** Jacob **6** Marley
Eber
son: **5** Peleg
Eberhard-Faber: **6** pencil
part: **5** point **6** eraser
Eberle: **3** Ray
Eberly: **3** Bob
Ebert: **5** rater, Roger **9** Friedrich
emulate ~: **4** rate
Eboli: **4** city, town
locale: **5** Italy
ebon: **3** jet **4** dark **5** black, sable **9** coal-black, unlighted
ebonize: **5** shade **6** darken, smudge **7** blacken
ebony: **4** dark, tree **5** black, color **8** hardwood, jet-black **9** coal-black
relative: **3** jet **4** inky, onyx **5** raven, sable **14** sooty. persimmon
Ebony: **3** mag **8** magazine
rival: **3** Jet **7** Essence
Ebony and Ivory (1982 song)
artist: Paul McCartney, Stevie Wonder
Ebony Eyes (1961 song)
artist: Everly Brothers
Ebony Tower, The
author: John Fowles
Ebro: **3** río **5** river
locale: **5** Spain **6** Aragón
___ E. Brown: **3** Joe
Ebsen, Buddy: **5** actor
film: Breakfast at Tiffany's (1961) Davy Crockett... (1955)
TV: Barnaby Jones, The Beverly Hillbillies
ebullience: **3** joy, zip **4** zest **5** bliss **6** gaiety, gayety **7** delight, ecstasy, elation, rapture **8** buoyance, buoyancy, euphoria, felicity, vitality, vivacity **9** agitation, animation, happiness **10** enthusiasm, excitement, exuberance, exuberancy, friskiness, liveliness
ebullient: **4** agog **5** sunny, zippy **6** bouncy, elated, hearty, yeasty **7** chipper, excited, gushing, zestful **8** animated, effusive **9** explosive, exuberant, vivacious
be ~: **7** enthuse
EC
member: **3** Den., Eng., Ger., Nor. **4** Ital.
part of ~: **3** Eur.
E.C.: **5** Segar **7** Bentley
écarté: **4** game **8** card game
E casta al par di neve!
singer: **5** Tonio
ecce: **6** behold
ecce ___: **4** homo
Ecce Homo
painter: George Grosz
eccentric: **3** odd **4** card, coot, eery, geek, kook, luny, zany **5** balmy, batty, crank, dippy, dotty, eerie, flaky, gonzo, kooky, loony, loopy, nutty, outré, potty, queer, wacko, wacky, weird, wiggy **6** atypic, codger, far-out, flakey, freaky, fruity, galoot, geezer, kookie, looney, quaint, quirky, weirdo, whacky **7** bizarre, deviant, erratic, galloot, oddball, offbeat, strange, touched, unusual **8** aberrant, abnormal, atypical, crackpot, freakish, original, peculiar, singular, uncommon **9** anomalous, character, crotchety, divergent, fantastic, irregular, laughable, off-center, queer duck, quizzical, unnatural, unscrewed, vagarious, whimsical **10** capricious, off-the-wall, outlandish, unbalanced, unorthodox
Eccentricities of a Nightingale, The
author: Tennessee Williams
eccentricity: **3** tic **4** kink **5** quirk **6** foible, oddity **7** anomaly, oddness **8** crotchet **9** mannerism
ecclesia: **5** synod **6** church **7** council **8** assembly
Ecclesiastes preceder: **8** Proverbs
ecclesiastic: **4** abbé **5** abbot, padre, prior, vicar **6** bishop, cleric, father, parson, pastor, priest **8** clerical, minister, preacher
ecclesiastical: **4** holy **5** pious **8** churchly, clerical, hieratic, pastoral **9** religious
adjective: **5** papal
assembly: **5** synod
deg.: **3** Th.D.
district: **3** see **7** diocese, prelacy **9** bishopric **10** episcopacy
headdress: **5** miter
law: **5** canon
office: **6** curacy
title: **3** rev. **4** msgr. **5** Rt. Rev.
wear: **5** amice, orale, pilei
see also church
ecclesiastics: **6** clergy
ecdysis: **7** molting
ECG: **4** test **5** chart
concern: **5** heart
user: **2** MD **4** hosp.
echelon: **4** rank, tier **5** class, grade, level, order **7** ranking **8** position
___ echelon: **3** top **4** rear
echelons: **9** hierarchy
echidna: **6** animal, mammal
feature: **5** spine
food: **3** ant
Echidna
daughter: **6** Sphinx
echinoderm: **9** sea urchin
echo: **3** ape **4** copy, ring, roll **5** mimic, recur, sound **6** answer, bounce, do like, go like, mirror, parrot, repeat **7** imitate, iterate, rebound, recount, reflect, resound, run over, thunder, vibrate **8** imitator, make like, parallel, reaction, response **9** duplicate, imitation, parroting, reiterate, reproduce **10** bounce back, reflection, repetition
area: **5** cañon, gorge **6** canyon, valley
ender: **4** gram **5** virus **8** location **10** cardiogram
Echo: **3** car **4** auto **5** nymph, oread **6** Toyota **10** automobile
daughter: **4** lynx
lover: **3** Pan
echoer: **5** mimic **6** parrot, yes-man **7** copycat
Echoes
author: Maeve Binchy
Echoi
composer: Lukas Foss
echoic: **9** emulative, imitative **10** resounding
echoing: **8** resonant
echolocation device: **5** sonar
Echo's Bones
author: Samuel Beckett
Eckhart: **5** Aaron **8** Johannes
Eckstine: **5** Billy
éclair: **4** cake **6** pastry **7** dessert
emporium: **6** bakery
éclat: **4** dash, fame, pomp **5** flair, glory, kudos **6** dazzle, praise, renown, repute **7** acclaim, fanfare, success **8** applause, eminence, plaudits, prestige, splendor **9** celebrity **10** brilliance
eclectic: **8** rarefied
eclipse: **3** cap, top **4** hide, veil **5** cover, outdo **6** exceed, shadow, show up **7** becloud, blot out, obscure, surpass **8** outshine, outstrip, outweigh **9** adumbrate, darkening, shadowing, transcend **10** extinguish, overshadow, put to shame, tower above
feature: **5** umbra **6** corona
maybe: **4** omen
___ eclipse: **5** lunar, solar, total
Eclipse: **3** car **4** auto **10** Mitsubishi
eclipsed: **5** inner **6** hidden, unseen, veiled **7** cloaked, clouded, covered **8** shielded, shrouded **9** concealed, disguised, incognito, out of view, unexposed **10** cloistered, tucked away, undercover
eclogue: **4** idyl **5** idyll, verse **8** pastoral
Eclogues
author: Vergil, Virgil
character: **4** Amor **5** Delia
ecodisaster: **5** spill
eco-friendly, be: **5** reuse
école: **6** French, school
attender: **5** élève
kin: **5** lycée
session: **5** lecon **6** classe
___ école: **5** haute
École ___ Beaux-Arts: **3** des
ecol. no-no: **3** CFC
ecological: **5** green
adjective: **5** seral
grouping: **5** biome, biota
hazard: **5** radon
ecology: **7** science **9** bionomics
concern: **3** air **5** ozone, water
org.: **3** EPA
practice ~: **5** reuse
Econoline: **3** van **4** Ford
Econo Lodge: **5** motel
alternative: *see* motel
economic: **6** fiscal **8** monetary **9** budgetary, financial, pecuniary **10** commercial, industrial, mercantile
decline: **4** bust **5** slump **9** recession **10** depression
global ~ grp.: **3** WTO
prefix: **5** socio
rise: **4** boom **5** spurt **6** growth, upturn **7** upsurge, upswing **10** prosperity
stat: **3** CPI, GDP, GNP **5** index
economic ___: **4** good **5** cycle, model
economical: **3** low **5** chary, cheap, spare **6** frugal, modest, on sale, stingy **7** bargain, cut-rate, low-cost, prudent, sparing, thrifty **8** a good buy, moderate, uncostly, ungiving **9** dirt cheap, efficient, half-price, low-priced, penny-wise, penurious,

EC

practical, provident, scrimping 10 avaricious, dime a dozen, marked down, methodical, prudential, reasonable, time-saving, unwasteful, work-saving
  be ~: 5 reuse
  not ~: 8 wasteful
economics: 7 banking, finance, science 10 Wall Street
  concern: 5 money
  prefix for ~: 5 macro, micro
  __ economics: 4 home
economize: 4 save 5 skimp, stint 6 scrape, scrimp 7 cut down, lay away 8 conserve 9 save money 10 cut corners, underspend
economy: 4 size 6 saving, thrift 8 prudence 9 frugality, restraint, scrimping 10 efficiency
  class: 5 coach
  size: 3 big 5 jumbo, large
ecophobe fear: 4 home
__ e Core: 5 Anema
eco-rich: 8 abundant
écossaise: 5 dance
ecosystem part: 5 fauna, flora
Ecotrin: 9 analgesic 10 painkiller
  alternative: ***see*** pain reliever brand
Eco, Umberto: 6 writer 7 Italian
  work: Apocalypse Postponed
    Baudolino
    Foucault's Pendulum
    Il nome della rosa
    Il pendolo di Foucault
    The Island of the Day Before
    The Limits of Interpretation
    Misreadings
    The Name of the Rose
    A Theory of Semiotics
__ E. Coyote: 4 Wile
ecru: 3 tan 5 beige, brown, color 6 suntan 7 neutral 8 eggshell 10 light brown
  relative: ***see*** brown color
ecstasy: 3 joy 5 bliss 6 heaven, raptus, trance 7 delight, elation, emotion, passion, rapture 8 delirium, euphoria, felicity, lyricism, paradise 9 happiness 10 ebullience, exaltation, joyfulness
  opposite: 5 agony
ecstatic: 4 glad, high, rapt, wild 5 happy, merry 6 blithe, cheery, elated, jovial, joyful, joyous, upbeat 7 gleeful, glowing, pleased, radiant, tickled 8 beatific, blissful, cheerful, euphoric, exultant, floating, jubilant, mirthful, thrilled 9 delighted, delirious, emotional, gladdened, overjoyed, rapturous, rejoicing, rhapsodic, very happy 10 enraptured, flying high
  exclamation: 5 whoop, zowie
  make ~: 5 elate, liven 6 lift up, please, thrill 7 delight, elevate, gladden, hearten, satisfy 9 enrapture, transport 10 exhilarate
  wax ~: 4 rave
ecto- ending: 5 -plasm
ectomorphic: 4 lean, slim, trim
ecto- opposite: 4 endo, ento
ectype: 3 fax 4 copy, dupe 5 clone, ditto, mimeo, repro, xerox 6 carbon 7 replica, reprint, tracing 8 likeness 9 duplicate, facsimile, look-alike, photocopy, Photostat 10 mimeograph, transcript 12 reproduction
Ecuador: 6 nation 7 country
  bay: 5 Manta
  bird: 4 yeni
  capital: 5 Quito
  city: 5 Manta, Quito 6 Ambato, Cuenca 7 Machala, Milagro 9 Guayaquil 10 Portoviejo
  gulf: 9 Guayaquil
  Indian: 6 Jivaro
  islands: 9 Galápagos
  language: 6 Jivaro
  money: 5 sucre 6 condor
  mountain: 10 Chimborazo
  neighbor: 4 Peru 8 Colombia
  org.: 3 OAS
  river: 4 Napo
  tennis pro: 6 Segura
  volcano: 6 Sangay 8 Cotopaxi
  writer: 5 Adoum 8 Montalvo
  see also Spanish
ECU issuer: 3 EEC
ecumenical: 6 cosmic 8 catholic, cosmical 9 inclusive, universal, worldwide
ed.
  request: 3 SAE 4 SASE
  __ ed: 4 phys 6 driver 7 driver's
Ed: 3 Ott 4 Ames, Koch, Wood, Wynn 5 Asner, horse, Lopat, Sneed, Walsh 6 Begley, Harris, Lauter, McBain, Nelson, Norton, O'Neill 7 Bradley, Bullins, McMahon 8 Flanders, Marinaro, Sullivan 9 Delahanty, Kranepool
  son: 6 Keenan
Eda: 6 LeShan
edacious: 5 unfed 6 greedy, hungry 7 peckish, piggish, starved 8 esurient, famished, ravenous 9 insatiate, voracious 10 gluttonous
edacity: 5 greed 6 hunger 8 gluttony
Edam: 5 Dutch 6 cheese
  alternative: ***see*** cheese
Edberg: 5 Swede 6 Stefan 9 tennis pro
  rival: 5 Lendl 6 Agassi
Edd: 4 Hall 5 Roush 6 Byrnes
Eddie: 3 Foy 4 Egan, Yost 5 Bauer, Lopat, Mekka, Money, Plank, Shore 6 Albert, Arcaro, Cantor, Condon, Felson, Fisher, Hodges, Holman, Murphy, Stanky, Vedder 7 Bracken, Brigati, Cochran, Collins, Haskell, Heywood, Holland, Mathews, Munster, Rabbitt 8 Anderson, Van Halen 9 Kendricks
  cop character: 4 Axel
  __ Eddie Felson: 4 Fast
eddo: 4 taro
  product: 3 poi
eddy: 4 tide, turn, wash 5 draft, surge, swirl, whirl, whorl 6 rotate, vortex 7 current 8 backflow 9 dust devil, maelstrom, whirlpool
Eddy: 5 Duane, Grant 6 Arnold, Duchin, Merckx, Nelson
eddying: 6 aswirl
Eddy, Nelson: 5 actor
  film: Bitter Sweet (1940)
    Maytime (1937)
    Phantom of the Opera (1943)
    Rosalie (1937)
    Rose Marie (1936)
Ede: 4 town
  locale: 7 Holland 11 Netherlands
Edel, Leon: 6 writer 10 biographer
  subject: James, Cather, Thoreau
Edelman: 4 Herb 6 Gerald
Edelstein: 4 Lisa
edelweiss: 5 plant 6 flower
Edelweiss
  composer: Oscar Hammerstein, Richard Rodgers
Eden: 6 utopia 7 Anthony, Arcadia, Barbara, Elysium, nirvana 8 paradise 9 Shangri-la 10 Phillpotts
  event: 4 fall
  exile: 3 Eve 4 Adam
  he went east of ~: 4 Cain
  place east of ~: 3 Nod
Eden, Anthony: 3 sir 4 earl
  earldom: 4 Avon
  predecessor: 9 Churchill
  successor: 9 Macmillan
Eden, Barbara: 7 actress
  character: 5 genie
  spouse: Michael Ansara
  TV: Harper Valley PTA, I Dream of Jeannie
edenic: 5 ideal 7 Utopian 8 blissful, heavenly
Eden Prairie: 4 city, town
  locale: 9 Minnesota
Eder: 5 river
  locale: 7 Germany
Ederle: 5 Trudy 7 swimmer 8 Gertrude
Edessa: 4 city, town, Urfa
  locale: 6 Greece
__ ed Euridice: 5 Orfeo
__ E. Dewey: 6 Thomas
Edgar: 5 award, Cayce, Cecil, Degas, Guest, opera 6 Adrian, Bergen, Selwyn, Winter 7 Kennedy, Wallace 8 Bronfman, Buchanan, Martinez 9 Burroughs
  composer: Giacomo Puccini
Edgar __ Burroughs: 4 Rice
Edgar Allan: 3 Poe
Edgard: 6 Varèse
__ Edgar Hoover: 4 John
Edgar Lee: 7 Masters
edge: 3 end, hem, lip, rim, tip 4 brim, curb, lead, line, odds, side, trim, whet 5 blade, bound, brink, creep, crust, frame, grind, ledge, leg up, limit, sidle, skirt, start, strop, verge 6 border, defeat, flange, fringe, limbus, margin, slip by, tipoff 7 contour, molding, nose out, outline 8 boundary, decorate, frontier, handicap, keenness, leverage, purchase, slip past, surround, trimming 9 advantage, extremity, head start, outskirts, perimeter, periphery, precipice, sharpness, squeeze by, threshold, upper hand
  cutting ~: 4 lead 8 up-to-date, vanguard
  ender: 4 ways, wise
  gain an ~ on: 5 one up
  improve an ~: 4 hone, whet 5 grind, strop 7 sharpen
  in: 3 add, fit 5 enter 6 arrive 9 interpose, interrupt
  ocean ~: 4 sand 5 beach, coast 8 littoral, seacoast 10 waterfront
  on ~: 4 avid, keen, sour 5 antsy, eager, jumpy, nervy, tense, testy 6 jangly, uneasy 7 excited, fidgety, jittery, nervous, psyched, uptight, worried 8 fluttery, hopped up, restless 9 expectant, ill at ease, impatient, perturbed, tremulous, unsettled 10 raring to go
  on the ~: 4 iffy 5 minor 7 minimal 8 marginal 10 borderline, negligible, peripheral
  (out): 3 win 4 nose
  (past): 5 sidle
  pole along an ~: 4 rail 7 railing
  projecting ~: 4 eave 6 flange
  starter: 4 hard 7 feather 8 straight
  take the ~ off: 4 ease, lull 5 blunt 6 lessen, pacify, smooth, soothe, temper 8 mitigate, tone down
  to the ~: 7 outward, sideway 8 sideways, sidewise
edge __: 3 out
__ edge: 5 on the 7 cutting
__-edge: 4 gilt 7 leading
__ Edge: 6 Jagged, River's
edged: 4 keen 5 honed, sharp 7 fringed 9 sarcastic, trenchant
__-edged: 3 two 4 gilt, hard 5 sharp 6 double
edgeless: 4 curt 5 blunt, frank, gruff, plain, short, vocal 6 abrupt, direct 7 brusque 8 straight, succinct, unsubtle 9 outspoken 10 forthright, free-spoken, from the hip, point-blank, unpolished
Edge of Heaven, The (1987 song)
  artist: George Michael
Edge of Night, The (CBS/ABC): 4 soap 9 soap opera
Edge of Seventeen (1982 song)
  artist: Stevie Nicks
Edge of the Sea, The
  author: Rachel Carson
Edge of the Storm, The
  author: Augustín Yañez
edger: 4 tool 6 chisel 7 trimmer
Edge, The
  author: Dick Francis
__ Edge, The: 6 Razor's, River's
edgewise: 5 end on 7 sideway 8 sideways 9 laterally
Edgeworth, Maria: 5 Irish 6 writer
edginess: 7 fidgets, tension 9 tightness 10 impatience, inquietude
edging: 3 hem 4 lace, tape, trim 5 picot 6 border, fringe, ribbon
edgy: 5 antsy, itchy, jumpy, tense, testy, wired 6 fretty, ireful, jangly, snappy, touchy, uneasy 7 anxious, excited, fretful, jittery, keyed up, nervous, restive, uptight 8 fluttery, fretsome, restless, skittish, snappish 9 all nerves, excitable, ill at ease, impatient, irritable, querulous, tremulous, unsettled 10 high-strung
edible: 4 food, good 5 yummy 6 vittle 8 esculent, fit to eat, non-toxic 9 nutritive, palatable, toothsome, vegetable, wholesome 10 comestible, digestible, nourishing
  become ~: 5 ripen
  bulb: 4 leek 5 camas, onion 6 camass
  no longer ~: 5 stale
  root: 3 oca, oka, yam 4 beet, taro 6 carrot
  seaweed: 4 agar 5 arame, dulse, laver 8 agar-agar

seed: 3 nut 4 chia 5 piñon 6 cashew, walnut
trendy ~: 4 tofu 8 bean curd
tuber: 3 oca, oka
edibles: 4 diet, fare, food, grub, meat 6 viands 7 aliment, produce, victual 8 victuals 9 provender 10 provisions, sustenance
edict: 3 act, law 4 fiat, rule, word 5 canon, irade, order, ukase 6 decree, firman, ruling 7 command, mandate, precept, statute 8 sentence 9 directive, manifesto, ordinance 10 injunction, regulation
Edict of __: 6 Nantes
Edie: 5 Adams, Falco 6 Magnus 7 McClurg 8 Brickell, Sedgwick
author: Jean Stein
edifice: 5 tower 8 building 9 structure 10 skyscraper
edify: 5 brief, coach, guide, teach, tutor 6 direct, inform, school, uplift 7 benefit, educate, raise up 8 illumine, initiate, instruct 9 enlighten, inculcate 10 illuminate
edifying: 9 rewarding, wholesome
Edina: 4 city, town
locale: 9 Minnesota
Edinburgh: 4 city, port, town
city near ~: 5 Perth 6 Dundee
locale: 8 Scotland
Edipo
composer: Modest Mussorgsky
Edirne: 4 city, town
locale: 6 Turkey
Edison: 4 city, town 6 Thomas
locale: 9 New Jersey
Edison __: 6 effect
Edison Lighthouse
song: Love Grows (1970)
Edison, Thomas: 8 inventor
birthplace: 4 Ohio 5 Milan
contemporary: 5 Tesla
middle name: 4 Alva
sneezer in ~'s first film: 3 Ott
Edisto: 4 isle 5 river 6 island
locale: 4 S. Car.
edit: 3 cut 4 dele, omit, redo, thin, trim 5 adapt, alter, amend, emend 6 censor, doctor, insert, mark up, polish, redact, refine, revise, rework 7 arrange, correct, improve, massage, rewrite, scissor, shorten, tighten, touch up 8 annotate, condense, copyread, fine-tune, rephrase 9 expurgate, proofread 10 blue-pencil, bowdlerize
a film: 3 cut, dub 5 recut, redub
out: 4 dele 5 bleep 6 censor, delete 8 cross out 9 expurgate
problems: 6 errata
starter: 4 copy
edited, not: 5 rough, uncut
Edith: 4 Head, Piaf 5 Evans, Meeks 6 Bunker, Wilson 7 Sitwell, Wharton 8 Hamilton
cousin: 5 Maude
husband: 6 Archie
editing: 8 revision 10 correction, emendation
edition: 3 ver. 4 book 5 issue 6 volume 7 reprint, version 8 printing 10 reprinting
Bible ~: 3 KJV, RSV 5 Douay 7 Vulgate
limited ~ perhaps: 5 print
magazine ~: 3 iss. 5 issue
newspaper ~: 5 extra, final
__ edition: 5 first 7 bulldog, limited
__ Edition: 6 Inside
editor: 4 Pohl 6 Monroe, Strand, writer 7 Bradlee, emender, Greeley, newsman, Perkins, reviser, Shapiro 8 compiler, polisher, redactor, rewriter 9 annotator, collector, Podhoretz, Tina Brown, wordsmith 10 Ben Bradlee, diaskeuast, Perry White
compilation: 6 errata
concern: 3 mss. 4 text, typo 5 style 6 errata
notation: 4 dele, stet 5 caret
req.: 3 SAE 4 SASE
__ editor: 3 art 4 city, copy, text
editorial: 5 input, piece, prose 6 column 7 article, comment, opinion, writing 8 critique 10 commentary, exposition
editorialist: 5 press 6 author, scribe, writer 7 analyst 8 reporter 9 columnist 10 journalist
editor in __: 5 chief
Edmond: 4 city, town 5 Hoyle 6 Dantes, O'Brien 7 Fischer, Rostand 8 Goncourt
locale: 8 Oklahoma
Edmonds: 4 city, town 5 Kevon
locale: 10 Washington
Edmonton: 4 city, town
locale: 6 Canada 7 Alb. Alta., Alberta
newspaper: 3 Sun 7 Journal
team: 6 Oilers
Ed, Mr.: 5 horse, steed
Edmund: 4 Kean, Lowe 5 Burke, Gwenn 6 Halley, Muskie, Waller, Wilson 7 Blunden, Hillary, Husserl, Spenser, Stedman 8 Goulding
Edmund Fitzgerald cargo: 3 ore
Edmunds: 4 Dave
Edna: 4 Best 5 Chase 6 Ferber, Millay, O'Brien 7 Everage, Stengel 8 Buchanan 9 Purviance
Edna __ Oliver: 3 May
Edo: 7 de Waart 8 Nigerian
home: 6 Africa 7 Nigeria
today: 5 Tokio, Tokyo
Edom
capital of ~: 5 Petra
kingdom near ~: 4 Moab
Edomites ancestor: 4 Esau
Édouard: 4 Lalo 5 Manet 8 Glissant, Vuillard
see also French
Edsel: 3 car 4 auto, Ford 5 lemon 10 automobile
model: 5 Pacer 6 Ranger 7 Bermuda, Corsair, Roundup 8 Citation, Villager
Edsel Ford Range
locale: 10 Antarctica
Edsels
song: Rama Lama Ding Dong (1961)
Ed Sullivan Show routine: 3 act
Ed TV (1999 film)
cast: Jenna Elfman, Woody Harrelson, Matthew McConaughey
director: Ron Howard
Eduard: 5 Benes, Franz 6 Mörike 7 Buchner 9 Bernstein
Eduardo: 7 Barrios, da Silva 8 Marquina
see also Spanish
educ.
institution: 2 HS 3 JHS, sch. 4 acad., coll., inst., univ.
union: 3 AFT, NEA, UFT
educate: 4 form, rear 5 coach, edify, groom, teach, train, tutor 6 inform, school 7 break in, nurture, smarten 8 instruct 9 catechize, cultivate, enlighten 10 evangelize
educated: 4 wise 6 taught, versed 7 erudite, learned 8 cultured, lettered, literate, prepared 9 scholarly 10 cultivated
guess: 3 est. 7 opinion, surmise 8 estimate, forecast, judgment 9 appraisal, reckoning, valuation 10 assessment, conjecture, evaluation, prediction, projection
__-educated: 4 self, well
Educating Rita (1983 film)
cast: Michael Caine, Julie Walters
education: 5 light, study 6 lesson 7 culture, reading, tuition 8 coaching, guidance, learning, literacy, pedagogy, teaching, training, tutoring 9 catechism, direction, erudition, grounding, knowledge, paedagogy, schooling 10 background, discipline, refinement, upbringing
basic ~ letters: 3 RRR
public ~ pioneer: 4 Mann
recipient: 5 pupil, tutee 7 learner, student, trainee
__ education: 5 adult 6 driver, higher
educational: 8 cultural, didactic 9 pedagogic 10 didactical
institution: 6 lyceum, school 7 academy, college
org.: 2 HS 3 JHS, PTA, sch. 4 acad., coll., inst., univ.
pursuit: 6 degree 7 diploma, master's 9 doctorate, sheepskin
Education of __ K*A*P*L*A*N, The: 5 Hyman
educator: 4 dean 5 coach, tutor 6 mentor 7 teacher, trainer 8 lecturer 9 abecedary, professor 10 instructor
educe: 5 infer 6 derive, elicit, recall 7 develop, draw out, extract, work out 8 bring out 9 draw forth
Edvard: 5 Grieg, Munch
Edward: 3 Fox 4 Coke, Lear 5 Abbey, Albee, Asner, Cline, Doisy, Elgar, Gorey, Heath, Hicks, Lewis, Tatum, Young, Zwick 6 Albert, Arnold, Gibbon, Hopper, Jenner, Ludwig, Norton, Teller 7 Bernays, Buzzell, Dmytryk, Furlong, Kendall, Mulhare, Purcell 8 Appleton, Flanagan, Herrmann, Hoagland, Sedgwick, Steichen, Villella, Woodward 10 FitzGerald
Edward __: 3 VII 4 Bear
Edward __ Horton: 7 Everett
Edward __-Lytton: 6 Bulwer
Edward __ Olmos: 5 James
Edward __ Robinson: 9 Arlington
Edward Cardinal __: 4 Egan
Edward D. __ Jr.: 4 Wood
Edward Everett __: 4 Hale
Edward G.: 8 Robinson
Edwardian __: 3 Era
__ Edward Island: 6 Prince
Edward James: 5 Olmos
Edward M.: 7 Kennedy
Edward R.: 6 Murrow
Edwards: 3 AFB, Gus 5 Blake, Cliff, Jorge, Ralph, Tommy, Vince 7 Anthony 8 Jonathan
Edwards, Blake: 8 director
film: Breakfast at Tiffany's (1961)
Darling Lili (1970)
Days of Wine and Roses (1962)
The Great Race (1965)
Micki + Maude (1984)
Operation Petticoat (1959)
The Party (1968)
The Pink Panther (1964)
A Shot in the Dark (1964)
SOB (1981)
Sunset (1988)
The Tamarind Seed (1974)
That's Life! (1986)
Victor/Victoria (1982)
spouse: Julie Andrews
Edward Scissorhands (1990 film)
cast: Johnny Depp, Vincent Price, Winona Ryder, Dianne Wiest
director: Tim Burton
hands: 6 shears
Edwards, Cliff nickname: Ukulele Ike
Edwards, Jorge: 6 writer 7 Chilean
Edwards, Tommy
song: It's All in the Game (1958)
Edwards, Vince: 5 actor
TV: Ben Casey
Edward the Confessor: 5 saint
Edwin: 4 Land, Muir 5 Abbey, Booth, Drake, Drood, Krebs, Meese, Moses, Starr 6 Hubble, McCain, Newman 7 Fischer, Hubbell, Markham, O'Connor 8 McMillan 9 Armstrong
Ed Wood (1994 film)
cast: Patricia Arquette, Johnny Depp, Martin Landau, Bill Murray, Sarah Jessica Parker
director: Tim Burton
role: 4 Bela 5 Orson 6 Lugosi, Welles
Edy's: 8 ice cream
alternative: *see* ice cream
e.e.: 8 cummings
EE: 4 shoe, wide 5 width
awarder: 3 MIT, RPI
EEC
member: 3 Den., Eng., Ger., Nor. 4 Ital.
money: 3 ecu 4 euro
part of ~: 3 Eur. 4 Comm., Econ.
prefix: 4 Euro-
EEE: 4 shoe, wide 5 width
eek: 4 yipe 6 a mouse
eel: 4 fish, grig, snig 5 anago, moray, unagi 6 conger 7 lamprey, seafood 8 wriggler 9 ichthyoid 10 spitchcock
emulate an ~: 5 slide 7 slither
ender: 4 worm 5 grass
like an ~: 6 apodal 7 apodous
mud ~: 5 siren 9 amphibian 10 salamander
young ~: 4 grig 5 elver
__ eel: 3 mud 4 cusk, pike, sand 5 glass, moray
eellike fish: 6 gunnel
eelpot: 4 trap
eelpout: 4 fish, quab
eelworm: 4 nema
eely: 7 elusive, elusory, wriggly 8 slippery, slithery

e'en: 4 dusk 7 evening, gloamin' 8 gloaming, twilight 9 nightfall
not ~ once: 4 ne'er
eensie-___: 7 weensie
eensy: 4 tiny 9 itty-bitty, miniature
eensy-___: 6 weensy
eeny follower: 5 meeny
EEOC
part of ~: 3 Emp. 4 Comm. 5 Equal
e'er: 2 ay 3 aye 5 alway
not quite ~: 3 oft
eerie: 3 odd 5 queer, scary, weird 6 atypic, crawly, creepy, freaky, occult, quirky, spooky, unreal 7 bizarre, deviant, eidolic, fearful, ghostly, haunted, macaber, macabre, offbeat, strange, uncanny, unusual 8 aberrant, atypical, chilling, eldritch, freakish, haunting, peculiar, spectral, uncommon 9 anomalous, divergent, eccentric, fantastic, ghostlike, grotesque, irregular, unearthly, unnerving 10 mysterious, outlandish, paranormal, unorthodox
feeling: 6 déjà vu
sound: 4 moan
Eero: 8 Saarinen
to Eliel: 3 son
...eether and ___ eyether: 4 I say
Eeyore: 6 donkey
creator: A.A. Milne
friend: 3 owl, Roo 4 Pooh
E.F.: 6 Hutton
eff.: 3 apt.
efface: 4 rase, raze 5 erase 6 cancel, delete, rub out 7 blot out, expunge, wipe out 8 cross out, wear away 9 eliminate, eradicate, extirpate, sponge out 10 do away with, extinguish, obliterate, scratch out
___-effacing: 4 self
effect: 2 do 3 get 4 earn, look, show 5 cause, clout, drift 6 action, create, fulfil, impact, import, induce, obtain, render, result, secure, splash, thrust, upshot 7 achieve, actuate, compass, display, execute, fallout, fulfill, meaning, outcome, perform, procure, produce, product, pull off, purport, realize 8 bring off, carry out, complete, conclude, generate, occasion 9 actualize, aftermath, get across, implement, influence, outgrowth, put across 10 accomplish, bring about, consummate, give rise to, importance, impression, perpetrate, possession, put through
appreciable ~: 4 dent, mark 10 impression
be in ~: 4 hold, last, take 5 apply, carry, stand 6 endure, remain 7 carry on, contain, control, include, persist 8 stand for
carry into ~: 4 obey
combining form: 4 -ergy
go into ~: 6 kick in
have an ~: 4 take, tell, work
have an ~ on: 6 impact 8 register 9 influence 10 impression
have the opposite ~: 6 recoil 7 rebound 8 backfire 9 boomerang 10 bounce back
in ~: 5 truly, valid 6 active, almost, nearly, really, verily 8 actually 9 basically, so to speak, virtually 10 implicitly
not in ~: 4 null
put into ~: 4 vote 5 enact, order 8 legalize 9 establish, institute, legislate
starter: 5 after
take ~: 4 tell, work 5 enure, inure, set in 6 happen
to no ~: 4 vain 6 futile, hollow, in vain 7 inutile, sterile, useless 8 gainless 9 for naught, fruitless, pointless, thankless 10 profitless, unavailing
___ effect: 4 Bohr, side, take 5 sound 6 Edison, ripple 7 Doppler
effective: 4 able, neat 5 quick, smart, sound, valid 6 active, cogent, potent, strong, up to it, useful 7 capable, current, in force, operant, telling, working 8 adequate, forceful, powerful 9 competent, efficient, expedient, on the ball, operative, practical, sovereign, trenchant 10 compelling, convincing, impressive, infallible, persuasive, powerhouse, productive, proficient
be ~: 6 pan out 7 work out
cost-~: 6 doable 9 lucrative 10 worthwhile
date in law: 4 nisi
effectively: 4 well
effectiveness: 5 avail, clout, force, power, punch, teeth, vigor 6 weight 7 potence, potency, success 8 strength, validity
lose ~: 4 pall
effector: 4 doer
effects: 4 gear 5 goods, stuff 6 assets, things 8 chattels, holdings, property 9 trappings 10 belongings
___ effects: 7 optical, special 8 personal
effectual: 5 quick, sound 6 aidful, benign, useful 7 helpful, telling 8 positive, powerful, remedial, salutary 9 achieving, efficient, favorable 10 conclusive, fulfilling, infallible, persuasive, productive, successful, worthwhile
effectually: 6 almost 9 just about, virtually
effectuate: 2 do 4 work 5 cause 6 commit, fulfil 7 execute, fulfill, perform, produce, realize 8 carry out, complete, transact 9 implement 10 accomplish, bring about, consummate, make happen
effendi: 3 sir 4 boss 5 title
in India: 5 saheb, sahib
effervesce: 4 fizz, foam, rave 5 exult, froth, spume 6 bubble, simmer 7 delight, enthuse, rejoice, sparkle
effervescence: 3 gas, joy, vim 4 fizz, foam, glee, zing 5 froth 6 gaiety, gayety 7 bubbles 8 bubbling, buoyance, buoyancy, frothing, vitality, vivacity
effervescent: 5 alive, fizzy, happy, jolly, light, merry, perky, zingy 6 bouncy, breezy, bubbly, frothy, joyful, joyous, lively, yeasty 7 buoyant, excited, gleeful, zinging 8 animated, jubilant, mirthful, spirited 9 sprightly, vivacious
make ~: 6 aerate 7 freshen 9 oxygenate, ventilate
effete: 4 puny, weak, worn 5 frail, spent, wimpy 6 anemic, atonic, barren, feeble, flabby, flimsy 7 anaemic, fragile, wimpish, worn-out 8 decadent, delicate, depleted, helpless, outmoded, pithless 9 exhausted, faltering, infertile, powerless, sissified 10 vulnerable
efficacious: 6 aidful, benign, potent, useful 7 capable, helpful 8 adequate, positive, powerful, puissant, remedial, salutary 9 effectual, favorable 10 productive, worthwhile
be ~: 4 take
efficacy: 5 avail, force, power 7 potence, potency, utility 8 strength, validity 10 capability
efficiency: 4 ease 5 skill 7 ability, economy, faculty, know-how, prowess 8 adequacy, facility 9 abundance, adeptness, expertise, readiness 10 capability, competence, competency
efficient: 3 apt 4 able, deft, good, lean, neat 5 adept, brisk, can-do, handy, slick 6 adroit, au fait, expert, nimble, prompt, up to it, useful 7 capable, regular, skilled, trained 8 adequate, dextrous, graceful, masterly, methodic, seasoned, skillful, thorough 9 competent, conducive, dexterous, effective, effectual, masterful, organized, practical, practiced, qualified 10 economical, methodical, productive, proficient, profitable, systematic
___-efficient: 4 cost, fuel
efficiently: 4 ably, well
effigy: 5 dummy, image, model 6 statue 7 picture 8 likeness, straw man
effloresce: 3 bud 4 grow 5 bloom 6 flower, sprout, thrive 7 blossom, burgeon, develop, prosper, succeed 8 flourish, fructify
effluence: 7 outflow 8 emission, emptying 9 discharge, emanation 10 outpouring
effluent: 4 flow, gush 6 oozing 7 outflow 9 discharge, emanation, exudation 10 exhalation
effluvial: 4 fumy 5 gassy 8 vaporous
effluvious: 7 odorous
effluvium: 3 gas 4 fume, odor, reek 5 miasm, vapor 6 miasma, stench 7 exhaust 10 exhalation
efflux: 7 outflow 8 emission 9 discharge, emanation 10 outpouring
ef follower: 3 gee
effort: 3 bid, job, try 4 care, deed, dint, feat, pain, push, shot, stab, toil, work 5 drive, essay, fling, force, labor, oomph, pains, sweat 6 action, strain 7 attempt, measure, trouble, venture 8 endeavor, exercise, exertion, industry, striving, struggle 9 diligence, operation 10 enterprise
best ~: 3 all
exert minimal ~: 5 glide, slide 6 cruise
futile ~: 5 waste
make an ~: 3 try 4 toil, work 5 exert, lay to, sweat 6 bother, strive, tackle 7 trouble 8 struggle
move without ~: 5 coast, glide, slide
reduce ~: 5 relax
with no ~: 6 easily, simply 7 lightly 9 leisurely, naturally
___ effort: 4 A for, E for
effortful: 6 uphill 7 hard-won, labored 9 difficult, laborious, strenuous 10 formidable
effortless: 4 easy, glib, soft 5 a snap, cushy, light 6 facile, fluent, simple, smooth 7 no sweat 8 dextrous, duck soup, painless, untaxing 9 dexterous, no problem 10 child's play, unexacting
effortlessly: 4 well 7 handily, lightly, readily 9 hands down 10 swimmingly
effortlessness: 4 ease
effrontery: 3 lip 4 face, gall, guff, sass 5 brass, check, cheek, crust, nerve 7 license 8 audacity, boldness, chutzpah, defiance, rudeness, temerity 9 arrogance, assurance, brashness, impudence, insolence, smart talk 10 brazenness, cheekiness, disrespect, incivility
effulgence: 4 glow 5 blaze, gleam, light, shine 6 luster 7 aureola, aureole, sparkle 8 radiance, radiancy, splendor 10 brightness, brilliance
effulgent: 5 lucid, nitid 6 bright 7 beaming, radiant 8 luminous, lustrous 9 brilliant
effuse: 4 emit, gush, pour 5 exude, spirt, spout, spurt 7 diffuse, emanate, flow out, pour out, profuse, secrete 9 ooze forth, pour forth, scattered, spread out
effusion: 5 spirt, spurt, surge 7 torrent
effusive: 4 avid, warm 5 gushy, mushy 6 hearty, lavish 7 fulsome, gushing, profuse 9 ebullient, expansive, exuberant, talkative 10 bigmouthed, unreserved
be ~: 7 enthuse
Efik
home: 6 Africa 7 Nigeria
kin: 6 Ibibio
E-flat: 3 key 8 major key
equivalent: 6 D-sharp
EFL cousin: 3 ESL
Efrem: 9 Zimbalist
Efron: 3 Zac
eft: 4 newt 9 amphibian 10 salamander
Efuru
author: Flora Nwapa
___-E. Fyne: 4 Sylk
e.g.: 4 abbr. 10 for example
E.G.: 8 Marshall
egad: 3 fie, gee 4 darn, drat, oath, oh my, rats, yipe 5 yikes, yipes 6 zounds 9 expletive
in German: 3 ach
___, égalité, fraternité: 7 liberté
Egan: 5 Eddie 6 Pierce, Walter 7 Richard
Egbert: 4 king 5 Saxon
Eger: 4 city, Ohre, town 5 river
locale: 7 Germany, Hungary

Egeria: 5 nymph 8 asteroid
husband: 4 Numa
egest: 4 spew, spue 5 expel, exude 7 cast off, cast out, spew out 8 disgorge, perspire 9 discharge
egesta: 5 sweat, tears
egg: 3 roe 4 cell, chap, ovum, prod, seed, urge 5 taunt 6 embryo, fellow, gamete, needle, origin, urge on 7 oospore, provoke
Australian ~: 4 goog
bad ~: 3 cad, cur 5 rogue 6 rotter 7 dirtbag, stinker, villain 9 nogoodnik, scoundrel
beater: 5 whisk
cell: 4 ovum 5 ootid
combining form: 2 oo-, ov- 3 ovi-, ovo-
concoction: 3 nog 6 omelet, quiche 8 omelette
contents: 5 fetus 6 embryo, foetus
deposit: 5 spawn
distibutor: 5 bunny, dairy 6 rabbit
ender: 3 cup, nog 4 head 5 fruit, plant, shell 6 beater
examiner: 5 sexer
golden ~ producer: 5 goose
good ~: 6 mensch
goose ~: 3 nil, zip 4 nada, none, null, zero 5 zilch, zippo 6 cipher, naught, nought 7 nothing
holder: 4 case, nest 5 crate 6 carton
immature ~: 5 ovule 6 oocyte
insect ~: 3 nit
lay an ~: 4 bomb, bust, fail, flop, lose, slip, trip 5 flunk 6 blow it, falter 7 blunder, founder, go under, go wrong, misstep, stumble, wash out 8 fall flat, flounder 9 strike out
layer: 3 hen 4 bird
like ~ whites: 6 beaten
nest ~: 3 IRA 5 cache, funds, means, store 7 reserve, savings 9 resources
on: 4 abet, coax, goad, prod, push, spur, urge 5 annoy, impel, press 6 fillip, incite, kindle, prompt, stir up 7 actuate, agitate, incense, provoke 8 motivate 9 encourage, instigate
part: 4 yolk 5 glair, white 6 glaire
prepare an ~: 3 fry 4 boil 5 devil, poach, shirr 8 scramble
produce an ~: 3 lay
quantity: 3 doz. 5 dozen
rating: 6 grade A
size: 5 jumbo, large 10 extra large
egg ___: 3 nog 4 case, cell, roll 5 cream, salad, timer, white
egg ___ soup: 4 drop
egg ___ yung: 3 foo
___ egg: 3 ant, bad 4 good, nest 5 goose, lay an 6 Easter, Scotch
egg and ___: 4 dart
egg and ___ race: 5 spoon
Egg and I, The (1947 film)
cast: Claudette Colbert, Percy Kilbride, Fred MacMurray, Marjorie Main
dog: 5 Sport
Eggar: 8 Samantha
eggbeater: 5 mixer 6 copter, gadget
___-egg blue: 6 robin's
egg-cream ingredient: 4 milk 5 sirup, syrup 7 seltzer
egg drop: 4 soup
egg-dyeing time: 6 Easter
egger: 4 moth
Eggert: 6 Nicole
egg foo ___: 4 yong, yung
egghead: 3 ace 4 dork, geek, nerd, whiz, wonk 5 brain 6 genius 7 prodigy, scholar, thinker 8 Einstein, hairless, highbrow, longhair, virtuoso 9 intellect, know-it-all, professor 10 mastermind
pride: 2 IQ 4 mind 5 brain, ideas 6 brains 9 intellect
eggheaded: 5 smart 6 bright 9 brilliant
eggnog: 5 drink 8 beverage, cocktail
ingredient: 3 egg, rum 4 milk 6 brandy, cloves, nutmeg 7 liqueur, vanilla
egg on one's ___: 4 face
eggplant: 6 veggie 9 vegetable
appetizer: 8 caponata
color: 4 puce 6 purple
relative: *see* purple color
egg roll: 9 appetizer
time: 6 Easter
eggs: 3 ova, roe 5 dairy 6 caviar 7 caviare
color Easter ~: 3 dye
companion: 3 ham 4 hash 5 bacon, steak, toast 7 sausage 9 home fries
fish ~: 3 roe 6 caviar
goose ~: 3 OOO 4 OOOO 5 OOOOO
group of ~: 6 clutch
in Latin: 3 ova
like robins' ~: 4 blue 6 bluish 7 blueish
lobster ~: 3 roe
walking on ~: 4 wary 5 alert, chary, leery 7 careful, heedful, mindful, prudent 8 cautious, delicate, vigilant, watchful 9 tentative 10 deliberate
walk on ~: 6 tiptoe 9 pussyfoot
eggs ___ suisse: 3 à la
...eggs ___ basket: 5 in one
___ Eggs and Ham: 5 Green
Eggs Benedict, prepare: 5 poach
egg-shaped: 4 ooid, oval 5 ovate, ovoid, round 7 oviform 8 lopsided 9 ellipsoid 10 elliptical
eggshell: 4 ecru 5 color, white
relative: *see* white color
egg-timer filler: 4 sand
eggy: 4 rich 9 yellowish
Egham: 4 city, town
locale: 6 Surrey
Egil: 5 Krogh
egis: 5 favor 6 shield, surety 7 support 8 auspices, guaranty, umbrella 9 patronage, safeguard 10 protection
eglantine: 5 plant 6 flower
Eglevsky, André: 6 dancer 7 danseur
specialty: 6 ballet
Egmont
author: Goethe
ego: 4 self, soul 5 pride 6 psyche, vanity 7 big head, conceit 8 bovarism, identity 9 arrogance, self-image 10 narcissism, self-esteem, self-regard
alter ~: 3 pal 4 ally, chum, mate 5 buddy, crony 6 backer, cohort, friend 7 comrade, consort, partner 8 intimate, playmate, sidekick, soul mate 9 associate, companion, confidant 10 bosom buddy, compatriot
companion: 2 id
trip: 5 pride 6 vanity
ego ___: 4 trip 5 ideal
___ ego: 5 alter
Ego and the Id, The
author: Sigmund Freud
egocentric: 4 vain 6 stuffy 7 selfish 9 conceited 10 big-talking, egoistical, self-loving
egoism: 5 pride 6 vanity 7 conceit, hauteur 9 arrogance 10 narcissism, self-esteem
egoist: 4 snob 8 braggart 10 narcissist, self-seeker, self-server
egoistical: 4 smug, vain 5 proud 7 selfish 9 conceited, hubristic 10 egocentric, self-loving
Egoist, The
author: George Meredith
Egon: 7 Schiele
egotism: 5 pride 6 vanity 7 conceit, hauteur 9 arrogance 10 narcissism
egotist: 7 showoff
obsession: 4 self
egotistic: 7 fustian, haughty, pompous, selfish 8 arrogant, assuming, boastful, snobbish 9 grandiose 10 complacent, disdainful
egotistical: 4 smug, vain 5 proud 7 haughty, pompous, selfish, stuck-up 8 affected, boastful, cocksure, inflated, prideful, puffed up, snobbish
egregious: 4 foul, rank 5 gross, utter 6 wicked 7 extreme, glaring 8 flagrant, grievous, uncommon 9 atrocious, monstrous, nefarious, notorious 10 deplorable, immoderate, outrageous, scandalous
egress: 4 door, exit, gate 5 go out, leave 6 escape, exodus, outlet, way out 7 exiting 9 departure 10 withdrawal
egression: 4 exit 6 escape 7 parting, walkout 9 departure 10 decampment, evacuation
egret: 4 bird 5 heron, wader 9 marsh bird 10 cattle bird
cousin: 4 ibis
emulate an ~: 4 wade
Eguren, José Maria: 4 poet 8 Peruvian
Egypt: 6 nation 7 country
ancient city: 4 Sais 5 Tanis 6 Abydos, Thebes
ancient ~ lighthouse: 6 Pharos
ancient ~ sacred flower: 5 lotus
and Syr., once: 3 UAR
Arabic name of ~: 4 Misr
archeological site: 5 Luxor 6 Amarna, Karnak
bay: 6 Abukir
bird: 4 ibis
bushel: 5 ardeb
capital: 5 Cairo
carriage: 6 gharri, gharry
cat of ~ mythology: 4 Bast
Christian: 4 Copt
city: 4 Giza, Qena, Suez 5 Aswan, Asyut, Benha, Cairo, Luxor, Tanta 6 Assiut, Assuan 7 Assouan 8 Port Said 10 Alexandria
cobra: 3 asp 6 uraeus
conquerors of ~: 6 Hyksos
cotton: 3 sak
dam: 5 Aswan
desert: 6 Libyan, Sahara 7 Arabian
dyestuff: 5 henna
father: 3 Ham
god: 2 Ra 3 Bes, Set 4 Aten, Aton, Nunu, Ptah, Seth 5 Horus, Sebek, Thoth 6 Amon-Ra, Anubis, Osiris 7 Taueret
goddess: 3 Mut, Nut 4 Bast, Isis, Maat 6 Hathor 7 Sekhmet 8 Nephthys
god of wisdom: 5 Thoth
group: 10 Arab League
gulf: 5 Akaba, Aqaba
home: 6 Africa
image in ~ art: 3 asp
it's n. of ~: 3 Eur. 5 Medit.
king: 3 Tut 4 Fuad 5 Menes 6 Farouk, Ramses 7 Rameses
lake: 6 Nasser
language: 6 Arabic, Coptic
money: 5 asper 7 piaster, piastre 8 millieme
month: 4 Ahet
neighbor: 3 Isr., Leb. 5 Libya, Sudan 6 Israel
Nobelist in Literature: 7 Mahfouz
Nobelist in Peace: 5 Sadat
opera set in ~: 4 Aïda
peasant: 6 fellah
peninsula: 5 Sinai
port: 4 Suez 5 Cairo 8 Port Saïd 10 Alexandria
president: 5 Sadat 6 Nasser 7 Mubarak
province: 6 Faiyum
queen: 4 Cleo
river: 4 Nile
sacred bull: 4 Apis
scientist: 7 Ptolemy
solar disk: 4 Aten, Aton
source of ocher: 6 dakhla
strip between Israel and ~: 4 Gaza
temple site: 6 Karnak
tree: 7 ambatch
waterwheel: 5 sakia
wind: 7 khamsin
writer: 9 el Saadawi
Egyptian: 4 Arab 5 dance 8 language
Egyptologist: 5 Young 6 Petrie 7 Belzoni
symbol: 5 glyph
eh: 3 huh 4 what 5 query
E. Howard ___: 4 Hunt
Ehrlichman: 4 John
Ehrlich, Paul: 8 Nobelist
Ehud: 5 Barak 6 Olmert
Eichhorn: 4 Lisa
eider: 4 bird, duck, fowl 10 diving duck
ender: 4 down
relative: **see** duck
eider ___: 4 down, duck
eiderdown: 5 fluff, quilt 7 bedding 8 coverlet, coverlid 9 comforter
eidolic: 5 eerie 6 spooky 7 ghostly, haunted 10 phantasmal, wraithlike
eidolon: 5 ghost, ideal 6 fantom 7 phantom 8 delusion 10 apparition

Eiffel: 8 language 9 Alexandre
alternative: *see* computer language
Eiffel Tower
locale: 5 Paris
Eiger: 3 alp 4 peak 5 mount 8 mountain
locale: 4 Alps 6 Europe 11 Switzerland
Eiger Sanction, The (1975 film)
cast: Jack Cassidy, Clint Eastwood, George Kennedy
director: Clint Eastwood
setting: 4 Alps
eight
base ~: 5 octal
behind the ~ ball: 6 in a fix, in a jam 7 trapped, unlucky
bells: 4 noon 6 midday
bits: 4 byte
combining form: 3 oct- 4 octa-, octo-
composition for ~: 5 octet 7 octette
cube root of ~: 3 two
figure of ~: 4 knot
furlongs: 2 mi. 4 mile
gills: 2 qt. 5 quart
group of ~: 5 octad, octet 6 octave 7 octette
half a figure ~: 3 ess
homophone for ~: 3 ait, ate
in French: 4 huit
in German: 4 acht
in Italian: 4 otto
in Japanese: 5 hachi
in Latin: 4 octo
in Portuguese: 4 oito
in Spanish: 4 ocho
ounces: 3 cup
pints: 3 gal. 6 gallon
prefix: 4 octa-, octo-
quarter of ~: 3 two
quarts: 4 peck
to Mohs: 5 topaz
eightball: 4 game
maneuver: 5 massé
requirement: 3 cue
Eight Bells
artist: Winslow Homer
Eight Cousins
author: Louisa May Alcott
Eight Days a Week (1965 song)
artist: Beatles
eighteen-wheeler: 4 semi 5 truck
eighth: 5 grade 6 octave
every ~ day: 5 octan
letter: 5 aitch
mo.: 3 Aug. 6 August
eighth ___: 4 note, rest
Eighth Commandment, The
author: Lawrence Sanders
Eighth Day, The
author: Thornton Wilder
Eighth Wonder of the World, The: 4 Kong
eight-legged creatures: 6 octopi
Eight Men Out (1988 film)
cast: John Cusack, Clifton James, Christopher Lloyd, Charlie Sheen, David Strathairn, D.B. Sweeney
director: John Sayles
Eight Mortal Ladies Possessed
author: Tennessee Williams
eightpenny ___: 4 nail
___ eights: 5 crazy
eights, do figure: 5 skate
eight-track ___: 4 tape
eighty: 9 fourscore
___-eighty: 3 one
Eighty-Eight: 3 car 4 auto, Olds 10 automobile, Oldsmobile
Eighty-Five Poems
author: Louis MacNeice
eighty-six: 3 nix 4 boot, drop, kill, toss 5 chuck, ditch, eject, scrap 6 bounce 7 let go of 9 dispose of, throw over 10 disqualify
eighty-sixed: 4 beat, fini, over, shot, sunk 5 kaput 6 done in, no more, ruined, undone 7 all over, belly-up, defunct, done for, extinct, totaled, wrecked 8 finished, washed-up, wiped out 9 destroyed 10 demolished
Eikenberry, Jill: 7 actress
spouse: Michael Tucker
Eilat: 4 city, port, town
locale: 6 Israel
Eilbacher: 4 Lisa
Eileen: 4 Ford 6 Fulton 7 Brennan, Farrell, Heckart
Eilers: 5 Sally
ein: 3 one 6 German
in French: 3 une
in Italian: 3 uno
in Spanish: 3 uno
Eine ___ in Venedig: 5 Nacht
Eine Kleine Nachtmusik
composer: Wolfgang Amadeus Mozart
Einsam in trüben Tagen
singer: 4 Elsa
eins doubled: 4 zwei
Einstein: 3 ace 4 whiz 5 brain 6 Albert, genius 7 egghead, prodigy, thinker 8 highbrow, virtuoso 9 intellect 10 mastermind
Einstein, Albert: 8 Nobelist 9 physicist
birthplace: 3 Ger., Ulm 7 Germany
colleague: Neils Bohr
forte: 4 math 7 physics
part of an ~ equation: 4 mass
see also German
einsteinium: 7 element
Eire: 6 Old Sod 7 Ireland 9 Innisfail, Innisfree
___ Éireann: 4 Dáil 6 Seanad
Eisaku: 4 Sato
eisen: 4 iron 6 German
Eisenhower: 3 Ike 5 David, Mamie 6 Dwight, Milton
Eisenhower ___: 6 jacket
Eisenhower, Dwight D.: president
alma mater: 4 USMA 9 West Point
birthplace: 5 Texas 7 Denison
cabinet member: 5 Gates, Hobby, McKay, Weeks 6 Benson, Dulles, Durkin, Folsom, Herter, Rogers, Wilson 7 McElroy 8 Anderson, Brownell, Flemming, Humphrey, Mitchell
former occupation: 7 general, soldier
home: 6 Kansas 7 Abilene 10 Gettysburg
HQ in '45: 5 Reims 6 Rheims
middle name: 5 David
nickname: 3 Ike
opponent: 9 Stevenson
real first name: 5 David
V.P.: 5 Nixon
wife: 5 Mamie
work: At Ease
Eisenhut: 3 alp
Eisenstaedt: 6 Alfred, photog
Eisenstein, Sergei: 8 director
film: Alexander Nevsky (1938) Potemkin (1925)
'E' Is for Evidence
author: Sue Grafton
Eisley: 7 Anthony
Eisner: 7 Michael
either: 3 too 4 also, both, each 6 as well 8 likewise 9 whichever 10 this or that
or both: 5 and/or
eject: 3 rid 4 boot, bump, dump, emit, fire, oust, pump, rout, spew, spue, vent, void 5 debar, empty, evict, expel, exude, issue, purge, spout 6 banish, bounce, depose, disbar, launch, propel, remove, squirt 7 bail out, cast off, cast out, diffuse, dismiss, emanate, exclude, extrude, give off, kick out, radiate, spit out, toss out, turn out, unloose 8 disgorge, dislodge, displace, drive off, force out, get rid of, heave out, jettison, relegate, shoot out, throw off, throw out 9 discharge, eighty-six, eliminate, eradicate, send forth 10 dispossess
ejecta: 4 lava
ejection: 4 cast 8 emission, eruption, exorcism 9 discharge, exclusion, expulsion 10 deposition, evacuation, unfrocking
ejection ___: 4 seat 7 capsule
ejector ___: 4 seat
Ekberg: 5 Anita, Swede
eke: 5 skimp 6 make do, scrape 7 augment, scratch, squeeze, stretch 10 supplement, underspend
out: 6 make do, manage 7 squeeze 8 scrape by 10 supplement
___ E. Kelley: 5 David
Ekelöf, Gunnar: 4 poet 7 Swedish
EKG: 4 test 5 chart
concern: 5 heart
user: 2 MD 4 hosp.
___ E. King: 3 Ben
Ekland: 5 Britt
spouse: Peter Sellers
Ekwensi, Cyprian: 6 writer 8 Nigerian
el: 2 RR 8 railroad
cousin: 3 the
follower: 2 em
initials: 3 CTA
locale: 3 Chi 4 Loop 7 Chicago
preceder: 3 kay
stop: 3 sta., stn. 7 station
el ___: 4 toro 6 cheapo
El ___: 3 Cid 4 Niño, Paso 5 Greco, Norte, Super 6 Diario, Dorado 7 Capitan 8 Cordobés
El ___ Brujo: 4 Amor
El ___, CA: 4 Toro
El ___ Campeador: 3 Cid
El ___ Grande: 6 Rancho
El ___ Mexico: 5 Salón
El ___ Pasa: 6 Condor
El ___, TX: 4 Paso
E.L.: 8 Doctorow
elaborate: 4 rich 5 fancy, ritzy, showy 6 detail, expand, flashy, florid, frilly, glitzy, knotty, lavish, ornate, unfold 7 amplify, clarify, complex, develop, explain, flowery, for show, opulent, specify, work out 8 detailed, involved, thorough 9 ambitious, decorated, discourse, embellish, embroider, expatiate, extensive, garnished, interpret, intricate, luxuriant, luxurious, perfected, sumptuous 10 complicate, flamboyant, ornamental, ornamented, overworked, prodigious
inlay: 4 buhl 5 boule 6 boulle
on: 4 list, show, tell 6 detail, lay out, report, reveal, sketch 7 itemize, narrate, portray, recount, specify 8 describe, set forth, spell out 9 delineate, embellish, enumerate, make clear
elaboration, without: 6 simply
Elaine: 3 May 5 Zayak 7 Stewart, Stritch
Elaine, the lily ___: 4 Maid
El Al: 7 airline
destination: 3 Lod
El Alamein: 6 battle
Elam: 4 Jack
capital of ~: 4 Susa
father: 4 Shem
grandfather: 4 Noah
___ el Amarna: 3 Tel
élan: 3 vim, zip 4 brio, dash, fire, life, snap, soul, zest, zing 5 ardor, flair, flash, gusto, oomph, spunk, style, verve, vigor 6 bounce, energy, esprit, gaiety, gayety, pizazz, psyche, spirit 7 abandon, panache, pizzazz, sparkle 8 activity, buoyance, buoyancy, fervency, flourish, vitality, vivacity 9 animation 10 enthusiasm, excitement, exuberance, get-up-and-go, liveliness, vital spark
eland: 6 animal, mammal 8 antelope
land: 5 veldt
relative: *see* antelope
elanet: 4 hawk, kite 10 bird of prey
Elantra: 3 car 4 auto 7 Hyundai
elapid: 5 cobra, snake 6 animal 7 reptile
elapse: 2 go 3 fly 4 flow, go by, pass 5 fly by, lapse 6 expire, pass by, roll by, roll on, run out, slip by 7 glide by, slide by 8 slip away, tick away 9 glide away, intervene, transpire
elapsed: 4 gone, past 6 lapsed
Elara: 4 moon
planet: 7 Jupiter
elastic: 4 soft 6 limber, lissom, spongy, supple 7 lissome, plastic, pliable, springy 8 flexible, stretchy, yielding 9 resilient
device: 6 bungee
fabric: 7 spandex
elastic ___: 6 clause
___ elastic: 3 gum
elasticity: 4 give, tone 6 bounce, spring
Elat: 4 city, port, town
locale: 6 Israel
elate: 4 send 5 cheer, liven 6 buoy up, lift up, perk up, please, puff up, thrill, tickle, turn on 7 delight,

elevate, gladden, happify, hearten, lighten, overjoy, satisfy **9** enrapture, inebriate, make happy **10** exhilarate, intoxicate
elated: 4 glad, high, sent **5** happy **6** cheery, flying, joyful, joyous **7** beaming, gleeful, pleased **8** blissful, bubbling, ecstatic, enthused, euphoric, exultant, in heaven, jubilant, sanguine **9** ebullient, overjoyed, rapturous, rejoicing, rhapsodic **10** flying high, triumphant
be ~: 4 glow **5** exult **9** walk on air
elaterid: 3 dor **4** dorr **6** beetle, insect
Elath: 4 city, town
locale: 6 Israel
elation: 3 joy **4** glee, zest **5** bliss **6** gaiety, gayety **7** delight, ecstasy, emotion, jollity, rapture, triumph **8** euphoria, felicity, optimism **9** happiness, joviality, lightness **10** ebullience, exultation, jubilation
show ~: 4 beam **5** exult **7** light up
Elayne: 7 Boosler
Elba: 4 isle **5** Idris **6** island
Elbe: 5 river
city on the ~: 5 Pirna **7** Dresden, Hamburg
locale: 7 Germany
river to the ~: 4 Eger, Iser, Ohre **6** Moldau, Vltava
Elbert: 4 peak **5** mount **7** Hubbard **8** mountain
locale: 7 Rockies **8** Colorado
elbow: 4 bump, poke, prod, push **5** hinge, joint, nudge, shove **6** jostle, justle, thrust **7** flexure **8** shoulder **9** push aside
armor: 6 couter
at one's ~: 4 near **5** close, handy, ready, utile **6** nearby, useful **7** close by **9** available **10** accessible, convenient
bend an ~: 3 sip **4** swig, tope **5** drink, snort **6** imbibe, tipple
bender: 3 sot **4** lush **5** toper
counterpart: 4 knee
ender: 4 room
grease: 4 work **6** effort **8** exertion
locale: 3 arm
room: 5 space **6** leeway
use ~ grease: 3 ply **4** buff **5** apply, scour, sweat, wield **6** employ, polish, strain **7** trouble, try hard, utilize **8** put forth
elbow __: 4 room **6** grease
__ elbow: 6 tennis
elbow grease: 4 toil
use ~: 5 exert, scrub
elbowing, like: 4 rude **7** uncouth
elbowroom: 3 way **4** play **5** scope, space **6** leeway **7** freedom **8** latitude **9** free space, open space
elbows: 5 pasta **7** noodles **8** macaroni
out at the ~: 5 broke, needy, seedy **6** bad off, hard up, ill off, in need, in want, shabby **7** pinched **8** badly off, bankrupt, beggarly, indigent, strapped **9** destitute, insolvent, moneyless, penniless, penurious **10** pauperized, straitened
rub ~: 3 mix **6** hobnob **9** socialize **10** fraternize
up to one's ~: 4 full **5** awash **7** crowded **8** brimming
__ elbows with: 3 rub
elbow-to-elbow: 3 SRO **5** dense, tight **6** packed **7** cramped, crowded, teeming **8** brimming, populous, squeezed **9** chock-full, jam-packed **10** wall-to-wall
elbow-to-fingertip distance: 5 cubit
Elbridge: 5 Gerry
Elbrus: 4 peak **5** mount **8** mountain
locale: 6 Europe, Russia **8** Caucasus
Elburz: 5 range
locale: 4 Asia, Iran
El Cajon: 4 city, town
locale: 10 California
El Capitan: 4 peak **5** mount, train **8** mountain
composer: John Philip Sousa
locale: 8 Yosemite **10** California
Elcar: 4 Dana
El Centro: 4 city, town
locale: 10 California
El Cerrito: 4 city, town
locale: 10 California
El Cid
foe: 4 Moor
El Cid (1961 film): 4 epic
cast: Charlton Heston, Sophia Loren
director: Anthony Mann
El Condor: 4 peak **5** mount **8** mountain
locale: 5 Andes **9** Argentina
El Condor Pasa (1970 song)
artist: Simon and Garfunkel
El Cordobés: 6 torero **7** matador **8** toreador
see also Spanish
eld: 4 yore **9** antiquity **10** days of yore, yesteryear
elder: 4 tree **5** doyen, genro, older, shrub **6** cleric, senior **8** superior **9** firstborn, matriarch, patriarch, presbyter **10** golden ager
ender: 4 care **5** berry
marsh ~: 3 iva
relative: 6 abelia **8** snowball
elder __: 6 hostel
__ elder: 3 box
Elder: 3 Lee
Elder __: 4 Edda
elderberry: 4 wine **5** fruit
Elder, Katie brood: 4 sons
elderly: 3 old **4** aged **5** aging **6** ageing **7** ancient, wizened **8** grizzled **9** geriatric, getting on, senescent, up in years, venerable **10** gray-haired
Elders: 8 Joycelyn
eldest: 4 heir **9** born first, firstborn
in law: 4 aine
eldest, Jr.'s maybe: 3 III
Eldorado: 3 car **4** auto **8** Cadillac
artist: 3 ELO
author: Edgar Allan Poe
El Dorado
treasure: 3 oro
see also Spanish
Eldridge: 3 Roy **7** Cleaver **8** Florence
Eldridge, Roy: 9 trumpeter
genre: 4 jazz
eldritch: 4 eery **5** eerie, weird
__ e Leandro: 3 Ero
Eleanor: 4 Bron **5** Rigby, Smeal **6** Parker, Porter, Powell, Steber **7** Hibbert **9** Roosevelt
mother-in-law: 4 Sara
successor: 4 Bess
to Franklin: 4 wife
to Teddy: 5 niece
Eleanor and Franklin
author: Joseph Lash
Eleanor of __: 9 Aquitaine
Eleanor Rigby (1966 song)
artist: Beatles
Eleanor Roosevelt, __ Roosevelt: 3 née
Eleazar
father: 5 Aaron
elec.: 3 pwr.
charge: 3 neg., pos.
company: 4 util.
cooler: 2 AC
device: 4 rheo
measure: 3 amp, kwh
elect: 3 opt **4** make, name, pick, take, vote **5** go for **6** accept, assign, choice, choose, chosen, decide, opt for, prefer, select, vote in **7** chooses, pick out, vote for **8** handpick, nominate, settle on **9** designate, determine, single out **10** decide upon, settle upon
ender: 3 ion **5** orate
elected: 9 preferred, voluntary
be ~: 3 win **5** get in
ones: 3 ins
try to get ~: 3 run
election: 4 race **5** event **6** choice, option, voting **7** primary **8** choosing, decision **9** balloting, franchise, selection **10** nomination, referendum
campaign for ~: 5 stump
committee: 6 caucus **8** congress
district: 3 pct. **4** ward **8** precinct
ender: 3 eer
losers: 4 outs
need: 4 poll **6** ballot
participant: 5 voter
result: 5 tally
selection: 5 slate **9** candidate
tactic: 5 smear
time: 3 Nov. **4** fall **8** November
winners: 3 ins
Election (1999 film)
cast: Matthew Broderick, Reese Witherspoon
Election Day: 3 Tue. **4** Tues.
Election Day (1985 song)
artist: Arcadia
electioneer: 4 back, hype, plug, push **5** stump **6** talk up **7** advance, canvass, promote, support **8** campaign, plump for, politick
elective: 5 class **6** course **7** seminar **8** optional
electoral __: 4 vote **7** college
Electoral College member: 5 proxy
electorate: 5 party **6** public, voters
elector ender: 3 ate
Electra: 3 car, cat **4** auto, font **5** Buick **6** Carmen, Pleiad **8** typeface
author: Euripides, Sophocles
brother: 7 Orestes
daughter: 4 Iris
father: 5 Atlas **9** Agamemnon
husband: 7 Pylades
lover: 4 Zeus
sister: 9 Iphigenia
son: 5 Medon **9** Strophius
Electra __: 7 complex
Electra, Carmen: 5 model **7** actress
spouse: Dave Navarro, Dennis Rodman
Electrasol: 9 detergent
alternative: 3 Joy **4** Ajax, Dawn **7** Cascade **8** Sunlight **9** Palmolive
electric: 5 kicky **7** charged, dynamic, voltaic **8** exciting, stirring **9** automatic, thrilling
company: 4 util. **7** utility
device: 5 relay **6** switch
discharge: 3 arc
meter: 5 gauge
power network: 4 grid
sign: 4 neon
starter: 6 dynamo
swimmer: 3 eel
electric __: 3 arc, car, eel, eye, ray **4** blue, cell, flux, glow, wave **5** field, light, meter, motor, organ, razor, storm **6** charge, guitar **7** circuit, current
__ Electric: 7 General
electrical: 9 automated, motorized **10** electronic, mechanized
conductor: 4 wire **5** shunt **6** dynode
connector: 4 plug
cord in Britain: 4 flex
junction: 3 wye
problem: 5 short, surge
switch: 5 on/off
unit: 3 amp, mho, ohm **4** volt, watt **5** farad, gauss **7** coulomb **8** ampere. mV
electrical __: 5 storm
Electric Avenue (1983 song)
artist: Eddy Grant
Electric Blue (1988 song)
artist: Icehouse
electric-dart firer: 5 taser
electric eel: 4 fish
electric guitar hookup: 3 amp
Electric Horseman, The (1979 film)
cast: Jane Fonda, Willie Nelson, Valerie Perrine, Robert Redford
director: Sydney Pollack
electrician: 5 wirer
film ~: 6 gaffer
need: 6 pliers
electricity: 2 AC, DC **5** juice, power **7** current, utility, voltage
demand for ~: 4 load
generator: 3 eel, ray
install ~: 4 wire
__ electricity: 6 static
Electric Kool-Aid Acid Test, The
author: Tom Wolfe
electric-plug projection: 5 prong
electric slide: 5 dance
electrify: 3 awe **4** fire, send, stir, wire **5** rouse, shock **6** arouse, charge, dazzle, excite, thrill **7** enthuse **8** energize, surprise **9** galvanize, go over big, magnetize, stimulate, transport **10** invigorate
electrifying: 7 vibrant **8** dramatic, striking **9** arresting, thrilling
fish: 3 eel, ray
electrochemistry: 7 science
electrode: 5 anode **7** cathode
bridge: 3 arc
of an ~: 6 anodal, anodic **8** cathodic
electro ending: 4 lyte

Electrolux: 3 vac **6** vacuum
competitor: 5 Kirby, Oreck **6** Eureka, Hoover
electrolysis migrator: 5 anion
electromagnetic
amplifier: 5 maser
storm: 6 aurora
unit: 5 abohm
electromotive force unit: 4 volt
electron: 6 lepton **8** particle
charge: 3 neg., pos. **8** negative, positive
free ~: 3 ion
gainer: 5 anion
high speed ~: 4 beta
site: 4 atom
tube: 5 diode
electron __: 3 gun **4** lens, tube
electron-__: 4 volt
__ electron: 4 free **7** valence
electronic: 6 hi-tech **9** automated, automatic
control system: 5 servo
info source: 5 CD/ROM
instrument: 4 Moog **5** synth
not ~: 5 print
reading: 4 scan
signal: 4 beep, blip, page **5** bleep
summoner: 5 pager **6** beeper
electronic __: 4 mail **5** brain, music
electronic music pioneer: 3 Eno
electronics: 7 science
company: 3 JVC, NEC, RCA **4** Acer, Aiwa, Koss, Sony **5** Casio, Epson, Sanyo, Sharp **6** Quasar, Yamaha, Zenith **7** Emerson, Hitachi, Philips, Pioneer, ProScan, Samsung, Toshiba **8** Magnavox, Sylvania **9** Panasonic
device: 5 diode
electron tube part: 5 anode
__ E. Lee: 4 Robt. **6** Robert
eleemosynary: 7 liberal **10** almsgiving, altruistic, beneficent, benevolent, charitable, gratuitous
Elegaic Stanzas
author: William Wordsworth
elegance: 4 luxe, ritz **5** charm, class, flair, grace, poise, style, taste **6** beauty, luxury, polish **7** culture, dignity, hauteur **8** breeding, delicacy, felicity, grandeur, lushness, nobility, noblesse, poshness, splendor **9** gentility, good looks **10** refinement
elegant: 4 chic, fine, haut, lacy, luxe, nice, posh **5** clean, fancy, grand, haute, plush, ritzy, slick, smart, swank, swell, swish **6** august, chichi, classy, deluxe, dressy, modish, ornate, proper, spruce, superb, urbane **7** courtly, dashing, genteel, opulent, refined, shapely, stately, stylish, voguish **8** artistic, debonair, decorous, esthetic, finished, gorgeous, graceful, handsome, highbred, highbrow, ladylike, majestic, polished, splendid, superior, tasteful **9** beautiful, classical, debonaire, dignified, exquisite, glamorous, high-toned, in fashion, luxurious, processed, sumptuous **10** artistical, cultivated, debonnaire, majestical
not ~: 5 crass, tacky
elegant fowl, Lear's: 3 owl
Elegants
song: Little Star (1958)
elegiac: 3 sad **5** bleak **6** dismal, somber **7** doleful **8** dolorous, funereal, mournful **9** sorrowful, woebegone **10** lugubrious, melancholy
elegit: 4 writ
elegy: 4 poem **5** dirge **6** lament, plaint **7** requiem **8** threnody
Elegy Written in a Country Churchyard
author: Thomas Gray
__ eleison: 5 kyrie
Elektra: 8 asteroid
element: 3 tin **4** gold, iron, item, lead, link, neon, part, unit, zinc **5** argon, boron, facet, field, iodin, piece, radon, state, xenon **6** aspect, barium, carbon, cerium, cesium, cobalt, copper, curium, detail, domain, erbium, factor, helium, indium, iodine, member, milieu, nickel, osmium, oxygen, radium, silver, sodium, sphere, streak, sulfur **7** arsenic, bismuth, bohrium, bromine, cadmium, caesium, calcium, dubnium, feature, fermium, gallium, habitat, hafnium, hahnium, hassium, holmium, iridium, krypton, lithium, mercury, niobium, portion, rhenium, rhodium, section, silicon, sulphur, terbium, thulium, uranium, wolfram, yttrium **8** actinium, aluminum, antimony, astatine, chlorine, chromium, europium, fluorine, francium, hydrogen, lutetium, material, nitrogen, nobelium, platinum, polonium, rubidium, samarium, scandium, selenium, tantalum, thallium, titanium, tungsten, vanadium **9** aluminium, americium, berkelium, beryllium, component, germanium, lanthanum, magnesium, manganese, neodymium, neptunium, palladium, plutonium, potassium, ruthenium, strontium, tellurium, ytterbium, zirconium **10** dysprosium, gadolinium, ingredient, lawrencium, molybdenum, particular, phosphorus, promethium, technetium **11** californium, einsteinium, mendelevium **12** protactinium **13** rutherfordium
class: 5 metal **8** nonmetal
component: 4 atom
distinguishing ~: 4 qual. **7** quality
form: 7 isotope
having one ~: 5 unary
ID: 4 at. no.
inactive ~: 4 neon **5** argon, radon, xenon **6** helium **7** krypton
in alchemy: 3 air **4** fire **5** earth, water
magnetic ~: 6 cobalt
out of one's ~: 4 asea, lost **5** at sea
radioactive ~: 5 radon **6** curium, radium **7** bohrium, dubnium, fermium, hassium, thorium, uranium **8** actinium, astatine, francium, nobelium, polonium **9** americium, berkelium, neptunium, plutonium **10** lawrencium, meitnerium, promethium, seaborgium, technetium **11** californium, einsteinium, mendelevium **12** protactinium **13** rutherfordium
rare earth ~: 6 cerium, cesium, erbium **7** caesium, holmium, terbium, thulium, yttrium **8** europium, lutetium, samarium, scandium **9** neodymium, ytterbium **10** dysprosium, gadolinium, promethium **12** praseodymium
suffix: 3 -ium
unit: 4 atom **8** particle
Element: 3 SUV **5** Honda
elemental: 5 basic **6** earthy **7** organic, primary **8** integral, ultimate **9** component, essential, intrinsic **10** primordial, underlying
state: 3 gas **5** solid **6** liquid **7** gaseous
elementary: 4 easy **5** basal, basic, plain **6** facile, simple **7** initial, primary **8** duck soup, original **9** beginning, essential, incipient, primitive, uncomplex **10** child's play, simplified, substratal, underlying
particle: 4 muon **5** meson, quark **6** baryon, lepton
elementary __: 6 school
elements: 6 matter **7** climate, weather
basic ~: 4 ABCs
one of the four ~: 3 air **4** fire **5** earth, water
safe from the ~: 6 indoor, inside **7** indoors
Elements
author: Euclid
elements by atomic number:
1 - hydrogen (H)
2 - helium (He)
3 - lithium (Li)
4 - beryllium (Be)
5 - boron (B)
6 - carbon (C)
7 - nitrogen (N)
8 - oxygen (O)
9 - fluorine (F)
10 - neon (Ne)
11 - sodium (Na)
12 - magnesium (Mg)
13 - aluminum (Al)
14 - silicon (Si)
15 - phosphorus (P)
16 - sulfur/sulphur (S)
17 - chlorine (Cl)
18 - argon (Ar)
19 - potassium (K)
20 - calcium (Ca)
21 - scandium (Sc)
22 - titanium (Ti)
23 - vanadium (V)
24 - chromium (Cr)
25 - manganese (Mn)
26 - iron (Fe)
27 - cobalt (Co)
28 - nickel (Ni)
29 - copper (Cu)
30 - zinc (Zn)
31 - gallium (Ga)
32 - germanium (Ge)
33 - arsenic (As)
34 - selenium (Se)
35 - bromine (Br)
36 - krypton (Kr)
37 - rubidium (Rb)
38 - strontium (Sr)
39 - yttrium (Y)
40 - zirconium (Zr)
41 - niobium (Nb)
42 - molybdenum (Mo)
43 - technetium (Tc)
44 - ruthenium (Ru)
45 - rhodium (Rh)
46 - palladium (Pd)
47 - silver (Ag)
48 - cadmium (Cd)
49 - indium (In)
50 - tin (Sn)
51 - antimony (Sb)
52 - tellurium (Te)
53 - iodine (I)
54 - xenon (Xe)
55 - cesium (Cs)
56 - barium (Ba)
57 - lanthanum (La)
58 - cerium (Ce)
59 - praseodymium (Pr)
60 - neodymium (Nd)
61 - promethium (Pm)
62 - samarium (Sm)
63 - europium (Eu)
64 - gadolinium (Gd)
65 - terbium (Tb)
66 - dysprosium (Dy)
67 - holmium (Ho)
68 - erbium (Er)
69 - thulium (Tm)
70 - ytterbium (Yb)
71 - lutetium (Lu)
72 - hafnium (Hf)
73 - tantalum (Ta)
74 - tungsten/wolfram (W)
75 - rhenium (Re)
76 - osmium (Os)
77 - iridium (Ir)
78 - platinum (Pt)
79 - gold (Au)
80 - mercury (Hg)
81 - thallium (Tl)
82 - lead (Pb)
83 - bismuth (Bi)
84 - polonium (Po)
85 - astatine (At)
86 - radon (Rn)
87 - francium (Fr)
88 - radium (Ra)
89 - actinium (Ac)
90 - thorium (Th)
91 - proactinium (Pa)
92 - uranium (U)
93 - neptunium (Np)
94 - plutonium (Pu)
95 - americium (Am)
96 - curium (Cm)
97 - berkelium (Bk)
98 - californium (Cf)
99 - einsteinium (Es)
100 - fermium (Fm)
101 - mendelevium (Md)
102 - nobelium (No)
103 - lawrencium (Lr)
104 - rutherfordium (Rf)
105 - hahnium/dubnium (Ha/Db)
106 - seaborgium (Sg)
107 - bohrium (Bh)
108 - hassium (Hs)
109 - meitnerium (Mt)
110 - darmstadtium (Ds)
111 - roentgenium (Rg)
112 - copernicium (Cn)
Elements of Style, The
author: E.B. White

Elements of Style, The author: William Strunk Jr.
Elena: **6** Bechke, Bonner, Valova **7** Verdugo **9** Nikolaidi
in English: **5** Ellen, Helen
Eleni
author: Nicholas Gage
writer: **12** Nicholas Gage
Eleni (1985 film)
cast: Linda Hunt, John Malkovich, Kate Nelligan
director: Peter Yates
Eleniak, Erika: **7** actress
TV: Baywatch
Elenore (1968 song)
artist: Turtles
Eleonora: **4** Duse
author: Edgar Allan Poe
elephant: **5** Dumbo, Jumbo, mount **6** animal, mammal **9** pachyderm
counterpart: **6** donkey
dinner: **6** baobab
ender: **3** ine, oid
feature: **3** ear **4** tusk **5** trunk
female: **3** cow
fictional ~: **5** Babar **6** Horton
GOP ~ creator: Thomas Nast
group: **4** herd
home: **3** zoo **6** big top, circus
Kipling, Rudyard ~: **5** Hathi
lone ~: **5** rogue
male: **4** bull
owner: **4** raja
party: **3** GOP
prehistoric ~: **7** mammoth **8** stegodon **9** dinothere
seat: **6** houdah, howdah
sound: **6** bellow **7** trumpet
trap: **5** kheda **6** keddah, khedah
young: **4** calf
__ elephant: **3** sea **4** pink **5** rogue, white **6** Indian **7** African, Asiatic
Elephant Boy (1937 film)
cast: Sabu
elephantine: **3** big **4** huge, vast **5** giant, great, jumbo, large **7** hulking, immense, lumpish, mammoth, massive, sizable, titanic **8** colossal, enormous, gigantic, king-size, oversize, sizeable, towering, whapping, whopping **9** Herculean, humongous, monstrous, overlarge, ponderous **10** gargantuan, monumental, prodigious, stupendous, tremendous
Elephant Man, The (1980 film)
cast: Anne Bancroft, Sir John Gielgud, Anthony Hopkins, John Hurt
director: David Lynch
Elephant of the Celebes
artist: Max Ernst
elephant's-ear: **4** taro
Eleuthera
locale: **7** Bahamas
Eleutherius: **4** pope **7** pontiff
elev.: **2** mt. **3** alt., hgt., mtn.
elevate: **4** bump, buoy, hike, lift, rise **5** boost, cheer, deify, elate, ensky, exalt, grace, heave, hoist, raise, set up **6** bump up, buoy up, enrich, haul up, hike up, jack up, jerk up, lift up, move up, perk up, praise, prefer, refine, uphold, uplift **7** advance, dignify, enhance, ennoble, further, glorify, hearten, improve, inspire, magnify, promote, raise up, upgrade, upheave, upraise **8** heighten, levitate, nominate **9** intensify, transport
elevated: **4** high, tall **5** grand, great, lofty, moral, noble **6** aerial, alpine, high up, superb **7** eminent, ethical, exalted, soaring, stately, sublime, uprisen **8** empyreal, empyrean, rarefied, towering, upraised, virtuous **9** dignified, honorable, righteous **10** high-minded, upstanding
area: **4** mesa **5** ridge **7** plateau **8** highland
dwelling: **4** aery, eyry **5** aerie, eyrie **9** tree house
elevation: **4** hill, hump, rise, side **5** boost, knoll, level, raise, ridge **6** ascent, glacis, height, zenith **7** hillock, plateau, rampart, stature **8** altitude, eminence, grandeur, mountain, nobility, platform **9** acclivity, loftiness, promotion, sublimity, upgrading **10** apotheosis, exaltation, high ground, levitation, preferment, prominence
elevator: **4** lift, shoe **5** hoist
alternative: **5** stair **9** escalator
button: **2** up **4** down, stop **8** door open **9** door close
compartment: **3** cab, car
contents: **5** grain, wheat
inventor: **4** Otis
music: **5** Muzak
passage: **5** shaft
sound: **5** whish
stop: **4** deck **5** floor, level, story **6** cellar **9** mezzanine
take the ~: **4** go up, rise **5** climb **6** ascend
elevator __: **3** car **4** shoe
__ elevator: **5** grain **7** service
élève
locale: **5** école, lycée
__ Eleven: **6** Ocean's **7** Chapter
elevenses: **3** tea
eleventh-day gift: **6** pipers
eleventh-hour: **4** late **5** tardy **7** belated, delayed, overdue **10** behind time, last-minute, unpunctual
elf: **3** fay, hob, imp **4** nixy, peri, pixy **5** faery, fairy, gnome, nisse, nixie, ouphe, pixie **6** faerie, goblin, kobold, sprite **7** brownie, gremlin **8** toymaker **9** hobgoblin **10** leprechaun
ender: **4** lock
product: **3** toy
Elf (2003 film)
cast: Edward Asner, James Caan, Zooey Deschanel, Will Ferrell
elfin: **3** fey **6** impish, little, petite **7** puckish **8** prankish **9** fairylike, sprightly, undersize **10** diminutive, leprechaun
elfish: **5** small **6** impish **8** spritely
Elfman: **5** Danny, Jenna
Elfman, Jenna: **7** actress
TV: Dharma & Greg
E.L. Fudge
alternative: ***see*** cookie brand
Elg: **5** Taina
Elgar, Edward: **7** British **8** composer
work: The Apostles
The Black Knight
Cockaigne
Coronation Ode
Enigma Variations
The Kingdom
Pomp and Circumstance
Elgart: **3** Les **5** Larry
Elgin: **4** city, town **5** watch **6** Baylor
alternative: ***see*** wristwatch
locale: **8** Illinois
Elgin Marbles
locale: **6** Athens
El Greco: **6** artist **7** painter
birthplace: **5** Crete **6** Candia
home: **5** Spain **6** Toledo
museum: **5** Prado
Eli: **4** Bush **5** Lilly, Terry, Yalie **7** Bulldog, Manning, Wallach, Whitney
cheer: **5** boola
rival: **6** Cantab
Elia: **4** Lamb **5** Kazan
product: **5** essay
Elias: **4** Howe **5** Corey **7** Canetti
elicit: **3** get, pry **4** draw, milk **5** cause, educe, evoke, fetch **6** arouse, derive, dig out, obtain, prompt, recall **7** draw out, extract, get from, provoke, trigger **8** bring out, occasion **9** call forth **10** bring forth
elide: **4** omit, slur **5** blend **6** delete, excise, ignore **7** abridge, curtail **8** cut short, leave out, pass over, slur over, suppress **9** gloss over, slide over, strike out, syncopate
Elie: **4** Abel, Saab **6** Wiesel **8** Ducommun, Nadelman
Eliel's son: **4** Eero
Eliezer
parent: **5** Moses **8** Zipporah
eligible: **3** fit **5** unwed **6** in line, single, suited, vested, worthy **8** wifeless **9** qualified, unmarried **10** acceptable, employable, privileged
make ~: **6** enable, permit **7** empower, entitle, intitle, qualify **8** christen **9** authorize, designate, privilege **10** legitimize
Eligius: **5** saint
Elihu: **4** Root, Yale
friend: **3** Job
Elijah: **4** Wood **5** McCoy **8** Muhammad
anathema for ~: **4** Baal
in Russian: **4** Ilya
in the Douay: **5** Elias
Elijah's __: **3** cup **5** chair
Elimelech
wife: **5** Naomi
eliminate: **2** ax **3** axe, lop, rid **4** dele, drop, omit, oust, slay, x out **5** clear, eject, erase, evict, expel, purge **6** cancel, cut out, defeat, delete, efface, put out, reject, remove, screen, uproot **7** blot out, cast out, discard, dismiss, exclude, rule out, scratch, take out, wipe out **8** count out, drive out, get rid of, knock out, leave out, phase out, stamp out, throw out **9** close down, discharge, dispose of, disregard, eradicate, extirpate, liquidate, polish off, terminate **10** annihilate, disqualify, do away with, extinguish, invalidate
elimination: **3** ebb **4** test **5** letup **6** fading, relief, waning **7** anodyne, decline **8** decrease, quelling, stoppage **9** abatement, abolition, annulment, deduction, lessening, reduction, tempering, weakening **10** arrestment, diminution, prevention, subsidence
Eliminator
artist: ZZ Top
Elinor: **4** Glyn **5** Wylie **7** Donahue
Elio: **5** Petri **6** Chacon **8** Fiorucci
__ Eli Olds: **6** Ransom
Elion, Gertrude: **8** Nobelist
Eliot: **2** T.S. **4** Ness **6** George **7** Janeway
Eliot, George: **5** alias **6** writer **7** British
homeland: England
real last name: Evans
work: Adam Bede
Daniel Deronda
Felix Holt
Middlemarch
The Mill on the Floss
The Radical
Romola
Silas Marner
__ Eliot Morison: **6** Samuel
Eliot, T.S.: **4** poet **6** writer **7** British **8** Nobelist **10** playwright
birthplace: **7** St. Louis
colleague: Ezra Pound
first name: **6** Thomas
middle name: **7** Stearns
work: Ash Wednesday
Aunt Helen
The Cocktail Party
A Cooking Egg
The Family Reunion
The Hollow Men
The Love Song of J. Alfred Prufrock
Murder in the Cathedral
Portrait of a Lady
The Sacred Wood
The Waste Land
Eliphaz
parent: **4** Adah, Esau
Elis
see Yale
Elisabeth: **4** Shue
Eli's Coming (1969 song)
artist: Three Dog Night
Elise: **4** Neal **8** Kimberly **9** Christine
__ Elise: **3** Für
Eliseo: **5** Diego
Elisha: **4** Cook, Otis
Elisheba
husband: **5** Aaron
Elissa: **4** Dido **5** Landi
elite: **3** top **4** best, font, pick, type **5** A-list, cream, haves, noble, prime, upper **6** aristo, choice, chosen, flower, gentry, jet set, select, tip-top **7** favored, in crowd, in-group, society **8** literati, nobility, old money, selected, top-class, top-notch **9** blue blood, exclusive, gilt-edged, haut monde, highbrows, high-class, top drawer, topflight **10** blue bloods, first-class, glitterati, illuminati, main liners, privileged, upper-class, upper crust, world-class
alternative: ***see*** point size
__ elite: **5** power
Elite: **3** car, Reo **4** auto, font **8** typeface
Elite Syncopations: **3** rag

elitist: **4** snob **7** pompous **8** highbrow **10** high-hatter
elixir: **4** cure **5** tonic **6** liquid, liquor, nectar, potion, remedy **7** arcanum, cure-all, nostrum, panacea **8** medicine, pick-me-up, solution **10** invigorant, medication
__ Eli Yale: **5** Bingo
Eliza: **6** Dushku **9** Doolittle
composer: Thomas Arne
where ~ urged Dover: **5** Ascot
Elizabeth: **4** city, Dole, Peña, town **5** Allen, Arden, Bowen, Kenny, queen, ruler, Seton **6** Ashley, Hurley, Jolley, Taylor **7** Berkley, Hartman, Perkins, Shannon **8** Gilbreth, McGovern **9** Blackwell **10** Montgomery
in Germany: **4** Ilse
in Spanish: **6** Isabel
locale: **9** New Jersey
Elizabeth __ Browning: **7** Barrett
Elizabeth __ Seton: **3** Ann
Elizabeth __ Stanton: **4** Cady
Elizabethan: **3** Age, Era **6** sonnet
epithet: **4** Bess
Elizabeth and __: **5** Essex
Elizabeth Appleton
author: John O'Hara
Elizabeth Arden: **6** makeup
alternative: *see* cosmetic brand
Elizabeth I: **5** queen, royal, ruler, Tudor
father: **5** Henry
mother: **6** Boleyn
Elizabeth II: **5** queen, royal, ruler **7** Windsor
award bestowed by ~: **3** OBE
child: **4** Anne **6** Andrew, Edward **7** Charles
father: **6** George
spouse: **6** Philip
to Edward VIII: **5** niece
Elizabeth II, Queen: **4** boat, ship **5** liner
milieu for ~: **3** sea **5** ocean
__ Elizabeth Mastrantonio: **4** Mary
Elizabeth the Queen
author: Maxwell Anderson
Elizondo, Hector: **5** actor
TV: Chicago Hope
elk: **4** deer **6** animal, mammal, wapiti
ender: **5** hound
feature: **4** horn **6** antler
female: **3** cow
male: **4** bull
relative: *see* deer
young: **4** calf
Elk: **5** range, river
city on the ~: **10** Charleston
Elke: **6** Sommer
Elk Grove: **4** city, town
locale: **8** Illinois
Elkhart: **4** city, town
locale: **7** Indiana
elkhound: **3** dog **5** canid **6** canine
Elkins: **5** Aaron
Elkin, Stanley: **6** writer
Elko: **4** city, town
locale: **6** Nevada
Elks: **4** BPOE **5** lodge
Elkton: **4** city, town
locale: **8** Maryland
ell: **4** wing **5** annex, joint **8** addition
build an ~: **5** add on
Ella: **5** Joyce, Logan **6** Grasso, Raines **7** Cinders **10** Fitzgerald
contemporary: **4** Lena
specialty: **4** scat
Ella Enchanted (2004 film)
cast: Cary Elwes, Vivica A. Fox, Anne Hathaway
Ellas: **6** Greece
elle: **3** she **6** French
Elle: **3** mag **5** model **10** Macpherson
rival: **5** Cosmo, Vogue
Elle et lui
author: George Sand
Ellen: **4** Drew, Page **5** Corby, Terry **6** Barkin, Greene, Pompeo **7** Burstyn, Glasgow, Goodman **9** Cleghorne, DeGeneres
in French: **6** Elaine
in Italian: **5** Elena
in Russian: **6** Yelena
in Spanish: **5** Elena
__-Ellen: **4** Vera
__ Ellen Ewing: **3** Sue
Eller: **4** aunt
Ellerbee: **5** Linda
Ellery
colleague: **3** Rex **4** Erle **6** Agatha
Ellesmere: **4** isle **6** island
Ellie: **5** Ewing **6** Kemper **9** Greenwich
to J.R.: **4** mama
Ellie __: **4** Rhee
Elliman, Yvonne
song: If I Can't Have You (1978)
Ellington: **4** Duke **6** Mercer
contemporary: **5** Basie **9** Armstrong
Ellington, Duke: **6** Edward **7** pianist
genre: **4** jazz
Ellio's: **5** pizza
alternative: **5** Jeno's, Tony's **7** Celeste, Totino's **8** DiGiorno **9** Tombstone **10** Freschetta
Elliot: **4** Cass **8** Mama Cass
Elliott: **3** Bob, Sam **4** Cass **5** Chris, Gould, Missy **6** Nugent **7** Denholm **8** Mama Cass
Elliott, Missy
song: Get Ur Freak On (2001)
Hot Boyz (1999)
Make It Hot (1998)
Not Tonight (1997)
One Minute Man (2001)
Trippin' (1998)
Elliott, Sam: **5** actor
spouse: Katharine Ross
ellipse: **5** curve, orbit **9** sinuosity
part: **3** arc
ellipsis component: **3** dot
elliptic: **4** oval **5** ovoid **9** egg-shaped
elliptical: **4** oval **5** ovate, ovoid, round, terse **6** curved, oblong **7** egglike **9** egg-shaped **10** oval-shaped
Ellis: **4** Bell, isle **5** Burks, Jimmy, Perry **6** island **7** Shirley **8** Havelock, Marsalis, Patricia
Island locale: **3** NYC
Ellison: **5** James, Ralph **6** Harlan
Ellison, Harlan: **6** writer
genre: **5** sci-fi
Ellison, Ralph: **6** writer
work: Going to the Territory
Invisible Man
Shadow and Act
Ellis, Shirley
song: The Clapping Song (1965)
The Name Game (1965)
The Nitty Gritty (1963)
Ellsberg: **6** Daniel
Elly __ Clampett: **3** May
elm: **4** tree, wych **8** hardwood **9** shade tree
fruit: **6** samara
tree: **7** zelkova **9** hackberry
Elm: **2** st. **6** street
Elman: **5** Ziggy **6** Mischa
Elman, Mischa: **7** Russian **9** violinist
Elm City collegian: **3** Eli **5** Yalie **7** Bulldog
__ elm disease: **5** Dutch
Elmer: **4** Fudd, Rice, Valo **5** Flick **6** Gantry, Sperry **9** Bernstein, Nordstrom
mate: **5** Elsie
to Bugs: **3** doc
Elmer Gantry: **4** film **5** novel
author: Sinclair Lewis
cast: Shirley Jones, Burt Lancaster
Elmer's __: **4** Glue, Tune
Elmhurst: **4** city, town
locale: **8** Illinois
Elmira: **4** city, town
locale: **7** New York
El Misti: **7** volcano
fallout: **3** ash
locale: **4** Peru **5** Andes
Elmo: **5** Roper, saint **6** Muppet **7** Lincoln, Zumwalt
on Eek the Cat: **3** elk
street: **6** Sesame
El Monte: **4** city, town
locale: **10** California
Elmore: **7** Leonard
__ Elmo's fire: **5** Saint
Elmwood Park: **4** city, town
locale: **8** Illinois
ELO
song: Don't Bring Me Down (1979)
Evil Woman (1975)
Hold on Tight (1981)
Shine a Little Love (1979)
Telephone Line (1977)
Xanadu (1980)
elocution: **5** voice **6** speech **7** diction, oratory **8** delivery, rhetoric, verbiage **9** eloquence, utterance **10** expression, vocalizing
elocutionist: **6** orator
eloge: **6** eulogy **8** encomium **9** panegyric
elohim: **3** God **7** Creator, Jehovah
eloign: **4** flee **5** elope, leave **6** beat it, decamp, desert, escape, go AWOL, run off **7** abscond, duck out, run away, vamoose **9** cut and run, disappear, skedaddle, sneak away, steal away **10** fly the coop, make a break
Eloisa to Abelard
author: Alexander Pope
Eloise's dog: **6** Weenie
Elon
son-in-law: **4** Esau
elongate: **6** extend **7** enlarge, lengthy, stretch **8** lengthen **9** string out
elongated: **7** lengthy **8** drawn out, expanded, extended
shape: **4** oval **7** ellipse
elongation: **4** limb, wing **5** annex **6** branch, growth, length **7** adjunct **8** addition, appendix, increase, widening **9** appendage, expansion, extension, inflation **10** attachment, distension, perpetuity, projection, stretching, supplement
elongator: **5** stilt
elope: **3** run **4** bolt, flee **5** leave **6** decamp, escape, run off **7** abscond, run away, take off **8** skip town, slip away, sneak off **9** steal away
eloper: **5** lover, Romeo **6** Juliet **8** lothario **9** inamorato
need: **2** JP **6** ladder
of rhyme: **4** dish **5** spoon
eloquence: **4** rhet. **7** diction, fluency, oratory **8** facility, rhetoric **9** elocution, gift of gab, loquacity, readiness, wittiness **10** expression, volubility
eloquent: **4** glib **5** vivid, vocal **6** fluent, moving **7** graphic **8** poignant, readable, stirring, touching **9** graphical, talkative **10** articulate, expressive, impressive, meaningful, oratorical, passionate, persuasive, rhetorical
wax ~: **3** act **4** gush **5** orate **7** carry on, overact, perform, playact **9** dramatize
El Paso: **4** city, town
athletes: **6** Miners **9** Longhorns
campus: **4** UTEP
fort: **5** Bliss
locale: **5** Texas
river: **9** Rio Grande
El Paso (1959 song)
artist: Marty Robbins
__ El Paso: **3** Old
El Prado: **5** museo **6** museum
Elroy: **6** Hirsch, Jetson
pet: **5** Astro
Els: **5** Ernie
Elsa: **7** Klensch, lioness, Maxwell, Morante, Peretti **10** Lanchester, Martinelli
dad: **4** lion
raiser: **7** Adamson
El Salón Mexico
composer: Aaron Copland
El Salvador: **6** nation **7** country
city: **5** Apopa **8** Santa Ana **9** Mejicanos, San Miguel, Soyapango
currency: **5** colón
Indian: **5** Lenca
neighbor: **8** Honduras **9** Guatemala
org.: **3** OAS
see also Spanish
Elsa's Dream: **4** aria
else: **4** more **5** if not, other **7** besides, further, instead **9** different, otherwise **10** additional, in addition
before anything ~: **5** first **6** maiden, mainly **7** chiefly, initial, leading, lead-off, opening, pioneer, premier, to start **8** above all, earliest, foremost, original **9** in advance, inaugural, initially, primarily, primitive, prototype **10** originally
ender: **5** where
everything ~: **4** rest **9** remainder
nothing ~ but: **5** fully **6** really, wholly
or ~: **9** otherwise
or ~ in music: **5** ossia
something ~: **4** neat **5** doozy, grand, novel, other **6** marvel,

unique 7 another, unusual 9 wonderful
somewhere ~: 4 away, gone 6 absent
__ else fails...: 5 If all
Els, Ernie: 6 golfer
milieu: 5 links 6 course
org.: 3 PGA
elsewhere: 3 off, out 4 away, gone 5 not in 6 abroad, absent 7 missing, not here 8 vanished 9 out of here 10 on vacation
direct ~: 5 refer
Elsie: 3 cow 5 Janis 8 Dinsmore
comment from ~: 3 low, moo
spouse: 5 Elmer
Elsie Venner
author: Oliver Wendell Holmes
Elton: 4 John
eluant: 7 solvent
Éluard, Paul: 4 poet 6 French
elucidate: 4 show 5 gloss, solve, state 6 set out, unfold 7 clarify, clear up, explain, resolve 8 describe, illumine, simplify, spell out 9 bring home, enlighten, exemplify, explicate, expound on, get across, interpret, make plain, translate 10 account for, illuminate, illustrate
elucidation: 5 gloss, light 7 comment 8 exegesis, solution
elude: 4 defy, duck, flee, foil, lose, shun 5 avoid, dodge, evade, parry, shake, shirk, skirt 6 baffle, escape, eschew, outrun, outwit, thwart 7 mystify, retreat 8 confound, get out of, shake off, sidestep, slip past, throw off 9 frustrate, get around 10 circumvent, get clear of
Elul: 5 month 6 Hebrew
predecessor: 2 Av
successor: 6 Tishri
elusive: 3 sly 4 cagy, eely 5 cagey 6 shifty, tricky 7 evasive, furtive 8 baffling, puzzling, slippery 9 deceitful, deceptive 10 intangible, mysterious
one: 3 eel 6 dodger
elute: 7 extract, wash out
elver: 3 eel 4 fish 5 moray 8 glass eel
Elvin: 5 Hayes, Jones 6 Bishop
Elvira (1981 song)
artist: Oak Ridge Boys
Elvis: 4 idol 6 Stojko 7 Presley 8 Costello
daughter: 4 Lisa
like ~ ' shoes: 4 blue 5 suede
recording: 4 oldy 5 oldie
elvish: 5 short, small 6 impish
Elway, John: 2 QB 11 quarterback
sport: 8 football
Elwes, Cary: 5 actor
film: Glory (1989)
Hot Shots! (1991)
Kiss the Girls (1997)
Lady Jane (1985)
The Princess Bride (1987)
Robin Hood: Men in Tights (1993)
Twister (1996)
Elwood: 4 Dowd
friend: 5 pooka 6 Harvey, rabbit
Ely: 3 Joe, Ron 4 city, isle, town 10 Culbertson
locale: 3 Nev. 6 Nevada
Elyria: 4 city, town
locale: 4 Ohio

__ Élysées: 6 Champs
elysian: 8 beatific, empyreal, empyrean 9 ambrosial, celestial
Elysian Fields: 6 utopia
Elysium: 4 Eden 6 heaven 7 Nirvana, rapture, Valhall, Walhall 8 paradise, Valhalla, Walhalla 9 Shangri-la
Elytis, Odysseus: 4 poet 5 Greek 6 writer 8 Nobelist
em: 3 ltr. 6 letter
follower: 2 en
preceder: 2 el
em __: 4 dash, pica, quad
__ 'em: 3 sic 4 hold
Em
to Dorothy: 4 aunt
E.M.: 7 Forster
emaciate: 5 dry up 6 wither 7 atrophy, shrivel 9 waste away 10 degenerate
emaciated: 4 bony, lank, lean, puny, thin 5 boney, gaunt 6 ill-fed, meager, peaked, skinny 7 haggard, starved 8 starving, underfed 9 atrophied 10 attenuated
e-mag: 5 Slate 7 webzine
e-mail: 3 msg. 4 memo 7 message
address part: 3 com, dot, edu, org
alternative: 3 fax 6 letter
ancestor: 5 telex
angry ~: 5 flame
command: 4 send 5 reply
guffaw: 3 LOL
header: 4 from
need: 5 modem
nuisance: 4 spam
prepare to check ~: 5 log in
server: 3 AOL
emanate: 4 emit, flow, gush, rise, spew, spue, stem 5 arise, eject, expel, exude, issue 6 derive, effuse, spring 7 cast out, diffuse, give off, proceed, radiate 8 flow from, throw off 9 arise from, come forth, discharge, originate, send forth
emanation: 4 aura, beam, flow, glow, gush, odor, vibe 5 aroma, light, smell, vibes 6 efflux, oozing 7 arising, flowing, gushing, issuing, outflow 8 effluent, emerging, issuance 9 beginning, discharge, effluence, emergence, exudation, radiation 10 derivation, exhalation
emancipate: 4 free, save 5 loose 6 loosen, redeem 7 deliver, manumit, release 8 liberate 9 unshackle 10 disenthral
emancipation: 7 freedom, liberty, release 8 delivery 9 salvation
emancipator: 6 savior 7 saviour
__ 'em and weep: 4 read
Emanuel: 2 Ax 4 Rahm 6 Lasker, Leutze 10 Swedenborg
embank: 4 dike 5 guard 6 defend, secure, shield 7 protect
embankment: 3 dam 4 berm, dike, wall 5 berme, levee, mound, shore 6 escarp 7 defense, landing, rampart 10 breakwater
build an ~: 5 revet
embar: 5 block 6 hinder, lock up 8 imprison
embargo: 3 ban, bar 4 stop, veto 6 forbid, outlaw 7 barrier, boycott, exclude 8 blockage, disallow, sanction 9 exclusion, interdict, restraint 10 keeping out
Embargo, The
author: William Cullen Bryant
embark: 2 go 4 sail, ship 5 begin, leave, start 6 set off, set out 7 emplane, entrain, head out, jump off, set sail, ship out, take off 8 approach, go aboard, set forth, start off 9 get to work, leave port, undertake
on: 5 begin, enter 6 assume, launch, tackle 8 commence
embarkation: 5 start 6 origin
embarked: 6 aboard 7 en route, on board 9 in transit, traveling
embarrass: 3 vex 4 faze 5 abash, shame 6 humble, rattle, show up, unglue 7 chagrin, fluster, mortify, nonplus 9 discomfit, dumbfound, humiliate 10 compromise, demoralize, discomfort, discompose, disconcert, disgruntle
embarrassed: 3 red 6 ablush 7 abashed, bashful 8 blushing, red-faced, sheepish
embarrassing: 6 sticky, touchy 7 awkward 8 delicate, ticklish 9 offensive
episode: 5 gaffe, scene 7 faux pas
embarrassment: 5 shame 6 fiasco, strait, unease 7 chagrin, faux pas, scandal 8 distress 9 abashment
exclamation of ~: 4 oops 6 whoops
show ~: 5 blush 6 redden
embarrassment of __: 6 riches
embassy: 7 mission 8 legation 9 consulate, residence
at times: 6 asylum
worker: 3 amb. 4 aide 6 consul, legate
embattle: 3 arm 5 beset, equip 7 besiege, fortify 8 mobilize 10 militarize
embay: 8 surround
embed: 3 fix, put, set 4 bury, nest, root, sink 5 imbue, infix, inlay, lodge, plant, stick 6 insert, instal, thrust 7 deposit, drive in, engrain, implant, ingrain, install, stuff in 8 hammer in, thrust in
embedded: 3 set 4 firm, hard 5 dense, fixed, inset 6 nailed, rooted, steely, welded 7 adamant, secured 8 anchored, cemented, concrete, fastened, hardened, hard-line, ironclad 9 condensed, screwed in, tightened 10 compressed, deep-rooted, stationary
embellish: 4 deck, do up, gild, trim 5 adorn, array, color, fudge, grace 6 bedeck, blazon, detail, enrich, expand, jazz up 7 dress up, encrust, enhance, festoon, flatter, garnish, gussy up, incrust, magnify, spiff up, varnish 8 beautify, brighten, decorate, misquote, ornament, spruce up 9 elaborate, embroider, glamorize, overstate 10 exaggerate, illustrate
embellished: 4 tall 5 fancy, showy 6 flashy, florid, frilly, glitzy, lavish, ornate 7 flowery, opulent 9 decorated, elaborate, garnished, luxurious, sumptuous
embellishment: 4 note, trim 5 frill 6 fillip 7 garnish, gilding, roulade 8 flourish, froufrou, ornament 9 adornment
ember: 3 ash 4 coal 6 cinder 7 hot coal
embezzle: 3 rob 4 loot 5 filch, steal 6 pilfer, thieve 7 purloin 8 peculate 9 defalcate
embezzlement: 5 theft 6 misuse 7 larceny 8 filching, skimming, stealing
embezzler: 5 thief
dread: 3 aud. 5 audit
embitter: 4 sour 5 anger, upset 6 rankle 7 envenom 8 acerbate, alienate, irritate 9 acidulate, aggravate, disaffect, frustrate 10 disappoint
embittering: 7 onerous
emblazon: 4 deck, do up, trim 5 adorn, color 6 jazz up 7 display, gussy up 8 beautify, brighten, decorate, ornament, spruce up
emblem: 3 tag 4 flag, logo, mark, seal, sign 5 badge, crest, patch, stamp, token, totem 6 banner, device, ensign, figure, symbol 7 imprint, insigne, pennant 8 colophon, hallmark, heraldry, insignia, standard 9 adumbrate, trademark 10 coat of arms, decoration, fleur-de-lis
in heraldry: 6 device
emblematic: 5 typic 6 iconic 7 typical 8 iconical, symbolic 10 figurative, indicative, symbolical
...emblem of the __ love: 5 land I
embodied: 4 real 8 tangible 9 incarnate, touchable
embodiment: 4 form 5 image, model, shape 6 avatar, symbol 7 epitome, example, picture 8 exemplar, specimen 9 archetype, formation 10 apotheosis, collection, expression
embody: 4 have 5 cover, merge, shape, unite 6 codify, typify 7 combine, contain, express, include 8 comprise, manifest, organize, stand for 9 encompass, exemplify, integrate, personify, represent, symbolize 10 amalgamate, assimilate, constitute, illustrate
embog: 4 mire 6 bemire
embolden: 4 abet, buoy, goad, spur, stir 5 boost, cheer, rouse, steel 6 arouse, buck up, stir up 7 fortify, hearten, inspire, psych up 8 energize, enspirit, inspirit, motivate, psyche up 9 encourage, enhearten 10 invigorate, revitalize, strengthen
embonpoint: 3 big 5 large, obese 9 corpulent 10 well-padded
emboss: 5 carve, raise 7 encrust, impress, incrust 8 decorate, ornament
embossing tool: 4 seal
embouchure: 3 lip, rim 5 mouth
embow: 4 arch
embrace: 3 hug 4 grip, hold, lock, love 5 admit, adopt, clasp, cling, cover, crush, greet, let in, press, seize, touch 6 accept, caress, choose, clinch, clutch, cuddle,

enfold, infold, nuzzle, take in, take on, take up **7** contain, enclose, espouse, inclose, include, involve, squeeze, welcome **8** comprise, deal with, encircle, surround **9** encompass, keep close
Embraceable You
composer: George Gershwin, Ira Gershwin
Embraced by the Light
author: Betty Eadie
__-embracing: 3 all
embrasure: 6 recess
embrocate: 3 oil **5** apply **6** anoint **9** lubricate
embrocation: 6 lotion **8** lenitive, liniment, ointment
embroider: 3 sew **4** deck, gild, trim **5** color, fudge **6** bedeck, blow up, overdo, play up, puff up, stitch **7** falsify, gussy up, lay it on, magnify **8** beautify, decorate, misquote, ornament **9** dramatize, elaborate, embellish, overstate **10** aggrandize, exaggerate
maybe: 3 fib, lie **7** falsity, untruth **9** falsehood, mendacity **10** taradiddle
embroidered: 6 ornate
embroidery: 5 craft **6** crewel **9** adornment, arabesque **10** decoration, needlework
archaic ~: 5 brede
loop: 5 picot
purchase: 5 spool **6** needle, thread **10** pin cushion
thread: 5 floss
trim: 6 eyelet
embroil: 4 mire **5** snarl **6** enmesh, entrap, immesh, inmesh, tangle **7** ensnare, insnare, involve, quarrel **8** entangle
embryo: 3 egg **4** germ, seed **5** fetus, ovule **6** foetus **7** nucleus **8** rudiment
ender: 7 genesis
membrane: 6 amnion
nourishment for an ~: 4 yolk
embryology: 7 science
embryonic: 5 early, fetal **6** foetal, little **7** initial **8** evolving, germinal, immature, original **9** incipient, potential
area: 6 anlage
emcee: 4 host **9** officiate **10** auctioneer, ringmaster
jointly: 6 cohost
line: 5 intro
need: 3 mic **4** mike
place: 4 dais **6** podium **7** lectern, rostrum **8** platform
quiz show ~: 5 asker
__ 'em, cowboy: 4 Ride
Emden: 4 city, port, town
locale: 7 Germany
emeer: 4 Arab **5** Osman, ruler **6** leader, Othman, prince **7** Kuwaiti **8** kingfish **9** chieftain, commander, potentate
emend: 3 fix **4** edit, mend **5** right **6** redact, reform, repair, revise **7** correct, improve, rectify, touch up **10** fiddle with
emendation: 6 change **7** editing, rewrite **8** revision **9** polishing, redaction **10** alteration, correction
emerald: 3 gem **5** beryl, color, green, jewel, virid **6** grassy **7** mineral **8** gemstone
alternative: ***see*** point size
ersatz ~: 5 paste
month: 3 May
name meaning ~: 9 Esmeralda
relative: ***see*** green color **10** aquamarine
surface: 5 facet
Emerald __: 4 City, Isle
Emerald City
visitor: 4 lion, Toto **6** Tin Man **7** Dorothy **9** scarecrow
Emerald Isle: 4 Eire, Erin **7** Ireland
from the ~: 5 Irish
Emerald Point __: 3 NAS
emerge: 4 dawn, exit, loom, peep, peer, rise, show **5** arise, begin, bob up, break, pop up, spirt, spurt **6** appear, crop up, fade in, loom up, result, spring, sprout, stream **7** come out, develop, peep out, surface **8** break out, spring up, stand out **9** come forth, grow out of, originate, transpire **10** issue forth
as: 6 become
(from): 4 come
emergence: 4 dawn, rise **5** birth **6** origin **7** genesis, infancy **9** emanation **10** appearance, incipience
emergency: 4 need, pass **5** event, pinch, spare **6** crisis, crunch, plight, strait **7** stopgap, straits **8** exigence, exigency, juncture, meltdown, zero hour **9** crossroad, extremity, necessity **10** compulsion, difficulty, occurrence
fund: 7 nest egg, reserve
money: 5 scrip
signal: 3 SOS **5** alarm, flare, siren
worker: 3 EMT **5** medic **9** paramedic
emergency __: 4 boat, exit, room **5** brake
Emergency (NBC drama)
cast: Robert Fuller (Dr. Kelly Brackett)
Julie London (Dixie McCall)
Randolph Mantooth (John Gage)
Kevin Tighe (Roy DeSoto)
Bobby Troup (Dr. Joe Early)
dog: 5 Boots
producer: Jack Webb
Emeril: 7 Lagasse
Emeril exclamation: 3 bam
emeritus: 3 ret. **4** retd. **5** title **7** retired **9** professor
Emerson: 2 TV **3** Roy **4** Faye **5** TV set **10** Fittipaldi, television
alternative: ***see*** electronics company
Emerson, __ and Palmer: 4 Lake
Emerson, Ralph Waldo: 4 poet **6** writer **8** essayist
alma mater: Harvard
essay topic: 3 art
hometown: Boston
work: May-Day
Nature
Self-Reliance
Emerson, Roy: 7 netster **9** tennis pro
milieu: 5 court
emery: 7 mineral **8** abrasive, corundum
board: 4 file
emery __: 5 board, cloth, wheel
émeute: 4 riot **6** tumult **8** outbreak, uprising, violence
EMF unit: 4 volt
__ 'em High: 4 Hang
EMI: 5 label
emigrant: 5 alien **7** refugee **8** colonist **10** expatriate
emigrate: 5 leave **6** depart **7** migrate **10** transplant
emigration: 6 exodus, moving **8** trekking **9** departure **10** relocation, resettling
émigré: 5 exile **7** refugee **9** foreigner **10** expatriate
hope: 6 asylum
Emil: 5 Sitka **6** Gilels, Kocher, Ludwig, Scaria **7** Zátopek **8** Jannings **10** von Behring
Emile: 6 Hirsch **7** Francis **8** Ardolino, Berliner, de Becque, Griffith
see also French
Émile: 4 Zola
see also French
Emilia
creator: 11 Shakespeare
husband: 4 Iago
work featuring ~: 7 Othello
Émilie: 6 Dionne
Emilio: 5 Pucci, Segrè **7** Estefan, Estevez **8** Pericoli
Emily: 4 Post **5** Balch, Blunt, Lloyd **6** Brontë **7** Saliers **9** Deschanel, Dickinson
to Charlotte: 3 sis
Eminem: 6 rapper
eminence: 4 fame, hill, name, note, rise **5** éclat, glory, honor, title **6** esteem, height, leader, renown, repute, status, zenith **7** dignity, stature, success **8** altitude, grandeur, luminary, mountain, nobility, prestige, standing **9** authority, celebrity, elevation, greatness, loftiness, magnitude, personage **10** high ground, importance, kingliness, notability, prominence, reputation
__ eminence: 4 gray, grey
Éminence __: 5 grise
eminent: 3 big **4** high, loft **5** famed, grand, great, noble, noted, upper **6** august, famous **7** big-name, big-time, exalted, notable, storied **8** elevated, esteemed, glorious, immortal, renowned, singular, splendid, superior **9** big-league, dignified, honorable, important, prominent, topflight, well-known **10** celebrated
eminent __: 6 domain
eminently: 7 greatly **9** extremely **10** especially, remarkably, strikingly
emir: 4 Arab **5** Osman, ruler **6** gerent, leader, Othman, prince **7** Kuwaiti **8** kingfish **9** chieftain, commander, potentate
emirate: 5 Ajman, Dibai, Dubai, Katar, Qatar **6** Kuwait
resident: 4 Arab **6** Qatari **7** Kuwaiti
emissary: 3 amb., spy **5** agent, envoy **6** bearer, consul, deputy, legate, nuncio **7** carrier, courier **8** delegate, diplomat **9** appointee, go-between, messenger, negotiant **10** ambassador, interceder
emission: 5 issue **6** efflux **7** venting **8** ejection, issuance **9** discharge, effluence, exudation, radiation **10** exhalation
emissions watchdog: 3 EPA
emit: 4 beam, gush, ooze, pour, reek, send, shed, spew, spue, vent, void **5** eject, eruct, erupt, expel, exude, issue, loose, shine, shoot, sound, spill, spout **6** effuse, evolve, exhale, let off, put out, squirt, stream **7** cast out, diffuse, emanate, extrude, give off, give out, radiate, release, secrete, send out **8** shoot out, throw off, throw out **9** broadcast, cast forth, discharge, give forth, send forth
coherent light: 4 lase
EMK: 3 sen., Ted **7** Kennedy
Emlyn: 8 Williams
Emma: 4 Peel **5** Calvé, Eames, Samms **6** Bovary, Bunton, Lathen **7** Goldman, Lazarus, Roberts, Tennant, Willard **8** Hamilton, Thompson **9** Woodhouse
author: Jane Austen
portrayer: 3 Uma **5** Diana
successor on The Avengers: 4 Tara
Emma (1996 film)
cast: Toni Collette, Jeremy Northam, Gwyneth Paltrow, Greta Scacchi
Emmanuel: 5 Lewis **9** Rosenthal
Emmanuelle: 5 Béart
Emmeline: 9 Pankhurst
Emmenthaler: 5 Swiss **6** cheese
Emmerich: 4 Noah **6** Roland
emmet: 3 ant, bug **6** insect **7** pismire
Emmett: 5 Kelly
Emmitt: 5 Smith
Emmy: 5 award **6** Rossum
Emmylou: 6 Harris
Emo: 7 Philips
emollient: 4 aloe, balm **5** cream, salve **6** lotion **7** lenient, unction, unguent **8** balsamic, lenitive, liniment, ointment, soothing **9** demulcent
emolument: 3 fee, pay **4** tips, wage **5** wages **6** income, profit, salary **7** payment, revenue, stipend **8** benefice, earnings, gratuity **10** honorarium, recompense
Emona: 4 font **8** typeface
Emory University site: 7 Atlanta, Georgia
__ E. Mosley: 5 Roger
emote: 3 act **4** gush **7** carry on, enthuse, ham it up, overact, perform, playact **9** dramatize, play a role
for a photo: 3 mug
emoter: 3 ham **5** actor **6** hot dog **7** actress, overact
emotion: 3 awe, ire, joy **4** fear, hate, love, mood, rage, soul, zeal **5** agony, anger, angst, ardor, grief, heart, odium, pique, pride, scorn, shame, spite, wrath **6** animus, bathos, desire, enmity, fervor, hoopla, malice, pathos, rancor, sorrow, spirit, thrill, warmth **7** concern, despair, disgust, ecstasy, elation, empathy, feeling,

ill will, impulse, offense, outrage, passion, remorse, sadness, umbrage **8** acrimony, loathing, lyricism, sympathy, vexation **9** affection, agitation, animosity, antipathy, happiness, intensity, petulance, revulsion, sensation, sentiment, vehemence **10** abhorrence, enthusiasm, excitement, melancholy, repugnance
burst of ~: **5** spasm
combining form: **4** thym- **5** thymo-
feel ~: **5** throb
Hindu ~: **4** rasa
negative ~: **4** rage **5** odium, pique, scorn, spite, wrath **6** animus, enmity, malice, rancor **7** disgust, ill will, offense, outrage, umbrage **8** acrimony, loathing, vexation **9** animosity, antipathy, petulance, revulsion **10** abhorrence, repugnance
outburst of ~: **6** fantod
sans ~: **5** dryly, icily
show ~: **3** cry **4** rage, vent **5** react
touch the ~ of: **4** move **6** affect
emotional: **3** gut **4** warm **5** fiery, inner, mushy, teary **6** ardent, fervid, heated, moving, tender **7** fervent, lyrical, mawkish, nervous, soulful, zealous **8** dramatic, ecstatic, exciting, poignant, stirring, touching, visceral **9** affecting, affective, disturbed, excitable, fanatical, impetuous, impulsive, intuitive, sensitive, thrilling **10** histrionic, hot-blooded, hysterical, irrational, passionate, responsive, subjective
event: **5** drama
heat: **3** ire **4** fury, rage **5** pique, wrath **6** choler, enmity **7** offense, outrage **10** antagonism
onrush: **4** pang **5** throe
outburst: **3** cry, sob **4** bawl, wail, weep **5** scene **6** lament, scream
overly ~: **4** agog **5** gushy, lurid, mushy
tone: **4** mood
Emotional Rescue (1980 song)
artist: Rolling Stones
Emotion in Motion (1986 song)
artist: Ric Ocasek
emotionless: **3** icy **4** cold, cool **5** aloof **6** chilly, remote **7** glacial **9** withdrawn
one: **6** icicle
__ emotions: **5** mixed
Emotions (song)
artist: Mariah Carey, Destiny's Child, Brenda Lee
emotive: **4** avid **8** touching **10** histrionic
empale: **6** pierce **8** transfix
empanada: **9** appetizer
empath
skill: **3** ESP **9** intuition, telepathy
empathetic: **4** warm **6** caring **9** vicarious **10** responsive
empathic: **8** merciful **10** responsive
empathize: **4** grok **5** bleed, mourn **6** grieve, lament, relate, suffer
empathy: **4** pity **7** emotion, rapport **8** affinity, sympathy **9** good vibes **10** compassion, friendship
have ~: **4** care, heed, mind **5** worry **6** regard, regret, relate
7 anguish, concern **8** distress, interest **9** give a darn
lacking ~: **3** icy **4** hard, mean **5** cruel, rigid, rough, stern, tough **6** bitter, brutal, severe, strict, unkind **7** austere, callous, harshly, hostile **8** despotic, grueling, indurate, pitiless, rocklike, ruthless, savagely, severely, stubborn, wearying **9** difficult, insensate, merciless, obstinate, stringent, unbending, unfeeling, unsparing, viciously **10** adamantine, inflexible, pitilessly, relentless, unmerciful, unpleasant
Empedocles on Etna
author: Matthew Arnold
emperor: **4** czar, male, tsar, tzar **5** noble, ruler **6** dynast, gerent, sultan **7** monarch, viceroy **8** dictator, imperial **9** potentate, sovereign
Roman ~: **4** Nero **6** Caesar
Emperor and Galilean
author: Henrik Ibsen
Emperor Concerto
composer: Ludwig van Beethoven
Emperor Jones, The
author: Eugene O'Neill
character: **3** Lem **6** Brutus
Emperor of Ice Cream, The
author: Wallace Stevens
Emperor of the North (1973 film)
cast: Ernest Borgnine, Lee Marvin
Emperor's New Groove, The (2000 film)
voice cast: John Goodman, Eartha Kitt, David Spade
__ Emperor, The: **4** Last
Emperor Waltz
composer: Johann Strauss
empery: **5** realm **6** domain **8** dominion
emphasis: **4** tone **5** force, slant **6** accent, import, stress, weight **8** priority **9** attention, intensity **10** importance, insistence, prominence
exclamation of ~: **3** gee, wow **4** gosh **5** by gum, golly **6** far out **8** by cracky
give ~: **6** accent, play up, stress **7** bracket, feature, point up **9** highlight, italicize, punctuate, reinforce **10** accentuate, underscore
musical ~: **3** sfz. **9** sforzando
emphasize: **5** press, voice **6** accent, assert, harp on, play up, stress **7** dwell on, feature, impress, iterate **8** headline, insist on **9** dramatize, dwell upon, highlight, intensify, italicize, make clear, pronounce, punctuate, reinforce, reiterate, spotlight, underline **10** accentuate, articulate, exaggerate, illustrate, make a point, make much of, underscore
emphatic: **4** firm, loud **6** all-out, strong **7** decided, dynamic, express **8** absolute, accented, definite, explicit, forceful, powerful, resolute, stressed, striking, vehement, vigorous **9** assertive, energetic, insistent, trenchant **10** conclusive, definitive, expressive, pronounced, resounding, unswerving, unwavering, vociferant
be ~: **6** assert, demand, insist
turndown: **5** never, no how, no sir, no way
type: **6** italic **7** italics
emphatically: **4** hard, very **7** greatly
empire: **4** rule, sway **5** realm **6** domain, nation **7** dynasty, kingdom **8** dominion **9** supremacy, territory
ancient ~ builder: **4** Inca, Maya **5** Incan, Mayan
builder: **5** baron, mogul **6** bigwig, tycoon **7** magnate **9** financier, plutocrat **10** capitalist
former ~: **4** USSR
Empire: **5** apple
author: Gore Vidal
relative: *see* apple
__ Empire: **5** Roman **7** British, Ottoman
Empire of the Sun (1987 film)
cast: Christian Bale, John Malkovich, Miranda Richardson
director: Steven Spielberg
Empire State Bldg. site: **3** NYC **4** NY NY
Empire Strikes Back, The (1980 film)
cast: Carrie Fisher, Harrison Ford, Mark Hamill, Billy Dee Williams
composer: John Williams
planet: **4** Hoth
empirical: **7** factual **9** practical, pragmatic
emplane: **5** board, get on **6** embark **8** go aboard
employ: **3** ply, put, use **4** hire, turn, work **5** apply, exert, spend, treat, wield **6** commit, engage, enlist, handle, hire on, occupy, resort, retain, sign on, sign up, take on **7** charter, exploit, harness, operate, utilize **8** exercise, keep busy, work with **9** make use of, put to work **10** commission, fall back on, manipulate
employable: **6** usable **7** useable **8** eligible **10** accessible
employed: **4** busy **5** in use **6** active, at work, on duty **7** working **8** laboring, occupied, on the job **9** on the move
be ~: **4** help, moil, plod, tend, toil, work **5** grind, labor, sweat **8** endeavor, exercise, plug away **9** grind away, moonlight **10** apprentice
be ~ by: **5** serve **7** work for
__-employed: **4** self
employee: **4** hand, hire **5** agent, clerk, labor **6** earner, worker **7** laborer, staffer **8** commuter, hireling, operator **9** assistant, hired hand, jobholder **10** apprentice, wage earner
badge: **6** ID card
entry-level ~: **5** clerk, gofer **6** gopher
health plan: **3** HMO, PPO
ID, often: **3** SSN
IRS ~: **3** fed
last words: **5** I quit
live-in ~: **4** maid **5** nanny **6** au pair, butler
reward: **4** perk **5** bonus, raise
transferred ~ benefit: **4** relo **10** relocation
underpaid ~: **5** slave **6** drudge
employees: **4** help **5** staff, union **9** personnel
employer: **4** boss, firm **5** hirer **6** master **7** company, manager **8** brass hat **10** management, supervisor
like some ~s: **5** bossy **8** arrogant, despotic **9** imperious **10** autocratic, commanding, oppressive, tyrannical
temp's ~: **4** firm **6** agency, office **7** company **10** department
employment: **3** job, use **4** line, post, work **5** labor, place, trade, usage **6** billet, sphere **7** pursuit, service, station **8** adoption, business, exercise, handling, position, vocation **9** appliance, avocation, enrolment, operation, signing on, situation **10** assignment, commission, enlistment, enrollment, livelihood, occupation, profession
change ~ frequently: **6** job-hop
gainful ~: **4** post, work **8** position
proof of ~: **5** badge **6** ID card
seek ~: **5** apply **8** petition
employment-data agcy.: **3** BLS
Emporia: **4** city, town
locale: **6** Kansas
emporium: **4** mart, shop **5** bazar, store **6** bazaar, market, outlet **8** boutique
event: **4** sale **8** closeout **9** clearance
empower: **4** gird, tone, vest **5** allow, build, shore, steel **6** anneal, assign, beef up, commit, enable, harden, invest, permit, prop up, temper, tone up **7** bolster, brace up, build up, burgeon, develop, enhance, entitle, entrust, fortify, intitle, intrust, license, qualify, shore up, stiffen, toughen, warrant **8** accredit, bourgeon, buttress, delegate, deputize, energize, indurate, nominate, sanction, vitalize **9** authorize, intensify, reinforce **10** capacitate, commission, constitute, invigorate, strengthen
empowered: **4** able **6** vested **10** privileged
empress: **4** Lady **5** noble, queen, ruler **6** gerent **7** monarch **8** imperial **9** potentate, sovereign
emptiness: **4** need, void **6** vacuum **7** vacancy, vacuity **8** solitude **9** blankness **10** desolation, exhaustion, hollowness, loneliness
emptor: **5** buyer **6** patron, vendee **7** end user **8** consumer, customer
__ emptor: **6** caveat
empty: **3** dry, gut, tip **4** bare, dull, dump, flat, idle, null, pump, vain, vent, void **5** blank, clear, drain, eject, expel, inane, leach, purge, scoop, silly, spend, spill, strip, tired, unfed, unlet, use up, vapid **6** absent, barren, decant, devoid, finish, glassy, hollow, hungry, jejune, lonely, unload, vacant, vacate **7** all gone, consume, deflate, deplete, exhaust, fatuous, insipid, lighten, pour out, sold out, starved, sterile, trivial, untaken,

vacated, vacuous 8 clean out, deflated, depleted, deserted, desolate, disgorge, evacuate, famished, finished, ill-spent, lifeless, out of gas, ravenous, starving, unburden, unfilled 9 abandoned, discharge, evacuated, excavated, exhausted, frivolous, fruitless, senseless, valueless, worthless 10 groundless, unoccupied, unprofound
be on ~: 6 run out
combining form: 3 ken- 4 keno-
in one gulp: 4 chug 5 swill 6 guzzle
(into): 3 run 4 flow 6 stream
leave ~: 6 vacate
leave no part ~: 4 cram, fill, pack, sate 5 crowd 6 occupy, top off 7 jam-pack, pervade, satiate 8 brim over, permeate
literally, ~ hand: 6 karate
near ~: 3 low 4 down 5 below, lower, lowly, under 6 meager, paltry, sparse, sunken 7 nominal, reduced, shallow 8 depleted, subsided, uncostly 9 in the pits 10 down and out, marked down, rock-bottom
(of): 3 rid
of water: 4 bail 7 draw off 8 drain off
out: 4 dump 5 purge 6 hollow
space: 3 vac. 6 vacuum 8 headroom 9 clearance
words: 3 gas, pap, rot 4 bunk, wind 5 prate, stuff, tripe 6 bunkum, humbug 7 blarney, bombast, fustian, hogwash, malarky, palaver 8 buncombe, claptrap, malarkey, nonsense 9 gibberish, moonshine 10 mumbo jumbo

empty __: 6 nester
empty __ syndrome: 4 nest
empty-__: 6 handed, headed
empty-headed: 4 daft 5 dizzy, giddy, goofy, inane, silly, thick 6 vacant 7 flighty, shallow, vacuous 8 ignorant
emptying: 4 flow, gush, ooze 5 burst, spill, spurt 7 seepage 8 ejection, emission, eruption, outburst, unlading 9 departure, discharge, effluence, excretion, explosion, expulsion, exudation, purgation, secretion, unloading 10 evacuation, withdrawal
Empty Nest (NBC sitcom)
cast: Dinah Manoff (Carol Weston) Kristy McNichol (Barbara Weston) Richard Mulligan (Dr. Harry Weston)
dog: 8 Dreyfuss
__ empty stomach: 4 on an
empyreal: 5 lofty, noble 7 elysian, exalted, sublime 8 elevated, ethereal, heavenly, majestic, ultimate 9 ambrosial, celestial, ineffable 10 majestical
empyrean: 3 sky 5 azure 6 heaven 8 ethereal, heavenly, paradise, ultimate 9 celestial, firmament 10 atmosphere
__ 'em, Rover!: 3 Sic
__ Ems, Germany: 3 Bad
EMT: 5 medic 9 paramedic
destination: 2 ER 4 hosp.
part of ~: 3 Med. 4 Emer., Tech.
procedure: 3 CPR
emu: 4 bird 5 biped 6 Aussie, ratite
relative: 4 kiwi, rhea
emulate: 3 ape 4 copy 5 equal, mimic, rival 6 follow, mirror 7 dress as, imitate, pattern, reflect 9 take after
emulating: 3 à la 4 like
emulative: 5 apish, rival 6 copied, echoic 9 imitative, mimicking, simulated 10 derivative, reflective, secondhand, unoriginal
emulator: 4 aper 5 rival, sheep, toady 6 yes man 7 Babbitt, epigone 8 assenter, imitator 10 conformist
remark: 5 ditto, me too
emulsifying agent: 5 algin 8 lecithin
emulsion: 5 cream, paint 8 solution
en __: 3 ami 4 bloc, dash, quad 5 garde, masse, route, suite 7 famille, passant
en __ air: 5 plein
En __: 5 Vogue
En __!: 5 garde
enable: 2 OK 3 let 4 fund, okay 5 allow, equip 6 permit, turn on 7 empower, entitle, intitle, license, qualify 8 accredit, activate, energize 9 authorize 10 capacitate, commission, facilitate
enact: 3 tax 4 make, pass, vote 5 order, stage 6 ordain, recite 7 achieve, perform, portray 8 carry out, legalize, recreate, transact 9 dramatize, establish, institute, interpret, legislate, prescribe 10 perpetrate
enacted: 5 legal 6 lawful, passed 7 decreed, ordered 8 enforced, enjoined, mandated, ordained 9 legalized, statutory 10 authorized, legislated
enactment: 3 law 7 measure, passage, playing, statute 9 depiction, execution, ordinance, portrayal 10 playacting, regulation
enamel: 5 color, glaze, gloss, inlay, japan, paint 6 finish, polish, veneer 7 coating, encrust, incrust, lacquer, varnish 9 champlevé, cloisonné 10 nail polish
crack, as ~: 5 craze
ender: 4 ware
neighbor: 6 dentin 7 dentine
target: 4 nail
enamelware: 4 tole
enamor: 5 charm 6 endear, entice 7 bewitch, enchant, enthral, inthral 8 enthrall, entrance, inthrall 9 captivate, enrapture, fascinate, infatuate, sweet-talk
enamored: 4 fond 6 loving 7 smitten
be ~ of: 4 love 5 fancy 6 dote on
of: 6 caring, doting, loving, tender 7 adoring, amatory, amorous 8 intimate, mad about, romantic 10 captivated, infatuated
enantiosis: 5 irony 6 satire 7 sarcasm
Enberg: 4 Dick
en bloc: 6 in full 8 as a whole, together 10 altogether
enc.: 3 env., SAE 4 SASE
part: 3 vol.
encage: 3 box 6 coop up, lock up 7 confine
encaged: 4 pent 6 pent up
encamp: 6 settle 7 bivouac 8 settle in 10 pitch a tent
encampment: 5 étape 7 bivouac, tentage 8 barracks, garrison
South African ~: 5 lager 6 laager
encapsulate: 5 sum up 6 digest 7 abridge, sheathe, shorten 8 condense 9 summarize
encarmine: 6 redden
encarnadine: 6 redden
encase: 3 box 4 pack, wrap 5 box in, box up, cover, crate, frame, house 6 pack up 7 close in, confine, enclose, envelop, inclose, package, protect, sheathe 8 preserve, surround
enceinte: 8 pregnant 9 expectant, expecting, with child
Enceladus: 4 moon
planet: 6 Saturn
encephalogram: 4 x-ray
enchain: 4 bind 5 rivet 6 fetter 7 engross, manacle, shackle, trammel 8 enfetter, handcuff, hold fast 9 captivate
enchant: 3 hex, wow 4 draw, grip, lure, send, take 5 charm 6 allure, appeal, disarm, enamor, engage, entice, please, ravish, thrill, tickle, turn on 7 attract, beguile, bewitch, delight, enthral, inthral 8 bedazzle, enthrall, entrance, inthrall, intrigue, transfix 9 captivate, carry away, delectate, enrapture, fascinate, hypnotize, inebriate, mesmerize, spellbind 10 intoxicate
enchanted: 3 fey 5 magic 6 enrapt 7 magical 9 bewitched, delighted, gladdened, possessed 10 fascinated, spellbound
be ~ by: 4 feel, like, love 5 adore, fancy, go for, prize 6 admire, dote on, regard, revere 7 care for, cherish, cling to, fall for, idolize, long for, romance, worship 8 be mad for, hold dear, treasure, venerate 9 delight in
state: 5 spell
Enchanted (1959 song)
artist: Platters
Enchanted (2007 film)
cast: Amy Adams, Patrick Dempsey
__ Enchanted: 4 Ella
Enchanted April (1991 film)
cast: Joan Plowright, Miranda Richardson
setting: 5 Italy
__ Enchanted Evening: 4 Some
enchanter: 6 wizard 7 charmer 8 conjurer, conjuror, magician, sorcerer 9 bewitcher
enchanting: 4 fair, glam 5 magic, siren, spell 6 lovely, quaint 7 darling, lovable, magical, sirenic, winning, winsome 8 loveable, pleasant, pleasing, romantic 9 appealing, beguiling, endearing, glamorous, ravishing, sirenical, thrilling 10 attractive, bewitching, delectable, delightful, entrancing, intriguing
enchantment: 4 love 5 charm, magic, spell 6 allure 7 ecstasy, rapture, sorcery 9 magnetism
enchantress: 4 vamp 5 Aeaea, Circe, Kirke, Medea, siren, witch 7 charmer, Lorelei 9 sorceress
enchilada
filling: 5 chile, chili 6 chilli
sauce: 5 salsa
whole ~: 3 all 4 A to Z 8 entirety
__ enchilada: 3 big 5 whole
enchiridion: 5 bible, guide 8 handbook
Encina, Juan del: 4 poet 7 Spanish 10 playwright
Encinitas: 4 city, town
locale: 10 California
Encino: 4 city
locale: 10 California
Encino Man (1992 film)
cast: Sean Astin, Brendan Fraser, Pauly Shore
encircle: 3 orb 4 band, coil, gird, girt, hoop, lock, loop, ring, wind, wrap 5 bower, fence, girth, hem in, orbit, siege, twine 6 begird, define, emball, engird, gird in 7 besiege, compass, embrace, enclose, environ, inclose 8 cincture, surround 9 close in on, encompass, enwreathe
encirclement: 5 siege
encircling: 7 ambient
Encke's __: 5 comet
encl.: 3 env., SAE 4 SASE
enclad: 7 clothed
enclave: 4 area 7 country 8 district 9 territory
enclose: 3 hem, pen 4 cage, case, fold, gird, hold, lock, ring, shut, veil, wall, wrap 5 bower, box up, cover, fence, frame, hedge, hem in 6 begird, circle, coop up, cordon, corral, define, encase, engird, immure, incase, insert, intern, lock in, seal in, shut in, wall in 7 compass, confine, contain, embrace, envelop, environ, impound, include, rope off, seclude, shelter 8 blockade, block off, encircle, fence off, surround 9 encompass
enclosed: 5 inner 6 herein, indoor
enclosure: 3 pen, sty 4 area, cage, cell, coop, yard 5 booth, court, frame, hutch 6 aviary, corral, insert 7 chamber, fencing 8 stockade 9 birdhouse, courtyard 10 quadrangle
encode: 8 disguise, scramble
encoded: 6 secret
encoil: 4 wind
encomiastic: 7 glowing 9 adulatory, approving, favorable, laudatory, praiseful 10 eulogistic, flattering
encomium: 4 pean 5 eloge, honor, kudos, paean 6 eulogy, homage, praise, salute 7 acclaim, plaudit, tribute 8 accolade, citation, flattery, good word, plaudits 9 extolment, laudation, panegyric 10 compliment, exaltation
encompass: 4 gird, have, loop, ring, span 5 cover, hem in, range, reach 6 begird, circle, define, embody, engird, girdle, imbody, take in 7 contain, embrace, enclose, envelop, environ, inclose, include 8 cincture, comprise, encircle, sur-

round **9** enwreathe **10** comprehend
encompassed by: 4 amid **5** among, 'twixt **6** amidst **7** between, betwixt
encompassing: 5 round **6** around **7** all over, ambient **9** embracing **10** encircling, enveloping
__-encompassing: 3 all
encore: 3 bis **4** more **5** again, rerun **6** repeat **7** reprise **8** once more **9** extra song **10** repetition
request an ~: 4 clap **5** cheer **7** applaud
Encore: 7 channel
alternative: *see* movie channel
encounter: 3 see **4** bout, face, find, flap, fray, meet, spot, tilt **5** brush, clash, fight, run-in, scrap, set-to, shock, stand, taste **6** action, attack, battle, combat, rumpus **7** contest, dispute, hit upon, liaison, meeting, quarrel, receive, run into, undergo **8** argument, bump into, chance on, come upon, conflict, confront, happen on, meet with, skirmish, squabble, struggle **9** clash with, collision, discovery, get to know, interview, reception, run across **10** alight upon, chance upon, come across, contention, engagement, experience, fall in with, happen upon, meet up with, rendezvous
encounter __: 5 group **7** session
__ Encounter: 5 Brief
__ Encounters...: 5 Close
encourage: 3 aid **4** abet, back, buoy, coax, feed, goad, help, prod, push, spur, stir, urge **5** boost, cheer, drive, egg on, rally, rouse, steel **6** advise, ask for, assist, buck up, buoy up, excite, exhort, foment, foster, incite, invite, praise, prop up, second, solace, spur on, succor, uphold **7** advance, animate, applaud, bolster, cheer up, comfort, console, endorse, enliven, forward, further, gladden, hearten, help out, indorse, inspire, lighten, nurture, promote, psych up, pull for, root for, support **8** advocate, embolden, energize, enspirit, imbolden, inspirit, reassure, revivify, sanction, side with **9** cultivate, galvanize, get behind, instigate, reinforce, smile upon, subsidize **10** exhilarate, predispose, revitalize, strengthen
falsely: 6 lead on
in evil: 6 incite **7** collude **9** instigate
encouragement: 3 aid **4** help, lift, spur **5** boost, cheer **6** succor, urging **7** backing, comfort, support **8** advocacy, optimism, sanction, stimulus
cry: 3 olé, rah, yay, yea, yes **4** c'mon, good **5** huzza **6** chin up, hoorah, hooray, hurrah, hurray, huzzah, let's go **7** attaboy **8** alley-oop, attagirl
encouraging: 4 rosy **6** bright, upbeat **7** hopeful **8** probable **9** promising **10** supportive
not ~: 4 dark **5** bleak, dusky **6** dismal, dreary, gloomy, somber **7** doleful, ominous **8** hopeless **9** miserable, saddening, saturnine, sorrowful, woebegone **10** depressing
encrinite: 6 fossil
encroach: 5 poach **6** invade, meddle **7** violate **8** trespass **9** intrude on, penetrate
on: 4 raid **5** storm, usurp **6** assail, breach, infest, invade, maraud, occupy, ravage **7** overrun, pillage, plunder, violate **8** permeate, trespass **9** penetrate
encroachment: 6 attack, inroad **8** invasion, trespass **9** incursion, violation
encrust: 4 cake **8** solidify
encrypted: 5 coded **6** in code
encrypting org.: 3 NSA
encryption: 4 code **6** cipher
encumber: 3 lay, tax **4** clog, fill, load **5** block, cramp, delay, tie up **6** burden, fetter, hamper, hand up, hinder, hogtie, hold up, impede, lumber, saddle **7** oppress, perplex **8** handicap, obstruct, overload, slow down **9** hamstring, weigh down
encumbered: 5 taxed **7** charged, fraught **8** burdened, hampered, weighted **9** laden. full, oppressed **10** loaded down
encumbrance: 3 bar **4** debt, drag, duty, lien, load, onus **6** burden, weight **7** barrier **8** handicap, obstacle **9** liability
encumbrances: 4 gear **5** goods
encyclopedia: 3 ref., set **7** Grolier **9** Americana, reference, World Book **10** Britannica
book: 3 vol. **5** index **6** volume
medium: 5 CD/ROM **6** online
encyclopedic: 4 a to z, vast, wide **5** broad **7** general **8** complete, far-flung, sweeping **9** expansive, extensive, universal **10** exhaustive, widespread
end: 3 aim, tip, top, use **4** butt, cusp, doom, drop, edge, goal, halt, heel, last, lees, lift, quit, rear, ruin, stop, stub, tail **5** abort, bound, cease, close, dregs, final, finis, lapse, limit, omega, point, quash, reach, sew up, stump **6** bottom, cut off, demise, desist, epilog, expire, expiry, finale, finish, inning, intent, lay off, motive, object, payoff, period, quench, reason, result, run out, settle, target, tipoff, top off, upshot, vanish, windup, wrap up **7** abolish, adjourn, athlete, break up, call off, closing, closure, destroy, due date, extreme, get done, kiss off, last act, mission, outcome, passing, purpose, quietus, remnant, residue, resolve, selvage, sign off, undoing **8** abrogate, blow over, boundary, break off, close out, complete, conclude, curtains, cut short, deadline, dissolve, epilogue, get rid of, intermit, knock off, last gasp, last word, leave off, pack it in, rearmost, round off, round out, selvedge, shut down, stamp out, surcease, swan song, terminal, terminus, twilight, ultimate **9** cessation, close down, culminate, disappear, extremity, finish off, intention, interrupt, objective, punchline, remainder, ruination, terminate **10** aspiration, borderline, call it a day, completion, conclusion, consummate, denouement, do away with, expiration, extinguish, finish line, limitation, put through, relinquish, resolution
at: 4 abut
bad ~: 4 doom
combining form: 3 tel- **4** tele-, telo-
ender: 3 pin **4** game, long, most, note, play, ways, wise **5** brain, paper, point
in music: 4 fine
of a series: 5 omega **6** finale
starter: 4 book, week, year
to the ~ in Latin: 5 ad fin.
to the ~ in music: 6 al fine
end __: 3 man, men, run, use **4** game, user, zone **5** paper, plate, table
end __ high note: 3 on a
end __ line: 5 of the
end __ road: 5 of the
end __ world: 5 of the
end-__: 3 all
__ end: 3 the **4** at an, dead, tail **5** in the, loose, split, tight **6** bitter, living
__-end: 3 low **4** high, open, rear, year **5** front **6** closed
__ End: 4 Dead, East, West **5** Land's **6** Stoney, World's **7** Howards
end-all: 3 ult. **8** ultimate
endanger: 4 risk **5** peril **6** chance, hazard, menace **7** imperil, lay open **8** overhang, threaten **10** compromise, jeopardize
endangered: 4 rare **6** at risk **7** at stake **10** in jeopardy
endangered __: 7 species
endangerment: 4 risk **5** peril **8** jeopardy
endear: 5 charm **6** enamor **7** attract, win over **10** ingratiate
endeared: 5 amour **6** adored, prized **7** beloved, revered **8** cared for, esteemed, hallowed, idolized, precious **9** cherished, venerated, worshiped
endearing: 7 lovable, winning, winsome **8** loveable **10** enchanting
endearment: 3 hon **5** honey **7** pet name **8** fondness **9** affection, sweet talk **10** attachment, attraction
British term of ~: 3 luv
term of ~: 3 hon, pet **4** baby, dear, love **5** angel, honey, kiddo, sugar, sweet **7** cara mia, darling **8** snookums **10** sweetheart
endeavor: 3 aim, bid, try **4** seek, shot, stab, toil **5** assay, essay, labor, offer, trial **6** effort, intend, strain, strive, take on **7** attempt, venture **8** activity, exertion, striving, struggle **9** undertake **10** enterprise
Endeavour org.: 4 NASA
ended: 3 o'er, out **4** done, fini, gone, over, past **7** all over, through **8** complete, over with **9** completed
__-ended: 4 open
endemic: 5 local **6** native **8** catching, regional **10** aboriginal, indigenous
__-ender: 6 bitter
Ender, Kornelia: 7 swimmer
Endgame
author: Samuel Beckett
end in __: 4 a tie **5** a draw
ending: 4 coda, last, stop **5** close, final, finis, omega **6** epilog, finale, finish, sequel, upshot, windup, wrap-up **7** closing, closure, last act, outcome **8** epilogue, last page, surcease, swan song, terminus **9** cessation, summation **10** completion, conclusion, denouement, desistance, expiration, resolution
__ ending: 5 happy
__-ending: 5 never
Ending Up
author: Kingsley Amis
end is __, The: 4 near
endive: 4 herb **6** veggie **9** vegetable
__ endive: 6 French **7** Belgian
__ End Kids: 4 Dead
endless: 3 big **4** much, vast **6** eonian, eterne, myriad, steady, untold **7** abiding, eternal, heaping, lasting, nonstop, tedious, undying **8** constant, enduring, infinite, timeless, unbroken, unending, unwaning **9** ceaseless, continual, countless, deathless, incessant, limitless, perennial, perpetual, unbounded, unceasing, unfailing, unlimited **10** continuous, enervating, innumerous, persistent, unnumbered
Endless Love (song)
artist: Mariah Carey, Lionel Richie, Diana Ross, Luther Vandross
endlessly: 4 ever **7** forever, on and on **8** evermore **9** eternally
endlessness: 6 length **8** eternity **9** immensity
Endless Nights (1987 song)
artist: Eddie Money
Endless Sleep (1958 song)
artist: Jody Reynolds
Endless Summers Nights (1988 song) artist: Richard Marx
endman: 7 Mr. Bones
endnotes phrase: 6 et alia, et alii
endo-: 5 inner
ending: 5 plasm
opposite: 3 exo-
endocrine: 5 gland
endodontist deg.: 3 DDS, DMD
end of __: 5 an era
__ end of one's rope: 5 at the
end-of-page abbreviation: 3 PTO
end-of-scene direction: 4 exit **6** exeunt
end-of-semester
event: 4 exam, test **5** final
end of the __: 4 line
End of the Battle, The
author: Evelyn Waugh
End of the Innocence, The (1989 song)
artist: Don Henley
End of the Road (1992 song)
artist: Boyz II Men
End of the Road, The
author: John Barth
End of the Romance, The
artist: Erté
__ end of the stick, the: 5 short
End of the World, The (1963 song)
artist: Skeeter Davis

end-of-week cry: 4 TGIF
end on __ note: 5 a high
Endor
beast: 4 Ewok
dweller: 5 witch
endorse: 2 OK 3 ink, let 4 back, okay, sign 5 boost, favor 6 affirm, defend, permit, praise, ratify, second, uphold 7 approve, certify, commend, confirm, promote, support, sustain, warrant, witness 8 accredit, attest to, champion, notarize, sanction, stump for, validate, vouch for 9 authorize, autograph, encourage, get behind, guarantee, indemnify, recommend, subscribe 10 go to bat for, speak up for, stand up for, underwrite
endorsed: 3 OK'd 4 OK'ed 6 okayed 8 official 9 preferred
item: 5 check 7 voucher
endorsement: 2 OK 4 amen, okay, plug 7 backing, go-ahead, support 8 adoption, advocacy, approval, sanction 9 reference
endorser: 6 backer, master, patron 7 apostle, paladin 8 advocate, champion, crusader, defender, exponent 9 paraclete, proponent, supporter
at times: 3 xer
endorsing: 3 for, pro 9 agreement
endow: 4 fund, give, vest, will 5 award, bless, crown, endue, equip, found, grant, indue 6 accord, bestow, confer, donate, enrich, invest, supply 7 finance, furnish, prepare, qualify, sponsor, support 8 bequeath, confer on 9 establish, subsidize 10 contribute, underwrite
endowed with, be: 4 have 5 boast 7 possess
endowment: 4 boon, fund, gift 5 award, flair, grant 6 bounty, legacy, talent 7 ability, bequest, faculty, funding, largess, present, quality, subsidy 8 aptitude, bestowal, capacity, donation, largesse 9 allowance, attribute, provision 10 capability, foundation, investment
recipient: 4 heir 5 donee
end-run: 6 outwit 8 outsmart
ends
at loose ~: 6 adrift 8 dallying, drifting, wavering 9 uncertain, unsettled
make ~ meet: 3 eke 4 live, save 5 skimp, stint 7 subsist
odds and ~: 4 bits, misc., olio, rest 5 melee, scrap, trash 6 debris, job lot, jumble, litter, medley, scraps, things 7 mélange, remnant, rubbish, rummage 8 et cetera, leavings, leftover, remnants, snatches, snippets 9 fragments, leftovers, potpourri, remainder 10 miscellany
partner: 4 odds
where ~ meet: 4 seam
__ ends: 5 loose, split
__ ends of the earth: 5 to the
Endsville
see wonderful
end-table item: 4 lamp 5 clock, radio
End, The (1978 film)
cast: Dom DeLuise, Sally Field, Burt Reynolds
__ end to: 5 put an
endue: 5 crown, endow, honor 6 assume, bestow, clothe, instal, invest 7 install, instate, provide 9 transfuse
endurable: 7 livable 8 liveable 9 tolerable 10 sufferable
endurance: 3 vim 4 dint, grit, guts, thew, will 5 brawn, force, heart, might, moxie, pluck, power, spunk, thews, vigor 6 energy, mettle, muscle 7 bravery, courage, fitness, muscles, potence, potency, prowess, stamina 8 capacity, lifetime, patience, tenacity, vitality 9 allowance, beefiness, constancy, existence, fixedness, fortitude, gutsiness, hardiness, huskiness, longevity, puissance, restraint, stability, stoutness, suffering, tolerance, toughness 10 brawniness, brute force, continuity, durability, indulgence, mightiness, permanence, resistance, resolution, robustness, sturdiness, submission, sufferance, toleration
endure: 2 go 4 bear, bide, go on, have, hold, last, live, lump, stay, take 5 abide, brave, brook, exist, stand, stick 6 accept, bear up, hang on, hold on, hold up, keep on, linger, live on, manage, permit, remain, resist, stay on, submit, suffer, wear on 7 carry on, hold out, make out, outlast, persist, prevail, receive, ride out, stomach, subsist, survive, sustain, swallow, undergo, wait out, weather 8 continue, cope with, meet with, stand for, sweat out, tolerate, wear well 9 go through, persevere, put up with, withstand 10 get through, sit through, stick it out, tough it out
enduring: 3 old 4 firm, sure 5 fixed, stoic, tight 6 stable, steady, strong 7 abiding, chronic, endless, eternal, lasting, nonstop, passive, patient, stoical, undying 8 constant, lifelong, residual, timeless, unending, unwaning 9 ceaseless, chronical, continual, incessant, indelible, long-lived, memorable, perennial, permanent, perpetual, steadfast, unabating, unceasing 10 changeless, habituated, inerasable, inveterate, monumental, persistent, unchanging, undecaying, unwavering
enduringly: 4 ever 6 always 7 finally, forever, for good, lasting 8 evermore 9 endlessly, eternally 10 unendingly
enduro: 4 test 8 auto race
Endust: 6 polish
alternative: 6 Behold, Pledge 10 Liquid Gold, Old English
endways: 7 upright 10 lengthways, lengthwise
Endymion: 4 poem
author: John Keats
lover: 6 Selene
mother: 6 Calyce
parent: 4 Zeus 6 Calyce
son: 5 Epeus, Paeon 7 Aetolus 9 Narcissus
End Zone
author: Don DeLillo
ENE: 3 dir. 5 point 9 direction
opposite: 3 WSW
__ en el Rancho Grande: 4 Alla
enemies
like some ~: 5 sworn
make ~: 5 anger 6 enrage, fire up, madden 7 incense, inflame, provoke 8 irritate 9 displease, infuriate 10 exasperate
Enemies, A Love Story (1989 film)
cast: Anjelica Huston, Lena Olin, Ron Silver
enemy: 3 foe 4 them 5 rival 6 bad guy, foeman 7 bad guys, defamer, hostile, invader, nemesis, opposer, traitor, villain 8 attacker, betrayer, opponent, saboteur 9 adversary, aggressor, assailant, combatant, detractor, ill-wisher, other side, terrorist 10 antagonist, competitor, opposition
join the ~: 4 turn 6 defect, desert, run out 7 forsake, pull out, sell out
meet one's ~: 4 face 6 attack, engage, line up, take on 7 assault 9 fight with
opposite: 4 ally
starter: 4 arch
survey: 5 recon
...enemy, and they __: 4 is us 7 are ours
Enemy at the Gates (2001 film)
cast: Joseph Fiennes, Ed Harris, Jude Law, Rachel Weisz
Enemy Below, The (1957 film)
vessel: 3 sub 5 U-boat
Enemy Gods, The
author: Oliver La Farge
Enemy Mine (1985 film)
cast: Louis Gossett Jr., Dennis Quaid
Enemy of the People, An
author: Henrik Ibsen
character: 4 Kiil 5 Ejlif, Petra 6 Morten 7 Hovstad
Enemy of the State (1998 film)
cast: Lisa Bonet, Gene Hackman, Will Smith, Jon Voight
__ Enemy, The: 6 Public 7 Violent
energetic: 4 busy, go-go, hale, live, racy, spry 5 alive, astir, brisk, fresh, hardy, lusty, peppy, perky, quick, smart, vital, zesty, zippy 6 active, at work, bouncy, hearty, lively, rugged, snappy, strong, virile, yeasty 7 animate, driving, dynamic, hyped-up, intense, kinetic, rousing, vibrant, willing, working, zestful 8 animated, bustling, emphatic, forceful, grooving, powerful, spirited, tireless, untiring, vigorous 9 ambitious, assiduous, combative, exuberant, sprightly, strenuous, vivacious 10 expressive, full of life, productive, red-blooded, undeterred, unflagging, unwearying
one: 4 doer 6 dynamo
energetically: 4 hard 5 madly 8 mightily
energize: 4 fuel, gird, pump, stir, tone 5 brace, build, hop up, liven, pep up, power, shore, steel 6 anneal, beef up, enable, excite, harden, jazz up, prop up, pump up, temper, tone up, turn on, vivify 7 actuate, animate, bolster, brace up, build up, burgeon, develop, empower, enhance, enliven, fortify, inspire, juice up, liven up, quicken, refresh, shore up, stiffen, toughen 8 activate, bourgeon, buttress, embolden, enspirit, imbolden, indurate, inspirit, motivate, vitalize 9 electrify, encourage, galvanize, intensify, jump-start, reinforce, stimulate 10 invigorate
energizer: 5 tonic 8 pick-me-up 9 stimulant
energy: 3 pep, vim, zap, zip 4 brio, dash, dint, élan, fire, fuel, life, push, soul, thew, zeal, zest, zing 5 ardor, brawn, drive, force, juice, labor, might, moxie, oomph, power, punch, steam, thews, verve, vigor 6 action, bounce, bustle, muscle, pizazz, spirit, starch 7 fitness, muscles, pizzazz, potence, potency, stamina, voltage 8 activity, exertion, fervency, gumption, industry, momentum, strength, vitality, vivacity 9 animation, beefiness, élan vital, endurance, fortitude, hardiness, huskiness, intensity, puissance, stoutness, toughness 10 brawniness, brute force, enterprise, enthusiasm, exuberance, get up and go, horsepower, initiative, liveliness, mightiness, resolution, robustness, sturdiness
biochemical ~ source: 3 ATP
Buddhist: 5 prana
bundle of ~: 6 dynamo
burst of ~: 5 spasm, spirt, spurt
center: 6 chakra
channel: 4 nadi
dynamo's ~: 3 EMF
field: 4 aura 8 ambience 9 emanation 10 atmosphere
full of ~: 4 go-go 5 alive, lusty, peppy, vital
lacking ~: 4 lazy, logy 6 effete 7 languid 8 listless
lack of ~: 6 anemia, anergy 7 anaemia
lose ~: 3 sag 4 tire, wilt
meas.: 3 BTU
nuclear ~ watchdog: 3 AEC
sap, as ~: 4 tire 5 drain, leach, use up 6 expend, lessen 7 deplete, exhaust, fatigue, suck dry, tire out 8 diminish, wear down 10 debilitate, devitalize, impoverish
science of ~: 7 physics
source: 3 sun 4 atom, carb, fuel 5 hydro
unit: 2 eV 3 cal. 4 ft. lb. 5 joule 7 calorie 9 degree-day, foot-pound
energy __: 4 band 5 audit, level
__ energy: 4 wind 5 clean, solar 6 atomic 7 kinetic, nuclear
__-energy: 4 high
enero: 3 mes 5 month 7 January, Spanish
enervate: 3 sag, sap 4 flag, jade, tire, wane 5 blunt, weary 6 impair, reduce, shrink, soften, weaken 7 deplete, depress, exhaust,

fatigue, tire out, unnerve, vitiate, wear out 8 enfeeble 9 attenuate, indispose, undermine 10 debilitate, devitalize, emasculate

enervated: 4 limp, logy, weak 5 faint, spent, tired, weary 6 done in, feeble 7 far-gone, languid, run-down, worn out 8 listless, out of gas 9 enfeebled, exhausted, lethargic, nerveless, paralyzed, prostrate, washed-out 10 gone to seed, knocked out, languorous, on the ropes, out of shape, spiritless

enervating: 6 taxing 7 tedious 8 tiresome

enervation: 6 anemia 7 anaemia, fatigue, frazzle, malaise 9 weariness 10 exhaustion, feebleness

Enesco, Georges: 8 Romanian, Rumanian 9 Roumanian, violinist

enfant terrible: 3 imp 4 brat 5 devil, scamp

enfeeble: 3 sag, sap 4 flag, tire, wane 5 blunt, waste, weary 6 impair, reduce, shrink, soften, weaken 7 deplete, exhaust, fatigue, tire out, unnerve, vitiate, wear out 8 enervate, paralyse, paralyze 9 attenuate, indispose, undermine 10 debilitate, devitalize

enfeebled: 6 infirm 7 injured

enfetter: 3 pin, tie 4 bind, bond, link, weld, wrap, yoke 5 affix, clamp, hitch, tie up 6 attach, bundle, cement, fasten, hook up, secure, tether 7 conjoin, connect, enchain, shackle, tighten

Enfield: 5 rifle

enfilade: 5 salvo 6 volley 7 barrage

enfin: 6 at last 7 finally 8 in the end

enflame: 3 bug, get, irk, vex 4 bait, gall, rage, rile, roil 5 anger, annoy, chafe, grate, peeve, pique, rouse, upset 6 abrade, bother, harass, offend, plague, rankle, ruffle 7 bedevil, disturb, provoke, torment, trouble 8 irritate 9 aggravate, displease, excoriate 10 exasperate

enfold: 3 hug, lap 4 hold, veil, wrap 5 cinch, clasp, press 6 clinch, clutch, swathe, wrap up 7 embrace, envelop, squeeze 8 surround 9 keep close

enforce: 3 use 5 apply, order, press 6 decree, demand, direct, enjoin, impose, invoke 7 command, entreat 9 implement, proscribe

enforceable: 4 just 5 legal, legit, licit, valid 6 kosher, lawful, proper 7 allowed, decreed 8 judicial 9 allowable, juridical, justified, statutory, warranted 10 authorized, legitimate, prescribed, sanctioned

enforcement: 6 duress 8 coercion, exaction
- **power:** 5 teeth

Enforcer, The: 5 Nitti

enfranchisement: 4 vote 6 choice 7 liberty 8 autonomy, decision, sanction, suffrage 10 liberation

eng.
- **part:** 4 carb.
- **school:** 4 tech.
- ***see also*** engine, engineering

Eng.: 4 lang., subj.
- **course:** 3 lit.
- **neighbor:** 3 Ire. 4 Scot.
- ***see also*** British, English

Eng. __: 3 Lit.

engage: 3 use 4 book, busy, face, grab, grip, hire, lock, meet, mesh, rent 5 apply, charm, enrol, lease, order, tie up 6 absorb, allure, appeal, arrest, assail, attack, commit, employ, enlist, enroll, line up, occupy, retain, secure, sign on, sign up, take on 7 appoint, assault, attract, betroth, charter, enchant, engross, enthral, immerse, inthral, involve, promise, recruit, reserve, takes on 8 activate, affiance, backbite, contract, enthrall, entrance, interest, inthrall, keep busy, switch on, take part 9 captivate, fascinate, fight with, interlace, interlock, intermesh, preoccupy, put to work 10 commission, monopolize
- **an entertainer:** 4 hire 5 set up 6 line up, pick up 7 procure 8 register, schedule
- **in:** 3 ply 4 have, wage 6 pursue, tackle, take up 7 address 8 practice 9 undertake
- **(in):** 8 take part

engaged: 4 busy 5 in use 6 active, at work, in gear, intent, signed, tied up 7 focused, working 8 involved, occupied, plighted, reserved 9 committed, on the move, operating, spoken for, wrapped up 10 performing
- **in:** 4 up to
- **(in):** 7 dealing
- **one:** 6 fiancé 7 fiancée
- **one ~ in (suffix):** 3 -eer

engagement: 3 gig, job, vow 4 bout, date, duel, duty, fray, meet, oath, pact, work 5 brush, clash, fight, match, stand, stint, troth, tryst 6 action, battle, combat, errand, pledge, wooing 7 booking, contest, meeting, promise 8 conflict, contract, skirmish 9 assurance, betrothal, blind date, courtship, encounter, enrolment, interview, situation 10 absorption, commission, commitment, enrollment, enterprise, invitation, obligation, rendezvous

engagement __: 4 ring

engaging: 4 nice 5 sweet 6 lovely, pretty 7 amiable, darling, likable, lovable, winning, winsome 8 charming, inviting, loveable, pleasant, pleasing, readable 9 appealing 10 attractive, delightful

En garde! follower: 4 duel

Engel: 6 Lehman, Marian 7 Georgia

Engels: 9 Friedrich

Engels, Friedrich
- **colleague:** Karl Marx

engender: 4 bear, give, make, sire 5 beget, breed, bring, cause, hatch, plant, rouse, spark, spawn 6 arouse, create, foment, incite, induce, instil, lead to 7 develop, instill, produce, provoke 8 generate, occasion 9 instigate, propagate, stimulate 10 bring about, give rise to

engine: 4 tool, V-six 5 means, motor, turbo, V-four 6 barney, device, diesel, fanjet, V-eight, Wankel 7 machine, turbine 8 auto part, catapult, outboard, turbojet 9 apparatus, fire truck, generator, implement, machinery, mechanism 10 instrument, locomotive, powerhouse, power train
- **additive:** 3 STP
- **cover:** 4 hood
- **gun an ~:** 3 rev 4 race
- **housing:** 3 pod
- **meas.:** 2 hp 3 rps
- **part:** 3 cam, cyl., fan 4 pump 8 cylinder
- **problem:** 5 no oil
- **small ~:** 6 donkey
- **sound:** 3 hum, pur 4 chug, ping, purr, putt, roar 5 cough, knock, vroom 6 varoom

engine __: 5 block, house 7 company

__ engine: 3 gas, ion, jet 4 fire 5 steam 6 diesel, rotary, search, Wankel

Engine Engine #9 (1965 song)
- **artist:** Roger Miller

engineer: 3 rig 4 plan, plot, tech. 5 build, set up, stage 6 create, devise, direct, manage 7 arrange, builder, concoct, conduct, finagle, operate, planner 8 conceive, contrive, designer, maneuver, organize 9 construct, fashioner, machinate, negotiate, originate 10 bring about, manipulate, mastermind, put through
- **furry ~:** 6 beaver

__ engineer: 4 port 5 civil 6 flight, marine, mining

__-engineer: 7 reverse

engineering
- **branch:** 4 mech. 5 civil 10 mechanical
- **datum:** 4 spec 6 detail
- **feat:** 3 dam 4 dike 6 bridge
- **subject:** 4 math, phys. 7 physics
- **toy:** 4 Lego
- **univ.:** 3 MIT, RPI

__ engineering: 7 genetic

Engineers school: 6 Lehigh

Engine Number 9 (1970 song)
- **artist:** Wilson Pickett

__-engine red: 4 fire

engird: 4 ring, wind 6 circle 7 enclose, environ, inclose 8 encircle, surround 9 encompass

England: 4 isle 6 Albion
- **ancient god:** 3 Tiu
- **archaeologist:** 5 Evans 6 Petrie
- **astronomer:** 6 Halley 8 Herschel 9 Eddington
- **biochemist:** 6 Sanger 7 Hopkins
- **biologist:** 6 Huxley
- **biophysicist:** 7 Hodgkin
- **botanist:** 5 Banks
- **bovine:** 5 Devon 6 Jersey, Sussex 7 Red Poll 8 Guernsey, Hereford 10 Lincoln Red
- **boys' school:** 4 Eton
- **cathedral city:** 3 Ely
- **cheese:** 7 Chester, Stilton 8 Cheshire
- **chemist:** 4 Davy 5 Black, Boyle, Soddy 6 Dalton, Perkin, Ramsay 7 Crookes, Hodgkin 9 Cavendish, Priestley
- **city:** 4 Bath, Ryde, York 5 Blyth, Crewe, Derby, Dover, Egham, Leeds, Luton, Otley, Poole, Rugby 6 Batley, Bolton, Bootle, Dudley, Eccles, Exeter, Havant, Jarrow, Kendal, London, Oldham, Ossett, Oxford, Seaham, Slough, Stroud, Widnes, Yeovil 7 Banbury, Berwick, Bexhill, Bristol, Burnley, Cannock, Crawley, Ipswich, Margate, Norwich, Reading, Staines, Sunbury, Swindon, Telford, Walsall, Watford 8 Bradford, Brighton, Coventry, Hastings, Hereford, Plymouth 9 Cambridge, Leicester, Liverpool, Rotherham, Sheffield, Stockport, Worcester 10 Birmingham, Chelmsford, Colchester, Eastbourne, Gloucester, Manchester, Nottingham, Sunderland 11 Bournemouth
- **clergyman:** 6 Wesley
- **combining form:** 5 Anglo-
- **composer:** 4 Arne 5 Elgar, Holst, Lawes 7 Britten
- **country festival:** 3 ale
- **county:** 4 Beds, Kent, Oxon 5 Berks, Bucks, Cambs, Devon, Essex, Hants, Herts, Hunts, Lancs, Leics, Lincs, Middx, Notts, Salop, Warks, Wilts, Worcs, Yorks 6 Derbys, Dorset, Durham, Gloucs, Staffs, Surrey, Sussex 7 Norfolk, Rutland, Suffolk 8 Cheshire, Cornwall, Hereford, Somerset 9 Berkshire, Hampshire, Middlesex, Northants, Wiltshire, Yorkshire 10 Cumberland, Derbyshire, Lancashire, Shropshire
- **courtier:** 6 Sidney 7 Raleigh 8 Suckling
- **dance:** 6 morris
- **designer:** 6 Morris
- **diarist:** 5 Pepys
- **dukedom:** 4 York
- **Egyptologist:** 5 Young 6 Petrie
- **essayist:** 4 Lamb 5 Lewis, Pater, Powys 6 Pinero, Steele 9 Priestley, Stapledon
- **explorer:** 4 Cook, Ross 5 Cabot, Davys, Drake 6 Baffin, Hudson 7 Dampier, Gilbert, Hawkins, Hillary, Raleigh
- **French port nearest ~:** 6 Calais
- **garden feature:** 4 maze
- **geneticist:** 5 Crick 6 Galton
- **geologist:** 5 Lyell
- **historian:** 7 Toynbee, Walpole 8 Runciman, Strachey
- **humanist:** 4 More
- **humorist:** 9 Wodehouse
- **hymn writer:** 5 Watts 6 Wesley
- **illustrator:** 6 Potter
- **invader of ~:** 5 Saxon 6 Norman
- **island:** 3 Ely, Man 5 Wight 6 Jersey 8 Guernsey
- **journalist:** 5 Smart
- **king:** 4 Edwy, John 5 Edgar, Edred, Henry, James 6 Alfred, Canute, Edmund, Edward, Egbert, George, Harold, Henry I, Henry V, James I 7 Charles, Edward I, Edward V, George I, George V, Henry II, Henry IV, Henry VI, James II, Richard,

EN

Stephen, William **8** Charles I, Edward II, Edward IV, Edward VI, Ethelred, George II, George IV, George VI, Henry III, Henry VII, Richard I, William I **9** Athelstan, Charles II, Edward III, Edward VII, Ethelbald, Ethelbert, Ethelwulf, George III, Henry VIII, Richard II, William II, William IV **10** Edward VIII, Richard III, William III
lake: **8** Grasmere **10** Windermere
lexicographer: **7** Johnson **9** Partridge
mathematician: **7** Russell **9** Whitehead
money: **3** mil **5** broad, groat, noble, unite **6** guinea, tester, teston **7** carolus, jacobus, testoon **9** rose-noble
natural historian: **3** Ray **6** Darwin **7** Wallace
neighbor: **4** Eire **5** Wales **7** Ireland **8** Scotland
network: **3** BBC
of ancient ~: **6** Anglic
pamphleteer: **5** Paine
philosopher: **4** Ryle **5** Locke **7** Russell, Spencer **9** Stapledon, Whitehead
physicist: **5** Boyle, Bragg, Hooke, Joule **6** Kelvin, Newton **7** Crookes, Faraday, Thomson, Tyndall **8** Blackett, Chadwick, Rayleigh **9** Cavendish, Eddington **10** Rutherford
physiologist: **6** Adrian
pianist: **4** Hess
playwright: **5** Eliot, Nashe, Orton, Peele **6** Morgan, Pinero, Pinter, Rowley, Rudkin, Savage, Steele, Storey, Wesker **7** Chapman, Marlowe, Nichols, Osborne, Shaffer, Shirley, Webster, Whiting **8** Rattigan, Sheridan, Stoppard **9** Middleton, Priestley, Wycherley **11** Shakespeare
poet: **4** Owen, Pope, Read **5** Donne, Eliot, Monro, Peele, Powys, Raine, Rowse, Smart, Smith, Swift, Wyatt **6** Morris, Sidney, Symons, Waller **7** Chapman, Marlowe, Marvell, Peacock, Quarles, Raleigh, Sassoon, Shelley, Sitwell, Skelton, Southey, Spender, Spenser **8** Lovelace, Overbury, Richards, Rossetti, Suckling, Tennyson **9** Sackville, Southwell, Swinburne **10** Wordsworth **11** Shakespeare **13** Sackville-West
port: **4** Hull **5** Dover **6** London **8** Falmouth, Newhaven, Penzance, Plymouth, Sandwich, Weymouth **9** Liverpool, Newcastle **10** Colchester, Folkestone, Portsmouth
professor's deg.: **4** Lit.D.
publisher: **7** Newbery
queen: **4** Anne, Mary **5** Mary I **6** Mary II **8** Victoria **9** Elizabeth **10** Elizabeth I **11** Elizabeth II
racetrack: **5** Ascot, Epsom
ritual: **3** tea
river: **3** Cam, Usk, Wye **4** Aire, Avon, Leam, Ouse, Tyne **5** Leame, Tamar, Trent **6** Thames
royal house: **4** York **5** Blois, Tudor **6** Stuart **7** Hanover, Windsor **8** Normandy **9** Lancaster **11** Plantagenet
saint: **4** Bede **5** Alban, Baeda **6** Anselm **7** Dunstan **8** Boniface, Cuthbert **10** Thomas More **18** Edward the Confessor
satirist: **4** Pope **5** Nashe, Swift **9** Thackeray
scientist: **3** Ray **4** Davy, Snow **5** Banks, Black, Boyle, Bragg, Crick, Evans, Hooke, Joule, Lyell, Soddy, Young **6** Adrian, Dalton, Darwin, Galton, Halley, Huxley, Kelvin, Newton, Perkin, Ramsay, Sanger **7** Crookes, Faraday, Hodgkin, Hopkins, Thomson, Tyndall, Wallace **8** Blackett, Chadwick, Herschel, Rayleigh **9** Cavendish, Eddington, Priestley **10** Rutherford
sea: **5** Irish, North
spa: **4** Bath
to America: **4** ally
writer: **3** Pym **4** Amis, Lamb, Lear, More, Rhys, Ryle, Snow, Wain, West **5** Lewis, Locke, Mason, Menen, Moore, Murry, Orczy, Paine, Pater, Pepys, Powys, Reade, Rolfe, Shute, Watts, Waugh, White, Woolf, Young **6** Browne, Burney, Clarke, Conrad, Milton, Morgan, Morris, Orwell, Petrie, Potter, Powell, Ruskin, Sansom, Sayers, Sterne, Storey, Symons, Walton, Warner, Warton, Wilson **7** Dickens, le Carré, Marryat, Marston, Maugham, Meynell, Mitford, Montagu, Painter, Peacock, Renault, Russell, Shelley, Sitwell, Spencer, Stephen, Stewart, Surtees, Tolkien, Toynbee, Walpole **8** Christie, Lawrence, Macaulay, Matineau, Meredith, Mortimer, Quennell, Runciman, Sillitoe, Smollett, Strachey, Trollope, Williams **9** du Maurier, Masefield, Massinger, Mitchison, Partridge, Priestley, Pritchett, Radcliffe, Stapledon, Thackeray, Whitehead, Wodehouse **10** Muggeridge, Richardson **11** Shakespeare
see also British, Great Britain
England __: **6** Swings
__ England: **3** New
England Swings (1965 song)
artist: Roger Miller
Englewood: **4** city, town
locale: **7** Florida **8** Colorado **9** New Jersey
English: **4** Alex, spin **8** language
body ~: **6** motion
deg.: **4** Lit.B.
homework: **5** essay, theme, vocab. **10** vocabulary
horn: **3** cor **4** reed
in plain ~: **6** namely **8** straight
English __: **3** elm, ivy, Lit, pea, red, yew **4** horn **6** muffin, saddle, setter, sonnet **7** Channel
English __ spaniel: **3** toy **6** cocker
__ English: **3** Old **4** body **5** king's **6** pidgin, queen's **7** reverse
English at the North Pole, The
author: Jules Verne
English Channel
feeder: **3** Exe **4** Orne **5** Seine, Somme
gulf: **6** St. Malo
isle: **5** Wight **6** Jersey **8** Guernsey
town: **5** Dover, Poole **6** Dieppe
English Derby
locale: **5** Epsom
English horn
kin: **4** oboe, reed
Englishman: **4** Brit **6** Briton
exclamation: **4** I say **8** good show
English muffin
alternative: **4** roll **5** bagel, bialy, toast **9** croissant
English Patient, The (1996 film)
cast: Juliette Binoche, Willem Dafoe, Ralph Fiennes, Kristen Scott Thomas
role: **4** Hana
setting: **6** Sahara
English setter: **3** dog **5** canid **6** canine
English Suites
composer: J.S. Bach
Englund: **6** Robert
englut: **4** gulp **6** guzzle **8** wolf down
engorge: **4** bolt, glut, sate, wolf **5** raven, stuff **6** devour **8** gulp down **10** gobble down
oneself on: **3** eat **4** bolt **6** devour, feed on, finish, ingest, relish **7** consume, feast on, put away, scarf up **8** chow down, gobble up, wolf down **9** polish off, scarf down **10** gormandize
engr.
kind of ~: **4** mech.
sch.: **3** MIT, RPI
engrain: **8** entrench
engrave: **4** etch **5** carve, chase, infix, print, stamp **6** chisel, incise, instil **7** impress, imprint, instill, scratch **8** inscribe **9** mezzotint
engraved pillar: **5** stela, stele
engraver: **5** Dürer **6** etcher **7** jeweler **8** lapidary **10** lapidarist
need: **5** burin **6** dabber, stylus
engraving: **5** print **7** etching, picture, woodcut **8** intaglio **9** mezzotint **10** impression, lithograph
engross: **4** grip, hold, hook **5** rivet, write **6** absorb, arrest, engage, engulf, ingulf, occupy, take up **7** beguile, bewitch, consume, enchain, enthral, immerse, inthral **8** enthrall, interest, inthrall, transfix **9** captivate, enrapture, entertain, fascinate, preoccupy **10** monopolize
engrossed: **4** busy, deep, lost, rapt **6** intent **7** focused, wound up **8** caught up, held fast, obsessed, occupied **9** assiduous, impressed, intrigued, submerged, undivided, wrapped up **10** captivated, enthralled, fascinated, interested, really into, thoughtful, up to here in
engrossing: **8** readable **9** absorbing, consuming, obsessing **10** compelling, intriguing
engrossment: **4** grip, lure, stir **6** allure, regard, turn-on **7** concern, dousing, dunking, passion, pastime **8** interest, intrigue **9** attention, curiosity, diversion, immersion **10** absorption, attraction, enthusiasm, excitement, motivation, saturating, saturation, submerging
engulf: **4** bury, sink **5** drown, flood, swamp, whelm **6** absorb, deluge, devour **7** consume, engross, envelop, immerse, overrun, swallow **8** inundate, overflow, overtake, submerge, surround **9** overwhelm, snow under, swallow up
enhance: **4** gild, gird, lift, tone **5** add to, adorn, amend, boost, build, exalt, fix up, grace, raise, shore, steel **6** anneal, become, bedeck, beef up, better, enrich, harden, polish, prop up, reform, temper, tone up **7** amplify, augment, benefit, bolster, brace up, build up, burgeon, develop, elevate, empower, flatter, fortify, garnish, improve, magnify, shape up, sharpen, shore up, spice up, stiffen, touch up, toughen, upgrade **8** beautify, bourgeon, buttress, decorate, energize, heighten, increase, indurate, spruce up, vitalize **9** embellish, glamorize, intensify, meliorate, reinforce **10** ameliorate, complement, invigorate, strengthen, supplement
enhancement: **4** gain, plus **5** bonus, extra **8** addition, increase **10** supplement
enhancer
flavor ~: **3** MSG **4** herb, salt **5** spice
enhancing: **8** cosmetic **10** decorative, ornamental
enhearten: **4** stir **5** rouse **6** arouse, buck up, stir up **7** inspire **8** embolden, enspirit, imbolden, inspirit, motivate, psyche up
Enid: **4** city, town **6** Blyton, Markey **7** Bagnold
husband: **7** Geraint
locale: **8** Oklahoma
Enid Is Sleeping (1990 film)
cast: Jeffrey Jones, Elizabeth Perkins, Judge Reinhold
enigma: **4** crux, knot, prob. **5** poser, vexer **6** puzzle, riddle, secret, sphinx, teaser **7** arcanum, baffler, boggler, mystery, paradox, problem, puzzler, stumper **8** question **9** conundrum **10** mind-bender, perplexity
Enigma (2001 film)
cast: Jeremy Northam, Dougray Scott, Kate Winslet
director: Michael Apted
Enigma, An
author: Edgar Allan Poe
enigmatic: **4** dark **5** mirky, murky, vague **6** arcane, mystic **7** complex, cryptic, obscure, unclear **8** abstruse, Delphian, esoteric, nebulous, puzzling, stealthy, ulterior **9** ambiguous, confusing, cryptical, difficult, secretive **10** indistinct, inexplicit, mysterious, perplexing

Enigma Variations
composer: Edward Elgar
enisle: **6** maroon, strand **7** isolate, seclude **8** set apart **10** place apart, quarantine
Eniwetok: **4** isle **5** atoll **6** island
event: **5** A-test, N-test
test subject: **5** H-bomb
enjoin: **3** ban, bar, bid, put **4** tell, urge, warn **5** debar, force, order, plead, press **6** adjure, decree, demand, direct, forbid, impose, indite, ordain **7** command, counsel, dictate, enforce, inhibit, require **8** call upon, preclude, prohibit, restrain **9** prescribe, proscribe, recommend
enjoinment: **7** refusal
enjoy: **3** dig, own, use **4** grok, have, like, love **5** adore, boast, dig in, eat up, fancy, go for, lap up, revel, savor, taste **6** dote on, relish, savour, wallow **7** have fun, possess, rejoice, revel in **8** cotton to, dote upon, flip over, thrill to **9** delight in, get high on, have a ball, luxuriate **10** appreciate, experience, have a blast
enjoyable: **3** fun **5** jolly, kicky, merry, nifty, sweet **6** lively, lovely **7** likable, welcome **8** heavenly, pleasant, pleasing, readable **9** agreeable, delicious, flavorful, marvelous, palatable **10** delectable, delightful, gratifying, preferable, relishable, satisfying
enjoyment: **3** fun **4** kick, life, love, play, zest **5** gusto, sport **6** luxury, relish, thrill **7** rapture **8** felicity, pleasure **9** amusement, diversion, happiness, merriment, ownership **10** indulgence, possession, recreation, relaxation
exclamation of ~: **3** yum **6** yum-yum
Enjoy the Silence (1990 song)
artist: Depeche Mode
Enke, Karin: **6** skater
enkindle: **4** burn **5** light, rouse, spark **6** arouse, ignite **7** inspire **9** catch fire, impassion
enl.: **4** incr.
see also enlarge, enlist
enlace: **3** tie **4** bind **5** braid, twine, twist **6** bind up, corset, thread **8** surround, tangle up **9** interfold, interlock **10** intertwine, interweave
En-lai: **4** Zhou
enlarge: **3** add, pad, wax **4** grow, puff **5** add on, add to, bloat, boost, build, bulge, mount, raise, swell, widen **6** accrue, beef up, blow up, dilate, expand, extend, gather, jack up, puff up, pump up, ramble, recite, spread **7** add on to, advance, amplify, augment, balloon, broaden, burgeon, develop, distend, fill out, inflate, magnify, stretch, thicken, upsurge **8** bourgeon, elongate, escalate, heighten, increase, lengthen, multiply, snowball **9** branch out, expatiate, intumesce, reinforce, spread out **10** aggrandize, exaggerate, strengthen
a hole: **4** ream
enlarged: **5** puffy, tumid **7** swollen
enlargement: **4** incr. **6** blowup, growth, spread **7** buildup **8** addition, increase, swelling
maybe: **5** inset
enlighten: **5** brief, edify, guide, solve, teach, train **6** inform, school, wise up **7** apprise, apprize, educate **8** acquaint, advise of, disabuse, initiate, instruct **9** catechize, elucidate, exemplify, undeceive **10** illuminate
enlightened: **3** hep, hip **4** wise **5** aware, right, savvy **6** with it **7** knowing, learned, liberal, mindful, refined, tuned in **8** profound, rational **9** cognizant, in the know, plugged in
one: **5** arhat **6** Buddha
enlightening: **5** lucid, vivid **6** bright **7** evident, fulgent, refined **8** artistic, cultural, luminous, lustrous **9** brilliant, effulgent, elevating, enriching, graspable, inspiring, refulgent, uplifting
enlightenment: **4** info, life **5** light **6** wisdom **7** culture, liberty
Zen ~: **6** satori
enlink: **3** tie, wed **4** bind, bond, join, meet, mesh, yoke **5** annex, hitch, unite **6** adjoin, attach, bridge, cement, cohere, couple, fasten, hook up **7** combine, conjoin, connect **8** meld with **9** affiliate, interface
enlist: **3** get **4** hire, join, levy **5** draft, enrol, enter **6** assign, call up, employ, engage, enroll, induct, join up, muster, obtain, secure, sign on, sign up, take on **7** appoint, procure, recruit **8** initiate, mobilize, persuade, register, shanghai **9** conscribe, conscript, volunteer **10** commission
again: **4** reup
enlisted one: **2** GI **3** PFC **5** GI Joe **7** private, recruit, soldier, warrior
enlistment: **6** sign-up **9** enrolment, mustering **10** employment, enrollment
enliven: **4** buoy, fire, wake **5** awake, cheer, color, hop up, pep up, rally, renew, rouse, spark, spice, waken **6** arouse, awaken, buck up, buoy up, excite, fire up, jazz up, perk up, pick up, pump up, turn on, vivify, wake up **7** animate, brace up, cheer up, fortify, freshen, gladden, hearten, inspire, juice up, punch up, quicken, refresh, spice up **8** activate, brighten, energize, enspirit, inspirit, vitalize **9** encourage, entertain, galvanize, impassion, stimulate **10** exhilarate, intoxicate, invigorate, rejuvenate, strengthen
en masse: **6** bodily, wholly **8** in unison, mutually, together **10** altogether, completely
enmesh: **3** net **4** hook, mire, trap **5** catch, snare, snarl, twine **6** entrap, tangle **7** embroil, ensnare, entwine, insnare, intwine, involve, related **8** entangle, tangle up **9** interlace **10** intertwine
enmity: **3** ire, war **4** feud, hate **5** anger, odium, spite, venom **6** animus, grudge, hatred, malice, rancor, spleen **7** dislike, ill will **8** acrimony, aversion, bad blood, loathing **9** animosity, antipathy, hostility, nastiness, prejudice **10** abhorrence, alienation, antagonism, bitterness, unkindness
Enna: **4** city, town
locale: **5** Italy
ennea-: **4** nine
preceder: **4** octo-
successor: **3** dec-
ennead: **4** nine **5** Muses, nonet
less one: **5** octad
one of a mythical ~: **4** Clio **5** Erato **6** Thalia, Urania **7** Euterpe **8** Calliope **9** Melpomene **10** Polyhymnia **11** Terpsichore
Ennio: **9** Morricone
Ennis: **4** city, town **7** Skinnay
locale: **5** Texas **7** Ireland
ennoble: **5** crown, deify, exalt, honor **6** praise **7** elevate, magnify, promote **10** aggrandize
ennui: **4** tire **6** apathy, tedium **7** boredom, languor **8** doldrums, flatness, monotony **9** lassitude, weariness **10** melancholy
causing ~: **5** ho-hum
exhibit ~: **4** yawn
Ennui
author: Langston Hughes
Eno: **5** Brian
Enoch: **5** Arden, Light
cousin: **4** Enos
father: **4** Cain **5** Jared
grandmother: **3** Eve
son: **4** Irad **6** Lamech
Enoch Arden: **4** poem
author: Alfred Tennyson
enoki: **8** mushroom
Enola Gay: **5** plane **6** bomber **8** airplane
payload: **5** A-bomb **6** Fat Man
enormity: **4** bulk, evil, size **6** horror **7** bigness, outrage **8** atrocity, evilness, hugeness, rankness, vastness, vileness **9** depravity, flagrancy, greatness, grossness, immensity, magnitude **10** infinitude
enormous: **3** big **4** huge, vast **5** bulky, giant, great, gross, jumbo, large **6** cosmic, mighty **7** hulking, immense, mammoth, massive, sizable, titanic **8** colossal, cosmical, gigantic, king-size, oversize, sizeable, spacious, terrific, towering, whapping, whopping **9** excessive, fantastic, Herculean, humongous, monstrous, overlarge, whalelike **10** astronomic, gargantuan, monumental, prodigious, stupendous, tremendous
enormously: **4** a lot, much, very **6** vastly **7** big time **9** in a big way, like crazy **10** incredibly
Enormous Radio, The
author: John Cheever
Enormous Room, The
author: e.e. cummings
Enos: **5** Mills **6** Barton, Cabell **9** Slaughter
father: **4** Seth
grandfather: **4** Adam
grandmother: **3** Eve
Enosh
see Enos
enough: **5** ample, amply, uncle **6** fairly, plenty, rather **8** abundant, adequate **9** bounteous, bountiful, plenteous, plentiful **10** abundantly, acceptable, acceptably, moderately, reasonably, sufficient, unbearable
already: **4** OK OK
barely ~: **5** light, scant
be ~: **2** do **4** suit, work **5** get by, serve **6** render **7** fulfill, perform, realize, satisfy, suffice, work out
be good ~: **2** do **4** pass, suit, work **5** avail, get by, serve **6** answer **7** content, deliver, qualify, satisfy, suffice **10** hit the spot
good ~: **4** fine **7** up to par **8** adequate, very well **9** tolerable **10** acceptable
more than ~: **5** ample, spare, undue **6** excess, galore, oodles
not good ~: **7** lacking, wanting **8** inferior **9** deficient, half-baked, imperfect **10** inadequate, incomplete
old ~: **5** of age
old ~ to know better: **5** adult, grown, of age **6** mature **7** grown-up
sure ~: **7** sincere **10** absolutely, guaranteed
well ~: **4** so-so **9** tolerably **10** acceptably, adequately, fairly well
__ enough: **4** good, sure **5** oddly
Enough (2002 film)
cast: Bill Campbell, Juliette Lewis, Jennifer Lopez
director: Michael Apted
Enough!: **5** can it, I give, uncle **6** no more, quit it, stop it
__ Enough and Time: **5** World
Enough Rope
author: Dorothy Parker
enounce: **5** state
en passant: **7** by the by **8** by the way **9** in passing
capture: **4** pawn
enplane: **5** board, get on, hop on
__-en-Provence: **3** Aix
Enquirer: **5** paper **9** newspaper
locale: **10** Cincinnati
Enquiry
author: Dick Francis
enrage: **3** ire **4** rile **5** anger, steam, upset **6** fire up, ireful, madden, rile up, tee off, work up **7** enflame, incense, inflame, make mad, provoke, steam up, tick off **8** irritate, make boil **9** displease, infuriate, make angry **10** exasperate
enraged: **3** hot, mad **4** ired, sore **5** angry, cross, huffy, irate, livid, riled, wroth **6** fierce, fuming, ireful, raging, raving, red-hot **7** angered, boiling, furious, ranting, violent **8** choleric, incensed, inflamed, volcanic, white-hot, wrathful **9** indignant, resentful, splenetic **10** aggravated, infuriated
enrapt: **6** joyful **7** all eyes **8** absorbed, caught up, turned on **9** attentive, delighted, enchanted, entranced **10** captivated, enthralled, fascinated, mesmerized, spell-bound, starry-eyed, transfixed

enrapture: **4** send **5** charm, elate, rivet **6** allure, enamor, ravish **7** attract, beatify, beguile, bewitch, delight, enchant, engross, enthral, inthral **8** enthrall, entrance, inthrall **9** captivate, fascinate, spellbind, transport
enraptured: **4** rapt **6** joyful, joyous **7** far gone **8** blissful, ecstatic, held fast, jubilant **9** bewitched **10** fascinated, infatuated
enravish: **7** beatify **8** enthrall **9** enrapture
enrich: **4** lard **5** add to, adorn, build, endow, fix up **6** better, fatten, fulfil, polish, reform, uplift **7** build up, develop, elevate, enhance, fortify, fulfill, improve, shape up, sharpen, sweeten, upgrade **8** decorate, ornament, spruce up **9** cultivate, embellish, fertilize, make finer, meliorate **10** aggrandize, ameliorate, supplement
enrichment: **7** enhance **8** flourish, ornament **9** accessory, adornment, bedecking **10** complement, completion, decoration, festooning, garnishing, supplement
Enrico: **5** Fermi **6** Caruso **9** Colantoni
in English: **5** Henry
Enright: **3** Dan, Ray
Enrique in English: **5** Henry
enrobe: **4** garb **5** dress **6** attire, clothe **7** cover up
enrobed: **4** clad
enroll: **3** reg. **4** join, list **5** admit, draft, enter, learn, start **6** accept, engage, enlist, join up, line up, muster, record, sign on, sign up, wrap up **7** recruit **8** register **9** chronicle, subscribe
enrollment: **9** accession, admission, induction, reception **10** acceptance, employment, engagement, enlistment, initiation
__ enrollment: **4** open
enroot: **3** fix **5** plant **6** attach, foster **7** develop, implant **8** take hold **9** establish
__ en Rose: **5** La Vie
en route: **6** aboard, coming, midway **7** driving **8** embarked, motoring, on the way **9** advancing, in transit, on the road, traveling
on a ship: **4** asea **5** at sea
__ en scène: **4** mise
ensconce: **3** set, sit **4** bury, hide **5** cache, cover, plant, stash **6** instal, locate, nestle, occupy, settle **7** conceal, install, shelter, situate, snuggle **8** stow away, tuck away **9** establish, sequester
enseal: **5** stamp **8** notarize
ensemble: **4** band, cast, garb, suit, togs, trio **5** array, choir, dress, group, nonet, octet, suite **6** attire, chorus, livery, outfit, septet, sestet, sextet, troupe **7** clothes, company, costume, octette, quartet, quintet **8** entirety, glee club, sextette, totality **9** aggregate, gathering, orchestra, quintette, vocalists **10** assemblage, collection, Sunday best
furniture ~: **5** suite
leading part: **5** primo
musical ~: **4** band, orch., trio **5** choir, combo, nonet, octet **6** chorus, sestet, sextet **7** octette, quartet **8** sextette **9** orchestra, vocalists
__ ensemble: **4** tout
Ensenada: **4** city, town
locale: **6** Mexico
enshrine: **5** adore, bless, ensky, exalt **6** hallow, revere **7** cherish **8** remember, sanctify, treasure **9** care about **10** consecrate, hold sacred
enshroud: **4** bury, hide, mask, veil, wrap **5** cloak, cover **7** conceal
enshrouded: **6** covert, hidden, mystic, secret, unseen **9** concealed, covered up, incognito, invisible **10** tucked away, undercover, under wraps
ensign: **4** flag, rank **5** badge **6** banner, colors, emblem, sailor **7** pennant **8** gonfalon, standard, streamer **9** banderole
asst.: **3** CPO
evil ~: **4** Iago
org.: **3** USN
Ensign Pulver (1964 film)
cast: Burl Ives, Tommy Sands
ensilage: **5** straw
ensile: **5** store
ensky: **4** hail, laud, lift **5** bless, boost, crown, deify, exalt, extol, honor, raise **6** esteem, praise, revere **7** acclaim, commend, dignify, elevate, ennoble, glorify, idolize, lionize, magnify, promote, worship **8** enshrine, enthrone, eulogize **9** celebrate, recommend **10** aggrandize, compliment
enslave: **4** tame **9** indenture, subjugate
enslavement: **4** yoke **6** chains **9** servitude
ensnare: **3** bag, get, nab, net **4** grab, hook, lure, mesh, mire, snag, take, trap **5** catch, snarl, trick **6** enmesh, entrap, immesh, inmesh, rope in, suck in, tangle **7** capture, deceive, embroil, mislead **8** entangle, inveigle
ensorcelled: **5** magic **7** magical **8** wizardly, wizardry **9** bewitched **10** bewitching, enchanting, entrancing, miraculous
Ensor, James: **6** artist **7** painter
homeland: **7** Belgium
ensoul: **4** love **5** adore, prize, savor, value **6** admire, dote on, esteem, revere **7** care for, cherish, idolize, worship **8** enshrine, hold dear, treasure, venerate
ensue: **5** arise, occur, trail **6** follow, happen, result **7** go after, proceed, succeed **8** come next **9** arise from, come after, eventuate, intervene, supervene, transpire **10** come to pass
ensuing: **4** next **5** after, later **6** behind, coming, serial **8** eventual, in back of **9** following, resultant **10** consequent, subsequent, succeeding, successive
ensure: **3** ice **4** lock, mind, seal **5** cinch, guard **6** lock in, lock up, secure **7** certify, confirm, protect, warrant **8** attest to, make safe, nail down **9** guarantee, safeguard
ensured: **3** gtd. **7** certain **10** guaranteed
ENT
part of ~: **3** ear **4** nose **6** throat
entablature part: **6** frieze
entail: **4** mean **5** cause, imply **7** call for, include, involve, require
entangle: **3** net **4** hook, mesh, mire, snag, trap **5** catch, mix up, ravel, snare, snarl, twine **6** burden, enmesh, entrap, hamper, immesh, impede, inmesh, jumble, muddle, puzzle, tangle **7** confuse, embroil, ensnare, entwine, insnare, intwine, involve, perplex **8** bewilder **9** implicate, interlace **10** complicate, intertwine, interweave
entangled: **6** knotty, tricky **7** complex **8** abstruse, tortuous **9** Byzantine, difficult, elaborate, intricate **10** convoluted, perplexing
entanglement: **3** web **4** knot, mesh, mess, node, trap **5** mix-up, skein, snare, snarl, tieup **6** affair, cobweb, jumble, muddle, tangle **7** liaison, pitfall **8** disorder, intrigue, quagmire **9** labyrinth
Entebbe: **4** city, town
action: **4** raid
locale: **6** Uganda
entendre
double ~: **3** pun **8** wordplay
__ entendu: **4** bien
entente: **4** bloc, pact **6** accord, treaty **7** compact, concord **8** alliance **9** agreement
__ Entente: **6** Triple
enter: **3** key, log **4** book, come, go in, join, type **5** begin, enrol, get in, input, key in, pop in, probe, reach **6** access, appear, arrive, blow in, bust in, come in, drop in, ease in, edge in, enlist, enroll, fill in, go into, horn in, invade, join up, jump in, move in, muster, pierce, pile in, record, roll in, rush in, show up, sign on, sign up, slip in, step in, type in, walk in, worm in **7** barge in, break in, burst in, crowd in, drive in, ingress, intrude, punch in, put down, set down, sneak in, turn out **8** breeze in, come into, commence, embark on, enroll in, initiate, inscribe, mark down, pass into, register, set about, set out on **9** penetrate, set foot in **10** inaugurate, infiltrate, take part in
a harbor: **4** dock **5** put in
a highway: **5** merge
allow to ~: **5** admit, greet, let in **6** accept **7** embrace, receive, welcome
a plea: **3** sue
cyberspace: **5** log on
data: **4** type **5** input, key in **6** type in
how actors ~: **5** on cue
into: **4** join, open **5** begin, start, study **6** assume, launch **7** analyze, kick off, lead off, partake **8** commence, consider, get going, initiate **9** originate, undertake **10** inaugurate, scrutinize
one by one: **6** file in
enter __: **4** into, upon
__ Enter: **5** Do Not
Enter neighbor: **5** Shift
enterprise: **3** job, try **4** dash, firm, plan, push, task, zeal **5** cause, drive, pluck, quest, trade, vigor **6** action, affair, daring, effort, energy, hustle, outfit, spirit **7** attempt, company, concern, courage, crusade, project, pursuit, venture **8** activity, ambition, audacity, boldness, business, campaign, endeavor, gumption, industry **9** adventure, alertness, eagerness, foresight, happening, operation, readiness **10** engagement, enthusiasm, expedition, experiment, get-up-and-go, initiative
lack of ~: **5** sloth
__ enterprise: **4** free
Enterprise: **4** city, town **9** car rental **10** auto rental
alternative: ***see*** car rental
journey: **4** trek
letters: **3** NCC, USS
locale: **7** Alabama
officer: **4** Data, Sulu, Troi **5** Bones, McCoy, Scott, Spock, Uhura **6** Chekov
speed: **4** warp
Enterprise (UPN sci-fi)
cast: Scott Bakula (Capt. Jonathan Archer)
John Billingsley (Dr. Phlox)
Jolene Blalock (T'Pol)
John Fleck (Silik)
Dominic Keating (Lt. Malcolm Reed)
Anthony Montgomery (Ens. Travis Mayweather)
Linda Park (Ens. Hoshi Sato)
Connor Trinneer (Cmdr. Trip Tucker)
dog: **7** Porthos
__ Enterprise: **3** USS **4** Free
enterprising: **4** bold, busy, go-go, spry **5** astir, eager, perky **6** active, at work, daring, lively **7** dashing, driving, dynamic, zealous **8** animated, aspiring, bustling, diligent, hustling, intrepid, vigorous **9** assiduous, energetic, sprightly
Enter Sandman (1991 song)
artist: Metallica
entertain: **4** bear, fete, host **5** amuse, charm, cheer, lodge, put up, treat **6** absorb, divert, harbor, listen, occupy, please, regale, tickle **7** beguile, comfort, delight, disport, engross, enliven, enthral, gratify, harbour, inthral, receive, welcome **8** distract, enthrall, interest, inthrall **9** captivate, knock dead, make merry, recognize, socialize, spring for, stimulate, think over, titillate **10** anticipate, cogitate on, deliberate, keep in mind
an idea: **4** muse **5** study **6** ponder **7** reflect **8** cogitate, consider, mull over, ruminate **9** think over **10** deliberate, introspect
entertainer: **2** DJ **4** host, mime, name **5** actor, clown, comic, mimer **6** amuser, dancer, deejay, singer **7** acrobat, actress **8** comedian, humorist, musician, thespian **9** ballerina, chanteuse, performer

10 comedienne
engage an ~: 4 book, hire 5 set up 6 line up, pick up 7 procure 8 register, schedule
medieval ~: 4 bard, poet 8 minstrel
entertainers' union: 3 SAG 5 AFTRA
Entertainer, The: 3 rag
Entertainer, The (1974 song)
artist: Marvin Hamlisch
entertaining: 3 fun 5 funny, jolly, light, merry, witty 6 clever, lively, moving, social 7 piquant, rousing 8 humorous, pleasant, readable, stirring 9 laughable
entertainment: 3 fun 4 play, show 5 party, sport 6 affair, frolic 7 delight, pastime, revelry 8 pleasure 9 reception 10 recreation
center: 6 arcade
center component: 2 TV 3 VCR 5 TV set 9 DVD player
charge: 5 cover
choice: 4 show 5 movie, revue 6 comedy, review 7 theater
conglomerate: 3 MCA 4 Sony 6 Viacom
home ~ letters: 3 VHS
inflight ~: 5 movie
__ Entertainment: 5 That's
Entertainment Tonight
host: 4 Hart, Tesh
__ Entertain You: 5 Let Me
Enter the Dragon (1973 film)
cast: Bruce Lee
Enter the Matrix
company: 5 Atari
enthrall: 4 grab, grip, hook, send 5 charm, rivet 6 absorb, enamor, engage, ravish 7 attract, beatify, beguile, bewitch, enchant, engross, satisfy 8 entrance, interest 9 captivate, enrapture, entertain, fascinate, hypnotize, indenture, infatuate, knock dead, mesmerize, preoccupy, spellbind, subjugate, transport
enthralled: 4 agog, rapt 6 enrapt 8 held fast 9 attentive, engrossed, possessed 10 fascinated
enthralling: 7 lovable 8 loveable, readable
enthrallment: 7 slavery
enthrone: 4 king, seat 5 ensky, exalt 6 invest 7 glorify, instate, raise up
enthuse: 4 gush, rave, send 5 drool, emote, flush, psych 6 excite, fire up, thrill, work up 7 get into, impress, psych up 8 interest 9 electrify, go on about 10 bubble over, effervesce, get excited
enthused: 4 keen 6 elated, fervid, gung-ho 7 fervent 8 inspired
about: 5 big on
enthusiasm: 3 vim, zip 4 dash, élan, fire, life, zeal, zest, zing 5 ardor, drive, gusto, mania, oomph, spark, verve, vigor 6 energy, esprit, fervor, relish, spirit 7 ardency, avidity, emotion, passion, rapture 8 alacrity, ambition, delirium, devotion, fervency, interest, keenness, optimism, vivacity 9 animation, eagerness, élan vital, fieriness, intensity, obsession, transport, vehemence 10 conviction, ebullience, enterprise, excitement, exuberance, fanaticism, initiative, joyfulness
combining form: 5 -mania
lack of ~: 5 ennui 6 apathy, tedium 7 boredom, languor 8 doldrums, monotony 9 lassitude, weariness
show ~: 5 eat up, lap up 10 effervesce
enthusiast: 3 fan, nut 4 buff, jock 5 fiend, freak, lover 6 addict, maniac, rooter, votary, zealot 7 admirer, devotee, fanatic 8 adherent, partisan 9 proponent, supporter 10 aficionado, monomaniac
combining form: 4 -phil 5 -phile
enthusiastic: 3 hot, mad 4 agog, avid, busy, gaga, keen, spry, warm, wild 5 afire, astir, eager, fiery, het up, manic, peppy, perky, rabid, ready, wired 6 ablaze, active, aflame, ardent, at work, fervid, gung ho, hearty, intent, lively, pumped, rah-rah, yeasty 7 anxious, athirst, bananas, devoted, dynamic, earnest, excited, fervent, fired up, glowing, gushing, keyed up, psyched, willing, working, zealous 8 animated, bustling, effusive, juiced up, sanguine, spirited, thrilled, tireless, vigorous, youthful 9 assiduous, dedicated, energetic, rhapsodic, sprightly
about: 4 into 6 all for, keen on
affirmative: 6 yes yes
not ~: 4 loth 5 loath, tepid
sort: 5 tiger
entice: 4 bait, coax, draw, hook, lure, pull, wile 5 decoy, shill, snare, tempt 6 allure, appeal, arouse, beckon, cajole, draw in, enamor, entrap, lead on, pull in, rope in 7 attract, beguile, enchant, mislead, wheedle 8 appeal to, interest, inveigle, persuade 9 fascinate, sweet-talk, tantalize
enticement: 4 bait, hook, lure, trap 5 decoy, savor, snare 6 allure, carrot, come-on 8 cajolery 9 incentive, mousetrap, sweetener 10 allurement, attraction, inducement, invitation, persuasion, temptation
enticer: 4 vamp 5 lurer
enticing: 4 sexy 6 lovely 8 alluring, inviting, tempting 9 beautiful, covetable, desirable 10 attractive, delectable, persuasive, voluptuous
entire: 3 all 4 full 5 gross, round, sound, total, uncut, utter, whole 6 intact 7 perfect, plenary, radical 8 absolute, all-in-one, complete, finished, integral, livelong, outright, the works, thorough, unbroken 9 aggregate, full-dress, inclusive, inviolate, undamaged, undivided, universal, unlimited, unreduced, untouched 10 continuous, exhaustive, in one piece, unabridged
combining form: 3 hol- 4 holo-, toti-
scale: 4 A to Z 5 field, gamut, range, reach, scope, sweep 6 extent 7 breadth 8 panorama, spectrum
entirely: 3 all 4 just, only, well 5 fully, plumb, quite, right, sheer 6 bodily, in full, in toto, purely, solely, wholly 7 totally, utterly 8 whole hog 9 every inch, like a book, perfectly, to the hilt 10 absolutely, altogether, completely, thoroughly, to the limit, to the teeth
not ~: 6 in part, mostly, partly, sort of
use ~: 5 eat up 7 exhaust 9 polish off
entirety: 3 all, sum 5 gross, total, whole 6 corpus 8 ensemble, totality 9 aggregate 10 opera omnia
entitle: 3 dub 4 call, name 5 allow, label, title 6 enable, permit 7 baptize, empower, qualify, warrant 8 christen, nickname 9 authorize, designate, privilege 10 legitimize
entitled: 6 vested
entitled to, be: 4 earn, rate 5 merit 7 deserve
entitlement: 3 due 4 dibs 5 right, title 7 license 9 privilege
org.: 3 SSA
entity: 3 ens 4 body, item, unit 5 being, thing, whole 6 matter, nature, object 7 article, essence, reality, someone 8 creature, organism, presence, quiddity 9 actuality, existence, something 10 individual
single ~: 4 unit 5 monad
starter: 3 non
entom.: 3 sci.
entomb: 6 inhume
entomological stage: 4 pupa 5 imago, larva
entomologist accessory: 3 net
entomology: 7 science
branch of ~: 11 myrmecology
study: 7 insects
entomophobe fear: 7 insects
entourage: 5 court, staff, suite, train 6 escort 7 company, cortege, retinue 9 courtiers, followers, following, hangers-on, retainers 10 associates, attendants, companions, sycophants
entr'__: 4 acte
entrain: 5 board, get on, hop on 6 depart, embark 8 go aboard
entrammel: 3 tie 5 tie up
entrance: 3 way, wow 4 adit, door, gate, grip, hall, ramp 5 charm, inlet, lobby, mouth, start, way in 6 access, advent, allure, dazzle, disarm, enamor, engage, influx, portal, ravish, thrill 7 arrival, attract, beguile, bewitch, delight, doorway, enchant, enthral, gateway, ingress, inthral, passage, postern 8 anteroom, enthrall, hatchway, inthrall 9 admission, beginning, captivate, carry away, enrapture, fascinate, hypnotize, inception, inebriate, mesmerize, spellbind, threshold, transport, vestibule 10 admittance, appearance, initiation, intoxicate, passageway
allow ~: 5 let in 6 lead in 7 receive
curved ~: 4 arch
ender: 3 way
estate ~: 6 portal 7 doorway, ingress
fee: 4 ante
hall: 5 foyer, lobby 6 atrium 9 vestibule
hotel ~ feature: 6 awning, canopy 8 overhang
in France ~: 5 porte
mine ~: 4 adit
requirement: 4 exam, test
stairway: 5 stoop
entranced: 4 lost, rapt 6 enrapt 8 held fast 9 bewitched, delighted, gladdened 10 fascinated
entrancement: 3 hex 5 spell
entrancing: 5 magic 7 lovable, magical 8 heavenly, loveable, magnetic 9 glamorous 10 enchanting, magnetical
entrant: 6 novice 8 aspirant, beginner, initiate, neophyte, newcomer 9 candidate 10 competitor, contestant, tenderfoot
entrants: 5 field 7 entries, runners 8 nominees 10 applicants, candidates
entrap: 3 bag, net 4 hook, lure, mire, take, trap 5 box in, catch, decoy, set up, snare, sting, tempt, trick 6 allure, ambush, draw in, enmesh, entice, immesh, inmesh, lay for, lead on, reel in, rope in, suck in, tangle 7 beguile, capture, deceive, embroil, ensnare, insnare 8 entangle, inveigle 10 circumvent
Entrapment (1999 film)
cast: Sean Connery, Ving Rhames, Catherine Zeta-Jones
director: Jon Amiel
entreat: 3 ask, beg, sue, woo 4 pray, seek, urge 5 plead, press 6 adjure, appeal, exhort, invoke 7 beseech, implore, request, solicit 8 appeal to, petition 9 impetrate, importune, plead with 10 supplicate
entreaty: 4 plea, suit 6 appeal, demand, desire, prayer 7 coaxing, request 8 petition 9 wheedling 10 invocation
make an ~: 3 ask, beg 4 seek, urge 5 plead, probe, query 6 appeal 7 beseech, implore, inquire, request 8 call upon, petition
entrechat: 4 jump, leap
entrée: 2 in 3 cod, ham 4 bass, beef, chop, crab, dish, duck, fish, lamb, meal, meat, pork, pull, ribs, sole, stew, tuna, veal 5 chops, clams, filet, liver, roast, scrod, squab, steak, tacos, trout, way in 6 access, course, cutlet, dinner, pot pie, salmon, shrimp, ticket, turkey 7 chicken, codfish, doorway, halibut, ingress, lasagna, lasagne, lobster, mussels, oysters, ravioli, sea bass, serving, venison, welcome 8 beef stew, bluefish, fresh ham, lamb stew, main dish, meat loaf, open door, osso buco, passport, pheasant, pork loin, pot roast, scallops 9 admission, crab cakes, fried fish, influence, lamb chops, leg of lamb, meatballs, pork chops, roast duck, roast pork, smoked ham, spaghetti, spare ribs, swordfish, tortillas, veal chops 10 admittance, Cornish hen, enchi-

ladas, fettuccine, main course, rack of lamb, red snapper, stroganoff, tenderloin, tortellini, veal cutlet
Boston ~: 5 scrod 6 schrod
brunch ~: 6 omelet 8 omelette
equine ~: 5 straw
French ~: 4 roti, veau
garnish: 5 cress 7 parsley
give ~ to: 6 take in
list: 4 menu
topping: 5 garni, gravy, sauce
entrench: 3 fix, peg, pin, set, tie 4 bind, bond, camp, glue, lock, nail, nest, root, stay, tack, weld 5 embed, imbed, infix, lodge, paste, perch, plant, roost, squat, stick 6 anchor, cement, enroot, fasten, harden, hole up, secure, settle 7 implant, ingrain, install, instill, station, stiffen, tighten 8 nail down, position, rigidify, solidify 9 establish, stabilize, thumbtack
entrenched: 3 set 9 confirmed 10 inveterate
become ~: 5 dig in
entre nous: 7 sub rosa 8 in secret, secretly 9 between us, privately
entrepreneur: 6 backer, tycoon 7 founder 8 promoter
letters: 3 DBA, SBA
entropy: 5 chaos, decay 7 decline 9 mobocracy
entrust: 4 lend, vest 5 leave, trust 6 assign, charge, commit, invest 7 commend, confide, consign, empower, present 8 accredit, delegate, hand over, relegate, turn over 9 surrender 10 commission
entry: 3 way 4 adit, door, gate, item 5 way in 6 access, portal, record 7 doorway, ingress 8 hatchway, notation, register 9 admission, threshold, vestibule 10 admittance
acct. ~: 2 cr.
ender: 3 way
fee: 4 ante 5 stake
forbid ~: 3 bar
gain ~: 4 come 5 get in 6 arrive, come in, show up
grant ~ to: 5 admit, greet 6 accept 7 include, receive, welcome
illegal ~: 6 bag job 8 trespass
ledger ~: 4 item, loss 5 asset, debit 6 credit
make an ~: 4 note 6 notate
permit ~: 5 let in 7 allow in
requirement: 5 badge 6 ID card
entry ___: 4 card, form, word 5 blank
Entry of Christ Into Brussels
artist: James Ensor
entryway: 4 door, gate 6 access, portal 7 ingress, postern 9 vestibule
Entwhistle: 4 John
entwine: 4 coil, curl, join, knit, lace, lock, wind 5 braid, plait, snake, snarl, twist, weave 6 enmesh, immesh, inmesh, spiral, splice 7 sinuate 8 entangle 9 corkscrew, interlace 10 interweave
___ Enuff: 4 Tuff
Enugu's country: 6 Biafra
enumerate: 3 add 4 cite, list, name, tell 5 add up, count, state, sum up, tally, total 6 detail, figure, number, recite, reckon, record, run off 7 itemize, mention, recount, run down, specify, tick off 8 spell out, tabulate 9 calculate, inventory, keep count, keep score 10 count noses
enumeration: 5 count, tally 6 census, litany 7 recital
enunciate: 3 say 5 speak, state, utter, voice 6 affirm, intone 7 declare, express 8 proclaim, set forth, vocalize 9 pronounce 10 articulate, promulgate
enunciation: 5 voice 6 speech 8 delivery
enure: 6 harden, season 7 break in, toughen 8 accustom 9 acclimate, condition, get used to, habituate, withstand 10 take effect
(to): 6 harden
env.: 3 SAE 4 SASE
contents: 3 enc., ltr. 4 encl.
designation: 5 PO Box
see also envelope
enveil: 4 bury, wrap 5 cloak, cover, dress, guise, hider, layer 6 clothe, encase, screen, shield, shroud 7 conceal, enclose, envelop, obscure, protect 8 disguise, enshroud, traverse 9 adumbrate 10 spread over
envelop: 3 hug, lap 4 fold, hide, veil, wind, wrap 5 cloak, cover 6 circle, encase, enfold, engulf, enwrap, incase, infold, ingulf, inwrap, muffle, wrap up 7 besiege, blanket, conceal, enclose, inclose, smother 8 muffle up, surround 9 close in on, encompass
envelope: 5 cover 6 jacket, packet 7 wrapper 8 covering 9 container, portfolio 10 atmosphere, integument
abbr.: 3 att. 4 addr., attn.
earth's ~: 3 air 5 ether 6 aether
letters: 4 SWAK
need: 3 gum 4 glue 5 stamp
number: 3 Zip
open an ~: 4 slit
part: 4 flap 5 clasp
phrase: 6 care of
shape: 4 rect. 9 rectangle
wet an ~: 4 lick, seal
envelopment: 5 siege
envenom: 4 sour 8 embitter, imbitter
enviable: 5 lucky 7 desired 8 superior 9 covetable, desirable, excellent, fortunate
assignment: 4 plum
envious: 5 green 7 jealous 8 covetous 9 green-eyed, malicious, resentful 10 begrudging
be ~: 4 lust, seek 5 covet, crave 6 desire 7 ache for, itch for, long for, wish for 8 aspire to, yearn for 9 hanker for, thirst for
environ: 4 area, ring 6 circle, engird 7 enclose, inclose 8 encircle, surround 9 encompass
environment: 4 aura 5 state, world 6 milieu, nature, sphere 7 climate, context, element, habitat, setting, terrain 8 ambiance, ambience, backdrop, vicinity
combining form: 3 eco-
cultureless ~: 5 wilds 6 desert 9 wasteland 10 wilderness
organism modified by ~: 4 ecad
rapid growth ~: 3 den 4 nest 6 cradle, hotbed
science of ~: 7 ecology
environmental: 8 physical
agcy.: 3 DNR, EPA
problem: 4 smog 6 litter 9 pollution
science: 4 ecol. 7 ecology 8 oecology
environment-minded: 5 green
environs: 4 area 6 region, suburb 7 compass, grounds, suburbs 8 confines, purlieus, vicinity 9 outskirts 10 boundaries
envisage: 4 plan 5 fancy, think 7 foresee, imagine, picture, predict, realize 8 conceive, consider, envision 9 visualize 10 anticipate
envisaging: 4 idea, view 5 image, start 6 design, notion, origin, outset, theory, vision 7 infancy, inkling, opinion, reading, thought 8 creation, ideality 9 beginning, cognition, formation, imagining, invention, launching 10 cogitating, conception, exposition, impression, initiation
envision: 3 see 5 fancy, think 7 foresee, imagine, picture, predict, project, realize 8 conceive, envisage 9 fantasize, visualize 10 anticipate
En Vogue
song: Don't Let Go (1996)
Free Your Mind (1992)
Hold on (1990)
My Lovin' (1992)
Whatta Man (1994)
envoy: 3 amb. 5 agent, vicar 6 bearer, consul, deputy, legate, nuncio 7 apostle, attaché, carrier, courier 8 delegate, diplomat, emissary, minister 9 appointee, go-between, messenger 10 ambassador, interceder
envy: 3 sin 4 wish 5 covet 6 resent 8 begrudge, coveting, jealousy
enwind: 4 coil, curl, kink, loop 5 braid, crimp, curve, helix, snake, swirl, twirl, twist, whorl 6 spiral, tangle 7 wreathe 9 corkscrew 10 intertwine
enwrap: 6 shroud 7 envelop, swaddle 8 bundle up, surround
enwreathe: 3 arc 4 arch, coil, curl, gird, hoop, knot, loop, ring, roll 5 curve, twirl, twist, whorl 6 circle, girdle, spiral 7 circuit, scallop 8 encircle 9 encompass
Enya homeland: Ireland
Enzo: 3 car 4 auto 7 Ferrari, Stuarti
enzyme: 5 lyase, renin 6 lipase, pepsin 7 pepsine
genetic ~: 5 DNAse, RNAse
suffix: 3 ase
enzymes, science of: 8 zymology
eoan: 7 auroral
Eocene: 5 Epoch
eohippus: 5 horse 6 equine
Eola
locale: 5 Texas
Eolus: 4 peak 5 mount 8 mountain
locale: 7 Rockies 8 Colorado
E.O.M. item: 4 bill 7 invoice 9 statement
eon: 3 age 4 ages 6 period 7 century, dog's age 8 eternity, long time 10 time period
Buddhist ~: 5 kalpa
Hindu ~: 4 yuga
eonian: 7 endless, eternal 8 infinite, unending 9 boundless, limitless, unbounded, unlimited 10 without end
Eos
brother: 6 Helios
equivalent: 6 Aurora
lover: 4 Ares 5 Orion 8 Astraeus, Cephalus, Tithonus
parent: 4 Thea, Thia 8 Hyperion
sister: 6 Selene
son: 5 Eurus, Notus 6 Boreas, Memnon 7 Adymnus 8 Emathion, Phaethon, Zephyrus
eosin: 3 dye 6 red dye
EPA
concern: 3 AQI, mpg, PCB 4 ecol., smog
part of ~: 3 Env. 6 Agency 10 Protection
eparch: 6 bishop 7 prefect 8 praefect
EPCOT site: 3 Fla. 7 Florida, Orlando
épée: 5 blade, sport, sword 9 swordplay
alternative: 4 foil
move: 5 lunge
wield an ~: 5 fence, parry
Épernay's river: 5 Marne
ephah fraction: 4 omer
ephahs, ten: 3 kor
ephemeral: 5 brief, short 6 mortal 7 passing 8 episodic, fleeting, flitting, meteoric, temporal, volatile 9 fugacious, momentary, temporary, transient 10 episodical, evanescent, short-lived, transitory, unenduring
Ephesians preceder: 9 Galatians
ephod: 8 vestment
Ephron: 4 Nora 5 Delia, Henry
Ephron, Nora: 8 director
film: Bewitched (2005)
Michael (1996)
Sleepless in Seattle (1993)
You've Got Mail (1998)
spouse: Carl Bernstein
epi: 6 finial
ender: 4 cure 6 center
epi-: 4 near, over, upon
epic: 4 huge, poem, saga, tale 5 grand, story, verse 6 epopee, heroic 7 Homeric 8 fabulous, heroical, sweeping 9 grandiose, narrative 10 monumental
Greek ~: 5 Iliad 6 Aeneid 7 Odyssey
hero of a Hindu ~: 4 Rama
Norse ~: 4 edda, saga
of ~ proportions: 3 big 4 huge, vast 5 giant, great, gross, heavy, jumbo, large 6 cosmic 7 immense, mammoth, massive, monster, titanic 8 colossal, enormous, gigantic, oversize, spacious, terrific, towering, whopping 9 extensive, herculean, humongous, monstrous, walloping 10 gargantuan, monumental, overweight, prodigious, tremendous
poetry: 6 epopee 8 epopoeia
reciter: 4 bard

epical: **5** grand, great **6** heroic **8** heroical, majestic **9** grandiose **10** impressive, majestical
epicarp: **4** peel
Epicene
  author: Ben Jonson
epicure: **5** eater **6** foodie **7** gourmet **8** gourmand **10** gastronome
  delicacy: **5** snail, viand **8** escargot
epicurean: **7** sensual **8** sensuous **9** bon vivant, libertine, luxurious, sybaritic **10** gastronome, gluttonous, hedonistic, sensualist, voluptuous
epidemic: **4** rife **6** plague **7** rampant **8** catching, outbreak **9** infection **10** infectious, widespread
epidemiology HQ: **3** CDC
epidermis: **4** pelt, skin
  dermis plus ~: **5** cutis
  opening: **5** stoma
epidote: **3** gem **7** zoisite
epigone: **3** ape **5** mimic, phony **6** copier, monkey, parrot, shadow **7** copycat **8** emulator, follower, imitator, impostor **10** plagiarist
epigram: **3** saw **4** quip **5** moral, motto, truth **6** bon mot, saying **7** proverb **8** aphorism, laconism **9** witticism
epigrammatic: **5** brief, meaty, pithy, short, terse, witty **7** concise, pointed **8** succinct **9** ingenious **10** to the point
  tale: **4** myth, tale, yarn **5** fable, story **6** legend **7** parable **8** allegory
epigraph: **5** motto **6** legend, rubric
epilogue: **3** end **4** coda **6** ending, finale, sequel, wrap-up **9** afterword **10** conclusion, postscript
epimeliad: **5** nymph
Epimetheus: **4** moon **5** giant, Titan
  brother: **5** Atlas **10** Prometheus
  planet: **6** Saturn
Épinal: **4** city, town
  locale: **6** France, Vosges
épinglé: **6** fabric
epinicion: **3** ode **4** poem
epiphany: **7** insight **10** appearance, perception
Epiphany figures: **4** Magi
epiphyte: **5** plant
episcopal: **5** papal **8** churchly, clerical, pastoral, prelatic, priestly **9** canonical, religious **10** pontifical, rabbinical
episcopate: **3** see **7** diocese, prelacy
episode: **5** event, scene, story, thing **6** affair, matter **7** chapter **8** incident, occasion **9** adventure, happening, interlude **10** experience, occurrence
  histrionic ~: **7** tantrum **8** outburst
  violent ~: **5** quake **10** earthquake
episodic: **8** rambling **9** ephemeral **10** digressive
epistle: **6** letter **7** message, missive
  apostle: **4** Paul
  appendage: **2** PS **3** PPS
Epistle to Dr. Arbuthnot
  author: Alexander Pope
epistolize: **5** write **9** drop a line, drop a note **10** correspond
epitaph: **5** elegy **6** legend
  starter: **4** here
Epitaph: **5** paper **9** newspaper
  locale: **9** Tombstone
Epitaph for a Spy
  author: Eric Ambler
epithalamic: **6** bridal **7** marital, nuptial **8** conjugal
epithet: **4** name **5** curse, label, title **6** insult **8** cognomen, nickname **9** expletive, sobriquet
  mild ~: **4** dang, egad, rats **5** egads
epitome: **3** sum **4** type **5** ideal, model **6** digest **7** essence, paragon, summary **8** abstract, exemplar, paradigm, synopsis **9** archetype **10** abridgment, apotheosis, compendium, conspectus, embodiment
epitomize: **5** sum up **6** detail, typify **8** contract, stand for **9** exemplify, represent, symbolize **10** illustrate
epizootic: **8** catching **9** pestilent, spreading **10** contagious, infectious
E Pluribus Unum: **5** Latin, motto
epoch: **3** age, era **4** time **6** period **7** vintage **10** generation
  Cenozoic ~: **6** Eocene
  N. Amer. geologic ~: **5** Erian
  of an ~: **4** eral
  Pleistocene ~: **6** ice age
  Tertiary Period ~: **6** Eocene
Epoch: **6** Eocene **7** Miocene
epochal: **8** periodic **9** momentous
epode: **4** poem **5** verse
  like an ~: **6** heroic **8** heroical
Epodes
  author: Horace
eponym: **4** name **8** namesake
  noted ~: **7** Romulus **8** Quisling, Shrapnel
epopee: **4** epic **5** Iliad **7** Odyssey
__ époque: **5** belle
E. Power __: **5** Biggs
epoxy: **5** resin **6** cement **8** adhesive
Eppa: **5** Rixey
Epperly: **4** peak **5** mount **8** mountain
  locale: **10** Antarctica
Epps: **4** Omar
epsilon: **5** Greek **6** letter
  follower: **4** zeta
  preceder: **5** delta
Epsom: **3** spa
  event: **5** Derby **9** horse race
  locale: **7** England
Epsom __: **4** salt **5** Downs, salts
Epsom and __: **5** Ewell
Epstein: **3** Rob **5** Brian, Jacob
equable: **4** calm, cool, even, mild **5** level, quiet **6** low-key, mellow, placid, sedate, serene, stable, steady **7** amiable, at peace, pacific, relaxed, stoical, uniform, unmoved **8** amicable, composed, constant, laid-back, moderate, peaceful, tranquil **9** collected, easygoing, impassive, quiescent, temperate, unexcited, unextreme, unruffled, unvarying **10** consistent, phlegmatic, true to type, unagitated, unchanging, untroubled
equal: **3** iso-, tie **4** even, fair, like, peer, same, tied **5** alike, level, match, reach, rival, total, touch **6** come to, fellow, on a par, square **7** abreast, add up to, compeer, emulate, identic, matched, sum up to, uniform **8** amount to, balanced, confrere, one to one, parallel, rank with, unbiased **9** duplicate, identical, impartial, objective **10** comparable, coordinate, correspond, evenhanded, fifty-fifty, homologous, synonymous, tantamount
  be ~ to: **3** can **5** rival **7** emulate
  combining form: **3** iso- **4** pari-
  footing: **3** par
  make ~: **5** level
  not ~ to: **5** unfit **6** unable **9** incapable
  on an ~ footing: **4** fair **5** level **6** square **7** uniform **8** balanced, matching **10** fifty-fifty
  out: **6** cancel, offset **7** redress, rescind **10** balance out, counteract, neutralize
  portion: **4** half **9** bisection
  score: **3** tie
  to: **4** like **5** ready **8** as good as
  to the task: **3** fit **4** able, deft, keen **5** adept **6** adroit, expert, gifted **7** knowing, skilled **9** competent, masterful, qualified **10** proficient
  without ~: **5** alone **6** single, unique **8** peerless
equal __: **4** sign, time
Equal __ Amendment: **6** Rights
equality: **3** lib, par **6** parity **7** balance, isonomy **8** evenness, fairness, fair play, likeness, sameness, symmetry
  org. promoting ~: **4** CORE **5** NAACP
equalize: **4** even **5** level, match **6** even up, offset, square **7** balance **8** square up **9** stabilize **10** commeasure, recompense
equalizer: **3** gun
equally: **4** both **5** alike, as one **9** uniformly
equals __: **4** sign
equal-sided: **6** square **7** rhombic
equanimity: **4** calm **5** peace, poise **6** aplomb, temper **7** ataraxy, balance **8** calmness, coolness, patience, serenity **9** assurance, composure, placidity, sangfroid **10** confidence, detachment, neutrality, sedateness, steadiness
equate: **5** level, liken, match **7** balance, compare **8** parallel **9** associate, correlate, make alike **10** correspond
equation: **5** ratio **7** formula **10** proportion
  part: **3** var. **8** variable
equator: **4** line
  capital near the ~: **5** Quito
  deg. above the ~: **4** N. Lat.
  dist. from the ~: **3** lat. **8** latitude
equatorial: **3** hot **5** humid **6** sultry, torrid, tropic **8** steaming, stifling, tropical **10** sweltering
Equatorial __: **6** Guinea **7** Current
__ Equatorial Africa: **6** French
Equatorial Guinea: **6** nation **7** country
  capital: **6** Malabo
  neighbor: **5** Gabon **8** Cameroon
  people: **3** Fan **4** Fang **6** Pangwe **7** Pahouin
equerry: **4** page **5** groom **8** horseman
equestrian: **5** rider **6** cowboy, gaucho, jockey, knight, lancer **7** Cossack, cowgirl, dragoon **8** buckaroo, horseman **10** cavalryman
  mishap: **5** spill
  need: **4** crop, tack **5** habit
  sport: **4** polo
equiangular figure: **6** isogon, square
Equiano, Olaudah: **6** writer **8** Nigerian
equi- cousin: **3** iso-
equidistant: **6** median, middle **8** parallel
equilateral figure: **5** rhomb **6** square **7** rhombus
equilibrium: **3** par **4** calm **5** poise **6** aplomb, stasis **7** ataraxy, balance **8** calmness, coolness, serenity, symmetry **9** equipoise
equine: **3** ass, bay, cob, dun, nag **4** Arab, barb, colt, foal, hack, jade, mare, moke, mule, plug, pony, roan **5** bronc, burro, filly, horse, horsy, kiang, mount, pacer, paint, pinto, steed, zebra **6** bronco, cayuse, dapple, dobbin, donkey, gee-gee, horsey, hunter, jumper, onager, quagga, sorrel, tarpan **7** Arabian, bobtail, charger, courser, cow pony, gelding, hackney, jackass, mustang, palfrey, piebald, trooper, trotter, unicorn **8** chestnut, chigetai, destrier, eohippus, palomino, polo pony, skewbald, stallion **9** appaloosa, dziggetai, packhorse, Percheron **10** Clydesdale, Lippizaner
  African ~: **5** zebra **6** quagga
  armor: **4** bard
  Asian ~: **5** kiang **6** onager **8** chigetai **9** dziggetai
  comment: **4** bray **5** neigh **6** heehaw, whinny
  dad: **4** sire
  entrée: **3** hay **4** oats **5** straw
  extinct ~: **6** quagga
  loquacious ~: **4** Mr. Ed
  mom: **4** mare **5** filly
  ornery ~: **3** ass **4** mule **5** burro
  restraint: **4** rein
  shade: **4** roan
  small ~: **3** ass **4** pony **5** burro
  stockade: **3** pen **6** corral **9** enclosure
  TV ~: **4** Fury, Mr. Ed **8** Mister Ed
  see also horse
equinoctial __: **4** line, year **5** point, rains, storm **6** circle
equinox
  month: **3** Mar., Sep. **4** Sept. **5** March **9** September
  sign: **5** Aries
__ equinox: **4** fall **6** spring, vernal
equip: **3** arm, fit, rig **4** deck, gear, gird **5** array, endow, ready, rig up, stock, train **6** enable, fit out, gear up, get set, outfit, purvey, rig out, supply **7** appoint, deck out, furnish, plenish, prepare, provide, qualify, satisfy, turn out **8** accouter, accoutre, embattle **9** condition, provision
  ender: **3** age
  with weapons: **7** fortify **8** embattle
equipage: **3** rig **4** gear **6** outfit **7** baggage **8** carriage **9** munitions
equipment: **3** kit, rig **4** gear **5** means, plant, stuff, thing, tools **6** tackle **7** baggage, devices **8** fittings, fix-

tures, supplies, utensils **9** apparatus, furniture, implement, machinery, trappings **10** appliances, belongings, facilities, instrument, provisions
  change the ~: **5** refit
equipment design
  science of ~: **10** ergonomics
equipoise: **5** level **6** aplomb, stasis **7** balance **8** evenness, symmetry **9** stability **10** equanimity, sedateness
equipped: **4** able **5** armed, ready **9** qualified
__-equipped: **3** ill **4** well
__ Equis: **3** Dos
equitable: **3** due **4** even, fair, just **5** right **6** proper, square **7** correct, ethical **8** balanced, deserved, straight, unbiased **9** impartial, objective, uncolored, unslanted **10** evenhanded, impersonal, reasonable
equitableness: **5** right **6** virtue **7** justice, redress **8** evenness, fairness, fair play, justness, morality **9** rectitude **10** due process, lawfulness
equity: **5** right **6** assets **7** justice **8** fairness, fair play, justness, property
__ equity: **5** sweat
__ Equity: **6** Actors'
__ equity loan: **4** home
Equity member: **5** actor **9** performer
equivalence: **3** tie **5** match **6** parity **7** balance **8** evenness, identity, likeness, sameness, synonymy
equivalent: **4** akin, even, like, same, such **5** alike, level, rival **6** agnate, allied, on a par **7** cognate, kindred, similar **8** matching, parallel **9** alternate, analogous, duplicate, identical **10** carbon copy, comparable, coordinate, dead ringer, homologous, reciprocal, substitute, synonymous, tantamount
  be ~ to: **6** offset
  is ~ (to): **6** amount
  make ~: **5** level **6** equate **7** balance
  to: **4** akin, like, same **5** equal **6** in kind, on a par, same as **7** close to, equal to, related, similar, uniform **8** as good as, matching, parallel **9** analogous, identical, virtually **10** comparable, compatible, resembling, synonymous, tantamount
  word: **3** syn. **7** synonym
equivalently: **4** akin, same **5** alike, equal **6** on a par **7** cognate, equally, related, the same, uniform **8** in common **9** analogous, identical, similarly, uniformly **10** comparable, comparably, equivalent, the same way
equivocal: **4** hazy, open **5** fuzzy, muzzy, vague **7** clouded, dubious, evasive, muddled, oblique, unclear **8** doubtful, ulterior **9** ambiguous, tenebrous, uncertain, undecided **10** ambivalent, apocryphal, borderline, clear as mud, indefinite, indistinct, inexplicit, left-handed, misleading, suspicious, unexplicit, unverified
  linker: **3** but **5** and/or
equivocate: **3** haw, lie **5** dodge, evade, fence, hedge, skirt, stall, swing, waver **6** waffle **7** quibble, whiffle **8** footdrag, hesitate, misquote, simulate **9** hem and haw, oscillate, pussyfoot, run around, stonewall **10** double-talk, mince words, tergiverse
equivocating: **5** lying **6** shifty **7** evasive
equivocation: **5** shift **7** evasion **9** runaround **10** hesitation
  without ~: **6** flatly **9** sincerely **10** foursquare
equivocator: **4** liar **6** fibber **7** deluder **8** deceiver, perjurer **9** chameleon, con artist, falsifier, trickster **10** fabricator
  response: **5** maybe
equivoque: **3** pun **8** wordplay
equus: **3** ass, nag **4** Arab, colt, foal, mare, mule, pony, roan **5** burro, filly, horse, pinto, steed, zebra **6** donkey, equine, Morgan **7** gelding, mustang, trotter **8** Shetland, stallion **10** Clydesdale
Equus: **4** play
  author: Peter Shaffer
  character: **4** Alan, Dora **6** Dysart, Strang
er
  relative: **2** uh, um
Er: **7** element **10** elem.. erbium
  68 for ~: **4** at. no.
ER
  command: **4** stat
  part: **4** emer., room **9** emergency
  procedure: **3** CPR, EKG
  setting: **3** ICU
  staffer: **2** Dr., MD, RN **3** EMT **5** nurse **6** doctor
  supply: **2** IV **4** sera **5** serum
  unit: **2** cc.
ER (NBC drama)
  cast: George Clooney (Dr. Douglas Ross)
  Anthony Edwards (Dr. Mark Greene)
  Laura Innes (Dr. Kerry Weaver)
  Eriq LaSalle (Dr. Peter Benton)
  Julianna Margulies (Carol Hathaway)
  Noah Wyle (Dr. John Carter)
  setting: Chicago
era: **3** age, day **4** time **5** cycle, epoch **6** period **7** vintage **10** generation, time period
  bygone ~: **4** past, then **7** old days
  in this ~: **3** now **5** today **9** currently
  many ~s: **3** age, eon **4** aeon, ages **6** period **8** long time
  of the same ~: **6** coeval **10** coexistent, coincident
Era: **5** Mogul **6** Moslem, Muslim **7** Baroque **8** Cambrian, Cenozoic, Colonial, Gaslight, Mesozoic, Sassanid **9** Christian, detergent, Mycenaean, Paleozoic, Victorian
  alternative: ***see*** detergent
__ Era: **6** Common, Gaslit
ERA: **4** stat
  part of ~: **3** Avg. **4** Runs **5** Equal **6** Earned, Rights **7** Average **9** Amendment
  proponent: **3** NOW
__ Era and Out the Other: **5** In One
eradicate: **3** rid **4** lose, rase, raze **5** eject, erase, purge, trash **6** banish, delete, efface, excise, remove, rub off, rub out, uproot **7** abolish, blot out, destroy, expunge, lighten, mow down, pluck up, root out, weed out, wipe out **8** demolish, stamp out **9** eliminate, extirpate, liquidate, shoot down **10** annihilate, deracinate, do away with, extinguish, obliterate
eradication: **4** dele **7** erasure, removal **8** deletion **9** abatement, pulling up, uprooting **10** demolition, extinction, pulling out, rooting out, rubbing out, tearing out
Era of __ Feeling: **4** Good
erase: **3** cut, rub **4** dele, slay, trim, undo, wipe, X out **5** annul, clean, clear, purge, scrub **6** cancel, cut out, delete, efface, excise, forget, negate, remove, revoke, rub off, rub out, strike **7** abolish, blot out, destroy, expunge, nullify, scissor, scratch, take out, wipe out **8** blank out, bleep out, get rid of, stamp out **9** eliminate, eradicate, expurgate, extirpate, sponge out, strike out **10** annihilate, extinguish, obliterate, scratch out
eraser: **6** art gum, rubber **9** eliminate
  like a blackboard ~: **5** dirty, dusty **7** powdery, unclean **8** unwashed
  material: **3** gum
  use an ~: **4** X out **6** cancel, cut out, delete, excise, remove, rub out **7** expunge, scratch, wipe out **8** black out **9** eliminate, strike out
__ eraser: **3** gum
Eraser (1996 film)
  cast: James Caan, James Coburn, Arnold Schwarzenegger, Vanessa Williams
Eraserhead (1978 film)
  director: David Lynch
Erasmus, Desiderius: **5** Dutch **6** writer **8** humanist
Erastus: **6** Thomas
erasure: **8** deletion **10** effacement
__ erat demonstrandum: **4** quod
__ erat faciendum: **4** quod
Erato: **4** Muse
  colleague: ***see*** Muse
  lover: **8** Heracles
  parent: **4** Zeus **9** Mnemosyne
Eratosthenes: **10** astronomer
Erbe: **7** Kathryn
Erbil: **4** city, town
  locale: **4** Irak, Iraq
erbium: **7** element
Erdman: **4** Paul
Erdrich, Louise: **6** writer
  subject: Chippewa
ere: **3** ago **4** once **5** afore, prior **6** before, gone by **7** earlier, prior to **9** in the past, preceding **10** previously, previous to
  ender: **3** now **4** long **5** while
...ere __ Elba: **4** I saw
ereb: **3** eve **6** Hebrew
Erebus: **4** peak **5** mount **7** volcano **8** mountain
  daughter: **6** Hemera **7** Hespera, Nemesis
  locale: **10** Antarctica
  parent: **3** Nyx **5** Chaos
  son: **6** Charon, Hypnos
erect: **4** form, lift, make, rear **5** build, forge, found, frame, on end, pitch, plumb, put up, raise, set up, sheer, stand, steep **6** create, uprear **7** fashion, produce, upraise, upright **8** assemble, initiate, standing, straight, vertical **9** construct, establish, fabricate, institute **10** upstanding
  be ~: **5** stand
Erector __: **3** Set
__ erectus: **4** Homo
...ere I saw __: **4** Elba
erelong: **4** anon, soon **10** in good time
eremite: **4** monk **5** loner **6** hermit **7** isolato, recluse **8** anchoret, solitary **9** anchoress, anchorite
eremitic: **4** line **5** alone **7** recluse **8** isolated, solitary **9** reclusive **10** antisocial
erenow: **4** once **5** afore, as yet **6** before **7** long ago **9** in the past **10** heretofore, previously
Eretz __: **6** Israel **7** Yisrael
erev: **3** eve **6** sunset **9** day before
Erewhon: **6** utopia
  author: Samuel Butler
  character: **4** Yram **5** Senoj, Thims **6** Strong, Ydgrun, Zulora
ergate: **3** ant
ergo: **4** then, thus **5** hence **9** as a result, therefore
ergo-: **4** work
ergonomics: **7** science
ergophobe fear: **4** work
__, ergo sum: **6** cogito
ergot: **4** mold **6** fungus, mildew
Erhard: **6** Werner
  discipline: **3** Est
Eri
  father: **3** Gad
Eric: **4** Bana, Idle, Thal, Till, Utne **5** Berne, Blore, Davis, Lutes, Scott **6** Ambler, Burdon, Carmen, Heiden, Hoffer, Holder, Kandel, Knight, Rochat, Rohmer, Stoltz **7** Braeden, Clapton, Cornell, Fleming, Lindros, Portman, Roberts **8** Bogosian, Mitchell, Sevareid **9** Dickerson, Lustbader, McCormack, Partridge, Weissburg, Wieschaus
  son: **4** Leif
Eric __: **6** the Red
Eric __ Lustbader: **3** Van
erica: **4** tree **5** heath, shrub **7** heather **9** evergreen
  relative: ***see*** heath family shrub
Erica: **4** Jong, Kane
Erich: **5** Fromm, Segal **6** Kunzel **7** Kleiber **9** Leinsdorf
Erich __ Korngold: **8** Wolfgang
Erich __ Remarque: **5** Maria
Erich __ Stroheim: **3** von
Ericson, Leif: **5** Norse **6** Viking **8** explorer
Ericsson: **5** phone **9** cell phone
  alternative: **5** Nokia **6** Nextel **8** Motorola
Eric the Red: **5** Norse **6** Viking **8** explorer
Erie: **4** city, lake, port, town **5** canal, Mills, tribe **6** Indian **7** Amerind **9** Great Lake
  locale: **4** Penn. **5** Penna. **6** Canada

neighbor: 5 Huron
vessel: 5 laker
Erie Canal
city: 6 Albany
craft: 5 barge
Erie Lackawanna: 2 RR 3 rwy. 8 railroad
Erik: 5 Bruhn, Satie 7 Darling, Erikson, Estrada 8 Lindberg 9 Karlfeldt
Erik ___ Karlfeldt: 4 Axel
Erika: 6 Morini, Slezak 7 Eleniak
Erik Dorn
author: Ben Hecht
___-Erik Hexum: 3 Jon
Erikson: 4 Erik
Eriksson: 4 Leif
Erin: 4 Eire, Gray 5 Davis, Moran 6 Old Sod 7 auld sod, Ireland 8 Hibernia 9 Innisfail, Innisfree
tongue: 4 Erse 6 Gaelic
Erin Brockovich (2000 film)
cast: Albert Finney, Julia Roberts
director: Steven Soderbergh
Erin go ___!: 5 bragh
Erinyes: 6 Furies
Eriq: 7 LaSalle
Eris
daughter: 3 Ate 5 Lethe
parent: 3 Nyx 4 Hera, Zeus
twin: 4 Ares
Eritrea: 6 nation 7 country
bovine: 5 Barka
capital: 6 Asmara
neighbor: 5 Sudan 8 Djibouti, Ethiopia
people: 4 Afar, Beja 7 Danakil
Erle: 6 Kenton 7 Gardner
colleague: 3 Rex 6 Agatha, Ellery
Erle ___ Gardner: 7 Stanley
Erle C. ___: 6 Kenton
Erlenmeyer ___: 5 flask
Erl-King, The
author: Goethe
Erma: 7 Bombeck
ermine: 3 fur 4 coat, pelt, wrap 5 stoat 6 animal, weasel
relative: *see* weasel
Ermine, The
author: Jean Anouilh
Ermont: 4 city, town
locale: 6 France
-er, more than: 3 -est
ern: 4 bird 5 eagle 7 seabird 8 sea eagle 9 shorebird 10 bird of prey
starter: 4 east, west 5 north, south
Ern: 8 Westmore
Erna: 6 Berger 7 Brodber
Ernani: 5 opera
composer: Giuseppe Verdi
erne: 4 bird 5 eagle 7 seabird 8 sea eagle 9 shorebird 10 bird of prey
Ernest: 4 Ball, Gold, Papa, Tubb 5 Bloch, Gallo, Renan, Seton, Truex 6 Dowson, Lehman, Solvay, Walton 7 Worrell 8 Ansermet, Borgnine, Chausson, Hollings, Lawrence, Thompson, Torrence 9 Hemingway 10 Rutherford, Shackleton
nickname: 4 Papa
Ernest Goes to ___: 4 Camp
Ernest J. ___: 6 Gaines
Ernest K. ___: 4 Gann
Ernesto: 6 Moneta, Sábato 7 Guevara 8 Cardinal, Maserati
nickname: 3 Che
see also Spanish
Ernie: 3 Els 4 K-Doe, Pyle 5 Banks, Bilko, Shore 6 Fields, Hudson, Kovacs, Muppet, Nevers 7 Freeman, Maresca 8 Stautner 10 Bushmiller
colleague: 4 Bert 5 Piggy 6 Kermit 7 Big Bird
___ Ernie Ford: 9 Tennessee
Ernie K-___: 3 Doe
Erno: 5 Rubik
Ernst: 3 Ken, Max 4 Mach, Toch 5 Chain, Ruska 6 Jünger 7 Fischer, Haeckel, Richard 8 Cassirer, Lubitsch
Ernst, Max: 6 artist 7 painter
homeland: 7 Germany
Ernst & Young
staffer: 3 aud., CPA 4 acct. 7 auditor
erode: 3 eat, sap 4 rust, wear 5 chafe, decay, eat at 6 ablate, abrade, damage, lessen, ravage, weaken 7 consume, corrode, crumble, eat away, eat into, rub away, rub down, wash out 8 undercut, wear away, wear down 9 break down, grind down, undermine 10 chip away at
eroded: 3 ate 4 worn 8 timeworn
Eroica: 8 symphony
composer: Ludwig van Beethoven
key: 5 E-flat
Eros: 3 god 4 Amor 5 Cupid 6 libido 7 love god 8 amoretto, asteroid
brother: 7 Anteros, Anterus
daughter: 7 Volupta
equivalent: 4 Amor 5 Cupid
lover: 6 Psyche
parent: 3 Nyx 5 Chaos 9 Aphrodite
Eros and Civilization
author: Herbert Marcuse
erose: 6 ragged, uneven 8 windworn
erosion: 4 wear 7 wearing 8 abrasion, decrease 9 attrition, corrosion
cause of ~: 4 tide, wind 5 river, water
result: 5 gully 6 canyon, gulley
erosive: 7 caustic, wearing 8 abrading, abrasive 9 attritive, consuming, corrosive
erotic: 3 hot 4 blue, lewd, racy, sexy 5 funky, spicy 6 loving, rated X, risqué, spicey, steamy, sultry, torrid, X-rated 7 amatory, naughty, sensual 8 alluring, magnetic, romantic 9 amatorial 10 magnetical, voluptuous
Erotica (1992 song)
artist: Madonna
err: 3 sin 4 flub, goof, miss, muff, slip, trip 5 botch, fluff, lapse, misdo, snafu, stray 6 blow it, bobble, booboo, bungle, detour, foozle, foul up, fumble, go awry, mess up, misadd, miscue, slip up, wander 7 blunder, deviate, do wrong, go wrong, louse up, misdeal, misplay, misstep, mistake, snarl up, stumble 8 bollix up, go astray, misjudge, misspeak, misspell, slip a cog 9 misbehave, mishandle, mismanage, misreckon 10 transgress
errand: 3 job 4 task, trip 5 chore 7 mission 10 assignment, commission, engagement
assign to an ~: 4 send
do an ~: 3 run
helpful ~: 3 aid 5 favor 7 service 8 courtesy, goodwill, kindness
on an ~: 3 out 4 away
runner: 4 page 5 gofer 6 gopher, legman 9 messenger
___ errand: 4 on an 5 fool's
errant: 4 wild 5 stray, wrong 6 roving 7 aimless, deviant, naughty, offbase, roaming, wayward 8 fallible, questing, rambling, straying, vagabond 9 deviating, itinerant, off-course, off-target, traveling, wandering 10 journeying, meandering, off the mark, unorthodox, unreliable
___-errant: 6 knight
errantly: 3 off 5 amiss 6 astray
errare humanum ___: 3 est
errata: 5 goofs, slips, typos 6 boners, lapses 7 boo-boos 8 bloopers, mistakes 9 misprints 10 corrigenda
free of ~: 5 clean 7 correct, perfect 8 accurate
erratic: 3 odd 5 flaky, fluid, moody, queer, wacky, weird, wrong 6 chancy, fickle, flakey, patchy, quaint, random, roving, spotty, uneven, whacky, zigzag 7 aimless, bizarre, mutable, oddball, protean, strange, wayward 8 freakish, on-and-off, peculiar, periodic, rambling, shifting, sporadic, unstable, unsteady, variable, volatile, wavering 9 arbitrary, eccentric, fluctuant, haphazard, irregular, mercurial, spasmodic, uncertain, vagarious, wandering, whimsical 10 capricious, changeable, discursive, flickering, inconstant, meandering, nonuniform, outlandish, sporadical, unbalanced, undirected, unreliable, willy-nilly
move: 3 zag, zig 5 weave
erratum: 4 typo 7 mistake 8 misprint 10 inaccuracy
erring: 5 wrong 6 adrift, astray, faulty 7 peccant 8 fallible, mistaken 9 incorrect 10 inaccurate
___ 'er rip!: 3 Let
Errol: 4 Leon 5 Flynn 6 Le Cain, Morris
Erroll: 6 Garner
erroneous: 3 bad 5 false, wrong 6 all wet, faulty, flawed, untrue 7 inexact, invalid, unsound 8 improper, mistaken, specious, spurious 9 defective, falsified, incorrect, misguided, unfounded 10 fallacious, ill-founded, inaccurate, mendacious, ungrounded, unreliable
conviction: 5 frame 6 bum rap
erroneously: 4 awry 5 afoul, amiss, badly, wrong 7 wrongly 8 erringly, faultily 9 foolishly 10 mistakenly, out of joint, unsuitably
error: 3 bad, bug, sin 4 flaw, foul, goof, miss, slip, trip, typo 5 boner, fault, fluff, gaffe, lapse, snafu, wrong 6 barney, boo-boo, defect, glitch, howler, lapsus, miscue, slipup 7 blooper, blunder, erratum, fallacy, falsity, faux pas, louse-up, misdeed, misplay, misstep, mistake, stumble 8 misprint, omission, solecism, trespass 9 deviation, misbelief, oversight, veniality 10 inaccuracy, infraction
check for ~s: 5 proof
free from ~: 5 right 6 aright 7 correct 8 debugged, disabuse
in ~: 5 false, wrong 6 all wet, astray, faulty, untrue 7 inexact, unsound 8 specious 10 inaccurate, ungrounded
make an ~: 4 muff
margin for ~: 4 room 5 range, slack, space 6 leeway 8 latitude 9 elbowroom 10 room to move
partner: 5 trial
remover: 6 eraser
see the ~ of ways: 6 repent
service ~: 5 fault
show the ~ of one's ways: 6 reason
sports ~: 4 balk, foul 5 fault
errorless: 4 just 5 exact, right, valid 7 correct, factual, precise 8 accurate, flawless, unerring 9 faultless 10 immaculate, impeccable
error-prone: 5 human 6 clumsy 8 careless
ersatz: 4 fake, mock, sham 5 bogus, false, phony, put-on 6 forged, phoney, pseudo, unreal 7 assumed, feigned, plastic, stopgap 8 spurious 9 imitation, imitative, simulated, synthetic, unnatural 10 artificial, fabricated, fictitious, fraudulent, substitute
not ~: 4 real
Erse: 6 Celtic, Gaelic 8 language
Erskine: 4 John 8 Caldwell
erst: 4 once 6 whilom 7 quondam 8 formerly
ender: 5 while
erstwhile: 3 old 4 late, once, past 6 bygone, former 7 old-time, onetime, quondam 8 previous 9 preceding 10 previously
Erté: 6 artist 7 Russian
style: 4 deco
Ertegun: 5 Ahmet
eruct: 4 burp, emit 5 belch
erudite: 4 wise 5 savvy, smart 6 brainy 7 bookish, learned, sapient 8 academic, cerebral, educated, highbrow, lettered, literary, literate, longhair, pedantic, profound, well-read 9 scholarly 10 pedantical
erudition: 4 info, lore 5 savvy 6 brains, wisdom 7 culture, letters, reading 8 learning, literacy 9 education, knowledge 10 refinement
___ 'er up!: 4 Fill
erupt: 4 blow, emit, gush, rage, spew, spue, vent 5 burst, go off, spirt, spout, spurt 6 blow up, go boom 7 explode, rupture, spew out 8 boil over, break out, detonate, have a fit, shoot off 9 discharge, pour forth 10 break forth, shoot forth
erupter: 7 volcano
erupting: 6 aburst
eruption: 4 gust, rash 5 blast, burst, noise, spasm, spirt, spurt 6 blowup 8 ejection, outbreak, outburst, paroxysm, upheaval 9 discharge, explosion

fallout: 3 ash 4 lava 5 ember 6 cinder
ervil: 5 vetch
Ervin: 3 Sam
Erving, Julius: 3 Dr. J
milieu: 5 court
org.: 3 NBA
sport: 10 basketball
Erwin: 3 Stu 5 Neher 6 Rommel, Stuart
Erykah: 4 Badu
erythrocyte: 4 cell 7 red cell 9 blood cell, corpuscle
erythrophobe fear: 3 red 8 blushing
Erz: 5 range
locale: 6 Europe 7 Germany
Es: 4 elem. 7 element 11 einsteinium
99 for ~: 4 at. no.
Esa-___ Salonen: 5 Pekka
Esai: 7 Morales
Esaki, Leo: 8 Nobelist 9 physicist, scientist
Esa-Pekka: 7 Salonen
Esau
father-in-law: 4 Elon
grandson: 4 Omar
parent: 5 Isaac 7 Rebekah
son: 5 Jalam, Korah, Reuel 7 Eliphaz
twin: 5 Jacob
wife: 4 Adah 6 Judith 8 Basemath, Mahalath 10 Oholibamah
Esc: 3 key
Escalade: 3 SUV 8 Cadillac
Escalante: 5 Jaime
escalate: 4 go up, grow, leap, rise, soar 5 add to, arise, build, climb, mount, raise, swell, widen 6 ascend, expand, extend, jack up, move up, spread, step up 7 advance, amplify, augment, broaden, build up, enlarge, magnify, scale up 8 heighten, increase 9 go forward, increment, intensify 10 supplement
escalation: 4 leap, rise 6 spread 7 buildup 8 increase 9 inflation
escalator
alternative: 5 stair, steps 8 elevator
direction: 4 down 5 lower 10 descending
essentially: 5 stair
part: 4 axle, step 5 motor, tread
escalator ___: 6 clause
Escales
composer: Jacques Ibert
escallop: 4 bake, cook 5 brown, shell, steam 8 seashell
Escamillo: 6 torero 8 toreador 11 bullfighter
see also Spanish
escapade: 4 game, joke, lark 5 antic, caper, fling, prank, sport 6 frolic, gambol 7 exploit, rollick
Escapade (1990 song)
artist: Janet Jackson
escape: 2 go 3 fly, lam, run 4 bolt, duck, evac., flee, leak, lose, ooze, seep, shun, skip 5 avert, avoid, break, dodge, elope, elude, evade, lam it, leave, skirt 6 decamp, depart, desert, egress, flight, get out, outlet, refuge, run off, run out, tunnel, vanish, way out 7 abscond, bailout, bust out, dodging, duck out, elusion, evasion, getaway, go south, leakage, make off, mystify, pastime, retreat, run away, slip off 8 breakout, cut loose, fugitate, get out of, light out, loophole, magic act, skip town, slip away, throw off, turn tail 9 avoidance, break away, break jail, cut and run, departure, disappear, salvation, steal away 10 break loose, circumvent, fly the coop, get clear of, ivory tower, take flight
artist: 7 Houdini 8 magician
button: 5 eject
cut off from ~: 4 trap 5 hem in 6 corner
from: 5 avoid, evade 8 shake off
means of ~: 3 out 4 exit 6 ladder
vehicle: 3 pod
escape ___: 3 pod 5 hatch, valve, wheel 6 artist, clause
___ escape: 4 fire 6 narrow
Escape: 3 SUV 4 Ford
Escape (1979 song)
artist: Rupert Holmes
escaped: 4 free, wild 5 loose 7 at large 10 on the loose
escapee: 5 fleer, hider 6 dodger, émigré 7 refugee, runaway 8 defector, deserter, fugitive, renegade
like an ~: 5 loose 7 at large 8 on the run
Escape From Alcatraz (1979 film)
cast: Clint Eastwood, Patrick McGoohan
director: Don Siegel
Escape from Freedom
author: Erich Fromm
Escape From New York (1981 film)
cast: Ernest Borgnine, Donald Pleasence, Kurt Russell, Lee Van Cleef
director: John Carpenter
escapist: 7 dreamer, ostrich 8 idealist 9 fantasist 10 daydreamer, nonrealist
escargot: 5 snail 9 appetizer
escarole
alternative: 6 endive
escarp: 5 cliff 9 precipice 10 embankment
eschew: 4 duck, shun, skip 5 avoid, dodge, elude, evade, forgo, shirk 6 abjure, bypass, forego, give up 7 abstain, boycott, dislike, forbear, refrain, shy from 8 flee from, forswear, keep from, renounce, swear off 9 foreswear 10 circumvent
Escobar
see Spanish
Escoffier: 4 chef 7 Auguste
see also French
Escondido: 4 city, town
locale: 10 California
escort: 3 see, ush 4 date, lead, seat, show, take, walk 5 bring, fetch, guard, guide, lover, scout, see in, steer, train, usher 6 attend, convoy, duenna, go with, lead in, squire 7 conduct, retinue, step out 8 chaperon, guardian 9 accompany, attendant, bodyguard, boyfriend, chaperone, companion, entourage, protector, safeguard offering: 3 arm 4 limb 9 extremity
Escort: 3 car 4 auto, Ford 10 automobile
escorting: 4 with
escorts: 5 train 7 retinue
escritoire: 4 desk 5 table 7 rolltop 9 secretary
accessory: 3 pen
escrow: 4 care 5 aegis, owner 6 charge 7 custody 9 oversight 10 possession, protection
escudo: 4 coin 5 money
country: 8 Portugal 9 Cape Verde
escuela child: 4 niña, niño 10 estudiante
esculent: 4 good 5 tasty 6 edible
escutcheon: 4 seal 5 plate 6 shield
border: 4 orle
mark: 4 blot 5 stain
ESE: 3 dir. 5 point 9 direction
opposite: 3 WNW
___ e sempre: 3 ora
___, es, est: 3 sum
Esfahan: 4 city, town
locale: 4 Iran
ESG
part of ~: 4 Erle 7 Gardner, Stanley
Eshkol, Levi: 7 Israeli
predecessor: 9 Ben-Gurion
successor: 4 Meir
Esiason, Boomer: 2 QB 11 quarterback
sport: 8 football
eskers: 4 osar 6 ridges
Eskimo: 5 Aleut, Inuit, Yupik 6 Innuit, Inupik 8 Aleutian
ancient ~ culture: 6 Dorset
coat: 6 anorak
home: 4 iglu 5 igloo 6 Alaska, Arctic
knife: 3 ulu
language: 5 Aleut, Inuit 6 Innuit, Inupik 8 Aleutian
pole: 5 totem
relative: 5 Aleut 8 Aleutian
vehicle: 4 sled 5 kayak, umiak
Eskimo ___: 3 Pie
ESL: 6 course
cousin: 3 EFL
part of ~: 3 Eng. 4 Lang. 6 Second
Esme
author: Saki
Esmeralda pet: 4 goat
___ Esme-with Love and Squalor: 3 For
___ Esmond: 5 Henry
esne: 4 serf 6 thrall
place: 4 fief 5 manor
Eso Beso (1962 song)
artist: Paul Anka
esophagus: 3 maw 6 gullet, throat 7 pharynx
esoteric: 4 deep 6 arcane, hidden, inside, mystic, occult, Orphic, secret 7 cryptic, learned, obscure, private 8 abstruse, mystical, profound, rarefied 9 cryptical, difficult, enigmatic, innermost, recondite 10 mysterious, unknowable
esoterics: 6 cabala, kabala 7 cabbala, kabbala
ESP: 9 intuition, telepathy 10 sixth sense
espalier: 5 train
España: 5 Spain 6 nación
esparto: 5 grass
especial: 3 def, rad 4 aces, A-one, boss, braw, cool, dece, fine, gear, keen, neat, nice, phat, tuff 5 dandy, ducky, grand, great, marvy, neato, nobby, prime, slick, super, swell 6 bang on, bang-up, bonzer, bosker, choice, divine, dreamy, far-out, gnarly, groovy, lovely, peachy, single, slap-up, spot on, superb, terrif, tiptop, unreal, whizzo, wicked 7 amazing, awesome, capital, corking, perfect, ripping, skookum, stellar, sublime 8 dazzling, eximious, fabulous, favorite, five-star, four-star, frabjous, glorious, heavenly, jim-dandy, slam-bang, smashing, splendid, standout, sterling, stick-out, superior, terrific, top-level, top-notch, very good, wondrous 9 bodacious, Endsville, excellent, exemplary, exquisite, first-rate, high-grade, hunky-dory, marvelous, sollicker, top-flight, wonderful 10 first-class, hotsy-totsy, individual, jack-a-dandy, occasional, out of sight, particular, peachy-keen, phenomenal, remarkable, stupendous, super-duper
especially: 4 such, very 5 extra 6 mainly, namely 7 chiefly, notably 8 above all, markedly, signally, uniquely 9 curiously, eminently, expressly, primarily, specially, strangely, supremely, unusually 10 abnormally, peculiarly, remarkably, singularly, strikingly, uncommonly
Esperanto: 6 tongue 8 language
espial: 6 notice 8 exposure, sighting 9 detection, discovery, unmasking 10 uncovering
espionage: 6 spying
name in ~: 4 Hari, Mata
org.: 3 CIA, KGB
starter: 7 counter
esplanade: 4 mall, path, walk 7 walkway
ESPN: 7 channel, network
alternative: *see* cable channel
fare: 6 sports
feature: 3 NBA
Espoo: 4 city, town
locale: 7 Finland
esposa de su padre: 5 madre
Esposito: 4 Phil 9 Giancarlo
Esposito, Phil
milieu: 3 ice 4 rink 5 arena 6 hockey
org.: 3 NHL
espousal: 5 match, troth 7 support, wedding 8 adoption, advocacy, marriage, nuptials 9 betrothal, fosterage, promotion
espouse: 3 wed 4 back 5 adopt, marry 6 defend, take on, take up 7 embrace, promote, support 8 advocate, champion 10 speak up for, stand up for
espouser: 5 urger 9 proponent, supporter
espresso: 3 joe 4 java 5 drink, latte 6 coffee 8 beverage
place: 4 café 6 bistro, eatery 10 restaurant
esprit: 3 vim, wit 4 brio, dash, élan, life, mood, zing 5 verve, vigor 6 morale, spirit, temper 7 sparkle

8 vivacity 9 animation, élan vital, intuition, mother wit 10 cleverness, enthusiasm, liveliness
de corps: 6 morale
__ esprit: 4 jeu d'
espy: 3 see 4 find, spot, view 5 sight, watch 6 behold, descry, detect, notice, remark 7 discern, glimpse, make out, observe, witness 8 discover, smell out 9 lay eyes on, recognize
Espy: 4 Mike 7 Willard
-esque cousin: 3 -ine, -ish, -oid 4 -like
esquire: 4 male
Esquivel: 5 Laura
ess: 5 curve, sigma 8 curlicue, curlycue, sibilant
curve: 4 ogee
follower: 3 tee
preceder: 2 ar
__ es Salaam: 3 Dar
essay: 3 aim, bid, try 4 Op-Ed, seek, test 5 paper, prose, theme, tract, trial 6 effort, intend, strive, thesis, tryout 7 article, attempt, venture, writing 8 critique, endeavor, struggle, treatise 9 give it a go, undertake 10 experiment, exposition, literature, think piece
Essay __, An: 5 on Man
Essay Concerning Human Understanding, An
author: John Locke
essayist: 5 Royce 6 author, scribe, writer 8 novelist 9 Podhoretz, wordsmith
alias: 4 Elia
Argentinian ~: 6 Sábato
British ~: 4 Lamb 5 Lewis, Pater, Powys 6 Pinero, Steele 9 Priestley, Stapledon
Czech ~: 9 Skvorecky
Ecuadorian ~: 8 Montalvo
French ~: 5 Péguy 7 Reverdy, Rolland, Romains
German ~: 4 Mann
Mexican ~: 5 Reyes
Nigerian ~: 7 Soyinka
West Indian ~: 7 Naipaul
Essay on Criticism, An
author: Alexander Pope
Essay on Man, An
author: Alexander Pope
Essays of Elia
author: Charles Lamb
esse: 4 to be 5 being 6 entity 7 reality 9 actuality, existence
form of ~: 3 est 4 erat
esse __ percipi: 3 est
esse __ videri: 4 quam
Essen: 4 city, town
locale: 7 Germany
river: 4 Ruhr
essence: 3 nub, sum 4 atar, aura, body, core, crux, germ, gist, knub, meat, odor, otto, pith, root, soul 5 aroma, athar, attar, basis, being, drift, fiber, heart, ottar, point, scent, smell, tenor 6 center, entity, flavor, kernel, marrow, nature, spirit 7 epitome, keynote, nucleus, perfume, summary, texture 8 backbone, key point, main idea, quiddity 9 character, flavoring, lifeblood, necessity, substance 10 bottom line, sine qua non
in ~: 5 per se 6 nearly 8 innately 9 basically, primarily, virtually 10 implicitly
of roses: 4 atar, otto 5 athar, attar, ottar
__ essence: 5 of the
Essence: 3 mag 8 magazine
rival: 3 Jet 5 Ebony
Essenes: 4 sect
essential: 3 key 4 high, main, must, need 5 basic, chief, inner, prime, typic, vital 6 inmost, needed, staple, urgent 7 capital, central, crucial, minimal, needful, organic, pivotal, primary, radical, typical 8 cardinal, foremost, inherent, integral, material, required 9 condition, elemental, groceries, important, intrinsic, mandatory, necessary, necessity, principal, principle, requisite, right-hand, substance, vital part 10 bottom line, brass tacks, congenital, deep-seated, elementary, imperative, sine qua non, substratal, underlying
be ~: 6 inhere
beginning: 5 quint
mineral: 4 iron, zinc
oil: 4 atar, otto 5 athar, attar, ottar
part: 3 nub 4 core, knub, meat, pith 5 heart, vital
essential __: 3 oil
essential __ acid: 5 amino, fatty
essentially: 5 per se 6 mainly, mostly, purely 8 above all, in effect 9 primarily, virtually
essentials: 4 ABCs
esses, mispronounce: 4 lisp
Essex: 3 car 4 auto, city, earl, town 5 David, shire 6 county 10 automobile
city: 10 Chelmsford, Colchester
locale: 7 England 8 Maryland
rival: 3 Reo
Essex __: 5 Junto, table
Essex, David
song: Rock On (1974)
Esso
competitor: 4 Arco
est __ in nobis: 4 deus
est.: 5 guess 6 approx. 9 valuation
establish: 3 fix, lay, set 4 base, form, make, rule, seat, show 5 argue, begin, build, enact, endow, erect, forge, found, learn, plant, prove, put up, set at, set up, start 6 create, define, enroot, impose, instal, invest, locate, occupy, ratify, reason, settle, verify 7 arrange, certify, confirm, develop, find out, install, instate, pioneer, produce, specify, station, support 8 assemble, ensconce, entrench, identify, organize, validate 9 ascertain, authorize, construct, determine, fabricate, formalize, formulate, hammer out, inculcate, institute, introduce, legislate, originate, predicate, preordain, prescribe, stabilize 10 constitute, generalize, inaugurate, strengthen
as fact: 6 verify 7 certify, confirm, warrant 8 document, validate 9 ascertain, determine
established: 3 set 4 sure 5 known, set at, sound, tight, usual 6 formal, lawful, proper, rooted, secure, stable 7 certain, regular 8 definite, habitual, official, ordinary, orthodox, standard 9 prevalent, steadfast 10 prevailing
be ~ in: 6 occupy
fact: 5 axiom, given 7 premise 9 postulate
get ~: 5 set in 6 locate, settle 8 make good, take root
less ~: 5 newer
not yet ~: 3 new 5 unset
position: 4 base 6 anchor 7 support 8 foothold, lodgment 9 beachhead 10 bridgehead, foundation
establishment: 3 ins 4 firm 5 abode, house, joint, plant, setup, start 6 office, outfit, regime, system 7 company, concern, factory 8 business, creation, founding, old guard, quarters 9 stability
frontier ~: 3 bar, inn 6 saloon 7 barroom 10 restaurant
happy hour ~: 3 pub 6 saloon, tavern 7 taproom 8 alehouse, taphouse
roadside ~: 3 inn 5 diner, motel, stand
seedy ~: 4 dive 5 joint
Establishment, The
author: Howard Fast
__ Estacado: 5 Llano
estado: 5 state 7 Spanish
estamin: 6 fabric 8 material
estancia: 5 ranch
estate: 4 land, park, rank, seat, Tara 5 acres, caste, class, dacha, manor, means, press, ranch, villa 6 assets, clergy, datcha, domain, legacy, nobles, spread, status, wealth, Xanadu 7 acreage, chateau, demesne, fortune, grounds, mansion, station 8 hacienda, holdings, net worth, property 9 Chartwell, farmstead, Graceland, homestead, patrimony, residence 10 belongings, Brideshead, journalism, Monticello, plantation
document: 4 will
English ~ feature: 4 maze
entrance: 4 gate 6 portal 7 doorway, ingress
first ~: 6 clergy, curate 7 prelacy 8 ministry 9 pastorate, rabbinate 10 priesthood
fourth ~: 5 press
measure: 4 acre
medieval ~: 4 fief, odal 5 manor
of India: 5 taluk 7 talooka
plus: 5 asset
real ~: 3 lot 4 land 6 assets, ground 7 acreage, grounds 8 property
real ~ abbr.: 2 rm. 3 EIK, MLS 4 bdrm.
sharer: 4 heir 6 coheir
staffer: 4 cook, maid 5 valet 6 butler
estate __: 3 tax 8 planning
estate-__: 7 bottled
__ estate: 4 real
Estates __: 7 General
estates, like many: 5 gated
__ est celare artem: 3 ars
est deus in __: 5 nobis
Estée Lauder: 6 makeup
alternative: *see* cosmetic brand
esteem: 4 fame, like, love, rank, rate 5 exalt, extol, favor, honor, kudos, prize, think, value 6 admire, credit, extoll, homage, honors, praise, reckon, regard, repute, revere 7 cherish, idolize, respect, tribute, valuing, worship 8 approval, consider, eminence, good name, hold dear, hold high, look up to, prestige, treasure, venerate 9 adoration, care about, recommend, reverence 10 admiration, appreciate, importance, popularity, reputation, set store by, veneration
don't ~: 5 scorn
gain ~: 4 rate 6 enamor, endear
lower in ~: 5 shame 6 debase, defile, demean, vilify 7 cheapen, degrade, deprave, devalue, profane, put down, vitiate 8 disgrace, dishonor, take down 9 humiliate, shoot down, undermine 10 adulterate
__-esteem: 4 self
Esteem: 3 car 4 auto 6 Suzuki
esteemed: 4 dear 5 noted 7 beloved, eminent 8 glorious, renowned, valuable 9 honorable, reputable, venerable
Estefan: 6 Emilio, Gloria
Estefan, Gloria
home: 5 Miami
song: 1-2-3 (1988)
Anything for You (1988)
Bad Boy (1986)
Can't Stay Away From You (1988)
Coming Out of the Dark (1991)
Conga (1985)
Don't Wanna Lose You (1989)
Here We Are (1990)
Music of My Heart (1999)
Rhythm Is Gonna Get You (1987)
Words Get in the Way (1986)
Estelí: 4 city, town
locale: 9 Nicaragua
Estella to Miss Havisham: 4 ward
Estelle: 5 Getty 6 Harris 7 Parsons
ester: 6 borate, malate, oleate 7 acetate, citrate, cyanate, lactate, nitrate, nitrite, oxalate, stearin, sulfate, sulfite, toluate 8 benzoate, glycerin, stearate, stearine, tartrate, urethane 9 banana oil, carbonate, glutamate, glyceride, glycerine 10 benzocaine, salicylate
Esterhaus: 4 Phil
__ est errare: 7 humanum
Estes: 3 Bob, Rob 5 Shawn, Simon 8 Kefauver
running mate: 5 Adlai
Estes, Bob: 6 golfer
Estes Park: 4 city, town
locale: 8 Colorado
Estes, Simon: 4 bass 6 singer 8 baritone
specialty: 5 opera
Estevez, Emilio: 5 actor
father: Martin Sheen
film: The Breakfast Club (1985)
The Mighty Ducks (1992)
Mission: Impossible (1996)
Repo Man (1984)
Stakeout (1987)

St. Elmo's Fire (1985)
Young Guns (1988)
spouse: Paula Abdul
Esther: 5 Rolle 6 Forbes 8 Phillips, Williams
composer: George Frideric Handel
cousin: 8 Mordecai
festival: 5 Purim
foe: 5 Haman
follower: 3 Job
husband: 6 Xerxes 9 Ahasuerus
preceder: 3 Neh. 8 Nehemiah
esthetic: 8 tasteful
Esth neighbor: 4 Lett
est, id: 3 viz. 5 to wit 6 namely, that is
estimable: 4 good 5 solid 6 worthy 8 laudable 9 admirable, deserving, excellent, exemplary, honorable, meritable, praisable, reputable, respected, venerable 10 calculable, creditable
estimate: 3 set 4 call, deem, make, rank, rate 5 assay, gauge, guess, judge, price, sum up, think, weigh 6 assess, deduce, figure, reckon, regard, size up, survey 7 measure, opinion, predict, project, suppose, surmise 8 appraise, evaluate, forecast, judgment 9 appraisal, calculate, reckoning, valuation 10 assessment, conjecture, evaluation, prediction, projection
expenses: 6 ration 8 allocate 9 apportion
financial ~: 5 quote 6 budget 9 quotation
estimated: 5 rough 7 inexact
estimation: 5 favor, stock, worth 6 belief, regard 7 opinion, respect, thought, valuing 8 judgment, standing 9 adoration, appraisal, character, ciphering, measuring, reckoning, valuation, viewpoint 10 admiration, arithmetic, assessment, comparison, evaluation, impression, veneration
estimator phrase: 4 or so
estivation: 5 sleep
Estonia: 6 nation 7 country
capital: 7 Tallinn
chess master: 3 Nei
city: 5 Narva, Tartu 6 Tallin 7 Tallinn
from ~: 6 Baltic
lake: 6 Peipus
money: 5 kroon
neighbor: 6 Latvia, Russia
once: 3 SSR
Estonian: 4 Balt 8 language
estop: 3 ban, bar 5 block
EST, part of: 3 std. 4 time 7 Eastern
__ est percipi: 4 esse
Estrada: 4 Erik
estrange: 6 divide 8 disunite, separate 9 disaffect 10 antagonize
estranged: 6 bitter, lonely 10 friendless, unfriendly
estrangement: 4 feud, rift 5 break, split 6 breach, schism 7 rupture 8 disunity, division
estray: 4 dogy 5 dogey, dogie 8 wanderer
Estrela, Serra da: 5 range
estrin: 7 hormone
estuary: 3 arm, bay, ria 5 fiord, firth, fjord, frith, inlet, marsh, mouth
surge: 5 eager, eagre
Esultate!: 4 aria
esurience: 3 yen 4 itch, lust, need, want, wish 5 greed 6 desire, hunger, thirst 7 avarice, craving, longing 8 appetite, rapacity, venality, yearning 9 eagerness, hankering 10 famishment
esurient: 5 unfed 6 greedy, hungry 7 peckish, starved 8 edacious, famished, ravenous 9 insatiate, voracious
ESV: 3 van 8 Cadillac
Eszterhas: 3 Joe
et __: 3 seq., sqq., vir 4 alia, alii, seqq., uxor 6 cetera
et __ genus omne: 3 hoc
ET: 5 alien, dance, Orkan 6 Vulcan 7 Martian 8 Venusian
vehicle: 3 UFO
eta: 5 Greek 6 letter
follower: 5 theta
preceder: 4 zeta
ETA: 5 guess
part of ~: 3 arr., est. 4 time 7 arrival 9 estimated
place: 3 sta., stn. 4 sked 5 depot, sched. 7 station
étagère piece: 5 china, curio, dodad, objet 6 doodad
e-tailer offering: 3 CDs 5 books, music
big ~ season: 4 Xmas
et al.: 9 and others
part of ~: 4 alia, alii
relative: 3 etc.
et alia
cousin: 3 etc.
etamine: 6 fabric 8 material
etaoin __: 6 shrdlu
étape: 7 bivouac 9 warehouse 10 encampment
__ États-Unis: 3 Les
etc.: 7 and so on 10 and so forth
category: 4 misc.
cousin: 4 et al. 6 et alia, et alii
etch: 4 draw 5 carve, stamp 6 incise 7 cut into, engrain, engrave, impress, imprint, ingrain, scratch 8 inscribe 9 delineate 10 illustrate
Etch a __: 6 Sketch
__ et Chandon: 4 Moet
etched in __: 5 stone
etcher: 4 Goya, Graf 5 Goyen 6 artist 8 engraver, Whistler
need: 4 acid 5 glass 6 stylus
__-et-Cher: 4 Loir
etching: 3 art 5 print 7 drawing, picture 9 engraving, mezzotint
ETD: 5 guess
part of ~: 3 arr., dep., est. 4 time 9 departure, estimated
place: 3 sta., stn. 4 sked 5 depot, sched. 7 station
__ et Decorum Est: 5 Dulce
été: 6 French, saison, summer
__ E. Tee: 3 Lil
eternal: 4 ever, vast 6 eonian, steady 7 abiding, ageless, endless, lasting, undying 8 almighty, enduring, immortal, infinite, timeless, unending, unwaning 9 ceaseless, continual, deathless, incessant, perennial, perpetual, Sisyphean, unceasing, unfailing 10 unchanging
Eternal __: 4 City 5 Flame
Eternal City, The: 4 Roma, Rome
Eternal Fire
author: Calder Willingham
eternally: 3 e'er 4 ever 5 no end 6 always 7 forever 8 evermore, for keeps 9 endlessly, regularly 10 unendingly
Eternal Sunshine of the Spotless Mind (2004 film)
cast: Jim Carrey, Kirsten Dunst, Kate Winslet
Eternal, the: 3 God 4 Lord
eterne: 7 ageless, endless, forever 8 timeless, unending 9 ceaseless, perpetual
eternity: 3 eon 4 aeon, ages, time 7 century, forever
Ethan: 4 Coen 5 Allen, Canin, Frome, Hawke 8 Phillips
ethane: 3 gas 4 fuel
Ethan Frome
author: Edith Wharton
character: 3 Ned 5 Zeena 6 Mattie 7 Zenobia
ethanol to dimethyl ether: 6 isomer
Ethel: 5 Mertz 6 Merman, Waters, Wilson 7 Kennedy 9 Barrymore
brother: 4 John 6 Lionel
Diana Barrymore, to ~: 5 niece
husband: 4 Fred
Ethelbert: 5 Nevin
Ethelred the __: 7 Unready
ether: 3 sky 7 heavens 10 anesthetic
ethereal: 4 airy 5 filmy, light 6 aerial, dainty, divine 7 angelic, sublime, tenuous 8 delicate, empyreal, empyrean, gossamer, heavenly, supernal 9 ambrosial, angelical, celestial, exquisite, ineffable, lightsome, spiritual, unearthly, unworldly 10 immaterial, intangible, unphysical
Etheridge: 6 Knight 7 Melissa
ethic: 6 morals 9 principle, tradition
__ ethic: 4 work 7 Puritan
ethical: 4 fair, fine, good, just, nice, okay 5 clean, great, legit, moral, noble, right, sound 6 decent, honest, humane, proper, square, trusty 7 upright 8 all right, elevated, laudable, pleasant, pleasing, splendid, straight, superior, virtuous 9 admirable, agreeable, equitable, excellent, high-toned, honorable, reputable, righteous, veracious, wholesome, wonderful 10 acceptable, beneficial, creditable, high-minded, principled, scrupulous, upstanding
Ethical Culture
originator: Felix Adler
ethically: 9 honorably 10 virtuously
ethics: 4 code 5 mores 6 belief, values, virtue 7 decency, honesty 8 morality, precepts, standard 9 integrity 10 conscience, honestness, principles
lacking ~: 6 amoral
Ethiopia: 6 nation 7 country
ancient city: 4 Axum 5 Aksum, Meroe
bishop: 4 abba
bovine: 5 Barka, Boran, Horro
capital: 10 Addis Ababa
city: 5 Adowa, Harar 10 Addis Ababa
fossil site: 5 Hadar
lake: 4 Tana 5 Abaya, Tsana
language: 6 Somali
money: 4 birr, cent
mountain: 4 Batu, Guna 5 Gughe 9 Ras Dashan
neighbor: 5 Kenya, Sudan 7 Eritrea, Somalia 8 Djibouti
people: 4 Afar 5 Galla, Oromo, Tigré 6 Amhara, Sidamo, Somali 7 Danakil
primate: 6 gelada, grivet
province: 4 Shoa
royal name: 5 Haile
runner: 6 Bikila
title: 3 Ras
volcano: 7 Erta-Ale
waterfall: 6 Fincha
ethmoid: 4 bone
locale: 5 skull 7 cranium 9 braincase
ethnic: 6 native, racial, tribal 8 cultural, national 10 indigenous
group: 4 race 5 tribe
prefix: 4 poly- 5 Italo-
suffix: 3 -ese
ethnic __: 4 food 5 pride
ethnobotany: 4 lore 5 tales 6 fables 7 beliefs, customs, legends 8 doctrine, folklore, teaching 9 mythology 10 traditions
ethnology: 4 race 5 mores 6 custom, values 7 culture, customs, science, society 8 folklore, folkways
study: 8 cultures
ethos: 5 mores 7 culture 8 folkways 9 character, standards
without ~: 3 bad 5 wrong 6 amoral, wicked
ethyl: 3 gas 4 fuel
acetate: 5 ester
ender: 3 -ene
hydride: 6 ethane 8 dimethyl
ethylene __: 6 glycol
Étienne
in English: 6 Steven 7 Stephen
see also French
etiolate: 4 fade 6 blanch, bleach, whiten 7 wash out 8 enfeeble
etiquette: 4 code, form 6 custom 7 decency, decorum, dignity, fashion, manners, p's and q's 8 ceremony, civility, courtesy, niceties, protocol 9 amenities, formality, gentility, politesse, propriety, suavities 10 convention, deportment, politeness, seemliness
error: 4 no-no 5 gaffe 7 faux pas
name: 3 Amy 4 Post 5 Emily 7 Letitia 8 Baldrige 10 Vanderbilt
__ et labora: 3 ora
__-et-Loir: 4 Eure
__-et-Loire: 5 Indre, Maine, Saône
__ et lui: 4 Elle
__ et lumière: 3 son
__ et mon droit: 4 Dieu
Etna: 4 cone 7 volcano 10 Mongibello
emulate ~: 4 spew, spue 5 erupt
locale: 5 Italy 6 Europe
output: 3 ash 4 lava
view from ~: 6 Ionian
__ et noir: 5 rouge
ETO
commander: 3 DDE
nickname: 3 Ike

part: 3 Eur. 7 Theater 8 European 10 Operations
étoile: 4 star 6 dancer 9 ballerina
when ~ s come out: 4 nuit
Eton: 6 collar, jacket, school
like an ~ collar: 5 stiff
ref. for ~: 3 OED
rival: 6 Harrow
river: 6 Thames
Eton __: 6 collar, jacket 7 College
Etonian parent: 5 mater, pater
__ et orbi: 4 urbi
étouffée: 4 stew
__ et quarante: 6 trente
__-être: 4 bien, peut
Etruscan: 8 Etrurian, language
city founded by ~s: 5 Siena
god: 5 Tinia
town: 4 Veii 5 Adria
Etruscan Places
author: D.H. Lawrence
ETs: 6 aliens 8 Martians
ETS exam: 3 GRE, SAT 4 GMAT, LSAT, PSAT
Etta: 4 Kett 5 Candy, James, Jones, Place
E.T. The Extra-Terrestrial (1982 film)
cast: Drew Barrymore, Peter Coyote, Henry Thomas, Dee Wallace
composer: John Williams
director: Steven Spielberg
dog: 6 Harvey
Etting: 4 Ruth
Ettore: 7 Bugatti
in English: 6 Hector
Et tu, __?: 5 brute
Et tu time: 4 Ides
__ et tuum: 4 meum
__ et ubique: 3 hic
étude: 5 music, study
Étude __ Major: 3 in E
etui: 4 case
__-et-un: 5 vingt
__ et Veritas: 3 Lux
__-et-Vilaine: 4 Ille
etymology: 4 root 6 origin, source 7 descent 8 ancestry 9 beginning 10 derivation, extraction, provenance
etymon: 4 root 6 origin
Eu: 4 elem. 7 element 8 europium
63 for ~: 4 at. no.
Eubanks: 3 Bob, Kev 5 Kevin
Eubie: 5 Blake
eucalyptus: 4 tree, yate
eater: 5 koala
ether in ~ oil: 6 cineol
relative: 5 guava 6 myrtle 7 cajeput
yield: 3 gum 4 kino 5 resin
Eucerin: 6 lotion
alternative: 4 Keri 5 Curel, Nivea 6 Aveeno 7 Jergens, Pacquin 9 Lubriderm
Eucharist: 4 rite 9 communion, sacrament
box: 3 pix, pyx
bread: 5 wafer
plate: 5 paten
rite: 4 Mass
table: 5 altar
euchre: 4 game 5 cheat 7 swindle 8 card game, hoodwink
kin: 6 écarté
Euclid: 4 city, town
locale: 4 Ohio
work: 8 Elements
Euclidean __: 8 geometry
Eudora: 5 Welty
Eugene: 4 city, Debs, List, pope, town 5 Field, Fodor, Roche, Ysaye 6 O'Neill, Wigner 7 Burdick, Istomin, Ormandy, pontiff 8 Goossens, McCarthy
athletes: 5 Ducks
in Russian: 7 Yevgeni, Yevgeny
locale: 3 Ore. 6 Oregon
Eugene __: 4 Aram 6 Onegin
Eugène: 3 Sue 7 Ionesco 9 Delacroix
Eugene Aram
author: Edward Bulwer-Lytton
Eugene Onegin: 5 novel, opera
author: Aleksandr Pushkin
character: 4 Olga 5 Tanya
composer: Peter Tchaikovsky
Eukanuba: 7 dog food
alternative: *see* pet food brand
Eula: 6 Varner
Eulabus: 4 pope 7 pontiff
Eulalie
author: Edgar Allan Poe
__ Eulenspiegel: 4 Till
Euler, Leonhard: 13 mathematician
eulogize: 4 laud 5 bless, ensky, exalt, extol, honor 6 extoll, praise 7 acclaim, applaud, glorify, lionize, magnify 9 celebrate, recommend 10 panegyrize
eulogy: 5 eloge, psalm 6 praise, speech 7 acclaim, oration, plaudit, tribute 8 accolade, encomium 9 extolment, laudation, panegyric 10 exaltation
Eumenides
author: Aeschylus
Eunice: 7 Shriver
brother: 3 JFK, Ted
daughter: 5 Maria
son: 7 Timothy
euphemism: 8 delicacy 9 inflation, pomposity 10 floridness
swearer's ~: 4 dang, darn, drat
euphemistic: 4 mild 5 vague 8 indirect, softened
euphonic: 5 sweet 6 dulcet
euphonious: 5 in key, sweet 6 dulcet, in tune 7 lyrical, melodic, musical, tuneful 8 sonorous 9 melodious, well-tuned 10 harmonious
euphonium: 4 horn, tuba, wind
euphony: 4 tune 5 music 6 melody 7 harmony
euphoria: 3 joy 4 glee 5 bliss 7 delight, ecstasy, elation, rapture 8 felicity 9 happiness 10 ebullience, exaltation, exultation, joyousness, jubilation
euphoric: 4 glad 5 giddy, happy, merry 6 blithe, cheery, elated, jovial, joyful, joyous, upbeat 7 beaming, gleeful, pleased, tickled 8 blissful, cheerful, ecstatic, exultant, jubilant, mirthful, thrilled 9 delighted, overjoyed, rapturous, rejoicing
state: 4 high 5 happy, tipsy 6 elated, joyful, pumped 7 psyched, soaring 9 exuberant 10 optimistic
Euphrates: 5 river
it joins the ~: 6 Tigris
locale: 4 Irak, Iraq 5 Syria 6 Turkey
river to the ~: 5 Murat 6 Khabur
Euphrosyne: 5 Grace 8 asteroid
colleague: 6 Aglaia, Thalia
euphuistic: 5 wordy 7 orotund, pompous, verbose 8 inflated 9 bombastic, grandiose, rhapsodic 10 big-talking, flamboyant, long-winded, rhetorical
eupnea: 4 puff 6 breath 9 breathing 10 exhalation, inhalation
Eur.: 4 cont.
alliance: 4 NATO
former ~ country: 3 GDR
historic ~ realm: 3 HRE
nation: 3 Aus., Lux., Rus., Swe. 4 Aust., Belg., Bulg., Gr. Br., Gt. Br., Holl., Icel., Lith., Neth., Norw., Swed.
south of ~: 3 Afr. 5 Medit.
speedometer reading in ~: 3 kph
Eurasia
bird: 4 smew, tern
language family: 6 Altaic
range: 4 Alai 5 Urals
sea: 5 Black 7 Caspian
shrub: 6 daphne 8 mezereon, mezereum, oleander, oleaster, tamarisk
Eure-et-__: 4 Loir
Eureka: 3 vac 4 city, town 5 motto 6 vacuum
author: Edgar Allan Poe
locale: 10 California
rival: 5 Kirby, Oreck 6 Hoover 10 Electrolux
Eureka!: 3 aha, cry, hah, oho
Euripides: 5 Greek 10 playwright
work: Alcestis
Andromache
Bacchae
Cyclops
Electra
Hecuba
Helen
Hippolytus
Ion
Iphigenia in Aulis
Medea
Orestes
The Trojan Women
euro: 4 coin 5 money 8 wallaroo 9 marsupial
competitor: 3 dol. 6 dollar
country: 5 Italy, Malta, Spain 6 Cyprus, France, Greece 7 Austria, Belgium, Finland, Germany, Holland, Ireland 8 Portugal, Slovakia, Slovenia 10 Luxembourg 11 Netherlands
replacer: 4 lira, mark 5 franc 6 peseta 7 drachma, guilder
Euro __: 6 Disney
Euromoney: 3 ecu
Europa: 4 moon 8 asteroid
brother: 5 Cilix 6 Cadmus, Thasus 7 Phineus, Phoenix
father: 6 Agenor 10 Telephassa
lover: 4 Zeus
planet: 7 Jupiter
sister: 4 Asia 6 Cadmus
son: 5 Minos 8 Sarpedon
Europe: 8 Old World 9 continent
airline: 3 KLM, SAS 5 MALEV 6 Iberia
bird: 4 chat, lark, rook, ruff, shag, smew 5 ousel, ouzel, saker, serin, tarin, twite 6 chough, cuckoo, hoopoe, lanner, linnet, siskin 7 babbler, graylag, greylag, jackdaw, lapwing, pochard, redwing, skylark, sunbird, wagtail, waxbill 8 coturnix, dotterel, eagle owl, garganey, hawfinch, ringdove, starling, whinchat, woodchat, woodlark 9 bullfinch, cormorant, fieldfare, francolin, goldfinch, ossifrage, stonechat 10 greenfinch, turtledove
boot: 5 Italy
buy from ~: 6 import
capital: 4 Bern, Kiev, Oslo, Riga, Roma, Rome, Wien 5 Berne, Minsk, Paris, Praha, Sofia, Vaduz, Vilna 6 Athens, Berlin, Dublin, Lisboa, Lisbon, London, Madrid, Moscow, Prague, Skopje, Sofiya, Tirana, Tiranë, Vienna, Warsaw, Zagreb 7 Belfast, Cardiff, Den Haag, Nicosia, Tallinn 8 Belgrade, Brussels, Chisinau, Helsinki, Sarajevo, The Hague, Valletta 9 Amsterdam, Bucharest, Edinburgh, Ljubljana, Stockholm 10 Bratislava, Copenhagen
car: 3 BMW 4 Fiat, Opel, Saab, Yugo
coal region: 4 Saar
ctry.: 3 Alb., Den., Eng., Ger., Ire., Nor., Rom. 4 Ital.
defense org.: 4 NATO
do ~: 4 tour
fish: 3 dab, ide 4 blay, boce, dory, ling, rudd 5 bleak, brill, guasa, loach, pargo, perch, tench 6 barbel, beluga, maigre, turbot, weever, zander 7 gudgeon, pigfoot 8 John Dory, pilchard 10 bitterling
former money: 4 lira, mark 5 ducat, franc 6 markka, peseta 7 drachma, pistole 9 schilling
grass: 7 esparto
gulf: 7 Bothnia
herb: 6 borage, lovage
in ~: 6 abroad 7 touring 8 overseas
it's s. of ~: 3 Afr. 5 Medit. 6 Africa
lake: 5 Onega
language: 3 Ger. 4 Erse, Ital. 5 Czech, Dutch, Greek, Irish 6 Danish, French, German, Polish 7 English, Finnish, Flemish, Italian, Latvian, Russian, Spanish, Swedish 8 Albanian, Estonian, Romanian 9 Hungarian, Icelandic, Norwegian 10 Lithuanian, Portuguese
language group: 6 Finnic
money: 4 euro 5 zloty 6 forint
mountain: 3 alp 4 Rysy, Zupo 5 Aneto, Eiger, Kekes, Korab, Teide 6 Castor, Ecrins, Elbrus, Elbruz, Estats, Musala, Posets, Snezka 7 Aragats, Bernina, Olympus, Triglov 8 Ben Nevis, Jungfrau 9 Mont Blanc, Monte Rosa 10 Matterhorn, Monte Corno
mountains: 4 Alps 5 Urals 8 Pyre-

nees **9** Apennines
nation: 3 Aus., Lux., Rus., Swe. **4** Aust., Belg., Bulg., Eire, Erin, Gr. Br., Gt. Br., Holl., Icel., Lith., Neth., Norw., Swed. **5** Italy, Spain **6** Bosnia, España, France, Greece, Latvia, Monaco, Norway, Poland, Russia, Serbia, Sweden, Turkey **7** Albania, Andorra, Austria, Belarus, Belgium, Croatia, Denmark, England, Estonia, Finland, Germany, Holland, Hungary, Iceland, Ireland, Moldova, Romania, Ukraine **8** Bulgaria, Portugal, Slovakia, Slovenia **9** Lithuania **11** Netherlands, Switzerland, Vatican City **13** Liechtenstein
neighbor: 4 Asia
old ~ country: 4 USSR **6** Latium
peninsula: 5 Italy **6** Iberia
region: 5 Scand. **6** Kosovo **7** Balkans
river: 3 Aar, Bug, Cam, Dal, Dee, Don, Inn, Lek, Lot, Lys, Oka, San, Tay, Ume, Usk, Wye **4** Aare, Adda, Aire, Aube, Avon, Cher, Doon, Drin, Ebro, Eder, Eger, Elbe, Ille, Isar, Kama, Maas, Main, Miño, Neva, Oder, Odra, Ohre, Oise, Oulu, Ouse, Prut, Ruhr, Saar, Sava, Styr, Taff, Tees, Tyne, Ural, Waal, Yser **5** Adige, Aisne, Boyne, Clyde, Desna, Dnepr, Doubs, Douro, Drava, Drina, Dvina, Isère, Kuban, Loire, Marne, Memel, Meuse, Minho, Mures, Narew, Neman, Onega, Peene, Piave, Rhine, Rhone, Saône, Seine, Siret, Somme, Tagus, Tiber, Tisza, Trent, Tweed, Volga, Warta, Weser **6** Allier, Danube, Dnestr, Donets, Glomma, Humber, IJssel, Isonzo, Liffey, Mersey, Moldau, Morava, Neckar, Neisse, Niemen, Pripet, Sambre, Severn, Struma, Thames, Thjórs, Vardar, Vltava, Yarrow **7** Derwent, Dnieper, Garonne, Livenza, Maritsa, Moselle, Pechora, Rubicon, Schelde, Scheldt, Shannon, Trebbia, Vistula **8** Berezina, Dniester, Dordogne, Guadiana, Volturno
rodent: 6 suslik **7** hamster, mole rat, souslik
sea: 5 North **6** Baltic
starter: 3 Pan- **4** Indo-
tree: 4 sorb, wych **5** rowan
volcano: 4 Etna **8** Vesuvius **9** Santorini, Stromboli
weasel: 5 fitch, sable **6** ermine **7** foumart, polecat **8** foulmart
yard: 5 meter

European: 4 Balt, Brit, Dane, Esth, Finn, Gael, Lett, Pole, Serb, Slav, Turk **5** Greek, Swede, Swiss **6** German **7** Belgian, Bosnian, Italian, Latvian, Russian, Serbian, Slovene **8** Albanian, Austrian, Croatian, Estonian, Moldovan, Romanian, Spaniard **9** Bulgarian, Frenchman, Hungarian, Norwegian, Slovakian, Slovenian, Ukrainian **10** Lithuanian, Monegasque
European __: 4 plan **5** Union
__-European: 4 Indo
Europeans, The
author: Henry James
europium: 7 element
Eurovan: 2 VW **10** Volkswagen
Eurus
mother: 3 Eos
Euryale: 6 Amazon
father: 4 Ares **5** Minos
lover: 8 Poseidon
sister: 6 Medusa
son: 5 Orion
Euryclea
mother: 3 Ops
Eurydice
husband: 6 Nestor **7** Orpheus
lover: 5 Eneas **6** Aeneas
son: 5 Etias
Eurythemis
daughter: 4 Leda
Eurythmics
song: Here Comes the Rain Again (1984)
Sweet Dreams (1983)
Would I Lie to You? (1985)
Eusebius: 4 pope **7** pontiff
Eustace: 5 saint
Eustache: 9 Deschamps
Eustachian tube site: 3 ear
Eustachius: 5 saint
Eustatius, St. neighbor: 4 Saba
Eustis: 4 city, town
locale: 7 Florida
__ Eustis, VA: 4 Fort
Euterpe: 4 Muse
area: 3 mus. **5** music
parent: 4 Zeus **9** Mnemosyne
sister: 4 Clio **5** Erato **6** Thalia, Urania **8** Calliope **9** Melpomene **10** Polyhymnia **11** Terpsichore
Euwe, Max forte: 5 chess
Eva: 5 Gabor, Green, Novak, Perón **6** Bartok, Duarte, Marton **7** Tanguay
sister: 5 Magda **6** Zsa Zsa
Eva __ Saint: 5 Marie
__ Eva: 6 Little
EVA: 9 spacewalk
org.: 4 NASA
evacuate: 2 go **4** void **5** drain, empty, leave, purge, use up **6** decamp, depart, get out, remove, unload **7** consume, deplete, exhaust, pull out
evacuated: 4 bare **5** empty **6** barren
evacuation: 4 exit **6** exodus **7** retreat **8** ejection, emptying **9** catharsis, clearance, departure, discharge, expulsion, purgation **10** withdrawal
evade: 4 duck, flee, jump, loaf, lose, shun **5** avoid, dodge, elude, fudge, hedge, parry, shirk, skirt, sneak **6** bypass, cop out, escape, eschew, ignore, put off, refuse **7** abstain, disobey, fend off, neglect, quibble, shy from **8** flee from, get out of, keep from, shake off, sidestep, throw off **9** get around, hem and haw, pussyfoot, sneak away **10** circumvent, equivocate, escape from, get clear of, work around
a haymaker: 3 bob **4** duck **5** weave
the issue: 6 waffle **10** equivocate
the seeker: 4 hide
evader: 5 cheat **7** escapee **8** deserter **9** goldbrick
work ~: 5 idler **6** loafer, truant **7** goof-off, shirker, slacker **8** fainéant **9** do-nothing, lazybones **10** ne'er-do-well
evaluate: 3 try, vet **4** case, rank, rate, sift **5** assay, check, gauge, grade, judge, price, think, weigh **6** assess, ponder, reckon, review, screen, size up, survey, try out **7** analyze, balance, inspect, measure **8** appraise, check out, classify, estimate, factor in, keep tabs, look over **9** criticize, figure out, pick apart
evaluation: 4 test **5** stock **6** rating **7** opinion **8** analysis, estimate, feedback, judgment **9** appraisal, criticism, probation, valuation **10** assessment, estimation
evaluator: 5 judge **6** critic, expert, pundit **7** analyst, arbiter, scholar **8** reviewer **9** authority
Eva Luna
author: Isabel Allende
Eva Marie __: 5 Saint
Evan: 4 Bayh **6** Hunter, Mecham
Evan-__: 6 Picone
Evan Almighty (2007 film)
cast: Steve Carell, Morgan Freeman, Lauren Graham
Evander: 9 Holyfield
evanesce: 4 fade, melt **6** vanish **8** dissolve, fade away, vaporize **9** disappear, dissipate, evaporate
evanescent: 5 brief, short **6** mortal **7** passing, trivial **8** fleeting, flitting, temporal **9** ephemeral, momentary, temporary, transient **10** intangible, unenduring
Evangeline: 4 poem
author: Henry Wadsworth Longfellow
character: 5 Basil, Mowis **7** Gabriel, Lilinau
setting: 6 Acadia
evangelist: 8 minister, preacher
Evangelista: 5 Linda **10** Torricelli
evangelize: 5 drill, teach, train **6** preach **7** educate **8** instruct **9** catechize
Evans: 3 Gil, Ray **4** Dale, Gene, Greg, Joan, Paul, peak **5** Chris, Edith, Faith, Janet, Linda, Madge, mount **6** Arthur, Dwight, Harold, Oliver, Robert, Walker **7** Connell, Darrell, Maurice, Rowland **8** mountain
locale: 7 Rockies **8** Colorado
partner: 5 Novak
Evans, Arthur: 12 archeologist
excavation site: 5 Crete **6** Candia
Evans, Dale
horse: 10 Buttermilk
spouse: Roy Rogers
Evans, Darrell
sport: 8 baseball
Evans, Edith: 4 Dame
__ Evans Hughes: 7 Charles
Evans, Janet: 7 swimmer
Evans, Linda: 7 actress
spouse: John Derek
Evans, Mary Ann
pseudonym: George Eliot
Evans, Robert
spouse: Phyllis George, Ali MacGraw, Catherine Oxenberg
Evanston: 4 city, town
athletes: 8 Wildcats
locale: 8 Illinois
Evansville: 4 city, town
locale: 7 Indiana
sch.: 3 USI
Evans, Walker collaborator: 4 Agee
evaporate: 3 dry **4** boil, fade **5** dry up **6** dry out, vanish **7** distill **8** decrease, dissolve, evanesce, fade away, peter out **9** anhydrate, dehydrate, desiccate, disappear, dissipate **10** dehumidify
evaporated __: 4 milk
evaporation: 5 decay **6** fading **8** drying up **9** abatement
residue: 4 salt
evasion: 3 lie **4** ruse, tale **5** dodge, shift, trick **6** cop-out, escape, excuse **7** dodging, elusion, pretext, quibble **8** pretense, shirking, shunning, trickery **9** avoidance, runaround **10** subterfuge
__ evasion: 3 tax
evasive: 3 coy, sly **4** cagy **5** cagey, dodgy, vague **6** shifty, tricky **7** cunning, devious, elusive, elusory, furtive, oblique, unclear **8** slippery **9** ambiguous, casuistic, deceitful, deceptive, equivocal, insincere, unwilling **10** inexplicit, misleading, roundabout, unexplicit, unobliging
phrase: 4 not I **5** not me
tactic: 3 zag, zig **6** end run
eve: 5 brink, verge **6** sunset **9** nighttime, threshold
Hebrew ~: 4 ereb, erev
opposite: 4 morn
Eve: 5 Arden, Curie, Plumb **6** Queler **7** Merriam **10** Harrington
composer: Jules Massenet
domain: 4 Eden
grandson: 4 Enos **5** Enoch
husband: 4 Adam
son: 4 Abel, Cain, Seth
source: 3 rib
tempter: 5 apple, snake **7** serpent
Eve __ Agnes, The: 4 of St.
Eve __ Mark, The: 4 of St.
Evel: 7 Knievel **9** daredevil
Evelina
author: Fanny Burney
Evelyn: 4 John, King, Lear, Wood **5** Keyes, Waugh **6** Ankers **7** Ashford, Venable
Evelyne: 5 Accad
even: 3 tie, yet **4** calm, cool, fair, flat, just, tied **5** align, aline, equal, flush, level, match, plane, still **6** honest, in a tie, on a par, placid, serene, smooth, square, stable, steady **7** balance, equable, flatten, regular, uniform **8** balanced, composed, constant, equalize, matching, moderate, parallel, peaceful, smoothly, so much as, straight, tranquil, unbiased, unbroken **9** equitable, identical, impartial, smooth out, stabilize, temperate, unextreme, uniformly, unruffled, unvarying **10** all the more, consistent, deadlocked, dependable, equivalent, fifty-fifty, nose to nose, rhythmical, straighten, true to type,

unagitated, unchanging, unwavering
a little: **3** any **5** at all
chance: **6** tossup
come out ~: **3** tie **7** balance
ender: **4** fall, song, tide **6** handed
get ~: **3** fix, tie **5** repay, spite **6** avenge **7** pay back, requite, revenge **9** pay in kind, retaliate
if: **3** tho, yet **5** altho, while **6** albeit, though, whilst **7** despite **8** although **9** supposing
nearly ~: **5** close, tight **8** not quite, round off, round out **9** proximate
not ~: **3** odd **4** nary
not ~ close: **4** cold **5** wrong **6** all wet **7** distant **8** mistaken **9** erroneous **10** inaccurate
not ~ once: **4** ne'er **5** never
not ~ one: **4** nada **5** zilch
now: **3** yet **5** still
on an ~ keel: **4** calm **5** alike, equal, level **6** in line, smooth, stable, steady **7** aligned, equable, lined up, matched, regular **8** balanced, constant, parallel, straight, unbroken **9** identical **10** comparable, consistent, equivalent
once: **4** ever **5** at all **9** at any time **10** at any point
one: **3** any **4** a bit **5** at all **7** a little
opposite: **4** morn
out: **5** level **6** spread **7** balance, flatten, redress
(out): **7** average
so: **3** yes, yet **5** still **10** all the same
stay ~: **6** keep up **8** maintain, preserve
supposing: **6** though
temper: **8** patience **9** composure **10** sedateness
up: **3** tie **4** tied, trim **5** align, aline, level, plane **6** square **7** balance **8** equalize
even __: **5** money
even __ speak: **4** as we
even-__: **6** steven
__ even: **3** get **5** break, odd or
...__ even a mouse: **3** not
evenhanded: **4** fair, just **5** equal **6** honest, square **7** neutral, upright **8** balanced, straight, unbiased **9** equitable, impartial, objective, uncolored, unslanted
evenhandedness: **6** equity **7** justice **8** fairness, fair play, justness **9** rightness **10** lawfulness
evening: **3** e'en **4** dark, dusk, nite **5** night **6** sunset **7** sundown **8** gloaming, twilight **9** nightfall, nighttime
draw toward ~: **5** laten
each ~: **7** nightly
ender: **4** wear
have an ~ meal: **3** sup **4** dine **5** feast
hour: **2** p.m. **3** six **4** nine **5** eight, seven
in French: **4** soir
in Italian: **4** sera
meal: **6** dinner, repast, supper
part of the ~: **5** shank
party: **6** soiree
star: **5** Venus **6** planet, Vesper
wear: **3** PJs, tux **4** gown **5** dress, stole **6** formal
evening __: **3** bag **4** gown, star **5** dress **6** prayer, school **7** clothes
__ evening: **4** good
Evening __: **4** Star **5** Class, Shade
Evening at Pops
network: **3** PBS
Evening Class
author: Maeve Binchy
Evening Shade (CBS sitcom)
cast: Ossie Davis (Ponder Blue) Marilu Henner (Ava Newton) Hal Holbrook (Evan Evans) Burt Reynolds (Wood Newton)
setting: **3** Ark. **8** Arkansas
Evening Star
author: Edgar Allan Poe
Evening Star, The: **5** novel
author: Larry McMurtry
Evening with Richard Nixon, An
author: Gore Vidal
__ even keel: **4** on an
evenly: **5** alike, right **9** pari passu, uniformly
__ even more than anyone...: **3** E is
evenness: **7** balance, isonomy, justice **8** equality, monotony, symmetry **9** composure, equipoise **10** legibility
Even Now (song)
artist: Barry Manilow, Bob Seger
evensong: **4** hymn **6** vesper **7** vespers
even-steven, go: **3** tie **5** split
event: **2** do **4** bash, bout, case, expo, fair, fete, gala, game, meet, race **5** big do, match, mixer, party, pro-am, scene, state, thing **6** affair, discus, mishap, prelim, slalom **7** benefit, contest, episode, holiday, javelin, shot put **8** accident, birthday, calamity, election, fortuity, high jump, incident, landmark, long jump, marathon, occasion **9** box social, emergency, happening, milestone, pole vault, situation, spectacle, triathlon **10** barnburner, casus belli, centennial, experience, graduation, occurrence, phenomenon, tournament
blessed ~: **5** birth
host: **2** MC **5** emcee
important ~: **4** rite **8** landmark **9** milestone
in any ~: **5** still **6** anyhow, anyway **7** at least **9** at any rate **10** regardless
in that ~: **4** then **9** therefore
in the ~: **9** given that
main ~: **4** bout, duel **5** fight, match, round **7** contest, feature **8** showcase **9** headliner, highlight **10** engagement
sporting ~: **4** bout, bowl, dash, game, meet, race **5** fight, match, relay, rodeo **6** discus **10** prizefight
__ event: **4** main **5** field, in any, media, track **7** blessed
even-tempered: **4** cool **6** placid **7** equable, patient **8** tranquil
not ~: **5** moody
eventful: **7** fateful **8** pregnant **9** memorable, momentous
even the __: **5** score
Even the Nights Are Better (1982 song)
artist: Air Supply
eventide: **5** night **6** sunset **8** twilight **9** nightfall, nighttime
events: **4** proc. **6** doings **8** goings-on **10** happenings
course of ~: **4** tide
current ~: **4** news
order of ~: **7** program
past ~: **6** annals **7** account, history **9** chronicle, olden days, posterity, recountal
events list: **4** sked **5** sched., slate
eventual: **4** last **5** final, later **6** coming, future, latter **7** ensuing **8** terminal, ultimate, upcoming **9** resulting **10** concluding, consequent, inevitable, subsequent
eventuality: **4** case **5** state **6** result, upshot
eventualize: **5** occur **6** result
eventually: **3** yet **4** anon, soon, then **5** after **6** at last, in a bit, in time, not now, one day **7** by and by, finally, for good, later on, someday **8** after all, in a while, in the end, sometime **9** afterward, hereafter **10** before long, ultimately
eventuate: **2** go **4** rise **5** begin, ensue, occur **6** follow, happen, pan out, result **7** turn out **9** come about, take place, terminate, transpire **10** come to pass
even-up: **10** fifty-fifty
Eve of Destruction (1965 song)
artist: Barry McGuire
Eve of St. Agnes, The: **4** poem
author: John Keats
Eve of St. Mark, The
author: Maxwell Anderson
eve. preceder: **3** aft
ever: **3** too **5** at all, no how **6** always **7** for good **8** even once, for keeps, in any way, sometime, unending **9** at any time, endlessly, eternally **10** at all times, at any point, constantly, enduringly, for all time, invariably, unendingly
and anon: **3** oft
as ~: **6** always, surely **10** invariably
ender: **4** more **5** glade, green, where, which **6** glades **7** bearing, lasting **8** blooming
hardly ~: **6** little, rarely, seldom **8** scarcely
not ~: **4** ne'er **5** never
partner: **4** anon
since: **4** as of, from
so: **4** very **5** quite **9** extremely
so much: **4** a lot, many **6** highly **7** greatly
starter: **3** for, how, who **4** what, when, whom **5** which
Ever After (1998 film)
cast: Drew Barrymore, Anjelica Huston
Everage: **4** Dame, Edna
ever and __: **4** anon **5** again
Everest: **3** mtn. **4** peak **5** mount **8** mountain
conqueror: **6** Norgay **7** Hillary
guide: **6** Sherpa
locale: **4** Asia **5** Nepal, Tibet **6** Xizang **7** Sitsang **9** Himalayas
Everett: **4** Chad, city, town **5** Betty **6** Rupert, Sloane
locale: **10** Washington
__ Everett Horton: **6** Edward
__ Ever Fall in Love: **3** If I
everglades: **5** marsh, swamp
Everglades: **4** park
inhabitant: **4** ibis **5** egret
locale: **3** Fla. **7** Florida
evergreen: **3** fir, yew **4** atle, pine, wood **5** athel, boldo, cacao, erica, furze, hakea, olive, piñon, plant, thuja, thuya, toyon **6** alerce, balsam, laurel, longan, loquat, lungan, spruce **7** arbutus, cypress, juniper **8** gardenia **9** sapodilla **10** arborvitae, sandalwood
African ~: **4** akee
Chilean ~: **5** maqui
forest: **5** taiga
genus: **5** picea
like an ~: **4** piny **5** firry, piney
New Zealand ~: **5** kauri
oak: **4** holm, ilex
shrub: **3** box, kat, qat **4** khat **5** erica, gorse, hakea, heath, holly, maqui, pyxie, salal, toyon **6** aucuba, dahoon, kalmia, myrtle, nardin, privet **7** arbutus, boxwood, juniper, mahonia, nandina, skimmia **8** camellia, cassiope, rosemary **9** firethorn, sugarbush
Evergreen State: **4** Wash. **10** Washington
Everhart: **5** Angie
everlasting: **6** always, eterne **7** abiding, endless, eternal, undying **8** almighty, constant, enduring, immortal, infinite, timeless, unending **9** ceaseless, deathless, perennial, permanent, perpetual, unceasing
Everlasting Love (1974 song)
artist: Carl Carlton
Everlasting Love, An (1978 song)
artist: Andy Gibb
everlastingly: **5** no end
Everlasting Mercy, The
author: John Masefield
Everly Brothers: **3** Don, duo **4** Phil
song: All I Have to Do Is Dream (1958)
Bird Dog (1958)
Bye Bye Love (1957)
Cathy's Clown (1960)
Crying in the Rain (1962)
Devoted to You (1958)
Ebony Eyes (1961)
I Kissed You (1959)
Let It Be Me (1960)
Problems (1958)
So Sad (1960)
That's Old Fashioned (1962)
Wake Up Little Susie (1957)
Walk Right Back (1961)
When Will I Be Loved (1960)
evermore: **6** always **9** endlessly, eternally, from now on **10** enduringly, henceforth, unendingly
__ Ever Need Is You: **4** All I
ever-present: **7** chronic **9** chronical **10** ubiquitous
Evers: **6** Johnny, Medgar **7** Charles
everse: **9** overthrow
Evers, Johnny: **3** Cub
__ ever so humble...: **4** Be it
evert: **6** refute **7** reverse
Evert, Chris: **7** netster **9** tennis pro
milieu: **5** court
spouse: Greg Norman

every: 3 all, per 4 each 5 whole
12 mos.: 4 yrly. 6 yearly
24 hours: 4 a day 5 daily
60 minutes: 5 horal 6 hourly
any and ~: 3 all
bit: 4 to a T 5 fully 6 wholly 7 exactly, totally 10 throughout
eighth day: 5 octan
ender: 3 day, man, one 4 body 5 place, thing, where
evening: 7 nightly
inch: 5 fully 6 wholly 7 totally, utterly 8 entirely 10 completely, thoroughly
in prescriptions: 3 omn.
make ~ effort: 6 strive 8 struggle
morning: 5 daily 7 diurnal, regular, routine 9 quotidian
now and then: 6 seldom 8 periodic, sporadic 9 sometimes 10 occasional
other: 9 alternate
show ~ sign of: 4 seem 6 appear
which way: 5 messy, mussy 6 hectic, untidy 7 chaotic, haywire, jumbled, lawless, riotous, tangled 8 anarchic, confused, pell-mell 10 anarchical, disjointed, disordered, disorderly, topsy-turvy, tumultuous
win ~ game: 5 sweep 7 clean up
with ~ option: 4 full, rich 5 flush, tight 6 loaded, packed 7 crowded, replete, stuffed 8 brimming, cram-full 9 chock-full, jam-packed 10 wall-to-wall
every ___: 3 bit, day 4 inch 5 other
every ___ and then: 3 now
every ___ in a while: 4 once
every ___ jack: 3 man
every ___ son: 7 mother's
every ___ way: 5 which
Every ___ has his day: 3 dog
Every ___ of My Heart: 4 Beat
Every ___ Way But Loose: 5 Which
Every ___ You Take: 6 Breath
Every Beat of My Heart (1961 song)
artist: Gladys Knight and the Pips
everybody: 3 all 4 y'all 5 world 9 one and all
opposite: 5 no one
Everybody (song)
artist: Backstreet Boys, Tommy Roe
Everybody Has an ___: 4 Aura
Everybody Hurts (1993 song)
artist: R.E.M.
Everybody Loves a Clown (1965 song)
artist: Gary Lewis and the Playboys
Everybody Loves a Lover (1958 song)
artist: Doris Day
Everybody Loves Me But You (1962 song)
artist: Brenda Lee
Everybody Loves Raymond (CBS sitcom)
cast: Peter Boyle (Frank Barone) Brad Garrett (Robert Barone) Patricia Heaton (Debra Barone) Doris Roberts (Marie Barone) Ray Romano (Ray Barone)
dog: 7 Shamsky
Everybody Loves Somebody (1964 song)
artist: Dean Martin
Everybody Ought to Have a ___: 4 Maid
Everybody Plays the Fool (song)
artist: Main Ingredient, Aaron Neville
Everybody's All-American (1988 film)
cast: Timothy Hutton, Jessica Lange, Dennis Quaid
Everybody's Somebody's Fool (1960 song)
artist: Connie Francis
Everybody's Talkin' (1969 song)
artist: Nilsson
Everybody Wants to Rule the World (1985 song)
artist: Tears for Fears
Every Breath You Take (1983 song)
artist: Police, Sting
everyday: 5 lowly, plain, stock, typic, usual 6 common, normal, vulgar, wonted 7 average, diurnal, general, generic, humdrum, mundane, natural, prosaic, regular, routine, trivial, typical 8 frequent, habitual, informal, ordinary, orthodox, standard 9 customary, generical, prosaical, quotidian 10 accustomed, pedestrian, prevailing, uninspired, widespread
not ~: 4 rare
Everyday People (1969 song)
artist: Sly and the Family Stone
Every Heartbeat (1991 song)
artist: Amy Grant
Every hero becomes ___ at last: 5 a bore
Every Kinda People (1978 song)
artist: Robert Palmer
___ Every Little Star: 5 I Told
Every Little Step (1989 song)
artist: Bobby Brown
Every Little Thing She Does Is Magic (1981 song)
artist: Police
every man ___: 4 jack
Every Man in His Humour
author: Ben Jonson
every now and ___: 4 then 5 again
every once ___ while: 3 in a
everyone: 3 all 4 y'all 5 world 6 public
in music: 5 tutti
Everyone But Thee and Me
author: Ogden Nash
Everyone Says I Love You (1996 film)
cast: Alan Alda, Woody Allen, Goldie Hawn, Julia Roberts
director: Woody Allen
Every Rose Has Its Thorn (1988 song)
artist: Poison
every so ___: 5 often
everything: 3 all 5 whole, works 6 the lot 8 the works, universe 9 aggregate
counting ~: 5 in all 6 in toto, wholly 7 totally 10 altogether, completely
despite ~: 10 regardless
else: 4 rest
in French: 4 tout 5 toute
in Spanish: 4 todo 5 todos
take ~: 3 hog 7 possess 10 monopolize
everything ___ place: 5 in its
Everything (1989 song)
artist: Jody Watley
Everything I Own (1972 song)
artist: Bread
Everything Is Beautiful (1970 song)
artist: Ray Stevens
Everything's Coming Up Roses
composer: Stephen Sondheim, Jule Styne
Everything She Wants (1985 song)
artist: George Michael
Everything that Rises Must Converge
author: Flannery O'Connor
Everything That Touches You (1968 song)
artist: Association, The
Everything to Gain
author: Jimmy Carter
Everything Your Heart Desires (1988 song)
artist: Daryl Hall and John Oates
everywhere: 7 all over, overall 9 all around 10 far and wide, high and low, near and far, pole to pole, throughout, ubiquitous
look ~: 4 comb, rake, seek, sift, sort 5 probe, scour, sweep 6 forage, search 7 examine, inspect, ransack, rummage
prefix: 4 omni-
every which ___: 3 way
Every Which Way But Loose (1978 film)
beast: 5 Clyde, orang
cast: Beverly D'Angelo, Clint Eastwood, Geoffrey Lewis, Sondra Locke
Every Woman in the World (1980 song)
artist: Air Supply
___ Every Woman Knows: 4 What
___ Eve, The: 4 Lady
Evian: 3 spa 5 water
alternative: 4 Naya 7 Perrier 8 Aquafina 9 Arrowhead
see also French
Évian-___-Bains, France: 3 Les
evict: 4 boot, oust 5 eject, expel 6 banish, bounce, put out, remove 7 boot out, dismiss, exclude, kick out, shut off, shut out, toss out, turn out 8 dislodge, displace, force out, throw out 9 eliminate 10 dispossess
eviction: 6 ouster 9 dismissal, exclusion, expulsion
evidence: 4 clew, clue, data, give, hint, lead, look, mark, show, sign 5 basis, proof, prove, token, trace 6 denote, evince, record, reveal 7 confirm, display, exhibit, grounds, signify, symptom, witness 8 document, indicate, manifest 9 affidavit, reference, testimony 10 deposition, illustrate, indication, smoking gun
combustion ~: 3 ash 5 ashes, flame, smoke
crime scene ~: 3 DNA 5 print
hear ~: 3 try 4 deem, rule 5 gauge, judge 6 assess, decide, decree, deduce, settle, size up 7 discern, examine, mediate 8 appraise, consider, evaluate, moderate, sentence 9 arbitrate, determine
in ~: 7 obvious
minimal ~: 5 shred
offer ~: 5 prove, quote, swear 6 adduce, attest 7 testify 8 attest to
___ evidence: 6 state's 7 hearsay
evident: 4 open, real 5 clear, lucid, naked, overt, plain, vivid 6 cogent, marked, patent 7 express, glaring, obvious, outward, seeming, visible 8 apparent, clear-cut, distinct, explicit, luminous, manifest, palpable, tangible 9 axiomatic, graspable, prominent 10 noticeable, observable, pronounced, spelled out, undeniable
be ~: 4 look, loom, show 5 pop up 6 appear, crop up, emerge, happen, show up, turn up 7 surface 8 look as if, look like, spring up
make ~: 5 prove
___-evident: 4 self
evidently: 8 markedly 9 doubtless, obviously, outwardly, seemingly 10 apparently, manifestly, officially, ostensibly
Evigan: 4 Greg
evil: 3 bad, ill, low, sin 4 base, dark, foul, harm, mean, ugly, vice, vile 5 cruel, nasty, wrong 6 guilty, horrid, infamy, malice, malign, no good, poison, sinful, unholy, unkind, wicked 7 badness, baleful, baneful, beastly, corrupt, crooked, demonic, devilry, harmful, hateful, heinous, hideous, hurtful, immoral, impiety, lawless, malefic, outrage, satanic, Stygian, unclean, vicious 8 atrocity, baseness, criminal, daemonic, damnable, demoniac, depraved, devilish, deviltry, diabolic, enormity, fiendish, foulness, ignominy, infamous, iniquity, meanness, mischief, sinister, spiteful, vileness, villainy, wrongful 9 demonical, depravity, diabolism, execrable, indecency, injurious, loathsome, malicious, malignity, miscreant, monstrous, nefarious, offensive, rancorous, repugnant, revolting, satanical, turpitude, vandalism 10 corruption, diabolical, immorality, inexpiable, iniquitous, maleficent, malevolent, misconduct, opprobrium, perfidious, pernicious, perversity, sinfulness, traitorous, villainous, virtueless, wantonness, wickedness, wrongdoing
combining form: 4 male-
do ~: 9 misbehave
encourage in ~: 4 abet 6 incite 7 collude 9 instigate
ender: 4 doer 5 doing
eye: 3 hex 4 jinx, look 5 curse, glare, scowl 7 sorcery
free from ~: 5 purge 6 purify 8 exorcise, exorcize
in French: 3 mal
look: 4 leer
one: 4 ogre 5 baddy, demon, devil, ghoul, Satan 6 baddie, daemon,

daimon, diablo **7** Lucifer **9** arch-fiend
repeller: **5** charm, spell **6** amulet **7** periapt **8** talisman
speak ~ of: **4** slur **5** smear **6** defame, impugn, malign, smirch, vilify **7** asperse, put down, rip into, run down, slander **8** backbite, badmouth, belittle, besmirch, tear down, throw mud **9** criticize, denigrate, deprecate, disparage, fling dirt **10** calumniate, depreciate, speak ill of, throw mud on
ways: **4** hoax **5** guile, wiles **7** con game, cunning, knavery, roguery **8** deviltry, flimflam, mischief, trickery, villainy **9** chicanery **10** dishonesty, subterfuge, wrongdoing
evil __: **3** eye
Evil __: **4** Ways **5** Woman
__ Evil: **5** See No
evildoer: **4** perp **5** devil, felon, fiend, Satan **6** bad guy, sinner **7** hellion, villain **8** criminal, gangster **9** miscreant **10** lawbreaker
evildoing: **3** sin **4** vice **7** outrage **8** iniquity
Evil Empire: **4** USSR
evil-minded: **4** mean **5** catty, nasty, petty, snide **6** ornery, wicked **7** harmful, hateful, hostile, hurtful, jealous, vicious **8** fiendish, vengeful, venomous **9** green-eyed, malicious **10** bad-natured, malevolent, pernicious, vindictive
evil-smelling: **4** rank **5** funky **6** rancid
...evil that __ do...: **3** men
Evil Ways (1970 song)
artist: Santana
Evil Woman (1975 song)
artist: ELO
evince: **4** have, show **5** argue, prove **6** reveal, unfold **7** display, exhibit, reflect, signify **8** evidence, indicate, manifest, proclaim **9** make clear, make plain **10** illustrate
Evita (1996 film): **7** musical
cast: Antonio Banderas, Madonna, Jonathan Pryce
director: Alan Parker
role: **3** Che **4** Juan **5** Perón
Evita (musical)
composer: Andrew Lloyd Webber, Tim Rice
evocative: **8** arousing, kindling, stirring **9** awakening, remindful **10** rekindling, suggestive
evoke: **4** draw **6** arouse, call up, elicit, induce, invite, recall, summon **7** conjure, extract, suggest **8** bring out, occasion **9** call forth, conjure up, draw forth, stimulate **10** bring forth
evolution: **6** change, growth **7** process **8** progress **9** expansion, flowering, formation, gestation, unfolding **10** maturation, perfection, transition
Evolution: **3** car **4** auto **10** Mitsubishi
evolutionary
rung on the ~ ladder: **3** ape, man **5** human **6** apeman
evolve: **4** come, emit, grow **5** ripen **6** change, mature, mutate, unfold **7** advance, develop, give off, perfect, shape up, work out **8** progress **9** come about, formulate, originate
into: **6** become **8** emerge as
evolving: **5** early **7** initial, ongoing **8** germinal, immature **9** embryonic, incipient
Evonne: **9** Goolagong
rival: **5** Chris
Évora: **4** city, town
locale: **8** Portugal
Ev'rybody's Got __ But Me: **5** a Home
__ Ev'ry Mountain: **5** Climb
Ev'ry Time __ Goodbye: **5** We Say
evulse: **3** pry **4** cull, mine, pull, take, yank **5** evoke, glean, leach, pluck, wrest, wring **6** derive, elicit, obtain, remove, select, siphon, uproot **7** distill, draw out, extract, weed out **8** bring out
E.W.: **7** Scripps
Ewa: **4** city, town
locale: **6** Hawaii
Ewan: **8** McGregor
Ewbank, Weeb: **5** coach
sport: **8** football
ewe: **3** she **6** female **7** bleater
baby: **4** lamb
covering: **4** wool
homophone: **3** yew, you
mate: **3** ram
milieu: **3** lea **5** field, grass **6** meadow **7** pasture **9** grassland
sound: **3** baa, maa **5** bleat
Ewell: **3** Tom
ewer: **3** jug **5** basin **6** vessel **7** pitcher **8** oenochoe **9** container
adjunct: **4** bowl **5** basin **6** vessel
use a ~: **4** pour
__ E. Westlake: **6** Donald
Ewing: **2** J.R. **3** Pam **4** Buck, city, Gary, Jock, Lucy, town **5** Bobby, Ellie **6** Valene **7** Patrick
concern: **3** oil
J.R. ~ foe: **5** Cliff **6** Barnes
locale: **9** New Jersey
Ewing, Patrick org.: **3** NBA
Ewings, The
author: John O'Hara
Ewok: **5** alien
ally: **4** Jedi
home: **5** Endor
Ew-w-w!: **3** ick, ugh **5** gross, yecch
ex: **6** former **7** divorcé **8** divorcée, previous
ex __: **5** parte **6** libris **7** officio
ex __ facto: **4** post
ex, __, zee: **3** wye
ex-: **4** late, past **8** outgoing
exacerbate: **4** sink, slip, sour **5** add to, decay, slide **6** worsen **7** enflame, inflame **8** compound **9** aggravate, infuriate, intensify **10** degenerate, exasperate, retrogress
exact: **3** tax **4** fine, firm, just, levy, nice, same, true **5** clear, force, fussy, level, right, rigid, seize, sound, stiff, valid, wrest, wring **6** actual, coerce, compel, dead-on, demand, direct, extort, impose, proper, severe, strict, wrench **7** call for, careful, command, correct, express, factual, finicky, inflict, literal, perfect, precise, refined, regular, require, right on, solicit **8** absolute, accurate, clear-cut, definite, distinct, faithful, finiking, finnicky, flawless, inerrant, methodic, on target, on the dot, rigorous, specific, straight, thorough, truthful, unerring, verbatim **9** definable, demanding, errorless, faultless, identical, on the nose, unbending, veracious **10** impeccable, infallible, insist upon, methodical, meticulous, nailed down, on the money, particular, scrupulous, unmistaken
retribution: **6** avenge **7** get even **9** retaliate
exacta: **3** bet **5** wager
locale: **3** OTB **5** track
player: **6** better, bettor **7** gambler, wagerer **8** gamester
exacting: **4** firm, hard **5** bossy, cruel, fussy, harsh, picky, rigid, stern, stiff, tight, tough **6** severe, strict, taxing, trying **7** austere, careful, exigent, finicky, hard-won, onerous, precise, prudent, Spartan, weighty **8** captious, cautious, critical, despotic, exigeant, finiking, finnicky, hard-line, rigorous, thorough, tiresome **9** assiduous, attentive, demanding, difficult, draconian, imperious, judicious, observant, stringent, unbending, unfeeling, unsparing **10** burdensome, despotical, enervating, fastidious, inflexible, iron-fisted, meticulous, nitpicking, no-nonsense, oppressive, particular, scrupulous, tyrannical, unamenable
exaction: **3** fee, tax **4** duty, levy, toll **6** assess, charge, custom, excise, impose, impost, tariff **10** collection
exactitude: **5** right, rigor, truth **7** clarity **8** accuracy, fidelity, veracity **9** precision **10** conformity, factuality
exactly: **3** due, pat **4** just, to a T **5** plumb, sharp, smack, spang **8** directly, for a fact, on the dot, straight, verbatim **9** literally, literatim, on the nose, precisely **10** for certain, on the money, unerringly
in Latin: **10** ad litteram
not ~: **5** about, kinda, sorta **6** in a way, kind of, sort of
exactness: **4** care **5** right, rigor **8** accuracy, fidelity, veracity **9** austerity, precision **10** definitude, perfection, regularity, strictness
exaggerate: **3** lie, pad **4** puff **5** add to, boast, boost, color, fudge **6** blow up, expand, overdo, puff up **7** amplify, build up, enlarge, inflate, lay it on, magnify, stretch **8** go too far, misquote, overplay, overrate **9** aggravate, dramatize, embellish, embroider, emphasize, fabricate, intensify, misreport, overstate **10** caricature
exaggerated: **4** tall **5** campy, hammy, undue **6** lavish, too-too **8** overdone, strained
exaggeration: **3** fib **4** hype, puff, rhet., tale, yarn **7** blarney, stretch **8** rhetoric, travesty
comic ~: **4** camp **5** farce
exalt: **4** hail, laud, lift **5** adore, bless, boost, crown, deify, ensky, extol, honor, raise **6** esteem, extoll, lift up, praise, puff up, revere, salute, uplift **7** acclaim, advance, applaud, build up, commend, dignify, elevate, enhance, ennoble, flatter, glorify, idolize, inflate, lionize, magnify, promote, worship **8** enshrine, enthrone, eulogize, heighten, inshrine, inthrone, sanctify **9** celebrate, recommend, reverence **10** aggrandize, compliment, panegyrize
exaltation: **5** glory, honor, kudos **6** eulogy, homage, praise, salute **7** acclaim, ecstasy, hosanna, plaudit, rapture, tribute **8** accolade, encomium, euphoria, flattery, good word **9** adoration, animation, elevation, extolment, laudation, loftiness, panegyric, promotion, reverence, transport, upgrading, uplifting **10** apotheosis, excitement, idolzation, joyousness, jubilation
exalted: **4** high **5** grand, great, lofty, noble, noted, royal **6** august, divine, lordly, superb **7** eminent, gleeful, praised, sublime **8** elevated, empyreal, empyrean, glorious, imposing, inspired, majestic, rarefied, superior **9** dignified, high-flown, honorable, top-drawer, unrivaled **10** majestical, unrivalled
exam: **4** oral, quiz, test **5** final **7** checkup, midterm, midyear **8** physical **9** true-false **10** ultrasound
base: **4** text **6** course **8** textbook
British ~: **6** A level, tripos
choice: **4** true **5** false
coll. senior's ~: **3** GRE **4** GMAT, LSAT, MCAT
for immigrants: **5** TOEFL
format: **4** test **5** essay, paper **9** true/false
for would-be teachers: **3** NTE
future doctor's: **4** MCAT
H.S. ~: **3** SAT **4** PSAT
medical ~: **3** ECG, EEG, EKG, MRI **4** x-ray **8** physical
prepare for an ~: **4** cram **5** learn, study **6** master
score: **4** mark, rank **5** grade **6** rating
take an ~: **3** sit
__ exam: **3** bar **4** oral **6** dental
examination: **4** look, oral, quiz, scan, test **5** assay, audit, check, final, probe, proof, study, trial **6** review, survey **7** battery, checkup, enquiry, inquest, inquiry, midterm, perusal, pop quiz, reading **8** analysis, checking, grilling, once-over, scrutiny **9** going-over
combining form: **4** -opsy
conduct an ~: **5** delve, probe **8** research
IRS ~: **3** aud. **5** audit
quick ~: **4** peek **7** look-see
visual ~: **4** gaze, leer, peek, scan, seek **5** sight, study, watch **6** aspect, gander, glance, review, survey **7** display, exhibit, glimpse, look-see, viewing

8 once-over, scrutiny 9 beholding 10 inspection
examine: 3 eye, see, spy, try, vet 4 case, comb, quiz, read, scan, sift, test, view 5 assay, audit, check, grill, judge, plumb, probe, prove, query, study, sum up, think, touch, weigh 6 browse, go into, go over, handle, look at, peer at, peruse, ponder, reason, review, sample, screen, search, survey, winnow 7 analyze, canvass, collate, compare, dig into, dissect, explore, inspect, observe 8 appraise, check out, consider, factor in, look into, look over, overhaul, pick over, pore over, question 9 catechize, criticize, delve into, go through, interview, pick apart 10 scrutinize
carefully: 4 look, pore
__-examine: 5 cross
examiner: 6 censor, tester 7 analyst, auditor, quizzer 8 reviewer 9 inspector 10 accountant, inquisitor, questioner
future ~: 5 augur, sibyl 6 medium, oracle 7 diviner, palmist, prophet, psychic 8 haruspex 9 theurgist 10 forecaster, foreteller, soothsayer
example: 4 case, noun 5 gauge, ideal, light, model, piece 6 sample 7 display, epitome, paragon, pattern, problem, warning 8 citation, instance, paradigm, specimen, standard 9 archetype, precedent, prototype 10 embodiment, stereotype
follow the ~ of: 3 ape 4 copy 5 equal, mimic, rival 6 mirror 7 emulate, imitate, pattern, reflect 9 take after
for ~: 3 say, viz. 4 thus 5 to wit 6 such as
give an ~: 4 cite, name 5 offer, quote 7 specify 8 point out, spell out 9 enumerate
helpful ~: 6 lesson, sermon 7 precept
starter: 7 counter
__ example: 3 for 4 as an 5 set an
exanimate: 6 bummed 7 defunct, extinct 8 dejected, downcast, lifeless 9 bummed-out 10 dispirited, spiritless
ex animo: 9 sincerely
exarch: 6 bishop
exasperate: 3 get, ire, vex 4 gall, rile, roil, tire, wear 5 anger, annoy, chafe, grate, peeve, pique, upset, weary 6 bother, enrage, madden, nettle, offend, put out, rankle, tee off 7 agitate, distress, enflame, incense, inflame, provoke 8 acerbate, irritate 9 aggravate, displease, infuriate, make waves 10 exacerbate
exasperated: 3 hot, mad 4 ired, sore 5 angry, cross, fed up, huffy, irate, livid, testy, tired, wroth 6 fuming, ireful, raging, raving, red-hot 7 enraged, furious, ranting 8 choleric, wrathful 9 indignant, resentful, splenetic
sound ~: 4 sigh
exasperating: 6 trying 7 naughty 8 tiresome 9 annoyance, vexatious
exasperation: 3 ire 4 care, fury, rage 5 anger, pique, upset, wrath 7 umbrage 8 vexation 9 annoyance
exclamation of ~: 6 enough, sheesh 8 honestly
Excalibur: 5 hotel, sword
locale: 5 Vegas 8 Las Vegas
excavate: 3 dig 4 grub, mine, sink 5 delve, dig up, gouge, scoop 6 burrow, deepen, dig out, hollow, quarry, tunnel 7 unearth 8 gouge out, scoop out 9 hollow out, undermine
excavated: 5 empty 6 sunken 7 concave 8 indented 9 depressed 10 scooped out
excavation: 3 dig, pit 4 hole, mine 5 ditch, gouge 6 burrow, cavity, dugout, hollow, quarry, trench 7 foxhole 9 shoveling 10 depression, unearthing
mine ~: 5 stope
excavator: 5 miner 6 dredge 7 backhoe
find: 3 ore 4 gold 5 relic, shard 6 fossil
Excedrin: 9 analgesic 10 painkiller
alternative: *see* pain reliever brand
exceed: 3 cap, top 4 beat, best, pass 5 break, outdo, tower 6 better, go past, outrun 7 eclipse, outpace, overrun, run over, surpass 8 go beyond, outclass, outshine, outstrip, outweigh, overrate, overstep, surmount 9 rise above, transcend 10 put to shame, tower above
the limit: 5 speed
exceeding: 4 more 5 above, undue 8 superior
exceedingly: 4 most, much, very 5 madly, no end, quite 6 ever so, highly, hugely, really 7 awfully, greatly 8 terribly
excel: 3 ace, cap, top 4 lead, lick, pass 5 outdo, shine, trump 6 do well 7 surpass 8 go to town, outclass, outshine, outstrip, outweigh, stand out 9 transcend 10 overshadow
in: 6 master
Excel: 3 car 4 auto 7 Hyundai
excellence: 5 merit, value, worth 6 virtue 7 quality 8 goodness, nobility 9 greatness, supremacy 10 classicism, perfection, superbness
artistic ~: 5 vertu, virtu
standard of ~: 3 par 5 ideal 9 beau idéal
__ excellence: 3 par
Excellency: 5 title
excellent: 3 top 4 aces 5 crack, legit, moral, neato, noble, sharp, solid 6 golden, goodly, proper, select, worthy 7 ethical, vintage 8 all right, laudable, pleasant, pleasing 9 agreeable, certified, reputable, sovereign 10 acceptable, attractive, beneficial, creditable
in hip-hop: 3 rad 4 phat
more ~: 5 finer 6 better, fitter 7 greater 8 improved, stronger, superior, upgraded, worthier
player: 3 ace, pro 4 whiz 6 expert, master, talent 8 virtuoso 10 specialist
see also wonderful
excellent adventure participant: 3 Ted 4 Bill
excellent instrument: 3 pen
excellently: 4 well
Excellent Woman
author: Barbara Pym
excelsior
alternative: *see* point size
Excelsior: 5 motto 6 ballet
composer: Romualdo Marenco
except: 3 ban, bar, but 4 less, omit, save 5 debar, minus 6 all but, reject, unless 7 barring, besides, lacking, rule out, short of, without 8 disallow, leave out, omitting, pass over 9 apart from, aside from, excluding, other than, outside of, rejecting 10 leaving out
exception: 5 quirk 6 oddity 7 anomaly, barring, variant 8 omission 9 allowance, anomalism, condition, debarment, departure, deviation, exclusion, expulsion, privilege, rejection, variation 10 difference
take ~: 5 demur 6 differ 7 dissent, protest, quarrel
take ~ to: 4 mind 5 cavil 6 object, oppose, resent 8 question 9 challenge, deprecate
without ~: 3 all 5 every, fully 6 always, to a man, wholly 8 entirely 10 completely
exceptional: 3 odd 4 eery, rare 5 eerie, weird 6 atypic, banner, freaky, quirky, signal, single 7 bizarre, deviant, notable, oddball, offbeat, special, strange, uncanny, unusual 8 aberrant, abnormal, advanced, atypical, freakish, isolated, peculiar, singular, uncommon 9 anomalous, divergent, eccentric, irregular, recherché, unheard of 10 unorthodox
see also wonderful
exceptionally: 4 much, very 5 extra 6 highly, rarely 7 greatly
excerpt: 4 cite, clip, part, pick 5 glean, quote 6 choose, select 7 extract, passage, pick out, portion 8 citation, fragment, pericope 9 quotation, selection, sound bite
excerpts: 8 analecta, analects
excess: 4 glut, hype, much, orgy, rest 5 flood, slack, waste 7 backlog, license, nimiety, overage, padding, remnant, residue, surfeit, surplus, too much 8 leftover, overflow, overkill, overload, plethora 9 decadence, profusion, redundant, remainder 10 immoderacy, indulgence, lavishness, oversupply, redundancy, sybaritism
baggage: 4 load 6 weight 9 unwelcome
fill to ~: 4 cloy, sate 5 stuff 9 overstuff
in ~: 5 spare
indulge to ~: 4 cloy, glut 5 gorge, stuff 7 surfeit 8 overfill 10 gormandize
in French: 4 trop
in ~ of: 4 over 7 besides 8 more than
excessive: 3 big 4 high, long, over, rank, rich 5 gross, heavy, large, steep, stiff, ultra, undue 6 costly, garish, lavish, wanton 7 glaring, intense, onerous, profuse, radical, rampant, sky-high, too many, too much 8 enormous, needless, overdone, overmuch, prodigal, terrific 9 boundless, expensive, exuberant, indulgent, limitless, luxuriant, out of hand, overblown, overboard, plethoric, redundant, unbounded 10 dissipated, exorbitant, immoderate, inordinate, outrageous, profligate, undeserved, untempered
make ~ demands on: 3 tax
prefix: 4 over- 5 hyper-, ultra-
take ~ pride: 4 brag 5 boast, gloat
talker: 6 gossip, magpie, yakker 7 windbag 8 prattler 10 chatterbox
excessively: 3 too 4 oh so, very 5 madly, quite, super 6 overly, unduly 7 awfully 8 to a fault
exchange: 4 deal, mart, sell, swap, swop, talk 5 bandy, shift, trade 6 barter, cash in, deal in, invert, market, redeem, rotate, seesaw, switch 7 dealing, replace, reverse, shuffle, shuttle, wrangle 8 commerce, flip-flop, take back, treasury 9 interplay, liquidate, take turns, tit for tat, transpose 10 buy and sell, conversion, quid pro quo, substitute
blows: 3 box 4 duel, spar, swat 5 argue, brawl, brush, fight, punch, run-in, whack 6 attack, battle, bicker, combat, go at it, oppose, rumble, take on, tussle 7 assault, contend, contest, mix it up, quarrel, scuffle, vie with, wage war, wrangle, wrestle 8 do battle 9 altercate, slug it out, square off 10 fisticuffs, tangle with
chips: 6 cash in, redeem
currency ~ abbr.: 3 USD
futures ~ for short: 4 Merc
give in ~: 3 pay 5 repay
letters: 3 OTC
medium of ~: 4 bill, cash, coin 5 dough, funds, money, moola 6 dinero, moolah, specie 7 cabbage 8 currency 9 banknotes 10 green stuff
of a sort: 5 Q and A 7 inquiry
of ideas: 4 chat, talk 6 confab, dialog, parley, powwow 8 colloquy, dialogue 9 discourse, tête-à-tête 10 conference, discussion
premium: 4 agio
start of an ~: 3 tit
stock ~: 4 mart 6 market
verbal ~: 4 quip, talk 7 jesting, joshing, kidding, ribbing, teasing 8 chitchat, repartee 9 small talk, table talk
words: 3 gab, rap, yak, yap 4 chat, talk 5 prate, speak 6 banter, gossip, parley 7 prattle 8 converse, dialogue 9 tête-à-tête, touch base 10 chew the fat, conference

exchange __: **4** rate, vows **7** student
__ exchange: **4** post **5** stock **7** foreign
exchangeable: **8** tradable **9** swappable **10** commutable, reciprocal, returnable, switchable
__ exchanger: **4** heat
exchequer: **4** fisc **5** purse **6** coffer **8** treasury, war chest
excise: **3** cut, tax **4** dele, duty, levy, trim, X out **5** elide, erase **6** censor, cut off, cut out, delete, exsect, impost, lop off, remove, resect, tariff **7** blot out, expunge, exscind, scissor **8** cross out, exaction **9** eradicate, expurgate, surcharge **10** blue-pencil, scissor out, scratch out
excision: **3** cut **7** removal **8** deletion **9** resection
  combining form: **4** -tomy **6** -ectomy
excitability: **6** temper
excitable: **4** edgy **5** antsy, fiery, itchy, jumpy, nervy, tense, testy **6** feisty, touchy, uneasy **7** anxious, jittery, keyed up, nervous, peevish, restive, uptight **8** agitated, restless, skittish, troubled, volatile **9** alarmable, concerned, emotional, hotheaded, ill at ease, impatient, impetuous, impulsive, irascible, mercurial, sensitive **10** high-strung, hot-blooded, hysterical, intolerant, passionate, short-fused
excitant: **4** spur
excite: **3** get **4** abet, fire, grab, move, prod, rile, send, stir, wake, whet **5** hop up, key up, liven, pique, prime, rev up, rouse, spark, touch, upset, waken, worry **6** arouse, awaken, incite, kindle, ruffle, stir up, thrill, tickle, turn on, wake up, whip up, work up **7** agitate, animate, delight, disturb, enflame, enliven, enthuse, ferment, fluster, inflame, inspire, juice up, provoke, quicken, thrills **8** energize, enspirit, inspirit, interest, intrigue, motivate **9** electrify, encourage, fascinate, galvanize, instigate, stimulate, titillate, transport **10** invigorate
excited: **3** ape, hot, mad **4** agog, edgy, high, warm **5** afire, amped, astir, eager, het up, hyper, jumpy, manic, tense, upset, wired **6** aflame, burbly, fervid, gung-ho, hectic, jangly, joyful, joyous, on edge, piqued **7** burning, fervent, fired up, frantic, keyed up, nervous **8** animated, feverish, fluttery, frenetic, frenzied, in a tizzy, inspired, jubilant, maniacal, skittish, up in arms **9** delirious, ebullient, exuberant, hot to trot, rapturous, wrought up **10** breathless, in an uproar, passionate
  about: **4** into **5** up for **7** taken by **8** obsessed, turned on
  answer: **6** I do I do
  cry: **5** whoop
  get ~: **4** flip, rave **5** go ape, hop up, key up **6** arouse, tingle **7** bristle, enthuse
  get too ~ over: **4** gush **5** drool **7** enthuse
  not ~: **5** blasé, bored, jaded, weary **7** unmoved **9** apathetic **10** nonchalant, world-weary
  state: **3** fit **4** flap, stew **6** dither, lather, tumult **9** commotion, confusion
__ Excited: **4** I'm So
excitedly in music: **7** agitato
excitement: **3** ado **4** buzz, fire, fuss, heat, jazz, kick, life, stir, to-do **5** fever, furor, hoo-ha, kicks, mania, punch, shock, spice, tizzy **6** action, dither, fervor, flurry, frenzy, hoopla, hoorah, hooray, hubbub, hurrah, hurray, raptus, tumult **7** arousal, emotion, ferment, jollies, turmoil **8** activity, fervency, interest **9** adventure, agitation, animation, commotion, confusion, eagerness, intensity, melodrama, sensation **10** ebullience, enthusiasm, exaltation, exuberance, hullabaloo, impatience, incitement, motivation
  exclamation of ~: **3** ooh, yow **4** arra, oh oh **5** arrah, blimy, hoo-ha **6** blimey, hoo-hah
  full of ~: **4** agog, keen **5** aboil, eager **7** psyched **9** expectant **10** breathless
  show ~: **4** rave **6** bubble **7** delight, enthuse, rejoice, sparkle **10** effervesce
exciter, atom: **5** maser
exciting: **5** heady, juicy, kicky **6** hectic, moving, yeasty **7** zestful **8** dramatic, electric, readable, romantic **9** arresting, emotional, glamorous, thrilling **10** impressive, in an uproar, intoxicant, rip-roaring
  not ~: **4** blah, drab, dull, flat, tame **5** banal, bland, ho-hum, tripe, vapid **6** boring **7** fustian, insipid, languid **8** lifeless, sluggish **9** apathetic, lethargic, wearisome **10** dullsville, flavorless, lackluster, monotonous, spiritless
excl.
  not: **4** incl.
exclaim: **3** cry **4** call, howl, roar, yell **5** blurt, shout, utter, whoop **6** bellow, cry out, holler **7** call out **8** burst out, shout out
...exclaim __ drove out of sight: **4** as he
exclamation: **2** ah, aw, eh, ha, hi, ho, oh, ow, uh **3** aah, ack, aha, arf, bah, bam, boo, boy, brr, cry, duh, fie, gee, grr, haw, heh, hey, huh, ick, nix, och, oho, olé, oof, ooh, pah, pow, rah, rot, say, tsk, tut, ugh, why, wow, yah, yay, yea, yes, yow, yum, zzz **4** ahem, ahoy, alas, amen, arra, bosh, ciao, darn, dear, drat, ecce, egad, evoe, good, gosh, ha-ha, hail, heck, help, hush, jeez, mush, nuts, oh-oh, okay, oops, ouch, oyes, oyez, pfft, pfui, phew, phoo, pish, poof, pooh, posh, ptui, rats, roar, scat, shoo, ta-da, ta-ta, tush, uh-oh, uh-uh, well, wham, whee, whew, yeah, yell, yeow, yipe, yo-ho, yuck **5** achoo, alack, arrah, avast, banco, bingo, blimy, brava, bravo, egads, faugh, fudge, golly, goody, great, hallo, hello, hillo, ho-hum, hooey, hoo-ha, howdy, hullo, humph, huzza, later, nerts, nertz, peace, phfft, prost, pshaw, right, salud, scram, shame, shout, shush, skoal, sooey, sorry, ta-dah, te-hee, uh-huh, voilà, whoof, whoop, yecch, yipes, zooks, zowie **6** ahchoo, begone, behold, bellow, blimey, by Jove, clamor, crikey, cripes, encore, enough, eureka, giddap, goodie, good-oh, gotcha, hachoo, halloa, halloo, hallow, haw-haw, hilloa, holler, hoo-hah, hoorah, hooray, hotcha, hot dog, hulloo, hurrah, hurray, huzzah, indeed, jiminy, ka-boom, la-de-da, la-di-da, l'chaim, outcry, phooey, presto, prosit, ptooey, rather, righto, shalom, sheesh, sholom, shucks, tee-hee, thanks, touché, tsk tsk, tut-tut, whammo, whizzo, whoops, yippee, yoicks, yoo-hoo, yum-yum, zounds **7** attaboy, big deal, brother, by jingo, caramba, cheerio, gangway, giddyap, giddyup, goldarn, goldurn, goodbye, heave ho, heigh-ho, holy cow, horrors, hosanna, hushaby, jeepers, jimminy, kerchoo, l'chayim, lehayim, Odzooks, rubbish, whoopee, whoopie **8** alley-oop, all right, attagirl, by cracky, farewell, for shame, Gadzooks, gracious, holy moly, honestly, lackaday, lah-di-dah, lechayim, scramola, welladay, wellaway, whatever **10** hallelujah
  acclamation: **4** hail
  attention-getter's ~: **3** hey, say **4** ahem, ahoy, ecce, help, yo-ho **5** hello **6** behold, yoo-hoo
  baccarat ~: **5** banco
  Brit's: **4** I say **5** blimy **6** blimey, good-oh, rather, righto, whizzo **7** cheerio
  campy ~: **3** oof **5** zowie
  canine ~: **3** arf, grr
  cartoon brawl ~: **3** oof
  casino ~: **5** banco
  church: **7** hosanna
  collision: **4** wham
  courtroom ~: **4** oyes, oyez
  cowboy ~: **5** howdy **6** giddap **7** giddyap, giddyup
  dog ~: **3** arf, grr **4** bark
  during winter: **3** brr
  ecstatic ~: **5** whoop, zowie
  Emeril ~: **3** bam
  explosive ~: **3** pow **6** ka-boom
  face-slapper's ~: **5** fresh
  fencing ~: **6** touché
  fight ~: **3** oof
  fox hunting ~: **5** hallo, hullo **6** halloa, halloo, hallow, hilloa, hulloo, yoicks
  fox hunting`~: **5** hillo
  French ~: **5** voilà
  fumbler's ~: **4** oops
  Furby ~: **4** whee
  Greek ~: **4** evoe
  Hebrew ~: **6** l'chaim **7** l'chayim, lehayim **8** lechayim
  hippie ~: **5** peace **6** far out
  hog-calling ~: **5** sooey
  Iditarod ~: **4** mush
  interrogatory ~: **3** huh **4** what
  Irish ~: **3** och **4** aroo, arra, orra **5** arrah, orrow
  klutz's ~: **4** oh oh
  Latin ~: **4** ecce
  magician's ~: **5** voilà **6** presto
  nautical ~: **4** ahoy **5** avast **7** heave ho
  near-miss ~: **4** whew
  of acceptance: **3** def, rad **4** cool, fine, good, neat, nice, okay, phat **5** dandy, ducky, great, neato, super **6** dreamy, far-out, gnarly, groovy, peachy, terrif, wicked **7** amazing, awesome, stellar **8** terrific **9** bodacious, fantastic, hunky-dory, marvelous **10** out of sight, peachy-keen, super-duper
  of acclamation: **5** hallo **6** hurrah, huzzah
  of admiration: **5** great **6** good-oh, touché
  of affectation: **6** la-de-da, la-di-da **8** lah-di-dah
  of affirmation: **3** yay, yea, yes **4** yeah **6** rather
  of agreement: **3** boy **4** amen, okay **5** uh-huh **6** by Jove, good-oh **7** by jingo
  of alert: **7** gangway
  of amazement: **6** crikey
  of amusement: **4** ha-ha **5** te-hee **6** haw-haw, tee-hee
  of anger: **7** caramba, goldarn, goldurn
  of annoyance: **3** bah, duh, fie, tsk, tut **4** heck **6** tsk tsk, tut-tut
  of anticipation: **4** oh oh
  of apology: **5** sorry
  of appreciation: **5** great, huzza **6** hoorah, hooray, hurrah, hurray, huzzah, thanks
  of approval: **2** da, ja, sí **3** aye, boy, olé, oui, yay, yea, yep, yes, yup **4** amen, fine, good, okay, what, yeah **5** brava, bravo, good-o, goody, great, natch, roger, uh-huh, zowie **6** by Jove, encore, gladly, goodie, good-oh, indeed, rather, righto, whizzo, you bet, yowzah **7** attaboy, by jingo, go ahead, indeedy, mais oui, quite so, ten-four **8** all right, as you say, attagirl, of course, thumbs up, to be sure, very much, very well **9** be my guest, certainly, darn right, naturally, sure thing, you betcha, you said it **10** absolutely, by all means, definitely, sure enough, that's right
  of assent: **3** yes **4** yeah **5** right **6** rather, righto
  of astonishment: **4** jeez, whew **5** zowie **6** by Jove, crikey, cripes **7** by jingo, caramba, holy cow **8** holy moly
  of aversion: **3** ack, ick, ugh **4** yuck **5** yecch
  of awe: **3** boy, gee **4** gosh **5** golly, hello **6** jiminy **7** jeepers, jimminy
  of bewilderment: **3** hey, huh **7** holy cow
  of boredom: **5** ho-hum **7** heigh-ho
  of chagrin: **4** oh-oh, oops, uh-oh **6** whoops
  of concern: **4** alas, oh-oh, uh-oh **5** alack

of confirmation: 5 uh-huh
of confusion: 3 hey, huh
of contempt: 3 aha, bah, boo, boy, huh, pah, tsk, tut, yah 4 pfui, phoo, pish, pooh, posh, tush 5 faugh, ho-hum, humph, pshaw, shame 6 phooey, tsk tsk, tut-tut 8 for shame
of defiance: 3 yah 4 nuts 5 nerts, nertz
of delight: 3 aah 4 good, whee 5 goody 6 goodie, hotcha, hot dog
of derision: 3 aha, fie, yah 4 ha-ha, nuts 5 hello, nerts, nertz, te-hee 6 haw-haw, la-de-da, la-di-da, tee-hee 7 big deal 8 lah-di-dah
of disagreement: 3 rot 4 bosh, uh-uh 7 rubbish
of disappointment: 4 darn, drat, jeez, rats 5 fudge, zooks 6 shucks, zounds 7 brother, horrors, Odzooks 8 Gadzooks
of disapproval: 3 boo, fie, och 4 nuts, pooh, posh, uh-uh 5 hooey, nerts, nertz, pshaw 7 big deal
of disbelief: 3 huh, pah 4 pooh, posh, rats, what 5 hooey, humph, pshaw, zooks 6 zounds 7 Odzooks 8 Gadzooks, honestly
of discomfort: 2 ow 3 ack, ick, oof, ugh, yow 4 ouch, phew, yeow, yuck 5 yecch
of discovery: 6 eureka
of disdain: 3 bah, pah, tsk, tut 4 egad, pooh, posh, tush 5 egads, pshaw, shame 6 tsk tsk, tut-tut 8 for shame
of disgust: 3 ack, fie, huh, ick, pah, rot, ugh, yah 4 bosh, darn, drat, heck, nuts, pfui, phew, phoo, pooh, posh, rats, yech, yuck 5 faugh, fudge, nerts, nertz, pshaw, yecch, zooks 6 phooey, shucks, zounds 7 brother, goldarn, goldurn, Odzooks, rubbish 8 Gadzooks
of dismay: 2 ow 3 yow 4 alas, oops, ouch, whew, yeow 5 alack 6 crikey, whoops 7 caramba, horrors 8 gracious, honestly
of displeasure: 2 ow 3 boy, yow 4 ouch, yeow
of dissatisfaction: 4 uh-uh
of distaste: 3 ack, ick, rot, ugh 4 bosh, yuck 5 yecch 7 rubbish
of distress: 4 dear
of doubt: 3 hah 5 humph
of embarrassment: 4 oops 6 whoops
of emphasis: 3 gee 4 gosh 5 golly 8 by cracky
of encouragement: 3 olé, rah 5 huzza 6 hoorah, hooray, hurrah, hurray, huzzah 7 attaboy 8 alley-oop, attagirl
of enjoyment: 3 yum 6 yum-yum
of exasperation: 6 enough, sheesh 8 honestly
of excitement: 3 oho, ooh, yow 4 arra, evoe 5 arrah, blimy, hoo-ha, huzza, whoof, wowee 6 blimey, hoo-hah, hoorah, hooray, hurrah, hurray, huzzah, yippee 7 heigh-ho, whoopee, whoopie
of exhaustion: 4 phew
of exhortation: 8 alley-oop
of failure: 4 pfft 5 phfft
of fanfare: 4 ta-da 5 ta-dah
of farewell: 4 ciao, ta-ta 5 later, peace 6 shalom, sholom 7 cheerio, good-bye 8 farewell
of fright: 4 yipe 5 yipes
of frustration: 6 sheesh
of gratitude: 6 thanks
of greeting: 4 hail 5 hello, howdy 6 shalom, sholom
of grief: 4 alas 5 alack
of horror: 3 ack, ick, ugh 4 yuck 5 yecch
of impact: 3 pow 4 wham 6 whammo
of impatience: 3 tsk, tut, yah 4 phew, pish, pooh, posh, tush 5 pshaw, shame 6 enough, tsk tsk, tut-tut 8 for shame
of indifference: 8 whatever
of irony: 3 aha 6 indeed 7 big deal
of joy: 3 aah, yay, yea, yes, yow 4 evoe, whee, yeah 5 huzza 6 hoorah, hooray, hot dog, hurrah, hurray, huzzah, yippee 7 whoopee, whoopie 8 all right
of laughter: 4 ha-ha 5 te-hee 6 haw-haw, tee-hee
of melancholy: 7 heigh-ho
of pain: 2 ow 3 yow 4 ouch, yeow, yipe 5 yipes
of pity: 4 alas 5 alack 8 lackaday
of pleasure: 3 gee, hey, ooh, wow, yes 4 gosh, yeah 5 golly, zowie 6 whizzo, yippee 7 whoopee, whoopie 8 all right
of praise: 5 brava, bravo 6 encore 7 hosanna
of puzzlement: 3 gee 4 gosh 5 golly 6 jiminy 7 jeepers, jimminy
of regret: 3 och 4 alas, rats 5 alack, sorry 6 shucks 7 Odzooks 8 Gadzooks, lackaday
of rejection: 4 heck, pfui, phoo 6 phooey
of relief: 4 phew, whew 8 gracious
of reproach: 3 tch, tsk, tut 4 pfui, phoo, tush, well 6 phooey, tsk tsk, tut-tut
of repugnance: 3 ack, ick, ugh 4 yuck 5 yecch
of satisfaction: 3 ooh, yum 5 uh-huh, voilà 6 yum-yum
of snoring: 3 zzz
of sorrow: 4 alas 5 alack 8 lackaday, welladay, wellaway
of success: 5 voilà
of suddenness: 5 bingo
of support: 3 yay, yea
of surprise: 3 aah, aha, gee, hey, huh, och, oho, say, why, wow, yow 4 arra, dear, egad, gosh, jeez, my my, oops, phew, uh-oh, well, yipe 5 arrah, blimy, egads, golly, hello, hoo-ha, whoof, wowie, yipes 6 blimey, by Jove, crikey, cripes, hoo-hah, indeed, jiminy, whoops 7 brother, by jingo, caramba, goldarn, goldurn, heavens, heigh-ho, holy cow, horrors, jeepers, jimminy 8 by cracky, gracious, holy moly
of triumph: 3 aha, olé 5 hoo-ha, voilà 6 eureka, gotcha, hoo-hah, yippee 7 whoopee, whoopie
of understanding: 4 okay 5 right 6 righto
of unhappiness: 4 alas 5 alack 8 lackaday
of weariness: 4 blah 5 ho-hum 7 heigh-ho 10 dullsville
of wonder: 3 boy, gee, wow 4 gosh 5 golly, hello 6 jiminy, whizzo 7 jeepers, jimminy
old-time ~: 4 egad 5 egads, mercy, pshaw 6 zounds
palindromic ~: 3 aha, hah, oho, wow
pig-calling ~: 5 sooey
sailor's ~: 4 ahoy 5 avast 7 heave ho
Scottish ~: 3 och
Spanish ~: 5 salud 6 arriba
to a dog team: 4 mush
to a horse: 3 haw 6 giddap 7 giddyap, giddyup
toast ~: 5 prost, salud, skoal 6 l'chaim, prosit 7 cheerio, l'chayim, lehayim 8 lechayim
Valley Girl ~: 5 oh wow
warning ~: 3 grr, nix 4 ahem, oh-oh, uh-oh 7 gangway
Western ~: 5 howdy, wahoo
wistful ~: 4 ah me, alas 5 oh gee
with a drum roll: 4 ta-da 5 ta-dah

exclamation __: 4 mark 5 point
exclude: 3 ban, bar 4 omit, oust, shun, shut, skip, tabu, veto 5 block, debar, eject, evict, expel, spurn 6 bounce, delete, disbar, exempt, forbid, ignore, outlaw, pass on, rebuff, reject, remove 7 disdain, dismiss, embargo, keep out, lock out, prevent, rule out, say no to, shut off, shut out 8 count out, disallow, drive out, force out, get rid of, leave out, pass over, preclude, prohibit, throw out, turn down 9 blackball, blacklist, cast aside, eliminate, foreclose, freeze out, interdict, ostracize, proscribe, repudiate 10 disinherit, monopolize
excluded: 5 apart 6 exempt 9 nonliable, unwelcome
excluding: 3 bar 6 except 7 besides 9 apart from, aside from
none: 3 all 5 fully, whole 6 entire, solely, wholly 7 totally, utterly 8 complete, entirely, everyone 9 everybody 10 completely, everything
exclusion: 3 ban, bar 4 skip, tabu 6 ouster 7 boycott, embargo, lockout, ousting, refusal, removal 8 ejection, eviction, omission 9 blackball, debarment, debarring, discharge, dismissal, exception, expulsion, interdict, occlusion, ostracism, rejection 10 preclusion, prevention, relegation, separation, suspension
reason: 4 no ID
__ exclusion principle: 5 Pauli
exclusive: 4 posh, sole 5 elite, ritzy, scoop, smart, swank, swish 6 classy, closed, deluxe, inside, modish, narrow, select, single, swanky, unique 7 private, special, stylish 8 clannish, cliquish, personal, singular, snobbish, unshared 9 sectarian, undivided 10 individual, particular, privileged, restricted, segregated, upper-crust
group: 4 club 5 elect, elite 6 clique
of: 5 minus 6 except 7 besides, without 8 omitting 9 apart from, aside from, other than 10 leaving out
exclusively: 3 all 4 only 5 alone 6 purely, solely, wholly 8 entirely
excogitate: 9 hammer out, speculate 10 deliberate
excommunicate: 3 ban, bar 4 oust 5 eject, expel 6 banish 7 cast out 9 ostracize, proscribe
excommunication, grounds for: 6 heresy
ex-con: 7 parolee
excoriate: 4 damn, flay, gall, skin, zing 5 abuse, chafe, roast, scold, strip 6 abrade, assail, attack, berate, rebuke, scathe, scrape, vilify 7 censure, condemn, lambast, reprove, scourge, upbraid 8 chastise, denounce, lambaste, reproach, strip off, tear into 9 castigate, criticize
excrete: 4 pass 5 egest, expel, sweat 6 remove 8 perspire, throw off
excruciate: 4 rack 5 abuse 6 harrow 7 agonize, torment, torture 8 maltreat, mistreat
excruciating: 5 acute, sharp 6 severe 7 intense, painful, racking, searing 8 grueling, piercing, stabbing 9 torturous
exculpate: 5 clear 6 acquit, pardon 7 absolve, forgive, release 9 discharge, exonerate, vindicate
exculpation: 4 plea 5 alibi, reply, story 6 answer, excuse, reason, retort 7 defense 8 response 9 rejoinder
excurse: 6 ramble
excursion: 3 run 4 hike, ride, tour, trip, turn 5 drive, jaunt, sally 6 cruise, junket, outing, picnic, ramble, safari, travel 7 journey 9 round trip, wandering 10 digression, expedition
Excursion: 3 SUV 4 Ford
excursionist: 8 wayfarer
__ excursion module: 5 lunar
excursive: 7 aimless 8 rambling 9 desultory, wandering 10 digressive, tangential
excusable: 6 venial 7 tenable 9 allowable, not too bad, plausible 10 condonable, defensible, forgivable, pardonable, reasonable, remittable, vindicable
excuse: 3 out 4 call, free, plea, tale 5 alibi, clear, I can't, let go, remit, spare, story 6 acquit, cop-out, exempt, let off, pardon, reason, wink at 7 absolve, condone, defense, evasion, forgive, justify, pretext, release, warrant 8 bear with, occasion, overlook, pretense, tolerate 9 rationale, vindicate, whitewash 10 sour grapes
like a poor ~: 4 lame, thin, weak 6 feeble 10 inadequate

me: 5 sorry 6 whoops
(oneself): 6 absent
excused: 4 free 5 spare 6 exempt, let off 7 cleared 8 absolved, excluded, released 10 off the hook, privileged
Excuse me!: 3 say 4 ahem, oops 6 yoo-hoo
Excuse me?: 3 huh 4 what
excusez-__: 3 moi
exec: 3 CEO 4 boss, veep 6 bigwig, gerent, leader, top dog, veepee 7 captain, manager 8 director, higher-up, kingfish, official, superior 9 authority, big cheese, commander 10 head honcho
account ~: 3 rep
business: 3 mgt. 4 mgmt. 10 management
car: 4 limo
corp. ~: 2 GM, VP 3 CEO, CFO, COO, dir., mgr., mgt. 4 mgmt., mngr., pres., prez, veep 5 admin., treas. 6 veepee
deg.: 3 MBA
helper: 4 aide, asst., secy. 5 steno 9 assistant, secretary
magazine ~: 6 editor 9 publisher
schedule: 6 agenda
exec. __: 3 dir.
__ exec.: 4 acct.
execrable
see awful
execrate: 4 hate 5 abhor 6 detest, loathe 7 despise, dislike 9 abominate, blaspheme
execration: 4 hate 6 hatred 9 blasphemy, damnation, profanity 10 abhorrence
execute: 5 apply, stage 6 effect, finish, fulfil 7 achieve, fulfill, perform, pull off, put over 8 bring off, carry out, complete, dispense, transact 9 discharge, implement 10 accomplish, administer, consummate, effectuate, mastermind, perpetrate, put through, take care of
as vengeance: 5 wreak
perfectly: 4 nail
executed: 4 done 7 wrought
deftly ~: 4 neat 5 clean, nifty 6 clever
execution: 5 doing 6 action 9 discharge, enactment, operation, rendering, technique, treatment 10 completion, expression, fulfilling
Executioner's Song, The
author: Norman Mailer
executive: 3 CEO 4 boss 5 brass, chief, mogul 6 gerent, honcho, leader, ruling, top dog, tycoon 7 captain, headman, manager, officer 8 big wheel, brass hat, director, governor, higher-up, kingfish, managing, official, overseer, superior 9 authority, commander, directing, governing, key player, organizer 10 government, head honcho, leadership, management, managerial, supervisor
department heads: 5 board 7 Cabinet, council 8 advisors 9 committee 10 brain trust, counselors
extra: 4 perk 5 bonus
executive __: 5 order
__ executive: 5 chief 7 account
Executive __: 5 Suite 7 Mansion
executive-branch dept.: 3 Agr., NSA, NSC, OMB
Executive Decision (1996 film)
cast: Halle Berry, Kurt Russell, Steven Seagal
__ executive officer: 5 chief
executives: 4 head 5 board, brass, panel, suits 6 bosses, regime 7 cabinet, council 8 top brass, trustees 9 authority, committee, directors, employers, overseers, syndicate 10 management
executor: 5 agent 7 trustee 8 guardian, watchdog 9 custodian
concern: 4 heir, will 6 estate
exedra: 4 seat 5 bench, chair
exegesis: 7 remarks 8 analysis, critique, treatise 9 criticism, editorial 10 commentary, exposition
exemplar: 4 hero, type 5 gauge, ideal, light, model 6 lesson, symbol 7 epitome, paragon, pattern 8 original, paradigm, specimen, standard 9 archetype, precedent, prototype 10 embodiment, touchstone
exemplary: 4 nice, pure 5 clean, model, moral 7 classic, upright 8 innocent, laudable 9 blameless, faultless, guiltless, honorable, righteous, wholesome 10 creditable, inculpable
see also wonderful
exempli __: 5 causa 6 gratia
exemplification: 4 case 6 sample 8 instance, occasion, specimen 9 precedent, situation 10 occurrence
exemplify: 4 cite 6 depict, embody, imbody, typify 7 display 8 stand for 9 elucidate, enlighten, epitomize, interpret, personify, represent, symbolize 10 illuminate, illustrate
exempt: 4 free 5 clear, spare 6 excuse, immune, let off 7 absolve, cleared, exclude, excused, forgive, release, relieve 8 absolved, excluded, released 9 nonliable, not liable 10 off the hook, privileged, vindicated
(from): 4 free 6 spared
__-exempt: 3 non, tax
exemption: 5 right 7 liberty, license, release 9 acquittal, condition, discharge, franchise, privilege 10 absolution
exercise: 3 irk, jog, try, use, vex 4 gall, have, toil, walk, work 5 annoy, apply, chafe, drill, labor, put in, sport, teach, theme, train, upset, wield, worry 6 action, bother, chin-up, effort, employ, get fit, lesson, resort, ritual, tone up, tune up 7 agitate, disturb, exploit, keep fit, operate, perturb, provoke, trouble, utilize, workout 8 activity, aerobics, distress, limber up, movement, practice, pump iron, put forth, rehearse, training 9 isotonics, operation 10 daily dozen, discipline, employment, gymnastics, isometrics, recitation, recreation
attire: 6 shorts, sweats, T-shirt 7 leotard, tank top 9 sweatband
floor ~: 5 event
judgment: 4 deem, feel, hold, rate, view 5 think 6 assume, reckon, regard 7 believe, imagine, presume, suppose, surmise 8 consider
martial arts ~: 4 kata
meditation ~: 4 yoga
need: 3 mat 5 bench, water 7 barbell, mirrors, trainer 8 dumbbell, Nautilus 9 treadmill
one's franchise: 4 pick, vote 5 elect 6 choose, opt for, select, vote in 7 vote for 10 decide upon
place: 3 gym, spa 4 club, YMCA, YWCA 10 health club
result: 4 ache 5 speed 6 growth 7 agility, fitness 8 leanness, strength, wiriness
target: 3 abs 4 flab, hips, neck, pecs 5 delts, quads, thigh 6 biceps, calves, glutes 7 triceps 8 forearms, shoulder 9 spare tire 10 hamstrings, midsection
training ~: 5 drill 8 maneuver
workout: 3 dip 4 curl 5 press, shrug, sit up, squat 6 chin-up, push-up 7 routine 10 bench press
exercise __: 4 bike 5 price 7 bicycle
exercises: 5 drill 9 athletics, maneuvers
exert: 3 ply 4 push 5 apply, spend, sweat, wield 6 employ, put out, strain, strive 7 trouble, try hard, utilize 8 put forth, put to use 9 make use of 10 put forward
minimal effort: 5 coast, glide, slide 6 cruise
oneself: 3 try 4 moil, push, work 5 labor 6 bother, strain, strive 8 bust a gut, endeavor, go all out, struggle
pressure: 6 extort, lean on 7 squeeze
exertion: 4 dint, toil, work 5 labor, pains, sweat 6 action, effort, energy, strain 7 travail, trouble 8 activity, endeavor, hard work, industry, striving, struggle 9 diligence
Exeter: 4 city, town
locale: 5 Devon 7 England
exeunt __: 5 omnes
ex facto: 8 actually
exfoliate: 4 molt, peel, shed 5 flake 8 flake off, laminate, scale off, throw off
ex-GI: 3 vet
garb: 5 mufti 7 civvies
org.: 3 VFW
exhalation: 3 air, gas 4 odor, sigh 5 steam, vapor 6 breath 8 emission 9 effluvium, emanation
exhale: 4 blow, emit, puff, sigh 6 let out 7 blow out, breathe, give off, respire 10 breathe out
Exhale (1995 song)
artist: Whitney Houston
exhaust: 3 eat, sag, sap, tax, use 4 flag, jade, lose, milk, poop, tire, wane, wear 5 bleed, blunt, drain, eat up, empty, spend, use up, weary 6 finish, impair, reduce, run out, shrink, soften, unload, weaken 7 burn out, consume, deflate, deplete, fatigue, play out, poop out, suck dry, tire out, vitiate, wear out 8 bleed dry, enervate, enfeeble, evacuate, overwork, run out of, squander, wear down 9 attenuate, dissipate, effluvium, indispose, prostrate, run ragged, tucker out, undermine 10 debilitate, devitalize, run through
emanation: 4 fume
opposite: 6 intake
exhaust __: 3 fan 4 pipe
exhausted: 3 dry, out 4 bare, beat, gone, limp, weak, worn 5 all in, empty, faint, spent, tired, trite, weary, wiped 6 barren, bushed, dished, effete, sapped, vacant, winded 7 all gone, at an end, drained, far-gone, gulping, haggard, run-down, worn out 8 careworn, dog-tired, frazzled, out of gas 9 bone-weary, dead tired, destitute, enervated, infertile, prostrate, washed-out 10 breathless, dissipated, knocked out, prostrated, squandered
exhausting: 4 hard 5 tough 6 tiring, uphill 7 arduous, hard-won, onerous, tedious 8 grueling, tiresome 9 demanding, difficult, fatiguing, laborious, murderous, strenuous 10 enervating
exhaustion: 6 anemia 7 anaemia, fatigue, frazzle 9 emptiness, lassitude, tiredness, weariness 10 absorption, bankruptcy, enervation, feebleness
exclamation of ~: 4 phew 6 I'm beat
exhaustive: 3 big 4 A to Z, full 5 total, uncut, whole 6 all-out, entire, global, minute 7 in-depth, plenary 8 complete, detailed, profound, sweeping, thorough, whole hog 9 extensive, full-blown, full-dress, full-range, full-scale, intensive, out-and-out, searching, unreduced 10 definitive, soup to nuts, unabridged
exhaustively: 4 A to Z, hard 7 in depth
exhibit: 3 air 4 bare, bear, have, leak, look, show, wear 5 array, exude, sight, sport 6 detail, evince, expose, flaunt, lay out, parade, reveal, unmask, unveil 7 bespeak, display, divulge, feature, lay bare, let slip, present, produce, reflect, roll out, show off, signify, trot out, uncover 8 disclose, evidence, manifest, register, showcase, specimen 9 advertise, make clear, make known, make plain, promenade, put on view 10 illustrate, make public, wave around
exhibition: 4 expo, fair, show 5 array, scene, sight 6 airing, museum 7 display, pageant, showing 9 fireworks, spectacle 10 appearance, exposition
hall: 5 salon 7 gallery 8 pavilion
exhibition __: 4 game
exhibitionist: 7 showoff
exhilarate: 4 buoy, lift, send 5 boost, cheer, elate, flush, liven, pep up, rouse 6 buoy up, lift up, perk up, revive, thrill, uplift 7 animate, boost up, cheer up, delight, enliven,

gladden, refresh, satisfy **8** enspirit, inspirit **9** encourage, make happy, stimulate **10** invigorate
exhilarated: **4** high **5** happy **8** inspired
exhilarating: **4** racy **5** brisk, heady **6** yeasty **7** bracing **8** electric, exciting, stirring **10** refreshing
exhilaration: **3** joy **4** glee **5** bliss, gusto **6** gaiety, gayety **7** delight, elation, rapture **8** euphoria, felicity, optimism **9** happiness **10** ebullience
EX
exhort: **3** bid **4** goad, prod, spur, urge, warn **5** press **6** advise, charge, incite, preach, prompt **7** beseech, caution, counsel, entreat **8** admonish, call upon, harangue, persuade, press for **9** encourage, recommend
exhortation: **4** talk **6** charge, sermon, speech, urging **7** caution, counsel, goading, warning **8** entreaty, harangue
exhume: **5** dig up **7** unearth **8** disinter
exigency: **3** jam, law **4** lack, need, pass, want **5** pinch **6** crisis, plight, scrape **7** dilemma, urgency **8** distress, hardship, pressure, quandary, zero hour **9** emergency, necessity, requisite **10** difficulty, occurrence
exigent: **4** dire **5** acute, grave **6** urgent **7** burning, crucial, hurry-up, instant **8** critical, exacting, pressing **9** clamorous, demanding, important **10** imperative, oppressive
exiguity: **4** lack, need **6** dearth **7** absence, deficit, paucity, poverty **8** scarcity, shortage, sparsity **9** depletion, shortfall, shrinkage **10** deficiency, inadequacy, meagerness, scantiness, slightness
exiguous: **4** poor, thin **5** small, spare **6** meager, minute, paltry, scanty, skimpy, slight, sparse **7** limited, slender, tenuous **10** inadequate, negligible
exiguousness: **4** lack, need, want **6** dearth **7** absence, paucity, poverty **8** scarcity, shortage, sparsity **9** scantness **10** deficiency, inadequacy, meagerness
exile: **4** oust **5** expel **6** banish, deport, pariah, punish, uproot **7** cast out, outcast, refugee, turn out **8** deportee, diaspora, displace, drive out, Napoleon, relegate, renegade **9** dismissal, expulsion, ostracism, ostracize, proscribe, transport **10** banishment, expatriate
site: **4** Elba **8** St. Helena
Exiles
author: James Joyce
Exile, The
author: Pearl S. Buck
exist: **2** be **3** are, lie **4** fare, go on, last, live, stay **5** abide, dwell, get by, occur **6** endure, remain, reside **7** breathe, subsist, survive **8** continue, get along
did not ~: **5** wasn't
didst ~: **4** wert
does not ~: **4** isn't
do not ~: **5** aren't
ender: **3** ent **4** ence
generally: **7** prevail
in great numbers: **4** teem **5** crowd, swarm, swell **6** abound, infest, thrive **8** flourish, overflow
just ~: **4** loaf **7** go to pot, subsist **8** go to seed, languish, stagnate, vegetate
naturally: **5** dwell **6** inhere **7** inhabit
existed: **3** was **4** been, were
existence: **4** esse, life **5** being **6** entity, living **7** reality **8** lifetime, presence, survival **9** actuality, animation, endurance, real world **10** occurrence, permanence
bring into ~: **4** cast, form, make, rear **5** beget, breed, hatch, order, set up, spawn, train **6** cook up, create, effect, father, invent, mature **7** arrange, bring up, compose, concoct, develop, outline, pioneer, produce, think up, turn out **8** assemble, conceive, engineer, generate, initiate **9** actualize, construct, establish, fabricate, hammer out, originate, take shape **10** give life to, mastermind
combining form: **3** ont- **4** onto-
come into ~: **5** begin, start **6** grow up, spring **9** originate
in ~: **4** live **5** alive **6** actual, living, viable **7** organic, working **9** breathing, conscious
in French: **3** vie
in Latin: **4** esse
span of ~: **4** days, life **5** years **6** course, period **8** lifetime
existent: **4** live **5** alive **6** actual, living **8** physical **9** something **10** unimagined
Existential Essays
author: Colin Wilson
existentialist, French: **4** Gide **5** Camus, Genet **6** Sartre
existing: **4** real **5** alive **6** actual, extant, living **8** standing **10** unimagined
not ~: **6** irreal
exit: **2** go **4** door, gate, quit, vent **5** adieu, go out, leave, scram, split **6** beat it, decamp, depart, egress, emerge, exodus, get out, go away, outlet, refuge, retire, way out **7** doorway, getaway, goodbye, head out, leaving, move out, off-ramp, opening, passage, pull out, push off, retreat, take off, turnoff, walk out **8** farewell, hatchway, hightail, porthole, shove off, slip away, withdraw **9** departure, disappear, egression, take a hike **10** evacuation, fire escape, passageway, retirement, shuffle off, withdrawal
mine ~: **4** adit
poll participant: **5** voter
quickly: **3** hie, lam **4** flee **5** lam it
exit __: **4** poll, ramp
Exit: **4** sign **8** road sign
Exit Laughing
author: Irvin S. Cobb
exit-ramp
sight: **5** diner, motel **10** gas station
word: **3** Slo
Exit the King
author: Eugène Ionesco
__ Exit to Brooklyn: **4** Last
Exit to Eden
author: Anne Rice
__ ex machina: **4** deus
exo-: **5** outer **7** outside **8** external
opposite: **4** endo-, ento-
exobiology: **7** science
exocarp: **4** peel
exocrine __: **5** gland
exodus: **4** exit **6** egress, flight, hegira, hejira **7** leaving, retreat **8** trekking **9** defection, departure, desertion, egression, migration **10** emigration, evacuation, relocation, resettling, withdrawal
Exodus: **4** film, song **5** novel
artist: Ferrante and Teicher
author: Leon Uris
cast: Lee J. Cobb, John Derek, Peter Lawford, Sal Mineo, Paul Newman, Eva Marie Saint
character: **3** Ari **5** Aaron, Moses **6** Joshua
director: Otto Preminger
feast of the ~: **5** seder
follower: **3** Lev. **5** Levit. **9** Leviticus
food: **5** manna
idol: **4** calf
locale: **5** Egypt **6** Midian, Red Sea
mountain: **5** Horeb, Sinai
preceder: **3** Gen. **7** Genesis
verb: **5** shalt
Exodus Theme (1961 song)
artist: Mantovani
Exon: **5** James
exonerate: **5** clear, remit **6** acquit, let off, pardon **7** absolve, forgive, release **9** allow to go, disburden, discharge, exculpate, vindicate, whitewash
exonerated: **10** off the hook, vindicated
exorbitance: **4** glut, orgy, posh **5** frill, ritzy, waste **6** excess, luxury, wealth **7** nimiety, surfeit, surplus **8** elegance, hedonism, opulence, overflow, plethora, splendor **9** affluence, decadence, profusion **10** high living, immoderacy, indulgence, lavishness, prosperity, redundancy
exorbitant: **4** dear, high, rich, tall **5** large, pricy, steep, stiff, undue **6** costly, pricey **7** extreme **9** excessive, expensive, overboard **10** at a premium, high-priced, immoderate, inordinate, out of sight, outrageous
interest: **5** usury
exorcise: **5** expel, purge, rid of **6** purify, remove **7** cast out, dismiss **8** drive out
exorcism: **4** rite **5** spell **6** ritual **8** ejection
target: **5** demon **6** daemon, daimon
Exorcist, The (1973 film)
cast: Linda Blair, Ellen Burstyn, Lee J. Cobb, Jason Miller, Max von Sydow
director: William Friedkin
role: **5** Regan
exordium: **5** onset, start **6** advent, outset **7** kickoff, leadoff, preface, prelude **8** foreword, preamble **9** inception
exoteric: **4** open **5** outer **6** public **7** outside, outward **8** external
exotic: **3** odd **4** rare **5** alien **6** arcane, scanty, scarce **7** curious, foreign, new wave, strange, unknown, unusual **8** imported, romantic, uncommon **9** fantastic, glamorous, recherché **10** avant-garde, hard to find, outlandish, unfamiliar
expand: **3** enl., pad, wax **4** boom, grow, open, rise **5** add on, add to, bloat, boost, build, bulge, plump, splay, swell, widen **6** beef up, blow up, bulk up, deepen, dilate, extend, fan out, fatten, gather, let out, puff up, pump up, spread, unfold **7** amplify, augment, balloon, bolster, broaden, build up, burgeon, develop, distend, drag out, enlarge, fill out, inflate, magnify, open out, prolong, radiate, stretch, thicken, upsurge **8** bourgeon, elongate, escalate, flesh out, heighten, increase, lengthen, multiply, mushroom, protract **9** branch out, diversify, elaborate, embellish, expatiate, get bigger, intumesce, outspread, spread out **10** aggrandize, exaggerate, grow larger, liberalize
a compressed file: **5** unzip
expanse: **4** area, belt, land, room **5** field, orbit, range, reach, realm, scope, sheet, space, sweep, tract, width **6** extent, length, radius, region, spread **7** acreage, breadth, stretch, surface **8** clearing **9** immensity, largeness, magnitude, territory
of land: **4** land, lots **5** acres, tract
sandy ~: **5** beach **6** desert, Sahara
treeless ~: **5** pampa
vast ~: **3** sea **5** ocean
expansion: **5** boost, space **6** growth, length, spread **7** buildup **8** addition, dilation, increase, swelling **9** diffusion, evolution, extension, inflation, unfolding, unfurling **10** distension, elongation, maturation, prosperity
expansion __: **4** card, slot, team
expansive: **3** big **4** free, open, vast, wide **5** ample, broad, gushy, large, roomy **6** genial, lavish **7** affable, gushing **8** effusive, far-flung, friendly, outgoing, sociable, spacious, sweeping, thorough **9** capacious, extensive, garrulous, inclusive, resilient, talkative **10** big-mouthed, commodious, gregarious, loquacious, stretching, unreserved, voluminous, widespread
view: **5** vista
expatiate: **5** speak, spout **6** expand, ramble, recite **7** amplify, descant, discant, enlarge **8** perorate **9** discourse, elaborate, explicate, prerorate **10** dissertate
expatiation: **4** talk **7** descant, discant, monolog **9** discourse, monologue
expatriate: **5** exile, expel **6** banish, deport, émigré **7** outcast, refugee **8** deportee, displace, emigrant, relegate **9** ostracize, proscribe, transport

expect: 4 hope, look, rely, wait 5 await, think, trust 6 assume, bank on, intend, reckon, rely on 7 believe, count on, hope for, look for, presume, propose, require, suppose, surmise, suspect, wait for 8 theorize, watch for 9 count upon 10 anticipate, hang out for, understand
lead to ~: 7 promise
like you'd ~: 5 usual 6 as ever, normal 7 typical
too much: 8 overrate
expectancy: 4 hope 8 suspense 9 assurance 10 assumption, confidence, conjecture, impatience, likelihood, prediction
__ expectancy: 4 life
expectant: 4 agog, atip 5 alert, eager, ready 6 gravid, on edge 7 anxious, hopeful 8 enceinte, pregnant, watchful 9 confident, presuming 10 breathless, in suspense, optimistic
expectation: 4 hope 5 hunch, trust 6 belief 7 outlook, thought 8 optimism, prospect 9 prognosis
contrary to ~: 5 oddly
in ~ of: 5 until
of the worst: 9 pessimism
__ Expectations: 5 Great
expectations, like some: 5 unmet
expected: 3 due 5 typic, usual 6 coming, likely 7 regular, typical 8 oncoming, probable, upcoming
as ~: 4 duly 5 on cue 8 of course
is ~ to: 5 ought 6 should
not as ~: 5 oddly
result: 3 par 4 norm
sooner than ~: 5 early 9 in advance, premature
expecting: 6 gravid 8 enceinte, pregnant 9 confident
be ~: 4 wait 5 await 8 watch for 10 anticipate
expectorate: 4 spit
expediency: 5 means, shift, worth 6 agency, device, method, resort, tactic 7 benefit, fitness, utility 8 prudence, resource, strategy 9 advantage, diplomacy, readiness
with ~: 4 fast 5 apace 7 quickly, rapidly, swiftly 8 in no time, speedily 9 hurriedly, posthaste
expedient: 3 fit 4 meet, plan 5 means, shift, trick 6 agency, device, method, refuge, resort, tactic, timely, useful 7 fitting, measure, politic, prudent, sleight, stopgap, vehicle 8 artifice, recourse, resource, strategy, suitable 9 advisable, desirable, effective, judicious, makeshift, necessary, opportune, practical, pragmatic, stratagem 10 beneficial, convenient, instrument, jury-rigged, profitable, seasonable, substitute, subterfuge, time-saving, worthwhile
expedite: 4 ease, push, rush 5 hurry, speed 6 assist, hasten, step up 7 forward, further, quicken, speed up 9 fast-track 10 accelerate, facilitate
expedition: 4 tour, trek, trip 5 haste, hurry, jaunt, quest, sally, speed 6 junket, outing, safari, search, travel, voyage 7 caravan, crusade, journey 8 alacrity, campaign, celerity, dispatch, rapidity, velocity 9 cavalcade, excursion, explorers, fleetness, quickness, readiness, swiftness 10 enterprise, promptness, travellers
need: 5 scout
sponsor: 3 NGS
__ expedition: 7 fishing
Expedition: 3 SUV 4 Ford
expeditious: 4 fast 5 brisk, fleet, hasty, quick, rapid, swift 6 flying, prompt, racing, snappy, speedy 7 express, hurried, instant 8 punctual 9 breakneck 10 double-time
expeditiously: 3 PDQ 4 fast, soon 5 apace 6 presto 7 fleetly, rapidly, swiftly 8 in a flash, in a jiffy, in no time, pell-mell, promptly 9 forthwith, instantly, like a shot, posthaste
expeditiousness: 5 haste 8 celerity, dispatch
expel: 3 ban, bar, can, rid 4 boot, dump, emit, fire, oust, rout, sack, spew, spue, vent, void 5 chase, egest, eject, empty, evict, exile, exude, issue, purge, shoot, spout 6 banish, deport, punish, remove 7 boot out, cashier, cast out, diffuse, dismiss, drum out, emanate, exclude, excrete, extrude, give off, kick out, radiate, turn out 8 disgorge, dislodge, displace, drive out, exorcise, exorcize, force out, get rid of, jettison, relegate, throw off, throw out 9 blackball, discharge, eliminate, order to go, ostracize, send forth 10 dispossess, expatriate
expend: 3 pay, use 4 lose 5 drain, put in, spend, use up 6 finish, lavish, lay out, outlay, pay out 7 consume, deplete, fork out, play out 8 disburse, shell out, squander 9 dissipate 10 run through
expendable: 6 excess 7 useless 8 needless, unneeded 10 disposable, unrequired
one: 4 pawn
expenditure: 3 use 4 cost 5 outgo, price 6 charge, outlay, upkeep 7 payment
acknowledgment: 3 rct. 7 receipt
monthly ~: 4 rent
expense: 3 fee, tax 4 cost, fare 5 debit, outgo, price, value 6 amount, charge, damage, outlay, tariff, towage 7 damages, payment, payroll 8 overhead
at the ~ of yours truly: 4 on me
bear the ~: 3 pay 5 treat
incidental ~: 3 tip
office ~: 4 rent 5 lease 8 overhead
receipt: 3 vou. 7 voucher
spare the ~ of: 5 grant, offer 6 afford, bestow, impart, render 7 furnish, provide
expense __: 7 account
__ expense: 4 at no 7 spare no
expenses: 5 outgo 6 outlay, upkeep 8 overhead
after ~: 3 net
cut ~: 4 save 5 skimp
estimate ~: 6 budget, ration 8 allocate 9 apportion
keep ~ low: 4 save 6 scrape, scrimp 8 conserve, roll back 9 economize 10 cut corners
net plus ~: 5 gross
__-expenses-paid: 3 all
expensive: 4 dear, high, posh, rich 5 fancy, pricy, ritzy, steep, stiff, swank 6 costly, deluxe, lavish, pricey, swanky 7 sky-high, upscale 8 precious, splendid, valuable 9 big-ticket, excessive, luxurious, priceless, sumptuous 10 at a premium, exorbitant, high-priced, out of sight, overpriced
not as ~: 4 less
Expensive People
author: Joyce Carol Oates
experience: 3 see 4 face, have, know, live, meet, view 5 enjoy, event, savor, share, skill, stand, taste 6 fall on, record, sample, suffer, wisdom 7 episode, know-how, receive, sustain, undergo, witness 8 exposure, fall upon, incident, intimacy, maturity, meet with, practice, stand for, training 9 actuality, adventure, awareness, encounter, get to know, go through, happening, knowledge, seasoning 10 background, empiricism, occurrence, upbringing
bad ~: 4 drag 6 bummer 9 nightmare
combining form: 7 empirio- 8 empirico-
gain ~: 3 see 5 glean, learn, study 6 absorb, master, pick up, soak up, take in 7 catch on, find out 8 discover, pore over 9 ascertain, brush up on, get word of 10 apprentice, get down pat, understand
units of ~: 5 sensa
experienced: 3 ace, old 4 deft, ripe, wise 5 adept, slick 6 adroit, au fait, expert, mature, nimble, versed 7 capable, knowing, learned, skilled, trained, veteran, worldly 8 broken-in, dextrous, familiar, graceful, masterly, prepared, seasoned, skillful 9 competent, dexterous, efficient, masterful, qualified 10 proficient
less ~: 5 newer
not ~: 3 raw 4 naif 5 naive
old-style: 5 verst 6 verste, werste
one: 3 pro, vet 6 old pro 7 old hand
Experience keeps __ school: 5 a dear
experiential: 7 empiric, factual 9 empirical, practical, pragmatic
experiment: 3 try 4 test 5 essay, prove, study, trial 6 sample, tryout 7 attempt, venture 8 rehearse, trial run 9 procedure, rehearsal, shakedown, speculate 10 dissection, enterprise, futz around
atomic ~: 5 A-test, N-test
combining form: 7 empirio- 8 empirico-
room: 3 lab
experimental: 4 beta, test 5 novel, pilot, trial 8 unproved 9 tentative
animal: 3 rat 6 lab rat 9 guinea pig
experimentalize: 4 test
Experimental Novel, The
author: Émile Zola
experimentation: 8 research
Experiment in Autobiography
author: H.G. Wells
__ Experiment, The: 6 Harrad
expert: 3 ace, apt, dab, pro, wiz 4 able, deft, good, guru, sage, whiz 5 adept, crack, great, handy, maven, mavin, ready, savvy, sharp, slick 6 adroit, artist, au fait, critic, facile, master, nimble, old pro, pundit, savant, source, versed, wizard 7 adviser, advisor, capable, hotshot, knowing, learned, maestro, old hand, prodigy, skilled, trained, veteran 8 dextrous, graceful, masterly, schooled, seasoned, skillful, superior, virtuoso 9 authority, black belt, competent, dexterous, efficient, evaluator, masterful, practiced, qualified, unrivaled 10 master hand, proficient, specialist, unrivalled, well-versed
combining form: 7 -meister
ender: 3 -ise
group: 5 panel
in England: 3 dab
expert __: 6 system 7 witness
expertise: 3 art, job 4 ease 5 craft, forte, knack, savvy, skill 6 aplomb 7 ability, aptness, faculty, fluency, know-how, mastery, prowess 8 artistry, deftness 9 adeptness, dexterity, expertise, knowledge 10 competence, department, efficiency, profession, virtuosity
field of ~: 4 area, turf 5 niche
expertly: 4 neat, well 8 worthily
expiate: 5 atone, purge 6 purify, remedy 7 rectify, redress 8 atone for 9 make up for 10 make amends, recompense
expiation: 6 amends, ransom, remedy 7 penance, redress 8 righting 9 atonement, indemnity 10 reparation
expiration: 3 end 5 close 6 ending, finish 9 cessation, departure 10 completion, conclusion
avoid ~: 5 renew
expiration __: 4 date
expire: 3 end 4 quit, stop 5 cease, close, lapse 6 elapse, run out 7 succumb 8 conclude 9 terminate 10 breathe out
expired: 3 out 4 over 6 lapsed, no more, run out 7 elapsed 10 terminated
not ~: 5 valid
expiry: 3 end 5 close 6 ending, finish 9 cessation, departure 10 completion, conclusion
explain: 4 show, tell 5 argue, brief, clear, gloss, prove, solve, state, teach 6 answer, decode, defend, define, recite, record, refine, set out, unfold 7 analyze, clarify, clear up, justify, resolve 8 annotate, construe, decipher, describe, simplify, spell out, untangle 9 adumbrate, elaborate, elucidate, expound on, interpret, make clear, put across, translate 10 account for, illuminate, illustrate, understand
away: 5 gloze 8 minimize 9 gloss over
further: 3 add, say 5 sum up

6 reckon 7 include, throw in 8 figure in 9 enumerate, interject
in Britain: 4 rede
explain __: 4 away
explanation: 3 key 4 plea 5 alibi, basis, cause, gloss, light 6 answer, excuse, reason 7 account, comment, defense, meaning, preface 8 exegesis, solution 9 narration, rationale, statement
seeker's query: 3 why
start of an ~: 4 look 5 id est
__-explanatory: 4 self
explanatory note: 7 comment
expletive: 5 curse 7 epithet 8 cuss oath, cuss word 9 swear word
delete an ~: 5 bleep 6 censor
mild ~: 3 boy 4 drat, durn, egad, heck 5 egads, golly, pshaw
explicable: 7 soluble 9 countable 10 calculable
explicate: 6 unfold 8 describe 9 bring home, elucidate, expatiate, expound on, interpret, make clear, make plain, translate 10 illustrate
explication: 5 essay, paper, prose, theme, tract 6 reason, report, thesis 8 critique, exegesis, treatise 9 discourse, monograph, rationale, reasoning, statement 10 annotation, commentary, discussion, exposition
explicit: 4 firm, open, real 5 clear, lucid, plain, sharp, vivid 6 actual, cogent, direct, formal, honest, in view, patent, public 7 evident, exposed, express, graphic, obvious, precise, visible 8 absolute, apparent, clear-cut, concrete, definite, distinct, emphatic, manifest, palpable, positive, readable, specific, tangible, unhidden, unsubtle, unveiled 9 downright, graphical, graspable, outspoken 10 definitive, observable, point-blank, spelled out, unshrouded, well-marked
explicitly: 5 plain, to wit 9 expressly, purposely 10 definitely, point-blank
explicitness: 7 clarity 8 accuracy, lucidity 9 certainty, precision 10 directness, exactitude
explode: 3 pop 4 blow, boom, fire, rage, rave, roar 5 belie, blast, burst, erupt, go off, shoot, sound 6 blow up, debunk, go boom, refute, set off 7 confute, flare up, shatter, smolder, thunder 8 backfire, detonate, disprove, dynamite, have a fit, mushroom, shoot off, smoulder 9 blow a fuse, discharge, discredit, fulminate, shoot down 10 hit the roof, invalidate, prove wrong
exploit: 3 act, tap, use 4 coup, deed, feat, gest, gull, milk, soak, work 5 abuse, apply, doing, geste, stunt, trick 6 action, employ, handle, misuse, play on, prey on, rip off 7 develop, harness, utilize 8 cash in on, escapade, exercise, play upon, profit by 9 adventure, victimize 10 manipulate
daring ~: 4 gest 5 geste, stunt
exploitable: 4 easy 6 usable 7 useable
exploitation: 5 abuse, using 6 misuse
exploited: 7 put upon 8 economic, monetary 9 for-profit 10 commercial, marketable, mercantile, profitable
exploits
in Latin: 8 res geste
tale of heroic ~: 4 saga
exploration: 5 probe, quest 7 enquiry, inquiry
exploratory mission: 5 probe, recon
explore: 2 do 4 hike, roam, rove, seek, sift, tour, view 5 assay, plumb, probe, range, scout 6 forage, go into, search, survey, travel 7 dig into, examine, pioneer, ransack, rummage 8 look into, research, traverse 9 delve into, range over 10 knock about, scrutinize
explorer: 5 diver, scout 7 pioneer 8 traveler, vagabond, wanderer 10 adventurer, pathfinder
Africa ~: 4 Park 5 Baker, Speke 6 Burton 7 Johnson, Stanley 11 Livingstone
Antarctic ~: 4 Byrd, Ross 5 Scott 6 Mawson 8 Amundsen 10 Shackleton
Arctic ~: 3 Rae 4 Ross 5 Davys, Peary 6 Bering, Nansen, Nobile 7 Barents 9 Rasmussen
Australia ~: 6 Mawson 8 Flinders 9 Vancouver
British ~: 3 Rae 4 Cook, Ross 5 Baker, Cabot, Davys, Drake, Parry, Scott, Speke 6 Baffin, Burton, Hudson, Mawson 7 Dampier, Gilbert, Hawkins, Markham, Raleigh, Stanley 8 Flinders, Franklin 9 Frobisher, Vancouver 10 Shackleton
Canada ~: 6 Joliet 7 Cartier, Gilbert, Jolliet 9 Champlain
Caribbean ~: 7 Hawkins 8 Columbus
China ~: 4 Polo
circumnavigation ~: 4 Gray 5 Drake 8 Magellan
Danish ~: 6 Bering 9 Rasmussen
Dutch ~: 6 Tasman 7 Barents
Easter Island ~: 9 Heyerdahl
Florida ~: 6 de Soto 11 Ponce de León
French ~: 5 Salle 7 Cartier, Nicolet 8 Cousteau 9 Champlain, David-Neel
German ~: 7 Wegener
Greenland ~: 7 Ericson
Guiana ~: 7 Raleigh
India ~: 6 da Gama
Italian ~: 4 Polo 7 Nobilei 8 Columbus, Vespucci
Mars ~: 5 probe
Mexico ~: 4 Peck 6 Cortés
Mississippi River ~: 6 Joliet 7 Jolliet, La Salle
Mount Everest ~: 6 Norgay 7 Hillary
need: 3 map 6 octant 7 compass, sextant
New Zealand ~: 6 Tasman
North America ~: 5 Cabot 6 Hudson 8 Columbus
Northwest Passage ~: 5 Parry 6 Baffin 7 Gilbert 8 Franklin 9 Frobisher
Norwegian ~: 6 Nansen 7 Ericson 8 Amundsen 9 Heyerdahl
objective: 5 trade
Pacific Ocean ~: 6 Balboa 9 Vancouver
Peru ~: 7 Pizarro
Portuguese ~: 6 Cabral, da Gama 8 Magellan
Rocky Mountains ~: 4 Pike
Scottish ~: 4 Park, Ross 11 Livingstone
South America ~: 4 Peck 5 Cabot 6 Cabral 8 Vespucci
South Seas ~: 4 Cook 5 Davys 6 Tasman 7 Dampier, Johnson 9 Heyerdahl, Vancouver
Spanish ~: 6 Balboa, Cortés 7 Pizarro 8 Coronado 11 Ponce de León
Swedish ~: 5 Hedin
Tibet ~: 5 Hedin 9 David-Neel
underground ~: 5 caver 9 spelunker
underwater ~: 5 Beebe 8 Cousteau
Venetian ~: 4 Polo
Viking ~: 4 Eric, Leif 7 Ericson
Virginia ~: 7 Raleigh
Western ~: 4 Gray 5 Clark, Lewis 6 Balboa 7 Fremont 8 Coronado
Explorer: 3 SUV 4 Ford 5 Scout 8 Boy Scout
org.: 3 BSA
explorers, ancient: 5 Norse 7 Vikings
explosion: 3 pop 4 bang, boom, roar 5 blast, burst, crack, noise, salvo, spirt, spurt 6 blowup, firing, report 7 blowout, flare-up, tantrum 8 backfire, eruption, outbreak, outburst, upheaval 9 discharge 10 combustion, concussion, demolition, detonation, percussion
cause: 5 spark
outlawed ~: 5 A-test, N-test
explosive: 3 TNT 4 ammo, bomb, live, mine 5 nitro, shell 6 amatol, charge, unsafe 7 grenade, missile 8 dynamite, munition, volatile 9 booby trap, dangerous, detonator, ebullient, fireworks, fulminant, gunpowder, hazardous, impetuous, pineapple, unsettled 10 ammunition, convulsive, detonative, propellant
ingredient: 5 niter
sign: 6 danger, hazard
small ~ sound: 4 poof
sound: 3 pow 4 bang, blam, boom, wham 5 blast 6 kaboom
__ explosive: 3 low 4 high 7 plastic
expo: 4 fair, show 10 World's Fair
Expo: 3 van 4 NLer 10 baseballer, Mitsubishi
Expo '67 site: 6 Canada, Quebec 8 Montreal
Expo '98 site: 6 Lisbon 8 Portugal
exponent: 5 power, urger 6 backer 7 booster, support 8 advocate, champion, defender, endorser, partisan, promoter 9 proponent, supporter
algebraic ~: 5 index
export: 4 ship 7 send off, ship out, smuggle 10 ship abroad
exporter: 8 merchant
exports: 5 cargo, goods 7 freight, tonnage 8 shipment
Expos: 4 nine, team
1990s manager: 4 Alou
home: 8 Montreal
org.: 3 MLB, NLE
rival: *see* baseball team
sport: 8 baseball
expose: 3 air, ope, out 4 bare, leak, nail, news, show, slur 5 admit, catch, strip 6 betray, debunk, denude, detect, let out, refute, reveal, show up, unfold, unmask, unveil 7 display, divulge, exhibit, lay bare, lay open, let slip, show off, uncover, unearth, weather 8 bring out, disclose, disprove, give away, ridicule, smell out, smoke out 9 discredit, make known, put on view 10 make public
to the atmosphere: 6 aerate
exposé: 5 story 6 baring 7 scandal, tell-all 9 unmasking, unveiling 10 confession, disclosure, revelation, unbosoming, uncovering
Exposé
members: Curless, Jarado, Bruno
song: Come Go With Me (1987)
I'll Never Get Over You (1993)
Let Me Be the One (1987)
Point of No Return (1987)
Seasons Change (1987)
Tell Me Why (1989)
What You Don't Know (1989)
When I Looked at Him (1989)
exposed: 3 raw 4 bare, nude, open 5 clear, naked, outer, plain, prone 6 at risk, drafty, in view, liable, on view, patent, public 7 in peril, obvious, subject, visible 8 apparent, clear-cut, explicit, helpless, in danger, manifest, unhidden, unveiled 9 on display, unguarded 10 accessible, observable, unshielded, unshrouded, vulnerable
exposition: 4 fair, show 5 essay, paper, prose, theme, tract 6 reason, report, thesis 7 display 8 critique, exegesis, treatise 9 construal, criticism, discourse, discovery, editorial, monograph, rationale, reasoning, spectacle, statement, voice-over 10 annotation, commentary, conception, county fair, discussion, exhibition, literature, production
ex post __: 5 facto
expostulate: 3 say 6 reason 7 protest
expostulation: 6 rebuke
exposure: 4 leak, risk 5 peril 6 airing, baring, danger, espial 7 display 8 betrayal, jeopardy 9 detection, divulging, liability, unmasking 10 experience, revelation, uncovering
measure: 3 rad, rem 5 curie
to injury: 4 risk 5 peril 6 hazard, menace 8 jeopardy
__ exposure: 4 time 6 double
expound: 5 orate, solve, state, teach 7 clarify, comment, lecture, present 8 proclaim, set forth, spell out 9 interpret, talk about 10 promulgate
on: 4 tell 5 state 6 detail, relate, report, unfold 7 explain, write up

8 describe, set forth 9 chronicle, elucidate, explicate, make clear
expounder: 5 agent 6 backer 7 apostle, booster, paladin, sponsor 8 advocate, champion, crusader, promoter 9 proponent, supporter
express: 3 air, put, say 4 aver, fast, look, mail, show, sign, talk, tell, vent 5 brisk, clear, couch, exact, fleet, hasty, opine, plain, quick, rapid, speak, spell, state, swift, train, utter, vivid, voice 6 act out, assert, cogent, convey, denote, direct, embody, flying, formal, imbody, phrase, proper, racing, relate, reveal, speedy 7 add up to, breathe, certain, declare, deliver, evident, forward, hurried, instant, nonstop, obvious, precise, purport, reflect, signify, special 8 apparent, clear-cut, definite, describe, distinct, emphatic, explicit, indicate, manifest, palpable, proclaim, register, set forth, specific, vocalize 9 breakneck, enunciate, graspable, personify, predicate, represent, symbolize, verbalize 10 articulate, considered, definitive, deliberate, double-time, individual, particular, spelled out, unmediated, well-marked
ability to ~ oneself: 5 oracy
alternative: 5 local
freely: 4 vent 6 unload
grief: 3 cry, rue, sob 4 keen, moan, pine, sigh, wail, weep 6 lament, sorrow
jubilance: 4 hoot, yell 5 cheer, shout 6 holler, hurrah, scream, shriek 7 exclaim
one's preference: 4 vote 6 choose
opposite: 5 local
train: 3 ltd. 7 limited
express __: 4 lane 5 train
__ express: 3 air 4 pony
Express __: 4 Mail
__ Express: 4 Nova, Ohio, Pony 6 Berlin, Orient 7 Federal
expressed: 4 oral, said 5 vocal 6 spoken, verbal
expression: 3 mug 4 face, grin, look, mien, pout, term, word 5 idiom, smile, smirk, sneer, token 6 phrase, slogan, speech, visage 7 grimace, wording 8 language, locution 9 assertion, character, elocution, eloquence, execution, narration, rendition, statement, utterance 10 commentary, definition, embodiment, indication, intonation
__-expression: 4 self
Expressionism, prefix with: 3 neo
expressionless: 5 blank, stony 6 glassy, stolid, stoney, vacant, wooden 7 deadpan, neutral, vacuous 8 fish-eyed
expressive: 4 rich 5 showy, vivid, vocal 6 fluent, lively, loving, moving 7 graphic, lyrical, soulful, telling 8 artistic, colorful, dramatic, eloquent, emphatic, poignant, spirited, stirring, striking, touching 9 brilliant, energetic, graphical, ingenious, pictorial, revealing 10 articulate, artistical, indicative, meaningful, passionate, responsive, revelatory, suggestive, thoughtful
expressiveness: 4 brio, fire 6 warmth 7 emotion, passion, rapture 8 lyricism, rhapsody 9 intensity
expressly: 6 namely, wholly 8 for a fact 9 decidedly, on purpose, pointedly, precisely, purposely, specially 10 absolutely, apparently, definitely, distinctly, especially, explicitly, far and away, manifestly, positively
expressway: 2 rd. 3 fwy., hwy., tpk. 4 belt, pike, road, tnpk. 7 freeway, highway, parkway, thruway 8 turnpike 10 interstate, throughway
like an ~: 5 laned
Express Yourself (1989 song)
artist: Madonna
exprobate: 3 rag 4 flay 5 chide, scold 6 berate, preach, punish, rank on, rebuke, tirade 7 censure, declaim, lecture, reprove, tell off 8 admonish, harangue, moralize 9 reprimand, sermonize
expropriate: 4 take 5 annex, seize, usurp 6 assume 7 deprive, impound, preempt 8 take over 10 commandeer
expulse: 4 oust 8 relegate 9 ostracize
expulsion: 4 cast 5 exile, purge 6 ouster 7 deposal, ousting, removal 8 ejection, eviction 9 banishing, debarment, discharge, dismissal, exception, exclusion, extrusion, ostracism 10 banishment, deportment, driving out, evacuation, forcing out, keeping out, relegation, suspension
expunge: 3 cut, zap 4 dele, X out 5 clean, erase, purge 6 cancel, delete, efface, excise, remove, revoke, rub off, rub out 7 abolish, blot out, destroy, root out, scissor, take out, wipe out 8 white out 9 eradicate, sponge out, strike out 10 annihilate, blue-pencil, obliterate
don't ~: 4 stet
expurgate: 3 cut 4 dele, edit 5 bleep, erase, purge 6 censor, delete, excise 7 cleanse, clean up, scissor 8 bleep out, sanitize 10 blue-pencil, bowdlerize
expurgated: 3 cut 7 partial, refined, sketchy 10 incomplete
exquisite: 5 acute 6 dainty, subtle 7 elegant, for show, intense 8 delicate, esthetic, ethereal, luscious, piercing, poignant, tasteful 9 thrilling, virtuosic 10 attractive, consummate, delectable, fastidious, immaculate, impeccable, meticulous, ornamental
see also wonderful
exquisiteness: 5 class, grace, merit, style, value, worth 6 beauty, luxury 7 finesse, glamour 8 artistry, delicacy, elegance, fineness, radiance 9 fragility, lightness, propriety 10 daintiness, loveliness, refinement
exsanguine: 3 wan 4 pale 5 pasty 6 anemic, sallow 7 anaemic
exscind: 4 X out 5 erase 6 censor, cut out, delete, lop off, remove 7 blot out, expunge 8 cross out 9 expurgate 10 scissor out, scratch out
exsect: 6 cut out, excise, remove
ex-senior: 4 alum, grad 7 alumnus 8 graduate
exsiccate: 5 parch 6 dry out 9 anhydrate, dehydrate
__ Ex's Live in Texas: 5 All My
ex-soldiers' org.: 3 VFW
ext.
not ~: 3 int.
extant: 4 left 5 alive, in use 6 living, modern, with us 7 current, not lost, ongoing, present 8 existing, up-to-date 9 remaining, surviving
Extasy, The
author: John Donne
extemporaneous: 4 snap 5 ad hoc, ad-lib 6 casual 7 offhand
performance: 6 improv
extempore: 5 ad-lib 6 vamped 7 offhand 8 informal 9 impromptu, whipped up 10 improvised, informally, off-the-cuff, unscripted
extemporize: 5 ad-lib 6 fake it, wing it 7 toss off
extend: 3 add, jut, lie, pad, run 4 give, grow, lend 5 add to, award, boost, build, grant, offer, range, reach, renew, swell, widen 6 bestow, deepen, dilate, expand, impart, ramble, sprawl, spread, unfold 7 augment, broaden, carry on, compass, develop, drag out, draw out, enlarge, hold out, magnify, pervade, present, proffer, prolong, stretch 8 continue, elongate, escalate, go beyond, heighten, increase, lengthen, multiply, overhang, protract, protrude, reach out, stick out 9 branch out, hold forth, keep going, spread out, string out 10 aggrandize, strengthen, stretch out, supplement
(above): 5 tower
a lease: 5 relet
along: 7 overlap
a subscription: 5 renew
outward: 3 jut 4 lean, poke 5 bulge 7 poke out, project 8 overhang, protrude, stand out, stick out
over: 4 span 5 cross, reach 6 bridge 8 go across
throughout: 4 fill 7 pervade
extended: 4 long, more, open, wide 5 broad 7 lengthy 8 drawn-out, far-flung, sweeping, very long 9 capacious, elongated, spread out 10 large-scale
not ~: 5 terse
note, in music: 5 longa
extended __: 6 family
extension: 3 arm 4 limb, loan, size, span, wing 5 add-on, annex, delay, phone, reach, scope, sweep 6 branch, growth, radius, spread 7 adjunct 8 addendum, addition, appendix, increase, widening 9 accession, accessory, appendage, expansion, inflation 10 attachment, broadening, continuity, dilatation, distension, elongation, perpetuity, projection, stretching, supplement
building ~: 3 ell 4 wing 5 annex
extension __: 4 bolt, cord, rule, tube 5 agent, field 6 course, ladder
extensive: 3 big 4 full, good, huge, long, open, rife, vast, wide 5 ample, broad, great, hefty, large, roomy 7 blanket, copious, full-out, immense, lengthy, massive, sizable 8 far-flung, handsome, pandemic, profound, sizeable, spacious, sweeping, thorough, whole-hog 9 boundless, capacious, elaborate, expansive, full-dress, full-scale, important, inclusive, pervasive, prevalent, universal, unlimited, wholesale, worldwide 10 commodious, exhaustive, large-scale, protracted, soup to nuts, voluminous, wall to wall, widespread
extensively: 4 a lot 7 in depth, largely 10 far and wide
extensiveness: 6 length 7 breadth 9 amplitude
extent: 4 area, bulk, deal, land, size, span, time 5 ambit, gamut, limit, point, range, reach, scale, scope, space, sweep, tract, width 6 amount, bounds, degree, leeway, length, radius, spread, volume 7 breadth, compass, expanse, horizon, measure, stretch 8 distance, duration, latitude 9 amplitude, dimension, immensity, incidence, largeness, magnitude, territory 10 dimensions
comparative ~: 5 ratio
greatest ~: 3 end, max, rim 4 brim, edge 5 brink, limit 6 fringe, height, period 7 ceiling, extreme, maximum 8 confines, end point 9 outskirts, parameter, perimeter, periphery 10 bottom line, boundaries
horizontal ~: 7 breadth
linear ~: 4 span 5 orbit, range 6 course, length, radius 7 breadth, expanse, measure, purview, section, segment 8 diameter, distance, longness 9 longitude
of great ~: 4 vast
of variation: 5 range
to a great ~: 4 much 6 ever so 7 largely 8 markedly
to a greater ~: 4 more
to any ~: 3 any 4 ever 5 at all
to a smaller ~: 4 less 5 fewer, lower, minor 7 limited, reduced, without 8 inferior 9 excepting, secondary, shortened 10 diminished
to some ~: 3 any 5 quite 6 in a way, in part, kind of, partly, rather, sort of 8 slightly 9 partially
to the ~ that: 5 until 7 as far as
extenuate: 5 gloze 6 lessen 7 forgive, lighten 8 decrease, diminish, downplay, minimize, mitigate, moderate, palliate 9 attenuate 10 debilitate
extenuated: 4 lean, long, thin 5 gaunt, lanky, rangy 6 gangly,

EX

meager, skinny, twiggy **7** scrawny, slender, stringy **8** beanpole, rawboned **9** beanstalk
extenuation: 4 plea **9** softening **10** mitigation
exterior: 4 face **5** front, outer, shell **6** facade, veneer **7** outdoor, outside, outward, surface **10** peripheral
combining form: 3 epi- **4** ecto-
exterminate: 3 rid **5** erase **6** ravage, remove, rub out, uproot **7** abolish, blot out, destroy, wipe out **8** stamp out **9** liquidate
exterminator
company: 5 Orkin
do an ~ job: 5 spray **8** fumigate
target: 3 ant, rat **4** pest **5** roach
extern: 2 dr., MD **6** doctor **9** physician
external: 5 outer **7** foreign, outside, outward, surface, visible **8** exoteric, outlying, skin-deep **10** peripheral
combining form: 2 ex- **3** ect-, exo- **4** ecto-
in anatomy: 5 ectal
externalize: 3 air **8** manifest **9** personify
extinct: 4 gone, late, lost **5** kaput, passé **6** bygone **7** archaic, defunct **8** obsolete, outmoded, vanished **9** exanimate
become ~: 4 fade **6** die off, die out, vanish
bird: 3 moa **4** dodo
not ~: 4 left **5** alive **6** extant, living **7** current, ongoing **9** remaining, surviving
reptile: 8 dinosaur
wild ox: 4 urus
extinction: 4 doom, ruin **10** desolation
extinguish: 3 end, out **4** kill **5** abate, douse, dowse, erase, outen, quash, quell, snuff **6** efface, put out, quench, ravage, squash, stifle **7** abolish, blot out, blow out, destroy, eclipse, obscure, put down, silence, smother, squelch, turn off, wipe out **8** snuff out, stamp out, suppress **9** eliminate, eradicate, extirpate, suffocate, terminate **10** annihilate, obliterate
__ extinguisher: 4 fire
extinguishing, needing: 6 ablaze
extirpate: 3 rid **4** rase, raze **5** erase, pluck, purge, quash **6** cut out, efface, pull up, remove, uproot **7** abolish, blow out, destroy, extract, pull out, root out, wipe out **8** demolish **9** eliminate, eradicate **10** annihilate, deracinate, extinguish
extol: 4 hail, laud, tout **5** bless, cry up, deify, ensky, exalt, honor **6** esteem, praise, puff up, salute, talk up **7** acclaim, applaud, commend, flatter, glorify, worship **8** eulogize, hand it to, sanctify **9** brag about, celebrate, publicize, recommend **10** compliment, panegyrize
extolment: 5 glory, honor, kudos, paean **6** eulogy, homage, praise **7** acclaim, hosanna, rapture, tribute **8** accolade, citation, encomium, plaudits **9** adoration, elevation, laudation, loftiness, panegyric, promotion, reverence **10** apotheosis, compliment, exaltation, exultation, idolzation
extort: 3 pry **4** levy, milk **5** bleed, bully, exact, force, gouge, mulct, screw, wrest, wring **6** coerce, wrench **7** squeeze, swindle **9** blackmail, shake down
extortion: 5 force, graft, theft **6** racket **7** squeeze, swindle **8** coercion, thievery, venality **9** blackmail, shakedown **10** compulsion, corruption, oppression, protection
extortionate: 5 undue **8** exacting, usurious **9** excessive, expensive, out-of-line, rapacious **10** avaricious, exorbitant, outrageous
extortioner: 9 profiteer **10** armtwister
extra: 4 left, more, over, part, perk, plus, role, supe, supp. **5** added, bonus, fresh, frill, gravy, minor, other, spare **6** backup, doubly, margin, player, second, unused **7** adjunct, further, premium, reserve, residue, surplus, trivial **8** addendum, addition, dividend, leftover, markedly, needless, optional, picayune, residual, trifling, unneeded **9** accessory, ancillary, auxiliary, in reserve, lagniappe, newspaper, redundant, unusually **10** additional, attachment, especially, noticeably, remarkably, supplement, uncommonly, unconsumed
effort: 5 oomph
give a little ~: 6 slap on, tack on, toss in **8** increase
prefix: 5 super-
something ~: 5 bonus, frill, gravy **6** encore **8** addition
valuable ~: 4 perk **5** bonus, lucre **6** reward **8** dividend
extra __ attraction: 5 added
extra-__ olive oil: 6 virgin
Extra: 10 chewing gum
alternative: ***see*** chewing gum
extra-base hit: 5 homer **6** double, triple **7** home run
__ extra cost: 4 at no
extract: 3 get, pry, tax **4** cite, clip, copy, cull, draw, milk, mine, pull, take, text, yank **5** educe, elute, evoke, glean, leach, pluck, quote, wrest, wring **6** avulse, decoct, derive, elicit, evulse, flavor, liquid, liquor, nectar, obtain, recall, remove, select, siphon, syphon, uproot **7** distill, draw out, excerpt, jerk out, passage, portion, snippet, squeeze, summary, weed out **8** bring out, citation, jerk away, solution **9** decoction, extirpate, flavoring, quotation **10** distillate
__ extract: 7 vanilla
extraction: 5 birth, roots, stock **6** origin, strain **7** descent, lineage, pulling, removal **8** ancestry, avulsion, evulsion, pedigree, wresting, wringing **9** etymology, evocation, forebears, genealogy, parentage, uprooting, wrenching **10** derivation, separation, withdrawal
extractor: 6 gadget, juicer
extracts: 6 pieces **7** sayings **8** analecta, analects, excerpts, passages **9** citations **10** quotations, selections
extradite: 3 bag, get, nab **4** grab **5** catch, grasp, seize **6** arrest, collar, detain, pick up, take in **7** capture **9** apprehend, surrender
extra-long: 4 maxi
__ extra mile: 5 go the
extramundane: 9 spiritual
extraneous: 5 outer **7** foreign, outside **9** extrinsic, inapropos, pointless, redundant, unrelated **10** accidental, additional, immaterial, inapposite, incidental, irrelevant, out of place, peripheral
extraordinarily: 4 very **6** highly, rarely **9** unusually
extraordinary: 4 eery, nice **5** eerie, queer, weird **6** atypic, freaky, quirky, signal **7** bizarre, deviant, intense, magical, oddball, offbeat, strange, uncanny, unusual **8** aberrant, abnormal, atypical, freakish, historic, peculiar, singular, towering, uncommon **9** anomalous, arresting, divergent, eccentric, irregular, memorable, unearthly, unnatural **10** miraculous, unorthodox
not ~: 5 usual
person: 6 genius
thing: 3 pip **4** oner **5** doozy **6** doozie
see also wonderful
extrapolate: 7 project
extrasensory: 7 psychic **10** telepathic
extraterrestrial: 5 alien **7** Martian **8** Venusian
extraterrestrial life, science of: 10 exobiology
Extra, The
author: Hal Porter
extravagance: 5 frill, waste **6** excess, luxury
extravagant: 4 high, rank, rich, wild **5** campy, fancy, large, outré, steep, stiff, undue **6** absurd, costly, lavish, wanton **7** opulent, profuse, rampant, ruinous, splashy **8** prodigal, romantic, wasteful **9** excessive, luxuriant, luxurious, sumptuous **10** immoderate, profligate, rhetorical
be ~: 5 spend **7** splurge
extravagantly: 4 very **6** unduly **7** largely
extravaganza: 4 gala, play **5** event **6** parade **7** pageant **9** spectacle
extreme: 3 end, far, nth, ult. **4** dire, high, last, rank, rare **5** brink, gross, limit, outré, polar, rough, sharp, sheer, steep, stiff, ultra, undue, utter, verge **6** arrant, far-out, fringe, mortal, severe, strong, utmost **7** drastic, fanatic, glaring, intense, outside, profuse, radical **8** advanced, farthest, flagrant, furthest, profound, remotest, terminal, terrible, terrific, ultimate, uncommon **9** desperate, draconian, egregious, fanatical, fantastic, nth degree, outermost **10** exorbitant, immoderate, inordinate, irrational, outrageous, undeserved, untempered
other ~: 8 opposite
to the ~: 4 very
unction: 4 rite
extreme __: 7 unction
extremely: 3 far, too **4** most, much, oh so, over, very, well **5** madly, no end, quite, super **6** ever so, highly, hugely, overly, plenty, rarely, unduly, vastly **7** acutely, awfully, greatly, notably, only too, utterly **8** insanely, markedly, overmuch, powerful, severely, terribly **9** eminently, immensely, in a big way, intensely, radically, unusually, violently **10** incredibly, remarkably, strikingly, thoroughly, uncommonly
in music: 5 assai, molto
prefix: 5 ultra-
Extreme Machines network: 3 TLC
Extreme Prejudice (1987 film)
cast: Nick Nolte
__ Extremes: 5 I Go to
extremes, go to: 6 overdo
extremist: 3 rad **5** ultra **6** zealot **7** diehard, fanatic, radical **8** agitator, ultraist **9** sectarian
'70s ~ grp.: 3 SLA
group: 4 cult, sect **7** faction
extremity: 3 arm, end, leg, rim, tip, toe **4** butt, claw, edge, foot, hand, limb, need, pole, tail **5** brink, digit, verge **6** apogee, border, finger, margin, member, plight, strait, tipoff **8** boundary **9** acuteness, adversity, appendage, emergency, requisite
extricate: 4 free, save **5** clear, loose, untie **6** loosen, redeem, rescue, unbind **7** bail out, deliver, recover, release **8** dislodge, liberate, untangle **9** disburden, disengage **10** disinvolve
extrication: 6 escape **9** salvation
extrinsic: 5 alien, outer **6** exotic **7** foreign, outside, strange, unusual **9** redundant, unrelated **10** additional, immaterial, inapposite, incidental, irrelevant, out of place, peripheral, unfamiliar
extrovert: 5 mixer **8** outgoing **9** character
extrude: 4 emit **5** eject, expel **8** force out, press out, stick out
exuberance: 3 pep, vim, zip **4** élan, glee, life, zest, zing **5** ardor, gusto, juice, spark, verve, vigor **6** bounce, energy, fervor, pepper, plenty, spirit **7** abandon **8** buoyance, buoyancy, hilarity, lushness, plethora, richness, vitality **9** abundance, affluence, animation, eagerness, élan vital, happiness, plenitude, profusion **10** ebullience, enthusiasm, excitement, friskiness, get up and go, lavishness, liveliness, luxuriance
exclamation of ~: 6 yippee **7** whoopee, whoopie
exuberant: 3 gay **4** high, lush, rank, rich **5** aglow, eager, zingy, zippy **6** ardent, bouncy, fecund, hearty, lavish, lively, yeasty **7** buoyant, chipper, copious, excited, fertile, fulsome, gushing, liberal, opulent, profuse, rampant, teeming, zestful, zinging **8** abundant, animated,

cheerful, effusive, fruitful, grooving, prodigal, prolific, spirited, vigorous **9** bountiful, ebullient, energetic, excessive, luxuriant, plenteous, plentiful, sparkling, sprightly, vivacious **10** frolicsome, passionate, rollicking
be ~: 9 walk on air
make ~: 4 gush, rave, send **5** elate, psych **6** excite, fire up, thrill, work up **7** enthuse, impress **8** interest **9** electrify **10** bubble over, effervesce
yell: 5 wahoo, yahoo **6** yippee **7** whoopee
exudate: 4 ooze
exudation: 4 ooze **8** effluent, emission **9** discharge, emanation
exude: 4 drip, emit, flow, leak, ooze, reek, seep, shed, spew, spue **5** bleed, drain, egest, eject, expel, issue, spout, sweat **6** effuse, reek of **7** cast out, diffuse, display, emanate, exhibit, flow out, give off, ooze out, project, radiate, secrete, send out, trickle **8** perspire, throw off **9** discharge, give forth, percolate, send forth
exult: 4 brag, crow **5** cheer, gloat, glory, revel **7** delight, rejoice, triumph **8** jubilate **9** celebrate, make merry, walk on air **10** effervesce, jump for joy
exultance: 7 triumph
exultant: 4 glad **5** happy, merry **6** blithe, cheery, elated, jovial, joyful, joyous, upbeat **7** gleeful, pleased, tickled **8** blissful, cheerful, cheering, ecstatic, euphoric, jubilant, mirthful, reveling, thrilled **9** delighted, gladdened, overjoyed, rejoicing **10** flying high, triumphant
be ~: 5 preen **9** walk on air
cry: 3 aha, oho **5** huzza, whoof, wowee **6** at last, hoorah, hooray, hurrah, hurray, huzzah, yippee **7** heigh-ho, whoopee, whoopie
exultation: 3 joy **4** glee **5** glory **7** delight, elation, triumph **8** euphoria, reveling **9** happiness, jubilance, merriment, rejoicing, transport **10** joyousness, jubilation
exuviate: 4 molt, shed
Exxon
bad news for ~: 5 spill
it merged with ~: 5 Mobil
old name for ~: 4 Esso
rival: 4 Arco **5** Amoco, Shell **6** Conoco
Exxon Valdez: 5 oiler **6** tanker
E.Y.: 7 Harburg
__ Eyck: 6 Jan van
Eydie: 5 Gorme
husband: 5 Steve
eye: 3 orb, see **4** glom, leer, look, ogle, scan, spot, tail, view **5** organ, sight, stare, study, watch **6** gape at, gawk at, gaze at, goggle, leer at, look at, notice, peek at, peeper, peer at, regard, size up, survey, take in, vision **7** examine, glimpse, inspect, measure, oversee, stare at **8** appraise, check out, glance at, look upon **9** flirt with **10** get a load of, needle hole, perception, rubberneck, scrutinize
ailment: 3 sty **4** stye
apple of one's ~: 3 pet **5** pearl **7** darling **8** favorite
bat an ~: 4 wink **5** blink
bat of an ~: 4 jiff **5** jiffy **6** minute, second
be a private ~: 3 spy **4** espy, find, spot **5** dig up, hit on **6** detect, expose, unmask **7** make out, uncover **8** discover, pinpoint, smell out **9** ascertain, stumble on, track down
black ~: 4 blot, slur **5** mouse, odium, stain **6** bruise, insult, shiner **7** slander
bull's ~: 4 mark **8** specific
camera ~: 4 lens
catch the ~: 8 stand out
cock the ~: 6 squint
color: 4 blue, gray, grey **5** brown, green, hazel
combining form: 4 ocul-, opto- **5** oculo- **8** ophthalm- **9** ophthalmo-
cover: 3 lid **4** wool
doctor: 7 oculist
drop: 4 tear
eagle ~: 5 stare, vigil, watch **6** acuity **7** lookout **8** scrutiny
ender: 3 cup, let, lid **4** ball, bolt, brow, hole, hook, lash, lift, shot, sore, spot, wash, wear, wink **5** glass, liner, patch, piece, shade, sight, stalk, teeth, tooth **6** bright, strain **7** dropper, glasses, witness
evil ~: 3 hex **4** jinx, look **5** curse, glare **7** sorcery
eye for an ~: 7 revenge **8** reprisal **9** vengeance
fish ~: 4 gaze
give a black ~: 4 slur **5** libel, shame, smear **6** defame, vilify **8** mistreat
give the ~: 4 leer, ogle **5** stare
give the evil ~: 5 scowl
glad ~: 4 wink
hook and ~: 8 fastener
in a pig's ~: 5 never
inflammation: 6 iritis
in French: 4 oeil
insect ~ lens: 5 facet
in the wink of an ~: 4 anon, soon **7** quickly **9** momentary
irritant: 4 mote
it colors the ~: 4 iris
it has an ~: 5 storm
jaundiced ~: 4 bias **6** enmity **7** bigotry **8** aversion **9** antipathy **10** chauvinism, fanaticism, favoritism, narrowness, partiality
keep an ~ on: 4 boss, mark, mind, tend **5** guard, scout, study, watch **6** advert, attend, detect, direct, follow, look at, manage, notice **7** baby-sit, discern, monitor, observe, oversee **8** chaperon, shepherd **9** look after, supervise **10** administer, ride herd on, scrutinize
layer: 4 uvea
look in your ~: 3 ray **4** beam **5** gleam, glint **6** glance **7** glimmer, glisten, sparkle, twinkle
makeup: 4 kohl **5** liner **6** shadow **7** mascara
mind's ~: 6 memory
muscle: 6 rectus
my ~: 5 no way **8** forget it
nerve: 5 optic
network: 3 CBS
not bat an ~: 8 keep cool **9** stay loose
of an ~ layer: 5 uveal
offend the ~: 5 clash
of the ~: 5 optic
of the storm: 4 calm, lull **6** center
opener: 5 shock
opening: 4 slit
part: 4 iris, lens, uvea **5** white **6** cornea
partner: 4 hook
private ~: 3 tec **4** dick **6** shamus **7** gumshoe **9** detective
protector: 3 lid **4** lash **5** visor, vizor
public ~: 9 spotlight
run one's ~ over: 4 skim
see eye to ~: 4 gybe, jibe **5** agree **6** accede, accord, assent, comply, concur **7** approve, consent, go along **8** coincide **9** acquiesce, harmonize
shadow: 4 kohl
shape: 6 almond
signal: 4 wink **5** blink
socket: 5 orbit
starter: 3 big, red **4** buck, dead, fish, frog, moon, pink, shut, wall **5** watch **6** golden, silver
the bull's-eye: 3 aim **5** aim at, point **6** target
to a poet: 3 orb
to the ~: 7 outward **9** outwardly **10** ostensibly
turn a blind ~ to: 8 overlook
watchful ~: 5 vigil **7** lookout **8** guidance, tutelage, wardship **9** oversight
weather ~: 5 vigil, watch
wink of the ~: 4 jiff **5** jiffy, trice **6** moment **7** eyewink, instant
with an ~ out: 4 wary **5** alert, awake, ready, sharp **7** all ears, careful, heedful, mindful, on guard **8** cautious, keen-eyed, vigilant, watchful **9** attentive, expectant, observant, wide-awake **10** on one's toes, perceptive
eye __: 5 chart, drops, rhyme **6** appeal, doctor, shadow, socket **7** contact
eye-__: 7 opening, popping
eye-__ coordination: 4 hand
__ eye: 4 evil, glad **5** black, bull's, eagle, mind's, naked **7** private, weather
__-eye: 3 red **4** cat's
Eye __: 5 Guess
Eye __ Needle: 5 of the
Eye __ Tiger: 5 of the
eyeball: 3 spy **4** face, leer, peer, view **5** check, stare **6** assess, regard, verify **7** observe, witness **8** look hard
bender: 5 op art
covering: 6 cornea
eyebrow: 4 hair
shape: 3 arc, bow **4** arch **5** curve **8** crescent
eyebrow __: 6 pencil
__ eyebrows: 5 raise
eye-catching: 4 bold **8** gorgeous, striking, stunning
__-eyed: 3 bug, cat, doe, dry, pie **4** blue, cold, dewy, hawk, lynx, moon, open, sloe, wide, wild **5** Argus, beady, blear, clear, cross, eagle, misty, sharp, teary **6** bleary, bright, gimlet, glassy, goggle, googly, squint, starry
__ Eyed Girl: 5 Brown
__-Eyed Jacks: 3 One
__-eyed monster: 5 green
__ Eye dog: 6 Seeing
__-eyed pea: 5 black
eyed starter: 3 bog, pop **4** cock, moon, wall
__-eyed Susan: 5 black
eyeful: 4 load **5** sight, views **6** beauty, looker, pretty, vision **7** dazzler, stunner **8** good look, knockout
get an ~: 3 see **4** gaze **7** observe
eyeglass: 4 lens **5** loupe
eyeglasses: 5 specs **8** bifocals, cheaters, horn-rims, pince-nez **10** spectacles
part: 4 lens **5** frame
support: 3 ear
taped ~ wearer: 4 nerd
__-eye gravy: 3 red
Eye Guess: 8 game show
host: Bill Cullen
...__ eye in the house: 4 a dry
Eye in the Sky (1982 song)
artist: Alan Parsons Project
__ Eye Is on the Sparrow: 3 His
eyelash: 4 hair **6** cilium
by an ~: 4 just **6** barely, hardly **8** narrowly, scarcely
flutter: 3 bat **4** wink **5** blink **6** twitch **9** nictitate
__ eyelash: 5 bat an
eyelashes
bat ~: 5 flirt
__ eyelashes: 5 false
Eyeless in Gaza
author: Aldous Huxley
eyelet: 4 loop **7** grommet **8** peephole **10** buttonhole
eyelid: 6 winker **7** blinker
feature: 4 lash
inflammation: 3 sty **4** stye
eyeliner: 4 kohl **6** makeup
site: 3 lid
__ eye movement: 5 rapid
Eye of newt and __ frog: 5 toe of
Eye of the Tiger (1982 song)
artist: Survivor
eyeopener: 4 news **5** shock **6** coffee **8** pick-me-up, surprise **10** revelation
eyepiece: 4 lens
eyer: 5 flirt, ogler **6** viewer **7** witness **8** observer, surveyor **9** spectator **10** peeping Tom
eyes: 5 sight **9** baby blues
all ~: 6 enrapt **9** attentive **10** fascinated
big ~: 6 hunger
cover the ~: 7 obscure **9** blindfold, obfuscate
easy on the ~: 4 fair **6** lavish, lovely **8** dazzling, gorgeous, handsome, imposing, stunning **9** beautiful, exquisite, ravishing, sumptuous **10** attractive
feast for the ~: 6 beauty, vision **7** dazzler, stunner **8** knockout

feast one's ~: 3 eye, spy 4 gaze, look, ogle, peer, view 5 sight, stare, watch 6 behold, look at, regard 7 examine, eyeball, inspect, observe 8 look upon 10 scrutinize
food with ~: 4 spud
have ~ for: 4 itch, like, pant, pine, want, wish 5 covet, crave, fancy, go for, yearn 6 desire, hanker, hunger, obsess, pursue, thirst 7 long for 8 aspire to, languish
having ~ in verse: 5 orbed
keep one's ~ peeled: 5 stare, watch
lay ~ on: 3 spy 4 espy, view 5 stare
like some ~: 4 evil 5 beady, teary
make ~ at: 3 eye 4 leer, ogle 5 flirt, stare, tease 7 eyeball 8 coquette
open one's ~: 4 wake 5 edify, teach, waken 6 awaken 8 disabuse, illumine
pull the wool over one's ~: 3 con, lie, rob, sap 4 bilk, butt, dupe, have, hoax, jerk, prey, trap 5 cheat, fraud, shaft, trick 6 delude, fleece, lead on, outwit, rip off, rope in, suck in, take in 7 beguile, buffalo, chicane, deceive, defraud, mislead, swindle, two-time, wheedle 8 bulldoze, flimflam, hoodwink, inveigle, outsmart, sucker in 9 bamboozle, disinform, scapegoat
raise, as ~: 6 cast up
rivet one's ~: 5 focus 6 fixate, obsess, zero in 9 preoccupy
roll the ~: 4 leer, look, ogle 5 stare 6 goggle
scrunch the ~: 6 squint
shut one's ~ to: 6 ignore, wink at 9 disregard
with ~ open: 4 wary 5 awake 7 mindful 8 vigilant, watchful

eyes-__: 4 only
__ eyes: 3 all 4 make 5 snake 6 goo-goo, sheep's
Eyes __ Shut: 4 Wide
__ Eyes: 3 Sad 4 Dark, Lyin', Sexy 5 Angel, Banjo, Ebony, Green, Irish, Naked, Short, These, Tiger
eyeshade: 5 visor, vizor
eyeshot: 3 ken 4 peek, view 5 sight 10 visibility
eyesight: 6 vision 10 perception
Eyes of Darkness, The
author: Dean Koontz
Eyes of Laura Mars (1978 film)
cast: Faye Dunaway, Tommy Lee Jones
__ eyes on: 3 lay
eyes-only: 6 secret
eyesore: 4 mess 5 sight 6 blight, fright, litter 7 blemish
__-eye steak: 3 rib
Eyes Wide Shut (1999 film)
cast: Tom Cruise, Nicole Kidman, Sydney Pollack
director: Stanley Kubrick
Eyes Without a Face (1984 song)
artist: Billy Idol
eyeteeth
give one's ~ (for): 4 pant 5 yearn
Eye, The (2008 film)
cast: Jessica Alba
__ Eye, The: 6 Bluest
eye-to-brain link: 6 nerves
eye to eye
see ~: 5 agree 10 think alike
seeing ~: 5 as one
eyetooth: 6 canine
__-eye view: 5 bird's, worm's
eyewash
acid: 5 boric 7 boracic
natural ~: 4 tear
see also baloney
eyewear: 5 specs 6 shades 7 glasses, goggles 8 bifocals, contacts 9 trifocals 10 spectacles
eyewear, piece of: 4 lens
eyewink: 4 jiff 5 flash, jiffy, trice 6 moment 7 instant
eyewitness: 3 see 4 seer, view 5 watch 6 looker, viewer 7 observe, watcher, witness 8 beholder, looker-on, observer, onlooker 9 bystander, firsthand, spectator
words: 4 I saw
eyra: 3 cat 5 felid 6 feline, jaguar 7 wildcat 10 jaguarundi
relative: ***see*** feline
Eyre: 4 Jane, lake
locale: 9 Australia
eyrie
see aerie
eyry
see aerie
E.Z.C.: 6 Judson
Ezekiel follower: 6 Daniel
Ezer
father: 7 Ephraim
E-Z formula: 3 ABC
e-zine: 5 Slate
Ezio: 5 Pinza
composer: George Frideric Handel
Ezra: 5 Pound, Stone 6 Benson 7 Cornell
follower: 3 Neh. 8 Nehemiah
preceder: 10 Chronicles
EZ Streets (CBS drama)
cast: Ken Olin (Cameron Quinn)
Ezzard: 7 Charles

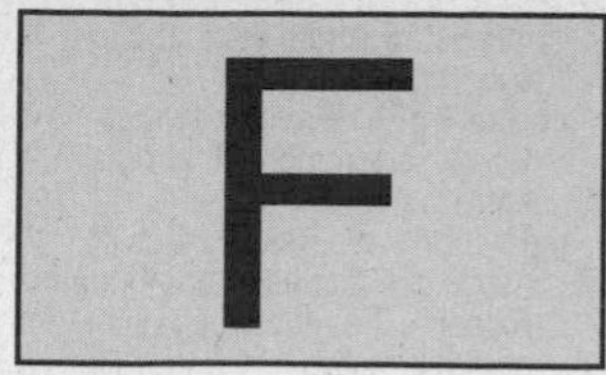

__.45: 4 Colt
__ + 4: 3 ZIP
4-H
part: 4 head 5 hands, heart 6 health
participant: 5 youth
4th-qtr.
follower: 2 OT
4 Seasons of Loneliness (1997 song) artist: Boyz II Men
4/1 activity: 5 prank
5th Avenue: 3 bar 5 candy 8 candy bar 9 chocolate
alternative: *see* candy brand
5K: 4 race
14
creature with ~ legs: 6 isopod
__-14: 6 carbon
40 __ and a Mule: 5 Acres
__ 40: 3 Top
40-decibel unit: 4 sone
42nd Parallel, The
author: John Dos Passos
trilogy: 3 USA
42nd Street (1933 film)
cast: Warner Baxter, George Brent, Bebe Daniels, Ruby Keeler, Dick Powell
director: Lloyd Bacon
45
player: 5 phono
surface: 5 A-side, B-side, side A, side B
45 __: 3 RPM
45-rpm, long: 2 EP
__ 48: 5 Lower
48HRS. (1982 film)
cast: Eddie Murphy, Nick Nolte, Annette O'Toole
director: Walter Hill
49-day period in Judaism: 4 omer
49ers: 6 eleven
div.: 3 NFC
home: 12 San Francisco
rival: *see* NFL team
50 Cent: 6 rapper
50 First Dates (2004 film)
cast: Drew Barrymore, Adam Sandler
50 Ways to Leave Your Lover (1976 song)
artist: Paul Simon
__ 57: 5 Heinz
400: 5 elite
magazine: 6 Forbes
name: 5 Astor
401(k)
alternative: 4 ESOP
cousin: 5 Keogh
500: 5 elite
magazine: 7 Fortune
500 __: 5 rummy
500 Hats of Bartholomew Cubbins, The
author: Dr. Seuss
1400: 5 two p.m.
1488 (2007 film)
cast: Jon Cusack, Samuel L. Jackson
1492
caravel: 4 Niña 5 Pinta 10 Santa Maria
departure harbor: 5 Palos
1521
conqueree: 5 Aztec
1588 loser: 6 Armada
5,000 Nights at the Opera
author: Rudolf Bing
5280 feet: 4 mile
F: 3 key 4 clef, elem., mark 5 false, grade 6 letter 7 element 8 fluorine 10 Fahrenheit
9 for ~: 4 at. no.
avoid an ~: 4 pass
equivalent: 6 E-sharp
in phonetic alphabet: 7 Foxtrot
in physics: 5 farad
measure: 3 deg. 6 degree
worth an ~: 3 bad 5 awful, lousy, woful 6 woeful 8 dreadful, horrible, terrible 9 atrocious 10 abominable, horrendous
F __: 4 clef, star 5 layer, Troop 6 region
F __ foxtrot: 4 as in
F. __ Abraham: 6 Murray
F. __ Bailey: 3 Lee
F. __ Fitzgerald: 5 Scott
'F' __ Fugitive: 5 Is for
F-16: 5 Viper
counterpart: 3 MiG
home: 3 AFB
F1 neighbor: 3 ESC
fa: 4 note
follower: 3 sol 4 so la 5 sol la 6 so la ti 7 sol la ti
preceder: 2 mi 4 re mi 6 do re mi
fa-__: 4 la-la
__-fa: 3 sol
FAA
concern: 3 saf. 6 safety
department: 3 DOT
part: 3 Fed. 5 Admin. 7 Federal 8 Aviation
fab
see wonderful
Fab: 9 detergent
alternative: *see* detergent
Fab __: 4 Four
Fabares, Shelley: 7 actress
song: Johnny Angel (1962)
spouse: Mike Farrell
TV: Coach, The Donna Reed Show
Fabergé
glaze: 6 enamel
object: 3 egg
Fab Four
name: 4 John, Paul 5 Ringo, Starr 6 George, Lennon 8 Harrison 9 McCartney
see also Beatles
Fabi: 3 Teo
Fabian: 4 pope 6 singer 7 pontiff
last name: Forte
fable: 4 myth, tale, yarn 5 conte, story 6 apolog, legend 7 fiction, parable, recital 8 allegory, apologue 9 fairy tale, folk story
author: 4 Esop 5 Aesop
ending: 5 moral
figure: 3 ant, fox 4 hare 8 tortoise
moral ~: 6 apolog 8 apologue
fabled: 5 noted 6 famous, unreal 7 storied 8 mythical 9 legendary 10 fictitious
fables: 4 lore
__ Fables: 6 Aesop's, Flower, Modern
Fables for Our Time
author: James Thurber
Fables in Slang
author: George Ade
Fabray: 3 Nan 7 Nanette
fabric: 3 aba, net, rep 4 abba, duck, felt, ikat, lace, lamé, lawn, leno, mesh, poly, repp, silk, wool 5 baize, batik, blend, chino, cloth, crape, crash, crepe, denim, dhoti, dhuti, Dynel, fiber, frisé, gauze, gazar, Honan, Kasha, kente, khaki, Kodel, linen, lisle, lisse, loden, moire, ninon, nylon, pekin, piqué, plaid, plush, ramie, rayon, satin, scrim, serge, stuff, suede, surah, tammy, terry, toile, tweed, twill, voile, wigan 6 alpaca, Angora, armure, barege, battik, Bengal, bouclé, burlap, camaca, camaka, camoca, canvas, chally, chintz, coburg, cotton, coutil, crepon, Dacron, damask, dhooti, dimity, faille, fleece, gloria, jersey, linsey, madras, make-up, merino, mohair, moreen, muslin, oxford, plissé, pongee, poplin, ratiné, samite, sateen, saxony, stamin, tammie, tartan, tricot, tussah, tusseh, tusser, tussor, tussur, velour, velvet, vicuña, wadmal 7 batiste, brocade, buckram, bunting, cambric, challie, challis, charvet, Cheviot, chiffon, dhootie, drugget, duvetyn, épinglé, estamin, etamine, fishnet, flannel, foulard, fustian, galatea, gingham, Gore-Tex, grogram, hickory, jaconet, kashmir, khaddar, mockado, Mogador, nankeen, netting, oilskin, organdy, organza, ottoman, paisley, percale, sarsnet, satinet, silesia, spandex, tabaret, tabinet, taffeta, textile, ticking, tiffany, tussore, velours, Viyella, worsted 8 algerine, barathea, bayadere, Burberry, canotier, cashmere, casimere, casimire, Celanese, chambray, chenille, corduroy, cretonne, diamante, homespun, Indienne, jacquard, marcella, marocain, material, Milanese, moleskin, moquette, nainsook, oilcloth, organdie, paduasoy, popeline, prunella, prunelle, prunello, sanglier, sarcenet, sarsenet, shalloon, shantung, tabbinet, tarlatan, Venetian, whipcord, wild silk 9 astrakhan, Bengaline, bombazeen, bombazine, calamanco, cassimere, charmeuse, cothamore, crinoline, flannelet, framework, gabardine, georgette, Glen plaid, grenadine, grosgrain, henrietta, horsehair, matelassé, Naugahyde, paramatta, percaline, polyester, sailcloth, satinette, sharkskin, silkaline, structure, velveteen 10 balbriggan, broadcloth, Irish tweed, marseilles, peau de soie, seersucker, tattersall
acid-washed ~: 5 denim
ancient silk ~: 6 byssus
attachment: 4 snap 6 button, Velcro, zipper
bit of ~: 3 rag 5 scrap 6 swatch
blouse ~: 4 silk
border: 3 hem 4 seam 6 edging, fringe
camel hair ~: 3 aba 4 abba
canvas ~: 5 wigan 9 sailcloth
carpet ~: 5 frisé, plush
coarse ~: 3 aba 4 abba 5 chino, denim 6 burlap, linsey
coat ~: 5 serge 6 saxony 8 Burberry 9 cothamore
corded ~: 3 rep 4 repp
cotton ~: 3 rep 4 duck, lawn, repp 5 baize, chino, crape, crepe, dhoti, dhuti, khaki, piqué, plush, scrim, terry, toile, voile 6 canvas, chally, chintz, damask, dhooti, dimity, gloria, madras, moreen, muslin, oxford, pongee, poplin, sateen, wadmal 7 buckram, bunting, cambric, challie, challis, dhootie, duvetyn, etamine, flannel, foulard, fustian, galatea, gingham, jaconet, khaddar, nankeen, oilskin, organdy, percale, satinet, silesia, ticking, tiffany, Viyella 8 Burberry, chambray, corduroy, Indienne, marcella, moleskin, nainsook, oilcloth, organdie, shantung, tarlatan 9 crinoline, flannelet, gabardine, paramatta, percaline, sailcloth, satinette, silkaline, velveteen 10 balbriggan, marseilles, seersucker
crepe ~: 8 marocain
crinkled ~: 5 crape, crepe, lisse
curtain ~: 4 lace, leno 5 ninon, voile 6 chintz, dimity, moreen 7 tabaret 8 cretonne
delicate ~: 4 lace 5 tulle
dress ~: 5 crash, voile 6 coburg, dimity
durable ~: 5 chino, denim, khaki
elastic ~: 5 Lycra 7 spandex
embossed ~: 9 matelassé
feature: 3 nap 4 pile, wale
feltlike ~: 5 baize
filmy ~: 5 gauze, lisse, tulle
flax ~: 5 linen 7 fustian
fold: 6 crease
fuzz: 3 nap 4 lint
gather ~: 5 shirr
gauzy ~: 3 net 4 leno 5 lisse, tulle
glazed ~: 4 cire 5 tammy 6 chintz, tammie
glossy ~: 4 lamé, silk 5 ramee, ramie, satin 6 sateen 7 taffeta 8 diamante
goat ~: 3 aba 4 abba 5 Kasha 7 kashmir 8 cashmere
gown ~: 4 lamé, silk 5 satin, tulle
hand-dyed ~: 5 batik 6 battik
heavy ~: 4 wool 5 denim, loden 6 burlap, canvas, crepon 8 cretonne
hose ~: 5 lisle, nylon
lightweight ~: 5 voile
linen ~: 4 lawn 5 toile 6 canvas, damask 7 cambric 8 chambray, marcella 10 seersucker
looped ~: 5 frise
measure: 3 ell 4 bolt, yard 6 denier

mesh ~: 3 net 4 leno 5 gauze 7 fishnet, netting, tiffany 8 tarlatan
metallic ~: 4 lamé
mohair ~: 7 grogram 8 sanglier
muslin ~: 4 mull
napped ~: 5 baize 7 flannel
natural ~: 4 silk, wool 6 cotton
nonwoven ~: 4 felt 5 suede
nylon ~: 5 satin, tulle 6 gloria, jersey, tricot, velvet 7 chiffon, organza, taffeta 8 Milanese 9 grenadine, sailcloth
open ~: 3 net 4 lace, leno, mesh 5 scrim, tulle
pattern: 4 dots 5 twill
patterned ~: 5 plaid, print 6 madras, tartan 7 gingham
poplin-like ~: 9 Bengaline
puckered ~: 6 plisse
quilted ~: 5 cloky 6 cloque
rayon ~: 3 rep 4 repp 5 moire, piqué, satin, surah, tulle, voile 6 chally, faille, jersey, pongee, poplin, velvet 7 challie, challis, charvet, chiffon, duvetyn, foulard, Mogador, organza, ottoman, silesia, taffeta 8 Celanese, chenille, marocain, Milanese, popeline, shantung 9 grenadine, sharkskin 10 seersucker
reversible ~: 6 damask
ribbed ~: 3 rep 4 cord, repp 5 pique, twill 6 faille, poplin, tricot 7 épinglé 8 corduroy 9 grosgrain
sheer ~: 4 lawn, leno 5 gauze, ninon, toile, voile 6 barege, dimity 7 batiste, chiffon 9 georgette
sheet ~: 4 pima 6 cotton
shirt ~: 4 pima, silk 5 nylon 6 cotton, Madras 9 polyester
silk ~: 3 rep 4 repp 5 crape, crepe, gazar, Honan, moire, pekin, piqué, plush, satin, surah, tulle, voile 6 armure, camaca, camaka, camoca, damask, faille, gloria, jersey, pongee, poplin, samite, tricot, tussah, tusseh, tusser, tussor, tussur, velvet 7 charvet, chiffon, duvetyn, foulard, grogram, Mogador, organza, ottoman, sarsnet, tabaret, tabinet, taffeta, tussore 8 chambray, chenille, marocain, Milanese, paduasoy, popeline, sarcenet, sarsenet, tabbinet 9 charmeuse, grenadine 10 peau de soie
silklike ~: 5 ramee, ramie
silky ~: 6 fleece
soft ~: 6 chally 7 challie, challis
striped ~: 7 gingham 8 bayadere
suit ~: 4 wool 5 serge, tweed, twill
summer ~: 5 linen, voile
sweater ~: 4 wool 5 Orlon
synthetic ~: 4 poly 5 Arnel, Dynel, Kodel, Lycra, nylon, Orlon, rayon 6 Ban-Lon, Dacron 7 Gore-Tex, spandex 9 gabardine, polyester
taffeta ~: 6 faille
tie ~: 4 repp, silk 7 charvet, Mogador
tie-dyed ~: 4 ikat 5 batik 6 battik
towel ~: 5 crash, terry
transparent ~: 5 toile
twill ~: 5 chino, denim, serge 6 coburg, coutil, oxford 7 Cheviot, estamin, foulard, hickory, nankeen, silesia, Viyella 8 canotier, casimere, casimire, moleskin, prunella, prunelle, prunello, shalloon, Venetian 9 bombazeen, bombazine, cassimere, gabardine, henrietta, paramatta, sharkskin 10 broadcloth
upholstery ~: 5 frise 6 damask, velour 7 tabaret, velours 8 moquette 9 horsehair, Naugahyde
veil ~: 3 net 6 barege
velvet ~: 5 panne
velvetlike ~: 6 velour 7 mockado, velours 8 moquette
vinyl ~: 9 Naugahyde
waterproof ~: 5 loden 7 Gore-Tex, oilskin 8 oilcloth
wavelike ~: 5 moire
wax-glazed ~: 4 cire
whitener: 6 bluing 7 blueing
wool ~: 3 rep 4 felt, repp 5 baize, Kasha, khaki, plush, serge, tweed, voile 6 alpaca, Angora, armure, chally, damask, gloria, jersey, kersey, merino, mohair, moreen, poplin, saxony, stamin, tartan, tricot, vicuña, wadmal 7 bunting, challie, challis, Cheviot, drugget, duvetyn, flannel, grogram, paisley, tabinet, Viyella, worsted 8 algerine, homespun, marocain, shalloon, tabbinet, Venetian, whipcord 9 astrakhan, calamanco, grenadine, henrietta, paramatta 10 Irish tweed
wool-like ~: 7 satinet 9 satinette
worker: 4 dyer
worker's concern: 6 dye lot
worsted ~: 5 serge 6 wadmal 7 estamin, etamine 8 casimere, casimire, sanglier, Venetian 9 cassimere, gabardine, sharkskin
woven ~: 4 knit, mesh, wool 5 linen 8 barathea
wrinkle-resistant ~: 5 Orlon 6 Dacron
see also material
fabricate: 4 fake, make 5 build, draft, erect, feign, forge, frame, fudge, put up, shape, weave 6 cook up, create, devise, invent, make up, whip up 7 compose, concoct, falsify, fashion, imagine, prepare, produce, trump up, turn out 8 assemble, simulate 9 construct, establish, formulate, structure 10 brainstorm, exaggerate
fabricated: 4 fake, made, sham 5 bogus, false, phony, put-on 6 ersatz, made-up, phoney, pseudo, unreal 8 mythical, spurious 9 imitation, synthetic, unfounded, unnatural 10 artificial, fictitious, fraudulent
fabrication: 3 fib, lie 4 fake, hoax, myth, tale, yarn 5 rumor, story 6 deceit 7 fiction, forgery, product, untruth 8 assembly, creation, pretense 9 structure
fabricator: 4 liar 5 maker 6 framer 7 builder, creator, devisor, drafter 9 assembler
Fabric, Bent
song: Alley Cat (1962)
fabrics, like some: 5 sheer 6 fleecy 7 natural 9 synthetic
fabric softener: 5 Downy 6 Bounce 7 Snuggle 9 Cling Free 10 Final Touch
Fabrizi: 4 Aldo
fabulist: 3 Ade 4 Esop, liar 5 Aesop 9 George Ade
fabulous
see wonderful
Fabulous Baker Boys, The (1989 film)
cast: Beau Bridges, Jeff Bridges, Michelle Pfeiffer
director: Steve Kloves
facade: 3 act 4 mask, pose, sham, wall 5 cloak, decoy, front, guise, put-on, shell 6 veneer 7 outside, surface 8 disguise, exterior, pretense 9 semblance 10 appearance, false front, masquerade
face: 3 air, mug 4 defy, font, line, look, meet, puss, risk, show, side 5 brave, front, guide, nerve, plane, pride, shell 6 accost, aspect, engage, give on, kisser, take on, turn to, veneer, visage 7 display, encrust, eyeball, front on, grimace, incrust, outside, profile, surface 8 boldness, confront, cope with, exterior, features, laminate, overlook 9 encounter, front onto, impudence, semblance, stand up to, withstand 10 appearance, effrontery, experience, expression, look toward, reckon with, turn toward
about ~: 4 turn 5 U-turn 6 switch 8 reversal 9 one-eighty
boldly: 4 dare, defy 5 brave 8 confront 9 stand up to
card: 4 jack, king 5 honor, queen
combining form: 6 -hedron, prosop- 7 prosopo-
cover: 4 mask, veil 6 domino
down: 4 defy 6 oppose 9 challenge
ender: 4 down 5 cloth, plate
fall flat on one's ~: 4 fail, flop
familiar ~: 6 patron 7 devotee, habitué, visitor 8 customer 10 frequenter
fly in the ~ of: 4 dare, defy 6 oppose 7 disobey
for ~ value: 5 at par
get in one's ~: 5 annoy 6 accost, bother 8 confront 9 challenge
in Spanish: 4 cara
it has a ~: 5 clock, watch
lacking ~ value: 5 no par
loss of ~: 5 shame, stain, taint 6 stigma 8 disgrace, dishonor, ignominy 9 abashment, disrepute
make a ~: 3 mug 4 moue 5 scowl, smirk, sneer, wince
make a long ~: 4 mope, pout, sulk 5 brood
off: 5 argue, brawl, clash, fight, scrap 6 bicker, debate 7 contend, dispute, mix it up, quarrel, wrangle 8 squabble 9 lock horns
on the ~ of it: 9 evidently, outwardly, seemingly 10 apparently, ostensibly
part: 3 ear, eye, jaw, lip 4 chin, hair, nose 5 cheek, mouth, naris 6 dimple 7 eyebrow, eyelash, nostril 8 philtrum
put on a happy ~: 4 beam, grin 5 smile
red in the ~: 6 ablush
see face to ~: 5 greet 7 run into 8 bump into, confront 9 run across
shape: 4 oval 5 ovate, ovoid, round 8 elliptic 10 elliptical
show one's ~: 5 pop in, visit 6 appear, arrive, attend, blow in, drop in, emerge, roll in, turn up 7 check in, clock in, punch in, turn out 8 breeze in
slap in the ~: 4 slam, slur 5 smear 6 rebuke, slight 7 affront, obloquy, offense, repulse 9 aspersion, cheap shot, rejection 10 backbiting, defamation, detraction, opprobrium
slapper's shout: 5 fresh
starter: 3 dog 4 bold, club, pale, type 5 black, dough, inter, light, white
take at ~ value: 4 rely 5 bet on, trust 6 accept, assume, bank on, commit, credit, expect, lean on, look to, rely on 7 believe, consign, count on, entrust, presume, suppose, swear by 8 depend on, rely upon
the day: 4 rise, wake 5 arise, awake, get up 6 awaken
up to: 5 admit 8 confront, cope with, deal with 10 meet head on
vertical ~: 4 crag, hill 5 bluff, cliff 8 mountain 9 precipice
wear a long ~: 4 fret, moon, pine, pout, sulk 5 brood, droop 6 grieve, lament
with a long ~: 4 glum, mopy 5 mopey
with a straight ~: 7 for real 9 seriously, sincerely
face __: 3 bow 4 card, down, gear, mask, time, up to 5 angle, cloth, facts, towel, value 6 powder
face-__: 3 off 4 down, lift, nail 6 harden, saving
__ face: 4 baby, left, long, lose, save 5 about, beach, false, make a, poker, right, smile 6 smiley 7 working
__-face: 5 about, kissy, volte
Face __ Manchu, The: 4 of Fu
__ Face: 4 Baby 5 Angel, Funny
faced
combining form: 6 -hedral
starter: 4 bare 5 shame
__-faced: 3 pie, red, sad, two 4 baby, bald, bold, full, lean, long, moon, open, rock 5 glass, hairy, horse, Janus, pasty, pitch, poker, round, steel, stone, stony, white 6 brazen, double, quarry, rubber, smooth 7 freckle
__-faced lie: 4 bald
facedown: 5 prone
__-faced sandwich: 4 open
__-Faced Woman: 3 Two

face in the misty light, The: 5 Laura
face-lift
  give a ~: 5 fix up, rehab, renew 6 revamp, update 7 remodel, restore, touch up 8 overhaul, renovate, spruce up 9 modernize, refurbish
___ Face Nelson: 4 Baby
face-off: 5 set-to, start 6 launch 7 opening 9 beginning, inception
Face/Off (1997 film)
  cast: Joan Allen, Nicolas Cage, John Travolta
  director: John Woo
Face of Fear, The
  author: Dean Koontz
___ face of it: 5 on the
face powder mineral: 4 talc
___ Faces Life: 6 Portia
___ Faces of Eve, The: 5 Three
facet: 4 side 5 phase, plane, thing 6 aspect 7 element, feature, respect, surface 9 attribute
face that launched a thousand ships, The: 5 Helen
face the ___: 5 music
___ Face the Music and Dance: 4 Let's
Face the Nation (CBS news)
  former host: 5 Stahl
facetious: 4 flip 5 comic, droll, funny, silly, witty 6 jocose, joking, jovial 7 amusing, comical, jesting, jocular, joshing, kidding, playful, satiric, waggish 8 farcical, flippant, humorous 9 frivolous, laughable, ludicrous, sarcastic, satirical, sprightly, whimsical 10 indecorous, irreverent, nonserious, ridiculous
  be ~ with: 3 kid 4 twit 5 tease
facetiously: 5 in fun 7 as a joke, as a lark 8 for a joke
facetiousness: 3 wit 5 humor 6 comedy, levity 8 jocosity 10 jocularity
face-to-face: 6 direct, head-on, openly 7 vis-à-vis 8 directly, opposite 10 unmediated
  see ~: 4 meet
face-up: 6 supine
facial: 7 mudpack
  expression: 4 grin 5 scowl, smile, smirk 7 grimace
  feature: 3 ear, eye, jaw, lip 4 chin, hair, nose 5 beard, cheek, mouth 6 dimple, eyelid 7 eyebrow, eyelash 8 philtrum
  see also face
facial ___: 5 angle, index, nerve 6 tissue
___ facie: 5 prima
facile: 3 ace, pat 4 able, deft, easy, glib 5 adept, handy, light, quick, vocal 6 adroit, expert, fluent, simple, smooth 7 flowing 8 dextrous, skillful 9 dexterous 10 child's play, effortless, elementary, proficient
facileness: 4 ease
facilitate: 3 aid 4 ease, help 5 favor, speed 6 assist, enable, grease, smooth 7 further, lighten, make for, promote, speed up 8 expedite, simplify
facilitation: 3 aid 4 help 6 assist 10 assistance
facilities: 4 gear 9 equipment
facility: 3 art 4 bent, ease 5 knack, skill, touch 6 office, talent 7 ability, amenity, faculty, fluency, freedom, know-how, prowess, sleight 8 aptitude, capacity, hang of it 9 dexterity, eloquence, readiness, technique 10 adroitness, capability, efficiency, green thumb, smoothness
  health-care ~: 8 hospital 9 infirmary 10 dispensary
facing: 5 front 6 across, lining, toward, veneer 7 against, coating, towards 8 covering, opposite 10 decoration
Facing the Flag
  author: Jules Verne
facsimile: 4 copy, stat, twin 5 clone, ditto, image, mimeo, model, Xerox 6 double, ectype 7 replica 8 knockoff, likeness 9 duplicate, look-alike, miniature, photocopy, Photostat 10 carbon copy, dead ringer, transcript
fact: 5 datum, given, known, thing, truth 6 gospel, truism, verity 7 finding, reality 9 actuality, certainty, certitude, principle 10 particular, phenomenon
  assumed as ~: 5 given 9 axiomatic 10 postulated, understood
  contrary to ~: 5 false 6 untrue 9 incorrect 10 fabricated, fallacious, fictitious, inaccurate
  due to the ~ that: 7 whereas
  ending: 3 oid, ory
  establish as ~: 5 prove 6 verify 7 certify, confirm, warrant 8 document, validate 9 ascertain, determine
  for a ~: 3 yes 4 amen, sure 5 quite, truly 6 and how, easily, indeed, really, simply, surely, to a tee 7 exactly, flat out, in truth, right on 9 assuredly, certainly, decidedly, doubtless, expressly, hands down, in reality, on the nose 10 absolutely, by all means, definitely, positively
  in spite of the ~ that: 6 albeit, though 8 although 10 even though
  not based on ~: 6 untrue 7 invalid 8 spurious 9 erroneous, unfounded 10 fallacious, groundless
  numerical ~: 4 stat
  old-style: 5 sooth
  state as ~: 4 aver 5 posit
  take as ~: 6 accept, assume 7 believe, suppose, surmise 9 postulate
fact-finding: 8 research
faction: 3 set 4 band, bloc, camp, cell, clan, club, crew, cult, part, ring, sect, side, team, wing 5 cabal, cadre, crowd, group, junto, lobby, party, split 6 caucus, circle, clique, schism, strife 7 coterie, discord, in-group 8 disunity, intrigue, offshoot 9 coalition 10 disharmony, dissension, persuasion
factional: 8 partisan 9 divergent, sectarian, sectional
factious: 6 unruly 7 defiant, wayward 8 contrary, disloyal, indocile, mutinous, perverse, stubborn 9 alienated, bellicose, dissident, insurgent, obstinate 10 disorderly, rebellious, refractory
factitious: 4 fake, mock, sham 5 bogus, faked 8 affected 9 contrived, insincere, pretended, simulated, unnatural 10 artificial, fictitious
___ facto: 4 ipso
facto, de: 10 unimagined
fact of ___: 4 life
factor: 4 part 5 agent, cause, piece, thing 6 agency, detail, medium 7 element, feature, portion, quality, steward 9 appointee, component, go-between 10 ingredient, instrument
  in: 5 weigh 6 assess 7 analyze, examine 8 appraise, consider, evaluate
  pivotal ~: 3 key 5 hinge 7 fulcrum
  supporting ~: 4 crux, root 5 basis, cause 6 motive, reason 7 footing, grounds, premise, pretext 8 evidence 9 criterion, principle 10 assumption, foundation
___ factor: 4 load, risk, unit 5 chill, fudge, noise 6 common, filter, Rhesus, safety 7 culture
factorage: 7 percent 10 commission
factory: 4 mill, shop 5 forge, plant 6 office 7 foundry 8 business
  built in a ~: 3 mfd.
  converted ~ space: 4 loft
  figure: 3 mgr. 7 foreman, manager
  group: 5 union
  make in a ~: 3 mfr.
  modernize a ~: 5 refit
  owners' org.: 3 NAM
  period: 5 shift
  right from the ~: 3 new 5 fresh 8 brand-new
  second: 5 irreg. 9 irregular
  store: 6 outlet
  work: 3 mfg.
factotum: 4 aide 5 agent, do-all 6 drudge, lackey, slavey 7 lacquey 8 handyman 9 gal Friday, man Friday 10 girl Friday
facts: 4 data, dope, info, poop 5 proof, score, truth 7 details, lowdown, reality 8 material 9 knowledge 10 brass tacks
  absorb ~: 4 cram 5 learn 6 soak up, take in 7 drink in 8 memorize
  alter ~: 3 lie 5 fudge
  bare ~: 7 outline
___ facts: 4 bare, face
Facts of Life, The (NBC sitcom)
  cast: Mindy Cohn (Natalie Green) Kim Fields (Tootie Ramsey) Nancy McKeon (Jo Polniaczek) Charlotte Rae (Edna Garrett) Lisa Whelchel (Blair Warner)
factual: 4 just, real, true 5 exact, frank, legit, right, valid 6 actual, honest, kasher, kosher, square 7 correct, empiric, genuine, precise, upright 8 absolute, accurate, concrete, credible, flawless, positive, straight, truthful, unbiased, unerring, verified 9 authentic, empirical, errorless, unadorned, veracious, veritable 10 forthright, historical, on the level, scrupulous, unmistaken
factuality: 5 right, truth 8 accuracy, fidelity, veracity 9 precision 10 exactitude
factually: 5 truly
factum: 5 truth
facula: 7 sunspot
faculties: 4 mind, wits 5 sense 6 brains, reason, wisdom 8 judgment, lucidity, sagacity, sapience 9 intellect 10 perception
  with full ~: 4 sane 5 sober, sound 8 composed, rational, sensible 9 collected, judicious, practical, pragmatic, temperate 10 controlled
faculty: 4 bent, gift, head 5 flair, knack, power, profs, sense, skill, staff, touch 6 talent 7 ability, aptness, know-how 8 aptitude, capacity, facility, hang of it, instinct, penchant, teachers 9 academics, dexterity, endowment, lecturers, personnel 10 adroitness, capability, efficiency, green thumb, proclivity, professors, propensity
  head: 4 dean
  member: 4 prof 7 teacher 8 lecturer 9 professor 10 instructor
Faculty, The (1998 film)
  cast: Jordana Brewster, Josh Hartnett, Salma Hayek, Elijah Wood
fad: 3 bug 4 mode, pogs, rage 5 craze, mania, style, thing, trend, vogue 7 in thing, lambada, novelty, pet rock 8 hot pants, Hula-Hoop, lava lamp, mood ring 9 streaking 10 dernier cri
  doll: 5 troll
faddish: 3 hip, hot, mod, new, now 4 chic 5 smart 6 latest, modish, red-hot, trendy, with-it 7 à la mode, current, dashing, in vogue, popular, stylish 8 last-word, up-to-date 9 happening 10 all the rage
___-faddle: 6 fiddle
fade: 3 die, dim, dip, ebb 4 coif, flag, melt, pale, pass, thin, tire, wane, wear, wilt 5 abate, decay, peter, waste, weary 6 blanch, bleach, blench, die out, hairdo, lessen, recede, vanish, weaken, whiten, wither 7 becloud, decline, decolor, die down, dwindle, relapse, tail off, thin out, wash out 8 coiffure, decrease, dissolve, etiolate, evanesce, get tired, languish, melt away, peter out, slack off, taper off, tone down, trail off 9 attenuate, disappear, evaporate, fizzle out 10 decolorize
  ender: 3 out 4 away
  in: 4 loom 6 appear, emerge
Fade Away (1981 song)
  artist: Bruce Springsteen
faded: 3 dim 4 dark, drab, dull, pale, weak 5 dusky, faint, fuzzy, light, mirky, murky, seedy, stale, tacky 6 bleary, blurry, shabby 7 shadowy 9 colorless, washed-out 10 indistinct, lackluster, lusterless
fade-in: 4 shot
fade-out technique: 4 iris
Fadiman: 7 Clifton
fading: 4 weak 5 decay 9 on the wane

away: 3 ebb 5 decay 6 ebbing 7 abating 8 decaying 9 abatement
faerie: 3 elf 6 sprite
Faerie Queene, The: 4 epic, poem
author: Edmund Spenser
character: 3 Ate, Una 4 Alma, Atin, Jove, Lucy 5 Diana, Venus 6 Adonis, Elissa, Merlin, Serena 7 Proteus 8 Gloriana
division: 5 canto
Faeroe Islands
capital: 8 Tórshavn
locale: 3 Atl. 8 Atlantic
Fagin: 5 crook 10 pickpocket
Fahd, King: 4 Arab
faith: 5 Islam
Fahey: 4 Jeff, John
Fahr.: 4 temp.
not ~: 3 Cel.
Fahrenheit: 6 Daniel 7 Gabriel
measure: 3 deg. 6 degree
Fahrenheit 451: 4 film 5 novel
author: Ray Bradbury
cast: Julie Christie, Cyril Cusack, Oskar Werner
director: François Truffaut
fail: 2 go 3 die, lag, sag 4 bomb, bust, flop, flub, fold, lose, miss, muff, sell, sink, tire, wane, wilt 5 close, decay, flunk, peter, yield 6 blow it, desert, fizzle, go bust, shrink, slight, weaken 7 abandon, conk out, decline, default, forsake, founder, go kaput, go under, go wrong, let down, lose out, mistake, neglect, poop out, relapse, wash out 8 backfire, collapse, fall down, fall flat, flounder, go astray, languish, lay an egg, peter out 9 backslide, break down, fall short, fizzle out, go belly up, strike out 10 be defeated, disappoint, go bankrupt, go downhill, run aground
bound to ~: 5 no-win
don't ~: 3 win 7 succeed
ender: 3 ure
prefix: 3 for-
to do: 4 miss, omit, shun, skip, snub 5 evade, scorn, shirk, spurn 6 bypass, forget, ignore, pass by 7 let pass, neglect 8 brush off, let slide, overlook, pass over 9 disregard, gloss over
to keep: 5 use up, waste 6 divest, mislay 7 forfeit 8 misplace, squander 9 dissipate 10 run through
to keep up: 4 drag, flag, poke 5 dally, tarry, trail 6 dawdle, falter, linger, loiter 7 fall off, slacken 8 hang back, lose time, straggle 10 dillydally, lose ground
without ~: 6 always, indeed, really, surely 9 certainly 10 absolutely, by all means, definitely, infallibly, invariably, positively
fail-__: 4 safe, soft
__-fail: 4 pass
__ Fáil: 3 Lia
failed
to: 5 didn't
failing: 3 shy 4 flaw, vice, weak 5 decay, fault, guilt, lapse, short 6 defect, foible, poorly, skimpy 7 decline 8 drawback, weakness 9 blind spot, deficient, worsening 10 deficiency, faultiness, inadequacy, inadequate, inefficacy
grade: 2 ef
that: 4 else 9 otherwise
faille: 4 silk 6 fabric 7 taffeta
fail-safe: 4 sure 7 certain 8 inerrant, reliable, unerring 9 foolproof, goofproof 10 infallible, undoubtful
Fail-Safe: 4 film 5 novel
author: Eugene Burdick, Harvey Wheeler
Fail-Safe (1964 film)
cast: Henry Fonda, Walter Matthau, Fritz Weaver
director: Sidney Lumet
fails to be: 4 ain't, isn't
failure: 3 bum, dog, dud 4 bomb, bust, flop, loss, miss, muff, rout, ruin, slip 5 crash, lapse, lemon, loser, slump, smash, wreck 6 bungle, defeat, fiasco, turkey 7 also-ran, debacle, default, misstep, reverse, tragedy, undoing, washout 8 collapse, downfall, shortage 9 breakdown, defaulter, oversight 10 bankruptcy, inadequacy, insolvency, misfortune, nonpayment, nonsuccess
exclamation: 4 pfft 5 phfft
prefix: 3 mis-
to act, in law: 6 laches
Failure to Launch (2006 film)
cast: Kathy Bates, Matthew McConaughey, Sarah Jessica Parker
fain: 5 ready 6 gladly
Fain: 5 Sammy 6 Ferris
faineance: 5 sloth 6 acedia, torpor 7 inertia, languor, laxness 8 idleness, laziness, otiosity 9 indolence, torpidity 10 stagnation
fainéant: 4 logy 6 torpid 7 shirker 8 indolent, slothful 9 do-nothing, goldbrick, shiftless 10 ne'er-do-well
faint: 3 dim, low, wan 4 dull, hazy, pale, slim, soft, tire, weak, wilt 5 bated, dizzy, faded, fuzzy, light, muted, piano, plotz, quail, queer, quiet, swoon, tired, vague, wispy, woozy 6 far off, feeble, go limp, hushed, sickly, silent, slight, subtle, weaken 7 distant, languid, muffled, obscure, outside, pass out, slender, starved, subdued, syncope, tenuous, unclear, wispish 8 blackout, collapse, cowardly, dampened, deadened, keel over, languish, lifeless, listless, murmured, starving, timorous, unlikely 9 enervated, exhausted, toned down, whispered 10 ill-defined, indistinct, turned down
become ~: 3 die, dim, ebb 4 fade, melt, pale, wane 6 die out, fizzle, recede, vanish 7 die away, dwindle, slacken, subside, tail off 8 diminish, evanesce, fade away, melt away, peter out, slack off, taper off, trail off 9 attenuate, fizzle out
feeling ~: 5 woozy
heart: 8 cold feet, timidity 9 cowardice
fainthearted: 4 meek, weak 5 cowed, mousy, timid, wimpy 6 afraid, craven, mousey, scared, trepid, yellow 7 abashed, alarmed, anxious, chicken, daunted, fearful, gutless, nervous, panicky, spooked, wimpish 8 cowardly, fearsome, hesitant, recreant, timorous 9 petrified, spineless, terrified, tremulous 10 frightened
faintheartedness: 4 fear
fainting: 6 aswoon
faintly: 6 hardly 7 lightly, scantly 8 scarcely, slightly
fair: 3 due 4 even, expo, just, mart, mild, nice, okay, okeh, okey, open, show, so-so, tidy 5 balmy, bazar, blond, bonny, clean, clear, equal, legal, legit, light, right, sound, sunny, white 6 bazaar, blonde, bonnie, bright, circus, comely, decent, fiesta, honest, in play, lawful, likely, lovely, market, medium, modest, not bad, pretty, proper, serene, square 7 average, clement, condign, ethical, logical, upright 8 adequate, all right, balanced, carnival, deserved, festival, gorgeous, handsome, mediocre, middling, moderate, ordinary, passable, rightful, sporting, straight, sunshiny, tolerant, unbiased 9 beautiful, cloudless, equitable, honorable, impartial, objective, palatable, promising, righteous, temperate, tolerable, tow-haired, tow-headed, unclouded, uncolored, unnotable, unslanted 10 aboveboard, acceptable, attractive, enchanting, evenhanded, exhibition, exposition, legitimate, on the level, pretty good, principled, reasonable, scrupulous
amount: 4 half, some
and square: 4 even, just 6 honest
don't play ~: 5 cheat
ender: 3 way 4 lead 5 water 6 ground, leader
local ~: 5 feria
mark: 3 cee
name meaning ~: 9 Guinevere
not ~: 4 foul 5 dirty, shady 6 biased, skewed, unjust 7 corrupt, crooked, partial 8 partisan, stinking 9 dishonest 10 subjective
offering: 4 ride
play: 6 equity 7 justice 8 equality
religious ~ of India: 4 mela
shake: 6 chance 9 equitable 10 likelihood
to middling: 4 okay, so-so 8 mediocre, moderate 9 tolerable
fair __: 3 off, sex 4 ball, copy, game, play 5 catch, shake, trade 6 dinkum 7 housing
fair-__: 6 haired, minded, spoken
fair-__ agreement: 5 trade
fair-__ boy: 6 haired
fair-__ friend: 7 weather
fair-__ law: 5 trade
fair-__ value: 6 market
__ fair: 3 fun 5 craft 6 county, world's
__ fair...: 4 All's
Fair __: 4 Deal
__ Fair: 4 All's 5 State 6 Vanity, World's
Fair, A.A., real first name: 4 Erle
fair and __: 6 square
Fair as __, when only one...: 5 a star
Fairbanks: 4 city, town 5 Chuck 7 Charles, Douglas
locale: 6 Alaska
newspaper: 9 News-Miner
road to ~: 5 Alcan
Fairbanks Jr., Douglas: 5 actor
spouse: Joan Crawford
Fairbanks Sr., Douglas: 5 actor
film: The Black Pirate (1926)
The Iron Mask (1929)
The Mark of Zorro (1920)
Mr. Robinson Crusoe (1932)
The Thief of Bagdad (1924)
spouse: Mary Pickford
Fairchild: 6 Morgan
Fair Deal monogram: 3 HST
__-faire: 6 savoir 7 laissez
Fairest of the Fair, The
composer: John Philip Sousa
Fairfax: 4 city, town
locale: 8 Virginia
Fairfield: 4 city, town
locale: 4 Conn., Ohio 10 California
fairground: 5 field
employee: 5 carny 6 carney
prize: 4 doll 6 kewpie 8 goldfish
fair-haired: 3 pet 5 blond 6 blonde, chosen 7 darling, favored, popular 9 fortunate, preferred 10 privileged
one's nickname: 5 Sandy 7 blondie
fair-haired __: 3 boy
fair-hiring letters: 3 EEO, EOE 4 EEOC
fair lance, name meaning: 6 Rowena
Fairlane: 3 car 4 auto, Ford 10 automobile
Fairleigh Dickinson: 6 school
athletes: 7 Knights
locale: 7 Teaneck 9 New Jersey
fairly: 5 clean, quite 6 enough, kind of, pretty, rather, sort of 8 by rights, somewhat 10 moderately, more or less
good: 4 so-so 6 decent, not bad 7 average 8 adequate, all right, bearable, mediocre, middling, moderate, ordinary, passable 9 tolerable 10 acceptable, admissible, reasonable, sufficient
in Latin: 9 pari passu
well: 4 so-so 9 tolerably 10 acceptably, adequately
Fair Maid of Perth, The
composer: Georges Bizet
fair-market __: 5 price, value
fair-minded: 4 just, sane 7 neutral 9 impartial, unslanted
fairness: 5 honor, right 6 equity 7 decency, honesty, justice, probity 8 equality 9 balminess, good faith, integrity 10 moderation
Fair Penitent, The
author: Nicholas Rowe
fair-skinned: 5 light
fairs, like state: 6 annual
__ Fair, The: 4 Holy 5 Horse
fair-trade __: 3 law
Fairuza: 4 Balk

fairway
see golf
fair-weather friend: 4 user 5 phony
fairy: 3 elf, fay, imp 4 peri, pixy 5 pixie 6 sprite 7 brownie 10 leprechaun
concern: 5 tooth
ender: 4 land
godmother: 5 donor 6 backer, patron 10 benefactor
Irish ~: 4 shee, sidh 5 sidhe
king: 6 Oberon
like a ~: 3 fey 4 tiny 5 elfin, teeny 6 elfish, elvish, teensy 9 sprightly
queen: 3 Mab 7 Titania
story: 4 lore, myth, tale 5 fable 6 legend 7 fantasy, fiction 8 allegory, delusion, folktale 9 falsehood, invention
tale: 4 yarn 5 story 7 romance
fairy __: 4 lamp, lily, ring, tale, wand 5 glove, green, stone, story 6 shrimp 9 godmother
__ fairy: 5 tooth
__-fairy: 4 airy
fairyland: 9 unreality
Fairy-Land
author: Edgar Allan Poe
fairy-slipper: 5 plant 6 flower
fairy tale
character: 3 elf, imp 4 nixy, ogre, pixy 5 giant, gnome, nixie, pixie, troll 6 goblin, kobold, sprite 7 brownie, gremlin, monster 9 hobgoblin 10 leprechaun
locale: 3 hut 6 castle, forest
word: 4 ever, once 5 after 7 happily
fairy-tale: 8 fanciful, mythical, romantic
Fairytale (1974 song)
artist: Pointer Sisters
__ Fairy Tales: 6 Grimm's
__ fait: 5 tout à
fait accompli: 4 fact 5 given 7 reality 9 actuality, certainty
fait, au: 4 deft 5 slick 6 adroit, expert, nimble, posted, proper, versed 7 abreast, capable, skilled, trained 8 decorous, dextrous, graceful, informed, masterly, seasoned, skillful 9 competent, dexterous, efficient, masterful, qualified 10 conversant, proficient, well-versed
faites __ jeux: 3 vos
faith: 3 rel. 4 sect 5 creed, dogma, piety, stock, tenet, trust 6 belief, credit, fealty, virtue 7 loyalty 8 credence, doctrine, fidelity, reliance, religion, theology 10 allegiance, confidence, conviction, dependance, dependence, persuasion, principles
articles of ~: 5 canon, creed, dogma 6 belief, tenets 8 doctrine, ideology, religion 9 teachings 10 persuasion, principles
bad ~: 5 fraud 6 deceit, dupery 7 perfidy 8 betrayal, quackery 9 deception, duplicity, hypocrisy, treachery 10 dishonesty, disloyalty
break ~: 4 sell 7 sell out 8 go back on
colleague: 4 hope 7 charity
good ~: 5 honor, truth 6 candor 7 decency, honesty, probity 8 fairness, veracity 9 frankness, integrity, sincerity
have ~: 7 believe
in good ~: 5 truly 7 frankly 8 candidly, for keeps, heartily, honestly 9 earnestly, genuinely, seriously, sincerely 10 aboveboard, truthfully
keeping the ~: 6 upbeat 7 hopeful, wishful 8 aspiring, sanguine, trusting 9 confident, expectant 10 optimistic
keep the ~: 7 abide by 8 adhere to, carry out
lack of ~: 5 doubt 8 distrust, mistrust, wariness 9 disbelief, misgiving, suspicion 10 skepticism
lose ~: 7 despair 10 give up hope
name meaning ~: 4 Vera
take on ~: 5 trust 6 accept, assume 7 believe
unquestioning, as ~: 8 mindless 9 oblivious, senseless
see also religion
faith __: 4 cure 6 healer
__ faith: 3 bad 4 good 5 act of 6 animal
Faith: 4 Ford, Hill 5 Evans, Percy 7 Daniels, Popcorn
Faith (1987 song)
artist: George Michael
__ faith and credit: 4 full
faithful: 4 fast, good, holy, just, nice, true 5 exact, liege, loyal, right, sound 6 ardent, devout, loving, steady, trusty 7 careful, correct, devoted, dutiful, literal, precise, sincere, staunch 8 accurate, constant, hard-core, obedient, reliable, resolute, true-blue, virtuous, yeomanly 9 allegiant, authentic, dedicated, honorable, realistic, steadfast, unfailing 10 convincing, dependable, unwavering
be ~: 6 adhere
keep ~ to: 4 heed, obey 6 adhere, follow 7 abide by, conform, fulfill, observe, respect, stand by 8 carry out 9 discharge, stick with 10 comply with
__ Faithful: 3 Old
Faithfull: 8 Marianne
faithfully: 9 honorably 10 unerringly
faithfulness: 5 honor, right, troth, trust 6 fealty, virtue 7 loyalty 8 devotion, fidelity
faithless: 5 false 6 fickle, rotten, untrue 7 corrupt, unloyal 8 cheating, disloyal, forsworn, recreant, two-faced 9 deceitful, dishonest, insincere, skeptical, two-timing 10 capricious, changeable, inconstant, perfidious, traitorous, unfaithful, unreliable, untruthful
Faithless (2000 film)
director: Liv Ullmann
faithlessness: 6 deceit 7 perfidy, sellout, treason 8 betrayal 9 deception, desertion, duplicity, treachery, two-timing 10 disloyalty, infidelity
Faith No More
song: Epic (1990)
Faith of Our Fathers: 4 hymn
Faith, Percy: 9 conductor
fake: 3 bad, lie, rig 4 copy, faux, hoax, imit., juke, mock, sham 5 actor, bluff, bogus, cheat, color, decoy, false, feign, forge, fraud, fudge, phony, pseud, put on, quack, quasi, setup, spoof 6 affect, assume, ersatz, forged, invent, phoney, play at, poseur, pseudo, unreal 7 assumed, bluffer, charade, falsify, feigned, forgery, pretend, trump up 8 affected, disguise, hoodwink, imposter, impostor, invented, simulate, spurious 9 charlatan, concocted, contrived, deception, deceptive, dissemble, fabricate, falsified, falsifier, hypocrite, imitation, imposture, improvise, insincere, invention, mare's nest, pretended, pretender, simulated, synthetic 10 artificial, fabricated, factitious, fictitious, fraudulent, mountebank, unreliable
in ice hockey: 4 deke
it: 3 act 4 pose, sham 5 ad-lib, feign 6 affect 7 playact, posture, pretend, show off 8 simulate 9 improvise, put on airs 10 grandstand, masquerade, put on an act
not ~: 4 real 5 legit 6 actual, square 7 genuine 8 bona fide, truthful 9 authentic 10 legitimate
out: 4 deke, fool, hoax 5 bluff, outdo, trick 6 outwit 7 pretend 8 outsmart
prove ~: 6 debunk 9 shoot down
fake __: 3 fur, out 4 book
fake-book notation: 5 chord 6 chords, melody
faked: 4 mock 5 put-on, set-up 6 pseudo 8 spurious 9 impromptu 10 artificial, factitious, fictitious
fake-ID user: 4 teen 5 minor 10 adolescent
faker: 5 fraud, phony, pseud, quack 6 forger, phoney 8 imposter, impostor 9 charlatan, falsifier, hypocrite, pretender 10 mountebank
fakery: 4 sham 6 deceit 8 flimflam, pretense
fakir: 5 Hindu 6 beggar, Hindoo, Muslim 7 ascetic, dervish 9 mendicant, religious
income: 4 alms
Fala: 3 dog, pet 7 Scottie
owner: 3 FDR 9 Roosevelt
falafel: 5 snack
bean: 4 fava
bread: 4 pita
Falana: 4 Lola
falcate: 6 curved, hooked 8 crescent
Falco, Edie: 7 actress
film: Judy Berlin (2000)
Laws of Gravity (1991)
Sunshine State (2002)
TV: Oz, The Sopranos
falcon: 4 bird, hawk 5 saker 6 lanner, merlin, tercel 7 kestrel 9 peregrine 10 bird of prey
cover a ~'s eyes: 4 seel
feature: 3 neb 4 beak, claw
home: 4 nest
hunter: 5 Spade
leash: 4 lune
like a ~: 6 hooded
relative: 4 kite 8 caracara
strap: 4 jess
young: 4 eyas
__ falcon: 5 saker 7 prairie
Falcon: 3 car 4 auto, Ford 10 automobile, footballer
Falcon Crest (CBS drama)
cast: Ana Alicia (Melissa)
Abby Dalton (Julia Cumson)
Robert Foxworth (Chase Gioberti)
Margaret Ladd (Emma Channing)
Lorenzo Lamas (Lance Cumson)
David Selby (Richard Channing)
Susan Sullivan (Maggie Gioberti)
Jane Wyman (Angela Channing)
valley: 7 Tuscany
Falconer
author: John Cheever
falconry: 5 sport 7 hawking
leash: 4 lune
Falcons: 4 team 6 eleven
home: 7 Atlanta
org.: 3 NFC, NFL
rival: *see* NFL team
sport: 8 football
__ Falcon, The: 7 Maltese
falderal
see baloney
Faldo, Nick: 6 golfer
Faline: 4 deer, toon
friend: 5 Bambi
Falkenburg, Jinx
spouse: Tex McCrary
Falklands: 4 isls. 5 isles 7 islands
Falk, Peter: 5 actor
TV: Columbo
fall: 3 cut, dip, ebb, sag, set 4 dive, drip, drop, ease, flag, flop, lull, plop, rain, ruin, sink, slip, thud, tilt, trip, wane 5 abate, crash, lapse, let up, lower, occur, pitch, reach, slide, slope, slump, spill, swoop, thump, yield 6 autumn, defeat, give up, go down, happen, header, lessen, plunge, recede, relent, season, topple, tumble 7 cascade, crumble, decline, descend, descent, drop off, dwindle, founder, give way, plummet, stumble, subside, succumb, tail off, tip over 8 collapse, decrease, diminish, downturn, drop down, keel over, lowering, moderate, nosedive 9 abatement, backslide, come about, dwindling, hairpiece, lessening, overthrow, perdition, plump down, reduction, surrender, take place 10 come to pass, diminution, hit the dirt
apart: 3 rot 6 go awry 8 collapse, disunite 9 break down, decompose
asleep: 3 nap, nod 4 doze, rest 5 droop 6 catnap, drowse, snooze 7 drop off 8 drift off
at the feet of: 6 grovel
back: 3 ebb 5 lapse 6 recede, retire 7 regress, relapse, retreat 8 withdraw 10 lose ground
back on: 3 use 6 employ, look to, resort, take to 8 call upon, resort to, retire to 9 count upon, make use of, retreat to 10 withdraw to
back (on): 5 count 6 depend
behind: 3 lag 5 trail

cause of a ~: 6 hubris, hybris
clumsily: 4 trip
color: 4 rust
cousin: 3 wig 6 toupee
do a ~ chore: 4 rake
down: 4 fail 7 give way 8 collapse 10 disappoint
down on: 4 fail 6 sadden 7 sell out 8 embitter, imbitter 10 disappoint, disenchant
ender: 3 off, out 4 back, fish 5 board
event: 5 frost
fader: 3 tan
flat: 4 bomb, bust, fail, flop, lose, miss, slip, trip 5 crash, flunk 6 blow it, falter 7 blunder, founder, go under, go wrong, misfire, misstep, stumble, wash out 8 collapse, flounder, lay an egg 9 strike out
flower: 3 mum 5 aster
for: 3 buy 4 love 7 swallow
forward: 5 pitch
from grace: 3 err, sin 5 lapse, stray 7 do wrong, offense 8 iniquity 9 backslide 10 transgress
from the sky: 4 hail, rain, snow 5 sleet
gathering: 4 crop 6 leaves
guy: 3 sap 4 butt, dupe, lamb, mark, prey 5 chump, patsy, raker 6 pigeon, stooge, sucker 9 scapegoat
heir to: 3 get, own 4 gain 6 obtain 7 acquire, inherit, receive, succeed 8 come into, take over
ill with: 3 get 5 catch
in: 4 come, sink 6 arrive 8 collapse, come down 9 break down 10 fraternize
into place: 4 form, jell 5 click
in with: 4 join, meet 5 enter 6 sign on, sign up 7 run into 8 bump into, chance on, come upon, take part 9 accompany, encounter, run across 10 chance upon, come across
let ~: 4 drop, shed 5 spill
let ~ between the cracks: 4 omit 6 forget, ignore 7 neglect 8 overlook 9 disregard
like a ~ day: 5 brisk, crisp
month: 3 Dec., Nov., Oct., Sep. 4 Sept. 7 October 8 December, November 9 September
off: 3 dip, ebb, lag 4 curb, drop, flag, slip, slow, wane 5 erode, lower, slide, slump 6 lessen, reduce, shrink, worsen 7 curtail, cut down, dwindle, regress 8 diminish, peter out, slow down 10 degenerate
off the wagon: 5 drink, lapse 7 regress 9 backslide
on: 5 go for 6 assail, attack 7 assault, run into 8 meet with 10 experience
on one's knees: 7 bow down, worship 9 genuflect, prostrate 10 pay tribute
opposite: 4 rise
out: 5 scrap, sleep 7 quarrel, wrangle 8 squabble
over: 4 trip 5 swoon 7 pass out
planting: 4 bulb
preceder: 4 trip 5 pride
protection: 3 net
rise and ~: 4 toss 6 billow, rhythm
short: 4 fail, lack, lose, miss 7 let down
sign: 5 Libra 7 Scorpio 11 Sagittarius
silent: 5 quiet 6 shut up 7 be quiet 8 pipe down 9 keep still
sound of a ~: 5 splat
starter: 3 dew, ice, pit 4 dead, down, even, foot, land, prat, rain, snow, wind 5 night, short, water
through: 4 fail, flop 6 fizzle 7 founder, misfire 8 collapse
to: 7 get busy
upon: 4 raid 5 lunge 6 pounce, strike
worker: 5 raker

fall __: 3 for, guy, off, out 4 away, back, down, flat, foul, line, upon, wind 5 apart, front, short, under 6 behind 7 through, webworm
fall __ bed: 4 into 5 out of
fall __ grace: 4 from
fall __ line: 4 into 5 out of
fall __ on: 4 back
fall __ to: 4 back, prey
fall __ upon: 4 back
fall __ wayside: 5 by the
fall-__ position: 4 back
__ fall: 3 ash 4 free
Fallaci: 6 Oriana
fallacious: 3 bad 5 false, not so, phony, wrong 6 faulty, phoney, untrue 7 inexact, invalid, unsound 8 deluding, delusive, delusory, illusive, illusory, mistaken, specious, spurious 9 beguiling, deceitful, deceiving, deceptive, erroneous, illogical, incorrect, sophistic, unfounded 10 fictitious, fraudulent, ill-founded, inaccurate, irrational, misleading, reasonless, ungrounded, unreasoned
fallacy: 5 error 6 deceit 7 falsity, sophism, untruth 8 delusion, illusion 9 casuistry, deception, sophistry 10 invalidity
Falla, Manuel de: 7 Spanish 8 composer
work: The Three-Cornered Hat
fall by the __: 7 wayside
__ fall down: 3 All
fallen: 4 flat 6 ruined, shamed 9 collapsed, disgraced, prostrate 10 dishonored
angel: 5 devil, Satan 6 Belial, diablo 7 evil one, Lucifer 9 Beelzebub
starter: 4 chap, chop 5 crest
fall from __: 5 grace
Fall From Grace
author: Andrew Greeley
Fall Guy, The (ABC adventure)
cast: Douglas Barr (Howie Munson) Lee Majors (Colt Seavers) Markie Post (Terri) Heather Thomas (Jody Banks)
fallibility: 7 errancy 8 humanity
fallible: 5 human 6 broken, errant, erring, faulty, flawed, marred 7 damaged, unsound 8 careless, impaired 9 defective, imperfect 10 unreliable
falling: 4 down 7 descent
apart: 5 shaky 7 rickety, run-down 8 decrepit 9 crumbling 10 ramshackle, tumbledown
for anything: 4 naif 5 green, naive 6 simple, unwary 8 gullable, gullible, trusting 9 accepting, believing, credulous 10 uncritical
keep from ~: 4 hold, lift, prop 5 boost, brace, carry, shore, stake 6 assist, buoy up, hold up, prop up 7 bolster, fortify, shore up, support 8 buttress 9 reinforce, stabilize, undergird 10 strengthen
like ~ off a log: 4 easy, snap 6 facile, picnic, simple 7 no sweat 8 no bother 9 no problem, no trouble 10 child's play, effortless, elementary
sound: 4 plop
falling __: 4 band, door, down, star 5 apart 6 action, rhythm 7 weather
falling __ log: 4 off a
Falling (1963 song)
artist: Roy Orbison
Falling in Love (1984 film)
cast: Robert De Niro, Harvey Keitel, Meryl Streep
director: Ulu Grosbard
Falling in Place
author: Ann Beattie
falling-off: 4 wane 5 slump 7 decline 8 decrease
falling-out: 3 row 4 feud, fuss, rift, spat, tiff 5 clash, fight, run-in 6 breach 7 dispute, quarrel, wrangle 9 imbroglio 10 difficulty
minor ~: 4 spat, tiff 5 scrap 8 squabble
__ falling, The: 5 sky is
__ Fall in Love: 4 Let's 5 When I
fall into __: 3 bed 4 line 5 a trap
falloff: 3 dip 4 drop 5 slide, slump 7 decline 8 contract, decrease, slowdown 9 abatement
Fall of Hyperion, The
poet: John Keats
Fall of Moondust, A
author: Arthur C. Clarke
Fall of the House of Usher, The
author: Edgar Allan Poe
fall on __ ears: 4 deaf
Falloppio: 8 Gabriele
fallout: 6 effect, result 7 outcome 9 aftermath
fall out of __: 3 bed 4 line
fallow: 4 idle 6 barren, unused, yellow 7 dormant, sterile 8 inactive, unfarmed, unplowed, unseeded, untilled 9 unplanted
lie ~: 4 idle 8 languish, stagnate
Fall River: 4 city, town
locale: 4 Mass.
Falls: 4 Mesa 5 Angel 6 Iguaçu 7 Iguassú, Kalambo, Niagara 8 Victoria, Yosemite
__ Falls Conference: 6 Seneca
__ Falls, Idaho: 4 Twin
__ Falls, NY: 5 Glens
Fall, The
author: Albert Camus
fall through the __: 6 cracks
Falmouth: 4 city, port, town
locale: 4 Mass.
false: 4 fake, foul, mock, sham 5 bogus, lying, not so, phony, wrong 6 ersatz, faulty, forged, hollow, made-up, off-key, phoney, pseudo, tricky, unreal, untrue 7 assumed, corrupt, crooked, devious, feigned, in error, inexact, invalid, plastic, unloyal, unsound 8 affected, cooked-up, delusive, disloyal, forsworn, guileful, improper, libelous, mistaken, mythical, recreant, specious, spurious, strained, suborned, two-faced 9 concocted, contrived, deceitful, deceptive, disguised, dishonest, erroneous, faithless, illogical, imaginary, incorrect, insincere, pretended, simulated, synthetic, trumped-up, two-timing, unfounded, unnatural 10 artificial, fabricated, fallacious, fictitious, fraudulent, groundless, ill-founded, inaccurate, inconstant, mendacious, misleading, perfidious, substitute, traitorous, unfaithful, ungrounded, unreliable, untruthful
accusation: 4 slur 5 smear 6 bum rap 7 calumny
appearance: 3 act 4 mask 5 guise 10 camouflage
at times: 3 ans. 6 answer
bear ~ witness: 3 lie 5 libel 7 perjure 9 dissemble
claim: 4 hoax 5 frame, smear 6 canard
combining form: 5 pseud- 6 pseudo-
declare ~: 4 deny 5 rebut 6 impugn, reject 7 disavow, gainsay 8 disclaim, renounce 9 repudiate 10 contradict, controvert
friend: 5 enemy, Judas, knave, snake 7 traitor 8 betrayer, informer 9 informant
front: 3 act 4 airs, mask, pose, sham, show 5 bluff, guise 6 facade 8 disguise
give a ~ impression: 4 hoke 5 belie 6 lead on
god: 4 Baal, idol 10 juggernaut
handle: 5 alias 6 anonym 7 moniker, pen name 9 pseudonym, stage name 10 nom de plume
move: 4 trip 5 boner 7 misstep, mistake
notion: 4 myth 7 fantasy 8 delusion, illusion
play ~: 4 sell 7 sell out 8 go back on
put on a ~ front: 3 lie 7 cover up, deceive, mislead 9 misdirect, misinform 10 steer wrong
report: 3 lie 4 tale 5 libel, smear 7 calumny, slander, untruth 10 imputation
show ~: 5 belie, rebut 6 debunk, refute 7 confute 10 prove wrong
witness: 4 liar
false __: 3 rib 4 aloe, card, cast, dawn, face, idol, move, pond, step 5 alarm, color, front, fruit, start, teeth, topaz 6 acacia, aralia, arrest, bottom, colors, indigo, ipecac, memory, mildew 7 horizon, vampire, witness
falsehood: 3 fib, lie 4 myth, sham, tale 5 rumor, story 6 canard, deceit, dupery 7 fiction, untruth,

whapper, whopper **8** pretense **9** deception, duplicity, fairy tale, half-truth, invention, mendacity **10** dishonesty, distortion, imputation
False Memory
author: Dean Koontz
__ false move...: 3 One
falseness: 3 lie **6** deceit **9** desertion, improbity **10** disloyalty, infidelity
False Prophet
author: Faye Kellerman
__-false test: 4 true
falsetto: 4 male **6** singer
sing ~: 5 yodel, yodle
falsification: 3 lie **4** hoax **7** forgery **8** pretense
falsified: 3 bad **5** wrong **7** corrupt, crooked **8** doctored **9** erroneous, incorrect **10** fraudulent
falsifier: 4 liar **5** faker, fraud **6** forger
falsify: 3 lie, rig **4** fake, hoke **5** color, forge, fudge, twist **6** deacon, doctor, invent, juggle, suborn **7** distort, perjure, phony up **8** disguise, misquote, misstate **9** dissemble, embroider, fabricate
falsity: 3 fib, lie **4** sham **5** error, fraud **6** canard, deceit, dupery **7** fallacy, perfidy, untruth **9** deception, duplicity, mendacity, treachery **10** dishonesty, inaccuracy, infidelity, invalidity
Falstaff: 5 opera **7** Sir John
composer: Edward Elgar, Giuseppe Verdi
friend: 3 Hal
like ~: 5 heavy, obese, stout **6** fleshy, portly, rotund, stocky **8** thickset **9** corpulent **10** abdominous
quaff: 3 ale
role: 4 Anne, Ford, Page **5** Caius **6** Fenton, Pistol **7** Quickly **8** Bardolph, Nannetta
setting: 7 England, Windsor
song: 4 aria
where ~ premiered: 5 Milan
falter: 3 lag, sag **4** balk, bomb, bust, flop, halt, limp, lose, reel, slip, trip **5** flunk, lurch, quail, waver **6** blow it, boggle, bumble, hobble, linger, recoil, teeter, topple, totter, wabble, weaken, wobble **7** blunder, founder, go under, go wrong, misstep, scruple, stagger, stammer, stumble, stutter, wash out **8** be unsure, fall flat, flounder, hang back, hesitate, lay an egg **9** hem and haw, strike out, vacillate
faltering: 4 lame, puny, weak **5** frail, shaky, wimpy **6** anemic, atonic, effete, feeble, fickle, flabby, flimsy, infirm **7** anaemic, fragile, halting, wimpish **8** delicate, helpless, hesitant, pithless, wavering **9** doddering, hesitancy, ill at ease, irregular, powerless, tentative, uncertain **10** ambivalent, hesitation, incoherent, indecisive, irresolute, vulnerable, weak-willed, wishy-washy
falteringly, move: 6 totter **7** stagger
Faltermeyer: 6 Harold
Faludi: 5 Susan
Falwell: 5 Jerry
fam.
see family
Fam and Yam
author: Edward Albee
fame: 4 mark, name, note **5** éclat, glory **6** credit, renown, repute **7** acclaim, laurels, stardom, success **8** eminence, prestige **9** celebrity, notoriety, spotlight **10** importance, notability, popularity, prominence, reputation
attain ~: 6 arrive
Fame (song)
artist: David Bowie, Irene Cara
Fame (TV drama)
cast: Debbie Allen (Lydia Grant)
Cynthia Gibb (Holly Laird)
Carlo Imperato (Danny Amatullo)
Nia Peeples (Nicole Chapman)
Gene Anthony Ray (Leroy Johnson)
famed: 5 great, noted **7** eminent, notable, storied **8** glorious, historic, laureate, renowned **9** legendary, prominent **10** celebrated, preeminent
familial: 6 lineal **9** ancestral **10** affiliated
familia member: 3 tía, tío **4** niña, niño **5** madre, padre **7** hermana, hermano
familiar: 3 old **4** cosy, cozy, dull, mate **5** aware, close, cozey, cozie, known, nervy, thick, usual **6** chatty, chummy, common, friend, genial, posted, social, versed, vulgar, wise to **7** abreast, affable, cordial, general, natural, popular, relaxed, routine **8** amicable, friendly, habitual, informal, informed, intimate, ordinary, sociable **9** au courant, cognizant, customary, easygoing, prevalent, well-known **10** accustomed, acquainted, buddy-buddy, conversant, dullsville, palsy-walsy, proverbial
be ~ with: 4 know **9** recognize
face: 6 patron **7** devotee, habitué, regular, visitor **8** customer **10** frequenter
get ~: 6 orient
less ~: 5 newer
not ~: 5 alien **7** foreign, strange, unknown, unusual **10** outlandish
not yet ~ with: 5 new to
too ~: 4 dull, flat **5** banal, corny, hokey, stale, tired, trite, vapid **6** common, jejune, old hat **7** clichéd, insipid, prosaic, routine **8** bromidic, ordinary, shopworn, timeworn **9** hackneyed **10** pedestrian, uninspired, unoriginal, warmed-over
with: 4 onto, upon **6** at home, used to **10** conversant, proficient, well-versed
familiarity: 4 ease **5** grasp, sense **6** déjà vu **7** freedom, liberty, license, mastery **8** intimacy, openness
familiarize: 5 enure, inure **6** ground, inform, orient **8** accustom, acquaint, initiate
Familiar Quotations
author: John Bartlett
famille member: 4 fils, mère, père **5** frère, oncle, soeur, tante
family: 3 ilk, kin **4** clan, kids, kind, line, race, sort, type **5** brood, class, folks, group, house, stock, young **6** lineal, litter, origin, people, strain **7** kindred, kinfolk, lineage, progeny **8** kinfolks, kinsfolk **9** household, offspring, posterity, relatives **10** hereditary
member: 2 ma, pa **3** bro, dad, kin, mom, pop, rel., sis **4** aunt, gram **6** cousin, father, gramps, mother, sister **7** brother, grandma, grandpa **8** relative
room item: 2 TV **3** VCR **5** TV set
vehicle: 3 car **4** auto **5** sedan
family __: 3 man **4** fare, hour, name, plan, room, time, tree **5** Bible, court, leave, style **6** circle, doctor, values
__ family: 5 birth, first, heath, joint, royal **7** blended, nuclear
__-family: 6 single
Family (ABC drama)
cast: Meredith Baxter-Birney (Nancy Maitland)
James Broderick (Doug Lawrence)
Gary Frank (Willie Lawrence)
Kristy McNichol (Buddy Lawrence)
Sada Thompson (Kate Lawrence)
Family __: 3 Man **4** Feud, Plot, Ties **6** Affair, Circle, Circus
Family __, A: 6 Affair **7** Fortune
Family __, The: 3 Man, Way **6** Circle, Moskat **7** Arsenal, Reunion
__ Family: 4 Holy **5** Mama's, Poppy, We Are
Family Affair (1971 song)
artist: Sly and the Family Stone
Family Affair (CBS sitcom)
cast: Sebastian Cabot (Mr. French)
Kathy Garver (Cissy)
Anissa Jones (Buffy)
Brian Keith (Bill Davis)
Johnnie Whitaker (Jody)
dog: 6 Oliver
Family Arsenal, The
author: Paul Theroux
Family Business (1989 film)
cast: Matthew Broderick, Sean Connery, Dustin Hoffman
director: Sidney Lumet
Family Circle, The
author: André Maurois
Family Circus, The: 5 comic **7** cartoon
artist: Bil Keane
cat: 8 Kittycat
character: 3 Bil **4** Thel **5** Billy, Dolly, Jeffy
dog: 3 Sam **5** Barfy
mischief-maker: 5 Not Me
Family Feud: 8 game show
host: Louie Anderson, Ray Combs, Richard Dawson, Richard Karn
Family Man (1983 song)
artist: Hall and Oates
Family Man, The (2000 film)
cast: Nicolas Cage, Don Cheadle, Téa Leoni
director: Brett Ratner
Family Matters
kid: 5 Urkel
Family Moskat, The
author: Isaac Bashevis Singer
Family of Charles IV
artist: Francisco de Goya
Family Plot (1976 film)
cast: Karen Black, Bruce Dern, William Devane, Barbara Harris
director: Alfred Hitchcock
Family Reunion, The
author: T.S. Eliot
__ Family Robinson: 5 Swiss
__ Family Singers: 5 Trapp
family-size: 3 big **5** giant, jumbo, large
Family Stone, The (2005 film)
cast: Claire Danes, Diane Keaton, Rachel McAdams
__ Family, The: 3 Abe **5** Hogan, Royal **6** Addams **7** Aldrich
Family Ties (NBC sitcom)
cast: Justine Bateman (Mallory Keaton)
Meredith Baxter-Birney (Elyse Keaton)
Michael J. Fox (Alex P. Keaton)
Michael Gross (Steve Keaton)
Tina Yothers (Jennifer Keaton)
__ Family Values: 6 Addams
famine: 4 lack, need, want **6** dearth **7** paucity, poverty
opposite: 5 feast
relief: 4 food
famine-stricken: 5 unfed
famish: 6 starve
famished: 5 empty, unfed **6** hungry **7** peckish, starved **8** edacious, esurient, ravenous, starving **9** insatiate, voracious
famishment: 6 hunger **7** edacity **8** appetite, voracity **9** appetence, esurience
Famke: 7 Janssen
famous: 4 star **5** great, known, noted **6** fabled, signal **7** eminent, leading, notable, popular, salient, storied **8** glorious, historic, immortal, laureate, renowned **9** acclaimed, legendary, memorable, notorious, prominent, topflight, well-known **10** celebrated, noteworthy, preeminent, proverbial, publicized, remarkable
become ~: 6 arrive **7** succeed
person: 4 lion, star **7** notable **9** celebrity, dignitary
Famous Amos: 6 cookie
competitor: ***see*** cookie manufacturer
Famous Dave's
rival: ***see*** restaurant chain
famously: 4 well **7** greatly
fan: 3 nut **4** buff **5** fiend, freak, hound, lover, whiff **6** addict, adorer, blower, cooler, maniac, rooter, unfold **7** admirer, air-cool, cool off, devotee, groupie, support **8** adherent, disciple, follower, partisan **9** propeller, spectator, strike out, supporter **10** aficionado, enthusiast, ventilator
be a ~: 4 root
club focus: 4 idol
combining form: 5 rhipi- **6** rhipid- **7** rhipido- **8** flabelli-
creation: 6 breeze
disenchanted ~: 5 booer

display: 4 wave
ender: 3 dom, jet 4 fare, tail, wort 5 light
jazz ~: 3 cat 6 bopper, hepcat
like a ~ belt: 4 taut 5 tight
mag: 4 zine
noise: 3 rah 5 cheer
opposite: 5 hater
out: 6 expand, spread, unfold 7 scatter 8 disperse
part: 5 blade, grill, motor
setting: 3 low 4 high 5 on low 6 medium
sound: 4 whir 5 whirr

fan __: 3 out 4 belt, club, mail, palm, roof, worm 5 delta, vault 6 letter, window

fan-__: 3 tan 6 tailed

__ fan: 3 sea 4 tail 7 ceiling, exhaust

fanatic: 3 bug, nut 5 bigot, crank, demon, fiend, freak, ultra 6 addict, daemon, daimon, maniac, zealot 7 devotee, groupie, radical, touched, zealous 8 activist, inflamer, militant, partisan, ultraist 9 demagogue, extremist, sectarian 10 aficionado, enthusiast
ender: 3 ism
feeling: 4 zeal

fanatical: 3 mad 4 avid, wild 5 crazy, fiery, manic, rabid, ultra 6 crazed, fervid, gung-ho, raving 7 burning, extreme, fervent, intense, radical, rampant, zealous 8 dogmatic, frenzied, obsessed, wild-eyed 9 credulous, emotional, obsessive, obstinate, possessed 10 dogmatical, headstrong, immoderate, intolerant, prejudiced

fanatically: 4 very 7 greatly, rabidly 9 extremely, zealously

fanaticism: 4 zeal 6 frenzy 8 zealotry 9 contumacy, extremism, injustice, intensity, monomania, obstinacy, prejudice 10 chauvinism, dedication, enthusiasm, narrowness, partiality

fancied: 5 liked, loved 7 desired 9 imaginary, preferred

fancier: 5 liker 6 rooter 7 admirer, devotee 8 follower

fanciful: 4 tall 5 ideal 6 dreamy, irreal, quaint, unreal 8 baseless, delusive, illusive, illusory, quixotic 9 dreamlike, fairy-tale, idealized, imaginary, vagarious, visionary, whimsical 10 capricious, chimerical, fictitious, improbable, quixotical

fanciness: 4 chic 5 swank, vogue

fancy: 3 yen 4 chic, fine, haut, idea, lacy, like, love, posh, rich, urge, want, whim, will, wish 5 adore, covet, crave, dream, enjoy, favor, gaudy, haute, jazzy, quirk, ritzy, showy, swank, taste, think 6 chichi, choice, deluxe, desire, dressy, flashy, flossy, frilly, glitzy, lavish, liking, ornate, prefer, reckon, relish, spiffy, swanky, vagary 7 adorned, believe, caprice, care for, chimera, dream of, dream up, elegant, for show, imagine, impulse, opulent, passion, picture, realize, suppose, surmise, think up, thought, wish for 8 chimaera, crotchet, daydream, envisage, envision, fondness, penchant, pleasure, yearn for, yearning 9 decorated, elaborate, expensive, hankering, intricate, luxuriant, luxurious, obsession, pipe dream, sumptuous, visualize 10 conceive of, custom-made, decorative, ornamental, ornamented, partiality, preference, propensity, woolgather
affair: 2 do 4 ball, bash, gala 7 banquet, shindig 8 function, wingding
Dan: 4 dude 5 swell 10 jack-a-dandy
digs: 5 manor 6 estate 7 chateau, mansion 10 plantation
display: 4 ritz
dress: 6 finery 9 caparison
fabric: 4 lamé, silk 5 satin
flight of ~: 6 revery 7 reverie
not ~: 5 bleak, plain, stark 6 barren, severe 7 austere 9 unadorned
passing ~: 3 fad 4 rage, urge, whim 5 craze, mania, quirk 6 notion, vagary 7 caprice, impulse 8 crotchet
tickle one's ~: 5 amuse, cheer 6 divert, please, tickle 7 delight 9 entertain, titillate

fancy __: 3 Dan 4 dive, fern 5 dress 6 diving

fancy-__: 4 free 5 pants

__ fancy: 7 passing

Fancy __!: 4 that

Fancy Feast: 7 cat food
alternative: *see* pet food brand

Fancy Free: 6 ballet
choreographer: 7 Robbins
composer: Leonard Bernstein

Fancy that!: 3 gee

fandangle: 5 frill 9 adornment 10 decoration

fandango: 5 dance
instrument: 6 guitar
kin: 6 bolero 9 malaguena

fandom: 9 followers

fane: 6 church, temple

Faneuil Hall
locale: 6 Boston

fanfare: 3 ado 4 pomp 5 blare, éclat, noise, tusch 6 hoopla, hoorah, hooray, hurrah, hurray, parade 7 tantara 8 ballyhoo, flourish 9 publicity
verbal ~: 4 ta-da 5 ta-dah

Fanfare for Fred
composer: PDQ Bach

Fanfare for the Common Cold
composer: PDQ Bach

Fanfare for the Common Man
composer: Aaron Copland

fanfaron: 6 gascon 7 boaster, fanfare 8 blowhard, braggart 9 big talker

fanfaronade: 6 hot air 7 big talk, bluster, bombast, bravado 8 boasting, bragging 9 gasconade

fang: 5 tooth 7 incisor

fanion: 4 flag

Fannie: 5 Flagg, Hurst 6 Farmer

Fannie __: 3 Mae

Fanning: 5 Shawn 6 Dakota

Fanny: 5 Brice 6 Burney, Kemble
author: Erica Jong

Fanny and Alexander (1983 film)
director: Ingmar Bergman

Fanny's First Play
author: George Bernard Shaw

fanon: 4 cape 5 orale 7 maniple

Fanon: 6 Frantz

fans: 6 circle 8 groupies 9 entourage, followers, following

Fanshawe
author: Nathaniel Hawthorne

Fansler: 4 Kate

Fanta: 9 soft drink
alternative: *see* soft drink

fantabulous
see wonderful

fantail: 4 bird 6 pigeon 7 warbler

fan-tan: 4 game 6 sevens 8 card game

fantasia: 5 music

Fantasia
creature: 4 faun
dancer: 5 hippo
hippo's wear in ~: 4 tutu

fantasist: 7 dreamer 8 escapist, idealist 10 daydreamer

fantasize: 4 moon 5 dream 7 imagine, picture 8 daydream, envision 10 woolgather

fantastic: 3 odd 4 A-one, eery, huge 5 crazy, eerie, great, super, weird 6 absurd, atypic, exotic, far-out, freaky, groovy, irreal, quirky, superb, unreal 7 awesome, bizarre, deviant, extreme, massive, oddball, offbeat, strange, surreal, uncanny, unusual 8 aberrant, abnormal, atypical, enormous, fabulous, freakish, peculiar, romantic, splendid, terrific, uncommon 9 anomalous, delicious, different, divergent, eccentric, excellent, fictional, first-rate, grotesque, humongous, imaginary, irregular, laughable, ludicrous, marvelous, monstrous, whimsical, wonderful, wunderbar 10 artificial, capricious, chimerical, far-fetched, fictitious, first-class, incredible, irrational, monumental, outlandish, out of sight, phenomenal, prodigious, ridiculous, stupendous, tremendous, unfamiliar, unorthodox
trip the light ~: 4 step 5 dance, party, rumba, tango, waltz 6 cha-cha, rhumba 7 cut a rug

Fantastic Four (2005 film)
cast: Jessica Alba, Michael Chiklis, Chris Evans, Ioan Gruffudd

Fantasticks, The: 4 film 7 musical
character: 4 Matt 5 Luisa 7 El Gallo
composer: Tom Jones, Harvey Schmidt

Fantasticks, The (1995 film)
director: Michael Ritchie

Fantastic Mr. Fox
author: Roald Dahl

Fantastic Voyage (1966 film)
cast: Stephen Boyd, Edmond O'Brien, Donald Pleasence, Raquel Welch
director: Richard Fleischer
route: 5 aorta

Fantastic Voyage (1994 song)
artist: Coolio

Fantastik: 7 cleaner
alternative: 5 Brite, Lysol 6 Top Job 7 Lestoil, Mr. Clean, Pine Sol 9 Step Saver

fantasy: 4 myth 5 dream 6 mirage, revery, vision 7 chimera, figment, reverie, romance 8 chimaera, daydream, delusion, illusion 9 dreamland, fairy tale, invention, pipe dream, unreality 10 apparition
ender: 4 land

Fantasy (1995 song)
artist: Mariah Carey

Fantasy Island (ABC drama)
cast: Ricardo Montalban (Mr. Roarke)
Hervé Villechaize (Tattoo)
prop: 3 lei
sighting: 5 plane

Fante home: 5 Ghana 6 Africa

Fan, The (1996 film)
cast: Ellen Barkin, Robert De Niro, Wesley Snipes
director: Tony Scott

__ fan tutte: 4 Così

fanzine: 3 mag

FAO __: 7 Schwarz

far: 3 off 4 much, very 5 miles, quite 6 remote, way off 7 distant, extreme, foreign, greatly, outside 8 a long way, outlying, very much 9 a ways away, decidedly, extremely 10 out of reach
afield: 4 away, awry 5 amiss 6 astray 9 off course 10 off the mark
and away: 5 truly 6 easily, surely 8 of course 9 certainly, decidedly, doubtless, expressly, obviously 10 absolutely, by all means, definitely, positively, undeniably
and wide: 6 afield 7 broadly, largely 10 everywhere
apart: 3 few 4 rare 6 meager, scarce, seldom, sparse 7 limited, unusual 8 isolated, sporadic, uncommon 9 irregular, scattered, spasmodic, uncrowded 10 infrequent, occasional, sporadical, unfrequent
as ~ as: 4 up to 5 until
away: 6 remote 7 oversea 8 overseas
by ~: 6 easily 7 clearly, plainly 8 very much 9 hands down, obviously
combining form: 3 tel- 4 tele-, telo-
cry: 7 long way 8 distance
cry from: 6 unlike
down: 4 deep 6 buried 9 cavernous
ender: 4 away 6 seeing 7 sighted
few and ~ between: 4 rare, thin 5 scant 6 scanty, scarce, skimpy, sparse, spotty 7 unusual 8 uncommon 9 scattered 10 hard to find, infrequent
go ~: 4 last 5 get on 7 advance, succeed 8 get ahead, progress
go as ~ as: 5 reach
gone: 3 mad 6 in love 7 charmed, smitten 8 beguiled, besotted, obsessed 9 bewitched, possessed 10 captivated, crazy about, enraptured, fascinated, infatuated, spellbound
go so ~: 6 gather, take it 7 presume, suppose, surmise

go too ~: 4 hype 6 overdo, pile on 7 belabor, lay it on, stretch 8 overplay 9 overstate 10 exaggerate
look ~ and wide: 5 scour
near and ~: 7 all over 9 all around 10 everywhere
not ~: 4 near, nigh 5 close, handy 6 at hand, nearby 7 close by 8 adjacent, next door, proximal 9 alongside 10 convenient, near-at-hand
on the ~ side of: 6 across 7 athwart
partner: 4 away, near, wide
point: 3 end
push too ~: 3 tax 4 task, tire, wear 6 impose, strain, weaken 7 oppress, wear out 8 overload, overtask, overwork 9 weigh down 10 overburden
so ~: 3 yet, YTD 5 as yet, by now 6 to date 7 till now, up to now 8 hitherto, until now 10 heretofore
thus ~: 8 until now
far __: 3 cry 5 piece 6 afield
far __ from me: 4 be it
far-__: 3 off, out 4 gone 5 famed, flung, point 7 fetched
__ far: 4 thus
...far __ can see: 3 as I
Far __: 4 East, West 7 Eastern, Islands, Tortuga, Western
Far __, The: 4 Side 5 Field 7 Country
Faracy: 9 Stephanie
Faraday, Michael: 9 physicist, scientist
far and __: 4 away, near, wide
Far and Away (1992 film)
cast: Tom Cruise, Thomas Gibson, Nicole Kidman
director: Ron Howard
Far and Near
author: Pearl S. Buck
farandole: 5 dance
faraway: 4 lost 6 yonder 7 distant, foreign, strange, unknown 8 outlying
far be it __ me: 4 from
...far beyond those of __ men: 6 mortal
farce: 4 camp, joke, play, sham 5 drama, humor, put-on 6 comedy, parody, satire 7 burlesk, charade, mockery 8 nonsense, pretense, ridicule, travesty 9 absurdity, burlesque, slapstick 10 buffoonery, caricature
farceur: 3 wag, wit 4 zany 5 clown, comic, joker 7 pierrot 8 comedian, funnyman, kibitzer
farcical: 4 rich 5 droll, funny, silly 6 jocose 7 amusing, comical, jocular, satiric, waggish 8 humorous 9 facetious, laughable, ludicrous, satirical, whimsical 10 ridiculous
fardel: 6 bundle, burden
fare: 2 do, go 4 diet, eats, food, grub, live, meal, meat, menu, pass, ride, toll 5 exist, get by, get on, meals, price, rider 6 charge, income, manage, tariff 7 aliment, cuisine, edibles, expense, make out, passage, proceed, rations, turn out, victual, vittles 8 eatables, get along, progress, victuals 9 passenger 10 gastronomy, provisions, sustenance
bill of ~: 4 menu 5 carte, table
bland ~: 3 pap
carrier: 3 cab 4 hack, taxi 7 taxicab
counter: 5 meter
ender: 4 well
reduced ~: 4 diet
starter: 3 air, car, fan, war 4 work 5 field, thoro 8 thorough
thee well: 3 bye 4 ciao, ta ta 5 adieu, adios, aloha, later, peace 6 bye-bye, shalom, sholom, so long 7 cheerio, goodbye 8 sayonara 9 Abyssinia
well: 7 prosper 8 hit it big
fare-__-well: 3 you 4 thee
__ fare: 3 air 6 family
Far East
see Asia
Farentino: 5 James 6 Debrah
Farentino, James
spouse: Elizabeth Ashley, Debrah Farentino, Michele Lee
farer: 7 voyager 8 traveler, vagabond
starter: 3 sea, way 5 space
__ fare-thee-well: 3 to a
farewell: 3 bye 4 ciao, exit, ta ta 5 adieu, adios, aloha, congé, later, leave, peace 6 bye-bye, congée, shalom, sholom, so long 7 cheerio, goodbye, parting, sendoff 8 sayonara 9 Abyssinia, departure 10 separation
bid ~: 4 wave
in French: 5 adieu
in Hawaiian: 5 aloha
in Italian: 4 ciao
in Latin: 3 ave 4 vale
in Spanish: 5 adios
Farewell, My Lovely
author: Raymond Chandler
Farewell My Youth
writer: Arnold Bax
Farewell Symphony
composer: Joseph Haydn
Farewell to Arms, A: 4 film 5 novel
author: Ernest Hemingway
cast: Gary Cooper, Helen Hayes, Adolphe Menjou
character: 5 Piani 6 Ettore 7 Moretti
farfalle: 5 pasta 7 bow ties, noodles
alternative: *see* pasta
__ far, far better...: 5 It is a
far-fetched: 4 tall 7 dubious 8 strained 9 fantastic, illogical, recondite, unnatural 10 improbable, incredible, suspicious
far-flung: 3 big 4 vast, wide 5 broad, roomy 6 global, remote 7 distant 8 extended, outlying, spacious, sweeping 9 capacious, expansive, extensive 10 large-scale, widespread
Far From Heaven (2002 film)
cast: Patricia Clarkson, Dennis Haysbert, Julianne Moore, Dennis Quaid
Far From Over (1983 song)
artist: Frank Stallone
Far From the Madding Crowd: 4 film 5 novel
author: Thomas Hardy
cast: Alan Bates, Julie Christie, Peter Finch, Terence Stamp
character: 3 Jan, Oak 4 Troy 5 Liddy, Lydia
director: John Schlesinger
Fargo: 4 city, town 5 Donna
locale: 4 N. Dak.
Fargo (1996 film)
cast: Steve Buscemi, William H. Macy, Frances McDormand, Harve Presnell
director: Joel Coen
__ Fargo: 5 Wells
Fargo, Donna
song: Funny Face (1972)
far-gone: 4 shot, worn 5 spent, tired, weary 6 bushed, dished, used up 7 drained, wearied, worn out 8 depleted, dog-tired, fatigued, tired out, weakened 9 enervated, exhausted 10 dissipated
Far Hills NJ org.: 4 USGA
farina: 4 meal 5 flour, grain 6 cereal, starch
Farina: 6 Dennis
farinaceous: 5 mealy 6 floury
faring starter: 3 sea, way
Faris: 4 Anna
Farley: 5 Chris, Mowat 6 Walter 7 Granger
Farlow: 3 Tal
farm: 4 land, plow, till, work 5 abode, croft, dairy, plant, ranch, rural 6 grange, spread 8 property 9 cultivate, homestead, sharecrop 10 plantation
animal: 3 ant, cow, ewe, hen, hog, pig, ram, sow, tom 4 boar, calf, foal, goat, lamb, mare, mule 5 chick, horse, piggy, swine 6 heifer, piggie, pullet 7 chicken
animals: 4 oxen 5 stock 6 cattle
baby: 4 calf, foal, lamb 5 chick 6 piglet
barrier: 4 rail
basket: 4 skep
building: 4 barn, shed, silo
bundle: 5 sheaf
call: 5 sooey
connection: 4 yoke
dept.: 3 Agr.
do a ~ job: 3 hoe, sow 4 plow, reap 6 ensile
enclosure: 3 pen, sty 6 corral, pigpen, pigsty
ender: 4 land, yard 5 house, stead, woman, women
equipment maker: 5 Deere
fat ~: 3 spa 6 resort
feed: 4 mash 6 forage
fit to ~: 6 arable 7 fertile 8 plowable, tillable 10 cultivable
gate: 5 stile
give birth on the ~: 4 yean 5 calve
horse: 6 dobbin
implement: 3 hoe 4 fork, plow 5 churn 6 harrow
machine: 4 trac 5 baler, sower 6 seeder 7 combine, tractor
mother: 3 ewe, hen, sow 4 mare
package: 4 bale
product: 4 corn, crop, eggs, milk, oats 5 wheat 6 barley 7 sorghum
show: 4 fair
small ~: 5 croft
soil: 4 dirt, land, loam 5 earth
sound: 3 baa, moo 4 oink 6 heehaw
South American ~: 5 finca
Soviet ~: 5 artel
trough: 6 feeder
unit: 4 acre, bale
vehicle: 4 cart, dray, wain 5 wagon
water supply: 4 well
worker: 4 hand
farm __: 3 out 4 belt, club, hand, team 6 system
__ farm: 3 ant, fat, fur 4 bird, dirt, fish, tank, tree, work 5 dairy, stock, strip, stump, truck 6 county, oyster
...farm, __: 5 E-I-E-I-O
Farm __: 3 Aid 6 Bureau
farmed, not: 6 fallow
farmer: 4 Abel, hick 5 sower 6 cheese, grower, plower, reaper, rustic, tiller 7 hayseed, planter 8 gardener 9 harvester 10 agronomist, cornhusker, cultivator
addr.: 3 RFD
concern: 4 soil
friend: 4 rain
group: 4 co-op 6 Grange
in Dutch: 4 Boer
name meaning ~: 5 Bauer 6 George 7 Granger
need: 3 hoe 4 plow, rake, seed
often: 4 hoer 5 sower
org.: 3 ADA
place: 4 dell
wake-up call: 4 crow
farmer __: 6 cheese
farmer __ dell: 5 in the
__ farmer: 4 dirt 6 tenant
Farmer: 4 Gary 5 James 6 Fannie 7 Frances
Farmer in the Dell, The: 4 song
character: 3 cat, rat 4 wife 5 nurse 6 cheese
syllables: 4 hi-ho
Farmer, James org.: 4 CORE
farmers' __: 6 market
Farmers
competitor: *see* insurance company
Farmers' Allminax humorist: 4 Shaw
Farmer's Almanac fare: 6 trivia 7 weather 8 forecast
__ Farmers of America: 6 Future
Farmer Takes a Wife, The
author: Marc Connelly
farmhand: 5 baler 6 worker 7 laborer
farming: 3 agr. 7 growing, reaping, seeding, tillage 8 agronomy 9 geoponics, threshing 10 harvesting
agency: 4 USDA
combining form: 4 agri-, agro-
deg.: 3 MSA 4 M.Agr.
major: 5 aggie
science of ~: 11 agriculture
unfit for ~: 3 dry 4 arid, sere 5 dusty 6 barren, desert, torrid 7 bone-dry, parched 9 waterless
__ farming: 4 tank 5 ocean, strip 7 dryland
farmland: 3 lea, ley 4 soil 5 field
Mayan ~: 5 milpa
unit: 4 acre
farmlike: 5 rural 6 rustic 7 bucolic 8 pastoral
farmstead: 4 land 5 ranch 6 estate 7 acreage 8 hacienda 10 plantation

Farm, The
artist: Joan Miró
__ far niente: 5 dolce
Farnum: 6 Dustin **7** William
faro: 4 game **8** card game
Faroes: 4 isls. **5** isles **7** islands
far-off: 4 away **5** faint **6** dreamy, remote **7** distant, unknown **8** outlying
Far Off Place, A: 4 book, film
author: Laurens Van der Post
cast: Ethan Randall, Maximilian Schell, Reese Witherspoon
Faron: 5 Young
Farouk's father: 4 Fuad
far-out
see bizarre, wonderful
Farr: 5 Jamie **7** Felicia
farrago: 4 hash, mess **6** jumble, medley **7** mélange **8** mishmash **9** potpourri **10** hodgepodge, miscellany, salmagundi
Farragut: 5 David **7** admiral
org.: 3 USN
Farrah: 7 Fawcett
ex: 3 Lee
Farrar: 8 Margaret **9** Geraldine
__ Farrar: 4 Brat
Farrar, Geraldine: 4 diva **6** singer **7** soprano
specialty: 5 opera
far-reaching: 3 big **4** deep, vast, wide **5** broad, roomy **7** general **8** pandemic, profound, spacious, sweeping **9** capacious, expansive, extensive, momentous, wholesale **10** widespread
view: 5 sweep, vista **8** panorama
Farrell: 4 Mike **5** Colin, Terry **6** Eileen, Glenda, Sharon **7** Charles, Suzanne
Farrell, Charles: 5 actor
TV: My Little Margie
Farrell, Eileen: 6 singer **7** soprano
specialty: 5 opera
Farrell, James T.: 6 writer
work: Studs Lonigan
Farrell, Mike: 5 actor
spouse: Shelley Fabares
Farrell, Suzanne: 6 dancer **8** danseuse **9** ballerina
Farrelly: 5 Bobby, Peter
Farr, Felicia: 7 actress
spouse: Jack Lemmon
farrier: 5 smith
did a ~ job: 4 shod
item: 4 rasp, shoe **5** anvil **9** horseshoe
tool: 4 rasp
Farr, Jamie feature: 4 nose
farrow: 3 pig **6** litter
Farrow: 3 Mia **4** John, Tisa
Farrow, Mia: 7 actress
film: Alice (1990)
Another Woman (1988)
Broadway Danny Rose (1984)
Crimes and Misdemeanors (1989)
The Great Gatsby (1974)
Hannah and Her Sisters (1986)
Husbands and Wives (1992)
A Midsummer Night's Sex Comedy (1982)
The Purple Rose of Cairo (1985)
Radio Days (1987)
Rosemary's Baby (1968)
Secret Ceremony (1968)
See No Evil (1971)
Shadows and Fog (1992)
Zelig (1983)
spouse: Woody Allen, André Previn, Frank Sinatra
TV: Peyton Place
farseeing: 4 keen, wise **6** astute, shrewd **7** prudent **8** cautious, discreet, watchful **9** astucious, prescient **10** longheaded
Far Side, The: 5 comic **7** cartoon
animal: 3 cow
artist: Gary Larson
farsighted: 4 wise **6** shrewd **7** prudent **8** rational, sensible **9** judicious, prescient, provident, sagacious **10** cool-headed, discerning, perceptive
farsightedness: 6 vision
Farsi speaker: 5 Irani
farther: 4 more **5** other **6** yonder **7** outside
ender: 4 most
__ farther: 4 go no
farthest: 3 ult. **4** last **6** utmost **7** extreme, outside **8** ultimate **9** uttermost
point: 3 end **5** brink, limit **6** apogee, border, fringe **7** extreme **8** frontier **9** extremity, periphery
farthing: 4 coin **5** money
fasces: 4 rods **5** staff **6** bundle
fascia: 4 band, belt **8** hair band
fascinate: 4 bait, draw, grip, lure, take **5** charm, rivet, tempt **6** absorb, allure, appeal, arrest, dazzle, disarm, enamor, engage, entice, excite, ravish, thrill **7** attract, beguile, bewitch, delight, enchant, engross, enthral, inthral **8** enthrall, entrance, interest, inthrall, intrigue, transfix **9** captivate, enrapture, hypnotize, infatuate, mesmerize, overpower, overwhelm, spellbind, stimulate, tantalize, titillate, transport **10** intoxicate
fascinated: 4 agog, rapt **6** enrapt **7** all eyes, far gone, smitten **8** held fast **9** attentive, attracted, bewitched, delighted, enchanted, engrossed, entranced, impressed **10** captivated, enraptured, enthralled, hypnotized, infatuated, interested, mesmerized, spellbound, tantalized, titillated, transfixed
be ~ with: 4 love
by: 4 into **6** in love **10** crazy about
fascinating: 5 juicy **7** amazing, lovable, winning, winsome **8** inviting, loveable, magnetic, readable, romantic, striking, tempting **10** magnetical
Fascinating Rhythm
composer: George Gershwin, Ira Gershwin
fascination: 4 lure, pull **5** charm, magic, mania, spell **6** allure, appeal, hang-up, wonder **7** charism, lovable, romance **8** charisma, loveable, mystique **9** immersion, magnetism, obsession
fascinator: 5 scarf
fascism: 7 tyranny **9** autocracy, brutality, despotism **10** oppression
fashion: 3 cut, fit, ton, way **4** chic, form, kind, look, make, mode, mold, rage, sort, vein, work **5** adapt, build, craft, draft, erect, forge, frame, model, retro, shape, stamp, style, trend, usage, vogue **6** adjust, cook up, create, custom, design, devise, figure, invent, make up, manner, method, tailor **7** costume, dream up, in thing, pattern, prepare, produce **8** assemble, contrive, demeanor, practice **9** construct, etiquette, fabricate, sculpture **10** convention, dernier cri, stereotype
accessory: 3 bag, boa, tie, wig **5** scarf
after a ~: 6 in a way **7** somehow
brief ~: 3 fad
British ~ plate: 4 toff
figure: 5 model **8** designer **9** couturier
in ~: 3 hot **4** chic **5** smart, swank **6** dapper, dressy, modish, swanky, trendy **7** à la mode, current, dashing, elegant, popular, stylish, voguish **8** up-to-date **9** au courant **10** all the rage
initials: 3 YSL **4** DKNY
in this ~: 4 thus **6** like so, thusly **7** that way
item: 3 bag, tie, wig **5** A-line, scarf, skirt **6** blouse
latest ~: 10 dernier cri
length: 4 maxi, midi, mini
mecca: 5 Paris
name: 4 Dior, Oleg **5** Karan, Klein, label **6** Lauren **7** Cassini, Versace
out of ~: 3 old **5** dated, passé **6** démodé, old hat **7** has-been **8** obsolete **9** hackneyed, out-of-date
plate: 3 fop **4** dude **5** dandy **7** coxcomb
plate opposite: 5 frump
fashion __: 5 plate **9** statement
__ fashion: 3 in a **4** high **6** after a **7** Bristol
fashionable: 3 hep, hip, hot, mod, new, now **4** chic, posh, tony **5** class, natty, sharp, sleek, smart, swank, swell, swish, toney, vogue **6** chichi, classy, dressy, flossy, modish, rakish, snappy, swanky, trendy, with it **7** à la mode, current, dashing, elegant, genteel, in style, in vogue, popular, stylish, voguish **8** handsome, up-to-date **10** all the rage
group: 6 jet set
__-fashioned: 3 new, old **4** full
__ Fashioned Love Song: 5 An Old
fashioner: 5 maker **7** creator, deviser, planner **8** designer, engineer, inventer, inventor **9** architect, contriver **10** mastermind, originator
Fassbinder: 6 Rainer
fast: 3 PDQ, set **4** firm, held, lewd, sure, true **5** apace, brisk, close, fixed, fleet, glued, hasty, loose, loyal, quick, rapid, sharp, swift, tight **6** ardent, firmly, flying, presto, pronto, racing, rakish, secure, snappy, speedy, stable, steady, strong, sudden **7** abiding, abstain, cursory, dashing, express, fixedly, fleetly, hastily, hurried, instant, quickly, raffish, rapidly, staunch, swiftly, tightly **8** attached, constant, faithful, fastened, fleeting, flitting, full tilt, go hungry, in a flash, in a jiffy, in no time, keep from, promptly, resolute, securely, spanking, speedily, true blue, unbroken, uncurbed **9** breakneck, hurriedly, immovable, immovably, like a shot, posthaste, steadfast **10** double-time, harefooted, hypersonic, in high gear, profligate, supersonic, ultrasonic, unwavering
and loose: 4 rash, wild **5** hasty **6** amoral, unruly, unwise **7** corrupt, immoral **8** careless, feckless, headlong, heedless, reckless **9** corrupted, foolhardy, imprudent, negligent **10** incautious, indiscreet
approaching: 4 near, nigh **5** close **6** at hand, coming, in view **7** brewing, in store, looming, pending **8** imminent, in the air, on the way **9** impending, in the wind
break ~: 3 eat
car: 2 GT **5** racer **6** hot rod
combining form: 5 tachy-
ender: 4 back, ball
exit: 3 lam
flyer: 3 jet, SST
follower: 6 Easter
food: 4 nosh **5** snack
get no place ~: 3 lag **4** drag, flag, idle, limp, loaf, loll, plod, poke **5** dally, delay, tarry **6** dabble, dawdle, diddle, loiter **7** fall off, fritter, slacken **8** hang back, straggle **9** waste time **10** dilly-dally, lose ground, mess around, wait around
get there ~: 3 run **4** dash, rush, tear, whiz, zoom **5** hurry, speed, whisk **6** hasten, scurry **7** scamper
go ~: 3 fly, hie, run, zip **4** dash, race, tear, zoom **5** hurry, scoot, speed **6** hot-rod, hurtle, hustle, sprint
go too ~: 4 rush, tear, whiz, zoom **5** speed **6** barrel
held ~: 4 rapt **7** charmed, gripped **8** absorbed, beguiled, immersed **9** delighted, engrossed, entranced **10** captivated, enraptured, enthralled, fascinated, hypnotized, spellbound
hold ~: 5 cling, seize, stick **6** adhere, cohere **7** enchain
hold ~ to: 4 obey **6** follow **7** abide by, observe, respect **10** comply with
in music: 5 mosso
make ~: 3 fix, peg, tie **4** bind, lock, moor, nail **5** hitch, latch, rivet, truss
not as ~: 6 slower
one: 4 hoax **5** cheat, fraud **6** dupery, humbug **7** swindle **8** trickery **9** deception
on one's feet: 5 agile, fleet
on the uptake: 3 apt **5** adept, savvy, sharp, smart **6** adroit, astute, bright, clever, cogent,

gifted, shrewd **7** capable **8** incisive **9** observant
partner: 5 loose
pull a ~ one: 3 con **4** fool **5** cheat, outdo, trick **6** delude, outwit **7** deceive, defraud, mislead, swindle **8** flimflam, hoodwink, outsmart **9** bamboozle
starter: 5 stead
talk: 4 bull, bunk, jive **5** prate **6** banter, hot air, humbug, patter **7** baloney, blarney, blather **8** malarkey **9** banana oil **10** applesauce, balderdash
time: 4 Lent
too ~: 4 rash **5** brash, hasty **6** abrupt, madcap **8** careless, headlong, heedless, pell-mell, reckless, slapdash **9** foolhardy, impetuous, impulsive
traveler: 7 bad news
fast __: 3 day, ice, one **4** buck, food, lane, time **5** break, track **6** asleep, dollar, motion, worker **7** forward
fast __ get-out: 5 as all
fast-__: 3 cut **4** talk **5** count **6** moving
__ fast: 4 make
__ fast!: 5 Not so
__ fast and loose: 4 play
Fast and the Furious, The (2001 film)
cast: Jordana Brewster, Vin Diesel, Michelle Rodriguez, Paul Walker
director: Rob Cohen
fastball: 4 heat **5** pitch **6** heater
fast-breeder __: 7 reactor
Fast Car (1988 song)
artist: Tracy Chapman
Fast Eddie: 6 Felson
need: 3 cue **5** chalk, stick
portrayer: Paul Newman
shot: 5 carom, massé
fasten: 3 fix, peg, pin, set, sew, tag, tie, zip **4** band, belt, bind, bolt, bond, clip, do up, glue, hook, join, knot, lace, link, lock, moor, nail, seal, shut, snap, tack, tape, weld, yoke **5** affix, annex, brace, chain, clamp, clasp, close, hitch, infix, latch, leash, paste, rivet, screw, stick, tie up, truss, zip up **6** adhere, anchor, append, attach, batten, begird, buckle, button, cement, cleave, clinch, cohere, couple, hook on, hook up, lace up, secure, solder, staple, tether **7** connect, mortice, mortise, tie down, tighten **8** button up **9** stabilize, thumbtack
again: 5 repeg, repin, retie, rezip
at sea: 4 lash **5** belay
securely: 4 bolt, moor **5** rivet, tie up **6** batten
fastened: 4 fast, firm **5** tight **6** secure
fastener: 3 nut, tie **4** bolt, bond, brad, hook, lock, nail, snap, stud, T-nut **5** catch, clamp, clasp, latch, rivet, screw, T-bolt, U-bolt **6** buckle, button, cap nut, Velcro **7** bracket **10** attachment, hook and eye
door ~: 4 bolt, hasp, hook **5** latch
metal ~: 4 bolt, brad, nail **5** screw, U-bolt
needing two nuts: 5 U-bolt
__ fastener: 3 zip **4** snap **5** press, slide
fasteners: 8 hardware
fastening: 3 tie **4** link, lock **5** clasp, latch **8** vinculum **10** attachment, connection
Faster __ speeding bullet: 5 than a
Faster!: 4 c'mon **5** hurry
faster, make: 6 hasten **7** quicken, speed up
fast food: 4 bite **5** snack
drink: 4 cola, soda **5** shake
fare: 3 sub **4** hero, taco **5** chile, chili, frank, fries, pizza **6** Big Mac, burger, chilli, hot dog, wiener **7** Whopper
place: 3 KFC **4** deli **5** Arby's **6** Subway, Wendy's **7** Blimpie **8** Pizza Hut **9** McDonald's, Roy Rogers **10** Burger King
symbol: 4 arch
Fast, Howard: 6 writer
work: April Morning
Citizen Tom Paine
The Crossing
The Dinner Party
The Establishment
Freedom Road
The Immigrants
The Legacy
Max
The Naked God
The Pledge
The Second Generation
Spartacus
fastidious: 4 neat, nice, prim, tidy, trim **5** chary, fussy, kempt, picky **6** choosy, dainty, prissy, spruce **7** bookish, careful, choosey, finical, finicky, groomed, mincing, orderly, precise, prudent, prudish, refined **8** cautious, exacting, finiking, finnicky, precious, rigorous, thorough, well-kept **9** assiduous, attentive, demanding, difficult, disgusted, exquisite, judicious, observant, shipshape, squeamish, stickling **10** meticulous, particular, scrupulous
fastidiousness: 4 care **9** diligence, exactness, precision
fasting
period: 4 Lent
Fastlove (1996 song)
artist: George Michael
Fast Money
genre: talk
guest: trader
network: CNBC
topic: finance
fast-moving object: 4 blur
fastness: 4 fort, keep **5** speed, tower **6** castle, refuge **7** bastion, bulwark, citadel, rampart, redoubt **8** fortress, garrison, presidio **10** stronghold
__ fast one: 5 pull a
fast-talk: 4 snow
fast-talking: 4 glib, oily **5** slick **6** artful, prolix, smooth **8** slippery **10** loquacious
Fast Times at Ridgemont High (1982 film)
cast: Phoebe Cates, Jennifer Jason Leigh, Sean Penn, Judge Reinhold, Ray Walston
director: Amy Heckerling
fast-track: 4 push **5** speed **6** hasten **7** quicken, speed up **8** expedite **10** accelerate, facilitate
fast-tracker: 5 comer
fat: 4 gras, lard, rich, soft, suet **5** lardy, lipid, obese, plump, pudgy, stout, thick **6** grease, lipids, paunch, portly, rotund, stocky, stubby **7** weighty **8** splendid **10** abdominous
avoider of rhyme: 5 Sprat
cat: 5 mogul, nabob **6** tycoon **7** big shot, Pooh-bah **9** moneybags, plutocrat **10** man of means
cats: 4 rich **5** haves
chew the ~: 3 gab, jaw, rap, yak **4** chat, talk **5** speak **8** converse
combining form: 3 lip- **4** adip-, lipo-, sebi-, sebo- **5** adipo-, lipar-, stear-, steat- **6** liparo-, stearo-, steato-
cook in ~: 3 fry
farm: 3 spa **6** resort
full of ~: 4 oily **5** lardy, suety **6** greasy **7** buttery
in French: 4 gras
low in ~: 4 lean
margarine ~: 5 olein **6** oleine
mouth: 7 tattler **10** taleteller, tattletale
starter: 6 butter, marrow
substitute: 5 Olean **7** Olestra
fat __: 3 cat, lip **4** cell, city, farm, meat, pine **6** chance
fat __ land, the: 5 of the
fat __ the fire, the: 4 is in
fat-__: 4 free **6** witted **7** soluble
__ fat: 5 trans
__-fat: 3 low
Fat __: 4 City
Fata __: 7 Morgana
Fatagaga collagist: 3 Arp
Fatal Attraction (1987 film)
cast: Anne Archer, Glenn Close, Michael Douglas
director: Adrian Lyne
role: 4 Alex
Fatal Cure
author: Robin Cook
fatale, femme: 4 vamp **5** flirt, siren, vixen
fat-cat: 7 wealthy
Fat chance!: 3 hah, nah, naw, nay, nix, non **4** nein, nope, nyet, uh-uh **5** I won't, ixnay, never, nohow, no way **6** no deal, noways, nowise **7** I refuse **8** forget it, I will not, negative, negatory **9** by no means, I think not **10** count me out, not a chance, thumbs down
Fat City (1972 film)
cast: Jeff Bridges, Stacy Keach
director: John Huston
fate: 3 lot **4** luck **5** karma **6** chance, kismat, kismet **7** destiny, fortune, outcome, portion **8** fortuity, Lady Luck **10** divine will, foreordain, providence
Greek goddess of ~: 5 Moira
Norse ~ goddess: 3 Urd **4** Norn
tragic ~: 4 doom, ruin **8** downfall **9** cataclysm, ruination
fated: 5 bound **6** doomed **8** destined, impelled **9** necessary **10** inevitable, in the cards, in the stars
__-fated: 3 ill
fateful: 6 tragic **7** crucial, direful, doomful, ominous, ruinous **8** critical, decisive, eventful, tragical **9** important, momentous **10** calamitous, disastrous, portentous
Fate Is the Hunter
author: Ernest K. Gann
Fates: 4 trio **9** threesome
one of the ~: 6 Clotho **7** Atropos **8** Lachesis
fat-free: 4 skim **7** skimmed
__ Fat Greek Wedding: 5 My Big
__ Fatha Hines: 4 Earl
fathead
see ninny
...__ fat hen: 4 a big
father: 2 he, pa **3** dad, man, pop **4** curé, draw, male, papa, sire **5** beget, daddy, padre, pappy, poppa, spawn, title **6** cleric, create, curate, old man, origin, parent, parson, pastor, priest, source **7** founder, kinsman **8** ancestor, begetter, forebear, inventer, inventor, minister, preacher, relative, reverend **9** clergyman, confesser, confessor, patriarch, propagate, religious, reproduce **10** originator
brother: 3 unc, unk **5** uncle
combining form: 4 patr- **5** patri-, patro-
ender: 4 hood, land, less
expectant ~ supply: 5 cigar
first ~: 4 Adam
in Arabic: 3 abu
in French: 4 père
in Spanish: 5 padre
related on ~'s side: 6 agnate
starter: 3 god **4** fore, step **5** grand
father __: 5 image **6** figure
father-__: 5 in-law
__ father: 3 den **4** city, room **5** birth **6** church, desert, foster
Father (1998 song)
artist: LL Cool J
Father __: 4 Time **5** Brown, Goose **6** Figure, Murphy
Father __ Best: 5 Knows
Father __ Bride: 5 of the
Father __ Sarducci: 5 Guido
__ Father: 3 Our **4** Holy
Father Christmas: 5 Santa **6** St. Nick **9** Saint Nick **10** Santa Claus, St. Nicholas
Father Figure (1988 song)
artist: George Michael
Father Goose
author: L. Frank Baum
Father Goose (1964 film)
cast: Leslie Caron, Cary Grant, Trevor Howard
fatherhood: 9 parentage, paternity
Fatherhood
author: Bill Cosby
father-in-__: 3 law
Father Knows Best (CBS/NBC/ABC sitcom)
cast: Lauren Chapin (Kathy 'Kitten' Anderson)
Elinor Donahue (Betty 'Princess' Anderson)
Billy Gray (Bud Anderson)
Jane Wyatt (Margaret Anderson)
Robert Young (Jim Anderson)
fatherland: 4 home **5** roots
fatherless one: 3 Eve **4** Adam
fatherly: 4 kind **8** parental, paternal **10** protective

Father Murphy (NBC drama)
cast: Moses Gunn (Moses Gage) Merlin Olsen (John Murphy)
Father of the Bride (1950 film)
cast: Joan Bennett, Elizabeth Taylor, Spencer Tracy
director: Vincente Minnelli
Father of the Bride (1991 film)
cast: Diane Keaton, Steve Martin, Martin Short
director: Charles Shyer
role: 5 Ellie
Fathers and Sons
author: Ivan Turgenev
Father's Day
gift: 3 tie 5 razor, shirt
month: 3 Jun. 4 June
Father Time feature: 5 beard 6 scythe
__ Father, who art...: 3 Our
fathom: 3 get, ken, see 4 know 5 gauge, grasp, plumb, solve 6 divine, figure, follow, intuit 7 cognize, discern, make out, resolve, six feet 8 perceive 9 apprehend, figure out, penetrate 10 appreciate, comprehend, understand
hard to ~: 6 arcane, occult 8 esoteric, mystical 9 recondite 10 mysterious
fathomable: 5 lucid 8 knowable, luminous
fathomless: 4 deep, vast 7 abysmal 8 profound 9 cavernous, unsounded 10 bottomless, unknowable
fatidic: 6 mantic 7 Delphic 8 Delphian, oracular, sibyllic 9 prescient, prophetic, sibylline, vaticinal, visionary 10 portentous, prognostic
fatigue: 3 sag, sap 4 bore, bush, flag, jade, poop, sink, tire, wane, wear 5 blunt, drain, weary 6 anemia, fizzle, impair, overdo, reduce, shrink, soften, strain, weaken 7 anaemia, boredom, burnout, conk out, deplete, exhaust, frailty, languor, poop out, tire out, vitiate, wear out 8 debility, enervate, enfeeble, knock out, languish, overtire, peter out, puniness, weakness, wear down 9 attenuate, fragility, lassitude, prostrate, tiredness, tucker out, undermine, weariness 10 debilitate, devitalize, enervation, exhaustion, feebleness
sign of ~: 4 sigh, yawn
yield to ~: 3 sag 4 flag 5 droop, slump 6 slouch
__ fatigue: 6 battle, combat
fatigued: 4 beat, worn 5 all in, drawn, spent, tired, weary, wiped 6 aweary, done in, droopy, sleepy, wasted 7 haggard, languid, rundown, worn out 8 careworn, dogtired, out of gas 9 played out, washed-out 10 knocked out
fatigues: 3 ODs 5 drabs 6 khakis 7 uniform
fatiguing: 4 hard 5 stiff 6 trying 7 tedious 8 tiresome 9 laborious 10 enervating, exhausting
Fatima
father: 8 Muhammad
husband: 3 Ali
Fatman
partner: 4 Jake
Fat Man: 5 A-bomb
Fats: 6 Domino, Waller 7 Navarro
__ Fats: 9 Minnesota
fatsia: 4 tree 5 shrub
family: 7 ginseng
fatten: 4 feed 5 bloat, plump, stuff, swell 6 beef up, enrich, expand 7 broaden, build up, distend, fill out, thicken 8 increase, overfeed, round out
fattening: 4 rich 7 caloric
fatty: 4 oily, rich 5 lardy 6 lipoid 7 adipose 8 lipoidal
acid: 3 DHA 5 oleic
not ~: 4 lean
substance: 5 lipid, sebum 6 lipide
fatty __: 3 oil 4 acid
Fatty: 8 Arbuckle
__-fatty acid: 5 trans
fatuitous: 5 inane, silly 6 absurd 7 asinine, foolish 10 ridiculous
fatuity: 5 folly 6 lunacy 7 foolery 8 nonsense 9 absurdity, asininity, silliness
fatuous: 4 dull, soft 5 corny, crazy, dense, empty, hokey, inane, jerky, passé, sappy, silly, stale, trite, vapid, wacky 6 absurd, common, doting, jejune, old hat, screwy, whacky 7 asinine, clichéd, foolish, humdrum, idiotic, prosaic, puerile, unsound, witless 8 bromidic, cockeyed, mindless, outdated, outmoded, specious 9 brainless, hackneyed, illogical, ludicrous, prosaical, senseless, untenable 10 boneheaded, chimerical, groundless, ridiculous, uninspired, unoriginal, weak-minded
fatuus, ignis: 6 mirage 7 chimera, eidolon, fantasm, figment 8 chimaera, delusion, phantasm 9 obsession
Faubourg St. Honore
artist: Erté
faucet: 3 tap 4 bibb 5 valve 6 spigot 7 petcock 8 stopcock
problem: 4 drip, leak 7 trickle
Faulkner, William: 6 writer 8 Nobelist
work: Absalom, Absalom!
As I Lay Dying
The Bear
Go Down, Moses
The Hamlet
Light in August
The Marble Faun
The Reivers
Requiem for a Nun
Sanctuary
Sartoris
Soldier's Pay
The Sound and the Fury
fault: 3 sin 4 blot, flaw, miss, onus, rift, slip, vice 5 blame, error, guilt, lapse, shift, speck, wrong 6 accuse, defect, foible, miscue, slip-up 7 blemish, blunder, failing, misdeed, mistake, offense 8 drawback, peccancy, trespass, weakness 9 criticize, oversight 10 deficiency, inaccuracy, misconduct, negligence, wrongdoing
activity: 5 quake, seism 6 tremor
at ~: 5 wrong 6 guilty, liable 7 to blame 8 blamable, culpable, mistaken 9 blameable 10 in the wrong
be at ~: 3 err 5 act up 7 do wrong, go wrong 8 go astray 9 misbehave 10 transgress
ender: 6 finder
find ~: 3 hit, nag, pan 4 carp 5 blame, cavil, gripe, knock, nag at, scold 6 accuse, jibe at, pick at 7 cavil at, censure, condemn, grumble, nitpick, put down, quarrel, quibble 8 complain 9 criticize, make a fuss, pick apart, pull apart, reprehend, shoot down 10 vituperate
hold at ~: 5 blame, decry, scold 6 accuse, charge, finger, indict, rebuke 7 censure, condemn, reprove, upbraid 8 denounce, reproach 9 criticize, implicate, reprimand 10 denunciate, take to task, vituperate
to a ~: 6 unduly 7 too much 8 overmuch
fault __: 4 line, zone 5 block, plane, scarp 7 breccia
__ fault: 3 to a 4 foot 5 comma 6 double, ground, normal, strike, thrust 7 gravity, reverse
faultfinder: 4 prig 5 momus, shrew 6 carper, censor, chider, critic, grouch 7 caviler 8 quibbler 9 nitpicker, termagant 10 fussbudget
faultfinders: 4 momi
faultfinding: 7 carping, fretful, peevish 8 captious, critical, fretsome, petulant
faultiness: 4 flaw 6 defect 7 failing 10 inadequacy, inefficacy
faultless: 3 pat 4 just, nice, pure 5 clean, exact, ideal, model, right, sound 7 correct, perfect, sinless 8 absolute, accurate, flawless, inerrant, innocent, peerless, spotless, unbroken, unerring, unmarred 9 blameless, crimeless, errorless, exemplary, exquisite, foolproof, guilt-free, guiltless, stainless, undamaged, unspotted, unsullied, virtuosic 10 consummate, immaculate, impeccable, inculpable, infallible
faultlessness: 8 accuracy 9 precision 10 exactitude
faults, crust between: 5 horst
__ fault with: 4 find
faulty: 3 bad 4 awry, lame, poor, thin, weak 5 amiss, false, leaky, lousy, wrong 6 broken, erring, feeble, flawed, marred, skimpy, untrue 7 botched, cracked, damaged, halting, ill-done, in error, inexact, invalid, lacking, limited, sketchy, unsound, wanting 8 fallible, impaired, mistaken, slipshod, specious 9 defective, deficient, erroneous, illogical, imperfect, imprecise, incorrect, sophistic, untenable 10 fallacious, inaccurate, inadequate, not working, out of order
most ~: 5 worst
faun: 5 satyr 9 libertine
fauna: 6 beasts 7 animals
category: 4 aves
collection: 3 zoo
counterpart: 5 flora
devoid of ~: 5 bleak, stark 6 barren 8 desolate, lifeless
regional ~ and flora: 5 biota
__ Faun, The: 6 Marble
Fauntleroy, Little Lord name: 5 Errol
Fauré, Gabriel: 6 French 8 composer
Faust: 4 play 5 opera
author: Goethe
composer: Charles Gounod
Faustino: 5 David
Faust Symphony
composer: Franz Liszt
__ Faustus: 6 Doktor
Fauvist
painter: Alice Bailly, Georges Braque, André Derain, Raoul Dufy, Henri Matisse, Jean Puy
faux: 4 fake, imit., mock 9 imitation 10 artificial
faux __: 3 pas
faux pas: 4 slip, trip 5 boner, error, gaffe, lapse, wrong 6 bêtise, booboo, howler, slip-up 7 blooper, blunder, misstep, mistake 9 gaucherie, indecorum 10 infraction
follower: 4 oops
make a ~: 3 err 4 flub, goof, muff, slip, trip 5 botch, lapse, stray 6 bungle, foul up, fumble, mess up, slip up 7 blunder, go wrong, louse up, misstep, stumble 8 go astray
fava __: 4 bean
Favaloro: 4 René
favor: 3 aid 4 back, boon, egis, gift, good, help, lean, like, spur, turn 5 aegis, fancy, go for, grace, spoil, token, vogue 6 accept, assist, choose, esteem, oblige, opt for, pamper, prefer, regard, reward 7 approve, backing, benefit, cater to, endorse, indorse, indulge, memento, present, promote, respect, root for, service, smile on, support 8 advocate, approval, courtesy, good turn, goodwill, keepsake, kindness, side with, stand for 9 approbate, approve of, benignity, patronize, privilege, recommend, smile upon, subscribe 10 admiration, estimation, facilitate, indulgence, lean toward, popularity, settle upon
curry ~: 3 woo 5 court 8 fawn over 9 get next to, insinuate, shine up to 10 ingratiate
in ~: 3 aye, yes 7 popular
in ~ of: 3 for, pro 6 all for, likely 9 payable to 10 supporting
not in ~ of: 3 con 4 anti
one side: 4 limp
out of ~: 5 in bad 7 scorned, shunned, unloved 8 despised, detested, disliked, unvalued, unwanted 9 unpopular, unwelcome
return the ~: 5 repay 7 pay back, requite
win the ~ of: 6 enamor, endear 7 attract
__ favor: 3 por 5 curry, party
favorable: 3 fit 4 good, kind, nice, ripe, rosy 5 happy, right 6 aidful,

benign, bright, golden, kindly, timely, useful **7** benefic, helpful, hopeful, welcome **8** amicable, friendly, pleasant, positive, remedial, salutary, suitable **9** agreeable, approving, assenting, benignant, congenial, effectual, fortunate, healthful, indulgent, laudatory, opportune, promising, receptive, welcoming, well-timed, wholesome **10** auspicious, beneficial, benevolent, charitable, commending, convenient, gratifying, heartening, productive, propitious, prosperous, reassuring, seasonable, successful, supportive, worthwhile
mention: **4** plug, puff, rave
most ~: **4** best **7** optimal, optimum
favorably: **4** well **5** right **8** very well **9** agreeably, cordially, helpfully, receptive, willingly **10** generously, graciously, positively, profitably, swimmingly
favored: **3** pet **5** blest, elite, lucky **6** chosen **7** darling, on a roll, popular **9** fortunate, on a streak, preferred **10** auspicious, fair-haired, felicitous, fortuitous, privileged
be ~ with: **3** own **4** have **5** boast, enjoy **7** possess
treatment: **4** bias **9** advantage, privilege, seniority **10** preference
__-favored-nation: **4** most
favoring: **3** for, pro **7** lenient **10** indulgence
favorite: **3** pet **4** idol, main, star **6** choice, likely **7** darling, dearest, popular **8** especial **9** best-loved, number one, preferred **10** honeybunch, preference
place: **5** haunt
thing: **3** pet
favorite __: **3** son
__ favorite: **6** odds-on
favorites, play: **4** side
__ Favorite Sport?: **4** Man's
favoritism: **4** bias **6** liking **8** inequity, nepotism **9** injustice, prejudice **10** friendship, partiality, preference, unfairness
show ~: **4** root, side
Favre, Brett: **2** QB
sport: **8** football
Fawcett, Farrah: **7** actress
spouse: Lee Majors
__ Fawkes Day: **3** Guy
Fawlty Towers: **5** hotel
Fawlty Towers (BBC sitcom)
creator: John Cleese
fawn: **3** tan **4** deer, dote **5** brown, color, cower, crawl, kotow, toady **6** animal, cringe, kowtow **7** lay it on **8** yearling **9** yellowish
over: **3** woo **5** adore, court, toady **6** stroke **7** adulate, flatter, kotow to **8** butter up, kowtow to, make up to, play up to **9** truckle to
parent: **3** doe **4** stag
relative: *see* brown color
Fawn: **4** Hall
fawner: **5** toady **6** flunky, jackal, lackey, yes man **7** flunkey, lacquey **8** adulator, bootlick, courtier, hanger-on, kowtower, servitor, truckler **9** flatterer, sycophant **10** bootlicker
fawners: **6** claque
fawning: **4** oily **6** abject, menial **7** servile, slavish **8** unctuous **9** adulatory, spineless **10** obsequious
fax: **4** copy, send **5** repro **6** ectype **7** deliver, message **8** telecopy, transmit **9** duplicate
ancestor: **5** telex
button: **4** send
header: **4** from
fax __: **5** modem
fay: **3** elf, imp **4** peri, pixy **5** fairy, gnome **6** sprite **7** brownie **10** leprechaun
Fay: **4** Wray **6** Weldon **7** Bainter, Vincent
Faye: **5** Alice **6** Herbie **7** Dunaway, Emerson **9** Kellerman
Faye, Alice: **7** actress
spouse: Phil Harris, Tony Martin
__ Faye Bakker: **5** Tammy
Fayetteville: **4** city, town
athletes: **10** Razorbacks
locale: **3** Ark. **4** N. Car. **8** Arkansas
Faylen: **5** Frank
faze: **3** vex **4** hurt, stun **5** abash, appal, daunt, get to **6** appall, bother, dismay, heckle, puzzle, rattle, ruffle **7** confuse, depress, fluster, inhibit, nonplus, perplex, perturb, shake up, unnerve **8** confound, frighten, irritate **9** discomfit, dumbfound, embarrass, give pause, take aback **10** discompose, disconcert
fazed: **5** upset **6** shaken **7** abashed, nervous **8** agitated, unstrung **9** flustered **10** confounded
FBI: **4** agcy. **6** agency
'70s ~ sting: **6** Abscam
British ~: **3** CID
counterpart: **3** CIA
datum: **5** crime
department: **7** Justice
high-tech ~ tool: **3** DNA
letters in an ~ file: **3** aka
member: **3** agt., Fed **4** G-man **5** agent
part: **3** Bur., Fed., Inv. **6** Bureau **7** Federal
FBI Story, The (1959 film)
cast: Murray Hamilton, Vera Miles, James Stewart
director: Mervyn LeRoy
FBI, The (ABC drama)
cast: Philip Abbott (Arthur Ward) Efrem Zimbalist Jr. (Inspector Lewis Erskine)
__ F.B. Morse: **6** Samuel
__ F. Buckley Jr.: **7** William
FCC: **4** agcy. **6** agency
concern: **2** TV **5** radio **8** airwaves
part: **3** Fed. **4** Comm. **7** Federal **10** Commission
FDA: **4** agcy. **6** agency
department: **3** HHS
figure: **3** RDA
part: **4** Drug, Food **5** Admin.
FDIC: **4** agcy. **6** agency
part: **3** Dep., Fed., Ind. **7** Deposit, Federal **9** Insurance
FDR: **3** Dem. **4** pres.
org.: **3** NRA, OPA, PWA, REA, RFC, SSA, TVA, WPA
successor: **3** HST
see also Franklin Delano Roosevelt
Fe: **4** elem., iron **5** metal **7** element
26 for ~: **4** at. no.
__ Fe: **5** Santa
fealty: **5** faith, honor **6** homage **7** loyalty **8** devotion, fidelity **10** allegiance
fear: **4** funk **5** alarm, angst, avoid, dread, panic, quail, qualm, worry **6** dismay, fright, horror, phobia, stress, terror, unease **7** anxiety, bugaboo, concern, jitters, respect, shudder, suspect, willies **8** cold feet, distress, fret over, mistrust, timidity **9** cowardice, misgiving, reverence, trepidity **10** insecurity
combining form: **4** phob- **5** phobo- **6** -phobia
ender: **4** some
fill with ~: **3** cow **5** alarm, daunt, scare
for ~ that: **4** lest **9** perchance
hide in ~: **5** cower, quail, quake **6** cringe, recoil, shrink **7** tremble
overcome with ~: **3** cow **4** faze **5** bully **6** dismay, menace **7** terrify, unnerve **8** paralyze **10** demoralize, intimidate, scare stiff
respectful ~: **3** awe
show ~: **3** hie, run **5** cower, quail, quake, wince **6** cringe, recoil, shrink **7** tremble
Fear __ Out: **7** Strikes
__ Fear: **4** Cape **5** Storm **6** Mortal, Primal, Sudden
fearer combining form: **5** -phobe
fearful: **3** shy **4** dire, eery, grim **5** awful, eerie, funky, jumpy, leery, mousy, pavid, timid, weird **6** afraid, craven, gun-shy, mousey, phobic, scared, trepid, uneasy, yellow **7** alarmed, anxious, baleful, chicken, daunted, ghastly, hideous, jittery, macaber, macabre, nervous, ominous, panicky, quivery, spooked, uptight, wimpish, worried **8** cowardly, dreadful, fearsome, grievous, hesitant, horrible, horrific, recreant, sheepish, shocking, skittish, terrible, terrific, timorous **9** appalling, atrocious, concerned, diffident, flinching, frightful, ill-omened, monstrous, nerveless, petrified, shrinking, spineless, terrified, tremulous, weak-kneed **10** disquieted, formidable, frightened, horrendous, horrifying, petrifying, solicitous, tremendous
fearfulness: **5** alarm, dread, panic **6** fright, phobia, terror **7** anxiety **8** timidity **9** cowardice, trepidity **10** faint heart
fearing combining form: **6** -phobic
Fear in the Night (1947 film)
director: Maxwell Shane
fearless: **4** bold, game **5** brave, cocky, gutsy, nervy, stout **6** awless, brassy, daring, gritty, heroic, plucky, spunky **7** assured, aweless, dashing, defiant, doughty, gallant, impavid, leonine, staunch, valiant **8** heroical, intrepid, resolute, spirited, stalwart, unafraid, valorous **9** audacious, confident, dauntless, dreadless, unabashed, undaunted **10** courageous, mettlesome, undismayed
be ~: **4** dare
Fearless (1993 film)
cast: Jeff Bridges, Rosie Perez, Isabella Rossellini
director: Peter Weir
Fearless Fosdick
creator: Al Capp
fearlessness: **4** grit **5** nerve, pluck, valor **6** mettle **7** bravery, heroism, prowess **8** audacity
Fear Nothing
author: Dean Koontz
fearnought: **4** coat **6** jacket **8** overcoat
Fear of Fifty
author: Erica Jong
Fear of Flying
author: Erica Jong
fears, allay: **5** quell **6** assure **10** conciliate
fearsome: **4** dire **5** funky, scary, timid **6** scared, trepid, unsafe **7** abashed, alarmed, anxious, chicken, daunted, nervous, panicky, spooked **8** cowardly, hesitant, timorous **9** frightful, ill-omened, petrified, terrified **10** frightened
Fear Strikes Out (1957 film)
cast: Karl Malden, Anthony Perkins
feasible: **3** fit **4** sane **5** utile **6** doable, likely, viable **7** earthly, fitting **8** credible, possible, probable, suitable, workable **9** plausible, potential, practical, thinkable **10** achievable, attainable, imaginable, realizable, reasonable, worthwhile
make ~: **3** let **6** enable, permit **7** empower, license, qualify **9** authorize
feasibly: **5** maybe **7** perhaps **8** possibly **9** perchance
feast: **3** eat **4** dine, fete, gala, luau, meal **5** party, Seder **6** dinner, regale, repast, spread **7** banquet, blowout, holiday, holy day **8** clambake, potlatch **9** celebrate, festivity, luxuriate, Pentecost
British ~: **3** ale
day: **7** jubilee
eyes on: **3** spy **4** view **5** sight, watch **6** behold, look at, regard **7** examine, inspect **8** look upon
for the eyes: **6** beauty, vision **7** dazzler, stunner **8** knockout
Hawaiian ~: **4** luau
Jewish ~: **5** Seder
love ~: **5** agape
on: **3** eat **4** love **5** adore, eat up, fancy, favor, savor **6** devour **7** consume, put away, scarf up **8** gobble up, wolf down **9** polish off, scarf down
one's eyes: **4** gaze, look, ogle, peer, view **5** stare **6** behold **7** observe **10** scrutinize
opposite: **6** famine
upon: **3** eat **7** indulge **9** delight in, luxuriate
feast __: **3** day
feast __ famine: **3** or a
__ feast: **4** love **7** movable

Feast
of Lights observer: 3 Jew
of Lots: 5 Purim
of Lots book: 6 Esther
Feast at Solhaug, The
author: Henrik Ibsen
Feast of ___: 4 Lots 5 Ashes, Fools, Weeks 6 Booths, Lights
Feast of All Saints
author: Anne Rice
Feast of Ashes choreographer: 5 Ailey
Feast of Saint ___: 5 Agnes
Feast of St. Nicholas, The
artist: Jan Steen
feast one's ___ on: 4 eyes
feat: 3 act 4 coup, deed 5 geste, stunt, thing 6 action, effort, stroke 7 exploit, triumph, victory 8 conquest 9 adventure 10 attainment
feather: 5 penna, pinna, plume, quill 6 fletch, pinion, pompon 7 plumule 8 plumelet
barb: 4 herl
bird's flight ~: 5 remex
birds of a ~: 7 cohorts, cronies 10 colleagues
combining form: 3 pen- 4 pinn-, pter-, ptil- 5 penni-, penno-, pinni-, ptero-, ptilo- 7 pinnati-
cut: 2 do 9 hairstyle
ender: 3 bed 4 bone, edge, head 5 brain 6 stitch, weight
full ~: 6 finery 8 glad rags 9 caparison
in one's cap: 4 fame 5 award, badge, glory, honor, kudos, medal, prize 6 credit, praise, renown, reward, trophy 7 acclaim, laurels, triumph, victory 8 accolade, citation, gold star, prestige 10 decoration
light as a ~: 4 airy, soft 5 wispy 6 creamy, dainty, flossy, slight 7 wispish 8 gossamer 10 weightless
neck ~: 6 hackle, heckle 7 hatchel
one's nest: 4 save 6 do well, make it, thrive 7 advance, develop, make out, prosper, succeed, triumph 8 conserve, flourish, go places, grow rich, hit it big, make good, progress
part: 5 shaft 6 rachis 7 rhachis
starter: 3 pin
stiff ~: 5 alula, quill
stole: 3 boa
feather ___: 3 bed, key 4 palm, shot, star, worm 5 grass, tract 6 duster 7 banding
___ feather: 3 gay, sea 5 water, white 6 flight, sickle 7 contour
featherbed: 4 idle, laze, loll 5 dog it, shirk 6 dawdle 7 goof off, slacken 8 lollygag, malinger, slack off 9 goldbrick 10 fool around
featherbrain
see ninny
featherbrained
see foolish
feathered: 5 plumy
feathered friend
see bird
Feathered Serpent, The
author: Scott O'Dell
featherheaded: 4 daft, dopy, soft, zany 5 daffy, dippy, dizzy, dopey, empty, giddy, goofy, inane, nutty, sappy, silly, wacky 6 absurd, jejune, simple, unwise, whacky 7 asinine, comical, doltish, fatuous, flighty, foolish, puerile, vacuous, witless 8 anserine, anserous, childish, farcical, ignorant, immature, mindless, trifling 9 brainless, dim-witted, fatuitous, foolhardy, frivolous, half-baked, illogical, ill-suited, imprudent, laughable, ludicrous, nitwitted, pointless, senseless 10 addlepated, boneheaded, cockamamie, half-witted, ill-advised, irrational, ridiculous
feather in one's ___: 3 cap
feather one's ___: 4 nest
feathers: 4 down, tuft 5 fluff 7 plumage
cover with ~: 6 fledge
drop ~: 4 molt, shed 5 moult
fuss and ~: 3 ado 4 stir 5 furor 6 bother, bustle, clamor, flurry, hoopla, hubbub, rumpus, tumult, uproar 7 fanfare, trouble, turmoil 8 activity, busyness 9 commotion, confusion 10 difficulty, excitement, hullabaloo
partner: 3 tar 4 fuss
ruffle ~: 3 irk, vex 4 miff 5 annoy, peeve 6 bother, nettle 8 irritate
starter: 5 horse
trim ~: 5 preen
tuft of ~: 3 ear
___ Feathers: 5 Horse 6 Pigeon
featherweight: 4 soft 5 light, wispy 6 creamy, dainty, flossy, slight 7 wispish 8 gossamer 9 lightsome
weapon: 3 jab 4 fist 5 punch
see also boxing
feathery: 4 soft 5 light, wispy 6 creamy, dainty, flossy, slight 7 wispish 8 gossamer 9 lightsome 10 weightless
flower: 8 tamarisk
palm: 5 assai
scarf: 3 boa
feats, flaunt one's: 4 brag 5 boast, spout, vaunt 7 lay it on, show off, swagger, talk big 9 gasconade
feature: 4 have, item, star 5 facet, movie, phase, point, story, thing, think, trait 6 aspect, column, detail, factor, play up, regard, stress, virtue 7 article, display, earmark, element, exhibit, point up, quality, realize, show off 8 hallmark, headline, landmark, property, showcase 9 attribute, component, emphasize, headliner, highlight, lineament, main event, specialty, spotlight, underline 10 accentuate, ingredient, particular, underscore
feature ___: 4 film 5 story
feature-___: 6 length
___ feature: 4 main 6 double, triple
features: 3 mug, pan 4 face, mien, puss 5 looks 6 nature, visage 10 appearance, lineaments
featuring: 9 promoting 10 displaying, headlining, presenting
Feb.: 2 mo.
see also February
febrero: 3 mes 7 Spanish 8 February
febrile: 3 hot 7 boiling, pyretic 8 feverish, roasting 9 scorching
February: 2 mo. 5 month
14 figure: 4 Amor, Eros 5 Cupid
birthstone: 8 amethyst
follower: 3 Mar. 5 March
like a ~ day: 5 brisk, crisp, nippy
plea: 6 be mine
preceder: 3 Jan. 7 January
sign: 4 Fish 6 Pisces 8 Aquarius
February 13: 4 ides
February 5: 5 nones
FEC: 4 agcy. 6 agency
part: 3 Fed. 4 Comm., Elec. 7 Federal 8 Election 10 Commission
feckless: 4 lazy 5 inept 6 futile 7 aimless, unready, useless 8 carefree, reckless 9 shiftless, uncareful, worthless 10 unbothered, unthinking
one: 5 idler, rogue, scamp 6 rascal 8 scalawag 9 do-nothing, reprobate 10 ne'er-do-well
fecund: 4 rich 7 fertile, teeming 8 fruitful, prolific 9 exuberant, luxuriant 10 productive
___ Fecunditatis: 4 Mare
fecundity: 8 richness 9 abundance, fertility 10 luxuriance
fed.: 4 natl.
agency: 3 ATC, ATF, BEP, BLS, CDC, CIA, DEA, DOD, DOT, EPA, FAA, FBI, FCC, FDA, FEC, FTC, GAO, GPO, GSA, HHS, HUD, INS, IRS, NEA, NIH, NPS, NRC, NSA, NSC, NSF, NWS, OMB, SBA, SEC, SSA, SSS 4 CPSC, EEOC, FDIC, FEMA, NASA, NLRB, NOAA, NTSB, OSHA, USCG, USDA, USIA, USPS 6 Amtrak
agent: 4 G-man, narc, nark, T-man 5 narco
airport monitor: 3 FAA
airport service: 3 ATC
arts sponsor: 3 NEA
auditor: 3 GAO
building agcy.: 3 HUD
clean-up org.: 3 EPA
collection org.: 3 IRS
employee: 3 agt.
grant giver: 3 NSF
hush-hush group: 3 NSA
inspector: 4 USDA
lender: 3 SBA
medical detectives: 3 CDC
meteorology agcy.: 3 NWS
money overseer: 3 OMB
pension org.: 3 SSA
press: 3 GPO
stipend: 3 SSI
watchdog org.: 3 EPA, FDA
wellness org.: 3 NIH
___-fed: 4 clip, corn, well 5 spoon, stall 6 bottle
Fed: 4 G-man, Ness, T-man 5 agent
Fed. ___: 5 Res. Bd., Res. Bk.
___-fed beef: 4 corn
Fedders
alternative: 5 Rheem, Sears, Trane 6 Lennox 7 Carrier, Kenmore 9 Friedrich
federal: 6 public, united 8 national
agent: 4 G-man, narc, nark, T-man
deficit: 4 debt
issuance: 4 bond 5 T-bill, T-bond, T-note
make a ~ case of: 6 overdo
federal ___: 4 case 5 court
Federal ___: 4 Hill 5 party 7 Express
Federal ___ Bank: 4 Land 7 Reserve
Federal ___ Board: 7 Reserve
Federal ___ Commission: 5 Power, Trade
Federal ___ note: 7 Reserve
Federal Chamber of Deputies
locale: 6 Mexico
___ federalism: 3 new 5 world
Federalist ___: 5 Party
Federal Reserve ___: 4 Bank, note 5 Board 6 System
Federal Theater Project sponsor: 3 WPA
Federal Way: 4 city, town
locale: 10 Washington
federate: 4 band 5 merge, unify 6 league 7 conjoin
federation: 4 bloc, gild, ring 5 guild, state, union 6 league 7 academy 8 alliance 9 anschluss, coalition, syndicate 10 trade union
___ Federation: 7 Russian
Federico: 7 Fellini
in English: 9 Frederick
Federico ___ Lorca: 6 García
Federko, Bernie
milieu: 3 ice 4 rink 5 arena
org.: 3 NHL
FedEx
rival: 3 DHL, UPS
send by ~: 4 rush 8 expedite
units: 3 lbs.
won't deliver to it: 5 P.O. box
Fedor: 4 tsar
fedora: 3 hat 6 topper 8 snap-brim
fabric: 4 felt
feature: 6 crease
Fedora highlight: 4 aria
___-fed press: 3 web
fed up: 3 low 4 sick 5 jaded, tired, vexed, weary 6 ireful 9 disgusted
fed-up one's shout: 6 enough
fee: 3 pay, tip 4 ante, bite, cost, dues, fine, levy, rate, toll, wage 5 price, wages 6 charge, income, salary, tariff, tipoff 7 charges, expense, payment, percent, premium, stipend, tuition 8 retainer 9 emolument, reckoning, surcharge 10 assessment, commission, honorarium, recompense
hourly ~: 4 rate
payer: 6 client, patron 8 customer
usage ~: 3 tax 4 duty, levy 6 charge, impost, tariff, towage 10 assessment
fee ___: 4 tail 6 simple
fee-___-service: 3 for
___ fee: 4 user 5 green, legal 6 greens 7 advance, capping, finder's, license
Fee ___ foe fum: 3 fie
feeble: 3 low, wan 4 lame, limp, poor, puny, sick, slim, tame, thin, weak 5 dotty, faint, frail, lousy, slack, timid, unfit, wimpy, woful 6 anemic, atonic, effete, faulty, flabby, flimsy, infirm, paltry, sickly, simple, skimpy, slight, tender, woeful 7 anaemic, fragile, lacking, languid, mawkish, slender, wimpish 8 decrepit, delicate, helpless, pathetic, pithless, weakened 9 enervated, faltering, nerveless, powerless, spineless, unhealthy

10 inadequate, pathetical, vulnerable
in a ~ manner: 5 wanly
make ~: 6 weaken 8 enervate 9 attenuate 10 debilitate, devitalize
feeble-minded: 3 dim 4 daft, slow 5 dense, thick 6 oafish, simple 9 brainless, dimwitted, nitwitted 10 half-witted
feebleness: 6 anemia 7 anaemia, fatigue, frailty, malaise 8 debility, puniness, weakness 9 fragility, frailness, inability, infirmity, lassitude 10 effeteness, enervation, etiolation, exhaustion, flimsiness, inadequacy, incapacity, infirmness, sickliness, unwellness
feed: 3 hay 4 corn, fuel, grub, keep, live, meal, oats, slop, tend 5 cater, grain, grass, graze, serve, stoke, straw 6 barley, fatten, fodder, forage, foster, signal, silage, supply 7 aliment, augment, bolster, cater to, nourish, nurture, provide, support, sustain, victual, vittles 8 chow down 9 encourage, pasturage, provender 10 strengthen, take care of
animal ~: 4 bran, mash 6 fodder, forage
chicken ~: 4 mash 6 change 8 pittance
don't ~: 6 famish, starve
ender: 3 bag, lot 4 back, hole 5 stock, stuff 7 through
lines to: 3 cue 6 prompt
off one's ~: 3 ill 4 sick 6 ailing, laid up, unwell
on: 3 eat 6 devour 7 consume
(on): 4 prey
the fire: 4 fuel, stir 5 stoke
the kitty: 4 ante 5 wager 6 chip in, kick in
too well: 4 cloy, glut, sate 5 gorge, stuff 7 surfeit 8 overfill 10 gormandize
feed __: 3 bag 5 grain
__ feed: 3 red 4 bird 7 chicken, gravity, tractor
__-feed: 4 hand 5 creep, float, spoon, stall 6 bottle
Feed __, starve...: 5 a cold
feedback: 5 input, reply 6 answer 7 comment 8 reaction, rebuttal, response 9 criticism 10 evaluation
give ~: 5 react, reply 6 answer 7 respond 9 get back to
nonverbal ~: 5 vibes
feedback __: 4 loop
feedbag
don the ~: 3 eat, sup
morsel: 3 oat
feeder: 5 river 6 trough 8 waterway 9 confluent, tributary
English Channel ~: 3 Exe
sound: 4 peep 5 chirp, tweet
feeder __: 4 line, road
__ feeder: 4 bird 5 creep, sheet, snake 6 bottom, filter
feeding __: 3 cup 6 frenzy
feeding combining form: 6 -trophy
feed the __: 5 kitty
Fee, fi, foe, __!: 3 fum
feel: 3 air, paw, see 4 aura, deem, hold, love, mood, tone 5 flair, frisk, grope, react, savor, sense, think, touch 6 finger, flavor, handle, intuit 7 believe, discern, presume, suppose, surmise, suspect, texture, undergo 8 ambiance, ambience, consider, perceive, theorize 9 semblance, sensation 10 atmosphere, conjecture, have a hunch, impression, manipulate
don't ~ so good: 3 ail 4 ache
in one's bones: 4 know
feel __: 3 for, out 4 like, up to
feel-__: 4 good
feeler: 4 hint, palp 5 offer, organ 6 palpus, sensor 7 advance, antenna, inquiry 8 overture, proposal, tentacle 10 invitation, suggestion
animal ~: 4 palp 6 palpus
put out a ~: 5 probe 7 inquire
feeling: 3 air 4 aura, idea, mood, soul, view 5 guess, heart, hunch, sense 6 belief, notion, pathos, spirit, theory 7 emotion, impulse, opinion, passion, posture, sensate, texture, thought 8 attitude, instinct, judgment, reaction 9 affection, awareness, intuition, semblance, sensation, sensitive, sentiment, suspicion, undertone 10 conviction, impression, perception
bored ~: 5 blahs 6 apathy
combining form: 5 patho-, -pathy 8 esthesio- 9 aesthesio-
down: 3 low, sad 4 blue, glum 5 moody, mopey, woful 6 broody, dreary, gloomy, morose, somber, woeful 7 doleful, unhappy 8 dejected, downcast, mournful, troubled 9 depressed, heartsick, miserable, plaintive, saturnine, sorrowful 10 despondent, dispirited, melancholy
eerie ~: 6 déjà vu
faint: 5 woozy
fellow ~: 4 pity 6 lenity 7 charity 8 clemency, easiness, humanity, kindness, lenience, mildness, patience, softness, sympathy 9 tolerance 10 compassion, generosity, gentleness, indulgence, moderation, tenderness
fervid ~: 5 ardor
for the unfortunate: 6 warmth 7 empathy 8 sympathy 10 compassion, kindliness, tenderness
friendless: 7 forlorn 8 forsaken, isolated, lonesome
funny ~: 5 hunch 7 portent 9 suspicion
good: 3 fit 4 fine, hale, well 5 happy, hardy, husky, sound 6 hearty, robust, strong 7 chipper, healthy, up to par 8 blooming, thriving, vigorous 9 in the pink 10 able-bodied
good ~: 3 joy 4 ease, glee 6 relief, solace, thrill 7 comfort 8 sympathy 9 happiness, well-being
guilty: 5 sorry 6 rueful 7 ashamed 8 contrite, penitent 9 chastened, regretful, repentant 10 apologetic, remorseful
guilty ~: 5 shame
gut ~: 5 hunch 8 bad vibes, instinct 9 suspicion
gut-wrenching ~: 4 fear 5 dread 7 anxiety
happy ~: 3 joy 4 glee 5 bliss, cheer, mirth 6 gaiety 7 delight, ecstasy, elation, jollity 8 euphoria, gladness 9 merriment 10 exultation, joyfulness, joyousness, jubilation
harsh ~: 4 gall, hate 5 spite, venom 6 enmity, grudge, hatred, malice, rancor, spleen 7 cruelty, ill will, umbrage 8 acrimony, bad blood, contempt 9 animosity, antipathy, hostility, vengeance 10 resentment
haunted-house ~: 4 fear 5 alarm, angst, panic 6 fright, horror, terror
have a ~: 5 sense, smell 6 intuit 7 believe
ho-hum ~: 5 ennui 6 tedium, torpor 7 boredom, languor 8 lethargy 9 lassitude
ill ~: 4 bile, hate 5 odium, pique, scorn, spite, venom, wrath 6 animus, enmity, grudge, hatred, malice, rancor, spleen 7 discord, disdain, disgust, dudgeon, umbrage 8 acerbity, acrimony, aversion, bad blood, distaste, loathing 9 animosity, antipathy, harshness, hostility, malignity, mordacity, revulsion, vengeance, virulence 10 abhorrence, antagonism, bitterness, execration, repugnance, resentment
impervious to ~: 5 aloof, stoic 6 stolid 7 unmoved 9 apathetic, impassive
intense ~: 5 ardor
intensity of ~: 4 heat 5 ardor 6 fervor 7 passion 10 fervidness
lack of ~: 8 numbness
longing ~: 4 ache, pang 7 craving 9 hankering
negative ~: 3 ire 4 fury, hate, rage 5 anger, odium, pique, scorn, spite, wrath 6 animus, choler, enmity, malice, rancor 7 disdain, disgust, dislike, dudgeon, ill will, offense, outrage, umbrage 8 acrimony, aversion, distaste, loathing, vexation 9 agitation, animosity, antipathy, hostility, petulance, revulsion 10 abhorrence, antagonism, execration, irritation, repugnance, resentment
no pain: 4 numb 5 tipsy
no stress: 6 at ease 7 content, relaxed 8 carefree, composed, tranquil
not ~ well: 3 ill 4 sick 6 ailing, queasy
of unease: 4 fear 5 alarm, angst, panic 6 dismay, fright, horror, phobia, terror 10 foreboding
one's oats: 5 happy, jolly, merry 6 frisky, impish, lively 7 coltish, naughty, playful, puckish, teasing, waggish 8 mirthful, prankish, skittish, sportive 9 fun-loving, lightsome, sprightly, vivacious, whimsical 10 frolicsome, rollicking
remove ~: 4 dull 6 benumb, deaden
restless ~: 4 itch 7 craving 8 yearning 9 hankering
scared ~: 4 fear 5 alarm, angst, dread, panic 6 fright, horror, terror 7 anxiety
shared ~: 5 unity 7 empathy, rapport 8 affinity, sympathy
sinking ~: 7 portent
sore: 4 achy 5 angry
tender ~: 4 pity 5 heart, mercy 6 lenity 7 charity, empathy, quarter 8 clemency, kindness, lenience, sympathy 9 sentiment, tolerance 10 compassion, condolence, humaneness
the strain: 5 tense
vindictive ~: 3 ire 4 bile, fury, hate, rage 5 anger, wrath 6 rancor, spleen 7 dudgeon, outrage, umbrage 8 acrimony, vexation 10 resentment
walking-on-air ~: 3 joy 7 ecstasy, elation, rapture 8 euphoria, gladness 9 happiness
warm ~: 4 love 5 ardor 8 fondness 9 adoration, affection 10 tenderness
without ~: 4 numb 9 insensate
with strong ~: 5 hotly
world-weary ~: 6 apathy, tedium 7 boredom, languor 9 lassitude
feeling no __: 4 pain
feeling one's __: 4 oats
feelings: 8 sympathy
evoke good ~: 6 endear
feign ~: 3 act 5 emote 7 playact
hard ~: 5 anger 6 grudge, hatred 7 offense
have hard ~: 6 resent
hurt one's ~: 6 insult, offend 7 torment 8 distress
reveal one's ~: 4 avow, tell 5 admit, allow, let on 6 fess up 7 concede, confess, divulge 8 disclose 9 make known
wounded ~: 5 pique 6 insult 7 affront, offense, outrage, umbrage 9 indignity 10 resentment
Feelings (1975 song)
artist: Morris Albert
feel in one's __: 5 bones
Feelin' Stronger Every Day (1973 song)
artist: Chicago
feel no __: 4 pain
feel one's __: 4 oats
Feel So Good (1997 song)
artist: Mase
Feels So Good (1978 song)
artist: Chuck Mangione
__-feely: 6 touchy
feet: 5 meter
5280 ~: 4 mile
cold ~: 4 fear 5 alarm, panic 8 timidity 9 cowardice 10 faint heart
dead on one's ~: 5 tired
drag one's ~: 3 lag 4 idle, laze, loaf 5 amble, dally, mosey, stall, tarry 6 dawdle, linger, loiter, put off 7 saunter 8 lollygag, obstruct, straggle 9 waste time 10 dilly-dally
fall at the ~ of: 5 kneel 6 grovel 9 prostrate

fast on one's ~: 5 agile, fleet
get back on one's ~: 7 rebound, recover
get cold ~: 5 quail, waver 6 falter, wobble 8 hang back, hesitate 9 hem and haw, vacillate
get off one's ~: 3 lie, sit 4 loll, rest 5 relax 6 lounge, repose, sprawl 7 recline 10 stretch out
get one's ~ wet: 4 ford, open, wade 5 begin, slosh, start 6 launch, paddle, splash, tackle 7 kick off, lead off 8 commence, get going, set forth 9 enter into, strike out 10 inaugurate, plunge into
get to one's ~: 4 rise, wake 5 arise, awake, stand, waken 6 awaken, jump up, wake up 7 stand up
give one's ~ a rest: 3 sit 5 relax
have cold ~: 5 cower, quail, quake 6 cringe, falter, flinch, recoil, shrink 7 tremble 10 chicken out
having cold ~: 5 jumpy, timid 6 afraid, craven, scared, yellow 7 chicken, daunted, fearful, panicky, spooked, wimpish 8 cowardly, fearsome, recreant, sheepish, timorous 9 nerveless, spineless, terrified, tremulous 10 frightened
having no ~: 6 apodal 7 apodous
kiss the ~ of: 5 adore, deify, honor 6 admire, dote on, revere 7 cherish, glorify, idolize, worship 8 venerate
lay at one's ~: 4 give 5 offer 6 tender 7 present, propose
leave one's ~: 3 hop 4 jump, leap 5 bound
light on one's ~: 4 deft, spry 5 agile, lithe 6 nimble 7 lissome 8 graceful, spirited, vigorous 9 energetic, vivacious
off one's ~: 3 ill 4 sick 6 ailing, infirm, laid up, sickly, unwell 7 unsound 9 afflicted, bedridden 10 indisposed
on one's ~: 5 erect 6 arisen 8 standing
put back on one's ~: 4 cure, heal, mend 5 treat
put one's ~ up: 4 laze, loaf, loll, rest 5 relax 6 repose, unwind 7 lay back, lie down, recline, sit back, take ten 8 take five 10 settle back, take a break, take it easy
put on one's ~: 4 help 5 boost 6 assist, buck up 7 bolster, support, sustain 10 facilitate
six ~: 6 fathom
sweep off one's ~: 4 lure 5 besot, charm, tempt 6 allure, entice, rope in 7 attract, beguile, bewitch, enchant 8 entrance 9 captivate, fascinate, infatuate
three ~: 4 yard
three ~ plus: 5 meter, metre
walk on bare ~: 3 pad
__ feet: 4 cold, flat 5 board
__-feet: 5 crow's
feet of __: 4 clay
Feiffer, Jules: 10 cartoonist
feign: 3 act 4 fake, mock, pose, seem, sham 5 bluff, put on 6 affect, assume, fake it, invent, play at 7 imitate, phony up, pretend, profess 8 disguise, make as if, simulate 9 dissemble, fabricate
feelings: 3 act 7 playact
feigned: 4 fake, mock, sham 5 bogus, false, phony, put-on 6 ersatz, forged, phoney, pseudo, unreal 7 assumed 8 affected, spurious 9 imitation, insincere, pretended, synthetic, unnatural 10 artificial, fictitious, fraudulent
feijoa: 5 shrub
relative: 5 ramee, ramie 6 myrtle
__ Fein: 4 Sinn
Feinstein: 6 Dianne 7 Michael
org.: 3 Sen. 6 Senate
Feinstein, Michael: 6 singer 7 pianist
feint: 4 deke, hoax, juke, ploy, ruse, sham, trap, wile 5 bluff, dodge, fraud, trick 6 deceit, device, dupery, gambit, humbug 7 gimmick, pretext, snow job, swindle 8 artifice, pretense 9 chicanery, deception, imposture 10 subterfuge
fencer's ~: 5 appel
rink ~: 4 deke
feist: 3 cur, dog 4 mutt 5 canid 6 canine 7 mongrel
feistiness: 4 grit, guts 5 heart, moxie, nerve, pluck, spunk 6 daring, mettle 7 bravado 8 audacity, chutzpah, gumption, tenacity, true grit 9 fortitude, gutsiness, toughness 10 pluckiness
feisty: 4 game 5 alive, peppy, surly, tough 6 active, bubbly, fretty, frisky, lively, ornery, plucky, spunky, touchy, unruly 7 defiant, naughty, scrappy, waspish, wayward, zestful 8 contrary, snappish, spirited, stubborn 9 difficult, excitable, irascible, irritable, splenetic, truculent 10 high-strung, hotblooded, out of sorts, pugnacious, rebellious, unamenable
not ~: 4 tame
Feldman: 5 Corey, Marty 6 Morton
Feldman, Marty: 5 actor 8 comedian
in Young Frankenstein: 4 Igor
Feldon: 4 Leah 7 Barbara
Feldshuh: 5 Tovah
feldspar: 7 mineral
mineral: 7 granite
opalescent ~ gem: 9 moonstone
Felicia: 4 Farr
Feliciano, José
song: Light My Fire (1968)
felicitate: 9 recommend 10 compliment
__ Félicité, Que.: 3 Ste.
felicitous: 3 apt, fit 4 just 5 blest, happy, lucky, right 6 timely 7 apropos, blessed, charmed, favored, fitting, germane, on a roll 8 apposite, relevant 9 befitting, fortunate, on a streak, opportune, pertinent, well-timed 10 applicable, auspicious, convincing, fortuitous, propitious, seasonable, well-chosen
felicity: 3 joy 4 glee 5 bliss, mirth 7 delight, ecstasy, elation, rapture 8 elegance, euphoria, pleasure 9 enjoyment, happiness, merriment, well-being 10 ebullience, jubilation
Felicity: 7 Huffman, Kendall
Felicity (WB drama)
cast: Scott Foley (Noel Crane)
Keri Russell (Felicity Porter)
Scott Speedman (Ben Covington)
feline: 3 cat, pet, sly 4 eyra, lion, lynx, puma, puss, wily 5 catty, fossa, kitty, liger, ounce, tabby, tiger, tigon 6 bobcat, calico, cougar, jaguar, kitten, margay, ocelot, serval, sneaky, tiglon 7 bay lynx, caracal, catlike, cheetah, cunning, leonine, leopard, panther, Siamese 8 Garfield, lynxlike, sneaking, stealthy 9 catamount, grimalkin 10 jaguarundi
Africa: 4 lion 6 serval 7 caracal, cheetah, leopard
Asia: 4 lion 5 ounce, tiger 7 cheetah, leopard
attractor: 6 catnip
Central America: 6 margay
drink like a ~: 5 lap up
forest ~: 4 lynx
hybrid: 5 liger, tigon 6 tiglon
India: 7 caracal
like a ~: 5 furry
Mexico: 6 ocelot
nemesis: 6 canine
nocturnal: 6 serval
North America: 4 lynx, puma 6 cougar 7 panther 9 catamount
often: 5 pawer
play with like a ~: 5 paw at
sound: 3 mew 4 meow 5 miaou, miaow, miaul
South America: 4 puma 6 cougar, margay, ocelot 7 panther
spotted: 5 ounce 6 jaguar, ocelot, serval 7 leopard
striped: 5 tiger
tawny: 4 puma 6 cougar 7 panther
tropical: 4 eyra 10 jaguarundi
see also cat
Felipe: 4 Alou
brother: 5 Jesus, Matty
in English: 6 Philip
son: 6 Moises
see also Spanish
__ Felipe: 3 San
felis: 3 cat
felis __: 3 leo
felis pardalis: 6 ocelot
Felix: 3 cat 4 pope 5 Adler, Bloch, Silla, Ungar, Unger 6 Salten 7 pontiff 8 Hoffmann
creator: Neil Simon
like ~: 4 neat, tidy 7 orderly 10 fastidious
roomie: 5 Oscar
Felix Holt
author: George Eliot
Feliz __ Nuevo!: 3 Año
fell: 2 ax 3 axe, hew 4 chop, down, hack, moor, slid, ugly 5 level 7 cut down, inhuman, saw down 8 backslid, chop down, declined, dreadful, inhumane, pull down, went down 9 bring down, collapsed, knock down, plummeted, prostrate, shoot down, throw down 10 strike down
Fell: 6 Norman
__ Fell: 3 If I 5 A Tear
fella
see fellow
__ Fell, A: 4 Tear 7 Blossom
Fell, Dr. Gideon creator: John Dickson Carr
felled: 4 hewn
feller: 2 he 3 boy, bud, cat, egg, guy, lad, man, sir 4 bean, chap, dude, gent, male 5 bloke, buddy 6 mister, person 7 brother 9 gentleman
tree ~: 3 saw 5 axman 6 axeman
see also fellow
Feller, Bob: 6 hurler, Indian 7 pitcher
Fellini, Federico: 7 Italian 8 director
film: 8 1/2 (1963)
Amarcord (1974)
The Clowns (1971)
I Vitelloni (1953)
La Dolce Vita (1960)
La Strada (1954)
Roma (1972)
film composer: Nino Rota
__ Fell on Alabama: 5 Stars
__ Fell Out of Heaven: 5 A Star
fellow: 2 he 3 boy, bud, cat, egg, guy, him, lad, mac, man, sir 4 beau, chap, dude, gent, male, peer 5 bloke, buddy, equal, hubby 6 cohort, mister, person, suitor 7 compeer, comrade 8 coworker, lecturer, roommate 9 associate, companion, professor 10 reciprocal
ender: 3 man, men 4 ship
feeling: 4 pity 6 lenity 7 charity 8 clemency, easiness, humanity, kindness, lenience, mildness, patience, softness, sympathy 9 tolerance 10 compassion, generosity, gentleness, indulgence, moderation, tenderness
fraternal ~: 3 Elk 4 Lion 5 Moose
funny ~: 3 wag, wit 4 hoot
in Australia: 4 mate
in England: 4 mate
in France: 8 monsieur
in Germany: 4 Herr
in Spain: 5 señor
Jamaican ~: 3 mon
regular ~: 3 Joe
starter: 3 bed 6 school
that ~: 3 him
unnamed ~: 3 bub, him, mac
young ~: 3 boy, kid, lad, tad 4 tike, tyke 5 sprig 6 shaver
__ fellow: 3 old 4 good
__ Fellow: 3 Odd
fellow's
that ~: 3 his
fellowship: 4 club, gild 5 amity, grant, guild 6 league 7 company, coterie, society, subsidy 8 alliance, sodality 9 allowance, communion 10 affability, kindliness
__ Fellow, The: 5 Quare
__-fellow-well-met: 4 hail
__ fell swoop: 5 at one, in one
felon: 3 con 4 perp 5 crook, lifer, thief 6 outlaw, rascal, robber 7 burglar, convict 8 arsonist, assassin, criminal, evildoer, internee, jailbird, kidnaper, offender, prisoner, yardbird 9 kidnapper, miscreant, purloiner 10 delinquent, lawbreaker, malefactor
aid a ~: 4 abet

certain ~: 4 yegg 5 lifer 8 arsonist
computer ~: 6 hacker
released ~: 5 ex-con
felonious: 4 tabu 5 taboo, wrong 6 banned, guilty 7 illegal, illicit 8 criminal, improper, outlawed, unlawful, verboten, wrongful 9 forbidden 10 prohibited
felony: 5 arson, crime, wrong 7 assault, battery, offense, robbery, treason 8 burglary 10 grand theft, kidnapping
Felson: 5 Eddie 9 Fast Eddie
felt: 5 cloth 6 fabric 8 material
combining form: 3 pil- 4 pilo-
deeply ~: 5 inner 8 visceral 9 emotional
hat: 3 fez 6 fedora
imitation ~: 5 baize
starter: 5 heart
surface: 3 nap
felt __: 3 pen 4 side 6 marker
felt-tip: 3 pen
felucca: 4 boat, ship 5 craft 6 vessel
fem.: 6 gender
flier: 3 WAF
neither masc. nor ~: 4 neut.
not ~: 4 masc., neut.
title: 3 Mrs.
female: 3 cow, dam, doe, ewe, gal, hen, her, Mrs., pen, she, sow 4 aunt, girl, lady, lass, maid, miss, wife 5 filly, madam, woman 6 Amazon, damsel, gender, lassie, madame, maiden, matron, missis, missus, mother, sister 7 womanly 8 daughter, ladylove 9 inamorata, matriarch, muliebral, young lady
brazen ~: 5 hussy 7 Jezebel
campus ~: 4 coed
combining form: 3 gyn- 4 gyne-, gyno-, -gyny 5 gynec-, thely- 6 gyneco-, -gynous
palindromic ~: 3 Ada, Ava, Eve, Lil, Nan 4 Anna 6 Hannah
relative: 3 mom 4 aunt, mama 5 mamma, momma, niece 6 mother 7 grandma 9 great-aunt 10 grandniece
young ~: 3 kid 4 girl, lass, maid, teen 5 minor 6 damsel, lassie, maiden 8 Fraülein, teenager
FEMA part: 3 Fed., Mgt. 4 Agcy., Emer., Mgmt. 6 Agency 7 Federal 9 Emergency 10 Management
feminine: 6 gender 7 womanly 8 ladylike 9 muliebral
accessory: 5 purse 7 handbag 10 pocketbook
principle: 3 yin 5 anima
pronoun: 3 her, she 4 hers 7 herself
suffix: 3 -ess, -ina, -ine 4 -enne, -etta, -ette, -euse, -trix
feminine __: 5 rhyme 6 ending 7 caesura
Feminine Mystique, The
author: Betty Friedan
feminist
cause: 3 ERA
grp.: 3 NOW
monogram: 3 ECS, SBA
femme: 10 Parisienne
canonized ~: 3 ste.
fatale: 4 vamp 5 flirt, siren, vixen
unmarried ~: 4 mlle.
femme __: 6 fatale
femme fatale: 7 man-trap
femoral __: 6 artery
__ femoris: 6 biceps
femur: 4 bone 9 thighbone
joiners: 4 ilia
locale: 3 leg 5 thigh
neighbor: 5 tibia
-tibia connector: 4 knee 7 kneecap, patella
fen: 3 bog 4 mire, sink 5 marsh, money, swamp 6 morass, muskeg 8 quagmire
100 ~: 4 yuan
fence: 3 buy, hem, pen 4 coop, duel, rail, sell, wall 5 bound, dodge, hedge, limit, parry 6 corral, girdle, paling, picket, robber 7 barrier, confine, defense, enclose, inclose, pickets, railing, rampart 8 encircle, palisade, restrict, separate, sidestep, simulate, stockade, surround 9 barricade 10 equivocate
alternative: 5 hedge
defense: 4 barb
get off the ~: 3 act, opt 6 choose, decide
go over the ~: 6 defect, desert, run out 7 abscond
in: 3 pen 6 define 7 impound 8 surround
material: 4 wire, wood 6 picket
off: 7 enclose, inclose, shut off, shut out 9 partition
on the ~: 4 torn 5 fluid, shaky, timid 6 fickle, unsure 7 dubious, neutral, not sure 8 detached, doubtful, hesitant, lukewarm, volatile, waffling, wavering 9 dithering, spineless, tentative, uncertain, undecided, unsettled, weak-kneed 10 ambivalent, changeable, hesitating, hot-and-cold, indecisive, irresolute, nonaligned, of two minds, wishy-washy
opening: 4 gate
part: 4 pale, post, rail
sit on the ~: 5 waver 7 abstain, quibble 8 hesitate 9 pussyfoot
steps: 5 stile
sunken ~: 4 ha-ha
supplier: 5 thief 7 burglar
fence-__: 3 off 6 sitter 7 mending
__ fence: 4 rail, rock, snow, sunk, worm 5 on the, snake, spite 6 dogleg, paling, picket 7 Cyclone
fenced
area: 3 pen, sty 4 coop 6 corral
in: 4 pent 8 confined, cooped up 9 corralled
not ~: 4 open 8 unclosed 10 accessible
__ Fence Me In: 4 Don't
fencer: 8 Olympian 9 swordsman
__ fences: 4 mend
Fences: 4 play 5 drama
author: August Wilson
character: 3 Jim 4 Bono, Cory, Rose, Troy 5 Lyons 6 Maxson 7 Gabriel, Raynell
__ Fences: 6 Picket
fence-sit: 5 hedge, waver 6 dither, waffle 7 abstain, whiffle 8 hesitate, straddle 9 hem and haw, vacillate
fence-sitting response: 5 maybe 7 perhaps 8 possibly 9 it could be, it might be
fence-straddling: 8 hesitant, wavering 9 undecided 10 indecisive, irresolute, wishy-washy
fencing: 5 sport 7 hedging 9 enclosure, swordplay
area: 5 piste
art of ~: 4 épée
hit: 5 punto
Japanese ~: 5 kendo
match: 4 duel
move: 4 volt 5 appel, feint, lunge, parry 6 fleche, remise, thrust 7 passado, riposte 8 balestra
shout in ~: 7 en garde
sword part: 6 foible
term: 4 épée, foil 5 feint, lunge, parry, piste, saber, sixte 6 foible, quarte, quinte, rapier, remise, thrust, tierce, touché 7 en garde, riposte, seconde, septime
weapon: 4 épée, foil 5 blade, saber, sword
fend: 6 shield 8 get along 9 safeguard
off: 5 avert, avoid, deter, dodge, evade, parry, repel, stave 6 offend, rebuff, sicken 7 deflect, disgust, repulse 8 alienate 9 force back
(off): 4 hold, ward 5 drive
fend __: 3 off
fend __ oneself: 3 for
fender: 6 bumper, shield 8 auto part, mudguard 10 wheel guard
crumpled ~: 6 damage
flaw: 4 ding
in Britain: 4 wing
material: 6 chrome
fender __: 4 pile 6 bender
Fender: 3 Leo 6 Freddy
fender-bender: 4 dent 5 crash, wreck 6 mishap, pileup 7 smashup 8 accident 9 collision
fenestra: 6 window
feng __: 4 shui
Fenice: 4 font 8 typeface
__ Fenimore Cooper: 5 James
__ Fe, NM: 5 Santa
Fenn: 4 John 8 Sherilyn
fennel: 4 herb 5 plant, spice 9 flavoring, seasoning
unit: 5 stalk
__ fennel: 3 dog 4 wild 5 giant, sweet
fenny: 5 boggy 6 marshy, swampy
Fenrir
father: 4 Loki
fenugreek: 5 spice
Fenway Park: 5 arena
locale: 6 Boston
nickname: 3 Yaz
team: 3 Sox 5 Bosox 6 Red Sox
Feodor: 5 Lynen 9 Chaliapin
in English: 8 Theodore
fer
not ~: 4 agin
feral: 4 wild 5 rabid 6 animal, brutal, fierce, savage 7 beastly, bestial, untamed, vicious 8 ravenous, unbroken 9 barbarous, rapacious, raptorial, unbridled
not ~: 4 tame
Ferber, Edna: 6 writer
collaborator: Kaufman
work: Cimarron
Come and Get It
Dawn O'Hara
Dinner at Eight
Giant
The Girls
Great Sun
Ice Palace
A Kind of Magic
One Basket
A Peculiar Treasure
The Royal Family
Saratoga Trunk
Show Boat
So Big
Stage Door
Ferde: 5 Grofé
fer-de-lance: 5 snake, viper
Fer-de-Lance
author: Rex Stout
Ferdinand: 3 Rey 4 Cohn, Foch 6 Marcos 7 Buisson, Porsche 8 Magellan, Zeppelin 9 de Lesseps
land: 5 Spain
wife: 6 Imelda
Ferdinand the Bull creator: Munro Leaf
Ferenc: 6 Molnár
Fergie: 5 Sarah 7 Jenkins
ex: 4 Andy 6 Andrew
former sister-in-law: 4 Anne
Ferguson: 3 Jay 5 Craig, Sarah 7 Jenkins, Maynard
opponent: 6 Plessy
Ferguson, Maynard: 9 trumpeter
genre: 4 jazz
feria: 4 fair 7 Spanish
ferine: 5 rabid 6 savage 7 beastly, untamed 8 unbroken 9 unbridled
ferity: 7 cruelty 8 savagery 10 inhumanity
Ferlin: 5 Husky
Ferlinghetti, Lawrence: 6 writer
work: Her
fermata: 4 hold 5 pause
Fermat's __ theorem: 4 last
ferment: 3 row 4 brew, flap, foam, mess, mold, stew, stir, to-do 5 chaos, froth, furor, rouse, storm, yeast 6 bedlam, clamor, excite, flurry, frenzy, hubbub, incite, mayhem, outcry, rumble, seethe, simmer, stir up, tumult, unrest, uproar, work up 7 anarchy, distill, enflame, inflame, provoke, rampage, smolder, turmoil 8 brouhaha, disarray, disquiet, smoulder, upheaval, uprising 9 agitation, commotion, confusion, imbroglio, intensity 10 excitement, turbulence
combining form: 3 zym- 4 zymo-
in a ~: 5 astir 8 bustling
fermentation
byproduct: 6 alegar
science of ~: 7 zymurgy
fermented: 4 hard, sour 9 alcoholic
beverage: 3 ale 4 beer 5 cider, lager
mash: 4 wort
milk drink: 5 kefir
palm sap: 4 arak 6 arrack
partly ~ grape juice: 4 stum
fermenting: 5 barmy, foamy 6 frothy, yeasty
fungi: 5 yeast
tank: 3 vat
Fermi, Enrico: 7 Italian 8 Nobelist 9 physicist
concern: 4 atom
fermium: 5 metal 7 element

fern: **4** nito **5** plant **6** osmund **7** bracken, osmunda, wall rue, woodsia **8** moonwort, polypody, staghorn **9** rock brake **10** cliff brake, fiddlehead, houseplant, maidenhair, pepperwort, spleenwort, Venus's-hair
combining form: **6** pterid- **7** pterido-
future ~: **5** spore
leaf: **5** frond
spore cluster: **5** sorus
spore clusters: **4** sori
stalk: **5** stipe
Fernand: **5** Léger
Fernando: **3** Rey **5** Lamas, Tatis **7** Arrabal, Bujones **10** Valenzuela
in English: **9** Ferdinand
see also Spanish
Fernando (1976 song)
artist: ABBA
__ Fernando Valley: **3** San
FernGully...The __ Rainforest: **4** Last
Fernwood 2-Night (syndicated sitcom)
cast: Frank DeVol, Martin Mull, Fred Willard
ferocious: **4** grim, mean, wild **5** cruel, harsh, nasty, rabid, rough **6** animal, brutal, fierce, lupine, savage, unkind, wanton **7** beastly, brutish, callous, hurtful, inhuman, tigrish, untamed, vicious, violent, wolfish **8** barbaric, fiendish, inhumane, pitiless, ravenous, ruthless, sadistic, tigerish, unbroken, vehement, vengeful **9** barbarous, cutthroat, frightful, merciless, monstrous, predatory, rapacious, truculent, unbridled, unpitying, voracious, vulturous **10** implacable, relentless, sanguinary, unmerciful, vindictive
not ~: **4** meek, mild, tame **5** mousy, quiet **6** broken, docile, gentle, mellow **7** passive, pliable **8** lamblike, sheepish, yielding **9** compliant, easygoing, tractable **10** submissive
ferociously: **4** hard
ferocity: **4** fury, heat, rage **7** cruelty **8** savagery, violence, wildness **9** barbarity, brutality **10** fierceness, inhumanity
symbol of ~: **4** lion **5** tiger
Ferrante: **6** Arthur
Ferrante & Teicher: **8** pianists
song: Exodus (1960) Tonight (1961)
Ferrara: **4** Abel
family name: **4** Este
Ferrare: **8** Cristina
Ferrari: **3** car **4** auto, Dino, Enzo **10** automobile
model: **3** GTO **4** Enzo **6** Modena **7** Mondial **9** Maranello **10** Testarossa
Ferraro: **9** Geraldine
Ferré: **7** Rosario
Ferrell: **4** Will **8** Conchata
Ferrer: **3** Mel **4** José **6** Miguel
Ferrera: **7** America
Ferrer, José: **5** actor
film: The Caine Mutiny (1954) Cyrano de Bergerac (1950, AA) The Great Man (1956) Miss Sadie Thompson (1953) Moulin Rouge (1952) Ship of Fools (1965) State Fair (1962) Whirlpool (1949)
spouse: Rosemary Clooney, Uta Hagen
Ferrer, Mel: **5** actor
spouse: Audrey Hepburn
ferret: **3** pet **4** root **5** snoop **6** animal, mammal, search, weasel **7** ransack
female: **4** jill
male: **3** hob
out: **3** pry **4** find, seek, spot **5** dig up, scour, scout, trace **6** locate, search **7** unearth **8** discover **9** ascertain, determine, penetrate, track down
(out): **4** hunt **6** search
relative: **4** mink **5** fitch, otter, ratel, sable, skunk, stoat, tayra **6** badger, ermine, marten **7** foumart, polecat **8** carcajou, foulmart, kolinsky, muishond **9** wolverine
young: **3** kit
ferrety: **6** prying, snoopy **8** invasive **9** intrusive
ferric: **4** iron **6** steely **8** metallic
compound: **4** rust
deficiency: **6** anemia **7** anaemia
mineral: **8** hematite
ferric __: **5** oxide
ferriferous rock: **3** ore
Ferrigno: **3** Lou
role: **4** Hulk
Ferris Bueller's Day Off (1986 film)
cast: Matthew Broderick, Jeffrey Jones, Alan Ruck, Mia Sara
director: John Hughes
Ferris wheel: **4** ride
cry: **4** whee
operator: **5** carny **6** carney
ferrite: **4** iron
ferrous: **4** iron **6** steely **8** metallic
ferrous __: **5** oxide **7** sulfate, sulfide
Ferruccio: **6** Busoni
ferry: **3** lug, ply, tow **4** bear, boat, cart, pack, take, tote **5** carry **6** convey, packet **7** shuttle **8** transfer **9** chauffeur, transport
ender: **4** boat
locale: **5** river
operate a ~: **3** ply
operator: **5** plier, plyer, poler
slip: **4** dock, pier **5** berth
__ Ferry, WV: **7** Harpers
fertile: **4** lush, rich **5** loamy **6** arable, fecund **7** teeming **8** abundant, creative, fruitful, original, prolific **9** bountiful, exuberant, inventive, luxuriant, plenteous, plentiful **10** generative, productive
area: **5** oasis
Fertile Crescent
country: **4** Irak, Iraq
river: **6** Tigris **9** Euphrates
fertility: **8** richness **9** abundance, fecundity **10** luxuriance
god: **4** Baal
goddess: **4** Isis **7** Astarte
fertilize: **5** mulch **6** enrich **7** compost **8** fructify **9** cultivate, germinate, pollinate, propagate
__-fertilize: **5** cross
fertilizer: **5** humus **7** compost **9** plant food
brand: **5** Ortho
clay ~: **4** marl
ingredient: **4** urea **5** niter, nitre
ferule: **4** whip **6** cudgel **9** truncheon
fervency: **4** brio, élan, zeal **5** ardor, gusto, verve, vigor **6** energy, spirit **7** passion **8** vivacity **9** eagerness **10** enthusiasm, excitement, heartiness
fervent
see fervid
fervently: **5** hotly, madly **6** wildly **7** greatly **8** ardently **9** furiously, intensely, like crazy, seriously **10** recklessly
fervid: **3** hot **4** avid, keen, warm **5** eager, fiery, itchy, rabid **6** ablaze, ardent, devout, hearty, heated, hectic, loving, red-hot, strong, torrid **7** amatory, burning, devoted, earnest, excited, flaming, glowing, intense, serious, sincere, valuing, zealous **8** animated, enthused, hopped up, vehement, wild-eyed **9** amatorial, emotional, fanatical, heartfelt, impetuous **10** hot-blooded, inspirited, passionate
fervor: **4** fire, heat, love, lust, soul, zeal, zest **5** ardor, flame, gusto, oomph, verve, vigor **6** desire, warmth **7** ardency, emotion, passion **8** alacrity, delirium, devotion, keenness, strength, vitality **9** animation, eagerness, inner fire, intensity, monomania, sincerity **10** conviction, devoutness, enthusiasm, excitement, exuberance, heartiness, liveliness
fescue: **5** grass
roll out the ~: **3** sod
fess (up): **3** own **4** give
Fess: **6** Parker
fess up: **3** bow, let, own **4** avow, fold, quit **5** admit, agree, allow, grant, let on, yield **6** accede, accept, accord, cave in, reveal **7** concede, tell all **9** come clean, recognize, surrender **10** capitulate, understand
fest: **2** do **4** ball, bash, fete, gala **5** blast, party **6** affair **7** shindig **8** function, wingding
follower: **3** oon
starter: **3** fun, gab **4** slug, song, talk
festal: **3** fun, gay **4** gala **5** happy, jolly, merry **6** joyful, joyous, lively **7** special **8** cheerful **9** convivial
fester: **3** irk, rot, vex **4** gall **5** chafe **6** rankle **7** smolder **8** irritate, smoulder, stagnate
Fester: **5** uncle
Morticia, to ~: **5** niece
festina __: **5** lente
Festiva: **3** car **4** auto, Ford **10** automobile
festival: **4** fair, fete, gala **6** fiesta, gaiety, gayety **7** holiday, jubilee, revelry **8** carnival, jamboree
Afro-American ~: **6** Kwanza **7** Kwanzaa
Celtic harvest ~: **6** lammas
English country ~: **3** ale
Greek ~: **5** delia
Hindu ~: **4** holi **6** Dewali, Divali, Diwali
Jewish ~: **5** Purim
Muslim ~: **6** Bairam
Old English ~: **6** lammas
outdoor ~: **6** kermis
preceder: **3** eve
showing: **4** film **5** movie
spring ~: **6** Easter
Vietnamese ~: **3** Tet
Festival in Cannes (2002 film)
cast: Anouk Aimée, Greta Scacchi, Maximilian Schell
festivals, Roman: **4** ludi
festive: **3** gay **4** gala **5** happy, jolly, merry **6** cheery, jocund, jovial, joyful, joyous, lively **7** gleeful, special **8** jubilant, mirthful **9** convivial
occasion: **4** fete **5** party **6** affair
festivity: **2** do **3** fun, hop **4** ball, bash, fete, gala, prom **5** blast, dance, feast, mirth, party, revel, roast **6** affair, fiesta, gaiety, gayety **7** blowout, jollity, jubilee, pageant, revelry, shindig, triumph **8** clambake, function, goings-on, hilarity, jamboree, pleasure, wingding **9** amusement, happiness, joviality, merriment, revelment **10** joyfulness, masquerade, recreation
festoon: **4** deck, hang, swag, trim **5** adorn, crown, drape **6** bedeck, wreath **7** garland, garnish **8** decorate, ornament **9** embellish **10** decoration
festoso: **3** gay **5** happy, merry **6** bright, jovial, joyful **7** gleeful **8** cheerful, mirthful
feta: **5** Greek **6** cheese
fetch: **3** get **4** draw, earn, take, tote **5** bring, carry, go for, go get, shlep **6** convey, elicit, escort, obtain, schlep, shlepp **7** bring in, deliver, produce, realize, schlepp, sell for **8** retrieve **9** transport
something to ~: **5** stick
up: **4** halt, stop **5** brake **6** arrive
__-fetched: **3** far
fetching: **6** comely, lovely, pretty **7** lovable, winning, winsome **8** adorable, alluring, charming, gorgeous, handsome, loveable, pleasing, stunning, tempting **9** covetable, desirable **10** attractive
Fetchit: **6** Stepin
fete: **2** do **4** ball, bash, fest, gala **5** bazar, big do, event, feast, honor, party, roast **6** bazaar, fiesta, soiree **7** banquet, blowout, jubilee, lionize, shindig **8** clambake, festival, function, wingding **9** celebrate, entertain, festivity
fetid: **4** foul, olid, rank **5** stale **6** frowsy, frowzy, rancid, rotten, smelly, stinky, strong **7** noisome, noxious, odorous, reeking, squalid, unclean **8** inedible, mephitic, stinking **10** malodorous
fetidness: **4** odor, reek **5** smell, stink **6** stench **7** malodor **9** redolence
fetish: **3** obi **4** juju **5** charm, mania, obeah, quirk, thing **6** amulet, grigri **8** fixation, greegree, gris-gris **9** obsession
fetlock: **5** joint
neighbor: **4** hoof
fetor: **4** reek **5** smell, stink
__ Fe Trail: **5** Santa
fetter: **3** tie **4** bind, bond, curb, gyve,

hold 5 chain, leash, tie up 6 hamper, hand up, hinder, hobble, hogtie, pinion 7 confine, enchain, manacle, repress, shackle, trammel 8 encumber, handcuff, handicap, restrain, restrict 9 hamstring, restraint
fetters: 5 bonds, irons 6 chains 7 bondage 8 shackles, trammels 9 captivity, handcuffs
fettle: 4 form, trim 5 shape, state 6 health, kilter 7 fitness, spirits 8 wellness 9 condition
in fine ~: 4 hale, trim, well 5 hardy, right, sound 6 robust 7 healthy
fettuccine: 5 pasta 7 noodles
alternative: *see* pasta
topper: 5 pesto
fettuccine __: 7 Alfredo
__ feu: 5 grand, petit
__-feu: 5 pot-au
Feuchtwanger, Lion: 6 German, writer 10 playwright
feud: 3 row 4 spat 5 brawl, claim, clash, fight 6 battle, bicker, debate, enmity, fracas, go at it, grudge, strife 7 contend, discord, dispute, quarrel, rivalry, rupture, wrangle 8 argument, bad blood, conflict, disunity, friction, squabble, vendetta 9 bickering, disaccord, have words, hostility 10 antagonism, bone to pick, contention, difference, disharmony, dissension, falling-out, litigation
__ feud: 5 blood
__ Feud: 6 Family
feudal: 8 medieval 9 mediaeval
bigwig: 4 lord 5 baron, liege, mesne, thane, thegn
defense: 4 moat
holding: 4 fief 6 castle
Japanese ~ lord: 6 daimio, daimyo
tenure: 5 feoff
term of respect: 4 sire
territorial division: 4 vill
warrior: 5 ninja
worker: 4 esne, serf 5 liege 6 corvée 7 subject
feuder perhaps: 4 clan
feuding: 6 at odds, battle, debate 7 dispute, dissent, rivalry 8 conflict, friction 9 hostility, on the outs 10 disharmony, dissidence, opposition
__-feuille: 5 mille
fever: 4 ague, heat 5 craze 6 frenzy, lather 7 passion, pyrexia 9 intensity 10 excitement
chills and ~: 4 ague
combining form: 5 febri-, pyret- 6 pyreto-
ender: 3 few 4 weed, wort
gold ~: 7 avarice
having spring ~: 6 draggy 7 languid 8 sluggish 9 lethargic
run a ~: 3 ail
running a ~: 3 ill 4 sick 6 ailing, unwell 10 indisposed
fever __: 4 heat, tree, twig 5 pitch
__ fever: 3 hay 4 buck, gold, run a 5 cabin 6 spring, yellow 7 Potomac
Fever
author: Robin Cook
Fever (song)
artist: Peggy Lee, McCoys
__ Fever: 5 Night 6 Boogie, Jungle, Pac-Man 9 White Line
Fever, A
author: John Donne
feverish: 3 hot, ill 4 sick 6 heated, hectic 7 burning, excited, febrile, frantic, furious, keyed up, pyretic 8 agitated, frenetic, frenzied, restless 10 in an uproar
feverishness: 4 heat, zeal
février: 4 mois 5 month 6 French 8 February
follower: 4 mars
preceder: 7 janvier
few: 6 scarce 7 handful, not many, pronoun 9 hardly any 10 infrequent, occasional, scattering, smattering, sprinkling
a ~: 4 some 7 several 8 one or two 10 two or three
and far between: 4 rare, thin 5 scant 6 scanty, scarce, skimpy, sparse, spotty 7 unusual 8 uncommon 9 scattered 10 hard to find, infrequent
combining form: 4 olig- 5 oligo-, pauci-
give or take a ~: 5 about
hoist a ~: 4 swig, tope 5 drink, quaff 6 guzzle, imbibe
in a ~ cases: 6 rarely, seldom 9 sometimes
in a ~ minutes: 4 anon, soon 5 later 7 erelong, shortly 8 directly 9 presently 10 before long
known by ~: 4 deep 6 mystic, occult 8 esoteric, mystical 9 recondite 10 mysterious
more than a ~: 4 many 5 loads 6 a lot of, divers, gobs of, lots of, myriad, umteen, untold 7 a host of, a slew of, copious, heaps of, no end of, piles of, profuse, scads of, umpteen 8 a bunch of, abundant, an army of, manifold, numerous, oodles of, scores of, umpsteen 9 a passel of, bountiful, countless 10 zillions of
of ~ words: 4 curt 5 brief, crisp, pithy, short, terse 6 snappy 7 brusque, clipped, concise, laconic 8 succinct 9 trenchant 10 aphoristic, to the point
org. for a ~ good men: 4 USMC
starter: 5 fever
Few __ Men, A: 4 Good
few and __ between: 3 far
__ Few Dollars More: 4 For a
fewer: 4 less
fewest: 5 least
Few Figs From Thistles, A
author: Edna St. Vincent Millay
Few Good Men, A (1992 film)
cast: Kevin Bacon, Tom Cruise, Demi Moore, Jack Nicholson, Kiefer Sutherland
director: Rob Reiner
Few Green Leaves, A
author: Barbara Pym
fewness: 4 lack 6 dearth 7 paucity 8 scarcity, shortage, sparsity 10 deficiency, inadequacy, meagerness
__ few rounds: 3 go a
fey: 5 elfin 6 impish 7 magical, pixyish, playful, puckish, strange 8 pixieish 9 enchanted, fairylike, visionary, whimsical
Fey: 4 Tina
Feydeau, Georges: 6 French 10 playwright
Feynman, Richard: 8 Nobelist 9 physicist
fez: 3 cap, hat
feature: 6 tassel
Fez: 4 city, town
city near ~: 6 Meknes
locale: 3 Mor. 7 Morocco
section of ~: 6 Casbah, Kasbah
FFA study: 3 agr.
fff: 4 loud 6 loudly
FHA: 4 agcy. 6 agency, lender
department: 3 HUD
loan: 4 mtge. 8 mortgage
part: 3 Fed. 5 Admin. 7 Federal, Housing
__-fi: 3 sci
fiancé: 3 man 4 beau, love 7 beloved 8 intended 9 betrothed, inamorato
fiancée: 4 love 5 woman 7 beloved 8 intended 9 betrothed, inamorata
fiasco: 3 dud 4 bomb, bust, flop, loss, mess 6 defeat, mishap, turkey 7 blunder, debacle, failure, misstep, stumble, washout 8 disaster, downfall 10 nonsuccess
fiat: 5 edict, irade, order, ukase 6 decree, dictum, firman 7 command, dictate, mandate 9 ordinance
fiat __: 3 lux 5 money
Fiat: 3 car 4 auto 7 Italian 10 automobile
fib: 3 lie 4 tale 5 story 6 dupery, invent 7 falsity, untruth 8 white lie 9 deception, falsehood, fish story, invention, mendacity 10 inveracity, taradiddle
fibber: 4 liar
admission: 5 I lied
Fibber McGee and Molly: 9 radio show
fibbing: 5 lying 10 mendacious, untruthful
fiber: 3 nap 4 fuzz, hair, hemp, yarn 5 nylon, Orlon, sisal 6 Dacron, fabric, nature, strand, thread 7 essence, quality, tendril 8 filament, strength 9 substance
agave ~: 5 istle, ixtle, sisal
carpet ~: 4 kemp 5 istle, ixtle
coconut-husk ~: 4 coir
cordage ~: 4 hemp 5 istle, ixtle, sisal
ender: 4 fill 5 board, glass, scope
hemp ~: 5 abaca, oakum
hemplike ~: 4 sunn 5 sisal
moral ~: 4 grit, guts, will 5 pluck, spine, spunk, valor 6 mettle, spirit 7 bravery, courage 8 backbone, firmness, tenacity 9 fortitude, toughness 10 resolution
rope ~: 4 bast, coir, hemp, jute 5 abaca, istle, ixtle, oakum, sisal
source: 3 oat 4 bean, bran, flax 6 cereal, legume
strong ~: 6 Kevlar
see also fabric
fiber __: 3 pen 5 optic 6 bundle, optics
Fiber __: 3 One
fiberglass bundle: 4 batt
fiber of the gods: 6 alpaca
Fiber One
competitor: *see* cereal
fiber-optics pulse: 5 laser
fiber-rich cereal: 4 bran 10 bran flakes, raisin bran
fibril: 4 hair 8 filament
fibrous: 3 raw 4 ropy 5 ropey, tough 7 stringy
fibula: 4 bone
combining form: 6 perono-
locale: 3 leg
neighbor: 5 tibia
FICA
ID: 3 SSN
org.: 3 SSA
fiche: 9 microfilm
fickle: 5 light, moody 6 uneven 7 erratic, flighty, mutable, unloyal, wayward 8 hesitant, skittish, ticklish, unstable, unsteady, variable, volatile, wavering 9 arbitrary, faithless, faltering, frivolous, lightsome, mercurial, uncertain, vagarious, whimsical 10 ambivalent, capricious, changeable, coquettish, inconstant, irresolute, unfaithful, unreliable, weak-willed, wishy-washy
be ~: 4 vary 6 change 9 hem and haw
fiction: 3 lie 4 myth, tale, yarn 5 drama, fable, genre, novel, prose, rumor, story 6 legend 7 romance, untruth, western 9 fairy tale, falsehood, fish story, invention, narrative, potboiler 10 inveracity
genre: 4 play, pulp 5 drama, novel 6 comedy, Gothic 7 mystery, romance, tragedy, western 8 whodunit 9 fairy tale
inferior ~: 5 bilge, trash 6 drivel 7 garbage
like pulp ~: 5 lurid
opposite: 4 fact
__ fiction: 4 pulp 7 science
__ Fiction: 4 Pulp
fictional
see fictitious
fictitious: 4 fake, sham 5 bogus, faked, false, phony, put-on 6 ersatz, fabled, fantom, forged, made-up, mythic, phoney, pseudo, unreal, untrue 7 assumed, feigned, phantom 8 cooked-up, fanciful, imagined, mythical, spurious 9 concocted, deceptive, dishonest, fantastic, imaginary, imitation, pretended, simulated, synthetic, trumped-up 10 apocryphal, artificial, chimerical, fabricated, factitious, fallacious, fraudulent, improvised, misleading
name: 5 pseud. 9 pseudonym
ficus: 3 fig 4 tree 5 shrub 6 banian, banyan
relative: 3 fig 4 upas 5 ramon 6 antiar, fustic 8 mulberry 10 breadfruit
fiddle: 3 toy 4 play, poke 6 dabble, monkey, putter, string, tamper, tinker, violin 8 fool with 9 muck about 10 mess around, play around
around: 4 idle, laze, loaf, loll 5 dally, relax, shirk 6 dawdle, linger 7 goof off, hang out 8 lollygag, malinger, slack off 9 goldbrick

ender: 4 head 6 sticks
famous ~: 5 Amati, Strad
stick: 3 bow
with: 3 rig 5 alter 6 adjust 7 correct 8 overhaul
(with): 3 toy 4 fool, mess, play 6 monkey, tamper, tinker
see also violin
fiddle __: 3 bow 4 away 7 pattern
fiddle-__: 5 de-dee 6 faddle, footed
__ fiddle: 4 bass, bull, nun's 6 second
fiddle-de-dee
see baloney
fiddle-faddle
see baloney
Fiddle-faddle!: 3 bah 4 drat, pooh, rats 5 pshaw, shoot 6 darn it
Fiddle-Faddle
composer: Leroy Anderson
fiddler __: 4 crab 6 beetle
fiddler crab: 3 uca
Fiddler of Dooney, The
author: William Butler Yeats
Fiddler on the Roof (1971 film): 7 musical
cast: Norma Crane, Leonard Frey, Topol
character: 5 Chava, Golde, Hodel, Lazar, Motel, Tevye, Yente 6 Mielka 7 Perchik, Tzeitel
director: Norman Jewison
setting: 6 Russia, shtetl 8 Anatevka
violinist: Isaac Stern
Fiddler on the Roof (musical)
composer: Jerry Bock, Sheldon Harnick
fiddlers' king: 4 Cole
Fiddlesticks!: 3 bah 4 drat, pooh, rats 5 pshaw, shoot 6 darn it
__ fide: 4 bona, mala
fide, bona: 4 good, just, real, true 5 legit, right, valid 6 actual, honest, kasher, kosher, lawful 7 genuine, literal, regular, sincere 8 official, rightful, verified 9 authentic, heartfelt, veritable
Fidel: 6 Castro
brother: 4 Raul
friend: 3 Che
home: 4 Cuba 6 Habana, Havana
see also Spanish
__ Fideles: 6 Adeste
Fidelio: 5 opera
composer: Ludwig van Beethoven
role: 5 Rocco 7 Leonore 8 Fernando, Jacquino 9 Florestan
setting: 5 Spain 6 prison 7 Seville
__ Fidelis: 6 Semper
fidelity: 4 love 5 faith, piety, rigor, troth 6 fealty, homage, lealty 7 honesty, loyalty, realism 8 accuracy, devotion 9 constancy, exactness, fixedness, integrity, precision 10 allegiance, exactitude, factuality, observance
model of ~: 4 Enid
pledge of ~: 5 troth
__ fidelity: 4 high
fidget: 4 stir 6 jitter, squirm
fidgets: 6 nerves, unrest 7 anxiety, jitters, malaise, willies 8 disquiet, edginess 10 impatience, inquietude, uneasiness
fidgety: 5 antsy, hyper, itchy, jumpy, tense 6 jangly, on edge, uneasy 7 jittery, nervous, restive 8 fluttery, restless, skittish 9 unsettled 10 high-strung
fidla: 6 string, zither
origin: 7 Ireland
Fidler: 5 Jimmy
fido: 4 coin
Fido: 3 dog, pet 6 bowwow, canine
command to ~: 3 beg, sic, sit 4 down, heel, stay 5 fetch, sit up
pal: 4 Spot 5 Rover
see also dog
Fidrych: 4 Mark 5 Tiger 6 hurler 7 pitcher
Fie!: 3 bah 5 shame
Fiedler: 4 John 6 Arthur
Fiedler, Arthur: 9 conductor
group: 10 Boston Pops
fief
see feudal
field: 3 job, lea, ley, lot, sod 4 area, land, park, walk 5 arena, array, catch, gamut, green, orbit, patch, plain, range, realm, scope, space, sward, topic, tract, veldt, world 6 answer, career, domain, ground, handle, meadow, métier, region, sphere, swarth 7 acreage, compass, diamond, element, entries, expanse, grounds, pasture, purview, reply to, runners, section, stadium, terrain, tillage 8 business, cropland, cup of tea, deal with, entrants, farmland, gridiron, nominees, play area, precinct, province, retrieve, vineyard, vocation 9 avocation, bailiwick, grassland, ranchland, specialty, territory 10 applicants, candidates, department, discipline, fairground, occupation, playground, profession, walk of life
combining form: 4 agro-
day: 4 bash 5 binge, fling, revel, spree 6 junket 10 recreation
divider: 5 fence, hedge
ender: 4 fare, work 5 stone, strip 6 worker
home ~: 4 turf
house: 3 gym 9 gymnasium
of honor event: 4 duel
of reference: 3 run 4 area, play, span, sway, view 5 ambit, gamut, orbit, range, reach, realm, scale, scope, space, sweep, width 6 extent, margin, radius, sphere 7 breadth, compass, expanse, horizon, purview, subject 8 confines, latitude 9 amplitude, dimension
of view: 3 ken 5 range, reach, scope, sight, vista 7 compass, eyeshot, horizon, purview
partner: 5 track 6 stream
rice ~: 5 paddy
starter: 3 air, mid 4 back, down, mine 6 battle
the question: 5 reply 6 answer 7 respond
unit: 4 acre
worker: 5 agent, baler 6 farmer
field __: 3 bed, day, pea 4 army, coil, corn, crop, goal, hand, lark, lens, line, mint, stop, trip 5 event, grade, guide, house, mouse, poppy, trial 6 hockey, jacket, magnet, ration, theory 7 captain, cricket, current, glasses, marshal, officer, spaniel, sparrow, winding
field-__: 4 test 5 strip
field-__ microscope: 3 ion
__ field: 3 gas, ice, oil, old 4 coal, gold, left, open, root, skew 5 force, prime, right, short 6 broken, center, flying, scalar, vector, visual 7 landing, ordered, playing
Field: 5 Betty, Sally 6 Eugene, Rachel 7 Chelsea 8 Marshall
__ Field: 6 Ebbets 7 Wrigley
Field and __: 6 Stream
Fieldcrest product: 5 linen, sheet, towel
__ fielder: 4 left 5 right 6 center
Fielder: 4 Cook 5 Cecil
fielder's __: 6 choice
fieldfare: 4 bird
Fielding: 5 Helen, Henry
Fielding, Henry: 6 writer 7 British 10 playwright
work: Amelia
Tom Jones
Tom Thumb
field mouse
predator: 3 cat, owl
field of __: 4 fire, view 5 force, honor 6 vision
Field of Dreams (1989 film)
cast: Kevin Costner, James Earl Jones, Burt Lancaster, Ray Liotta, Amy Madigan
director: Phil Alden Robinson
setting: 4 Iowa
Field of Ice, The
author: Jules Verne
Field of Thirteen
author: Dick Francis
Fields: 2 W.C. 3 Kim, Mrs. 4 Shep 5 Debbi, Ernie, Totie 6 Gracie 7 Dorothy
vaudeville partner: 5 Weber
__ Fields: 3 Mrs. 6 London 7 Elysian
Field, Sally: 7 actress
film: Absence of Malice (1981)
The End (1978)
Forrest Gump (1994)
Hooper (1978)
Mrs. Doubtfire (1993)
Murphy's Romance (1985)
Norma Rae (1979, AA)
Not Without My Daughter (1991)
Places in the Heart (1984, AA)
Punchline (1988)
Smokey and the Bandit (1977)
Soapdish (1991)
Stay Hungry (1976)
Steel Magnolias (1989)
Surrender (1987)
TV: The Flying Nun
Fields, The
author: Conrad Richter
__ Fields, The: 7 Killing
Fields, W.C.: 5 actor 8 comedian
costar: 3 Mae 4 West 5 Leroy
film: The Bank Dick (1940)
The Big Broadcast of 1938 (1938)
David Copperfield (1935)
If I Had a Million (1932)
International House (1933)
It's a Gift (1934)
The Man on the Flying Trapeze (1935)
Million Dollar Legs (1932)
Mississippi (1935)
Mrs. Wiggs of the Cabbage Patch (1934)
My Little Chickadee (1940)
Never Give a Sucker an Even Break (1941)
The Old-Fashioned Way (1934)
Poppy (1936)
Six of a Kind (1934)
Tillie and Gus (1933)
You Can't Cheat an Honest Man (1939)
You're Telling Me (1934)
foil: Baby Leroy
persona: 3 sot 5 souse
__ Field, The: 3 Far 5 Onion
__ field theory: 7 quantum, unified
fieldwork: 5 redan
fiend: 3 fan, imp, nut 4 ogre 5 beast, brute, demon, devil, freak, knave, rowdy 6 addict, daemon, daimon, diablo, maniac, meanie, savage, zealot 7 dastard, devotee, fanatic, monster, villain 8 evildoer 9 barbarian, hellhound 10 aficionado, enthusiast
ender: 3 ish
starter: 4 arch
fiendish: 4 evil, mean 5 cruel, harsh, nasty 6 animal, brutal, fierce, savage, unkind, wanton, wicked 7 beastly, brutish, callous, demonic, hellish, hurtful, inhuman, satanic, vicious 8 barbaric, daemonic, demoniac, devilish, diabolic, infernal, inhumane, obsessed, pitiless, ruthless, sadistic, vengeful 9 atrocious, cutthroat, demonical, ferocious, malicious, merciless, monstrous, nefarious, possessed, satanical, truculent 10 diabolical, maleficent, vindictive
fiendishness: 6 malice 7 cruelty, tyranny 8 ferocity, savagery 9 barbarism, brutality, harshness
Fiennes: 5 Ralph 6 Joseph
Fiennes, Ralph: 5 actor
film: The Avengers (1998)
The English Patient (1996)
The Prince of Egypt (1998)
Quiz Show (1994)
Red Dragon (2002)
Schindler's List (1993)
fierce: 4 mean, wild 5 angry, cruel, feral, harsh, nasty, rough, sharp 6 animal, ardent, bitter, brutal, heated, lupine, raging, raving, savage, severe, stormy, strong, unkind, wanton 7 beastly, brutish, callous, enraged, furious, hurtful, inhuman, intense, lawless, tigrish, untamed, vicious, violent 8 barbaric, fiendish, grueling, inhumane, menacing, piercing, pitiless, ruthless, sadistic, terrific, tigerish, vehement, vengeful, venomous 9 agonizing, barbarous, cutthroat, desperate, ferocious, merciless, monstrous, truculent, turbulent, unpitying 10 formidable, passionate, relentless, tumultuous, unpeaceful, vindictive
emotion: 5 wrath
one: 5 shark, tiger 6 dragon, savage 7 bearcat, panther
something ~: 5 madly 6 wildly 7 rabidly 9 excitedly, furiously, intensely, violently 10 frenziedly

stare: 5 glare
Fierce Creatures (1997 film)
cast: John Cleese, Jamie Lee Curtis, Kevin Kline
fiercely: 4 hard 5 gonzo, madly 6 keenly 7 like mad 8 insanely 9 viciously 10 vehemently
fierceness: 4 fury, zeal 5 ardor 8 ferocity, violence 9 brutality, intensity
fieriness: 4 heat 9 vehemence 10 enthusiasm
Fierstein: 6 Harvey
fiery: 3 hot 5 lurid, proud, spicy 6 ablaze, aflame, ardent, fervid, heated, red-hot, spicey, torrid 7 blazing, boiling, burning, fervent, flaming, flaring, intense, peppery, violent 8 choleric, in flames, spirited, vehement, white-hot 9 emotional, excitable, fanatical, hotheaded, irritable, scorching 10 hot-blooded, passionate, sweltering
particle: 5 ember, spark 6 cinder
stack: 4 pyre
Fiesque
composer: Édouard Lalo
fiesta: 4 bash, fair, fete, gala 5 party 6 gaiety, gayety 7 holiday, jubilee, revelry 8 festival 9 festivity
Fiesta: 3 car 4 auto, Ford, Olds 8 Bowl game 10 Oldsmobile
Fiesta __: 4 Bowl, ware
Fiesta Bowl
letters: 4 NCAA
locale: 4 Ariz. 5 Tempe 7 Arizona
fiesta de __: 5 toros
Fie, thou dishonest __!: 5 Satan
fife: 4 wind 8 woodwind 10 instrument
accompaniment: 4 drum 5 taber, tabor 6 tabour
Fife: 6 Barney
Fifi: 6 D'Orsay
dog often named ~: 6 poodle
see also French
fifteen
comb. form: 8 pentadec- 9 pentadeca-
fifth
anniversary gift: 4 wood
columnist: 5 snake 7 traitor 8 quisling, turncoat
combining form: 5 quint- 6 quinti-
in a series: 5 part V
name meaning ~: 7 Quentin
person: 4 Seth
fifth __: 5 force, wheel 6 column, estate
Fifth __: 3 Ave. 6 Avenue
Fifth __, The: 3 Son 6 Column, Monkey 7 Element
Fifth Avenue: 3 car 4 auto 8 Chrysler 10 automobile
store: 4 Saks
__ Fifth Avenue: 4 Saks
Fifth Column, The
author: Ernest Hemingway
Fifth Dimension
members: Davis, LaRue, McCoo, McLemore, Townson
song: Aquarius/Let the Sunshine In (1969)
I Didn't Get to Sleep at All (1972)
If I Could Reach You (1972)
One Less Bell to Answer (1970)
Stoned Soul Picnic (1968)
Up, Up and Away (1967)
Wedding Bell Blues (1969)
Fifth Element, The (1997 film)
cast: Ian Holm, Milla Jovovich, Gary Oldman, Bruce Willis
cat: 7 Sweetie
director: Luc Besson
fifth-grader: 5 'tween
Fifth of Beethoven, A (1976 song)
artist: Walter Murphy
fifth-rate: 4 poor 5 awful, lousy 6 cheesy, crumby, crummy 8 inferior
Fifth Republic nation: 6 France
Fifth Son, The
author: Elie Wiesel
Fifties, The
author: David Halberstam
fifty
minutes past: 5 ten of, ten to
percent: 4 half
fifty-fifty: 4 even, luck 5 equal 6 even-up 10 compromise, likelihood
go ~: 5 halve, share, split
Fifty-four-forty or __: 5 Fight
Fifty Million Frenchmen: 7 musical
composer: Cole Porter
song: 5 Paree
fig: 4 iota, tree, whit 5 fruit, shrub 8 least bit 9 fruit tree
bar: 6 cookie
ender: 4 wort
relative: 4 upas 5 ficus, ramon 6 antiar, fustic 8 mulberry 10 breadfruit
tree: 2 bo 5 bodhi, ficus, papal, pipal 6 banian, banyan, peepul
fig __: 4 leaf, wasp
fig.: 2 no. 4 stat.
three-D ~: 3 sph.
__ fig: 4 Java, wild 5 moldy 6 Indian, Smyrna 7 Barbary, weeping
Figaro: 3 cat 6 barber 7 cat food
alternative: *see* pet food brand
love: 6 Rosina
tune: 4 aria
Figgis, Mike: 8 director
fight: 3 box, row, vie, war 4 bout, buck, claw, defy, duel, feud, fray, fuss, riot, spar, tiff, tilt, to-do 5 argue, brawl, brush, clash, match, melee, mix-up, rebel, repel, run-in, scrap, set-to, siege, sport, trial, valor 6 action, affray, attack, barney, battle, bicker, combat, debate, defend, fracas, go at it, hassle, oppose, racket, resist, rumble, strife, strive, take on, tumult, tussle 7 assault, carry on, contend, contest, dispute, grapple, lawsuit, lay into, mix it up, protest, quarrel, rivalry, scuffle, vie with, wage war, wrangle, wrestle 8 argument, campaign, conflict, do battle, object to, skirmish, squabble, struggle, tug-of-war 9 altercate, challenge, duke it out, encounter, have words, hostility, imbroglio, light into, militancy, pugnacity, scrimmage, square off, wrangling 10 aggression, buckle down, contention, dissension, donnybrook, engagement, falling-out, fisticuffs, free-for-all, make a stand, opposition, put up a fuss, resistance, tangle with, tournament
back: 5 react, rebel, reply 6 mutiny, resist 7 respond
ender: 5 truce
ending: 2 KO 3 TKO
exclamation: 3 oof, pow
for: 6 defend 8 champion, keep safe
(for): 3 vie
knight ~: 4 duel, list 6 charge, combat 7 contest, tourney 10 tournament
minor ~: 4 spat, tiff
off: 5 repel 6 defeat 7 repulse
over: 3 sue 5 argue 6 defend 7 contest 8 litigate, question
poster word: 6 versus
put up a ~: 6 resist 7 dissent 8 struggle
ready to ~: 5 armed 7 hawkish, martial, warlike 8 militant 9 bellicose, combative 10 aggressive, pugnacious
rigged ~: 5 setup
site: 4 ring 5 arena 8 coliseum
starter: 3 cat, dog, gun 4 bull, cock, fire, fist 5 prize
train for a ~: 4 spar
unit: 3 rnd. 5 round
verbal ~: 4 spat 5 fight, set-to 6 debate 7 dispute, polemic, quarrel, rhubarb 8 argument, polemics, squabble 9 bickering, encounter 10 war of words
verbally: 5 argue, claim, plead 6 appeal, bicker, debate, dicker, haggle, oppose, reason 7 contend, dispute, dissent, protest, quarrel, quibble, wrangle 8 disagree, hash over, maintain, squabble 9 lock horns 10 controvert, deliberate
with: 4 meet 6 assail, attack, engage, take on 7 assault
fight __: 3 off 5 it out, shy of
fight __ and nail: 5 tooth
__ fight: 3 sea 5 proxy
fighter: 3 pug 5 boxer 6 knight 7 bruiser, soldier, warrior 8 crusader, pugilist 9 aggressor, assailant, combatant, contender, disputant, gladiator, mercenary 10 antagonist, competitor, contestant
dirty ~: 5 biter
org.: 3 WBA, WBC
starter: 3 gun, jet 4 bull, fire 5 prize
__ fighter: 3 jet 4 club, tank 6 escort, street 7 freedom
__-fighter: 5 crime
Fighter of the Century award-winner: 3 Ali
__ Fighters: 3 Foo
fight fire __ fire: 4 with
Fight for Your Right (1987 song)
artist: Beastie Boys
fighting: 3 war 4 at it 5 angry, at war 6 battle, combat, strife 7 hawkish, hostile, martial, warfare, warlike 8 conflict, militant, violence 9 bellicose, combative 10 aggressive, fisticuffs, pugnacious, resistance
combining form: 5 -machy
force: 4 army, navy 5 troop 6 armada 7 marines
in ~ trim: 4 wiry 5 tough 6 strong
fighting __: 4 cock, fish 5 chair, words 6 chance
Fighting __: 5 Angel, Irish 6 French, Illini, Tigers
Fighting Angel
author: Pearl S. Buck
__ fighting fish: 7 Siamese
Fighting Irish: 3 NDU 9 Notre Dame
__ Fighting Ships: 5 Jane's
Fighting Tigers: 3 LSU
__ fightin' words!: 5 Them's
fight it __: 3 out
__ fight no more forever: 5 I will
fight-or-__ response: 6 flight
fights
site of many ~: 5 Vegas 8 Las Vegas
where some ~ are aired: 5 pay TV
Fight the Power (1975 song)
artist: Isley Brothers
fight tooth and __: 4 nail
figment: 5 dream 6 fantom 7 chimera, fantasy, phantom 8 chimaera, creation, daydream, delusion, illusion 9 invention
Fig Newtons
alternative: *see* cookie brand
__ Figs From Thistles: 4 A Few
figuration: 6 sketch 7 outline
figurative: 8 symbolic 9 pictorial 10 denotative, emblematic, metaphoric, signifying
language: 7 imagery, similes 9 allusions, metaphors
figure: 3 add, bod, sum 4 body, doll, form, line, mull, rate 5 add up, build, count, digit, frame, gauge, price, quote, shape, sum up, tally, thing, torso, total, tot up 6 assess, cipher, decide, do sums, emblem, fathom, number, ponder, reckon, settle, sketch, statue, symbol, worthy 7 anatomy, chassis, compute, contour, diagram, dope out, fashion, integer, measure, notable, numeral, outline, pattern, predict, presume, profile, suppose, work out 8 appraise, estimate, keep tabs, physique, portrait, quantity, ruminate, standard, tabulate 9 calculate, celebrity, character, determine, dignitary, enumerate, keep score, make sense, personage, quotation, speculate
action ~: 3 toy 4 doer, doll 5 GI Joe
ballpark ~: 5 guess 8 estimate 9 appraisal 10 assessment, guestimate
bottom-line ~: 3 net, sum 5 count, score, tally, total 6 amount 9 aggregate, reckoning
combining form: 3 eid- 4 eido-
do ~ eights: 5 skate
ender: 4 head
geometric ~: 4 rect. 5 rhomb, solid 6 circle, square 7 hexagon, octagon, rhombus 8 pentagon, triangle 9 rectangle, trapezoid
in: 3 add 4 form
of speech: 5 idiom, image, trope 6 simile 8 metaphor
on: 4 plan 5 hatch 6 devise 7 concoct, plan for 8 block out, envisage 10 prepare for

out: 2 do 3 get, see 4 find 5 crack, infer, learn, solve, think 6 decode, deduce, fathom, reason, reckon 7 analyze, discern, unravel 8 decipher, evaluate 9 determine, penetrate, speculate 10 understand
(out): 4 suss, work
preliminary ~: 3 est. 8 estimate
public ~: 4 name, star 5 celeb 7 big name, notable 8 eminence, luminary, somebody 9 celebrity, dignitary, personage, superstar
starter: 5 trans
three-D ~: 4 cone, cube 5 solid 6 sphere 7 pyramid

figure __: 3 out 5 eight 6 skater 7 skating
__ figure: 3 lay 4 cut a 5 noise, stick, Venus 6 father, mother, public, school
figure eight
half: 3 ess
where to do a ~: 3 ice 4 rink
figurehead: 4 tool 5 front 6 puppet 9 nonentity, straw boss 10 mouthpiece
spot: 4 prow
figure of __: 6 speech
figures: 3 nos. 4 data 5 count, tally
check the ~: 5 readd
figure skater: 3 Ito 4 Kwan, Witt 5 Baiul, Heiss, Henie, Kulik 6 Button, Hamill, Hughes 7 Boitano, Cousins, Fleming 8 Albright, Hamilton, Lipinski 9 Midori Ito, Yamaguchi 10 Carol Heiss, Dick Button, Sonja Henie
British: 7 Cousins
German: 4 Witt
Japanese: 9 Midori Ito
jump: 4 axel, lutz
Norwegian: 10 Sonja Henie
Russian: 5 Kulik
Ukrainian: 5 Baiul
figure skating: 5 sport
figurine: 4 doll, idol 5 model 6 Hummel 9 statuette
Hawaiian ~: 4 tiki
material: 4 jade, lava, onyx
figuring: 6 adding 8 addition, counting, tallying 9 ciphering, reckoning 10 arithmetic
Fiji: 4 isls. 5 isles 6 nation 7 country, islands
capital: 4 Suva
island: 3 Gau 4 Koro 6 Ovalau 7 Kandavu, Taveuni 8 Viti Levu 9 Vanua Levu
money: 4 cent 6 dollar
neighbor: 5 Samoa, Tonga
Fijian: 10 Melanesian
golfer: 10 Vijay Singh
fila: 7 threads
filament: 4 hair 5 cilia, fiber, fibre, floss, kapok, twine 6 cobweb, fibril, strand, string, thread 7 tendril 8 fibrilla, gossamer
filbert: 3 nut 4 tree 5 hazel, shrub
cousin: 5 pecan
filch: 3 cop, rob 4 crib, glom, lift, take 5 pinch, poach, swipe 6 pilfer, pocket, rip off, snitch, thieve 7 purloin, ransack 8 embezzle, scrounge
filcher: 5 crook, thief 7 burglar 9 purloiner
filching: 5 theft 8 burglary, thievery
file: 3 row 4 hone, line, rasp, slot, sort, tier, tool, walk, whet 5 grate, grind, index, order, queue, train 6 abrade, docket, folder, record, scrape, series, smooth, string 7 arrange, catalog, dossier, put away, rub down, sharpen, suspend 8 classify, register 9 catalogue, portfolio 10 categorize, emery board, pigeonhole, procession
a claim: 3 sue 8 litigate
as a complaint: 5 lodge
away: 4 drop, save 5 defer, delay, shunt, table 6 ignore, put off, shelve 8 lay aside 10 pigeonhole
(by): 5 march
coarse ~: 4 rasp
holder: 6 folder 7 dossier 9 portfolio
in single ~: 4 arow
label: 3 tab, XYZ 4 misc., name
partner: 4 rank
rank and ~: 5 crowd, plebs 6 masses, people, proles, public, rabble 9 hoi polloi, plebeians
subject: 4 case
suit: 9 go to court
target: 4 nail
unit: 6 drawer
file __: 4 band, card 5 clerk, dance 6 folder, server 7 cabinet, footage
__ file: 4 nail 5 round 6 chrono, Indian, master, single 7 rat-tail, spindle, tickler
__-file: 4 flat 5 cross, end-of
filé: 6 powder 9 thickener
filer: 5 clerk 8 taxpayer 10 manicurist
files: 6 annals, record 7 archive, records 8 archives 10 chronicles
like some ~: 6 coarse
__-Files: 4 The X
filet: 3 cut 4 bone, lace 5 steak 6 debone 10 tenderloin
filet __: 4 lace 6 mignon
Filet-__: 5 O-Fish
__ File, The: 6 Odessa
filet mignon: 4 meat 5 steak
filet of __: 4 sole
filial: 5 sonly 6 loving 7 devoted, dutiful, sonlike 8 obedient 10 daughterly, respectful
filibeg: 4 kilt 5 skirt
filibuster: 3 gab 5 delay, run on, stall, tarry 6 impede, speech 8 footdrag, lose time 9 hindrance, talkathon 10 opposition, vocalizing
filigree: 3 web 4 lace, lacy 7 lattice 10 decoration
filigreed: 4 lacy 6 frilly
filing month: 3 Apr. 5 April
filings, metal: 5 swarf
Filipino: 4 Moro 8 language
Filippo: 5 Lippi
fill: 3 mob 4 cram, jade, lade, load, pack, plug, sate 5 crowd, gorge, imbue, spend, steep, stock, stuff 6 load up, make up, occupy, plug up, pump up, supply, top off 7 congest, inflate, jam-pack, pervade, process, satiate, satisfy, surfeit 8 brim over, capacity, flesh out, permeate 9 overstuff, replenish
a position: 4 hire 6 employ, engage, retain, sign on, sign up, take on
in: 3 sub 4 post, tell, temp, warn 5 brief, enter, prime, ready 6 act for, advise, double, inform, notify 7 apprise, apprize, prepare, replace 8 complete, flesh out, pinch-hit, round off, round out 9 alternate, change off, interject, share with 10 substitute
in (for): 3 sub 5 cover 10 substitute
out: 3 pad, wax 4 grow 5 swell 6 blow up, expand, fatten, mature, puff up 7 enlarge 8 complete, round off 10 supplement
starter: 4 land, over 5 fiber
the bill: 3 fit 4 suit 5 cater, serve 6 please 7 qualify, satisfy
the hold: 4 lade, load, stow 5 lay in
the tank: 4 fuel 5 gas up
thing to ~ out: 4 form 5 blank
to excess: 4 cloy, cram, heap, jade, sate 5 stuff
to overflowing: 4 load, pack, pile 5 amass, mound 6 lavish 9 stockpile
up: 4 fuel, lade 5 gorge 6 inpour 7 recruit
up on: 3 eat
fille: 4 girl 6 French
friend: 4 amie
parent: 4 mère, père
__ fille: 5 jeune
filled: 3 fed 4 rife 5 laden 6 loaded 7 crowded, fraught, replete, teeming 8 abundant, brimming 9 abounding, chock-full
not ~ in: 5 blank, clean, empty 6 vacant 8 unmarked
filled __: 4 gold, milk
__-filled: 4 gold
filled-out: 5 beefy, burly, buxom, obese, plump, pudgy, pursy, round, stout, tubby 6 chubby, chunky, fleshy, portly, rotund, stocky 9 corpulent 10 overweight
__-filled room: 5 smoke
filler: 6 insert 8 stuffing
conversation ~: 2 er, um 4 I see 5 I mean
fillet: 3 cut 4 bone, fish, meat 5 strip 6 debone, ribbon 10 hair ribbon
comb. form: 4 taen- 5 taeni- 6 taenio-
narrow ~: 6 listel
fill-in: 4 temp 7 stopgap 9 alternate, surrogate 10 jury-rigged, substitute
filling: 4 rich, weft 5 beefy, inlay 6 vitals 7 amalgam, batting, caloric, innards, padding, wadding 8 contents, stuffing
tooth ~: 5 crown
filling __: 3 out 7 station
filling station freebie, once: 3 air, map
fillip: 3 tap 4 flip, goad, poke, prod, push, snap, spur 5 egg on, flick, tonic 6 arouse, prompt, strike 8 get going 9 stimulate 10 incitement
Fillmore, Millard: 9 president
former occupation: 6 lawyer
home: 7 Buffalo, New York
wife: 7 Abigail 8 Caroline
fill one's __: 5 shoes
fill the __: 4 bill
fill to the __: 4 brim
filly: 4 foal, mare 5 horse 6 animal, equine, female
food: 4 oats
parent: 4 mare 8 stallion
film: 3 pic 4 cine, mist, rust, scum, show, skin, veil, wash 5 flick, layer, movie, scale, sheet, shoot 6 cinema, patina, patine, powder, record, talkie 7 coating, picture 8 membrane 9 celluloid, photoplay 10 photograph, production
big shot: 5 mogul
cast-of-thousands ~: 4 epic
combining form: 4 cine-
container: 3 can
crew member: 4 grip, tech 6 editor, gaffer 7 best boy 8 stunt man
developing abbr.: 3 enl.
developing compound: 6 amidol
ender: 3 dom 4 card, goer 5 going, maker, strip 6 making 7 setting
feat: 5 stunt
fragment: 4 clip
light: 5 klieg
performers' org.: 3 SAG
processing site: 3 lab
rating org.: 4 MPAA
session: 5 shoot
specification: 3 ASA 5 speed
studio: 3 Fox, MGM 6 Disney 7 Miramax, New Line 8 Columbia 9 Paramount, Universal 10 Dreamworks, Warner Bros.
unit: 4 reel, take
film __: 4 clip, gate, noir, pack 5 badge, speed 7 library
__ film: 3 art 4 cult, disc, disk, roll, thin 5 pilot, sheet, sound 6 safety 7 feature, nitrate
filmgoer, G-rated: 5 minor
filmmaker: 6 auteur 8 director
films: 3 pix 6 cinema
like some ~: 4 gory 6 G-rated, R-rated
filmy: 4 fine, thin 5 gauzy, light, sheer, wispy 6 limpid 7 chiffon, wispish 8 cobwebby, delicate, ethereal, finespun, gossamer 10 cobweblike, diaphanous
fabric: 5 gauze, lisse, tulle
Filofax: 3 log 5 diary 7 daybook, journal 8 calendar
fils: 3 son 6 French
parent: 4 mère, père
filter: 4 leak, ooze, seep, sift 5 clean, drain, leach, sieve, unmix 6 osmose, purify, refine, screen, strain, winnow 7 distill, trickle 8 auto part, permeate, purifier, separate 9 penetrate, percolate
in: 4 seep 8 permeate 9 penetrate, percolate
like some ~s: 5 linty
spotlight ~: 3 gel
filth: 4 crud, dirt, gunk, mire, muck, smut 5 grime, trash 6 grunge, refuse 7 garbage 8 impurity 9 pollution, profanity, vulgarity 10 corruption, defilement, impurities
filthy: 4 foul, lewd, ugly, vile 5 black, dirty, germy, grimy, mangy, muddy, nasty, sooty 6 cruddy, crumby, crummy, fouled, grubby, grungy, impure, mangey, ribald,

rotten, smutty, soiled, sordid, vulgar **7** corrupt, profane, smudged, squalid, stained, tainted, unclean, unswept **8** befouled, begrimed, maculate, polluted, slovenly, stagnant, unwashed **9** blackened, loathsome, low-minded, lubricous, tarnished **10** bedraggled, besmirched, despicable, germ-ridden, insanitary, scurrilous, unsanitary
lucre: **4** pelf
make ~: **4** foul, soil **5** dirty, spoil, stain, sully, taint **6** befoul, defile **7** corrupt, pollute, vitiate **9** desecrate **10** adulterate
filthy __: **4** rich **5** lucre
filtrate: **4** ooze, seep **5** leach **9** percolate
filum: **6** thread
fin: **4** bill, five, limb **5** fiver, pinna **6** dorsal **7** airfoil, ventral **8** five-spot, pectoral
change for a ~: **4** ones **7** singles
combining form: **6** pteryg- **7** pterygo-
ender: **4** back, fish
starter: **3** bow **4** lobe, tail **6** thread
fin __: **3** ray **4** keel **5** whale
__ fin: **4** skid, swim, tail **6** caudal, dorsal, pelvic **7** adipose, ventral
finagle: **4** plot **5** cheat, trick **6** outwit, scheme, wangle **7** connive, finesse, swindle, wheedle **8** contrive, engineer, freeload, intrigue, maneuver, outsmart, scrounge **9** machinate **10** manipulate
final: **3** end, net, ult. **4** exam, last, test **6** ending, latest, latter, utmost **7** closing, parting, supreme **8** absolute, crowning, decisive, definite, eventual, terminal, ultimate **9** finishing, last-ditch **10** concluding, conclusive, definitive, overriding, peremptory, unarguable, undisputed
ender: **3** ist, ity
make ~: **5** close, sew up **6** clinch **8** finalize **10** consummate
not ~: **6** unfirm **9** provisory, tentative, uncertain, undecided, unsettled **10** indecisive, unfinished
not ~ in law: **4** nisi
reckoning: **3** end **6** result, upshot **7** outcome **9** punch line **10** bottom line, conclusion, denouement, resolution, settlement
starter: **4** semi **7** quarter
tend to ~ details: **5** mop up
word: **4** amen
final __: **3** cut **5** cause
Final __: **4** Four **5** Touch
Final Analysis (1992 film)
cast: Kim Basinger, Richard Gere, Eric Roberts, Uma Thurman
Final Countdown, The (1980 film)
cast: Kirk Douglas, Charles Durning, James Farentino, Katharine Ross, Martin Sheen
dog: **7** Charlie
finale: **3** end **4** coda, last **5** close, grand **6** climax, ending, epilog, windup, wrap-up **7** last act **8** curtains, end piece, epilogue, last gasp, terminus **10** conclusion, denouement, resolution
__ finale: **5** grand
Final Four
event: **4** semi **5** round, semis
org.: **4** NCAA
final frontier, The: **5** space
finalize: **4** jell, seal **5** sew up, tie up **6** clinch, decide, settle, wind up, wrap up **7** work out **8** complete, conclude, nail down, round off, round out **10** consummate
finally: **3** yet **4** last **6** at last, lastly **7** forever, for good **8** after all, in the end **10** eventually, for all time, ultimately
finals
prelim: **4** semi **5** semis
prepare for ~: **4** cram **5** study **6** bone up, review
Final Touch
alternative: **5** Downy **6** Bounce **7** Snuggle **9** Cling Free
finance: **4** back, fund **5** endow, stake **6** defray, pay for **7** banking, sponsor, support **8** bankroll, maintain **9** budgeting, economics, subsidize **10** capitalize, investment, underwrite, Wall Street
company: **6** lender
degree: **3** MBA
govt. ~ org.: **3** OMB
world ~ org.: **3** IMF
finance __: **4** bill **6** charge **7** company
__ finance: **4** high
financer: **6** backer, friend, patron **7** sponsor **9** supporter **10** benefactor
finances: **5** means, money, purse **6** income **8** monetary
science of ~: **9** economics
financial: **6** fiscal **8** economic, monetary **9** budgeting, pecuniary **10** commercial
aid: **5** grant **6** credit **7** alimony, backing, pension, subsidy, support **8** donation **9** allowance, endowment, patronage **10** assistance, fellowship, honorarium
aid criterion: **4** need **5** merit **6** income
analysis tool: **5** chart, graph
asset: **4** bond, cash **5** stock
average: **3** Dow **5** S and P
crisis: **5** panic
estimate: **5** quote **9** quotation
hedger: **3** arb
item: **5** asset **6** credit
market: **3** OTC **4** AMEX, NYSE **5** Comex
officer: **2** tr. **5** treas. **9** treasurer
plan: **6** budget
publication: **3** WSJ **6** Forbes **7** Barron's, Fortune
records: **5** books
reserve: **6** buffer **7** cushion
resources: **5** means, purse **10** pocketbook
service: **6** escrow
standing: **5** worth **8** net worth
transaction: **4** loan
U.S. ~ capital: **3** NYC
wiz: **3** CPA **4** acct. **10** accountant
financial __: **3** aid **7** planner
financier: **5** baron **6** backer, banker, broker, tycoon **7** magnate, sponsor **8** investor **9** moneybags **10** bankroller, capitalist, grubstaker, speculator
Financier, The
author: Theodore Dreiser
financing: **5** funds **7** capital, funding **9** patronage **10** investment
__ financing: **3** APR **4** debt **6** bridge **7** deficit
finback: **5** minke, whale **8** cetacean
relative: **3** orc, sei **6** beluga, narwal **7** cowfish, dolphin, grampus, narwhal, rorqual **8** narwhale, porpoise
finca: **5** ranch
finch: **4** bird **5** junco, serin, tarin, twite **6** canary, linnet, siskin, towhee, whidah, whydah **7** bunting, redpoll, sparrow, waxbill **8** grosbeak **9** grassquit, seedeater
color: **4** gold **5** green **6** yellow
home: **4** nest
relative: **9** crossbill
starter: **3** haw **4** bull, gold **5** green
__ finch: **4** Java, pine, rosy **5** grass, house, zebra **6** purple, weaver
Finch, Peter: **5** actor
film: Far From the Madding Crowd (1967)
Father Brown (1954)
Flight of the Phoenix (1966)
Network (1976, AA)
The Nun's Story (1959)
The Pumpkin Eater (1964)
Sunday, Bloody Sunday (1971)
Windom's Way (1957)
find: **3** get **4** espy, gain, meet, rule, spot **5** dig up, judge, prove, scour, sight, trace **6** attain, collar, corral, detect, locate, look up, notice, obtain, strike, supply, turn up **7** achieve, acquire, bargain, discern, good buy, hit upon, make out, observe, procure, recover, rout out, run into, scare up, scout up, uncover, unearth **8** arrive at, bump into, chance on, come upon, discover, great buy, identify, perceive, pinpoint, rustle up, scout out, smell out, smoke out **9** ascertain, calculate, detection, determine, discovery, encounter, ferret out, figure out, light upon, recognize, run across, stumble on, track down **10** chance upon, come across, happen upon
again: **7** get back, recover
archaeologist's ~: **4** abri, bone, ruin **5** mound, relic, ruins, shard, sherd, stela, stele **6** fossil
be unable to ~: **6** mislay **7** misfile **8** misplace
fault: **3** hit, nag, pan **4** carp **5** blame, cavil, gripe, knock, nag at, scold **6** accuse, jibe at, pick at **7** cavil at, censure, condemn, grumble, nitpick, put down, quarrel, quibble **8** complain **9** criticize, make a fuss, pick apart, pull apart, reprehend, shoot down **10** vituperate
hard to ~: **4** rare **6** exotic, scanty, scarce **8** uncommon
in flagrante delicto: **5** catch
obnoxious: **4** hate **6** loathe **7** despise **8** execrate **9** abominate
out: **3** see **4** hear, seek, tell **5** catch, glean, learn, solve **6** verify **7** unearth **8** discover **9** ascertain, determine, establish, get word of **10** understand
(out): **4** hunt
the key to: **5** crack **6** decode, fathom, unlock **7** clear up, explain, hit upon, unravel, work out **8** decipher, get right, untangle **9** figure out, interpret, puzzle out **10** account for
try to ~: **4** hunt, seek **5** trace, track, trail **6** gun for, pursue **7** fish for, go after, hunt for, look for, scout up **8** quest for, run after, scout out, sniff out **9** track down
underground ~: **3** oil **4** coal **7** mineral **9** petroleum
find __: **3** out
find __ with: **5** fault
fin-de-__: **6** siècle
__ finder: **4** fact **5** depth, range
finders __: **7** keepers
finder's __: **3** fee
finder starter: **4** path, view **5** fault, water
finding: **4** fact **6** decree, result, ruling **7** verdict **8** decision, judgment **9** deduction, discovery **10** conclusion, resolution
Finding Forrester (2000 film)
cast: F. Murray Abraham, Sean Connery, Anna Paquin
director: Gus Van Sant
__-finding mission: **4** fact
Finding Nemo (2003 film)
character: **4** Dory, Gill **5** Bruce, Crush, Nigel, Peach **6** Marlin
studio: **5** Pixar
voice cast: Albert Brooks, Willem Dafoe, Ellen DeGeneres, Geoffrey Rush
Finding Neverland (2004 film)
cast: Julie Christie, Johnny Depp, Dustin Hoffman, Radha Mitchell, Kate Winslet
Finding the Sun
author: Edward Albee
Findlay: **4** city, town **5** Maude
locale: **4** Ohio
Findley, Timothy: **6** writer **8** Canadian
__ Finds Andy Hardy: **4** Love
fine: **4** levy, thin **5** acute, exact, fancy, filmy, gauzy, moral, mulct, noble, quite, sharp, sheer, slick, smart, sunny **6** agreed, amerce, indeed, narrow, ornate, pretty, proper, punish, select, subtle, surely, you bet **7** damages, elegant, ethical, exactly, forfeit, fragile, go ahead, netlike, penalty, perfect, powdery, precise, refined, slender, stellar, suits me, ten-four **8** all right, as you say, becoming, delicate, distinct, esthetic, gossamer, handsome, penalize, pleasant, pleasing, skillful, tasteful, thumbs up, very good, very well **9** admirable, agreeable, be my guest, certainly, darn right, gilt-edged, high-grade, naturally, okey-dokey, precisely, reputable, sensitive, sure thing, you betcha, you said it **10** absolutely, accept-

able, amercement, assessment, beneficial, by all means, cobweb-like, creditable, definitely, diaphanous, first-class, forfeiture, good enough, positively, punishment, reparation, sure enough, swimmingly, that's right
alternative: 4 jail
check the ~ print: 4 pore, read 5 study 8 pore over
combining form: 4 lept- 5 lepto-
in ~ fettle: 4 hale, trim, well 5 hardy, right, sound 6 robust 7 healthy
medievfine: 4 wite
not ~: 3 raw 4 rude 5 crude, rough, tacky 6 coarse, common, rustic 8 plebeian 9 inelegant, tasteless 10 uncultured
point: 6 detail, nicety, nuance 9 punctilio
print: 5 terms 7 details, proviso, strings 9 condition, provision 10 conditions
punish by ~: 5 mulct 6 amerce 8 penalize
set a ~: 4 levy 6 assess, impose
see also wonderful
fine __: 3 art 4 arts, comb, nail 5 print 6 bouche
fine-__: 3 cut 4 draw, spun, tune 5 drawn, grain 7 grained
fine-__ comb: 5 tooth 7 toothed
Fine: 5 Larry 6 Sylvia
Fine __, A: 4 Mess 7 Madness, Romance
Fine!: 4 okay, sure 6 you bet
__ Fine: 5 He's So, I Feel
__-Fine: 3 My-T
__ Fine Day: 3 One
fine kettle of fish: 4 mess
Fine Madness, A (1966 film)
cast: Sean Connery, Jean Seberg, Joanne Woodward
fineness: 4 luxe 6 virtue 7 texture 8 delicacy, grandeur 10 refinement
unit: 5 karat
Fine Old Conflict, A
author: Jessica Mitford
finer: 6 better 8 superior
make ~: 6 better, enrich 7 enhance, improve, sweeten 9 embellish 10 supplement
Fine Romance, A
composer: Dorothy Fields, Jerome Kern
Finer Things, The (1987 song)
artist: Steve Winwood
finery: 5 array, silks 6 attire, satins 7 clothes, formals, jewelry, regalia 8 frippery, glad rags 9 adornment, caparison, trappings 10 Sunday best
eschewing ~: 5 plain
finespun: 4 lacy 5 filmy, gauzy, light, sheer 6 subtle 7 refined, tissuey 8 cobwebby, delicate, gossamer 9 gauzelike 10 diaphanous
finesse: 3 art 4 tact, wile 5 bluff, craft, guile, savvy, skill, trick 6 acumen, jockey, polish, wangle 7 ability, beguile, finagle, gimmick, know-how, mastery 8 artifice, artistry, delicacy, maneuver, subtlety, urbanity 9 adeptness, dexterity, diplomacy, smartness, stratagem 10 adroitness, artfulness, cleverness, competence, craftiness, discretion, manipulate, refinement
Finesse: 7 shampoo
alternative: 4 Flex, Pert 5 Prell, Suave, Wella 7 Pantene
finest: 3 top 4 best 5 cream 9 top-drawer, topflight
__ Finest Hour: 5 Their
fine-tooth __: 4 comb
fine-tune: 4 edit, hone 5 alter, tweak 6 adjust 8 modulate 9 calibrate
finfoot: 4 bird
Fingal's __: 4 Cave
finger: 4 feel, make, name, pick 5 blame, digit, pinky, point, rat on, thumb, touch 6 dactyl, give up, handle, member, pilfer, pinkie, turn in 7 pointer, specify, toy with 8 identify, pinpoint 9 appendage, designate, implicate, recognize 10 manipulate
combining form: 6 dactyl-, digiti- 7 dactylo-
crook a ~: 6 beckon, entice, invite, signal, summon
ender: 3 tip 4 nail, pick 5 board, print, spell 7 breadth
food: 6 canapé 9 antipasto, appetizer
in the ribs: 3 jab 4 poke, prod 5 nudge 6 tickle
lay a ~ on: 5 touch
lift a ~ for: 4 help
opposite: 3 toe
part: 4 nail 7 cuticle, knuckle
point a ~ at: 5 blame 6 accuse, charge
problem: 6 agnail
put one's ~ on: 4 find 5 place 6 locate, recall 7 find out, specify 8 discover, identify, remember 9 bring back
put the ~ on: 4 name 6 betray, give up, tattle
put the ~ (on): 3 rat 4 tell 6 inform, snitch
shake a ~: 3 wag
sound: 4 snap
starter: 4 fore, lady
wrap around one's little ~: 3 use 6 misuse 7 control 10 manipulate
finger __: 3 man 4 bowl, food, gate, hole, mark, post, wave 5 grass, paint 6 puppet 7 reading
__ finger: 4 ring 5 index, lift a, third 6 little, middle 7 trigger
Finger __: 5 Lakes
fingerboard ridge: 4 fret
__-fingered: 5 light 6 sticky
__-fingered fastball: 5 split
__ Finger Exercise: 4 Five
finger-in-door reaction: 2 ow 3 yow 4 ouch, yeow
__ finger in the pie: 5 have a
Finger Lake: 5 Keuka 6 Cayuga, Owasco, Seneca 11 Canandaigua, Skaneateles
fingernail: 4 claw 5 talon 6 ungual, unguis
base: 4 lune
crescent: 6 lunula, lunule
in Spanish: 3 uña
polish: 5 glaze, paint 6 enamel 7 lacquer, varnish
finger-paint: 3 dab 4 daub 5 smear
__ fingerprint: 3 DNA 6 latent 7 genetic
fingerprint line: 5 ridge, whorl
fingers
get one's ~ on: 3 bag, nab 4 grab, grip, take 5 catch, grasp, seize, snare, steal 6 secure, snatch 7 acquire, plunder, receive 8 glom on to 9 lay hold of
keep one's ~ crossed: 4 hope, wish 5 dream 6 aspire, expect 7 look for 10 anticipate
middle ~: 5 medii
slip through one's ~: 4 flee, skip 6 escape, run off, run out 7 abscond, bail out, duck out, get away, make off, run away, slip off 8 slip away 9 break away, steal away 10 fly the coop
starter: 6 butter
tap one's ~: 4 drum
work one's ~ to the bone: 5 slave
__ fingers: 5 green 6 sticky
__ Fingers: 6 Vienna
Fingers, Rollie: 6 hurler 7 pitcher
fingertip: 3 pad
fingertips
at one's ~: 4 near 5 ready
have at one's ~: 4 know 5 grasp 6 fathom 7 cognize 10 comprehend
use one's ~: 4 feel 5 touch
finger-to-lips sound: 3 shh
finger wave: 4 coif 6 hairdo 8 coiffure
fini: 4 done, over 5 ended, kaput 6 sewn up 7 all over, settled, through 8 achieved 9 concluded
finial: 3 cap, epi, top
Finian's Rainbow (1968 film)
cast: Fred Astaire, Petula Clark, Tommy Steele
director: Francis Ford Coppola
Finian's Rainbow (musical)
composer: Yip Harburg, Burtone Lane
finicky: 4 neat 5 exact, fussy, picky 6 choosy, dainty, prissy 7 careful, choosey, mincing, precise, prudent, prudish 8 captious, cautious, critical, exacting, precious, rigorous, thorough 9 assiduous, attentive, demanding, difficult, judicious, observant, querulous, squeamish 10 fastidious, meticulous, nitpicking, particular, scrupulous
cat on TV: 6 Morris
eater: 3 cat
finis: 3 end 4 last 6 ending, windup 7 through 10 conclusion
finish: 2 do, go 3 end, wax, zap 4 best, coat, do in, gild, halt, last, quit, rout, ruin, slay, stop, wrap 5 cease, close, crown, drain, empty, end up, glaze, gloss, mop up, sew up, sheen, shine, spend, stain, use up 6 clinch, defeat, devour, enamel, ending, expend, finale, fulfil, luster, patina, patine, polish, refine, result, run out, settle, smooth, veneer, windup, wrap up 7 abolish, achieve, adjourn, break up, closing, closure, coating, consume, deplete, destroy, execute, exhaust, fulfill, get done, lacquer, last act, perfect, perform, play out, resolve, surface, varnish, wipe out, work out 8 complete, conclude, curtains, dispatch, hang it up, pack it in, round off, round out, shut down, surcease, terminus, transact, vaporize 9 cessation, culminate, discharge, dispose of, go through, polish off, terminate 10 accomplish, call it a day, completion, conclusion, consummate, denouement, desistance, expiration, get through, go the route, put through, refinement, resolution, run through
a course: 3 eat
ahead of: 6 defeat
at: 4 abut 5 verge 8 border on, neighbor
behind: 6 lose to
dull ~: 3 mat 5 matte
first: 3 win 4 best 7 succeed, triumph
in the money: 3 win 4 show 5 place
last: 4 lose
line: 4 tape, wire
off: 3 eat, end 4 do in 5 eat up, mop up, use up 8 abrogate, close out, surcease 9 liquidate 10 annihilate
perfectly: 3 ace
photo ~: 3 mat, tie 4 stat 5 gloss, matte
second: 4 fail, lose 5 place 9 fall short
starter: 5 photo
third: 4 lose, show
finish __: 4 coat, line
__ finish: 5 photo 7 English, Holland
finish'd: 3 o'er
finished: 3 out 4 done, gone, lost, over, past, thru 5 empty, kaput, spent, suave, tired, total, whole 6 done in, entire, undone, urbane 7 all over, at an end, decided, elegant, plenary, through, wrecked 8 complete, cultured, flawless, over with, realized, thorough, washed-up 10 devastated, exhaustive
with: 5 rid of
__-finished: 4 half
finishing: 4 last 5 final 6 sequel 10 completion, definitive
finishing __: 4 coat, nail 5 touch 6 school
Finish What Ya Started (1988 song)
artist: Van Halen
finite: 6 mortal 7 limited 9 definable 10 measurable
finite __: 4 verb 6 clause 7 decimal
finito: 4 done, over 5 ended, kaput 6 sewn up 7 all over, settled, through 8 achieved 9 concluded
fink: 3 rat 4 nark, sing 5 namer, snake 6 canary, snitch, tattle, weasel 7 blabber, stoolie, tattler, tipster, traitor 8 fat mouth, informer, squealer, turncoat 9 miscreant 10 taleteller, tattletale
be a ~: 5 rat on 6 squeal, tattle, turn in 7 sell out
on: 4 name 6 betray, give up, tattle, turn in
starter: 3 rat
__ Fink: 4 Mike, Ratt 6 Barton

Finkel: **6** Fyvush
Finland: **4** gulf **6** nation **7** country
architect: **5** Aalto
bath: **5** sauna
capital: **8** Helsinki
city: **4** Oulu **5** Espoo, Lahti, Turku, Vaasa **6** Kuopio, Vantaa **7** Tampere **8** Helsinki **9** Jyväskylä
combining form: **5** Fenno-
conductor: **7** Salonen
former money: **5** penni **6** markka
Gulf of ~ feeder: **4** Neva
islands: **5** Aland
lake: **4** Nasi **5** Enare, Inari **6** Saimaa
legislature: **9** Eduskunta
money: **4** euro
native: **4** Lapp
neighbor: **6** Norway, Russia, Sweden
Nobelist in Chemistry: **8** Virtanen
Nobelist in Literature: **9** Sillanpöö
phone maker: **5** Nokia
poet: **8** Runeberg
port: **4** Pori **5** Vaasa **8** Helsinki
runner: **5** Nurmi **10** Paavo Nurmi
to Finns: **5** Suomi
writer: **4** Kivi **5** Canth **8** Haavikko **9** Sillanpää
Finlandia
composer: Jean Sibelius
Finlayson: **5** James
Finley: **7** Charlie **8** Charlie O.
Finley Peter __: **5** Dunne
__ Finn: **4** Huck **6** Mickey **7** Phineas
Finnair
competitor: **3** SAS
finnan __: **6** haddie **7** haddock
finnan haddie: **4** fish
__-finned: **4** soft **5** spiny
Finnegans Wake
author: James Joyce
character: **3** ALP, Ann, HCE **4** Anna, Jaun, Shem, Yawn **5** Chuff, Dolph, Glugg, Jerry, Kevin, Shaun **6** Isobel **8** Humphrey **9** Earwicker **10** Plurabelle
last word: **3** the
Finney: **4** Jack **6** Albert
Finney, Albert: **5** actor
film: Erin Brockovich (2000)
Murder on the Orient Express (1974)
Scrooge (1970)
Shoot the Moon (1982)
Tom Jones (1963)
Two for the Road (1967)
Under the Volcano (1984)
Wolfen (1981)
Finn, Huck: **4** teen
craft: **4** raft
father: **3** Pap
__-Finnic: **4** Ugro
Finnic language: **4** Mari
Finnish: **8** language
see also Finland
__-Finnish War: **5** Russo
Finno-__: **5** Ugric **6** Ugrian
Finno-__ War: **5** Russo
Finsteraarhorn: **3** Alp
Finsterwald, Dow: **6** golfer
Fiona: **5** Apple **10** Hutchinson
Fionnula: **8** Flanagan
fiord: **3** bay **4** cove, gulf **5** bight, cliff, firth, frith, inlet
locale: **4** Oslo **6** Norway
Fiore: **6** Robert
Fiorello: **9** La Guardia
Fiorello!
author: Jerome Weidman
Fiorentino, Linda: **7** actress
Fiorucci: **4** Elio
fir: **4** tree **6** balsam **7** conifer **9** evergreen
kin: **4** pine **6** spruce **7** hemlock **8** tamarack
product: **4** cone
__ fir: **7** Douglas
fire: **2** ax **3** axe, can, rid, zip **4** boot, brio, dash, drop, élan, fury, hurl, oust, sack, send, stir, zeal, zing **5** ardor, blaze, drive, eject, expel, flame, gusto, heave, let go, light, liven, pitch, rally, rouse, salvo, shell, shoot, sling, spark, verve, vigor **6** arouse, attack, energy, excite, fervor, flames, hearth, incite, launch, lay off, let fly, set off, spirit, stir up, volley **7** animate, barrage, burning, cashier, dismiss, drum out, enflame, enliven, explode, inferno, inflame, inspire, passion, provoke, sniping, turn out **8** afflatus, detonate, displace, enspirit, fervency, ignition, inspirit, lyricism, motivate, pink-slip, shelling, touch off, vivacity **9** animation, cannonade, discharge, eagerness, electrify, fusillade, galvanize, impassion, intensity, scorching, terminate **10** combustion, enthusiasm, excitement, heartiness, intoxicate, liveliness
add fuel to the ~: **4** spur, stir **5** rouse **6** whip up, work up **7** agitate **9** stimulate
aftermath: **3** ash
antiaircraft ~: **4** flak **5** flack
artillery ~: **5** salvo **7** barrage **9** cannonade, fusillade
at: **6** strafe
(at): **5** snipe
back: **5** rebut, reply **6** answer, retort **7** counter, respond **9** rejoinder
ball of ~: **3** sun **4** star **6** dynamo **7** hustler **8** tireless **9** ambitious, energetic
be on ~: **4** burn **5** blaze **7** smolder
bit of ~: **5** spark
breathe ~: **4** boil, fume, rage, stew **5** storm **6** see red, seethe **7** smolder **10** hit the roof
breather: **6** dragon
breathing ~: **3** hot, mad **5** angry, irate, livid, riled, surly, vexed, wroth **6** fuming, ireful, piqued, raging, red-hot **7** angered, annoyed, berserk, boiling, enraged, furious, steamed **8** incensed, inflamed, provoked, up in arms, volcanic, worked up, wrathful **9** indignant, irritated, seeing red, ticked off **10** infuriated
calm the ~: **4** damp
catch ~: **4** burn **6** ignite, kindle, set off **8** enkindle **10** incinerate
ceremonial ~: **4** pyre
chief: **7** marshal
combining form: **3** pyr- **4** igni-, pyro-
crime: **5** arson
destroy, as by ~: **3** gut
dog name: **4** Spot
ender: **3** arm, box, bug, dog, fly, man, men **4** ball, base, bird, boat, bomb, brat, clay, damp, lock, plug, side, trap, wall, weed, wood, work **5** board, brand, break, brick, drake, fight, flood, guard, house, light, place, power, proof, stone, storm, water **7** cracker, fighter
escape: **4** exit **6** ladder
feed the ~: **4** fuel, stir
fighter: **4** rain **5** water
from ~: **7** igneous
goddess: **6** Birgit
got the ~ going again: **5** relit
hang ~: **4** pend
hanging ~: **6** put off **7** abeyant, delayed, pending **9** postponed, undecided, unsettled **10** in abeyance, up in the air
indicator: **5** smoke
inner ~: **3** vim **4** zeal, zest **5** ardor, drive, oomph, verve **6** fervor **7** longing, passion **8** ambition **9** intensity **10** fanaticism, initiative
iron in the ~: **3** gig, job **4** task **5** chore **7** project, venture **8** activity **10** assignment
light a ~ under: **4** goad, stir **5** rouse, spark **6** arouse, bestir, excite, incite, stir up, wake up, whip up, work up **7** animate, inspire, provoke **8** motivate **9** galvanize, stimulate
no ball of ~: **5** idler, sloth **7** laggard, slacker
off: **3** lob **4** cast, hurl, send, toss **5** chuck, fling, heave, pitch, shoot, throw **6** launch, let fly, propel
offshoot: **6** cinder
on ~: **3** hot **6** ablaze, aflame, flambé **7** burning
open ~: **5** blast, shoot **7** bombard
playing with ~: **5** risky **8** perilous, reckless
play with ~: **4** dare, risk **9** take a risk
pottery: **4** bake
prepare to ~: **3** aim **4** cock
pull out of the ~: **4** save **5** spare **6** rescue
put on the ~: **4** heat, warm **6** heat up, warm up
ready to ~: **5** armed **6** cocked, loaded
residue: **3** ash **4** soot
rod: **5** poker
safety activity: **5** drill
set ~ to: **3** lit **5** light **6** kindle
sign: **5** Aries, smoke
signal: **4** bell, gong **5** alarm
starter: **3** fox, gun **4** back, camp, drum, spit, wild **5** brush, cross, flint, match, shell, spark **8** kindling
tend a ~: **4** poke **5** stoke
truck: **6** engine
truck adjunct: **5** siren
up: **3** rev **4** boil, goad, heat, rile, spur, wake **5** anger, pique, rouse, start, waken **6** arouse, enrage, incite, kindle, thrill **7** actuate, enflame, enliven, enthuse, incense, inflame, inspire, outrage **9** galvanize, impassion, instigate, stimulate **10** accelerate
upon: **5** beset, blast, blitz, shell, shoot **6** attack, strike **7** barrage, besiege, bombard **9** broadside, cannonade
with many irons in the ~: **4** at it, busy **6** active, hectic, lively **7** on the go, swamped **8** bustling, immersed **9** engrossed
fire __: **3** ant, hat, off, pot, red **4** area, away, boss, clay, code, door, hose, iron, line, opal, pink, sale, ship, sign, wall **5** alarm, chief, drill, point, tower, truck **6** beetle, blight, cherry, engine, escape, screen, temple **7** balloon, brigade, company, control, curtain, gilding, hydrant, marshal, setting, station, support
fire-__: **4** cure, plow **5** eater **6** polish
fire-__ red: **6** engine
__ fire: **3** red, sea **4** hang, slow **5** brush, catch, cross, crown, Greek, quick, set on, under, watch **6** liquid **7** council, hostile, Kentish
__-fire: **4** sure **5** cease, rapid **6** center **7** central
Fire (song)
artist: Arthur Brown, Ohio Players, Pointer Sisters
Fire __ Time, The: **4** Next
__ Fire: **4** Cold, I'm on, Sure **5** Under **7** Chicago, Eternal
Fire and Ice
author: Robert Frost
Fire and Rain (1970 song)
artist: James Taylor
firearm: **3** gat, gun, Uzi **4** heat **5** piece, rifle **6** heater, musket, pistol, roscoe, weapon **7** handgun, shotgun **8** revolver
lobby: **3** NRA
part: **6** barrel, breech
fireball: **3** sun **6** bolide, dynamo **7** zealous **8** live wire **9** lightning
Firebird: **3** car **4** auto **7** Pontiac **10** automobile
Firebird, The: **6** ballet
composer: Igor Stravinsky
firebox innards: **5** alarm
firebrand: **7** hellion, hothead, radical **8** agitator, flambeau, inflamer, ultraist **9** demagogue **10** incendiary
firebrat: **3** bug **6** insect
firebug: **4** pyro **5** torch **8** arsonist **10** incendiary, pyromaniac
crime: **5** arson
firecracker
noise: **3** pop **4** bang **5** burst, crack **9** explosion
part: **4** fuse
__ Firecracker: **4** Miss
__-fired: **3** all, gas **4** hell **7** biscuit
firedamp: **3** gas **7** coal gas
firedog: **7** andiron
fired up: **3** lit **4** avid, keen **5** eager, wired **6** aflame, gung-ho, rah-rah, yeasty **7** demonic, excited, zealous **8** daemonic, inspired **9** demonical
again: **5** relit
fire-eating: **4** bold **5** brave, gutsy **9** combative, undaunted **10** courageous

fire-engine __: 3 red
fire escape sign: 4 Exit
fire-extinguishing agent: 5 halon
firefighter
concern: 5 arson
need: 3 axe 4 foam, hose 6 helmet, ladder
often: 5 hoser
volunteer ~: 4 vamp
Fireflies
author: Rabindranath Tagore
firefly: 3 bug 6 beetle, insect
like a ~: 3 lit 5 aglow 6 bright
output: 4 glow 5 glint
Firefly Summer
author: Maeve Binchy
Fire From Heaven
author: Mary Renault
__ Fire Girl: 4 Camp
Firehouse
author: David Halberstam
Fire in the Ashes
author: Theodore H. White
Fire Lake (1980 song)
artist: Bob Seger
Fire Next Time, The
author: James Baldwin
Firenze: 4 city, town 8 Florence
locale: 5 Italy 6 Italia
river: 4 Arno
fireplace: 5 ingle, stove 6 hearth 9 inglenook 10 hearthside
fuel: 3 log 4 wood 6 gas log
part: 3 hob 4 flue, vent 5 grate 6 ashpit
receptacle: 6 ashcan, ashpan
remnant: 3 ash 5 ember
site: 5 cabin, lodge 6 chalet 7 cottage
tool: 5 poker
vent: 6 airway 7 chimney 10 smokeshaft
firepower: 4 arms, guns 6 rifles 7 weapons 8 matériel, ordnance, weaponry 9 munitions
provide ~ to: 3 arm 7 fortify 8 embattle
fire-retardant acid: 5 boric 7 boracic
fireside: 4 home 5 abode, ingle 6 casual, hearth, low-key, social 7 amiable, cordial, domicil 8 domicile, dwelling, friendly, home life, informal, laid-back, sociable 9 easygoing, homestead, inglenook, residence 10 family life, habitation, hearthside
fireside __: 4 chat
Firestarter: 4 film 5 novel
author: Stephen King
cast: Drew Barrymore, George C. Scott, Martin Sheen
Firestone: 3 Roy 6 Harvey
__ fire to: 3 set
firewater: 6 liquor, whisky 7 alcohol, spirits, whiskey 9 aqua vitae, inebriant
__ fire with fire: 5 fight
firewood: 4 fuel 8 kindling
amount: 4 cord, rick 6 armful
chopping ~: 5 chore
hauler: 4 cart
make ~: 3 cut, hew 4 chop
make ~ smaller: 5 resaw
season ~: 3 age, dry
firework: 6 fizgig
revolving ~: 5 wheel
fireworks: 4 rage, show 5 noise 6 hoopla, thrill 7 dispute 9 explosive, sparklers 10 exhibition
compound in ~: 5 niter
igniter: 4 punk 6 amadou
name: 6 Grucci
reaction to ~: 3 awe, ooh
time: 4 July 5 night
firing: 8 kindling 9 discharge, explosion
on all cylinders: 4 sane
rocket ~: 7 liftoff
firing __: 3 pin 4 line 5 glass, range
firkin: 3 keg, tub 4 cask 6 barrel 9 butter tub, container
firm: 2 co. 3 set 4 bent, corp., fast, hard, iron, snug, sure, taut, true 5 bossy, cruel, dense, exact, fixed, house, loyal, picky, rigid, rocky, solid, sound, stern, stiff, stony, tight, tough 6 agency, all-out, bolted, braced, flinty, harden, intent, nailed, outfit, rooted, secure, severe, stable, static, steady, steely, stoney, strict, strong, sturdy, tone up, welded 7 abiding, adamant, al dente, austere, certain, compact, company, concern, decided, diehard, hard-set, riveted, secured, settled, Spartan, staunch, stiffen 8 anchored, business, cemented, concrete, constant, decisive, definite, despotic, embedded, emphatic, employer, enduring, exacting, explicit, fastened, forceful, hardened, hard-line, hellbent, immobile, implicit, ironclad, obdurate, positive, reliable, resolute, rigorous, soldered, stubborn, unmoving 9 assertive, condensed, demanding, draconian, immovable, immutable, impliable, inelastic, nonporous, obstinate, permanent, screwed in, stabilize, steadfast, stringent, tightened, unbending, unsparing 10 adamantine, compressed, conclusive, consistent, deep-rooted, despotical, determined, enterprise, foursquare, hard-bitten, hard-packed, impervious, inflexible, invariable, iron-fisted, iron-willed, motionless, no-nonsense, oppressive, peremptory, persistent, purposeful, stationary, tyrannical, unchanging, unflagging, unshakable, unswerving, unwavering, unyielding
control: 4 grip 5 grasp 6 clench, clinch 7 command, mastery
ender: 4 ware
expanding ~: 5 hirer
foundation: 4 rock
high-tech ~: 6 dot-com
make ~: 3 fix, pin, tie 4 bind, bond, gird, lock, nail, root, weld 5 brace, build, plant, rivet, shore, steel 6 anchor, cement, enroot, fasten, harden, secure, tone up 7 bolster, build up, fortify, implant, shore up, stiffen, tighten, toughen 8 buttress, entrench, nail down, rigidify, solidify 9 reinforce, stabilize 10 straighten, strengthen
not ~: 4 soft, weak 5 boggy, saggy, slack, unset 7 flaccid 8 yielding
stand ~: 6 insist, resist 7 persist 9 persevere, withstand
up: 3 gel, set 4 jell, tone 6 anneal, harden 8 nail down, solidify 9 stabilize 10 strengthen
__ firm: 3 CPA 6 member
firmament: 3 sky 5 azure, skies 6 heaven 7 heavens 8 empyrean
in the ~: 5 above, aloft 6 high up, on high
firman: 4 fiat 5 edict, order, ukase 6 decree, dictum 7 command, mandate 9 directive, manifesto 10 injunction
firma, terra: 4 land, soil 5 earth 6 ground
firmly: 4 fast, hard 5 tight 8 severely 9 immovably, like a rock
firmness: 4 will 5 nerve, valor 6 fixity 7 courage, density, purpose, resolve 8 backbone, decision, hardness, obduracy, rigidity, solidity, strength, tenacity 9 assurance, certainty, constancy, fixedness, obstinacy, stability, willpower 10 conviction, durability, moral fiber, resolution
exemplar of ~: 4 vise
lacking ~: 4 limp, soft 6 droopy, flabby, floppy, pliant 7 flaccid, pliable 8 drooping
lose ~: 3 sag
Firm of Girdlestone, The
author: Arthur Conan Doyle
Firm, The (1993 film)
cast: Tom Cruise, Gene Hackman, Jeanne Tripplehorn
director: Sydney Pollack
dog: 7 Hearsay
firn: 4 névé, snow
Firpo, Luis: 5 boxer
first: 4 A-one, base, head, main, tops 5 ahead, chief, front, least, older, prime 6 choice, maiden, rather, select, superb, top dog, utmost, victor, virgin 7 forward, in front, initial, leading, lead-off, opening, optimal, optimum, pioneer, premier, primary, ranking, supreme, to start 8 champion, dominant, earliest, foremost, greatest, headmost, in the van, original, primeval, topnotch, top-rated, virginal 9 beginning, immediate, in advance, inaugural, inceptive, initially, number one, numero uno, paramount, primaeval, primarily, primitive, principal, prototype, uttermost 10 aboriginal, beforehand, consummate, originally, preeminent, primordial, super-duper
combining form: 4 arch-, prot- 5 arche-, archi-, proto-
in music: 5 primo
starter: 4 head
first __: 3 aid, off 4 base, dark, dibs, down, gear, lady, lien, mate, name, post 5 class, floor, light, night, thing, water 6 cousin, estate, family, fruits, papers, person, strike 7 baseman, edition, officer, quarter, reading
first-__: 4 born, come, foot, hand, line, rate, time 5 class, timer 6 degree, string, termer
first-__ cover: 3 day
first-__ kit: 3 aid
first-__ mail: 5 class
first-__ movie: 3 run
__ first: 6 double, safety
First __: 4 Lady, Lord, Love 5 Alert, Blood, Cause, Class, World 6 Empire, Flight, Knight, Reader 7 Chamber, Nighter
First __ Club, The: 5 Wives
First __ Ever I Saw..., The: 4 Time
First __, first...: 5 in war
First __ I see tonight...: 4 star
First __ Sin, The: 6 Deadly
First __, The: 4 Noel, Time 5 Night 6 Circle, Legion
First __ War: 5 World 6 Balkan
first aid
giver: 3 EMT
item: 4 tape 5 gauze, iodin, sling 6 eyecup, ice bag, iodine 7 ice pack
job: 3 cut 4 gash
plant: 4 aloe
first-aid __: 3 kit
First Amendment lobbyist: 4 ACLU
first and __: 3 ten 4 last
first baseman
famous ~: 3 Who
Hall of Fame ~: 4 Foxx, Mize 5 Anson, Perez, Terry 6 Cepeda, Gehrig, Murray, Sisler 7 Leonard, McCovey 8 Cap Anson 9 Bill Terry, Greenberg, Killebrew, Lou Gehrig, Tony Perez 10 Jimmie Foxx, Johnny Mize
First Blood (1982 film)
cast: David Caruso, Richard Crenna, Brian Dennehy, Sylvester Stallone
firstborn: 5 elder, older 6 eldest, oldest, senior
name meaning ~: 6 Winona
First Cause, the: 4 Lord
First Circle, The
author: Aleksandr Solzhenitsyn
first-class: 3 top 4 A-one, best, fine, good, tops 5 crack, dandy, elite, grand, great, prime, primo, sharp, slick, super, swell 6 choice, deluxe, goodly, grade A, lavish, select, tiptop, worthy 7 capital, private, stellar, supreme 8 fabulous, five-star, four-star, splendid, sterling, superior, topnotch, very good 9 excellent, fantastic, important, topflight, unrivaled, wunderbar 10 unrivalled
first-class __: 4 mail
__ first class: 6 airman 7 private
First Daughter
1960s ~: 4 Luci 5 Julie, Lynda 6 Tricia 8 Caroline
1970s ~: 3 Amy 5 Susan
1980s~: 7 Maureen
1990s ~: 7 Chelsea
2000s ~: 5 Jenna, Malia, Sasha 7 Barbara
first-day __: 5 cover
First Deadly Sin, The: 5 novel
author: Lawrence Sanders
first-degree, in math: 5 monic
First Dog
1940s: 4 Fala
1960s: 3 Her, Him
1990s: 5 Buddy 6 Millie
first-down yardage: 3 ten

- **first-family member:** 3 Eve 4 Abel, Adam, Cain, Seth
- **First Flight**
  - **author:** Maxwell Anderson
- **first-grade lesson:** 4 ABCs 8 alphabet
- **first-grader's shout:** 4 me me
- **firsthand:** 6 direct 8 intimate, original 9 immediate 10 eyewitness, unmediated
- **First Knight (1995 film)**
  - **cast:** Sean Connery, Richard Gere, Julia Ormond
  - **director:** Jerry Zucker
- **First Lady**
  - **of the Theater:** 10 Helen Hayes
- **First Lady of**
  - **song:** 4 Ella
- **first-line players:** 5 A-team
- **___ first-name basis:** 3 on a
- **First Nighter:** 9 radio show
- **First Night, The (1998 song)**
  - **artist:** Monica
- **First Noel, The:** 5 carol
- **first-of-month payment:** 4 rent
- **___, first-out:** 6 last-in 7 first-in
- **first-pitch preceder:** 6 anthem
- **first-place medal:** 4 gold
- **first-quality:** 5 prime
  - **not ~:** 3 irr. 5 irreg. 9 irregular
- **first-rate:** 9 top-drawer
  - ***see also*** wonderful
- **first-sight phenomenon:** 4 love
- **First State:** 3 Del. 8 Delaware
- **first-string players:** 5 A-team
- **First Time Ever I Saw Your Face, The (1972 song)**
  - **artist:** Roberta Flack
- **first-timer:** 4 tyro 6 newbie, rookie 7 trainee 8 beginner, initiate, newcomer 10 tenderfoot
- **First Wives Club, The (1996 film)**
  - **cameo role:** 5 Ivana
  - **cast:** Goldie Hawn, Diane Keaton, Bette Midler, Maggie Smith
  - **dog:** 5 Roach
  - **members:** 4 exes
  - **setting:** 3 NYC 9 Manhattan
- **First World ___:** 3 War
- **first-year**
  - **cadet:** 4 pleb 5 plebe
  - **law student:** 4 one L
  - **student:** 5 frosh 8 freshman
- **___ first you don't...:** 4 If at
- **firth:** 3 bay 4 gulf 5 fiord, fjord, inlet, mouth
- **Firth:** 5 Colin, Peter
- **___ Firth:** 5 Moray 6 Solway
- **Firth of ___:** 3 Tay 4 Lorn 5 Clyde, Forth
- **Firth of Clyde**
  - **island:** 5 Arran
  - **port:** 3 Ayr
  - **river to the ~:** 4 Doon
- **Firth of Lorn port:** 4 Oban
- **Firth of Tay port:** 6 Dundee
- **fisc:** 6 coffer 8 treasury 9 exchequer
- **fiscal:** 8 economic, monetary 9 budgetary, financial, pecuniary
  - **beneficiary:** 5 payee
  - **period:** 2 yr. 3 qtr. 4 year 7 quarter
  - **plan:** 6 budget
- **fiscal ___:** 4 plan, year 5 agent 6 period, policy
- **Fischer:** 4 Hans 5 Bobby, Edwin, Ernst 6 Edmond 7 Hermann
- **Fischer, Bobby forte:** 5 chess
- **Fischer-Dieskau:** 6 German 8 baritone, Dietrich
  - **forte:** 6 lieder
- **'F' Is for Fugitive**
  - **author:** Sue Grafton
- **fish:** 3 ayu, cat, cod, dab, eel, fry, gar, ged, ide, ihi, koi, orf, ray, sey, tai 4 barb, bass, blay, boce, boga, bret, brit, carp, cero, char, chub, chum, coho, cusk, dace, dory, drum, dupe, fugu, game, goby, hake, hiku, huss, jack, jocu, lija, ling, loro, mado, mapo, masu, meat, mero, mola, opah, orfe, parr, pega, peto, pike, pogy, pout, quab, raad, rudd, ruff, sama, scad, sesi, shad, skil, sole, spet, tope, tuna, ulua 5 akule, angle, betta, bleak, bolti, bream, brill, chiro, chopa, cisco, cobia, coney, danio, elver, grope, grunt, guasa, guppy, hilsa, jurel, loach, lotte, manta, moray, pargo, perch, porgy, sargo, saury, scrod, seine, shark, skate, smelt, smolt, snook, sprat, tench, tetra, torsk, trawl, troll, trout, tunny, wahoo 6 aimara, anabas, barbel, beluga, beshow, bichir, bigeye, blenny, bonaci, bonito, bowfin, burbot, caplin, caribe, conger, cuchia, cunner, darter, entrée, grilse, groper, gunnel, hapuku, hilsah, inanga, louvar, maigre, marlin, medaka, minnow, mullet, nonnat, piraña, Pisces, plaice, plakat, pollan, puffer, puneca, remora, roughy, saithe, salele, salema, salmon, saurel, savola, schrod, sea eel, search, sennet, shiner, sucker, tandan, tarpon, tautog, testar, tetard, tiñosa, tomcod, turbot, weever, wrasse, zander 7 alewife, alfiona, anchovy, bacalao, barbudo, bloater, bluefin, cabezon, capelin, cavalla, corbina, corvina, crappie, croaker, eelpout, escolar, finspot, flycast, garlopa, garpike, gourami, graysby, grindle, grouper, grunion, gudgeon, gurnard, gwyniad, haddock, halibut, helleri, herring, inconnu, lamprey, lingcod, margate, mojarra, mooneye, nibbler, oldwife, opaleye, pigfoot, piranha, pollack, pollock, pomfret, pompano, ronquil, rummage, sand dab, sardine, scalare, sculpin, sea bass, snapper, sockeye, sterlet, sweeper, tilapia, torpedo, walleye, whapuku, whiting, wolf-eel 8 albacore, anableps, arapaima, baysmelt, bigmouth, bloodfin, bluegill, bluehead, brisling, bullhead, cabrilla, card game, characin, chimaera, crevalle, dragonet, flathead, flounder, gambusia, gilthead, grayling, halfbeak, halfmoon, hiwi hiwi, John Dory, mackerel, mahimahi, manta ray, medregal, menhaden, mulloway, nannygai, palometa, pearleye, pilchard, sea bream, sea horse, sea raven, skipjack, stingray, sturgeon, tommycod, topsmelt, trevally, tubenose, wrymouth 9 amberjack, argentine, barracuda, barreleye, blue shark, Dover sole, eelblenny, feel about, greenling, grenadier, lake trout, martinico, mudminnow, neon tetra, pikeperch, red mullet, sand lance, schnapper, sea urchin, spikedace, surfperch, swordtail, threadfin, topminnow, tubesnout, whitebait, yellowfin 10 bitterling, blanquillo, brook trout, brown trout, coelacanth, pikeblenny, red snapper, sandroller, silverside, squaretail, tiger shark, troutperch, whale shark, white cloud, white shark, yellow jack, yellowtail
  - **Africa:** 5 bolti 6 anabas, bichir 7 tilapia 8 characin 10 coelacanth
  - **alternative:** 4 fowl
  - **appendage:** 6 barbel
  - **appetizer:** 3 lox 7 ceviche
  - **aquarium ~:** 3 orf 4 barb, orfe 5 danio, guppy, platy, tetra 6 medaka 7 gourami, helleri, scalare 8 bloodfin 9 neon tetra, swordtail
  - **Arizona ~:** 9 spikedace
  - **Asia:** 5 betta, loach, tench 6 anabas 7 gourami, sterlet
  - **Atlantic:** 3 cod, sey 4 cero, cusk, hake, jack, mapo 5 lotte, porgy, saury, snook 6 gunnel, saithe, tarpon, tautog, tomcod 7 cavalla, croaker, graysby, haddock, halibut, herring, margate, pollack, pollock, pomfret, torpedo, whiting 8 mackerel, sea raven, wrymouth 9 amberjack
  - **Australian:** 4 mado 6 groper, roughy, tandan 8 mulloway, nannygai, trevally 9 schnapper
  - **bag-shaped ~ trap:** 4 fyke
  - **bait:** 4 lure, worm 5 sprat
  - **bait ~:** 4 chub, dace
  - **balancer:** 3 fin
  - **basslike ~:** 4 boga 5 snook 6 salele
  - **big ~:** 6 lunker
  - **bin for salting ~:** 5 kench
  - **blackish ~:** 5 sable
  - **boned ~:** 5 filet
  - **bottom-feeding ~:** 7 eelpout
  - **Brazil:** 5 piaba 8 arapaima
  - **breakfast ~:** 3 lox
  - **bright:** 4 opah 5 tetra
  - **bring in a ~:** 3 net 4 land
  - **by jigging:** 3 dib
  - **California:** 7 alfiona, finspot, grunion, sculpin 8 halfmoon 10 yellowtail
  - **canned ~:** 4 tuna 6 salmon 8 sardines
  - **Caribbean ~:** 10 yellow jack
  - **catcher:** 3 net 4 hook 5 seine
  - **cave-dwelling ~:** 3 eel
  - **Central American:** 7 helleri 9 swordtail
  - **chunk-light ~:** 4 tuna
  - **clean a ~:** 3 gut 5 scale
  - **cold-water ~:** 5 smelt
  - **collation:** 5 sushi 7 sashimi
  - **combining form:** 5 pisci- 6 ichthy- 7 ichthyo-
  - **cut:** 6 fillet
  - **cyprinoid ~:** 3 ide
  - **deep-sea ~:** 8 pearleye 9 barreleye, grenadier
  - **deli ~:** 4 chub
  - **delicacy:** 3 roe
  - **dish:** 3 roe 5 sushi 6 caviar, kipper 7 ceviche, gravlax, sashimi 8 lutefisk, matelote 9 carbonado
  - **eellike ~:** 6 cuchia, gunnel
  - **eggs:** 3 roe 6 caviar
  - **elongated:** 3 eel 4 ling
  - **emulate ~:** 4 swim
  - **ender:** 3 eye, gig, net 4 bowl, hook, meal, pond, tail, wife 5 plate 6 monger
  - **Europe:** 3 dab, ide 4 blay, boce, dace, dory, ling, rudd, ruff 5 bleak, brill, guasa, loach, pargo, perch, tench 6 barbel, beluga, maigre, turbot, weever, zander 7 gudgeon, pigfoot 8 John Dory, pilchard 10 bitterling
  - **eye:** 4 gaze
  - **fierce ~:** 5 shark
  - **fighting ~:** 5 betta
  - **filet ~:** 4 sole
  - **finder:** 5 sonar
  - **finless ~:** 3 eel
  - **flat ~:** 3 ray
  - **food:** 4 alga, bait
  - **food ~:** 3 cod, ide 4 bass, hake, mahi, scup, shad, sole, tuna 5 jurel, trout 6 bonaci, bonito
  - **for:** 4 seek 5 probe 6 pursue
  - **(for):** 4 hunt 5 grope 6 search
  - **freshen a ~ tank:** 6 aerate
  - **freshwater ~:** 3 gar, ide 4 bass, carp, chub, dace, pike, rudd 5 bream, cisco, loach, perch, roach, tench, trout 6 darter
  - **fry:** 4 meal 6 picnic
  - **game ~:** 4 bass, cero, tuna, ulua 5 trout, wahoo 6 marlin, tarpon 7 cavalla, walleye 9 barracuda
  - **ganoid ~:** 3 gar 6 bowfin 7 grindle
  - **go ~:** 8 card game, kids' game
  - **Great Lakes ~:** 4 chub 5 cisco, smelt 7 bloater
  - **group:** 5 shoal 6 school
  - **haul:** 4 take 5 catch
  - **Hawaii:** 4 ulae, ulua 5 akule, moano 8 mahimahi
  - **herringlike ~:** 4 pogy, shad 7 anchovy, mooneye
  - **holder:** 5 creel 6 kettle
  - **how to pack ~:** 5 in ice
  - **illegally:** 5 poach
  - **India:** 5 danio, hilsa 6 cuchia, hilsah
  - **Japan:** 3 ayu, koi, tai 4 fugu, masu 5 cobia 6 medaka
  - **kettle of ~:** 3 fix, jam 4 spot 5 snarl 6 fiasco, muddle, pickle, plight, scrape, tangle 7 dilemma, problem, screwup, trouble, turmoil 8 bad scene 9 deep water, mare's nest
  - **lake ~:** 4 bass 5 trout
  - **leftover:** 5 spine
  - **like ~:** 5 finny, scaly
  - **like a cold ~:** 5 aloof 6 chilly 7 distant 8 detached 9 apathetic, impassive 10 unfriendly, unsociable
  - **like a ~ hook:** 5 sharp 6 barbed 7 pointed
  - **long ~:** 3 eel
  - **long-jawed ~:** 3 gar
  - **lung:** 4 gill

lure a ~: 3 dap
marinated ~ appetizer: 7 ceviche
Mediterranean: 5 porgy 6 nonnat 7 anchovy 8 gilthead
Mexico: 7 garlopa 8 anableps
net: 5 seine, trawl
New England: 5 scrod 6 schrod
New Zealand: 3 ihi 4 hiku 6 hapuku, inanga 7 whapuku 8 hiwi hiwi
oil acid: 3 DHA
one way to ~: 5 troll
out of water: 6 misfit 7 oddball 8 maverick
Pacific ~: 5 sargo 6 beshow, bigeye, tomcod 7 cabezon, corbina, corvina, halibut, herring, nibbler, opaleye, pomfret, ronquil, sand dab, wolf-eel 8 baysmelt, flathead, palometa, topsmelt, tubenose 9 greenling, surfperch, tubesnout
parrot ~: 4 loro
part: 4 gill
Philippine ~: 9 martinico
plate: 5 scale
predator: 3 ern 4 bear, erne
prepare ~: 4 bone 6 debone, fillet
puffer ~: 4 fugu
rainbow ~: 5 smelt
raw ~: 5 sushi
relish: 4 alec
sardine ~: 5 sprat
sauce: 4 alec
scaleless ~: 3 eel
science of: 11 ichthyology
scored and broiled ~: 9 carbonado
Scotland: 3 ged
shadlike ~: 7 alewife 8 menhaden
sharp-snouted ~: 5 saury
sharp-toothed ~: 5 moray
silvery ~: 4 blay, mola 5 bleak, bream, smelt 6 shiner 7 grunion, mojarra, mooneye 8 baysmelt, bloodfin, topsmelt 9 argentine
smallmouth ~: 4 bass
smoked ~: 3 eel 6 kipper, salmon 7 herring
snakelike ~: 3 eel 5 moray 7 lamprey
sound: 4 plop
South America: 6 aimara 7 piranha, scalare 8 bloodfin, characin
spear: 3 gig
Sri Lanka: 5 danio
starter: 3 bat, box, cat, cod, cow, dog, fin, gar, hag, hog, mud, oar, pig, pin, pup, rat, red, saw, sun 4 bait, bill, blow, blue, boar, bone, cave, coal, craw, deal, fall, file, flat, frog, goat, gold, gray, grey, king, lady, lion, lump, lung, milk, monk, moon, numb, pipe, rock, rose, sail, sand, star, stud, suck, tile, toad, weak 5 angel, black, blind, cling, cramp, devil, frost, glass, globe, goose, jelly, jewel, sable, shell, snake, snipe, spade, spear, stock, stone, swell, sword, trunk, viper, white 6 angler, archer, butter, candle, damsel, dollar, guitar, lizard, mutton, needle, paddle, parrot, ribbon, rudder, shrimp, silver, tongue 7 rooster, surgeon, trigger 8 squirrel
stew: 8 matelote
story: 3 fib, lie 4 tale, yarn 7 fiction
story teller: 6 fibber 8 deceiver
striped ~: 4 bass
sushi ~: 3 eel
Tasmania: 6 inanga
trap: 3 net 4 weir
troll for ~: 5 drail
tropical ~: 3 pet 4 loro, mola, opah, scad 5 chiro, manta, moray, tetra 6 louvar, salema, tiñosa, wrasse 9 barracuda 10 pikeblenny, squaretail
try for a ~: 4 cast
unhatched ~: 3 egg
unicorn ~: 4 unie
warm-water game ~: 5 cobia
West Indies: 6 bigeye
white ~: 5 scrod 6 schrod
with a charge: 3 eel
young ~: 3 fry

fish __: 3 fry, out 4 bowl, cake, crow, duck, farm, fork, hawk, meal, pole 5 flake, flour, knife, louse, slice, stick, story, wheel 6 doctor, ladder, tackle, warden 7 culture
fish __ bait: 5 or cut
fish __ fowl: 3 nor
fish __ of water: 3 out
__ fish: 3 pan, tin 4 bony, cold, food, game, tuna 5 clown, green, pilot, rough, sport, trash 6 basket, bottom, flying, ground 7 anemone, bellows, buffalo, gefilte, jawless, rainbow, walking
Fish: 4 Phil, sign 6 Pisces 7 Stanley 8 Hamilton
month: 3 Feb., Mar. 5 March 8 February
successor: 3 Ram
the ~: 4 sign 5 dance 6 Pisces
__ Fish: 6 Rumble 7 Passion
fish-and-chips quaff: 3 ale
Fishburne, Laurence: 5 actor
film: Akeelah and the Bee (2006)
Boyz N the Hood (1991)
The Matrix (1999)
The Matrix Reloaded (2003)
Mystic River (2003)
Othello (1995)
School Daze (1988)
What's Love Got to Do With It (1993)
Fish Called Wanda, A (1988 film)
cast: John Cleese, Jamie Lee Curtis, Kevin Kline, Michael Palin
director: Charles Crichton
fisher: 5 pekan 6 angler, marten
starter: 4 king
Fisher: 3 Bud, Ham, M.F.K. 4 Fred, Gail, Toni 5 Eddie, Joely 6 Carrie 7 Dorothy, Frances, Stevens, Terence
rival: 4 Aiwa, Sony 7 Marantz, Pioneer
Fisher-__: 5 Price
Fisher, Carrie: 7 actress
film: The 'burbs (1989)
The Empire Strikes Back (1980)
Garbo Talks (1984)
Hannah and Her Sisters (1986)
Return of the Jedi (1983)
Shampoo (1975)
Soapdish (1991)
Star Wars (1977)
When Harry Met Sally... (1989)
mother: Debbie Reynolds
spouse: Paul Simon
Fisher, Eddie
daughter: Carrie, Joely
song: Cindy, Oh Cindy (1956)
Count Your Blessings (1954)
Dungaree Doll (1955)
Heart (1955)
I Need You Now (1954)
Oh! My Pa-Pa (1953)
spouse: Debbie Reynolds, Connie Stevens, Elizabeth Taylor
__ Fisher Hall: 5 Avery
Fisher King, The (1991 film)
cast: Jeff Bridges, Amanda Plummer, Mercedes Ruehl, Robin Williams
director: Terry Gilliam
fisherman: 5 eeler 6 angler, seiner 7 trawler, troller 8 piscator
at times: 5 lurer 6 baiter
Newfoundland ~: 6 banker
see also fishing
fisherman's __: 4 bend, knot, ring 7 platter
Fisherman's __: 5 Wharf
fisherman's bend: 4 knot
Fisher, M.F.K.: 6 writer
subject: 4 food
Fisher-Price product: 3 toy
__ Fishers, The: 5 Pearl
fisheye __: 4 lens
fishhook: 4 gaff
attachment: 5 snell
part: 4 barb
__ fishin': 4 gone
fishing: 5 sport
boat: 4 dory 5 smack 6 lugger, whaler 7 coaster, trawler
bob ~ bait: 3 dib
boot: 5 wader
Dutch ~ boat: 6 dogger
expedition: 6 search 8 research
float: 4 cork 6 bobber, dobber
footwear: 5 wader
garment: 5 oiler
gear: 3 bob, net, rod 4 lure, reel 6 fly rod, tackle
gear name: 5 Orvis
grounds off the Shetlands: 4 Haaf
guide: 5 gilly 6 gillie
hope: 4 bite
line: 5 snell, troll
line material: 3 gut
lure: 3 fly, jig 4 plug 5 spoon, troll 6 dry fly
need: 3 net, rod 4 bait, line, lure, reel 5 creel, seine
net: 5 seine, trawl
reel, in Britain: 4 pirn
reel part: 5 spool
Scottish ~ boat: 6 baldie
spot: 4 lake, pier, pond 5 creek, wharf 6 stream
start ~: 4 cast
take: 4 haul 5 catch 6 keeper
fishing __: 3 rod 4 line, pole, trip, worm 5 banks, smack 6 ground
__ fishing: 3 ice 4 spin
__-fishing: 3 fly
Fish Magic
artist: Paul Klee
fishnet: 6 fabric
fiber: 5 olona
fishnets: 7 hosiery
like ~: 5 meshy
__ fish nor fowl: 7 neither
fish or __ bait: 3 cut
fish out of __: 5 water
__ fish out of water: 5 like a
__ fish sandwich: 4 tuna
fish sauce, literally: 6 catsup 7 ketchup
fish story: 3 lie 4 tale
teller: 4 liar
fishtail: 3 wag 4 palm, skid 9 oscillate
fishtank need: 6 filter
fish-to-be: 3 ova, roe
__ fish to fry: 5 other
fishwife: 5 scold, shrew 6 virago 7 needler 9 henpecker, Xanthippe
fishy: 5 queer 7 dubious, suspect 9 unethical 10 incredible, suspicious
Fisk, Carlton: 7 catcher
gear for ~: 4 mitt
fission: 7 parting 8 dividing, division 9 severance, splitting
experiment: 5 A-test
fission __: 4 bomb
__ fission: 6 binary 7 nuclear
fissionable: 6 atomic 8 atomical
material: 4 atom
fissure: 3 cut, gap 4 hole, leak, reft, rent, rift, slit, tear, vent 5 abyss, break, chasm, chink, cleft, crack, gorge, gully, split 6 breach, cranny, ravine 7 crevice, opening, rupture 8 cleavage, crevasse, fracture 10 interstice
fist: 4 duke, grab, grip, hand 5 clasp, grasp, seize 6 clench, clutch, import
ender: 5 fight
hit without a ~: 4 knee, slap
make a ~: 6 clench
material: 4 iron
product: 3 jab 4 sock 5 punch 6 one-two 8 haymaker, uppercut 10 roundhouse
shake a ~ at: 8 threaten
__ fist: 6 mailed 7 monkey's
F.I.S.T. (1978 film)
cast: Peter Boyle, Melinda Dillon, Sylvester Stallone, Rod Steiger
director: Norman Jewison
__-fisted: 3 ham, two 4 hard 5 close, tight 6 narrow
fistfight: 4 bout 5 scrap 6 tussle
memento: 6 bruise, fat lip, shiner 8 black eye
prelude, perhaps: 5 shove
Fistful of Dollars (1964 film): 5 oater
cast: Clint Eastwood
director: Sergio Leone
fistic: 10 pugilistic
fisticuff: 4 bang, blow, shot 5 clout, punch, smack, thump, whack 6 pummel
fisticuffs: 4 bout 5 fight 6 boxing 7 quarrel 8 pugilism
fists, fight with: 3 box
fit: 2 go 3 apt, arm, rig, set, tic 4 able, good, gybe, hale, jibe, just, lean, meet, sane, suit, tiff, trim, well 5 adapt, agile, agree, alter, apply, burly, clock, equip, hardy, match, mount, prime, ready, right, serve, shape, sound, spasm, spate, spell,

spirt, spurt, throe, throw, toned, tough, try on **6** adjust, attack, become, belong, brawny, change, concur, decent, dither, edge in, frenzy, modify, proper, robust, rugged, seemly, square, strong, tailor, timely, up to it, usable, useful, worthy **7** apropos, capable, conform, correct, fashion, furnish, healthy, in shape, livable, measure, provide, qualify, seizure, tantrum, useable **8** accouter, accoutre, adequate, apposite, athletic, decorous, dovetail, eligible, feasible, laughter, liveable, muscular, outbreak, outburst, paroxysm, powerful, prepared, regulate, relevant, rightful, stalwart, suitable, vigorous **9** advisable, competent, expedient, favorable, harmonize, hysterics, interlock, in the pink, opportune, qualified, reconcile, strapping, up to snuff, wholesome **10** able-bodied, applicable, compatible, conniption, convenient, correspond, felicitous, go together, propitious, reasonable, well-suited
as seen ~: **4** duly
be ~ for: **4** suit **6** beseem **7** behoove
check for ~: **5** try on
cut to ~: **4** trim **5** adapt **6** tailor
for a queen: **5** regal, royal **9** luxurious
get ~: **3** jog **6** tone up **7** work out **8** exercise
have a ~: **4** boil, flip, fume, rage, rant, rave **5** erupt, freak, panic, steam, storm **6** blow up, lose it **7** explode, run riot, run wild **8** boil over, freak out, run amuck **9** go berserk, overreact **10** hit the roof
in: **2** go **4** gybe, jibe **5** blend, chime, yield **6** belong, cohere, relate **7** conform **9** make sense
in with: **2** go **4** gybe, jibe, mesh **5** agree, blend **6** accord, attune, belong, square **7** conform **8** dovetail **9** correlate, harmonize **10** coordinate, correspond
keep ~: **3** run **8** exercise
make ~: **4** suit **5** adapt, alter, amend **6** adjust, recast, remold, revamp, revise, tailor **7** correct, reshape **8** fine-tune, renovate
of temper: **3** ire, pet **4** huff, pout, rage, snit **5** blast, blaze, flash, scene, storm, surge **6** access, attack, flurry, frenzy, outcry, tirade **7** flare-up, tantrum, torrent **8** eruption, outbreak, outburst, paroxysm, upheaval **9** discharge, explosion, hysterics **10** conniption, outpouring
out: **3** rig **4** garb, gear, wear **5** array, dress, equip, ready **6** attire, clothe, gear up, get set **7** appoint, bedrape, furnish, prepare, provide **8** accouter, accoutre **9** caparison, provision
(out): **4** turn
physically ~: **4** trim **5** sound **6** robust **7** healthy
render ~: **10** capacitate
see ~: **5** deign **6** please **10** condescend
starter: **5** retro
to be tied: **3** mad **4** wild **5** angry, irate, livid, vexed **6** fuming, heated, piqued, raging, red-hot **7** boiling, enraged, furious, intense, steamed, violent **8** incensed, up in arms, wrathful **9** bummed-out, indignant **10** hysterical, infuriated
to farm: **6** arable **7** fertile **8** plowable, tillable **10** cultivable
together: **4** gybe, jibe, mesh, nest **6** hook up
up: **3** rig **4** deck **5** dress, equip **6** attire, bedeck, clothe, rig out, supply **7** deck out, furnish **8** accouter, accoutre **9** caparison
fit __: **4** to a T **6** to a tee, to kill
fit __ fiddle: **3** as a
fit __ king: **4** for a
fit __ T: **3** to a
fit __ tee: **3** to a
fit __ tied: **4** to be
__ fit: **5** drive, force, hissy, press
fit as a __: **6** fiddle
fitch: **6** weasel
relative: **4** mink **5** otter, ratel, sable, skunk, stoat, tayra **6** badger, ermine, ferret, marten **7** foumart, polecat **8** carcajou, foulmart, kolinsky, muishond **9** wolverine
Fitch: **3** Val **4** John **5** Clyde, rater
best rating: **3** AAA
rival: **5** S and P **6** A.M. Best, Moody's
fit for __: **5** a king **6** a queen
fitful: **5** jerky, jumpy, moody **6** patchy, uneven **8** off and on, restless, unstable, unsteady, variable **9** desultory, irregular, spasmodic, uncertain **10** capricious
fitfully: **8** off and on **9** piecemeal
fitness: **3** vim **4** dint, form, thew, trim **5** brawn, force, might, power, shape, thews, vigor **6** energy, fettle, health, muscle **7** aptness, muscles, potence, potency, stamina, utility **8** adequacy, aptitude, strength, vitality, wellness **9** condition, congruity, endurance, fortitude, hardiness, propriety, puissance, readiness, relevancy **10** brute force, competence, consonance, expediency, pertinence
center: **3** gym, spa **4** YMCA
equipment: **3** wts. **7** weights **8** Nautilus **9** dumbbells, treadmill
pro: **7** trainer
suffix: **7** -ability, -ibility
fits
by ~ and starts: **6** spotty **9** gradually, piecemeal
where one ~ in: **5** niche
fits and __: **6** starts
fitted: **8** suitable **9** qualified **10** tailor-made
out: **5** armed, ready
fitter: **6** better, tailor **8** clothier **9** couturier **10** dressmaker
__ fitter: **3** gas **4** pipe **5** steam
fitting: **3** apt, due, pat **4** good, just, meet, part, well **5** happy, piece, right **6** cogent, decent, proper, seemly, timely **7** adjunct, apropos, condign, correct, fixture, germane **8** apposite, becoming, decorous, deserved, feasible, relevant, rightful, suitable **9** accessory, advisable, agreeable, component, deserving, expedient, opportune, pertinent, praisable **10** adjustment, applicable, attachment, compatible, felicitous
measurement: **5** waist **6** inseam
not ~: **5** unapt **9** ill-suited **10** inapposite, malapropos, out of place, unsuitable
place: **5** niche
starter: **4** form, pipe **5** steam
tightly: **4** snug
use a ~ room: **5** try on
fitting __: **4** room
__ fitting: **3** gas **4** pipe **5** curve
__-fitting: **5** close, loose
fittingly: **4** well **5** right **9** correctly **10** adequately
fittings: **4** gear **8** fixtures, hardware **9** equipment
Fittipaldi, Emerson: **5** racer **9** auto racer
milieu: **5** track
fit to __: **4** a tee, kill
fit to be __: **4** tied
Fitzgerald: **4** Ella, Tara **5** Barry, Zelda **6** F. Scott, Pegeen **9** Geraldine
forte: **4** scat
FitzGerald, Edward: **4** poet **7** British
translated him: **4** Omar **7** Khayyám
Fitzgerald, F. Scott: **6** writer
first name: Francis
wife: Zelda
work: The Great Gatsby
The Last Tycoon
Tales of the Jazz Age
Tender Is the Night
This Side of Paradise
Fitzwater: **6** Marlin
five: **3** fin **6** number **7** respite
combining form: **4** pent- **5** penta- **6** quinqu- **7** quinque-
dollars: **3** fin
group of ~: **6** pentad **7** quintet **8** cinquain
high ~: **8** greeting
in dice: **6** cinque
in French: **4** cinq
in German: **4** fünf
in Italian: **6** cinque
in Portuguese: **5** cinco
in Spanish: **5** cinco
o'clock shadow: **7** stubble
one of ~: **5** sense, sight, smell, taste, touch **7** hearing
take ~: **4** rest **5** break, pause, relax **6** recess, rest up **8** intermit
to Mohs: **7** apatite
five __: **6** senses
five __ shadow: **6** o'clock
five-__: **4** spot, star **6** finger, gaited
five-__ chili: **3** way **5** alarm
five-__ fire: **5** alarm
five-__ plan: **4** year
five-__ transmission: **5** speed
__ five: **4** hang, take **6** nine to
__-five: **4** high
Five __: **7** Corners, Nations
Five __ in a Balloon: **5** Weeks
Five __ Named Moe: **4** Guys
Five __ Pieces: **4** Easy
Five __ Pips, The: **6** Orange
__ Five: **3** Big **4** Jive, Take **5** Count
five-alarmer: **4** fire **5** blaze
five-and-__: **3** ten **4** dime
five-and-ten: **5** store **8** emporium
five-card stud: **4** game **8** card game
five-centime piece: **3** sou
Five Civilized __: **6** Tribes **7** Nations
Five Days in Paris
author: Danielle Steel
five-digit number: **3** zip **7** zip code
Five Easy Pieces (1970 film)
cast: Susan Anspach, Karen Black, Fannie Flagg, Jack Nicholson
director: Bob Rafelson
Five Families
author: Oscar Lewis
Five Finger Exercise
author: Peter Shaffer
five-franc coin: **3** écu
Five Guys Named __: **3** Moe
five hundred __: **5** rummy
five-in-a-row game: **4** keno **5** bingo, pente
Five Minutes More
composer: Sammy Cahn, Jule Styne
Five Nations: **6** Cayuga, Mohawk, Oneida, Seneca **8** Onandaga
foe: **5** Huron
__ Five-O: **6** Hawaii
five o'clock shadow: **5** beard **7** stubble
Five Orange Pips, The
author: Arthur Conan Doyle
fiver: **3** fin **4** bill
change for a ~: **4** ones
part: **3** dol. **4** buck **6** dollar
fivesome: **7** quintet **9** quintette
five-spot: **3** fin
Five Stairsteps
song: O-o-h Child (1970)
five-star
monogram: **3** DDE
name: **3** Ike **4** Omar
see also wonderful
__-Five Theses: **6** Ninety
Five thousand years __...: **5** agone
five-way __: **5** chile, chili
Five Weeks in a Balloon
author: Jules Verne
Five Women
author: Rona Jaffe
Five W's, one of the: **3** who, why **4** what, when **5** where
five-year __: **4** plan
fix: **3** jam, lay, peg, pin, rig, set, tie **4** bind, bond, cook, cure, glue, lock, make, mend, mess, moor, nail, nuke, plot, rank, root, site, spay, spot, stop, tack, tune, vamp, weld **5** align, aline, amend, bribe, debug, embed, emend, focus, frame, imbed, limit, lodge, paste, patch, place, plant, price, prove, ready, right, rig up, rivet, see to, set up, solve, stamp, stare **6** adjust, anchor, arrest, assess, attach, buy off, cement, corner, decide, define, doctor, enroot, fasten, get set, harden, instal, instil, juggle, locate, make up, ordain, pickle, plight, punish, remedy, repair, replan, revamp, revise, scrape, secure, settle, square, tamper, tinker, tune up, wangle, whip up **7** agree on,

arrange, correct, corrupt, dilemma, engrain, implant, imprint, ingrain, install, instill, patch up, pay back, prepare, rebuild, rectify, resolve, restore, specify, stay put, stiffen, tighten, touch up, work out **8** arrive at, conclude, entrench, get ready, hot water, make fast, maneuver, nail down, overhaul, position, put right, quagmire, quandary, regulate, rigidify, set right, solidify, solution **9** deep water, determine, do justice, establish, formalize, inculcate, microwave, plan ahead, preordain, reconcile, stabilize, sterilize, thumbtack, tight spot **10** difficulty, manipulate, prearrange, recompense, straighten, tamper with
a hole: **4** mend **5** patch **6** repair
clumsy ~: **5** kluge **6** kludge
firmly: **3** tie **4** etch, glue, moor, nail **5** embed, imbed, rivet **6** anchor, attach, fasten, secure **7** enchain, engrain, ingrain **8** bolt down, make fast
get a ~ on: **6** locate **8** identify, pinpoint **9** determine
in a ~: **5** stuck **7** stymied, trapped, up a tree **8** besieged, cornered, strapped, troubled **10** up the creek
in the mind: **4** etch **5** learn **8** remember
something to ~: **5** wagon
starter: **5** trans
up: **4** mend, redo, tidy, vamp **5** primp, renew **6** adjust, better, doctor, enrich, instal, polish, reform, revamp, supply **7** arrange, correct, enhance, furbish, furnish, install, mollify, provide, rectify, restore, sharpen **8** ornament, renovate **9** meliorate, reconcile, refurbish **10** ameliorate
upon: **4** pick **5** elect, favor **6** choose, opt for, prefer, select **9** single out
(upon): **6** decide
__ fix: **3** in a **5** quick **7** running
Fix: **4** Paul
fixate: **4** dote **5** focus **6** obsess, zero in **7** stick on **9** preoccupy, stabilize
(on): **6** center
fixation: **5** craze, mania, thing **6** fetich, fetish, hang-up **7** complex **9** monomania, obsession
fixative: **3** gum **4** bond, glue **5** paste **6** cement **7** stickum **8** adhesive, mucilage
fixe
idée ~: **5** mania, thing **9** obsession
__ fixe: **4** idée, prix **5** blanc
fixed: **3** set **4** fast, firm, sure **5** given, right, rigid, solid, staid, stiff, tight, usual **6** frozen, glassy, intent, narrow, rooted, secure, stable, static, steady, strong **7** abiding, adamant, certain, decided, focused, limited, precise, rebuilt, regular, uniform **8** absolute, absorbed, constant, definite, enduring, immobile, implicit, ironclad, methodic, prepared, resolute, standing, stubborn **9** definable, good as new, immovable, ingrained, iron-jawed, permanent, steadfast, tenacious, unbending, unmovable, unpliable **10** back online, deep-seated, definitive, gridlocked, inflexible, invariable, mechanical, methodical, motionless, persistent, prevailing, purposeful, stationary, unchanging, unflagging, unwavering, unyielding
at ~ intervals: **6** cyclic, hourly, weekly, yearly **7** monthly, regular **8** cyclical, periodic **9** recurrent, recurring
become ~: **5** lodge **6** freeze, harden **7** stiffen **8** rigidify
for: **3** set **6** all set **8** geared up
(for): **5** ready
idea: **3** bug **6** hang-up **7** craving **9** monomania, obsession
look: **4** gaze **5** stare
not ~: **5** fluid **7** mutable **8** flexible, variable **9** adaptable, malleable, mercurial, unsettled **10** changeable, indefinite
order: **4** plan **5** setup **6** method, scheme, system **7** pattern, process, routine **8** practice **9** mechanism, operation, procedure, structure, technique
points: **4** loca, loci
routine: **3** rut **4** rote **7** rat race **8** monotony **9** treadmill
fixed __: **3** oil **4** cost, idea, sign, star **5** asset, price, trust **6** charge **7** capital
fixed-__: **4** wing **5** price **6** income, length
fixed-__ mortgage: **4** rate
fixedly: **4** fast, hard **8** intently, steadily **9** immovably
fixedness: **7** loyalty **8** devotion, fidelity, firmness **9** adherence, certainty, constancy, diligence, eagerness, endurance, fortitude, frequency, integrity, stability **10** allegiance, attachment, continuity, doggedness, permanence, regularity, resolution, steadiness, trustiness, uniformity
fixer: **5** agent **6** broker **7** liaison **8** diplomat, mediator, repairer **9** go-between, moderator, repairman **10** negotiator
fixer-__: **5** upper
Fixer, The
author: Bernard Malamud
fixing: **7** binding, curbing **8** limiting **9** confining **10** adjustment
__ fixing: **4** gold **5** price
Fixing __: **5** a Hole
fix-it __: **4** shop
Fix-it, Mr.: **8** handyman, repairer **9** repairman
fixity: **8** firmness **9** constancy, stability **10** permanence
fix one's __: **5** wagon
fixture: **4** lock **7** fitting **9** accessory, appliance, component
fixtures: **4** gear **8** fittings, hardware, plumbing, supplies **9** apparatus, equipment, machinery, trappings **10** facilities
fixup: **6** repair
Fixx: **3** Jim **5** James
fizz: **4** foam, hiss, soda **5** drink, froth **6** bubble, bubbly **7** bubbles, hissing, seltzer, sparkle **8** beverage, bubbling, club soda **9** champagne **10** effervesce, tonic water
add ~ to: **6** aerate
ingredient: **3** gin
lacking ~: **4** flat **5** still
__ fizz: **5** royal **6** golden, silver
fizzle: **3** die **4** fail, flop **6** sizzle **7** fatigue, founder, go kaput, misfire, sparkle, sputter **8** collapse
out: **4** fade, fail **8** languish, trail off
fizzler: **3** dud **4** bomb, bust, flop **7** failure, washout
fizzling sound: **4** pfft **5** pffft, phfft
fizzy: **5** foamy **6** bubbly
drink: **4** cola, soda **7** seltzer **8** club soda, root beer **10** tonic water
remedy: **5** Bromo
F-J connector: **3** GHI
fjord: **3** arm, bay **4** cove, gulf **5** basin, bight, firth, frith, inlet **7** estuary
country, to its people: **5** Norge
locale: **3** Nor. **4** Norw., Oslo **6** Norway
__ Fjord: **4** Oslo
F-K connector: **4** GHIJ
__ F. Kennedy: **4** John **6** Robert
FL
see Florida
Fla.
it borders ~: **3** Ala., Atl.
living in ~ maybe: **3** ret. **4** retd.
time: **3** EDT, EST
see also Florida
flab: **6** tissue **9** spare tire
flabbergast: **4** daze, stun **5** abash, amaze, floor, shock, throw **6** boggle, puzzle **7** astound, nonplus, stagger, stupefy **8** astonish, blow away, bowl over, confound, surprise **9** dumbfound, overwhelm **10** disconcert
flabbergasted: **4** agog
flabbiness: **5** atony **6** atonia
flabby: **3** lax **4** limp, puny, soft, weak **5** baggy, frail, loose, slack, unfit, wimpy **6** anemic, atonic, droopy, effete, feeble, flimsy **7** anaemic, flaccid, fragile, untoned, wimpish **8** delicate, drooping, helpless, pithless, toneless **9** faltering, powerless **10** out of shape, vulnerable
become ~: **6** go soft
flaccid: **3** lax **4** limp, soft, weak **5** baggy, loose, slack **6** droopy, flabby, floppy **7** hanging, sagging, untoned **8** dangling, drooping
flack: **8** promoter **9** publicity **10** press agent
concern: **5** image
Flack, Roberta
song: The Closer I Get to You (1978)
Feel Like Makin' Love (1974)
The First Time Ever I Saw Your Face (1972)
Killing Me Softly With His Song (1973)
Set the Night to Music (1991)
Tonight, I Celebrate My Love (1983)
Where Is the Love (1972)
flacon: **5** flask **6** bottle **9** container
flag: **3** ebb, lag, sag, sap, std., tab **4** fade, fall, hail, iris, jack, jade, name, sign, sink, tire, wane, wilt **5** abate, alert, blunt, droop, peter, plant, slump, trail, weary **6** banner, burgee, colors, emblem, ensign, flower, impair, loiter, pennon, reduce, shrink, signal, soften, weaken **7** decline, deplete, exhaust, fall off, fatigue, pennant, thin out **8** bookmark, enervate, enfeeble, get tired, gonfalon, languish, Old Glory, peter out, standard, streamer, taper off, tricolor, wave down **9** attenuate, banderole, undermine, Union Jack **10** debilitate, devitalize, Jolly Roger
American ~ color: **3** red **4** blue **5** white
blue ~: **5** plant **6** flower
country with a five-sided ~: **5** Nepal
down: **4** hail
ender: **3** man, men **4** pole, ship **5** staff, stick, stone
feature: **4** star **6** stripe
holder: **4** pole
maker: **4** Ross **9** Betsy Ross
military ~: **6** colors, ensign
nation with a green ~: **5** Libya
pirate ~ emblem: **5** skull **10** crossbones
raise a red ~: **4** warn **5** alert **6** tip off **7** caution
red ~: **6** caveat
roll up a ~: **4** furl
show a white ~: **9** surrender
small ~: **6** fanion, guidon
symbol on Pakistan's ~: **4** lune
wave a red ~: **6** enrage **7** caution **8** forewarn
waver: **4** gale, wind **5** jingo **7** patriot
white ~: **5** pause, truce **7** respite **9** armistice, cease-fire, surrender **10** moratorium, submission
yacht ~: **6** burgee
flag __: **4** rank, seat, smut **7** officer, station
flag-__: **5** waver **6** waving
__ flag: **3** red **4** blue, code, mail **5** black, green, guest, house, pilot, prize, sweet, water, white **6** powder, prayer, racing, yellow **7** crimson, protest
Flag __: **3** Day
__ Flag: **5** Black
Flag Day grp.: **3** VFW
flagellate: **4** flog, lash, whip **5** birch, strap **6** switch **7** scourge **9** horsewhip
flagellation: **7** lashing **8** birching, flogging, whipping **9** scourging, strapping, switching
flagellum: **5** organ
Flagg: **5** Hazel **6** Fannie **7** Colonel
flagging: **3** ebb **4** lazy, limp, weak **5** seedy, tired, weary **6** wilted **10** knocked out
flagitious: **4** vile **7** heinous **8** unlawful **9** nefarious
flag of __: **5** truce
flagon: **3** jug **5** crock, flask **6** bottle, carafe **7** amphora **8** decanter
filler: **3** ale **4** wine
flagpole: **4** mast, pole **5** staff
run up the ~: **4** test **5** hoist, raise
topper: **5** eagle
flagpole __: **6** sitter
flagrancy: **6** horror **8** atrocity, enormity **9** grossness, immensity, magnitude

flagrant: **4** open, rank **5** awful, gross, utter **6** arrant, brazen, patent **7** blatant, extreme, glaring, heinous, obvious, rampant **8** dreadful, grievous, shameful, shocking, striking, unsubtle **9** atrocious, barefaced, egregious, flaunting, monstrous, nefarious, out-and-out, shameless **10** noticeable, outrageous, scandalous
flagrante delicto
find in ~: **4** nail **5** catch
in ~: **9** red-handed
Flags of Our Fathers (2006 film)
cast: Ryan Phillippe, Paul Walker
director: Clint Eastwood
Flagstad, Kirsten: **6** singer **7** soprano
specialty: **5** opera
flagstaff: **4** pole
Flagstaff: **4** city, town
locale: **7** Arizona
flagstone: **4** slab
lay ~s: **4** pave
...__ flag was still there: **3** our
flail: **3** hit, tan **4** bash, beat, club, flap, flog, hurt, slug, sock **5** knock, smack, smite **6** batter, pommel, pummel, strike, thrash, thwack, writhe **7** scourge **9** cast about, horsewhip, truncheon
flair: **3** zip **4** bent, chic, dash, élan, feel, gift, head, nose, turn **5** éclat, forte, knack, oomph, style, taste, touch, verve **6** glamor, pizazz, splash, talent **7** ability, aptness, faculty, glamour, know-how, panache, pizzazz, promise **8** aptitude, artistry, elegance, hang of it **9** endowment, ingenuity **10** green thumb
Flair: **3** pen **7** felt tip
flak: **3** rap **6** outcry **7** dissent, protest **8** friction **9** criticism **10** complaints, opposition
flak __: **4** suit, vest **6** jacket
flake: **3** bit **4** chip, ditz, kook, peel, zany **5** scale **6** maniac, sliver, weirdo **7** oddball, peel off, shaving, speckle **8** laminate, splinter **9** character, exfoliate, screwball **10** desquamate
combining form: **5** lepid-, -lepis **6** lepido-
off: **4** molt, peel, shed **9** exfoliate
starter: **4** snow
flakes: **4** snow, soap **6** cereal **8** dandruff
__ flakes: **4** corn, soap
flaky: **3** odd, off **4** daft, zany **5** batty, dizzy, goofy, kooky, nutty, wacky, weird **6** absurd, kookie, screwy, whacky **7** erratic, jocular, oddball **8** aberrant, peculiar **9** eccentric, laminated, senseless **10** irrational, off-the-wall, unreliable
not ~: **4** sane, wise **5** lucid, sober, sound **6** steady **7** logical, prudent **8** balanced, rational, sensible, together **9** practical, pragmatic, realistic **10** reasonable, thoughtful
flam: **4** hoax, ruse **7** swindle **9** deception
flambé: **5** afire, burnt **6** burned, on fire **7** ignited
flamboyant: **3** big **4** loud **5** gaudy, jazzy, showy, swank, vivid **6** flashy, florid, ornate, rococo, snazzy, swanky **7** dashing, flowery, splashy **8** splendid **9** bombastic, brilliant, elaborate, glamorous, grandiose, luxuriant **10** peacockish, rhetorical, theatrical
flame: **2** jo **3** joe, pet **4** baby, beau, burn, dear, fire, glow, jill, love, zeal **5** amour, angel, ardor, blaze, chéri, color, cooky, cutey, cutie, deary, ducky, e-mail, flare, flash, honey, leman, light, lover, lovey, novia, novio, shine, sugar, swain, sweet, wooer **6** bon ami, chérie, cookie, dautie, dearie, fervor, orange, steady, sweets **7** beloved, darling, dearest, dear one, flare up, passion, pigsney, reddish, schatzi, squeeze, sweetie, tootsie **8** chouchou, cutie pie, dowsabel, dulcinea, ladylove, lovebird, macushla, paramour, precious, snookums, sugar pie, sweetums, truelove **9** bonne amie, boyfriend, coruscate, dreamboat, inamorata, inamorato, petit chou, valentine **10** girlfriend, heartthrob, honeybunch, incandesce, mavourneen, pilot light, sweetheart, sweetie pie, turtledove
color: **3** red **4** blue **6** orange, yellow
ender: **3** out **5** proof **7** thrower
fancier: **4** moth
name meaning ~: **6** Brenda
relative: **5** henna **7** pumpkin, saffron **8** hyacinth **9** tangerine **10** terra cotta
up: **4** fume **6** get hot, see red, seethe
__ flame: **3** old
__ Flame: **4** Blue **5** My Old **7** Eternal
Flame and Shadow
author: Sara Teasdale
flamenco: **5** dance **7** alegras
flames: **4** fire **5** blaze **8** wildfire
felonious ~: **5** arson
in ~: **5** afire, fiery **6** ablaze **7** burning
Flames: **3** six **4** team
home: **7** Calgary
milieu: **3** ice **4** rink
org.: **3** NHL
rival: ***see*** hockey team
sport: **6** hockey
Flame, The (1988 song)
artist: Cheap Trick
flaming: **3** hot, red **5** afire, fiery, livid, lurid **6** ablaze, alight, ardent, fervid, red-hot, torrid **7** fervent, flaring, intense, zealous **9** brilliant **10** combustion, infuriated, passionate
Flaming __: **4** Star **7** Feather
flamingo: **4** bird, pink
kin: **5** stork
relative: **4** nude **5** melon **6** damask, salmon **7** apricot **9** carnation
Flamingo Kid, The (1984 film)
cast: Richard Crenna, Matt Dillon, Hector Elizondo, Jessica Walter
director: Garry Marshall
Flamingo Road (1949 film)
cast: Joan Crawford, Sydney Greenstreet
director: Michael Curtiz
Flaming Star: **4** film, song
artist: Elvis Presley
cast: Barbara Eden, Steve Forrest, Elvis Presley
director: Don Siegel
flammable: **8** burnable **9** ignitable **10** incendiary
gas: **6** ethane **8** dimethyl
__ Flam Man, The: **4** Flim
flan: **7** custard, dessert, pudding
ingredient: **3** egg **4** yolk
like ~: **4** eggy
Flanagan: **5** Tommy **6** Edward, Father **8** Fionnula
Flanders: **2** Ed **3** Ned
language: **7** Flemish
locale: **7** Belgium, Holland
medieval capital: **5** Lille
town: **5** Aalst, Alost
Flanders __: **5** poppy
__ Flanders: **4** Moll
__ Flanders, A: **5** Dog of
flange: **3** lip, rib, rim **4** brim, edge, ring **5** bezel, ridge **6** collar **8** shoulder
flank: **4** meat, side **5** skirt, steak **6** haunch
combining form: **5** lapar- **6** laparo-
muscle: **5** psoas
muscles: **5** psoae, psoai
flank __: **5** speed, steak
flanker __: **4** back
flanking: **4** side **7** lateral **8** sideward, sideways, sidewise
flannel: **5** cloth **6** fabric **7** fustian **8** material
feature: **3** nap
fiber: **4** wool **6** cotton
in America: **9** washcloth
item: **3** PJs **5** shirt **7** pajamas **9** nightgown
see also baloney
flannel __: **4** cake **5** plant
flannels: **5** pants **6** slacks **8** trousers
Flannery: **5** Susan **7** O'Connor
flap: **3** ado, bat, ear, tab, tag, wag **4** beat, fold, fuss, lobe, loll, riot, spat, stew, stir, to-do, wave **5** flail, furor, lapel, panic, shake, swing, tizzy, valve **6** billow, dither, flurry, fracas, hassle, hubbub, lather, pother, ruckus, thrash, tumult, uproar **7** agitate, aileron, bluster, clutter, ferment, flutter, overlap, scandal, turmoil, twitter, wrangle **8** argument, brouhaha, conflict, rowdydow, squabble **9** agitation, commotion, confusion, encounter **10** hullabaloo
airplane ~: **6** elevon
cap ~: **6** earlap
ender: **4** jack **6** doodle
gummed ~: **4** seal
one's gums: **3** gab, gas, jaw, rap, yak, yap **4** blab, chat, gush, talk **5** prate, run on, speak, spout **6** babble, gabble, gibber, jabber, natter, parley, yammer **7** blabber, blather, chatter, maunder, prattle, twaddle **8** converse, ramble on, spout off **9** go on and on **10** yakkety-yak
starter: **3** ear
tent ~: **3** fly
flap __: **4** door **5** hinge, valve
__ flap: **3** mud **5** split **6** Fowler **7** landing
flapdoodle
see baloney
flapjack: **4** cake **7** hotcake, pancake **10** battercake
acronym: **4** IHOP
in French: **5** crepe
mix: **6** batter
order: **5** stack
flapper dance: **10** Charleston
flapping: **5** loose **7** beating, darting **8** flitting
stopped ~: **3** lit **4** alit
flaps, let down the: **4** slow
flare: **3** lip **4** boil, snap **5** blaze, flame, gleam, light, shine, spark, splay, torch, widen **6** beacon, signal, spread **7** blaze up, broaden, flicker, shimmer **8** outburst
send up a ~: **4** warn **5** alert **6** signal
up: **4** boil, rage, rave, rise **5** blaze, flame **6** ignite **7** bristle, explode, surface
warning ~: **5** fusee, fuzee
__ flare: **5** solar
flare-up: **4** gust **5** blaze **7** offense, tantrum **8** outbreak, outburst **9** explosion, hysterics
flaring: **3** hot **5** afire, fiery, lurid **6** ablaze, aflame, heated **7** blazing, burning, flaming
flash: **3** ray **4** beam, bolt, élan, jiff, look, snap, tick, wink, zoom **5** blaze, blink, burst, éclat, flame, gleam, glint, jiffy, light, scoop, shine, shoot, spark, speed, telex **6** dazzle, flaunt, glance, minute, moment, pizazz, recall, regard, second, signal, thrill **7** display, flicker, glimmer, glimpse, glisten, glitter, impulse, instant, lighten, radiate, reflect, release, shimmer, show off, sparkle, twinkle **8** outbreak, outburst, shoot out, telegram **9** container, coruscate, fulgurate, lightning, recollect, sensation **10** incandesce
ender: **3** gun **4** back, cube, over **5** board, light
flood: **5** spate **8** overflow
gone in a ~: **9** momentary
in a ~: **3** PDQ **4** fast **5** apace **6** presto **7** fleetly, hastily, quickly, rapidly, swiftly **8** pell-mell, speedily **9** forthwith, hurriedly, instantly, like a shot, on the spot, posthaste
news ~: **6** notice **8** bulletin, dispatch **10** communiqué, revelation
of lightning: **4** bolt
on: **6** recall **9** recognize, recollect
on and off: **5** blink
producer: **4** bulb **6** camera
flash __: **4** bulb, burn, card, lamp, tube **5** flood, point **6** memory **7** picture, welding
flash __ pan: **5** in the
flash-__: **4** lock **6** freeze **7** forward
__ flash: **3** in a, red **4** blue, news, open **5** green **6** bounce **7** bounced
Flash: **6** Gordon
Flashdance (1983 film)
cast: Jennifer Beals, Michael Nouri, Lilia Skala

director: Adrian Lyne
dog: 5 Grunt
role: 4 Alex
song: 6 Maniac
Flashdance ... What a Feeling (1983 song)
artist: Irene Cara
Flash Gordon: 6 serial
cast: Buster Crabbe (Flash Gordon)
foe: 4 Ming
locale: 5 Mongo
flashiness: 4 ritz 5 glitz, style
flashing: 5 light 6 ablaze, bright 8 meteoric 9 momentary
flash in the ___: 3 pan
flashlight, British: 5 torch
flashy: 3 lit 4 bold, loud 5 aglow, fancy, gaudy, jazzy, ritzy, shiny, showy, swank, tacky 6 ablaze, brazen, bright, florid, frilly, garish, glitzy, lavish, ornate, rakish, snazzy, swanky, tawdry, tinsel, vulgar 7 beaming, blatant, blazing, fulgent, glaring, glowing, lambent, opulent, radiant, shining 8 colorful, dazzling, gleaming, glittery, luminous, lustrous 9 brilliant, decorated, elaborate, flaunting, glamorous, luxurious, sparkling, sumptuous, tasteless 10 flamboyant, ornamented, theatrical
one: 4 dude 5 sport
flask: 4 vial 5 phial 6 beaker, bottle, carafe, flacon, flagon 7 canteen 9 container
drink from a ~: 4 swig 5 snort 6 guzzle, imbibe
flat: 3 pad 4 arid, blah, co-op, drab, dull, even, home, mild, poor, room, shoe, tame, two-D 5 abode, banal, bland, condo, empty, flush, ho-hum, house, level, matte, needy, plane, prone, stale, suite, trite, vapid 6 boring, draggy, dreary, fallen, jejune, off-key, planar, rental, smooth, supine, walk-up 7 blowout, habitat, housing, insipid, lodging, lowland, planate, prosaic, regular, shallow, tedious, unwaxed 8 absolute, complete, lifeless, outright, puncture, quarters, sea-level, tiresome, unlively, unsalted 9 apartment, colorless, container, penniless, pointless, prosaical, prostrate, recumbent, residence, tasteless 10 absolutely, dullsville, flavorless, horizontal, lackluster, lusterless, monotonous, pedestrian, spiritless, unelevated, unexciting, uninspired, warmed-over
area: 5 pampa, plain, plane, shelf 7 prairie
broke: 4 poor 8 deprived 9 destitute, penniless, penurious
cause: 4 nail, tack 5 glass, shard
combining form: 4 plan-, plat- 5 plani-, plano-, platy-
container: 4 tray 5 plate 7 platter
dweller: 6 lessee, lodger, renter, roomer, tenant 7 boarder 8 occupant, resident
ender: 3 bed, car, top 4 boat, feet, fish, foot, iron, land, ware, ways, wise, work, worm 5 bread 6 bottom, footed, lander
fall ~: 4 bomb, bust, fail, flop, lose, miss, slip, trip 5 crash, flunk 6 blow it, falter 7 blunder, founder, go under, go wrong, misfire, misstep, stumble, wash out 8 collapse, flounder, lay an egg 9 strike out
finish: 3 mat 5 matte
fix a ~: 5 patch 6 repair
fixer's tool: 4 jack
in nothing ~: 3 PDQ 4 fast 5 apace 6 presto 7 fleetly, hastily, quickly, rapidly, swiftly 8 pell-mell, promptly, speedily 9 forthwith, hurriedly, instantly, like a shot, posthaste
lack: 3 air
leave ~: 4 jilt, quit 6 desert
lying ~: 5 level, prone 6 face up, supine 8 face down 9 recumbent 10 horizontal
make ~: 4 even 5 level 8 straight
not ~: 5 foamy, hilly, on key, sharp, steep
nothing ~: 6 minute, moment, second
on one's back: 6 beaten, laid up 7 forlorn 8 helpless 9 abandoned, destitute, powerless 10 friendless
out: 5 plain, swift, total, utter 7 hastily, rapidly, swiftly, totally 8 absolute, decisive, for a fact, promptly, specific, whole hog 9 decidedly, full blast, no mistake 10 conclusive, definitive, positively, thoroughly, unarguable
payment: 4 rent
sign: 5 to let
tire: 8 puncture
flat ___: 3 bug, out 4 arch, back, bond, feet, knot, race, sour, tire 5 light 6 sennit, silver
flat ___ board: 3 as a
flat ___ pancake: 3 as a
flat-___: 3 out, saw 4 file, knit 6 footed, rolled 7 earther, grained
flat-___ boat: 6 bottom
flat-___ plotter: 3 bed
flat-___ press: 3 bed
___ flat: 3 mud 4 fall, salt, wing 5 adobe, tidal 6 alkali, double, French, granny 7 service
flat as a ___: 5 board 7 pancake
flatbed ___: 5 truck 7 trailer
flatboat: 3 ark 4 scow 5 barge
flat-bottomed boat: 4 dory, junk, punt, raft, scow 5 barge
flatfish: 3 dab 4 sole 5 brill 6 plaice, turbot 7 halibut, sand dab 8 flounder 9 Dover sole
flatfoot: 3 cop 6 copper 7 officer
flat-footed: 4 open 5 frank 6 candid, direct 7 unready 10 forthright, unprepared
flathead: 4 fish 5 screw 7 catfish
flatland: 5 plain, plane, table
South American ~: 5 pampa
Flatliners (1990 film)
cast: Kevin Bacon, William Baldwin, Julia Roberts, Kiefer Sutherland
flatness: 3 rut 5 ennui 6 tedium 7 boredom 8 banality, dullness, monotony, vapidity 10 insipidity, uniformity
flat on one's ___: 4 back
flats: 5 pumps, shoes 7 loafers, sandals 8 sneakers
Flatt: 6 Lester
flat-tasting: 4 blah 5 bland 7 insipid 10 flavorless
flatten: 2 KO 3 lay 4 deck, even, iron, kayo, rase, raze, ruin 5 crush, floor, grade, level, plane, press, smash, wreck 6 abrade, debunk, ground, lay low, smooth, spread, squash, unfold 7 deflate, depress, even out, iron out, mow down, plateau, roll out, trample, unbuild 8 beat down, bulldoze, compress, demolish, knock out, level out, puncture 9 knock down, prostrate, spread out
flattened
slightly ~: 6 oblate
flatter: 4 coax, hail, laud, puff, suit 5 adorn, exalt, extol, honor, toady 6 become, cajole, extoll, fawn on, praise, puff up, salute, stroke 7 acclaim, adulate, applaud, commend, enhance, glorify, lay it on, wheedle 8 beautify, blandish, bootlick, butter up, decorate, fawn over, gush over, inveigle, kowtow to, make up to, ornament, play up to, soft-soap, suck up to 9 embellish, glamorize, shine up to, sweet-talk 10 complement, compliment, look good on, overpraise, panegyrize
in a way: 4 copy 7 imitate
oneself: 4 brag 5 boast, pride
flatterer: 5 toady 6 fawner, flunky, lackey, yes man 7 booster, flunkey, lacquey 8 adulator, courtier, kowtower, servitor 9 sycophant
flatterers: 6 claque
flattering: 4 oily 7 candied 8 specious 9 laudatory
flattery: 3 oil 5 honor, kudos, smarm 6 homage, praise, salute 7 acclaim, blarney, coaxing, palaver, plaudit, puffery, tribute 8 accolade, cajolery, encomium, good word, soft soap, stroking 9 adulation, laudation, panegyric, wheedling 10 compliment, exaltation
flat-tire cause: 4 nail, tack 5 glass, shard
Flatt, Lester: 9 guitarist
partner: Earl Scruggs
flattop: 4 coif, mesa 6 hairdo 7 frigate, warship 8 coiffure, man-of-war 9 hairstyle 10 battleship
flatware: 4 fork 5 knife, spoon 6 silver
Flaubert, Gustave: 6 French, writer
character: 4 Emma
homeland: France
work: Madame Bovary
flaunt: 4 show 5 boast, flash, strut 6 dangle, parade 7 display, exhibit, show off, trot out 8 brandish, flourish, proclaim 9 advertise, brag about, broadcast, promenade 10 grandstand, wave around
one's feats: 4 brag 5 boast, spout, vaunt 7 lay it on, show off, swagger, talk big 9 gasconade
flaunting: 5 gaudy 6 flashy 7 blatant, fustian 8 flagrant
flautist: 5 piper
Flava ___ Ear: 4 in Ya
flavor: 3 air 4 feel, hint, lime, mint, odor, salt, tang, tone, zest, zing 5 lemon, pep up, sapor, savor, spice, style, taste 6 infuse, orange, pepper, relish, season, spirit 7 essence, extract, quality, vanilla 8 infusion, licorice, overtone, sapidity, sourness, tartness 9 character, chocolate, Rocky Road, saltiness, seasoning, spiciness, sweetness, undertone 10 bitterness, strawberry
cool ~: 4 mint
enhancer: 3 MSG 4 herb, salt 5 spice
half a ~: 5 tutti 6 frutti
have the ~: 5 smack
sharp ~: 3 nip, zip 4 bite, kick, tang, zest, zing 6 relish 8 piquancy, pungency 9 spiciness
flavor ___ month: 5 of the
flavored: 5 tinct
highly ~: 5 spicy, tangy, zesty 6 savory, strong 7 peppery, piquant, pungent, zestful
flavorful: 4 rich 5 sapid, spicy, tangy, tasty, yummy, zesty 6 savory, spicey, toothy 7 piquant, pungent 8 luscious 9 ambrosial, delicious, enjoyable, nectarous, palatable, toothsome 10 appetizing, delectable
flavoring: 4 herb, zest 5 sauce, spice 6 fennel, relish 7 essence, extract 9 condiment, seasoning
sans ~: 5 basic, plain 7 regular 8 straight 9 unadorned
flavorless: 4 blah, dull, flat 5 bland, vapid 6 watery 7 insipid 8 unsalted, unsavory 9 savorless, tasteless
flavorsome: 4 rich 5 sapid, spicy, tangy, tasty, yummy, zesty 6 savory, spicey, toothy 7 piquant, pungent 8 luscious 9 ambrosial, delicious, enjoyable, nectarous, palatable, toothsome 10 appetizing, delectable
flaw: 3 bug 4 blot, kink, scar, spot, typo, vice, wart 5 crack, error, fault, speck 6 defect, foible, glitch 7 blemish, failing, pitfall, scratch 8 drawback, weakness 9 deviation 10 deficiency, faultiness, inadequacy
minor ~: 4 dent, nick
___ flaw: 6 tragic
flawed: 3 irr. 5 irreg. 6 broken, faulty, impure, marred 7 damaged, lacking, unsound 8 fallible, impaired 9 defective, deficient, erroneous, imperfect, incorrect, sophistic, untenable
flawless: 4 good, just, nice, perf., pure 5 clean, exact, ideal, model, right, sound, valid 7 correct, factual, optimum, perfect, precise 8 absolute, accurate, finished, inerrant, peerless, spotless, unbroken, unerring, unmarred 9 faultless, foolproof, just right, undamaged, unsullied, untouched, virtuosic 10 consummate, immaculate, impeccable, infallible

flawlessly: 3 pat 4 to a T 6 to a tee 9 perfectly
flawlessness: 6 purity 9 precision 10 perfection
flax: 5 plant 6 flower
dampen ~: 3 ret
ender: 4 seed
fabric: 5 linen 7 fustian
name meaning ~: 5 Linus
pod: 4 boll
starter: 4 toad
flaxen: 3 tow 4 tawn 5 blond, color, sandy 6 blonde, golden, yellow 7 aureate 8 xanthous 9 yellowish
relative: *see* yellow color
flaxen-haired: 4 fair 5 blond 6 blonde
flaxlike fiber: 5 ramee, ramie
flay: 3 pan 4 lash, pare, peel, skin, slam, whip 5 blast, roast, strip 6 attack, berate, fleece, jump on, rip off 7 chew out, defraud, lambast, lecture, swindle 8 chastise, lambaste, strip off 9 castigate, criticize, excoriate, fustigate, light into, shoot down, skin alive
flea: 3 bug 4 pest 5 biter 6 chigoe, hopper, insect, jigger, vermin 7 chigger
ender: 3 bag, pit 4 bane, bite
genus: 5 tunga
in one's ear: 3 tip 4 clue, hint 6 tip-off 7 glimmer, inkling, whisper 10 glimmering, suggestion
market: 5 bazar 6 bazaar
market stipulation: 4 as is
market transaction: 6 resale
flea __: 6 beetle, circus, collar, market
flea-__: 6 bitten 7 flicker
__ flea: 3 cat, dog 4 sand 5 beach, water 6 chigoe, jigger
Flea __ Ear, A: 5 in Her
fleabag: 5 hotel 9 flophouse
like a ~: 5 dingy, ratty, seedy 6 crummy, shabby, shoddy, sordid 7 squalid 8 decrepit
flea in one's __: 3 ear
Flea, The
author: John Donne
fleck: 3 bit, dab, dot 4 mark, mote, snip, spot 5 point, speck 6 dapple, mottle 7 speckle, stipple 8 particle
flecked: 6 dotted 7 dappled, mottled, spotted 8 freckled, spangled, speckled, stippled
flection: 3 bow 4 bend, fold 5 angle
Fledermaus: 3 bat
__ Fledermaus: 3 Die
__-fledged: 4 full
fledgling: 4 tiro, tyro 5 chick, owlet, young 6 cygnet, eaglet, newbie, novice, rookie 7 budding, learner, new hand, recruit, trainee 8 beginner, duckling, neophyte, nestling 9 greenhorn, youngster 10 apprentice, catechumen, tenderfoot
comment: 5 cheep
home: 4 nest
flee: 2 go 3 fly, lam, run 4 bail, blow, bolt, jump, scat, skip 5 break, elope, elude, evade, lam it, leave, scoot, scram, skirr, split 6 beat it, bug out, cut out, decamp, depart, desert, escape, get out, go AWOL, hasten, run off, skidoo 7 abscond, get away, go south, make off, retreat, run away, scamper, scatter, skip out, take off, vamoose 8 cheese it, clear out, fugitate, run for it, skip town, slip away, turn tail, withdraw 9 cut and run, disappear, hotfoot it, scurry off, skedaddle 10 break loose, fly the coop, get clear of, hightail it, make tracks, scamper off, take flight
from: 4 duck, shun 5 avoid, dodge, evade, shirk 6 bypass, eschew 7 abstain 10 circumvent
to a J.P.: 5 elope 6 run off 8 slip away
unable to ~: 5 at bay, treed 7 trapped 8 cornered 9 powerless
F. Lee __: 6 Bailey
fleece: 2 do 3 abb, con, rob 4 bilk, burn, clip, coat, flay, gull, hoax, hose, milk, nick, pelt, pile, rook, ruin, take, wool 5 bleed, cheat, cozen, fluff, gouge, mulct, shaft, shear 6 denude, fabric, hustle, prey on, rip off, rope in 7 deceive, defraud, plunder, swindle 8 flimflam, hoodwink 9 bamboozle, victimize 10 overcharge
product: 4 yarn
source: 3 ewe, ram 5 llama, sheep 6 alpaca, vicuña
__ Fleece: 6 Golden
fleeced: 5 burnt, shorn 6 burned
fleece-seeking ship: 4 Argo
fleecing: 4 scam 5 bunco, theft 8 thievery
fleecy: 4 soft 5 downy, furry, nappy, plush, wooly 6 fluffy, woolly 7 squishy, velvety 8 cushiony, woollike 9 sheeplike
fleeing: 3 run 7 in a rush, retreat 8 on the run
fleer: 4 grin, jeer, mock 5 scoff, smirk, sneer 6 deride, heehaw 7 escapee, grimace 8 ridicule 9 make fun of, poke fun at 10 horselaugh
Fleer
rival: 5 Topps
fleet: 4 fast, navy, spry 5 agile, brisk, hasty, quick, rapid, swift 6 argosy, armada, convoy, flying, nimble, racing, snappy, speedy, sudden 7 brigade, express, hurried, instant 8 flitting, flotilla, meteoric 9 breakneck 10 double-time, harefooted, hypersonic, supersonic, ultrasonic
initials: 3 USN, USS
member: 3 cab 4 boat, ship, taxi
of the ~: 3 nav. 5 naval
VIP: 3 adm. 7 admiral
worker: 4 hack 6 cabbie 7 trucker
fleet __: 7 admiral
Fleet __: 6 Street
__ Fleet: 5 Jo Van
fleet-footed: 5 agile
fleeting: 4 fast 5 brief, short 6 little 7 cursory, passing 8 meteoric, temporal 9 ephemeral, fugacious, momentary, temporary, transient 10 evanescent, short-lived, transitory, unenduring
fleetly: 3 PDQ 4 fast, soon 5 apace 6 presto 7 hastily 8 in a flash, in a jiffy, in no time, pell-mell 9 forthwith, hurriedly, instantly, like a shot, posthaste
fleetness: 5 haste, hurry, speed 8 alacrity, celerity, dispatch, rapidity, velocity 9 quickness, swiftness 10 expedition, promptness, speediness
Fleet Street: 5 press
Fleetwood: 3 car 4 auto, Mick 8 Cadillac
Fleetwood Mac
members: Nicks, McVie, Buckingham
song: Big Love (1987)
Don't Stop (1977)
Dreams (1977)
Go Your Own Way (1977)
Hold Me (1982)
Little Lies (1987)
Sara (1979)
Tusk (1979)
You Make Loving Fun (1977)
Fleischer: 3 Ari, Max, Nat 7 Richard
Fleischmann's: 4 oleo 9 margarine
alternative: 6 Parkay, Shedd's 7 Promise 8 Imperial
Fleisher: 4 Leon
Flem: 6 Snopes
Fleming: 3 Art, Ian 4 Eric 5 Peggy, Renée 6 Andrew, Rhonda, Victor 9 Alexander
valve: 5 diode
__ Fleming: 5 Rhoda
Fleming, Ian: 6 writer 7 British
alma mater: 4 Eton
character: Bond, Oddjob
homeland: England
work: Casino Royale
Chitty Chitty Bang Bang
Diamonds Are Forever
Dr. No
For Your Eyes Only
From Russia, With Love
Goldfinger
Live and Let Die
The Living Daylights
The Man With the Golden Gun
Moonraker
Octopussy
On Her Majesty's Secret Service
The Spy Who Loved Me
Thunderball
A View to a Kill
You Only Live Twice
Fleming, Peggy: 6 skater
Fleming, Renée: 6 singer 7 soprano
specialty: 5 opera
Fleming, Victor: 8 director
film: Captains Courageous (1937)
Dr. Jekyll and Mr. Hyde (1941)
Gone With the Wind (1939, AA)
Red Dust (1932)
Test Pilot (1938)
Tortilla Flat (1942)
Treasure Island (1934)
The Way of All Flesh (1927)
The Wizard of Oz (1939)
Flemish: 8 language
cartographer: 8 Mercator
medieval ~ capital: 5 Lille
painter: 6 Rubens 7 Bruegel, van Dyck, van Eyck 8 Brueghel
poet: 7 Gezelle
Flemish Feast in an Inn
artist: Jan Steen
flesh: 4 pulp, skin 6 muscle 8 humanity 9 humankind
and blood: 3 kin 4 aunt, life, soul 5 being, uncle 6 cousin, family, sister 7 brother, kinfolk, sibling 8 relation, relative
combining form: 3 cre- 4 creo-, kreo-, sarc- 5 creat-, sarco- 6 creato-
in the ~: 4 here 6 bodily
like the ~ proverbially: 4 weak
make one's ~ crawl: 5 chill, panic, scare, spook 7 horrify, petrify, terrify 8 frighten 9 terrorize
out: 3 pad 4 fill 5 color 6 expand, fill in 7 inflate
press the ~: 5 lobby, stump 8 campaign, politick 10 shake hands
starter: 5 horse
thorn in the ~: 4 pain, pest 6 bother, gadfly, hassle 8 irritant, nuisance 9 annoyance
flesh __: 3 fly 5 color, wound
__ flesh: 5 goose, in the
flesh and __: 5 blood
Flesh and Blood
author: Jonathan Kellerman
fleshiness: 7 obesity 9 adiposity, bulkiness, plumpness, pudginess, stoutness 10 corpulence, portliness
fleshy: 4 soft 5 beefy, fubsy, heavy, obese, plump, pudgy, pursy, stout 6 chubby, portly, pyknic, rotund, stocky, zaftig, zoftig 7 adipose, paunchy, weighty 8 roly-poly, sensuous 9 corpulent, filled-out 10 overweight, well-padded
fruit: 4 pepo, pome 5 papaw
root: 5 tuber
fletch: 5 plume 7 feather
Fletch (1985 film)
cast: Joe Don Baker, Chevy Chase, Tim Matheson
director: Michael Ritchie
Fletcher: 6 Knebel, Louise, Markle 9 Christian, Henderson
Fletcher, Jessica doctor friend: 4 Seth
fleur-de-__: 3 lis, lys
fleur-de-lis: 4 iris 5 plant 6 emblem, flower
__-fleuve: 5 roman
__ Flew Over the Cuckoo's Nest: 3 One
flex: 3 bow, sag 4 arch, bend, curl, kink, loop 5 crook, curve, hunch, slump, stoop, yield 6 camber, slouch
ender: 4 time
one's muscles: 8 threaten
flex __: 5 point
Flex: 7 shampoo
alternative: 4 Pert 5 Prell, Suave, Wella 7 Finesse, Pantene
flexed, easily: 5 lithe
flexibility: 4 give, play 6 leeway, spring 7 freedom, pliancy
flexible: 3 lax 4 easy, kind, limp, mild, open, soft, wiry 5 fluid, lithe, loose, slack 6 aidful, clayey, gentle, kindly, limber, lissom, pliant, spongy, supple 7 clayish, clement, elastic, helpful, liberal, lissome, plastic, pliable, ruthful, sparing, springy 8 bendable, laid-back, merciful, moldable, obedient, obliging, placable, tolerant, yielding 9 adaptable, assuasive, compliant, easygoing, forgiving,

indulgent, lightsome, lithesome, malleable, resilient, tractable, versatile **10** adjustable, forbearing, permissive, unexacting, unhardened
 not ~: **4** firm **5** fixed, rigid, stern, stiff **6** flinty, mulish, steely, strict **7** adamant **8** hard-line, indurate, ironclad, obdurate, resolute, stubborn **9** hidebound, obstinate, pig-headed, steadfast, stringent **10** bullheaded, implacable
Flexible Flyer: **4** sled
 inventor: Samuel Allen
flexor: **6** biceps, muscle
flexuous: **4** wavy **5** snaky **6** curved, zigzag **7** sinuous, turning, winding **8** twisting **10** circuitous, convoluted, meandering
flexure: **3** arc, bow **4** bend, fold, turn **5** angle, crook, elbow **7** bending, curving **9** curvature, sinuosity
flibbertigibbet: **3** oaf **4** ditz, fool, jerk **5** dummy, dunce, ninny, snoop, yenta **6** gossip, lubber, nitwit **7** dullard, jackass, meddler **8** busybody, quidnunc **9** blockhead, simpleton **10** nincompoop
flic: **3** cop **6** French **9** policeman
flick: **3** dab, pat, pic, tap **4** film, lick, show, snap, tick, wink **5** movie, oater, throw, touch, whisk **6** fillip **7** picture **10** tearjerker
 minor ~: **6** B movie
 something to ~: **5** wrist
 see also film, movie
Flicka: **4** mare **5** horse
Flick, Elmer: **6** Indian **10** outfielder
flicker: **3** ray **4** lick, wink **5** blink, flare, flash, gleam, shake, shine, spark, waver **7** glimmer, glisten, glitter, shimmer, sparkle, twinkle **9** luminesce
 ender: **4** tail
__-flicker: **4** flea
flickering: **6** spotty, uneven **7** erratic, glowing, lambent **8** sporadic **9** irregular, spasmodic
flicks: **3** pix **6** cinema
__ fliegende Holländer: **3** Der
flier: **2** ad **3** ace **5** pilot **6** airman, insert, raffle **7** aviator, leaflet, war hero **8** aeronaut, circular, handbill, pamphlet
 see also airline, bird
flies
 as the crow ~: **6** direct, in a row, linear, unbent **7** unbowed **8** directly, straight **10** unswerving
 catch ~: **4** shag, yawn
 no ~ on: **3** hip **5** alert, sharp, smart **7** knowing **9** wide-awake **10** perceptive
 to spiders: **4** diet, fare, prey
Flies, The
 author: Jean-Paul Sartre
flight: **3** lam, run **4** trip **6** escape, exodus, hegira, hejira, red-eye, voyage **7** fleeing, getaway, journey, retreat, running, shuttle, soaring **8** aviation, movement, stairway, stampede **9** departure **10** volitation
 abbr.: **3** arr., dep., ETA, ETD
 advisory team: **3** ATC
 board: **4** sked **5** sched. **8** schedule
 crew member: **3** nav. **4** capt. **5** pilot **7** captain **9** navigator
 delayer: **3** fog **4** snow **5** storm **8** blizzard
 dir.: **3** ENE, ESE, NNE, NNW, SSE, SSW, WNW, WSW
 ender: **6** worthy
 in ~: **5** aloft **8** on the run **9** on the wing
 inducer: **4** fear
 of fancy: **6** revery **7** reverie
 part: **5** riser, stair
 path: **6** ascent
 pertaining to ~: **4** aero
 prefix: **3** aer- **4** aero-
 put to ~: **4** rout **5** panic, repel **7** overrun, repulse, scatter **8** chase out, stampede
 record: **3** log
 regulator: **3** FAA
 route: **3** arc
 science of ~: **11** aeronautics
 sudden ~: **3** lam **6** escape **7** getaway
 support: **5** newel
 take ~: **2** go **3** run **4** bolt, flee, wing **6** decamp, escape **7** abscond, retreat **8** fugitate, withdraw **9** disappear
 top-~: **4** A-one
 unit: **4** step
 word: **4** mach
flight __: **3** bag, cap, pay **4** deck, line, path, plan, suit **5** arrow, nurse, strip **6** leader **7** control, feather, officer, surgeon
__ flight: **4** free, take, test **5** put to, space **6** direct **7** capital, contact, nonstop
__-flight: **3** top
flight-accident investigators: **4** NTSB
flightiness: **5** mirth **6** levity **8** hilarity, nonsense **9** frivolity, merriment
flightless bird: **3** emu, moa **4** dodo, emeu, rhea **7** penguin
Flightplan (2005 film)
 cast: Jodie Foster, Peter Sarsgaard
flighty: **4** wild, zany **5** dizzy, giddy, light, moody, silly **6** fickle, giggly **7** aimless, wayward **8** flippant, skittish, volatile **9** frivolous, lightsome, mercurial, vagarious **10** capricious
flimflam: **2** do **3** con, gyp **4** bilk, burn, dupe, fool, gull, hoax, hose, jazz, jive, nick, pooh, rook, scam, sham, take **5** bunco, cheat, fraud, pluck, shaft, trash, trick **6** chisel, deceit, dupery, fakery, fleece, kibosh, piffle, rip off, take in **7** beguile, deceive, defraud, swindle **8** trickery, trumpery **9** bamboozle, deception, four-flush, gibberish, imposture, unethical, victimize
 see also baloney
Flim Flam Man, The (1967 film)
 cast: Sue Lyon, Michael Sarrazin, George C. Scott
 director: Irvin Kershner
flimflammed
 easily ~: **5** naive
flimsy: **4** lame, poor, puny, slim, soft, thin, weak **5** frail, gauzy, light, shaky, sheer, slack, tinny, wimpy **6** anemic, atonic, cheesy, effete, feeble, flabby, meager, papery, sleazy, slight, unfirm, wabbly, wobbly **7** anaemic, chiffon, fragile, rickety, shallow, tenuous, trivial, unsound, wimpish **8** baseless, decrepit, delicate, gossamer, helpless, pithless, wretched **9** breakable, faltering, frangible, powerless, rinky-dink **10** cobweblike, diaphanous, improbable, inadequate, jerry-built, nondurable, ramshackle, tumbledown, vulnerable
Flin __, Manitoba: **4** Flon
flinch: **4** balk, jump **5** baulk, cower, quail, start, wince **6** blanch, blench, cringe, recoil, shrink **7** shy away **8** draw back, withdraw **10** shrink back
 from: **4** hate **6** detest, loathe **7** despise
flinching: **3** coy, shy **4** meek **5** chary, timid **7** abashed, bashful, fearful **8** hesitant, sheepish **9** blenching, diffident, reluctant, shrinking, unassured, withdrawn
flinders: **6** pieces **7** slivers **9** fragments, splinters
fling: **2** go **3** lob, peg, sow, try **4** cast, hurl, lark, send, shot, slam, stab, toot, toss **5** binge, chuck, crack, dance, heave, pitch, shoot, sling, spree, throw, trial, whack, whirl **6** effort, gamble, launch, let fly, propel **7** attempt, deliver, liaison, project, rampage, romance, scatter, splurge, venture **8** catapult
 dirt: **4** slur **5** libel, smear, sully, taint **6** defame, impugn, malign, vilify **7** asperse, slander, traduce **8** besmirch, throw mud **9** disparage **10** calumniate
 have a ~: **5** binge, revel, spree **6** cavort, frolic, gambol **7** carouse, roister, rollick **8** cut loose **9** celebrate, make merry, whoop it up
 take a ~: **4** risk **6** gamble, hazard **7** venture **9** speculate
flint: **4** rock **5** silex, stone **6** quartz, silica **7** adamant, lighter, mineral
 ancient ~: **6** eolith
 creation: **5** spark
 ender: **4** head, lock
 starter: **3** gun **4** skin
 successor: **5** match
 tool: **5** burin
 work with ~: **4** knap
Flint: **4** city, town
 locale: **8** Michigan
flintlock: **3** arm, gun **5** fusil, rifle **6** musket
Flintstones, The (ABC sitcom)
 boss: Slate
 pet: Dino
 setting: Bedrock
 voice cast: Bea Benaderet (Betty Rubble)
 Mel Blanc (Barney Rubble)
 Don Messick (Bamm Bamm Rubble)
 Alan Reed (Fred Flintstone)
 Jean Vander Pyl (Wilma Flintstone, Pebbles Flintstone)
flinty: **4** firm, hard **5** cruel, rigid, rocky, stern, stony, tough **6** steely, stoney **7** hard-set, ice-cold **8** indurate, obdurate **9** impliable, unpitying **10** inflexible, iron-willed, unmerciful, unyielding
flip: **3** lob **4** cast, pert, rave, rude, snap, toss **5** chuck, crack, drink, fresh, go ape, nervy, pitch, sassy, saucy, throw, upend **6** awless, brazen, cheeky, go wild, invert, jaunty, lose it, snippy, tumble **7** aweless, go crazy, uncivil **8** beverage, cocktail, coiffure, go postal, have a fit, impolite, impudent, insolent, snippety **9** blow a fuse, facetious, frivolous, go bananas, go berserk, go bonkers, hairstyle, out of line **10** hit the roof, irreverent, nonserious, somersault
 a coin: **6** choose
 coin ~ choice: **5** heads, tails
 ender: **4** book
 ingredient: **3** egg **4** wine **6** liquor, nutmeg
 one's lid: **4** rage **8** freak out
 over: **5** adore, enjoy, upend **10** appreciate
 (over): **6** go wild
 side: **6** option **7** reverse **8** opposite **9** inversion **10** antithesis
 talk: **3** lip **4** guff, sass
 through: **4** read, scan, skim **6** browse **8** look over
 (through): **4** leaf, page
flip __: **4** side **5** a coin, chart
flip-__: **4** flap, flop
flip-__ circuit: **4** flop
Flip: **6** Wilson **8** Phillips
flip chart holder: **5** easel
flip-flop: **4** shoe **5** hedge, shift, thong, U-turn, waver **6** change, invert **7** quibble, reverse, whiffle **8** apostasy, exchange, footwear, reversal, variance **9** about-face, back-pedal, inversion, transpose, turnabout **10** conversion, turnaround
flip one's __: **3** lid, wig
flippancy: **4** sass **5** cheek, humor **6** levity **8** pertness **9** cockiness, freshness, frivolity, impudence, lightness, sauciness **10** cheekiness, disrespect, impishness, jocoseness, volatility
 flippant: **4** pert, rude **5** fresh, nervy, sassy, saucy, smart **6** awless, brassy, brazen, cheeky, impish, jaunty, snippy **7** aweless, flighty, uncivil **8** impolite, impudent, insolent, snippety **9** facetious, out of line **10** irreverent
 be ~ with: **3** kid **4** josh **5** tease
flippantly: **6** mildly **7** lightly **8** casually **10** carelessly, heedlessly
flipped: **4** amok **5** amuck, manic **7** berserk, bonkers, frantic, haywire, unglued **8** frenetic, frenzied, maniacal **9** delirious **10** bewildered
 out: **6** raging, raving **9** wrought-up
flipper: **3** oar **5** pinna **6** paddle
Flipper (NBC adventure)
 cast: Luke Halpin (Sandy Ricks)
 Brian Kelly (Porter Ricks)
 Tommy Norden (Bud Ricks)
 pelican: Pete
 title character: **7** dolphin
flip-up __: **5** visor
flirt: **3** toy **4** eyer, minx, vamp, wink

5 dally, ogler, tease, toyer, vixen 6 coquet, lead on, masher, teaser, trifle 7 toy with, trifler 8 coquette 9 libertine 10 make eyes at, trifle with
weapon: 5 hanky 6 hankie
with: 3 eye 4 ogle 6 gaze at, look at 7 stare at
flirtation: 4 idyl 5 idyll 7 romance 9 dalliance
flirtatious: 3 coy 7 playful, teasing
gesture: 4 wink
flit: 3 fly, gad, hie, rip, run, zip 4 dart, dash, race, rush, sail, skip, tear, whiz, zoom 5 drift, glide, hover, hurry, leave, scoot, shake, speed, steal, sweep, whisk 6 barrel, gallop, hasten, hustle, move it, rocket, scurry 7 floor it, flutter, hop to it, quicken, scamper 8 gad about, hurry off, step on it, volitate 9 hotfoot it, shake a leg, skedaddle 10 get a move on, hightail it
by: 5 glide 6 elapse
flitter: 4 hang 5 float, hover, shake
flitting: 4 fast 5 brief, fleet, quick, rapid, short 7 beating, darting 8 flapping 9 ephemeral, momentary, temporary, transient 10 evanescent, shortlived, transitory, unenduring
flivver: 3 car 4 auto 5 crate 6 jalopy 10 automobile, rattletrap
part: 5 choke
Flix: 7 channel
alternative: *see* cable channel
offering: 4 film 5 movie
Flo: 5 Hyman 8 Ziegfeld
boss: 3 Mel
coworker: 4 Vera 5 Alice
float: 3 bob 4 boat, buoy, hang, sail, skim, swim, waft, wash 5 drift, glide, hover, range 6 wander 8 beverage, levitate, volplane 10 underwrite
don't ~: 4 sink
fishing ~: 4 cork 6 bobber, dobber
ingredient: 4 soda 5 syrup 8 ice cream
nautical ~: 7 caisson
place: 6 parade 7 pageant
to the top: 4 rise
float __: 5 a loan
floatability: 8 buoyance, buoyancy
floater: 4 loan 5 tramp 7 release, vagrant 8 outsider, wanderer
flume ~: 3 log
pond ~: 3 pad
floating: 4 asea 5 aswim, at sea, awash, light, loose 6 adrift, natant 7 buoyant, movable, unfixed 8 ecstatic, moveable, shifting, variable 9 lightsome, unsettled
platform: 4 boat, raft 5 barge
floating __: 3 rib 4 dock, gang, vote 5 heart, point, stock
__-floating: 4 free
Floating City, A
author: Jules Verne
floating island: 7 dessert
Float like a butterfly boxer: 3 Ali
__ Floats: 4 Hope
floaty: 7 buoyant
flock: 3 mob 4 army, bevy, herd, host, mass, meet, pack, pile 5 brood, bunch, covey, crowd, drove, group, laics, laity, press, stock, swarm, troop 6 gaggle, gather, huddle, legion, parish, rabble, throng 7 collect, company 8 assemble, assembly, converge 9 gathering, multitude 10 collection, congregate, worshipers
area: 4 nave
far from the ~: 4 lost 6 astray
funds from the ~: 5 tithe
hangout: 3 lea, ley 5 field 6 meadow 7 pasture
leader: 3 ram
leave the ~: 5 stray
member: 3 ewe 4 lamb 5 sheep 6 layman
of fowl: 5 skein
of mallards: 4 sute
of the ~: 4 laic 6 laical 7 secular 8 temporal
priest's ~: 4 fold 5 laity 6 parish
sound: 3 baa, maa 5 bleat
together: 3 mob 4 band, gang, herd 5 bunch, crowd, group, rally, swarm, troop 6 gather, muster, throng 7 cluster, collect, convene 8 assemble 9 aggregate 10 congregate
Flockhart: 7 Calista
role: Ally McBeal
flocks: 4 lots 5 hosts, loads, scads 6 crowds, droves, hoards, oodles, scores, swarms 7 legions, throngs 8 millions 9 livestock
floe: 3 ice 8 ice sheet
flog: 3 hit, tan 4 beat, belt, cane, drub, hurt, hype, lash, lick, sell, whip, whup 5 flail, smite, spank, whack, whomp 6 cudgel, larrup, paddle, punish, strike, thrash 7 lambast, promote, scourge, trounce 8 lambaste 9 castigate, horsewhip, publicize 10 flagellate
flogging: 6 hiding 7 lashing, tanning 8 flailing, whipping 9 switching, thrashing 10 punishment
flood: 4 glut, gush, load, pour, rain, rush, soak, spew, spue, tide 5 crowd, drown, flush, light, shock, spate, surge, swamp, swarm 6 bounty, deluge, drench, engulf, excess, ingulf, inrush, myriad, onrush, stream 7 cascade, congest, freshet, overrun, surplus, torrent 8 brim over, downpour, drencher, inundate, irrigate, overflow, plethora, submerge 9 abundance, avalanche, cataclysm, overwhelm, profusion 10 inundation, outgushing, outpouring, oversupply
control: 3 dam 4 dike 5 levee 10 embankment
control initials: 3 TVA
ender: 3 lit 4 gate 5 light, water
follower: 5 light
protect from ~: 4 dike 6 embank
residue: 3 mud
stage: 3 ebb 5 crest
survivor: 3 Ham 4 Noah, Shem 7 Japheth
the market: 4 glut 10 oversupply
flood __: 4 lamp, tide, wall 5 plain 7 control
__ flood: 5 flash
Flood: 4 Curt
flooded: 5 awash 6 packed 7 crowded, replete 8 brimming
floodgate: 4 door 5 hatch 6 sluice
floods, site of annual: 4 Nile
Flood, The
author: Günter Grass
floodwater, like: 5 silty
flooey: 4 awry 5 amiss, askew
floor: 3 awe 4 deck, jolt, kayo, stun 5 addle, amaze, level, nadir, quota, shock, story, stump, throw, upset 6 baffle, bottom, cellar, defeat, lay low, puzzle 7 astound, confuse, conquer, flatten, landing, mystify, nonplus, perplex, stagger, startle, stupefy, unnerve 8 astonish, basement, bewilder, blow away, bowl over, confound, knock out, low point, surprise 9 dumbfound, knock down, mezzanine, overwhelm, prostrate, underside
access: 5 stair
bottom ~: 6 cellar 8 basement
cleaner: 3 vac 5 broom 6 mopper, vacuum 7 sweeper
clean the ~: 3 mop 5 sweep 6 vacuum
covering: 3 mat, rug, wax 4 lino, tile 6 carpet 8 linoleum
do the ~: 3 wax
ender: 5 board 6 walker
fix a ~: 5 repeg
hit the ~ hard: 5 stomp
in French: 5 étage
installer: 5 tiler
it: 3 fly, hie, rip, run, zip 4 dart, dash, flit, race, rush, tear, zoom 5 hurry, scoot, speed 6 barrel, gallop, hasten, hustle, rocket, scurry 7 quicken, scamper 9 get moving, shake a leg, skedaddle 10 get a move on, get hopping
mark: 5 scuff
model: 4 demo
mop the ~ with: 4 beat, rout
plan: 5 chart 6 design, layout, sketch 7 diagram, drawing, outline 9 blueprint, visual aid
space: 4 area
support: 4 beam, stud 5 joist 6 header
take the ~: 4 talk 5 orate, speak, spout 6 recite 7 lecture 9 hold forth, sermonize, speechify
top ~: 4 loft 5 attic 6 garret
walk the ~: 4 pace
floor __: 3 pan 4 lamp, loom, plan, show 5 model, price 6 broker, leader, pocket, sample, trader 7 furnace, manager
floor-__: 4 work 6 length, manage 7 through
__ floor: 3 fly, sea 4 deep 5 blind, first, plank 6 ground, second 7 selling
floorboards
like some ~: 6 creaky
sound: 5 creak
flooring: 7 parquet
material: 5 vinyl
piece: 4 tile 5 board, plank
flooring __: 3 saw 4 brad
floor model warning: 4 as is
floor plan: 6 design, layout 7 drawing
designation: 3 den, lav 4 bdrm., door 5 attic 6 closet 7 bedroom, kitchen 8 basement, bathroom, lavatory 10 family room, living room
floor-show unit: 3 act
floors, like some: 4 waxy
flop: 3 dog, dud, sag 4 bomb, bust, drop, fail, fall, loll, lose, loss, play, slip, trip 5 droop, flunk, lemon, loser, slump 6 blow it, bounce, dangle, defeat, falter, fiasco, fizzle, mishap, sprawl, topple, tumble, turkey, turn in 7 blunder, debacle, failure, fizzler, founder, go kaput, go under, go wrong, misstep, stumble, washout 8 backfire, collapse, disaster, downfall, fall flat, flounder, lay an egg, plop down 9 strike out 10 nonsuccess
ender: 5 house, sweat
inclined to ~: 5 loppy 6 droopy
opposite: 3 hit 5 smash 6 winner 7 sellout, success, triumph 9 sensation
sound: 4 pfft 5 pffft, phfft
flop-__: 5 eared
__ flop: 5 belly
__-flop: 4 flip
flophouse: 5 hotel 7 fleabag
floppy: 4 disk, limp 5 baggy, slack 6 droopy 7 flaccid, hanging, sagging 8 dangling, diskette 10 ill-fitting
alternative: 5 CD-ROM
contents: 4 data
prepare a ~: 6 format
user: 2 PC 3 Mac 4 mini 5 micro 6 laptop 8 computer, notebook
floppy __: 4 disk
Flopsy brother: 5 Mopsy, Peter
Floptical __: 4 disk
flora: 6 plants 9 plant life 10 vegetation
fauna and ~: 5 biome, biota
migration: 6 ecesis
study: 6 botany
Flora: 5 Nwapa 6 Robson
flora and __: 5 fauna
floral: 7 botanic, flowery, verdant 8 blossomy
see also flower
__ Flor and Her Two Husbands: 4 Dona
Florek: 4 Dann
Florence: 4 city, town 6 Kelley 7 Ballard, Harding 8 Chadwick, Eldridge, Lawrence 9 Henderson
locale: 5 Italy 7 Alabama 8 Kentucky 10 California
palace: 5 Pitti
river: 4 Arno
town near ~: 5 Lucca, Prato, Siena
Florence __-Joyner: 8 Griffith
Florentine: 5 onion
poet: 5 Dante
__ Florentine: 3 à la
florescence: 3 bud 5 bloom 6 flower 7 blossom 9 flowerage, flowering 10 blossoming
floret: 3 bud 5 bloom 7 blossom
Florey: 6 Howard, Robert
floribunda: 4 rose 5 plant 6 flower
florid: 3 red 5 flush, ruddy, showy 6 blowsy, blowzy, flashy, ornate, rococo 7 baroque, blowsed, blowzed, flushed 8 colorful, reddened, rubicund, sanguine 9 beetfaced, elaborate, luxuriant 10 decorative, flamboyant, ornamented, rhetorical

Florida: 5 state
acquisition: 3 tan
bay: 5 Tampa 8 Biscayne 9 Apalachee, Pensacola
capital: Tallahassee
city: 4 Leto, Ojus 5 Brent, Davie, Largo, Miami, Ocala, Ocoee, Tampa 6 Apopka, De Land, Eustis, Naples, Oviedo, St. Pete, Stuart, Sunset, Weston, Wright 7 Brandon, Captiva, Deltona, Dunedin, Hialeah, Holiday, Jupiter, Kendall, Key West, Lantana, Margate, Miramar, Norland, Orlando, Palm Bay, Perrine, Sanford, Sanibel, St. Cloud, Sunrise, Tamarac, Tamiami 8 Aventura, Bellview, East Lake, Lakeland, Lakeside, Oak Ridge, Palm City, Pinewood, Sarasota, Ybor City 9 Boca Raton, Bradenton, Cape Coral, Carol City, Egypt Lake, Englewood, Ferry Pass, Fort Myers, Hollywood, Homestead, Immokalee, Kissimmee, Lake Worth, Melbourne, Mount Dora, Northdale, North Port, Palm Coast, Pensacola, Pine Hills, Plant City, Rockledge, Vero Beach 10 Bal Harbour, Boca del Mar, Citrus Park, Clearwater, Cocoa Beach, Cooper City, Dania Beach, Fort Pierce, Golden Gate, Greenacres, Hallandale, Land O'Lakes, Lauderhill, Miami Beach, Miami Lakes, North Miami, Palm Harbor, Panama City, Plantation, Port Orange, Punta Gorda, Spring Hill, Titusville, University, Warrington, Wellington, Winter Park 11 Delray Beach
conference: 3 SEC
county: 3 Bay, Lee 4 Clay, Dade, Gulf, Lake, Leon, Polk 5 Duval, Pasco 6 Citrus, De Soto, Glades, Orange, Sumter 7 Alachua, Flagler, Osceola, Volusia 8 Sarasota 9 Miami-Dade
dwelling: 5 condo
explorer: 6 de Soto 11 Ponce de León
footballer: 4 'Nole 5 Gator 8 Seminole
golf course: 5 Doral
Indian: 5 Miami 8 Mikasuki, Seminole
islands off ~: 7 Bahamas
islet: 3 cay, key
key: 4 isle, West 5 Largo 6 island 8 Biscayne, Longboat
lake: 10 Okeechobee
national park: 8 Biscayne 10 Everglades
neighbor: 7 Alabama, Georgia
one way to ~: 6 Amtrak
port: 5 Miami, Tampa 9 Pensacola
pro team: 4 Bucs, Heat 7 Jaguars, Marlins 8 Dolphins, Panthers 9 Lightning 10 Buccaneers
school: 7 Stetson
state gem: 9 moonstone
state mammal: 7 panther
state marine mammal: 7 manatee
state reptile: 9 alligator
state saltwater fish: 8 sailfish
state saltwater mammal: 8 porpoise
state shell: 10 horse conch
state tree: 8 palmetto
state wildflower: 9 coreopsis
theme park: 5 Epcot

Florida ___: 4 Keys, moss, room 6 Strait 7 Current
Florida State athletes: 5 'Noles 9 Seminoles
Florida State conference: 3 ACC
Florida Strait, city on the: 6 Havana
floridness: 9 euphemism, inflation, pomposity
florilegium: 8 analecta, analects
florin: 4 coin 5 Dutch, money 6 gilder, gulden 7 guilder
florist
need: 3 pot 4 vase
offering: 3 bud 5 bloom, roses 7 bouquet
floristics: 6 botany
Florsheim offering: 4 shoe
floss: 4 fuzz 8 corn silk, filament 9 adornment
___ floss: 5 candy 6 dental
flossing advocates' org.: 3 ADA
flossy: 4 chic 5 downy, fancy, fuzzy, silky, slick 6 dressy, fluffy, frilly, satiny, silken, smooth 7 stylish, velvety, voguish 8 feathery, gossamer 9 gossamery, gussied up
flotation ___: 6 device
flotilla: 4 navy 5 fleet, group 6 argosy, armada 10 naval force
flotsam: 5 lagan, ligan 6 debris, jetsam, jetsom 8 wreckage
partner: 6 jetsam, jetsom
flotsam and ___: 6 jetsam
flounce: 4 toss 5 frill, strut, sweep 6 fringe, prance, ruffle
flounder: 3 dab 4 bomb, bust, fail, fish, flop, keel, lose, sink, slip, sole, toss, trip 5 botch, flunk, grope, lurch, pitch, slosh, waver 6 blow it, falter, fumble, muddle, plaice, plunge, squirm, totter, wallow 7 blunder, founder, go under, go wrong, misstep, stumble, wash out 8 fall flat, hesitate, lay an egg, struggle 9 cast about, feel about, hit bottom, strike out
in water: 6 splash
floundering: 4 asea 5 at sea, gawky, inept 6 clumsy, gauche, klutzy, oafish 7 awkward, gawkish, halting, unhandy 8 bumbling, bungling, cloddish, tactless, ungainly 9 all thumbs, graceless, lumbering, maladroit, stumbling, unskilled 10 blundering, left-handed, ungraceful, unskillful
flour: 4 meal, mill 6 farina, powder
coat with ~: 6 dredge
combining form: 6 aleuro-
container: 3 bag 4 sack
make ~: 5 grind
Mexican corn ~: 4 masa
mixture: 5 dough 6 batter
process ~: 4 sift
product: 4 cake, roll 5 bread
sack weight: 5 ten lb.
sifter: 5 sieve
source: 3 oat, rye, soy 5 grain, grist, wheat
___ flour: 3 soy 4 cake, clay, corn, fish, rock 5 bread 6 gluten, graham, patent
flourish: 2 go 3 win 4 boom, curl, dash, élan, grow, live, rise, show, wave 5 bloom, sweep, swing, swish, vaunt, verve, wield 6 abound, dangle, do well, flaunt, hack it, make it, pan out, paraph, spiral, stroke, thrive 7 blossom, burgeon, develop, display, fanfare, luck out, make out, prevail, prosper, succeed, swagger, tantara, triumph, work out 8 bourgeon, brandish, curlicue, curlycue, get ahead, go places, hit it big, make good, mushroom 9 luxuriate, make it big 10 decoration, strengthen
printing ~: 5 serif, swash 6 paraph
trumpet ~: 5 tusch 7 fanfare, tantara
flourishing: 4 hale, lush, rank, well 5 palmy 6 golden, robust 7 healthy, roaring, verdant, well-off 8 blooming, fruitful, thriving, vigorous 9 luxuriant 10 prosperous
floury: 5 mealy 7 powdery 8 granular
flout: 4 defy, gibe, jibe, mock 5 rebel, scoff, scorn, sneer, spurn 6 deride, ignore, insult, oppose, resist, revolt 7 disobey, scoff at, violate 9 disregard, go against, repudiate
flow: 3 run 4 gush, leak, move, ooze, pass, pour, purl, roll, rush, seep, stem, thaw, tide, wash 5 drift, exude, glide, issue, river, slide, spate, spirt, spurt, surge, swell, trend 6 abound, course, elapse, influx, liquid, motion, onrush, rhythm, series, spread, spring, squirt, stream 7 cascade, current, emanate, glide by, passage, process, trickle 8 fluidity, kinetics, movement, sequence, unfreeze 9 arise from, circulate, discharge, emanation, originate 10 continuity, outpouring, passageway
back: 3 ebb 4 fade, wane 5 abate 6 recede 7 dwindle, subside 8 slack off 9 retrocede
cash ~: 6 income 7 revenue 8 receipts
combining form: 4 -rhea, rheo- 5 -rrhea
ebb and ~: 4 flux, tide, wash 5 swing 6 billow 7 current 9 fluctuate, oscillate
(from): 5 arise 6 derive, result, spring 7 emanate, proceed 9 originate
go with the ~: 4 cope, roam, rove 5 agree, drift, get by, glide, mosey, yield 6 assent, give in, make do, manage, ramble, wander 7 make out, meander, saunter 9 acquiesce
heavy ~: 4 gush 5 flood, spate 6 stream 7 torrent 9 waterfall 10 inundation, outpouring
let ~: 4 open
measure: 3 amp, gph, gpm 5 cusec 6 ampere
opposite: 3 ebb
out: 4 spew, spue 5 bleed, drain, exude, spirt, spurt 6 effuse
outward ~: 3 ebb 4 tide 6 efflux, reflux 9 abatement, discharge, recession
over: 4 brim, well 5 spill
slowly: 4 ooze, seep 5 leach
starter: 3 air, mud 4 over, work
stop the ~: 3 dam 4 stem 5 block, check 6 arrest, cut off, stanch 8 hold back
together: 3 mix 4 join, meld 5 blend, merge, unify, unite 7 combine 8 converge 9 integrate
volcano ~: 4 lava 5 magma
flow ___: 5 chart, sheet
___ flow: 3 ash 4 cash, gene
___ Flow: 5 Scapa
flow-chart command: 4 go to
flower: 3 mum 4 boom, flag, flax, glad, iris, lily, pink, posy, rose, sego 5 agave, aster, bloom, bluet, broom, camas, cream, daisy, elite, lehua, lilac, lotus, pansy, peony, phlox, plant, poppy, prime, stock, tansy, tulip, vetch, viola, yucca 6 acacia, annual, arnica, azalea, betony, cactus, camass, cosmos, crocus, dahlia, heyday, heydey, indigo, lupine, mallow, mature, maypop, mimosa, mullen, myrtle, orchid, oxalis, salvia, smilax, spirea, teasel, teazel, teazle, thrift, violet, yarrow, zinnia 7 aconite, anemone, arbutus, begonia, berseem, blossom, bulrush, burgeon, calypso, catalpa, cattail, comfrey, cowslip, day lily, dog rose, dogwood, figwort, foxtail, freesia, fuchsia, gentian, heather, hogweed, jasmine, jonquil, lobelia, mayweed, mullein, petunia, produce, prosper, ragwort, rambler, saffron, saguaro, spiraea, tea rose, thistle, trefoil, vanilla, verbena 8 aconitum, ageratum, amaranth, arethusa, asphodel, best part, bluebell, blue flag, boltonia, bourgeon, camellia, camomile, clematis, cyclamen, daffodil, dianthus, duckweed, erigeron, fireweed, foxglove, gardenia, geranium, gladiola, gloxinia, harebell, hawkweed, hawthorn, hepatica, hibiscus, hyacinth, japonica, laburnum, larkspur, lavender, magnolia, marigold, mosspink, moss rose, oleander, ornament, pilewort, primrose, rain lily, reed mace, rockrose, snowball, snowdrop, sweet pea, tamarisk, tidytips, trillium, tuberose, veronica, viburnum, wild rose, wistaria, wisteria 9 amaryllis, arrowhead, artichoke, bloodroot, buttercup, calendula, calla lily, candytuft, carnation, celandine, chamomile, cineraria, cockscomb, colicroot, columbine, corydalis, dandelion, edelweiss, eglantine, fairy lily, forsythia, gladiolus, goldenrod, ground ivy, groundsel, hollyhock, horehound, horsemint, hydrangea, impatiens, jessamine, mayflower, monkshood, narcissus, ohia lehua, Oswego tea, perennial, portulaca, pussy-toes, pyrethrum, rafflesia, redfescue, rudbeckia, safflower, santonica, snowberry, snow plant, sunflower, swamp pink, tiger lily, water lily, wolfsbane,

woundwort **10** aspidistra, bitterroot, bluebonnet, bluebottle, buttonbush, coneflower, cornflower, damask rose, delphinium, Easter lily, fleur-de-lis, floribunda, frangipani, gaillardia, goatsbeard, heliotrope, Indian pipe, marguerite, mignonette, mock orange, motherwort, nasturtium, oxeye daisy, pennyroyal, periwinkle, poinsettia, ranunculus, snapdragon, stamen site, sweetbriar, sweetbrier, wallflower, zephyr lily
ancient Egyptian sacred ~: **5** lotus
aquatic ~: **5** lotus **8** duckweed **9** arrowhead, water lily
arrangement: **4** posy **5** spray **7** bouquet, ikebana, nosegay
arranging: **3** art
asterlike ~: **8** boltonia
bearded ~: **4** iris
bell-shaped ~: **5** tulip
blue ~: **4** flag, flax, iris **5** camas **6** camass, indigo, lupine, violet **7** aconite, gentian **8** aconitum, ageratum, boltonia, harebell, larkspur, veronica **9** columbine, ground ivy, hydrangea **10** cornflower, delphinium, periwinkle
brown ~: **7** bulrush, cattail **8** reed mace **10** aspidistra
bulbous ~: **4** glad **5** tulip
Central America: **6** dahlia
child: **5** hippy **6** hippie **8** bohemian, longhair
clove-scented ~: **4** pink
cluster: **5** ament, umbel **6** catkin
combining form: **4** anth-, flor- **5** antho-, flori-
corsage ~: **3** mum
cut ~: **4** stem
daisylike ~: **5** aster
dark-centered ~: **9** sunflower
desert ~: **5** agave, yucca **7** saguaro
display: **5** spray **7** bouquet, corsage
fall ~: **3** mum **5** aster
fragrant ~: **4** lily, pink, rose **5** lilac, stock **7** jasmine, tea rose **8** dianthus, gardenia, hyacinth, lavender, magnolia, moss rose, tuberose **9** carnation, jessamine, narcissus **10** damask rose, Easter lily, frangipani, heliotrope, mock orange, wallflower
funnel-shaped ~: **6** azalea
garden ~: **4** glad, iris, rose **5** aster, phlox, tulip, viola **6** azalea
garland: **3** lei
girl, often: **5** niece
green ~: **6** smilax **7** figwort **8** pilewort **10** mignonette
Hawaiian: **5** lehua
in ~: **6** abloom
in a Buddhist mantra: **5** lotus
in French: **5** fleur
in full ~: **4** ripe **6** bloomy, mature **7** matured **8** blooming
in Italian: **5** fiore
lavender ~: **4** lily **6** orchid, thrift **8** trillium, wistaria, wisteria **9** candytuft
lily-family ~: **5** yucca
location: **3** bed, pot, urn **4** vase **6** garden
meadow ~: **5** bluet
new ~: **3** bud
nursery rhyme ~: **4** posy
oak-tree ~: **5** ament **6** catkin
of chivalry: **6** knight
of forgetfulness: **5** lotus
oil: **4** atar, otto **5** athar, attar, ottar
orange ~: **5** poppy, tulip **6** cosmos **7** day lily **8** hawkweed, marigold **9** calendula **10** nasturtium, wallflower
orchidlike ~: **4** iris
pansylike ~: **5** viola
parasol-like ~: **5** umbel
part: **4** stem **5** ovule, petal, sepal, stalk **6** anther, carina, pistil, stamen
pink ~: **4** lily **5** lotus, peony **6** cosmos, lupine, mallow, mimosa, spirea, thrift **7** arbutus, begonia, dog rose, dogwood, freesia, rambler, spiraea, tea rose **8** arethusa, asphodel, camellia, geranium, hawthorn, larkspur, moss rose, oleander, tamarisk, wild rose **9** amaryllis, candytuft, corydalis, eglantine, hollyhock, hydrangea, mayflower, snowberry, water lily **10** bitterroot, bluebottle, cornflower, damask rose, delphinium, poinsettia, sweetbriar, sweetbrier
pink and white ~: **8** dianthus
pinkish-purple ~: **8** fireweed
potential ~: **4** seed
prickly ~: **6** teasel, teazel, teazle **7** thistle
purple ~: **3** mum **4** flag, iris **5** lilac, tulip, vetch **6** betony, crocus, maypop, orchid, violet **7** figwort, heather, saffron, thistle **8** boltonia, erigeron, foxglove, hepatica, hyacinth, lavender, wistaria, wisteria **9** candytuft, cockscomb, monkshood, wolfsbane **10** bluebottle, coneflower, cornflower, heliotrope, motherwort, pennyroyal
purple-red ~: **7** fuchsia **8** amaranth, cyclamen
rayed ~: **5** aster
red ~: **3** mum **4** lily **5** lehua, peony, poppy, tulip **6** cosmos, salvia **7** day lily, rambler **8** camellia, geranium, japonica, marigold, oleander, rockrose, tamarisk **9** amaryllis, candytuft, cockscomb, hollyhock, ohia lehua, Oswego tea, snow plant, woundwort **10** gaillardia, nasturtium, poinsettia
red-orange ~: **9** tiger lily
sepals: **5** calyx
showy ~: **3** mum **4** flag, iris, lily, rose **5** canna, lehua, lotus, pansy, peony, phlox, poppy, tulip **6** azalea, dahlia, orchid, salvia **7** day lily, fuchsia **8** hibiscus **9** calla lily, hollyhock, ohia lehua, tiger lily **10** delphinium, poinsettia, snapdragon
signature: **4** odor **5** aroma, scent **7** bouquet **9** fragrance
spring ~: **6** crocus
stalk: **4** stem **5** scape
starlike ~: **5** aster
starter: **3** cup, day, may, sun **4** ball, bell, cone, corn, foam, mist, moon, star, twin, wall, wand, wild, wind **5** bunch, globe, shell, straw **6** cuckoo **7** passion
thorny ~: **4** rose
top: **6** corona
varicolored ~: **4** glad, rose **5** canna, pansy, phlox, stock, viola **6** azalea, dahlia, oxalis, zinnia **7** anemone, comfrey, lobelia, petunia, verbena **8** clematis, gladiola, gloxinia, hibiscus, rain lily, sweet pea **9** carnation, cineraria, fairy lily, gladiolus, impatiens, portulaca, pyrethrum **10** floribunda, frangipani, snapdragon, zephyr lily
visitor: **3** bee
white ~: **3** mum **4** flag, iris, lily **5** camas, daisy, lilac, lotus, peony, poppy, tulip, yucca **6** camass, crocus, lupine, mallow, maypop, myrtle, spirea, thrift, violet, yarrow **7** aconite, arbutus, catalpa, dog rose, dogwood, freesia, hogweed, jasmine, jonquil, mayweed, rambler, saguaro, spiraea **8** aconitum, ageratum, asphodel, boltonia, camellia, erigeron, gardenia, hawthorn, hepatica, hyacinth, larkspur, magnolia, oleander, rockrose, snowball, snowdrop, tamarisk, trillium, tuberose, viburnum, wistaria, wisteria **9** arrowhead, bloodroot, calla lily, candytuft, colicroot, edelweiss, horehound, hydrangea, jessamine, mayflower, narcissus, pussytoes, water lily **10** bluebottle, buttonbush, cornflower, delphinium, Easter lily, fleur-de-lis, goatsbeard, Indian pipe, marguerite, mock orange, oxeye daisy, poinsettia, ranunculus, spider lily
white and yellow ~: **8** camomile **9** calla lily, chamomile
willow ~: **5** ament **6** catkin
with a face: **5** pansy
with a white spathe: **5** calla **8** arum lily
world's largest ~: **9** rafflesia
wormwood ~: **9** santonica
wreath: **3** lei **4** haku **7** garland
yellow ~: **3** mum **4** flag, iris, lily **5** broom, tulip **6** acacia, arnica, cosmos, crocus, mullen, orchid, violet, yarrow **7** berseem, cowslip, day lily, freesia, jonquil, mullein, ragwort, tea rose **8** asphodel, daffodil, hyacinth, laburnum, marigold, primrose, rockrose, tidytips **9** buttercup, calendula, celandine, colicroot, corydalis, dandelion, forsythia, goldenrod, groundsel, horsemint, narcissus **10** goatsbeard, marguerite, nasturtium, ranunculus, wallflower
yellow-rayed ~: **9** coreopsis, owl's claws, rudbeckia, sunflower **10** coneflower, gaillardia
flower __: **3** bed, box, bud, bug, fly **4** girl, head **5** child, power **6** beetle
__ flower: **3** cut, ray, wax **4** coat, disk, musk, rock **5** state, tunic **6** basket, calico, monkey, tassel **7** balloon, pinxter, popcorn, trumpet
Flower: **4** toon **5** skunk
Flower __ Song: **4** Drum
__ Flower: **6** Cactus
flower bed: **4** plot **6** garden
covering: **5** humus, mulch **7** compost
foundation: **4** soil
smooth the ~: **4** rake
Flower Drum Song (1961 film): **7** musical
cast: Nancy Kwan, James Shigeta, Jack Soo, Miyoshi Umeki
composer: Oscar Hammerstein, Richard Rodgers
director: Henry Koster
flowered combining form: **7** -anthous, -florous
Flower Fables
author: Louisa May Alcott
flowering: **5** prime **6** abloom, growth, spring **8** blooming, progress **9** evolution
Flowering Judas
author: Katherine Anne Porter
Flowering Peach, The
author: Clifford Odets
flowerless plant: **4** fern, moss
Flower Petal Gown
sculptor: Erté
flowerpot
locale: **4** sill **5** ledge, shelf
flowers: **6** posies
encourage larger ~: **6** disbud
gather ~: **4** pick **5** pluck
goddess of ~: **5** Flora
in German: **5** rosen
in Italian: **5** fiori
like some ~: **6** abloom, annual **9** perennial
raise ~: **6** garden
ring of ~: **3** lei
Flowers: **7** Wayland
Flowers for Algernon
author: Daniel Keyes
Flowers in the __: **5** Attic
Flower Song: **4** aria
flowery: **5** showy **6** floral, ornate, rococo **7** pompous, stilted, verbose **9** elaborate, luxuriant, overblown **10** flamboyant, ornamented, rhetorical
language: **7** bombast **8** rhetoric **9** eloquence
name meaning ~: **6** Anthea **8** Florence
necklace: **3** lei
perfume: **4** atar, otto **5** athar, attar, ottar
recess: **5** bower
Flow Gently, Sweet __: **5** Afton
flowing: **4** soft **6** active, facile, legato, liquid, smooth **7** current, running **8** graceful, readable **9** emanation, plentiful **10** integrated
of ~ water: **5** lotic
rock: **4** lava **5** magma
together: **7** meeting **9** confluent **10** convergent
__ flowing with milk and honey: **5** A land

___-flown: 4 high
Floyd: 3 Ray 4 King 6 Cramer, Mutrux 9 Patterson
___ Floyd: 4 Pink
Floyd, Ray: 6 golfer
fl. oz., one-sixth: 3 tsp.
flu: 3 bug 6 grippe 7 ailment
  cause: 5 virus
  down with the ~: 3 ill 4 sick 6 ailing, unwell 10 indisposed
  have the ~: 3 ail 4 ache
  like some ~: 5 viral
  shot: 4 hypo
  symptom: 4 ache, ague 5 chill, cough, fever
___ flu: 4 blue 5 Asian, swine 8 Hong Kong
flub: 3 err 4 boot, fail, goof, miss, muff, slip 5 boner, botch, error, fluff, lapse 6 blow it, boggle, bungle, foozle, foul up, fumble, goof up, mess up, miscue, slip-up 7 blunder, mistake, screwup 9 mishandle, mismanage
___ Flubber: 5 Son of
flubdub
  see baloney
fluctuate: 4 lick, sway, vary, yo-yo 5 pulse, range, shake, shift, swing, waver 6 change, seesaw, teeter 7 vibrate 9 alternate, hem and haw, oscillate, vacillate 10 ebb and flow
fluctuating: 5 fluid, shaky 6 spotty, uneven, zigzag 7 erratic, mutable, protean, varying 8 floating, periodic, unstable, unsteady, variable 9 mercurial, uncertain, vagarious 10 changeable
fluctuation: 4 sway 5 shift 6 bounce, change, motion 8 variance 9 variation, vibration 10 undulation
flue: 4 duct, pipe, tube, vent 6 airway 7 air duct, channel, chimney 10 air passage, smokeshaft, smokestack
  material: 3 ash 4 soot
  part: 6 damper
fluency: 4 ease 5 grace 8 facility, fluidity 9 eloquence, liquidity, readiness 10 smoothness
fluent: 4 easy, glib 5 vocal 6 facile, liquid, smooth 8 eloquent, graceful, readable, skillful 9 talkative 10 articulate, effortless, expressive, loquacious, well-spoken, well-versed
fluff: 3 err, nap 4 down, flub, fuzz, lint, muff, slip 5 error 6 bobble, fleece, fumble, miscue, slipup 7 blooper, blunder, misstep, mistake, stumble 8 feathers 9 eiderdown
  cluster: 4 tuft
  full of ~: 5 linty
  up: 5 plump, tease, whisk
fluffy: 4 airy, soft 5 downy, furry, fuzzy, light, nappy, plush 6 creamy, fleecy, flossy, napped 7 squishy, velvety 8 cushiony 9 lightsome
Fluffy: 3 cat, pet 6 feline
flügelhorn: 4 wind 10 instrument
  cousin: 6 cornet 7 trumpet
fluid: 3 liq., oil, sap, tea 4 ooze, soft 5 juice, runny, water 6 coffee, liquid, liquor, mobile, molten, nectar, serous, smooth, watery 7 aqueous, erratic, mutable, protean, running 8 flexible, shifting, solution, unstable, variable, wavering 9 adaptable, liquefied, malleable, mercurial, revocable, uncertain, unsettled 10 changeable, indefinite
  body ~: 5 blood, humor, lymph, serum
  container: 3 sac
  not ~: 3 set 4 firm 5 fixed, solid 6 secure, stable, static 8 constant, definite 10 definitive, unchanging
  of blood ~: 6 serous
  plant ~: 3 sap 5 juice, latex, serum
  rock: 4 lava
fluid ___: 4 dram 5 drive, ounce 6 drachm
___ fluid: 5 brake
fluidity: 4 ease, flow, flux 7 fluency 9 liquidity 10 smoothness
  unit: 3 rhe
fluidize: 4 melt, thaw 7 defrost, liquefy, liquify 8 dissolve 10 deliquesce
fluid-ounce fraction: 5 minim
fluids, medical: 4 sera
fluke: 4 luck, tail 5 quirk 6 hazard 8 accident, fortuity 9 mischance 10 fortuitous, lucky break
fluky: 3 odd 6 chance, random 7 oddball 9 hit-or-miss, unplanned 10 contingent, fortuitous, unexpected
flume: 5 chute 6 ravine, sluice, trough 7 channel, conduit 8 spillway 10 water slide
  floater: 3 log
flummery: 7 custard, dessert
  see also baloney
flummox: 4 fool, stun 5 addle 6 puzzle, rattle 7 confuse, nonplus 8 confound
flummoxed: 4 asea, lost 5 at sea 7 baffled, out of it, puzzled 8 confused 9 mystified, perplexed 10 bewildered
___-flung: 3 far
flunk: 4 bomb, bust, fail, flop, lose, slip, trip 6 blow it, falter 7 blunder, founder, go under, go wrong, misstep, stumble, wash out 8 fall flat, flounder, lay an egg 9 strike out
  don't ~: 4 pass
  letter: 2 ef 3 eff
flunkey
  see flunky
flunky: 4 aide, pawn, tool 5 gofer, groom, toady, valet 6 butler, fawner, gopher, helper, jackal, lackey, menial, minion, yes man 7 footman, lacquey, servant 8 adulator, courtier, follower, hanger-on, henchman, hireling, kowtower, retainer, servitor, truckler 9 assistant, flatterer, sycophant, underling 10 bootlicker, handshaker, hatchet man
fluorescent: 4 bulb, lamp, tube 5 light
  lamp filler: 5 argon
  paint: 6 Day-Glo
fluoride: 4 salt
Fluorigard: 9 mouthwash
  alternative: 3 Act 4 Plax 5 Scope 6 Signal 7 Lavoris 9 Listerine
fluorine: 3 gas 7 element, halogen
  source of ~: 8 fluorite
fluorite: 7 mineral
  rare white ~: 8 cryolite
  to Mohs: 4 four
fluoroscope: 4 x-ray
flurries: 4 snow 6 powder, precip
flurry: 3 ado 4 blow, flap, fuss, gust, puff, rush, snow, stir, to-do 5 furor, haste, hurry, spasm, spirt, spurt, upset, whirl 6 action, breeze, bustle, hoopla, pother, rattle, ruffle, tumult 7 confuse, disturb, ferment, fluster, nonplus, perturb, turmoil, unhinge 8 bewilder, brouhaha, outburst, unsettle 9 commotion, confusion 10 discompose, disconcert, excitement
flush: 4 even, flat, full, glow, hand, rich, tint, wash 5 blush, clean, flood, level, rinse, scour, spurn 6 arouse, drench, florid, lavish, loaded, monied, redden, smooth 7 animate, cleanse, enthuse, inspire, moneyed, opulent, redness, wealthy, well-off 8 abundant, affluent, generous, in clover, inundate, prodigal, rosiness, squarely, well-to-do 9 abounding, ruddiness, well-fixed 10 exhilarate, in the dough, in the money, intoxicate, privileged, propertied, prosperous, well-heeled
  game: 4 stud 5 poker
  out: 4 hunt 5 chase, clean, erase, expel, purge, rinse, trace, track 6 ambush, banish, pursue, uproot 7 cleanse 8 exorcise 9 eliminate, overthrow
flush ___: 4 girl, left 5 right
___ flush: 5 royal 6 monkey 8 straight
___-Flush: 4 Sani
flushed: 3 red 4 pink, rosy, warm 5 livid, ruddy 6 florid 7 reddish 8 blushing, rubicund, sanguine
___-flusher: 4 four
Flushing Meadows
  locale: 3 NYC 4 Ashe, Shea 6 Queens 7 New York 9 Citi Field
  sport: 6 tennis 8 baseball
  team: 4 Mets
fluster: 4 faze 5 abash, addle, get to, mix up, shake, spook, throw, upset 6 bother, excite, flurry, lather, muddle, rattle, ruffle, stir up, work up 7 agitate, confuse, disturb, nonplus, perplex, perturb, unhinge, unnerve 8 befuddle, bewilder, confound, disquiet, psych out, unsettle 9 discomfit, embarrass, frustrate, give a turn 10 discompose, disconcert
flustered: 5 fazed 7 nervous 8 unstrung 9 unsettled 10 bewildered, distraught
flute: 4 fife, kink, wind 5 crimp, nguru, quena, titzu 6 crease, fujara, groove 7 shiwaya, talinka, tonette 9 corrugate
  architectural ~: 5 stria
  combining form: 3 aul- 4 aulo-
  cousin: 4 oboe 7 piccolo
  play a ~: 4 blow 5 trill
  player: 5 piper
___ flute: 4 alto 6 fipple
Flute-Player, The
  role: 5 Elena
___ Flute, The: 3 Tin 5 Magic
Flutie, Doug: 2 QB
  sport: 8 football
fluting: 5 crimp, stria 6 crease, groove 7 channel
flutist: 4 Mann 6 Galway, Rampal 10 Herbie Mann
flutter: 3 ado, bat, fly, wag 4 bate, beat, flap, flit, fuss, lick, stir, wave, wink 5 blink, drift, hover, shake, throb, waver 6 ripple, ruffle, rustle, shiver, teeter, thrill, tremor, twitch 7 pulsate, tremble, vibrate 8 volitate 9 palpitate, toss about
fluttering sound: 5 trill
fluttery: 5 tense 6 jangly
flux: 3 run 4 rush, thaw, tide 6 change, liquid, motion, unrest 7 process, torrent 8 fluidity, kinetics, movement 10 alteration, ebb and flow, mutability, transition
  magnetic ~ unit: 5 gauss, tesla
fly: 2 go 3 bug, hie, rip, run, zip 4 bolt, dart, dash, flap, flee, flit, gnat, go by, lure, move, pest, race, ride, rush, sail, skim, skip, soar, tear, whiz, wing, zoom 5 break, dance, glide, hover, hurry, leave, midge, pop up, scoot, skirr, speed, sweep, swoop, whisk, zip by 6 ascend, aviate, barrel, decamp, dobson, elapse, escape, gallop, hasten, hustle, insect, move it, pass by, rocket, run off, scurry, skidoo, spring, travel, tsetse, tzetze, wing it, zipper 7 abscond, floor it, flutter, get away, hop to it, journey, make off, quicken, run away, scamper, skip out, take off, vamoose 8 clear out, glossina, hightail, levitate, make time, slip away, step on it, take wing, volation, volitate, volplane 9 barnstorm, cut and run, disappear, go swiftly, hotfoot it, make haste, shake a leg, skedaddle, steal away 10 bluebottle, get a move on, get hopping, hightail it
  advance on a ~ ball: 5 tag up
  African: 6 tsetse, tzetze 8 glossina
  alone: 4 solo
  artificial ~: 4 herl, lure
  at: 3 hit 6 assail, attack, pounce 7 assault, lay into 9 light into, pitch into
  (at): 4 have 6 strike 7 lash out
  by: 4 flow, pass 6 elapse 8 slip away, tick away 9 transpire
  cast a ~: 4 fish 5 angle
  catcher: 3 web 5 honey
  close a ~: 5 zip up
  combining form: 3 myi- 4 myio- 5 musci-
  down: 5 light, swoop 6 alight
  eater: 4 frog
  ender: 3 boy, way 4 away, boat, leaf, trap 5 blown, paper, sheet, speck, wheel, whisk 6 weight 7 catcher
  fishing ~: 4 lure
  fling a ~: 4 cast
  go ~ a kite: 5 scram, split 6 beat it, begone 7 buzz off, get lost, take off 9 take a hike
  half a ~: 3 tse

high: 4 soar
hit a ~: 4 loft, swat
house ~: 4 pest 8 irritant
in: 4 land 5 light 6 alight
in the face of: 4 dare, defy 6 oppose 7 disobey
in the ointment: 3 rub 4 flaw, kink, snag 5 catch, hitch, snafu 6 defect, kicker 7 problem 8 drawback
Japanese: 3 hae
let ~: 3 lob 4 cast, fire, hurl, send, toss 5 chuck, fling, heave, pitch, shoot, sling, throw 6 launch, propel 7 fire off
low: 4 buzz
off the handle: 4 rage, rant, snap 5 freak, go ape
on the ~: 7 hastily, quickly, swiftly 8 in a hurry, in motion, speedily 9 hurriedly
open: 4 gush 5 burst, erupt 7 explode
pop ~: 5 bloop 6 looper
starter: 3 bar, day, gad, may, med, saw 4 blow, deer, fire, gall, shad, shoo 5 catch, green, horse, house, stone, white 6 butter, damsel, dobson, dragon
swatter material: 4 mesh
the coop: 4 flee, skip 6 decamp, escape 7 abandon, abscond, go south, vamoose 8 fugitate, jump bail 9 break away
tier: 6 angler 9 fisherman
to a spider: 4 prey
trajectory: 3 arc
trap: 3 web 5 mouth 6 cobweb
when donkeys ~: 5 nohow, no way 8 forget it 9 fat chance 10 impossible, not a chance
without an engine: 5 glide
fly __: 3 ash, net, rod 4 ball, book, high, line, loft, rail 5 block, floor, front, sheet 6 agaric 7 casting, gallery, swatter
fly __ face of: 5 in the
fly __ ointment: 5 in the
fly __ teeth of: 5 in the
fly __ the handle: 3 off
fly-__: 4 cast, over 7 fishing
__ fly: 3 bee, bot, dry, dun, let, pop, sac, wet 4 blow, deer, frit, heel, tent, true 5 black, crane, drake, flesh, fruit, horse, March, on the, screw, shore 6 flower, hackle, pomace, robber, spider, stable, tsetse, tzetze, warble 7 cluster, harvest, Hessian, soldier, syrphid, tachina, vinegar
__, fly!: 4 Shoo
Fly: 5 river
constellation: 5 Musca
River locale: 9 New Guinea
Fly __ an Eagle: 4 Like
Fly __ the Moon: 4 Me to
__ Fly Away: 3 I'll 4 Let's
flyboy: 3 ace 5 pilot 6 airman 7 aviator 8 aeronaut
org.: 3 AFB 4 USAF
fly-by-__: 4 wire 5 night
fly-by-night: 5 shady 6 shifty 9 transient, trustless, unethical 10 improvised, short-lived, unreliable
fly-cast: 4 fish
fly casting: 5 sport
flycatcher: 4 bird 5 pewee 6 phoebe 7 fantail 8 kingbird
flyer: 3 ace 4 bill 5 pilot, wager 6 airman, gamble 7 aviator, handout, leaflet, war hero 8 brochure, circular, handbill, pamphlet 9 broadside, navigator
fast ~: 3 SST
take a ~: 4 risk 6 gamble 7 venture
see also airline, bird
__ Flyer: 5 Radio
Flyers: 3 six 4 team
milieu: 3 ice 4 rink
org.: 3 NHL
rival: *see* hockey team
sport: 6 hockey
flyers, frequent: 6 jet set
fly-fish: 3 dap
fly-fishing: 5 sport
flying: 4 fast, high 5 aloft, avian, brisk, fleet, hasty, quick, rapid, swift, volar 6 aerial, elated, racing, speedy, travel, volant 7 express, hurried, instant, soaring 8 airborne, aviation, in the air, volitant 9 breakneck, galloping, momentary, on the wing 10 double-time, hypersonic, navigation, supersonic, ultrasonic, volitation
colors: 7 success, triumph, victory
emulate a ~ saucer: 5 hover
formation: 3 vee 7 echelon
go ~: 4 soar 6 aviate
high: 3 gay 4 glad 5 happy, merry, sunny 6 blithe, chirpy, elated, golden, joyful, joyous, upbeat 7 beaming, buoyant, chipper, content, gleeful, glowing, pleased, radiant, tickled 8 blissful, carefree, cheerful, ecstatic, exultant, gladsome, grooving, jubilant, laughing, sanguine, thrilled, unbeaten 9 contented, delighted, fortunate, gratified, lightsome, overjoyed 10 optimistic, successful, triumphant, unbothered
in heraldry: 6 volant
machine: 4 giro 6 copter 8 autogiro
saucer: 3 UFO
with ~ colors: 4 fine, well 5 great 6 easily 7 handily 8 adroitly, smoothly, very well 9 hands down 10 skillfully, swimmingly
woe: 6 jet lag
flying __: 3 fox, jib 4 boat, bomb, bond, fish, frog, kite, mare, moor, wing 5 field, filly, jenny, lemur, mouse, robin, shear, squad, start 6 boxcar, bridge, carpet, circus, colors, column, saucer, tackle
Flying __: 4 Home 6 Finish, Tigers 7 Dustbin, Machine
Flying __, The: 3 Nun 6 Deuces, Saucer
Flying __ to Rio: 4 Down
Flying Cloud: 3 car, Reo 4 auto
__ flying colors: 4 with
Flying Deuces, The (1939 film)
cast: Oliver Hardy, Stan Laurel
Flying Down to Rio (1933 film)
cast: Fred Astaire, Dolores Del Rio, Ginger Rogers
studio: 3 RKO
Flying Dutchman, The: 4 boat, ship 5 opera
character: 4 Erik, Mary 5 Senta 6 Daland
composer: Richard Wagner
setting: 6 Norway
Flying Finish
author: Dick Francis
Flying Finn, The: Paavo Nurmi
Flying Fortress: 5 plane 6 bomber
crew: 6 airmen
Flying Grasshopper
ingredient: 5 vodka
Flying Hero Class
author: Thomas Keneally
Flying High (1931 film)
cast: Bert Lahr
Flying Machine
song: Smile a Little Smile for Me (1969)
Flying Nun, The (ABC sitcom)
cast: Sally Field (Sister Bertrille) Alejandro Rey (Carlos Ramirez)
setting: convent, Puerto Rico
fly in the __ of: 4 face 5 teeth
fly into __: 5 a rage
Fly Like an Eagle (song)
artist: Seal, Steve Miller Band
Fly Me to the __: 4 Moon
Flynn: 3 Joe 5 Errol 7 Raymond
__ Flynn Boyle: 4 Lara
Flynn, Errol: 5 actor
film: Adventures of Don Juan (1949)
The Adventures of Robin Hood (1938)
Captain Blood (1935)
The Charge of the Light Brigade (1936)
The Dawn Patrol (1938)
Desperate Journey (1942)
Dive Bomber (1941)
Dodge City (1939)
Edge of Darkness (1943)
Gentleman Jim (1942)
Kim (1950)
Objective, Burma! (1945)
The Prince and the Pauper (1937)
The Private Lives of Elizabeth and Essex (1939)
San Antonio (1945)
The Sea Hawk (1940)
The Sisters (1938)
They Died With Their Boots On (1941)
spouse: Lili Damita
__ Fly Now: 5 Gonna
fly off the __: 6 handle
flypaper: 4 lure
__-fly pie: 4 shoo
__ fly rule: 7 infield
flyspeck: 3 dot 4 iota, mote, spot 5 point
fly the __: 4 coop
Fly, The (1961 song)
artist: Chubby Checker
Fly, The (1986 film)
cast: Geena Davis, Jeff Goldblum
flytrap: 3 web 5 plant
feature: 5 hinge
__ flytrap: 5 Venus
fly under the __: 5 radar
__ Fly With Me: 4 Come
Fm: 4 elem. 7 element, fermium
100 for ~: 4 at. no.
FM: 4 band 5 radio
celeb: 2 DJ 6 deejay
choice: 3 sta., stn. 7 station
part: 4 Freq. 9 Frequency 10 Modulation
F. Murray __: 7 Abraham
FNMA: 4 agcy. 6 agency
concern: 4 loan
part: 3 Fed., Nat. 4 Assn., Mtge., Natl. 7 Federal 8 Mortgage, National
f-number: 4 stop
foal: 4 colt 5 filly, horse 6 animal, equine
food: 3 hay 4 oats 6 fodder
like a ~: 5 leggy
parent: 3 dam 4 mare, sire
foam: 4 fizz, head, suds, surf, wave 5 froth, spray, spume 6 aerate, bubble, burble, gurgle, lather, seethe, simmer 7 bubbles, ferment 9 whitecaps 10 effervesce, frothiness
at the mouth: 4 rage, rave 6 see red, seethe 8 freak out
preceder: 5 styro
foam __: 5 glass, metal 6 rubber
__ foam: 3 sea 7 plastic
foam-ball brand: 4 Nerf
foaming: 4 wild 5 soapy, sudsy 6 bubbly, frothy, yeasty 7 furious, lathery 8 agitated 9 turbulent
at the mouth: 4 wild 5 manic, rabid, upset 6 raging 7 frantic, unglued 8 agitated, frenzied, maniacal, unstrung, vehement 9 bummed-out, fanatical 10 freaked out, hysterical
foamy: 5 barmy, soapy, sudsy 6 frothy, yeasty 7 fizzing, lathery 8 burbling, unrinsed 10 carbonated, fermenting
fob: 5 chain
off: 5 foist
(off): 4 palm
fob __: 3 off
__ fob: 5 watch
FOB
not ~: 3 COD
part: 4 Free 5 Board
focal: 7 central, pivotal 10 overriding
point: 3 hub 4 node, pith 6 center 8 cynosure 9 highlight
points: 4 loca, loci
focal __: 4 area 5 plane, point, ratio 6 length
focalize: 5 unify 6 center 8 converge
Foch: 4 Nina 9 Ferdinand
fo'c's'le: 4 deck
say ~: 5 elide
focus: 3 fix, hub, nub 4 core, join, knub, look, meet, pith 5 angle, heart, level, merge, nexus, slant, stare, think, train, unite 6 adjust, center, direct, fixate, gather, home in, hone in, middle, nucleus, target, zero in, zoom in 7 keynote 8 assemble, converge, cynosure, look hard, polestar 9 highlight, limelight, spotlight, substance 10 centralize, ground zero
centers of ~: 4 loca, loci
in ~: 5 clear, sharp 8 viewable
lose ~: 4 blur 5 blear, cloud, muddy
main ~: 4 gist 5 tenor, theme, topic
on: 6 look at, take up, tend to 7 address 8 consider, deal with, mull over 10 take care of, think about

out of ~: 4 hazy 5 fuzzy 6 bleary, blurry 10 indistinct
perhaps: 4 zoom
focus __: 5 group
__ focus: 4 back, deep, soft
__-focus: 4 auto
Focus: 3 car 4 auto, Ford 10 automobile
focused: 4 rapt 5 fixed 6 intent 7 engaged, riveted 8 absorbed, hellbent, immersed 9 attentive, engrossed, wrapped up
fodder: 3 hay 4 corn, feed, food, grub, oats 5 grain, straw 6 clover, forage, leaves, silage, stalks 7 sorghum 10 cornstalks
__ fodder: 6 cannon
Fodor, Eugene: 9 violinist
foe: 4 anti, side 5 enemy, rival 7 invader, nemesis 8 attacker, opponent 9 adversary, aggressor, assailant, combatant, ill-wisher 10 antagonist, challenger, competitor, opposition
foeman: 4 anti, side 5 enemy, rival 7 invader, nemesis 8 attacker, opponent 9 adversary, aggressor, assailant, combatant, ill-wisher 10 antagonist, challenger, competitor, opposition
foetid: 4 foul, olid, rank 5 stale 6 frowsy, frowzy, rancid, rotten, smelly, stinky, strong 7 noisome, noxious, odorous, reeking, squalid, unclean 8 inedible, mephitic, stinking 10 malodorous
fog: 3 dim 4 blur, daze, haze, mist, smog, soup 5 brume, cloud, muddy, smaze, spray, vapor 6 muddle 7 becloud, confuse, obscure, pea soup, steam up 8 haziness, moisture 9 murkiness, obfuscate, pea-souper
ender: 3 bow, dog 4 horn 5 bound
in a ~: 4 asea, hazy, lost 5 at sea, dazed 7 out of it, puzzled 8 confused 9 perplexed, spaced out 10 bewildered
like ~: 3 wet 5 dense, misty
starter: 5 petti
up: 4 blur
fog __: 3 gun 4 bank, drip 5 light 6 forest, signal
__ fog: 3 dry, ice 4 tule 5 black, steam 6 frozen, ground
Fog
author: Carl Sandburg
__ Fog: 6 London
fogbow: 3 arc 6 seadog
Fogelberg, Dan
song: Hard to Say (1981)
Leader of the Band (1981)
Longer (1980)
Same Old Lang Syne (1980)
Fogerty: 4 John
fogey: 4 dodo 6 codger, geezer 7 diehard 8 mossback 10 fuddy-duddy
__ fogey: 3 old
foggy: 3 wet 4 hazy 5 fuzzy, mirky, misty, murky, thick, vague 6 blurry, steamy 7 blurred, brumous, clouded, obscure, sunless, unclear 8 confused, nebulous, obscured, overcast, socked in 9 unfocused 10 indistinct
become ~: 4 blur 5 bedim, blear, cloud 6 muddle
Foggy __: 6 Bottom
Foggy Day, A
city: 6 London
composer: George Gershwin, Ira Gershwin
Fog, The (1980 film)
cast: Adrienne Barbeau, Jamie Lee Curtis, Hal Holbrook, Janet Leigh
director: John Carpenter
fogy: 4 dodo 6 codger, geezer 7 diehard 8 mossback 10 fuddy-duddy
__ fogy: 3 old
fogyish: 5 fusty, passé, stale 6 stodgy 7 archaic, diehard 8 obsolete, outdated 9 old-school, out-of-date 10 antiquated
foible: 3 tic 4 flaw, kink, vice 5 fault, lapse, quirk 6 defect, oddity 7 failing, frailty 8 bad habit, gambling, weakness 9 mannerism
foie gras: 5 liver 10 goose liver
foil: 4 beat, dash, defy, stop, wrap 5 avert, blade, cheat, check, cross, elude, metal, patsy, shake, stimy, stump, stymy, sword 6 baffle, bollix, defeat, hamper, outwit, rapier, scotch, stooge, stymie, thwart 7 buffalo, counter, prevent, ward off 8 contrast, laminate, outflank, preclude, shake off 9 frustrate, get around, hamstring, undermine 10 antithesis, circumvent, complement, counteract, disappoint
alternative: 4 épée 5 saber, sabre, Saran
kitchen ~: 5 Alcoa 8 Reynolds
like a ~: 5 blunt
material: 3 tin 5 metal 8 aluminum
starter: 3 air, jet 6 cinque 7 counter
use a ~: 5 fence
__ foil: 3 tin 4 gold 6 chaton, silver
Foiled again!: 3 bah
foist: 6 impose 7 force on, palm off, pass off 9 insinuate
Fokine: 6 Michel
Fokker: 5 plane 7 Anthony 8 airplane, warplane
foe: 4 Spad
folate: 3 vit. 7 vitamin 8 B vitamin
fold: 3 lap, pen, ply 4 bend, bust, fail, flap, give, ruck, tire, tuck, wrap 5 close, crimp, laity, plait, pleat, ridge, ruche, yield 6 crease, dog-ear, double, fess up, go bust, parish, pucker, relent, rumple, submit, wrap up 7 concede, crinkle, disband, dog's-ear, enclose, envelop, flexure, go broke, go under, inclose, plicate, succumb, wrinkle 8 collapse, flection, shut down 9 corrugate, surrender 10 capitulate, double over
anatomical ~: 5 plica 6 dewlap
cloth ~: 5 plait, pleat 6 crease
coat ~: 5 lapel
combining form: 5 ptych- 6 ptycho-
dweller: 3 ewe 4 lamb 5 sheep
in: 3 add
leave the ~: 4 roam 5 stray 6 depart, wander
over: 4 tuck
page ~: 6 dog-ear
starter: 3 pin 4 bill, gate, mani, many 5 blind, sheep 6 center 7 several
up: 2 go 4 bust, shut 5 close, yield
foldaway: 3 bed, cot
folder: 4 file 6 jacket, packet 7 dossier 8 pamphlet 9 portfolio
change the ~: 6 refile
words: 5 I'm out
__ folder: 4 file
folderol
see baloney
folding: 7 compact 8 portable
art: 7 origami
folding __: 4 door, rule 5 chair, money, table
folds
arrange in ~: 5 drape, plait, pleat
__ folds: 5 vocal
Foley: 3 Red, Tom 4 Axel, Dave 5 James 6 Thomas
Folgers: 6 coffee
alternative: 5 Sanka, Yuban 7 Melitta, Nescafé, Savarin 9 Hills Bros.
foliage: 4 leaf 5 frond 6 leaves 7 herbage, leafage, verdure 8 greenery 10 vegetation
destroy ~: 6 denude
full of ~: 5 dense, leafy 6 in leaf
folic acid: 3 vit. 7 vitamin 8 B vitamin
Folies Bergère
dance: 6 cancan
locale: 5 Paris 6 France
folio: 4 leaf, page
folium: 5 layer 6 lamina
folk: 5 music, stock 6 humans, people, public 7 lineage 8 relative 10 population
ender: 3 mot, way 4 lore, moot, mote, tale, ways
hero: 4 icon, idol 9 celebrity
history: 4 lore 5 tales 6 fables 7 legends 9 tradition 10 traditions
like ~ songs: 4 anon., trad.
music instrument: 5 banjo
starter: 3 kin, men 4 work 5 towns, women 6 gentle
story: 4 tale 5 fable 6 legend 9 tradition
wisdom: 3 saw 5 adage, gnome, maxim, moral 6 byword, dictum, saying, slogan, truism 7 epigram, proverb 8 aphorism, apothegm 9 platitude 10 apophthegm
folk __: 3 art 4 mass, rock, song, tale 5 dance, music, story 6 singer 7 singing, society
folk dance: 3 jig 4 hora, jota, reel
Hungary: 7 csardas, czardas
Portugal: 4 fado
Serbia: 4 kolo
Ukraine: 5 gopak, hopak
Folkestone: 4 port
locale: 7 England
folkie: 4 Arlo, Baez, Joni 5 Dylan 6 Seeger 7 Guthrie 8 Bob Dylan, Joan Baez 10 Pete Seeger
instrument: 6 guitar
folklore: 4 myth 6 legend 7 culture
being: 3 elf 4 ogre 5 gnome, troll
folks: 3 kin 4 clan, ones 6 family, humans, people 7 parents 9 relatives
different ~: 4 rest 6 others
__ folks: 4 just
__ Folks: 3 Li'l 7 Oldtown
__ Folks at Home: 3 Old
Folks That Live on the Hill, The
author: Kingsley Amis
folksy: 4 cosy, cozy, homy 5 cozey, cozie, homey, plain 6 casual, earthy, low-key, modest, rustic, simple 7 natural 8 down-home, homespun, informal 10 unaffected, unassuming
folktale: 4 myth 5 story 6 legend 10 fairy story
folkways: 5 ethos, mores 6 custom, values 7 culture, customs, manners, society 9 ethnology, tradition
Follett, Ken: 6 writer
figure: 3 spy
work: Code to Zero
A Dangerous Fortune
Eye of the Needle
The Hammer of Eden
Hornet Flight
Jackdaws
The Key to Rebecca
Lie Down With Lions
The Man From St. Petersburg
The Modigliani Scandal
Night Over Water
On Wings of Eagles
Paper Money
The Pillars of the Earth
A Place Called Freedom
The Third Twin
Triple
follicle: 3 sac
__ follicle: 4 hair
Follies: 7 musical
composer: Stephen Sondheim
__ Follies: 3 Ice
Follies fellow: Flo Ziegfeld
follow: 3 dig, dog, get, pan, see, tag 4 copy, grok, heed, mind, obey, tail 5 act on, adopt, bow to, catch, chase, ensue, grasp, mimic, segue, spy on, stalk, trace, track, trail, watch 6 absorb, accept, bend to, comply, dangle, do like, fathom, fulfil, go next, happen, mirror, pursue, result, rotate, take in 7 abide by, act upon, agree to, catch on, defer to, emulate, fulfill, go after, imitate, make out, monitor, observe, pattern, proceed, realize, reflect, replace, respect, succeed 8 adhere to, carry out, come next, displace, join with, listen to, live up to, practice, run after, supplant 9 accompany, apprehend, arise from, come after, conform to, consent to, cultivate, eventuate, grow out of, supersede, supervene, take after, track down 10 appreciate, comply with, comprehend, happen next, hold fast to, keep in step, toe the line, understand
as advice: 4 heed, obey 5 act on
closely: 3 ape, dog 5 hound, stalk 7 emulate, imitate
don't ~: 4 lead 9 supervise 10 show the way
(from): 4 come 5 arise
one's nose: 3 gad 4 roam, rove 6 ramble 7 meander, traipse 9 gallivant

orders: **4** heed, mind, obey **5** act on, bow to **6** accept, bend to, listen, submit **7** abide by, agree to, defer to, observe, stick to **8** adhere to, carry out **9** conform to, consent to, truckle to **10** comply with, keep in step, toe the line
secretly: **4** tail **5** spy on **6** shadow
the example of: **3** ape **4** copy **5** equal, mimic, rival **6** mirror **7** emulate, imitate, pattern, reflect **9** take after
through: **2** do **4** go on, last **6** attain, effect, finish, linger **7** carry on, deliver, execute, get done, persist, realize, succeed **8** bring off, carry out, complete, continue, plug away **9** discharge, keep going **10** accomplish, bring about, consummate, tough it out
up: **5** probe **6** pursue **8** check out, look into
follow __: **3** out **4** shot, suit **5** along **7** through
follower: **3** fan, nut **4** buff, tail **5** freak, pupil, sheep **6** addict, cohort, flunky, helper, minion, rooter **7** acolyte, admirer, apostle, convert, copycat, devotee, fancier, flunkey, groupie, servant **8** adherent, believer, courtier, disciple, henchman, imitator, partisan, retainer, servitor, sidekick **9** attendant, layperson, proselyte, supporter, worshiper **10** aficionado
(suffix): **3** -ist, -ite
followers: **6** fandom, school **7** fan club **9** entourage
whom ~ follow: **3** ldr. **6** leader
__ Follow Him: **5** I Will
following: **4** cult, fans, next, then **5** after, later **6** behind, circle, coming, latter, public, school, serial **7** cortege, coterie, ensuing, later on, patrons, pursuit **8** groupies, in back of, regulars **9** adherents, afterward, attendant, clientele, deducible, entourage, hangers-on, imitative, in pursuit, patronage, posterior, presently, proximate, resulting **10** coming next, consequent, dependents, henceforth, in search of, sequential, subsequent, succeeding, successive, supporters, thereafter
and the ~: **5** et seq.
and those ~: **6** et seqq.
closely: **6** at heel
not ~: **4** lost **5** ahead, prior **7** earlier **10** beforehand
prefix: **3** epi-
that: **4** next, then **5** later **9** thereupon **10** afterwards
the ~ ones: **4** seqq.
__ following: **4** cult
Following the Equator
author: Mark Twain
follow one's __: **4** nose
follows
as ~: **4** thus
it ~ that: **4** ergo, then, thus **5** hence **9** therefore
Follows: **5** Megan
Follow That Dream: **4** film, song
artist: Elvis Presley
cast: Elvis Presley
follow the __: **6** leader
Follow the Fleet (1936 film)
cast: Fred Astaire, Ginger Rogers, Randolph Scott
composer: Irving Berlin
studio: **3** RKO
follow the leader: **4** game
player: **4** aper
follow-through: **3** end **6** ending **10** conclusion, resolution
follow-up: **3** seq. **6** sequel
folly: **6** idiocy, lunacy **7** fatuity, foolery, inanity, madness **8** daftness, nonsense, rashness **9** absurdity, craziness, dottiness, frivolity, goofiness, silliness **10** imprudence
curse one's ~: **3** rue **6** bemoan, bewail, lament, regret, repent
__ Folly: **7** Fulton's, Seward's, Talley's
__ folly to be wise: **3** 'tis
Folsom: **4** city, town
locale: **10** California
Folsom Prison Blues (1968 song)
artist: Johnny Cash
Fomalhaut: **4** star
foment: **4** abet, brew, spur **5** hop up, impel, raise, rouse **6** arouse, foster, incite, kindle, stir up, whip up, work up **7** aggress, agitate, enflame, inflame, promote, provoke, stirs up **8** engender **9** encourage, impassion, instigate, stimulate
anew: **5** resow
fomenter: **8** agitator, inflamer **9** demagogue
fond: **4** warm **6** caring, doting, loving, tender **7** adoring, amatory, amorous, kissing, valuing **8** friendly, intimate, parental, romantic **9** amatorial
ardently ~: **4** gaga **5** giddy **7** smitten
au ~: **6** wholly **7** in depth, totally **8** from A to Z, in detail, whole hog **9** to the full **10** completely, thoroughly, to the limit
be ~ of: **4** like, love **5** adore, enjoy, go for **6** dote on, revere **7** care for, cherish, idolize, worship **8** hold dear, treasure
be too ~: **4** dote
gesture: **3** hug **4** kiss **6** caress
of: **4** into **6** keen on, soft on **7** stuck on, sweet on **9** partial to **10** cherishing, in love with
(of): **8** enamored
overly ~ one: **5** doter
Fonda: **4** Jane **5** Henry, Peter **7** Bridget
Fonda, Bridget: **7** actress
aunt: **4** Jane
film: Aria (1987)
City Hall (1996)
Doc Hollywood (1991)
It Could Happen to You (1994)
The Road to Wellville (1994)
Scandal (1989)
A Simple Plan (1998)
Single White Female (1992)
Fonda, Henry: **5** actor
film: 12 Angry Men (1957)
Advise & Consent (1962)
The Best Man (1964)
A Big Hand for the Little Lady (1966)
Blockade (1938)
The Cheyenne Social Club (1970)
Drums Along the Mohawk (1939)
Fail-Safe (1964)
Fort Apache (1948)
The Fugitive (1947)
The Grapes of Wrath (1940)
How the West Was Won (1962)
Jesse James (1939)
Jezebel (1938)
The Lady Eve (1941)
The Longest Day (1962)
Madigan (1968)
The Magnificent Dope (1942)
The Male Animal (1942)
Mister Roberts (1955)
My Darling Clementine (1946)
Once Upon a Time in the West (1968)
On Golden Pond (1981, AA)
The Ox-Bow Incident (1943)
The Return of Frank James (1940)
Sex and the Single Girl (1964)
Spawn of the North (1938)
The Story of Alexander Graham Bell (1939)
Tales of Manhattan (1942)
There Was a Crooked Man... (1970)
The Tin Star (1957)
Too Late the Hero (1970)
The Trail of the Lonesome Pine (1936)
Warlock (1959)
Welcome to Hard Times (1967)
The Wrong Man (1957)
Young Mr. Lincoln (1939)
You Only Live Once (1937)
Yours, Mine and Ours (1968)
spouse: Margaret Sullavan
Fonda, Jane: **7** actress
film: Agnes of God (1985)
Any Wednesday (1966)
Barbarella (1968)
Barefoot in the Park (1967)
California Suite (1978)
Cat Ballou (1965)
The China Syndrome (1979)
Coming Home (1978, AA)
The Electric Horseman (1979)
Georgia Rule (2007)
Julia (1977)
Klute (1971, AA)
Monster-in-Law (2005)
Nine to Five (1980)
Old Gringo (1989)
On Golden Pond (1981)
Period of Adjustment (1962)
Stanley & Iris (1990)
Steelyard Blues (1973)
Sunday in New York (1963)
They Shoot Horses, Don't They? (1969)
niece: **7** Bridget
spouse: Tom Hayden, Ted Turner, Roger Vadim
fondant: **5** candy **6** bonbon **10** confection
Fonda, Peter: **5** actor
film: 92 in the Shade (1975)
Dirty Mary Crazy Larry (1974)
Easy Rider (1969)
Futureworld (1976)
The Hired Hand (1971)
The Limey (1999)
Nadja (1994)
Outlaw Blues (1977)
Split Image (1982)
Ulee's Gold (1997)
title role: **4** Ulee
Fond du Lac: **4** city, town
locale: **3** Wis. **4** Wisc. **9** Wisconsin
__ fond farewell: **4** bid a
fondle: **3** pat, paw **5** touch **6** caress, cosset, stroke
fondness: **4** love **5** fancy, taste **6** desire, liking, regard, relish **7** passion **8** affinity, appetite, devotion, penchant, soft spot, weakness **9** affection **10** attachment, endearment, partiality, preference
fondu: **4** bend
fondue: **3** dip **6** cheese **9** appetizer
Fong: **5** Hiram
font: **4** City, Elan, face, pica, root, Saga, Skia, type, Zeal **5** Abadi, agate, Aldus, Arial, Basel, basin, Bembo, Boton, Dante, Delta, Devin, Didot, Dutch, elite, Emona, Gamma, Goudy, Imago, Kabel, Kalix, Norma, pearl, print, Romic, Sabon, Savoy, Swiss, Times, Weiss, Wilke **6** Aldine, Amasis, Apollo, Auriol, Avenir, Batang, Bodoni, Bulmer, Caslon, Catull, Caxton, Cerigo, Cooper, Corona, Cosmos, Delima, Dialog, Esprit, Fenice, Futura, Gareth, Geneva, Glypha, Gothic, Guardi, Joanna, Legacy, loving, Lucida, Maxima, Melior, Minion, Modern, Monaca, Myriad, Nofret, Odense, Optima, Orator, origin, Praxis, Quorum, Romana, Serifa, source, Syndor, Syntax, Tahoma, Utopia, Zurich **7** Amerigo, Barmeno, Bauhaus, Bergamo, Berling, Bookman, Calisto, Candida, Centaur, Century, Courier, Cremona, Cushing, Diotima, Electra, Formata, Korinna, Leawood, Matisse, Memphis, Origami, Pacella, Panache, Peignot, Photina, Plantin, Poetica, Present, Sassoon, Shannon, Spartan, Tiepolo, Tiffany, Univers, Vectora, Verdana, Walbaum **8** Broadway, Caecilia, Cantoria, Carniola, Compacta, Concorde, Fournier, Frutiger, Galliard, Garamond, Giovanni, Hadriano, Meridien, Minister, Novarese, Palatino, Perpetua, Playbill, Rockwell, Slimbach, Souvenir, typeface, wellhead **9** Helvetica **10** Avant Garde, Times Roman, wellspring
baptismal ~: **5** laver
widths: **3** ems, ens
Fontaine: **3** Fox **4** Joan **5** Frank
Fontaine, Joan: **7** actress
film: The Bigamist (1953)
Casanova's Big Night (1954)
The Constant Nymph (1943)
A Damsel in Distress (1937)
The Devil's Own (1966)
Frenchman's Creek (1944)
From This Day Forward (1946)
Gunga Din (1939)
Ivanhoe (1952)

Jane Eyre (1944)
Letter From an Unknown Woman (1948)
Rebecca (1940)
Suspicion (1941, AA)
This Above All (1942)
Voyage to the Bottom of the Sea (1961)
sister: Olivia de Havilland
spouse: Brian Aherne
Fontanne, Lynn: **7** actress
spouse: Alfred Lunt
Fonteyn, Margot: **4** Dame **6** dancer **8** danseuse **9** ballerina
attire: **4** tutu
fulcrum: **3** toe
fontina: **6** cheese
food: **4** chow, diet, dish, eats, fare, fuel, grub, meal, meat, mess, need **5** board, bread, table, viand **6** edible, fodder, intake, ration, snacks, viands **7** aliment, cookery, cooking, cuisine, edibles, goodies, rations, support, victual, vittles **8** supplies, victuals **9** groceries, nutriment, nutrition, provender **10** gastronomy, provisions, sustenance
additive: **3** dye, MSG
chain bottom: **4** alga
Chinese ~: **4** pu pu **6** lo mein, mei fun, won ton **7** chow fun, egg roll, pea pods **8** bean curd, chop suey, chow mein, dumpling, snow peas, spare rib **9** fried rice, roast pork **10** egg foo yung, moo shu pork, Peking duck, spring roll
combining form: **4** sito-
ender: **5** stuff
exclamation: **3** yum **6** yum-yum
label stat: **4** nt. wt. **5** net wt.
starter: **3** sea
store: **4** deli **6** market **7** grocery
supply ~: **5** cater
thickener: **4** agar **8** agar-agar
wrap: **4** foil **5** cello **10** cellophane
food __: **3** web **4** bank, fish, mill **5** chain, court, grain, stamp **6** coupon, vessel **7** pyramid, science, service, vacuole
__ food: **4** baby, fast, junk, soul **5** plant **6** ethnic, finger, frozen, health, rabbit **7** comfort, natural
Food and __ Administration: **4** Drug
__ food cake: **5** angel **6** devil's
Food, Glorious Food musical: **6** Oliver!
foodie: **7** epicure, gourmet **10** gastronome
Food Network
host: **4** chef
food processor: **6** enzyme **9** Cuisinart
setting: **4** chop **5** purée
__ Foods: **4** Best **5** Tyson **7** General
food storage brand: **4** Glad **5** Hefty **6** Ziploc **8** Reynolds **9** Saran Wrap
foodstuff: **4** meat **6** viands **7** aliment, produce, victual **8** victuals
foofaraw: **3** ado **4** riot, to-do **5** hooha **6** hoopla
fool: **3** ass, con, kid, nit, oaf, sap **4** boob, bozo, clod, dolt, dope, dupe, gink, goof, gowk, gull, hoax, jerk, jive, joke, juke, loon, scam, simp, snow, trap, twit, yo-yo, zany **5** bluff, booby, cheat, chump, clown, cluck, cozen, dummy, dunce, hocus, joker, let on, loser, ninny, patsy, put on, schmo, spoof, stump, trick **6** delude, dimwit, galoot, jester, lead on, lubber, lummox, nitwit, outfox, pigeon, putter, rope in, schmoe, stooge, sucker, suck in, take in, trip up, turkey **7** beguile, buffoon, bungler, chicane, coxcomb, deceive, dessert, dingbat, dullard, fake out, fathead, flummox, fribble, galloot, halfwit, jackass, mislead, pierrot, pinhead, pretend, saphead, swindle, two-time **8** bonehead, dumbbell, flimflam, hoodwink, meathead, numskull, pettifog, pushover **9** bamboozle, birdbrain, blockhead, disinform, four-flush, harebrain, harlequin, ignoramus, lamebrain, numbskull, schlemiel, simpleton, victimize **10** dunderhead, nincompoop, noodlehead, silly billy
around: **4** futz, joke, loaf, play **5** dally **6** cavort, dabble, dawdle, frolic, gambol, linger, monkey, trifle **7** goof off **9** misbehave, waste time
away: **3** sap **4** laze **5** drain, trash **6** burn up **7** deplete, fribble, play out **8** squander **9** dissipate
away time: **4** idle, laze, loaf, loll **5** dally, dream, shirk, stall **6** dawdle, loiter, lounge **7** hang out **8** malinger, slack off **9** goldbrick **10** dillydally, knock about
ender: **5** hardy, proof
make a ~ of: **6** outwit **8** outsmart, ridicule
month: **3** Apr. **5** April
no ~: **5** truly **6** really **7** for real
nobody's ~: **4** keen **5** savvy, sharp, slick, smart **6** adroit, artful, astute, brainy, bright, clever, crafty, shrewd **7** knowing **8** lynx-eyed **9** observant, on the ball **10** discerning, insightful, perceptive
old ~: **4** coot
old-style: **4** mome
play for a ~: **3** con, use **4** bilk, dupe, gull, hoax, rook, snow, take **5** cheat, trick **6** delude, entrap, outwit, rip off, take in **7** deceive, defraud, ensnare, fake out, finagle, mislead, snooker, swindle **8** flimflam, hoodwink, outsmart, sucker in **9** bamboozle, victimize **10** manipulate
play the ~: **5** amuse, clown
starter: **3** tom
(with): **3** toy **4** play **6** fiddle, monkey, tinker **9** interfere **10** mess around
fool __: **3** hen **4** away **6** around
__ fool: **5** April
Fool __ as I, A: **4** Such
Fool __ Hill, The: **5** on the
__ Fool: **3** I'm a **5** Henry, She's a **7** Nobody's
foolable: **4** naif **5** green, naive **6** unwary **7** artless **8** gullible, lamblike, trustful, trusting, wide-eyed **9** credulous, guileless
__ Fool Believes: **5** What a
fooled by, not: **4** onto
foolery: **3** fun **4** jest **5** antic, caper, folly **6** antics **7** fatuity **8** jocosity, zaniness **9** silliness
starter: **3** tom
foolhardiness: **5** haste **8** temerity
foolhardy: **3** mad **4** bold, rash, wild **5** brash, hasty, risky, silly **6** daring, madcap, unwise **8** headlong, heedless, reckless **9** audacious, breakneck, daredevil, desperate, idiotical, impetuous, imprudent, uncareful, venturous **10** headstrong, ill-advised, incautious, out on a limb
exploit: **5** stunt
Fool (If You Think It's Over) (1978 song)
artist: Chris Rea
fooling: **3** fun **7** hijinks, mockery **8** falderal, falderol, folderol, nonsense **9** high jinks, horseplay **10** buffoonery
no ~: **5** frank **6** candid, honest, really **7** earnest **8** honestly **9** sincerely **10** forthright, on the level
foolish: **3** mad **4** daft, dopy, dumb, idle, soft, wild, zany **5** balmy, daffy, dense, dippy, dizzy, dopey, dotty, goofy, goony, goosy, inane, kooky, nutty, sappy, silly, wacky **6** absurd, gooney, goosey, kookie, madcap, obtuse, simple, stupid, unwise, whacky **7** asinine, doltish, fatuous, idiotic, puerile, vacuous, witless **8** headless, ill-spent, mindless **9** brainless, dim-witted, fatuitous, frivolous, half-baked, imprudent, insensate, lightsome, ludicrous, misguided, senseless **10** cockamamie, half-witted, ill-advised, incautious, indiscreet, irrational, ridiculous, sophomoric, unprofound, unthinking, weak-minded
not ~: **4** sage, wise **5** canny, sharp, smart **6** astute, clever, shrewd **7** careful, logical, politic, prudent, sapient, tactful **8** rational, sensible **9** judicious, provident, sagacious **10** discerning, insightful, perceptive, reasonable
render ~: **5** besot
talk: **3** yap **4** guff, yaup, yawp **5** trash **6** drivel **7** blather, blether
__-foolish: **5** pound
Foolish __: **4** Beat **5** Games, Heart, Wives
Foolish Beat (1988 song)
artist: Debbie Gibson
Foolish Games (1997 song)
artist: Jewel
Foolish Little Girl (1963 song)
artist: Shirelles
foolishness
see baloney
__ Foolish Things: **5** These
Fool me __, shame...: **4** once
Fool me twice, shame __: **4** on me
Fool on the Hill, The (song)
artist: Beatles, Sérgio Mendes
foolproof: **4** safe, sure **7** certain, perfect **8** fail-safe, flawless, inerrant, reliable, sure-fire, unerring **9** faultless **10** infallible, undoubtful
fool's __: **3** cap **4** gold **6** errand **8** paradise
Fools
author: Neil Simon
fool's-cap feature: **4** bell
__ Fools' Day: **3** All **5** April
Fools Die
author: Mario Puzo
fools ender: **3** cap
__ fool's errand: **3** on a
__ Fools Fall in Love: **5** Why Do
fool's gold: **6** pyrite **10** iron pyrite
Fool's Gold (2008 film)
cast: Kate Hudson, Matthew McConaughey
fool's paradise: **6** revery **7** reverie **8** delusion
Fools Rush In (1963 song)
artist: Ricky Nelson
Fool Such __, A: **3** as I
Fool Such as I, A (1959 song)
artist: Elvis Presley
Fool There Was, A (1915 film)
cast: Theda Bara
foot: **3** dog, pad, paw, pes **4** base, hoof, iamb, unit **5** nadir, socle **6** bottom, dactyl, member, plinth, podium, reckon, tootsy **7** anapest, spondee, tootsie, trotter **8** ambulate, anapaest, pedestal **9** extremity, underside **10** foundation
anatomical ~: **3** pes
ancestor: **5** cubit
animal ~: **3** paw **4** hoof
athlete's ~: **5** tinea
bone: **5** talus **6** tarsus
bones: **4** tali **5** tarsi
classical metric ~: **5** paeon
combining form: **3** ped-, pod- **4** -pede, pedi-, pedo-, podo-
covering: **4** shoe, sock **5** socks **9** stockings
division: **4** inch
ender: **3** age, boy, man, men, pad, way **4** ball, bath, fall, gear, hill, hold, long, mark, note, pace, path, race, rest, rope, slog, sore, step, wall, wear, work **5** board, cloth, loose, print, stalk, stall, stone, stool **6** bridge, lights, locker
go on ~: **4** hoof, walk **5** leg it **6** hoof it
grind under ~: **7** trample
it: **4** hike, trek, walk **5** march **6** stroll **9** take a walk
lever: **5** pedal
of the ~: **5** podal
one on ~: **3** ped. **6** walker **10** pedestrian
part: **3** pad, toe **4** arch, heel, inch, sole **6** big toe, instep
pedal: **5** lever **7** treadle
poetic ~: **4** iamb **6** dactyl **7** anapest, pyrrhic, spondee, trochee **8** anapaest
problem: **4** gout **6** bunion
put one's ~ down: **4** step, walk **5** tread **6** demand, insist **7** protest **9** stand firm
rabbit's ~: **5** charm **6** amulet **8** talisman
set ~ in: **5** enter, get to, reach **6** come to **8** arrive at
shoot oneself in the ~: **3** err **4** flub, goof **5** gum up **6** blow it,

bungle, foul up, fumble, goof up, mess up **7** blunder, louse up **9** mishandle, mismanage
soldier: **2** GI **3** pvt. **5** grunt **7** private, recruit, veteran, warrior
starter: **3** hot, web **4** bare, crow, flat, fore **5** Black, colts, goose, light, pussy, splay, under **6** tender
support: **6** insole
the bill: **3** pay **5** spend, treat **6** defray
width: **3** AAA, EEE **4** AAAA, EEEE
wiper: **3** mat
foot ___: **4** line, race, rule **5** brake, fault, level, score **6** doctor, warmer **7** soldier
foot ___ door: **5** in the
foot-___: **3** ton **5** pound **6** candle **7** lambert
___ foot: **3** bar, bun, ice, pad, web **4** ball, claw, club, cord, duck, hoof, lead, tern, tube **5** board, drake, front, melon, snake, spade, stump, under, whorl **6** cloven, French, runner, scroll, square, trifid **7** bracket, presser, rabbit's, slipper, Spanish
___-foot: **3** cat **4** acre **5** cock's, crow's, first **6** second, single
___ Foot: **3** Big
___ footage: **4** file **5** stock
footage, square: **4** area
football: **4** game **5** sport
15 min. of ~: **3** qtr. **7** quarter
1-pt. ~ play: **3** PAT
2-pt. ~ play: **3** saf. **6** safety
3-pt. ~ play: **2** FG **9** field goal
6-pt. ~ play: **2** TD **9** touchdown
area: **7** end zone **8** midfield, sideline
boo-boo: **6** fumble
charge: **5** blitz
conference: **3** AFC, NFC **4** Amer., Natl. **8** American, National
defunct ~ grp.: **3** AFL
equipment: **6** helmet
fastener: **5** lacer
field: **4** grid **5** arena **8** gridiron
filler: **3** air
flag ~ team: **5** eight, octad
formation: **6** huddle
foul: **4** clip, hold
game duration: **4** hour
Hall of Fame coach: **4** Levy, Noll **5** Allen, Brown, Grant, Halas, Neale, Shula, Stram **6** Ewbank, Landry, Madden **7** Gillman, Pollard **8** Bud Grant, Don Shula, Lombardi, Marv Levy **9** Chuck Noll, Paul Brown, Tom Landry **10** John Madden, Sid Gillman, Weeb Ewbank
Hall of Fame player: **4** Dean, Huff, Lary, Lott, Monk, Page **5** Allen, Brown, Ditka, Eller, Green, Groza, Hayes, Irvin, Jones, Olsen, Shell, Smith, Swann, White **6** Bethea, Butkus, Carson, Casper, Csonka, Grange, Greene, Harris, Hirsch, Lofton, Nevers, Payton, Refnro, Sayers, Taylor, Thomas, Thorpe, Wehrli, Wright **7** Alworth, Art Monk, Dorsett, Gifford, Hampton, Hornung, Largent, Sam Huff, Sanders, Simpson, Tippett, Woodson **8** Alan Page, Art Shell, Bob Brown, Bob Hayes, Campbell, Fred Dean, Jim Brown, Lou Groza, Matthews, McDaniel, Nagurski, Nitschke, Stenerud, Yale Lary **9** Carl Eller, Dickerson, Hickerson, Jim Thorpe, Joe Greene, Lynn Swann, Marchetti, Mel Renfro, Mike Ditka, O.J. Simpson, Red Grange, Zimmerman **10** Bruce Smith, Buoniconti, Dan Hampton, Dave Casper, Dick Butkus, Gale Sayers, Robustelli, Ronnie Lott, Stallworth
Hall of Fame quarterback: **4** Moon **5** Baugh, Elway, Fouts, Kelly, Starr, Young **6** Aikman, Blanda, Dawson, Graham, Griese, Marino, Tittle, Unitas **7** Luckman, Montana **8** Bradshaw, Dan Fouts, Friedman, Jim Kelly, Staubach, Y.A. Tittle **9** Bart Starr, Bob Griese, Dan Marino, John Elway, Jurgensen, Len Dawson, Tarkenton **10** Joe Montana, Otto Graham, Sammy Baugh, Sid Luckman, Steve Young, Warren Moon
Hall of Fame site: **4** Ohio **6** Canton
honor: **6** All-Pro
huddle phrase: **5** on two
infraction: **7** holding, offside **8** clipping
job: **5** coach
kick: **4** punt
kind of ~: **4** Nerf
like arena ~: **6** indoor
maneuver: **4** rush, snap **5** blitz, block, sneak **6** end run **7** hand-off, reverse **8** drop kick, pitch-out
official: **3** ref **5** zebra **7** referee **8** linesman
part: **4** lace
pass: **4** bomb **6** aerial, looper, spiral **7** lateral
path: **3** arc
play: **3** run **4** down, pass, punt, rush **6** end run
political ~: **5** issue **7** problem
position: **2** LB, LG, LT, RB, RG, RT **3** end, LFB, LHB, OLB, RFB, RHB **4** back **5** guard **6** center, tackle **7** flanker, lineman **8** fullback, halfback **9** left guard **10** right guard **11** quarterback
pro team: **4** Jets, Rams **5** Bears, Bills, Colts, Lions **6** Browns, Chiefs, Eagles, eleven, Giants, Niners, Ravens, Saints, Texans, Titans **7** Bengals, Broncos, Cowboys, Falcons, Jaguars, Packers, Raiders, Vikings **8** Chargers, Dolphins, Panthers, Patriots, Redskins, Seahawks, Steelers **9** Cardinals **10** Buccaneers
reference: **8** playbook
relative: **5** rugby
score: **2** TD **4** goal **6** safety **9** field goal
season: **4** fall **6** autumn
setback: **4** loss **8** turnover
shaped like a ~: **5** ovate, ovoid
shirt: **6** jersey
shoe part: **5** cleat
shutout line score: **4** OOOO
stadium: **4** bowl
stand: **3** tee
star: **4** Moon, Rote **5** Elway, Favre, Kosar, Simms, Smith **6** Aikman, Barber, Flutie, Marino **7** Esiason, Sanders **8** Kyle Rote **9** Dan Marino, John Elway, Phil Simms **10** Brett Favre, Doug Flutie, Testaverde, Tiki Barber, Troy Aikman, Warren Moon
starter: **7** kickoff
stat: **3** int., TDs, yds. **5** yards **6** points **7** tackles
team: **6** eleven
term: **3** end, ref **4** back, bomb, down, gain, goal, pass, punt, rush, sack, snap **5** blitz, block, sneak, spike, zebra **6** aerial, All-Pro, center, end run, fumble, huddle, onside, punter, safety, spiral, tackle **7** convert, end zone, flanker, hand-off, holding, kickoff, lateral, lineman, offside, penalty, pigskin, quarter, referee, reverse, time-out **8** clipping, crossbar, drop kick, fullback, goal line, goalpost, halfback, halftime, hang time, hash mark, linesman, midfield, pitch-out, playbook, receiver, sideline, turnover
tiebreaker: **2** OT **8** overtime
yardage: **4** gain
yell: **3** rah
___ football: **4** flag **5** arena, touch
footballer
former pro ~: **5** LA Ram
Foot Book, The
author: Dr. Seuss
foot-drag: **4** loaf **5** dally, delay, stall, tarry **6** dawdle **8** obstruct **10** dilly-dally, equivocate, filibuster
foot-dragger: **7** holdout
foot-dragging: **4** lazy, poky **7** gradual, halting, impeded, lagging, languid, loafing **8** crawling, creeping, dallying, dawdling, delaying, dilatory, drawn-out, hesitant, plodding, slothful, sluggish, stalling, toddling **9** leisurely, lethargic, prolonged, snaillike, unhurried **10** deliberate, protracted
Foote: **6** Horton, Shelby
___-footed: **3** fin, web **4** flat, slow, sure, wing **5** fleet, heavy, light, loose **6** fiddle
footed combining form: **6** -podous
footfall: **4** step
___ foot forward: **4** best
footgear
see footwear
foothold: **4** base, grip **6** anchor **7** support **8** lodgment, purchase **9** beachhead **10** bridgehead, foundation
foot-in-___: **5** mouth
___ foot in: **3** set
footing: **4** base, hold, rank **5** basis, grade, plane, stage, state, terms **6** status **7** quality, station, support **8** position, purchase, standing **9** situation **10** foundation
equal ~: **3** par
lose one's ~: **4** fall, slip, trip
on an equal ~: **4** even, fair **5** level **6** square **7** uniform **8** balanced, matching **10** fifty-fifty
foot in the ___: **4** door
foot-leg connector: **5** ankle
footless: **4** apod **6** apodal **7** apodous
footlet: **3** Ped **7** hosiery
Footlight Parade (1933 film)
cast: Joan Blondell, James Cagney, Ruby Keeler, Dick Powell
footlights: **5** stage **7** theater, theatre
footlike part
combining form: **4** -pode **6** -podium
footlocker: **5** trunk
footloose: **4** free **8** carefree, restless, vagabond
one: **5** rover
Footloose (1984 film)
cast: Kevin Bacon, John Lithgow, Lori Singer, Dianne Wiest
director: Herbert Ross
role: **3** Ren
Footloose (1984 song)
artist: Kenny Loggins
footman: **5** valet **6** flunky, lackey **7** flunkey, lacquey
attire: **6** livery
footnote: **7** comment, mention **8** annotate **10** annotation
abbr.: **3** vid. **4** et al., ibid., idem **5** et seq., op. cit. **6** loc. cit.
make a ~: **4** cite
phrase: **6** et alia, et alii
user: **5** citer
word: **6** ibidem
___-foot oil: **5** neat's
footpad: **5** thief **7** brigand **10** highwayman
footpath: **4** lane, walk **5** track, trail **7** walkway
foot-pound
relative: **3** erg **5** joule
footprint: **4** clew, clue, step **5** spoor, trace, track **10** impression
footprints: **5** track, trail
footrace end: **4** tape
footrest: **4** rail **5** stool **7** hassock, ottoman
footsie, play: **5** flirt
footstep: **4** pace **5** tread **6** stride
combining form: **4** ichn- **5** ichno-
footstool: **4** seat **7** hassock, ottoman
foot the ___: **4** bill
footway: **4** lane, path **5** trail
footwear: **3** pac **4** boot, cack, clog, geta, mule, pump, shoe **5** heels, sabot, sling, socks, spike, stogy, thong, wader **6** bootee, bootie, brogan, brogue, buskin, chukka, galosh, gillie, kiltie, loafer, oxford, patten, rubber, sandal, stogie, wedgie **7** chopine, ghillie, gumboot, high-low, jodhpur, ski boot, slipper, sneaker, wingtip **8** balmoral, flip-flop, moccasin, plimsoll, sneakers, Top-Sider **9** ankle boot, high heels, Mary Janes, sling-back, spike heel **10** clodhopper, wellington, white bucks
ankle-length ~: **6** chukka **7** high-low, jodhpur
baby ~: **6** bootee, bootie
backless ~: **4** mule **5** thong **8** flip-flop

calf-length ~: 7 gumboot
canted ~: 6 wedgie
canvas ~: 7 sneaker 8 plimsoll, Top-Sider
casual ~: 10 white bucks
deerskin ~: 8 moccasin
divided-toe ~: 5 thong 8 flip-flop
dressy ~: 5 heels 9 high heels 10 spike heels
golfer ~: 6 kiltie
heavy ~: 5 stogy 6 stogie 10 clod-hopper
heelless ~: 8 moccasin
Indian ~: 8 moccasin
infant ~: 6 bootee, bootie
knee-length ~: 10 wellington
knitted ~: 6 bootee, bootie
ladies ~: 8 balmoral
leather ~: 8 Top-Sider 10 welling-ton
light ~: 7 slipper
liner ~: 3 pac
low-cut ~: 4 pump 6 gillie, oxford, sandal 7 ghillie, slipper 9 ankle boot
low-heeled ~: 6 brogue 9 Mary Janes
moccasinlike ~: 6 loafer
open-backed ~: 5 sling 9 sling-back
oxford ~: 10 white bucks
perforated pattern ~: 7 wingtip
plastic ~: 7 ski boot
provided ~ to: 4 shod
rubber ~: 7 gumboot, sneaker 8 Top-Sider
rubber-soled ~: 8 plimsoll
shiny ~: 9 Mary Janes
slip-on ~: 6 loafer
soft-soled ~: 4 cack
stiff ~: 7 ski boot
strapless ~: 4 pump
sturdy ~: 4 boot 6 oxford
suede ~: 6 chukka
thick-soled ~: 4 clog 5 sabot 6 buskin, chopin, patten 7 chopine
tongueless ~: 6 gillie 7 ghillie
walking ~: 8 balmoral
waterproof ~: 4 boot 5 wader 6 galosh, rubber
wooden ~: 4 geta 5 sabot
work ~: 6 brogan
see also boot, shoe

__ foo yung: 3 egg
foozle: 3 err 4 flub, goof, muff, slip 5 botch 6 bungle, foul up, fumble, goof up, mess up 7 blunder, louse up 9 mishandle, mismanage
fop: 4 dude 5 blade, dandy, swell 7 coxcomb, peacock, preener 8 macaroni, popinjay 9 pretty boy 10 jack-a-dandy
like a ~: 4 vain 9 conceited
foppish: 5 dandy 6 la-de-da, la-di-da 8 lah-di-dah
for: 3 aye, pro 5 since 6 behind 7 because, through, whereas 8 favoring 9 being that, endorsing, in favor of, in honor of, in place of 10 inasmuch as, in behalf of, on behalf of, supporting, supportive
for __: 3 fun 4 free, good, life, love, real, rent, sure 5 a song, a time, keeps, short 7 certain, example, openers
for __ by owner: 4 sale
for __ intents and purposes: 3 all
for __ it's worth: 3 all 4 what
for __ life: 4 dear
for __ matter: 4 that
for __ measure: 4 good
for __ or for worse: 6 better
for __ or money: 4 love
for __ out loud: 6 crying
for __ the world: 3 all
__ for: 3 ask, gun, opt, pop 4 call, fall, feel, go in, look, make, pass, pull, send, take, what 5 put in, shoot, speak, stand, vouch 6 spring 7 account, bargain
__-for: 7 uncared, unhoped
...for __, for poorer: 6 richer
...for __ of woman born: 4 none
For __: 3 You 5 Annie, A' That, Kicks
For __ a jolly...: 3 he's
For __ be Queen...: 4 I'm to
For __ Dollars More: 4 a Few
For __ Eyes Only: 4 Your
For __ in My Life: 4 Once
For __ is the Kingdom...: 5 thine
For __ jolly...: 4 he's a
For __ know...: 4 all I
For __ Know: 5 All We
For __ My Gal: 5 Me and
For __ of a nail...: 4 want
For __ Sake: 5 Pete's 7 Heaven's
For __ the Bell Tolls: 4 Whom
For __ us a child is born: 4 unto
For __ waves of grain: 5 amber
For __ We Know: 3 All
For __-With Love and Squalor: 4 Esme
__ For: 5 To Die
for a __: 4 song 6 wonder
For a __ Dollars More: 3 Few
__ for Adano: 5 A Bell
__ for a Day: 4 King, Lady 5 Queen
__ for a fall: 4 ride
For a Few Dollars More (1966 film)
cast: Clint Eastwood, Lee Van Cleef
director: Sergio Leone
__ for Africa: 3 USA
forage: 3 hay 4 comb, feed, hunt, raid, root, seek 5 prowl, scour 6 browse, fodder, ravage, search 7 aliment, explore, look for, plunder, ransack, rummage 8 scrounge 9 cast about
food: 3 hay 6 rustle
grass: 5 sorgo 6 millet, sorgho 7 setaria
plant: 3 ers 5 emmer, ervil, vetch 6 clover, cowpea
plant of Asia: 3 urd
store ~: 6 ensile
__ for a Heavyweight: 7 Requiem
__ for a king: 3 fit
__ for alarm: 5 cause
__ for Alibi: 3 A Is
for all __ and purposes: 7 intents
__-for-all: 4 free
for all one is __: 5 worth
__ for All Seasons: 4 A Man
for all the __: 5 world
For All We Know (1971 song)
artist: Carpenters
__ for a loop: 5 knock, throw
Foran: 4 Dick
For Annie
author: Edgar Allan Poe
__ for apple: 3 A is
__ for apples: 3 bob
__ for a rainy day: 4 save
for argument's __: 4 sake
__ for a ride: 4 take
For A' That
author: Robert Burns
foray: 4 raid, trip 5 sally, storm 6 attack, inroad, maraud, ravage, sortie 7 assault, descent, overrun, venture 8 invasion 9 incursion, irruption
make a ~: 7 plunder
Foray: 4 June
forbear: 4 omit, shun 5 avoid, forgo, remit, spare 6 desist, eschew, forego, relent, resist 7 abstain, back off, decline, refrain 8 keep back, keep from, renounce, with-hold 9 sacrifice 10 desist from, pro-genitor
__ for bear: 6 loaded
forbearance: 4 pity 5 mercy 6 lenity, pardon 8 clemency, kindness, lenience, patience 9 restraint, tol-erance 10 temperance
forbearing: 3 lax 4 easy, kind, meek, mild, soft 5 loose 6 chaste, gentle, kindly 7 clement, lenient, patient, ruthful, sparing 8 flexible, laid-back, merciful, parental, placable, tolerant 9 assuasive, compliant, easygoing, forgiving, indulgent 10 charitable, living with, permis-sive, thoughtful, unexacting
forbears: 7 kinfolk, lineage 8 kin-folks, kinsfolk
__ for beauty: 5 an eye
Forbes: 3 mag 5 Bryan, Steve 6 Esther 7 Malcolm 8 magazine
alternative: 7 Barron's, Fortune
forbid: 3 ban, bar, nix 4 deny, halt, stop, tabu, veto, warn 5 block, debar, say no, taboo 6 abjure, censor, enjoin, hinder, impede, outlaw, reject 7 embargo, exclude, forfend, inhibit, prevent, rule out 8 disallow, forefend, obstruct, pre-clude, prohibit, restrain, restrict 9 foreclose, forestall, interdict, pro-scribe
forbiddance: 3 ban 4 veto 7 boycott, embargo 8 sanction 9 exclusion
forbidden: 4 tabu 5 taboo 6 banned, vetoed 7 illegal, illicit 8 criminal, improper, outlawed, smuggled, unlawful, verboten, wrongful 9 felo-nious, off-limits 10 closed-down, contraband, not allowed, prohib-ited, proscribed
thing: 4 no-no 5 taboo
forbidden __: 5 fruit
Forbidden __: 4 City 6 Planet
Forbidden City: 4 Lasa 5 Lassa, Lhasa
occupant: 3 emp. 7 emperor
forbidden fruit: 5 apple
locale: 4 Eden
Forbidden Paradise (1924 film)
cast: Pola Negri
Forbidden Planet (1956 film)
cast: Anne Francis, Leslie Nielsen, Walter Pidgeon
forbidding: 4 dark, dour, grim, ugly 5 gaunt, stern, tough 6 odious, severe, strict 7 hostile, ominous, refusal 8 daunting, menacing, sin-ister 9 abhorrent, glowering, offen-sive, repellent, repulsive 10 cen-sorship, off-putting, unfriendly, unpleasant
look: 5 glare, scowl 6 glower
__ for Bonzo: 7 Bedtime
__ for Burglar: 3 B Is
__ for business: 4 open
force: 3 pry, ram, vim 4 army, bind, cram, crew, dint, drag, fury, gist, goad, kick, make, push, soul, thew 5 agent, brawn, brunt, cadre, clout, corps, draft, drive, exact, jimmy, might, order, power, press, punch, seize, sinew, squad, staff, thews, troop, twist, vigor, wring 6 coerce, compel, demand, detail, duress, effort, energy, enjoin, extort, impact, impose, insist, legion, muscle, oblige, propel, reduce, spirit, stress, thrust, wrench 7 assault, brigade, command, dragoon, fitness, gravity, impetus, impulse, inflict, muscles, oppress, pin down, potence, potency, require, sandbag, squeeze, stamina, violate, voltage 8 bust open, coercion, division, dynamism, efficacy, emphasis, gumption, keep down, momentum, obligate, pressure, regiment, salesmen, shanghai, soldiers, squadron, stimulus, strength, valid-ity, vitality 9 authority, battalion, beefiness, blackmail, break open, conscript, constrain, crack open, endurance, extortion, fortitude, hardiness, huskiness, influence, intensity, operation, puissance, stoutness, strong-arm, substance, toughness, will power 10 brawni-ness, compulsion, detachment, horsepower, importance, mighti-ness, oppression, pressurize, robustness, sturdiness
at full ~: 5 amain
back: 5 repel 6 defeat, put off, rebuff 7 fend off, repulse, ward off 8 drive off 9 drive away
be in ~: 4 hold, rule 5 stand
brute ~: 3 vim 4 dint, thew 5 brawn, might, power, thews, vigor 6 energy, muscle 7 fitness, muscles, potence, potency, stamina 8 strength, violence, vitality 9 beefiness, endurance, fortitude, hardiness, huskiness, puissance, stoutness, tough-ness 10 brawniness, mighti-ness, robustness, sturdiness
destructive ~: 4 bane 7 scourge
down: 4 sink 7 depress 8 sub-merge
driving ~: 4 birr, urge 6 engine 7 impetus
fighting ~: 3 GIs 4 army, navy 5 fleet 6 armada 7 cavalry, marines, sailors 8 military, sol-diers
forward: 5 impel
get by ~: 3 pry 5 bully, exact, gouge, usurp, wrest, wring 6 coerce, extort, wrench 7 squeeze 9 blackmail, shake down
hostile ~: 3 foe 5 enemy 7 invader, villain 8 attacker, opponent 9 adversary, assailant, combatant, other side

10 antagonist, opposition
hypothetical ~: 4 odyl 5 odyle
in: 3 jam 6 insert, thrust 7 intrude, squeeze 9 interject, interpose, interrupt
in ~: 5 valid 6 active, at work 7 working 9 effective, operative
lacking ~: 4 limp, weak 6 effete, feeble 8 weakened 9 enervated, powerless
life ~: 3 Tao 6 spirit
main ~: 5 brunt
mystical ~: 5 karma 6 kismet
naval ~: 6 argosy 8 flotilla
obtain by ~: 3 pry 5 bully, exact, gouge, usurp, wrest, wring 6 coerce, extort, wrench 7 squeeze 9 blackmail, shake down
(on): 5 foist
open: 3 pry 5 jimmy, lever 7 crowbar
out: 4 oust, pump 5 eject, evict, expel 6 depose 7 dismiss, exclude, extrude 8 dislodge, displace, supplant
physical ~: 4 main
starter: 3 per 4 work 7 counter
strike with ~: 3 hit, ram 4 beat, push, slam 5 smash 6 batter, hammer
take by ~: 5 usurp, wrest, wring 6 extort, ravish, wrench
taken by ~ old-style: 4 reft
task ~: 6 detail 9 committee 10 detachment
tour de ~: 4 coup, feat 5 stunt 7 classic, exploit, triumph
unit: 4 dyne 6 newton
upon: 4 vent 5 visit, wreak 6 impose 7 inflict, unleash 8 carry out 9 knock down 10 bring about, perpetrate
vital ~: 4 soul 5 anima, being 6 energy, psyche, spirit 8 vivacity
with great ~: 4 hard 7 harshly, heavily 8 brutally, fiercely, intently 9 earnestly, intensely, violently, zealously 10 gruelingly, powerfully, rigorously, vehemently, vigorously
work ~: 5 labor, staff 9 personnel

force __: 3 cup, fit 4 play, pump 5 field 7 majeure
force-__: 3 out 5 draft
__ force: 3 air 4 gale, life, task, weak, work 5 color, fifth, labor, third, vital 6 police, strike, strong 7 buoyant, landing, Lorentz
__-force: 3 ton 4 main 5 pound
__ Force: 3 Air 5 Brute 6 Magnum 7 Driving
forced: 5 bound, stiff 7 labored, stilted 8 affected, coercive, grudging, impelled, strained 9 contrived, insincere, laborious, mandatory, stringent, unnatural, unwilling 10 artificial, begrudging, compulsive, compulsory, obligatory, unobliging
be ~: 6 have to
is ~ to: 4 must
forceful: 4 bold, firm, hale, iron, wiry 5 beefy, burly, hardy, hefty, hunky, husky, lusty, nervy, stout, tough 6 active, all-out, brawny, cogent, hearty, mighty, potent, robust, rugged, sinewy, steely, stocky, strong, sturdy, virile 7 doughty, drastic, driving, dynamic, intense, telling, violent 8 athletic, decisive, dominant, emphatic, indurate, muscular, positive, powerful, puissant, resolute, stalwart, striking, vehement, vigorous 9 assertive, Atlantean, effective, energetic, herculean, insistent, masterful, strapping, stringent, trenchant, well-built 10 able-bodied, commanding, conclusive, iron-willed, passionate, persuasive, red-blooded, take-charge, unswerving, unwavering
one: 6 dynamo
forcefulness: 5 power, punch, vigor 6 energy, weight
forceless: 4 meek, weak 5 timid 6 feeble 8 cowardly 10 irresolute, submissive
force of __: 5 habit
__ Force One: 3 Air
force one's __: 4 hand
forceps: 4 tool 6 pliers
forces
furnish new ~ to: 5 reman
join ~: 4 pool 5 merge, unite 6 club up, gang up, league 9 cooperate 10 assist with
science of ~: 9 mechanics
__ forces: 5 armed
__ Forces: 7 Special
Force, The
champion of ~: 4 Jedi
dark side of ~: 4 evil
Forché, Carolyn: 4 poet
forcible: 6 strong 7 telling, violent 8 striking
forcibly: 4 hard 7 greatly 8 mightily, severely, strongly 9 intensely 10 powerfully
__ for Columbine: 7 Bowling
__ for Corpse: 3 C Is
For crying __ loud!: 3 out
ford: 4 span, wade 5 cross 8 go across 10 wade across
Ford: 3 car, LTD 4 auto, Doug, John, Lita, Paul 5 Betty, Faith, Frick, Glenn, Henry 6 Anitra, Eileen, Gerald, Whitey 7 Mercury, Richard, Wallace 8 Harrison 10 automobile
alternative: *see* automobile
make: 7 Lincoln, Mercury
model: 3 LTD 5 Cobra, Edsel, Focus, Pinto, Probe, Ranch, 'Stang, T-Bird, Tempo, Tudor 6 Aspire, Bronco, Custom, Del Rio, Escape, Escort, Falcon, Fiesta, Fusion, Futura, Model A, Model B, Model T, Ranger, Squire, Taurus, Torino 7 Contour, Festiva, Galaxie, Grabber, Granada, Mustang 8 Aerostar, Explorer, Fairlane, Fairmont, Mainline, Maverick, Parklane, Skyliner, Sunliner, Victoria, Windstar 9 Econoline, Excursion, Town Sedan 10 Customline, Expedition, Ranch Wagon 11 Thunderbird
Ford __ better idea: 4 has a
Ford __ Ford: 5 Madox
__ for Danger: 5 Green
__ for Danny Fisher, A: 5 Stone
__ Ford Coley: 4 John
__ Ford Coppola: 7 Francis
Ford, Doug: 6 golfer
__ for Deadbeat: 3 D Is
for dear __: 4 life
Ford Explorer: 3 SUV
Ford, Ford Madox: 6 writer 7 British
Ford, Gerald: 9 president
alma mater: 8 Michigan
birth name: 10 Leslie King
birthplace: 3 Neb. 4 Nebr. 5 Omaha
child: 4 Jack 5 Susan 6 Steven 7 Michael
former occupation: 6 lawyer
home: 8 Michigan
middle name: 7 Rudolph
opponent: 6 Carter
running mate: 4 Dole
vacation spot: 4 Vail
V.P.: 3 NAR 11 Rockefeller
wife: 5 Betty
Ford, Glenn: 5 actor
film: Gilda (1946)
Jubal (1956)
spouse: Eleanor Powell
Fordham: 6 school
athletes: 4 Rams
locale: 5 Bronx 7 New York
Ford, Harrison: 5 actor
film: Air Force One (1997)
Blade Runner (1982)
Clear and Present Danger (1994)
Crossing Over (2009)
The Devil's Own (1997)
The Empire Strikes Back (1980)
The Frisco Kid (1979)
The Fugitive (1993)
Indiana Jones and the Kingdom of the Crystal Skull (2008)
Indiana Jones and the Last Crusade (1989)
Indiana Jones and the Temple of Doom (1984)
The Mosquito Coast (1986)
Patriot Games (1992)
Presumed Innocent (1990)
Raiders of the Lost Ark (1981)
Regarding Henry (1991)
Return of the Jedi (1983)
Sabrina (1995)
Six Days Seven Nights (1998)
Star Wars (1977)
What Lies Beneath (2000)
Witness (1985)
Working Girl (1988)
spouse: Melissa Mathison
Ford, Henry son: 5 Edsel
__ for dinner?: 5 What's
Ford, John: 8 director
film: 3 Bad Men (1926)
3 Godfathers (1948)
Airmail (1932)
Cheyenne Autumn (1964)
Donovan's Reef (1963)
Dr. Bull (1933)
Drums Along the Mohawk (1939)
Flesh (1932)
Fort Apache (1948)
Four Men and a Prayer (1938)
Four Sons (1928)
The Fugitive (1947)
The Grapes of Wrath (1940, AA)
Hangman's House (1928)
How Green Was My Valley (1941, AA)
How the West Was Won (1962)
The Hurricane (1937)
The Informer (1935, AA)
The Iron Horse (1924)
Judge Priest (1934)
The Last Hurrah (1958)
The Long Gray Line (1955)
The Long Voyage Home (1940)
The Lost Patrol (1934)
The Man Who Shot Liberty Valance (1962)
Mary of Scotland (1936)
Mister Roberts (1955)
Mogambo (1953)
My Darling Clementine (1946)
The Prisoner of Shark Island (1936)
The Quiet Man (1952, AA)
Rio Grande (1950)
The Searchers (1956)
Sergeant Rutledge (1960)
She Wore a Yellow Ribbon (1949)
Stagecoach (1939)
Steamboat 'Round the Bend (1935)
The Sun Shines Bright (1953)
They Were Expendable (1945)
Wagon Master (1950)
Wee Willie Winkie (1937)
The Whole Town's Talking (1935)
Young Cassidy (1965)
Young Mr. Lincoln (1939)
Ford Madox __: 4 Ford 5 Brown
fordo: 7 destroy
__ Ford Range: 5 Edsel
Ford, Tennessee Ernie
song: Ballad of Davy Crockett (1955)
Sixteen Tons (1955)
Ford, Whitey: 6 hurler, Yankee 7 pitcher
fore: 3 bow 4 head 5 front
at the ~: 5 ahead 7 in front
be at the ~: 4 lead
combining form: 6 antero-
ender: 4 lady, word 6 father 7 quarter
opposite: 3 aft
starter: 5 there, where 6 hereto 7 thereto 8 hereunto 9 thereunto
fore-__: 5 check 7 topmast, topsail
__ fore: 5 to the
__ for Each Other: 4 Made
fore and __: 3 aft
forearm: 7 prepare
bone: 4 ulna 6 radius
bones: 5 radii, ulnae
of a ~ bone: 5 ulnar
forebear: 6 father, mother 9 ascendant, matriarch, patriarch, precursor 10 antecedent, originator, procreator, progenitor
forebears: 5 roots, stock 7 descent, lineage 8 ancestry, heritage, pedigree 9 ancestors, bloodline, genealogy 10 extraction, family tree
forebode: 7 betoken, portend, predict, presage, promise 8 prophesy, threaten
foreboding: 4 care, omen, sign 5 dread, qualm 6 augury, threat 7 anxiety, ominous, portent, presage, warning 8 bad vibes, dis-

quiet, mistrust, prophecy, sinister **9** misgiving, prenotion **10** prediction, prognostic
forecast: 3 tip **4** look, sign **5** augur, hunch **6** augury, tip-off **7** betoken, outlook, predict, presage, project **8** estimate, prophecy, prophesy **9** adumbrate, prognosis **10** anticipate, prediction, projection
agcy.: 4 NOAA
aid: 5 radar
letters: 3 THI
line: 5 front **6** isobar **8** isotherm
weather ~: 3 dry, fog, hot, icy, wet **4** cold, cool, damp, fair, gale, hail, haze, mild, rain, warm **5** clear, humid, sleet, storm, sunny **6** cloudy
forecaster: 4 seer **5** augur, sibyl **6** oracle **7** diviner, prophet **9** predictor **10** soothsayer
foreclose: 3 bar **5** block, debar, deter **6** forbid, hinder, impede, refuse, reject **7** exclude, lock out, prevent, shut out **8** blockade, obstruct, preclude
forefather: 8 ancestor **9** precursor **10** antecedent, progenitor
forefathers: 5 roots **7** kinfolk **8** kinfolks, kinsfolk
forefend: 4 stop **5** avert, block, debar **6** enjoin, forbid **7** prevent **8** stave off **9** interdict
forefoot: 3 paw
forefront: 3 van **4** head, lead **8** vanguard
forego: 4 lead **7** precede **9** surrender
foregoing: 4 past **5** above, prior **6** former **7** earlier **8** anterior, previous **9** precedent, preceding **10** antecedent
foregone: 4 past **5** prior **6** former **7** earlier **8** previous
foreground: 5 front
forehead: 4 brow **5** front
feature: 5 ridge **6** furrow
Hindu's ~ mark: 5 tilak
insect ~: 5 frons
slapper's comment: 3 duh
foreign: 3 far **5** alien **6** exotic, remote **7** distant, faraway, outside, oversea, strange, unknown **8** external, imported, offshore, overseas **9** nonnative, peregrine **10** extraneous, immaterial, irrelevant, outlandish, unexplored, unfamiliar
affairs: 8 politics **9** diplomacy **10** statecraft
agent: 3 spy
like some ~ words: 3 fem. **4** masc., neut. **6** neuter **8** feminine **9** masculine
matter: 5 taint **8** impurity
merchandise: 6 import
name meaning ~: 7 Barbara
not ~: 6 native **8** domestic, internal **9** home-grown **10** indigenous
representative: 5 envoy **6** consul, legate **8** delegate, diplomat, emissary, minister **10** ambassador
foreign __: 3 aid, car **4** bill **6** legion, office, policy **7** affairs, mission, service
foreign-__: 4 born, flag
Foreign Affairs
author: Alison Lurie
foreigner: 5 alien **6** émigré, gaijin **7** refugee, visitor **8** newcomer, outsider, stranger **9** immigrant, outlander
name meaning ~: 7 Wallace
foreign exchange
cost: 4 agio
listing: 3 yen **4** euro, peso **5** pound, zloty
foreknowledge: 3 ESP **4** sign **6** vision **8** prophecy **10** prescience
foreland: 4 cape, head **5** point **10** promontory
foreleg: 4 calf, shin
forelimb: 4 wing
foreman: 4 boss **7** manager **8** director, superior **10** supervisor
deck ~: 4 bo's'n **5** bosun
group: 4 jury
Foreman, George: 5 boxer
foe: 3 Ali
match: 4 bout **5** fight
milieu: 4 ring **5** arena
punch: 3 jab **4** left **5** right **8** uppercut
stat: 2 KO **3** TKO
foremost: 3 top **4** A-one, arch, best, head, lead, main, tops **5** chief, first, front, prime **6** mainly, master, top dog, urgent **7** central, highest, leading, premier, primary, supreme **8** above all, champion **9** essential, number-one, paramount, primarily, principal, prominent, topflight, worthiest **10** preeminent
combining form: 4 prot- **5** proto-
member: 4 dean **5** doyen
forenoon: 2 a.m. **4** morn **7** morning
forensic: 4 moot **5** legal **8** judicial, juristic **9** debatable, dialectic, juridical, polemical **10** juristical, rhetorical
site: 3 lab
foreordain: 4 doom, fate **7** destine **9** destinate, determine **10** prearrange, predestine
foreordained: 5 bound, fated **6** doomed **8** destined **10** inevitable
forepart: 3 bow **4** head, prow **5** front **8** anterior
__ for error: 6 margin
forerunner: 5 pacer **6** augury, herald, leader, parent **7** portent **8** ancestor, original **9** announcer, harbinger, initiator, messenger, precursor, prototype **10** antecedent, antecessor, indication, originator, progenitor, prognostic
foresail: 3 jib
foresee: 5 think **7** predict **8** envisage, envision, prophesy **10** anticipate, reckon with
foreseeable: 4 near
foreshadow: 4 bode, hint, mean **5** augur **7** betoken, portend, predict, presage, promise **8** prophesy, threaten **9** adumbrate, prefigure
foreshadowing: 4 sign **6** threat **7** portent **9** prophetic
foreshow: 4 bode, mean, omen, warn **5** augur **6** herald **7** auspice, betoken, point to, portend, predict, presage, promise, signify **8** antecede, prophesy **9** adumbrate, prefigure **10** vaticinate
foresight: 6 vision, wisdom **9** canniness, provision **10** discretion, enterprise, leadership, perception, precaution, prescience, providence
foresighted: 5 canny **6** shrewd **7** prudent **9** provident **10** discerning
For Esme-With Love and Squalor
author: J.D. Salinger
forest: 4 park, wood **5** Arden, grove, wilds, woods **6** nature, timber **8** Sherwood, wildwood, woodland **9** backwoods **10** timberland, wilderness
clearing: 5 glade
combining form: 3 hyl- **4** hylo-
commodity: 4 pulp
creature: 3 doe **4** bear, deer, fawn, hare, hart, lynx, stag **6** badger
crown: 6 canopy
deity: 3 Pan
floor: 5 humus
growth: 4 moss **6** lichen
like a ~ floor: 5 ferny
like some ~s: 4 lush **5** firry, piney
like the earth in a ~: 5 rooty
national ~: 4 Gila, Inyo, Pike **5** Boise, Delta, Dixie, Huron, Modoc, Ocala, Ozark, Routt, Tahoe, Teton, Tonto, Twain, Uinta, Wayne **6** Apache, Ashley, Carson, Cibola, Custer, De Soto, Helena, Kaibab, Lassen, Marion, Ochoco, Oconee, Oglala, Ottawa, Pawnee, Pisgah, Plumas, Sabine, Salmon, Shasta, Sierra, Sumter, Umpqua, Winema **7** Angeles, Arapaho, Bighorn, Bridger, Caribou, Challis, Chugach, Conecuh, Fremont, Hoosier, Houston, Klamath, Lincoln, Malheur, Nicolet, Olympic, Osceola, Payette, Pinchot, San Juan, Santa Fe, Sequoia, Shawnee, Siuslaw, Targhee, Tongass, Trinity, Wasatch **8** Angelina, Bankhead, Cherokee, Chippewa, Coconino, Colville, Croatoan, Crockett, Eldorado, Fishlake, Flathead, Gallatin, Hiawatha, Humboldt, Kootenai, Manistee, Nez Perce, Okanogan, Ouachita, Prescott, Sawtooth, Shoshone, Superior, Tombigee, Tuskegee, Uwharrie **9** Allegheny, Bienville, Deschutes, Kisatchie, Roosevelt, Talladega, Wenatchee
nymph: 5 dryad
old-style: 5 weald
rain ~: 5 biome, selva **6** jungle
ranger, at times: 5 guide
region: 5 taiga
sprite: 3 elf
unit: 4 tree
way: 4 lane, path **8** footpath
forest __: 5 green **6** ranger **7** reserve
__ forest: 4 rain
Forest: 8 Whitaker
Forest __: 7 Service
__ Forest: 3 New **4** Wake **5** Black, Lee De **6** Epping **7** Argonne, Waltham **8** Sherwood
forestage: 5 apron
forestall: 4 stop **5** avert, deter, parry **6** forbid, hinder, hogtie, thwart **7** obviate, prevent, rule out, ward off **8** obstruct, preclude **9** frustrate **10** anticipate, get ahead of
forestalling: 4 veto
__ Forest cake: 5 Black
forested: 5 woody **6** silvan, sylvan, wooded, woodsy **8** arboreal
Forester: 3 car **4** auto **6** Subaru
Forester, C.S.: 6 writer **7** British
first name: Cecil
work: The African Queen, Sink the Bismarck!
forester tool: 3 axe **7** hatchet
forestry: 7 science
study: 5 trees
tool: 3 axe
foretaste: 6 hansel **7** handsel, warning **10** anticipate
foretell: 3 see **4** bode, look, mean, warn **5** augur, spell **6** divine **7** betoken, portend, predict, presage **8** prophesy, soothsay **9** adumbrate **10** anticipate
foreteller: 4 seer **5** augur **10** soothsayer
foretelling: 5 vatic **6** augury, occult, oracle, vision **8** mystical, oracular, prophecy **9** prescient, prophetic, sibylline **10** auspicious, divination, portentous, prediction
forethought: 4 care **7** caution **10** precaution
foretoken: 4 bode, omen, sign **5** augur **6** augury, herald **7** portend, portent, presage, promise, warning **9** harbinger, prefigure
foretop ender: 4 mast, sail **7** gallant
forever: 4 ages **5** etern **6** always, eterne **7** finally, lasting **8** eternity **9** endlessly, eternally, indelibly **10** enduringly, unendingly
and a day: 3 eon **4** aeon, ages **8** long time
in verse: 5 etern **6** eterne
lasting ~: 6 eonian
now and ~: 8 immortal, timeless, unending **9** perpetual
take ~: 4 drag **5** dally, stall, tarry **6** dawdle **10** dillydally
forever __ day: 4 and a
Forever
author: Judy Blume
Forever (song)
artist: Mariah Carey, Kiss, Little Dippers
Forever __: 5 Amber, Young **6** Female
Forever __ Girl: 4 Your
__ Forever: 6 Batman
Forever Amber (1947 film)
cast: Linda Darnell, Richard Greene, Cornel Wilde
director: Otto Preminger
forever and __: 4 a day
Forever Young (1988 song)
artist: Rod Stewart
Forever Young (1992 film)
cast: Jamie Lee Curtis, Mel Gibson, Elijah Wood
director: Steve Miner
Forever Your Girl (1989 song)
artist: Paula Abdul
__ for Evidence: 3 E Is

forewarn: 3 tip 5 alert 6 advise, inform, tip off 7 apprise, apprize, caution, portend, presage 8 admonish, prophesy, threaten
forewarning: 4 omen, sign 5 alarm 6 advice, augury, caveat 7 caution, portent, presage 9 foretoken, predictor
foreword: 5 intro, proem 6 prolog 7 preface, prelude 8 exordium, overture, preamble, prologue
__ for Fears: 5 Tears
forfeit: 4 cede, drop, dump, fine, lose, pawn, sell, shed 5 chuck, ditch, forgo, yield 6 forego, give up 7 abandon, forsake, penalty 8 forswear, get rid of, give over, hand over, jettison, part with, throw out 9 cast aside, dispose of, foreswear, sacrifice, surrender, throw away 10 punishment, relinquish
ender: 3 ure
Forfeit
author: Dick Francis
forfeited: 4 lost
forfeits: 4 game 8 card game
game with ~: 3 loo
variety: 3 loo
forfeiture: 4 cost, fine, loss 5 mulct 7 penalty
forfend: 6 forbid 7 obviate, prevent, rule out 8 preclude, prohibit
__ for Fire: 5 Quest
__ for Five: 5 Table 6 Dinner
__ for Fugitive: 3 F Is
forgather: 4 meet 5 group 6 muster 7 convene 8 assemble 10 congregate, rendezvous
forge: 4 fake, form, make, mint, mold, push 5 build, craft, draft, erect, frame, lunge, put up, shape, shove, stove 6 beetle, charge, create, design, devise, pirate, plunge, smithy, thrust 7 develop, factory, falsify, fashion, foundry, furnace, phony up, produce 8 assemble, simulate, smithery 9 construct, establish, fabricate, formulate, give shape, hammer out, ironworks, steamroll, strongarm
ahead: 5 march 7 advance, recover 8 continue, progress 9 go forward
need: 4 fire 5 anvil
site of Vulcan's ~: 4 Etna 5 Aetna
worker: 5 smith 10 blacksmith
__ forge: 4 drop
forged: 4 fake, mock, sham 5 bogus, false, phony, put-on 6 ersatz, phoney, pseudo, unreal 7 assumed, feigned 8 spurious 9 imitation, simulated, synthetic 10 artificial, fabricated, fictitious, fraudulent
__ Forge, PA: 6 Valley
forger: 5 faker, fraud 8 imitator, swindler 9 falsifier
forgery: 4 copy, fake, sham 5 phony 6 phoney 9 imitation
forget: 4 lose, miss, omit, skip 5 leave 6 ignore, slight 7 let slip, neglect 8 discount, overlook, pass over, space out, write off 9 disregard 10 draw a blank
about: 4 drop, skip 8 write off
don't ~: 8 remember
forgive and ~: 6 make up, settle 9 reconcile 10 make amends, shake hands
hard to ~: 6 catchy
it: 2 no 3 nah, naw, nay, nix, non 4 nein, nope, nyet, uh-uh 5 I won't, ixnay, never, nohow, no sir, no way 6 no deal, no dice, no soap, noways, nowise 7 I refuse 8 I will not, negative, negatory, no matter 9 by no means, fat chance, I think not, never mind 10 count me out, not a chance, thumbs down
one's lines: 4 go up 5 choke, fluff 6 freeze 7 go blank 10 draw a blank
where it is: 4 lose 6 mislay 7 misfile 8 misplace
forget-__: 5 me-not
forgetful: 3 lax 5 slack 6 remiss 7 unaware 8 careless, mindless 9 airheaded, amnemonic, negligent, oblivious, unheedful, unmindful, unwitting 10 abstracted, distracted, neglectful, out to lunch, ungrateful
forgetfulness: 5 lapse 7 amnesia, neglect 8 oblivion
flower of ~: 5 lotus
river of ~: 5 Lethe
Forget Him (1963 song)
artist: Bobby Rydell
forget-me-not: 5 plant 6 flower
Forget Paris (1995 film)
cast: Billy Crystal, Joe Mantegna, Debra Winger
director: Billy Crystal
forgivable: 6 venial 9 allowable, excusable, tolerable 10 pardonable
forgive: 4 pity 5 purge, remit, spare 6 acquit, excuse, exempt, let off, pardon, wink at 7 absolve, condone, let it go, let pass, release 8 allow for, bear with, laugh off, overlook, reprieve, take back 9 exculpate, exonerate, extenuate
and forget: 6 make up, settle 9 reconcile 10 make amends, shake hands
don't ~ and forget: 6 avenge
...__ forgiven!: 5 all is
forgiveness: 5 grace, mercy 6 lenity, pardon 7 amnesty, quarter 8 clemency, immunity, reprieve 9 remission
ask ~: 5 atone 6 repent
__ forgive those...: 4 as we
forgiving: 3 lax 4 easy, kind, mild, soft 5 loose 6 gentle, kindly, tender 7 clement, lenient, patient, ruthful 8 flexible, laid-back, merciful, placable, tolerant 9 assuasive, brotherly, compliant, easygoing, indulgent 10 charitable, forbearing, permissive, unexacting
__ for Glory: 5 Bound
forgo: 4 cede, drop, dump, miss, quit, sell, shed, shun, skip 5 chuck, ditch, spare, waive, yield 6 abjure, eschew, give up, pass on, pass up, resist, sit out 7 abandon, abstain, forbear, forsake, refrain 8 abdicate, get rid of, hand over, jettison, keep from, leave out, part with, renounce, sign away, swear off, throw out 9 cast aside, dispose of, do without, sacrifice, surrender, throw away 10 desist from, relinquish
a right: 5 waive 6 give up 8 sign away 10 relinquish
__ for Godot: 7 Waiting
forgoing: 5 sober, staid
for good __: 7 measure
For goodness __!: 4 sake
For goodness sake!: 4 oh my
forgotten: 4 gone, lost, past 5 passé 6 buried, bygone, erased, lapsed 7 omitted 8 out of use 9 abandoned, blown over, repressed 10 blanked out, blotted out, left behind, suppressed, unrecalled
be ~: 4 pass 7 subside 8 blow over
something ~: 5 lapse 8 omission 9 oversight
Forgotten, The
author: Faye Kellerman
__ for granted: 4 take
__ for Gumshoe: 3 G Is
For heaven's __!: 4 sake
for here, not: 4 to go
__ for her eyes, with...: 3 E is
For He's a Jolly Good Fellow end: 4 deny
__: For Hire: 7 Spenser
__ for Hollywood: 6 Hooray
__ for Homicide: 3 H Is
__ for Innocent: 3 I Is
__ for it: 3 ask
__ for Judgment: 3 J Is
fork: 4 part, turn 5 split 6 bisect, branch, divide, ramble, recess 7 diverge, utensil 8 disburse, separate, shell out 9 bifurcate, branch off, implement, tableware, tributary 10 divergence, silverware
ender: 4 ball, lift
like a ~: 5 tined 7 pronged
over: 3 pay 4 cede, deal, give 5 relay, remit, spend, yield 6 expend, pay out, render 7 cough up, deliver 8 shell out 9 surrender 10 relinquish
part: 4 tine 5 prong
partner: 5 knife
shape: 3 vee, wye
site: 4 road 5 river
starter: 3 hay 5 pitch
use a ~: 3 eat, sup 4 chew, dine 5 feast 7 consume, partake
__ fork: 4 fish 5 salad 6 dinner, oyster, sucket, tuning 7 carving, dessert
forkball: 5 pitch
forked: 5 split, tined 6 cloven, zigzag 7 furcate, pronged 8 furcated 9 bifurcate, lightning
speak with ~ tongue: 3 fib, lie 4 dupe 5 bluff, fudge, guile 6 delude 7 deceive, falsify, mislead 8 misspeak 9 dissemble, misinform
__ for keeps: 4 play 7 playing
forkful: 4 bite
For Kicks
author: Dick Francis
__ for Killer: 3 K Is
forklift: 5 truck
forks: 4 ware 9 tableware 10 dinnerware, silverware
__ for Lawless: 3 L Is
__-for-leather: 4 hell
__ for Lefty: 7 Waiting
__ for Life: 4 Lust, Zest
for life in Latin: 7 ad vitam
__ for Living: 6 Design
forlorn: 3 low, sad 4 blue, down, mopy 5 alone, drear, gaunt, mopey 6 abject, bereft, dismal, dreary, gloomy, lonely, tragic 7 doleful, hangdog, in a funk, pitiful, unhappy, wistful 8 deprived, deserted, desolate, downcast, forsaken, helpless, homesick, hopeless, lonesome, pitiable, tragical, wretched 9 cheerless, depressed, desperate, heartsick, miserable, woebegone 10 despairing, despondent, lugubrious
feeling: 7 despair
forlorn __: 4 hope
__ for Love: 3 All 6 Hooray, Lookin'
For Love of __: 3 Ivy
For Love of the Game (1999 film)
cast: Kevin Costner, Kelly Preston, John C. Reilly
director: Sam Raimi
for love or __: 5 money
form: 3 bod, ilk 4 body, brew, cast, kind, make, mode, mold, rear, rite, sort, trim, type 5 blank, build, class, erect, forge, found, frame, model, order, setup, shape, stamp, state, style, teach, thing, torso, train, usage 6 appear, beetle, cook up, create, custom, design, devise, fettle, figure, health, invent, make up, manner, mature, medium, method, ritual, scheme, school, sketch, system 7 anatomy, arrange, bring up, compose, concoct, conduct, contour, decorum, develop, dream up, educate, fashion, fitness, liturgy, outline, pattern, process, produce, profile, shape up, turn out, variety 8 assemble, behavior, block out, ceremony, complete, comprise, conceive, contrive, document, figure in, generate, instruct, likeness, organize, physique, practice, protocol, symmetry 9 character, construct, establish, etiquette, framework, give shape, hammer out, lineament, originate, paperwork, placement, propriety, semblance, structure, take shape, tradition 10 appearance, bring about, constitute, convention, embodiment, observance, regulation, silhouette
a gully: 4 flow, gush 5 erode
a judgment: 3 fix 4 rule 6 choose, decide 7 appoint 8 finalize, sentence 9 determine, establish, negotiate
a notion: 5 think 6 ideate
assume the ~ of: 6 become 8 turn into
a union: 4 bond, join, yoke 5 marry, merge 7 combine, make one 9 integrate 10 tie the knot
bad ~: 8 improper, unseemly 9 graceless 10 indecorous, indelicacy, indelicate, out of order, unsuitable
combining form: 5 -morph

6 morpho-
derived ~: 7 variant
ending: 3 ula 5 ative
fill out a ~: 5 apply
good ~: 7 manners 8 protocol 9 propriety
in its original ~: 5 uncut 6 intact 8 complete 10 unabridged
pertaining to ~: 5 modal
qualification ~: 4 exam, test
return to ~: 5 rally 7 get well, rebound, recover 8 snap back 10 bounce back, convalesce, recuperate, spring back
starter: 3 ovi, uni
take ~: 4 jell 5 shape 8 incubate
vague ~: 4 blob, glob, lump, mass, spot 5 smear 6 smudge 7 splotch
without ~: 5 vague 8 nebulous 9 amorphous, shapeless 10 indefinite

FO

form __: 4 drag, nail, stop, word 5 class, genus 6 letter
__ form: 3 art 4 life, slip 5 bound, dance, entry 6 binary, racing, sonata, speech 7 clipped, derived, ternary
__-form: 4 free, wave
__ forma: 3 pro
formable: 7 ductile, plastic, pliable 9 malleable, shapeable
formal: 4 ball, gown, prim 5 aloof, dance, legal, staid, stiff 6 dressy, lordly, polite, proper, ritual, solemn, stodgy, strict, stuffy, tuxedo 7 bookish, correct, courtly, express, nominal, orderly, regular, stately, stilted 8 academic, affected, black-tie, decorous, explicit, highbred, ladylike, literary, official, reserved, starched 9 dignified, unbending 10 ceremonial, liturgical, methodical, prescribed, systematic
act: 4 rite 6 ritual 8 ceremony
address: 3 sir 4 ma'am 5 madam
affair: 4 ball, fete, meal, prom 5 feast, levee, party 6 repast, spread 7 banquet
agreement: 4 pact 6 accord, treaty 7 charter, compact, concord 8 contract, protocol 9 concordat 10 convention
attire: 3 tux 4 gown, tuck 5 tails 6 tuxedo 7 cutaway 8 black tie, white tie
ender: 4 wear
greeting: 3 bow 6 curtsy
opposite: 6 casual
overly ~: 4 prim 5 stiff
starter: 4 semi
wear of old: 4 toga
__ for Malice: 3 M Is
formalist: 4 prig 6 purist 7 fusspot, puritan 8 bluenose 9 nitpicker 10 fuddy-duddy
formalistic: 8 academic 9 pedagogic 10 scholastic
formalities: 6 ritual 7 decorum, red tape 8 ceremony, protocol 9 etiquette, politesse, propriety
formality: 4 pomp, rite 6 custom, ritual, starch 7 decorum, liturgy, p's and q's, reserve 8 ceremony, protocol 9 academism, austerity, etiquette, gentility, politesse, procedure, propriety, solemnity, tradition 10 classicism, convenance, convention, observance, solemnness, stereotype
formalize: 3 fix 4 name 5 shape 6 define, settle 7 specify 8 nail down, restrict, spell out 9 establish
formals: 6 finery 7 regalia 9 trappings
Forman, Milos: 8 director
film: Amadeus (1984, AA)
Man on the Moon (1999)
One Flew Over the Cuckoo's Nest (1975, AA)
Ragtime (1981)
Taking Off (1971)
__ for Man, so stealthily betrayed: 4 Alas
format: 4 look, plan 5 array, setup, shape 6 layout, makeup, scheme 7 arrange, pattern 8 organize 9 structure 10 appearance, dimensions
Formata: 4 font 8 typeface
formation: 6 design, layout, makeup 7 deposit, genesis 8 creation, grouping 9 evolution, synthesis 10 conception, embodiment, generation, production
combining form: 6 -plasty 7 -poiesis
__ formation: 4 back 6 flight
formative: 6 pliant 7 seminal 8 immature, moldable, original 9 inventive, malleable, sensitive
years: 5 teens, youth
__ for Me: 3 You 4 Good, Send
For Me and My Gal (1942 film)
cast: Judy Garland, Gene Kelly, George Murphy
director: Busby Berkeley
__-formed: 3 ill
former: 3 old 4 late, past 5 olden, older, prior 6 bygone, bypast, whilom 7 ancient, earlier, old-time, one-time, quondam 8 anterior, foregone, old-style, outgoing, previous 9 erstwhile, foregoing, preceding
combining form: 6 proter- 7 protero-
opposite: 6 latter
formerly: 3 ago, nee 4 erst, once, then 6 before 7 already, earlier, long ago 8 until now 9 at one time, in the past 10 beforetime, heretofore, originally, previously
form-fitting: 4 firm, snug, taut 5 rigid, stiff
formic acid producer: 3 ant
formicary: 4 nest
dweller: 3 ant 5 emmet 6 ergate
Formicidae member: 3 ant
formidability: 5 brawn, clout, might, power, punch, sinew, vigor 6 muscle 7 potency, prowess 8 strength, vitality 9 puissance 10 browniness
formidable: 4 dire, grim, hard, ugly 5 awful, great, heavy, rough, stiff, tough 6 fierce, knotty, mighty, potent, rugged, sticky, strong, thorny, trying, uphill 7 arduous, awesome, fearful, mammoth, onerous, serious 8 colossal, daunting, dreadful, grueling, horrible, horrific, imposing, menacing, powerful, shocking, terrible, terrific, toilsome 9 ambitious, appalling, dangerous, demanding, difficult, dismaying, effortful, frightful, herculean, laborious, strenuous 10 impressive, iron-willed, oppressive, petrifying, staggering, terrifying, tremendous
__-forming: 4 acid 5 habit
formless: 4 soft 9 amorphous, shapeless 10 unfinished
Formosa: 3 str. 4 isle 6 island, strait, Taiwan
island near ~: 4 Mazu 5 Matsu 6 Quemoy
__ for Mrs. Pollifax: 5 A Palm
formula: 3 law 4 milk, rule 5 usage 6 method, recipe 7 liturgy, precept, routine, theorem 8 equation 9 blueprint, principle, procedure 10 directions, stereotype
catcher: 3 bib
food ~: 6 recipe
formula __: 4 unit 6 weight
__ formula: 4 wing 5 Hero's 6 Euler's, Frenet 7 Kekulé's
Formula __: 3 One
Formula 409: 7 cleaner
alternative: 5 Brite, Lysol 6 Top Job 7 Lestoil, Mr. Clean, Pine Sol 9 Fantastik, Step Saver
Formula One car: 5 racer
formulate: 3 map, put 4 draw, make, plan 5 build, couch, draft, forge, frame, hatch, write 6 codify, cook up, create, define, derive, detail, devise, draw up, evolve, invent, make up, map out, phrase 7 compose, concoct, develop, dream up, prepare, set down, think up, work out 8 conceive, contrive, legalize, organize, tabulate, theorize 9 construct, establish, fabricate, originate
formulation: 3 ism 4 idea 6 belief, system, theory, thesis 7 concept, opinion, premise, surmise, theorem, thought 8 argument, creation, doctrine, position 9 postulate, rationale 10 assumption, conception, conjecture, hypothesis, philosophy, principium
__ for Murder: 5 Dial M
__ for My Baby: 3 One
__ for news: 4 nose
__ for Noose: 3 N Is
__-for-nothing: 4 good
For Once in My Life (1968 song)
artist: Stevie Wonder
__ for one...: 3 All
__ for One More: 4 Room
__ for oneself: 4 fend
__ for one's money: 4 a run
__ for One Year, A: 5 Widow
__ for Outlaw: 3 O Is
__ for Peace: 5 Atoms
__ for Peril: 3 P Is
For Pete's __!: 4 sake
For Pete's Sake (1974 film)
cast: Estelle Parsons, Michael Sarrazin, Barbra Streisand
director: Peter Yates
__-for-profit: 3 not
__ for Quarry: 3 Q Is
__ for Red October, The: 4 Hunt
Forrest: 4 Gump 5 Gregg, Steve 6 Nathan, Sawyer, Tucker 8 Frederic
Forrestal: 5 James
__ Forrester: 7 Finding
Forrest, Frederic: 5 actor
film: Hammett (1983)
The Rose (1979)
Forrest Gump (1994 film)
cast: Sally Field, Tom Hanks, Haley Joel Osment, Gary Sinise, Robin Wright
character: 3 Dan 5 Bubba, Jenny
director: Robert Zemeckis
locale: 3 Ala., Nam 7 Alabama, Vietnam
for richer, for __: 6 poorer
__ for Ricochet: 3 R Is
forsake: 4 cede, drop, dump, fail, jilt, quit, sell, shed 5 chuck, ditch, forgo, leave, spare, spurn, yield 6 abjure, betray, defect, desert, disown, forego, give up, maroon, reject, strand 7 abandon, cast off, disavow, discard, forfeit, scuttle 8 disclaim, forswear, get rid of, give up on, go back on, hand over, jettison, part with, renounce, run out on, swear off, throw out 9 cast aside, dispose of, foreswear, repudiate, surrender, throw away, throw over, walk out on 10 relinquish
forsaken: 4 left, lone, lorn 5 alone, stark 6 jilted, lonely 7 cast off, forlorn, given up, ignored, in a funk, outcast, run-down, spurned, unloved 8 derelict, deserted, desolate, disowned, helpless, isolated, marooned, solitary, untended 9 abandoned, renounced 10 repudiated
child: 4 waif
starter: 3 god
forsaker: 7 heretic, runaway, traitor 8 apostate, betrayer, defector, deserter, renegade, turncoat 10 iconoclast, schismatic
forsaking: 8 apostasy 9 defection, desertion, sundering
__ for Sale: 4 Love 6 Beauty, Heroes
for sale by __: 5 owner
__ for Scandal, The: 6 School
__-for-service: 3 fee
For shame!: 3 fie, tsk, tut 4 my my 6 tsk tsk
__ for Silence: 3 S Is
__ for size: 5 try on
forsooth: 9 yea verily
__ for sore eyes, a: 5 sight
__ for Space: 3 S Is
__ for St. Cecilia's Day: 3 Ode
Forster: 2 E.M. 6 Robert
Forster, E.M.: 6 writer 7 British
work: Howards End
A Passage to India
A Room With a View
__ for Strings: 6 Adagio
__ for Success: 5 Dress
...__ for Superman!: 4 a job
For sure!: 5 oh yes 6 you bet
forswear: 3 lie 4 cede, deny, drop, dump, jilt, sell, shed 5 chuck, ditch, forgo, leave, spurn, yield 6 abjure, desert, disown, eschew, forego, give up, maroon, pass up, recall, recant, reject 7 abandon, cast off, disavow, forfeit, forsake, perjure, retract 8 disclaim, get rid of, hand

over, jettison, part with, renounce, run out on, throw out, withdraw **9** cast aside, dispose of, repudiate, surrender, throw away, walk out on **10** relinquish
forswearing: 6 denial **8** apostasy **9** disavowal, rejection **10** refutation
forsworn: 5 false **6** untrue **7** unloyal **8** disloyal **9** deceitful, faithless, two-timing **10** unfaithful
Forsyte Saga, The
author: John Galsworthy
character: 3 Jon, Val **4** June, Mont **5** Belby, Boris, Fleur, Holly, Irene, James, Jolly **6** Dartie, Jolyon, Philip, Soames **7** Annette, Lamotte, Swithin, Timothy **8** Bosinney, Winifred
dog: 9 Balthasar
novel: In Chancery, To Let
Forsyth: 4 Bill **9** Frederick
Forsythe, John: 5 actor
TV: Bachelor Father, Charlie's Angels, Dynasty
forsythia: 5 plant, shrub **6** flower
relative: 5 lilac, olive **7** jasmine **9** jessamine
fort: 4 post **5** redan **6** castle, refuge **7** citadel, defense, rampart, redoubt **8** fastness, garrison, presidio **9** acropolis **10** stronghold
Alabama: 6 Rucker
Alaska: 10 Richardson
Arizona: 8 Huachuca
California: 3 Ord **5** Irwin
Colorado: 6 Carson
ditch: 4 moat
El Paso: 5 Bliss
ender: 5 night
Georgia: 6 Gordon **7** Benning **9** McPherson
gold ~: 4 Knox
hold the ~: 4 stay **6** defend, remain, uphold **7** carry on, stand by **8** maintain
Kansas: 5 Riley
Kentucky: 4 Knox **8** Campbell
Louisiana: 4 Polk
Maryland: 5 Meade **7** Detrick, McHenry
New Jersey: 3 Dix **8** Monmouth
New York: 4 Drum **8** Hamilton
Niagara: 4 Erie
North Carolina: 5 Bragg
Oklahoma: 4 Sill
opening: 4 gate
South Carolina: 7 Jackson
Texas: 5 Bliss **10** Sam Houston
Virginia: 3 Lee **6** Eustis, Monroe
Washington: 5 Lewis
Fort __: 3 Dix, Lee, Ord **4** Drum, Erie, Hood, Knox, Mims, Myer, Polk, Sill **5** Bliss, Boise, Bragg, Henry, Irwin, Lewis, Meade, Meigs, Riley **6** Apache, Carson, Casper, Devens, Eustis, Gordon, McNair, Monroe, Orange, Rucker, Sumter **7** Belvoir, Benning, Detrick, Jackson, Kearney, Laramie, McHenry, Pickens, Pulaski, Stewart
Fort __ Dam: 4 Peck
Fort __, FL: 5 Myers
Fort __ Houston: 3 Sam
Fort __, IN: 5 Wayne
Fort __, Ont.: 4 Erie
Fort Apache (1948 film): 5 oater
cast: John Agar, Ward Bond, Henry Fonda, Shirley Temple, John Wayne
director: John Ford
Fortas: 3 Abe
forte: 3 law
__ for tat: 3 tit
Fort Bliss site: 6 El Paso
Fort Bragg: 4 city, town
locale: 4 N. Car. **10** California
Fort Collins: 4 city, town
athletes: 4 Rams
locale: 3 Col. **8** Colorado
school: 3 CSU
Fort Courage group: 6 F Troop
Fort-de-France: 4 city, town
locale: 10 Martinique
Fort Dodge: 4 city, town
locale: 4 Iowa
forte: 3 job **4** gift, loud **5** flair, noisy, thing **6** loudly, métier, talent **7** blaring, booming, jarring, pealing, rackety, raucous, reboant, roaring **8** crashing, long suit, piercing, plangent, rumbling, sonorous, strength, strident, turned up **9** big-voiced, clamorous, deafening, expertise, specialty **10** boisterous, resounding, stentorian, strepitous, strong suit, thundering, uproarious, vociferous
opposite: 5 piano
__ forte: 5 mezzo
Fort Erie: 4 city, town
locale: 6 Canada **7** Ontario
forth: 3 out **4** away **5** ahead, along **6** onward **7** onwards, outward
ender: 4 with **5** right **6** coming
starter: 5 hence **6** thence
__ forth: 3 put, set **4** call, hold, send **5** and so, bring
for that __: 6 matter
forthcoming: 3 TBA **4** near, nigh **5** on tap **6** at hand, future **7** awaited, in store, pending **8** gracious, oncoming **9** proximate
for the __: 4 best **5** birds, nonce **6** asking **7** present
for the __ being: 4 time
for the __ of it: 3 fun **4** heck
for the __ of Pete: 4 love
for the __ part: 4 most
__ for the books: 3 one
For the Boys (1991 film)
cast: James Caan, Bette Midler, Patrick O'Neal, George Segal
director: Mark Rydell
grp.: 3 USO
__ for the buck: 4 bang
__ for the Common Man: 7 Fanfare
__ for the course: 3 par
for the fun __: 4 of it
for the heck __: 4 of it
__ for the Holidays: 4 Home
For the life __,...: 4 of me
For the Love of Money (1974 song)
artist: O'Jays
__ for the Memory: 6 Thanks
__ for the mill: 5 grist
__ for the million things...: 3 M is
__ for the Misbegotten: 5 A Moon
__ for the money: 4 in it
__ for the money...: 3 One
for the most __: 4 part
__ for the only one I see: 3 O is
__ for the poor: 4 alms
__ for the Prosecution: 7 Witness
__ for the ride: 5 along
__ for the road: 3 one
__ for the Road: 3 Two
__ for the Seesaw: 3 Two
__ for the show: 3 Two
__ for the Silver Lining: 4 Look
__ for the tears...: 3 T is
for the time __: 5 being
for the time being in Latin: 10 pro tempore
__ for the Tsar: 5 A Life
for this, literally: 5 ad hoc
__ for Three Oranges, The: 4 Love
forthright: 4 bold, open **5** bluff, blunt, frank, legit, plain, vocal **6** candid, direct, honest, infelt, square **7** factual, forward, natural, sincere, up-front, upright **8** credible, definite, directly, like it is, out-front, straight, truthful **9** outspoken, veracious **10** aboveboard, flat-footed, four-square, free-spoken, from the hip, on the level, scrupulous, unmediated, unreserved, unreticent
be ~: 4 aver, avow **6** affirm, assert **7** declare **8** proclaim, speak out **10** asseverate
not ~: 3 sly **4** foxy, wily **5** cagey, slick, snaky **6** covert, crafty, impish, secret, shifty, sneaky, tricky **7** crooked, cunning, devious, evasive, furtive, roguish **8** delusive, guileful, stealthy **9** conniving, deceitful, deceptive, designing, dishonest, insidious
forthrightly: 6 openly **8** directly **10** foursquare
forthwith: 3 now, PDQ **4** anon, ASAP, soon **5** apace, today **6** at once, presto **7** fleetly, hastily, quickly, rapidly, swiftly **8** directly, in a flash, in a jiffy, in no time, pell-mell, promptly, right now, right off, speedily **9** at present, hurriedly, instantly, like a shot, posthaste, presently, right away, summarily **10** at this time, here and now, this minute
fortification: 4 keep, wall **5** redan, tower **6** buffer, castle **7** barrier, bastion, buildup, bulwark, citadel, defense, outpost, rampart **8** garrison, palisade, presidio, stockade
slope: 5 talus
fortified: 5 armed **6** secure, sturdy
place: 7 bastion, bulwark, citadel, parapet, rampart **8** fortress **10** breastwork, stronghold
fortify: 3 arm, man **4** gird, lace, prop, tone **5** brace, build, rally, ready, renew, rouse, shore, steel **6** anneal, arouse, beef up, enrich, harden, prop up, step up, temper, tone up **7** bolster, brace up, build up, bulwark, burgeon, develop, empower, enhance, enliven, hearten, prepare, protect, punch up, refresh, restore, shore up, stiffen, support, sustain, toughen **8** bourgeon, buttress, embattle, embolden, energize, imbolden, indurate, vitalize **9** intensify, reinforce **10** invigorate, strengthen, supplement
fortifying: 4 cool **5** brisk, crisp, fresh **7** bracing, healthy, rousing **8** vigorous **10** energizing, refreshing
__ for time: 4 play
Fortín: 4 city, town
locale: 6 Mexico **8** Veracruz
__ for Tinhorns: 5 Fugue
fortis
opposite: 5 lenis
__ fortis: 4 aqua
fortitude: 3 vim **4** dint, grit, guts, thew **5** brawn, force, heart, might, moxie, nerve, pluck, power, spine, spunk, thews, valor, vigor **6** energy, mettle, muscle, spirit, starch, virtue **7** bravery, courage, fitness, heroism, muscles, potence, potency, prowess, stamina **8** backbone, boldness, decision, patience, strength, tenacity, true grit, valiance, valiancy, vitality **9** beefiness, braveness, composure, constancy, endurance, fixedness, gutsiness, hardihood, hardiness, huskiness, puissance, stoutness, tolerance, toughness **10** brawniness, brute force, confidence, mightiness, moral fiber, resolution, robustness, sturdiness
Fort Knox: 4 city, town **8** treasury
filler: 4 gold **6** ingots **7** bullion
locale: 3 Ken. **8** Kentucky
Fort Lauderdale: 4 city, town
locale: 3 Fla. **7** Florida
Fort Lee: 4 city, town
locale: 9 New Jersey
Fort Leonard __: 4 Wood
Fort Myers: 4 city, town
city near ~: 6 Naples
locale: 3 Fla. **7** Florida
fortnighter: 3 bag **7** luggage **8** suitcase
fortnight, half a: 4 week
fortnights, two: 5 month
__ for Tomorrow: 6 Search
__ for Tots: 4 Toys
Fort Peck __: 3 Dam
Fort Pierce: 4 city, town
locale: 3 Fla. **7** Florida
Fortran: 8 language
alternative; ***see*** computer language
developer: 3 IBM
__ for Trespass: 3 T Is
fortress: 4 aery, eyry, keep **5** aerie, eyrie, tower **6** castle, refuge **7** bastion, chateau, citadel, defense, redoubt **8** fastness, garrison, presidio **9** acropolis **10** stronghold
Crusades ~: 5 Haifa
defense: 4 moat
extension: 5 redan
mountain ~: 4 aery, eyry **5** aerie, eyrie
North African ~: 6 Casbah, Kasbah
__ Fortress: 6 Flying
Fortress Around Your Heart (1985 song)
artist: Sting
__ for trouble: 3 ask **6** asking
Fort Sill
locale: 4 Okla. **8** Oklahoma
Fort Smith: 4 city, town
locale: 3 Ark. **8** Arkansas
fortuitous: 3 odd **5** blest, fluke, fluky, lucky **6** chance, flukey, random

7 blessed, charmed, favored, oddball, on a roll 9 arbitrary, haphazard, on a streak, opportune, unplanned 10 accidental, auspicious, contingent, felicitous, incidental, unforeseen, unintended
fortuitously: 7 luckily 8 by chance
fortuity: 4 luck 5 event, fluke 6 chance, hazard 7 fortune 8 accident, long shot
fortunate: 4 good, well 5 blest, happy, lucky 6 chance, in luck 7 blessed, charmed, favored, helpful, hopeful, on a roll, wealthy, well-off 8 affluent, enviable, well-to-do 9 favorable, on a streak, opportune, promising 10 auspicious, convenient, fair-haired, felicitous, flying high, profitable, propitious, prosperous, successful, triumphant, victorious
fortune: 3 hap, lot, wad 4 fate, luck, mint, pile 5 karma, means 6 chance, cookie, estate, kismat, kismet, oracle, riches, wealth 7 destiny, portion, success 8 fortuity, gold mine, opulence, opulency, treasure 9 abundance, affluence 10 prosperity, providence
good ~: 4 luck 5 break, fluke 7 godsend, welfare 8 blessing, windfall 9 well-being 10 lucky break, prosperity
holder: 6 cookie
ill ~: 3 woe 5 trial 6 misery, mishap 7 bad luck, tragedy, travail, trouble 8 bad break, calamity, disaster, distress, hardship 9 adversity, hard times, mischance, tough luck 10 affliction, hard knocks
partner: 4 fame
sharer: 6 coheir
soldier of ~: 4 merc 9 mercenary 10 adventurer
fortune __: 6 cookie, hunter, teller
Fortune
rival: 6 Forbes 7 Barron's
Fortune 500 firm: 3 AOL, CVS, Dow, IBM, NCR, UPS 4 Nike 5 Aetna, Aflac, Alcoa, Apple, Avnet, Chubb, Cigna, Cisco, Exxon, FedEx, Heinz, Intel, Kmart, Kodak, Lilly, Loews, Lowe's, Merck, Qwest, Sears, Sysco, Tyson, Xerox 6 Abbott, Altria, Amazon, Boeing, Clorox, Costco, Disney, DuPont, Hilton, Hormel, Humana, Kroger, Lauder, Mattel, Nextel, Oracle, Pfizer, Sprint, Target, Unocal, Viacom 7 Aramark, Bank One, Best Buy, Borders, Cinergy, ConAgra, Corning, Gannett, Harrah's, Hershey, Kellogg, Keyspan, Lexmark, MetLife, PepsiCo, Rite Aid, Safeway, Sara Lee, Staples, Tenneco, Toys R Us, Verizon, Visteon, Walmart 8 Allstate, Auto Zone, Coca-Cola, Gillette, Goodrich, J.C. Penney, Marriott, Motorola, Navistar, Raytheon, Wachovia, Walgreen 9 BellSouth, Brunswick, Citigroup, Fannie Mae, Home Depot, Honeywell, McDonald's, Microsoft, Office Max, Starbucks, State Farm, Whirlpool 10 Albertson's, Freddie Mac, McGraw-Hill, Radio Shack, Wells Fargo
Fortune Cookie, The (1966 film)
cast: Jack Lemmon, Walter Matthau
director: Billy Wilder
fortuneless: 4 poor 5 broke 8 dirt poor, strapped 9 destitute, insolvent, penniless 10 stone-broke, straitened
fortune-teller: 4 seer 5 augur, sibyl 6 medium, oracle, reader 7 adviser, advisor, diviner, palmist, prophet, psychic
reading: 4 palm 5 tarot 6 I Ching 10 tarot cards
words: 4 I see
fortune-telling: 6 augury 8 prophecy 9 astrology, palmistry 10 prediction
Fort Wayne: 4 city, town
county: 5 Allen
locale: 3 Ind. 7 Indiana
__ for Two: 3 Tea 7 Trouble
Fort Worth: 4 city, town
county: 7 Tarrant
locale: 3 Tex. 5 Texas
river: 7 Trinity
school: 3 TCU
forty: 8 twoscore
one of the back ~: 4 acre
taking ~ winks: 6 asleep
winks: 3 nap 4 doze, rest 5 sleep 6 catnap, snooze 7 slumber
forty __: 5 winks
forty-__: 5 niner
__ forty: 4 back
forty-five: 3 gun 6 pistol 7 firearm 8 revolver
Forty Miles of Bad Road (1959 song)
artist: Duane Eddy
Forty Modern Fables
author: George Ade
forty-niner: 5 miner
quest: 4 gold 6 riches
stakeout: 4 mine 5 claim
Forty-Second Street
composer: Al Dubin, Harry Warren
Forty Thieves
foe: 3 Ali
forum: 4 talk 5 arena, court, organ 6 debate, powwow 8 assembly, colloquy, tribunal 9 symposium 10 conference
Forum: 5 arena
garb: 4 toga 5 tunic
language: 5 Latin
official: 5 edile 6 aedile 7 senator
site: 4 Rome
__ for Undertow: 3 U Is
__ for Us: 5 A Time
For want of __...: 5 a nail, a shoe
forward: 3 aid, out 4 abet, back, bold, gear, head, help, mail, pert, post, rude, send, ship 5 ahead, along, brash, early, first, fresh, front, hurry, nervy, pushy, relay, remit, route, sassy, saucy, speed, unshy 6 better, brassy, brazen, cheeky, convey, daring, foster, hasten, incite, onward, second, unruly, wilful 7 advance, athlete, consign, deliver, express, freight, further, in front, leading, nurture, promote, reroute, restive, support, willful 8 advanced, anterior, assuming, champion, dispatch, expedite, immodest, impudent, indocile, into view, transfer, transmit 9 advancing, assertive, audacious, barefaced, bumptious, encourage, in advance, intrusive, obtrusive, officious, pigheaded, premature, shameless, transport 10 accelerate, aggressive, forthright, precocious
bring ~: 3 lay 6 adduce 7 advance, produce
come ~: 5 offer 7 advance 8 progress 9 volunteer
drive ~: 5 impel
go ~: 4 gain, push 5 march 6 hasten, move on 7 achieve, advance, further, improve, press on, proceed, shape up 8 continue, escalate, get ahead, progress 10 accelerate, accomplish, forge ahead, gain ground, move onward, shoot ahead
jerk ~: 4 jump 5 heave, lunge, pitch
lean ~: 4 bend 5 stoop 7 bow down
look ~ to: 4 wait 5 await 6 expect 8 envision, see ahead, watch for
not ~: 3 coy, shy 4 meek 5 quiet, timid 6 demure, modest 7 bashful 8 backward, reserved, reticent, retiring, sheepish, skittish 9 diffident, shrinking, withdrawn 10 unassuming
push ~: 4 goad, move, prod, spur, urge 5 boost, drive, press, sally, shove, speed 6 attack, incite, induce, prompt, propel, stir up 7 actuate, inspire 8 motivate 9 influence, instigate, stimulate 10 accelerate
put ~: 3 lay 4 move, pose 5 offer, raise 6 assert, submit, turn in 7 advance, declare, present, produce, propose, suggest, support 8 propound 9 introduce, postulate, recommend, volunteer
rush ~: 5 lunge, lurch, pitch, surge 6 charge
starter: 5 hence 6 thence 8 straight
urge ~: 4 goad, move, poke, prod, push, spur 5 drive, press, shove 6 compel, incite, induce, prompt, propel, thrust, turn on 7 inspire, quicken 8 mobilize, motivate, persuade, pressure, railroad 9 instigate
forward __: 4 dive, pass 7 echelon
__ forward: 3 put, set 4 come, fast 5 bring, carry, power 6 center, inside 7 outside
__-forward: 5 flash
__ Forward: 5 Pay It 6 Spring
__ forwarding: 4 call
forward-looking dept.: 5 R and D
forwardness: 5 brass, cheek, nerve 6 hutzpa 7 chutzpa, hutzpah, license 8 audacity, boldness, chutzpah, temerity 9 brashness, impudence, insolence 10 effrontery
forward pass in football: 6 aerial
__ forward to: 4 look
For what __ worth...: 3 it's
For Whom the Bell Tolls: 4 film 5 novel
author: Ernest Hemingway
cast: Ingrid Bergman, Gary Cooper, Katina Paxinou, Akim Tamiroff
character: 4 Golz 5 André, Maria, Marty, Pablo, Pilar 6 Andrés, Eladio, Karkov, Rafael 7 Anselmo
director: Sam Wood
setting: 5 Spain
for whose benefit in Latin: 7 cui bono
__ for you!: 4 Good
__ for You: 3 All 4 Just 5 Crazy, I'd Lie, I Do It, I Feel
For You (1964 song)
artist: Ricky Nelson
For You I Will (1997 song)
artist: Monica
For Your Eyes Only: 4 film, song 5 novel
artist: Sheena Easton
author: Ian Fleming
cast: Roger Moore, Topol
director: John Glen
__ for Your Life: 3 Run
For Your Love (song)
artist: Peaches and Herb, Yardbirds
__ for your thoughts: 5 penny
__ for Zero: 3 Z Is
Fosbury, Dick: 10 high jumper
foss: 4 moat
Foss: 5 Lukas
fossa: 3 cat, pit 6 feline
fosse: 4 dike, moat 6 trench 7 foxhole
Fosse, Bob: 8 director
film: All That Jazz (1979) Cabaret (1972, AA) Lenny (1974) Sweet Charity (1969)
forte: 5 dance
spouse: Gwen Verdon
Fossey, Dian subject: 3 ape 7 gorilla
fossil: 3 old 5 amber, copal, relic 7 crinite 8 ammonite, calamite, obsolete 9 belemnite, coprolite, encrinite, nummulite, protoavis, stone lily, trilobite 10 fuddy-duddy, graptolite
combining form: 3 -ite 4 -lite, -lyte 5 oryct- 6 orycto-
Ethiopian ~ site: 5 Hadar
fuel: 3 gas, oil 4 coal
impression: 4 fern
repository: 3 bog, tar 5 amber, copal, resin 6 tar pit
fossil __: 3 gum 4 fuel
Fossil: 5 watch
alternative: *see* wristwatch
fossilize: 3 age 6 ossify 7 petrify 8 indurate
fossil tracks, science of: 9 ichnology
Foss, Lukas: 9 conductor
foster: 4 abet, back, feed, keep, rear, tend 5 boost, breed, nurse, raise, spark 6 arouse, defend, enroot, foment 7 advance, develop, forward, further, nourish, nurture, promote, protect, shelter, sponsor, support, sustain 8 champion, min-

ister **9** cultivate, encourage, patronize **10** speak up for, take care of
child: 4 ward **7** adoptee
foster __: 3 son **4** care, home **5** child **6** father, mother, parent, sister **7** brother
Foster: 3 Hal, Meg **4** Phil, Rube **5** Jodie **6** Brooks, Norman **7** Preston, Stephen
fosterage: 8 adoption, espousal **10** acceptance
__ Foster Dulles: 4 John
Foster Grants: 6 shades **10** sunglasses
Foster, Jodie: 7 actress
alma mater: 4 Yale
film: The Accused (1988, AA)
Anna and the King (1999)
Backtrack (1989)
The Brave One (2007)
Carny (1980)
Contact (1997)
Five Corners (1988)
Flightplan (2005)
Freaky Friday (1977)
The Hotel New Hampshire (1984)
Inside Man (2006)
Little Man Tate (1991)
Maverick (1994)
Nell (1994)
Panic Room (2002)
The Silence of the Lambs (1991, AA)
Sommersby (1993)
Stealing Home (1988)
Taxi Driver (1976)
Foster, Stephen: 8 composer
song: Beautiful Dreamer
De Camptown Races
Jeanie With the Light Brown Hair
Oh! Susanna
Old Black Joe
Old Dog Tray
Old Folks at Home
Uncle Ned
Foucault's Pendulum
author: Umberto Eco
foul: 3 ill **4** base, blue, evil, grim, lewd, poor, rank, soil, ugly, vile **5** awful, dirty, error, false, fetid, grimy, gross, lousy, nasty, shady, smear, stain, sully, taint, woful **6** breach, clog up, coarse, crud up, crumby, crummy, defile, dismal, filthy, foetid, grungy, horrid, impure, no fair, odious, rancid, rotten, smelly, smudge, smutty, sordid, stinky, stormy, tangle, unfair, unjust, vulgar, wicked, woeful **7** abusive, accurst, baleful, baneful, beastly, begrime, besmear, blacken, corrupt, crooked, doleful, ghastly, hateful, heinous, low blow, noisome, noxious, odorous, offense, pollute, profane, reeking, squalid, sullied, tainted, tarnish, unclean, unswept, vicious **8** accursed, besmirch, dreadful, God-awful, grievous, horrible, indecent, infamous, inferior, mephitic, polluted, shameful, stagnant, stinking, terrible, unsavory, unwashed, wretched **9** abhorrent, appalling, atrocious, defective, dishonest, egregious, execrable, frightful, inclement, insidious, loathsome, low-minded, miserable, monstrous, nefarious, notorious, offensive, repellent, repugnant, repulsive, revolting, violation **10** abominable, despicable, detestable, disastrous, disgusting, horrendous, indelicate, infraction, iniquitous, insanitary, maleficent, malodorous, scandalous, undeserved, unpleasant, villainous
caller: 3 ref, ump **6** umpire **7** referee
language: 4 oath **5** curse **7** cursing, cussing **8** cussword, swearing **9** obscenity, profanity, swearword **10** execration, expletives
mood: 4 snit
not ~: 4 fair, just **6** proper **7** ethical **8** rightful **9** honorable **10** acceptable
odor: 4 reek **5** smell, stink **6** stench **9** effluvium
play: 4 harm **5** wrong **6** dupery, murder **8** inequity, violence
ring ~: 4 butt, knee
spot: 3 sty **5** hovel, sewer **6** pigpen, pigsty **8** pesthole
up: 3 err, mar **4** flub, goof, muff, ruin **5** botch, cross, misdo **6** blight, blow it, boggle, bollix, bungle, derail, foozle, injure, jumble, muddle **7** blunder, confuse, disturb **8** confound, obstruct **9** mishandle, mismanage **10** complicate, disconcert
(up): 3 mix **4** mess, trip
foul __: 3 tip **4** ball, line, play, pole, shot **6** matter
foulard: 3 tie **5** ascot **6** cravat, fabric **7** necktie **8** neckwear **10** four-in-hand
fouled: 5 dirty, grimy, sooty **6** filthy, grubby, grungy, soiled **8** maculate, slovenly **10** unsanitary
foulmouthed: 4 lewd **5** dirty **6** filthy, ribald, smutty, vulgar **7** obscene, profane **8** indecent **10** scurrilous
foulness: 4 evil **5** stink **9** indecency, pollution **10** corruption
Foul Play (1978 film)
cast: Chevy Chase, Goldie Hawn, Burgess Meredith, Dudley Moore
dog: 7 Chaucer
foul-smelling: 4 olid, rank **5** acrid, fetid **6** foetid
foul-up: 4 goof, slip **5** boner, snafu **6** muddle **9** mare's nest
found: 4 base, form **5** begin, build, endow, erect, plant, set up, start **6** create, launch **7** pioneer, start up, support **8** commence, generate, get going, initiate, organize **9** establish, institute, originate **10** constitute, inaugurate
a perch: 3 lit, sat **4** alit
as ~: 6 in situ
at this place: 6 herein
be ~: 5 occur **6** appear, crop up, show up, turn up **9** take place
by chance: 5 lit on
nowhere to be ~: 4 away, AWOL, gone, lost **6** absent **7** far away, missing **8** vanished
opposite: 4 lost
starter: 4 dumb
found __: 3 art **4** poem **5** money **6** object
foundation: 3 bed **4** ABCs, base, core, foot, root, seat **5** basis, cause, start, stays **6** bottom, corset, ground, makeup, museum, origin **7** academy, bedrock, charity, footing, grounds, support **8** backbone, creation, foothold, occasion, training, validity **9** authority, criterion, endowment, framework, institute, principle, underside **10** brass tacks, derivation, groundwork, hypothesis, settlement, substratum
exec: 3 dir. **4** pres. **8** director **9** president
firm ~: 4 rock
garment: 5 stays **6** corset, girdle
lay the ~: 5 begin, set up, start **6** launch **7** develop, kick off, prepare **8** commence **9** establish, institute, introduce, originate **10** inaugurate
material: 6 cement **8** concrete
support a ~: 6 bestow, donate **10** contribute
without ~: 8 baseless **10** groundless
Foundation
author: Isaac Asimov
__ Foundation: 4 Ford **6** Hillel
foundational: 7 radical
founded: 3 est. **4** estd. **5** estab.
__-founded: 3 ill **4** well
founder: 4 bomb, bust, fail, fall, flop, lose, sink, slip, trip **5** flunk, wreck **6** blow it, falter, father, fizzle, go down **7** blunder, creator, go under, go wrong, misstep, pioneer, stagger, stumble, succumb, wash out **8** collapse, designer, fall flat, flounder, lay an egg, submerge **9** architect, break down, hit bottom, initiator, organizer, strike out **10** benefactor, originator
foundered: 7 aground **8** marooned, stranded **10** high and dry
founders' __: 4 type **6** shares
Founders __: 3 Day
Founding __: 7 Fathers
foundling: 4 waif, ward **5** stray **6** orphan **10** ragamuffin
foundry: 4 mill **5** forge, plant **6** office **7** factory **9** ironworks
do ~ work: 6 anneal
form: 4 mold
material: 5 metal, steel
refuse: 4 slag
sound: 5 clang
fount: 4 fund, mine, well **5** store **6** origin **7** bubbler **10** wellspring
fountain: 3 jet **4** mine, well **5** spirt, spout, spurt, store **6** geyser, origin, source, spring, stream **8** wellhead **9** reservoir **10** wellspring
coin count: 5 three
coin in a ~: 4 cent, euro, lira
ender: 4 head
fare: 4 Coke, cola, cone, malt, soda **5** Pepsi, shake **6** frappe
freebie: 5 straw
New England soda ~: 3 spa
Rome ~: 5 Trevi
sound: 6 gurgle
fountain __: 3 pen **5** grass, plant
__ fountain: 3 ink **4** soda **5** Trevi, water
fountainhead: 4 germ, well **5** birth, maker **6** father, mother, origin, source, spring **7** builder, creator **10** wellspring
Fountainhead, The: 4 film **5** novel
author: Ayn Rand
cast: Gary Cooper, Raymond Massey, Patricia Neal
character: 5 Roark **6** Toohey, Wynand
director: King Vidor
Fountain of Age, The
author: Betty Friedan
Fountain of Youth site: 6 Bimini
Fountain Overflows, The
author: Rebecca West
Fountain, Pete: 11 clarinetist
genre: 4 jazz **9** Dixieland
Fountains of Paradise, The
author: Arthur C. Clarke
four: 7 quartet
a.m.: 7 wee hour
combining form: 4 tetr- **5** quadr-, tetra- **6** quadri-, quadru-, quater-, tessar- **7** tessara-, tessera-
divide into ~: 7 quarter
ender: 4 some, teen **5** score
in French: 6 quatre
in German: 4 vier
in Italian: 7 quattro
in Japanese: 3 shi
in Portuguese: 6 quatro
in Spanish: 6 quatro
often: 3 par
three or ~: 4 a few, some **7** several
to Mohs: 8 fluorite
four __: 4 bits, o'cat
four __ cat: 3 old
four __ kind: 3 of a
four-__: 3 way **4** a-cat, spot, star **5** color, cycle **6** bagger, banger, handed, legged, stroke **7** channel, flusher, striper
four-__ bed: 6 poster
four-__ clover: 4 leaf
four-__ fire: 5 alarm
four-__-floor: 5 on-the
four-__ harmony: 4 part
four-__ highway: 4 lane
four-__ word: 6 letter
__ four: 5 front, petit
__-four: 3 ten **5** two-by
Four __: 4 Aces, Lads, Sons, Tops **5** Preps, Walls **7** Corners, Friends, Seasons
Four __ in a Jeep: 5 Jills
Four __ in Three Acts: 6 Saints
__ Four: 3 Fab **5** Final
Four Apostles
painter: Altrecht Dürer
four-bagger: 5 homer **7** home run
Four Christmases (2008 film)
cast: Robert Duvall, Sissy Spacek, Vince Vaughn, Reese Witherspoon
Four Corners state: 4 Utah **7** Arizona **8** Colorado **9** New Mexico
__-four-dollar question: 5 sixty
four-door: 3 car **4** auto **5** sedan **10** automobile
alternative: 5 coupé

Four Feathers, The
author: A.E.W. Mason
four-flush: 5 bluff 6 take in 9 disinform, dissemble
fourflusher: 4 fake, sham 5 faker, fraud, knave, quack, rogue 6 rascal 7 bluffer, cheater 8 deceiver, imposter, impostor, swindler 9 pretender
four-footed: 9 quadruped
specialist: 3 DVM, vet
__-four-forty or Fight: 5 Fifty
fourgon: 3 van 5 wagon 7 tumbril
Four-H __: 4 Club
Four Horsemen, one of the: 3 War 5 Death 6 Famine 10 Pestilence
Four-H part: 4 head 5 hands, heart 6 health
Four Hundred Blows, The (1959 film)
director: François Truffaut
Fourier, Jean: 9 physicist
four-in-hand: 3 tie 5 ascot 6 cravat 7 foulard, necktie 8 neckwear
Four Jills in __: 5 a Jeep
Four Lads
song: Moments to Remember (1955)
No, Not Much! (1956)
Put a Light in the Window (1957)
Standing on the Corner (1956)
There's Only One of You (1958)
Who Needs You (1957)
four-leaf clover purpose: 4 luck
four-letter
use ~ words: 4 cuss 5 swear 9 blaspheme
word: 4 cuss, oath 5 curse 9 expletive, profanity
words: 7 cursing, cussing 8 swearing 9 blasphemy, profanity
word substitute: 5 bleep
four-letter __: 4 word
four-minute __: 4 mile
four of __: 5 a kind
four-on-the-__: 5 floor
four-page sheet: 5 folio
four-part __: 7 harmony
fourpence: 5 groat
fourpenny __: 4 nail
four-petaled flower in heraldry: 10 quatrefoil
fourposter: 3 bed
topping: 6 canopy
Four Quartets: 4 poem
author: T.S. Eliot
fours
go on all ~: 5 crawl, creep, slink 7 clamber, slither, wriggle
not on all ~: 5 erect 7 upright 8 standing, straight, vertical
plus ~: 5 pants 8 breeches, knickers, trousers
__ fours: 3 all 4 plus 5 on all
Four Saints in Three Acts
composer: Virgil Thomson
librettist: Gertrude Stein
fourscore: 6 eighty
Fourscore and seven years __: 3 ago
Four Seasons: 5 hotel
alternative: *see* hotel
leader: Frankie Valli
song: Big Girls Don't Cry (1962)
Bye, Bye, Baby (1965)
Candy Girl (1963)
C'mon Marianne (1967)
Dawn (1964)
December 1963 (1976)
I've Got You Under My Skin (1966)
Let's Hang On (1965)
Rag Doll (1964)
Ronnie (1964)
Save It for Me (1964)
Sherry (1962)
Stay (1964)
Tell It to the Rain (1966)
Walk Like a Man (1963)
Who Loves You (1975)
Working My Way Back to You (1966)
Four Seasons, The
composer: Antonio Vivaldi
Four Seasons, The (1981 film)
cast: Alan Alda, Carol Burnett, Len Cariou, Sandy Dennis, Rita Moreno, Jack Weston
director: Alan Alda
__-four seven: 6 twenty
four-sharp key: 6 E major
four-sided figure: 4 rect. 6 square 7 rhombus 9 rectangle, trapezoid
foursome: 4 team 6 tetrad 7 quartet
member: 6 golfer
foursquare: 4 firm 5 frank 6 candid, direct 8 resolute, resolved 9 outspoken, steadfast 10 forthright, from the hip, unwavering, unyielding
four-star
review: 4 rave
see also wonderful
four-striper: 7 captain, officer, skipper 9 commander
Four Strong Winds (1964 song)
artist: Bobby Bare
__ Fourteen Points: 7 Wilson's
fourth: 4 part 7 portion, quarter 8 fraction
combining form: 5 quart- 6 tetart- 7 tetarto-
in a series: 5 delta
man: 4 Seth
person: 4 Abel
fourth __: 4 gear, wall 6 estate
fourth-__: 4 rate 5 class
Fourth Deadly Sin, The
author: Lawrence Sanders
fourth-down option: 4 kick, pass, punt
Fourth Hand, The
author: John Irving
fourth hitter in baseball: 7 clean-up
Fourth of July: 4 date 7 holiday
item: 4 flag, punk 8 sparkler
sound: 4 bang
fourth-quarter follower: 2 OT 8 overtime
fourth-rate: 4 poor 5 lousy 6 cheesy, crumby, crummy 8 inferior, lowgrade
Four Tops
leader: Levi Stubbs
song: Ain't No Woman (1973)
Baby I Need Your Loving (1964)
Bernadette (1967)
I Can't Help Myself (1965)
It's the Same Old Song (1965)
Keeper of the Castle (1972)
Reach Out I'll Be There (1966)
Standing in the Shadows of Love (1966)
Four Weddings and a Funeral (1994 film)
cast: Hugh Grant, Andie MacDowell, Kristin Scott Thomas
director: Mike Newell
four-wheel __: 5 drive
four-wheeler: 6 go-cart, go-kart
Four Zoas, The
author: William Blake
Fouts, Dan: 2 QB
sport: 8 football
fowl: 3 hen 4 bird, duck, game, meat, nene, smew, swan, teal 5 biddy, birds, brant, capon, drake, ducks, eider, geese, goose, Pekin, poult, quail, Rouen, scaup, skein, snipe 6 bantam, Brahma, Cayuga, chukar, grouse, Houdan, peahen, pullet, scoter, Sussex, turkey 7 chicken, Cornish, Dorking, gadwall, graylag, Leghorn, mallard, peacock, pintail, pochard, poultry, redhead, rooster, sea duck, widgeon 8 Araucana, curassow, garganey, gray duck, Langshan, mandarin, musk duck, oldsquaw, pheasant, Shanghai, shoveler, surf duck, woodcock, wood duck 9 black duck, broadbill, Dominique, goldeneye, goosander, greenhead, merganser, Orpington, partridge, ruddy duck, snow goose, sprigtail, Wyandotte 10 bufflehead, canvasback, surf scoter, tufted duck, wild turkey
abode: 4 coop, nest 5 roost
fill a ~: 5 stuff
place: 5 roost
sound: 5 cluck 6 cackle
starter: 3 bat, pea, sea 4 moor, wild 5 water
fowler: 6 hunter
Fowler: 3 Jim 6 Robert 7 William
Fowles, John: 6 writer 7 British
work: The Aristos
The Collector
The Ebony Tower
The French Lieutenant's Woman
The Magus
Mantissa
fox: 3 fur, top 4 asse 5 canid, grape, ready, trick 6 animal, canine, corsac, fennec, mammal, outwit 7 deceive 8 outflank, outsmart
African ~: 4 asse 6 fennec
baby ~: 3 kit
ender: 4 fire, hole, tail, trot 5 glove, hound
female ~: 5 vixen
flying ~: 6 kalong
home: 3 den 4 lair 6 burrow
hunter coat: 5 pinks
hunter cry: 4 hark 5 hallo, hillo, hullo 6 halloa, halloo, hallow, hilloa, hulloo, yoicks
like a ~: 3 sly 4 wily 5 cagey 6 crafty, shrewd 7 cunning 8 guileful
like the ~ hunting set: 5 horsy 6 horsey
male: 3 dog
prey: 3 hen 7 chicken
relative: *see* canine
scent: 5 spoor
sound: 4 bark
sour fruit: 5 grape
tail: 5 brush
young: 3 cub, kit, pup
fox __: 4 bolt, trot 5 brush, grape, snake 6 hunter 7 hunting, sparrow, terrier
__ fox: 3 dog, kit, red, sea 4 blue, Cape, gray, grey 5 black, cross, white 6 Arctic, flying, silver
Fox: 3 car, net 4 auto 5 James, Jorja, Megan, tribe 6 Edward, George, Indian, Mulder, Nellie, Nelson, studio 7 Amerind, Matthew, network 8 Fontaine, language, Samantha 10 automobile, Volkswagen
comedy series: 5 MAD TV
creation: 4 film 5 movie
documentary: 4 Cops
rival: 3 ABC, CBS, MGM, NBC, PBS 5 The CW 6 Disney 7 Miramax, New Line 8 Columbia 9 Paramount, Universal 10 DreamWorks, Warner Bros.
sitcom: 3 Roc
__ Fox: 4 Br'er 6 Little
Fox and the Grapes, The
source: 4 Esop 5 Aesop
Fox and the Hound, The (1981 film)
director: Richard Rich
Foxes of Harrow, The
author: Frank Yerby
__ Foxes, The: 6 Little
Foxfire
author: Joyce Carol Oates, Anya Seton
foxglove: 5 plant 6 flower 7 blossom
Foxglove Saga, The
author: Auberon Waugh
foxhole: 3 pit 4 foss 5 ditch, fosse 6 dugout, trench 9 earthwork 10 depression, excavation
deepen a ~: 5 redig
entrée: 4 Spam
Foxhound: 3 dog 5 canid 6 canine
foxiness: 5 craft, wiles 8 keenness
Fox in Socks
author: Dr. Seuss
Fox, Michael J.: 5 actor
film: Back to the Future (1985)
Back to the Future Part II (1989)
Back to the Future Part III (1990)
Bright Lights, Big City (1988)
Doc Hollywood (1991)
Life With Mikey (1993)
The Secret of My Success (1987)
Stuart Little (1999)
Teen Wolf (1985)
film (voice): Atlantis: The Lost Empire (2001)
spouse: Tracy Pollan
TV: Family Ties, Spin City
foxtail: 5 grass, plant 6 flower
fox terrier: 3 dog 5 canid 6 canine
__ Fox, The: 6 Desert
fox trot: 5 dance
Foxwoods: 6 casino
Foxworth: 6 Robert
Foxworthy: 4 Jeff
Foxx: 4 Inez, Redd 5 Jamie 6 Jimmie
Foxx, Jamie: 5 actor
film: Ali (2001)
Collateral (2003)
Dreamgirls (2006)
Ray (2004, AA)
The Soloist (2009)

foxy: **3** sly **4** arch, sexy, wily **5** brown, canny, sharp, slick **6** adroit, artful, astute, clever, crafty, pretty, shifty, shrewd, tricky **7** cunning, devious, furtive, knavish, reddish, vulpine **8** alluring, guileful, scheming, slippery **9** astucious, conniving, deceitful, deceptive, glamorous, insidious, sagacious, yellowish
in a ~ fashion: **5** slyly
relative: ***see*** brown color
Foxy __: **4** Loxy **5** Brown
Foxy Brown (1974 film)
cast: Pam Grier
Foy: **5** Eddie
foyer: **4** hall **5** lobby **7** ingress **8** anteroom, corridor **9** concourse, vestibule
spread: **3** rug **6** carpet
__ Foyle: **5** Kitty
__-Foy, Que.: **3** Ste.
Foyt, A.J.: **5** racer **9** auto racer
contemporary: **5** Unser
milieu: **5** track
Fozzie: **4** bear **6** Muppet
friend: **6** Kermit
Fr: **4** elem. **7** element **8** francium
87 for ~: **4** at. no.
Fr.
see France
Fra: **4** monk **5** title **8** Angelico **9** religious
Fra __ Lippi: **5** Lippo
frabjous
see wonderful
fracas: **3** ado, row **4** feud, flap, fray, riot, tilt, to-do **5** brawl, brush, clash, fight, melee, mix-up, noise, run-in, scrap, set-to **6** affray, battle, mayhem, racket, rumpus, shindy, tumult, tussle, uproar **7** dispute, quarrel, rhubarb, ruction, scuffle, wrangle **8** brouhaha, conflict, disorder, skirmish, squabble **9** bickering, confusion, scrimmage **10** donnybrook, free-for-all
fraction: **2** pt. **3** bit, cut **4** bite, half, part, unit **5** chunk, fifth, ninth, piece, ratio, share, sixth, slice, tenth, third **6** eighth, fourth, morsel, trifle **7** modicum, one-half, portion, quarter, section, segment, seventh **8** division, fragment, one-fifth, one-ninth, one-sixth, one-tenth, one-third **9** one-eighth, one-fourth, two-fifths, two-ninths, two-thirds **10** five-ninths, five-sixths, four-fifths, four-ninths, nine-tenths, one-quarter, one-seventh, proportion
term: **3** LCD
fractional: **5** light **7** divided, partial **9** dispersed, piecemeal, sectional, segmented **10** incomplete
prefix: **4** demi-, hemi-, nano-, semi- **5** centi-, milli-
fractious: **4** mean **5** cross, huffy, surly, testy **6** crabby, ornery, snappy, touchy, unruly, wilful **7** fretful, grouchy, naughty, peevish, waspish, willful **8** captious, fretsome, perverse, petulant, snappish, stubborn **9** crotchety, difficult, insurgent, irascible, irritable, querulous, splenetic **10** disorderly, intolerant, out of sorts, refractory, unamenable
fracture: **3** gap **4** bust, rend, rent, rift, rive, snap **5** break, burst, cleft, crack, crash, laugh, smash, split **6** breach, injury, regale, schism, sunder **7** fissure, rupture, shatter **8** cleavage, splinter
detector: **4** X-ray
glacier ~: **4** gulf, rift **5** chasm **7** crevice
treat a ~: **3** set
Fracture (2007 film)
cast: Ryan Gosling, Anthony Hopkins
fractured: **4** torn **6** broken **7** cracked
Fra Diavolo
composer: Daniel Auber
__ Fra Diavolo: **7** lobster
Fraggle Rock
dog: **8** Sprocket
fragile: **4** fine, puny, slim, thin, weak **5** frail, sheer, wimpy **6** anemic, atonic, dainty, effete, feeble, flabby, flimsy, slight, tender **7** anaemic, brittle, crumbly, friable, rickety, slender, unsound, wimpish **8** decrepit, delicate, helpless, pithless **9** breakable, faltering, frangible, powerless **10** nondurable, vulnerable
fragility: **6** anemia **7** anaemia, fatigue, frailty **8** debility, delicacy, puniness, weakness **9** frailness, infirmity **10** feebleness, flimsiness, unwellness
fragment: **3** bit **4** bite, chip, clip, iota, part, snip, whit, wisp **5** break, burst, chunk, crash, crumb, piece, relic, scrap, shard, share, sherd, shred, slice, smash, split, trace **6** gobbet, morsel, sample, shiver, sliver, snatch **7** crumble, excerpt, flinder, granule, modicum, oddment, portion, remnant, section, shatter, split up **8** clipping, disunify, disunite, fraction, landmark, molecule, particle, splinter **9** come apart **10** come undone
fragmentary: **3** odd **5** light **7** oddball, partial **9** piecemeal
fragmentation: **4** rent, rift **5** break, cleft, crack, split **6** schism **7** discord **8** cleavage, disunion, division, fracture **9** dichotomy **10** divergence
Fragments
author: Edward Albee
Fragonard: **4** Jean
fragrance: **4** atar, balm, nose, odor, otto **5** aroma, athar, attar, ottar, scent, smell, spice **7** bouquet, cologne, perfume **9** redolence
hint of ~: **5** whiff
without ~: **8** odorless **9** unscented
YSL ~: **5** Opium
fragrant: **5** balmy, olent, spicy, sweet **6** savory, spicey **7** odorous, perfumy **8** aromatic, perfumed, redolent **9** ambrosial, delicious **10** delectable
compound: **5** ester
flower: **4** lily, pink, rose **5** lilac, phlox, stock **7** jasmine, tea rose **8** dianthus, gardenia, hyacinth, lavender, magnolia, moss rose, tuberose **9** carnation, jessamine, narcissus **10** damask rose, Easter lily, frangipani, heliotrope, mock orange, wallflower
hardly ~: **4** olid
herb: **4** mint
make ~: **5** cense
oil: **4** atar, otto **5** athar, attar, ottar
ointment: **4** nard
plant: **5** thyme
resin: **4** tolu **5** elemi **6** balsam
root: **5** orris
shrub of Asia: **4** gumi
tree: **3** fir **4** pine **5** aloes, cedar **6** storax
vine of Hawaii: **5** maile
__ fraîche: **5** crème
fraidy-cat: **4** wimp **5** sissy **6** coward, craven **7** chicken, cowards, dastard, quitter, wimpish **8** poltroon, recreant **9** jellyfish
frail: **4** puny, sick, weak **5** reedy, wimpy **6** anemic, atonic, dainty, effete, feeble, flabby, flimsy, infirm, mortal, slight, tender **7** anaemic, brittle, fragile, invalid, rickety, tenuous, unsound, wimpish **8** delicate, helpless, pithless **9** breakable, faltering, frangible, powerless, unhealthy **10** vulnerable
not ~: **3** fit **4** hale **5** hardy, sound, stout, tough **6** brawny, robust, rugged, sinewy, strong, sturdy, virile **7** healthy **8** athletic, muscular, thriving, vigorous **9** strapping **10** able-bodied
something ~: **4** wisp
frailty: **4** vice **5** lapse **6** anemia, foible **7** anaemia, fatigue **8** debility, delicacy, puniness, weakness **9** fragility, infirmity **10** feebleness, flimsiness, insecurity
fraise: **5** scarf **10** strawberry
Frakes, Jonathan: **5** actor
spouse: Genie Francis
Fra Lippo Lippi: **4** poem
author: Robert Browning
Fram
rival: **3** STP
frame: **3** fix, map, mat, rim **4** body, cage, case, edge, form, make, mold, plan, plot, rack, tidy, trim **5** build, couch, draft, erect, forge, hatch, model, mount, pin on, set up, shape, shell, stage, stand **6** border, bum rap, casing, cook up, design, devise, draw up, encase, figure, fringe, incase, indite, invent, make up, map out, phrase, timber **7** anatomy, arrange, chassis, compose, concoct, dream up, enclose, fashion, inclose, lattice, outline, prepare, produce, project **8** assemble, block out, conceive, contrive, mounting, organize, physique, scaffold, skeleton, trimming **9** construct, enclosure, fabricate, formulate, implicate, structure **10** constitute
a photo again: **5** remat
bed ~: **5** stead
car ~: **7** chassis
cartoon ~: **3** cel **4** cell
door ~: **4** sash
ender: **4** work
film ~: **3** cel **4** cell **5** slide
fireplace ~: **5** grate
insert: **4** lens **5** photo **7** picture **8** painting
of mind: **4** mood, vein **5** humor, state **6** spirit, temper **7** outlook, posture **8** attitude **9** mentality
of reference: **4** idea, side, view **5** angle, light, slant, stand **6** aspect, stance, system **7** horizon, opinion, outlook, posture **8** attitude, position **9** viewpoint **10** estimation, philosophy, standpoint
picture ~ juncture: **5** miter, slant **8** diagonal
ship ~: **4** hull
spacecraft ~: **6** gantry
starter: **3** air **4** main
structural ~: **5** truss
weaver's ~: **4** slay, sley **6** sleigh
window ~: **4** sash **6** casing
__ frame: **4** open, time **6** freeze
__ Framed Roger Rabbit: **3** Who
Frame, Janet: **6** writer
framer: **5** maker **7** builder, creator, devisor, drafter, planner **8** composer **9** assembler **10** fabricator
frames: **5** specs **7** glasses **10** spectacles
in a game: **3** ten
frame-up: **4** plot **6** racket, scheme **10** conspiracy
framework: **4** core, form, grid, plan, sash **5** cadre, setup, shell **6** casing, fabric, nature, scheme **7** chassis, outline, setting **8** skeleton **9** bare bones, structure **10** background, foundation
metal ~: **5** grate
part: **5** truss
framing __: **6** chisel, square
Framingham: **4** city, town
locale: **4** Mass.
framing need: **3** mat
Frampton, Peter
song: Do You Feel Like We Do (1976)
I'm In You (1977)
Show Me the Way (1976)
Fran: **5** Healy **7** Allison **8** Drescher, Lebowitz **9** Tarkenton
partner: **5** Kukla, Ollie
franc: **4** coin **5** money
part of a ~: **3** sou
replacement: **4** euro
__ franca: **6** lingua
__ française: **3** à la
__ Française: **7** Comédie
France: **5** Nuyen, repub. **6** nation **7** Anatole, country **8** republic
ancient ~: **4** Gaul
appetizer: **9** escargots, macédoine
astronomer: **7** Laplace **8** Lagrange
ballet dancer: **6** Béjart
bay: **6** Biscay
biologist: **6** Carrel
bovine: **6** Aubrac, Herens, Salers, Vosges **7** Alberes **8** Limousin **9** Charolais
cap: **5** beret
capital: **5** Paris
car: **5** Simca **7** Peugeot, Renault
card game: **6** belote **7** belotte
cathedral city: **5** Reims **6** Rheims
cheese: **4** Brie **5** banon **7** gervais, Gruyère **9** Camembert, Port Salut, Roquefort **10** Neufchâtel

11 Pont l'Évêque
chemist: 4 Lehn 5 Curie 6 Perrin 7 Moissan, Pasteur 9 Berthelot, Gay-Lussac, Lavoisier
city: 3 Dax, Pau 4 Agde, Agen, Albi, Ales, Auch, Bron, Caen, Évry, Issy, laon, Lens, Loos, Lyon, Metz, Nice, Orly, Rezé, Riom, St. Lô 5 Arles, Arras, Blois, Bondy, Brest, Cenon, Cergy, Creil, Dijon, Douai, Dreux, Gagny, Laval, Lille, Lomme, Lunel, Lyons, Mâcon, Massy, Melun, Muret, Nancy, Nîmes, Niort, Ornes, Paris, Reims, Rodez, Rouen, Sedan, Tours, Tulle, Vichy 6 Amiens, Angers, Anglet, Annecy, Bastia, Bezons, Calais, Cannes, Cholet, Clichy, Colmar, Denain, Dieppe, Drancy, Épinal, Ermont, Évreux, Fécamp, Fréjus, Grigny, Guéret, Hyéres, Istres, Le Mans, Meudon, Millau, Nantes, Nevers, Pantin, Pessac, Poissy, Rennes, Rheims, Roanne, Sevran, Sèvres, St. Malo, Tarbes, Toulon, Troyes, Vannes, Vanves, Verdun, Vertou, Vesoul, Voiron, Yerres 7 Ajaccio, Alençon, Avignon, Bayonne, Belfort, Béziers, Castres, Chablis, Draveil, Dunkirk, Forbach, Le Havre, Limoges, Orléans, Roubaix, St.-Denis, Talence, Taverny, Valence, Vierzon 8 Biarritz, Bordeaux, Chartres, Grenoble, Poitiers, Soissons, St.-Mihiel, Toulouse 9 Cherbourg, Marseille, St.-Étienne 10 Marseilles, Strasbourg
combining form: 5 Gallo- 6 Franco-
conductor: 5 Morel, Münch 6 Boulez 7 Monteux 9 Leibowitz, Rosenthal
couturier: 4 Dior
dance: 5 gavot 6 branle, cancan 7 bourrée, favotte 9 cotillion, farandole, passepied, quadrille
department: 3 Ain, Lot, Var 4 Aube, Aude, Cher, Eure, Gard, Gers, Jura, Nord, Oise, Orne, Tarn 5 Aisne, Doubs, Drôme, Indre, Isère, Loire, Marne, Meuse, Rhone, Somme, Yonne 6 Allier, Ariège, Cantal, Creuse, Landes, Loiret, Lozère, Manche, Nièvre, Sarthe, Savoie, Vendée, Vienne, Vosges 7 Ardèche, Aveyron, Bas-Rhin, Corrèze, Côte-d'Or, Essonne, Gironde, Hérault, Mayenne, Moselle 8 Ardennes, Calvados, Charente, Dordogne, Haut-Rhin, Morbihan, Val-d'Oise, Vaucluse, Yvelines 9 Finistère, Puy-de-Dôme 10 Deux-Sèvres, Haute-Corse, Haute-Loire, Haute-Marne, Haute-Saône, Loir-et-Cher, Val-de-Marne 11 Eure-et-Loire
dialect: 6 Creole
diplomat: 5 Perse
director: 4 Tati 5 Vadim 6 Renoir 8 Truffaut 10 Jean Renoir, Roger Vadim
entomologist: 5 Fabre
essayist: 5 Péguy 7 Reverdy, Rolland, Romains
existentialist: 4 Gide
explorer: 5 Salle 6 Joliet 7 Cartier, Jolliet 8 Cousteau 9 Champlain, David-Neel
film award: 5 César
flutist: 6 Rampal
former colony: 4 Chad, Laos, Mali, Togo 5 Benin, Gabon, Haiti, Niger 6 Acadia, Canada, Guinea 7 Algeria, Morocco, Senegal, Tunisia, Vietnam 8 Cambodia, Cameroon, Djibouti 9 Louisiana 10 Ivory Coast, Madagascar, Mauritania
gulf: 5 Lions 6 St. Malo
historian: 5 Taine 9 Froissart
humanist: 8 Rabelais
impressionist: 5 Degas, Manet, Monet
journalist: 7 Prévost
lake: 6 Geneva
land measure: 6 arpent
language: 6 Basque
legislature: 5 sénat
mathematician: 6 Pascal 7 Laplace 8 Lagrange
medieval ~ poem: 3 lai
money: 3 écu, sol, sou 4 euro 5 franc, liard, livre, louis, obole, oboli 6 decime, obolus, teston 7 centime, testoon 8 louis d'or, napoleon
mountain: 4 Jura 6 Ecrins, Mézenc, Vosges 8 Cévennes, Pyrenees 9 Mont Blanc, Puy-de-Dôme, Savoy Alps
natural historian: 6 Buffon, Cuvier 7 Lamarck
neighbor: 5 Italy, Spain 6 Monaco 7 Andorra, Belgium, Germany 10 Luxembourg
Nobelist in Chemistry: 4 Lehn 7 Moissan 11 Joliot-Curie
Nobelist in Economics: 6 Allais, Debreu
Nobelist in Literature: 4 Gide 5 Camus, Perse, Simon 6 du Gard, France, Sartre 7 Bergson, Mauriac, Mistral, Rolland 9 Prudhomme
Nobelist in Medicine: 5 Jacob, Lwoff, Monod 6 Carrel, Richet 7 Dausset, Laveran, Nicolle 11 Metchnikoff
Nobelist in Peace: 5 Passy 6 Briand, Cassin 7 Balluet, Buisson, Jouhaux, Renault 9 Bourgeois 10 Schweitzer
Nobelist in Physics: 4 Néel 5 Curie 6 Perrin 7 Kastler 8 de Gennes, Lippmann 9 Becquerel, de Broglie, Guillaume
org.: 4 NATO
Oscar: 5 César
painter: 3 Arp 4 Dufy 5 Corot, Degas, Léger, Manet, Monet 6 Braque, Ingres, Renoir, Seurat, Tanguy, Tissot 7 Bonheur, Cézanne, Duchamp, Gauguin, Matisse, Utrillo 8 Dubuffet 9 Delacroix
palace: 6 Elysée
philosopher: 4 Weil 5 Taine 6 Pascal, Sartre 7 Bergson 8 Maritain, Rousseau, Voltaire
physicist: 4 Néel 5 Curie 6 Ampère, Franck, Perrin 7 Coulomb, Fourier, Fresnel, Kastler, Réaumur 8 de Gennes, Foucault, Lippmann 9 Becquerel, de Broglie, Gay-Lussac, Guillaume 11 Joliot-Curie
playwright: 5 Camus, Genet, Hardy, Jarry, Sagan 6 Gréban, Grévin, Musset, Racine, Sardou, Scribe 7 Anouilh, Feydeau, Garnier, Ionesco, Molière, Régnard, Rolland, Romains, Rostand, Sedaine 8 Salacrou, Sarraute 9 Corneille
poem: 6 dizain
poet: 4 Char 5 Bodel, Jacob, Jouve, Marot, Péguy, Perse, Scève 6 Breton, Desnos, Éluard, France, Grévin, Musset, writer 7 Boileau, Chénier, Heredia, Michaux, Mistral, Prévert, Queneau, Régnier, Reverdy, Rimbaud, Ronsard 8 Chartier, Soupault 9 Corneille, Deschamps, Desportes, Froissart, Lamartine, Prudhomme 10 Baudelaire
port: 4 Caen, Nice, Sète 5 Brest 6 Calais, Cannes, Dieppe, St. Malo, Toulon 7 Dunkirk, Le Havre 8 Bordeaux, Boulogne 9 Cherbourg, Marseille 10 La Rochelle, Marseilles
provincial: 5 style
region: 5 Corse, Savoy 6 Alsace, Artois, Centre 8 Auvergne, Bretagne, Brittany, Limousin, Lorraine, Normandy, Picardie 9 Aquitaine, Bourgogne 10 Rhône-Alpes
resort: 3 Pau 4 Midi, Nice 5 Evian 6 Cannes, Dinard, Menton, St. Malo 7 Riviera 8 Biarritz, St. Tropez 9 Côte d'Azur, Deauville, Le Touquet, Trouville
revolutionary: 5 Marat
river: 3 Lot, Lys 4 Aire, Aube, Aude, Cher, Eure, Ille, Leie, Oise, Orne, Yser 5 Aisne, Doubs, Isère, Loire, Marne, Meuse, Rhone, Saône, Sarre, Seine, Selle, Somme, Yonne 6 Allier, Escaut 7 Garonne, Moselle 8 Dordogne
rocket: 6 Ariane
royal house: 5 Capet 6 Valois 7 Bourbon, Orleans
royal name: 5 Henry, Louis 6 Philip 7 Charles
saint: 5 Denis, Denys, Giles 6 Ansgar, Fiacre 7 Bernard, Louis IX 8 Lawrence 9 Genevieve, Joan of Arc 10 Bernadette
scientist: 5 Curie, Fabre 6 Ampère, Buffon, Carrel, Cuvier, Franck, Pascal, Perrin 7 Coulomb, Fourier, Fresnel, Lamarck, Laplace, Pasteur, Réaumur 8 Foucault, Lagrange 9 Berthelot, Gay-Lussac, Lavoisier
sculptor: 3 Arp 5 Rodin 8 Dubuffet
shrine: 7 Lourdes
silk center: 4 Lyon 5 Lyons
site of Roman ruins in ~: 5 Arles
skier: 5 Killy
soprano: 4 Pons 5 Calvé 7 Crespin
southern ~ wind: 7 mistral
take ~ leave: 4 flee
tennis pro: 7 Lacoste
Tour de ~: 4 race
Tour de ~ entrant: 5 biker
underground: 6 Maquis
vowel sound: 5 nasal
water: 3 eau 5 Evian, Vichy
waterfall: 8 Gavarnie
wine: 4 Moët 5 Gamay, Mâcon, Médoc, Tavel, Yquem 6 claret, Graves 7 aligoté, Chablis, Musigny, Pommard, Vouvray 8 Bordeaux, Cabernet, Muscadet, Sancerre 9 champagne, Meursault 10 Beaujolais, Chambertin, Montrachet
wine region: 5 Loire, Médoc, Rhone
writer: 3 Sue 4 Aymé, Gary, Gide, Hugo, Loti, Sade, Sand, Weil, Zola 5 Butor, Camus, Dumas, Duras, Giono, Green, Hémon, Perse, Renan, Sagan, Simon, Taine, Verne 6 Aragon, Balzac, Barrès, Belloc, Boulle, Céline, Cixous, Daudet, du Gard, France, Guitry, Lesage, Marcel, Pascal, Proust, Sartre 7 Anouilh, Aubigné, Bergson, Bourget, Claudel, Cocteau, Colette, Duhamel, Mauriac, Maurois, Mérimée, Mistral, Prévost, Queneau, Rolland, Romains, Scudéry, Simenon 8 Bataille, Beauvoir, Bernanos, Cendrars, d'Aubigné, Flaubert, Goncourt, Gringore, Huysmans, Maritain, Perrault, Proudhon, Rabelais, Rousseau, Sarraute, Stendhal, Voltaire 9 Giraudoux, Montaigne, Prudhomme 10 La Fontaine, Maupassant, Oldenbourg 11 Montesquieu, Sainte-Beuve
see also French

__ France: 3 Air, New 5 Ile de 7 Marie de
France, Anatole: 4 poet 6 French, writer 8 Nobelist
work: The Bloom of Life
L'Etui de nacre
Penguin Island
The Red Lily
Thaïs
Frances: 3 Dee 4 Alda 6 Bavier, Farmer, Fisher, Harper 7 Perkins, Willard 8 Goodrich 9 Lockridge, McDormand 10 Sternhagen
Frances (1982 film)
cast: Jessica Lange, Sam Shepard, Kim Stanley
Francesca: 7 Cabrini
Francesco: 5 Berni 6 Arrivi 9 Borromini
in English: 7 Francis
Francesco Rinaldi: 10 pasta sauce
alternative: 4 Ragú 5 Prego 6 Prince 8 Classico 10 Newman's Own 11 Aunt Millie's
Frances Hodgson __: 7 Burnett

Franchi: 6 Sergio
sister: Dana Valery
franchise: 4 vote 5 right 6 agency, ballot, patent, permit, voting 7 charter, liberty 8 election, suffrage 9 authority, exemption, privilege
exercise one's ~: 4 vote 5 elect
exerciser: 5 voter
Franchise Affair, The
author: Josephine Tey
franchisee: 6 dealer, seller, vendor 8 merchant, retailer
Franchot: 4 Tone
Franciosa: 4 Tony 7 Anthony
Franciosa, Tony: 5 actor
spouse: Shelley Winters
Francis: 3 Fry, Kay 4 Anne, Dick, mule 5 Aston, Bacon, Cleve, Crick, Drake, Emile, Genie, Missy 6 Arlene, Baring, Connie, Galton, Marion, Ouimet, Xavier 7 de Sales, Lederer, Parkman, Poulenc, Quarles 8 Beaufort
imitate ~: 4 bray
in Italian: 9 Francesco
in Spanish: 9 Francisco
Francis __ Coppola: 4 Ford
Francis __ Key: 5 Scott
Francis, Arlene: 7 actress
spouse: Martin Gabel
Franciscan: 5 friar
founder's home: 6 Assisi
org.: 3 OFM
Francisco: 4 Goya 6 Franco, Madero 7 Pizarro 8 Coronado
in English: 7 Francis
Francisco __ de Goya: 4 José
__ Francisco: 3 San
Francis, Connie
song: Among My Souvenirs (1959)
Breakin' in a Brand New Broken Heart (1961)
Don't Break the Heart That Loves You (1962)
Everybody's Somebody's Fool (1960)
Frankie (1959)
Lipstick on Your Collar (1959)
Mama (1960)
Many Tears Ago (1960)
My Happiness (1958)
My Heart Has a Mind of Its Own (1960)
Second Hand Love (1962)
Stupid Cupid (1958)
Together (1961)
Vacation (1962)
When the Boy in Your Arms (1961)
Where the Boys Are (1961)
Who's Sorry Now (1958)
__ Francisco River: 3 Sao
Franciscus: 5 James
Francis de Sales: 5 saint
Francis, Dick: 6 writer 7 British
former job: jockey
homeland: England
locale: 5 Ascot
work: 10 Lb. Penalty
Banker
Blood Sport
Bolt
Bonecrack
Break in
Comeback
Come to Grief
The Danger
Dead Cert
Decider
Driving Force
The Edge
Enquiry
Field of Thirteen
Flying Finish
Forfeit
For Kicks
High Stakes
Hot Money
In the Frame
Knockdown
Longshot
Nerve
Odds Against
Proof
Rat Race
Reflex
Risk
Second Wind
Shattered
Slay Ride
Smokescreen
Straight
To the Hilt
Trial Run
Twice Shy
Whip Hand
Wild Horses
Francis Ford __: 7 Coppola
Francis, Genie
spouse: Jonathan Frakes
Francis of __: 5 Paula, Sales 6 Assisi
Francis of Assisi: 5 saint
Francis Scott __: 3 Key
Francistown: 4 city
locale: 8 Botswana
Francis X. __: 7 Bushman
Francis Xavier: 5 saint
francium: 5 metal 7 element
Franck: 5 César, James
Franco: 4 John, Nero 5 James 6 Harris 7 Corelli 9 Francisco, Sacchetti 10 Modigliani, Zeffirelli
François: 5 Jacob 6 Villon 7 Boucher, Mauriac 8 Duvalier, Rabelais, Truffaut 9 Mitterand
see also French
__-François Champollion: 4 Jean
Françoise: 5 Sagan
see also French
François le Champi
author: George Sand
Franco, John: 3 Met 6 hurler 7 pitcher
francolin: 4 bird
Franco-Prussian __: 3 War
frangible: 4 weak 5 frail 6 flimsy 7 brittle, crumbly, fragile, rickety, unsound 8 delicate 9 breakable 10 nondurable
frangipane: 6 pastry
ingredient: 3 egg 5 cream, sugar 6 almond
frangipani: 4 tree 5 plant, shrub 6 flower
relative: 5 orris 7 dogbane, karanda 8 oleander
frank: 4 meat, open 5 bluff, blunt, brusk, legit, naked, plain, vocal, weeny 6 abrupt, candid, direct, honest, hot dog, infelt, simple, square, weenie, wiener, wienie 7 artless, brusque, factual, genuine, natural, sincere, up-front, upright 8 credible, impolite, outfront, straight, tactless, truthful 9 downright, guileless, ingenuous, outspoken, unfeigned, unguarded, veracious 10 aboveboard, flatfooted, forthright, foursquare, freespoken, from the hip, indelicate, on the level, point-blank, scrupulous, to the point, unaffected, unreserved, unreticent
be ~: 5 level
ender: 6 pledge 7 incense
too ~: 9 impolitic, unguarded 10 indiscreet
see also frankfurter, hot dog
Frank: 2 Oz 4 Anne, Bank, Cady, Gary, Ilja 5 Baker, Beard, Capra, DeVol, Libby, Lloyd, Mills, O'Hara, Perry, Yerby, Zappa 6 Bidart, Bonner, Borman, Burnet, Chance, Coraci, Faylen, Howard, Ifield, Lawton, McHugh, Melvin, Morgan, Norris, Sutton, Tanana, Thomas, Tuttle, Whaley 7 Borzage, Gifford, Gorshin, Herbert, Kellogg, Launder, Loesser, Lovejoy, McCourt, O'Connor, Shorter, Sinatra, Tashlin 8 Crosetti, Fontaine, Gilbreth, Langella, Marshall, Robinson, Sargeson, Stallone, Sullivan, Wedekind 9 Slaughter
comics partner: 6 Ernest
daughter: 4 Tina 5 Nancy
ex: 3 Ava, Mia 5 Nancy
in German: 5 Franz
outlaw brother: 5 Jesse
pal: 4 Dean 5 Sammy
Frank & __: 5 Ollie
Frank __ Wright: 5 Lloyd
Frank, Anne hideout: 5 attic
__ Frank Baum: 5 Lyman
Franken: 2 Al
Franken Berry
competitor: *see* cereal
Frankenheimer, John: 8 director
Frankenstein
assistant: 4 Igor
author: Mary Shelley
milieu: 3 lab
monster name: 4 Adam
Frankenstein (1931 film)
cast: Mae Clarke, Colin Clive, Boris Karloff
__ Frankenstein: 5 Son of, Young
Frankfort: 4 city, town 7 capital
campus: 3 KSU
locale: 3 Ken. 8 Kentucky
Frankfurt: 4 city, town
city near ~: 5 Hanau, Mainz
locale: 7 Germany
river: 4 Main, Oder, Odra
frankfurter: 3 dog 4 meat 5 Kahn's, weeny 6 Armour, hot dog, weenie, wiener, wienie 8 Ball Park 10 Oscar Mayer
accompaniment: 3 bun 5 chili, kraut, works 6 relish 7 mustard 10 sauerkraut
covering: 4 skin 6 casing
see also hot dog
Frankfurter: 5 Felix 6 German
Frankie: 5 Carle, Laine, Lymon, Valli 6 Avalon, Frisch
Frankie and Johnny (1966 song)
artist: Elvis Presley
frankincense: 5 resin 8 olibanum 9 fragrance
partner: 4 gold 5 myrrh
Frankish: 8 language
Franklin: 3 Ben 4 Carl, city, John, town 5 Adams, Cover, Miles 6 Aretha, Bonnie, Kameny, Pierce, Sidney 8 Benjamin, Pangborn 9 Roosevelt, Schaffner
bill: 5 C-note
cousin: 5 Teddy 8 Theodore
Eleanor, to ~: 4 wife
flier: 4 kite
invention: 3 DST
locale: 9 Tennessee, Wisconsin
mother: 4 Sara
note: 3 cee
opponent: 3 Alf 6 Thomas 7 Wendell
Franklin __: 5 stove
Franklin __ Roosevelt: 6 Delano
Franklin, Aretha
nickname: The Queen of Soul
song: Baby I Love You (1967)
Bridge Over Troubled Water (1971)
Chain of Fools (1967)
Day Dreaming (1972)
Freeway of Love (1985)
The House That Jack Built (1968)
I Knew You Were Waiting (1987)
I Never Loved a Man (1967)
I Say a Little Prayer (1968)
A Natural Woman (1967)
Respect (1967)
Rock Steady (1971)
Since You've Been Gone (1968)
Spanish Harlem (1971)
Think (1968)
Until You Come Back to Me (1973)
Who's Zoomin' Who (1985)
Franklin Gothic: 4 font
franklinite: 7 mineral
Franklin P. __: 5 Adams
Frank Lloyd __: 6 Wright
frankly: 5 truly 6 openly, simply 8 directly, straight 9 sincerely 10 point-blank
Frankly, my dear... sayer: 5 Rhett
frankness: 6 candor 7 honesty, naiveté 8 veracity 9 good faith, innocence, sincerity
Franks
king: 6 Clovis
of the ~: 5 Salic
Frank's Campaign
author: Horatio Alger
Frann: 4 Mary
Franny and Zooey
author: J.D. Salinger
cat: 9 Bloomberg
__, Fran & Ollie: 5 Kukla
Frans: 4 Hals 9 Sillanpää
frantic: 3 mad 4 wild 5 hyper, manic, upset, wired 6 hectic 7 burning, demonic, excited, keyed up, unglued 8 agitated, daemonic, feverish, frenetic, frenzied, in a tizzy, maniacal, vehement, worked up 9 at wits' end, delirious, demonical, desperate, last-ditch 10 corybantic, distraught, distressed, flipped out, hysterical, in an uproar, infuriated

frantically: 4 hard 5 madly 7 like mad
Frantz: 5 Fanon
Franz: 4 Boas 5 Haydn, Kafka, Kline, Lehár, Liszt 6 Arthur, Dennis, Eduard, Waxman, Werfel 7 Klammer 8 Schubert
 in English: 5 Frank
 see also German
Franz __ Haydn: 6 Joseph
Franz __ Land: 5 Josef
Franz, Dennis: 5 actor
 TV: NYPD Blue
frap: 4 bind, wrap
frappé: 4 iced 5 drink, shake 6 frozen 7 chilled, dessert 9 milkshake
Frascati: 4 wine 5 white
 origin: 5 Italy
Fraser: 4 Dawn 5 Neale, river 7 Antonia, Brendan
Fraser, Antonia: 6 writer 7 British
 spouse: Harold Pinter
Fraser, Brendan: 5 actor
 film: Bedazzled (2000)
  Blast From the Past (1999)
  Dudley Do-Right (1999)
  Encino Man (1992)
  George of the Jungle (1997)
  Gods and Monsters (1998)
  Mrs. Winterbourne (1996)
  The Mummy (1999)
  School Ties (1992)
  Still Breathing (1998)
Fraser, Dawn: 7 swimmer
Fraser, Neale: 7 netster 9 tennis pro
 milieu: 5 court
Frasier (NBC sitcom)
 cast: Peri Gilpin (Roz Doyle)
  Kelsey Grammer (Dr. Frasier Crane)
  Jane Leeves (Daphne Moon)
  John Mahoney (Martin Crane)
  David Hyde Pierce (Dr. Niles Crane)
 dog: Eddie
 Niles' wife: Maris
 setting: Seattle, Washington
frat
 see fraternity
frater: 3 bro, pal 4 chum, mate 5 buddy, crony 6 friend 7 comrade
fraternal: 4 true 5 loyal 6 caring 7 devoted, related 9 brotherly
 group: 4 BPOE, Elks, IOOF 5 Lions, Lodge 7 Kiwanis 10 Odd Fellows
fraternal __: 4 twin 7 society
fraternity: 3 set 4 clan, club 5 house, order, union 7 academy, coterie 8 quarters
 delivery: 3 keg
 fee: 4 dues
 house alternative: 4 dorm
 inspection: 4 rush
 letter: 2 mu, nu, pi, xi 3 chi, eta, phi, psi, rho, tau 4 beta, iota, zeta 5 alpha, delta, gamma, kappa, omega, sigma, theta 6 lambda 7 epsilon, omicron, upsilon
 one in a ~: 3 mem. 6 member 7 brother
 opposite: 3 sor. 8 sorority
 party: 4 stag 5 mixer
 party attire: 4 toga 5 sheet
 quarters: 5 house
 recruit: 5 frosh 6 rushee 8 freshman
 wear: 3 pin
fraternity __: 5 house
Fraternity __: 3 Row
fraternize: 3 mix 6 fall in, hobnob, mingle 7 consort, hang out 9 associate, socialize
Fratianne, Linda: 6 skater
fratricide victim: 4 Abel
Frau: 3 Mrs. 5 title, woman 6 German
 husband: 4 Herr
fraud: 3 con, job 4 fake, hoax, ruse, scam, sham 5 cheat, crook, faker, feint, guile, phony, put-on, quack, rogue, shark, sting, theft, trick 6 bad guy, deceit, dupery, forger, hoaxer, humbug, hustle, phoney, racket, rascal, rip-off, robber 7 bluffer, chicane, con game, falsity, fast one, sharper, sharpie, snow job, swindle 8 artifice, bad faith, deceiver, flimflam, imposter, impostor, swindler, thievery, trickery 9 charlatan, chicanery, deception, duplicity, falsifier, hypocrisy, hypocrite, imposture, improbity, mare's nest, pretender, racketeer, treachery 10 corruption, hanky-panky, hocus-pocus, imposition, mountebank, plagiarism, subterfuge
 check for ~: 5 audit 6 go over 7 examine, inspect 9 go through 10 scrutinize
 ending: 5 ulent
 monitoring agcy.: 3 FTC
 obtain by ~: 5 grift
fraudulence: 6 deceit 7 falsity 8 cheating, pretense 9 chicanery, duplicity, imposture, treachery 10 dishonesty, subterfuge
fraudulent: 4 fake, mock, sham 5 bogus, false, phony, put-on 6 ersatz, forged, phoney, pseudo, shifty, unreal 7 assumed, corrupt, crooked, devious, feigned 8 criminal, spurious, thieving, thievish 9 deceitful, deceptive, dishonest, falsified, imitation, simulated, swindling, synthetic, underhand 10 artificial, fabricated, fallacious, fictitious
 not ~: 4 good 5 legit, valid 6 kosher, lawful 7 genuine 9 authentic
fraught: 5 heavy, laden, risky 6 filled 7 replete, stuffed 8 brimming 9 bristling
Fraülein: 4 girl, lass, maid, miss 5 title 6 damsel, German, lassie, maiden 7 colleen 8 señorita 9 young lady 10 young woman
Fraunhofer, Joseph von: 9 physicist, scientist
Frawley, William: 5 actor
 TV: I Love Lucy, My Three Sons
 TV wife: Vivian Vance
fray: 3 row, rub 4 riot, tear, wear 5 brawl, clash, fight, melee, mix-up, scrap, set-to, shred, storm 6 action, barney, battle, combat, fracas, ragged, ruckus, rumble, rumpus, tussle 7 contest, frazzle, quarrel, scuffle, unravel, wear out 8 brouhaha, conflict, skirmish, slugfest, struggle 9 encounter, imbroglio 10 donnybrook, engagement, free-for-all
 above the ~: 5 aloof
 ready for the ~: 5 armed
frayed: 4 worn 5 tatty 6 ragged, shabby 10 threadbare
Frayn, Michael: 6 writer 7 British 10 playwright
 work: Alphabetical Order
  Copenhagen
  Donkey's Years
  Headlong
  A Landing on the Sun
  Look, Look
  Make and Break
  Noises Off
  Now You Know
  Spies
  Sweet Dreams
  The Trick of It
Frazer: 3 Dan 5 James
Frazier: 3 Joe 4 Walt 6 Marvis
Frazier, Joe: 5 boxer
 foe: 3 Ali
 milieu: 4 ring
Frazier, Walt
 milieu: 5 court
 org.: 3 NBA
 sport: 10 basketball
frazzle: 4 fray, poop, tear 5 shred 7 poop out, remnant, tire out, wear out 8 knock out 9 prostrate, tucker out 10 come undone, enervation, exhaustion
 worn to a ~: 4 beat 5 jumpy, tired, weary, wired 6 bushed, dished, done in 7 drained, run-down, uptight, wound up 8 dog-tired, fatigued, in a tizzy, unnerved 9 enervated, exhausted, played out 10 distressed
frazzled: 4 worn 6 ragged 9 exhausted, prostrate
freak: 3 bug, fan, nut, odd 4 buff, rage, rave 5 fiend, go ape 6 addict, lose it, mutant, zealot 7 admirer, anomaly, devotee, fanatic, flip out, go crazy, monster, oddball, unhinge, unusual 8 follower, have a fit, mutation 9 go berserk 10 aberration, aficionado, enthusiast
 out: 4 rave 5 go ape, upset 6 go nuts, lose it 8 have a fit
 (out): 3 wig
 out on: 3 dig 4 like 5 enjoy, savor 6 relish 10 appreciate
freak __: 3 out
freaked out: 3 hot, mad 4 ired, sore 5 cross, huffy, irate, livid, manic, riled, upset, wroth 6 fuming, ireful, raging, raving, red-hot 7 bananas, furious, lunatic, ranting 8 choleric, maniacal, wrathful 9 indignant, resentful, splenetic, wrought-up
freakish: 3 odd 4 eery, wild 5 eerie, outré, weird 6 atypic, far-out, quirky, way-out 7 bizarre, deviant, erratic, oddball, offbeat, strange, surreal, unusual 8 aberrant, abnormal, atypical, peculiar, uncommon 9 anomalous, divergent, eccentric, fantastic, grotesque, irregular, monstrous, unnatural 10 outlandish, unorthodox
freak of __: 6 nature
__ Freak On: 5 Get Ur
Freaky Friday (1977 film)
 cast: John Astin, Jodie Foster, Barbara Harris
Freaky Friday (2003 film)
 cast: Jamie Lee Curtis, Lindsay Lohan
__ Freans: 4 Peek
Freberg: 4 Stan
freckle: 3 dot 4 spot 5 speck 7 lentigo
freckle-__: 5 faced
freckled: 6 dotted 7 dappled, flecked, mottled, spotted 8 speckled
Freckle Juice
 author: Judy Blume
Fred: 3 Ebb 4 Lynn, Ward 5 Allen, Clark, Dryer, Hoyle, Mertz, Niblo 6 Grandy, Gwynne, Noonan, Piscop, Rogers, Savage, Stolle, Waring 7 Astaire, Couples, McGriff 8 Friendly, Newmeyer, Schepisi 9 de Cordova, MacMurray, Zinnemann 10 Flintstone
 dancing partner: 3 Cyd 6 Barrie, Ginger
 pet: 4 Dino
 sister: 5 Adele
 to Pebbles: 3 Dad
 wife: 5 Wilma
Fred __: 6 Basset
Freda: 5 Payne
freddie: 5 dance
Freddie: 5 Patek 6 Prinze 7 Mercury
Freddie __: 3 Mac
Freddie and the Dreamers
 song: I'm Telling You Now (1965)
Freddy: 3 Adu 6 Cannon, Fender 8 Reynolds
 street: 3 Elm
Frederic: 5 Cohen 6 Dannay 7 Forrest, Manning 9 Remington
Frédéric: 5 Passy 6 Chopin 7 Mistral 9 Bartholdi
Frederica von __: 5 Stade
Frédéric Joliot-__: 5 Curie
Frederick: 4 city, town 5 Loewe, North, Rolfe, Soddy 6 Church, Delius, Reines, Sanger 7 Banting, Forsyth, Hopkins, Marryat, Olmsted, Robbins 8 Douglass
 in German: 9 Friedrich
 in Italian: 8 Federico
 locale: 8 Maryland
Fredericksburg: 6 battle
 winner: 3 Lee
Frederick the __: 5 Great
Fredericton: 4 city, town
 locale: 6 Canada
Frederik: 4 Pohl
Fredo: 8 Corleone
Fredric: 5 March
free: 3 big, rid 4 idle, open, save, undo, wild 5 clear, let go, loose, saved, spare, spell, unjam, unled, unpin, untie 6 acquit, excuse, exempt, gratis, lavish, let off, let out, liquid, loosen, pardon, parole, public, purify, ransom, redeem, rescue, spring, unbind, uncage, unhand, unpaid, untied, unused, unwind, vacant 7 absolve, as a gift, at large, bail out, deliver, dismiss, escaped, liberal, lighten, manumit, off-duty, pro bono, release, relieve, rescued, through, unbound, unchain, unleash, untaken,

untwine **8** absolute, at no cost, costless, cut loose, detached, generous, informal, let loose, liberate, not in use, prodigal, released, reprieve, separate, set loose, unbarred, unburden, unfetter **9** at leisure, at liberty, available, disburden, discharge, disengage, expansive, extricate, footloose, leisurely, liberated, nonliable, on one's own, on the cuff, out of work, outspoken, unchained, uncoerced, unengaged, unhitched, unimpeded, unshackle, unsparing, voluntary **10** autonomous, bighearted, democratic, disengaged, emancipate, for nothing, liberalize, munificent, off the hook, on the house, on the loose, permissive, privileged, self-ruling, unattached, unconfined, unemployed, unfettered, unhampered, unhindered, unoccupied, unreserved, unreticent, unshackled, vindicated
and easy: **3** lax **5** homey, light, loose **6** breezy, casual, folksy, mellow **7** lenient, offhand, patient, relaxed **8** informal, laid back, outgoing, tolerant **9** indulgent, leisurely **10** forbearing, nonchalant, off-the-cuff, open-minded, permissive, unaffected
ender: **3** dom, man, men, way **4** boot, born, form, hand, hold, load **5** board, lance, mason, stone, style, wheel **6** handed, holder, lancer, loader, martin **7** hearted, masonry, thinker **8** standing, wheeling
from: **5** rid of
(from): **6** exempt, immune **7** absolve
from evil: **5** purge **6** purify **8** exorcise, exorcize
from (prefix): **3** dis-
go ~: **4** walk **6** get out
hand: **5** swing **6** leeway **7** bigness, largess **8** largesse, latitude **10** generosity, liberality
home ~: **10** in the clear
not ~: **4** busy **6** costly **7** engaged **8** occupied
of: **6** beyond **7** lacking
(of): **3** rid **6** devoid, divest
set ~: **5** clear, let go, loose, unpen, untie **6** loosen, ransom, redeem, rescue, unbind, unhand **7** absolve, manumit, release, unloose **8** liberate **9** discharge **10** unhindered
space: **4** play, room **6** leeway **9** elbowroom
starter: **4** care, germ **5** hands
ticket: **4** comp, pass **11** Annie Oakley
time: **4** ease **6** recess, repose **7** holiday, leisure, liberty **8** vacation **9** idle hours **10** recreation, relaxation, sabbatical
up: **3** let **4** open **8** liberate
will: **6** choice, option **8** volition
work ~: **4** undo **5** untie **6** unbind **7** release, unhitch, unloose **9** disengage
free __: **3** air, bid **4** city, fall, gold, hand, jazz, kick, list, port, rein, ride, will, zone **5** agent, beach, goods, house, lance, liver, lunch, press, reach, rider, sheet, space, throw, trade, verse, world **6** ascent, charge, church, diving, energy, flight, safety, school, silver, socage, speech, spirit, weight **7** balloon, coinage, company, radical, thought
free __ bird: **3** as a
free-__: **4** form **5** blown, bored, range **6** handed, living, spoken **7** cutting, hearted, swimmer
free-__-all: **3** for
free-__ zone: **4** fire **5** trade
__ free: **3** for, set **4** home
__-free: **3** ice, tax **4** duty, post, rent, scot **5** fancy, heart **7** carrier
Free __: **4** Bird, Kirk, Ride **5** Willy **6** French
Free-__ Party: **4** Soil
__ Free: **4** Born
free and __: **4** easy **5** clear
Free and Accepted __: **6** Masons
free as __: **5** a bird
Free as a Bird (1995 song)
artist: Beatles
freebie: **4** comp, gift, pass **7** handout, premium **8** giveaway
office ~: **4** perk, plus **5** bonus **7** benefit **8** dividend **10** perquisite
restaurant ~: **4** roll, salt **5** bread, jelly, sugar, syrup, water **6** catsup, napkin, pepper **7** catchup, ketchup, mustard **8** doggy bag **9** bowser bag, doggie bag
Freebie and the __: **4** Bean
freeboot: **4** loot, raid, sack **5** spoil, strip **6** harrow, maraud, pirate, ravage, rip off **7** despoil, pillage, plunder, ransack **8** prey upon **9** depredate, devastate **10** lay waste to
freebooter: **6** looter, pirate, raider, viking **7** brigand, corsair **8** marauder, pillager **9** buccaneer, plunderer, privateer
__-free call: **4** toll
Freed: **4** Alan, Herb **6** Arthur
__ free delivery: **5** rural
Freedent: **3** gum **10** chewing gum
alternative: **5** Extra, Orbit **7** Dentyne, Trident **8** Carefree, Chiclets **10** Doublemint, Juicy Fruit
freedman: **4** laet
freedom: **3** lib. **5** leave, power, range, right, scope **6** laxity, leeway, parole, rescue, safety **7** abandon, ability, leisure, liberty, license, passage, release **8** autarchy, autonomy, facility, immunity, latitude, security **9** democracy, elbowroom, privilege, salvation, tolerance **10** indulgence, liberation, permission, redemption
combining form: **8** eleuther- **9** eleuthero-
from care: **4** ease **5** peace **8** calmness, serenity **9** composure
in Swahili: **5** uhuru
of movement: **4** room **5** range, scope **6** leeway **8** latitude **9** elbowroom
freedom __: **5** march, rider **7** fighter
freedom __ city: **5** of the
freedom __ press: **5** of the
freedom __ seas: **5** of the
Freedom: **5** apple
relative: *see* apple
Freedom (1985 song)
artist: George Michael
__ Freedom: **3** Cry **5** Sweet
Freedomland (2006 film)
cast: Edie Falco, Samuel L. Jackson, Julianne Moore
freedom of __: **6** choice, speech **8** religion
Freedom of Choice
artist: Devo
Freedom of Information __: **3** Act
freedom of the __: **4** city, seas **5** press
Freedom Road
author: Howard Fast
Freedom Road (1979 film)
cast: Muhammad Ali
__ Freedoms: **4** Four
Freedom Writers (2007 film)
cast: Patrick Dempsey, Scott Glenn, Hilary Swank
__ Free Europe: **5** Radio
free-floating: **6** adrift **7** aimless **8** goalless, unmoored **10** unanchored
free-flowing: **6** lavish **7** fulsome, gushing, profuse **8** effusive **9** expansive
free-for-all: **3** row **4** fray, riot **5** brawl, fight, furor, melee, mix-up, scrap, storm **6** affray, barney, battle, fracas, racket, tussle **7** ruction, scuffle **8** brouhaha, scramble, struggle **10** donnybrook
__-free gasoline: **4** lead
Freeh: **5** Louis
free-handed: **6** giving **7** liberal **8** generous **9** unselfish **10** benevolent, charitable, munificent, ungrudging, unstinting
free-hearted: **4** open **7** liberal **8** generous **10** ungrudging, unreserved
Freeh, Louis
org.: **3** FBI
freehold: **4** land, plot **5** tract **6** parcel **8** property
Freehold: **4** city, town
locale: **9** New Jersey
freeholder: **8** landlord
freeing: **7** release **8** delivery **9** discharge
freelance: **4** work **8** non-staff
assignment: **3** job
instructor: **5** tutor
payment: **3** fee
freelancer: **5** indie **6** jobber, writer
encl.: **4** SASE
Free Lance, The
composer: John Philip Sousa
freeload: **3** beg, bum **5** cadge, leech, mooch **6** sponge **7** finagle, wheedle **8** scrounge **9** panhandle
freeloader: **5** leech **6** cadger, sponge **7** sponger **8** deadbeat, parasite
freely: **5** ad lib **6** at will, gladly **7** lightly, readily **9** naturally, voluntary
freeman: **5** ceorl
Freeman: **4** Joan, Mona **5** Bobby, Ernie **6** Crofts, Gosden, Morgan **8** Kathleen
Freeman, Morgan: **5** actor
film: Amistad (1997)
The Bonfire of the Vanities (1990)
Bopha! (1993)
Bruce Almighty (2003)
The Bucket List (2007)
Clean and Sober (1988)
Dark Knight (2008)
Deep Impact (1998)
Desert Blue (1999)
Driving Miss Daisy (1989)
Evan Almighty (2007)
Feast of Love (2007)
Glory (1989)
Hard Rain (1998)
High Crimes (2002)
Hurricane Streets (1998)
Invictus (2009)
Kiss the Girls (1997)
Lean on Me (1989)
Million Dollar Baby (2004, AA)
Nurse Betty (2000)
Outbreak (1995)
Robin Hood: Prince of Thieves (1991)
Se7en (1995)
The Shawshank Redemption (1994)
The Sum of All Fears (2002)
An Unfinished Life (2005)
Unforgiven (1992)
Wanted (2008)
free on __: **5** board
Freeport: **4** city, town
locale: **7** New York **8** Illinois
Free Press: **5** paper **9** newspaper
locale: **7** Detroit **8** Winnipeg
freer: **6** savior **7** saviour **9** liberator
__-free refrigerator: **5** frost
Freer Gallery display: **3** art
freesia: **4** irid **5** plant **6** flower
free-spoken: **4** open **5** blunt, frank, vocal **6** candid **8** out-front **9** ingenuous **10** forthright, from the hip, unreserved
__ Free State: **5** Congo, Irish **6** Orange
freestone: **5** fruit, peach
freestyle: **8** swimming
freethinker: **5** pagan **7** heathen, infidel, radical
religion: **5** deism
freethinking: **7** radical **8** doubting, maverick **9** quizzical, skeptical **10** avant-garde, rebellious
Freetown: **4** city, port **7** capital
locale: Sierra Leone
free-trade __: **4** zone
freeway: **4** road **5** route **6** artery **10** interstate
clogger: **3** car, van **4** auto, semi **5** truck **7** traffic **10** automobile
enter a ~: **5** merge
feature: **4** exit, lane, ramp **8** entrance, rest stop
problem: **3** jam **4** smog **6** detour **8** accident
system, to tourists: **4** maze
see also highway
Freeway of Love (1985 song)
artist: Aretha Franklin
freewheel: **5** coast, glide
Free Willy (1993 film)
animal: **4** orca **5** whale
cast: Michael Madsen, Lori Petty
Free Your Mind (1992 song)
artist: En Vogue

freeze: 3 ice 4 cool, halt, numb, stop 5 chill, frost, ice up, pause, store 6 arrest, benumb, harden, hold up, ossify, shelve, shiver 7 congeal, ice over, process, stiffen, suspend, terrify, thicken 8 glaciate, paralyse, paralyze, preserve, prohibit, solidify, stop cold 9 cessation, stabilize 10 inactivate, stand still, suspension
combining form: 4 cryo-
deep ~: 6 ice age
out: 3 ban, bar 4 stop 5 block 6 bounce, enjoin 7 dismiss, exclude 8 blockade, disallow, obstruct, prohibit, restrain 9 barricade, discharge 10 disqualify
over: 5 ice up
starter: 4 anti
(to): 5 stick
up: 5 panic
freeze __: 3 out 4 on to 5 frame 7 etching
freeze-__: 3 dry 4 etch 5 dried, frame
__ freeze: 3 dry 4 deep, land
__-freeze: 5 flash, quick, sharp
Freeze!: 4 halt, stop 6 hold it 8 don't move
Freeze foe, Mr.: 6 Batman
freezeout: 4 game 8 card game
freezer: 6 cooler, icebox
name: 5 Amana 6 Maytag 7 Kenmore 9 Whirlpool
product: 3 ice 7 ice cube
freezer __: 4 burn
freezing: 3 icy, raw 4 cold 5 chill, gelid, nippy, polar 6 arctic, biting, bitter, chilly, frigid, frosty, wintry 7 chilled, glacial, ice-cold, numbing, shivery, wintery 8 piercing, Siberian
temperatures: 5 teens
freezing __: 4 rain 5 point 7 drizzle
Fregonese: 4 Hugo
Frehley: 3 Ace
Freida: 5 Pinto
freight: 4 haul, load, send, ship 5 cargo, goods 6 lading 7 forward, imports, payload, traffic 8 carriage, contents, shipment 9 wagonload
agcy.: 3 ICC
bearing ~: 5 heavy, laden 6 packed
carrier: 3 van 4 semi 5 barge, train, truck 6 boxcar, coaler 8 railroad
hopper: 4 hobo
weight: 3 lbs., ton 4 tons 5 pound 6 pounds
freight __: 3 car, ton 5 agent, house, train 6 engine
__ freight: 3 air 4 dead, hop a
freighter: 4 boat, ship 6 vessel 7 steamer 9 transport
destination: 3 POC 4 port 10 port of call
Freight Train Blues (song)
artist: Roy Acuff, Bob Dylan
__ Freischütz: 3 Der
Fremont: 4 city, town
locale: 8 Nebraska 10 California
Frémont, John C.: 8 explorer
French: 4 lang. 5 bread, Nicki 6 course, Gallic, Harold, Victor 7 Marilyn, Stewart 8 dressing, language
door part: 4 sash
explorer: 7 Nicolet
fries: 4 side 8 side dish
fries in Britain: 5 chips
historian: 5 Renan
possessive: 4 a moi
Resistance center: 4 Lyon 5 Lyons
Revolution figure: 5 Marat
speaking nation: 4 Chad, Mali, Togo 5 Benin, Gabon, Gabun, Haiti, Niger 6 Canada, Guinea, Rwanda 7 Algeria, Burundi, Comoros, Morocco, Reunion, Senegal, Tunisia, Vanuatu 8 Cameroon, Dominica, Sjibouti 9 Mauritius 10 Ivory Coast, Madagascar, Mauritania, Saint Lucia, Upper Volta 11 Switzerland
see also France
French __: 3 bed, dip, fry, kid 4 Alps, arch, bean, chop, cuff, door, flat, foot, harp, heel, horn, roll, roof, rose, seam 5 bread, chalk, Congo, curve, drain, fries, India, leave, pitch, roast, Shore, Sudan, toast, twist, Union 6 endive, Guiana, Guinea, pastry, polish, Suites, system, window 7 Academy, bulldog, cruller, Morocco, Oceania, pancake, Quarter 8 dressing
French __ Indies: 4 West
French __ soup: 5 onion
French-__: 3 cut 5 style 6 polish
French-__ potatoes: 5 fried
__ French: 3 law, Old 4 Free 6 Middle, Modern, Norman
French and Indian __: 3 War
French Chef, The: Julia Child
French Connection, The (1971 film)
cast: Gene Hackman, Tony Lo Bianco, Fernando Rey, Roy Scheider
cop: 4 narc, nark
director: William Friedkin
highlight: 5 chase
inspiration: 4 Egan
setting: 3 NYC 7 New York
French, Daniel Chester: 6 artist 8 sculptor
French Equatorial __: 6 Africa
French Foreign __: 6 Legion
French Guiana
capital: 7 Cayenne
Indian: 6 Galibi
neighbor: 6 Brazil 8 Suriname
__ French hens...: 5 three
French Indochina part: 4 Anam, Laos 5 Annam 6 Tonkin 7 Vietnam 8 Cambodia
French Leave
author: P.G. Wodehouse
French Lieutenant's Woman, The: 4 film 5 novel
author: John Fowles
cast: Jeremy Irons, Leo McKern, Meryl Streep
director: Karel Reisz
French onion: 4 soup
French Open: 6 tennis 7 tourney
seven-time ~ champ: 5 Evert
French Polynesia
capital: 7 Papeete
island: 3 Hao 4 Anaa, Eïao, Rapa, Reao, Ua Pu 5 Tahaa 6 Hatutu, Hiva Oa, Mooréa, Rurutu, Tahiti, Tubuai, Ua Huka 7 Huahine, Makatéa, Raïatéa, Tahuata 8 Fakarava, Fatu Hiva, Nuku Hiva, Raevavae, Rangiroa, Rimatara 9 Mangareva
islands: 7 Austral, Gambier, Society, Tuamotu 9 Marquesas
French Powder Mystery, The
author: Ellery Queen
French Quarter (1978 film)
director: Dennis Kane
French Revolution
calendar month: Brumaire, Floréal, Frimaire, Fructidor, Germinal, Messidor, Nivôse, Pluviôse, Prairial, Thermidor, Vendémiaire, Ventôse
figure: 5 Marat
French roast: 6 coffee
French's: 7 mustard
alternative: 7 Gulden's 10 Grey Poupon
French Sudan today: 4 Mali
French Suites
composer: J.S. Bach
French toast: 5 bread 9 breakfast
French twist: 4 coif 6 hairdo 8 coiffure
French West __: 6 Africa, Indies
French White House: 6 Élysée
French words
a: 3 une
academy: 5 école
according to the custom: 7 à la mode
adverb: 3 ici, mal, que 4 très 5 quand
affirmative: 3 oui
after: 5 après
ait: 3 île
all together: 7 en masse
among: 5 entre
are: 4 êtes
area: 4 aire
arm: 4 bras
article: 3 les, une
aunt: 5 tante
back: 3 dos
badly: 3 mal
be: 4 être
below: 4 à bas
between: 5 entre
between ourselves: 9 entre nous
beverage: 3 thé, vin 4 café, lait
bias: 9 parti pris
black: 4 noir 5 noire
born: 3 née
brainstorm: 4 idée
bread: 4 pain
bridge: 4 pont
by the way: 9 en passant
cabbage: 4 chou
cake: 6 gateau
carefree: 9 sans souci
cat: 4 chat 5 tigre
cheer: 4 vive
cleric: 4 abbé
coffee: 4 café
color: 4 bleu, brun, noir 5 blanc, jeune, noire, rouge 7 blanche
conjunction: 2 et 3 que
count: 5 comte
cup: 5 tasse
customary: 7 de règle
dance: 3 bal 5 valse
day: 4 jour
day of the week: 5 jeudi, lundi, mardi 6 samedi 8 dimanche, mercredi, vendredi
dear: 4 cher
decadent: 11 fin de siècle
denial: 3 non
dessert: 5 glacé
direction: 3 est, sud 4 nord 5 ouest
distance: 5 metre 9 kilomètre
donkey: 3 ane
down with: 4 à bas
duke: 3 duc
earth: 5 terre
east: 3 est
eight: 4 huit
eleven: 4 onze
enjoy your meal: 10 bon appétit
entrée: 4 roti, veau
evil: 3 mal
exclamation: 3 zut 5 voilà 8 zut alors
eye: 4 oeil
failed: 6 manqué
fashionable society: 9 beau monde
fat: 4 gras
father: 4 père
fine arts: 9 beaux arts
five: 4 cinq
flower: 3 lis
four: 6 quatre
fourteen: 8 quatorze
friend: 3 ami 4 amie
golden: 3 d'or
good: 3 bon
goodbye: 5 adieu 8 au revoir
green: 4 vert
greeting: 5 salut 7 bon jour, bon soir
harm: 3 mal
head: 4 tête
health: 5 santé
hearsay: 7 oui-dire
Help!: 4 à moi
here: 3 ici
hers: 3 ses
high: 4 haut 5 haute
hint: 3 mot
his: 3 ses
holy: 5 sacre
holy woman: 3 ste. 6 sainte
hook: 4 croc
ill: 3 mal
in: 4 dans
inexpensive: 9 bon marché
infinitive: 4 être
in harmony: 9 en rapport
interrogative: 4 quel, quoi 5 quand
in the home of: 4 chez
into: 4 dans
island: 3 île
key: 3 clé 4 clef
kind: 3 bon
king: 3 roi
lady: 3 mme. 6 madame
land: 5 terre
latest fashion: 10 dernier cri
legislature: 5 sénat
life: 3 vie
lily: 3 lis
love: 5 amour
love letter: 10 billet doux
low: 3 bas
maid: 5 bonne
May: 3 mai
me: 3 moi

milk: 4 lait
mine: 4 à moi
miss: 4 mlle.
mister: 8 monsieur
model of excellence: 9 beau idéal
monk: 5 frère
month: 3 mai 4 août, juin, mars 5 avril 7 février, janvier, juillet, octobre 8 décembre, novembre 9 septembre
mother: 4 mère
Mrs.: 3 Mme.
Ms.: 4 Mlle.
my: 3 mes, moi
naked: 9 au naturel
name: 3 nom
nine: 4 neuf
ninny: 3 ane
no: 3 non
noon: 4 midi
not: 3 pas
nothing: 4 rien
notice: 4 avis
notion: 4 idée
noun: 3 nom
number: 2 un 3 dix, six 4 cent, cinq, deux, huit, neuf, onze, sept 5 douze, mille, seize, trois, vingt 6 quatre, quinze, treize, trente 8 quarante, quatorze, soixante 9 cinquante
obligatory: 9 de rigueur
obsession: 8 idée fixe
one: 2 un
on foot: 5 à pied
opinion: 4 avis
our: 3 nos
pancake: 5 crepe
pet peeve: 9 bête noire
possessive: 3 mes, mon, ses, tes, toi 5 notre
precipitation: 5 neige, pluie
preposition: 3 des 4 avec, dans, sans 5 entre
priest: 4 abbé
pronoun: 3 lui, mes, moi, qui, ses, soi, tes, toi, une 4 à moi, elle, nous, tien, vous 5 notre
pseudonym: 10 nom de plume
queen: 5 reine
rabble: 8 canaille
rain: 5 pluie
reason to exist: 11 raison d'être
relative: 4 mère, père 5 frère, oncle, soeur, tante 7 cousine
right?: 9 n'est-ce pas?
salt: 3 sel
school: 5 école, lycée
sea: 3 mer
seasickness: 8 mal de mer
season: 3 été 5 hiver 7 automne 9 printemps
see you soon: 8 à bientôt
seven: 4 sept
she: 4 elle
silk: 4 soie
since: 3 des
snow: 5 neige
so-called: 9 soi-disant
social error: 7 faux pas
soft: 3 bas
soldier: 5 poilu
some: 3 des
so much the better: 9 tant mieux
so much the worse: 7 tant pis
soul: 3 âme
spoken: 3 dit
star: 6 étoile
state: 4 état
step: 3 pas
stocking: 3 bas
street name starter: 3 rue 5 rue de
student: 5 élève
summer: 3 été
tea: 3 thé
ten: 3 dix
that's life: 9 c'est la vie
the: 3 les
theater: 4 cine
thirteen: 6 treize
thou: 3 toi
three: 5 trois
toast: 5 salut
to be: 4 être
too much: 6 de trop
to the left: 7 à gauche
to the point: 7 à propos
treason: 11 lèse majesté
turnabout: 9 volte-face
twelve: 5 douze
two: 4 deux
uncommon: 9 recherché
upon: 3 sur
up-to-date: 9 au courant
veal: 4 veau
very: 4 très
vineyard: 3 cru
water: 3 eau
well: 4 bien
well-versed: 6 au fait
when: 5 quand
wine: 3 vin
with: 4 avec
without: 4 sans
woman: 5 femme
word: 3 mot
year: 2 an 5 année
yes: 3 oui 7 mais oui
you: 4 vous
your: 3 tes, toi 5 votre

Freneau, Philip: 4 poet
frenetic: 3 mad 5 hyper, wired 6 hectic 7 excited, frantic, keyed up, unglued, zealous 8 agitated, feverish, frenzied, in a tizzy, maniacal, worked up 9 at wits' end, delirious 10 corybantic, distraught, distressed, flipped out, in an uproar
frenetically: 7 like mad
frenum
locale: 6 tongue
frenzied: 3 mad 4 amok, wild 5 amuck, hyper, irate, manic, rabid, wired 6 ablaze, heated, hectic, raging 7 burning, demonic, excited, frantic, hog-wild, keyed up, unglued 8 agitated, daemonic, feverish, frenetic, in a furor, in a tizzy, maniacal, white-hot, wild-eyed, worked up 9 at wits' end, delirious, demonical, desperate, fanatical, last-ditch, possessed, unscrewed, wrought-up 10 corybantic, distraught, distressed, flipped out, hysterical, in an uproar, infuriated, passionate
frenzy: 3 fit, row 4 fury, fuss, rage, to-do 5 fever, furor, mania, panic, spasm, tizzy 6 lather, madden, ruckus, rumble, rumpus 7 ferment, mad rush, passion, rampage, ruction, turmoil 8 delirium, hysteria, outburst, paroxysm 9 agitation, vehemence 10 excitement, fanaticism
__ frenzy: 7 feeding
Frenzy (1972 film)
director: Alfred Hitchcock
Freon: 3 gas 7 coolant
freq.
not: 3 occ.
frequency: 5 pitch 9 abundance, constancy, fixedness, iteration, pulsation 10 commonness, prevalence, recurrence, regularity, repetition
unit: 2 Hz 3 kHz, mHz 5 hertz 9 kilocycle, kilohertz, megahertz
frequent: 4 many 5 haunt, usual, visit 6 common, resort 7 generic, profuse, regular, routine 8 everyday, habitual, iterated, manifold, numerous, ordinary, periodic, repeated, unwaning 9 a good many, continual, customary, generical, hang out at, patronize, prevalent, recurrent 10 hang around, persistent, reiterated, widespread
frequent __: 5 flier, flyer
frequent-__ miles: 5 flier, flyer
frequented spot: 5 haunt 7 hangout, retreat
frequenter: 6 patron 7 habitué, regular
frequently: 3 oft 4 much 5 often 6 mostly 7 as a rule, usually 8 ofttimes 9 generally, many a time, many times, regularly, sometimes, very often 10 habitually, oftentimes, ordinarily, repeatedly
not ~: 6 seldom
frère: 4 monk 6 French 7 brother
mère's ~: 5 oncle
Frère Jacques word: 4 vous
Fresca: 3 pop 4 soda 9 soft drink
alternative: *see* soft drink
Freschetta: 5 pizza
alternative: 5 Jeno's, Tony's 6 Ellio's 7 Celeste, Totino's 8 DiGiorno 9 Tombstone
fresco: 3 art 5 mural 8 painting 10 watercolor
base: 5 gesso 7 plaster
do a ~: 5 paint
opposite: 5 secco
fresh: 3 new, raw 4 airy, anew, bold, cool, dewy, flip, good, keen, late, mint, more, naif, orig., pert, pure, rosy, rude, spry, wise 5 added, alert, brisk, clean, clear, crisp, extra, green, hardy, lippy, naive, nervy, novel, other, ruddy, sassy, saucy, sharp, smart, sweet, vital, windy, young 6 active, awless, bouncy, brazen, breezy, bright, callow, cheeky, chilly, clever, daring, latest, lively, modern, modish, recent, red-hot, rested, snippy, unused, virgin 7 artless, aweless, bracing, chipper, current, forward, glowing, healthy, just out, like new, offbeat, revived, uncivil, unfaded, unjaded, untried, unusual, updated, verdant 8 brand-new, creative, flippant, impolite, impudent, insolent, inspired, neoteric, original, snippety, undimmed, unsoiled, unversed, unwilted, up-to-date, vigorous, virginal, youthful 9 energetic, ingenious, inventive, out of line, sparkling, sprightly, unskilled, unspoiled, untainted, untouched, untrained, unwearied 10 additional, bright-eyed, fortifying, innovative, irreverent, newfangled, refreshing, ungracious
air: 5 ozone 7 outside 8 outdoors
get ~: 4 sass 8 mouth off, talk back 10 answer back
not ~: 3 old 5 stale, trite 6 canned, frozen
talk: 3 lip 4 guff, sass 5 cheek, mouth, sauce 9 impudence, insolence, sauciness
with ~ vigor: 5 newly
fresh __: 3 air 4 gale 5 water 6 breeze
fresh __ daisy: 3 as a
Fresh __: 3 Air
Fresh __ of Bel Air: 6 Prince
Fresh Air (NPR talk)
host: Terry Gross
fresh as a __: 5 daisy
freshen: 3 air 4 wake 5 renew, rouse, waken 6 aerate, air out, perk up, purify, revive 7 cleanse, enliven, refresh, restore 8 spruce up 9 deodorize, ventilate 10 invigorate, revitalize
up: 4 wash
__ freshener: 3 air 6 breath
freshet: 5 flood, spate 6 stream 10 inundation
freshly: 4 anew, just 5 newly 6 lately 8 recently
freshman: 4 pleb, year 5 plebe, pupil 6 newbie, novice, rookie 7 student 8 beginner 9 collegian, greenhorn, undergrad
see also college
Freshman, The (1990 film)
cast: Marlon Brando, Matthew Broderick, Penelope Ann Miller, Maximilian Schell
freshness: 3 lip 4 glow, sass 5 bloom, sauce, shine, vigor, youth 7 novelty, sparkle 9 cleanness, clearness, flippancy, greenness, innocence 10 brightness, callowness, uniqueness
check for ~: 5 sniff
lose ~: 4 wilt 5 droop, go bad, spoil 6 wither 7 shrivel
words on a ~ label: 5 use by
freshness __: 4 date
Fresh Prince of Bel Air (NBC sitcom)
cast: James Avery (Philip Banks) Will Smith (Will Smith)
freshwater
fish: 3 gar, ide 4 bass, carp, chub, dace, pike, rudd 5 bream, cisco, loach, perch, roach, tench, tetra, trout 6 darter
mussel: 4 clam, unio 5 naiad
Fresnay: 6 Pierre
Fresno: 4 city, town
athletes: 8 Bulldogs
locale: 10 California
newspaper: 3 Bee
school: 3 FSU
Fresno State conference: 3 WAC
__ Fresnos, TX: 3 Los
fret: 3 irk, nag, vex 4 fume, fuss, goad, mope, pine, rile, stew

5 annoy, brood, harry, mourn, peeve, pique, sweat, worry 6 bother, harass, nettle, offend, pother, rankle, repine, ruffle 7 agonize, anguish, disturb, provoke, torment, trouble 8 disquiet, distress, irritate 9 displease
over: 3 rue 4 fear 5 dread, worry 6 bemoan, regret 8 mistrust
fret ___: 3 saw
fretful: 4 edgy 5 cross, fussy, huffy, jumpy, tense, testy, whiny 6 crabby, cranky, ornery, touchy, uneasy, whiney 7 carping, peevish, prickly, restive, worried 8 captious, caviling, critical, fluttery, petulant, restless, snappish 9 crotchety, fractious, impatient, irritable, querulous, splenetic 10 irritating, out of sorts
fretfulness: 4 care 6 nerves, temper 7 anxiety, chagrin 8 disquiet
fretting, stop: 5 relax 8 calm down
fretty: 4 edgy 5 cross, huffy, surly, testy 6 crabby, feisty, grumpy, ornery, snappy, touchy 7 grouchy, waspish 8 snappish 9 crotchety, irritable 10 out of sorts
fretwork: 7 lattice 9 adornment 10 decoration
Freud: 4 Anna 6 Lucian 7 Clement, Sigmund
contemporary: 4 Jung 5 Adler
stage: 4 oral
topic: 2 id 3 ego 5 dream
see also German
Freud (1962 film)
cast: Montgomery Clift, Larry Parks, Susannah York
director: John Huston
Freudian ___: 4 slip
Freud, Sigmund: 6 writer 8 Austrian 12 psychiatrist
contemporary: Adler, Jung
work: The Ego and the Id
The Interpretation of Dreams
Totem and Taboo
Frewer: 4 Matt
Frey, Glenn
group: The Eagles
song: The Heat Is On (1985)
You Belong to the City (1985)
Fri.: 3 day
follower: 3 Sat.
man ~: 4 asst.
preceder: 3 Thu. 4 Thur. 5 Thurs.
to Sat.: 4 yest.
see also Friday
friable: 5 crisp, flaky, light, loamy, short 6 crispy, crusty 7 brittle, fragile, powdery
friar: 4 abbé, monk 5 padre 6 priest 7 brother, recluse 8 monastic 9 Carmelite, Dominican, mendicant, religious 10 Franciscan, monastical
Hindu ~: 5 sadhu
home: 4 cell 5 abbey 8 cloister 9 monastery
Friar ___: 4 Tuck 5 Minor
___ Friar: 4 Gray 5 Black, White
Friars Club event: 5 roast
friary: 5 abbey 8 cloister 9 monastery
fribble: 3 toy 4 fool, play 5 waste 6 geegaw, gewgaw, trifle 7 trinket 8 fool away, gimcrack 9 bagatelle, frivolity 10 gamble away
Fribourg, from: 5 Swiss
fricassee: 3 fry 4 cook, meat
Frick: 4 Ford
collection: 3 art
Fricke: 5 Janie
Fricker, Brenda Oscar: My Left Foot
friction: 3 rub 4 feud, flak, wear 5 clash, flack 6 ruckus, rumpus, strife 7 chafing, discord, dispute, grating, quarrel, rasping, rivalry, rubbing, trouble 8 abrasion, bad blood, conflict, grinding, scraping, traction 9 animosity, bickering, hostility, wrangling 10 antagonism, contention, discontent, disharmony, dissension, irritation, opposition, resentment, resistance
combining form: 5 tribo-
easer: 3 lub., oil 9 lubricant
friction ___: 3 saw 4 head, pile, tape 5 drive, layer, match 6 clutch 7 gearing, welding
frictionless: 6 smooth
Frid: 8 Jonathan
Frida: 5 Kahlo
Frida (2002 film)
cast: Antonio Banderas, Salma Hayek, Ashley Judd, Alfred Molina, Geoffrey Rush
Friday: 3 cop, Joe, man, sgt. 4 Webb 8 sergeant
creator: Daniel Defoe
man ~: 4 aide, hand 6 deputy, helper 8 adjutant, factotum 9 assistant, secretary 10 lieutenant
partner: 5 Smith 6 Gannon
quest: 5 facts
___ Friday: 3 gal, guy, man 4 girl, Good 6 casual, Freaky
Friday Foster (1975 film)
cast: Pam Grier
___ Friday's: 3 T.G.I.
Friday the ___ Slept Late: 5 Rabbi
Friday the 13th (1980 film)
cast: Kevin Bacon, Harry Crosby, Adrienne King, Betsy Palmer
prop: 3 axe
role: 5 Jason
___ Frideric Handel: 6 George
fridge: 6 cooler, icebox 9 appliance
see also refrigerator
___-fried: 3 pan 4 deep, stir
Fried ___ Tomatoes: 5 Green
Friedan, Betty: 6 writer 8 activist
work: The Feminine Mystique
The Fountain of Age
It Changed My Life
Life So Far
The Second Stage
Fried Green Tomatoes (1991 film)
cast: Kathy Bates, Mary Stuart Masterson, Mary-Louise Parker, Jessica Tandy
director: Jon Avnet
Fried Green Tomatoes...
author: Fannie Flagg
Friedkin, William: 8 director
film: The Birthday Party (1968)
The Boys in the Band (1970)
The Brink's Job (1978)
The Exorcist (1973)
The French Connection (1971, AA)
The Night They Raided Minsky's (1968)
Rules of Engagement (2000)
spouse: Lesley-Anne Down, Sherry Lansing, Jeanne Moreau
Friedman: 5 Kinky 6 Jerome, Milton
Friedman, Bruce Jay: 6 writer
work: Scuba Duba
Stern
Tokyo Woes
Friedman, Milton: 8 Nobelist 9 economist
___-fried potatoes: 3 pan 4 home 6 French
Friedrich: 6 Engels, Hebbel 7 Bergius, Froebel, Rückert 9 Nietzsche, Serturner
alternative: 5 Rheem, Trane 6 Lennox 7 Carrier, Fedders
collaborator: 4 Karl
in English: 9 Frederick
___-fried steak: 7 chicken
Friel, Brian: 5 Irish 10 playwright
home: 4 Eire
Friels: 5 Colin
friend: 3 bro, pal 4 ally, beau, chum, mate 5 amigo, buddy, crony 6 backer, cohort, frater, patron 7 compeer, comrade, consort, partner 8 advocate, alter ego, familiar, intimate, neighbor, playmate, roommate, sidekick, soulmate 9 associate, classmate, colleague, companion, confidant, proponent, soulmates, supporter 10 benefactor, bosom buddy, compatriot, connection, schoolmate, well-wisher
in French: 3 ami 4 amie
in Spanish: 5 amiga, amigo
starter: 3 boy 4 girl
friend ___ court: 5 of the
Friend: 6 Quaker
pronoun: 3 thy 4 thee, thou 5 thine
friend in ___, A: 4 need
friendless: 4 lone 5 alone 6 lonely 8 lonesome, solitary 9 abandoned, alienated, estranged 10 ostracized, unattached
feeling ~: 6 lonely 7 forlorn 8 forsaken, isolated, lonesome
friendliness: 5 amity 6 comity, warmth 7 welcome 8 goodness, goodwill, open arms 10 affability
express ~: 5 smile
friendly: 4 fond, good, homy, kind, nice, warm 5 close, homey, sweet, thick 6 allied, benign, chatty, chummy, clubby, decent, genial, hearty, kindly, loving, polite, social 7 affable, amiable, cordial, helpful, likable, lovable 8 amicable, familiar, gracious, intimate, loveable, outgoing, peaceful, pleasant, sociable 9 attentive, congenial, convivial, expansive, favorable, peaceable, receptive, welcoming 10 beneficial, benevolent, buddy-buddy, gregarious, hospitable, neighborly, personable, solicitous
skies flier: 6 United
friendly ___: 4 fire
___-friendly: 3 eco 4 user
Friendly: 4 Fred
Friendly Islands: 5 Tonga
Friendly Persuasion: 4 film, song
artist: Pat Boone
cast: Gary Cooper, Marjorie Main, Dorothy McGuire, Anthony Perkins
director: William Wyler
music: Dimitri Tiomkin
Friendly's: 8 ice cream
alternative: 4 Edy's 7 Breyer's 9 Good Humor 10 Dairy Queen, Häagen-Dazs, Turkey Hill
rival: *see* restaurant chain
friend of the ___: 5 court 6 family
Friend or ___?: 3 foe
friends
and neighbors: 4 kith
be ~ with: 4 know
group: 6 circle, clique
make ~: 4 bond 7 connect
see old ~: 5 reune
___ friends: 5 among
Friends (NBC sitcom)
cast: Jennifer Aniston (Rachel Green)
Courteney Cox (Monica Geller)
Lisa Kudrow (Phoebe Buffay)
Matt LeBlanc (Joey Tribbiani)
Matthew Perry (Chandler Bing)
David Schwimmer (Ross Geller)
Friends follower: 6 Romans
friendship: 4 bond, love 5 amity, peace, unity 6 accord, comity, warmth 7 concord, empathy, harmony, rapport, society, support 8 affinity, alliance, devotion, goodwill, intimacy, sodality 9 affection, agreement, closeness, coalition, good vibes 10 amiability, attachment, attraction, consonance, favoritism, partiality, solidarity
Friendship
composer: Cole Porter
Friends of ___ Coyle, The: 5 Eddie
___ Friend, The: 3 Boy 4 Girl
...friend who never made ___: 4 a foe
fries: 4 side 8 side dish
future ~: 4 spud 5 tater 6 potato
partner: 6 burger 9 hamburger
topping: 6 catsup 7 ketchup
___ fries: 4 home 6 French, German 7 cottage, country
Friesland Museum site: 5 Emden
Frietchie: 7 Barbara
frigate: 4 boat, ship 7 carrier, cruiser, flattop, gunboat 8 corvette, man-of-war 9 destroyer 10 battleship
Frigga: 5 Norse 7 goddess
husband: 4 Odin 5 Othin
son: 5 Baldr 6 Balder
fright: 4 fear, funk, mess, scar 5 alarm, dread, panic, scare, shock, sight 6 dismay, horror, terror 7 eyesore, startle 9 terrorize, trepidity
exclamation: 4 yipe 5 yikes, yipes
sound of ~: 4 gasp
fright ___: 3 wig
___ fright: 4 mike 5 stage
frighten: 3 awe, cow 4 faze 5 alarm, appal, chill, daunt, deter, haunt, panic, repel, scare, shake, shock, spook, unman 6 appall, dismay, menace, rattle 7 horrify, petrify, startle, terrify, unhinge, unnerve 8 disquiet, scare off, threaten, unstring 9 give a turn, give pause, terrorize 10 discomfort, disconcert, discourage, intimidate, scare stiff
frightened: 5 funky, jumpy, pavid,

shaky, timid 6 afeard, afraid, aghast, gun-shy, scared, trepid, yellow 7 afeared, anxious, chicken, fearful, jittery, nervous, panicky, shivery, spooked, uptight, worried 8 cowardly, fearsome, hesitant, in a panic, recreant, timorous 9 petrified, spineless, terrified, tremulous 10 terrorized

frightening: 4 eery, grim 5 awful, dread, eerie, lurid, scary 6 creepy, horrid, spooky 7 dreaded, fearful, ghastly, hideous, macaber, macabre, ominous 8 alarming, chilling, daunting, dreadful, fearsome, gruesome, horrible, menacing, terrible 9 unearthly
  exclamation: 3 boo
  vision: 8 bad dream 9 nightmare

frightful: 4 dire, foul, gory, grim, poor, ugly 5 awful, dread, gross, hairy, lousy, lurid, scary, woful 6 crumby, crummy, dismal, grisly, horrid, morbid, odious, rotten, spooky, woeful 7 accurst, baleful, baneful, beastly, doleful, dreaded, fearful, ghastly, heinous, hideous, macaber, macabre, ominous, ungodly, vicious 8 accursed, alarming, chilling, daunting, dreadful, fearsome, God-awful, grievous, gruesome, horrible, inferior, menacing, shameful, stinking, terrible, terrific, wretched 9 abhorrent, appalling, atrocious, defective, execrable, ferocious, insidious, loathsome, miserable, monstrous, offensive, repellant, repellent, revolting, unsightly 10 abominable, despicable, detestable, disastrous, disgusting, formidable, horrendous, petrifying, unpleasant
  combining form: 4 dino-

frigid: 3 icy, raw 4 cold, cool 5 aloof, chill, gelid, nippy, polar, stiff 6 arctic, biting, bitter, chilly, frosty, frozen, wintry 7 chilled, distant, glacial, ice-cold, numbing, passive, shivery, wintery 8 freezing, hibernal, indurate, loveless, Siberian 9 below zero 10 insociable, unagitated
  time: 6 ice age

Frigid: 4 Zone
  ender: 4 aire

Frigidaire
  alternative: *see* appliance brand

frigidity: 4 cold 5 chill 7 iciness 8 coldness, gelidity 10 frozenness

frijol: 4 bean 6 legume

frijoles refritos, make: 5 refry

frill: 4 trim 5 dodad, extra 6 doodad, luxury, ruffle 7 amenity, flounce, garnish 8 froufrou, gimcrack, ornament, trimming 9 adornment, fandangle 10 decoration
  not a ~: 9 necessity, requisite 10 obligation 11 requirement

frills, cut the: 8 simplify

frilly: 4 lacy 5 fancy, gaudy, showy 6 chichi, dressy, flashy, flossy, glitzy, lavish, ornate 7 adorned, opulent 9 decorated, elaborate, gussied up, luxurious, sumptuous 10 decorative, ornamental, ornamented
  trim: 5 jabot, ruche

Friml: 6 Rudolf 8 composer

fringe: 3 hem, rim 4 brim, edge, trim 5 brink, frame, limit, skirt, verge 6 border, edging, margin, ricrac, suburb 7 extreme, flounce 8 rickrack, surround, trimming 9 outskirts, perimeter, periphery 10 borderline
  benefit: 4 boon, perk, plus 5 bonus 6 reward
  beyond the ~: 5 outré 7 bizarre, offbeat 8 freakish 10 outlandish
  combining form: 6 thysan- 7 thysano-
  on a golf course: 5 apron

fringe __: 4 area, tree 7 benefit

fringed item: 5 shawl 6 surrey

frippery: 6 finery, geegaw, gewgaw 7 clothes, jewelry 9 adornment 10 decoration, Sunday best

Frisbee: 3 fad, toy 4 disc, disk
  company: 5 Wham-o
  inspiration: 6 pie tin

Frisch: 3 Max 4 Karl 5 Frank 6 Ragnar 7 Frankie

Frisco: 4 city, town
  see also San Francisco

Frisco Kid, The (1979 film)
  cast: Harrison Ford, Gene Wilder
  director: Robert Aldrich

frisé: 6 fabric 8 material
  bichon ~: 3 dog, pet 6 canine

frisk: 3 hop 4 feel, jump, lark, leap, play, romp, skip 5 caper, check, dance, touch 6 bounce, cavort, frolic, gambol, prance, search 7 inspect, pat down, rollick 9 shake down

Friskies: 7 cat food
  alternative: *see* pet food brand

friskiness: 3 pep, zip 4 élan, zest, zing 5 spark, verve 6 bounce, fervor 7 abandon, devilry, hijinks, knavery 8 buoyancy, deviltry, mischief, vitality 9 high jinks, rascality 10 ebullience, enthusiasm, exuberance, jauntiness, liveliness, tomfoolery

frisky: 4 spry 5 peppy, zesty, zippy 6 active, bouncy, feisty, jaunty, lively 7 coltish, playful, romping, zestful 8 spirited, sporting, sportive 9 gamboling, kittenish 10 frolicsome, rollicking

__ frites: 6 pommes

Frito: 4 nosh 5 snack 8 corn chip

Frito-__: 3 Lay

frittata: 6 omelet 8 omelette
  base: 3 egg

fritter: 4 cake, laze 5 spend 6 churro, lavish, loiter, pastry, putter, trifle 9 throw away, while away
  away: 3 sap 4 idle, loaf 5 drain, trash, use up, waste 6 burn up, linger, loiter, lounge 7 consume, deplete, fribble, play out 8 squander 9 dissipate

__ fritter: 4 corn

fritto __: 5 misto

fritz
  go on the ~: 5 act up
  on the: 5 kaput 6 blooey, blooie, broken 7 damaged 9 defective, disrepair 10 broken-down, out of order

Fritz: 4 Lang 5 Busch, Haber, Loewe, Pregl 6 Leiber, Reiner, Weaver 7 Lipmann, Mondale 8 Kreisler
  comics brother: 4 Hans
  see also German

Fritzi to Nancy: 4 aunt

frivol: 5 waste 6 trifle 7 deplete 8 squander 9 bagatelle, dissipate 10 triviality

frivolity: 4 glee, jest 5 folly, mirth 6 gaiety, gayety, levity, whimsy 7 abandon, fribble, gayness, whimsey 8 dallying, nonsense, trifling, zaniness 9 diversion, flippancy, giddiness, lightness, puerility, silliness 10 triviality, volatility

frivolous: 4 flip, idle, vain 5 empty, giddy, inane, light, petty, silly 6 fickle, giggly, madcap, yeasty 7 flighty, foolish, puerile, shallow, trivial 8 childish, ill-spent, juvenile, skittish, trifling 9 arbitrary, facetious, pointless, senseless, whimsical 10 coquettish, nonserious, unprofound
  be ~ with: 3 rib 4 jest, josh 5 tease
  in a ~ way: 4 idly
  novel: 5 fluff

frizz: 4 curl, kink 5 crimp 8 make wavy

Frizzell: 5 David, Lefty

frizzle: 4 curl, sear 6 scorch, sizzle

frizzy: 5 curly, fuzzy, kinky 6 permed
  top: 4 Afro

fro: 4 away, back 6 hairdo 8 backward
  move to and ~: 3 wag 4 sway, wave 5 waver

__ fro: 5 to and

Frobe: 4 Gert

Frobisher: 3 bay 6 Martin

frock: 4 coat, gown 5 dress, smock 6 jacket, kirtle, ordain 7 clothes, garment, instate 10 Sunday best
  wearer: 4 monk 5 friar, padre 6 priest 7 brother

frock __: 4 coat

Frodo: 6 hobbit 7 Baggins
  quest: 4 ring
  uncle: 5 Bilbo

froe: 4 tool 7 cleaver

frog: 5 ranid 6 anuran, hopper, Kermit, peeper 7 crapaud, croaker, tadpole 8 polliwog, pollywog 9 amphibian
  combining form: 4 rani- 7 batrach- 8 batracho-
  cousin: 4 newt, toad
  dish: 4 legs
  ender: 3 eye, man, men 4 fish 5 mouth 6 hopper
  feature: 4 wart
  genus: 4 rana
  in one's throat: 4 rasp 7 scratch
  like a ~: 5 warty 6 croaky
  pad: 4 lily
  snack: 3 fly
  sound: 5 croak 6 ribbit
  starter: 4 bull, leap
  tree ~: 4 hyla
  young: 7 tadpole 8 polliwog, pollywog

frog __: 4 kick, lily, spit 7 sticker

__ frog: 4 bell, rain, tree, true, wood 6 chorus, flying, horned, robber, tailed 7 barking, cricket, leopard

Frog and the Ox, The source: 4 Esop 5 Aesop

froggy: 5 husky, raspy 6 croaky, hoarse 7 grating, throaty 8 croaking, gravelly, guttural

frogman: 5 diver
  gear: 4 mask, tank 5 scuba, spear 6 oxygen 7 goggles, wet suit

frogmouth: 4 bird

Frogner Park city: 4 Oslo

Frogs and __...: 6 snails

frogskin: 4 bill, buck 6 dollar 7 smacker 8 banknote, simoleon 9 greenback

frogskins
  see moolah

Frogs, The
  author: Aristophanes

__-froid: 4 sang 5 chaud

frolic: 3 fun, joy 4 lark, play, romp, trip 5 antic, caper, dance, frisk, jaunt, mirth, prank, revel, sport, spree 6 cavort, gaiety, gambol, gayety, junket, prance 7 carouse, have fun, hijinks, rollick 8 escapade 9 amusement, have a ball, high jinks, joviality, make merry, merriment, whoop it up 10 fool around, recreation, shenanigan, skylarking
  ender: 4 some

frolicking: 6 at play

frolicsome: 3 fun, gay 4 spry 5 antic, jolly, merry 6 frisky, impish, jaunty, jovial, lively 7 coltish, gleeful, jesting, jocular, playful, roguish 8 sporting, sportive 9 exuberant, gamboling, hilarious, kittenish, sprightly, vivacious 10 rollicking

from: 4 as of 5 off of 6 born in 8 starting
  in German: 3 von
  starter: 5 there, where

from __: 4 A to Z 7 scratch

from __ one: 4 year

from __ to nuts: 4 soup

from __ to post: 6 pillar

from __ to riches: 4 rags

from __ to stern: 4 stem

from __ worse: 5 bad to

from __ Z: 3 A to

__ from: 4 hail 5 apart, aside

...from __ shining...: 5 sea to

From __ day forward: 4 this

From __ Moment On: 4 This

From __ shining...: 5 sea to

From __ to Eternity: 4 Here

From __ With Love: 6 Russia

From __ You: 4 Me to

from A __: 3 to Z

From a Distance (1990 song)
  artist: Bette Midler

__ from afar: 4 come 7 worship

__ from Alabama...: 5 I come

__ From Aloes, A: 6 Lesson

__ From a Mall: 6 Scenes

__ From a Marriage: 6 Scenes

Froman: 4 Jane

from bad to __: 5 worse

From Bauhaus to Our House
  author: Tom Wolfe

From Bed to Worse
  author: Robert Benchley

__ From Brazil, The: 4 Boys

__ From Brooklyn, The: 3 Kid

__ from Chelsea: 5 Elsie

From Death to Morning
  author: Thomas Wolfe

Frome: 5 Ethan
From Far, From Eve and Morning
author: A.E. Housman
__ **from grace:** 4 fall
from head __: 5 to toe
__ **From Heaven:** 3 Far 5 A Gift 7 Pennies
from here __: 4 on in 5 on out
From Here to Eternity: 4 film 5 novel
author: James Jones
cast: Montgomery Clift, Deborah Kerr, Burt Lancaster, Donna Reed, Frank Sinatra
__ **From Ipanema, The:** 4 Girl
Frommer: 6 Arthur
Fromm, Erich: 6 writer
work: The Art of Loving
Man For Himself
__ **From Muskogee:** 4 Okie
__**, from New York...:** 4 Live
from one's __: 5 heart
.....__ from our sponsor: 5 a word
from pillar to __: 4 post
from rags to __: 6 riches
From Russia With Love: 4 film 5 novel
author: Ian Fleming
cast: Pedro Armendariz, Daniela Bianchi, Sean Connery, Bernard Lee, Lotte Lenya, Lois Maxwell, Robert Shaw
director: Terence Young
__ **From Snowy River, The:** 3 Man
from soup to nuts: 5 gamut
from stem to __: 5 stern
__ **From Syracuse, The:** 4 Boys
from the __: 5 get-go, heart
from the __ up: 6 ground
From the __ of Montezuma: 5 halls
from the beginning in Latin: 5 ab ovo 8 ab initio 9 ab origine
__ **from the blue:** 4 bolt
__ **from the Bridge:** 5 A View
From the Corner of His Eye
author: Dean Koontz
__ **From the Crypt:** 5 Tales
From the Earth to the Moon
author: Jules Verne
__ **from the hip:** 5 shoot
__ **from the horse's mouth:** 5 right
__ **From the Madding Crowd:** 3 Far
__ **from the past:** 5 blast
__ **From the Portuguese:** 7 Sonnets
__ **from the rooftops:** 5 shout
From the Terrace: 5 novel
author: John O'Hara
__ **From the Underground:** 5 Notes
__ **From the Vienna Woods:** 5 Tales
From this __ forward: 3 day
From This Moment on
composer: Cole Porter
From This Moment On (1998 song)
artist: Shania Twain
__ **From U.N.C.L.E., The:** 3 Man 4 Girl
__ **from under:** 3 out
From where __...: 4 I sit
from year __: 3 one
frond: 4 leaf 5 blade, bract 7 foliage
holder: 4 fern, palm, stem
front: 3 act, bow, van 4 face, fore, head, lead, look, mask, meet, mien, pose, show, side 5 blind, cover, first, guise, put-on 6 border, facade, face on, facing, give on, veneer 7 air mass, bearing, cover-up, display, forward, leading, obverse, outside, pretext 8 advanced, anterior, demeanor, disguise, exterior, forehead, foremost, forepart, headmost, overlook, presence, vanguard 9 beginning, coalition, semblance 10 appearance, figurehead, foreground, masquerade, pretension
be in ~: 4 lead
boat ~: 3 bow 4 prow
combining form: 4 fore- 6 antero-
ender: 3 age, ier 4 ward 5 wards
false ~: 3 act 4 airs, mask, pose, sham, show 5 bluff, guise 6 facade 8 disguise
for: 7 endorse, promote 8 nominate 9 recommend 10 put forward
in ~: 4 best, tops 5 afore, ahead, first 6 onward 7 forward, leading, onwards, optimal, supreme 8 peerless 9 at the fore, nonpareil, paramount, unequaled, unrivaled 10 preeminent, unrivalled
in ~ of: 6 before 7 prior to 9 preceding
in ~ of (prefix): 3 pre-, pro- 4 ante-, fore-
man: 5 scout 7 bird-dog 8 outrider
money: 7 advance
neither ~ nor back: 4 side
office: 9 directors 10 executives, management
on: 4 face, look 8 overlook
out-~: 5 frank, on top, plain 6 candid, direct, honest, square 7 sincere, winning 8 boastful, exultant, straight, truthful, unbeaten 9 guileless, honorable, in the lead, veracious 10 forthright, on the level
put on a false ~: 3 lie 7 cover up, deceive, mislead 9 misdirect 10 steer wrong
put up a ~: 3 lie 4 pose, sham 7 pretend 9 misinform
starter: 3 bow 4 lake 5 beach, break, ocean, river, shore, store, water 6 battle
front __: 4 desk, dive, door, foot, four, line, nine, page, room 5 bench, court, money 6 burner, loader, matter, office, runner, window
front-__: 3 end 4 line, load, rank 5 drive
front-__ drive: 5 wheel
__ **front:** 3 bow, fly, ice, out, sea 4 cold, drop, fall, home, warm, wave, yoke 5 block, false, oxbow, polar, shirt, shock, slant, swell 6 united 7 people's, popular
__**-front:** 3 out
Front __ Farrell: 4 Page
frontal: 6 head-on 10 face-to-face
frontal __: 4 bone, lobe 5 gyrus 7 cyclone
__**-frontal:** 4 full
front and __: 6 center
front-end
job: 5 toe-in
front-end job: 9 alignment, alinement
frontier: 4 edge 5 brink, limit 6 border, remote, sticks 7 boonies, outback 8 boundary 9 backwoods, boondocks 10 hinterland
adventurer: 5 scout
dwelling: 5 cabin
establishment: 3 bar, inn 6 saloon 7 barroom 10 blacksmith, restaurant
outpost: 4 fort
transportation: 5 buggy, horse, stage 8 carriage 10 stagecoach
Frontier: 3 car 4 auto 6 Nissan
__ **Frontier:** 3 New 5 On the
frontiersman: 5 Boone 7 pioneer, settler 8 colonist, Crockett, emigrant 9 immigrant 10 inhabitant
fronting: 6 toward 7 towards 8 opposite
fronton: 5 court
basket: 5 cesta
sport: 7 jai alai
front page
box: 3 ear
item: 4 news 5 event, title
word: 5 extra
front-page: 3 big 6 of note 7 notable 9 important, momentous 10 meaningful, noteworthy
Front Page Farrell: 9 radio show
Front Page, The: 4 play
author: Ben Hecht
character: 5 Hildy 6 Mollie
Front Page, The (1974 film)
cast: Carol Burnett, Jack Lemmon, Walter Matthau
director: Billy Wilder
front-runner: 4 star 6 choice, leader 7 darling 8 favorite 9 number one
Front, The (1976 film)
cast: Woody Allen, Herschel Bernardi, Zero Mostel
director: Martin Ritt
front-wheel __: 5 drive
Froot Loops
competitor: *see* cereal
frosh: 4 pleb 5 plebe 7 student
see also college, freshman
frost: 3 nip 4 cold, cool, hoar, rime 6 freeze, whiten 8 coldness 9 crispness
again: 5 reice
combining form: 4 crym- 5 crymo-
covered: 3 icy 4 rimy 5 hoary
ender: 3 bit 4 bite, fish, line, work 6 bitten
kin: 3 dew
melt the ~: 5 deice
over: 5 ice up
remover: 6 deicer
starter: 4 hoar 5 perma
victim: 3 bud
frost __: 5 grape, heave, point, smoke 6 flower
frost-__ refrigerator: 4 free
__ **frost:** 5 black, white 6 silver 7 killing
...frost __ the punkin: 4 is on
Frost: 4 Jack 5 David, Sadie 6 Robert
Frost __: 4 Belt
Frost at Midnight
author: Samuel Taylor Coleridge
frostbitten: 4 numb
Frost, David: 3 Sir
frosted: 3 icy 5 glacè, white 6 pearly
Frosted __-Wheats: 4 Mini
Frosted Flakes
competitor: *see* cereal
Frosted Mini-Wheats
competitor: *see* cereal
frosting: 5 glaze, icing 7 topping 8 covering
apply ~: 3 ice
Frost/Nixon (2008 film)
cast: Kevin Bacon, Frank Langella, Michael Sheen
director: Ron Howard
Frost, Robert: 4 poet
contemporary: 5 Auden
work: The Axe-Helve
Birches
Canis Major
The Death of the Hired Man
Fire and Ice
The Gift Outright
The Hill Wife
Hyla Brook
In a Poem
In a Vale
Into My Own
A Late Walk
Mending Wall
The Most of It
Mowing
Not to Keep
Once by the Pacific
The Oven Bird
Pan With Us
A Peck of Gold
The Road Not Taken
Stopping by Woods on a Snowy Evening
Storm Fear
To E.T.
Tree at My Window
The Tuft of Flowers
The Witch of Coos
frosty: 3 icy, raw 4 cold, cool, iced 5 chill, gelid, nippy, polar 6 arctic, biting, bitter, chilly, frigid, frozen, wintry 7 chilled, glacial, ice-cold, numbing, shivery, wintery 8 freezing, Siberian 10 unagitated
Frosty accessory: 4 pipe
froth: 4 barm, fizz, foam, head, scum, suds, surf 5 spray, spume 6 aerate, bubble, burble, gurgle, lather, seethe, simmer 7 bubbles, ferment, slobber 10 effervesce
up: 4 boil, fizz, foam 6 bubble, gurgle, simmer 7 blister 9 percolate 10 effervesce
frothy: 5 barmy, foamy, light, soapy, sudsy 6 beaten, bubbly, yeasty 7 foaming, lathery 8 untaxing 10 fermenting
froufrou: 5 frill 6 gewgaw 7 trinket 8 ornament 9 adornment 10 decoration
frown: 4 lour, pout, sulk 5 glare, lower, scowl 6 glower 7 grimace
upon: 4 mind, veto 5 shame 6 object, oppose, refuse 7 censure, run down, scoff at 8 belittle, reproach, turn down 9 criticize, discredit, disparage
frowned on: 4 tabu 5 taboo 10 not allowed
frowning: 5 angry, stern, surly 6 morose, sullen 8 lowering, scowling 9 glowering
frowzy: 4 rank 5 dirty, dowdy, fetid, fusty, moldy, musty, stale 6 foetid, frumpy, rancid, shabby, sloppy,

smelly, stinky, unneat, untidy **7** noisome, unkempt **8** slovenly **10** bedraggled, disheveled, malodorous
frozen: **3** icy, raw **4** cold, iced, numb **5** at bay, chill, fixed, gelid, glacé, nippy, polar, stiff **6** arctic, biting, bitter, chilly, frappé, frigid, frosty, rooted, wintry **7** chilled, glacial, ice-cold, numbing, shivery, stopped, wintery **8** freezing, immobile, Siberian **9** immovable, petrified, suspended, unpliable **10** motionless, stock-still
dessert: **3** ice **5** bombe **6** frappé, gelati, gelato **7** sherbet **8** ice cream
fall: **4** snow **5** sleet
not ~: **5** fresh
rain: **4** hail **5** sleet
region: **6** icecap
water: **3** ice **6** icicle
frozen __: **3** fog **4** food **6** assets, yogurt **7** custard, pudding
__-frozen: **4** deep
Frozen (1998 song)
artist: Madonna
frozen-faced: **5** rocky, stony **6** flinty, stoney **7** deadpan **8** hardened, ruthless **9** heartless, merciless **10** inflexible
fructify: **4** bear **5** bloom, fruit **7** blossom **9** fertilize
fructose: **5** sugar
glucose, to ~: **6** isomer
frug: **5** dance
frugal: **5** chary, light, spare **6** Lenten, skimpy **7** careful, prudent, sparing, thrifty **8** ungiving **9** penny-wise, provident **10** abstemious, economical, unwasteful
be ~: **4** save **5** reuse, skimp, stint **6** scrape **9** economize
one: **5** saver
too ~: **4** mean, near **5** cheap, tight **6** greedy, stingy **7** miserly **9** penurious
Frugal Gourmet, The: Jeff Smith
frugality: **6** thrift **7** economy **9** parsimony, scrimping **10** abstinence, moderation, providence, stinginess
fruit: **3** fig, nut, pay **4** akee, bael, crop, date, kaki, kiwi, lime, pear, plum, pome, sloe, sorb, ugli **5** acorn, apple, berry, cacao, cubeb, drupe, grape, guava, lemon, mamey, mango, maqui, melon, nopal, olive, papaw, peach, prune, salal **6** annona, banana, casaba, cherry, citron, citrus, dahoon, durian, jujube, loquat, maypop, orange, papaya, pawpaw, pomelo, profit, quince, raisin, result, return, reward, sapota, tangor, tomato **7** acerola, apricot, atemoya, avocado, benefit, bilimbi, cassaba, chayote, coconut, cumquat, currant, genipap, harvest, kumquat, marasca, outcome, produce, product, pumpkin, results, saguaro, satsuma, tangelo **8** barberry, bayberry, bergamot, bilberry, canistel, cowberry, dewberry, dogberry, doom palm, doum palm, eggfruit, fructify, hawthorn, mandarin, may apple, mirliton, mulberry, pitahaya, plantain, rambutan, sea grape, shaddock, sweetsop, tamarind, teaberry **9** Anjou pear, bearberry, blueberry, carambola, cherimoya, cranberry, freestone, hackberry, love apple, manzanita, muscadine, muskmelon, nectarine, persimmon, pineapple, raspberry, sapodilla, tangerine, tomatillo **10** blackberry, calamondin, clingstone, cloudberry, elderberry, gooseberry, granadilla, grapefruit, loganberry, mangosteen, strawberry, watermelon
acid: **6** citric
Asian ~: **6** durian, loquat **7** bilimbi **8** rambutan, tamarind **9** carambola
autumn ~: **4** pear
bananalike ~: **8** plantain
banned ~ spray: **4** Alar
banyan ~: **3** fig
basket for dried ~: **5** frail
bear ~: **5** bloom, ripen **6** thrive, unfold **7** blossom, prosper **8** fructify
berrylike ~: **5** cubeb
black ~: **5** olive
blue ~: **7** genipap
bog ~: **9** cranberry
bramble ~: **10** blackberry
breakfast ~: **5** melon **6** banana
brown ~: **3** fig
cactus ~: **5** nopal **7** saguaro **8** pitahaya
candlemaking ~: **8** bayberry
cashew family ~: **5** mango
center: **4** core
Central American ~: **9** sapodilla
chayote ~: **8** mirliton
cherrylike ~: **7** acerola **9** hackberry
chicle-yielding ~: **9** sapodilla
Chilean ~: **5** maqui
Chinese ~: **6** loquat
chocolate ~: **5** cacao
citrus ~: **4** lime **5** lemon **6** citron, orange **7** kumquat **8** shaddock **9** tangerine **10** grapefruit
combining form: **4** -carp **5** carpo-, fruct- **6** fructi-
compote ~: **4** pear
concoction: **5** salad
cookie ~: **3** fig
covering: **4** peel, rind, skin
cucumber-shaped ~: **7** bilimbi
cupped ~: **5** acorn
desert ~: **4** date
dish: **3** pie
downy ~: **5** peach
dreamy ~ of Greek myth: **5** lotus
dried ~: **5** prune **6** raisin
drink: **3** ade **5** cider, juice, punch **6** frappé **7** limeade **8** lemonade
dry ~: **3** nut **5** regma
East Indian ~: **5** cubeb **10** mangosteen
egg-shaped ~: **5** mango **8** may apple **10** granadilla
egg-sized ~: **4** kiwi
elm family ~: **9** hackberry
ender: **3** age **4** cake, wood
fancier: **3** Eve **4** Adam
flaw: **6** bruise
fleshy ~: **4** pepo, pome **5** papaw
fuzzy ~: **4** kiwi **5** peach
Georgia ~: **5** peach
gingerbread-flavored ~: **8** doom palm, doum palm
grapefruitlike ~: **8** shaddock
green ~: **5** grape, olive **9** cherimoya **10** gooseberry
hair: **6** villus
hairs: **5** villi
hard ~: **6** quince
holder: **4** stem
Indian ~: **4** bael **5** cubeb **10** mangosteen
innards: **4** pulp
Itaian ~: **8** bergamot
Jamaican ~: **4** akee
Japanese persimmon ~: **4** kaki
juicy ~: **5** berry, mango, melon **6** orange **8** tamarind **10** mangosteen
leathery ~: **5** cacao
lemonlike ~: **6** cedrat, citron
like fake ~: **3** wax **5** waxed
like some ~: **5** acerb, pulpy, tangy
melonlike ~: **5** papaw
Mexican ~: **7** chayote **8** eggfruit **9** sapodilla, tomatillo
musky ~: **9** muscadine
oblong ~: **5** mango
orchard ~: **4** pear **5** apple
oval ~: **8** rambutan
Pacific Coast ~: **5** salal **9** manzanita
palm ~: **4** date
pear-shaped ~: **3** fig **4** bael **7** chayote
prepare ~: **4** core, pare, peel **6** deseed
prickly ~: **6** durian **8** hawthorn **10** gooseberry
problem: **3** rot
producer: **4** tree
product: **3** jam **5** cider, jelly, juice **6** nectar
pulpy ~: **5** drupe
purple ~: **4** sloe **8** mulberry **10** elderberry
red ~: **7** saguaro **8** hawthorn, rambutan **9** cranberry **10** loganberry
ribbed ~: **5** cacao
ripener: **6** ethene
rose ~: **3** hip
rot: **4** blet
rowan ~: **4** sorb
sandy beach ~: **8** sea grape
service tree ~: **4** sorb
shrub ~: **5** berry **6** annona **8** barberry **9** bearberry, blueberry
single-seeded ~: **5** akene, drupe **6** achene
slot-machine ~: **5** lemon **6** cherry
sour ~: **4** lime, sloe **5** lemon **7** bilimbi
Spain: **4** pina
starter: **3** egg **4** jack **5** bread, grape
stewed ~: **5** grunt, sauce
sticky ~: **3** fig **4** date
summer ~: **4** plum **5** melon
tart ~: **4** sloe **5** berry **9** crab apple, cranberry
thick pod ~: **8** tamarind
thick rind ~: **6** citron
tree: **3** fig **4** palm, pear, sorb **5** apple, papaw **6** annona, orange
tropical ~: **3** fig **4** akee, date, ugli **5** guava, mango, melon **6** banana, papaya **7** genipap, soursop **8** sea grape, sweetsop **9** cherimoya
vine ~: **5** melon **7** chayote
waxy ~: **8** bayberry
West Indies ~: **5** mamey **6** annona **7** acerola
white ~: **8** bayberry **9** cherimoya
wild ~: **10** blackberry
wild grape ~: **9** muscadine
wintergreen ~: **8** teaberry
wrinkly ~: **4** ugli
yellow ~: **4** bael **5** guava **6** dahoon, loquat, papaya, quince **8** may apple, sweetsop **9** carambola, jackfruit **10** cloudberry
fruit __: **3** bat, cup, fly, jar **4** tree **5** knife, ranch, sugar
__ fruit: **3** hen, key **4** bear, star, true **5** false, spore, stone **6** fleshy, simple **7** miracle
__ Fruit: **5** Juicy **7** Strange
fruit cup: **7** dessert **9** appetizer
morsel: **4** pear **6** cherry, orange
fruitful: **4** rich **6** fecund, useful **7** copious, fertile, profuse, teeming **8** abundant, blooming, prolific **9** exuberant, inventive, lucrative, luxuriant, plenteous, plentiful, rewarding, well-spent **10** beneficial, blossoming, productive, profitable, successful, worthwhile
fruitfulness: **6** bounty, plenty, wealth **8** opulence **9** abundance, affluence, fecundity, profusion **10** luxuriance
fruition: **6** result **7** harvest, success **8** maturity, ripeness **10** attainment, completion, perfection
at ~: **4** ripe
bring to ~: **5** ripen **7** realize **8** complete
fruit juice: **8** beverage
fruit-juice name: **5** Mott's
fruitless: **4** idle, vain **5** empty, no-win **6** barren, futile, hollow, in vain **7** inutile, sterile, useless **8** gainless **9** for naught, infertile, pointless, thankless, to no avail **10** profitless, to no effect, unavailing, unprolific
fruitlessly: **6** in vain
Fruit of the Loom
product: **4** sock **5** brief, short **6** T-shirt
rival: **5** Hanes
fruits: **4** crop **7** harvest, produce
science of ~: **8** pomology
__ fruits: **5** first
fruit salad: **6** medals
Fruits of the Earth, The
author: André Gide
frumpy: **4** drab **5** dowdy, tacky **6** blowsy, frowsy, frowzy, shabby, unneat **7** unkempt **8** slovenly **9** unstylish **10** bedraggled
frustrate: **3** nip **4** balk, dash, defy, foil, mock, stop **5** avert, baulk, block, cheat, cross, elude, stimy, stump, stymy **6** arrest, blight, defeat, hamper, hang up, hinder, hogtie, impede, negate, outwit, resist, scotch, stymie, thwart **7** counter, fluster, inhibit, nonplus, nullify, prevent, redress, ward off **8** handcuff, obstruct, outflank, pre-

FR

clude, sabotage 9 discomfit, displease, forestall, hamstring, interfere, tantalize, undermine 10 circumvent, counteract, disappoint, disconcert, discourage, dishearten, neutralize
frustrated: 9 inhibited, resentful, up the wall 10 embittered
sound: 4 sigh 6 sheesh
frustration: 6 defeat 7 chagrin, failure, setback 8 headache
frustule: 5 shell 8 seashell
Frutiger: 4 font 8 typeface
__-frutti: 5 tutti
fry: 4 cook, heat, sear 5 brown, sauté, singe 6 rebuke, sizzle 7 cookout, frizzle 8 pan-broil 9 fricassee
ender: 3 pan
fish ~: 4 meal 6 picnic
small ~: 3 boy, tad, tot 4 fish 5 child, kiddy, youth
fry __: 4 cook
__ fry: 4 fish 5 small 6 French
__-fry: 3 pan 4 deep, stir 6 batter 7 chicken
Fry: 7 Francis, Stephen
Fry, Christopher: 7 British 10 playwright
work: The Lady's Not for Burning
Frye, David: 4 aper
Frye, Deacon show: 4 Amen
__ fryer: 4 deep
fryer, Cantonese: 3 wok
frying
medium: 3 oil 4 lard 6 Crisco
pan: 3 wok 6 spider, vessel 7 skillet
frying __: 3 pan
frypan: 3 wok 6 spider 7 skillet 8 cookware, gridiron
F. Scott: 10 Fitzgerald
Fs, get: 4 fail
F-sharp
equivalent: 5 G-flat
FSU conference: 3 ACC
ft.: 4 lgth., meas.
3280.8 ~: 2 km. 3 kil.
6 ~ at sea: 3 fth.
Ft. __, FL: 5 Myers
Ft. __, IN: 5 Wayne
FTC part: 3 Fed. 4 Comm. 5 Trade 7 Federal 10 Commission
FTO: 3 car 4 auto 10 Mitsubishi
F Troop (ABC sitcom)
cast: Ken Berry (Capt. Wilton Parmenter)
Melody Patterson (Wrangler Jane)
Larry Storch (Cpl. Randolph Agarn)
Forrest Tucker (Sgt. Morgan O'Rourke)
Indians: Hekawi
location: Fort Courage
structure: 4 fort, tipi 5 tepee 6 teepee
ft./sec. measure: 3 vel. 8 velocity
Ft. Worth campus: 3 TCU
__ fu: 4 kung
Fu __: 6 Manchu
Fuad successor: 5 Faruk 6 Farouk
fubsy: 5 beefy, obese, plump, pudgy, pursy, stout 6 chubby, fleshy, portly, pyknic, rotund, stocky, zaftig, zoftig 7 adipose, paunchy 8 roly-poly 9 corpulent 10 overweight
fuchsia: 3 red 4 pink 5 color, plant, shrub 6 flower, purply 8 purplish
relative: *see* red color
fucoid: 7 seaweed
Fudd: 5 Elmer
fuddle: 6 muddle, puzzle 7 confuse, nonplus, perplex 8 bewilder 9 inebriate
fuddled: 5 at sea, dazed, dizzy, tipsy 6 addled 7 rattled 8 confused 10 bewildered, confounded, taken aback
fuddy-duddy: 4 dodo, fogy, poop, prig, prim 5 fogey 6 fossil, geezer, square 9 formalist 10 fussbudget
fudge: 3 gas, lie, pad, rot 4 blah, bosh, bull, bunk, drat, fake, guff, jazz, jive, pooh, tosh 5 bilge, candy, cheat, color, dodge, evade, hedge, hokum, hooey, prate, slant, snack, stuff, trash, tripe 6 bunkum, bushwa, doctor, drivel, footle, gabble, gammon, gibber, havers, hot air, humbug, jabber, jargon, kibosh, piffle 7 baloney, blarney, blather, blether, boloney, bushwah, dessert, distort, eyewash, falsify, flannel, flubdub, fustian, garbage, hogwash, inanity, pretend, quibble, rubbish, twaddle 8 buncombe, claptrap, falderal, falderol, flimflam, flummery, folderal, folderol, nonsense, slipslop, tommyrot, trumpery 9 banana oil, chocolate, embellish, embroider, fabricate, gibberish, kidstakes, moonshine, overstate, poppycock, rigmarole, sweetmeat 10 applesauce, balderdash, bilge water, codswallop, confection, double-talk, exaggerate, flapdoodle, galimatias, Jabberwock, mumbo jumbo, rigamarole, taradiddle, understate
flavor: 5 maple, mocha
like ~: 5 gooey
Oh ~!: 3 bah, rot 4 pooh, tosh 5 pshaw 6 phooey
fudge __: 6 factor, ripple, sundae
__ fudge: 7 vanilla
Fudge-a-mania
author: Judy Blume
fudge ripple: 8 ice cream
alternative: *see* ice cream flavor
fuel: 3 gas, LNG, oil 4 coal, coke, feed, food, logs, peat, wood 5 gas up, juice, LP gas, stoke 6 energy, ethane, fill up, hexane, incite, kindle, petrol, tank up 7 coal gas, gasohol, impetus, nourish, propane, stoke up 8 dimethyl, energize, firewood, gasoline, kerosene, kindling, matériel, stimulus 10 ammunition, natural gas, propellant, sustenance
additive: 6 deicer
add ~ to the fire: 4 spur, stir 5 rouse, stoke 6 whip up, work up 7 agitate 9 stimulate
alternative ~: 4 wind 6 ethane 7 gasohol 8 dimethyl, sunlight
auto ~ mixer: 4 carb 10 carburetor
bottled ~: 5 LP gas
camper's ~: 3 LPG
car ~: 3 gas 8 gasoline
carrier: 4 tank 5 oiler 6 coaler
cartel: 4 OPEC
efficiency abbr.: 3 EPA, mpg
fireplace ~: 4 logs, wood
fossil ~: 3 gas, oil 4 coal
funny-car ~: 5 nitro
furnace ~: 4 coal, coke
gas: 6 butane, ethane 8 dimethyl
heating ~: 3 gas, oil 4 coal
indicator: 5 gauge 8 gas gauge
industrial ~: 4 coal, coke
lamp ~: 3 oil 8 kerosene
lighter ~: 6 butane
measure: 6 gallon, octane
organic ~: 6 biogas
plane ~: 5 avgas
rocket ~: 3 LOX
rocket ~ ingredient: 5 nitro
source: 4 peat
starter: 3 syn
train ~: 4 coal
truck ~: 6 diesel
fuel __: 3 oil, rod 4 cell 7 economy
__ fuel: 3 hog 6 diesel, fossil 7 nuclear
Fuentes: 5 Daisy 6 Carlos
Fuentes, Carlos: 6 writer 7 Mexican
work: Aura
The Hydra Head
The Old Gringo
Fuentes del Valle: 4 city, town
locale: 6 Mexico
fugacious: 8 fleeting, volatile 9 ephemeral
Fuga Meshuga
composer: PDQ Bach
Fugard, Athol: 6 writer 10 playwright 12 South African
work: The Abbess
The Blood Knot
Boesman and Lena
Captain's Tiger
The Cell
The Coat
Hello and Goodbye
The Island
The Last Bus
A Lesson From Aloes
Nongogo
Playland
The Road to Mecca
Tsotsi
Valley Song
Fugger: 5 Jakob
fuggy: 5 stale 7 airless
__ fugit: 6 tempus
fugitate: 3 fly, run 4 bail, blow, bolt, flee, skip 5 leave, scoot, scram, split 6 bug out, cut out, decamp, depart, escape, run off, skidoo 7 abscond, get away, make off, run away, scamper, skip out, vamoose 8 turn tail 9 cut and run, hotfoot it, skedaddle 10 fly the coop, make tracks, take flight
fugitive: 5 rover 6 outlaw 7 at large, escapee, outcast, passing, runaway 8 criminal, renegade, temporal, volatile 9 momentary, temporary, transient 10 transitory
Fugitive, The (1993 film)
cast: Harrison Ford, Tommy Lee Jones, Sela Ward
director: Andrew Davis
Fugitive, The (ABC drama)
cast: David Janssen (Richard Kimble)
Barry Morse (Lt. Philip Gerard)
narrator: William Conrad
Fugitive Trail, The
author: Zane Grey
fugu: 4 fish 10 puffer fish
locale: 5 Japan
fugue: 5 music
composer: 4 Bach
part: 6 answer
relative: 5 canon
Fugue for Tinhorns
composer: Frank Loesser
__ Fugue, The: 5 Art of
Fujairah
locale: 3 UAE
Fuji: 4 city, film, town 6 camera 7 volcano
alternative: *see* camera
flow: 4 lava
like ~: 5 snowy
locale: 4 Asia 5 Japan 6 Honshu
neighbor: 5 Asama
opening: 6 crater
Fujimori: 7 Alberto
land: 4 Peru
__-ful: 5 chock
Fu la sorte dell'armi: 4 duet
fulcrum: 4 axis 5 hinge, pivot 6 center
it turns on a ~: 5 lever
oar ~: 5 thole
Fulda tributary: 4 Eder
fulfill: 2 do 4 heed, meet, mind, obey 5 bow to, crown, serve 6 accept, attain, bend to, effect, enrich, finish, follow, redeem, supply 7 abide by, achieve, agree to, delight, execute, gratify, observe, perform, realize, respect, satisfy, succeed, suffice 8 adhere to, carry out, complete, conclude, listen to, make good 9 conform to, consent to, discharge, implement 10 accomplish, complement, comply with, consummate, effectuate, make good on
an obligation: 5 pay up 6 square 7 satisfy 10 remunerate
fulfilled: 7 content 9 compassed, completed, concluded, delighted, gladdened, gratified, perfected, performed, satisfied 10 actualized, dispatched
be ~: 5 occur 6 happen 8 come true
not ~: 5 unmet
fulfilling: 9 effectual, execution, rewarding 10 gratifying
__-fulfilling prophecy: 4 self
fulfillment: 3 end 5 kicks 8 exercise, fruition 10 perfection
Fulgencio: 7 Batista
fulgent: 3 lit 5 aglow, shiny 6 ablaze, bright, flashy 7 beaming, blazing, glowing, lambent, radiant, shining 8 dazzling, gleaming, luminous, lustrous 9 brilliant, sparkling
Fulghum: 6 Robert
fulgurate: 3 run, zip 4 bolt, dart, dash, race, rush, tear, whiz, zoom 5 flash, hurry, scoot, speed 6 hasten, scurry, sprint 7 scamper
fuliginous: 5 sooty
full: 3 all, big, fed, SRO 4 deep, rich, wide 5 ample, awash, broad, flush, laden, large, plump, puffy, round, sated, thick, total, whole 6 all-out, choate, cloyed, entire, gorged,

imbued, jammed, loaded, minute, packed, utmost **7** copious, crammed, crowded, glutted, maximum, orotund, plenary, profuse, replete, rounded, stuffed, teeming **8** absolute, abundant, affluent, brimming, bursting, complete, detailed, generous, implicit, integral, itemized, livelong, occupied, resonant, satiated, sonorous, thorough, whole-hog **9** abounding, bounteous, extensive, inclusive, jam-packed, plenteous, satisfied, surfeited, undivided, unlimited **10** at capacity, blow-by-blow, exhaustive, sufficient, unabridged, voluminous
amount: **3** all **4** body **5** total, whole **8** entirety, the works, totality **9** aggregate
at ~ gallop: **4** fast **5** apace **7** hastily, quickly, rapidly, swiftly **8** pell-mell, speedily **9** posthaste
blast: **6** in toto, wholly **7** flat out, totally, utterly **8** entirely **9** to the hilt **10** completely, thoroughly, to the limit
ender: **4** back
feather: **6** finery **8** glad rags
growth: **5** prime **8** majority **9** adulthood
having a ~ plate: **4** busy
in ~: **5** uncut **6** wholly **7** totally **8** as a whole, entirely **10** completely, thoroughly, to the limit
in ~ flower: **6** mature **7** matured **8** blooming
in music: **6** grosso
not at ~ power: **5** on low
of fat: **4** oily **6** greasy **7** buttery
of fun: **5** jolly, merry **8** sporting, sportive
of ginger: **4** game **5** peppy **6** active, frisky, lively, spunky **7** scrappy **8** spirited
of holes: **5** leaky **6** flawed, porous, ragged
of jeopardy: **4** iffy **5** dicey, hairy **6** chancy, daring, touchy, tricky, unsafe **7** fraught, parlous, unsound **8** perilous, ticklish **9** dangerous, daredevil, desperate, foolhardy, hazardous, uncertain **10** touch-and-go
of substance: **4** rich **5** meaty, pithy **7** weighty **8** profound
of (suffix): **3** -ose
of vigor: **4** hale **5** alert, perky, zippy **6** active, bubbly, feisty, lively, potent, robust, strong, sturdy, virile **7** dashing, dynamic, healthy, vibrant, zestful **8** animated, muscular, powerful, spirited **9** energetic, sprightly, strenuous, vivacious
of vim: **4** go-go, spry **5** alert, alive, brisk, lusty, peppy, perky, vital, zesty, zingy, zippy **6** active, bright, bubbly, feisty, frisky, lively **7** dashing, dynamic, healthy, piquant, playful, vibrant, zinging **8** animated, skittish, spirited, vigorous, youthful **9** energetic, sparkling, sprightly, vivacious
poke ~ of holes: **6** riddle **8** puncture
range: **4** A to Z **5** gamut, sweep **7** breadth **8** spectrum
supply: **7** satiety, surfeit **8** plethora **9** plenitude **10** saturation
tilt: **4** fast **5** swift **7** rapidly, swiftly
turn: **5** orbit **6** circle **10** revolution
type of ~ house: **6** aces up
with ~ faculties: **4** sane **5** sound **8** composed, rational, sensible **9** collected, judicious, practical, pragmatic, temperate **10** controlled
full __: **4** moon, sail, stop, tilt, time, word **5** blast, blood, dress, frame, house, marks, rhyme, speed, swing, twist **6** circle, cousin, gainer, nelson
full __ air: **5** of hot
full __ and credit: **5** faith
full-__: **3** cut **4** bore, line, size, term **5** blown, dress, faced, grain, grown, power, scale, sized, timer **6** bodied, length, rigged **7** blooded, figured, fledged, frontal, mouthed, service
full-__ press: **5** court
__-full: **4** cram, half **5** chock, choke, chuck
Full __ ahead!: **5** speed, steam
Full __ and Empty Arms: **4** Moon
Full __ Jacket: **5** Metal
Full __, The: **5** Monty
fullback: **7** athlete, gridder **10** footballer
attempt: **4** gain, goal **5** carry
full-blooded: **5** hardy, sound **6** hearty, robust, unmixt, virile **7** unmixed **8** powerful, purebred, vigorous
full-blown: **4** aged **6** all-out, mature **9** unlimited **10** exhaustive
full-bodied: **4** rich **6** mellow, potent, robust, strong
full-court __: **5** press
full-dress: **4** A to Z **5** total **6** all-out, entire, minute **7** in-depth **8** complete, detailed, profound, sweeping, thorough **9** extensive, intensive, out-and-out, searching **10** definitive, exhaustive
Fuller: **3** Roy **4** Loie **5** Bobby **6** Alfred, Robert, Samuel **7** Charles **8** Margaret
Fuller __: **5** Brush
Fuller, Margaret: **6** writer
Fuller, R. Buckminster: **8** engineer **9** architect
creation: **4** dome
first name: Richard
Fullerton: **4** city, town
locale: **10** California
full faith and __: **6** credit
full-figured: **5** beefy, buxom, fubsy, heavy, obese, plump, pudgy, pursy, stout **6** chubby, fleshy, portly, pyknic, rotund, stocky, zaftig **7** adipose, paunchy **8** roly-poly **9** corpulent **10** overweight
full-flavored: **4** good, nice, rich **5** spicy, tangy, tasty, yummy **6** savory, spicey **7** piquant **8** luscious, pleasing, tempting **9** ambrosial, delicious, palatable, toothsome **10** appetizing, delectable
full-fledged: **5** adult, of age, prime, whole **6** all-out, mature **7** ripened
full-grown: **3** big **4** ripe **5** adult, of age, prime **6** mature **7** ripened
Full House (ABC sitcom)
cast: Candace Cameron (D.J. Tanner)
David Coulier (Joey Gladstone)
Lori Loughlin (Becky Donaldson)
Ashley and Mary-Kate Olsen (Michelle Elizabeth Tanner)
Bob Saget (Danny Tanner)
John Stamos (Jesse Cochran)
Jodie Sweetin (Steph Tanner)
dog: **5** Comet
full-length: **5** uncut **8** complete
Full Metal Jacket (1987 film)
cast: Adam Baldwin, Vincent D'Onofrio, Matthew Modine
director: Stanley Kubrick
setting: **3** Hué, Nam **7** Vietnam
Full Moon and __ Arms: **5** Empty
fullness: **7** breadth, satiety **8** maturity
full of __: **4** life **5** beans **7** baloney **8** malarkey
full of __ air: **3** hot
full of combining form: **3** -ous
full-out: **5** total **9** extensive, unlimited
full-range: **4** A to Z **5** whole **10** exhaustive
full-scale: **6** all-out **9** extensive, unlimited **10** exhaustive
full-size: **4** ripe **5** adult, grown **6** mature **7** grown-up, ripened
full speed __: **5** ahead
full steam __: **5** ahead
full-strength: **4** neat, pure **8** straight **9** undiluted
fully: **3** all **4** well **5** in all, plumb, quite **6** bodily, in toto, openly, wholly **7** in depth, totally, utterly **8** entirely, from A to Z, outright, whole hog **9** all the way, every inch, inside out, perfectly, to the hilt **10** altogether, completely, thoroughly, to the teeth
fulminate: **4** boil, fume, lash, rage, rail **5** decry, knock **6** berate, vilify **7** censure, condemn, declaim, explode, protest, put down, smolder, thunder, upbraid **8** bloviate, denounce, detonate, smoulder **9** castigate **10** animadvert, denunciate, intimidate, vituperate
fulmination: **4** rant **5** abuse **6** screed, sermon, tirade **7** censure, ranting **8** diatribe, harangue, jeremiad, outburst **9** invective, philippic **10** revilement
fulsome: **4** oily **7** profuse **8** effusive **9** exuberant, overblown
Fulton: **5** Sheen **6** Eileen, Robert
Fulton, Robert power: **5** steam
Fulton's __: **5** Folly
fumarole: **4** hole, vent
fumble: **3** err **4** drop, flub, goof, miss, muff **5** botch, fluff, grope **6** bobble, boggle, bollix, bumble, bungle, foozle, mess up, slip-up **7** blunder, botch up, louse up **8** flounder, hesitate, misfield **9** feel about, mishandle, mismanage
fumbler: **2** ox **3** oaf **4** clod, lout **5** klutz
exclamation: **4** oops
fumbling: **5** crude, green, inept, unapt **6** clumsy, gauche, klutzy, oafish **7** awkward **8** bumbling, bungling, cloddish, inexpert **9** all thumbs, incapable, maladroit **10** amateurish, hesitation, unskillful
fume: **3** gas **4** boil, burn, fret, pout, rage, rant, rave, reek, stew **5** chafe, smoke, steam **6** blow up, see red, seethe, simmer **7** bristle, flame up, smolder **8** have a fit, smoulder **9** fulminate
fumes: **3** gas **5** vapor **9** effluvium
fumet: **4** soup
fumigant: **8** cleanser **9** germicide **10** antiseptic
fumigate: **6** purify **9** disinfect, sterilize
fumigation target: **4** ants **7** roaches **8** termites
fuming: **3** hot, mad **4** ired, sore, stew **5** angry, cross, huffy, irate, livid, riled, smoky, upset, wroth **6** ablaze, galled, ireful, peeved, raging, red-hot **7** enraged, furious, steamed **8** choleric, incensed, inflamed, maddened, outraged, volcanic, wrathful **9** indignant, irritated, resentful, splenetic **10** freaked out, infuriated
one: **5** rager
over: **5** mad at
fumy: **5** gassy, smoky **7** miasmic **8** aeriform, vaporous, volatile **9** effluvial
fun: **3** joy **4** kick, lark, play, romp **5** happy, humor, kicks, kicky, merry, mirth, sport **6** festal, frolic, gaiety, gayety, joking, laughs, thrill **7** amusing, foolery, hijinks, jesting, jollies, jollity, pastime, revelry **8** clowning, good time, jocosity, laughter, nonsense, pleasant, pleasure **9** amusement, convivial, diversion, diverting, enjoyable, enjoyment, festivity, high jinks, horseplay, merriment, sprightly **10** buffoonery, frolicsome, jocularity, liveliness, recreation, relaxation, tomfoolery
a lot of ~: **4** hoot, howl, kick **5** blast
ender: **4** fest, ster
for ~: **6** in jest **7** as a joke, on a lark, on a whim
full of ~: **5** jolly, merry **8** sporting, sportive
good clean ~: **4** lark **6** frolic
have ~: **5** enjoy **6** frolic, regale **7** carouse
having ~: **3** gay **5** happy, jolly, merry **6** elated, genial, joyful, joyous **7** buoyant, chipper, content, gleeful, playful **8** cheerful, laughing, mirthful **9** contented, convivial, vivacious
in ~: **7** as a lark **8** for a joke, jokingly **9** playfully, teasingly **10** humorously
make ~ of: **3** kid, rag **4** bait, gibe, jape, jeer, jibe, jive, mock, razz, twit **5** fleer, mimic, taunt, tease **6** banter, deride, go like **7** lampoon, laugh at, run down, scoff at **8** ridicule
no ~: **3** sad **5** bleak **6** dismal, dreary, gloomy, somber **7** joyless **8** hopeless **9** cheerless, dejecting **10** depressing,

lugubrious, melancholy
poke ~ at: 3 kid, rag, rib 4 jeer, mock, ride, twit 5 fleer, roast, scoff, taunt, tease 6 deride, needle 7 put down 8 ridicule
say in ~: 3 kid 4 fool, gibe, jape, jest, joke, josh 5 clown, crack 9 kid around
fun __: 4 fair 5 house
__ fun: 3 for
Funafuti: 4 city, town 5 atoll 7 capital
locale: 6 Tuvalu
funambulist: 7 acrobat
fun and __: 5 games
__ fun at: 4 poke
function: 2 do, go 3 act, job, run, use 4 duty, fest, fete, gala, goal, part, role, task, work 5 party, place, sense, serve 6 affair, behave, object, office, sphere 7 concern, mission, operate, perform, purpose, service, utility 8 activity, business, capacity, practice, province 9 festivity, gathering, objective, operation, reception 10 department, occupation
(as): 4 work 5 serve
ender: 5 ality
find another ~ for: 5 reuse
starter: 3 mal
(suffix): 3 -ive, -ure
VCR ~: 6 delete
function __: 3 key 4 word 5 space
functional: 5 handy, utile 6 usable, useful 7 useable 8 operable 9 operative, practical
functionary: 5 agent 8 official 10 bureaucrat
functioned as: 3 was
functioning: 4 live 5 alive 6 active, in gear 7 running, working 9 mechanism, operative
not ~: 4 dead 5 kaput 6 broken, busted, faulty 7 haywire 9 defective 10 broken-down, inoperable, on the blink, on the fritz, out of order
or not: 4 as is
well: 5 right, sound 7 running 8 accurate 9 effective, in the pink, up to snuff 10 unimpaired
fund: 4 back, mine, pool 5 endow, fount, hoard, kitty, money, stake, stock, store 6 defray, enable, pay for, source, supply 7 finance, reserve, sponsor, support 8 bankroll, treasury 9 endowment, grubstake, patronize, reservoir, subsidize 10 capitalize, repository, storehouse, underwrite
rainy day ~: 7 nest egg, reserve, savings
fund-__: 6 raiser 7 raising
__ fund: 4 load 5 hedge, index, money, slush, trust 6 growth, mutual, no-load 7 imprest, pension, sinking, welfare
fundamental: 3 key, law 4 main, root, rule 5 axiom, basal, basic, major, prime, vital 6 bottom, innate, primal, staple 7 central, crucial, initial, minimal, organic, primary, radical, theorem 8 cardinal, integral, rudiment, standard, ultimate 9 necessary, necessity, principle, requisite
fundamentally: 5 per se 6 au fond, wholly 7 at heart 9 primarily, virtually
fundamentals: 4 ABCs, text 6 basics 8 alphabet
funding: 7 capital 9 endowment, financing, patronage
fund-raiser: 3 PTA 4 gala 5 bazar, bingo, drive 6 appeal, bazaar, raffle 7 benefit 8 bake sale, cake sale, telethon
suffix: 4 thon
funds: 3 nut, oof 4 cash, gelt, jack, kail, kale, loot, peag, pelf, pool 5 bills, bread, bucks, dough, lucre, means, money, moola, mopus, pesos, purse, rhino, sewan 6 assets, budget, dinero, do-re-mi, mammon, mazuma, monies, moolah, seawan, silver, specie, wampum, wealth 7 backing, cabbage, capital, dollars, lettuce, nest egg, ooftish, profits, revenue, savings, scratch, shekels 8 bankroll, cold cash, currency, hard cash, proceeds, smackers 9 affluence, banknotes, financing, frogskins, long green, resources, simoleons 10 collateral, greenbacks, green stuff
emergency ~ source: 3 ATM
household ~: 6 budget 9 piggy bank
in need of ~: 5 broke 6 busted 7 pinched
research ~: 5 grant 9 endowment 10 fellowship
source: 4 loan 6 backer
Fundy: 3 bay
locale: 6 Canada
funereal: 6 solemn, somber 7 serious 10 lugubrious
Fun, Fun, Fun (1964 song)
artist: Beach Boys
car: 5 T-bird
fungicide: 5 zineb 6 captan
fungo __: 3 bat
fungus: 3 cep 4 koji, mold, rust, smut 5 ergot, morel, mould, mucor, plant, slime, yeast 6 agaric, blewit, lichen, mildew, torula 7 amanita, blewitt, blueleg, bluette, boletus, candida, chytrid, truffle 8 basidium, blue mold, botrytis, death cap, gray mold, mushroom, pig's ears, puffball, snow mold 9 bread mold, earth star, matsu-take, slime mold, sooty mold, sparassis, stinkhorn, toadstool, wheat rust
alga and ~: 6 lichen
combining form: 3 myc- 4 myco- 6 -mycete
grain ~: 4 smut
pouch: 3 sac
science of ~: 8 mycology
spore-case clusters: 5 telia
spores: 5 oidia
spore sac: 5 ascus 6 aecium
fun-house figure: 5 ghost, spook, witch
Funhouse, The
author: Dean Koontz
Funicello, Annette: 7 actress
costar: 6 Avalon
film: Back to the Beach (1987)
Beach Blanket Bingo (1965)
Beach Party (1963)
Bikini Beach (1964)
Muscle Beach Party (1964)
Pajama Party (1964)
The Shaggy Dog (1959)
song: O Dio Mio (1960)
Tall Paul (1959)
TV: Mickey Mouse Club
__ Fun in the Summertime: 3 Hot
funk: 4 fear, mood 5 gloom, panic, quail, scare, slump, smell 6 fright, stench, terror 7 bad mood, sadness 8 doldrums, frighten 9 trepidity 10 depression, heavy heart, melancholy
be in a ~: 4 fret, moon, mope, pine, pout, sulk 5 brood 6 lament
go into a ~: 4 fret, mope, sulk 5 worry 7 agonize 8 languish 10 introspect
in a ~: 4 blue, down, lorn 6 gloomy, morose 7 forlorn, joyless, unhappy 8 dejected, desolate, downcast, forsaken, wretched 9 cheerless, depressed, miserable 10 despondent, devastated, melancholy
put into a ~: 6 bum out, deject, sadden 7 depress 8 dispirit, distress 10 discourage, dishearten
Funk: 5 Isaac
__ Funk: 5 Grand
Funkdafied (1994 song)
artist: Da Brat
__ Funk Railroad: 5 Grand
funky: 3 hip, sad 4 rank 5 campy, weird 6 afraid, earthy, modish, quirky, scared, smelly, stinky 7 fearful, noisome, offbeat, sensual, soulful, stylish 8 fearsome, mournful 9 blues-like, terrified 10 frightened, melancholy
Funky Broadway (1967 song)
artist: Wilson Pickett
funky chicken: 5 dance
Funky Cold Medina (1989 song)
artist: Tone Loc
funky pigeon: 5 dance
fun-loving: 5 jolly, merry 7 playful 9 convivial, kittenish 10 rollicking
funnel: 6 convey, hopper 7 channel 8 transmit 10 smokestack
combining form: 5 choan- 6 choano-
funnel __: 4 cake 5 cloud
funnel-shaped: 5 conic 7 conical
flower: 6 azalea
funnier than, be: 3 top
funnies: 6 comics, strips
funniness: 3 wit 4 gags 5 farce, humor, jests, jokes 6 comedy, joking, levity, whimsy 7 jesting 8 clowning, drollery, raillery 9 amusement 10 buffoonery, comicality, jocularity, tomfoolery, wisecracks
react to ~: 4 howl, roar 5 laugh 6 giggle, titter 7 chuckle, crack up
funny: 3 odd, wry 4 rich, zany 5 antic, comic, droll, jolly, light, queer, silly, weird, witty, wrong 6 absurd, har-har, ironic, jocose, quaint 7 amusing, bizarre, comedic, comical, curious, jesting, jocular, oddball, playful, riotous, risible, strange, unusual, waggish 8 farcical, humorous, mirthful, peculiar, puzzling 9 diverting, facetious, hilarious, laughable, ludicrous, priceless, slapstick, whimsical 10 gut-busting, hysterical, perplexing, ridiculous, suspicious, uproarious
act ~: 5 amuse
business: 5 antic, caper, humor, trick 6 levity 7 hijinks 8 mischief, trickery 9 high jinks
fare: 5 farce, humor 6 comedy, satire 9 burlesque, slapstick
feeling: 5 hunch 7 portent 9 suspicion
person: 3 wag 4 card, hoot, riot, zany 5 clown, comic 6 scream 8 comedian
thing: 4 howl, joke, quip, riot 5 crack 6 gasser, hot one, scream
very ~: 4 rich 6 absurd 7 amusing, comical 8 farcical, humorous 9 diverting, hilarious, laughable, ludicrous, slapstick 10 gut-busting, ridiculous, rollicking, uproarious
funny __: 3 car 4 bone, book, ha-ha 5 money, paper
__ funny!: 4 Very
Funny __: 4 Face, Girl, Lady
Funny!: 4 ha-ha
funny bone
locale: 5 elbow
Funny Face (1957 film): 7 musical
cast: Fred Astaire, Audrey Hepburn, Kay Thompson
composer: George Gershwin, Ira Gershwin
director: Stanley Donen
setting: 5 Paris 6 France
Funny Face (1972 song)
artist: Donna Fargo
Funny Girl (1968 film)
cast: Omar Sharif, Barbra Streisand
director: William Wyler
song: 6 People
song subject: 4 Rose 5 Sadie
subject: Fanny Brice
Funny Girl (musical)
composer: Bob Merrill, Jule Styne
funnyman: 3 wag, wit 4 card 5 clown, comic, cutup, joker 6 jester, kidder, scream 7 buffoon, farceur, gagster, punster 8 comedian, humorist, quipster 9 prankster
__ funny, McGee!: 5 T'aint
__ Funny That Way: 4 She's
Funny Thing Happened..., A: 7 musical
composer: Stephen Sondheim
Funny Way of Laughin' (1962 song)
artist: Burl Ives
__ fun of: 4 make
Funt: 5 Allen, Peter
command: 5 smile
need: 6 camera
Fun With Dick and Jane (1977 film)
cast: Jane Fonda, Ed McMahon, George Segal
dog: 4 Spot
Fun With Dick and Jane (2005 film)
cast: Alec Baldwin, Jim Carrey, Téa Leoni
__ fuoco: 3 con

fur: 3 fox 4 coat, down, fuzz, hair, mink, pelt, skin, wolf, wool 5 lapin, otter, sable, stole 6 beaver, coyote, ermine, kit fox, marten, nutria, pelage, rabbit, racoon, red fox 7 blue fox, garment, karakul, krimmer, leopard, minever, miniver, raccoon 8 bearskin, sea otter 9 astrakhan, sheepskin, silver fox 10 chinchilla
in heraldry: 4 vair 8 tincture
lose ~: 4 shed
magnate: 5 Astor
piece: 3 boa 4 pelt, wrap 5 stole
rabbit ~: 4 cony 5 coney, lapin
fur __: 4 coat, farm, seal
__ fur: 4 fake
Für __: 5 Elise
furbish: 4 buff 5 adorn, clean, fix up, glaze, renew, shine 6 polish 7 burnish, gussy up, improve, restore 8 brighten, decorate, renovate, spruce up
Furby: 3 toy
exclamation: 4 whee
maker: 6 Hasbro
furcate: 5 forky 6 forked
Für Elise
composer: Ludwig van Beethoven
Furies: 5 Dirae 7 Erinyes 9 Eumenides
one of the ~: 6 Alecto 7 Megaera 9 Tisiphone
Furillo: 3 cop 4 Carl
__ Furioso: 7 Orlando
furioso opposite: 5 dolce
furious: 3 hot, mad 4 ired, sore, wild 5 angry, cross, huffy, irate, livid, riled, upset, vexed, wroth 6 ablaze, fierce, fuming, heated, hectic, ireful, peeved, piqued, raging, raving, red-hot, savage, stormy 7 boiling, enraged, foaming, intense, rampant, ranting, steamed, violent 8 blustery, choleric, feverish, incensed, inflamed, maddened, outraged, up in arms, vehement, white-hot, worked up, wrathful 9 bummed-out, indignant, irritated, rapacious, resentful, seeing red, splenetic, turbulent, wrought up 10 freaked out, hopping mad, hysterical, in an uproar, passionate
be ~: 4 boil, burn, fume, rage, rave 5 steam 6 blow up, see red, seethe 7 smolder 9 fulminate
make ~: 3 ire 5 peeve 6 enrage, madden
one: 5 raver
with: 5 mad at
furiously: 4 hard 5 madly 7 like mad 9 fervently, like crazy, viciously 10 vehemently
furl: 4 roll, wind 6 curl up, roll up, wrap up 10 wind around
furlong: 6 length 7 measure
eight ~s: 4 mile
fraction: 4 foot, yard
furlough: 3 axe, can 4 boot, drop, oust, pass, sack 5 leave, let go, R and R 6 bounce, layoff 7 cashier, dismiss, drum out, liberty, release 8 get rid of, pink-slip, vacation 9 discharge, terminate 10 shore leave
furnace: 4 kiln 5 forge, stove 6 boiler, burner, cupola, heater
button: 5 reset
duct: 4 flue 6 leader
feed a ~: 4 fuel 5 stoke
fleck: 3 ash
fuel: 4 coal
like a ~: 3 hot 5 fiery 6 torrid 7 blazing, intense
part: 6 damper
room: 6 cellar 8 basement
unit: 3 BTU
worker: 5 firer 6 stoker
__ furnace: 3 arc, gas 5 blast, floor, solar
Furness: 5 Betty
furnish: 3 fit, rig 4 gear, give, lend 5 array, cater, endow, equip, fix up, offer, stock, yield 6 afford, bestow, clothe, fit out, gear up, instal, invest, outfit, purvey, render, rig out, supply 7 advance, appoint, deck out, install, prepare, produce, provide, satisfy, turn out 8 accouter, accoutre, decorate, dispense 9 provision 10 administer
Furnished Room, The
author: O. Henry
furnishings: 4 gear 5 décor, goods 8 equipage, fittings, fixtures
__ furnishings: 4 home
furniture: 3 bed 4 crib, desk, sofa 5 bench, chair, chest, couch, hutch, stool, table 6 buffet, bureau, glider, rocker, settee 7 cabinet, commode, dresser, highboy, rolltop, seating, sofa bed 8 bookcase, credenza, cupboard, love seat, recliner, wardrobe 9 appliance, davenport, equipment, secretary, sideboard 10 breakfront, possession
bedroom ~: 5 chest, table 6 bureau 8 credenza, end table 10 breakfront, cedar chest, chiffonier, night table
buildup: 4 dust
chain: 4 IKEA
den ~: 4 desk, sofa 6 settee 8 bookcase
detail: 5 inlay
dining-room ~: 5 hutch, table 7 cabinet 8 credenza 10 breakfront
feature: 3 leg, wax 5 stain 6 finish, polish 8 baluster
leg decoration: 3 ear
living-room ~: 4 sofa 5 table 7 ottoman
material: 4 wood 6 bamboo, wicker
measurement: 5 width
mover: 3 van 5 truck, U-Haul
nursery ~: 4 crib 6 cradle 8 bassinet
office ~: 4 sofa 5 couch, divan, table 6 lounge, settee 7 cabinet, rolltop 8 credenza 9 davenport, secretary, sectional 10 escritoire
ornament: 5 acorn 6 finial
patio ~: 5 chair, table 6 chaise 8 umbrella
porch ~: 6 glider
protector: 4 tarp 5 doily, stain 6 doyley 7 Formica 9 slipcover, tarpaulin 10 upholstery
school ~: 4 desk
set: 5 suite 8 ensemble
style: 4 Adam 6 Empire 7 modular 8 colonial, Sheraton
trim: 5 skirt
wheel: 6 caster
wood: 3 koa, oak 4 acle, pine, teak 5 alder, cedar, ebony, maple 6 cherry, gaboon 8 mahogany
worker: 5 caner
__ furniture: 5 patio
furniture polish: 6 Behold, Endust, Pledge 10 Liquid Gold, Old English
furor: 3 ado, row 4 flap, fuss, rage, stir, to-do 5 mania, scene, stink, storm 6 bustle, flurry, frenzy, hoopla, hubbub, ruckus, squall, tumult, uproar 7 ferment, tempest, turmoil 8 brouhaha, paroxysm 9 agitation, commotion, hue and cry, maelstrom, sensation, vehemence, whoop-de-do 10 excitement, free-for-all, hullabaloo, hurly-burly
in a ~: 4 wild 5 manic, rabid 6 crazed, raging 7 berserk 8 frenzied, unhinged 9 ferocious 10 hysterical
Furphy, Joseph: 6 writer 10 Australian
furrier offering: 3 fox 4 mink, pelt, wrap 5 otter, sable, stole 6 ermine 9 silver fox 10 chinchilla
furrow: 3 cut, row, rut 4 knit, line, plow, seam 5 ditch, gouge, plica, ridge, score 6 crease, groove, gutter, hollow, pucker, rabbet, rimple, sulcus, trench, trough 7 channel, crinkle, wrinkle 9 corrugate 10 depression
narrow ~: 5 stria
furry: 4 soft 5 downy, fuzzy, hairy, nappy, plush 6 fleecy, fluffy, shaggy 7 hirsute, squishy, unshorn, velvety 8 cushiony
Furst: 7 Stephen
further: 3 aid, and, too, yet 4 also, ease, else, help, more, push, then 5 added, again, boost, extra, lobby, other, speed 6 assist, back up, better, beyond, foster, hasten, incite, second, to boot, yonder 7 advance, benefit, besides, elevate, forward, nurture, promote, support 8 advocate, champion, expedite, increase, likewise, moreover 9 cultivate, encourage, go forward 10 accelerate, additional, facilitate
ender: 4 more, most
in time: 4 anon 5 after, later 8 eventual 9 afterward 10 thereafter
say ~: 3 add
without ~ ado: 3 now, PDQ 6 at once 8 promptly, right now 9 forthwith, right away
__ further: 4 go no
__ further ado: 7 without
furtherance: 3 aid 6 course 7 advance, support
in ~ of: 3 for 10 supporting
furthermore: 3 and, too, yet 4 also, plus 5 again 6 as well, to boot 7 besides 8 likewise
furthermost: 3 top 4 last 5 final, prime 6 all-out 7 extreme, highest, leading, maximal, supreme 8 absolute, farthest, greatest, ultimate 9 sovereign 10 preeminent
furthest: 4 last 7 extreme, outmost, outside 8 ultimate 9 uttermost
from the hole, in golf: 4 away
point: 3 end 4 edge 5 limit 7 extreme 8 boundary 9 extremity
furtive: 3 sly 4 foxy, wily 6 artful, covert, crafty, hidden, masked, secret, shifty, slinky, sneaky, tricky, unseen, veiled 7 cloaked, cunning, elusive, elusory, evasive, private, sub rosa 8 guileful, hush-hush, obscured, scheming, secluded, shrouded, skulking, slinking, sneaking, stealthy 9 backstair, concealed, deceitful, disguised, insidious, secretive, underhand 10 backstairs, undercover, under wraps, unreliable
glance: 4 peek, peep
in a ~ manner: 5 slyly
one: 5 skunk, snake, sneak 6 rascal, weasel 9 scoundrel
org.: 3 CIA
whisper: 3 pst 4 psst
furtively: 7 asquint, on the QT, sub rosa 8 on the sly, secretly
fury: 3 ire 4 fire, heat, rage 5 anger, force, storm, wrath 6 frenzy, temper 7 outrage, passion, rampage, umbrage 8 acrimony, asperity, ferocity, rabidity, savagery, violence 9 intensity, vehemence 10 fierceness, resentment, turbulence, unkindness
fill with ~: 6 enrage
Fury: 3 car 4 auto 6 Alecto 7 Megaera 8 Plymouth 9 Tisiphone 10 automobile
__ Fury: 5 Black, Son of 7 Blanche, Captain
furze: 5 gorse, shrub 7 bramble
like a ~: 5 spiny
Fusco Brothers, The dog: 4 Axel
Fusco, Paul
role: 3 ALF
fuscous: 4 gray, grey 5 dusky 8 browning
fuse: 3 mix, wed 4 bond, join, meld, melt, thaw, weld, wick 5 blend, merge, smelt, stick, unify, unite 6 cement, cohere, mingle, solder 7 combine, lighter 8 coalesce, intermix 9 commingle, integrate 10 amalgamate, synthesize
blow a ~: 4 flip, rage, rave 5 storm 6 see red 7 explode 10 hit the roof
problem: 5 short
short ~: 6 temper 9 surliness
unit: 3 amp 6 ampere
with a short ~: 9 excitable
fuse __: 3 box
__ fuse: 5 blow a, short
fusee: 5 flare, match 7 lighter
fuselage: 4 body 7 chassis
fusil: 3 gun 6 musket, weapon 9 flintlock
fusile: 6 melted, molten 7 founded, smelted
fusillade: 4 fire 5 burst, salvo, storm 6 volley 7 barrage 9 discharge 10 outpouring
fusilli: 5 pasta 7 noodles
alternative: *see* pasta

fusion: **5** blend, union, unity **7** mixture **9** admixture, composite, synthesis
target: **4** atom
fusion __: **4** bomb **7** reactor
__ fusion: **4** cell, cold **7** nuclear
__-fusion: **4** jazz
fuss: **3** ado, nag, row **4** flap, fret, kick, spat, stew, stir, to-do, wail **5** fight, furor, hoo-ha, noise, scene, stink, storm, sweat, whine **6** bother, bustle, clamor, flurry, frenzy, grouse, hassle, hoo-hah, hoopla, hubbub, kickup, lather, pother, racket, ruckus, rumpus, strife, tumult, unrest, uproar **7** clutter, dispute, fanfare, flutter, grumble, quarrel, scuffle, trouble, turmoil, whimper **8** activity, argument, busyness, complain, disorder, squabble **9** agitation, bellyache, bickering, commotion, complaint, confusion, objection **10** difficulty, excitement, falling out, hullabaloo
ender: **3** pot **6** budget
kick up a ~: **3** cry **4** yell **5** gripe, groan, shout, whine **6** holler, shriek, yammer **7** grumble, protest, screech **8** complain **9** bellyache, raise Cain
make a ~: **4** balk, beef, carp, kick, mind, moan, rail, rant, sigh, wail, weep, yell **5** act up, baulk, cavil, demur, fight, gripe, groan, growl, mourn, whine **6** clamor, grouch, grouse, holler, mutter, repine, squawk, squeal, yammer **7** grumble, protest, quarrel, trouble, whimper **8** complain, sound off **9** bellyache, find fault
over dress: **5** preen, primp, prink
with one's hair: **5** groom, preen
without ~: **6** calmly
fussbudget: **4** prig **5** biddy **8** quibbler, stickler **9** nitpicker **10** fuddy-duddy
fussy: **4** nice, prim **5** exact, picky **6** choosy, dainty, ornate, prissy **7** bookish, careful, choosey, finical, finicky, fretful, mincing, nervous, precise, prudent, prudish **8** cautious, critical, exacting, finiking, finnicky, fretsome, pedantic, rigorous, thorough **9** assiduous, attentive, demanding, difficult, judicious, observant, querulous, squeamish, stickling **10** fastidious, meticulous, nitpicking, particular, pedantical, scrupulous, unamenable
dresser: **3** fop **5** dandy **7** coxcomb **8** popinjay **10** jack-a-dandy
fustian
see baloney
fustigate: **5** cavil, roast, scold **6** attack, berate, punish, rail at **7** condemn, lay into **8** backbite, badmouth, chastise, denounce **9** criticize, disparage, light into, reprehend **10** denunciate
fusty: **4** rank **5** moldy, musty, passé, stale **6** frowsy, frowzy, rancid **7** archaic, fogyish **8** mildewed, obsolete, outdated, out of use **9** old-school, out-of-date **10** antiquated, malodorous
futhark: **8** alphabet
character: **4** rune
like ~: **5** runic
futile: **4** idle, null, vain **5** no use, nowin **6** hollow, in vain, otiose, stupid **7** sterile, useless **8** feckless, hopeless, nugatory **9** for naught, fruitless, pointless, thankless, to no avail, valueless, worthless **10** for nothing, profitless, unavailing
futilely: **6** vainly **9** uselessly
futon: **3** bed **6** daybed **7** sofa bed **8** mattress
Futura: **3** car **4** auto, font, Ford **8** typeface **10** automobile
future: **4** time, to be **5** later **6** coming, offing **7** by and by, destiny **8** eventual, imminent, intended, tomorrow, ulterior, upcoming **9** commodity, impending, potential **10** days to come, subsequent, unrealized
at a ~ time: **3** yet **5** later **7** someday **10** eventually, ultimately
examiner: **4** seer **5** augur, sibyl **6** medium, oracle **7** diviner, palmist, prophet, psychic **8** haruspex **9** theurgist **10** forecaster, foreteller, soothsayer
generations: **4** seed **5** heirs, issue **7** progeny **8** children **9** posterity
groom: **4** beau **6** fiancé **8** intended **9** betrothed
in the ~: **3** yet **4** anon, soon, then **5** after, ahead, hence, later **7** by and by, later on, someday **8** evermore, sometime **9** afterward, hereafter **10** before long, eventually, ultimately
life: **9** hereafter, next world **10** afterworld
save for ~ use: **7** lay away
sign of the ~: **4** omen **6** augury, herald **7** portent, presage **9** foretoken, harbinger
future __: **5** shock, tense **7** perfect
future __, the: **5** is now
Future __ of America: **7** Farmers
Future Indefinite
author: Noël Coward
Future Is in Eggs, The
author: Eugène Ionesco
futures market: **4** Merc **5** COMEX
item: **3** oil, rye **4** corn, eggs, gold, hogs, lard, lead, oats, zinc **5** cocoa, sugar, wheat **6** barley, cattle, coffee, copper, cotton, lumber, onions, silver **7** plywood **8** crude oil, flaxseed, gasoline, platinum, potatoes **9** pork belly **10** heating oil, natural gas, soybean oil
Futureworld (1976 film)
cast: Yul Brynner, Blythe Danner, Peter Fonda, Arthur Hill
futurity __: **4** race **6** stakes
futz around: **4** idle **8** lollygag, slack off **9** waste time **10** experiment
fuze: **7** lighter **9** detonator
see also fuse
fuzz: **3** cop, fur, nap **4** down, hair, lint **5** beard, fiber, floss, fluff, kapok **6** copper, police **8** whiskers **9** detective
full of ~: **5** linty
fuzzy: **3** dim **4** dark, hazy **5** blear, downy, dusky, faded, faint, foggy, furry, hairy, linty, mirky, misty, muddy, murky, muted, nappy, vague, wooly **6** bleary, blurry, flossy, fluffy, frizzy, napped, woolly **7** blurred, frizzly, hirsute, obscure, shadowy, unclear, unshorn **9** equivocal, imprecise, unfocused **10** ill-defined, indefinite, indistinct, inexplicit, out of focus, unexplicit, unspecific
fruit: **4** kiwi **5** peach
make ~: **4** blur, roil, veil **5** bedim, befog **7** becloud, obscure
warm ~: **6** praise **10** compliment
fuzzy __: **3** set **4** math **5** logic
Fuzzy: **7** Zoeller
fuzzy-headed
see foolish
Fuzzy-Wuzzy
author: Rudyard Kipling
Soudan, to ~: **3** 'ome
Fuzzy-Wuzzy __ bear: **4** was a
Fuzzy-Wuzzy __ fuzzy...: **5** wasn't
F.W.: **7** de Klerk **9** Woolworth
FWIW
part of ~: **3** for, its **4** what **5** worth
fwy. cousin: **3** tpk.
F/X (1986 film)
cast: Bryan Brown, Brian Dennehy, Diane Venora
FYI, part of: **3** for **4** your **11** information
Fyodor: **4** czar, tsar **7** Gladkov, Sologub **9** Chaliapin
in English: **8** Theodore
Fyvush: **6** Finkel
__ F. Zanuck: **6** Darryl

g.: **4** gram, meas.
G: 3 key **4** clef, thou **6** letter, rating **8** thousand
Anglo-Saxon ~: 4 yogh
a thousand ~s: 3 mil **7** million
equivalent: 6 E minor
in phonetic alphabet: 4 Golf
one ~: 4 thou **7** gravity
rater: 4 MPAA
G __ go: 4 as in
G. __ Liddy: 6 Gordon
__ G: 5 Kenny, super
'G' __ Gumshoe: 5 Is for
Ga: 4 elem. **7** element, gallium
31 for ~: 4 at. no.
Ga.
airline based in ~: 3 DAL
neighbor: 3 Ala., Fla. **8** N. Car. Tenn.
zone: 3 EDT, EST
see also Georgia
gab: 3 jaw, rap, say, yak, yap **4** blab, chat, chin, talk, yack **5** prate, run on, speak **6** confer, drivel, gibber, gossip, jabber, natter, parley, patter, pop off, rattle, yammer **7** blabber, blather, blether, chatter, palaver, prattle, schmoos **8** babbling, chitchat, converse, ramble on, rattle on, schmoose, schmooze **9** table talk, touch base **10** chew the fat, chew the rag, yackety-yak, yakkety-yak
ender: 4 fest
gift of ~: 8 rhetoric **9** eloquence, loquacity, wittiness **10** volubility
line of ~: 5 pitch, spiel **6** patter
starter: 6 baffle
gabardine: 5 twill **6** fabric **8** material
gabber: 10 motormouth
gabbing: 5 noisy **8** babbling
gabble
see jabber
gabby: 4 long **5** wordy **6** chatty, prolix **7** diffuse, lengthy, unterse, verbose, voluble **8** grasping, rambling **9** bombastic, garrulous, talkative **10** bigmouthed, discursive, long-winded, loquacious, palaverous
Gabby: 5 Hayes **8** Hartnett
Gabe: 4 Dell **6** Kaplan
Gabel, Martin
spouse: Arlene Francis
gable
house with a ~: 6 A-frame
topper: 6 finial
Gable, Clark: 5 actor
film: Boom Town (1940)
The Call of the Wild (1935)
China Seas (1935)
Command Decision (1948)
Dancing Lady (1933)
A Free Soul (1931)
Gone With the Wind (1939)
Hold Your Man (1933)
The Hucksters (1947)
Idiot's Delight (1939)
It Happened One Night (1934, AA)
Manhattan Melodrama (1934)
The Misfits (1961)
Mogambo (1953)
Mutiny on the Bounty (1935)
Possessed (1931)
Red Dust (1932)
Run Silent, Run Deep (1958)
San Francisco (1936)
Soldier of Fortune (1955)
Strange Cargo (1940)
Strange Interlude (1932)
Teacher's Pet (1958)
Test Pilot (1938)
Too Hot to Handle (1938)
spouse: Carole Lombard
Gabler: 5 Hedda
__ Gables, FL: 5 Coral
Gabon: 6 nation **7** country
capital: 10 Libreville
money: 5 franc
neighbor: 5 Congo **8** Cameroon
people: 3 Fan **4** Fang **6** Pangwe **7** Pahouin
gaboon: 4 tree **5** viper **6** okoume
Gabor: 3 Eva **5** Jolie, Magda **6** Dennis, Zsa Zsa
Gabor, Dennis: 8 Nobelist **9** physicist
Gaborone: 4 city, town **7** capital
locale: 8 Botswana
Gabor, Zsa Zsa: 7 actress
spouse: George Sanders
Gabriel: 4 Dell **5** angel, Byrne, Fauré, Okara, Peter, saint **6** Marcel **8** Lippmann **9** archangel **10** Fahrenheit
Gabriel __ Márquez: 6 García
Gabriela: 7 Mistral **8** Carteris, Sabatini
see also Spanish
__ Gabriel, CA: 3 San
Gabriele: 9 D'Annunzio, Falloppio
Gabriel Hounds, The
author: Mary Stewart
Gabrielle: 3 Roy **5** Anwar, Reece
__ Gabriel Mountains: 3 San
Gabriel, Peter
song: Big Time (1987)
Sledgehammer (1986)
__ Gabriel Rossetti: 5 Dante
Gaby: 8 Hoffmann, Sabatini
gad: 4 flit, roam, rove **5** drift **6** cruise, ramble, wander **7** meander, saunter **8** ambulate, wanderer **9** gallivant, run around **10** knock about, window-shop
ender: 3 fly **5** about
Gad
brother: 3 Dan **4** Levi **5** Asher, Judah **6** Joseph, Reuben, Simeon **7** Zebulun **8** Benjamin, Issachar, Naphtali
parent: 5 Jacob **6** Zilpah
sister: 5 Dinah
son: 3 Eri **5** Haggi
gadabout: 4 goer **5** nomad, rover **7** rambler **8** runagate, traveler, vagabond, wanderer, wayfarer **9** jet-setter, transient, wayfaring
__-Gadda-Da-Vida: 3 In-a
gadfly: 3 bug **4** pest **6** critic, insect **8** irritant, nuisance, provoker **9** annoyance
gadget: 4 tool **5** dodad, gismo, gizmo, pager, thing **6** device, doodad, whosis, widget **7** gimmick, machine, novelty, trinket, utensil **9** apparatus, appliance, can opener, doohickey, implement, invention, machinery, mechanism **10** instrument
kitchen ~: 5 corer, dicer, parer, ricer, timer **6** baster, beater, grater
gadid: 3 cod **7** codfish
gadolinium: 5 metal **7** element
Gadsden: 4 city, town
locale: 7 Alabama
Purchase boundary river: 4 Gila
gadwall: 4 bird, duck, fowl
relative: *see* duck
Gadzooks!: 4 egad, oath **5** egads **6** zounds
Gaea
daughter: 4 Ceto, Rhea, Thia **5** Aetna, Dione, Pheme **6** Creusa, Phoebe, Tethys, Themis **7** Eurybia **9** Charybdis, Mnemosyne
father: 5 Chaos
husband: 6 Uranus
son: 4 Anax, Ceto **5** Arges, Argus, Arion, Coeus, Crius, Manes, Mimas, Orion, Titan **6** Agrius, Caerus, Cronos, Cronus, Hyllus, Leitus, Nereus, Phlyus, Pontus, Typhon, Uranus **7** Antaeus, Brontes, Cecrops, Clytius, Iapetus, Oceanus, Phorcus, Thaumas **8** Hyperion, Steropes
Gael: 4 Celt, Scot **6** Greene **10** Highlander
garb: 4 kilt
republic: 4 Eire **7** Ireland
Gaelic: 4 Erse, Manx **8** language
people: 5 Irish
__ Gaelic: 5 Irish, Scots **6** Scotch
Gaels school: 4 Iona
Gaetano: 9 Donizetti
gaff: 4 boom, hook, spar **7** javelin
stand the ~: 4 cope, last **5** brook **6** endure, hang on, keep on, stay on **7** carry on, hold out, outlast, survive, weather **9** put up with **10** get through, stick it out
gaffe: 4 goof, slip **5** boner, error, lapse **6** boo-boo, howler, slip-up **7** blooper, blunder, faux pas, misstep, mistake **8** solecism **9** gaucherie, indecorum
golf ~: 4 baff, hook **5** slice
make a ~: 3 err **6** slip up **7** blunder
vocal ~: 4 flub, gaff, goof **5** error, gaffe, lapse **7** blooper, misstep
gaffer: 4 hick, rube **6** rustic **9** graybeard
workplace: 3 set **10** soundstage
gag: 3 tie **4** cork, hush, jape, jest, joke, quip, stop **5** caper, crack, humor, prank, quiet, trick **6** muffle, muzzle, shut up, stifle **7** hot foot, repress, silence, squelch **8** mischief, one-liner, pretense, restrain, silencer, suppress, throttle **9** April fool, keep still, tongue-tie, wisecrack, witticism **10** shenanigan
response, informally: 4 laff
starter: 5 lolly
gag __: 3 law **4** line, rule **5** order **6** reflex
__ gag: 5 sight **7** running
gaga: 4 daft **5** crazy, dizzy, dotty, giddy, goony, loopy **7** bananas, bonkers, bug-eyed, smitten **8** lovesick **9** bewitched **10** infatuated, out to lunch
be ~ over: 5 adore
Gaga: 4 Lady
Gagarin: 4 Yuri **9** cosmonaut
follower: 5 Titov
gage: 4 bond, pawn **5** glove, token, trial **6** pledge, surety **7** deposit, hostage **8** gauntlet, security **9** challenge
green ~: 4 plum
Gage, Nicholas
work: Eleni
gaggle: 3 set **5** flock, geese
noise: 4 honk
Gag me with a spoon!: 3 ugh
gags: 9 funniness **10** jocoseness
gagster: 3 wag **5** clown, joker **6** amuser **8** funnyman **9** leg-puller
Gahagan, Helen
role: 3 She
spouse: Melvyn Douglas
Gahan: 6 Wilson
gaiety: 3 fun, joy **4** glee **5** cheer, humor, mirth, revel, sport **6** fiesta, frolic **7** elation, jollity, rapture, revelry, sparkle **8** buoyance, buoyancy, festival, gladness, hilarity, pleasure, radiance, radiancy, vivacity **9** animation, festivity, frivolity, geniality, good humor, happiness, jocundity, joviality, lightness, merriment **10** blitheness, brightness, ebullience, joyousness, liveliness, risibility
gaijin: 9 foreigner
Gai-Jin
author: James Clavell
Gail: 3 Max **5** Davis **6** Borden, Devers, Fisher, Godwin, O'Grady, Sheehy **7** Patrick, Russell **8** Goodrich
gaily: 6 gladly **7** merrily
gain: 3 bag, get, net, win **4** earn, find, have, land, make, mend, plus, reap, sake **5** annex, avail, boost, lucre, reach, score, seize **6** accept, attain, garner, gather, growth, look up, obtain, output, perk up, pick up, profit, rack up, return, secure, snatch, spoils **7** accrual, achieve, acquire, advance, benefit, bring in, buildup, capture, harvest, improve, inherit, procure, prosper, realize, receive, recover, recruit, revenue, triumph **8** addition, earnings, get ahead, increase, interest, proceeds, progress, purchase, receipts, winnings **9** accretion, go forward, increment **10** accomplish, accumulate, annexation, appreciate, attainment, percentage, prosperity, recuperate
altitude: 4 go up, rise **5** climb **6** ascend
a victory: 4 beat, earn, sway, take **5** score, upset **7** achieve, conquer, edge out, prevail, realize, succeed, triumph, trounce **8** overcome **9** overwhelm
ender: 3 say **4** said
entry: 4 come **6** arrive, show up
experience: 3 see **5** glean, study **6** absorb, master, pick up, soak

up, take in **7** catch on, find out **8** discover, pore over **9** ascertain, brush up on **10** apprentice, get down pat, understand
ground: 6 pick up **7** advance **8** get ahead, progress **9** go forward
on: 5 reach **7** catch up, close in **8** approach, do better, overtake **9** catch up to
time: 5 dally, delay, stall **6** put off **8** postpone **9** temporize
unlawfully: 3 rob **5** steal **6** thieve **8** shoplift
weight: 4 grow **5** swell, widen **6** expand, fatten, spread **7** broaden, enlarge, fill out, thicken
with difficulty: 5 wrest
__ gain: 7 capital
Gain: 9 detergent
alternative: ***see*** detergent
gainer: 4 dive
place: 4 pool
__ gainer: 4 full, half
Gaines: 4 Bill
mag: 3 Mad
Gaines, Ernest J.: 6 writer
Gainesville: 4 city, town
athletes: 6 Gators
locale: 7 Florida, Georgia
neighbor: 5 Ocala
gainful: 6 useful **8** salutary **9** lucrative, rewarding **10** beneficial, productive, profitable, well-paying, worthwhile
employment: 3 job **4** post, work **8** position
gainly: 8 graceful
gainsay: 4 deny **5** belie **6** impugn, negate, oppose, refute **7** disavow, dispute **8** disclaim **9** disaffirm, repudiate **10** contradict, contravene, controvert, disconfirm
gainsaying: 6 denial **7** opposed **8** negation, negative, opposing
Gainsborough, Thomas: 6 artist **7** British, painter
homeland: 7 England
work: 3 oil **7** Blue Boy **8** portrait
gains, ill-gotten: 4 loot, pelf **5** booty, grift, lucre
gainst: 6 contra **7** counter **8** contrary, opposite **9** opposed to
gait: 3 jog, run **4** clip, lope, pace, rate, step, trot, walk **5** amble, march, speed, strut, tread **6** canter, gallop, stride **8** carriage, galopade, rapidity **9** gallopade
antelope ~: 4 stot
horse's ~: 4 lope, pace, trot **6** canter, gallop
gaiter: 4 spat **5** putty **6** puttee, puttie **7** gambado, legging
Gaithersburg: 4 city, town
locale: 8 Maryland
Gaius: 7 Macenas **9** Petronius
garment: 4 toga
gal: 3 she **4** lady, lass **5** woman **6** female, madame, person
Friday: 4 asst. **6** helper **9** assistant
gunsel's ~: 4 moll
of song: 3 Sal
palindromic ~: 3 Ada, Ava, Eve, Lil, Nan **4** Anna **6** Hannah
partner: 3 guy
see also woman
gal __: 3 pal **6** Friday
gal.
fraction: 2 oz., pt., qt.
Gal.
follower: 3 Eph.
gala: 2 do **3** hop **4** ball, bash, fest, fete, prom **5** big do, blast, dance, feast, party, revel, roast, showy **6** affair, festal, fiesta, soiree **7** benefit, blowout, festive, jubilee, pageant, shindig, special **8** clambake, festival, function, jamboree, wingding **9** convivial, festivity **10** fund-raiser
wear: 3 tux **4** gown **5** tails **6** tuxedo
Gala
relative: ***see*** apple
galactic
distance unit: 4 lt. yr. **9** light year
time period: 3 age, eon **4** aeon
galago
see bush baby
Galahad: 3 Sir **4** hero
father: 8 Lancelot
garb: 5 armor
go against ~: 4 list, tilt **5** joust
like ~: 4 pure **6** chaste, devout **8** spotless, virtuous **9** exemplary, lily-white, stainless, uncorrupt
mother: 6 Elaine
weapon: 5 lance
__ Galahad: 3 Kid, Sir
Galant: 3 car **4** auto **10** Mitsubishi
__ galante: 4 fête
Galápagos: 4 isls. **5** isles **7** islands
beast: 6 iguana
Gala Performance
artist: Erté
Galarraga, Andres
sport: 8 baseball
Galatea: 4 moon **6** Nereid
lover: 4 Acis
parent: 5 Doris **6** Nereus
planet: 7 Neptune
Galatia capital: 6 Angora, Ankara
Galatians follower: 9 Ephesians
galax: 9 coltsfoot **10** beetleweed
Galaxie: 3 car **4** auto, Ford **10** automobile
galaxy: 6 cosmos **8** Milky Way **10** star system
starter: 4 meta
unit: 4 star **6** planet
Galaxy Quest (1999 film)
cast: Tim Allen, Alan Rickman, Sigourney Weaver
Galba: 5 Roman **6** Caesar
garment: 4 toga
predecessor: 4 Nero
see also Latin
Galbraith, J.K. subj.: 4 econ.
gale: 4 blow, gust, wind **5** blast, noser, storm **6** squall **7** cyclone, tempest **9** windstorm
out of the ~: 4 alee
Gale: 4 Zona **5** Storm **6** Gordon, Sayers **7** Dorothy, Garnett
dog: 4 Toto
Gale __ Hurd: 3 Ann
Galeao Airport
locale: 3 Rio
galena: 3 ore, PbS **7** lead ore, mineral
Galena: 4 city, town
locale: 8 Illinois
Galesburg: 4 city, town
locale: 8 Illinois
Gale, Zona: 6 writer
work: Miss Lulu Bett
Galibi: 6 Indian **7** Amerind
Galilean tetrarch: 5 Herod
Galilee: 3 sea
locale: 6 Israel **7** Mideast
town: 4 Acre, Cana
__ Galilee: 5 Man of, Sea of
Galileo: 5 probe **7** Galilei **10** astronomer
home: 4 Pisa **5** Italy
launcher: 4 NASA
Gal in __, A: 6 Calico
Galina: 7 Ulanova
__ gal in Kalamazoo: 5 I got a
gall: 3 bug, get, irk, vex **4** bait, bile, burn, pain, rage, rile, roil, wear **5** anger, annoy, brass, chafe, cheek, crust, grate, harry, nerve, peeve, pique, sauce, scuff, spite, upset, venom **6** abrade, bother, fester, harass, offend, plague, pother, put out, rancor, rankle, ruffle, scrape **7** bedevil, disturb, dudgeon, enflame, hauteur, inflame, provoke, torment, trouble **8** audacity, boldness, chutzpah, exercise, irritate, temerity **9** aggravate, arrogance, brashness, displease, excoriate, impudence, insolence, sauciness **10** bitterness, brazenness, effrontery, exasperate, irritation, resentment
bladder neighbor: 5 liver
combining form: 4 chol- **5** chole-, cholo-
ender: 3 fly, nut **5** stone **7** bladder
starter: 3 nut
gall __: 7 bladder
Gallagher: 4 Tess **5** Helen, Peter **7** Gateley
partner: 5 Shean
Galla home: 5 Kenya **6** Africa **8** Ethiopia
gallant: 4 bold, game, kind **5** brave, grand, gutsy, lofty, nervy, noble, suave, swain, wooer **6** awless, daring, gritty, heroic, kindly, knight, plucky, polite, spunky, urbane **7** aweless, courtly, dashing, defiant, doughty, heedful, impavid, mindful, stately, staunch, tactful, valiant **8** fearless, glorious, gracious, heroical, highbred, intrepid, knightly, obliging, resolute, splendid, stalwart, unafraid, valorous, well-bred **9** attentive, audacious, courteous, dauntless, dignified, dreadless, honorable, inamorato, libertine, sensitive, undaunted, unfearful, unfearing, unselfish **10** chivalrous, courageous, jack-a-dandy, thoughtful, undismayed
country ~: 5 swain
starter: 3 top **7** foretop
Gallant Lords of Bois-Dori, The
author: George Sand
Gallant, Mavis: 6 writer **8** Canadian
gallantry: 4 tact **5** heart, honor, nerve, pluck, poise, valor **6** daring, mettle **7** bravery, courage, heroism, prowess **8** audacity, boldness, civility, courtesy, nobility, urbanity, valiance, valiancy **9** deference, derring-do **10** attentions, politeness, resolution
Gallatin: 4 city, town **6** Albert
locale: 9 Tennessee
Gallaudet communication: 3 ASL
galled: 5 angry, irate, riled, vexed **6** fuming, piqued **7** annoyed, steamed **8** incensed **9** indignant, irritated, ticked off
Gallegos, Rómulo: 6 writer **10** Venezuelan
galleon: 4 boat **6** argosy, vessel **8** sailboat
cargo: 3 oro
need: 4 boom, mast, pole, post, spar **6** mizzen, timber **8** flagpole
worker: 5 rower
gallery: 4 hall, loge, tier **5** salon **6** arcade, loggia, lyceum, museum **7** balcony, hearers, ingress **8** audience, showroom **9** listeners, mezzanine, onlookers, witnesses **10** spectators
display: 3 art **5** easel, op art
__ gallery: 6 peanut, rogue's
__ Gallery: 5 Night
gallet: 4 chip **5** spall, stone
galley: 4 boat, ship **5** proof **6** bireme **7** kitchen, trireme **8** sailboat **10** manuscript
ancient ~: 6 bireme **7** trireme
directive: 4 dele, stet
glitch: 4 typo **7** erratum **8** misprint
implement: 3 oar
space in a ~: 4 quad **6** em quad, en quad
stall a ~: 6 becalm
worker: 3 oar **5** rower **6** editor, writer **8** redactor
galley __: 5 proof, slave
galleys, work on: 4 edit
Gallia __ omnis...: 3 est
Galliano flavoring: 5 anise
galliard: 5 dance
Gallic: 6 French
Gallico: 4 Paul
Galli-Curci, Amelita: 6 singer **7** soprano
specialty: 5 opera
__ Gallienne: 5 Eva Le
Galligan: 4 Zach
gallimaufry: 4 hash, olio, stew **6** jumble, medley, ragout **7** farrago, mélange, mixture **8** mishmash **9** potpourri **10** hodgepodge, miscellany, salmagundi
galling: 6 bitter **7** onerous **8** abrasive, worrying **10** irritating
gallinipper: 3 bug **6** insect
gallinule: 4 bird
Gallipoli: 9 peninsula
author: Alan Moorehead
cape: 6 Helles
locale: 6 Turkey
Gallipoli (1981 film)
cast: Mel Gibson
director: Peter Weir
gallium: 5 metal **7** element
gallivant: 3 gad **4** roam, rove **5** drift, jaunt, range, stray, tramp **6** cruise, ramble, trapes, wander **7** meander, traipse **8** ambulate, gad about **9** run around **10** knock about
gallivanting: 6 errant, roving **7** roaming **9** wandering
Gallo: 4 Bill **5** Julio **6** Ernest
gallon: 4 meas. **7** measure
fraction: 2 oz., pt., qt. **4** pint **5** ounce, quart

___-gallon: **4** half
___-gallon hat: **3** ten
gallop: **3** fly, hie, rip, run, zip **4** bolt, dart, dash, flit, gait, pace, race, ride, rush, step, tear, zoom **5** hurry, scoot, speed **6** barrel, canter, hasten, hustle, move it, rocket, scurry, sprint **7** floor it, hop to it, quicken, scamper **8** step on it **9** go swiftly, hotfoot it, shake a leg, skedaddle **10** get a move on, hightail it
  at full ~: **4** fast **5** apace **7** hastily, quickly, rapidly, swiftly **8** pell-mell, speedily **9** posthaste
  ender: **3** ade
  relative: **3** jog **4** trot **6** canter
___ gallop: **3** at a
galloper: **5** horse
galloping: **5** rapid, swift **6** flying, speedy **9** whirlwind
Galloping Gourmet, The: Graham Kerr
Galloway: **3** Don
Gallup: **4** city, town **6** George
  activity: **4** poll
  colleague: **5** Roper **6** Harris
  locale: **9** New Mexico
galoot: **2** ox **3** ape, lug, oaf **4** bozo, dolt, goon, lout **5** klutz **6** big ape, codger, lubber **7** bumpkin, jackass, Palooka **9** eccentric, harebrain
galop: **5** dance, music
  ender: **3** ade
galore: **4** much **5** à gogo, amply **7** all over, aplenty, liberal, profuse, to spare **9** in a big way, in bunches **10** in quantity
galosh: **4** boot, shoe **6** rubber **8** footwear, overshoe
  relative: **4** boot **5** wader **8** overshoe
Galsworthy, John: **6** writer **7** British **8** Nobelist **10** playwright
  group founded by: PEN
  heroine: **5** Irene
  work: The Forsyte Saga
    To Let
Galton, Francis: **10** geneticist
galumph: **4** plod **5** stump **6** lumber
galumphing: **6** clumsy **7** awkward **9** ponderous **10** cumbersome
Galvani: **5** Luigi
galvanic ___: **4** cell **7** battery
galvanization material: **4** zinc
galvanize: **4** fire, jolt, move, prod, spur, stir, wake, zinc **5** hop up, pique, prime, rouse, shock, spark, waken **6** arouse, awaken, excite, fire up, thrill **7** animate, enliven, inspire, provoke, quicken, startle **8** dynamize, energize, enspirit, inspirit, motivate **9** electrify, encourage, impassion, stimulate **10** invigorate
galvanized ___: **4** iron **5** steel
galvanometer measure: **3** amp **7** current
Galveston: **3** bay **4** city, port, town
  locale: **5** Texas
Galveston (1969 song)
  artist: Glen Campbell
Galway: **4** city, town **5** James **7** Kinnell
  island group: **4** Aran **5** Arans
  locale: **4** Eire, Erin **7** Ireland
Galway, James: **5** Irish **7** flutist **8** flautist
gam: **4** limb **5** shank, visit **7** meeting
Gam: **4** Rita
Gamal ___ Nasser: **5** Abdel
Gamay: **3** red **4** wine **5** grape **7** red wine
  origin: **6** France
  relative: *see* wine
gambado: **4** jump, spat **5** antic, caper, prank **6** gaiter, puttee **7** legging
Gambia: **5** river **6** nation **7** country
  bovine: **5** N'dama
  capital: **6** Banjul
  language: **7** Malinke
  money: **5** butut **6** dalasi
  neighbor: **7** Senegal
gambit: **4** plan, plot, ploy, ruse, trap, wile **5** feint, shift, trick **6** device **7** gimmick, sleight **8** artifice, maneuver, strategy **9** stratagem
Gambit: **8** game show
  host: Wink Martindale
gamble: **3** bet, lay **4** dare, dice, play, risk, shot, stab **5** flier, fling, flyer, stake, wager **6** chance, hazard **7** venture **8** chance it, long shot, make book **9** speculate **10** go for broke, jeopardize, take a flyer
  away: **4** blow, lose **5** waste **6** misuse **7** fribble **8** squander **9** dissipate **10** run through
  badly: **4** lose
  on: **5** trust **7** believe
  (on): **4** bank, rely **5** count **6** depend
gambled: **7** at stake
gambler: **5** sport **6** better, bettor, punter, risker **7** plunger, wagerer **8** gamester **9** bookmaker, risk-taker **10** adventurer, speculator
  consideration: **4** edge, odds **7** chances **8** handicap
  cube: **3** die
  loss: **5** shirt
  mecca: **3** OTB **4** Reno **5** Tahoe, Vegas **6** casino, Nevada **8** Las Vegas
  need: **4** luck **5** stake
  pass: **5** no bet
  pot: **5** chips, kitty
Gambler, The
  author: Fyodor Dostoyevsky
Gambler, The (1978 song)
  artist: Kenny Rogers
gambling
  establishment: **5** house **6** casino
  game: **3** loo **4** faro, keno **5** beano, bingo, craps, lotto, monte, poker **6** fan-tan **7** lottery **8** baccarat **9** blackjack, twenty-one
  stake: **4** ante
gambling ___: **3** den
gambol: **4** joke, lark, play, romp, skip **5** caper, dance, frisk, revel, sport, spree **6** cavort, frolic, prance, spring **7** carry on, roister, rollick **8** recreate **9** have a ball, whoop it up **10** fool around
gamboling: **6** frisky, lively **7** coltish, playful **8** sportive **10** frolicsome
Gambon: **7** Michael
gambrel ___: **4** roof
game: **3** gin, job, lay, loo, tag, toy, uno, war **4** bold, Clue, faro, keno, lame, Myst, play, ploy, Pong, pool, prey, Risk, ruse, skat, stud **5** beano, bingo, brave, chess, craps, darts, eager, event, ghost, gutsy, hardy, jacks, Jotto, lotto, match, monte, nervy, omber, Pedro, pente, pitch, poker, prank, ready, rummy, shogi, skeet, Sorry, spoof, sport, stake, tarok, trade, trick, wager, whist **6** awless, belote, Boggle, bridge, casino, daring, écarté, euchre, fan-tan, feisty, go fish, gritty, hearts, heroic, hockey, Pac-Man, plucky, quarry, quoits, racket, spunky, squash, Tetris **7** aweless, belotte, canasta, Careers, contest, cricket, croquet, curling, defiant, doughty, gallant, marbles, old maid, Othello, pachisi, pastime, pinball, pursuit, seven-up, snooker, staunch, tenpins, valiant, venison, willing **8** amenable, baccarat, baseball, charades, checkers, cribbage, disposed, dominoes, draughts, escapade, fearless, football, heroical, intrepid, leapfrog, mah-jongg, Monopoly, ninepins, pachinko, parchesi, parchisi, peekaboo, resolute, ringtoss, Scrabble, skittles, softball, spirited, sporting, sportive, stalwart, Stratego, strategy, unafraid, valorous, vocation **9** amusement, audacious, blackjack, dauntless, diversion, dodgeball, dreadless, specialty, tic-tac-toe, twenty-one, undaunted, unfearful, unfearing, water polo **10** chuck-a-luck, courageous, Donkey Kong, jackstraws, livelihood, mettlesome, post office, profession, recreation, ring-a-levio, tetherball, tournament, undismayed, volleyball
  African board ~: **3** bao
  animal: **3** elk **4** deer **5** moose, rhino
  anybody's ~: **5** close **10** nip and tuck
  ball ~: **5** bocce, bocci, lotto, rugby **6** squash **7** jai alai **9** situation
  beat the ~: **3** win **7** triumph
  be ~ for: **5** allow **6** accede
  bird: **4** fowl **5** quail **6** grouse **8** pheasant
  board ~: **4** Clue, keno, Risk **5** chess, pente, shogi, Sorry **7** Careers, Othello, Reversi **8** checkers, Monopoly, Scrabble, Stratego
  board square: **5** start
  card ~: **3** gin, loo, uno, war **4** faro, jass, skat, stud **5** beano, monte, omber, Pedro, poker, rummy, tarok, whist **6** belote, bridge, casino, écarté, euchre, fan-tan, go fish, hold 'em **7** belotte, canasta **8** baccarat **9** blackjack, twenty-one
  center: **4** mall **6** arcade **7** gallery
  computer ~: **4** Doom, Myst, Pong **6** Pac-Man, Tetris **10** Donkey Kong
  computer ~ maker: **3** NES **4** Sega **5** Atari **7** Genesis **8** Nintendo
  con ~: **4** hoax, lure, scam **5** bunco, dodge, fraud, sting **6** dupery, humbug, racket **7** knavery **8** trickery **9** deception **10** illegality
  counting ~: **3** nim
  cry: **4** I win
  dice ~: **5** craps **7** Yahtzee **8** Monopoly **10** backgammon
  dish: **5** salmi **6** salmis
  ender: **4** cock, some, ster **6** keeper
  factor: **4** luck **5** skill
  fish: **4** bass, cero, tuna, ulua **5** trout, wahoo **6** marlin, tarpon **7** cavalla, walleye **9** barracuda
  five-in-a-row ~: **4** keno **5** bingo, pente
  (for): **3** hot **5** ready
  gambling ~: **3** loo **4** faro, keno **5** beano, bingo, craps, lotto, monte, poker **6** écarté, fan-tan **8** baccarat **9** blackjack, twenty-one
  get in the ~: **4** ante **6** ante up
  go after ~: **4** hunt **5** chase, stalk, track **6** forage
  golf ~: **5** round
  item: **3** die **4** cube **5** board
  kids' ~: **3** tag, war **4** I spy **5** catch, jacks, potsy, t-ball **6** Cootie, go fish **9** hopscotch
  knocking ~: **3** gin **5** rummy
  lawn ~: **4** polo **5** bocci, roque **6** tennis
  little ~: **4** plot, trap **5** cabal **6** racket, scheme **8** intrigue **9** coalition, collusion, treachery **10** complicity, connivance, conspiracy, disloyalty
  make ~ of: **3** rag **4** gibe, jeer, jibe, mock **5** taunt, tease **7** scoff at **8** ridicule
  mallet ~: **4** polo **5** roque **7** croquet
  name in ~ shows: **3** Pat **4** Alex, Merv
  name of the ~: **5** point **7** meaning, reality
  net ~: **6** hockey, tennis **8** Ping Pong **9** badminton
  New Year's ~: **4** Bowl **8** Rose Bowl **10** Cotton Bowl, Orange Bowl
  numbers ~: **4** keno **5** beano, bingo, lotto **7** lottery
  one: **5** trier
  opener: **3** bet **4** ante **5** stake, wager
  outdoor ~: **4** golf, polo **6** tennis **7** croquet **8** baseball, football, softball
  park: **3** zoo
  participant: **4** side, team **6** player
  piece: **3** man **4** pawn **6** domino
  plan: **4** idea, plan, ruse **5** model **6** design, scheme **8** scenario, strategy, time line **9** blueprint
  play the ~: **5** yield **6** accept **7** conform, go along **9** cooperate **10** keep in step, toe the mark
  pub ~: **4** pool **5** darts **9** billiards
  punting ~: **5** rugby **6** soccer **8** football
  racket ~: **6** squash, tennis **8** Ping Pong **9** badminton
  run a ~ on: **2** do **3** con **4** bilk, burn, clip, dupe, fool, gull, hoax, rook, scam, snow **5** cheat, gouge, hocus, set up, shaft, sting, trick **6** fleece, hustle, rip off, rope in, take in **7** deceive, defraud, fake

out, swindle 8 flimflam, hoodwink 9 bamboozle, four-flush, shake down, victimize
shell ~: 5 cheat 7 swindle 8 trickery 9 collusion
starter: 3 end 4 ball
still in the ~: 4 live 5 alive
take out of the ~: 5 bench
unit: 3 set
what the ~ may be: 5 afoot
win every ~: 5 sweep 7 clean up
with a jackpot: 7 lottery
word ~: 5 ghost, Jotto 6 Boggle 8 Scrabble
game __: 3 law 4 bird, fish, fowl, park, plan, room, show 5 point 6 theory, warden
game, __, match: 3 set
__ game: 3 big, con, end, war 4 ball, bowl, card, draw, fair, long, love, mind, mug's, skin, word 5 board, no-hit, Ponzi, shell, short, small, video 6 arcade, parlor, pepper, rubber 7 numbers, perfect, waiting, zero-sum
__ Game: 5 He Got 7 All-Star
Game Boy
man: 5 Mario
rival: 4 Sega
GameCube
rival: 4 Xbox
__ game in town, the: 4 only
game is __, The: 5 afoot
gamekeeper: 6 warden
gamelan instrument: 4 gong
gameness: 4 grit 5 nerve, pluck, spunk 6 mettle
game of __: 5 skill 6 chance
games: 5 sport 9 athletics, merriment 10 recreation
companion: 3 fun
ender: 3 man, men
play ~: 3 toy 6 manage, trifle 8 maneuver 9 machinate 10 manipulate
Roman ~: 4 ludi
six ~: 3 set
war ~: 5 drill
__ games: 3 war 4 mind, play
Games __ Play: 6 People
__ Games: 4 Mind 6 Nemean, Summer, Winter 7 Foolish, Olympic, Patriot, Pythian 8 Goodwill
Games for the Superintelligent
author: Jim Fixx
game show
group: 5 panel
name: 3 Pat 4 Alex, Wink 5 Vanna
sound: 4 ding 6 buzzer
winnings: 3 car 4 cash, loot, trip 5 prize 6 cruise
worker: 2 MC 4 host 5 emcee, model
__-game show: 3 pre
Game Show Network
program: 5 Lingo
gamesmanship, practice: 5 psych
gamesome: 6 jaunty
Games People Play
author: Eric Berne
Games People Play (song)
artist: Alan Parsons Project, Joe South, Spinners
gamester: 6 better, bettor 7 gambler
emulate a ~: 3 bet, lay 4 ante, play, risk 5 hedge, stake, wager 6 gamble, hazard, parlay 8 make book 9 challenge
gamete: 3 egg 4 germ, seed 8 germ cell
source: 5 monad
Game, The
author: A.S. Byatt
Game, The (1997 film)
cast: Carroll Baker, Michael Douglas, Sean Penn
__ Game, The: 3 Gin, War 4 Name 5 Lion's, Match 6 Circle, Crying, Dating, Dinner, Mating, Pajama
game-winning __: 3 RBI
gamin: 3 imp, kid 4 waif 6 urchin 10 jackanapes, ragamuffin
gaming __: 5 table
gamma: 5 Greek 6 letter
follower: 5 delta
preceder: 4 beta
gamma __: 3 ray
gamma ray product: 3 ion
gammon
see baloney
gamophobe fear: 7 wedlock 8 marriage 9 matrimony
gamp: 6 brolly 8 umbrella
Gam, Rita: 7 actress
spouse: Sidney Lumet
gamut: 4 A to Z, span 5 field, range, reach, scale, scope, sweep 6 extent 7 breadth, compass 8 panorama, spectrum 9 full-range
...gamut of emotions from __: 4 A to B
gamy: 4 rank 6 rancid, risque 7 corrupt, tainted 10 malodorous
__ Gan: 5 Ramat
Gance: 4 Abel
gander: 2 he 4 bird, look, male, peek, peep, view 5 goose 6 glance 7 glimpse 8 once-over
take a ~: 3 eye 4 look, scan, view
Gandhi: 5 Sonia 6 Indira 7 Mahatma 8 Mohandas
Gandhi (1982 film)
cast: Candice Bergen, John Gielgud, Ben Kingsley
Gandhi, Indira father: 5 Nehru
Gandhi, Mahatma: 5 Hindu 6 Hindoo
associate: 5 Nehru
foe: 3 Raj
home: 5 India
Gandolfini, James: 5 actor
TV: The Sopranos
__ Gandolfo: 6 Castel
gandy __: 6 dancer
ganef: 5 crook, rogue, thief 6 rascal 8 chiseler, swindler 9 scoundrel
job: 5 heist
gang: 3 lot, mob, set 4 band, clan, club, crew, herd, Jets, pack, ring, team 5 bunch, covey, crowd, group, hands, horde, junto, posse, squad, troop 6 clique, league, muster, outfit, rabble, Sharks, troupe 7 cluster, company, coterie, in-group, society 9 syndicate 10 assemblage
around: 4 herd, meet 5 bunch, crowd, flock, group, rally, swarm 6 gather, muster 7 bunch up, collect, compile, convene, hang out 8 assemble 9 forgather 10 congregate, rendezvous
ender: 3 way 4 land, plow, ster 5 plank, punch 6 buster
member: 4 goon, hood 5 biker, tough
see the old ~: 5 reune 6 remeet
territory: 4 turf
up: 5 group 8 assemble 10 join forces
up on: 4 rush 5 blitz 6 attack 7 assault 8 overcome
weapon: 3 gat 4 shiv 5 knife
gang __: 4 up on
__ gang: 4 road 5 chain
__ Gang: 3 Our 5 Andy's, Chain
...gang aft __: 5 agley
__ gangbusters: 4 like
Ganges: 5 river
city on the ~: 5 Patna 7 Benares
dress: 4 sari 5 saree
locale: 5 India
river to the ~: 5 Jumna 6 Yamuna
gangland girl: 4 moll
ganglia: 6 nerves
gangling: 4 lank, lean, long, tall, thin 5 lanky, leggy, rangy 6 meager, skinny 7 awkward, spindly, stringy 8 rambling, rawboned 10 long-legged
gangly: 4 lank, lean, slim, tall, thin, wiry 5 lanky, rangy, spare 6 dainty, meager, skinny, slight, slinky, svelte, twiggy 7 awkward, gracile, scraggy, scrawny, slender, spidery, spindly, willowy 9 sylphlike
Gang of __: 4 Four
gangplank: 4 ramp 6 access
use the ~: 6 debark
Gangs of New York (2002 film)
cast: Daniel Day-Lewis, Cameron Diaz, Leonardo DiCaprio
director: Martin Scorsese
gangsta __: 3 rap
Gangsta Lean (1993 song)
artist: D.R.S.
Gangsta's Paradise (1995 song)
artist: Coolio
gangster: 4 goon, hood, thug 5 crook, tough 6 bandit, gunsel, outlaw 7 brigand, hoodlum, mobster, ruffian 8 evildoer, hooligan, tough guy 9 desperado, racketeer
ender: 3 dom
girl: 4 moll
gangsters: 3 mob 5 Mafia 9 syndicate 10 underworld
__ Gang, The: 7 Capital
gangway: 4 ramp, walk 5 aisle 7 ingress
gannet: 4 bird 5 booby, solan 7 seabird 8 sea goose
Gannon University
locale: 4 Erie
ganoid fish: 3 gar 6 bowfin 7 grindle
Gant: 3 Ron 6 Eugene
gantline: 4 rope
Gant, Ron
sport: 8 baseball
Gantry: 5 Elmer
Ganymede: 4 moon
planet: 7 Jupiter
gaol: 4 jail 6 prison 7 bastile 8 bastille
gaoler: 5 guard 6 jailer, warden 7 turnkey
GAO part: 3 Gen., Off. 5 Acctg. 6 Office 7 General 10 Accounting
gap: 4 gulf, hole, lull, open, pass, rest, rift, vent, void, yawn 5 break, chasm, cleft, crack, gorge, gulch, gully, lapse, pause, space, split 6 breach, cavity, cesura, cranny, divide, gulley, hiatus, hollow, lacuna, ravine, recess, vacuum 7 caesura, crevice, interim, opening, respite, vacancy, vacuity 8 aperture, cleavage, distance, division, fracture, interval, omission, weakness 9 clearance, disparity, interlude 10 difference, divergence, interspace, interstice, passageway, separation
bridge the ~: 3 aid 6 assist 8 tide over 9 help along 10 see through
filler: 4 shim
generation ~: 4 gulf 5 break, split 10 alienation
in time: 4 stay 5 delay, hitch, pause, stall 6 holdup 7 respite, setback 8 interval, reprieve, slowdown, stoppage 9 deferment, extension, interlude 10 standstill, suspension
narrow the ~: 4 gain, near 5 close 7 catch up, close in 8 approach, overtake
starter: 4 stop
__ gap: 5 water 6 gender 7 missile
Gap
The ~: 5 store
gape: 3 see 4 gawk, gaze, look, open, peer, rift, yawn 5 split, stare 6 goggle, marvel 10 separation
at: 3 eye 4 view 5 watch
make ~: 3 awe 4 daze, rock, stun 5 amaze, floor 6 bemuse, boggle, dazzle, thrill 7 astound, nonplus 8 astonish, blow away, bowl over, confound, transfix 9 dumbfound, take aback
gaper: 4 clam
gaping: 4 awed, open, vast, wide 5 broad 6 amazed, astare, rictus 7 yawning 8 wide open 9 cavernous 10 slack-jawed
hole: 3 maw 5 abyss, chasm
gar: 4 fish 8 billfish 10 needlefish
ender: 4 fish, pike
garage: 4 shop 5 depot 6 hangar
bus ~: 4 barn
do ~ work: 4 lube 5 align, aline
item: 4 jack, tool 5 gizmo 6 gadget 7 machine, vehicle 9 implement
occupant: 3 bus, car 4 auto
sale sign: 4 as is, sold
sign: 4 Exit, Park 5 Enter
smudge: 3 oil
garage __: 4 band, sale
garage-__ opener: 4 door
Garagiola: 3 Joe
Garamond: 4 font 8 typeface
Garand: 3 gun 5 rifle 6 weapon
garb: 4 duds, gear, gown, rags, wear 5 array, cover, drape, dress, getup, habit, robes 6 attire, clothe, enrobe, fit out, livery, outfit, rig out, suit up, tog out 7 apparel, bedrape, clothes, costume, deck out, garment, raiment, threads, toggery, uniform 8 accouter, accoutre, clothing, covering, ensemble, garments, glad rags 9 trappings, vestments 10 canoni-

cals, habiliment, Sunday best
ender: **3** age
see also clothing, garment
garbage: **4** junk **5** dregs, dross, filth, offal, scrap, swill, trash, waste **6** debris, litter, refuse, rubble **7** residue, rubbish **8** detritus, leavings **9** scrapings, sweepings
collector: **6** ashman
disposal button: **5** reset
holder: **4** dump **5** barge **6** ashcan **8** landfill, trash can
pickup place: **4** curb
taking out the ~: **3** job **4** duty, task **5** chore **9** housework
see also baloney
garbage __: **3** bin, can
garbanzo: **4** bean **6** legume **8** chickpea
garbed: **4** clad **6** decent
Garber: **6** Victor **7** Matthew
garble: **4** slur, warp **5** color, mix up, slant, twist **6** doctor, jumble **7** confuse, distort **8** misquote, scramble
Garbo, Greta: **7** actress, Swedish
film: Anna Christie (1930)
Anna Karenina (1935)
Camille (1937)
Conquest (1937)
Flesh and the Devil (1927)
Grand Hotel (1932)
The Kiss (1929)
Mata Hari (1932)
Ninotchka (1939)
Queen Christina (1933)
Two-Faced Woman (1941)
A Woman of Affairs (1928)
what ~ wanted to be: **5** alone
Garbo Talks (1984 film)
cast: Anne Bancroft, Carrie Fisher
director: Sidney Lumet
Garcia: **4** Gary **5** Jerry
García: **4** Andy **6** Sergio
García Lorca, Federico: **4** poet **6** writer **7** Spanish
__ García Márquez: **7** Gabriel
Garciaparra: **5** Nomar
García, Sergio: **6** golfer
garçon: **6** server, waiter
Garda: **4** lago, lake
locale: **5** Italy
Gard capital: **5** Nîmes
__-garde: **5** avant **7** arrière
garde, avant: **6** exotic **8** original
garden: **3** bed, dig, hoe **4** plot, till, weed, yard **5** court, patch **7** outdoor **8** outdoors **9** cultivate, flower bed
access: **4** gate **7** postern
area: **3** bed **4** path, plot **5** arbor, patch
bane: **4** weed
Biblical ~: **4** Eden
climber: **3** ivy
combining form: **4** -etum
container: **3** pod **4** hull, husk **5** shuck **6** jacket **8** seed case **10** integument
crawler: **4** worm
dweller: **3** Eve **4** Adam **5** brink
feature: **3** row **4** maze, rock **5** arbor **6** gazebo
flower: **4** glad, iris, lily, rose **5** aster, bloom, pansy, peony, phlox, tulip, viola **6** azalea, hybrid
hazard: **3** bur **5** brier, spine, thorn **7** bramble, prickle, spicule, sticker
lead up the ~ path: **7** deceive
like an unkempt ~: **5** weedy
material: **4** loam, soil **5** earth
of Eden: **6** utopia
pest: **4** coon, mole, slug **5** aphid, aphis **6** earwig **7** raccoon
products brand: **5** Ortho
spray: **5** zineb **6** fogger
tool: **3** hoe **4** hose, rake **5** edger, spade **6** dibble
variety: **5** usual **8** ordinary, standard
veggie: **3** pea **4** beet, cuke, kail, kale **5** chard **6** carrot, tomato
work in the ~: **3** hoe, sow **4** rake, seed, weed **5** spade
garden __: **3** pea **4** path **5** party, salad
garden-__: **7** variety
__ garden: **3** tea **4** beer, rock, roof **5** truck **7** botanic, victory
Garden: **3** MSG **4** Mary
org.: **3** NBA
__ Garden: **4** Rose **5** Olive **6** Covent, Secret
Gardena: **4** city, town
locale: **10** California
Garden City: **4** town
locale: **7** New York
gardener: **6** farmer, grower **9** caretaker **10** cultivator
at times: **4** hoer **5** hoser, raker
concern: **4** lawn, soil **5** plant, shrub
first ~: **4** Adam
purchase: **4** bulb, lime, seed **5** humus **6** barrow
sci.: **4** hort.
tool: **3** hoe **4** hose, rake **5** edger, spade **6** dibble
Garden Grove: **4** city, town
locale: **10** California
gardenia: **4** tree **5** plant, shrub **6** flower **9** evergreen
relative: **5** ixora **6** bluets, coffee, ipecac, madder **8** cinchona **9** bouvardia
Gardenia: **7** Vincent
Garden, Mary: **6** singer **7** soprano
specialty: **5** opera
Garden of __, The: **4** Eden **5** Allah
Garden of Earthly Delights
artist: Hieronymous Bosch
Garden of Earthly Delights, A
author: Joyce Carol Oates
Garden of the Finzi-Continis, The (1971 film)
cast: Helmut Berger, Dominique Sanda
director: Vittorio De Sica
__ Garden of Verses, A: **6** Child's
Garden Party (1972 song)
artist: Ricky Nelson
Garden Party, The
author: Václav Havel, Katherine Mansfield
__ Gardens: **3** Kew **5** Busch **6** Tivoli
__ Gardens of Babylon: **7** Hanging
Gardens of Stone (1987 film)
cast: James Caan, Anjelica Huston, James Earl Jones, Mary Stuart Masterson, D.B. Sweeney
director: Francis Ford Coppola
Garden State
see New Jersey
__ Garden, The: **6** Secret
garden-variety: **5** plain, stock **6** common **7** average, humdrum, prosaic **9** prosaical
Gardiner: **8** Reginald
Gardner: **3** Ava, Rea **4** city, Erle, John, peak, town **5** McKay, mount **8** mountain
locale: **10** Antarctica
word in many ~ titles: **4** Case
Gardner, Ava: **7** actress
film: The Barefoot Contessa (1954)
The Killers (1946)
Mogambo (1953)
The Night of the Iguana (1964)
On the Beach (1959)
Seven Days in May (1964)
Show Boat (1951)
The Snows of Kilimanjaro (1952)
The Sun Also Rises (1957)
spouse: Mickey Rooney, Artie Shaw, Frank Sinatra
Gardner, Erle Stanley: **6** writer
character: Della, Perry, Mason, Street, Burger
pseudonym: A.A. Fair
Gardner, John: **4** poet **6** writer
work: Grendel
Gare de __: **4** l'Est
Gare Saint-Lazare
painter: Claude Monet
Garfield: **3** cat, pet **4** city, John, town **5** Allen, comic, James, strip **6** feline
cat: **6** Arlene
Garfield (comic strip)
artist: Jim Davis
character: **3** Jon, Liz **4** Odie **6** Arlene
Garfield County, seat of: **4** Enid
Garfield Heights: **4** city, town
locale: **4** Ohio
Garfield, James: president
assassin: **7** Guiteau
had one: **5** beard
home: **4** Ohio
middle name: **5** Abram
opponent: **7** Hancock
V.P.: **6** Arthur
wife: **8** Lucretia
Garfunkel, Art
song: All I Know (1973)
Garfunkel partner: **5** Simon
Gargan: **7** William
Gargantua: **5** giant
Gargantua and Pantagruel
author: François Rabelais
gargantuan: **3** big **4** cast, huge, vast **5** giant, great, jumbo, large **7** hulking, immense, mammoth, massive, sizable, titanic **8** colossal, enormous, gigantic, king-size, oversize, sizeable, towering, whapping, whopping **9** difficult, herculean, humongous, leviathan, monstrous, overlarge **10** monumental, prodigious, stupendous, super-duper, tremendous
gargoyle: **4** ogre **7** monster
garibaldi: **5** shirt
Garibaldi: **8** Giuseppe
birthplace: **4** Nice
garish: **4** loud **5** cheap, crude, gaudy, showy, tacky **6** flashy, tawdry, tinsel, vulgar **7** blatant, glaring, kitschy **8** overdone **9** excessive, tasteless
light: **4** neon
garishness: **5** glare
garland: **3** lei **4** swag **6** anadem, reward, wreath **7** chaplet, coronet, festoon
Garland: **4** city, Judy, town **6** Hamlin **7** Beverly
locale: **5** Texas
Garland, Hamlin: **6** writer
Garland, Judy: **6** singer **7** actress
costar: **4** Lahr **5** Haley **6** Bolger, Rooney
film: A Child Is Waiting (1963)
The Clock (1945)
Easter Parade (1948)
For Me and My Gal (1942)
Girl Crazy (1943)
The Harvey Girls (1946)
In the Good Old Summertime (1949)
Judgment at Nuremberg (1961)
Love Finds Andy Hardy (1938)
Meet Me in St. Louis (1944)
Pigskin Parade (1936)
The Pirate (1948)
A Star Is Born (1954)
Summer Stock (1950)
The Wizard of Oz (1939)
Ziegfeld Follies (1946)
Ziegfeld Girl (1941)
spouse: Vincente Minnelli, David Rose
garlic: **5** bread, spice **6** allium **9** condiment, seasoning
California ~ center: **6** Gilroy
cousin: **4** leek **5** onion **7** shallot
-flavored mayonnaise: **5** aioli
prepare: **5** mince
segment: **5** clove
garlic __: **4** salt **5** bread
Garlits, Don: **5** racer **9** auto racer
milieu: **5** track
garment: **3** aba, alb, fur, tog **4** abba, cape, coat, garb, gown, kilt, maxi, mini, robe, sack, sari, suit, toga, tutu, vest, wear **5** A-line, apron, cloak, dress, frock, getup, jeans, oiler, pants, parka, robes, saree, shawl, shirt, skirt, skort, smock, stole, tunic **6** anorak, attire, blouse, bodice, caftan, halter, jumper, kaftan, kimono, kirtle, livery, outfit, sarong, things, tights **7** apparel, chemise, costume, dashiki, leotard, raiment **8** camisole, covering, trousers **9** housecoat, trappings, underwear
African ~: **4** bubu **5** kanzu **6** boubou **7** dashiki
alter a ~: **3** hem **6** take in **7** take out
ancient Greek ~: **6** chiton, peplos, peplus **7** chlamys
attachment: **3** tag
clerical ~: **5** Rabat
draped ~: **4** sari **5** saree
fastener: **4** snap **5** patte **6** button, Velcro, zipper
fisherman's ~: **5** oiler
foundation ~: **5** stays **6** corset, girdle
Indian: **4** sari **5** lungi, saree **6** lungee, lungyi

insert: **5** godet
judicial ~: **4** gown, robe
loose ~: **3** aba **4** abba, robe, sack **5** cloak **6** jumper
Mideast: **3** aba **4** abba, haik, izar **5** burga, burka, haick **6** burkha, chadar, chador, jubbah **7** bourkha, chaddar, chuddar
outer ~: **3** fur **4** coat, robe **5** cloak, parka, stole **6** anorak, jacket **8** raincoat
part: **4** pouf, tuck, vent, yoke **5** bosom, waist **6** revere, revers
Polynesian ~: **5** pareo, pareu **8** lava-lava
Roman: **4** toga **5** stola
size: **2** sm., XL **3** lge., med., XXL **5** large, small **6** medium **10** extra large
Turkish ~: **6** caftan, kaftan
under a chasuble: **3** alb
upper ~: **6** jerkin **9** waistcoat
Victorian ~: **6** girdle
with a hood: **4** cowl
woman's ~: **5** dress, middy, skirt, skort **6** blouse, bodice
worker: **6** hemmer, tailor
see also clothes, clothing

garment __: **3** bag
garments: **4** duds, garb, gear, togs, wear **5** array, dress, get-up, robes **6** attire, livery, outfit **7** apparel, clothes, raiment, threads **8** wardrobe **10** habiliment, Sunday best
Garn: **4** Jake **7** senator **9** astronaut
Garneau, Hector: **4** poet **8** Canadian
garner: **3** get, net, win **4** cull, earn, gain, hold, keep, reap, save **5** amass, cache, glean, hoard, lay by, lay up, put by, store **6** corral, gather, retain, roll up, save up **7** acquire, bring in, collect, compile, deposit, harvest, lay away, put away, store up **8** assemble, cumulate, hang onto, hold onto, maintain, put aside, scrape up, stow away **9** stockpile **10** accumulate
Garner: **4** John **5** James **6** Erroll **8** Jennifer **9** John Nance
Garner, Erroll: **7** pianist **8** composer
genre: **4** jazz
Garner, James: **5** actor
film: The Americanization of Emily (1964)
Duel at Diablo (1966)
Marlowe (1969)
Maverick (1994)
Murphy's Romance (1985)
My Fellow Americans (1996)
Skin Game (1971)
Space Cowboys (2000)
Sunset (1988)
Support Your Local Gunfighter (1971)
Support Your Local Sheriff (1969)
The Thrill of It All (1963)
Victor/Victoria (1982)
TV: Maverick, The Rockford Files
Garner, Jennifer: **7** actress
film: 13 Going on 30 (2004)
Catch and Release (2006)
Elektra (2005)
Ghosts of Girlfriends Past (2009)
The Invention of Lying (2009)
Juno (2007)
The Kingdom (2007)
TV: Alias
garnet: **3** gem, red **5** color **6** pyrope **7** mineral **9** almandine, demantoid
month: **7** January
relative: ***see*** red color
synthetic ~: **3** yag
Garnett: **3** Tay **4** Gale
garnish: **3** top **4** deck, gild, lard, lime, trim **5** adorn, aspic, caper, cress, frill, grace, lemon, olive **6** attach, bedeck, set off **7** enhance, festoon, gussy up, parsley, spiff up **8** beautify, decorate, ornament, spruce up, trimming **9** adornment, embellish **10** decoration
Gibson ~: **5** onion
martini ~: **5** olive
garnished: **9** decorated, elaborate **10** ornamented
Garofalo, Janeane: **7** actress
film: Bye Bye, Love (1995)
Clay Pigeons (1998)
Cop Land (1997)
The Independent (2001)
The Minus Man (1999)
Mystery Men (1999)
Reality Bites (1994)
The Truth About Cats and Dogs (1996)
Wet Hot American Summer (2001)
Garonne: **5** river
city on the ~: **8** Bordeaux, Toulouse
locale: **6** France
river to the ~: **3** Lot
__-Garonne: **5** Haute, Lot-et
__-garou: **4** loup
garpike: **4** fish
garret: **4** loft **5** attic **6** dormer **7** atelier, mansard **8** top floor
Garret: **6** Hobart
Garrett: **3** Pat **4** Brad, Leif, Wang **5** Betty **6** Morris
Garrett, Betty: **7** actress
spouse: Larry Parks
TV: Laverne & Shirley
Garrett, Leif
song: I Was Made for Dancin' (1978)
Garrick: **5** David, Utley
Garrick Gaieties, The: **7** musical
composer: Lorenz Hart, Richard Rodgers
garrison: **4** base, camp, fort, post **6** casern, occupy **7** caserne, citadel, defense, station **8** barracks, fastness, fortress **10** encampment, stronghold
Garrison: **3** Jim **7** Keillor
Garroway: **4** Dave, host **5** emcee
signoff: **5** peace
Garr, Teri: **7** actress
film: The Black Stallion (1979)
Dumb & Dumber (1994)
Head (1968)
Mr. Mom (1983)
Oh, God! (1977)
Tootsie (1982)
Young Frankenstein (1974)
garrulity: **8** babbling **9** jabbering, loquacity, prattling, prolixity, verbosity, wordiness **10** blathering, chattering, chattiness, volubility
garrulous: **4** glib, long **5** gabby, talky, windy, wordy **6** chatty, prolix **7** diffuse, gushing, lengthy, unterse, verbose, voluble **8** babbling, rambling **9** bombastic, expansive, gossiping, prattling, talkative **10** bigmouthed, chattering, discursive, long-winded, loquacious, motormouth, palaverous
Garry: **5** Moore **6** Maddox **7** Trudeau **8** Kasparov, Marshall **9** Shandling
__ Garry Shandling's Show: **3** It's
Garson: **5** Greer, Kanin
Garson, Greer: **7** actress
film: Goodbye, Mr. Chips (1939)
Julia Misbehaves (1948)
Julius Caesar (1953)
Madame Curie (1943)
Mrs. Miniver (1942, AA)
Mrs. Parkington (1944)
Pride and Prejudice (1940)
Random Harvest (1942)
Sunrise at Campobello (1960)
The Valley of Decision (1945)
garter __: **5** snake
garter tosser: **5** groom
Garth: **6** Brooks, Jennie
Garver: **5** Kathy
Garvey: **5** Steve **6** Marcus
Garvey, Steve
sport: **8** baseball
Gary: **4** city, Cole, Hart, town **5** Busey, Ewing, Frank, Lewis, Numan, Owens, Sandy **6** Becker, Carter, Cooper, Farmer, Garcia, Grimes, Larson, Oldman, Player, Romain, Sinise, Snyder, Wright **7** Coleman, Collins, Glitter, Merrill, Puckett **8** Burghoff, Graffman, Lockwood, Lorraine
locale: **3** Ind. **7** Indiana
Gary __ and the Playboys: **5** Lewis
Gary __ and the Union Gap: **7** Puckett
Gary, Romain: **6** French, writer
Gary U.S. __: **5** Bonds
Garza García: **4** city, town
locale: **6** Mexico **9** Nuevo León
gas: **3** air **4** fuel, fume, neon **5** argon, ethyl, fluid, Freon, fumes, mouth, ozone, radon, steam, vapor, xenon **6** butane, corona, ethane, ethene, helium, ketene, oxygen, petrol **7** ammonia, krypton, methane, premium, propane, regular, tankful, utility **8** chlorine, ethylene, firedamp, fluorine, high-test, hydrogen, nitrogen, road sign, unleaded **9** effluvium, great time, isobutene, wordiness **10** anesthetic, exhalation, fossil fuel
appliance: **5** grill, range, stove **8** barbecue
asset: **6** octane
bill unit: **5** therm **6** therme
combining form: **3** aer-, atm- **4** aero-, mano-
company: **4** util. **7** utility
consumption fig.: **3** mpg
ender: **3** bag **5** house, light, tight, works
fill with ~: **4** fuel **6** aerate
gauge reading: **4** full, half **5** empty **8** half-full
guzzler: **3** car **4** auto, heap **5** crate **6** jalopy, wheels **7** clunker, vehicle **9** limousine **10** automobile
holder: **4** main, pump, tank
inert ~: **4** neon **5** argon, radon, xenon **7** krypton
in physics: **5** state
meter: **5** gauge **9** indicator
natural ~: **8** resource
natural ~ component: **6** ethane **8** dimethyl
noble ~: **4** neon **5** argon, radon, xenon **7** krypton
old ~ brand: **4** Esso **7** Flying A **8** Sinclair
out of ~: **4** beat, worn **5** empty, weary **7** worn-out **8** fatigued **9** enervated, exhausted **10** knocked out
pump ~: **4** fill, fuel **6** fill up, refuel, tank up
quantity: **3** gal. **6** gallon
run out of ~: **3** sag **4** drop, flag, fold, tire, yawn **5** stall, weary **6** fizzle **7** dwindle, poop out **8** collapse, overwork
station former freebie: **3** air, map
step on the ~: **4** rush **5** hurry, spank **7** speed up **10** accelerate
word on old ~ pumps: **5** ethyl
see also baloney, gasoline

gas __: **3** jet, law, log, tax **4** coal, main, mask, pump, tank, tube, well **5** meter, pedal, range **6** burner, engine, fitter **7** furnace, guzzler, station, turbine
gas-__: **5** fired **7** guzzler
__ gas: **3** air **4** blue, coal, tear **5** inert, marsh, noble, out of, swamp **6** leaded **7** natural **8** unleaded
__-gas: **3** bio
gasbag: **4** bore **8** blowhard **9** blusterer **10** chatterbox
gascon: **7** boaster, showoff **8** blowhard, braggart, fanfaron **9** know-it-all, swaggerer
ender: **3** ade
gasconade: **4** brag **5** boast, pride **6** hot air **7** bluster, bombast, bravado, talk big **8** boasting
gash: **3** cut **4** hurt, rent, rift, slit, stab, tear **5** gouge, score, slash, slice, wound **6** incise, injury, lesion **7** scratch **8** incision, lacerate **10** interspace, laceration
gashed: **4** torn **7** incised **9** lacerated
gasify: **8** vaporize
Gaskell, Elizabeth Cleghorn: **6** writer **7** British
gasket: **4** ring, seal **5** O-ring
blow a ~: **4** rage, rant **5** freak, go ape
gaslight: **7** lantern
Gaslight (1944 film)
cast: Ingrid Bergman, Charles Boyer, Joseph Cotten
director: George Cukor
Gaslight __: **3** era
gasohol: **4** fuel
gasoline: **4** fuel **5** petro **6** diesel, hi-test, no-lead, petrol **7** premium, regular **8** high-test
additive: **4** lead **5** ethyl
dispenser: **4** pump
measure: **6** gallon
name: **4** Gulf, Hess **5** Amoco, Exxon, Shell, Sohio **6** Sunoco **7** Chevron

platform: **6** island
rating: **6** octane
see also gas
Gasoline __: **5** Alley
gasp: **4** pant, puff, sigh **6** breath, inhale, wheeze **7** breathe **10** inhalation
comics ~: **3** ulp
last ~: **3** end **6** finale, windup, wrap-up **10** conclusion
Gaspar and others: **4** Magi
gasping: **7** gulping
gasser: **4** joke, riot **6** scream **9** wise-crack **10** rib-tickler
Gasser, Herbert: **8** Nobelist
Gassman, Vittorio: **5** actor
spouse: Shelley Winters
gassy: **4** fumy **6** chatty **7** bloated, miasmic **8** aeriform, boastful, vaporous, volatile **9** bombastic, effluvial
Gastein: **5** falls **9** waterfall
locale: **7** Austria
Gasteyer: **3** Ana
gasthaus: **3** inn **6** German
gastronome: **6** foodie **7** epicure, gourmet **8** gourmand **9** epicurean
gastronomy: **4** fare, food, menu **5** table **6** dishes **7** cookery, cooking, cuisine
gastropod: **4** slug **5** murex **6** limpet
gat: **3** gun, rod **5** piece **6** heater, pistol, roscoe **7** firearm
gata: **5** shark
Gatam
grandfather: **4** Esau
gate: **3** way **4** door, exit, take **5** entry, lucre, stile, torii, valve **6** access, egress, portal, profit, wicket **7** barrier, doorway, ingress, postern, revenue, turnout **8** earnings, entrance, entryway, proceeds, receipts **9** threshold, turnstile **10** attendance
closer: **3** bar **4** bolt, hasp, hook, lock **5** catch, latch **7** padlock
design: **5** grill **6** grille
ender: **3** way **4** fold, post **5** crash, house **6** keeper
figure: **3** att. **4** take **10** attendance
give the ~: **4** oust **5** spurn
make it through the ~: **5** get in
squeaker: **5** hinge, pivot
starter: **4** tail, toll **5** flood, South, water
starting ~: **4** post
gate-__: **7** crasher
gate-__ table: **3** leg **6** legged
gâteau: **4** cake **6** French
__ Gate Bridge: **6** Golden
gate-crasher: **7** invader **8** intruder **10** trespasser
gatehouse: **5** lodge
gatekeeper: **5** guard, usher **6** porter, sentry **7** lookout, monitor **8** sentinel
gateleg __: **5** table
gater starter: **4** tail
Gates: **4** Bill **5** Larry **7** Horatio **8** McFadden
__ Gates: **4** Iron **6** Pearly
Gates fo the Forest, The
author: Elie Wiesel
Gates of Heaven (1978 film)
director: Errol Morris
Gates of the Arctic: **4** park
locale: **6** Alaska
gateway: **3** ent. **4** arch **5** lobby **6** portal **7** ingress, postern **8** entrance
Japanese ~: **5** torii
Gateway: **2** PC **8** computer
rival: **3** IBM **4** Dell, Sony **5** Apple **7** Toshiba
Gateway Arch: **8** landmark
architect: **8** Saarinen
locale: **7** St. Louis **8** Missouri
gather: **3** wax **4** band, call, cull, draw, earn, gain, grow, herd, join, levy, loom, mass, meet, pick, pile, pull, rake, reap, rise, save, take, tuck **5** amass, bring, build, bunch, crowd, flock, focus, glean, group, hoard, infer, merge, pluck, raise, rally, reune, scoop, sop up, stock, swarm, swell, think, troop, unite **6** accrue, assume, corral, deduce, derive, draw in, expand, garner, huddle, ingest, load up, muster, obtain, osmose, pick up, pile up, pucker, rake in, reason, reckon, rustle, select, soak up, suck up, summon, take in, take it, throng **7** acquire, believe, bunch up, cluster, collate, collect, compile, convene, convoke, drink in, enlarge, harvest, imagine, marshal, pick out, predict, presume, procure, receive, recruit, reunite, round up, scare up, stack up, suppose, surmise, suspect, swallow **8** assemble, conclude, converge, heighten, hold on to, increase, mobilize, muster up, rustle up, scrape up **9** aggregate, intensify, stockpile **10** accumulate, assimilate, congregate, rendezvous, understand
fabric: **5** shirr
flowers: **4** pick, snip **5** pluck
garment: **4** tuck **5** plait, pleat
leaves: **4** rake **6** rake up **7** clean up
on a surface: **4** sorb **6** adsorb
resources: **6** enlist, enroll, muster **7** procure, round up **8** mobilize
roses: **3** cut **4** clip
starter: **4** wool
__ gather: **3** So I
gatherer: **7** hoarder, pack rat **9** collector
__-gatherer: **6** hunter
gathering: **3** bee, mob, tea **4** band, bash, be-in, bevy, body, crop, fete, heap, herd, levy, mass **5** bunch, crowd, drove, flock, group, horde, mixer, party, rally, roast, swarm, troop **6** affair, caucus, huddle, klatch, love-in, muster, parley, powwow, rabble, throng **7** cluster, company, council, harvest, meeting, reunion, roundup, session, turnout **8** assembly, audience, clambake, conclave, congress, ensemble, function, imminent, jamboree, luncheon, visitors **9** aggregate, concourse, impending, listeners, reception, stockpile **10** assemblage, attendance, collection, concursion, conference, confluence, convention, cumulation, delegation
combining form: **4** -fest
dust: **4** idle
place: **5** haunt, lobby, venue
social ~: **3** bee **5** salon **6** affair, soiree
starter: **4** news, wool
Gathering __, The: **5** Storm
...gathering nuts __: **5** in May
Gathering Storm, The
author: Winston Churchill
...gathers no __: **4** moss
Gather Together in My Name
author: Maya Angelou
__-gatherum: **6** omnium
gating starter: **4** tail
Gatlin: **4** Rudy **5** Larry, Steve
Gatlin Brothers: **4** trio
Gatling: **3** gun **7** Richard
descendant: **3** Uzi
__ gato: **5** una de
gato, big: **5** tigre
gator: **6** animal **7** reptile
cousin: **4** croc **9** crocodile
home: **4** moat **5** swamp
Gator
ender: **3** ade
Gatorade: **5** drink **9** soft drink
Gator Bowl site: **3** Fla. **7** Florida
__ Gatos, CA: **3** Los
Gatsby: **3** Jay
portrayer: Alan Ladd, Robert Redford
__ Gatsby, The: **5** Great
Gattaca (1997 film)
cast: Ethan Hawke, Jude Law, Uma Thurman
GATT successor: **5** NAFTA
Gatún: **4** lake
locale: **6** Panama
Gatwick: **7** airport
locale: **7** England
gauche: **4** left **5** crude, gawky, inapt, inept, rough, tacky, wrong **6** clumsy, coarse, oafish, rustic, wooden **7** awkward, gawkish, ill-bred, unadept, uncouth **8** bumbling, fumbling, ignorant, tactless, unsubtle **9** graceless, ham-handed, impolitic, inelegant, maladroit **10** outlandish, unbecoming, uncultured, unpolished, unskillful
__ gauche: **4** rive
gaucherie: **4** muff **5** gaffe **7** blunder, crudity, faux pas
gaucho: **6** cowboy, herder **7** cowpoke **8** horseman, wrangler **10** equestrian
gear: **4** bola **5** reata
home: **3** Arg. **5** pampa **6** pampas **9** Argentina
roundup: **5** rodeo
see also Spanish
gauchos: **5** pants **8** knickers, trousers
gaud: **4** bead **6** geegaw, gewgaw **7** trinket **9** bagatelle
Gaudí: **7** Antonio
gaudiness: **5** glitz **6** kitsch **7** glitter
gaudy: **4** loud, neon **5** fancy, showy, tacky, vivid **6** bright, flashy, frilly, garish, glitzy, ornate, shoddy, tawdry, tinsel, vulgar **7** glaring, kitschy, splashy **8** colorful **9** flaunting, tasteless **10** flamboyant
not ~: **4** drab
gauge: **4** dial, make, mark, norm, test **5** basis, check, count, guide, judge, meter, model, plumb, scale, tally, value, weigh **6** assess, fathom, figure, number, reckon, screen, size up **7** compute, example, measure, pointer, project **8** appraise, check out, estimate, evaluate, exemplar, gas meter, keep tabs, quantify, standard **9** ascertain, barometer, bench-mark, calculate, calibrate, criterion, determine, guideline, indicator, yardstick **10** touchstone
auto ~: **3** odo **4** tach **8** odometer **10** tachometer
reading: **5** level **6** status **8** altitude **9** elevation
__ gauge: **4** rain
Gauguin, Paul: **6** artist, French **7** painter
half a ~ book title: **3** Noa
hangout: **6** Tahiti
Gaul
ancient people of ~: **4** Remi
city: **5** Lyons **6** Alesia
language: **8** Frankish
today: **6** France
Gauls, to Romans: **3** foe **5** enemy
gaunt: **4** bony, grim, lank, lean, thin **5** bleak, boney, drawn, lanky, spare **6** dismal, dreary, ill-fed, meager, skinny **7** angular, forlorn, haggard, scraggy, scrawny, sterile **8** angulose, angulous, desolate, rawboned **9** emaciated **10** forbidding
gauntlet: **4** gage, test **5** glove, trial **9** challenge
throw down the ~: **4** dare, defy **9** challenge **10** make a stand
Gauntlet, The (1977 film)
cast: Clint Eastwood, Pat Hingle, Sondra Locke
director: Clint Eastwood
Gauss: **4** Karl
Gautama: **6** Buddha **10** Shakyamuni
birthplace: **7** Lumbini
cousin: **6** Ananda
enemy: **4** Mara
horse: **7** Kantaka
lifesaver: **6** Sujata
meditation spot: **6** bo tree
mother: **9** Queen Maya
son: **6** Rahula
wife: **9** Yasodhara
Gautier: **4** Dick **9** Théophile
gauze: **4** mesh **5** weave **6** fabric **7** chiffon **8** gossamer
fabric: **3** net **4** leno **5** lisse, tulle **6** cotton
like ~: **4** wove **5** woven
gauzy: **4** fine, lacy, thin **5** filmy, light, lucid, sheer **6** flimsy **8** delicate, finespun, gossamer **10** cobweb-like, diaphanous, see-through
Gave __ through the night...: **5** proof
gavel: **6** hammer, mallet, tapper
title: **3** sir **5** madam **9** your honor
user: **5** chair, judge **8** chairman
user demand: **5** order
gavel-down word: **4** gone, sold
gavial: **4** croc **6** animal **7** reptile **9** crocodile
Gavilan: **3** Kid
Gavin: **4** John, Muir **7** MacLeod, Maxwell
Gaviscon: **7** antacid
alternative: ***see*** antacid
gavotte: **5** dance, music
__ Gavotte: **5** Ascot

___-Gavras: 5 Costa
Gavrilo: 7 Princip
Gawain: 3 Sir 6 knight
need: 5 armor, lance
gawd: 4 oath
gawk: 3 see 4 gape, gaze, look, ogle, peer 5 stare 6 goggle 10 rubberneck
at: 3 eye 4 view
gawker: 5 ogler 10 rubberneck
gawking: 6 astare
gawky: 4 lank, thin 6 clumsy, gauche, klutzy, oafish, wooden 7 awkward, loutish, unadept, uncouth 8 bumbling, bungling, lubberly, ungainly 9 all thumbs, graceless, lumbering, maladroit, stumbling, unskilled 10 leadfooted, unskillful
gawp: 4 ogle 5 stare
gay: 5 happy, jolly, light, merry, riant, sunny, vivid, witty 6 blithe, bouncy, bright, cheery, chirpy, festal, jocund, jovial, joyful, joyous, lively, rakish 7 chipper, festive, gleeful, jocular, radiant, raffish, romping 8 animated, carefree, cheerful, debonair, giggling, jubilant, laughing, mirthful, sporting, sportive 9 convivial, debonaire, exuberant, lightsome, sprightly, vivacious 10 debonnaire, flying high, frolicsome, rollicking
blade: 4 dude 5 swell 10 jack-a-dandy
in music: 7 festoso
starter: 4 nose
Gay: 4 John 6 Brewer, Talese
Gay ___: 5 Paree 7 Divorce
___ Gay: 5 Enola
Gay Divorcee, The (1934 film): 7 musical
cast: Fred Astaire, Ginger Rogers
music: Cole Porter
Gaye: 4 Nona 6 Marvin
Gaye, Marvin
song: Ain't Nothing Like the Real Thing (1968)
Ain't That Peculiar (1965)
Got to Give It Up (1977)
How Sweet It Is to Be Loved by You (1964)
I Heard it Through the Grapevine (1968)
I'll Be Doggone (1965)
Inner City Blues (1971)
Let's Get It On (1973)
Mercy Mercy Me (1971)
Pride and Joy (1963)
That's the Way Love Is (1969)
Too Busy Thinking About My Baby (1969)
Trouble Man (1972)
What's Going On (1971)
You're All I Need to Get By (1968)
Your Precious Love (1967)
___ Gay Hamilton: 4 Lisa
___ Gay Harden: 6 Marcia
Gayheart: 4 Lucy
Gay, John: 4 poet 7 British 10 playwright
work: The Beggar's Opera
Gay, John work: The Beggar's Opera
Gayle: 7 Crystal 9 Hunnicutt
Gayle, Crystal
sister: Loretta Lynn
song: Don't It Make My Brown Eyes Blue (1977)
You and I (1982)
Gaylord: 5 Mitch, Perry 6 Nelson 7 Ravenal
Gaynes: 6 George
gayness: 3 joy 4 glee 5 mirth 6 gaiety, levity 7 jollity, revelry 8 hilarity, laughter 9 frivolity, happiness, lightness, merriment
Gay Nineties: 3 era
like the ~: 6 gaslit
Gaynor: 5 Janet, Mitzi 6 Gloria
Gaynor, Gloria
song: I Will Survive (1979)
Never Can Say Goodbye (1974)
Gay Purr-ee
composer: Harold Arlen, Yip Harburg
gaz.: 2 bk. 3 ref.
Gaza: 5 strip
grp.: 3 PLO
resident: 4 Arab
gaze: 3 see 4 gape, gawk, look, peek, peep, peer, view 5 stare, watch 6 regard 7 fish eye 10 rubberneck
at: 3 eye, see 4 leer, ogle 5 watch 6 behold, regard 9 flirt with
crystal ~: 4 scry
dreamily: 4 moon 5 yearn 9 fantasize 10 woolgather
starter: 4 star
wide-eyed: 4 gape 5 stare 6 goggle, marvel, wonder
gazebo: 5 kiosk 8 pavilion 9 belvedere
gazehound: 3 dog 5 canid 6 canine
gaze in ___: 3 awe
gazelle: 3 goa 5 ariel, loper 6 animal, mammal 8 antelope
gait: 4 stot
relative: *see* antelope
gazer: 9 spectator
crystal ~: 4 seer 5 sibyl 6 oracle 7 psychic
starter: 4 star
___ gazer: 7 crystal
gazette: 5 paper 7 journal 8 magazine 9 newspaper
Gazette: 5 paper 9 newspaper
locale: 8 Montreal
gazetteer: 4 book 9 reference
abbr.: 3 isl., mts., str. 4 N. Lat., terr.
data: 4 area
gazing: 6 astare
starter: 4 star
gazpacho: 4 sopa, soup
ingredient: 3 oil 4 cuke 5 onion 6 garlic, tomato 7 vinegar 8 cucumber
like ~: 4 cold, cool 7 chilled
Gazzara, Ben: 5 actor
spouse: Janice Rule
TV: Run for Your Life
G.B.
part of ~: 3 Eng. 4 Brit., Scot.
___ G. Biv: 3 Roy
GBS: 4 Shaw
home: 3 Ire.
___ G. Carroll: 3 Leo
Gd: 4 elem. 7 element 10 gadolinium
64 for ~: 4 at. no.
Gdansk: 4 city, port, town 6 Danzig
locale: 6 Baltic, Poland
gds.: 4 mdse.
producer: 3 mfr.
Ge: 4 elem. 7 element 9 germanium
32 for ~: 4 at. no.
GE
part of ~: 3 Gen. 4 Elec.
subsidiary: 3 NBC, RCA
gear: 3 cog, kit, low, rig 4 duds, garb, rags, suit, togs, wear 5 adapt, array, dress, drive, equip, goods, habit, robes, stuff, thing, tools 6 adjust, attire, fit out, outfit, pinion, tackle, tailor 7 apparel, baggage, clothes, costume, effects, forward, furnish, harness, luggage, prepare, reverse, rigging, threads 8 accouter, accoutre, clothing, cogwheel, covering, equipage, fittings, garments, material, sprocket 9 apparatus, caparison, equipment, machinery, trappings 10 belongings, instrument, Sunday best
element: 5 tooth
ender: 3 box 5 shift, wheel
starter: 4 foot, head
up: 7 prepare
gear ___: 3 box 4 down
___ gear: 3 low 4 high
gears: 8 workings 9 machinery, mechanism
change ~: 5 shift
like ~: 6 cogged
what ~ do: 4 lock, mesh 5 catch 6 engage
___ gears: 5 shift 6 switch
gearshift: 3 box
position: 3 low 4 park 5 first, third 6 second 7 neutral, reverse
sequence: 5 PRNDL
gear-tooth cutter: 3 hob
Geary: 7 Anthony, Cynthia
Geb
child: 4 Isis 6 Osiris
Geber
father: 3 Uri
gecko: 5 tokay 6 animal, lizard 7 reptile
cousin: 5 skink
G.E. College Bowl: 8 game show
host: Allen Ludden, Robert Earle
Geddes: 4 Anne
Gedrick: 5 Jason
gee: 3 wow 4 gosh, thou 5 golly 6 cripes, jiminy 7 jimminy
follower: 5 aitch
one-tenth of a ~: 3 cee
opposite: 3 haw
preceder: 2 ef
Gee ___!: 4 whiz
geebung: 4 tree 5 shrub
geegaw: 5 curio 6 bauble, doodad, trifle 7 trinket 8 gimcrack, ornament 9 bagatelle 10 knickknack
gee-gee: 5 horse 6 equine
geek: 4 dolt, nerd, tech, wonk 5 dweeb 6 techie, tekkie, weirdo 7 buffoon, egghead, oddball 9 eccentric
computer ~: 4 guru, nerd
geeky: 5 nerdy, unhip
Geelong: 4 city, port, town
locale: 9 Australia
Geena: 5 Davis
Geer, Will: 5 actor
TV: The Waltons
___ Gees: 3 Bee
geese: 4 fowl 5 birds 7 poultry
group: 5 flock, skein 6 gaggle
like some ~: 4 wild
Geeson: 4 Judy
geezer: 4 coot, cuss, fogy 5 fogey 6 codger 9 eccentric, graybeard 10 fuddy-duddy
query: 2 eh
Geffen: 5 David
gefilte ___: 4 fish
Gehrig: 3 Lou 4 Yank 6 Yankee 9 Iron Horse
contemporary: 4 Ruth 5 Combs 6 Dickey 7 Lazzeri 8 DiMaggio
Gehringer: 7 Charlie
___ gehts?: 3 Wie
Geiberger: 2 Al 5 Brent
Geiberger, Brent: 6 golfer
GEICO
competitor: *see* insurance company
Geiger counter, set off a: 4 emit
Geiger, Hans: 6 German 9 physicist
Geils: 6 Jerome
Geils Band, J.
song: Centerfold (1981)
Freeze-Frame (1982)
Geisel pen name: 5 Seuss
geisha: 5 woman 8 Japanese
accessory: 3 fan, obi
garb: 6 kimono
purse: 4 inro
serving: 3 cha, tea 4 sake
zither: 4 koto
Geissler tube illuminant: 4 neon
gel: 3 set 4 clot, goop 6 firm up, harden 7 colloid, congeal, stiffen, thicken 8 coalesce, solidify 9 coagulate, semisolid, take shape
lab ~: 4 agar 8 agar-agar
___ gel: 6 silica
gelada
relative: *see* primate
Gelasius: 4 pope 7 pontiff
gelastic: 9 laughable, ludicrous
gelate: 3 set 4 clot, jell 6 curdle, harden 7 clabber, clobber, congeal, stiffen, thicken 8 solidify 9 coagulate
gelatin: 5 Jell-O 7 dessert
Chinese ~: 4 agar 8 agar-agar
move like ~: 5 shake 6 jiggle, shimmy, wiggle 7 wriggle
shaper: 4 mold
substitute: 4 agar 8 agar-agar
gelatinize: 3 set 4 jell 7 congeal, stiffen, thicken 8 solidify 9 coagulate
gelatinous: 4 soft 5 thick 7 jellied, viscose, viscous 9 glutinous, jelly-like 10 coagulated
gelato: 3 ice 7 dessert 8 ice cream
alternative: 6 sundae 7 parfait, spumone, spumoni, tortoni 8 snowball
Gelbart: 5 Larry
Gelderland commune: 3 Ede
gelding: 5 horse 6 equine
Geldof: 3 Bob
gelée: 3 goo 5 aspic
Geleon father: 3 Ion
Gelett: 7 Burgess
gelid: 3 icy 4 cold, cool, rimy 5 chill 6 arctic, bitter, chilly, frigid, frosty, frozen, wintry 7 glacial, ice-cold, wintery 8 freezing
period: 6 ice age
gelidity: 4 cold 5 chill 9 frigidity

Gellar, Sarah Michelle: 7 actress
film: I Know What You Did Last Summer (1997)
Scooby-Doo (2002)
spouse: Freddie Prinze Jr.
TV: Buffy the Vampire Slayer
Geller: 3 Uri 5 Bruce
gelling agent: 4 agar 8 agar-agar
Gell-Mann, Murray: 8 Nobelist 9 physicist
Gelsey: 8 Kirkland
gelt
see moolah
Gelusil: 7 antacid
alternative: *see* antacid
gem: 3 ice 4 jade, onyx, opal, rock, ruby, sard 5 agate, angel, balas, beaut, beryl, bijou, boule, coral, dandy, honey, jewel, lapis, paste, pearl, prize, stone, topaz 6 baguet, bauble, garnet, jasper, muffin, zircon 7 cat's-eye, diamond, emerald, jewelry, kunzite, paragon, peridot, sardine, sardius 8 amethyst, baguette, cabochon, marquise, ornament, rara avis, sapphire, sparkler, treasure 9 amazonite, briolette, carnelian, moonstone, nonpareil, tiger's-eye, turquoise 10 aquamarine, birthstone, bloodstone, rhinestone, tourmaline
alternative: *see* point size
amethyst ~: 8 hyacinth
artificial ~: 5 paste
bed: 5 bezel
beryl ~: 7 emerald 9 morganite 10 aquamarine
blue ~: 7 azurite, euclase 8 sapphire 9 turquoise 10 aquamarine, tourmaline
brown ~: 7 zoisite 10 staurolite
carved ~: 5 cameo
chalcedony ~: 4 onyx, sard
clear ~: 6 zircon 7 peridot 9 tanzanite 10 tourmaline
corundum ~: 4 ruby 5 topaz 8 sapphire
ender: 5 stone
feldspar ~: 9 moonstone
garnet ~: 6 pyrope 9 almandine
green ~: 4 jade 7 emerald, euclase, peridot 8 nephrite 9 demantoid, hiddenite 10 tourmaline
holder: 5 prong
jade ~: 8 nephrite
like some ~s: 3 set 5 unset
milky ~: 4 opal
mount a ~: 3 set 6 collet
nephrite ~: 4 jade
opaque ~: 9 turquoise
orange ~: 4 sard 5 balas 7 sardine, sardius
oyster ~: 5 pearl
pink ~: 7 zoisite
quartz ~: 7 citrine 8 amethyst
red ~: 4 ruby 5 balas 6 garnet, pyrope, spinel 8 spinelle 9 rhodolite, rubellite 10 ruby spinel
shape: 4 oval, pear 5 round
silica ~: 4 opal
silicate ~: 6 circon, garnet 9 rhodolite 10 tourmaline
surface: 4 face 5 culet, facet, plane
tool: 3 dop 5 loupe
tourmaline ~: 9 rubellite
unfaceted ~: 4 opal 5 pearl
unit: 2 ct. 5 carat
violet ~: 8 amethyst
white ~: 8 sardonyx
yellow ~: 7 citrine
Gemayel: 4 Amin
Gemini: 3 duo, two 4 sign 5 Twins 6 Castor, Pollux
astronaut: 5 Scott, White, Young 6 Aldrin, Borman, Cernan, Conrad, Cooper, Gordon, Lovell 7 Collins, Grissom, Schirra 8 McDivitt, Stafford 9 Armstrong
follower: 4 crab 6 Cancer
month: 3 Jun., May 4 June
mother: 4 Leda
org.: 4 NASA
predecessor: 6 Taurus
rocket: 5 Agena
successor: 6 Cancer
Gemini Contenders, The
author: Robert Ludlum
Gemini Dream (1981 song)
artist: Moody Blues
Gemma: 4 star
gemologist: 7 jeweler 8 lapidary
gemology: 7 science
gems: 6 bijoux, jewels 7 jewelry 9 heirlooms, valuables
__ Gems: 6 Screen
gemsbok: 4 oryx 6 animal, mammal 8 antelope
relative: *see* antelope
Gem State: 5 Idaho
gemstone
see gem
gen.: 3 DDE, ldr., off. 5 R.E. Lee
Gen-__: 3 X'er
Gen.
follower: 4 Exod.
__ Gen.: 3 Att., Maj. 4 Atty., Brig., Comp., Surg.
Gena: 8 Rowlands
Gena __ Nolin: 3 Lee
gendarme: 6 French 7 officer 9 policeman
what a ~ upholds: 3 loi
gender: 3 fem., sex 4 male, masc., neut. 6 female, neuter 8 feminine 9 masculine
not restricted by ~: 4 coed
suffix: 3 -ess 4 -enne, -ette
gender __: 3 gap 4 role 6 bender
gender-__: 7 neutral
gene: 6 allele
component: 3 DNA, RNA
determinant: 5 trait
locate a ~: 3 map
sites: 4 loca, loci
Gene: 4 Mako, Saks 5 Autry, Barry, Evans, Kelly, Krupa 6 Markey, Nelson, Pitney, Shalit, Siskel, Tunney, Upshaw, Wilder 7 Cornish, Hackman, Littler, Rayburn, Raymond, Sarazen, Simmons, Tierney, Vincent 8 Chandler, Lockhart 9 McDaniels
genealogy: 5 class, roots 7 descent, lineage 8 ancestry, pedigree 9 bloodline, forebears, parentage 10 derivation, extraction
carving: 5 totem
subject:: 3 fam., lin. 4 desc., tree 6 family 7 lineage 8 ancestor, pedigree 10 descendant
word: 3 née 4 born
Gene Anthony __: 3 Ray
general: 3 lax 4 rank, rife, wide 5 broad, loose, total, typic, usual, vague 6 common, global, leader, normal, public 7 blanket, diffuse, inexact, liberal, officer, overall, plenary, popular, regular, routine, typical 8 accepted, catholic, everyday, familiar, habitual, ordinary, sweeping 9 all-around, customary, imprecise, inclusive, panoramic, pervasive, prevalent, universal, worldwide 10 collective, indefinite, prevailing, undetailed, unspecific, widespread
address: 3 sir
appearance: 3 air 6 facies
assistant: 3 ADC 4 aide 8 adjutant
combining form: 3 cen- 4 caen-, ceno-, coen- 5 caeno-, coeno-
command: 6 at ease
condition: 5 state 6 repair, status
denial: 5 no sir
designation: 4 star
idea: 4 core, crux, gist, meat, pith 5 heart, point, tenor 6 kernel, marrow, thrust, upshot 7 essence, purport 9 substance
in ~: 6 mainly 7 as a rule, overall, usually 8 as a whole, normally 9 routinely 10 by and large, on the whole, ordinarily
org. with a secretary ~: 4 NATO 5 the UN
practitioner: 3 doc 5 medic 6 doctor, medico 8 sawbones 9 physician
public: 3 mob 4 folk, herd 5 world 6 masses, people, rabble 7 society 8 populace, riffraff 9 bourgeois, citizenry, hoi polloi, multitude, plebeians
sense: 4 gist, tone, vein 5 drift, tenor, theme, trend 6 burden, intent 7 essence, meaning, purport 9 substance
store: 4 mart 6 market, outlet 8 emporium
transport: 4 jeep
general __: 4 rule 5 staff, store 6 orders, strike 7 officer, partner
__ general: 5 major 6 consul 7 one-star, surgeon, two-star 8 attorney, five-star, four-star 9 brigadier, three-star 10 lieutenant
__-general: 5 agent, vicar
General __: 5 Court, Foods, Mills 6 Motors 8 Electric
General __ Army: 5 of the
General __ chicken: 4 Tso's
__ General: 7 Estates
General Foods brand: 5 Sanka
General Hospital (ABC): 9 soap opera
extra: 2 RN 5 nurse
generalist: 8 polymath
generality: 4 rule 9 half-truth, principle
generalization: 3 law 6 reason
generalize: 6 reason 9 establish, postulate, speculate
generalized: 5 vague
generally: 3 oft 5 about, often 6 mainly, mostly 7 as a rule, at large, chiefly, largely, roughly, usually 8 all in all, as a rule 9 in the main, on average, popularly, primarily, regularly, routinely, typically 10 altogether, by and large, frequently, habitually, on the whole, ordinarily
General Mills
cereal: 3 Kix 4 Trix 5 Total 6 Kaboom 7 Harmony 8 Boo Berry, Cheerios, Corn Chex, Fiber One, Rice Chex, Wheaties 9 Wheat Chex 10 Cocoa Puffs 11 Cookie Crisp, Lucky Charms
General Motors: 8 carmaker 9 automaker
birthplace: 5 Flint
brand: 3 Geo 4 Olds, Opel 5 Buick, Chevy 6 Saturn 7 Pontiac 8 Cadillac 9 Chevrolet 10 Oldsmobile
general-obligation __: 4 bond
General of the __: 4 Army 6 Armies
General Re
competitor: *see* insurance company
Generals and Majors (1980 song)
artist: XTC
General's Daughter, The
author: Nelson DeMille
General's Daughter, The (1999 film)
cast: Timothy Hutton, Madeleine Stowe, John Travolta
General Seeger
author: Ira Levin
generalship: 5 skill 7 tactics
General, The (1927 film)
cast: Buster Keaton
General William Booth Enters Into Heaven
author: Vachel Lindsay
generate: 4 form, make 5 breed, cause, found, hatch, set up, spawn, yield 6 create, effect, induce, whip up, work up 7 achieve, develop, perform, produce, trigger 8 engender, initiate, multiply 9 institute, introduce, originate, propagate, send forth 10 accomplish, bring about, give rise to
generated (from), be: 4 stem
generation: 3 age, day, era 4 span, time 5 epoch, years 6 period 7 bearing 8 age group, breeding, creation, spawning 9 begetting, beginning, formation, offspring 10 production
gap: 4 gulf, rift 5 break, split 10 alienation
generation __: 3 gap
Generation __: 3 X-er
__ Generation: 4 Beat, Lost
generations, future: 4 seed 5 heirs, issue 7 kinfolk, progeny 8 children, kinfolks, kinsfolk 9 posterity
generative: 7 fertile 8 original, prolific
generator: 5 motor 6 dynamo, engine, origin
__ generator: 3 ion
generic: 5 usual 6 common, no-name 7 blanket, grouped, routine 8 catholic, everyday, frequent, ordinary 9 unbranded 10 collective, nonbranded, widespread
generis, sui: 6 unique 10 unexampled

generosity: **5** mercy **6** lenity, virtue **7** charity, largess **8** free hand, goodness, goodwill, kindness, largesse, lenience, nobility **9** greatness, nobleness, profusion, readiness **10** almsgiving, liberality
generous: **3** big **4** free, full, kind, much, nice, tidy **5** ample, flush, large, lofty, noble, roomy, sweet **6** decent, giving, kindly, lavish, loving, plenty **7** copious, helpful, liberal, profuse **8** abundant, handsome, merciful, princely, prodigal, spacious, sporting, sportive **9** bounteous, bountiful, capacious, luxuriant, plenteous, plentiful, unselfish, unsparing **10** altruistic, beneficent, benevolent, bighearted, charitable, free-handed, hospitable, humanistic, munificent, openhanded, thoughtful, ungrudging, unstinting
be ~: **4** give **5** share **6** donate, lavish
name meaning ~: **6** Kareem
not ~: **4** mean **5** cheap, close, tight **6** greedy, narrow, skimpy, stingy **7** miserly, sparing, thrifty **8** grasping **9** penurious
one: **5** donor, sport
words: **4** on me
generous __ fault: **3** to a
generously: **7** largely **9** favorably **10** handsomely
Genesee: **5** river
locale: **7** New York
genesis: **4** dawn, rise, seed **5** basis, birth, cause, onset, roots, start, sunup **6** advent, day one, origin, outset, source, spring **7** coinage, dawning, infancy, morning, opening, sunrise, trigger **8** babyhood, creation, daybreak, daylight, nascence, nascency **9** beginning, emergence, formation, inception, invention, square one **10** beginnings, brainchild, break of day, conception, derivation, first light, foundation, generation, initiation
starter: **4** meta **6** embryo
Genesis
author: Delmore Schwartz
Genesis (Bible book)
bird: **4** dove
follower: **6** Exodus
fruit: **5** apple
locale: **4** Eden, Edom **5** Sodom **6** Ararat, Goshen
name: **3** Eve, Ham **4** Abel, Adam, Cain, Enos, Esau, Noah, Seth, Shem **5** Isaac, Jacob, Sarah **7** Abraham
to Deuteronomy: **4** Tora **5** Torah
vessel: **3** ark
Genesis (music group)
album: **6** Abacab
leader: Phil Collins
song: I Can't Dance (1992)
In Too Deep (1987)
Invisible Touch (1986)
Land of Confusion (1986)
That's All! (1983)
Throwing It All Away (1986)
__ Genesis: **4** Sega
genet: **3** cat **6** animal, mammal
genetic: **6** inbred, innate, racial **9** ancestral **10** hereditary
enzyme: **5** DNAse, RNAse
factor: **5** trait
material: **3** DNA, RNA **4** mRNA
product: **5** clone
product combining form: **7** Franken-
starter: **4** meta
genetic __: **3** map **4** code
geneticist: **5** Crick **6** cloner, Galton, Watson
genetics: **7** science
pioneer: **6** Mendel
study: **8** heredity
Genet, Jean: **6** French **10** playwright
work: The Balcony
The Maids
Miracle of the Rose
Our Lady of the Flowers
The Screens
Geneva: **4** city, font, lake, town **8** typeface
lake: **5** Leman
locale: Switzerland
river: **5** Rhone
Geneva Convention concern: **3** POW, war
Genevieve: **3** Ste. **5** saint **6** Bujold, sainte
__ Genevieve, MO: **3** Ste.
Genghis Khan
follower: **5** horde, Tatar **6** Mongol
genial: **4** kind, mild, nice, warm **5** close, happy, jolly, merry, suave, sunny **6** benign, blithe, cheery, chirpy, chummy, clubby, gentle, hearty, jocund, jovial, joyful, joyous, kindly, smooth, upbeat **7** affable, amiable, chipper, cordial, likable, lovable **8** amicable, cheerful, familiar, friendly, gracious, intimate, likeable, loveable, outgoing, pleasant, sociable **9** agreeable, convivial, easygoing, expansive **10** benevolent, buddy-buddy, hospitable, neighborly, solicitous
geniality: **6** gaiety, gayety, warmth **7** amenity **9** good cheer, happiness, joviality, pleasance, sunniness **10** affability, amiability, cheeriness, cordiality, good nature, heartiness, kindliness
genie: **3** jin **4** djin, jinn **5** djinn, Jafar, jinni **6** djinni, spirit
home: **4** lamp
offering: **4** wish
portrayer: **4** Eden
summon a ~: **3** rub
Genie: **7** Francis
Genie in a Bottle (1999 song)
artist: Christina Aguilera
Genitrix
author: François Mauriac
genius: **3** ace **4** gift, head, mind, soul, whiz **5** brain, knack, smart **6** acumen, marvel, master, spirit, talent, wisdom, wizard **7** egghead, prodigy, prowess **8** afflatus, artistry, Einstein, highbrow, longhair, virtuoso **9** intellect **10** astuteness, brilliance, mastermind
group: **5** Mensa
stroke of ~: **4** coup, feat **7** exploit, triumph
Genius, The
author: Theodore Dreiser
genl.: **3** off.
employer: **3** USA **4** USAF
Genn: **3** Leo
Gennaro: **5** Peter
__ Gennaro: **3** San
Genoa: **3** jib **4** city, gulf, port, town **6** salami
locale: **5** Italy
genoise: **4** cake
genome mapping company: **6** Celera
genomic __: **3** DNA
Genova: **4** city, town
locale: **5** Italy
genre: **3** ilk **4** kind, sort, type **5** brand, class, group, order, style **6** school **7** fiction, variety **8** category **9** character
book ~: **4** biog. **5** drama, farce, how-to, sci-fi **7** fiction **9** biography
fiction ~: **4** pulp **6** Gothic **7** romance
film ~: **5** drama, sci-fi **6** action, comedy, horror
music ~: **3** bop **4** folk, funk, glam, rock **5** bebop, disco, R and B, swing **6** gospel, grunge, hip-hop
gens du __: **5** monde
gent: **3** guy, him, nob **4** chap, dude, male **5** bloke **6** feller, fellow, mister, squire
genteel: **4** nice, prim **5** civil, haute, noble **6** la-de-da, la-di-da, polite, prissy, proper, urbane **7** courtly, elegant, prudish, refined, stilted, stylish **8** cultured, highborn, highbred, ladylike, lah-di-dah, mannerly, polished, well-bred **9** courteous **10** chivalrous, cultivated
gentian: **5** plant **6** flower
gentian __: **6** violet
__ gentian: **5** green, horse **6** bottle, closed, yellow **7** fringed
gentility: **6** polish **7** amenity, culture, decorum **8** breeding, civility, courtesy, elegance, niceties, noblesse **9** blue blood, etiquette, formality, high birth, propriety **10** politeness, refinement, upper class, upper crust
gentle: **3** lax **4** calm, cool, easy, kind, meek, mild, nice, soft, tame **5** balmy, light, loose, lowly, muted, noble, quiet, sweet, timid **6** benign, decent, docile, genial, humane, hushed, irenic, kindly, mellow, placid, polite, sedate, serene, smooth, soothe, subdue, tender **7** affable, amiable, clement, gradual, lenient, pacific, patient, pliable, ruthful, sparing, subdued, tactful **8** dovelike, flexible, gracious, harmless, highborn, humanize, irenical, ladylike, laid-back, lamblike, maternal, merciful, moderate, parental, peaceful, placable, pleasant, tolerant, tranquil, untaxing, well-bred **9** agreeable, assuasive, compliant, courteous, easygoing, forgiving, indulgent, leisurely, peaceable, sensitive, temperate, tractable **10** altruistic, benevolent, forbearing, permissive, unagitated, unexacting, unhardened
ender: **3** man, men **4** folk **5** woman, women **6** people, person
make ~: **4** tame **6** mellow, soften **8** civilize, humanize
not ~: **4** mean, rude **5** cruel, harsh, rigid, rough, sharp, stern **6** brutal, savage, severe, unkind **7** abusive, austere **8** pitiless, ruthless **9** heartless, merciless **10** hard-boiled, oppressive, relentless
one: **4** lamb
runner: **5** loper
slope: **4** rise **6** glacis **9** acclivity
touch: **3** hug, pat **6** caress, cuddle, stroke **7** embrace, snuggle
gentle __ lamb: **3** as a
Gentle __ Mind: **4** on My
gentle as __: **5** a lamb
Gentle Ben: **4** bear
like ~: **4** tame **6** ursine
gentleman: **3** guy, him, sir **4** male **5** noble **6** feller **7** grown-up **9** patrician
country ~: **3** esq. **7** esquire
friend: **4** beau **5** flame, lover, swain, wooer **6** steady, suitor **7** admirer, gallant **8** paramour **9** inamorato
gentleman's ~: **5** valet **6** butler **7** servant
in German: **4** herr
in India: **3** sri
in Portuguese: **3** dom **6** senhor
in Spanish: **3** don **5** señor
no ~: **3** cad **4** heel, rake, roué
that ~'s: **3** his
gentleman __: **6** caller, friend
gentleman __ road: **5** of the
gentleman-__: **6** farmer
Gentleman __: **3** Jim
gentleman-at-__: **4** arms
Gentleman Is a Dope, The
composer: Oscar Hammerstein, Richard Rodgers
gentlemanly: **4** kind **5** civil, noble **6** polite, urbane **7** genteel, refined, tactful **8** gracious, mannerly, obliging, pleasant, well-bred **9** courteous **10** respectful, thoughtful
Gentleman's Agreement (1947 film)
author: Laura Z. Hobson
cast: John Garfield, Celeste Holm, Gregory Peck
director: Elia Kazan
gentlemen: **3** he's **6** Messrs.
Gentlemen, __ your engines: **5** start
__ Gentlemen Marry Brunettes: **3** But
__ Gentlemen of Verona: **3** Two
Gentlemen Prefer Blondes: **7** musical
composer: Leo Robin, Jule Styne
Gentlemen Prefer Blondes (1953 film)
author: Anita Loos
cast: Marilyn Monroe, Jane Russell
director: Howard Hawks
gentleness: **5** mercy **6** lenity **8** clemency, lenience, morality **9** balminess

GE

Gentle on My Mind (1968 song)
artist: Glen Campbell
gentlewoman: **4** lady **5** madam, noble **6** female **9** patrician
gently: **4** easy, soft **5** light **8** gingerly
gentrify: **4** redo **7** improve **8** make over, renovate
gentry: **5** elite, lords **7** society **8** nobility, patroons **10** haute monde, landowners, upper class, upper crust
Gentry, Bobbie
song: Ode to Billy Joe (1967)
genu: **4** knee **5** Latin
genuflect: **4** bend **5** kneel, knell **7** bow down, worship **9** pay homage **10** pay tribute
genuine: **4** auth., good, pure, real, sure, true **5** frank, legit, naïve, pucka, pukka, right, solid, valid **6** actual, candid, honest, infelt, kasher, kosher, proved, proven **7** artless, earnest, factual, for real, natural, serious, sincere, up-front **8** absolute, accurate, bona fide, innocent, original, positive, verified **9** authentic, certified, guileless, heartfelt, intrinsic, realistic, unfeigned, veracious, veritable **10** legitimate, true-to-life, unaffected, unimagined
not ~: **4** imit., sham **5** acted, phony **6** irreal, phoney, pseudo **9** imitation
pass off as ~: **5** foist **7** palm off
genuineness: **4** fact **5** truth **7** honesty, reality **8** validity, veracity **9** sincerity
genus: **4** kind, sort, type **5** brand, class, order, style, taxon **7** variety **8** category
gen-Xer's parent: **6** boomer
Geo: **3** car **4** auto **5** Chevy, Metro, Storm **7** Tracker **9** Chevrolet **10** automobile
model: **5** Metro, Prizm, Storm **6** Sprint **7** Firefly, Tracker
geode: **4** rock **5** stone **7** mineral
cavity: **3** vug **4** vugg, vugh
geodesic __: **4** dome
geodesy: **7** science
geodetic __: **6** survey
geoduck: **4** clam **7** bivalve, mollusk
Geoffrey: **4** Rush **5** Beene, Lewis **7** Chaucer **9** Wilkinson
Geoffrion, Bernie
milieu: **3** ice **4** rink **5** arena
nickname: Boom Boom
org.: **3** NHL
geog.: **3** sci. **7** science
__ geog.: **4** phys.
geographer: **5** Hedin **6** Strabo **9** Pausanias
geographic
datum: **4** area **9** elevation
feature: **4** hill, isle, mesa, peak **5** butte, islet, river **6** canyon, island, stream, valley **8** mountain
region: **5** biome
geography: **6** layout **7** science **10** topography
abbr.: **2** mt. **3** alt., Atl., isl., lat., mtn., Pac., riv., str., ter. **4** sq mi., terr.
study: **5** Earth
geol.: **3** sci.
geologic __: **4** time
geological
epoch: **6** Eocene **7** Miocene **8** Pliocene **9** Oligocene, Paleocene
era: **8** Cenozoic, Mesozoic **9** Paleozoic
formation: **4** dome, mesa **5** butte, fault **6** folium, geyser
period: **3** eon, era **4** aeon **5** epoch, stade **7** Permian, stadial **8** Cambrian, Devonian, Jurassic, Silurian, Tertiary, Triassic **10** Archeozoic, Cretaceous, Ordovician, Quaternary
sample: **4** core
suffix: **3** -ite **4** -lite, -lith, -zoic
geologist, British: **5** Lyell
geom.: **3** sci. **4** math.
term: **2** sq. **3** ang., cir., ctr., sph., sqr.
geomancer: **7** prophet
geometry: **4** math
assignment: **5** proof
corner: **5** angle **6** vertex
father: **6** Euclid
figure: **3** cir. **4** cone, rect. **5** prism, rhomb, solid, torus **6** circle **7** hexagon, nonagon, octagon, rhombus **8** heptagon, pentagon, triangle **9** rectangle, trapezoid
line: **3** arc **4** axis, side **5** x-axis, y-axis, z-axis
measure: **3** vol. **4** area **6** volume
points: **4** loca, loci
suffix: **3** -gon
symbol: **2** pi
__ geometry: **5** plane, solid
geophysics: **7** science
study: **5** earth
geophyte: **5** plant
geoponics: **7** farming, science
Georg: **3** Ohm **5** Hegel, Solti **6** Kaiser, Wittig **7** Bednorz, Büchner **8** Telemann
Georg __ Brown: **7** Sanford
George: **3** Ade, Boy, Fox, Pal **4** Bush, Kell, lake, Olah, Raft, Sand, Wald, Will **5** Allen, Baker, Boole, Brent, Brett, Burns, Cates, Cohan, Cukor, Dewey, Eliot, Gamow, Gobel, Grosz, Halas, Innes, Jones, Lopez, Lucas, Meade, Mikan, Minot, Monck, Moore, Owens, Peele, saint, Segal, Snell, Susan, Szell, Takei, Wendt, Wythe **6** Abbott, Archer, Arliss, Beadle, Benson, Blanda, Carlin, Crabbe, Custer, Dallas, Gallup, Gaynes, Gervin, Gladys, Handel, Inness, Jessel, Jetson, McAfee, McCrae, Miller, Murphy, O'Brien, Orwell, Palade, Patton, Porter, Putnam, Reeves, Romney, Seaton, Sidney, Sisler, Stefan, Stokes, Strait, Stubbs, Tobias **7** Akerlof, Axelrod, Barbara, Chapman, Clinton, Clooney, Dzundza, Eastman, Foreman, Gissing, Herbert, Hurrell, Kennedy, Lazenby, Lindsey, Maharis, Mallory, McManus, Michael, O'Hanlon, Peppard, Phyllis, Pollock, Sanders, Seferis, Stevens, Stigler, Thomson, Waggner, Wallace, Whipple **8** Bancroft, Berkeley, Chakiris, Farquhar, Gershwin, Goethals, Grinnell, Grizzard, Hamilton, Harrison, Herriman, Macready, Marshall, McGinnis, McGovern, Meredith, Plimpton, Shearing **9** Bredehorn, Hitchings, McClellan, Santayana, Thorogood, Vancouver **10** Balanchine, Montgomery, Stephenson, Washington
brother: **3** Ira
couldn't tell it: **4** a lie
Gracie, to ~: **4** wife **6** costar **7** partner
in Russian: **4** Yuri
in Spanish: **5** Jorge
Martha, to ~: **4** wife
opponent: **4** Bill, Ross
predecessor: **3** Ron
successor: **4** Bill
who was a she: **4** Sand **5** Eliot
W.'s brother: **3** Jeb
George __: **3** III
George __ Carver: **10** Washington
George __ Custer: **9** Armstrong
George __ Handel: **8** Frideric
George __ Hill: **3** Roy
George __ Jungle: **5** of the
George __ Shaw: **7** Bernard
__ George: **8** Gorgeous
__ George Apley, The: **4** Late
George Armstrong __: **6** Custer
George Bernard __: **4** Shaw
George C. __: **5** Scott
__ George do it: **3** let
George Gordon __ Byron: **4** Lord, Noel
George I
mother: **4** Anne
George Jean __: **6** Nathan
George, Lloyd
contemporary: Vladimir Lenin
George M!: **7** musical
cast: Joel Grey, Bernadette Peters
subject: **5** Cohan
George of the Jungle (1997 film)
cast: Brendan Fraser, Leslie Mann
elephant: **4** Shep
George, Phyllis
spouse: Robert Evans
George Roy __: **4** Hill
Georges: **4** Pire **5** Bizet, Perec, Sorel **6** Braque, Cuvier, Danton, Enesco, Enescu, Köhler, Seurat **7** Charpak, Duhamel, Feydeau, Rouault, Simenon **8** Bataille, Bernanos, Lemaître **10** Clemenceau
see also French
Georges __: **4** Cinq
George S. __: **6** Patton **7** Kaufman
George, Saint
emulate: **4** slay
foe: **6** dragon
George, Stefan: **4** poet **6** German
__ George's War: **4** King
Georgetown: **4** city, port **7** capital
athletes: **5** Hoyas
conference: **7** Big East
educator: **6** Jesuit
locale: **2** D.C. **5** Texas **6** Guyana **7** Caymans **10** Washington
George V: **4** king
wife: **4** Mary
George W. __: **4** Bush
George Washington __: **5** Cable **6** Bridge, Carver
George Washington __ here: **5** slept
Georgia: **4** font **5** Engel, Gibbs **7** O'Keeffe **8** typeface
politician: **4** Nunn
Georgia (country)
capital: **7** Tbilisi
city: **5** Redan **6** Batumi **7** Kutaisi, Rustavi, Tbilisi
it's south of ~: **4** Iran
money: **4** lari
mountains: **8** Caucasus
neighbor: **6** Russia, Turkey **7** Armenia **10** Azerbaijan
once: **3** SSR
river: **4** Rion **5** Rioni
Georgia (state)
capital: **7** Atlanta
city: **4** Rome **5** Macon **6** Albany, Athens, Clarke, Dalton, Duluth, Newnan, Plains, Smyrna, Tucker **7** Atlanta, Augusta, Candler, Griffin, MacAfee, Roswell **8** Columbus, Dunwoody, Kennesaw, La Grange, Mableton, Marietta, Martinez, Norcross, Richmond, Savannah, Valdosta **9** East Point **10** Alpharetta, Hinesville, Statesboro
conference: **3** SEC
county: **4** Bibb, Cobb, Dade **5** Dooly, Glynn, Lamar, Macon, Peach, Rabun, Troup, Upson **6** De Kalb, Elbert, Fulton, Lanier, Oconee, Schley, Sumter, Toombs, Twiggs
fruit: **5** peach
he went down to ~: **5** devil
Indian: **5** Creek
neighbor: **7** Alabama, Florida **9** Tennessee
nickname: **10** Peach State
river: **5** Coosa
state crop: **6** peanut
state fossil: **10** shark tooth
state game bird: **8** bobwhite
state gem: **6** quartz
state insect: **8** honeybee
state marine mammal: **10** right whale
state mineral: **10** staurolite
state tree: **7** live oak
state wildflower: **6** azalea
university: **5** Emory
University of ~ site: **6** Athens
Georgia __: **4** Tech
Georgia __ Mind: **4** on My
Georgia-__: **7** Pacific
Georgia Boy
author: Erskine Caldwell
__ Georgia Brown: **5** Sweet
Georgia Dome: **5** arena
Georgia on My Mind (1960 song)
artist: Ray Charles
Georgia Peach: Ty Cobb
Georgia Tech
conference: **3** ACC
grad: **4** engr. **8** engineer
locale: **7** Atlanta
georgic: **4** idyl **5** idyll, rural
Georg Sanford __: **5** Brown
Georgy Girl: **4** film, song
artist: Seekers
cast: Alan Bates, James Mason, Lynn Redgrave
geothermal spout: **6** geyser
Gephardt: **4** Dick **7** Richard

Ger.: 4 lang., Teut.
neighbor: 3 Aus., Pol. **4** Aust.
see also Germany
Geraint: 3 Sir **6** knight
wife: 4 Enid
Gerald: 4 Ford **6** Levert **7** Edelman, McRaney
in Italian: 7 Gennaro
Gerald __ Horst: 3 Ter
Geraldine: 4 Page **6** Brooks, Farrar **7** Chaplin, Ferraro **10** Fitzgerald
portrayer: 4 Flip
Geraldo: 6 Rivera
colleague: 4 Phil **5** Oprah
geranium: 3 red **5** color, plant **6** flower
relative: *see* red color
Gerard: 3 Gil **6** Butler, Debreu
Gerard __ Borch: 3 Ter
Gerard __ Hopkins: 6 Manley
Gérard: 9 Depardieu
Gerard, Gil: 5 actor
spouse: Connie Sellecca
Gerardus: 6 't Hooft **8** Mercator
gerbil: 3 pet **6** animal, mammal, rodent
female: 3 doe
male: 4 buck
relative: *see* rodent
young: 3 pup
gerent: 4 boss, czar, emir, exec, head, khan, king, lord, rani, shah, suit **5** chief, mogul, pasha, queen, rajah, royal, ruler **6** caliph, dynast, kaiser, leader, mikado, prince, satrap, shogun, sultan, top dog **7** czarina, emperor, empress, manager, monarch, pharaoh, viceroy **8** dictator, director, governor, maharani, official, oligarch, overlord, overseer, princess, suzerain **9** chieftain, commander, executive, maharajah, potentate, sovereign, straw boss **10** supervisor
Gere, Richard: 5 actor
film: Chicago (2002)
The Cotton Club (1984)
Days of Heaven (1978)
Final Analysis (1992)
First Knight (1995)
The Hoax (2007)
The Jackal (1997)
Looking for Mr. Goodbar (1977)
Nights in Rodanthe (2008)
An Officer and a Gentleman (1982)
Pretty Woman (1990)
Primal Fear (1996)
Runaway Bride (1999)
Shall We Dance? (2004)
Sommersby (1993)
Unfaithful (2002)
Yanks (1979)
spouse: Cindy Crawford, Carey Lowell
Gerhard: 6 Domagk, Groote **8** Herzberg
in English: 6 Gerard
Gerhardus: 8 Mercator
Geri: 9 Halliwell
geriatric: 3 old **4** aged **5** aging **6** ageing **7** ancient, elderly, wizened **8** grizzled **9** getting on, senescent, up in years
germ: 3 bud, bug **4** cell, root, seed **5** spark, strep, virus **6** embryo, gamete, kernel, origin, source **7** essence, keynote, microbe, nucleus **8** pathogen, rudiment **9** bacterium, beginning
cell: 4 seed **5** spore **6** gamete
combining form: 6 bacter- **7** bacteri- **8** bacterio-
ender: 4 free
fighter: 4 drug **5** serum **7** vaccine
__ germ: 5 wheat
Germaine: 5 Greer
German: 4 Teut. **6** Teuton **7** Deutsch **8** Berliner, language, Teutonic **9** Hamburger
archaeologist: 10 Schliemann
astronomer: 6 Kepler
auto: 2 VW **3** BMW **4** Audi, Opel **6** Beetle **8** Mercedes **10** Volkswagen
bacteriologist: 4 Koch
ballet dancer: 5 Jooss
biologist: 8 Weismann
botanist: 4 Cohn
bovine: 4 Glan **6** Angeln **8** Gelbvieh
camera: 5 Leica
canal: 4 Kiel
capital: 6 Berlin
cheese: 8 bierkäse
chemist: 4 Hahn, Kuhn **6** Bunsen, Müller, Nernst
city: 3 Aue, Ulm **4** Bonn, Gera, Hamm, Jena, Kiel, Köln, Unna **5** Baden, Düren, Emden, Essen, Fürth, Gotha, Hagen, Halle, Herne, Mainz, Neuss, Pirna, Riesa, Trier, Worms **6** Aachen, Berlin, Bremen, Dessau, Erfurt, Kassel, Lübeck, Munich, Siegen, Treves, Witten **7** Bottrop, Coblenz, Cologne, Dresden, Hamburg, Hanover, Koblenz, Krefeld, Leipsic, Leipzig, München, Münster, Potsdam, Rostock **8** Augsburg, Bayreuth, Chemnitz, Dortmund, Duisburg, Mannheim, Nürnberg, Solingen, Würzburg **9** Frankfurt, Karlsruhe, Magdeburg, Nuremberg, Offenbach, Oldenburg, Osnabrück, Stuttgart, Wiesbaden, Wolfsburg, Wuppertal **10** Düsseldorf, Heidelberg, Oberhausen
coal region: 4 Saar
composer: 4 Bach **6** Schütz
conductor: 4 Foss **5** Busch, Masur **6** Rudolf, Walter **8** Damrosch **9** Klemperer **11** Furtwängler
dance: 7 ländler
engraver: 5 Dürer
environmentalist: 5 Green
essayist: 4 Mann
figure skater: 4 Witt
first ~ president: 5 Ebert
former money: 3 pfg. **4** mark **5** taler **6** heller, thaler **7** pfennig **8** kreutzer **9** rix-dollar
former region: 4 Saxe **5** Lippe **6** Alsace
former ~ ruler: 6 kaiser
geophysicist: 7 Wegener
golfer: 6 Langer
gun: 5 Luger
historian: 8 Schiller
industrial region: 4 Ruhr, Saar
John: 4 Hans **6** Johann
journalist: 8 Remarque
leader: 4 Kohl **5** Ebert **6** Brandt, Erhard, Merkel **7** Schmidt **8** Adenauer, Bismarck, Schroder
legislature: 9 Bundesrat, Bundestag
liqueur: 6 kümmel
magazine: 5 Stern
mathematician: 5 Gauss **6** Kepler
money: 4 euro, mark **5** taler **6** thaler **7** pfennig
mountain range: 3 Erz **4** Harz, Rhön
natural historian: 4 Baer
neighbor: 6 France, Poland **7** Austria, Belgium, Denmark **10** Luxembourg
Nobelist in Chemistry: 4 Hahn, Kuhn **5** Alder, Bosch, Diels, Eigen, Haber, Huber **6** Michel, Nernst, Wittig **7** Bergius, Buchner, Fischer, Ostwald, Wallach, Wieland, Windaus, Ziegler **9** Butenandt, von Baeyer, Zsigmondy **10** Staudinger **11** Deisenhofer, Willstötter
Nobelist in Economics: 6 Selten
Nobelist in Literature: 4 Böll, Mann **5** Grass, Hesse, Heyse **6** Eucken **7** Mommsen **9** Hauptmann
Nobelist in Medicine: 4 Koch **5** Lynen, Neher **6** Domagk, Köhler, Kossel, Lorenz **7** Ehrlich, Sakmann, Spemann, Warburg **8** Meyerhof **9** von Frisch **10** von Behring
Nobelist in Peace: 6 Brandt, Quidde **10** Stresemann
Nobelist in Physics: 4 Paul, Wien **5** Bothe, Braun, Hertz, Ruska, Stark **6** Binnig, Franck, Jensen, Planck **7** Bednorz, Dehmelt, Röntgen, von Laue **8** Einstein, Ketterle **9** Mössbauer, von Lenard **10** Heisenberg **11** von Klitzing
org.: 4 NATO
painter: 5 Dürer, Ernst **7** Holbein
philosopher: 8 Spengler **9** Nietzsche
physicist: 3 Ohm **4** Born **5** Hertz, Ruska, Stern **6** Binnig, Nernst, Planck **8** Einstein, Roentgen **9** Kirchhoff **10** Fahrenheit, Fraunhofer, Heisenberg
pianist: 5 Bülow
plane: 5 Stuka
playwright: 4 Holz **5** Sachs **6** Brecht, Grabbe, Hebbel, Kaiser **7** Büchner, Freytag, Gutzkow, Horvath **8** Gryphius, Schiller **9** Hauptmann, Sudermann, Zuckmayer
poet: 4 Holz **5** Brant, Celan, Heine, Hesse, Rilke, Sachs, Storm **6** Brecht, Dehmel, George, Hebbel, Mörike **7** Fontane, Rückert **8** Brentano, Chamisso, Gryphius, Schiller, Schlegel **9** Nietzsche
port: 4 Kiel **5** Emden **6** Bremen, Lübeck **7** Hamburg, Münster, Rostock **8** Cuxhaven
reformer: 6 Luther
region: 3 Bav. **4** Prus. **5** Baden, Hesse **6** Saxony **7** Bavaria, Prussia **8** Saarland **9** Rhineland
river: 3 Ems **4** Eder, Eger, Elbe, Isar, Main, Naab, Oder, Odra, Ohre, Oste, Ruhr **5** Fulda, Rhine, Weser
scientist: 3 Ohm **4** Baer, Born, Cohn, Hahn, Koch, Kuhn **5** Gauss, Hertz, Ruska, Stern **6** Binnig, Bunsen, Kepler, Müller, Nernst, Planck **7** Wegener **8** Einstein, Roentgen, Weismann **9** Kirchhoff **10** Fahrenheit, Fraunhofer, Heisenberg, Schliemann
silver: 6 albata
socialist: 4 Marx
soprano: 6 Berger **7** Lehmann
spa: 3 Ems **5** Baden **6** Bad Ems
speed skater: 4 Enke
sub: 5 U-boat
swimmer: 4 Otto **5** Ender
toast in ~: 6 prosit
valley: 4 Ruhr, Saar **5** Mosel
violinist: 6 Mutter
wine: 4 hock, Sekt **7** Auslese, cabinet, Moselle **8** cold duck **10** Hochheimer
wine region: 5 Rhine
writer: 4 Benn, Böll, Mann, Marx **5** Arnim, Grass, Grimm, Hesse, Heyse, Raabe, Zweig **6** Döblin, Goethe, Heinse, Jünger, Kleist, Luther, Walser **7** Fontane, Freytag, Gutzkow, Hoffman, Johnson, Novalis, Richter, Wieland **8** Borchert, Remarque, Spengler, Wedekind **10** Schliemann
WWII naval base: 5 Emden
see also Germany
German __: 3 ivy **7** measles, Requiem
germane: 3 apt **5** ad rem **6** proper, timely **7** apropos, fitting, logical, on point, related **8** apposite, material, on target, relative, relevant, suitable **9** pertinent **10** applicable, felicitous, to the point
not ~: 5 inapt **10** extraneous, immaterial, irrelevant, out of place
not ~ to: 6 beside
Germania
author: Tacitus
Germanic
god: 3 Tiu
goddess: 4 Norn
invader: 4 Goth, jute
germanium: 5 metal **7** element
Germann: 4 Greg
German Requiem
composer: Johannes Brahms
German shepherd: 3 dog **5** canid **6** canine
in Britain: 8 Alsatian
German silver: 5 alloy
component: 4 zinc **6** copper, nickel
Germantown: 4 city
locale: 4 Penn.
German words
a: 3 ein **4** eine **5** einem, einer, eines
above: 4 über

ago: 3 vor
and: 3 und
article: 3 das, dem, den, der, die, ein 4 eine
before: 3 vor
beyond: 4 über
cordial: 6 kümmel
count: 4 graf
east: 3 ost
eat: 5 essen
eleven: 3 elf
exclamation: 3 ach 6 himmel
from: 3 von
goblin: 6 kobold
I: 3 ich
league: 4 bund
me: 3 mir
mister: 4 herr
mouse: 4 maus
Mrs.: 4 frau
my: 4 mein 5 meine
near: 4 nahe
nine: 4 neun
no: 4 nein
old one: 4 alte
one: 3 ein 4 eins
our: 5 unser
over: 4 ober, über
possessive: 4 mein 5 meine
preposition: 3 aus, bei, mit, von 4 ober, ohne, über
pronoun: 3 ich, mir, sie, uns 4 mein 5 einer, meine, unser
roses: 5 rosen
salad: 5 salat
salt: 4 salz
sausage: 5 wurst
son: 4 sohn
song: 4 lied
songs: 6 lieder
star: 5 stern
state: 5 staat
the: 3 das, der, die
three: 4 drei
toast: 5 prost
us: 3 uns
very: 4 sehr
with: 3 mit
without: 4 ohne
you: 3 sie
Germany: 6 nation 7 country 8 republic
__ Germany: 4 East, West
germfree: 4 pure 5 clean 6 axenic, washed 7 aseptic, sterile 8 hygienic, pristine, sanitary, unsoiled 10 antiseptic, immaculate
germicide: 8 cleanser, fumigant 10 antiseptic
germinal: 5 early 8 evolving 9 embryonic
Germinal
author: Émile Zola
germinate: 3 bud 4 grow 5 begin, bloom, shoot 6 sprout 7 blossom, burgeon, develop 8 bourgeon, take root, vegetate 9 fertilize, originate, pullulate
germination: 6 growth
germ-related: 5 viral
germ-ridden: 5 dirty 6 filthy, soiled 7 tainted 9 unhealthy 10 unsanitary
germs: 7 bacilli 8 bacteria, microbes 9 pathogens
absence of ~: 7 asepsis
germy: 5 dirty 6 filthy, septic 7 unclean 8 infected 10 unsanitary
not ~: 4 pure 5 clean 7 aseptic, sterile 8 purified, sanitary 10 sterilized, uninfected
Gernreich: 4 Rudi
Gernsback, Hugo: 6 writer
genre: sci-fi
Geronimo: 5 chief 6 Apache, Indian
Gerontion
poet: T.S.Eliot
Gerrit: 6 Graham
Gerry: 5 Adams 6 Cooney, Goffin 7 Ferraro, Marsden 8 Elbridge, Mulligan, Rafferty
Gerry and the Pacemakers
song: Don't Let the Sun Catch You Crying (1964)
Ferry Cross the Mersey (1965)
How Do You Do It? (1964)
gerrymander: 3 fix, rig 10 manipulate, tamper with
Gershon: 4 Gina
Gershwin, George: 8 composer
biographer: 4 Ewen
brother: 3 Ira
colleague: Harold Arlen, Irving Berlin, Jerome Kern, Oscar Levant
heroine: 4 Bess
musical: Crazy for You
Funny Face
Girl Crazy
Lady, Be Good!
La La Lucille
Let 'Em Eat Cake
Of Thee I Sing
Oh, Kay!
Pardon My English
Porgy and Bess
Primrose
Strike Up the Band
Tip-Toes
portrayer: Robert Alda
song: Bess, You Is My Woman
Bidin' My Time
But Not for Me
Clap Yo Hands
Could You Use Me?
Delishious
Do Do Do
Do It Again
Embraceable You
Fascinating Rhythm
A Foggy Day
Funny Face
How Long Has This Been Going On?
I Got Plenty o' Nuthin'
I Got Rhythm
I'll Build a Stairway to Paradise
Isn't It a Pity?
It Ain't Necessarily So
I've Got a Crush on You
I Was Doing All Right
Let's Call the Whole Thing Off
Liza
Love Is Here to Stay
Love Is Sweeping the Country
Love Walked In
The Man I Love
Maybe
Mine
My Cousin in Milwaukee
My One and Only
Nice Work if You Can Get It
Nobody but You
Of Thee I Sing
Oh, Lady Be Good
Rialto Ripples
Somebody Loves Me
Someone to Watch Over Me
Soon
Strike Up the Band
Summertime
Swanee
Sweet and Low-Down
'S Wonderful
That Certain Feeling
They All Laughed
They Can't Take That Away From Me
Who Cares
Wintergreen for President
A Woman Is a Sometime Thing
work: An American in Paris
Concerto in F
Cuban Overture
Rhapsody in Blue
Second Rhapsody
Gert: 5 Frobe
Gertrude: 4 Berg 5 Elion, saint, Stein 6 Ederle 8 Lawrence
friend: 5 Alice
son: 6 Hamlet
Gertz: 4 Jami
Gerulaitis: 5 Vitas 7 netster 9 tennis pro
gerund end: 3 ing
gervais: 6 cheese
Gervais: 5 Ricky
Gervin, George
org.: 3 NBA
sport: 10 basketball
gest: 4 deed, feat 7 exploit
__ gestae: 3 res
gestation: 6 growth 9 evolution, gravidity, pregnancy 10 incubation, maturation
stage: 5 fetus 6 foetus
geste: 4 deed, feat 7 exploit 9 adventure
__ Geste: 4 Beau
gesticulate: 4 sign, wave 6 beckon, motion, signal
gesture: 3 bow, nod 4 beck, mime, sign, wave, wink 5 shrug, V sign 6 action, beckon, curtsy, motion, salute, signal 7 curtsey 8 laughter, movement 9 pantomime 10 indication
affectionate ~: 3 hug 4 kiss 6 caress
Buddhist ~: 5 mudra
flirtatious ~: 4 wink
of approval: 3 nod, vee 5 V sign
of greeting: 4 wave
peace ~: 3 vee 5 V sign
polite ~: 3 bow 6 curtsy 7 curtsey
gesturing performer: 4 mime 5 clown, mimer, mimic
gesundheit evoker: 5 achoo 6 ahchoo, hachoo, sneeze 7 kerchoo
get: 3 bag, bug, buy, cop, dig, irk, nab, net, see, vex, win 4 burn, coax, draw, earn, find, gain, gall, grab, hail, have, kids, know, land, make, nail, reap, rile, snag, stir, sway, take, trap, urge 5 amuse, anger, annex, annoy, bring, catch, fetch, glean, grasp, learn, peeve, pique, press, reach, ready, score, seize, sense, solve, upset 6 absorb, accept, access, affect, arouse, arrest, attain, become, bother, buy out, collar, come by, defeat, derive, effect, elicit, enlist, excite, fathom, follow, garner, induce, line up, nettle, obtain, outwit, pick up, prompt, rack up, rankle, secure, snap up, stir up, wangle 7 abscond, achieve, acquire, agitate, bring in, build up, buy into, capture, chalk up, contact, enflame, ensnare, extract, harvest, impress, inherit, insnare, nonplus, perturb, procure, progeny, provoke, realize, receive, scare up, wheedle, win over 8 come to be, contract, convince, invest in, irritate, perceive, persuade, pull down, purchase, receipts, retrieve, rustle up 9 aggravate, apprehend, catch on to, extradite, figure out, influence, intercept, lay hold of, overpower 10 accomplish, appreciate, comprehend, exasperate, fall heir to, understand
across: 5 speak 6 convey, effect 9 bring home, elucidate, make clear 10 illustrate
a fix on: 6 locate 8 identify, localize 9 determine
ahead: 3 win 4 gain, grow 5 go far 6 make it, pan out, thrive 7 advance, luck out, make out, prevail, prosper, triumph, work out 8 flourish, go places, grow rich, hit it big, make good, progress 9 go forward 10 gain ground
a hold of: 4 call, meet 5 phone, reach 6 talk to 7 contact, liaison, speak to 8 approach 9 check with, telephone, touch base
a kick out of: 3 dig, use 4 like 5 enjoy, go for 6 relish 8 flip over, thrill to 9 delight in, get high on, indulge in
a load of: 3 eye, see, spy 4 look, peek, peep, peer, view 5 watch 6 behold, glance, listen, look at, notice, regard 7 glimpse, observe, witness 10 sneak a look
a loan: 6 borrow
a loan on: 4 pawn 6 pledge
along: 2 do 3 mix 4 fare, fend, live 5 agree, exist 6 make do, manage 7 make out, subsist 8 go places
a move on: 2 go 3 fly, hie, rip, run, zip 4 dart, dash, flit, race, rush, stir, tear, zoom 5 hurry, scoot, spank, speed 6 barrel, gallop, hasten, hustle, rocket, scurry 7 floor it, hop to it, quicken, scamper, speed up 8 step on it 9 hotfoot it, shake a leg, skedaddle 10 hightail it
an A on: 3 ace
an earful: 4 heed 6 listen, take in 7 receive 8 discover, listen in, listen to 9 eavesdrop 10 understand
an eyeful: 3 see 4 gaze 7 observe
angry: 4 fume, snap 6 rear up, see red
around: 4 foil, pass, shun 5 avoid, dodge, elude, evade, shirk, skirt, visit 6 bypass, outwit 8 outsmart,

overcome **9** circulate, negotiate, prevail on, socialize **10** circumvent
as far as: 5 reach
a shot: 4 snap **10** photograph
at: 5 annoy, bribe, imply, reach **6** access, locate, obtain **7** suggest **8** intimate **9** influence, insinuate
a tan: 3 sun **4** bask **8** sunbathe
a taste of: 3 try **6** sample
away: 2 go **3** fly **4** exit, flee **5** break **6** depart, escape **8** fugitate, run for it, withdraw **10** break loose
away from: 5 elude, evade, leave **8** shake off, throw off
back: 5 reply **6** avenge, recoup, redeem, regain **7** rebound, reclaim, recover, respond, salvage **8** retrieve **9** reacquire, recapture
back at: 5 react, repay **7** revenge **9** pay in kind, retaliate
behind: 4 back, hype, plug, push **6** hype up, second, talk up **7** approve, endorse, indorse, promote, sponsor, support **8** sanction **9** encourage, guarantee, subscribe **10** rally round
better: 3 age **4** heal, mend **5** rally **6** look up, pick up **7** rebound, recover **10** recuperate
bigger: 3 wax **4** grow **6** expand
bored: 4 tire
boring: 4 pale, pall
bushed: 4 flag, tire
busy: 3 act **4** move **6** fall to, jump in, tackle **7** hop to it, pitch in **9** take steps **10** buckle down
but good: 4 nail
by: 2 do **4** cope, fare, live, pass **5** exist **6** hack it, make do, manage **7** make out, qualify, satisfy, suffice, survive
by force: 3 pry **5** exact, usurp, wrest, wring **6** extort, wrench
by trickery: 4 gull **5** cheat, mulct **6** extort, fleece **7** defraud, swindle
clear of: 4 duck, flee, lose **5** avoid, dodge, elude, evade, skirt **6** escape **7** fend off **8** sidestep **10** circumvent
cold feet: 5 quail, waver **6** falter, wobble **8** hang back, hesitate **9** hem and haw, vacillate
coverage for: 6 ensure, insure **7** protect, warrant **9** indemnify
cozy: 6 curl up, nestle **7** snuggle
cracking: 3 hie **4** rush **5** begin, start **6** go to it **7** pitch in **8** commence
crowned: 4 rule **5** reign **6** accede
dark: 5 laten **7** becloud
darker: 5 laten
dirty: 4 soil
done: 3 end **4** cook **5** mop up **6** finish **7** achieve **10** put through
down: 4 duck, land **5** dance, light, party **6** alight, boogie **7** jump off **8** dismount
down on one knee: 3 woo
down pat: 5 learn **6** master **9** ascertain
down to basics: 6 lay out **7** explain **8** simplify, spell out **9** make plain
down to brass tacks: 6 detail **7** account, itemize, specify **9** make clear, stipulate
down to business: 5 start **7** shape up
duded up: 5 groom, preen, primp, prink
due to ~: 5 in for
established: 6 locate, settle **8** make good, take root
even: 5 repay, spite **6** avenge **7** pay back, requite, revenge **9** retaliate
excited: 4 flip **5** go ape **6** arouse, tingle **7** bristle, enthuse
extra life from: 5 reuse
fail to ~: 4 miss
familiar: 6 orient
fat: 4 gain **6** thrive
fit: 6 tone up **8** exercise
fresh: 4 sass **8** mouth off, talk back **10** answer back
F's: 4 fail
go ~: 5 bring, fetch **6** obtain **8** retrieve
going: 4 move, open, roll **5** begin, crank, found, rouse, start **6** fillip, launch, let rip, set off, set out **7** kick off, lead off, pitch in, speed up **8** commence, initiate, organize, set about, set forth **9** enter upon, originate **10** inaugurate
gratis: 5 leech **8** freeload, scrounge
hard to ~ to: 3 dim **4** dull, slow **5** dense, thick **6** obtuse, simple, stolid **9** pigheaded
help from: 6 lean on
hep: 6 wise up
higher: 4 rise, soar **6** ascend, move up **7** take off
high on: 4 like, love **5** enjoy, savor **6** relish **9** delight in **10** appreciate
hitched: 3 wed **5** elope, marry **10** tie the knot
hold of: 4 grab, have **5** catch, grasp, reach **6** locate, obtain **7** acquire, possess, receive **8** come into **9** ascertain
hopping: 3 fly, hie, run, zip **4** dart, dash, move, rush, tear **5** hurry, scoot **6** bustle, hasten, hustle, scurry **7** floor it, quicken **8** step on it **9** make haste, shake a leg **10** lose no time, make tracks
horizontal: 4 laze
hot: 7 flame up
in: 4 come **5** enter, reach **6** arrive, show up
in a dragnet: 3 nab **4** bust, grab, nail, trap **5** catch, pinch, seize **6** arrest, collar, corner, pick up, pull in, snatch **7** capture **9** apprehend
in a sting: 6 entrap
in line: 4 wait
in one's face: 5 annoy **6** accost, bother **8** confront **9** challenge
in one's hair: 3 bug, irk, vex **4** gall, rile **5** annoy, peeve, pique **6** madden, nettle, pester, plague, ruffle **7** provoke, tick off **8** irritate **9** aggravate **10** exasperate
in one's head: 5 grasp, learn, study **6** absorb, master, pick up, soak up **7** find out **8** discover, memorize **10** understand
in return: 4 earn, gain, reap **5** clear **6** derive, garner, profit, secure, take in **7** bring in, collect, harvest, receive **8** gather in
in shape: 3 jog **4** hone, tone **5** train **7** rebound, recover, work out
in someone's hair: 3 irk **4** rile **5** peeve, upset
in sync: 6 attune **10** coordinate
in the act: 7 partake
in the game: 4 ante
in the way of: 4 clog **5** deter **6** hamper, hinder, impair, impede, impose **8** handicap, obstruct
into: 3 don **6** absorb, access **7** enthuse
(into): 4 seep
into a dither: 4 fret, fuss, stew **5** sweat, worry **7** agonize
into line: 4 heed, obey **6** comply, follow, submit **7** conform, observe
into mischief: 5 act up, cut up **8** go astray **9** misbehave **10** fool around, roughhouse
in touch: 5 reach **7** contact, respond
in with: 9 associate, cultivate, insinuate, shine up to **10** ingratiate
it: 3 dig, see **7** catch on, realize **10** comprehend, understand
it together: 4 plan **5** set up **7** arrange **8** organize **10** coordinate
just ~ by: 6 eke out, make do **7** squeeze
larger: 3 wax **4** grow **5** build, swell, widen **6** dilate, expand **7** augment, broaden, develop, fill out, magnify **8** increase
licked: 4 lose
lost: 2 go **4** scat **5** scram, split, stray **6** beat it, begone, bug off, wander **7** push off **8** withdraw **10** go fly a kite
lower: 3 ebb **4** drop, wane **6** lessen, recede **7** decline, dwindle, retreat, subside, tail off **8** decrease, diminish, fall back, slack off
mad: 5 anger **6** blow up, rear up **10** hit the roof
melodramatic: 3 act **5** emote **7** carry on, overact
misty: 3 cry, sob **4** weep **7** blubber **9** shed tears
money: 6 cash in, redeem **9** liquidate
money for: 4 sell
more out of: 5 reuse
moving: 3 hie **4** roll, stir **5** speed, start **6** bestir **7** speed up **8** hightail, run along
next to: 3 woo **7** flatter, promote **8** butter up **9** cultivate, shine up to **10** curry favor
no place fast: 3 lag **4** drag, flag, idle, limp, loaf, loll, plod, poke **5** dally, delay, tarry **6** dabble, dawdle, diddle, loiter **7** fall off, fritter, slacken **8** hang back, straggle **9** inch along, poke along, waste time **10** dillydally, lose ground, mess around, wait around
nosy: 3 ask, pry
off: 6 alight, debark **7** descend, detrain **8** dismount **9** disembark
off one's chest: 3 say **4** tell **5** spill **6** relate, unload **7** confess, confide, recount, tell all, unbosom **8** unburden
off one's feet: 3 sit **4** loll, rest **6** lounge, repose, sprawl **7** recline **10** stretch out
off the fence: 3 act, opt **6** choose, decide
off the ground: 5 begin
off the hook: 4 save **5** spare **6** rescue
off the point: 5 drift, stray **6** ramble, wander **7** deviate, digress, diverge **8** divagate
off the stage: 4 exit
off the track: 5 stray **6** derail, ramble **7** digress
older: 3 age
on: 3 age, bug **4** bait, fare, ride, wear **5** agree, board, go far, mount, taunt **6** harass, thrive **7** make out, proceed **8** progress
on a horse: 6 gallop, travel **7** journey
on a soapbox: 5 orate **6** preach **7** address, declaim, lecture **8** harangue, proclaim
on board: 6 embark
one's act together: 5 rally
one's dander up: 3 ire, irk **4** rile **5** anger, peeve **7** bristle
one's feet wet: 4 ford, open, wade **5** begin, slosh, start **6** launch, paddle, splash, tackle **7** kick off, lead off **8** commence, get going, set forth **9** enter into, strike out **10** inaugurate, plunge into
one's fingers on: 3 bag, nab **4** grab, grip, take **5** catch, grasp, seize, snare, steal **6** secure, snatch **7** acquire, plunder, receive **8** glom on to **9** lay hold of
one's goat: 3 irk, vex **4** miff, rile **5** anger, peeve, upset **6** enrage, rankle
one's hands on: 3 get **4** grab, have **5** catch, seize, snare **6** obtain **7** acquire, possess, receive **9** latch onto
one's just deserts: 4 earn, rate **5** merit **7** deserve **10** have coming
one's second wind: 5 rally
on it: 5 hop to
on one's case: 3 bug, nag **4** carp, harp **6** badger **9** find fault
on one's feet: 5 stand
on one's nerves: 3 irk **4** rile **5** grate, peeve, upset
on the bandwagon for: 4 back **5** boost **7** espouse, promote, sponsor, support **8** advocate, champion
on the horn: 4 buzz, call, dial, ring **5** phone **6** call up, dial up, ring up **7** contact **9** telephone
on the wagon: 4 quit

on with it: 7 proceed
organized: 4 plan, plot 5 chart, frame, set up 6 lay out, map out 7 outline, prepare, project, propose, work out 8 engineer, rough out, schedule, think out 9 formulate 10 mastermind
out: 2 go 4 exit, flee, quit 5 be off, break, issue, leave, scram, split 6 beat it, begone, decamp, depart, escape 7 bail out, buzz off, publish, run away, skiddoo, take off, vamoose 8 evacuate, hightail, withdraw 9 broadcast, skedaddle, take a hike 10 high-tail it
out from under: 6 recoup 7 recover 8 liberate
out of: 4 doff, duck, peel, shed 5 avoid, dodge, elude, evade, shake, shirk, strip 6 escape 7 disrobe, slip off, take off 8 sidestep
out of bed: 4 rise, wake 5 arise, rouse, waken
out of here: 2 go 5 leave, scram 6 move it 7 vamoose 8 run along, shove off 9 move along, take a hike 10 hit the road
out of line: 4 defy, riot, rise 5 act up, rebel 6 mutiny, oppose, resist, revolt, rise up 7 disobey, dissent, protest 9 make waves, misbehave
out of sight: 4 hide 6 lie low 9 take cover
out of the way: 4 duck 5 dodge 8 sidestep
out to ~: 5 after
over: 7 recover 9 negotiate
past: 4 beat 5 clear, outdo, steer 6 detour 8 maneuver, outstrip, overtake 9 negotiate
pleasure from: 3 dig 4 like, love, want 5 adore, eat up, enjoy, fancy, go for, savor 6 desire, dote on, relish 9 delight in, indulge in 10 appreciate, be mad about
promoted: 4 rise
psyched: 7 enthuse
ready: 3 fix 4 gird, pack, prep 5 brace, groom, ready, ripen 6 gear up 7 prepare, psych up 8 mobilize 10 square away
real: 6 come on, wise up
revenge on: 3 fix 5 set up 6 punish 7 pay back
rid of: 2 ax 3 axe, can, end, zap 4 boot, cede, drop, dump, junk, lose, oust, sack, sell, shed, toss 5 chuck, ditch, drain, eject, erase, expel, forgo, let go, purge, scrap, yield 6 banish, bounce, forego, give up, lay off, remove, unload 7 abandon, cashier, discard, dismiss, drum out, exclude, forfeit, forsake, release, wipe out 8 exorcise, exorcize, forswear, furlough, hand over, jettison, part with, pink-slip, shake off, stamp out, throw out, unburden 9 cast aside, discharge, eliminate, foreswear, liquidate, surrender, terminate, throw away 10 do away with, relinquish
rid (of): 6 divest
rid of knots: 4 undo 6 loosen 8 untangle
right: 5 solve 6 unlock 7 explain, unravel, work out 8 decipher 9 figure out, puzzle out
satisfaction from: 3 dig 4 like 5 boast, eat up, enjoy, go for, savor 6 dote on, wallow 7 revel in 8 flip over, thrill to 9 delight in 10 appreciate
set: 3 fix 4 prep 5 equip, prime, ready 6 fit out, gear up, warm up 7 arrange, prepare 8 mobilize, organize, rehearse 10 pave the way, square away
sidetracked: 5 stray 6 ramble, wander 7 digress, meander
situated: 3 set 5 dwell, lodge, perch, roost 6 locate, orient, settle
sleepy: 3 nod 4 doze, tire 5 droop 6 drowse
slippery: 5 ice up 6 freeze
smaller: 6 lessen, reduce, shrink 7 dwindle, shrivel 8 contract, diminish
smart: 4 sass 5 learn 8 mouth off 9 give lip to
soft: 4 melt, thaw 6 loosen, warm up 7 defrost 8 unfreeze 10 deliquesce
somewhere: 6 arrive
started: 4 move 5 crank 7 proceed, take off 8 turn over
steamed up: 4 boil, burn, fume, stew 5 froth 6 see red, seethe, simmer 7 bristle, smolder
straight A's: 5 excel
stuck: 4 mire 5 lodge 6 fixate, wallow
support for, as an idea: 4 sell
tangled: 3 mat 4 knot 5 snarl, twist
the ball rolling: 5 begin, cause, start 8 commence
the best of: 3 win 5 one-up, trump, unarm, upset, worst 6 defeat, master, outwit, subdue 7 conquer 8 outsmart, overcome 9 overpower
the gold: 3 win
the goods on: 3 pin 4 nail, trap
the hang of: 3 see 5 learn 6 master
the hard way: 3 pry 5 wring 6 extort, wrench
the impression: 4 feel 5 think 6 divine, intuit, pick up, reason 7 believe, discern 8 perceive 10 understand
the job done: 4 work 6 hack it
the jump on: 5 outdo 7 prevail, surpass 8 dominate, outstrip
the knack of: 5 grasp, learn 6 pick up 7 excel in
the lead out: 3 hie 4 move, rush, tear 5 erase, hurry 6 hasten
the lowdown: 5 learn
the message: 3 see 4 hear 8 perceive
the punch line: 4 grin, howl, roar 5 laugh 6 giggle, guffaw 7 chortle, chuckle, crack up, snicker, snigger
there: 4 land 5 light, reach 6 arrive, attend, blow in, make it, pull in, roll in, show up, sign in, turn up 7 check in, clock in, fetch up, hit town 8 breeze in 9 disembark, touch down 10 drop anchor
there fast: 3 run, zip 4 dash, rush, tear, whiz, zoom 5 hurry, speed, whisk 6 hasten, scurry 7 scamper
the same answer: 5 agree
the show on the road: 5 begin 6 launch 7 lead off 8 commence
the upper hand: 4 beat, bury, drub, rout, stun 5 cream, crush, drown, quell, smash, total, trash, upset, waste 6 defeat, subdue 7 clobber, conquer, oppress, put away, stagger, take out, torpedo, trounce 8 bear down, blow away, bulldoze, overcome, roll over, shellack, suppress, vanquish 9 overthrow, subjugate 10 take care of
the word: 4 hear 5 learn
the wrong idea: 3 err 7 presume 8 misjudge 9 underrate
through: 5 reach, solve 6 endure, finish 7 survive, weather 8 complete 10 accomplish
through one's head: 5 grasp, learn 7 discern 9 recognize 10 appreciate, comprehend, understand
through to: 5 reach, touch 8 register
tired: 4 fade, flag, jade 5 droop, weary 8 languish, peter out, slow down
to: 3 irk 4 faze, rile 5 anger, annoy, bribe, eat at, peeve, reach, upset 6 access, affect, attain, bother, pester, rattle, tamper 7 agitate, contact, fluster, trouble, unnerve 8 arrive at, distress, unsettle 9 aggravate, influence 10 disconcert
together: 4 mass, meet 5 amass, merge, rally, troop, unite 6 confer 7 combine, compile, convene 9 socialize 10 rendezvous
to know: 3 see 4 hear, meet, read 5 dig up, glean, grasp, greet, learn, reach, study 6 link up, master, peruse, pick up, take in, turn up 7 connect, contact, discern, find out, run into, uncover, unearth, welcome 8 approach, deal with, discover, pore over, smoke out 9 ascertain, catch on to, determine, encounter, forgather 10 experience, rendezvous, understand
too excited over: 4 gush 7 enthuse
to one's feet: 4 rise, wake 5 arise, awake, stand, waken 6 awaken, jump up, wake up 7 stand up
too personal: 3 pry, spy 5 snoop, stare 6 butt in, horn in, meddle 7 intrude, obtrude, wiretap 8 question 9 interfere
to the bottom of: 5 plumb, solve 6 fathom 9 penetrate
to the top: 3 win 5 score 6 arrive 7 achieve, make out, prosper, succeed 8 carry off, flourish, go places, make good 10 accomplish, do all right
to work: 5 begin, start 6 dive in, embark, set off, set out 7 lead off, proceed 8 commence, set about, set forth
try to ~ answers: 3 ask 4 pump, quiz 5 grill, query 7 canvass, consult, inquire, request
under one's skin: 3 ire, irk, vex 4 rile 5 annoy, pique, upset
under way: 4 open, sail, send 5 begin, speed, start 6 launch, set off, set out 7 kick off, lead off, proceed 8 commence, initiate, set forth 9 enter upon, originate, strike out 10 inaugurate
up: 4 rise, stir, wake 5 arise, awake, hatch, rouse, stand, waken 6 awaken, outfit 7 costume, roll out, turn out 8 lose a lap 10 hit the deck
up and go: 3 pep, vim 4 exit, life, push, snap 5 drive, leave, oomph, vigor 6 bounce, energy, starch 8 ambition, gumption, vitality, vivacity 10 exuberance
upright: 5 stand
upset: 4 burn, fume, lose, pout, stew 6 blow up, seethe, simmer 7 bristle, smolder
used to: 5 adapt, enure, inure 6 attune 7 break in 8 accustom, cope with 9 acclimate, reconcile
vibes: 4 feel, know, mind, read 5 grasp, smell 6 absorb, divine, intuit, notice, pick up, reason, take in 7 believe, catch on, discern, observe, realize 8 perceive 9 apprehend 10 anticipate, get the idea, have a hunch, understand
well: 4 heal, mend 5 rally 6 recoup 7 rebound, recover 10 recuperate
wind of: 4 hear 5 learn, scent, smell 6 pick up 7 find out 8 discover 9 ascertain
wise: 9 smarten up
get __: 3 off, out, set 4 away, back, down, even, into, over, to it, wise 5 about, after, ahead, along, going, ready, rid of, there 6 across, around 7 nowhere, through
get __ a good thing: 4 in on
get __ at: 4 back
get __ awakening: 5 a rude
get __ deal: 4 a raw
get __ for: 5 a feel
get __ for effort: 3 an A, an E
get __ for one's money: 4 a run
get __ good thing: 5 in on a
get __ holding the bag: 4 left
get __ in edgewise: 5 a word
get __ in one's stomach: 5 a knot
get __ in one's throat: 5 a lump
get __ in the face: 5 a slap
get __ it: 4 with
get __ lease on life: 4 a new
get __ line: 4 into
get __ of: 3 rid 4 hold, wind 5 a hold, a load
get __ of one's own medicine: 5 a dose
get __ on: 5 a bead, a jump, a move
get __ one's skin: 5 under
get __ on the right foot: 3 off
get __ on the wrist: 5 a slap

GE

get __ on the wrong foot: 3 off
get __ out of: 5 a bang, a kick, a rise
get __ shape: 4 into
get __ start: 5 a late
get __ stick: 5 on the
get __ the act: 4 into
get __ the ground floor: 4 in on
get __ the right foot: 5 off on
get __ the wrong foot: 5 off on
get __ to: 6 around
get __ to cases: 4 down
get __ together: 5 it all
get __ trouble: 4 into
get __ up: 4 a leg
get __ with: 4 away, even
get __ writing: 4 it in
get-__ card: 4 well
get-__-go: 5 up-and
Get __: 3 Off 4 a Job, Back, Down, Here, It On 5 Crazy, Happy, Ready, Smart 6 Carter, Closer, Shorty
Get __!: 4 on it, real 5 a grip, a life, Bruce
Get __ back!: 5 off my
Get __ behind me...: 4 thee
Get __ it!: 4 with
Get __ of that!: 5 a load
Get __ of yourself!: 5 a hold
Get __ the Church...: 4 Me to
Get __ up: 4 a leg
Get __ Ya-Ya's Out!: 3 Yer
geta: 4 clog, shoe 8 footwear
get a __: 5 leg up
get a __ lease on life: 3 new
get a __ of: 4 load
get a __ on: 4 bead, move 6 handle, wiggle
get a __ out of: 4 bang
get a __ up: 3 leg
Get a __: 3 Job
Get a __!: 4 grip, life
Get a __ of that!: 4 load
Get a __ on!: 4 move
Get a Job: 4 oldy 5 oldie 6 doo-wop
syllable: 3 sha
Get a Job (1958 song)
artist: Silhouettes
Get a Leg Up (1991 song)
artist: John Cougar Mellencamp
Get a load of that!: 4 look
get an __ effort: 4 A for, E for
get a new __ on life: 5 lease
get around __: 4 to it
getaway: 3 lam 4 exit, tour, trip 5 break 6 escape, flight, resort 8 breakout, vacation 9 departure 10 decampment
make a ~: 3 fly, run 4 bolt, flee, flit, skip 5 elude, evade 6 decamp, escape 7 abscond 8 jump bail, shake off 9 cut and run, disappear, skedaddle 10 fly the coop, hightail it
weekend ~: 5 B and B
Get away!: 4 shoo
Getaway, The (1972 film)
cast: Ali MacGraw, Steve McQueen
director: Sam Peckinpah
Get Back (1969 song)
artist: Beatles
__ Get By: 3 I'll
Get Carter (2000 film)
cast: Rachael Leigh Cook, Miranda Richardson, Sylvester Stallone
Get Closer (1976 song)
artist: Seals and Crofts
get down to __: 5 cases
Get Down Tonight (1975 song)
artist: KC and the Sunshine Band
get-go: 5 onset, start 9 beginning, square one
Get going!: 4 move 6 move it
Get Happy
composer: Harold Arlen, Ted Koehler
Get Here (1991 song)
artist: Oleta Adams
...get her poor dog __: 5 a bone
get in __ ground floor: 5 on the
get in one's __: 3 way 4 face, hair
get in on the __ floor: 6 ground
__ Get in the Way: 5 Words
get into __: 4 line
get into the __: 3 act
get it __ together: 3 all
Get it?: 3 dig, see
__ Get It for You Wholesale: 4 I Can
get left holding the __: 3 bag
Get lost!: 4 scat, shoo 5 scoot, scram, split 6 beat it, begone, bug off
Get Me to the Church on Time
composer: Alan Jay Lerner, Frederick Loewe
Get off my __!: 4 case
Get Off My Cloud (1965 song)
artist: Rolling Stones
get off on the __ foot: 5 right, wrong
get one's __: 4 goat 6 number
get one's __ in a row: 5 ducks
get one's __ in the door: 4 foot
get one's __ into: 5 teeth
get one's __ together: 3 act
get one's __ up: 7 hackles
get one's ducks in a __: 3 row
get one's foot in the __: 4 door
get one's teeth __: 4 into
get on one's __: 6 nerves
get on one's __ horse: 4 high
get on the __: 5 stick
Get on the Bus (1996 film)
cast: Ossie Davis, Charles S. Dutton
director: Spike Lee
__ get-out: 3 all
Get Outta My Dreams... (1988 song)
artist: Billy Ocean
Get real!: 4 as if, c'mon
Get Shorty: 4 film 5 novel
author: Elmore Leonard
cast: Danny DeVito, Gene Hackman, Rene Russo, John Travolta
director: Barry Sonnenfeld
__ Gets in Your Eyes: 5 Smoke
Get Smart (2008 film)
cast: Alan Arkin, Steve Carell, Anne Hathaway
Get Smart (NBC/CBS sitcom)
cast: Don Adams (Maxwell Smart, Agent 86)
Barbara Feldon (Agent 99)
Edward Platt (The Chief)
foe: 4 KAOS 9 Siegfried
robot: Hymie
__ Get Started: 5 I Can't
get the __: 4 gate, hook 5 point 7 message
get the __ of: 4 best, hang
get the __ of it: 5 worst
get the __ on: 4 drop, jump
get the __ on the road: 4 show
get the __ out: 4 lead
Get thee __ nunnery: 3 to a
get the lead __: 3 out
get the show on the __: 4 road
get the worst __: 4 of it
__ get this straight...: 5 Let me
Gettin' __ Wit It: 5 Jiggy
getting
means of ~ there: 4 belt, lane, path, pike, road, ship 5 guide, route, trail 6 access, artery, avenue, detour, street 7 channel, freeway, highway, parkway, passage, roadway, thruway, viaduct 8 shortcut, turnpike 9 boulevard, itinerary 10 expressway, throughway
nowhere: 6 in a rut
on: 4 aged 5 aging 6 ageing 7 ancient, elderly, wizened 8 grizzled 9 geriatric, senescent, up in years
warm: 4 near 5 close 7 close by
getting __ years: 4 on in 7 along in
__ Getting to Be a Habit...: 5 You're
Getting to Know You: 4 song
composer: Oscar Hammerstein, Richard Rodgers
singer: 4 Anna
Getting Up and Going Home
author: Robert Anderson
Gettin' Jiggy Wit It (1998 song)
artist: Will Smith
Gett Off (1991 song)
artist: Prince
get-together: 3 bee, mtg. 4 gala, sess. 5 mixer, party, rally 6 caucus, huddle, powwow 7 meeting, reunion, session 8 assembly, function
Getty: 5 J. Paul 6 Gordon 7 Estelle 9 Balthazar
product: 3 gas, oil
rival: 4 Gulf 5 Amoco, Exxon, Mobil, Shell 6 Texaco 7 Chevron
Gettysburg: 6 battle
addresser: 3 Abe 7 Lincoln
general: 3 Lee 5 Meade
locale: 4 Penn.
soldier: 3 reb
Gettysburg (1993 film)
cast: Tom Berenger, Jeff Daniels, Martin Sheen
Gettysburg Address ender: 5 Earth
get under one's __: 4 skin
getup: 3 rig 4 garb, suit, togs 5 array, dress, robes 6 attire, livery, outfit 7 apparel, clothes, costume, garment, turnout 8 clothing, garments 9 trappings 10 Sunday best
get-up-and-go: 3 pep, vim, zip 4 life, push, zest, zing 5 drive, moxie, oomph, vigor 6 energy, hustle 8 gumption, vitality 9 élan vital 10 enterprise, initiative
having no ~: 4 dull, idle, lazy, logy 5 inert, slack, tired 7 languid, loafing, out of it, passive 8 dilatory, feckless, flagging, indolent, lifeless, slothful, sluggish 9 apathetic, lethargic, sedentary, shiftless 10 slow-moving
Get Ur Freak On (2001 song)
artist: Missy Elliott
get-well __: 4 card
Get Yer __ Out: 5 Ya-Ya's
__ Get You Into My Life: 5 Got to
__ Get Your Gun: 5 Annie
Getz, Stan
genre: 4 jazz
instrument: 3 sax 9 saxophone
song: Desafinado (1962)
The Girl From Ipanema (1964)
gewgaw: 3 toy 4 gaud 5 dodad 6 bangle, bauble, doodad, trifle 7 fribble, trinket 8 frippery, gimcrack, kickshaw, nicknack, ornament 9 adornment, bagatelle, brummagem, plaything 10 decoration, knickknack
Gewürztraminer: 4 wine 5 white
origin: 6 France 7 Germany
geyser: 3 jet 5 spirt, spurt 6 gusher, spring 8 fountain, water jet 9 hot spring
Gezelle, Guido: 4 poet 7 Flemish
G-factor: 6 weight
G-flat: 4 note 8 black key
G. Gordon __: 5 Liddy
Ghana: 6 nation 7 country
capital: 5 Accra, Akkra
city: 4 Tema 5 Accra, Akkra 6 Kumasi, Obuasi, Tamale
export: 5 cocoa
fabric: 5 kente
language: 3 Ewe, Gbe, Twi 4 Tshi 7 Ashanti
money: 4 cedi 6 pesewa
neighbor: 4 Togo 10 Ivory Coast
Nobelist in Peace: 5 Annan
people: 3 Ewe 4 Akan 5 Fante 6 Asante 7 Ashanti
poet: 8 Anyidoho
river: 5 Volta
writer: 5 Aidoo, Armah 7 Awoonor
__ ghanouj: 4 baba
__ G. Harding: 6 Warren
ghastly: 3 wan 4 ashy, foul, gory, grim, pale, poor 5 ashen, awful, lousy, lurid, weird, woful 6 crumby, crummy, dismal, grisly, horrid, morbid, odious, pallid, rotten, woeful 7 accurst, baleful, baneful, beastly, doleful, fearful, heinous, hideous, macaber, macabre 8 accursed, dreadful, ghoulish, God-awful, grievous, gruesome, horrible, inferior, shameful, shocking, stinking, terrible, wretched 9 abhorrent, appalling, atrocious, defective, execrable, frightful, insidious, loathsome, miserable, offensive, repellent, revolting, unearthly 10 abominable, despicable, detestable, disastrous, disgusting, horrendous, horrifying, petrifying, terrifying
Ghats: 5 range 9 mountains
locale: 4 Asia 5 India
Ghent: 4 city, town
locale: 7 Belgium
river: 3 Lys 4 Leie 7 Schelde, Scheldt
gherkin: 6 pickle, veggie 9 vegetable
Gherman: 5 Titov
ghetto: 4 slum 6 barrio, region 7 quarter 9 inner city
__ Ghetto: 5 In the
Ghetto Supastar (1998 song)
artist: Mya
ghibli: 4 wind
ghillie: 4 shoe 8 footwear

ghost: 4 game, soul 5 shade, spook, umbra, write 6 author, fantom, spirit, wraith 7 banshee, banshie, eidolon, fantasm, phantom, specter 8 illusion, phantasm, presence, word game 10 apparition, substitute
costume: 5 sheet
do a ~ job: 5 haunt
ender: 4 weed 5 write 6 writer
German ~: 6 kobold
white as a ~: 3 wan
word: 3 boo
ghost __: 4 crab, moth, town, word 5 dance, image, story 6 shrimp, writer
ghost __ chance: 3 of a
Ghost
(1990 film) role: Oda Mae
Ghost (1990 film)
cast: Whoopi Goldberg, Demi Moore, Patrick Swayze
director: Jerry Zucker
__ Ghost: 4 Holy
Ghost and Mrs. Muir, The (1947 film)
cast: Rex Harrison, George Sanders, Gene Tierney
Ghostbusters: 4 film, song
artist: Ray Parker Jr
cast: Dan Aykroyd, Bill Murray, Harold Ramis, Sigourney Weaver
director: Ivan Reitman
goo: 5 slime
role: 4 Egon
Ghost Goes West, The (1935 film)
cast: Robert Donat
Ghostley: 5 Alice
ghostlike: 3 wan 4 eery, pale 5 eerie, weird 6 spooky 7 eidolic, haunted, macaber, macabre, uncanny 8 spectral 9 invisible, spiritual, unearthly 10 immaterial, phantasmal, wraithlike
ghostly: 10 unphysical
ghost of a __: 6 chance
Ghost of Christmas __: 4 Past 7 Present
Ghost of the Buffaloes, The
author: Vachel Lindsay
Ghost Rider (2007 film)
cast: Nicolas Cage, Eva Mendes
Ghosts: 4 play
author: Henrik Ibsen
character: 5 Helen 6 Alving, Oswald, Regina
Ghosts of Girlfriends Past (2009 film)
cast: Jennifer Garner, Matthew McConaughey
Ghosts of Mississippi (1996 film)
cast: Alec Baldwin, Whoopi Goldberg, Craig T. Nelson, James Woods
director: Rob Reiner
Ghost, The
author: Danielle Steel
Ghost Writer, The
author: Philip Roth
ghoul: 5 demon 6 daemon, daimon 7 monster 8 bogeyman 9 archfiend, hobgoblin
greeting: 3 boo
ghoulish: 4 sick 6 creepy, morbid 7 ghastly, macaber, macabre 9 unearthly
G.I.: 3 NCO, PFC, pvt., rct. 4 Yank 5 grunt 6 airman 7 dogface, draftee, private, recruit, soldier, veteran, warrior
1950's ~ ally: 3 ROK
address: 3 APO
captured ~: 3 POW
clothing: 3 ODs 5 drabs 6 khakis
command: 4 halt 6 at ease
cop: 2 MP
doing ~ kitchen duty: 4 on KP
female: 3 WAC 4 WAAC
former ~: 3 vet 5 Amvet
group: 4 unit 5 troop 7 brigade 8 division 9 battalion
hangout: 3 USO
ID: 2 SN 6 dogtag
Joe: 3 toy 4 doll
Joe maker: 6 Hasbro
meal: 3 MRE 4 mess, Spam 7 K-ration
money: 5 scrip
need: 4 ammo
offender: 4 AWOL
org. for former ~s: 3 VFW
part of ~: 4 govt. 5 issue
source, once: 3 SSS
supplier: 2 PX
unaccounted-for ~: 3 MIA
see also army, military, soldier
G.I. __: 3 Joe 4 Bill, Jane 5 Blues
Gia: 5 Scala 7 Carides
Giacomo: 7 Puccini 8 Casanova 9 Meyerbeer
Giacosa, Giuseppe: 7 Italian 10 playwright
collaborator: Puccini
Giaever, Ivar: 8 Nobelist 9 physicist
Gia Lan Airport site: 5 Hanoi
Giamatti: 4 Bart, Paul
Giambattista: 4 Vico 6 Basile, Marino
Giancarlo: 8 Esposito, Giannini
Gian Carlo __: 7 Menotti
Gianlorenzo: 7 Bernini
Gianni: 7 Versace
Giannini: 2 A.P. 9 Giancarlo
giant: 3 big 4 huge, ogre, tall, vast 5 Atlas, great, jumbo, large, titan, whale 6 Amazon, Bunyan, witigo 7 Goliath, hulking, immense, mammoth, massive, monster, sizable, titanic, windigo 8 behemoth, colossal, colossus, enormous, gigantic, king-size, oversize, sizeable, towering, whapping, whopping 9 cyclopean, herculean, humongous, leviathan, monstrous, overlarge 10 family-size, gargantuan, monumental, Paul Bunyan, prodigious, stupendous, tremendous
Biblical ~: 7 Goliath
fictional ~: 9 Gargantua 10 Pantagruel
mental ~: 3 ace 4 whiz 5 brain 6 genius 7 egghead, prodigy, thinker 8 Einstein, highbrow, virtuoso 10 mastermind
of Greek myth: 4 Rhea, Thia 5 Argus, Atlas, Coeus, Crius, Dione, Orion 6 Cronus, Phoebe, Tethys, Themis, Typhon 7 Cyclops, Eurybia, Iapetus, Oceanus 8 Hyperion 9 Menoetius, Mnemosyne 10 Epimetheus, Polyphemus, Prometheus
of Norse myth: 4 Norn, Ymer, Ymir 5 Jotun
red ~: 4 Mira, star 5 S star 7 Antares
syllable: 3 fee, fie, fum
to Jack: 3 foe
giant __: 5 panda, steps 6 slalom 7 redwood, sequoia
__ giant: 3 red 4 blue 6 mental
Giant: 4 film, NLer 5 NFLer, novel 10 baseballer, footballer
author: Edna Ferber
cast: Carroll Baker, James Dean, Rock Hudson, Elizabeth Taylor
composer: Dimitri Tiomkin
director: George Stevens
Hall-of-Famer: 3 Ott 4 Mays 5 Rusie, Terry 6 Cepeda, McGraw, Mel Ott 7 Hubbell, McCovey 8 Marichal 9 Amos Rusie, Bill Terry, Mathewson 10 John McGraw, Willie Mays
ranch: 5 Reata
__ Giant: 5 Green 6 Gentle, Jersey, Little
Giant Raft
author: Jules Verne
Giants: 4 nine 6 eleven
home: 7 New York
org.: 3 MLB, NFC, NLW
rival: ***see*** baseball team, NFL team
giant-screen technology: 4 Imax
Giants in the Earth
author: Ole Rölvaag
character: 3 Ole 4 Hans, Holm 5 Beret, Peder, Seier, Sofie
__ giant slalom: 5 super
gib: 3 cat 6 tomcat
Gib.: 3 str.
Gibb: 4 Andy 5 Barry, Robin 7 Cynthia, Maurice
brother: 6 Bee Gee
Gibb, Andy
song: Desire (1980)
Don't Throw It All Away (1978)
An Everlasting Love (1978)
I Just Want to Be Your Everything (1977)
Shadow Dancing (1978)
Thicker Than Water (1977)
Gibb, Barry
song: Guilty (1980)
gibber: 3 gab, yak 4 rant 6 babble, footle, gossip, prater 7 blather, blether, chatter, palaver, prattle 8 chit-chat, ramble on 9 table talk
gibberish: 4 wind 5 Babel 7 chatter, inanity, palaver 8 babbling 10 empty words
see also baloney
gibbon: 6 animal, mammal 7 primate
Malay ~: 3 lar
relative: ***see*** primate
Gibbon, Edward: 6 writer 7 British 9 historian
Gibbons: 5 Leeza 6 Cedric
Gibbs: 5 Marla, Terri 7 Georgia
Gibbs, Georgia
nickname: Her Nibs
song: Dance With Me Henry (1955)
Tweedle Dee (1955)
gibe: 3 dig, dis, jab, rag 4 barb, hoot, jape, jeer, jest, mock, quip, slam, slap, slur, snub, twit 5 abuse, agree, decry, flout, libel, roast, scoff, scorn, sneer, spurn, swipe, taunt, tease 6 defame, deride, dump on, heckle, impugn, jibe at, malign, offend, rebuff, slight, vilify 7 affront, asperse, calumny, catcall, degrade, disdain, mockery, obloquy, offense, putdown, rank out, sarcasm, slander, traduce 8 belittle, brickbat, contempt, denounce, derision, ridicule, scoffing, vilipend 9 aspersion, cheap shot, contumely, denigrate, discredit, disparage, humiliate, make fun of 10 calumniate, defamation, disrespect, opprobrium
giblets part: 5 heart, liver 7 gizzard
Gibraltar: 4 city, port, town 6 colony, strait
denizen: 3 ape 10 Barbary ape
landmark: 4 rock
locale: 6 Iberia
neighbor: 5 Spain 7 Morocco
port near ~: 4 Adra 5 Cadiz, Ceuta
__ Gibraltar: 6 Rocket, Rock of
Gibran, Kahlil: 4 poet 6 writer 8 Lebanese
work: The Prophet
Gibson: 3 Bob, Don, Mel 4 Hoot, Josh, Kirk 5 Henry 6 Althea, Debbie, desert, Thomas 7 Deborah, William
garnish: 5 onion
Gibson __: 4 girl 6 Desert
Gibson, Althea: 7 netster 9 tennis pro
milieu: 5 court
Gibson, Bob: 6 hurler 7 pitcher 8 Cardinal
Gibson, Debbie
song: Foolish Beat (1988)
Lost in Your Eyes (1989)
Only in My Dreams (1987)
Out of the Blue (1988)
Shake Your Love (1987)
Gibson, Don
song: Oh Lonesome Me (1958)
Gibson, Josh: 7 catcher, slugger
Gibson, Mel: 5 actor
film: Air America (1990)
Bird on a Wire (1990)
The Bounty (1984)
Braveheart (1995, AA)
Conspiracy Theory (1997)
Forever Young (1992)
Gallipoli (1981)
Hamlet (1990)
Lethal Weapon (1987)
Mad Max (1979)
The Man Without a Face (1993)
Maverick (1994)
The Patriot (2000)
Ransom (1996)
Road Warrior (1981)
Tequila Sunrise (1988)
We Were Soldiers (2002)
What Women Want (2000)
The Year of Living Dangerously (1983)
Gibson, William: 6 writer
giddiness: 6 levity 8 nonsense 9 frivolity
giddy: 4 gaga, wild 5 ditzy, dizzy, light, silly 6 awhirl, giggly, punchy 7 flighty 8 euphoric, skittish, unstable, volatile 9 brainless, frivolous,

impulsive, lightsome, slaphappy **10** capricious, inconstant, nonserious
be ~: **4** reel, swim **5** swirl
Gide, André: **6** French, writer **8** Nobelist
work: The Counterfeiters
The Fruits of the Earth
If It Die
Strait Is the Gate
Gideon: **5** judge
author: Paddy Chayefsky
placement: **5** Bible
Gideon's __: **7** Trumpet
Gidget (1959 film)
cast: James Darren, Sandra Dee
Gielgud, John: **3** Sir **5** actor
film: Arthur (1981, AA)
Becket (1964)
The Elephant Man (1980)
Gandhi (1982)
Julius Caesar (1953)
Murder on the Orient Express (1974)
Richard III (1955)
Time After Time (1985)
role: **4** Lear
Gifford, Frank
sport: **8** football
Gifford, Kathie Lee
spouse: Frank Gifford
gift: **3** tip **4** alms, bent, boon, dole, head, nose, turn **5** award, bonus, favor, flair, forte, goody, grant, knack, power, skill, token, treat **6** bounty, genius, goodie, legacy, reward, talent, tipoff **7** ability, aptness, benefit, bequest, charity, faculty, freebee, freebie, godsend, handout, largess, premium, present, proffer, subsidy **8** aptitude, bestowal, capacity, courtesy, donation, giveaway, gratuity, instinct, kickback, largesse, offering, penchant, souvenir **9** allowance, endowment, lagniappe **10** green thumb
acknowledge a ~: **5** thank
as a ~: **4** free **6** gratis **8** costless **10** for nothing, on the house
baby shower ~: **7** bootees, booties
card word: **3** for **4** from
container: **3** box **7** package
ender: **4** ware
Father's Day ~: **3** tie **5** razor, shirt
feature: **3** bow
giver: **5** donor
make a ~: **5** grant, offer **6** bestow, confer, donate **8** bequeath **10** contribute
name meaning ~: **4** Dora **6** Nathan
naughty child's Christmas ~: **4** coal
of gab: **8** rhetoric **9** eloquence, loquacity, wittiness **10** volubility
of the Magi: **4** gold **5** myrrh **12** frankincense
prepare a ~: **4** do up, tape, wrap
receiver: **5** donee
recipient's question: **5** for me
reveal a ~: **4** open **5** unbox
small ~: **5** favor, goody, token, treat **7** memento **8** keepsake, surprise
temporary ~: **4** loan **6** credit **7** advance **9** extension
time: **4** yule **8** birthday **9** Christmas **10** Father's Day, Mother's Day
wrap: **5** paper **6** tissue
gift __: **3** tax **4** wrap **5** of gab
Gift __ Magi, The: **5** of the
__ Gift: **4** It's a
gifted: **3** apt **4** able **5** blest, smart **6** adroit, brainy, clever **7** skilled **8** creative, talented **9** brilliant, ingenious, inventive, promising, versatile **10** precocious, proficient
one: **3** wiz **4** whiz **6** genius
__ gift horse in the mouth: **5** look a
...giftie __ us..., the: **3** gie
gift of __: **3** gab
gift of God
name meaning ~: **7** Dorothy, Matthew **8** Dorothea, Matthias, Theodore **9** Nathaniel
Gift of the Magi, The
author: O. Henry
character: **3** Jim **5** Della
device: **5** irony
gift: **3** fob **5** combs
Gift Outright, The
author: Robert Frost
Gift, The
author: Danielle Steel
Gift, The (2000 film)
cast: Cate Blanchett, Katie Holmes, Keanu Reeves
director: Sam Raimi
gig: **3** job **4** boat, show, work **7** booking, calling, concert, javelin, recital, rowboat **8** carriage **10** engagement
do a ~: **4** play **6** appear **7** perform
Gig: **5** Young
gigantic: **3** big **4** huge, vast **5** giant, great, jumbo, large **6** mighty **7** hulking, immense, mammoth, massive, monster, sizable, titanic **8** colossal, enormous, king-size, oversize, sizeable, terrific, towering, whapping, whopping **9** cyclopean, herculean, humongous, monstrous, overlarge, whalelike **10** gargantuan, monumental, prodigious, stupendous, tremendous
giggle: **4** ha-ha, he-he **5** laugh, tehee **6** cackle, guffaw, heehee, teehee, titter **7** break up, chortle, chuckle, crack up, snicker, snigger **8** laughter
giggling: **3** gay **5** happy, merry **7** gleeful **8** cackling, cheerful, laughing, laughter, mirthful **9** chuckling, tittering **10** snickering, sniggering
giggly: **5** dizzy, giddy, silly **6** jejune **7** flighty **8** immature **9** frivolous
Gigi: **7** Perreau
composer: Alan Jay Lerner, Frederick Loewe
Gigi (1958 film)
cast: Leslie Caron, Maurice Chevalier, Hermione Gingold, Louis Jourdan
director: Vincente Minnelli
Gigi (novel)
author: Colette
__ Gigio: **4** Topo
Gigli (2003 film)
cast: Ben Affleck, Jennifer Lopez, Al Pacino
__ Gigolo: **5** Just a
gigue: **5** dance
G.I. Jane (1997 film)
cast: Anne Bancroft, Demi Moore, Viggo Mortensen
director: Ridley Scott
Gil: **5** Evans **6** Gerard, Hodges, Morgan **7** Bellows **10** Scott-Heron
Gil __: **4** Blas
Gila: **5** Golan, river
monster: **6** animal, lizard **7** reptile
monster's home: **6** desert **7** Arizona
river locale: **7** Arizona **9** New Mexico
Gilbert: **3** Rod **4** Cass, John, Ryle, Sara, town **5** Cates, Lewis **6** Parker, Roland, Stuart, Walter **7** Melissa **8** Humphrey **9** Gottfried, O'Sullivan
Gilbert __ Chesterton: **5** Keith
Gilbert and __ Islands: **6** Ellice
Gilbert, Cass: **9** architect
Gilbert, Melissa
spouse: Bruce Boxleitner
Gilberto: **6** Astrud
Gilbert, Rod
milieu: **3** ice **4** rink **5** arena
org.: **3** NHL
Gilberts: **4** isls. **5** isles **7** islands
Gilbert, Walter: **7** chemist **8** Nobelist
Gilbert, William S.: **3** Sir **6** writer **7** British **8** lyricist **10** playwright
partner: Arthur Sullivan
work: The Gondoliers
The Grand Duke
HMS Pinafore
Iolanthe
The Mikado
Patience
The Pirates of Penzance
Princess Ida
Ruddigore
The Sorcerer
Trial by Jury
Utopia, Ltd.
The Yeoman of the Guard
Gil Blas
author: Alain Lesage
Gilbreth: **5** Frank **9** Elizabeth
gild: **4** deck **5** adorn **6** aurify, bedeck, finish **7** aureate, dress up, encrust, enhance, garnish, incrust, overlay, varnish **8** beautify, brighten, decorate, ornament **9** embellish, embroider
Gilda: **6** Radner
Gilda (1946 film)
cast: Glenn Ford, Rita Hayworth
director: Charles Vidor
gilded: **4** doré, rich **6** ornate **7** aureate
Gilded __, The: **3** Age **4** Lily
Gilder, Nick
song: Hot Child in the City (1978)
Gildersleeve: **5** nabob
like: **5** great
nickname: **4** Mort
__ Gildersleeve, The: **5** Great
gilding: **4** trim **9** adornment **10** decoration
__ gilding: **3** oil **4** fire **5** honey **6** parcel **7** amalgam
gild the __: **4** lily
Gilead: **4** peak **5** mount **8** mountain
balm of ~: **5** resin **6** balsam
locale: **4** Asia **6** Jordan **7** Mideast
Gilels, Emil: **7** pianist, Russian
Giles: **5** saint **6** Warren
Giles Goat-Boy
author: John Barth
__-Giles system: **4** Wade
Gilford: **4** Jack
Gilgamesh: **4** king **8** Sumerian
gilguy: **4** rope
gill: **5** organ **8** breather
combining form: **7** branchi- **8** branchio-
cousin: **4** lung
ender: **3** net
starter: **4** blue
gill-__: **6** netter
Gill: **5** Vince **6** Johnny **7** Brendan
Gillan: **3** Ian
Gillespie, Dizzy: **9** trumpeter
genre: **3** bop **4** jazz **5** bebop
Gillespie partner: **5** Tibbs
Gillette: **4** King **5** Anita, razor
alternative: **3** Bic **6** Schick
model: **4** Atra
Gilley, Mickey
cousin: Jerry Lee Lewis, Jimmy Swaggart
Gilliam: **3** Stu **5** Terry
Gilliam, Terry: **5** actor **8** comedian
film: The Adventures of Baron Munchausen (1989)
Brazil (1985)
The Fisher King (1991)
Monty Python's The Meaning of Life (1983)
Time Bandits (1981)
Twelve Monkeys (1995)
Gillian: **8** Anderson
Gilliat: **6** Sidney
Gillies, Clark
milieu: **3** ice **4** rink **5** arena
org.: **3** NHL
Gilligan home: **3** hut **4** isle
Gilligan's Island (CBS sitcom)
boat: **6** Minnow
cast: Jim Backus (Thurston Howell III)
Bob Denver (Gilligan)
Alan Hale (Skipper)
Russell Johnson (The Professor)
Tina Louise (Ginger Grant)
Natalie Schafer (Lovey Howell)
Dawn Wells (Mary Ann Summers)
feature: **6** lagoon
Gillis: **5** Dobie
Gillman, Sid: **5** coach
sport: **8** football
gills
eight ~: **5** quart
four ~: **4** pint
green around the ~: **3** ill **6** queasy, queazy
one with ~: **4** fish
stuff to the ~: **7** satiate
__ gills: **5** to the
Gill, Vince
spouse: Amy Grant
Gilman: **6** Alfred **7** Dorothy **9** Charlotte
Gilman, Alfred: **8** Nobelist
Gilman, Charlotte: **6** writer
Gilmore, Artis
milieu: **5** court
org.: **3** NBA
sport: **10** basketball

Gilmore Girls (WB/CW comedy/drama)
cast: Alexis Bledel (Rory Gilmore) Luke Danes (Scott Patterson) Lauren Graham (Lorelai Gilmore)
Gilpin: **4** Peri
Gilroy: **4** city, town
locale: **10** California
specialty: **6** garlic
gilt: **3** sow **5** color **6** golden **8** gold leaf **10** decoration
gilt-__: **4** edge **5** edged
gilt-edged: **4** A-one, fine **5** elite **7** optimum
gilthead: **4** fish
Gimbel
rival: **4** Macy
...gimble in the __: **4** wabe
gimcrack: **5** frill **6** bauble, geegaw, gewgaw, tawdry **7** fribble, trinket **8** nicknack, whim-wham **9** bagatelle **10** decoration, knick-knack
gimel: **6** Hebrew, letter
follower: **5** dales, dalet **6** daleth
preceder: **3** bes, bet **4** beth
gimlet: **3** awl **4** tool **5** drink **8** beverage, cocktail
cousin: **5** auger
ingredient: **3** gin **4** lime **5** vodka **9** lime juice
use a ~: **4** bore, ream **5** drill, gouge **6** pierce **8** puncture
gimme: **4** putt **5** tap-in
Gimme a break!: **4** c'mon **6** sheesh
Gimme a Break (NBC sitcom)
cast: Nell Carter (Nell Harper) Dolph Sweet (Carl Kanisky)
Gimme Shelter (1970 film)
cast: Melvin Belli, Jefferson Airplane, Rolling Stones
gimmick: **4** lure, ploy, ruse, wile **5** dodge, feint, gizmo, stunt, trick **6** deceit, device, dupery, gadget, gambit, scheme **7** finesse, sleight **8** artifice, maneuver, strategy **9** deception, imposture, mechanism, stratagem **10** motivation
adman ~: **5** promo, tie-in
gin: **4** game, trap **5** crank, drink, rummy, snare **6** liquor **7** machine, schnaps **8** beverage, card game, schnapps, windlass
bathtub ~: **5** hooch **6** hootch
drink: **5** sling **6** Gibson, gimlet, rickey **7** martini
flavoring: **4** sloe
lover: **3** sot
mill: **3** bar, pub **6** saloon, tavern **7** barroom **8** taphouse
partner: **5** tonic
product: **6** cotton
use a ~: **6** deseed
gin __: **4** fizz, mill **5** block, joint, rummy **6** rickey
__ gin: **4** pink, sloe **6** cotton **7** bathtub
Gina: **7** Gershon **8** Thompson
see also Italian
gin and __: **5** tonic
__ gin fizz: **4** sloe **5** Ramos
Ging: **4** Jack
ginger: **4** zest **5** brown, color, spice, taste **7** reddish, redhead **9** yellowish
ale: **5** mixer **8** beverage **9** soft drink
ender: **4** root, snap **5** bread
full of ~: **4** game **5** peppy **6** active, feisty, frisky, lively, spunky **7** scrappy **8** spirited
like ~: **3** hot **5** fiery, spicy, zesty, zippy **6** spicey **7** pungent **8** fragrant
relative: ***see*** brown color
ginger __: **3** ale, jar **4** beer, lily, snap
__ ginger: **4** wild **5** white **6** canton **7** Jamaica
Ginger: **6** Rogers
partner: **4** Fred
predecessor: **5** Adele
Ginger __: **3** Pye
__ ginger ale: **7** pale-dry
gingerbread: **4** cake, palm, trim **6** geegaw, gewgaw **8** ornament
gingerbread __: **3** man **4** palm, plum **5** house
Ginger Bread (1958 song)
artist: Frankie Avalon
Gingerbread Lady, The
author: Neil Simon
gingerly: **6** gently **7** lightly **9** carefully **10** cautiously
Ginger Pye
author: Eleanor Estes
gingersnap: **5** cooky **6** cookie
gingery: **5** spicy **6** spicey **8** spirited
gingham: **5** cloth **6** fabric **8** material
alternative: **6** calico
gingiva: **3** gum
gingko __: **6** biloba
Gingold: **8** Hermione
Gingrich: **4** Newt
Gin & Juice (1994 song)
artist: Snoop Doggy Dogg
gink: **4** fool
ginkgo: **4** tree
ginkgo __: **6** biloba
Ginnie __: **3** Mae
Ginny Fizz: **4** Wade
Gino: **8** Vannelli **9** Marchetti
gin rummy: **4** game **8** card game
Ginsberg, Allen: **4** poet
friend: Kerouac
genre: Beat
work: Howl
Ginsburg: **4** Ruth
ginseng: **4** herb
relative: **3** ivy, udo **4** nard **6** fatsia
Ginza
light: **4** neon
locale: **5** Japan, Tokio, Tokyo
money: **3** sen, yen
Ginzburg, Natalia: **6** writer **7** Italian
Gioacchino: **7** Rossini
giocoso: **8** jokingly **10** humorously
Giorgio: **6** Armani **7** Bassani, Moroder
__, Giorgio: **3** Yes
Giorgos: **7** Seferis
__ giorno!: **4** Buon
Giotto: **6** artist **7** Italian, painter **8** sculptor
contemporary: **5** Dante
place to see ~ paintings: **6** Assisi
Giovanna in English: **4** Jane, Joan
Giovanni: **3** Don **4** font **5** Nikki **6** Ribisi **7** Bellini, Belzoni, Pascoli, Pontano, Tiepolo **8** typeface **9** Boccaccio **10** Palestrina
in English: **4** John
see also Italian
__ Giovanni: **3** Don
Giovanni's Room
author: James Baldwin
Gipper
portrayer: **6** Reagan
giraffe: **6** animal, mammal
cousin: **5** okapi
favorite tree: **6** acacia
feature: **4** neck
female: **3** cow
home: **3** zoo **5** veldt **6** Africa
male: **4** bull
young: **4** calf
__ Girardeau, MO: **4** Cape
girasol: **4** opal
Giraudoux, Jean: **6** French, writer
gird: **3** tie **4** band, belt, hoop, loop, ring, tone, wind **5** brace, build, equip, hem in, ready, shore, steel **6** anneal, beef up, bind up, circle, harden, prop up, secure, temper, tone up **7** bolster, brace up, build up, burgeon, develop, empower, enclose, enhance, fortify, inclose, prepare, shore up, stiffen, support, toughen **8** bourgeon, buttress, cincture, encircle, energize, indurate, surround, vitalize **9** encompass, enwreathe, intensify, reinforce **10** invigorate, strengthen
girded: **5** armed
girder: **4** beam, I-bar **5** brace, H-beam, I-beam, joist, L-beam, T-beam **6** rafter, timber
fastener: **4** weld **5** rivet
material: **5** steel
girdle: **4** band, belt, cord, loop, ring, sash **5** fence, stays **6** corset **8** cincture, lingerie, surround **9** encompass, enwreathe, waistband
gird one's __: **5** loins
girl: **3** kid **4** lass, maid, teen **5** minor, missy, woman **6** damsel, female, lassie, maiden **7** sapling **8** daughter, fräulein, juvenile, ladylove, teenager **9** inamorata, young lady, youngster **10** adolescent, bobbysoxer, demoiselle, young woman
baby ~ clothes color: **4** pink
ender: **3** ish **6** friend
Friday: **4** asst. **9** assistant
name meaning ~: **4** Cora **7** Colleen
starter: **3** bar, bat, cow **4** atta, copy, news, play, show **5** choir, paper, sales **6** school
see also girlfriend
girl __: **4** talk **5** guide, scout **6** Friday, wonder
__ girl: **3** bar, bat, bus, old **4** ball, copy, show **5** altar, cover, Teddy **6** chorus, flower, Gibson, office, pompom, script **7** glamour, working
__ girl!: **4** Atta, It's a
Girl __: **3** Shy **4** on TV **5** Crazy, Happy, Scout **7** Watcher
Girl __, A: **5** Like I
Girl __ Golden West: **5** of the
Girl __ Help It, The: **4** Can't
Girl __ Ipanema, The: **4** From
Girl __ Marry, The: **5** That I
Girl __, The: **6** Friend **7** Hunters
__ Girl: **3** Bad, Hey **4** City, Rich, That **5** Black, Candy, China, Cover, Funny, Just a, Party, The It, Young **6** Barbie, Bobby's, Georgy, Island, Single, Surfer, Uptown, Valley, Whirly **7** Diamond, Jessie's, Working
Girl, 20
author: Kingsley Amis
Girl, a Guy, and __, A: **4** a Gob
__ Girl Blue: **6** Little
Girl Can't __ It, The: **4** Help
Girl Crazy (1943 film): **7** musical
cast: Judy Garland, Mickey Rooney
composer: George Gershwin, Ira Gershwin
director: Norman Taurog
__ Girl Friday: **3** His
girlfriend: **4** date **5** woman **7** admirer **8** intimate **9** companion **10** confidante
in French: **4** amie
see also sweetheart
Girl From Ipanema, The (1964 song)
artist: Stan Getz
girlhood: **5** youth
Girl Hunters, The
author: Mickey Spillane
Girl I'm Gonna Miss You (1989 song)
artist: Milli Vanilli
Girl, Interrupted (1999 film)
cast: Angelina Jolie, Brittany Murphy, Winona Ryder
cat: **4** Ruby
director: James Mangold
__ Girl in Town: **3** New
girlish: **5** young **8** juvenile, youthful **10** adolescent
__ Girl Is Like a Melody, A: **6** Pretty
Girl Is Mine, The (1982 song)
artist: Michael Jackson, Paul McCartney
Girl Like I, A
author: Anita Loos
Girl Like You, A (1967 song)
artist: Rascals
__ Girl Marries: **5** When a
__-girl network: **3** old
Girl of the Golden West
composer: Giacomo Puccini
Girl on TV (1999 song)
artist: LFO
girls
for boys and ~: **4** coed **6** unisex
girl's
that: **4** hers
Girls __ Out: **4** Nite
Girls __ Want to Have Fun: **4** Just
__ Girls: **3** Bad, Les **5** Cover, Spice **7** Buffalo
__ Girls Are Easy: **5** Earth
girls' club: **4** YWCA, YWHA
Girl Scouts
founder: Juliette Low
__ Girls Don't Cry: **3** Big
Girls! Girls! Girls! (1962 film)
cast: Elvis Presley, Stella Stevens
Girls, Girls, Girls (1987 song)
artist: Mötley Crüe
Girls Just Want to Have Fun (1984 song)
artist: Cyndi Lauper
Girls, The
author: Edna Ferber
__ Girls, The: **6** Golden, Harvey
Girl That I Marry, The
composer: Irving Berlin

__ Girl, The: 7 Country, Goodbye
__ Girl Wants: 5 What a
Girl With the Hatbox, The (1927 film)
cast: Anna Sten
Girl You Know It's True (1989 song)
artist: Milli Vanilli
Girl, You'll Be a Woman Soon (1967 song)
artist: Neil Diamond
giro: 8 aircraft
Girolamo: 10 Fracastoro, Savonarola
Gironde, river to the: 7 Garonne
Gironella, José Maria: 6 writer 7 Spanish
Giroux partner: 6 Farrar, Straus
girth: 4 band, bulk, size 5 cinch, waist, width 8 encircle
girtline: 4 rope
girt starter: 3 sea
G.I.'s: 4 unit 5 troop 6 grunts 8 infantry
Giscard D'Estaing: 6 Valéry
Gisele: 8 Bündchen 9 MacKenzie
'G' Is for Gumshoe
author: Sue Grafton
Gish: 7 Dorothy, Lillian 8 Annabeth
Gish, Lillian: 7 actress
film: The Birth of a Nation (1915) Intolerance (1916) The Whales of August (1987)
gismo: 5 dodad, gizmo 6 doodad, gadget, thingy, whosis, widget 7 doodads 9 doohickey, invention 10 instrument
gist: 3 nub 4 body, core, crux, idea, knub, meat, pith 5 drift, force, heart, point, sense, tenor, theme 6 center, kernel, marrow, spirit, thrust, upshot 7 essence, keynote, meaning, purport, summary 8 main idea 9 main point, substance
git: 4 scat, shoo 5 scram 6 beat it 7 amscray, vamoose 9 skedaddle
git-__-git: 5 up-and
Gitano: 5 jeans, pants 6 denims
Gitarzan (1969 song)
artist: Ray Stevens
Gitchee __: 5 Gumee
git-go: 5 start 6 day one, origin, outset 9 beginning, inception
Giuliani: 4 Rudy 7 Rudolph
Giuseppe: 5 Belli, Verdi 6 Parini 7 Giacosa, Mazzini 8 Fiorelli 9 Garibaldi
in English: 6 Joseph
see also Italian
give: 3 pay, put, sag, tip 4 cede, fold, hand, lend, mete, play, show, will 5 allow, apply, award, endow, grant, issue, offer, relax, remit, serve, spare, spend, stage, utter, yield 6 accord, afford, ante up, assign, bestow, cave in, commit, confer, convey, credit, devote, donate, extend, fork up, hand in, heap on, impart, lavish, lay out, pony up, ration, relent, render, supply, tender 7 concede, consign, crumple, deal out, deliver, dish out, display, divvy up, dole out, furnish, hand out, lay upon, let have, mete out, offer up, pass out, present, produce, proffer, provide 8 bequeath, collapse, disburse, dispense, engender, evidence, fork over, hand down, hand over, heap upon, indicate, manifest, minister, set forth, shell out, transfer, turn over 9 looseness, parcel out, subscribe, surrender, vouchsafe 10 administer, contribute, distribute, elasticity, lavish upon, relinquish, resilience
a bad name: 7 asperse, slander 8 backbite
a black eye: 4 slur 5 libel, shame, smear 6 defame, vilify
a boost to: 4 help 6 assist 7 further, promote
a break: 4 save 5 spare, spell
a Bronx cheer: 4 jeer, mock 5 sneer, taunt
a darn: 4 care, heed, mind 5 sweat, worry 6 bother, object, regret, tend to 8 remember 9 make a fuss, watch over
a deposition: 4 avow 6 allege, assert, attest 7 certify, declare
a face-lift: 5 fix up, rehab, renew 6 revamp, update 7 remodel, restore, touch up 8 overhaul, renovate, spruce up 9 modernize, refurbish
a going-over: 7 lecture
a hand: 4 abet, clap 6 assist 7 bail out, relieve
a handle: 3 dub 8 christen
a hand to: 6 deal in 7 applaud
a hard time: 3 irk, nag, vex 5 tease, upset 6 harass, hassle 7 torment
a jingle: 4 call, dial 5 phone 6 ring up 9 touch base
a job to: 4 hire 6 employ, engage, sign on, take on
a lecture: 4 talk 5 edify, orate, speak, spout, teach, tutor 6 advise, inform 7 address, declaim, deliver, educate, expound, instill 8 initiate, instruct 9 discourse, hold forth, inculcate, interpret, pound into, sermonize
a leg up: 3 aid 4 help 5 boost, hoist 6 assist, succor 9 encourage
a lift to: 3 aid 5 cheer, elate, raise 6 assist, pick up 7 enliven 8 reassure
a little extra: 3 add 6 slap on, tack on, toss in 8 increase
a medal to: 4 cite 5 honor 8 decorate
an account: 4 tell 6 recite, relate 7 narrate
a name to: 3 dub, tag 4 call, term 5 label, title 7 baptize 8 christen
an audience: 4 hear 6 listen
and take: 4 swap, swop 5 bandy, share, trade 8 exchange
an edge to: 4 hone, whet 5 grind 7 sharpen
an encore performance: 5 rerun
an example: 4 cite, name 5 offer, quote 7 specify 8 point out, spell out 9 enumerate
an opinion: 3 say 5 speak, state, voice 6 assert, remark 7 chime in, observe 8 maintain, propound
an oration: 4 talk 5 speak, spout 7 declaim 9 hold forth, speechify
an ovation: 4 clap 5 cheer, honor 6 praise 7 acclaim, applaud
an overview: 5 sum up 6 digest 7 outline 8 condense 9 synopsize
a party: 6 regale 7 splurge 9 entertain
a party for: 4 fete 5 honor 7 lionize 9 celebrate, entertain
a pep talk: 4 urge 6 charge, exhort 9 encourage
a piece of one's mind: 5 scold 6 berate 7 lecture 8 admonish
a pink slip: 2 ax 3 axe, can 4 fire, sack 6 lay off
a poor review to: 3 pan
a poser to: 5 throw 6 baffle, puzzle 7 buffalo, mystify, perplex 8 confound
approval: 6 accede
a rain check: 5 defer, delay 6 put off 7 suspend 8 postpone
a reading: 6 recite, render 7 narrate 9 dramatize, interpret
a reason for: 4 show 6 defend 7 clarify, clear up, explain, justify 8 spell out 9 expound on, make clear
a recital: 4 play, sing 5 dance 7 perform
as an example: 4 cite
a talk: 5 orate, speak 6 preach 7 address, declaim, deliver, expound, lecture 9 discourse, hold forth
a talking-to: 5 scold 6 berate
a thumbs-up to: 4 laud, rate 7 approve 9 recommend
a tip to: 4 warn 5 alert 6 advise, clue in, fill in, inform 7 apprise, let know 8 acquaint, forewarn
attention: 4 heed 6 listen, regard
a turn: 5 alarm, scare, shake, shock, spook, throw 6 dismay, rattle 7 fluster, startle, unnerve 8 affright, frighten, surprise, unsettle 9 take aback 10 disconcert, intimidate
authority to: 4 name 6 assign, charge, commit, depute, invest, ordain 7 appoint, consign, empower, entrust, intrust, license 8 accredit, delegate, deputize, hand over, relegate, turn over 9 authorize, designate 10 commission
away: 4 blab, leak, sell 5 let on, spill 6 betray, expose, reveal, tattle 7 divulge, sell out, uncover 8 disclose
a wide berth to: 4 shun 5 avoid, elude, evade, scorn, skirt 6 eschew 8 flee from, sidestep 10 circumvent, recoil from, shrink from
back: 5 repay 6 refund, return 7 reflect, replace, restore
birth to: 4 bear, have 5 begin, breed, spawn 6 create, parent 7 deliver 8 engender, generate, initiate 9 originate 10 bring forth
confidence to: 6 affirm, assure 7 hearten
consent: 2 OK 3 let 4 okay 5 agree, allow, grant, yield 6 accede, accord, assent, cave in, comply, concur, permit 7 concede 9 acquiesce, cooperate 10 come around
cover: 6 shield
credence to: 7 believe
don't ~ up: 4 keep, save 5 amass, cache, hoard, stock 6 insist, retain 8 withhold 10 accumulate
ear to: 4 care, hear, heed, mind, obey 6 attend, follow, listen, notice 7 abide by, observe 8 consider 10 bear in mind, be guided by, take care of, toe the line
emphasis: 6 accent, play up, stress 7 bracket, feature, point up 9 highlight, italicize, punctuate, reinforce, underline 10 accentuate, underscore
ender: 4 away, back
evidence: 5 swear 6 attest 7 testify, witness
expression to: 4 vent 5 voice
feedback: 5 react, reply 6 answer 7 respond 9 get back to
forth: 3 say 4 emit, shed 5 exude 7 deliver, reflect
ground: 6 retire 7 retreat 8 withdraw
grounds for: 5 prove 7 justify, testify, warrant
guns to: 7 fortify
heed to: 4 mind 6 harken, listen
in: 3 bow 4 melt 5 yield 6 accede, assent, comply, relent, submit 7 consent, succumb 9 acquiesce, lighten up, surrender 10 capitulate
incentive: 4 fire, goad, move, prod, spur, urge, whet 5 goose, impel, prime, rouse, spark, tempt 6 arouse, bestir, excite, induce, prompt, propel, stir up 7 inspire, quicken 8 energize, motivate, persuade 9 galvanize, stimulate
in return: 3 pay 6 avenge, reward 7 get even, requite 9 retaliate
insight to: 5 edify 7 clarify 8 instruct 9 elucidate
in to: 5 humor, spoil 6 coddle, cosset, dote on, pamper, pander 7 gratify, indulge
it a whirl: 3 try 4 test 7 attempt
it to: 4 beat, whip 5 pound
joy to: 5 elate
just deserts: 5 spite 6 avenge 7 get even, hit back, pay back, requite 9 get back at, stick it to
leave: 2 OK 3 let 4 okay 5 allow, grant 6 accede, free up, permit 7 approve, concede, endorse, license 8 sanction 9 authorize 10 say the word
lessons to: 5 edify, teach, train 8 instruct
life to: 4 form, sire 5 beget, breed, build, erect, forge, found, hatch, model, shape, spawn, start 6 author, create, design, devise, effect, father 7 compose, develop, dream up, fashion, imagine, produce, think up 8 conceive, engender, engineer, generate, occasion, organize 9 actualize, construct, establish, institute, originate 10 mastermind

lip to: 4 sass 8 get smart, mouth off, talk back 10 answer back
little: 4 save 5 skimp 6 scrape, scrimp, slight 8 conserve, roll back, withhold 9 economize 10 cut corners
money for: 3 buy
no choice: 5 force 6 coerce, compel
no ground: 5 force, order, press 6 demand, insist 8 pressure 9 stand firm
not about to ~: 4 firm 5 rigid, solid, tight, tough 6 flinty, secure, stable, steely, sturdy 7 adamant, diehard, staunch 8 hard-line, hellbent, resolute, stubborn 9 obstinate, steadfast, unbending 10 determined, inflexible, unshakable, unswerving, unwavering, unyielding
notice: 4 quit, warn 5 leave 6 resign
not ~ the time of day: 3 cut 4 shun, snub 5 spurn 6 ignore, rebuff, slight 8 brush off
odds: 3 fix, lay 6 gamble 8 make book 9 speculate
off: 4 beam, emit, send, spew, spue 5 eject, expel, exude, issue, yield 6 evolve, exhale 7 cast out, diffuse, emanate, radiate, release, secrete 9 discharge, send forth
off an odor: 4 reek 5 smell, stink
off light: 4 glow 5 gleam, shine
on: 4 face 5 front 8 overlook
one's blessing: 5 agree 6 concur, permit 7 approve, consent 9 acquiesce 10 condescend
one's consent: 2 OK 4 okay, okeh, okey
one's feet a rest: 5 relax
one's stamp of approval: 2 OK 4 okay, pass 5 bless 6 ratify 7 certify, confirm, consent, endorse, license 8 sanction, validate 9 authorize, sign off on
one's word: 3 vow 4 aver 5 swear 6 assure, attest 7 promise
orders: 4 boss, head, lead, rule, tell 5 steer 6 advise, charge, enjoin, govern, manage 7 command, dictate, oversee, preside 8 dominate 9 officiate, prescribe, supervise 10 administer, mastermind, ride herd on, run the show
or take: 6 nearly 7 roughly 9 virtually
out: 4 deal, dole, emit, mete, tell, tire, wilt 5 allot, grant, issue, share 6 assign, ration, reveal 7 radiate, release 8 dispense, proclaim 9 apportion
over: 4 quit 5 yield 7 forfeit 8 dedicate, leave off
partner: 4 take
pause: 3 cow 4 faze 5 alarm, daunt, deter, shake 6 bemuse, dismay 7 overawe, unnerve 8 bewilder, dispirit, frighten 10 demoralize, discourage, dishearten, intimidate
permission: 3 let 5 allow, grant 6 accede, enable, permit 7 approve, certify, endorse, license 8 sanction 9 authorize
pleasure to: 5 amuse, elate 7 gratify
power to: 6 enable 7 entitle, license 9 authorize
prominence: 6 play up 7 feature 9 publicize, spotlight
proof: 4 aver 5 prove, swear 6 assure, attest, depone, verify 7 bear out, certify, confirm, declare, stand by, testify, warrant, witness 8 vouch for
quarter: 4 pity 5 spare 6 relent
quarters to: 4 rent 5 board, house, lodge, put up 6 billet, harbor, take in 7 shelter 9 entertain
refuge: 4 hide, save 6 foster, harbor, rescue, shield 7 protect, shelter 8 insulate 9 look after, safeguard
rise to: 5 beget, breed, cause, spawn 6 effect, induce, prompt 7 inspire, produce, trigger 8 engender, generate, occasion 10 bring about
shape: 4 cast, form, mold 5 forge, model 6 design, sculpt 7 fashion, whittle
shelter: 4 hide 5 house 6 harbor, shield 7 conceal, protect
slack: 6 relent
stars to: 4 rate 6 size up 8 classify, evaluate
support: 4 abet 5 endow 6 assist
testimony: 5 swear, vouch 6 assert, depone, depose 7 certify, declare, warrant, witness
thanks: 5 bless 6 praise 10 appreciate
the boot to: 2 ax 3 axe, can 4 fire, oust, sack 6 depose 7 dismiss
the brush: 4 snub 6 slight
the bum's rush to: 4 boot 6 bounce 7 boot out, cast out, kick out, turn out 8 throw out 9 chase away
the business to: 3 bug, nag, rag 4 haze, ride 5 harry, hound 6 badger, harass, hassle, heckle, needle, plague 8 browbeat
the cold shoulder: 4 snub 5 spurn 6 ignore, rebuff, slight
the evil eye: 5 scowl
the eye: 4 leer
the eye to: 4 ogle 5 stare
the gate: 4 oust 5 spurn
the go-ahead: 2 OK 4 okay 5 agree, allow 6 accede, enable 7 approve, endorse, indorse
the high sign: 3 tip 4 warn 5 alert 6 advise, signal, tip off 7 caution 8 forewarn
the impression: 4 look, seem 5 imply, sound 6 appear 7 suggest 8 intimate, resemble 9 insinuate, sound like 10 appear to be
the lie to: 4 deny 5 rebut 6 differ, impugn, negate, refute 7 confute, counter, dispute, gainsay 8 disprove 9 overthrow
the low-down: 3 cue, tip 4 leak, talk, tell, warn 5 brief, spill, steer 6 advise, impart, let out, reveal, tip off 7 caution, confide, divulge, lay bare 8 disclose
the meaning of: 6 define 7 explain 8 spell out 9 interpret
the nod: 4 okay 5 admit, adopt, allow, go for 6 accept, assent, comply, concur 7 consent, include, sign off, welcome 8 sanction, stand for 9 recognize
the once-over: 3 eye 4 ogle, peek, scan, skim 6 survey 7 inspect 8 check out
the raspberry: 3 boo 4 hiss, hoot, jeer, mock 5 fleer, taunt 6 deride, heckle 7 catcall 9 make fun of
the runaround: 5 stimy, stymy 6 stymie
the rundown: 5 brief 6 fill in, inform, report, update 7 apprise
the show away: 4 blab, leak, talk 5 spill 6 tattle
the slip: 4 foil, lose 5 avoid, dodge, elude, evade, leave 8 shake off, throw off
the third degree: 4 pump, quiz 5 grill 8 question
the word: 6 advise
the wrong idea: 4 dupe, fool, gull, hoax, scam, snow 5 bluff, cheat, put on, shaft, trick 6 delude, lead on, rope in, suck in, take in 7 confuse, deceive, defraud, mislead 8 hoodwink, inveigle, misguide, throw off 9 disinform, misinform 10 lead astray
thumbs-down: 3 nix, pan 4 rate, veto 6 refuse, refute, reject
thumbs-up: 2 OK 4 okay 6 accept 7 approve
too much: 4 cloy, glut, sate 5 gorge 7 surfeit
twenty lashes: 4 cane, drub, flog, whip 5 flail 6 larrup 7 scourge
unwanted advice: 6 kibitz, meddle
up: 4 bail, cede, drop, dump, fall, kick, lose, name, quit, sell, shed, stop 5 cease, chuck, ditch, forgo, spare, waive, yield 6 comply, eschew, fess up, forego, lay off, relent, resign, vacate 7 abandon, bail out, concede, discard, forfeit, forsake, lay down, let go of, refrain, sell out 8 abdicate, forswear, get rid of, hand over, jettison, leave off, part with, renounce, say uncle, sign away, squeal on, throw out 9 cast aside, dispose of, foreswear, lose heart, sacrifice, surrender, throw away 10 capitulate, relinquish
up hope: 7 despair 9 lose heart
up on: 4 drop, quit 5 ditch 7 abandon, discard, forsake, scuttle 8 write off 9 back out of, pull out of
voice to: 3 air 4 talk, vent 5 speak, utter 7 pour out
walking papers: 3 axe, can 4 fire
way: 3 sag 4 fall, move, snap 5 budge, burst, defer, split, yield 6 buckle, cave in, relent, retire, tumble, weaken 7 crumble, crumple, succumb 8 collapse, fall down, withdraw 9 lighten up 10 come undone
what for: 3 rag 4 flay, rail, ream 5 abuse, baste, chide, scold 6 assail, berate, jump on, preach, rail at, rebuke, vilify 7 bawl out, censure, chasten, chew out, lecture, reprove, tell off, upbraid 8 admonish, chastise, denounce, lace into, lambaste, reproach, sail into, tear into 9 castigate, criticize, dress down, excoriate, fulminate, light into, reprehend, reprimand 10 denunciate, tongue-lash, vituperate
words to: 3 say 4 tell 5 speak, utter, voice 6 assert 7 express 8 proclaim 9 enunciate, verbalize 10 articulate
work to: 4 hire 6 employ, engage, sign on, take on
wrong information: 3 lie 7 cover up, deceive, mislead 8 misguide, misstate 9 misdirect, misinform 10 lead astray, steer wrong

give __: 3 off, out, way 4 a rap, away, back, it to, over 5 a damn, a darn, a hang, a hoot, an ear, chase, it a go 6 ground
give __ berth to: 5 a wide
give __ for: 4 it up
give __ for one's money: 4 a run
give __ go: 3 it a
give __ of confidence: 5 a vote
give __ rein to: 4 free, full
give __ shot: 3 it a
give __ time: 5 a hard
give __ to: 4 rise, vent 5 a hand, birth
give __ to Cerberus: 4 a sop
give __ try: 3 it a
give __ up: 4 a leg
give __ whirl: 3 it a
Give __ a Chance: 5 Peace
Give __ break!: 3 me a, us a
Give __ day...: 6 us this
Give __. Don't pollute: 5 a hoot
Give __ rest!: 3 it a
Give __ Sailor: 3 Me a
Give __ Simple Life: 5 Me the
give a __: 4 darn, hang, hoot 5 leg up
give a __ berth to: 4 wide
give a __ up: 3 leg
Give a __ Horse He Can Ride: 4 Man a
Give all thou __: 5 canst
give an __: 3 ear
give and __: 4 take
give-and-take: 6 banter 10 reciprocal
Give a Rouse
author: Robert Browning
giveaway: 4 gift, sign, slip 7 freebee, freebie, premium 8 betrayal 10 disclosure
AAA ~: 7 road map
give a wide __ to: 5 berth
giveback: 6 refund 10 concession
Give 'Em Hell, Harry! (1975 film)
cast: James Whitmore
give free __ to: 4 rein
give full __ to: 4 rein
Give it __!: 3 a go 4 a try 5 a rest, a shot 6 a whirl

Give me __!: 4 five
Give me __ ship...: 5 a tall
Give Me Love (1973 song)
artist: George Harrison
Give Me One Reason (1996 song)
artist: Tracy Chapman
Give Me the Night (1980 song)
artist: George Benson
Give me your __...: 5 tired
Give My Regards to Broadway
composer: George M. Cohan
given: 3 apt, set 4 fact 5 axiom, fixed 6 liable, stated 7 assumed, nominal, premise, settled 9 axiomatic, postulate, specified 10 agreed upon, understood
be ~: 7 receive
that: 2 if 8 assuming, provided 9 providing, subject to, supposing 10 in the event
(to): 6 liable, likely 10 accustomed
to (suffix): 3 -ose
given __: 4 name
__-given: 3 God
Givens, Robi: 7 actress
Givens, Robin
spouse: Mike Tyson
__ Given Sunday: 3 Any
give one's __: 3 all
give or take: 5 about
Give Peace a Chance (1969 song)
artist: John Lennon
giver: 5 donor 6 backer 7 donator, grantor 9 supporter 10 benefactor
no ~: 5 miser
verdict ~: 4 jury 5 panel, peers 8 tribunal 9 veniremen
Giverny
artist: Claude Monet
giver opposite: 5 taker
__ gives?: 4 What
...gives us __ the right: 5 to see
give the __: 3 axe, eye 4 gate, slip 5 lie to, shake
give the __ his due: 5 devil
give the __ to: 3 lie 4 slip
give-up: 6 refund
__ Give Up the Ship: 4 Don't
giving: 4 good, kind 7 largess, liberal, plastic 8 generous, gracious, largesse 9 unselfish 10 charitable, free-handed, humanistic, munificent, openhanded, ungrudging
one: 5 donor
starter: 3 mis
__-giving: 4 life
Giving Him Something He Can Feel (1992 song)
artist: En Vogue
Giving You the Best That I Got (1988 song)
artist: Anita Baker
Giza: 4 city, town
locale: 5 Egypt
river: 4 Nile
gizmo: 4 tool 5 dodad, thing 6 device, doodad, gadget, thingy, whosis, widget 7 gimmick, machine, novelty, whatsis 9 apparatus, doohickey, invention 10 instrument
gizzard: 3 maw 4 craw 5 belly, organ 6 gullet 7 stomach
Gjellerup, Karl: 4 poet 6 Danish, writer 8 Nobelist
Gjetost: 6 cheese
Gk.
see Greek
G.K.: 10 Chesterton
glabella: 4 bone
locale: 4 face
glabrous: 4 bald 5 naked, shorn, stark 6 shaven 8 hairless
glacé: 4 iced 6 frozen, glazed 7 candied 8 lustrous, slippery
__ glacés: 7 marrons
glacial: 3 icy, raw 4 cold, cool, mean, slow 5 aloof, chill, gelid, nasty, nippy, polar, surly 6 arctic, biting, bitter, chilly, frigid, frosty, frozen, ornery, remote, wintry 7 hateful, hostile, ice-cold, wintery 8 contrary, freezing, inimical, piercing, spiteful 9 bellicose, malicious, withdrawn 10 malevolent, pugnacious, unagitated, unfriendly
glaciate: 3 ice 6 freeze
glacier: 3 ice
Alaskan ~: 4 Muir
basin: 3 cwm
era: 6 ice age
field: 4 firn, névé
fracture: 4 gulf, rift 5 abyss, chasm 7 crevice
hill: 4 paha
ice pinnacle: 5 serac
in a ~'s path: 5 stoss
marking: 5 stria
mass: 4 berg 7 iceberg
polar ~: 6 icecap
ridge: 4 kame 5 arête, esker, serac 7 moraine
ridges: 4 osar
Glacier: 4 park
locale: 7 Montana
Glacier Bay: 4 park
locale: 6 Alaska
sight: 4 berg
glacis: 4 bank, hill, rise 5 grade 6 ascent 7 hillock, incline, upgrade 8 gradient, hillside 9 acclivity, elevation
glad: 5 happy, merry, plant, ready 6 blithe, cheery, elated, flower, jovial, joyful, joyous, upbeat 7 content, crowing, gleeful, pleased, radiant, tickled 8 blissful, cheerful, ecstatic, euphoric, exultant, jubilant, mirthful, thrilled 9 delighted, gratified, lightsome, overjoyed, rejoicing 10 flying high, rollicking
be ~: 5 enjoy, exult 7 delight, rejoice 9 celebrate
ender: 4 some
I'm ~ that's over: 4 whew
make ~: 5 cheer, elate, liven 6 lift up, please, thrill 7 content, delight, gratify, hearten, lighten, overjoy, satisfy 9 enrapture 10 exhilarate, intoxicate
rags: 4 garb, togs 5 array 6 finery 9 caparison
glad __: 3 eye 4 hand, rags
Glad: 4 wrap
alternative: 5 Hefty, Saran 6 Ziploc 8 Reynolds
Glad All Over (1964 song)
artist: Dave Clark Five
gladden: 5 cheer, elate, liven 6 divert, please, thrill, turn on 7 cheer up, console, delight, enliven, gratify, happify, hearten, lighten, satisfy 8 brighten, enspirit, inspirit 9 encourage 10 exhilarate
gladdened: 4 rapt 5 happy 6 joyous 7 charmed, gleeful, radiant 8 blissful, ecstatic, exultant, jubilant 9 delighted, delirious, enchanted, entranced, fulfilled, gratified, overjoyed, rhapsodic 10 captivated
glade: 5 space 8 clearing
Glade
alternative: 6 Wizard 7 Airwick, Renuzit 8 Stick-Ups
glades starter: 4 ever
gladiator: 3 pug 5 boxer 7 fighter, warrior 8 pugilist 9 combatant
item: 3 net 5 sword 6 shield
venue: 4 Rome 5 arena
see also Latin
Gladiator (2000 film)
cast: Russell Crowe, Joaquin Phoenix, Oliver Reed
director: Ridley Scott
setting: 4 Rome 5 arena
gladiatorial: 7 warlike 8 militant
Gladiator, The
composer: John Philip Sousa
gladiolus: 4 irid 5 plant 6 flower
base: 4 corm
Gladkov, Fyodor: 6 writer 7 Russian
gladly: 4 fain, lief 5 gaily, lieve 6 freely, warmly 7 happily, readily 8 cheerily, heartily, joyfully, joyously 9 precisely 10 cheerfully, with relish
see also of course
gladness: 3 joy 4 glee 5 bliss, cheer, mirth 6 gaiety, gayety 7 rapture 8 pleasure 9 happiness, jocundity, lightness 10 risibility
gladsome: 5 happy 6 blithe 8 cheering, pleasant, pleasing 10 flying high
Gladstone: 4 city, town 7 William
Disraeli, to ~: 5 rival
locale: 8 Missouri
prep school: 4 Eton
Gladstone __: 3 bag
__ glad to see you!: 3 Am I
Gladys: 6 Cooper, George, Knight
glair: 8 egg white
surroundings: 4 yolk
glairy: 7 viscose, viscous
glam: 5 glitz 8 alluring 10 enchanting
Glamis title: 5 thane, thegn
glamor
see glamour
glamorize: 4 deck 5 adorn, array 6 bedeck 7 dress up, enhance, flatter 8 beautify, prettify 9 embellish, smarten up
glamorous: 4 foxy, sexy 5 kicky, swank 6 classy, exotic, flashy, lovely, swanky 7 elegant 8 alluring, charming, dazzling, exciting, magnetic, romantic 10 attractive, bewitching, enchanting, entrancing, flamboyant, glittering, magnetical
in London: 5 dishy
not ~: 5 plain, stark
woman: 3 fox 5 siren 9 temptress
Glamorous Life, The (1984 song)
artist: Sheila E.
glamour: 5 charm, flair, glitz, spell, style 6 allure, appeal, beauty 7 charism, glitter, romance 8 charisma, mystique 9 good looks, magnetism 10 attraction, loveliness
glamour __: 3 boy 4 girl, puss
Glamour: 3 mag 8 magazine
founder: Condé Nast
rival: 4 Elle 5 Vogue
glance: 4 gaze, leaf, lick, look, peek, peep, skip, view 5 carom, flash, gleam, glint, graze, sight, sweep 6 aperçu, bounce, careen, carrom, gander, look-in, regard, squint 7 deflect, glimmer, glimpse, glisten, look-see, rebound, shimmer, sparkle, twinkle 8 ricochet 10 reflection, sneak a look
at: 3 eye 4 skim 5 watch 6 advert, browse 10 get a load of
at a ~: 6 easily 7 quickly 9 right away 10 apparently
off: 5 graze, parry 6 bounce, divert 7 deflect 8 ricochet
over: 4 scan, skim 6 peruse
quick ~: 4 peep 6 gander 7 glimpse, look-see
(through): 5 thumb
__ glance: 3 at a
gland: 5 liver 6 spleen, thymus 7 adrenal, thyroid 8 pancreas, salivary 9 endocrine, pituitary
combining form: 4 aden- 5 adeno-
ending: 4 ular
sac: 6 acinus
sweat ~: 4 pore 6 outlet 7 opening, orifice
__ gland: 4 salt, silk 5 lymph, preen, renal, scent, sweat 6 pineal, thymus 7 adrenal, carotid, Cowper's, parotid, thyroid
glare: 5 blaze, frown, light, lower, scowl, shine, stare 6 dazzle, glower, goggle 7 evil eye, glisten, glitter 8 radiance, radiancy 9 dirty look 10 brilliance, garishness, incandesce
protector: 5 visor, vizor
glaring: 4 open, rank 5 gaudy, gross, lurid, overt, showy, stark, utter, vivid 6 arrant, astare, brazen, crying, flashy, garish, patent, strong 7 blatant, blazing, evident, extreme, obvious, visible 8 apparent, blinding, flagrant, grievous, manifest, shocking, unsubtle 9 audacious, barefaced, egregious, excessive, nefarious, obtrusive, prominent 10 noticeable, outrageous
Glasgow: 4 city, port, town 5 Ellen
locale: 8 Scotland
river: 5 Clyde
Glasgow, Ellen: 6 writer
glasnost initials: 4 USSR
Glaspell, Susan: 6 writer
work: Alison's House
glass: 3 cup 4 lens, pane 5 drink 6 beaker, bottle, goblet, jigger, mirror 7 crystal, snifter, trinket, tumbler 9 reflector
champagne ~: 5 flute
combining form: 4 hyal-, vitr- 5 hyalo-, vitri-, vitro-
container: 3 jar 4 pony, tube, vial 5 ampul, cruet, flask, phial, pipet 6 ampule, beaker, bottle, goblet, jigger 7 ampoule, pipette, snifter, tumbler 8 test tube

create ~: **4** blow
eel: **5** elver
ender: **3** ine **4** fish, ware, work, wort **5** maker **6** making
fitted with ~: **5** paned
fragment: **5** shard, sherd **6** cullet
imperfection: **5** stria
looking ~: **6** mirror
made of ~: **6** hyalin **7** hyaline
optical ~: **4** lens **5** loupe **6** ocular **7** monocle **8** eyepiece **9** magnifier
oven: **4** lehr
partly fused ~: **4** frit **5** fritt
sound: **4** ting
source: **4** sand
starter: **3** eye, spy **4** hour, wine **5** fiber **7** weather
test-tube ~: **5** Pyrex
treat ~: **6** anneal, temper **7** toughen
volcanic ~: **8** obsidian
window ~: **4** pane **5** sheet
glass __: **3** eel, jaw **6** blower **7** ceiling
glass-__: **5** faced
__ glass: **3** art, cut **4** lead, milk, opal, shot, spun **5** opera, plate, sheet **6** safety, tinted **7** looking, stained, Steuben, Tiffany
Glass: **3** Ira, Ron **6** Carter, Philip
Glass __: **4** Bell **5** Tiger
Glass __, The: **3** Key, Web **4** Harp, Lake **5** House, Onion
Glass Bead Game, The
author: Hermann Hesse
Glass Bell
author: Anaïs Nin
Glass Bottom Boat, The (1966 film)
cast: Doris Day, Arthur Godfrey, Rod Taylor
dog: **8** Vladimir
glass cleaner: **6** Windex
glassed-in: **5** paned
glasses: **4** spex **5** specs **6** frames, shades **7** goggles **8** bifocals, cheaters, contacts, horn rims, pince-nez, stemware **9** lorgnette, tableware, trifocals **10** spectacles
alternative: **5** Lasik
big name in ~: **4** Lomb **6** Bausch, Pearle
hoist ~: **5** drink, honor, toast **6** pledge
rose-colored ~: **4** hope **8** idealism, optimism **10** positivism
starter: **3** eye, sun
__ glasses: **4** nose **5** field, opera **6** granny **7** aviator, reading
Glass House, The (2001 film)
cast: Bruce Dern, Diane Lane, Leelee Sobieski
Glass Key, The: **5** novel
author: Dashiell Hammett
character: **3** Ned **4** Farr, Opal, Shad **5** O'Rory **6** Madvig
Glass Lake, The
author: Maeve Binchy
glassmaking: **5** craft
material: **4** sand **5** borax, ceria, silex
rod: **5** punty **6** pontil
Glass Menagerie, The: **4** play
author: Tennessee Williams
character: **3** Tom **5** Laura **6** Amanda **9** Wingfield
Glass of Blessings
author: Barbara Pym
Glass Plus
alternative: **6** Windex
glassy: **3** icy **4** cold, dull, void **5** blank, clear, dazed, empty, fixed, lucid, shiny, sleek, slick **6** hyalin, smooth, vacant, vitric **7** crystal, hyaline **8** lifeless, lustrous, polished, slippery, vitreous **9** burnished, lubricous **10** mirrorlike, poker-faced, reflective
it may be ~: **5** stare
glassy-eyed: **4** dull **6** vacant, wooden **8** lifeless
Glassy Sea, The
author: Marian Engel
Glaswegian: **4** Scot
glatt __: **6** kosher
Glavine, Tom: **6** hurler **7** pitcher
glaze: **4** coat **5** color, cover, gloss, icing, sheen, shine, sirup, syrup **6** enamel, finish, luster, patina, patine, polish, smooth **7** burnish, coating, encrust, furbish, incrust, lacquer, overlay, varnish **8** covering, frosting **9** sugarcoat
base: **4** frit **5** fritt
glazed: **3** icy **5** glacé, slick **6** glossy, smooth **8** lustrous, slippery
fabric: **4** cire **5** tammy **6** chintz, tammie
food: **5** donut **8** doughnut
glazier need: **4** pane **5** putty
Glazunov: **9** Aleksandr, Alexander
Glazunov, Alexander ballet: Raymonda
gleam: **3** ray **4** beam, glow, wink **5** flare, flash, glint, gloss, light, sheen, shine, spark **6** glance, luster **7** flicker, glimmer, glisten, glitter, lighten, radiate, shimmer, sparkle, twinkle **8** radiance, radiancy **9** coruscate, irradiate, luminesce, scintilla **10** brightness, brilliance, effulgence, incandesce, luminosity
gleaming: **3** lit **5** aglow, lucid, shiny **6** ablaze, ashine, bright, flashy, glossy **7** fulgent, lambent, radiant **8** luminous, lustrous, spotless **9** brilliant, refulgent
glean: **3** get **4** cull, pick, reap, sift **5** amass, infer, learn **6** deduce, derive, garner, gather, obtain, pick up, select, winnow **7** collect, excerpt, extract, find out, harvest, pick out, salvage **8** conclude, discover, scrape up **9** ascertain, get to know **10** accumulate
gleaning: **4** crop
Gleason: **5** James **6** Jackie
Gleason, Jackie: **5** actor **8** comedian
character: Ralph Kramden
costar: **4** Kean **6** Carney, MacRae **7** Meadows **8** Randolph
film: Gigot (1962)
The Hustler (1961)
Nothing in Common (1986)
Requiem for a Heavyweight (1962)
Smokey and the Bandit (1977)
Soldier in the Rain (1963)
TV: The Honeymooners, The Life of Riley
glee: **3** joy **4** song **5** cheer, mirth **6** gaiety, gayety **7** delight, elation, gayness, jollity **8** euphoria, felicity, gladness, hilarity, laughter, pleasure **9** frivolity, happiness, jocundity, joviality, lightness, merriment **10** exuberance, exultation, joyfulness, joyousness, jubilation, liveliness, risibility
cry of ~: **3** hah, yay **4** I win, whee **5** whoop **6** gotcha
fill with ~: **5** elate
for ~ clubs: **5** lyric **6** choral
name meaning ~: **4** Hoyt
show ~: **4** beam, grin **5** smile **7** sparkle
with ~: **5** gaily, gayly
glee club: **6** chorus **7** singers **8** ensemble **9** vocalists
member: **4** alto, bass **5** tenor **7** soprano **8** baritone
gleeful: **3** gay **4** boon, glad **5** happy, jolly, merry, riant **6** blithe, cheery, elated, jocund, jovial, joyful, joyous, upbeat **7** exalted, festive, jocular, pleased, tickled **8** blissful, cheerful, ecstatic, euphoric, exultant, giggling, grooving, jubilant, laughing, mirthful, thrilled **9** delighted, gladdened, lightsome, overjoyed, rejoicing **10** flying high, frolicsome, triumphant
gleek: **4** game **8** card game
Gleem: **10** toothpaste
alternative: *see* toothpaste
glen: **4** dale, dell, vale **5** combe, coomb, gorge **6** coombe, dingle, valley
Glen: **4** John **8** Campbell
plaid: **6** fabric **7** pattern **8** material
Glen __: **5** check, plaid **6** Burnie
__ Glen: **3** Tam **7** Watkins
Glen Burnie: **4** city, town
locale: **8** Maryland
Glen Cove: **4** city, town
locale: **7** New York **10** Long Island
Glenda: **7** Farrell, Jackson
Glendale: **4** city, town
locale: **7** Arizona **10** California
Glendale Heights: **4** city, town
locale: **8** Illinois
Glendora: **4** city, town
locale: **10** California
Glendora (1956 song)
artist: Perry Como
Glen Ellyn: **4** city, town
locale: **8** Illinois
Glengarry: **3** cap, hat
Glengarry Glen Ross: **4** film, play
author: David Mamet
cast: Alan Arkin, Alec Baldwin, Ed Harris, Jack Lemmon, Al Pacino, Kevin Spacey
Glenmont: **4** city, town
locale: **8** Maryland
Glenn: **4** Ford, Frey, John **5** Close, Gould, Scott **6** Miller **7** Corbett, Curtiss, Seaborg **8** Medeiros **9** Yarbrough
Glenne: **6** Headly
Glenn, John: **7** senator **9** astronaut
state: **4** Ohio
Glenn Miller Story, The (1954 film)
cast: June Allyson, James Stewart
Glenview: **4** city, town
locale: **8** Illinois
Gless: **6** Sharon
glib: **3** pat **4** oily **5** slick, suave, vocal **6** artful, facile, fluent, prolix, smooth **7** offhand, verbose, voluble **8** eloquent, slippery **9** garrulous, insincere, rehearsed, talkative **10** articulate, effortless, loquacious, rhetorical
talk: **4** jive
glide: **3** fly, run, ski **4** flit, flow, move, roll, sail, scud, skee, skid, skim, slip, soar, waft **5** coast, drift, float, skate, slide, slink, sneak, steal, sweep, waltz **6** chassé, stream **7** slither **8** levitate, volitate, volplane
ballroom ~: **6** chassé
by: **4** flow, pass **6** elapse, roll on
downward: **5** sweep, swoop
on snow: **3** ski **4** skee
(through): **6** breeze
glide __: **4** path
glider: **4** seat **8** aircraft
locale: **5** lanai, porch **7** veranda **8** verandah
on a ~: **5** aloft
use a ~: **3** fly **4** lift, soar
wood: **5** balsa
__ glider: **4** hang
__ gliding: **4** hang
glim: **4** lamp **5** light **7** lantern
glimmer: **3** ray **4** glow, hint, wink **5** blink, flash, gleam, glint, light, shine, speck, trace **6** glance **7** flicker, glisten, glitter, inkling, shimmer, sparkle, twinkle, vestige **9** coruscate, luminesce, scintilla, suspicion **10** suggestion
glimmer __: **3** ice
glimmering: **4** hint, idea **5** shiny **6** ashine **7** inkling
glimpse: **3** eye, see, spy **4** espy, look, peek, peep, spot, view **5** flash, sight, watch **6** apercu, descry, detect, gander, glance, notice, peek at, peer at, squint, take in **7** discern, look-see, make out **8** check out, discover **10** get a load of, sneak a look
Glinda: **5** witch
Glinka, Mikhail: **7** Russian **8** composer
work: A Life for the Tsar
Russlan and Ludmilla
glint: **3** ray **5** flash, gleam, gloss, light, sheen, shine, spark **6** glance, luster **7** glimmer, glisten, glitter, inkling, shimmer, sparkle, twinkle **9** scintilla
glinty: **8** lustrous **9** sparkling
glissade: **4** slip, step **5** slink **7** slither
Glissant, Édouard: **6** writer **10** Martinican
glisten: **4** glow **5** flash, glare, gleam, glint, shine **6** glance **7** flicker, glimmer, glitter, shimmer, sparkle, twinkle **9** coruscate, luminesce **10** incandesce
glistening: **5** shiny, sleek **6** ashine, glossy **8** lustrous, slippery **9** refulgent
glitch: **3** bug **4** flaw, kink, snag, typo **5** error, hitch, snafu **6** defect, mishap **7** erratum, misfire, problem, setback **9** hindrance **10** deficiency
galley ~: **4** typo **7** erratum **8** misprint
glitter: **3** ray **4** beam, glow, show, wink **5** blink, flash, glare, gleam,

glint, glitz, light, sheen, shine, spark **6** glamor, luster, tinsel **7** flicker, glamour, glimmer, glisten, radiate, shimmer, spangle, sparkle, twinkle **8** radiance, radiancy, splendor **9** coruscate, gaudiness, irradiate, luminesce, pageantry, showiness **10** brightness, brilliance

glitter __: **3** ice
Glitter: **4** Gary
glitterati: **5** elite **6** celebs, jet set
glittering: **5** beady, shiny **6** aglint, bright, flashy, tawdry **7** radiant **8** dazzling, splendid **9** brilliant, glamorous, refulgent
fabric: **4** lamé **8** diamante
glitz: **4** glam **5** shine **6** glamor **7** glamour, glitter, sparkle **9** gaudiness, showiness **10** flashiness
glitzy: **5** fancy, gaudy, showy **6** flashy, frilly, lavish, ornate, tawdry **7** opulent **9** decorated, elaborate, luxurious, sumptuous **10** ornamented
sign: **4** neon
Glo-__: **4** Coat
__-Glo: **3** Day
gloaming: **3** e'en **4** dusk **7** evening **8** twilight **9** nightfall
gloat: **4** brag, crow **5** boast, exult, preen, revel, savor **7** rub it in, swagger, triumph **9** whoop it up
(in): **6** wallow
over: **5** savor **6** relish **9** rejoice in
gloating: **4** smug **5** proud **8** arrogant, puffed-up **10** complacent
glob: **3** wad **4** bead, blob, hunk, lump, mass **5** chunk, clump **6** dollop **8** mountain
ender: **3** ule
global: **4** intl. **5** total, world **7** earthly, general, overall **8** catholic, far-flung, sweeping **9** all around, spherical, universal, worldwide **10** exhaustive
speck: **3** isl. **4** isle **5** islet **6** island
global __: **7** village, warming
Global: **5** mover
rival: **6** Allied, United
Global Positioning __: **6** System
globe: **3** map, orb **4** ball **5** Earth, world **6** planet, sphere
ender: **4** fish, trot **6** flower
Globe: **5** paper **9** newspaper
locale: **6** Boston
Globe and Mail: **5** paper **9** newspaper
locale: **7** Toronto
globefish: **6** puffer
globelike: **5** round **9** spherical
globetrot: **4** roam, tour **5** range **6** travel, wander **7** journey
globetrotter: **5** rover **7** pilgrim, tourist **8** gadabout, traveler, wanderer, wayfarer **9** jet-setter, sightseer
woe: **6** jet lag
__ Globetrotters: **6** Harlem
globetrotting: **6** roving, travel **7** on the go, roaming **8** voyaging **9** on the move, wandering, wayfaring **10** jet-setting, journeying
globular: **5** orbed, round **6** rotund **7** bulbous, orotund, rounded **9** spherical **10** ball-shaped
globule: **4** ball, bead, blob, drop, tear **5** round **6** bubble, sphere **7** dewdrop, driblet **8** spheroid, spherule, teardrop
__ globulin: **4** beta **5** alpha, gamma
glockenspiel: **4** lyra
component: **5** chime
glögg ingredient: **4** wine
glom: **3** eye **4** lift **5** filch, grasp, seize, steal, swipe **6** pilfer
on to: **5** catch, grasp **6** attain
(onto): **4** grab **5** latch
glom __: **4** onto
gloom: **3** woe **4** dark, funk, mirk, murk, pall **5** blues, dolor, grief, night, shade **6** misery, shadow, sorrow **7** anguish, despair, dimness, malaise, sadness **8** darkness, distress, doldrums, glumness, the blues **9** adumbrate, blackness, bleakness, dejection, heartache, murkiness, obscurity, pessimism **10** depression, desolation, dreariness, heavy heart, infelicity, loneliness, melancholy, somberness, woefulness
partner: **4** doom
gloominess: **3** woe **5** shade **7** dim view, sadness **8** glumness **9** pessimism **10** depression, desolation, heavy heart, loneliness, woefulness
__ gloom of night...: **3** nor
gloomy: **3** bad, dim, dun, low, sad **4** blue, dark, dour, down, glum, gray, grey, grim, lour, ugly **5** black, bleak, drear, dusky, grave, heavy, leady, livid, loury, mirky, moody, murky, sorry, sulky, surly, unlit, woful **6** broody, cloudy, crabby, dismal, dreary, leaden, lowery, moping, mopish, morbid, morose, somber, sullen, woeful **7** doleful, forlorn, hangdog, in a funk, joyless, obscure, ominous, shadowy, unhappy, way down **8** darkened, dejected, desolate, downbeat, downcast, hopeless, liverish, lonesome, lowering, negative, overcast, troubled, wretched **9** bummed out, cheerless, depressed, heartsick, lightless, mirthless, miserable, saddening, saturnine, sorrowful, tenebrous, unhopeful, unlighted, woebegone **10** chapfallen, depressing, despondent, dispirited, lugubrious, melancholy, oppressive, out of sorts, tenebrific
atmosphere: **4** pall
be ~: **4** mope
make ~: **6** dampen, darken, deject, sadden, shadow **7** depress, obscure **8** dispirit **9** bring down **10** demoralize, discourage, dishearten
one: **3** Gus **4** mope **5** moper **7** killjoy **9** pessimist, worrywart
Gloomy __: **3** Gus
Gloomy Dean, The: **4** Inge
glop: **3** goo **4** gunk, mess, muck, mush, ooze **5** slime **6** dollop
gloppy: **7** jellied
gloria: **4** halo
Gloria: **4** hymn **5** Henry **6** Bunker, Gaynor, Loring, Stivic, Stuart **7** De Haven, Estefan, Grahame, Steinem, Swanson **10** Vanderbilt
mom: **5** Edith
Gloria (song)
artist: Laura Branigan, Shadows of Knight
Gloria in Excelsis __: **3** Deo
Gloria Patri ending: **4** amen
glorification: **5** honor **6** eulogy **7** hosanna **8** encomium
glorify: **4** hail, laud, sing, tout **5** adore, bless, deify, ensky, exalt, extol, grace, honor **6** admire, extoll, praise, revere, salute **7** acclaim, applaud, commend, elevate, flatter, idolize, lionize, magnify, worship **8** canonize, enthrone, eulogize, inthrone, sanctify, venerate **9** celebrate, recommend **10** aggrandize, compliment, panegyrize
gloriole: **4** aura, halo, ring **5** glory **6** circle, corona, nimbus **7** aureola, aureole **8** radiance, radiancy
gloriosa __: **4** lily
glorious: **4** nice **5** famed, noble, noted, palmy, proud **6** august, famous, golden, heroic **7** eminent, exalted, gallant, honored, radiant, shining **8** gorgeous, heroical, idolized, lustrous, majestic, renowned **9** venerable, well-known **10** celebrated, majestical, triumphant
starter: **4** vain
see also wonderful
glory: **4** fame **5** éclat, exult, honor, kudos, revel, state **6** credit, honors, praise, renown, wallow **7** dignity, laurels, majesty, rapture, rejoice, triumph **8** eminence, gloriole, grandeur, jubilate, nobility, prestige, splendor **9** celebrity, greatness, sublimity **10** exaltation, exultation, importance, reputation
starter: **4** vain
__ glory: **7** morning
Glory (1989 film)
cast: Matthew Broderick, Cary Elwes, Morgan Freeman, Denzel Washington
director: Edward Zwick
Glory __: **4** Days, Road
__ Glory: **3** Old **7** Morning
Glory Days (1985 song)
artist: Bruce Springsteen
Glory of Love (1986 song)
artist: Peter Cetera
Glory of the Yankee Navy, The
composer: John Philip Sousa
Glory Road
author: Bruce Catton
gloss: **3** rub **4** buff, coat, lick, note **5** color, glaze, gleam, glint, input, paint, sheen, shine **6** enamel, finish, luster, makeup, polish, remark, smooth, veneer **7** burnish, comment, explain, lacquer, shimmer, touch up, varnish **8** annotate **9** comment on, elucidate, interpret, silkiness, translate, whitewash **10** annotation, brightness, brilliance
over: **4** coat, omit **5** elide, gloze, mince **7** neglect **8** leave out, palliate, play down, shrug off **9** underplay, whitewash
put a ~ on: **3** rub, wax **4** buff **5** shine **6** polish **7** burnish
__ gloss: **3** lip
glossa: **6** tongue
glossary: **4** list **5** lexis, vocab. **7** lexicon **10** vocabulary
glossy: **5** light, nitid, photo, print, shiny, silky, sleek, slick **6** bright, glazed, satiny, silken, smooth **8** gleaming, lustrous, magazine, polished **9** brilliant, burnished, lubricous **10** glistening, photograph
material: **5** satin **6** enamel, sateen **7** taffeta
not ~: **3** mat **5** matte **10** lusterless
glottal __: **4** stop
glottis starter: **3** epi
Gloucester: **4** city, port, town
cape: **3** Ann
king: **4** Lear
locale: **4** Mass. **6** Canada **7** England, Ontario
Gloucestershire: **6** county
city: **6** Stroud
locale: **7** England
neighbor: **4** Avon
glove: **4** gage, mitt **8** gauntlet
alternative: **4** muff
boxing ~ of ancient Rome: **6** cestus
game: **6** boxing
hand in ~: **4** deep **5** close, solid, thick, tight **6** allied, chummy, united **7** unified **8** friendly, in league **10** buddy-buddy, palsy-walsy
insert: **4** hand
material: **3** kid **5** latex **7** leather
part: **4** palm **5** thumb **6** finger
starter: **3** fox
wearer: **5** boxer **8** pugilist
glove __: **3** box
__ glove: **4** golf **6** boxing, velvet
glove-box item: **3** map **6** deicer **10** flashlight
Glover: **4** John **5** Danny **6** Savion **7** Crispin
Glover, Danny: **5** actor
film: Angels in the Outfield (1994)
Bat*21 (1988)
Bopha! (1993)
The Color Purple (1985)
Grand Canyon (1991)
Lethal Weapon (1987)
Places in the Heart (1984)
Saw (2004)
The Shaggy Dog (2006)
Shooter (2007)
Silverado (1985)
To Sleep With Anger (1990)
__ gloves: **3** kid
glow: **4** aura, burn, tint **5** flame, flush, gleam, light, sheen, shine, spark, sweat **6** luster, redden, thrill **7** glimmer, glisten, glitter, light up, radiate, shimmer, sparkle, twinkle **8** lambency, perspire, radiance, radiancy **9** freshness, luminesce **10** brightness, brilliance, complexion, effulgence, luminosity, refulgence
ender: **4** worm
enjoy the ~: **4** bask
make ~: **5** shine **6** polish **7** burnish, cheer up, light up **8** brighten, illumine **10** illuminate
starter: **3** air **5** after, night **7** counter
Glow-__: **4** Worm
glower: **4** look, pout, sulk **5** frown, glare, scowl, stare

glowing: **3** lit, red **4** avid, keen, rosy, warm **5** eager, fresh, happy, light, lit up, ruddy, shiny, sunny, vivid **6** ablaze, ardent, ashine, bright, fervid, flashy, sweaty **7** fervent, fulgent, lambent, radiant, vibrant, zealous **8** blooming, ecstatic, luminous, lustrous, sanguine, splendid **9** adulatory, brilliant, laudatory, refulgent, rhapsodic **10** flickering, flying high, passionate
  bit: **5** ember, spark
glowworm: **3** bug **6** insect
gloxinia: **5** plant **6** flower
gloze: **7** justify **8** minimize, palliate **9** extenuate, gloss over, underplay
Gluck: **4** Alma **6** Louise **9** Christoph
Glück: **6** Louise
Gluck, Alma: **7** soprano
  spouse: Efrem Zimbalist
Gluck, Christoph ballet: Don Juan
glucose: **5** sugar
  to lactose: **6** isomer
glue: **3** fix, gum **4** bond, join, tack **5** affix, epoxy, paste, resin, stick **6** adhere, attach, cement, cohere, Elmer's, fasten **7** stickum **8** adhesive, fixative, mucilage
glue __: **3** gun
glued: **4** fast **8** watchful **9** attentive
gluey: **5** gummy, pasty, tacky **6** clayey, sticky, viscid **7** clayish, viscose, viscous **8** adhesive, cohesive **9** glutinous
glum
  not ~: *see* cheerful
  see also gloomy
Glumdalclitch: **5** giant
glumness: **3** woe **5** blues, dumps, gloom, mopes **7** despair, sadness **8** cynicism, doldrums **9** dejection, moodiness, pessimism **10** depression, gloominess, heavy heart, low spirits, melancholy
glut: **4** cloy, cram, load, sate **5** flood, gorge, stuff, weary **6** excess **7** congest, engorge, nimiety, satiate, satiety, satisfy, surfeit, surplus **8** inundate, overfeed, overfill, overload, plethora, saturate **9** overstock, plenitude, profusion, repletion **10** gormandize, inundation, oversupply, saturation
gluten source: **4** corn **5** grain, wheat
glutinous: **4** ropy **5** gluey, gummy, ropey, slimy **6** sticky, viscid **7** viscose, viscous **10** gelatinous
glutted: **3** fed **4** full **5** blasé, sated **7** replete **8** satiated
glutton: **3** hog, pig **5** eater **6** gorger **7** gobbler **8** gourmand **9** overeater
  delight: **5** feast **6** buffet
gluttonize: **5** gorge **10** gormandize
gluttonous: **5** piggy **6** greedy, piggie **7** gorging, hoggish, lustful, piggish, starved **8** covetous, edacious, ravenous **9** epicurean, insatiate, rapacious, voracious **10** insatiable, omnivorous, quenchless
gluttony: **3** sin **7** edacity, license **8** voracity
glyceride: **5** ester, olein **6** oleine
glycerin: **5** ester
  starter: **5** nitro
Glyn, Elinor: **6** writer **7** British
Glynis: **5** Johns
Glynn: **6** Turman
Glynnis: **7** O'Connor
glyph: **10** pictograph
  prefix for ~: **5** petro
gm.: **2** wt. **4** meas.
GM: **4** boss **8** carmaker **9** automaker
  former ~ rival: **3** AMC
  home: **4** Mich.
  part: **3** gen., mgr. **6** Motors **7** General
  workers' org.: **3** UAW
  see also General Motors
GMA
  rival: **5** Today
G-man: **3** agt., fed **4** narc, nark **5** agent **8** FBI agent
GMAT: **4** exam, test
GMC: **3** van **5** truck
  model: **5** Jimmy, Yukon **6** Denali, Safari, Savana **7** Vandura **8** Suburban **9** Starcraft
gnar
  see gnarl
gnarl: **4** bump, knot, knur, lump, spur **5** growl, snarl, twist **6** deform, knot up **7** contort, distort **8** swelling
gnarled: **5** lumpy, rough **6** knobby **7** knurled
gnarly: **6** knobby **7** twisted
  see also wonderful
gnash: **5** chomp, grate, grind, snarl
gnat: **3** bug, fly **4** pest **5** biter, midge, punky **6** insect, punkie **7** no-see-um
  combining form: **5** culic- **6** culici-
  group: **5** swarm
  like a ~: **5** pesky, pesty **10** bothersome
gnatcatcher: **4** bird
gnaw: **3** eat **4** bite, chew **5** champ, chomp, eat at, munch, tease **6** crunch, nibble **9** eat away at, masticate
  at: **4** bite **5** worry **6** bother, plague **7** corrode
  on: **4** bite **5** eat at **9** masticate
gnawed away: **5** erose
gneiss: **7** mineral
GNMA: **6** lender
  concern: **4** loan **8** mortgage
  part of ~: **3** Gov., Nat. **4** Assn., Govt., Mtge., Natl. **8** Mortgage, National
gnome: **3** elf, fay, saw **4** rule **5** moral, troll **6** byword, dictum, goblin, kobold, midget, sprite **7** gremlin, proverb **8** aphorism, laconism **10** leprechaun
gnomic: **5** terse **9** axiomatic **10** synopsized
G-note: **4** thou
GNP: **4** stat
  part: **3** Nat. **4** Natl., Prod. **5** Gross **7** Product **8** National
  topic: **4** econ. **9** economics
gnu: **6** animal, mammal **8** antelope **10** wildebeest
  milieu: **3** zoo **5** veldt **6** Africa
  relative: *see* antelope
go: **3** fit, fly, hie, pep, try, zip **4** bear, exit, fail, fare, flee, game, gybe, jibe, mesh, move, part, pass, push, quit, shot, snap, stab, take, test, time, turn, work, zest **5** abide, agree, allow, be off, blend, break, brook, crack, drive, fit in, fling, lam it, leave, match, mosey, occur, oomph, reach, refer, scram, split, stand, verve, vigor, whack, whirl, zip by **6** attend, beat it, belong, bug out, decamp, depart, elapse, embark, endure, energy, escape, finish, fold up, get out, happen, move it, pan out, pass by, permit, pop off, push on, repair, run off, set off, set out, spirit, suffer, thrive, travel, vanish **7** abscond, advance, attempt, blend in, carry on, conform, crumble, develop, get away, get lost, head out, hop to it, journey, make off, make out, migrate, move off, move out, operate, perform, persist, potence, potency, proceed, pull out, push off, ride off, run away, skip out, step out, stomach, succeed, take off, turn out, vamoose **8** collapse, continue, dovetail, evacuate, flourish, function, hightail, run along, set forth, shove off, slip away, tick away, tolerate, vitality, vivacity, withdraw **9** animation, consent to, disappear, eventuate, harmonize, move along, put up with, steal away, take a hike, take a turn, transpire **10** assist with, correspond, get a move on, green light, hightail it, hit the road, sally forth, shuffle off, step lively, take flight
  aboard: **4** ship **6** embark **7** emplane, entrain, set sail, ship out **9** leave port
  about: **6** tackle **8** shoulder **9** undertake
  abroad: **4** tour **6** travel **8** sightsee, vacation
  across: **4** ford, span **5** reach **6** bridge **7** connect, stretch **8** pass over, traverse
  adrift: **3** err
  a few rounds: **4** spar **5** fight
  after: **4** seek **5** chase, ensue, set at, trail **6** assail, attack, follow, have at, pursue, rebuke, strive **7** succeed **9** track down
  after game: **4** hunt **5** chase, stalk, track **6** forage
  against: **4** foil **5** flout **6** hinder, offset, oppose, thwart **7** infract, obviate, prevent, redress **9** frustrate **10** contravene, counteract, neutralize
  against the grain: **3** bug, get, irk, try, vex **4** gall, rile **5** annoy, peeve, pique, upset **6** bother, nettle, offend, rankle, ruffle **7** grate on, provoke **8** irritate **9** aggravate **10** exasperate
  ahead: **4** pass **5** begin, start **6** set off, set out, surely **7** advance, lead off, proceed **8** set forth
  ahead of: **4** lead **7** precede, presage **8** antecede **9** introduce
  ahead with: **5** act on **6** follow
  aimlessly: **4** rove
  all out: **3** try **5** speed **6** strain, strive **8** struggle
  allow to ~: **4** free **5** loose **6** acquit, let off, pardon, parole **7** cashier, dismiss, release, set free **8** liberate **9** discharge, exonerate, muster out, terminate
  all systems ~: **5** ready **8** prepared
  all the way: **4** last **6** endure, hold on, linger **7** carry on, survive **8** continue, plug away **9** hang tough, keep going, persevere, stand firm **10** tough it out
  along: **5** agree, say OK **6** accede, assent, behave, comply, concur, say yes **7** approve, consent **8** join with **9** accompany, acquiesce, cooperate, play along **10** assist with
  along with: **4** obey **5** abide, humor, yield **6** accept, relent, second **7** agree to, approve, endorse, indorse, indulge, support **8** overlook, tolerate **9** subscribe
  ape: **4** flip, rage, rant, rave, snap **5** crack, freak **6** lose it **8** freak out
  around: **4** spin, turn, wind **5** orbit, skirt **6** bypass, circle, rotate **7** revolve
  as far as: **5** reach
  ashore: **4** land **6** arrive, debark **9** disembark
  astray: **3** err, sin **4** fail **6** derail, ramble, wander **9** backslide, misbehave
  at: **6** assail, attack
  at it: **4** feud **5** brawl, fight **6** battle, tussle **7** grapple, mix it up, quarrel
  at top speed: **3** run **4** dash, race, rush, tear, whiz **5** scoot **6** gallop, scurry, sprint, streak **7** scamper
  away: **4** exit **5** leave, scram, split **6** beat it, decamp, depart, recede, retire, skidoo, vacate, vanish **7** head out, pull out, skiddoo **8** run along, separate, shove off **10** shuffle off
  away from: **4** drop, quit **5** leave **6** desert **7** abandon, forsake **8** run out on **9** throw over, walk out on
  AWOL: **4** flee **6** desert **7** abscond **9** play hooky
  awry: **3** err **9** break down, fall apart
  back: **3** ebb **4** turn **6** recede, return, revert **7** regress, retreat, revisit **9** retrocede, weasel out
  back and forth: **3** wag **4** jolt, reel, rock, roll, sway, toss, yo-yo **5** hedge, hover, lurch, pitch, shake, shift, swing, waver **6** careen, dither, jiggle, jounce, seesaw, teeter, waffle, wobble **7** vibrate **8** fence-sit, hesitate, straddle **9** alternate, fluctuate, hem and haw, oscillate, pussyfoot, vacillate
  back on: **3** lie **4** deny **5** belie, renig **6** betray, cop out, renege **7** disavow, forsake, retract **9** play false, repudiate **10** break faith
  back on one's word: **5** unsay **6** recant, renege **7** retract **9** weasel out, worm out of
  backwards: **7** reverse **8** flip-flop
  bad: **3** rot **4** turn **5** decay, spoil
  ballistic: **4** flip, rage, rant, snap, vent **5** freak **6** lose it
  bananas: **4** flip, rage, rant, rave, snap **6** lose it
  bankrupt: **4** bust, fail, fold, sink
  before: **7** precede **8** antecede, run ahead

belly-up: 4 fail, fold 6 topple
berserk: 4 flip, rage, riot, snap 5 freak, panic 6 lose it 7 rampage, run wild 8 have a fit
beyond: 3 top 4 pass 5 break 6 exceed, extend 7 overlap, overrun, run over, surpass 8 overstep 9 cut across, transcend
bonkers: 4 flip, rant, rave, snap 5 crack 6 lose it
boom: 5 erupt 7 explode, thunder 8 detonate 9 discharge
by: 3 fly 4 pass, snub 6 elapse, roll on
by air: 3 fly 6 aviate, fly out
by shanks' mare: 4 slog, walk 5 leg it, march 6 foot it, hoof it, trudge
cause to ~: 6 betake
come and ~: 5 recur 9 alternate, oscillate
counter to: 4 defy 5 flout, rebel 6 ignore 7 disobey, violate 9 disregard 10 contravene
crazy: 4 flip, rage, rant, rave, snap 5 freak 7 rampage
don't ~: 4 bide, stay 6 loiter
don't ~ together: 3 jar 5 clash 6 jangle
down: 3 dip, ebb, set 4 dive, drop, fall, lose, sink, wane 5 abate, slide, slump, swoop 6 plunge, topple 7 descend, founder, plummet, subside 9 hit bottom, surrender
downhill: 3 ski 4 fail, sink 5 slide, slump 6 worsen 7 decline 10 degenerate
down the tubes: 4 fail
easy: 5 let up, relax 10 take it slow
easy on: 4 pity 5 spare 6 relent 7 absolve, release 9 lighten up
far: 4 last 5 get on 7 advance, succeed 8 get ahead, progress
fast: 3 fly, hie, run, zip 4 race, tear, zoom 5 speed 6 hot rod, hurtle, hustle
fifty-fifty: 5 share, split
first: 4 head, lead 5 guide, usher 7 conduct, lead off, pioneer, precede 9 spearhead 10 trailblaze
fish: 4 game 8 card game
fly a kite: 5 scram, split 6 beat it, begone 7 buzz off, get lost, take off 9 take a hike
for: 3 opt, vie 4 like, love, okay 5 admit, adopt, adore, allow, crave, elect, enjoy, favor, fetch 6 accept, admire, assent, attack, choose, comply, desire, fall on, have at, leap at, prefer, ratify, relish, revere 7 cherish, idolize, include, realize, welcome, worship 8 fall upon, hold dear, treasure 9 put up with, recognize, sign off on 10 concur with, give the nod
(for): 7 contend
for a ride: 6 travel
for broke: 4 dare, risk 6 gamble, hazard, strain, strive 7 serious 9 persevere
force to ~: 4 send 5 exile
for it: 3 try 4 dare 6 tackle 9 persevere
forth: 5 leave, sally, split 7 advance, head out
for the gold: 3 dig, run, vie 4 mine, race 5 rival 6 battle, strive 7 compete, contend
for the jugular: 3 vie 7 compete, contend 8 bear down
forward: 4 gain, push 5 march 6 hasten, move on 7 achieve, advance, further, improve, press on, proceed, shape up 8 continue, escalate, get ahead, progress 10 accelerate, accomplish, forge ahead, gain ground, move onward, shoot ahead
from pillar to post: 3 gad 4 roam, rove 5 drift 6 ramble, wander
furtively: 4 lurk, slip 5 creep, prowl, skulk, slink, snake, sneak, steal 6 crouch 7 slither
get: 5 bring, fetch 6 obtain 8 retrieve
get up and ~: 3 pep, vim 4 life, push, snap 5 drive, leave, oomph, vigor 6 bounce, energy, starch 8 ambition, gumption, vitality, vivacity 10 exuberance
great guns: 5 excel 8 flourish
hand over hand: 5 climb, scale 6 ascend, shinny 7 clamber
have a ~ at: 3 try 5 essay 6 take on 7 address, attempt
have another ~: 5 retry
headlong: 4 rush, trip 6 careen
head over heels: 4 fall, slip 5 lurch 6 plunge, sprawl, topple, tumble 7 stumble
head to head: 3 pit, vie 4 play 5 fight, match, rival 6 oppose, take on 7 compete, contend 8 struggle 9 challenge
hellbent for leather: 6 careen, hasten, hurtle 7 rampage 8 stampede
here and there: 3 gad 4 roam, rove, trek 5 drift, range 6 ramble, travel, wander 7 explore, journey, meander, traipse 9 bat around, bum around, gallivant, run around 10 knock about
hog-wild over: 5 enjoy
hungry: 6 starve
in: 5 enter 6 arrive
in advance: 5 usher 6 herald 7 precede, presage 8 antecede, run ahead 10 anticipate
in search of: 4 seek 5 quest 6 aspire, gun for, pursue 7 hunt for, long for, look for 8 yearn for 9 track down
into: 4 sift 5 enter, probe, treat 6 choose, select 7 discuss, examine, explore, touch on 9 touch upon, undertake
(into): 5 delve
into a funk: 4 fret, mope, sulk 5 brood, worry 7 agonize 8 languish 10 introspect
into detail: 4 list 5 brief, gloss 6 lay out 7 analyze, clarify, explain, itemize, specify 8 annotate, describe, spell out 9 blueprint, elaborate, elucidate, enumerate, expound on, make clear, put across
into hysterics: 4 flip, rant, snap 8 get angry
in with: 4 pool 5 share
kaput: 3 die 4 fail, flop, fold 6 fizzle 7 conk out 8 backfire 9 break down
let ~: 2 ax 3 axe, can 4 axed, boot, drop, fire, free, miss, omit, oust, sack, weep 5 clear, fired, freed, loose, relax, spare, throw, untie, waive, yield 6 acquit, bounce, canned, excuse, ignore, lay off, let off, loosen, relent, sprang, spring, sprung, unhand, untied 7 abandon, cashier, dismiss, drum out, forgive, manumit, neglect, release, set free 8 cut loose, furlough, get rid of, liberate, overlook, pink-slip, released 9 discharge, disengage, dismissed, liberated, sacrifice, surrender, terminate, turn loose 10 discharged, relinquish
let it ~: 6 excuse, pardon 8 laugh off, overlook
let ~ of: 4 drop, dump, shed 5 ditch, spurn 6 give up, unload 7 abandon, discard, toss out 8 renounce 9 eighty-six, repudiate, throw away 10 relinquish
let oneself ~: 5 relax, unlax 6 rest up, unwind 7 lay back, sit back 8 loosen up, slack off 9 hang loose 10 settle back, take it easy
let's ~: 4 c'mon 7 vamanos
like: 3 ape 4 copy, echo, mime, mock 5 mimic 7 imitate 9 make fun of, pantomime 10 caricature
like a shot: 3 fly, hie, rip, run 4 race, rush, whiz 5 hurry, speed 6 hurtle, streak
limp: 3 sag 4 wilt 5 droop, faint, swoon 6 weaken 7 crumple, pass out, shrivel 8 black out, keel over
make ~: 7 operate
make a ~ of it: 6 thrive
missing: 6 vanish 9 disappear
native: 5 adapt 7 blend in 9 integrate 10 assimilate
near: 8 approach
next: 6 follow 7 succeed
off: 4 blow, ring 5 burst, erupt, leave, spoil 6 depart 7 explode 8 detonate
off-course: 3 err, yaw, zag 4 roam, rove, skid, slue, tack, turn, veer 5 drift, lurch, range, slide, stray, swing 6 divert, ramble, swerve, wander 7 deflect, deviate, digress, diverge, maunder, meander 8 sideslip, straggle
off on a tangent: 5 stray 6 ramble, wander 7 digress
on: 3 add 4 last 5 exist, reach, spout 6 endure, happen, resume 7 persist 8 continue 9 persevere
on about: 4 gush, rail, rant, rave 6 stress 7 belabor, enthuse 8 harangue 10 effervesce, hammer home, rhapsodize
on a diet: 4 lose 6 reduce 8 slim down 10 lose weight
on a jag: 5 spree 7 splurge
on all fours: 5 crawl, creep, slink 7 clamber, slither, wriggle
on and on: 3 yak 4 rant, rave 5 drone, spout 6 babble, jabber, ramble
on a spree: 5 binge, revel 7 carouse
on bended knee: 3 beg, sue 4 urge 5 crawl 7 beseech, declare, entreat, implore 8 petition 9 importune 10 supplicate
one better: 3 top 5 outdo 7 surpass
(one's way): 4 wend
on foot: 4 hoof, walk 5 leg it
on stage: 3 act 5 enter 7 perform
on strike: 5 rebel 6 resist, revolt 7 protest
on the ~: 4 busy, spry 6 active 8 restless, tireless 9 traveling, wayfaring
on the air: 6 report 7 network 8 announce, televise 9 advertise, broadcast, publicize 10 make public
on the fritz: 5 act up
on the lam: 4 bolt, flee 6 bug out
on the road: 4 tour
on the wagon: 4 quit, stop 6 eschew 7 abstain, refrain 8 renounce 9 do without
on with: 6 pick up, resume 7 persist, proceed 8 continue, maintain, return to 9 persevere 10 recommence
order to ~: 4 fire, mail, oust, post, send, ship 5 exile, expel, route 6 assign, banish, deport, direct, put out 7 cast out, consign, turn out 8 dispatch, displace, drive out, transfer 9 dismissal, ostracize, transport 10 expatriate
out: 3 ebb 4 date, exit 5 leave 6 egress, recede 9 socialize
out of business: 4 fail, fold 6 fold up
out of control: 4 yell 5 erupt, freak, storm 6 blow up, careen, rail at, scream 7 explode, rampage, run wild 8 boil over, have a fit, run amuck 9 blow a fuse, go berserk 10 hit the roof, kick up a row
out on a limb: 5 guess 6 hazard 7 venture
out with: 3 see 4 date 5 court
out with a whimper: 6 fizzle
over: 4 read 5 audit, cross, study 6 pan out, review 7 examine, inspect, iterate, rectify 8 practice, question, rehearse, traverse 9 reiterate
over again: 5 recap 6 repeat 9 reiterate
over and over: 3 nag 6 harp on, repeat, stress 7 iterate 9 emphasize, reiterate
over big: 3 wow 5 score 6 please, thrill, turn on 7 impress 8 blow away 9 electrify
over lightly: 4 leaf, scan, skim 6 riffle 8 glance at
over the fence: 5 vault 6 defect, desert, escape, run out 7 abscond
over the hill: 3 lam 4 bolt, flee 6 desert, run off 7 abscond, bail out, run away 8 break out
over the wall: 3 run 4 bolt, flee, jump, leap, skip 5 bound

6 desert, run off, run out 7 abscond, bail out, get away, make off, run away 8 cut loose, slip away, turn tail 9 cut and run, steal away 10 fly the coop
partner: 4 come, stop 5 get up
partners: 5 unite 6 hook up, team up 9 affiliate, associate 10 join up with
past: 4 omit, skip 6 exceed 9 overshoot
pell-mell: 4 bolt, race, rush, tear, whiz, zoom 5 lunge, speed 6 charge, hurtle
pfft: 4 fail
pitapat: 4 beat 5 pound, throb 7 flutter 9 palpitate
places: 3 win 4 rise 6 hack it, make it, pan out, thrive 7 advance, luck out, make out, prevail, prosper, succeed, triumph, work out 8 flourish, get ahead, get along, hit it big, make good 10 do all right
postal: 4 flip, rage, rant, snap
preceder: 6 get set
public with: 3 air 4 bare, leak, talk 5 admit, spill, voice 6 betray, expose, report, reveal 7 divulge, publish 8 disclose, give away 9 broadcast, make known
quickly: 3 hie, run 4 race, rush, zing 5 scoot, skirr, speed 6 hustle
raring to ~: 4 avid, keen 5 eager, itchy, ready 6 all set, on edge 9 hot to trot 10 inspirited
ready to ~: 3 set 6 at hand 7 in store 9 available 10 obtainable
refuse to ~: 4 balk, stop 5 baulk, demur 6 recoil
see: 5 visit
separate ways: 4 fork, part 5 leave, split 7 break up, disband, diverge, pull out, scatter, split up 10 say goodbye
slowly: 4 ease, inch, plod 5 crawl, creep
smoothly: 3 fly 4 flow, sail, skim, soar 5 coast, drift, float, glide, slide, sweep 6 cruise
so far: 6 gather, take it 7 suppose, surmise
soft: 4 melt, thaw 6 relent 8 languish
sour: 4 ruin, turn 5 addle, spoil, taint 6 curdle, mildew 7 acidify
south: 4 bolt, flee, quit 5 split 6 beat it, decamp, defect, escape 7 abscond, make off, pull out, skip out, vamoose 9 cut and run, disappear, skedaddle, steal away 10 fly the coop, high-tail it, make a break
stale: 3 rot 4 mold, rust, tire 5 decay 7 crumble 8 stagnate
steady with: 3 pin, see, woo 4 date
stealthily: 5 slink, steal 7 slither
straight: 6 reform 7 shape up
swiftly: 3 fly, run 4 bolt, dart, flee 5 hurry, scoot, scram 6 gallop, hasten, scurry, sprint, streak 7 scamper
the distance: 4 last 6 endure, finish, strive 7 persist 8 keep at it
through: 4 sift 5 audit, brave, rifle, spend, use up 6 endure, finish, lavish, misuse, search, suffer 7 consume, examine, inspect, ransack, receive, undergo 8 permeate, rehearse, squander 9 penetrate, withstand 10 experience
through one's head: 5 occur 6 dawn on
through the roof: 4 grow, rise, soar 5 mount, surge 6 ascend 7 burgeon, mount up 8 escalate, increase 9 intensify 10 appreciate
to: 4 join 5 reach, visit 6 attend, resort 7 head for
to bat for: 3 aid 4 back, help 6 assist, defend 7 endorse, indorse, stick by, support 8 advocate, champion 10 rally round, speak up for
to bed: 3 lie 6 retire, turn in 7 sack out 10 hit the sack
to court: 3 sue 6 appeal 7 contest, dispute 8 file suit, litigate 9 prosecute
toe-to-toe: 5 fight
to extremes: 6 overdo
together: 3 fit 4 gybe, jibe, suit 5 agree, blend, click, match, rhyme 6 belong 9 accompany
to it: 5 begin, start 7 pitch in
to law: 3 sue, try 6 accuse, appeal, indict, summon 7 arraign, contest, dispute 8 file suit, litigate 9 fight over, prosecute 10 put on trial
too far: 4 hype 6 overdo, pile on 7 belabor, lay it on, stretch 8 overplay 9 overstate 10 exaggerate
too fast: 4 tear, whiz, zoom 5 speed 6 barrel
to pieces: 3 rot 5 panic 7 crumble 8 collapse, languish 9 break down 10 degenerate
to pot: 4 rust 5 spoil 8 vegetate
to press: 7 let roll
to see: 5 pop in, visit 6 attend, call on, drop by, look up, stop in, travel 7 sojourn, swing by 8 pay a call, stay with
to seed: 3 rot 4 rust 5 decay 8 stagnate, vegetate
to sleep: 3 nap 4 rest 6 retire, turn in 7 lie down, sack out 8 abdicate 9 hit the hay 10 hit the sack
to the dogs: 4 sink 5 decay 7 decline 9 fall apart 10 degenerate
to the mat for: 4 back 5 stake, vouch 7 endorse, promote, sponsor, support, warrant 8 champion 9 get behind 10 underwrite
to town: 5 excel 7 prosper
touch and ~: 6 unsafe, unsure, urgent 8 perilous 9 debatable, uncertain
toward: 7 advance, make for 8 approach
under: 4 bomb, bust, fail, flop, fold, lose, sink, slip, trip 5 close, flunk 6 blow it, falter, perish 7 blunder, founder, misstep, stumble, succumb, wash out 8 fall flat, flounder, lay an egg, submerge 9 hit bottom, strike out
undercover: 3 spy 4 hide 6 hole up, lie low
underground: 6 hole up, lie low 7 descend
underwater: 3 dip 4 dive, swim 5 drown, scuba 6 fall in 7 capsize, descend, founder, immerse 8 submerge 9 scuba-dive, shipwreck
unused: 4 stay 6 remain
up: 4 incr., rise, shin, soar 5 arise, climb, mount, scale 6 ascend, aviate 8 escalate
up against: 4 abut, defy, face 6 combat, oppose 8 confront, struggle
up in smoke: 4 burn, fail 6 ignite
up to: 8 approach, draw near 10 move toward
well: 5 blend 6 pan out, result 7 succeed, turn out
whole hog: 4 jump, leap, push, rush, sink 6 hurtle, plunge
wild: 4 flip, rave 5 crack
with: 3 see 4 date, pick, take 6 belong, choose, escort, opt for, select 9 accompany
(with): 7 conform
without: 4 miss, want 5 avoid 6 eschew
with the flow: 4 cope, roam, rove 5 adapt, agree, drift, get by, glide, mosey, yield 6 assent, give in, manage, ramble, wander 7 make out, meander, saunter 9 acquiesce
wrong: 3 err 4 bomb, bust, flop, lose, slip, trip 5 flunk, misdo, stray 6 blow it, falter 7 blunder, founder, misstep, stumble, wash out 8 fall flat, flounder, lay an egg 9 misbehave, strike out

go __: 3 ape, far, for, off, out 4 at it, away, bust, down, fish, into, over, to it, with 5 about, after, ahead, along, Dutch, for it, in for, to pot, under, wrong 6 around, native, places, postal 7 against, bananas, begging, belly-up, through
go __ a kite: 3 fly
go __ better: 3 one
go __ board: 5 by the
go __ broke: 3 for
go __ detail: 4 into
go __ diet: 3 on a
go __ dogs: 5 to the
go __ flames: 4 up in
go __ for: 5 to bat
go __ guns: 5 great
go __ half-cocked: 3 off
go __ hog: 5 whole
go __ hotcakes: 4 like
go __ it: 3 for
go __ kite: 4 fly a
go __ length: 4 on at
go __ mat: 5 to the
go __ of one's way: 3 out
go __ of style: 3 out
go __ on: 4 back 5 light
go __ one's way: 5 out of
go __ saying: 7 without
go __ smoke: 4 up in
go __ style: 5 out of
go __ the deep end: 3 off
go __ the gold: 3 for
go __ the hammer: 5 under
go __ the line: 4 down
go __ the motions: 7 through
go __ the roof: 7 through
go __ the window: 3 out
go __-up: 5 belly
go __ wall: 5 to the
go __ way: 5 a long
go __ wayside: 5 by the
go __ with: 3 out 5 along 6 public
go-__: 3 fer 4 cart, kart, slow 5 ahead, devil, train 6 getter 7 between
__ go: 3 let 5 on the
__ go!: 4 Let's 5 Way to
__-go: 3 get, git
Go __: 4 Fish, Home, West
Go __ It on the Mountain: 4 Tell
Go __ Little Girl: 4 Away
Go __, Moses: 4 Down
Go __, young man: 4 West
Go __ Your Dance: 4 Into
Go __ your father: 3 ask
Go, __!: 4 team
goa: 6 mammal 7 gazelle 8 antelope
relative: *see* antelope
go a __ way: 4 long
Goa: 5 state
garment: 4 sari 5 saree
locale: 5 India
goad: 3 egg, nag 4 fret, prod, push, spur, urge 5 annoy, bully, drive, egg on, force, hop up, hound, impel, liven, pique, prick, rouse, taunt, tease, worry 6 arouse, badger, bother, coerce, exhort, fillip, fire up, harass, incite, needle, nettle, noodge, prompt, propel, stir up, whip up 7 impetus, impulse, provoke, quicken 8 catalyst, embolden, imbolden, irritate, motivate, stimulus, talk into 9 encourage, impassion, incentive, instigate, stimulate 10 cattle prod, incitement, inducement, motivation
__ go again!: 4 Let's 5 Here I 6 Here we
go-ahead: 2 OK 3 nod 4 okay, word 5 leave 6 assent, permit, signal 7 consent, license, mandate, warrant 8 approval, sanction 9 clearance 10 green light, permission
give the ~: 2 OK 3 nod 4 okay 5 agree, allow, clear 6 accede, enable 7 approve
Go ahead!: 5 shoot, try me
Go ahead... __ my day!: 4 make
goal: 3 aim, end, job, obj. 4 hope, mark 5 cause, dream, ideal, point, score 6 design, intent, object, reason, target 7 meaning, mission, purpose 8 ambition, function 9 intention, objective, touchdown 10 aspiration, ground zero
lofty ~: 6 vision
set a lofty ~: 4 hope, wish 5 dream 6 aspire
ultimate ~: 6 end-all
goal __: 4 line, post
__ goal: 5 field 6 career
Goalby, Bob: 6 golfer
goalie: 6 player 7 athlete 9 net-keeper
concern: 4 puck
feat: 4 save
fool the ~: 4 deke

game: 6 hockey, soccer 7 lacrosse
get past the ~: 5 score
milieu: 3 ice, net 4 rink 6 crease
org.: 3 NHL
protection: 4 mask
goalless: 6 adrift
go a long __: 3 way
goal-oriented: 5 telic
goals
like some ~: 5 lofty, unmet
go-anywhere vehicle: 3 ATV
goat: 4 ibex, meat, tahr, thar 5 bovid, patsy 6 Angora, animal, butter, lecher, mammal, target 7 markhor 8 easy mark, markhoor, omnivore 9 Capricorn, livestock
antelope: 5 goral, serow
Asian ~: 4 ibex, tahr, thar 7 markhor 8 markhoor
assault like a ~: 4 butt
baby: 3 kid 8 yeanling
bear a ~: 4 yean
cheese: 4 feta 6 chèvre 7 chevret, crottin
combining form: 5 capri-
ender: 4 fish, skin 6 sucker
fabric: 3 aba 4 abba 5 Kasha 7 kashmir 8 cashmere
feature: 5 beard
female: 3 doe 5 nanny
foot: 4 hoof
get one's ~: 3 irk, vex 4 miff, rile 5 anger, peeve, upset 6 enrage, rankle
male: 4 buck 5 billy
meat: 6 chevon
noise: 3 maa 4 blat 5 bleat
old ~: 4 roué 9 libertine 10 profligate
relative: 5 sheep
starter: 5 scape
__ goat: 5 billy, nanny 6 Angora
__ go at: 5 have a
Goat: 4 sign 7 January 8 December 9 Capricorn
follower: 11 Water Bearer
month: 3 Dec., Jan. 7 January 8 December
predecessor: 6 Archer
__ Goat-Boy: 5 Giles
goatee: 4 hair, tuft 5 beard 8 whiskers
get rid of a ~: 4 snip 5 shave
site: 4 chin
goatfish: 5 moana 6 mullet
goat-footed
deity: 3 Pan 5 satyr
goatish: 6 caprid 7 caprine, hircine, lustful 9 lubricous 10 libidinous
__ go at it: 5 have a
goatskin: 3 kid 5 mocha, suede 6 galyak 7 leather 8 cordovan
goatsucker: 4 bird 8 nightjar 9 nighthawk
relative: 5 potoo 9 frogmouth
Go away!: 4 scat, shoo 5 scram 6 beat it
Go Away Little Girl (song)
artist: Steve Lawrence, Donny Osmond
gob: 3 tar, wad 4 hunk, lump, mass, pile, salt, swab, swob 5 bunch, chunk, clump 6 dollop, sailor, sea dog, seaman, swabby 7 crewman, jack tar, mariner, matelot, matelow, portion, swabbie 8 deckhand, mouthful, seafarer 10 bluejacket
see also nautical, sailor
gobbet: 3 bit 4 lump, mass 5 piece 8 fragment
gobble: 3 eat 4 bolt, cram, gulp, wolf 5 gorge, scarf, stuff 6 devour, guzzle, inhale, suck up 7 put away, scarf up, swallow 8 wolf down 9 grab a bite, scarf down 10 gormandize
up: 3 eat, use 4 wolf 5 eat up 6 devour, obtain 7 consume, engorge, feast on
gobbledegook
see baloney
gobbler: 3 tom 4 male 5 eater 6 turkey 7 glutton
Gobel: 6 George
go-between: 3 agt. 5 agent, envoy, fixer, proxy 6 broker, deputy, factor 7 arbiter, liaison, referee 8 attorney, emissary, mediator 9 appointee, messenger, middleman, negotiant 10 arbitrator, connection, interagent, interceder, matchmaker, negotiator, peacemaker
be a ~: 6 liaise
Gobi: 6 desert
like the ~: 3 dry 4 arid 5 sandy
site: 4 Asia 8 Mongolia
goblet: 3 cup 5 glass, grail, mazer 7 chalice, snifter 8 stemware 9 wineglass
part: 4 stem
Scottish ~: 4 tass
sound: 4 ting
goblin: 3 elf, imp 4 nixy, pixy 5 demon, gnome, nixie, ouphe, pixie, spook 6 daemon, daimon, kobold, sprite 7 brownie, bugbear, gremlin
German ~: 6 kobold
greeting: 3 boo
in Scandinavian folklore: 5 nisse
starter: 3 hob
__ go bragh: 4 Erin
gobs: 4 a lot, lots, much, peck, slew 5 ocean
of: 4 many 6 divers, myriad, umteen, untold 7 copious, profuse, umpteen 8 abundant, manifold, numerous, umpsteen 9 bountiful, countless, quite a few
goby: 4 fish
go-by: 6 rebuff
go by the __: 5 board 7 wayside
god: 5 deity, maker 6 daemon 8 divinity
bellicose ~: 4 Ares, Mars
combining form: 3 the- 4 theo-
Egyptian ~: 3 Bes, Set 4 Ptah, Seth 5 Horus, Sebek, Thoth 6 Amon-Ra, Anubis, Osiris 7 Taueret
ender: 3 son 4 head, send 5 child 6 father, mother, parent 8 children, daughter, forsaken
goat-footed ~: 5 satyr
Greek ~: 3 Pan 4 Ares, Eros, Zeus 5 Hades 6 Aeolus, Apollo, Charon, Helios, Hermes, Hypnos, Icarus 8 Cerberus, Dionysus, Poseidon 10 Hephaestus
Hindu ~: 4 Agni, Kama, Siva, Soma, Yama 5 Indra, Shiva, Surya 6 Brahma, Varuna, Vishnu 7 Ganesha, Hanuman, Krishna
in Latin: 3 deo
Islamic ~: 5 Allah
Japanese ~: 5 Inari
love ~: 4 Amor, Eros 5 Cupid
Norse ~: 4 Frey, Loki, Odin, Thor 5 Aegir, Njord, Othin 6 Balder 7 Forseti
Phoenician ~: 4 Baal
Roman ~: 3 Dis 4 Mars 5 Cupid, Janus, Pluto 6 Apollo, Saturn, Vulcan 7 Bacchus, Jupiter, Mercury, Neptune 8 Silvanus
solar ~: 4 Aten, Aton 6 Apollo
starter: 4 demi
sylvan ~: 3 Pan 5 satyr
tutelary ~: 3 lar
Vedic ~: 4 Agni, Kama, Siva, Soma, Yama 5 Indra, Shiva, Surya 6 Brahma, Varuna, Vishnu 7 Ganesha, Hanuman, Krishna
woodland ~: 5 satyr
God: 4 Lord 5 Allah, Jahve, Jahwe, Yahve, Yahwe 6 Jahveh, Jahweh, Yahveh, Yahweh 7 Creator, Jehovah 8 Almighty, divinity
ender: 5 speed
God __: 5 bless, knows
God __ America: 5 Bless
God __ Co-Pilot: 4 Is My
God __ the Queen: 4 Save
God-__: 5 awful, given 7 fearing
__ God: 5 act of, man of, Son of
__ God!: 5 Thank
God and Mammon
author: François Mauriac
God and Man at __: 4 Yale
Godard: 7 Jean-Luc
Godavari: 5 river
God-awful
see awful
God Bless America
composer: Irving Berlin
God bless us __ one: 5 every
God bless you
preceder: 5 achoo 6 ahchoo, hachoo, sneeze 7 kerchoo
__ God Brown, The: 5 Great
godchild: 4 ward
__ God Created Woman: 3 And
Goddard: 4 Mark 6 Robert 8 Paulette
Goddard, Paulette: 7 actress
spouse: Charles Chaplin, Burgess Meredith, Erich Maria Remarque
Goddard, Robert: 9 physicist, rocketeer
Godden: 5 Rumer
goddess: 5 deity 8 divinity
Egyptian ~: 3 Mut, Nut 4 Bast, Isis, Maat 6 Hathor 7 Sekhmet 8 Nephthys
Greek ~: 3 Eos 4 Hebe, Hera, Iris, Nike 5 Aeaea, Circe, Kirke 6 Athena, Athene, Hecate, Hekate, Hestia, Medusa, Selene 7 Artemis, Demeter 9 Aphrodite 10 Persephone
Hindu ~: 4 Devi, Kali, Usha 5 Durga, Ushas 7 Lakshmi, Parvati 9 Sarasvati
in Latin: 3 dea
Japanese ~: 9 Amaterasu
Norse ~: 3 Hel 5 Freya, Frigg
Roman ~: 3 Ops 4 Juno 5 Ceres, Diana, Flora, Venus, Vesta 6 Aurora 7 Fortuna, Minerva
Vedic ~: 4 Devi, Kali, Usha 5 Durga, Ushas 7 Lakshmi, Parvati 9 Sarasvati
goddesses
Greek ~: 6 Furies, Gorgon, Graces
Norse ~: 5 Norns
go-devil: 4 sled
Godey's Lady's Book editor: 4 Hale
godfather: 3 don
Godfather Part III, The (1990 film)
cast: Andy García, George Hamilton, Diane Keaton, Joe Mantegna, Al Pacino, Talia Shire, Eli Wallach
director: Francis Ford Coppola
Godfather Part II, The (1974 film)
cast: John Cazale, Robert De Niro, Robert Duvall, Diane Keaton, Al Pacino, Talia Shire, Lee Strasberg
director: Francis Ford Coppola
Godfather, The
author: Mario Puzo
Godfather, The (1972 film)
cast: Marlon Brando, James Caan, John Cazale, Robert Duvall, Diane Keaton, Al Pacino, Talia Shire
composer: Nino Rota
director: Francis Ford Coppola
God-fearing: 5 pious 6 devout 9 religious
godforsaken: 6 lonely, remote 8 deserted, desolate, stranded 9 miserable
Godfrey: 5 Peter 6 Arthur 9 Cambridge 10 Hounsfield
in German: 9 Gottfried
__ Godfrey: 5 My Man
Godfrey, Arthur: 4 host 5 emcee
instrument: 3 uke 7 ukulele
God-given: 6 innate
godhood: 8 divinity
God in Ruins, A
author: Leon Uris
Go directly to __: 4 Jail
Godiva: 4 Lady 5 rider
God Knows
author: Joseph Heller
godless: 5 pagan 7 impious, profane 9 atheistic
godlike: 6 deific, divine 8 almighty 9 celestial 10 omnipotent
make ~: 5 adore, deify, exalt, extol 7 elevate, glorify, worship 8 sanctify, venerate 10 consecrate
godliness: 4 zeal 5 piety 8 divinity 10 devoutness
godly: 4 holy 5 pious 6 deific, devout, divine, sacred 7 angelic, saintly 9 ambrosial, angelical, pietistic, religious, righteous
God Makers, The
author: Frank Herbert
godmother
fairy ~: 5 donor 6 backer, patron 10 benefactor
often: 4 aunt 8 relative
__ godmother: 5 fairy
go down in __: 6 flames

Go Down, Moses
author: William Faulkner
go down the __: **4** line
godparent: **7** sponsor
Godplayer
author: Robin Cook
God Rest Ye Merry, Gentlemen: **4** noel **5** carol
gods
in Latin: **3** dei
Norse ~: **5** Aesir, Vanir
Roman household ~: **5** Lares **7** Penates
God's __: **4** acre, Word **5** penny **6** plenty **7** country
God Said, 'HA!' (1999 film)
cast: Julia Sweeney
God Save the Queen: **6** anthem
God's Country (1985 film)
director: Louis Malle
God-Seeker, The
author: Sinclair Lewis
godsend: **4** boon, gift, luck **7** benefit **8** blessing, surprise, windfall **10** lucky break
God shed His grace on __: **4** thee
God's Little Acre: **5** novel
author: Erskine Caldwell
Gods Must Be Crazy, The (1981 film)
character: **4** Xixo
director: Jamie Uys
Gods of the Lightning
author: Maxwell Anderson
God's Other Son
author: Don Imus
Godspeed: **5** adieu
God strengthens, name meaning: **7** Ezekiel
__ God's Wife, The: **7** Kitchen
Godthab: **4** city, town
locale: **9** Greenland
Godunov: **5** Boris **9** Alexander
see also Russian
Godunov, Boris: **4** czar, tsar
Godwin Austen: **3** mtn. **4** peak **5** mount **8** mountain
locale: **4** Asia
Godwin, Gail: **6** writer
godwit: **4** bird **9** shorebird
Godzilla: **7** monster **8** behemoth, dinosaur
foe: **5** Rodan **6** Mothra
setting: **5** Japan, Tokio, Tokyo
Godzilla (1998 film)
cast: Hank Azaria, Matthew Broderick
director: Roland Emmerich
Godzilla's Revenge (1969 film)
director: Ishiro Honda
Goen: **3** Bob
goer: **7** habitué **8** attendee, gadabout, traveler
starter: **4** film, play **5** movie **7** theater, theatre
__ goes!: **4** Here
__ Goes On: **4** Life
__ Goes On, The: **4** Beat
...goes out like __: **5** a lamb
__ goes there?: **3** Who
__ Goes to College: **5** Bonzo
__ Goes to Jail: **6** Ernest
__ Goes Visiting: **4** Pooh
Goethals, George: **8** engineer
Goethe, Johann Wolfgang von: **4** poet **6** German, writer
work: The Erl-King
Faust

gofer: **4** aide, page **5** grunt **6** flunky, helper, lackey, runner **7** flunkey, lacquey **8** henchman **9** assistant, errand boy, messenger
job: **6** errand
sports ~: **5** caddy **6** bat boy, caddie
Goffin: **5** Gerry
go fish: **4** game **8** card game
alternative: **3** war **7** old maid
Go fly __!: **5** a kite
go for __: **4** a dip **5** a spin, broke **7** the gold
Go For The Goal
author: Mia Hamm
Gog and __: **5** Magog
__ go gentle...: **5** Do not
go-getter: **4** doer **5** mover, tiger **6** dynamo **7** hustler **8** live wire
no ~: **5** sloth
goggle: **3** eye **4** gape, gawk, leer, look, ogle **5** glare, stare **6** marvel
box: **2** TV **5** TV set **10** television
goggle-eyed: **6** astare **7** staring
Gogi: **5** Grant
__ go, girl!: **3** You
go-go: **5** pushy, zippy **6** active, lively **7** buzzing, driving, dynamic, jumping **9** energetic **10** aggressive
music: **5** disco
go-go __: **6** dancer
gogo, à: **6** galore
Gogol
genre: **7** realism
Gogol, Nikolai: **6** writer **7** Russian
work: Dead Souls
Diary of a Madman
The Inspector General
The Overcoat
Taras Bulba
Go-Go's
leader: Belinda Carlisle
song: Vacation (1982)
We Got the Beat (1982)
go great __: **4** guns
Go Home (1985 song)
artist: Stevie Wonder
go in __: **3** for **4** with
Goin' __ My Head: **5** Out of
going: **7** current, parting, running, working **9** departure
around: **5** faddy **6** trendy **7** current, popular **9** in the news **10** widespread
away: **6** easily **9** departure
easy on: **3** lax **4** mild, soft **6** benign, gentle, humane **7** clement, lenient, liberal, sparing **8** allowing, excusing, merciful, obliging, tolerant, yielding **9** condoning, forgiving, indulgent, pampering, pardoning **10** charitable, permissive
get ~: **4** move, open, roll **5** begin, crank, found, rouse, start **6** fillip, launch, let rip, set off, set out **7** kick off, lead off, pitch in, speed up **8** commence, initiate, organize, set about, set forth **9** enter upon, originate **10** inaugurate
is ~ to: **4** will
keep ~: **5** run on **6** extend, hold on, push on **7** persist, subsist, sustain **8** maintain, progress, protract, tide over **9** persevere **10** perpetuate
keep one ~: **3** aid **6** assist **9** help

along **10** see through
nowhere: **4** lost **6** adrift, in a rut **9** pointless
on: **5** afoot **6** serial **7** present **8** underway **10** in progress
on and on: **5** gabby, windy, wordy **6** chatty, prolix, turgid **7** gushing, lengthy, tedious, verbose, voluble **8** babbling, inflated, rambling **9** bombastic, garrulous, jabbering, talkative **10** bigmouthed, blathering, long-winded, loquacious
set ~: **6** launch
starter: **3** sea **4** easy, film, play **5** dance, movie, ocean **6** church **7** concert, theater, theatre **8** thorough
strong: **5** palmy **7** booming, healthy, roaring, rolling **8** thriving **9** advancing, doing well **10** prospering, prosperous, successful
going __: **3** ape **4** rate **7** concern
going-__: **4** over
__ going: **3** get
__-going: **4** easy, slow **6** steady
Going __: **4** Home, Solo **5** My Way
Going __,...: **4** once
Going Back to Cali (1988 song)
artist: LL Cool J
Going, going, __: **4** gone
Going in Style (1979 film)
cast: George Burns, Art Carney, Lee Strasberg
director: Martin Brest
Going My Way (1944 film)
cast: Bing Crosby, Barry Fitzgerald
director: Leo McCarey
__ going on?: **5** What's
going-over: **6** rebuke **7** lecture **9** rehearsal **10** upbraiding
Going Solo
author: Roald Dahl
goings-on: **6** action, doings, events **7** revelry **8** business, occasion, partying **9** festivity **10** happenings
Going to a Go-Go (1966 song)
artist: Miracles
...going to St. Ives, __...: **4** I met
Going to the Territory
author: Ralph Ellison
Goin' Out of My Head (1964 song)
artist: Little Anthony and the Imperials
Goin' Out of My Head... (1968 song)
artist: Lettermen
Goin' South (1978 film)
cast: Christopher Lloyd, Jack Nicholson, Mary Steenburgen
director: Jack Nicholson
go into __: **6** detail
__ go, into the...: **5** Off we
go it __: **5** alone
goiter treatment: **5** iodin **6** iodine
go-kart: **5** racer
Golan: **4** Gila **7** Menahem
Golan Heights
locale: **3** Isr. **6** Israel
Gola, Tom
milieu: **5** court
org.: **3** NBA
sport: **10** basketball
gold: **5** aurum, medal, metal, money **6** riches, wealth, yellow **7** bullion, element, laurels **8** treasure **9** valuables
alloy: **8** electrum
Biblical kingdom of ~: **5** Ophir
black ~: **3** oil
braid: **5** orris
coat with ~: **4** gild **5** plate
combining form: **3** aur- **4** auri- **5** chrys- **6** chryso-
compound: **6** aurate
container: **3** pan, pot **4** mint
containing ~: **5** auric **6** aurous
digger: **5** miner
ender: **4** fish **5** brick, field, finch, smith, stone **6** beater, thread
fabric: **4** lamé
fake ~: **6** ormolu, pyrite
fever: **5** greed **7** avarice
get the ~: **3** win
go for the ~: **3** dig, run, vie **4** mine, race **5** rival **6** battle, strive **7** compete, contend
imitation ~: **6** ormolu
in Spanish: **3** oro
item: **3** bar **5** ingot, medal
leaf: **4** gilt
measure: **2** ct., kt. **3** pwt. **5** carat, karat
medalist: **4** hero **5** first **6** victor, winner **8** champion
mine: **4** lode **5** cache, stock, store **6** source, supply, wealth **7** bonanza, cash cow, deposit, fortune, reserve **8** windfall **10** mother lode
oak leaf wearer: **3** maj. **5** major
old ~: **5** amber, color, tawny **6** yellow **7** saffron
old ~ coin: **4** rial **5** dobla, ducat, krone, mohur, riyal **6** aureus
ore: **9** sylvanite
partner: **5** myrrh **12** frankincense
record: **3** hit **5** smash **7** success, triumph **9** sensation
relative: *see* yellow color
seek ~: **3** dig, pan
solid ~: **7** optimum **8** splendid **9** marvelous
source: **3** ore **4** lode, mine, seam, vein **6** pocket, streak **7** stratum
star: **5** award, prize **6** trophy **7** laurels
the ~: **7** triumph, victory
gold __: **4** bond, dust, foil, lamé, leaf, mine, note, rush, star **5** fever, medal, plate **6** digger **7** bullion
gold-__: **6** filled, plated
__ gold: **3** old **5** black, fool's, pot of **6** filled, good as, liquid
Gold: **5** Missy **6** Andrew, Ernest, Tracey **7** Herbert
Gold __: **5** Coast
Gold __, The: **3** Bug **4** Rush
__ Gold: **4** Inca, Rold **5** Irish, Ulee's **6** Desert
Golda: **4** Meir
colleague: **4** Abba **5** Moshe
Gold, Andrew
song: Lonely Boy (1977)
Goldberg: **4** Adam, Rube **5** Jonah **6** Arthur, Whoopi
Goldbergs, The (radio/TV sitcom)
cast: Gertrude Berg
Goldberg Variations
composer: J.S. Bach

Goldberg, Whoopi: 7 actress
film: Boys on the Side (1995)
The Color Purple (1985)
Corrina, Corrina (1994)
Deep End of the Ocean (1999)
Ghost (1990, AA)
Ghosts of Mississippi (1996)
How Stella Got Her Groove Back (1998)
Kingdom Come (2001)
The Long Walk Home (1990)
Moonlight and Valentino (1995)
The Player (1992)
Rat Race (2001)
Sister Act (1992)
Soapdish (1991)
TV: Hollywood Squares, Star Trek: The Next Generation, The View
Goldblum, Jeff: 5 actor
film: Between the Lines (1977)
The Big Chill (1983)
Earth Girls Are Easy (1989)
The Fly (1986)
Independence Day (1996)
Into the Night (1985)
Jurassic Park (1993)
The Lost World: Jurassic Park (1997)
Nine Months (1995)
spouse: Geena Davis
goldbrick: 3 veg 4 loaf 5 dog it, idler, shirk 6 loafer, lounge, truant 7 goof-off, shirker, slacker 8 fainéant, loiterer, malinger, parasite, slack off 9 do-nothing, lazybones 10 ne'er-do-well
in Britain: 5 sculk, skulk
goldbricking: 4 lazy
Goldbrick Variations
composer: PDQ Bach
gold bronze: 5 alloy
component: 3 tin 4 lead, zinc 6 copper
Gold Bug, The
author: Edgar Allan Poe
__ Gold Cadillac, The: 5 Solid
gold-chained actor: 3 Mr. T
Gold Coast: 5 Ghana
capital: 5 Accra, Akkra
tribe: 4 Akra
Gold Coast, The
author: Nelson DeMille
goldcup: 5 shrub
family: 10 nightshade
Gold Diggers of 1933 (1933 film)
cast: Joan Blondell, Ruby Keeler
director: Mervyn LeRoy
golden: 4 A-one, dore, gilt 5 auric, blond, flaxy, happy, lucky, tawny, wheat 6 aurous, blonde, bright, flaxen, joyful, joyous, yellow 7 aureate, radiant, shining 8 blissful, glorious, precious, valuable 9 brilliant, excellent, favorable, opportune, promising 10 auspicious, delightful, flying high, propitious
age: 6 heyday
ager: 5 elder 6 senior
ager grp: 4 AARP
aster: 5 plant 6 flower
brown: 5 hazel
calf: 10 juggernaut
cowrie: 5 shell 8 seashell
egg producer: 5 goose
ender: 3 eye, rod 4 seal
in French: 3 d'or
name meaning ~: 5 Gilda
oldie: 4 song, tune 6 melody
rule word: 4 unto 6 others
touch man: 5 Midas
golden __: 3 age, lab 4 ager, calf, mean, rule 5 eagle, goose, oldie, years 7 jubilee, wedding
golden-__: 5 brown
golden-__ corn: 5 eared
Golden: 4 city, town 5 Harry
locale: 8 Colorado
Golden __: 3 Boy 4 Gate, Horn 5 Horde 6 Fleece
Golden __ Bridge: 4 Gate
Golden __, The: 3 Ass 4 Bear, Boat, Bowl, Hind, Seal 5 Girls
Golden __ Warriors: 5 State
Golden Apples of the Sun, The
author: Ray Bradbury
Golden Apples, The
author: Eudora Welty
Golden Arches: 9 McDonald's
favorite: 6 Big Mac
Golden Bear: 8 Nicklaus
Golden Bears: 4 U. Cal., UCLA
Golden Boat, The
author: Rabindranath Tagore
Golden Bowl, The
author: Henry James
Golden Bowl, The (2001 film)
cast: Kate Beckinsale, Nick Nolte, Uma Thurman
director: James Ivory
Golden Boy: 7 musical
author: Clifford Odets
character: 3 Joe, Tom 4 Moon 5 Eddie, Lorna, Moody
composer: Lee Adams, Charles Strouse
Golden Calf, The
artist: Erté
Golden Cockerel, The: 5 opera
Golden Corral
rival: *see* restaurant chain
Golden Crisp: 6 cereal
competitor: *see* cereal
Golden Delicious: 5 apple
relative: *see* apple
Golden Eagles: 9 Marquette
golden-eared __: 4 corn
Golden Earring
song: Twilight Zone (1983)
goldeneye: 4 bird, duck, fowl 8 whistler
relative: *see* duck
GoldenEye (1995 film)
cast: Joe Don Baker, Pierce Brosnan, Judi Dench, Famke Janssen
golden fizz: 5 drink 8 beverage, cocktail
ingredient: 3 gin 4 soda 5 vodka 7 egg yolk 10 lemon juice
Golden Fleece
land: 7 Colchis
princess: 5 Medea
seeker: 5 Jason
ship: 4 Argo
source: 5 Aries
Golden Gate: 4 park, town 6 bridge
Golden Gate Bridge, county north of the: 5 Marin
Goldengirl (1979 film)
cast: Susan Anton, Leslie Caron, James Coburn
Golden Girls, The (NBC sitcom)
cast: Bea Arthur (Dorothy Zbornak)
Estelle Getty (Sophia Petrillo)
Rue McClanahan (Blanche Devereaux)
Betty White (Rose Nylund)
setting: 5 Miami 7 Florida
Golden Globe: 5 award
Golden Grahams: 6 cereal
competitor: *see* cereal
golden-haired: 4 fair 5 blond, light, sandy 6 blonde, flaxen 9 tow-headed
Golden Harvest, The
author: Jorge Amado
Golden Hind: 4 boat, ship
captain: 5 Drake
Golden Horde member: 5 Tatar
Golden Hurricanes school: 5 Tulsa
Golden Jubilee
composer: John Philip Sousa
Golden Legend, The
author: Henry Wadsworth Longfellow
Golden Nugget
locale: 5 Vegas
golden retriever: 3 dog 5 canid 6 canine
goldenrod: 5 plant 6 flower, yellow
relative: *see* yellow color
__ Golden Slippers: 5 Oh Dem
Golden Spike state: 4 Utah
Golden State
see California
Golden Temple worshiper: 4 Sikh
Golden Years (1976 song)
artist: David Bowie
goldfinch: 4 bird
Goldfinger: 4 film, song 5 Auric, novel
artist: Shirley Bassey
author: Ian Fleming
cast: Honor Blackman, Sean Connery, Shirley Eaton, Gert Frobe, Bernard Lee, Lois Maxwell, Harold Sakata
goldfish: 3 pet 4 carp
at a carnival: 5 prize
relative: 4 dace
Goldfish, The
artist: Paul Klee
Goldie: 4 Hawn
colleague: 3 Dan 4 Alan, Arte, Lily, Ruth
goldilocks: 5 plant
Golding, William: 6 writer 7 British 8 Nobelist
work: Lord of the Flies
Goldman: 4 Emma 7 William
Goldman __: 5 Sachs
Goldmark: 5 Peter
gold-medal position: 5 first
Goldoni, Carlo: 7 Italian 10 playwright
gold piece, ten-dollar: 5 eagle
Gold Rush
figure: 5 miner, niner
implement: 6 cradle
locale: 6 Alaska, Juneau 10 California
Gold Rush, The (1925 film)
cast: Charles Chaplin
Goldsboro: 4 town 5 Bobby
locale: 4 N. Car.
Goldsmith: 5 Jerry 6 Oliver
Goldsmith, Oliver: 6 writer 7 British
work: The Deserted Village
She Stoops to Conquer
The Vicar of Wakefield
Goldthwait: 6 Bobcat
Goldwater: 5 Barry
Goldwyn: 4 Tony 6 Samuel
colleague: 5 Mayer
__-Goldwyn-Mayer: 5 Metro
Goldwyn's Folly: 4 Sten
golem: 5 droid, robot 9 automaton
Goleta: 4 city, town
locale: 10 California
golf: 4 game 5 sport
alert: 4 fore
area: 3 tee 5 apron, green, rough 6 fringe 7 fairway
bad shot in ~: 4 baff
baff a ~ ball: 4 loft
ball feature: 6 dimple
ball material: 6 balata
ball position in ~: 3 lie
bet in ~: 6 Nassau
club: 4 iron, wood 5 cleek, spoon, wedge 6 driver, mashie, putter 7 brassie, niblick
club part: 3 toe 4 head, hose, sole 5 hosel, shaft 6 flange
coup: 3 ace 5 eagle
course: 5 links
course feature: 6 dogleg
course material: 3 sod 4 lawn, turf 5 grass, sward
course piece: 3 sod 5 divot
cup: 5 Ryder
distance a ~ ball rolls: 3 run
do ~ course work: 5 resod
easy ~ shot: 5 tap in
Florida ~ course: 5 Doral
furthest from the hole, in ~: 4 away
game: 5 round
gear: 3 tee 4 ball, club, iron, wood 5 cleek, spoon, visor, vizor, wedge 6 driver
get ready to play ~: 5 tee up
gofer: 5 caddy 6 caddie
goof: 4 hook 5 shank, slice
group: 8 foursome
half the ~ course: 3 out 4 nine
hazard: 4 sand, trap 6 bunker
hole edge: 3 lip
hole in one: 3 ace
instructor: 3 ace, pro
locale: 5 green, links, rough 6 hazard
match-play ~ score: 5 one up
motion: 6 waggle
official: 7 starter
org.: 3 PGA 4 LPGA, USGA
position: 3 lie
rental: 4 cart
score: 3 ace, par 5 bogey, bogie, eagle 6 birdie
shoe feature: 5 cleat
shot: 4 chip, putt 5 drive, pitch
target: 3 cup, pin 4 hole
term: 3 ace, cup, lie, par, tee 4 away, baff, chip, club, draw, fade, fore, hook, iron, loft, putt, wood, yips 5 apron, bogey, caddy, cleek, divot, dormy, drive, eagle, gimme, green, halve, honor, hosel, links, pitch, pro-am, rough, slice, wedge 6 birdie, bunker, caddie, dimple, dogleg, dormie, driver, duffer, fringe, hazard, marker, mashie, Nassau, putter, stroke, stymie, waggle 7 address, brassie,

fairway, niblick, starter
8 approach, backspin, best ball, duck hook, foursome, handicap, mulligan, sand trap
vehicle: 4 cart
woe: 4 hook 5 slice 6 bad lie, stymie 8 duck hook
golf __: 3 bag, tee 4 ball, cart, club 5 glove, links, widow 6 course
__ golf: 6 midget 9 miniature
Golf: 2 VW 3 car 4 auto 10 Volkswagen
Golf Begins at Forty
author: Sam Snead
golfer: 3 Els, Pak 4 Aoki, Berg, Daly, Ford, Hoch, Kite, Lema, Love, Lyle, Mann, Mize, Toms, Wall, Webb, Weir, Wood 5 Aaron, Baugh, Beman, Boros, Burke, Coody, Duval, Estes, Faldo, Floyd, Hagen, Hogan, Irwin, Jones, Lopez, Pavin, Price, Rawls, Singh, Smith, Snead, Stacy, Suggs, Woods 6 Alcott, Archer, Armour, Brewer, Caponi, Carner, Casper, Daniel, García, Goalby, Harmon, Haynie, Hinkle, Janzen, Keiser, Langer, Mallon, Miller, Morgan, Nelson, Norman, O'Meara, Ouimet, Palmer, Picard, Player, Rankin, Sluman, Sutton, Watson, Wright 7 Art Wall, athlete, Azinger, Couples, Demaret, Guldahl, Inkster, Littler, Masters, Mediate, Sarazen, Se Ri Pak, Sheehan, Stadler, Stewart, Tom Kite, Trevino, Venturi, Wadkins, Woosnam, Zoeller 8 Crenshaw, Doug Ford, Ernie Els, Isao Aoki, John Daly, Nicklaus, Olazabal, Ray Floyd, Sam Snead, Tony Lema, Zaharias 9 Amy Alcott, Bob Goalby, Gay Brewer, Geiberger, Gil Morgan, Hal Sutton, Lee Janzen, Lon Hinkle, Meg Mallon, Mickelson, Nick Faldo, Nick Price, Patty Berg, Scott Hoch, Sorenstam, Stevenson, Tom Watson 10 Baker-Finch, Beth Daniel, Corey Pavin, Deane Beman, Gary Player, Greg Norman, Ian Woosnam, Jeff Sluman, Judy Rankin, Ken Venturi, Laura Baugh, Lee Trevino, Mark O'Meara, Middlecoff, Tiger Woods, Vijay Singh 11 Ballesteros
at times: 4 teer
Australian ~: 6 Norman 9 Stevenson 10 Baker-Finch
average, to a ~: 3 par
bad ~: 6 duffer, hacker
British ~: 5 Faldo
Fijian ~: 5 Singh
German ~: 6 Langer
Japanese ~: 4 Aoki
Korean ~: 3 Pak
nickname: 3 Sam 5 Arnie, Tiger
South African ~: 3 Els 5 Price 6 Player
Spanish ~: 6 García 11 Ballesteros
Swedish ~: 9 Sorenstam
Welsh ~: 7 Woosnam
Golgi __: 4 body
Golgi, Camillo: 8 Nobelist
Goliath: 5 giant, he-man
hometown: 4 Gath
to David: 3 foe 5 enemy
Golightly: 5 Holly
Golino: 7 Valeria
golly: 3 gee, wow 4 gosh 6 my gosh, my oh my 7 gee whiz, jeepers 8 well well
__ Golly, Miss Molly: 4 Good
Go, Lovely Rose
author: Edmund Waller
__ Go Lover: 5 Let Me
__-go-lucky: 5 happy
Gombrowicz, Witold: 6 Polish, writer
Gomer: 4 Pyle
cousin: 6 Goober
grandfather: 4 Noah
husband: 5 Hosea
rank: 3 PFC
Gomer Pyle, U.S.M.C. (CBS sitcom)
cast: Jim Nabors (Pvt. Gomer Pyle)
Frank Sutton (Sgt. Vince Carter)
Gomez: 5 Lefty 6 Addams
cousin: 3 Itt
uncle: 6 Fester
wife: 4 Tish 8 Morticia
see also Spanish
Gomez, Lefty: 6 Yankee 7 pitcher
Gomorrah neighbor: 5 Sodom
Gompers: 6 Samuel
-gon
starter: 4 deca, hexa, nona, octa, poly 5 penta 6 dodeca
__ Gonçalo, Brazil: 3 Sao
Goncharov, Ivan: 6 writer 7 Russian
Goncourt: 5 Jules 6 Edmond
Goncourt, Edmond: 6 French, writer
Goncourt, Jules: 6 French, writer
Gondar's province: 6 Amhara
gondola: 4 boat
maneuver a ~: 4 pole
place: 5 canal 6 Venice
worker: 5 poler
Gondoliers, The
composer: W.S. Gilbert, Arthur Sullivan
role: 4 Inez, Luiz 5 Tessa
gone: 3 off, out 4 away, AWOL, left, lost, over, past, quit, shot, worn 5 ended, moved, not in, spent, split 6 absent, lapsed, passed, run off, used up 7 defunct, dried up, eaten up, elapsed, extinct, lacking, missing, sold out, worn-out 8 decamped, departed, depleted, finished, obsolete, vamoosed, vanished 9 destroyed, dissolved, elsewhere, exhausted, forgotten, out of here, traveling, withdrawn 10 by the board, cleared out, dissipated, on vacation
all ~: 3 out 5 empty, spent 9 exhausted 10 dissipated, squandered
astray: 4 lost 7 mislaid, missing 9 misplaced
bad: 3 off 4 rank, sour 6 rancid, rotten, turned 7 curdled 8 vinegary
be ~: 4 flit, quit 5 leave, split 6 beat it, cut out, defect, go away 7 drop out, head out, make off, pull out, push off, ride off, ship out, skip out, walk out 8 check out, clear out, light out, run along, shove off, slip away, step down 9 disappear, take a hike 10 give notice
by the boards: 3 out 5 dated, fusty, hoary, passé, stale 6 démodé, old hat 7 archaic, outworn 8 obsolete, outdated, outmoded 9 forgotten, moss-grown, out-of-date 10 antiquated, superseded
days ~ by: 4 once, past 5 of old 6 before
far ~: 3 mad 6 in love 7 charmed, smitten 8 beguiled, besotted, obsessed 9 bewitched, possessed 10 captivated, crazy about, enraptured, fascinated, infatuated, spellbound
haywire: 5 kaput 10 broken-down, on the blink, on the fritz, out of order, out of whack
in a flash: 9 momentary
long ~: 3 ago 4 late, over, yore 6 former 7 old-time, one-time 8 finished, obsolete 9 forgotten, out-of-date, preceding, yesterday 10 historical, out of style, yesteryear
starter: 3 dog
to seed: 4 soft 5 passé, ratty 9 enervated 10 dissipated
__ gone: 3 all, far 4 real
Gone (1957 song)
artist: Ferlin Husky
Gone __ the Wind: 4 With
__ Gone A-Hunting: 6 Daddy's
goner: 8 lame duck 9 lost cause
like a ~: 4 lost, sunk 6 doomed, ruined, undone 7 done for 8 luckless
name: 3 mud
Goneril
father: 4 Lear
sister: 5 Regan 8 Cordelia
Gone Till November (1998 song)
artist: Wyclef Jean
Gone With the Wind: 4 film 5 novel
author: Margaret Mitchell
cast: Olivia de Havilland, Clark Gable, Leslie Howard, Victor Jory, Evelyn Keyes, Vivien Leigh, Hattie McDaniel, Butterfly McQueen, Thomas Mitchell
character: 5 Ellen, Frank, India, Mammy, O'Hara, Rhett 6 Ashley, Butler, Gerald, Wilkes 7 Charles, Kennedy, Melanie, Suellen 8 Hamilton, Pittypat, Scarlett 10 Bonnie Blue
director: Victor Fleming
music: Max Steiner
setting: 4 Tara 7 Atlanta, Georgia
gonfalon: 4 flag 6 banner, ensign
gong: 3 kin 4 bell, peal, ring, toll 5 chime, clang, knell 6 jangle, jingle, kenong, tam-tam 7 resound 10 percussion
Góngora, Luis de: 4 poet 7 Spanish
Gong Show, The: 8 game show
host: Chuck Barris
regular: 4 Farr
Gonna Fly Now (1977 song)
artist: Bill Conti
film: 5 Rocky
__ Gonna Give You Up: 5 Never
Go Now! (1965 song)
artist: Moody Blues
Gonzaga: 6 school 10 university
athletes: 4 Zags 8 Bulldogs
locale: 7 Spokane 10 Washington
Gonzales: 6 Pancho, Speedy
see also Spanish
Gonzales, Pancho: 7 netster 9 tennis pro
milieu: 5 court
Gonzales, Speedy: 4 toon 5 mouse
Gonzalez: 5 Elian
gonzo: 7 bizarre 9 eccentric
goo: 4 glop, gunk, muck, ooze 5 paste, slime 6 liquid 8 baby talk
goober: 4 rube 6 peanut
goober __: 3 pea
Goober: 4 Pyle
cousin: 5 Gomer
Goobers: 5 candy
good: 3 apt, fit, use 4 able, kind, meet, neat, pure, real, sake, tidy, well 5 adept, avail, bully, crack, favor, fresh, great, legal, legit, licit, loyal, moral, right, smart, solid, sound, tasty, valid, yummy 6 adroit, benign, chaste, choice, clever, decent, edible, expert, giving, honest, humane, kasher, kindly, kosher, lawful, polite, proper, savory, seemly, stable, toothy, up to it, useful, virtue, worthy 7 benefit, capable, correct, dutiful, eatable, ethical, fitting, genuine, healthy, helpful, honesty, likable, orderly, probity, saintly, sizable, skilled, upright, welcome, welfare 8 accurate, adequate, all right, becoming, bona fide, dextrous, esculent, faithful, flawless, friendly, gracious, innocent, interest, mannerly, merciful, morality, obedient, obliging, orthodox, pleasant, pleasing, positive, reliable, salutary, sizeable, skillful, splendid, sterling, suitable, talented, very well, virtuous 9 admirable, advantage, agreeable, allowable, authentic, blameless, competent, covetable, delicious, desirable, dexterous, efficient, extensive, favorable, fortunate, guiltless, healthful, honorable, incorrupt, lucrative, opportune, palatable, qualified, rectitude, reputable, righteous, shipshape, sprightly, unspoiled, untainted, up to snuff, well-being, wholesome, .wonderful 10 acceptable, admissible, altruistic, auspicious, beneficent, beneficial, benevolent, charitable, comestible, convenient, creditable, dependable, gratifying, inculpable, in the rules, law-abiding, legitimate, proficient, respectful, salubrious, satisfying, upstanding, usefulness, worthwhile
as ~ as: 6 almost, nearly 7 equal to 8 rivaling 9 virtually 10 tantamount
as ~ as won: 5 on ice 7 assured 10 guaranteed
as new: 5 fixed 6 healed 8 repaired, restored 9 unspoiled
at a ~ clip: 5 apace
be ~ enough: 2 do 4 pass, suit, work 5 avail, get by, serve 6 answer 7 content, deliver, qualify, satisfy, suffice 10 hit the spot

be ~ for: 3 aid 4 help, suit 5 edify, serve 6 assist 7 benefit, enhance, further, improve 9 agree with
be on ~ terms with: 4 know
between prime and ~: 6 choice
bit: 4 some 5 quite 6 rather
breeding: 6 polish 7 conduct, culture, decorum, manners, p's and q's 8 behavior, courtesy, urbanity 9 etiquette, politesse 10 deportment, politeness, refinement
buddy: 3 bro, pal 4 CBer 5 crony
but ~: 4 a lot, very 5 mucho 6 highly, hugely, plenty 9 decidedly 10 thoroughly
buy: 4 deal, find 5 cheap 6 on sale 7 bargain, cut-rate 9 dirt cheap, low-priced 10 economical, marked down
cheer: 8 optimism 9 geniality, happiness
citizen: 5 voter 7 patriot
clean fun: 6 frolic
condition: 5 order 6 health, kilter 7 fitness
create ~ will: 6 endear
deal: 4 lots 5 steal 6 plenty 7 bargain
deed: 8 kindness 10 kindliness
eating: 4 fare, menu 7 cuisine
ender: 3 bye 4 will 7 hearted
enough: 4 fine 8 very well 9 tolerable 10 acceptable
fairly ~: 2 OK 4 fair, so-so 6 decent, not bad 7 average 8 adequate, all right, bearable, mediocre, middling, moderate, ordinary, passable 9 tolerable 10 acceptable, admissible, reasonable, sufficient
faith: 5 honor, truth 6 candor 7 decency, honesty, probity 8 fairness, veracity 9 frankness, integrity, sincerity
feeling: 4 ease 6 relief, solace, thrill 7 comfort 8 sympathy 9 happiness, well-being
feeling ~: 3 fit 4 fine, hale, well 5 happy, hardy, husky, sound 6 hearty, robust, strong 7 chipper, healthy, up to par 8 blooming, thriving, vigorous 9 in the pink 10 able-bodied
find ~: 4 like
for ~: 6 at last 7 finally, forever 8 after all, in the end 10 eventually, ultimately, unendingly
for growing: 7 fertile 8 plowable, tillable
form: 7 manners 8 protocol 9 propriety
for ~ measure: 4 free 6 gratis 7 as a gift 8 as a bonus 9 as an extra 10 in addition, on the house
for nothing: 3 bad 4 evil 6 abject, dismal, rotten 7 pitiful 8 wretched 9 miserable, worthless 10 deplorable, despicable, detestable
for something: 5 handy, utile 6 useful 9 practical
fortune: 4 luck 7 welfare 9 well-being 10 prosperity
full of ~ cheer: 5 merry
general ~: 4 weal
get but ~: 4 nail
grade: 5 B plus
guy: 4 hero
habits: 6 ethics, morals 7 decency, virtues 9 integrity, rectitude 10 principles
hand: 5 flush 8 straight 10 royal flush
have a ~ time: 5 enjoy, party, revel 6 cavort 7 carouse, skylark 8 cut loose, live it up 9 celebrate, make merry, whoop it up
humor: 3 joy 5 mirth 6 gaiety, gayety 9 happiness
in a ~ mood: 5 happy, jolly, riant 6 cheery 7 chipper 8 cheerful, sanguine
in ~ condition: 3 fit 4 neat, well 5 hardy, right, sound 7 healthy 9 untouched
in ~ faith: 5 truly 7 frankly 8 candidly, for keeps, heartily, honestly 9 earnestly, genuinely, seriously, sincerely 10 aboveboard, truthfully
in French: 3 bon
in Italian: 4 bene
in Latin: 4 bene
in ~ shape: 3 fit 4 neat, tidy, trim 5 hardy, sound 6 robust, spruce 7 healthy 8 vigorous
in ~ taste: 6 decent, seemly, snappy 8 tasteful
in the ~ old days: 4 once, past 6 before 7 earlier, long ago, time was, way back 8 back when, formerly, years ago 10 previously
in ~ time: 4 anon, soon 5 early 6 prompt, timely 7 by and by, erelong, shortly 8 punctual 9 presently 10 beforehand, before long
judgment: 5 sense 6 sanity, wisdom
least ~: 5 worst
life: 6 luxury 7 comfort, leisure 9 affluence 10 bed of roses, prosperity
look: 6 eyeful
look ~ on: 3 fit 4 suit 6 become 7 flatter
looks: 4 plus 5 class 6 beauty 7 glamour 8 elegance 9 advantage 10 loveliness
make ~: 3 pay, win 5 atone, pay up, repay 6 arrive, do well, fulfil, hack it, pan out, pay for, recoup, redeem, refund, settle, thrive 7 deliver, fulfill, luck out, pay back, prevail, prosper, realize, recover, rectify, satisfy, succeed, triumph, work out 8 atone for, flourish, get ahead, go places, hit it big, square up 9 indemnify, reimburse 10 accomplish, do all right, recompense
make ~ on: 5 repay 6 fulfil, remedy 7 correct, fulfill, realize 8 carry out, set right 10 accomplish
manners: 5 couth 8 civility, courtesy 9 propriety
many: 8 frequent, numerous
name: 3 rep 5 asset, honor, worth 6 credit, esteem, regard, repute 8 prestige, standing 9 character 10 reputation
name meaning ~: 6 Agatha, Bonnie
nature: 6 gaiety, warmth 9 geniality, joviality, pleasance, sunniness 10 affability, amiability, cheeriness, cordiality, kindliness
no ~: 4 evil, junk 5 lousy 7 useless 10 virtueless
not ~: 3 bad 4 evil, poor
not as ~: 5 worse
not ~ enough: 7 lacking, wanting 8 inferior 9 deficient, half-baked, imperfect 10 inadequate, incomplete
not feel ~: 3 ail 4 hurt
not in ~ humor: 4 dour, glum, ugly 5 cross, gruff, huffy, irate, sulky, surly, testy 6 crabby, cranky, gloomy, grumpy, morose, ornery, sullen 7 grouchy, hostile, peevish 8 frowning, growling, perverse, snappish 9 crotchety, irritable 10 out of sorts, ungracious
old days: 4 past, yore 7 earlier, history, long ago 8 back when 9 yesterday 10 yesteryear
on ~ terms: 4 kind 5 close, thick 6 chummy, clubby, genial, kindly 7 affable, amiable, cordial 8 amicable, friendly, intimate, outgoing, peaceful, sociable 9 convivial 10 benevolent, buddy-buddy, neighborly, solicitous
on the ~ side of: 6 in with
opinion: 6 esteem, regard 7 respect 8 approval, prestige 10 reputation
point: 4 plus 5 asset 6 virtue
pretty ~: 4 fair, so-so, tidy
prospects: 4 hope 7 promise
public ~: 4 weal
put in a ~ word for: 4 laud, plug 8 champion 9 recommend
put in ~ shape: 4 tidy 5 fix up 6 neaten 10 straighten
relations: 5 amity, peace 6 comity 7 concord, harmony 8 goodwill 10 cordiality, fellowship, friendship
review: 4 rave
right arm: 8 backbone, linchpin
sense: 3 wit 5 logic 10 discretion
showing ~ judgment: 4 sane, wise 5 lucid, sober, sound 6 steady 7 logical, prudent 8 all there, balanced, moderate, rational, sensible, together 9 judicious, practical, pragmatic, realistic 10 discerning, fair-minded, reasonable, thoughtful
spirits: 4 glee 5 cheer, mirth 6 gaiety, levity 7 elation, jollity, rapture 8 euphoria, gladness, hilarity 9 happiness, joviality, merriment, well-being 10 enthusiasm, exuberance, joyfulness
stretch of ~ luck: 3 run
stroke of ~ fortune: 4 luck 5 break, fluke 7 godsend 8 blessing, windfall 10 lucky break
taste: 4 tact 5 taste 7 culture
time: 3 fun 4 lark, romp 5 blast
times: 3 fun, ups 10 prosperity
to eat: 4 rich 5 spicy, tasty, yummy 6 delish, savory, toothy 8 heavenly, luscious 9 delicious, flavorful, palatable, succulent, toothsome 10 appetizing, delectable
too ~ for: 10 unworthy of
too much of a ~ thing: 4 glut 5 flood 6 excess 7 surfeit, surplus 8 overload 10 indulgence, oversupply
turn: 5 favor 8 kindness 10 kindliness
very ~: *see* wonderful
vibes: 4 bond 5 unity 6 accord 7 concord, empathy, harmony, rapport 8 affinity 9 agreement, communion 10 friendship
vision: 8 keenness
will: 5 unity 7 harmony 8 kindness 9 readiness, tolerance 10 friendship
wishes: 7 benison, devoirs, regards 8 blessing 10 salutation
with ~ grace: 6 freely, gladly, warmly 7 happily, readily 8 cheerily, heartily 9 willingly 10 cheerfully
with ~ heart: 4 bold 5 brave 6 daring, gritty, plucky, spunky 7 doughty, gallant, valiant 8 intrepid, valorous 9 dauntless 10 courageous
with tools: 4 able 5 adept, handy 6 adroit 7 skilled 8 skillful
with words: 3 pat 4 glib, oily 5 slick, suave 6 artful, facile, fluent, smooth 7 voluble 8 eloquent, slippery 10 articulate, loquacious
word: 4 plug 5 honor, kudos 6 eulogy, homage, praise, salute 7 acclaim, plaudit, tribute 8 accolade, encomium, flattery 9 laudation, panegyric, reference 10 compliment, exaltation
see also wonderful

good __: 3 day, egg, Joe, use 4 life, luck, news, time, word 5 as new, buddy, cheer, faith, humor, looks, night, ol' boy, or bad, speed, title, usage, vibes 6 fellow, morrow, nature 7 evening, morning, offices
good __ boy: 3 old, ole
good __ days: 3 old
good __ nothing: 3 for
good __ was had by all, A: 4 time
good-__: 3 bye 5 sized 7 hearted, looking, natured
good-__ Charlie: 4 time
__ good: 3 for 4 make 5 to the
__-good: 4 feel
Good __: 4 Book, News 5 Times 6 Friday
Good __!: 4 idea 5 gravy, grief
Good __ Hard to Find, A: 5 Man is
Good __ Hunting: 4 Will
Good __, Miss Molly: 5 Golly
Good __, The: 3 Son 4 Deed, Life 5 Earth, Fairy, Fight 6 Doctor, Mother
Good __, Vietnam: 7 Morning
Goodacre, Jill
spouse: Harry Connick Jr.

Goodall: 4 Jane
subject: 3 ape
good and __: 5 ready
Good and __: 6 Fruity, Plenty
Good and Fruity: 4 nosh 5 candy, snack
Good and Plenty: 4 nosh 5 candy, snack
good as __: 3 new 4 gold
Good as Gold
author: Joseph Heller
Good Book: 5 Bible
__ Good Boy Does Fine: 5 Every
goodbye: 4 ciao, exit, ta-ta, vale 5 adieu, adios, aloha, later, leave, peace, see ya 6 bye-bye, shalom, sholom, so long 7 cheerio, parting 8 au revoir, farewell, sayonara, toodle-oo 9 departure
in French: 5 adieu
in Hawaiian: 5 aloha
in Italian: 4 ciao
in Latin: 3 ave 4 vale
in Spanish: 5 adios
kiss ~: 3 rid 4 lose 5 eject, spend 7 abandon, forsake 8 forswear 9 foreswear
say ~: 4 part 5 leave 6 go home
silent ~: 4 wave
Goodbye (song)
artist: Night Ranger, Spice Girls
Goodbye, Columbus: 4 film 7 novella
author: Philip Roth
cast: Richard Benjamin, Jack Klugman, Ali MacGraw
Goodbye Cruel World (1961 song)
artist: James Darren
Goodbye Girl, The (1977 film)
cast: Quinn Cummings, Richard Dreyfuss, Marsha Mason
director: Herbert Ross
Goodbye, Janette
author: Harold Robbins
Goodbye, Mr. Chips: 4 film 5 novel
author: James Hilton
cast: Robert Donat, Greer Garson, Paul Henreid
director: Sam Wood
Goodbye's All We Got Left (1987 song)
artist: Steve Earle
Good-Bye to All That
author: Robert Graves
Goodbye to Berlin
author: Christopher Isherwood
Goodbye to Love (1972 song)
artist: Carpenters
Goodbye Yellow Brick Road (1973 song)
artist: Elton John
__ Good Care of My Baby: 4 Take
__ good cheer!: 4 Be of
Good Christian Men, Rejoice: 5 carol
__ good conscience: 5 in all
good deed
doer: 4 hero 8 Boy Scout
org.: 3 BSA
__ good deed: 3 do a
Good Deed, The
author: Pearl S. Buck
Good Doctor, The
author: Neil Simon
Good Earth, The: 4 film 5 novel
author: Pearl S. Buck
cast: Paul Muni, Luise Rainer
character: 3 Liu 4 O-Lan 5 Ching 6 Nung En 7 Nung Wen 8 Wang Lung
sequel: 4 Sons
Gooden, Dwight: 6 hurler 7 pitcher
nickname: 3 Doc
Good enough!: 4 okay 6 It'll do
Good Enough (1992 song)
artist: Bobby Brown
Goodeve: 5 Grant
__ good example: 4 set a
__ good faith: 5 act in
__ Good Feeling: 5 Era of
GoodFellas (1990 film)
boss: 3 don
cast: Lorraine Bracco, Robert De Niro, Ray Liotta, Joe Pesci, Paul Sorvino
director: Martin Scorsese
group: 5 Mafia
Goodfellow: 3 AFB 5 Robin
Good for Me (1992 song)
artist: Amy Grant
good-for-nothing: 3 bum, cad, low 4 heel, punk 5 brute, churl, crook, fiend, idler, knave, leech, loser, louse, quack, rogue, rowdy, scamp, snake, sorry 6 bad boy, bad egg, bad guy, con man, crummy, loafer, rascal, rotter, varlet, weasel 7 bounder, goof-off, ignoble, laggard, lowlife, moocher, shirker, shyster, slacker, stinker, useless, varmint, wastrel 8 blighter, bootless, chiseler, deadbeat, derelict, fainéant, feckless, inferior, layabout, parasite, picaroon, prodigal, recreant, scalawag, slugabed, sluggard, spalpeen, swindler, unworthy, wretched 9 charlatan, do-nothing, goldbrick, lazybones, miserable, no-account, reprobate, scallawag, scallywag, scoundrel, valueless, worthless 10 malingerer, mountebank, ne'er-do-well, scapegrace
good for what __ you: 4 ails
__ Good Friends: 4 Such
Good Golly, Miss Molly (1958 song)
artist: Little Richard
Good grief!: 4 egad, oh my 5 egads
good-hearted: 4 kind 6 kindly 8 generous, gracious 9 unselfish
Good Hearted Woman (1976 song)
artist: Willie Nelson
Good Hope: 4 cape
locale: 3 RSA 6 Africa
Good Housekeeping award: 4 seal
Good Humor: 8 ice cream
alternative: *see* ice cream
good-humored: 4 easy, mild 5 funny, sweet 7 affable 8 amicable, cheerful, pleasant
goodie: 3 yay 4 gift 5 candy, cooky, snack, sweet, treat 6 cookie 7 present
goodie __: 3 bag
goodies: 4 eats, food, loot 5 snack 6 reward 8 junk food
Gooding: 4 Cuba, Omar
Gooding Jr., Cuba: 5 actor
film: As Good as It Gets (1997)
Boyz N the Hood (1991)
Daddy Day Camp (2007)
Instinct (1999)
Jerry Maguire (1996, AA)
Losing Isaiah (1995)
Men of Honor (2000)
Pearl Harbor (2001)
Radio (2003)
Rat Race (2001)
What Dreams May Come (1998)
Good Intentions
poet: Ogden Nash
Good job!: 5 bravo
Good King Wenceslas: 5 carol
Good Life, The (1963 song)
artist: Tony Bennett
__ good light: 3 in a
__, Good-Lookin': 3 Hey
good-looking: 4 cute, fair, nice 5 bonny 6 bonnie, comely, dreamy, lovely, pretty 7 winsome 8 alluring, gorgeous, handsome, striking, stunning 9 ravishing 10 attractive
guy: 4 hunk 6 Apollo
Good Lord!: 4 egad 5 egads
Good Lovin' (1966 song)
artist: Rascals
Good Luck Charm (1962 song)
artist: Elvis Presley
Good Luck, Miss Wyckoff
author: William Inge
good-luck piece: 5 charm 6 amulet, scarab 8 talisman
goodly: 3 big 4 tidy 5 ample, large, prime 6 choice, select 7 quality, sizable 8 sizeable, superior, top-notch 9 excellent, first-rate, top-drawer 10 first-class
number: 4 gobs, lots, many, tons 5 heaps, horde, piles, scads 6 divers, legion, myriad, oodles, plenty, scores, throng, untold 7 jillion, no end of, umpteen 8 numerous 9 abundance, countless, multitude, thousands, uncounted
part of: 4 most
Goodman: 3 Ace 4 Dody, John 5 Benny, Ellen 6 Dickie
Goodman, Benny: 11 clarinetist
genre: 4 jazz
instrument: clarinet
portrayer: 5 Allen
__ Goodman Brown: 5 Young
Good Man is Hard to Find, A
author: Flannery O'Connor
Goodman, John: 5 actor
film: Always (1989)
Arachnophobia (1990)
The Babe (1992)
Barton Fink (1991)
The Big Lebowski (1998)
Blues Brothers 2000 (1998)
Bringing Out the Dead (1999)
Coyote Ugly (2000)
King Ralph (1991)
Matinee (1993)
One Night at McCool's (2001)
Punchline (1988)
Sea of Love (1989)
film (voice): The Emperor's New Groove (2000)
Monsters, Inc. (2001)
TV: Roseanne
good man, name meaning: 7 Evander
__ good measure: 3 for
__ Good Men: 4 A Few
Good Morning America
alternative: 5 Today
Good Morning, America
author: Carl Sandburg
Good Morning, Dearie: 7 musical
composer: Jerome Kern
Good Morning, Midnight
author: Jean Rhys
Good Morning Starshine (1969 song)
artist: Oliver
show: 4 Hair
Good Morning, Vietnam (1987 film)
cast: Forest Whitaker, Robin Williams
director: Barry Levinson
Good Morrow, The
author: John Donne
Good Mother, The (1988 film)
cast: Ralph Bellamy, Diane Keaton, Liam Neeson, Jason Robards
director: Leonard Nimoy
good-natured: 4 easy, kind, mild, nice 5 jolly, sweet 6 genial, jovial, kindly, polite 7 affable, amiable, cordial, helpful, lenient, likable 8 friendly, gracious, obliging, sociable, tolerant 10 personable
one: 5 sport
Good Neighbor __: 3 Sam 6 Policy
goodness: 4 oh my, oh no, pity 5 heart, honor, merit, right, worth 6 dear me, my word, oh dear, virtue 7 decency, honesty, probity 8 kindness, morality 9 integrity, rectitude 10 excellence, generosity, humaneness, kindliness
honest to ~: 5 truly 6 actual, indeed, really
my ~: 4 gosh 6 dear me 7 heavens
__ goodness: 5 thank
Goodness __!: 8 gracious
Good News (1947 film)
cast: June Allyson, Peter Lawford
Goodnight (1965 song)
artist: Roy Orbison
Goodnight __: 5 Irene 6 Ladies
Good night, __: 4 Chet 5 David
Good Night, and Good Luck (2005 film)
cast: George Clooney, Robert Downey, Jr., David Strathairn
director: George Clooney
Goodnight girl: 5 Irene
Goodnight Tonight (1979 song)
artist: Paul McCartney
good ol' __: 3 boy
Good Queen __: 4 Bess
Goodrich: 2 B.F. 4 Gail 7 Frances
Goodrich, Gail
milieu: 5 court
org.: 3 NBA
sport: 10 basketball
goods: 4 gear, line, load, loot, mdse, ware 5 booty, cargo, order, proof, skill, stock, stuff, wares 6 assets, estate, lading, spoils, tackle, things, wealth 7 effects, freight, imports, produce, product 8 chattels, material, property 9 knowledge, materials, resources, trappings, vendibles, wagonload 10 belongings, right stuff
custodian of ~: 6 bailee
deliver the ~: 7 perform
delivery of ~: 7 receipt
get the ~ on: 3 pin 4 nail, trap
move ~: 4 hawk, push, sell, vend 5 pitch, trade 6 barter, handle,

hustle, market, peddle, retail, unload **7** auction, promote, traffic **9** wholesale
sell a bill of ~: 2 do **3** con, rob **4** bilk, burn, clip, dupe, fool, gull, have, hoax, nick, rook, scam, take, trim **5** cheat, cozen, fraud, gouge, mulct, pluck, set up, shaft, stiff, sting, trick **6** diddle, extort, fleece, hustle, outwit, rip off, sucker **7** deceive, defraud, finagle, sandbag, swindle **8** flim-flam, hoodwink, outsmart **9** bamboozle, four-flush, shake down, victimize **10** run a game on
stolen ~: 4 loot, swag **5** booty **6** spoils **7** plunder
stolen ~ outlet: 5 fence
the ~: 4 dope, info, news, word **7** lowdown
thrown overboard: 5 lagan, ligan
transfer illegal ~: 4 push **7** bootleg, smuggle
yard ~: 5 cloth, stuff **6** fabric **8** material, textiles
__ goods: 3 dry **4** case, free, gray, grey, hard, soft, wash, yard **5** brown, dress, piece, white **7** capital, durable
Good Seasons: 8 dressing
alternative: 8 Wish-Bone **9** Seven Seas
Good Shepherd, The (2006 film)
cast: Alec Baldwin, Matt Damon, William Hurt, Angelina Jolie
director: Robert De Niro
__ Good Ship Lollipop: 5 On the
good-sized: 3 lge. **4** tidy **5** ample, large
Goodson: 4 Mark
good-tasting: 5 tasty, yummy **6** savory **8** luscious, tempting **9** ambrosial, delicious, flavorful, palatable, succulent, toothsome **10** appetizing, delectable
good-tempered: 4 calm, easy, kind, mild, warm **5** sunny, sweet **6** breezy, genial, gentle, mellow, placid, serene **7** affable, amiable, equable, lenient, patient, relaxed **8** amenable, carefree, obliging, outgoing, peaceful, pleasant, tolerant, tranquil **9** easygoing, forgiving, indulgent, peaceable **10** forbearing, unexacting
Good, the Bad, and the Ugly, The: 4 film, song **5** oater **7** western
artist: Hugo Montenegro
cast: Clint Eastwood, Lee Van Cleef, Eli Wallach
director: Sergio Leone
Good Thing (song)
artist: Fine Young Cannibals, Paul Revere and the Raiders
__ good time: 5 all in
good-time Charlie: 5 sport
Good Time Charlie's Got the Blues (1972 song)
artist: Danny O'Keefe
Good Times (1979 song)
artist: Chic
Good Times (CBS sitcom)
cast: John Amos (James Evans)
Esther Rolle (Florida Evans)
Jimmie Walker (J.J. Evans)
catchword: Dynomite
setting: Chicago, Illinois
__ good to be true: 3 too
__ good turn: 3 do a
Good Vibrations (song)
artist: Beach Boys, Marky Mark and the Funky Bunch
good victory, name meaning: 6 Eunice
good walk spoiled, A: 4 golf
goodwill: 5 amity, favor **6** comity **7** charity, concord, rapport **8** altruism **9** sincerity, tolerance **10** cordiality, friendship, generosity
...good will __: 5 to men
Goodwill Games venue: 5 track
Good Will Hunting (1997 film)
cast: Ben Affleck, Matt Damon, Minnie Driver, Robin Williams
director: Gus Van Sant
setting: 3 MIT
Goodwin: 3 Kia
...good witch __ bad witch?: 3 or a
Good work!: 4 nice **5** bravo
goody: 4 gift **5** bonus, candy, cooky, snack, treat **6** cookie, tidbit
often: 4 oldy **5** oldie
two-shoes: 4 prig **5** prude **7** puritan **9** nice Nelly
Goody!: 3 yay, yea, yum **5** oh boy
Goodyear: 4 city, town **7** Charles
craft: 5 blimp
home: 5 Akron
locale: 7 Arizona
goody-goody: 4 prig, prim **5** moral, pious, prude **6** prissy **7** prudish, puritan **8** priggish, virtuous **9** nice Nelly
Goody Goody (1957 song)
artist: Frankie Lymon and the Teenagers
goody-two-shoes: 4 prim **5** sissy **6** demure, proper, stuffy **7** prudish **8** overnice, precious **9** sissified, squeamish, Victorian **10** fastidious, tight-laced
Goody Two Shoes (1982 song)
artist: Adam Ant
gooey: 4 icky, oozy **5** gummy, slimy, tacky, thick **6** creamy, sticky, viscid **7** maudlin, mawkish, viscose, viscous **8** adhesive
stuff: 4 glob, glop, ooze **5** slime
goof: 3 err **4** flub, slip, type **5** boner, botch, error, gaffe, lapse, mix up, snafu, wrong **6** blow it, boo-boo, bungle, foozle, foul up, fumble, mess up, slip up **7** blunder, clinker, erratum, jackass, louse up, mistake, screw up **9** indecorum, mishandle, mismanage
data-entry ~: 4 typo
ender: 4 ball **5** proof
off: 3 veg **4** idle, laze, loll **5** coast, dog it, relax, shirk, slack, tarry **6** dawdle, linger, lounge, putter **7** hang out, slacken **8** lallygag, lollygag, malinger **9** bum around **10** featherbed, fool around, mess around
off, in Britain: 5 sculk, skulk
up: 4 flub **5** botch **6** blow it, boggle, bungle, foozle, mess up **7** blunder **9** mishandle, mismanage
goof-__: 3 off
__ go of: 5 make a
goofball: 4 bozo, nerd **5** dufus **6** doofus **7** bungler, jackass
go off __-cocked: 4 half
goof-off: 5 idler **6** loafer **7** slacker **8** loiterer **9** do-nothing, goldbrick, lazybones **10** ne'er-do-well
goofproof: 4 safe, sure **8** fail-safe, reliable **10** dependable
goofs: 6 errata
goof-up: 5 lapse **7** mistake
goofy: 4 loco, zany **5** daffy, dippy, ditzy, dotty, flaky, goosy, inane, kooky, nutty, silly, wacky **6** absurd, flakey, kookie, screwy, whacky **7** comical, foolish **10** ridiculous, weak-minded
__ goo gai pan: 3 moo
Google: 6 Barney **7** Web site
specialty: 6 search
googly-__: 4 eyed
googol, suffix for: 4 plex
goo-goo: 8 baby talk
make ~ eyes at: 4 ogle **5** flirt **8** check out
Goo Goo Dolls
song: Iris (1998)
Name (1995)
Slide (1998)
Goolagong, Evonne: 7 netster **9** tennis pro
goon: 3 ape **4** boor, hood, thug **5** rowdy, tough **6** galoot, gunsel, lummox **7** bruiser, galloot, gorilla, hoodlum, ruffian **8** gangster, hooligan, tough guy **9** roughneck
goon __: 5 squad
go on __: 5 a diet, a tear **6** record
Go on...: 3 and
go one __: 6 better
gooney: 4 bird **5** silly **9** albatross
Goonies 'R' Good Enough, The (1985 song)
artist: Cyndi Lauper
goony: 3 mad **4** bird, gaga **5** sappy, silly, wacky **6** absurd, madcap **7** foolish **9** half-baked, ludicrous, senseless **10** ridiculous
goop: 3 gel, tar **4** gunk **6** liquid
goopy: 5 yucky **7** viscose, viscous
goose: 4 bird, dolt, fowl, lift, meat, nene, poke, prod, push, spur **5** biped, brant, ninny, pique, raise, silly **6** dimwit, Embden, honker, outwit **7** graylag, greylag, jackass, pinhead **8** motivate, outsmart **9** harebrain, simpleton **10** nincompoop
arctic ~: 5 brant
cousin: 4 swan
down garment: 4 vest
egg: 3 nil, zip **4** nada, none, null, zero **5** zilch, zippo **6** cipher, naught, nought **7** nothing
eggs: 3 OOO **4** OOOO **5** OOOOO
ender: 4 fish, foot, neck **5** berry
formation: 3 vee
genus: 5 anser
group: 5 flock **6** gaggle
have ~ bumps: 6 shiver, thrill
Hawaiian ~: 4 nene
like a ~: 8 anserine
male: 6 gander
sea ~: 5 solan **6** gannet
snow ~ genus: 4 chen
something for the ~: 5 sauce
sound: 4 honk, yang **6** cackle
young: 7 gosling
goose __: 3 egg **4** down, skin, step **5** bumps, flesh **6** grease **7** pimples
__ goose: 4 snow **6** Canada, golden
Goose: 5 Tatum **6** Goslin **7** Gossage
Goose __: 3 Bay
__ Goose: 4 Grey **6** Father, Mother, Spruce
Goose and Tomtom
author: David Rabe
gooseberry: 5 fruit, shrub
Chinese ~: 4 kiwi
Hawaiian ~: 4 poha
wild ~: 8 dogberry
gooseberry fool: 7 dessert
goose bumps
have ~: 6 tingle
raising ~: 4 eery **5** eerie, scary, weird **6** creepy, occult, spooky **7** ghostly, macabre, uncanny **9** unearthly **10** mysterious
Goosebumps: 10 book series
author: R.L. Stine
like ~: 4 eery **5** eerie
__-goose chase: 4 wild
goosefoot plant: 5 orach **6** orache
gooseneck __: 4 lamp
goosenecker: 9 spectator
__-goosey: 6 loosey
Goossens, Eugene: 9 conductor
goosy: 4 daft **5** balmy, daffy, dotty, goofy, inane, kooky, nutty, sappy, silly, wacky **6** simple **7** asinine, foolish, witless **9** brainless, half-baked, senseless **10** half-witted
go out of __: 5 style
go out of one's __: 3 way
go out the __: 6 window
go out with __: 5 a bang
GOP: 5 party **10** Republican
birthplace: 5 Ripon
elephant creator: Thomas Nast
member: 3 Rep.
opponent: 3 Dem.
org.: 3 RNC
part of ~: 3 Old **5** Grand, Party
gopher: 6 animal, mammal, rodent
gig: 6 errand
relative: *see* rodent
gopher __: 4 ball, wood
__ Gophers: 6 Golden
Gopher State: 4 Minn. **9** Minnesota
Gorbachev: 5 Raisa **7** Mikhail **8** Nobelist
realm: 4 USSR
see also Russian
Gorcey: 3 Leo **7** Bernard
__ Gorda, FL: 5 Punta
Gordian knot: 5 poser
undoer's reward: 4 Asia
Gordie: 4 Howe
Gordimer, Nadine: 6 writer **8** Nobelist **12** South African
Gordius
problem for ~: 4 knot
son: 5 Midas
__ Gordo: 5 Cerro
Gordon: 4 Gale, Jeff, Jump, Ruth **5** Barry, Flash, Gekko, Keith, Parks, Scott **6** Dexter, MacRae, Stuart **7** Douglas, Jenkins, Michael **9** Lightfoot
Gordon __: 6 setter
Gordon, Dexter: 11 saxophonist
genre: 4 jazz
Gordon, Flash: 4 hero
alma mater: 4 Yale
milieu: 5 space
partner: 4 Dale

__ Gordon, GA: 4 Fort
Gordon, Ruth: 7 actress
film: Harold and Maude (1972)
Maxie (1985)
Rosemary's Baby (1968, AA)
spouse: Garson Kanin
Gordy: 5 Berry
gore: 4 stab 5 panel, stick 6 empale, gusset, impale, pierce 9 penetrate
Gore: 2 Al 5 Vidal 6 Lesley, Tipper 7 Michael
interest: 4 ecol. 7 ecology
Gore, Lesley
song: It's My Party (1963)
Judy's Turn to Cry (1963)
She's a Fool (1963)
You Don't Own Me (1964)
Goren, Charles forte: 6 bridge
Gore-Tex: 6 fabric 8 material
Gorey: 6 Edward
gorge: 3 eat, gap 4 bolt, cloy, fill, glen, glut, gulf, gulp, hole, pass, rift, sate, wolf 5 abyss, binge, cañon, chasm, cleft, dig in, gulch, gully, stuff 6 arroyo, canyon, devour, fill up, gobble, guzzle, hollow, pig out, ravine, valley 7 consume, fissure, Olduvai, overeat, satiate, satisfy, surfeit 8 crevasse 10 gluttonize, gormandize
gorged: 3 fed 4 full 7 replete
Gorge of the __: 3 Aar 4 Aare
gorgeous: 4 cute, fair, rich 5 bonny, plush, showy 6 bonnie, comely, lavish, lovely, pretty 7 elegant, sublime, winsome 8 adorable, alluring, dazzling, fetching, glorious, handsome, imposing, pleasing, splendid, striking, stunning 9 beautiful, exquisite, luxurious, ravishing, sumptuous 10 attractive
one: 4 hunk 6 Adonis, Apollo 8 knockout
Gorgeous __: 6 George
gorgeousness: 6 dazzle 7 glitter 8 splendor
gorger: 7 glutton
gorget: 6 wimple
gorging: 7 hoggish 9 voracious 10 gluttonous
Gorgon: 3 hag 6 Medusa
mother: 4 Ceto
Gorgonzola: 6 cheese
gorilla: 3 ape 4 goon, thug 5 biped 6 animal 7 primate
like a ~: 5 apish, hairy
relative: *see* primate
small ~: 6 apelet
Gorillas in the Mist (1988 film)
cast: Bryan Brown, Julie Harris, Sigourney Weaver
director: Michael Apted
__ Goriot: 4 Père
Gorki: 4 city, town 5 Maxim 6 Maksim
locale: 6 Russia
river: 3 Oka 5 Volga
Gorky: 5 Maxim 6 Maksim 7 Arshile, Russian
Gorky Park (1983 film)
cast: Brian Dennehy, William Hurt, Lee Marvin
director: Michael Apted
Gorman: 5 Cliff
gormandize: 3 eat 4 cloy, glut, sate 5 binge, gorge, stuff 6 devour, gobble 7 overeat, satiate, surfeit 10 gluttonize
gormandizer: 5 eater 7 glutton, gobbler
Gorme, Eydie
song: Blame It on the Bossa Nova (1963)
spouse: Steve Lawrence
__-go-round: 5 merry
gorp: 5 snack 8 trail mix
eater: 5 hiker
gorse: 4 whin 5 brush, furze, shrub 7 bramble
like a ~: 5 spiny 7 prickly
locale: 4 moor
Gorshin: 5 Frank
Gortner: 6 Marjoe
Gorton: 5 Slade
gory: 3 raw, red 5 lurid 6 bloody, grisly 7 ghastly, graphic, macabre, violent 8 gruesome 9 frightful 10 horrifying
Gosden, Freeman
role: 4 Amos
Gosdin: 4 Vern
Gosford Park (2001 film)
cast: Bob Balaban, Alan Bates, Kristin Scott Thomas
director: Robert Altman
gosh: 3 gee, wow 4 oath, oh my 5 golly 6 jiminy 7 heavens, jeepers, jimminy 10 my goodness
preceder: 3 omi
goshawk: 4 bird
Goshen: 4 city, town
locale: 7 Indiana
__ Goshen!: 5 Land o'
gosling: 4 bird
parent: 5 goose 6 gander
Gosling: 4 Ryan
Goslin, Goose: 10 outfielder
gospel: 4 fact 5 dogma, genre, music, truth 6 truism, verity 8 doctrine 9 actuality
take as ~: 3 buy 6 accept, credit, rely on 7 believe, swallow, swear by
gospel __: 5 music, truth 6 brunch
Gospel: 4 John, Luke, Mark 5 truth 7 Matthew, the Word
Gospels follower: 4 Acts
Gossage, Goose: 6 hurler 7 pitcher
gossamer: 3 web 4 airy, fine, lacy, thin 5 filmy, gauze, gauzy, light, sheer, wispy 6 flimsy, flossy 7 netlike, tenuous, weblike 8 delicate, ethereal, feathery, filament, finespun 9 lightsome 10 cobweblike, diaphanous
Gosselin: 3 Jon 4 Kate
`Gosselin`
kids: 5 eight
Gossett: 3 Lou 5 Louis
Gossett Jr., Louis Oscar: An Officer and a Gentleman
gossip: 3 gab, jaw, mud, wag, yak, yap 4 blab, buzz, chat, chin, dirt, dish, dope, info, poop, talk, word 5 juice, prate, rumor, snoop, story, yenta 6 babble, earful, gabble, gibber, latest, ramble, report, rumors, tattle, yakker 7 babbler, blather, blether, chatter, hearsay, meddler, palaver, prattle, scandal, schmoos, tattler, whisper 8 busybody, chitchat, dish dirt, fat mouth, idle talk, prattler, quidnunc, schmoose, schmooze 9 loose talk, small talk, table talk 10 backbiting, chatterbox, chew the rag, dirty linen, noise about, taleteller, tattletale
column subject: 4 item, star 5 actor, celeb 7 actress, notable 8 luminary 9 celebrity, headliner, personage
ender: 6 monger
like a ~'s tongue: 4 awag
like some ~: 4 idle
spread ~: 3 gab, yak 5 bandy
tidbit: 4 item, tale 5 on dit, rumor
Gossip From the Forest
author: Thomas Keneally
gossiping: 5 prate 9 garrulous 10 scandalous
gossipmonger: 5 yenta 7 meddler 8 busybody, quidnunc
gossipy: 5 abuzz, juicy, newsy 6 blabby, chatty 9 talkative 10 bigmouthed, loquacious
Gosta Berlings Saga
author: Selma Lagerlöf
Got __ O' Livin' To Do: 4 a Lot
Got __ There: 4 to Be
Got __ With an Angel: 5 a Date
__ Got a Brand New Bag: 5 Papa's
__ Got a Crush on You: 3 I've
Got a Date With an __: 5 Angel
__ Got a Friend: 5 You've
__ Got a Gal in Kalamazoo: 3 I've
Got a Hold of Me (1984 song)
artist: Christine McVie
Gotama __: 6 Buddha
__ Got a Name: 3 I've
__ Got a Secret: 3 I've
__ Got a Way: 4 She's
gotcha: 3 aha, hah, oho 4 I dig, I see, trap 7 mistake 10 understood
Go, team!: 3 rah, yay, yea
Göteborg: 4 city, port, town
locale: 6 Sweden
Go Tell __ the Mountain: 4 It on
Go Tell It on the Mountain
author: James Baldwin
Goth: 5 genre, style 9 barbarian
foe: 5 Roman
kin: 3 Hun
target: 4 Rome
Gotha: 4 city, town
locale: 7 Germany
Gotham
see New York City
Gotham City
defender: 6 Batman
Gotham City (1997 song)
artist: R. Kelly
Gothamite: 4 NYer 9 New Yorker
__ go there: 4 Don't
gothic: 5 crude 8 barbaric 9 barbarous
Gothic: 4 font 5 style 6 quaint 8 medieval, typeface 9 mediaeval
architectural feature: 5 gable, ogive 6 flèche 8 gargoyle
Gothic __: 4 arch 5 armor, novel
Gothika (2003 film)
cast: Halle Berry, Robert Downey Jr.
go through the __: 4 roof 7 motions
__ got it!: 3 I've
Got it!: 4 I dig, I see
Got it?: 3 See
Gotland: 4 isle 6 island
locale: 6 Baltic, Sweden
__ Got Mail: 5 You've
Got me!: 6 I dunno
Got My Mind Set on You (1987 song)
artist: George Harrison
__ Got Noboby: 5 I Ain't
go to __: 3 pot 4 seed, town 5 press, waste 6 pieces
go to __ for: 3 bat
go-to-__: 7 meeting
go to one's __: 4 head
go to the __: 3 mat 4 dogs, wall
__ Got Sixpence: 3 I've
__ Gotta Be Me: 3 I've
__ Gotta Crow: 3 I've
__ gotta do what...: 5 A man's
__ Gotta Have It: 4 She's
__-gotten gains: 3 ill
Götterdämmerung: 5 opera
composer: Richard Wagner
role: 4 Norn 5 Hagen 7 Gunther, Gutrune 8 Alberich 9 Siegfried, Waltraute 10 Brünnhilde
setting: 5 Rhine 7 Germany
Gottfried: 4 Benn 5 Brian 6 Keller 7 Gilbert
in Lohengrin: 4 swan
sister: 4 Elsa
__ Got the Sun in the Morning: 3 I've
__ Got the Whole World...: 3 He's
__ Got the World on a String: 3 I've
Gottlieb: 4 Mark 7 Daimler
Got to Be There (1971 song)
artist: Michael Jackson
Got to Get You Into My Life (song)
artist: Beatles, Earth, Wind & Fire
Got to Give It Up (1977 song)
artist: Marvin Gaye
__ Got Tonight: 4 We've
__ Got You Under My Skin: 3 I've
gouache: 3 art 5 paint 7 picture
Gouda: 4 city, town 6 cheese
kin: *see* cheese
locale: 7 Holland 11 Netherlands
Goudy: 4 font 8 typeface
gouge: 3 cut, dig, pit, rut 4 bilk, bore, gash, hole, nick, rook 5 cheat, notch, scoop, score 6 burrow, chisel, dredge, extort, fleece, furrow, groove, shovel, trench, tunnel 7 channel, defraud, swindle 8 excavate 9 victimize 10 excavation, overcharge, run a game on
out: 4 bore, rout 8 excavate
gouging, interest: 5 usury
goulash: 3 mix 4 stew 6 jumble 7 mélange, mixture 8 mishmash 9 casserole, potpourri 10 hodgepodge
Gould: 3 Jay 5 Glenn, Shane 6 Harold, Morton 7 Chester, Elliott
Gould, Chester character: 4 Dick, Tess 5 Tracy 9 Trueheart
__ Gould Cozzens: 5 James
Gould, Elliott: 5 actor
film: Bob & Carol & Ted & Alice (1969)
Bugsy (1991)
Capricorn One (1978)
Little Murders (1971)
MASH (1970)
Ocean's 11 (2001)
The Silent Partner (1978)
spouse: Barbra Streisand
Gould, Glenn: 7 pianist 8 Canadian, musician

Goulding: 3 Ray 6 Edmund
Gould, Jay railroad: 4 Erie
Gould, Shane: 7 swimmer
Goulet, Robert
spouse: Carol Lawrence
go under the __: 6 hammer
Gounod: 7 Charles
contemporary: 4 Lalo 5 Bizet
opera: 5 Faust
go up in __: 5 smoke 6 flames
gourami: 3 pet 4 fish 6 anabas
__ gourami: 7 kissing
gourd: 4 pepo 5 melon 6 ipu ipu, noggin, veggie 7 shekere 8 calabash 9 vegetable
kin: 6 squash 7 pumpkin
musical instrument: 5 guiro
sponge ~: 5 loofa, luffa 6 loofah
gourmand: 5 diner, eater 7 epicure, glutton 10 gastronome
gourmandism: 7 cookery, cuisine 8 gluttony 10 gastronomy
gourmandize: 3 eat 4 dine 5 feast
gourmet: 6 foodie 7 epicure 9 bon vivant 10 gastronome
treat: 6 luxury 8 ambrosia, delicacy
govern: 3 run 4 curb, head, lead, rule, sway, tame 5 pilot, reign, steer 6 direct, handle, head up, manage, subdue 7 command, conduct, contain, control, dictate, oversee, preside 8 dominate, hold sway, regulate, restrain, rule over 9 determine, officiate, reign over, supervise 10 administer, predispose
governable: 8 obedient 9 compliant, malleable, tractable 10 manageable, submissive
governed: 5 ruled, under 7 subject 9 subject to 10 answerable, controlled
be ~ by: 4 obey
governess: 4 amah, ayah, nana 5 nanny, nurse 6 duenna, nannie 8 tutoress 9 nursemaid
fictional ~: 4 Anna, Eyre 7 Poppins
like ~ novels: 6 Gothic
governing: 4 main 5 major, prime 7 leading, primary 9 executive, number one, paramount, principal 10 preeminent
body: 5 board, panel 7 council 8 trustees 9 directors 10 commission, executives, management
__-governing: 4 self 7 nonself
government: 4 rule 5 power, state, taxer, union 6 regime 7 command, control 8 dominion, politics, Uncle Sam 9 authority, direction, dominance, executive, restraint, supremacy 10 domination, management, presidency, regulation, statecraft, Washington
agent: 4 G-man, narc, nark, T-man
bite: 3 tax
combining form: 5 -archy, -cracy
head: 2 p.m. 4 pres. 9 president
local ~ unit: 2 tp. 3 twp. 8 township
of ~: 5 polit. 9 political
official: 5 envoy 6 consul, legate 8 delegate, diplomat, emissary, minister 10 ambassador
official in India: 5 dewan, diwan
provisional ~: 5 junta
rules of ~: 3 law 10 due process
rules, to some: 4 maze 6 jungle, morass 7 red tape 9 labyrinth
seat of ~: 7 capital
security: 5 E bond, T-bill, T-bond, T-note
veteran: 3 pol
government-in-__: 5 exile
governor: 4 boss, head 5 chief, ruler 6 gerent, leader, master, top dog, warden 7 manager 8 director, official 9 executive, organizer 10 supervisor
Algerian ~: 3 dey
governor __: 7 general
Governors __: 6 Island
govt.
'40s ~ agcy.: 3 OPA
agcy.: 3 ATF, BEP, BLS, CDC, CIA, DEA, DOD, DOT, EPA, FAA, FBI, FCC, FDA, FEC, FTC, GAO, GPO, GSA, HHS, HUD, INS, IRS, NEA, NIH, NPS, NRC, NSA, NSC, NSF, NWS, SBA, SEC, SSA, SSS 4 CPSC, EEOC, FDIC, FEMA, NASA, NLRB, NOAA, NTSB, OSHA, USCG, USDA, USIA, USPS 6 Amtrak
agency: 3 bur. 4 dept.
agt.: 3 Fed
assistance fund: 3 SSI
bank underwriter: 4 FDIC
document: 3 lic.
employee: 3 agt.
flight regulator: 3 FAA
investigation grp.: 3 ATF
investigator: 4 G-man, T-man
lender: 3 FHA 4 FNMA, GNMA
local ~ unit: 3 twp.
meteorology agcy.: 3 NWS
news source: 4 USIA
-owned: 4 natl.
purchasing org.: 3 GSA
representative: 3 amb.
research sponsor: 3 NSF
seed-money agency: 3 SBA
shortwave service: 3 VOA
spending watchdog: 3 GAO, OMB
training program: 4 CETA
undercover group: 3 NSA
see also government
Gowdy: 4 Curt
Gower: 4 John 8 Champion
wife: 5 Marge
Gower, John: 4 poet 7 British
Go West (1940 film)
cast: Chico Marx, Groucho Marx, Harpo Marx
Go West, Young Man (1936 film)
cast: Randolph Scott, Mae West
go whole __: 3 hog
go without __: 6 saying
go-with-the-flow: 6 pliant 7 pliable 8 flexible, moldable 9 adaptable, malleable, tractable
gowk: 3 sap 4 clod, dolt, dope, fool 5 cluck, dummy, dunce, klutz, ninny 6 dimwit, lummox, nitwit 7 dullard, half-wit 8 dumbbell, lunkhead 9 blockhead, simpleton 10 dunderhead, nincompoop
gown: 4 garb, robe 5 dress, frock, habit, tunic 6 formal, kimono, kirtle 7 costume, garment
fabric: 4 lamé, silk 5 satin, tulle
like some ~s: 6 beaded, dressy
occasion: 4 prom
part: 5 train
renter: 3 snr. 6 senior
Roman ~: 5 stola
starter: 5 night
__ gown: 6 bridal, cap and 7 evening, wedding
Goya, Francisco: 6 artist, etcher 7 painter, Spanish
locale: 5 Prado
subject: 4 Alba, Maja
Go Your Own Way (1977 song)
artist: Fleetwood Mac
Gozzi, Carlo: 7 Italian 10 playwright
gp.: 3 org. 4 assn.
GP: 2 dr., MD 3 doc 6 doctor 9 physician
exam for future ~s: 4 MCAT
expertise: 4 anat.
horse ~: 3 DVM
org.: 3 AMA
reference: 3 PDR
GPA part: 3 avg. 5 grade, point 7 average
GPO
concern: 3 ltr. 4 mail
part: 6 Office 8 Printing 10 Government
GQ: 3 mag 8 magazine
Gr.
see Greece
grab: 3 get, nab 4 fist, glom, grip, hook, land, nail, snag, snap, take, tear, trap 5 catch, clasp, grasp, pluck, seize, usurp 6 arrest, clinch, clutch, collar, corral, engage, jump at, kidnap, obtain, please, regale, snap up, snatch, tackle 7 acquire, capture, ensnare, enthral, grapple, impress, insnare, inthral, latch on, possess, procure, receive, seizure 8 enthrall, glom on to, interest, inthrall, intrigue, take over 9 apprehend, extradite, get hold of, latch onto, lay hold of, stimulate, titillate 10 confiscate, lay hands on, usurpation
a bite: 3 eat 4 nosh 5 lunch, snack 6 gobble, nibble 7 munch on, put away, scarf up 8 chow down, wolf down 9 have a meal, scarf down
a chair: 3 sit 4 park 5 perch 8 plop down
a plane: 6 hijack 8 highjack
away: 3 nab 4 snag 6 abduct, kidnap, snatch 7 capture
bag: 3 mix 7 mixture 9 patchwork
smash and ~: 4 loot 5 rifle 7 plunder
some z's: 4 doze 5 sleep 6 catnap, drowse, nod off, snooze 7 drop off, slumber
the check: 3 buy 5 treat 6 pay for, pick up
grab __: 3 bag, bar 4 line, rope
grab __ to eat: 5 a bite
Grabbe, Christian: 6 German 10 playwright
grabber: 5 cleat, proof, talon 6 pliers 7 mystery
grabbiness: 5 greed 7 avarice 8 cupidity, rapacity
grabby: 6 greedy 7 selfish 9 mercenary 10 avaricious
Grable, Betty: 5 pinup 7 actress
spouse: Jackie Coogan, Harry James
grabs, up for: 4 iffy, open 6 chancy, unsure 7 anyone's, to be had 9 ambiguous, available, uncertain, unsettled 10 accessible, indefinite, obtainable, unoccupied, unresolved
grab the __ by the horns: 4 bull
grace: 4 deck 5 adorn, balon, charm, favor, honor, mercy, poise, style 6 allure, ballon, beauty, bedeck, pardon, polish, prayer, set off 7 culture, dignify, elevate, enhance, fluency, garnish, glorify, quarter, smile on 8 beautify, blessing, breeding, clemency, decorate, elegance, kindness, lenience, leniency, ornament, reprieve, urbanity 9 embellish, lightness, smile upon, tolerance 10 invocation, loveliness, refinement, suppleness
coup de ~: 4 blow 5 ender 9 final blow
embodiment of ~: 4 swan
fall from ~: 3 err, sin 5 lapse, stray 7 do wrong, offense 8 iniquity 9 backslide 10 transgress
follower: 5 dig in
lack of ~: 9 gaucherie
name meaning ~: 3 Ann 4 Anna, Anne 6 Hannah
say ~: 4 pray 6 invoke
starter: 3 dis 5 scape
under pressure: 4 cool, tact 5 poise 6 aplomb 7 dignity 8 presence 9 assurance, composure, diplomacy, sang-froid 10 confidence, equanimity
with good ~: 6 freely, gladly, warmly 7 happily, readily 8 cheerily, heartily 9 willingly 10 cheerfully
word: 4 amen 5 bless
grace __: 3 cup 4 note 6 period
__ grace: 6 saving
Grace: 4 Mark 5 Jones, Kelly, Moore, Paley, Slick 6 Aglaia, Bumbry, Maggie, Thalia, Topher 7 Van Owen 8 Coolidge 9 Metalious, Mirabella 10 Euphrosyne
ender: 4 land
__ & Grace: 4 Will
Grace Abounding
author: John Bunyan
graceful: 4 airy, deft, neat, nice, trim 5 agile, clean, light, lithe, slick 6 adroit, au fait, dainty, expert, fluent, gainly, limber, lissom, lovely, nimble, poised, pretty, smooth, supple, svelte 7 capable, elegant, flowing, lissome, refined, shapely, skilled, tactful, trained, willowy 8 artistic, delicate, dextrous, esthetic, masterly, seasoned, skillful, tasteful 9 aesthetic, competent, dexterous, efficient, lightsome, lithesome, masterful 10 artistical, proficient, statuesque
one: 4 peri, swan 5 sylph 6 impala

Graceland: 6 estate
locale: 4 Tenn. 7 Memphis 9 Tennessee
name: 4 Aron 5 Elvis
graceless: 4 rude 5 crude, gawky, inept, rough, stiff, unapt 6 clumsy, clunky, coarse, gauche, klutzy, oafish 7 awkward, boorish, corrupt, gawkish, loutish, unadept, uncouth 8 barbaric, bumbling, bungling, improper, ungainly, unpoised 9 all thumbs, barbarian, barbarous, inelegant, lumbering, maladroit, ponderous, shameless, stumbling, tasteless, unskilled 10 indecorous, outlandish, uncultured, unmannered, unskillful
one: 2 ox 3 lug, oaf 4 boor, clod, lout 5 klutz 6 lummox 7 bumbler, bungler, fumbler, palooka 8 meathead 10 stumblebum
Grace, Mark
sport: 8 baseball
...grace of God __: 3 go I
graces
social ~: 7 manners 9 propriety
Grace Under Fire (ABC sitcom)
cast: Brett Butler (Grace Kelly)
Grace Van __: 4 Owen
gracias: 5 danke 6 thanks 7 spasibo 8 thank you
response: 6 de nada
Gracie: 5 Allen 6 Fields 7 Charlie
to George: 4 wife 6 costar 7 partner
Gracie __: 7 Mansion
gracile: 4 lank, lean, slim, thin, wiry 5 lanky, spare 6 dainty, gangly, skinny, slight, slinky, svelte, twiggy 7 scraggy, scrawny, slender, spidery, willowy 8 gangling 9 sylphlike
gracious: 3 big 4 good, kind, nice, warm 5 civil, noble, suave 6 benign, decent, genial, gentle, giving, kindly, polite, tender, urbane 7 affable, amiable, clement, cordial, courtly, dutiful, gallant, heedful, lenient, mindful, refined, sparing, stately, tactful, willing 8 amenable, amicable, debonair, friendly, highbred, ladylike, likeable, mannerly, merciful, obliging, pleasant, pleasing, sociable, yielding 9 agreeable, attentive, compliant, congenial, courteous, debonaire, favorable, indulgent, sensitive, tractable, unselfish 10 altruistic, beneficent, benevolent, bighearted, charitable, chivalrous, debonnaire, diplomatic, hospitable, neighborly, propitious, respectful, submissive, thoughtful
be ~: 5 bless, smile, thank 6 praise
Gracious!: 4 egad, oh no 5 egads
graciousness: 5 heart 8 kindness, sympathy 10 compassion
grackle: 3 daw 4 bird
call: 3 caw 5 croak 6 squawk
grad: 4 alum 6 reuner 7 alumnus, student
achievement: 3 deg. 6 degree
degree: 2 MS 3 Ed.D., MFA, Ph.D
future ~: 2 jr., sr. 3 jnr., snr. 6 junior, senior
sch. exam: 3 GRE 4 GMAT, LSAT
school major: 3 law 4 math
tech ~: 2 EE, IE, ME 4 engr.
gradation: 4 rank, step 5 level, order, scale, shade, stage 6 degree, series 8 sequence 9 variation 10 difference, divergence, succession
grade: 3 bee, cee, dee 4 hill, mark, ramp, rank, rate, sift, sort, step, tier, tilt 5 A plus, B plus, class, C plus, D plus, level, pitch, score, slant, slope, stage 6 A minus, assort, B minus, C minus, degree, divide, D minus, glacis, league, rating, screen, status 7 echelon, flatten, footing, incline, measure, quality, station, stratum, variety 8 category, classify, evaluate, graduate, standard 9 acclivity
A: 4 best 5 prime 8 four-star, topnotch 9 egg rating, topflight 10 first-class, milk rating
adjuster: 4 plus 5 minus
bad ~: 2 ef 5 D plus 6 D minus
good ~: 5 A plus, B plus
junior-high ~: 5 ninth 6 eighth 7 seventh
make the ~: 3 win 4 pass 5 ace it, cut it, score 6 arrive, hack it, pan out, thrive 7 luck out, prevail, prosper, qualify, satisfy, succeed, triumph, work out 8 flourish, get ahead, go places 9 measure up 10 pass muster
middling ~: 5 C plus 6 C minus
not make the ~: 4 bomb, fail, flop, fold 7 lose out 8 fall flat 9 fall short
range: 4 elhi
receive a high ~ on: 3 ace
starter: 4 down 5 retro
steak ~: 5 prime 6 choice
up to ~: 8 adequate, suitable 10 acceptable, sufficient
grade __: 6 school
grade __ average: 5 point
__ grade: 3 pay
__-grade: 3 low 4 high
Grade: 3 Lew
Grade A product: 4 eggs, milk
grade-schooler: 3 kid 5 child 9 youngster
gradient: 4 ramp, rise, tilt 5 pitch, slant, slope 6 glacis 7 incline 9 acclivity, declivity
grad-to-be: 2 sr. 3 snr. 6 senior
gradual: 4 poky, slow 6 draggy, gentle, steady 7 halting, impeded, lagging, languid 8 bit by bit, crawling, creeping, dawdling, dilatory, dragging, drawn-out, hesitant, plodding, slothful, sluggish, toddling 9 by degrees, leisurely, lethargic, piecemeal, prolonged, snaillike, unhurried 10 deliberate, protracted, step-by-step
decrease: 5 slump 7 decline, falloff 8 downturn, slowdown 9 downtrend 10 slackening
gradually: 8 bit by bit 9 by degrees, leisurely, piecemeal, regularly 10 constantly, inch by inch, moderately, step by step
graduate: 4 alum, pass, rank, sort 5 grade, group, order 6 alumna, doctor, master 7 alumnus, arrange, mark off, promote, student 8 bachelor, classify, conferee 9 calibrate, diplomate 10 measure out
assistant: 7 teacher 8 lecturer 10 instructor
deg.: 3 DDS, LLD, MBA, MFA, MPA, Sc.D.
garb: 3 cap 4 gown
work: 5 paper 6 thesis 9 discourse 10 exposition
graduate __: 6 school
Graduate, The (1967 film)
cast: Anne Bancroft, Dustin Hoffman, Katharine Ross
character: 3 Ben 6 Elaine
director: Mike Nichols
hotel: 4 Taft
graduation: 5 event 8 ceremony, sequence
month: 4 June
Grady: 3 Don
Graeco-__: 5 Roman
Graf: 4 Hans 6 Steffi
rival: 5 Seles
see also German
Graf __: 4 Spee
Graff: 5 Ilene
graffiti: 7 doodles, marring 9 scribbles 10 defacement
apply ~: 3 mar 5 spray 6 deface
artist's addition: 5 beard 6 goatee
to some: 3 art
Graffman, Gary: 7 pianist
Graf, Hans: 9 conductor
Graf, Steffi
spouse: Andre Agassi
graft: 3 bud 4 cion, join, loot 5 bribe, scion, shoot 6 boodle, payoff, payola, racket, splice, spoils 7 bribery, implant, jobbery 8 kickback, venality 9 extortion, hush money 10 corruption, transplant
recipient: 4 host, tree 5 plant
grafted, in heraldry: 4 enté
grafter: 6 rascal, robber
Grafton: 3 Sue
Grafton, Sue: 6 writer
sleuth: Kinsey Millhone
work: 'A' Is for Alibi
'B' Is for Burglar
'C' Is for Corpse
'D' Is for Deadbeat
'E' Is for Evidence
'F' Is for Fugitive
'G' Is for Gumshoe
'H' Is for Homicide
'I' Is for Innocent
'J' Is for Judgment
'K' Is for Killer
'L' Is for Lawless
'M' Is for Malice
'N' Is for Noose
'O' Is for Outlaw
'P' Is for Peril
'Q' Is for Quarry
'R' Is for Ricochet
'S' Is for Silence
'T' Is for Trespass
'U' Is for Undertow
'Z' Is for Zero
graham __: 5 flour 7 cracker
Graham: 4 Bill, Hill, Kerr, Nash, Otto, town 5 Billy, Larry 6 Gerrit, Greene, Lauren, Martha, Parker 7 Chapman, Heather, Sheilah, Stedman 9 Katharine
__ Graham Bell: 9 Alexander
Graham, Billy: 3 rev. 8 reverend
Graham, Bob state: 3 Fla. 7 Florida
Grahame: 6 Gloria 7 Kenneth
Grahame, Kenneth: 6 writer 7 British
character: 4 Mole, Toad 5 Otter
work: The Wind in the Willows
Graham, Heather: 7 actress
film: Austin Powers: The Spy Who Shagged Me (1999)
Boogie Nights (1997)
Bowfinger (1999)
Lost in Space (1998)
Sidewalks of New York (2001)
Graham, Otto: 2 QB
sport: 8 football
Graig: 7 Nettles
grail: 3 cup 6 goblet, trophy 7 chalice
seeker: 6 knight
__ Grail: 4 Holy
grain: 3 bit, dot, jot, oat, rye 4 atom, bran, corn, drop, feed, iota, malt, masa, milo, mite, mote, oats, ragi, rice, seed, whit 5 crumb, durra, durum, grits, kasha, ounce, raggy, scrap, shred, spark, speck, stone, trace, wheat 6 barley, bulgur, cereal, farina, fodder, groats, hegari, hominy, kernel, millet, morsel, raggee, tittle 7 basmati, einkorn, minimum, modicum, polenta, scruple, smidgen, smidgin, sorghum, texture 8 cornmeal, couscous, feterita, molecule, particle, semolina, smidgeon, wild rice 9 brown rice, buckwheat, scintilla, white rice
beard: 3 awn 6 arista
bearded, as ~: 5 awned
bundle: 5 sheaf, shock, stack
cereal ~: 3 oat, rye 4 corn 5 wheat 6 barley
chaff: 5 palea
combining form: 4 cocc-, sito- 5 cocci-, cocco-, grani-
disease: 4 smut 5 ergot
ear: 5 spica
gather ~: 4 reap
go against the ~: 3 bug, get, irk, try, vex 4 gall, rile 5 annoy, peeve, pique, upset 6 bother, nettle, offend, rankle, ruffle 7 grate on, provoke 8 irritate 9 aggravate 10 exasperate
goddess of ~: 5 Ceres
grinder: 4 mill 5 quern
ground ~: 4 meal 5 flour, grist
holder: 3 bin 4 crib, silo 5 barge
husks: 4 bran 5 chaff
implement: 5 flail
like some ~: 4 oaty 5 oaten
prefix: 5 multi-
product: 5 flour
sorghum: 4 milo 5 doura, durra, kafir 6 dourah, hegari
spike: 3 ear
store ~: 6 ensile
unprocessed ~: 5 grist
whiskey ~: 3 rye 4 corn
__-grain: 4 fine, full 5 whole
__-Grain: 5 Nutri
__-grained: 4 fine, flat 5 close, cross 6 coarse

__ grain of salt: 5 with a
grains: 6 powder
60 ~: 4 dram
grainy: 6 coarse, gritty **7** powdery **8** gravelly **9** unrefined
gram: 4 nana, unit **8** chickpea
starter: 4 deca, deka, echo, kilo, logo, mono, sono, tele **5** audio, cable, milli, penta
Grambling: 6 school **7** college
athletes: 6 Tigers
locale: 9 Louisiana
Gramm: 3 Lou **4** Phil
gramma: 5 grass
grammar: 6 syntax **9** structure **10** morphology
abbr.: 3 inf., obj. **4** neut., poss. **5** irreg.
case: 6 dative
concern: 4 word **5** usage **6** custom **7** diction, lexicon, wording **8** phrasing
connector: 6 copula
do a ~ task: 5 parse
Lat. ~ case: 3 abl., acc.
no-no: 4 ain't
subject: 4 noun, verb **6** adverb **7** article, pronoun **9** adjective
grammar __: 6 school
Grammer: 5 Billy **6** Kelsey
Grammer, Kelsey: 5 actor
film: 15 Minutes (2001)
TV: Cheers, Frasier
Grammy: 5 award
category: 3 pop, rap **4** jazz **5** album, R and B
org.: 5 NARAS
gramp's
son: 2 pa **3** dad **6** father
wife: 4 gran, nana
grampus: 3 orc **5** whale **8** cetacean
family: 3 gam
relative: ***see*** cetacean
grams
1000 ~: 4 kilo
28.35 ~: 5 ounce
gran: 4 nana
Gran __: 5 Chaco **7** Canaria
Gran __ Omologato: 7 Turismo
Granada: 3 car **4** auto, city, Ford, town
city near ~: 4 Jaen
locale: 5 Spain
Granatelli: 4 Andy
Granby: 4 city, town
locale: 6 Canada, Québec
grand: 4 epic, lush, main, posh, rich, thou **5** chief, G-note, large, lofty, noble, noted, piano, prime, proud, regal, royal, swank, swish **6** august, bang on, cosmic, deluxe, epical, finale, heroic, lavish, lordly, scenic, solemn, swanky **7** elegant, eminent, exalted, gallant, highest, Homeric, leading, massive, opulent, pompous, stately, supreme **8** cosmical, elevated, glorious, heroical, imperial, imposing, kinglike, majestic, palatial, scenical, Steinway **9** ambitious, dignified, luxurious, principal, sumptuous, wonderful **10** impressive, majestical, monumental, preeminent, remarkable, statuesque
combining form: 3 meg- **4** mega- **5** megal- **6** megalo-
design: 6 scheme **8** game plan, scenario, strategy
display: 4 pomp, show **5** state **7** fanfare, panoply **8** ceremony, heraldry **9** pageantry
ender: 3 dad, kid, sir, son **4** aunt, baby, sire **5** child, daddy, niece, stand, uncle **6** father, master, mother, nephew, parent **7** stander **8** daughter
occasion: 4 ball, bash, fete, gala, prom **5** feast, party **6** affair, fiesta **7** blowout, jubilee, pageant, shindig **8** festival, wingding
opening: 5 debut **7** kickoff **8** premiere
slam: 5 homer **7** success, triumph, victory **9** landslide
thousand ~: 3 mil **7** million
view: 5 sight, sweep, vista **7** horizon, scenery **8** panorama, prospect **9** landscape
see also wonderful
grand __: 3 feu, fir **4** chop, coup, duke, jeté, jury, slam, tier, tour **5** duchy, juror, march, opera, piano, prize, theft, vizir **6** finale, vizier **7** duchess, larceny, marshal, opening
grand __ homer: 4 slam
__ grand: 4 baby **6** parlor **7** concert
Grand: 5 Canal, river
Canal locale: 5 Italy **6** Venice
city on the ~: 7 Lansing
river locale: 8 Michigan
Grand __: 3 Cru, Pre **4** Bank, Funk, Lama, Prix, Turk **5** Banks, Canal, Hotel, Manan, Mufti, Teton **6** Bahama, Canary, Canyon, Cayman, Kabuki, Master **7** Guignol, Marnier
Grand __ Dam: 6 Coulee
Grand __ Island: 6 Bahama
Grand __, MI: 6 Rapids
Grand __ National Park: 5 Teton
Grand __, ND: 5 Forks
Grand __, NS: 3 Pré
Grand __ of the Republic: 4 Army
Grand __ Opry: 3 Ole
Grand __ Party: 3 Old
Grand __ Plaza: 4 Army
Grand __ Railroad: 4 Funk
Grand __ Suite: 6 Canyon
Grand Alliance, The
author: Winston Churchill
Grandbois, Alain: 4 poet **8** Canadian
Grand Canal worker: 5 poler
Grand Canyon: 4 park **5** gorge
emotion: 3 awe
feature: 3 rim
locale: 4 Ariz. **7** Arizona
transport: 5 burro **6** copter
Grand Canyon (1991 film)
cast: Danny Glover, Kevin Kline, Steve Martin, Mary McDonnell
director: Lawrence Kasdan
Grand Canyon State
see Arizona
Grand Canyon Suite
composer: Ferde Grofé
Grand Cayman: 4 isle **6** island
Grand Central
locale: 3 NYC **7** New York **9** Manhattan
grandchildren
watch the ~: 3 sit
Grand Coulee: 3 dam
locale: 10 Washington
granddaughter: 5 woman **7** kinsman
Grand Duke's father: 4 czar, tsar, tzar
Grand Duke, The
composer: W.S. Gilbert, Arthur Sullivan
grande __: 4 dame
__ Grande: 3 Rio **4** Casa
grandee: 3 don **4** rank **5** title
grander: 6 better **8** superior
Grande-Terre: 4 isle **6** island
locale: 10 Guadeloupe
grandeur: 4 pomp **5** glory, state, style **7** dignity, majesty **8** elegance, eminence, fineness, nobility, opulence, opulency, richness, splendor **9** celebrity, elevation, greatness, largeness, loftiness, magnitude, sublimity **10** augustness, brilliance, kingliness
grandfather: 3 kin, man **4** male **7** kinsman **8** ancestor
grandfather __: 5 clock **6** clause
__-grandfather: 5 great
grandfathered: 6 exempt
grandfatherly: 4 kind **6** doting **10** protective
Grand Forks: 4 city, town
locale: 4 N. Dak.
Grand Funk
song: Bad Time (1975)
The Loco-Motion (1974)
Some Kind of Wonderful (1974)
We're an American Band (1973)
Grand Hotel: 4 film **5** novel
author: Vicki Baum
cast: John Barrymore, Wallace Beery, Joan Crawford, Greta Garbo
character: 4 Otto
director: Edmund Goulding
studio: 3 MGM
__ Grand Hotel: 3 MGM
grandiloquence: 7 bombast, fustian **8** rhetoric **9** pomposity
grandiloquent: 5 lofty, tumid, windy **6** florid, lavish, turgid **7** flowery, fustian, orotund, pompous, stilted, swollen, verbose **8** elevated, inflated **9** overblown
be ~: 4 talk **5** orate, speak, spout **6** preach **7** address, declaim, lecture **8** harangue, sound off **9** discourse, hold forth, sermonize, speechify
grandiose: 4 epic **5** large, lofty, noble, showy **6** august, cosmic, epical, heroic, lordly **7** fustian, orotund, pompous, splashy, stately, utopian **8** affected, cosmical, heroical, imposing, splendid **9** ambitious, bombastic, egotistic, high-flown, luxurious, monstrous **10** euphuistic, flamboyant, impressive, monumental, rhetorical, theatrical, unfeasible
Grand Island: 4 city, town
locale: 8 Nebraska
Grand Junction: 4 city, town
locale: 8 Colorado
grandly: 9 in a big way
grandma: 4 nana
Grandma Moses: 4 Anna
Grand Marnier: 5 drink **8** beverage
Grand Marquis: 3 car **4** auto, Merc **7** Mercury **10** automobile
Grandmaster __: 5 Flash
grandmother: 3 kin **5** woman **6** female **7** kinsman **8** ancestor
first ~: 3 Eve
__-grandmother: 5 great
grandmotherly: 4 kind **5** sweet **6** loving **9** indulgent **10** bighearted, protective, solicitous
__ Grand Night for Singing: 4 It's a
grand old __: 3 man
Grand Old __: 5 Party
grand old name: 4 Mary
Grand Ole __: 4 Opry
Grandpa: 5 Jones
emulate ~: 4 dote
grandparent: 5 doter **6** adorer **7** kinsman **8** relative
of a ~: 4 aval
Grand Prairie: 4 city, town
locale: 5 Texas
Grand Prix: 3 car **4** auto **7** Pontiac
competitor: 5 racer
site: 6 Le Mans
Grand Rapids: 4 city, town
county: 4 Kent
locale: 8 Michigan
grand slam: 5 homer **7** home run
grandson: 4 cion **5** scion **7** kinsman **10** descendant
maybe: 3 III
__-grandson: 5 great
grandstand: 4 brag, pose, show **5** boast, strut **6** fake it, hot dog **7** show off, swagger **8** flaunt it, showboat **9** bleachers
level: 4 tier
maneuver: 4 wave
sound: 4 hoot, roar, yell **5** shout **6** scream
grandstand __: 4 play
grandstander: 3 ham **6** hotdog **9** daredevil
Grand Teton: 4 park
locale: 7 Wyoming
Grand Theft __: 4 Auto
Grand Tour
locale: 3 Eur. **6** Europe
Grandview: 4 city, town
locale: 8 Missouri
Grandy: 4 Fred
grange: 4 farm **9** homestead
Granger: 6 Farley **7** Stewart **8** Hermione
Grange, Red
sport: 8 football
Granger, Stewart: 5 actor
spouse: Jean Simmons
Grani: 5 horse, steed **6** equine
granite: 4 gray, grey, rock **6** aplite **7** mineral
ender: 4 ware
in ~: 3 set
quarry locale: 5 Barre
Granite City: 4 city, town
locale: 8 Illinois
granitelike: 4 hard **8** indurate
Granit, Ragnar: 8 Nobelist
granny: 4 knot, nana **5** nanna **9** matriarch
companion: 5 gramp **6** gramps
daughter: 4 aunt **5** aunty
garment: 5 shawl **6** bonnet
granny __: 4 flat, knot **5** dress **7** glasses
Granny Dan
author: Danielle Steel

Granny Smith: **4** pome **5** apple
relative: *see* apple
granola: **6** cereal
ingredient: **4** bran, date, nuts, oats, rice **5** honey **6** raisin
like ~: **4** oaty **5** chewy, oaten
__ grano salis: **3** cum
Gran Paradiso: **3** alp
Gran Sport: **3** car **4** auto **5** Buick
grant: **3** let, own **4** alms, avow, cede, dole, gift, give, lend, send, vest **5** admit, allot, allow, award, endow, let on, offer, spare, waive, yield **6** accede, accept, accord, afford, assume, bestow, bounty, confer, convey, donate, extend, fess up, permit, render, reward, supply **7** agree to, backing, bequest, charity, concede, confess, funding, give out, handout, license, pension, present, provide, stipend, subsidy, suppose **8** allocate, bestowal, bestow on, donation, gratuity, largesse **9** allotment, allowance, authorize, consent to, endowment, give leave, patronage, privilege, recognize, subscribe, vouchsafe **10** allocation, contribute, fellowship
a mortgage: **4** lend, loan
applicant: **5** asker
criterion: **4** need **5** merit
entry to: **5** admit, greet, let in **6** accept **7** include, receive, welcome
fed. ~ giver: **3** NSF
permission: **3** let **5** agree, allow, yield **6** permit **7** approve, concede, empower, entitle, license **8** sanction **9** acquiesce, authorize
recipient: **5** donee
grant-__: **5** in-aid
__ grant: **4** land
Grant: **3** Amy, Bud, Lee, Lou **4** Cary, Earl, Eddy, Gogi, Hugh, Show, Wood **5** Kirby, Shaud **6** Tinker **7** Goodeve, Kathryn, Ulysses **8** Jennifer, Ulysses S., Williams
colleague: **5** Meade
feature: **5** beard
foe: **3** Lee **5** R.E. Lee
Grant, Amy
song: Baby Baby (1991)
Every Heartbeat (1991)
Good for Me (1992)
The Next Time I Fall (1986)
That's What Love Is for (1991)
spouse: Vince Gill
Grant, Bud: **5** coach
sport: **8** football
Grant, Cary: **5** actor
film: Arsenic and Old Lace (1944)
The Awful Truth (1937)
The Bachelor and the Bobby-Soxer (1947)
The Bishop's Wife (1947)
Blonde Venus (1932)
Bringing Up Baby (1938)
Charade (1963)
The Eagle and the Hawk (1933)
Father Goose (1964)
The Grass Is Greener (1960)
Gunga Din (1939)
His Girl Friday (1940)
Holiday (1938)
Houseboat (1958)
I'm No Angel (1933)
Indiscreet (1958)
In Name Only (1939)
I Was a Male War Bride (1949)
The Last Outpost (1935)
Monkey Business (1952)
Mr. Blandings Builds His Dream House (1948)
Mr. Lucky (1943)
My Favorite Wife (1940)
Night and Day (1946)
None but the Lonely Heart (1944)
North by Northwest (1959)
Notorious (1946)
Only Angels Have Wings (1939)
Operation Petticoat (1959)
Penny Serenade (1941)
People Will Talk (1951)
The Philadelphia Story (1940)
Room for One More (1952)
She Done Him Wrong (1933)
Suspicion (1941)
Sylvia Scarlett (1935)
The Talk of the Town (1942)
The Toast of New York (1937)
To Catch a Thief (1955)
Topper (1937)
Walk, Don't Run (1966)
spouse: Dyan Cannon, Barbara Hutton
__-grant college: **3** sea **4** land
granted: **3** yes **5** legal **6** indeed, though **8** very well **9** axiomatic
permission ~: *see* of course **3** oui **4** okay **5** uh-huh **6** agreed, gladly **7** go ahead, mais oui, ten-four **8** all right, thumbs up, very well **9** be my guest **10** by all means, sure enough
take for ~: **5** posit **6** assume **7** believe, presume, suppose **9** postulate
taken for ~: **5** given, tacit **6** unsaid **7** assumed **8** implicit, unspoken, unstated, unvoiced **9** axiomatic **10** understood
grantee: **4** heir **7** heiress, legatee **9** inheritor
Grant, Gogi
song: Suddenly There's a Valley (1955)
The Wayward Wind (1956)
Grant, Hugh: **5** actor
film: About a Boy (2002)
Bridget Jones's Diary (2001)
Did You Hear About the Morgans? (2009)
Four Weddings and a Funeral (1994)
Impromptu (1991)
Love Actually (2003)
Music and Lyrics (2007)
Nine Months (1995)
Notting Hill (1999)
Sense and Sensibility (1995)
Small Time Crooks (2000)
Two Weeks Notice (2002)
grant-in-__: **3** aid
granting: **2** if **8** provided
that: **3** tho **6** though
Grant, Kathryn: **7** actress
spouse: Bing Crosby
Grantland: **4** Rice
Grant, Lee Oscar: Shampoo
Grant, Lou: **5** Asner
emulate ~: **4** edit
wife: **4** Edie
Grant Moves South
author: Bruce Catton
grantor: **5** angel, donor, giver **6** backer, patron **8** altruist, bestower **9** supporter **10** benefactor
Gran Torino (2008 film)
cast: Clint Eastwood
director: Clint Eastwood
Grant's __: **4** Tomb
Grants Pass: **4** city, town
locale: **6** Oregon
Grant Takes Command
author: Bruce Catton
Grant, Ulysses S.: **9** president
alma mater: **4** USMA **9** West Point
former occupation: **7** general, soldier
home: **4** Ohio
middle name: **7** Simpson
opponent: **7** Greeley, Seymour
publisher: **5** Twain
real first name: **5** Hiram
V.P.: **6** Colfax, Wilson
wife: **5** Julia
granular: **5** mealy **6** gritty **7** powdery **8** gravelly
snow: **4** firn, névé
granulate: **4** mill **5** crush, grate, grind **6** powder **7** atomize, crumble **9** comminute, pulverize, triturate
granulated: **6** gritty **8** gravelly
granulated __: **5** sugar
granule: **3** bit **4** bead, mite **5** crumb, speck **6** pellet **8** fragment, particle
Granville: **5** Hicks **6** Bonita
grape: **3** fox, red **4** fern **5** color, fruit, gamay, pinot, skunk, Tokay **6** Merlot, Muscat, purple, purply **7** Catawba, Concord, Niagara **8** Cabernet, Grenache, malvasia, muscatel, purplish **9** muscadine, Sauvignon, zinfandel **10** Chardonnay
brandy: **4** marc
disease: **6** coleur
ender: **4** shot, vine **5** fruit
holder: **4** vine
partly fermented ~ juice: **4** stum
pit: **6** acinus
plant: **4** vine
product: **4** wine
purchase: **5** bunch **7** cluster
relative: *see* red color
seeker of fable: **3** fox
stuffed ~ leaf: **5** dolma
tartar: **5** argal, argol
valley: **4** Napa
wild ~ fruit: **9** muscadine
grape __: **3** ivy **4** fern, Nehi **5** sugar
__ grape: **7** Concord
Grape __: **4** Nuts
grapefruit: **4** tree **6** citrus
hybrid: **4** ugli **7** tangelo
league locale: **3** Fla. **7** Florida
like ~ juice: **6** acidic
relative: **8** bergamot
serving: **4** half
topper: **5** sugar **6** cherry
see also citrus
grapefruit __: **6** league
Grapefruit
author: Yoko Ono
grapefruitlike fruit: **8** shaddock
Grape-Nuts: **6** cereal
competitor: *see* cereal
grapes
crush ~: **5** stomp, tramp, tread
first cultivator of ~: **6** Oeneus
like sour ~: **6** acidic
sour ~: **6** excuse, reason **9** rationale
__ grapes: **4** sour
Grapes of Wrath, The: **4** film **5** novel
author: John Steinbeck
cast: John Carradine, Jane Darwell, Henry Fonda
character: **3** Ivy, Tom **4** Casy, Ella, Joad, Noah, Okie **5** Aggie, Sairy **6** Feeley, Ruthie
director: John Ford
grapevine: **4** buzz, talk **5** rumor **6** report **7** hearsay
combining form: **5** ampel- **6** ampelo-
product: **4** buzz, news, tale, talk, word **5** rumor **6** canard, earful, gossip, report **7** hearsay, whisper
graph: **3** map **4** draw, grid, plot **5** chart, table **7** diagram **8** bar chart, pie chart **9** visual aid
draw points on a ~: **4** plot
ender: **3** -ite
line: **4** axis **5** x-axis, y-axis, z-axis
points: **4** loca, loci
starter: **3** iso, odo, oro **4** auto, logo, para, tele **5** mimeo, phono, photo **6** corona, shadow
statistical ~: **5** ogive
graph __: **5** paper
__ graph: **3** bar, pie **6** circle
graphic: **4** gory **5** clear, lucid, lurid, vivid **6** lively, visual **7** drawing, precise, telling **8** colorful, definite, detailed, distinct, eloquent, explicit, incisive, luculent, readable, stirring, striking, viewable **9** pictorial, realistic, trenchant **10** expressive
starter: **3** geo **4** ideo, xero **5** ortho, photo
graphic __: **4** arts **5** novel **6** design
graphical __ interface: **4** user
graphite: **6** carbon **7** mineral **8** plumbago
remover: **6** eraser
grapnel: **4** hook **5** hitch
grapple: **4** cope, grab, hook, lock **5** clash, fight, grasp, seize **6** battle, go at it, snatch, tackle, take on, tussle **7** contend, scuffle, vie with, wrestle **8** do battle, struggle **9** lay hold of, pitch into, titillate
with: **4** face **9** withstand
(with): **4** deal
grappling __: **4** hook, iron
graptolite: **6** fossil
gras: **3** fat **6** French
__ gras: **4** foie
__ Gras: **5** Mardi
Grasmere: **4** lake
locale: **7** England
grasp: **3** dig, get, ken, see, wit **4** fist, glom, grab, grip, have, hold, hook, keep, know, land, lock, snap, take, wits **5** ahold, catch, clasp, learn, reach, seize, sense **6** absorb, acumen, attain, clench, clinch, clutch, collar, corral, fathom,

GR

follow, handle, intuit, master, pick up, secure, snatch, take in **7** catch on, cognize, command, compass, grapple, make out, mastery, purview, reading, realize **8** clutches, glom on to, judgment, perceive, relate to **9** apprehend, awareness, get hold of, handclasp, knowledge, lay hold of, penetrate **10** appreciate, comprehend, perception, understand
hard to ~: **4** deep, eely **6** arcane **8** slippery
graspable: **5** clear, lucid, plain, vivid **6** cogent **7** evident, express, obvious **8** apparent, distinct, explicit, luminous, manifest, palpable **10** spelled out
grasp at __: **6** straws
grasping: **4** avid **5** gabby, itchy, tight **6** greedy, stingy **7** miserly, selfish, wishful **8** covetous, desirous, ravenous, ungiving **9** mercenary, penurious, rapacious, voracious **10** avaricious
sort: **5** taker
grass: **3** lea, ley, sod **4** feed, lawn, turf, yard **5** Bahia, plant, sward **6** bamboo, fescue, meadow, swarth, zoysia **7** pasture, verdure **10** vegetation
African ~: **4** teff **6** kikuyu, napier **7** esparto
Asian cereal ~: **4** ragi **5** raggy **6** raggee
bamboolike ~: **4** cane
cereal ~: **3** oat, rye **4** rice **5** grain, wheat
change the ~: **5** resod
clump: **4** tuft
cutter: **5** mower
cut the ~: **3** mow **4** trim
eat ~: **4** feed **5** graze
eater: **3** cow
ender: **4** land **5** roots **6** hopper
European ~: **7** esparto
fodder ~: **5** sorgo **6** sorgho
forage ~: **7** setaria
for thatching: **5** cogon
fungus: **4** smut
genus: **3** poa, zea
Indian ~: **4** kans **7** vetiver **8** khuskhus
invader: **4** weed
lawn ~: **6** fescue, redtop, zoysia **7** festuca
leaf of ~: **5** blade
like ~ in the morning: **3** wet **4** damp, dewy **5** moist
like tall ~: **5** reedy
marsh ~: **4** reed
Mexican basket ~: **5** otate
moor ~: **4** nard
of temperate regions: **5** brome
pasture ~: **5** grama **6** fescue, redtop **7** festuca
path: **5** swath **6** swathe
prickly ~: **7** sandbur
rye ~: **6** darnel
scatter ~: **3** ted
second ~ crop: **5** rowen
snake in the ~: **5** knave, rogue, sneak **7** traitor **8** turncoat **9** scoundrel
sod ~: **5** Bahia
stalk: **4** cane, reed
starter: **3** cut, eel, rib, rye **4** bent, blue, crab, knot, wire, worm **5** bunch, lemon **6** carpet, hopper, pepper, ripple **7** sparrow
swamp ~: **5** sedge
tropical ~: **5** Bahia, cogon **6** bamboo **7** Bermuda
grass __: **5** skirt, snake, stain, widow
__ grass: **3** cut, elk, oat, rye **4** crab **5** Bahia, lemon, marsh **6** Bahama **7** Bermuda
Grass: **4** poem **6** Günter
author: Carl Sandburg
Grass __, The: **4** Harp
grass-animal name: **4** Chia
Grass, Günter: **6** German, writer **8** Nobelist
work: The Call of the Toad
Cat and Mouse
Dog Years
The Flood
The Rat
The Tin Drum
Grass Harp, The: **4** book, film
author: Truman Capote
cast: Piper Laurie, Walter Matthau, Sissy Spacek
grasshopper: **3** bug **5** drink **6** insect, locust **8** beverage, cocktail
colleague: **3** ant
ingredient: **5** cream
sound: **5** chirr, churr, trill **6** chirre
young: **5** nymph
Grass Is Always Greener Over the Septic Tank, The
author: Erma Bombeck
grassland: **3** lea, ley, sod **4** veld **5** biome, campo, field, green, llano, plain, sward, veldt **6** meadow, pampas, swarth **7** lowland, pasture, prairie, savanna, verdure **8** savannah
Grassle: **5** Karen
Grasso: **4** Ella
Grass Roots
song: Let's Live for Today (1967)
Midnight Confessions (1968)
Sooner or Later (1971)
grass-roots musician: **5** folky **6** folkie
grass skirt
accessory: **3** lei
dance: **4** hula
__ Grass, The: **5** Sea of
grassy: **5** green **7** emerald, verdant **9** verdurous
area: **4** lawn, yard **5** campo, llano, sward **6** meadow, swarth
border: **5** verge
__ grata: **3** non **7** persona
grata, persona non: **3** bum **5** tramp **6** pariah **7** outcast **8** derelict **9** miscreant, reprobate
grate: **3** irk, jar, rub, vex **4** file, gall, rasp, rile **5** annoy, chafe, clash, creak, gnash, grind, mince, peeve, pique, shred **6** abrade, hearth, nettle, powder, rankle, scrape **7** enflame, inflame, lattice, provoke, scratch **8** gridiron, irritate, levigate **9** aggravate, granulate, pulverize **10** exasperate
contents: **3** ash **5** ember **6** cinder
locale: **9** fireplace
on: **3** irk, vex **4** rasp, rile **6** bother
residue: **3** ash **5** ember **6** cinder
grated cheese: **6** Romano **8** Parmesan
grateful: **7** obliged **8** beholden, indebted, relieved, thankful
feel ~ to: **3** owe **10** appreciate
Grateful Dead
label: **6** Arista
member: Jerry Garcia, Phil Lesh, Bob Weir Weir
song: Touch of Grey (1987)
gratefulness: **6** thanks
__ gratia: **3** Dei **7** exempli
__ Gratia Artis: **3** Ars
__ gratias: **3** deo
gratification: **3** joy **4** kick **5** pride **6** luxury **7** comfort, rapture
__ gratification: **7** instant
gratified: **4** glad **5** happy, proud **6** joyful, joyous **7** content **8** jubilant, relieved, thankful **9** contented, delighted, fulfilled, gladdened **10** complacent, flying high
be ~ by: **4** like
not ~: **5** unmet
gratify: **4** sate **5** cheer, humor **6** coddle, divert, fulfil, oblige, pamper, pander, please, regale, thrill, tickle **7** appease, cater to, content, delight, fulfill, gladden, hearten, indulge, satiate, satisfy **8** give in to **9** delectate, entertain, make happy
gratifying: **4** good **5** sweet **6** lovely **7** welcome **8** pleasant, pleasing, readable, tasteful **9** agreeable, covetable, delicious, desirable, enjoyable, favorable, indulgent, luxurious, rewarding **10** delectable, delightful, fulfilling, satisfying
grating: **4** grid **5** grill, gruff, harsh, noisy, raspy, rough, roupy **6** grille, hoarse, off-key, shrill **7** irksome, jarring, lattice, rasping, raucous **8** abrasion, annoying, friction, grinding, guttural, jangling, scraping, strident, worrying **9** cacophony, dissonant, unmusical **10** discordant, irritating, stridulent, unpleasant
noise: **5** creak **6** squeak, squeal
gratis: **4** free **7** as a gift **8** costless **9** on the cuff **10** for nothing, on the house
get ~: **3** bum **5** leech **8** freeload, scrounge
provide ~: **4** comp
gratitude: **5** thanx **6** thanks **10** obligation
gratuitous: **5** undue **6** unpaid **7** unasked **8** baseless, mindless, needless **9** causeless, unfounded, uninvited, unmerited, voluntary **10** chargeless, for nothing, groundless, inordinate, reasonless, unasked-for, undeserved, unprovoked
gratuity: **3** tip **4** gift, perk, toke **5** bonus, grant, token **6** reward **7** present, stipend **8** donation, largesse, offering **9** emolument, lagniappe, sweetener
Grauman: **3** Sid
Grau, Shirley Ann: **6** writer
grave: **3** bad, sad **4** dire, dour, grim, ugly **5** acute, heavy, major, sober, staid, tempo, vault **6** accent, gloomy, incise, severe, solemn, somber, urgent **7** crucial, exigent, heinous, learned, ominous, onerous, pensive, serious, subdued, weighty **8** critical, exigeant, grievous, perilous **9** desperate, hazardous, momentous, ponderous, unsmiling **10** inexpiable, portentous, thoughtful
faster than ~: **5** largo
gravel: **4** grit, rock **5** stone **7** pebbles **8** detritus
gravelly: **5** harsh, raspy, rocky, roupy, sandy, stony **6** froggy, grainy, gritty, hoarse, pebbly, stoney **7** rasping, shingly, throaty **8** croaking, granular, guttural **10** granulated, laryngitic
voice: **5** grate **7** scratch
gravely: **8** for keeps, severely, terribly **9** seriously
graven: **6** carved **7** incised **8** sculpted
image: **4** idol
graven __: **5** image
Gravenstein: **5** apple
relative: *see* apple
Graves: **4** wine **5** Peter **6** Robert
origin: **6** France
Graves, Peter: **5** actor
brother: James Arness
film: Airplane! (1980)
TV: Fury, Mission: Impossible
Graves, Robert: **4** poet **6** writer **7** British
work: Good-Bye to All That
I, Claudius
The White Goddess
graveyard __: **5** shift, watch
gravid: **8** enceinte, pregnant **9** expectant, expecting, with child
gravidity: **9** gestation
gravitate: **4** lean, tend **5** trend **7** conduce, incline
(toward): **4** lean, tend **5** verge
gravity: **4** heft, one G **5** force **6** import, moment, weight **7** concern, urgency **8** severity **9** acuteness, heaviness **10** importance
defy ~: **4** lift
respond to ~: **3** sag **4** drop, fall, sink **6** plunge, topple **7** plummet
__ gravity: **4** zero **5** law of
gravity-powered vehicle: **4** luge, pung, sled **6** sleigh **8** toboggan
Gravity's Rainbow
author: Thomas Pynchon
gravy: **3** jus **4** perk **5** bonus, lucre, money, sauce **6** juices, profit, reward **7** jobbery, revenue **8** dividend **9** condiment
dip in ~: **3** sop
flaw: **4** lump
holder: **4** boat
ingredient: **4** roux **5** broth, flour, liver **6** giblet
like bad ~: **5** lumpy
train: **7** success
gravy __: **4** boat **5** train
__ gravy: **3** pan **4** beef, dish, milk **6** giblet, red-eye **7** chicken
__ Gravy: **4** Wavy
gray: **3** age, ash, old **4** ashy, drab, dull, hoar, pale **5** ashen, color, dingy, dusky, hoary, mirky, mousy, murky, shade, slaty, smoky **6** cloudy, gloomy, leaden, mousey, shadow, somber **7** clouded, granite, neutral, peppery, silvery,

sunless **8** darkened, gunmetal, lowering, overcast **9** cinereous
become ~: **3** age
bluish ~: **5** merle, pearl, slate **8** platinum
brownish ~: **4** drab **5** beige, putty, taupe **7** fuscous **8** charcoal
color: **3** ash **4** ashy, dove, drab, opal **5** beige, dusty, merle, pearl, putty, slate, steel, taupe **6** silver **7** grizzly **8** charcoal, gunmetal, platinum
combining form: **4** poli- **5** glauc-, polio- **6** glauco-
cover the ~ again: **5** redye
ender: **3** lag **4** fish, mail **5** beard
matter: **4** head, mind **5** brain **9** mentality
name meaning ~: **5** Lloyd
use the ~ matter: **5** think **6** ideate
yellowish ~: **4** drab **5** putty
gray __: **4** area **5** goods, power, scale **6** market, matter
__ gray: **3** ash **5** steel
Gray: **3** Asa **4** Erin **5** Billy, Dobie, Linda, Simon **6** Coleen, Harold, Robert, Thomas **8** Spalding
monogram: **3** CSA
subject: **4** anat. **7** anatomy
work: **3** ode **5** elegy
Gray __: **4** Lady **5** Friar **7** Panther
Gray, Asa: **8** botanist **9** scientist
graybeard: **4** sage **6** codger, gaffer, geezer **7** old-time **9** patriarch, venerable
Gray, Dorian
what ~ didn't do: **3** age
gray-haired: **4** aged **5** hoary **6** senior **7** elderly, wizened **8** grizzled **9** venerable
grayish: **3** wan **4** ashy, pale **5** livid **6** pallid **7** cindery **9** colorless
color: **3** dun **4** ecru, nude, sage **5** Alice, beige, flaxy, loden, lovat, sepia, slate **6** chammy, flaxen, indigo, oyster, reseda, shammy, shamoy **7** celadon, chamois **8** mulberry
graylag: **4** bird, fowl **5** goose
genus: **5** anser
relative: **4** nene **5** brant **9** snow goose
__ Gray Line, The: **4** Long
grayling: **4** fish
Gray, Robert: **8** explorer
Gray, Simon: **7** British **10** playwright
Grayson: **4** Dick **7** Kathryn
Grayson, Dick to Bruce Wayne: **4** ward
Grayson, Kathryn: **7** actress
film: Anchors Aweigh (1945)
Kiss Me Kate (1953)
Rio Rita (1942)
Show Boat (1951)
Gray, Thomas: **4** poet **7** British
alma mater: **4** Eton
work: Elegy Written in a Country Churchyard
Graz: **4** city, town
locale: **7** Austria
graze: **3** eat, rub **4** chew, feed, kiss, lick, rake, skim, skin, skip, wear, wing **5** brush, chafe, shave, touch **6** abrade, browse, glance, nibble, scrape **7** pasture, scratch **9** glance off, masticate
grazer: **3** cow, ewe **4** bull, calf, goat, herd, lamb **5** sheep
Graziano, Rocky: **5** boxer
foe: **4** Zale
milieu: **4** ring
grazie: **6** thanks **7** Italian, spasibo **8** thank you
response: **5** prego
grazing area: **3** lea, ley **4** veld **5** range, veldt
Grazing in the Grass (song)
artist: Friends of Distinction, Hugh Masekela
Gr. Br.: **5** the UK
locale: **3** Eur.
part: **3** Eng. **4** Scot.
grease: **3** fat, lub., oil, sop **4** lard, lube **5** bribe **6** buy off, payoff, reward **7** jobbery, rake-off **8** kickback, leverage **9** drippings, lubricant, lubricate **10** facilitate, recompense
a palm: **5** bribe, get to **6** buy off, pay off, suborn **7** corrupt **9** lubricate
combining form: **4** sebi-, sebo-
deposit: **4** crud **5** filth, grime
elbow ~: **4** toil, work **6** effort **8** exertion
ender: **4** wood **5** paint, proof
remove ~: **5** defat
the wheels: **4** ease **6** smooth **8** expedite **10** facilitate
use elbow ~: **3** ply **4** buff **5** apply, scour, scrub, sweat, wield **6** employ, polish, strain **7** trouble, utilize **8** put forth
wool ~: **5** suint
grease __: **3** cup, gun **4** wool **5** paint **6** monkey, pencil
__ grease: **4** axle **5** elbow, goose
Grease: **4** film, song
artist: Frankie Valli
cast: Eve Arden, Stockard Channing, Jeff Conaway, Didi Conn, Olivia Newton-John, John Travolta
character: **5** Sandy
prop: **4** comb
Grease __ word: **5** is the
greasepaint: **6** makeup **7** pancake **9** cosmetics **10** foundation, maquillage
greasy: **4** oily **5** lardy, slick, slimy **8** slippery, unctuous **9** lubricous **10** lubricated, lubricious, oleaginous
residue: **4** gunk, ooze **5** grime, slime
Greasy: **5** Neale
greasy spoon: **4** café **5** diner **6** eatery **10** restaurant
patron: **5** eater
sign: **4** eats
great: **3** big **4** huge, star, tall, vast **5** adept, ample, bulky, famed, giant, grand, jumbo, large, legit, lofty, mondo, moral, noble, noted **6** adroit, august, epical, expert, famous, heroic, proper, signal, strong **7** eminent, ethical, exalted, hulking, immense, intense, mammoth, massive, notable, sizable, titanic **8** abundant, colossal, elevated, enormous, gigantic, glorious, heroical, infinite, king-size, laudable, masterly, oversize, peerless, pleasant, pleasing, profound, renowned, sizeable, skillful, spacious, towering, whopping **9** agreeable, dignified, extensive, Herculean, honorable, humongous, important, memorable, monstrous, overlarge, prominent, reputable, superstar, unlimited, unrivaled, virtuosic, wonderful, wunderbar **10** beneficial, celebrated, consummate, creditable, formidable, gargantuan, high-minded, monumental, prodigious, swimmingly, tremendous, voluminous
combining form: **3** meg- **4** macr-, magn-, mega- **5** macro-, magni-, megal- **6** megalo-
ender: **4** coat **7** hearted
in music: **6** grosso
name meaning ~: **5** Grant
not ~: **4** fair, okay, so-so
prefix: **4** maxi-, mega- **5** macro-
see also wonderful
great __: **3** ape, auk **4** guns **6** circle
great __ heron: **4** blue **5** white
great __ owl: **4** gray **6** horned
great __ shark: **4** blue **5** white
great-__: **4** aunt **5** niece, uncle **6** nephew
Great __: **3** War **4** Bear, Dane, Rift **5** Lakes, Scott, White **6** Circle, Divide, Plains, Schism **7** Britain, Smokies, Society
Great __ Bay: **5** South
Great __ Brown, The: **3** God
Great __ Desert: **4** Salt **5** Sandy
Great __ Detective, The: **5** Mouse
Great __ Hope, The: **5** White
Great __ Lake: **4** Salt **5** Slave
Great __ Mountains: **5** Smoky
Great __ of China: **4** Wall
Great __ of Fire: **5** Balls
Great __ Pepper, The: **5** Waldo
Great __ Reef: **7** Barrier
Great __ Robbery, The: **5** Train
Great __ Spot: **3** Red
Great __, The: **3** Lie, Man **4** Race **5** Brain, Lover **6** Caruso, Escape, Gatsby, Shadow **7** Garrick, McGinty
Great __ Valley: **4** Rift
Great __ Way: **5** White
Great American Novel, The
author: Philip Roth
great-aunt: **3** kin **5** woman **7** kinsman **9** kinswoman
Great Australian __: **5** Bight
Great Balls of Fire (1957 song)
artist: Jerry Lee Lewis
Great Barrier Island: **4** Otea
Great Barrier Reef essentially: **5** coral
Great Basin: **4** park **6** desert
language: **5** Piute **6** Paiute
locale: **3** Nev. **6** Nevada
Great Bear: **4** lake
locale: **6** Canada
Great Beyond, The (1999 song)
artist: R.E.M.
great blue __: **5** heron
Great Britain: **4** isls. **5** isles **7** islands
see also England
Great Caesar's __!: **5** ghost
Great Caruso, The (1951 film)
cast: Mario Lanza
Great Circle
author: Conrad Aiken
Great Commoner, The: **4** Pitt
Great Compromiser, The: **4** Clay
Great Dane: **3** dog **5** canid **6** canine
Great Debaters, The (2007 film)
cast: Kimberly Elise, Nate Parker, Denzel Washington, Forest Whitaker
director: Denzel Washington
Great Dictator, The (1940 film)
cast: Charles Chaplin, Paulette Goddard, Jack Oakie
director: Charles Chaplin
greater: **3** lgr. **4** more **5** major **6** better, larger **8** superior
become ~: **3** wax **4** grow **6** accrue, expand, mature **7** augment, enlarge, magnify **8** escalate, increase, multiply
in seniority: **5** elder, older **9** first-born
make ~: **3** pad **4** feed, hike **5** add to, boost, swell, widen **6** beef up, expand, extend, jack up **7** amplify, augment, build up, develop, enhance, enlarge, inflate, magnify, scale up **8** heighten, increase, lengthen **9** intensify **10** aggrandize, strengthen, supplement
part: **4** bulk, mass **8** majority **9** plurality
than: **4** over **5** above **6** beyond **8** superior **9** exceeding, upwards of **10** surpassing
Greater __ York: **3** New
Great Escape, The (1963 film)
cast: Charles Bronson, James Coburn, James Garner, David McCallum, Steve McQueen, Donald Pleasence
greatest: **3** top **4** A-one, arch, best, most, tops **5** first, major, prime **6** utmost **7** leading, maximum, optimum, primary, supreme, topmost **8** champion, ultimate **9** marvelous, principal, topflight, uppermost, uttermost **10** preeminent
extent: **3** end, max, rim **4** brim, edge, most **5** brink, limit **6** fringe, height, period **7** ceiling, extreme, maximum **8** confines, end point **9** outskirts, parameter, perimeter, periphery **10** bottom line, boundaries
Greatest Generation, The
author: Tom Brokaw
subject: **4** WWII
greatest hits album phrase: **6** best of
Greatest Love of All (1986 song)
artist: Whitney Houston
Greatest Show on Earth, The (1952 film)
cast: Charlton Heston, Betty Hutton, Dorothy Lamour, James Stewart
director: Cecil B. DeMille
Greatest Story Ever Told, The (1965 film)
cast: Carroll Baker, Jose Ferrer, Van Heflin, Charlton Heston, Angela Lansbury, Sidney Poitier, Claude Rains, Telly Savalas, Max von Sydow, John Wayne, Shelley Winters, Ed Wynn

Greatest, The: **3** Ali
Great Expectations: **5** novel
author: Charles Dickens
character: **3** Pip **4** Abel **5** Biddy, Clara **6** Pirrip **7** Estella
Great Expectations (1998 film)
cast: Anne Bancroft, Chris Cooper, Ethan Hawke, Gwyneth Paltrow
Great Falls: **4** city, town
locale: **7** Montana
Great Forest, The
artist: Max Ernst
Great Gatsby, The: **4** film **5** novel
author: F. Scott Fitzgerald
cast: Karen Black, Bruce Dern, Mia Farrow, Robert Redford
character: **3** Jay, Tom **4** Nick **5** Baker, Daisy, Meyer **6** George, Jordan, Myrtle, Wilson **8** Buchanan, Carraway **9** Wolfshiem
Great God Brown, The
author: Eugene O'Neill
greathearted: **3** big **5** noble **6** heroic, humane **7** gallant, valiant **8** generous **9** unselfish **10** benevolent, charitable, high-minded
Great Impostor, The (1961 film)
cast: Tony Curtis, Karl Malden, Raymond Massey, Edmond O'Brien
Great Lake: **4** Erie **5** Huron **7** Ontario **8** Michigan, Superior
canals: **3** Soo
cargo: **3** ore
fish: **4** chub, coho **5** cisco, cohoe, smelt **6** salmon **7** bloater
Indian: **4** Cree, Erie **5** Miami
native language: **6** Ojibwa **7** Ojibway **8** Chippewa
of a ~: **5** Erian
port: **6** Duluth
state: **4** Ohio **8** Michigan
when the ~ s were formed: **6** ice age
Great Leap Forward proponent: **3** Mao
greatly: **3** far **4** a lot, most, much, very, well **5** quite **6** highly, hugely, vastly **7** largely, notably **8** famously, markedly, mightily, terribly, very much **9** eminently, extremely, fervently, glaringly, immensely, intensely, like crazy, supremely **10** abundantly, enormously, ever so much, incredibly, powerfully, remarkably, strikingly
Great Mosque
locale: **5** Mecca
Great Muppet Caper, The (1981 film)
director: Jim Henson
Great Nebula
locale: **5** Orion
Great Neck: **4** city, town
locale: **7** New York **10** Long Island
greatness: **4** note, size **5** glory, honor **7** dignity **8** eminence, enormity, grandeur, nobility **9** abundance, amplitude, celebrity, immensity, intensity, loftiness, magnitude, sublimity **10** excellence, generosity, importance, prominence, worthiness
Great Opposer, The: **5** Borah
Great Outdoors, The (1988 film)
cast: Dan Aykroyd, Annette Bening, John Candy
Great Pacificator, The: **4** Clay
Great Plains
dwelling: **4** tipi **5** tepee **6** teepee
Indian: **3** Kaw, Oto **4** Crow, Otoe **5** Caddo, Kansa, Kiowa, Osage **6** Dakota, Pawnee, Quapaw, Siouan **7** Arapaho **8** Arapahoe, Cheyenne, Comanche, Kickapoo **9** Blackfoot
Great Pretender, The (1955 song)
artist: Platters
Great Pyramid site: **4** Giza **5** Egypt
Great Pyrenees: **3** dog **5** canid **6** canine
Great Race, The (1965 film)
cast: Tony Curtis, Peter Falk, Jack Lemmon, Natalie Wood
composer: Henry Mancini
director: Blake Edwards
Great Railway Bazaar, The
author: Paul Theroux
Great Red ___: **4** Spot
Great Rift Valley
locale: **5** Kenya
Great Salt: **6** desert
locale: **4** Utah
Great Salt Lake
locale: **4** Utah
river to the ~: **4** Bear
Great Sandy: **6** desert
locale: **9** Australia
Great Seal
bird: **5** eagle
word on the ~: **4** ordo **5** novus
Great Shadow, The
author: Arthur Conan Doyle
Great Slave: **4** lake
locale: **6** Canada
Great Smoky Mountains: **4** park **5** range
locale: **9** Tennessee
Great Sun
author: Edna Ferber
Great Train Robbery, The: **4** film **5** novel
cast: Sean Connery, Lesley-Anne Down, Donald Sutherland
director: Michael Crichton
Great Trek participant: **4** Boer
great-uncle: **3** kin **7** kinsman **8** relative
Great Victoria: **6** desert
locale: **9** Australia
Great Waldo Pepper, The (1975 film)
cast: Robert Redford, Susan Sarandon
director: George Roy Hill
Great Wall
dynasty: **3** Qin **4** Chin
locale: **4** Asia **5** China
Great weeds do grow ___: **5** apace
great white
relative: **4** mako
great white ___: **5** heron, shark
Great White ___: **3** Way **6** Father
Great White Hope, The (1970 film)
cast: Jane Alexander, James Earl Jones
director: Martin Ritt
Great White North: **6** Canada
Great White Way light: **4** neon
great work in Latin: **10** magnum opus
Great Ziegfeld, The (1936 film)
cast: Myrna Loy, William Powell, Luise Rainer
Gréban, Arnoul: **6** French **10** playwright
grebe: **4** bird **5** diver **8** dabchick, didapper **9** helldiver
Grecian: **9** classical
Greco: **4** José **5** Buddy
Greco-Roman
alternative: **4** sumo
wrestling: **5** sport
GRE cousin: **4** LSAT
Greece: **5** Ellas **6** Hellas, nation **7** country
capital: **6** Athens
cheese: **4** feta
city: **6** Athens, Edessa, Patros **7** Piraeus **8** Iráklion, Peiraeus
combining form: **5** Greco- **6** Graeco- **7** Helleno-
conductor: **11** Mitropoulos
food: **4** feta, gyro, lamb **5** olive **8** moussaka, olive oil
former money: **5** lepta **6** drachm, lepton **7** drachma **9** didrachma
from ~: **6** Balkan
god: **6** Nereus
guerrilla: **6** klepht
gulf: **6** Aegina, Patras **7** Laconia, Saronic **8** Messinia, Salonika
infantry: **6** evzone
instrument: **8** bouzouki
island: **3** Cos, Ios, Kos **4** Milo **5** Corfu, Crete, Delos, Leros, Melos, Milos, Naxos, Paros, Samos, Thera, Thira, Zante **6** Candia, Euboea, Lemnos, Lesbos, Patmos, Skiros, Skyros **8** Santorin **9** Santorini
islands: **6** Ionian
language: **5** Koine **8** Hellenic
leftist coalition: **3** EAM
legislature: **5** boule
letter: **2** mu, nu, pi, xi **3** chi, eta, phi, psi, rho, tau **4** beta, iota, zeta **5** alpha, delta, gamma, kappa, omega, sigma, theta **6** lambda **7** epsilon, omicron, upsilon
liqueur: **4** ouzo
money: **4** euro
mountain: **4** oros, Ossa **5** Athos **6** Pindus **7** Olympus
mountains: **4** Oeta **6** Pindus
musical note: **4** nete
neighbor: **6** Turkey **7** Albania **8** Bulgaria **9** Macedonia
Nobelist in Literature: **6** Elytis **7** Seferis
org.: **4** NATO
peninsula: **5** Morea
philosopher: **8** Diogenes **9** Aristotle
poet: **4** Bion **5** Arion **6** Hesiod, Ibycus **7** Agathon, Alcaeus **8** Anacreon
political movement: **6** enosis
port: **5** Aulis, Corfu, Pilos, Pylos **6** Patras, Rhodes **7** Piraeus **8** Peiraeus
river: **4** Arta
saint: **5** Cyril
sea: **5** Egean **6** Aegean, Ionian
township: **4** deme
tycoon: **3** Ari **7** Onassis
underground: **4** ELAS
verb form: **6** aorist
volcano: **9** Santorini
vowel: **3** eta **4** iota **5** omega **7** omicron, upsilon
wine: **7** malmsey, retsina
Greece (ancient)
architect: **6** Scopas
architectural style: **5** Ionic
astronomer: **10** Hipparchus **11** Aristarchus **12** Eratosthenes
author: **4** Esop **5** Aesop, Homer
boat: **6** galley
carved image: **6** xoanon
carved images: **5** xoana
chorus part: **5** epode
city: **4** Arta, Elea **5** Argos, Pella, polis, siris, Tegea **6** Tiryns **7** Eleusis
clan: **6** phyles
colonnade: **4** stoa
colony: **4** Elea **5** Cumae, Ionia **6** Aeolia, Aeolis
dialect: **5** Doric, Ionic **6** Aeolic
district: **6** Phocis
dreamy fruit of ~ myth: **5** lotus
drinking cup: **5** cylix, kylix
drinking horns: **5** rhyta
epic: **5** Iliad **6** Aeneid **7** Odyssey
exclamation: **4** evoe
garment: **5** tunic **6** chiton, peplos, peplus **7** chlamys
geographer: **6** Strabo **9** Pausanias
god: **3** Pan **4** Ares, Eros, Zeus **5** Hades, theos, Titan **6** Aeolus, Apollo, Charon, Helios, Hermes, Hypnos, Icarus **8** Cerberus, Dionysus, Poseidon **10** Hephaestus
goddess: **3** Ate, Eos **4** Hebe, Hera, Iris, Nike **5** Aeaea, Circe, Kirke **6** Athena, Athene, Hecate, Hekate, Hestia, Medusa, Selene **7** Artemis, Demeter **9** Aphrodite **10** Persephone
goddesses: **6** Furies, Gorgon, Graces
goddess of discord: **4** Eris
goddess of fate: **5** Moira
goddess of peace: **5** Irene
goddess of wisdom: **6** Athena, Athene
god of love: **4** Eros
god of ridicule: **5** Momus
hero struggle: **4** agon
instrument: **4** lyre
jug: **4** olpe
magistrate: **6** archon
marketplace: **5** agora
mathematician: **10** Pythagoras
messenger of the gods: **4** Iris
money: **4** mina, obol **6** stater, talent
personification of the sea: **6** Pontos, Pontus
philosopher: **8** Plotinus, Socrates **10** Pythagoras
physician: **5** Galen
playwright: **8** Menander **9** Aeschylus, Euripides, Sophocles **12** Aristophanes
poet: **6** Ritsos **9** Simonides **11** Homer Pindar **15** Sappho Aeschylus

provincial governor: 6 eparch
queen of the gods: 4 Hera
region: 6 Achaea, Actium, Attica
rhetorician: 6 Zoilus
sanctuary: 5 secos, sekos
scientist: 6 Strabo 9 Pausanias 10 Archimedes, Hipparchus 11 Aristarchus 12 Eratosthenes
sculptor: 5 Myron 6 Scopas
stanza: 5 epode
statue: 4 Kore
storyteller: 4 Esop 5 Aesop
strongman: 5 Atlas
temple: 4 naos 6 hieron
temple detail: 4 anta
theater: 5 odeon, odeum
theaters: 4 odea
tribe: 6 phyles
underworld river: 4 Styx 5 Lethe
valley: 5 Nemea
verse form: 4 epos
war god: 4 Ares
weight: 5 oboli 6 obolus
wine pitcher: 4 olpe
writer: 5 Homer, Plato 6 Zoilus 8 Plotinus, Plutarch, Xenophon 9 Aeschylus

greed: 4 lust 6 hunger 7 avarice, avidity, edacity 8 cupidity, rapacity, venality, voracity 9 esurience, gold fever 10 grabbiness
exemplar of ~: 5 Midas

greedy: 4 avid 5 itchy, piggy, tight 6 grabby, hungry, piggie, stingy 7 craving, hoggish, lustful, miserly, piggish, selfish, swinish, thirsty 8 covetous, edacious, esurient, grasping, ravenous, ungiving 9 mercenary, penurious, predatory, rapacious, voracious 10 avaricious, gluttonous, insatiable, possessive, skinflinty
be ~: 4 envy, want 5 covet 7 burn for 8 begrudge
one: 3 hog, pig 5 harpy, taker
person's demand: 5 gimme

Greek: 5 Attic 6 Cretan 7 Hellene, Spartan 8 language 9 classical
group: 4 frat 8 sorority 10 fraternity
see also Greece

Greek __: 3 god 5 cross, salad

Greek alphabet:
1st - alpha
2nd - beta
3rd - gamma
4th - delta
5th - epsilon
6th - zeta
7th - eta
8th - theta
9th - iota
10th - kappa
11th - lambda
12th - mu
13th - nu
14th - xi
15th - omicron
16th - pi
17th - rho
18th - sigma
19th - tau
20th - upsilon
21st - phi
22nd - chi
23rd - psi
24th - omega

Greek/Roman god equivalents:
Aphrodite - Venus
Apollo - Apollo
Ares - Mars
Artemis - Diana
Athena - Minerva
Ceres - Demeter
Cronos - Saturn
Dionysus - Bacchus
Eos - Aurora
Eros - Amor, Cupid
Hades - Pluto
Helios - Sol
Hephaestus - Vulcan
Hera - Juno
Hermes - Mercury
Hestia - Vesta
Irene - Pax
Persephone - Proserpina
Poseidon - Neptune
Rhea - Ops
Zeus - Jupiter, Jove

Greek Tycoon, The
model: 3 Ari 7 Onassis

Greeley: 4 city, town 6 Andrew, editor, Horace
direction: 4 west
emulate ~: 4 edit
locale: 8 Colorado

Greeley, Andrew: 6 writer
character: Ryan, McGrail
work: The Bishop at Sea
The Cardinal Sins
Cardinal Virtues
Fall From Grace
Irish Eyes
Irish Gold
Irish Lace
Irish Love
Irish Mist
Irish Stew!
Irish Whiskey
A Midwinter's Tale
Patience of a Saint
Rite of Spring
Wages of Sin
White Smoke

green: 3 new, pea, raw 4 aqua, jade, lawn, lime, lush, naif, Nile, park, sick 5 field, fresh, kelly, leafy, loden, moola, naive, olive, plaza, young 6 boyish, callow, common, grassy, in leaf, moolah, newish, simple, tender, unripe 7 avocado, emerald, envious, jealous, puerile, verdant 8 fumbling, gullable, gullible, ignorant, immature, inexpert, innocent, juvenile, unartful, untested, unversed, unwilted, youthful 9 beardless, credulous, grassland, ingenuous, sprouting, untrained, unworldly, vegetable 10 chartreuse, ecological, unpolished, unseasoned, unskillful
around the gills: 3 ill 6 queasy, queazy
beverage: 3 tea 5 hyson
bluish ~: 4 aqua, cyan, jade, Nile 5 beryl 6 myrtle 9 turquoise 10 aquamarine
brownish ~: 5 breen, olive
card holder: 5 alien 7 refugee 8 emigrant, newcomer 9 foreigner, immigrant 10 noncitizen
cheese: 7 sapsago
color: 3 pea 4 aqua, cyan, jade, lime, Nile, sage 5 beryl, breen, kelly, loden, olive, virid 6 myrtle, reseda 7 avocado, celadon, emerald, verdant 9 pistachio, turquoise 10 aquamarine, chartreuse
combining form: 4 verd- 5 chlor-, verdo- 6 chloro-
cover: 5 baize
ender: 3 fly, way 4 back, belt, gage, head, horn, mail, room, sand, sick, side, wood 5 brier, finch, heart, house, shank, stone, sward 6 grocer, market, swarth 7 grocery
feature: 3 pin 4 flag, hole
fix the ~: 5 resod
flower: 6 smilax 7 figwort 8 pilewort 10 mignonette
fruit: 4 pear 5 grape, olive
gage: 4 plum
gemstone: 4 jade
give the ~ light: 2 OK 4 okay 5 agree, allow 6 accede, enable 7 endorse, indorse
grayish ~: 4 sage 5 lovat 6 reseda 7 celadon
in French: 4 vert
in heraldry: 4 vert
light: 2 go, OK 3 yes 4 okay, word 5 leave 6 assent, permit, signal 7 go-ahead, license, mandate, warrant 8 approval, sanction 9 clearance 10 acceptance
not ~: 4 ripe 6 mature 7 ripened, skilled 8 seasoned 10 well-versed
one: 4 tyro 6 novice, rookie 7 recruit, trainee 8 beginner, neophyte, newcomer 9 fledgling 10 apprentice, tenderfoot
opposite: 3 tee
org.: 3 PGA
shoot for the ~: 4 chip 5 slice
shot: 4 putt
spot: 5 oasis 6 garden
starter: 4 ever 6 winter
stroke: 4 putt
stuff: ***see*** moolah
thumb: 4 gift 5 flair, knack, touch 6 talent
turn ~ over: 4 envy 5 covet 8 begrudge
vegetable: 3 pea 4 kail, kale 5 chard, cress 7 cabbage, lettuce, parsley, spinach
village ~: 4 park 5 plaza 6 common, square
yellowish ~: 3 pea 4 jade, sage 5 olive 9 pistachio 10 chartreuse

green __: 3 pea, tea 4 bean, card 5 light, onion, power, stuff, thumb 6 pepper

green-__ monster: 4 eyed

__ green: 3 pea, sea 4 jade, lime, long, Nile 5 kelly, olive, Paris, salad 6 forest 7 emerald, putting

Green: 2 Al 3 Eva, Guy 4 city, Paul, town 5 Henry, Hetty, Mitzi, Nigel, range 6 Johnny, Julien
land: 4 Eire, Erin 7 Ireland
locale: 4 Ohio 7 Vermont

Green __: 3 Bay, Day 4 Card, Eyes 5 Acres, Beret, Giant, Grass, party, Stamp

Green __ and Ham: 4 Eggs

Green __ Packers: 3 Bay

Green __, The: 3 Hat, Man, Ray 4 Mile 6 Hornet

__ Green: 6 Gretna

Green Acres (CBS sitcom)
cast: Eddie Albert (Oliver Douglas)
Pat Buttram (Mr. Haney)
Mary Grace Canfield (Ralph Monroe)
Eva Gabor (Lisa Douglas)
Tom Lester (Ed Dawson)
Sid Melton (Alf Monroe)
Alvy Moore (Hank Kimball)
cow: Eleanor
dog: 6 Mignon 7 Cynthia
pig: Arnold
structure: 4 barn

Green, Adolph collaborator: 6 Comden

Green, Al
song: Call Me (1973)
Here I Am (1973)
I'm Still in Love With You (1972)
Let's Stay Together (1971)
Look What You Done for Me (1972)
Put a Little Love in Your Heart (1988)
Sha-La-La (1974)
You Ought to Be With Me (1972)

__ Green Apples: 6 Little

Greenaway: 4 Kate 5 Peter

greenback: 4 bill, buck 5 money 6 dollar 7 smacker 8 banknote, frogskin, simoleon

greenbacks
see moolah

Greenbaum, Norman
song: Spirit in the Sky (1970)

Green Bay: 4 city, port, town
city near ~: 6 Antigo
locale: 9 Wisconsin
quarterback: 5 Starr
team: 7 Packers

green bean: 6 legume, veggie 9 vegetable

Greenbelt: 4 city, town
locale: 8 Maryland

Green Beret: 7 soldier
like a ~: 5 elite
org.: 4 Army 6 U.S. Army

Greenberg: 5 Bryan

Greenberg, Hank: 5 Tiger 7 slugger

Greenberg, Uri Zvi: 4 poet 6 Hebrew

Greenbrier: 3 car 4 auto 5 Chevy 9 Chevrolet 10 automobile

Green Card (1990 film)
cast: Gérard Depardieu, Andie MacDowell, Bebe Neuwirth
director: Peter Weir

Greene: 3 Bob, Joe 4 Gael 5 Ellen, Lorne 6 Graham, Robert, Shecky 7 Mean Joe, Michele, Richard
costar: 6 Landon 7 Blocker, Roberts

Green Eggs and Ham
author: Dr. Seuss
character: 3 Sam 6 Sam-I-Am

Greene, Graham: 6 writer 7 British
work: Brighton Rock
A Gun for Sale
The Heart of the Matter
Our Man in Havana
The Third Man

GR

Greene, Joe
sport: 8 football
Greene, Lorne
song: Ringo (1964)
TV: Bonanza
Greene, Robert: 6 writer 7 British
greenery: 7 foliage, verdure
bit of ~: 5 plant, sprig
chew the ~: 5 graze
conceal with ~: 6 embosk
urban ~: 4 lawn 6 common, square 7 reserve 8 preserve
green-eyed: 7 envious, jealous 9 invidious, malicious 10 suspicious
monster: 4 envy
Greenfields (1960 song)
artist: Brothers Four
greenfinch: 4 bird
Green Gables girl: 4 Anne
greengage: 4 plum
relative: 4 sloe 6 cherry, damson 9 myrobalan
Green Giant
competitor: 5 Libby 6 Libby's 8 Birdseye, Del Monte
__ Green Giant: 5 Jolly
Green Grass of Wyoming, The
author: Mary O'Hara
Green, Green Grass of Home (1967 song)
artist: Tom Jones
Green Hat, The
author: Michael Arlen
Green Hills of Africa
author: Ernest Hemingway
greenhorn: 4 babe, lamb, naif, tiro, tool, tyro 5 newie 6 intern, novice 7 amateur, dabbler, interne, learner, new hand, recruit 8 beginner, freshman, neophyte, newcomer, putterer 9 fledgling, simpleton 10 apprentice, dilettante, tenderfoot, uninitiate
like a ~: 3 new
social ~: 4 nerd
Green Hornet, The: 9 radio show
aide: 4 Kato
alter ego: 4 Reid 5 Britt
greenhouse: 7 nursery
area: 6 hotbed
do a ~ chore: 5 repot
like a ~: 5 humid, moist 6 steamy
greenhouse __: 3 gas 6 effect
Greening of America, The
author: Charles A. Reich
greenish color: 4 aqua, cyan, lime, Nile, teal 5 hazel, lemon 6 acacia, citron, cobalt, sallow 7 luteous, peacock 8 cerulean 9 champagne, robin's-egg, turquoise 10 aquamarine
Green, Julien: 6 French, writer
Greenland: 3 sea 4 isle 6 island
air base: 5 Thule
bay: 6 Baffin
bovine: 6 muskox
capital: 7 Godthab
explorer: 7 Ericson
garb: 5 parka 6 anorak
native: 5 Inuit 6 Eskimo, Innuit, Inupik
sea: 8 Labrador
settlement: 4 Etah
sight: 5 fiord, fjord 6 icecap
__ Greenleaf Whittier: 4 John
green light
give the ~: 2 OK 3 let 4 okay 5 allow, clear 6 enable 7 approve
greenling: 4 fish
Green Mansions: 4 film 5 novel
author: W.H. Hudson
cast: Audrey Hepburn, Anthony Perkins
character: 4 Abel, Rima, Runi 5 Nuflo
Green Man, The
author: Kingsley Amis
Green Mare, The
author: Marcel Aymé
Green Mile, The (1999 film)
author: Stephen King
cast: Michael Clarke Duncan, Tom Hanks, Bonnie Hunt
director: Frank Darabont
Green Mountain
Boy: 5 Allen, Ethan
locale: 7 Vermont
range: 6 Hoosac
greenness: 5 youth 7 naiveté, verdure 8 verdancy, viridity 9 credulity, freshness, innocence 10 callowness, immaturity
Greenock: 4 city, port, town
locale: 8 Scotland
greenockite: 3 ore 7 mineral
Green Onions (1962 song)
artist: Booker T. and the MGs
Green Pastures, The
author: Marc Connelly
character: 4 Lawd
Greenpeace concern: 4 ecol., nuke 5 A-test 7 ecology
Green Ray, The
author: Jules Verne
Green Ripper, The
author: John D. MacDonald
Green River (1969 song)
artist: Creedence Clearwater Revival
greenroom: 6 lounge
greens: 5 salad 6 veggie 7 produce 10 rabbit food, vegetables
ender: 6 keeper
game: 4 golf
greens __: 3 fee
__ greens: 5 salad 6 turnip 7 collard
Greensboro: 4 city, town
locale: 4 N. Car.
greenskeeper's job, do a: 3 mow 6 aerate
Greenspan, Alan: 9 economist
org.: 3 Fed, FRS
spouse: Andrea Mitchell
subj.: 3 GNP 4 econ. 7 economy
green-stamp company: 5 S and H
Greenstreet: Sydney: 5 actor
costar: 5 Lorre
greensward: 3 sod 4 lawn, turf
Green Tambourine (1967 song)
artist: Lemon Pipers
__ Green Tomatoes: 5 Fried
Greenville: 4 city, town
athletes: 7 Pirates
city near ~: 6 Easley
college: 3 ECU 5 Thiel
locale: 5 Texas
__ Green Was My Valley: 3 How
Green Wave: 6 Tulane
Greenway: 6 Aurora
Greenwich: 4 city, town 5 Ellie
locale: 4 Conn. 7 England
river: 6 Thames
Greenwich __: 4 Time 7 Village
Greenwich __ Time: 4 Mean
Greenwich Village
neighbor: 4 Soho 7 Tribeca
sch.: 3 NYU
green with __: 4 envy
Greenwood: 3 Lee 4 city, Joan, town
locale: 7 Indiana
greeny: 3 cub 6 novice 7 recruit, trainee 8 beginner, neophyte 10 apprentice, tenderfoot
Greer: 3 Hal 4 Jane 6 Garson 8 Germaine
Greer, Germaine: 6 writer
greet: 3 bow, hug, nod, see 4 hail, meet 5 let in, nod to, see in, shake 6 accost, herald, salaam, salute, wave to 7 embrace, receive, usher in, welcome 8 high-five 9 recognize
the day: 4 rise, wake 5 arise, awake, get up, waken 6 awaken
the moon: 3 bay 4 howl 7 ululate
the villain: 3 boo 4 hiss, jeer 8 sibilate
warmly: 3 hug 5 ask in
greeting: 2 hi 3 hey, nod 4 ciao, hail, hiya, oh hi 5 aloha, hello, howdy 6 curtsy, halloa, how now, salaam, salute, shalom, sholom, yo dude 7 bon jour, regards, welcome 8 high five 9 reception 10 how do you do, pleasantry, salutation
Australian: 4 g'day
British: 4 'ello 5 hullo
formal ~: 3 bow 6 curtsy
French: 5 salut
gesture: 3 nod 4 wave
Hawaiian ~: 5 aloha
hippie ~: 5 peace
Indian ~ in oaters: 3 how
infant: 4 dada, mama
Maori ~: 5 hongi
nautical: 4 ahoy
reunion ~: 3 hug
warm ~: 3 hug 4 kiss 7 embrace
Zen ~: 6 gassho
greeting card
feature: 4 poem 5 rhyme, verse 8 doggerel
like some ~ verses: 4 zany 5 corny, inane, mushy, sappy, silly 6 drippy, slushy, sticky 7 maudlin, mawkish 8 overdone
word: 4 Noel, yule 5 happy
greetings: 7 regards, tidings 8 respects
Greetings ___...: 4 from
Greetings org.: 3 SSS
Greg: 4 Lake 6 Evigan, Gumbel, Kinner, LeMond, Maddux, Morris, Norman 7 Germann, Kinnear 8 Louganis, Luzinski, Mullavey
TV wife: 6 Dharma
__ & Greg: 6 Dharma
gregarious: 6 clubby, social 7 affable, cordial 8 friendly, outgoing, sociable 9 convivial, expansive 10 hospitable, personable
type: 5 mixer 6 joiner 7 mingler 9 extrovert 10 socializer
Gregg: 4 John 6 Allman 7 Forrest
grego: 4 coat 6 jacket
Gregor: 6 Mendel
Gregorian
chant notation: 4 neum 5 neume
cycle: 4 year
preceder: 6 Julian
tune: 5 chant
Gregorian __: 5 chant 8 calendar
Gregory: 4 Dick, Peck, pope 5 Corso, Hines, saint 6 Abbott, Horace, La Cava, Martin, Ratoff, Sierra 7 Cynthia, pontiff 8 Harrison
Gregory, Horace: 4 poet
__ Gregson Wagner: 7 Natasha
greige: 6 undyed 10 unbleached
Greist, Kim: 7 actress
__ gré, mal gré: 3 bon
gremlin: 3 elf, imp 4 bogy 5 gnome 6 goblin, kobold, sprite 8 barghest 9 hobgoblin
Gremlin: 3 AMC, car 4 auto 10 automobile
Gremlins (1984 film)
cast: Hoyt Axton, Phoebe Cates, Zach Galligan
director: Joe Dante
dog: 6 Barney
Grenache: 5 grape
Grenada: 4 isle 6 island, nation 7 country
capital: 9 St. George's
money: 4 cent 6 dollar
org.: 3 OAS
grenade: 4 bomb, frag 5 shell 9 explosive
__ grenade: 4 hand
grenades: 4 ammo 9 munitions 10 ammunition
grenadier: 4 fish
grenadine: 5 syrup 6 fabric 8 material
Grenadines: 4 isls. 5 isles 7 islands
locale: 9 Caribbean
Grendel: 4 ogre
ancestor: 4 Cain
author: John Gardner
Grenoble: 4 city, town
city near ~: 4 Lyon 5 Lyons
department: 5 Isère
locale: 6 France
river: 5 Isère
Greschner, Ron
spouse: Carol Alt
Gresham: 4 city, town
locale: 6 Oregon
Gresham's __: 3 law
Greta: 5 Garbo 7 Scacchi
Gretchen: 3 Mol
Grete: 5 Waitz
Gretel
brother: 6 Hansel
see also German
Gretna: 4 city, town
locale: 9 Louisiana
Gretna Green, go to: 5 elope
Gretzky, Wayne
emulate ~: 5 skate
milieu: 3 ice 4 rink 5 arena
nine-time award: 3 MVP
org.: 3 NHL
quest: 4 goal
team: 6 Oilers
workplace: 3 ice 4 rink
grey: 3 ash 4 ashy, drab, hoar 5 ashen, dingy, hoary, smoky 6 cloudy, gloomy, leaden, somber 7 silvery, sunless 8 lowering, overcast 9 cinereous
ender: 3 hen, lag 5 hound
see also gray
Grey: 3 Nan 4 Earl, Jane, Joel, Lita, Zane 8 Jennifer, Virginia

Grey __: **6** Poupon
__ Grey: **5** Agnes
Grey Cup grp.: **3** CFL
Grey Goose: **5** vodka
competitor: **4** Skyy **5** Popov, Stoli **6** Rodnik, Starka **7** Absolut **8** Smirnoff
__ Grey Goose, The: **3** Ole
greyhound: **3** dog **5** canid, racer **6** canine
Greyhound: **3** bus
alternative: **6** Amtrak
get off the ~: **5** debus
greyhound racing: **5** sport
greyish: **3** wan **4** ashy, pale **5** ashen, livid, pasty, waxen **6** pallid
Grey, Jane: **4** Lady
Grey, Joel Oscar: Cabaret
greylag: **4** bird
Grey Poupon: **7** mustard
alternative: **7** French's, Gulden's
Grey's Anatomy (ABC drama)
cast: Justin Chambers (Alex Karev)
Katherine Heigl (Isobel 'Izzie' Stevens)
T.R. Knight (George O' Malley)
Sandra Oh (Cristina Yang)
Ellen Pompeo (Meredith Grey)
Greystoke: **4** lord **6** Tarzan
playmate: **3** ape
__ Grey tea: **4** Earl
Grey, Zane: **6** writer
genre: western
work: Arizona Ames
Arizona Clan
Black Mesa
Call of the Canyon
Code of the West
Desert Gold
The Desert of Wheat
The Dude Ranger
The Fugitive Trail
Knights of the Range
The Last of the Plainsmen
The Last Trail
The Last Wagon Train
The Lone Star Ranger
Lost Pueblo
The Man of the Forest
The Maverick Queen
The Mysterious Rider
Nevada
The Rainbow Trail
Riders of the Purple Sage
Robbers' Roost
Rogue River Feud
Shadow on the Trail
The Spirit of the Border
Stranger From the Tonto
Sunset Pass
The Thundering Herd
To the Last Man
The Trail Driver
Twin Sombreros
Under the Tonto Rim
The U.P. Trail
Valley of Wild Horses
West of the Pecos
Wildfire
Wild Horse Mesa
Wyoming
GRF: **4** Ford
predecessor: **3** RMN
successor: **3** JEC
grid: **5** graph **6** matrix **7** grating, lattice, network **9** framework, grillwork
ender: **4** iron, lock
see also football, gridiron
gridder
see football, gridiron
griddle: **3** pan **4** cook
ender: **4** cake
hot off the ~: **3** new **5** fresh
griddlecake: **8** flapjack
gridiron: **5** field, grate **6** frypan **7** stadium
action: **4** fake, juke, kick, pass, play, punt **5** blitz, catch, sneak **6** end run, fumble, huddle, tackle **7** penalty **9** field goal, scrimmage, touchdown
arbiter: **3** ref **5** zebra **7** referee
defunct ~ grp.: **4** USFL
gear: **3** tee **6** helmet
group: **3** AFC, NFC, NFL, sqd. **4** line, NCAA **5** squad **6** huddle
honor: **6** All-Pro
injury site: **4** knee
no-no: **4** clip
opportunity: **4** down
position: **2** FB, HB, LG, LH, LT, RB, RG, RT **3** ctr., end, RFB, RHB **5** guard **6** back. QB, center, tackle **8** fullback, half-back
quota: **6** eleven
setback: **4** loss
stat: **2** TD **3** int. **9** touchdown
two ~ periods: **4** half
unit: **4** yard
see also football
gridlock: **3** cog, jam **5** jam-up **6** holdup, logjam **7** impasse, traffic **8** blockage, prohibit, stoppage **9** stalemate **10** bottleneck, congestion, standstill, traffic jam
unit: **3** car **4** auto
gridlocked: **5** fixed, stuck **6** packed, static **7** stalled, stopped **8** immobile **9** congested
Grieco: **7** Richard
grief: **3** rue, woe **4** ache, dole, pain **5** agony, dolor, gloom, trial, worry **6** lament, misery, regret, sorrow **7** anguish, despair, emotion, remorse, sadness, trouble **8** distress, hardship, mourning, troubles, vexation **9** dejection, heartache, suffering **10** affliction, depression, desolation, heartbreak, heavy heart, loneliness, melancholy, woefulness
come to ~: **4** fail **5** abort **7** founder, misfire **8** miscarry
exclamation: **4** alas **5** alack
express ~: **3** cry, rue, sob **4** keen, moan, pine, sigh, wail, weep **5** mourn **6** lament, sorrow
feel ~ for: **4** pity **10** sympathize
Grief
author: Elizabeth Barrett Browning
grief-stricken: **3** sad **4** down **6** morose **7** hurting, unhappy **8** dejected, overcome, troubled **9** plaintive, woebegone
be ~: **3** cry, sob **4** wail, weep **5** mourn **6** lament **9** break down, shed tears
Grieg, Edvard: **8** composer
home: **4** Oslo **6** Norway
work: Holberg Suite
Peer Gynt
Grier: **3** Pam **5** Rosey **9** Roosevelt
Griese, Bob: **2** QB
sport: **8** football
grievance: **4** beef, hurt **5** gripe, score, stink, wrong **6** bygone, grouse, grudge, injury, matter, plaint, squawk **7** affront, protest **8** big stink, distress, hardship, inequity, jeremiad **9** annoyance, ax to grind, bellyache, complaint, indignity, injustice, objection **10** affliction, difficulty, resentment
grieve: **3** rue **4** ache, hurt, moan, mope, pain, pine, wail, weep **5** bleed, brood, crush, mourn, upset, wound **6** bemoan, bewail, injure, lament, regret, sadden, sorrow, suffer **7** afflict, agonize, trouble **8** distress, languish **10** feel sorrow, take it hard
for: **4** pity **6** bemoan, bewail
grieving: **3** sad **4** hurt, sore **5** sorry, tears, woful **6** lament, sorrow, woeful **7** doleful, injured, keening, unhappy **8** mourning **9** heartsick, sorrowful **10** despondent
grievous: **3** sad **4** dire, foul, grim, poor, ugly **5** awful, grave, gross, heavy, lousy, sorry, tough, woful **6** bitter, crumby, crummy, dismal, horrid, mortal, odious, rotten, severe, taxing, tragic, unfair, woeful **7** accurst, baleful, baneful, beastly, doleful, fearful, ghastly, glaring, harmful, heinous, hurtful, onerous, painful, piteous, pitiful, serious, weighty **8** accursed, damaging, dolorous, dreadful, flagrant, God-awful, horrible, inferior, mournful, shameful, shocking, stinking, terrible, tragical, wretched **9** abhorrent, agonizing, appalling, atrocious, defective, egregious, execrable, frightful, harrowing, ill-omened, injurious, insidious, loathsome, miserable, monstrous, offensive, plaintive, revolting, sorrowful, upsetting **10** abominable, calamitous, deplorable, despicable, detestable, disastrous, disturbing, horrendous, lamentable, oppressive, outrageous, unbearable, villainous
Grievous Sin
author: Faye Kellerman
Griffey Jr., Ken
sport: **8** baseball
griffin: **7** monster
part: **4** lion **5** eagle
Griffin: **4** city, Merv, town **5** Dunne **6** Archie
locale: **7** Georgia
Griffith: **2** D.W. **4** Andy, Hugh, Park **5** Clark, Emile **7** Melanie
Griffith, Andy: **5** actor
film: A Face in the Crowd (1957)
No Time for Sergeants (1958)
TV: The Andy Griffith Show, Matlock
Griffith, D.W.: **8** director
film: The Birth of a Nation (1915)
Intolerance (1916)
rival: **4** Ince
Griffith, Emile: **5** boxer
milieu: **4** ring
Griffith-Joyner, Florence: **6** runner
Griffith, Melanie: **7** actress
film: Another Day in Paradise (1998)
Body Double (1984)
The Bonfire of the Vanities (1990)
Crazy in Alabama (1999)
Lolita (1997)
Nobody's Fool (1994)
Pacific Heights (1990)
Paradise (1991)
Shining Through (1992)
Stormy Monday (1988)
Working Girl (1988)
mother: Tippi Hedren
spouse: Antonio Banderas, Steven Bauer, Don Johnson
__ griffon: **7** Belgian
grifter: **5** cheat, shark **6** con man **7** hustler **8** swindler
brainchild: **4** scam
Grifters, The (1990 film)
cast: Annette Bening, John Cusack, Anjelica Huston
director: Stephen Frears
grig: **3** eel
home: **6** eelery
trap: **6** eelpot
grigri: **5** charm **6** amulet, fetich, fetish
grill: **3** ask **4** cook, heat, pump, quiz, sear, test **5** broil, query, roast, toast **6** sizzle **7** brasier, brazier, examine, hibachi, lattice, torture **8** barbecue, question **9** catechize, interview, lunchroom **10** restaurant, rotisserie
ender: **3** age **4** room, work
partner: **3** bar
remnant: **3** ash **5** ember **6** cinder
site: **4** yard **5** patio
treat: **3** rib **5** cabob, frank, kabab, kabob, kebab, kebob, steak **6** burger, hot dog **7** chicken
__ grill: **3** gas **5** mixed **8** barbecue
grille: **7** grating **8** auto part **10** cowcatcher
material: **6** chrome
protector: **3** bra
Grillparzer, Franz: **8** Austrian **10** playwright
grillwork: **4** grid
grim: **3** bad **4** dark, dire, dour, foul, glum, poor **5** awful, bleak, cruel, gaunt, grave, harsh, lousy, lurid, mirky, murky, no-win, sorry, stark, stern, sulky, woful **6** crumby, crummy, dismal, dogged, gloomy, grisly, horrid, morbid, morose, odious, rotten, savage, severe, somber, strict, sullen, tragic, woeful **7** accurst, austere, baleful, baneful, beastly, doleful, fearful, ghastly, hangdog, hideous, inhuman, macaber, macabre, ominous, serious, unhappy **8** accursed, dreadful, God-awful, grievous, gruesome, hopeless, horrible, inferior, inhumane, lowering, resolute, ruthless, shameful, sinister, stinking, terrible, tragical, wretched **9** abhorrent, appalling, atrocious, cheerless, defective, depressed, execrable, ferocious,

frightful, insidious, loathsome, merciless, miserable, offensive, revolting, unpitying, woebegone **10** abominable, deplorable, depressing, despicable, detestable, disastrous, forbidding, formidable, horrendous, implacable, iron-willed, lamentable, relentless, unpleasant, unyielding
  not ~: **4** pink, rosy **6** bright, upbeat **7** glowing, hopeful **8** cheerful, pleasing, sanguine **9** favorable, promising **10** auspicious, optimistic
grimace: **3** mug **4** face, moue, pout **5** fleer, frown, scowl, smirk, sneer, snoot, wince **10** contortion, expression
  word said with a ~: **2** ow **3** yow **4** ouch, yeow
grimalkin: **3** cat **5** felid, kitty, tabby **6** feline
grime: **4** crud, dirt, gunk, muck, smut, soil, soot **5** filth **6** grunge, smooch, smudge, smutch **8** impurity
  remover: **4** soap **8** cleanser **9** detergent
Grimes: **4** Gary **5** Tammy **6** Martha **8** Burleigh
___ Grimes: **5** Peter
Grimes, Tammy: **7** actress
  daughter: Amanda Plummer
  spouse: Christopher Plummer
Grimley: **2** Ed
Grimm: **5** Jacob **7** Wilhelm
  character: **3** elf **4** ogre **5** gnome, troll
Grimm, Jacob: **6** German, writer
Grimm, Wilhelm: **6** German, writer
Grimson: **3** Stu
grimy: **4** foul **5** dingy, dirty, dusty, messy, mucky, muddy, smoky, sooty **6** filthy, fouled, grubby, grungy, soiled, sordid **7** muddied, smeared, smudged, squalid, stained, tainted, unclean, unswept **8** befouled, maculate, polluted, slovenly, unwashed **9** blackened, tarnished **10** bedraggled, besmirched, lusterless, unsanitary
grin: **4** beam **5** fleer, laugh, smile, smirk, sneer **6** simper **9** say cheese **10** expression
  and bear it: **4** cope, take **5** stick **6** adjust, submit **7** stomach **8** overlook
  like some ~s: **6** boyish, impish
Grin, Aleksandr: **6** writer **7** Russian
Grin and Bear It
  senator: **5** Snort
Grinch: **4** ogre **6** meanie
  creator: Dr. Seuss
  dog: **3** Max
  victim: **3** Who
grind: **3** job, rub, rut **4** chew, edge, file, grit, hone, mash, mill, plod, rasp, task, toil, wear, whet, wonk, work **5** annoy, chore, crush, gnash, grate, hound, labor, mince, munch, pound, slave, study, sweat, usual **6** abrade, crunch, harass, pestle, plague, powder, scrape, smooth, tedium **7** atomize, crumble, crumple, drudger, oppress, rat race, routine, sharpen, slavery, torment, travail, trouble **8** drudgery, hard work, keep down, levigate, struggle, tireless **9** comminute, granulate, grunt work, lucubrate, persecute, pulverize, triturate, tyrannize **10** livelihood
  against: **3** bug, irk, rub, vex **4** gall, wear **5** annoy, chafe, erode, grate **6** abrade, bother, harass, nettle, scrape **7** enflame, incense, inflame, provoke **8** exercise, irritate **10** exasperate
  an ax: **4** edge, file, hone, whet **5** strop **7** sharpen
  away: **4** plod, read, toil, work **5** labor, slave, study **6** drudge **9** lucubrate
  ax to ~: **6** agenda **9** grievance, obsession
  daily ~: **3** job, rut **4** work **5** labor **6** groove **7** routine
  down: **4** wear **5** erode
  ender: **5** stone
  underfoot: **5** crush, worst **6** defeat **7** flatten, trample
grind ___ halt: **3** to a
___ grind: **4** drip
grinder: **4** hero, mill **5** hoagy, molar, tooth **6** hoagie, pestle **8** sandwich
___ grinder: **4** meat **5** organ
grinding: **4** hard **7** grating, onerous, raucous **8** abrasive, friction **10** oppressive
  in need of ~: **4** dull **5** blunt
  machine: **5** lathe
  substance: **5** emery
  tooth: **5** molar
Grinding It Out
  author: Ray Kroc
grindle: **4** fish, tuna **6** bowfin
Grinnell: **6** George
grip: **3** ken **4** case, fist, grab, hold, keep, lock, snap, take, vise **5** ahold, brace, catch, cinch, clamp, clasp, grasp, rivet, seize **6** arrest, clench, clinch, clutch, engage, snatch, valise **7** command, embrace, enchant, engross, enthral, inthral, mastery, squeeze, tighten **8** clutches, enthrall, entrance, foothold, interest, inthrall, suitcase, traction **9** fascinate, handclasp, handshake, hypnotize, lay hold of, mesmerize, spellbind, stagehand **10** perception, possession
  loosen one's ~: **4** free **5** let go **6** unhand **7** release, set free **9** disengage
  starter: **4** hand
  tight ~: **3** hug **4** lock **6** clinch, clutch **7** bear hug, squeeze
___ grip: **3** key **6** pistol
___ grip!: **4** Get a
___-Grip: **4** Poli
gripe: **3** nag **4** beef, carp, crab, kick, moan, pain, pang, sulk **5** groan, peeve, whine **6** charge, grouch, grouse, kvetch, mutter, plaint, repine, squawk, yammer **7** grumble, protest, quibble **8** complain **9** annoyance, bellyache, complaint, find fault, grievance, make a fuss
  about nothing: **3** nag **4** carp **5** cavil, whine **6** bicker, grouse **7** nitpick, quibble **8** pettifog
griper: **5** grump **6** grouch, kvetch, moaner **7** crybaby **8** grumbler **10** malcontent
grippe: **3** bug, flu **5** virus **9** influenza
gripped: **4** rapt **8** held fast, obsessed, ravished **10** spellbound
gripper: **4** vise **5** cleat, tongs **6** C-clamp, pliers
gripping: **6** moving **8** readable **9** thrilling
grips with, come to: **4** face **6** handle, tackle **8** cope with, deal with **9** encounter **10** meet head on
gris-gris: **5** charm **6** amulet, fetish
Grisham, John: **6** writer
  profession: **3** law
  work: The Appeal
    The Associate
    Bleachers
    The Brethren
    The Broker
    The Chamber
    The Client
    The Firm
    Ford County
    The King of Torts
    The Last Juror
    The Partner
    The Pelican Brief
    The Rainmaker
    Runaway Jury
    Street Lawyer
    The Summons
    Testament
    A Time to Kill
Gris, Juan: **6** artist **7** painter, Spanish
grisly: **4** gory, grim, ugly **5** awful, livid, lurid **6** horrid, morbid **7** ghastly, hideous, macaber, macabre **8** dreadful, gruesome, horrible, shocking, terrible **9** appalling, frightful **10** abominable, horrendous, horrifying, petrifying, terrifying
Gris-Nez: **4** cape
  locale: **6** France
Grissom: **3** Gus **6** Virgil **9** astronaut
grist ender: **4** mill
grist for the ___: **4** mill
gristly: **5** tough **7** stringy
grit: **4** guts, sand **5** grind, heart, moxie, nerve, pluck, spine, spunk, valor **6** daring, gravel, mettle, powder, spirit, starch **7** bravery, courage, prowess, resolve, stamina **8** abrasive, backbone, gameness, gumption, tenacity, valiance, valiancy **9** endurance, fortitude, gutsiness, hardiness, toughness, willpower **10** confidence, doggedness, durability, feistiness, moral fiber, pluckiness, spunkiness
  one's teeth: **5** steel **6** clench
  true ~: **4** guts **5** pluck, spunk **9** fortitude
___ Grit: **4** True
grits: **5** grain **6** cereal
  prepare ~: **4** boil
___ grits: **4** corn **6** hominy
gritty: **4** bold, game **5** brave, gutsy, hardy, nervy, sandy, tough **6** awless, daring, dogged, grainy, heroic, plucky, spunky **7** aweless, defiant, doughty, gallant, powdery, staunch, valiant **8** abrasive, fearless, granular, gravelly, heroical, indurate, intrepid, resolute, sandlike, scratchy, spirited, stalwart, unafraid, valorous **9** audacious, dauntless, dreadless, steadfast, tenacious, undaunted, unfearful **10** courageous, determined, granulated, lusterless, mettlesome, undismayed, unflagging
___-gritty: **5** nitty
grivet: **6** mammal **7** primate
  relative: *see* primate
Grizabella: **3** cat
  creator: T.S. Eliot
Grizzard: **5** Lewis **6** George
grizzle: **6** whiten
grizzled: **3** old **4** aged **5** aging, hoary **6** ageing **7** ancient, elderly, wizened **9** geriatric, getting on, senescent, up in years **10** gray-haired
Grizzlies: **4** five
  home: **7** Memphis
  org.: **3** NBA
  rival: *see* NBA team
grizzly: **4** bear, gray, grey **5** ursid
  home: **3** den **4** lair
  relative: *see* gray color
  young ~: **3** cub
Grk.: **4** lang.
gro.
  fraction: **3** doz.
groan: **3** nag **4** carp, crab, howl, moan, sigh **5** creak, gripe, whine **6** grouse, kvetch, lament, mutter, plaint, repine, sorrow, squawk, yammer **7** grumble, screech **8** complain, vocalize **9** bellyache, make a fuss
  about: **4** moan **6** bemoan, bewail, lament, regret **7** deplore
groaner: **3** pun
groat: **4** coin **5** money **9** fourpence
groats: **4** oats **5** grain, kasha, wheat **6** cereal
___ G. Robinson: **6** Edward
grocer: **6** dealer, seller, vendor **8** merchant, purveyor, retailer **10** shopkeeper
groceries: **4** food **10** essentials, provisions
  remove the ~: **5** unbag
grocery: **3** mkt. **4** mart **6** bodega, market **9** food store
  bags: **6** armful
  bars: **3** UPC
  box fig.: **5** net wt.
  buy: **3** can, ham, pop, tea, tin **4** beef, chop, eggs, food, kail, kale, meat, milk, rice, salt **5** limes, pasta, pears, roast, sugar, viand **6** apples, cereal, lemons **7** cookies, oranges **9** detergent
  chain letters: **3** IGA
  coupon value: **5** cents
  holder: **3** bag, box, jar **4** case **5** quart **6** bottle, carton
  list abbr.: **3** doz.
  need: **4** bags **5** scale
  section: **4** deli, lane **5** aisle, dairy
  starter: **5** green
  trip: **6** errand
grocery ___: **4** cart **5** store
Grodin, Charles: **5** actor
  film: The Heartbreak Kid (1972)

Ishtar (1987)
It's My Turn (1980)
King Kong (1976)
The Lonely Guy (1984)
Midnight Run (1988)
Seems Like Old Times (1980)
grody: **5** dirty, seedy **6** sleazy **8** slovenly
Grody __ max!: **5** to the
Groening: **4** Matt
parent: **5** Homer, Marge
Grofé, Ferde: **8** composer
work: Grand Canyon Suite
Hollywood Suite
Mark Twain Suite
Mississippi Suite
New England Suite
grog: **3** ale **5** booze, drink, quaff **6** liquor **7** alcohol, spirits **8** beverage **10** intoxicant
ingredient: **3** rum
shop: **6** tavern **7** barroom **8** taphouse
groggy: **5** dazed, dizzy **6** sleepy **9** heavy-eyed, somnolent
grogram: **6** fabric **8** material
Groh: **5** David
grok: **3** dig **5** enjoy **6** follow **8** relate to **9** empathize **10** appreciate, comprehend
Grolier's: **3** enc. **4** ency. **5** encyc.
grommet: **6** eyelet
Gromyko: **6** Andrei
groom: **4** clip, comb, hand, male, mate, prep, tend, tidy, wash **5** brush, clean, curry, drill, preen, prime, primp, ready, train, tutor, vower **6** flunky, lackey, spouse, tidy up **7** educate, equerry, flunkey, husband, lacquey, nurture, prepare, shape up, spiff up **8** benedict, horseman, neaten up, newlywed, prettify, pretty up, spruce up **9** make ready, smarten up
acquisition: **5** in-law
area: **6** stable
buy: **4** band, ring
future ~: **4** beau **6** fiancé **8** intended **9** betrothed
of India: **4** sice, syce **5** saice
partner: **5** bride
response: **3** I do
starter: **5** bride
wear: **3** tux **4** tuck **10** cummerbund
groomed: **4** tidy, trim **5** natty, sleek, slick, smart **6** all set, dapper, primed, spruce **10** fastidious, immaculate
__-groomed: **4** well
grooming aid: **4** comb
groove: **3** cut, rut, sit **4** dado, kerf, line, rote, slot **5** canal, crimp, ditch, flute, gouge, habit, notch, ridge, score, stria, track, trail **6** crease, furrow, gutter, hollow, incise, rabbet, trench **7** channel, fluting, rapport, routine **8** accustom, habitude **9** corrugate **10** daily grind, depression, interspace
barrel ~: **5** croze
bowstring ~: **4** nock
carpenter ~: **4** dado
shaft ~: **6** keyway
sliding door ~: **5** regle
small ~: **4** nurl **5** knurl, stria
Groovin' (1967 song)
artist: Rascals

grooving: **5** happy, merry, peppy, perky **6** joyful **7** gleeful **8** animated, carefree, cheerful, jubilant, laughing, mirthful **9** energetic, exuberant, sprightly **10** flying high, optimistic
groovy
see wonderful
Groovy Kind of Love, A (song)
artist: Phil Collins, Mindbenders
grope: **3** paw **4** feel, fish **5** probe, touch **6** fumble, search **8** flounder **9** cast about, feel about
groper: **4** fish **5** pawer
Gropius, Walter: **6** German **9** architect
Grosbard, Ulu: **8** director
grosbeak: **4** bird **8** cardinal, hawfinch
beak: **3** neb, nib
grosgrain: **5** cloth **6** fabric **8** material
gross: **3** all, big, low, raw, sum **4** earn, foul, huge, icky, lewd, loud, make, rank, rude, sick, ugly **5** awful, bulky, crass, crude, heavy, large, nasty, sheer, stark, total, utter, whole, yucky **6** coarse, entire, patent, profit, ribald, rotten, scuzzy, take in, unmeet, vulgar **7** blatant, boorish, bring in, extreme, glaring, hateful, heinous, hideous, loutish, massive, obvious, sizable, uncouth, weighty **8** abnormal, apparent, complete, degraded, dreadful, enormous, entirety, flagrant, grievous, horrible, improper, indecent, manifest, outright, pull down, receipts, shameful, shocking, sizeable, sum total, terrible, totality, unsavory, unseemly, unsubtle, unwieldy, wretched **9** aggregate, appalling, downright, egregious, excessive, frightful, grotesque, inelegant, loathsome, low-minded, lubricous, monstrous, nefarious, offensive, out-and-out, repellant, revolting, tasteless, unrefined, unsightly, unwieldly **10** abominable, disgusting, immoderate, indecorous, indelicate, inordinate, lascivious, outrageous, overweight, scurrilous, uncultured, uninviting, unpleasant
fraction: **5** dozen
not ~: **3** net **6** profit **8** take-home
out: **5** appal, repel **6** appall, offend, revolt, sicken **7** disgust
gross __: **3** out, ton **6** income, profit, weight **7** anatomy, revenue
Gross: **4** Arye, Mary, Milt **5** Henry **7** Michael
Gross!: **3** ick, ugh **4** yech, yuck **5** yecch
Gross Anatomy (1989 film)
cast: Christine Lahti, Matthew Modine, Daphne Zuniga
gross domestic __: **7** product
Grosse __: **3** Ile
Grosse __, MI: **6** Pointe
Grosse Pointe Blank (1997 film)
cast: Alan Arkin, Dan Aykroyd, Joan Cusack, John Cusack, Minnie Driver
Grosset partner: **6** Dunlap
Grossglockner: **3** alp
Grossman: **3** Rex
gross national __: **7** product

grossness: **8** enormity, ribaldry **9** bawdiness, brutality, crudeness, indecency, vulgarity
grosso: **4** full **5** great
__ Grosso: **4** Mato
Gros Ventre: **5** tribe
grosz: **5** money
Grosz: **6** George
groszy, 100: **5** zloty
Grote: **5** Jerry, Reber
grotesque: **3** odd **4** eery, ugly, wild **5** antic, eerie, gross, weird **6** absurd **7** bizarre, hideous, macabre, strange, surreal **8** aberrant, freakish **9** distorted, fantastic, ludicrous, malformed, misshapen, monstrous, unnatural, whimsical **10** outlandish, ridiculous
grotto: **4** cave, cove **5** antre, bower **6** alcove, cavern, recess **7** hideout
grotty: **5** dirty, seedy **8** wretched
grouch: **4** carp, crab, moan **5** churl, crank, gripe, growl, grump, shrew, whine **6** griper, grouse, kvetch, moaner, mutter, whiner **7** grouser, growler, grumble **8** complain, grumbler, sorehead, sourball, sourpuss **9** bellyache, make a fuss **10** bellyacher, complainer, crosspatch, curmudgeon, malcontent
look: **5** scowl
grouchiness: **4** bile **6** spleen, temper
Groucho: **3** wit **4** host, Marx **5** emcee
brother: **5** Chico, Gummo, Harpo, Zeppo
cap: **5** beret
glance from ~: **4** leer
specialty: **3** pun **5** ad-lib
grouchy: **4** sour **5** cross, gruff, moody, rough, sulky, surly, testy **6** crabby, cranky, crusty, fretty, grumpy, ireful, morose, ornery, snappy, touchy **7** bearish, huffish, kvetchy, peevish, waspish **8** choleric, churlish, growling, grumpish, liverish, petulant, snappish **9** crotchety, fractious, irascible, irritable, querulous, splenetic **10** out of sorts
be ~: **4** bark, vent **5** growl, grunt, snarl **7** grumble **8** complain
ground: **3** bed, sod **4** base, dirt, land, root, site, soil, turf, zone **5** basis, coach, earth, field, level, lower, patch, teach, train, tutor, venue **6** bottom, inform, keep in, punish, reason, region, school, sphere **7** confine, flatten, powdery, premise, prepare, qualify, support, terrain, topsoil **8** acquaint, initiate, instruct, restrict **9** landscape, principle, pulverize, underside **10** foundation, real estate, terra firma
break ~: **4** plow **5** begin **7** kick off
breaker: **3** hoe **5** spade
breaking new ~: **5** fresh, novel **6** clever **7** unusual **8** creative, inspired, original, singular **9** ingenious, inventive **10** innovative
breeding ~: **6** hotbed
combining form: **3** geo- **5** chame- **6** chamae-

cover: **3** sod **4** lawn, snow, tarp **5** ajuga, grass, mulch, plant, sedum
cover ~: **3** fly, hie, run **4** rush **5** speed **6** travel **8** progress
ender: **3** hog, nut, out **4** ball, mass, side, sill, work **5** cover, speed, swell, water **6** keeper, stroke **7** breaker **8** breaking
gain ~: **6** pick up **7** advance **8** get ahead, progress **9** go forward
get off the ~: **5** begin, start
give ~: **6** retire **7** retreat **8** withdraw
give no ~: **5** force, order, press **6** demand, insist **8** pressure **9** stand firm
giving no ~: **8** stubborn
grain: **4** meal **5** flour, grist
happy hunting ~: **6** heaven, utopia **7** Arcadia, Elysium **9** Shangri-la
high ~: **4** hill, rise **5** knoll, ridge **7** plateau **8** eminence, mountain **9** acclivity, elevation **10** prominence
hit the ~: **3** lit **4** alit, fell, land **5** light **6** alight
hold one's ~: **4** stay **6** adhere, endure, remain, take it **7** persist, stay put
leave the ~: **3** fly **4** rise, soar **5** arise, climb, vault **6** ascend, rocket **7** balloon, take off **8** levitate
lose ~: **3** lag **4** slip **5** slide **7** regress **8** fall back
near the ~: **3** low **5** below **7** beneath **8** crouched, low-lying
on slippery ~: **4** iffy **5** dicey, hairy, risky **6** chancy, daring, touchy, tricky, unsafe **7** fraught **8** ticklish **9** dangerous, desperate, foolhardy, hazardous **10** precarious, touch-and-go
on solid ~: **6** ashore
piece of ~: **3** lot **4** area **5** field, range, tract **7** section, terrain
plan: **3** map **5** chart, draft **6** design, layout, scheme, sketch, survey **7** diagram, outline, program, rundown **8** proposal, scenario **9** blueprint, framework, rough idea **10** rough draft
rising ~: **4** bank, hill **5** slope **7** incline **8** gradient
rule: **6** policy **7** precept **9** guideline
run into the ~: **6** overdo **7** belabor, overuse **8** overplay
starter: **4** back, camp, fair, play **5** above, below **6** battle
stomping ~: **4** turf **5** haunt **6** domain, locale, region, sphere **7** hangout, quarter **8** locality **9** territory
toward the ~: **3** low **4** down **5** below **10** underneath
wet ~: **3** bog **5** marsh
zero: **4** goal **5** focus **6** target **8** bull's-eye **9** objective
ground __: **3** fog, ice, ivy **4** ball, coat, crew, rule, zero **5** cover, floor, glass, level, rules, water **6** stroke **7** control

GR

__ **ground:** 4 gain, give, high, home, lose 5 break, cover 6 common, middle 7 hunting, neutral, proving
__**-ground:** 5 air-to 7 dumping
groundbreaking: 3 new 5 novel 7 radical
grounded: 6 ashore 7 learned 8 stranded
nautically: 6 neaped
__**-grounded:** 4 well
grounder, botched: 5 error
groundhog: 6 animal, digger, mammal, rodent
relative: *see* rodent
Groundhog Day (1993 film)
cast: Chris Elliott, Andie MacDowell, Bill Murray
director: Harold Ramis
Groundhog Day month: 3 Feb. 8 February
grounding: 8 training 9 education 10 background, upbringing
groundless: 4 idle, null 5 empty, false, inane, silly, wacky, wrong 6 absurd, screwy, wanton, whacky 7 fatuous, unsound 8 baseless, cockeyed, needless, specious 9 causeless, illogical, imaginary, senseless, unfounded, untenable 10 bottomless, chimerical, gratuitous, ungrounded, unprovoked
ground-level: 3 low 4 flat 5 short 10 unelevated
__**-ground missile:** 5 air-to
groundnut: 5 tuber 6 veggie 9 vegetable
ground-round serving: 5 patty 6 pattie
grounds: 3 lot, why 4 area, call, land, lees, park, root 5 basis, cause, dregs, field, proof, realm, tract 6 campus, domain, estate, motive, reason, sphere 7 acreage, country, deposit, habitat, premise, pretext, residue, terrain 8 district, environs, evidence, leavings, occasion, premises, property, sediment, validity 9 rationale, settlings, territory, testimony, wherefore 10 foundation, legitimacy, real estate
ender: 6 keeper
for a suit: 4 tort 5 abuse, crime, libel, smear, wrong 6 attack 7 calumny, slander 10 defamation
give ~ for: 5 incur, prove 7 justify, testify
house and ~: 5 manor, ranch 6 estate 8 premises, property 10 plantation
school ~: 4 quad 6 campus
__ **grounds:** 6 parade
groundsel: 4 weed 5 plant 6 flower
groundskeeper
at times: 5 mower, raker
concern: 5 shrub
groundswell: 5 flood, surge 6 onrush 10 outpouring
__**-ground wheat:** 5 stone
groundwork: 3 bed 4 base 5 basis 7 support 8 research, training 10 background, foundation, substratum
lay the ~: 4 plan 5 draft, found, frame, set up, shape, start 6 create, draw up, launch 7 develop, pioneer, prepare, provide 8 initiate 9 establish, formulate, institute, introduce, spearhead 10 anticipate, trailblaze
group: 3 lot, org., set 4 assn., band, bevy, bloc, body, clan, clot, club, crew, cult, gang, herd, link, lump, mass, pack, pool, rank, sect, sort, team, tier, type, unit 5 batch, bunch, chain, class, clump, corps, covey, crowd, flock, genre, order, party, posse, squad, suite, troop 6 assort, bundle, cartel, circle, clique, clutch, corral, divide, family, gang up, gather, huddle, league, legion, muster, outfit, parcel, passel, school, series, throng 7 arrange, battery, brigade, bunch up, cluster, collect, combine, company, consort, coterie, faction, marshal, platoon, round up, scare up, society, species 8 assemble, assembly, category, classify, ensemble, flotilla, graduate, organize, separate 9 aggregate, associate, coalition, committee, concourse, forgather, gathering, syndicate 10 assemblage, assortment, categorize, collection, concursion, congregate, contingent, cumulation, distribute, pigeonhole
ender: 5 think
__ **group:** 3 age, rap 4 peer, rock, user 5 blood, focus, study, youth 7 control, support
grouped: 5 joint 6 mutual 7 generic, unified 8 combined, communal, compiled, conjoint 9 assembled, composite, concerted, generical 10 collective, cumulative
grouper: 4 fish, mero 5 guasa
groupie: 3 fan, nut 4 buff 7 admirer, devotee, fanatic 8 follower, hanger-on 9 sycophant 10 aficionado
need: 4 hero, icon, idol 7 darling, pop star 8 luminary 9 celebrity, superstar
grouping: 4 tier 5 class 6 league 7 bracket 8 category, division, sequence 9 formation
symbol: 5 paren.
Group, The (1966 film)
author: Mary McCarthy
cast: Candice Bergen, Joan Hackett, Elizabeth Hartman
director: Sidney Lumet
groupthink: 4 talk 10 conference, discussion
grouse: 4 beef, bird, carp, crab, fowl, fuss, moan, sulk 5 cavil, gripe, groan, whine 6 grouch, kvetch, mutter, plaint 7 grumble, protest 8 complain, game bird 9 bellyache, complaint, grievance, make a fuss, ptarmigan, sprigtail
female ~: 6 gorhen
relative: *see* fowl
grouser: 6 grouch, kvetch 8 sorehead
grousing: 7 peevish 9 grumbling, querulous
grout: 6 cement, filler, mortar 7 plaster
user: 5 tiler
grouty: 5 sulky, surly, testy
grove: 4 mott, park, wood 5 copse, motte, stand, woods 6 bosket, forest, timber 7 bosquet, coppice, orchard
__ **grove:** 6 orange
grovel: 3 beg 5 cower, crawl, kotow, toady 6 cringe, kowtow 7 eat crow 8 bootlick 9 prostrate
Grove, Lefty: 6 hurler 7 pitcher
groveler: 5 toady 6 lackey 7 lacquey 8 kowtower 9 sycophant
groveling: 6 abject, menial 7 servile, slavish 8 cringing, toadying, toadyish 9 kowtowing 10 obsequious, submissive
__ **Grove, NJ:** 5 Penns
Grover: 9 Cleveland 10 Washington
vice president: 5 Adlai
Grover __ Alexander: 9 Cleveland
Groves of Academe, The
author: Mary McCarthy
__ **Grove Village, IL:** 3 Elk
grow: 3 age, sow, wax 4 rise, till 5 add to, bloat, bloom, build, mount, plant, raise, ripen, shape, swell, widen 6 accrue, beef up, deepen, dilate, evolve, expand, extend, gather, mature, spread, spring, sprout, step up, thrive, unfold 7 accrete, advance, amplify, augment, balloon, broaden, build up, burgeon, develop, enlarge, fill out, inflate, magnify, mount up, prosper, quicken, recover, stretch 8 bourgeon, escalate, flourish, get ahead, heighten, increase, incubate, lengthen, maturate, multiply, progress, snowball, vegetate 9 branch out, germinate, increment, luxuriate, propagate 10 accumulate, appreciate, burst forth, gain weight, liberalize, supplement
accustomed: 5 adapt, inure 6 adjust, harden, orient 7 conform 9 acclimate, reconcile 10 assimilate, come around
dim: 4 fade 6 darken 7 blacken
dull: 4 fade, pale
into: 4 turn 7 advance 8 progress
larger: 3 wax 5 widen 6 expand
older: 3 age 4 grow 6 mature 7 develop
on: 6 accept, affect 9 influence
out of: 5 arise, issue 6 derive, emerge, follow, result 7 proceed 9 arise from, originate
profusely: 4 riot 5 bloom 6 abound, thrive 7 burgeon, run riot 8 flourish 9 luxuriate
rapidly: 4 boom 5 swell 6 thrive 7 burgeon, explode, shoot up 8 flourish, mushroom
rich: 4 gain 5 get on, score 6 arrive, batten, do well, profit 7 burgeon, make out, prosper, succeed 8 flourish, get ahead, go places, hit it big, make good 9 make money
smaller: 3 ebb 4 wane 6 lessen, narrow, shrink 7 decline, deflate, drop off, dwindle 8 contract, decrease, diminish
stronger: 5 rally, train 6 arouse, perk up, pick up, revive 7 get well, improve, rebound, recover, shape up 8 come back 9 get better 10 bounce back, come around, recuperate, rejuvenate, turn around
together: 4 knit, mend 7 entwine
up: 5 arise 6 appear, mature 7 develop 9 come of age 10 burst forth
weary: 4 flag, jade, pall, tire 8 peter out
white: 4 fade 6 blanch, bleach 8 etiolate
grow __: 4 into
grower: 6 farmer 7 planter 8 gardener 10 agronomist, cultivator
starter: 4 wine, wool
growing: 5 alive, young 7 farming, ongoing, rampant 8 blooming, thriving
business: 4 farm
early: 4 rath 5 rathe
good for ~: 6 arable 7 fertile 8 plowable, tillable
medium: 4 dirt, loam, soil 5 earth 6 ground 7 topsoil
org.: 3 UFW
out: 5 enate
room: 4 acre
season: 3 spr. 6 spring
together: 9 confluent
vigorously: 4 rank, wild 7 rampant 8 prolific 9 exuberant, luxuriant 10 junglelike
years: 5 teens, youth 7 boyhood 8 girlhood 9 childhood 10 immaturity, pubescence
growing __: 5 pains
Growing Pains (ABC sitcom)
cast: Kirk Cameron (Mike Seaver) Tracey Gold (Carol Seaver) Joanna Kerns (Maggie Seaver) Jeremy Miller (Ben Seaver) Alan Thicke (Dr. Jason Seaver)
Growing Up in New Guinea
author: Margaret Mead
growl: 4 bark, gnar, howl, moan, roar, roll, snap 5 gnarl, gnarr, grunt, snarl 6 bellow, grouch, mutter, rumble 7 grumble, thunder 8 complain 9 make a fuss 10 vituperate
source: 5 belly, tummy 7 stomach
growler: 6 grouch, kvetch 7 pitcher
grow like __: 5 a weed
growling: 5 gruff, surly, testy 6 grumpy, ornery, touchy 7 bearish, grouchy, peevish, uncivil 8 snappish 9 irascible, irritable, querulous 10 out of sorts
grown: 3 big 5 adult 6 mature 8 full-size 9 full-sized
starter: 4 home, moss
together: 6 adnate
up: 3 big 4 ripe 5 adult, of age 6 mature 9 developed
grown-__: 3 ups
__**-grown:** 4 full 5 shade
__ **Grown Accustomed to Her Face:** 3 I've
grown-up: 3 man 4 lady 5 adult, woman 6 mature, mister, person 9 gentleman
__ **grow on:** 5 one to
__ **Grows in Brooklyn:** 5 A Tree

growth: **4** boom, gain, hike, incr., life, rise **5** boost, surge, swell **6** upping, waxing **7** accrual, advance, buildup, process, stature, success **8** increase, progress, widening **9** beefing up, evolution, expansion, extension, flowering, gestation, sprouting **10** incipience, maturation, production, prosperity, transition
combining form: **3** aux- **4** auxo- **6** auxamo-, -trophy
full ~: **5** prime **8** majority, maturity **9** adulthood
new ~: **4** twig, wand **5** shoot, sprig
rapid ~ environment: **3** den **4** nest **6** cradle, hotbed
rings: **6** annuli
season's ~: **4** crop **5** yield **7** harvest
slow ~: **5** stunt
spell: **4** boom **5** spirt, spurt
underground ~: **5** radix, tuber **7** radicle, rhizome
unwelcome ~: **4** weed
__ Grow Too Old to Dream: **5** When I
__ Grow Up: **5** I Won't, When I
Groza, Lou
sport: **8** football
Groza, Lou sport
nickname: **3** Toe
grp.: **3** org. **4** assn. **5** assoc.
grub: **3** bug, dig **4** chow, eats, fare, feed, food, meal, meat, nosh, plod, root, slog, toil, wonk **5** delve, labor, larva, scour, shove, slave, snack **6** burrow, drudge, fodder, insect, search, uproot **7** aliment, edibles, rations, rummage, uncover, unearth, victual, vittles **8** excavate, scrounge, victuals **9** provender **10** provisions, sustenance
ender: **5** stake
grownup ~: **6** beetle
Grub __: **6** Street
grubber starter: **5** money
grubby: **5** dirty, grimy, messy, muddy, nasty, seedy, sooty, tacky **6** filthy, fouled, grungy, soiled, sordid, unneat **7** smudged, stained, tainted, unkempt, unswept **8** befouled, begrimed, maculate, polluted, slovenly, unwashed **9** blackened, tarnished **10** besmirched, unsanitary
grubstake: **4** fund **7** funding, sponsor **9** guarantee, subsidize
grubstaker: **7** sponsor **9** financier, guarantor **10** benefactor
grudge: **4** feud **5** score, spite, stint, venom **6** animus, enmity, hatred, malice, rancor **7** dislike, ill will, umbrage **8** bad blood **9** animosity, antipathy, grievance **10** bitterness, resentment
bear a ~: **6** resent
carrying a ~: **3** mad **4** sore **6** bitter
have a ~ against: **4** hate **5** spite **6** detest **7** despise
__ grudge: **5** bear a
grudging: **4** sour **6** forced, stingy **7** jealous **8** ungiving **9** reluctant, unwilling **10** unfriendly, unobliging, vindictive
gruel: **7** oatmeal **8** flummery, porridge
oatmeal ~: **6** burgoo
grueling: **4** hard **5** hairy, harsh, rough, stiff, tough **6** brutal, fierce, severe, taxing, thorny, trying, uphill **7** arduous, hard-won, onerous, racking **8** crushing, toilsome **9** demanding, difficult, herculean, laborious, punishing, strenuous, torturous **10** enervating, exhausting, formidable, oppressive
gruesome: **4** gory, grim, vile **5** awful, lurid **6** creepy, grisly, horrid, morbid **7** ghastly, hideous, macaber, macabre, squalid **8** horrible, horrific, shocking, terrible **9** appalling, frightful, monstrous, repugnant **10** abominable, disgusting, horrendous, horrifying, petrifying, terrifying
gruff: **4** curt, rude **5** blunt, brusk, harsh, husky, raspy, rough, short, surly **6** abrupt, coarse, crabby, croaky, crusty, grumpy, hoarse, ireful, morose, snappy, snippy, sullen **7** bearish, boorish, brusque, grating, grouchy, loutish, raucous, throaty, uncivil **8** churlish, growling, grumpish, guttural, impolite, inurbane, snippety, tactless **9** truculent **10** ill-humored, unfriendly, ungracious, unmannerly
sound ~: **4** bark, snap, yell **5** growl, snarl **6** bellow
Gruffudd: **4** Ioan
grumble: **4** bark, beef, carp, crab, fuss, kick, moan, mope, pule, snap **5** gripe, groan, growl, snarl, whine **6** grouch, grouse, kvetch, mumble, murmur, mutter, repine, rumble, snivel, squawk, yammer **7** protest **8** complain **9** bellyache, complaint, find fault, make a fuss
grumbler: **4** bear, crab **5** shrew **6** chider, griper, grouch, kvetch, moaner **7** crybaby, grouser **8** sourball **9** termagant **10** bellyacher, curmudgeon
grumbling: **7** carping **8** grousing, petulant **9** grouching, irritable, muttering, nattering, querulous **10** discontent
Grumman: **5** Leroy
grump: **4** bear, crab, mope, sulk **5** crank **6** grouch, whiner **8** complain, sorehead, sourball, sourpuss **10** bellyacher, complainer, curmudgeon, malcontent
Grumpier Old Men (1995 film)
cast: Ann-Margret, Jack Lemmon, Sophia Loren, Walter Matthau, Burgess Meredith
grumpiness: **4** bile **5** spite, venom **6** rancor, spleen, temper **8** acrimony
grumpy: **5** cross, gruff, huffy, moody, sulky, surly, testy **6** crabby, cranky, fretty, ornery, sullen, touchy **7** bearish, bilious, griping, grouchy, huffish, kvetchy, peevish, pettish, prickly, waspish **8** churlish, growling, liverish, petulant, snappish **9** crotchety, grumbling, irritable, querulous, splenetic, truculent **10** out of sorts
be ~: **4** fret, mope, sulk **5** brood, chafe **6** kvetch
expression: **5** frown, glare, scowl **7** grimace **9** dirty look
mood: **4** huff, snit, stew **5** pique **6** temper
Grumpy: **5** dwarf
colleague: *see* dwarf
Grumpy Old Men (1993 film)
cast: Ann-Margret, Jack Lemmon, Walter Matthau, Burgess Meredith
__ Grundy: **3** Mrs.
grunge: **4** dirt **5** filth, grime, trash **7** rubbish
grungy: **3** bad **4** foul, vile **5** dirty, grimy, messy, sooty **6** cruddy, filthy, fouled, grubby, shoddy, sloppy, soiled, trashy, unneat **7** rundown, smudged, stained, tainted, unkempt, unswept **8** befouled, begrimed, maculate, polluted, slovenly, untended, unwashed, wretched **9** blackened, tarnished **10** besmirched, disgusting, disheveled, unsanitary
grunion: **4** fish **10** silverside
grunt: **4** fish, hand, oink, snap **5** croak, gofer, growl, sargo **6** gopher, mutter **7** dessert, laborer, soldier **9** reckoning
sound: **3** oof, ugh
work: **4** moil, toil **5** grind, labor, sweat **7** travail **8** drudgery
grunt __: **4** work
grunter: **3** hog, pig **5** swine
grunts: **3** GIs **8** dogfaces, infantry, soldiers
Grusin: **4** Dave
Gruyère: **6** cheese
coat: **4** rind
grysbok: **6** animal, mammal **8** antelope
relative: *see* antelope
GSA part: **3** Gen. **4** Serv. **5** Admin. **7** General **8** Services
G-sharp: **5** A-flat
GSO: **4** aide, asst.
Gstaad: **6** resort
gear: **3** ski **4** skee
locale: **4** Alps **11** Switzerland
G-String Murders, The
author: Gypsy Rose Lee
G-suit buyer: **4** NASA
GT: **3** car
like a ~: **6** sporty
maker: **4** Opel
Gt. Brit.
locale: **3** Eur.
part of ~: **3** Eng., Ire. **4** Scot.
GTE: **2** co.
employee: **4** oper.
rival: **3** ITT
GTI: **2** VW **3** car **4** auto **10** automobile, Volkswagen
GTO: **3** car **4** auto **7** Ferrari, Pontiac
like a ~: **6** sporty
part of ~: **4** Gran **7** Turismo
G.T.O. (1964 song)
artist: Ronny & the Daytonas
guacamole: **3** dip **9** appetizer
partner: **4** chip
source: **7** avocado
guacharo: **4** bird
Guadalajara: **4** city, town
locale: **6** Mexico **7** Jalisco
see also Spanish
Guadalcanal: **4** isle **6** island
island near ~: **4** Savo
Guadalquivir: **5** river
city on the ~: **7** Córdoba, Seville
locale: **5** Spain
Guadalupe: **4** city, town **5** range
city on the ~: **7** San Jose
locale: **6** Mexico **9** Nuevo León, Zacatecas
see also Spanish
Guadalupe Mountains: **4** park
locale: **5** Texas
Guadeloupe: **4** isle **6** island
capital: **10** Basse-Terre
writer: **5** Condé
Guam: **3** ter. **4** isle, terr. **6** island
capital: **5** Agana
Guanabara: **3** bay
locale: **3** Rio **6** Brazil
guanaco: **6** animal, mammal
like the ~: **6** Andean
relative: **5** camel, llama **6** alpaca, vicuña **8** Bactrian **9** dromedary
Guantanamera (1966 song)
artist: Sandpipers
Guantánamo: **3** bay **4** city, town **5** Gitmo
locale: **4** Cuba
guar __: **3** gum
guar.: **4** cert.
Guaraldi, Vince: **7** pianist
genre: **4** jazz
__-Guarani: **4** Tupi
guarantee: **3** ice, vow **4** aver, bond, oath, pawn, seal, word **5** cinch, swear, vouch **6** affirm, assure, attest, avouch, cosign, ensure, insure, pledge, secure, surety **7** certify, confirm, endorse, indorse, promise, protect, sponsor, warrant **8** attest to, contract, make sure, reassure, security, vouch for, warranty **9** agreement, answer for, assurance, certainty, get behind, grubstake, insurance, stipulate, sure thing, testament, undertake **10** collateral, commitment, stand up for, underwrite
the outcome: **3** peg, rig **5** frame, set up **6** buy off, cement, doctor **8** nail down **9** formalize, plan ahead, preordain **10** manipulate, prearrange, tamper with
with no ~: **4** as is
guaranteed: **4** sure **5** on ice **7** certain, for sure **8** definite, in the bag, positive, sure-fire **9** certified, confirmed, protected, warranted **10** conclusive, sure enough
guarantor: **6** backer, patron **7** sponsor **10** grubstaker
guaranty: **4** egis, pawn **6** pledge **7** warrant **8** warranty
guard: **4** egis, mind, save, tend **5** aegis, armor, cover, watch **6** attend, buffer, convoy, defend, embank, ensure, escort, gaoler, keeper, patrol, picket, police, screen, secure, sentry, shield, warden **7** athlete, baby-sit, bouncer, bulwark, defense, lookout, observe, protect, rampart, shelter, soldier, support, ward off, watcher **8** chaperon, defender, preserve, security, sentinel, shepherd, treasure, watchman **9** accompany, chaperone, look after, protector, safeguard, supervise **10** doorkeeper, gatekeeper, protection

against: 5 avoid 6 beware 8 watch out
against (prefix): 3 par- 4 para-
be on ~: 4 mind 5 watch 6 patrol 7 look out
cry: 4 halt, stop 6 freeze
drop one's ~: 3 nap
ender: 3 ant 4 rail, room 5 house
keep ~: 5 watch 6 defend, picket, police 7 protect
off ~: 4 rash 6 unwary 7 unalert 8 careless, heedless, reckless, unawares 9 negligent, unmindful 10 incautious, not careful, unthinking, unvigilant, unwatchful
old ~: 7 veteran 8 warhorse
on ~: 4 wary 5 alert, awake, leery 7 heads-up, heedful, wakeful 8 keen-eyed, prepared, vigilant, watchful
post: 4 gate
put on ~: 4 warn 5 alarm, alert, awake, scare 6 arouse, clue in, inform, notify, tip off 7 apprise, caution, forearm, prepare 8 acquaint, forewarn
route: 6 rounds
starter: 3 mud, van 4 body, fire, life, safe 5 black 6 splash
throw off ~: 4 stun 5 shake 7 astound, nonplus, stagger 8 astonish, bowl over, surprise 9 discomfit, dumbfound, take aback 10 disconcert

guard __: 3 dog, pin 4 band, cell, duty, hair, post, ring
__ guard: 3 off, old 4 nose, rear, shin, snow 5 color, honor, point, stand 6 bumper, palace, splash
__ Guard: 3 Old, Red 5 Coast, Right, Swiss
__-guard cutter: 5 coast
guarded: 4 cagy, safe, wary 5 cagey, canny, chary, leery 6 unsure 7 careful, dubious, prudent 8 cautious, discreet, doubtful, doubting, hesitant, vigilant, watchful 9 skeptical, uncertain 10 suspicious
guardedness: 10 weather eye
guardhouse: 4 brig, jail 6 lockup, prison
guardian: 5 angel 6 escort, keeper, parent, savior, sitter 7 curator, paladin, saviour, sponsor 8 Cerberus, chaperon, defender, executor, overseer, sentinel, shepherd, tutelary, watchdog 9 attendant, chaperone, custodian, preserver, protector 10 baby sitter, doorkeeper, supervisor
charge: 4 ward 5 child, minor 6 orphan 7 adoptee, protege
spirit: 3 Lar 5 angel 6 daemon, genius
spirits: 5 Lares
guardian __: 5 angel
Guardian Angel
cap: 5 beret
founder: Curtis Sliwa
guardianship: 4 care, egis, ward 5 aegis, trust, watch 7 custody, keeping 9 oversight 10 protection
Guarding Tess (1994 film)
cast: Nicolas Cage, Shirley MacLaine

Guardino: 5 Harry
Guard of Honor
author: James Gould Cozzens
Guare, John: 6 writer
work: The House of Blue Leaves
Lydie Breeze
Marco Polo Sings a Solo
Rich and Famous
Six Degrees of Separation
Guarneri
kin: 5 Amati, Strad
Guatemala: 6 nation 7 country
ancient city of ~: 5 Tikal
capital: 9 Guatemala
city: 5 Cobán, Mixco, Zunil 6 Flores, Jalapa, Salamá, Sololá, Zacapa 7 Cuilapa
garment: 6 huipil
Indian: 3 Mam 4 Maya
lake: 6 Izabal, Yzabal 7 Atitlán
money: 6 quezal 7 quetzal
native language: 5 Mayan
neighbor: 3 Mex. 6 Belize, Mexico 8 Honduras 10 El Salvador
Nobelist in Literature: 8 Asturias
Nobelist in Peace: 3 Tum
org.: 3 OAS
river: 5 Hondo
volcano: 5 Fuego, Tacan 6 Pacaya
writer: 8 Asturias
see also Spanish
guava: 4 tree 5 fruit, shrub
relative: 6 myrtle 7 cajeput 10 eucalyptus
Guayaquil: 4 city, gulf, port, town
locale: 7 Ecuador
Guber: 5 Peter
Gucci: 4 Aldo
guck: 4 dirt 5 slime 6 sludge
gudgeon: 4 fish 6 socket
Gudrun
brother: 6 Gunnar
husband: 4 Atli
Guelph: 4 city, town
locale: 6 Canada 7 Ontario
guerdon: 5 prize 6 reward, trophy 10 remunerate
Guernica: 5 mural
artist: Pablo Picasso
guernsey: 5 shirt
Guernsey: 3 cow 4 bull, isle 6 bovine, cattle, island
exclamation: 3 moo
neighbor: 4 Sark
Guernsey __: 4 lily
guerra opposite: 3 paz
guerre, nom de: 4 name 5 alias 6 anonym 8 cognomen 9 pseudonym
Guerrero: 5 Pedro, state 7 Mexican
city: 5 Taxco 8 Acapulco
guerrilla: 3 huk 6 Contra, klepht 7 soldier 8 partisan 9 warmonger
1970's ~ grp.: 3 SLA
guerrilla __: 7 warfare
guess: 3 est., say 4 call, shot, stab 5 dance, hunch, infer, judge, opine, think 6 assess, assume, belief, deduce, divine, notion, reckon, theory 7 daresay, feeling, imagine, opinion, predict, presume, suppose, surmise, suspect, thought, venture 8 estimate, judgment, theorize 9 reckoning, speculate, suspicion, take a shot 10 assumption, conjecture, hypothesis, prediction, projection
ender: 4 work
word: 5 about
words: 4 or so
__-guess: 6 second
Guess __!: 5 again
Guess __?: 3 who 4 what
Guess?
competitor: 6 Gitano
__ Guess: 3 Eye
Guess Who
song: American Woman (1970)
Clap for the Wolfman (1974)
Laughing (1969)
No Time (1970)
Share the Land (1970)
These Eyes (1969)
Guess Who (2005 film)
cast: Ashton Kutcher, Bernie Mac, Zoe Saldana
Guess Who's Coming to Dinner (1967 film)
cast: Katharine Hepburn, Sidney Poitier, Spencer Tracy
director: Stanley Kramer
guesswork: 7 surmise 9 suspicion 10 conjecture
guest: 6 caller, client, lodger, renter, roomer, tenant 7 boarder, company, invitee, visitor 8 customer 9 partygoer, sojourner, transient 10 vacationer
be a ~ at: 5 visit 6 attend
ender: 5 house
paying ~: 5 liver 6 lodger, patron
room: 3 den
starter: 5 house
take in a ~: 5 greet 6 invite 7 receive, welcome
unwanted ~: 3 ant, bug, fly, nag 4 bore, drag, drip, flea, gnat, pain, pest, pill 5 creep, mouse 6 drop-in, insect 7 termite 8 headache, housefly, mosquito, nuisance 9 cockroach
__ guest: 4 be my
Guest: 2 C.Z. 3 Val 5 Edgar 6 Judith 8 Cornelia
Guest, Christopher
spouse: Jamie Lee Curtis
guesthouse: 3 inn 5 lodge 6 hostel 7 auberge
guest of __: 5 honor
Guest of Reality
author: Pär Lagerkvist
guests: 7 callers, company 8 assembly, visitors
desirable ~: 5 A-list
have ~: 4 fete, host 5 eat in, put up 6 regale 9 entertain, make merry, socialize
where honored ~ sit: 4 dais 6 podium 7 rostrum 8 platform
Guevara: 3 Che 7 Ernesto
guff: 3 lip 4 sass 5 mouth, sauce 8 back talk 9 impudence, insolence 10 effrontery
see also baloney
guffaw: 4 ha-ha, hoot, howl, laff, roar 5 laugh 6 cackle, giggle, haw-haw, heehaw, titter 7 break up, chortle, chuckle, crack up, snicker, snigger 8 laughter 10 belly laugh, horse laugh
e-mail ~: 3 LOL
Guggenheim: 5 Peggy
Gugino: 5 Carla

Guglielmo: 7 Marconi
in English: 7 William
__ Guiana: 5 Dutch 6 French 7 British
Guiana explorer: 7 Raleigh
Guiana Indian: 6 Arawak
guidance: 3 aid 4 hand, help 6 advice 7 conduct, control, warning 8 training, tutelage 9 direction, education, influence 10 assistance, counseling, leadership, management, regulation
lacking ~: 5 unled
guide: 3 aid 4 face, guru, head, helm, help, lead, menu, show, take, warn 5 bible, bring, edify, gauge, index, pilot, point, refer, route, scout, shape, steer, swing, teach, train, tutor, usher 6 advise, attend, beacon, convoy, direct, docent, escort, handle, jockey, leader, lead in, lead to, manage, manual, mentor, pundit, school, Sherpa 7 adviser, advisor, channel, conduct, control, counsel, go first, monitor, pattern, pioneer, support, teacher, usher in 8 chaperon, cicerone, handbook, instruct, landmark, lodestar, navigate, paradigm, regulate, shepherd, workbook 9 abecedary, accompany, attendant, chaperone, companion, conductor, counselor, directory, enlighten, indicator, influence, vade mecum 10 instructor, lead the way, pathfinder, show the way, trailblaze
ender: 4 book, line, post, word
group: 4 tour
naval ~: 10 lighthouse, watchtower
to a chair: 4 seat 5 usher
tour ~: 3 map 6 docent
guide __: 3 dog 4 rail, rope, word
__ guide: 4 girl 5 field
guidebook: 5 bible 6 manual 8 Baedeker 9 itinerary, vade mecum
guided __: 4 tour 7 missile
guided by, be: 4 heed 6 follow
guideline: 4 rule 5 bylaw, gauge 6 policy 7 precept 8 standard 9 direction, parameter 10 ground rule
guidepost: 4 sign 5 pylon
guiding: 5 polar 9 sovereign
light: 4 guru 6 beacon 8 cynosure, lodestar, polestar 10 apotheosis
principle: 3 saw 5 adage, axiom, credo, maxim, moral, motto, tenet 6 belief, byword, dictum, saying, slogan, war cry 7 epigram, precept, proverb 8 aphorism 9 battle cry, platitude, watchword
Guiding Light, The (CBS): 4 soap 9 soap opera
character: 4 Nola
Guido: 4 Reni 7 Gezelle 10 Cavalcanti
high note: 3 e la
in English: 3 Guy
see also Italian
Guido __: 7 d'Arezzo
guidon: 4 flag
Guidry, Ron: 6 hurler 7 pitcher
guild: 4 club 5 order, union 6 league 7 society 8 congress 10 federation, fellowship, trade union

ender: 4 hall
medieval ~: 5 hansa, hanse
Guildenstern
friend: 6 Hamlet
guilder: 4 coin 5 money 6 florin
guile: 3 art, lie 4 jive, ruse 5 craft, fraud, wiles 6 acumen, deceit, dupery 7 cunning, finesse, knavery, slyness 8 artifice, trickery, wiliness 9 chicanery, deception, dirty pool, duplicity, smartness, treachery 10 artfulness, cleverness, craftiness, dishonesty, trickiness
guileful: 3 sly 4 cagy, foxy, wily 5 cagey, canny, false, lying, slick, snaky 6 artful, crafty, shifty, shrewd, sneaky, subtle, tricky 7 crooked, cunning, devious, furtive, vulpine 8 delusive, slippery 9 deceitful, deceptive, dishonest, insidious, insincere, underhand 10 mendacious, untruthful
guileless: 4 naif, open, pure 5 frank, naive 6 callow, candid, honest, infelt, simple 7 artless, genuine, natural, sincere 8 innocent, lamblike, out-front, truthful, unartful 9 childlike, ingenuous, unguarded, unstudied 10 aboveboard, unaffected
one: 4 lamb, naif
guilelessness: 6 candor 7 naiveté 8 openness 9 credulity, innocence 10 simplicity
Guillaume: 6 Robert 7 Charles
in English: 7 William
see also French
Guillaume, Charles: 8 Nobelist 9 physicist
Guillaume, Robert: 5 actor
film: Lean on Me (1989)
TV: Benson, Soap
guillemot: 4 bird 5 murre
kin: 3 auk
Guillén, Jorge: 4 poet 7 Spanish
Guillén, Nicolás: 4 poet 5 Cuban
Guillermin: 4 John
Guillermo: 5 Vilas
in English: 7 William
guilt: 3 sin 4 onus 5 blame, fault, lapse, shame, wrong 6 infamy 7 failing, misstep, offense, remorse 8 disgrace, dishonor, iniquity 9 liability 10 misconduct, repentance
admission of ~: 6 I did it 8 mea culpa
admit ~: 9 apologize, beg pardon 10 make amends
guilt __: 4 trip
guiltiness: 9 collusion 10 complicity, connivance, conspiracy
guiltless: 4 good, pure 5 clean, clear 7 sinless 8 innocent, spotless, unsoiled, virtuous 9 blameless, crimeless, exemplary, faultless, righteous, unsullied, untainted 10 exculpated, immaculate, impeccable, inculpable, in the clear
guilty: 4 evil 5 wrong 6 liable, sinful, unholy, wicked 7 at fault, verdict 8 blamable, criminal, culpable 9 blameable, convicted, felonious, red-handed 10 delinquent, iniquitous, in the wrong
feel ~: 3 rue 6 regret, repent
feeling ~: 5 sorry 6 rueful 7 ashamed 8 contrite, penitent 9 chastened, regretful, repentant 10 apologetic, remorseful
find ~: 3 hit, rap 4 damn, defy, hiss 5 blame, chide, decry, knock, sneer 6 outlaw, punish, rail at 7 censure, condemn, convict, deplore, dislike, reprove, upbraid 8 denounce, penalize, reproach, sentence 9 castigate, criticize, deprecate, excoriate, fulminate, imprecate, proscribe, reprehend 10 come down on, vituperate
not ~: 7 sinless 8 innocent 9 acquitted, blameless, faultless, untainted 10 inculcable, inculpable, in the clear
one: 4 perp 5 crook, felon 7 culprit 8 criminal
guilty __: 5 as sin
__ guilty: 5 plead
Guilty (1980 song)
artist: Barry Gibb, Barbra Streisand
Guilty by Suspicion (1991 film)
cast: Annette Bening, Robert De Niro, George Wendt, Patricia Wettig
Guilty Pleasures
author: Lawrence Sanders
Guinan: 5 Texas
guinea: 4 coin 5 money
guinea __: 3 hen, pig 4 fowl
Guinea: 4 gulf 6 nation 7 country
bovine: 5 N'dama
capital: 7 Conakry
city: 6 Kankan 7 Conakry, Konakri
coin: 4 syli
Gulf of ~ port: 5 Lagos
Gulf of ~ republic: 5 Ghana
neighbor: 4 Mali 7 Liberia, Senegal 10 Ivory Coast
people: 6 Kpelle 7 Malinka, Malinke 8 Mandingo, Mandinka
river to the Gulf of ~: 5 Niger
__ Guinea: 3 New
Guinea-Bissau: 6 nation 7 country
capital: 6 Bissau
money: 4 peso
neighbor: 7 Senegal
guinea fowl, young: 4 keat, keet
guinea pig: 3 pet 4 cavy 6 animal, mammal, rodent 7 subject
female: 3 doe, sow
home: 3 lab 4 cage
male: 4 buck
relative: *see* rodent
young: 3 pup
Guinevere lover: 8 Lancelot 9 Launcelot
Guinier: 4 Lani
Guinness: 4 Alec 5 drink 7 brewery 8 beverage
brew: 3 ale 5 stout
Guinness, Alec: 3 Sir 5 actor
film: All at Sea (1958)
The Bridge on the River Kwai (1957, AA)
Captain's Paradise (1953)
Damn the Defiant! (1962)
Doctor Zhivago (1965)
The Fall of the Roman Empire (1964)
Father Brown (1954)
The Horse's Mouth (1958)
Kind Hearts and Coronets (1949)
The Ladykillers (1955)
The Lavender Hill Mob (1951)
Lawrence of Arabia (1962)
The Man in the White Suit (1951)
The Mudlark (1950)
Murder by Death (1976)
Oliver Twist (1948)
The Prisoner (1955)
The Promoter (1952)
The Quiller Memorandum (1966)
Scrooge (1970)
Star Wars (1977)
The Swan (1956)
Tunes of Glory (1960)
Guinness Book
entry: 4 feat
suffix: 3 est
superlative: 4 most
guipure: 4 lace
guise: 4 look, mask, mien, pose, role, show, veil 5 cloak, cover, front, shape 6 aspect, attire, facade, outfit, veneer 7 costume, posture, pretext 8 demeanor, likeness, pretense 9 semblance 10 appearance, camouflage, complexion, false front, masquerade
starter: 3 dis
Guisewite: 5 Cathy
guitar: 5 Dobro, Strat 6 cither, cuatro, ramkie, string 7 cittern, gittern
adjunct: 3 amp 4 capo, pick
ancestor: 4 lute
cousin: 3 uke 5 banjo
diagram: 5 chord
effect: 4 wawa 6 wah wah
ender: 3 ist 4 fish
like a loud ~: 5 amped
part: 4 fret, neck 5 waist
play a ~: 5 pluck, strum, thrum
sound: 5 twang
__ guitar: 5 steel
Guitar: 6 Bonnie
guitarist: 4 Byrd, King, Paul 5 Charo, Flatt 6 Atkins, B.B. King 7 Clapton, Diddley, Hendrix, Les Paul, Segovia 8 Ritenour 9 Bo Diddley 10 Chet Atkins, Montgomery
blues ~: 4 King 7 Diddley
jazz ~: 4 Byrd 10 Montgomery
Spanish ~: 5 Charo 7 Segovia
Guitarist, The
artist: Édouard Manet
Guiteau: 7 Charles
Guitry, Sacha: 6 French, writer 10 playwright
Gujarat garment: 4 sari 5 saree
gulag: 6 prison 7 Russian
Gulag Archipelago, The
author: Aleksandr Solzhenitsyn
Gulager: 3 Clu
gulch: 3 gap 4 rift, wadi, wady 5 cañon, gorge, gully 6 arroyo, canyon, coulee, gulley, ravine, trench 7 channel
__-gulch: 3 dry
Guldahl, Ralph: 6 golfer
gulden: 5 Dutch, money 6 florin
Gulden's: 7 mustard
alternative: 7 French's 10 Grey Poupon
gulf: 3 bay, gap, pit 4 cove, hole, rift, void 5 abyss, bayou, bight, cañon, chasm, cleft, depth, fiord, firth, fjord, frith, gorge, gully, inlet, sound, split 6 breach, canyon, gulley, hiatus, lacuna, lagoon, ravine 7 vacuity 8 crevasse 10 profundity
Adriatic: 6 Venice 7 Trieste 8 Quarnero
Aegean: 5 Izmir, Saros 6 Africa, Guinea 7 Argolis, Saronic 8 Salonika
Argentina: 8 San Jorge 9 San Matias
Atlantic: 6 Guinea, Mexico 8 San Jorge 9 San Matias
Baltic: 4 Riga 6 Danzig 7 Bothnia, Finland
Canada: 7 Boothia 10 St. Lawrence
Caribbean: 6 Darien, Gonâve 7 San Blas 8 Gonaïves, Honduras
Central America: 6 Panama 7 Fonseca 8 Honduras
Chile: 5 Penas
China: 5 Bohai, Pohai 8 Liaodong, Liaotung
Costa Rica: 8 Papagayo
Ecuador: 9 Guayaquil
English Channel: 6 St. Malo
France: 5 Lions 6 St. Malo
Greece: 6 Aegina, Patras 7 Laconia, Saronic 8 Messinia, Salonika
Haiti: 6 Gonâve 8 Gonaïves
Indian Ocean: 6 Mannar
Ionian: 4 Arta 6 Patras 7 Corinth, Laconia, Lepanto, Taranto 8 Messinia
Italy: 5 Genoa 6 Venice 7 Taranto, Trieste
Ivory Coast: 6 Guinea
Mediterranean: 5 Gabès, Lions, Sidra
Mexico: 8 Campeche
Mideast: 4 Aden, Oman, Suez 5 Akaba, Aqaba, Sidra 7 Arabian, Persian
Myanmar: 8 Martaban
New Guinea ~: 5 Papua
Pacific: 5 Davao, Papua, Penas 6 Alaska 7 Fonseca 8 Papagayo 9 Guayaquil 10 California
Panama: 7 San Blas
Philippines: 5 Davao, Panay
Poland: 6 Danzig
Red Sea: 4 Suez
Russia: 8 Taganrog
Scandinavia: 7 Bothnia
Sea of Azov: 8 Taganrog
South America: 9 Guayaquil
South China Sea: 4 Siam 6 Tonkin 8 Thailand
Spain: 5 Cádiz
Tunisia: 5 Gabès
Turkey: 5 Izmir
Tyrrhenian Sea: 5 Gaeta
Venezuela: 5 Paria 9 Maracaibo
Yugoslavia: 8 Quarnero
Gulf: 3 gas 8 gasoline
rival: 5 Amoco, Exxon, Getty, Mobil 6 Sunoco 7 Chevron
Gulf __: 3 Oil, War 5 Coast 6 States, Stream

__ Gulf: 7 Arabian, Persian
Gulf Coast
city: 5 Tampa 6 St. Pete 8 Sarasota
Gulf of __: 4 Aden, Arta, Oman, Oran, Riga, Siam, Suez 5 Akaba, Aqaba, Cadiz, Lions, Papua, Saros, Sidra, Tunis 6 Alaska, Cambay, Guinea, Mexico, Panama 7 Argolis, Bothnia, Corinth, Finland, Fonseca, Lepanto
Gulf of Aden
country: 5 Yemen
vessel: 3 dau, dow 4 dhow
Gulf of Bothnia
river to the ~: 3 Dal, Ume 4 Oulu
Gulf of Cádiz, river to the: 8 Guadiana
Gulf of California
river to the ~: 5 Yaqui 8 Colorado
Gulf of Finland, river to the: 4 Neva
Gulf of Guinea
capital: 5 Accra, Akkra
island: 7 Sao Tomé
Gulf of Mexico
bay: 5 Tampa 6 Mobile 9 Galveston, Pensacola
city: 5 Tampa
river to the ~: 5 Pearl 6 Pánuco, Sabine 8 Suwannee 9 Rio Grande
Gulf of Tonkin, river to the: 3 Red
Gulf of Trieste, river to the: 6 Isonzo
Gulfport: 4 city, port, town
locale: 4 Miss.
neighbor: 6 Biloxi
Gulf Stream, The
painter: Winslow Homer
Gulf War
ally: 5 Saudi, Syria
city: 5 Basra, Busra 6 Busrah
figure: 4 amir, emir 5 ameer, emeer
foe: 4 Irak, Iraq
missile: 4 Scud
participant: 4 Arab
gull: 3 con, gyp, mew, mug, sap 4 bilk, bird, dupe, fool, hoax, mark, prey, rook, take 5 cheat, chump, cozen, hocus, mulct, patsy, sting, trick 6 fleece, fulmar, outwit, pigeon, rope in, sea mew, sucker, take in, target, victim 7 deceive, defraud, exploit, jackass, mislead, seabird, swindle 8 flimflam, hoodwink, outsmart 9 bamboozle, four-flush, kittiwake, scapegoat, schlemiel, shorebird, victimize
ender: 4 wing
genus: 5 larus
like a ~: 6 larine
perch: 4 buoy
relative: 4 skua, tern
gullet: 3 cut, maw 4 craw, crop 5 ditch 6 ravine, throat, trench 7 channel, gizzard, pharynx 9 esophagus 10 oesophagus
gullibility: 7 naiveté 9 credulity, greenness
gullible: 4 easy, naif 5 green, naive 6 simple, stupid 8 innocent, trusting 9 credulous
not ~: 3 sly 4 foxy, wary, wily, wise 5 acute, cagey, canny, quick, slick, smart 6 astute, clever, crafty, shrewd 7 careful, cunning, guarded, knowing, prudent 8 cautious, watchful
person: 3 sap 4 butt, dupe, fool, mark, tool 5 chump, patsy, yokel 6 pigeon, sucker 8 pushover
Gullible's Travels
author: Ring Lardner
Gulliver's Travels: 5 novel 6 satire
author: Jonathan Swift
character: 5 Yahoo
land: 6 Laputa
Gullstrand, Allvar: 8 Nobelist
gully: 3 gap 4 gulf, rift, wadi, wady 5 cañon, chasm, ditch, gulch 6 arroyo, canyon, ravine, trench, trough 7 channel, culvert 8 crevasse
form a ~: 4 flow, gush, wash 5 erode
in Britain: 4 sike, syke
__ gully: 5 hully
gullywasher: 4 rain 5 flood, spate, storm 6 deluge, precip 7 monsoon, torrent 8 downpour, drencher 9 rainstorm 10 cloudburst
gulp: 3 eat 4 bolt, chug, pant, puff, swig, wolf 5 choke, drink, gorge, quaff, scarf, swill 6 breath, devour, englut, gobble, guzzle, imbibe, inhale 7 breathe, consume, draught, scarf up, swallow 8 chug-a-lug, mouthful, wolf down 9 knock back, scarf down 10 inhalation
big ~: 4 belt, swig 7 swallow
down: 4 bolt, chug 6 ingest 7 engorge
empty in one ~: 5 swill 6 guzzle
__ Gulp: 3 Big
gulping: 6 winded 7 anxious, gasping, panting 9 exhausted 10 breathless
gum: 4 bond, glue, seal, tree 5 paste, resin 6 cement, clog up 7 Bazooka, gingiva 8 adhesive, fixative, mucilage
arabic: 6 acacia
arabic tree: 5 babul
art ~: 6 eraser
by ~: 4 oath
ender: 4 ball, drop, shoe, wood
like some ~: 5 minty
non-elastic ~: 6 balata
resin: 4 kino 5 myrrh 6 copalm
source: 4 guar 6 chicle
starter: 6 bubble
tree denizen: 3 bee 5 drone
up: 3 jam 4 muff 5 botch, snarl, spoil 6 bungle 9 mishandle, mismanage
up the works: 3 err 4 flub, mess, slip 5 botch, fluff 6 boggle, bumble, bungle, fumble, mess up, slip up 7 blunder, stumble 9 mishandle, mismanage
use ~: 4 chew 5 erase 9 masticate
gum __: 6 acacia, arabic, eraser
gum __ works: 5 up the
__ gum: 4 guar 6 bubble, spirit 7 chewing
__-gum: 3 dad
Gumbel: 4 Greg 6 Bryant
gumbo: 4 soup, stew 6 bisque, patois
ingredient: 4 file, ocra, okra, okro 5 thyme
like ~: 5 Cajan, Cajun
gumboot: 4 shoe 8 footwear
Gumby
horse: 5 Pokey
material: 4 clay
gumdrops: 5 candy, sweet 10 confection
__-gummed: 3 dad
Gummo: 4 Marx
brother: 5 Chico, Harpo, Zeppo 7 Groucho
gummy: 4 icky 5 gluey, gooey, muddy, thick 6 clayey, sticky, viscid 7 clayish, jellied, viscose, viscous 8 adhesive 9 glutinous
Gump: 3 Min 4 Andy 7 Forrest, Worsley
dog: 4 Buck
Gumps, The
cat: 4 Hope
dog: 4 Buck
gumption: 4 grit, guts, push 5 drive, force, moxie, nerve, pluck, spine, spunk 6 energy, hustle, starch 7 bravery, courage 8 industry 9 ingenuity 10 enterprise, feistiness, get up and go, initiative, shrewdness
gums: 3 ula
be good to your ~: 5 brush, floss
combining form: 3 ulo- 6 gingiv- 7 gingivo-
flap one's ~: 3 gab, gas, jaw, rap, yak, yap 4 blab, chat, gush, talk 5 prate, run on, speak, spout 6 babble, gabble, gibber, jabber, natter, parley, yammer 7 blabber, blather, chatter, maunder, prattle, twaddle 8 converse, ramble on, spout off 9 go on and on 10 yakkety-yak
gumshoe: 2 PI 3 tec 4 dick, lurk 5 sneak, snoop 6 shamus 7 snooper 9 detective
quest: 4 clue 5 proof
gum up the __: 5 works
gun: 3 aim, cap, gat, man, men, pop, rev, rod, Uzi 4 ammo, bang, blow, boat, Bren, Colt, draw, fire, hand, kick, load, lock, play, room, shot, Sten, thug, wale 5 aim at, chase, fight, flash, flint, Luger, metal, piece, point, proof, rifle, round, salvo, shoot, sight, skeet, smith, spray, stock, taser, vroom 6 ack ack, barrel, Bertha, breech, cannon, cotton, muzzle, powder, pursue, report, runner, search, weapon 7 barrage, fighter, notable, slinger 8 air rifle 9 Big Bertha, dignitary, equalizer, flintlock, forty-five 10 accelerate, six-shooter
jumping the ~: 7 too soon 8 too early 9 overhasty 10 half-cocked
gun __: 3 dog, for 4 crew, deck, moll, room 7 control
gun-__: 3 shy 6 toting
__ gun: 3 air, big, cap, ray, top, zip 4 Bren, burp, glue, stun 5 hired, spear, spray, Tommy, water 6 grease, squirt, staple 7 Gatling, machine, smoking
__-gun: 3 six
__ Gun: 3 Top
gunboat: 7 frigate, warship 8 man-of-war 10 battleship
Gunfight at the O.K. Corral (1957 film): 5 oater 7 western
cast: Kirk Douglas, Rhonda Fleming, Burt Lancaster, Jo Van Fleet
gunfighter dare: 4 draw
__ Gun for Hire: 4 This
Gunga Din: 4 film, poem
author: Rudyard Kipling
cast: Douglas Fairbanks Jr., Joan Fontaine, Cary Grant
director: George Stevens
setting: 5 India
studio: 3 RKO
gung-ho: 4 avid, into, keen, warm 5 can-do, eager 6 ardent, rah-rah, red-hot 7 anxious, excited, fired up, keyed up, zealous 8 enthused, spirited 9 fanatical, hot to trot 10 inspirited, passionate
quality: 3 pep, zip 4 élan, fire, push, zeal, zest 5 drive, gusto, oomph, punch, verve 6 energy, fervor, relish, spirit 7 passion 8 alacrity, dispatch, interest, keenness 9 animation, assiduity, diligence, eagerness, intensity, readiness 10 ebullience, enterprise, enthusiasm, exuberance, heartiness, initiative
Gung Ho (1986 film)
cast: Michael Keaton, George Wendt
director: Ron Howard
gunk: 3 goo 4 blob, crud, dirt, glop, goop, muck, ooze 5 grime, slime 8 sediment
gunky: 4 icky, oozy 5 muddy, thick 6 sticky
gunman: 6 sniper 7 shooter 9 desperado
gunmetal: 4 gray, grey 5 alloy, color
component: 3 tin 4 zinc 6 copper
relative: *see* gray color
Gunn: 3 Ben 4 Thom 5 Moses, Peter
Gunnar: 6 Ekelöf, Myrdal, Nelson
gunnel: 4 fish 6 blenny 7 railing
gunner: 7 soldier
need: 4 ammo
gunning for: 5 after
Gunn, Peter: 3 tec 6 sleuth 7 gumshoe 9 detective 10 private eye
girlfriend: 4 Edie
Gunn, Thom: 4 poet 7 British
gunny-__: 3 bag
gunny ender: 4 sack
gunnysack: 3 bag 4 poke
material: 4 jute 6 burlap
gunpowder: 3 tea 9 explosive 10 ammunition
chemical: 5 niter
holder: 3 keg
igniter: 5 spark
Gunpowder __: 4 Plot
guns: 4 arms 7 battery 8 materiel, weaponry 9 artillery, firepower, munitions
alternative: 6 butter
get new ~: 5 rearm
give ~ to: 3 arm 7 fortify
go great ~: 5 excel 8 flourish
sticking to one's ~: 3 set 4 firm 5 dug in 6 dogged, steely, strong 7 adamant, decided, do-or-die 8 hard-line, locked in, resolute, stubborn 9 iron-jawed, steadfast, tenacious 10 unswayable, unyielding

stick to one's ~: **6** insist **7** persist **9** persevere
— guns: **5** great
— Guns: **5** Young
gunsel: **4** goon, thug **5** tough **7** hoodlum, mobster **8** criminal, gangster, hooligan **9** racketeer
gal: **4** moll
gig: **5** heist
gun-shy: **5** balky, chary, timid **6** afraid, scared **7** chicken, dubious, fearful, nervous **8** hesitant **9** reluctant **10** frightened
Gun Shy (2000 film)
cast: Sandra Bullock, Liam Neeson, Oliver Platt
gunslinger: **6** outlaw **9** desperado
command: **4** draw **5** reach
unit: **5** notch
Gunslinger, The
author: Stephen King
Gunsmoke (CBS western)
bartender: **3** Sam
cast: James Arness (Matt Dillon)
Amanda Blake (Kitty Russell)
Ken Curtis (Festus Haggen)
Burt Reynolds (Quint Asper)
Milburn Stone (Doc Adams)
Dennis Weaver (Chester Goode)
deputy: **5** Newly
setting: Dodge City, Kansas
Guns N' Roses
leader: Axl Rose
song: Don't Cry (1991)
November Rain (1992)
Paradise City (1989)
Patience (1989)
Sweet Child o' Mine (1988)
Welcome to the Jungle (1988)
Guns of August, The: **4** book, film
author: Barbara Tuchman
director: Nathan Kroll
Guns of Navarone, The
author: Alistair MacLean
Guns of Navarone, The (1961 film)
cast: David Niven, Gregory Peck, Anthony Quinn
composer: Dimitri Tiomkin
gunter: **4** sail
Günter: **5** Grass **6** Blobel
see also German
— Gun, The: **5** Naked
Gunther —-Williams: **5** Gebel
Gunther, John: **6** writer
work: Death Be Not Proud
Inside Africa
Inside Asia
Inside Australia
Inside Europe Today
Inside Russia Today
Inside South America
Inside U.S.A.
Gunton: **3** Bob
gunwale: **7** railing
pin: **5** thole
— Gun Will Travel: **4** Have
Guofeng: **3** Hua
guppy: **3** pet **4** fish
—-gurdy: **5** hurdy
Gurganus, Allan: **6** writer
work: Oldest Living Confederate Widow Tells All
gurgle: **3** coo, lap **4** foam, purl **5** froth **6** babble, bubble, murmur, ripple, splash
Gurkha land: **5** Nepal
— Gurley Brown: **5** Helen
gurney: **3** cot **4** cart **9** stretcher
guru: **4** lama, sage, seer, tech **5** guide, Hindu, maven, mavin, rishi, swami, swamy, tutor **6** cleric, expert, Hindoo, leader, master, mentor, pundit, techie, tekkie **7** teacher **9** abecedary, authority, preceptor **10** specialist, technician
discipline: **4** yoga
home: **6** ashram, asrama
student: **5** chela
title: **4** yogi **5** yogin
Gus: **4** Kahn **5** Meins **7** Grissom, Van Sant
gloomy ~: **4** mope **5** moper **9** pessimist, worrywart
gush: **3** jet, run, yak **4** emit, flow, go on, pour, rave, rush, spew, spue, wash **5** burst, drool, emote, erupt, flood, issue, prate, river, spate, spirt, spout, spurt, surge, swell **6** babble, deluge, effuse, jabber, rattle, spring, stream **7** blabber, blather, blether, cascade, chatter, emanate, enthuse, pour out, prattle, run over, torrent **8** outbreak, outburst, overflow, well over **9** discharge, emanation, pour forth, send forth, spillover, upwelling **10** bubble over, outpouring
over: **6** praise **7** adulate, flatter, lionize
gusher: **6** geyser **7** oil well
go for a ~: **5** drill **7** wildcat
gushing: **4** oily **5** wordy **6** hearty **7** mawkish, unterse, verbose **8** effusive **9** ebullient, emanation, expansive, exuberant, garrulous **10** pleonastic, unreserved
gushy: **7** maudlin, mawkish **8** effusive **9** expansive
writing: **4** slop
gusset: **4** gore **5** plait, pleat **6** insert
gussied up: **4** chic **5** natty **6** chichi, dapper, flossy, spiffy **7** adorned, duded up
gussy up: **4** deck, doll **5** adorn, preen, primp, prink **7** furbish, garnish **8** decorate, emblazon **9** embellish, embroider, refurbish
gust: **4** blow, gale, puff, rush, waft, wind **5** blast, burst, draft, storm, whiff **6** breeze, flurry, squall **7** cyclone, flare-up, outrush **8** eruption, outburst
Gustafsson, Lars: **4** poet **7** Swedish
Gustav: **5** Hertz, Holst **6** Mahler **7** Freytag **9** Kirchhoff **10** Stresemann
Gustave: **4** Doré **5** Klimt **6** Eiffel **7** Courbet **8** Flaubert
— Gustav Jung: **4** Carl
Gustavus —: **8** Adolphus
gusto: **3** pep, vim, zip **4** brio, élan, fire, zeal, zest, zing **5** ardor, savor, spice, taste, verve **6** fervor, relish, spirit **7** delight, passion **8** appetite, fervency, pleasure **9** eagerness, enjoyment **10** enthusiasm, exuberance
with ~: **7** eagerly, readily
gusty: **5** windy **6** breezy, stormy
gut: **3** tum **4** sack **5** belly, clean, empty, inner, rifle, strip, tummy **6** innate, inside, paunch, ravage **7** abdomen, destroy, pillage, plunder, ransack, stomach **8** clean out, decimate, potbelly, visceral **9** depredate, emotional, intuitive **10** deep-seated, midsection
ender: **6** bucket
feeling: **5** hunch **8** bad vibes, instinct **9** suspicion
section: **5** ileum
starter: **3** cat, rot **4** hind
— gut!: **4** Sehr
gut-busting: **4** rich **5** funny **7** comical, riotous **8** humorous **9** hilarious, priceless **10** hysterical, uproarious
Gutenberg: **8** Johannes
partner: **4** Fust
Gutenberg —: **5** Bible
Gutenberg Galaxy, The
author: Marshall McLuhan
Guthrie: **2** A.B. **4** Arlo, city, town **5** Janet, Woody **6** Tyrone **7** Carlene
locale: **8** Oklahoma
Guthrie, A.B.: **6** writer
genre: western
work: The Way West
Guthrie, Arlo
father: Woody
song: Alice's Restaurant (1967)
The City of New Orleans (1972)
gutless: **6** craven, yellow **7** wimpish **8** cowardly **9** spineless
guts: **4** grit **5** heart, moxie, nerve, pluck, spice, spine, spunk, valor **6** daring, mettle, spirit, starch **7** bravery, courage, innards, insides, prowess, stamina, viscera **8** audacity, backbone, boldness, gumption, strength, tenacity, true grit, vitality **9** endurance, fortitude, substance **10** durability, feistiness, moral fiber, resolution
gutsy: **4** bold, game **5** brave, nervy **6** awless, brazen, daring, gritty, heroic, plucky, spunky, strong **7** assured, aweless, defiant, doughty, gallant, impavid, staunch, valiant **8** fearless, heroical, intrepid, resolute, spirited, stalwart, unafraid, valorous **9** audacious, dauntless, dreadless, undaunted, unfearful **10** courageous, iron-willed, mettlesome, undismayed
one: **4** hero
gutta percha: **3** gum
alternative: **6** balata
source: **5** latex **9** sapodilla
Guttenberg: **5** Steve
gutter: **4** duct **5** chute, ditch, drain, least **6** cullis, furrow, groove, sluice, trench, trough **7** channel, conduit, culvert **9** rainspout
ender: **5** snipe
site: **4** curb, eave
guttersnipe: **4** waif **5** gamin **6** beggar
guttural: **3** low **4** deep **5** gruff, harsh, husky, raspy, velar **6** hoarse **7** grating, rasping, throaty **8** gravelly
sound: **5** grunt
gut-wrenching
feeling: **4** fear **5** angst, dread **7** anxiety
Gutzkow, Karl: **6** German, writer **10** playwright
Gutzon: **7** Borglum
guy: **2** he **3** bud, cat, him, lad, man, sir **4** chap, dude, gent, josh, male, twit **5** bloke, buddy, cheat, fella, hubby, quack, shark, taunt, tease **6** bilker, con man, feller, fellow, mister, person **7** brother, grifter, hustler, scammer **8** swindler **9** defrauder, gentleman
bad ~: **4** ogre **6** meanie **7** villain
in Australia: **4** mate
in Britain: **4** mate
partner: **3** gal **4** doll
that ~: **3** him
tough ~: **4** hood **7** hoodlum
typical ~: **3** Joe **7** Joe Blow **9** Joe Doakes **10** Joe Six-Pack
see also man
guy —: **6** Friday
— guy: **4** fall, wise
Guy: **5** Buddy, Green **6** Fawkes, Kibbee **7** Jasmine, Lafleur, Laroche, Madison, Ritchie **8** Hamilton, Lombardo, Mitchell, Williams
in Italian: **5** Guido
Guyana: **6** nation **7** country
city: **10** Georgetown
Indian: **6** Arawak
money: **4** cent **6** dollar
native language: **6** Arawak
neighbor: **6** Brazil **8** Suriname **9** Venezuela
org.: **3** OAS
waterfall: **8** Kaieteur
writer: **6** Harris
Guy de —: **10** Maupassant
Guy Fawkes Day month: **3** Nov. **8** November
Guy Mannering
author: Walter Scott
guys: **3** hes
bad ~: **4** them **5** enemy
just for ~: **4** stag
Guys — Dolls: **3** and
— Guys: **4** Wise **5** Tough
Guys and Dolls: **4** play **7** musical
composer: Frank Loesser
locale: **4** Cuba **6** Havana **7** New York
role: **3** Sky **5** Sarah **6** Nathan **7** Detroit **8** Adelaide **9** Masterson
song: **5** Sue Me
Tony winner: **4** Alda
Guys and Dolls (1955 film)
cast: Vivian Blaine, Marlon Brando, Stubby Kaye, Jean Simmons, Frank Sinatra
source: Damon Runyon
— Guys Don't Dance: **5** Tough
guy's, that: **3** his
— Guy, The: **4** Fall, Tall **5** Cable, Other **6** Lonely
Guy Thing, A (2003 film)
cast: Selma Blair, Jason Lee, Julia Stiles
guzzle: **3** eat **4** bolt, chug, gulp, swig, tope, wolf **5** drink, gorge, quaff, scarf, slurp, swill **6** devour, englut, gobble, imbibe, inhale, tipple **7** consume, scarf up, swallow **8** chugalug, wolf down **9** hoist a few, knock back, scarf down
Guzzle, King land: **3** Moo
guzzler: **3** sot **4** lush **5** souse, toper **7** tippler
comment: **3** hic

gas ~: 3 car 4 heap 5 crate 6 jalopy 7 clunker 9 limousine 10 automobile
__ guzzler: 3 gas
Gwen: 6 McCrae, Verdon 7 Stefani
Gwendolyn: 6 Brooks 7 Bennett
Gwenn: 6 Edmund
Gwinnett: 6 Button
GWTW
see Gone With the Wind
GWU
locale: 4 Wash.
Gwyn: 4 Nell
Gwyneth: 7 Paltrow
former boyfriend: 4 Brad
mother: 6 Blythe
role: 4 Emma
Gwynne: 4 Fred
Gwynn, Tony
sport: 8 baseball
Gyllenhaal: 4 Jake 6 Maggie 7 Stephen
gym: 3 spa 5 arena 6 lyceum, phys. ed. 10 field house, health club, hippodrome
apparatus: 5 horse
black belt: 4 dojo
compartment: 6 locker
event: 3 hop 4 gala, prom 5 dance
exercise: 5 shrug, sit-up
gear: 3 wts. 7 weights 8 Nautilus
iteration: 3 rep
muscles: 3 abs 5 delts, quads 6 biceps 7 triceps
output: 5 sweat 6 effort
site: 4 YMCA, YMHA, YWCA, YWHA
surface: 3 mat
teacher deg.: 3 BPE
wear: 5 shoes 6 shorts, sneaks, sweats, T-shirt 7 leotard, tank top 8 sneakers
gym __: 4 shoe, suit 6 shorts
__ gym: 6 jungle
gymnasium
see gym
gymnast: 6 Korbut, Retton, turner 7 acrobat, athlete, tumbler, vaulter 8 Comaneci 9 aerialist 10 Olga Korbut
competition: 4 meet
concern: 4 form, tone 9 condition
device: 4 beam 5 horse
goal: 3 ten
like a ~: 4 spry 5 agile, lithe 9 lithesome
maneuver: 4 flip 5 nip-up, split, vault 6 aerial
need: 3 mat 5 rosin
gymnastics: 5 sport 7 workout 8 exercise, tumbling, vaulting 10 aerobatics
Gymnopédies
composer: Erik Satie
gynephobe fear: 5 women
Gynt, Peer
creator: Henrik Ibsen
mother: 3 Ase
gypsum: 7 mineral, plaster
to Mohs: 3 two
gypsy: 5 nomad, rover 7 migrant, nomadic, outcast 8 bohemian, traveler, vagabond, wanderer 9 journeyer, migratory
language: 6 Romani, Romany 7 Rommany
male ~: 3 rom
revenge: 5 curse
Spanish ~: 6 gitano
gypsy __: 3 cab 4 moth
Gypsy (1962 film): 7 musical
cast: Karl Malden, Rosalind Russell, Natalie Wood
director: Mervyn LeRoy
dog: 8 Chow Mein
Gypsy (musical)
composer: Stephen Sondheim, Jule Styne
Gypsy __: 7 Rose Lee
Gypsy __, The: 5 Baron, Moths
Gypsy Girl
artist: Frans Hals
Gypsy Man (1973 song)
artist: War
Gypsys, Tramps & Thieves (1971 song)
artist: Cher
Gypsy Woman (song)
artist: Brian Hyland, Crystal Waters
__ Gyra: 5 Spyro
gyrate: 4 jink, roll, spin, turn 5 dance, shake, twirl, wheel, whirl 6 circle, rotate 7 revolve, shudder 9 pirouette
gyration: 4 gyre, roll, spin 5 swirl, twirl, whirl 6 spiral 7 rolling 8 rotation, spinning, swirling, twirling, wheeling, whirling 9 pirouette, swiveling 10 revolution
gyre: 4 ring 5 wheel 6 circle, vortex
gyrene: 6 Marine 7 soldier
gyro: 5 Greek 8 sandwich
need: 4 lamb, pita, spit
gyroscope: 5 rotor 10 stabilizer
cousin: 3 top
imitate a ~: 4 spin 6 rotate
part: 4 axis
gyve: 5 chain 6 fetter 7 shackle, trammel

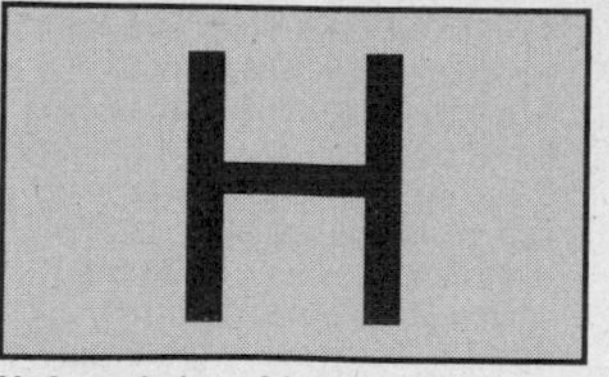

H: **3** eta **4** elem. **6** letter **7** vitamin **8** hydrogen
1 for ~: **4** at. no.
in phonetic alphabet: **5** Hotel
position: **6** eighth
H __ hat: **4** as in
H-__: **4** bomb, hour
H. __ Brown: **3** Rap
H. __ Haggard: **5** Rider
H. __ Perot: **4** Ross
'H' __ Homicide: **5** Is for
H2O: **5** water
__-ha: **3** hoo
Ha!: **3** oho **4** I bet
__ Haag: **3** Den
Häagen-Dazs: **8** ice cream
alternative: ***see*** ice cream
Haakon VI son: **4** Olaf, Olav
Haarlem: **4** city, town
locale: **7** Holland
Haas: **5** Lukas
Habakkuk: **4** book
follower: **9** Zephaniah
preceder: **5** Nahum
habanera: **5** dance
habeas corpus: **4** writ **5** trial
haberdasher: **6** tailor **8** clothier **9** outfitter
deparment: **4** men's
offering: **3** hat, tie **4** sock **5** scarf, shirt **6** bowtie, cravat **7** necktie
Haber, Fritz: **7** chemist **8** Nobelist
habile: **4** deft **5** adept **6** adroit, clever **7** skilled **8** masterly, skillful **9** dexterous, ingenious, inventive, masterful **10** proficient, well-versed
habiliment: **4** garb, gear **5** dress, getup, habit **6** attire, outfit, things **7** apparel, clothes **8** clothing **9** machinery, trappings, vestments **10** Sunday best
__ habilis: **4** homo
habit: **3** rut, way **4** bent, garb, gear, gown, rote, wont **5** dress, quirk, trait, usage **6** attire, custom, groove, livery, praxis **7** apparel, costume, routine, uniform **8** accouter, accoutre, penchant, practice, tendency, vestment **9** addiction, mannerism **10** canonicals, convention, habiliment, propensity
bad ~: **4** vice **6** foible
be in the ~ of: **4** tend
in the ~: **7** grooved **10** accustomed
in the ~ of: **6** likely, used to **8** disposed, inclined
kick the ~: **4** quit, stop **5** cease **6** desist, lay off **8** renounce
part: **4** veil
riding ~: **4** togs
wearer: **3** nun
habitable: **7** livable **8** liveable
habitant: **7** denizen, resider **8** indigene, resident
habitat: **3** pad **4** co-op, digs, flat, home, nest, site, turf **5** abode, condo, house, place, range, roost **6** domain, locale, medium **7** domicil, element, grounds, housing, lodging, shelter, terrain **8** domicile, dwelling, quarters **9** apartment, biosphere, residence, territory
establishment in a new ~: **6** ecesis
prefix: **3** eco-
habitation: **7** lodging, mansion **8** fireside, quarters **9** occupancy, residence
elevated ~: **4** aery, eyry **5** aerie, eyrie
habits: **4** ways **6** praxes **8** behavior **10** ins and outs
good ~: **6** ethics, morals **7** decency, virtues **8** morality **9** integrity, rectitude **10** principles
habitual: **5** typic, usual **6** common, normal, steady, wonted **7** chronic, general, natural, regular, routine, typical **8** accepted, constant, everyday, familiar, frequent, knee-jerk, ordinary, orthodox, repeated, standard, unwaning **9** automatic, chronical, confirmed, continual, customary, ingrained, practiced, prevalent, recurrent, unabating **10** accustomed, deep-seated, inveterate, mechanical, methodical, persistent, prevailing, systematic
manner: **3** way
habitually: **3** oft **5** often **7** usually **9** generally, many a time, naturally **10** frequently
habituate: **5** enure, haunt, inure, train **6** adjust, harden **7** break in **8** accustom, indurate **9** acclimate, condition **10** discipline
habituated: **7** abiding **8** enduring **9** confirmed, ingrained **10** deep-rooted, deep-seated, inveterate
habitude: **4** wont **5** usage **6** custom, groove **7** routine **8** practice **9** tradition
habitué: **4** goer, user **6** addict, patron **7** devotee, visitor **8** customer **10** frequenter
hacienda: **4** casa **5** house, ranch **6** estate **7** mansion **9** farmstead **10** plantation
material: **5** adobe
room: **4** sala
Hacienda __, CA: **3** Hts.
hack: **3** axe, cab, cut, hew, rip **4** chop, fell, jade, maim, ride, take, taxi **5** cabby, cough, horse, labor, mince, slash, slice, split **6** cabbie, cabmen, common, driver, drudge, equine, jackal, mangle **7** pickaxe, plodder, scissor, taxicab, vehicle **8** hireling, inferior, mutilate **9** detractor, transport **10** second-rate
ender: **3** saw **4** work **5** berry **6** butter
it: **4** pass **5** get by **6** manage, thrive **7** make out, prosper, qualify, succeed **8** flourish, go places, make good **9** measure up **10** do all right, make the cut, pass muster
off: **2** ax **3** axe **5** sever **7** cut down **8** chop down
rider: **4** fare
Hack: **6** Wilson **7** Shelley
hackberry: **4** tree **5** fruit, shrub
cousin: **3** elm **7** zelkova
family: **3** elm
Hackensack: **4** city, town
locale: **9** New Jersey
hacker: **3** axe **4** user **6** golfer **10** cyber-crook
creation: **4** code **5** virus
headache: **3** bug
like a ~: **5** nerdy
purchase: **2** PC **4** disk **8** computer
Hackett: **4** Joan **5** Bobby, Buddy **6** Albert
hackie: **5** cabby **6** cabbie, driver **9** cab driver **10** taxi driver
hackle: **3** cut **6** mangle
hackles: **4** hair **5** anger
raise one's ~: **3** bug, get, irk, try, vex **4** fret, gall, miff, rile **5** annoy, chafe, grate, harry, peeve, pique **6** abrade, bother, harass, hector, needle, nettle, pester, plague, rankle, ruffle **7** disturb, provoke **8** irritate **9** aggravate, displease
where ~ rise: **4** nape
hackly: **5** rough **6** jagged, uneven **9** irregular
Hackman, Gene: **5** actor
film: Absolute Power (1997)
All Night Long (1981)
Behind Enemy Lines (2001)
the Birdcage (1995)
Bite the Bullet (1975)
Bonnie and Clyde (1967)
Cisco Pike (1972)
Class Action (1991)
The Conversation (1974)
Crimson Tide (1995)
Downhill Racer (1969)
Enemy of the State (1998)
The Firm (1993)
The French Connection (1971, AA)
Get Shorty (1995)
The Gypsy Moths (1969)
Heartbreakers (2001)
Heist (2001)
Hoosiers (1986)
I Never Sang for My Father (1970)
Mississippi Burning (1988)
Night Moves (1975)
No Way Out (1987)
The Poseidon Adventure (1972)
Postcards From the Edge (1990)
Prime Cut (1972)
The Quick and the Dead (1995)
Riot (1969)
The Royal Tenenbaums (2001)
Runaway Jury (2003)
Scarecrow (1973)
Superman (1978)
Superman II (1980)
Twice in a Lifetime (1985)
Twilight (1998)
Under Fire (1983)
Unforgiven (1992, AA)
Welcome to Mooseport (2004)
Wyatt Earp (1994)
film (voice): Antz (1998)
hackney: **5** coach, horse **6** equine **8** carriage
hackneyed: **3** old **4** dull, worn **5** banal, corny, hokey, moldy, musty, passé, stale, stock, tired, trite, vapid **6** common, jejune, old hat **7** clichéd, fatuous, humdrum, prosaic, worn-out **8** bromidic, outdated, outmoded, timeworn, well-used **9** moth-eaten, out-of-date, played out, prosaical, quotidian **10** antiquated, dullsville, overworked, pedestrian, threadbare, uninspired, unoriginal
expression: **6** cliché
hacksaw: **4** tool
Hacky Sack company: **5** Wham-o
Had __ and couldn't keep her: **5** a wife
__ Had a Hammer: **3** If I
__ Had a Million: **3** If I
__ had a secret love: **5** Once I
Haddam: **4** city, town
locale: **4** Conn.
__ haddie: **6** finnan
haddock: **3** cod **4** fish **5** scrod **6** schrod
__ had 'em: **4** Adam
Hades: **3** Dis **4** hell **5** abyss, limbo, Orcus, Pluto **7** Avernus, inferno **9** perdition **10** lower world, underworld
brother: **4** Zeus **8** Poseidon
dog: **8** Cerberus
entrance: **6** Averno
equivalent: **5** Pluto
parent: **4** Rhea **6** Cronos, Cronus
place enroute to ~: **6** Erebus
river: **4** Styx **5** Lethe
sister: **4** Hera **6** Hestia **7** Demeter
wife: **10** Persephone
Hades Factor, The
author: Robert Ludlum
__ had it!: **3** I've
hadj: **4** trek, trip **10** pilgrimage
__ had my way...: **3** If I
hadn't, wish you: **3** rue
Hadrian: **5** Roman **6** Caesar
Hadrian's Wall, south of: **6** Anglia
hadron: **8** particle
component: **5** quark
Haendel: **3** Ida
Hafey: **5** Chick
Hafez: **4** poet **7** Al-Assad, Persian
Haffner Symphony
composer: Wolfgang Amadeus Mozart
hafnium: **5** metal **7** element
haft: **6** handle
hag: **5** crone, harpy, witch **6** beldam, gorgon **7** beldame **8** harridan
assembly: **5** coven
ender: **4** fish
Hagar: **5** Sammy
Hägar the Horrible: **5** comic **10** comic strip
daughter: **4** Honi
dog: **5** Snert
wife: **5** Helga
Hagen: **3** Uta **4** city, Jean, town **5** Earle **6** Walter
locale: **7** Germany
Hagen, Uta: **7** actress
award: **4** Tony
spouse: José Ferrer
Hagen, Walter: **6** golfer
Hagerstown: **4** city
locale: **8** Maryland
Hagerty, Julie: **7** actress
film: Airplane! (1980)

Lost in America (1985)
Noises Off (1992)
What About Bob? (1991)
haggadah time: 5 seder 8 Passover
Haggai: 4 book
follower: 9 Zechariah
preceder: 9 Zephaniah
haggard: 3 wan 4 lean, pale, thin, worn 5 drawn, gaunt, spare, tired 6 ill-fed, peaked 7 starved, worn-out 8 careworn, fatigued, starving, weakened, worn-down 9 emaciated, exhausted
Haggard: 5 Merle, Rider 6 H. Rider
Haggard, H. Rider: 6 writer 7 British
character: 6 Ayesha
first name: Henry
work: Allan Quatermain
Ayesha
King Solomon's Mines
Nada the Lily
She
Haggerty: 3 Dan
haggle: 5 argue 6 barter, bicker, dicker 7 bargain, quarrel, wrangle 9 have words, negotiate 10 horse-trade
point: 5 price
hagiology subject: 3 ste., sts. 5 saint
Hagler, Marvin: 5 boxer
milieu: 4 ring
Hagman, Larry: 5 actor
costar: 4 Eden
mother: Mary Martin
TV: Dallas, I Dream of Jeannie
Hague, The: 4 city, town 7 capital
locale: 7 Holland 11 Netherlands
__-hah: 3 hoo
ha-ha: 5 laugh 6 cackle, giggle, guffaw, titter 7 break up, chortle, chuckle, crack up 8 laughter
Hahn: 4 Otto 6 Hilary
Hahn, Hilary: 9 violinist
Hahn, Otto: 7 chemist 8 Nobelist
hai: 3 yes 8 Japanese
__ H'ai: 4 Bali
Haid: 7 Charles
Haida: 5 tribe 6 Indian 7 Amerind 8 language
Haifa: 4 city, port, town
locale: 3 Isr. 6 Israel
port north of ~: 4 Acre
Haig: 2 Al 9 Alexander
former command: 4 NATO
Haight-Ashbury city: 6 Frisco
haiku: 4 poem 5 verse 6 poetry
birthplace: 5 Japan
kin: 5 tanka
hail: 3 ave, get, ice 4 flag, laud, rain 5 cheer, exalt, extol, greet, hallo, hillo, honor, hullo, huzza, salvo, storm 6 accost, call to, extoll, halloa, halloo, hallow, hilloa, hoorah, hooray, hulloo, hurrah, hurray, huzzah, praise, salute, shower, signal, summon, yell to 7 acclaim, applaud, approve, barrage, call for, commend, flatter, glorify, torrent, welcome, yell for 8 flag down, greeting, wave down 9 recognize 10 compliment, panegyrize, salutation
ender: 5 stone, storm
(from): 4 come 9 originate
in Latin: 3 ave
something to ~: 3 cab 4 taxi 7 taxicab
hail __: 4 a cab, from
hail-__-well-met: 6 fellow
Hail __: 4 Mary
Hail __ Chief: 5 to the
Hail __ pass: 4 Mary
Hail, Caesar!: 3 ave
Haile Selassie: 9 Ras Tafari
Hailey, Arthur: 6 writer
work: Airport
Detective
The Evening News
The Final Diagnosis
Hotel
In High Places
The Moneychangers
Overload
Runway Zero-Eight
Strong Medicine
Wheels
hail-fellow well met: 5 mixer 7 mingler 9 extrovert 10 socializer
Hail Mary __: 4 pass, play
Hail Mary counter: 6 rosary
Haim: 5 Corey
Haines: 5 Randa
Haing: 4 Ngor
Haiphong: 4 city, town
locale: 3 Nam 7 Vietnam
hair: 3 bun, fur, mop, wig 4 fuzz, lock, mane, pelt 5 beard, fiber, locks, pilus, tress 6 cilium, goatee, strand, toupee 7 bristle, cowlick, eyebrow, eyelash, minimum, tresses 8 coiffure, filament, sideburn, whiskers 9 moustache
adornment: 3 bow
animal ~: 3 fur 4 coat
appliance: 5 drier, dryer 6 blower
application: 3 dye, gel 5 frost, spray
arrange ~: 4 comb, do up 5 tease
band: 6 fascia
by a ~: 6 barely 8 narrowly
cause of a bad ~ day: 4 wind
color: 3 dye, red 4 gray, grey, tint 5 black, blond, brown, henna, rinse, trait, white 6 auburn, blonde 8 brunette
combining form: 3 pil- 4 pili-, pilo- 5 chaet-, crini-, trich- 6 chaeto-, -tricha, tricho-
covering: 3 hat, net
curl one's ~: 5 alarm, scare, spook 7 horrify, terrify 8 frighten
cut ~: 5 layer, shave
cutter: 5 razor 6 barber
dryer setting: 5 on low
ender: 3 cut, dos, pin 4 ball, line, worm 5 brush, cloth, piece, spray, style, weave 6 cutter, spring, streak 7 breadth, dresser 8 splitter
facial ~: 5 beard 8 mustache, whiskers 9 moustache
foundation: 5 scalp
fuss with one's ~: 5 groom, preen, primp
gel amount: 4 glob
get in one's ~: 3 bug, irk, vex 4 gall, rile 5 annoy, peeve, pique, upset 6 madden, nettle, pester, plague, ruffle 7 provoke, tick off 8 irritate 9 aggravate 10 exasperate
having ~ like horses: 5 maned
in one's ~: 5 pesky 7 irksome 8 annoying 9 obnoxious, vexatious 10 bothersome, irritating, nettlesome
interwoven ~: 5 braid, plait, queue 7 pigtail 8 ponytail
let one's ~ down: 4 undo 5 unpin 6 relate 8 unburden
like some ~: 4 wavy 5 curly, silky 6 frizzy
long ~: 3 mop 4 mane
lose ~: 4 bald, molt, shed 5 moult
microscopic ~: 6 cilium
neck ~: 7 hackles
problem: 4 knot 5 snarl 6 tangle
quality: 4 body 6 luster
quantity: 4 curl, hank, lock, tuft, wisp 5 shock, tress
remover: 4 Nair, Neet 10 depilatory
ribbon: 6 fillet
root ~: 6 fibril
shirt: 7 penance 9 penitence 10 contrition
shirt wearer: 6 atoner
shop: 5 salon
short ~: 7 bristle, whisker
splitter: 4 part
spray name: 5 Adorn
starter: 4 long, wire 5 cross, horse, short
style: 2 DA, do 3 bob, bun, cut, 'fro 4 Afro, burr, coif, conk, fade, flip, perm, pouf, puff, punk, shag, updo 5 bangs, braid, butch, queue, twist 6 braids, marcel, Mohawk, plaits 7 beehive, chignon, crew cut, flattop, natural, pageboy, topknot, upsweep 8 bouffant, brush cut, coiffure, cold wave, cornrows, ducktail, Dutch bob, pigtails, pin curls, pixie cut, ponytail, razor cut, ringlets 9 headdress, permanent, pompadour, poodle cut, scalp lock, spit curls 10 cornbraids, dreadlocks, feather cut, finger wave, Psyche knot
stylist, at times: 4 dyer
transplanted ~: 4 plug
treat ~: 3 dye, set 4 tint 5 rinse, tease
where ~ rises: 4 nape
with no ~ out of place: 4 neat, tidy 5 natty, sleek, slick, smart 6 dapper, spruce 7 orderly 8 spotless 9 shipshape
hair __: 3 net 5 shirt, spray, style 7 stylist, trigger
hair __ dog: 5 of the
hair-__: 6 raiser 7 raising
__ hair: 3 big, by a 5 angel, turn a 6 camel's
Hair: 7 musical
character: 3 Hud 4 Woof 6 Berger, Claude, Crissy, Sheila 7 Jeannie
lyricist: 4 Rado
producer: 4 Papp
song: 3 Air
Hair (1969 song)
artist: Cowsills
__ hair coat: 6 camel's
haircream holder: 4 tube
Haircut
author: Ring Lardner
__ hair day: 3 bad
hairdo: 2 DA 3 bob, bun, cut, 'fro 4 Afro, coif, conk, fade, flip, perm, pouf, puff, punk, shag, updo 5 bangs, braid, butch, queue, twist 6 braids, marcel, Mohawk, plaits 7 beehive, chignon, crew cut, flattop, natural, pageboy, topknot, upsweep 8 bouffant, brush cut, coiffure, cold wave, cornrows, ducktail, Dutch bob, pigtails, pin curls, pixie cut, ponytail, razor cut, ringlets 9 headdress, permanent, pompadour, poodle cut, scalp lock, spit curls 10 cornbraids, dreadlocks, feather cut, finger wave, Psyche knot
feature: 4 part 5 roach, swirl
like a punk ~: 5 spiky
hairdresser: 6 barber 7 friseur, stylist 8 coiffeur
at times: 4 dyer
haired: 6 pilose, pilous
starter: 4 long, wire 5 short
__-haired: 4 fair 5 white
__-haired boy: 4 fair
__-haired terrier: 4 wire
hairless: 4 bald 5 pelon, shorn 6 shaved, shaven, smooth 7 egghead 8 glabrate, glabrous
__ hairless: 7 Mexican
hairnet: 5 snood
hair of the __: 3 dog
...hair on my __...: 6 chinny
hairpiece: 3 rug, wig 4 fall 6 toupee
hairpin: 6 bodkin
curve: 3 zag, zig
hair-raising: 4 eery 5 eerie, scary 6 creepy 7 fearful 8 chilling, exciting 9 thrilling, unearthly
hairs
ender: 7 breadth
fruit ~: 5 villi
split ~: 5 cavil 6 niggle 7 nitpick, quibble 8 pettifog
starter: 5 cross
use the cross ~: 3 aim 5 sight
__ hairs: 5 cross, split
hairsplitting: 4 fine 7 carping 8 caviling, finespun, pedantic 10 pedantical
Hairspray (1988 film)
cast: Sonny Bono, Ruth Brown, Divine
director: John Waters
role: 4 Edna
Hairspray (2007 film)
cast: Nikki Blonsky, Michelle Pfeiffer, John Travolta, Christopher Walken
hairstyle
see hairdo
hairy: 4 hard 5 bushy, furry, fuzzy, pilar, risky, rough, scary, tough 6 chancy, comate, pilose, pilous, shaggy, sticky, unsafe 7 bearded, bristly, hirsute, parlous, pileous, unshorn 8 critical, grueling, perilous, unshaven 9 dangerous, difficult, frightful, hazardous, uncertain, whiskered 10 abominable, jeopardous, precarious, touch-and-go
combining form: 4 dasy-
no longer ~: 5 shorn
one: 3 ape
Hairy Ape, The
author: Eugene O'Neill
hairy-chested: 5 macho, manly 6 virile 9 masculine

hairy one
Biblical ~: 4 Esau
Haiti: 6 nation 7 country
city: 6 Delmas 9 Carrefour
gulf: 6 Gonâve 8 Gonaïves
island off ~: 6 Gonâve
language: 6 Creole, French
money: 3 gde. 6 gourde
org.: 3 OAS
practice: 5 vodun 6 voodoo
rum: 5 tafia 6 taffia
Haje: 9 Khrystyne
hajj destination: 5 Mecca
Haj, The
author: Leon Uris
hake: 4 fish
hakea: 4 tree 5 shrub 9 evergreen
Hakeem: 8 Olajuwon
Hal: 5 Ashby, Chase, David, Greer, Leroy, March, Roach, Smith 6 Foster, Linden, Porter, Prince, Salwen, Sutton, Walker, Wallis 7 Hartley, Ketchum, Needham 8 Holbrook, McIntyre, Williams 9 Newhouser 10 Fittipaldi
Halas, George: 5 coach
sport: 8 football
halberd
medieval ~: 5 vouge
Halberstam, David: 6 writer
subject: 6 Jordan 7 Vietnam 8 baseball
work: The Amateurs
The Best and the Brightest
The Breaks of the Game
The Fifties
Firehouse
October 1964
Playing for Keeps
The Powers That Be
The Reckoning
Summer of '49
War in a Time of Peace
halcyon: 4 bird, calm 5 happy, palmy, quiet 6 joyful, serene 7 at peace 8 carefree, peaceful, tranquil 10 harmonious, untroubled
Haldan: 8 Hartline
Haldane: 7 Richard
Haldeman: 2 H.R.
hale: 3 fit 4 iron, trim, well, wiry 5 beefy, burly, hardy, hefty, hunky, husky, lusty, right, sound, stout, tough, whole 6 brawny, hearty, mighty, potent, robust, rugged, sinewy, steely, stocky, strong, sturdy, virile 7 doughty, healthy, in shape, up to par 8 athletic, forceful, indurate, muscular, powerful, puissant, stalwart, vigorous 9 Atlantean, energetic, Herculean, in the pink, strapping, well-built 10 able-bodied, red-blooded
partner: 6 hearty
Hale: 4 Alan 5 Irwin 6 Nathan, Philip 7 Barbara
hero: 5 Nolan
Hale-__: 4 Bopp
Haleakala: 4 park 6 crater
locale: 4 Maui 6 Hawaii
Hale, Barbara: 7 actress
son: William Katt
TV: Perry Mason
Hale-Bopp: 5 comet
__ Hale Broun: 7 Heywood
__ Halen: 3 Van
Hale, Nathan: 3 spy
alma mater: 4 Yale
Halen, Eddie Van: 8 musician
spouse: Valerie Bertinelli
haleness: 6 health
ha-Levi: 5 Judah
Haley: 4 Alex, Bill, Jack
costar: 4 Lahr 6 Bolger 7 Garland
Haley __ Osment: 4 Joel
Haley, Alex: 6 writer
ancestor: Kinte
work: The Autobiography of Malcolm X
Roots
Haley and His Comets, Bill
song: Burn That Candle (1955)
Rock Around the Clock (1955)
See You Later, Alligator (1956)
Shake, Rattle and Roll (1954)
Haley Jr., Jack
spouse: Liza Minnelli
half: 5 piece 6 handle, moiety 9 bisection
ender: 3 way 4 back, time, tone 5 pence, penny 6 cocked 7 hearted
in music: 5 mezzo
prefix: 4 demi-, hemi-, semi-
half __: 3 pay 4 bath, cent, dime, note, pint, rest, size, sole, step, tone 5 crown, eagle, hitch, shell, title, twist 6 dollar, gainer, nelson, sister 7 brother
half-__: 3 caf, wit 4 full, hour, inch, life, mast, mile, moon, note, pint, sole, turn 5 baked, pound, right, truth 6 asleep, cocked, gallon, joking
half-__ over: 4 seas
__ half: 5 other 6 better 7 shelter
Half __ Bay, CA: 4 Moon
Half __ is better...: 5 a loaf
half-and-half: 6 evenly
amount: 2 pt. 4 pint
part: 3 ale 4 milk 5 cream 6 porter
half-asleep: 4 dozy, logy 5 tired 6 drowsy 9 heavy-eyed
half-awake
see half-asleep
halfback: 7 athlete, gridder 10 footballer
move: 4 juke 5 feint 6 end run
__ half bad: 3 not
half-baked: 4 daft 5 batty, goony, goosy, silly 7 foolish, shallow, vacuous, wanting, witless 9 brainless, senseless 10 boneheaded, dilettante, ill-advised, indiscreet, sophomoric, unfinished, weak-minded
half-cocked
see half-baked
__ half-cocked: 5 go off
half-cup: 4 gill
half dollar: 4 coin 5 money
word: 3 God 4 unum 5 trust 6 States, United 7 America, liberty 8 pluribus
half-done: 7 sketchy 10 incomplete, unfinished
half-gainer: 4 dive
half-goat, half-man: 3 Pan 4 faun 5 satyr
half-grown: 5 young 6 callow 8 immature 10 adolescent, developing
halfhearted: 4 cold, cool, tame 5 tepid 7 passive 8 grudging, hesitant, listless, lukewarm
half-hour at sea: 4 bell
Half-Lives
author: Erica Jong
half-moon: 3 arc 4 lune
Half Moon: 4 boat, ship
captain: 6 Hudson
half-note feature: 4 stem
half-off event: 4 sale
halfpenny: 4 coin 5 money 6 bawbee
half-pint: 3 boy, kid, lad 4 runt 5 child, sprig, youth 6 peewee 8 juvenile 9 stripling, youngster
serving: 3 ale 4 beer 5 stout
half-price: 5 cheap 6 on sale 7 cutrate, low-cost, reduced 10 economical, marked down, reasonable
half-seas __: 4 over
half-serpent, half-woman: 5 lamia
halftime entertainer: 4 band
Half Time rapper: 3 Nas
halftone: 5 print
Halftrack: 4 Amos 7 general
half-truth: 4 myth 9 falsehood 10 generality
half turn in ballet: 7 déboulé
halfway: 3 mid 4 mean 5 midst 6 almost, in part, median, middle, nearly, partly 7 partial 9 partially
meet ~: 7 mediate 9 arbitrate, negotiate, reconcile 10 conciliate
point: 6 center, median, middle
__ halfway: 4 meet
halfway house program: 5 rehab
half-wit
see ninny
halibut: 4 fish, sole
Halifax: 4 city, port, town
clock setting: 3 AST
locale: 6 Canada 10 Nova Scotia
newspaper: 4 News 6 Herald
school: 9 Dalhousie
halite: 7 mineral 8 rock salt
melter: 4 snow
halitosis: 9 bad breath
cause: 5 onion 6 garlic
fighter: 5 Scope 9 Listerine
hall: 5 foyer, lobby, odeon, odeum 6 lyceum, museum, palace 7 gallery, ingress, mansion, passage, theater, theatre, walkway 8 anteroom, ballroom, corridor 9 classroom, concourse, dormitory, residence, vestibule 10 auditorium, passageway, schoolroom
activity: 5 study
concert ~: 5 arena, odeon, odeum, venue 7 theater, theatre
dance ~: 5 disco
decker: 5 holly
dining ~: 4 mess
ender: 3 way 4 mark
entrance ~: 5 foyer, lobby 9 vestibule
exhibition ~: 5 salon 8 pavilion
in Spanish: 4 sala
lecture ~: 6 lyceum 10 auditorium
mess ~: 10 dining room
of justice: 5 court
preceder: 4 town
starter: 4 gild 5 dance, guild, White
hall __: 4 tree 7 monitor
__ hall: 3 rec 4 beer, city, mess, pool, town 5 bingo, dance, music, study 6 dining, hiring 7 borough
Hall: 3 Edd, Gus, Jon 4 Fawn 5 Annie, Daryl, Huntz, Jerry, Monty, Peter 6 Deidre, Donald 7 Arsenio, Juanita 8 Bartlett 9 Alexander, Radclyffe
partner: 5 Oates
__ Hall: 4 City 5 Annie, Seton 6 Nassau 7 Faneuil, Kingdom, Tammany
Hallandale: 4 city, town
locale: 7 Florida
Hall and Oates
song: Adult Education (1984)
Did It in a Minute (1982)
Everything Your Heart Desires (1988)
Family Man (1983)
I Can't Go For That (1981)
Kiss on My List (1981)
Maneater (1982)
Method of Modern Love (1985)
One on One (1983)
Out of Touch (1984)
Private Eyes (1981)
Rich Girl (1977)
Sara Smile (1976)
Say It Isn't So (1983)
She's Gone (1976)
You Make My Dreams (1981)
Hall, Arsenio: 2 MC 4 host 5 emcee
Halle: 4 city, town 5 Berry
locale: 7 Germany
river: 5 Saale
hallelujah: 4 amen, pean 5 huzza, paean, shout 6 hoorah, hooray, hurrah, hurray, huzzah 7 hosanna 8 alleluia
Hallelujah, __ Bum: 3 I'm a
Hallelujah, Baby!: 7 musical
composer: Jule Styne
Halley, Edmund: 10 astronomer
Halley's __: 5 comet
Halliburton: 4 Erle
Halliwell: 4 Geri 6 Leslie
Hall, Jerry
spouse: Mick Jagger
hallmark: 4 seal, sign 5 badge, brand, stamp, trait 6 emblem, symbol 7 feature 8 property, sure sign 9 indicator 10 indication
Hallmark __: 5 Cards
Hall, Monty: 2 MC 4 host 5 emcee
offering: 4 deal
hallo: 3 cry 4 call, hail, yell 5 shout 6 call to, cry out 7 address, exclaim 8 greeting 9 call out to 10 salutation
Hall of __: 4 Fame 5 Famer
Hall of Fame
baseball ~ executive: 4 Kuhn 5 Frick, Giles, Veeck 6 Barrow, Landis, Manley, Rickey, Yawkey 7 Johnson, O'Malley 8 Chandler, Griffith, MacPhail, Spalding 9 Bill Veeck, Bowie Kuhn, Ford Frick, Tom Yawkey 10 Ban Johnson, Effa Manley
baseball ~ manager: 4 Mack 5 Lopez, Selee 6 Alston, Hanlon, Harris, McGraw, Weaver 7 Al Lopez, Huggins, Lasorda, Stengel 8 Anderson, Durocher, McCarthy, Williams 9 McKechnie, Ned Hanlon 10 Connie Mack, Earl Weaver, Frank Selee, John McGraw, Southworth

baseball ~ player: 3 Day, Fox, Ott 4 Babe, Bell, Cobb, Dean, Doby, Fisk, Ford, Foxx, Hoyt, Mays, Mize, Rice, Ruth, Ryan, Wynn, Yogi 5 Aaron, Anson, Banks, Bench, Boggs, Brett, Brock, Carew, Combs, Doerr, Evers, Flick, Gomez, Grove, Gwynn, Irvin, Kiner, Klein, Lemon, Paige, Perez, Reese, Rixey, Roush, Rusie, Smith, Spahn, Terry, Vance, Waner, Wheat, Young, Yount 6 Bender, Carter, Cepeda, Cronin, Cuyler, Dihigo, Feller, Foster, Frisch, Gehrig, Gibson, Gordon, Goslin, Hunter, Kaline, Koufax, Lajoie, Mantle, Mel Ott, Morgan, Murray, Musial, Niekro, Palmer, Ripken, Seaver, Sisler, Snider, Sutter, Sutton, Ty Cobb, Wagner, Wilson 7 Appling, Ashburn, Averill, Bunning, Carlton, Collins, Cy Young, Fingers, Gossage, Hornsby, Hubbell, Jackson, Jenkins, Jim Rice, Johnson, Lazzeri, Leon Day, Mathews, McCovey, Medwick, Molitor, Puckett, Rizzuto, Roberts, Ruffing, Sam Rice, Schmidt, Speaker, Stearns, Traynor, Vaughan, Waddell, Wilhelm 8 Al Kaline, Aparicio, Babe Ruth, Bob Lemon, Boudreau, Cap Anson, Clemente, Cochrane, DiMaggio, Drysdale, Edd Roush, Lou Brock, Marichal, Marquard, Robinson, Rod Carew, Sandberg, Stargell, Williams, Winfield 9 Alexander, Amos Rusie, Bill Terry, Bob Feller, Bob Gibson, Cal Ripken, Dandridge, Dizzy Dean, Don Sutton, Early Wynn, Eckersley, Eppa Rixey, Greenberg, Hank Aaron, Henderson, Jim Palmer, Joe Cronin, Joe Gordon, Joe Morgan, Killebrew, Larry Doby, Lou Gehrig, Mathewson, Mazeroski, Nap Lajoie, Nellie Fox, Newhouser, Nolan Ryan, Paul Waner, Radbourne, Slaughter, Tom Seaver, Tony Gwynn, Tony Perez, Wade Boggs, Waite Hoyt, Yogi Berra, Zack Wheat 10 Bobby Doerr, Campanella, Charleston, Chuck Klein, Dazzy Vance, Duke Snider, Earle Combs, Elmer Flick, Ernie Banks, Gary Carter, Hack Wilson, Jim Bunning, Jimmie Foxx, Joe Medwick, Josh Gibson, Kiki Cuyler, Lefty Gomez, Lefty Grove, Lloyd Waner, Monte Irvin, Ozzie Smith, Phil Niekro, Pie Traynor, Ralph Kiner, Red Ruffing, Robin Yount, Rube Foster, Stan Musial, Whitey Ford, Willie Mays 11 Yastrzemski

baseball ~ umpire: 4 Klem 6 Chylak, Conlan 7 Barlick, Hubbard 8 Bill Klem 9 Al Barlick

basketball ~ player: 3 Iba, Yow 4 Bing, Bird, Daly, Gola, Reed, Rupp, West 5 Barry, Brown, Cousy, Ewing, Hayes, Issel, Lucas, Mikan, Olson 6 Baylor, Cowens, Dumars, Erving, Gervin, Holman, Jordan, Kay Yow, Knight, Lanier, Malone, McAdoo, Meyers, Monroe, Parish, Pettit, Stokes, Thomas, Twyman, Unseld, Walton, Wooden, Worthy 7 Barkley, Bellamy, Bradley, Dantley, Drexler, Frazier, Hank Iba, Holzman, Johnson, Russell, Schayes, Tom Gola, Wilkens, Wilkins 8 Auerbach, Bob Cousy, Dan Issel, Dave Bing, Goodrich, Havlicek, Heinsohn, Maravich, Olajuwon, Petrovic, Robinson, Stockton, Thurmond 9 Ann Meyers, Archibald, Bob Knight, Bob Lanier, Bob McAdoo, Bob Pettit, Chuck Daly, Jerry West, Larry Bird, Lute Olson, Nat Holman, Rick Barry, Robertson, Wes Unseld 10 Adolph Rupp, Bill Walton, Carnesecca, Dave Cowens, Earl Monroe, Elvin Hayes, Jack Twyman, Jerry Lucas, John Wooden, Larry Brown, Red Holzman, Willis Reed 11 Abdul-Jabbar, Chamberlain, DeBusschere

football ~ coach: 4 Levy, Noll 5 Allen, Brown, Grant, Halas, Neale, Shula, Stram 6 Ewbank, Landry, Madden 7 Gillman, Pollard 8 Bud Grant, Don Shula, Lombardi, Marv Levy 9 Chuck Noll, Paul Brown, Tom Landry 10 John Madden, Sid Gillman, Weeb Ewbank

football ~ player: 4 Dean, Huff, Lary, Lott, Monk, Page 5 Allen, Brown, Ditka, Eller, Green, Groza, Hayes, Irvin, Jones, Olsen, Shell, Smith, Swann, White 6 Bethea, Butkus, Carson, Casper, Csonka, Grange, Greene, Harris, Hirsch, Lofton, Nevers, Payton, Refnro, Sayers, Taylor, Thomas, Thorpe, Wehrli, Wright 7 Alworth, Art Monk, Dorsett, Gifford, Hampton, Hornung, Largent, Sam Huff, Sanders, Simpson, Tippett, Woodson 8 Alan Page, Art Shell, Bob Brown, Bob Hayes, Campbell, Fred Dean, Jim Brown, Lou Groza, Matthews, McDaniel, Nagurski, Nitschke, Stenerud, Yale Lary 9 Carl Eller, Dickerson, Hickerson, Jim Thorpe, Joe Greene, Lynn Swann, Marchetti, Mel Renfro, Mike Ditka, O.J. Simpson, Red Grange, Zimmerman 10 Bruce Smith, Buoniconti, Dan Hampton, Dave Casper, Dick Butkus, Gale Sayers, Robustelli, Ronnie Lott, Stallworth

football ~ quarterback: 4 Moon 5 Baugh, Elway, Fouts, Kelly, Starr, Young 6 Aikman, Blanda, Dawson, Graham, Griese, Marino, Tittle, Unitas 7 Luckman, Montana 8 Bradshaw, Dan Fouts, Friedman, Jim Kelly, Staubach, Y.A. Tittle 9 Bart Starr, Bob Griese, Dan Marino, John Elway, Jurgensen, Len Dawson, Tarkenton 10 Joe Montana, Otto Graham, Sammy Baugh, Sid Luckman, Steve Young, Warren Moon

hockey ~ player: 3 Orr, Roy 4 Duff, Fuhr, Howe, Hull, Park 5 Bossy, Neely 6 Coffey, Dionne, Mikita, Murphy, Parent, Plante, Potvin 7 Bourque, Federko, Francis, Gilbert, Gillies, Gretzky, Lafleur, Langway, Lemieux, Messier, Richard, Sawchuk, Stevens, Worsley 8 Anderson, Bathgate, Bobby Orr, Brad Park, Cam Neely, Dick Duff, Esposito, Larionov, MacInnis, Trottier 9 Bobby Hull, Geoffrion, Grant Fuhr, Kharlamov, Mike Bossy 10 Al MacInnis, Gordie Howe, Guy Lafleur, LaFontaine, Patrick Roy, Paul Coffey, Rod Gilbert, Stan Mikita

Hall of Fame for Great Americans
site: 3 NYU

Hall-of-Famer: 5 great

hallow: 5 bless, honor 6 anoint, devote, revere 7 respect 8 dedicate, enshrine, inshrine, sanctify, venerate 10 consecrate

hallowed: 4 holy 5 blest 6 sacred, solemn 7 beloved 9 inviolate
place: 6 church, shrine 9 sanctuary

Halloween
activity: 5 prank 6 booing
animal: 3 bat, cat
decor: 5 skull 6 cobweb 7 pumpkin
like ~: 4 eery 5 eerie, scary
month: 3 Oct. 7 October
option: 5 treat, trick
reaction: 6 fright
sound: 3 boo 4 moan
treat: 5 candy
wear: 3 wig 4 mask, wart 5 fangs, ghost, sheet, spook 6 goblin

Halloween (1978 film)
cast: Jamie Lee Curtis, Donald Pleasence
director: John Carpenter

Halloween H20 (1998 film)
cast: Adam Arkin, Jamie Lee Curtis, Josh Hartnett, Michelle Williams

Hallow ender: 3 een

__ Hallows' Eve: 3 All

Hall, Radclyffe: 6 writer 7 British

halls of ivy: 6 school 7 academy, college

Hallström: 5 Lasse

hallucinate: 7 imagine 8 daydream

hallucination: 5 dream 6 fantom, mirage, vision 7 phantom 8 delusion 9 nightmare

hallucinatory: 6 unreal 8 fanciful, illusory 9 fantastic, imaginary

__ Hall University: 5 Seton

hallux: 3 toe 6 big toe

hallway: 5 aisle, lobby 7 ingress, passage 8 corridor 9 vestibule

halo: 4 aura, ring 6 circle, corona, gloria, nimbus 7 aureola, aureole 8 gloriole

halogen: 6 iodine 7 bromine 8 astatine, chlorine, fluorine
compound: 6 iodate
suffix: 3 ide, ine

halogen __: 4 lamp

Halpin: 4 Luke

Halsey: 4 Bull 5 Brett 7 admiral, William
org.: 3 USN

Hals, Frans: 5 Dutch 6 artist 7 painter

halt: 3 bar, end 4 kill, lame, limp, quit, rest, stay, stop, wait 5 block, brake, break, cease, check, close, letup, lie to, pause, stall, tie up, truce, waver 6 arrest, becalm, cesura, cool it, cutoff, desist, dither, falter, finish, forbid, freeze, hiatus, hold up, lay off, loiter, period, pull up, recess, remain, stifle, tackle, thwart, wind up, wrap up 7 adjourn, break up, caesura, fetch up, impasse, prevent, refrain, squelch, stammer, stumble, suspend, ward off 8 break off, conclude, deadlock, hesitate, hold back, intermit, knock off, leave off, obstruct, pack it in, paralyse, paralyze, prohibit, shut down, stoppage, surcease 9 cessation, close down, intercept, interlude, interrupt, terminate, vacillate 10 call it a day, knock it off, standstill, suspension
at sea: 5 avast

Halt!: 4 whoa 5 avast
caller: 6 sentry

halted: 5 still 6 at rest, static 8 stagnant, unmoving 10 motionless

halter: 3 top 4 curb, rein 5 check, shirt 6 blouse, bodice, bridle, tether 7 control, harness, trammel 9 restraint

halter __: 3 top

halting: 4 poky, slow 6 clumsy, draggy, faulty 7 awkward, gradual, impeded, labored, lagging, languid, unadept 8 bumbling, dilatory, drawn-out, hesitant, slothful, sluggish, toddling, unsteady, wavering 9 faltering, imperfect, leisurely, lethargic, maladroit, prolonged, snaillike, stumbling, tentative, uncertain, unhurried 10 deliberate, indecisive, protracted

haltingly: 7 loathly 8 bit by bit
speak ~: 6 mumble 7 sputter, stumble, stutter

halvah: 4 nosh 5 candy, snack
ingredient: 5 honey, sugar 6 sesame

halve: 5 split 6 bisect, divide 7 divvy up, split up

halved: 5 in two

halves
go ~: 5 share 6 divide
two ~: 4 buck 5 whole 6 dollar, single 7 one-spot, smacker 8 simoleon

halyard: 4 line

ham: 4 meat 5 actor 6 emoter, gammon, hotdog, player 7 actress, cold cut, overact, showoff 10 prosciutto

alternative: 3 BLT 4 tuna 8 tuna fish 9 roast beef 10 corned beef
baked ~ insert: 5 clove
cut: 4 hock
device: 5 radio
ender: 4 burg, ster 6 burger, string, strung
it up: 3 act 4 play 5 emote 7 overact, perform 8 overplay
mate: 3 rye 4 eggs 5 Swiss
place: 4 deli 5 stage 7 theater, theatre
prepare ~: 4 cure 5 glaze, mince, slice
product: 4 Spam
relative: 4 pork
salad ingredient: 4 mayo 6 pickle
source: 3 pig 5 swine 6 porker
theft: 5 scene
word: 4 over 5 roger
ham __: 4 it up 5 on rye
ham-__: 6 fisted, handed
__ ham: 5 daisy 6 picnic, Polish, spiced 7 country 8 Virginia
Ham: 6 Fisher
brother: 4 Shem 7 Japheth
father: 4 Noah
son: 3 Put 4 Cush, Kush 5 Egypt 6 Canaan
Hama: 4 city, town
locale: 5 Syria
hamadryad: 5 nymph
ham and __: 4 eggs 6 cheese
Haman nemesis: 6 Esther
hamate: 4 bone 9 wrist bone 10 hook-shaped
Hambletonian gait: 4 trot
Hamburg: 4 city, port, town
city north of ~: 4 Kiel
locale: 7 Germany
river: 4 Elbe
hamburger: 4 meat 5 patty 6 pattie 8 sandwich
holder: 3 bun
topping: 5 onion 6 catsup, pickle, relish, tomato 7 ketchup, lettuce
Hamburger: 6 German
Hamburger __: 6 Helper
Hamden: 4 city, town
locale: 4 Conn.
Hamel: 3 Ray 8 Veronica
Hamelin visitor: 3 rat 5 piper
Hamer: 5 Rusty 6 Robert
ham-handed: 6 clumsy, gauche 7 unadept
one: 3 oaf 5 klutz, pawer 6 galoot, lummox 7 botcher, bungler, fumbler 8 stumbler
Hamhung: 4 city, town
locale: 10 North Korea
Hamill: 4 Mark, Pete 7 Dorothy
Hamill, Dorothy: 6 skater
Hamill, Mark: 5 actor
film: The Big Red One (1980) The Empire Strikes Back (1980) Return of the Jedi (1983) Star Wars (1977)
Hamilton: 3 Guy, Roy 4 city, Emma, Fish, John, Neil, Russ, town 5 Edith, Linda, Luske, river, Scott, Smith 6 Donald, George, Jordan, Murray 7 Lisa Gay 8 Margaret 9 Alexander
athletes: 7 Raiders
bill: 3 ten
-Burr meeting: 4 duel
foe: 4 Burr
locale: 3 Ont. 4 Ohio 6 Canada 7 Bermuda, Ontario 9 New Jersey 10 New Zealand
River locale: 8 Labrador
school: 7 Colgate 8 McMaster
Hamilton Beach
competitor: 5 Oster
Hamilton, Donald: 6 writer
spy: Matt Helm
Hamilton, Emma: 4 Lady
Hamilton, George: 5 actor
film: Love at First Bite (1979) Your Cheatin' Heart (1964)
Hamilton, Joe Frank & Reynolds
song: Don't Pull Your Love (1971) Fallin' in Love (1975)
Hamilton, Linda: 7 actress
spouse: James Cameron
__ Hamilton, NY: 4 Fort
Hamilton, Scott: 6 skater
__ Hamilton Woman: 4 That
Hamish in English: 5 James
Hamite: 6 Berber, Nimrod
hamlet: 3 vil. 4 burg, dorp, town 5 place, thorp 6 suburb, thorpe 7 village 8 Dogpatch 9 community 10 settlement
old-style: 5 thorp 6 thorpe
Hamlet: 4 Dane, play 5 drama 7 tragedy
aromatic plant: 3 rue
author: William Shakespeare
catch: 3 rub
character: 5 Osric 6 Hamlet 7 Horatio, Laertes, Ophelia 8 Bernardo, Claudius, Gertrude, Polonius, Reynaldo 9 Francisco, Marcellus 10 Fortinbras 11 Rosencrantz 12 Guildenstern
emulate ~: 6 avenge
exclamation: 3 fie 4 alas
father: 5 ghost
language: 6 Danish
locale: 8 Elsinore
opener: 4 Act I
phrase: 4 to be
prop: 5 arras, skull
quintet: 4 acts
to Gertrude: 3 son
what ~ smelled: 4 a rat
Hamlet (1948 film)
cast: Laurence Olivier
Hamlet (1990 film)
cast: Alan Bates, Helena Bonham Carter, Glenn Close, Mel Gibson, Ian Holm, Paul Scofield
director: Franco Zeffirelli
Hamlet, The
author: William Faulkner
Hamlin: 5 Harry 7 Garland, Vincent 8 Hannibal
Hamlin, Harry
spouse: Lisa Rinna, Nicollette Sheridan
Hamm: 3 Mia 4 city, town
locale: 4 Ruhr 7 Germany
Hammarskjöld, Dag: 7 Swedish 8 diplomat, Nobelist
predecessor: 3 Lie
successor: 6 U Thant
hammer: 3 hit, ram 4 bang, beat, bone, club, drub, lash, nail, pelt, slam, tool, whip 5 gavel, knock, pound, pulse, smite, stamp, whack, whomp 6 batter, beetle, defeat, mallet, pommel, pummel, sledge, strike, thrash, wallop 7 clobber, lambast, trounce 8 lambaste
drop the ~: 4 fire 5 shoot
ender: 4 head, lock
head: 3 tup
heavy ~: 4 mall, maul
home: 7 belabor, dwell on 9 go on about
hurler: 4 Thor
in: 5 embed, imbed
into: 5 drill 7 impress, ingrain 9 inculcate
judge's ~: 5 gavel
locale: 3 ear
obliquely: 3 toe
out: 4 form 5 forge 9 construct, establish, negotiate 10 accomplish, bring about, excogitate
part: 4 claw, peen
partner: 4 claw 5 tongs 6 chisel, sickle
sound: 3 bam
starter: 4 jack, trip 6 sledge, yellow
stirrup and ~ partner: 5 anvil
target: 4 gong, nail
throw: 5 event
hammer __: 4 mill, pond 5 throw
__ hammer: 3 air 4 claw
Hammer: 2 M.C. 3 Jan 4 Mike 6 Armand
hammer and __: 5 tongs 6 sickle
hammerhead: 4 bird 5 shark
feature: 4 claw
relative: 4 mako
Hammerin' Hank: 5 Aaron
Hammer, Jan
song: Miami Vice Theme (1985)
Hammer, Mike: 3 tec 6 shamus, sleuth 7 gumshoe 9 detective 10 private eye
hammer-on-thumb cry: 2 ow 3 yow 4 ouch, yeow
hammers are thrown, where: 4 meet
Hammerstein II, Oscar: 8 lyricist
collaborator: Jerome Kern, Richard Rodgers, Sigmund Romberg
musical: Allegro Carousel Flower Drum Song The King and I Me and Juliet Oklahoma! Pipe Dream Show Boat The Sound of Music South Pacific
Hammett (1983 film)
cast: Peter Boyle, Frederic Forrest, Marilu Henner
director: Wim Wenders
Hammett, Dashiell: 6 writer
dog: 4 Asta
first name: Samuel
friend: 7 Hellman, Lillian
sleuth: 3 Sam 4 Nick, Nora 5 Spade 7 Charles
work: The Continental Op The Dain Curse The Glass Key The Maltese Falcon The Thin Man
hammock
rigging: 5 clews
use a ~: 3 lie 4 bask, idle, laze, loaf, loll, rest 5 relax 6 dawdle, lounge, repose 7 goof off 10 take it easy
weave: 3 net
Hammond: 4 city, town 5 Peter 6 Albert
locale: 7 Indiana
product: 3 map 5 atlas, organ
hammy: 5 stagy 6 stagey 8 affected, overdone 10 theatrical
ham on __: 3 rye
hamper: 3 bin, tie 4 bind, clog, curb, foil, load, rein, slow, snag, stop 5 block, brake, check, cramp, crimp, delay, leash, limit, stall, stimy, stymy, tie up 6 baffle, basket, dampen, fetter, hang up, hinder, hobble, hogtie, hold up, hurdle, impede, rein in, retard, slow up, stymie, thwart 7 confine, inhibit, prevent, shackle, trammel 8 encumber, entangle, handicap, obstruct, preclude, prohibit, restrain, restrict, sabotage, slow down, straiten 9 container, frustrate, hamstring, weigh down 10 receptacle
contents: 4 wash 7 laundry
in the ~: 5 dirty 7 unclean
Hampshire: 3 pig 5 sheep, Susan, swine 6 county
city: 6 Havant
locale: 7 England
Hampton: 3 Dan 4 city, town 5 James 6 Lionel
locale: 8 Virginia
Hampton __, VA: 5 Roads
Hampton Court feature: 4 maze
Hampton, Dan
sport: 8 football
Hampton Inn: 5 motel
alternative: *see* motel
Hampton, Lionel: 12 vibraphonist
genre: 4 jazz
Hampton Roads: 6 battle
locale: 8 Virginia
Hamptons route: 4 LIRR
hamster: 3 pet 6 animal, mammal, rodent
female: 3 doe
home: 4 cage
male: 4 buck
relative: *see* rodent
young: 3 pup
hamstring: 4 foil, maim 5 block, check, cramp 6 fetter, hamper, hang up, hinder, hobble, hogtie, hold up, impair, impede, tendon, thwart 7 disable, inhibit, prevent, shackle 8 encumber, handicap, obstruct, restrain, restrict 9 frustrate
site: 3 leg 5 thigh
Hamsun, Knut: 6 writer 8 Nobelist 9 Norwegian
Han: 4 Solo 5 river 6 Indian 7 Amerind, dynasty
city on the ~: 5 Seoul
River locale: 5 China, Korea
Hana: 4 city, town 10 Mandlikova
locale: 4 Maui 6 Hawaii
Hancock: 4 John 6 Herbie
Hancock (2008 film)
cast: Jason Bateman, Will Smith, Charlize Theron
Hancock, Herbie: 7 pianist
genre: 4 jazz

hand: 3 paw **4** aide, duke, fist, give, help, lift, mitt, peon, serf, side, span, unit **5** boost, clerk, grunt, labor, leg up, offer, reach, slave, yield **6** assist, helper, jobber, member, relief, sailor, tender, worker **7** artisan, crewman, employe, jack tar, laborer, ovation, present, proffer, servant, support, tribute **8** applause, donation, employee, guidance, hireling, kindness **9** attendant, extremity **10** apprentice, assistance, crewperson, roustabout, wage earner, working man
a line: 10 ingratiate
and glove: 6 allied, united **7** unified **8** friendly, in league
at ~: 4 near, nigh **5** close, ready **6** nearby, next to, usable **7** close-by, in store, looming, present, useable **8** adjacent, imminent, next door **9** available, bordering, impending, proximate, ready to go **10** accessible, convenient, in the cards, obtainable
at ~ , poetically: 4 nigh **5** anear
at the ~ of: 3 per **7** through
back: 6 return
be at ~: 4 loom
big ~: 5 kudos **6** praise **7** ovation, plaudit **8** accolade, applause, cheering **9** standing O
by ~: 8 manually
clenched ~: 4 fist
combining form: 5 chiro- **6** cheiro-
covering: 4 mitt, muff **5** glove **6** mitten
dab ~: 8 skillful
deck ~: 6 sailor **7** jack tar
done by ~: 6 manual
down: 4 give, will **5** leave, relay **6** impart, pass on, render **7** deliver **8** bequeath, transmit
empty ~ , literally: 6 karate
ender: 3 bag, car, gun, off, out, saw, set **4** ball, bill, book, cart, clap, cuff, fast, grip, held, hold, made, maid, pick, rail, sell, some, work, wove **5** blown, clasp, craft, print, shake, spike, stand, woven **6** barrow, cuffed, maiden, spring **7** breadth, crafted, wringer, writing **8** kerchief
extend one's ~ to: 5 greet
field ~: 4 peon
follower: 5 shake
free ~: 5 swing **6** leeway **7** bigness, largess **8** largesse, latitude **10** generosity, liberality
get the upper ~: 4 beat, best, bury, drub, rout, stun **5** cream, crush, drown, quell, smash, total, trash, upset, waste **6** defeat, subdue **7** clobber, conquer, oppress, put away, stagger, take out, torpedo, trounce **8** bear down, blow away, bulldoze, dominate, overcome, roll over, shellack, suppress, vanquish **9** overpower, overthrow, subjugate **10** take care of
give a ~ to: 3 aid **4** abet, clap, help **6** assist, deal in, step in **7** applaud, bail out, pitch in, relieve, sustain **9** cooperate
go ~ over hand: 5 climb, scale **6** ascend, shinny **7** clamber
hand in ~: 7 jointly **8** together
have a ~ in: 5 share, split **6** divide **7** split up **9** partake of
have the upper ~: 4 boss, head, lead, rule **5** reign **6** direct, govern, manage **7** command, control, dictate, prevail, triumph **8** overrule **9** subjugate, tyrannize **10** monopolize, run the show
helping ~: 5 break, leg up, start
hide in the ~: 4 palm
hired ~: 6 jobber, worker **7** employe **8** employee **9** jobholder
holder: 5 wrist
hold out one's ~: 3 beg **5** cadge, hit up, mooch **8** freeload **9** impetrate, mendicate, panhandle **10** supplicate
in: 4 give **5** offer **6** pass on, render, submit, tender **7** deliver, present **8** turn over
in ~: 7 secured
in glove: 4 deep **5** close, solid, thick, tight **6** chummy **10** buddy-buddy, palsy-walsy
in hand: 7 jointly **8** together
iron ~: 5 rigor **7** cruelty, tyranny **8** coercion, hardness, severity **9** austerity, autocracy, brutality, despotism, harshness, sternness **10** oppression, severeness, strictness
items on ~: 5 these
it to: 4 laud **5** extol **6** admire, praise **7** applaud, commend **10** compliment
keep on ~: 4 have, save **5** carry, stock, store **9** inventory
matter at ~: 3 job **5** theme, topic **7** subject
menacing ~: 4 fist
milieu: 4 farm **5** ranch
motion: 4 clap, wave **5** wring
new ~: 4 babe, lamb, naif, tiro, tyro **6** intern, novice **7** learner, recruit **8** beginner, freshman, neophyte **9** fledgling, greenhorn **10** tenderfoot
off: 4 send **5** relay **7** forward **8** transmit
old ~: 3 ace, pro, vet **4** whiz **5** adept **6** expert, master, wizard **7** hotshot, veteran **8** virtuoso **10** specialist
on: 4 send **5** relay **7** forward **8** transmit
on ~: 4 here **5** ready, there **6** with us **7** present **9** available
one is dealt: 3 lot **4** life
on the other ~: 3 but, yet **4** else **5** if not **7** however **9** otherwise
out: 4 deal, dole, give, mete **5** allot, award, issue, spend **6** assign, bestow, divide, donate, ration **7** divvy up **8** disburse, dispense **10** contribute, distribute
out of ~: 5 rowdy **6** unruly, wanton **7** rampant **9** excessive, unbridled, unchecked
over: 3 pay **4** cede, drop, dump, give, pass, sell, shed **5** chuck, ditch, forgo, relay, waive, yield **6** forego, fork up, give up, render, resign, supply, turn in **7** abandon, commend, consign, cough up, deliver, drop off, entrust, forfeit, forsake, intrust, present **8** delegate, forswear, get rid of, jettison, part with, relegate, shell out, transfer, turn over **9** cast aside, dispose of, foreswear, surrender **10** relinquish
part: 4 palm **5** digit, thumb **6** finger
poker ~: 4 pair **5** flush **6** aces up **7** ace high, two pair **8** straight **9** full house **10** royal flush
pork belly, in ~: 6 actual
ranch ~: 5 groom **6** cowboy, drover **8** buckaroo, wrangler
right ~: 6 dexter
seek the ~ of: 3 woo **5** court **6** pursue
set one's ~ to: 4 sign
sleight of ~: 5 magic, trick **9** dexterity
starter: 3 cow, off **4** back, deal, dock, fore, free, long, over **5** first, short, stage, third, under **6** before, behind, second
stock on ~: 3 inv. **9** inventory
take a ~: 6 butt in, step in **7** barge in, mediate **9** intercede, intervene
take by the ~: 4 lead **5** guide, steer, usher **6** assist, direct, escort, lead in **7** bolster, conduct **9** encourage
throw in one's ~: 4 quit **5** yield **6** submit **7** concede **9** surrender
tip one's ~: 4 show, tell **6** expose, reveal **7** divulge, lay bare, lay open, uncover **8** disclose **9** make known
truck: 5 dolly **6** barrow
try one's ~: 5 essay **7** attempt, venture **9** have a go at, take a shot
up: 6 fetter **7** inhibit **8** encumber
upper ~: 4 edge **7** control, victory **9** advantage, authority, dominance
with an iron ~: 4 hard **6** firmly **7** harshly, roughly, sternly **8** severely, strictly **10** rigorously
wringer: 4 ruer
wringer word: 4 alas
hand __: 3 off, out **4** down, it to, over, tool **5** brake, drill, truck **6** letter, puppet, signal **7** grenade
hand __ fist: 4 over
hand-__: 4 feed, held, knit, ride, walk, wash **5** blown, carry **6** tailor **7** deliver, launder
__ hand: 3 dab, old, pat **4** deck, farm, free, glad, hour, iron, whip **5** cap in, field, hat in, hired, lend a, out of, right, sweep, upper **6** minute, second **7** helping
__-hand: 4 glad **5** first, hat-in
Hand: 6 Rollin **7** Learned
hand and __: 4 foot **5** glove
handbag: 4 tote **5** pouch, purse **6** clutch **8** carryall, reticule **10** pocketbook
like some ~s: 6 beaded
part: 5 strap
handball: 4 game **5** sport
need: 4 wall **5** glove
handbill: 5 flier, flyer **6** dodger **7** leaflet **8** brochure, circular **9** broadside, throwaway
handbook: 4 text **5** bible, guide **6** manual, primer **8** Baedeker **9** companion, directory, vade mecum **10** compendium
handcart: 6 barrow
handclasp: 4 grip **5** grasp, shake **7** squeeze
__-hand coordination: 3 eye
handcrafted: 8 homemade
hand-cream ingredient: 4 aloe
handcuff: 4 bind, bond, iron **5** chain, run in **6** fetter, hinder, impede, pinion, thwart **7** enchain, inhibit, manacle, shackle **8** restrain, restrict **9** frustrate
holder: 5 wrist
handcuffed: 8 helpless **9** powerless
handcuffs: 5 irons **6** chains **7** fetters **8** manacles, shackles, trammels **9** bracelets
__ handcuffs: 6 golden **7** Chinese
hand-dyed fabric: 5 batik **6** battik
handed
down: 10 bequeathed, hereditary
starter: 3 off **4** back, bare, even, iron, open
__-handed: 3 ham, red **4** free, hard, high, left, sure **5** clean, empty, heavy, light, right, short **6** single, steady
__-handedly: 4 high **6** single
Handel, George Frideric: 6 German **8** composer
work: Admeto
Alcina
Arianna
Atalanta
Berenice
Esther
Ezio
Hercules
Israel in Egypt
Jephtha
Joshua
Messiah
Nero
Orlando
Ottone
Rinaldo
Samson
Saul
Semele
Serse
Solomon
Susanna
Teseo
Theodora
Tolomeo
Water Music
Xerxes
__ Hand for the Little Lady: 4 A Big
handful: 3 few **4** lump, some **6** strong **7** several **10** scattering, smattering, sprinkling
a ~ of: 5 scant **6** meager, paltry **7** limited **8** one or two
maybe: 4 brat
more than a ~: 4 gobs, lots, many, much, tons **5** heaps, piles, scads **6** oodles, plenty, scores **7** copious, umpteen **8** abundant,

numerous 9 bountiful, multitude, thousands
Handful of Dust, A
author: Evelyn Waugh
handgun: 5 Luger 6 pistol 7 firearm 8 revolver
see also gun
Handi-__: 5 Wipes
handicap: 4 edge, odds 5 block, limit, minus, tie up 6 burden, fetter, hamper, hinder, hogtie, hurdle, impede, impost, points 7 barrier, inhibit, oppress, penalty, prevent 8 drawback, encumber, hold back, obstacle, penalize, restrain, restrict, weakness 9 advantage, detriment, hamstring, head start, hindrance, liability 10 impairment, impediment, incapacity, limitation
in boxing: 8 glass jaw
handicapper hangout: 3 OTB 5 track
handicraft: 4 work 10 production
gaudy ~: 6 kitsch
handicraftsman: 7 artisan 9 carpenter
handily: 4 neat 6 deftly, easily, nimbly 7 capably 8 adroitly, facilely, very well 10 swimmingly
hand in __: 5 glove
__ hand in: 5 have a
handiness: 5 skill 7 ability 9 dexterity, readiness 10 adroitness, cleverness, nimbleness, usefulness
Hand in Glove
author: Ngaio Marsh
Hand in My Pocket (1995 song)
artist: Alanis Morissette
Handi-Wipes, like: 5 moist
handiwork: 4 work 5 doing 7 product 8 creation
handkerchief
dance: 9 siciliano
material ~: 6 cotton, Madras
place: 5 purse 6 pocket
handle: 3 ear, ply, run, try, use 4 ansa, bail, feel, haft, half, hilt, hold, knob, meet, name, sell, take, tend, test, work 5 alias, carry, check, crank, field, grasp, guide, helve, see to, serve, stand, steer, stock, strap, title, touch, trade, treat, wield 6 byname, deal in, direct, employ, finger, govern, holder, jockey, manage, pick up, retail, tiller 7 command, conduct, control, examine, exploit, moniker, operate, preside, process, support, surname, survive, trade in, utilize, work out 8 cognomen, cope with, deal with, dominate, maneuver, monicker, nickname, receipts, regulate, stand for, transact 9 negotiate, officiate, sobriquet, supervise, traffic in 10 administer, manipulate, reckon with, take care of
an order: 4 fill, lade, load, pack 6 make up, supply 7 process, satisfy
archeologist's ~: 4 ansa
as questions: 5 field 7 reply to
badly: 5 abuse
capably: 5 wield
easy to ~: 3 yar 4 yare
ender: 3 bar
false ~: 5 alias 7 moniker, pen name 9 pseudonym, stage name 10 nom de plume
fly off the ~: 4 rage, rant, snap 5 freak, go ape
gently: 4 baby 6 caress
give a ~: 3 dub 4 name 8 christen
hard to ~: 5 bulky, spiny 7 awkward 10 cumbersome
having a ~: 5 eared 6 ansate
knife ~: 4 grip, haft, hilt
Latin words ~: 4 ansa
long ~: 5 shaft
problems: 4 cope
roughly: 3 paw 4 mall, maul 5 paw at 6 misuse 8 mistreat
starter: 3 man, mis, pan 5 stick
sword ~: 4 hilt
tool ~: 4 haft 5 helve, shaft, snath 6 snathe
word above a ~: 4 pull, push
__ Handle a Woman: 5 How to
__ handle on: 4 get a 5 have a
handler: 5 agent 8 promoter
starter: 3 pan 5 stick
__ handles: 4 love
handle with __: 4 care
handle with __ gloves: 3 kid
Handlin: 5 Oscar
handling: 3 use 5 usage 7 conduct, running 9 oversight, treatment 10 employment, management, regulation
rough ~: 5 abuse 6 misuse
hand-lotion ingredient: 4 aloe
__ Hand Luke: 4 Cool
Hand-Made Fables
author: George Ade
handmaiden: 6 female 7 servant 9 attendant
Handmaid's Tale, The
author: Margaret Atwood
__-hand man: 5 right
hand-me-down: 3 rag 4 used 6 reused 8 preowned
hand-me-downs: 4 togs 7 apparel, clothes, raiment, threads 8 garments
Hand of Bridge, A
composer: Samuel Barber
Hand of God, The
sculptor: Auguste Rodin
__ Hand of God, The: 4 Left
__ hand on: 4 lay a
hand-operated: 6 manual
handout: 3 tip 4 alms, dole, gift 5 flyer, grant 6 notice, tipoff 7 charity, freebee, freebie, present, release 8 brochure, bulletin, circular, pamphlet 9 broadside, publicity, throwaway 10 free sample, propaganda
seek a ~: 3 beg 5 cadge
hand over __: 4 fist
handpick: 4 cull, take 5 elect 6 choose, select 8 nominate 9 designate, single out
handpicked: 6 choice, select 9 preferred
handrail: 4 post 8 banister
ballet ~: 3 bar 5 barre
post: 5 newel
__ Hand Rose: 6 Second
hands: 4 crew, gang, help, team 5 corps, squad, staff, troop 6 outfit 7 company
can't lay one's ~ on: 8 misplace
clean ~: 7 probity 9 innocence
down: 5 by far 6 easily 8 for a fact, very well 9 no contest 10 absolutely, positively, swimmingly, undeniably
get one's ~ on: 3 get 4 find, grab, have 5 catch, seize, snare 6 collar, locate, obtain, snatch 7 acquire, possess, procure, receive 9 latch onto
good with one's ~: 6 adroit
it has ~ and a face: 5 clock, watch
join, as ~: 4 grip
laying on of ~: 8 blessing
move on one's ~ and knees: 4 inch 5 crawl, creep, slink, sneak, steal 7 clamber, slither, wriggle
putty in one's ~: 8 yielding 9 malleable, tractable
shake ~: 3 run 4 meet 5 agree, greet, reach 6 make up 7 receive
shake ~ on: 4 seal 5 close 6 clinch, settle 7 confirm 8 finalize
shaking ~: 6 custom, ritual 9 formality 10 convention
show of ~: 4 vote
sit on one's ~: 7 abstain
speak with one's ~: 4 sign
use one's ~: 4 mime, wave 6 beckon, signal 7 gesture 9 pantomime
wash one's ~ of: 6 disown 7 abandon, bail out, disavow, forsake 8 forswear, renounce 9 foreswear, repudiate
win ~ down: 5 sweep 7 conquer, prevail, succeed, triumph, trounce 8 blow away, dominate, vanquish, walk over
with ~ on hips: 6 akimbo
with ~ tied: 5 at bay 8 helpless 9 powerless
hands-__: 4 down
hands-__ policy: 3 off
__ hands: 5 clean, shake 6 change 7 dishpan
Hands (1998 song)
artist: Jewel
Hands Across the Sea
composer: John Philip Sousa
hands-free __: 5 phone
handshake: 4 grip 5 clasp 6 clench 7 welcome
__ handshake: 6 golden
handshaker: 5 toady 6 flunky, lackey, minion, yes man 7 flunkey 9 candidate, job-hunter, sycophant 10 politician
Hands off!: 3 hey
handsome: 4 cute, fair, fine, tidy 5 ample, bonny, hunky, large, sharp 6 bonnie, comely, dapper, lavish, lovely, pretty 7 elegant, liberal, sizable, stylish, winsome 8 abundant, adorable, alluring, becoming, clean-cut, fetching, generous, gorgeous, pleasing, princely, sizeable, striking, stunning, tasteful 9 beautiful, bounteous, bountiful, extensive, plentiful, ravishing, unsparing 10 attractive, munificent
dark and ~ companion: 4 tall
name meaning ~: 7 Kenneth
one: 4 hunk 6 Adonis, Apollo
Handsome __ handsome does: 4 is as
handsomely: 4 well 9 liberally 10 abundantly, generously
handsomeness: 5 charm 6 beauty, glamor 7 glamour 8 elegance 9 good looks
__ hands on deck!: 3 all
Hands to Heaven (1988 song)
artist: Breathe
Hand That Rocks the Cradle, The (1992 film)
cast: Ernie Hudson, Rebecca De Mornay, Annabella Sciorra
hand-to-__: 5 mouth
Hand to Hold on to (1982 song)
artist: John Cougar Mellencamp
handwrite: 3 pen 4 sign 8 inscribe 9 autograph
handwriting: 6 scrawl, script 7 writing 8 printing
feature: 5 slant
on the wall: 4 omen, sign 7 portent, warning
see the ~ on the wall: 7 predict
handwriting-on-the-wall book: 6 Daniel
handy: 4 able, deft, easy, near 5 adept, close, of use, ready, utile 6 adroit, expert, nearby, nimble, useful, wieldy 7 capable, close by, helpful, skilled 8 adjacent, dextrous, portable, prepared, skillful 9 available, dexterous, efficient, practical, versatile 10 accessible, beneficial, convenient, functional, proficient, time-saving
come in ~ for: 3 aid
ender: 3 man
to: 4 near
handy-__: 4 andy 5 dandy
Handy: 2 W.C.
Handycam maker: 4 Sony
handyman: 5 do-all 6 jobber 7 Mr. Fix-it 8 factotum
do a ~ job: 3 fix 6 repair 7 restore 8 renovate
need: 4 tool, vise 6 pliers, wrench
Handy Man (song)
artist: Jimmy Jones, James Taylor
handyman's __: 7 special
Hanes
competitor: 3 BVD 5 Leggs 6 Jockey
Haney: 5 Carol
Hanff: 6 Helene
hang: 3 sag 4 pend, stay, wait 5 drape, float, hover, pin up, swing 6 dangle, depend 7 festoon, suspend 8 levitate
about: 4 stay 6 dangle
a left: 4 turn
around: 4 bide, laze, loll, lurk, stay, wait 5 abide, haunt, tarry 6 dangle, dawdle, linger, loiter, lounge, remain 8 frequent 9 associate, socialize 10 hover about
around for: 5 await 6 expect
back: 3 lag 4 poke 5 trail 6 boggle, falter, loiter, shrink 8 hesitate
(by): 5 stand, stick
don't ~ onto: 4 lose
down: 3 lop, sag 5 droop, trail 6 dangle
ender: 3 dog, out, tag 4 nail, over
fire: 4 pend
five: 4 surf

get the ~ of: 3 see 4 know 5 learn 6 master
in: 3 try 4 last, stay, take 5 abide 6 be cool, endure 7 persist, sustain 8 continue 9 persevere, withstand
in the breeze: 3 air, dry 6 air-dry
it up: 4 quit, stop 6 finish, resign
let it all ~ out: 4 bare 6 reveal, unveil 7 divulge, lay bare 8 disclose, manifest 9 make known 10 make public
loose: 4 loll 5 relax
loosely: 3 lop 5 drape, droop
of it: 5 flair, knack, skill, trick 6 method 7 ability, faculty, know-how, mastery 8 facility 9 technique
on: 4 last 5 cling, pivot, stand 6 adhere, endure, linger 7 outlast, subsist 8 stand for 9 be patient 10 stick it out
(on): 4 rest 6 depend
one's hat: 4 live 5 dwell 6 locate, reside
on one's words: 6 listen
onto: 4 hold, keep, save 5 amass, cache, hoard, put by, store 6 garner, retain, save up 7 put away 8 maintain, put aside 10 accumulate
open: 4 gape, yawn
out: 3 mix 4 idle, laze, loaf, stay 5 haunt 6 linger, loiter, mingle, remain 7 consort, goof off 9 pal around, socialize 10 congregate, fraternize, wait around
out at: 5 haunt, visit 8 frequent 9 patronize
out one's shingle: 6 settle
out with: 3 mix 6 hobnob, mingle 9 socialize 10 fraternize
over: 4 loom 5 sling 8 threaten
(over): 4 arch
starter: 4 over 5 strap
suspended: 5 float, hover
ten: 4 surf
the lip: 4 mope, pout, sulk 5 brood
together: 4 ally 5 unite 6 cleave, cohere, hook up, pair up 7 combine, partner 8 assemble, coalesce 9 cooperate, integrate 10 close ranks, join forces
tough: 6 take it 7 persist 9 persevere, withstand
up: 4 clog, slow 5 block, spite, stimy, stymy 6 cut off, detain, hamper, hobble, hold up, impede, retard, shelve, stymie 7 ring off, set back 8 hold over, obstruct, restrict, slow down 9 frustrate, hamstring 10 bottleneck, disconnect
hang ___: 3 out, ten 4 back, fire, five, it up, on to, time 5 a left, loose, tough 6 around, glider 7 gliding
hang ___ balance: 5 in the
___ hang: 5 care a, give a
___-hang: 5 cliff
Hang ___ Index: 4 Seng
hang a ___: 4 left 5 right
hangar: 4 shed 6 garage 7 shelter
tenant: 3 jet 4 bird 5 blimp, plane
hangdog: 3 sad 4 blue, down, grim 5 mopey, woful 6 abject, broody, gloomy, woeful 7 doleful, forlorn 8 dejected, downcast 9 bummed-out, cheerless, depressed, long-faced, plaintive, sorrowful, woebegone 10 chapfallen, despondent, dispirited, melancholy
look: 4 pout
Hang 'em High (1968 film)
cast: Ed Begley, Clint Eastwood, Inger Stevens
Hang 'Em High (1968 song)
artist: Booker T. and the MGs
hanger
material: 4 wire 7 plastic
place: 6 closet
starter: 5 cliff, crape, paper, strap
support: 3 rod
___ hanger: 4 coat
hanger-on: 5 leech 6 fawner, jackal, lackey, sponge 7 lacquey, sponger 8 henchman, kowtower 9 sycophant
hangers-on: 5 suite 6 circle 7 coterie, retinue 8 groupies 9 entourage, following, retainers 10 attendants
hang glide: 4 soar
hang gliding: 5 sport
finished ~: 3 lit 4 alit
Hang in ___!: 5 there
hanging: 4 limp 5 baggy, loose, slack 6 droopy, floppy 7 drapery, flaccid, pendant, pendent, pending 8 overhead 9 pendulous, suspended
back: 3 shy 5 balky, chary 7 fearful 8 hesitant, wavering 9 reluctant, skeptical, tentative 10 wishy-washy
by a thread: 5 risky 6 unsafe 9 uncertain
fire: 6 put off 7 abeyant, delayed, pending 9 postponed, undecided, unsettled 10 in abeyance, up in the air
in the balance: 6 at risk
keep ~: 5 tease, worry 6 entice, lead on 7 torment 8 interest 9 fascinate, frustrate, tantalize, titillate
leave ~: 4 jilt, quit 6 desert, maroon 7 abandon, forsake
loose: 6 at ease 7 relaxed 8 carefree, composed, tranquil
loosely: 4 alop
on every word: 4 rapt
starter: 5 paper, strap
together: 5 sound
tough: 3 set 7 adamant 8 stalwart
wall ~: 5 arras, litho, pin-up, tapis 6 cobweb, sconce 8 tapestry
___ hanging: 4 wall
Hanging ___ of Babylon: 7 Gardens
Hanging Up (2000 film)
cast: Diane Keaton, Lisa Kudrow, Walter Matthau, Meg Ryan
director: Diane Keaton
hang in the ___: 7 balance
Hangin' Tough (1989 song)
artist: New Kids on the Block
hang-loose: 9 easygoing
Hangman, The
author: Pär Lagerkvist
Hang on!: 4 whoa
___ Hang On: 4 Let's
Hang on Sloopy (1965 song)
artist: McCoys
hangout: 3 bar, den 4 dive, nest, site, spot 5 haunt, joint, place 6 resort 7 purlieu 10 rendezvous
hangover: 6 clamor, uproar 7 anguish 8 distress 10 uneasiness
have a ~: 4 ache
remedy: 5 Bromo
hangs
where one ~ one's hat: 3 pad 4 home 5 house 7 lodging 8 domicile, dwelling 9 residence
___ Hangs High, The: 5 Noose
hang-tough: 5 stern 10 relentless
hang-up: 3 rub 4 snag 5 block, delay, hitch, mania, quirk, thing 6 phobia 7 complex, problem 8 fixation, obstacle 9 obsession 10 difficulty, impediment, inhibition
hank: 4 coil, knot, loop, roll 5 piece, skein, twist 6 length
Hank: 3 Iba 4 Snow 5 Aaron, Bauer 6 Azaria 7 Ballard, Ketcham, Locklin 8 Williams 9 Greenberg
hanker: 4 ache, itch, long, need, pine, sigh, want, wish 5 yearn 7 long for 8 languish, yearn for
for: 4 like, seek, want 5 covet, crave
hankering: 3 yen 4 ache, achy, itch, love, urge, want, will, wish 5 fancy, letch 6 desire, hunger, hungry, pining, thirst 7 craving, longing 8 appetite, yearning 9 adoration, affection 10 aspiration, attachment
Hanks: 3 Tom 5 Colin, Nancy
Hanks, Tom: 5 actor
film: Angels & Demons (2009)
Apollo 13 (1995)
Bachelor Party (1984)
Big (1988)
The Bonfire of the Vanities (1990)
The 'burbs (1989)
Cast Away (2000)
Catch Me if You Can (2002)
Charlie Wilson's War (2007)
The Da Vinci Code (2006)
Dragnet (1987)
Forrest Gump (1994, AA)
The Green Mile (1999)
Joe Versus the Volcano (1990)
The Ladykillers (2004)
A League of Their Own (1992)
The Man With One Red Shoe (1985)
The Money Pit (1986)
Nothing in Common (1986)
Philadelphia (1993, AA)
The Polar Express (2004)
Punchline (1988)
Road to Perdition (2002)
Saving Private Ryan (1998)
Sleepless in Seattle (1993)
Splash (1984)
Terminal (2004)
that thing you do! (1996)
Turner & Hooch (1989)
Volunteers (1985)
You've Got Mail (1998)
film (voice): Toy Story (1995)
spouse: Rita Wilson
TV: Bosom Buddies
hanky
place: 5 purse 6 pocket
use a ~: 4 wipe
hanky-panky: 5 antic, cheat, fraud 6 dupery 7 knavery 9 chicanery, dalliance, deception, fourberie 10 dishonesty, subterfuge, tomfoolery
Hanky Panky (song)
artist: Madonna, Tommy James and the Shondells
Hanna: 4 Mark 7 William
Hanna-Barbera dog: 5 Astro
Hannah: 4 Page 5 Adams, Daryl, Moore 6 Arendt, Glasse
like ~'s heart: 4 hard
son: 6 Samuel
Hannah and Her Sisters (1986 film)
cast: Woody Allen, Michael Caine, Mia Farrow, Carrie Fisher, Barbara Hershey, Lloyd Nolan, Maureen O'Sullivan, Daniel Stern, Max von Sydow, Dianne Wiest
director: Woody Allen
Hannah, Daryl: 7 actress
film: Legal Eagles (1986)
The Pope of Greenwich Village (1984)
The Real Blonde (1998)
Roxanne (1987)
Splash (1984)
Steel Magnolias (1989)
A Walk to Remember (2002)
Wall Street (1987)
Wildflowers (1999)
Hannibal: 6 Hamlin, Lecter
crossed them: 4 Alps
where ~ was defeated: 4 Zama
Hannibal (2001 film)
cast: Giancarlo Giannini, Anthony Hopkins, Ray Liotta, Julianne Moore
director: Ridley Scott
Hannigan: 6 Alyson
Hannigan, Miss charge: 5 Annie
Hanoi: 4 city, town 7 capital
Hilton resident: 3 POW
locale: 7 Vietnam
New Year in ~: 3 Tet
Hanover: 4 city, town
athletes: 8 Big Green
locale: 7 Germany
school: 9 Dartmouth
___ Hanover: 4 Bret
Hans: 3 Arp 4 Blix, Graf 5 Bethe, Henze, Krebs, Sachs 6 Geiger 7 Brinker, Conried, Dehmelt, Driesch, Fischer, Holbein, Memling, Oersted, Spemann
in English: 4 John
see also German
Hans ___ Bülow: 3 von
Hansberry, Lorraine: 6 writer
work: A Raisin in the Sun
To Be Young, Gifted and Black
Hans Brinker
author: Mary Mapes Dodge
Hans Christian Andersen (1952 film)
cast: Danny Kaye
director: Charles Vidor
role: 4 Doro, Otto 5 Niels
Hanseatic League
member: 4 Hamm 5 Halle 6 Lubeck
Hansel
see German
Hansel and Gretel: 5 opera
need: 4 oven
setting: 6 forest
Hansel & Gretel & Ted & Alice
composer: PDQ Bach

Hänsel und Gretel: **5** opera
Hansen: **5** Liane, Patti
hansom: **3** cab
relative: **6** chaise
Hanson: **4** Lars **6** Curtis, Howard
members: Isaac, Taylor, Zac
song: I Will Come to You (1997) MMMBop (1997)
Hans von __: **5** Bülow
Hants: **6** county
locale: **7** England
Hanukkah
month: **6** Kislev
need: **7** menorah
pancake: **5** latke
prayer: **6** Hallel
top: **7** dreidel
Hanya: **4** Holm
haole: **7** tourist **8** Hawaiian
gift for a ~: **3** lei
greeting: **5** aloha
hap: **3** lot **4** luck **6** chance **7** fortune **8** accident **10** occurrence
ender: **6** hazard
starter: **3** may
__ Hap-Hap-Happy Day: **4** It's a
haphazard: **5** loose **6** casual, chance, random **7** aimless, cursory, erratic, offhand **8** careless, pell-mell, reckless, slapdash, slipshod **9** arbitrary, desultory, hit-or-miss, irregular, vagarious **10** accidental, contingent, designless, disorderly, fortuitous, incidental, nonuniform, unexpected, unintended, unthinking, unthorough, willy-nilly
haphazardly: **6** anyhow **8** at random, by chance, pell-mell **9** any old way
hapless: **5** curst, hexed, sorry, woful **6** cursed, jinxed, tragic, woeful **7** unblest, unlucky **8** ill-fated, luckless, tragical, wretched **9** miserable, unblessed, unfavored **10** ill-starred
one: **5** schmo **6** schmoe
happen: **2** go **4** come, fall, go on **5** arise, break, ensue, occur, pop up **6** appear, arrive, befall, betide, crop up, follow, pan out, result **7** come off, develop, proceed, turn out, work out **8** come over, come to be, come true **9** come about, eventuate, intervene, take place, transpire **10** come to pass, take effect
about to ~: **6** at hand, coming **7** in store, pending **8** imminent
again: **5** recur **6** repeat, return
be about to ~: **4** loom **6** impend
bound to ~: **4** sure **7** certain, cinched **8** definite, in the bag, positive **10** guaranteed, inevitable
cause to ~: **4** spur **5** incur, spark **6** incite, prompt, set off **7** produce, trigger **8** generate, motivate, touch off **9** stimulate **10** bring about
ender: **6** chance, stance
let ~: **5** allow **6** permit **8** sanction, tolerate
let it ~: **6** give in, give up, relent **7** back off **9** acquiesce **10** capitulate
make ~: **5** cause **7** realize **8** occasion **10** bring about, effectuate
next: **5** ensue **6** follow
to: **6** befall, betide **7** betides **8** come over
upon: **4** find, meet **6** locate, strike **7** run into, stumble **8** bump into **9** encounter **10** come across
with: **9** accompany
__ happened was ...: **4** What
happening: **4** case **5** afoot, event, faddy, scene, thing **6** action, actual, affair, modish **7** episode **8** accident, incident, occasion, underway **9** adventure, milestone **10** enterprise, experience, in progress, occurrence, phenomenon, proceeding
after: **5** later
chance ~: **5** fluke, quirk **8** accident, fortuity
dreadful ~: **4** blow **7** tragedy **8** calamity, disaster **10** misfortune
keep from ~: **4** foil **5** avert, block **6** stifle, stymie, thwart **7** fend off, forfend, head off, hold off, prevent, ward off **8** hold back, obstruct, stave off **9** forestall, interrupt
now: **4** live **7** current, running
sudden ~: **5** burst **7** flare-up **8** outbreak
what's ~: **6** action **8** activity
__ happening?: **5** What's
happenings: **6** doings, events **8** business, goings-on
Happenings
song: I Got Rhythm (1967) See You in September (1966)
Happening, The (1967 song)
artist: Supremes
__ happens: **4** as it
happenstance: **4** luck **5** fluke **6** chance **8** accident, fortuity
__ happen to you...: **5** It can
Happiest Day, The
author: Edgar Allan Poe
Happiest Girl in the Whole U.S.A., The (1972 song)
artist: Donna Fargo
happify: **5** cheer, elate **6** thrill **7** delight, gladden, hearten
happily: **4** well **6** gladly **7** luckily, with joy **9** agreeably, willingly **10** swimmingly
...happily __ after: **4** ever
happiness: **3** joy **4** glee, life, luck, play, weal **5** bliss, cheer, mirth **6** gaiety, gayety, heaven, utopia **7** comfort, delight, ecstasy, elation, emotion, gayness, rapture, success, triumph, welfare **8** euphoria, felicity, gladness, good luck, hilarity, optimism, pleasure, radiance, radiancy **9** beatitude, enjoyment, festivity, geniality, good cheer, good humor, jocundity, joviality, merriment, rejoicing, well-being **10** cheeriness, ebullience, exuberance, exultation, jubilation, prosperity
fill with ~: **5** elate
name meaning ~: **7** Gwyneth
name meaning ~ bringer: **8** Beatrice
paradigm of ~: **4** clam
sound of ~: **2** ah
Happiness __ Warm Puppy: **3** Is a
happy: **3** apt, fun, gay **4** gaga, glad, high, warm, well **5** aglow, blest, jolly, lucky, merry, perky, ready, riant, sunny, tipsy **6** blithe, bright, cheery, chirpy, elated, festal, genial, golden, jovial, joyful, joyous, lively, timely, upbeat **7** beaming, blessed, buoyant, chipper, content, festive, fitting, gleeful, glowing, halcyon, jocular, playful, pleased, radiant, tickled **8** blissful, carefree, cheerful, ecstatic, euphoric, exultant, giggling, gladsome, grooving, jubilant, laughing, mirthful, sanguine, suitable, thrilled **9** contented, convivial, delighted, delirious, favorable, fortunate, gladdened, gratified, lightsome, opportune, overjoyed, promising, rejoicing, satisfied, vivacious, well-timed **10** accidental, convenient, felicitous, flying high, nonchalant, optimistic, propitious, rollicking, successful, triumphant
days: **5** toast **6** kampai
feel ~: **4** live **5** enjoy, exult, glory, revel **7** delight, rejoice, triumph **8** jubilate **9** celebrate, make merry, walk on air **10** effervesce
feeling: **3** joy **4** glee **5** bliss, cheer, mirth **6** gaiety **7** delight, ecstasy, elation, jollity **8** euphoria, gladness **9** merriment **10** exultation, joyfulness, joyousness, jubilation
hour: **7** respite
hour establishment: **3** pub **6** saloon, tavern **7** taproom **8** alehouse, taphouse
hunting ground: **6** heaven, utopia **7** Arcadia, Elysium **8** paradise **9** Shangri-la
look ~: **4** grin **5** smile
make ~: **5** cheer, elate **6** please **7** beatify, gladden, gratify, sweeten **8** brighten **10** exhilarate
medium: **7** balance **8** midpoint **10** compromise
name meaning ~: **3** Ida **5** Felix **7** Felicia
name meaning ~ friend: **5** Edwin **6** Edwina
name meaning ~ guardian: **6** Edward
name meaning ~ hall: **5** Edsel
name meaning ~ protection: **6** Edmond, Edmund
name meaning ~ spear: **5** Edgar
name meaning ~ war: **5** Edith **6** Edythe
not ~: **3** sad **4** blue **5** upset
sound: **2** ah **5** chirp
starter: **4** slap
happy __: **4** hour **6** camper, ending **7** warrior
happy __ clam: **3** as a
happy __ ground: **7** hunting
happy __ lark: **3** as a
__-happy: **7** trigger
Happy: **5** dwarf **8** Chandler
colleague: *see* dwarf
Happy (1972 song)
artist: Rolling Stones
Happy __: **4** Days, Meal, Talk **6** Trails
Happy __ Are Here Again: **4** Days
Happy, __: **5** Texas
__ Happy: **3** Get **4** Girl, Love
happy as __: **5** a clam, a lark
Happy Birthday
writer: **4** icer
Happy Birthday __: **5** to You
Happy Birthday, Sweet Sixteen (1961 song)
artist: Neil Sedaka
Happy Days (ABC sitcom)
cast: Tom Bosley (Howard Cunningham)
Ron Howard (Richie Cunningham)
Erin Moran (Joanie Cunningham)
Donny Most (Ralph Malph)
Pat Morita (Arnold)
Marion Ross (Marion Cunningham)
Anson Williams (Potsie Weber)
Henry Winkler (Arthur 'Fonz' Fonzarelli)
catchphrase: Sit on it
dog: **6** Spunky
hangout: Arnold's
setting: Milwaukee
Happy Days Are Here Again
composer: Milton Ager
Happy Feet
composer: Milton Ager
Happy Feet (2006 film)
voice cast: Hugh Jackman, Nicole Kidman, Brittany Murphy, Robin Williams, Elijah Wood
__ Happy Fella, The: **4** Most
happy-go-lucky: **5** merry **6** blithe, casual **8** carefree, cheerful
Happy Hollisters
cat: **9** White Nose
dog: **3** Zip
Happy Hooligan: **5** comic **10** comic strip
cartoonist: **5** Opper
dog: **4** Flip
happy hour: **6** recess
charge: **6** bar tab
establishment: **3** bar
order: **3** ale **4** beer, wine **5** drink, lager
perch: **5** stool
happy hunting __: **6** ground
Happy New __: **4** Year
Happy Organ, The (1959 song)
artist: Dave Cortez
Happy Prince and Other Tales, The
author: Oscar Wilde
__ happy returns: **4** many
Happy Talk
composer: Oscar Hammerstein, Richard Rodgers
Happy Together (1967 song)
artist: Turtles
Happy Trails
artist: Dale Evans, Roy Rogers
Happy Warrior, The: Al Smith
Hapsburg
see German
hara-__: **4** kiri
Harald III, city founded by: **4** Oslo
Harald, King father: **4** Olaf, Olav
harangue: **3** nag **4** rant, rave, talk **5** orate, spiel, spout **6** berate, exhort, preach, rail at, rant at, raving, screed, sermon, speech, tirade **7** chew out, declaim, inveigh, lecture, monolog, oration, ranting, venting **8** bloviate, diatribe,

jeremiad, perorate, spouting **9** discourse, go on about, hold forth, monologue, philippic **10** peroration, vocalizing
Harare: 4 city, town **7** capital
locale: 8 Zimbabwe
harass: 3 bug, dog, irk, nag, ply, rag, try, vex **4** bait, fret, gall, goad, pain, ride, roil, tire **5** annoy, bedog, beset, bully, chafe, get on, grind, harry, hit on, hound, nag at, press, spite, taunt, tease, upset, weary, worry **6** accost, badger, bother, hassle, heckle, hector, maraud, needle, nettle, noodge, pester, pick on, plague, pother, pursue, put out, rankle, rattle, ruffle **7** afflict, bedevil, besiege, bombard, disturb, henpeck, oppress, rip into, torment, trouble **8** aggrieve, browbeat, disquiet, distress, irritate **9** beleaguer, importune, persecute **10** discompose, intimidate
harasser: 4 pest **6** nudnik
harassment: 8 hounding **9** annoyance, badgering, bothering, pestering, provoking **10** difficulty, irritation
Harbach: 4 Otto
Harbin: 4 city, town
locale: 5 China
harbinger: 4 omen, sign **5** augur **6** augury, herald, leader, signal **7** portent, presage **9** foretoken, messenger, precursor, predictor **10** forerunner, indication
harbinger of __: 6 spring
harbor: 3 bay **4** bear, cove, dock, hide, hold, pier, port **5** basin, berth, board, cover, haven, house, jetty, lodge, put up, wharf **6** asylum, marina, refuge, resort, secure, shield **7** conceal, domicil, landing, lodging, mooring, protect, quarter, retreat, seaport, secrete, shelter **8** domicile **9** anchorage, entertain, safeguard, sanctuary **10** protection
city: 2 pt. **3** spt. **4** port **7** seaport
ender: 3 age **6** master
enter a ~: 4 dock **5** put in
expert: 5 pilot
locale: 4 cove, dock, pier **5** inlet, jetty
machine: 6 dredge
out of the ~: 4 asea **5** at sea
sound: 4 toot
vessel: 3 hoy, tow, tug **4** boat, scow **5** barge, ferry **7** tugboat
harbor __: 4 seal **6** master
__ harbor: 3 air **4** safe
Harbor __: 6 Lights
__ Harbor: 3 Bar, Sag **5** Pearl
harborage: 5 haven **6** refuge **7** shelter **9** anchorage, sanctuary
Harbor Lights (1959 song)
artist: Platters
__ Harbour, FL: 3 Bal
Harburg: 2 E.Y. **3** Yip
hard: 4 firm, iron, mean **5** bossy, cruel, dense, hairy, heavy, madly, picky, rigid, rocky, rough, solid, stale, stern, stiff, stony, thick, tough **6** avidly, bitter, brutal, firmly, flinty, keenly, knotty, packed, rugged, severe, steely, stoney, strict, strong, thorny, tiring, trying, unjust, unkind, uphill **7** arduous, austere, callous, eagerly, harshly, heavily, hostile, intense, labored, onerous, operose, painful, roughly, serious, sharply, Spartan, toilful, wearing **8** ardently, bitterly, brutally, concrete, despotic, doggedly, exacting, fiercely, forcibly, granitic, grinding, grueling, indurate, intently, leathery, pitiless, puzzling, resolute, rigorous, rocklike, ruthless, savagely, severely, strongly, stubborn, terrible, tiresome, toilsome, urgently, vigorous, wearying **9** alcoholic, ambitious, arduously, austerely, compacted, demanding, difficult, draconian, earnestly, fatiguing, fermented, furiously, herculean, insensate, insoluble, intensely, laborious, merciless, obstinate, onerously, painfully, realistic, recondite, seriously, stonelike, strenuous, stringent, unbending, unfeeling, unpitying, unpliable, unsparing, viciously, violently, zealously **10** adamantine, burdensome, compressed, despotical, diligently, exhausting, formidable, gruelingly, impervious, inflexible, iron-fisted, no-nonsense, oppressive, perplexing, pitilessly, powerfully, relentless, rigorously, ruthlessly, sedulously, solidified, studiously, thoroughly, tyrannical, unmerciful, unpleasant, untiringly, unyielding, vehemently, vigorously
and fast: 3 set
as nails: 5 rigid, tough **6** steely, strong **9** unbending
as rock: 7 lithoid **9** lithoidal
blow: 4 gale, gust **5** blast, storm **6** squall **7** cyclone, tempest **9** windstorm
breathe ~: 4 gasp, pant, puff **5** heave
by: 4 near, next, nigh **5** close
candy: 4 drop **5** charm, lolly
case: 4 hull, husk, thug **5** shell **8** carapace **10** integument
cash: 4 gelt, loot **5** bread, bucks, dough, funds, money, moola **6** dinero, moolah **7** capital, dollars, lettuce, scratch **8** bankroll, currency, smackers **9** banknotes, simoleons **10** green stuff
combining form: 5 scler- **6** sclera-, sclero-
come down ~: 4 pour, rain, teem
come down ~ on: 6 punish **8** admonish
don't work very ~: 4 laze **7** goof off **8** slack off
ender: 3 hat, pan, top **4** back, ball, core, edge, hack, head, line, news, tack, ware, wire, wood **5** board, bound, cover, heads, stand **6** headed **7** hearted **8** scrabble
feelings: 5 anger **6** grudge, hatred **7** offense
get the ~ way: 3 pry **5** wrest, wring **6** extort, wrench
give a ~ time: 6 hassle
give a ~ time to: 3 irk, nag, vex **5** tease, upset **6** harass **7** torment
hat: 5 labor **6** helmet
have ~ feelings: 6 resent
hit: 4 blow, slap
hit ~: 4 belt, slam, slug, wham **5** paste, smack, smite, whack, whomp
knocks: 3 woe **7** bad luck, travail, trouble **9** adversity, mischance, tough luck **10** misfortune
labor: 4 toil **5** sweat **7** travail **8** drudgery, exertion
look ~: 4 gape, gawk, gaze, peer **5** focus, glare, rivet, stare **7** eyeball
luck: 6 mishap **7** setback, trouble **8** bad break, calamity **9** adversity, mischance, suffering **10** misfortune
not ~: 4 easy, soft **5** mushy **6** cuddly, fleecy, fluffy, simple, spongy, supple **7** no sweat, pliable, snuggly, squishy **8** cushiony, no bother, painless **9** no problem, no trouble **10** child's play, effortless, unexacting
not yet ~: 5 unset
one working ~: 5 plier, plyer
playing ~: 7 serious
pull ~: 3 tug **4** jerk, yank **5** pluck **6** wrench
put: 8 strained
question: 5 poser **6** enigma, puzzle, riddle, teaser **7** problem, stumper **9** conundrum
requiring ~ labor: 7 arduous, onerous **8** grueling **9** strenuous **10** exhausting, oppressive
sell: 5 spiel **6** patter **8** cajolery **10** persuasion
starter: 3 die **4** blow
stuff: 4 rock **5** metal, sauce **6** liquor, whisky **7** alcohol, spirits, whiskey **9** inebriant
take it ~: 3 cry, sob **4** bawl, howl, keen, moan, mope, wail, weep **5** brood, mourn **6** bemoan, bewail, grieve, lament
think ~: 5 focus **6** fixate
time: 6 hassle, ordeal, rebuff, rebuke **8** distress **9** rejection **10** upbraiding
times: 3 woe **5** slump **9** adversity, recession **10** depression, woefulness
to find: 4 rare **6** exotic, scanty, scarce **8** uncommon
to get to: 3 dim **4** dull, slow **5** thick **6** obtuse, simple, stolid **9** pigheaded
to please: 5 fussy, picky **6** choosy **7** choosey, finicky **8** finiking, finnicky **9** querulous
to see: 3 dim **4** hazy **5** faint, fuzzy, murky, muzzy, vague **6** bleary, blurry, far-off, opaque **7** blurred, clouded, muddled, obscure, shadowy, unclear **8** nebulous **10** indistinct
to understand: 4 mazy **5** tough **6** knotty, opaque, sticky, thorny, tricky **7** complex, obscure, unclear **8** abstruse, baffling, puzzling **9** difficult, intricate **10** formidable, mystifying, perplexing
to use: 7 awkward **8** affected, unwieldy **9** ponderous **10** cumbersome
up: 4 poor **5** broke, needy **6** bad off, ill off, in need, in want **7** pinched **8** badly off, bankrupt, beggarly, indigent, strapped **9** desperate, destitute, insolvent, moneyless, penniless, penurious **10** down and out, pauperized, straitened
work: 4 moil, toil **5** grind, sweat **7** travail **8** drudgery, exertion, industry **10** punishment
work ~: 4 moil, push, slog, toil **5** exert, labor, slave **6** drudge, hustle, strain **9** persevere
worker: 4 doer **5** demon, grind, plier, plyer **6** dynamo **7** hustler
hard __: 3 bop, hat, put **4** case, cash, coal, copy, core, disk, head, line, news, rock, sell, sign, time **5** candy, cider, court, drive, goods, labor, stuff, water, wheat **6** cheese, palate, rubber **7** landing, science
hard __ rock: 3 as a
hard __ to crack: 3 nut
hard __ to hoe: 3 row
hard-__: 3 hat, put, set **4** bill, boil, laid, nose, spun **5** asset, edged, knock, liner, nosed, shell, wired **6** bitten, boiled, fisted, handed **7** hitting, pressed
hard-__ clam: 5 shell
hard-__ crab: 5 shell
__-hard: 3 die **4** blow
Hard __: 4 Rain **5** Times, to Get, to Say
Hard __!: 4 alee **5** aport
Hard __ Cafe: 4 Rock
Hard __ Night, A: 4 Day's
hard-and-fast: 6 strict **7** binding **8** exacting **9** stringent, unbending **10** unyielding
hard-and-fast __: 4 rule
hard as __: 5 a rock, nails
hardback: 4 book
__ hardball: 4 play
Hardball broadcaster: 5 MSNBC
hard-bitten: 4 firm **5** balky, rigid, sober, stern, stony, tough **6** dogged, mulish, ornery **7** adamant **8** contrary, hellbent, indurate, obdurate, resolute, stubborn **9** immovable, obstinate, pigheaded, practical, pragmatic, steadfast, tenacious, unbending **10** bullheaded, inflexible, unromantic, unshakable
hard-boiled: 5 harsh, stern, tough **7** callous **9** heartless, practical, pragmatic, realistic **10** determined, iron-willed, unromantic
Hard Candy
author: Tennessee Williams
Hard Cash
author: Charles Reade
hard cider: 5 drink **8** beverage
hard-copy creator: 3 ptr. **7** printer
hard-core: 5 stern **8** faithful **10** unyielding
hardcover: 4 book
part: 5 spine
Hard Day's Night A: 4 film, song
artist: Beatles
cast: George Harrison, John Lennon, Paul McCartney, Ringo Starr
director: Richard Lester

hard-driving: **5** type A **6** virile **8** vigorous
not ~: **5** type B
har-de-har-har: **5** laugh
harden: **3** dry, fix, gel, set **4** cake, clot, firm, gird, jell, tone **5** adapt, build, enure, inure, set in, shore, steel, train **6** adjust, anneal, beef up, cement, curdle, firm up, freeze, gelate, ossify, prop up, season, settle, temper, tone up **7** bolster, brace up, build up, burgeon, calcify, coarsen, congeal, develop, empower, enhance, fortify, petrify, shore up, stiffen, thicken, tighten, toughen, vitrify **8** accustom, bourgeon, buttress, energize, indurate, solidify, vitalize **9** acclimate, coagulate, habituate, intensify, reinforce, vulcanize **10** amalgamate, invigorate, strengthen
(to): **5** enure, inure
hardened: **3** old, set **4** cold, firm, numb **5** cruel, set in, stiff, stony, tough **6** steely, stoney **7** callous **8** indurate, leathery, obdurate, uncaring **9** impassive, impliable, insensate, obstinate, unbending, unfeeling, unpliable **10** inveterate
starter: **4** case
Harden, Marcia Gay Oscar: Pollock
__ Harder: **5** We Try
Harder They Fall, The (1956 film)
cast: Humphrey Bogart, Rod Steiger
Hard Habit to Break (1984 song)
artist: Chicago
hardhack: **5** shrub
relative: *see* rose family plant
hardheaded: **5** stern, stiff **8** stubborn **9** impliable, practical, pragmatic **10** hard-bitten, iron-willed
Hard Headed Woman (1958 song)
artist: Elvis Presley
hardhearted: **4** cold, mean **5** cruel, stern, stony **6** stoney, unkind **7** brutish, callous, inhuman **8** obdurate, pitiless, ruthless, uncaring **9** merciless, unfeeling
Hard Hearted Hannah
composer: Milton Ager
hardihood: **5** valor **7** prowess **9** fortitude **10** confidence
Hardin: **2** Ty
hardiness: **3** vim **4** dint, grit, thew, will **5** brawn, force, might, power, thews, valor, vigor **6** energy, health, muscle **7** bravery, courage, fitness, muscles, potence, potency, stamina **8** audacity, boldness, strength, tenacity, vitality **9** endurance, fortitude, puissance, tolerance **10** brute force, resolution, robustness
Harding: **3** Ann **5** Tonya **6** Warren **8** Florence
Harding, Warren G.: **9** president
former occupation: **9** publisher
home: **4** Ohio **6** Marion
middle name: **8** Gamaliel
opponent: **3** Cox **4** Debs
V.P.: **8** Coolidge
wife: **8** Florence
Hardison: **6** Kadeem
hard-line: **4** firm **5** bossy, cruel, picky, rigid, stern, tough **6** severe **7** austere, Spartan **8** despotic, exacting, orthodox, rigorous **9** demanding, draconian, stringent, unbending, unsparing **10** despotical, inflexible, iron-fisted, iron-willed, no-nonsense, oppressive, tyrannical, unyielding
hardliner: **4** hawk
Hard Lines
poet: Ogden Nash
hard-luck guy: **5** patsy
hardly: **4** just, only **6** adverb, barely, little, seldom **7** faintly, not a bit, not much, scantly **8** not at all, not often, scarcely, slightly **9** by no means, not likely
hardly __: **4** ever
Hardly __ is now alive...: **4** a man
__ hardly wait!: **4** I can
hardness: **5** rigor **7** density **8** firmness, iron hand, rigidity **9** harshness, stiffness, toughness **10** difficulty, inclemency, strictness
epitome of ~: **5** nails
of heart: **5** odium **6** animus, enmity, hatred, rancor **7** ill will **8** acrimony **9** animosity **10** antagonism, resentment
hard-nosed: **4** mean **5** harsh, stern, tough **6** mulish, severe, strong, wilful **7** adamant, willful **8** resolute, stubborn **9** immovable **10** headstrong, iron-willed, unyielding
not ~: **3** lax
hard nut to __: **5** crack
hard-packed: **4** firm **5** dense, solid, thick, tight **6** jammed **7** compact, crammed, crowded **9** condensed **10** compressed
hard-place
alternative: **4** rock
hard-pressed: **7** harried **8** burdened, harassed **9** oppressed, pressured **10** overloaded
Hard Rain (1998 film)
cast: Minnie Driver, Morgan Freeman, Randy Quaid, Christian Slater
Hard Road to Glory, A
author: Arthur Ashe
Hard Rock __: **4** Cafe
hard row __: **5** to hoe
hard-set: **4** firm **5** rigid, stern, stiff, tough **6** flinty, mulish, steely, strict **7** adamant **8** immobile, indurate, obdurate, resolute, stubborn **9** immovable, obstinate, pigheaded, steadfast, stringent, unbending **10** bullheaded, implacable, inflexible, unyielding
hard-shell: **4** clam, crab **5** stern **9** confirmed **10** headstrong
hard-shelled: **5** stern, stout, tough **6** feisty, robust, steely, strict, strong **7** adamant, callous, staunch **8** obdurate, resolute, rigorous, stubborn **9** merciless, obstinate, resilient, resistant, stringent, tenacious, unbending **10** courageous, formidable, pugnacious
hardship: **3** woe **4** care, toil **5** grief, rigor, trial **6** burden, misery, mishap, sorrow, strait **7** poverty, tragedy, travail, trouble **8** calamity, disaster, distress, drudgery, exigence, exigency, obstacle **9** adversity, austerity, grievance, privation, suffering **10** affliction, difficulty, discomfort, ill fortune, infelicity, misfortune, oppression
face ~: **4** cope
__ hard times: **6** fall on
Hard Times
author: Charles Dickens
Hard to Kill (1990 film)
cast: Kelly LeBrock, Steven Seagal
hardtop: **3** car **4** auto **5** sedan **10** automobile
Hard to Say (1981 song)
artist: Dan Fogelberg
Hard to Say I'm Sorry (song)
artist: Az Yet, Peter Cetera, Chicago
hardware: **3** PCs **5** metal, tools **8** fittings, fixtures, plumbing, printers, trinkets **9** computers, fasteners **10** implements
install new ~: **5** refit
item: **3** awl, nut **4** bolt, nail, tack, T-nut **5** screw, t bolt, U-bolt
hardware __: **5** store
__ Hardware: **3** Ace
Hardwicke: Cedric: **3** Sir **5** actor
hard-won: **5** rough, tough **6** thorny, trying, uphill **7** arduous **8** exacting, grueling, toilsome **9** difficult, effortful, laborious **10** exhausting
hardwood: **3** ash, elm, oak **4** poon, teak, tree **5** cedar, ebony, larch, lehua, maple **6** jarrah, locust, timber, wandoo **7** wallaba **8** mahogany
block: **5** rabot
Hawaiian ~: **4** ohia **5** lehua
hard-working: **4** busy, spry **5** astir, perky **6** active, lively **7** dynamic, working **8** animated, bustling, diligent, sedulous, studious, tireless **9** assiduous, dedicated, energetic, motivated, sprightly
hardy: **3** fit **4** able, game, hale, iron, well, wiry **5** beefy, burly, fresh, hefty, hunky, husky, lusty, right, solid, sound, stout, tough **6** brawny, gritty, hearty, mighty, potent, robust, rugged, sinewy, steely, stocky, strong, sturdy, virile **7** capable, doughty, healthy, staunch **8** athletic, forceful, indurate, muscular, powerful, puissant, seasoned, stalwart, vigorous **9** Atlantean, energetic, Herculean, in the pink, resilient, strapping, tenacious, well-built **10** able-bodied, courageous, iron-willed, red-blooded, unflagging
starter: **4** fool
Hardy: **3** Joe **4** Andy **5** Ollie **6** Oliver, Thomas **9** Alexandre
partner: **6** Laurel
Hardy __: **4** Boys
Hardy Boys
character: **4** Chet
Hardy's
rival: *see* restaurant chain
Hardy, Thomas: **4** poet **6** writer **7** British
setting: Wessex
villain: **4** Alec
work: The Dynasts
Far From the Madding Crowd
Jude the Obscure
The Mayor of Casterbridge
The Return of the Native
Tess of the d'Urbervilles
The Woodlanders
hare: **3** hie **4** cony **5** coney, speed **6** animal, malkin, mammal, mawkin **7** leveret **9** lagomorph
and hounds: **4** game
combining form: **3** lag- **4** lago-
ender: **4** bell **7** brained
female: **3** doe
like a March ~: **3** mad
male: **4** buck
name meaning ~: **4** Haas
tail: **4** scut
to hounds: **4** prey
young: **7** leveret
__ hare: **5** March
Hare
constellation: **5** Lepus
Hare __: **7** Krishna
hare and hounds: **4** game
harebell: **5** plant **6** flower
harebrain
see ninny
harebrained
see foolish
harefooted: **4** fast **5** fleet, quick, rapid **6** snappy, speedy
Hare Krishna
offering: **5** chant
harem: **6** zenana **7** odalisk **8** seraglio **9** odalisque
jewelry: **6** anklet
members: **5** wives
one with a ~: **5** sheik **6** shaikh, sheikh
room: **3** oda **4** odah
harem __: **5** pants
Hargitay: **6** Mickey **7** Mariska
har-har: **5** comic, droll, funny **7** amusing, comical, risible **8** humorous **9** hilarious, laughable, ludicrous
Hari: **4** Mata **6** Rhodes
haricot: **4** bean, stew **6** legume, veggie **9** vegetable
haricot bean: **6** veggie **9** vegetable
Haring: **5** Keith
hark: **4** hear, heed **6** attend, listen **9** bend an ear **10** give head to
back: **6** recall **8** look back **9** recollect, reminisce
harkening
name meaning ~: **6** Simeon
Harkin: **3** Tom
Hark, the Herald Angels Sing: **4** noel **5** carol
Harlan: **4** John **7** Ellison
Harland: **7** Sanders
Harlem: **5** river
locale: **3** NYC **7** New York
theater: **6** Apollo
__ Harlem: **7** Spanish
Harlem Shuffle (1986 song)
artist: Rolling Stones
harlequin: **4** duck, fool, zany **5** clown **6** jester, motley **7** buffoon, pierrot **10** motley fool
ender: **3** ade
Harlequin __: **7** Romance
Harlequin's Carnival, The
painter: Joan Miró
Harley: **3** hog **4** bike **5** cycle **10** motorcycle
alternative: **5** Honda **6** Yamaha **8** Kawasaki
partner: **8** Davidson
Harline: **5** Leigh

Harlingen: **4** city, town
locale: **5** Texas
Harlin, Renny: **8** director
spouse: Geena Davis
Harlow: **4** Jean **6** Shalom
Harlow, Jean: **6** blonde **7** actress
film: Bombshell (1933)
China Seas (1935)
Dinner at Eight (1933)
Hell's Angels (1930)
Hold Your Man (1933)
Platinum Blonde (1931)
The Public Enemy (1931)
Red Dust (1932)
Red-Headed Woman (1932)
harm: **3** ill, mar **4** beat, evil, hurt, loss, maim, pain, ruin **5** abuse, break, crack, lay up, spite, spoil, wound, wreck, wrong **6** bruise, damage, deface, defile, impair, injure, injury, malign, mess up, mishap, misuse, molest, muck up, poison **7** corrupt, offense, vitiate **8** aggrieve, breakage, disserve, foul play, ill-treat, lacerate, maltreat, mischief, mistreat, sabotage **9** adversity, detriment, mishandle, mismanage, prejudice, vandalism, vandalize **10** defacement, defilement, impairment, misfortune
cause ~ to: **3** mar **4** maim, ruin **5** abuse, spoil, stain, wound, wrong **6** batter, bruise, damage, deface, defile, impair, injure, mangle, ravage **7** corrupt, pollute, scratch, tarnish **9** undermine
free from ~: **4** safe
in French: **3** mal
protection from ~: **6** asylum, refuge, safety **7** shelter **9** sanctuary
__ harm: **4** do no **6** bodily
harmed: **4** hurt **7** injured **9** aggrieved
easily ~: **9** sensitive
harmful: **3** bad, ill **4** dire, evil **5** lousy, toxic **6** costly, lethal, malign, nocent, sinful, unsafe **7** adverse, baleful, baneful, hurtful, malefic, nocuous, noisome, noxious, ruinous **8** damaging, grievous, inimical, menacing, sinister, virulent **9** injurious, malicious, pestilent, poisonous, unhealthy **10** calamitous, corrupting, disastrous, incendiary, maleficent, pernicious, subversive
not ~: **4** mild **6** benign, gentle **7** healthy **9** healthful
thing: **4** bane **5** curse **6** blight, plague, poison **7** scourge **8** calamity **9** detriment
Harmful Intent
author: Robin Cook
harmfully: **3** ill **5** wrong **9** seriously
harmless: **4** kind, safe, sage, tame **6** benign, gentle, secure **8** innocent, nontoxic, reliable **9** innocuous, innoxious
make ~: **5** unarm **6** defang, defuse, defuze, dehorn, disarm **7** disable
__ harmless: **4** save
Harmon: **3** Tom **4** Anne, Mark **5** Angie, Kelly **6** Claude **9** Killebrew
Harmon, Angie: **5** model **7** actress
spouse: Jason Sehorn
Harmon, Claude: **6** golfer
Harmonia: **5** nymph
brother: **6** Deimos, Phobus
daughter: **5** Agave **9** Hippolyte
husband: **6** Cadmus
parent: **4** Ares **9** Aphrodite
harmonic: **5** tonal
harmonica: **4** wind **10** instrument, mouth organ
maker: **6** Hohner
part: **4** reed
player: **5** Adler
harmonious: **4** calm **5** in key, on key, sweet **6** in step, in tune **7** cordial, halcyon, lyrical, melodic, musical, regular, tuneful **8** amicable, balanced, esthetic, in accord, of a piece, peaceful, sonorous, tasteful **9** accordant, according, agreeable, classical, congenial, congruent, congruous, consonant, in concert, melodious, of one mind, simpatico, symphonic, unanimous, well-tuned **10** compatible, concordant, concurrent, consistent, euphonious, like-minded, rhythmical, synchronal, true to type
make ~: **4** tune **9** reconcile
relationship: **4** sync **5** unity
sounds: **5** music
harmonium: **8** keyboard **10** instrument
harmonize: **2** go **3** fit **4** gybe, jibe, mesh, sing, tune **5** agree, blend, chime, fit in, match, synch **6** accord, attune, belong, cohere, square, tune up **7** comport, compose, conform **8** dovetail, modulate **9** chime with, cooperate, correlate, integrate, reconcile **10** coordinate, correspond, proportion
Harmon, Mark: **5** actor
spouse: Pam Dawber
TV: Chicago Hope, St. Elsewhere
harmony: **4** calm, sync, tune **5** amity, blend, chord, music, order, peace, quiet, sound, synch, triad, unity **6** accord, comity, melody, unison **7** concert, concord, euphony, keeping, kinship, oneness, rapport **8** diapason, good will, serenity, symmetry, symphony **9** agreement, communion, congruity, consensus, good vibes, unanimity **10** conformity, friendship, proportion
be in ~: **4** gybe, jibe **5** agree
in ~: **5** at one **6** jibing **10** compatible, like-minded
name meaning ~: **4** Alan **5** Allan, Allen
one in ~: **6** agreer
part: **4** alto, bass **5** tenor **7** soprano
restore ~: **7** mediate **9** reconcile **10** conciliate
harm's way: **5** peril **6** danger **8** jeopardy
in ~: **6** unsafe
out of ~: **2** OK **4** safe, snug **6** secure **8** harbored, home-free, shielded **9** protected, sheltered
harness: **3** use **4** curb, gear, rein, tame, yoke **5** apply, check, hitch, strap **6** couple, employ, halter, hook up, inspan, rein in, tether **7** contain, control, exploit, utilize **8** mobilize, restrain **9** constrain
gear: **4** tack
part: **3** bit **4** curb, hame, rein **5** strap, trace **6** bridle
sharers: **4** team
harness __: **4** race **5** hitch, horse **6** racing
harnessed: **4** tame **5** yoked
harness racing: **5** sport
gait: **4** trot
horse: **5** pacer **7** trotter
need: **5** sulky
Harney: **4** peak **5** mount **8** mountain
locale: **4** S. Dak. **10** Black Hills
Harnick: **7** Sheldon
Harold: **4** Gray, Rome, Teen, Urey **5** Arlen, Bloom, Evans, Gould, Kroto, Lloyd, Monro, Ramis **6** Baines, Becker, Clarke, French, Melvin, Pinter, Sakata, Varmus, Wilson **7** Brodkey, Kushner, Robbins, Russell **9** Macmillan
author: Edward Bulwer-Lytton
__ Harold: **6** Childe
Harold and Maude (1972 film)
cast: Bud Cort, Ruth Gordon
Harold in Italy
composer: Hector Berlioz
__ Harold's Pilgrimage: **6** Childe
harp: **3** nag **4** carp **5** bolon **6** string **8** clarsach, complain **10** tongue-lash
cousin: **4** lyre
on: **3** nag **4** push **5** press, rub in **6** ramble, repeat, stress **7** belabor, iterate **9** emphasize, reiterate
(on): **5** dwell **6** fixate
player: **5** angel
play the ~: **5** strum
sky ~: **4** Lyra
starter: **4** auto
tuner: **5** wrest
__ harp: **4** Jew's
harper: **3** nag **8** minstrel, musician
Harper: **3** Lee **4** Tess **7** Frances, Jessica, Stephen, Valerie
partner: **3** Row **7** Collins
Harper (1966 film)
cast: Lauren Bacall, Julie Harris, Paul Newman, Shelley Winters
Harper, Frances: **6** writer
work: Iola Leroy
__ Harper Lee: **5** Nelle
Harper's: **3** mag **8** magazine
cartoonist: **4** Nast
Harper's Bazaar: **3** mag **8** magazine
artist: Erté
Harpers Ferry
event: **4** raid
locale: **3** W.Va.
Harper, Valerie: **7** actress
TV: The Hogan Family, The Mary Tyler Moore Show, Rhoda
Harper Valley P.T.A. (1968 song)
artist: Jeannie C. Riley
Harpies' sister: **4** Iris
Harpo: **4** Marx
brother: **5** Chico, Gummo, Zeppo **7** Groucho
harpoon: **5** lance, spear **7** javelin
harpsichord: **7** cembalo **8** keyboard **10** instrument
harpsichordist: **9** Landowska
__ Harp, The: **5** Grass
Harp Weaver and Other Poems, The
author: Edna St. Vincent Millay
harpy: **3** hag **5** shrew, vixen **6** chider, virago **8** harridan, predator **9** henpecker, termagant, Xanthippe
like a ~: **6** grabby, greedy **7** hoggish, piggish **8** covetous, edacious, esurient, grasping **9** penurious **10** avaricious, gluttonous
Harrah: **4** Bill, Toby **7** William
Harrah's: **6** casino
Harrah, Toby
sport: **8** baseball
Harrelson: **3** Bud **5** Woody
Harrelson, Woody: **5** actor
film: Ed TV (1999)
The Hi-Lo Country (1998)
Indecent Proposal (1993)
Kingpin (1996)
Play It to the Bone (1999)
White Men Can't Jump (1992)
TV: Cheers
harridan: **3** hag, nag **5** crone, harpy, scold, shrew **6** beldam, chider, virago **7** beldame **8** battle-ax **9** battle-axe, henpecker, termagant
harried: **5** tense **9** pressured **10** overworked
harrier: **4** bird **5** bully, racer **6** runner
Harrier: **3** dog **5** canid **6** canine
Harriet: **3** spy **6** Monroe, Nelson, Tubman **7** Lothrop **8** Hilliard, Matineau **9** MacGibbon
husband: **5** Ozzie
son: **4** Rick **5** David, Ricky
Harriet Beecher __: **5** Stowe
Harrigan
composer: George M. Cohan
Harriman: **6** Pamela **7** Averell
Harrington: **3** Eve, Pat **7** Michael
Harris: **2** Ed **3** Lou, Mel **4** Neil, Phil, Rolf **5** Bucky, Julie, Major, Steve, Yulin **6** Franco, Wilson **7** Barbara, Emmylou, Estelle, Richard, William **8** Jonathan, Thurston
Harris __: **5** Tweed
Harrisburg: **4** city, town **7** capital
county: **7** Dauphin
locale: **4** Penn.
Harris, Ed: **5** actor
film: Absolute Power (1997)
The Abyss (1989)
Apollo 13 (1995)
A Beautiful Mind (2001)
Enemy at the Gates (2001)
Glengarry Glen Ross (1992)
Jacknife (1989)
Knightriders (1981)
Nixon (1995)
Paris Trout (1991)
Places in the Heart (1984)
Pollock (2000)
Radio (2003)
The Right Stuff (1983)
The Rock (1996)
State of Grace (1990)
Sweet Dreams (1985)
The Third Miracle (1999)
The Truman Show (1998)
spouse: Amy Madigan
Harris, Franco
sport: **8** football
Harris, Joel Chandler: **6** writer
character: Remus
honorific: Brer
work: The Tar-Baby

Harris, Mel: 7 actress
TV: thirtysomething
Harrison: 3 Rex 4 city, Ford, town 6 George 7 Gregory, Wilbert 8 Benjamin, Jennilee
in Star Wars: 3 Han
locale: 7 New York 8 Michigan
Harrison, Benjamin: 9 president
alma mater: 5 Miami
former occupation: 6 lawyer
home: 4 Ohio 7 Indiana
opponent: 9 Cleveland
V.P.: 6 Morton
wife: 8 Caroline
Harrison, George
song: All Those Years Ago (1981)
Give Me Love (1973)
Got My Mind Set on You (1987)
Isn't It a Pity (1970)
My Sweet Lord (1970)
What Is Life (1971)
Harrison, Gregory: 5 actor
TV: Trapper John, M.D.
Harrison, Rex: 3 Sir 5 actor
film: Anna and the King of Siam (1946)
Blithe Spirit (1945)
Cleopatra (1963)
Doctor Dolittle (1967)
The Ghost and Mrs. Muir (1947)
Major Barbara (1941)
My Fair Lady (1964, AA)
Storm in a Teacup (1937)
The Yellow Rolls-Royce (1964)
son: 4 Noel
spouse: Lilli Palmer
Harrison, Wilbert
song: Kansas City (1959)
Harrison, William Henry: 9 president
former occupation: 7 soldier
home: 4 Ohio
opponent: 8 Van Buren
V.P.: 5 Tyler
wife: 4 Anna
Harris, Phil
spouse: Alice Faye
Harris, Richard: 5 actor
film: The Cassandra Crossing (1977)
Cry, the Beloved Country (1995)
Hawaii (1966)
Man in the Wilderness (1971)
Robin and Marian (1976)
This Sporting Life (1963)
Unforgiven (1992)
song: MacArthur Park (1968)
Harris, Thurston
song: Little Bitty Pretty One (1957)
Harris Tweed: 6 fabric 8 material
Harris, Wilson: 6 writer 8 Guyanese
Harrod's conveyance: 4 lift
Harrold: 7 Kathryn
harrow: 4 disk, loot, pain, rack, rake, rend, rive, sack, till 6 ravage, strike 7 agonize, anguish, break up, despoil, pillage, plunder, torment, torture 8 distress, freeboot 9 cultivate, depredate 10 excruciate
blade: 4 disc, disk
Harrow: 6 school
rival: 4 Eton
harrowing: 6 tragic 7 painful, parlous, racking 8 alarming, chilling, dolorous, grievous, terrible, tragical 9 agonizing, appalling, dangerous, murderous, torturous, traumatic 10 disturbing, petrifying, terrifying, tormenting
Harrumph!: 3 bah, tut 4 ahem 5 pshaw
harry: 3 irk, nag, rag, rob, vex 4 fret, gall, raid, ride, sack 5 annoy, hound, strip, tease, upset, worry 6 badger, bother, harass, hassle, maraud, molest, noodge, pester, plague, pother, pursue, ravage 7 afflict, bedevil, disturb, oppress, perturb, pillage, plunder, ransack, torment, trouble 8 aggrieve, distress, irritate 9 beleaguer, devastate, persecute 10 discompose
Harry: 4 Cohn, Lime, Reid 5 Caray, Carey, James 6 Chapin, Debbie, Golden, Hamlin, Hooper, Jackée, Lauder, Morgan, Truman, Warren 7 Connick, Deborah, Houdini, Langdon, Nilsson, Shearer, Simeone, Von Zell 8 Anderson, Beaumont, Blackmun, Guardino, Helmsley, Kemelman, Matinson, Reasoner 9 Belafonte, Markowitz, Martinson 10 Blackstone
successor: 3 Ike
wife: 4 Bess
Harry __ Stanton: 4 Dean
__ Harry: 5 Dirty
Harry and Tonto (1974 film)
cast: Ellen Burstyn, Art Carney
Harry in Your Pocket (1973 film)
cast: James Coburn, Michael Sarrazin, Trish Van Devere
__ Harry Lee: 10 Light-Horse
__ Harry Met Sally ...: 4 When
Harry Potter
cat: 5 Snowy, Tufty 6 Mr. Paws 7 Tibbles 9 Mrs. Norris
dog: 6 Fluffy
owl: 5 Errol
Harry Potter and the Chamber of Secrets (2002 film)
cast: Kenneth Branagh, Richard Griffiths, Rupert Grint, Richard Harris, Daniel Radcliffe, Emma Watson
director: Chris Columbus
Harry Potter and the Goblet of Fire (2005 film)
cast: Ralph Fiennes, Rupert Grint, Daniel Radcliffe, Emma Watson
Harry Potter and the Half-Blood Prince (2009 film)
cast: Michael Gambon, Rupert Grint, Daniel Radcliffe, Emma Watson
Harry Potter and the Order of the Phoenix (2007 film)
cast: Ralph Fiennes, Rupert Grint, Daniel Radcliffe, Emma Watson
Harry Potter and the Prisoner of Azkaban (2004 film)
cast: Rupert Grint, Gary Oldman, Daniel Radcliffe, Alan Rickman, Emma Thompson, Emma Watson
Harry Potter and the Sorcerer's Stone (2001 film)
cast: Rupert Grint, Richard Harris, Daniel Radcliffe, Emma Watson
composer: John Williams
director: Chris Columbus
Harry, Prince: 5 royal 7 Windsor
aunt: 4 Anne
parent: 5 Diana 7 Charles
uncle: 6 Andrew, Edward
harsh: 3 bad, raw 4 acid, grim, mean, rude 5 acerb, acrid, crude, cruel, gruff, heavy, husky, nasty, noisy, raspy, rigid, rough, sharp, stark, stern, stiff, tough 6 animal, biting, bitter, brutal, coarse, craggy, fierce, hoarse, jagged, morose, off-key, rugged, savage, severe, strict, unkind, wanton, wintry 7 abusive, acerbic, arduous, austere, beastly, callous, caustic, cragged, drastic, grating, hooting, hurtful, intense, jarring, onerous, raucous, Spartan, uncivil, vicious, wintery 8 abrasive, asperous, barbaric, clashing, despotic, exacting, fiendish, gravelly, grueling, guttural, inhumane, jangling, no picnic, pitiless, punitive, rigorous, ruthless, sadistic, scathing, strident, tactless, terrific, vengeful 9 cutthroat, dissonant, draconian, ferocious, hard-nosed, heartless, impliable, inclement, merciless, monstrous, stringent, truculent, unfeeling, unmusical, unpitying, unsparing 10 astringent, despotical, discordant, hard-boiled, inexorable, iron-willed, irritating, oppressive, relentless, ungracious, unpleasant, vindictive
criticism: 4 slam 5 blast 6 attack, earful, rebuke 7 censure, lecture, obloquy, reproof 8 berating, reproach, reproval 9 aspersion, reprimand, talking-to 10 bawling-out, upbraiding
cry: 3 caw 4 yaup, yawp
feeling: 4 gall 5 spite 6 enmity, hatred, malice, rancor, spleen 7 ill will, umbrage 8 acrimony, bad blood, contempt 9 animosity, antipathy, hostility, vengeance 10 resentment
in sound: 6 shrill 7 blaring, grating, raucous 8 piercing, strident 10 clangorous, discordant, screeching
not ~: 3 lax 4 calm, kind, mild 5 balmy 6 benign, genial, gentle, kindly, placid, remiss, serene, tender 7 affable, amiable, clement, lenient, pacific, patient, subdued, tactful 8 laid-back, merciful, moderate, peaceful, tolerant, tranquil, yielding 9 easygoing, sensitive, temperate 10 neglectful, permissive
old-style: 5 asper
harshly: 4 hard 5 rough 8 severely 9 viciously
harshness: 5 rigor 6 rancor 7 cruelty, discord 8 acrimony, asperity, hardness, iron hand, severity, violence 9 austerity 10 bitterness, coarseness, dissonance, oppression, unkindness
hart: 4 deer, stag 6 animal
mate: 4 hind
part: 6 antler
Hart: 4 Gary, Mary, Moss 5 Bobby, Corey, Crane, Doris, Larry, Roxie 6 Johnny, Lorenz 7 Bochner, Dolores, Roxanne
Hartack, Bill: 6 jockey
milieu: 5 track
__ Hart Benton: 6 Thomas
hartebeest: 4 tora 6 animal, mammal 8 antelope
relative: *see* antelope
Harte, Bret: 6 writer
collaborator: Twain
work: Ah Sin
The Luck of Roaring Camp
The Outcasts of Poker Flat
Hartford: 4 city, town
competitor: *see* insurance company
locale: 4 Conn.
newspaper: 7 Courant
Hartley: 2 L.P. 3 Bob, Hal 8 Mariette
__-Hartley Act: 4 Taft
Hart, Lorenz: 8 lyricist
collaborator: Richard Rodgers
musical: Babes in Arms
The Boys From Syracuse
By Jupiter
A Connecticut Yankee
Dearest Enemy
The Garrick Gaieties
The Girl Friend
Heads Up!
Higher and Higher
I'd Rather Be Right
I Married an Angel
Jumbo
On Your Toes
Pal Joey
Peggy-Ann
Present Arms
Simple Simon
Spring Is Here
Too Many Girls
Hartman: 3 Dan 4 Lisa, Mary, Phil 5 David 9 Elizabeth
Hartman, Dan
song: I Can Dream About You (1984)
Hartman, Lisa: 7 actress
spouse: Clint Black
Hart, Moss: 6 writer 10 playwright
collaborator: Kaufman, Weill, Berlin, Porter
spouse: Kitty Carlisle
work: Act One
Lady in the Dark
The Man Who Came to Dinner
Once in a Lifetime
You Can't Take It With You
Hartnett: 4 Josh 5 Gabby
Hartnett, Josh: 5 actor
film: Black Hawk Down (2001)
The Faculty (1998)
Pearl Harbor (2001)
hart's-tongue: 4 fern
Hart's War (2002 film)
cast: Colin Farrell, Terrence Howard, Bruce Willis
Hart to Hart (ABC adventure)
cast: Stefanie Powers (Jennifer Hart)
Lionel Stander (Max)
Robert Wagner (Jonathan Hart)
dog: Freeway
__ Harum: 6 Procol
harum-scarum: 4 rash 5 giddy, hasty 6 daring 7 chaotic, erratic, flighty 8 careless, reckless
haruspex: 4 seer 5 augur 7 diviner, prophet 10 soothsayer
Harvard: 3 sch. 4 coll., John, peak, univ. 5 mount 7 college 8 mountain
art museum: 4 Fogg

athletes: 7 Crimson
deg.: 3 MBA
league: 3 Ivy
locale: 4 Mass. 7 Rockies, Sawatch 8 Colorado 9 Cambridge
motto: 7 Veritas
neighbor: 3 MIT
rival: 4 Yale
student: 6 Cantab
Harvard __: 4 Yard 5 beets, chair
Harvarder
rival: 3 Eli
Harve: 8 Presnell
harvest: 3 get 4 crop, cull, gain, pick, reap, stow 5 amass, cache, crops, fruit, glean, hoard, pluck, stash, store, yield 6 garner, gather, output, pile up, profit 7 collect, produce, reaping 8 fruition 9 garnering, gathering 10 accumulate, vegetables
Celtic ~ festival: 6 lammas
clean up after ~: 5 glean
farm ~: 4 corn 5 wheat
festival: 6 Kwanza
goddess: 3 Ops 5 Ceres
leavings: 5 chaff
machine: 5 baler 6 reaper
time: 3 Oct. 4 fall, Sept. 6 autumn 7 October 9 September
unit: 5 sheaf 6 bushel
harvest __: 4 moon
__ Harvest: 6 Random
harvestable: 4 ripe
harvester: 6 farmer, reaper
harvester __: 3 ant
Harvest Home
author: Thomas Tryon
Harvest Poems
author: Carl Sandburg
Harvey: 4 Paul 5 Wiley 6 Keitel, Korman, Penick 7 Anthony, William 8 Laurence 9 Fierstein, Firestone
Harvey (1950 film)
cast: Peggy Dow, Josephine Hull, James Stewart
character: 4 Dowd, Veta 6 Elwood
director: Henry Koster
Harvey Girls, The (1946 film)
cast: Ray Bolger, Judy Garland
Harvey, Laurence: 5 actor
film: The Alamo (1960)
Butterfield 8 (1960)
Darling (1965)
I Am a Camera (1955)
The Manchurian Candidate (1962)
Room at the Top (1959)
Summer and Smoke (1961)
Harvey Wallbanger: 5 drink 8 beverage, cocktail
ingredient: 5 vodka 8 Galliano
Harz: 5 range 9 mountains
locale: 6 Europe 7 Germany
has-__: 4 been
Has 1,001 __: 4 uses
__ Has a Birthday: 6 Eeyore
has-been: 5 loser, passé 8 outdated, outmoded 9 out-of-date
Hasbro product: 5 Furby, G.I. Joe 8 Scrabble
Hasbrouck __, NJ: 3 Hts.
Hasek, Jaroslav: 5 Czech 6 writer
hasenpfeffer: 4 stew
__ has fleas: 5 My dog
hash: 4 mess, muss, olio, stew 5 mince 6 jumble, litter, medley, muddle, ragout 7 farrago, mélange, mixture 8 mishmash, scramble 9 leftovers, patchwork, potpourri 10 assortment, hodgepodge, miscellany, salmagundi
house: 5 diner 6 eatery 10 restaurant
make ~: 5 mince
make a ~ of: 4 flub, goof, muff 5 botch, gum up 6 bungle, foul up, goof up, mess up 7 louse up 9 mishandle, mismanage
over: 5 argue 6 debate, review 7 discuss 10 kick around
propel ~: 5 sling
slinger: 4 chef, cook
hash __: 3 out 4 mark 5 house 6 browns
hash-__: 7 slinger
__ Hashanah: 4 Rosh
Hashemite kingdom: 6 Jordan
hashhouse
client: 5 diner, eater 7 luncher
need: 5 grill
order: 4 eggs
sign: 4 Eats
see also diner, restaurant
Hasidic: 6 Jewish
leader: 5 rabbi, rebbe
mysticism: 6 cabala, kabala 7 cabbala, kabbala
__ has it...: 5 Rumor
Haskell: 5 Eddie
__ Has Landed, The: 5 Eagle
Has Man a Future?
author: Bertrand Russell
hasn't: 5 lacks, needs
hasp: 4 lock 5 catch, latch 7 bracket
Hassam, Childe: 6 artist 7 painter
hassar: 4 fish 7 catfish
Hasselbeck: 4 Matt 9 Elisabeth
Hasselhoff: 5 David
hassle: 3 bug, nag, row, vex 4 flap, fuss, rile, to-do 5 annoy, fight, harry, hound, mix up, press, run-in, scrap, trial, upset, whirl, worry 6 badger, bicker, bother, burden, clamor, harass, hubbub, lather, noodge, pester, plague, stress, strife, tsuris, tumult, tussle, uproar 7 dispute, problem, quarrel, quibble, rhubarb, trouble, tsouris, turmoil, wrangle 8 argument, hard time, headache, irritant, nuisance, pressure, squabble, struggle, vexation 9 annoyance, commotion, tight spot 10 difficulty, hullabaloo
Hasso: 5 Signe
hassock: 4 pouf 5 squab 7 cricket, cushion, ottoman, taboret 8 footrest, tabouret 9 footstool
hasta __: 5 luego 6 mañana 7 la vista
hasta la vista: 3 bye 4 ciao, ta-ta 5 adieu, adios, aloha, later 6 bye-bye, shalom, so long 7 cheerio, goodbye 8 au revoir, farewell, sayonara, toodle-oo
hasta luego
see hasta la vista
haste: 4 dash, rush 5 hurry, press, speed 6 bustle, flurry, hustle, scurry 7 urgency 8 alacrity, celerity, dispatch, rapidity, rashness, velocity 9 briskness, fleetness, quickness, swiftness 10 expedition, impatience, promptness
in ~: 7 quickly, rapidly, swiftly 8 on the run, speedily 9 hurriedly
in great ~: 5 amain
make ~: 3 fly, hie, run, zip 4 rush 5 hurry, scoot, speed 7 quicken 8 hightail, scramble 10 get hopping
product: 5 waste
without ~: 4 slow 6 calmly, casual, lazily, slowly 7 relaxed 8 casually, laid-back 9 gradually, leisurely, unhurried
__ haste: 4 make
Haste makes waste: 5 adage
hasten: 3 fly, hie, rip, run, zip 4 bolt, dart, dash, flee, flit, push, race, rush, skip, tear, zoom 5 bound, hurry, press, scoot, shoot, speed, whisk 6 barrel, bustle, gallop, hustle, move it, rocket, scurry, sprint, step up 7 advance, floor it, forward, further, hop to it, quicken, scamper, speed up 8 dispatch, expedite, hightail, scramble, snap to it, step on it 9 go forward, go swiftly, hotfoot it, shake a leg, skedaddle 10 accelerate, get a move on, get hopping, hightail it, make tracks
hastily: 3 PDQ 4 fast, soon 5 apace, madly, quick, short 6 presto 7 briefly, flat out, rapidly, swiftly 8 chop-chop, in a flash, in a hurry, in a jiffy, in no time, on the fly, on the run, pell-mell, promptly 9 forthwith, headfirst, instantly, like a shot 10 in high gear
Hastings: 4 city, town 5 Alcee 6 battle
locale: 6 Sussex 7 England 8 Nebraska
Hast thou __ the Jabberwock?: 5 slain
__ Has Two Faces, The: 6 Mirror
hasty: 3 lax 4 fast, rash, rush 5 blind, brash, brief, brisk, fleet, quick, rapid, swift 6 abrupt, flying, little, madcap, prompt, racing, remiss, rushed, sloppy, snappy, speedy, sudden, unwary 7 cursory, express, hurried, instant, quickie 8 careless, headlong, heedless, pell-mell, reckless, slapdash, slipshod, tactless, unsubtle 9 breakneck, desperate, foolhardy, impatient, impetuous, imprudent, impulsive, momentary, negligent, premature, unadvised, uncareful, unmindful, whirlwind 10 double-time, hypersonic, ill-advised, incautious, indiscreet, nonchalant, supersonic, unthinking
make a ~ escape: 5 lam it
retreat: 3 lam 6 escape, flight 7 getaway
hasty __: 7 pudding
__ hasty retreat: 5 beat a
hat: 3 cap, lid, tam 4 kepi, topi 5 beret, derby, gibus, miter, toque 6 beaver, bicorn, boater, bonnet, bowler, cloche, fedora, helmet, hennin, Panama, sailor, topper, trilby, turban 7 bicorne, burnous, chapeau, leghorn, petasus, pillbox, porkpie, skimmer, Stetson, tricorn 8 burnoose, coonskin, covering, headgear, jipijapa, snap-brim, sombrero, tricorne 9 sou'wester, stovepipe, sunbonnet, ten-gallon 10 pith helmet
attachment: 4 veil
bad ~: 3 cad 5 knave, scamp, skunk 6 rascal 8 picaroon, recreant, scalawag 9 reprobate, scoundrel 10 blackguard, ne'er-do-well, scapegrace
brass ~: 4 boss 6 top dog 7 manager 8 employer, superior 9 executive 10 supervisor
brimless ~: 3 tam 5 beret, toque
broad-brimmed ~: 5 terai
decoration: 5 plume
ender: 3 box, pin 4 band 5 check
felt ~: 3 fez 5 terai
flat ~: 3 tam 5 beret
French ~: 5 beret
hang one's ~: 4 live 5 dwell 6 locate, reside
hard ~: 5 labor 6 helmet
holder: 4 head
jaunty ~: 3 cap
material: 4 felt 5 straw 6 beaver
military ~: 4 kepi 5 busby, shako 6 helmet
old ~: 4 dull 5 corny, dated, dowdy, hokey, musty, passé, stale, trite, vapid 6 common, jejune 7 archaic, clichéd, fatuous, humdrum, outworn, prosaic 8 bromidic 9 hackneyed, played out, prosaical 10 antiquated, out of style, uninspired, unoriginal
part: 4 brim 5 visor, vizor 6 earlap
pass the ~: 3 beg 7 collect, solicit
Pope's ~: 5 miter
soft ~: 3 tam 5 beret
starter: 4 hard
straw ~: 6 boater
sun ~: 4 topi 5 topee
tip one's ~ to: 4 hail 5 cheer, greet, honor 6 praise, salute 7 applaud, commend 10 compliment
tipper's word: 4 ma'am
under one's ~: 6 hidden 7 private 9 concealed
where one hangs one's ~: 3 pad 4 home 5 abode, house 7 lodging 8 domicile, dwelling 9 residence
woman's ~: 5 toque 6 Breton, cloche
hat __: 4 tree 5 check, dance, trick
__ hat: 3 old, red, tin, top, war 4 fire, hard, high, silk 5 brass, opera, straw 6 cocked, cowboy, Panama 7 pillbox
__-hat: 4 hard, high
__ Hat: 3 Top
Hatari! (1962 film)
cast: Red Buttons, Elsa Martinelli, John Wayne
composer: Henry Mancini
director: Howard Hawks
hatch: 3 lay 4 brew, door, make, plan, plot 5 brood, cause, frame, get up, sit on, spawn 6 cook up,

create, derive, design, devise, invent, make up, scheme, spring, whip up, work up **7** concoct, dream up, ingress, opening, prepare, produce, think up, trump up **8** conceive, contrive, engender, generate, incubate, trapdoor **9** floodgate, formulate, machinate, originate, reproduce **10** brainstorm, bring forth, come up with
as an idea: **4** brew, form **6** cook up, create, devise, invent, make up **7** concoct, develop, dream up
down the ~: **5** toast
ender: **3** way **4** back
starter: **3** nut **5** cross
__ hatch: **5** booby **6** escape
Hatch: **5** Orrin **6** Wilbur
hatchback: **3** car **4** auto **10** automobile
cousin: **5** sedan
hatched: **4** born
Hatcher, Teri: **7** actress
costar: **4** Cain
role: **4** Lane, Lois
TV: Lois & Clark
hatchery
sound: **4** peep **5** cheep, chirp, tweet
unit: **3** egg
__ hatchery: **4** fish
__ Hatches the Egg: **6** Horton
hatchet: **2** ax **3** axe **4** tool **5** hewer **8** tomahawk
aborigine ~: **4** mogo
bury the ~: **5** agree **6** make up, pardon **7** forgive **9** negotiate, reconcile
handle: **4** haft
man: **5** firer **6** flunky **7** flunkey **8** henchman
use a ~: **3** cut, hew **4** chop
hatchet __: **3** job, man
hatchetlike tool: **3** zax
hatchling: **4** baby, bird **5** chick
home: **4** nest
identifier: **5** sexer
hatchlings: **5** brood, covey
Hatch, Orrin: **7** senator
state: **4** Utah
hatchway: **4** door, exit **5** entry **6** portal **8** entrance
__-hat cymbals: **4** high
__ hat dance: **7** Mexican
hate: **4** loth **5** abhor, dread, loath, odium, scorn, spite, venom, wrath **6** animus, detest, enmity, loathe, malice, rancor, spleen **7** bigotry, contemn, deplore, despise, disdain, disgust, dislike, ill will **8** aversion, distaste, execrate, loathing **9** abominate, animosity, antipathy, deprecate, disrelish, hostility, revulsion **10** abhorrence, antagonism, execration, flinch from, repugnance, resentment
combining form: **3** mis- **4** miso-
old-style: **5** spise
opposite: **4** love
hate __: **4** mail **5** crime
hated: **7** unloved **9** unpopular
hateful: **4** cold, cool, evil, foul, mean, vile **5** awful, catty, cruel, curst, gross, lousy, nasty, snide, surly **6** bitter, chilly, cursed, horrid, malign, odious, ornery, remote, unkind **7** accurst, blasted, cutting, glacial, heinous, hideous, hostile, inhuman, satanic, vicious **8** abrasive, accursed, annoying, contrary, infamous, inhumane, inimical, shocking, spiteful, terrible, venomous, virulent **9** abhorrent, bellicose, execrable, invidious, loathsome, malicious, obnoxious, offensive, rancorous, repellent, repugnant, repulsive, revolting, satanical, truculent **10** abominable, confounded, despicable, detestable, disgusting, malevolent, pugnacious, vindictive
hatefulness: **5** spite, wrath **6** malice, rancor **7** disgust
hater: **5** bigot **9** miscreant **10** misogynist
work ~: **5** drone **6** loafer, rascal, truant **7** dawdler, laggard, shirker, slacker **8** parasite **9** donothing, goldbrick, lazybones **10** ne'er-do-well
__-hate relationship: **4** love
Hatfield: **4** Mark
to a McCoy: **3** foe **5** enemy
Hatfields: **4** clan
hath: **4** owns
hatha-__: **4** yoga
Hathaway: **4** Anne **5** Donny, Henry, shirt
competitor: **4** Izod
on Steve Allen's show: **3** Nye
Hathaway, Anne: **7** actress
film: Becoming Jane (2007)
Bride Wars (2009)
Brokeback Mountain (2005)
The Devil Wears Prada (2007)
Ella Enchanted (2004)
Get Smart (2007)
The Princess Diaries (2001)
Rachel Getting Married (2008)
Hathaway, Donny
song: The Closer I Get to You (1978)
Where Is the Love (1972)
hat-in-hand type: **6** beggar **8** deadbeat **9** mendicant **10** panhandler, supplicant
Hatlo, Jimmy: **10** cartoonist
hatrack: **7** antlers
hatred: **5** odium, pique, scorn, spite, venom **6** animus, enmity, grudge, malice, phobia, rancor, spleen **7** disdain, disgust, dislike, ill will **8** acrimony, aversion, bad blood, contempt, distaste, ignominy, loathing **9** animosity, antipathy, hostility, militancy, repulsion, revulsion **10** abhorrence, antagonism, bitterness, execration, repugnance, unkindness
Hats Off to Larry (1961 song)
artist: Del Shannon
hatter: **8** milliner
__ Hatter: **3** Mad
__ Hatteras, NC: **4** Cape
Hatters: **7** Stetson
__ Hat, The: **5** Green
Hattie: **8** McDaniel
__ Hattie: **6** Panama
Hattiesburg: **4** city, town
locale: **4** Miss.
school: **3** USM
hat-trick part: **4** goal
__ Hat, White Tie and Tails: **3** Top
Hauer: **6** Rutger
haughtiness: **4** airs **5** pride, scorn **6** hubris, hybris
haughty: **3** big **4** smug, vain **5** aloof, cocky, lofty, proud, regal **6** lordly, sniffy, snooty, stuffy **7** fustian, pompous, stately, stuck-up **8** arrogant, assuming, boastful, cavalier, kinglike, scornful, snobbish, superior **9** big-headed, conceited, egotistic, hubristic, imperious **10** disdainful, hoity-toity
be ~: **4** snub **7** disdain
one: **4** snob
response: **5** never, sniff
haul: **3** bag, lug, tow, tug **4** cart, drag, draw, load, loot, move, pack, pelf, pull, ship, swag, take, tote **5** booty, bring, cargo, carry, catch, heave, prize, shlep, trail, truck **6** bagful, convey, lading, schlep, shlepp **7** freight, plunder **8** cart away, transfer **9** transport
away: **3** tow **4** drag **9** transport
heist ~: **4** take **5** booty **7** plunder
in: **3** nab **4** take **6** arrest
in for the long ~: **6** stable **7** abiding, durable, lasting **8** enduring **9** permanent, unabating
long ~: **4** trek **6** battle **7** journey, odyssey **8** struggle **10** pilgrimage
off on: **4** belt, slug, swat **5** punch, smash, thump, whack **6** assail, attack, strike, wallop **7** assault, bombard, clobber, lay into **8** lace into **9** light into
on board: **4** lade, load
over the coals: **5** roast
short ~: **3** hop, run **5** jaunt **6** outing **7** day trip
starter: **3** box **4** down, keel
up: **4** heft, lift **5** boost, hoist, raise **7** elevate
haul __: **3** off
__ haul: **4** long **5** short
haulable: **7** movable **8** portable
hauler: **3** van **4** cart, dray, semi, tram, wain **5** toter, truck, wagon **7** trucker **8** teamster
British ~: **5** lorry
haul in one's __: **5** horns
haul over the __: **5** coals
haunch: **3** hip **4** rump, side **5** flank, thigh
haunt: **3** bar, den, dog, vex **4** dive, lair, nest, site **5** beset, hound, joint, lodge, prowl, shade, spook, stalk, visit **6** fantom, locale, madden, obsess, plague, prey on, pursue **7** bedevil, besiege, hangout, phantom, purlieu, retreat, terrify, torment, trouble, weigh on **8** frequent, frighten, locality **9** clubhouse, habituate, hang out at, terrorize **10** hang around, rendezvous, scare stiff
haunted: **4** eery **5** eerie **7** ghostly **8** obsessed **9** possessed, unearthly
like a ~ house: **5** eerie **6** creepy, spooky **7** macabre **8** chilling
Haunted __, The: **4** Mesa
haunted-house
feature: **5** ghost, spook **6** cobweb
feeling: **4** fear **5** alarm, angst, dread, panic **6** fright, horror, terror
sound: **4** moan **5** creak
Haunted Palace, The
author: Edgar Allan Poe
haunting: **4** eery **5** eerie, weird **6** spooky **7** nagging **9** memorable, nostalgic, obsessive, recurrent **10** persistent
haus: **5** abode, house **6** German
the lady of the ~: **4** frau
Hauser: **5** Wings
haut __: **5** monde
Haut-__: **4** Rhin
hautboy: **4** oboe, reed, wind **10** instrument
haute: **4** chic **5** fancy, swank **6** chichi, classy, lavish, swanky **7** elegant, genteel, refined, stylish, voguish **9** luxurious
monde: **6** gentry, jet set **7** society, who's who **10** upper class, upper crust
haute __: **5** école, monde **7** couture, cuisine
Haute-__: **5** Loire, Marne, Saône
haute couture
designer: **4** Dior
magazine: **4** Elle **5** Vogue
__ Haute, IN: **5** Terre
Hautes-__: **5** Alpes
Haute-Savoie
range: **5** Alpes
spa: **5** Evian
hauteur: **4** airs, gall **5** nerve, pride **6** vanity **7** conceit, dignity, disdain, egotism **8** audacity, contempt, elegance, noblesse **9** arrogance, pomposity **10** narcissism, self-esteem
show ~ toward: **4** snub
with ~: **5** icily
haut monde: **5** elite
Havana: **4** city, port, town **5** cigar, smoke **7** capital
castle: **5** Morro
locale: **4** Cuba
see also Spanish
Havana (1990 film)
cast: Alan Arkin, Lena Olin, Robert Redford
director: Sydney Pollack
Havana Brown: **3** cat **5** felid **6** feline
Havanese: **3** dog **5** canid **6** canine
__ Havasu City: **4** Lake
have: **3** con, eat, get, own **4** bear, dupe, gain, hold, keep, land, rook, take **5** beget, carry, cheat, enjoy, grasp, ought, solve, stock, trick, wield **6** embody, endure, evince, imbody, obtain, outfox, outwit, permit, pick up, retain, secure, suffer, take in **7** acquire, carry on, contain, deceive, deliver, exhibit, feature, include, involve, possess, procure, receive, subsume, swindle, two-time, undergo **8** comprise, engage in, exercise, hoodwink, maintain, outsmart, tolerate **9** bamboozle, encompass, get hold of, latch onto, partake of, put up with, victimize **10** experience, keep on hand, monopolize
a ball: **4** romp **5** party **9** celebrate
a bug: **3** ail
a crush on: **4** like **5** adore
a long face: **4** mope, pout
a look at: **3** eye, see

H A

a yearning: 4 ache
bills: 3 owe
coming: 4 earn 5 merit
dinner: 3 eat, sup 5 feast
down cold: 4 know
importance: 4 rate 6 matter
literally: 6 habeas
no doubts: 4 know
relevance: 6 relate
the nerve: 4 dare
words: 5 argue 6 bicker
have __: 4 a cow, a fit 5 a ball, a care, a go at, a seat, a talk, had it, it out, words
have __ a mind to: 4 half
have __ at: 3 a go 5 a shot
have __ day: 5 an off
have __ for: 4 a yen, eyes, it in 5 a feel, a need, an eye, no use
have __ for news: 5 a nose
have __ good authority: 4 it on
have __ in: 4 a say 5 a hand
have __ in common: 4 a lot
have __ in one's bonnet: 4 a bee
have __ in one's eyes: 5 stars
have __ in the hole: 5 an ace
have __ mind to: 5 a good, half a
have __ of: 4 none
have __ of tea: 5 a spot
have __ on: 4 pity
have __ on one's shoulder: 5 a chip
have __-see: 5 a look
have __ spot for: 5 a soft
have __ to: 5 a mind
have __ to eat: 5 a bite
have __ to grind: 4 an ax 5 an axe
have __ to pick: 5 a bone
have __ to play: 5 a role
have __ to the ground: 5 an ear
have __ up one's sleeve: 5 an ace
have __ with: 4 an in, a way, done, to do 5 a word
have-__: 3 not
Have __ and safe holiday: 5 a sane
Have __ and sane holiday: 5 a safe
Have __ day!: 5 a good, a nice 6 a great
Have __ girl for you!: 5 I got a
Have __ news for you!: 4 I got
Have __ Will Travel: 3 Gun
have a __: 4 ball, go at, seat 5 heart
have a __ at: 4 shot 5 whack
have a __ for news: 4 nose
have a __ in: 4 hand
have a __ in one's bonnet: 3 bee
have a __ in the pie: 6 finger
have a __ it: 4 go at
have a __ mind to: 4 good
have a __ on: 6 handle
have a __ one's bonnet: 5 bee in
have a __ skin: 4 thin 5 thick
have a __ stand on: 5 leg to
have a __ to pick: 4 bone
have a __ with: 3 way 4 word
Have a __ day!: 4 good, nice 5 great
have a bee in one's __: 6 bonnet
have a bone to __: 4 pick
have a finger in the __: 3 pie
have a go __: 4 at it
have a good __ to: 4 mind
have an __ for: 3 eye
have an __ grind: 4 ax to 5 axe to
have an __ one's sleeve: 5 ace up
have an __ the ground: 5 ear to
have an __ to grind: 3 axe
have an __ to the ground: 3 ear
have an ax to __: 5 grind
have an ear to the __: 6 ground
Have a nice __!: 3 day
have a nose __ news: 3 for
__ Have Another Cup of Coffee: 4 Let's
Have a taste!: 5 try it
have a thick __: 4 skin
have a thin __: 4 skin
have a way __: 4 with
have a word __: 4 with
__ have been changed..., The: 5 names
__ have ears, The: 5 walls
have eyes __: 3 for
__ have eyes for: 4 only
__ Have Eyes for You: 5 I Only
Have Gun Will Travel (CBS western)
cast: Richard Boone (Paladin)
have half __ to: 5 a mind
have it __: 3 out 4 made 5 in for
have it in __: 3 for
Have I Told You Lately (1993 song)
artist: Rod Stewart
have it on __ authority: 4 good
__ have it, The: 4 ayes, nays
Havel: 5 river
city on the ~: 6 Berlin 7 Potsdam
locale: 7 Germany
Havel, Václav: 4 poet 5 Czech 10 playwright
work: The Garden Party
Letters to Olga
The Memorandum
haven: 4 port 5 cover, oasis 6 asylum, harbor, refuge, resort, shield 7 harbour, hideout, retreat, sanctum, shelter 9 anchorage, harborage, hermitage, sanctuary 10 ivory tower, protection, safe harbor
safe ~: 4 nest
__ haven: 3 tax 4 safe
__ Haven: 3 New 4 West 6 Winter
have no __ for: 3 use 5 words
__ Have No Bananas: 5 Yes! We
have-not: 6 beggar, pauper 8 indigent 9 mendicant
__ Have Nothing: 4 I Who
condition: 7 poverty
Havens: 6 Richie
haven't: 4 lack
Haven't Got Time for the Pain (1974 song)
artist: Carly Simon
have one's __: 3 say 5 eye on 6 number
have one's __ about one: 4 wits
have one's __ court: 5 day in
have one's __ crossed: 7 fingers
have one's __ on: 3 eye
have one's __ set on: 5 heart
have one's __ tied: 5 hands
have one's fingers __: 7 crossed
have one's hands __: 4 tied
have one's heart __ on: 3 set
Haverhill: 4 city, town
locale: 4 Mass.
Haver, June
spouse: Fred MacMurray
Havers: 5 Nigel
haversack: 3 bag 4 pack 6 kitbag 8 knapsack 9 duffelbag
haves: 4 rich 5 elite 6 jet set 7 fat cats
one of the ~: 5 nabob 6 tycoon 7 magnate 9 plutocrat
have stars in one's __: 4 eyes
have the __ laugh: 4 last
have the __ of: 4 best
have the __ of it: 5 worst
have the __ on: 4 drop, jump 5 goods
have the last __: 5 laugh
have the worst __: 4 of it
__ have to?: 3 Do I
__ have to do!: 4 It'll
__ Have to Do Is Dream: 4 All I
__ have you: 4 what
...have you __ wool?: 3 any
Have You __ Her?: 4 Seen
Have You Ever? (1998 song)
artist: Brandy
Have You Ever Really Loved a Woman? (1995 song)
artist: Bryan Adams
Have You Ever Seen the Rain (1971 song)
artist: Creedence Clearwater Revival
Have You Never Been Mellow (1975 song)
artist: Olivia Newton-John
Have Yourself a __ Little Christmas: 5 Merry
Have You Seen Her (1971 song)
artist: Chi-Lites
Have You Seen Her (1990 song)
artist: M.C. Hammer
Have You Seen Your Mother, Baby? (1966 song)
artist: Rolling Stones
Have you two __?: 3 met
__ Having a Baby: 4 She's
__ having fun yet?: 5 Are we
Having My Baby (1974 song)
artist: Paul Anka
Havlicek, John: 5 cager
milieu: 5 court
org.: 3 NBA
sport: 10 basketball
havoc: 4 mess, ruin 5 chaos, waste 6 mayhem 7 carnage, debacle 8 calamity, disorder, shambles, wreckage 9 cataclysm, confusion, mobocracy, ruination 10 desolation
cause ~: 5 wreak, wreck
wreak ~ on: 4 loot, raid, ruin, sack 5 rifle, spoil, strip, waste, wreck 6 harrow, maraud, ravage 7 despoil, destroy, pillage, plunder, ransack 9 depredate, desecrate, devastate, vandalize
__ havoc: 3 cry 5 wreak
Havoc: 4 June
sister: 3 Lee 9 Gypsy Rose
Havoline
competitor: 3 STP
Havre de Grace: 4 city, town
locale: 8 Maryland
haw: 5 dally, demur 8 hesitate, turn left 10 dillydally, equivocate
cousin: 2 er, uh, um
direction: 4 left
ender: 4 king 5 finch, thorn
hem and ~: 4 sway, vary 5 dodge, evade, hedge, shift, stall, waver 6 falter, waffle 7 quibble, stammer, whiffle 8 hesitate 9 fluctuate, pussyfoot, vacillate 10 equivocate
opposite: 3 gee
partner: 3 hem
Haw.
once: 3 ter. 4 terr.
see also Hawaii
__ Haw: 3 Hee
Hawaii: 4 isle, saga 5 novel, state 6 island
author: James A. Michener
bird: 2 oo 4 nene, omao 5 alala, koloa, shama 7 elepaio
carving: 4 tiki
carving material: 4 lava
celebration: 6 Lei Day
city: 3 Ewa 4 Aiea, Hana, Hilo 6 Kailua 7 Kahului, Kaneohe, Waimalu, Waipahu 8 Honolulu, Mililani
coffee region: 4 Kona
conference: 3 WAC
County seat: 4 Hilo
dance: 4 hula 8 hula-hula
director: George Roy Hill
dish: 3 poi
dress: 4 mumu 6 muumuu
feast: 4 luau
first governor: 4 Dole
fish: 4 mano, ulae 5 akule, moano 8 mahimahi
flower: 5 lehua
goodbye: 5 aloha
goose: 4 nene
gooseberry: 4 poha
hardwood: 4 ohia 5 lehua
hark: 4 mano
hello: 5 aloha
honcho: 6 kahuna
honeycreeper: 4 iiwi
honey-eater: 2 oo
hors d'oeuvre: 4 pupu
instrument: 3 uke 7 ukulele
island: 4 Maui, Oahu 5 Kauai, Lanai
islet: 6 Laysan
long, in ~: 3 loa
major employer: 4 Dole
mountain: 5 Mauna
national park: 9 Haleakala
native: 6 kanaka
necklace shell: 4 puka
neckpiece: 3 lei
nickname: 10 Aloha State
non-native: 5 haole
not at all, in ~: 4 aole
once: 3 ter. 4 terr. 9 territory
port: 4 Hilo 8 Honolulu
region: 4 Kona
shark: 4 mano
shrub: 4 poha 5 aalii, akala, olona
state bird: 4 nene
state flower: 8 hibiscus
state gem: 10 black coral
steep slope: 4 pali
tree: 3 koa 5 kukui, lehua
tuna: 3 ahi
vine: 5 maile
volcano: 7 Kilauea 8 Mauna Loa
waterfall: 5 Akaka
wind: 4 Kona
Hawaii __: 5 Five-O
__ Hawaii: 4 Blue
Hawaiian __: 3 Eye 5 Punch, shirt
Hawaiian Punch
rival: 3 HiC
Hawaiian Wedding Song, The (1959 song)
artist: Andy Williams
Hawaii Five-O (CBS drama, song)
artist: Ventures
cast: Jack Lord (Steve McGarrett)

James MacArthur (Danny Dano/Danno Williams)
setting: 4 Oahu **8** Honolulu
villain: Wo Fat
hawfinch: 4 bird
haw-haw: 5 laugh **6** guffaw
___ Haw-Haw: 4 Lord
hawing, hemming and: 8 hesitant, waffling, wavering **9** dithering, equivocal, tentative, undecided, unsettled **10** ambivalent, indecisive, irresolute, of two minds, on the fence, unresolved, up in the air, wishy-washy
hawk: 4 bird, kite, push, sell, vend **5** buteo **6** elanet, falcon, market, osprey, peddle, tercel **7** buzzard, harrier, kestrel, lookout, solicit **9** advertise, hardliner, warmonger **10** bird of prey
attack like a ~: 5 swoop **7** descend, plummet **9** sweep down
female: 3 hen
home: 4 aery, eyry, nest **5** aerie, eyrie
leash: 4 lune
male: 7 tiercel
opposite: 4 dove
relative: 5 eagle
starter: 5 Black, night
trap: 6 bownet
young: 4 eyas
hawk-___: 4 eyed
___ hawk: 3 war **7** chicken
___ Hawk: 5 Black, Kitty
Hawke: 5 Ethan **10** Youngblood
Hawke, Ethan: 5 actor
film: Alive (1993)
Dead Poets Society (1989)
Floundering (1994)
Gattaca (1997)
Great Expectations (1998)
A Midnight Clear (1992)
Reality Bites (1994)
Tape (2001)
Training Day (2001)
White Fang (1991)
spouse: Uma Thurman
hawker: 5 crier **6** pedlar, pedler, seller, vender, vendor **7** peddler **8** huckster, pitchman **10** proclaimer
starter: 3 jay
talk: 5 spiel
Hawkes: 4 John **7** Chesney
Hawkeye: 5 Iowan **6** Pierce
milieu: 4 MASH
portrayer: Alan Alda, Donald Sutherland
Hawkeye State: 4 Iowa
Hawking: 7 Stephen
alma mater: 6 Oxford
Hawkins: 4 Jack, John **5** Sadie **7** Coleman
Hawkins, Coleman: 11 saxophonist
genre: 4 jazz
___ Hawkins Day: 5 Sadie
Hawkins, Jack: 5 actor
spouse: Jessica Tandy
hawkish: 7 hostile, martial, warlike **8** militant **9** bellicose, combative **10** aggressive, pugnacious
___ Hawk, NC: 5 Kitty
Hawks: 4 five, team **6** Howard
former home: 4 Omni
home: 7 Atlanta, Georgia
org.: 3 NBA
rival: ***see*** NBA team
sport: 10 basketball
hawksbill: 6 animal **7** reptile
hawkshaw: 3 tec **6** shamus, sleuth **7** gumshoe **9** detective
Hawks, Howard: 8 director
film: The Big Sleep (1946)
Bringing Up Baby (1938)
Gentlemen Prefer Blondes (1953)
Hatari! (1962)
His Girl Friday (1940)
Red River (1948)
Rio Bravo (1959)
Rio Lobo (1970)
Sergeant York (1941)
To Have and Have Not (1944)
___ Hawk, The: 3 Sea
___ Hawk War: 5 Black
hawkweed: 5 plant **6** flower
___-Hawley: 5 Smoot
Hawn, Goldie: 7 actress
daughter: Kate Hudson
film: Bird on a Wire (1990)
Butterflies Are Free (1972)
Cactus Flower (1969, AA)
Death Becomes Her (1992)
Everyone Says I Love You (1996)
The First Wives Club (1996)
Foul Play (1978)
The Out-of-Towners (1999)
Overboard (1987)
Private Benjamin (1980)
Seems Like Old Times (1980)
Shampoo (1975)
The Sugarland Express (1974)
There's a Girl in My Soup (1970)
Wildcats (1986)
TV: Rowan and Martin's Laugh-In
hawser: 4 line, rope **5** cable **10** anchor rope, towing rope
bend: 4 knot
hawthorn: 4 tree **5** fruit, plant **6** flower
relative: 4 pear, plum, rose **5** apple, peach **6** almond, cherry, medlar, quince **7** apricot **8** oiticica **10** blackthorn
Hawthorne: 5 Nigel **9** Nathaniel
Hawthorne, Nathaniel: 6 writer
friend: Emerson, Thoreau, Melville
town: 5 Salem
work: The Blithedale Romance
Fanshawe
The House of the Seven Gables
The Marble Faun
The Old Manse
The Scarlet Letter
Twice-Told Tales
Young Goodman Brown
hay: 4 feed **5** straw **6** fodder, forage, redtop **7** alfalfa, timothy **9** pasturage
area: 3 mow **4** loft
ask for ~: 5 neigh
bit: 3 awn **4** wisp
bundle: 4 bale **5** stack
bundler: 5 baler
cut ~: 3 mow
ender: 3 mow **4** cock, fork, loft, rack, rick, ride, seed, wire **5** maker, stack
fever reaction: 5 achoo **6** ahchoo, hachoo **7** allergy, kerchoo
hit the ~: 5 crash, sleep **6** retire, turn in **7** sack out **9** go to sleep
pitch, as ~: 4 fork
preserve ~: 6 ensile
second ~ crop: 5 rowen
hay ___: 4 rake **5** baler, fever
___ hay: 4 make
Hay: 3 Ian **4** John
___ Hay: 5 Antic
Hayakawa: 2 S.I. **6** Sessue
Hayden: 3 Tom **6** Robert **7** Carruth, Melissa, Michael **8** Sterling
org.: 3 CIA
Hayden, Tom
org.: 3 SDS
spouse: Jane Fonda
Haydn: 6 Joseph **7** Richard
Haydn, Joseph: 8 Austrian, composer
nickname: 4 Papa
work: Clock Symphony
The Creation
Drum Roll Symphony
Farewell Symphony
Military Symphony
Surprise Symphony
Toy Symphony
Hayek, Salma: 7 actress
film: The Faculty (1998)
Frida (2002)
Timecode (2000)
Wild Wild West (1999)
Hayes: 3 Bob **4** Bill, Lucy **5** Billy, Elvin, Gabby, Helen, Isaac, Woody
product: 5 modem
Hayes, Bill
song: The Ballad of Davy Crockett (1955)
Hayes, Bob: 6 runner **8** sprinter
Hayes, Elvin: 5 cager
milieu: 5 court
org.: 3 NBA
sport: 10 basketball
Hayes, Helen: 7 actress
film: Airport (1970, AA)
Anastasia (1956)
A Farewell to Arms (1932)
The Sin of Madelon Claudet (1931, AA)
spouse: Charles MacArthur
Hayes, Isaac
song: Theme from Shaft (1971)
Hayes, Rutherford B.: 9 president
feature: 5 beard
former occupation: 6 lawyer
home: 4 Ohio **7** Fremont
middle name: 8 Birchard
opponent: 6 Tilden
V.P.: 7 Wheeler
wife: 4 Lucy
Hayley: 5 Mills
hayloft: 3 mow
locale: 4 barn
haymaker: 4 sock **5** punch **6** wallop **8** uppercut
evade a ~: 3 bob **4** duck
land a ~: 2 KO
target: 3 jaw
throw a ~: 5 swing
Haymarket Square event: 4 riot
Haymes, Dick: 6 singer
spouse: Joanne Dru, Rita Hayworth
haymow: 4 loft
Haynes: 4 Todd **5** Abner, Lloyd **7** Marques
Haynie, Sandra: 6 golfer
hayrick: 5 mound
Hays: 4 Will **6** Robert
Haysbert: 6 Dennis
hayseed: 3 oaf **4** boor, hick, rube **5** yokel **6** farmer, lummox, rustic **7** bumpkin, plowboy **9** hillbilly **10** clodhopper
haystack: 4 rick **5** mound
item: 6 needle
Haystacks
painter: Claude Monet
Hayward: 4 city, town **5** Louis, Susan **6** Leland
locale: 10 California
Hayward, Leland
spouse: Margaret Sullavan
Hayward, Susan: 7 actress
film: Ada (1961)
I'll Cry Tomorrow (1955)
I Want to Live! (1958, AA)
The Snows of Kilimanjaro (1952)
With a Song in My Heart (1952)
haywire: 4 amok **5** amuck **6** broken **7** berserk, bonkers, chaotic, flipped, unglued **8** confused **9** defective **10** broken-down, disordered, out of order, out of whack, upside-down
gone ~: 5 kaput **10** on the blink, on the fritz, out of order, out of whack
Hayworth, Rita: 7 actress
film: Blood and Sand (1941)
Cover Girl (1944)
Gilda (1946)
The Lady From Shanghai (1948)
Miss Sadie Thompson (1953)
My Gal Sal (1942)
Pal Joey (1957)
Separate Tables (1958)
The Strawberry Blonde (1941)
You'll Never Get Rich (1941)
You Were Never Lovelier (1942)
spouse: Dick Haymes, Aly Khan, Orson Welles
hazan: 6 cantor
hazard: 3 lay **4** dare, game, luck, play, risk **5** fluke, peril, stake, wager **6** chance, danger, gamble, menace, threat **7** iceberg, imperil, pitfall, thin ice, trouble, venture **8** accident, endanger, fortuity, jeopardy, unsafety **9** adventure, hot potato, postulate, speculate, undertake **10** go for broke, impediment, insecurity, jeopardize
a guess: 5 opine **7** suppose, surmise, suspect **9** speculate
driving ~: 3 fog, ice **4** mist **5** glare, sleet
garden ~: 3 bur **5** brier, spine **7** bramble, prickle, spicule, sticker
golf ~: 4 lake, trap **5** water **6** bunker
navigation ~: 3 fog **4** berg, floe, reef **5** shoal
Hazard (1992 song)
artist: Richard Marx
hazardous: 3 icy **5** dicey, grave, hairy, risky, rocky, tight **6** chancy, unsafe, wicked **7** parlous, unsound **8** insecure, perilous **9** dangerous, desperate, difficult, explosive, uncertain, unhealthy **10** precarious, touch-and-go
not ~: 4 safe

hazardous __: 5 waste
hazardousness: 7 gravity
__ Hazard Perry: 6 Oliver
haze: 3 fog 4 film, mirk, mist, murk, pall, smog 5 brume, bully, roast, taunt, vapor 6 badger, dry fog, hector, muddle, shadow 7 dimness 8 ridicule 9 fogginess, obscurity, vagueness 10 overshadow
Haze: 6 Lolita
__ Haze: 6 Purple
hazel: 3 nut 4 tree 5 acorn, brown, color, shrub 6 cobnut 7 filbert 8 nutbrown
cousin: 5 alder, birch 7 dogwood 8 hornbeam
ender: 3 nut
relative: *see* brown color
tree: 6 cobnut 7 filbert
__ hazel: 5 witch
Hazel: 4 maid 5 comic
cartoonist: 3 Key
dog: 6 Smiley
Hazel (NBC/CBS sitcom)
cast: Whitney Blake (Dorothy Baxter)
Shirley Booth (Hazel Burke)
Don DeFore (George Baxter)
hazelnut: 7 filbert 8 ice cream
alternative: *see* ice cream flavor
haziness: 3 fog 4 blur, smog
hazing target: 4 pleb 5 frosh, plebe
hazy: 3 dim 4 soft 5 dizzy, faint, foggy, fuzzy, mirky, misty, muddy, murky, muzzy, smoky, vague 6 addled, bleary, blurry, cloudy, in a fog, opaque, steamy 7 blurred, clouded, muddled, obscure, shadowy, sunless, unclear 8 confused, nebulous, obscured, overcast 9 befuddled, equivocal, imprecise, uncertain, unfocused 10 bewildered, ill-defined, indefinite, indistinct, inexplicit, obfuscated, out of focus, unexplicit, unspecific
become ~: 4 blur
make ~: 4 blur 5 bedim, befog, blear, cloud, muddy, smear 7 becloud, obscure 9 adumbrate
Hazy Shade of Winter (song)
artist: Bangles, Simon and Garfunkel
HBO: 7 channel
alternative: *see* movie channel
offering: 5 movie
receiver: 2 TV 5 TV set
H.C.: 6 Potter 7 McNeile
HCl: 4 acid
__-H Club: 4 Four
hdg.: 3 dir.
compass ~: 3 ENE, ESE, NNE, NNW, SSE, SSW, WNW, WSW
ship ~: 3 SbE
hd. of state: 3 ldr. 4 pres.
he: 3 guy, man, sir 4 chap, male, pron. 5 bloke 6 feller, fellow, gander, Hebrew, letter, mister 7 pronoun 9 gentleman
and she: 4 they
not ~: 3 she
predecessor: 6 daleth
successor: 3 vav, vaw, waw
he-__: 3 man, men
He: 3 gas 4 elem. 6 helium 7 element
2 for ~: 4 at. no.
He (song)
artist: Al Hibbler, McGuire Sisters, Righteous Brothers
He __ Game: 3 Got
He __ heavy...: 4 ain't
He __ you when you're sleeping...: 4 sees
H.E.: 5 Bates
head: 3 ldr., mgr., run, tip, top 4 acme, apex, bent, boss, dean, dome, foam, fore, gift, lead, main, mind, pate, peak, pres., rule, stem, suds, tend, turn 5 act on, brain, chief, crest, crown, first, flair, front, froth, guide, knack, prime, ruler, skill, skull, title 6 apogee, bigwig, climax, direct, genius, gerent, govern, height, honcho, lather, leader, legend, manage, master, noggin, noodle, origin, sconce, senior, source, summit, talent, tipoff, top dog, vertex 7 ability, act upon, captain, coconut, command, conduct, control, cranium, faculty, forward, go first, highest, latrine, leading, lead off, manager, officer, oversee, premier, supreme, topmost 8 antecede, aptitude, big wheel, capacity, chairman, champion, cocoanut, director, dominate, foreland, foremost, forepart, governor, kingfish, light out, overseer, superior, vanguard 9 braincase, chieftain, commander, forefront, intellect, mentality, organizer, president, principal, supervise 10 administer, gray matter, management, preeminent, promontory, supervisor
a ~: 3 per 4 each
and shoulders: 4 bust
away: 3 ebb 4 fade, flag, wane 5 abate 6 die out, ease up, recede, reflux 7 decline, die down, dwindle, ease off, slacken, subside, tail off 8 decrease, diminish, withdraw
bend the ~: 3 nap, nod 4 doze 6 drowse
big ~: 3 ego
bone: 3 jaw 7 maxilla 8 mandible
cavity: 5 naris, sinus 7 nostril
combining form: 6 cephal- 7 cephalo-, -cephaly 8 -cephalic 9 -cephalous
come to a ~: 5 crest 6 climax 9 culminate
cooler: 6 ice bag 7 ice pack
count: 5 tally 6 census
covering: 3 cap, hat, tam 4 cowl, hair, hood 5 scarf, shawl
crowned ~: 4 czar, king, tsar, tzar 5 ruler 7 monarch
dept. ~: 3 mgr. 4 boss 7 manager
ender: 3 man, set, way 4 ache, achy, band, fast, gear, hunt, lamp, land, line, lock, long, most, race, rest, room, sail, ship, shot, wear, wind, word, work 5 board, dress, first, light, liner, phone, piece, scarf, shake, space, stall, stand, stock, stone, water 6 cheese, hunter, master, spring, strong, waiter, worker 7 counter, hunting, quarter, scarves 8 foremost, mistress, quarters 9 quartered
for: 4 go to, move 5 steer 6 lead to, repair
(for): 3 aim 4 bear, make
for the bottom: 4 sink
for the hills: 2 go 3 fly, lam, run 4 bolt, flee 5 break, leave, scram 6 beat it, bug out, decamp, depart, desert, escape, get out 7 abscond, make off, retreat, run away, take off, vamoose 8 clear out 9 disappear, skedaddle 10 fly the coop, hightail it, hit the road
get in one's ~: 5 grasp, learn, study 6 absorb, master, pick up, soak up 7 find out 8 discover, memorize 10 understand
get through one's ~: 5 grasp, learn 7 discern, realize 9 recognize 10 appreciate, comprehend, understand
go head to ~: 3 pit, vie 4 play 5 fight, match, rival 6 oppose, take on 7 compete, contend 8 struggle 9 challenge
go ~ over heels: 4 fall, flip, slip 5 lurch 6 plunge, sprawl, topple, tumble 7 stumble
go through one's ~: 5 occur 6 dawn on
have a ~ start: 4 lead 7 precede
have in one's ~: 4 know
hit upside the ~: 3 wap 4 beat, whap, whop
honcho: 4 boss, exec, king, prex, prez 5 chief, prexy 7 manager 8 higher-up, official, overseer 9 commander, executive, key player
hurt: 4 ache
in England: 4 noll
in French: 4 tête
it's over your ~: 3 hat 4 hair, roof
lose one's ~: 4 flip 5 freak, panic 6 blow up 7 explode, flip out 8 freak out, have a fit
make one's ~ swim: 3 awe 5 amaze 6 dazzle 7 impress
meet ~ on: 8 confront, cope with, deal with, face up to
movement: 3 nod 5 shrug
off: 5 avert, catch, quell 7 inhibit, prevent 8 preclude 9 intercept, interpose
off the top of one's ~: 5 ad-lib 9 extempore, impromptu, unplanned 10 improvised, unprepared
of state: 5 ruler
of steam: 5 force
of the class: 3 ace 4 best
opposite: 3 toe 4 tail
ornament: 5 crown, tiara 6 anadem, diadem, wreath 7 coronet
out: 2 go 4 exit, move, sail 5 be off, leave, scram, split 6 beat it, be gone, decamp, depart, embark, go away, run off, set off 7 abscond, go forth, push off, retreat, ride off, take off, vamoose 8 run along, set forth, shove off, slip away, withdraw 10 shuffle off
over heels: 4 gaga 6 in love 7 smitten 8 absorbed 9 intensely 10 completely, thoroughly
over one's ~: 4 high 5 above, aloft 6 high up, on high 7 skyward 8 skywards 10 up in the air, up in the sky
part: 3 ear, eye, lip 4 chin, hair, nose, pate 5 scalp
per ~: 4 a pop, each 5 a shot 6 apiece, a throw, singly
remove ~ covering: 5 unhat
start: 4 edge, jump 5 leg up 8 handicap
starter: 3 air, big, bow, cat, egg, fat, god, hot, jar, pin, red, sap, tow, war 4 bald, bill, bone, bulk, bull, dead, drum, fore, hard, hogs, long, mast, meat, over, rail, skin, soft, sore, well 5 arrow, beach, black, block, cross, flint, green, river, snake, spear, steel, swell, thick, trail 6 barrel, bridge, bubble, copper, dragon, fiddle, figure, hammer, knight, letter, logger, mutton, shovel, shower, sleepy, spring, timber, turtle, wooden 7 chuckle, feather, knuckle, leather, thunder 8 fountain
support: 4 neck
swelled ~: 3 ego 5 pride, quirk 6 egoism, vanity 7 conceit, egotism, hauteur, swagger 8 self-love, smugness 9 arrogance, immodesty, vainglory 10 pretension, stuffiness
tilt, as the ~: 4 cock
top of a bird's ~: 6 pileus
toward: 7 make for
(toward): 4 move
trip: 6 revery, vision 7 reverie
up: 3 run 5 chair, climb 6 direct, govern 7 control, preside 8 antecede
use one's ~: 5 think 6 reason 8 cogitate 9 cerebrate
with one's ~ together: 4 sane 5 lucid, sober 8 rational
head __: 3 dip, off, pin 4 cold, trip, wind 5 count, start, table, to toe 7 lettuce
head __ heels: 4 over
__ head: 4 hard 7 chapter, running, swelled, talking
Head: 3 Roy 5 Edith 6 Bessie, Howard, Murray
Head (1968 film)
cast: Teri Garr, Monkees
Head __ Class: 5 of the
__ Head: 7 Diamond
headache: 4 bane, pest, task 5 worry 6 bother, hassle, megrim, misery 7 problem, trouble 8 irritant, migraine, nuisance, quagmire, vexation 9 annoyance, hindrance 10 difficulty
remedy: 3 APC 5 Advil, Bromo 6 Anacin, ice bag 7 aspirin, ice pack
__ headache: 5 sinus
head and shoulders __: 5 above
headband: 5 snood 6 diadem 7 coronet
headband cord, Arab: 4 agal
headcloth: 5 scarf 8 kerchief, mantilla
headdress: 3 cap, taj 4 coif, pouf 5 scarf, tiara 6 bonnet, hairdo, turban 8 coiffure, kaffiyeh, kerchief
clerical ~: 5 miter, mitre

headed
for: **5** off to **6** toward **7** towards
starter: **3** hot, pig, red, sap, tow **4** bare, hard, long, soft **5** level, light, swell **6** mutton
__-headed: **3** red **4** cool, hard, soft, weak, wild **5** clear, empty, fuzzy, giddy, sober, wrong **6** bubble
__-Headed League, The: **3** Red
__ Headed Woman: **4** Hard
Head 'em off at the __!: **4** pass
header: **4** beam, dive, fall, trip **5** spill, title **6** plunge **7** attempt, stumble
starter: **6** double, triple
take a ~: **4** fall, risk **6** topple, tumble
headfirst: **6** rashly **7** hastily **9** hurriedly **10** heedlessly, recklessly
headgear: **3** fez, hat, tam **5** beret, crown, tiara **6** bonnet, diadem, helmet **7** homburg
heavenly ~: **4** halo
see also hat
headhunter
come-on: **5** no-fee
company: **4** agcy. **6** agency
slot: **3** job
heading: **4** name, tack, west **5** label, route, title, track **6** course, legend **7** bearing, caption **8** category, tendency **9** direction **10** trajectory
calendar ~: **3** Apr., Aug., Dec., Feb., Fri., Jan., Jul., Jun., Mar, May, Mon., Nov., Oct., Sat., Sun., Thu., Wed. **4** Sept., Thur. **5** Thurs.
ship ~: **3** ENE, ESE, NbE, NbW, NNE, NNW, SbE, SSE, SSW, WNW, WSW **4** NEbE, NebN
__ Head Island: **6** Hilton
headland: **3** ras **4** cape, hill, mull, ness **5** bluff, point **10** prominence, promontory
headless: **6** stupid **7** aimless, foolish, idiotic, witless **8** mindless, unguided **9** brainless, idiotical, senseless **10** half-witted, leaderless, rudderless, undirected, ungoverned
Headley, Heather
role: **4** Aida
headlight
holder: **5** bezel
setting: **3** dim **4** high
headline: **4** lead, news, star **5** title **6** banner, stress **7** caption, feature **8** screamer, showcase **9** emphasize, publicize
like some ~s: **5** lurid
scream, as a ~: **5** blaze
headliner: **4** hero, name, star **7** feature
Headlines comic: **4** Leno
headlong: **4** rash **5** amain, brash, hasty, quick, swift **6** abrupt, daring, rushed, speedy, sudden **7** hurried, rushing **8** pell-mell, reckless **9** breakneck, dangerous, daredevil, desperate, foolhardy, impatient, impetuous, impulsive, uncareful, whirlwind **10** passionate
go ~: **4** rush, trip **6** careen, tumble
Headlong
author: Michael Frayn
Headlong Hall
author: Thomas Peacock
Headly, Glenne: **7** actress
film: Dick Tracy (1990)
Dirty Rotten Scoundrels (1988)
Making Mr. Right (1987)
Mr. Holland's Opus (1995)
spouse: John Malkovich
headman: **4** boss **5** chief, ruler **6** bigwig, honcho, leader, top cat, top dog **7** kingpin, manager, skipper **8** big wheel, director, kingfish **9** big cheese, commander, executive **10** supervisor
headmaster: **4** dean **8** director **9** principal
headmost: **5** chief, first, front, prime **7** leading, premier, primary, supreme **8** cardinal, foremost **9** paramount, principal
__ Head, NC: **4** Nags
head of __: **5** state
Head of State (2003 film)
cast: Bernie Mac, Tracy Morgan, Chris Rock
Head of the Class (ABC sitcom)
cast: Khrystyne Haje (Simone Foster)
Howard Hesseman (Charlie Moore)
head-on: **6** direct **7** frontal **8** opposing **10** face-to-face, unmediated
strike ~: **3** ram **4** butt **5** smash **6** batter
head-over-__: **5** heels
Head over Feet (1997 song)
artist: Alanis Morissette
Head Over Heels (1985 song)
artist: Tears for Fears
headpiece: **3** wig **5** tiara **6** anadem
headquarters: **4** base, seat, site **6** center, office **7** address, offices, station **8** barracks **9** residence
headrest: **7** cushion
headroom: **4** room **5** space **9** allowance, clearance, open space **10** empty space
__ Headroom: **3** Max
heads
alternative: **5** tails
bump ~: **6** debate **7** wrangle **8** struggle
count ~: **3** add **4** tote **5** add up, tally, total **6** reckon, tote up
family ~: **3** mas, pas
make ~ or tails of: **3** see **6** fathom, follow, pick up **9** figure out **10** comprehend, understand
put ones' ~ together: **6** confer **10** brainstorm
up: **7** look out, warning, watch it **8** watch out **9** be careful
-up situation: **6** danger
__ heads: **4** bump **5** count
Heads __,...: **4** I win
__ Heads: **7** Crowned, Talking
headset: **4** ears **5** phone **7** outlook
Heads I win, tails you __: **4** lose
head-splitting: **5** forte, noisy **7** blaring, booming, jarring, pealing, rackety, raucous, reboant, roaring **8** crashing, piercing, plangent, rumbling, sonorous, strident, turned up **9** big-voiced, clamorous, deafening **10** boisterous, resounding, stentorian, strepitous, thundering, uproarious, vociferous
headstrong: **4** rash **5** brash, stiff, tough **6** mulish, ornery, unruly, wilful **7** adamant, naughty, piggish, wayward, willful **8** contrary, indocile, obdurate, perverse, stubborn **9** desperate, fanatical, foolhardy, hard-nosed, hard-shell, imprudent, impulsive, obstinate **10** determined, refractory, self-willed, unyielding
heads-up: **4** wary **5** alert, aware **7** on guard **8** vigilant, watchful **9** wide-awake **10** on one's toes, on the stick
Heads Up!: **7** musical
composer: Lorenz Hart, Richard Rodgers
head to __: **3** toe
Head to Toe (1987 song)
artist: Lisa Lisa and Cult Jam
head-turner: **5** cutey, cutie
headway: **3** way **4** dent **5** space, speed **6** leeway **7** advance **8** progress
make ~: **4** gain, sail **5** go far **7** advance, shape up
headwear
see hat
heady: **4** racy **5** kicky **6** strong **8** dizzying, exciting **9** thrilling **10** intoxicant
He Ain't Heavy, He's My Brother (1970 song)
artist: Hollies
heal: **4** cure, knit, mend **5** nurse, treat **6** doctor, remedy **7** get well, patch up, rebound, recover, restore **8** minister **9** get better **10** convalesce, recuperate
Heald: **7** Anthony
healed: **6** better **9** good as new
healer: **3** doc **5** curer, medic **6** doctor, medico, mender, shaman **9** physician, therapist
name meaning ~: **5** Jason
org.: **3** AMA
__ healer: **5** faith
Healey: **2** Ed **4** Jeff
healing: **7** therapy **8** curative, remedial, sanative **9** on the mend, treatment **10** corrective
combining form: **5** iatro-, -iatry **7** -iatrics
sign of ~: **4** scab
substance: **4** aloe, balm **5** salve **6** arnica
waters: **3** spa
healing __: **4** arts
health: **4** form, luck, trim **5** shape, vigor **6** fettle **7** fitness, hygiene, welfare **8** haleness, strength, wellness **9** condition, hardiness, salubrity, soundness, toast word, well-being **10** robustness
bad ~: **7** illness **8** sickness **9** infirmity
booster: **3** vit. **7** mineral, vitamin
care facility: **6** clinic **8** hospital **9** infirmary
club: **3** gym, spa **9** gymnasium
food buy: **4** bran, kelp, tofu **5** carob **8** bean curd
good ~: **4** pink, tone **5** asset, vigor
hazard: **5** radon
ill ~: **6** malady **7** ailment, disease **9** infirmity **10** affliction, unwellness
improve in ~: **4** gain, heal, mend **5** rally **6** pick up **7** get well, rebound, recover **9** come along, get better **10** bounce back, convalesce, recuperate
in good ~: **4** well **5** right, sound
in poor ~: **3** ill **4** sick **6** sickly, unwell **7** unsound
mental ~: **6** sanity
org.: **3** CDC, FDA **6** HMO. PPO
professional: **2** MD, RN **3** LPN
regain one's ~: **4** heal **7** get well, rebound, recover **8** snap back **9** get better **10** convalesce, recuperate
restore to ~: **4** cure, heal, mend **5** fix up, treat **6** doctor, remedy **7** patch up
Roman goddess of ~: **5** Salus
science of ~: **8** medicine
to your ~: **5** salud, salut, skoal, toast **6** cheers, prosit **7** l'chayim **9** happy days
health __: **3** spa **4** care, club, code, food
__ health: **3** ill **6** mental, public
healthful: **4** good, pure **6** benign **7** outdoor **8** curative, salutary, sanative, sanitary **9** favorable, wholesome **10** beneficial, nutritious, salubrious
healthier: **6** better
__ Health Organization: **5** World
healthy: **3** fit **4** good, hale, safe, sane, spry, tidy, trim, well **5** fresh, hardy, lusty, sound, tonic, whole **6** active, benign, robust, septic, strong, sturdy, virile **7** bracing, chipper, up to par **8** all right, athletic, blooming, hygienic, muscular, salutary, sanatory, sanitary, thriving, vigorous **9** in the pink, wholesome **10** able-bodied, beneficial, bright-eyed, fortifying, mitigative, nourishing, nutritious, salubrious, unimpaired
hue: **4** pink
looking: **4** rosy **5** ruddy
make ~: **4** cure, heal
mind: **6** sanity
more ~: **6** better
not ~: **3** ill **4** sick **6** ailing, anemic, laid up, sickly, unwell **8** below par, feverish, infected **9** afflicted, bedridden **10** indisposed, out of shape
state: **4** weal
healthy __ horse: **3** as a
healthy-looking: **7** flushed, glowing **8** sanguine
Heaney, Seamus: **4** poet **5** Irish **8** Nobelist
heap: **3** car, lot, wad **4** auto, carn, load, lots, lump, mass, mint, pack, peck, pile, raft **5** amass, bunch, cairn, crate, drift, hoard, mound, ocean, stack, wreck **6** bagful, bundle, huddle, jalopy, jungle, lavish, myriad, pileup **7** buildup, bunch up, clunker, numbers, smother **8** mountain **9** abundance, aggregate, amassment, congeries, gathering, great deal, multitude, profusion, stockpile **10** accumulate, automobile, collection, cumulation, rattletrap
combining form: **5** cumul- **6** cumuli-, cumulo-
kudos on: **5** extol, honor **6** admire, praise, puff up, stroke **7** acclaim,

approve, build up, commend, flatter, lionize **8** hand it to **10** compliment
on: 4 give **6** assign, bestow, confer
refuse ~: 8 junkyard
starter: 5 scrap
top of the ~: 4 acme, A-one, best **5** elite
up: 4 load, pile **5** amass, stack **10** accumulate
__ heap: 3 ash **5** scrap
heaped: 5 thick **6** jammed **7** replete **8** abundant **9** abounding, aggregate, jam-packed
heaping: 6 myriad, untold **7** endless **9** countless
heaps: 4 a lot, lots, many, much **6** oceans, oodles, plenty **10** inundation
of: 6 divers, myriad, umteen, untold **7** copious, profuse, umpteen **8** abundant, manifold, numerous, umpsteen **9** bountiful, countless, quite a few
hear: 3 try **4** heed **5** catch, learn, sense **6** descry, harken, listen, pick up, take in **7** find out, learn of, receive **8** discover, listen in, listen to **9** apprehend, ascertain, eavesdrop, get wind of, get word of **10** adjudicate, understand
cases: 3 try **5** judge
eager to ~: 7 all ears **9** attentive
ender: 3 say
fail to ~: 4 miss
not ~ of: 4 deny **5** spurn **6** ignore, oppose, rebuff, reject **7** disdain, dismiss **8** brush off, disallow **9** disregard
of: 10 learn about
out: 4 heed **6** attend, listen **9** lend an ear
so all can ~: 5 aloud **6** loudly **8** viva voce
the alarm: 4 rise, stir **5** arise, awake, get up, waken **6** awaken, bestir, wake up
ye: 4 oyes, oyez
hear __ drop: 4 a pin
hearable: 5 aloud **7** sensory **9** sensorial
__ Hear a Waltz?: 3 Do I
heard
make oneself ~: 5 shout, speak **6** assert, insist **7** declare, speak up **8** sound off, speak out
something ~: 5 sound
__ Heard That Song Before: 3 I've
hearer: 5 judge
hearers: 5 crowd **7** gallery **8** audience
Hear, hear!: 4 amen **6** I agree
hearing: 5 sense, trial **6** review, tryout **7** earshot, enquiry, inquiry, meeting, session **8** audience, audition **9** listening **10** conference, discussion, perception
combining form: 4 acou- **5** acouo-, audio-
court ~: 4 oyer
of ~: 4 otic **5** aural **6** audial
organ: 3 ear
problem: 6 earwax, otitis, otosis
within ~: 4 near **5** close **6** at hand, nearby **7** close by
hearing __: 3 aid, dog
hearing-__ dog: 3 ear
hearing impaired
device: 3 TDD
lang. for the ~: 3 ASL
__ Hear It for the Boy: 4 Let's
hearken: 4 heed, mark **6** attend, listen **7** look out, pay heed **8** take heed **9** bend an ear, lend an ear
Hearn: 5 Chick **6** George **8** Lafcadio
Hearn, Lafcadio: 6 writer
work: Chita
Youma
Hear no __...: 4 evil
__ Hears a Who: 6 Horton
hearsay: 4 buzz, news, talk, word **5** noise, rumor **6** gossip, report, tattle **7** scandal **9** grapevine
in French: 7 oui-dire
Hearst: 5 Patty
captor: 3 SLA
heart: 3 hub, nub **4** core, crux, gist, grit, guts, knub, meat, pith, seat, soul, will **5** focus, midst, moxie, nerve, organ, pluck, point, spunk, valor **6** center, inside, kernel, marrow, mettle, middle, morale, nature, recess, spirit, ticker, warmth **7** bravery, courage, emotion, essence, feeling, keynote, meaning, nucleus, prowess, purport, stamina **8** backbone, boldness, goodness, interior, kindness, sympathy **9** endurance, fortitude, gallantry, innermost, main point, sincerity, substance, valentine **10** compassion, confidence, durability, humaneness, resolution, tenderness
all ~: 4 kind **6** kindly, tender **8** merciful **10** altruistic, benevolent, charitable, personable
and soul: 4 pith **6** wholly **7** essence **8** entirely **10** completely, thoroughly
at ~: 5 truly **6** really **8** innately **9** basically, in reality
at the ~ of: 6 amidst
bleeding ~: 5 plant **6** flower
break one's ~: 4 jilt **6** bum out, sadden **7** depress, let down **8** dispirit, distress **10** disappoint, dishearten
chambers: 5 atria
chart: 3 ECG, EKG
combining form: 5 cardi- **6** -cardia, cardio- **7** -cardium
cross one's ~: 3 vow **4** avow **5** swear **6** pledge **7** promise
eat one's ~ out: 4 fret, mope **5** mourn **6** grieve, lament, sorrow
ender: 4 ache, beat, burn, felt, land, leaf, sick, wood, worm **5** break, throb **6** broken, string **7** rending, warming **8** breaking
essentially: 4 pump
faint ~: 8 cold feet, timidity **9** cowardice
hardness of ~: 5 odium **6** animus, enmity, hatred, rancor **7** ill will **8** acrimony **9** animosity **10** antagonism, resentment
have a ~: 4 care
have a broken ~: 5 mourn
have a change of ~: 6 recant **7** retract, reverse **8** pull back, withdraw **9** back-pedal
heavy ~: 3 woe **4** funk **5** blues, dolor, gloom, grief **6** misery, pathos, sorrow **7** anguish, sadness **8** distress, doldrums, glumness **9** dejection **10** depression, gloominess, melancholy
hurt: 4 ache **5** dolor, grief **6** misery **7** anguish **8** distress
in French: 5 coeur
it comes from the ~: 5 blood
know by ~: 4 cite **6** retain **8** memorize
learn by ~: 4 know **8** memorize, remember
line: 4 vein **5** aorta **6** artery
lose ~: 4 mope **5** quail **6** give up **7** despair, despond **10** give up hope
lose one's ~ to: 4 love
name meaning ~: 4 Hugh
near to one's ~: 6 adored, prized **7** beloved, darling **8** cared for, endeared **9** cherished, treasured, worshiped
of a ~ chamber: 6 atrial
of the ~: 7 cardial
of the matter: 3 nub **4** crux, gist, knub **5** nexus, point
part: 5 valve **6** atrium **7** auricle **9** ventricle
rate: 5 pulse
set one's ~ on: 4 wish **5** yearn **6** desire
sick at ~: 3 sad **4** blue, glum **5** moody, mopey, woful **6** gloomy, morose, woeful **7** doleful **8** dejected, dolorous, downcast, grieving, mournful, troubled **9** cheerless, depressed, miserable, saturnine, sorrowful, woebegone **10** despondent, dispirited, melancholy
starter: 3 CPR **5** green, sweet **6** purple
take ~: 6 perk up **7** cheer up **10** brighten up
take to ~: 4 heed, obey **6** follow **7** abide by, observe, respect **8** adhere to
take to one's ~: 6 endear
tug at the ~: 4 move **6** affect
where the ~ is: 4 home
with a heavy ~: 5 sadly
with all one's ~: 5 truly **8** candidly **9** sincerely
with good ~: 4 bold, game **5** brave **6** daring, gritty, plucky, spunky **7** doughty, gallant, valiant **8** intrepid, valorous **9** dauntless **10** courageous
heart __ matter: 5 of the
heart-__: 7 rending
__ heart: 4 take **5** have a **6** broken
Heart
song: Alone (1987)
Magic Man (1976)
Never (1985)
Nothin' at All (1986)
Tell It Like It Is (1980)
These Dreams (1986)
What About Love? (1985)
Who Will You Run To (1987)
Heart __ Lonely Hunter, The: 3 is a
__ Heart: 4 Dear **6** Clara's, Purple, Sacred
heartache: 3 woe **4** pain **5** agony, dolor, gloom, grief, worry **6** misery, regret, sorrow **7** anguish, despair, sadness, torment, trouble **8** distress, the blues **9** dejection, suffering **10** depression, desolation, loneliness, melancholy, woefulness
__ Heartache: 4 It's a
Heartaches by the Numbers (1959 song)
artist: Guy Mitchell
Heartache Tonight (1979 song)
artist: Eagles
heart and __: 4 soul
Heart and Soul (1983 song)
artist: Huey Lewis and the News
Heart and Soul (1987 song)
artist: T'Pau
Heart Attack (1982 song)
artist: Olivia Newton-John
heartbeat: 5 pulse, throb
quickener: 6 crisis
sound: 5 thump
Heartbeat
author: Danielle Steel
Heartbeat (1986 song)
artist: Don Johnson
Heartbeat - It's a Lovebeat (1973 song)
artist: DeFranco Family
heartbreak: 3 woe **5** agony, dolor, grief, trial **6** misery, regret, sorrow **7** anguish, despair, sadness, torment **8** distress **9** dejection, suffering **10** affliction, bitterness, depression, desolation, loneliness, woefulness
Heartbreak __: 5 Hotel, House, Ridge
Heartbreaker (song)
artist: Mariah Carey, Jay-Z, Dionne Warwick
__ Heartbreaker: 5 She's a
Heartbreakers (2001 film)
cast: Gene Hackman, Jennifer Love Hewitt, Ray Liotta, Sigourney Weaver
Heartbreak Hotel (song)
artist: Faith Evans, Whitney Houston, Elvis Presley, Kelly Price
Heartbreak House
author: George Bernard Shaw
character: 4 Addy, Dunn **5** Ellie, Hessy
heartbreaking: 3 sad **4** dire **5** sorry, woful **6** bitter, moving, tragic, woeful **7** joyless, piteous, pitiful **8** dolorous, grievous, pathetic, poignant, touching, tragical **10** lamentable, pathetical
Heartbreak Kid, The (1972 film)
cast: Eddie Albert, Charles Grodin, Cybill Shepherd
director: Elaine May
role: 5 Lenny
Heartbreak Ridge (1986 film)
cast: Clint Eastwood, Marsha Mason
heartbroken: 3 sad **4** blue, down, glum **5** sorry, woful **6** gloomy, morose, somber, woeful **7** crushed, doleful, joyless, unhappy **8** dejected, dismayed, downcast, grieving, mournful, troubled, wretched **9** bummed-out, cheerless, depressed, miserable,

sorrowful, woebegone **10** chapfallen, dispirited, melancholy
one: **5** piner
heartburn: **5** agita
cause: **3** gas
remedy: **4** Tums **6** Maalox, Pepcid, Riopan, Zantac **7** Gelusil, Lactaid, Mylanta, Rolaids **8** Gaviscon **11** Alka-Seltzer, Pepto-Bismol
Heartburn (1986 film)
cast: Jeff Daniels, Jack Nicholson, Meryl Streep
director: Mike Nichols
__-hearted: **3** big **4** cold, free, good, iron, open, soft, warm **5** black, faint, false, heavy, stony, stout **6** simple, single, tender **7** chicken
hearted starter: **4** down, free, good, half, hard, kind, lion, open, soft **5** great, light, stone, stony, stout, whole **6** broken, tender
hearten: **4** buoy, stir **5** cheer, elate, liven, rouse, steel **6** arouse, assure, buck up, buoy up, please, solace, stir up, thrill **7** cheer up, comfort, condole, console, delight, elevate, enliven, fortify, gladden, gratify, happify, inspire, lighten **8** brighten, embolden, enspirit, imbolden, inspirit, motivate, psyche up, reassure, revivify **9** encourage **10** strengthen
heartening: **6** cheery, joyful, joyous, upbeat **7** hopeful **8** cheerful, jubilant **9** favorable **10** optimistic
heartfelt: **4** dear, deep, real, true, warm **6** ardent, devout, fervid, honest **7** earnest, fervent, genuine, sincere **8** bona fide, profound **9** unfeigned **10** passionate
Heart Full of Soul (1965 song)
artist: Yardbirds
hearth: **4** fire, home **5** grate, ingle **8** fireside **9** fireplace
ender: **3** rug **4** side **5** stone
goddess: **5** Vesta
like an unswept ~: **4** ashy
residue: **3** ash **6** cinder
Roman ~ protector: **3** Lar
Roman ~ protectors: **5** Lares
tend the ~: **5** stoke
tool: **5** poker
__-hearth: **4** open
hearthstone, use a: **5** scour
heartily: **4** well **6** avidly, gladly, warmly **8** ardently **9** cordially, sincerely, zealously
heartiness: **4** fire, zest **5** vigor **6** fervor **9** eagerness, geniality **10** cordiality
Heart in Hand (1962 song)
artist: Brenda Lee
Heart is a Lonely Hunter, The
author: Carson McCullers
character: **4** Biff, Jake, Mick **5** Alice **6** Portia, Spiros
heartland unit: **4** acre
heartless: **4** cold **5** cruel, harsh, stony **6** brutal, savage, stoney, unkind, wicked **7** callous, inhuman **8** pitiless, ruthless, uncaring **9** barbarous, impassive, merciless, unfeeling, unpitying **10** hard-boiled, unmerciful
one: **4** ogre **5** beast, brute **6** animal, savage, tyrant **9** barbarian
Heartlight (1982 song)
artist: Neil Diamond
heart of __: **4** gold, palm
Heart of a Woman, The
author: Maya Angelou
Heart of Darkness
author: Joseph Conrad
Heart of Dixie: **3** Ala. **7** Alabama
Heart of Glass (1979 song)
artist: Blondie
Heart of Gold (1972 song)
artist: Neil Young
Heart of Midlothian, The
author: Walter Scott
Heart of Rock & Roll, The (1984 song)
artist: Huey Lewis and the News
Heart of Stone (1965 song)
artist: Rolling Stones
Heart of the Hunter, The
author: Laurens Van der Post
Heart of the Matter, The
author: Graham Greene
Heart of the Night (1979 song)
artist: Poco
heartrending: **3** bad, sad **4** dire **5** sorry, woful **6** moving, tragic, woeful **7** doleful, pitiful **8** dolorous, grievous, pathetic, poignant, touching, tragical **9** harrowing, plaintive **10** pathetical
hearts: **4** game, suit **8** card game
at times: **5** trump
ender: **4** ease
starter: **6** lonely
two ~: **3** bid
Hearts Afire (CBS sitcom)
cast: Edward Asner (George Lahti)
Markie Post (Georgie Hartman)
John Ritter (John Hartman)
hearts and __: **7** flowers
__ Hearts and Coronets: **4** Kind
__ Hearts Dance: **5** Sweet
heart's desire: **4** love, will **7** darling
heart's-ease: **5** pansy
heartsick: **3** low, sad **4** blue, down, glum **5** woful **6** aching, broody, gloomy, morose, somber, woeful **7** doleful, forlorn, joyless, unhappy **8** dejected, downcast, grieving, mournful, troubled **9** bummed out, cheerless, miserable, sorrowful, woebegone **10** chapfallen, dispirited, melancholy
be ~: **4** ache
be ~ about: **3** rue **5** mourn **6** bemoan, bewail, lament, regret
one: **5** piner
heartsickness: **3** woe **5** agony, angst, gloom, grief, worry **6** misery, sorrow **7** anguish, anxiety, despair **9** dejection **10** depression, desolation, melancholy
Hearts on Fire (1981 song)
artist: Randy Meisner
heartstring sound: **4** zing
heartstrings, tug on the: **4** stir
__ Hearts Were Young and Gay: **3** Our
heartthrob
see sweetheart
heart-to-heart: **4** chat **5** frank **6** candid, honest
heart-to-heart __: **4** talk
Heart to Heart (1982 song)
artist: Kenny Loggins
heartwarming: **4** good **9** rewarding **10** delightful, fulfilling, gratifying, satisfying
hearty: **3** fit **4** avid, hale, iron, warm, well, wiry **5** beefy, burly, eager, hardy, hefty, hunky, husky, jolly, lusty, sound, stout, tough **6** ardent, brawny, cheery, devout, fervid, genial, jovial, mighty, potent, robust, rugged, sinewy, steely, stocky, strong, sturdy, virile **7** affable, cordial, doughty, earnest, fervent, gushing, profuse, sincere, zealous **8** animated, athletic, cheerful, effusive, forceful, friendly, indurate, muscular, powerful, puissant, stalwart, vehement, vigorous **9** Atlantean, convivial, ebullient, energetic, exuberant, Herculean, strapping, unfeigned, vivacious, well-built **10** able-bodied, passionate, red-blooded, rollicking, unreserved
partner: **4** hale
Hear ye!: **4** oyes, oyez
heat: **3** fry **4** bake, boil, char, fury, race, rage, sear, warm **5** anger, ardor, broil, fever, grill, roast, scald, singe, toast **6** fervor, fire up, police, scorch, stress, summer, temper, warmth, warm up **7** firearm, hotness, passion, swelter, torrefy, torrify **8** calidity, calorify, ferocity, melt down, pressure, violence, warmness **9** carbonize, fieriness, intensity, surliness, torridity, vehemence **10** caloricity, excitement, fervidness, sultriness
body ~: **7** pyrexia
combining form: **3** pyr- **4** pyro- **5** therm- **6** calori-, thermo-, -thermy
conductor: **4** coil
dead ~: **3** tie **4** draw
emotional ~: **3** ire **4** fury, rage **5** anger, pique, wrath **6** choler, enmity **7** offense, outrage **10** antagonism
ender: **5** proof
feel the ~: **4** bask **8** sunbathe
join with ~: **4** bond, fuse, melt, weld **6** solder
measure: **3** BTU, cal., deg. **4** kcal. **6** degree **7** calorie
mind's ~: **4** zeal **5** ardor **6** fervor **7** avidity, passion
one in a ~: **4** vier **6** runner **8** sprinter
react to ~: **6** expand
shriveled from ~: **3** dry **4** sere **7** parched **10** desiccated
source: **3** sun **4** coal, fire **6** boiler
suffer from the ~: **4** wilt **5** sweat **7** shrivel, swelter
take the ~ off: **4** ease **5** allay, let up, relax **6** lessen, relent **7** lighten, slacken **8** mitigate, moderate **9** alleviate, disburden
unit: **5** therm **7** calorie
up: **4** boil, cook, nuke, warm **6** arouse **8** escalate **9** impassion, intensify, reinforce
heat __: **3** gun **4** lamp, pump, sink, wave **5** index **6** shield
heat __!, The: **4** is on
heat-__: **4** seal **5** treat
__ heat: **4** dead **5** solar, steam, white **6** latent **7** prickly, radiant
Heat: **4** five
home: **5** Miami
org.: **3** NBA
rival: *see* NBA team
Heat (1995 film)
cast: Robert De Niro, Val Kilmer, Al Pacino, Jon Voight
director: Michael Mann
Heat __: **4** Wave
__ Heat: **3** Red **4** Body, City **5** Steam, White
Heat and the Clouds, The
artist: Erté
heated: **3** hot **4** warm **5** angry, fiery, irate, upset **6** ablaze, bitter, fervid, fierce, hectic, ireful, raging, stormy, torrid **7** burning, fervent, flaring, furious, intense, thermal, violent **8** feverish, frenzied, vehement, volcanic, wrathful **9** emotional, indignant **10** in an uproar, infuriated, passionate
slightly ~: **5** tepid **8** lukewarm
__-heated: **5** steam
heater: **3** gat, gun, rod **5** stove **6** boiler, pistol, roscoe **7** furnace **8** auto part, fastball, radiator
lab ~: **4** etna
pack a ~: **4** tote **5** carry
__ heater: **5** space, water
heath: **4** moor **5** erica, plain, shrub **6** meadow **7** lowland **9** scrubland
family shrub: **5** erica, salal **6** azalea, kalmia, sorrel **7** arbutus, madrone, rhodora **8** cassiope, cowberry **9** blueberry, deerberry
genus: **5** erica
Heath: **3** bar, Ted **5** candy **6** Edward, Ledger **8** candy bar **9** chocolate
alternative: *see* candy brand
__ Heath: **5** Egdon
Heathcliff: **3** cat **4** toon **7** musical **8** Huxtable
Heath, Edward: **2** P.M. h
predecessor: **6** Wilson
successor: **6** Wilson
heathen: **5** pagan **7** infidel, profane **9** barbarian
ender: **3** dom
heather: **5** color, erica, plant **6** flower, purple **7** pinkish
relative: *see* purple color
where ~ grows: **4** moor
Heather: **6** Graham, Thomas **7** Menzies, O'Rourke, Rattray **8** Locklear **10** Langenkamp
Heather on the Hill, The
composer: Alan Jay Lerner, Frederick Loewe
Heathers (1989 film)
cast: Shannen Doherty, Winona Ryder, Christian Slater
Heatherton: **3** Ray **4** Joey
Heathrow arr., former: **3** SST
heating
conduit: **4** duct
fuel: **3** oil **4** coal
unit: **5** therm **6** burner, therme
heating __: **3** pad
__ heating: **5** panel, solar, steam
Heat Is On, The (1985 song)
artist: Glenn Frey

Heat of the Day, The
author: Elizabeth Bowen
Heat of the Moment (1982 song)
artist: Asia
Heat of the Night (1987 song)
artist: Bryan Adams
___ Heat of the Night: 5 In the
Heaton: 8 Patricia
heat-resistant
alloy: 6 cermet 7 ceramal
material: 5 Pyrex 6 boride
___ Heat, The: 3 Big
Heat Wave
composer: Irving Berlin
Heat Wave (song)
artist: Martha & the Vandellas, Linda Ronstadt
heave: 3 lug, pry, tug 4 cast, fire, haul, heft, hurl, keel, lift, move, pant, puff, pull, roll, sigh, spew, spue, toss, wash, wave 5 boost, bulge, chuck, fling, hoist, lurch, pitch, raise, roust, sling, surge, swell, throw 6 billow, launch, let fly, plunge, propel, thrust, well up 7 elevate, project 8 catapult, jettison
at sea: 5 scend
out: 4 boot, bump, rout 5 eject, evict, expel 6 banish, bounce, depose 7 cast off 8 drive off, get rid of 9 eliminate 10 dispossess
heave-ho: 4 boot 9 discharge, dismissal
give the ~: 3 axe, can 4 boot, fire, oust 6 depose
heaven: 3 sky 5 azure, bliss 6 utopia 7 Arcadia, ecstasy, Elysium, nirvana, rapture 8 empyrean, paradise 9 cloud nine, firmament, happiness, Shangri-la
ender: 4 ward 5 wards
food from ~: 5 manna
highest ~: 8 empyrean
in ~: 4 glad, over 5 above, aloft, happy, merry 6 blithe, cheery, elated, jovial, joyful, joyous, upbeat 7 gleeful, pleased, tickled 8 blissful, cheerful, ecstatic, euphoric, exultant, jubilant, mirthful, thrilled 9 delighted, ebullient, overjoyed, rapturous, rejoicing, rhapsodic
like ~: 5 above, aloft
made in ~: 5 ideal 7 perfect, utopian 9 exemplary, nonpareil
manna from ~: 4 boon 7 godsend 8 blessing, windfall
on earth: 4 Eden
opposite: 5 Hades
queen of ~: 4 Hera
search high ~: 4 comb 6 forage 7 ransack
vault of ~: 3 sky 8 empyrean
heaven ___: 5 knows
heaven ___ me: 4 help
heaven-___: 4 born, sent
___ heaven: 3 hog 5 thank 6 peanut 7 seventh
Heaven (song)
artist: Bryan Adams, Warrant
___ Heaven: 5 Cry to 7 Seventh
___ heaven and earth: 4 move
Heaven Can Wait (1978 film)
cast: Warren Beatty, Dyan Cannon, Julie Christie, Jack Warden
director: Warren Beatty
___ Heaven for Little Girls: 5 Thank
Heaven Help Me (1989 song)
artist: Dean Estus, George Michael
Heaven Help Us All (1970 song)
artist: Stevie Wonder
Heaven Is a Place on Earth (1987 song)
artist: Belinda Carisle
Heaven Knows (1979 song)
artist: Donna Summer
Heaven Knows, Mr. Allison (1957 film)
cast: Deborah Kerr, Robert Mitchum
director: John Huston
heavenly: 5 tasty, yummy 6 astral, divine, dreamy, edenic, toothy 7 angelic, darling 8 alluring, almighty, beatific, blissful, empyreal, empyrean, ethereal, seraphic, supernal 9 ambrosial, angelical, celestial, delicious, enjoyable, good to eat, ineffable, nectarous, rapturous, succulent 10 delectable, entrancing, seraphical
see also wonderful
heavenly hash: 8 ice cream
alternative: *see* ice cream flavor
Heaven Makers, The
author: Frank Herbert
heavens: 3 sky 5 ether 6 aether 9 firmament 10 atmosphere
combining form: 4 uran- 5 urano-
survey the ~: 4 gaze
Heavens ___!: 5 above
Heavens!: 4 egad, gosh, oh my, oh no 5 egads, mercy 6 dear me 10 my goodness
___ heaven's sake!: 3 For
Heavens to ___!: 5 Betsy
heavenward: 5 above
heavier-___-air: 4 than
heavily: 4 hard
in music: 7 pesante
heaviness: 4 heft, mass 6 weight 7 boredom, gravity 8 dullness, pressure
determine the ~ of: 5 weigh
heaving sound: 5 grunt
heavy: 3 big, sad 4 deep, hard, huge, logy, rich 5 ample, beefy, dense, grave, gross, harsh, hefty, laden, leady, obese, prime, rough, solid, squat, stiff, stout, thick, tough 6 bad guy, broody, chunky, dismal, fleshy, gloomy, knotty, leaden, portly, severe, sleepy, solemn, stodgy, stolid, stuffy, sullen, sultry, taxing, torpid, zaftig, zoftig 7 arduous, complex, fraught, labored, languid, lumpish, massive, onerous, sensual, serious, tedious, weighty 8 abstruse, abundant, dejected, downcast, grievous, listless, profound, sluggish, tiresome, toilsome, unwieldy, weighted 9 corpulent, depressed, difficult, excessive, impassive, laborious, lethargic, momentous, ponderous, recondite, sorrowful, strenuous, unwieldly, wearisome 10 burdensome, cumbersome, despondent, enervating, formidable, melancholy, oppressive, overweight, passionate, well-padded
be ~: 5 weigh
blow: 4 welt 5 thump, whomp 6 wallop
coat: 5 parka, wamus 6 anorak, ulster, wammus, wampus
combining form: 4 bary- 5 gravi-
ender: 3 set 6 weight
fabric: 4 wool 5 denim, loden 8 cretonne
heart: 3 woe 4 funk 5 blues, dolor, gloom, grief 6 misery, pathos, sorrow 7 anguish, sadness 8 distress, doldrums, glumness 9 dejection 10 depression, gloominess, melancholy
hitter: 4 czar 5 mogul
hot and ~: 6 ardent
jacket: 5 wamus 6 ulster, wammus, wampus
knock: 4 slam, thud 5 clonk, clunk, thunk
load: 4 onus 6 burden, weight
metal: 4 iron, lead 5 armor, brass, music
not ~: 4 lean, puny, slim, thin, trim 5 light, spare 6 dainty, flimsy, gentle, scanty, skinny, slight, sparse, svelte, twiggy 7 slender, willowy 8 delicate, ethereal, feathery, gossamer 9 gossamery
sound: 4 thud, wham 5 clonk, clunk, thump, thunk
weight: 3 ton
weigh ~ upon: 5 worry 6 burden, plague, sadden 7 oppress, torment 8 distress 10 dishearten
heavy ___: 4 seas 5 cream, metal, water 6 hitter 7 lifting, traffic
heavy-___: 4 duty 5 laden 6 footed, handed 7 hearted
___-heavy: 3 top
heavy-duty: 3 big 6 hearty, potent, robust, rugged, strong 7 durable 8 powerful, well-made 9 well-built
heavy-eyed: 4 dozy 5 yawny 6 drowsy, groggy, sleepy 9 somnolent 10 half-asleep
heavy-footed: 5 gawky 6 clumsy, klutzy 7 awkward, hulking 8 clunking, ungainly 9 lumbering, maladroit
heavy-handed: 4 hard 5 bossy, harsh, unfit 6 clumsy, gauche, severe 7 awkward, uncouth 8 despotic, lubberly 9 draconian, graceless, maladroit, ponderous 10 autocratic, despotical, ironfisted, oppressive, tyrannical, ungraceful
one: 3 ape, oaf 6 galoot, lummox
heavy-hearted: 3 sad 4 blue 5 sorry 7 crushed, forlorn, unhappy 8 dejected, downcast, mournful 9 depressed, long-faced, miserable, sorrowful 10 chapfallen, melancholy
be ~: 4 moan, mope, pine 5 brood, mourn 6 grieve, lament 7 agonize 8 languish
heavy hydrogen
discoverer: Harold Urey
heavy-load mover: 5 dolly, truck
heavy-metal: 4 rock 5 music
heavyset: 3 big 5 squat 6 chunky, rugged, stocky, stubby
Heavy Traffic (1973 film)
director: Ralph Bakshi
heavyweight: 3 big, VIP 5 biggy, boxer, hefty 6 biggie, big gun, bigwig 7 big name, big shot, massive, notable 8 big wheel, powerful, somebody, superior, wrestler 9 dignitary, important, personage, ponderous
see also boxing
___ heavyweight: 5 light
Hebb, Bobby
song: Sunny (1966)
hebdomad: 4 week 6 septet
Hebe: 8 asteroid
brother: 4 Ares
husband: 8 Heracles
parent: 4 Hera, Zeus
Hebert: 3 Jay 6 Lionel
Hébert, Anne: 4 poet 8 Canadian
hebetude: 5 sloth 6 torpor 7 languor 8 laziness, lethargy 9 indolence, torpidity
hebetudinous: 4 logy 5 heavy 6 torpid
Hebrew: 5 Isaac, Jacob 6 Danite, Jewish, Levite 7 Abraham, Solomon 8 language 9 Israelite
bushel: 4 epha, omer 5 ephah
dance: 4 hora
day in ~: 3 yom
dry measure: 4 epha, omer 5 ephah
eve: 4 ereb, erev
exclamation ~: 6 l'chaim 7 l'chayim, lehayim 8 lechayim
feast: 5 seder
holiday: 5 Purim 8 Passover
judge: 3 Eli
king: 4 Saul 5 David 7 Solomon
law: 4 Tora 5 Torah
letter: 2 he, pe 3 bes, bet, heh, kof, mem, nun, peh, sin, tau, tav, taw, tet, vav, vaw, waw, yod 4 alef, ayin, beth, caph, heth, kaph, koph, qoph, resh, sadi, shin, teth, yodh 5 aleph, cheth, gimel, lamed, sadhe, tsade, tsadi, zayin 6 daleth, lamedh, samech, samekh
lyre: 4 asor
measure: 3 hin, kor
month: 2 Av 4 Adar, Elul, Iyar 5 Nisan, Sivan, Tevet 6 Kislev, Shevat, Tammuz, Tishri 7 Heshvan
people: 4 Sion, Zion
poet: 6 Bialik 8 Alterman 9 Greenberg
prayer: 5 shema
priest: 5 Aaron
prophet: 4 Amos, Ezra 5 Elias, Hosea, Moses
queen: 6 Esther
sacrifice: 6 corban, korban
scholar: 5 rabbi, rebbe
tribe: 3 Dan 4 Levi
underworld: 5 Sheol
writer: 5 Agnon
Hebrew National: 5 frank 6 hot dog, wiener
alternative: 5 Kahn's 6 Armour 8 Ball Park 10 Oscar Mayer
Hebrews: 4 book
follower: 5 James
preceder: 8 Philemon
Hebrides: 4 isls. 5 isles 7 islands

island: 4 Iona, Mull, Skye, Uist 5 Barra, Islay
language: 4 Erse
locale: 8 Scotland
__ Hebrides: 5 Inner, Outer
Hebrides Overture
composer: Felix Mendelssohn
Hebron grp.: 3 PLO
Hecate: 8 conjurer, sorcerer
daughter: 5 Aeaea, Circe, Kirke, Medea 6 Scylla 8 Apsyrtus
Heche, Anne: 7 actress
film: John Q (2002)
The Juror (1996)
Return to Paradise (1998)
Six Days Seven Nights (1998)
The Third Miracle (1999)
Volcano (1997)
Wag the Dog (1997)
TV: Men in Trees
Hecht, Ben: 6 writer 10 playwright
work: The Front Page
heck: 4 darn, drat, rats 6 phooey 7 dickens 9 all get-out
Heckart, Eileen Oscar: Butterflies Are Free
heckelphone
cousin: 4 oboe
Heckerling, Amy: 8 director
film: Clueless (1995)
Fast Times at Ridgemont High (1982)
Look Who's Talking (1989)
heckle: 3 boo, dis, nag, rag 4 bait, faze, gibe, hiss, jeer, jibe, mock, razz, ride, slam, slur, snub 5 abuse, annoy, decry, hound, libel, scorn, spurn, taunt 6 badger, bother, defame, deride, dump on, harass, impugn, malign, needle, noodge, offend, pester, pick on, plague, rattle, rebuff, slight, vilify 7 affront, asperse, catcall, degrade, disdain, disrupt, disturb, put down, rank out, shout at, slander, torment, traduce 8 belittle, denounce, ridicule, vilipend 9 denigrate, discomfit, discredit, disparage, humiliate 10 calumniate, disconcert, disrespect
Heckle: 4 toon 6 magpie
colleague: 6 Jeckle
heckler: 4 pest 5 booer
missile: 3 egg 6 tomato
hectare cousin: 4 acre
hectic: 4 busy, wild 5 crazy, wooly 6 fervid, heated, rushed, woolly 7 chaotic, excited, frantic, furious, hurried, riotous 8 agitated, animated, confused, exciting, feverish, frenetic, frenzied 9 turbulent 10 boisterous, disordered, in an uproar, rip-roaring, tumultuous
hector: 3 cow, irk, nag, vex 4 haze, jeer, ride, roil 5 annoy, bully, hound, peeve, scold, tease, worry 6 badger, harass, needle, noodge, pester, pick on, plague, pother 7 bluster, henpeck, swagger 8 bludgeon, browbeat, bulldoze, bullyboy, domineer 9 persecute, strong-arm, terrorize, tyrannize 10 intimidate
Hector: 4 hero 6 Trojan 7 Babenco, Berlioz, Garneau 8 Elizondo
brother: 5 Paris 6 Pammon 7 Helenus, Polites, Troilus 8 Antiphus
home: 4 Troy
in Italian: 6 Ettore
parent: 5 Priam 6 Hecuba 7 Priamus
sister: 6 Creusa, Iliona 7 Laodice 8 Polyxena 9 Cassandra
slayer of ~: 8 Achilles
son: 8 Astyanax
wife: 10 Andromache
Hector __ Camacho: 5 Macho
...Hector __ a pup: 3 was
Hector Servadac
author: Jules Verne
Hecuba: 6 Trojan
author: Euripides
brother: 5 Asius
daughter: 6 Creusa, Iliona 7 Laodice 8 Polyxena 9 Cassandra
home: 4 Troy
husband: 5 Priam 7 Priamus
son: 5 Paris 6 Hector, Pammon 7 Helenus, Polites, Troilus
Hedaya: 3 Dan
Hedda: 6 Gabler, Hopper
Hedda Gabler
author: Henrik Ibsen
character: 4 Thea 5 Brack 6 Eilert 7 Tessman
Heder: 3 Jon
hedge: 3 pen 4 bush, duck, ring 5 avoid, delay, dodge, evade, fence, fudge, hem in, skirt, stall, wager, waver 6 corral, offset, privet, screen, waffle 7 barrier, confine, enclose, inclose, shuffle, thicket, whiffle 8 boundary, flip-flop, hesitate, sidestep, surround 9 hem and haw, pussyfoot, runaround, shrubbery, stonewall, temporize, vacillate 10 equivocate
arrangement: 4 maze
cut the ~: 4 snip, trim 5 prune
ender: 3 hog, hop, row
expert: 3 arb
something to hedge: 3 bet 4 risk
trimmer: 6 shears
hedge __: 4 fund
hedged in: 4 pent
hedgehog: 6 animal, mammal
cousin: 4 mole
feature: 5 spine
female: 3 sow
like a ~: 5 spiny 7 bristly, prickly
male: 4 boar
video-game ~: 5 Sonic
young: 3 pup
hedges: 9 shrubbery
hedging one's bets: 4 sage, wary, wise 5 chary, leery 7 careful, guarded, politic, prudent 8 cautious 9 judicious, provident, sagacious, tentative
Hedin, Sven: 7 Swedish 8 explorer 10 geographer
Hedison: 5 David
He done __ wrong: 3 her
hedonism: 6 luxury 10 indulgence, profligacy, sybaritism
hedonist: 5 pagan 8 sybarite 9 bon vivant, libertine 10 sensualist, voluptuary
hedonistic: 7 sensual 8 Lucullan, sensuous 9 epicurean, indulgent, luxurious
He Don't Love You (1975 song)
artist: Tony Orlando & Dawn
He don't plant __...: 6 taters
Hedren, Tippi: 7 actress
daughter: Melanie Griffith
film: The Birds (1963)
Marnie (1964)
-hedron starter: 5 penta-
__ he drove out of sight...: 3 ere
Hedy: 6 Lamarr
__-hee: 3 tee
heebie-jeebies: 6 nerves 7 anxiety, fidgets, jitters, shivers, willies
heed: 3 ear 4 care, hark, hear, look, mind, obey 5 bow to, study, watch 6 accept, advert, attend, bend to, concur, follow, fulfil, hollow, listen, notice, regard 7 abide by, agree to, caution, concern, defer to, fulfill, hearken, hear out, observe, respect, thought 8 adhere to, carry out, consider, listen to, listen up 9 alertness, attention, conform to, consent to, give a darn, give ear to, hearken to, lend an ear, vigilance 10 bear in mind, cognizance, comply with, observance, solicitude, take note of, take notice, toe the line
don't ~: 6 ignore 7 disobey
give ~ to: 4 mind 6 listen
giving no ~: 4 deaf
take ~: 4 mark, mind, tend 5 watch 6 advert, attend, beware, harken, listen, notice 7 hearken, observe, respect 8 listen to, watch out
take ~, old-style: 4 reck
the alarm: 4 rise, wake 5 awake, get up, waken 6 awaken
heedful: 4 kind, wary 5 alert, awake, aware, canny, chary, ready 6 kindly, polite 7 careful, gallant, mindful, on guard, prudent, tactful, wakeful 8 cautious, gracious, obliging, vigilant, watchful 9 attentive, observant, regardful, sensitive, unselfish 10 meticulous, on one's toes, protective, solicitous, thoughtful
heedfulness: 7 caution, concern 9 chariness 10 precaution
heedless: 4 deaf, rash, rude 5 blind, brash, hasty, loose, nervy, slack 6 blithe, madcap, remiss, unruly, unwary, wanton 7 boorish, selfish, unaware 8 careless, impolite, listless, mindless, reckless, slovenly, tactless, uncaring 9 daredevil, foolhardy, impetuous, imprudent, incurious, negligent, oblivious, unadvised, uncareful, unguarded, unhearing, unmindful 10 incautious, indiscreet, neglectful, regardless, ungracious, unthinking
heedlessly: 7 lightly 8 absently, pell-mell 9 headfirst
heedlessness: 5 haste 6 laxity 7 neglect 8 lethargy
Heeger, Alan: 7 chemist 8 Nobelist
heehaw: 4 bray 5 fleer 6 guffaw 7 snicker, snigger 8 laughter 10 horselaugh
Hee Haw (TV variety)
host: Roy Clark, Buck Owens
humor: 4 corn
mascot: 3 ass 6 donkey
radio station: KORN
heehee: 5 laugh 6 giggle, titter 7 chuckle, snicker
heel: 3 cad, cur, end, tag, tip 4 jerk, list, rear, tilt, toad, worm 5 churl, knave, louse, rogue, scamp, slant, sneak 6 bad guy, plunge, rascal, rotter 7 dastard, lowlife, recline, remnant, residue, villain 9 miscreant, reprobate, scoundrel, vulgarian 10 blackguard
Achilles ~: 8 weakness
at ~: 5 close 6 at hand, nearby
attachment: 3 tap
bring to ~: 4 tame
down at ~: 5 needy
ender: 3 tap 4 ball, post, work 5 piece
high ~: 4 pump 5 spike
light of ~: 4 fast 5 fleet, quick, rapid, swift 6 nimble, speedy
over: 3 tip 4 list 5 pitch 6 careen
partner: 3 toe 4 sole
__ heel: 5 Cuban, spike, stack, wedge 8 stiletto
__ Heel: 3 Tar
heel-and-__: 3 toe
heeler: 3 dog, pol 5 canid 6 canine 8 politico 10 politician
__ heeler: 4 ward
heeling, nautically: 5 alist
heels: 4 shoe 8 footwear
cool one's ~: 4 wait 5 tarry 8 sit tight
dig in one's ~: 4 balk 6 refuse, resist
down at the ~: 4 poor, worn 5 broke, needy, seedy 6 bad off, hard up, ill off, in need, in want 7 pinched 8 badly off, bankrupt, beggarly, indigent, strapped 9 destitute, insolvent, moneyless, penniless, penurious 10 pauperized, straitened
go for, as the ~: 5 nip at
go head over ~: 4 fall, slip, trip 5 lurch 6 plunge, sprawl, topple, tumble 7 stumble
head over ~: 4 gaga 6 in love 7 smitten 8 absorbed 9 intensely 10 completely, thoroughly
kick up one's ~: 4 lark, romp 5 caper, jaunt, revel 6 cavort, frolic, gambol, prance 7 carouse, rollick 9 make merry, whoop it up
lay by the ~: 3 bag, nab 4 bust, grab, nail 5 catch, pinch, run in, seize 6 arrest, collar, detain, pick up, pull in, snap up, snatch 7 capture 9 apprehend
on the ~ of: 5 after 6 behind 9 following
take to one's ~: 3 fly, hie, run 4 flee 5 lam it
__ heels of: 5 on the
__ Heel State: 3 Tar
Heep: 5 Uriah
emulate: 4 fawn
Heflin: 3 Van 6 Howell
Hefner: 4 Hugh 8 Christie
Hefner, Hugh prop: 4 pipe, robe
heft: 4 bulk, lift, mass 5 heave, hoist, raise, weigh 6 haul up, import, lift up, pounds, weight 7 gravity, hoist up, raise up 9 bulkiness, heaviness, substance 10 importance
Hefti: 4 Neal

hefty: 4 hale, iron, wiry 5 ample, bulky, burly, hardy, heavy, hulky, hunky, large, lusty, solid, tough 6 brawny, hearty, leaden, mighty, potent, robust, rugged, severe, sinewy, steely, strong, sturdy, taxing, virile 7 doughty, hulking, massive, onerous, sizable, weighty 8 athletic, colossal, forceful, indurate, muscular, powerful, puissant, sizeable, stalwart, thumping, tiresome, unwieldy, vigorous, whapping, whopping 9 Atlantean, extensive, Herculean, ponderous, strapping, unwieldly, well-built 10 able-bodied, burdensome, cumbersome, oppressive, red-blooded, tremendous
chunk: 4 slab
guy: 4 hulk
see also obese
Hefty: 4 wrap
alternative: 4 Glad 5 Saran 6 Ziploc 8 Reynolds
Hegel, Georg: 11 philosopher
hegemony: 4 rule, sway 5 power 7 command, control, primacy 8 dominion 9 supremacy 10 domination, leadership
hegira: 6 exodus, flight 7 journey
He Got Game (1998 film)
cast: Milla Jovovich, Denzel Washington
director: Spike Lee
Hegyes: 6 Robert
heh: 5 laugh 6 Hebrew, letter
predecessor: 6 daleth
successor: 3 vav, vaw, waw
Heidegger, Martin: 11 philosopher
Heidelberg: 4 city, town
locale: 7 Germany
river: 6 Neckar
Heidelberg __: 3 man
Heiden, Eric: 6 skater
Heidi: 5 Bohay, novel
author: Johanna Spyri
home: 4 Alps
Heidt, Horace: 10 bandleader
heifer: 3 cow 4 calf 6 animal, bovine, cattle, mammal
dehorned ~: 5 muley 6 mulley
hangout: 3 lea, ley 4 farm
heifers: 4 kine
Heifetz, Jascha: 9 violinist
colleague: 5 Elman
teacher: 4 Auer
height: 3 alt., tip, top 4 acme, apex, cusp, elev., head, hill, peak, rise, size 5 crest, crown, level, limit, pitch 6 apogee, climax, heyday, heydey, length, summit, tip-top, vertex, zenith 7 ceiling, maximum, stature 8 altitude, eminence, mountain, pinnacle, solstice, tallness, ultimate 9 dimension, elevation, largeness, loftiness, precipice 10 prominence
combining form: 3 acr- 4 acro-
enhancer: 4 lift 5 stilt
how ~ may be measured: 5 y-axis
name meaning ~: 3 Eli
of fashion: 3 hem 4 rage
of the same ~: 4 even 5 level 6 square 8 parallel
opposite: 5 depth 6 length
prefix: 4 alti-
rocky ~: 3 tor 4 crag 5 cliff
to a cager: 5 asset
heighten: 3 wax 4 grow, lift, rise 5 add to, bloat, boost, build, exalt, mount, raise, rouse, swell 6 beef up, dilate, expand, extend, gather, spread 7 amplify, augment, boost up, broaden, build up, burgeon, develop, elevate, enhance, enlarge, improve, inflate, magnify, raise up, spice up 8 bourgeon, escalate, increase, multiply 9 intensify 10 accentuate, aggrandize, strengthen
__ Heights: 5 Golan 6 Shaker 7 Liberty, Pacific
heights, reach the: 4 soar 5 climb
Heimskringla: 4 saga
Hein: 3 Mel
Heine, Heinrich: 4 poet 6 German
homeland: Germany
work: Atta Troll
Almansor
Heineken: 4 beer
alternative: ***see*** beer
Heinie: 6 Manush
heinous: 3 bad 4 base, evil, foul 5 awful, curst, grave, gross, nasty 6 crying, cursed, odious, unholy, wicked 7 accurst, beastly, ghastly, hateful, hideous, ignoble, satanic, vicious 8 accursed, flagrant, grievous, horrible, infamous, shameful, shocking 9 abhorrent, atrocious, execrable, frightful, monstrous, nefarious, offensive, repellant, repellent, revolting, satanical 10 abominable, detestable, flagitious, horrendous, horrifying, inexpiable, iniquitous, outrageous, scandalous, villainous, virtueless
heinousness: 4 evil, vice 6 horror, infamy 7 outrage 8 atrocity, ignominy, iniquity, villainy 9 flagrancy, indecency 10 corruption, opprobrium
Heinrich: 4 Böll, Mann 5 Heine, Hertz 6 Rohrer, Schütz 7 Wieland 10 Schliemann
in English: 5 Henry
see also German
Heinsohn, Tom
milieu: 5 court
org.: 3 NBA
sport: 10 basketball
Heinz: 6 catsup 7 ketchup
alternative: 5 Hunt's 8 Del Monte
product: 4 food 5 beans 7 pickles
see also German
heir: 4 cion 5 owner, scion, sprig 7 devisee, grantee, heritor, legatee 9 inheritor, offspring, successor 10 descendant
concern: 4 will 6 estate
ender: 3 dom, ess 4 loom
fall ~ to: 3 get, own 4 gain 6 obtain 7 acquire, inherit, receive, succeed 8 come into, take over
homophone: 3 air, ere
maybe: 3 son 5 niece 6 eldest, nephew 8 daughter
to the throne: 6 dynast
heiress: 4 cion 5 owner, scion 7 devisee, grantee, heritor, legatee 9 inheritor, successor
Heiress, The (1949 film)
cast: Montgomery Clift, Olivia de Havilland, Ralph Richardson
heirloom: 5 relic 6 legacy 7 antique, bequest 8 valuable
heirs: 4 kids, seed 5 issue 7 kinfolk, progeny 8 children, kinfolks, kinsfolk 9 posterity
proverbial ~: 4 meek
Heisenberg, Werner: 8 Nobelist 9 physicist, scientist
Heisman Trophy: 5 award
sport: 8 football
Heiss, Carol: 6 skater
heist: 3 job, rob 4 lift 5 caper, crime, steal, swipe, theft 6 holdup, pilfer, rip-off, thieve 7 bank job, break-in, larceny, robbery, stickup 8 burglary, thievery 9 pilferage
heister: 5 crook, ganef, thief
stuff: 4 haul, loot, take 5 booty 7 plunder
Heist (2001 film)
cast: Danny DeVito, Gene Hackman, Delroy Lindo
director: David Mamet
hejira: 6 exodus, flight 7 journey, odyssey 9 migration 10 pilgrimage
__ Hejirae: 4 Anno
Hekawi: 5 tribe 7 Indians
__ He Kissed Me: 4 Then
Hekla: 7 volcano
locale: 7 Iceland
Hel
father: 4 Loki
held: 4 fast 6 jailed 7 captive, reputed 8 obsessed 10 spellbound
back: 5 sat on 6 pent-up 9 in reserve
be ~ by: 8 belong to
dear: 8 valuable
down: 5 under 6 pinned
fast: 4 rapt 7 charmed, gripped 8 absorbed, beguiled, immersed 9 engrossed, entranced 10 captivated, enraptured, enthralled, fascinated, hypnotized, spellbound
in ballet: 5 tendu
it may be ~: 4 mayo
off: 5 at bay 6 caught 8 cornered 9 powerless
starter: 4 hand, with
up: 4 late 5 tardy 7 overdue 8 detained
Held, Anna
spouse: Flo Ziegfeld
__ Heldenleben: 3 Ein
Helen: 4 Hunt, Kane, Mack, play 5 Hayes, Price, Reddy, saint, Trent, Wills 6 Keller, Mirren, Morgan, Shaver, Slater, Thomas 7 Gahagan, Traubel 8 Fielding, MacInnes, O'Connell, Van Slyke
abductor: 5 Paris
attendant of ~: 7 Adraste
author: Euripides
brother: 6 Castor, Pollux
city: 4 Troy 5 Ilium
daughter: 8 Hermione 9 Iphigenia
husband: 5 Paris 8 Menelaus
lover: 7 Theseus
parent: 4 Leda, Zeus
suitor: 4 Ajax 5 Thoas 8 Menelaus, Odysseus, Peneleus 10 Antilochus
Helen __ Brown: 6 Gurley
Helen __ Douglas: 7 Gahagan
Helen __ Jackson: 4 Hunt
Helen __ Moody: 5 Wills
Helen __ Slyke: 3 Van
Helena: 4 city, town 5 falls 9 waterfall 10 Rubinstein
locale: 7 Montana
rival: 5 Estée
Helena __ Carter: 6 Bonham
Helene: 4 moon 5 Hanff 6 Curtis
planet: 6 Saturn
Hélène: 6 Çixous
author: Émile Zola
see also French
Helene Curtis
rival: 4 Avon, Pert 5 Prell
Helen Gahagan __: 7 Douglas
Helen Gurley __: 5 Brown
Helen Hunt __: 7 Jackson
Helen of __: 4 Troy
Helens, Mt. St.: 4 peak 7 volcano
clock setting: 3 PDT, PST
locale: 4 Wash. 10 Washington
Helenus: 4 seer
brother: 5 Paris 6 Hector
parent: 5 Priam 6 Hecuba 7 Priamus
twin: 9 Cassandra
Helen Van __: 5 Slyke
Helen Wheels (1973 song)
artist: Paul McCartney
Helen Wills __: 5 Moody
Helfgott, David: 7 British, pianist
Helga: 4 toon
daughter: 4 Honi
husband: 5 Hägar
Helgenberger: 4 Marg
helical: 5 spiry 6 coiled, curled, spiral 7 whorled
Helice
husband: 3 Ion
helicon: 4 horn, tuba, wind 10 instrument
helicopter: 7 chopper 8 aircraft 9 eggbeater 10 whirlybird
Army ~: 6 Apache
like some ~ rescues: 6 air-sea
part: 5 rotor
sound: 4 whir 5 whirr
heliophobe fear: 3 Sun
Helios: 3 god
daughter: 3 Aex 5 Aeaea, Circe
equivalent: 3 Sol
parent: 4 Thia 8 Hyperion
sister: 3 Eos 6 Selene
heliotrope: 5 color, plant 6 flower, purple 7 reddish
relative: ***see*** purple color
heliport site, often: 4 roof
helium: 3 gas 7 element
like ~: 5 inert
helix: 4 coil, curl 5 screw, twist, whorl 6 spiral, volute 9 corkscrew
double ~: 3 DNA
single ~: 3 RNA
hell: 5 abyss, Hades 6 misery, ordeal 7 anguish, inferno, torment 9 nightmare, suffering 10 underworld
denizen: 5 demon, devil 6 daemon, daimon
ender: 3 box, cat 4 bent, hole 5 diver, hound 6 bender
feature: 4 fire 6 flames 7 inferno
like ~: 6 ablaze
like a bat out of ~: 5 manic
like a rare day in ~: 4 cold, cool 6 chilly 8 freezing
raise ~: 5 party 9 celebrate, make merry

raising ~: **4** wild **5** noisy, rowdy **6** unruly **7** lawless, naughty, raucous **9** turbulent **10** boisterous, disorderly, tumultuous
starter: **4** rake
sure as ~: **5** truly **9** certainly, doubtless **10** absolutely, definitely, positively
to pay: **7** censure, penalty **10** discipline, punishment
to Sherman: **3** war
hell __: **4** week **5** to pay
hell-__: **4** bent **5** fired **6** raiser
hell-__-leather: **3** for
__ hell: **5** raise, War is
Hell __ Heroes: **5** Is for
Hell __ no fury...: **4** hath
hellbent: **4** firm **6** driven, intent **8** obsessed, resolute, resolved, stubborn **9** steadfast, tenacious **10** determined, hard-bitten, persistent, unwavering
go ~ for leather: **4** tear **5** speed **6** careen, hasten, hurtle **7** rampage **8** stampede
(on): **3** set
helldiver: **4** bird **5** grebe
Hellene: **5** Greek
capital: **6** Athens
Hellenic: **8** language **9** classical
see also Greece
heller: **5** money, rowdy **7** ruffian
helleri: **4** fish
Heller, Joseph: **6** writer
work: Catch-22
Closing Time
God Knows
Good as Gold
Something Happened
He'll Have to Go (1960 song)
artist: Jim Reeves
hellhound: **5** beast, brute, fiend, knave **6** savage **7** dastard, monster **9** barbarian
hellion: **3** imp **4** brat **5** demon, rowdy **6** daemon, daimon **7** inciter, monster **8** agitator, evildoer, inflamer, recreant, renegade **9** firebrand **10** holy terror, instigator
hellish: **5** cruel, nasty **6** savage, wicked **7** accurst, demonic, satanic, vicious **8** accursed, daemonic, devilish, diabolic, fiendish, horrible, infernal, terrible **9** atrocious, barbarous, demonical, monstrous, murderous, nefarious, satanical **10** abominable, diabolical, malevolent, petrifying, unpleasant
Hellman: **5** Monte **7** Lillian
Hellman, Lillian: **6** writer **10** playwright
friend: Dashiell Hammett
work: The Children's Hour
The Little Foxes
Maybe
Pentimento
Toys in the Attic
Watch on the Rhine
Hellmann's: **4** mayo **10** mayonnaise
hello: **4** ahoy, hi ya **5** aloha, howdy **7** welcome **8** greeting **9** greetings **10** salutation
Aussie ~: **4** g'day
Hawaii ~: **5** aloha
Navajo ~: **6** yateeh
returnee ~: **6** I'm home
say ~: **5** greet
silent ~: **3** nod **4** wave
warm ~: **3** hug **4** kiss **7** embrace
Hello (1984 song)
artist: Lionel Richie
Hello __: **5** Again, It's Me, Walls **7** Goodbye
Hello __!: **5** Dolly
Hello __ Lou: **4** Mary
Hello __ Me: **3** It's
Hello, __!: **5** Dolly **6** Eeyore
Hello, __ Be Going: **5** I Must
Hello, __ Lovers: **5** Young
Hello, __ You: **5** I Love
Hello Again (1983 song)
artist: Neil Diamond
Hello and Goodbye
author: Athol Fugard
Hello, Dolly!: **7** musical
composer: Jerry Herman
Hello, Dolly! (1964 song)
artist: Louis Armstrong
Hello, Dolly! (1969 film)
cast: Michael Crawford, Walter Matthau, Barbra Streisand
director: Gene Kelly
role: **4** Levi
Hello, Eeyore!
author: A.A. Milne
Hello Goodbye (1967 song)
artist: Beatles
Hello, I Love You (1968 song)
artist: Doors
Hello It's Me (1973 song)
artist: Todd Rundgren
Hello Mary Lou (1961 song)
artist: Ricky Nelson
Hello Mudduh, Hello Fadduh! (1963 song)
artist: Allan Sherman
__ hell or high water: **4** come
Hello Walls (1961 song)
artist: Faron Young
Hello, Young Lovers
composer: Oscar Hammerstein, Richard Rodgers
hell's __: **5** bells
Hell's __: **5** Angel **6** Angels, Canyon **7** Kitchen
Hell's Angel: **5** biker
Hell's Angels (1930 film)
cast: Jean Harlow
director: Howard Hughes
Hells Canyon state: **5** Idaho
hell to __: **3** pay
Hellzapoppin' (1941 film)
cast: Mischa Auer, Chic Johnson, Ole Olsen, Martha Raye
helm: **4** lead **5** guide, reins, steer, wheel **6** rudder, tiller **7** control
dir.: **3** ENE, ESE, NNE, NNW, SSE, SSW, WNW, WSW
position: **4** alee **8** aweather
take the ~: **5** steer **6** direct, manage **8** navigate
Helm: **4** Matt
Helmer, Nora creator: Henrik Ibsen
helmet: **3** hat **4** topi **5** armet, terai **6** casque **7** basinet, hard hat **8** headgear
adornment: **5** plume **7** feather
name meaning ~: **4** Elmo
one with a ~: **5** miner
part: **5** visor, vizor
pith ~: **3** hat **4** topi **5** topee
plume: **5** crest
prickly ~: **5** shell **8** seashell
__ helmet: **4** pith **5** crash
Helm, Matt: **3** spy
Helmond: **9** Katherine
Helms: **5** Bobby, Jesse
successor: **4** Dole
Helms, Bobby
song: Jingle Bell Rock (1957)
My Special Angel (1957)
Helms, Jesse: **3** sen. **7** senator
Helmsley: **5** Harry, Leona
helmsman: **5** pilot **6** sailor **7** captain, jack tar, mariner, skipper **8** seafarer **9** navigator
direction: **4** alee **5** aport **8** aweather
Helmut: **4** Kohl **6** Berger **7** Schmidt
see also German
Héloïse
see French
Héloise and Abélard
author: George Moore
Heloise tidbit: **4** hint
helot: **4** serf **7** bondman, villein
cousin: **4** esne
helotry: **4** yoke
he loves in Latin: **4** amat
help: **3** aid, SOS, use **4** abet, back, boon, ease, hand, lift **5** aides, asset, boost, favor, guide, hands, labor, maids, serve, slave, speed, staff, tutor **6** advice, assist, better, buck up, jobber, join in, Mayday, profit, relief, remedy, second, soothe, succor, uphold, wait on, worker **7** backing, benefit, bolster, butlers, comfort, forward, further, improve, offices, pitch in, promote, redress, relieve, servant, service, sponsor, stand by, support, sustain, utility, workers, work for **8** abetment, deputies, guidance, kindness, minister, mitigate, palliate, recourse, servants, stump for, tide over, wait upon **9** alleviate, cooperate, disburden, employees, encourage, intercede, lend a hand, patronage, smile upon, stimulate, subsidize **10** ameliorate, assistance, assistants, attendants, facilitate, go to bat for, hired hands, see through, stick up for
ask for ~, maybe: **4** pray
be of ~: **5** avail, serve
beyond ~: **4** sunk **5** kaput **6** doomed **7** done for
can't ~ but: **4** must **6** have to, should **7** ought to
ender: **4** less, mate, meet
for the needy: **4** alms **7** charity
get ~ from: **6** lean on
household ~: **4** cook, maid **5** nanny, valet **6** au pair, butler, nannie
in crime: **4** abet **7** collude
in the kitchen: **3** dry, mop **4** wash **5** clean, clear **6** sponge
name meaning ~: **4** Ezra
one beyond ~: **5** goner
oneself to: **3** nip **4** take **6** pocket
online ~ source: **3** FAQ
puzzle ~: **4** hint
the cause: **6** chip in, donate **10** contribute
to make up: **6** pacify, soothe **7** appease, assuage, mediate, mollify, placate, reunite, satisfy, sweeten, win over **9** arbitrate, intervene, reconcile **10** compromise, conciliate
with costs: **6** defray
with homework: **5** tutor
without ~: **5** alone **7** forlorn, unaided **8** forsaken, isolated, solitary **9** abandoned **10** unassisted
with the dishes: **3** dry **4** wipe
worthy of ~: **5** needy **8** indigent **9** destitute, penniless, penurious **10** down-and-out
help __: **3** out
__-help: **4** self
Help __ Its Way: **4** Is on
Help!: **3** SOS **4** film, song **6** Mayday
artist: Beatles
cast: George Harrison, John Lennon, Paul McCartney, Ringo Starr
director: Richard Lester
in French: **4** à moi
helper: **4** aide, ally, asst., hand, mate, page, temp **5** aides, gofer, labor **6** backer, backup, cohort, deputy, flunky, gopher, lackey, patron, second **7** abetter, abettor, acolyte, adjunct, adviser, advisor, flunkey, lacquey, partner, recruit, servant, sponsor **8** adherent, adjutant, follower, henchman **9** accessory, assistant, attendant, auxiliary, coadjutor, gal Friday, man Friday, secretary, supporter, volunteer **10** accomplice, apprentice, coadjutant, girl Friday, lieutenant
kitchen ~: **4** tool **7** utensil **9** appliance
name meaning ~: **6** Alexis
name meaning ~ of men: **9** Cassandra
office ~: **4** temp **5** clerk, gofer **6** gopher **9** assistant, gal Friday, man Friday, secretary **10** girl Friday
phrase: **5** let me
protégé ~: **6** mentor
__ helper: **6** Santa's **7** mother's
__ Helper: **4** Tuna
helpful: **4** good, kind, nice **5** handy, of use, utile **6** benign, caring, decent, kindly, timely, usable, useful **7** useable **8** flexible, friendly, generous, obliging, positive, remedial, salutary, suitable, valuable **9** covetable, desirable, effectual, favorable, fortunate, operative, opportune, practical, symbiotic, unselfish **10** applicable, beneficial, benevolent, convenient, invaluable, neighborly, productive, profitable, supportive, thoughtful, time-saving, worthwhile
be ~: **3** aid **6** assist **7** pitch in
example: **5** model **6** lesson
hint: **3** tip **6** advice, tipoff **7** inkling, pointer, warning **10** suggestion
helpful __: **4** hint
helpfulness: **5** value **7** benefit **8** function **9** advantage, relevance, usability **10** assistance
helping: **4** part **5** plate, share, slice **6** ration **7** portion
hand: **5** break
helping __: **4** hand
helpless: **4** puny, weak **5** at bay,

frail, naked, wimpy **6** anemic, atonic, clumsy, effete, feeble, flabby, flimsy, pinned, unable **7** anaemic, exposed, forlorn, fragile, unadept, wimpish **8** delicate, forsaken, pithless, stranded, up a creek **9** abandoned, dependant, dependent, destitute, faltering, incapable, powerless, prostrate **10** handcuffed, impuissant, unequipped, vulnerable
one: **4** dupe, lamb **5** patsy **6** sucker **7** fall guy **8** easy mark, innocent, pushover
render ~: **4** bind **5** unarm **6** fetter, hamper, hobble, hogtie **8** restrain **9** hamstring
__ helpless as a kitten...: **4** I'm as
helplessness, show: **5** shrug
__ Help Lovin' Dat Man: **4** Can't
helpmate: **4** mate, wife **5** bride **6** spouse **7** husband, partner
Help Me (1974 song)
artist: Joni Mitchell
helpmeet: **4** wife **6** spouse **7** husband
Help Me Make It Through the Night (1971 song)
artist: Sammi Smith
Help Me, Rhonda (1965 song)
artist: Beach Boys
__ Help Myself: **5** I Can't
__ Help Us: **6** Heaven
help-wanted
letters: **3** EEO, EOE, SOS
notices: **3** ads
__ help you?: **4** Can I, May I
Helsinki: **4** city, port, town **7** capital
hot spot: **5** sauna
lake northwest of ~: **4** Nasi
locale: **7** Finland
suburb: **5** Espoo
Helsinki __: **4** Pact
helter-skelter: **5** about **6** hectic **7** chaotic **8** pell-mell, reckless **10** disorderly
helve: **6** handle
__-Helve, The: **3** Axe
Helvetica: **4** font **8** typeface
hem: **3** rim **4** edge, seam, tack, tuck **5** fence, skirt, verge **6** border, edging, fringe, margin **7** enclose, inclose **9** perimeter, periphery
and haw: **2** um **4** sway, vary **5** dodge, evade, hedge, shift, stall, waver **6** falter, waffle **7** quibble, stammer, whiffle **8** hesitate **9** fluctuate, pussyfoot, vacillate **10** equivocate
change a ~: **5** alter, lower, raise, resew
cousin: **2** er, uh, um
ender: **4** line, lock **6** stitch
in: **3** pen **4** gird, ring, wall **5** beset, bound, hedge, limit **6** begird, circle, corner **7** compass, confine, enclose, inclose **8** encircle, restrain, restrict, surround **9** constrain, encompass
make a ~: **3** sew
material: **6** edging
partner: **3** haw
prepare a ~: **5** baste, pin up
he-man: **4** hunk, stud **5** atlas, macho **6** Samson, Tarzan **7** bruiser, Goliath **8** Hercules, tough guy **10** powerhouse
like a ~: **5** macho **6** brawny, strong, virile **8** muscular, vigorous **9** masculine, strapping
no ~: **4** wimp **5** sissy, weeny **8** weakling
He-Man
sister: **5** She-Ra
hematite: **3** ore **7** mineral
hemi-: **4** half
hemidemisemiquaver: **4** note
hemimorphite: **3** ore
Hemings: **5** Sally
Hemingway, Ernest: **6** writer **8** Nobelist
granddaughter: **6** Mariel **7** Margaux
nickname: Papa
work: Death in the Afternoon
A Farewell to Arms
The Fifth Column
For Whom the Bell Tolls
Green Hills of Africa
Islands in the Stream
A Moveable Feast
The Old Man and the Sea
The Snows of Kilimanjaro
The Sun Also Rises
To Have and Have Not
Hemingway, Mariel: **7** actress
hemlock: **4** tree **5** toxin **6** conium
home: **4** nest
poison in ~: **5** conin
relative: **3** fir **4** pine **6** spruce **8** tamarack
hemmed
in: **4** girt
hemmed in: **4** pent **5** bound **6** narrow **7** cramped, limited **8** confined **10** restrained, restricted
hemmer: **6** tailor
interjection: **2** er, uh, um
hemming and hawing: **8** hesitant, waffling, wavering **9** dithering, equivocal, tentative, undecided, unsettled **10** ambivalent, indecisive, irresolute, of two minds, on the fence, unresolved, up in the air, wishy-washy
Hemmings: **5** David
hemoglobin
shortage: **6** anemia **7** anaemia
Hémon, Louis: **6** French, writer
hemophobe fear: **5** blood
hemp: **4** bast **5** bhang, fiber
fabric: **6** canvas
fiber: **5** abaca, oakum
Indian ~ shrub: **4** pooa **5** pooah
moisten ~: **3** ret
product: **4** rope **5** twine **6** opiate
Russian ~: **4** rine
hemplike fiber: **4** sunn **5** sisal
Hempstead: **4** city, town
athletes: **5** Pride
locale: **7** New York **10** Long Island
school: **7** Hofstra
Hemsley, Sherman sitcom: **4** Amen
hen: **3** she **4** bird, fowl **5** biddy, layer **6** bantam, female, pullet **7** brooder, clucker, Leghorn, poulard, poultry **8** busybody, poularde
act the mother ~: **4** fuss
ender: **3** bit **4** bane, coop, peck
family: **5** brood
lack: **5** teeth
like a wet ~: **3** mad **5** irate
product: **3** egg
sound: **5** cluck **6** cackle
starter: **3** pea **4** grey, moor
hen __: **5** party
__ hen: **3** mud **4** fool, sage **6** guinea, mother
henbane: **5** toxin **6** poison
henbit: **4** weed
hence: **4** away, ergo, then, this, thus **6** avaunt, onward, thence **7** onwards **8** from here **9** as a result, from now on, hereafter, therefore, therefrom, thereupon
ender: **5** forth **7** forward
henceforth: **6** onward, thence **7** onwards **8** evermore, from here **9** following, from now on, hereafter
henchman: **4** aide, ally, pawn **5** gofer **6** backup, cohort, deputy, flunky, gopher, helper, jackal, lackey, stooge **7** abetter, abettor, adjunct, flunkey, lacquey **8** adherent, follower, hanger-on, sidekick **9** accessory, assistant, attendant, bodyguard, coadjutor, colleague, companion, supporter **10** accomplice, apprentice, coadjutant
be a ~: **4** abet
Henderson: **3** Joe **4** city, town **6** Arthur, Rickey, Skitch **8** Fletcher, Florence
locale: **6** Nevada **8** Kentucky
Henderson, Fletcher: **7** pianist
genre: **4** jazz
Henderson, Rickey
sport: **8** baseball
theft: **4** base
Henderson the Rain King
author: Saul Bellow
Hendrik: **7** Lorentz, van Loon **10** Conscience
Hendrix, Jimi: **9** guitarist
genre: **4** rock
Hendry: **3** Ian
Hendryx: **4** Nona
henhouse: **4** coop **5** roost
sound: **5** cluck **6** cackle
Henie, Sonja: **6** skater
home: **4** Oslo **6** Norway
Henley: **3** Don **4** Beth **5** shirt **7** William
need ~: **3** oar
participant: **5** rower
Henley __: **7** Regatta
Henley, Beth: **6** writer **10** playwright
work: Abundance
Am I Blue
Crimes of the Heart
The Debutante Ball
Impossible Marriage
The Lucky Spot
The Miss Firecracker Contest
Henley, Don
song: All She Wants to Do is Dance (1985)
The Boys of Summer (1984)
Dirty Laundry (1982)
The End of the Innocence (1989)
Leather and Lace (1981)
Sometimes Love Just Isn't Enough (1992)
Henley-on-__: **6** Thames
Henley, William: **4** poet **7** British **10** playwright
work: Invictus
Henn: **6** Carrie
henna: **3** dye **4** tree **5** color, rinse, shrub **6** orange **7** hair dye, reddish
apply ~: **3** dye **4** tint **6** redden
apply more ~: **5** redye
relative: **5** flame **7** pumpkin, saffron **8** hyacinth **9** tangerine **10** terra cotta
user: **4** dyer
Henner, Marilu: **7** actress
role: **3** Ava **5** Nardo **6** Elaine
TV: Evening Shade, Taxi
hennery: **4** coop
Henning: **4** Doug **8** magician
Henny: **8** Youngman
hen of the woods: **6** fungus
henpeck: **3** nag **4** carp, ride **5** annoy, bully, hound, scold **6** badger, berate, bother, harass, hector, needle, noodge, pester, pick on **7** torment **8** domineer, irritate
henpecker: **3** nag **5** harpy, scold, shrew **6** beldam, chider, kvetch, ogress, virago, whiner **7** caviler, rebuker, reviler **8** fishwife, harridan, spitfire **9** termagant, Xanthippe **10** castigator, complainer
Henreid, Paul: **5** actor
film: Casablanca (1942)
Goodbye, Mr. Chips (1939)
Now, Voyager (1942)
Henri: **7** Bergson, Matisse, Michaux, Moissan **8** Rousseau
see also French
Henri __-Bresson: **7** Cartier
Henrich: **4** Yank **5** Tommy **6** Yankee
Henri de __-Lautrec: **8** Toulouse
henrietta: **6** fabric **8** material
Henrik: **3** Dam **5** Ibsen
Henriksen: **5** Lance
Henry: **3** Pye **4** Buck, Clay, Dale, Ford, King, Luce, Rous **5** Adams, Bacon, Fonda, Green, Gross, James, Lawes, Levin, Moore, Percy, Royce, Silva, Taube, Tudor **6** Cavill, Czerny, Draper, Gibson, Gloria, Hudson, Jaglom, Joseph, Justin, Koster, Kravis, Miller, Picard, Robert, Selick, Thomas **7** Higgins, Kendall, Mancini, Patrick, Purcell, Travers, Winkler **8** Bessemer, Clarence, Fielding, Hathaway, Maudslay, Shrapnel, Wilcoxon **9** Armstrong, Cavendish, Kissinger **10** Morgenthau
in French: **5** Henri
in German: **8** Heinrich
in Italian: **6** Enrico
in Spanish: **7** Enrique
son: **5** Edsel
Henry __: **4** VIII **6** Esmond
Henry __ Beecher: **4** Ward
Henry __ Lodge: **5** Cabot
Henry __ Longfellow: **9** Wadsworth
Henry __ Perot: **4** Ross
Henry __ Stanley: **6** Morton
Henry __ Thoreau: **5** David
__ Henry: **4** Fort, John **5** After
Henry and Cato
author: Iris Murdoch
Henry Cabot __: **5** Lodge
__ Henry Dana: **7** Richard
Henry David __: **7** Thoreau
Henry Esmond
author: William Makepeace Thackeray
__ Henry Harrison: **7** William
__ Henry Hoover: **3** Lou
Henry IV
author: William Shakespeare

Henry James
author: Rebecca West
Henry, John drove it: 5 steel
Henry & June (1990 film)
cast: Uma Thurman, Fred Ward
role: 3 Nin **5** Anaïs **6** Miller
Henry Morton __: 7 Stanley
Henry, O.: 6 writer
real name: Porter
work: The Furnished Room
The Gift of the Magi
The Last Leaf
The Ransom of Red Chief
The Trimmed Lamp
Henry, Patrick: 6 orator
Henry the __: 9 Navigator
Henry V: 3 Hal **9** Prince Hal
author: William Shakespeare
Henry V (1989 film)
cast: Brian Blessed, Kenneth Branagh, Derek Jacobi
director: Kenneth Branagh
Henry VI
author: William Shakespeare
Henry VI founded it: 4 Eton
Henry VIII
daughter: 5 Mary I
desire: 3 son
like ~: 5 obese, stout **6** portly, rotund **9** corpulent
wife: 4 Anne, Parr **6** Boleyn, Howard **9** Catherine
wife count: 3 six
Henry Wadsworth __: 10 Longfellow
Henry Ward __: 7 Beecher
Hensley: 6 Pamela
Henson, Jim: 8 director **9** puppeteer
creation: 4 Bert **5** Ernie, Oscar **6** Kermit, Muppet **7** Big Bird **9** Miss Piggy
film: The Dark Crystal (1982)
The Great Muppet Caper (1981)
Labyrinth (1986)
__ hen's teeth: 6 rare as
Henstridge, Natasha: 7 actress
film: Bounce (2000)
Species (1995)
The Whole Nine Yards (2000)
Hentoff: 3 Nat
hep: 4 cool, in on, onto, wise **5** aware, savvy **6** posted, versed, wise to, with it **7** current, knowing, mindful, tuned in **8** apprised, informed **9** cognizant, in the know, plugged in **10** conversant
ender: 3 cat
get ~: 6 wise up
to: 4 up on **9** in the know, wise about
hepatic: 5 renal
hepatic __: 4 duct
hepatica: 5 plant **6** flower
__ Hepatica: 3 Sal
hepatologist concern: 5 liver
Hepburn, Audrey: 7 actress
film: Breakfast at Tiffany's (1961)
Charade (1963)
Funny Face (1957)
Green Mansions (1959)
How to Steal a Million (1966)
Love in the Afternoon (1957)
My Fair Lady (1964)
The Nun's Story (1959)
Robin and Marian (1976)
Roman Holiday (1953, AA)
Sabrina (1954)
They All Laughed (1981)
Two for the Road (1967)
The Unforgiven (1960)
Wait Until Dark (1967)
real first name: 4 Edda
spouse: Mel Ferrer
Hepburn, Katharine: 7 actress
costar: 5 Tracy
film: Adam's Rib (1949)
The African Queen (1951)
Alice Adams (1935)
A Bill of Divorcement (1932)
Bringing Up Baby (1938)
Desk Set (1957)
Guess Who's Coming to Dinner (1967, AA)
Holiday (1938)
Keeper of the Flame (1943)
The Lion in Winter (1968, AA)
The Little Minister (1934)
Little Women (1933)
Long Day's Journey Into Night (1962)
Love Affair (1994)
Mary of Scotland (1936)
Morning Glory (1933, AA)
On Golden Pond (1981, AA)
Pat and Mike (1952)
The Philadelphia Story (1940)
Quality Street (1937)
The Rainmaker (1956)
Rooster Cogburn (1975)
Stage Door (1937)
State of the Union (1948)
Suddenly, Last Summer (1959)
Summertime (1955)
Sylvia Scarlett (1935)
Without Love (1945)
Woman of the Year (1942)
A Woman Rebels (1936)
nickname: 4 Kate
hepcat: 4 dude **6** daddy-o **7** hipster, swinger
Hephaestus
equivalent: 6 Vulcan
mother: 4 Hera
Hepplewhite: 5 style **6** George
hepta-: 5 seven
follower: 4 octa-, octo-
preceder: 3 hex- **4** hexa-
heptad: 4 seas **5** seven **6** dwarfs
plus one: 5 octad
heptarch: 5 ruler
Hepworth: 7 Barbara
her: 3 she **4** pron. **5** woman **6** female **7** pronoun
ender: 4 self **5** story
his and ~: 5 their
like ~: 4 poss.
not ~: 3 him
her __: 4 nibs
Her: 3 dog **6** beagle, canine
owner: 3 LBJ
predecessor: 4 Fala
Her __ Georgia Gibbs: 4 Nibs
Her __ Highness: 5 Royal **6** Serene
Her __ Too: 4 Town
Hera: 7 goddess
brother: 4 Zeus **5** Hades
daughter: 4 Eris, Hebe **8** Pasithea
equivalent: 4 Juno
husband: 4 Zeus
lover: 8 Dionysus
parent: 4 Rhea **6** Cronos, Cronus
rival: 4 Leda
sister: 6 Hestia **7** Demeter
son: 4 Ares **10** Hephaestus
__ Her About It: 4 Tell
Heracles: 8 Argonaut
captive: 4 Iole
child: 5 Creon, Iobes, Lydus, Teles **6** Pallas **8** Laomedon **9** Antiochus **10** Antimachus
labor site: 5 Nemea
one of twelve for ~: 5 labor
parent: 4 Zeus **7** Alcmena
quest: 6 girdle
ship: 4 Argo
twin: 8 Iphicles
wife: 4 Hebe **6** Megara
Heraclitus: 5 Greek **11** philosopher
__ Her Again: 4 I Saw
herald: 4 mean, omen, sign, tout **5** augur, crier, greet, robin, spell, token, usher **6** bearer, leader, signal **7** courier, declare, portend, presage, prophet, swallow, trumpet, usher in **8** announce, antecede, ballyhoo, foreshow, proclaim **9** advertise, announcer, broadcast, foretoken, harbinger, make known, messenger, precursor, publicize, town crier **10** forerunner, indication, missionary, proclaimer
Herald: 5 paper **9** newspaper
locale: 5 Miami **6** Boston **7** Calgary, Halifax
heraldry: 4 pomp **5** badge, crest **6** design, device, emblem, symbol **7** insigne **8** blazonry, ceremony, insignia, splendor **9** pageantry
heraldry terms
arrangement: 10 coat of arms
background: 5 field
band: 4 orle **5** fesse
bearing: 6 charge **8** ordinary
black: 5 sable
blue: 5 azure
border: 7 bordure
center: 9 fess point **10** fesse point
centerless: 6 voided
center point of lower half: 7 nombril
coat of arms: 5 crest **6** blazon
coat of arms panel: 9 hatchment
color: 8 tincture
device: 7 bearing
diagonal band: 4 bend
diamond: 7 lozenge
dragon: 6 wyvern
emblem: 6 device
flying: 6 volant
footless bird: 7 martlet
four-petaled flower: 10 quatrefoil
fur: 4 vair **8** tincture
gold: 2 or
green: 4 vert
horizontal band: 3 bar
horned giraffe: 10 camelopard
inverted V: 7 chevron
left: 8 sinister
lion: 7 leopard
lion-eagle: 7 griffin
looking backward: 9 regardant
lower part: 4 base
lying down: 7 dormant **8** couchant
metal: 8 tincture
narrow horizontal: 5 label **6** fillet
one of four divisions: 7 quarter
purple: 7 purpure
rearing up: 7 rampant
red: 5 gules
repeated pattern: 4 semé
ribbon with motto: 6 scroll **9** banderole
right: 6 dexter
rising: 7 issuant
shield: 4 enté **10** escutcheon
shortened diagonal band: 5 baton
side view: 7 gardant **8** guardant
silver: 6 argent
sprinkled: 4 semé
St. Andrew's cross: 7 saltire
three-petaled flower: 7 trefoil
three-petaled iris: 10 fleur-de-lis
triangle: 5 gyron
upper right: 6 canton
walking: 7 passant
wavy: 4 onde, undé
wedge: 4 pile
white: 6 argent
wide horizontal band: 4 fess **5** fesse
wide vertical band: 4 pale
wreath: 5 torse
Herat: 4 city, town
locale: 11 Afghanistan
herb: 3 rue **4** balm, dill, mint, sage **5** anise, basil, chive, cumin, plant, thyme **6** borage, catnip, endive, fennel, lovage, savory **7** bay leaf, caraway, chervil, chicory, mustard, oregano, parsley **8** angelica, cardamom, cilantro, marjoram, rosemary, tarragon **9** coriander, flavoring, horehound, lemon balm, medicinal, seasoning, spearmint, vegetable **10** peppermint
aromatic ~: 4 dill, mint, nard, sage **5** anise, tansy, thyme **6** catnip, fennel, hyssop
Asian ~: 5 orach **6** orache
ender: 3 age, ose
European ~: 6 borage, lovage
healing ~: 6 arnica
Japanese ~: 3 udo
kitchen ~: 4 dill, sage **5** anise, basil, chive, cumin, thyme **6** fennel **7** oregano, parsley **8** cilantro, marjoram, rosemary
like a certain ~: 4 sagy **5** minty
medicinal ~: 4 sage **5** urena
perennial ~: 5 orpin **6** asarum
remedy: 5 jalap
starter: 3 cow, pot
herb __: 3 tea
Herb: 4 Caen **5** Freed **6** Alpert **7** Edelman, Pennock, Shriner, Stempel, Woodley
herbage: 7 foliage, verdure **10** vegetation
dried ~: 3 hay
herbal __: 3 tea
__ Herb Brown: 5 Nacio
Herber: 5 Arnie
Herbert: 3 Lom **4** Agar, Gold, Read, Ross **5** Brown, Frank, saint, Simon, Swope **6** Gasser, George, Hoover, Victor, Wilcox, Xavier **7** Asquith, Kroemer, Marcuse, Spencer **8** Anderson, Hauptman, Marshall, Zbigniew
Herbert __ Karajan: 3 von
Herbert, Frank: 6 writer
genre: sci-fi
work: The Dragon in the Sea
Dune
The God Makers
The Heaven Makers

Herbert, George: 4 poet 5 Welsh
Herbert, Victor: 8 composer
org. cofounded by: 5 ASCAP
Herbert, Xavier: 6 writer 10 Australian
Herbert, Zbigniew: 4 poet 6 Polish
__ herbes: 5 fines
herbicide: 3 DDT 6 poison
target: 4 weed
Herbie: 2 VW 3 car 4 auto, Faye, Mann 7 Hancock, Love Bug 10 Volkswagen
Herbie: Fully Loaded (2005 film)
cast: Matt Dillon, Michael Keaton, Lindsay Lohan
herbivore: 5 rhino, vegan 7 gorilla
Hercule: 6 Poirot
creator: Agatha Christie
herculean: 3 big 4 hale, hard, huge, iron, vast, wiry 5 beefy, brave, burly, giant, great, hardy, hefty, hunky, husky, jumbo, large, lusty, stout, tough 6 brawny, hearty, heroic, mighty, potent, robust, rugged, sinewy, steely, stocky, strong, sturdy, virile 7 arduous, doughty, hulking, immense, mammoth, massive, onerous, sizable, titanic, valiant 8 athletic, colossal, enormous, forceful, gigantic, grueling, heroical, indurate, king-size, muscular, oversize, powerful, puissant, sizeable, stalwart, toilsome, towering, vigorous, whapping, whopping 9 Atlantean, difficult, humongous, laborious, overlarge, strapping, strenuous, well-built 10 able-bodied, courageous, formidable, gargantuan, iron-willed, monumental, prodigious, red-blooded, stupendous, tremendous
not ~: 4 puny, tiny, weak 5 frail 6 feeble 8 trifling 9 pint-sized 10 diminutive
Hercules: 4 city, hero, town 5 he-man
captive: 4 Iole
constellation near ~: 4 Lyra
labor site: 5 Nemea
locale: 10 California
one of twelve for ~: 5 labor
quest: 6 girdle
wife: 4 Hebe 6 Megara
see also Heracles
Hercules... (TV adventure)
cast: Kevin Sorbo (Hercules)
herd: 3 mob 4 bevy, gang, mass, pack, tend 5 bunch, covey, crowd, drive, drove, flock, group, horde, press, rally, steer, stock, swarm, troop 6 cattle, corral, gather, huddle, people, rabble, throng 7 bunch up, cluster, collect, grazers, numbers, oversee, roundup, wrangle 8 assemble, shepherd 9 gathering, livestock, multitude 10 assemblage, collection, congregate
cattle: 5 drive
ID: 5 brand
member: 3 cow 5 sheep, steer
orphan: 4 dogy 5 dogey, dogie
ride ~ on: 3 run 4 mind, tend 5 drive 6 direct 7 conduct, oversee 9 supervise, trample on, tyrannize 10 administer
sound: 3 baa, low, moo
starter: 3 cow 4 neat 5 swine
stray: 5 rogue
herder: 6 collie, cowboy, gaucho 8 sheepdog
herding __: 3 dog
__ herd on: 4 ride
herds: 4 kine
herdsman: 6 cowboy, drover 7 cowpoke
constellation: 6 Boötes
first ~: 4 Abel
hut: 6 chalet
here: 6 hither, in town, on hand, with us 7 on board, on Earth, present 9 attending 10 at this time
again: 4 back
and now: 5 today 6 at once 7 quickly 8 promptly, right off 9 at present, forthwith, presently, right away 10 at this time, this minute
and there: 5 about 6 around 7 in spots 8 rambling 9 irregular, sometimes, somewhere
around ~: 6 nearby
ender: 4 into, unto, upon, with 5 about, after
from ~: 5 hence
get out of ~: 2 go 5 leave, scram 6 move it 7 vamoose 8 run along, shove off 9 move along, take a hike 10 hit the road
go ~ and there: 3 gad 4 roam, rove, trek 5 drift, range 6 ramble, travel, wander 7 explore, journey, meander, traipse 9 bat around, bum around, gallivant, run around 10 knock about
in French: 3 ici
in Latin: 3 hic
it's neither ~ nor there: 5 limbo 7 nowhere
not ~: 4 gone 5 there 6 absent 9 elsewhere
out of ~: 3 off 4 away, gone 6 yonder 9 elsewhere
partner: 3 now 5 there
see ~: 4 look, wait
the ones ~: 5 these
up to ~: 6 excess 7 satiety, surfeit 8 bellyful, plethora
here __ now: 3 and
__ here!: 4 Same 6 They're
Here __!: 3 I am, I go 4 goes, we go 5 we are
Here __ Come Again: 3 You
Here __ Mr. Jordan: 5 Comes
Here __ nothing!: 4 goes
Here __ the Judge: 5 Comes
Here __, there...: 4 a moo
Here __ the Sun: 5 Comes
Here!: 6 try one
hereabout: 4 near
to a poet: 5 anear
hereafter: 4 anon, soon, then 5 hence 6 in a bit, in time 7 by and by, later on, someday 8 in a while, sometime 9 after this, from now on, next world 10 afterworld, before long, eventually, henceforth, otherworld, ultimately
here and __: 3 now 5 there
Here and Now (1990 song)
artist: Luther Vandross
here and there in Latin: 6 passim
hereby: 4 thus 9 as a result, in this way
Here Comes Santa Claus
artist: Gene Autry
Here Comes the __: 3 Sun
Here Comes the Judge (1968 song)
artist: Shorty Long, Pigmeat Markham
Here Comes the Rain Again (1984 song)
artist: Eurythmics
Here comes trouble: 4 oh-oh, uh-oh
Here Come the Warm Jets
composer: Brian Eno
Heredia, José Maria de: 4 poet 6 French
hereditary: 5 genic 6 family, inborn, inbred, innate, lineal, racial 7 genetic 9 ancestral, genetical, ingrained, intrinsic 10 bequeathed, derivative, handed down
cause of ~ variation: 6 allele
factor: 4 gene
identification: 5 genom 6 genome
letters: 3 DNA, RNA
ruler: 4 king 6 dynast
heredity: 4 line 7 descent, lineage 8 ancestry, genetics
science of ~: 8 genetics
Hereford: 3 cow, pig 4 bull, city, town 5 swine 6 bovine, cattle, county
city: 9 Worcester
locale: 7 England
Herefordshire: 6 county
locale: 7 England
Here I Am (song)
artist: Air Supply, Al Green
Here I Go Again (1987 song)
artist: Whitesnake
herein: 3 enc. 8 enclosed
ender: 5 after 6 before
hereinafter: 8 evermore 9 from now on 10 henceforth
Here Is Your War
author: Ernie Pyle
Here it is!: 4 ta-da 5 ta-dah, voila
Herek: 7 Stephen
Here Lies
author: Dorothy Parker
__ here nor there: 7 neither
Herens: 3 cow 4 bull 6 bovine, cattle
Here on Gilligan's __: 4 isle
__ Here, Private Hargrove: 3 See
Here's __: 4 Lucy
Here's __!: 3 how 6 Johnny
Here's looking at you!: 5 toast
Here's Lucy (CBS sitcom)
cast: Desi Arnaz Jr. (Craig Carter)
Lucie Arnaz (Kim Carter)
Lucille Ball (Lucy Carter)
Gale Gordon (Harrison Carter)
Here's mud in your eye!: 5 toast
Here's to you!: 5 salud, skoal, toast 6 cheers
heresy: 7 dissent 9 blasphemy, rebellion, sacrilege 10 dissension
heretic: 5 rebel 7 infidel 8 agitator, forsaker, maverick, renegade 9 dissenter, dissident, protester 10 iconoclast, malcontent
heretical: 7 deviant 9 atheistic, differing, dissident, heterodox, miscreant, sectarian, skeptical 10 dissenting, idolatrous, schismatic, unorthodox
hereto: 3 yet 5 as yet 6 before 8 until now
ender: 4 fore
__ Here to Eternity: 4 From
heretofore: 3 ago, née 4 once 5 as yet, so far 6 erenow 7 already, earlier 8 formerly, hitherto, until now 9 at one time, preceding 10 previously
mentioned: 5 above
hereupon: 4 anon, soon 7 ere long, shortly 9 presently 10 before long
Here We Are (1990 song)
artist: Gloria Estefan
Here With Me (1988 song)
artist: REO Speedwagon
Here You Come Again (1977 song)
artist: Dolly Parton
heritage: 5 birth, roots 6 legacy, origin 8 ancestry, pedigree 9 tradition 10 birthright
heritor: 4 heir 7 heiress, legatee
herky-__: 5 jerky
herm: 4 bust
Her Majesty: 5 queen
Herman: 4 Babe, Bang, Wouk 5 Billy, Jerry, Woody 6 Keiser, Pee-wee 7 Munster 8 Melville
hermana: 6 sister 7 Spanish
father's ~: 3 tía
Herman, Jerry: 8 composer
musical: Hello, Dolly!
La Cage Aux Folles
Mack & Mabel
Mame
Hermann: 5 Broch, Hesse 6 Muller 7 Fischer 9 Sudermann 10 Staudinger
hermano: 7 brother, Spanish
father's ~: 3 tío
Herman, Pee-wee
persona: 4 nerd
Herman's Hermits
leader: Peter Noone
song: Can't You Hear My Heartbeat (1965)
Dandy (1966)
I'm Henry VIII, I Am (1965)
Just a Little Bit Better (1965)
Leaning on the Lamp Post (1966)
Listen People (1966)
Mrs. Brown You've Got a Lovely Daughter (1965)
A Must to Avoid (1966)
Silhouettes (1965)
There's a Kind of Hush (1967)
Wonderful World (1965)
Herman, Woody: 10 bandleader
genre: 4 jazz
instrument: clarinet, sax
hermeneutics: 8 exegesis
Hermes: 3 Pan
equivalent: 7 Mercury
half-brother: 4 Ares
invention: 4 lyre
parent: 4 Maia, Zeus
son: 3 Pan 6 Faunus 7 Daphnis
hermetic: 5 tight 6 hidden, occult 7 recluse 8 profound, secluded 9 leakproof, nonporous, reclusive, recondite 10 impervious
Hermione: 7 Gingold 8 asteroid, Baddeley
hermit: 4 crab, monk 5 loner 6 cookie 7 ascetic, eremite, isolato,

recluse **8** anchoret, solitary **9** anchorite, religious **10** solitarian, stay-at-home
ender: 3 age
home: 3 hut
like a ~: 5 alone **8** eremitic, solitary **9** reclusive, withdrawn **10** antisocial, cloistered, unsociable
hermit __: 4 crab
hermitage: 5 haven **6** refuge **7** retreat, shelter **8** cloister, hideaway **9** sanctuary, seclusion
Hermitage figure: 4 czar, tsar, tzar
hermitic: 5 alone **8** solitary **9** reclusive **10** antisocial
__ Hermits: 7 Herman's
Hermon: 4 peak **5** mount **8** mountain
locale: 4 Asia **5** Syria
Hermosillo: 4 city, town
locale: 6 Mexico, Sonora
see also Spanish
__ Her Name With Pride: 5 Carve
Hernán: 6 Cortés, Cortez
Hernando: 6 Cortés, Cortez, de Soto
see also Spanish
Hernando's Hideaway: 4 song **5** tango
composer: Richard Adler, Jerry Ross
Hernani
author: Victor Hugo
Herndon: 4 city, town
locale: 8 Virginia
Herne: 4 city, town
locale: 7 Germany
region: 4 Ruhr
Herne, James A.: 6 writer **10** playwright
Herne's __, The: 3 Egg
Herne's Egg, The
author: William Butler Yeats
hero: 3 sub **4** idol, lead, lion, part, role, star **5** hoagy, model, po boy **6** hoagie, savior, victor, winner **7** good guy, grinder, paragon, poor boy, saviour, torpedo, warrior **8** champion, cynosure, exemplar, lead role, luminary, male lead, sandwich **9** conqueror, headliner, lifesaver, role model, submarine, superstar **10** leading man
ender: 3 ine, ism
journey: 5 quest **6** voyage **7** crusade, mission **9** adventure **10** expedition
starter: 4 anti
trait: 4 grit, guts, will **5** moxie, nerve, pluck, valor **6** daring, mettle **7** bravery, courage **8** audacity, backbone, boldness, gumption, strength, tenacity **9** brashness, fortitude, gallantry **10** confidence
work: 4 deed
hero __: 7 worship
Hero
lover: 7 Leander
Hero (1992 film)
cast: Joan Cusack, Geena Davis, Andy García, Dustin Hoffman
Hero (1993 song)
artist: Mariah Carey
Hero and Leander
author: Christopher Marlowe
Herod: 4 king
kingdom: 6 Judaea
niece: 6 Salome
Herod __: 7 Agrippa, Antipas
heroes
like some ~: 5 macho
__ Heroes: 6 Hogan's, Kelly's
heroic: 4 bold, epic, game **5** brave, grand, great, gutsy, nervy, noble, stout **6** awless, daring, epical, gritty, mighty, plucky, spunky **7** aweless, defiant, doughty, gallant, Homeric, impavid, staunch, valiant **8** fearless, glorious, immortal, intrepid, resolute, stalwart, unafraid, valorous **9** audacious, dauntless, dreadless, grandiose, herculean, undaunted, unfearful, unfearing **10** chivalrous, courageous, mettlesome, undismayed
achievement: 4 coup, deed, feat **7** exploit, triumph, victory **8** conquest
not ~: 3 shy **4** meek, weak **5** mousy, timid **6** afraid, craven, yellow **7** chicken, daunted, fearful, wimpish **8** cowardly, sheepish, timorous **9** dastardly, nerveless, spineless **10** frightened, irresolute, submissive
poem: 4 epic, epos **5** epode **6** epopee **8** epopoeia
tale: 4 edda, epic, gest, saga **5** geste
heroic __: 3 age **4** poem **5** drama, meter, tenor, verse **6** stanza **7** couplet
__-heroic: 4 mock
heroics: 5 deeds **6** rescue **9** derring-do
Heroide
composer: Max Reger
Heroides
author: Ovid
heroine: 4 star
answer to a villain: 5 never
heroism: 5 pluck, valor **6** daring, rescue **7** bravery, courage, prowess **8** boldness, valiance, valiancy **9** fortitude, gallantry
heron: 4 bird **5** egret, wader **7** bittern **8** boatbill **9** marsh bird, shorebird **10** wading bird
cousin: 4 ibis **5** crane, stork
home: 4 nest **5** marsh, swamp **7** lowland, wetland **9** swampland
__ heron: 4 blue
__ Her on Monday: 4 I Met
Hero of Lake Erie, The: 5 Perry
hero-worship: 5 exalt **7** adulate, glorify, idolize, lionize
herpetology: 7 science
branch of ~: 9 ophiology
study: 7 reptile **10** amphibians
herpetophobe fear: 8 reptiles
...__ her poor dog a bone: 5 to get
Herr: 5 title **6** German, mister
wife: 4 Frau
Herrick, Robert: 4 poet **7** British
Herriman: 6 George
feline: Krazy Kat
herring: 4 brit, fish, shad, sild **5** sprat **6** kipper **7** sardine **8** brisling
barrel: 4 cade
ender: 4 bone
red ~: 4 ploy, ruse **5** decoy **9** diversion **10** camouflage
young ~: 4 brit **9** whitebait
__ herring: 3 red **7** pickled
__ Herring: 6 Albert
herringbone: 6 coutil, fabric
herringbone __: 5 tweed, weave **6** stitch
herringlike fish: 4 pogy, shad
Herriot, James: 3 vet **4** Scot **6** writer
Herrmann: 6 Edward **7** Bernard
Herrmann, Bernard: 8 composer
film score: Citizen Kane
The Day the Earth Stood Still
The Man Who Knew Too Much
Marnie
North by Northwest
Psycho
Vertigo
Her Royal Majesty (1962 song)
artist: James Darren
hers: 4 pron. **7** pronoun
his or ~ item: 5 towel
in French: 3 ses
like ~: 4 poss.
not ~: 3 his **5** yours
Herschbach, Dudley: 7 chemist **8** Nobelist
Herschel: 4 John **6** Walker **7** William **8** Bernardi
Herschel, John: 7 British **10** astronomer
Herschel, William: 3 Sir **7** British **10** astronomer
Hersey, John: 6 writer **7** British
work: A Bell for Adano
Hiroshima
The Wall
Hershey: 6 Alfred, Milton **7** Barbara
alternative: *see* candy brand
brand: 4 Rolo **6** Kit-Kat
product: 3 bar **4** kiss **5** candy **8** candy bar **9** chocolate
st.: 4 Penn.
Hershey, Alfred: 8 Nobelist
Hershfield cartoon character: 4 Abie
Hershiser, Orel: 6 hurler **7** pitcher
Hersholt: 4 Jean
__ Her Standing There: 4 I Saw
Hertel: 5 Peter
Hertfordshire: 6 county
city: 7 Watford
locale: 7 England
__ Her to Heaven: 5 Leave
Her Town Too (1981 song)
artist: James Taylor
Herts: 6 county
locale: 7 England
Hertz: 6 Gustav **8** Heinrich **9** car rental **10** auto rental
alternative: *see* car rental
Hertz, Gustav: 8 Nobelist **9** physicist
Hertz, Heinrich: 9 physicist
Hertzian __: 4 wave
hertz starter: 4 kilo-, mega-, tera-
Hervey: 5 Allen, Irene, Jason
Hervey, Irene
spouse: Allan Jones
Herzberg, Gerhard: 7 chemist **8** Nobelist
Herzegovina partner: 6 Bosnia
Herzl: 7 Theodor
Herzog: 6 Werner, Whitey
author: Saul Bellow
he's: 4 boys **5** bucks, bulls, stags **6** drakes
He's __: 4 Mine **5** So Shy
He's __ nowhere man: 5 a real
He's __ Picker: 4 a Rag
He Said, She Said (1991 film)
cast: Kevin Bacon, Elizabeth Perkins, Sharon Stone
He's a Rebel (1962 song)
artist: Crystals
He Sees You When You're Sleeping
author: Mary Higgins Clark
He's Got the Whole World __ Hands: 5 in His
Heshvan: 5 month **6** Hebrew
predecessor: 6 Tishri
successor: 6 Kislev
Hesiod: 4 poet **5** Greek
hesistantly: 8 bit by bit **9** piecemeal **10** step by step
hesitancy: 4 stop **5** break, doubt, pause **8** stopping **9** faltering, timidness **10** diffidence, indecision
hesitant: 3 shy **4** loth, poky, wary, weak **5** balky, chary, loath, timid **6** afraid, averse, draggy, fickle, gun-shy, scared, trepid, unsure **7** abashed, alarmed, anxious, chicken, daunted, dubious, fearful, gradual, guarded, halting, impeded, lagging, languid, nervous, panicky, spooked, uneager **8** cautious, cowardly, crawling, creeping, dawdling, delaying, dilatory, doubtful, doubting, dragging, drawn-out, fearsome, lukewarm, plodding, slothful, sluggish, timorous, toddling, wavering **9** diffident, faltering, flinching, leisurely, lethargic, petrified, prolonged, reluctant, skeptical, snaillike, tentative, terrified, uncertain, undecided, unhurried, unwilling **10** ambivalent, deliberate, frightened, indecisive, indisposed, irresolute, protracted, suspicious, uninclined, unobliging, unresolved, weak-willed, wishy-washy
remark: 5 maybe **7** perhaps **8** possibly
sounds: 2 er, uh, um
hesitate: 3 haw, hem **4** balk, halt, wait **5** baulk, dally, defer, delay, demur, hedge, pause, waver **6** boggle, falter, fumble, linger, recoil, seesaw, shrink, totter, waffle **7** hold off, scruple, shy away, stagger, stammer, stumble, stutter, whiffle **8** flounder, hang back, hold back, pull back, question **9** hem and haw, oscillate, pussyfoot, vacillate **10** dillydally, equivocate
hesitating: 8 doubtful **9** skeptical **10** indecisive, irresolute
hesitation: 5 delay, demur, doubt, pause, qualm **7** dubiety, scruple **8** delaying, demurral, fumbling, wavering **9** dubiosity, faltering, misgiving, stumbling **10** averseness, diffidence, indecision, reluctance, skepticism, stammering, stuttering
exclamation: 3 why
show ~: 5 waver **6** falter, wobble **9** hem and haw, vacillate
sound: 2 er, uh, um
without ~: 6 flatly **7** readily **8** directly **9** willingly
word of ~: 4 well
hesitation __: 5 waltz

He's Just Not That Into You (2009 film)
cast: Ben Affleck, Jennifer Aniston, Drew Barrymore, Scarlett Johansson
He's making __...: 5 a list
He's Mine (song)
artist: Mokenstef, Platters
Hesperia: 4 city, town 5 nymph
father: 5 Atlas
locale: 10 California
Hess: 4 Leon, Myra 6 Rudolf, Victor, Walter
__ Hess: 7 Amerada
Hess, Dame Myra: 7 British, pianist
Hesse
river: 4 Eder
see also German
Hesse, Hermann: 4 poet 6 German, writer 8 Nobelist
work: The Glass Bead Game
Siddhartha
Steppenwolf
Hesseman, Howard: 5 actor
TV: Head of the Class, WKRP in Cincinnati
Hessian __: 4 boot
He's So Fine (1963 song)
artist: Chiffons
He's So Shy (1980 song)
artist: Pointer Sisters
Hess, Victor: 8 Nobelist 9 physicist, scientist
Hess, Walter: 8 Nobelist
Hester's mark: 4 red A
He's the Greatest Dancer (1979 song)
artist: Sister Sledge
He's the Wiz and he lives __: 4 in Oz
Hestia: 7 goddess
brother: 4 Zeus 5 Hades 8 Poseidon
equivalent: 5 Vesta
mother: 4 Rhea
parent: 4 Rhea 6 Cronos, Cronus
sister: 4 Hera 7 Demeter
Heston, Charlton: 5 actor
adversary: 3 ape
film: Ben-Hur (1959, AA)
The Buccaneer (1958)
El Cid (1961)
The Greatest Show on Earth (1952)
The Hawaiians (1970)
The Omega Man (1971)
Planet of the Apes (1968)
Pony Express (1953)
The President's Lady (1953)
The Ten Commandments (1956)
Touch of Evil (1958)
Will Penny (1968)
org: 3 NRA
role: 5 Moses
heterodox: 7 lawless 8 abnormal 9 dissident, heretical
heterodoxy: 9 disaccord 10 disharmony, dissension, dissidence
heterogeneity: 3 mix 7 mélange, mixture, variety 9 diversity, potpourri 10 miscellany
heterogeneous: 4 misc., mixt 5 mixed 6 motley, unlike, varied 7 diverse, various 8 assorted, multiple
heterophyte: 5 plant
heth: 6 Hebrew, letter
predecessor: 5 zayin
successor: 3 tet 4 teth
He that __ clean hands...: 4 hath
Hetty: 5 Green
het up: 4 agog 5 afire, angry, irate, riled 7 excited 8 agitated, in a state, in a tizzy, incensed 9 in a lather, indignant, perturbed
heurige: 4 wine 5 white 9 white wine
origin: 7 Austria
heuristic: 9 inquiring 10 analytical
__ Heusen: 3 Van
hew: 2 ax 3 axe, cut 4 chop, crop, fell, hack 5 sever, shape 6 chisel, cleave, saw off 7 cut down 8 chop down, chop wood 9 sculpture
anew: 5 recut
__-hew: 5 rough
HEW
part: 4 Educ. 6 Health 7 Welfare 9 Education
successor: 3 HHS
he was, in Latin: 4 erat
hewer: 3 axe 6 axeman 7 hatchet
He Will Break Your Heart (1960 song)
artist: Jerry Butler
Hewitt: 3 Don 8 Jennifer
Hewitt, Jennifer Love: 7 actress
film: Heartbreakers (2001)
I Know What You Did Last Summer (1997)
TV: Ghost Whisperer, Party of Five
Hewlett: 7 William
Hewlett-Packard
competitor: 3 IBM 5 Epson
product: 2 PC 7 printer 8 computer
hewn: 6 felled 8 rough-cut
__-hewn: 5 rough
He wouldn't harm __: 4 a fly 5 a flea
hex: 3 pox 4 jinx 5 charm, curse, magic, spell 6 voodoo, whammy 7 bewitch, enchant, evil eye, sorcery 10 hocus-pocus
halter: 6 amulet
sign locale: 4 barn
hex __: 4 sign
hex-: 3 six
halved: 3 tri-
predecessor: 4 pent-
successor: 4 sept-
hexa-: 3 six
plus two: 4 octa-, octo-
predecessor ~: 5 penta-
successor: 5 septi-
hexad: 3 six 6 sextet 8 sextette
half a ~: 4 trio 5 triad 6 triple
hexade: 3 six
hexahedron: 3 die 4 cube
hexane: 4 fuel 7 solvent
hexapod: 3 bug 6 insect
hexed: 7 accurst, hapless 8 accursed, luckless
hexing: 5 spell
hexone: 7 solvent
hexose: 5 sugar
Hexum: 7 Jon-Erik
hey: 8 greeting
ender: 3 day
follower: 6 diddle
hey __: 4 rube
Hey __: 4 Girl, Jude, Mr. D.J. 5 Lover, Paula, There
Hey __ Lonely Girl: 5 There
Hey!: 3 cry, pst 4 ahoy, psst 6 listen
say ~: 4 yell
Hey, __!: 3 you
Hey, __ Me Over: 4 Look
heyday: 4 acme, peak, pink, time 5 prime 6 flower, height, zenith 8 pinnacle 9 golden age
Heyerdahl, Thor: 8 explorer 9 Norwegian
island destination: 6 Easter
transport: 3 Ra I 4 raft, Ra II 7 Kon-Tiki
word in a ~ title: 3 Aku
Hey Girl (1971 song)
artist: Donny Osmond
Hey, Good __: 6 Lookin'
__ Hey Hey Kiss Him Goodbye: 4 Na Na
Hey Jude (1968 song)
artist: Beatles
__ Hey Kid: 3 Say
Hey, kids! What time __?: 4 is it
Hey Lover (1995 song)
artist: LL Cool J
Heymans, Corneille: 8 Nobelist
Hey Mr. D.J. (1993 song)
artist: Zhané
Hey Nineteen (1980 song)
artist: Steely Dan
Hey there!: 4 ahoy
Hey There (1954 song)
artist: Rosemary Clooney
Hey There Lonely Girl (1970 song)
artist: Eddie Holman
Heyward, DuBose: 6 writer
work: Porgy
Porgy and Bess
Heywood: 4 John 5 Broun, Eddie 6 Thomas
Heywood __ Broun: 4 Hale
Heywood, John: 4 poet 7 British
Heywood, Thomas: 7 British 10 playwright
Hey you!: 3 pst 4 ahoy, psst
Hezekiah's mother: 3 Abi
Hf: 4 elem. 7 element, hafnium
72 for ~: 4 at. no.
Hg: 4 elem., merc. 7 mercury
80 for ~: 4 at. no.
H.G.: 5 Wells
hgt.: 2 mt. 3 alt., mtn. 4 elev.
HGTV: 7 channel
alternative: *see* cable channel
hgwy.: 2 rt. 3 rte.
HHH: 7 Liberal 8 Humphrey
boss: 3 LBJ
he defeated ~: 3 RMN
org. cofounded by ~: 3 ADA
HHS
agency: 3 CDC, FDA, NIH, SSA
part: 5 Human 6 Health 8 Services
hi-__: 3 res 4 tech
Hi: 5 aloha, hello 6 shalom 8 greeting
say ~ to: 5 greet
wife: 4 Lois
Hi, __!: 3 Mom
Hi-__, Hi-Lo: 4 Lili
HI
see Hawaii
Hialeah: 4 city, town
locale: 7 Florida
transaction: 5 wager
Hi and Lois: 5 comic, strip 10 comic strip
dog: 4 Dawg
kid: 3 Dot 4 Chip 5 Ditto 6 Trixie
hiatus: 3 gap 4 gulf, halt, lull, rift 5 break, lapse, pause, space 6 breach, lacuna, layoff, recess 7 interim, respite 8 interval, omission 9 cessation, interlude 10 sabbatical
Hiawatha: 4 poem 6 Indian
author: Henry Wadsworth Longfellow
boat: 5 canoe
hibachi: 7 brasier, brazier
feature: 5 grate
residue: 3 ash
Hibbert: 7 Eleanor
Hibbing: 4 city, town
locale: 9 Minnesota
Hibbler, Al
song: Unchained Melody (1955)
hibernal: 6 chilly, frigid, wintry 7 wintery
hibernate: 4 hide, idle, rest 5 sleep 6 hole up 8 stagnate 10 lie dormant
place to ~: 3 den 4 lair
hibernating: 6 asleep, dozing 7 dormant, napping 8 dreaming 9 sacked out, somnolent
hibernation: 5 sleep
Hibernia: 4 Eire, Erin 7 Ireland
Hibernian: 4 Celt 5 Irish
Hiberno-__: 5 Saxon
hibiscus: 4 tree 5 plant 6 flower
cousin: 4 ocra, okra, okro 6 mallow
hic __: 5 jacet
hic, __, hoc: 4 haec
hiccup: 5 spasm 6 reflex 7 setback 10 difficulty
hick: 3 oaf 4 boor, rube 5 rural, yokel 6 farmer, gaffer, rustic 7 bumpkin, hayseed, plowboy 9 backwater, hillbilly 10 clodhopper, provincial
Hickey: 7 William
Hickman: 6 Darryl, Dwayne
Hickok: 4 Bill 8 Wild Bill
hickory: 3 nut 4 tree 6 fabric
tree: 5 pecan 6 hognut, pignut, walnut 9 butternut
__ Hickory: 3 Old
Hickory Dickory __: 4 Dock
Hickox: 7 Douglas
Hicks: 4 John 6 Edward 9 Catherine, Granville
Hicks, Granville: 6 writer
Hicks, John: 8 Nobelist 9 economist
Hicksville: 4 city, town
locale: 7 New York 10 Long Island
Hidalgo: 4 city, town 5 state
locale: 6 Mexico 9 Chihuahua
see also Spanish
hidden: 4 dark, deep, lost 5 blind, inner, leafy, perdu, privy 6 arcane, buried, covert, inward, latent, masked, mystic, occult, perdue, secret, unseen, untold, veiled 7 cloaked, clouded, covered, cryptic, furtive, obscure, on the QT, private, shadowy, unknown 8 abstruse, eclipsed, esoteric, hermetic, hush-hush, isolated, mystical, obscured, screened, secluded, shielded, shrouded, ulterior, withheld 9 concealed, cryptical, disguised, incognito, innermost, in the dark, invisible, nonpublic, out of view, potential, recondite, unexposed, unnoticed 10 cloistered, mysterious, out of sight, tucked away, undercover, underlying,

under wraps, undetected, undivulged, unrevealed, unviewable
combining form: **4** adel- **5** adelo-, crypt-, krypt- **6** crypto-, krypto-
drawback: **4** snag, trap **5** catch
not ~: **5** clear, overt, plain **6** patent **7** obvious, visible **8** apparent, manifest **10** observable
supply: **5** cache, hoard, stash
wait while ~: **4** lurk
hidden __: **3** tax **6** agenda
hiddenite: **3** gem **8** gemstone
Hidden Valley: **8** dressing
alternative: **8** Wish-Bone **9** Seven Seas **11** Good Seasons
Hidden Valley __: **5** Ranch
hide: **4** bury, lurk, mask, pelt, skin, veil, whip, wrap **5** cache, cloak, couch, cover, cower, ditch, shade, sneak, spank, stash, store **6** closet, harbor, hole up, hush up, inhume, lie low, pocket, screen, shield, shroud **7** becloud, blot out, conceal, cover up, eclipse, envelop, harbour, leather, obscure, protect, seclude, secrete, shelter, shut off, smuggle **8** covering, disguise, ensconce, enshroud, hold back, salt away, sock away, stow away, suppress, tuck away, withhold **9** adumbrate, dissemble, hibernate, keep quiet, obfuscate, sequester, take cover, whitewash **10** camouflage, integument, interweave, keep secret
away: **4** save **5** stash, store **9** sequester
brushed ~: **5** suede
cure ~s: **3** tan
don't ~: **5** pop in **6** appear, show up, turn up **7** turn out
ender: **3** out **4** away **5** bound
from: **5** avoid
in fear: **5** cower, quail **6** cringe, shrink **7** tremble
in the hand: **4** palm
partner: **4** hair, seek
place to ~: **4** hole, lair **5** haven **6** refuge **7** retreat, shelter **9** safe house, sanctuary
starter: **3** cow, raw **5** horse
tan a ~: **5** spank **6** punish
untanned ~: **3** kip
hide __: **3** out **4** away
hide __ hair: **3** nor
hide-__-seek: **5** and-go
Hide-__: **4** A-Bed
hide and seek: **4** game
cheat at ~: **4** peek
phrase: **5** not it **7** you're it
spot: **4** base
word: **5** ready
Hide and Seek (2005 film)
cast: Robert De Niro, Dakota Fanning, Famke Janssen
hideaway: **3** den, mew **4** aery, cave, eyry, lair, nest, nook **5** aerie, eyrie, villa **6** asylum, burrow, corner, covert, lounge, refuge, resort **7** retreat, shelter **9** hermitage, nightclub, sanctuary, seclusion **10** ivory tower
hideaway __: **3** bed
Hideaway
author: Dean Koontz
hidebound: **5** rigid, stiff, tight **6** little, narrow **9** bourgeois, impliable, parochial **10** inflexible, intolerant, provincial
Hideki: **5** Irabu
hide nor __: **4** hair
Hideo: **4** Nomo
hide one's __: **4** head
hideous: **4** evil, grim, ugly **5** awful, gross, lurid **6** grisly, horrid, morbid, odious **7** beastly, fearful, ghastly, hateful, heinous, macaber, macabre **8** dreadful, gruesome, horrible, shocking, terrible, wretched **9** appalling, frightful, grotesque, loathsome, monstrous, offensive, repellant, repellent, repugnant, repulsive, revolting, unsightly **10** abominable, detestable, disgusting, horrendous, horrifying, petrifying, terrifying, unpleasant
hideout: **3** den **4** lair, nest, nook **5** cover, haven **6** corner, grotto, refuge **7** shelter **9** safe house, sanctuary **10** ivory tower
hider: **8** stowaway
hidey-hole: **5** cache
hiding: **7** beating, masking, secrecy, veiling **8** cloaking, covering, flogging **9** screening, seclusion, secretion, shielding, thrashing **10** out of sight
come out of ~: **4** show **6** appear, emerge **7** peep out, surface **10** break cover
nothing: **4** bare, open **5** frank, overt, plain **7** exposed, obvious **8** wide-open
place: **3** den **4** lair **5** cache, cover, haven, niche **6** recess, refuge
hie: **2** go **3** fly, rip, run, zip **4** dart, dash, flit, hare, pelt, race, rush, tear, trot, zoom **5** hurry, scoot, scram, shoot, spank, speed **6** barrel, gallop, hasten, hustle, move it, repair, rocket, run off, scurry **7** dash off, floor it, hop to it, quicken, scamper, take off, tear off **8** hightail, light out, make time, step on it **9** get moving, go quickly, hotfoot it, make haste, shake a leg, skedaddle **10** double-time, get a move on, get hopping, hightail it, make tracks
hiemal: **4** cold **6** wintry **7** wintery
hierarchy: **4** rank **5** order, scale **7** ranking **8** echelons **9** apparatus
level: **4** rank, rung
hieratic: **8** clerical, priestly **10** sacerdotal
hieroglyphics: **4** code **6** cipher **7** writing **9** ideograms **10** characters, cryptogram
Hieronymus: **5** Bosch
hi-fi: **5** phono **6** stereo **8** Victrola **10** phonograph
buy: **2** LP **3** amp **5** tuner **6** stereo
Higgins: **4** Jack **5** Henry **6** Bertie
Higgins, Bertie
song: Key Largo (1982)
__ Higgins Clark: **4** Mary
Higgins, Henry creator: George Bernard Shaw
higgle: **6** dicker, palter **7** bargain
high: **3** big **4** dear, rank, tall **5** above, aloft, happy, light, lofty, noble, pricy, steep, stiff, tight, tipsy, upper **6** aerial, alpine, costly, elated, flying, joyful, lordly, piping, pricey, pumped, rancid, shrill, strong, treble **7** crucial, eminent, exalted, excited, extreme, psyched, soaring, soprano, stately, sublime **8** cheerful, ecstatic, elevated, hovering, piercing, powerful, towering, upraised **9** essential, excessive, expensive, exuberant, important, prominent **10** at a premium, exorbitant, malodorous, optimistic, overpriced, up in the air
abode: **4** aery, eyry **5** aerie, eyrie
aim ~: **5** dream **6** aspire
and dry: **7** aground **8** cast away, deserted, marooned, stranded **9** abandoned
and low: **7** all over **10** everywhere
and mighty: **5** lofty **7** haughty, pompous **8** arrogant, dogmatic, snobbish **10** dogmatical
ball: **3** lob **5** pop-up
beams: **7** brights
be in ~ spirits: **4** crow **5** exult **6** bubble **7** enthuse, rejoice **9** make merry **10** effervesce, jump for joy
birth: **9** blue blood, gentility **10** upper class, upper crust
blow sky ~: **5** rebut **6** refute **8** disprove **9** discredit, shoot down **10** invalidate
combining form: **3** alt- **4** alti-
command: **5** brass **10** management
country: **4** mesa **5** butte, Nepal, Tibet **6** Xizang **7** plateau, Sitsang
degree of insight: **5** depth **6** acuity, acumen, wisdom **8** sagacity **10** astuteness
dudgeon: **3** ire **4** rage **5** anger, wrath **7** umbrage
ender: **3** boy, way **4** ball, born, bred, brow, jack, land, life, rise, road, tail **5** chair, flier, flyer, lands, light **6** binder, flying, handed, lander **7** lighter
five: **4** slap **8** greeting
fly ~: **4** soar
flying ~: **3** gay **4** glad **5** happy, merry, sunny **6** blithe, cheery, chirpy, elated, golden, joyful, joyous, upbeat **7** beaming, buoyant, chipper, content, gleeful, glowing, pleased, radiant, tickled **8** blissful, carefree, cheerful, ecstatic, exultant, gladsome, grooving, jubilant, laughing, sanguine, thrilled, unbeaten **9** contented, delighted, fortunate, gratified, lightsome, overjoyed **10** optimistic, successful, triumphant, unbothered
get ~ on: **4** like, love **5** enjoy, savor **6** relish **9** delight in **10** appreciate
give the ~ sign: **3** tip **4** warn **5** alert **6** advise, signal, tip off **7** caution **8** forewarn
ground: **4** hill, rise **5** knoll, ridge **7** plateau **8** eminence, mountain **9** acclivity, elevation **10** prominence
heel: **4** pump **5** spike
hit ~ into the air: **4** loft
hit the ~ spots: **4** skim **8** simplify
hold ~: **4** love **5** adore, honor **6** esteem
in alcohol: **4** hard
in ~ dudgeon: **5** irate
in ~ gear: **4** fast **5** apace **7** hastily, quickly, rapidly, swiftly **8** speedily **9** hurriedly
in music: **3** alt
in place names: **4** Alta
in ~ style: **3** mod **4** chic **5** natty, swank **6** classy, dapper, dressy, modish **7** à la mode, dashing, elegant, voguish
IQ: **10** braininess
jinks: **4** lark **5** caper, prank, spree **7** fooling, revelry **8** mischief **9** vandalism
jump: **5** event
leave ~ and dry: **4** jilt **6** desert, maroon, strand **8** abdicate
live ~ on the hog: **4** bask **5** revel **6** thrive **7** indulge, rollick **8** flourish **9** luxuriate
living: **6** luxury, wealth **8** opulence, splendor **9** affluence **10** prosperity
look ~ and low: **4** hunt, seek **5** scour **6** search **7** ransack, rummage
low to ~: **5** range
mark: **5** A plus
mountain: **3** alp
muckamuck: **6** honcho
name meaning ~ peace: **8** Humphrey
noon: **6** zenith **8** meridian
not ~: **3** low **4** deep, down **5** lowly
not as ~: **5** below, lower, under
note: **3** e la
old time: **4** lark **5** caper, fling, revel, spree **6** frolic, gambol, picnic **7** rollick
on ~: **4** over **5** above, aloft, lofty **8** overhead
on one's ~ horse: **6** snooty **7** haughty
opinion: **6** esteem, regard **7** respect **9** reverence **10** admiration
partner: **3** dry, low
pitched too ~: **5** sharp
place: **6** heaven **9** firmament
point: **3** top **4** acme, apex, peak **5** crest **6** climax, zenith **10** prominence
pt.: **2** mt. **3** mtn.
raise ~: **4** heft, hike, lift **5** extol **6** hike up **7** build up, elevate, ennoble, glorify, idolize, lionize, worship
rate ~: **4** like, love **5** adore, enjoy, favor, go for **6** admire, prefer, relish, revere **7** cherish, idolize **8** hold dear, venerate **10** appreciate
rating: **4** A-one, one-A
regard: **4** love **6** esteem **10** attachment
repute: **4** fame **5** éclat, glory **6** renown **7** acclaim **8** eminence, prestige **9** celebrity
roller: **7** spender **8** prodigal **10** big spender

search ~ heaven: 4 comb 6 forage 7 ransack, rummage
seas: 5 ocean
sign: 4 wink 5 alarm, alert 6 motion
society: 5 elite 6 bon ton, jet set 8 nobility
spirits: 3 joy, pep 4 élan, glee, life, mood 5 mirth 6 gaiety, gayety, levity 7 elation, jollity 8 buoyance, buoyancy, euphoria, felicity, hilarity
spot: 4 acme, apex, peak 5 attic, crest, crown, tower 6 climax, payoff, summit, zenith 8 capstone, pinnacle 10 denouement
standing: 4 note 5 glory, honor 6 esteem, renown 7 acclaim, dignity 8 eminence, prestige 9 celebrity, greatness, magnitude, reverence 10 importance, prominence
temperature: 4 heat 5 fever
time: 4 noon 5 spree 6 at last
to a ~ degree: 4 very 5 quite 6 deeply, rather, vastly 7 acutely, greatly 8 terribly 9 decidedly, extremely, seriously, supremely, unusually 10 enormously, especially, profoundly, remarkably, thoroughly, uncommonly
tops: 6 sneaks 8 sneakers
up: 5 aloft, lofty 8 elevated, towering
value: 4 perk, plum 5 bonus, price, prize 6 bounty 7 premium 8 dividend 10 perquisite
water alternative: 4 hell
high __: 3 bar, hat, tea 4 beam, gear, jump, mass, noon, road, seas, sign, tide, time, wire 5 horse, jinks, liver, style, water 6 ground, jumper, priest, relief, roller, school 7 command, concept, fashion, finance, hurdles, profile, society, spirits, treason
high __ hog: 5 on the 6 off the
high __ kite: 3 as a
high-__: 3 end, hat 4 five, rise, risk, step, tech, test 5 class, count, flown, grade, level, power, speed, toned 6 energy, handed, income, minded, necked, octane, priced, strung, ticket 7 pitched, powered, rolling, tension, voltage
high-__ act: 4 wire
high-__ cymbals: 3 hat
high-__ district: 4 rent
high-__ lipoprotein: 7 density
high-__ mark: 5 water
high-__ poker: 3 low
high-__ sneakers: 3 top
__ high: 3 fly 4 ride 6 Azores 7 Bermuda, Pacific
__-high: 3 ace, sky 4 hole, knee, type 5 waist
High __: 3 Tor 4 Mass, Noon, Wall 5 Court, Hopes 6 Church, Crimes, Enough, Sierra, Stakes 7 Anxiety, Holiday, Rollers, Society
High __ Day: 4 Holy
High __ Drifter: 6 Plains
High __ Shoes: 6 Button
High __ the Mighty, The: 3 and
__ High: 3 How, Sky 4 Aces 6 Cooley 7 Natural
high-altitude: 4 tall 6 alpine 8 towering
high and __: 3 dry, low 6 mighty
high-and-mighty: 4 vain 5 proud 6 stuffy 8 cavalier, snobbish, superior
High and the Mighty, The (1954 film)
cast: Laraine Day, Robert Stack, Claire Trevor, John Wayne
composer: Dimitri Tiomkin
director: William Wellman
writer: 4 Gann
High Anxiety (1977 film)
cast: Mel Brooks, Madeline Kahn, Harvey Korman, Cloris Leachman
director: Mel Brooks
high as __: 5 a kite
highball: 5 drink 8 beverage, cocktail, libation 10 intoxicant
ingredient: 3 rye
highborn: 5 noble, royal 6 gentle 7 genteel 9 patrician 10 upper-class
unfit for the ~: 4 non-U
highboy: 5 chest 7 dresser 9 furniture
highbred: 5 noble, royal 6 august, formal, polite 7 courtly, elegant, gallant, genteel, refined 8 cultured, decorous, gracious, polished 9 dignified 10 chivalrous, respectful
highbrow: 3 ace 4 sage, snob, whiz 5 brain, snoot 6 august, brainy, genius, proper, savant 7 bookish, egghead, elegant, elitist, erudite, learned, prodigy, refined, scholar, stately, thinker 8 academic, cerebral, cultured, decorous, Einstein, longhair, studious, virtuoso 9 dignified, intellect, scholarly 10 mastermind
highbrows: 5 elite 8 literati 10 illuminati, upper-crust
High Button Shoes: 7 musical
composer: Jule Styne
high-caliber: 8 superior
highchair: 4 seat
hazard: 5 spill
part: 4 tray
user: 3 tot 6 infant
high-class: 4 A-one, best, chic, luxe, posh, rich 5 elite, ritzy 6 choice, deluxe 7 stylish, supreme, voguish 8 ladylike, superior
High Crimes (2002 film)
cast: Morgan Freeman, Ashley Judd, Amanda Peet
__ High Dam: 5 Aswan
higher: 4 more 5 upper 6 senior
get ~: 4 rise, soar 6 ascend, move up 7 take off
make ~: 4 hike 5 boost, raise 6 jack up 7 elevate 8 increase
of ~ rank: 6 senior 8 superior
prefix: 5 super-, supra-
than: 4 over, past 5 above 6 beyond 9 upwards of
higher-__: 3 ups
Higher and Higher: 7 musical
composer: Lorenz Hart, Richard Rodgers
Higher and Higher (song)
artist: Rita Coolidge, Jackie Wilson
Higher Ground (1973 song)
artist: Stevie Wonder
Higher Love (1986 song)
artist: Steve Winwood
higher-quality: 6 better
higher-up: 4 boss, exec 5 chief 6 honcho, leader, top dog 7 big shot, manager 8 big wheel, kingfish, overseer, superior 9 authority, executive 10 head honcho, supervisor
highest: 3 nth, top, ult. 4 A-one, best, head, most, tops 5 chief, grand, prime 6 utmost 7 leading, maximum, optimum, premier, primary, supreme, topmost 8 foremost, ultimate 9 principal, sovereign, uppermost, uttermost
of the ~ order: 6 curule
point: 3 tip, top 4 acme, apex, peak 5 crest, crown, limit 6 apogee, summit, zenith 7 maximum 8 pinnacle 10 prominence
prefix: 4 arch-
highest-quality: 4 A-one, best, tops 5 first, primo
__-High-Everything-Else: 4 Lord
highfalutin: 5 artsy 6 august, la-di-da 7 pompous, stately 8 affected, lah-di-dah, mannered
manner: 4 airs
type: 4 snob
high-five: 5 greet
exchange a ~: 5 exult
slapper: 4 palm
sound: 4 slap
high-flown: 5 lofty, showy 6 ornate 7 exalted, fustian, pompous, stilted 8 inflated 9 bombastic, grandiose 10 rhetorical
__ high gear: 4 into
high-grade
see wonderful
high-handed: 5 proud 6 lordly 8 despotic 9 arbitrary, imperious 10 despotical, peremptory
high-handedness: 7 cruelty, tyranny 8 coercion 9 autocracy, despotism 10 oppression
high-hat: 4 snob, snub 5 scorn, snoot 6 stuffy 7 cymbals 8 snobbish, superior 10 percussion
look: 5 sneer
high-hatter: 4 snob 5 snoot
high-heel: 4 shoe 8 footwear
High Holy __: 3 Day
High Hopes (1959 song)
animal: 3 ant, ram
artist: Frank Sinatra
composer: Sammy Cahn, Jimmy Van Heusen
high-income: 8 well-paid 9 lucrative 10 profitable
high-IQ club: 5 Mensa
high jump: 5 event, sport
high jumper: 6 Brumel 7 Fosbury
highland: 4 hill 7 plateau
Highland
see Scotland
Highlander: 3 SUV 4 Celt, Gael, Scot 6 Toyota
Highlander (1986 film)
cast: Sean Connery, Roxanne Hart, Christopher Lambert
Highland fling: 5 dance
Highland Park: 4 city, town
locale: 8 Illinois, Michigan
highlands: 5 peaks 9 mountains
like the ~: 5 hilly
Highlands
see Scotland
high-level: 7 crucial 8 critical, historic 9 big-league, important, momentous, paramount
highlight: 4 peak 5 focus, light 6 accent, play up, stress 7 feature, point up 8 best part 9 emphasize, punctuate, spotlight, underline 10 accentuate, focal point, illuminate, illustrate, underscore
hockey ~: 5 fight
highlighted, be: 8 stand out
highlights: 5 recap 6 wrap-up 7 summary 8 synopsis
high-low: 4 game, shoe 5 poker 8 card game, footwear
high-low-jack: 4 game 8 card game
alias: 5 pitch 7 seven-up 9 old sledge
highly: 4 a lot, much, very, well 5 mucho, quite 6 deeply, hugely, plenty, vastly 7 but good, greatly 8 terribly, very much, very well 9 decidedly, extremely, immensely 10 profoundly, remarkably, thoroughly, to the quick
highly-wrought: 4 posh 5 fancy, plush, showy, swank 6 flashy, frilly, glitzy, lavish, ornate, swanky 7 elegant, opulent 8 splendid 9 decorated, elaborate, intricate, luxurious, sumptuous 10 decorative, munificent, ornamented
high-minded: 4 just 5 great, lofty, moral, noble 6 honest 7 ethical, liberal, refined, stately, upright 8 elevated, knightly, virtuous 9 honorable 10 chivalrous
high-mindedness: 6 ethics, purity, virtue 7 decency, honesty, probity 8 fairness, morality, nobility 9 character, integrity, rectitude 10 generosity, temperance
high-muck-a-muck: 3 VIP 4 boss, king 5 mogul, nabob
Highness: 5 title
__ Highness: 3 Her 4 Your 8 Royal. His
High Noon (1952 film): 5 oater 7 western
cast: Lloyd Bridges, Gary Cooper, Katy Jurado, Grace Kelly
composer: Dimitri Tiomkin
singer: Frankie Laine
__ high off the hog: 3 eat
high on the __: 3 hog
high-pH substance: 3 lye 6 alkali
high-pitched: 5 fluty, reedy, sharp 6 shrill 8 piercing
sound: 4 ting 5 whine 6 squawk, squeak
High Plains Drifter (1973 film): 5 oater
cast: Clint Eastwood
director: Clint Eastwood
High Point: 4 city, town
locale: 4 N. Car.
high-powered: 5 type A 6 active, mighty, potent, robust 7 driving, dynamic, intense, pushing 8 force-

ful, hustling, vigorous **9** attacking, energetic **10** aggressive, compelling
not ~: **5** type B
high-priced: **4** dear, rich **5** steep, stiff **6** costly **8** precious, valuable **9** expensive **10** at a premium, exorbitant
high-principled: **4** true **6** honest **7** ethical **8** reliable, virtuous **9** veracious
high-priority: **7** crucial **8** critical, pressing
high-profile: **3** big **4** star **5** famed **6** famous **7** eminent, popular **8** renowned **9** important, prominent, well-known **10** celebrated
high-quality: **5** prime **6** grade A **9** excellent
high-ranking: **5** noble **6** august **7** eminent
one: **6** aristo
high-rise: **5** lofty, tower **7** edifice **8** building
locale: **3** urb **4** city
support: **4** I-bar
unit: **5** condo **9** apartment
high-risk: **4** spec
High Rollers: **8** game show
host: Alex Trebek
high school
class: **3** alg., art, bio., Eng., gym, mus., sci. **4** chem., math, shop, trig **5** music **6** home ec **7** algebra, biology, English, history, physics, science **8** geometry **9** chemistry
dance: **3** hop **4** prom
equiv.: **3** GED
keepsake: **2** yb. **8** yearbook
misfit: **4** geek, nerd **7** egghead
safety org.: **4** SADD
school student: **10** adolescent
sport: **4** golf **5** track **6** soccer, tennis **7** bowling **8** baseball, football, lacrosse **9** wrestling **10** basketball
student: **4** teen **5** minor **6** teener
High School Cadets, The
composer: John Philip Sousa
High School Confidential (1958 song)
artist: Jerry Lee Lewis
High Sierra (1941 film)
cast: Humphrey Bogart, Ida Lupino
director: Raoul Walsh
dog: **4** Pard
Highsmith, Patricia: **6** writer
work: Strangers on a Train
The Talented Mr. Ripley
High Society (1956 film): **7** musical
cast: Bing Crosby, Celeste Holm, Grace Kelly, Frank Sinatra
composer: Cole Porter
high-speed number: **4** Mach
high-spirited: **5** alive, peppy, vital **6** frisky, jaunty, lively, snappy **7** dashing, dynamic, vibrant **8** animated, vigorous **9** energetic, vivacious
__ High Stadium: **4** Mile
High Stakes
author: Dick Francis
__ high standard: **4** set a
high-strung: **4** edgy **5** hyper, itchy, jumpy, tense, wired **6** feisty, jangly, uneasy **7** anxious, fidgety, jittery, keyed up, nervous, restive, shook up, uptight **8** agitated, fluttery, restless, shaken up, skittish, stressed, troubled **9** concerned, excitable, ill at ease, impatient, irascible, irritable, sensitive, unrestful **10** all shook up
hightail it: **2** go **3** fly, hie, lam, rip, run, zip **4** bolt, dart, dash, flee, flit, race, rush, scat, tear, zoom **5** hurry, scoot, scram, speed **6** barrel, decamp, gallop, get out, hasten, hustle, rocket, scurry **7** abscond, go south, make off, quicken, scamper, take off **8** shove off **9** get moving, make haste, shake a leg, skedaddle **10** get a move on
high-tech: **6** modern **10** electronic
company: **6** dot-com
memo: **3** fax **5** e-mail
high-temperature: **3** hot
high-test: **3** gas **8** gasoline
__ High the Moon: **3** How
high-toned: **4** chic, tony **5** moral, put on, ritzy, suave, toney **6** classy, la-de-da, la-di-da, urbane **7** elegant, ethical **8** affected, lah-di-dah **9** honorable, insincere, uncorrupt **10** aboveboard
Hightower: **7** Rosella
high-water mark: **4** acme, apex, peak **5** crest **6** apogee, summit, zenith **8** meridian, pinnacle
highway: **3** way **4** pike, road **5** route **6** artery **7** freeway, ingress, thruway **8** main road, toll road, turnpike **10** expressway, interstate, throughway
abbr. on ~ overpasses: **3** max
agcy.: **3** DOT
alert: **5** flare, fusee, fuzee
ancient ~: **3** via
crosser, maybe: **4** deer
enter a ~: **5** merge
feature: **4** exit, lane, ramp **6** stripe **8** shoulder
fee: **4** toll
hanging: **4** sign
hazard: **3** ess
headache: **3** jam **5** delay, tie up **8** accident, slowdown **10** bottleneck, congestion, traffic jam
improve a ~: **5** widen
like some ~s: **5** laned
Maine-to-Florida ~: **5** US one
marker: **4** cone **5** pylon
material: **3** tar **7** asphalt **8** concrete
Minneapolis-to-Fargo ~: **5** US ten
noisemaker: **4** horn
sight: **3** car **4** auto, semi **5** truck
sign: **3** SLO **4** eats, Exit, hill, slow **5** arrow
starter: **5** super
stop: **5** diner, motel
US-to-Alaska ~: **5** Alcan
worker: **5** paver
see also road
highway __: **6** patrol **7** robbery
__ highway: **7** divided
__ Highway: **5** Alcan
highwayman: **4** thug **5** thief **6** bandit, looter **7** brigand, footpad **8** marauder
Highwayman, The: **4** poem
author: Alfred Noyes
heroine: **4** Bess
Highway to Heaven (NBC drama)
cast: Victor French (Mark Gordon) Michael Landon (Jonathan Smith)
High Window, The
author: Raymond Chandler
high-wire
garb: **6** tights
insurance: **3** net
high-wire __: **3** act
Higuchi Ichiyo: **4** poet **6** writer **8** Japanese
hi-hat: **7** cymbals **10** percussion
Hi, Hi, Hi (1972 song)
artist: Paul McCartney
Hi-Ho
competitor: ***see*** cracker
Hi, honey, __!: **6** I'm home
hijack: **3** rob **4** take **5** seize, steal, usurp **6** kidnap **7** plunder **8** take over **10** commandeer
Hijack (1975 song)
artist: Herbie Mann
hijacker: **5** thief **6** bandit, robber **9** kidnapper
hijinks: **3** fun **5** caper **6** frolic **7** fooling **9** horseplay
hike: **2** up **4** jack, jump, lift, rise, roam, snap, trek, trip, walk **5** add to, boost, jaunt, leg it, march, raise, tramp, tromp **6** foot it, growth, jack up, jerk up, junket, mark up, pull up, ramble, stroll, trudge, wander **7** amplify, augment, elevate, explore, journey, magnify **8** addition, backpack, increase, progress **9** excursion, inflation **10** hit the road
starter: **5** hitch
take a ~: **2** go **4** blow, exit, part, quit **5** leave **6** begone, get out **8** light out, withdraw **10** go fly a kite
__ hike: **5** take a
Hiken: **3** Nat
hiker: **6** center **10** backpacker, pedestrian
need: **3** map **4** pack **5** trail **8** backpack
path: **5** trail
snack: **4** gorp **7** berries
Hikmet, Nazim: **4** poet **7** Turkish
Hilaire: **6** Belloc
Hilario: **4** Nene
hilarious: **4** rich **5** funny, jolly, merry **6** har-har, jovial **7** comical **8** humorous **9** convivial, laughable, priceless, very funny **10** frolicsome, gut-busting, ridiculous, rollicking, uproarious
one: **4** riot **6** scream
hilarity: **3** joy **4** glee **5** cheer, mirth, revel **6** comedy, gaiety, gayety, levity **7** gayness, jollity, revelry **8** jocosity, laughter, partying **9** festivity, happiness, jocundity, joviality, jubilance, merriment **10** exuberance, joyfulness, recreation
Hilary: **4** Duff, Hahn, pope **5** saint, Swank **7** pontiff
Hilda: **5** Solis **8** asteroid **9** Doolittle
__-Hilda: **5** Broom
Hildebrand: **5** saint
Hildegarde: **4** Neff
Hilfiger: **5** Tommy
Hi-Lili, __: **4** Hi-Lo
hill: **3** tor **4** dune, mesa, rise **5** bluff, butte, cliff, grade, knoll, mound, ridge, slope, stack **6** barrow, glacis, height, upland **7** incline, rampart, upgrade **8** eminence, headland, highland, landmark **9** acclivity, elevation **10** high ground, prominence, promontory
arctic ~: **5** pingo
bottom: **4** foot
broad-topped ~: **4** loma
builder: **3** ant
companion: **4** dale
crest: **4** brow
ender: **3** ock, top **4** side **5** billy, crest
glacial ~: **4** paha
go over the ~: **3** lam **4** bolt, flee **6** desert, escape, run off **7** abscond, bail out, run away **8** break out
hollow: **6** corrie
isolated ~: **4** mesa **5** butte **9** tableland **10** prominence
king of the ~: **5** on top
large ~: **8** mountain
of beans: **6** trifle
over the ~: **3** old **5** passé **7** ancient, fogyish **9** out-of-date **10** antiquated, out of style
rolling ~: **4** wold
rounded ~: **4** knob **5** morro
sand ~: **4** dune
Scottish ~: **4** brae
slope: **4** side
small ~: **4** dune **5** knoll, mound
starter: **3** ant **4** down, foot, mole
Hill: **3** Dan, Joe, Sam **5** Anita, Benny, Faith **6** Arthur, Bunker, Graham, Lauryn, Steven, Walter **7** Capitol, Rowland **9** Archibald, Blueberry
group: **6** Senate
Hill __ Blues: **6** Street
__ Hill: **3** Nob, Sam **4** Boot **6** Beacon, Breed's, Bunker **7** Capitol, Mission, Notting
__-Hill: **6** McGraw
__ hill and dale: **3** o'er
Hillary: **5** Waugh **6** Brooke, Edmund **7** Clinton
to Bill: **4** wife
Hillary Clinton, __ Rodham: **3** née
Hillary, Edmund: **3** Sir **8** explorer
emulate ~: **5** climb
locale: **5** Nepal **7** Everest
__ Hillbillies, The: **7** Beverly
hillbilly: **3** oaf **4** hick, rube **5** yokel **6** rustic **7** bumpkin, hayseed
parent: **3** maw, paw
hill-builder, small: **3** ant **5** emmet
Hillel: **5** rabbi
__ Hillel: **4** Beth
Hillenbrand: **4** Shea
Hiller: **5** Wendy **6** Arthur
Hillerman: **4** John
Hill, Faith
song: Breathe (1999)
It's Your Love (1997)
Mississippi Girl (2005)
This Kiss (1998)
spouse: Tim McGraw
Hillis, Margaret: **9** conductor
Hill, Lauryn
song: Doo Wop (1998)
__ Hill, NC: **6** Chapel

hillock: 4 rise 5 knoll, mound, ridge 6 glacis 7 hummock 9 acclivity, elevation 10 prominence
hill of __: 5 beans
hills: 8 outdoors
chain of ~: 5 ridge
head for the ~: 2 go 3 fly, run 4 bolt, flee 5 break, leave, scram 6 beat it, bug out, decamp, depart, desert, escape, get out 7 abscond, make off, retreat, run away, take off, vamoose 8 clear out 9 disappear, skedaddle 10 fly the coop, hightail it, hit the road
like the ~: 3 old
old as the ~: 6 creaky 7 ancient 9 venerable 10 antiquated
Hills: 5 Carla
__ Hills: 5 Black 6 Holmby 7 Beverly
__ Hills 90210: 7 Beverly
Hills Beyond, The
author: Thomas Wolfe
Hills Bros.: 6 coffee
alternative: 5 Sanka, Yuban 7 Folgers, Melitta, Nescafé, Savarin
hillside: 5 slope 6 glacis 9 acclivity
Hillside: 4 city, town
locale: 9 New Jersey
__ Hills of Rome: 5 Seven
Hill, Steven: 5 actor
TV: Law & Order, Mission: Impossible
Hill Street Blues (NBC drama)
cast: Michael Conrad (Sgt. Phil Esterhaus)
Charles Haid (Off. Andy Renko)
Veronica Hamel (Joyce Davenport)
Ken Olin (Det. Harry Garibaldi)
Daniel J. Travanti (Capt. Frank Furillo)
Michael Warren (Off. Bobby Hill)
character: 3 cop
producer: MTM
Hill Street Blues Theme, The (1981 song)
artist: Mike Post
hilltop: 5 crest 7 outdoor
sight: 5 vista 8 panorama 9 landscape
Hilltoppers
song: Marianne (1957)
Only You (1955)
Hill Wife, The
author: Robert Frost
hilly: 6 rugged, uneven 7 rolling
not ~: 4 flat 5 level 6 planar 7 planate
Hilo: 4 city, port, town
locale: 6 Hawaii
Hi-Lo Country, The (1998 film)
cast: Patricia Arquette, Billy Crudup, Sam Elliott, Woody Harrelson
director: Stephen Frears
hilsa: 4 fish
hilt: 4 haft 6 handle
to the ~: 5 fully 6 wholly 7 totally 8 entirely 9 all the way 10 completely
__ hilt: 5 to the
Hilton: 5 hotel, James, Nicky 6 Conrad
alternative: ***see*** hotel
__ Hilton: 5 Hanoi
Hilton Head Island: 4 city, town
locale: 4 S. Car.
Hilton-Jacobs: 8 Lawrence
Hilton, James: 6 writer 7 British
work: Goodbye, Mr. Chips
Lost Horizon
Random Harvest
hilum extension: 4 aril
him: 3 guy, man, sir 4 gent, male, poem 6 fellow 7 pronoun 9 gentleman
author: e.e. cummings
ender: 4 self
not ~: 3 her
Him (1980 song)
artist: Rupert Holmes
Himalayan: 3 cat 5 felid 6 feline
Himalayas: 5 range
aromatic ~ plant: 4 nard
bovine: 3 yak 5 takin
cedar: 6 deodar 7 deodara
city: 4 Lasa 5 Lassa, Lhasa
country: 3 Nep. 5 India, Nepal, Tibet 6 Bhutan, Xizang 7 Sitsang
goat: 4 tahr, thar
home: 4 Asia
legend: 4 yeti
mountain: 3 Api 4 Mana 5 Kabru, Kamet 6 Cho Oyu, Kangto, Lhotse, Makalu, Nunkun, Nuptse, Trisul 7 Everest, Manaslu, Pyramid, Trisuli 8 Anapurna, Baruntse, Chamlang, Changtzu, Dunagiri, Pauhunri, Tent Peak 9 Ama Dablam, Annapurna, Badrinath, Nanda Devi, Nepal Peak, Sia Kangri 10 Chomo Lhari, Dhaulagiri, Himalchuli, Kula Kangri
river from the ~ to the Ganges: 5 Jumna
sheep: 6 bharal 7 burrhel
Himalia: 4 moon 5 nymph
planet: 7 Jupiter
Himes, Chester: 6 writer
work: Cotton Comes to Harlem
If He Hollers Let Him Go
Hi, Mom! (1970 film)
cast: Robert De Niro
director: Brian De Palma
Him With His Foot in His Mouth
author: Saul Bellow
hind: 3 doe, roe 4 back, deer, rear 6 animal, rustic 7 peasant, red deer 8 rearmost 9 aftermost
ender: 3 gut 4 most 5 brain, sight 7 quarter 8 quarters
mate: 4 hart, stag
on one's ~ legs: 5 erect
part: 6 breech
rise on the ~ legs: 4 rear
__ Hind: 6 Golden
Hindemith, Paul: 6 German 8 composer
Hindenburg: 4 Paul
Hindenburg __: 4 line
hinder: 3 bar, dam, jam, tie 4 clog, curb, rein, slow, stay, stem, stop 5 block, box in, brake, check, cramp, crimp, cross, debar, delay, deter, embar, limit, stall, stimy, stunt, stymy, tie up 6 arrest, burden, cumber, dampen, detain, fetter, forbid, hamper, hobble, hogtie, hold up, impair, impede, oppose, rein in, resist, retard, slow up, stymie, thwart 7 confine, inhibit, occlude, prevent, set back, trammel 8 encumber, handcuff, handicap, hold back, obstruct, preclude, prohibit, restrain, sabotage, slow down, straiten 9 foreclose, forestall, frustrate, hamstring, interdict, interrupt, posterior, prejudice 10 bottleneck, counteract, disconcert, discourage
in law: 5 debar
Hindi: 5 Indic 8 language
cousin: 4 Urdu
king, in ~: 4 raja
see also Hindu
hindmost: 4 back, last, rear 6 latter 9 posterior
part: 4 back, rear
hindrance: 3 bar, rub 4 care, clog, curb, drag, load, snag, wall 5 block, brake, catch, check, delay, hitch, minus 6 burden, glitch, hurdle, kicker 7 baggage, barrier, setback, trammel 8 drawback, handicap, headache, obstacle, weakness 9 albatross, cumbrance, detention, deterrent, detriment, impedance, liability, millstone, restraint 10 constraint, difficulty, filibuster, impediment, inhibition, limitation
hindsight: 6 recall 10 retrospect
phrase: 6 if only
word: 6 coulda, woulda 7 shoulda
Hindu: 4 guru, Jain, Sikh 5 faker, fakir, faqir, Jaina, swami, swamy 6 faquir 7 Brahmin
aphorism: 5 sutra
archeological site: 6 Ellora
ascetic: 4 yogi 5 faker, fakir, faqir, sadhu, swami, swamy, yogin 6 faquir
caste: 4 jati 5 Sudra, Varna
class: 5 caste
Creator: 6 Brahma
Destroyer: 5 Shiva
devotion: 6 bhakti
discipline: 4 yoga
doctrine: 6 dharma
emotion: 4 rasa
eon: 4 yuga
festival: 6 Dewali, Divali, Diwali
forehead mark: 5 tilak
garb: 4 sari 5 saree
god: 4 Agni, Kama, Mara, Siva, Soma, Yama 5 Indra, Shiva, Surya 6 Brahma, Varuna, Vishnu 7 Ganesha, Hanuman, Krishna
goddess: 4 Devi, Kali, Usha 5 Durga, Ushas 7 Lakshmi, Parvati 9 Sarasvati
god of love: 4 Kama
hero of a ~ epic: 4 Rama
holy work: 4 Veda
honcho: 4 raja 5 nawab, rajah
language: 3 Skr, Skt. 4 Skrt. 5 Vedic 8 Sanskrit
leader: 5 Nehru 6 Gandhi
loincloth: 5 dhoti, dhuti 6 dhooti 7 dhootie
lute: 5 sarod, sitar
mantra: 2 om 3 aum
melody: 4 raga
monarchy: 5 Nepal
monk: 5 sadhu
month: 4 Magh
nectar of the gods: 6 amrita 7 amreeta
noble: 4 raja, rani 5 rajah, ranee
of a ~ philosophy: 5 yogic
of ~ scripture: 5 Vedic
pilgrimage place: 4 Gaya, Puri
Preserver: 6 Vishnu
religious society: 5 samaj
retreat: 6 ashram, asrama
sacred river: 6 Ganges
sage: 4 guru 5 rishi
sentiment: 4 rasa
shirt: 5 kurta
soul: 4 atma 5 atman
spring festival: 4 holi
teacher: 4 guru 5 swami, swamy
temple: 6 ashram
title: 3 sri 4 babu, shri 5 baboo
village chief: 5 patel
worship: 4 puja
Hinduism: 3 rel. 8 religion
Hindustani: 8 language
derivative: 4 Urdu
Hines: 4 Earl 6 Cheryl, Connie, Duncan, Jerome 7 Gregory
__ Hines: 6 Duncan
Hines, Earl Fatha: 7 pianist
genre: 4 jazz
Hines, Gregory: 5 actor 6 dancer
film: The Cotton Club (1984)
The Preacher's Wife (1996)
Renaissance Man (1994)
Tap (1989)
The Tic Code (2000)
milieu: 3 tap
Hines, Jerome: 4 bass 5 basso
hinge: 4 base, knee, rest 5 elbow, joint, pivot 6 depend, swivel 7 fulcrum 8 junction, juncture
anatomical ~: 4 knee 5 elbow 7 knuckle
door ~ site: 4 jamb 5 jambe
(on): 4 rely, rest, turn 6 depend
hinged fastener: 4 hasp
Hinge of Fate, The
author: Winston Churchill
Hingis, Martina: 7 netster 9 tennis pro
milieu: 5 court
Hingle: 3 Pat
Hinkle, Lon: 6 golfer
Hinky __ Parlay Voo: 5 Dinky
hinny: 6 animal, equine, mammal
mother: 3 ass
opposite: 4 mule
Hinshelwood, Cyril: 7 chemist 8 Nobelist
hint: 3 cue, tip 4 clew, clue, lead, lick, seem, sign, talk, tang, tint, warn, wind, wisp 5 imply, infer, let on, point, scent, shade, spark, taste, tinge, token, touch, trace, whiff 6 breath, feeler, flavor, little, prompt, remind, shadow, streak, tipoff, trifle 7 connote, glimmer, inkling, make out, pointer, portend, promise, soupçon, suggest, symptom, vestige, warning, whisper 8 allude to, allusion, evidence, indicate, innuendo, intimate, mnemonic, overtone, reminder, spoonful 9 adumbrate, indicator, insinuate, reference, scintilla, suspicion, undertone 10 foreshadow, glimmering, imputation, indication, intimation, sprinkling, suggestion

at: 4 mean 5 imply 6 advert, allude, broach 7 connote, mention, purport, suggest 8 allude to, intimate, lead up to
give a ~: 3 tip 5 let on, steer
helpful ~: 6 advice, tipoff 7 inkling, pointer, warning 10 suggestion
in French: 3 mot
__ hint: 5 drop a, take a
hinted at: 5 tacit 7 implied 8 unvoiced 9 intimated
hinter ender: 4 land 5 lands
hinterlands: 4 bush 5 wilds 6 inland, sticks 7 country 8 frontier 9 backwater, backwoods
Hinton, S.E.: 6 writer
names: 5 Susan 6 Eloise
work: Big David, Little David
The Outsiders
The Puppy Sister
Rumble Fish
Taming the Star Runner
Tex
That Was Then, This Is Now
hip: 3 hot, mod 4 chic, cool, in on, wise 5 aware, faddy, funky, joint, savvy, smart 6 astute, chichi, far-out, haunch, modish, posted, trendy, versed, wise to, with it 7 current, in style, in vogue, knowing, mindful, stylish, tuned in, voguish 8 apprised, informed 9 astucious, cognizant, in the know, plugged in 10 all the rage, conversant
about: 4 onto
be ~: 5 swing
bone: 5 ilium 6 pelvis
boot: 8 overshoe
combining form: 4 coxa- 5 ischi-, ischo-
cow's ~ joint: 5 thurl
ender: 4 bone, ster
follower: 6 hooray
from the ~: 4 open 5 bluff, blunt, frank, plain 6 candid, direct, honest 7 up-front 8 like it is, straight, truthful 9 outspoken 10 aboveboard, forthright, foursquare, free-spoken, unreserved
joint: 4 coxa
muscle: 5 psoas
muscles: 5 psoae, psoai
neighbor: 5 thigh
of the ~ bone: 5 iliac
part: 6 haunch
swiveler: 5 Elvis
talk: 4 jive
to: 7 aware of
hip __: 4 boot, roof 5 joint
hip-__: 3 hop 7 huggers
__ hip: 4 rose
hipbones: 4 ilia
Hip hip __!: 6 hooray
hip-hop: 3 rap 5 music
excellent, in ~: 3 def, rad 4 phat
Hip Hop Hooray (1993 song)
artist: Naughty by Nature
hiphuggers: 5 pants 6 slacks 8 trousers
Hipparchus: 5 Greek 10 astronomer
hippety-hop: 4 jump, leap, skip 5 bound 6 spring
hippie: 8 bohemian, longhair
adornment: 4 ankh
ender: 3 dom
gathering: 4 be-in 6 love-in
gesture: 5 V sign
greeting: 5 peace
home: 3 pad
money: 5 bread
phrase: 5 dig it 6 far out
Hippocratic __: 4 oath
hippodrome: 4 ring 5 arena 7 theater, theatre 8 coliseum 9 colosseum, gymnasium
hippo ender: 5 drome 6 campus
Hippolyte: 5 Taine 6 Amazon
parent: 4 Ares 8 Harmonia
Hippolytus: 4 pope 7 pontiff
author: Euripides
Hippomenes
wife: 8 Atalanta
hippophobe fear: 6 horses
hippopotamic: 3 big
hippopotamus: 5 beast 6 animal, mammal
female: 3 cow
hangout: 5 river
home: 3 zoo 6 Africa
male: 4 bull
young: 4 calf
Hippopotamus, The
poet: T.S. Eliot
hippy: 3 big 4 wide 5 broad
dance: 4 hula
__ hips: 4 rose
hipster: 3 cat 6 hepcat
address: 6 daddy-o
no ~: 4 nerd
hips, with hands on: 6 akimbo
Hip to Be Square (1986 song)
artist: Huey Lewis and the News
Hirakata: 4 city, town
locale: 5 Japan
Hiram: 6 Powers, Walker
Hiram, King home: 4 Tyre
hircine: 7 goatish 8 goatlike
hire: 3 pay 4 book, rent, take 5 lease, price, put on 6 employ, engage, enlist, line up, retain, sign on, sign up, take on 7 charter 9 put to work, situation 10 commission
opposite: 6 lay off
hired
car: 3 cab 4 limo, taxi 7 taxicab 9 limousine
gun: 4 goon, thug
hand: 6 jobber, worker 7 employe 8 employee 9 jobholder
just ~: 3 new, raw 5 green 9 untrained
hired __: 3 gun 4 hand
hireling: 4 hack, hand, tool 5 labor, venal 6 flunky 7 employe, flunkey, laborer, servant 8 employee 9 mercenary
hirer: 4 boss 7 manager 8 employer, superior 10 supervisor
Hires: 4 soda 5 drink 8 beverage, root beer 9 soft drink
rival: 4 Dad's
hiring __: 4 hall
hiring fairness agcy.: 3 OEO
Hirobumi: 3 Ito
Hiroshima: 4 city, port, town
author: John Hersey
locale: 5 Japan
river: 3 Ota
Hiroshima, __ Amour: 3 Mon
Hirsch: 4 Judd 5 Elroy, Emile 9 Crazylegs
Hirsch, Crazylegs
sport: 8 football
Hirschfeld: 2 Al
daughter: 4 Nina
Hirsch, Judd: 5 actor
TV: Taxi
hirsute: 5 furry, fuzzy, hairy, pilar 6 pilose, pilous, shaggy 7 bearded, unshorn 8 unshaven 9 whiskered
Hirt, Al: 9 trumpeter
song: Java (1964)
his: 4 pron. 7 pronoun
and hers: 5 their 6 theirs
Honor: 5 judge, mayor 6 jurist 10 magistrate
in French: 3 ses
like: 4 poss.
not ~: 4 hers 5 yours
or hers item: 5 towel
his __: 4 nibs
His __ Friday: 4 Girl
His __ Highness: 5 Royal
His __ on the Sparrow: 5 Eye Is
Hi, sailor!: 4 ahoy
his and __: 4 hers
His Eye __ the Sparrow: 4 Is On
'H' Is for Homicide
author: Sue Grafton
His Girl Friday (1940 film)
cast: Ralph Bellamy, Cary Grant, Rosalind Russell
His Latest Flame (1961 song)
artist: Elvis Presley
His Master's Voice company: 3 RCA
Hispanic: 6 Latina, Latino
neighborhood: 6 barrio
nickname: 4 Paco
see also Spanish
Hispaniola: 4 boat, isle, ship 6 island
part: 5 Haiti 6 Dom. Rep.
hispid: 5 spiny 7 bristly
hiss: 3 boo 4 fizz, jeer, razz, spit, whiz 5 decry 6 deride, heckle, sizzle, wheeze 7 catcall, condemn, whisper, whistle 8 ridicule, sibilant, sibilate 9 sibilance 10 sibilation
Hiss: 5 Alger
hisser: 5 snake 7 serpent
hissing: 4 fizz
hissy fit: 4 snit
hist.: 4 subj.
Histoire de Ma Vie
author: George Sand
Historiae
author: Tacitus
historian: 6 Nevins, Shirer, Sparks 7 Parkman 8 annalist, recorder 9 archivist 10 chronicler 11 Schlesinger
British ~: 6 Gibbon
English ~: 7 Toynbee, Walpole 8 Runciman, Strachey
French ~: 5 Renan, Taine 9 Froissart
German ~: 8 Schiller
military: 5 Foote 6 Catton 7 Ambrose, Weigley
natural ~: 3 Ray 4 Baer 6 Buffon, Cuvier, Darwin, Gesner 7 Agassiz, Lamarck, Wallace
Roman ~: 4 Livy 7 Sallust, Tacitus 9 Suetonius
Scottish ~: 7 Carlyle
tribal ~: 5 griot
Welsh ~: 7 Nennius
word: 3 ago 6 before
historic: 5 famed 6 famous 7 notable 8 renowned 9 important, memorable, momentous, red-letter, well-known 10 celebrated, monumental, remarkable
event: 5 first
org.: 3 DAR
starter: 3 pre
historical: 4 past 6 actual 7 factual 8 archival 9 authentic, classical, important 10 chronicled, documented, unimagined, verifiable
of an ~ time: 4 eral
period: 3 age, era 6 decade
piece: 3 bio
records: 6 annals 7 archive 9 chronicle
sight: 5 ruins 6 marker 8 landmark, monument
souvenir: 5 relic 7 antique 8 artifact
historical __: 5 novel
history: 3 ago 4 life, past 5 genre, story 6 annals, record, report 7 account 9 chronicle, narrative, olden days, posterity, recountal 10 background, literature, upbringing
ancient ~: 4 over, past, yore 8 years ago 9 olden days 10 yesteryear
bit of ~: 5 relic
book verb: 3 did, was 4 were
case ~: 4 file 6 record, report 7 dossier 8 document, specimen 10 background
class fixture: 5 globe
family ~: 4 line 5 birth, blood, roots, stock 6 origin, strain 7 descent, lineage 8 ancestry, heredity, heritage, pedigree 9 genealogy 10 derivation, extraction
folk ~: 4 lore 5 tales 7 legends 9 tradition
homework: 5 essay
Muse of ~: 4 Clio
oral ~: 4 myth 5 sagas, tales 7 beliefs, customs, legends, sayings 8 folklore 10 traditions
oral ~ keeper: 5 griot
personal ~: 3 bio 6 memoir, résumé 7 memoirs, profile
segment: 3 era
teacher's question: 4 when
work ~: 4 vita 6 résumé
__ history: 4 case, life, oral 7 ancient, natural
History of Mr. Polly, The
author: H.G. Wells
History of New York, A
author: Washington Irving
History of Rome
author: Livy
History of the Standard Oil Company
author: Ida Tarbell
__ History of Time, A: 5 Brief
History of Western Philosophy, A
author: Bertrand Russell
histrionic: 5 stagy 6 stagey 7 emotive 8 dramatic, thespian 9 bombastic, emotional 10 theatrical
episode: 5 scene 7 tantrum 8 outburst
histrionics: 6 acting 9 dramatics 10 stagecraft

hit: **2** KO **3** bop, jab, jag, pop, ram, rap, win **4** bang, bash, beat, belt, blow, bump, butt, cane, clip, club, cuff, drub, flog, hurt, kayo, lace, lash, lick, mall, maul, pelt, slam, slap, sock, swat, verb **5** abuse, brain, clout, crack, flail, fly at, homer, knock, lunge, occur, pound, punch, reach, serve, shoot, smack, smash, solve, swipe, thump, touch, whack, wound **6** attain, batter, berate, buffet, cudgel, defame, double, hammer, impact, larrup, malign, murder, single, strike, stroke, thrash, thwack, triple, wallop, winner **7** censure, clobber, condemn, lambast, offense, put down, rough up, sellout, success, triumph, victory **8** arrive at, arrive in, bang into, bludgeon, come upon, denounce, lambaste, reaction, uppercut **9** castigate, collision, crash into, criticize, denigrate, knock into, sensation, sideswipe, smash into **10** bestseller, calumniate, crunch into, gold record
  abbr.: **3** SRO
  a fly, perhaps: **3** bat
  a high ball: **3** fly **4** loft
  alternative: **4** miss, walk
  and rebound: **5** carom **6** carrom
  a sour note: **5** clash **6** jangle
  back: **5** react, reply **6** answer, resist **7** counter, revenge **9** retaliate
  below the belt: **4** knee
  between infield and outfield: **5** bloop
  big ~: **3** win **5** homer, smash **6** winner **7** home run, success, triumph, victory
  bottom: **4** fall, sink **6** go down, plunge **7** founder, go under **8** flounder, submerge
  box-office ~: **4** boff **5** boffo, smash **7** boffola, success
  broadside: **3** ram
  extra-base ~: **5** homer **6** double, triple **7** home run **9** grand slam
  fail to ~: **4** miss
  hard: **4** pelt, slam, slug, wham **5** paste, smack, smite, whack, whomp
  in baseball: **5** homer **6** double, single, triple **7** home run
  it big: **6** arrive, do well **7** make out, prosper, succeed, triumph **8** fare well, flourish, get ahead, go places, make good
  it off: **4** jibe **5** agree, click **9** harmonize
  lightly: **3** tap **5** touch
  like a ton of bricks: **3** jar **4** jolt, kayo, stun **5** shock **6** bedaze **7** astound, flummox, horrify, nonplus, outrage, stagger, stupefy, terrify **8** astonish, bewilder, blow away, bowl over, knock out, unsettle **9** dumbfound, overpower, overwhelm, take aback **10** discompose
  list: **5** chart
  location, often: **5** side A
  make a ~: **5** score **7** succeed, triumph
  make ~ the ceiling: **5** anger **6** madden, offend **7** incense, outrage **9** infuriate
  old-style: **4** smit
  on: **6** detect **7** solicit, think of **8** smell out **9** run across
  on the noggin: **4** conk
  opposite: **4** flop **6** turkey
  or miss: **6** random
  out: **5** blast **6** assail, attack **7** censure **9** light into
  outfield ~: **3** fly
  pinch ~: **7** replace
  precisely: **4** nail
  ready to ~: **5** at bat
  send: **5** e-mail
  soft ~: **4** bunt
  softly: **4** bump **5** nudge
  starter: **4** mega
  the big time: **6** arrive, thrive **7** prosper, succeed
  the books: **4** cram, read **5** study **6** master
  the brakes: **4** slow **6** ease up, hold up, rein in **7** ease off **8** hold back, moderate, slow down **10** decelerate
  the bricks: **2** go **4** exit, move **5** leave **6** beat it, depart, go away, move on **7** make off, pull out, push off, take off **8** shove off, slip away **10** shuffle off
  the ceiling: **4** rage, rant, snap **5** freak **6** seethe
  the deck: **4** wake **5** arise, awake, get up, waken
  the dirt: **4** fall **5** slide **6** topple
  the floor hard: **5** stamp
  the ground: **3** lit **4** alit, fall, fell, land **5** light **6** alight, landed
  the hay: **5** crash, sleep **6** retire, turn in **7** sack out
  the high spots: **4** skim **8** simplify
  the horn: **4** blow, honk
  the jackpot: **3** win **5** score **7** prosper, succeed
  the + key: **3** add
  the low spots: **4** slum
  the mall: **4** shop **6** browse
  the road: **2** go **4** blow, hike, rove, scat, tour, walk, went **5** leave, scram, start **6** beat it, decamp, depart, set off, set out **7** push off, take off **8** hightail, set forth
  the roof: **4** flip, rage, rant, rave, snap **5** storm **6** blow up, bridle, get mad, see red **7** explode **9** blow a fuse, throw a fit
  the sack: **5** sleep **6** retire, turn in
  the skids: **4** fail, sink **7** decline
  the sky: **3** fly **4** soar **6** aviate
  the slopes: **3** ski **4** skee
  the spot: **6** please **7** satisfy, suffice
  the switch: **4** kill, stop **5** douse, light **6** kindle, turn on **7** turn off **8** activate **9** throw open
  the track: **3** jog, run **4** trot
  the trail: **3** run **4** tour **5** start **6** depart, set off, set out **7** take off **8** campaign, set forth
  town: **4** come **5** get in, pop up, reach **6** arrive **8** get there
  up: **3** beg **7** request, solicit **8** question **9** impetrate
  upon: **4** find **5** catch, solve **6** locate, turn up **7** uncover **8** discover **9** encounter, run across
  upside the head: **3** wap **4** whap, whop

hit ___: **4** home, upon **5** a snag, it big, it off **6** parade
hit ___ note: **5** a sour
hit ___ spot: **5** a sore
hit-___: **6** or-miss
___ hit: **3** leg **4** base **5** pinch, smash **7** infield, one-base, scratch, two-base
___-hit: **6** switch
hit a ___: **4** snag
hit a ___ nerve: **3** raw
Hitachi: **2** TV **5** TV set **10** television
  alternative: *see* electronics company
hit-and-___: **3** run **4** miss
hitch: **3** rub, tie, tug **4** bind, hook, join, kink, knot, limp, link, moor, ride, snag, term, tour, yank, yoke **5** block, catch, delay, pause, snafu, spell, strap, thumb, tie up **6** attach, couple, fasten, glitch, hang-up, holdup, hook on, hook up, inspan, kicker, mishap, secure, splice, tether **7** conjoin, connect, grapnel, harness, problem, setback, trouble **8** drawback, make fast, obstacle, sentence **9** hindrance **10** difficulty, impediment, thumb a ride, tour of duty
  do another ~: **4** reup
  ender: **4** hike
  on: **4** join, link, yoke **5** annex, unite **6** attach, cohere, couple, hook up **7** combine, conjoin, connect
  without a ~: **6** easily **7** handily **10** swimmingly
hitch ___: **5** a ride
___ hitch: **4** half **5** clove
Hitch (2005 film)
  cast: Kevin James, Eva Mendes, Will Smith
Hitchcock, Alfred: **3** Sir **8** director
  designer: **4** Head
  film: The 39 Steps (1935)
    The Birds (1963)
    Blackmail (1929)
    Dial M for Murder (1954)
    Family Plot (1976)
    Foreign Correspondent (1940)
    Frenzy (1972)
    The Lady Vanishes (1938)
    Lifeboat (1944)
    The Man Who Knew Too Much (1934, 1956)
    Marnie (1964)
    Mr. and Mrs. Smith (1941)
    North by Northwest (1959)
    Notorious (1946)
    Psycho (1960)
    Rear Window (1954)
    Rebecca (1940)
    The Ring (1927)
    Rope (1948)
    Sabotage (1936)
    Saboteur (1942)
    Shadow of a Doubt (1943)
    Spellbound (1945)
    Strangers on a Train (1951)
    Suspicion (1941)
    To Catch a Thief (1955)
    Topaz (1969)
    Torn Curtain (1966)
    The Trouble With Harry (1955)
    Vertigo (1958)
    The Wrong Man (1957)
    Young and Innocent (1937)
  performance: **5** cameo
  wife: **4** Alma
hitched
  get ~: **3** wed **5** marry **10** tie the knot
  get ~ in a hurry: **5** elope
hitchhike: **4** ride **5** dance, thumb
hitchhiker: **5** rider, tramp **7** drifter **8** traveler, vagabond **9** passenger
  need: **4** lift **5** thumb
  site: **4** berm **5** berme
  words to a ~: **5** get in, hop in
hitching ___: **4** post
hitching area: **5** altar **6** chapel
Hitchings, George: **8** Nobelist
Hitchy-___: **3** Koo
Hitch your wagon to ___: **5** a star
Hite: **5** Shere
hi-tech: **6** modern **10** electronic
hither: **4** here **8** over here
  come ~: **6** allure **10** attraction, enticement
  ender: **4** most, ward **5** wards
  move ~ and thither: **3** gad **4** roam **6** ramble, wander **7** meander, traipse **8** ambulate, nomadize **9** bum around, gallivant, globetrot
  partner: **3** yon
___-hither: **4** come
hither and ___: **3** yon **7** thither
hitherto: **3** yet **5** so far **6** before, ere now, of late **7** thus far **8** until now **9** at one time, to this day **10** heretofore, previously
  unknown: **5** fresh, novel **7** offbeat **8** original **9** different **10** innovative, newfangled
hit it ___: **3** big, off
hitless stretch: **5** slump
Hit Me With Your Best Shot (1980 song)
  artist: Pat Benatar
hit one's ___: **6** stride
hit-or-miss: **5** fluky **6** casual, chance, flukey, random **7** aimless **8** slipshod, sporadic **9** haphazard, irregular, makeshift **10** improvised, nonuniform, sporadical, unthorough, willy-nilly
___ Hit Parade: **4** Your
hitter: **7** batsman
  bull's-eye ~: **4** dart **5** arrow **6** archer
  chance: **5** at bat
  heavy ~: **5** mogul **7** big shot
  pinch ~: **3** sub **9** surrogate **10** substitute
  problem: **5** slump
  stat: **2** HR **3** RBI
___ hitter: **4** pull **5** heavy, pinch **6** switch
hit the ___: **3** hay **4** deck, road, roof, sack, silk, spot, wall **5** books **7** ceiling, jackpot
hit the ___ on the head: **4** nail
hit the ___ running: **6** ground
hit the ___ spots: **4** high
Hit the ___ Jack: **4** Road
hit the high ___: **5** spots **6** points
Hit the road!: **3** git **4** scat, shoo **5** scram **6** beat it
Hit the Road Jack (1961 song)
  artist: Ray Charles
hitting: **5** at bat

__-hitting: 4 hard
__-Hittite: 4 Indo
hive: 4 nest 6 apiary 8 vespiary
group: 5 swarm
resident: 3 bee 5 drone, queen
sound: 3 hum 4 buzz 5 drone
hives: 4 rash 5 uredo
Hive, The
author: Camilo José Cela
hiwi hiwi: 4 fish
Hi-yo Silver, __!: 4 away
H.J. __: 3 Res. 5 Heinz
Hjalmar: 7 Bergman 9 Söderberg
H.L.: 7 Mencken
HLA __: 4 gene 7 antigen
__ H. Macy: 7 William
HMO: 8 WellCare 10 BlueChoice
alternative: 3 PPO
concern: 8 wellness
employee: 2 Dr., MD, RN 3 doc 5 nurse 6 doctor
part: 3 org. 5 maint. 6 health
requirement: 5 copay
Hmong: 4 Miao 8 language
HMS part: 3 her, his 4 ship 8 majesty's
H.M.S. Pinafore
character: 4 Dick, Hebe 5 Ralph 7 Deadeye
composer: W.S. Gilbert, Arthur Sullivan
fleet: 5 navee
ho-__: 3 dad, hum
__ ho!: 4 Land 5 Heave
__-ho: 4 gung 5 heave, heigh
Ho: 3 Don 4 elem. 7 element, holmium
67 for ~: 4 at. no.
home, once: 5 Hanoi
Ho __: 7 Chi Minh
HO __: 5 gauge
Hoad, Lew: 7 netster 9 tennis pro
milieu: 5 court
Hoag: 4 Tami
hoagie: 3 sub 4 hero 5 po' boy 7 grinder 8 sandwich 9 submarine
ingredient: 3 ham 4 mayo, tuna 5 onion 6 cheese, pepper, pickle, tomato, turkey 7 chicken, lettuce 9 roast beef
where to get a ~: 4 deli
hoagy
see hoagie
Hoagy: 10 Carmichael
__-ho and a bottle...: 4 Yo-ho
hoar: 4 rime 5 frost
like ~: 3 icy
hoard: 4 fund, heap, hold, keep, mass, mine, pile, save, stow 5 amass, buy up, cache, lay by, lay up, put by, stack, stash, stock, store, trove 6 garner, gather, obtain, pile up, retain, save up, scrimp, supply, wealth 7 collect, harvest, lay away, put away, reserve 8 conserve, gather up, hang onto, hold onto, maintain, put aside, salt away, sock away, stow away, treasure, treasury 9 abundance, amassment, inventory, stash away, stockpile 10 accumulate, collection, cumulation
private ~: 5 cache, stash 7 reserve 9 stockpile
hoarder: 5 miser, saver 7 pack rat 8 gatherer
cry: 4 mine, more
hoards: 4 lots, tons 5 loads, scads 6 droves, oodles, scores 7 throngs 8 billions, millions
hoarfrost: 4 rime
hoariness: 9 antiquity
hoarse: 5 gruff, harsh, husky, raspy, rough, roupy 6 croaky, croupy, froggy 7 breathy, cracked, grating, raucous, throaty 8 croaking, gravelly, guttural 10 laryngitic
sound ~: 4 frog, rasp 5 croak
hoary: 3 old 4 dull, gray, grey 5 musty, passé, white 6 age-old 7 ancient, antique, revered 8 grizzled, out of use, timeworn, well-used 9 out-of-date, venerable, venerated, weathered 10 antiquated, dullsville, gray-haired
hoax: 2 do 3 con, lie 4 dupe, fake, flam, fool, gull, quiz, rook, ruse, scam, sham, snow 5 cheat, dodge, feint, fraud, hocus, prank, put on, set up, spoof, sting, trick 6 canard, deceit, delude, dupery, fleece, humbug, hustle, outwit, rope in, scheme, take in 7 chicane, con game, deceive, defraud, fake out, fast one, knavery, mislead, snow job, swindle 8 artifice, flimflam, hoodwink, outsmart, trickery 9 bamboozle, deception, disinform, four-flush, imposture, mare's nest, victimize 10 imposition, run a game on, subterfuge
like a ~: 4 fake 5 bogus, false, phony 6 unreal, untrue 8 delusive 9 concocted, contrived 10 fabricated, untruthful
pull a ~: 5 bluff, cheat, feign, put on 7 deceive, mislead, pretend
hoaxer: 5 fraud 6 Barnum
Hoax, The (2007 film)
cast: Richard Gere, Marcia Gay Harden, Alfred Molina
hob: 3 elf, peg
ender: 3 nob 4 nail 6 goblin
game: 6 quoits
Hoban, James: 9 architect
Hobart: 4 city, town 6 Garret
locale: 7 Indiana 8 Tasmania 9 Australia
river: 7 Derwent
Hobbes, Thomas: 7 British 11 philosopher
hobbit: 5 Frodo
community: 5 Shire
foe: 3 orc
like ~ feet: 5 furry
Hobbit, The
author: J.R.R. Tolkien
character: 5 Bilbo 7 Baggins, Gandalf
hobble: 3 lag 4 bind, curb, limp 5 cramp, leash, skirt 6 dodder, falter, fetter, hamper, hang up, hinder, hogtie, impede, linger, tether 7 trammel 8 restrict 9 hamstring
hobble __: 5 skirt
hobbledehoy: 2 ox 3 lug, oaf 4 boob, boor, clod, dolt, fool, jerk, lout, rube, yo-yo 5 chump, churl, dunce, ninny 6 duffer, galoot, lummox, nitwit 7 botcher, bumbler, bungler, dullard, fathead, fumbler, jackass, saphead, tomfool 8 bonehead, lunkhead, meathead 9 birdbrain, blockhead, blunderer, schlemiel, simpleton 10 dunderhead, stumblebum
Hobbs: 4 city, town
locale: 9 New Mexico
hobby: 3 bag 7 pastime, pursuit 8 activity, interest, sideline 9 avocation, diversion, specialty 10 recreation
ender: 3 ist 5 horse
shop buy: 3 kit 5 model
Hobby: 9 Oveta Culp
hobbyist: 3 fan 4 buff 7 devotee
hobgoblin: 3 elf, imp 4 goby 5 bogey, bogie, bogle, ghoul 6 boggle, sprite 7 brownie, bugbear, gremlin
Hobie Cat
need: 4 wind
hobnob: 3 mix 5 party 6 mingle 7 consort, schmoos 8 schmoose, schmooze 9 associate, pal around, rub elbows, socialize 10 chum around, fraternize
hobo: 3 bum, vag 5 nomad, tramp 6 beggar 7 drifter, migrant, outcast, vagrant 8 derelict, traveler, vagabond, wanderer 9 sundowner, transient 10 ragamuffin
blanket: 6 bindle
dinner: 4 stew
home: 5 shack 6 jungle
transport: 4 rail 6 boxcar
Hoboken: 4 city, port, town
locale: 9 New Jersey
Hobson: 5 Laura 7 Valerie
Hobson-__: 6 Jobson
Hobson, Laura Z.: 6 writer
work: Gentleman's Agreement
Hobson's choice: 4 bind 5 horse
Hoc __ in votis: 4 erat
__ hoc, ergo propter hoc: 4 post
Hochheimer: 4 wine
origin: 7 Germany
Ho Chi Minh City: 4 city, port, town
locale: 7 Vietnam
river: 6 Saigon
Ho Chi Minh Trail
locale: 3 Nam 4 Laos
Hoch, Scott: 6 golfer
hock: 4 debt, pawn, wine 5 ankle 6 pledge 9 Rhine wine
be in ~: 3 owe
ender: 4 shop
get out of ~: 6 cash in, redeem
horse's ~: 5 ankle
in ~: 6 pawned 7 obliged 8 beholden, indebted 9 obligated
origin: 7 Germany
starter: 3 ham 5 holly
hockey: 4 game 5 sport
area: 4 cage, goal 6 crease
birthplace: 6 Canada
Boston team: 6 Bruins
Buffalo team: 6 Sabres
Calgary team: 6 Flames
Edmonton team: 6 Oilers
extra period: 2 OT 8 overtime
gear: 3 net 4 puck 5 stick
Hall-of-Famer: 3 Orr, Roy 4 Duff, Fuhr, Howe, Hull, Park 5 Bossy, Neely 6 Coffey, Dionne, Mikita, Murphy, Parent, Plante, Potvin 7 Bourque, Federko, Francis, Gilbert, Gillies, Gretzky, Lafleur, Langway, Lemieux, Messier, Richard, Sawchuk, Stevens, Worsley 8 Anderson, Bathgate, Bobby Orr, Brad Park, Cam Neely, Dick Duff, Esposito, Larionov, MacInnis, Trottier 9 Bobby Hull, Geoffrion, Grant Fuhr, Kharlamov, Mike Bossy 10 Al MacInnis, Gordie Howe, Guy Lafleur, LaFontaine, Patrick Roy, Paul Coffey, Rod Gilbert, Stan Mikita
highlight: 5 brawl, fight
Houston team: 5 Aeros
infraction: 5 icing
locale: 4 rink 5 arena
Los Angeles team: 5 Kings
Philadelphia team: 6 Flyers
player: 4 wing 6 center, goalie, iceman
ploy: 4 deke
prize: 3 cup 10 Stanley Cup
protection: 3 pad 4 mask
San Jose team: 6 Sharks
shutout line score: 3 OOO
sportscaster cry: 5 score
stat: 4 goal 6 assist
surface: 3 ice
team: 3 six 4 Wild 5 Blues, Kings, Stars 6 Bruins, Devils, Flames, Flyers, Oilers, Sabres, Sharks 7 Canucks, Coyotes, Rangers 8 Capitals, Panthers, Penguins, Red Wings, Senators 9 Avalanche, Canadiens, Islanders, Lightning, Predators, Thrashers 10 Blackhawks, Hurricanes, Maple Leafs
Winnipeg team: 4 Jets
__ hockey: 3 ice 5 field 6 roller, street
__-Hockey: 3 Nok
Hockney: 5 David
hocus: 4 dupe, fool, gull, hoax 5 trick 6 take in 7 deceive 8 hoodwink
hocus-pocus: 3 hex 5 fraud, magic, spell, trick 6 dupery 7 sorcery 8 trickery 9 chicanery, conjuring, deception, gibberish, imposture, rigmarole 10 dishonesty, imposition, invocation, mumbo jumbo, open sesame
hod: 7 carrier 9 container
__ hod: 4 coal
Hodding: 6 Carter
__ Hodesh: 4 Rosh
Hodge: 2 Al
hodgepodge: 3 mix 4 hash, mess, misc., olio 6 jumble, litter, medley 7 clutter, farrago, goulash, mélange, mixture 8 mishmash, mixed bag, pastiche, shambles 9 confusion, patchwork, potpourri 10 assortment, collection, cumulation, miscellany, salmagundi
Hodges: 3 Gil 4 Mike 5 Eddie
Hodges, Gil
sport: 8 baseball
Hodgkin, Alan: 8 Nobelist 12 biophysicist
Hodgkin, Dorothy: 7 chemist 8 Nobelist
__ Hodgson Burnett: 7 Frances
Hodiak: 4 John
Ho, Don: 6 singer 8 Hawaiian
hoe: 3 dig 4 till, tool 6 garden 9 cultivate 10 cultivator
cousin: 4 rake 6 harrow
ender: 4 cake, down

long row to ~: **4** task **5** grind **6** burden
starter: **4** back
target: **4** clod, weed
__ hoe: **4** back
hoedown: **5** dance
date: **3** gal
instrument: **6** fiddle
prop: **3** hay **4** bale
hoeing, in need of: **5** weedy
Hoek: **3** Ren
Hoff: **3** Syd
Hoffa: **5** Jimmy **8** Portland
Hoffa (1992 film)
cast: Armand Assante, Danny DeVito, Jack Nicholson, J.T. Walsh
director: Danny DeVito
Hoffa, Portland
spouse: Fred Allen
Hoffer, Eric: **6** writer
Hoffman: **3** E.T.A. **5** Abbie **6** Dustin **7** Malvina, William
Hoffman, Dustin: **5** actor
film: Agatha (1979)
All the President's Men (1976)
American Buffalo (1996)
Billy Bathgate (1991)
Family Business (1989)
The Graduate (1967)
Hero (1992)
Hook (1991)
Ishtar (1987)
Kramer vs. Kramer (1979, AA)
Last Chance Harvey (2008)
Lenny (1974)
Little Big Man (1970)
Marathon Man (1976)
Midnight Cowboy (1969)
Outbreak (1995)
Papillon (1973)
Rain Man (1988, AA)
Runaway Jury (2003)
Sleepers (1996)
Sphere (1998)
Straight Time (1978)
Straw Dogs (1971)
Tootsie (1982)
Wag the Dog (1997)
Hoffman, E.T.A.: **6** German, writer
Hoffmann: **4** Gaby **5** Cecil, Felix, Roald
Hoffmann, Roald: **7** chemist **8** Nobelist
Hoffman, Philip Seymour: **5** actor
film: Capote (2005, AA)
Charlie Wilson's War (2007)
Doubt (2008)
Patch Adams (1998)
Synecdoche, New York (2008)
Hoffman, William play: **4** As Is
Hofmann, Josef: **6** Polish **7** pianist
Hofstadter: **6** Robert **7** Richard
Hofstra: **10** university
athletes: **5** Pride
locale: **7** New York **9** Hempstead **10** Long Island
hog: **3** pig, sow **4** bike, boar **5** cycle, shoat, shote, shott, swine **6** animal, barrow, Harley, oinker, porker, tusker **7** glutton, grunter, peccary, possess **8** dominate **9** razorback **10** monopolize, motorcycle
call: **5** sooey
ender: **3** tie **4** back, fish, wash, weed
feed: **4** mast, slop **5** swill
go whole ~: **4** jump, leap, push, rush, sink **6** hurtle, plunge
home: **3** pen, sty **4** farm
in ~ heaven: **5** happy **6** cheery, elated, joyful, joyous **7** gleeful **8** blissful, ecstatic, euphoric, exultant, jubilant **9** ebullient, overjoyed
live high on the ~: **4** bask **5** revel **6** thrive **7** indulge, rollick **8** flourish **9** luxuriate
love: **3** mud
rider: **5** biker
starter: **4** sand, wart **5** hedge **6** ground
whole ~: **5** fully **7** flat out, in depth, totally **8** entirely, from A to Z, in detail **9** inside out, up-and-down **10** completely, thoroughly, to the limit
young ~: **5** shoat, shote, shott
see also pig
hog __: **6** heaven
hog-__: **3** tie **4** wild
__ hog: **4** road
__-hog: **5** whole
Hogan: **3** Ben **4** Hulk, Paul
Hogan, Ben: **6** golfer
rival: **5** Snead
Hogan Family, The (NBC/CBS sitcom)
cast: Jason Bateman (David Hogan)
Sandy Duncan (Sandy Hogan)
Valerie Harper (Valerie Hogan)
Jeremy Licht (Mark Hogan)
Hogan, Hulk: **8** wrestler
hogan material: **3** sod
Hogan, Paul
spouse: Linda Kozlowski
Hogan's __: **4** Goat **6** Heroes
Hogan's Heroes (CBS sitcom)
cast: John Banner (Sgt. Schultz)
Robert Clary (Cpl. LeBeau)
Bob Crane (Col. Hogan)
Richard Dawson (Cpl. Newkirk)
Ivan Dixon (Sgt. Kinchloe)
Larry Hovis (Sgt. Carter)
Werner Klemperer (Col. Klink)
group: **4** POWs
setting: stalag, Germany
Hogarth, William: **6** artist **7** British, painter
subject: **4** rake
hogback: **5** ridge, spine
Hogg: **3** Ima **5** James
hoggish: **6** greedy **7** gorging, lustful, piggish, porcine, selfish, swinish **9** rapacious **10** avaricious, gluttonous
hoggishness: **5** greed **7** avarice, avidity **8** cupidity, gluttony, rapacity, venality **9** esurience
hognose: **5** adder, snake
hognut: **4** tree **7** hickory
hogs: **5** stock **9** livestock
ender: **4** head
slopping the ~: **5** chore
hogshead: **3** keg, tub **4** cask, unit **6** barrel
hogtie: **4** bind **6** fetter, hamper, hinder, hobble, impede, pinion, thwart **7** confine, contain, inhibit, shackle, truss up **8** encumber, handicap, restrain **9** constrain, frustrate, hamstring **10** immobilize
hogwash
see baloney
hog-wild: **5** manic, rabid **7** berserk **8** frenzied, maniacal **10** hysterical
go ~ over: **5** eat up, enjoy, lap up
ho ho: **5** laugh
Ho Ho: **4** cake, nosh **5** snack
ho-hum: **4** blah, drab, dull, flat, mild, so-so **5** bland **6** boring, stuffy **7** insipid, mundane, nowhere, prosaic, routine, tedious **8** tiresome **9** prosaical, wearisome **10** dullsville, lackluster, monotonous, pedestrian, unexciting
feeling: **5** ennui **6** apathy, tedium, torpor **7** boredom, languor **8** lethargy **9** lassitude
same old ~: **3** rut **7** rat race, routine **9** treadmill
hoick shouter: **6** hunter
hoi polloi: **3** mob **4** ruck **6** masses, people, public, rabble **8** populace, riffraff
one of the: **5** prole **6** worker
hoist: **4** heft, lift, rear **5** boost, crane, heave, raise, sling **6** haul up, lift up, pick up, tackle, uphold, uplift, uprear **7** derrick, elevate, upheave, upraise
a few: **4** tope **5** drink **6** imbibe
chain: **3** tye
device: **5** crane, sling, winch
glasses: **5** drink, honor, toast **6** pledge
marina ~: **5** davit
hoist by one's own __: **6** petard
hoisted, nautically: **5** atrip
hoity-toity: **5** proud **6** la-de-da, la-di-da, uppity **7** haughty, pompous **8** arrogant, highbrow, lah-di-dah, snobbish **9** conceited, hubristic **10** disdainful
act ~: **5** snoot
group: **5** elite **6** gentry, jet set **7** society **8** old money **10** blue bloods, glitterati, main liners, upper crust
one: **4** snob **5** snoot **7** elitist **8** highbrow **9** swellhead
hoke: **4** mock **5** alter **6** jazz up **7** deceive, falsify, phony up **10** manipulate
hokey: **4** dull, mock **5** banal, corny, passé, phony, stale, trite, vapid **6** common, jejune, old hat, phoney **7** clichéd, fatuous, humdrum, mawkish, prosaic **8** bromidic, cornball, outdated, outmoded, shopworn **9** contrived, hackneyed, prosaical **10** uninspired, unoriginal
stuff: **4** corn
Hokkaido: **4** isle **6** island
city: **5** Otaru **6** Ebetsu, Kitami **7** Kushiro, Obihiro, Sapporo
islands off ~: **5** Kuril
locale: **4** Asia **5** Japan
native: **4** Ainu
volcano: **3** Usu **4** Akan **6** Oshima
hokum
see baloney
Holbein, Hans: **6** artist, German **7** painter
Holberg, Ludvig: **6** Danish, writer
Holberg Suite
composer: Edvard Grieg
Holbrook: **3** Hal **4** city, town
locale: **7** New York **10** Long Island
Holbrook, Hal: **5** actor
film: All the President's Men (1976)
Capricorn One (1978)
The Fog (1980)
Magnum Force (1973)
Wall Street (1987)
spouse: Dixie Carter
TV: Evening Shade
Holcroft Covenant, The
author: Robert Ludlum
hold: **3** den, hug, own, tie **4** aver, avow, bear, deem, feel, grip, have, jail, keep, last, prop, save, seat, stay, take, view, vise **5** amass, apply, brace, cache, carry, claim, clasp, grasp, hoard, house, judge, opine, press, put by, seize, sense, shore, stand, store, think, tie up, wield **6** absorb, accept, adhere, affirm, allege, arrest, assert, assume, clench, clinch, clutch, coop up, cork up, cradle, cuddle, defend, detain, endure, enfold, fetter, garner, handle, harbor, immure, infold, lock up, nelson, occupy, reckon, regard, remain, retain, save up, shelve, tenure **7** believe, bolster, carry on, conduct, confine, contain, control, convene, embrace, enclose, fermata, footing, harbour, impound, inclose, include, observe, operate, persist, possess, presume, put away, receive, repress, reserve, shore up, squeeze, stay put, support, suspect, sustain **8** bottle up, buttress, continue, dominion, hang onto, imprison, location, maintain, purchase, put aside, restrain, set aside, stand for, transfix, underpin **9** influence, persevere **10** accumulate, monopolize, possession
a brief for: **6** defend, second **7** approve, endorse, indorse, support **8** champion, sanction, side with
a meeting: **3** sit **4** call, meet **5** rally **6** confer, gather, muster, summon **7** convene, convoke **8** assemble **10** congregate
a powwow: **6** confer, huddle, parley **7** commune, palaver **8** converse **10** deliberate
a reading: **5** drill **6** review **8** practice, rehearse **9** go through **10** run through
as an opinion: **4** deem, feel, view **5** think **6** assume, reckon, regard **7** believe, presume, suppose, surmise **8** consider
at bay: **5** parry, repel **7** fend off, repulse, ward off **8** stave off
at fault: **5** blame **6** accuse, finger **7** censure, condemn, reprove **8** denounce, reproach **9** criticize, implicate, reprimand **10** take to task
back: **3** dam **4** curb, halt, hide, save, slow, stay, stem, stop **5** check, demur, deter, leash, stint, tarry **6** arrest, bridle,

HA

detain, hinder, impede, refuse, rein in, slow up **7** confine, contain, control, inhibit, prevent, prolong, repulse, reserve, trammel **8** handicap, hesitate, restrain, slow down, stave off, suppress, withhold **9** constrain, keep at bay **10** discourage, keep a lid on, keep in line
back a year: **4** fail **5** flunk
catch ~ of: **3** nab **4** grab, hook, land, nail, snag **5** seize **6** arrest, collar, corral, snap up, snatch **7** capture, ensnare **9** apprehend, latch onto
contents: **5** cargo, goods **7** freight, tonnage **8** shipload
dear: **4** like, love **5** adore, go for, honor, prize, value **6** esteem, revere **7** care for, cherish, idolize, worship **8** remember, stand for, treasure **9** care about
dominion: **4** rule **5** reign **6** direct, govern **7** command, control, oversee
don't ~: **5** let go
down: **3** pin **6** anchor, manage **7** inhibit **8** restrict
down a job: **4** earn, work
ender: **3** all, out **4** back, fast, over
fast: **5** cling, seize, stick **6** adhere, cohere **7** enchain
fast to: **6** follow **7** abide by **10** comply with
filler: **5** lader
fill the ~: **4** load, stow **5** lay in
fondly: **3** hug **4** love **5** press **6** caress, cosset, cuddle, dandle, nestle, nuzzle **7** embrace, snuggle, squeeze
for later: **4** keep, save
for ransom: **6** abduct, hijack, kidnap, pirate
forth: **4** talk **5** offer, orate, speak, spout **6** extend, recite **7** advance, declaim, lecture, narrate, proffer **8** bloviate, harangue, perorate **9** discourse
gently: **3** hug **6** cradle
get ~ of: **4** call, grab, have, meet **5** catch, phone, reach **6** locate, obtain, talk to **7** acquire, contact, liaison, possess, receive, speak to **8** approach, come into **9** ascertain, check with, telephone, touch base
hard to ~: **4** eely
in: **6** stifle **7** contain, repress, tighten **8** bottle up, suppress
in check: **4** keep, rein **6** govern **7** control
in contempt: **5** sneer, spurn
in custody: **6** detain, immure, intern **8** imprison
in music: **7** fermata
in trust: **6** escrow
in view: **3** eye, see, spy **4** espy, spot **5** watch **7** discern **8** perceive **10** get a load of
it: **4** stop **5** cease **6** desist
it down: **4** hush **5** quiet **6** hush up, muffle, muzzle, stifle **7** repress **8** restrain, suppress
it ~ s water: **3** cup **4** vase
it won't ~ water: **3** net **5** sieve **8** colander
lay ~ of: **3** get, nab **4** grab, grip, jerk, land, pull, snag, stop, take **5** catch, clasp, grasp, seize, twist, usurp, wrest **6** clinch, clutch, snatch **7** capture, grapple **8** come into
like a sword: **5** wield
loosen one's ~: **4** free **5** let go, untie **6** let off **7** release, set free **9** disengage
low: **4** hate **5** abhor **6** detest, loathe **7** despise, dislike **8** execrate **9** abominate
off: **5** delay, parry, repel, stall **6** offend, put off, rebuff, refuse, shelve, sicken **7** adjourn, disgust, prevent, repulse, suspend **8** alienate, hesitate, postpone
(off): **4** fend
off for: **5** await
office: **5** serve **6** act for **7** serve as **8** speak for **9** represent **10** administer
on: **4** bide, wait **5** abide, cling, stick **6** endure **7** persist, stand by **8** continue **9** keep going, persevere **10** stay a while
on ~: **8** inactive
one's attention: **5** rivet **6** absorb, arrest **7** bewitch, engross **8** enthrall, transfix **9** captivate, enrapture, fascinate, preoccupy
one's ground: **4** stay **5** stick **6** adhere, endure, remain, take it **7** persist, stay put
one's horses: **4** rein, wait
one's own: **4** cope **5** get by **6** manage **7** make out
one's tongue: **6** shut up **7** keep mum, silence **8** be silent
on to: **4** cull, keep, save **5** amass, cache, hoard, lay by, put by, stack, store **6** accrue, detain, garner, gather, pile up, rack up, retain, save up **7** collect, compile, possess, procure, put away, shelter, store up **8** assemble, maintain, put aside, salt away **9** aggregate, stockpile **10** accumulate
other views: **6** differ **7** dissent **8** disagree
out: **5** offer, reach **6** endure, extend, refuse, resist **7** present, proffer, survive **9** withstand
out one's hand: **3** beg **5** cadge, hit up, mooch **8** freeload **9** impetrate, mendicate, panhandle **10** supplicate
over: **5** defer, delay **6** detain, hang up, hold up, put off, shelve **7** prolong **8** postpone, protract
place in the ~: **4** fill, lade, pack, stow
prepare to ~ out: **5** dig in
put on ~: **5** defer, table **6** recess, shelve **7** suspend **8** postpone
rapt: **5** charm **6** absorb, engage **7** enchant, engross, immerse **8** enthrall, entrance **9** fascinate, preoccupy
responsible: **5** blame, thank **6** assign
sacred: **5** exalt **6** hallow **8** enshrine, inshrine, sanctify **10** consecrate
scoreless: **5** skunk
something to ~: **4** mayo
spellbound: **5** charm **7** enchant **8** enthrall, entrance, transfix **9** captivate, fascinate, hypnotize, mesmerize
starter: **3** toe **4** foot, free, hand, root, with **5** choke, house, lease, stoke **6** strong **8** strangle
sway: **4** head, rule **5** reign **6** direct, govern, manage **7** command, control, prevail **8** dominate, overrule
take ~: **3** fix **5** set in **6** enroot
take ~ of: **3** bag, nab **4** bust, grab, grip, nail, snag **5** catch, grasp, pinch, seize, snare **6** abduct, arrest, collar, detain, hijack, obtain, secure, snap up, snatch, tackle **7** capture, impound, overrun, procure, receive **8** carry off **9** apprehend, overwhelm **10** commandeer, confiscate
the attention of: **4** grab, grip, lure **5** catch, rivet, tempt **6** absorb, divert, engage, entice, occupy **7** attract, engross, impress, involve **8** enthrall, interest **9** entertain, fascinate, tantalize, titillate
the deed to: **3** own **7** possess
the fort: **4** stay **6** defend, remain, uphold **7** carry on, stand by **8** maintain
the phone: **4** wait **6** cool it **7** stand by **8** mark time, sit tight
the reins: **4** rule **5** guide, reign **6** direct, govern **7** command, control, oversee
the scepter: **4** rule **5** reign **6** govern **7** command
tight: **5** clamp, clasp, cling **6** clench **7** squeeze
to: **6** pursue **7** abide by, believe **8** obligate
up: **3** rob **4** halt, last, prop, rein, slow, wear **5** block, brace, delay, laten, raise, steal, waive **6** detain, endure, freeze, hamper, hinder, impede, rein in, retard, shelve, thwart, verify, waylay **7** bolster, display, set back, support, suspend **8** blockade, encumber, obstruct, postpone, prohibit **9** hamstring, interrupt, recommend, stonewall, undergird
up to ridicule: **4** mock, twit **5** sneer, taunt **6** dump on, insult **7** disdain, lampoon, put down **8** belittle, satirize **9** burlesque **10** caricature
water: **4** wash **5** add up **6** cohere **9** make sense
with: **5** grant **6** accept, affirm **7** believe **10** set store by
wrestling ~: **4** lock **6** nelson
hold __: **3** off, out **4** back, down, over, sway, with **5** at bay, forth, water
__ hold: **4** take
hold a __ to: **6** candle
holdall: **3** bag **6** duffel, kitbag **8** backpack, knapsack
hold 'em: **4** game **5** poker **8** card game
Holden: **3** Ron **4** Eben **7** William
Holden, William: **5** actor
film: Born Yesterday (1950)
The Bridge on the River Kwai (1957)
The Bridges at Toko-Ri (1955)
The Country Girl (1954)
Executive Suite (1954)
The Fleet's In (1942)
Love Is a Many Splendored Thing (1955)
Network (1976)
Our Town (1940)
Picnic (1955)
Sabrina (1954)
S.O.B. (1981)
Stalag 17 (1953, AA)
Sunset Blvd. (1950)
The Towering Inferno (1974)
The Wild Bunch (1969)
Wild Rovers (1971)
holder: **3** urn **4** rack, vase **5** owner, stein **6** handle, tenant **7** bracket **8** canister, occupant, oven mitt **9** container **10** proprietor, receptacle
starter: **3** gas, job, pen, pot **4** bond, card, copy, free, land **5** house, lease, place, share, stake, stock, title **6** candle, office, policy
Holder: **4** Eric
Hold Her Tight (1972 song)
artist: Osmonds
holding: **4** land **5** asset, title **6** tenure **7** keeping, logical **8** monopoly **9** occupancy, ownership
be in a ~ pattern: **4** pend, wait
company: **4** corp. **6** cartel
one left ~ the bag: **4** dupe, goat **5** chump, patsy **6** sucker, victim **7** cat's-paw, fall guy **9** scapegoat
pattern: **5** delay
starter: **4** with **5** share, stock
holding __: **3** pen **4** sway, tank **7** company, pattern
Holding On (1988 song)
artist: Steve Winwood
Holding Out for a Hero (1984 song)
artist: Bonnie Tyler
holdings: **5** means **6** assets, estate, wealth **7** effects **8** property **9** resources **10** belongings, securities
vast ~: **5** realm **6** empire **7** kingdom **8** dominion **9** territory
Hold it!: **3** hey **4** stop, whoa
Hold Me (song)
artist: Fleetwood Mac, K.T. Oslin
Hold Me Now (1984 song)
artist: Thompson Twins
Hold Me Tight (1968 song)
artist: Johnny Nash
Hold My Hand (song)
artist: Don Cornell, Hootie and the Blowfish
__ hold of: **3** get
Hold on!: **3** hey **4** stop, whoa **6** one sec
Hold On (1990 song)
artist: En Vogue, Wilson Phillips
Hold on a __!: **3** sec
hold one's __: **3** own **5** peace **6** ground, horses, tongue

Hold On! I'm a Comin' (1966 song)
artist: Sam and Dave
Hold on Tight (1981 song)
artist: ELO
Hold On to the Nights (1988 song)
artist: Richard Marx
holdout: 4 mule
Holdridge: 3 Lee **6** Cheryl
holds barred, no: 8 absolute, straight **9** limitless
Hold That Blonde (1945 film)
cast: Veronica Lake
hold the __: 3 bag **4** fort, line, mayo **5** phone
Hold the Line (1978 song)
artist: Toto
holdup: 3 jam, job **4** snag, wait **5** crime, delay, heist, hitch, theft **7** mugging, problem, robbery, setback, stickup, trouble **8** burglary, gridlock, lateness, stoppage, thievery **10** bottleneck, difficulty, impediment
man: 5 thief **6** mugger, robber
Hold What You've Got (1965 song)
artist: Joe Tex
Hold your __!: 4 fire **6** horses
Hold You Tight (1991 song)
artist: Tara Kemp
hole: 3 gap, jam, pit, rip **4** cave, gulf, lair, leak, nook, sink, slit, slot, spot, tear, vent, void, well **5** abyss, break, chasm, crack, ditch, gorge, gouge, niche, space **6** breach, burrow, cavern, cavity, cranny, crater, hollow, kennel, lacuna, locale, pickle, plight, pocket, recess, refuge, trench, tunnel **7** chamber, crevice, dungeon, fissure, opening, orifice, vacuity **8** aperture, locality, puncture, quagmire **9** concavity, sanctuary **10** depression, excavation, interspace, interstice, standstill
air ~: 4 vent
be in the ~: 3 owe
black ~ once: 4 star
combining form: 5 -trema
finish a ~: 4 putt
fix a ~: 4 darn, mend **5** patch **6** repair
furthest from the ~ in golf: 4 away
gaping ~: 3 maw **5** abyss, chasm
in one: 3 ace **7** triumph
in the ground: 3 pit **4** cave, well **6** cavern, crater
in the head: 5 mouth, naris, sinus **7** nostril
in the wall: 4 vent **6** outlet, refuge **7** hideout, retreat, shelter **8** hideaway **9** sanctuary
make a ~: 3 dig **4** bore **5** drill, gouge **6** burrow, dredge **8** excavate **9** hollow out
make a new ~: 5 redig
maker: 3 awl **4** moth **5** auger, borer **6** gimlet
needle ~: 3 eye
one in the ~: 4 ower
out: 4 putt
pipe ~: 4 leak **5** crack, drain
put another ~ in the cask: 5 retap
shoelace ~: 6 eyelet
start a ~: 5 tee up
starter: 3 arm, eye, fox, key, man, pin, pot **4** blow, bolt, bore, feed, hell, knee, knot, loop, peep, pest, port, post, sink, worm **5** chuck, cubby, hawse, stoke, thumb, touch **6** button, pigeon
subpar ~: 6 birdie
Swiss cheese ~: 3 eye
up: 4 hide, wait **5** lodge **6** lie low **7** conceal, hide out **9** hibernate **10** lie dormant
water ~: 4 pond, well
watering ~: 3 bar, pub **4** pond, well **5** haunt, oasis **6** bistro, lounge, saloon, tavern
wear a ~ in the rug: 4 pace
widen a ~: 4 ream
hole __: 3 saw **4** card **5** in one
hole __ wall: 5 in the
__ hole: 3 air, dry **5** black, glory, in the, water **6** finger
__-hole: 5 hidey
__ Hole: 7 Jackson
hole in __: 3 one
__ hole in one's pocket: 5 burn a
hole in the __: 4 wall
__ Hole of Calcutta: 5 Black
holes
18 ~: 5 round
cheese with ~: 5 Swiss
full of ~: 5 leaky, mothy **6** flawed, porous, ragged
in ~: 6 ragged **8** tattered **9** moth-eaten **10** threadbare
poke full of ~: 6 refute, riddle **8** puncture **9** perforate
Holes (2003 film)
cast: Shia LaBeouf, Jon Voight, Sigourney Weaver
holey: 5 leaky **6** porous **9** moth-eaten
holiday: 4 rest, stay, tour **5** break, event, feast, leave, visit **6** fiesta, recess **7** jubilee, leisure, liberty, time off **8** festival, vacation **10** recreation
annual ~: 6 Fourth
Asian ~: 3 Tet
cheer: 3 nog
Christian: 6 Advent, Easter
exhibit: 6 crèche
extravaganza: 6 parade
helper: 3 elf
Italian ~: 5 festa
Jewish: 5 Purim **8** Passover **9** Yom Kippur
Jewish ~ dinner: 5 seder
Jewish ~ eve: 4 ereb, erev
month: 3 Dec. **8** December
month without a ~: 6 August
preceder: 3 eve
purchase: 3 fir
quaff: 6 eggnog
quick ~: 5 jaunt
season: 4 Noel, Xmas, yule
song: 4 noel **5** carol
suitable for a ~: 6 festal
take a ~: 4 loaf, rest, slow **5** break, pause, relax **6** unwind **8** recreate, slack off, slow down, vacation
visitor: 5 Santa **6** St. Nick **10** Santa Claus
word: 5 happy
see also Christmas
__ holiday: 4 bank **5** legal, Roman **7** busman's
Holiday: 6 Billie
Holiday (1938 film)
cast: Cary Grant, Katharine Hepburn
director: George Cukor
Holiday (1983 song)
artist: Madonna
Holiday __: 3 Inn **5** on Ice
__ Holiday: 4 High **5** Roman
Holiday Inn: 5 motel
alternative: ***see*** motel
Holiday Inn (1942 film)
cast: Fred Astaire, Bing Crosby
composer: Irving Berlin
Holiday, The (2006 film)
cast: Jack Black, Cameron Diaz, Jude Law, Kate Winslet
holier-than-thou: 4 smug **6** stuffy **7** pompous, stuck-up **8** arrogant, snobbish, superior **9** conceited
holiness: 5 piety **8** divinity, sanctity
Holiness, his: 4 pope **7** pontiff
Holland: 3 Tom **4** city, Neth., town **5** Brian, Eddie **11** Netherlands
born in ~: 5 Dutch
locale: 8 Michigan
Holland __ Line: 7 America
hollandaise: 5 sauce
Hollander: 6 Nicole
Hollander, Lorin: 7 pianist **9** conductor
holler: 3 cry, yap **4** bawl, call, hoot, howl, rant, rave, roar, wail, yell, yelp, yowl **5** cheer, go ape, shout, storm, whoop **6** bellow, clamor, scream, shriek, squawk, squeal **7** bluster, carry on, declaim, exclaim, screech, sing out, ululate **8** bloviate, complain, freak out, shout out **9** make a fuss, raise Cain **10** hit the roof, vociferate
hollering: 5 noisy
__ hollers,...: 4 If he
Holliday: 3 Doc **4** Judy **5** Polly **8** Jennifer
pal: 4 Earp
Holliday, Judy: 7 actress
film: Adam's Rib (1949)
Bells Are Ringing (1960)
Born Yesterday (1950, AA)
Phffft! (1954)
Holliday, Polly
role: 3 Flo
Hollies
song: The Air That I Breathe (1974)
Bus Stop (1966)
Carrie-Anne (1967)
He Ain't Heavy, He's My Brother (1970)
Long Cool Woman (1972)
Stop Stop Stop (1966)
Holliman: 4 Earl
Hollings: 6 Ernest
Hollis: 5 Stacy
hollow: 3 gap, pit, rut **4** dale, dell, dent, dull, heed, hole, idle, sink, vain, vale, void **5** basin, cleft, empty, false, gorge, muted, niche, notch, scoop, tubal **6** absent, cavity, cranny, crater, dig out, dimple, dingle, furrow, futile, groove, pocket, recess, sunken, untrue, vacant, valley **7** concave, muffled, useless, vacuity **8** empty out, excavate, lifeless, scoop out, sinkhole, unfilled **9** cup-shaped, deceitful, depressed, excavated, fruitless, illogical, insincere, pointless, worthless **10** artificial, depression, excavation, unreliable
not: 5 solid
out: 3 dig **6** burrow **8** excavate **9** undermine
place: 4 cave, hole **5** ditch, gorge **6** cavern, cavity, crater, trench, tunnel **7** chamber **10** depression
secluded ~: 4 dell
small ~: 4 dent **6** areola, areole
sound: 5 clunk, thunk
__ Hollow: 6 Sleepy
Holloway: 7 Stanley **8** Sterling
Hollow Hills, The
author: Mary Stewart
Hollow Men, The
author: T.S. Eliot
holly: 4 tree **5** shrub
ender: 4 hock
feature: 5 berry
genus: 4 ilex
sea ~: 6 eryngo
season: 4 Xmas, Yule
shrub: 4 ilex **5** yapon **6** yaupon **8** inkberry
Holly: 4 Near **5** Buddy **6** Hunter, Lauren **7** Palance
Holly __: 4 Holy
Holly and the Crickets, Buddy
song: Oh, Boy! (1957)
Peggy Sue (1957)
That'll Be the Day (1957)
hollyhock: 5 plant **6** flower
Holly Holy (1969 song)
artist: Neil Diamond
__-Holly Johnson: 4 Lynn
Holly, Lauren: 7 actress
film: Beautiful Girls (1996)
Dumb & Dumber (1994)
spouse: Jim Carrey
hollylike tree: 4 holm
Hollywood: 4 city, town
clashers: 4 egos
figure: 3 rep **4** star **5** actor, agent, celeb **8** director, producer **9** celebrity
industry: 6 cinema, movies
locale: 7 Florida **10** California
magnate: 4 Cohn **5** Mayer **7** Goldwyn
publicity frame: 5 still
release: 5 movie
studio: 3 Fox, MGM, RKO **6** Warner **8** Columbia **9** Paramount
walk-on: 5 extra
workplace: 3 set **6** studio **10** soundstage
Hollywood __ of Fame: 4 Walk
__ Hollywood: 3 Doc **5** Going
Hollywood Argyles
song: Alley-Oop (1960)
Hollywood Boulevard
crosser: 4 Vine
embedment: 4 star
Hollywood Ending (2002 film)
cast: Woody Allen, Téa Leoni, Debra Messing, Treat Williams
director: Woody Allen
Hollywoodland (2006 film)
cast: Ben Affleck, Adrien Brody, Bob Hoskins, Diane Lane
Hollywood Nights (1978 song)
artist: Bob Seger
Hollywood Squares, The: 8 game show
answer: 5 agree **8** disagree

former regular: 3 Cox 5 Lynde 6 Weaver
host: Peter Marshall, John Davidson, Tom Bergeron
non-win: 3 OOX, OXO, OXX, XOO, XOX, XXO
ploy: 5 bluff
star complement: 4 nine
win: 3 OOO, XXX
Hollywood Suite
composer: Ferde Grofé
Hollywood Swinging (1974 song)
artist: Kool and the Gang
Holm: 3 Ian 5 Hanya 7 Celeste, Eleanor
Holman: 3 Nat 4 Hunt 5 Eddie
Holman, Eddie
song: Hey There Lonely Girl (1970)
Holman, Nat
milieu: 5 court
org.: 3 NBA
sport: 10 basketball
Holm, Celeste: 7 actress
film: All About Eve (1950)
Champagne for Caesar (1950)
Gentleman's Agreement (1947, AA)
High Society (1956)
Holmes: 5 Clint, Katie, Larry 6 Oliver, Rupert 8 Sherlock
O.W. ~ carriage: 4 shay
Holmes, Clint
song: Playground in My Mind (1973)
Holmes, Larry: 5 boxer
milieu: 4 ring
Holmes, Oliver Wendell: 4 poet
work: The Autocrat of the Breakfast-Table
The Chambered Nautilus
Elsie Venner
Old Ironsides
The Wonderful One-Hoss Shay
Holmes, Rupert
song: Escape (1979)
Him (1980)
Holmes, Sherlock: 6 sleuth 9 detective
adverb for ~: 5 afoot
brother: 7 Mycroft
clue: 3 ash
colleague: 6 Watson
creator: Arthur Conan Doyle
foe: 8 Moriarty
friend: 5 Irene
girl: 5 Elsie
home: 6 London 7 Baker St.
landlady: 6 Hudson
portrayer: Basil Rathbone
prop for ~: 4 pipe
quest: 4 clew, clue
task for ~: 4 case
holmium: 7 element
holm oak: 4 ilex
Holocaust documentary: 5 Shoah
hologram maker: 5 laser
holographic __: 4 will
holography tool: 5 laser
Holstein: 3 cow 4 bull 6 bovine, cattle
comment: 3 moo
home: 4 barn
part: 5 udder
holster item: 3 gun, rod 5 piece 6 pistol, roscoe, weapon 7 firearm 8 revolver 9 forty-five

Holst, Gustav
work: The Planets
Holt: 3 Tim 8 Victoria
Holt, Laura partner: 6 Steele
Holtz: 3 Lou
Holub, Miroslav: 4 poet 5 Czech
holy: 5 blest, godly, pious 6 devout, divine, sacred, solemn 7 angelic, blessed, sainted, saintly 8 faithful, hallowed, numinous, reverent, seraphic 9 angelical, celestial, inviolate, religious, righteous, spiritual 10 inviolable, sacrosanct, sanctified, seraphical
combining form: 4 hagi-, hier- 5 hagio-, hiero-
ender: 3 day 5 stone
name meaning ~: 4 Olga 5 Helga
terror: 3 imp 4 brat
holy __: 3 cow, day, oil, war 4 moly 5 Moses, water 6 orders, terror
Holy __: 3 Ark, See 4 Land, Rood, Week, Writ 5 Bible, Cross, Ghost, Grail
Holy __!: 3 cow 4 moly 5 smoke 6 Toledo 8 mackerel
Holy __ Empire: 5 Roman
Holy __, The: 3 War 4 Fair
__ Holy: 5 Holly
Holy Ark
locale: 4 shul 5 schul 9 synagogue
Holy cow!: 3 gee, wow 4 egad, gosh, yipe 5 egads, yikes, yipes
Holy Cross
athletes: 9 Crusaders
locale: 4 Mass. 9 Worcester
__ Holy Day: 4 High
Holy Fair, The
author: Robert Burns
Holy Father: 4 pope 7 pontiff
Holyfield, Evander: 5 boxer
milieu: 4 ring
rival: 5 Tyson
Holy Land: 4 Sion, Zion 5 Judea 6 Judaea
Holy mackerel!: 3 gee, wow 4 egad 5 egads, golly
Holyoke: 4 city, town
locale: 4 Mass.
Holy One: 4 Lord
Holy Roman Empire
founder: 4 Otto
Holy smoke!: 3 gee, wow 4 egad, oath 5 egads, golly
Holy Toledo!: 3 gee, wow 4 egad 5 egads, golly
Holy War, The
author: John Bunyan
holy-water basin: 4 font 5 stoup
Holy Week ends it: 4 Lent
Holz, Arno: 4 poet 6 German 10 playwright
Holzman, Red: 5 coach
org.: 3 NBA
sport: 10 basketball
homage: 4 pean 5 honor, kudos, paean 6 esteem, fealty, praise, regard, salute 7 acclaim, loyalty, plaudit, respect, tribute, worship 8 accolade, devotion, encomium, fidelity, flattery, good word 9 adoration, adulation, deference, laudation, obeisance, panegyric, reverence 10 admiration, allegiance, exaltation
pay ~ to: 4 hail 5 exalt, honor 6 attend, praise, revere, salute 7 glorify 9 genuflect
Homage to Clio
author: W.H. Auden
Homage to Mistress Bradstreet...
author: John Berryman
Homage to Picasso
painter: Juan Gris
Homage to the Square: 5 op art
hombre: 4 game 8 card game
Hombre (1967 film)
cast: Richard Boone, Fredric March, Paul Newman
director: Martin Ritt
homburg: 3 hat 7 chapeau 8 headgear
alternative: *see* hat
__ Homburg: 3 Bad
home: 3 hut, pad 4 base, co-op, digs, flat, land, nest, site, soil, turf 5 abode, cabin, condo, house, joint, local, lodge, manor, place, roost, villa 6 castle, hearth, locale, palace, refuge 7 address, chez moi, cottage, domicil, habitat, housing, lodging, mansion, shelter 8 bungalow, crash pad, domestic, domicile, dwelling, fireside, interior, internal, locality, lodgment, property, quarters 9 apartment, dormitory, household, residence, townhouse 10 birthplace, fatherland, native land
ender: 3 boy 4 body, bred, land, made, port, room, sick, spun, town, ward, work 5 bound, buyer, grown, maker, owner, stead, wards 6 coming, making 7 builder, stretch 8 steading
in French: 6 maison
in Spanish: 4 casa
large ~: 6 castle, estate, palace 7 mansion
lofty ~: 4 aery, eyry 5 aerie, eyrie
not ~: 3 out 4 away
on the range: 5 ranch
site: 4 plot
see also house
home __: 3 row, run 4 base, brew, free, page, port, rule 5 fries, front, plate, stand, video 6 center, office
home __ loan: 6 equity
home __ potatoes: 5 fried
home-__: 4 brew, care 5 style
__ home: 3 hit 5 bring, motor, not at, solar 6 mobile
__-home: 4 down
Home __: 5 Alone, Depot
Home __ Baker: 3 Run
Home __ Brave: 5 of the
Home __ Range: 5 on the
Home __ the Holidays: 3 for
Home, __!: 5 James
__ Home: 5 Going, I'll Be 6 Coming, Daddy's, Flying 7 Harvest
Home Again host: 4 Vila
__ Home Alabama: 5 Sweet
Home Alone (1990 film)
cast: Macaulay Culkin, John Heard, Catherine O'Hara, Joe Pesci, Daniel Stern
composer: John Williams
director: Chris Columbus
kid: 5 Kevin
homebody: 5 loner 7 recluse 9 introvert

homeboy: 3 bud, pal 4 chum 5 amigo, crony 6 friend
homebuyer option: 5 condo
homecoming: 6 return 7 arrival
attend ~: 5 reune
celebrant: 4 alum, grad 6 alumna 7 alumnus
Homecoming, The: 4 play
author: Harold Pinter
home delivery terr.: 3 rte.
Home Depot
rival: 5 Lowe's
home-district
some ~ appropriations: 4 pork
home equity __: 4 loan
Home for the Holidays (1954 song)
artist: Perry Como
home-free: 4 safe
home fries: 8 potatoes
homegirl: 3 bud, pal 4 chum 5 amiga, crony 6 friend
homegrown: 5 local 6 native 8 domestic 10 indigenous, provincial
home heating need: 3 gas, oil
Homeier: 2 G.V. 4 Skip
Home Improvement (ABC sitcom)
cast: Tim Allen (Tim Taylor)
Debbe Dunning (Heidi)
Patricia Richardson (Jill Taylor)
setting: Detroit
show: Tool Time
__ home is his castle: 5 A man's
homeland: 4 soil 5 roots 7 country
homeless: 5 stray 6 exiled, lonely 7 vagrant 8 derelict, indigent, stranded, unhoused, vagabond
one: 4 waif 5 gamin, stray 6 pauper 7 vagrant
homelike: 4 cozy, snug 5 comfy 7 livable 8 intimate
home-loan org.: 3 FHA 4 FNMA, GNMA
homemade: 5 crude, rough 6 rustic, simple 9 inelegant, makeshift 10 amateurish
liquor: 4 jake 5 hooch 6 hootch 9 moonshine
homemaker, at times: 4 cook 5 sewer 6 duster, ironer, washer
home of the brave: 3 USA
Home on the Range (2004 film)
voice cast: Roseanne Barr, Judi Dench
Home on the Range beast: 4 deer 7 buffalo 8 antelope
homeowner
new ~: 6 lienee
paper: 4 deed
payment: 4 mtge. 8 mortgage
pride: 4 lawn 5 grass 8 backyard
__-home pay: 4 take
homer: 3 hit, run 5 tater 6 dinger 7 triumph 9 grand slam 10 four-bagger
hitter's run: 4 trot
king: 5 Aaron
trying for a ~: 5 at bat
two-run ~ requirement: 5 one on
Homer: 4 city, poet, town 5 Greek 7 Simpson, Winslow
grunt: 3 doh
instrument: 4 lyre
locale: 6 Alaska
neighbor: 3 Ned

opus: 4 epic, epos 5 Iliad 7 Odyssey
partner: 6 Jethro
wife: 5 Marge
see also Greek
Homeric: 4 epic 5 grand 6 heroic 8 heroical 9 classical 10 monumental
Homeric __: 6 simile
Homeric Greek: 6 Argive
home ruler, name meaning: 5 Henry
home run
see homer
Home Run __: 5 Baker
Homer, Winslow: 6 artist 7 painter
home: 5 Maine
__ Homes and Gardens: 6 Better
home security device: 5 alarm
Home Shopping Network
rival: 3 QVC
homesick: 7 forlorn 8 lonesome
homesite: 3 lot
HOMES part: 4 Erie 5 Huron 7 Ontario 8 Michigan, Superior
homespun: 5 plain 6 fabric, folksy, rustic, simple 8 ordinary 10 provincial, unpolished
homestead: 4 farm, soil 5 ranch 6 estate, grange, settle 8 fireside
Homestead: 4 city, town
locale: 7 Florida
Homestead Act
measure: 4 acre
offering: 4 land
homesteader: 5 liver 6 nester, sooner 7 pioneer, settler 8 colonial, colonist, squatter
tract: 5 claim
Home, Sweet Home
composer: John Howard Payne
starter: 3 mid
__ home the bacon: 5 bring
Home to Harlem
author: Claude McKay
__ home to roost: 4 come
home video format: 3 DVD, VHS 4 Beta
__ Homeward, Angel: 4 Look
Homeward Bound (1966 song)
artist: Simon and Garfunkel
homework: 4 task 6 lesson 10 assignment
do ~: 5 study 9 grind away
do elementary-school ~: 3 add
English ~: 5 essay, theme
help with ~: 5 tutor
homey: 4 cosy, cozy, nice, snug, warm 5 comfy, cozey, cozie 6 casual, earthy, folksy, rustic, simple 7 livable, natural, relaxed 8 friendly, informal, inviting, liveable, pleasant 9 household 10 unaffected
homilize: 5 orate 6 preach
homily: 3 ser. 4 talk 6 cliché, lesson, saying, sermon, speech 7 oration 8 teaching 9 discourse 10 admonition, vocalizing
homing __: 6 pigeon
hominy: 4 samp 5 grain, grits
homme: 3 man 6 French
homme d'__: 4 état
homme du __: 5 monde
__ homo: 4 ecce
Homo __: 7 erectus, habilis, sapiens
Homo erectus: 5 biped
homogeneous: 4 akin, even, like 5 alike 6 allied 7 cognate, kindred, of a kind, similar, uniform 8 constant, parallel 9 analogous, unanimous 10 comparable, equivalent
homogenize: 3 mix 5 blend 9 integrate 10 amalgamate, assimilate
homogenized product: 4 milk
homogenous: 6 on a par 9 analogous, identical, unvarying 10 comparable, consistent, homologous, true to type
Homolka: 5 Oscar
homologize: 6 absorb 9 integrate 10 assimilate
homologous: 4 like 5 equal 9 analogous 10 equivalent, homogenous
homo sapiens: 3 man 5 biped, human 6 people
Homs: 4 city, town
locale: 5 Syria
hon: 3 luv 4 babe, dear 5 deary, sugar, toots 6 dearie 7 darling, pet name, sweetie 8 snookums 10 endearment, sweetheart, sweetie pie
honcho: 3 VIP 4 boss, head, jefe, king, lord, prex, prez 5 chief, Mr. Big, nabob, prexy, wheel 6 bigwig, kahuna, top dog 7 big shot, headman 8 big wheel, director, higher-up, kingfish, overseer, superior 9 big kahuna, commander, executive, organizer
head ~: 8 higher-up 9 key player
Hond.
neighbor: 3 Nic. 4 Guat.
see also Honduras
Honda: 3 car 4 auto 6 import 8 Soichiro 10 automobile
model: 3 CRV 5 Acura, civic, Pilot 6 Accord, Del Sol 7 Element, Odyssey, Prelude 8 Passport
rival: *see* automobile
Honduras: 4 gulf 6 nation 7 country
Indian: 4 Maya 5 Lenca 7 Miskito
money: 7 lempira
native: 4 Maya
neighbor: 9 Guatemala, Nicaragua 10 El Salvador
org.: 3 OAS
town in ~: 4 Tela
see also Spanish
hone: 4 file, whet 5 grind, strop, train 6 refine 7 improve, perfect, sharpen 8 fine-tune, oilstone, practice, rehearse 9 acuminate, whetstone
in: 5 focus
honed: 4 keen 5 edged, sharp 9 sharpened
Honegger: 6 Arthur
contemporary: 5 Satie
honest: 4 even, fair, good, just, open, true 5 blunt, frank, legit, moral, naïve, plain, right 6 actual, candid, decent, direct, proper, simple, square, trusty, worthy 7 artless, ethical, factual, genuine, serious, sincere, unfaked, up-front, upright, veridic 8 bona fide, credible, explicit, innocent, out front, reliable, straight, truthful, unbiased, virtuous 9 downright, guileless, heartfelt, honorable, impartial, ingenuous, objective, reputable, righteous, unfeigned, unslanted, veracious, veridical 10 aboveboard, believable, evenhanded, forthright, from the hip, high-minded, inviolable, law-abiding, legitimate, on the level, point-blank, reasonable, scrupulous, unaffected, upstanding
be ~: 5 level 6 face it
to goodness: 5 truly 6 indeed, really
Honest __: 3 Abe 4 John
Honest!: 5 no lie 6 I swear
honestly: 5 clean, right, truly 6 openly, really, simply 8 directly 9 honorably, sincerely 10 point-blank, virtuously
honestness: 5 truth 6 ethics, virtue 7 probity 8 morality, veracity 9 character, integrity, principle, rectitude
honest-to-__: 3 God
honest-to-goodness: 4 real, true 5 legit, plumb, valid 6 actual, kasher, kosher, proven, really 7 certain, factual, for real, genuine 8 absolute, accurate, bona fide, straight 9 authentic, confirmed, downright, heartfelt, in reality, out-and-out, seriously, sincerely 10 definitely
honesty: 4 good 5 honor, right 6 candor, ethics, virtue 7 loyalty, probity 8 fairness, fidelity, goodness, morality, openness, veracity 9 bluntness, frankness, good faith, integrity, rectitude, sincerity 10 candidness, trustiness
exemplar of ~: 3 Abe 7 Lincoln
of dubious ~: 5 shady 7 corrupt, crooked, devious 8 slippery, unsavory 9 notorious, unethical
Honesty (1979 song)
artist: Billy Joel
Honesty __ best policy: 5 is the
honey
badger: 5 ratel
color: 4 gold 5 amber
drink: 4 mead
ender: 3 bee, dew 4 comb, moon 5 berry, eater 6 suckle 7 creeper
factory: 4 comb, hive 6 apiary
in prescriptions: 3 mel
land of milk and ~: 6 utopia 7 Arcadia, Erewhon 8 paradise 9 Shangri-la
like ~: 5 sweet 6 sticky
maker: 3 bee
source: 6 clover
see also sweetheart
honey __: 3 bee, bun 7 mustard
Honey (1968 song)
artist: Bobby Goldsboro
Honey (1997 song)
artist: Mariah Carey
Honey __: 4 Fitz
Honey __ Cheerios: 3 Nut
__-Honey: 4 Bit-o
Honey and Salt
author: Carl Sandburg
honeybee: 3 bug 6 insect
honeybunch
see sweetheart
Honey Bunches of Oats
competitor: *see* cereal
honeycomb: 6 pierce 9 penetrate
material: 3 wax
unit: 4 cell
Honeycomb (1957 song)
artist: Jimmie Rodgers
Honey Comb: 6 cereal
competitor: *see* cereal
honeycreeper: 4 bird, iiwi
honeydew: 5 fruit, melon
kin: 6 casaba 7 cassaba
honey Dijon: 8 dressing
Honeydrippers
song: Sea of Love (1984)
honeyeater: 3 tui 4 bird 9 friarbird
honey-eating bird: 2 oo 3 iao
honeyed: 5 sweet 6 sugary 7 candied 9 adulatory 10 saccharine
Honey Fitz daughter: 4 Rose
Honey, I Shrunk the Kids (1989 film)
cast: Matt Frewer, Rick Moranis, Marcia Strassman
honeymoon
locale: 5 Aruba 6 Hawaii 7 Niagara
honeymooner: 5 bride, groom 8 newlywed
Honeymooners, The (CBS sitcom)
cast: Art Carney (Ed Norton) Jackie Gleason (Ralph Kramden) Audrey Meadows (Alice Kramden) Joyce Randolph (Trixie Norton)
dog: 5 Lucky
laugh: 3 har
prop: 6 icebox
setting: 7 New York 8 Brooklyn
Honeymoon Festivel, The
author: Marian Engel
Honeymoon in Vegas (1992 film)
cast: James Caan, Nicolas Cage, Sarah Jessica Parker
Honey Nut Cheerios
competitor: *see* cereal
honeysuckle: 5 plant 6 flower
shrub: 5 elder 6 abelia 8 snowball
Honeysuckle Rose (1980 film)
cast: Dyan Cannon, Amy Irving, Willie Nelson
honey-tongued: 4 glib, oily 5 slick, suave 6 artful, facile, smooth 8 eloquent 9 garrulous
Honey West ocelot: 5 Bruce
Hong Kong: 4 isls. 5 isles 7 islands
boat: 4 junk
locale: 4 Asia 5 China
money: 4 cent 6 dollar
neighbor: 5 Macao, Macau
river: 5 Pearl
Hong Kong __: 3 flu
honi __ qui mal y pense: 4 soit
Honi: 5 Coles
Honiara: 4 city, town 7 capital
locale: 8 Solomons
honied: 5 sweet
honk: 4 beep, blow, bray, toot, yang 5 blare, blast, noise 6 tootle
honker: 4 horn 5 goose 8 motorist
honkers: 5 geese, skein 6 gaggle
Honk if you...
locale: 6 bumper
Honky Cat (1972 song)
artist: Elton John
honky-tonk: 3 bar 5 joint, music 6 tavern 8 taphouse 9 nightclub
Honkytonk Man (1982 film)
cast: Clint Eastwood
director: Clint Eastwood

Honky Tonk Women (1969 song)
artist: Rolling Stones
Honolulu: 4 city, port, town
athletes: 8 Warriors
greeting: 5 aloha
locale: 4 Oahu **6** Hawaii
newspaper: 10 Advertiser
palace: 6 Iolani
shindig: 4 luau
suburb: 4 Aiea
honor: 4 fete, hail, laud, name, palm, sing **5** adore, award, bless, crown, endue, exalt, extol, glory, grace, indue, kudos, medal, merit, prize, raise, toast **6** admire, credit, esteem, extoll, fealty, hallow, homage, praise, regard, renown, revere, reward, salute, trophy, virtue **7** acclaim, adulate, applaud, commend, decency, dignify, dignity, ennoble, flatter, glorify, honesty, laurels, lionize, loyalty, magnify, observe, plaudit, probity, respect, tribute, worship **8** accolade, decorate, eminence, encomium, eulogize, fairness, flattery, good name, goodness, good word, live up to, look up to, morality, nobility, ornament, prestige, venerate, veracity **9** adoration, adulation, celebrate, celebrity, character, deference, gallantry, greatness, integrity, laudation, liquidate, panegyric, privilege, recognize, rectitude, reverence, sincerity **10** admiration, compliment, consecrate, decoration, exaltation, panegyrize, veneration
an IOU: 3 pay **5** pay up, repay **6** refund, settle **7** pay back **8** make good, settle up, square up **9** reimburse **10** remunerate
battle of ~: 4 duel
card: 3 ace, ten **4** king
in ~ of: 3 for **5** after
place of ~: 4 dais
put on the ~ system: 5 trust
sense of ~: 6 ethics, morals, values **7** probity **8** morality **9** character, integrity, rectitude **10** conscience, principles
with a title: 3 dub **6** knight
with insults: 5 roast
word of ~: 3 vow **4** oath, word **6** pledge **7** promise
honor __: 4 card, roll **5** guard **6** system **7** society
honor __ thieves: 5 among
honor-__: 5 bound
__ honor: 4 your
Honor: 8 Blackman
his ~: 5 judge, mayor **6** jurist **10** magistrate
Honor __ Father: 3 Thy
__ Honor: 7 Prizzi's
honorable: 4 fair, good, just, true **5** clean, great, moral, noble, right, sound **6** august, decent, honest, trusty, worthy **7** eminent, ethical, exalted, gallant, notable, sincere, upright **8** elevated, esteemed, faithful, knightly, reliable, sterling, straight, truthful, unsoiled, virtuous **9** dignified, estimable, exemplary, high-toned, reputable, righteous, venerable **10** chivalrous, creditable, high-minded, scrupulous, upstanding
honorable __: 7 mention
honorably: 4 well **5** right **7** morally **8** honestly, properly **9** carefully, ethically, uprightly **10** dependably, faithfully, virtuously
honorarium: 3 fee, pay **7** payment, subsidy **9** allowance, emolument
honorary: 6 unpaid **7** nominal, titular **10** unsalaried
honor-bound: 6 liable **7** obliged **8** beholden, indebted **9** obligated
Honoré: 6 Balzac **7** Daumier
honored: 5 noted, proud **7** storied, welcome **8** glorious, laureate **9** venerable **10** preeminent
where ~ guests sit: 6 podium **7** rostrum **8** platform
__-honored: 4 time
honorific: 5 title **7** address
female ~: 4 ma'am **5** madam
Japanese ~: 3 san
honoris __: 5 causa
Honorius: 4 pope **7** pontiff
__ honor, I will do my...: 4 On my
honors: 5 glory, kudos, prize **6** esteem, laurel, praise **7** acclaim, laurels
confer ~: 5 award
do the ~: 7 present, preside **9** officiate
__ honors: 5 do the
honor society
concern: 3 GPA
letter: 3 phi **4** beta **5** kappa
Honor Thy Father
author: Gay Talese
Honourable Schoolboy, The
author: John le Carré
Honshu: 4 isle **6** island
cape: 3 Oma
city: 3 Ise, Ito, Ome, Ota, Tsu, Ube, Uji, Yao **4** Ageo, Anjo, Fuji, Gifu, Hino, Hofu, Iida, Kobe, Kofu, Kure, Mito, Nara, Noda, Otsu, Seto, Soka, Tama, Toda, Ueda, Zama **5** Abiko, Akita, Aomon, Asaka, Chiba, Chofu, Daito, Ebina, Fuchu, Fukui, Handa, Ikeda, Ikoma, Iruma, Itami, Iwaki, Izumi, Kioto, Kiryu, Kyoto, Minoo, Niiza, Ogaki, Omiya, Osaka, Oyama, Sakai, Suita, Tokio, Tokyo, Urawa, Yaizu **6** Nagano, Nagoya, Toyota, Yamato **7** Hitachi, Komatsu, Machida, Matsudo **8** Fukuyama, Kawasaki, Yokohama, Yokosuka **9** Hiroshima
lake: 3 Omi
locale: 4 Asia **5** Japan
port: 3 Ito, Ube **4** Kobe, Kure **5** Akita, Aomon, Chiba, Osaka
river: 3 Ota
volcano: 4 Fuji **5** Asama, Azuma, Oyama **6** Bandai, Chokai, Ontake **7** Adatara
Honus: 6 Wagner
hoo-__: 3 hah
__-hoo: 3 boo, yoo
hooch: 5 booze, sauce **6** liquor, redeye, whisky **7** alcohol, bootleg, spirits, whiskey **9** moonshine **10** bathtub gin, intoxicant
holder: 3 jug
maker: 5 still
slug of ~: 4 belt
hood: 3 ape **4** cowl, goon, mask, punk, thug, yegg **5** tough **6** outlaw **7** brigand, capuche, mobster, ruffian **8** gangster, hooligan, tough guy
combining form: 8 calyptri-, calyptro-
ender: 4 mold, wink
garment with a ~: 4 cowl **5** parka
in Britain: 3 yob **6** bonnet
it's under the ~: 5 motor **6** engine **10** power train
starter: 3 boy, god, man **4** baby, girl, lady **5** adult, angel, child, monks, saint, state, woman **6** father, knight, matron, mother, parent, priest, sister **7** brother
weapon: 3 gat **4** shiv **5** piece **6** roscoe
wearer: 4 monk **5** cobra, friar, viper
'hood: 4 area **8** vicinity
man in the ~: 5 mista
Hood: 2 mt. **3** mtn. **4** peak **5** Darla, mount **6** Thomas **8** mountain
locale: 6 Oregon **8** Cascades
__ Hood: 4 Fort **5** Mount, Robin
hooded: 9 cucullate
garment: 5 capot, grego, parka **6** anorak, capote, duffle
hoodlum: 3 ape **4** goon, punk, thug **5** rowdy, tough **6** gunsel, outlaw, vandal **7** brigand, mobster, ruffian **8** criminal, gangster, hooligan **9** miscreant, racketeer **10** delinquent
hoodoo: 4 jinx **5** curse, magic **7** bad luck **10** witchcraft
Hood, Robin
colleague: 4 Will **7** Scarlet **8** Scarlett **9** Alan-a-Dale, Friar Tuck **10** Allan-a-Dale, Little John
girlfriend: 10 Maid Marian
portrayer: 5 Errol
quaff: 3 ale
weapon: 3 bow **5** arrow
hood-shaped petal: 5 galea
Hood, Thomas: 4 poet **7** British
__ Hood, TX: 4 Fort
hoodwink: 3 con, gyp **4** bilk, burn, dupe, fake, fool, gull, have, hoax, nick, scam, snow, take **5** cheat, cozen, hocus, lie to, trick **6** befool, delude, euchre, fleece, lead on, outwit, suck in, take in **7** beguile, buffalo, deceive, defraud, mislead, pretend, swindle, two-time **8** outsmart, pettifog **9** bamboozle, disinform, four-flush, victimize
Hoodwinked (2006 film)
voice cast: Jim Belushi, Glenn Close, Anne Hathaway
hoodwinking: 4 hoax, scam **5** fraud, guile, put-on, sting, trick **6** deceit, dupery, humbug, racket, rip-off **7** fast one, swindle **8** flimflam, trickery **9** chicanery, duplicity, imposture **10** hocus-pocus
hooey
see baloney
hoof: 4 foot, step **6** unguis **8** ambulate
it: 4 walk **5** dance **8** tap-dance
worker: 5 shoer
__ hoof: 5 on the **6** cloven
hoofbeat: 4 clop
hoofed animal: 3 pig **5** horse, tapir
hoofer: 6 dancer **7** Astaire, O'Connor **9** Gene Kelly, tap dancer
Hooft, Gerardus 't: 8 Nobelist **9** physicist
hoo-ha: 3 ado, din **4** fuss, stir, to-do **5** noise, tizzy **6** clamor, outcry, racket, ruckus, rumpus, uproar **7** rhubarb **8** foofaraw **9** commotion, maelstrom **10** excitement, hullabaloo, hurly-burly
hook: 3 bag, net **4** barb, bend, draw, gaff, grab, land, lift, lock, lure, trap, turn **5** angle, catch, curve, grasp, hitch, latch, punch, snare, swipe, tempt **6** allure, arrest, collar, enmesh, entice, entrap, fasten, immesh, inmesh, locate, pilfer, pull in, rope in, secure, tackle, Velcro **7** attract, capture, deceive, engross, ensnare, enthral, graplin, grapnel, grapple, insnare, inthral, win over **8** appeal to, convince, crotchet, entangle, enthrall, fastener, grapline, interest, inthrall, intrigue, inveigle, persuade **9** grapeline, stimulate, titillate **10** inducement
alternative: 3 jab **5** clasp
and eye: 5 latch **8** fastener
attachment: 4 bait, worm **5** snell
by ~ or by crook: 7 somehow, someway **8** someways
cheap ~: 4 nail
combining form: 3 onc- **4** onch-, onci-, onco- **5** oncho- **6** ancylo-, ankylo- **7** anchylo-
deliverer: 4 fist
destination, often: 5 rough
ender: 4 nose, worm
fishing ~: 4 gaff
get off the ~: 4 save **5** spare **6** rescue
grab with a ~: 4 gaff
in French: 4 croc
leaded ~: 5 drail
let off the ~: 5 unpeg **6** exempt **7** absolve **9** exonerate
off the ~: 4 free **6** exempt **7** cleared **9** acquitted **10** exonerated, vindicated
on: 3 add, tie **4** link, yoke **5** affix, hitch **6** attach, couple, fasten **7** connect
opposite: 5 slice
partner: 3 eye **6** ladder
prepare a ~: 4 bait
starter: 3 eye, pot, sky **4** bill, fish **6** button, tenter
target: 3 jaw
trolling ~: 5 drail
up: 3 tie **4** bind, dock, join, link, pair, yoke **5** annex, hitch, unite **6** attach, cohere, couple, fasten, instal, plug in **7** combine, conjoin, connect, harness, hitch on, install **8** assemble **9** affiliate **10** go partners
up again: 5 rerig
up with: 4 join, meet **5** marry, unite **10** amalgamate
hook, __ and sinker: 4 line
__ hook: 4 meat **5** on the
__-hook: 3 sky
Hook (1991 film)
cast: Dustin Hoffman, Bob Hoskins, Julia Roberts, Robin Williams

character: 3 Pan 4 Nana, Smee 5 Peter 6 pirate 10 Tinker Bell
director: Steven Spielberg
hookah: 4 pipe 9 water pipe
Hook, Captain
alma mater: 4 Eton
nemesis: 3 Pan 4 croc 5 Peter
sidekick: 4 Smee
hooked: 7 crooked 8 aquiline, obsessed 9 dependant, dependent, possessed 10 spellbound
anatomical part: 5 uncus
on: 4 into
up: 6 allied, banded, linked, united 7 unified 8 in league 9 in cahoots, plugged in 10 affiliated, integrated
hooked __: 3 rug
Hooked on a Feeling (song)
artist: Blue Swede, B.J. Thomas
Hooker: 6 Joseph 7 John Lee
Hooke, Robert: 7 British 9 physicist
Hooke's __: 3 law
hook, line and __: 6 sinker
Hook of Holland: 4 port
Hooks: 3 Jan 5 Kevin 6 Robert
__ Hooks: 5 Use No
hook-shaped: 6 hamate
hookup: 3 tie 4 bond, link 6 scheme, system 7 circuit, liaison, linkage, linking, network 8 assembly, coupling, junction, juncture, vinculum 10 connecting, connection
hooky: 7 absence
play ~: 4 skip 6 go AWOL 7 abscond
playing ~: 4 AWOL 6 absent 7 missing
hooligan: 4 goon, hood, punk, thug 5 rogue, rowdy, tough 6 bad guy, bandit, gunsel, outlaw, rascal 7 hoodlum, mobster, ruffian 8 criminal, gangster, tough guy 10 delinquent, jackanapes
in Britain: 3 yob
hoop: 3 rim, toy 4 band, gird, loop, ring 5 skirt, wheel 6 basket, circle, wicket 7 earring 8 encircle, surround
edge: 3 rim
ender: 4 ster
group: 3 NBA 4 NCAA, WNBA
hanger: 3 net
like a ~: 4 oval 5 round 6 curved 8 circular
site: 3 ear
see also basketball
hoop __: 5 skirt
hoop-__: 4 de-do
__-Hoop: 4 Hula
Hooper: 4 Tobe 5 Harry
Hooper (1978 film)
cast: Sally Field, Burt Reynolds, Jan-Michael Vincent
director: Hal Needham
Hooperman dog: 6 Bijoux
hooper's concern: 6 barrel
hoopla: 3 ado 4 buzz, fuss, hype, stir, to-do 5 drama, furor 6 action, bustle, flurry, hubbub, lather, racket, ruckus, rumpus 7 buildup, emotion, fanfare, puffery 8 activity, ballyhoo, brouhaha, foofaraw, jamboree 9 commotion, fireworks, promotion, publicity 10 excitement, hullabaloo
Hoople: 4 Amos 5 Major
cry: 4 egad
hoopoe: 4 bird
home: 4 nest
hoops: 5 b-ball 7 baskets 10 basketball
hoopster: 5 cager
hooray: 3 olé, rah, yay 5 cheer 6 hot dog, yippee
for me: 4 ta-da 5 ta-dah
Hooray __ Hollywood: 3 for
Hooray for Hazel (1966 song)
artist: Tommy Roe
hoosegow: 3 can, jug, pen 4 cell, coop, jail, poky, stir 5 clink, pokey 6 cooler, lockup
Hoosier
see Indiana
Hoosier Poet, The: 5 Riley
Hoosiers (1986 film)
cast: Gene Hackman, Barbara Hershey, Dennis Hopper
hoot: 3 cry 4 bray, gibe, howl, jeer, jibe, kick, mock, roar, twit, yell 5 scorn, shout, whoop 6 deride, guffaw, holler, revile, scream, squawk 7 catcall, laugh at 8 particle, ridicule 10 rib-tickler, vociferate
and holler: 4 rant, rave, yell 5 go ape, storm 6 bellow 7 bluster, carry on, declaim 8 bloviate, freak out 9 raise Cain 10 hit the roof
at: 4 jeer, mock 5 scorn 6 deride
give a ~: 4 care, mind
hoot __: 3 owl
__ hoot: 5 care a, give a
Hoot: 6 Gibson
hoot and __: 6 holler
hootch
see hooch
hootchy-kootchy: 5 dance
hooter: 3 owl
Hootie and the Blowfish
song: Hold My Hand (1994)
Let Her Cry (1995)
Only Wanna Be With You (1995)
hooting: 4 loud 5 harsh, noisy 9 clamorous
Hoover: 3 dam, vac 6 J. Edgar, vacuum 7 Herbert
competitor: 5 Kirby, Oreck 6 Eureka 10 Electrolux
Hoover Dam
city near ~: 5 Vegas 8 Las Vegas
lake: 4 Mead
locale: 3 Nev. 6 Nevada
Hoover, Herbert: 9 president
alma mater: 8 Stanford
birthplace: 4 Iowa
former occupation: 8 engineer
former specialty: 6 mining
opponent: 5 Smith
V.P.: 6 Curtis
wife: 3 Lou
Hoover, J. Edgar
employee: 4 G-man
org.: 3 FBI
hooves, like some: 10 cloven. shod
hop: 4 gala, jump, leap, skip, tour, trip, verb 5 bound, dance, frisk, jaunt 6 bounce, hurdle, junket, spring 8 jump over, leap over 9 festivity
ballet ~: 9 temps levé
ender: 4 sack 6 scotch
off: 4 land 6 alight 7 descend 8 dismount
on: 5 board, catch 7 enplane, entrain
out of bed: 4 wake 5 arise, awake, get up, waken 6 awaken, wake up
over: 4 jump 5 bound 6 hurdle
starter: 3 bar, car, day 4 bell 5 hedge
to: 2 go 3 act, fly, hie, rip, run, zip 4 dart, dash, flit, move, race, rush, tear, zoom 5 scoot, speed 6 barrel, gallop, hasten, hustle, move it, rocket, scurry 7 get busy, pitch in, quicken, scamper 9 shake a leg, skedaddle 10 get a move on
up: 4 goad, spur, stir 5 rouse, waken 6 arouse, bestir, excite, foment, incite, vivify 7 enliven, inflame, inspire, provoke 8 energize, inspirit, motivate 9 galvanize, instigate, stimulate 10 invigorate
hop __: 4 to it 6 clover
hop, __ and a jump: 4 skip
hop-__-thumb: 3 o'-my
__ hop: 3 bad 4 sock 5 bunny, lindy
__-hop: 3 hip, jet, job 4 bell 5 table 6 island
Hop __: 4 Sing 5 on Pop
Hop __!: 4 to it
__ Hop: 5 At the
Hopalong Cassidy: 6 cowboy
star: William Boyd
hope: 4 goal, look, wish 5 dream 6 aspire, desire, expect, intent, resort, virtue 7 believe, longing, look for, promise, propose, purpose, thought 8 ambition, daydream, optimism, prospect, yearning 9 intention 10 anticipate, aspiration, expectancy, woolgather
companion: 5 faith 7 charity
ender: 3 ful 4 less 5 fully
for: 4 need, want, wish 5 crave 6 aspire, desire, expect 7 dream of 8 aspire to 10 anticipate
(for): 4 long, pine, wish 5 yearn
give false ~: 6 lead on
give up ~: 7 despair 9 lose heart
name meaning ~: 5 Nadia
Roman goddess of ~: 4 Spes
(to): 4 mean 6 aspire
trace of ~: 5 gleam
hope __: 5 chest
hope __ hope: 7 against
__ hope: 5 ray of
Hope: 2 A.D. 3 Bob 5 Davis, Lange 7 Anthony
costar: 6 Crosby, Lamour
Hope __: 6 Floats 7 diamond
__ Hope: 5 Ryan's 7 Chicago
Hope, Bob: 5 actor 8 comedian
film: Alias Jesse James (1952)
Beau James (1957)
The Big Broadcast of 1938 (1938)
Casanova's Big Night (1954)
The Cat and the Canary (1939)
Caught in the Draft (1941)
The Facts of Life (1960)
Fancy Pants (1950)
The Ghost Breakers (1940)
The Great Lover (1949)
The Lemon Drop Kid (1951)
Let's Face It (1943)
Monsieur Beaucaire (1946)
My Favorite Blonde (1942)
My Favorite Brunette (1947)
My Favorite Spy (1951)
Never Say Die (1939)
The Paleface (1948)
The Princess and the Pirate (1944)
Road to Bali (1952)
The Road to Hong Kong (1962)
Road to Morocco (1942)
Road to Rio (1947)
Road to Singapore (1940)
Road to Utopia (1945)
Road to Zanzibar (1941)
The Seven Little Foys (1955)
Son of Paleface (1952)
Star Spangled Rhythm (1942)
sponsor: 3 USO 8 Chrysler
spouse: 7 Dolores
Hope/Crosby
destination: 3 Rio 4 Bali 6 Utopia 7 Morocco 8 Hong Kong, Zanzibar 9 Singapore
locale: 4 road
Hope Floats (1998 film)
cast: Sandra Bullock, Harry Connick Jr., Gena Rowlands
director: Forest Whitaker
hopeful: 4 rosy 5 lucky 6 bright, likely, timely, upbeat 7 nominee, wannabe, wishful 8 aspirant, aspiring, desirous, possible, sanguine, trustful, trusting 9 applicant, candidate, confident, expectant, favorable, fortunate, inspiring, job-hunter, opportune, presuming, promising, well-timed 10 auspicious, beneficial, contestant, convenient, heartening, inspirited, optimistic, propitious
be ~: 4 rely 5 trust 6 assume, bank on 7 believe, count on, entrust, presume 8 depend on, gamble on, rely upon
hopefulness: 8 optimism
Hope Is the Thing With Feathers: 4 poem
author: Emily Dickinson
hopeless: 4 dark, grim, lost, vain 5 black, bleak, inept, no use, no-win, woful 6 abject, dismal, futile, gloomy, tragic, woeful 7 forlorn, useless 8 ill-fated, reckless, tragical, wretched 9 desperate, for naught, in despair, miserable, saddening 10 depressing, impossible, infeasible, irremedial, out of reach, unavailing, unfeasible, up the creek
case: 5 goner
Hopelessly Devoted to You (1978 song)
artist: Olivia Newton-John
hopelessness: 7 despair, sadness 9 pessimism
__ Hopes: 4 High
hopes, dash: 6 dismay, thwart 7 let down 10 disappoint, dishearten
Hop-Frog
author: Edgar Allan Poe
Hopi: 5 tribe 6 Indian 7 Amerind 8 language
prayer stick: 4 paho
sunken chamber: 4 kiva
hoping: 10 optimistic
__ hoping!: 5 Here's

Hopkin, Mary
song: Those Were the Days (1968)
Hopkins: **2** Bo **5** Johns, Telma **6** Miriam **7** Anthony **9** Frederick
Hopkins, Anthony: **3** Sir **5** actor
film: Amistad (1997)
Beowulf (2007)
The Bounty (1984)
Bram Stoker's Dracula (1992)
The Elephant Man (1980)
Fracture (2007)
Hannibal (2001)
Howards End (1992)
The Human Stain (2003)
Instinct (1999)
The Mask of Zorro (1998)
Meet Joe Black (1998)
Nixon (1995)
Red Dragon (2002)
The Remains of the Day (1993)
The Road to Wellville (1994)
Shadowlands (1993)
The Silence of the Lambs (1991, AA)
Titus (1999)
__ Hopkins Gallaudet: **6** Thomas
Hopkins, Gerard Manley: **4** poet **7** British
__ Hopkins Joyce: **5** Peggy
Hopkinsville: **4** city, town
locale: **8** Kentucky
hop-o'-my-__: **5** thumb
Hop on Pop
author: Dr. Seuss
hopped up: **4** avid **5** angry, eager, hyper **6** fervid, on edge, stormy **7** anxious, burning, furious **8** vehement
hopper: **3** bin, 'roo **4** flea, frog, toad **6** funnel, rabbit **7** coal car **8** kangaroo **9** container **10** receptacle
filler: **4** coal
starter: **4** clod, frog, leaf, tree **5** grass
__ hopper: **3** job
Hopper: **5** Hedda **6** Dennis, DeWolf, Edward **7** William
Hopper, Dennis: **5** actor
film: Backtrack (1989)
Black Widow (1987)
Blue Velvet (1986)
Colors (1988)
Easy Rider (1969)
Hoosiers (1986)
Paris Trout (1991)
Red Rock West (1993)
Rumble Fish (1983)
Speed (1994)
True Romance (1993)
Waterworld (1995)
spouse: Michelle Phillips
Hopper, Edward: **6** artist **7** painter
Hopper, Hedda trademark: **3** hat
Hoppe, Willie game: **4** pool **9** billiards
hopping
animal: **4** hare **6** rabbit **8** kangaroo
be ~ mad: **4** boil, burn, fume, rage, rave, stew **6** blow up, see red, seethe
get ~: **3** fly, hie, run, zip **4** dart, dash, move, rush, tear **5** hurry, scoot **6** bustle, hasten, hustle, scurry **7** floor it, quicken **8** step on it **9** make haste, shake a leg **10** make tracks
mad: **4** sore **5** angry, cross, huffy, irate, livid, vexed **6** ireful **7** furious **9** irritated
hops
beverage: **3** ale **4** beer **5** stout **6** porter
kiln: **4** oast
stem: **4** bine
hopscotch: **4** game **5** potsy **6** wander
Hopscotch (1980 film)
cast: Ned Beatty, Glenda Jackson, Walter Matthau, Sam Waterston
hop, skip __ jump: **4** and a
hor.
not ~: **4** vert.
hora: **5** dance
Horace: **4** Mann, poet **5** Heidt, odist, Roman **7** Greeley, Gregory, McMahon, Walpole **8** satirist
author: Pierre Corneille, George Sand
contemporary: **4** Ovid
work: Ars Poetica
Epodes
Odes
Satires
Horae Lyricae
author: Isaac Watts
Horae, one of the: **4** Dike **5** Irene **7** Eunomia
__ hora es?: **3** Qué
horal: **6** hourly
horas, 24: **3** día
Horatian __: **3** ode
Horatio: **4** Dane **5** Alger, Gates **6** Nelson
horde: **3** mob **4** army, bevy, gang, herd, host, many, mass, pack **5** crowd, crush, drove, loads, press, swarm, tribe, troop **6** legion, myriad, rabble, throng **7** legions, numbers **9** gathering, multitude
member: **3** Hun
__ Horde: **6** Golden
hordeolum: **3** sty
Horeb: **4** peak **5** mount **8** mountain
Horgan, Paul: **6** writer
horizon: **5** range, reach, scope, vista **6** extent **7** compass, purview, setting **9** viewpoint
be on the ~: **6** impend **8** forebode, threaten
fall below the ~: **3** set
on the ~: **4** afar, nigh **5** ahead **8** imminent
Horizon: **3** car **4** auto **8** Plymouth
__ Horizon: **4** Lost
horizontal: **4** flat **5** level, plane, prone **6** smooth **8** straight **9** accumbent, prostrate, recumbent
band: **6** fascia
bar: **4** rail **5** event
extent: **5** scope **7** breadth
get ~: **4** laze
opposite: **4** vert. **8** vertical
supporter: **4** beam **5** joist **6** rafter **8** crossbar **10** crosspiece
horizontally: **4** flat **6** across **10** side to side
Hormel
competitor: **6** Armour
product: **4** Spam
hormone: **4** ACTH **5** auxin, kinin **6** estrin, ligand **7** insulin
combining form: **5** kinin-
producer: **5** gland
Hormuz: **3** str. **6** strait
nation on the Strait of ~: **4** Iran
horn: **4** tuba **5** bugle, cornu, pager, phone **6** antler, beeper, claxon, cornet, honker, klaxon **7** helicon, trumpet **8** auto part, trombone **9** euphonium, telephone **10** cornucopia, sousaphone
accessory: **4** mute **6** damper
big ~: **4** tuba **9** euphonium **10** sousaphone
blow one's own ~: **4** brag, crow **5** boast, vaunt **7** talk big
combining form: **4** -corn **5** cerat-, kerat- **6** cerato-, kerato-
crescent-moon ~: **4** cusp
effect: **6** wah-wah
ender: **4** beam, bill, book, pipe, pout, tail, worm, wort **6** blende
English ~: **3** cor **4** reed
get on the ~: **4** buzz, call, dial, ring **5** phone **6** call up, dial up, ring up **7** contact **9** telephone
Greek drinking ~: **6** rhyton
harsh ~: **6** claxon, klaxon
hit the ~: **4** blow, honk
in: **3** pry **5** crash, enter **6** impose, meddle, tamper **7** intrude, obtrude **8** trespass **9** insinuate, interfere, interpose, interrupt, intervene
in Latin: **5** cornu
man with a ~: **5** Harpo **6** Al Hirt, Alpert **7** Satchmo **9** Armstrong, Harpo Marx
nautical: **6** typhon
orchestra ~: **4** alto
play the ~: **4** blow, toot
rims: **7** glasses **8** cheaters **10** spectacles
sound: **4** beep, honk
sound the ~: **4** beep, blow, honk, toot
starter: **3** big, fog, ink, leg, sax, tin **4** buck, bull, long, shoe **5** green, prong, short, stink
horn-__ glasses: **6** rimmed
__ horn: **3** air **4** alto, bass, bull, long, post, ram's **5** tenor **6** French, powder, saddle **7** English
__ Horn: **4** Cape **6** Golden, Trader
hornbeam: **4** tree **5** shrub
relative: **5** alder, birch, hazel
hornbill: **4** bird
home: **4** nest
hornblende: **7** mineral
Hornblower, Horatio: **7** captain
milieu: **3** sea **5** ocean
ship: **5** Lydia
wife: **5** Maria
Horne: **4** Lena **5** James **7** Marilyn
solo: **4** aria
horned __: **3** owl **4** frog, toad
Horned Frogs' sch.: **3** TCU
horned giraffe in heraldry: **10** camelopard
Horne, Lena: **6** singer
film: Cabin in the Sky (1943)
Stormy Weather (1943)
Horne, Marilyn: **4** diva **5** mezzo **6** singer **7** soprano
specialty: **4** aria **5** opera
Horner: **3** Bob **4** Jack **5** James
Horner, Jack: **5** eater
last words: **3** am I
treat: **3** pie
hornet: **3** bug **4** pest, wasp **6** insect **7** stinger
home: **4** nest
kin: **4** wasp
Hornet: **3** AMC, car **4** auto **6** Hudson
Hornets: **4** five, team
home: **9** Charlotte
org.: **3** NBA
rival: *see* NBA team
sport: **10** basketball
hornet's nest: **3** ado, fix **4** mess, stir **5** furor **6** clamor, pickle, rumpus, scrape, tumult, uproar **7** travail, trouble, turmoil **8** quagmire, quandary
__ Hornet, The: **5** Green
Horney: **5** Karen
hornless: **7** acerous
cattle: **5** muley **6** mulley
horn of __: **6** plenty
hornpipe: **4** wind **5** dance, music **6** alboka **8** clarinet
horn-rims: **7** glasses **8** cheaters **10** eyeglasses
horns
Greek drinking ~: **5** rhyta
lock ~: **4** spar **5** argue, clash **6** debate **7** compete, contend, quarrel, wrangle **8** conflict, struggle **9** have words, square off
Hornsby: **5** Bruce **6** Rogers
nickname: **5** Rajah
Hornsby and the Range, Bruce
song: Mandolin Rain (1987)
The Valley Road (1988)
The Way It Is (1986)
hornswoggle: **3** con **4** dupe, fool, gull, have, rook, snow **5** cheat **6** suck in, take in **7** swindle **8** hoodwink **9** bamboozle
Hornung, Paul
sport: **8** football
horologist: **7** jeweler **10** watchmaker
horology: **7** science
study: **4** time
horoscope: **5** chart **8** forecast **10** prediction
do a ~: **4** cast
__ horoscope: **5** natal
Horovitz: **4** Adam
Horovitz, Israel: **10** playwright
Horowitz, Vladimir: **7** pianist
horrendous
see awful
horrible: **4** dark, dire, foul, grim, poor, ugly, vile **5** awful, cruel, dread, gross, lousy, lurid, nasty, woful **6** crumby, crummy, dismal, grisly, odious, rotten, woeful **7** accurst, baleful, baneful, beastly, doleful, dreaded, fearful, ghastly, heinous, hellish, hideous, macaber, macabre, satanic, squalid, ungodly **8** accursed, dreadful, God-awful, grievous, gruesome, inferior, shameful, shocking, stinking, terrible, terrific, wretched **9** abhorrent, appalling, atrocious, defective, execrable, frightful, insidious, loathsome, miserable, monstrous, nefarious, obnoxious, offensive, repellent, revolting, satanical **10** abominable, despicable, detestable, disastrous, formidable, horrendous, outrageous, petrifying, scandalous, terrifying, unpleasant

horrid: 4 dire, evil, foul, grim, ugly, vile 5 awful, nasty, yucky 6 grisly, morbid, odious 7 ghastly, hateful, hideous, noisome, satanic, squalid, ungodly, vicious 8 dreadful, gruesome, terrible 9 appalling, atrocious, frightful, offensive, repugnant, revolting, satanical, unsightly 10 abominable, detestable, disgusting, petrifying, unpleasant

horrific: 4 dire 5 awful, weird 7 fearful 8 dreadful, gruesome, shocking, terrific 9 appalling, execrable 10 formidable

horrified: 6 aghast

horrify: 5 alarm, appal, chill, scare, shake, shock 6 appall, offend, revolt 7 disgust, petrify, terrify 8 affright, frighten, unstring 9 terrorize 10 scandalize, scare stiff

horrifying: 4 gory 5 lurid, scary 6 grisly 7 fearful, ghastly, heinous, hideous 8 gruesome, shocking, terrible 9 appalling, atrocious, monstrous 10 deplorable, petrifying

horripilating: 4 eery 5 eerie, scary 6 creepy, spooky 7 bizarre, macabre, strange, uncanny 8 haunting 9 grotesque

Horrocks: 4 Jane

horror: 4 fear 5 alarm, dread 6 fright, phobia, terror 7 monster 8 aversion, enormity 9 revulsion, trepidity 10 abhorrence, repugnance
- **cause ~:** 5 appal 6 appall 7 horrify, terrify 8 frighten 9 terrorize
- **exclamation:** 2 oy 3 ack, ick, ugh 4 yuck 5 yecch
- **like ~ films:** 4 eery, gory 5 eerie

horror ___: 4 film 5 movie, story

Horrors!: 3 ugh 4 oh my, oh no

horror-struck: 6 aghast, scared 7 shocked, stunned 8 appalled 10 speechless

hors d'___: 4 état 6 oeuvre

hors de ___: 6 combat

hors d'oeuvre: 4 whet 5 snack, taste 6 canapé, caviar 7 caviare 9 appetizer
- **garnish:** 5 caper
- **Hawaiian ~:** 4 pupu
- **spread:** 4 pâté 5 liver

horse: 3 bay, cob, dun, nag, pet 4 Arab, barb, colt, foal, hack, jade, mare, moke, plug, pony, roan 5 bronc, filly, mount, neddy, pacer, paint, pinto, steed 6 animal, bronco, cayuse, dapple, dobbin, equine, gee-gee, hunter, jumper, mammal, Morgan, mudder, sorrel, tarpan 7 Arabian, bobtail, broncho, charger, courser, cow pony, gelding, hackney, mustang, palfrey, piebald, trooper, trotter 8 bangtail, buckskin, chestnut, claybank, destrier, eohippus, galloper, palomino, polo pony, Shetland, skewbald, stallion 9 appaloosa, broodmare, Percheron 10 chess piece, Clydesdale, Indian pony, Lippizaner
- **agile ~:** 7 cow pony
- **ailment:** 5 colic
- **ancestor:** 8 eohippus
- **and wagon:** 3 rig
- **ankle:** 4 hock
- **Arabian-descended ~:** 7 mustang
- **Arabian-related ~:** 4 barb
- **armor:** 5 barde
- **around:** 4 joke, play 5 act up, caper 6 cavort, gambol
- **Australian ~:** 4 moke 5 neddy, waler
- **Austrian ~:** 10 Lippizaner
- **back the wrong ~:** 4 fail, lose
- **bi-colored ~:** 7 piebald 8 skewbald
- **blanket:** 5 manta
- **brake:** 4 rein
- **carriage ~:** 7 hackney
- **cavalry ~:** 7 charger, trooper
- **charley ~:** 4 kink 5 cramp, crick, spasm
- **chestnut:** 6 conker
- **clip a ~ mane:** 5 roach
- **color:** 3 bay, dun 5 pinto 8 chestnut
- **combining form:** 4 hipp- 5 hippo- 6 -hippus
- **command:** 3 gee, haw 4 whoa 6 giddap 7 giddyap, giddyup
- **could eat a ~:** 7 starved 8 ravenous, starving
- **dark ~:** 8 opponent, underdog 9 candidate 10 competitor, contestant
- **doctor:** 3 DVM, vet
- **draft ~:** 9 Percheron 10 Clydesdale
- **dressage ~:** 10 Lippizaner
- **eat like a ~:** 5 chomp, gorge 10 gormandize
- **ender:** 3 fly, man, men 4 back, hair, hide, mint, play, race, shoe, tail, weed, whip 5 flesh, laugh, leech, power, woman, women 6 racing, radish 8 feathers
- **farm ~:** 6 dobbin
- **father:** 4 sire, stud
- **female:** 3 dam 4 mare 5 filly
- **foot:** 4 hoof
- **fresh team of ~s:** 5 relay
- **gear:** 3 bit 4 rein 6 bridle, halter, saddle
- **genus:** 5 equus
- **get on a ~:** 4 ride 6 gallop, travel 7 journey
- **golden coat ~:** 8 palomino
- **grayish-brown ~:** 3 dun
- **groom a ~:** 5 curry
- **group of ~s:** 4 span, team
- **guiding rope:** 5 longe
- **hair:** 4 mane
- **handicap:** 6 impost
- **handler:** 5 groom
- **harness racing ~:** 5 pacer 7 trotter
- **height measure:** 4 hand
- **high-spirited ~:** 5 steed
- **hock:** 5 ankle
- **home:** 4 barn 6 corral, stable
- **horse sport:** 4 polo 6 racing
- **Indian ~:** 6 cayuse
- **in horse racing:** 3 dam 4 mare, sire 5 filly, pacer 6 maiden, mudder 7 trotter
- **jump:** 6 curvet
- **jumping ~:** 6 hunter
- **laugh:** 4 howl, roar 6 guffaw
- **left, to a ~:** 3 haw
- **leg part:** 6 gaskin
- **like a ~:** 5 maned 6 hoofed
- **male ~:** 8 stallion
- **marking:** 5 blaze
- **meal:** 3 hay 4 feed, oats 6 fodder
- **noise:** 4 clop 5 neigh, snort 6 whinny
- **of a different color:** 3 new 5 novel
- **old ~:** 3 nag 4 hack, jade, moke, plug
- **on one's high ~:** 7 haughty 8 up in arms
- **opera:** 5 drama, oater
- **pace:** 4 gait, lope, pace, trot 6 canter, gallop
- **part of a ~ collar:** 4 hame
- **player hangout:** 3 OTB 5 track
- **race:** 4 pace, trot 5 derby
- **ranch ~:** 7 cow pony
- **range ~:** 6 cayuse
- **reddish-brown ~:** 3 bay 6 sorrel 8 chestnut
- **relative:** *see* equine
- **restrainer:** 5 trave
- **rider:** 6 jockey 10 equestrian
- **right, to a ~:** 3 gee
- **rump:** 5 croup
- **saddle ~:** 4 hack, pony 5 mount, steed 7 hackney, palfrey 9 Appaloosa
- **sense:** 5 savvy 6 acumen, brains, reason, wisdom 7 insight 8 judgment, prudence, sagacity 9 ingenuity, reasoning, sharpness 10 astuteness, perception, shrewdness
- **short-legged ~:** 3 cob
- **small ~:** 4 pony 8 polo pony 10 Indian pony
- **soldier:** 6 lancer
- **soldiers:** 7 cavalry
- **sometimes:** 5 loper
- **spotted ~:** 5 paint, pinto 6 dapple
- **starter:** 3 saw, sea, war 4 cock, fire, pack, race, stud, work 5 hobby 7 clothes
- **steppes ~:** 6 tarpan
- **stocky ~:** 3 cob
- **stopper:** 4 whoa
- **stubborn ~:** 6 balker
- **swift ~:** 4 Arab, barb 7 Arabian, courser
- **tend the ~:** 5 brush, groom
- **thick-set ~:** 3 cob
- **tie a ~:** 5 hitch 6 tether
- **tooth:** 4 tush
- **trade:** 4 deal 9 negotiate
- **trainer's aid:** 4 whip
- **training:** 6 manège
- **TV talking ~:** 4 Mr. Ed
- **where ~ races start:** 4 gate
- **white mane ~:** 8 palomino
- **wild ~:** 5 bronc 6 bronco, brumby, ladino, tarpan 7 broncho, mustang
- **young:** 4 colt, foal 5 filly
- ***see also*** equine, horses and riders

horse ___: 3 fly 4 race, show 5 laugh, opera, sense, trade 6 around, collar, racing, trader

horse ___ different color: 3 of a

___ horse: 3 sea 4 cart, dark, high, iron 5 coach, light 6 pommel, saddle, Trojan 7 Arabian, charley, quarter, rocking, walking

___ horse!: 4 Get a

___ Horse: 5 Crazy

horse and ___: 4 cart 5 buggy

horse-and-buggy: 3 era 5 passé 8 obsolete, outmoded
- **users:** 5 Amish

___ horseback: 5 man on

horse chestnut tree: 7 buckeye

horse-donkey offspring: 5 hinny

horse-drawn
- **carriage:** 6 calash, fiacre, hansom 7 caleche
- **vehicle of India:** 5 tonga

horsefeathers
- *see* baloney

Horsefeathers!: 3 bah 5 nerts, nertz, pshaw

Horse Feathers (1932 film)
- **cast:** Chico Marx, Groucho Marx, Harpo Marx, Zeppo Marx, Thelma Todd

___-Horse Harry Lee: 5 Light

Horsehead: 6 Nebula

horsehide: 4 ball 8 baseball

horselaugh: 6 guffaw

horseless carriage: 3 car 4 auto 7 vehicle 10 automobile

horseman: 5 groom, rider 6 cowboy, gaucho, hussar, jockey, knight, lancer, ostler 7 Cossack, cowgirl, dragoon, equerry, hostler 8 buckaroo, cavalier 10 cavalryman, equestrian
- **Hungarian ~:** 6 hussar
- **Mexican ~:** 6 charro

Horseman of the Apocalypse: 3 War 5 Death 6 Famine 10 Pestilence

Horseman Pass By
- **author:** Larry McMurtry

horsemen, army: 3 cav. 7 cavalry

horsemint: 5 plant 6 flower

horse of a different ___: 5 color

horseplay: 3 fun 5 prank, sport 6 antics, capers, pranks 7 fooling, hijinks 8 clowning
- **like ~:** 5 rowdy

horsepower: 5 drive, force, power, punch, vigor 6 effort, energy, muscle 7 impetus, potency, voltage 8 dynamism, strength 9 toughness
- **booster:** 5 turbo
- **coiner:** 4 Watt
- **fraction:** 4 watt

horse-pulled vehicle: 4 cart, dray 5 buggy 8 carriage

horse race: 4 pace 5 Derby 7 Belmont 9 Preakness

horse racing: 5 sport
- **announcer:** 6 caller
- **area:** 4 rail 5 track 7 paddock
- **bet:** 4 show 5 place 6 exacta, parlay 8 perfecta, quinella, trifecta
- **devotee:** 8 railbird
- **horse:** 3 dam 4 mare, sire 5 filly, pacer 6 maiden, mudder 7 trotter
- **measure:** 4 mile 6 length 7 furlong
- **term:** 3 dam, win 4 mare, nose, odds, show, sire, tout, turf 5 filly, groom, pacer, place, purse, silks, sulky 6 caller, exacta, length, maiden, mudder, odds-on, parlay, sloppy 7 furlong, inquiry, paddock, scratch,

stretch, trotter **8** blinkers, dead heat, long shot, perfecta, post time, quinella, railbird, trifecta
tie: 8 dead heat
winnings: 5 purse
worker: 5 groom
horseradish: 5 spice **6** relish **9** condiment
horses: 5 stock **9** livestock
group of ~: 4 team
hold one's ~: 4 wait
play the ~: 3 bet
Horses and Men
author: Sherwood Anderson
horses and riders
Achilles: 7 Xanthus
Alexander the Great: 10 Bucephalus
Autry, Gene: 8 Champion
Bellerophon: 7 Pegasus
Ben-Hur: 5 Rigel **6** Altair **7** Antares **9** Aldebaran
Caligula: 9 Incitatus
Cisco Kid: 6 Diablo
Custer, George: 8 Comanche
Evans, Dale: 10 Buttermilk
Grant, Ulysses S.: 10 Cincinnati
Lee, Robert E.: 9 Traveller
Lone Ranger: 6 Silver
Mix, Tom: 4 Tony
Muhammad: 7 Alborak
Napoleon: 7 Marengo
Odin: 8 Sleipner, Sleipnir
Quixote, Don: 9 Rocinante, Rosinante
Rogers, Roy: 7 Trigger
Rogers, Will: 8 Soapsuds
Sigurd: 5 Grani
Tonto: 5 Scout
Turpin, Dick: 9 Black Bess
Wellington, Duke of: 10 Copenhagen
horseshoe: 5 charm **6** amulet
place: 4 hoof
projection: 4 calk
sound: 4 clop
horseshoe ___: 4 crab **6** magnet
___ Horseshoe: 6 Golden
Horseshoe Falls
locale: 6 Canada **7** Ontario
horseshoer: 5 smith **7** farrier **10** blacksmith
horseshoes: 4 game **5** sport
game like ~: 6 quoits
play ~: 4 toss
score: 6 leaner, ringer
sound: 5 clang
horseshoe-shaped fastener: 5 U-bolt
horse's mouth: 6 expert, origin, source **9** authority **10** originator
Horse's Mouth, The
author: Joyce Cary
horse's neck: 5 drink **8** beverage, cocktail
ingredient: 6 whisky **9** ginger ale, lemon peel
horsetail: 4 rush **5** plant
___-horse town: 3 one
horse-trade: 4 deal **6** haggle
horsewhip: 4 flog, lash, whip **5** flail **7** scourge **10** flagellate
Horse Whisperer, The: 4 film **5** novel
author: Nicholas Evans
cast: Sam Neill, Robert Redford, Kristin Scott Thomas, Dianne Wiest
director: Robert Redford
Horse With No Name, A (1972 song)
artist: America
horsewoman: 5 rider **6** jockey
Horsley: 3 Lee
Horst: 5 Louis **7** Störmer **8** Buchholz
horsy: 6 equine
Hortense: 8 Calisher
horticultural art: 6 bonsai
horticulture: 6 botany **7** science
study: 6 fruits, plants **7** gardens **10** vegetables
horticulturist: 8 gardener
mixture: 5 mulch
topic: 6 botany
Horton: 5 Foote, Peter, Smith **6** Johnny, Robert **9** Who hearer
creator: Dr. Seuss
Horton Hatches the Egg
author: Dr. Seuss
Horton Hears a Who
author: Dr. Seuss
Horton Hears a Who! (2008 film)
voice cast: Carol Burnett, Steve Carell, Jim Carrey
Horton, Johnny
song: The Battle of New Orleans (1959)
North to Alaska (1960)
Sink the Bismarck (1960)
Horus: 3 god **8** Egyptian
parent: 4 Isis **6** Osiris
Horvath, Odon von: 6 German **10** playwright
Hosain, Attia: 6 Indian, writer
hosanna: 4 hymn, laud, pean **5** paean **6** praise **8** hallejah **10** exaltation, hallelujah
hose: 4 pipe, tube **5** cheat, socks, water **6** drench, nylons, siphon, syphon, tights, tubing **7** anklets, argyles, legwear, mislead, wet down **8** flimflam, footwear, lingerie, wash down **9** stockings
plastic: 3 PVC
use a ~: 3 wet **4** wash **5** douse, dowse, spray, water
see also hosiery
hose ___: 4 down
___ hose: 4 fire **5** panty
Hosea: 4 book **7** Prophet
follower: 4 Joel
in the Douay Bible: 4 Osee
preceder: 6 Daniel
wife: 5 Gomer
hosiery: 4 sock, tabi **5** socks **6** anklet, argyle, bootee, bootie, nylons **7** anklets, footlet, woolens **8** crew sock, fishnets, knee-high, knee-sock, stocking, tube sock **9** ankle sock, kneehighs, stockings **10** bobbysocks, thigh-highs
brand: 4 Peds **5** L'eggs
fabric: 5 lisle, nylon
filler: 3 leg **4** foot
holder: 6 garter
item: 6 anklet
Japanese ~: 4 tabi
like some ~: 5 meshy, sheer
measure: 6 denier
mishap: 3 run **4** kink, snag
part: 3 toe **4** heel
shade: 4 ecru, nude **5** taupe
hosing: 5 abuse **6** con job **7** calumny **8** reproach **10** debasement, impugnment
Hoskins, Bob: 5 actor
film: Cousin Bette (1998)
Hook (1991)
Mermaids (1990)
Nixon (1995)
Sweet Liberty (1986)
Who Framed Roger Rabbit (1988)
role: 4 Smee
Hosni: 7 Mubarak
hosp.
see hospital
hospice: 5 lodge **6** hostel, imaret **9** infirmary
hospitable: 4 kind, open, warm **6** genial, kindly, social **7** cordial **8** amenable, amicable, friendly, generous, gracious, obliging, sociable **9** bountiful, convivial, courteous, receptive, welcoming **10** accessible, charitable, gregarious, neighborly, open-minded, responsive
be ~: 4 host **5** ask in, ask up **6** invite
not ~: 5 aloof, stony **6** chilly, frosty **7** hostile **10** unfriendly
hospital: 6 clinic **7** sick bay **9** infirmary **10** sanatorium
amt.: 2 cc.
Brit. ~ coverage: 3 NHI
cart: 6 gurney
delivery: 4 baby
device: 2 IV
do a animal ~ job: 4 spay
employee: 2 dr., MD, RN **3** EMT, LPN **5** nurse **6** intern **7** interne, orderly **8** resident
extension: 4 wing
facility: 2 ER, IC, OR **3** CCU, ICU, MRI **4** ward **5** pre-op
furniture: 3 bed
popular ~ name: 5 Mercy
reference: 3 PDR **5** chart
routine: 6 rounds
scourge: 5 staph
sign: 5 quiet
supply: 4 sera **5** blood, drugs, serum **8** medicine
test: 3 ECG, EEG, EKG
wear: 4 gown
hospital ___: 3 bed **6** corner
___ hospital: 5 field
___ Hospital: 7 General
hospital-cornered: 4 neat
hospitality: 5 cheer **6** warmth **7** welcome **8** kindness
recipient: 5 guest
show one's ~: 9 entertain
hospitality ___: 4 room **5** suite
hospitalization: 9 treatment
hospitalize: 5 lay up **7** confine
Hospital Sketches
author: Louisa May Alcott
Hospital, The (1971 film)
cast: Diana Rigg, George C. Scott
hoss: 5 mount **6** cayuse
Hoss: 9 Radbourne **10** Cartwright
brother: 3 Joe **4** Adam **9** Little Joe
father: 3 Ben
host: 2 MC **3** mob **4** army, mass, raft, slew **5** array, bunch, cater, crowd, emcee, flock, horde, ocean, owner, press, swarm, troop **6** anchor, keeper, legion, myriad, throng **7** manager, numbers, receive **8** hotelier **9** entertain, innkeeper, moderator, multitude, profusion **10** proprietor
a party: 5 throw
counterpart: 5 guest
ender: 3 age, ess
generous ~: 5 sater
music-show ~: 2 DJ, VJ **6** deejay, veejay
of: 6 divers, myriad, umteen, untold **7** copious, profuse, umpteen **8** abundant, manifold, numerous, umpsteen **9** bountiful, countless, quite a few
play ~: 5 ask in, emcee, see in, treat **9** entertain
preference: 5 A-list
request: 4 RSVP
roast ~: 2 MC **5** emcee, Friar
hostage: 4 gage, pawn **6** surety **7** captive **8** internee, leverage, prisoner, security
taker: 6 captor
take ~s: 6 abduct
Hostage, The
author: Brendan Behan
hostel: 3 inn **4** khan **5** hotel, lodge **6** bethel **7** hospice, lodging, shelter **8** lodgment **10** guesthouse
Turkish ~: 6 imaret
___ hostel: 5 elder, youth
hosteler: 9 innkeeper
hostelry: 3 inn **5** hotel, lodge **6** tavern **7** lodging
hostess
bar ~: 5 B-girl
Japanese ~: 6 geisha
Washington ~: 5 Mesta
Hostess with the Mostes': 5 Mesta
hostile: 3 icy, ill **4** cold, cool, hard, mean **5** angry, catty, chill, enemy, nasty, stony, surly **6** averse, bitter, chilly, malign, ornery, stoney, sullen **7** adverse, glacial, hateful, hawkish, martial, ominous, opposed, scrappy, warlike **8** clashing, contrary, fighting, inimical, militant, opposing, spiteful, venomous, viperous, virulent **9** bellicose, malicious, oppugnant, rancorous, resentful, truculent, vitriolic, withdrawn **10** forbidding, jingoistic, malevolent, pugnacious, unamicable, unfriendly, unsociable
be ~ to: 4 hate **5** abhor **6** detest, loathe
in a ~ manner: 5 icily
look: 5 glare
make ~: 9 disaffect **10** antagonize
one: 3 foe **5** enemy
reaction: 4 flak **5** flack **6** outcry **7** dissent, protest **9** criticism
to: 3 con **6** down on **8** opposing **10** at odds with
hostilities: 3 war **6** unrest **7** warfare **8** fighting
begin ~: 5 set on, storm **6** attack, invade, strike **7** set upon
break in ~: 5 truce **9** cease-fire
engaged in ~: 5 at war
hostility: 3 ire, war **4** feud, hate **5** anger, fight, spite, venom **6** animus, battle, enmity, hatred, malice, rancor, spleen **7** discord, dislike, ill will, tension **8** aversion, bad blood, conflict, distaste, friction, meanness **9** animosity, antipathy, nastiness, virulence

10 abhorrence, aggression, antagonism, bitterness, contention, opposition, resentment
feel ~ toward: 4 hate 5 scorn 6 detest, loathe 7 deplore, despise, dislike 8 execrate 9 abominate
hostler: 8 horseman
Host, vessel containing the: 3 pix, pyx
hot: 3 hip, mad, red 4 ired, live, sore, warm 5 angry, cross, eager, fiery, huffy, irate, livid, lucky, riled, sharp, spicy, wroth, zesty 6 ardent, baking, erotic, fervid, fuming, heated, ireful, on fire, peeved, piping, piqued, raging, raving, spicey, steamy, stolen, stormy, strong, sultry, sweaty, toasty, torrid, touchy, trendy, tropic 7 blazing, boiling, burning, enraged, excited, faddish, febrile, fervent, flaming, flaring, furious, intense, in vogue, on a roll, peppery, piquant, popular, pungent, ranting, searing, sensual, smoking, steamed, summery, sweltry, thermal, violent, zealous 8 agitated, broiling, choleric, feverish, incensed, in demand, inflamed, maddened, outraged, ovenlike, parching, roasting, scalding, sizzling, spirited, steaming, tropical, up-to-date, valuable, vehement, wrathful 9 au courant, calescent, impetuous, indignant, irascible, irritable, irritated, lubricous, on a streak, resentful, scorching, splenetic 10 all the rage, blistering, equatorial, freaked out, infuriated, lascivious, marketable, much-wanted, passionate, sweltering
air: ***see*** baloney
and heavy: 6 ardent
and humid: 5 muggy 6 steamy, sultry, sweaty
baseball's ~ corner: 5 third
blow ~ and cold: 4 sway, vary 5 hedge, shift, waver 6 falter 9 fluctuate, vacillate
blowing ~ and cold: 6 fickle 7 erratic, flighty, mutable 8 variable, volatile 9 impulsive, mercurial, undecided 10 capricious, changeable, inconstant
combining form: 6 thermo-
crime: 5 arson
cuisine: 4 Thai 5 Hunan
diggety: 3 wow 5 huzza, oh boy, super 6 hoorah, hooray, hurrah, hurray, huzzah
drink: 3 tea 4 grog 5 cocoa, glogg, mocha, toddy 6 coffee
ender: 3 bed, box, dog 4 cake, foot, head, line, shot, spot 5 house 6 headed
foot: 3 gag 5 prank 8 mischief
(for): 4 game 5 ready
full of ~ air: 5 gassy, windy, wrong 9 talkative
goods: 4 loot 6 spoils 7 plunder
in ~ water: 7 trapped, up a tree 9 on the spot 10 on the ropes
lead: 3 tip 4 clew, clue
not ~: 4 cold, mild, warm 5 tepid 8 lukewarm, moderate, pleasant 9 temperate
not so ~: 4 cool, mild, sick, so-so 5 tepid
off the press: 3 fad, new 5 fresh 6 recent
on: 9 wild about
one: 4 riot 6 scream
pepper: 3 aji 5 chile, chili 6 chilli
pot: 4 stew
potato: 6 hazard
property: 8 valuable
red ~: 5 spicy, zesty 7 peppery, piquant, pungent 8 seasoned
rocks: 3 ice 4 lava 5 magma 6 basalt, pumice, scoria 8 obsidian
run ~ and cold: 4 yo-yo 5 hedge 6 dither, seesaw, waffle, wobble 8 straddle 9 hem and haw, pussyfoot, vacillate
sauce: 4 mole 7 Tabasco
sauce quality: 4 tang, zest, zing 5 punch, spice
spot: 3 spa, sun 4 hell, kiln, oven 5 sauna 6 boiler, desert
spring: 3 spa 4 bath 6 geyser, resort
stuff: 4 fire, lava 5 anger, chile, chili, salsa 6 chilli
time: 4 July 6 August, Jul. Aug., summer 7 dog days
tip: 4 clue, lead
toddy spice: 5 clove
topic: 5 issue 7 problem 8 argument
to trot: 4 avid 5 eager 6 gung ho 7 anxious, excited 10 raring to go
trend: 3 fad 4 rage 5 craze, mania, vogue 7 in thing
tub: 3 spa 5 sauna 7 Jacuzzi 9 whirlpool
under the collar: 4 sore 5 angry, het up, irate, riled, upset
water: 3 fix 4 bind 6 pickle 7 problem, trouble 9 deep water 10 difficulty
hot ___: 3 air, bed, cap, dog, pot, rod, tea, tub, war 4 cake, comb, lick, line, pack, pink, seat, shoe, shot, spot, tear, type, well 5 light, metal, money, pants, plate, sauce, stuff, toddy, water 6 button, corner, pepper, potato, rodder, spring, switch, tamale
hot ___ bun: 5 cross
hot ___ oven: 4 as an
hot ___ pistol: 3 as a
hot ___ sundae: 5 fudge
hot ___ the collar: 5 under
hot ___ trail: 5 on the
hot-___: 4 draw, roll, wire, work 6 button, dogger 7 blooded
hot-___ bottle: 5 water
hot-___ league: 5 stove
___ hot: 6 piping
___-hot: 3 red 5 white
Hot ___!: 5 Shots 7 Diggity
Hot ___ Houlihan: 4 Lips
Hot ___ in the Summertime: 3 Fun
Hot ___ National Park: 7 Springs
Hot ___, The: 4 Rock
hot-air ballooning: 5 sport
___, Hot and Blue!: 3 Red
hot-and-cold: 9 impulsive 10 indecisive, irresolute
___ hot and cold: 4 blow
hot and sour: 4 soup
hot as a ___: 6 pistol
hotbed: 3 den 4 nest 5 nidus 6 cradle 7 nursery
hot-blooded: 5 fiery, lusty 6 ardent, feisty, fervid, torrid 7 fervent, lustful 8 spirited 9 emotional, excitable, impetuous, impulsive 10 passionate
Hot Blooded (1978 song)
artist: Foreigner
Hot Boyz (1999 song)
artist: Eve, Missy Elliott, Nas, Q-tip
hot buttered ___: 3 rum
hotcake: 5 bread 8 flapjack
place: 4 IHOP
Hot Child in the City (1978 song)
artist: Nick Gilder
___ Hot Chili Peppers: 3 Red
Hotchner: 2 A.E.
hot chocolate: 8 beverage
hot cross bun: 6 pastry
time: 4 Lent
Hot cross buns, ___ penny, two...: 4 one a
Hot Diggity (1956 song)
artist: Perry Como
hot dog: 3 ham 4 brag, meat 5 Coney, frank, huzza, Kahn's, weeny 6 Armour, hoorah, hooray, hurrah, hurray, huzzah, weenie, wiener 7 showoff 8 Ball Park, stuntman 9 daredevil 10 grandstand, Oscar Mayer
covering: 4 skin 6 casing
expand, as a ~ dog: 5 plump
length, perhaps: 4 foot
partner: 3 bun 5 chile, chili, kraut, works 6 catsup, chilli, onions, relish 7 ketchup, mustard 10 sauerkraut
place: 5 stand 8 ballpark
hotel: 3 inn 4 Omni, Ritz 5 Hyatt, lodge, Penta, Plaza, Savoy 6 Hilton, hostel, resort, tavern, Westin 7 auberge, fleabag, lodging, pension, Wyndham 8 hostelry, lodgment, Marriott, Radisson, Sheraton 9 flophouse, roadhouse 10 DoubleTree 11 Crowne Plaza, Four Seasons
canine ~: 5 pound 6 kennel 7 shelter 8 doghouse
employee: 4 maid 5 valet 7 bellhop, bellman 9 concierge
ender: 3 ier 6 keeper
feature: 2 TV 3 bed, gym 4 safe 5 Bible, lobby, TV set 6 atrium, canopy 7 dresser 10 night table
features: 5 atria
floating ~: 4 ship 5 liner 10 cruise ship
group: 5 chain
Las Vegas ~: 3 MGM 7 Aladdin
lobby locale: 4 desk
London ~: 5 Savoy
New York City ~: 5 Plaza
offering: 3 bed 5 rooms, suite
Paris ~: 4 Ritz
patron: 5 guest 6 lodger
pest: 6 bedbug
price: 4 rate 8 rack rate
restriction: 6 no pets
seedy ~: 7 fleabag 9 flophouse
sign: 3 Ice 4 Exit
supply: 5 linen 6 sheets 7 bedding
unit: 2 rm. 4 room
visit: 4 rest, stay 7 holiday, respite, sojourn 8 stopover, vacation
youth ~: 6 hostel
Hotel (ABC drama)
cast: James Brolin (Peter McDermott)
Connie Sellecca (Christine Francis)
Hotel ___ Hampshire, The: 3 New
___ Hotel: 5 Grand
Hôtel ___ Invalides: 3 des
Hotel California (1977 song)
artist: Eagles
hôtel de ___: 5 ville
Hotel Happiness (1962 song)
artist: Brook Benton
hotelier: 4 host 8 landlord 9 innkeeper
Hotel New Hampshire, The: 4 film 5 novel
author: John Irving
cast: Beau Bridges, Jodie Foster, Rob Lowe
hotfoot: 4 hike, walk 5 prank
it: 3 fly, hie, rip, run, zip 4 bolt, dart, dash, flee, flit, race, rush, tear, zoom 5 scoot, speed 6 barrel, gallop, hasten, hustle, rocket, scurry 7 quicken, scamper 9 shake a leg, skedaddle 10 get a move on
reaction: 4 yeow
hot fudge ___: 6 sundae
Hot Fun in the Summertime (1969 song)
artist: Sly and the Family Stone
hothead: 8 inflamer 9 demagogue, firebrand
hotheaded: 4 rash, wild 5 brash, fiery, irate 6 madcap, touchy 7 violent 8 reckless, volatile 9 excitable, unadvised 10 ill-advised, incautious, passionate
hotheadedness: 6 temper
Hot l Baltimore, The
author: Lanford Wilson
Hot Legs (1978 song)
artist: Rod Stewart
hot-line situation: 6 crisis
Hot Lips: 5 nurse 8 Houlihan
portrayer: 4 Swit 9 Kellerman
Hot Money
author: Dick Francis
hot on the ___: 5 trail
hot pepper: 5 spice
Hotpoint: 9 appliance
alternative: ***see*** appliance
hot pot: 4 stew
Hot Rock, The (1972 film)
cast: Robert Redford, George Segal
hot rod: 3 car 4 auto, rush 5 motor, racer, speed 8 dragster 9 racing car 10 speed demon
part: 4 carb
propellant: 5 nitro
hotshot: 3 ace, VIP, wiz 4 smug, whiz 5 adept, biggy, comer 6 biggie, bigwig, dynamo, expert, wizard 7 old hand 8 cocksure, virtuoso 9 celebrity, personage

Hot Shots! (1991 film)
cast: Cary Elwes, Valeria Golino, Charlie Sheen
Hot Springs: 3 spa **4** city, park, town
locale: 3 Ark. **8** Arkansas
hotspur: 9 daredevil
hot-stove __: 6 league
Hot Stuff (1979 song)
artist: Donna Summer
__ Hot Summer, The: 4 Long
hotsy-totsy
see wonderful
hot-tempered: 5 angry, cross, fiery, huffy, irate, surly, testy **6** crusty, ornery, touchy **7** bearish, grouchy, peevish, peppery **8** choleric, liverish, snappish **9** irascible, irritable, querulous, splenetic **10** ill-humored
Hottentot tongue: 4 Nama
hot to __: 4 trot
__ hot to handle: 3 too
hot under the __: 6 collar
hot-water __: 6 bottle
hot-weather
quencher: 3 ade
stat: 3 THI
wear: 6 shorts **7** cut-offs **8** bermudas
Houdini: 5 Harry
Houdini (1953 film)
cast: Tony Curtis, Janet Leigh
Houk: 5 Ralph
Houlihan: 5 major, nurse **7** Hot Lips **8** Margaret
hound: 3 bug, dog, dun, fan, mut, nag, ply, vex **4** bait, goad, mutt, prod, ride, tail **5** annoy, bedog, beset, canid, chase, grind, harry, haunt, stalk **6** addict, badger, bark at, basset, beagle, bother, bowwow, canine, harass, hassle, heckle, hector, noodge, pester, plague, pursue **7** admirer, basenji, bird dog, bombard, coon dog, henpeck, mongrel, oppress, provoke, redbone, torment **8** distress, run after **9** importune, keep after, persecute **10** intimidate
for payment: 3 dun **9** keep after
hotel: 6 kennel
name: 4 Fido, Spot **5** Rover
quarry: 3 fox **4** duck, hare **7** raccoon
sound: 3 yip **4** woof
starter: 3 elk, fox **4** boar, buck, chow, coon, deer, gaze, grey, hell, news, stag, wolf **5** blood **6** sleuth
trail: 5 scent, spoor, track
hound __: 3 dog
__ hound: 4 rock **5** media **6** Afghan, basset **9** autograph
Hound __ Baskervilles, The: 5 of the
Hound Dog (1956 song)
artist: Elvis Presley
Hound-Dog Man
artist: Fabian
hounding: 6 bother **9** annoyance **10** harassment, irritation
Hound of the Baskervilles, The: 4 film **5** novel
author: Arthur Conan Doyle
cast: Nigel Bruce, Basil Rathbone
locale: 4 moor
hounds, ride to: 4 hunt
hound's-tooth __: 5 check
Hounsfield, Godfrey: 8 Nobelist

hour: 4 sext, time **5** nones, prime, terce **6** matins, moment, tierce **7** complin, set time, vespers **8** compline
afternoon: 3 one, two **4** five, four **5** one p.m., three, two p.m. **6** five p.m., four p.m. **7** three p.m.
canonical ~: 4 sext **5** matin, nones, terce **7** worship
ender: 4 long **5** glass
evening ~: 3 six, ten **4** nine **5** eight, seven, six p.m. **6** nine p.m. **7** eight p.m., seven p.m.
happy ~: 6 recess **7** respite
happy ~ establishment: 3 pub **6** saloon, tavern **7** taproom **8** alehouse, taphouse
in French: 5 heure
in Spanish: 4 hora
man of the ~: 4 hero, star **6** victor, winner **8** luminary
morning ~: 3 six, ten **4** nine **5** eight, seven, six a.m., ten a.m. **6** eleven, nine a.m. **7** eight a.m., seven a.m. **8** eleven a.m.
nearing the ~: 5 ten of, ten to **6** five of, five to
prime-time ~: 3 ten **4** nine **5** eight, ten p.m. **6** nine p.m. **7** eight p.m.
rush ~: 7 traffic
sound the ~: 4 peal, toll **5** chime
TV news ~: 3 six, ten **5** six p.m., ten p.m. **6** eleven **8** eleven p.m.
vacant ~: 6 recess **8** free time **9** spare time **10** recreation, relaxation
wee ~: 3 one, two **4** four, morn **5** night, one a.m., three, two a.m. **6** four a.m. **7** morning, three a.m.
witching ~: 8 midnight
zero ~: 4 D-day **6** crisis **7** due date **8** deadline, exigence, exigency, juncture **9** countdown, crossroad, emergency
hour __: 4 hand
hour-__: 4 long
__ hour: 4 rush, zero **5** happy, lunch **7** amateur
Hour Before Daylight, An
author: Jimmy Carter
hourglass: 5 timer **9** timepiece **10** timekeeper
figure feature: 5 waist
filler: 4 sand
part: 4 neck
Hour Glass, The
author: William Butler Yeats
hourly: 5 horal, often **8** periodic
hour-minute divider: 5 colon
__ Hour Photo: 3 One
hours
after ~: 4 late **5** night **9** nighttime
enter the wee ~: 5 laten
every 24 ~: 4 a day **5** daily, horal **7** diurnal
from now: 5 after, later **6** in time **7** by and by **8** in a while **9** afterward **10** thereafter
idle ~: 4 ease, rest **6** repose **7** holiday, leisure, time off **8** free time, vacation **9** spare time
in the wee ~: 5 early
wee ~: 9 nighttime
while away the ~: 4 idle, laze, loaf, loll **5** dally **6** dawdle, loiter **8** kill time, malinger, slack off **9** bum around, goldbrick, sit around, waste time **10** dillydally, fool around, knock about, take it easy
__ hours: 6 office **7** bankers'
__-hours: 5 after
Hours of Idleness
author: Lord Byron
Hours, The (2002 film)
cast: Nicole Kidman, Julianne Moore, Meryl Streep
__ Hours, The: 7 Gallant
__ Hour With You: 3 One
Housatonic: 5 river
locale: 4 Conn., Mass.
house: 3 hut, pad **4** clan, coop, digs, firm, flat, hold, home **5** abode, admit, cabin, condo, lodge, place, put up, ranch, roost, shack, Tudor **6** A-frame, billet, castle, chalet, encase, family, harbor, incase, outfit, shield, take in **7** address, Cape Cod, company, concern, contain, cottage, council, domicil, dynasty, habitat, harbour, lineage, mansion, quarter, shelter, station, vacancy **8** audience, bungalow, business, crash pad, domicile, dressing, dwelling, hacienda, lodgment, property, quarters **9** apartment, monastery, residence, structure **10** parliament, split-level
addition: 3 ell **4** wing **5** annex
and grounds: 5 manor, ranch **6** estate **8** property **10** plantation
away from the ~: 5 not in **9** elsewhere
big ~: 4 jail **5** manor **6** castle, estate, lockup, prison
big ~ resident: 3 con **5** crook, felon, lifer **7** convict **8** criminal, jailbird, prisoner, yardbird **10** lawbreaker
bird ~: 4 nest **6** aviary **9** enclosure
boarding ~: 5 hotel **7** lodging **8** lodgment
bring down the ~: 3 wow **5** amaze, level **6** topple **7** delight, flatten **8** bulldoze, demolish, entrance
clean ~: 5 purge, sweep
cleaner, in England: 4 char
country ~: 5 cabin, lodge, villa **6** chalet
covering: 5 paint **6** siding, stucco
dish of the ~: 9 specialty
drawing: 4 plan **6** layout
ender: 3 boy, fly, man, men, sat, sit, top **4** boat, coat, hold, keep, leek, maid, mate, room, ware, wife, work **5** bound, break, broke, dress, guest, plant, train, wares, wives **6** broken, holder, keeper, lights, master, mother, wifely, worker **7** husband, keeping, painter, sitting, warming **8** cleaning, wifelike
enlarge the ~: 5 add on
feature: 3 den **4** deck, door, hall, lawn, roof, stud, wall, yard **5** alarm, attic, gable, patio, porch **6** cellar, garage, screen, siding, stairs, window **7** bedroom, ceiling, kitchen, library, mailbox **8** backyard, basement, doorbell, driveway **10** living room, smoke alarm, welcome mat
field ~: 9 gymnasium
fix up an old ~: 5 rehab
fly: 8 irritant
hash ~: 5 diner **6** eatery **10** restaurant
haunted ~ feature: 5 ghost **6** cobweb
high ~: 4 aery, eyry **5** aerie, eyrie
ice ~: 4 iglu **5** igloo
in French: 6 maison
in Spanish: 4 casa
inspection concern: 5 radon
instant ~: 6 prefab
it may be on the ~: 5 drink
keep ~: 6 settle **7** clean up
large ~: 6 castle, estate, palace **7** chateau, mansion
level a ~: 4 rase, raze
like a ~ afire: 6 wildly **7** eagerly **8** fiercely **9** furiously **10** vigorously
like a haunted ~: 5 eerie, scary **6** creaky, creepy, spooky **7** macabre **8** chilling
manor ~: 7 chateau
movie ~: 5 odeon, odeum **7** theater, theatre **10** auditorium
not a new ~: 6 resale
of correction: 3 pen **4** jail, poky, stir **6** prison **7** slammer
of worship: 4 shul **5** schul **6** bethel, church **9** cathedral
on the ~: 4 free **6** gratis, unpaid **7** as a gift **8** costless **10** for nothing
opera ~: 5 odeon, odeum **7** theater, theatre **10** auditorium
opera ~ section: 3 row
out of the ~: 7 outdoor **8** alfresco, exterior
paper: 4 deed
pet: 3 cat, dog **4** bird, fish **6** canary, parrot **8** parakeet
public ~: 3 bar, inn, pub **5** lodge **6** saloon, tavern **7** barroom
room in a Roman ~: 6 atrium
rooming ~: 3 inn **5** hotel **7** lodging
safe ~: 6 asylum **7** hideout, retreat **9** sanctuary
shader: 3 elm, oak **4** tree
site: 3 lot **4** plot **5** tract **6** parcel
small ~: 3 hut **5** bower, cabin, hovel, hutch, shack **6** cabana, chalet, lean-to, shanty **7** cottage **8** bungalow
starter: 3 ale, bug, dog, fun, gas, hot, ice, mad, pot, tea **4** alms, bath, bird, boat, brew, bunk, chop, club, deck, doll, farm, fire, flop, gate, jail, long, play, poor, road, spec, toll, town, ware, work **5** block, court, glass, green, guard, guest, light, pilot, power, rough, round, smoke, state, steak, store, sugar, sweat, wheel **6** barrel, coffee, custom, mother, porter, school, spring, summer **7** charter, meeting, packing, station **8** boarding, clearing, counting
style: 5 ranch, Tudor **6** A-frame **7** Cape Cod **10** split-level
tree ~: 4 nest
upper ~: 6 Senate

wing: 3 ell
woman of the ~: 4 ma'am, wife 6 missis, missus
work: 5 chore
wrecker: 5 razer
see also home

house ___: 4 call, dick, rule 5 brand, of God, organ, party 6 arrest, doctor, sitter 7 manager, painter, slipper, trailer

___ house: 3 art, big, fun, row, sod 4 frat, full, hash, open, safe, town, tree, wire 5 chart, clean, coach, field, frame, lower, manor, movie, on the, opera, ranch, tract, Tudor, upper 6 coffee, custom, public 7 country, customs, halfway, meeting, rooming, station 8 discount

House
counterpart: 6 Senate
divider: 5 aisle
eye on the ~: 5 CSPAN
member: 3 rep.
vote: 3 nay, yea

House (Fox drama)
cast: Lisa Edelstein (Lisa Cuddy) Omar Epps (Eric Foreman) Hugh Laurie (Gregory House) Robert Sean Leonard (James Wilson)

House ___: 5 Calls, of Wax, Party
House ___, A: 7 Divided
House ___ a Home, A: 5 Is Not
House ___ Rising Sun: 5 of the
House ___ Seven Gables, The: 5 of the
___ House: 3 Our 4 Full, Hull 5 Blair, Bleak, Brick, Crazy, Noble, White 6 Animal, Random 7 Maxwell
___ House, A: 5 Doll's
___ house afire: 5 like a
House at Pooh Corner, The
author: A.A. Milne
House Beautiful topic: 5 decor
houseboat: 4 junk
Houseboat (1958 film)
cast: Cary Grant, Sophia Loren
housebound, make: 5 ice in
housebreak: 5 train
housebreaker: 5 crook, thief 6 robber 7 burglar, prowler 8 criminal, picklock, pilferer 9 plunderer
housebroken: 4 tame
House Calls (1978 film)
cast: Richard Benjamin, Art Carney, Glenda Jackson, Walter Matthau
housecat: 3 pet 5 tabby
housecleaning: 5 purge
housecoat: 4 robe 6 duster, kimono 7 garment
___ House cookies: 4 Toll
House Divided, A
author: Pearl S. Buck
housefly: 3 bug 4 pest 6 insect
genus: 5 Musca
houseguest, be a bad: 6 impose
household: 4 clan, home, homy 5 homey 6 family, ménage 8 domestic, ordinary 9 customary
animal: 3 cat, dog, pet 4 bird, fish
appliance: 2 TV 3 vac, VCR 4 iron, oven 5 drier, dryer, stove, TV set, waxer 6 fridge, vacuum, washer
appliance brand: 5 Amana, Norge 6 Bendix, Maytag, Tappan 7 Admiral, Jenn-Air, Kenmore 8 Hotpoint 9 Magic Chef, Whirlpool 10 Frigidaire, Kelvinator, KitchenAid
chore: 4 wash 7 ironing, laundry
funds: 6 budget
help: 4 maid 5 nanny 6 au pair, nannie
member: 3 cat, dad, dog, mom, pet, sis
name: 7 notable 8 somebody 9 celebrity
new ~ member: 3 pup 4 baby 5 puppy 6 infant, kitten
pest: 3 ant 5 roach
Roman ~ god: 3 Lar
Roman ~ gods: 5 Lares
see also home, house
household ___: 4 word 5 goods
householder: 5 liver 6 tenant 8 occupant, resident
House in Paris, The
author: Elizabeth Bowen
House Is Not ___, A: 5 a Home
housekeeper: 4 maid 7 servant 8 domestic
at times: 6 ironer
___ housekeeper: 6 live-in 7 sleep-in
___ Housekeeping: 4 Good
housekeeping, set up: 5 dwell
Houseman, John Oscar: The Paper Chase
house of ___: 3 God 5 cards, study 6 prayer 7 worship
House of ___: 3 Wax 4 Dior, Keys 5 Lords, Peers, Usher 7 Commons
House of ___, The: 4 Fear
House of Blue Leaves, The
author: John Guare
House of Commons
locale: 6 Canada
House of Dark Shadows (1970 film)
cast: Jonathan Frid
House of Dust
author: Conrad Aiken
House of Five Talents, The
author: Louis Auchincloss
House of Games (1987 film)
cast: Lindsay Crouse, Joe Mantegna
director: David Mamet
House of Lancaster symbol: 4 rose 7 red rose
House of Life, The
author: Dante Gabriel Rossetti
House of Lords
member: 3 sir 4 duke, earl, peer 5 baron 8 baroness, viscount
House of Mirth, The
author: Edith Wharton
House of the Dead, The
author: Fyodor Dostoyevsky
House of the Rising Sun (song)
artist: Animals, Frijid Pink
House of the Seven Gables, The: 4 film 5 novel
author: Nathaniel Hawthorne
cast: Vincent Price
character: 5 Maule 6 Phoebe, Venner
director: Joe May
site: 5 Salem
House of the Spirits, The
author: Isabel Allende
House of Thunder, The
author: Dean Koontz
House of Wax
role: 4 Igor
House of Wax (1953 film)
cast: Phyllis Kirk, Frank Lovejoy, Vincent Price
director: Andre de Toth
House of York
symbol: 4 rose 9 white rose
House on Hope Street, The
author: Danielle Steel
House on the Hill, The
author: Cesare Pavese
___ House on the Prairie: 6 Little
houseplant: 4 aloe, fern 5 areca 6 coleus
tend to a ~: 5 repot, unpot, water
Houser: 5 Jerry
___ House roll: 6 Parker
___ House Rules, The: 5 Cider
House That Jack Built, The (1968 song)
artist: Aretha Franklin
___ House, The: 3 Big, Red 5 Glass 6 Russia
housetop: 4 roof
sight: 4 vane
housewares name: 4 Ekco
housewarming gift: 5 plant
House Without a Key, The hero: 4 Chan
housework: 5 chore 6 sewing 7 cooking, dusting, ironing, laundry, mopping, washing 8 cleaning, sweeping 9 bedmaking, vacuuming 10 homemaking, laundering
do ~: 3 mop, sew 4 cook, dust, iron, wash 5 clean, sweep 7 launder
housing: 3 pad 4 coop, digs, flat, home 5 abode, condo, roost 6 billet, castle 7 domicil, habitat, mansion, shelter 8 covering, crash pad, domicile, dwelling, quarters 9 apartment, residence
development: 5 tract
housing ___: 5 start 7 project
___ housing: 4 fair, open 5 tract 6 public
Housman: 2 A.E. 8 Laurence
Housman, A.E.: 4 poet 7 British
first name: Alfred
work: From Far, From Eve and Morning
The Lent Lily
Loveliest of Trees
On the Idle Hill of Summer
On Wenlock Edge
A Shropshire Lad
To an Athlete Dying Young
When I Was One-and-Twenty
With Rue My Heart Is Laden
Houssay, Bernardo: 8 Nobelist 12 physiologist
Houston: 3 Sam 4 city, Matt, port, town 5 Cissy, David 6 Thelma 7 Whitney
athletes: 4 Owls 7 Cougars
county: 6 Harris
former ~ hockey player: 4 Aero
locale: 3 Tex. 5 Texas
newspaper: 9 Chronicle
org.: 4 NASA
school: 3 TSU 9 Rice. Rice U.
team: 6 Astros, Texans 7 Rockets
Houston-to-Dallas dir.: 3 NNW
Houston, Whitney
hometown: Newark
record label: 6 Arista
song: All the Man That I Need (1991)
Could I Have This Kiss Forever (2000)
Count on Me (1996)
Didn't We Almost Have It All (1987)
Exhale (1995)
Greatest Love of All (1986)
Heartbreak Hotel (1999)
How Will I Know (1985)
I Believe in You and Me (1996)
I Have Nothing (1993)
I'm Every Woman (1993)
I'm Your Baby Tonight (1990)
It's Not Right But It's Okay (1999)
I Wanna Dance With Somebody (1987)
I Will Always Love You (1992)
Love Will Save the Day (1988)
Miracle (1991)
My Love Is Your Love (1999)
One Moment in Time (1988)
Saving All My Love for You (1985)
So Emotional (1987)
Where Do Broken Hearts Go (1988)
You Give Good Love (1985)
spouse: Bobby Brown
Houyhnhnms subject: 5 Yahoo
HOV ___: 4 lane
hovel: 3 hut, sty 4 dump, shed 5 house, shack 6 lean-to, pigpen, pigsty, shanty 7 cottage, piggery, rathole
hover: 3 fly 4 flit, hang, loom, wait 5 float, pause, poise 6 impend, linger, loiter, remain 7 flitter, flutter 8 levitate, volitate 9 vacillate 10 wait around
about: 5 haunt 7 bedevil 8 frequent 9 habituate 10 hang around
ender: 5 craft
hovercraft: 3 ACV 4 boat
hovering: 4 high 5 above 8 elevated
Hovhaness, Alan: 8 composer
Hovis: 5 Larry
how: 6 the way 9 in what way
and ~: *see* of course 8 for a fact 9 you said it
do you do: 4 ciao, hail 5 aloha, hello, howdy 7 bon jour, welcome 8 greeting
ender: 4 ever 6 soever
find ~ many: 5 count
in French: 3 que 5 comme 7 combien, comment
in Spanish: 4 cómo
knows ~: 3 can
no ~: 3 nah, naw, nay, nix, non 4 ever, nein, nope, nyet, uh-uh 5 at all, I won't, ixnay, never 7 I refuse 8 forget it, I will not, negative, negatory, not at all 9 fat chance, I think not 10 count me out, not a chance, thumbs down
now: 2 hi 4 ciao 5 aloha, hello 6 shalom 7 bon jour
others see us: 9 depiction 10 appearance, conception, impression, perception, projection

so: 3 why
starter: 3 any 4 some
things are: 7 reality 9 condition, situation
how __: 4 come 6 and why
how __ do: 5 do you
how __ that: 5 about
__ how!: 3 And 5 Here's
__-how: 4 know
How
the West Was Won (1962 film): 4 epic
How __!: 4 true
How __?: 4 come
How __ Be Sure: 4 Can I
How __, brown cow: 3 now
How __ doing?: 3 am I
How __ Got Her Groove Back: 6 Stella
How __ Has This Been Going On?: 4 Long
How __ Is the Ocean: 4 Deep
How __ Is Your Love: 4 Deep
How __ it is!: 5 sweet
How __ love thee?: 3 do I
How __ Me Now: 5 U Like
How __ the little busy bee...: 4 doth
How __ the Moon: 4 High
How __ the War: 4 I Won
How __ things?: 3 are
How __ Want It: 3 Do U
How __ Was My Valley: 5 Green
How __ We Know: 6 Little
How __ you!: 4 dare
How __ you?: 3 are 5 about
How __ Your Mother: 4 I Met
How about that!: 3 gee 4 gosh
How Am I Supposed to Live Without You (1989 song)
artist: Michael Bolton
Howard: 3 Ken, Moe, Ron 4 duck, Duff, Fast, Keel, Koch 5 Adina, Clint, Curly, Dietz, Frank, Hawks, Jones, Rance, Ronny, Shemp, Stern, Temin, Zieff 6 Arliss, Carter, Cosell, Florey, Hanson, Hughes, Leslie, Morris, Sidney, Trevor 7 da Silva, Lindsay, Nemerov, Rollins 8 Hesseman, Terrence
athletes: 5 Bison
locale: 10 Washington
Howard K. __: 5 Smith
Howard, Leslie: 5 actor
film: Gone With the Wind (1939)
Intermezzo (1939)
Of Human Bondage (1934)
The Petrified Forest (1936)
Pygmalion (1938)
Romeo and Juliet (1936)
The Scarlet Pimpernel (1935)
role: 5 Romeo 6 Ashley, Wilkes
Howard, Ron: 5 actor 8 director
film: American Graffiti (1973)
Angels & Demons (2009)
Apollo 13 (1995)
Backdraft (1991)
A Beautiful Mind (2001, AA)
Cinderella Man (2005)
Cocoon (1985)
The Da Vinci Code (2006)
Ed TV (1999)
Far and Away (1992)
Frost/Nixon (2008)
Gung Ho (1986)
The Missing (2003)
The Music Man (1962)
Night Shift (1982)
The Paper (1994)
Parenthood (1989)
Ransom (1996)
The Shootist (1976)
Splash (1984)
Willow (1988)
role: 4 Opie 6 Taylor
TV: Andy Griffith Show, Happy Days
Howards End: 4 film 5 novel
author: E.M. Forster
cast: Helena Bonham Carter, Anthony Hopkins, Vanessa Redgrave, Emma Thompson
character: 4 Bast, Evie, Paul, Ruth 5 Annie, Helen, Henry, Juley, Tibby 6 Wilcox 7 Charles, Leonard 8 Margaret, Schlegel
director: James Ivory
Howard, Sidney: 6 writer 10 playwright
work: Lute Song
They Knew What They Wanted
__ Howard Taft: 7 William
How Are Things in Glocca __?: 5 Morra
How awful!: 4 alas 6 oh dear
howbeit: 3 yet 8 although
How Bizarre (1997 song)
artist: OMC
How Can __ Sure: 3 I Be
How Can I Be Sure (1967 song)
artist: Rascals
How Can We Be Lovers (1990 song)
artist: Michael Bolton
How Can You Mend a Broken Heart (1971 song)
artist: Bee Gees
How'd __?: 4 it go
How Deep Is the Ocean
composer: Irving Berlin
How Deep Is Your Love (song)
artist: Bee Gees, Dru Hill, Redman
How disgusting!: 3 ick, ugh 5 yecch
how do __: 5 you do
How do __ thee?: 5 I Love
How does that __ you?: 4 grab
How Do I Live (1997 song)
artist: LeAnn Rimes, Trisha Yearwood
How do I love thee?: 4 poem
author: Elizabeth Barrett Browning
How Do I Make You (1980 song)
artist: Linda Ronstadt
How do you __ relief?: 5 spell
how-do-you-do, fine: 6 plight
How Do You Do It? (1964 song)
artist: Gerry and the Pacemakers
How do you like them __?: 6 apples
howdy: 4 hiya 5 aloha, hello 7 bon jour, welcome 8 greeting
say ~: 5 greet 7 welcome
Howdy __: 5 Doody
__ Howdy Doody Time: 3 It's
Howe: 5 Elias 6 Gordie
on Cheers: 5 Alley
howe'er: 3 tho
Howe, Gordie
milieu: 3 ice 4 rink 5 arena
org.: 3 NHL
Howell: 5 Lovey 6 Heflin 8 Thurston
partner: 4 Bell
Howells, William Dean: 6 writer
work: The Rise of Silas Lapham
however: 3 but, tho, yet 4 only 5 still 6 though, withal 8 after all 9 per contra 10 all the same, for all that
How Great Thou __: 3 Art
How Green Was My Valley (1941 film)
cast: Donald Crisp, Anna Lee, Roddy McDowall, Maureen O'Hara, Walter Pidgeon
character: 3 Huw 4 Beth, Davy, Ivor, Owen 5 Ianto, miner 6 Gwilym, Iestyn, Marged 7 Bronwen, Ceinwen
director: John Ford
How High the __: 4 Moon
Howie: 6 Mandel, Meeker, Morenz
How Important Can It Be? (1955 song)
artist: Joni James
howitzer: 3 arm, gun 4 arty. 6 cannon 9 artillery
need: 4 ammo
nickname: 6 Bertha
howl: 3 bay, cry, sob 4 bark, bawl, hoot, keen, moan, riot, roar, sigh, wail, weep, yell, yelp, yowl 5 groan, growl, laugh, shout, storm, whine, whoop 6 bellow, clamor, guffaw, holler, lament, outcry, scream, shriek, squeal 7 blubber, exclaim, ululate 9 caterwaul 10 take it hard, vociferate
Howl
author: Allen Ginsberg
Howland: 4 Beth, isle 6 island
howler: 4 slip 5 error, gaffe 6 animal, coyote, mammal, monkey 7 blunder, faux pas, mistake, primate 10 inaccuracy
relative: *see* primate
Howlin' __: 4 Wolf
howling: 4 wild 6 stormy 8 laughter 9 turbulent
How Little We Know (1956 song)
artist: Frank Sinatra
How Long (1975 song)
artist: Ace, Pointer Sisters
How'm I doin'? asker: 4 Koch 6 Ed Koch
How now! __?: 4 a rat
How're you? response: 4 fine 6 I'm fine
How's __?: 6 things, tricks
How sad!: 4 alas 5 alack
Howser: 4 Dick 6 Doogie
How Sheba Sings the Song
author: Maya Angelou
How silly of me!: 3 duh
How soothing!: 3 aah
How Stella Got Her Groove Back (1998 film)
cast: Angela Bassett, Taye Diggs, Whoopi Goldberg
How sweet __!: 4 it is
How Sweet It Is (song)
artist: Marvin Gaye, James Taylor
How's Your Glass?
author: Kingsley Amis
How the Grinch Stole Christmas: 4 book, film
author: Dr. Seuss
cast: Christine Baranski, Jim Carrey, Bill Irwin, Jeffrey Tambor
director: Ron Howard
dog: 3 Max
How the Other Half Lives
author: Jacob Riis
How the Other Half Loves
author: Alan Ayckbourn
How the West Was Won (1962 film): 4 epic 5 oater
cast: Carroll Baker, Henry Fonda, Carolyn Jones, Gregory Peck, George Peppard, Robert Preston, Debbie Reynolds, James Stewart, Eli Wallach, John Wayne, Richard Widmark
how-to: 4 book
part: 4 step
How to __ a Million: 5 Steal
How to Lose a Guy in 10 Days (2003 film)
cast: Kate Hudson, Matthew McConaughey
How to Make an American Quilt (1995 film)
cast: Maya Angelou, Anne Bancroft, Ellen Burstyn, Winona Ryder
How to Marry a Millionaire (1953 film)
cast: Lauren Bacall, Betty Grable, Marilyn Monroe
How to Murder Your Wife (1965 film)
cast: Jack Lemmon, Virna Lisi
director: Richard Quine
How to Save Your Own Life
author: Erica Jong
How to Steal a Million (1966 film)
cast: Charles Boyer, Audrey Hepburn, Peter O'Toole
How to Succeed... (1967 film): 7 musical
cast: Michele Lee, Robert Morse, Rudy Vallee
composer: Frank Loesser
How to Write a Blackwood Article
author: Edgar Allan Poe
How was __ know?: 3 I to
How Will I Know (1985 song)
artist: Whitney Houston
hoya: 4 vine 5 plant, shrub
Hoyas: 10 Georgetown
hoyden: 4 bold, rude, snip, wild 5 rowdy 6 tomboy, unruly 10 boisterous
Hoyle: 4 Fred 6 Edmond
according to ~: 5 legal, legit, licit, valid 6 kosher, lawful 7 correct 8 bona fide, orthodox 9 allowable 10 admissible, authorized, meticulous, on the level, scrupulous
Hoyt: 5 Axton, Waite 7 Wilhelm
Hoyt, Waite: 6 hurler 7 pitcher
H.P.: 9 Lovecraft
HP product: 2 PC 3 ptr. 6 laptop 7 printer 8 computer
HQ: 4 base
hr.
see hour
H.R.: 8 Haldeman
Hrabal, Bohumil: 5 Czech 6 writer
H. Rap __: 5 Brown
Hrbek: 4 Kent
H&R Block staffer: 3 CPA
HRE part: 3 Emp., Rom. 4 Holy 5 Roman 6 Empire
HRH: 3 VIP 4 king 5 queen
award from ~: 3 OBE
part of ~: 3 Her, His 5 Royal 8 Highness

H. Rider __: **7** Haggard
H. Ross __: **5** Perot
H.S.
course: **2** PE **3** alg., bio., Eng., mus., sci. **4** biol., chem., geog., hist., math.
dropout's certificate: **3** GED
exam: **3** SAT **4** PSAT
head: **4** prin.
keepsake: **2** yb.
organization: **3** PTA
part of ~: **3** sch.
proficiency test: **3** GED
safety advocate: **4** SADD
student: **2** jr., sr. **3** jnr., snr.
see also high school
Hsing-Hsing: **5** panda
HSN: **8** shopping
alternative: **3** QVC **7** ShopNBC
HST: **3** Dem. **4** pres.
defeated him: **3** AES
predecessor: **3** FDR
successor: **3** DDE
see also Harry S Truman
ht.: **3** alt. **4** elev.
html: **8** language
alternative: ***see*** computer language
http
see Internet, Web
__ Huachuca, AZ: **4** Fort
Hua Kuo-__: **4** Feng
Huang He: **5** river
locale: **5** China
Huangpu, city on the: **8** Shanghai
hub: **4** core, seat **5** focus, heart, locus, Mecca, midst **6** center, kernel, middle **7** nucleus **8** polestar **10** focal point
ender: **3** cap
in the ~ of: **6** amidst
of activity: **3** ctr. **6** center
wheel ~: **4** nave
hub-and-__: **5** spoke
Hubba __: **5** Bubba
hubba-hubba: **6** clamor, uproar **10** hullabaloo
Hubba-hubba!: **3** wow **6** oo-la-la
Hubbard: **3** Cal, Kin **4** L. Ron, peak **5** mount **6** Elbert **8** mountain
Hubbard __: **6** squash
Hubbard, Mother: **5** dress
like ~: **3** old
like ~'s cupboard: **4** bare
pet: **3** dog
quest: **4** bone
Hubbell, Carl: **5** Giant **6** hurler **7** pitcher
teammate: **3** Ott
Hubble: **9** telescope
component: **4** lens
Hubble, Edwin: **10** astronomer
hubbly: **5** rough **6** coarse, uneven
hubbub: **3** ado, din **4** flap, fuss, stir, to-do **5** babel, furor, noise, whirl **6** bedlam, clamor, hassle, hoopla, hoorah, hooray, hurrah, hurray, jangle, lather, pother, racket, ruckus, rumpus, tumult, uproar **7** clangor, clutter, dispute, ferment, ruction, turmoil **8** brouhaha, disorder, rowdydow **9** commotion, confusion, hue and cry, maelstrom **10** clattering, excitement, hullabaloo, hurly-burly
hubby: **3** guy **4** mate **6** fellow, mister, spouse **7** husband
partner: **4** wife **6** missus
hubcap: **8** auto part
Hubert: **5** Booth, saint, Selby **7** van Eyck **8** Givenchy, Humphrey **9** Cornfield
comics wife: **5** Trudy
in Italian: **6** Uberto
Hubley: **6** Season
hub-rim connector: **5** spoke
hubris: **5** brass, cheek, nerve, pride **6** vanity **8** audacity, chutzpah **9** arrogance, cockiness, loftiness, pomposity **10** pretension
source: **3** ego
hubristic: **4** smug, vain **5** proud **6** snooty **7** haughty, pompous, stuck-up **8** arrogant, egoistic, snobbish **9** conceited, imperious **10** hoity-toity
hubs: **4** loca, loci
huck ender: **4** ster
huckleberry: **5** fruit, shrub
relative: ***see*** heath family shrub
Huckleberry Finn: **5** novel
author: Mark Twain
character: **3** Jim, Pap, Tom **9** Aunt Polly, Tom Sawyer
hucklebuck: **5** dance
huckster: **5** crier **6** barker, hawker, vender, vendor **10** mountebank, proclaimer
Hucksters, The (1947 film)
cast: Clark Gable, Sydney Greenstreet, Deborah Kerr
Hud (1963 film)
cast: Melvyn Douglas, Patricia Neal, Paul Newman
cinematographer: **4** Howe
director: Martin Ritt
Oscar-winner: **4** Neal
HUD
agency: **3** FHA
part: **4** Dept. **5** Urban **7** Housing **10** Department
place: **7** Cabinet
huddle: **4** heap, herd, mass, meet, mess, talk **5** bunch, chaos, crowd, flock, group **6** confab, confer, crouch, gather, hunker, jumble, nestle, parley, powwow, shrink, throng **7** bunch up, cluster, consult, meeting, palaver, session, snuggle **8** assemble, assembly, converge, disarray, disorder **9** confusion, gathering, touch base **10** assemblage, conference, discussion
count: **6** eleven
ender: **5** break
up: **6** crouch, cuddle, curl up, nestle **7** snuggle
...huddled __ yearning...: **6** masses
Hudibras
author: Samuel Butler
Hudson: **2** W.H. **3** bay, car, riv. **4** auto, city, Kate, Rock, town **5** Ernie, Henry, river **8** Jennifer, Rochelle **10** automobile
1920s ~ car: **5** Essex
competitor: **3** Reo **6** De Soto
locale: **4** Ohio
model: **4** Wasp **6** Big Boy, Hornet **7** Rambler **8** Super Six, Traveler **9** Commodore, Pacemaker **10** Great Eight, Terraplane
Hudson __: **3** Bay **6** Strait
Hudson Bay: **3** sea
locale: **6** Canada
river to ~: **6** Nelson, Thelon **9** Churchill
tribe: **4** Cree
Hudson, Henry: **7** British **8** explorer
Hudson, Kate: **7** actress
film: About Adam (2001)
Almost Famous (2000)
Desert Blue (1999)
The Four Feathers (2002)
mother: Goldie Hawn
Hudson River
canal: **4** Erie
city on the ~: **4** Troy **5** Nyack **6** Albany
locale: **7** New York
river to the ~: **6** Mohawk
sch.: **4** USMA
Hudson, Rock: **5** actor
film: All That Heaven Allows (1955)
The Ambassador (1984)
Battle Hymn (1957)
Come September (1961)
Darling Lili (1970)
A Gathering of Eagles (1963)
Giant (1956)
Ice Station Zebra (1968)
The Last Sunset (1961)
Lover Come Back (1961)
Magnificent Obsession (1954)
The Mirror Crack'd (1980)
Pillow Talk (1959)
Pretty Maids All in a Row (1971)
Send Me No Flowers (1964)
The Tarnished Angels (1958)
Written on the Wind (1956)
TV: McMillan and Wife
Hudson, W.H.: **6** writer **7** British
work: Green Mansions
Hudson, W.H. work: Green Mansions
Hudsucker Proxy, The (1994 film)
cast: Jennifer Jason Leigh, Paul Newman, Tim Robbins
director: Joel Coen
hue: **3** dye **4** cast, tint, tone **5** color, shade, tinct, tinge **6** chroma **7** pigment **8** tincture
and cry: **3** ado, din, row **5** alarm, furor, stink **6** clamor, hubbub, uproar **9** commotion **10** hullabaloo
partner: **3** cry
unbleached ~: **3** tan **5** brown
use a new ~: **5** redye
without ~: **3** wan **4** ashy, drab, dull, pale **5** ashen, faded, mousy, waxen, white **6** dreary, mousey **8** blanched, bleached **9** colorless, washed-out **10** achromatic
see also color
Hué: **4** city, town
city near ~: **6** Danang
locale: **3** Nam **7** Vietnam
was its capital: **4** Anam **5** Annam
hued: **5** vivid **7** vibrant **8** colorful **9** chromatic
Hues Corporation
song: Rock the Boat (1974)
Huey: **4** Long **5** Lewis **6** Newton
brother: **5** Dewey, Louie
Donald Duck, to ~: **4** unca
huff: **3** pet **4** pant, puff, rage, snit, stew, tiff **5** pique, snort, tizzy **7** bad mood, umbrage **10** irritation, resentment
and puff: **4** blow, gasp, pant
be in a ~: **4** mope, sulk **5** brood, grump, scowl **6** resent
in a ~: ***see*** angry
Huff: **3** Sam
huffer, fictional: **4** wolf **10** Big Bad Wolf
huffiness: **3** ire **4** snit **5** anger, wrath **6** dander, temper **9** pugnacity, short fuse, surliness
huffish: **4** curt **5** cross, testy **6** crabby, cranky, grumpy, snappy, touchy **7** grouchy, peevish, waspish **8** bullying, grumpish, insolent, snappish **9** irascible, irritable **10** blustering, out of sorts, swaggering
Huffman: **8** Felicity
Huff, Sam
sport: **8** football
huffy
see angry
hug: **4** hold, lock, love **5** clasp, crush, greet, press, touch **6** caress, clench, clinch, clutch, cradle, cuddle, enfold, infold, nestle **7** cling to, embrace, envelop, snuggle, squeeze, welcome **8** greeting **9** hold close, keep close
love letter ~s: **3** OOO
partner: **4** kiss
__ hug: **4** bear **5** bunny
huge: **3** big **4** vast **5** bulky, giant, great, gross, heavy, jumbo, large, massy, mondo **6** cosmic, mighty **7** hulking, immense, mammoth, massive, monster, oceanic, outsize, sizable, titanic **8** colossal, cosmical, enormous, gigantic, king-size, oversize, sizeable, spacious, terrific, towering, whapping, whopping **9** cavernous, cyclopean, extensive, fantastic, herculean, humongous, leviathan, monstrous, overlarge, oversized, ponderous, walloping **10** gargantuan, monumental, overweight, prodigious, stupendous, tremendous
amount: **4** lots, slew **5** scads **6** oodles, scores
poetically: **5** enorm
prefix: **4** mega-
seem ~: **4** loom **5** tower
hugely: **4** much, very **5** quite **6** highly, vastly **7** awfully, but good, greatly **9** extremely, in a big way **10** incredibly, thoroughly
hugeness: **4** size **8** enormity **9** amplitude, immensity, largeness, magnitude **10** infinitude
huggable: **6** cuddly **7** snuggly **10** cuddlesome
__-hugger: **4** tree
hugger-mugger: **4** mask, mess, veil **5** chaos, cloak, mussy **6** covert, jumble, muddle, secret **7** conceal, jumbled, muddled, secrecy, stealth **8** balled-up, confused, disarray, disorder, fouled-up **9** concealed, confusion **10** disorderly, in disarray, in disorder, keep secret, undercover
__-huggers: **3** hip

Huggies: **6** diaper
alternative: **4** Luvs **7** Drypers, Pampers
hugging: **6** in love, tender **7** amorous **8** romantic **10** passionate
Huggins: **3** Roy **6** Miller **7** Charles, William
Huggins, Charles: **8** Nobelist
Huggins, William: **10** astronomer
Hugh: **5** Capet, Downs, Grant **6** Hefner, Laurie, O'Brian, Wilson **7** Jackman, Lofting, Marlowe, Walpole **8** Beaumont, Griffith, Masekela **9** McElhenny **10** MacDiarmid
in Italian: **3** Ugo
Hughes: **3** Ken, Ted **4** John, Rudd **5** Jimmy, Sarah **6** Howard **7** Barnard **8** Langston
Hughes, Howard
airline: **3** TWA
spouse: Terry Moore, Jean Peters
Hughes, John: **8** director
film: The Breakfast Club (1985)
Ferris Bueller's Day Off (1986)
Planes, Trains & Automobiles (1987)
She's Having a Baby (1988)
Sixteen Candles (1984)
Uncle Buck (1989)
Weird Science (1985)
Hughes, Langston: **6** writer
collaborator: Hurston
work: Ask Your Mama
The Big Sea
Dream Deferred
Ennui
I, Too
I Wonder As I Wander
Jazzonia
Mule Bone
Po' Boy Blues
Sea Calm
Hughes, Sarah: **6** skater
Hughes, Ted: **4** poet **7** British
spouse: Sylvia Plath
Hughie: **8** Jennings
Hugli, city on the: **8** Calcutta
Hugo: **4** Ball **5** award, Black **6** Victor **7** De Vries, Grotius **9** Fregonese, Gernsback **10** Montenegro
contemporary: **5** Dumas
see also French
Hugo, Victor: **6** French, writer
work: Hernani
The Hunchback of Notre Dame
Les Misérables
__ Huguenots: **3** Les
Huguenot stronghold: **4** Caen
Huh?: **4** what
huit: **5** eight **6** French
follower: **4** neuf
preceder: **4** sept
Huitzilopochtli worshiper: **5** Aztec
hula: **5** dance
accessory: **3** lei
skirt material: **5** grass
strings: **3** uke
where to see a ~: **4** luau
hula __: **5** skirt
Hula __: **4** Bowl, Hoop
Hula Hoop: **3** fad **5** craze
company: **5** Wham-o
hula-hula: **5** dance
Hulce, Tom: **5** actor
film: Amadeus (1984)
Black Rainbow (1991)
Dominick and Eugene (1988)
Parenthood (1989)
hulk: **4** boat, loom **5** tower, wreck **9** shipwreck
like a ~: **5** beefy, bulky, burly, hefty, husky **6** brawny **7** massive **9** strapping
Hulk: **5** Hogan
hulking: **3** big **4** huge, vast **5** beefy, bulky, burly, giant, great, hefty, jumbo, large, stout **6** clumsy, sturdy **7** immense, mammoth, massive, sizable, titanic, weighty **8** colossal, enormous, gigantic, imposing, king-size, muscular, oversize, sizeable, towering, ungainly, unwieldy, whapping, whopping **9** Herculean, humongous, lumbering, overlarge, ponderous, strapping, unwieldly, whalelike **10** cumbersome, gargantuan, monumental, prodigious, stupendous, tremendous
Hulk, The (2003 film)
cast: Jennifer Connelly, Sam Elliott, Nick Nolte
director: Eric Bana
hull: **3** bur, pod **4** body, husk, peel, rind, skin **5** cover, crust, frame, shell, shuck, strip **6** bottom, casing **8** covering **10** integument
appendage: **3** fin
caulking: **5** oakum
interior: **4** hold
part: **3** rib **4** keel, wale **5** bilge
Hull: **4** city, port, town **5** Bobby, Isaac **7** Cordell **9** Josephine
locale: **6** Canada, Québec
Hull __: **5** House
hullabaloo: **3** ado, cry, din, row **4** flap, to-do **5** babel, furor, hoo-ha, mania, melee, noise, scene, whirl **6** bedlam, clamor, hassle, hoopla, hubbub, jangle, lather, outcry, pother, racket, ruckus, rumpus, tumult, uproar **7** clatter, ruction, turmoil **8** brouhaha, disorder, rowdydow **9** hue and cry **10** clattering, excitement, hubba-hubba
Hull, Bobby
milieu: **3** ice **4** rink **5** arena
org.: **3** NHL
Hull, Cordell: **8** Nobelist
Hull, Josephine Oscar: Harvey
hully gully: **5** dance
Hulme heroine: **3** nun
Hulot
portrayer: Jacques Tati
hum: **3** pur **4** buzz, purr, roll, sing, whir, whiz, zoom **5** croon, drone, sound, whirr **6** bustle, intone, mantra, mumble, murmur **7** mantram, operate, vibrate, whisper **9** bombinate, undertone
ender: **3** bug **4** drum
human: **4** body, soul, warm **5** being, biped, child, woman **6** mortal, person **7** primate **8** fallible, naked ape **9** character, Cro-Magnon, earthborn, earthling, incarnate **10** altruistic, error-prone, individual
act ~: **3** err
being: **4** life, soul **5** wight **6** person **10** individual
combining form: **5** homin- **6** homini- **7** anthrop- **8** anthropo-
dynamo: **4** doer **7** hustler **8** go-getter, live wire
ending: **3** oid
genus: **4** homo
it's ~: **5** to err
race: **3** man **4** life **5** Earth, world **6** people **7** mankind
resources: **5** staff **6** people **7** workers **9** employees, personnel, work force
rights org.: **3** ADL **4** ACLU **5** NAACP
score: **5** nails **6** digits
human __: **4** race **5** being, error **6** nature, rights **7** ecology
Human __ Project: **6** Genome
Human __, The: **6** Comedy
__ humana: **3** vox
Human Beast, The
author: Émile Zola
Human Comedy, The: **5** novel
author: Honoré de Balzac, William Saroyan
character: **4** Bess **5** Homer, Katey, Tobey **6** Lionel
Human Concretion
artist: Jean (Hans) Arp
humane: **4** good, kind, mild **5** noble **6** benign, caring, gentle, kindly, tender **7** clement, ethical, lenient, sparing **8** merciful, tolerant **9** unselfish **10** altruistic, benevolent, charitable, reasonable
org.: **4** SPCA **5** ASPCA
humane __: **7** society
humaneness: **5** heart **8** goodness **10** compassion
__ humani generis: **6** amicus
human-interest __: **5** story
__ humanism: **7** secular
humanist
British ~: **4** More
French ~: **8** Rabelais
humanistic: **6** giving **7** liberal **8** generous **9** classical, unselfish **10** benevolent, bighearted, charitable
humanitarian: **4** good, kind **6** giving, kindly **7** liberal **8** altruist, do-gooder, generous, merciful **9** unselfish
concern: **5** needy
no ~: **5** miser, piker **7** Scrooge **8** tightwad **9** skinflint **10** cheapskate, pinchpenny
__-humanité: **4** lèse
humanities: **4** arts **10** literature
class: **3** soc. **9** sociology
deg.: **3** LHD
humanity: **5** flesh, mercy, world **6** lenity, people **7** charity, society **8** kindness, lenience **9** tolerance
humanize: **4** ease **6** gentle, mellow, soften, temper **8** civilize
humankind: **5** flesh, world **7** society **9** community
Human Nature (1983 song)
artist: Michael Jackson
__ humano: **4** jure
Human Resources worker: **5** hirer
humans: **4** folk **5** folks **6** people
Human Touch (1992 song)
artist: Bruce Springsteen
humanum __ errare: **3** est
Humbard: **3** Rex
Humber: **5** river
locale: **7** England
source ~: **4** Ouse **5** Trent
humble: **3** low, shy **4** base, mean, meek, poor, puny, snub, sunk **5** abase, abash, lower, lowly, plain, shame, small, timid **6** abject, common, debase, demean, demote, demure, meager, measly, menial, modest, paltry, reduce, shabby, simple, squash, subdue **7** bashful, chasten, conquer, deflate, degrade, ignoble, lowborn, mortify, pitiful, put down, scrubby, servile, unknown **8** cast down, contrite, inferior, ordinary, plebeian, pull down, reserved, retiring, take down, vanquish, wretched, yielding **9** bring down, denigrate, diffident, discredit, embarrass, humiliate, miserable **10** inglorious, put to shame, respectful, soft-spoken, unassuming
abode: **5** hovel, shack **6** lean-to, shanty
not ~: **4** vain **5** cocky, proud **7** fustian, haughty, stuck-up **8** arrogant, boastful, cocksure, egoistic, puffed up **9** bigheaded, conceited **10** egocentric, swaggering
oneself: **4** sink **5** crawl, kneel, stoop **6** grovel
humble __: **3** pie **5** abode
humbled: **7** abashed, ashamed **8** penitent **9** awestruck, regretful **10** remorseful
meal for the ~: **4** crow
humbleness: **7** modesty, reserve **8** humility
__ humble pie: **3** eat
Humboldt: **3** bay **5** river **7** current
city on the ~: **4** Elko
river locale: **6** Nevada
Humboldt's Gift
author: Saul Bellow
humbug: **3** con **4** fake, hoax, ruse, scam, sham **5** bluff, feint, fraud, quack, sting **6** deceit, hustle **7** con game, fast one, snow job, swindle **8** artifice **9** hypocrite, imposture, silliness **10** subterfuge
see also baloney
__, humbug!: **3** Bah
Humbug!: **3** bah **5** pshaw
humdify: **6** dampen
humdinger: **3** pip, wow **4** lulu, oner **5** beaut, dandy, doozy, prize **6** beauty, doozie, pistol **7** whapper, whopper
humdrum: **4** arid, blah, drab, dull, tame **5** banal, bland, corny, hokey, passé, prosy, stale, trite, unfun, vapid **6** boring, common, dreary, jejune, old hat **7** clichéd, fatuous, insipid, mundane, nowhere, prosaic, routine, tedious **8** bromidic, dragging, everyday, mediocre, monotony, ordinary, outdated, outmoded, plodding, tiresome **9** hackneyed, ponderous, prosaical, wearisome **10** dullsville, enervating, monotonous, pedestrian, uneventful, uninspired, unoriginal
Hume: **4** Brit, John **5** David **6** Cronyn

HU

Hume, David: 8 Scottish 11 philosopher
humerus: 4 bone 7 arm bone
neighbor: 4 ulna
opposite: 5 femur
humid: 3 wet 4 damp, dank, dewy 5 close, moist, muggy, soggy, undry 6 clammy, hydric, steamy, sticky, sultry, sweaty 7 wettish 8 tropical 10 equatorial, sweltering
humidifier
output: 5 vapor
part: 5 grill 6 grille
humidify: 3 wet 4 damp, soak 5 water 6 dampen 7 moisten 8 saturate, sprinkle 10 moisturize
humidity: 7 swelter, wetness 8 dampness, dankness, dewiness, moisture 9 mugginess, sogginess 10 clamminess, steaminess, stickiness, sultriness
react to ~: 4 wilt
humidor: 3 box 9 container 10 receptacle
item: 5 cigar, claro 6 corona, Havana
humiliate: 3 rip 4 gibe, jeer, jibe, mock, sink, slam, slur, snub, sunk 5 abase, abash, abuse, break, decry, libel, lower, scorn, shame, spurn, taunt 6 debase, defame, demean, demote, deride, dump on, heckle, humble, impugn, insult, malign, offend, rebuff, reduce, slight, squash, subdue, vilify 7 affront, asperse, chasten, deflate, degrade, disdain, mortify, put down, rank out, run down, slander, traduce 8 belittle, cast down, denounce, disgrace, dishonor, pull down, ridicule, take down, vilipend 9 bring down, denigrate, discomfit, discredit, disparage, embarrass, shoot down 10 calumniate, dishearten, disrespect, put to shame
humiliated: 5 small 6 abject 7 abashed
humiliating: 4 base, vile 6 odious 8 humbling, infamous, shameful 9 degrading 10 belittling, derogatory, mortifying
humiliation: 3 dig 4 barb, gibe, jibe, slam, slap, slur, snub 5 abuse, libel, scorn, shame, taunt 6 rebuff, slight 7 affront, calumny, catcall, disdain, mockery, obloquy, offense, put-down, slander, undoing 8 contempt, disgrace, dishonor, ignominy, ridicule 9 abashment, cheap shot, contumely 10 disrespect, opprobrium
humility: 7 modesty 8 docility, meekness, timidity 9 lowliness, servility 10 demureness, submission
eschew ~: 4 brag, crow 5 boast, exult, gloat, vaunt 6 hotdog 7 bluster, show off, swagger, talk big 8 showboat 9 gasconade 10 grandstand
hummable: 6 catchy
hummer: 4 bird
Hummer: 7 vehicle
humming: 4 busy 5 abuzz 6 murmur
hummingbird
color of some ~ throats: 4 ruby
emulate a ~: 4 dart 5 hover, whirr
home: 4 nest
relative: 5 swift
sound: 5 whirr
Hummingbird (1955 song)
artist: Les Paul and Mary Ford
hummock: 4 rise 5 knoll, mound 7 hillock
hummus: 3 dip
humongous: 3 big 4 huge, vast 5 giant, great, jumbo, large, massy 7 hulking, immense, mammoth, massive, sizable, titanic 8 colossal, enormous, gigantic, king-size, oversize, sizeable, towering, whapping, whopping 9 fantastic, Herculean, overlarge 10 gargantuan, monumental, prodigious, stupendous, tremendous
prefix: 4 mega-
quantity: 3 sea 4 lots, raft 5 ocean, scads 6 oodles
humor: 3 fun, joy, wit 4 baby, gags, mood, tone, vein 5 farce, jests, jokes, spoil 6 banter, coddle, comedy, gaiety, gayety, joking, levity, makeup, nature, pamper, permit, please, spirit, temper, whimsy 7 cater to, gratify, indulge, jesting, kidding, mollify, whimsey 8 badinage, clowning, drollery, give in to, raillery, tolerate 9 amusement, flippancy, funniness 10 buffoonery, comicality, jocoseness, jocularity, tomfoolery, wisecracks, witticisms
bodily ~: 4 bile 5 blood 6 choler, phlegm 8 jocosity 9 silliness
country ~: 4 corn
dry ~: 4 salt
ending: 3 ous
good ~: 3 joy 5 mirth 6 gaiety, gayety 9 happiness
ill ~: 6 spleen 7 bad mood 9 testiness 10 crabbiness, crankiness, grumpiness, irritation, touchiness
like some ~: 5 crude 6 coarse, earthy, folksy
not in good ~: 4 dour, glum, ugly 5 cross, gruff, huffy, irate, sulky, surly, testy 6 crabby, cranky, gloomy, grumpy, morose, ornery, sullen 7 grouchy, hostile, peevish 8 frowning, growling, perverse, snappish 9 crotchety, irritable 10 out of sorts, ungracious
overwhelm with ~: 4 slay
response: 4 ha-ha
sardonic ~: 5 irony 7 sarcasm
sense of ~: 3 wit 9 wittiness 10 cleverness
without ~: 5 drily, dryly
__ humor: 3 ill 4 good 5 black 7 aqueous
Humoresque (1946 film)
cast: Joan Crawford, John Garfield, Oscar Levant
humoring: 7 coaxing, lenient 8 cajolery 9 wheedling 10 indulgence
humorist: 3 wag, wit 4 card, zany 5 clown, comic, cutup, joker 8 comedian, jokester, quipster, satirist 9 jokesmith 10 comedienne
humorless: 5 sober, staid 6 solemn, somber, stuffy 7 deadpan, serious 9 unamusing 10 no-nonsense, unhumorous
humorous: 4 camp, joky, nice, rich, zany 5 campy, comic, droll, funny, jokey, light, merry, silly, witty 6 harhar, ironic, jocose, jovial 7 amusing, comical, jesting, jocular, joshing, playful, waggish 8 farcical, humorous 9 facetious, hilarious, laughable, ludicrous, priceless, whimsical 10 capricious, gut-busting
dryly ~: 3 wry 5 droll 8 sardonic
in music: 5 buffa, buffo
remark: 3 gag, mot, pun 4 gibe, jest, joke, quip 5 crack 6 bon mot, zinger 8 one-liner 9 wisecrack, witticism
humorously: 5 in fun 7 as a joke, as a lark
in music: 7 giocoso
__ Humorum: 4 Mare
hump: 4 arch 5 bulge, mound 8 mountain, swelling 9 elevation 10 projection, protrusion
ender: 4 back
humpback: 5 whale
home: 3 sea 5 ocean 8 high seas
humped animal: 4 zebu 5 camel 8 Bactrian 9 dromedary
Humperdinck, Engelbert
song: After the Lovin' (1976) Release Me (1967)
Humphrey: 5 Doris 6 Bogart, Hubert, Muriel 7 Gilbert
Humphry: 4 Davy
Humpty Dumpty: 3 egg
like ~: 4 ooid, oval 5 obese, ovate, ovoid, round
Humpty Dumpty sat __ wall: 3 on a
humus: 3 mor 4 soil 5 mulch 7 compost 10 fertilizer
Humvee forerunner: 4 jeep
Hun: 6 Vandal 7 invader, ravager 8 marauder 9 barbarian
king: 4 Atli
Hunan: 7 cuisine
like ~: 3 hot 5 spicy
pan: 3 wok
hunch: 4 arch, bend, flex, idea 5 cower, guess, slump, squat, stoop 6 augury, crouch, hunker, notion, theory 7 feeling, inkling, portent, surmise 8 forecast, instinct 9 intuition, suspicion 10 assumption, conjecture, gut feeling, impression, prediction
have a ~: 4 feel 5 sense 6 intuit 7 predict, suspect 9 determine, speculate 10 anticipate
__ hunch: 3 on a
Hunchback of Notre Dame, The
author: Victor Hugo
Hunchback of Notre Dame, The (1923 film)
cast: Lon Chaney
Hunches in Bunches
author: Dr. Seuss
hundred: 6 centum 7 century
combining form: 4 cent-, hect-, hekt- 5 centi-, hecto-, hekto-
DC ~: 6 Senate
dollars: 5 C-note, C-spot 8 Franklin
ender: 6 weight
one in a ~: 4 cent
percent: 3 all 5 fully 6 in full, in toto, purely, wholly 7 cap-a-pie, totally, utterly 8 entirely, from A to Z 9 all the way, every inch, to the hilt 10 absolutely, completely, thoroughly, to the limit
sawbucks: 4 one G 5 G-note
years: 7 century 9 centenary
Hundred __ War: 5 Years'
Hundred __ Woods: 4 Acre
__ Hundred and One Dalmatians: 3 One
__ hundred rummy: 4 five
Hundred Secret Senses, The
author: Amy Tan
hundredth: 9 centenary
combining form: 4 cent- 5 centi-
part: 3 pct. 7 percent
Hundred Years' __: 3 War
__ Hundred Years of Solitude: 3 One
Hundred Years' War winner: 6 France
hung __: 4 jury
Hungaria
composer: Franz Liszt
Hungarian: 8 language
Hungarian __: 7 goulash
__-Hungarian Empire: 6 Austro
Hungarian Rhapsodies
composer: Franz Liszt
Hungary: 6 nation 7 country
airline: 5 MALEV
capital: 8 Budapest
cellist: 7 Starker
cheese: 8 Liptauer
city: 4 Eger, Gyor, Pécs, Raab 5 Tokay 6 Szeged 7 Miskolc 8 Budapest, Debrecen
composer: 5 Lehár
conductor: 5 Solti, Szell 6 Dorati, Reiner 7 Ormandy
dance: 7 csardas, czardas
Danube, in ~: 4 Duna
hero: 5 Arpad
horseman: 6 hussar
jam: 6 lekvar
lake: 7 Balaton
language: 5 Ugric
money: 5 pengo 6 filler, forint
mountain: 5 Kekes
neighbor: 3 Aus., Rom., Ukr. 4 Aust. 7 Austria, Croatia, Romania, Ukraine 8 Slovakia, Slovenia 10 Yugoslavia
Nobelist in Chemistry: 8 de Hevesy
Nobelist in Literature: 7 Kertész
Nobelist in Medicine: 12 Szent-Györgyi
org.: 4 NATO
poet: 6 József
river: 4 Eger, Raab, Raba 5 Tisza
saint: 7 Stephen 9 Elizabeth
sheepdog: 4 puli 6 kuvasz
sheepdogs: 5 pulik
violinist: 4 Auer 7 Joachim, Szigeti
wine: 5 tokay
writer: 6 Molnár
__-Hungary: 7 Austria
hunger: 3 yen 4 itch, long, lust, need, sigh, want, wish 5 greed, yearn 6 desire, thirst 7 craving, edacity, longing 8 appetite, cupidity, languish, munchies, voracity, yearning 9 appetence, eagerness, esurience, hankering, indigence 10 famishment, sweet tooth

cause ~: 6 famish
end one's ~: 3 eat
feeling of ~: 4 pang
for: 4 need, want
(for): 4 long, pant, pine 5 crave
reveal one's ~: 5 drool 8 salivate
symbol of voracious ~: 3 maw
__ hunger: 4 from
hungering: 7 longing, starved 8 starving
hunger strike, go on a: 4 fast
hungrily, eat: 4 wolf 6 devour, gobble, inhale 7 scarf up 9 scarf down
hungry: 5 eager, empty, itchy, unfed 6 greedy 7 longing, starved, thirsty, wishful 8 covetous, desirous, edacious, esurient, famished, ravenous, starving, unfilled 9 ambitious, hankering, insatiate, voracious
go ~: 4 fast 6 starve
no longer ~: 4 full 5 sated 6 gorged 7 glutted, stuffed 8 satiated 9 surfeited
hungry __ bear: 3 as a
Hungry __: 4 Eyes, Jack 5 Heart
Hungry Eyes (1987 song)
artist: Eric Carmen
Hungry Heart (1980 song)
artist: Bruce Springsteen
__ hungry I could...: 4 I'm so
Hungry Like the Wolf (1983 song)
artist: Duran Duran
hung up: 4 late 5 tardy 7 overdue, puzzled, worried 8 detained, obsessed
hunk: 3 gob, wad 4 clod, glob, lump, mass, part, slab, stud 5 batch, block, chunk, clump, he-man, macho, piece, scrap, slice, solid, wedge 6 Adonis, Apollo, looker, morsel, nugget 7 portion, section 8 beefcake, quantity
asset: 3 bod
of junk: 3 dud 5 crate, lemon
hunker down: 3 sit 4 bend, duck 5 hunch, squat, stoop 6 crouch, huddle
__ Hunk O' Love: 4 A Big
Hunkpapa: 5 tribe 6 Indian 7 Amerind
hunky: 4 hale, iron, wiry 5 beefy, burly, hardy, hefty, husky, lusty, stout, tough 6 brawny, hearty, mighty, potent, robust, rugged, sinewy, steely, stocky, sturdy, virile 7 doughty 8 athletic, forceful, handsome, indurate, muscular, powerful, puissant, stalwart, vigorous 9 Atlantean, Herculean, strapping, well-built 10 able-bodied, red-blooded
hunky-dory
see wonderful
Hunley: 5 Leann
Hunnicutt: 5 Gayle
hunt: 4 look, rake, root, seek 5 chase, probe, prowl, quest, scour, stalk, trace, track, trail 6 chivvy, forage, prey on, pursue, search 7 dragnet, look for, pursuit, ransack, rummage, seek out 8 run after, scout out, scrounge 9 chase down, come after, track down
and peck: 4 type
for: 4 seek, shop 6 look up, pursue 7 scout up 8 run after, scout out
(for): 3 dig 4 fish 5 quest 6 forage
goddess: 5 Diana
illegally: 5 poach
in the dark: 5 grope 6 fumble 9 feel about
on the ~: 9 piratical, predatory, raptorial, vulturous 10 predacious
(out): 4 find 6 ferret
partner: 4 peck
scavenger ~: 4 game
starter: 3 man 4 head
__-hunt: 3 job
Hunt: 3 Tim 5 Helen, Leigh, Linda, Peter 6 Bonnie, Holman, Marsha, Walter
__ Hunt: 3 Sea 5 Mouse
hunt and __: 4 peck
hunted: 4 mark, pawn, prey 5 patsy 6 pigeon, quarry, target, victim
hunter: 3 dog 5 canid, Diana, horse, jager, Orion, yager 6 canine, equine, jaeger, nimrod, seeker 7 Actaeon, pursuer, quester, shikari, stalker, tracker 8 Atalanta, Atalante, searcher, shikaree 9 Elmer Fudd, sportsman
attire: 3 cap 4 camo, topi, vest 5 topee
Biblical ~: 4 Cain, Esau
bird ~: 6 fowler
cabin: 5 lodge
cartoon ~: 4 Fudd 5 Elmer
conger ~: 5 eeler
fox ~ coat: 5 pinks
fox ~ cry: 4 hark, toho 5 hallo, hillo, hoick, hullo 6 halloa, halloo, hallow, hilloa, hulloo, yoicks
guide: 5 gilly 6 gillie 7 ghillie
mark: 4 game, prey 6 quarry
mythical ~: 5 Orion
need: 3 lic. 4 ammo 5 decoy, rifle 6 waders 7 license
org.: 3 NRA
post: 5 blind, stand
starter: 3 pot 4 head
track: 5 spoor
__ hunter: 3 fox 6 bounty 7 fortune
__-hunter: 3 job
Hunter: 3 Ian, Kim, Tab, Tim 4 Bill, Evan, peak, Ross, Tylo 5 Holly, mount 6 Nimrod, Rachel 7 Alberta, Catfish, Jeffrey 8 mountain
peak locale: 7 New York 9 Catskills
Hunter (NBC drama)
cast: Fred Dryer (Rick Hunter) Stepfanie Kramer (Dee Dee McCall)
employer: L.A.P.D.
Hunter, Catfish: 6 hurler 7 pitcher
Hunter, Evan: 6 writer
pseudonym: Ed McBain
real last name: Lombino
work: The Blackboard Jungle
Hunter Gets Captured..., The (1967 song)
artist: Marvelettes
Hunter, Holly: 7 actress
film: Always (1989)
Broadcast News (1987)
Copycat (1995)
Living Out Loud (1998)
Miss Firecracker (1989)
O Brother, Where Art Thou? (2000)
The Piano (1993, AA)
Raising Arizona (1987)
Hunter, Rachel
spouse: Rod Stewart
hunter's __: 4 moon, pink, robe 5 sauce
__ Hunters, The: 4 Girl 7 Mammoth
__ Hunter, The: 4 Deer
Hunt for Red October, The (1990 film)
cast: Alec Baldwin, Sean Connery, Scott Glenn
device: 5 sonar
Hunt, Helen: 7 actress
film: As Good as It Gets (1997, AA)
Cast Away (2000)
The Curse of the Jade Scorpion (2001)
Mr. Saturday Night (1992)
Pay It Forward (2000)
Trancers (1985)
Twister (1996)
The Waterdance (1992)
What Women Want (2000)
spouse: Hank Azaria
TV: Mad About You
hunting: 5 sport
happy ~ ground: 6 heaven, utopia 7 Arcadia, Elysium 8 paradise 9 Shangri-la
hunting __: 5 knife 6 ground
__ hunting: 3 fox, job 4 deer, duck
Hunting of the Snark, The
author: Lewis Carroll
Huntington: 4 town
locale: 7 New York 10 Long Island
Huntington Beach: 4 city, town
locale: 10 California
__ Hunt Jackson: 5 Helen
Hunt, Leigh: 4 poet 7 British
friend: John Keats, Percy Bysshe Shelley
work: Abou Ben Adhem
Huntley: 4 Chet
colleague: 8 Brinkley
Hunt, Linda Oscar: The Year of Living Dangerously
Hunts: 6 county
locale: 7 England
Hunt's: 6 catsup 7 ketchup
alternative: 5 Heinz 8 Del Monte
Huntsville: 4 city, town
locale: 3 Ala., Tex. 5 Texas 7 Alabama
Huntz: 4 Hall
milieu: 6 Bowery
Huon Gulf, port on: 3 Lae
Hupmobile: 3 car 4 auto 10 automobile
contemporary: 3 Reo
Huppert: 8 Isabelle
__-Hur: 3 Ben
Hurd: 7 Gale Ann
hurdle: 3 bar, hop, rub 4 jump, leap, lick, snag 5 bound, clear, minus, vault 6 hamper, spring 7 barrier, hop over 8 blockage, drawback, handicap, jump over, leap over, obstacle, overcome, surmount, weakness 9 barricade, detriment, hindrance, liability 10 difficulty, impediment
hurdler: 5 racer 6 runner 7 athlete
__ hurdles: 3 low 4 high
hurdy-gurdy: 8 keyboard 10 instrument
Hurdy Gurdy Man (1968 song)
artist: Donovan
hurl: 3 lob, peg 4 cast, fire, pelt, send, slam, toss 5 chuck, fling, heave, pitch, shoot, sling, throw 6 launch, let fly, propel 7 deliver, project 8 catapult, jettison
hurler: 7 catapul, pitcher
stat.: 3 ERA
hurley: 4 club
Hurley: 3 Liz 9 Elizabeth
Hurley, Elizabeth: 7 actress
film: Austin Powers... (1997)
Bedazzled (2000)
hurling: 4 game 5 sport
hurly-burly: 3 ado 4 flap, stir, to-do 5 chaos, furor, hoo-ha 6 bedlam, clamor, hubbub, pother, racket, ruckus, rumpus, squall, tumult, uproar 7 turmoil 8 brouhaha, upheaval 9 commotion, confusion 10 hullabaloo
Hurlyburly
author: David Rabe
Hurok: 3 Sol
Huron: 4 lake 5 tribe 6 Indian 7 Amerind 9 Great Lake
locale: 4 S. Dak. 6 Canada
neighbor: 4 Erie
hurrah: 3 cry, olé, rah, yay 4 hail, viva, vive, yell 5 bravo, cheer, huzza, whoop 6 banzai, hooray, hot dog, hubbub, huzzah, yippee 7 fanfare, way to go 9 commotion 10 boola boola, excitement, halleluhah, hot diggety
in Spanish: 3 olé
__ Hurrah, The: 4 Last
hurray preceder: 3 hip
hurricane: 4 blow, wind 5 storm 7 cyclone, lantern, monsoon, tempest, tornado, twister, typhoon
1960: 5 Donna
1964: 4 Dora
1970: 5 Celia
1972: 5 Agnes
1975: 6 Eloise
1989: 4 Hugo
1992: 5 Iniki 6 Andrew
1999: 4 Gert 6 Bertha
2005: 5 Wilma 7 Katrina
2008: 3 Ike
center: 3 eye
every other ~: 3 her, him
lamp part: 4 wick
like a ~ center: 4 calm 5 quiet 6 placid, serene 8 tranquil
remains: 6 debris, rubble
track: 4 path
water-wall: 5 surge
zone: 5 coast 9 shoreline
hurricane __: 4 deck, lamp
hurricane-__ wind: 5 force
Hurricanes: 3 six 4 team
home: 4 N. Car. 7 Raleigh
milieu: 3 ice 4 rink
org.: 3 NHL
rival: *see* hockey team
school: 5 Miami
sport: 6 hockey
Hurricane, The (1999 film)
cast: Liev Schreiber, Denzel Washington

hurried: **4** fast, rush **5** brief, brisk, fleet, hasty, quick, rapid, short, swift **6** abrupt, flying, hectic, racing, rushed, speedy, sudden **7** cursory, express, instant, rushing **8** headlong, pell-mell, slapdash **9** breakneck, impetuous **10** double-time, hypersonic, in an uproar, supersonic
hurriedly: **3** PDQ **4** fast **5** apace, madly, short **6** presto **7** briefly, fleetly, hastily, in haste, rapidly, swiftly **8** in a flash, in a jiffy, in no time, on the fly, on the run, pell-mell **9** forthwith, headfirst, instantly, like a shot, posthaste **10** in high gear
 leave ~: **4** dart, zoom **5** split **6** decamp **7** take off, vamoose
hurriedness: **3** zip **4** rush **5** haste, speed **6** hustle **8** alacrity, celerity, dispatch, rapidity, scramble, velocity **9** hastiness **10** expedition
hurry: **3** fly, hie, rip, run, zip **4** dart, dash, flit, move, pelt, race, rush, tear, trot, whiz **5** drive, haste, press, scoot, smoke, speed, whisk **6** barrel, bustle, flurry, gallop, hasten, hustle, rocket, scurry, step up **7** be quick, floor it, forward, quicken, scamper, urgency **8** alacrity, celerity, dispatch, expedite, hightail, make time, pressure, rapidity, stampede, step on it, velocity **9** fleetness, go swiftly, make haste, quickness, shake a leg, swiftness **10** accelerate, expedition, get a move on, make tracks, promptness, speediness
 in a ~: **7** hastily, quickly, rapidly, swiftly **8** speedily
 leave in a ~: **3** hie, run **4** bolt, flee, flit **6** decamp **9** bundle off
 old-style: **5** sessa
hurry __ wait: **5** up and
__ hurry: **3** in a **4** in no
Hurry!: **4** ASAP, c'mon, stat **6** come on, let's go
Hurry on Down
 author: John Wain
hurry-scurry: **3** ado **4** dash, fuss, rush, to-do **5** furor, haste, hasty **6** flurry, rushed **7** chaotic, flutter, hurried **8** agitated, confused, pell-mell **9** agitation, confusion
hurry-up: **4** dire, rush **5** acute **6** urgent **7** burning, crucial, exigent **8** pressing **9** important **10** compelling
hurry up and __: **4** wait
Hurst, Fannie: **6** writer
 work: Imitation of Life
Hurst, Fannie work: Imitation of Life
Hurston, Zora Neale: **6** writer
 collaborator: Hughes
 work: Dust Tracks on a Road
  Mule Bone
  Their Eyes Were Watching God
hurt: **3** ail, cut, hit, ill, mar, vex **4** ache, belt, blow, burn, faze, flog, gash, harm, kick, lash, loss, maim, mall, maul, miff, nick, ouch, pain, pang, scar, slap, slug, sore, stab, tear, whip, yeow, zing **5** abuse, break, burnt, crack, cramp, cut up, flail, lay up, pinch, pique, prick, punch, smart, spank, spite, spoil, sting, throb, upset, whack, wound, wreck, wrong **6** aching, batter, boo-boo, bruise, burned, damage, grazed, grieve, harmed, impair, injure, injury, in pain, lament, lean on, maimed, marred, mauled, mess up, miffed, nicked, offend, pained, piqued, pommel, pummel, punish, rankle, sadden, struck, suffer, tender, torn up, trauma **7** afflict, bruised, contuse, corrupt, crushed, damaged, injured, offense, rough up, scraped, scratch, slander, torment, torture, trample, trouble, unhappy, vitiate, wounded **8** aggrieve, battered, buffeted, busted up, contused, distress, grieving, impaired, insulted, lacerate, maltreat, mischief, offended, soreness **9** affronted, aggrieved, contusion, detriment, displease, disturbed, grievance, indignant, lacerated, miserable, prejudice, resentful, scratched, suffering, undermine **10** affliction, discomfort, distressed, laceration, resentment, traumatize
 easily ~: **6** touchy **8** skittish **9** sensitive **10** vulnerable
 for: **4** lack, miss, need, want **5** covet, crave **6** desire
 heart ~: **5** dolor, grief **6** misery **7** anguish **8** distress
 reaction: **2** ow **3** yow **4** ouch, yeow
 small ~: **6** boo-boo, bruise **7** scratch
Hurt: **4** John **7** William **8** Mary Beth
Hurt __: **5** So Bad
hurtful: **3** bad, ill **4** evil, mean **5** cruel, harsh, nasty, sharp, snide, toxic **6** aching, animal, bitter, brutal, fierce, lethal, malign, nocent, savage, unkind, wanton **7** baneful, beastly, callous, cutting, harmful, nocuous, noisome, noxious, vicious **8** abrasive, barbaric, damaging, fiendish, grievous, inhumane, inimical, pitiless, ruthless, sadistic, sinister, spiteful, vengeful **9** cutthroat, dangerous, ferocious, injurious, insulting, malicious, merciless, monstrous, poisonous, truculent, upsetting **10** afflictive, maleficent, pernicious, unmerciful, vindictive
hurting: **3** sad **4** achy, sore **6** in pain, misery, somber **7** painful, unhappy **8** wretched **9** irritated, miserable, sorrowful **10** lamentable
 for: **7** lacking
Hurting Each Other (1972 song)
 artist: Carpenters
hurtle: **3** ram **4** bolt, dart, jerk, jump, race, rush, tear, whiz, zoom **5** crash, lunge, shoot, speed **6** careen, charge, plunge **7** collide **8** catapult, leapfrog
Hurt Locker, The (2009 film)
 director: Kathryn Bigelow
__ Hurts: **4** Love
Hurt So Bad (song)
 artist: Lettermen, Little Anthony and the Imperials, Linda Ronstadt
Hurts So Good (1982 song)
 artist: John Cougar Mellencamp
__ Hurt, The: **3** Big
Hurt, William: **5** actor
 film: The Accidental Tourist (1988)
  Altered States (1980)
  The Big Chill (1983)
  Body Heat (1981)
  Broadcast News (1987)
  Children of a Lesser God (1986)
  The Doctor (1991)
  Gorky Park (1983)
  Kiss of the Spider Woman (1985, AA)
  Lost in Space (1998)
  Michael (1996)
  One True Thing (1998)
  Second Best (1994)
  Smoke (1995)
Hus: **3** Jan
husband: **4** keep, male, save **5** groom, hubby, store **6** mister, retain, spouse **7** consort, partner **8** benedict, helpmate, helpmeet **9** other half **10** bridegroom
 and wife: **3** duo **4** pair
 first ~: **4** Adam
 former: **2** ex **7** divorcé
 mate: **4** wife **6** missus
 starter: **5** house
 to-be: **6** fiancé **8** intended **9** betrothed
husbandless: **5** unwed **6** single **8** eligible **9** unmarried **10** unattached
husbandry: **6** thrift **7** farming **9** frugality
__ husbandry: **6** animal
Husbands and Wives (1992 film)
 cast: Woody Allen, Blythe Danner, Mia Farrow, Juliette Lewis, Liam Neeson, Sydney Pollack
 director: Woody Allen
hush: **3** gag **4** calm, lull, mute, stop **5** pause, peace, quiet, shush, still **6** muffle, muzzle, shut up, silent, soothe, stifle **7** cover up, secrecy, silence **8** pipe down, quietude, suppress **9** keep still, quiet down, stillness, voiceless **10** hold it down
 money: **5** bribe, graft **6** payoff **7** jobbery **8** kickback **9** blackmail
 up: **4** hide **5** quash, quell **6** stifle **7** conceal, cover up, smother, squelch **8** palliate, suppress **9** keep quiet **10** hold it down, keep secret
hush __: **5** money, puppy
Hush (1968 song)
 artist: Deep Purple
Hush!: **3** shh **5** bag it **6** shut up, stow it
hushed: **3** low **4** calm **5** faint, piano, quiet **6** gentle, silent **7** subdued **8** tranquil **9** noiseless, secretive, soundless **10** untroubled
 tone: **6** murmur **7** whisper
 up: **3** mum **4** calm **5** quiet **6** placid, silent **7** muffled, quieted, stilled **8** becalmed **9** quiescent **10** unspeaking
hush-hush: **5** close, privy **6** covert, hidden, masked, secret, unseen, veiled **7** furtive, private, silence, sub rosa **8** obscured, secluded, secretly, shrouded, stealthy **9** nonpublic, underhand **10** classified, restricted, undercover, under wraps
Hush ... Hush, Sweet Charlotte: **4** film, song
 artist: Patti Page
 cast: Mary Astor, Victor Buono, Joseph Cotten, Bette Davis, Olivia de Havilland, Bruce Dern, Agnes Moorehead
Hush Puppies mascot: **6** basset
Husing: **3** Ted
husk: **3** bur, pod **4** aril, bark, bran, case, hull, peel, rind, skin **5** chaff, shell, shuck, strip **7** outside **8** covering **10** integument
husker concern: **3** ear **4** corn
huskiness: **3** vim **4** dint, roup, thew **5** brawn, force, might, power, thews, vigor **6** energy, muscle **7** fitness, muscles, potence, potency, stamina **8** vitality **9** endurance, fortitude, puissance **10** brute force
husking __: **3** bee
husky: **3** big, dog **4** deep, hale, iron, well, wiry **5** beefy, burly, canid, gruff, hardy, harsh, hefty, hunky, lusty, raspy, rough, roupy, solid, stout, thick, tough **6** brawny, canine, chubby, chunky, croaky, hearty, hoarse, mighty, portly, potent, robust, rugged, sinewy, steely, stocky, strong, sturdy, virile **7** doughty, rasping, raucous, sizable, sled dog, throaty **8** athletic, croaking, forceful, guttural, indurate, muscular, powerful, puissant, scratchy, sizeable, stalwart, thickset, vigorous **9** Atlantean, corpulent, Herculean, strapping, well-built **10** able-bodied, red-blooded, well-padded
 command: **4** mush
 group: **4** team
 hangout: **5** Yukon **6** Alaska
 load: **4** sled
Husky, Ferlin
 song: Gone (1957)
huss: **4** fish
hussar: **7** dragoon **8** horseman
 blade: **5** saber
Hussein: **5** Waris
Hussein, King: **4** Arab **9** Jordanian
 wife: **4** Alia, Noor
Husserl, Edmund: **6** German **11** philosopher
Hussey: **4** Ruth **6** Olivia
hussy: **4** minx **7** Jezebel **8** spitfire
hustings: **5** stump **8** campaign
hustle: **3** fly, hie, mob, rip, rob, run, zip **4** dart, dash, flit, hoax, push, race, rush, scam, sell, tear, work, zoom **5** cheat, dance, fraud, haste, hurry, scoot, shove, spank, speed **6** barrel, bustle, dupery, fleece, gallop, hasten, humbug, move it, rocket, scheme, scurry **7** floor it, hop to it, quicken, request, scamper, solicit, swindle **8** activity, celerity, dispatch, gumption, hightail, shoulder, step on it, struggle, work hard **9** bundle off, deception, go quickly, hotfoot it, shake a leg, skedaddle **10** enterprise, get a move on, get hopping, get-up-and-go, hightail it
 and bustle: **4** to-do **5** hoo-ha **6** clamor, flurry, hoopla, hubbub, tumult, uproar **7** ferment, turmoil **8** activity, brouhaha, foofaraw

9 commotion 10 excitement, hullabaloo
do the ~: 5 dance, disco
partner: 6 bustle
hustler: 4 doer 5 cheat, shark 6 bilker, con man, dynamo 7 busy bee, grifter, scammer 8 go-getter, live wire, swindler 9 defrauder 10 ball of fire
Hustler, The (1961 film)
cast: Jackie Gleason, Piper Laurie, Paul Newman, George C. Scott
director: Robert Rossen
prop: 3 cue 4 rack
Hustle, The (1975 song)
artist: Van McCoy
phrase: 4 do it
Huston: 4 John 6 Walter 8 Anjelica
Huston, Anjelica: 7 actress
film: The Addams Family (1991)
Addams Family Values (1993)
The Dead (1987)
Enemies, A Love Story (1989)
Ever After (1998)
Gardens of Stone (1987)
The Grifters (1990)
Manhattan Murder Mystery (1993)
Prizzi's Honor (1985, AA)
The Royal Tenenbaums (2001)
The Witches (1990)
Huston, John: 8 director
film: The African Queen (1951)
The Asphalt Jungle (1950)
Beat the Devil (1954)
Casino Royale (1967)
Chinatown (1974)
The Dead (1987)
Fat City (1972)
Freud (1962)
Heaven Knows, Mr. Allison (1957)
In This Our Life (1942)
Key Largo (1948)
The Life and Times of Judge Roy Bean (1972)
The List of Adrian Messenger (1963)
The Maltese Falcon (1941)
Man in the Wilderness (1971)
The Man Who Would Be King (1975)
The Misfits (1961)
Moby Dick (1956)
Moulin Rouge (1952)
Myra Breckinridge (1970)
The Night of the Iguana (1964)
Prizzi's Honor (1985)
The Red Badge of Courage (1951)
The Treasure of the Sierra Madre (1948, AA)
Under the Volcano (1984)
The Unforgiven (1960)
We Were Strangers (1949)
Wise Blood (1979)
spouse: Evelyn Keyes
hut: 4 digs, dump, home, shed 5 bower, cabin, house, hovel, hutch, lodge, shack 6 billet, cabana, chalet, lean-to, shanty, wikiup 7 cottage, quonset, rathole, shelter, wickiup, wickyup 8 bungalow
follower: 3 one, two
ice ~: 4 iglu 5 igloo
Mexican ~: 5 jacal
Quonset ~: 8 barracks
sayer: 2 QB 11 quarterback
Shetland Islands ~: 4 skeo
__ hut: 6 Nissen 7 Quonset
__ Hut: 5 Pizza
hutch: 3 bin, box, cot, hut, pen 4 cage, coop 5 cabin, chest, shack 7 cabinet, confine, cottage 8 cupboard 9 container, enclosure, furniture
display: 5 china 6 dishes 8 ceramics
Hutch
portrayer: David Soul
Hutchence: 7 Michael
Hutchinson: 4 city, town 5 Fiona
locale: 6 Kansas
Hutchins, Will: 5 actor
film: Clambake (1967)
TV: Sugarfoot
Hutton: 2 E.F. 3 Jim 5 Betty 6 Ina Ray, Lauren, Robert 7 Barbara, Timothy
Hutton, Barbara
spouse: Cary Grant
Hutton, Jim: 5 actor
TV: Adventures of Ellery Queen
Hutton, Timothy: 5 actor
film: Beautiful Girls (1996)
City of Industry (1997)
Daniel (1983)
Deterrence (2000)
Everybody's All-American (1988)
The General's Daughter (1999)
Iceman (1984)
Ordinary People (1980, AA)
The Temp (1993)
spouse: Debra Winger
Hutu
foe: 4 Tusi 5 Tussi, Tutsi 6 Watusi 7 Watutsi
home: 6 Africa
Huxley: 6 Aldous, Andrew, Julian, Thomas
Huxley, Aldous: 6 writer 7 British
alma mater: Eton, Oxford
work: Antic Hay
Brave New World
Crome Yellow
Eyeless in Gaza
Point Counter Point
Huxley, Andrew: 7 British 8 Nobelist
Huxley, Julian: 3 Sir 7 British 9 biologist
work: Ants
Huxley, Thomas: 7 British 9 biologist
Huxtable: 3 Ada 4 Rudy, Theo 5 Clair, Cliff 6 Denise 7 Vanessa
Huxtable, Cliff
portrayer: Cos, Bill Cosby
Huygens, Christiaan: 5 Dutch 9 physicist 10 astronomer
Huysmans, Joris: 6 French, writer
huzzah: 3 cry, rah 4 hail, viva, vive, yell 5 bravo, cheer, shout 6 banzai, hoorah, hooray, hot dog, hurrah, hurray, yippee 7 way to go 8 accolade 10 boola boola, hallelujah, hot diggety
in Spanish: 3 olé
__ H. White: 8 Theodore
hwy.: 2 rd. 3 rte., tpk.
designer: 2 CE
intersection: 3 jct.
offense: 3 DWI
safety org.: 4 MADD
sign abbr.: 3 alt.
strip: 2 ln.
Hy: 8 Averback
hyacinth: 3 gem 5 color, plant 6 flower, orange 7 reddish 8 gemstone
home: 3 bed
relative: 5 flame, henna 7 pumpkin, saffron 9 tangerine 10 terra cotta
Hyakutake: 5 comet
hyaline: 5 clear 6 glassy 9 glasslike
hyalite: 4 opal 7 mineral
Hyams: 5 Leila, Peter
Hyannis: 4 city, town
course: 3 cod 5 scrod 6 schrod
locale: 4 Mass. 7 Cape Cod
Hyatt: 5 hotel
alternative: *see* hotel
Hyatt __: 7 Regency
hybrid: 3 cur, mix 4 mule 5 cross, liger, plant, tigon 6 tiglon 7 amalgam, beefalo, cattalo, mixture, mongrel 8 assorted 9 composite, cross-bred, immixture
bovine: 6 catalo 7 beefalo
cat: 5 liger, tigon
combining form: 4 noth- 5 notho-
tangerine ~: 4 Ugli
tree: 7 plumcot 8 limequat
hybrid __: 3 car 5 vigor
hybridize: 3 mix 5 cross 10 interbreed
Hyde, Mr., like: 4 evil
Hyde Park
initials: 3 FDR
locale: 6 London 7 England, New York
__ Hyde Pierce: 5 David
Hyderabad: 4 city, town
dress: 4 sari 5 saree
locale: 5 India
river: 5 Indus
sovereign: 5 Nizam
Hyde-White: 7 Wilfrid
Hydra: 7 monster, serpent
neighbor: 3 Leo 5 Libra 6 Antlia
number of heads: 4 nine
Hydra Head, The
author: Carlos Fuentes
hydrangea: 5 plant, shrub 6 flower
hydrant: 3 tap 4 plug 5 valve
hookup: 4 hose
__ hydrant: 4 fire
hydraulic __: 4 lift 5 brake
hydraulics: 7 science
study: 7 liquids
hydriad: 5 nymph
hydro: 10 power plant, water power
hydrocarbon: 4 amyl 5 arene, hexyl, tolan 6 alkane, butane, butene, cetane, ethane, hexane 8 dimethyl
ending: 3 -ane, -ene, -yne
radical: 5 alkyl
hydrochloric: 4 acid
hydrodynamics: 7 science
study: 7 liquids
hydroelectric: 5 power
org.: 3 TVA
project: 3 dam
hydrofluoric __: 4 acid
hydrofoil: 4 boat, ship 5 craft 6 vessel
hydrogen: 3 gas 7 element
hydrogen __: 3 ion 4 bomb
__ hydrogen: 5 heavy
hydrogeology: 7 science
hydrographic: 6 marine 7 oceanic, pelagic 8 maritime, nautical
hydrokinetics: 7 science
hydrology: 7 science
study: 5 water
hydrolyzed vegetable __: 7 protein
hydromassage facility: 3 spa
hydrometer scale: 5 Baume
hydrophobe fear: 5 water
hydrophobia: 5 lyssa 6 rabies
hydrophyte: 4 alga
hydroplane: 4 boat, skim 5 craft 6 vessel
part: 5 float
hydrostatics: 7 science
hydrous: 3 wet 6 liquid, watery 7 aqueous
Hydrox
rival: *see* cookie brand
hydroxide: 3 ion 4 base 6 alkali 7 antacid
potassium ~: 3 KOH
sodium ~: 4 NaOH
solution: 3 lye
hydroxyl: 3 ion
compound: 4 enol
Hydrus neighbor: 5 Mensa
hyena: 4 Lena 6 animal, mammal
kin: 6 jackal
Hyer: 6 Martha
hyetal: 5 rainy 7 pluvial, showery 8 pluvious
hygiene: 6 health 10 sanitation
__ hygiene: 4 oral 6 dental
hygienic: 5 clean 6 washed 7 aseptic, healthy, sterile 8 germ-free, pristine, sanitary, spotless, unsoiled 9 wholesome 10 antiseptic, immaculate, salubrious
__ hygienist: 6 dental
hygric: 3 wet 4 damp 5 humid, moist 6 watery
hyla: 8 tree frog, tree toad 9 amphibian
Hyla Brook
author: Robert Frost
Hyland: 5 Brian, Diana
Hyllus
wife: 4 Iole
Hyman: 3 Flo, Mac 4 Dick 5 Earle 8 Rickover
__ Hyman Award: 3 Flo
Hyman, Dick: 7 pianist
genre: 4 jazz
hymenopteran: 3 bee 6 insect
hymn: 3 ode 4 laud, lied, pean, poem, song 5 carol, dirge, motet, music, paean, psalm 6 anthem, choral, praise, Te Deum 7 chorale, hosanna 8 canticle, evensong
accompaniment: 5 organ
ender: 4 book
finale: 4 amen
of praise: 3 ode 4 pean 5 paean
opening: 6 adeste
singers: 5 choir, flock, laity
hymnal: 4 book
__ Hymn of the Republic, The: 6 Battle
Hymn to Apollo: 4 poem
author: Percy Bysshe Shelley
Hymn to Intellectual Beauty
author: Percy Bysshe Shelley
Hymn to Proserpine
author: Algernon Swinburne
Hynde: 8 Chrissie
hyoid: 4 bone
locale: 6 tongue

hype: **4** plug, puff, push, tout **5** lobby **6** hoopla, overdo, talk up **7** advance, buildup, promote, puffery, trumpet **8** ballyhoo, plugging **9** advertise, get behind, promotion, publicity, publicize, reinforce **10** propaganda
bit of ~: **4** plug **5** blurb, promo
up: **4** plug, push, stir, tout **5** rouse **6** arouse, bestir, incite **7** animate, enliven, inspire, promote, push for **8** ballyhoo, inspirit, motivate, vitalize **9** publicize, stimulate
hyped up: **5** zippy **6** lively **7** dynamic, kinetic, orotund, pompous **8** animated, inflated **9** bombastic, energetic, overblown **10** immoderate
hyper: **5** manic, tense, wired **6** jangly, lively **7** anxious, excited, fidgety, frantic, keyed up **8** fluttery, frenetic, frenzied, hopped up, restless, tireless, vehement **9** sprightly **10** high-strung, overactive, unwearying
not ~: **4** calm **5** staid **6** sedate **7** relaxed
hyperbola: **3** arc **5** curve
hyperbole: **5** trope **7** big talk **8** rhetoric **10** distortion
hyperbolize: **7** ham it up, overact **9** overstate **10** exaggerate
hypercritical: **7** carping **8** captious, exacting **9** squeamish
hypercriticize: **4** carp **5** cavil **7** nitpick, quibble **8** pettifog **10** split hairs
Hyperion: **4** moon **5** giant, Titan
author: John Keats, Henry Wadsworth Longfellow
daughter: **3** Eos
parent: **4** Gaea **6** Uranus
planet: **6** Saturn
sister: **4** Thia
son: **6** Helios
hyperphysical: **6** occult **8** ethereal **9** unearthly
hypersensitive: **6** touchy **7** waspish **8** allergic
hypersensitivity: **7** allergy
hypersonic: **4** fast **5** brisk, fleet, quick, rapid, swift **6** flying, speedy **9** breakneck
hypertrophic: **3** big
hyperventilate: **4** gasp, pant
hyphen cousin: **4** dash **6** em dash, en dash
Hypnos: **3** god
domain: **5** sleep
parent: **3** Nyx **6** Erebus
son: **8** Morpheus
hypnosis: **6** stupor, trance **8** numbness **9** mesmerism
hypnotic: **6** sleepy **8** magnetic, mesmeric, sedative **9** soporific **10** anesthetic, magnetical
state: **6** trance
hypnotism: **5** spell **9** magnetism
hypnotist: **9** mesmerist
word: **5** sleep
hypnotize: **4** grip, vamp **5** charm **6** dazzle **7** bewitch, enchant, enthral, inthral **8** enthrall, entrance, inthrall, transfix **9** captivate, fascinate, magnetize, mesmerize, spellbind
Hypnotize (1997 song)
artist: Notorious B.I.G.
hypnotized: **4** rapt **5** under **8** held fast **10** fascinated
hypo: **4** shot **6** needle **7** syringe **9** injection
bulb: **5** ampul **6** ampule **7** ampoule
contents: **4** sera
user: **2** dr., MD, RN **5** nurse **6** doctor
hypocrisy: **4** cant, sham **5** fraud **6** deceit, dupery **7** mockery **8** bad faith, pretense, quackery **9** casuistry, deception, duplicity, imposture, phoniness **10** dishonesty, imposition, lip service, pharisaism, pretension, sanctimony
hypocrite: **4** fake **5** cheat, faker, fraud, knave, phony, quack **6** con man, humbug, phoney, poseur, rascal **7** bluffer, two-face **8** deceiver, imposter, impostor, two-timer **9** charlatan, con artist, pretender **10** backslider, dissembler
hypocritical: **4** oily **5** false, phony **6** phoney **7** canting **8** affected, recreant, two-faced
act ~: **3** lie **7** deceive, mislead, pretend **8** simulate **9** dissemble, misinform
hypodermic: **6** needle **7** syringe
amt.: **2** cc.
hypothesis: **4** idea **5** guess, posit **6** belief, theory **7** concept, opinion, premise, surmise, thought **8** proposal **9** apriority, deduction, postulate, principle, rationale, reasoning **10** antecedent, assignment, assumption, conclusion, conjecture, contention, derivation, foundation, philosophy, suggestion
hypothesize: **5** guess, posit **6** assume, propose **7** explain, presume, suppose, surmise, think up **8** theorize **9** postulate, predicate, speculate **10** conjecture, put forward
hypothetical: **4** moot **5** ideal **6** unreal, what-if **7** assumed, guessed **8** abstract, academic, possible, supposed **10** indefinite, intangible
hyrax: **4** cony **5** coney **6** animal, dassie, mammal
Hyser: **5** Joyce
hyson: **3** tea **8** green tea
hysteria: **5** panic, shock, storm **6** frenzy, nerves **8** delirium
Hysteria (1988 song)
artist: Def Leppard
hysterical: **3** mad **4** wild **5** funny, irate, rabid **6** crazed, raging, raving **7** berserk, frantic, furious, hog-wild, nervous **8** frenzied, unnerved, vehement, wild-eyed **9** delirious, emotional, excitable, possessed, spasmodic **10** convulsive, distracted, distraught, ridiculous, uproarious
something ~: **4** hoot, howl, riot **5** laugh **6** scream
hysterics: **3** fit **4** rage **7** tantrum **8** outburst **10** conniption
go into ~: **4** rant, rave **7** run amok
Hyundai: **3** car **4** auto **10** automobile
headquarters: **5** Korea
model: **6** Accent, Scoupe, Sonata **7** Elantra, Santa Fe, Tiburon
rival: ***see*** automobile
Hywel: **7** Bennett

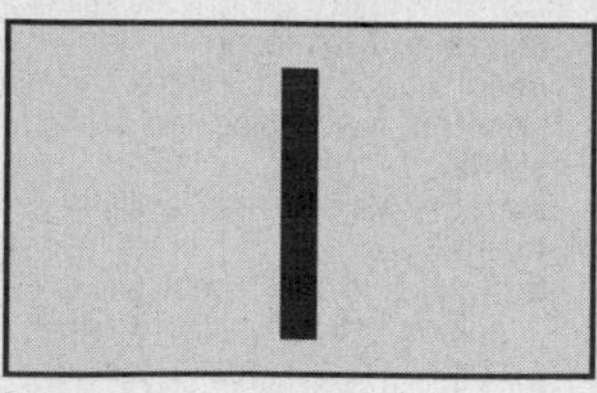

i
topper: 3 dot 6 tittle
I: 3 one 4 elem. 5 vowel 6 iodine, letter
53 for ~: 4 at. no.
Greek ~: 4 iota
in German: 3 ich
in Latin: 3 ego
in phonetic alphabet: 5 India
trouble: 3 ego 6 egoism 7 egotism
I __: 3 Spy 5 Am Sam, Ching
I __!: 3 say 5 dunno
I __ a crook: 5 am not
I __ a dream: 4 have
I __ a Kick Out of You: 3 Get
I __ a Little Prayer: 3 Say
I __ Always Love You: 4 Will
I __ a Male War Bride: 3 Was
I __ America Singing: 4 Hear
I __ a Mystery: 4 Love
I __ a Name: 3 Got
I __ Anyone Till You: 5 Hadn't
I __ a Parade: 4 Love
I __ a Piano: 4 Love
I __ a Place: 4 Know
I __ Around: 3 Get
I __ As I Wander: 6 Wonder
I __ a Song Coming On: 4 Feel
I __ a Symphony: 4 Hear
I __ a Tear: 5 Cried
I __ a Teenage Werewolf: 3 Was
I __ a thing to wear!: 6 haven't
I __ at the office: 4 gave
I __ Bad, and That Ain't Good: 5 Got It
I __ bad moon...: 4 see a
I __ Be Around: 5 Wanna
I __ been a contender!: 6 coulda
I __ Being a Girl: 5 Enjoy
I __ Be Loved By You: 5 Wanna
I __ Camera: 3 Am a
I __ Care: 4 Don't 6 Should
I __ differ!: 5 beg to
I __ Doing All Right: 3 Was
I __ Extremes: 4 Go to
I __ Fine: 4 Feel
I __ Follow Him: 4 Will
I __ for Animals: 5 Brake
I __ Fugitive...: 3 Am a
I __ gal in Kalamazoo: 4 got a
I __ Get It for You Wholesale: 3 Can
I __ Get Next to You: 4 Can't 5 Wanna
I __ Get No Satisfaction: 4 Can't
I __ Get Started: 4 Can't
I __ Got Nobody: 4 Ain't
I __ Grow Up: 4 Won't
I __ Have Danced All Night: 5 Could
I __ Have Eyes for You: 4 Only
I __ Help: 3 Can
I __ Help It: 4 Can't
I __ Help Myself: 4 Can't
I __ Her Again: 3 Saw
I __ Her Standing There: 3 Saw
I __ Hold Your Hand: 5 Wanna
I __ idea!: 5 had no
I __ Ideas: 3 Get
I __ Ike: 4 Like
I __ iodine: 4 as in
I __ It: 4 Dood, Like
I __ It Through the Grapevine: 5 Heard
I __ I Were in Love Again: 4 Wish
I __ kick from champagne: 5 get no
I __ Kick Out of You: 4 Get a
I __ Know: 5 Gotta
I __ Know What Time It Was: 5 Didn't
I __ Letter to My Love: 5 Sent a
I __ lineman for the county: 3 am a
I __ Little Prayer: 4 Say a
I __ Lucy: 4 Love
I __ Made for Dancin': 3 Was
I __ Made to Love Her: 3 Was
I __ Male War Bride: 4 Was a
I __ man with seven wives: 4 met a
I __ Men: 4 Hate
I __ my case!: 4 rest
I __ Mystery: 5 Love a
I __ my way: 5 did it
I __ my wits' end!: 4 am at
I __ Name: 4 Got a
I __ no kick from champagne...: 3 get
I __ Not Be Moved: 5 Shall
I __ of Jeannie: 5 Dream
I __ of You: 3 Beg
I __ Parade: 5 Love a
I __ Paris: 4 Love
I __ Piano: 5 Love a
I __ Pieces: 4 Go to
I __ Place: 5 Know a
I __ Plenty o' Nuthin': 3 Got
I __ Pretty: 4 Feel
I __ Promised You a Rose Garden: 5 Never
I __ Rainy Night: 5 Love a
I __ reason why not: 5 see no
I __ return: 5 shall
I __ Rhapsody: 5 Hear a
I __ Rhythm: 3 Got
I __ Right to Sing the Blues: 5 Gotta
I __ Rock: 3 Am a
I __ Rock and Roll Music: 3 Dig
I __ Said: 3 Am...I
I __ saw...: 5 came I
I __ Say No: 5 Cain't
I __ See Clearly Now: 3 Can
I __ See for Miles: 3 Can
I __ Song Coming On: 5 Feel a
I __ Song Go...: 4 Let a
I __ Stop Loving You: 4 Can't
I __ Stung: 3 Got
I __ Survive: 4 Will
I __ Symphony: 5 Hear a
I __ Teenage Were-wolf: 4 Was a
I __ tell a lie: 6 cannot
I __ That Emotion: 6 Second
I __ the Body Electric: 4 Sing
I __ the Earth Move: 4 Feel
I __ the Light: 3 Saw
I __ the Line: 4 Walk
I __ the Nightlife: 4 Love
I __ the Sheriff: 4 Shot
I __ the Songs: 5 Write
I __ the Stars: 5 Aim at
I __ the Sun in the Morning: 3 Got
I __ Three Lives: 3 Led
I __ to Be Happy: 4 Want
I __ to Cook Book: 4 Hate
I __ to differ!: 3 beg
I __ to Hold Your Hand: 4 Want
I __ to Live!: 4 Want
I __ to Pieces: 4 Fall
I __ to the Trees: 4 Talk
I __ Trouble: 4 Love
I __ vacation!: 5 need a
I __ Walrus: 5 Am the
I __ Wanna Cry: 4 Don't
I __ Wanna Stop: 4 Just
I __ Want to Be Right: 4 Don't
I __ Want to Celebrate: 4 Just
I __ We're Alone Now: 5 Think
I __ Write a Book: 5 Could
I __ You Babe: 3 Got
I __ You Knocking: 4 Hear
I __ you one!: 3 owe
I __ Your Love Tonight: 4 Need
I __ you so!: 4 told
I __ You Truly: 4 Love
I, __: 3 Too 4 Tina 5 Robot
I-__: 3 bar 4 beam
'I' __ Innocent: 5 Is for
...I __ a puddy tat!: 3 taw
...I __ not want: 5 shall
I-80: 3 rte. 5 route 7 highway 10 Interstate
city on ~: 4 Elko, Gary, Reno 5 Omaha 6 Moline 7 Chicago, Oakland, Teaneck 8 Cheyenne 9 Cleveland, Davenport, Des Moines, South Bend
runs through it: 3 Cal., Ill., Ind., Neb., Nev., Wyo. 4 Iowa, Nebr., Ohio, Penn., Utah 5 Calif. 6 Nevada 7 Indiana, Wyoming 8 Illinois, Nebraska 9 New Jersey 10 California
Ia.
see Iowa
Iacocca: 3 Lee 4 Lido
Iacta __ alea: 3 est
Iacta est __: 4 alea
Iago: 6 ensign 7 villain 8 Venetian
emulate ~: 3 lie 6 betray
in English: 5 James
wife: 6 Emilia
I agree!: 3 yep 4 amen 5 ditto, me too
Iain in English: 4 John
I Ain't __ Nobody: 3 Got
I Ain't Marching Anymore
artist: Phil Ochs
I Am __: 5 a Rock
I Am, __: 5 I Said
__ I Am: 4 Here, What
__-I-Am: 3 Sam
I Am a Rock (1966 song)
artist: Simon and Garfunkel
iamb: 4 foot
relative: 6 dactyl 7 anapest, pyrrhic, spondee, trochee
iambic
pentameter: 4 rime 5 meter, rhyme
I am here in Latin: 5 adsum
I Am...I Said (1971 song)
artist: Neil Diamond
I Am Legend (2007 film)
cast: Alice Braga, Will Smith
Iams: 7 dog food
alternative: *see* pet food brand
I Am Sam (2001 film)
cast: Sean Penn, Michelle Pfeiffer, Dianne Wiest
I am the __ of the sphere...: 5 owner
I Am Woman (1972 song)
artist: Helen Reddy
-ian
cousin: 3 ist, ite 4 ster
Ian: 3 Hay 4 Holm 5 Janis, Smith, Wolfe 6 Bannen, Gillan, Hendry, Hunter, McEwan, Wilmut 7 Fleming, McShane, Paisley, Woosnam, Ziering 8 Anderson, McKellen, Whitcomb 9 Charleson, Dalrymple 10 Baker-Finch, Ballantine, Carmichael, McNaughton, Richardson
in English: 4 John
I and Thou
author: Martin Buber
Ian, Janis
song: At Seventeen (1975)
Iapetus: 4 moon 5 giant, Titan
parent: 4 Gaea 6 Uranus
planet: 6 Saturn
son: 5 Atlas 10 Prometheus
__ I a stinker?: 4 ain't
iatric: 7 medical 8 curative, remedial, sanative 9 medicinal
iatrophobe fear: 7 doctors
Ibadan: 4 city, town
locale: 7 Nigeria
Iba, Hank: 5 coach
milieu: 5 court
org.: 3 NBA
sport: 10 basketball
I-bar: 4 beam
Ibarguren, Eva, née __: 5 Perón
Ibbetson: 5 Peter
I-beam: 4 beam 6 cursor
material: 5 steel
projection: 6 flange
i before e except after c: 4 rule
I beg of you: 6 please
I beg to differ!: 5 not so
I beg your pardon: 4 ahem
I Believe (1953 song)
artist: Frankie Laine
I Believe __: 5 in You
I Believe I Can Fly (1996 song)
artist: R. Kelly
I believe in Latin: 5 credo
I Believe in You and Me (1996 song)
artist: Whitney Houston
Iberia: 7 airline 9 peninsula
part of ~: 5 Spain 6 España 8 Portugal
river: 4 Ebro, Miño 5 Douro, Minho, Tagus
see also Portugal, Spain
Ibert: 7 Jacques
I bet!: 3 Hah
ibex: 4 goat 6 animal, mammal
relative: 4 tahr, thar 6 Angora 7 markhor 8 markhoor
ibid.: 4 same
relative: 5 op. cit.
ibis: 4 bird 5 wader 10 wading bird
relative: 5 stork 9 spoonbill
Ibiza: 4 isle 6 island
__, I Blew Up the Kid: 5 Honey
IBM: 2 co., PC 7 Big Blue, company 8 computer
early ~ computer model: 2 AT, XT
headquarters: 6 Armonk 7 New York
motto: 5 Think
part of ~: 3 Bus., Int. 4 Intl. 8 Business, Machines
rival: 3 DEC, Mac, NCR, NEC 5 Apple, Epson
Ibn: 4 Saud, Sina 7 al-'Arabi, Kahldun 8 Battutah, Taymiyah 9 al-Haytham
what ~ means: 5 son of
Ibn Saud: 4 Arab
Ibo: 8 language
home: 6 Africa 7 Nigeria
Ibsen, Henrik: 5 Norse 9 dramatist, Norwegian 10 playwright

character: 3 Ase 4 Nora
home: 4 Oslo
work: Brand
Catiline
A Doll's House
Emperor and Galilean
An Enemy of the People
The Feast at Solhaug
Ghosts
Hedda Gabler
John Gabriel Borkman
The Lady From the Sea
Lady Inger of Osteraad
The League of Youth
Little Eyolf
Love's Comedy
The Master Builder
Olaf Liljekrans
Peer Gynt
Pillars of Society
The Pretenders
Rosmersholm
St. John's Night
The Vikings at Helgeland
The Warrior's Barrow
When We Dead Awaken
The Wild Duck
ibuprofen: 5 NSAID
brand: 5 Advil
dose: 6 caplet
target: 4 ache, pain 5 cramp 8 headache, soreness
I burn, literally: 4 Etna 5 Aetna
Icahn: 4 Carl
I Cain't Say No
composer: Oscar Hammerstein, Richard Rodgers
I call 'em like I __: 5 see 'em
I came: 4 veni
I Can __ for Miles: 3 See
I Can Dream, __?: 5 Cant I
I Can Get It for You Wholesale: 5 novel
author: Jerome Weidman
I Can Help (1974 song)
artist: Billy Swan
__ I can help it!: 5 Not if
I cannot __ lie: 5 tell a
I Can Read With My Eyes Shut
author: Dr. Seuss
I Can See Clearly Now (1972 song)
artist: Johnny Nash
I Can See for Miles (1967 song)
artist: Who, The
I can't __ satisfaction: 5 get no
I can take __!: 5 a hint
I Can't Dance (1992 song)
artist: Genesis
I Can't Get Next to You (1969 song)
artist: Temptations
I Can't Go for That (1981 song)
artist: Hall and Oates
I can't hear you!: 6 louder 7 speak up
I Can't Help It (1980 song)
artist: Olivia Newton-John
I Can't Help Myself (1965 song)
artist: Four Tops
I Can't Make You Love Me (1992 song)
artist: Bonnie Raitt
I Can't Sleep Baby (1996 song)
artist: R. Kelly
I Can't Stand It (1981 song)
artist: Eric Clapton
I Can't Stop Loving You (1962 song)
artist: Ray Charles
I Can't Tell You Why (1980 song)
artist: Eagles
I Can't Wait (1986 song)
artist: Stevie Nicks, Nu Shooz
__ I care!: 4 As if
Icarian __: 3 Sea
Icarus: 8 asteroid
emulate ~: 3 fly 4 soar
parent: 7 Dedalus 8 Daedalus, Naucrate
Icarus Agenda, The
author: Robert Ludlum
ICBM: 4 MIRV 5 Atlas, Titan 7 Polaris
part of ~: 5 Inter 7 Missile 9 Ballistic
ICC concern: 3 trk.
ice: 3 gem 4 do in, floe, hail 5 chill, cinch, cubes, quiet, rocks, sew up 6 clinch, cooler, ensure, freeze, gelato, sorbet 7 dessert, glacier, jewelry 8 cool down, diamonds, glaciate 9 guarantee, sparklers 10 permafrost
break the ~: 5 begin, start 6 embark, launch 8 commence
coated with ~: 4 rimy 5 gelid
crystals: 6 frazil
cut some ~: 4 rate 5 count, weigh 6 matter
ender: 3 box, cap, man, men 4 berg, boat, fall 5 blink, bound, house, maker, scape 7 breaker
glacial ~: 4 firn 5 serac
house: 4 iglu 5 igloo
in German: 3 Eis
like ~: 4 cold 5 gelid, slick 6 frosty
liquor over cracked ~: 4 mist
mass: 4 berg, calf, floe 7 glacier
melter: 3 tea 4 rain, salt
on ~: 6 secure 7 assured, certain, chilled 8 confined, in the bag, put aside 9 in reserve 10 guaranteed, in abeyance, undoubtful
on ~ on: 8 chilling
on thin ~: 5 risky 6 unsafe 8 perilous 9 uncertain 10 precarious
out: 3 ban 4 thaw 7 boycott
palace: 4 rink 5 arena
pellets: 4 hail 5 sleet
perhaps: 4 numb
put on ~: 5 chill, delay, table 6 assure, shelve 7 confine, suspend 8 sentence
thin ~: 5 glaze 6 danger, hazard
tool: 3 awl 4 pick, tong 5 borer, tongs
travel on ~: 5 skate
unit: 4 cube
without ~: 4 neat 8 straight
ice __: 3 age, bag, cap, out 4 beer, blue, cave, cube, floe, milk, pack, pick, show 5 chest, cream, field, sheet, shelf, skate, storm, tongs, water 6 hockey, island, skater 7 dancing, fishing
ice-__: 4 cold
__ ice: 5 black, cut no
Ice __: 3 Age 4 Cube 6 Palace 7 Capades, Castles, Follies
Ice __ Zebra: 7 Station
__ Ice: 3 Dry 7 Vanilla
Ice Age (2002 film)
voice cast: Denis Leary, John Leguizamo, Ray Romano
iceberg: 6 hazard 7 lettuce
extremity: 3 tip
form an ~: 5 calve
iceboating: 5 sport
iceboat necessity: 4 sail
Icebound
author: Dean Koontz
icebox: 6 cooler, fridge 7 freezer
visit: 4 nosh, raid
icebreaker: 4 boat, ship 5 craft 6 vessel
Ice Brothers
author: Sloan Wilson
__ ice cap: 5 polar
Ice Capades
move: 4 axel, lutz
workplace: 4 rink 5 arena
Ice Castles (1979 film)
cast: Robby Benson, Colleen Dewhurst, Lynn-Holly Johnson
ice-cold: 5 algid, aloof, chill, gelid, polar, stony 6 arctic, bitter, brumal, flinty, frigid, frosty, frozen, stoney, wintry 7 cutting, glacial, wintery 8 freezing, Siberian 9 unfeeling
ice cream: 4 Edy's 5 dairy, treat 6 gelati 7 Breyer's, dessert 9 Friendly's, Good Humor 10 Dairy Queen, Häagen-Dazs, Turkey Hill
British ~ cone: 6 cornet
choice: 4 pint 6 flavor, gallon 10 half gallon
flavor: 5 lemon, mocha, peach 6 almond, banana, coffee, Jamoca, toffee 7 caramel, coconut, vanilla 8 cinnamon, hazelnut 9 bubblegum, chocolate, pineapple, pistachio, raspberry, rocky road, rum raisin 10 blackberry, cheesecake, Neapolitan, peppermint, strawberry
have ~: 3 eat 4 lick, nosh
holder: 4 cone 5 stick
ingredient: 4 agar 5 sugar 7 berries, guar gum 8 agar-agar
Italian ~: 6 gelati, gelato 7 spumone, spumoni, tortoni
pattern: 5 swirl
serving: 3 dip 4 glob 5 scoop
treat: 4 cone, malt, soda 5 bombe, float, shake 6 frappe, sundae
variety: 6 gelati, gelato, sundae 7 parfait, spumone, spumoni, tortoni 8 snowball
ice cream __: 3 pop 4 cone, soda, suit 5 chair, scoop 6 parlor, social
__ ice cream: 4 soft 6 French
ice cream soda: 8 beverage
Ice Cube music: 3 rap
iced: 4 cold 5 glacé 6 frappé, frosty, frozen 10 on the rocks
dessert: 4 cake 6 frappe
drink: 3 tea 6 cooler
ice dancing: 5 sport
iced tea addition: 4 mint 5 lemon
ice fishing: 5 sport
jig: 5 tip up
tool: 5 auger
Ice Follies venue: 4 rink 5 arena
ice hockey: 4 game 5 sport
area: 4 cage, rink 6 crease 7 red line 8 blue line
commit an ~ infraction: 4 knee
coup: 8 hat trick
fake: 4 deke
gear: 4 mask, puck 5 stick
infraction: 5 icing
machine: 7 Zamboni
need: 3 net 4 puck 5 arena
position: 4 wing 6 center, goalie
starter: 7 face-off
stat: 5 goals 6 points 7 assists
team: 3 six
term: 4 cage, deke, goal, puck, rink, wing 5 icing, stick 6 assist, center, crease, goalie, period 7 face-off, penalty, red line, time-out, Zamboni 8 blue line, hat trick, slap shot
see also hockey, NHL
Iceland: 4 isle 6 island, nation 7 country
bay: 4 Faxa, Huna
capital: 9 Reykjavík
legislature: 7 Althing
letter: 3 edh
locale: 3 Eur. 6 Europe
money: 5 aurar, eyrir, krona
moss: 6 lichen
Nobelist in Literature: 7 Laxness
of ~ poetry: 5 eddic
org.: 4 NATO
prose: 4 edda, saga
volcano: 5 Hekla 6 Krafla
Icelandair
competitor: ***see*** airline
Iceland Fisherman, An
author: Pierre Loti
Icelandic: 8 language
relative: 6 Danish
iceless: 4 neat 8 straight
Ice Maiden, The: 5 Evert 10 Chris Evert
iceman: 5 NHLer 10 jewel thief
Iceman Cometh, The: 4 play
author: Eugene O'Neill
Iceni: 5 tribe
Ice Palace
author: Edna Ferber
__ ices: 7 Italian
__ Ice Shelf: 4 Ross
ice-show venue: 4 rink 5 arena 8 coliseum
ice skating: 5 sport
figure: 5 eight
move: 4 axel, lutz
see also skating
Ice Station Zebra (1968 film)
cast: Ernest Borgnine, Jim Brown, Rock Hudson, Patrick McGoohan
Ice Storm, The (1997 film)
cast: Joan Allen, Kevin Kline, Christina Ricci, Sigourney Weaver
director: Ang Lee
Ice-T specialty: 3 rap
Ich __: 4 Dien
Ich __ dich: 5 liebe
Ich __ ein Berliner: 3 bin
Ichabod: 4 poem 5 Crane
author: John Greenleaf Whittier
foe: 4 Brom
grandfather: 3 Eli
like ~: 4 bony 5 boney
Ichiro: 6 Suzuki
ichnology: 7 science
ichorous: 6 liquid
ichthyoid: 3 eel
ichthyology: 7 science
study: 4 fish
ichthyophobe fear: 4 fish
icicle site: 4 eave
iciness: 4 cold 5 chill 9 frigidity
icing: 5 glaze 7 topping 8 frosting

add ~ to: 3 top
design: 4 rose 5 swirl
icing __ cake: 5 on the
Ici on __ français: 5 parle
ick: 3 ugh 4 yuck 5 gross
opposite: 3 yum 5 yummy 9 delicious
icky: 3 bad 5 gooey, gross, gummy, gunky, nasty, slimy, sweet, yucky 6 sticky, viscid 8 slovenly, unsavory 9 repellant, repellent, repugnant, repulsive, revolting 10 disgusting, uninviting, unpleasant
stuff: 3 goo 4 crud, glob, gook, muck, slop 5 slime 6 sludge
I, Claudius
author: Robert Graves
I, Claudius (BBC/PBS drama)
character: 4 Nero 5 Aelia, Julia, Livia, Macro
cast: Derek Jacobi
garment: 4 toga
I Come as a Thief
author: Louis Auchincloss
icon: 4 idol 5 image 6 emblem, statue, symbol 7 mandala, picture 8 likeness 10 simulacrum
element: 3 dot 5 pixel
figure: 5 orans, orant 6 orante
I Concentrate on You
composer: Cole Porter
iconic: 6 sacred 10 emblematic
iconoclast: 5 rebel 7 heretic, radical 8 bohemian, forsaker, maverick, renegade 9 dissenter, protester 10 malcontent
iconoclastic: 7 radical 8 renegade
I conquered: 4 vici
Icosa-, half of: 4 deca-
icosahedron's
one of an ~ twenty: 4 face
I could __ horse!: 4 eat a
I could __ unfold...: 5 a tale
I Could Fall in Love (1995 song)
artist: Selena
I Could Have Danced All Night
composer: Alan Jay Lerner, Frederick Loewe
I couldn't care __!: 4 less
I Could Write a Book
composer: Lorenz Hart, Richard Rodgers
I Cried __: 5 a Tear
I cried all the way to the __: 4 bank
I Cried a Tear (1958 song)
artist: LaVern Baker
ICU
amount: 2 cc.
apparatus: 2 IV
part of ~: 4 Care, Unit 9 Intensive
worker: 2 dr., MD, RN 3 LPN 5 nurse 6 doctor
icy: 3 raw 4 cold, rimy 5 algid, aloof, chill, gelid, hoary, nippy, polar, slick, stony 6 arctic, biting, bitter, chilly, frigid, frosty, frozen, glassy, glazed, remote, steely, stoney, wintry 7 distant, frosted, glacial, hostile, numbing, shivery, wintery 8 chilling, detached, freezing, loveless, reserved, slippery 9 hazardous, lubricous, undaunted, unfeeling 10 insociable, unamicable, unfriendly
treat an ~ road: 4 salt, sand
id: 4 that 6 libido
counterpart: 3 ego
est: 3 viz. 6 namely, that is
I'd __ Be Right: 6 Rather
I'd __ You to Want Me: 4 Love
ID: 3 SSN, tag 5 badge 6 dogtag, papers 8 passport
abbr.: 3 NMI
ask for an ~: 4 card
card datum: 3 DOB, hgt. 4 addr. 6 height 7 address
means of ~: 3 DNA
see also Idaho
ID __: 3 tag 4 card
__ ID: 5 photo 6 caller
Ida: 4 peak 5 mount, Wells 6 Cantor, Lupino 7 Tarbell 8 asteroid, Kaminska, Kavafian, McKinley, mountain
daughter: 5 Rhoda
Mt. ~ locale: 5 Crete 6 Candia
Ida, __ as Apple Cider: 5 Sweet
Ida.
neighbor: 3 Nev., Wyo. 4 Mont., Oreg., Wash.
see also Idaho
__-Ida: 3 Ore
Idaho: 4 spud 5 state, tater 6 potato
city: 5 Boise, Nampa 6 Moscow 7 Ketchum 8 Caldwell, Lewiston, Meridian 9 Pocatello, Sun Valley, Twin Falls
county: 3 Ada, Gem 5 Boise, Latah, Teton 6 Oneida
Indian: 7 Bannock, Kutenai
like ~: 6 inland
mountain: 5 Borah 6 Tetons 7 Wasatch
neighbor: 4 Utah 6 Canada, Nevada, Oregon 7 Montana, Wyoming 10 Washington
nickname: 8 Gem State
river: 5 Boise, Snake
school: 10 Boise State
senator: 5 Borah
start of ~ motto: 4 esto
state flower: 7 syringa
state gem: 10 star garnet
state horse: 9 Appaloosa
state tree: 9 white pine
waterfall: 8 Shoshone
Idaho Statesman: 5 paper 9 newspaper
locale: 5 Boise
Ida Red: 5 apple
relative: *see* apple
Ida, Sweet as __ Cider: 5 Apple
I'd be happy to!: 3 yes 4 fine, okay, sure 5 great, swell
I'd Be Surprisingly Good for You
musical: 5 Evita
I'd Do Anything for Your Love (1993 song)
artist: Meat Loaf
idea: 4 gist, plan, seed, text, view 5 fancy, hunch, point, theme, thing 6 belief, intent, motive, notion, reason, scheme, theory, thesis, vision 7 conceit, concept, feeling, inkling, opinion, purport, purpose, surmise, thought 8 game plan, instinct, proposal, scenario 9 intention, leitmotif, suspicion, viewpoint 10 brainchild, brainstorm, conception, conviction, glimmering, hypothesis, impression, perception, philosophy, reflection, suggestion
bad ~: 3 pap 5 folly
central ~ in music: 4 tema 5 motif
entertain an ~: 4 muse 5 study 6 ponder 7 reflect 8 cogitate, consider, meditate, mull over, ruminate 9 think over 10 deliberate, introspect
exchange: 4 chat, talk 6 confab, dialog, parley, powwow 8 colloquy, dialogue 9 discourse, tête-à-tête 10 conference, discussion
fixed ~: 3 bug 5 mania 6 hang-up 7 craving 9 monomania, obsession
get the ~: 3 see 5 sense 7 realize
get the wrong ~: 3 err 7 presume 8 misjudge 9 underrate
give the wrong ~: 4 dupe, fool, gull, hoax, scam, snow 5 bluff, cheat, put on, shaft, trick 6 delude, lead on, rope in, suck in, take in 7 confuse, deceive, defraud, mislead 8 hoodwink, inveigle, misguide, throw off 9 disinform, misinform 10 lead astray
have the same ~: 4 jibe 5 agree, match 6 concur 8 coincide 9 harmonize
main ~: 4 core, crux, gist, meat, pith 5 heart, motif, point, tenor 6 kernel, marrow, thrust, upshot 7 essence, keynote, purport 9 substance
man: 6 pundit 7 thinker 8 theorist
rough ~: 4 clew, clue 6 sketch 7 outline 10 ground plan
source: 4 germ, Muse, seed 5 spark 6 kernel
sudden ~: 4 whim 5 fancy 7 caprice, impulse 8 crotchet
whole ~: 6 motive, reason 7 purpose 9 rationale
idea __: 3 man
__ idea: 3 big
ideal: 4 best 5 cause, dream, model, right, typic 6 edenic, unreal, utmost, vision 7 eidolon, epitome, example, nonsuch, optimal, optimum, paragon, perfect, supreme, typical, utopian 8 absolute, abstract, exemplar, fanciful, flawless, nonesuch, paradigm, standard, ultimate, unproved 9 archetype, beautiful, exemplary, faultless, just right, nonpareil, principle, prototype, role model 10 apotheosis, archetypal, chimerical, consummate, intangible, perfection, touchstone
beau ~: 5 model 7 paragon 8 paradigm
ender: 3 ism, ist 5 istic
state: 6 utopia 10 perfection
__ ideal: 3 ego 4 beau
Ideal Husband, An
author: Oscar Wilde
idealist: 7 dreamer, utopian 8 escapist, optimist, romantic
need: 5 cause 7 crusade
idealistic: 6 dreamy 7 utopian 8 quixotic, romantic 9 unworldly, visionary 10 quixotical, unfeasible
ideality: 8 illusion 9 unreality 10 conception
idealized: 5 lofty 7 utopian 8 fanciful, quixotic 9 visionary 10 starry-eyed, unworkable
ideally: 6 at best 8 in theory 9 in thought
ideals: 6 morals, values 8 morality, standard
ideas
exchange of ~: 4 chat, talk 6 confab, dialog, parley, powwow 8 colloquy, dialogue 9 discourse, tête-à-tête 10 conference, discussion
open to new ~: 7 pliable 8 amenable, tolerant 9 acceptive, receptive, sensitive 10 hospitable, responsive
presentation of ~: 5 input
share ~: 10 brainstorm
__ Ideas: 4 I Get
ideate: 4 plan 5 opine, think 6 cook up, ponder 7 dream up, imagine, picture 8 conceive, daydream, theorize 10 brainstorm, conceive of
idée fixe: 5 mania, thing 9 obsession
idem: 7 as above
Identi-__: 3 Kit
identical: 4 even, like, same, twin 5 alike, equal, exact, level 6 cloned 7 similar, uniform 8 matching, selfsame 9 congruent, duplicate, lookalike 10 carbon copy, dead ringer, equivalent, homogenous, synonymous, tantamount, two of a kind
not ~: 5 other 6 unlike 7 unalike, unequal 8 distinct, separate 9 different, unrelated 10 dissimilar
to: 6 same as
twin: 5 sosie
identical __: 4 twin
identification: 3 tag 4 make, name, pass 5 badge, label 6 dog tag 8 labeling, passport, password
identified: 5 known
wrongly ~: 8 mistaken 9 incorrect 10 inaccurate
identifier: 5 brand, theme
identify: 3 peg, see, tab, tag 4 find, know, link, mark, name, spot, tell 5 label, place, smell 6 detect, finger, select 7 analyze, catalog, make out, pick out 8 bookmark, classify, diagnose, discover, pinpoint, point out, smell out 9 catalogue, determine, establish, preordain, recognize, single out 10 button down, categorize
a caller: 5 trace
with: 4 pity 6 be into 8 relate to
identity: 3 ego 4 self 8 likeness 9 character, integrity 10 uniqueness
a question of ~: 3 who
assumed ~: 5 cover 8 disguise
identity __: 4 card 6 crisis
Identity (2003 film)
cast: John Cusack, Ray Liotta, Amanda Peet
__ Identity, The: 6 Bourne
ideogram: 6 symbol 8 logogram 9 character 10 hieroglyph
ideology: 3 ism 4 line 5 credo, creed, dogma, tenet 6 belief, system 7 beliefs 10 philosophy, principles
Ides of March, The
author: Thornton Wilder
ides precursor: 5 nones
I'd hate to break up __: 4 a set
Idi __ Dada: 4 Amin
__ I Did for Love: 4 What
I didn't do it: 5 not me 6 denial
__ I didn't know!: 4 As if

I didn't need a __...: 5 shove
I Dig Rock and Roll Music (1967 song)
  artist: Peter, Paul and Mary
idiocy: 5 folly 6 lunacy 7 fatuity, inanity
idiom: 3 phr. 4 cant, jive, word 5 argot, lingo 6 jargon, patois, phrase, slogan, speech, tongue 7 dialect 8 language, localism, locution, parlance 10 expression, vernacular
idiomatic: 5 slang 6 common, vulgar 8 informal, regional 9 dialectal 10 colloquial, vernacular
idiosyncrasy: 3 tic, way 4 kink 5 habit, quirk, trait 6 foible, manner, oddity 7 feature 8 crotchet 9 mannerism
idiosyncratic: 3 odd 5 queer 6 quaint 7 oddball, offbeat, strange 8 peculiar
idiot: 3 ass, sap 4 bozo, dodo, dope, fool, jerk, twit, zany 5 booby, ninny 6 dimwit, lummox 7 bungler, jackass, pinhead 8 bonehead, numskull 9 blockhead, numbskull
  box: 2 TV 4 tube 5 TV set 10 television
idiot __: 3 box 4 card 5 board, light
idiot-__: 5 proof
idiotic
  see foolish
Idiot's Delight: 4 play
  author: Robert E. Sherwood
Idiots First
  author: Bernard Malamud
Idiot, The
  author: Fyodor Dostoyevsky
Iditarod: 4 race
  conveyance: 4 sled
  cry: 4 mush
  locale: 4 Nome 6 Alaska
  puller: 3 dog 5 husky
idle: 3 lag, lax, veg 4 free, laze, lazy, loaf, logy, loll, moon, mope, poke, rest, vain 5 amble, dally, empty, inert, mosey, not on, relax, slack, spend, stall, still, tarry 6 asleep, at rest, dawdle, draggy, fallow, futile, hollow, lay off, linger, loiter, lounge, otiose, torpid, unused 7 aimless, dormant, foolish, goof off, hang out, inutile, jobless, laid off, loafing, not used, off-duty, passive, resting, saunter, sitting, slacken, trivial, unsound, useless, vacuous 8 baseless, ill-spent, inactive, indolent, kill time, lollygag, malinger, mark time, misspent, not in use, slack off, slothful, sluggish, stagnant, stagnate, straggle, untilled, vagabond, vegetate 9 at leisure, do-nothing, for naught, frivolous, fruitless, hibernate, in neutral, lethargic, loitering, out of work, pointless, sedentary, senseless, shiftless, unfounded, unhelpful, valueless, waste time, worthless 10 dillydally, disengaged, groundless, irrelevant, mothballed, motionless, not serious, not working, on the shelf, stationary, take it easy, unavailing, unemployed, unoccupied
  be ~: 3 sit 4 loaf 5 relax
  hours: 4 ease, rest 6 repose 7 holiday, leisure, time off 8 free time, vacation 9 spare time
  make ~ conversation: 3 gab, yak 4 chat, chin
  not ~: 4 busy 7 working 8 occupied
  talk: 3 gab, gas, yap 4 wind 5 bilge, mouth, prate 6 babble, cackle, gossip 8 babbling, chitchat 9 loquacity
Idle: 4 Eric
idleness: 4 ease 5 sloth 6 acedia, torpor 7 inertia, languor 8 laziness, lethargy, otiosity 9 faineance, indolence, lassitude, torpidity 10 inactivity, stagnation
idler: 3 bum 5 drone, sloth 6 loafer, rascal, truant 7 dawdler, goof-off, laggard, shirker, slacker 8 layabout, parasite, slugabed, sluggard 9 do-nothing, goldbrick, lazybones, no-account 10 ne'er-do-well
  bane: 3 job 4 work
  opposite: 4 doer 6 dynamo
Idler, The
  author: Samuel Johnson
I'd Lie for You (1995 song)
  artist: Meat Loaf
I'd Like to Teach the World to Sing (1971 song)
  artist: Hillside Singers, New Seekers
idling: 9 in neutral
I'd Love You to Want Me (1972 song)
  artist: Lobo
idly: 4 easy 7 lightly 8 by chance, casually 9 leisurely
__ idly by: 5 stand
I do: 3 vow
  say ~: 3 wed 4 mate
  sayer: 4 wife 5 bride, groom 7 husband 10 bridegroom
  site: 5 altar
__ I Do: 3 But 4 Deed 6 What'll
I Do, I Do, I Do, I Do, I Do (1976 song)
  artist: ABBA
__ I doin'?: 4 How'm
__ I Do Is Dream of You: 3 All
I Do It for You (1991 song)
  artist: Bryan Adams
idol: 4 baal, hero, icon, ikon, joss, star, tiki 5 eikon 6 shrine 7 beloved, darling, pop star 8 false god, favorite, figurine, folk hero, loved one, luminary, megastar 9 celebrity, role model, sacred cow, superstar 10 golden calf, juggernaut
  Biblical ~: 4 Baal, calf
  Chinese ~: 4 joss
  Cockney ~: 3 'ero
  Hawaiian ~: 4 tiki
  worshiper: 5 pagan 7 heathen
__ idol: 4 teen 7 matinée
idolator: 5 pagan
idolatrous: 5 pagan 6 loving 9 heretical
idolatry: 5 honor 6 esteem, homage 7 respect, worship 8 devotion 9 adoration, reverence 10 admiration, veneration
Idol, Billy
  song: Cradle of Love (1990)
    Eyes Without a Face (1984)
    Mony Mony (1987)
    To Be a Lover (1986)
idolize: 4 like, love 5 adore, deify, exalt, go for 6 admire, dote on, esteem, revere 7 care for, cherish, glorify, lionize, worship 8 canonize, dote upon, hold dear, look up to, treasure, venerate 9 care about
idolized: 7 beloved 8 glorious, precious
Idomeneo
  composer: Wolfgang Amadeus Mozart
I do not __ for any crown...: 3 ask
I don't believe it: 4 bosh, nuts 5 my eye 6 phooey 7 baloney
I Don't Have the Heart (1990 song)
  artist: James Ingram
__ I Don't Have You: 5 Since
I don't know gesture: 5 shrug
I Don't Know How to Love Him (1971 song)
  artist: Helen Reddy
I don't think so!: 3 nah 4 nope
I Don't Wanna Cry (1991 song)
  artist: Mariah Carey
I Don't Wanna Fight (1993 song)
  artist: Tina Turner
I Don't Want __ the World on Fire: 5 to Set
I don't want to: 3 nah 4 nope
I Don't Want to Be Right (1972 song)
  artist: Luther Ingram
I Don't Want to Live Without You (1988 song)
  artist: Foreigner
I Don't Want to Miss a Thing (1998 song)
  artist: Aerosmith
I Don't Want to Walk Without You, Baby
  composer: Frank Loesser, Jule Styne
I Don't Want Your Love (1988 song)
  artist: Duran Duran
I doubt it: 4 game 8 card game
I'd Rather Be Right: 7 musical
  author: George S. Kaufman
  cast: George M. Cohan
  composer: Lorenz Hart, Richard Rodgers
  role: 3 FDR
I'd Really Love to See You Tonight (1976 song)
  artist: England Dan and John Ford Coley
I Dream of Jeannie (NBC sitcom)
  cast: Bill Daily (Capt. Roger Healey)
    Barbara Eden (Jeannie)
    Larry Hagman (Capt. Tony Nelson)
  dog: 10 Djinn Djinn
Idris: 4 Elba
I Drove All Night (1989 song)
  artist: Cyndi Lauper
Idu
  author: Flora Nwapa
...I'd've Baked __: 5 a Cake
idyll: 4 poem 5 verse 7 bucolic, eclogue, georgic, romance 8 pastoral 9 bucolical 10 flirtation
idyllic: 6 poetic, serene 8 pastoral, poetical, romantic
  locale: 3 lea, ley 4 Eden
Idylls of the King: 4 epic, poem
  author: Alfred Tennyson
  character: 3 Kay 4 Bors, Enid, Mark 5 Balan, Balin, Isolt, Uther, Ynoil 6 Arthur, Elaine, Gareth, Gawain, Merlin, Modred, Pellam, Vivien, Ygerne 7 Ettarre, Galahad, Geraint, Gorloïs, Lavaine, Lynette, Pelleas 8 Bedivere, Lancelot, Tristram 9 Guinevere, Launcelot, Percivale
i.e.: 3 viz. 5 id est, to wit 6 namely, that is
I eat what __: 4 I see
I Enjoy Being a Girl
  composer: Oscar Hammerstein, Richard Rodgers
Ieoh Ming __: 3 Pei
I, Etcetera
  author: Susan Sontag
__ I Ever Need Is You: 3 All
if: 3 yet 4 conj. 5 altho, doubt, maybe 6 in case, though 7 whether 8 although, granting, provided 9 condition, given that, providing, qualifier, supposing 10 for all that
  all goes right: 6 at best
  as ~: 4 like, that 5 quasi 8 just like 9 presuming, seemingly, so to speak 10 supposedly
  even ~: 3 tho 5 altho 6 albeit, though 8 although 9 supposing
  it were not for: 7 besides, without 8 omitting 9 apart from, aside from, excluding
  look as ~: 4 seem 6 appear
  make as ~: 3 act 4 pose 5 feign 7 pretend 8 simulate
  not: 3 but 4 else 9 otherwise
  not for: 3 but 6 except
  so: 4 then 10 in that case
if __ be: 4 need
if __ comes to shove: 4 push
__ if: 4 what
If (poem)
  author: Rudyard Kipling
  last word: 3 son
If (song)
  artist: Bread, Janet Jackson Jackson
If __: 4 I May 5 I Fell
If __ a Bell: 5 I Were
If __ a Carpenter: 5 I Were
If __ a Hammer: 4 I Had
If __ a Million: 4 I Had
If __ Answers: 4 a Man
If __ a Rich Man: 5 I Were
If __ be so bold...: 4 I may
If __ Came True: 6 Dreams, Wishes
If __ Could Read My Mind: 3 You
If __ Fall in Love: 5 I Ever
If __ Had a Brain: 5 I Only
If __ Hammer: 5 I Had a
If __ Have You: 5 I Can't
If __ I See You Again: 4 Ever
If __ I Would Leave You: 4 Ever
If __ King of the Forest: 5 I Were
If __ Knew Susie: 3 You
If __ make it there...: 4 I can
If __ Million: 5 I Had a
If __ My Way: 4 I Had
If __ Street Could Talk: 5 Beale
If __ the Circus: 4 I Ran
If __ the Zoo: 4 I ran
If __ Tuesday...: 3 It's
If __ were horses...: 6 wishes
If __ Would Leave You: 5 Ever I
If __ you...: 5 I were
If __ You: 4 I Had
If __ Your Woman: 5 I Were

If __ you were coming...: 5 I knew
if all __ fails: 4 else
__ I Fall in Love: 4 When
I Fall to Pieces (1961 song)
artist: Patsy Cline
If Anyone Falls (1983 song)
artist: Stevie Nicks
If Beale Street Could Talk
author: James Baldwin
__ if by land...: 3 One
IFC: 7 channel
alternative: ***see*** movie channel
I Feel Fine (1964 song)
artist: Beatles
I Feel for You (1984 song)
artist: Chaka Khan
I feel like __ again!: 4 a kid
I Feel Love (1977 song)
artist: Donna Summer
I Feel Pretty: 4 song **5** waltz
composer: Leonard Bernstein, Stephen Sondheim
I Feel So Bad (1961 song)
artist: Elvis Presley
I Feel the Earth Move (1971 song)
artist: Carole King
__ I Fell for You: 5 Since
If Ever __ You Again: 4 I See
If Ever I Would Leave You
composer: Alan Jay Lerner, Frederick Loewe
If Ever You're in My Arms Again (1984 song)
artist: Peabo Bryson
iffy: 5 risky, rocky **6** chancy, unsure **7** dubious, in doubt **8** doubtful, not final, variable **9** ambiguous, debatable, tentative, uncertain, undecided, unsettled **10** improbable, indefinite, precarious, unresolved, up for grabs, up in the air
If He Hollers Let Him Go
author: Chester Himes
If He Walked Into My Life show: 4 Mame
If I __: 4 Fell
If I __ Care: 5 Didn't
If I __ Hammer: 4 Had a
If I __ Rich Man: 5 Were a
If I __ the World: 5 Ruled
If I __ you...: 4 were
If I Can Dream (1968 song)
artist: Elvis Presley
__ if I can help it!: 3 Not
If I Can't Have You (1978 song)
artist: Yvonne Elliman
If I Could Build My Whole World Around You (1967 song)
artist: Marvin Gaye, Tammi Terrell
If I Could Turn Back Time (1989 song)
artist: Cher
Ifield: 5 Frank
If I Had a Hammer (song)
artist: Trini Lopez, Peter, Paul and Mary
If I Loved You
composer: Oscar Hammerstein, Richard Rodgers
I Finally Found Someone (1996 song)
artist: Bryan Adams, Barbra Streisand
If I Only Had a Brain
composer: Harold Arlen, Yip Harburg
If I Only Had the Nerve
singer: Bert Lahr
If I Ran the Circus
author: Dr. Seuss
If I Ran the Zoo
author: Dr. Seuss
If I rest, I __: 4 rust
If I Ruled the World (1965 song)
artist: Tony Bennett
If I Ruled the World rapper: 3 Nas
If it __ been for you...: 5 hadn't
If it __ broke...: 4 ain't
If It Die
author: André Gide
If It Makes You Happy (1996 song)
artist: Sheryl Crow
If it quacks like __...: 5 a duck
If it should rain, we'll __: 5 let it
If It's Tuesday, This Must Be Belgium (1969 film)
cast: Ian McShane, Suzanne Pleshette
If I've told you __,...: 4 once
If I Were __: 5 a Bell
If I Were __ Man: 5 a Rich
If I Were a Carpenter (1966 song)
artist: Bobby Darin
If I Were King of the Forest
composer: Harold Arlen, Yip Harburg
singer: Bert Lahr
If I Were Your Woman (1970 song)
artist: Gladys Knight and the Pips
If Morning Ever Comes
author: Anne Tyler
__ Ifni, Morocco: 4 Sidi
I forbid in Latin: 4 veto
I forgive you: 5 it's OK
I Fought the Law (1966 song)
artist: Bobby Fuller
I Found Someone (1988 song)
artist: Cher
if push __ to shove: 5 comes
ifs: 6 hedges **8** provisos
no ~ ands or buts: 6 really **7** exactly **9** precisely **10** absolutely, definitely, positively
If the __ fits...: 4 shoe
If This __ Love: 4 Isn't
If This Is It (1984 song)
artist: Huey Lewis and the News
If Tomorrow Comes
author: Sidney Sheldon
If We Only Have Love
composer: Jacques Brel
If wishes __ horses...: 4 were
if worst __ to worst: 5 comes
if you __: 4 dare **6** please
If you __...: 5 ask me
If You Asked Me to (1992 song)
artist: Celine Dion
If You Can Want (1968 song)
artist: Miracles
If You Could Read My Mind (1971 song)
artist: Gordon Lightfoot
If You Don't Know Me by Now (song)
artist: Harold Melvin and the Blue Notes, Simply Red
If You Go (1994 song)
artist: Jon Secada
If You Go Away
composer: Jacques Brel
If You Had My Love (1999 song)
artist: Jennifer Lopez
If You Knew Susie: 4 song
refrain: 6 oh oh oh
If You Knew Susie (1925 song)
artist: Eddie Cantor
If You Leave Me Now (1976 song)
artist: Chicago
If You Love Me (song)
artist: Brownstone, Olivia Newton-John
If You Love Somebody... (1985 song)
artist: Sting
If You Really Love Me (1971 song)
artist: Stevie Wonder
If you're ever in __...: 4 a jam
If You're Ready (1973 song)
artist: Staple Singers
I Get __: 5 Ideas
I Get a Kick Out of You
composer: Cole Porter
I Get Around (song)
artist: Beach Boys, Tupac
I get it: 3 aha, oho
__ I Get It Right: 3 'Til
I Get Lonely (1998 song)
artist: Blackstreet, Janet Jackson
I Get Weak (1988 song)
artist: Belinda Carlisle
Iggie's House
author: Judy Blume
Iggy: 3 Pop
I give up!: 5 uncle **6** enough, no more
Iglesias, Enrique
father: Julio
song: Bailamos (1999)
Iglesias, Julio
song: To All the Girls I've Loved Before (1984)
igloo: 3 hut **4** dome **5** abode
dweller: 3 Esk. **5** Inuit **6** Eskimo, Innuit, Inupik
igloo-shaped auto: 5 Pacer
Ignacy: 8 Krasicki **10** Paderewski
Ignatius: 5 saint
Ignatius of __: 6 Loyola
igneous
rock: 4 lava, sima **6** basalt, dunite, gabbro, norite, pumice **7** diorite, felsite, picrite, syenite **8** aphanite, dolerite, obsidian
rock source: 5 magma **7** volcano
ignis fatuus: 6 mirage **7** chimera, eidolon, fantasm, figment **8** chimaera, delusion, phantasm **9** obsession
ignitable: 9 flammable **10** incendiary
ignite: 4 burn, lick **5** light, shoot, spark, start **6** kindle, set off, turn on **7** enflame, flare up, inflame, light up, trigger **8** enkindle, set afire, touch off **9** catch fire, set ablaze, set aflame, set alight, set on fire **10** illuminate, incinerate
ignited: 3 lit **6** ablaze, flambé
again: 5 relit
igniter: 5 flint, spark
fireworks ~: 4 punk **6** amadou
ignition: 4 fire **7** lighter **10** combustion
awaiting ~: 4 dark **5** unlit
rocket ~: 7 liftoff
ignition system part: 3 cam **5** choke
ignoble: 3 low **4** base, mean, ugly, vile **5** lowly, seamy, small **6** abject, coarse, common, craven, humble, menial, modest, shabby, sordid, vulgar **7** caddish, corrupt, heinous, lowdown, miserly, servile, squalid **8** baseborn, degraded, infamous, inferior, ordinary, plebeian, shameful, unworthy, wretched **9** dastardly, low-minded **10** despicable, inglorious, outrageous, villainous
ignominious: 5 shady, sorry **6** abject, shoddy **7** ignoble **8** infra dig, shameful, unworthy **10** despicable
ignominy: 4 evil **5** odium, shame **6** hatred, infamy **8** contempt, disgrace, dishonor **9** disrepute, ill repute **10** opprobrium, virtueless, wickedness
ignoramus: 4 dope, dupe, loon, twit **5** klutz, ninny **6** stooge, sucker **7** bungler **9** barbarian, schlemiel **10** noodlehead
see also ninny
ignorance: 5 youth **7** naiveté **8** darkness **9** blindness, crudeness, denseness, disregard, innocence, nescience, vagueness **10** callowness, illiteracy, incapacity, obtuseness, simplicity
in an adage: 5 bliss
in Buddhism: 7 samsara
liberation from ~: 7 nirvana
sign of ~: 5 shrug
sound of ~: 3 duh
Ignorance __ excuse: 4 is no
ignorant: 3 raw **4** dark, naif **5** green, naive, silly, thick, young **6** gauche, simple, stupid, unread **7** lowbred, out of it, shallow, unaware **8** innocent, untaught **9** backwater, in the dark, unadvised, unknowing, unlearned, unmindful, untrained **10** uneducated, unfamiliar, uninformed, unschooled
not ~: 4 sage **5** smart **6** brainy **7** erudite, learned **8** cerebral **9** in the know, scholarly
of right and wrong: 6 amoral
ignore: 4 defy, miss, omit, shun, skip, snub **5** avoid, elide, evade, flout, rebel, scorn, skirt, spurn **6** bypass, forget, oppose, pass by, pass up, rebuff, refuse, reject, resist, revolt, slight, wink at **7** blink at, disobey, exclude, forsake, let go by, neglect, rule out, tune out, violate **8** brush off, discount, file away, laugh off, lay aside, overlook, overrule, pass over, pooh-pooh, shrug off, sneeze at **9** disregard **10** work around
ignoring: 6 rebuff **7** despite **9** disregard, in spite of
Igor: 4 aide, Tamm **6** prince, Ulanov **8** Moiseyev, Sikorsky **9** Markevich **10** Stravinsky
I got __ in Kalamazoo: 4 a gal
I Got __: 5 a Name
I Got a Name (1973 song)
artist: Jim Croce
I Gotcha (1972 song)
artist: Joe Tex
I Got Id (1995 song)
artist: Pearl Jam
I Go to Extremes (1990 song)
artist: Billy Joel
I Go to Pieces (1965 song)
artist: Peter and Gordon
I Got Plenty o' Nuthin'
composer: George Gershwin, Ira Gershwin
I Got Rhythm: 4 song
composer: George Gershwin, Ira Gershwin

I Got Stung (1958 song)
artist: Elvis Presley
I Gotta Know (1960 song)
artist: Elvis Presley
I Gotta Right to Sing the Blues
composer: Harold Arlen
I got the __ the morning...: **5** sun in
I Got the Feelin' (1968 song)
artist: James Brown
I Got the Sun in the Morning
composer: Irving Berlin
I Got You (1965 song)
artist: James Brown
I Got You Babe (1965 song)
artist: Sonny and Cher
__ I Grow to Old to Dream: **4** When
__ I Grow Up: **4** When
Iguaçu: **5** falls **9** waterfall
locale: **6** Brazil
iguana: **3** pet **6** animal, lizard **7** reptile
cousin: **5** agama, anole
fare: **6** insect
iguanodon: **8** dinosaur
Iguassú: **5** falls, river **9** waterfall
locale: **6** Brazil
I Guess That's Why They Call It the Blues (1983 song)
artist: Elton John
__ I had heard of Lucy Gray: **3** Oft
I hate __ to pieces!: **6** meeces
I Hate Men
composer: Cole Porter
I Hate Myself for Loving You (1988 song)
artist: Joan Jett and the Blackhearts
I hate to break up __: **4** a set
I Hate U (1995 song)
artist: Prince
I have __ walked...: **5** often
I have a dream
monogram: **3** MLK
speaker: **4** King
I Have a Rendezvous with Death
author: Alan Seeger
I have half __ to...: **5** a mind
I have no __!: **4** idea
I have not __ begun to fight: **3** yet
I Have Nothing (1993 song)
artist: Whitney Houston
I haven't __!: **5** a clue
__ I Have to Do Is Dream: **3** All
I Hear America Singing
author: Walt Whitman
I Hear a Symphony (1965 song)
artist: Supremes
I Heard a Rumour (1987 song)
artist: Bananarama
I Heard It Through the Grapevine (song)
artist: Marvin Gaye, Gladys Knight and the Pips
Ihimaera, Witi: **5** Maori **6** writer
I Honestly Love You (1974 song)
artist: Olivia Newton-John
IHOP: **5** chain **6** eatery **10** restaurant
freebie: **5** sirup, syrup
order: **2** OJ **5** stack **8** pancakes
part of ~: **4** Intl. **5** House
rival: *see* restaurant chain
II: **3** two **9** the Second
III: **5** three **8** the Third
father: **2** jr.
__ III: **5** Rambo, Rocky **7** Richard
__ II Men: **4** Boyz
I intended __: **5** an ode
'I' Is for Innocent
author: Sue Grafton
__ Il Society: **6** Menace
Ijssel: **5** river
attraction: **4** dike
locale: **7** Holland **11** Netherlands
town on the: **4** Edam
Ijsselmeer: **4** lake
locale: **7** Holland **11** Netherlands
I Just Called to Say I Love You (1984 song)
artist: Stevie Wonder
I Just Can't Stop Loving You (1987 song)
artist: Michael Jackson
I Just Fall in Love Again (1979 song)
artist: Anne Murray
I Just Want to Be Your Everything (1977 song)
artist: Andy Gibb
Ike: **3** DDE, gen. **6** Pappas, Turner **7** Clanton, general
alma mater: **4** Army, USMA
colleague: **3** Hap **4** Doug, Omar
command: **3** ETO **4** NATO
ex: **4** Tina
like ~: **4** bald
Mamie, to ~: **4** wife
opponent: **5** Adlai
see also Dwight D. Eisenhower
__ Ike: **5** Alibi, I Like
ikebana: **3** art
chrysanthemum, in ~: **4** kiku
home: **5** Japan
Ikhnaton: **7** pharaoh
river: **4** Nile
I kid __ not: **3** you
I Kid You Not
author: Jack Paar
Ikiru (1952 film)
director: Akira Kurosawa
I Kissed You (1959 song)
artist: Everly Brothers
__ I Kissed You: **3** 'Til
Ikkesh
son: **3** Ira
I knew it!: **3** aha
I Knew You Were Waiting (1987 song)
artist: Aretha Franklin, George Michael
I Know a Place (1965 song)
artist: Petula Clark
I Know What I Like (1987 song)
artist: Huey Lewis and the News
I Know What You Did Last Summer (1997 film)
cast: Sarah Michelle Gellar, Jennifer Love Hewitt, Ryan Phillippe, Freddie Prinze Jr.
I Know Why the Caged Bird Sings
author: Maya Angelou
Ikons, The
author: Lawrence Durrell
Il __ della rosa: **4** nome
IL
see Illinois
__ I lay me...: **3** Now
île: **6** Tahiti **10** Martinique
Ile-de-France river: **4** Oise
Ile de la Cité site: **5** Seine
I Led Three Lives (TV adventure)
cast: Richard Carlson (Herbert Philbrick)
Ile du __: **6** Diable
I Left My Heart in San Francisco (1962 song)
artist: Tony Bennett
Ilene: **5** Graff
Iler: **6** Robert
Iles __ Société: **4** de la
ileus: **5** colic
ilex: **4** tree **5** holly, shrub **7** holm oak
__ il faut: **5** comme
ILGWU: **5** union
chapter: **3** lcl. **5** local
do an ~ job: **3** sew **6** stitch
members: **5** labor
part of ~: **3** Int. **4** Intl. **5** Union **6** Ladies **7** Garment, Workers
Ilhéus: **4** city, town
locale: **6** Brazil
Ilia: **5** Kulik
iliac __: **6** artery
iliac starter: **5** sacro
Iliad: **4** epic, epos, poem **6** epopee **8** epopoeia
author: Homer
character: **4** Aias, Ajax, Ares, Hera, Iris, Zeus **5** Dolon, Eneas, Helen, Paris, Priam **6** Aeneas, Apollo, Athena, Athene, Hector, Hecuba, Nestor, Teucer, Thetis, Trojan **7** Antenor, Briseis, Calchas, Glaucus, Helenus, Machaon, Priamus **8** Achilles, Chryseis, Diomedes, Melelaus, Odysseus, Pandarus, Poseidon, Sarpedon **9** Agamemmon, Aphrodite, Cassandra, Deiphobus, Patroclus, Polydamus **10** Andromache, Hephaestus
locale: **4** Troy
Ilie: **7** Nastase
Iliescu: **3** Ion
__ I Lie to You?: **5** Would
I like __, except for meals: **4** eels
I Like __: **3** Ike
I Like Dreamin' (1976 song)
artist: Kenny Nolan
I Like It Here
author: Kingsley Amis
I Like It Like That (song)
artist: Dave Clark Five, Chris Kenner
I like your __: **5** style
I Like Your Kind of Love (1956 song)
artist: Andy Williams
ilium: **4** bone
locale: **3** hip **6** pelvis
Ilium: **4** Troy **5** Troia
feature: **5** tower
ilk: **4** form, kind, sort, type **5** brand, class, genre, stamp **6** family, nature, stripe **7** variety **8** category **9** character
of that ~: **4** akin **7** related, similar
Ilka: **5** Chase
ill: **3** bad, low **4** evil, foul, harm, hurt, sick **5** badly, rocky, wrong **6** ailing, infirm, injury, laid up, malady, malice, misery, peaked, poorly, queasy, queazy, unwell, wicked **7** adverse, badness, disease, harmful, hostile, hurtful, invalid, laid low, not well, ruinous, trouble, unsound **8** below par, calamity, damaging, diseased, feverish, inimical, sickness, sinister **9** adversely, afflicted, bedridden, depravity, harmfully, in a bad way, infirmity, injurious, malicious, miserable, unhealthy **10** affliction, indisposed, iniquitous, malevolent, misfortune, out of sorts, wickedness
at ease: **4** edgy **5** antsy, itchy, jumpy, tense **6** on edge **7** abashed, anxious, awkward, jittery, keyed up, nervous, restive, uptight, worried **8** agitated, restless, skittish, troubled **9** concerned, disturbed, excitable, faltering, unrelaxed, unsettled **10** disquieted, high-strung, out of place, suspicious
be ~ with: **3** get **4** have **5** catch **7** develop **8** contract
combining form: **3** dys-, mal-, mis-
feel ~: **3** ail
feeling: **4** bile, hate **5** odium, pique, scorn, spite, venom, wrath **6** animus, enmity, grudge, hatred, malice, rancor **7** discord, disdain, disgust, dudgeon, umbrage **8** acerbity, acrimony, aversion, bad blood, distaste, loathing **9** animosity, antipathy, harshness, hostility, malignity, mordacity, revulsion, vengeance, virulence **10** abhorrence, antagonism, bitterness, execration, repugnance, resentment
fortune: **7** bad luck **9** adversity
health: **6** malady **7** ailment, disease **8** sickness **9** infirmity **10** affliction, unwellness
humor: **3** ire **4** bile **6** spleen, temper **7** bad mood **8** acerbity **9** surliness, testiness **10** crabbiness, crankiness, grumpiness, irritation, touchiness
in French: **3** mal
less ~: **6** better
looking ~: **3** wan **4** ashy, pale **5** ashen
make ~: **5** repel, upset **6** infect, offend, poison, revolt, sicken **7** afflict
not ~: **4** ably, well **6** robust **7** adeptly, capably, healthy **8** expertly, properly **9** in the pink
off: **5** broke, needy **6** hard up, in need, in want **7** pinched **8** bankrupt, beggarly, indigent, strapped **9** destitute, insolvent, moneyless, penniless, penurious **10** down and out, pauperized, straitened
of ~ repute: **5** shady **8** infamous, shameful, unsavory **9** dishonest, notorious, unethical **10** scandalous
once: **5** amort
repute: **5** odium, shame **6** infamy **7** obloquy **8** disfavor, disgrace, dishonor, ignominy **9** disesteem, notoriety **10** opprobrium
speak ~ of: **5** abase **6** malign, vilify **7** asperse, run down **8** backbite **10** calumniate, villainize
temper: **4** bile
treatment: **4** harm **5** abuse
will: **4** hate **5** odium, spite, venom **6** animus, enmity, grudge, hatred, malice, rancor **8** acrimony, aversion, bad blood **9** animosity, antipathy, hostility, nastiness **10** antagonism, resentment, unkindness
(with): **4** down

ill __: **4** will, wind
ill-__: **3** off, use **4** bred **5** being, fated, timed **6** boding, omened, shapen, suited, wisher **7** natured
ill-__ gains: **6** gotten
Ill.
neighbor: **3** Ind., Ken., Wis. **4** Wisc.
see also Illinois
I'll __: **4** Wait **5** Get By
I'll __ 4 Ya: **6** Tumble
I'll __ at Your Wedding: **5** Dance
I'll __ By: **3** Get
I'll __ Manhattan: **4** Take
I'll __ monkey's uncle!: **3** be a
I'll __ my hat!: **3** eat
I'll __ Smile Again: **5** Never
I'll __ Tomorrow: **3** Cry
I'll __ You Halfway: **4** Meet
I'll __ Your Side: **4** Be by
I'll __ You There: **4** Take
ill-advised: **4** rash **5** brash, hasty, silly, wrong **6** madcap, stupid, unwary, unwise **7** foolish **8** improper, mistaken, reckless **9** foolhardy, half-baked, hotheaded, impolitic, imprudent, misguided, overhasty **10** incautious, indiscreet, ungrounded
I'll Always Love You (1988 song)
artist: Taylor Dayne
I'll be!: **3** wow **4** gosh **5** golly
I'll Be (1997 song)
artist: Foxy Brown, Jay-Z
I'll Be __ for Christmas: **4** Home
I'll Be Around (1972 song)
artist: Spinners
ill-behaved: **3** bad **6** bratty, unruly
I'll Be Home (1956 song)
artist: Pat Boone
I'll be loving you, __: **6** always
I'll Be Loving You (1989 song)
artist: New Kids on the Block
I'll Be Missing You (1997 song)
artist: Faith Evans, Puff Daddy
I'll Be Seeing You
author: Mary Higgins Clark
I'll be there __ long: **3** ere
I'll Be There (song)
artist: Mariah Carey, Escape Club, Jackson 5
I'll Be There for You (song)
artist: Mary J. Blige, Bon Jovi, Method Man
I'll Be Your Shelter (1990 song)
artist: Taylor Dayne
ill-boding: **4** dire **7** ominous **8** sinister
ill-bred: **3** low **4** rude **5** crude **6** gauche **7** bearish, boorish, caddish, loutish, raffish, uncivil, uncouth **8** impolite, impudent, inurbane, unpoised **9** ungallant **10** indecorous, unladylike, unmannerly
I'll Build a Stairway to Paradise
composer: Buddy DeSylva, George Gershwin, Ira Gershwin
ill-considered: **3** mad **4** luny, rash, wild, zany **5** crazy, hasty, inane, loony, sappy, silly, wacky, weird **6** absurd, looney, madcap, unwise, whacky **7** bizarre, fatuous, foolish, lunatic **9** fantastic, foolhardy, half-baked, imprudent, ludicrous, premature, senseless, unguarded **10** outrageous, ridiculous
ill-defined: **3** dim **4** hazy **5** faint, fuzzy, loose, vague **9** imprecise, unfocused **10** indistinct, inexplicit
ill-disposed: **6** averse, down on **7** adverse, against, hostile **8** spiteful **9** malicious **10** unfriendly
ill-done: **3** bad **4** poor **5** awful, lousy, sorry, wrong **6** faulty, woeful **8** dreadful, slipshod, terrible **9** atrocious, deficient, imperfect, incorrect, miserable, third-rate **10** inadequate
I'll do that!: **5** Let me
Illeana: **7** Douglas
grandfather: **6** Melvyn
...I'll eat __!: **5** my hat
illegal: **4** tabu **5** shady, taboo, wrong **6** banned **7** bootleg, crooked, illicit, sub rosa, wildcat **8** criminal, outlawed, smuggled, unlawful, verboten, wrongful **9** felonious, forbidden, unethical **10** actionable, contraband, indictable, not allowed, prohibited, proscribed, unlicensed
act: **3** sin **5** bribe, crime, usury **6** bag job **9** smuggling
inducement: **5** graft **6** grease, payoff, payola **8** kickback **9** hush money
make ~: **3** ban **6** forbid, outlaw
transfer ~ goods: **4** push **7** bootleg
illegality: **5** theft, wrong **6** racket **7** con game, misdeed, offense, swindle **8** cheating, thievery **9** violation **10** corruption, dishonesty, infraction
lure into ~: **6** entrap
illegible: **7** obscure, scrawly, unclear **8** scrawled **10** indistinct, unreadable
render ~: **5** smear
illegitimate: **3** bad **5** bogus **8** spurious, unlawful, wrongful
ill-fated: **4** poor **5** curst **6** cursed, doomed, jinxed, ruined, tragic **7** accurst, hapless, ominous, unblest, unhappy, unlucky **8** accursed, blighted, hopeless, luckless, tragical **9** unblessed, unfavored **10** disastrous, portentous
ill-favored: **4** ugly **9** unwelcome
ill-fed: **4** bony **5** gaunt **7** haggard, scrawny **9** emaciated
ill-fitting: **5** baggy, loose **6** floppy **7** sagging
ill-founded: **5** false, wrong **7** invalid, unsound **8** baseless **9** erroneous **10** fallacious, unreasoned
I'll Get By (1992 song)
artist: Eddie Money
I'll get right __!: **4** on it
ill-gotten gains: **4** pelf **5** booty, grift, lucre
I'll Have to Say I Love You in a Song (1974 song)
artist: Jim Croce
ill-humored: **4** dour **5** cross, gruff, moody, nasty, surly **6** crusty, morose, sullen **7** bilious, vicious, waspish **8** choleric, petulant, snappish **9** irritable, splenetic **10** out of sorts
be ~: **4** mope, pout, sulk **5** brood, gripe **6** grouse
one: **4** crab **5** crank, grump **6** grouch **8** sorehead, sourpuss **10** curmudgeon, malcontent
illiberal: **5** close **6** little, narrow, skimpy, stingy **7** insular, miserly **8** ungiving **9** bourgeois **10** intolerant
illiberality: **4** bias **6** racism **7** bigotry **9** injustice, prejudice **10** chauvinism, narrowness, partiality, unfairness
illicit: **4** tabu **5** dirty, taboo, wrong **6** banned **7** bootleg, illegal, lawless **8** criminal, improper, not legal, outlawed, unlawful, verboten, wrongful **9** felonious, forbidden **10** contraband, indictable, prohibited, unlicensed
scheme: **3** con **5** bunco **6** racket
illimitable: **3** big **4** vast **7** abysmal, endless **8** infinite **9** limitless, unlimited
Illini: **4** team
conference: **6** Big Ten
locale: **6** Urbana
Illinois: **5** river, state **6** Indian **7** Amerind
Benedictine College site: **5** Lisle
city: **4** Iola, Pana, Zion **5** Alton, Cairo, Elgin, Lisle, Niles, Olney, Pekin **6** Aurora, Berwyn, Cicero, Darien, De Kalb, Dolton, Galena, Gurnee, Harvey, Joliet, Macomb, Moline, Normal, Peoria, Quincy, Skokie, Urbana **7** Addison, Batavia, Burbank, Chicago, Decatur, Lansing, Lombard, Maywood, Oak Lawn, Oak Park, O'Fallon, Roselle, Wheaton **8** Bartlett, Bellwood, Danville, Elk Grove, Elmhurst, Evanston, Freeport, Glenview, Kankakee, MacHenry, Palatine, Rockford, Waukegan, Westmont, Wheeling, Wilmette **9** Algonquin, Belvidere, Champaign, Galesburg, Glen Ellyn, Loves Park, Mundelein, Oak Forest, Park Ridge, St. Charles, Villa Park, Woodridge, Woodstock **10** Belleville, Blue Island, Carbondale, Charleston, Des Plaines, East Moline, East Peoria, Lake Forest, Naperville, Northbrook, Orland Park, Park Forest, Rock Island, Romeoville, Schaumburg, Streamwood, Tinley Park
conference: **6** Big Ten
neighbor: **4** Iowa **7** Indiana **8** Kentucky, Missouri **9** Wisconsin
school: **6** DePaul, Loyola **7** Bradley
state fish: **8** bluegill
state flower: **6** violet
state mineral: **8** fluorite
state state bird: **8** cardinal
state tree: **8** white oak
illiteracy: **6** alexia **9** ignorance
illiterate: **6** simple, unread **9** benighted, inerudite, unlearned, untutored **10** solecistic, uneducated, unlettered, unschooled
Illiterate Digest, The
author: Will Rogers
ill-judged: **9** impolitic, imprudent **10** incautious
ill-kempt: **5** messy, tatty **6** ragged
I'll leave it __ you: **4** up to
ill-lit: **3** dim **4** dark **5** dingy, murky **7** obscure, shadowy
ill-looking: **3** wan **4** ashy, pale **5** ashen
Ill-Made Knight, The
author: T.H. White
ill-mannered: **4** loud, rude **5** crude, rough, surly, tacky **6** bratty, coarse, gauche, vulgar **7** boorish, caddish, loutish, lowbred, uncivil, uncouth **8** churlish, impolite, impudent, insolent
one: **2** ox **3** ass, cad, oaf **4** boob, boor, clod, goon, hick, lout, rube **5** brute, churl, clown, looby, yahoo, yokel **6** galoot, lummox, rustic **7** buffoon, bumpkin, hayseed, palooka, peasant **9** barbarian, vulgarian **10** philistine
ill-matched: **6** uneven, unfair **7** unequal **8** lopsided, one-sided
I'll Meet You Halfway (1971 song)
artist: Partridge Family
ill-natured: **4** acid, mean, sour **5** catty, nasty, sulky, surly **6** crabby, ornery, sullen, touchy, unkind **7** bearish, peevish, vicious **8** churlish, perverse, petulant, spiteful **9** crotchety, dyspeptic, irritable, malicious **10** malevolent, unfriendly, unpleasant
illness: **3** bug **5** spell, upset, virus **6** malady **7** ailment, disease, malaise, trouble **8** disorder, sickness **9** complaint, condition, infirmity **10** affliction, invalidism, unwellness
overcome ~: **5** rally **6** revive **7** get well, rebound, recover, shape up **9** get better **10** bounce back, come around, recuperate, turn around
Illness as Metaphor
author: Susan Sontag
illnesses, like some: **5** viral
I'll Never __ Again: **5** Smile
I'll Never Fall in Love Again (song)
artist: Tom Jones, Dionne Warwick
I'll Never Find Another You (1965 song)
artist: Seekers
I'll Never Love This Way Again (1979 song)
artist: Dionne Warwick
ill-off: **4** poor **5** broke, needy **6** bad off, busted, hard up, in need, in want **7** pinched **8** badly off, bankrupt, beggarly, dirt poor, homeless, indigent, strapped **9** destitute, insolvent, moneyless, penniless, penurious **10** down and out, pauperized, straitened
illogical: **3** mad **5** false, inane, nutty, sappy, silly, wacky **6** absurd, faulty, hollow, screwy, whacky **7** fatuous, invalid, unsound **8** cockeyed, mistaken, specious **9** casuistic, incorrect, pointless, senseless, sophistic, untenable **10** fallacious, far-fetched, groundless, irrational, irrelevant, off-the-wall, unreasoned
ill-omened: **4** dire **5** woful **6** cursed, doomed, jinxed, tragic, woeful **7** baleful, drastic, fearful, ruinous, unlucky **8** alarming, fearsome,

grievous, luckless, terrible **10** calamitous, disastrous
I'll Remember (1994 song)
artist: Madonna
I'll say!: **4** amen **6** sure is
ill-smelling: **4** gamy **5** funky, gamey **6** frowsy, frowzy
ill-spent: **4** idle **5** empty **7** foolish, trivial, unsound **8** wasteful **9** frivolous, pointless, valueless
ill-starred: **5** curst **6** cursed, jinxed, tragic **7** hapless, unblest, unhappy, unlucky **8** luckless, tragical **9** unblessed, unfavored **10** disastrous
ill-suited: **5** inapt, silly, unapt, unfit, wrong **8** improper, untimely **10** irrelevant, nongermane, unbecoming, unsuitable
I'll Take Manhattan
author: Judith Krantz
I'll take that as __: **3** a no **4** a yes
I'll Take You There (1972 song)
artist: Staple Singers
...I'll tell __ lies: **5** you no
ill-tempered: **4** mean, sour **5** acerb, angry, nasty, surly, testy, waspy **6** crabby, feisty, grumpy, morose, raving, snappy, touchy **7** annoyed, bearish, bilious, grouchy, huffish, ranting, vicious, waspish **8** churlish, grumpish, incensed **10** freaked out
person: **4** ogre **5** shrew **6** virago
see also angry
ill-timed: **8** improper **10** out of joint
ill-treat: **4** harm, mall, maul **5** abuse, wrong **6** injure, misuse **8** aggrieve **9** manhandle, persecute
I'll Tumble 4 Ya (1983 song)
artist: Culture Club
illume: **5** light **7** lighten **8** brighten
illuminate: **5** color, edify, light, shine, solve **6** ignite, inform, kindle **7** clarify, clear up, explain, lighten, light up **8** brighten **9** bring home, dramatize, elucidate, enlighten, exemplify, highlight, interpret, irradiate, make clear, spotlight **10** account for, floodlight, illustrate, incandesce
illuminated: **3** lit **5** aglow, light, lit up, shiny **6** ablaze, bright, flashy, gaslit **7** beaming, blazing, fulgent, glowing, lambent, radiant, shining, well-lit **8** dazzling, gleaming, luminous, lustrous **9** brilliant, sparkling
from below: **5** uplit
illuminati: **5** elite **8** literati **9** aesthetes, highbrows **10** upper-crust
illumination: **3** ray **4** beam, info, rays **5** beams, flame, flash, gleam, light **6** flames, gleams, lights **7** flashes
gas: **4** neon
source: **4** lamp **5** flare, light **6** beacon **10** flashlight
unit: **3** lux **4** phot, watt
units: **5** luces
illumine: **5** edify, light, shine **7** clarify, light up, radiate **8** brighten, instruct **9** elucidate, irradiate
illus.: **4** diag., pict.
ill-use: **4** harm **6** injure **8** aggrieve, maltreat, mistreat **9** brutalize
illusion: **4** myth **5** dream, ghost, magic, trick **6** mirage, vision **7** chimera, fallacy, fantasy, figment, mistake **8** chimaera, daydream, disguise, ideality **9** deception, dreamland, misbelief, nightmare, unreality **10** apparition
__ illusion: **7** optical
illusionist: **8** conjurer, magician
Illusionist, The (2006 film)
cast: Jessica Biel, Paul Giamatti, Edward Norton
illusive: **6** subtle **9** imaginary
illusory: **6** dreamy, fantom, irreal, unreal **7** phantom **8** apparent, fanciful **9** deceitful, deceptive, imaginary, visionary **10** chimerical, fallacious, ostensible, subjective
illustrate: **4** draw, etch, limn, show **5** paint, teach **6** adduce, depict, embody, evince, imbody, lay out, mirror, sketch, typify, unfold **7** clarify, clear up, display, exhibit, explain, get over, picture, point up, portray **8** describe, evidence, indicate, manifest, stand for **9** bring home, delineate, elucidate, embellish, emphasize, epitomize, exemplify, explicate, get across, highlight, interpret, make clear, make plain, personify, represent, spotlight, symbolize **10** allegorize, illuminate
illustrated: **7** graphic **9** decorated, graphical
Illustrated Man, The
author: Ray Bradbury
illustration: **3** art **4** case, icon, logo **5** chart, image, light, model, photo, plate, table **6** design, figure, sample, sketch **7** analogy, cartoon, drawing, etching, example, pattern, picture, tableau **8** citation, halftone, instance, painting, sampling, snapshot, specimen, vignette
illustrative: **5** typic **6** sample **7** graphic, typical **8** symbolic **9** graphical
illustrator: **4** Erté, Kent **5** Abbey **6** Potter **8** Rockwell
illustrious: **4** star **5** famed, grand, great, lofty, noble, noted, proud **6** famous, mighty, signal **7** eminent, exalted, notable, sublime **8** esteemed, glorious, immortal, laureate, renowned, splendid **9** legendary, memorable, well-known **10** preeminent
illustriousness: **5** glory **6** renown **8** eminence, nobility, prestige
I'll Wait (1984 song)
artist: Van Halen
ill wind nobody blows good, An: **4** oboe
ill-wisher: **3** foe **5** enemy, rival **6** foeman **7** defamer, invader, nemesis, opposer, traitor, villain **8** attacker, betrayer, opponent, saboteur **9** adversary, assailant, combatant, detractor, other side, terrorist **10** antagonist, competitor
Il mio tesoro: **4** aria
Il nome della rosa
author: Umberto Eco
ILO
headquarters: **6** Geneva
part of ~: **3** Int., Org. **4** Intl. **5** Labor
Iloilo: **4** city, port, town
locale: **5** Panay
town near ~: **4** Oton
Ilona: **6** Massey **7** Stoller
__ I Lost You: **4** When
I Love __: **4** Lucy **5** Paris **6** Louisa
I Love a Mystery: **9** radio show
I Love a Parade
composer: Harold Arlen
I Love a Piano
composer: Irving Berlin
I Love a Rainy Night (1980 song)
artist: Eddie Rabbitt
__ I Love Her: **3** And
I Love How You Love Me (song)
artist: Paris Sisters, Bobby Vinton
I love in Latin: **3** amo
I Love Lucy (CBS sitcom)
cast: Desi Arnaz (Ricky Ricardo) Lucille Ball (Lucy Ricardo) William Frawley (Fred Mertz) Vivian Vance (Ethel Mertz)
dog: **4** Fred **5** Butch
producer: **5** Arnaz **6** Desilu
I Love Music (1975 song)
artist: O'Jays
I Love Paris
composer: Cole Porter
I Love Rock 'n Roll (1982 song)
artist: Joan Jett and the Blackhearts
I Loves You, Porgy
singer: **4** Bess
__ I Love, The: **3** Man, One
I Love the Nightlife (1978 song)
artist: Alicia Bridges
I Love to __: **5** Laugh, Rhyme, Singa
I Love Trouble (1994 film)
cast: Nick Nolte, Julia Roberts
__ I Love You?: **5** Why Do
__, I Love You: **4** Baby **5** Hello
I Love You, Alice B. Toklas (1968 film)
cast: Peter Sellers, Leigh Taylor-Young, Jo Van Fleet
I Love You Because (1963 song)
artist: Al Martino
Il pendolo di Foucault
author: Umberto Eco
Il Penseroso
author: John Milton
Ilsa: **6** Laszlo
love: **4** Rick
Ilse: **9** Aichinger
Il Trovatore: **5** opera
composer: Giuseppe Verdi
prop: **5** anvil
role: **4** Inez, Ruiz **7** Leonora, Manrico
setting: **6** Aragon, Biscay
Ilyich: **4** Ivan
I'm __: **4** a Man, Easy **5** Sorry, Yours **7** Walking
I'm __ as Fast as I Can: **7** Dancing
I'm __ Baby Tonight: **4** Your
I'm __ boy!: **4** a bad
I'm __ Cowhand: **5** an Old
I'm __ Get You Sucka: **5** Gonna
I'm __ in Love With You: **5** Stone
I'm __ it!: **4** agin
I'm __ Mood for Love: **5** in the
I'm __ Rappaport: **3** Not
I'm __ sit right down...: **5** gonna
I'm __ VIII, I Am: **5** Henry
I'm __ Wild About Harry: **4** Just
I'm __ Woman: **5** Every
I'm __ You Now: **7** Telling
I'm __ your tricks!: **4** onto
I.M.: **3** Pei
Ima: **4** Hogg
I'm a __: **5** Loser
I'm a Believer (1966 song)
artist: Monkees
iMac: **5** Apple **8** computer
alternative: ***see*** computer
__, I'm Adam: **5** Madam
I Made It Throught the Rain (1980 song)
artist: Barry Manilow
image: **4** copy, icon, ikon, mold **5** eikon, model **6** double, effigy, mirror, notion, symbol, vision **7** concept, picture, realize, replica, thought **8** likeness, metaphor, portrait **9** adumbrate, depiction, facsimile, photocopy, semblance **10** appearance, conception, dead ringer, embodiment, envisaging, impression, perception, photograph, projection, reflection, simulacrum
combining form: **3** eid-, typ- **4** eido-, icon-, ikon-, typo- **5** eicon-, icono-, idolo-, ikono- **6** eicono-, eidolo-
computer-screen ~: **3** gif, jpg, tif **4** icon, jpeg **6** bitmap
crude ~: **6** effigy
darkroom: **3** neg. **8** negative
form an ~: **5** think **6** ideate
graven ~: **4** baal, idol
Greek carved ~: **6** xoanon
holy ~: **4** icon, ikon **5** eikon
indistinct ~: **4** blur
maker: **5** flack, PR man **6** camera, mirror **8** promoter
mental ~: **4** idea **6** memory, vision **7** thought
mirror ~: **4** refl. **10** reflection
radar ~: **3** pip **4** blip
reverse ~: **3** neg. **8** negative
spitting ~: **4** copy, twin **5** clone, match **6** double **7** picture **8** likeness **9** duplicate, look-alike **10** dead ringer
starter: **5** after
the very ~ of: **4** like
__ image: **4** body **5** ghost, spit 'n **6** graven, mirror
__-image: **4** self
imager: **3** MRI **6** artist
imagery: **7** similes **9** allusions, imaging, metaphors, picturing
imaginable: **6** doable, likely, viable **7** earthly **8** credible, feasible, possible, workable **9** plausible, potential, practical, thinkable **10** achievable, attainable, believable, calculable, convincing, supposable
imaginably: **5** maybe **7** perhaps **8** probably
imaginary: **5** false **6** dreamy, irreal, made-up, unreal **7** assumed, fancied **8** abstract, delusive, fabulous, fanciful, illusive, illusory, invented, mythical, notional, quixotic, spectral, supposed **9** deceptive, dreamed-up, dreamlike, fantastic, fictional, legendary, pretended, trumped-up, visionary, whimsical **10** apocryphal, chimerical, fictitious, groundless, phantasmal, phantasmic, quixotical
not ~: **4** real **5** solid **6** actual **7** genuine **8** concrete, existing, tangible **9** authentic, corporeal
Imaginary Friends
author: Alison Lurie

imagination: 4 myth 5 fancy 6 vision 7 fantasy, insight 8 artistry, daydream, ideality
figment of the ~: 6 fantom 7 phantom 8 illusion
product of the ~: 4 idea 5 dream 6 notion 7 thought
imaginative: 5 novel, slick, vivid 6 clever, dreamy, mental, poetic 7 cunning, fertile, fictive, offbeat, utopian 8 artistic, creative, fanciful, inspired, original, poetical, quixotic 10 artistical, quixotical
be ~: 4 coin 6 create, design, devise, make up 7 compose, concoct, dream up, fashion, think up 8 conceive, contrive 9 fabricate, formulate
imagine: 3 see 4 deem, take 5 dream, fancy, guess, infer, think 6 assume, cook up, create, deduce, devise, gather, ideate, invent, make up, reckon, take it 7 believe, dream of, dream up, picture, presume, pretend, realize, suppose, surmise, suspect, think of, think up 8 conceive, conclude, daydream, envisage, envision, theorize 9 conjure up, fabricate, fantasize, think of as, visualize 10 brainstorm, conjecture, understand, woolgather
old-style: 4 ween
Imagine (1971 song)
artist: John Lennon
Imagine __!: 4 that
imagined: 6 unreal, unseen 9 vicarious 10 fictitious
imagining: 7 imagery 8 daydream 10 conception, envisaging
I'm agin it!: 3 naw
imagist: 4 poet
imago: 3 bug 5 adult 6 insect
future ~: 4 pupa 5 pupae
Imago: 4 font 8 typeface
I'm a Little __: 6 Teapot
I'm Alive
artist: ELO
I'm all ears!: 6 Do tell
I'm Alright (1980 song)
artist: Kenny Loggins
imam: 5 calif, kalif, title 6 caliph, cleric, kaliph, khalif
deity: 5 Allah
text: 5 Koran, Quran
I'm a Man (1965 song)
artist: Yardbirds
I'm a man of means __ means...: 4 by no
Imamu __ Baraka: 5 Amiri
Iman: 5 model 10 supermodel
spouse: David Bowie
imaret: 3 inn 5 serai 7 hospice
I Married an Angel: 7 musical
composer: Lorenz Hart, Richard Rodgers
I'm a Stranger Here Myself
author: Alden Nowlan, Ogden Nash
I'm a Woman (1975 song)
artist: Maria Muldaur
Imax: 7 theater, theatre
imbalance: 6 nerves 9 disparity 10 inequality
imbed: 5 lodge, plant 6 anchor 7 implant
imbibe: 3 sip 4 belt, chug, down, gulp, swig, take, tope 5 drink, quaff 6 absorb, guzzle, ingest, tipple 7 consume, put away, swallow 8 toss back 9 hoist a few
imbiber: 3 sot 7 tippler
bill: 3 tab 6 bar tab
imbricate: 3 lap 7 overlap
__ Imbrium: 4 Mare
imbroglio: 3 row 4 fray, maze, riot, spat 5 brawl, fight, mix-up, run-in 6 crisis 7 dispute, ferment, quarrel 8 argument, brouhaha, disorder, quagmire, squabble 9 bickering, confusion, soap opera 10 complexity, difficulty, falling-out
I'm broke-it's __: 3 oke
imbrue: 4 soak, soil 5 dirty, douse, dowse, drown, souse, stain, sully, taint 6 defile, drench, infuse, stains 7 immerse, implant, suffuse 8 permeate, saturate
Imbruglia: 7 Natalie
imbue: 4 fill 5 bathe, color, infix, steep, teach, tinge 6 charge, drench, infuse, instil, invest 7 breathe, engrain, implant, ingrain, inspire, instill, pervade, suffuse 8 permeate, saturate 9 inculcate
with spirit: 6 ensoul, insoul
imbued: 4 full 5 awash 6 loaded 7 teeming 8 brimming 9 chock-full
I'm Coming Home (1974 song)
artist: Spinners
I'm Dancing as Fast as I Can
author: David Rabe
I'm Easy (1976 song)
artist: Keith Carradine
Imelda: 6 Marcos 8 Filipina
obsession: 5 shoes
I met __ with...: 4 a man
I'm Every Woman (song)
artist: Whitney Houston, Chaka Khan
IMF, part of: 3 Int. 4 Fund, Intl. 8 Monetary
I'm Free (song)
artist: Kenny Loggins, Who, The
I'm game!: 4 fine, let's, okay, sure
I'm glad that's over: 4 phew, whew
I'm Goin' Down (1985 song)
artist: Bruce Springsteen
I'm Gonna Be Strong (1964 song)
artist: Gene Pitney
I'm Gonna Get You Sucka (1988 film)
cast: Bernie Casey, Keenen Ivory Wayans
director: Keenen Ivory Wayans
I'm Gonna Love You Just... (1973 song)
artist: Barry White
I'm Gonna Make You Love Me (1968 song)
artist: Supremes, Temptations
I'm Henry VIII, I Am (1965 song)
artist: Herman's Hermits
__, I'm home!: 5 Honey
I'm in Love Again (1956 song)
artist: Fats Domino
I'm innocent!: 5 Not me
imitate: 3 ape 4 copy, echo, mock, sham 5 ditto, feign, mimic, spoof 6 assume, be like, borrow, do like, follow, go like, mirror, parody, parrot, pass as, repeat, send up 7 act like, burlesk, emulate, pattern, portray, pretend, reflect 8 make like, parallel, simulate 9 burlesque, duplicate, personate, replicate 10 borrow from, caricature
imitation: 4 copy, dupe, echo, fake, faux, mock, sham 5 apery, aping, bogus, clone, ditto, phony, put-on 6 acting, double, ersatz, forged, parody, phoney, pseudo, ringer, unreal 7 assumed, feigned, forgery, mimicry, mockery, replica, takeoff 8 knockoff, likeness, spurious, travesty 9 duplicate, imposture, parroting, photocopy, semblance, simulated, synthetic, unnatural 10 artificial, carbon copy, caricature, fabricated, fictitious, fraudulent, impression, patterning, reflection, simulacrum, simulation
in ~ of: 3 à la 4 like
not an ~: 4 orig. 8 original
suffix: 3 -een, -ine 4 -ette
Imitation
author: Edgar Allan Poe
Imitation of Life: 5 novel
author: Fannie Hurst
Imitations of Horace
author: Alexander Pope
imitative: 4 hack 5 apish 6 copied, echoic, ersatz, pseudo 7 copycat, mimetic 8 simulant 9 deceptive, emulative, following, mimicking, simulated 10 derivative, reflective, secondhand, threadbare, unoriginal
behavior: 5 apery
imitator: 3 ape 4 aper, echo 5 mimic, phony 6 copier, epigon, forger, monkey, parrot, phoney, shadow 7 copycat, epigone 8 emulator, follower, imposter, impostor 10 plagiarist
I'm Just a Singer (1973 song)
artist: Moody Blues
I'm Just Wild About Harry
composer: Eubie Blake, Noble Sissle
I'm Leaving It Up to You (1974 song)
artist: Donny and Marie Osmond
I'm listening: 4 go on 8 continue
I'm Livin' in Shame (1969 song)
artist: Supremes
I'm Losing You (1999 film)
cast: Rosanna Arquette, Salome Jens, Frank Langella, Andrew McCarthy
I'm Losing You (song)
artist: Rod Stewart, Temptations
immaculate: 4 neat, pure 5 clean, snowy, white 6 chaste, decent, virgin, washed 7 aseptic, groomed, perfect, sinless 8 flawless, germfree, hygienic, innocent, pristine, sanitary, spotless, unbroken, unmarred, unsoiled, virginal, virtuous 9 blameless, errorless, exquisite, faultless, guiltless, incorrupt, stainless, taintless, undamaged, undefiled, unspoiled, unsullied, untouched 10 antiseptic, impeccable, unpolluted
immalleable: 4 hard 5 stiff, stony
immanent: 7 central 8 intimate 9 innermost
Immanuel: 4 Kant, Lord
immaterial: 4 airy 6 dreamy, mental 7 foreign, ghostly, trivial 8 bodiless, ethereal, spectral 9 asomatous, celestial, disbodied, dreamlike, inapropos, no big deal, spiritual, unearthly 10 discarnate, extraneous, impalpable, inapposite, insensible, intangible, irrelevant, unembodied, unphysical, wraithlike
immature: 3 kid, raw 4 baby, rash, weak 5 crude, early, green, silly, small, young 6 boyish, callow, giggly, jejune, larval, little, tender, unripe, unwise 7 babyish, kiddish, puerile 8 childish, juvenile, underage, untested, youthful 9 beardless, childlike, dependent, embryonic, formative, half-grown, infantile, unsettled 10 adolescent, sophomoric, unfinished, unseasoned
immaturity: 5 youth 6 nonage 7 rawness 9 childhood, greenness, puerility 10 unripeness
immeasurable: 4 huge, much, vast 5 great, large 6 cosmic, myriad 7 abysmal, endless, immense 8 infinite, unending 9 boundless, countless, limitless, unlimited 10 gargantuan
time: 3 eon 4 aeon
void: 5 abysm, abyss
immeasurably: 5 by far 7 greatly
immediacy: 7 urgency 8 nearness, priority, vicinity 9 closeness, proximity 10 importance, precedence
immediate: 4 near 5 close, first, quick 6 direct, nearby, prompt, recent, snappy, speedy, sudden, urgent 7 current, instant, present, primary 8 adjacent, pressing, proximal 9 firsthand, intuitive, paramount, proximate 10 contiguous, convenient, imperative, near-at-hand, time-saving
area: 8 premises, presence, vicinity
needing ~ attention: 4 dire 5 acute 6 urgent 7 crucial, exigent, serious 8 critical, pressing 9 desperate, important 10 compelling, imperative
to a poet: 5 anear
vicinity: 5 midst 8 nearness 9 closeness, proximity
Immediate Family (1989 film)
cast: Glenn Close, Kevin Dillon, Mary Stuart Masterson, James Woods
immediately: 3 now, PDQ 4 anon, ASAP, stat 5 right, today 6 at once, presto, pronto 7 rapidly, readily 8 directly, hereupon, in a flash, in a jiffy, in a trice, on the dot, promptly, right now, right off 9 at present, forthwith, on the spot, presently, right away, summarily 10 at this time, here and now, this minute
immemorial: 3 old 5 olden 6 age-old 7 ageless, ancient
__ immemorial: 4 time
immense: 3 big 4 huge, vast 5 broad, bulky, giant, great, jumbo, large, massy, super 6 cosmic, mighty 7 hulking, mammoth, massive, sizable, titanic 8 colossal, cosmical, enormous, galactic, gigantic, king-size, oversize, sizeable, spacious, terrific, towering, whapping, whop-

ping **9** boundless, extensive, Herculean, humongous, limitless, monstrous, overlarge, unbounded, unlimited, whalelike **10** gargantuan, monumental, prodigious, stupendous, tremendous
immensely: **4** a lot, much, over **5** no end **6** highly, vastly **7** awfully, greatly **9** extremely, in a big way **10** incredibly
enjoy ~: **5** eat up, lap up, savor
immensity: **4** bulk, mass, size **5** space, width **6** extent **7** bigness, breadth, expanse, measure **8** enormity, hugeness, infinity, vastness **9** amplitude, bulkiness, greatness, largeness, magnitude **10** infinitude
immerse: **3** dip **4** bury, busy, dunk, sink, soak, wash **5** bathe, douse, dowse, drown, rinse, souse, steep **6** absorb, drench, embrue, engage, engulf, imbrue, ingulf, obsess, occupy, plunge, wallow **7** baptize, engross, involve **8** interest, inundate, saturate, submerge **9** preoccupy
immersed: **4** busy, deep, rapt **6** buried, intent, sunken, tied up **7** bound up **8** consumed, held fast **9** submerged, wrapped up **10** spellbound
immersion: **3** dip **7** bathing, dipping, dousing, ducking, dunking, sousing **8** infusion, plunging **9** attention **10** absorbtion, absorption, saturating, saturation, submerging
immesh: **6** tangle **8** tangle up
immigrant: **5** alien **7** pioneer **8** colonist, newcomer, stranger **9** foreigner
course: **3** ESL
exam: **5** TOEFL
island: **5** Ellis
Immigrants, The
author: Howard Fast
immigration concern: **5** quota
imminent: **4** near, nigh **5** close **6** at hand, coming, future, in view, nearby **7** brewing, in store, looming, nearing, pending **8** adjacent, in the air, oncoming, on the way, upcoming **9** bordering, gathering, impending, in the wind, proximate **10** coming soon, convenient, in the cards, in the works
be ~: **4** loom **6** impend **8** overhang, threaten
to a poet: **5** anear
imminently: **4** anon, soon **6** any day
immix: **4** meld, pool **5** blend, merge **6** mingle **7** combine **9** commingle, integrate **10** interweave
immixture: **5** blend **6** hybrid **7** amalgam **9** composite, synthesis
immobile: **4** firm **5** fixed, inert, rigid, stiff, still **6** frozen, nailed, rooted, static **7** hard-set, riveted **8** anchored, stagnant **9** steadfast **10** gridlocked, inexorable, motionless, stationary, stock-still
immobilize: **3** pin **5** stick **6** hogtie **7** petrify **8** paralyse, paralyze **9** overpower
immobilized: **3** set **6** frozen, rooted **7** riveted **9** paralytic **10** motionless
immoderacy: **4** glut **6** excess **7** surfeit **8** plethora **9** profusion
immoderate: **4** wild **5** gross, loose, steep, ultra, undue **6** lavish, wanton, wonton **7** drastic, extreme, hyped up, profuse, radical, ruinous, violent **8** dizzying, prodigal, ultraist, wasteful **9** egregious, excessive, expensive, fanatical, irregular, luxurious, overblown, unbridled, unthrifty **10** exorbitant, inordinate, profligate, unbalanced, untempered
immoderately: **3** too **4** very **6** overly, unduly **7** largely **8** to a fault
immoderation: **6** excess, luxury **7** license
immodest: **4** bold, lewd, racy, rank **5** lofty, nasty **6** brazen, coarse, risqué **7** forward **8** impudent, indecent, shameful, unseemly **9** barefaced, conceited, shameless, unashamed **10** big-talking, indelicate, suggestive
immodesty: **5** pride **7** conceit **9** indecency **10** narcissism
immoral: **3** bad **4** base, evil, lewd, vile **5** loose, nasty, wrong **6** sinful, smutty, unfair, unholy, wicked **7** corrupt, lustful, profane, vicious **8** depraved, improper, indecent, shameful, unchaste, wrongful **9** corrupted, debauched, dishonest, dissolute, low-minded, lubricous, miscreant, nefarious, shameless, unethical **10** dissipated, indelicate, iniquitous, lascivious, licentious, profligate, villainous, virtueless
act: **3** sin
sort: **3** cad **4** rake, roué **7** bounder **9** libertine **10** profligate
Immoralist, The
author: André Gide
immorality: **3** sin **4** evil, vice **5** wrong **8** iniquity, venality **9** depravity **10** corruption, degeneracy
immortal: **6** famous, heroic **7** eminent, eternal, undying **8** almighty, heroical, laureate, timeless, unending **9** deathless, legendary, perennial, permanent, perpetual **10** celebrated, monumental
name meaning ~: **7** Ambrose
Immortal Beloved (1994 film)
cast: Gary Oldman, Isabella Rossellini
immortalize: **5** deify **7** lionize **8** preserve **10** perpetuate
immovable: **3** set **4** fast, firm, iron **5** dug in, fixed, rigid, stuck **6** frozen, rooted, secure, static, steady **7** adamant, diehard, hard-set **8** locked in, obdurate, resolute, stubborn **9** dead set on, hard-nosed, immutable, impassive, obstinate, quiescent, steadfast **10** hard-bitten, inexorable, inflexible, invariable, motionless, set in stone, stationary, unshakable, unwavering, unyielding
immovably: **4** fast **6** firmly **7** fixedly, tightly **8** securely
immune: **6** exempt **8** free from **9** protected, resistant **10** impervious, privileged, vaccinated
immune-system element: **5** T-cell
immunity: **6** refuge, safety **7** freedom, liberty, license **8** security **9** privilege **10** protection
give ~ to: **6** excuse, exempt, let off
immunization
agents: **4** sera
device: **6** jet gun
letters: **3** DPT
immunize: **9** inoculate, vaccinate
immunological starter: **4** sero
immunologist: **4** Salk **5** Sabin
immunology adjective: **5** viral
immure: **4** hold, jail **6** detain, entomb, intern, lock up, punish, shut in, shut up, wall in, wall up **7** close in, close up, confine, enclose, impound, inclose, seclude **8** imprison
immured: **4** pent **6** pent up
immurement: **10** internment
immutable: **4** firm **6** stable **8** constant **9** immovable, permanent, perpetual, steadfast **10** changeless, inflexible, invariable, sacrosanct, unchanging, undecaying
I'm No Angel (1933 film)
cast: Cary Grant, Mae West
I'm not __ complain: **5** one to
I'm not half the __ used to be: **4** man I
I'm not kidding: **5** no lie, truly **6** no joke, really **7** for real **9** seriously
I'm Not Lisa (1975 song)
artist: Jessi Colter
Imogene: **4** Coca
cohort: **3** Sid
I'm OK-You're OK
author: Thomas A. Harris
I'm on Fire (1985 song)
artist: Bruce Springsteen
I'm outta here: **3** bye **4** ciao, ta-ta **5** adieu, later **6** so long **7** goodbye
imp: **3** elf, fay **4** brat, pixy, puck, tike, tyke **5** child, cutup, demon, devil, fairy, fiend, gamin, pixie, scamp **6** bad boy, daemon, daimon, goblin, rascal, sprite, urchin **7** brownie, gremlin, hellion **8** devilkin **9** hobgoblin **10** holy terror, jackanapes
impact: **3** hit, jar **4** bang, blow, jolt **5** brunt, clash, crash, crush, force, knock, punch, shock, smash, thump, touch **6** affect, crunch, effect, jounce, strike, wallop **7** contact, smash-up **8** bang into **9** aftermath, collision, crash into, influence, rear-ender **10** concussion, impression, percussion
on: **4** sway **5** alter **6** affect **9** influence
sound: **3** bam, pow **4** wham **5** kapow, smack, splat **6** whammo
__ Impact: **4** Deep **6** Sudden
impair: **3** mar, sag, sap **4** flag, harm, hurt, maim, tear, tire, wane **5** blunt, break, crack, spoil, wreck **6** damage, debase, deface, dilute, hinder, impair, injure, lessen, mangle, ravage, reduce, riddle, shrink, soften, weaken **7** corrupt, deplete, depress, devalue, disable, exhaust, fatigue, shatter, vitiate **8** enervate, enfeeble **9** attenuate, devaluate, hamstring, make worse, prejudice, undermine **10** adulterate, debilitate, devitalize
impaired: **4** hurt, sick, torn **5** rusty **6** broken, faulty, flawed **7** injured, lacking, unsound **8** fallible **9** defective, deficient, imperfect
impairment: **4** harm, loss, wear **5** abuse, decay **6** damage, injury **8** breakage, handicap, weakness **9** deformity, detriment **10** disability
impala: **6** animal, mammal **8** antelope
relative: *see* antelope
Impala: **3** car **4** auto **5** Chevy **9** Chevrolet
impale: **4** gore, stab **5** lance, spear, spike, stick **6** pierce, skewer, thrust **7** spindle, stick on, torture **8** puncture, transfix **9** penetrate **10** run through
Impaler, The: **4** Vlad
impalpable: **8** bodiless **9** imprecise, invisible **10** immaterial, indistinct, insensible, intangible, unapparent
impart: **4** give, lend, send, tell **5** allow, break, lends, teach **6** accord, afford, bestow, confer, convey, extend, inform, infuse, instil, pass on, recite, relate, render, report, reveal **7** breathe, confide, divulge, instill, mention, provide **8** advise of, announce, describe, disclose, hand down, transmit, vocalize **9** inculcate, make known **10** contribute
knowledge: **4** show **5** brief, coach, drill, edify, guide, teach, train, tutor **6** advise, ground, inform, school **7** educate, explain, instill, lecture **8** instruct **9** catechize, enlighten, inculcate, interpret
impartial: **4** even, fair, just, open **5** equal, sober **6** candid, honest, square **7** neutral **8** balanced, detached, judicial, moderate, rational, unbiased, unskewed **9** equitable, objective, unbigoted, uncolored, unslanted **10** evenhanded, fair-minded, impersonal, on-the-fence, open-minded, reasonable
not ~: **6** biased, myopic, skewed, unfair, unjust **7** bigoted **10** intolerant
impartiality: **6** equity **7** justice **8** fairness, fair play
impartially: **5** right
impartible: **8** catching **10** contagious
impassable: **6** closed **7** blocked **9** closed off **10** invincible, obstructed
impasse: **4** halt **6** corner, logjam, plight **7** dead end **8** cul-de-sac, deadlock, gridlock, quagmire, quandary, standoff **9** stalemate **10** blind alley, difficulty, standstill
at an ~: **5** mired, stuck
__ impasse: **4** at an
impassion: **4** fire, goad, spur, stir, wake **5** awake, rouse, spark **6** arouse, awaken, bestir, fire up, foment, heat up, incite, kindle, stir up, wake up, whip up, work up **7** actuate, agitate, animate, enliven, inflame, inspire, provoke **8** enkindle, inspirit, motivate, vitalize **9** galvanize, stimulate
impassioned: **3** hot, mad **4** keen **5** fiery, vivid **6** ablaze, ardent, fervid, fierce, hearty, heated, loving, moving, red-hot, torrid **7** amorous, blazing, burning,

earnest, excited, fervent, fired up, flaming, furious, glowing, intense, rousing, violent, zealous **8** animated, romantic, stirring, vehement **10** hot-blooded
impassive: 4 calm, cold, cool **5** aloof, blank, inert, quiet, staid, stoic, stony **6** at ease, bovine, low-key, mellow, placid, sedate, serene, stolid, stoney, wooden **7** amiable, at peace, callous, equable, languid, pacific, relaxed, stoical, unmoved **8** amicable, carefree, composed, hardened, laid-back, listless, peaceful, taciturn, tranquil **9** apathetic, bloodless, collected, easygoing, heartless, immovable, lethargic, nerveless, quiescent, temperate, unexcited, unfeeling, unruffled, unstirred **10** impervious, insensible, nonchalant, phlegmatic, poker-faced, spiritless, unaffected, unagitated, unreactive, untroubled
impassivity: 8 lethargy, stoicism
impatience: 5 haste **6** temper **7** anxiety, fidgets **8** edginess, rashness **9** agitation, annoyance, eagerness, hastiness, shortness, surliness, vehemence **10** excitement, expectancy, snappiness, uneasiness
sign of ~: 4 honk
impatiens: 5 plant **6** flower
impatient: 4 curt, edgy, rash **5** antsy, brusk, eager, hasty, itchy, quick, testy, type A, weary **6** abrupt, on edge, uneasy **7** anxious, brusque, chafing, fretful, restive **8** fretsome, headlong, petulant, restless **9** demanding, excitable, impetuous, indignant, irascible, irritable, straining **10** breathless, high-strung, intolerant, solicitous
how the ~ stand: 6 akimbo
not ~: 4 calm **5** type B **6** serene
one: 6 chafer
one's query: 4 when
remark: 3 tsk, tut, yah **4** c'mon, phew, pish, pooh, posh, tush **5** pshaw, shame **6** enough, let's go, move it, tsk tsk, tut-tut **8** for shame
impavid: 4 bold **5** brave, gutsy, nervy, stout **6** daring, heroic, plucky **7** doughty, gallant, valiant **8** fearless, heroical, intrepid, unafraid, valorous **9** dauntless, undaunted **10** courageous
impeach: 3 tax **6** accuse, charge, indict **8** denounce, question **9** inculpate
impeachment: 5 blame, trial **7** lawsuit
impeccable: 3 A-OK **4** pure **5** clean, exact, sound **7** correct, perfect, precise, sinless **8** absolute, accurate, flawless, inerrant, innocent, reliable, unerring, unflawed, unsoiled **9** blameless, errorless, exquisite, faultless, guiltless, incorrupt, stainless, virtuosic **10** consummate, immaculate, infallible
impecunious: 4 poor **5** broke, needy **6** bad off, busted, hard up, ill-off, in need, in want **7** pinched **8** badly off, bankrupt, beggarly, dirt poor, homeless, indigent, strapped **9** destitute, insolvent, moneyless, penniless, penurious **10** down and out, pauperized, straitened
impecuniousness: 4 need, want **7** beggary, poverty
impedance: 3 jam **4** clog **8** blockage, obstacle **9** hindrance, occlusion **10** bottleneck, congestion
impede: 3 bar, dam, jam **4** clog, curb, plug, rein, slow, stop **5** block, brake, check, choke, cramp, cross, dam up, delay, deter, stimy, stunt, stymy, tie up **6** bother, cut off, dampen, detain, forbid, hamper, hang up, hinder, hobble, hogtie, hold up, rein in, retard, slow up, stop up, stymie, thwart **7** congest, disrupt, inhibit, occlude, prevent, set back, trammel **8** close off, encumber, entangle, handcuff, handicap, hold back, obstruct, preclude, prohibit, restrain, restrict, slow down, straiten **9** foreclose, frustrate, hamstring, interdict, interfere, interrupt, stonewall **10** complicate, discourage, filibuster
legally: 5 estop
impeded: 4 poky, slow **6** draggy **7** gradual, halting, lagging, languid **8** crawling, creeping, dawdling, dilatory, dragging, drawn-out, hesitant, plodding, slothful, sluggish, toddling **9** leisurely, lethargic, snail-like **10** deliberate
impediment: 3 bar, rub **4** clog, curb, dike, drag, kink, snag, wall **5** block, check, cramp, delay, hitch, minus, thorn **6** burden, hang-up, hazard, holdup, hurdle, kicker **7** barrier, red tape, setback, shackle, trammel **8** blockade, blockage, drawback, handicap, obstacle, weakness **9** barricade, detention, deterrent, detriment, hindrance, liability, millstone, restraint, roadblock, stricture **10** bottleneck, dead weight, difficulty, inhibition
impedimenta: 4 gear **5** goods, stuff **6** things **7** baggage, luggage **8** equipage, materiel, supplies **9** equipment, trappings
impel: 4 cast, goad, make, move, poke, prod, push, spur, urge **5** boost, drive, egg on, press, shove, speed, throw **6** arouse, compel, foment, incite, induce, prompt, propel, stir up, thrust, turn on **7** actuate, inspire, press on, quicken **8** activate, mobilize, motivate, persuade, pressure, railroad **9** constrain, determine, influence, instigate, preordain, stimulate **10** accelerate, pressurize
impelled: 5 bound, fated **6** driven, forced **7** obliged **8** destined, required
impelling: 6 moving, urgent **8** forceful **10** persuasive
impend: 4 hang, loom, near **5** await, hover **6** menace **8** overhang, threaten
impending: 4 near, nigh **5** close **6** at hand, coming, future, nearby **7** brewing, in store, looming, nearing, ominous, pending **8** adjacent, imminent, lowering, menacing, oncoming, upcoming **9** dangerous, gathering, in the wind, proximate **10** convenient, inevitable, in the cards, in the works, portending
impenetrable: 4 firm, hard **5** dense, mirky, murky, solid, thick, tight **6** arcane, mystic, opaque, unseen **7** compact, obscure **8** abstruse, airtight, baffling, hardened, hermetic **10** fathomless, mysterious
impenitent: 8 indurate
imperative: 4 must **5** acute, state, vital **6** urgent **7** binding, burning, crucial, exigent, mandate **8** critical, exigeant, pressing, required **9** clamorous, essential, immediate, important, mandatory, necessary, necessity, requisite, strategic **10** autocratic, compulsory, obligatory, peremptory
Imperato: 5 Carlo
imperceptible: 4 slow, tiny, weak **5** faint, small, teeny **6** hidden, little, minute, slight, subtle, teensy, unseen **7** gradual, trivial
imperceptibly: 6 hardly **8** scarcely, slightly
imperceptive: 3 dim **5** crass, dense, thick **6** obtuse **8** mindless
imperfect: 3 bad, irr. **4** poor, sick **5** amiss, rough, tense **6** broken, faulty, flawed, marred, patchy **7** damaged, halting, ill-done, inexact, sketchy, unsound, wanting **8** below par, fallible, impaired, slipshod **9** defective, deficient, irregular **10** disfigured, inadequate, incomplete, unfinished
imperfection: 3 bug, mar **4** blot, dent, flaw, kink, spot, tear, vice, wart **5** fault, stain, taint **6** defect, foible, glitch **7** blemish, failing, frailty, problem **8** drawback, weakness
Imperfect Sympathies
author: Elia
imperial: 5 beard, grand, noble, regal, royal **6** kingly, lordly **7** emperor, empress, queenly, stately **8** despotic, imposing, kinglike, majestic, princely, splendid **9** dignified, monarchal, queenlike, sovereign **10** autocratic, despotical, majestical, tyrannical
volute: 5 shell **8** seashell
Imperial: 3 car **4** auto, oleo **8** Chrysler **9** margarine **10** automobile
alternative: 6 Parkay, Shedd's **7** Promise
Imperial Beach: 4 city, town
locale: 10 California
Imperial Woman
author: Pearl S. Buck
imperil: 4 risk **5** stake **6** hazard, menace **8** endanger, threaten **10** compromise, jeopardize
imperiled: 6 at risk **7** at stake **9** on the line **10** in jeopardy
imperilment: 4 risk **6** hazard **8** jeopardy
imperious: 3 big **5** bossy, proud, stern **6** kingly, lordly **7** haughty, pompous **8** arrogant, assuming, despotic, dogmatic, dominant, exacting, kinglike **9** arbitrary, demanding, dignified, hubristic, insistent, tyrannous **10** aggressive, autocratic, commanding, despotical, dogmatical, high-handed, iron-willed, oppressive, peremptory, tyrannical
imperiousness: 7 tyranny **9** autocracy, despotism **10** absolutism, oppression
imperishable: 7 abiding, eternal, lasting, undying **8** immortal, unfading **9** deathless, perennial, permanent, perpetual **10** changeless, undecaying
imperium: 5 power
impermanent: 5 brief, short **6** fickle, mortal **7** passing **8** fleeting, flitting, temporal, unstable **9** ephemeral, momentary, temporary, transient **10** evanescent, perishable, short-lived, transitory, unenduring
impermeable: 4 firm, hard, numb, safe **5** solid, thick, tight **6** immune **8** airtight, hermetic **9** impassive, nonporous, resistant, unstirred **10** unaffected, waterproof, watertight
impermissible: 5 taboo **6** banned **7** illegal, illicit **8** outlawed, unlawful, verboten **9** forbidden, off-limits **10** prohibited, proscribed
impersonal: 4 cold, cool **6** remote **7** neutral **8** abstract, detached **9** colorless, equitable, impartial, objective, uncolored, unslanted **10** poker-faced, unagitated, unfriendly
pronoun: 3 one
impersonate: 2 do **3** ape **4** play, pose **5** enact, mimic **6** assume, mirror, parody, pose as **7** act like, dress as, imitate, portray, pretend **8** double as, make like
impersonation: 4 copy, role **5** apery **6** acting
impersonator: 4 aper **5** mimic **8** imitator **9** look-alike
silent ~: 4 mime **5** mimer
impertinence: 3 lip **4** gall, guff, sass **5** cheek, crust, mouth, nerve, sauce **6** hutzpa, insult **7** chutzpa, hutzpah **8** audacity, back talk, boldness, chutzpah, pertness, rudeness, temerity
impertinent: 4 bold, flip, pert, rude, wise **5** brash, fresh, lippy, nervy, sassy, saucy, smart **6** brassy, brazen, cheeky **7** foreign, forward, off-base, uncivil, uncouth **8** arrogant, flippant, impolite, impudent, insolent **9** obtrusive, offensive, officious
one: 4 snip
imperturbability: 6 aplomb **8** patience, presence, stoicism
imperturbable: 4 calm, cool, even **5** sober, staid, stoic **6** assure, placid, sedate, serene, steady **7** assured, equable, patient, stoical **8** composed, tranquil **9** nerveless, unruffled
impervious: 4 firm, hard, numb, safe **5** solid, thick, tight **6** immune **8** airtight, hermetic **9** impassive, nonporous, resistant, unstirred **10** unaffected, waterproof, watertight
to feeling: 4 numb **5** aloof, stoic **6** stolid **7** unmoved **9** apathetic, impassive

impetrate: **3** ask, beg **5** cadge, hit up, mooch, plead **6** appeal, demand **7** beseech, entreat, implore, solicit **9** importune, mendicate, panhandle
impetration: **4** plea **6** appeal, demand **8** entreaty
impetuosity: **4** élan **5** haste **6** fervor **7** abandon **8** rashness **9** brashness, eagerness, hastiness, incaution **10** abruptness
impetuous: **3** hot **4** rash, wild **5** blind, brash, eager, hasty, quick **6** abrupt, fervid, sudden, unwary **7** dashing, hurried, rampant, rushing **8** headlong, heedless **9** desperate, emotional, excitable, explosive, foolhardy, impatient, impulsive, unbridled, unplanned, whirlwind **10** boisterous, hot-blooded, incautious, passionate, unexpected, unthinking
impetuously: **8** pell-mell **9** headfirst
impetus: **4** birr, fuel, goad, road, spur, urge **5** drive, force **6** reason, spring, thrust **7** advance **8** catalyst, momentum, progress, stimulus **9** incentive **10** horsepower, incitement, motivation
impiety: **3** sin **4** evil **9** blasphemy, profanity, sacrilege **10** disrespect, wickedness
impinge: **6** affect
upon: **5** touch **6** adjoin
impingement: **4** raid **5** foray **6** inroad **7** advance **8** invasion, trespass **9** incursion
impious: **6** unholy **7** godless, profane, ungodly, wayward **8** agnostic, apostate, diabolic **9** atheistic **10** diabolical, irreverent
impish: **3** fey, sly **5** elfin **6** bratty, elfish, elvish, jaunty, wicked **7** naughty, pixyish, playful, puckish, waggish **8** devilish, flippant, pixieish, prankish, rascally, sporting, sportive **10** frolicsome
act: **5** prank
one: **3** elf **4** pixy **5** pixie **6** sprite
impishness: **4** sass **5** cheek **8** mischief **9** flippancy, impudence, rascality, sauciness **10** cheekiness, tomfoolery
implacability: **4** hate **5** odium, spite **6** animus, enmity, hatred, malice, rancor **7** ill will **8** acrimony, bad blood **9** animosity, antipathy, hostility **10** bitterness, resentment
implacable: **4** grim, iron **5** cruel, rigid, stern **6** deadly, severe **7** hard-set, piggish **8** pitiless, ruthless, vengeful **9** ferocious, merciless, pigheaded, rancorous, unbending, unpitying **10** inexorable, inflexible, ironfisted, relentless, unyielding, vindictive
implant: **3** fix, set, sow **4** bury, root **5** embed, graft, imbed, imbue, infix, lodge, plant, set in, teach, train **6** embrue, enroot, imbrue, infuse, inject, insert, instil **7** engrain, impress, imprint, ingrain, inspire, instill **9** inculcate, influence, interject, interpose, pound into
tissue: **5** graft
implausible: **4** lame, tall, thin, weak **5** fishy **6** far-out, flimsy **7** dubious, suspect **8** doubtful, unlikely
implement: **2** ax **3** axe, hoe, mop, oar, saw, use **4** file, fork, plow, rake, tool **5** agent, apply, churn, corer, dicer, drill, flail, knife, means, parer, ricer, spoon, thing, whisk **6** agency, beater, device, effect, engine, fulfil, gadget, harrow, invoke, slicer **7** execute, fulfill, hayfork, machine, perform, realize, utensil, vehicle **8** carry out, dispense **9** actualize, apparatus, appliance, equipment **10** bring about, effectuate, instrument
ancient stone ~: **6** amgarn
combining form: **4** -labe
farm ~: **3** hoe **4** fork, plow, rake **5** churn, flail **6** harrow
kitchen ~: **5** corer, dicer, parer, ricer, whisk **6** beater, slicer
wherry ~: **6** paddle
see also tool
implementation: **8** exercise
implements: **3** kit **6** tackle **8** hardware **9** machinery
impliable: **4** firm **5** harsh, rigid, stern, stiff, stony **6** dogged, flinty, mulish, steely **7** adamant, piggish, starchy **8** hardened, obdurate, pitiless, resolute, stubborn **9** hidebound, obstinate, pigheaded, unbending **10** hardheaded, inflexible, unbendable, unyielding
implicate: **4** mire **5** blame, frame, rat on **6** accuse, charge, draw in, finger, tangle **7** connect, involve **8** entangle **9** associate, inculpate, insinuate **10** compromise, stigmatize
implication: **4** hint **5** drift, sense **7** meaning, purport **8** allusion, innuendo, overtone **9** reference, undertone
implicit: **4** firm, full **5** fixed, tacit, total **6** latent, silent, subtle, unsaid **7** certain, virtual **8** absolute, complete, connoted, definite, hinted at, indirect, inferred, inherent, unspoken, unvoiced **9** alluded to, intimated, potential, steadfast, suggested, unuttered **10** insinuated, undeclared, understood, unshakable
implicitly: **8** in effect **9** basically, in essence, so to speak, virtually
implied: **5** tacit **6** latent, silent, subtle, unsaid **7** certain, virtual **8** connoted, hinted at, indirect, inferred, inherent, unspoken, unvoiced **9** alluded to, intimated, potential, suggested, unuttered **10** insinuated, undeclared, understood
implode: **5** break, burst, smash, wreck **7** shatter
imploration: **4** plea **6** appeal **8** entreaty
implore: **3** ask, beg, sue **4** pray, urge **5** plead, press **6** adjure, appeal, demand, invoke **7** beseech, entreat, solicit **8** petition **9** impetrate, importune **10** supplicate
implosion: **5** burst **6** inrush
imply: **3** say **4** hint, mean, seem **5** get at, let on, point, spell **6** advert, allude, denote, entail, hint at **7** betoken, connote, involve, make out, purport, signify, suggest **8** indicate, intimate, lead up to, stand for **9** insinuate, predicate **10** presuppose
Imp of the Perverse, The
author: Edgar Allan Poe
impolite: **4** flip, pert, rude **5** blunt, brash, brusk, crude, frank, fresh, gruff, nervy, rough, sassy, saucy, short **6** abrupt, awless, brazen, candid, cheeky, coarse, oafish, snippy **7** aweless, boorish, brusque, ill-bred, loutish, lowbred, selfish, uncivil, uncouth **8** churlish, flippant, heedless, impudent, insolent, inurbane, snippety, tactless, unsubtle **9** out of line, outspoken, ungallant, unrefined **10** indecorous, indelicate, mannerless, ungracious, unmannerly, unthinking
look: **4** leer, ogle **5** sneer, stare
one: **4** boor, lout **5** ogler **6** starer
sound: **3** boo, hic **4** burp, jeer **5** belch **7** catcall **10** Bronx cheer
impolitic: **5** brash, unapt **6** gauche, unwise **8** tactless, unsubtle **9** ill-judged, imprudent, maladroit, misguided, unguarded **10** ill-advised, indiscreet
imponderable: **7** elusive, elusory **8** baffling, puzzling **10** mysterious
imponderous: **5** light, wispy **6** slight
import: **4** fist, heft **5** drift, point, sense, spell, value, worth **6** effect, moment, stress, thrust, weight **7** bearing, gravity, meaning, message, purport, purpose, signify **8** emphasis, Infiniti **9** intention, magnitude, substance
car: **3** BMW, Kia **4** Audi, Saab **5** Honda, Rolls, Volvo **6** Jaguar, Subaru, Suzuki **10** Mitsubishi, Rolls-Royce
importance: **4** fame, heft, note, pith, rank **5** force, glory, value, worth **6** effect, esteem, moment, status, stress, weight **7** concern, gravity, stature **8** eminence, emphasis, interest, position, prestige, priority, salience **9** attention, greatness, immediacy, influence, magnitude, relevance, substance **10** denotation, notability, precedence, prominence, reputation, usefulness
be of ~ old-style: **4** reck
have ~: **4** rate **5** count **6** matter
of no ~: **4** moot **5** minor, petty, small **6** little **7** trivial
person of ~: **3** VIP **4** lion **5** biggy, nabob **6** biggie, bigwig **7** magnate **8** luminary **9** plutocrat
person of no ~: **4** geek, nerd **5** dweeb **6** nobody **7** nebbish **9** nonentity
__ importance: **4** of no
Importance of Being Earnest, The
author: Oscar Wilde
important: **3** big, key **4** dear, high **5** acute, great, major, vital **6** needed, of note, staple, urgent **7** burning, crucial, earnest, eminent, exigent, fateful, hurry-up, notable, pivotal, primary, salient, serious, special, weighty **8** cardinal, critical, decisive, exigeant, historic, material, pregnant, pressing, relevant, required, valuable **9** big-league, essential, extensive, front-page, high-level, mandatory, memorable, momentous, necessary, operative, paramount, ponderous, principal, prominent, right-hand, something, strategic, top-drawer, well-known **10** celebrated, first-class, historical, imperative, impressive, meaningful, monumental, noteworthy, portentous, preeminent, remarkable, upper-class, worthwhile
be ~: **4** rate **5** weigh **6** matter
deem ~: **5** value **10** set store by
event: **8** landmark **9** milestone
less ~: **5** lower, minor **9** auxiliary, secondary **10** derivative, incidental, peripheral
most ~: **4** head **5** chief, grand **8** above all **9** principal, uppermost
most ~ part: **3** nub **4** body, core, crux, gist, knub, meat, pith **5** basis, heart, point **6** kernel, thrust **7** essence, keynote **10** bottom line
most ~ (prefix): **4** arch-
not ~: **4** mere, moot **5** minor, petty, small **6** little **7** trivial
one: **3** VIP **4** lion **5** biggy, nabob **6** biggie, bigwig **7** magnate **8** luminary **9** plutocrat
point: **6** factor **7** concern
time: **3** age, era **5** epoch
work: **4** opus **6** oeuvre **10** magnum opus
__-important: **3** all **4** self
imported: **6** exotic **7** foreign
imports: **5** cargo, goods **7** freight
importunate: **9** obtrusive
importune: **3** beg, dun, nag, sue, woo **4** coax, pray, urge **5** beset, court, hound, plead, press, tease, worry **6** appeal, badger, demand, harass, insist, pester, plague, work on **7** beseech, besiege, entreat, implore, solicit **9** impetrate **10** supplicate
impose: **3** lay, put, set, tax **4** levy, loom **5** exact, foist, force, order **6** assess, charge, compel, decree, demand, enjoin, meddle **7** be pushy, command, dictate, foist on, inflict, intrude, lay down, obtrude, presume **8** horn in on **9** establish, force upon, incommode, institute, prescribe, stipulate **10** administer, ask too much, promulgate, thrust upon
on: **5** wrong **6** lumber, put out **7** trouble
__-imposed: **4** self
imposed on, easily: **4** meek **5** timid
imposing: **3** big **5** grand, large, lofty, noble, proud, regal, royal, showy **6** august, lordly, mighty, solemn **7** awesome, exalted, hulking, massive, stately, sublime **8** gorgeous, imperial, kinglike, majestic, palatial, stirring, striking, towering **9** dignified, grandiose, luxurious, sumptuous **10** commanding, formidable, impressive, majestical, monumental, statuesque
residence: **5** manor, villa **6** castle, estate **7** mansion
imposition: **3** con, tax **4** drag, hoax, levy, onus, pain **5** fraud, trick **6** burden, demand **8** artifice **9** deception, hypocrisy, intrusion,

restraint **10** constraint, craftiness, hocus-pocus
impossible: 3 out **5** never, no how, no way, no-win **6** absurd, can't be **7** useless, utopian **8** hopeless **9** ludicrous, offensive, visionary **10** impassable, incredible, infeasible, outrageous, unfeasible, unworkable
dream: 5 quest
make ~: 4 veto **8** preclude, prohibit
__ Impossible: 3 It's
Impossible Marriage
author: Beth Henley
impost: 3 tax **4** duty, levy, toll **6** custom, excise, tariff **7** tribute **8** taxation, usage fee
Imposters, The (1998 film)
cast: Alfred Molina, Oliver Platt, Lili Taylor, Stanley Tucci
impostor: 4 fake, sham **5** actor, cheat, faker, fraud, mimic, phony, quack **6** con man, phoney, poseur **7** bluffer **8** imitator, swindler **9** charlatan, hypocrite, pretender **10** mountebank
imposture: 3 con **4** fake, hoax, ploy, ruse, sham, wile **5** cheat, feint, fraud, phony, put-on, spoof, trick **6** deceit, dupery, humbug, phoney **7** gimmick, snow job, swindle **8** artifice, flimflam, maneuver, pretense, trickery **9** deception, hypocrisy, imitation, stratagem **10** hocus-pocus, masquerade, pretension, subterfuge
impound: 3 pen **4** cage, hold, keep, take **5** seize **6** coop up, immure, intern, shut in, shut up **7** confine, enclose, fence in, inclose, interne **8** imprison, restrain, sentence **10** confiscate
impoverish: 4 bust, ruin, sink, undo **5** break, drain **6** beggar, reduce **7** deplete **8** bankrupt, straiten **9** pauperize
impoverished: 4 flat, poor **5** broke, needy, sorry **6** bad off, barren, bereft, hard up, ill-off, in need, in want, ruined **7** drained, pinched **8** badly off, bankrupt, beggarly, depleted, indigent, strapped **9** destitute, insolvent, miserable, moneyless, penniless, penurious **10** down and out, pauperized, straitened
impoverishment: 4 need **6** penury **7** poverty **8** exigency, exiguity, hardship **9** indigence, privation **10** insolvency
impractical: 4 wild **5** crazy **6** absurd, dreamy, insane, unreal **7** useless, utopian **8** abstract, chimeric, quixotic, romantic **9** visionary **10** chimerical, quixotical, ridiculous
impracticality: 5 folly
imprecate: 4 damn **5** curse **7** condemn
imprecation: 3 ban **4** jinx, oath **5** curse **6** darn it, hoodoo, prayer, whammy **7** evil eye **8** anathema
imprecise: 3 lax, off **4** hazy **5** fuzzy, loose, rough, vague **6** cloudy, faulty, untrue **7** general, inexact **8** careless, nebulous **9** ambiguous, incorrect **10** ill-defined, impalpable, inaccurate, indefinite, indistinct, inexplicit, uncritical, unspecific
impregnable: 4 firm **6** secure, strong
impregnate: 4 soak **5** souse, steep, tinge **8** permeate, saturate **9** percolate, transfuse
Impresario
author: Sol Hurok
impress: 3 awe, get, wow **4** dent, etch, grab, mark, move, sway **5** amaze, brand, draft, infix, print, stamp, touch **6** affect, arouse, dazzle, emboss, instil, strike, thrill **7** engrain, engrave, enthuse, implant, ingrain, inspire, instill, recruit **8** blow away, inscribe, interest, knock out, persuade, register, shanghai **9** conscript, drive home, emphasize, go over big, inculcate, influence, prevail on **10** hammer into, predispose
impressed: 7 touched **8** affected **9** engrossed **10** fascinated, interested
more than ~: 4 awed **5** in awe **6** amazed **7** floored, shocked
not ~: 5 stoic **6** awless **7** aweless
impressible: 4 soft **7** plastic, pliable **8** moldable **9** malleable
impression: 3 air **4** cast, dent, feel, idea, mark, mold, show, view **5** brand, hunch, image, print, sense, spoor, stamp, track **6** aperçu, belief, effect, impact, memory, notion, parody, result, send-up **7** concept, feeling, inkling, opinion, outline, pattern, reading, takeoff, thought **8** reaction, stamping **9** engraving, footprint, imitation, influence, sensation, suspicion **10** appearance, atmosphere, conception, conjecture, conviction, depression, estimation, masquerade, perception
get the ~: 4 feel **5** sense, think **6** divine, intuit, pick up, reason **7** believe, discern **8** perceive **10** understand
give a false ~: 4 hoke **5** belie **6** delude
give the ~: 4 look, seem **5** imply, sound **6** appear **7** suggest **8** intimate, resemble **9** insinuate, sound like **10** appear to be
have the ~: 4 feel **5** think **7** believe
lasting ~: 4 scar
make an ~: 5 score, stamp **8** register
wrong ~: 5 error **7** mistake
__ impression: 5 first
impressionable: 7 plastic **9** malleable **10** responsive
impressionist: 3 ape **4** aper **5** mimic
Impressionist: 5 Degas, Manet, Monet **6** Renoir **7** Cassatt, Utrillo
starter: 3 neo
Impression: Sunrise
artist: Claude Monet
impressive: 4 cool, deep **5** grand, great, noble, socko **6** august, epical, lavish, lordly, mighty, moving, potent, scenic, solemn, superb **7** awesome, massive, notable, rousing, salient, stately, telling **8** dramatic, eloquent, exciting, imposing, majestic, palatial, powerful, profound, scenical, splendid, stirring, striking, stunning, touching, towering, well done **9** absorbing, affecting, ambitious, arresting, effective, grandiose, important, inspiring, luxurious, momentous, monstrous, sumptuous, thrilling **10** believable, commanding, convincing, formidable, majestical, monumental, remarkable
group: 5 array
not ~: 4 puny **5** dinky **10** secondrate
Impressive!: 3 gee, wow **5** golly
impressiveness: 4 pomp **5** glory **7** majesty **8** elegance, grandeur, opulence, splendor **10** brilliance
imprest: 4 loan
Impreza: 3 car **4** auto **6** Subaru
imprimatur: 4 seal
imprint: 3 fix **4** etch, mark, name **5** infix, print, stamp, track **6** emblem, offset, symbol **7** engrain, engrave, implant, ingrain **8** inscribe **9** signature, trademark
imprison: 4 cage, hold, jail, shut **5** embar **6** arrest, closet, detain, immure, intern, lock in, lock up, punish, remand, shut in, shut up **7** confine, impound, interne, put away **8** restrain, sentence, stockade
imprisoned: 4 pent **6** jailed **7** captive
imprisonment: 6 arrest, chains **7** custody **9** restraint **10** internment
improbable: 4 iffy, lame, rare, slim, tall, thin, weak **6** flimsy, remote **7** dubious **8** doubtful, fanciful, unlikely **9** legendary, not likely, uncertain, unheard of **10** farfetched, incredible
improbity: 5 fraud **7** scandal **9** falseness **10** dishonesty, misconduct, wrongdoing
impromptu: 5 ad hoc, ad-lib, faked **6** casual, sudden, vamped, winged **7** offhand, stopgap **9** dashed-off, extempore, thrown-off, tossed-off, whipped-up **10** improvised, jury-rigged, off the cuff, unprepared, unscripted
improper: 4 lewd, racy, tabu **5** false, gross, inapt, nasty, taboo, unapt, undue, unfit, wrong **6** banned, risqué, smutty, unfair, unmeet, vulgar **7** awkward, bad form, illicit, ill-time, immoral, naughty, off-base **8** criminal, indecent, outlawed, unlawful, unseemly, untimely, untoward, verboten, wrongful **9** erroneous, felonious, forbidden, graceless, ill-suited, incorrect, inelegant, irregular, low-minded, shameless, tasteless, unethical, unfitting **10** discordant, ill-advised, inaccurate, indecorous, indelicate, irrelevant, malapropos, out of order, prohibited, scandalous, suggestive, unbecoming, undeserved, unsuitable
thing: 4 no-no **5** taboo **9** dirty pool
improperly: 3 too **5** amiss **6** overly, unduly **8** unfairly, unjustly **10** unsuitably
influence ~: 5 bribe, get at, get to
impropriety: 4 nono **5** fault, gaffe **7** license **9** gaucherie
improve: 3 age **4** edit, gain, help, hone, lift, mend, redo, rise **5** amend, boost, build, emend, raise, rally **6** adjust, better, enrich, look up, perk up, pick up, profit, purify, refine, reform, revamp, revise, step up, update, work up **7** advance, augment, benefit, build up, correct, develop, elevate, enhance, furbish, perfect, promote, recruit, rectify, restore, shape up, sharpen, spice up, touch up, upgrade **8** beautify, heighten, increase, overhaul, polish up, progress, regulate **9** cultivate, go forward, meliorate, modernize **10** ameliorate
an edge: 4 hone, whet **5** strop
in health: 4 gain, heal, mend **5** rally **6** pick up **7** get well, rebound, recover **9** come along, get better **10** bounce back, convalesce, recuperate
upon: 3 top **4** beat, best **5** outdo **6** better, exceed **7** eclipse, outpace, surpass **8** go beyond, outclass, outshine, outstrip, surmount **9** transcend **10** outperform, overshadow, tower above
improved partner: 3 new
improvement: 4 gain, rise **5** rally **6** growth **7** advance, buildup, headway, upgrade, upswing **8** comeback, increase, progress, recovery, revision
show ~: 4 gain, mend **5** rally **6** look up, pick up **7** advance, shape up **8** progress **9** come along, get better **10** recuperate
__-improvement: 4 self
__ Improvement: 4 Home
improvidence: 5 waste **7** neglect **8** rashness, temerity
improvident: 6 lavish, unwise, wanton **8** careless, prodigal, wasteful **9** excessive **10** immoderate, profligate
improving: 6 better **8** cosmetic **9** on the mend
improvisation: 5 ad-lib **6** acting
improvise: 3 rig **4** fake, vamp **5** ad-lib **6** devise, fake it, invent, make up, wing it **7** concoct, dash off, dream up, think up **8** contrive, knockoff **10** brainstorm
improvised: 5 ad hoc, ad-lib **6** vamped **7** offhand, stopgap **9** extempore, hit-or-miss, impromptu, makeshift, patchwork, unstudied, whipped up **10** fictitious, fly-by-night, jury-rigged, unprepared, unscripted
arrangement: 6 lashup
bit: 4 riff **5** ad-lib
improv offering: 3 gag **4** joke, quip, skit **5** ad-lib, comic **6** comedy **8** comedian, one-liner
imprudence: 4 slip **5** folly **8** rashness
imprudent: 3 lax, mad **4** rash, wild **5** brash, crazy, hasty, loose, silly, slack, unapt, wrong **6** madcap, remiss, sloppy, unwary, unwise **7** foolish **8** careless, heedless, reckless, slipshod, tactless **9** foolhardy, ill-judged, impolitic, misguided, negligent, overhasty, unadvised, uncareful, unguarded, unmindful **10** headstrong, ill-advised, incautious, indiscreet, nonchalant, unthinking

one: 3 oaf, sap 4 boob, clod, dolt, dope, dupe, fool, jerk, loon, twit 5 clown, cluck, dummy, dunce, joker, ninny, patsy 6 dimwit, lummox, nitwit, stooge, sucker, turkey 7 buffoon, bungler, dullard, fathead, halfwit, jackass 8 bonehead, dumbbell, numskull 9 birdbrain, blockhead, ignoramus, lamebrain, schlemiel, simpleton 10 dunderhead, nincompoop
impudence: 3 lip 4 face, gall, guff, sass 5 brass, cheek, crust, mouth, nerve, sauce 6 insult 8 audacity, back talk, boldness, chutzpah, defiance, pertness, rudeness, temerity 9 assurance, flippancy, insolence 10 confidence, disrespect, effrontery, impishness
impudent: 4 bold, flip, pert, rude, wise 5 brash, cocky, crude, fresh, lippy, nervy, rough, sassy, saucy, smart 6 arrant, awless, brashy, brassy, bratty, brazen, cheeky, coarse, daring, mouthy, snippy, vulgar 7 aweless, blatant, forward, ill-bred, uncivil, upstart 8 cocksure, flippant, immodest, impolite, insolent, overbold, snippety 9 audacious, barefaced, boldfaced, bumptious, officious, out-of-line, shameless, unabashed 10 irreverent, smart-mouth, ungracious, unmannerly
be ~: 4 sass 8 talk back
one: 4 brat, minx, snip 5 hussy, whelp 6 upstart
impugn: 3 tar, tax, zap 4 deny, gibe, jeer, jibe, mock, slam, slur, snub, zing 5 abuse, blast, cross, decry, knock, libel, query, scorn, smear, spurn, taunt, trash 6 assail, attack, charge, defame, deride, dump on, heckle, malign, negate, offend, oppose, rebuff, refute, slight, vilify 7 affront, asperse, censure, condemn, degrade, disavow, disdain, dispute, gainsay, put down, rank out, rip into, run down, slander, traduce 8 backbite, belittle, denounce, question, ridicule, vilipend 9 blaspheme, challenge, criticize, denigrate, disaffirm, discredit, disparage, humiliate, stick it to 10 calumniate, come down on, contradict, contravene, disrespect
impugnment: 5 abuse, libel 6 attack, hosing 7 affront, assault, calumny, obloquy, slander 8 derision, diatribe, outburst, reproach, scolding 9 aspersion, criticism, invective 10 assailment, backbiting, defamation, upbraiding
impuissant: 4 weak 6 unable 8 helpless 9 incapable, powerless
impulse: 3 yen 4 bent, goad, itch, spur, urge, whim 5 drive, fancy, flash, force, nisus 6 desire, motive, vagary 7 abandon, caprice, feeling, passion, resolve 8 instinct, momentum, stimulus, tendency 9 actuation 10 incitement, motivation
transmitter: 4 axon 5 axone
__ impulse: 4 on an 5 act on
Impulse: 3 car 4 auto 5 Isuzu
impulsion: 5 drive 6 thrust 10 constraint, motivation
impulsive: 4 rash 5 brash, giddy, hasty, moody 6 abrupt, madcap, sudden 7 offhand, rampant 8 careless, headlong, knee-jerk 9 automatic, daredevil, emotional, excitable, impetuous, intuitive, mercurial, momentary, unguarded, vagarious, whirlwind 10 capricious, changeable, headstrong, hot-and-cold, hot-blooded, incautious, passionate, unexpected, unprompted, unthinking
Impulsive (1990 song)
artist: Wilson Phillips
impulsively: 6 rashly 7 hastily 9 headfirst, hurriedly 10 heedlessly, recklessly
impulsiveness: 5 brass, haste
impunity: 9 exemption, indemnity
impure: 4 foul, lewd, vile 5 dirty 6 coarse, filthy, flawed, rancid, sordid 7 admixed, alloyed, corrupt, debased, defiled, diluted, profane, squalid, sullied, tainted, unclean 8 maculate, polluted, shameful, unchaste, vitiated 9 lubricous, unrefined 10 insanitary, licentious
make ~: 4 foul 5 dirty, sully, taint 6 debase, defile, poison 7 corrupt, degrade, pollute, vitiate 10 adulterate
impurity: 4 dirt 5 dross, filth, grime, stain, taint 6 poison 8 lewdness 9 infection, lubricity, pollutant, pollution 10 corruption, defilement
remove ~: 4 sift 5 clean 6 refine
imputable: 5 due to 7 owing to 8 blamable 9 blameable
imputation: 3 lie 4 blot, hint, slur, spot 5 abuse, blame, brand, curse, libel, smear, stain, taint 6 charge, smirch, stigma 7 blemish, calumny, censure, slander, tarnish, untruth 8 allusion, brickbat, citation, innuendo, reproach 9 aspersion, falsehood, invective 10 accusation
impute: 3 lay, tax 5 blame 6 accuse, adduce, allude, assign, attach, charge, credit 7 ascribe, make out, qualify 8 accredit 9 attribute, chalk up to, inculpate, insinuate
(to): 6 credit
Imre: 4 Nagy 7 Kertész
__ I'm Ready: 3 Yes
I'm Ready for Love (1966 song)
artist: Martha & the Vandellas
__ Imroth: 4 Anna
I'm Sitting on Top of the World (1926 song)
artist: Al Jolson
I'm So Excited (1982 song)
artist: Pointer Sisters
I'm So Into You (1993 song)
artist: SWV
I'm Sorry (song)
artist: John Denver, Brenda Lee, Platters
I'm so sorry!: 4 alas 5 alack
I'm Still __: 4 Here
I'm Still in Love With You (song)
artist: Al Green, New Edition
I'm Stone in Love With You (1972 song)
artist: Stylistics
I'm Telling You Now (1965 song)
artist: Freddie and the Dreamers
I'm That Kind of Guy (1989 song)
artist: LL Cool J
I'm the Only One (1994 song)
artist: Melissa Etheridge
..., __ I'm told: 4 or so
Imus: 3 Don 4 Fred
medium: 5 radio
I'm Walkin' (1957 song)
artist: Fats Domino, Ricky Nelson
__ I'm With You: 4 When
I'm Wondering (1967 song)
artist: Stevie Wonder
I'm working __!: 4 on it
I'm Your Angel (1998 song)
artist: Celine Dion, R. Kelly
I'm Your Baby Tonight (1990 song)
artist: Whitney Houston
I'm Your Man (1985 song)
artist: George Michael
__, I'm yours: 6 Take me
I'm Yours (1965 song)
artist: Elvis Presley
__ I'm Yours: 4 Baby
in: 3 hot, mod, now, tip 4 link, tony 5 faddy, funky, swish, toney, vogue 6 access, amidst, at home, chi-chi, entrée, latest, modish, tipoff, trendy, within 7 à la mode, current, liaison, popular, stylish, voguish 8 up-to-date 9 advantage, incumbent 10 all the rage
any way: 4 ever 5 at all
a while: 4 anon, soon 5 later
concert: 5 as one, at one 8 together
front: 5 ahead, first 7 leading
in French: 4 dans
one piece: 5 whole 6 entire, intact
perpetuity: 4 ever 7 forever 9 eternally
the ball park: 4 near 5 close 7 close by
the center: 4 amid 5 among 6 amidst, mongst 7 amongst
with: 4 amid 5 among 6 amidst, mongst 7 amongst
in __: 3 fun, tow, two 4 a bit, a box, a fog, a jam, a pet, a row, a rut, a sec, a way, esse, full, gear, half, hand, luck, part, play, situ, sync, time, toto, turn, vain 5 a bind, a daze, a hole, a rage, a rush, a snit, a spot, a stew, a walk, a word, brief, force, front, limbo, order, phase, print, shape, short, spots, stock, store, style, synch, tears, truth 6 camera, cement, charge, clover, common, detail, effect, person, public, spades, stages, tandem, unison
in __ act: 5 on the
in __ and starts: 4 fits
in __ case: 3 any
in __ conscience: 4 good
in __ course: 3 due
in __ day and age: 4 this
in __ ear...: 3 one
in __ event: 3 any
in __ eye: 5 a pig's
in __ fell swoop: 3 one
in __ fettle: 4 fine
in __ finish: 5 at the
in __ for: 4 line
in __ gear: 4 high
in __ good conscience: 3 all
in __ land: 4 la-la
in __ light: 4 a bad 5 a good
in __ of: 4 case, lieu, view 5 favor, light, place, spite, terms 6 excess
in __ of fact: 5 point
in __ of fire,...: 4 case
in __ of trouble: 5 a heap
in __ only: 4 name
in __ order: 5 short
in __ parentis: 4 loco
in __ part: 4 good
in __ probability: 3 all
in __ quo: 5 statu
in __ res: 6 medias
in __ rush: 4 a mad
in __ secret: 3 on a
in __ shakes: 3 two
in __ signo vinces: 3 hoc
in __ swing: 4 full
in __ that: 5 order
in __ the money: 5 it for
in __ time: 4 good
in __ to: 5 order 6 regard
in __ veritas: 4 vino
in __ water: 3 hot 4 deep
in __ way: 3 the 4 a bad 5 harm's
in __ words: 5 other
in-__: 3 box, law 4 goal, home, joke, kind 5 crowd, depth, group, house 6 basket 7 between, migrant, migrate, service
in-__-face: 4 your
in-__ movie: 6 flight
in-__ skating: 4 line
in.: 4 meas.
__ in: 3 all, cut, did, dig, eat, get, hem, key, lay, log, pay, pop, run, set, sit, tie 4 blow, butt, call, cash, cave, chip, clue, come, done, draw, drop, fall, fill, give, hang, horn, kick, lock, pile, plug, pull, rein, rope, send, shut, sign, sock, stay, step, suck, take, tuck, tune, turn, wade, work, zero, zoom 5 barge, break, bring, build, check, chime, close, count, phase, pitch, rub it, sleep, stand, throw, trade, write 6 breeze, factor, figure, listen
__-in: 3 run, sit, tap 4 cave, fade, iris, lead, love, shoo 5 carry
...in __ tree: 5 a pear
In: 4 elem. 6 indium 7 element
49 for ~: 4 at. no.
In __: 4 Neon 5 a Poem, a Vale, My Bed
In __?: 5 or out
In __ and out...: 6 one ear
In __ Arizona: 3 Old
In __ beginning...: 3 the
In __ Blood: 4 Cold
In __ eye!: 5 a pig's
In __ is truth: 4 wine
In __ of Folly: 6 Praise
In __ Our Life: 4 This
In __ Still Felt: 3 Joy
In __ Trust: 5 God We
In __ Yet Green: 6 Memory
__ In: 5 Let 'Em, Let Me
IN
see Indiana
in a __: 3 box, jam, row, rut, sec, way 4 bind, jiff, rush, snit, spot, stew, word 5 flash, jiffy, sense, state, tizzy, trice, while 6 dither, minute, pickle 7 fashion
in a __ age: 5 coon's
in a __ eye: 4 pig's
in a __ light: 3 bad 4 good
in a __ of speaking: 6 manner

Ina: **5** Balin, Souez **6** Claire **9** Coolbrith
In-a-__-Da-Vida: **5** Gadda
In a beautiful __-green boat: **3** pea
inability: **9** ineptness, unfitness **10** disability, feebleness, inadequacy, inaptitude, incapacity, inefficacy, ineptitude
__ in a blanket: **3** pig
__ in Able: **3** A as
__ in a Blue Dress: **5** Devil
__ in a blue moon: **4** once
__ in a Bottle: **4** Time **5** Genie **7** Message
inaccessible: **4** away **5** aloof **6** far-off, remote **7** distant, elusive, elusory, far away **10** impassable
inaccuracy: **3** lie **4** slip, tale, typo **5** error, fault **6** defect, howler **7** blunder, erratum, falsity, mistake **9** deception
inaccurate: **3** lax **4** wide **5** false, wrong **6** all wet, erring, faulty, untrue, way off **7** in error, inexact, off-base, unsound **8** improper, mistaken, slipshod, specious **9** defective, erroneous, imprecise, incorrect **10** apocryphal, discrepant, fallacious, ungrounded, unreliable
be ~: **3** err **7** go wrong
inaccurately: **5** wrong
In a cowslip's bell __: **4** I lie
inaction: **7** default, languor **8** lethargy **9** inertness, lassitude **10** standstill
inactivate: **4** stop **6** freeze, shelve **7** shut off, suspend **9** interrupt
inactive: **3** lax, old, ret. **4** calm, down, idle, lazy, logy, slow **5** inert, quiet, slack, still **6** asleep, at rest, draggy, fallow, latent, on hold, otiose, sleepy, static, torpid **7** abeyant, dormant, languid, passive, retired **8** indolent, slothful, sluggish, stagnant **9** lethargic, quiescent, sedentary, somnolent **10** disengaged, motionless, on the shelf, unemployed, unoccupied, unrealized
be ~: **4** laze, loaf, rest **5** relax
element: **4** neon **5** argon **7** krypton
not ~: **4** busy **5** astir **6** lively **8** bustling, in motion
inactivity: **4** ease, rest **5** sloth **6** repose, stasis, torpor **7** inertia, languor, latency, slumber **8** abeyance, dullness, idleness, laziness, lethargy **9** inertness, lassitude **10** depression, quiescence
period of ~: **4** calm, lull **6** hiatus, layoff, recess, stasis **7** respite, time-out **8** downtime **9** interlude
__ in a day's work: **3** all
inadequacy: **4** flaw, lack, need **6** dearth, defect **7** absence, deficit, failing, failure, paucity, poverty **8** drawback, scarcity, shortage, sparsity, underage, weakness **9** inability, inaptness, shortfall, unfitness **10** deficiency, faultiness, feebleness, incapacity, inefficacy, ineptitude, meagerness, scantiness, skimpiness
inadequate: **3** bad, low, shy **4** lame, poor, puny, slim, thin, weak **5** light, lousy, scant, short, small, sorry, unfit, woful **6** faulty, feeble, flimsy, meager, scanty, scarce, skimpy, sparse, stingy, unable, woeful **7** failing, ill-done, lacking, limited, miserly, pitiful, sketchy, slender, stinted, wanting **8** beggarly, exiguous, pathetic **9** defective, deficient, imperfect, incapable, spineless, too little **10** bush-league, incomplete, pathetical, unequipped
inadmissible: **8** improper, untimely **9** unethical, unwelcome **10** out of order
inadvertence: **4** goof, miss, slip **5** lapse **6** laxity, slip-up **7** mistake, neglect **8** omission
inadvertent: **6** chance **8** careless, heedless **9** negligent, unwitting
inadvertently: **8** absently, by chance
say ~: **5** blurt **8** blurt out
inadvisability: **5** folly
inadvisable: **5** folly **6** unwise **8** improper **9** unadvised
In-a-Gadda-Da-Vida (1968 song)
artist: Iron Butterfly
__ in a Gilded Cage: **5** A Bird
In a Gondola
author: Robert Browning
in-a-hurry
letters: **3** PDQ **4** ASAP
word: **3** now **4** fast, stat **7** quickly
__-in-aid: **5** grant
__ in Alabama: **5** Crazy
__ in a Lifetime: **4** Once **5** Twice
in all __ conscience: **4** good
__ in a Manger: **4** Away
__ in America: **4** Lost, Made, Only **6** Living
__ in a million: **3** one
inamorata
see sweetheart
inamorato
see sweetheart
__ in a name?: **5** What's
in and of __: **6** itself
In and Out of Love (1967 song)
artist: Supremes
inane: **5** batty, crazy, empty, vapid **6** jejune, screwy, simple, vacant **7** foolish, idiotic, insipid, inutile, shallow, unsound **8** cockeyed, specious **9** idiotical, illogical, laughable, pointless, untenable, worthless **10** amphigoric, groundless, nonserious, off the wall, pedestrian, unprofound, weak-minded
see also foolish
inanimate: **5** inert, still **8** lifeless, listless **9** insensate, quiescent, unfeeling **10** insentient, motionless, spiritless, unreactive
inanition: **6** torpor **7** languor, vacuity **8** lethargy
inanity
see baloney
in any __: **3** way **4** case **5** event
__-in apartment: **4** walk
In a pig's eye: **5** never, no how, no way
In a Poem
author: Robert Frost
__ in a poke: **3** pig **4** a pig
inappeasable: **4** hard **5** rigid **7** adamant **8** pitiless, vengeful
__ in apple: **3** A as
inapplicable: **5** unapt **8** improper **9** different, unrelated
inapposite: **5** inapt, unapt, unfit, wrong **7** off-base **8** unsuited **10** extraneous, immaterial, irrelevant, nongermane
inappreciable: **3** wee **4** tiny **5** minor, small, teeny **6** little, minute, slight, teensy **7** trivial **8** trifling
...in apprehension how like __: **4** a god
inappropriate: **3** bad **5** inapt, silly, unapt, undue, unfit, wrong **6** unwise **8** improper, mistaken, unseemly, untimely, untoward **9** ill-suited **10** irrelevant, out of order, unsuitable
inappropriately: **3** bad **5** afoul, amiss, badly, wrong **6** astray, rotten **7** wrongly **10** improperly
inapropos: **5** unapt **9** unrelated **10** extraneous, immaterial, irrelevant, out of place
inapt: **4** non-U **5** unfit, wrong **6** clumsy, gauche, unmeet **7** awkward, unhandy **8** improper, unfacile, unseemly, untimely **9** ill-suited, maladroit, unfitting, unskilled **10** inapposite, indecorous, irrelevant, malapropos, nongermane, out of place, unbecoming, unsuitable
Ina Ray: **6** Hutton
inarguable: **4** true **7** certain **8** absolute, concrete, decisive, definite, positive **10** conclusive, undisputed
Inari: **4** lake
locale: **7** Finland
__ in arms: **7** comrade
__ in Arms: **5** Babes
inarticulate: **3** mum, shy **5** muted, quiet **6** silent **7** bashful **8** nonvocal, reserved, reticent, taciturn, wordless **9** clammed up **10** tongue-tied
inarticulately, say: **6** mumble, mutter
inasmuch as: **3** for **5** since **7** because **9** therefore
__ in a teacup: **5** storm **7** tempest
__ in a teapot: **7** tempest
inattention: **6** laxity, slight **7** neglect **9** oversight
inattentive: **3** lax **4** lazy **5** blind, bored, slack **6** asleep, remiss, sloppy **7** faraway, unaware **8** careless, heedless, listless, mindless, reckless **9** negligent, unmindful
be ~: **3** nod **4** doze **5** sleep
one's response: **3** huh **4** what
inaudible: **4** weak **5** quiet **9** noiseless, soundless **10** indistinct
inaugural: **5** first **6** maiden **7** initial, leading, pioneer, premier **9** beginning, inceptive, induction **10** initiation
inaugurate: **4** open **5** begin, build, enter, found, set up, start, usher **6** induct, instal, launch **7** break in, install, instate, kick off, lead off, usher in **8** commence, dedicate, get going, initiate **9** enter upon, establish, institute, introduce, originate **10** commission
inauguration: **4** rise **5** debut, start **6** launch, origin **7** opening **8** starting
need: **4** oath **5** Bible
Inauguration __: **3** Day
inauspicious: **4** dire **5** curst **6** cursed, jinxed **7** baleful, baneful, hapless, ominous, unblest, unlucky **8** ill-fated, ill-timed, luckless, sinister, untimely **9** unblessed, unfavored **10** ill-starred, portentous
In a Vale
author: Robert Frost
__ in aviary: **3** A as
__ in a while: **4** once
in bad faith in Latin: **8** mala fide
__-in-Bay: **3** Put
in-between: **4** amid **5** among **6** amidst, mongst **7** amongst
state: **5** limbo
__ in Black: **3** Men
__ in Bloom: **4** Love
__ in Blue Jeans: **5** Venus
__ in B Minor: **4** Mass
inboard-outboard: **5** motor
__ in Bohemia, A: **7** Scandal
__ in bond: **7** bottled
__ in Boots: **4** Puss
inborn: **6** innate, native, rooted **7** chronic, natural **9** chronical, ingrained, intrinsic, intuitive **10** congenital, connatural, deep-seated, hereditary, indigenous
inbred: **6** native, rooted **7** genetic **8** inherent **9** genetical, ingrained, instilled, intrinsic **10** deep-seated, hereditary, indigenous
inbue: **5** embed, infix **7** engrain, implant, ingrain, instill **9** inculcate
__ in Bunches: **7** Hunches
Inca: **6** Andean, Indian, Kechua **7** Amerind, Kechuan, Quechua, Quichua **8** Quechuan **9** Atahualpa
city: **5** Cusco, Cuzco
counting device: **5** quipu
language: **6** Kechua **7** Kechuan, Quechua, Quichua **8** Quechuan
territory: **4** Peru **5** Andes
incalculable: **4** huge, iffy, vast **5** great **6** chancy, myriad, unsure, untold **7** endless **8** enormous, infinite **9** limitless, priceless, uncertain, unlimited
__ in Calico: **4** A Gal
incandesce: **4** burn, glow **5** blaze, flame, flash, glare, gleam, light, shine **7** glisten, shimmer, sparkle, twinkle **9** coruscate **10** illuminate
incandescence: **3** ray **4** beam, fire, glow **5** blaze, flame, flash, light, sheen, shine **6** luster **7** shimmer, sparkle, twinkle **8** radiance, radiancy, splendor
incandescent: **5** aglow, lucid **6** ablaze, bright, lucent **7** beaming, burning, fulgent, glowing, lambent, radiant, shining **8** luminous, lustrous
incandescent __: **4** lamp
incant: **3** say **5** chant **6** recite
incantation: **3** hex **5** chant, charm, magic, spell **6** voodoo **7** sorcery **8** wizardry **10** hocus pocus
start: **4** abra
incapable: **5** unapt, unfit **6** unable **8** fumbling, helpless **9** powerless, unskilled **10** impuissant, inadequate, unequipped, unskillful
is ~ of: **4** can't **6** cannot
incapacious: **6** narrow **7** cramped, limited **9** confining **10** compressed, contracted, restricted
incapacitate: **4** maim **5** lay up, wreck **6** hogtie **7** disable **8** paralyse, paralyze, sabotage

incapacitated: 5 unfit 6 unable 9 paralytic, powerless
incapacity: 8 handicap, weakness 9 ignorance, inability 10 disability, feebleness, inadequacy
incarcerate: 4 hold, jail 5 embar, seize 6 arrest, coop up, detain, immure, intern, lock up, punish, shut up 7 confine, impound, interne, put away 8 imprison, sentence
incarcerated: 4 pent 7 captive
incarceration: 6 arrest, chains, prison 7 custody
incarnate: 5 human 8 embodied, physical 9 personify 10 in the flesh, manifested
incarnation: 5 tulku 6 avatar 7 rebirth 10 embodiment
__ in case: 4 just
incautious: 3 lax 4 bold, rash, wild 5 brash, hasty 6 madcap, remiss, sloppy, unwary 7 foolish, unalert 8 careless, heedless, off-guard, reckless, slipshod 9 desperate, foolhardy, hotheaded, ill-judged, impetuous, imprudent, impulsive, negligent, unadvised, uncareful, unguarded, unmindful 10 ill-advised, indiscreet, neglectful, nonchalant, regardless, unthinking, unvigilant, unwatchful
incautiously: 9 any old way
incautiousness: 5 haste
Incaviglia: 4 Pete
inc. cousin: 3 LLC, ltd.
Ince: 6 Thomas
incendiarism: 5 arson 9 pyromania
incendiary: 7 firebug, harmful 8 arsonist, inflamer 9 dangerous, demagogic, demagogue, firebrand, flammable, ignitable, insurgent, seditious 10 pyromaniac, subversive
incense: 3 ire, irk 4 rile, roil 5 anger, aroma, chafe, egg on, peeve, pique, scent, smell, smoke, steam 6 bum out, burn up, enrage, fire up, madden, nettle 7 bouquet, enflame, inflame, outrage, perfume, provoke 8 irritate 9 displease, infuriate 10 exasperate
resin: 5 myrrh
starter: 5 frank
Incense and Peppermints (1967 song)
artist: Strawberry Alarm Clock
incensed: 3 hot, mad 4 ired, sore 5 angry, cross, het up, huffy, irate, livid, riled, upset, wroth 6 ablaze, fuming, galled, ireful, raging, raving, red-hot 7 enraged, furious, ranting, steamed 8 choleric, up in arms, white-hot, wrathful 9 indignant, resentful, splenetic, wrought up 10 infuriated
be ~: 4 boil, burn, fume, rage, stew 5 steam, storm 6 see red, seethe, simmer 7 bristle, smolder
incentive: 4 bait, goad, lure, prod, spur 5 bonus, drive, spark 6 carrot, come-on, motive, reason 7 impetus 8 catalyst, stimulus 9 rationale, stimulant 10 allurement, enticement, incitement, inducement, motivation, persuasion, temptation
give ~: 4 fire, goad, move, prod, spur, urge, whet 5 goose, impel, prime, rouse, spark, tempt 6 arouse, bestir, excite, induce, prompt, propel, stir up 7 inspire, quicken 8 energize, motivate, persuade 9 galvanize, stimulate
incept: 3 eat 6 take in 7 receive
inception: 4 dawn, rise 5 birth, git-go, onset, start 6 advent, origin, outset, source 7 genesis, kickoff, leadoff, opening 8 creation, entrance, exordium 9 beginning, threshold 10 derivation, initiation, provenance
inceptive: 5 early, first 7 initial, nascent, pioneer 8 earliest, original 9 beginning, inaugural, incipient 10 archetypal, innovative
incertitude: 7 dubiety 8 mistrust 9 dubiosity, suspicion
incessant: 6 steady 7 chronic, endless, eternal, lasting, nonstop, running, undying 8 constant, enduring, tireless, unbroken, unending, unwaning 9 ceaseless, chronical, continual, perennial, perpetual, unabating, unceasing 10 continuous, monotonous, persistent, relentless
incessantly: 4 ever 5 no end, on end
inch: 3 bit, lag 4 unit 5 crawl, creep, sidle 6 trifle 7 modicum
by inch: 6 slowly 8 bit by bit 9 gradually
ender: 4 meal, worm
every ~: 5 fully 6 wholly 7 totally, utterly 8 entirely 10 completely, thoroughly
fraction: 3 mil
multiple: 4 foot, mile, yard
__ inch: 5 cubic, every 6 column
__ in Charge: 7 Charles
__-in-cheek: 6 tongue
inches
20 ~: 5 cubit
36 ~: 4 yard
39+ ~: 5 meter, metre
nine ~: 4 span
__ in chief: 6 editor
__ Inch Nails: 4 Nine
inchoate: 8 unformed, unshaped 9 amorphous 10 incomplete
Inchon: 4 city, port, town
city near ~: 5 Seoul
locale: 10 South Korea
incidence: 4 area, rate 5 range, scope 6 extent 7 compass 10 occurrence
incident: 4 case 5 event, scene, thing 6 affair, matter 7 episode, related 8 activity, occasion 9 adventure, attendant, happening 10 experience, occurrence, phenomenon
unpleasant ~: 6 bummer, downer
incidental: 3 odd 4 side 5 minor, stray 6 casual, chance, random 7 related, trivial 9 ancillary, attendant, haphazard, secondary 10 accidental, concurrent, contingent, extraneous, fortuitous, occasional, subsidiary, synchronal
expense: 3 tip
incidentally: 3 BTW 7 by the by 8 by the way 9 in passing
Incident at Oglala (1992 film)
director: Michael Apted
Incident at Vichy
author: Arthur Miller
__ Incident, The: 5 Ox-Bow
__ in Cincinnati: 4 WKRP
incinerate: 3 ash 4 burn 5 torch 6 ignite 7 combust
incinerator: 6 boiler, burner 7 furnace
debris: 3 ash
incipience: 4 dawn, rise 5 debut, onset, start 6 growth, origin, outset 9 ascension, beginning, emergence
incipient: 7 budding, initial, nascent 9 beginning, embryonic, inceptive 10 commencing, developing, elementary, initiatory
incise: 3 cut 4 bite, etch, gash, nick, slit 5 carve, grave, lance, notch, score, slash, slice 6 chisel, sculpt 7 cut into, engrave, scratch 9 sculpture
incised: 3 cut 4 slit 5 cleft, split 6 carved, cloven, etched, gashed, graven, nicked 7 cut into, grooved, notched, slashed 8 engraved, sculpted
incision: 3 cut 4 gash, slit, stab 5 slash 10 laceration
combining form: 4 -tomy
incisive: 4 acid, keen 5 acerb, acute, sharp, terse 6 biting, bright, clever, gnomic, severe 7 acerbic, caustic, cutting, graphic, mordant, pointed, precise, pungent, satiric 8 definite, piercing, profound, sardonic, scathing 9 graphical, sarcastic, satirical, trenchant
incisiveness: 5 irony 6 acuity, acumen, satire 7 acidity, sarcasm 8 accuracy, judgment, keenness
incisor: 4 fang 5 biter, tooth
elongated ~: 4 tusk
neighbor: 5 molar 6 canine
Incitatus: 5 horse, steed 6 equine
rider: 8 Caligula
incite: 3 set 4 abet, bait, coax, fire, fuel, goad, move, prod, push, spur, stir, urge 5 cause, drive, egg on, hop up, impel, key up, raise, rouse, spark, tempt, wreak 6 arouse, ask for, excite, exhort, fire up, foment, induce, kindle, prompt, set off, stir up, urge on, whip up, work up 7 actuate, aggress, agitate, animate, enflame, ferment, forward, further, inflame, inspire, promote, provoke, psych up, quicken, trigger 8 engender, enspirit, inspirit, motivate, persuade 9 encourage, impassion, influence, instigate, stimulate 10 cause a riot
incitement: 3 jog 4 call, goad, itch, jolt, poke, prod, push, spur, urge 5 drive, prick 6 desire, fillip, motive, thrust 7 dictate, impetus, impulse 8 stimulus 9 agitation, annoyance, awakening, incentive 10 excitement, inducement, invitation
inciter: 7 demagog, hellion 8 agitator, inflamer 9 demagogue
incivility: 4 sass 6 insult 7 crudity 8 rudeness 9 indecency, insolence 10 disrespect, effrontery
inclemency: 4 cold 5 rigor 7 cruelty, rawness 8 hardness, severity 9 austerity
inclement: 3 bad, raw 4 cold, foul, wild 5 cruel, harsh, nasty, rainy, rough 6 bitter, rugged, savage, severe, stormy, unkind, wintry 7 callous, wintery 8 pitiless, rigorous, ruthless 9 draconian, merciless, turbulent, unfeeling, unpitying 10 tyrannical, unmerciful
weather: 4 rain 5 sleet, storm 7 showers 8 blizzard 9 rainstorm
inclination: 3 set 4 bend, bent, bias, cant, lean, list, tilt, will, wish 5 angle, fancy, grade, pitch, slant, slope, taste, trend 6 animus, liking 7 impulse, leaning, opinion 8 affinity, aptitude, attitude, gradient, penchant, pleasure, tendency, weakness 9 appetence, readiness, sentiment 10 partiality, proclivity, propensity
strong ~: 3 yen 4 itch, urge 7 craving, impulse 8 appetite, yearning 9 hankering
inclinatory: 4 awry 5 askew, atilt 6 canted, skewed, uneven 7 crooked, leaning, tilting 8 cockeyed, lopsided, one-sided, unsteady 10 off-balance, unbalanced
incline: 3 dip, tip 4 bend, bias, cant, hill, lean, list, ramp, rise, sway, tend, tilt, turn 5 chute, grade, level, pitch, ready, slant, slope, verge, way up 6 ascent, glacis 7 descent, dispose 8 gradient, motivate, persuade 9 acclivity, declivity, gravitate, prejudice 10 predispose
toward: 4 like, want 6 prefer
upward, nautically: 6 steeve
__ incline: 4 on an
inclined: 3 apt 4 bent, wont 5 atilt, bevel, leant, prone, ready 6 aslant, aslope, liable, likely 7 tending, willing 8 disposed, prepared
at sea: 5 alist
be ~: 4 lean, tend 5 slope
favorably ~: 7 partial
highly ~: 5 steep 6 abrupt
not ~: 5 balky, loath 6 averse 7 opposed, uneager 8 hesitant 9 reluctant, unwilling 10 indisposed
to (suffix): 3 -ish
inclined __: 5 plane
incl., not: 4 excl.
__-in closet: 4 walk
include: 3 add 4 bear, have, hold, okay, take 5 admit, adopt, allow, carry, co-opt, count, cover, go for, let in 6 append, assent, comply, deal in, embody, entail, imbody, insert, number, take in 7 build in, contain, embrace, enclose, inclose, involve, subsume, welcome 8 allow for, comprise, stand for 9 consist of, encompass, interject, put up with, recognize, sign off on 10 concur with, constitute, give the nod
don't ~: 4 drop, omit, shun, skip, snub 5 avoid, scorn 6 bypass, forget, pass by, pass up, reject 7 neglect 8 leave out, overlook 9 disregard
included
not ~: 3 out 5 apart, extra 6 absent
with: 4 amid 5 among, one of 6 amidst, mongst 7 amongst
including: 3 and 4 also, plus, with

8 as well as, counting 9 along with 10 containing
not ~: 4 sans 7 without
inclusion: 9 belonging, comprisal, insertion 10 admittance
inclusive: 4 A-to-Z, full, wide 5 broad, total 6 entire 7 blanket, general, overall, plenary 8 catchall, catholic, sweeping, umbrella 9 all-around, ball-of-wax, expansive, extensive 10 ecumenical, wall-to-wall
abbr.: 3 etc.
make more ~: 5 widen 6 expand, spread 7 augment, broaden, enlarge
pronoun: 3 our 4 ours
__-inclusive: 3 all
inclusiveness: 5 scope, width 7 breadth
incognita, terra: 6 enigma
incognito: 6 hidden, masked, secret 7 bearded, unknown 8 nameless 9 anonymous, concealed, disguised, unexposed 10 in disguise, undercover
incognizant: 4 deaf 7 napping, unaware 8 careless, heedless, off-guard
incoherent: 6 silent 8 rambling 9 delirious, faltering, wandering 10 breathless, discordant, disjointed, disordered, incomplete, irrational, maundering, stammering, stuttering, tongue-tied
incohesive: 5 messy 7 aimless, chaotic, jumbled, muddled 8 confused 10 disjointed, disordered
In Cold Blood: 4 book
author: Truman Capote
income: 3 fee, job, pay, rev. 4 alms, cash, fare, rent, tips, wage 5 lucre, means, money, wages, yield 6 living, payoff, profit, return, salary 7 annuity, revenue, royalty 8 cash flow, dividend, earnings, finances, proceeds, receipts 9 emolument, resources, royalties 10 IRS concern, livelihood
after taxes: 3 net
in French: 5 rente
investor ~: 3 div., int. 6 return 8 dividend, interest
opposite: 5 outgo 8 spending
source: 3 job 6 living 10 livelihood
income __: 3 tax
__ income: 3 net 4 real 5 gross 6 earned 7 accrued
__-income: 3 low 4 high 5 fixed 6 middle
incomer: 8 outsider, stranger 9 outlander
incommensurate: 6 uneven 7 unequal 8 lopsided 9 disparate, divergent 10 dissimilar, mismatched, unbalanced
incommode: 6 bother, burden, impose, put out 7 disturb, trouble 9 disoblige 10 discommode
incommodious: 4 boxy, tiny 5 teeny 6 narrow, teensy 7 cramped, irksome, unhandy, unroomy 8 confined
incommunicable: 5 privy 7 private 8 eyes-only, personal
incommunicado: 6 cut off, hidden 7 shut off 8 isolated, secluded, shielded 10 cloistered, tucked away
incommunicative: 3 mum, shy 4 curt, dumb, mute 5 brief, quiet, short, terse 6 silent 7 evasive, laconic 8 reserved, reticent, taciturn
incomparable: 4 best 5 ideal 6 unique 7 perfect, supreme 8 peerless, superior, ultimate, uncommon 9 matchless, priceless, unequaled 10 preeminent
incomparably: 5 by far 7 greatly
incompatibility: 6 rancor, strife, tussle 7 discord, dispute, dissent 8 bad blood, conflict, disunity, friction 9 antipathy, hostility 10 antagonism, contention, disharmony, dissension, dissonance, opposition
incompatible: 5 alien 6 motley, unlike 8 clashing, contrary 9 different, disparate, dissonant 10 discordant, dissimilar, mismatched
incompetence: 7 failure 8 weakness
incompetent: 3 raw 5 gawky, inapt, inept, unapt, unfit 6 clumsy, klutzy, oafish, unable 7 amateur, awkward, bungler, gawkish, useless 8 bumbling, bungling, feckless, helpless, inexpert, ungainly 9 all thumbs, graceless, lumbering, maladroit, stumbling, unskilled 10 unskillful
be ~: 9 mishandle, mismanage
incomplete: 6 broken 7 lacking, partial, sketchy, wanting 8 half-done 9 defective, deficient, imperfect 10 expurgated, fractional, inadequate, incoherent, unexecuted, unfinished
incompletely: 4 part 6 in part 8 somewhat
incomprehensible: 5 Greek, vague 6 arcane, opaque 7 cryptic, obscure, unclear 8 abstruse, baffling, nebulous, puzzling 9 confusing, cryptical, enigmatic, limitless, unlimited 10 fathomless, indistinct, perplexing
incompressible: 4 firm, hard 5 dense, solid, tight 7 compact
incomputable: 4 vast 6 untold 7 endless, immense, no end of 8 infinite
inconceivable: 8 hopeless, unlikely 9 marvelous, unheard-of 10 impossible, infeasible, out of reach
inconclusive: 4 weak 5 shaky 6 unsure 7 tenuous 10 inadequate
Inconel: 5 alloy
component: 4 iron 6 nickel 8 chromium
incongruity: 6 oddity 7 anomaly, illogic, paradox 8 conflict, variance
incongruous: 3 odd 4 rich 5 alien, inapt, wrong 6 absurd, ironic, unlike 7 unsound 8 improper, rambling, untimely 9 ill-suited, ludicrous, senseless 10 irrelevant, unsuitable
incongruousness: 5 irony
inconnu: 4 fish 8 stranger
inconsequential: 4 idle, null, punk, puny, tiny 5 dinky, light, minor, petty, scrub, small 6 frilly, measly, paltry, scanty, two-bit 7 nominal, trivial 8 picayune, trifling 9 valueless, worthless
inconsiderable: 4 slim, tiny 5 light, minor, small 6 little, minute, scanty, slight 7 nominal, trivial 8 trifling
inconsiderate: 4 rude 5 brash, crass, hasty, nervy, rough, short 6 madcap, shabby, unkind, wanton 7 boorish, selfish 8 careless, impolite, inurbane, reckless, tactless 9 negligent, thankless, unadvised
inconsideration: 6 laxity 7 laxness, neglect 8 omission 9 oversight 10 negligence, remissness
inconsistency: 7 anomaly, paradox 8 conflict, contrast, oxymoron, variance
inconsistent: 5 silly 6 at odds, fickle, spotty, unlike 7 erratic 8 contrary, opposite, unstable, variable 9 up-and-down
be ~: 4 sway, vary, yo-yo 5 swing, waver 9 fluctuate, hem and haw, oscillate, vacillate 10 ebb and flow, equivocate
inconsolable: 3 sad 4 blue, glum 5 woful 6 gloomy, morose, somber, woeful 7 doleful, forlorn, joyless, unhappy 8 dejected, desolate, downcast, troubled, wretched 9 bummed out, cheerless, desperate, heartsick, miserable, prostrate, sorrowful, woebegone 10 chapfallen, dispirited, melancholy
inconspicuous: 6 hidden, unseen 9 unnoticed 10 unobserved
inconstancy: 8 weakness
inconstant: 5 false, giddy 6 fickle, uneven, untrue 7 erratic, mutable, unloyal, wayward 8 disloyal, ticklish, unstable, unsteady, variable, volatile 9 faithless, irregular, mercurial, two-timing, uncertain, unsettled 10 capricious, changeable, nonuniform, perfidious, traitorous
incontestable: 4 real, sire, true 5 final, fixed, plain, solid 7 certain, evident, for sure 8 absolute, airtight, decisive, definite, positive 9 axiomatic
incontestably: 5 by far 9 going away, hands down
incontinent: 6 amoral 7 corrupt, immoral 8 depraved 9 corrupted, dissolute 10 licentious, lubricious, profligate
incontrovertible: 4 sure, true 5 clear 7 assured, certain, decided, settled 8 accurate, definite, in the bag, positive, resolved, surefire 10 conclusive, determined, guaranteed, unarguable, undeniable
inconvenience: 4 snag 5 trial 6 bother, hamper, hassle, put out 7 put upon, trouble 8 headache 9 liability
inconvenient: 3 bad 5 messy 7 awkward, unhandy 8 annoying, untimely, unwieldy 9 unwieldly
more than ~: 6 odious
Inconvenient Woman, An
author: Dominick Dunne
incorporate: 3 mix 4 fuse, have, join, link, pool 5 add to, annex, blend, co-opt, cover, merge, tie in, unite, weave 6 absorb, digest, embody, gather, imbody 7 combine, contain, embrace, include, subsume 8 coalesce, comprise, gather up 10 synthesize
incorporated: 4 mixt 5 mixed 6 united 9 municipal
incorporation: 3 mix 5 blend, union 6 merger 7 mixture
in corpore __: 4 sano
incorporeal: 6 unreal 7 ghostly 8 bodiless, spectral 9 spiritual, unworldly
incorrect: 3 bad, off 5 false, not so, wrong 6 erring, faulty, flawed, untrue, way off 7 ill-done, inexact, unsound 8 improper, mistaken, specious 9 erroneous, illogical, imprecise, unfitting 10 fallacious, inaccurate, ungrounded, unreliable, unsuitable
be ~: 3 err 4 flub, goof, slip 5 botch, lapse, stray 6 bungle, foul up, mess up, slip up 7 blunder, deviate, go wrong, louse up, stumble 8 go astray
marks ~: 3 xes
prefix: 3 mis-
incorrectly: 5 amiss, badly, wrong
incorrigible: 6 unruly, wicked 7 problem, wayward 8 indocile, indurate 9 scoundrel, shameless 10 rebellious
incorrupt: 4 good, pure 5 loyal, moral, noble 6 chaste, heroic, worthy 8 reliable 9 untouched 10 immaculate, impeccable
incorruptibility: 5 honor 6 virtue 7 honesty, loyalty, probity 8 morality, nobility
incorruptible: 4 fair, just, pure 5 moral 6 honest 7 upright 8 reliable, straight, virtuous 9 unselfish
In Country (1989 film)
cast: Joan Allen, Emily Lloyd, Bruce Willis
setting:: 3 Nam 7 Vietnam
incr.: 3 enl.
increase: 2 up 3 add, enl., wax 4 boom, bump, gain, go up, grow, hike, jump, leap, rise, whet 5 add to, boost, build, mount, raise, revup, run up, surge, swell, widen 6 accrue, deepen, expand, extend, fatten, gather, growth, jack up, jerk up, mark up, pick up, roll up, spread, step up, thrive, upturn, waxing 7 accrual, advance, amplify, augment, broaden, buildup, burgeon, develop, enhance, enlarge, further, improve, inflate, magnify, mount up, prolong, promote, prosper, quicken, recover, scale up, upgrade, upsurge, upswing 8 addition, bourgeon, escalate, heighten, lengthen, multiply, mushroom, progress, protract, snowball, swelling, widening 9 accretion, branch out, crescendo, expansion, extension, increment, inflation, intensify, luxuriate, propagate, pullulate, reinforce 10 accumulate, aggrandize, appreciate, broadening, burgeoning, cumulation, escalation, prosperity, strengthen, supplement
combining form: 3 aux- 4 auxo- 6 auxamo-
suddenly: 4 zoom 5 spike, surge, swell
__ increase: 4 on an 5 on the
Increase: 6 Mather

increased: 3 new 4 more 5 ran up, upped 10 additional
by: 3 and 4 plus
incredible: 5 fishy, great 6 absurd, unreal 7 amazing, awesome, surreal, suspect, uncanny 8 fabulous, glorious, unlikely 9 fantastic, ineffable, marvelous, untenable, wonderful 10 astounding, far-fetched, impossible, improbable, marvellous, outlandish, prodigious, ridiculous, superhuman
Incredible!: 3 wow 5 great, super
Incredible Hulk, The (2008 film)
cast: Edward Norton, Tim Roth, Liv Tyler
Incredible Hulk, The (CBS sci-fi)
cast: Bill Bixby (David Banner) Lou Ferrigno (The Hulk)
Incredible Journey, The
cat: 3 Tao
dog: 5 Luath 6 Bodger, Chance, Shadow
Incredibles, The (2004 film)
director: Brad Bird
voice cast: Holly Hunter, Craig T. Nelson
incredibly: 4 very 6 hugely, vastly 7 greatly 8 markedly, mightily, very much 9 extremely, immensely, intensely 10 abundantly, enormously, powerfully, remarkably, strikingly
incredulity: 5 doubt 6 wonder 8 distrust, mistrust, surprise, unbelief 9 suspicion
exclamation: 6 indeed, really 8 is that so 9 no kidding
incredulous: 5 leery 7 cynical, dubious 8 doubting 9 quizzical, skeptical
increment: 4 bump, gain, grow, rise, step 5 add to, boost, build, raise 6 profit, step up 7 augment, build up 8 addition, escalate, increase 9 accession, accretion, accrument 10 annexation, supplement
incrementally: 6 slowly 8 bit by bit
increscent: 9 on the rise 10 augmenting, cumulative, increasing
incriminate: 3 tax 4 name 5 blame, frame, rat on 6 accuse, charge, finger, give up, indict 8 denounce
incriminated: 6 guilty
incrimination: 5 blame, guilt
in crowd: 4 clan 5 elite 6 clique, jet set
'In' Crowd, The (1975 song)
artist: Ramsey Lewis
incrust: 3 set, tar 4 coat, face, gild, line, pave, tile 5 adorn, cover, glaze, inlay, japan, paint, plate 6 cement, emboss, enamel, stucco, veneer 7 lacquer, overlay, plaster, varnish 8 decorate, ornament 9 embellish, whitewash
incrustation: 4 crud, scab 5 scale, shell 6 casing 7 coating 8 covering
Inc. subject: 2 co. 7 company
incubate: 4 grow 5 brood, hatch, sit on 6 mature 7 develop, gestate, nurture 8 take form
incubation site: 4 nest
incubus: 4 onus 5 demon, fiend 6 daemon, daimon, spirit 9 archfiend, nightmare
inculcate: 3 fix, sow 5 drill, edify, imbue, infix, plant, teach 6 impart, infuse, instil 7 engrain, implant, impress, ingrain, instill 8 drum into, instruct 9 brainwash, break down, establish, pound into 10 hammer into
inculpable: 4 good 5 clean, moral 6 chaste 7 upright 8 innocent, spotless, virtuous 9 blameless, exemplary, faultless, guiltless 10 in the clear
inculpate: 3 tax 6 accuse, charge, impute, indict 7 arraign, impeach 9 implicate 10 take to task
incult: 4 rude, wild 6 coarse 7 boorish 9 unrefined
incumbency: 5 reign 6 regime, tenure
incumbent: 2 in 5 lying 6 inside 7 binding, in power, leaning, resting 8 lounging, occupant, official, reposing 10 inhabitant, politician
incur: 3 owe 4 draw 5 run up 6 afford 7 acquire, bring on, provoke 8 contract
incurable: 7 chronic 9 unfixable 10 inveterate, remediless
incuriosity: 5 ennui 6 apathy 7 boredom 8 coolness, lethargy 9 jadedness, lassitude, weariness
incurious: 4 cool 5 aloof, bored, jaded 8 heedless 10 nonchalant, unagitated
incursion: 4 raid 5 foray 6 attack, inroad 7 assault, descent 8 invasion 9 intrusion, irruption, onslaught 10 aggression
incus: 4 bone 5 anvil
locale: 3 ear
incuse: 5 stamp 8 hammer in
In days ___: 5 of old
indebted: 4 owed 5 bound 6 in hock, liable 7 obliged 8 beholden, grateful, thankful 9 obligated 10 answerable, honor-bound
be ~: 3 owe 5 owe to, thank 10 appreciate
one: 4 ower
indebtedness: 3 due 5 debit, debts 7 arrears, default, deficit 9 liability
indecency: 4 evil 7 crudity 8 foulness, lewdness, ribaldry, vileness 9 bawdiness, grossness, immodesty, indecorum, obscenity, vulgarity 10 coarseness, incivility, indelicacy
indecent: 3 low 4 base, blue, foul, lewd, racy, rude, vile 5 crude, dirty, gross, nasty, wrong 6 coarse, earthy, ribald, risqué, smutty, unmeet, vulgar, wicked, X-rated 7 immoral, obscene, profane, uncouth 8 immodest, improper, off-color, shameful, unseemly 9 low-minded, shameless 10 indecorous, indelicate, lascivious, scurrilous, suggestive, unbecoming
Indecent Obsession, An
author: Colleen McCullough
Indecent Proposal (1993 film)
cast: Woody Harrelson, Demi Moore, Robert Redford
director: Adrian Lyne
indecipherable: 3 dim 4 dark, hard 5 perdu, run-on, tough, vague 6 arcane, erased, hidden, knotty, perdue, secret, tricky, veiled 7 blotted, blurred, complex, cramped, cryptic, obscure, puzzing, smudged, tangled, unclear 8 abstract, abstruse, baffling, esoteric, involved, nebulous 9 cryptical
indecision: 5 doubt, qualm 7 dubiety 8 weakness 9 dubiosity, hesitancy 10 hesitation
sound of ~: 2 er, uh, um
indecisive: 4 weak 5 shaky, timid 6 unfirm, unsure 7 aimless, halting 8 doubtful, hesitant, lukewarm, waffling, wavering 9 astraddle, faltering, tentative, uncertain, undecided, unsettled, weak-kneed 10 borderline, changeable, hesitating, hot-and-cold, indefinite, irresolute, of two minds, on the fence, wishy-washy
be ~: 3 hem 5 waver 6 teeter 9 vacillate
indecorous: 4 base, rank, rude, vile 5 bawdy, crass, crude, gross, inapt, nasty, rough, unapt 6 coarse, common, ribald, risqué, unmeet, vulgar 7 boorish, ill-bred, loutish, lowbred, naughty, uncivil, uncouth 8 churlish, impolite, improper, indecent, inurbane, unseemly 9 facetious, graceless, tasteless, unrefined 10 indelicate
be ~: 5 act up 9 misbehave
indecorum: 4 goof, slip 5 boner, gaffe, lapse 6 slip-up 7 bad move, blunder, faux pas, misstep, stumble 8 bad taste, rudeness 9 indecency
indeed: 3 nay 4 amen 5 oh yes 6 it is so, verily 7 for real, granted, in truth 8 actually, for a fact, to be sure, very much 9 in reality, yea verily 10 admittedly, undeniably
see also of course
___, indeed!: 3 yes
indefatigability: 3 vim 4 grit, guts 5 might, moxie, power, vigor 6 energy, mettle 7 prowess, stamina 8 vitality 9 endurance, fortitude, gutsiness, hardiness 10 durability, resilience
indefatigable: 5 hardy 8 sedulous, tireless, untiring 9 laborious 10 unflagging
In Defense of Women
author: H.L. Mencken
indefinite: 3 lax 4 hazy, iffy, wide 5 broad, fluid, fuzzy, ideal, loose, vague 6 chancy, unsure 7 dubious, general, inexact, unclear, unfixed, unknown 8 abstract, confused, doubtful, nebulous 9 ambiguous, boundless, equivocal, imprecise, limitless, shapeless, tentative, uncertain, undecided, undefined, unlimited, unsettled 10 borderline, indecisive, indistinct, inexplicit, unexplicit, unresolved, unspecific, up for grabs, up in the air
amount: 3 any, few 4 many, some
answer: 5 maybe 7 perhaps 8 possibly, probably 9 it could be, it might be, perchance 10 imaginably
combining form: 4 myri- 5 myrio-
indefinitely: 4 ever 7 forever, sine die
indelible: 3 ink 7 lasting 8 enduring 9 ingrained, memorable, permanent 10 inerasable, unerasable
indelicacy: 7 bad form, crudity 8 bad taste, ribaldry, rudeness 9 indecency 10 coarseness, smuttiness
indelicate: 3 low 4 base, blue, foul, lewd, racy, rude, vile 5 bawdy, brusk, crass, crude, frank, gross, nasty, rough, salty, spicy 6 abrupt, candid, coarse, earthy, risqué, smutty, spicey, unmeet, vulgar, wicked 7 brusque, immoral, obscene, uncouth 8 immodest, impolite, improper, indecent, inurbane, off-color, tactless, unseemly 9 inelegant, offensive, outspoken, tasteless, ungallant, untactful 10 indecorous, outrageous, suggestive, unbecoming, unblushing
indemnify: 3 pay 5 atone, repay 6 ensure, insure, refund, return, reward, secure 7 certify, endorse, indorse, pay back, satisfy, warrant 8 make good 9 reimburse 10 compensate, make amends, recompense, remunerate
indemnity: 3 pay 6 pardon 7 damages, redress, warrant 8 impunity 9 expiation, insurance, jury award, privilege 10 commission, protection
___ indemnity: 6 double
indent: 5 notch 6 recess 9 serration
indentation: 3 cut, dip, pit, rut 4 bowl, dent, gash, hole, nick, sink 5 basin, cleft, niche, notch, score, stamp 6 cavity, crater, dimple, groove, hollow, recess 7 scallop, scollop 8 sinkhole
shoreline ~: 3 bay 4 cove, gulf 5 basin, bayou, bight, fiord, firth, fjord, inlet 6 lagoon 7 estuary
indented: 6 sunken 7 concave 8 serrated 9 depressed
indenture: 3 tie 4 bind, bond, deal, deed 5 lease 7 compact, enslave, enthral, inthral, slavery, voucher 8 contract, document, enthrall, inthrall 9 agreement
indentured ___: 7 servant
indentured one: 4 esne, serf
independence: 7 freedom, liberty, license 8 autarchy, autonomy, home rule, latitude, self-rule
Independence: 4 city, town
initials: 3 HST
locale: 8 Missouri
Independence ___: 3 Day 4 Hall
___ Independence: 5 War of
Independence Day (1996 film)
cast: Jeff Goldblum, Mary McDonnell, Bill Pullman, Randy Quaid, Will Smith
director: Roland Emmerich
dog: 6 Boomer
foe: 2 ET 5 alien
Independence Day time: 4 July 6 fourth, summer 9 the fourth
Independence Hall st.: 4 Penn.
independent: 4 free, rich 5 apart, proud, rebel 6 closed, strong 7 private, unaided, wealthy 8 maverick, opposite, separate, unallied 9 freelance, on one's own, sovereign, unrelated, voluntary 10 autonomous
make ~: 4 wean
of ~ means: 4 rich 5 flush 6 loaded 7 moneyed, opulent, upscale,

wealthy, well-off 8 affluent, thriving, well-to-do 10 in the chips, in the money, privileged, prosperous, successful, well-heeled
one: 5 loner 6 hermit
independently: 4 solo 5 alone, apart, per se, unled 6 singly 7 unaided 9 by oneself 10 unassisted
Independent Woman (2000 song)
artist: Destiny's Child
in-depth: 5 total 8 complete, thorough 9 full-dress, intensive, searching 10 exhaustive, soup to nuts
indescribable: 4 huge, vast 6 untold 7 immense 9 boundless
indestructible: 5 hardy 7 durable, lasting, undying 8 immortal 9 permanent 10 changeless
Buddhist symbol of the ~: 5 vajra
indeterminate: 4 gray, grey, wide 5 broad, loose, mousy, vague 6 mousey, unsure 7 dubious, general, inexact, unclear, unfixed, unknown 8 confused, doubtful, nebulous, possible 9 uncertain 10 unresolved
amount: 3 any, few 4 many, some
index: 4 clew, clue, DJIA, file, list, mark, sign, sort 5 guide, order, table, token 6 docket, roster, symbol, the Dow 7 arrange, pointer 8 classify, tabulate 9 benchmark, catalogue, directory, inventory 10 indication, tabulation
entry: 2 pg. 4 name, page 5 title
starter: 3 sub
index __: 4 card, fund 6 finger
__ index: 4 heat 5 thumb
__-indexed: 5 cross
indexing, word ignored in: 3 the
India: 3 ink 6 nation 7 country
aborigine: 4 Gond
actor: 4 Sabu
antelope: 5 sasin
bay: 6 Bengal
bovine: 3 Gir 4 arna, Rath, Siri, zebu 5 Dajal, Dangi, Deoni, gayal, Malvi, Rathi 6 Channi, Gaolao, Mewati, Nagori, Nimari, Ongole, Ponwar, Rojhan 7 Bachaur, Brahman, Brahmin, Sahiwal
bread: 3 nan
British rule: 3 raj
Buddhist king of ~: 5 Asoka
butter: 4 ghee
bwana, in ~: 5 saheb, sahib
camel: 4 oont
capital: 8 New Delhi
caste: 4 ahir
city: 4 Agra, Puna 5 Delhi, Mandi, Patan, Patna, Poona, Simla, Surat, Thana 6 Bhopal, Bombay, Ellora, Imphal, Indore, Jaipur, Kanpur, Madras, Mumbai, Pattan 7 Chennai, Jodhpur, Kolkata 8 Calcutta, New Delhi 9 Bangalore, Hyderabad
coat: 6 achkan, banian, banyan
conductor: 5 Mehta 10 Zubin Mehta
court: 6 adalat 7 adawlut
court officials: 5 omlah
criminal: 6 dacoit, dakoit
crocodile: 6 gavial
cymbals: 3 tal
dance: 6 kathak
deer: 4 axis 6 chital, sambar, sambur 7 sambhar, sambhur 9 barasingh
desert: 4 Tahr, Thar, Tuhr
district: 3 Goa 5 Daman
dog: 5 dhole
drum: 5 tabla
estate: 5 taluk 7 talooka
export: 3 tea
fabric: 6 Madras 7 khaddar
Father of ~: 6 Gandhi
feline: 7 caracal
forage crop: 3 urd
garment: 4 sari 5 lungi, saree 6 lungee, lungyi
Gateway to ~: 6 Bombay
gesture: 5 mudra
goat: 7 markhor 8 markhoor
government official: 5 dewan, diwan
grass: 7 vetiver 8 khus-khus
groom: 4 sice, syce 5 saice
invader: 5 Arian, Aryan
island: 3 Diu
language: 4 Pali, Tulu, Urdu 5 Hindi, Oriya, Tamil, Vedic 6 Telegu, Telugu 8 Sanscrit, Sanskrit 10 Hindustani
legislature: 6 Sansad
location: 4 Asia
maid: 4 ayah
memorial tower: 5 minah
millet: 5 doura, durra 6 dourah
mister: 3 sri 4 shri 5 saheb, sahib
Mogul capital: 4 Agra
money: 3 pie 4 anna, pice 5 mohur, paisa, rupee
mountain: 4 Mana 5 Ghats, Kamet 6 Trisul 7 Trisuli 8 Cardamom, Dunagiri, Pauhunri 9 Badrinath, Himalayas, Nanda Devi
music: 4 raga, tala 5 filmi
musket: 6 jingal 7 gingall
mystic: 5 faker, fakir, faqir 6 faquir
native: 4 Sikh 5 Hindu, Nahal, Parsi, Tamil 6 Hindoo, Lepcha
neighbor: 5 Burma, China, Nepal 6 Bhutan 8 Pakistan 10 Bangladesh
Nobelist: 3 Sen 5 Raman 6 Tagore
nursemaid: 4 amah
pants: 7 shalwar, shulwar
peasant: 4 ryot
peninsula: 6 Deccan
police club: 5 lathi 6 lathee
port: 4 Puri 6 Bombay, Cochin, Madras 8 Calcutta 10 Chittagong
primate: 5 loris 6 Bandar, rhesus 7 hoolock
princess of ~: 8 maharani 9 maharanee
reception: 6 durbar
religion: 4 Jain 5 Jaina 8 Hinduism
religious fair: 4 mela
river: 5 Indus, Jumna, Purna, Sarda 6 Ganges
riverbank steps: 4 ghat 5 ghaut
ruler: 4 raja, rana, rani 5 mogul, ranee
scarf: 5 rumal
sea: 7 Arabian
servant: 4 maty 5 matee
shawl: 5 pattu
shirt: 4 pooa 5 kurta, pooah 6 banian, banyan, khurta
shrub: 4 sola, sunn 5 cubeb 7 karanda
silkworm: 4 eria
sir: 5 saheb, sahib
sitarist: 7 Shankar
social stratum: 5 caste
soldier: 5 Sepoy
soup: 3 dal
spice: 5 curry
stable worker: 4 sice, syce 5 saice
state: 3 Goa 5 Assam, Bihar 6 Kerala, Orissa, Sikkim 7 Gujarat, Haryana, Manipur, Mizoram, Tripura 8 Nagaland
statesman: 5 Nehru 6 Gandhi 7 Shastri
story: 5 katha
stringed instrument: 4 vina 5 sitar, veena
temple: 4 rath 5 ratha
tree: 2 bo 3 bel 4 bael, pich, poon, teak 5 bodhi, ebony, mahua, mahwa, mohwa, mowra, papal, pipal 6 banian, banyan, deodar, mowrah, nutmeg, peepul 7 deodara, karanda, soursop 8 cinnamon
vehicle: 5 tonga 6 gharri, gharry
water container: 4 lota 5 lotah
weasel: 5 ratel
weight: 3 ser 4 tola
writer: 3 Rao 5 Anand, Desai, Iqbal, Mehta 6 Hosain, Moraes, Tagore 7 Bharati, Narayan, Rushdie 8 Kalidasa 9 Premchand 10 Markandaya
India __: 3 ink 5 paper 6 rubber
India.__: 4 Arie
__ India: 3 Air 6 Song of, Star of
__ India Company: 4 East
Indian: 3 Fox, Han, Kaw, Oto, Sac, Ute 4 ALer, Cree, Crow, Cuna, Erie, Eyak, Hopi, Inca, Iowa, Maya, Otoe, Pima, Pomo, Sauk, Seri, Tama, Taos, Tewa, Tiwa, Tupi, Yana, Yuma, Zuni 5 Ahtna, Asian, brave, Brulé, Caddo, Carib, Creek, Haida, Huron, Kansa, Kaska, Kiowa, Lenca, Lipan, Maidu, Makah, Miami, Miwok, Modoc, ocean, Omaha, Osage, Otomi, Piute, Ponca, Sioux, Taino, Teton, Unami, Washo, Wintu, Yaqui 6 Abnaki, Ahtena, Apache, Arawak, Aymara, Cayuga, Cayuse, Dakota, Feller, Galibi, Jivaro, Kechua, Laguna, Lengua, Lumbee, Mandan, Micmac, Mohave, Mohawk, Mojave, Munsee, Navaho, Navajo, Nootka, Oglala, Ojibwa, Oneida, Ottawa, Paiute, Papago, Patwin, Pawnee, Pequot, Plains, Pueblo, Quapaw, Salish, Santee, Seneca, Tanana, Toltec, Wintun, Yahgan, Yakima, Yokuts 7 Abenaki, Arapaho, Arikara, Atakapa, Bannock, Chibcha, Chilcat, Chilkat, Chinook, Choctaw, Chumash, Guarani, Huastec, Kechuan, Klamath, Koyukon, Kutchin, Kutenai, Mahican, Mazatec, Miskito, Mohegan, Mohican, Naskapi, Nipmuck, Ojibway, Quechua, Quichua, San Blas, Shawnee, Takelma, Tanaina, Tlingit, Washita, Wichita, Wyandot, Yankton, Yavapai, Yucatec, Zapotec 8 Arapahoe, Cahuilla, Caingang, Cherokee, Cheyenne, Chippewa, Comanche, Delaware, Hunkpapa, Illinois, Iroquois, Kickapoo, Kwakiutl, Malecite, Maricopa, Mikasuki, Missouri, Muskogee, Nez Percé, Onondaga, Ouachita, Puyallup, Quechuan, Sahaptin, Seminole, Squamish, Tarascan, Wabanaki, Wahpeton 9 Blackfoot, Chickasaw, Havasupai, Jicarilla, Karankawa, Menominee, Mescalero, Nanticoke, Penobscot, Saulteaux, Suquamish, Tehuelche, Tiger Lily, Tsimshian, Tuscarora, Wahpekute, Wampanoag, Winnebago, Wyandotte 10 Adirondack, Araucanian, Assiniboin, Athabaskan, Bellabella, Bellacoola, Chiricahua, Miniconjou, Potawatomi, Tarahumara
beads: 5 sewan
boat: 5 canoe
carving: 5 totem
corn: 5 maize
corn genus: 3 zea
dwelling: 4 tipi 5 hogan, tepee 6 teepee
fish: 5 danio, hilsa 6 cuchia, hilsah
footwear: 3 moc
friend: 5 netop
fruit: 4 bael
grass: 4 kans
greeting, in oaters: 3 how
Hall-of-Famer: 4 Doby, Wynn 5 Flick, Lemon 6 Feller, Lajoie 7 Speaker 8 Bob Lemon, Boudreau 9 Bob Feller, Early Wynn, Larry Doby, Nap Lajoie 10 Elmer Flick
horse: 6 cayuse
language family: 5 Numic
on the ~: 4 asea 5 at sea
paintbrush: 5 plant 6 flower
palindromic ~: 3 Oto
pipe: 5 plant 6 flower
pony: 6 cayuse
subdivision: 5 tribe
summer phenomenon: 4 haze
Territory, today: 4 Okla. 8 Oklahoma
Indian __: 4 club, corn, file 5 Ocean 6 summer
Indiana: 5 Jones, state 6 Robert
author: George Sand
basketballer: 5 Pacer
city: 4 Gary 5 Paoli 6 Carmel, Goshen, Hobart, Kokomo, Marion, Muncie 7 Elkhart, Fishers, Granger, Hammond, La Porte, Munster, Portage 8 Anderson, Columbus, Highland, Lawrence, Richmond 9 Fort Wayne, Greenwood, Lafayette, Mishawaka, New Albany, South Bend 10 Crown Point, Evansville, Terre Haute, Valparaiso
county: 4 Cass, Owen, Vigo 5 Parke 6 Jasper, Starke 7 Elkhart, La Porte
humorist: 3 Ade
Indian: 5 Miami
neighbor: 4 Ohio 8 Illinois, Kentucky, Michigan
politician: 4 Bayh
school: 3 NDU 6 Goshen, Purdue 9 Ball State, Notre Dame

Standard Oil of ~ today: 5 Amoco
state bird: 8 cardinal
state flower: 5 peony
state river: 6 Wabash
state stone: 9 limestone
__, Indiana: 5 Eerie
Indiana Jones and the Kingdom of the Crystal Skull (2008 film)
cast: Cate Blanchett, Harrison Ford
director: Steven Spielberg
Indiana Jones and the Last Crusade (1989 film)
cast: Sean Connery, Alison Doody, Denholm Elliott, Harrison Ford
director: Steven Spielberg
Indiana Jones and the Temple of Doom (1984 film)
cast: Kate Capshaw, Harrison Ford
director: Steven Spielberg
Indianapolis: 4 city, town
city near ~: 6 Kokomo
county: 6 Marion
newspaper: 4 Star
pro team: 5 Colts
river: 5 White
Indianapolis 500: 4 race
sound: 5 vroom 6 varoom
trouble: 5 crash 8 auto race
Indianapolis 500 winners:
2010 - Dario Franchitti
2009 - Helio Castroneves
2008 - Scott Dixon
2007 - Dario Franchitti
2006 - Sam Hornish, Jr.
2005 - Dan Wheldon
2004 - Buddy Rice
2003 - Gil de Ferran
2002 - Helio Castroneves
2001 - Helio Castroneves
2000 - Juan Montoya
1999 - Kenny Brack
1998 - Eddie Cheever Jr.
1997 - Arie Luyendyk
1996 - Buddy Lazier
1995 - Jacques Villeneuve
1994 - Al Unser Jr.
1993 - Emerson Fittipaldi
1992 - Al Unser Jr.
1991 - Rick Mears
1990 - Arie Luyendyk
1989 - Emerson Fittipaldi
1988 - Rick Mears
1987 - Al Unser
1986 - Bobby Rahal
1985 - Danny Sullivan
1984 - Rick Mears
1983 - Tom Sneva
1982 - Gordon Johncock
1981 - Bobby Unser
1980 - Johnny Rutherford
1979 - Rick Mears
1978 - Al Unser
1977 - A.J. Foyt
1976 - Johnny Rutherford
1975 - Bobby Unser
1974 - Johnny Rutherford
1973 - Gordon Johncock
1972 - Mark Donohue
1971 - Al Unser
1970 - Al Unser
1969 - Mario Andretti
1968 - Bobby Unser
1967 - A.J. Foyt
1966 - Graham Hill
1965 - Jim Clark
1964 - A.J. Foyt
1963 - Parnelli Jones
1962 - Rodger Ward
1961 - A.J. Foyt
1960 - Jim Rathmann
Indiana, Robert: 6 artist 9 pop artist
painting: 4 Love
Indiana University
athletes: 8 Hoosiers
conference: 6 Big Ten
locale: 4 Gary 6 Kokomo 8 Richmond 9 Fort Wayne, New Albany, South Bend
Indian Head: 4 cent, coin 5 penny
Indian Ocean
archipelago: 7 Comoros
bay: 6 Bengal 7 Delagoa
gulf: 6 Mannar
island: 5 Cocos 6 Comoro 8 Sri Lanka 9 Christmas, Mauritius 10 Madagascar, Seychelles
port: 6 Durban
river to the ~: 4 Juba, Tana 5 Tsana 6 Murray, Rovuma, Ruvuma 7 Limpopo, Zambezi
seaman: 6 lascar 7 lashkar
vessel: 3 dau, dow 4 dhow
wind: 7 monsoon
Indian Outlaw (1994 song)
artist: Tim McGraw
Indian Reservation (1971 song)
artist: Paul Revere and the Raiders
Indian Runner, The (1991 film)
cast: Valeria Golino, David Morse, Viggo Mortensen
director: Sean Penn
Indians: 3 ten 4 team
home: 9 Cleveland
org.: 3 ALC, MLB
rival: ***see*** baseball team
sport: 8 baseball
Indian Summer (1993 film)
cast: Alan Arkin, Matt Craven, Diane Lane
__ Indian Too: 4 I'm an
Indic: 4 Pali, Urdu 5 Hindi 7 Bengali 8 Sanscrit, Sanskrit 9 Sinhalese
lang.: 3 Skr., Skt. 4 Skrt.
indicate: 3 nod, peg, tab, tag 4 bode, give, hint, look, mark, mean, show, sign, wave 5 argue, augur, imply, let on, point, prove, spell 6 advert, attest, denote, evince, record, reveal, signal 7 add up to, bespeak, betoken, connote, display, express, pin down, point to, portend, promise, purport, reflect, signify, specify, suggest 8 announce, bookmark, evidence, intimate, manifest, pinpoint, point out, register, stand for 9 adumbrate, designate, predicate, symbolize, underline 10 illustrate
indication: 3 cue 4 clew, clue, hint, lead, mark, omen, sign, tick, wisp 5 index, proof, token, trace, track 6 augury, herald, signal, symbol 7 auspice, gesture, inkling, portent, presage, symptom, vestige, warning 8 bad vibes, evidence, hallmark, mnemonic, reminder 9 attribute, direction, harbinger, reference, signifier, testimony 10 denotation, directions, expression, forerunner, intimation, prognostic, suggestion
indicative: 7 augural 8 denotive 9 testatory 10 auspicious, denotative, diagnostic, emblematic, evidential, exhibitive, expressive, prognostic, suggestive
indicator: 4 clew, clue, dial, hint, mark, omen, sign 5 gauge, guide, meter, token 6 beacon, signal, symbol 7 pointer, warning 8 gas meter, hallmark 9 predictor 10 prediction
__ indicator: 4 turn 7 leading
indict: 3 sue, tax 4 name 5 blame 6 accuse, charge 7 arraign, censure, impeach 8 denounce 9 castigate, criminate, inculpate, prosecute
indictable: 7 illegal, illicit 8 criminal, unlawful 10 chargeable
indictment: 5 blame, trial 6 charge 7 lawsuit 9 detention, statement 10 accusation, allegation
Indienne: 6 fabric 8 material
__ Indies: 4 East, West
indifference: 5 ennui 6 apathy, laxity, slight, torpor 7 boredom, disdain, neglect 8 coldness, coolness, lethargy, stoicism 9 jadedness
exclamation: 8 whatever
show ~: 5 shrug
indifferent: 3 icy, lax 4 cold, cool, deaf, lazy, logy, so-so 5 aloof, blasé, blind, stoic, stony, tepid 6 amoral, chilly, remote, stolid, stoney 7 callous, distant, glacial, languid, neutral, stoical, unmoved 8 careless, detached, feckless, heedless, listless, lukewarm, mediocre, middling, ordinary, pitiless, scornful, uncaring 9 lethargic, negligent, tolerable, untouched, withdrawn 10 regardless
indifferently: 7 lightly 8 absently, casually, sloppily 10 carelessly, heedlessly
indigence: 4 lack, need, want 6 hunger, misery, penury 7 beggary, poverty, straits 8 distress 9 neediness, privation 10 bankruptcy
indigene: 5 local 6 native 7 citizen, dweller 8 habitant 9 aborigine 10 compatriot, countryman, inhabitant
indigenous: 4 wild 5 local 6 ethnic, inborn, inbred, innate, native 7 connate, endemic, natural 8 domestic, inherent, internal, regional 9 endemical, homegrown, inherited, primitive 10 aboriginal, congenital, connatural, unacquired
indigent: 4 poor 5 broke, needy, sorry 6 bad off, beggar, busted, hard up, ill-off, in need, in want, pauper 7 have-not, pinched 8 badly off, bankrupt, beggarly, deprived, homeless, strapped 9 destitute, insolvent, miserable, moneyless, penniless, penurious 10 down and out, pauperized, straitened
indigestion: 3 gas 5 agita
__ indigestion: 4 acid
indignant: 3 hot, mad 4 hurt, ired, sore 5 angry, cross, het up, huffy, irate, livid, riled, upset, wroth 6 fuming, galled, heated, ireful, miffed, peeved, piqued, raging, raving, red-hot 7 annoyed, boiling, enraged, furious, in a huff, ranting, steamed 8 burned up, choleric, incensed, inflamed, maddened, outraged, up in arms, wrathful 9 impatient, irritated, resentful, seeing red, splenetic, wrought up 10 displeased, freaked out, infuriated, intolerant
be ~: 4 boil, burn, fume, rage, rave 5 storm 6 blow up, see red, seethe 7 bristle, smolder 10 hit the roof
indignation: 3 ire 4 fury, rage 5 anger, pique, wrath 6 animus 7 offense, outrage, umbrage 9 annoyance
indignity: 3 cut 4 snub 6 insult 7 affront, offense 9 blasphemy, contumely, grievance 10 disrespect, opprobrium
indigo: 3 dye 4 anil, blue 5 color, plant 6 flower 7 grayish
relative: ***see*** blue color
__ Indigo: 4 Mood
Indigo Girls: 3 duo
Indio: 4 city, town
locale: 10 California
Indira: 6 Gandhi
attire: 4 sari 5 saree
father: 5 Nehru
son: 5 Rajiv
see also India
indirect: 4 side 5 snaky, tacit 6 sneaky, subtle, zigzag 7 devious, implied, sinuous, virtual 8 circular, tortuous 9 underhand, vicarious 10 collateral, meandering, roundabout, secondhand
indirectly: 7 sideway 8 sideways, sidewise 10 secondhand
let know ~: 4 hint 5 let on 6 allude, hint at 7 suggest 8 intimate, lead up to 9 insinuate
indiscernable: 3 dim 5 vague 6 cloudy, hidden, minute, slight 7 gradual, obscure, shadowy, unclear 8 nebulous
indiscreet: 4 rash 5 brash, hasty 6 stupid, unwary, unwise 7 foolish 8 careless, heedless, reckless, tactless 9 half-baked, impolitic, imprudent, misguided, unadvised, unguarded 10 headstrong, ill-advised, incautious
be ~: 4 blab, blat, tell 5 blurt 6 gossip, let out, reveal, squeal, tattle 7 divulge, let slip 8 disclose, give away
Indiscreet (1958 film)
cast: Ingrid Bergman, Cary Grant
director: Stanley Donen
role: 4 Anna
indiscretion: 4 goof, slip, trip 5 error, fault, folly, gaffe, guilt, lapse 6 bumble, foul-up, miscue, slip-up 7 faux pas, misstep, mistake, stumble 8 rashness
indiscriminate: 6 motley, random, wanton 9 wholesale
__ in Disguise: 4 Judy 5 Devil
indispensable: 3 key, nec. 5 basal, basic, major, vital 6 needed, urgent 7 crucial, needful, pivotal, primary 8 cardinal, integral, material, must-have, required 9 important, mandatory, necessary, requisite

thing: **4** must, need **8** must-have **9** essential, necessity, requisite **10** imperative, obligation, sine qua non

indispose: **3** ail **4** lame, maim **5** lay up, upset **6** sicken, weaken **7** disable, exhaust **8** enervate, enfeeble, paralyse, paralyze, sideline **10** discourage, dishearten

indisposed: **3** ill, low, shy **4** loth, sick **5** loath **6** afraid, ailing, averse, infirm, laid up, poorly, queasy, queazy, sickly, unwell **7** not well, out of it, uneager, unsound **8** below par, diseased, hesitant **9** afflicted, bedridden, reluctant, unwilling **10** out of sorts, uninclined

be ~: **3** ail

indisposition: **3** ill **6** malady **7** ailment, illness **8** distaste, headache, migraine, sickness, weakness **10** hesitation

indisputable: **4** real, sure, true **5** clear, plain **6** actual **7** certain, evident, obvious **8** absolute, accurate, airtight, decisive, in the bag, positive

indisputably: **6** easily **7** clearly **9** going away, hands down, literally

indissoluble: **4** firm **5** fixed, solid **6** stable, steady **7** abiding, binding, lasting **8** constant, enduring

indistinct: **3** dim **4** dark, hazy, pale, thin **5** dusky, faded, faint, foggy, fuzzy, light, mirky, misty, murky, muted, vague **6** arcane, bleary, blurry, cloudy, silent **7** bleared, blurred, cryptic, obscure, shadowy, unclear **8** abstruse, confused, darkened, nebulous, puzzling **9** ambiguous, confusing, cryptical, enigmatic, equivocal, hard to see, illegible, imprecise, inaudible, shapeless, uncertain, unfocused **10** ill-defined, impalpable, indefinite, inexplicit, out of focus, perplexing, unreadable

image: **4** blur

make ~: **4** blur, fade **5** befog, blear, cloud, fog up **7** becloud

indistinctness: **3** fog **4** blur, daze, haze, murk **5** blear, cloud, smear **6** muddle, smudge

indistinguishable: **4** akin, same **5** alike, equal **7** the same **8** fungible **9** identical **10** equivalent, synonymous

__ in Distress, A: **6** Damsel

indite: **3** pen **5** couch, draft, frame, write **6** enjoin, record **7** compose **8** inscribe

indium: **5** metal **7** element

49 for ~: **4** at. no.

indiv.: **4** pers., sing.

individual: **3** man, one, own **4** body, lone, self, sole, soul **5** alone, being, child, human, party, thing, woman **6** entity, mortal, person, proper, signal, single, unique **7** express, oddball, private, special, unalike, unusual, various **8** creature, discrete, distinct, especial, peculiar, personal, separate, singular, solitary, somebody, specific, specimen **9** character, different, exclusive, personage, singleton, something **10** dissimilar, human being, particular, respective

item: **4** unit **5** piece **6** detail, entity, module **7** article, element, section, segment

unspecified ~: **3** one **6** anyone

individualist: **5** loner, rebel **6** egoist

individuality: **4** soul **6** makeup, nature **8** identity

individualize: **4** name **6** detail **7** itemize, pin down, specify **9** stipulate

individually: **4** a pop, each **5** alone, apart **6** apiece, singly, solely **8** one by one **9** piecemeal

individuals: **4** folk **5** folks **6** people

indivisible: **3** one **5** solid, whole **6** atomic, single **8** atomical

literally, ~: **4** atom

Ind. neighbor: **3** Ill., Ken. **4** Mich.

see also Indiana

Indo-__: **5** Aryan

Indochina

country: **4** Laos **5** Burma **7** Myanmar, Vietnam **8** Cambodia, Thailand

language: **3** Lao **4** Thai **10** Vietnamese

native: **3** Tai **4** Laos, part, Thai **7** Vietnam **8** Cambodia, Thailand

__ Indochina: **6** French

indocile: **3** bad **4** wild **6** mulish, unruly, wilful **7** forward, opposed, restive, willful **8** contrary, factious, obdurate, perverse, stubborn **9** obstinate, pig-headed, resistant **10** headstrong, rebellious, refractory, self-willed

indoctrinate: **5** drill, imbue, infix, plant, teach, train **6** ground, infuse, instil, school **7** educate, implant, instill, program **8** initiate, instruct **9** prejudice

Indo-European: **5** Arian, Aryan

language: **5** Oscan

language family: **6** Italic

Indo-Iranian: **5** Arian, Aryan

indolence: **5** sloth **6** acedia, apathy, stupor, torpor **7** inertia, languor **8** dullness, hebetude, idleness, laziness, lethargy, loginess, otiosity **9** faineance, inertness, torpidity **10** stagnation

__ Indolence: **5** Ode on

indolent: **3** lax **4** idle, lazy, logy, slow **5** inert, slack **6** asleep, draggy, otiose, torpid **7** dormant, languid, passive **8** careless, dallying, fainéant, inactive, listless, slothful, sluggish **9** apathetic, do-nothing, leisurely, lethargic, negligent, sedentary, shiftless **10** disengaged, neglectful

be ~: **4** idle, laze, loaf, loll **5** dally, shirk **6** dawdle, loiter, lounge **7** goof off, hang out **8** kill time, lallygag, malinger, slack off, vegetate **9** bum around, do nothing, goldbrick, lie around, waste time **10** dillydally, fool around, knock about

indomitability: **4** grit, will **5** heart, moxie, nerve, pluck, spunk, valor **6** daring, mettle, spirit, starch **7** bravery, courage, heroism, prowess, resolve **8** audacity, backbone, boldness, firmness, gumption, rashness, temerity, tenacity

indomitable: **4** bold, firm, game **5** brave, gutsy, nervy, stoic, stout **6** awless, daring, dogged, gritty, heroic, mighty, plucky, spunky **7** aweless, defiant, doughty, gallant, staunch, stoical, valiant **8** fearless, heroical, intrepid, resolute, stalwart, unafraid, untiring, valorous **9** audacious, dauntless, dreadless, obstinate, undaunted, unfearful **10** courageous, unflagging

Indonesia: **4** isle **6** island, nation **7** country

bay: **6** Sarera

boat: **4** prao, prau, proa

bovine: **4** anoa

capital: **7** Jakarta **8** Djakarta

city: **5** Ambon, Bogor, Depok, Medan **6** Malang, Manado, Padang **7** Bandung, Jakarta, Mataram **8** Bengkulu, Djakarta, Semarang, Surabaya

export: **3** tea

island: **4** Bali, Biak, Java, Laut, Nias, Roti, Savu, Sawu **5** Ceram, Rotti, Spice, Sumba, Timor **6** Borneo, Butung, Lombok, Madura, Serang **7** Celebes, Sumatra **8** Krakatoa, Moluccas, Sulawesi

islands: **3** Aru **4** Aroe, Arru, Leti **5** Letti

money: **3** sen

native: **3** Ata **5** Malay

neighbor: **8** Malaysia

org.: **4** OPEC

primate: **5** orang **7** tarsier

sea: **5** Timor

until 1949: **3** ter. **4** terr. **9** territory

volcano: **5** Kelut, Raung **6** Dukono, Merapi, Semeru, Slamet **7** Kerinci **8** Gamalama

indoor: **8** enclosed

indoors: **6** within **8** enclosed **9** sheltered

In Dreams (1963 song)

artist: Roy Orbison

In Dreams (1999 film)

cast: Stephen Rea

In Dubious Battle

author: John Steinbeck

indubitable: **4** sure, true **5** right **6** actual **7** assured, certain, for sure, genuine **8** absolute, definite, positive **9** veritable

indubitably

see of course

induce: **3** get, put **4** coax, lead, lure, move, spur, sway, urge **5** bring, cause, evoke, impel, lobby, tempt **6** ask for, cajole, effect, incite, kindle, lead to, prompt **7** actuate, bring on, procure, produce, provoke, wheedle, win over **8** convince, engender, generate, inveigle, motivate, occasion, persuade **9** influence, instigate, prevail on, sweet-talk **10** bring about, give rise to, predispose

inducement: **4** bait, goad, hook, lure, spur, urge **5** bribe, cause, prize **6** carrot, come-on, motive, reason, reward **8** occasion, stimulus **9** incentive, sweet talk **10** attraction, enticement, incitement, invitation, temptation

illegal ~: **5** bribe, graft **6** grease, payoff, payola **8** kickback **9** hush money

induct: **5** admit, draft, enrol **6** enlist, enroll, instal **7** install, instate, receive, recruit, swear in **8** initiate, shanghai **9** conscript **10** inaugurate

induction: **5** logic **6** reason **8** judgment **9** accession, beginning, corollary, enrolment, inaugural, inference, reception **10** conclusion, conjecture, deducement, enrollment, initiation, ordination

motor pioneer: **5** Tesla

org.: **3** SSS

unit: **5** gauss

indulge: **4** baby, dote **5** favor, humor, revel, spoil, treat **6** coddle, cosset, dandle, dote on, pamper, pander, permit, please **7** cater to, delight, gratify, immerse, satiate, satisfy, yield to **8** dote upon, give in to, tolerate **9** luxuriate, spoon-feed

don't ~ in: **4** duck, shun, skip, snub **5** avoid, dodge, evade, scorn **6** bypass, eschew, ignore **8** sidestep

in: **2** do **4** like, play **9** partake of

oneself: **4** bask **5** enjoy, revel **6** wallow **7** delight **9** luxuriate

something to ~: **3** yen **4** urge, whim

to excess: **4** cloy, glut, sate **5** gorge, stuff **7** surfeit **8** overfill **10** gormandize

indulgence: **4** orgy **5** favor, leave **6** excess, lenity, luxury **7** babying, freedom, license **8** coddling, courtesy, favoring, hedonism, humoring, kindness, latitude, lenience, leniency, patience, spoiling **9** allowance, attention, endurance, enjoyment, pampering, privilege, satiation, tolerance **10** concession, debauchery, partiality, profligacy, sybaritism, toleration

brief ~: **5** binge, fling, spree

indulgent: **3** lax **4** easy, kind, mild, soft **5** loose **6** doting, gentle, kindly **7** clement, lenient, liberal, ruthful, sparing **8** flexible, gracious, laid-back, merciful, parental, placable, tolerant **9** assuasive, compliant, dissolute, easygoing, excessive, favorable, forgiving, luxurious **10** charitable, forbearing, gratifying, permissive, unexacting, unhardened, voluptuous

be ~: **4** baby, dote **5** cater, spoil **6** coddle

indurate: **3** set **4** bony, cold, gird, hale, hard, iron, tone, wiry **5** beefy, boney, build, burly, enure, hardy, hefty, hunky, husky, inure, lusty, rigid, rocky, shore, steel, stony, stout, tough, train **6** anneal, beef up, brawny, flinty, frigid, gritty, harden, hearty, mighty, ossify, potent, prop up, robust, rugged, season, sinewy, steely, stocky, stoney, strong, sturdy, temper, tone up, virile **7** bolster, brace up, build up, burgeon, calcify, callous, develop, doughty, empower, enhance, fortify, hard-set, petrify, shore up, stiffen, toughen, vitrify **8** accustom, athletic, bourgeon,

IN

buttress, concrete, energize, forceful, granitic, hardened, muscular, obdurate, powerful, puissant, recusant, stalwart, stubborn, vigorous, vitalize 9 acclimate, Atlantean, condition, fossilize, habituate, Herculean, intensify, obstinate, reinforce, strapping, unfeeling, vulcanize, well-built 10 able-bodied, adamantine, caseharden, hardbitten, impenitent, invigorate, redblooded, strengthen

Indus: 5 river 6 valley
city on the ~: 7 Karachi
constellation near ~: 4 Grus
locale: 5 Tibet 6 Xizang 7 Kashmir, Sitsang 8 Cashmere, Pakistan
river to the ~: 5 Kabul 6 Sutlej

industrial: 8 economic 9 automated, technical 10 mechanical, mechanized, vocational

industrialist: 3 mfr. 4 boss, czar 5 baron, mogul 6 tycoon 7 builder, magnate 8 producer

industrious: 4 busy 5 eager 6 active, intent, lively 7 dynamic, earnest, on the go, operose, zealous 8 diligent, sedulous, spirited, studious, tireless 9 assiduous, laborious, motivated
be ~: 4 work 8 plug away
insect: 3 ant, bee
name meaning ~: 5 Emily 6 Amelia

industry: 3 job, mfg. 4 care, toil, work, zeal 5 labor, trade, vigor 6 action, effort, energy 8 activity, business, commerce, exertion, gumption, hard work 9 assiduity, diligence 10 enterprise
captain of ~: 3 CEO 4 czar, exec 5 baron, mogul 6 tycoon 7 magnate 9 executive
watchdog org.: 4 OSHA

Industry is its motto: 4 Utah

indweller: 6 native 7 citizen, denizen 8 resident 10 inhabitant

indwelling: 9 ingrained, intrinsic 10 congenital, connatural

Indy 500
see Indianapolis 500

...in earth, __ is in heaven: 4 as it

inebriant: 4 beer 5 booze, drink, sauce, stock 6 liquor 7 alcohol, liqueur, potable 9 alcoholic, aqua vitae, firewater, hard stuff, moonshine 10 intoxicant

inebriate: 3 sot 4 stew 5 addle, besot, charm, crock, elate, souse, stone 6 fuddle, muddle, pickle, thrill 7 animate, bewitch, enchant, pollute, stupefy 8 befuddle, enspirit, entrance, inspirit

inebriated: 3 lit 5 drunk, tight, tipsy 9 irrigated, plastered

inebriating: 4 hard 6 strong 9 alcoholic, spiritous

inedible: 3 bad 4 sour 5 fetid, moldy, yucky, yukky 6 foetid, putrid, rotten, spoilt, turned 7 spoiled, tainted 9 uneatable 10 disgusting
mouthful: 3 gum 10 chewing gum

I Need Love (1987 song)
artist: LL Cool J

I Need You (1972 song)
artist: America

I Need Your Love Tonight (1959 song)
artist: Elvis Presley

ineffable: 6 divine 8 empyreal, empyrean, ethereal, heavenly 9 celestial, spiritual 10 delightful, incredible, untellable

ineffective: 4 idle, lame, vain, weak 5 inept, unfit 6 feeble, futile, in vain, otiose, paltry 7 inutile, useless 8 feckless, nugatory 9 spineless, worthless 10 unavailing

ineffectual: 3 wan 4 idle, lame, puny, vain, weak 5 empty, inept, mousy, small 6 feeble, futile, little, mousey, paltry, unable 7 inutile, limited, useless 8 feckless, nugatory 9 pointless, powerless, spineless, worthless 10 wishy-washy
make ~: 6 defang, hogtie, weaken
one: 3 oaf 4 boob, clod, nerd, wimp 5 dweeb, klutz 7 nebbish

inefficacious: 4 idle, lame, vain, weak 5 inept 6 feeble, futile, in vain, unable 7 inutile, useless 8 bootless 9 for naught, to no avail

inefficacy: 6 defect 7 failing 8 drawback 9 inability 10 faultiness, inadequacy

inefficient: 4 lame 5 inept 6 faulty, sloppy, unable 8 careless, slipshod, wasteful 9 illogical
be ~: 3 err 4 flub, goof 6 bungle, foul up, goof up, mess up 9 mishandle, mismanage

__ in Egypt: 6 Israel

inelaborate: 5 plain 6 humble, modest, simple, slight 7 limited 9 unadorned

inelastic: 4 firm, iron 5 rigid 6 steely 9 unbending 10 inflexible

inelegant: 5 crass, crude, gross, rough, tacky 6 clumsy, coarse, gauche, vulgar 7 awkward, boorish, unadept, uncouth 8 bungling, homemade, improper, unseemly 9 graceless, makeshift, primitive, tasteless, unrefined 10 amateurish, indelicate, uncultured, ungraceful, unpolished

ineligible: 5 unfit 8 unworthy 10 unequipped, unsuitable

ineluctable: 7 crucial 8 required 9 essential, necessary 10 imperative, obligatory

inept: 3 bad 4 poor, weak 5 dorky, nerdy, unfit 6 clumsy, gauche, klutzy, unable, unwise 7 artless, awkward, labored, unadept, unhandy, useless 8 bumbling, bungling, cloddish, feckless, fumbling, hopeless, inexpert, lubberly, tactless, ungainly 9 all thumbs, graceless, maladroit, unskilled 10 amateurish, unbecoming, undextrous, unskillful
one: 3 oaf 4 boob, clod, nerd, yoyo 5 dweeb 7 nebbish

inequality: 9 disparity, diversity, imbalance, injustice, prejudice, variation 10 difference, unevenness, unfairness, unjustness

inequitable: 6 unfair, unjust 7 unequal

inequity: 5 abuse, wrong 6 injury 8 foul play, nepotism 9 grievance, injustice 10 favoritism, unfairness

inerasable: 7 lasting 8 enduring 9 indelible, ingrained, permanent

inerrant: 4 sure 5 exact 7 certain 8 absolute, accurate, fail-safe, flawless, reliable 9 faultless, foolproof 10 dependable, impeccable, infallible

inert: 3 lax 4 idle, lazy, logy, numb, slow 5 quiet, slack, still 6 asleep, draggy, frozen, latent, leaden, static, stolid, torpid 7 dormant, languid, out cold, passive 8 immobile, inactive, indolent, lifeless, listless, slothful, sluggish, stagnant, unmoving 9 impassive, inanimate, insensate, lethargic, not moving, quiescent, sedentary 10 disengaged, insentient, motionless, stationary, stock-still, unreactive
be ~: 4 idle, laze, loaf 5 sleep 8 languish, stagnate, vegetate
gas: 4 neon 5 argon, radon, xenon 6 helium 7 krypton
material: 6 filler

inertia: 5 sloth 6 acedia, apathy, stupor, torpor 7 languor, laxness 8 doldrums, idleness, laziness, lethargy, otiosity, slowness 9 faineance, indolence, torpidity 10 inactivity, stagnation

inertness: 5 sloth 6 apathy, torpor 7 languor 8 dullness, inaction, lethargy 9 indolence, torpidity 10 inactivity

inerudite: 9 unlearned 10 illiterate, uncultured, uneducated, unschooled

inescapable: 4 sure 5 fated 7 certain, visible 8 destined 9 necessary, pervasive

in esse: 8 actually

inessential: 5 extra 7 surplus 8 needless 9 redundant

inestimable: 4 rare, vast 6 untold 7 endless, immense 8 infinite, manifold, peerless, precious, valuable 9 priceless

I never __ man...: 4 met a

I never __ purple cow: 4 saw a

I Never Loved a Man (1967 song)
artist: Aretha Franklin

I Never Sang for My Father: 4 play
author: Robert Anderson

I never saw __: 5 a moor

__ in Every Port: 5 A Girl

inevitable: 4 sure 5 fated 6 doomed 7 assured, certain, decided, decreed, settled 8 destined, eventual, in the bag, ordained 9 automatic, impending, necessary 10 compulsory, determined, for certain, inexorable, obligatory, prescribed, undeniable, undoubtful
the ~: 4 fate 5 karma 6 kismet 7 destiny

inevitably: 6 always, surely 7 for sure 9 certainly, decidedly 10 definitely, for certain, inexorably, invariably, positively

inexact: 3 lax, off 5 false, loose, rough, wrong 6 faulty, untrue 7 general, in error, off-base, unsound 8 specious 9 erroneous, imperfect, imprecise, incorrect 10 fallacious, inaccurate, indefinite, unspecific
be ~: 3 fib, lie 5 fudge 7 deceive
phrase: 4 or so

in excelsis __: 3 deo

inexcusable: 3 bad, low 5 cruel, wrong 6 unfair, unjust 7 immoral 8 criminal, grievous, improper 9 dishonest, unethical 10 unsporting

inexhaustible: 7 endless, lasting 8 enduring, infinite, tireless, untiring 9 limitless, plentiful, unfailing

inexorable: 4 sure 5 cruel, harsh, rigid, stern, stiff, stony 6 severe, stoney 7 adamant, dead set 8 destined, immobile, ironclad, obdurate, pitiless, resolute, stubborn 9 immovable, merciless, necessary, obstinate, unbending, unmovable, unpitying 10 adamantine, compulsory, implacable, inevitable, inflexible, relentless, set in stone, unyielding

inexpedient: 4 dumb 6 stupid, unwise 7 foolish, harmful 8 untimely 9 misguided 10 ill-advised

inexpensive: 3 low 5 cheap 6 budget, low-end, modest 7 bargain, cut-rate, low-cost, nominal 8 moderate 9 dirt-cheap, low-priced 10 affordable, dime a dozen, economical, reasonable
in French: 9 bon marché

inexperience: 5 youth 7 naiveté 9 greenness, ignorance, innocence

inexperienced: 3 new, raw 4 naif 5 fresh, green, inapt, inept, naive, unfit, young 6 boyish, callow, simple 7 amateur, puerile, untried, verdant 8 ignorant, immature, inexpert, innocent, unversed, youthful 9 beardless, untrained, untutored, unworldly
one: 3 pup 4 naif, tiro, tyro 5 puppy 8 untested
with: 5 new at

inexpert: 3 lay 5 crude, green, inept, unfit 6 clumsy, simple 7 awkward, unadept, unhandy 8 bumbling, bungling, fumbling 9 maladroit, unskilled, untrained, untutored 10 amateurish, blundering, lefthanded, unschooled, unseasoned, unskillful

inexpiable: 3 bad 4 evil, vile 5 awful, black, grave 6 mortal, sinful, wicked 7 capital, heinous, serious

inexplicable: 3 odd 5 eerie, vague, weird 6 spooky 7 strange, uncanny 8 baffling, peculiar, puzzling

inexplicit: 4 hazy 5 fuzzy, vague 7 evasive 9 ambiguous, deceptive, enigmatic, equivocal, imprecise, uncertain 10 ill-defined, indefinite, indistinct, misleading

inexpressible: 6 silent, untold 7 amazing, strange 8 wondrous

inexpressive: 4 cold, dead, dull, flat 5 blank, stony 6 boring, stoney 7 deadpan, passive, unmoved 8 lifeless

inextinguishable: 7 endless, eternal, lasting, undying 8 immortal, timeless, unending 9 ceaseless, incessant, perennial, permanent, perpetual, unceasing

inextricable: 6 knotty 7 complex, tangled 8 baffling, involved, puzzling

Inez: 4 Foxx

infallible: 4 sure, true 5 exact, right 7 certain, perfect 8 absolute, accurate, fail-safe, flawless, inerrant, reliable, surefire, unerring 9 agreeable, apodictic, effective, effectual, faultless, foolproof, unfailing 10 acceptable, dependable, impeccable, omniscient, unbeatable, undoubtful

infamous: 3 bad 4 dark, evil, foul, vile 5 shady 6 odious, rotten, wicked 7 corrupt, hateful, heinous, ignoble, vicious 8 ill-famed, shameful, shocking 9 miscreant, monstrous, nefarious, notorious, well-known 10 outrageous, villainous

infamy: 4 evil 5 guilt, odium, shame 7 obloquy, scandal 8 atrocity, contempt, disgrace, dishonor, ignominy, iniquity, villainy 9 disrepute, ill repute, notoriety 10 corruption, opprobrium, wickedness

__ Infamy: 5 Day of

infancy: 4 dawn, rise 5 birth, start 6 cradle 7 arising, genesis 8 babyhood, nascence 9 beginning, childhood, emergence 10 beginnings, conception

infant: 3 kid, tot 4 babe, baby 5 bairn, child, minor, young 6 little, rug rat, wee one 7 babyish, bambino, nascent, neonate, newborn, puerile, toddler, young 'un 8 childish, juvenile, nonvoter, original, youthful 9 little one
- **abandoned ~:** 4 waif 9 foundling
- **attention-getter:** 3 cry, wah 4 bawl
- **bed:** 4 crib 6 cradle 8 bassinet
- **fare:** 4 milk 7 formula 8 baby food
- **name meaning ~:** 6 Thelma
- **sound:** 3 goo 6 goo-goo, gurgle
- **tend to an ~:** 4 burp, feed 7 babysit
- **upset:** 5 colic
- **wear:** 6 bonnet, bootee, bootie, diaper
- **word:** 3 mom 4 dada, mama 5 mamma

infantile: 7 babyish, kiddish, puerile 8 childish, immature, juvenile

infantry: 3 GIs 4 army 6 grunts 8 dogfaces, soldiers
- **action:** 4 fray 6 attack, battle, charge, combat 7 warfare 8 fighting, skirmish 9 encounter 10 engagement
- **fare:** 4 Spam 7 rations
- **Greek ~:** 6 evzone
- **weapon:** 5 rifle 7 bayonet

infantryman: 2 GI 5 GI Joe, grunt 7 dogface, soldier

infatuate: 5 besot, charm, lover 6 allure, enamor, obsess 7 beguile, bewitch, enthral, inthral 8 enthrall, inthrall, stultify 9 captivate, fascinate

infatuated: 3 mad 4 gaga 5 crazy 6 in love, loving 7 charmed, far gone, smitten 8 beguiled, besotted, obsessed 9 bewitched, possessed 10 captivated, enraptured, enthralled, fascinated, spellbound
- **by:** 6 mad for 8 mad about 9 far gone on 10 crazy about

infatuation: 4 love, rage 5 craze, crush, furor, mania 7 passion 8 fixation 9 obsession

Infatuation (1984 song)
- **artist:** Rod Stewart

infeasible: 7 dubious 8 doubtful, hopeless, undoable, unlikely 10 impossible, out of reach

infect: 5 spoil, taint 6 blight, defile, poison 7 corrupt, make ill, pollute, vitiate

infected: 3 ill 4 sick 5 dirty, germy 7 corrupt 10 unsanitary
- **become ~ with:** 3 get 5 catch 7 develop 8 contract

infection: 3 bug 6 plague, poison 7 disease 8 epidemic, impurity 9 contagion
- **cause:** 4 germ 5 staph, strep, virus
- **type of ~:** 5 viral

infectious: 5 viral 8 catching, epidemic, virulent 9 pestilent, spreading 10 contagious, epidemical, inoculable
- **organism:** 3 bug 4 germ 7 microbe

infelicitous: 3 sad 4 poor 5 bleak, inapt, woful 6 gauche, gloomy, pained, woeful 7 awkward, forlorn, hapless, unhappy, unlucky 8 desolate, hopeless, ill-timed, improper, pitiable, sinister, wretched

infelicity: 3 woe 5 gloom 6 misery, sorrow, trials 7 bad luck, chagrin, despair, sadness, travail 8 hardship, troubles

infelt: 5 frank 6 candid 7 earnest, genuine, sincere 8 truthful 9 guileless, unfeigned 10 forthright, on the level

infer: 4 draw, hint 5 educe, glean, guess, judge, think 6 assume, deduce, derive, gather, intuit, reason, reckon, take it 7 imagine, make out, mention, presume, suggest, suppose, surmise 8 arrive at, conclude, construe, intimate 9 ascertain, interpret, reason out, speculate 10 conjecture, presuppose, understand
- **ender:** 4 ence 6 ential

inferable: 6 likely 9 deducible, derivable 10 consequent

inference: 5 educt, logic 6 reason 7 surmise, thought 8 allusion, overtone 9 corollary, deduction, induction 10 assumption, conclusion, conjecture

inferential: 6 cogent 7 a priori, logical, tenable 8 analytic, methodic, rational 9 deductive 10 methodical

inferior: 3 bad, low, off 4 foul, grim, hack, junk, less, mean, poor, punk 5 awful, below, cheap, lousy, lower, lowly, minor, scrub, small, sorry, under, woful, worse 6 cheapo, cheesy, common, crumby, crummy, dismal, horrid, humble, lesser, odious, rotten, second, shabby, shoddy, two-bit, woeful 7 accurst, baleful, baneful, beastly, doleful, ghastly, ignoble, subject, wanting 8 accursed, déclassé, dreadful, el cheapo, God-awful, grievous, horrible, low-grade, mediocre, middling, ordinary, shameful, stinking, terrible, wretched 9 abhorrent, appalling, atrocious, defective, deficient, execrable, fifth-rate, frightful, insidious, loathsome, miserable, offensive, revolting, secondary, third-rate 10 abominable, despicable, detestable, disastrous, fifth-class, fourth-rate, horrendous, low-quality, second-rate, third-class
- **of ~ quality:** 4 junk 5 cheap 7 schlock
- **product:** 3 dog 4 junk 5 trash, tripe 7 schlock
- **to:** 5 below, under 7 beneath 10 unworthy of
- **treat as ~:** 5 deign, stoop 6 demean 7 stoop to 9 patronize 10 condescend, look down on, talk down to

inferiority complex coiner: 5 Adler

infernal: 4 dark, evil 5 curst, stark 6 cursed, cussed, damned, nether, savage, wicked 7 accurst, blasted, demonic, hellish, satanic 8 accursed, daemonic, damnable, devilish, diabolic, fiendish 9 demonical, execrable, monstrous, nefarious, satanical 10 diabolical, malevolent

inferno: 4 fire, hell, pyre 5 Hades 10 underworld

Inferno, The: 4 poem 5 verse
- **division:** 5 canto
- **starter:** 3 nel
- **writer:** 5 Dante

inferred: 5 tacit 6 subtle, unsaid 7 implied 8 unvoiced 10 derivative, understood

infertile: 3 dry 4 sere 6 barren, desert, effete 7 sterile 8 infecund 9 exhausted, fruitless 10 unfruitful

infest: 6 abound, invade, riddle 7 overrun, pervade 10 run through

infestation: 6 blight

infested: 4 rife 5 mothy 7 overrun, profuse, rampant, replete, teeming 8 abundant, swarming 9 abounding, pervasive, prevalent

infidel: 5 pagan 7 atheist, heathen, heretic, sceptic, skeptic 8 agnostic 10 unbeliever

infidelity: 7 falsity 9 duplicity, falseness, treachery, two-timing 10 dishonesty, disloyalty, untrueness

infield
- **corner:** 4 base, home
- **covering:** 4 tarp
- **hit:** 4 bunt 5 bloop
- **stat:** 2 DP 6 assist, putout

infielder fluff: 5 error 6 bobble

infiltrate: 3 mix 4 soak 5 crack, enter, tinge 7 creep in, get into, sneak in 8 move into, pass into, permeate, worm into 9 insinuate, interject, penetrate, percolate 10 adulterate

infiltration: 4 raid 5 foray 6 attack, breach 7 assault, osmosis, transit 8 invasion, trespass 9 onslaught

infiltrator: 3 spy 4 mole 5 agent

in fine __: 6 fettle

infinite: 3 big 4 vast 5 great 6 cosmic, eonian, myriad, untold 7 endless, eternal, undying 8 absolute, almighty, cosmical, spacious, unending 9 boundless, countless, limitless, perpetual, unbounded, unlimited 10 innumerous, unnumbered, without end

infinite __: 6 baffle, series 7 decimal, product, regress

Infinite Plan, The
- **author:** Isabel Allende

infinitesimal: 3 wee 4 puny, tiny 5 bitty, small, teeny 6 atomic, little, minute, teensy 8 atomical, atomlike 9 itsy-bitsy, itty-bitty 10 teeny-weeny

Infiniti: 3 car 4 auto 6 import
- **alternative:** *see* automobile

__ infinitive: 5 split

infinitude: 8 enormity, hugeness, vastness 9 immensity

infinitum, ad: 5 no end 7 forever

infinity: 4 time 5 space 9 immensity, largeness, multitude

infirm: 3 ill 4 puny, sick, weak 5 anile, frail, shaky, slack 6 ailing, anemic, feeble, laid up, sickly, unwell, wabbly, wobbly 7 anaemic, invalid, languid, rickety, unsound 8 unsteady 9 afflicted, bedridden, doddering, enfeebled, faltering, powerless, unhealthy 10 indisposed

infirmary: 6 clinic 7 hospice, sick bay 8 hospital

infirmity: 3 ill 6 malady, unease 7 ailment, disease, frailty, illness, malaise 8 debility, disorder, sickness, syndrome, weakness 9 complaint, condition, fragility, frailness, ill health 10 affliction, disability, feebleness, sickliness, unwellness

__-in, first-out: 4 last 5 first

infix: 5 embed, imbed, imbue, lodge, rivet 6 fasten, infuse, inject, insert, instil 7 drive in, engrain, engrave, implant, impress, imprint, ingrain, instill 9 inculcate

in flagrante __: 7 delicto

inflame: 3 vex 4 fire, gall, rile, roil, stir 5 anger, annoy, chafe, grate, hop up, light, rouse, steam 6 arouse, enrage, excite, fire up, foment, ignite, incite, kindle, madden, rankle, whip up, work up 7 agitate, ferment, incense, inspire, provoke, steam up 8 enspirit, inspirit, irritate 9 aggravate, impassion, infuriate, instigate, stimulate 10 exacerbate, exasperate, intoxicate

inflamed: 3 hot, mad, red 4 ired, sore 5 angry, cross, huffy, irate, livid, puffy, riled, wroth 6 fuming, ireful, raging, raving, red-hot, tender 7 angered, enraged, furious, painful, ranting, swollen, violent 8 choleric, inspired, vehement, volcanic, white-hot, wrathful 9 indignant, irritated, resentful, splenetic 10 freaked out, infuriated, passionate

inflamer: 7 fanatic, hellion, hothead, inciter 8 agitator, fomenter 9 demagogue, firebrand 10 incendiary, instigator, politician

__ in flames: 4 go up

inflammation: 4 pain, rash 6 pimple 7 redness 8 swelling
- **joint ~:** 4 gout 9 arthritis
- **(suffix):** 4 -itis

inflate: 3 pad 4 fill, grow, puff, pump 5 bloat, boost, exalt, raise, swell, widen 6 aerate, beef up, blow up, dilate, expand, puff up, pump up 7 amplify, augment, balloon, broaden, build up, burgeon, distend, enlarge, magnify, puff out,

IN

stiffen, stretch, swell up **8** bourgeon, flesh out, heighten, increase, lengthen **9** intumesce, overstate **10** aggrandize, exaggerate

inflated: 3 big **4** vain **5** puffy, tumid, windy, wordy **6** prolix, turgid **7** fustian, hyped up, pompous, stilted, swollen, unterse, verbose **9** bombastic, high-flown, overblown **10** rhetorical

feeling: 3 ego **6** egoism **7** egotism

inflater: 4 pump

inflation: 4 hike, rise **7** buildup **8** increase, swelling **9** euphemism, expansion, extension, puffiness, recession **10** depression, distension, escalation, floridness

meas.: 3 CPI, psi

protection: 5 hedge

inflationary ___: 6 spiral

inflect: 4 vary **5** alter **6** change, intone, modify **7** decline **8** modulate, vocalize **9** conjugate

inflection: 4 tone **5** pitch, voice **6** accent, timbre **8** delivery, locution, tonality **9** variation **10** intonation, modulation

inflexibility: 5 rigor **6** starch **8** firmness, tautness, tenacity **9** toughness

inflexible: 3 set **4** firm, hard, iron, taut **5** balky, bossy, cruel, fixed, picky, rigid, stern, stiff, stony, tight, tough **6** dogged, flinty, mulish, narrow, ornery, severe, steely, stoney, strict, wilful, wooden **7** adamant, austere, decided, diehard, hardset, piggish, precise, Spartan, starchy, staunch, willful **8** contrary, despotic, exacting, hard-line, ironclad, obdurate, perverse, resolute, rigorous, starched, straight, stubborn **9** demanding, draconian, hidebound, immovable, immutable, impliable, inelastic, iron-jawed, obstinate, pigheaded, steadfast, stringent, tenacious, unbending, unpliable, unsparing **10** adamantine, despotical, determined, hardbitten, implacable, inexorable, intolerant, invariable, iron-fisted, iron-willed, no-nonsense, oppressive, relentless, tyrannical, unswayable, unyielding

inflict: 3 put **4** deal **5** apply, exact, force, visit, wreak **6** impose **7** deal out, deliver, mete out, subject **8** dispense **9** force upon **10** administer

infliction: 4 load **5** curse, worry **6** burden, ordeal **7** nemesis, penalty, scourge, torment, torture, trouble **8** disaster

inflictive: 5 penal **8** punitive

in-flight

announcement: 3 ETA **8** altitude

offering: 4 meal **5** drink, movie

inflorescence: 3 bud **5** bloom **6** floret, flower **7** blossom

inflow: 5 draft **6** afflux, feeder, influx **9** tributary

influence: 3 get **4** bend, bias, coax, drag, hold, lead, mold, move, pull, push, rule, sell, snow, sway, tint, turn, urge **5** act on, alter, bribe, budge, clout, force, get at, get to, guide, impel, juice, lobby, orbit, power, reach, reign, rouse, shape, slant, steer, swing, tempt **6** access, affect, agency, compel, credit, direct, effect, entrée, grow on, impact, incite, induce, manage, muscle, weight **7** act upon, channel, command, control, implant, impress, inspire, potence, potency, promote, squeeze, win over **8** dominion, grow upon, guidance, impact on, jaundice, leverage, override, overrule, persuade, pressure, prestige, purchase **9** advantage, argue into, authority, brainwash, determine, direction, dominance, instigate, magnetism, prejudice, prevail on, supremacy **10** ascendance, ascendancy, ascendence, ascendency, domination, importance, impression, leadership, manipulate, predispose, prominence, reputation

have ~: 4 rank, rate **5** count **6** matter

improperly: 5 bribe, get to

pervading ~: 4 aura **10** atmosphere

sphere of ~: 4 area **5** ambit, orbit, range **6** domain **8** dominion

try to ~: 4 coax, urge **5** lobby, press **6** lean on **8** pressure

under the ~: 3 lit **4** high **5** tight, tipsy

influential: 3 big **4** high **5** major **6** cogent, famous, moving, potent, strong **7** guiding, telling, weighty **8** dominant, powerful **9** important

one: 3 VIP **5** mover, nabob

people: 5 elite

influenza: 3 bug, flu **5** virus **6** grippe

influx: 4 flow, rush, wave **5** surge **6** inflow, stream **7** arrival, ingress, traffic **8** entrance, invasion **9** inpouring, intrusion, upwelling **10** inundation

info: 3 tip **4** data, dirt, dope, line, news, poop **5** facts, scoop **6** advice, earful, gossip, notice, report, skinny, wisdom **7** lowdown, message, tidings **8** learning, the goods **9** erudition, knowledge

info-gathering

mission: 5 recon

org.: 3 CIA, FBI

infomercial: 2 ad **5** promo

phrase: 5 try it **6** act now **7** call now

infomercials: 3 ads

in for ___ awakening: 5 a rude

inform: 3 say **4** post, sing, talk, tell, warn **5** alert, break, brief, cue in, edify, prime, spill, teach **6** advise, clue in, direct, fill in, ground, impart, notify, report, school, tip off, update **7** apprise, apprize, caution, counsel, educate, let in on, let know **8** acquaint, advise of, forewarn, instruct, relate to **9** enlighten, irradiate, touch base **10** illuminate, send word to

on: 3 rat **6** betray, finger, give up, squeal, turn in

informal: 4 cool, easy, free, homy **5** homey, loose, plain **6** breezy, casual, chatty, colloq., folksy, mellow, simple, slangy **7** natural, outdoor, relaxed, unfussy **8** down home, everyday, familiar, fireside, intimate, laid back, outgoing **9** easygoing, extempore, idiomatic **10** colloquial, off-the-cuff, unofficial

usage: 4 cant **5** argot, lingo **6** jargon, patois, pidgin **7** dialect **10** street talk, vernacular

informality: 4 ease **10** simplicity

informally: 5 ad-lib **9** extempore, on the side **10** off the cuff

informant: 3 rat **5** namer **6** canary, snitch, source, tattle **7** accuser, monitor, stoolie, tattler, tipster **8** betrayer **10** taleteller

information: 3 tip **4** data, dirt, dope, line, lore, news, word **5** facts, light, proof, scoop, thing **6** advice, earful, notice, report, tipoff, wisdom **7** lowdown, message, pointer, tidings **8** evidence, learning, material **9** testimony **10** literature

acquire ~: 4 read **5** glean, learn, study **6** absorb, pick up **7** find out

agency: 6 bureau

bit of ~: 3 tip **4** fact **5** datum

conductor: 5 nerve

digital ~ carrier: 7 databus

extract ~: 4 milk **7** debrief

give ~: 3 tip **5** brief **6** clue in, tip off

give wrong ~: 3 fib, lie **7** cover up, deceive, mislead **8** misguide, misstate **9** misdirect, misinform **10** lead astray

inside ~: 3 tip **4** dope **6** tipoff

seek ~: 3 ask **5** refer **7** enquire, inquire

seeker: 5 asker

share ~ with: 5 let in

source: 3 Net, Web **4** oper. **5** CD/ROM **7** library **8** Internet, operator **9** reference **10** dictionary

store ~: 4 file **5** enter **6** record **7** archive, catalog, put away **8** document, preserve, tabulate

unit: 3 bit **4** byte **8** gigabyte, megabyte

Information, ___!: 6 Please

informational meeting: 5 Q and A

Information, Please!: 9 radio show

Information, The

author: Martin Amis

informative: 5 newsy **6** chatty, social, useful **7** gossipy, helpful **10** newsworthy

informed: 3 hep, hip **4** onto, wise **5** aware, privy, savvy **6** au fait, posted, versed, wise to, with it **7** abreast, knowing, mindful, tuned in, versant **8** familiar, profound, sensible **9** au courant, cognizant, in the know, in the loop, judicious, plugged in **10** conversant

about: 4 up on **5** hep to, hip to

be ~ of: 4 hear, know **5** learn

stay ~: 6 keep up

informer: 3 rat, spy **4** fink, nark **5** namer, sneak **6** canary, tattle **7** accuser, stoolie, tattler, tipster, traitor **8** betrayer, fat mouth **10** taleteller, tattletale

British ~: 4 nark

turn ~: 4 sing **5** rat on, spill **6** betray, expose, fink on, give up, squeal **7** sell out **8** give away

Informer, The

author: Liam O'Flaherty

infra: 5 below, under **7** beneath **8** less than **10** underneath

opposite: 5 ultra

infra ___: 3 dig

___ infra: 4 vide

infract: 3 err, sin **5** break, lapse **6** breach **7** disobey, violate **9** go against **10** contravene, transgress

infraction: 3 sin **4** foul, slip **5** crime, error, lapse, wrong **6** breach **7** faux pas, offense **8** breaking, trespass **9** injustice, veniality, violation **10** illegality

in baseball: 4 balk

in basketball: 4 foul **7** palming

in bowling: 4 foul

in football: 7 holding, offside **8** clipping

in hockey: 5 icing **7** hooking, penalty **8** tripping

infrangible: 4 holy **6** divine, sacred **7** blessed **8** hallowed **9** enshrined **10** sanctified

infrared

light: 4 lamp

radiation: 4 heat

infrastructure: 4 base, root **5** basis, cadre **7** footing, support

infrequency: 6 rarity **7** fewness **8** rareness, scarcity **10** sparseness

infrequent: 3 few, occ. **4** rare **5** occas. **6** casual, meager, scarce, seldom, sparse **7** limited, several, unusual **8** far apart, isolated, sporadic, uncommon **9** irregular, scattered, spasmodic **10** occasional, sporadical

infrequently: 6 hardly, little, rarely, seldom **8** scarcely **10** hardly ever

infringe: 5 break **6** invade, meddle **7** presume, trample, violate **8** trespass **9** interrupt

on: 5 poach, usurp **6** butt in **8** displace **10** dispossess, plagiarize

infringement: 4 raid **5** drive, foray, sally **6** breach, inroad, sortie **7** evasion, ingress, misdeed, outrage, seizure **8** inequity, invasion, trespass **9** violation

___ in front!: 4 Down

in full ___: 5 swing

___ in full: 4 paid

infuriate: 3 ire **4** rile **5** anger **6** enrage, madden, tee off **7** enflame, incense, inflame, outrage, provoke **8** irritate **9** aggravate **10** exacerbate, exasperate

infuriated

be ~: 4 boil, fume, rage, rave **5** steam **6** blow up, rear up, see red, seethe **7** bristle, flare up **10** get excited

see also angry

infuriating: 5 pesky, pesty **7** irksome **9** vexatious **10** bothersome, nettlesome

infuriation: 3 ire **4** rage **5** anger, pique **6** choler **7** dudgeon, outrage **8** rabidity, vexation **9** petulance

infuse: 3 mix **4** brew, lade, load, soak **5** color, imbue, infix, steep **6** embrue, flavor, imbrue, impart, instil, invest **7** animate, breathe, engrain, implant, ingrain, inspire, instill, pervade **8** permeate, saturate **9** inculcate, inoculate, insinuate, introduce

infusion: 3 dip **4** bath, brew, soak **5** stain, tinge **6** flavor, liquor **8** color-

ing, steeping, tincture **9** immersion, injection **10** permeation, submersion
__ in G: **6** Minuet
Inga: **7** Swenson
Ingalls: **5** Laura
ingathering: **5** cache **7** harvest
__ in Gaza: **7** Eyeless
Inge: **6** Morath **7** William
Ingels, Marty
spouse: Shirley Jones
ingenious: **3** apt, sly **4** deft, neat **5** canny, fresh, nifty, novel, sharp, slick, smart **6** adroit, artful, astute, brainy, bright, clever, crafty, daedal, gifted, habile, shifty, shrewd, subtle **7** cunning, knowing, unusual **8** artistic, creative, dextrous, inspired, original, readable, skillful, talented **9** astucious, brilliant, deviceful, dexterous, inventive **10** artistical, discerning, expressive, innovative, innovatory
ingénue: **4** naif, role **6** player **7** actress
like an ~: **4** naif **5** naïve **6** demure
ingenuity: **3** art, wit **4** wits **5** craft, flair, skill **6** acumen, brains, talent **7** ability **8** gumption, judgment, resource **9** dexterity, smartness **10** cleverness
ingenuous: **4** naif, open **5** frank, green, naive, plain **6** candid, honest, simple, square **7** artless, natural, sincere, unjaded, up-front **8** innocent, trustful, trusting, truthful, unartful **9** childlike, guileless, outspoken, unguarded, unstudied, unworldly **10** free-spoken, unaffected, unreserved, unschooled
ingenuousness: **7** naiveté **9** greenness
Inger: **7** Stevens
Ingersoll-__: **4** Rand
ingest: **3** eat **4** down, take **5** drink, sop up **6** absorb, devour, digest, gather, imbibe, osmose, soak up, suck up **7** consume, partake, scarf up, swallow **8** chow down, gulp down, pack away **9** scarf down **10** assimilate
opposite: **5** egest
Inge, William: **6** writer **9** dramatist **10** playwright
dog: **5** Sheba
nickname: The Gloomy Dean
work: Bus Stop
Christian Mysticism
Come Back, Little Sheba
The Dark at the Top of the Stairs
Good Luck, Miss Wyckoff
The Last Pad
A Loss of Roses
Picnic
Splendor in the Grass
Summer Brave
Where's Daddy?
ingle: **6** hearth **8** fireside **9** fireplace
ender: **4** nook
__ inglese: **5** zuppa
Inglewood: **4** city, town
locale: **10** California, Washington
inglorious: **5** shady **6** humble, shoddy **7** ignoble **8** shameful, unworthy
ingloriousness: **5** odium, shame **6** infamy, malice **7** lowness, treason **8** disgrace, dishonor, vileness

Inglourious Basterds (2009 film)
cast: Christoph Waltz
__ in glove: **4** hand
Ingmar: **7** Bergman
collaborator: **4** Sven
protégé: **3** Liv
-ing, noun ending in: **6** gerund
in good __: **4** part, time
in good faith in Latin: **8** bona fide
__ in good health!: **5** Use it
__ in good stead: **5** stand
__ in good time: **3** all
ingot: **3** bar **4** slab **5** block, metal
ingrain: **3** fix **4** etch **5** embed, imbed, imbue, inbue, infix, lodge, rivet, steep, teach, train **6** infuse, inject, instil **7** implant, impress, imprint, instill **9** inculcate, insinuate, introduce, pound into **10** hammer into
ingrained: **5** fixed **6** etched, inborn, inbred, innate, rooted **7** built-in, chronic, infixed **8** habitual **9** chronical, confirmed, implanted, indelible, intrinsic **10** congenital, deep-rooted, deep-seated, habituated, hereditary, indwelling, in the blood, inveterate
activity: **5** habit
Ingram: **3** Rex **5** James **6** Luther
Ingram, James
song: Baby, Come to Me (1982)
I Don't Have the Heart (1990)
Somewhere Out There (1987)
ingratiate: **5** charm **6** endear **9** captivate, get in with, insinuate
oneself to: **3** woo **5** court, toady **6** kowtow **7** flatter, truckle **8** butter up, fawn over
ingratiating: **4** nice, oily **5** suave **6** smooth **7** candied
ingredient: **4** item, part **6** factor **7** element, feature **8** material **9** component
__ ingredient: **4** main **6** active
ingredients: **6** recipe **7** fixings **8** contents
Ingres, Jean: **6** artist, French **7** painter
inspirer: Edgar Degas
ingress: **3** way **4** adit, door, gate, hall, lane, path, road **5** enter, entry, foyer, hatch, lobby, means, porch, route, stile, way in **6** access, arcade, avenue, course, entrée, influx, inroad, portal, street, wicket **7** doorway, gallery, gangway, gateway, hallway, highway, opening, passage, pathway, portico, postern, roadway, walkway **8** anteroom, aperture, approach, corridor, driveway, entrance, entryway, invasion **9** admission, boulevard, intrusion, penetrate, threshold, turnstile, vestibule **10** admittance, passageway
Ingrid: **6** Thulin **7** Bergman
daughter: **3** Pia **8** Isabella
role: **4** Ilsa **5** Golda
__ in Grouchland: **4** Elmo
in-group: **3** set **4** clan, club, gang, ring **5** cabal, crowd, elite **6** circle, clique, outfit **7** coterie, faction
ingurgitate: **4** gulp **5** quaff **6** absorb, guzzle, imbibe **7** consume
inhabit: **5** dwell **6** inhere, live at, live in, locate, occupy, reside, settle, tenant **7** dwell at, dwell in, lodge in, sojourn **8** populate, reside in

inhabitable: **7** livable **8** liveable
inhabitant: **5** liver, local, voter **6** native, renter, roomer, tenant **7** citizen, denizen, dweller, resider, settler **8** colonist, indigene, occupant, resident **9** aborigine, addressee, incumbent, indweller **10** autochthon
locale: **4** digs, home **5** abode, house, place **7** lodging **8** domicile, dwelling, quarters **9** residence
of (suffix): **3** -ese, -ite, -ote
inhabitants: **4** folk **5** folks **6** people **7** country **10** population
inhalation: **4** drag, gasp, gulp, puff, toot **5** aroma, sniff, snort **6** breath **7** sniffle, snuffle **9** breathing **10** aspiration
combining form: **4** anem- **5** anemo-
involuntary ~: **3** hic
inhale: **3** eat **4** bolt, drag, gasp, gulp, puff, take **5** smell, smoke, sniff, snort, whiff **6** devour, draw in, gobble, guzzle, suck in, suck up, take in **7** breathe, consume, inspire, respire, swallow **8** wolf down **9** breathe in, scarf down **10** eat quickly, get some air
inhaler target: **6** asthma **10** congestion
__ in hand: **3** cap, hat **4** bird
__-in-hand: **4** four
__ in Harlem: **5** A Rage
inharmonious: **4** flat **5** harsh **6** atonal, off-key **7** grating, jarring, raucous **8** clashing, factious, jangling, negative, strident, tuneless **9** dissonant, unmusical
inharmoniousness: **5** clash **6** racket **7** discord **8** conflict, jangling, variance
inhere: **4** stay **5** abide, dwell **6** belong, make up, reside **7** inhabit
inherent: **4** born **5** basic **6** inbred, innate, latent, native **7** implied, natural, organic, radical **8** implicit **9** essential, innermost, potential **10** deep-seated, indigenous
inherently: **5** per se **8** by nature, innately **9** basically
inherit: **3** get, own **4** gain **6** obtain **7** acquire, receive, succeed **8** accede to, come into, take over **10** fall heir to
inheritance: **6** devise, estate, legacy **7** bequest **8** heirloom, heritage, property **9** patrimony **10** birthright
document: **4** will
factor: **4** gene
Inheritance, The
author: Louisa May Alcott
inherited: **6** native **9** ancestral **10** congenital, connatural, indigenous
inheritor: **4** cion, heir, seed **5** issue, scion **6** coheir **7** grantee, heiress, legatee, progeny **8** receiver
inheritors, Earth: **4** meek
Inheritors, The
author: Harold Robbins
Inherit the Wind (1960 film)
cast: Gene Kelly, Fredric March, Spencer Tracy, Dick York
director: Stanley Kramer

role: **5** Brady, Cates **7** Bertram **8** Drummond, Hornbeck
In Her Shoes (2005 film)
cast: Toni Collette, Cameron Diaz, Shirley MacLaine
inhibit: **3** bar **4** curb, faze, hold, slow, stop **5** avert, brake, check, cramp, crimp, delay, deter, limit, stimy, stint, stymy **6** arrest, bridle, dampen, detain, enjoin, forbid, hamper, hand up, hinder, hogtie, impede, retard, slow up, stymie **7** abolish, head off, prevent, refrain, repress, sandbag, silence, trammel **8** bottle up, handcuff, handicap, hold back, hold down, obstruct, preclude, prohibit, restrain, restrict, slow down, suppress, throttle **9** constrain, constrict, frustrate, hamstring, interdict **10** discourage, keep in line
inhibited: **6** pent-up, silent **7** hogtied **8** hampered **9** continent, repressed, withdrawn **10** frustrated
inhibition: **5** check **6** hang-up **7** scruple, trammel **8** neurosis **9** hindrance, restraint, reticence **10** constraint, impediment, prevention
inhibitions, abandon: **5** let go
in high __: **4** gear
__ in his heaven...: **4** God's
In His Image subject: **5** clone
__ in hoary winter's night: **3** As I
in hoc __ vinces: **5** signo
inhospitable: **3** icy **4** cold, cool, mean, rude **5** aloof, brusk, nasty, short, surly **6** chilly, ornery, remote, unkind **7** brusque, glacial, hateful, hostile **8** contrary, inimical, spiteful **9** bellicose, malicious, withdrawn **10** malevolent, pugnacious, unfriendly
in hot __: **5** water
inhuman: **4** fell, grim, mean **5** cruel **6** brutal, fierce, malign, savage, unkind **7** beastly, bestial, hateful, vicious **8** barbaric, devilish, fiendish, pitiless, ruthless **9** barbarian, barbarous, ferocious, heartless, monstrous, unfeeling **10** oppressive, outrageous, relentless
inhumane: **3** bad **4** fell, grim, mean **5** cruel, harsh, nasty **6** animal, brutal, fierce, malign, savage, unkind, wanton **7** beastly, bestial, callous, hateful, hurtful, vicious **8** barbaric, devilish, fiendish, pitiless, ruthless, sadistic, vengeful **9** barbarian, barbarous, cutthroat, ferocious, merciless, monstrous, truculent, unpitying **10** unmerciful, vindictive
inhumanity: **7** cruelty, outrage **8** atrocity, ferocity, savagery, violence **9** barbarism, barbarity, brutality
__ inhumanity to...: **4** man's
inhume: **4** bury, hide **5** cover **6** entomb **7** conceal, cover up
Inigo: **5** Jones
inimical: **3** icy, ill **4** cold, cool, mean **5** aloof, nasty, surly **6** averse, chilly, malign, ornery, remote **7** adverse, glacial, harmful, hateful, hostile,

hurtful, noxious, opposed, warlike 8 contrary, opposing, opposite, spiteful 9 bellicose, injurious, malicious, repugnant, withdrawn 10 malevolent, pugnacious, unfriendly

inimitable: 4 best, rare 6 unique 7 perfect, supreme 8 peerless, uncommon 9 matchless, nonpareil, unequaled, unmatched, unrivaled, virtuosic 10 consummate, unequalled, unexampled, unrivalled

inion: 4 bone

iniquitous: 3 bad, ill 4 base, evil, foul, vile 5 nasty 6 guilty, unholy, wicked 7 corrupt, heinous, immoral, satanic 8 unlawful 9 injurious, miscreant, nefarious, satanical 10 malevolent, villainous

iniquity: 3 sin 4 evil, vice 5 crime, guilt, wrong 6 infamy 7 devilry 8 baseness, deviltry 9 depravity, evildoing 10 corruption, immorality, miscreancy, sinfulness, wickedness, wrongdoing

__ iniquity: 5 den of

init.: 3 ltr.

__ in Italy: 6 Harold

__ in it for me?: 5 What's

initial: 2 OK 4 mark, okay, sign 5 basic, early, first, prime 6 letter, maiden, virgin 7 leading, nascent, opening, pioneer, premier, primary 8 earliest, original, virginal 9 beginning, embryonic, inaugural, inceptive, incipient 10 elementary

stage: 4 dawn 5 onset, start 6 outset 7 dawning, kickoff, opening 8 outbreak 9 beginning, inception

initialize a disk: 6 format

initially: 5 first 7 at first 9 primarily 10 at the start, originally

initiate: 3 set 4 haze, open, tiro, tyro 5 admit, begin, build, cause, coach, edify, enter, erect, found, newie, set up, start, teach, train 6 create, enlist, ground, induct, instal, invest, launch, take up 7 aggress, entrant, install, instate, kick off, lead off, learner, pioneer, receive, recruit, trigger, usher in 8 activate, ambition, beginner, commence, generate, get going, instruct, touch off 9 enlighten, enter upon, instigate, institute, introduce, originate, undertake 10 catechumen, inaugurate, lead the way, tenderfoot

initiation: 5 debut, intro, onset, start 6 origin 7 baptism, genesis, joining, opening 8 entrance 9 admission, beginning, enrolment, inaugural, inception, induction 10 conception, enrollment

initiative: 4 push, zeal 5 drive, moxie, punch, spunk, vigor 6 action, energy 8 ambition, dynamism, gumption, resource 9 eagerness 10 enterprise, enthusiasm, get-up-and-go, leadership

take the ~: 3 act 4 lead 9 spearhead, volunteer

initiator: 7 creator, founder 10 forerunner

initiatory: 5 first 6 maiden 7 opening 8 starting 9 inaugural, incipient

inject: 3 add 5 infix 6 insert, instil 7 breathe, engrain, implant, ingrain, instill 9 inoculate, insinuate, interpose, introduce, vaccinate

injected, not: 4 oral

injection: 4 hypo, shot 6 needle 8 infusion, medicine 10 medication

amt.: 2 cc.

reaction: 2 ow 4 ouch 5 wince

__ injection: 3 air 4 fuel

__ injector: 3 jet 4 fuel

in jest: 7 as a joke 8 jokingly 9 kiddingly

In Joy Still Felt

author: Isaac Asimov

injudicious: 4 dumb, rash 5 silly, wrong 6 stupid, unwise 7 foolish 8 careless, tactless 9 misguided, unadvised

injunction: 3 ban, law 4 word, writ 5 edict, order 6 decree, demand 7 command, dictate, mandate, precept, warning 8 sanction 9 directive, enjoinder 10 admonition

injure: 3 cut, mar 4 beat, harm, hurt, knee, maim, mall, maul, pain, ruin, scar, stab, tear, undo 5 abuse, break, crack, lay up, slash, spite, spoil, sting, wound, wrong 6 batter, bruise, damage, deface, foul up, grieve, impair, insult, malign, mangle, strain 7 contuse, disable, distort, slander, torture, trample, vitiate 8 aggrieve, distress, ill-treat, lacerate, maltreat, mistreat, mutilate 9 prejudice

slightly: 4 wing 6 bruise 7 scratch

injured: 3 cut 4 hurt 5 burnt, lamed, stung 6 abused, broken, burned, harmed, maimed, marred, ruined 7 cracked, damaged, grieved, libeled, mangled, misused, wounded, wronged 8 crippled, deformed, impaired, maligned, offended, traduced, vilified, weakened 9 aggrieved, blackened, enfeebled, lacerated, miserable, mutilated, slandered 10 denigrated, ill-treated, maltreated, mistreated

party: 6 sucker, victim 9 scapegoat

injurious: 3 bad, ill 4 evil 5 toxic 6 malign, nocent, unjust 7 abusive, adverse, baleful, baneful, harmful, hurtful, nocuous, noisome, noxious, ruinous 8 damaging, grievous, inimical, libelous, negative, sinister, virulent, wrongful 9 dangerous, insulting, malicious, pestilent, poisonous, unhealthy 10 calamitous, corrupting, defamatory, derogatory, disastrous, iniquitous, maleficent, pernicious, slanderous

act: 4 tort 5 wrong 9 violation

not ~: 4 safe 6 benign, gentle 8 harmless, nontoxic 9 innocuous

injury: 3 cut, ill 4 bite, burn, gash, harm, hurt, loss, nick, pain, pang, sore, welt 5 abuse, break, cramp, shock, sting, wound, wrong 6 booboo, bruise, damage, lesion, misuse, scrape, sprain, strain, trauma, twinge 7 affront, offense, outrage, scratch, umbrage 8 abrasion, breakage, distress, fracture, inequity, mischief, swelling 9 contusion, detriment, grievance 10 affliction, impairment, laceration, oppression

addition: 6 insult

exposure to ~: 4 risk 5 peril 6 danger, hazard, menace 8 jeopardy

minor ~: 4 welt 6 boo-boo, bruise, scrape 7 scratch 8 black eye 9 contusion

muscle ~: 4 pull, tear 6 sprain

result: 4 scab, scar

injustice: 4 bias 5 abuse, wrong 6 bum rap 7 offense, outrage 8 inequity 9 dirty deal, grievance, prejudice, violation 10 detraction, disservice, fanaticism, favoritism, inequality, infraction, negligence, oppression, partiality, unfairness, wrongdoing

do an ~: 4 harm 5 abuse 6 damage, ill-use, injure, misuse 7 torment 8 aggrieve, distress, ill-treat, maltreat, mistreat 9 mishandle, persecute

ink: 4 sign 5 India, sepia, write 7 endorse, indorse 9 publicity

debit ~: 3 red

dry ~: 5 toner

ender: 4 blot, horn, well 5 berry, stand

holder: 4 well 5 quill 8 fountain

Japanese ~: 4 sumi

red ~: 4 debt, loss 7 arrears, deficit 8 mortgage 9 arrearage, debenture, liability 10 obligation

sac: 5 organ

slinger: 6 writer 8 reporter 9 columnist 10 journalist, newswriter

source: 3 pen, soy 5 squid 7 octopus

spot: 4 blot 5 stain 6 blotch

user: 5 press 7 printer 9 newspaper

ink-__ printer: 3 jet

__ ink: 5 India

Inka __ Doo: 5 Dinka

Inkatha Party supporter: 4 Zulu

inkblot __: 4 test

inked: 3 sgd. 5 wrote 6 signed

inkle: 4 tape

material: 5 linen

inkling: 3 cue, tip 4 clew, clue, hint, idea, seed, sign, wind 5 glint, hunch, touch 6 notion, tipoff 7 glimmer 9 suspicion 10 conception, glimmering, impression, indication, intimation, suggestion

Inkster, Juli: 6 golfer

Ink Truck, The

author: William Kennedy

inkwell site of old: 4 desk

inky: 3 jet 4 dark, ebon 5 black, ebony, sooty 9 blackened, coalblack, lightless, unlighted 10 pitchblack

relative: 4 onyx 5 raven, sable

inky __: 3 cap

inlaid: 3 set 5 tiled 6 mosaic 7 studded 8 enameled, veneered 9 champlevé, checkered 10 ornamented

inland: 7 upriver 8 interior, internal 9 backwoods, upcountry

water: 4 lake

in-law: 6 affine 8 relative

offering: 5 dowry 6 dowery

__-in-law: 3 son 6 father, mother, parent, sister

In-Laws, The (1979 film)

cast: Alan Arkin, Peter Falk

In-Laws, The (2003 film)

cast: Candice Bergen, Albert Brooks, Michael Douglas

inlay: 3 set 4 tile 5 embed, imbed 6 insert, mosaic, tiling 7 checker, encrust, filling, incrust, parquet 10 decoration, tessellate

elaborate ~: 4 buhl 5 boule 6 boulle

material: 5 nacre

__ in left field: 3 out

inlet: 3 bay, ria 4 cove, gulf 5 basin, bayou, bight, fiord, firth, fjord, frith, mouth 6 laguna 7 estuary 8 entrance

__ Inlet: 4 Cook

...in like __: 5 a lion

in line __: 3 for

in-line __: 7 skating

__ in line: 4 next

In Living Color segment: 4 skit

in loc. __: 3 cit.

__ in Love: 4 Lost 5 Blume, I'm Not, Swann, Woman, Women, You're 7 Falling

__ in Love Again: 4 Back 7 Falling

__ in Love With Amy: 4 Once

__-in maid: 4 live

inmate: 3 con 5 lifer 7 convict, patient 8 jailbird, prisoner, resident, yardbird

in medias __: 3 res

In Memoriam

author: Alfred Tennyson

In Memory Yet Green

author: Isaac Asimov

__ in mind: 4 bear, have, keep

inmost: 6 center, innate, secret 7 deepest 9 essential, intrinsic

__ in motion: 3 set 6 poetry

__-in-mouth: 4 foot

__-in movie: 5 drive

__ in My Arms Again: 4 Back

__ in my backyard!: 3 Not

In My Dreams (1987 song)

artist: REO Speedwagon

__ in my memory lock'd: 3 'tis

In My Room (1963 song)

artist: Beach Boys

__ in My Shoes: 4 Sand

inn: 3 pub 5 B and B, hotel, lodge, motel, serai 6 hostel, imaret, posada, resort, saloon, Tabard, tavern 7 auberge, lodging 8 gasthaus, hostelry, lodgment, taphouse 9 roadhouse 10 guesthouse, restaurant

ender: 6 keeper

offering: 2 rm. 4 room

Turkish ~: 5 serai 6 imaret

waterfront ~: 5 botel 6 boatel

__ inn: 5 motor

Inn: 5 river

locale: 7 Austria, Germany

__ Inn: 4 Days 5 Gray's 6 Tabard 7 Holiday, Red Roof

Inn Album, The

author: Robert Browning

in name __: 4 only

innards: 4 guts 6 bowels, vitals 7 filling, viscera 8 contents, workings 9 mechanism

innate: **3** gut **4** born **5** basic **6** inborn, inmost, native **7** genetic, natural, organic, radical **8** born with, God-given, internal **9** genetical, ingrained, innermost, intrinsic, intuitive, unlabored, unlearned **10** congenital, hereditary, indigenous
innately: **5** per se **7** at heart **8** in itself **9** in essence, naturally
inner: **3** gut **6** center, clique, hidden, middle, secret, within **7** central, private **8** interior, internal, intimate, personal, visceral **9** emotional, essential, intrinsic, nonpublic, spiritual **10** deep-rooted, deep-seated
circle: **5** elite **6** clique
city: **3** urb **4** slum **6** barrio, ghetto, region **7** quarter
combining form: **3** eso- **4** endo-, ento-
ender: **4** most, sole, wear **6** spring
in anatomy: **5** ental
motivation: **4** urge **5** ardor, drive
not ~: **5** outer **7** outward **8** exterior, external
sanctum: **6** adytum
self: **4** soul **5** anima **6** psyche
voice: **8** superego **10** conscience
inner __: **3** ear, man **4** city, tube **5** child **6** circle **7** sanctum
Inner Circles
author: Alexander Haig
Inner City Blues (1971 song)
artist: Marvin Gaye
Inner Hebrides
cape: **5** Sleat
isle: **4** Eigg, Mull, Skye **5** Islay, Tiree, Tyree
innermost: **4** core, deep, pith **5** basic, heart, privy **6** center, depths, hidden, innate, marrow, secret, veiled **7** central, intense, organic, private **8** esoteric, immanent, inherent, intimate, personal, profound, recesses, visceral **9** out of view
part: **4** core **6** center **7** nucleus
Inner Sanctum, The: **9** radio show
Innerspace (1987 film)
cast: Kevin McCarthy, Dennis Quaid, Meg Ryan, Martin Short
director: Joe Dante
inner-tube
innards: **3** air
outsides: **4** tire
Innes: **5** Laura **7** Michael
Inness, George: **6** artist **7** painter
__ in New York: **5** A King **6** Autumn, Sunday
innie: **5** navel
opposite: **5** outie
inning: **5** frame
ender, often: **2** DP **9** strikeout
extra ~: **5** tenth
half an ~: **3** top **6** bottom
last ~ usually: **5** ninth
outs in an ~: **3** six
penultimate ~: **6** eighth
recap part: **6** no hits, no runs
unit: **3** out
__-inning stretch: **7** seventh
Innis: **3** Roy
org.: **4** CORE
Innisfail: **4** city, Eire, Erin, isle, town **7** Ireland
locale: **6** Canada **7** Ontario
Innisfree: **4** Eire, Erin, isle
innkeeper: **4** host **8** boniface, hosteler, hotelier, landlord
in Italian: **4** oste
in no __: **3** way **4** time
innocence: **5** youth **6** purity, virtue **7** naiveté, probity **9** frankness, freshness, greenness, ignorance, nescience, plainness, sincerity **10** candidness, clean hands, simplicity
remark of ~: **5** not me
__ Innocence, The: **5** Age of
innocent: **4** babe, good, lamb, naif, open, pure **5** clean, clear, green, legal, naive **6** boyish, chaste, cherub, honest, lawful, simple, victim, virgin **7** angelic, artless, genuine, natural, sincere, sinless, unjaded, upright **8** gullable, gullible, harmless, ignorant, lamblike, pristine, spotless, unartful, unsoiled, virginal, virtuous **9** angelical, blameless, childlike, exemplary, faultless, guileless, guilt-free, guiltless, ingenuous, innocuous, lily-white, not guilty, righteous, stainless, uncorrupt, unsullied, untainted, unwitting, unworldly, wholesome **10** immaculate, impeccable, inculcable, inculpable, in the clear, legitimate, unaffected, uninvolved
escapade: **4** lark **5** antic, caper, fling **6** frolic, gambol **7** rollick
find ~: **5** clear **6** acquit **9** vindicate
kid: **5** angel **6** cherub
not ~: **6** guilty, liable, sinful **7** at fault **8** culpable **10** in the wrong
innocent __ lamb: **3** as a
Innocent: **4** pope **7** pontiff
Innocent Man, An (1984 song)
artist: Billy Joel
Innocents Abroad, The
author: Mark Twain
innocuous: **4** mild, safe **5** banal, bland **6** pallid **7** insipid **8** harmless, innocent, painless **9** innoxious
Inn of the Sixth Happiness, The (1958 film)
cast: Ingrid Bergman, Robert Donat
In nomine __: **5** patri
innovate: **4** coin **5** alter **6** change, recast **7** remodel, restyle **8** renovate **9** modernize, originate, transform
innovation: **6** change **7** coinage, newness, novelty **9** departure, deviation, discovery, invention, modernism, variation **10** alteration, conversion, new wrinkle
innovative: **3** new **4** orig. **5** fresh, novel **6** clever **7** new-wave, unusual **8** creative, inspired, original **9** deviceful, inceptive, ingenious, inventive **10** avant-garde, newfangled
innovator: **7** creator, pioneer **8** inventer, inventor
prefix: **3** neo
innoxious: **4** safe **8** harmless, nontoxic **9** innocuous
Innsbruck: **4** city, town
locale: **3** Aus. **4** Alps, Aust. **5** Tirol, Tyrol **7** Austria
see also German
innuendo: **4** hint, slur, talk **5** smear **7** whisper **8** allusion, overtone **9** aspersion, reference **10** imputation, intimation, suggestion
Innuit: **6** Eskimo
innumerable: **4** many, more **6** a lot of, divers, gobs of, legion, lots of, myriad, umteen, untold **7** a host of, a slew of, copious, heaps of, no end of, piles of, profuse, scads of, umpteen **8** a bunch of, abundant, an army of, manifold, numerous, oodles of, prodigal, scores of, umpsteen **9** a passel of, bountiful, bunches of, countless, limitless, quite a few **10** zillions of
innumerous: **4** many **6** myriad, untold **7** endless, umpteen **8** infinite **9** countless, limitless, unlimited
Ino
brother: **9** Polydorus
father: **6** Cadmus
husband: **7** Athamas
sister: **5** Agave **6** Semele
inoculable: **8** catching **10** contagious, infectious
inoculant: **5** serum
inoculate: **6** infuse, inject, instil **7** instill **8** immunize **9** vaccinate
inoculation: **4** hypo, shot **6** needle **8** medicine
inoffensive: **4** calm, mild, safe **5** bland, clean, quiet **6** humble **7** neutral **8** friendly, harmless, innocent, pleasant, retiring
In Old Arizona: **5** oater
In Old Monterey: **5** oater
__ in on: **3** key, let **4** horn, look, move, zero **5** barge, close
in one __ and out...: **3** ear
in one __ swoop: **4** fell
__ in one: **4** hole
__-in-one: **3** all
in one's __ right: **3** own
__ in one's belfry: **4** bats
__ in one's bones: **4** feel
__ in one's bonnet: **4** a bee
__ in one's craw: **5** stick
__ in one's ear: **4** flea **5** a flea
__ in one's hair: **3** get
__ in one's horns: **4** draw, haul, pull
__ in one's own juice: **4** stew
__ in one's pants: **4** ants
__ in one's side: **5** thorn
__ in one's sleeve: **5** laugh
__ in one's throat: **4** lump
__ in one's ways: **3** set
__-i-noor Diamond: **3** Koh
inoperative: **4** no-go, null, void **6** broken, futile, unable, voided **7** inutile, invalid, revoked, useless **8** abortive, annulled, bootless, canceled, inactive, nugatory, reversed, set aside **10** out of order
inopportune: **5** unapt **7** adverse, awkward **8** improper, previous, untimely **9** premature
inordinate: **5** gross, steep, undue **6** lavish, wanton **7** copious, extreme, profuse, surplus, too much **8** a bit much, dizzying, needless, overmuch, wasteful **9** excessive, expensive, irregular, redundant **10** exorbitant, gratuitous, immoderate, irrational, outrageous, undeserved, untempered
inordinately: **3** too **4** over, very **6** overly, unduly **9** extremely
inordinateness: **4** glut **6** excess **7** surplus **8** plethora **9** profusion **10** immoderacy, lavishness, sybaritism
inositol to glucose: **6** isomer
In other words: **5** id est, I mean
Inoue Yasushi: **6** writer **8** Japanese
__ in Our Time: **5** Peace
In Our Time
author: Tom Wolfe
In & Out (1997 film)
cast: Joan Cusack, Matt Dillon, Kevin Kline, Tom Selleck
director: Frank Oz
Inouye, Daniel org.: **3** Sen.
__ in Paradise: **4** Ruby **5** To One **7** Trouble
__ in Paris: **5** April **6** Satori
__ in Peoria: **4** play
__-in period: **5** break
__ in Pink: **6** Pretty
__ in place: **3** run
in place in Latin: **6** in loco
__ in Plain Sight: **4** Hide
__ in point: **4** case **5** a case
in point of __: **4** fact
inpour: **6** fill up
In Praise of __: **5** Folly
In Praise of Johnny Appleseed
author: Vachel Lindsay
__ in progress: **4** work
__ In Provence: **5** A Year
input: **3** key **4** note, type **5** enter, gloss **6** advice, remark **7** comment, observe, opinion **8** critique, feedback, point out **9** criticism, editorial, interject, statement **10** discussion
inq.: **4** ques.
inquest: **5** panel **6** assize
inquietude: **5** angst **6** unrest **7** anxiety, fidgets, jitters, malaise **8** disquiet, edginess **10** discomfort
inquire: **3** ask, pry **4** quiz, seek, sift **5** apply, probe, query, scour **6** demand, meddle, wonder **7** request, solicit **8** look into, question **9** catechize
into: **4** test **5** assay, study **6** size up, try out **7** analyze, examine, explore **8** check out, evaluate **10** scrutinize
Inquirer: **5** paper **9** newspaper
inquiring: **4** nosy **5** nosey **7** curious **9** heuristic, quizzical, searching, wondering **10** analytical, interested
inquiry: **4** ques. **5** audit, check, probe, Q and A, query, quest, study **6** asking, demand, survey **7** hearing, pursuit, request **8** question, quizzing, research, scrutiny **10** inspection
judicial ~: **6** assize
make an ~: **3** ask **5** probe **8** look into
word of ~: **3** how, who, why **4** what, when **5** where
inquisition: **5** probe, trial **6** assize **7** enquiry, hearing, inquest, inquiry **8** grilling
Inquisition offense: **6** heresy
inquisitive: **4** nosy **5** nosey **6** prying, snoopy **7** big-eyed, curious **8** snooping **9** officious, quizzical
be ~: **3** ask **5** snoop **6** wonder
one: **5** asker, prier, pryer
inquisitor: **4** ogre **5** bully **6** tyrant **8** autocrat, dictator, examiner, martinet **9** oppressor **10** questioner
demand: **6** answer

__ in Red, The: 4 Lady 5 Woman
inroad: 4 raid 5 foray 7 advance, ingress, overrun 8 invasion, progress, trespass 9 incursion, intrusion, irruption, onslaught
__ in Rome...: 4 When
inrush: 5 flood 7 pouring 9 implosion
ins.
bank ~ initials: 4 FDIC, SBLI 5 FSLIC
health ~ choice: 3 HMO, PPO
payment: 4 prem.
see also insurance
INS: 4 agcy. 6 agency
part of ~: 4 Serv. 7 Service
insalubrious: 4 foul 5 dirty, fatal, toxic 6 deadly, jejune, lethal, septic, sickly 7 harmful, hurtful, noisome, noxious, unclean 8 damaging, virulent 9 unhealthy
ins and outs: 4 ways 5 bends, turns 6 curves, habits, traits, twists 7 customs, details 8 patterns, windings
insane: 3 mad 4 daft, wild 5 manic, wacky 6 fierce, whacky 7 extreme, fatuous, foolish, meshuga, touched, unsound 8 maniacal, meshugga 9 ludicrous, possessed, senseless, unscrewed 10 moonstruck, off-the-wall
insanitary: 4 foul 5 dirty, germy 6 filthy, impure, septic 7 dirtied, noxious, unclean 8 infected, polluted, unwashed
insatiable: 4 avid 6 greedy 7 lustful 8 esurient, ravenous 9 clamorous, demanding, insistent, rapacious, voracious 10 gluttonous, quenchless
desire: 4 lust, urge 5 greed 6 fervor, hunger, thirst 7 avidity, craving 8 cupidity 9 appetence
insatiate: 6 hungry 7 piggish, starved, wolfish 8 edacious, esurient, famished, ravenous, starving 9 voracious 10 gluttonous, omnivorous
__ in Scarlet, A: 5 Study
inscribe: 3 pen 4 etch, sign 5 enter, write 6 indite, record 7 address, engrave, impress, imprint 8 register, take down 9 autograph, handwrite
inscribed rock: 5 stela, stele
inscription: 3 tag 5 label, motto, title 6 legend, record 7 caption, epitaph, heading, message 8 memorial
like some old ~s: 5 runic
inscrutable: 5 blank 6 mystic 7 complex 8 esoteric, mystical 10 fathomless, mysterious
inseam measure: 4 lgth. 6 length
In Search of the Castaways
author: Jules Verne
insect: 3 ant, bee, bot, bug, dor, fly, nit 4 flea, gnat, grub, lice, mite, moth, pest, pupa, tick, tine, wasp 5 aphid, aphis, borer, cimex, cooty, drone, emmet, imago, larva, louse, midge, roach 6 bedbug, beetle, botfly, chafer, chigoe, chinch, cicada, cocoon, cootie, dayfly, earwig, gadfly, hornet, lo moth, larvae, locust, looper, maggot, mantid, mantis, mayfly, scarab, thrips, tussah, vermin, weevil 7 ant lion, billbug, blowfly, chigger, cricket, firefly, hexapod, katydid, ladybug, no-see-um, pismire, termite, viceroy 8 armyworm, conenose, firebrat, fruit fly, glowworm, honeybee, housefly, lacewing, mealybug, mosquito, muckworm, reduviid, silkworm, stinkbug, white ant, woodworm 9 arthropod, bumblebee, butterfly, chrysalis, cockroach, corn borer, damselfly, dobsonfly, doodlebug, dorbeetle, dragonfly, earthworm, saturniid, sheep tick, tarantula, woodborer 10 bluebottle, calicoback, deathwatch, digger wasp, froghopper, iguana fare, pear thrips, rose chafer, spittlebug, treehopper, woolly bear
busy ~: 3 ant, bee
cheek: 5 bucca
combining form: 6 entomo-
covering: 6 chitin
dorsal surface: 5 notum
eater: 4 frog, toad 8 aardvark
egg: 3 nit
eye lens: 5 facet
feeler: 4 palp 6 palpus
forehead: 5 frons
home:: 4 hive, nest 5 nidus
mouth parts: 5 labra
of an ~ nest: 5 nidal
of an ~ stage: 5 pupal 6 larval
part of an ~ stinger: 5 oopod
scale ~: 6 coccid
science: 5 entom. 10 entomology
sound: 5 chirr, churr 6 chirre
stage: 4 pupa 5 imago, larva 6 instar
stinging ~: 3 bee 4 wasp 6 hornet
upper plate: 5 notum
wing part: 5 jugum
wings: 4 alae
insecticide: 3 DDT 4 deet, neem 5 mirex, spray
brand: 4 Raid 9 Black Flag
Insect Play, The
author: Karel Capek
insects, parasitic: 4 lice
insecure: 4 weak 5 antsy, risky, shaky 6 uneasy, unfirm, unsafe, wabbly, wobbly 7 rickety, unsound 8 slippery, unstable 9 hazardous, uncertain, unsettled 10 precarious
insecurity: 4 fear, risk 5 doubt, peril 6 danger, hazard 7 anxiety, frailty, shyness 8 jeopardy, timidity, unsafety, wariness, weakness 9 misgiving, timidness 10 diffidence
insensate: 4 cold, dead, deaf, hard, numb 5 blind, inert 6 inured, zonked 7 callous, foolish, mineral, witless 8 hardened, lifeless, tuned out, uncaring 9 inanimate, unfeeling
insensibility: 4 daze 5 shock 6 stupor, trance 8 numbness
insensible: 7 unaware 8 lifeless, pitiless 9 apathetic, bloodless, impassive, unfeeling 10 immaterial, impalpable
insensitive: 4 hard, numb 5 aloof, blind, blunt, brusk, crass, stony, tough 6 abrupt, gauche, obtuse, stoney, unkind 7 boorish, brusque, callous 8 deadened, impolite, inurbane, tactless, uncaring 9 outspoken, unfeeling
one: 3 oaf 4 boor, clod 5 brute
insentient: 4 dead, numb 5 inert, under 6 zonked 7 mineral 8 comatose, deadened, lifeless 9 inanimate 10 unreactive
inseparable: 5 as one, close, solid, thick, whole 6 united 7 unified 8 attached
insert: 3 add, put, set 4 edit, root, stay, tuck 5 embed, flier, flyer, imbed, infix, inlay, place, plant, shove, stick, tenon 6 filler, gusset, inject, record 7 enclose, implant, inclose, include, obtrude, squeeze 8 shoehorn 9 enclosure, interject, interpose, introduce 10 put between, supplement
mark: 5 caret
inset: 5 panel
__ in sheep's clothing: 4 wolf 5 a wolf
in short __: 5 order
__ in show: 4 best
inside: 3 gut 4 core 5 belly, heart 6 at home, bowels, center, lining, middle, secret, vitals, within 7 central, indoors, innards, private 8 deep down, esoteric, interior, internal, inwardly 9 exclusive, incumbent, protected, sheltered 10 classified, restricted, tucked away
combining form: 4 endo-, ento-
nautically: 4 alow
turn ~ out: 6 forage 7 ransack, rummage
inside __: 3 job, out 4 joke, loop 5 story, track
__ inside: 5 Intel, on the
Inside __: 3 U.S.A. 4 Asia 6 Africa 7 Edition, Passage
Inside Africa
author: John Gunther
Inside Asia
author: John Gunther
Inside Australia
author: John Gunther
Inside Daisy Clover (1965 film)
cast: Roddy McDowall, Christopher Plummer, Robert Redford, Natalie Wood
Inside Europe Today
author: John Gunther
Inside Man (2006 film)
cast: Jodie Foster, Clive Owen, Denzel Washington
director: Spike Lee
inside-out: 5 messy 7 jumbled, muddled, upended 8 inverted 10 topsy-turvy
turn ~: 5 probe, rifle, scour 6 forage, search 7 examine, inspect, ransack, rummage 9 go through 10 scrutinize
Inside, Outside
author: Herman Wouk
insider: 5 shill 9 accessory 10 accomplice
former ~: 5 ex-con
signal: 4 wink
talk: 5 argot, idiom, lingo 6 jargon, patois
insider __: 7 trading
Insider, The (1999 film)
cast: Russell Crowe, Al Pacino, Christopher Plummer, Diane Venora
Inside Russia Today
author: John Gunther
insides: 4 guts 5 works 6 bowels, vitals 7 filling, viscera 8 contents, workings 9 mechanism
Inside South America
author: John Gunther
Inside the Atom
author: Isaac Asimov
Inside the Onion
author: Howard Nemerov
Inside the Third Reich
author: Albert Speer
Inside the Tornado
author: Geoffrey Moore
Inside U.S.A.
author: John Gunther
insidious: 3 sly 4 foul, foxy, grim, poor, wily 5 awful, lousy, slick, snaky, woful 6 artful, crafty, crummy, dismal, horrid, odious, rotten, shifty, sneaky, subtle, tricky, woeful 7 accurst, baleful, baneful, beastly, cunning, devious, doleful, furtive, ghastly, knavish 8 accursed, dreadful, God-awful, grievous, guileful, horrible, inferior, shameful, stealthy, stinking, terrible, wretched 9 abhorrent, appalling, atrocious, dangerous, deceitful, deceptive, defective, designing, dishonest, ensnaring, execrable, frightful, loathsome, miserable, offensive, revolting, underhand 10 abominable, despicable, detestable, disastrous, horrendous, intriguing, perfidious, traitorous
insight: 3 wit 4 wits 5 depth, light, sense 6 acumen, aperçu, vision, wisdom 8 epiphany, sagacity, sapience 9 awareness, intuition, knowledge 10 horse sense, luminosity, perception, profundity
give ~ to: 5 edify, teach, train 6 advise 7 clarify 8 illumine, instruct 9 elucidate
high degree of ~: 6 acuity, acumen, wisdom 8 sagacity 10 astuteness
meditation ~: 9 vipassana
mock phrase of ~: 4 ah so
__ in sight: 5 no end
insightful: 4 keen, wise 5 acute, alert, quick, savvy, sharp, smart 6 astute, brainy, shrewd 7 knowing, sapient 8 lynx-eyed, profound 9 astucious, sagacious 10 discerning, perceptive
insignia: 4 mark 5 badge, crest, label, patch 6 device, emblem, symbol 7 earmark 8 heraldry 10 coat of arms, decoration
Insignificance (1985 film)
cast: Gary Busey, Tony Curtis, Michael Emil, Theresa Russell
director: Nicolas Roeg
insignificant: 4 idle, mere, null, punk, puny, tiny 5 dinky, light, minor, petty, scrub, small, sorry, teeny 6 casual, humble, lesser, little, meager, measly, minute, paltry, scanty, slight, teensy 7 lowborn, minimal, nominal, tenuous, trivial 8 marginal, mediocre, nugatory, picayune, piddling, trifling 9 senseless, valueless, worthless

amount: 3 dot, jot 4 iota, whit 5 minim, speck 6 trifle
most ~: 5 least
one: 4 nerd, snip, twit 5 dweeb, twerp, twirp 7 nebbish
insincere: 4 fake, glib, sham 5 false, lying, phony, slick 6 forced, hollow, phoney, shifty, tricky, unreal, untrue 7 crooked, devious, evasive, feigned, knavish, mincing, plastic, unloyal 8 affected, delusive, guileful, two-faced, unctuous 9 deceitful, deceptive, dishonest, faithless, high-toned, pretended, unnatural 10 artificial, backhanded, factitious, mendacious, perfidious, unfaithful, untruthful
be ~: 5 flirt 6 trifle 8 lollygag 10 dillydally, fool around
insincerity: 4 cant, jive 5 guile, hokum, lying 6 bunkum, deceit 7 perfidy 8 bad faith, betrayal, buncombe, claptrap, flattery, pretense
insinuate: 3 say 4 hint, seem, slur, worm 5 foist, get at, imply 6 advert, allude, horn in, impute, infuse, inject, slip in, worm in 7 ascribe, connote, engrain, ingrain, make out, signify, suggest, wedge in, whisper 8 allude to, intimate, lead up to, muscle in 9 get in with, implicate, interject, interpose, introduce 10 curry favor, infiltrate, ingratiate
insinuating: 4 oily 5 snide 7 pointed 8 unctuous
insinuation: 4 hint, slur, talk 7 whisper 8 innuendo 9 reference 10 imputation
insipid: 3 dry 4 arid, blah, drab, dull, flat, mild, tame, weak 5 banal, bland, empty, ho-hum, inane, plain, stale, tired, trite, vapid 6 boring, jejune 7 humdrum, maudlin, mundane, prosaic, tedious 8 lifeless, ordinary, unlively, unsavory 9 colorless, innocuous, pointless, prosaical, tasteless, wearisome 10 dullsville, flavorless, lackluster, wishy-washy
become ~: 4 cloy, pall
one: 4 bore, drip, jerk, pest
insipidity: 6 anemia 7 anaemia, aridity, dryness 8 banality, dullness, flatness, limpness, monotony, thinness, vapidity, weakness
insist: 4 aver, avow, urge 5 claim, force, order, press 6 affirm, assert, demand, pester 7 command, contend, persist, protest, require, speak up 8 maintain, pressure, speak out 9 importune, persevere, stand firm 10 make a stand
ender: 3 ent 4 ence
on: 4 aver, urge 5 exact, press 6 assert, badger, demand, stress 7 require 9 challenge, emphasize, stipulate
insistence: 4 will 6 demand, stress, urging 7 goading 8 emphasis, pressure, prodding, spurring 9 assertion
insistent: 4 bent, dire 5 pushy, vocal 6 crying, dogged, urgent 7 adamant, burning 8 emphatic, forceful, pressing 9 assertive, clamorous, demanding, imperious, obstinate, pigheaded 10 continuous, insatiable, peremptory, persistent, vociferous

__ in smoke: 4 go up
in so __ words: 4 many
insociable: 3 icy 4 cold, cool 5 aloof, stiff 6 frigid, remote 7 distant 8 detached, reserved 10 unfriendly
__ in Socks: 3 Fox
insolence: 3 lip 4 gall, guff, sass 5 abuse, brass, cheek, mouth, nerve, pride, sauce 6 hutzpa, insult 7 chutzpa, hutzpah 8 audacity, back talk, boldness, chutzpah, contempt, defiance, pertness 9 arrogance, contumely, impudence 10 assumption, brazenness, disrespect, effrontery, incivility
insolent: 4 bold, flip, pert, rude, wise 5 brash, fresh, lofty, nervy, sassy, saucy, smart 6 awless, brassy, brazen, cheeky, snippy 7 abusive, aweless, defiant, huffish, uncivil 8 cavalier, flippant, impolite, impudent, off-based, snippety, superior 9 audacious, barefaced, insulting, offensive, out of line, shameless 10 disdainful, irreverent, ungracious
be ~: 4 sass 8 get smart, mouth off, talk back 10 answer back, disrespect
insoluble: 4 hard 6 thorny 7 obscure 8 baffling, puzzling 9 difficult 10 mysterious, mystifying, unresolved
insolvency: 4 ruin 6 penury 7 beggary, default, failure, poverty, straits 10 bankruptcy, nonpayment
insolvent: 4 poor 5 broke, needy 6 bad off, busted, hard up, ill-off, in need, in want, ruined 7 pinched 8 badly off, bankrupt, beggarly, deprived, indigent, in the red, strapped, wiped out 9 destitute, moneyless, penniless, penurious 10 down and out, foreclosed, on the rocks, out of money, pauperized, straitened
Insomnia
author: Stephen King
Insomnia (2002 film)
cast: Al Pacino, Hilary Swank, Maura Tierney, Robin Williams
insouciance: 8 airiness, buoyance, buoyancy, lethargy
insouciant: 8 carefree, listless 9 easygoing, unworried 10 nonchalant, unbothered, untroubled
__ in Space: 4 Lost
__ in Spain: 6 castle
__ in Spain, The: 4 Rain
inspan: 4 yoke 7 harness, hitch up
inspect: 3 eye, see, vet 4 case, comb, look, peer, scan, sift, view 5 audit, check, frisk, probe, study, touch 6 go over, patrol, peruse, review, sample, search, survey, try out 7 canvass, compare, dissect, examine, observe, oversee 8 appraise, check out, consider, evaluate, look into, look over, overhaul 9 go through, supervise 10 scrutinize
the joint: 4 look 5 spy on 6 survey 7 examine 8 check out 10 scrutinize
inspection: 4 look, scan, test, view 5 audit, check, probe, sight 6 review, search, survey 7 checkup, enquiry, inquiry, look-see, perusal, reading 8 analysis, once-over, scrutiny 9 inventory, maneuvers 10 dissection
__ inspection: 6 on-site
inspector: 5 judge 6 tester 7 auditor, checker, monitor 8 assessor, examiner, overseer, reviewer 10 supervisor
Inspector Gadget dog: 5 Brain
Inspector General, The
author: Nikolai Gogol
character: 4 Anna, Ivan, Luka 5 Anton, Marya
Inspector General, The (1949 film)
cast: Danny Kaye, Walter Slezak
inspiration: 3 awe 4 idea, muse, soul, spur, whim 5 fancy, flash, hunch, spark 6 breath, motive, notion, origin, thrill, vision 7 impulse, insight, rapture, thought 8 afflatus, stimulus 10 inhalation
for a poet: 4 Muse 5 Erato
romantic ~: 4 moon, rose 5 stars
inspirational phrase: 3 saw 5 adage, axiom, maxim, motto 6 saying, slogan 7 epigram, precept, proverb 8 aphorism
inspire: 3 awe 4 fire, move, push, spur, stir, sway, urge 5 amaze, boost, flush, hop up, imbue, impel, liven, rouse, sniff, spark, touch 6 affect, arouse, ask for, bestir, buck up, excite, fire up, incite, infuse, instil, kindle, motive, perk up, prompt, stir up, strike, thrill, turn on, work up 7 actuate, animate, cheer up, elevate, enflame, enliven, hearten, implant, impress, inflame, instill, lighten, provoke, quicken, trigger 8 embolden, enspirit, imbolden, inspirit, interest, motivate, occasion, psyche up, reassure, start off 9 encourage, enhearten, galvanize, impassion, influence, irradiate, stimulate 10 give rise to, invigorate, predispose
inspired: 4 avid 5 fresh, novel 6 clever 7 aroused, exalted, excited, fired up, kindled, sparked, unusual 8 animated, creative, enthused, inflamed, original, vivified 9 energized, enkindled, enlivened, heartened, ingenious, inventive 10 innovative, reanimated, revivified
inspiring: 6 moving, poetic 7 hopeful 8 luminous, original, poetical 10 impressive, intoxicant, passionate
__-inspiring: 3 awe
inspirit: 4 fire, stir 5 cheer, hop up, rally, rouse 6 arouse, buck up, excite, incite, kindle, stir up, turn on, vivify 7 animate, console, enflame, enliven, gladden, hearten, inflame, quicken, refresh 8 embolden, energize, imbolden, motivate, psyche up, reassure, vitalize 9 encourage, enhearten, galvanize, impassion, inebriate, stimulate 10 exhilarate, intoxicate, invigorate, regenerate, strengthen
inspirited: 4 avid, keen 5 eager 6 fervid, gung ho 7 anxious, fervent, fired up, hopeful, zealous, zestful 8 sanguine 9 promising, psyched up 10 optimistic, raring to go
inspissate: 7 stiffen, thicken 9 coagulate
inst.: 3 min., sch., sec., sem. 4 acad., coll., univ.
instability: 4 flux 5 anomy 6 anomie, danger 8 neurosis, weakness
install: 3 fit, fix, lay, put, set, sit 4 seat 5 crown, embed, endue, fix up, imbed, indue, lodge, mount, place, plant, put in, set up, stick 6 hook up, induct, invest, ordain, settle 7 appoint, deposit, furnish, instate, quarter, receive, station 8 ensconce, initiate, position 9 establish, institute, introduce 10 inaugurate, put in place
in office: 4 seat 6 enseat 7 swear in
installation: 4 base, fort, post 5 setup 7 fitting, station
installment: 3 pmt. 4 part, payt. 5 issue, piece 7 chapter, episode, payment, portion, premium, section 8 division
buying: 6 credit
installment __: 4 plan
instance: 4 case, item, time 5 piece 6 detail, sample 7 example 8 occasion, sampling, specimen 9 precedent, situation 10 occurrence
for ~: 3 say 5 to wit 6 namely 10 explicitly
instant: 3 bit, sec 4 dire, fast, jiff, tick, time, wink 5 brisk, flash, fleet, hasty, jiffy, point, quick, rapid, swift, trice 6 flying, minute, moment, prompt, racing, second, snappy, speedy, urgent 7 burning, clamant, exigent, express, hurried 8 exigeant, juncture, pressing 9 breakneck, immediate, on-the-spot, twinkling 10 double-time, hypersonic, supersonic
at that ~: 4 then
replay technique: 5 slo-mo
this ~: 3 now, PDQ 4 anon, fast, soon 5 apace, quick, right, today 6 at once, presto 7 quickly, rapidly, swiftly 8 directly, in a flash, in a jiffy, in no time, outright, pell-mell, promptly, right now, right off, speedily 9 at present, forthwith, like a shot, on the spot, posthaste, presently, right away 10 double-time, here and now
instant __: 6 camera, coffee, replay
__ instant: 4 in an
instantaneous: 4 snap 5 quick, rapid, swift 6 prompt 9 momentary
instantaneously: 3 now 4 anon, fast 5 apace 6 at once, presto 8 abruptly, directly, full tilt, in a jiffy, in a trice, in no time, suddenly
Instant Karma (1970 song)
artist: John Lennon
instantly: 3 PDQ 4 anon, soon 5 apace, right 6 at once, presto 7 quickly, rapidly, swiftly 8 directly, in a flash, in a jiffy, in no time, outright, pell-mell, promptly, right now, right off, speedily 9 forthwith, like a shot, on the spot, posthaste, right away 10 double-time, this minute

IN

instate: **4** seat **5** chair, crown, endue, frock, indue **6** induct, instal, invest, ordain **7** install, swear in **8** enthrone, initiate, inthrone **9** establish **10** inaugurate
in statu __: **3** quo
instead: **4** else **6** in lieu, rather **7** in place **8** on behalf **10** preferably
of: **4** over **10** rather than
instep: **4** arch
instigate: **3** set **4** abet, goad, spur, urge **5** cause, egg on, impel, raise, rouse, start **6** arouse, ask for, excite, fire up, foment, incite, induce, kindle, launch, needle, prompt, stir up, turn on, whip up, work up **7** actuate, enflame, inflame, provoke, steam up **8** engender, initiate, motivate, persuade, touch off **9** encourage, influence, make waves, stimulate **10** bring about, lead the way
instigation: **4** goad, prod, push, spur **5** cause **6** fillip, thrust, urging **7** dictate **9** incentive
instigator: **7** demagog, hellion **8** agitator, inflamer **9** demagogue
instill: **3** fix **5** imbue, infix, plant, teach **6** impart, infuse, inject **7** breathe, diffuse, engrain, engrave, implant, impress, inbreed, ingrain, inspire **8** engender, transmit **9** inculcate, inoculate, introduce, pound into
forcefully: **4** drub, drum
instinct: **4** gift, idea, nose, urge **5** hunch, knack, savvy, sense **7** faculty, feeling, impulse, know-how **8** aptitude **9** appetence, intuition **10** gut feeling, proclivity, sixth sense
having a killer ~: **5** cruel **6** brutal, savage **8** pitiless, ruthless **9** cutthroat, dog-eat-dog, ferocious
__ instinct: **3** gut
Instinct (1999 film)
cast: Cuba Gooding Jr., Anthony Hopkins, Donald Sutherland, Maura Tierney
__ Instinct: **5** Basic
instinctive: **3** gut **6** inborn, inbred, innate, native, reflex, rooted **7** natural **8** knee-jerk, visceral
feeling: **4** vibe **5** hunch, sense
institute: **4** open **5** begin, build, enact, erect, found, set up, start **6** create, impose, instal, launch, lyceum **7** academy, install, pioneer, society, usher in **8** generate, initiate **9** establish, introduce, originate, prescribe **10** come up with, foundation, inaugurate
__ Institute: **4** Salk **5** Pratt **6** Esalen
institution: **5** trust **6** museum **7** society **8** creation, localism
educational ~: **3** sch. **4** acad., coll., univ. **6** lyceum, school **7** academy, college
penal ~: **3** pen **4** jail **5** clink **6** prison **7** slammer **8** bastille, big house, hoosegow **9** calaboose
institutional: **4** cold, drab, dull, same **5** bland **7** inhuman, uniform **8** unvaried
__ in stone: **6** carved, etched
instr.: **4** prof.
instruct: **3** set **4** form, show, tell **5** brief, coach, drill, edify, guide, order, teach, train, tutor **6** advise, assign, charge, clue in, direct, ground, inform, notify, school **7** apprise, apprize, break in, command, counsel, educate, lecture, nurture, require **8** acquaint, illumine, initiate **9** catechize, enlighten, inculcate, prescribe
instruction: **4** info **5** drill, order **6** charge, homily, lesson **7** command, lecture, lessons, mandate, precept, tuition **8** coaching, drilling, guidance, pedagogy, teaching, training, tutelage **9** direction, paedagogy
manual: **5** how-to **8** handbook
unit: **4** step **6** lesson
Instruction Paintings
author: Yoko Ono
instructions: **6** method, recipe **7** formula **9** procedure **10** directions
instructor: **4** prof **5** coach, guide, tutor **6** didact, lector, master, mentor **7** adviser, advisor, pedagog, teacher, trainer **8** educator, lecturer **9** abecedary, counselor, pedagogue, preceptor, professor
__ instructor: **5** drill
instructors: **7** faculty
instructors' org.: **3** AFT, NEA, UFT
instrument: **3** sax, uke, way **4** fife, gear, gong, harp, horn, lute, lyre, Moog, oboe, pawn, tool, tuba, viol **5** agent, banjo, bongo, bugle, cello, dodad, flute, gismo, gizmo, kazoo, labor, means, organ, paper, piano, thing, viola **6** agency, chimes, cornet, device, doodad, engine, factor, fiddle, gadget, guitar, medium, puppet, tam-tam, tom-tom, violin, zither **7** alto sax, bagpipe, bassoon, celesta, channel, clavier, cymbals, helicon, machine, maracas, marimba, musette, ocarina, panpipe, piccolo, saxhorn, trumpet, ukulele, utensil, vehicle **8** altohorn, autoharp, bass drum, bass viol, calliope, castanet, clarinet, dulcimer, mandolin, melodeon, recorder, theremin, triangle, trombone **9** accordion, alpenhorn, apparatus, appliance, balalaika, equipment, euphonium, expedient, harmonica, harmonium, implement, mechanism, saxophone, testament, vibraharp **10** clavichord, concertina, contrabass, flugelhorn, hurdy-gurdy, kettledrum, sousaphone, squeezebox, tambourine, vibraphone **11** harpsichord
combining form: **4** -labe
instrument __: **5** panel
__ instrument: **4** reed, wind **5** brass
instrumental: **3** key **5** music, vital **6** active, of help, useful **7** helpful, pivotal **8** involved
instrumentalist: **5** fifer **6** bugler, oboist, player **7** cellist, drummer, flutist, harpist, pianist **8** banjoist, flautist, musician **9** guitarist, trumpeter, violinist
instrumentality: **4** help, mode, tool, ways **5** means **6** agency, device, method, system **7** channel, machine, vehicle **8** resource, strategy **9** operation
instruments
guided only by ~: **5** blind
__ Instruments: **5** Texas
insubordinate: **5** rebel **6** feisty, ornery, unruly **7** defiant, lawless, naughty, radical, wayward **8** contrary, factious, insolent, mutinous, stubborn **10** rebellious
be ~: **5** act up, be bad, cut up **7** carry on, go wrong **8** go astray **9** misbehave **10** fool around, transgress
insubordination: **6** heresy, mutiny, revolt **8** apostasy, audacity, contempt, defiance **9** contumacy, defection, impudence, insolence, rebellion **10** brazenness, effrontery
insubstantial: **4** airy, idle, poor, puny, slim, thin, weak **5** false, frail, light, trite **6** feeble, flimsy, porous, skimpy, slight, unreal **7** fragile, slender, tenuous, unsound **8** ethereal, illusive, illusory, skin-deep **9** transient
insufferable: **3** bad **4** hard **5** awful, lousy **7** painful **8** dreadful, horrible
one: **4** bore, drip, pain, pest, pill
insufficiency: **4** lack, need, want **5** minus **6** dearth **7** absence, beggary, deficit, paucity, poverty **8** exiguity, scarcity, shortage, sparsity **10** meagerness
insufficient: **3** shy **4** lame, poor, slim, weak **5** light, scant, short, small **6** little, meager, scanty, scarce, skimpy, sparse **7** failing, lacking, limited, sketchy, slender, unample, wanting
__ in sugar: **3** S as
insular: **6** closed, cut off, narrow **7** bigoted, limited, topical **8** confined, detached, isolated, secluded, separate **9** illiberal, parochial, sectarian **10** prejudiced, provincial, restricted
insulate: **6** shield **7** protect **8** cloister, separate **9** segregate, sequester
insulated, poorly: **6** drafty
insulation: **3** PVC **4** batt, down **5** kapok, Mylar
banned ~: **3** PCB **8** asbestos
insult: **3** cut, dig, dis **4** barb, jeer, mock, quip, slam, slap, slur, snub, zing **5** abase, abuse, crack, flout, libel, roast, scorn, shock, sneer, taunt, wound, wrong **6** debase, deride, dump on, injure, malign, offend, rebuff, slight **7** affront, blister, degrade, disgust, epithet, low blow, mockery, obloquy, offense, outrage, provoke, put down, slander **8** black eye, brickbat, derision, dishonor, rudeness **9** aspersion, cheap shot, contumely, humiliate, impudence, indignity, insolence, invective **10** antagonize, disrespect, incivility, opprobrium, scurrility, vituperate
Internet ~: **5** flame
insulted, feeling: **4** hurt **8** offended
insulting: **4** rude **5** snide **6** biting **7** abusive, hurtful, jeering, uncivil **8** derisive, insolent, inurbane **9** injurious, offensive, ungallant **10** defamatory, scurrilous
look: **4** gibe **5** smirk, sneer **7** snigger
insupportable: **4** weak **6** flawed **8** doubtful, specious **9** untenable
insuppressible: **4** wild **8** ebullient **10** full of life
insurance: **5** hedge **7** backing, promise, reserve, support **8** coverage, overhead, security **9** allowance, assurance, guarantee, indemnity, provision, safeguard **10** precaution, protection
addendum: **5** rider **9** amendment
center: **5** Omaha **8** Hartford
company: **3** AIG, Aon, AXA, CNA, Pru **4** MONY **5** Aetna, Amica, Chubb, GEICO, NYLIC **6** Kemper, Lloyd's, Safeco **7** Conseco, Farmers, Met Life, Sun Life **8** Allstate, Hartford **9** General Re, State Farm, Travelers **10** Nationwide, Prudential **11** John Hancock, New York Life **13** Liberty Mutual, Mutual of Omaha
concern: **4** loss, prem., risk **5** claim **7** premium
kind of ~: **3** car **4** auto, home, life, term **5** flood **6** health
office: **6** agency
org.: **3** HMO, PPO **4** FDIC **5** FSLIC
worker: **3** CLU **5** agent **7** actuary
__ insurance: **3** car **4** auto, fire, life, term **5** flood, group, theft, title **6** dental, excess, health, keyman, marine, mutual, social **7** no-fault
insure: **5** cover, sew up **6** clinch, defend, secure, shield **7** promise, protect **8** attest to **9** guarantee, indemnify, safeguard **10** underwrite
insurgence: **6** revolt **8** defiance, uprising **9** commotion, rebellion
insurgent: **5** rebel **6** anarch **7** lawless, radical, riotous **8** agitator, factious, frondeur, mutineer, mutinous, renegade, resister **9** anarchist, fractious, revolting, seditious **10** anarchical, incendiary, malcontent, rebellious, subversive, unpeaceful
starter: **7** counter
insurmountable: **8** hopeless **10** impassable, infeasible, out of reach
insurrection: **4** coup, riot **6** mutiny, revolt, unrest **8** disorder, outbreak, sedition, uprising **9** rebellion
insurrectionist: **5** rebel **7** heretic, radical, traitor **8** agitator, mutineer, renegade **9** dissenter, dissident, insurgent **10** malcontent
insusceptible: **3** icy **4** cold, cool, hard **5** stony **6** dead to, deaf to, flinty, frigid, inured, steely, stoney **7** callous
int.
not ~: **3** ext.
where ~ may appear: **4** stmt.
Int. __: **3** Rev.
intact: **4** mint **5** as one, solid, sound, uncut, whole **6** entire, unhurt, virgin **7** perfect, working **8** all there, complete, together, unbroken, unharmed, unmarked, virginal **9** inviolate, not broken, undamaged, uninjured, unscathed, untouched **10** in one piece, unabridged, unimpaired

intaglio: **7** carving, jewelry **9** engraving
counterpart: **5** cameo
stone: **4** onyx
intake: **4** diet, food **7** suction **8** air shaft, air valve **10** absorption
intake __: **5** valve
intangible: **5** ideal **6** dreamy, unreal **7** elusive, elusory **8** abstract, abstruse, bodiless, ethereal **9** invisible, spiritual **10** evanescent, immaterial, impalpable, indefinite, unapparent, unphysical, unviewable
__ in tango: **3** T as
...in tears amid the __ corn: **5** alien
integer: **2** no. **3** one, six, two **4** five, four, nine, unit **5** eight, seven, three **6** figure, number **7** numeral
integers, like some: **3** odd **4** even
Integra: **3** car **4** auto **5** Acura
integral: **3** sum **4** full **5** basic, total, vital, whole **6** choate, entire **7** organic, pivotal **8** complete **9** aggregate, elemental, essential, intrinsic, necessary, requisite, undivided
integrate: **3** mix, wed **4** fuse, join, knit, link, meld, mesh **5** blend, immix, merge, unify, unite **6** embody, imbody **7** combine, conjoin **8** coalesce, go native **9** associate, commingle, harmonize, interface, reconcile **10** amalgamate, assimilate, centralize, complement, constitute, coordinate, homogenize, proportion, synthesize
integrated: **6** joined, linked, meshed, smooth, united **7** flowing, unified **8** cohesive, complete, hooked up
integrated __: **3** bar **6** optics **7** circuit
integration: **5** blend, union **6** fusion **7** amalgam **9** synthesis
org. promoting ~: **4** CORE **5** NAACP
integrity: **5** asset, honor, right, truth, unity **6** ethics, purity, virtue **7** honesty, loyalty, probity **8** cohesion, fairness, fidelity, goodness, identity, morality, nobility, totality, veracity **9** character, coherence, constancy, fixedness, good faith, principle, rectitude, sincerity, soundness, stability, wholeness **10** entireness, honestness, perfection, principles, simplicity
integument: **3** pod **4** aril, bark, case, hide, hull, husk, rind, skin **5** crust, shell, shuck, testa **6** casing, sheath **7** coating, outside, peeling **8** covering, envelope, membrane, pellicle
Intel
rival: **3** AMD
intellect: **4** head, mind, nous, sage, soul, wits **5** brain, depth, savvy, sense **6** acuity, acumen, brains, genius, pundit, reason, smarts **7** ability, egghead, scholar, thinker **8** aptitude, Einstein, highbrow, judgment, sagacity **9** ingenuity, mentality **10** profundity
intellection: **4** idea, mind **5** brain, sense **6** acumen, brains, reason, senses **7** marbles **8** judgment, lucidity, sapience **9** mentality
intellectual: **3** ace **4** nerd, sage, whiz **5** brain, smart, sound **6** brainy, genius, mental, pundit **7** bookish, egghead, erudite, learned, prodigy, scholar, thinker **8** abstract, academic, cerebral, creative, Einstein, highbrow, longhair, profound, rational, studious, virtuoso **9** scholarly **10** mastermind
intellectualize: **5** think **6** ideate, reason **8** cogitate, ruminate **9** cerebrate
intelligence: **3** wit **4** head, info, mind, news, soul, wits, word **5** brain, depth, savvy, sense, skill **6** acuity, acumen, brains, esprit, genius, reason, report, sanity, smarts, wisdom **7** ability, lowdown, message, tidings **8** aptitude, judgment, keenness, sagacity, sapience **9** mentality
org.: **3** CIA, NSA
intelligence __: **4** test **5** agent
intelligent: **3** apt **4** able, keen, sage, sane, wise **5** quick, ready, sharp, smart, witty **6** astute, brainy, bright, clever, gifted, shrewd, strong **7** capable, knowing, liberal, logical, sapient **8** cerebral, highbrow, incisive, profound, rational, sensible, thinking **9** astucious, brilliant, ingenious, inventive, observant, sagacious **10** perceptive, reasonable
group: **5** Mensa
not ~: **3** dim **4** dull, dumb, slow **5** inane, silly **6** oafish, obtuse, simple **7** asinine, boorish, doltish, foolish, witless **8** ignorant **9** brainless, dimwitted, nitwitted, senseless **10** half-witted, illiterate, soft-headed
intelligentsia: **6** brains **7** savants **8** literati
intelligible: **4** open **5** clear, lucid, plain **6** limpid, simple **7** legible, obvious **8** coherent, distinct, knowable, luminous, readable, simplify
Intellivision
rival: **5** Atari
intemperance: **6** luxury
intemperate: **3** hot **4** wild **5** undue **6** bitter, lavish, severe, torrid, wanton **7** hoggish, lustful, piggish, raucous **8** prodigal, rigorous, tropical, uncurbed
be ~: **6** overdo **7** lay it on, run riot **8** overplay
intemperately: **3** too **4** very **6** unduly
intemperence: **4** lust **6** excess **8** gluttony, voracity
intend: **3** aim **4** mean, plan **5** aim to, essay, spell **6** aspire, design, expect **7** attempt, propose, purport, purpose, resolve, signify **8** endeavor **10** have in mind, have in view
to: **4** will **5** shall
intended: **5** meant **6** fiancé, future, wilful **7** fiancée, willful **8** plighted, promised **9** affianced, betrothed, voluntary **10** deliberate, purposeful, volitional
intense: **3** hot **4** avid, deep, hard, keen, loud, rich, warm, wild **5** acute, eager, fiery, great, harsh, lurid, sharp, type A, vivid **6** ardent, biting, bitter, devout, fervid, fierce, heated, marked, mortal, red-hot, severe, solemn, steady, strong, torrid, urgent **7** burning, cutting, dynamic, earnest, extreme, fervent, flaming, furious, soulful, vicious, violent, zealous **8** diligent, forceful, piercing, poignant, powerful, profound, stinging, strained, terrific, vehement, vigorous, wild-eyed **9** agonizing, desperate, energetic, excessive, exquisite, fanatical, innermost, steadfast, undivided **10** passionate, purposeful, unwavering
become less ~: **3** ebb **4** wane **5** abate **7** decline, subside, tail off
look: **3** eye **4** gaze, leer **5** glare, stare
not ~: **4** calm **5** type B **8** laid-back
intensely: **4** deep, hard **5** madly **6** keenly, vastly **7** greatly **8** forcibly, mightily, severely, terribly, urgently **9** extremely, fervently, like crazy, seriously **10** incredibly, powerfully, thoroughly
intensification: **5** surge, swell **6** growth, step-up, upturn, waxing **7** buildup, upsurge, upswing **8** increase, swelling, widening **9** crescendo, deepening **10** broadening, burgeoning
intensify: **4** boom, gird, rise, tone, whet **5** add to, boost, build, crank, mount, raise, revup, shore, spike, steel, swell **6** accent, anneal, beef up, deepen, gather, harden, heat up, prop up, step up, stress, temper, tone up **7** augment, bolster, brace up, build up, burgeon, develop, elevate, empower, enhance, fortify, magnify, quicken, scale up, sharpen, shore up, stiffen, toughen **8** bourgeon, brighten, buttress, compound, energize, escalate, heighten, increase, indurate, redouble, vitalize **9** aggravate, emphasize, reinforce **10** accentuate, aggrandize, exacerbate, exaggerate, invigorate, strengthen
intensity: **4** fire, fury, heat, kick, size, zeal **5** ardor, depth, fever, force, might, power, vigor **6** degree, energy, fervor, volume **7** emotion, ferment, passion, potence, potency, tension **8** devotion, emphasis, keenness, lyricism, severity, strength, violence **9** acuteness, diligence, greatness, high pitch, magnitude, sharpness, toughness, vehemence **10** enthusiasm, excitement, fanaticism, fierceness
lose ~: **3** ebb **4** wane **5** abate **7** subside
Intensity
author: Dean Koontz
intensive: **4** deep **6** all-out, severe **7** in-depth **8** complete, profound, thorough, whole hog **9** demanding, full-dress, out-and-out, speeded-up **10** exhaustive
__-intensive: **5** labor
intent: **3** aim, end, set **4** bent, firm, goal, hope, idea, keen, plan, rapt, will, wish **5** alert, bound, drift, eager, fixed, point, tenor **6** desire, motive, notion, object, spirit, target **7** dead-set, decided, earnest, engaged, focused, meaning, purport, purpose, riveted, settled **8** absorbed, ambition, decisive, hellbent, immersed, occupied, resolute, resolved, studious, volition, watchful **9** ambitious, attentive, committed, engrossed, iron-jawed, objective, steadfast, wrapped up **10** determined, purposeful, resolution, thoughtful
malicious ~: **5** spite **6** enmity, hatred, malice, rancor **7** cruelty, ill will, revenge **8** acrimony **9** animosity, hostility, vengeance
with the ~: **4** so as
intention: **3** aim, end **4** goal, hope, idea, plan, will, wish **5** angle, drift **6** animus, design, desire, import, motive, notion, object, reason, spirit, target **7** meaning, purport, purpose, resolve, thought **8** volition **10** resolution
intentional: **5** meant **6** wilful **7** advised, knowing, planned, studied, willful, willing, witting **8** designed, unforced **9** voluntary **10** purposeful
intently: **4** hard **6** firmly, keenly **7** alertly, closely, fixedly, sharply **8** steadily, urgently **9** seriously
intentness: **4** zeal **9** assiduity, attention, diligence, eagerness **10** absorption
__ intents and purposes: **5** to all **6** for all
inter __: **3** nos **4** alia, alii **5** alios, vivos
interact: **4** talk **6** relate **7** combine, connect, network **8** converse **9** cooperate, interface, touch base
interactive: **5** joint **6** mutual, shared **8** communal, conjoint **9** concerted **10** collective, reciprocal
interbreed: **3** mix **5** blend, cross **6** mingle **9** hybridize
intercede: **3** aid **4** help **5** mix in **6** assist, butt in, step in **7** barge in, intrude, mediate **9** arbitrate, intervene, negotiate, reconcile, take a hand
interceder: **5** agent, envoy **7** arbiter, liaison, referee **8** emissary, mediator **9** go-between, middleman **10** arbitrator, negotiator, peacemaker
intercept: **3** get **4** curb, halt, snag, stop, take **5** block, catch, check, seize **6** ambush, arrest, cut off, tackle, waylay **7** deflect, head off, prevent **8** obstruct, overhear **9** interpose, interrupt, shortstop **10** anticipate
intercession: **3** bid **4** plea, suit **6** agency, orison, prayer **8** intreaty, petition **9** mediation **10** assistance
intercessor: **3** ref, ump **5** judge **6** umpire **7** referee **10** arbitrator
interchange: **4** swap, swop **5** bandy, trade **6** barter, rotate, switch **7** liaison **8** exchange, language **9** take turns, transpose
sight: **5** diner, motel **10** gas station
interchangeable: **4** same **5** alike **7** related **8** fungible **10** reciprocal

intercom call: **4** page
interconnect: **6** adjoin, engage, relate
interconnection: **3** web **4** link **7** network
Inter-Continental: **5** hotel
  alternative: *see* hotel
intercourse: **5** trade, union **6** speech **7** contact, jobbing, rapping, talking, trading, traffic **8** colloquy, commerce
interdependent: **6** linked, mutual **7** related **10** reciprocal
interdict: **3** ban, bar **4** stop, tabu, veto **5** debar, taboo **6** censor, forbid, hinder, impede, outlaw **7** embargo, exclude, inhibit, prevent, repress **8** disallow, preclude, prohibit, restrain **9** exclusion, proscribe
interdicted: **5** taboo **7** crooked, illegal, illicit **8** criminal, unlawful, verboten **9** felonious, forbidden **10** not allowed
interdiction: **3** ban, bar **4** tabu, veto **7** embargo, refusal
interest: **4** care, gain, good, grab, grip, hook, lure, move, note, part, sake, side, stir, zest **5** amuse, catch, claim, hobby, piece, pique, right, rivet, rouse, share, snare, sport, stake, tempt, touch **6** absorb, affect, allure, arouse, arrest, behalf, divert, engage, entice, excite, matter, notice, occupy, perk up, please, points, profit, regard, return, strike, turn on **7** attract, benefit, concern, engross, enthral, enthuse, immerse, impress, inspire, inthral, involve, passion, pastime, portion, pursuit, revenue, welfare **8** activity, appeal to, dividend, enthrall, inthrall, intrigue, lifework, proceeds **9** advantage, affection, avocation, curiosity, diversion, entertain, fascinate, relevance, spotlight, stimulate, tantalize, titillate, well-being **10** absorption, attraction, enthusiasm, excitement, importance, motivation, percentage, prosperity, recreation, snoopiness
  common ~: **3** tie **4** bond, link
  devoid of ~: **4** blah, dull, flat **5** vapid **6** boring, jejune **7** insipid, prosaic **9** tasteless, wearisome **10** dullsville, flavorless, lackluster
  excessive ~: **5** usury
  factor: **3** pct. **4** rate **5** yield **7** percent
  have an ~ in: **3** own **4** hold **7** possess
  hold one's ~: **6** engage
  in the ~ of: **3** for
  lack of ~: **5** ennui **6** tedium **7** boredom
  lose ~: **3** nod **4** pale, pall, tire **5** weary
  paying ~: **5** owing **6** in debt
  personal ~: **5** share, stake **6** behalf **10** investment
  point of ~: **5** locus, scene, sight, vista **6** vision **7** display, exhibit **9** spectacle
  provide at ~: **4** lend, loan
  regard with ~: **4** gape, gawk, gaze **5** stare **10** rubberneck
  show lack of ~: **4** doze, yawn
  special ~ group: **3** soc. **5** guild, lobby **6** caucus **7** society
  strong ~: **4** zeal, zest **5** ardor, mania **6** fervor, thirst **7** craving, passion **8** devotion **9** intensity, obsession **10** dedication, enthusiasm
  take an ~ in: **4** like
  to a usurer: **3** vig **8** vigorish
  unit: **2** pt. **5** point
interest __: **4** rate
__ interest: **6** public, simple, vested **7** accrued, special
interested: **4** keen **5** drawn **6** caught **7** curious, liberal **9** attentive, attracted, concerned, engrossed, impressed, inquiring, observant, on the case, receptive **10** fascinated, implicated, prejudiced, responsive, stimulated
  be ~: **4** care **9** give a darn
  become ~: **5** sit up
  be ~ in: **5** watch **6** follow, take in **7** monitor, observe **9** cultivate
  too ~: **4** nosy **5** nosey **6** prying, snoopy **8** meddling, snooping **9** butting in, intrusive, obtrusive **10** meddlesome
  very ~: **4** avid **5** afire **6** ardent
interesting: **5** fresh, juicy, meaty, novel **6** clever, exotic **7** curious, unusual **8** creative, gripping, inspired, inviting, magnetic, original, readable **9** ingenious, inventive, memorable **10** innovative, magnetical
  not ~: **3** dry **4** blah **5** banal, ho-hum
__ interesting!: **4** Very
__-interest story: **5** human
interface: **4** link, talk **7** combine, connect, liaison **8** interact **9** integrate, touch base
interfere: **3** pry **4** nose, poke **5** mix in, snoop **6** butt in, horn in, impede, kibitz, meddle, step in, tamper **7** barge in, intrude, obtrude **8** conflict, obstruct **9** frustrate, interlope, interpose, interrupt, intervene **10** contravene, discommode, discourage
  with: **5** block, cross, delay **6** hamper, hinder, molest
  (with): **4** fool, mess
interference: **8** blocking, meddling, obstacle
  reception ~: **4** snow **6** static
  run ~ for: **4** help **6** assist **8** advocate
interfering: **4** nosy, rude **5** pushy **8** meddling **9** intrusive, obtrusive, officious **10** meddlesome
interfold: **5** weave **6** enlace, inlace
interim: **3** gap **4** wait **5** break, letup, pause, while **6** acting, breach, hiatus, lacuna, layoff, pro tem, recess **7** stopgap, time-out **8** breather, downtime, interval, meantime **9** makeshift, temporary, tentative **10** jury-rigged, pro tempore
  in the ~: **8** meantime **9** meanwhile
interior: **4** core, home, soul **5** heart, inner, midst **6** bowels, center, inland, inside, marrow, within **7** central, in-house, private **8** domestic, national
  combining form: **4** endo-, ento-
destroy the ~: **3** gut
Interior Dept. agcy: **3** BLM, NPS
Interiors (1978 film)
  cast: Diane Keaton, E.G. Marshall, Geraldine Page
  director: Woody Allen
interject: **3** add **5** input, put in **6** fill in, insert, jump in, thrust **7** comment, force in, implant, include, intrude, throw in **9** insinuate, interpose, interrupt, introduce, punctuate, squeeze in **10** infiltrate
interjection: **2** ah, aw, eh, ha, hi, ho, oh, ow, oy, uh **3** aah, ack, aha, arf, bah, bam, boo, boy, brr, cry, duh, fie, gee, grr, haw, heh, hey, huh, ick, nix, och, oho, olé, oof, ooh, pah, pow, rah, rot, say, tsk, tut, ugh, why, wow, yah, yay, yea, yes, yow, yum, zzz **4** ahem, ahoy, alas, amen, arra, bosh, ciao, darn, dear, drat, ecce, egad, evoe, good, gosh, ha-ha, hail, heck, help, hush, jeez, mush, nuts, oh-oh, okay, oops, ouch, oyes, oyez, pfft, pfui, phew, phoo, pish, poof, pooh, posh, ptui, rats, roar, scat, shoo, ta-da, ta-ta, tush, uh-oh, uh-uh, well, wham, whee, whew, whoo, word, yeah, yell, yeow, yipe, yo-ho, yuck **5** achoo, alack, arrah, avast, banco, bingo, blimy, brava, bravo, egads, faugh, fudge, golly, goody, great, hallo, hello, hillo, ho-hum, hooey, hoo-ha, howdy, hullo, humph, huzza, later, nerts, nertz, peace, phfft, prost, pshaw, right, salud, scram, shame, shout, shush, skoal, sooey, sorry, ta-dah, te-hee, uh-huh, voilà, whoof, whoop, yecch, yipes, zooks, zowie **6** ahchoo, begone, behold, bellow, blimey, by Jove, cheers, clamor, crikey, cripes, encore, enough, eureka, giddap, goodie, good-oh, gotcha, hachoo, halloa, halloo, hallow, haw-haw, hilloa, holler, hoo-hah, hoorah, hooray, hotcha, hot dog, hulloo, hurrah, hurray, huzzah, indeed, jiminy, ka-boom, la-de-da, la-di-da, l'chaim, outcry, phooey, presto, prosit, ptooey, rather, remark, righto, shalom, sheesh, sholom, shucks, tee-hee, thanks, touché, tsk tsk, tut-tut, whammo, whizzo, whoops, yippee, yoicks, yoo-hoo, yum-yum, zounds **7** attaboy, big deal, brother, by jingo, caramba, cheerio, gangway, giddyap, giddyup, goldarn, goldurn, good-bye, heave ho, heigh-ho, holy cow, horrors, hosanna, hushaby, jeepers, jimminy, kerchoo, l'chayim, lehayim, Odzooks, rubbish, whoopee, whoopie **8** alley-oop, all right, attagirl, by cracky, farewell, for shame, Gadzooks, gracious, holy moly, honestly, lackaday, lah-di-dah, lechayim, scramola, welladay, wellaway, whatever **10** hallelujah
  palindromic ~: **3** aha, hah, oho, wow
  see also exclamation
interlace: **3** mat, mix, tie **4** bind, join, knit, knot, lace **5** braid, plait, twine, weave **6** engage, enmesh, immesh, inmesh, mingle, splice, zigzag **7** combine, entwine, intwine **8** entangle
interlaced: **4** wove **5** woven
Interlaken river: **3** Aar **4** Aare
interlard: **5** admix, mix in **7** dress up, spice up
interlink: **4** join, link, mesh **5** unite **6** splice **7** connect **8** dovetail
interlock: **3** fit **4** knit, mesh **5** weave **6** engage, enlace, inlace **8** dovetail
interlocution: **4** chat, talk **6** confab, gossip, parley, powwow **7** chatter, palaver, schmoos **8** chitchat, converse, schmoose, schmooze
interlocutor: **2** MC **4** host **5** emcee
interlope: **3** pry **4** nose **5** snoop **6** tamper **7** intrude **8** trespass **9** interfere
interloper: **7** invader **8** kibitzer, outsider, stranger **10** trespasser
interlude: **3** gap **4** halt, lull, rest, wait **5** break, delay, pause, space, spell **6** hiatus, recess **7** episode, liaison, respite **8** downtime, interval, stoppage
intermediary: **3** rep **4** tool **5** agent, envoy, judge, means **6** broker, buffer, medium **7** channel, liaison, vehicle **8** delegate, emissary, mediator **9** appointee, messenger, middleman **10** peacemaker
intermediate: **6** center, medium, middle **7** average, neutral **8** moderate **9** appointee
  in law: **5** mesne
intermesh: **6** engage **8** activate
Intermezzo (1939 film)
  cast: Ingrid Bergman, Edna Best, Leslie Howard
  composer: Max Steiner
interminable: **4** dull, long **6** boring **7** endless, eternal, lengthy, nonstop, undying **8** constant, infinite, timeless, unending **9** perpetual, unlimited
interminably: **4** ever **5** no end, on end **7** forever, on and on
intermingle: **3** mix, wed **4** fuse, join, meld, mesh, pool **5** admix, blend, merge **6** mingle **7** combine **8** intermix
intermission: **4** lull, rest, stop, wait **5** break, lapse, let-up, pause, spell **6** layoff, recess **7** interim, leisure, respite, time-out **8** abeyance, breather, downtime, entr'acte, interval, stoppage
  follower: **5** Act II **6** act two
intermit: **3** end **4** halt, stay **5** break, cease, let up, pause, recur **6** arrest, recess **7** suspend, take ten **8** take five **9** interrupt, terminate
intermittent: **6** broken, uneven **8** frequent, off and on, on and off, periodic, sporadic **9** recurrent, spasmodic **10** sporadical
intermittently: **8** fitfully, off and on, on and off **9** piecemeal, sometimes
intermix: **4** fuse **5** alloy, blend, merge **6** mingle **7** shuffle **9** commingle **10** adulterate, assimilate
intermixture: **4** meld **5** alloy, blend, union **6** fusion, medley **7** amalgam, mélange, variety **8** mishmash,

mixed bag **9** composite, diversity, synthesis, variation **10** assortment, collection, concoction, miscellany
intern: 3 pen **4** cage, jail, keep, stay, tyro **5** gofer, medic, pupil, seize **6** detain, doctor, gopher, immure, lock up, novice, shut in **7** confine, enclose, impound, inclose, learner, new hand, student, trainee **8** imprison, resident, restrict **9** greenhorn, new doctor, physician **10** apprentice, tenderfoot
place: 4 ward **6** clinic **8** hospital
internal: 4 home **5** civic, inner **6** inland, innate, inside, inward **8** domestic, national **10** indigenous
combining form: 3 end-, ent- **4** endo-, ento-
internal __: 3 ear **5** audit, clock **7** revenue
Internal Affairs (1990 film)
cast: Andy García, Ricard Gere
internalize
anger: 4 boil, fret, fume **5** chafe **6** seethe
internalize anger: 4 stew **6** seethe
international: 5 alien, world **6** global **7** foreign, oversea **8** offshore, overseas **9** worldwide
international __: 3 law **4** unit
International __ Line: 4 Date
__ International: 7 Amnesty, Gideons
interne: 5 medic **6** doctor **9** physician
internecine: 4 gory **5** civil **6** bloody, deadly, family, mortal **7** ruinous **8** domestic, familial, internal
internee: 3 con **5** felon, lifer **7** captive, convict, hostage **8** criminal, detainee, jailbird, offender, prisoner, yardbird **10** lawbreaker
Internet: 3 Web, WWW **6** the Web **10** cyberspace
access method: 5 modem, Web TV
ad: 6 banner
addict, perhaps: 4 nerd
auction site: 4 eBay
banners: 3 ads
browse the ~: 4 surf
commerce: 5 e-tail **6** e-trade
company: 6 dot-com
convenience: 4 link
diary: 4 blog
insult: 5 flame
large ~ database: 5 Lexis, Nexis
letters: 3 URL, www **4** html, http
mag: 5 ezine
mag.: 5 e-zine
messages: 5 e-mail
name: 6 user ID
program: 6 applet
programming language: 4 Java
provider: 3 AOL **5** Yahoo!
query: 3 FAQ
search engine: 6 Google
separator: 3 dot
software: 3 app **6** applet **7** browser
start an ~ session: 5 log in, log on
suffix: 3 com, edu, gov, net, org
surfer: 4 user
surf the ~: 6 browse
internist: 2 MD **5** medic **6** doctor **9** physician
org.: 3 AMA
internment: 6 arrest **7** bondage, custody **9** captivity, detention **10** detainment, immurement

__ inter pares: 5 prima **6** primus
interpersonal __: 6 skills
interplay: 6 banter **8** exchange **9** tit for tat **10** networking
interpolation: 3 tag **5** ad lib, aside, rider **6** insert, prefix, suffix **7** adjunct, codicil **8** addendum, addition, footnote
word ~: 6 tmesis
Interpol HQ: 4 Lyon **5** Lyons
interpose: 3 pry **5** cut in, judge, stick **6** butt in, edge in, horn in, inject, insert, kibitz, meddle, step in, toss in, umpire, work in, worm in **7** barge in, head off, implant, mediate, referee, wedge in **8** chisel in, muscle in, sandwich **9** arbitrate, insinuate, intercept, interfere, interject, intervene, introduce **10** contravene
interposing: 4 nosy **5** nosey **6** prying, snoopy **8** snooping **9** intrusive
interpret: 4 limn, read, take **5** enact, gloss, infer, solve, state, teach, treat **6** decode, define, depict, recite, render **7** analyze, clarify, explain, expound, perform, portray **8** annotate, construe, decipher, simplify, spell out **9** criticize, delineate, elaborate, elucidate, exemplify, explicate, represent, translate **10** commentate, illuminate, illustrate, paraphrase, understand
interpretation: 4 spin **5** grasp, light, sense, slant **6** aspect **7** insight, meaning, reading, version **8** analysis, judgment **9** rendition
Interpretation of Dreams, The
author: Sigmund Freud
interpreter: 5 guide **6** critic, editor **7** decoder, exegete, prophet **8** cicerone, dragoman, exponent
Interpreter, The (2005 film)
cast: Catherine Keener, Nicole Kidman, Sean Penn
director: Sydney Pollack
interregnum: 3 gap **4** lull, rest **5** break, letup, pause **6** hiatus, lacuna, recess **7** interim, respite **8** abeyance, half time, interval
interrelationship: 4 bond, link **6** accord **7** concord, empathy, harmony, rapport **8** affinity, goodwill, sympathy **9** communion
__ in Terris: 5 Pacem
interrogate: 3 ask **4** pump, quiz **5** grill, probe, query, roast **6** go over **7** examine **8** question, work over
interrogation: 5 Q and A, query **6** asking **7** enquiry, inquiry, pumping **8** grilling, question
interrogative
adverb: 3 how **4** when **5** where
French ~: 4 quel, quoi
pronoun: 3 who, why **4** what, whom
Spanish ~: 3 qué **4** cómo **5** quíen
interrupt: 3 cut, end **4** halt, stop **5** barge, break, check, crash, cut in, delay, sever, stall **6** arrest, bother, bust in, butt in, cut off, divide, edge in, hinder, hold up, horn in, impede, jump in **7** barge in, break in, chime in, crowd in, disjoin, disturb, intrude, prevent, refrain, suspend **8** break off, cut short, disunite, infringe, intermit, obstruct, separate **9** intercept, interfere, interject, intervene, punctuate, shortstop **10** disconnect, inactivate
__, Interrupted: 4 Girl
interruption: 3 gap **4** halt, rift, stop **5** break, delay, lapse, letup, pause, space, split **6** breach, cutoff, detour, hiatus, lacuna, layoff **8** abeyance, blackout, break off, division, interval, obstacle, stoppage **10** disruption
cause: 5 pager
follow without ~: 4 flow **5** segue
polite ~: 4 ahem **8** pardon me
without ~: 5 on end **8** steadily
intersect: 3 cut **4** meet **5** cross **6** bisect, divide **8** converge, traverse **9** cut across, decussate **10** crisscross
intersection: 3 hub, jct. **4** link **5** joint **6** corner **7** meeting **8** crossing, junction, juncture
divider: 6 island
kind of ~: 3 tee
sign: 4 stop, walk **5** yield **8** don't walk
interspace: 3 cut, gap **4** gash, hole, mesh, rent, slit, slot **5** crack, space, split **6** cavity, cranny, groove, lacuna **7** opening **8** aperture
intersperse: 5 strew **7** scatter **9** punctuate
interstate: 2 rd. **3** rte. **4** pike, road **5** route **7** freeway, highway **8** national **10** expressway
access: 4 ramp
enter the ~: 5 merge
interruption: 6 bypass, detour
like an: 5 laned
sight: 3 car **4** auto, semi **5** truck
sign: 3 Gas **4** Exit
stopover: 3 inn **5** lodge, motel **10** motor court, motor lodge
see also freeway, highway
interstellar dist.: 4 lt. yr.
interstice: 3 gap **4** hole, slit **5** crack, space **6** areola, areole, lacuna **7** crevice, fissure, opening **8** aperture, interval
intertwine: 4 coil, knit, lace, mesh **5** braid, plait, twist, unite, weave **6** enlace, enmesh, immesh, inlace, inmesh, tangle **7** sinuate **8** entangle
intertwined: 4 wove **5** woven **7** related
interval: 3 gap, lag **4** lull, rest, span, term, time, wait **5** break, delay, lapse, letup, pause, point, space, spell **6** breach, hiatus, lacuna, layoff, length, period, radius, season **7** time-out **8** distance, downtime
musical ~: 4 step **5** fifth, ninth, sixth, third **6** fourth, octave **7** seventh, tritone
intervals
at ~: 6 slowly **8** off and on **9** gradually, piecemeal, sometimes **10** now and then, on occasion, step by step
at fixed ~: 6 cyclic, hourly, weekly, yearly **7** monthly, regular **8** cyclical, periodic **10** periodical
intervene: 5 ensue, mix in, occur **6** butt in, divide, elapse, happen, horn in, meddle, step in **7** barge in, intrude, mediate, obtrude **8** muscle in, separate **9** arbitrate, intercede, interfere, interpose, interrupt, negotiate, reconcile, supervene, take a hand **10** come to pass, conciliate
intervening: 6 middle **7** between, halfway
in law: 5 mesne
interview: 3 ask, see **4** poll, quiz, talk **5** grill, Q and A, visit **6** depose, talk to **7** examine **8** question, sound out **9** circulate, encounter, tête-à-tête, touch base **10** cattle call, conference, discussion, engagement
Zen ~: 7 dokusan
__ interview: 4 exit
interviewer: 4 host **5** asker, press **8** enquirer, inquirer, reporter
request: 2 CV **4** vita **6** résumé
Interview With the Vampire
author: Anne Rice
Interview With the Vampire... (1994 film)
cast: Antonio Banderas, Tom Cruise, Brad Pitt, Stephen Rea
interweave: 3 mix **4** hide, knit, lace, mesh, plat **5** blend, braid, cross, immix, plait, twine, twist, weave **6** enlace, inlace, mingle, relate, splice, tangle, tuck in **7** combine, entwine, intwine, wreathe **8** entangle **10** complicate
interwoven
hair: 5 plait, queue **7** pigtail **8** ponytail
intestinal: 9 abdominal
fortitude: 4 guts **5** nerve, pluck, spunk, valor **7** stamina **8** backbone, tenacity
intestine
combining form: 5 enter- **6** entero-
of the small ~: 5 ileac, ileal
part: 5 colon, ileum
in the __: 3 air, bag, end, red, way **4** dark, hole, hunt, know, loop, main, past, pink, soup, swim, wind, zone **5** black, cards, clear, flesh, least, money, wings, works **6** offing
in the __ boat: 4 same
in the __ luxury: 5 lap of
in the __ of: 4 name, wake **5** midst
in the __ of duty: 4 line
in the __ of luxury: 3 lap
in the __ of Morpheus: 4 arms
in the __ of time: 4 nick
in the __ run: 4 long **5** short
in the __ way: 5 worst
In the __: 5 Arena
In the __ of Fire: 4 Line
In the __ of the Night: 4 Heat **5** Still
__ In, The: 6 Fleet's
__ in the air: 6 castle **7** castles
In the Arena
author: Richard Nixon
__ in the arm: 4 shot
__ in the Attic: 4 Toys
__ in the back: 4 stab
in the back in Latin: 6 a tergo
__ in the bag!: 3 It's
__ in the balance: 4 hang
__ in the Balance: 5 Earth
__ in the Band, The: 4 Boys
In the Bar of a Tokyo Hotel
author: Tennessee Williams
In the Bedroom (2001 film)
cast: Sissy Spacek, Nick Stahl, Marisa Tomei

In the Beginning
author: Chaim Potok
in the blink ___ eye: 4 of an
___-in-the-bone: 4 bred
In the Boom Boom Room
author: David Rabe
___ in the Boondocks: 4 Down
___-in-the-box: 4 jack
___ in the bucket: 5 a drop
___ in the bud: 3 nip 5 nip it
In the Clap Shack
author: William Styron
In the Closet (1992 song)
artist: Michael Jackson
___ in the Clowns: 4 Send
___ in the cold: 3 out
___ in the Country: 4 A Day, Wild 6 A Month
___ in the Cradle: 4 Cat's
___ in the Crowd: 5 A Face
In the Cut (2003 film)
cast: Jennifer Jason Leigh, Mark Ruffalo, Meg Ryan
___ in the dark: 4 keep, leap, shot 7 whistle
___ in the Dark: 4 A Cry, Lady 5 A Shot, Piano 7 Dancing
___ in the Deep: 6 Asleep
___ in the Dell, The: 6 Farmer
___ in the door: 4 foot
___ in the Earth: 6 Giants
In The Evening
artist: Erté
in the event ___: 4 that
___ in the face: 4 blue
___ in the face of: 3 fly
___ in the Family: 3 All
___ in the fire: 4 iron 5 irons
In the Fire of Spring
author: Thomas Tryon
In the Frame
author: Dick Francis
In the Ghetto (1969 song)
artist: Elvis Presley
In the Good Old Summertime: 4 song 5 waltz
___ in the grass: 5 snake
___ in the Gray Flannel Suit, The: 3 Man 5 Horse
___ in the hand...: 5 A bird
___ in the Hat, The: 3 Cat
___ in the Head: 5 A Hole
___ in the Heart: 4 Deep 6 Places
___ in the Heart of Texas: 4 Deep
In the Heat of the Night (1967 film)
cast: Lee Grant, Warren Oates, Sidney Poitier, Rod Steiger
director: Norman Jewison
In the Heat of the Night (NBC/CBS drama)
cast: Carroll O'Connor (Bill Gillespie)
Howard Rollins (Virgil Tibbs)
setting: 4 Miss. 6 Sparta
___ in the hole: 3 ace
___ in the House: 5 Guest 6 Doctor
___ in the Iron Mask, The: 3 Man
___ in the Lake, The: 4 Lady
___ in the least: 3 not
___ in the Life: 4 A Day
in the line of ___: 4 duty
In the Line of Fire (1993 film)
cast: Clint Eastwood, John Malkovich, Rene Russo
in the long ___: 3 run
___ in the manger: 3 dog
___ in the market: 4 drug
In the Mecca
author: Gwendolyn Brooks
In the Midnight Hour (1965 song)
artist: Wilson Pickett
___ in the Money: 4 We're
___ in the moon: 3 man
___ in the Morning, No: 3 But
___ in the mouth: 4 down
___-in-the-mud: 5 stick
In the name of ___: 5 Allah
___! In the Name of Love: 4 Stop
In the Name of the Father (1993 film)
cast: Daniel Day Lewis, Emma Thompson
In the Navy (1979 song)
artist: Village People
___ in the neck: 4 pain 5 a pain
___ in the new year: 4 ring
___ in the Night: 5 Blues
___ in the ocean: 4 spit
___ in the ointment: 3 fly 4 a fly
___ in the Outfield: 6 Angels
___ in the Pacific: 4 Hell
___ in the pan: 5 flash
___ in the pants: 4 kick
___ in the Park With George: 6 Sunday
In the Penal Colony
author: Franz Kafka
...in the pot, ___ days old: 4 nine
___-in-the-pulpit: 4 jack
___ in the RAF: 5 A Yank
___ in the Rain: 6 Singin'
___ in there: 4 hang
___ in the reins: 4 draw
___ in the right direction: 5 a step
___ in the rough: 7 diamond
___-in-the-round: 7 theater, theatre
___ in the Ruins: 4 Love
___ in the Rye, The: 7 Catcher
___ in the Saddle: 4 Tall
in the same ___: 4 boat 6 breath
in the same place in Latin: 4 ibid.
___ in the shade: 4 made
___ in the sky: 3 pie
___ in the Sky: 3 Eye 5 Cabin 6 Spirit
___ In The Sky With Diamonds: 4 Lucy
___ in the Stars: 4 Lost 7 Written
...___ in the state of Denmark: 6 rotten
In the Still of the Nite (1992 song)
artist: Boyz II Men
___ in the Stone, The: 5 Sword
___ in the Stream: 7 Islands
___ in the street: 3 man 5 woman
___ in the Street: 7 Dancing
___ in the Streets: 5 Panic
In the Summertime (1970 song)
artist: Mungo Jerry
___ in the sun: 5 place 6 a place
___ in the Sun, A: 4 Walk 5 Place 6 Raisin
___ in the teeth of: 3 fly
___ in the tooth: 4 long
___ in the Underworld: 7 Orpheus
___ in the USA: 4 Born, made
In the Valley of Elah (2007 film)
cast: Tommy Lee Jones, Susan Sarandon, Charlize Theron
___ in the wall: 4 hole
___ in the Wall Gang: 4 Hole
___ in the water: 4 dead
___ in the Willows, The: 4 Wind
___ in the wind: 5 straw
___ in the Wind: 4 Dust 5 Voice 6 Blowin', Candle
___ in the Wine: 7 Bubbles
in the wink ___ eye: 4 of an
___ in the woods: 4 babe
___-in-the-wool: 4 dyed
in the worst ___: 3 way
In the Year 2525 (1969 song)
artist: Zager and Evans
in-thing: 6 latest, modish, trendy 7 faddish 8 up-to-date
in this ___ and age: 3 day
intimacy: 8 affinity 9 affection, closeness 10 experience, friendship
Intimacy
author: Jean-Paul Sartre
intimate: 3 bro, pal, say 4 chum, cosy, cozy, dear, deep, fond, hint, kind, mate, mean, near, pers., seem, snug, warm 5 bosom, buddy, close, cozey, cozie, crony, get at, imply, infer, inner, thick, tight 6 advert, allude, bon ami, chummy, clubby, friend, genial, hint at, inward, kindly, loving, secret, tip off 7 affable, amiable, compeer, comrade, connote, cordial, devoted, make out, mention, private, purport, signify, suggest, trusted, whisper 8 allude to, amicable, familiar, friendly, homelike, immanent, indicate, informal, lead up to, outgoing, personal, roommate, sociable 9 associate, boyfriend, companion, confidant, convivial, firsthand, innermost, insinuate, predicate 10 benevolent, bosom buddy, buddy-buddy, girlfriend, neighborly, solicitous
group: 4 club 6 circle, clique 7 coterie
intimated: 5 tacit 6 unsaid 8 hinted at, implicit, unspoken, unstated, unvoiced 9 alluded to
Intimate Exchanges
author: Alan Ayckbourn
intimately: 4 well 6 dearly, fondly, warmly 7 closely, privily 8 secretly
intimation: 3 cue 4 clew, clue, hint, sign, wind, word 5 tinge, touch, trace 6 shadow 7 inkling, warning 8 allusion, innuendo, overtone 9 suspicion 10 indication, suggestion
___ in Time: 4 Just 5 Steps
___ in time..., A: 6 stitch
___ in Time of Hesitation: 5 An Ode
intimidate: 3 awe, cow 5 alarm, bully, chill, daunt, deter, hound, psych, scare, shake, spook 6 coerce, dampen, harass, hector, lean on, menace, prey on, ruffle 7 bluster, buffalo, overawe, terrify, unnerve 8 bludgeon, browbeat, bulldoze, dispirit, dissuade, domineer, frighten, prey upon, psych out, threaten, unstring 9 constrain, fulminate, give a turn, give pause, strong-arm, terrorize, trample on, tyrannize 10 discourage, dishearten, pressurize, push around, scare stiff
intimidated: 5 timid 6 afraid, trepid 7 anxious, chicken, fearful, nervous, panicky 8 cowardly, fearsome, hesitant, timorous 9 awestruck
intimidating: 5 scary 6 feared 8 menacing 9 truculent
intimidation: 3 awe 4 fear, funk 5 alarm, dread 6 dismay, fright, terror, threat 7 tyranny 8 affright, bullying, coercion, daunting, pressure
intimidator: 5 bully, tough 8 hooligan
intl. alliance: 3 OAS 4 NATO
into: 7 taken by 8 beholden, hooked on, obsessed, pursuing, turned on 9 taken with, wild about 10 crazy about, involved in, obsessed by
in French: 4 dans
starter: 4 here 5 there, where
___ into: 3 buy, dig, eat, get, lay, lit, ram, rip, run, tap 4 bump, come, grow, lace, look, plow, plug, sail, tear, wade, work 5 break, build, delve, enter, light, pitch 6 breeze, plunge, settle
___ into account: 4 take
Into each ___...: 4 life
intolerable: 5 awful 7 extreme, onerous, painful, too much 8 a bit much, grievous 9 monstrous
one: 4 bore, drip, pain, pest, pill
Intolerable Cruelty (2003 film)
cast: George Clooney, Geoffrey Rush, Catherine Zeta-Jones
director: Joel Coen
intolerance: 4 bias 7 bigotry 8 jingoism, zealotry 9 prejudice
___ intolerance: 7 lactose
Intolerance (1916 film)
cast: Lillian Gish, Mae Marsh
director: D.W. Griffith
intolerant: 6 biased, narrow 7 bigoted 9 excitable, fanatical, fractious, hidebound, illiberal, impatient, indignant, irritable, jaundiced, short-fuse, unwilling 10 disdainful, inflexible, prejudiced, short-fused, xenophobic
one: 5 bigot
___ into line: 3 get 4 come, fall 5 bring
Into My Own
author: Robert Frost
intonated: 4 oral 5 vocal
intonation: 4 tone 5 sound, voice 6 accent 7 cadence, cadency 8 delivery 10 expression, inflection
intone: 3 hum, say 4 sing, talk 5 carol, chant, croon, drawl, mouth, speak, utter, voice 6 murmur, recite, warble 7 inflect, whisper 8 singsong, vocalize 9 enunciate, pronounce 10 articulate
In Too Deep (1987 song)
artist: Genesis
In Too Deep (1999 film)
cast: Omar Epps, LL Cool J, Nia Long, Stanley Tucci
___ into one's hands: 4 play
___ into one's head: 4 take
___ into one's own: 4 come
___ into play: 5 bring
___ into question: 4 call
___ into shape: 4 lick, whip
___ into the act: 3 get
___ into the ground: 3 run 5 drive
Into the Night (1985 film)
cast: Jeff Goldblum, Michelle Pfeiffer
director: John Landis
Into the Night host: 4 Dees
Into the Woods: 7 musical
composer: Stephen Sondheim

in toto: **10** completely
intoxicant: **4** grog, kava **5** booze, drink, heady, hooch, sauce **6** hootch, liquor, rotgut **7** alcohol, liqueur, spirits **8** cocktail, demon rum, exciting, highball, libation, potation, stirring **9** aqua vitae, inebriant, inspiring, thrilling
intoxicate: **4** fire, send, stew **5** addle, besot, charm, crock, elate, flush, rouse, souse, stone **6** arouse, excite, kindle, muddle, pickle, sozzle, thrill **7** animate, bewitch, enchant, enflame, enliven, inflame, plaster, pollute, stupefy **8** befuddle, enspirit, entrance, inspirit **9** fascinate
intoxicated: **3** lit **5** drunk, tight, tipsy
intoxicating: **5** heady **6** strong **7** rousing **8** exciting, stirring
intoxication: **6** frenzy **7** ecstasy, elation, madness **8** delirium
__ in Toyland: **5** Babes
intra __: **5** muros, vires, vitam
intractability: **7** resolve **8** defiance, firmness, hardness, rigidity, tenacity, wildness **9** obstinacy, toughness
intractable: **4** firm, grim **5** balky, tough **6** unruly, wilful **7** defiant, naughty, piggish, problem, wayward, willful **8** contrary, perverse, stubborn **9** obstinate, pigheaded, unbending
__ in trade: **5** stock
intransigence: **5** spunk **7** resolve **8** defiance, rigidity, tenacity **9** obstinacy **10** doggedness, resolution
intransigent: **4** firm **5** balky, rigid **6** mulish, ornery, wilful **7** adamant, diehard, piggish, radical, willful **8** contrary, obdurate, perverse, stubborn **9** obstinate, pigheaded, tenacious, unbending **10** inflexible
intransitive __: **4** verb
intrepid: **4** bold, game **5** brave, gutsy, macho, nervy, stout **6** awless, daring, gritty, heroic, plucky, spunky, steely **7** aweless, defiant, doughty, gallant, impavid, staunch, valiant **8** fearless, heroical, resolute, spirited, stalwart, unafraid, valorous **9** audacious, confident, dauntless, dreadless, nerveless, tenacious, undaunted, unfearful, unfearing **10** courageous, mettlesome, undismayed
be ~: **4** dare, defy
one: **4** hero **5** darer **7** heroine
Intrepid: **3** car **4** auto, boat, ship **5** Dodge **10** automobile, battleship
intrepidity: **4** grit, guts, sand, will **5** blood, heart, moxie, nerve, pluck, spunk, valor **6** daring, mettle, spirit, starch **7** bravery, courage, heroism, prowess, resolve **8** audacity, backbone, boldness, defiance, firmness, gumption, rashness, temerity, tenacity
intrepidness: **4** grit **5** nerve, pluck, valor
intricacy: **4** knot **9** confusion, labyrinth **10** complexity, knottiness
intricate: **5** fancy, tough **6** daedal, knotty, tricky **7** complex, tangled **8** abstruse, involved, tortuous **9** Byzantine, difficult, elaborate, entangled **10** convoluted
intrigue: **4** draw, grab, hook, plan, plot, pull, ruse, trap, wile **5** cabal, charm, dodge, pique, rivet **6** affair, cook up, devise, draw in, excite, lead on, racket, scheme **7** attract, collude, connive, delight, enchant, engross, faction, finagle, liaison, romance **8** artifice, conspire, contrive, interest, maneuver, trickery **9** captivate, chicanery, collusion, fascinate, machinate, stratagem, titillate **10** conspiracy
metaphorically: **3** web
Intrigue: **3** car **4** auto, Olds **10** automobile, Oldsmobile
intriguer: **5** snake **6** sharpy **7** plotter, schemer, wangler **8** finagler, slyboots
intriguing: **3** sly **4** wily **5** juicy **6** subtle **8** inviting, tempting **9** absorbing, designing, insidious **10** diplomatic, enchanting, engrossing
intrinsic: **3** own **4** born, real, true **5** basic, inner **6** inborn, inbred, inmost, innate, latent, native **7** built-in, central, genuine, natural, radical **8** integral, peculiar **9** component, elemental, essential, ingrained **10** congenital, connatural, deep-seated, hereditary, indwelling, underlying
be ~: **5** dwell **6** inhere, reside
intrinsically: **5** per se, truly **7** at heart
intro: **3** fwd. **4** pref., vamp **5** debut **6** lead-in, prelim, prolog **7** opening, prelude **8** foreword, overture, preamble, prologue **9** beginning **10** initiation
exclamation: **4** ta-da **5** ta-dah
introduce: **3** add, set **4** lead **5** begin, enter, offer, put in, raise, set up, start, usher **6** broach, infuse, inject, insert, instal, instil, launch, work in **7** bring up, engrain, ingrain, install, instill, kick off, lead off, pioneer, precede, preface, presage, present, propose, receive, roll out, suggest, throw in, usher in **8** antecede, bring out, commence, generate, initiate, set forth **9** establish, insinuate, institute, interject, interpose, make known, originate, recommend **10** inaugurate, pave the way, put forward
introduced to, be: **4** meet
introducer, act: **2** MC **4** host **5** emcee
introduction: **4** word **5** debut, entry, proem, start **6** access, entrée, influx, launch, lead-in, prolog **7** baptism, meeting, opening, preface, prelude **8** entrance, overture, preamble, prologue **9** reception
introductory: **3** new **5** early, first **7** initial, opening **8** original, starting **9** preceding
material: **4** ABCs **6** basics
introit: **4** song **5** psalm **6** anthem
introspect: **4** muse **5** brood **6** ponder **7** reflect **8** meditate, ruminate
introspection: **4** look **6** musing **7** thought **10** meditation, reflection, rumination
introspective: **4** rapt **5** moody **6** musing **7** pensive **8** absorbed, occupied, ruminant **9** engrossed
introvert: **5** loner **7** brooder, isolato **8** homebody **10** narcissist, wallflower
introverted: **3** shy **5** timid **6** demure **7** bashful **8** cautious, reserved, solitary **9** withdrawn
intrude: **3** pry **4** nose, poke **5** barge, cut in, enter, poach, snoop **6** butt in, horn in, impose, meddle, push in, tamper **7** barge in, presume **8** trespass **9** intercede, interfere, interject, interlope, interrupt, intervene **10** contravene
on: **4** raid **5** storm **6** assail, attack, invade, strike **7** assault, overrun **8** encroach, trespass
intruder: **5** alien **7** burglar, invader, meddler, prowler **8** outsider, stranger **9** aggressor **10** trespasser
intruding: **4** bold **7** forward **10** aggressive
intrusion: **6** attack, influx, inroad **7** ingress **8** invasion, overture, trespass **9** incursion **10** imposition
intrusive: **4** nosy **5** nosey, saucy **6** prying **7** ferrety, forward, salient **8** invasive, meddling **9** obtrusive, officious **10** aggressive, meddlesome
intuit: **3** see **4** feel, know **5** grasp, infer, sense **6** divine, fathom **7** realize **8** discover, perceive **9** apprehend **10** comprehend, have a hunch, understand
intuition: **3** ESP **4** vibe **5** hunch, sense **6** acumen, esprit, vision **7** feeling, insight, thought **8** instinct **10** divination, perception, sixth sense
intuitive: **3** gut **4** wise **5** acute **6** inborn, innate **7** natural **8** lynx-eyed, visceral **9** affective, automatic, emotional, immediate, impulsive **10** perceptive, subjective, understood
intumesce: **3** bag **5** belly, bloat, bulge, swell **6** blow up, expand, puff up **7** distend, enlarge, inflate **8** bubble up
Inuit: **3** Esk. **5** tribe **6** Eskimo
abode: **4** iglu **5** igloo
craft: **5** kayak, umiak
land: **7** Nunavut
outerwear: **6** anorak
inundate: **4** glut, pour, snow **5** drown, flood, flush, swamp, water **6** deluge, drench, engulf, ingulf **7** immerse, overrun, smother **8** overflow, submerge **9** overwhelm, snow under
inundation: **4** glut, tide, wave **5** flood, river, spate **6** deluge, influx, stream **7** cascade, freshet, monsoon, torrent **8** downpour, overflow **9** avalanche, cataclysm
an ~ (of): **4** lots, tons **5** heaps **7** barrels
inurbane: **4** rude **5** crass, gruff, surly **7** boorish, ill-bred, uncivil **8** impolite, tactless, unpoised, unsubtle **9** insulting, uncourtly, ungallant **10** indecorous, indelicate, ungracious, unladylike
inure: **5** train **6** season **7** break in, coarsen, toughen **8** accustom, indurate **9** acclimate, condition, habituate, withstand **10** take effect
(to): **5** adapt **6** harden **7** get used
inutile: **4** idle, null, vain **5** inane **6** futile **7** useless **8** bootless, unusable **9** for naught, fruitless, worthless **10** unavailing
invade: **4** loot, raid **5** blitz, crash, enter, storm **6** assail, attack, breach, infest, maraud, occupy, ravage, strike **7** assault, make war, overrun, pillage, plunder, violate **8** encroach, infringe, permeate, trespass **9** intrude on, penetrate **10** burglarize, encroach on, muscle in on, trespass on
privacy: **3** pry **4** nose, poke **5** mix in, snoop **6** horn in, impose, kibitz, meddle, worm in **7** barge in, break in, intrude, obtrude **9** interfere, intervene
invader: **3** foe, Hun **4** germ **5** alien, enemy **6** raider, vandal **8** attacker, intruder, marauder **9** aggressor, assailant, ill-wisher **10** encroacher, interloper, trespasser
ancient ~: **3** Hun **4** Goth, Jute, Moor **5** Horsa, Saxon, Tatar **6** Norman
invalid: **3** bad, ill **4** null, sick, void **5** false, frail, wrong **6** ailing, faulty, feeble, infirm, shut-in, sickly, untrue, unwell **7** laid low, patient, unsound **8** baseless, below par, nugatory **9** enfeebled, erroneous, illogical, sophistic, unfounded, unhealthy, worthless **10** fallacious, ill-founded, ungrounded, unreasoned
invalidate: **3** nix **4** ruin, undo, void **5** abate, annul, quash **6** cancel, negate, offset, refute, repeal, revoke, show up **7** abolish, confute, disable, explode, nullify, rescind, retract, reverse, vitiate **8** abrogate, disprove, dissolve, override, overrule, overturn **9** discredit, eliminate, overthrow **10** annihilate, circumduct, compensate, counteract, disqualify, neutralize, prove wrong
invalidation: **4** veto **6** denial, exposé, repeal **8** disproof, negation, overturn, rebuttal, reversal, voidance **9** discredit
invalidism: **7** frailty, illness **8** debility, sickness, weakness
invalidity: **7** fallacy, falsity, nullity, sophism **8** voidness, weakness
invaluable: **4** rare **6** worthy **7** helpful **8** precious, valuable **9** excellent, expensive, priceless
invariability: **5** habit **7** routine **8** evenness, fastness, firmness, habitude, monotony, sameness, solidity
invariable: **4** firm, same **5** fixed, rigid **6** smooth, stable, static **7** regular, uniform **8** constant, straight **9** immovable, immutable, perpetual, unfailing **10** changeless, consistent, inflexible, monotonous, true to type, unchanging, unrelieved, unwavering
invariably: **4** ever **6** always, as ever, surely **9** regularly **10** inevitably
invasion: **4** raid **5** foray, storm **6** attack, breach, influx, inroad **7** assault, descent, ingress **8** tres-

IN

pass 9 incursion, intrusion, irruption, offensive, onslaught, violation 10 occupation
site of '44: 5 Leyte
invasion of __: 7 privacy
Invasion of the Body Snatchers (1956 film)
cast: Kevin McCarthy, Dana Wynter
prop: 3 pod
Invasion of the Body Snatchers (1978 film)
cast: Brooke Adams, Leonard Nimoy, Donald Sutherland
Invasion of the Sea
author: Jules Verne
invasive: 5 pushy 6 prying, snoopy 7 ferrety 9 intrusive
invective: 5 abuse, scorn 6 insult, tirade 7 censure, lampoon, obloquy 8 berating, diatribe, jeremiad, reproach, swearing 9 aspersion, blasphemy, contumely, philippic 10 accusation, backbiting, impugnment, imputation, revilement, scurrility
bit of ~: 3 cut, dig 4 barb, gibe, oath 5 taunt 6 insult, needle, zinger
inveigh: 4 rail 6 revile 7 censure, declaim, protest 8 harangue
inveigle: 3 con 4 bait, coax, hook, lure, snow, trap 5 charm, decoy, shill, tempt 6 allure, cajole, disarm, entice, entrap, induce, lead on, rope in, stroke 7 beguile, ensnare, flatter, insnare, mislead, wheedle 8 blandish, maneuver, persuade 9 sweet-talk
inveiglement: 5 decoy, snare 7 coaxing
inveigler: 5 lurer 6 coaxer 7 cajoler, tempter 8 beguiler, swindler
__ in Venice: 5 Death
invent: 3 fib, lie 4 coin, fake, form, make, mint 5 feign, frame, hatch 6 cook up, create, design, devise, drum up, make up 7 concoct, dream up, falsify, fashion, imagine, pioneer, produce, think up, toss off, trump up, turn out 8 contrive, misstate, simulate 9 fabricate, formulate, improvise, originate 10 conceive of, mastermind
invented: 4 fake, made 6 unreal 8 mythical 9 imaginary, legendary
Inventing Memory
author: Erica Jong
invention: 3 fib, lie 4 fake, myth, sham, tale, yarn 5 dodad, gismo, gizmo, rumor 6 deceit, design, device, doodad, gadget 7 coinage, fantasy, fiction, figment, novelty, product, untruth 8 creation, pretense, tall tale 9 apparatus, causation, discovery, falsehood, tall story 10 brainchild, conception, concoction, creativity, fairy story, innovation
ancient ~: 5 wheel
mother: 4 idea 9 necessity
Inventions of the Monsters
artist: Salvador Dali
inventive: 4 orig. 5 fresh, novel, sharp, slick, smart 6 adroit, astute, brainy, bright, clever, gifted, habile, shifty 7 fertile, knowing, new wave, unusual 8 artistic, creative, dextrous, fruitful, inspired, original 9 astucious, brilliant, causative, demiurgic, deviceful, dexterous, formative, ingenious 10 artistical, avant-garde, innovative, productive
inventiveness: 3 art 8 resource 10 cleverness, creativity
inventor: 4 Bell, Eads, Land, Moog, Otis, Watt 5 Deere, maker, Morse, Nobel, Tesla, Volta 6 author, Bunsen, coiner, Diesel, Edison, father, Fulton, Geiger, Schick, Sperry, Tupper 7 builder, creator, Eastman, Gatling, Marconi, pioneer, Pullman 8 Bessemer, Bushnell, Daguerre, De Forest, designer, Foucault, Franklin, Gillette, Goodyear, Sikorsky, Zworykin 9 artificer, fashioner, Gutenberg, innovator, James Watt 10 Elisha Otis, Fahrenheit, originator
agcy.: 4 USPO
cry: 3 aha
monogram: 3 TAE
need: 4 idea 6 patent
inventory: 4 list 5 asset, hoard, index, stock, store, table, tally 6 record, roster, supply 7 account, backlog, catalog, inspect, itemize, reserve, summary 8 register, tabulate 9 catalogue, enumerate, keep count, reservoir, stock book, stockpile, summarize 10 inspection, keep on hand, tabulation
abbr.: 3 etc., gds., SKU, UPC 4 FIFO, LIFO 8 mdse.. whse.
in ~: 4 here 6 on hand 9 available
place: 5 shelf 9 stockroom, warehouse
unit: 3 SKU, UPC 4 item
inveracity: 3 fib, lie 6 deceit 7 fiction, untruth, whopper
Inverness: 4 cape, coat 6 jacket 8 overcoat 9 outerwear
attraction: 4 Ness
see also Scottish
inverse: 5 wrong 7 reverse 8 negation, opposite 10 antithesis, antithetic
inversely: 9 vice versa
inversion: 4 flip 6 switch 8 flip-flop, flip side, opposite, reversal 9 about-face, one-eighty, other side, turnabout 10 antithesis
invert: 4 flip, turn 5 upend, upset 6 upturn 7 capsize, reverse 8 exchange, flip-flop, overturn, turn over 9 transpose, turn about 10 turn around
inverted: 7 upended 8 backward 9 inside-out 10 topsy-turvy, upside-down
inverted V in heraldry: 7 chevron
invest: 3 put 5 cover, crown, endow, endue, imbue, indue, put in, put up, spend, stake, steep 6 attire, charge, infuse, instal, lay out, ordain 7 buy into, empower, entrust, furnish, go in for, install, instate, intrust, license 8 accouter, accoutre, bankroll, delegate, enthrone, initiate, inthrone, purchase, salt away, sanction 9 authorize, establish
in: 3 buy, get 6 obtain, pick up 7 acquire 8 purchase
invested: 6 at risk 7 at stake
investigate: 3 dig, pry, see, spy 4 case, comb, scan, seek, sift 5 assay, audit, check, cover, delve, go see, probe, scout, study 6 go into, search 7 analyze, dissect, enquire, examine, explore, feel out, inquire, inspect, ransack, run down 8 check out, consider, look into, look over, question, research, see about, stake out 9 enter into
investigation: 3 inq. 5 audit, check, probe, query, quest, study, trial 6 examen, review, search, survey 7 enquiry, hearing, inquest, inquiry, legwork, probing 8 analysis, question, research, scrutiny 9 going-over
investigative report: 6 exposé
investigator: 3 spy 4 G-man, narc, nark, T-man 5 agent 6 shamus, sleuth 7 analyst, auditor, gumshoe 8 enquirer, examiner, inquirer, Sherlock
job: 4 case 5 caper
investiture: 4 garb, robe 5 habit 6 attire, mantle 7 apparel, garment, raiment 8 chairing, crowning, frocking, vestment
investment: 3 buy 4 bond 5 asset, stake, stock 6 outlay 7 backing, capital, finance, venture 8 purchase 9 accession, endowment, financing, interests 10 commercial, smart money
for short: 2 CD 3 IRA, stk. 4 ESOP, REIT 5 R and D, T-bill, T-bond, T-note
insurance: 5 hedge
return: 3 int. 5 yield 6 income, profit 7 revenue 8 earnings, interest, proceeds
swindle: 5 Ponzi
world: 10 Wall Street
investment __: 4 bank 5 trust 6 banker
investments: 5 stock 7 savings 8 holdings 9 interests, portfolio
like venture capital ~: 5 dicey 6 chancy, daring, unsafe 9 uncertain 10 precarious
investor: 4 bear, bull 5 owner 6 backer, banker 9 financier 10 capitalist
activity, for short: 4 spec
bane: 4 loss 6 red ink
concern: 3 Dow 4 risk 5 yield
good news for an ~: 5 rally
mail-in: 5 proxy
inveterate: 3 old 4 avid 6 rooted 7 abiding, chronic, settled 8 constant, enduring, habitual, hardened, lifelong 9 chronical, confirmed, customary, incurable, ingrained, long-lived, perennial, permanent, unabating, unfixable 10 accustomed, congenital, continuing, deep-rooted, deep-seated, entrenched, habituated, persistent, persisting
Invictus
author: William Henley
invidious: 4 base 6 odious 7 hateful 8 annoying, libelous 9 green-eyed, loathsome, maligning, offensive, repugnant, slighting, vilifying 10 abominable, calumnious, defamatory, detestable, detracting, detractive, detractory, scandalous, slanderous
invidiousness: 4 hate 5 odium, scorn, spite, venom 6 animus, enmity, hatred, malice, rancor, spleen 7 disdain, disgust, dislike, ill will 8 acrimony, aversion, contempt, distaste, ignominy 9 animosity, antipathy, hostility, malignity, repulsion, revulsion 10 abhorrence, antagonism, execration, repugnance, resentment
invigorant: 5 tonic 6 bracer, elixir 7 cordial 8 pick-me-up 9 stimulant
invigorate: 4 gird, stir, tone 5 brace, build, hop up, liven, pep up, raise, rally, renew, rouse, shore, steel 6 anneal, beef up, buck up, excite, harden, perk up, pick up, prop up, revive, temper, tone up, turn on, vivify 7 bolster, brace up, build up, burgeon, develop, empower, enhance, enliven, fortify, freshen, inspire, liven up, punch up, quicken, refresh, shore up, stiffen, toughen 8 bourgeon, buttress, embolden, energize, enspirit, imbolden, indurate, inspirit, vitalize 9 electrify, galvanize, intensify, reinforce, stimulate 10 exhilarate, rejuvenate, revitalize, strengthen
invigorating: 5 brisk, crisp, fresh, tonic 6 lively 7 bracing, charged, healthy, outdoor 8 curative 10 refreshing
invincibility: 5 moxie, pluck, power, valor 6 mettle 7 stamina 9 fortitude, hardiness 10 resolution
invincible: 5 stout 8 almighty 9 dauntless, unfearing 10 impassable, inviolable, unbeatable, unyielding
Invincible (1985 song)
artist: Pat Benatar
Invincible Eagle, The
composer: John Philip Sousa
in vino __: 7 veritas
inviolability: 7 honesty, loyalty 8 holiness, sanctity, trueness
inviolable: 4 holy, safe, true 5 blest, loyal 6 honest, sacred, trusty 7 blessed 8 constant, reliable, true-blue, virtuous 10 invincible
inviolate: 4 holy, pure 5 blest, whole 6 entire, intact, sacred, unhurt 7 blessed 8 complete, hallowed, unbroken, unharmed, unmarred 10 sacrosanct
invisible: 5 perdu 6 covert, hidden, latent, minute, occult, perdue, unseen 7 ghostly 8 obscured, ulterior 9 concealed, deceptive, disguised, unseeable 10 impalpable, intangible, out of sight, tucked away, unapparent, undetected, unviewable, wraithlike
become ~: 4 fade 6 die out, vanish 7 die away 8 dissolve, evanesce, fade away, vaporize 9 disappear, dissipate, evaporate
combining form: 5 aphan- 6 aphano-
invisible __: 3 ink 5 fence
Invisible __: 3 Man
Invisible Cities
author: Italo Calvino

Invisible Friends
author: Alan Ayckbourn
Invisible Man
author: Ralph Ellison
setting: 3 NYC 6 Harlem 9 Manhattan
Invisible Man, The: 4 film 5 novel
author: H.G. Wells
cast: Una O'Connor, Claude Rains
character: 4 Ayde, Kemp
Invisible Touch (1986 song)
artist: Genesis
invitation: 3 bid 4 call, date, lure 5 offer 6 appeal, asking, feeler 7 request 8 overture, petition, proposal 9 challenge, prompting, rain check 10 allurement, attraction, engagement, enticement, incitement, inducement, suggestion, temptation
addendum: 3 BYO 4 BYOB, RSVP
go sans ~: 5 crash 7 barge in
word: 3 s'il 4 come, vous 5 plaît, where
invite: 3 ask, bid 4 lure, seek 5 ask in, evoke, tempt 6 ask out, beckon, call on, lead on, pick up, summon, ticket 7 attract, receive, request, welcome 8 petition 9 encourage
invited: 7 welcome
not ~: 5 unbid
invitee: 5 guest 7 visitor
invitees, top: 5 A-list
inviting: 4 cosy, cozy, homy, nice 5 homey 7 cordial, winning, winsome 8 alluring, charming, engaging, enticing, magnetic, pleasing, readable, tempting 9 appealing, beguiling 10 attractive, bewitching, delectable, delightful, intriguing, magnetical, persuasive
phrase: 6 call me
invocation: 5 grace 6 appeal, litany, prayer, speech 7 worship 8 blessing, entreaty 10 beseeching, hocus-pocus, mumbo jumbo
invoice: 3 tab 4 bill, list 9 reckoning, statement
abbr.: 3 amt. 7 ppd.. stmt.
add-on: 3 tax
stamp: 3 rcd. 4 paid 8 received
word: 3 net, pay 5 remit
invoke: 3 use 4 pray 5 apply 6 call on, pray to, summon 7 call for, conjure, enforce, entreat, implore, plead to, pray for, solicit 8 appeal to, call upon, petition, resort to, say grace 9 call forth, conjure up, implement
involuntary: 6 forced, reflex 7 natural 8 knee-jerk 9 mandatory, unwilling, unwitting
movement: 3 tic 5 start 6 shiver
noise: 3 hic 4 burp, gasp 6 hiccup 8 hiccough
involve: 4 have, mire 5 catch, cover, imply, snare, touch 6 absorb, affect, draw in, engage, enmesh, entail, immesh, inmesh, occupy 7 concern, contain, embrace, embroil, immerse, include, require 8 comprise, entangle, interest, persuade, relate to 9 implicate
involved: 4 rapt 6 active, knotty, lively, tricky 7 at stake, complex, engaged, prickly, tangled, verbose 8 abstruse, puzzling, tortuous 9 Byzantine, confusing, difficult, elaborate, intricate, recondite 10 convoluted, unsettling
become ~: 6 step in 7 mediate 9 intercede
be very ~: 6 wallow
person ~: 5 party
recently ~ with: 5 new to
with: 4 into, up to
involvement: 4 love, part, stew 5 stake 6 jumble, jungle 7 dilemma, farrago 8 interest, quandary 9 immersion, liability
__-in vote: 5 write
invulnerability: 6 safety 8 safeness, security
invulnerable: 4 safe 5 tight 6 secure
__ in wait: 3 lie
__-in-waiting: 4 lady, lord, maid
__ in war...: 5 First
inward: 6 hidden, secret, within 7 private 8 internal, intimate, personal 9 privately
inwardly: 6 inside, within 8 mentally, secretly 10 internally
__ in Winter, The: 4 Lion
__ in with: 4 fall
__ in Wonderland: 4 Alex 5 Alice
__ in wood: 4 aged
INXS
member: Hutchence, Pengilly, Beers, Farriss
song: Devil Inside (1988)
Disappear (1990)
Need You Tonight (1987)
Never Tear Us Apart (1988)
New Sensation (1988)
Suicide Blonde (1990)
What You Need (1986)
__ in Ya Ear: 5 Flava
__ in years: 5 along
__ in Yonkers: 4 Lost
in-your-__: 4 face
In your dreams!: 5 no how, no way
__ in Your Eyes: 4 Lost 6 Heaven
In Your Letter (1981 song)
artist: REO Speedwagon
__ in your mouth, not...: 5 Melts
In Youth I Have Known One
author: Edgar Allan Poe
Io: 4 moon, moth
planet: 7 Jupiter
__-I-O: 3 E-I-E
Ioan: 8 Gruffudd
I object!: 3 hey 4 stop 5 no way 6 hold it, stop it
__ iodide: 6 silver
iodine: 7 element, halogen 10 antiseptic
combining form: 3 iod- 4 iodo-
compound: 6 halide
source: 4 kelp 7 seafood
__ Iodine: 6 Little
Iola: 4 city, town
locale: 6 Kansas
Iola Leroy
author: Frances Harper
Iolani Palace
locale: 4 Oahu 6 Hawaii 8 Honolulu
Iolanthe: 8 operetta
character: 5 Celia, Fleta, Leila 6 Willis 7 Phyllis 8 Strephon
composer: W.S. Gilbert, Arthur Sullivan
Iolcos, ship from: 4 Argo
ion: 8 particle
chg.: 3 neg., pos.
source: 4 atom
Ion: 3 car 4 auto 6 Saturn, Tiriac 7 Iliescu
author: Euripides
parent: 6 Apollo, Creusa
wife: 6 Helice
ION
alternative: *see* cable channel
Iona: 4 isle 6 island, school
athletes: 5 Gaels
locale: 7 New York 8 Scotland
Ione: 4 Skye 5 nymph 8 sea nymph
Ionesco, Eugène: 6 French, writer 9 dramatist 10 playwright
homeland: Romania, France
work: Amédée
The Bald Soprano
The Chairs
Exit the King
The Future Is in Eggs
The Lesson
The New Tenant
Rhinoceros
A Stroll in the Air
Victims of Duty
Ionian: 3 sea 5 Homer 10 Heraclitus
ancient ~ city: 4 Teos
ancient ~ kingdom: 6 Epirus
Ionian __: 3 Sea
Ionian Sea
gulf: 4 Arta 6 Patras 7 Corinth, Laconia, Lepanto, Taranto 8 Messenia
island: 5 Corfu, Zante
locale: 5 Italy 6 Greece
view from ~: 4 Etna 5 Aetna
Ionic: 5 order 6 column 9 classical
not ~: 5 Doric 10 Corinthian
ionize: 6 charge
I Only Have Eyes for You: 4 song
composer: Al Dubin, Harry Warren
musical: 5 Dames
I Only Want to Be With You (1964 song)
artist: Dusty Springfield
ionosphere
part: 6 D layer, E layer, F layer
IOOF cousin: 4 BPOE, Elks 7 Kiwanis
iota: 3 bit, dot, jot, tad 4 atom, drop, mite, mote, spot, whit 5 crumb, grain, Greek, pinch, scrap, shred, skosh, speck, straw, trace 6 letter, morsel, tittle, wee bit 7 minimum, modicum, smidgen, smidgin 8 flyspeck, fragment, molecule, particle, smidgeon 9 little bit, scintilla
follower: 5 kappa
preceder: 5 theta
IOU: 3 tab 4 chit, debt, note 6 marker 8 mortgage 9 debenture, liability
honor an ~: 3 pay 5 pay up, repay 6 settle 7 pay back 8 make good, settle up, square up 9 reimburse 10 remunerate
receive an: 4 lend, loan
signer: 4 ower
write an ~: 3 owe 6 borrow
I Ought to Be in Pictures
author: Neil Simon
Iowa: 5 river, state 6 Indian 7 Amerind
athletes: 8 Hawkeyes
city: 4 Ames 5 Amana, Pella 6 Ankeny, Marion 7 Clinton, Dubuque, Ottumwa 8 Waterloo 9 Davenport, Des Moines, Fort Dodge, Mason City, Muscatine, Sioux City, Urbandale 10 Bettendorf, Burlington, Cedar Falls
conference: 6 Big Ten
crop: 4 corn
like ~: 6 inland
neighbor: 8 Illinois, Missouri, Nebraska 9 Minnesota, Wisconsin
painter from ~: 4 Wood
school: 3 Coe 5 Drake, Loras
state bird: 9 goldfinch
state flower: 8 wild rose
state rock: 5 geode
state tree: 3 oak
Iowa Baseball Confederacy, The
author: W.P. Kinsella
Iowa State
athletes: 8 Cyclones
conference: 9 Big Twelve
locale: 4 Ames
I Pagliacci
composer: Ruggiero Leoncavallo
role: 5 Beppe, Canio, Nedda, Tonio 6 Silvio
setting: 5 Italy 8 Calabria
Ipanema: 5 beach
locale: 3 Rio 6 Brazil
I pass: 5 no bet
Iphegenia in Brooklyn
composer: PDQ Bach
Iphigenia
brother: 7 Orestes
parent: 5 Helen 9 Agamemnon
sister: 7 Electra
Iphigenia in Aulis
author: Euripides
Iphigenie en Aulide
author: Jean Racine
iPod
model: 4 Nano
__ ipsa loquitur: 3 res
ipse __: 5 dixit
ipso: 6 itself
ipso __: 4 jure 5 facto
Ipswich: 4 city, town
locale: 4 Mass. 7 England, Suffolk
IQ: 6 brains 9 mentality 10 braininess
test developer: 5 Binet
I.Q. (1994 film)
cast: Walter Matthau, Tim Robbins, Meg Ryan
Iqaluit: 4 city, town
locale: 6 Canada 7 Nunavut
Ir: 4 elem. 7 element, iridium
77 for ~: 4 at. no.
Ira: 4 Wohl 5 Glass, Levin 6 Berkow, Remsen, Thomas 7 Wolfert 8 Aldridge, Gershwin 9 Magaziner
IRA: 7 nest egg, pension 8 Roth plan 10 tax shelter
accrual: 3 int. 8 interest
alternative: 4 ESOP 5 Keogh
investment: 2 CD
legislation: 5 ERISA
offerer: 4 bank 5 S and L
part of ~: 3 Acc., Ind., Rep., Ret. 4 Acct., Army 5 Irish 7 Account
__ IRA: 3 SEP 4 Roth
irade: 4 fiat 5 edict, order, ukase 6 decree, dictum
__ Irae: 4 Dies
Iráklion: 4 city, port, town 7 seaport
locale: 5 Crete 6 Candia, Greece
Iran: 6 nation 7 Barkley, country
ancient part of ~: 4 Elam

bovine: 5 Kurdi 6 Sarabi
capital: 6 Tehran 7 Teheran
city: 3 Qom, Qum 5 Ahvaz, Ahwaz, Rasht, Resht 6 Abadan, Shiraz, Tabriz, Tehran 7 Esfahan, Mashhad, Teheran
desert: 3 Lut 9 Dasht-e Lut, Great Salt
lake: 5 Urmia
language: 4 Pers. 5 Farsi, Parsi, Tajik 6 Tadjik, Tajiki 7 Persian, Tadzhik
money: 4 kran, rial 5 dinar
mountain: 6 Elburz, Zagros
mountain dweller: 4 Kurd
neighbor: 4 Irak, Iraq 6 Turkey 7 Armenia 8 Pakistan 10 Azerbaijan
org.: 4 OPEC
religion: 5 Baha'i
royal name: 4 Reza 7 Pahlavi, Pahlevi
title: 4 imam, shah 5 imaum
Iran-Contra grp.: 3 NSC
Irani: 7 Persian 8 Bani-Sadr, Khomeini 10 Rafsanjani
ancient ~: 4 Mede 5 Alani
neighbor: 4 Turk 5 Iraqi, Saudi
__-Iranian: 4 Indo
I ran out of gas: 5 alibi 6 excuse
Iraq: 6 nation 7 country
bovine: 5 Kurdi
capital: 6 Bagdad 7 Baghdad
city: 5 Arbil, Basra, Busra, Erbil, Irbil, Mosul 6 Arbela, Bagdad, Busrah, Kirkuk, Tikrit 7 Baghdad
desert: 6 Syrian
export: 3 oil 4 date
invaded it: 6 Koweit, Kuwait
minority: 4 Kurd
money: 4 fils 5 dinar
mountain: 6 Zagros
neighbor: 4 Iran 5 Syria 6 Jordan, Kuwait, Turkey
org.: 4 OPEC 10 Arab League
province: 5 Basra, Busra 6 Busrah
river: 6 Tigris
Iraqi: 4 Arab, Kurd 5 Asian 6 Arabic 8 language
neighbor: 4 Turk 5 Irani, Saudi
irascibility: 4 bile, gall 5 anger 6 spleen, temper 8 acerbity, asperity, edginess, ill humor, tartness
irascible: 3 hot 4 sour 5 angry, cross, huffy, moody, short, surly, testy 6 crabby, cranky, crusty, feisty, ireful, ogrish, ornery, snappy, snippy, touchy 7 bearish, bristly, grouchy, huffish, ogreish, peevish, peppery, uptight, waspish 8 choleric, growling, liverish, petulant, snappish, snippety 9 excitable, fractious, impatient, irritable, querulous, sarcastic, splenetic 10 high-strung, out of sorts
irate: 5 angry, surly, vexed, wroth 6 in a pet, raving, ticked 7 angered, annoyed, burning, in a huff, in a snit, nettled, ranting, ruffled, violent 8 agitated, burned up, frenzied, petulant, provoked, seething, steaming, volatile 9 hotheaded, indignant 10 freaked out, hysterical, pugnacious
see also angry
Irbil: 4 city, town
locale: 4 Irak, Iraq
ire: 3 vex 4 fury, rage 5 anger, annoy, upset, wrath 6 burn up, choler, dander, enmity, enrage, madden, nettle, spleen, temper 7 dudgeon, incense, offense, outrage, provoke, tick off, umbrage 8 irritate 9 hostility, huffiness, infuriate, surliness 10 exasperate, irritation, resentment
Ire.: 3 isl.
I read you!: 5 roger
ired: 3 hot, mad 4 sore 5 angry, cross, huffy, riled, vexed, wroth 6 peeved, piqued 7 annoyed, boiling, enraged, furious 8 choleric, incensed, inflamed, outraged, up in arms, vehement, wrathful 9 indignant, irritated, resentful, splenetic 10 infuriated
ireful: 4 edgy 5 angry, fed up, gruff, surly, testy 6 crabby, raving, touchy 7 annoyed, bearish, brusque, caustic, grouchy, mordant, peevish, ranting 8 petulant, snappish, venomous, virulent 9 irritable, trenchant 10 aggravated, freaked out
see also angry
Ireland: 4 Eire, Erin, isle, Jill, John 5 Kathy 6 island, nation 7 country
accent: 6 brogue
ancestor: 4 Celt, Gael
ballet dancer: 8 De Valois
bay: 5 Sligo 6 Dublin, Galway
bovine: 5 Kerry 6 Dexter
capital: 6 Dublin
city: 4 Cobh, Cork 5 Ennis, Sligo 6 Dublin, Galway, Tralee 7 Donegal, Shannon, Wexford 8 Limerick 9 Waterford
combining form: 7 Hiberno-
county: 4 Cork, Mayo, Tara 5 Cavan, Clare, Kerry, Louth, Meath, Sligo 6 Antrim, Armagh, Carlow, Dublin, Galway, Offaly 7 Donegal, Kildare, Leitrim, Wexford, Wicklow 8 Kilkenny, Laoighis, Limerick, Longford, Monaghan 9 Roscommon, Tipperary, Waterford, Westmeath
dagger: 5 skean, skene
dance: 3 jig
dramatist: 4 Shaw 6 O' Casey
exclamation: 3 och 4 aroo, arra, orra 5 arrah, orrow
fairy: 4 shee, sidh 5 sidhe
flutist: 6 Galway
goddess: 6 Birgit
island: 4 Aran 6 Achill
John, in ~: 4 Sean
knife: 5 skean, skene
lake: 5 lough, Neagh
language: 4 Erse 6 Celtic, Gaelic
luck: 4 cess
lullaby syllables: 5 loo-ra, too-ra
money: 4 punt 5 penny, pound
name part: 3 Mac 4 Fitz
national symbol: 4 harp
Nobelist in Literature: 4 Shaw 5 Yeats 6 Heaney 7 Beckett
Nobelist in Peace: 4 Hume 7 Trimble 8 Corrigan, MacBride, Williams
Nobelist in Physics: 6 Walton
old Greek name for ~: 5 Ierne
old ~ script: 4 ogam 5 ogham
parliament: 4 Dail
patron: 5 St. Pat 7 Patrick
philosopher: 7 Murdoch
playwright: 4 Shaw 5 Colum, Friel, Synge, Wilde, Yeats 6 O'Casey 8 Donleavy
poet: 5 Colum, Moore, Wilde, Yeats 6 Boland, O'Grady 7 Parnell 8 MacNeice 9 Kavanaugh
poetic name: 5 Irena
port: 4 Cobh, Cork 5 Derry 6 Dublin 7 Donegal 9 Waterford
product: 5 linen 7 whiskey
rebel: 5 O'more 6 Fenian
republic: 4 Eire
river: 4 Erne, Nore 5 Boyne
saint: 5 Aidan, Kevin
sea god: 3 Ler, Lir
seat of ancient kings: 4 Tara
spirit: 4 puca 5 pooka
symbol: 4 harp
word on ~ coins: 4 Eire
writer: 5 Behan, Joyce, Moore 6 Binchy, Crofts, Heaney, O'Brien 7 Beckett, Maturin, Murdoch, O'Connor 8 Carleton, Donleavy, O'Faolain 9 Edgeworth, O'Flaherty
Ireland, Jill
spouse: Charles Bronson, David McCallum
I Remember It Well: 4 song
composer: Alan Jay Lerner, Frederick Loewe
musical: 4 Gigi
I Remember Mama (1948 film)
cast: Barbara Bel Geddes, Irene Dunne
role: 4 Lars, Nels 5 Marta, Trina 6 Katrin
I Remember You (song)
artist: Frank Ifield, Skid Row
Irene: 4 Cara, Rich, Ryan 5 Dunne, Papas, Worth 6 Castle, Hervey 7 Bordoni
equivalent: 3 Pax
parent: 4 Zeus 6 Themis
Irène: 5 Jacob
Irène __-Curie: 6 Joliot
irenic: 4 mild 6 dovish, gentle 7 pacific 8 peaceful, tranquil 9 placating 10 diplomatic, mollifying, nonviolent
irid: 4 lily 7 freesia 8 gladiola 9 gladiolus
iridescence: 5 sheen, shine 6 dazzle, luster 7 glimmer, glisten, glitter, shimmer, sparkle
iridescent: 6 pearly 7 opaline 8 lustrous, nacreous 9 prismatic 10 opalescent, shimmering
gem: 4 opal
iridium: 5 metal 7 element
alloy: 7 platina
iris: 4 flag 5 plant 6 flower, sunbow 7 rainbow 10 fleur-de-lis
center: 5 pupil
combining form: 4 irid- 5 irido-
cover: 6 cornea
fragrant ~: 5 orris
locale: 3 eye
of the ~: 5 uveal
part: 4 uvea 6 areola, areole
South African ~: 4 ixia
Iris: 6 Rainer 7 Murdoch 8 asteroid
composer: Pietro Mascagni
parent: 7 Electra, Thaumas
sister: 4 Arce 5 Harpy
Iris (1998 song)
artist: Goo Goo Dolls
Iris (2001 film)
cast: Jim Broadbent, Judi Dench, Kate Winslet
director: Richard Eyre
__ & Iris: 7 Stanley
__ I Rise: 5 Still
Irises: 3 oil 7 van Gogh 8 painting
Irish: 3 sea 4 stew 6 dander, temper 9 Hibernian
Irish __: 3 jig, Sea 4 bull, moss, stew 5 linen, tweed 6 coffee, Gaelic, Rovers, setter, Spring, whisky 7 terrier, whiskey
Irish __ State: 4 Free
Irish coffee ingredient: 7 whiskey
Irish Eyes
author: Andrew Greeley
__ Irish Eyes Are Smiling: 4 When
Irish Gold
author: Andrew Greeley
Irish Lace
author: Andrew Greeley
Irish Love
author: Andrew Greeley
Irishman: 4 Celt, Gael
Irish Mist
author: Andrew Greeley
__ Irish Rose: 5 Abie's
Irish Sea
feeder: 3 Dee
island: 3 Man
river to the ~: 6 Mersey
Irish setter: 3 dog 5 canid 6 canine
Irish Spring: 4 soap
alternative: *see* soap
Irish Stew!
author: Andrew Greeley
Irish Whiskey
author: Andrew Greeley
Irish wolfhound: 3 dog 5 canid 6 canine
irk: 3 bug, eat, get, jar, try, vex 4 bait, fret, gall, miff, pain, rile, roil, tire, wear 5 annoy, chafe, get to, grate, harry, peeve, pique, steam, upset, weary 6 abrade, bother, fester, harass, hector, madden, needle, nettle, noodge, pester, plague, put out, rankle, ruffle, tee off, work up 7 afflict, disturb, incense, perturb, provoke, tick off, trouble 8 distress, exercise, irritate 9 aggravate, displease 10 discompose, run afoul of
ender: 4 some
irked: 4 sore 5 tired 9 resentful
easily ~: 4 edgy 5 cross, huffy, moody, surly, testy 6 crabby, cranky, crusty, grumpy, ireful, morose, ornery, snappy, sullen, touchy 7 bearish, grouchy, huffish, peevish, uptight, waspish 8 captious, choleric, petulant, snappish 9 crotchety, excitable, fractious, impatient, irascible, irritable, querulous, splenetic 10 out of sorts
irksome: 4 sore 5 pesky, pesty 6 thorny, trying, vexing 7 grating, onerous, tedious 8 annoying, tiresome, worrying 9 vexatious 10 in one's hair, irritating, unpleasant

one: 3 nag 4 drip, pain, pest, pill 5 creep 6 gadfly 7 annoyer 8 headache 9 tormentor
Irkutsk: 4 city, town
locale: 6 Russia
Irlene: 8 Mandrell
sister: 6 Louise 7 Barbara
Irma: 6 Thomas 8 Rombauer
Irma la Douce (1963 film)
cast: Jack Lemmon, Shirley MacLaine
director: Billy Wilder
I, Robot
author: Isaac Asimov
I, Robot (2004 film)
cast: Will Smith
IROC: 5 Chevy 6 Camaro 9 Chevrolet
I roll: 5 Volvo
iron: 4 club, cuff, firm, hale, hard, wiry 5 beefy, burly, chain, cleek, hardy, hefty, hunky, husky, lusty, mashy, metal, press, rigid, spoon, stout, tough, wedge 6 brawny, ferric, hearty, mangle, mashie, mighty, potent, robust, rugged, sinewy, smooth, steely, stocky, sturdy, virile 7 adamant, doughty, element, ferrite, ferrous, manacle, niblick, shackle 8 athletic, forceful, golf club, handcuff, indurate, muscular, obdurate, powerful, puissant, stalwart, stubborn, vigorous 9 Atlantean, Herculean, immovable, inelastic, merciless, smooth out, strapping, unbending, well-built 10 able-bodied, implacable, inflexible, red-blooded, relentless, unyielding
alloy: 5 Invar, Monel, steel 7 Elinvar, Inconel, Mumetal 8 cast iron, kamacite, Nichrome 9 Platinite 10 superalloy
alternative: 4 wood
angle ~: 4 L bar
bar of a sort: 5 U-bolt
cast ~: 5 alloy
clothes: 4 mail 5 armor
combining form: 5 ferri-, ferro-, sider- 6 sidero-
construction ~: 5 rebar
creation: 6 crease
deficiency: 6 anemia 7 anaemia
ender: 4 clad, ware, weed, wood, work 5 bound, smith, stone, works 6 handed, monger, worker
glassmaker's ~ rod: 5 punty 6 pontil
hand: 5 rigor 7 cruelty, tyranny 8 coercion, hardness, severity 9 austerity, autocracy, brutality, despotism, harshness, sternness 10 oppression, severeness, strictness
holder: 3 bag
hook: 4 gaff
horse sound: 4 chug
in German: 5 eisen
in the fire: 3 gig, job 4 task 5 chore 7 project, venture 8 activity
like ~: 6 dogged 7 adamant, durable 8 obdurate, resolute 9 obstinate, steadfast, tenacious, unbending 10 determined, relentless, unyielding
man: 5 robot 7 machine 9 automaton
number one ~: 5 cleek
on: 5 affix 6 attach
ore: 8 hematite, limonite, siderite, taconite 9 magnetite
out: 5 solve 6 smooth 7 arrange, flatten, resolve
oxide: 4 rust 9 corrosion
pigment: 4 heme 5 ocher, ochre
pump ~: 4 heft, lift 7 work out 8 exercise
source: 3 ore 5 liver
starter: 3 and, pig 4 flat, grid
use a branding ~: 4 sear
use a curling ~: 5 crimp
with ~: 6 ferric 7 ferrous
with an ~ hand: 4 hard 6 firmly 7 harshly, roughly, sternly 8 severely, strictly 10 rigorously
worker: 5 smith
work with ~: 4 weld 5 smelt 6 refine
iron ___: 3 out 4 hand, will 5 horse 6 maiden, pyrite 7 curtain
iron ___ fire: 5 in the
___ iron: 3 pig 4 cast, long, nine, tire 5 scrap, short, steam 6 waffle 7 curling, wrought 8 branding
Iron ___: 3 Age 4 Duke 5 Cross 7 Curtain
___ Iron: 5 Man of 7 Pumping
Iron Age culture: 6 La Tène
.... ___ iron bars a cage: 3 nor
Iron Butterfly
song: In-a-Gadda-Da-Vida (1968)
ironclad: 3 set 4 boat, firm, ship 5 fixed, rigid, tight 6 rooted, stable, static 7 certain, settled 8 constant, definite 9 permanent 10 changeless, inexorable, inflexible, unchanging, undoubtful, unwavering
ironclad ___: 5 alibi
ironfisted: 4 firm, hard 5 bossy, cruel, picky, rigid, stern, tough 6 severe, strict 7 austere, Spartan 8 despotic, exacting, hard-line, rigorous, ruthless 9 demanding, draconian, merciless, stringent, unbending, unpitying, unsparing 10 despotical, implacable, inflexible, no-nonsense, oppressive, tyrannical
one: 4 czar, tsar 6 despot, tyrant 8 autocrat, dictator 9 oppressor
Iron Giant, The (1999 film)
voice cast: Jennifer Aniston, Harry Connick Jr., Vin Diesel
ironhanded: 4 firm, hard 5 bossy, cruel, picky, rigid, stern, tough 6 severe, strict 7 austere, Spartan 8 despotic, exacting, hard-line, rigorous, ruthless 9 demanding, draconian, merciless, stringent, unbending, unsparing 10 despotical, implacable, inflexible, no-nonsense, oppressive, tyrannical
Iron Heel, The
author: Jack London
Iron Horse, The: 6 Gehrig
ironic: 3 dry, wry 4 arch 5 funny 7 satiric 8 humorous, sardonic 9 sarcastic, satirical 10 unexpected
Ironic (1996 song)
artist: Alanis Morissette
ironing: 5 chore 9 housework
challenge: 6 collar
obstacle: 6 button
ironing ___: 5 board
iron in the ___: 4 fire
iron-jawed: 3 set 5 fixed 6 intent, mulish 7 decided 8 resolute 9 unbending 10 inflexible, purposeful, unwavering, unyielding
Iron John
author: Robert Bly
Iron Man (2008 film)
cast: Jeff Bridges, Robert Downey, Jr., Terrence Howard, Gwyneth Paltrow
Ironman phase: 3 run 4 swim 7 cycling
Iron Mike: 5 Ditka
iron-on: 5 decal, patch 8 appliqué
jeans ~: 8 appliqué
iron oxide
pigment: 5 ocher, ochre
iron pumper: 5 he-man
pumper pride: 3 bod, pec 4 lats 6 biceps
routine: 4 curl
unit: 3 rep
iron pyrite: 7 mineral 9 fool's gold
irons: 5 bonds, cuffs 7 fetters 8 manacles, shackles 9 bracelets, handcuffs, restraint
carrier: 5 caddy 6 caddie
game with ~: 4 golf
put in ~: 6 fetter 7 enchain, manacle, shackle, trammel 8 handcuff
with many ~ in the fire: 4 at it, busy 6 active, hectic, lively 7 on the go, swamped 8 bustling, immersed 9 engrossed
Ironside (NBC drama)
cast: Barbara Anderson (Eve Whitfield)
Raymond Burr (Robert Ironside)
Don Galloway (Ed Brown)
Don Mitchell (Mark Sanger)
employer: SFPD
___ Ironsides: 3 Old
Iron & Silk (1990 film)
director: Shirley Sun
irons in the ___: 4 fire
Irons, Jeremy: 5 actor
film: Dead Ringers (1988)
Die Hard With a Vengeance (1995)
The French Lieutenant's Woman (1981)
Lolita (1997)
The Man in the Iron Mask (1998)
Reversal of Fortune (1990, AA)
Stealing Beauty (1996)
___-iron stomach: 4 cast
ironstone: 5 china 6 dishes, plates 8 ceramics 10 dinnerware
Ironweed: 4 film 5 novel
author: William Kennedy
cast: Carroll Baker, Jack Nicholson, Michael O'Keefe, Meryl Streep
iron-willed: 4 firm, grim 5 brave, cruel, gutsy, hardy, harsh, rigid, stern, stout 6 crusty, fervid, fierce, flinty, mighty, rugged, severe, steely, strong 7 austere, fervent, staunch 8 despotic, exacting, forceful, hard-line, powerful, resolute, ruthless, stubborn, vigorous 9 draconian, hard-nosed, herculean, imperious, steadfast, tenacious, unsparing 10 autocratic, bullheaded, courageous, formidable, hard-boiled, hardheaded, inflexible, relentless, unmerciful, unyielding
ironworks: 5 forge 6 smithy 7 foundry 8 smithery
device: 5 anvil
irony: 3 wit 5 trope 6 satire 7 sarcasm 10 enantiosis
exclamation: 3 aha 6 indeed 7 big deal
Iroquois: 5 Huron, tribe 6 Cayuga, Indian, Oneida 7 Amerind 8 Onondaga
enemy: 4 Erie
language: 4 Erie 5 Huron 6 Mohawk, Oneida, Seneca 8 Cherokee, Onondaga 9 Tuscarora
Iroquois League
member: 6 Cayuga, Mohawk, Oneida, Seneca 8 Onondaga 9 Tuscarora
irr.: 6 imperf.
irradiate: 4 beam 5 gleam, light, shine, teach 6 inform 7 glitter, inspire, lighten, light up, radiate, shimmer, sparkle 8 brighten, illumine 10 illuminate
irradiation: 3 ray 4 beam, glow, x-ray 5 light 8 radiance, radiancy
irrational: 3 mad 4 wild 5 flaky, kooky, queer, rabid, silly, wacky 6 absurd, flakey, kookie, unwise, whacky 7 extreme, foolish, unsound 8 mindless, unstable 9 arbitrary, brainless, delirious, emotional, fantastic, illogical, senseless, sophistic, unscrewed 10 cockamamie, disjointed, distraught, fallacious, ill-advised, incoherent, inordinate, off-the-wall, reasonless, ridiculous, unreasoned, unthinking
number: 4 surd
irrationality: 4 bosh 5 folly 6 drivel, idiocy, lunacy 7 fatuity, illogic, inanity, madness, oddness, prattle, twaddle 8 insanity, nonsense, wildness
Irrawaddy: 5 river
city on the ~: 3 Ava 9 Manadalay
locale: 5 Burma 7 Myanmar
river to the ~: 8 Chindwin
irreal: 6 dreamy 8 delusive, fanciful, illusory 9 fantastic, imaginary 10 chimerical
irreclaimable: 4 gone, lost
irreconcilable: 7 opposed 8 opposing, opposite
Irreconcilable Differences (1984 film)
cast: Drew Barrymore, Shelley Long, Ryan O'Neal
irrecoverable: 4 gone, lost 6 ruined 7 defunct, extinct, wrecked 8 consumed, vanished 9 destroyed 10 demolished, eradicated
irredeemable: 8 hopeless 10 beyond help
irreducible: 3 net
irrefragable: 4 firm, hard, sure 5 solid 8 hardened, rocklike
irrefutable: 4 sure 5 final, valid 6 proven 7 assured, certain 8 accurate, airtight, ironclad, luculent, positive
irreg., not: 3 std. 4 perf.
irregular: 3 odd 4 eery 5 bumpy,

eerie, erose, jerky, lumpy, queer, rough, weird **6** atypic, broken, casual, fitful, freaky, hackly, jagged, off-key, patchy, quirky, ragged, random, rugged, spotty, uneven, wabbly, way-out, wobbly, zigzag **7** aimless, bizarre, crooked, deviant, erratic, knurled, oddball, offbeat, strange, unalike, unequal, unusual **8** aberrant, abnormal, atypical, cockeyed, far apart, freakish, improper, lopsided, on-and-off, peculiar, periodic, rambling, shifting, sporadic, uncommon, unsteady, variable **9** amorphous, anomalous, desultory, different, dissonant, divergent, eccentric, faltering, fantastic, haphazard, hit-or-miss, malformed, off-center, recurrent, shapeless, spasmodic, unaligned, uncertain, unnatural, up-and-down, vagarious, zigzagged **10** capricious, changeable, disorderly, immoderate, inconstant, infrequent, inordinate, meandering, nonuniform, occasional, off-balance, out of order, sporadical, suspicious, unfrequent, unofficial, unorthodox, unpunctual, unreliable, willy-nilly
combining form: **4** anom- **5** anomo-
not ~: **4** even **5** level **6** smooth, stable, steady **7** uniform **8** balanced, constant, straight **9** unvarying **10** consistent, rhythmical, unwavering

IR

irregularity: **4** blip **5** quirk **6** defect, oddity **7** anomaly, caprice, oddness, variant **9** confusion
irregularly: **6** seldom **7** by turns **8** fitfully, off and on, on and off
irrelevant: **4** idle, moot **5** inapt, unapt **6** stupid **7** foreign, strange, trivial **8** improper, untimely **9** illogical, ill-suited, inapropos, pointless, unrelated **10** extraneous, immaterial, inapposite, nongermane, not germane, out of order, out of place, unsuitable
irreligious: **5** pagan **7** godless, heathen, impious, profane, ungodly **8** undevout
one: **5** pagan **7** atheist, heathen **10** unbeliever
irremedial: **5** no-win **6** ruined, undone **8** hopeless
irremissible: **8** required **9** de rigueur, essential, mandatory **10** compulsory, imperative, obligatory
irremovable: **4** firm **5** fixed, solid **6** rooted, secure **7** riveted
irreparable: **8** hopeless
irreplaceable: **4** rare **5** vital **6** needed, unique **9** priceless
irrepressible: **6** bouncy **7** buoyant **9** mercurial, resilient
irreproachable: **4** good, pure **5** clean **8** spotless **9** guiltless
irresilient: **4** limp **5** baggy, slack **6** droopy, flabby **7** flaccid **8** drooping **10** out of shape
irresistible: **5** siren **6** cogent **8** magnetic **10** magnetical
Irresistible Forces
author: Danielle Steel
irresolute: **4** torn, weak **5** timid **6** fickle, unsure **8** hesitant, lukewarm, wavering **9** faltering, spineless, tentative, uncertain, undecided, unsettled, weak-kneed **10** ambivalent, changeable, hesitating, hot-and-cold, indecisive, on the fence, weak-willed, wishy-washy
be ~: **5** waver **8** hesitate **9** vacillate
irresolution: **5** doubt **6** apathy **7** dubiety, frailty **8** softness, suspense, timidity, weakness **9** dubiosity, hesitancy **10** hesitation
irrespective: **7** despite **8** distinct, ignoring, separate
irresponsibility: **6** excess **7** license **8** audacity, boldness **10** indulgence, profligacy
irresponsible: **3** lax **4** rash, wild **5** giddy, hasty, loose, silly **6** fickle, remiss, sloppy, stupid, unwise **7** flighty **8** carefree, careless, derelict, feckless, immature, reckless, skittish, slipshod **9** imprudent, negligent, unmindful **10** incautious, nonchalant, unreliable, unthinking
one: **3** cad, cur **4** boor, heel, toad **5** knave, rogue, scamp, swine **6** rascal **9** miscreant, scoundrel, vulgarian **10** blackguard
irresponsive: **3** icy, mum **4** cold, cool, dull, mute **5** aloof, quiet **6** frigid, silent **7** languid, removed **8** detached, listless, reserved, reticent, taciturn
irretrievable: **4** gone, lost **8** past hope
one: **5** goner **9** lost cause
irreverence: **4** sass **5** sauce **7** impiety **9** profanity, sacrilege
irreverent: **4** flip **5** fresh, sassy, saucy **6** awless, cheeky, unholy **7** aweless, impious, mocking, profane, ungodly **8** derisive, flippant, impudent, insolent **9** facetious, out-of-line **10** unhallowed
irreversible: **4** lost **5** bleak **6** dismal, futile **7** useless **8** hopeless, ill-fated **9** desperate, permanent
irrevocable: **4** firm, lost, sure **5** final, fixed **7** certain, settled **8** constant, hopeless
damage: **4** ruin **7** debacle **8** calamity, disaster **9** cataclysm, perdition **10** extinction
irrigate: **3** wet **4** soak, wash **5** flood, spray, water **6** dampen, drench **7** moisten **8** sprinkle
irrigated: **3** lit **5** drunk, tipsy **6** stewed **8** besotted **10** inebriated
irrigation: **8** watering
device: **5** noria
need: **4** hose **5** water
needing ~: **3** dry **4** arid, sere **7** bone-dry, drained, parched, thirsty **9** shriveled, waterless **10** dehydrated, desiccated
project: **3** dam
irritability: **5** anger **6** choler, spleen, temper **8** acerbity, asperity, edginess, ill humor, tartness
irritable: **3** hot **4** edgy, sour **5** cross, fiery, huffy, moody, raspy, surly, testy, waspy **6** crabby, crusty, feisty, fretty, grumpy, ireful, morose, ornery, snappy, snippy, sullen, touchy **7** annoyed, bearish, bristly, fretful, grouchy, huffish, nervous, peevish, peppery, prickly, waspish **8** captious, choleric, fretsome, growling, grumpish, liverish, petulant, snappish, snarling, snippety **9** crotchety, difficult, dyspeptic, fractious, grumbling, impatient, irascible, querulous, resentful, sensitive, splenetic **10** high-strung, ill-humored, ill-natured, intolerant, out of humor, out of sorts
in Britain: **5** tilty
one: **4** crab **5** crank, grump **6** grouch **8** grumbler, sourball **10** curmudgeon
irritant: **3** bur **4** bore, load, pest **5** thorn, trial **6** bother, burden, gadfly, hassle, ordeal **8** headache, nuisance, pet peeve, sore spot, vexation **9** annoyance
starter: **7** counter
irritate: **3** bug, get, ire, irk, jar, nag, rag, rub, try, vex **4** bait, burn, faze, fret, gall, goad, miff, pain, rile, roil, tire **5** anger, annoy, chafe, grate, harry, peeve, pique, sting, upset, worry **6** abrade, bother, enrage, fester, harass, madden, needle, nettle, noodge, offend, pester, pother, put out, rankle, rattle, redden, ruffle, scrape, tee off **7** affront, bedevil, disturb, enflame, henpeck, incense, inflame, perturb, provoke, torment, trouble **8** distress, embitter, imbitter **9** aggravate, displease, infuriate **10** antagonize, discomfort, discompose, exasperate
irritated: **3** raw, red **5** angry, tired **6** chafed, pained, raving, tender **7** annoyed, burning, hurting, nettled, painful, plagued, ranting **8** harassed, pestered, smarting
state: **3** pet **4** huff, snit **5** pique
see also angry
irritating: **5** acrid, harsh, pesky, pesty **6** thorny, trying, vexing **7** burning, fretful, galling, grating, irksome **8** abrasive, annoying, fretsome, nettling, tiresome, worrying **9** annoyance, difficult, offensive, vexatious **10** bothersome, in one's hair
irritation: **3** ire **4** bile, gall, huff, itch, pest, tiff **5** anger, pique, trial, worry, wrath **6** bother, choler, nerves, spleen **7** dudgeon, offense, umbrage **8** acerbity, acrimony, friction, ill humor, slow burn, vexation **9** annoyance **10** difficulty, discomfort, harassment, unkindness
cause ~: **3** irk, vex **4** gall, rile **5** annoy, chafe, clash, grate, peeve, pique **6** abrade, nettle, rankle **7** inflame, provoke **9** aggravate **10** exasperate
show ~: **4** boil, fume, rage, rant, rave **5** chafe **6** blow up, seethe
irrupt: **7** break in, burst in **8** overflow
irruption: **4** raid **5** foray, sally **6** attack, inroad, sortie **8** invasion, outbreak **9** incursion
IRS: **4** agcy. **6** agency
action: **3** aud. **5** audit
busy month: **3** Apr. **5** April
concern: **3** IRA, tax **6** income
department: **8** Treasury
employee: **3** acc., agt., aud., CPA, fed **4** acct., T-man **5** agent
identifier: **3** SSN
part of ~: **3** Int., Rev., Svc. **4** Serv. **7** Revenue, Service **8** Internal
sheet: **4** form
web site suffix: **3** gov
IRT: **6** subway
kin: **3** BMT
locale: **3** NYC **7** New York
Irtysh: **5** river **8** Ob feeder
city on the ~: **4** Omsk
feeder: **3** Oma
locale: **5** China **6** Russia **10** Kazakhstan
river to the ~: **5** Tobol
Irvin: **4** Cobb **5** Monte **8** Kershner
Irvine: **4** city, town
locale: **8** Scotland **10** California
sch.: **3** UCI **4** U Cal.
Irving: **3** Amy **4** city, John, Reis, town **5** Stone **6** Berlin, Pichel, Rapper **7** Wallace **8** Cummings, Langmuir, Thalberg **10** Washington
locale: **5** Texas
snoozer: **3** Rip
Irving, Amy: **7** actress
film: Carrie (1976)
The Competition (1980)
Crossing Delancey (1988)
Honeysuckle Rose (1980)
Micki + Maude (1984)
Yentl (1983)
spouse: Steven Spielberg
Irving, Henry: **3** Sir
Irving, John: **6** writer
work: The Cider House Rules
The Fourth Hand
The Hotel New Hampshire
A Prayer for Owen Meany
A Son of the Circus
Trying to Save Piggy Sneed
The Water-Method Man
A Widow for One Year
The World According to Garp
Irvington: **4** city, town
locale: **9** New Jersey
Irving, Washington: **6** writer
work: A History of New York
The Legend of Sleepy Hollow
Rip Van Winkle
Irvin, Monte: **10** outfielder
Irwin: **4** Hale, Shaw **5** Allen, Corey **7** Winkler
__ Irwin, CA: **4** Fort
Irwin, Hale: **6** golfer
is: **4** verb
as ~: **7** unfixed **9** unchanged **10** unimproved
in Spanish: **4** esta
it ~ so: **4** amen
like it ~: **7** reality, sincere **8** candidly, veracity **9** situation, veracious **10** forthright, from the hip, truthfully
no longer ~: **3** was
not: **4** ain't
plurally: **3** are
that ~: **3** viz. **5** id est, to wit **6** namely
__ is: **4** that
...is __ itself: **4** fear
Is __ All There Is: **4** That
Is __ Crime: **3** It a
Is __ dagger...: **5** this a
Is __ fact?: **5** that a
Is __ so?: **4** that

Isaac: 4 Hull 5 Hayes, Stern, Watts 6 Asimov, Newton, Pitman 7 Albéniz
  brother: 7 Ishmael
  parent: 5 Sarah 7 Abraham
  son: 4 Esau 5 Jacob
  wife: 7 Rebekah
Isaac ___ Singer: 6 Merrit 8 Bashevis
Isaak: 5 Babel, Chris
___ Is a Battlefield: 4 Love
Isabeau
  composer: Pietro Mascagni
Isabel: 5 Jeans, Perón 6 Jewell 7 Allende, Sanford
  in English: 9 Elizabeth
  see also Spanish
Isabella: 4 poem 5 queen 10 Rossellini
  author: John Keats
  parent: 6 Ingrid 7 Roberto
  poet: 5 Keats
  spouse: Ferdinand
  vessel backed by: 4 Niña 5 Pinta 10 Santa Maria
Isabella d'___: 4 Este
Isabelle: 6 Adjani 7 Huppert
Isadora: 6 Duncan
Isadora (1968 film)
  cast: Vanessa Redgrave, Jason Robards
...is a friend ___: 6 indeed
Isaiah: 6 Berlin 7 prophet
  father: 4 Amoz
  follower: 8 Jeremiah
___, I Said: 3 I Am
___ is a jealous mistress: 3 Art
Isak: 5 Karen 7 Dinesen
___ Is All Around: 4 Love
___ is a Lonely Hunter, The: 5 Heart
___ Is a Many Splendored Thing: 4 Love
Isamu: 7 Noguchi
___ is an island: 5 No man
Isao: 4 Aoki
Isar: 5 river
  city on the ~: 6 Munich
  locale: 7 Austria, Germany
___ is as good...: 5 A miss
___ Is a Sometime Thing, A: 5 Woman
___ is a terrible thing to waste: 5 A mind
___ Is a Tramp, The: 4 Lady
I saw: 4 vidi
...___ I saw Elba: 3 ere
I Saw Her Again (1966 song)
  artist: Mamas & the Papas
I Saw Her Standing There (song)
  artist: Beatles
I Saw Him Standing There (1988 song)
  artist: Tiffany
I Saw the Light (1972 song)
  artist: Todd Rundgren
I Saw Three Ships: 4 noel 5 carol
___ I say...: 4 Do as
___ I Say: 5 What'd
I Say a Little Prayer (song)
  artist: Aretha Franklin, Dionne Warwick
___ I say more?: 4 Need
___ Is Beautiful: 4 Life
___ is believing: 6 seeing
___ Is Blue: 4 Love
ISBN: 2 ID
  part: 2 No. 3 Int., Std. 4 Book, Intl. 6 Number
___ Is Born, A: 4 Star 5 Child
___ Is Bustin' Out All Over: 4 June
___ is but a dream: 4 life
___ Iscariot: 5 Judas
___ is cast, The: 3 die
ischium: 4 bone
  locale: 6 pelvis
Ischl: 3 spa 6 resort
  locale: 7 Austria
I second that!: 4 amen
I Second That Emotion (1967 song)
  artist: Miracles
I see!: 3 aah, aha 4 ah so 5 got it, uh-huh
___ I See You, The: 4 More
___ Is Ended, The: 4 Song
___ Is Enough: 5 Eight
Isère: 5 river
  city on the ~: 8 Grenoble
  locale: 6 France
Is ev'rybody happy? asker: 5 Lewis
Isfahan
  locale: 4 Iran
___ is falling, The: 3 Sky
___ is father of the man, The: 5 child
...is fear ___: 6 itself
___ is forgiven: 3 all
___ is golden: 7 Silence
___ Is Green, The: 4 Corn
-ish: 4 like, near
  relative: 3 -oid 5 -esque, quasi-
Ish: 8 Kabibble
I Shall Not Be Moved
  author: Maya Angelou
Isham: 4 Mark 5 Jones
___ Is Here: 6 Spring
___ Is Here to Stay: 4 Love
Isherwood, Christopher: 6 writer 7 British 10 playwright
  colleague: W.H. Auden, Stephen Spender
  work: The Berlin Stories
    Goodbye to Berlin
    Lions and Shadows
    Mr. Norris Changes Trains
    Sally Bowles
___ Is High, The: 4 Tide
Ishikari Bay, city on: 5 Otaru
Ishmael: 4 Reed
  brother: 5 Isaac
  captain: 4 Ahab
  descendant: 4 Arab
  parent: 5 Hagar 7 Abraham
I Shot the Sheriff (1974 song)
  artist: Eric Clapton
I should say ___!: 3 not
___, I Shrunk the Kids: 5 Honey
Ishtar (1987 film)
  beast: 5 camel
  cast: Isabelle Adjani, Warren Beatty, Charles Grodin, Dustin Hoffman
  director: Elaine May
___ is human: 5 To err
Isiah: 6 Thomas
Isidor: 4 Rabi
isinglass: 4 mica
I Sing the Body Electric
  author: Ray Bradbury, Walt Whitman
...___ is in Heaven: 4 as it
___ is in the fire, the: 3 fat
___ Is in the Streets: 5 A Lion
Isis: 7 goddess
  animal sacred to ~: 3 cow
  brother: 3 Set 6 Osiris
  husband: 6 Osiris
  parent: 3 Geb, Nut
  son: 5 Horus
Is It a Crime (1985 song)
  artist: Sade
Is It Love (1986 song)
  artist: Mr. Mister
Is it soup ___?: 3 yet
Is It True (1964 song)
  artist: Brenda Lee
___ is just...: 5 A sigh
Isla de ___: 6 Pascua
Islam: 3 rel. 8 religion
  ablution: 4 wudu
  bridge to paradise: 5 sirat
  center: 5 Mecca 6 Medina
  coin: 5 dinar
  community: 4 umma 5 ummah
  decoration: 9 arabesque
  doctors: 5 ulema
  festival: 6 Bairam
  God of ~: 5 Allah
  holy book: 5 Koran, Quran
  law: 5 sunna
  leader: 4 amir, emir, imam 5 ameer, calif, emeer, imaum, kalif 6 caliph, kaliph, khalif
  messiah: 5 mahdi
  miracle: 5 miraj
  month: 4 Rabi 5 Rajab, Safar 6 Jumada, Shaban 7 Ramadan, Shawwal 8 Muharram 9 Dhu al-Qa'da 10 Dhu al-Hijja
  pilgrimage: 3 haj 4 hadj, hajj
  prayers: 4 raka 5 salah, salat
  republic: 4 Iran
  sect: 5 Sunni
  spirit: 3 jin 4 djin, jinn 5 djinn, jinni 6 djinni
  teacher: 5 mulla
  weight: 4 rotl
  weights: 5 artal
  see also Muslim
Islamabad: 4 city, town 7 capital
  locale: 3 Pak. 8 Pakistan
island: 3 ait, cay, Cos, key, Kos, Man, Yap 4 Aran, Bali, Cook, Cuba, Elba, eyot, Fiji, Guam, Iona, Java, Long, Maui, Milo, Oahu, Sark, Skye 5 Arran, Aruba, atoll, Capri, Cocos, Corfu, Crete, Delos, Ellis, Haiti, Hondo, Ibiza, Iviza, Kauai, Lanai, Leyte, Lundy, Luzon, Malta, Melos, Milos, Naxos, Panay, Samoa, Samos, Thera, Thira, Thule, Timor, Tonga, Wight 6 Baffin, Bahama, Bikini, Borneo, Canary, Candia, Cayman, Comoro, Cyprus, Easter, Hawaii, Hiva Oa, Honshu, Jersey, Jinmen, Kinmen, Kiushu, Kodiak, Kyushu, Lemnos, Madura, Midway, Parris, Patmos, Penang, Philae, Quemoy, Rhodes, Saipan, Savaii, Sicily, Staten, Sundas, Tahiti, Taiwan, Thanet, Tobago 7 Bahrain, Bahrein, Bali Ha'i, Bermuda, Celebes, Chinmen, Corsica, Curaçao, Formosa, Gotland, Grenada, Iceland, Ireland, Iwo Jima, Jamaica, La Palma, Liparis, Madeira, Majorca, Mindoro, Minorca, Mombasa, Mykonos, Nicobar, Norfolk, Oceania, Okinawa, Orkneys, Raiatea, Rapa Nui, Roanoke, Ryukyus, Sao Tomé, St. Croix, St. Lucia, Sumatra, Vanuatu, Wrangel 8 Alcatraz, Atlantis, Barbados, Bora Bora, Dominica, Eniwetok, Guernsey, Hokkaido, Hong Kong, Krakatoa, Mindanao, Moluccas, Pitcairn, Sakhalin, Sandwich, Santorin, Sardinia, Sri Lanka, St. Helena, St. Martin, St. Thomas, Sulawesi, Tasmania, Tenerife, Trinidad, Unalaska, Victoria, Viti Levu, Zanzibar 9 Ascension, Australia, Christmas, Ellesmere, Galápagos, Greenland, Indonesia, Innisfail, Innisfree, Manhattan, Mauritius, Nantucket, New Guinea, Rarotonga, Santorini, segregate, Singapore, St. George's, Stromboli, Teneriffe, Vancouver 10 Cape Breton, Guadeloupe, Hispaniola, Madagascar, Martinique, Montserrat, Puerto Rico, Saint Kitts, Upolu. Wight
  Aegean: 3 Cos, Ios, Kea, Kos, Zea 4 Keos, Milo 5 Chios, Crete, Delos, Khios, Melos, Milos, Samos 6 Candia, Icaria, Lemnos, Lesbos, Patmos, Rhodes, Rhodos, Skiros, Skyros 7 Mykonos 8 Cyclades
  Aegean ~: 5 Leros, Naxos, Paros, Thera 6 Euboea, Thasos 7 Syphnos, Tenedos
  Aleutian: 3 Rat 4 Adak, Atka, Attu 8 Unalaska
  Atlantic: 6 Faroes 7 Iceland, Ireland 8 St. Helena 9 Ascension, Greenland
  Balearic: 5 Ibiza, Iviza 7 Majorca, Menorca, Minorca
  Canada: 6 Baffin 8 Victoria 9 Ellesmere, Vancouver
  Canary: 6 Hierro 7 La Palma 8 Tenerife 9 Teneriffe
  Caribbean: 3 BWI 4 Saba 5 Aruba 7 Bahamas, Caymans
  Channel ~: 4 Sark 6 Jersey 8 Guernsey
  combining form: 4 neso- 5 -nesia
  coral ~: 3 cay, key
  Cyclades: 3 Kea, Zea 4 Keos, Milo 5 Delos, Melos, Milos, Naxos, Paros, Thera, Thira 8 Santorin 9 Santorini
  Cyclades ~: 3 Ios
  Dodecanese: 5 Leros 6 Patmos, Rhodes, Rhodos
  East China Sea: 4 Mazu 5 Matsu 6 Kiushu, Kyushu
  England: 3 Ely, Man 4 Sark 5 Wight 6 Jersey 8 Guernsey
  Greece: 3 Cos, Ios, Kos 4 Milo 5 Corfu, Crete, Delos, Leros, Melos, Milos, Naxos, Paros, Samos, Thera, Thira, Zante 6 Candia, Euboea, Lemnos, Lesbos, Skiros, Skyros 8 Santorin 9 Santorini
  Hawaiian: 4 Maui, Oahu 5 Kauai, Lanai
  Hebrides: 4 Iona, Mull, Skye
  Indian Ocean: 5 Cocos 6 Comoro 8 Sri Lanka 9 Christmas, Mauritius 10 Madagascar, Seychelles
  Indonesia: 4 Bali, Biak, Java, Laut, Leti, Nias, Roti, Savu, Sawu 5 Banka, Ceram, Letti, Rotti, Spice, Sumba, Timor 6 Bangka, Borneo, Butung, Lombok, Madura, Serang 7 Celebes,

Sumatra **8** Krakatoa, Moluccas, Sulawesi
in French: 3 île
Ionian Sea: 5 Corfu, Zante
Japan: 5 Hondo **6** Honshu, Kiushu **7** Okinawa, Shikoku **8** Hokkaido **13** Kyushu. Ryukyus
Leeward ~: 4 Saba **8** St. Martin **10** Guadeloupe, Montserrat
Malay: 5 Timor **6** Borneo, Sundas **9** Indonesia **10** East Indies
Mediterranean ~: 3 Sar. **4** Elba **5** Capri, Corfu, Crete, Malta **6** Candia, Cyprus, Sicily
nation: 5 Malta **6** Cyprus **7** Bermuda, Jamaica **8** Sri Lanka **9** Indonesia **10** New Zealand
New York: 4 Fire, Long **5** Coney, Ellis **6** Rikers, Staten **9** Manhattan
North Sea: 7 Frisian, Orkneys
Pacific: 3 Yap **4** Cook, Fiji, Guam, Niue, Reao, Savo, Truk, Wake **5** Hondo, Nauru, Palau, Samar, Samoa, Tonga, Upolu **6** Bikini, Easter, Hawaii, Hivaoa, Honshu, Midway, Saipan, Savaii, Tahiti **7** Oceania, Phoenix, Rapa Nui, Society, Vanuatu **8** Bora Bora, Eniwetok, Friendly, Gilberts, Hokkaido **9** Australia, Marquesas, Marshalls, New Guinea, Polynesia **10** Micronesia, New Zealand
Philippines: 4 Cebu, Jolo **5** Bohol, Leyte, Luzon, Panay, Samar **6** Negros **7** Mindoro **8** Mindanao, Visayans
river ~: 3 ait **4** eyot
Scotland: 4 Mull, Skye **5** Tiree, Tyree **8** Hebrides
small ~: 3 ait, cay, key **4** eyot
South China Sea: 6 Hainan, Taiwan **7** Formosa **8** Hong Kong **9** Singapore
Taiwan Strait: 4 Amoy **6** Jinmen, Kinmen, Quemoy **7** Chinmen **10** Pescadores
welcome: 3 lei **5** aloha
West Indies: 4 Cuba **5** Aruba, Haiti **6** Virgin **7** Jamaica **8** Antilles, Barbados, Windward **10** Hispaniola, Martinique, Puerto Rico
Windward ~: 7 Grenada, St. Lucia **8** Dominica **9** St. George's **10** Grenadines
see also Hawaii
island-__: 3 hop
__ island: 3 ice **4** heat **6** monkey, safety, speech **7** barrier, traffic
__ Island: 4 Fire, Long, Nim's, Wake **5** Coney, Ellis, Rhode **6** Baffin, Devil's, Easter, Parris, Staten **7** Baranof, Bedloe's, Fantasy, Liberty, Roanoke, Sanibel
__ Island Earth: 4 This
Islanders: 3 six **4** team
gear: 4 puck **5** stick
home: 7 New York
milieu: 3 ice **4** rink
org.: 3 NHL
rival: *see* hockey team
sport: 6 hockey
__ Island, FL: 5 Marco
Island Girl (1975 song)
artist: Elton John

__ Island Line: 4 Rock
__ Island National Park: 3 Elk
__ Island, NY: 4 City **5** Coney, Ellis **6** Rikers, Staten
Island of Dr. Moreau
author: H.G. Wells
Island of the Blue Dolphins
author: Scott O'Dell
Island of the Day Before, The
author: Umberto Eco
Island of the Fay, The
author: Edgar Allan Poe
__ Island Red: 5 Rhode
islands: 6 Azores, Faroes **7** Bahamas, Caymans, Faeroes, Ionians, Liparis, Oceania, Orkneys, Ryukyus **8** Andamans, Antilles, Canaries, Cyclades, Gilberts, Hebrides, Leewards, Marianas, Moluccas, Sandwich, Solomons, Visayans **9** Aleutians, Antipodes, Carolines, Falklands, Indonesia, Marquesas, Marshalls, Polynesia, Prilibofs **10** East Indies, Grenadines, Pescadores, Seychelles, West Indies
__ Islands: 3 Aru **4** Åran, Aroe, Arru, Cook, Fiji, Truk **5** Åland, Faroe, Spice, Sunda **6** Aegean, Bahama, Canary, Cayman, Ellice, Faeroe, Ionian, Kurile, Orkney, Virgin **7** Channel, Diomede, Leeward, Maldive, Mariana, Society, Solomon
__ Islands, AK: 3 Far **4** Near
Islands in the Stream
author: Ernest Hemingway
locale: 6 Bimini
Islands in the Stream (1983 song)
artist: Dolly Parton, Kenny Rogers
__ Island Sound: 4 Long
Island, The: 4 play **5** novel
author: Peter Benchley, Athol Fugard
Island, The (2005 film)
cast: Sean Bean, Scarlett Johansson, Ewan McGregor
__ Island With You: 4 On an
isle: 3 ait, cay, key **4** eyot
see also island
Isle __ National Park: 6 Royale
__ Isle: 5 Apple **6** Garden **7** Emerald, Presque
Isle of __: 3 Ely, Man **4** Skye **5** Capri, Pines, Wight
Isle of Man
language: 4 Manx
man: 4 Gael
Isle of Mull neighbor: 4 Iona
Isle of Wight city: 4 Ryde
Isle Royale: 4 park
locale: 8 Michigan
islet: 3 ait, cay, key **4** eyot **5** atoll
Isley: 6 O'Kelly, Ronald **7** Rudolph
Isley Brothers
song: Fight the Power (1975)
It's Your Thing (1969)
That Lady (1973)
Islip: 4 city, town
locale: 7 New York
ism: 5 creed, dogma, tenet **6** belief, school, system, theory **7** precept **8** doctrine, ideology, practice **9** principle **10** philosophy
Ismail: 8 Merchant
__ is me!: 3 Woe

__ Is Mine, The: 3 Boy **4** Girl
__ is more: 4 less
__ Is My Country: 4 This
__ is my shepherd..., The: 4 Lord
__ is my witness...: 5 As God
__ Is Not Enough: 4 Once **8** The World
__ Is Nothin' Like a Dame: 5 There
isn't: 4 ain't
Isn't __ bit like you and me?: 3 he a
Isn't __ Lovely?: 3 She
Isn't It a Pity (1970 song)
artist: George Harrison
Isn't It a Pity?
composer: George Gershwin, Ira Gershwin
Isn't It Romantic
composer: Lorenz Hart, Richard Rodgers
__ Isn't Love: 4 If It
__ Isn't So: 5 Say It
iso-: 4 equi-, same **5** equal
isobar: 4 line
Isocrates: 5 Greek **6** orator
isogon: 6 square **9** rectangle
isolate: 5 ice in, split **6** banish, cut off, detach, enisle, maroon, shut in, strand **7** confine, seclude **8** block off, close off, separate, set apart **9** disengage, keep apart, segregate, sequester **10** disconnect, quarantine
isolated: 4 lone, only, sole **5** alone, apart, aside, quiet, stray **6** atypic, far-out, hidden, lonely, narrow, random, remote, single, unique **7** insular, private, recluse, special, strange, unusual **8** abnormal, all alone, atypical, deserted, eremitic, far apart, forsaken, lonesome, secluded, separate, solitary, sporadic **9** abandoned, anomalous, nonpublic, reclusive, untypical, withdrawn **10** infrequent, sporadical
isolation: 7 privacy, secrecy **8** solitude **9** backwoods, seclusion **10** desolation, loneliness
isolation __: 5 booth
isolato: 5 loner **6** hermit **7** eremite, recluse **9** anchorite, introvert
isometrics: 7 regimen **8** exercise
__ Is on My Side: 4 Time
isonomy: 6 parity **7** balance **8** equality, evenness
isotonics: 7 regimen **8** exercise
ISP: 3 AOL **5** Yahoo! **9** Earthlink **10** Mindspring
option: 3 DSL
I 'spect I growed sayer: 5 Topsy
I Spy (2002 film)
cast: Famke Janssen, Malcolm McDowell, Eddie Murphy, Owen Wilson
I Spy (NBC drama)
cast: Bill Cosby (Alexander Scott) Robert Culp (Kelly Robinson)
Israel: 4 Sion, Zion **6** nation, Putnam **7** country **8** Horovitz
airline: 4 El Al
airport: 3 Lod **9** Ben-Gurion
Biblical name for ~: 6 Beulah, Canaan
bovine: 6 Baladi
capital: 9 Jerusalem
city: 3 Lod **4** Elat, Yafo **5** Eilat, Elath, Haifa, Jaffa **6** Ashdod, Bat Yam **7** Netanya, Tel Aviv **8** Nazareth **9** Beersheba, Jerusalem
dance: 4 hora **5** horah
desert: 5 Negeb, Negev
diplomat: 4 Eban
ender: 3 ite
gun: 3 Uzi
king: 4 Ahab, Elah, Jehu, Omri, Saul **5** David **7** Ahaziah, Solomon
lake: 7 Dead Sea
language: 3 Heb. **4** Hebr. **6** Hebrew
legislature: 7 Knesset
locale: 4 Asia **7** Mideast **8** Near East
money: 5 agora **6** agorot, shekel
mountain: 5 Tabor
native: 5 sabra
neighbor: 3 Leb., Syr. **5** Egypt, Syria **6** Jordan **7** Lebanon
Nobelist in Economics: 8 Kahneman
Nobelist in Literature: 5 Agnon
Nobelist in Peace: 5 Begin, Peres, Rabin
political party: 5 Likud, Mapam
port: 4 Acre, Yafo **5** Eilat, Elath, Haifa, Jaffa
sea: 4 Dead **7** Galilee
tribe of ~: 3 Dan, Gad **4** Levi **5** Asher, Judah **6** Joseph, Reuben, Simeon **7** Zebulun **8** Benjamin, Issachar, Naphtali
violinist: 7 Perlman **8** Zukerman
writer: 2 Oz **7** Amichai **9** Appelfeld
see also Hebrew
__ Israel: 5 Eretz
Israel in __: 5 Egypt
Israel in Egypt
composer: George Frideric Handel
__-Israeli relations: 4 Arab
Israelite: 3 Jew **6** Hebrew, Jewish
home: 6 Goshen
leader: 5 Moses **6** Joshua
Israel prime ministers:
2009- Benjamin Netanyahu
2006-09 Ehud Olmert
2001-06 Ariel Sharon
1999-01 Ehud Barak
1996-99 Benjamin Netanyahu
1995-96 Shimon Peres
1992-95 Yitzhak Rabin
1986-92 Yitzhak Shamir
1984-86 Shimon Peres
1983-84 Yitzhak Shamir
1977-83 Menachem Begin
1974-77 Yitzhak Rabin
1969-74 Golda Meir
1963-69 Levi Eshkol
1955-63 David Ben-Gurion
1954-55 Moshe Sharett
1948-54 David Ben-Gurion
Israfel
author: Edgar Allan Poe
__ is Rich: 6 Rabbit
__ Is Right, The: 5 Price
Issachar
brother: 3 Dan, Gad **4** Levi **5** Asher, Judah **6** Joseph, Reuben, Simeon **7** Zebulun **8** Benjamin, Naphtali
parent: 4 Leah **5** Jacob
sister: 5 Dinah
Issei: 8 Japanese **9** immigrant
child: 5 Nisei
Issel, Dan

milieu: 5 court
org.: 3 NBA
sport: 10 basketball
__ is silence, The: 4 rest
__ Is Sleeping: 4 Enid
Is so! rebuttal: 4 ain't 5 am not 6 are not
__ Is Spinal Tap: 4 This
...is still __...: 5 a kiss
__ Is Strange: 4 Love
issue: 3 run 4 cion, copy, emit, flow, give, gush, kids, mint, ooze, pour, rise, seed, send, sons, spew, spue, stem, text, vent 5 eject, expel, exude, heirs, point, print, query, scion, spawn, spirt, spurt, start, topic, young 6 emerge, get out, matter, put out, ration, scions, sequel, spring, stream, upshot 7 cast out, deal out, diffuse, dish out, divvy up, dole out, edition, emanate, give off, give out, hand out, kinfolk, mete out, outflow, pass out, problem, proceed, product, progeny, publish, radiate, release, send out, subject, trickle 8 argument, bring out, children, delivery, disburse, dispatch, dispense, emission, hot topic, kinfolks, kinsfolk, magazine, overflow, printing, question, throw off, transmit 9 arise from, circulate, daughters, grow out of, inheritor, offspring, originate, posterity, send forth 10 administer, contention, descendant, dispersion, distribute, promulgate, put forward
at ~: 4 open 10 in question
avoid the ~: 5 hedge, stall 6 waffle
cloud the ~: 5 befog 7 confuse 8 confound 9 obfuscate
for short: 3 pub
(from): 4 stem 5 arise 6 result
nettlesome ~: 5 thorn
no longer an ~: 4 dead, moot
not an ~: 4 moot 8 academic
point at ~: 5 theme, topic 8 argument, question
side: 3 con, pro
special ~: 5 extra 6 annual
take ~: 5 argue, clash 6 differ, oppose 7 quarrel, quibble 8 conflict, disagree
violently: 5 eruct, erupt
issued, soon to be: 3 NYP
Issus: 6 battle
__ Is Sweeping the Country: 4 Love
Issy: 4 city, town
locale: 6 France
-ist: 4 doer
cousin: 3 -ite, -nik, -yer 4 -ster
Istanbul: 4 city, port, town
area: 6 Galata
city near ~: 6 Edirne
it replaced ~: 6 Angora, Ankara
locale: 4 Asia 6 Europe, Turkey
I Started a Joke (1969 song)
artist: Bee Gees
Is that __?: 5 a fact
Is That All There Is (1969 song)
artist: Peggy Lee
Is that so?: 6 do tell, oh yeah, really
Is that your __ answer?: 5 final
__ Is the Army: 4 This
__ Is the Gate: 6 Strait
__ Is the Love: 5 Where
__ is the Message, The: 6 Medium
__ Is the Night: 6 Tender
Is There Something I Should Know (1983 song)
artist: Duran Duran
__ is the time...: 3 Now
__ is the winter...: 3 Now
Is this a dagger which __...: 4 I see
Is this seat __?: 5 taken
Is this the end of __?: 4 Rico
isthmus: 3 Kra 4 neck, Suez 6 Panama, strait 7 Corinth 10 land bridge
__ Is Tight: 4 Time
I Still Believe (1999 song)
artist: Mariah Carey
I Still See __: 5 Elisa
istle: 4 rope 5 fiber
source: 5 yucca
Istomin, Eugene: 7 pianist
__ Is Too Much With Us, The: 5 World
__ is to say: 4 that
ISU
conference: 9 Big Twelve
locale: 4 Ames
__ is up!, The: 3 jig
Isuzu: 3 car 4 auto 10 automobile
model: 5 Amigo, Axiom, Rodeo 6 Stylus 7 Impulse, Trooper 8 Ascender
__ Is Waiting, A: 5 Child
I swear!: 5 no lie 6 honest, really
__ is well: 3 All
__ Is Wild, The: 5 Joker
__ is yet to be, The: 4 best
__ Is Yet to Come, The: 4 Best
Is You __ Is You Ain't Ma Baby?: 4 Is or
__ Is Your Life: 4 This
__ Is You, The: 4 Song
it: 5 charm 6 appeal, neuter, seeker 7 charism 8 charisma
game: 3 tag
__ it: 3 bag, cut, dog, get, leg, mix 4 beat, cool, go at, go to, hoof, make, take, wing, with 5 catch, get to, go for, hop to, out of, rough, see to, watch 6 cheese
__ it!: 3 Bag, Can, Hit 4 Cool, Darn, I get, So be, Stow 5 Hop to, Prove
...it __ for thee: 5 tolls
It: 5 novel
author: Stephen King
It __ a dark...: 3 was
It __ as Well Be Spring: 5 Might
It __ a Thief: 5 Takes
It __ a Very Good Year: 3 Was
It __ Be Him: 4 Must
It __, be not afraid: 3 is I
It __ Be You: 5 Had to, Might
It __ Come Easy: 4 Don't
It __ Depends on You: 3 All
It __ Fair: 4 Isn't
It __ far far better thing...: 3 is a
It __ From Outer Space: 4 Came
It __ Happen to You: 5 Could 6 Should
It __ laugh: 4 is to
It __ Mean a Thing: 4 Don't
It __ Me Babe: 4 Ain't
It __ Necessarily So: 4 Ain't
It __ to Be Ignorant: 4 Pays
It __ to Be You: 3 Had
It __ Two: 5 Takes
It __ Very Good Year: 4 Was a
It.
see Italian
__ it a day: 4 call
__ It Again, Sam: 4 Play
__ it a go: 4 give
It Ain't __ Rain No Mo': 5 Gonna
It ain't a fit night out for man or __: 5 beast
It Ain't Hard To Tell rapper: 3 Nas
It Ain't Me Babe
composer: Bob Dylan
It Ain't Me Babe (1965 song)
artist: Turtles
It Ain't Necessarily So
composer: George Gershwin, Ira Gershwin
It Ain't Over 'Til It's Over (1991 song)
artist: Lenny Kravitz
Ital.: 4 lang.
see also Italian
Italia, city in: 4 Roma 6 Milano, Napoli, Torino 7 Firenze, Livorno, Venezia
Italian: 8 dressing, language
see also Italy
Italian __: 4 Alps, hand, ices 5 bread 6 sonnet, turnip
Italian Job, The (2003 film)
cast: Edward Norton, Charlize Theron, Mark Wahlberg
Italian Symphony
composer: Felix Mendelssohn
Italian words
apology: 5 scusa
art: 4 arte
asset: 4 bene
be: 3 ser
count: 5 conte
dear: 4 cara, caro
desk: 5 stipo
earth: 5 terra
eight: 4 otto
evening: 4 sera
farewell: 4 ciao
flower holder: 4 vaso
fruit: 5 oliva
good: 4 bene
goodbye: 4 ciao
holiday: 5 festa
holy man: 5 santo
innkeeper: 4 oste
ladder: 5 scala
lady: 5 donna
land: 5 terra
love: 5 amore
monk: 3 fra
month: 5 Marzo
moon: 4 luna
my: 3 mia, mio
noble: 5 conte
number: 3 due, sei, tre, uno 4 otto
off: 3 via
one: 3 una, uno
peak: 5 monte
road: 3 via
six: 3 sei
skill: 4 arte
street: 3 via
they: 4 esse, esso
three: 3 tre
two: 3 due
way: 3 via
wine: 4 vino
see also Italy
italicize: 6 stress 7 point up 9 emphasize, underline 10 accentuate
italics: 4 type
like ~: 6 aslant 7 slanted
what ~ show: 6 accent, stress
8 emphasis 10 importance
italic type: 6 aldine
I Talk to the Trees
composer: Alan Jay Lerner, Frederick Loewe
__ it all: 5 above
__-it-all: 4 know
It All Adds Up
author: Saul Bellow
__ it all hang out: 3 let
__ it all together: 3 get, put
Italo: 4 Tajo 5 Balbo, Svevo 7 Calvino 10 Montemezzi
Italy: 6 nation 7 country
ancient town: 4 Elea 5 Ostia
artist: 4 Reni 6 Giotto, Titian 7 Cellini, da Vinci, Raphael, Tiepolo 8 Angelico, del Sarto 9 Donatello 10 Botticelli, Modigliani, Tintoretto 12 Michelangelo
art patron: 4 Este
astronomer: 6 Piazzi 7 Galilei, Galileo
bass: 5 Pinza
bay: 6 Naples
bovine: 5 Oropa 8 Chianina
bowling: 5 bocce, bocci 6 boccia, boccie
brandy: 6 grappa
capital: 4 Roma, Rome
car: 4 Alfa, Fiat, Ghia 7 Bugatti, Ferrari 8 Maserati 9 Alfa Romeo
cheese: 6 Romano 7 fontina, ricotta 8 Bel Paese, Parmesan, pecorino 9 provolone 10 Gorgonzola, mascarpone, mozzarella
city: 3 Ven. 4 Asti, Atri, Bari, Enna, Iesi, Lodi, Pisa, Roma, Rome 5 Anzio, Cuneo, Eboli, Genoa, Lucca, Massa, Milan, Monza, Padua, Parma, Prato, Siena, Terni, Trent, Turin, Udine 6 Albino, Ancona, Assisi, Cesena, Genova, Milano, Modena, Naples, Napoli, Padova, Rimini, Torino, Trento, Venice, Verona 7 Bologna, Brescia, Catania, Cremona, Ferrara, Firenze, Leghorn, Livorno, Messina, Palermo, Perugia, Ravenna, Salerno, San Remo, Sassari, Taranto, Trieste, Venezia 8 Cagliari, Florence, Siracusa
commune: 4 Asti, Este, Oria, Todi 5 Paola, Riesi
conductor: 4 Muti 6 Abbado 9 Mantovani, Toscanini
dance: 5 ballo, gigue 10 bergamasca, saltarello, tarantella, villanella
explorer: 4 Polo 5 Cabot 6 Nobile 7 Belzoni 8 Columbus, Vespucci
film director: 5 Leone 6 De Sica 7 Fellini 8 Pasolini
food: 5 pasta 9 antipasto
fountain: 5 Trevi
fruit: 8 bergamot
gulf: 5 Genoa 6 Venice 7 Taranto, Trieste
ice cream: 6 gelati, gelato 7 spumone, spumoni, tortoni
island off ~: 3 Sar. 4 Elba, Lido 5 Malta 6 Sicily 7 Corsica 8 Sardinia

lake: 4 Como, Orta 5 Garda 6 Albano, Averno, Lugano 8 Maggiore 9 Trasimeno
language: 5 Oscan 6 Tuscan 7 Umbrian
last queen: 5 Elena
legislature: 6 Senate
magistrate: 4 doge
money: 4 euro, lira, lire, tari 5 scudi, scudo, soldi, soldo 6 florin 9 centesimo
mountain: 6 Cadore 7 Bernina 9 Apennines, Dolomites, Mont Blanc 10 Carnic Alps, Monte Corno
neighbor: 6 France 7 Austria 8 Slovenia 9 San Marino
news agency: 4 ANSA
newspaper: 6 Avanti
Nobelist in Chemistry: 5 Natta
Nobelist in Economics: 10 Modigliani
Nobelist in Literature: 2 Fo 7 Deledda, Montale 8 Carducci 9 Quasimodo 10 Pirandello
Nobelist in Medicine: 5 Bovet, Golgi 8 Dulbecco 14 Levi-Montalcini
Nobelist in Peace: 6 Moneta
Nobelist in Physics: 5 Fermi 6 Rubbia 7 Marconi
noble house: 4 Este
org.: 4 NATO
pet form of John: 4 Gino
physicist: 5 Fermi, Volta 7 Marconi 8 Avogadro 10 Torricelli
playwright: 5 Betti, Gozzi 6 Oriani 7 Giacosa, Goldoni, Rovetta 10 Pirandello
poet: 5 Belli, Berni, Tasso 6 Marino, Oriani, Parini, Pavese 7 Ariosto, Boiardo, Colonna, Folengo, Foscolo, Montale, Morante, Pascoli, Pontano 8 Carducci, Pasolini, Petrarch 9 Boccaccio, D'Annunzio, Quasimodo, Sacchetti 10 Cavalcanti
port: 4 Bari 5 Genoa, Ostia 6 Ancona, Naples, Venice 7 Leghorn, Livorno, Marsala, Messina, Palermo, Salerno, Trieste
pottery: 6 Faenza
region: 5 Aosta, Udine 6 Apulia
river: 2 Po 4 Arno, Nera, Sele 5 Adige, Oglio
royal house: 5 Savoy
saint: 5 Paolo, Pius X 7 Ambrose, Anthony, Francis, Gregory 8 Benedict 9 Catherine 10 Philip Neri
sauce: 5 pesto 6 tomato 8 marinara
scientist: 5 Fermi, Volta 6 Piazzi 7 Galilei, Galvani, Marconi 8 Avogadro 10 Torricelli
scooter: 5 Vespa
sculptor: 12 Michelangelo
sea: 6 Ionian 8 Adriatic, Ligurian 10 Tyrrhenian
shape: 4 boot
skier: 5 Tomba
soprano: 5 Freni, Patti 7 Tebaldi 8 Albanese 10 Galli-Curci, Tetrazzini
soup ingredient: 4 orzo
temple: 5 duomo
tenor: 6 Caruso 7 Corelli 9 Pavarotti
TV network: 3 RAI
violinmaker: 5 Amati 10 Stradivari
volcano: 4 Etna 5 Aetna 8 Vesuvius 9 Stromboli
waterfall: 4 Toce
wine: 5 corvo, Soave 6 Arneis, Barolo 7 Amarone, Barbera, Chianti, Marsala, Orvieto 8 Dolcetto, Frascati, spumante 9 Bardolino, lambrusco
wine measure: 4 orna
writer: 3 Eco 5 Dante, Svevo 6 Basile, Silone 7 Alberti, Alfieri, Aretino, Bassani, Calvino, Capuana, Cassola, Collodi, Deledda, Foscolo, Manzoni, Morante, Moravia, Rovetta 8 Ginzburg 18 Pico della Mirandola

__ It a Pity?: 4 Isn't
Itar-__: 4 Tass
__ it art?: 5 But is
Itasca: 4 lake
locale: 9 Minnesota
__ it a shot: 4 give
__ It as It Lays: 4 Play
__ it a try: 4 give
I taut I __ a puddy tat!: 3 taw
__ it away: 4 pack, take
__ It Bad: 4 I Got
__ it be?: 6 What'll
__ It Be: 3 Let
__ It Be Magic: 5 Could
__ It Be Me: 3 Let
__ it big: 3 hit 4 make
__ it by ear: 4 play
__ It Can Be Told: 3 Now
It can't be!: 4 oh no
It Can't Happen Here
author: Sinclair Lewis
itch: 3 yen 4 long, lust, need, urge, wish 5 yearn 6 desire, hanker, hunger, tickle, tingle 7 craving, impulse, longing, passion 8 appetite, pruritus, tingling, yearning 9 hankering, prickling 10 incitement, irritation
cause: 5 mange, tinea
combining form: 4 psor- 5 psoro-
for: 4 want 5 covet, crave
(for): 4 long, pant
scratch an ~: 5 react
It Changed My Life
author: Betty Friedan
itchy: 4 avid, edgy, keen 5 antsy, eager, jumpy, tense 6 fervid, greedy, hungry, tingle, uneasy 7 anxious, burning, craving, fidgety, jittery, keyed up, longing, nervous, restive, uptight, wishful, zealous 8 agitated, covetous, crawling, desirous, grasping, restless, scratchy, skittish, stinging, ticklish, tingling, troubled, yearning 9 concerned, excitable, ill at ease, impatient 10 high-strung, raring to go
__ it close to the vest: 4 play
It Could Happen to You (1994 film)
cast: Nicolas Cage, Bridget Fonda, Rosie Perez
It does __ good: 5 a body
It don't __ thing...: 5 mean a
It Don't Come Easy (1971 song)
artist: Ringo Starr
It Don't Matter to Me (1970 song)
artist: Bread
-ite: 4 rock 6 native
cousin: 3 -ese, -ist 4 -ster
item: 3 net 4 part, unit 5 entry, piece, thing 6 aspect, couple, detail, entity, object, regard 7 article, element, feature, subject 8 instance, specific 9 component 10 ingredient, particular
itemize: 4 cite, list 5 count, tally 6 detail, lay out, number, recite, record, relate, report, set out 7 catalog, mention, recount, specify 8 document, set forth, spell out 9 catalogue, enumerate, inventory, keep count
itemized: 4 full 8 detailed, thorough
items: 5 goods, stuff 7 rations 8 supplies 10 provisions
__-item veto: 4 line
iterate: 3 rpt. 4 echo 5 refer, resay 6 go over, harp on, rehash, repeat, retell, stress 7 dwell on, recount, restate, reutter, run over 8 practice, rehearse, return to 9 dwell upon, emphasize, reiterate 10 underscore
iterated: 8 frequent, manifold, numerous 9 recurrent
iteration: 3 rep 9 frequency 10 repetition
__ It for Me: 4 Save
__ It Forward: 3 Pay
__ it from me: 5 far be
It Girl, The: 3 Bow 8 Clara Bow
__ it goes: 5 And so
Ithaca: 4 city, town
athletes: 6 Big Red
locale: 7 New York
school: 7 Cornell
It Had to Be You
composer: Gus Kahn
I Thank You (1968 song)
artist: Sam and Dave
It Happened One Night (1934 film)
cast: Claudette Colbert, Clark Gable
director: Frank Capra
...I thee __: 3 wed
I, the Jury
author: Mickey Spillane
I think __!: 3 not
I Think I Love You (1970 song)
artist: Partridge Family
I Think We're Alone Now (song)
artist: Tiffany, Tommy James and the Shondells
It Hit Me Like a Hammer (1991 song)
artist: Huey Lewis and the News
I thought so!: 3 aha
I thought you'd never __!: 3 ask
It Hurts to Be in Love (1964 song)
artist: Gene Pitney
__ it in: 3 rub 4 pack
itinerant: 5 nomad, rover 6 arrant, errant, mobile, roving 7 drifter, migrant, nomadic, rambler, roaming, vagrant 8 rambling, stranger, traveler, vagabond, wanderer 9 journeyer, migratory, traveling, unsettled, wandering, wayfaring 10 ambulatory, journeying, travelling
itinerary: 3 rte. 4 beat, path, plan 5 route 6 course 7 circuit, journey, program 8 schedule 9 guidebook 10 travel plan
amend an ~: 5 remap
dizzying ~: 5 whirl 6 flurry
planner: 3 AAA
word: 3 via
itinerate: 4 rove 6 travel, wander
__ it is: 4 like
It is __ told...: 5 a tale
It Isn't Right (1956 song)
artist: Platters
it is so: 3 yes 4 amen 5 truly 6 indeed, verily 7 right on 10 positively
It is the __, and Juliet...: 4 east
__ it like it is: 4 tell
__ It Like That: 5 I Like
It'll be __ day in July...: 5 a cold
__ it made: 4 have
...__ it Memorex?: 4 or is
It Might as Well Be Spring
composer: Oscar Hammerstein, Richard Rodgers
It Might Be You (1983 song)
artist: Stephen Bishop
It might have __: 4 been
It must be him, __...: 3 or I
It Must Be Him (1967 song)
artist: Vikki Carr
__ it my way: 4 I did
It never __ but it pours: 5 rains
__-it note: 4 Post
__ It Now: 3 See 4 Cool 5 I Want
Ito: 4 Yuko 5 Lance 6 Midori, Robert 8 Hirobumi
__ it off: 3 hit 5 knock
I told you so!: 3 hah, see
Ito, Midori: 6 skater
__ it on: 3 get, lay 4 pour 5 bring
It Only Hurts for a Little While (1956 song)
artist: Ames Brothers
__ It on Rio: 5 Blame
__ it on the chin: 4 take
__ it on the lam: 4 take
__ it on the line: 3 lay
__ it on thick: 3 lay
I, Too
author: Langston Hughes
I topper: 3 dot 6 tittle
__ it or leave it: 4 take
__ it or lose it: 3 use
__ it or not: 4 like
__ it out: 4 dish, duke, hash, have 5 check, fight, sweat, tough
__ it over: 4 lord, talk
It Pays to Be Ignorant: 9 radio show
__ it quits: 4 call
__ it rich: 6 strike
__ it rich?: 4 Isn't
__ It Romantic?: 4 Isn't
It Runs in the Family (2003 film)
cast: Kirk Douglas, Michael Douglas
its: 6 neuter 7 pronoun
...it's __ work we go: 5 off to
It's __: 4 a Sin, Late, Over 5 a Gift, Magic
It's __!: 4 a boy, a hit 5 a date, a deal, a girl, Alive
It's __ a Long, Long Time: 4 Been
It's __ a Paper Moon: 4 Only
It's __ bag!: 5 in the
It's __ country!: 5 a free
It's __ for Me to Say: 3 Not
It's __ in the Game: 3 All
It's __, it's...: 5 a bird
It's __ Kiss: 5 in His

It's __ Late: 3 Too
It's __ Long, Long Time: 5 Been a
It's __ Love: 4 Only, You I, Your
It's __ Make Believe: 4 Only
It's __ Never: 5 Now or
It's __ Paper Moon: 5 Only a
It's __ point!: 5 a moot
It's __ Rock and Roll to Me: 5 Still
It's __ than you think: 5 later
It's __ the Game: 5 All in
It's __ the pale moon...: 3 not
It's __ thing: 4 a guy
It's __ time!: 5 about
It's __ to Tell a Lie: 4 a Sin
It's __ True: 3 All
It's __ Unusual: 3 Not
It's __ Unusual Day: 5 a Most
It's __-win situation!: 3 a no
It's a __!: 3 boy 4 bird, deal, girl 5 plane
It's a __ Tell a Lie: 5 Sin to
It's about __!: 4 time
It's a deal!: 4 done, okay
__ it safe: 4 play
It's a Gift (1934 film)
cast: W.C. Fields, Baby LeRoy
It's a Grand Night for Singing
composer: Oscar Hammerstein, Richard Rodgers
It's a Heartache (1978 song)
artist: Bonnie Tyler
It's all __: 5 an act
It's All __: 4 True
It's All About Me (1998 song)
artist: Mya
It's All About the Benjamins (1997 song)
artist: Lil' Kim, Lox, Notorious B.I.G., Puff Daddy
It's All Coming Back to Me Now (1996 song)
artist: Celine Dion
It's all in the __: 5 wrist
It's All in the Game
composer: Charles Dawes
It's All in the Game (1958 song)
artist: Tommy Edwards
It's All Over Now (1964 song)
artist: Rolling Stones
It's All Right (1963 song)
artist: Impressions
It's all the __ to me: 4 same
It's Almost Tomorrow (1955 song)
artist: Dream Weavers, Snooky Lanson
It's a Lovely Day Today
composer: Irving Berlin
It's Alright (1982 song)
artist: Yoko Ono
It's a Mad Mad Mad Mad World (1963 film)
cast: Edie Adams, Milton Berle, Sid Caesar, Jimmy Durante, Peter Falk, Buddy Hackett, Buster Keaton, Ethel Merman, Mickey Rooney, Dick Shawn, Phil Silvers, Spencer Tracy, Jonathan Winters
It's a Man's Man's Man's World (1966 song)
artist: James Brown
It's a Miracle (1975 song)
artist: Barry Manilow
It's a Mistake (1983 song)
artist: Men at Work
It's a Sin to Tell __: 4 a Lie
__ it's at: 5 where

It's a Wonderful Life (1946 film)
cast: Lionel Barrymore, Beulah Bondi, Thomas Mitchell, Donna Reed, James Stewart
composer: Dimitri Tiomkin
director: Frank Capra
role: 4 Bert, Mary 5 Billy, Ernie 6 Bailey, George, Potter, Violet 8 Clarence
studio: 3 RKO
It's been __!: 4 ages, real 5 great
It's Been a Long, Long Time
composer: Sammy Cahn, Jule Styne
It's clear!: 3 aha 4 I see
It's cold!: 3 brr
__, It's Cold Outside: 4 Baby
It's De-Lovely
composer: Cole Porter
It's Ecstasy... (1977 song)
artist: Barry White
itself
by ~: 5 alone, apart, per se 6 as such 10 separately
in: 8 innately
It's Gonna Take a Miracle (1982 song)
artist: Deniece Williams
It's grrrreat!
growler: 4 Tony
__-it shop: 3 fix
It shouldn't happen to __!: 4 a dog
It's Howdy Doody __: 4 time
It's Impossible (1970 song)
artist: Perry Como
It's in the __!: 3 bag
It's Just a Matter of Time (1959 song)
artist: Brook Benton
It's Late (1959 song)
artist: Ricky Nelson
It's Magic
composer: Sammy Cahn, Jule Styne
__ It's Me: 5 Hello
It's My Party (1963 song)
artist: Lesley Gore
It's My Turn (1980 film)
cast: Jill Clayburgh, Michael Douglas, Charles Grodin
It's My Turn (1980 song)
artist: Diana Ross
It's no __!: 3 use
It's Not for Me to Say (1957 song)
artist: Johnny Mathis
It's Not Over (1987 song)
artist: Starship
It's Not Right But It's Okay (1999 song)
artist: Whitney Houston
It's not the __ moon...: 4 pale
It's Not Unusual (1965 song)
artist: Tom Jones
__ It Snow: 3 Let
It's Now or Never (1960 song)
artist: Elvis Presley
...it's off to work __: 4 we go
It's okay with me!: 4 fine
It's only __!: 5 a game
It's Only a Paper Moon
composer: Harold Arlen, Yip Harburg, Billy Rose
It's Only Love (1985 song)
artist: Tina Turner
It's Only Make Believe (song)
artist: Glen Campbell, Conway Twitty

It's Only Rock 'n Roll (1974 song)
artist: Rolling Stones
It's Over (1964 song)
artist: Roy Orbison
It's So Easy (1977 song)
artist: Linda Ronstadt
It's So Hard to Say Goodbye... (1991 song)
artist: Boyz II Men
__ It's Spinach: 4 I Say
It's Still Rock and Roll to Me (1980 song)
artist: Billy Joel
It's still the same __ story...: 3 old
It's the __!: 3 law
It's the end of __!: 5 an era
It's the Hard-Knock Life show: 5 Annie
It's the Same Old Song (1965 song)
artist: Four Tops
It's Time to Cry (1959 song)
artist: Paul Anka
__ its toll: 4 take
It's Too Late (1971 song)
artist: Carole King
It's Too Soon to Know (1958 song)
artist: Pat Boone
__ it straight: 4 play
It's true!: 5 no lie
It's Up to You (1962 song)
artist: Ricky Nelson
itsy-bitsy: 3 wee 4 tiny 5 eensy, teeny 6 teensy 9 miniature, minuscule 10 diminutive
Itsy Bitsy Teenie Weenie... (1960 song)
artist: Brian Hyland
__ It's You: 4 Baby
It's You I Love (1957 song)
artist: Fats Domino
It's Your Love (1997 song)
artist: Faith Hill, Tim McGraw
It's Your Thing (1969 song)
artist: Isley Brothers
ITT: 2 co. 7 company
part of ~: 3 Int., Tel. 4 Intl., Tele.
rival: 3 GTE
__ it takes: 4 what
It takes __ know...: 5 one to
It takes __ o' livin'...: 5 a heap
It takes __ tango: 5 two to
It Takes a Thief (ABC drama)
cast: Malachi Throne (Noah Bain) Robert Wagner (Alexander Mundy)
__ it, the cops!: 6 Cheese
__ it the truth!: 4 Ain't
__ It Through the Rain: 5 I Made
__ it to: 3 put 4 give, hand 5 stick
__ It to Beaver: 5 Leave
__ it together: 3 get 4 keep
__ it to me!: 4 Sock
__ It to Me!: 5 Leave
__ It to the Limit: 4 Take
__ it to the Marines!: 4 Tell
__ It to Ya: 4 Wot's
itty-bitty: 3 wee 4 baby, puny, tiny 5 bitty, small, teeny, weeny 6 atomic, bantam, little, minute, peewee, petite, teensy 8 atomical, atomlike 9 miniature, pint-sized 10 diminutive, teeny-weeny, vest-pocket
__ it up: 3 ham, mix 4 camp, hang, live, pick 5 whoop

__ It Up: 3 Rip 4 Stir, Turn 5 Light, Shake 6 Living, Strike
Iturbi, José: 7 pianist, Spanish 8 composer 9 conductor
I Turn to You (2000 song)
artist: Christina Aguilera
It Walks by Night
author: John Dickson Carr
it was __ and stormy night: 5 a dark
It was __ killed the beast: 6 beauty
It was __ mistake!: 4 all a
It Was a Very Good Year (1966 song)
artist: Frank Sinatra
it was in Latin: 4 erat
It was twenty years __ today...: 3 ago
__ It With Music: 3 Say
...__ it would seem: 4 or so
It Would Take a Strong Strong Man (1988 song)
artist: Rick Astley
__ Itzá: 5 Petén 7 Chichén
Itzhak: 5 Rabin 7 Perlman
IU: 3 amt.
I understand!: 4 ah so 5 got it
Ivan: 4 czar, tsar, tzar 5 Bunin, Dixon, Klíma, Lendl 6 Boesky, Krylov, Passer, Pavlov 7 Reitman, Sokolov, Susanin 8 Turgenev 9 Goncharov, Karamazov, Mestrovic
in English: 4 John
son the Terrible: 6 Dmitri
see also Russian

Ivana: 5 Trump
daughter: 6 Ivanka
Ivanhoe: 4 hero 5 novel
author: Walter Scott
character: 5 Brian, Isaac, Lucas 6 Cedric, Rowena 7 Rebecca
contest: 4 tilt
weapon: 5 lance
Ivan IV
composer: Georges Bizet
Ivanov
author: Anton Chekhov
Ivanovic: 3 Ana
Ivanovna: 4 Anna
Ivan the __: 5 Great 8 Terrible
I've __!: 5 had it
I've __ Accustomed to Her Face: 5 Grown
I've __ a Crush on You: 3 Got
I've __ a Gal in Kalamazoo: 3 Got
I've __ a Secret: 3 Got
I've __ Be Me: 5 Gotta
I've __ Crow: 5 Gotta
I've __ Crush on You: 4 Got a
I've __ Date With an Angel: 4 Got a
I've __ Every Little Star: 4 Told
I've __ Feeling I'm Falling: 4 Got a
I've __ Gal in Kalamazoo: 4 Got a
I've __ had!: 4 been
I've __ it!: 3 had
I've __ robbed!: 4 been
I've __ Secret: 4 Got a
I've __ the World on a String: 3 Got
I've __ to London...: 4 been
I've __ Working on the Railroad: 4 Been
I've __ You Under My Skin: 3 Got
I've a feeling we're not in __ anymore: 6 Kansas
I've been __!: 3 had

I've Been Lonely Too Long (1967 song)
artist: Rascals
I've Come to ___ it Wealthily...: 4 Wive
I've Done Everything for You (1981 song)
artist: Rick Springfield
I've found it!: 6 eureka
I've Got ___ in Kalamazoo: 4 a Gal
I've Got a Crush on You
composer: George Gershwin, Ira Gershwin
I've Got a Gal in Kalamazoo
composer: Mack Gordon, Harry Warren
I've Got a Secret: 8 game show
host: Garry Moore, Steve Allen, Bill Cullen
I've Got a Tiger by the Tail (1965 song)
artist: Buck Owens
I've got it!: 3 Aha
I've Got Love on My Mind (1977 song)
artist: Natalie Cole
I've Gotta ___: 4 Be Me, Crow
I've Gotta Be Me (1969 song)
artist: Sammy Davis Jr.
I've Got the Music ___: 4 in Me
I've Got the World on a String
composer: Harold Arlen
I've Got to Get a Message to You (1968 song)
artist: Bee Gees
I've Got You ___: 4 Babe
I've Got You Under My Skin
artist: Four Seasons
composer: Cole Porter
I've Grown Accustomed to Her Face
composer: Alan Jay Lerner, Frederick Loewe
I've had ___ to here!: 4 it up
I've Heard That Song Before
composer: Sammy Cahn, Jule Styne
I've Never Been to Me (1982 song)
artist: Charlene
Iverson, Allen
milieu: 5 court
org.: 3 NBA
sport: 10 basketball
Ives: 4 Burl 5 James 7 Charles
___! I've Said It Again: 5 There
Ives, Burl: 5 actor 6 singer
film: The Big Country (1958, AA) Cat on a Hot Tin Roof (1958) East of Eden (1955)
song: Funny Way of Laughin' (1962) A Little Bitty Tear (1962)
I Vespri Siciliani
heroine: 5 Elena
I've Told Every Little Star
composer: Oscar Hammerstein, Jerome Kern
Ivey: 4 Dana 6 Judith
Ivins: 5 Molly
I Vitelloni (1953 film)
director: Federico Fellini
Ivo: 5 Robic 6 Andric
ivories: 4 keys 5 piano
tickle the ~: 4 play
ivory: 3 key 4 tusk 5 color, white 6 yellow 7 neutral 9 yellowish
relative: *see* white color
source: 4 tusk 6 walrus 8 elephant
tower: 4 lair 5 haven 6 asylum, escape, refuge 7 hideout, retreat 8 hideaway 9 sanctuary
ivory ___: 5 tower
Ivory: 4 soap 5 James 9 detergent
alternative: *see* soap
Ivory Coast: 6 nation 7 country
capital: 7 Abidjan
city: 4 Divo 5 Daloa 6 Anyama, Bouake 7 Abidjan, Korhogo
gulf: 6 Guinea
language: 4 Akan
money: 5 franc
neighbor: 4 Mali 5 Ghana 6 Guinea 7 Liberia
people: 4 Akan 6 Senufo 7 Malinka, Malinke 8 Mandingo, Mandinka
Ivory Snow: 9 detergent
alternative: *see* detergent
ivory-towered: 5 aloof 6 remote 7 distant, removed 8 academic, detached, quixotic, retiring, secluded 10 quixotical
___ Ivory Wayans: 6 Keenen
IV overseer: 2 RN 3 LPN
measure: 2 cc.
Ivry-___-Seine: 3 sur
ivy: 4 vine 5 plant 7 creeper
clump: 3 tod
emulate ~: 5 cling, creep, stick, twine
halls of ~: 6 school 7 academy, college
like ~: 4 viny 5 twiny, vined 6 twined
place: 4 wall
poison ~ genus: 4 rhus
poison ~ relative: 5 sumac 6 sumach
___ ivy: 6 Boston, poison
Ivy ___: 5 Three 6 League 7 Leaguer
Ivy League
city: 5 Phila. 6 Ithaca 7 Hanover, New York 8 New Haven 9 Cambridge, Princeton 10 Providence
school: 4 Penn., Yale 5 Brown 7 Cornell, Harvard 8 Columbia 9 Dartmouth, Princeton
team: 4 Elis 5 Bears, Lions 6 Big Red, Tigers 7 Crimson, Quakers 8 Big Green, Bulldogs
Ivy Leaguer: 3 Eli 5 Tiger, Yalie
Ivy Tree, The
author: Mary Stewart
I.W.: 4 Abel
I Walk the Line (1956 song)
artist: Johnny Cash
I Wandered Lonely as a Cloud: 4 poem
author: William Wordsworth
I Wanna Be Around (1963 song)
artist: Tony Bennett
I Wanna Be Down (1994 song)
artist: Brandy
I Wanna Dance With Somebody (1987 song)
artist: Whitney Houston
___ I Wanna Do: 3 All
I Wanna Get Next to You (1977 song)
artist: Rose Royce
I Wanna Go Back (1987 song)
artist: Eddie Money
I Wanna Love You Forever (1999 song)
artist: Jessica Simpson
I want ___ just like...: 5 a girl
I Want ___: 3 You 4 a Man
___ I want for Christmas...: 3 All
I want it ___!: 3 all
I Want It Now
author: Kingsley Amis
I Want It That Way (1999 song)
artist: Backstreet Boys
I want my ___!: 3 MTV 5 Maypo
I Want to Be Happy: 4 song
composer: Irving Caesar, Vincent Youmans
I Want to Be Wanted (1960 song)
artist: Brenda Lee
I Want to Hold Your Hand (1964 song)
artist: Beatles
I Want to Know What Love Is (1984 song)
artist: Foreigner
I Want to Walk You Home (1959 song)
artist: Fats Domino
I Want You Back (song)
artist: Jackson 5, 'Nsync
I Want You guy: 3 Sam 8 Uncle Sam
I Want You, I Need You, I Love You (1956 song)
artist: Elvis Presley
I Want Your Love (1979 song)
artist: Chic
I Want You to Want Me (1979 song)
artist: Cheap Trick
...I was born to ___ right!: 5 set it
I Was Doing All Right
composer: George Gershwin, Ira Gershwin
I Was Made for Dancin' (1978 song)
artist: Leif Garrett
I Was Made to Love Her (1967 song) artist: Stevie Wonder
___ I Was One-and-Twenty: 4 When
I Was the One (1956 song)
artist: Elvis Presley
___ I Were in Love Again: 5 I Wish
I Whistle a Happy Tune
composer: Oscar Hammerstein, Richard Rodgers
I will ___ and go now: 5 arise
I Will (1965 song)
artist: Dean Martin
I Will Always Love You (1992 song)
artist: Whitney Houston
I Will Come to You (1997 song)
artist: Hanson
I Will Follow Him (1963 song)
artist: Little Peggy March
I Will Remember You (1999 song)
artist: Sarah McLachlan
I Will Survive (1979 song)
artist: Gloria Gaynor
___ I win,...: 5 heads
I Wish (1976 song)
artist: Stevie Wonder
I Wish It Would Rain (1968 song)
artist: Temptations
I Wish It Would Rain Down (1990 song)
artist: Phil Collins
I Wish I Were in Love Again
composer: Lorenz Hart, Richard Rodgers
Iwo Jima: 4 isle 6 battle, island
terrain: 4 sand
I Woke Up in Love This Morning (1971 song)
artist: Partridge Family
I Wonder As I Wander
author: Langston Hughes
I Won't ___ Day Without You: 5 Last a
I Won't Back Down (1989 song)
artist: Tom Petty and the Heartbreakers
I Won't Dance
composer: Oscar Hammerstein, Otto Harbach, Jerome Kern
___ I Won the War: 3 How
I Won't Hold You Back (1983 song)
artist: Toto
I Would Die 4 U (1984 song)
artist: Prince
I wouldn't have ___ other way!: 5 it any
I Write the Songs (1975 song)
artist: Barry Manilow
ixnay: 2 no 3 nah, naw, nay, nix, non 4 nein, nope, nyet, uh-uh 5 I won't, never, no how, noway 6 no deal, no dice, noways, nowise 7 I refuse 8 forget it, I will not, negative, negatory 9 by no means, fat chance, I think not 10 count me out, not a chance, thumbs down
Ixtapa: 4 city, town 6 resort
locale: 6 Mexico 7 Jalisco
Iyar: 5 month 6 Hebrew
preceder: 5 Nisan 6 Nissan
successor: 5 Sivan
Iynx
mother: 4 Echo
Izmir: 4 city, gulf, port, town
locale: 6 Turkey
Izod product: 5 shirt
izzard: 3 zed
Izzy & ___: 3 Moe

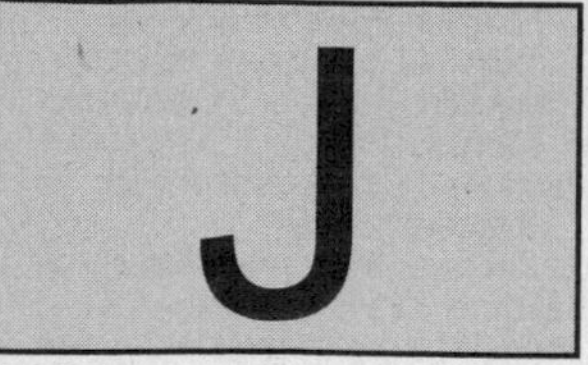

J: **6** letter
and others: **3** Drs.
in phonetic alphabet: **6** Juliet
position of ~: **5** tenth
topper: **3** dot **6** tittle
J __ John: **4** as in
J. __ Band: **5** Geils
J. __ Getty: **4** Paul
J. __ Hoover: **5** Edgar
J. __ Naish: **6** Carrol
J. __ Oppenheimer: **6** Robert
'J' __ Judgment: **5** Is for
ja
opposite: **4** nein
jab: **3** hit, rap, tap **4** blow, gibe, goad, jibe, knee, left, peck, poke, prod, slam, stab **5** elbow, lunge, nudge, prick, punch, right, shove, stick, taunt **6** jostle, justle, strike, thrust, thwack **8** puncture, uppercut **9** penetrate
target: **3** jaw, yap **4** chin, jowl **5** chops, mouth
Jabba the Hutt
like ~: **5** heavy, obese **9** corpulent **10** overweight, well-padded
jabber: **3** gab, gas, jaw, rap, yak, yap **4** blab, blah, chat, gush, rave, talk **5** noise, prate, run on **6** babble, drivel, mutter, patter, ramble, rattle, tattle **7** blather, chatter, maunder, prating, prattle, ranting, stammer, twaddle **8** chitchat, idle talk, nonsense **9** gibberish, go on and on, loquacity **10** maundering
see also baloney
jabbering: **5** noisy, prate, wordy **6** babble **7** unterse **8** babbling **9** garrulity **10** loquacious
Jabberwocky
start of ~: **4** 'Twas
word: **4** mome, 'twas, wabe **5** raths, toves **6** slithy
see also baloney
Jabir: **4** Arab **7** scholar **9** alchemist
jabiru: **4** bird **5** stork
jaborandi: **5** shrub
jabs
trade: **3** box **4** spar
jacal: **3** hut
jacamar: **4** bird
jacaranda: **4** tree
family: **7** catalpa
locale: **7** tropics
J'Accuse
author: Émile Zola
__ jacet: **3** hic
Jacinda: **7** Barrett
jacinth: **6** ligure
Jacinto: **9** Benavente
__ Jacinto: **3** San
jack: **3** oof **4** card, cash, fish, flag, gelt, hike, kail, kale, loot, male, peag, pelf, tool **5** bills, bread, bucks, dough, funds, knave, lucre, money, moola, mopus, pesos, raise, rhino, sewan **6** dinero, do-re-mi, lifter, mammon, mazuma, moolah, seawan, silver, specie, wampum, wealth **7** cabbage, capital, dollars, lettuce, ooftish, pennant, scratch, shekels **8** bankroll, cold cash, currency, face card, hard cash, smackers **9** banknotes, frogskins, long green, simoleons **10** greenbacks, green stuff
ender: **3** ass, daw, leg, pot **4** boot, stay **5** fruit, knife, light, plane, screw, shaft, snipe, stone, straw **6** hammer, rabbit **8** mackerel
in cards: **5** knave
in cribbage: **3** nob **4** nibs
locale: **5** trunk
preceder: **3** ten
starter: **3** sea, sky **4** boot, flap, high, skip, slap **5** amber, apple, black, cheap **6** lumber **7** cracker, steeple
up: **4** hike, lift **5** boost, raise **7** augment, elevate, enlarge, magnify **8** escalate, increase **10** accelerate, aggrandize
jack __: **6** cheese, rabbit
jack-__-box: **5** in-the
jack-__-pulpit: **5** in-the
jack-__-trades: **5** of-all
__ jack: **7** jumping
__-jack: **5** cheap
Jack: **3** Soo **4** Elam, Ging, Kemp, Lord, Paar, Webb **5** Benny, Black, Burke, Haley, Jones, Kelly, Kilby, Oakie, Scott, Sprat **6** Arnold, Bailey, Carson, Carter, Conway, Finney, Gelber, Horner, Kramer, Larson, Lemmon, London, Smight, Twyman, Wagner, Warden, Warner, Weston **7** Cardiff, Cassidy, Clayton, Couffer, Dempsey, Gilford, Hawkins, Higgins, Johnson, Kerouac, Klugman, LaLanne, Lambert, Palance, Siegler, Valenti **8** Anderson, Buchanan, Nicklaus, Thompson **9** Albertson, Nicholson, Teagarden **10** Williamson, Youngblood
adversary: **5** giant
Jackie, to ~: **4** wife
Jack (1996 film)
cast: Diane Lane, Jennifer Lopez, Robin Williams
director: Francis Ford Coppola
Jack __: **3** Tar **4** Rose **5** Frost
Jack __ could eat...: **5** Sprat
Jack __ terrier: **7** Russell
__ Jack: **5** Union **6** Hungry, Smilin' **7** Cracker, Wolfman
jack-a-dandy
see wonderful
jackal: **4** dupe, hack, tool **5** canid, drone, leech, slave, toady **6** animal, canine, drudge, fawner, flunky, lackey, minion, puppet, stooge, yes man **7** cat's-paw, doormat, flunkey, lacquey, wild dog **8** creature, hanger-on, henchman, parasite **10** accomplice
relative: ***see*** canine
Jackal, The: **5** alias **8** assassin
Jackal, The (1997 film)
cast: Richard Gere, Sidney Poitier, Bruce Willis
jackanapes: **3** imp, pup **4** brat, punk **5** devil, gamin, scamp **6** monkey, rascal, smarty **7** upstart, wannabe, wise guy **8** hooligan, wiseacre
Jack and Jill: **12** nursery rhyme
prop: **4** pail
Jack and the Beanstalk
syllable: **3** fie, fum
Jack Armstrong, the All-American Boy: **9** radio show
jackass: **5** burro, neddy, ninny **6** donkey, equine
mate: **5** jenny
relative: ***see*** equine
see also ninny
Jack-be-nimble
like ~: **3** fit **4** spry **5** agile **6** active, limber, lively **9** sprightly
__ Jack City: **3** New
jackdaw: **4** bird
Jackée: **5** Harry
jackeroo: **6** Aussie
jacker starter: **3** car, sea, sky **4** high
jacket: **3** mac, Mao, pod, tux **4** case, coat, Eton, skin, tuck, wrap **5** capot, frock, grego, jemmy, jibba, liner, loden, Nehru, parka, simar, tails, tunic, wamus **6** achkan, anorak, banian, banyan, blazer, bolero, bomber, capote, casing, coatee, duffle, duster, folder, jerkin, raglan, record, reefer, sheath, tabard, tuxedo, ulster, wammus, wampus **7** cagoule, car coat, cassock, cutaway, doublet, kuletuk, oilskin, paletot, peacoat, slicker, spencer, surcoat, surtout, topcoat, zamarra **8** benjamin, bush coat, chaqueta, covering, envelope, mackinaw, overcoat, polo coat, raincoat, sack coat **9** balmacaan, book cover, greatcoat, Inverness, macintosh, petersham, redingote, sou'wester, sport coat, storm coat **10** fearnought, macfarlane, mackintosh, potato skin, protection, trench coat
arctic ~: **5** parka **6** anorak
book ~ promo: **5** blurb **6** review
British ~: **5** jemmy, tunic **9** greatcoat
Canadian ~: **7** kuletuk
church ~: **7** cassock
close a ~: **3** zip **5** zip up
cowboy ~: **8** chaqueta
feature: **3** arm **4** snap **5** lapel **6** lining, peplum, zipper
formal ~: **3** tux **4** tuck **5** tails **6** tuxedo **7** cutaway
heavy ~: **5** wamus **6** anorak, ulster, wammus, wampus
hooded ~: **5** grego, parka **6** duffle
Indian ~: **6** achkan, banian, banyan
material: **5** suede, tweed **7** leather
medieval ~: **6** corset
Muslim ~: **5** jibba
opening: **4** slit, vent
pants and ~: **4** suit **6** outfit **8** ensemble
short ~: **5** grego **6** coatee, jerkin, reefer **8** sack coat
Spain ~: **7** zamarra
starter: **4** blue **6** strait **7** leather **8** straight
waterproof ~: **5** loden
woman's ~ of old: **5** simar
woolen ~: **8** mackinaw
yellow ~: **4** pest, wasp **6** insect
see also coat
__ jacket: **3** air, bed, Ike, Mao, pea **4** book, bush, dust, Eton, flak, life, mess **5** field, Nehru, shirt **6** battle, bomber, combat, dinner, safari, sports, yellow **7** smoking
__ Jack Flash: **6** Jumpin'
Jack Frost: **4** rime **6** winter
work: **6** icicle
jackfruit: **5** fruit
jackhammer: **3** bit **4** bore, tool **5** auger, drill
Jackie: **4** Chan **5** Mason **6** Coogan, Cooper, Mrs. JFK, Wilson **7** Collins, Gleason, Jackson, Kennedy, Onassis, Stewart **8** Robinson **9** DeShannon
sister: **3** Lee
to Ari: **4** wife
to Jack: **4** wife
to Roseanne: **3** sis
Jackie __-Kersee: **6** Joyner
Jackie Brown (1997 film)
cast: Pam Grier, Samuel L. Jackson, Michael Keaton
director: Quentin Tarantino
Jackie Robinson Story, The (1950 film)
cast: Ruby Dee, Jackie Robinson
jacking
starter: **3** car, sea, sky **4** high **5** black
jack-in-the-box: **3** toy
part: **3** lid
Jack in the Box
rival: ***see*** restaurant chain
jack-in-the-pulpit: **4** arum **5** aroid, plant **6** flower
cousin: **5** calla
jackknife: **6** fold up
jackknife __: **4** clam, dive
jackleg: **13** strikebreaker
Jackman: **4** Hugh
Jacknife (1989 film)
cast: Kathy Baker, Robert De Niro, Ed Harris
jack-of-all-trades: **5** do-all **6** jobber **8** factotum, handyman **10** generalist
jack-o'-lantern: **7** pumpkin
feature: **4** eyes, grin, nose **5** smile
make a ~: **5** carve
jack pine: **9** evergreen
jackpot: **3** pot **4** bank, pool **5** award, kitty, prize, total, whole **6** reward, stakes **8** windfall **10** mother lode
game with a ~: **5** lotto **7** lottery
hit the ~: **3** win **5** score **7** prosper, succeed
jackrabbit: **3** run, zip **4** hare, zoom **5** hurry **6** hasten
Jack Robinson
before one can say ~: **4** fast, soon **6** in a sec **7** quickly, rapidly
Jack Rose: **5** drink **8** beverage, cocktail
ingredient: **9** grenadine, lime juice **10** lemon juice
Jack Russell __: **7** terrier
jacks: **4** game
knucklebone in ~: **3** dib
Jacks: **5** Terry
__ Jacks: **5** Apple **7** One-Eyed
jacksnipe: **4** bird
Jackson: **2** Bo **3** Joe, Stu **4** Alan, Anne, city, Fort, Kate, Milt, Phil, Tito, town **5** Janet, Jesse, Laura,

Peter **6** Andrew, Browne, Glenda, Jackie, Joshua, La Toya, Marlon, Millie, Rachel, Rebbie, Reggie, Sherry **7** Mahalia, Maynard, Michael, Pollock, Shirley, Wilfred **8** Jermaine, Victoria **9** Stonewall
county: 5 Hinds
locale: 4 Mich., Miss., Tenn. **8** Michigan **9** Tennessee
resort near Mt. ~: 4 Vail
river: 5 Pearl
Jackson __: 3 Day **4** Hole
__ Jackson: 4 Fort **6** Action
Jackson 5
members: Jackie, Jermaine, Marlon, Michael, Randy, Tito
song: ABC (1970)
Dancing Machine (1974)
Enjoy Yourself (1976)
I'll Be There (1970)
I Want You Back (1969)
The Love You Save (1970)
Mama's Pearl (1971)
Never Can Say Goodbye (1971)
Shake Your Body (1979)
State of Shock (1984)
Sugar Daddy (1971)
Jackson, Andrew: president
former occupation: 6 lawyer **7** soldier
home: 9 Hermitage, Nashville, Tennessee
opponent: 4 Clay **5** Adams
predecessor: 5 Adams
successor: 8 Van Buren
V.P.: 7 Calhoun **8** Van Buren
wife: 6 Rachel
Jackson, Anne: 7 actress
spouse: Eli Wallach
Jackson, Glenda: 7 actress
film: Hopscotch (1980)
House Calls (1978)
Marat/Sade (1966)
Mary, Queen of Scots (1971)
Stevie (1978)
Sunday, Bloody Sunday (1971)
A Touch of Class (1973, AA)
Women in Love (1969, AA)
Jackson, Helen Hunt: 6 writer
work: Ramona
Jackson Hole: 4 city, town
county: 5 Teton
locale: 7 Wyoming
river: 5 Snake
Jackson, Janet
brother: 4 Tito **6** Jackie, Marlon **7** Michael **8** Germaine
sister: 6 La Toya
song: Again (1993)
All for You (2001)
Alright (1990)
Any Time, Any Place (1994)
Because of Love (1994)
The Best Things in Life... (1992)
Black Cat (1990)
Come Back to Me (1990)
Control (1986)
Doesn't Really Matter (2000)
Escapade (1990)
If (1993)
I Get Lonely (1998)
Let's Wait Awhile (1987)
Love Will Never Do (1990)
Miss You Much (1989)
Nasty (1986)
Rhythm Nation (1989)
Runaway (1995)
Scream (1995)
Someone to Call My Lover (2001)
State of the World (1991)
That's the Way Love Goes (1993)
Together Again (1997)
What's It Gonna Be (1999)
When I Think of You (1986)
You Want This (1994)
Jackson, Jesse: 3 rev. **8** reverend
onetime hairdo: 4 Afro
Jackson, Kate: 7 actress
role: Sabrina Duncan
spouse: Andrew Stevens
Jackson, Laura: 4 poet
Jackson, Michael
album: 3 Bad **8** Thriller
brother: 4 Tito **6** Jackie, Marlon **8** Germaine
hometown: 4 Gary
onetime do: 4 Afro
sister: 5 Janet **6** La Toya
song: Bad (1987)
Beat It (1983)
Ben (1972)
Billie Jean (1983)
Black or White (1991)
Dirty Diana (1988)
Don't Stop 'Til You Get Enough (1979)
The Girl Is Mine (1982)
Got to Be There (1971)
Human Nature (1983)
I Just Can't Stop Loving You (1987)
In the Closet (1992)
Man in the Mirror (1988)
Off the Wall (1980)
P.Y.T. (1983)
Remember the Time (1992)
Rockin' Robin (1972)
Rock With You (1979)
Say Say Say (1983)
Scream (1995)
She's Out of My Life (1980)
Smooth Criminal (1988)
Thriller (1984)
Wanna Be Startin' Somethin' (1983)
The Way You Make Me Feel (1987)
Will You Be There (1993)
You Are Not Alone (1995)
spouse: Lisa Marie Presley
trademark: glove
Jackson, Reggie: 10 outfielder
Jackson, Samuel L.: 5 actor
film: Black Snake Moan (2007)
Changing Lanes (2002)
Coach Carter (2005)
Deep Blue Sea (1999)
Die Hard With a Vengeance (1995)
Freedomland (2006)
Jackie Brown (1997)
Lakeview Terrace (2008)
The Negotiator (1998)
Pulp Fiction (1994)
Rules of Engagement (2000)
Shaft (2000)
Snakes on a Plane (2006)
Sphere (1998)
S.W.A.T. (2003)
A Time to Kill (1996)
White Sands (1992)
XXX (2002)
Jackson, Shirley: 6 writer
work: The Lottery
Jackson, Stonewall: 7 general
biographer: 4 Tate
Jacksonville: 4 city, port, town
county: 5 Duval
locale: 7 Florida **8** Arkansas
pro team: 7 Jaguars
river: 7 St. Johns
Jacks, Terry
song: Seasons in the Sun (1974)
jackstraws: 4 game
jack-tar: 3 gob **4** bo's'n, hand, salt, swab **5** bosun, middy **6** pirate, sailor, sea dog, seaman **7** boatman, crewman, mariner, matelot, old salt, recruit, skipper, swabbie **8** coxswain, deck hand, salty dog, seafarer, water dog **9** boatswain **10** bluejacket, midshipman
Jack Tar
composer: John Philip Sousa
Jack the __ Killer: 5 Giant
Jack the Bear (1993 film)
cast: Danny DeVito, Gary Sinise
Jaclyn: 5 Smith
colleague: 4 Kate **6** Farrah
Jacob: 3 cat, Max **4** Riis **5** Grimm, Irène, Smith **7** Epstein **8** François **9** Bronowski
daughter: 5 Dinah
father-in-law: 5 Laban
grandson: 3 Eri
in Italian: 8 Giacobbe
in Russian: 5 Yakov
parent: 5 Isaac **7** Rebekah
son: 3 Dan, Gad **4** Levi **5** Asher, Judah **6** Joseph, Reuben, Simeon **7** Zebulun **8** Benjamin, Issachar, Naphtali
son in the Douay Bible: 4 Aser
twin: 4 Esau
wife: 4 Leah **6** Rachel
__ Jacob Astor: 4 John
Jacobi: 3 Lou **5** Derek
Jacob, Max: 4 poet **6** French
Jacob's __: 4 Room **5** staff **6** ladder
Jacobsen, Jens: 6 Danish, writer
Jacobs Field player: 6 Indian
Jacobson: 4 Arne
Jacobson, Dan: 6 writer **12** South African
Jacob's Room
author: Virginia Woolf
Jacobsson: 4 Ulla
jacobus: 5 money
Jacobus __ Hoff: 4 van't
jaconet: 5 cloth **6** fabric **7** textile **8** material
Jacopo: 10 Tintoretto
jacquard: 5 cloth **6** fabric **7** textile **8** material
Jacquard __: 4 card, loom **5** weave
Jacqueline: 5 du Pré **6** Bisset, Susann **7** Cochran, Kennedy, Onassis
Jacqueline Kennedy, __ Bouvier: 3 née
jacquerie: 6 revolt
participant: 7 peasant
Jacques: 4 Brel, Tati **5** Ibert, Monod **6** Barzun, Chirac, Grévin, Plante **7** Cartier, Prévert **8** Bergerac, Clouseau, d'Amboise, Lipchitz, Maritain, Tourneur **9** Offenbach
see also French
Jacques-__ Cousteau: 4 Yves
__ Jacques: 5 Frère
__ Jacques Rousseau: 4 Jean
Jacques-Yves: 8 Cousteau
Jacquet: 3 Luc **8** Illinois
Jacta est __: 4 alea
Jacuzzi: 3 spa **6** hot tub
enjoy the ~: 4 soak
Jada __ Smith: 7 Pinkett
jade: 3 gem **4** bore, cloy, fill, flag, hack, pall, tire, wear **5** color, green, horse, weary **6** bluish, equine, weaken **7** blueish, exhaust, fatigue, mineral, overtax, poop out, satiate, satisfy, surfeit, tire out, vitiate, wear out **8** enervate, gemstone, nephrite, overwork, wear down **9** tucker out, yellowish **10** debilitate, devitalize
relative: *see* green color
work with ~: 5 carve **6** incise, sculpt **7** engrave
jade __: 5 green, plant
Jade: 6 Jagger
jaded: 4 sick, worn **5** blasé, bored, fed up, tired, weary **7** worn-out **10** world-weary
jadeite: 3 gem **8** gemstone
Jaden: 5 Smith
Jaeckel: 7 Richard
jaeger: 4 bird **6** hunter **7** seabird
relative: 4 skua **6** bonxie
Jafar: 5 genie
Jaffa: 4 city, town
locale: 6 Israel
Jaffa __: 6 orange
Jaffe: 3 Sam **4** Rona **7** Stanley
Jaffe, Sam: 5 actor
TV: Ben Casey
jag: 3 cut, hit, rip **4** nick, orgy, snag **5** binge, prick, spell, spree **6** bender **8** carousal, lacerate, splinter
go on a ~: 5 binge, spree **7** splurge
Jag
see Jaguar
jagged: 5 harsh, rocky, rough, sharp **6** broken, craggy, hackly, ragged, ridged, rugged, spiked, uneven, zigzag **7** cragged, notched, serrate, unlevel **8** serrated, unsmooth **9** irregular, lacerated **10** nonuniform
as a leaf: 5 erose
rock: 3 tor **4** crag **5** arête **8** pinnacle **10** escarpment
Jagged Edge (1985 film)
cast: Jeff Bridges, Glenn Close, Robert Loggia
Jagger: 4 Jade, Mick **6** Bianca
Jagger, Mick: 5 Stone **8** musician
spouse: Jerry Hall
Jaglom: 5 Henry
jaguar: 3 cat **4** eyra **5** felid **6** animal, feline, mammal **7** wildcat
relative: *see* feline
Jaguar: 3 car **4** auto **10** automobile
alternative: *see* automobile
model: 3 XJS, XKE, XKR
what a ~ symbolizes: 5 class **6** cachet, status **7** station **8** position, prestige, standing

Jaguars: **6** eleven
org.: **3** AFC
rival: *see* NFL team
jaguarundi: **3** cat **4** eyra **5** felid **6** animal, feline, mammal **7** wildcat
relative: *see* feline
Jahan, Shah built here: **4** Agra
jai alai: **4** game **5** sport
ball: **6** pelota
basket: **5** cesta
cloth: **5** cinta
court: **6** cancha **7** fronton
language: **6** Basque
need: **5** cesta **6** pelota
player: **8** pelotari
sash: **4** faja
shot: **5** chula
wall: **6** rebote
jail: **3** can, jug, nab, pen **4** bars, brig, cage, cell, coop, gaol, hold, poky, stir **5** clink, joint, pinch, pokey, run in, seize **6** arrest, cooler, detain, immure, lockup, prison, punish **7** bastile, confine, dungeon, hoosgow, put away, slammer **8** bastille, big house, hoosegow, imprison, restrain, sentence, stockade **9** calaboose, captivity **10** booby hatch, guardhouse
break ~: **6** escape **10** fly the coop
door sound: **5** clang
ender: **4** bird **5** break, house
in ~: **4** pent, sick **5** bound, close, local, on ice **6** laid up, pent-up, shut in **7** captive, insular, limited **8** confined
in Britain: **4** gaol, quod
-related: **5** penal
jailbird: **3** con **5** felon, lifer **6** inmate, outlaw, trusty **7** convict, parolee **8** internee, prisoner **9** miscreant
jailed: **4** held **7** captive **8** confined, locked up **9** in custody **10** imprisoned
jailer: **6** captor, gaoler, keeper, warden **7** turnkey
need: **3** key
Jailhouse Rock
artist: Elvis Presley
jailing: **4** bust **5** pinch **6** arrest, collar **7** custody **9** detention
jail-related: **8** punitive **10** corrective
Jaime: **6** Laredo **9** Escalante
see also Spanish
Jaime __ Bauer: **3** Lyn
j'aime in Latin: **3** amo
Jainism: **8** religion
Jaipur: **4** city, town
locale: **5** India
Jaja: **4** peak **5** mount **8** mountain
locale: **4** Asia **9** New Guinea
Jakarta: **4** city, port, town **7** capital
city near ~: **5** Bogor
locale: **4** Java **9** Indonesia
river: **6** Liwung
jake: **2** OK **4** fine, okay, okeh, okey **9** copacetic, first-rate, hunky-dory
Jake: **4** Garn **6** Kasdan **7** La Motta
Jake and the Fatman (CBS drama)
cast: William Conrad (Jason McCabe)
Joe Penny (Jake Styles)
dog: **3** Max
Jakes, John: **6** writer
__ Jakes, The: **3** Two
Jake's Thing
author: Kingsley Amis
Jake's Women: **4** film, play
author: Neil Simon
Jake's Women (1996 film)
cast: Alan Alda
Jakob: **4** Bohm **5** Boehm, Dylan **10** Wassermann
Jakob the Liar (1999 film)
cast: Alan Arkin, Bob Balaban, Robin Williams
Jalam
father: **4** Esau
jalap: **4** vine **9** cathartic
jalapeño: **5** spice **6** pepper **9** seasoning
hot stuff: **5** salsa **6** pepper **7** mustard **9** condiment, seasoning
Jaleel: **5** White
Jalisco: **5** state **7** Mexican
city: **4** Tala **5** Ameca, Jamay **6** Acatic, Ajijic, Autlán, Cocula, Guzmán, Ixtapa, Sayula, Tonalá, Tuxpan **7** Arandas, Ayotlán, Chapala, El Salto, La Barca, Ocotlán, Tequila, Zapopan
neighbor: **6** Colima
see also Spanish
jalopy: **3** car **4** auto, heap **5** crate, lemon, wreck **6** junker **7** clunker, junk car, vehicle **10** automobile, rattletrap
like a ~: **5** noisy, rusty **6** beat-up
Jalostotitlán: **4** city, town
locale: **6** Mexico **7** Jalisco
jalousie: **5** blind **7** shutter
Jalousie
composer: Jacob Gade
jalousie feature: **4** slat
jam: **3** box, fix, mob, ram **4** bind, clog, cram, hole, load, mess, pack, push, spot, stem **5** block, crowd, crush, delay, jelly, press, shove, snarl, sqush, stick, stuff, swarm, tie-up **6** corner, hinder, holdup, impede, pickle, plight, scrape, spread, squash, squish, squush, throng, thrust **7** congest, dilemma, force in, squeeze, squoosh, traffic **8** compress, deadlock, exigence, exigency, gridlock, obstruct, quagmire, quandary, slowdown, stoppage **9** conserves, deep water, impedance, multitude, overcrowd, overstuff, preserves, squeeze in, tight spot **10** bottleneck, confection, congestion, difficulty
holder: **3** jar
Hungarian ~: **6** lekvar
in: **4** pack **5** press, shove, wedge **7** bunch up **9** overcrowd
in a ~: **5** stuck **7** stymied, trapped, up a tree **8** besieged, cornered, strapped, troubled **10** up the creek
ingredient: **5** grape **6** pectin **7** apricot **10** strawberry
starter: **3** log
traffic ~: **4** clog **5** snarl, tie up **7** squeeze **8** blockage, clogging, crowding, gridlock, overflow **9** profusion **10** bottleneck, congestion
up: **3** dam **5** block, stick
jam __: **3** nut **7** session
jam-__: **4** pack **6** packed
__ jam: **3** ice, in a **7** traffic
__ Jam: **5** Pearl
Jamaal: **6** Wilkes
Jamaica: **4** isle **6** island, nation **7** country
athletes: **8** Red Storm
capital: **8** Kingston
city: **8** Kingston, Portmore **10** Montego Bay
export: **3** rum **5** sugar
fellow: **3** mon
fruit: **4** akee, ugli
locale: **3** BWI **10** West Indies
money: **4** cent **6** dollar
music: **3** ska
native: **5** Rasta **6** Arawak, Creole
org.: **3** OAS
school: **3** SJU **10** Saint John's
sect member: **5** rasta
tree: **8** milkwood
writer: **7** Brodber
Jamaica __: **3** Bay, Inn, rum **6** ginger
Jamal: **5** Ahmad
__-Jamal Warner: **7** Malcolm
JAMA reader: **2** dr., GP, MD
jamb: **4** beam, post, side **7** upright **8** doorpost **9** doorframe, sidepiece
ending: **4** oree
place: **6** window **8** casement
starter: **4** door
jambalaya: **5** carbo
country: **5** bayou
like ~: **6** creole
jambeau: **5** armor
jamboree: **4** bash, gala **5** party, rally, spree **6** hoopla **7** blowout, jubilee, shindig **8** festival, wingding **9** festivity, gathering **10** convention
org.: **3** BSA
participant: **5** scout, troop
shelter: **4** camp, tent
Jamboree (1999 song)
artist: Naughty by Nature, Zhané
James: **2** P.D. **3** bay, Fox, Orr **4** Agee, Best, Bond, Caan, Coco, Cook, Daly, Dean, Dunn, Etta, Exon, Fixx, Hogg, Ives, John, Joni, Mill, Olga, Ross, Watt **5** Algar, Avery, Baker, Beard, Black, Blish, Brady, Brown, Craig, Dewar, Drury, Ensor, Foley, Frank, Harry, Henry, Hoban, Horne, Ivory, Jesse, Jones, Joule, Joyce, Keach, Kevin, Mason, Meade, Noble, Purdy, Ralph, Randi, range, river, Sonny, Steve, Tobin, Tommy, Whale, Wolfe, Woods **6** Arness, Baxter, Brolin, Cagney, Coburn, Cronin, Darren, Dennis, Dickey, Doohan, Franck, Frazer, Galway, Garner, Hilton, Ingram, LeGros, Levine, McAvoy, McGraw, Monroe, Reston, Sheila, Spader, Sumner, Taylor, Tissot, Toback, Watson, Wright **7** Baldwin, Baskett, Beattie, Belushi, Boswell, Bridges, Cameron, Clavell, Clifton, Dearden, Ellison, Gleason, Hampton, Heckman, Herriot, Madison, Marsden, Merrill, Neilson, Shigeta, Shirley, Starley, Stewart, Thurber, William **8** Breasted, Buchanan, Callahan, Carville, Chadwick, Crichton, Cromwell, Garfield, Lovelock, Mirrlees, Naismith, Redfield, Schuyler, Whitmore **9** Broderick, Callaghan, Cleveland, Farentino, Finlayson, Forrestal, Goldstone, MacArthur, Patterson **10** Franciscus, Gandolfini
brother: **5** Jesus
city on the ~: **8** Richmond
follower: **5** Peter
in Irish: **6** Seamus
in Scottish: **6** Hamish
in Spanish: **4** Iago **5** Diego, Jaime
preceder: **7** Hebrews
River locale: **8** Virginia
river to the ~: **10** Appomattox
James __ Allen: **3** Van
James __ Beek: **6** Van Der
James __ Bennett: **6** Gordon
James __ Carter: **4** Earl
James __ Cooper: **8** Fenimore
James __ Cozzens: **5** Gould
James __ Flagg: **10** Montgomery
James __ Garfield: **5** Abram
James __ Heusen: **3** Van
James __ Johnson: **6** Weldon
James __ Jones: **4** Earl
James __ Lowell: **7** Russell
James __ Polk: **4** Knox
James __ Riley: **8** Whitcomb
James __ the Giant Peach: **3** and
James __ Whistler: **7** McNeill
__ James: **4** Beau
__, James!: **4** Home
James A. __: **5** Herne **8** Michener
James and the Giant Peach
author: Roald Dahl
James and the Shondells, Tommy
song: Crimson and Clover (1968)
Crystal Blue Persuasion (1969)
Hanky Panky (1966)
I Think We're Alone Now (1967)
Mirage (1967)
Mony Mony (1968)
Sweet Cherry Wine (1969)
__ James Audubon: **4** John
__ James Bible: **4** King
James Buchanan __: **4** Duke, Eads
James D. __: **6** Watson
James Earl __: **5** Jones
James Fenimore __: **6** Cooper
James Gordon __: **7** Bennett
James Gould __: **7** Cozzens
James, Harry: **10** bandleader
instrument: trumpet
spouse: Betty Grable
James, Henry: **6** writer
biographer: **4** Edel
friend: Howells
work: The Ambassadors
The American
The Aspern Papers
The Awkward Age
The Bostonians
Daisy Miller
The Europeans
The Golden Bowl
The Portrait of a Lady
The Princess Casamassima
Roderick Hudson
The Sacred Fount
The Spoils of Poynton
The Tragic Muse
The Turn of the Screw
Washington Square
What Maisie Knew
The Wings of the Dove

James II
daughter: 4 Anne
James J. __: 7 Corbett
James, Joni
song: How Important Can It Be? (1955)
You Are My Love (1955)
James K. __: 4 Polk
James L. __: 6 Brooks
James M. __: 4 Cain 6 Barrie
James McNeill __: 8 Whistler
James Montgomery __: 5 Flagg
__ James Olmos: 6 Edward
Jameson: 6 Parker
James, P.D.: 6 writer 7 British
first name: Phyllis
James Range
locale: 9 Australia
James Russell __: 6 Lowell
James T. __: 4 Kirk 7 Farrell
Jamestown: 4 city 6 colony
locale: 7 New York 8 St. Helena, Virginia
James Van __: 5 Allen 6 Heusen 7 Der Beek
__ James Version: 4 King
__ James Waller: 6 Robert
James Whitcomb __: 5 Riley
James, William: 11 philosopher
Jami: 5 Gertz
Jamie: 4 Farr, Foxx 5 Luner, Wyeth
Oscar role for ~: 3 Ray
Jamie Lee: 6 Curtis
parent: 4 Tony 5 Janet
jammed: 4 full, rife 5 close, dense, laden, thick, tight 6 heaped, loaded, packed 7 compact, crammed, crowded, replete, stuffed, teeming 8 brimming, populous, squeezed 9 chock-full, congested 10 compressed, hard-packed
jammer starter: 4 wind
jammies: 3 PJs 7 pajamas 9 nightwear, sleepwear
Jammu and __: 7 Kashmir
Jamoca: 8 ice cream
alternative: *see* ice cream flavor
jamoke: 3 joe, mud 4 java 6 coffee
jam-pack: 3 ram 4 cram, fill 5 crowd
jam-packed
see jammed
__-jams: 3 jim
jam session: 10 discussion
join a ~: 4 play 5 sit in
phrase: 4 riff
jam-up: 8 gridlock 10 bottleneck
Jan: 3 Hus 5 Berry, Brady, Hooks, Kadar, Kodes, Miner, Smuts, Steen 6 De Bont, Hammer, Morris, Murray, Neruda, Peerce 7 Clayton, Kubelik, van Eyck, Vermeer 8 Smithers, Stenerud, Sterling 9 Stevenson, Tinbergen
Jan & __: 4 Dean
Jan-__ Vincent: 7 Michael
Jan.: 2 mo.
follower: 3 Feb.
predecessor: 3 Dec.
Jan. 1
from ~ to now: 3 YTD
Jana: 7 Novotna
Janácek: 4 Leos 8 composer
Jan & Dean
members: Berry, Torrence
song: Baby Talk (1959)
Dead Man's Curve (1964)
Jennie Lee (1958)
The Little Old Lady (1964)
Surf City (1963)
Jane: 3 Ace, Doe, Roe 4 Eyre, Grey 5 Brody, Child, Fonda, Greer, March, Wyatt, Wyman 6 Addams, Austen, Bowles, Curtin, Froman, Jetson, Leeves, Marple, Morgan, Pauley, Powell 7 Campion, Clayson, Darwell, Goodall, Russell, Seymour 8 Horrocks, Morrison 9 Alexander, Krakowski
creator: Edgar Rice Burroughs
G.I. ~: 3 WAC
in Irish: 5 Shana
in Italian: 8 Giovanna
in Scottish: 5 Shona 6 Sheena
to Peter: 3 sis
__ Jane: 4 Baby, Lady 8 Calamity
__ & Jane: 7 Antonia
Janeane: 8 Garofalo
Jane Austen's Mafia! (1998 film)
cast: Christina Applegate, Lloyd Bridges
Jane Cunningham __: 5 Croly
Jane Eyre: 5 novel
author: Charlotte Brontë
character: 4 Reed 5 Abbot, Adele, Eliza, Grace, Maria, Poole 6 Bertha, Bessie
dog: 5 Pilot
__ Jane Grey: 4 Lady
__ Janes: 4 Mary
Jane's love: 6 apeman, Tarzan
Janesville: 4 city, town
locale: 9 Wisconsin
Janet: 4 Lynn, Reno 5 Blair, Evans, Frame, Leigh, Munro, Waldo 6 Dailey, Gaynor, Lennon 7 Guthrie, Jackson 8 Margolin
sister: 6 La Toya
Tony and ~ daughter: 5 Jamie
Janeway: 5 Eliot 7 Kathryn
jangle: 3 din, jar 4 gong, ring 5 babel, clang, clank, clash, clink, noise, sound 6 hubbub, racket, rattle, tinkle, tumult, uproar 7 clangor, clatter, discord, dispute, quarrel 8 argument 9 cacophony 10 dissonance, hullabaloo
jangled __: 6 nerves
jangling: 5 harsh 6 off-key, shrill 7 grating, jarring 8 clashing, strident 9 dissonant, unmusical 10 cacophonic, discordant, inharmonic, screeching
jangly: 4 edgy 5 drawn, hyper, jumpy, tense, wired 6 on edge 7 excited, fidgety, jittery, keyed up, nervous, uptight, wound up 8 agitated, fluttery, in a tizzy, unnerved 9 stressful, strung out, up the wall 10 high-strung
Janice: 4 Rule
Janie: 6 Fricke
Janie's Got a Gun (1989 song)
artist: Aerosmith
Janine: 6 Turner
Janis: 3 Ian 5 Elsie, Paige 6 Carter, Conrad, Joplin
janissary: 7 soldier
janitor: 6 porter 7 dustman, sweeper 8 watchdog 9 attendant, caretaker, custodian 10 doorkeeper
chore: 6 waxing 7 mopping, washing 8 cleaning, sweeping
need: 3 mop 5 Lysol
Janklow: 6 Morton
Jan-Michael: 7 Vincent
Jann: 6 Wenner
Janney: 7 Allison
Jannings, Emil Oscar: The Way of All Flesh
Janos: 7 Starker
Janowitz: 4 Tama
Janson Directive, The
author: Robert Ludlum
Janssen: 5 David, Famke
Janssen, David: 5 actor
TV: The Fugitive, Harry-O
Janssen, Famke: 7 actress
film: Celebrity (1998)
City of Industry (1997)
Don't Say a Word (2001)
GoldenEye (1995)
Love & Sex (2000)
Made (2001)
X-Men (2000)
Jansson, Tove: 6 writer 7 Finnish
__ Janszoon Tasman: 4 Abel
Januarius: 5 saint
January: 5 Jones, month
birthstone: 6 garnet
event: 4 sale 9 white sale
honoree's initials: 3 MLK
in Spanish: 5 enero
like a ~ day: 4 cold 5 brisk, crisp, nippy 6 frigid, frosty, frozen 8 freezing
sign: 4 Goat 8 Aquarius 9 Capricorn
to December: 4 year
warming: 4 thaw
January 13: 4 ides
January 5: 5 nones
Janus: 3 god 4 moon
daughter: 6 Canens
planet: 6 Saturn
son: 4 Fons
Janus-__: 5 faced
janvier: 4 mois 5 month 6 French 7 January
à décembre: 5 année
follower: 7 février
Janzen, Lee: 6 golfer
japan: 6 enamel 7 encrust, incrust, varnish
Japan: 3 sea 5 Nihon 6 nation, Nippon 7 country
ender: 3 ese
Mahayana school in ~: 3 Zen
rain, in ~: 3 ame
salmonlike fish of ~: 3 ayu
temple city of ~: 5 Kioto, Kyoto, Nikko
yes, in ~: 3 hai
Japan __: 3 wax 5 cedar 6 clover, Stream, tallow, Trench 7 Current
__ Japan: 5 Sea of
Japanese: 5 Asian 8 language
aborigine: 4 Ainu
admiral: 3 Ito
affirmative: 3 hai
airline: 3 ANA, JAL
apricot: 3 ume
art: 3 noh 6 bonsai
assassin: 5 ninja
auto: 5 Honda 6 Accord, Datsun, Nissan, Toyota
bay: 6 Sagami, Suruga
bean: 6 adzuki
bed: 3 mat 5 futon
beer: 5 Kirin
belt: 3 obi 6 hamaki
beverage: 3 tea 4 sake, saki
biologist: 6 Susumu
board game: 5 shogi
bovine: 5 Wagyu
bread: 3 pan
Buddhism of ~: 8 Mahayana
Buddhist monk of ~: 5 bonze
camera: 5 Canon, Nikon
cape: 3 Oma
capital: 5 Tokyo
capital, onetime: 3 Edo 4 Nara, Yedo 5 Yeddo
cartoon genre: 5 anime
celery: 3 udo
city: 3 Ise, Ome, Ota, Tsu, Ube, Uji, Usa, Yao 4 Ageo, Anjo, Fuji, Gifu, Hino, Hofu, Iida, Kobe, Kofu, Kure, Mito, Naha, Nara, Noda, Oita, Otsu, Saga, Seto, Soka, Tama, Toda, Ueda, Zama 5 Abiko, Akita, Asaka, Beppu, Chiba, Chofu, Daito, Ebina, Fuchu, Fukui, Handa, Ikeda, Ikoma, Iruma, Itami, Iwaki, Izumi, Kioto, Kiryu, Kochi, Kyoto, Minoo, Niiza, Ogaki, Omiya, Omuta, Osaka, Otaru, Oyama, Sakai, Suita, Tokio, Tokyo, Urawa, Yaizu 6 Akashi, Aomori, Atsugi, Ebetsu, Fujimi, Fukaya, Hadano, Himeji, Kadoma, Kasuga, Kitami, Kurume, Kuwana, Matsue, Misato, Mitaka, Nagano, Nagoya, Numazu, Sakado, Sakata, Sakura, Sasebo, Sayama, Sendai, Sukuka, Toyama, Toyota, Yamato, Yonago 7 Fukuoka, Hitachi, Komatsu, Matsudo, Mishima, Sapporo 8 Fukuyama, Hachioji, Kawasaki, Nagasaki, Yokohama 9 Hiroshima, Kagoshima
coat: 5 haori, happi
computer company: 3 NEC
conductor: 3 Oue 5 Ozawa
cooking ingredient: 4 miso
dance: 6 bugaku
delicacy: 4 fugu
diver: 3 ama
dog: 5 Akita
drama: 3 noh 6 kabuki
earthenware: 4 raku
elder statesman of ~: 5 genro
electronics giant: 4 Sony 5 Sanyo
emperor's title: 5 tenno
entertainer: 6 geisha
feudal lord: 6 daimio, daimyo
first-generation ~: 5 Issei
first prime minister: 3 Ito
fish: 3 koi, tai 4 fugu, masu 5 cobia 6 medaka
food: 3 eel 5 bento, ramen, sushi 6 larmen, ob ento, rumaki 7 sashimi, tempura 8 sukiyaki, teriyaki, yakitori
footwear: 4 geta, tabi, zori
fragrant-flowered ~ shrub: 4 gumi
gateway: 5 torii
gelatin: 4 agar 8 agar-agar
god: 5 Inari 9 Amaterasu
golfer: 4 Aoki
good morning in ~: 5 ohayo
hamlet: 4 mura
historical period: 5 Meiji

honorific: **3** san
hostess: **6** geisha
immigrant: **5** Issei, Nisei
ink: **4** sumi
iris: **5** plant **6** flower
island: **5** Hondo **6** Honshu, Kiushu, Kyushu, Ryukyu **7** Okinawa, Shikoku **8** Hokkaido
islands near ~: **5** Bonin **6** Kurils
lake: **3** Omi **4** Biwa
language: **4** Ainu
legislature: **4** Diet
locale: **4** Asia **6** Orient
martial art: **6** aikido, karate
mat: **6** tatami
measure: **3** sho
mercenary: **5** ninja
money: **3** rin, sen, yen
mountain: **4** Fuji **5** Oyama **8** Fujiyama
movie monster: **5** Rodan **8** Godzilla
mushroom: **5** enoki
neighbor: **5** China
Nobelist in Chemistry: **5** Fukui **6** Noyori, Tanaka **9** Shirakawa
Nobelist in Literature: **2** Oe **8** Kawabata
Nobelist in Medicine: **8** Tonegawa
Nobelist in Peace: **4** Sato
Nobelist in Physics: **5** Esaki **6** Yukawa **7** Koshiba **8** Tomonaga
overcoat: **4** mino
painter: **6** Sesshu
partition: **6** fusuma
pasta: **4** udon **5** ramen **6** larmen
perfume source: **5** rasse
persimmon: **4** kaki
physician: **8** Mori Ōgai
physicist: **5** Esaki **6** Yukawa
plum: **6** loquat
poem: **5** haiku, tanka
poet: **4** Issa **5** Basho, Buson **6** Yosano **7** Higuchi, Masaoka **8** Hagiwara **9** Shimazaki
porcelain: **5** imari
port: **4** Kobe, Kure, Naha, Oita **5** Akita, Kochi, Osaka, Otaru **6** Aomori **7** Niigata **8** Nagasaki, Yokohama **9** Amagasaki, Hiroshima, Kagoshima
radish: **6** daikon
red snapper: **3** tai
rice cake: **5** mochi
river: **3** Ota
robe: **6** kimono, yukata
royal: **3** emp.
sandal: **4** zori
sash: **3** obi
scientist: **5** Esaki **6** Susumu, Yukawa
screen: **5** shoji
script: **4** kana
sea: **5** China **6** Inland, Sagami **8** Japanese **9** East China
seaweed: **4** nori
shrub: **6** nardin, tobira **7** nandina
soup: **5** ramen **6** larmen
sport: **4** sumo **5** kendo
sports car: **5** Miata
spy: **5** ninja
stringed instrument: **4** koto
system of writing: **5** kanji
tangerine: **7** satsuma
theater: **3** noh **6** kabuki
tree: **4** kaki **6** hinoki
tub: **4** furo
vegetable: **3** udo
village: **4** mura
violinist: **6** Midori
volcano: **3** Aso, Usu **4** Akan, Fuji, Nasu **5** Asama, Azuma, Oyama, Unzen **6** Asosan, Bandai, Chokai, Ontake, Oshima **7** Adatara
war cry: **6** banzai
warrior: **7** samurai
watch: **5** Seiko
waterfall: **5** Kegon
wine: **4** sake, saki
winter sports center: **4** Arai **6** Nagano
writer: **4** Endo **5** Inoue **7** Abe Kobo, Higuchi, Mishima, Natsume **8** Kawabata, Mori Ōgai, Murasaki **9** Nagai Kafu, Yokomitsu **10** Dazai Osamu

Japanese __: **3** ivy, yew **6** beetle, radish **7** anemone, gelatin, lantern **9** persimmon
Japanese __ ceremony: **3** tea
Japanese-American: **5** Issei, Nisei
Japanese bobtail: **3** cat **5** felid **6** feline
Japanese Chin: **3** dog **5** canid **6** canine
__-Japanese War: **4** Sino **5** Russo
jape: **3** gag, rib **4** gibe, jest, jibe, joke, mock, quip **5** antic, caper, prank, taunt **7** lampoon, waggery **8** ridicule **9** kid around, make fun of, wisecrack **10** shenanigan, tomfoolery
japery: **5** jests, jokes, quips **7** mocking
Japheth
brother: **3** Ham **4** Shem
father: **4** Noah
son: **5** Gomer, Madai, Magog
japonica: **5** plant **6** flower
jar: **3** irk, pot **4** bang, bump, jerk, jolt, kick, olla, rock, stun, thud, vase **5** clash, crash, crock, cruse, flask, grate, shake, shock, smash, sound, start, thump **6** bottle, bounce, impact, jangle, jiggle, jostle, jounce, justle, nettle, offend, rattle, scream, vessel, wallop **7** agitate, amphora, disturb, shake up, startle, tremble **8** disquiet, irritate, surprise **9** buffeting, collision, container **10** concussion, discompose
contents: **3** jam **4** mayo **5** jelly
oil ~: **5** cruse
starter: **5** night
top: **3** cap, lid **5** cover
__ jar: **4** bell **5** mason **6** cookie, ginger, Leyden
Jardin des Tuileries: **4** parc
locale: **5** Paris **6** France
Jardine: **2** Al
jardiniere: **3** pot, urn **4** vase **7** amphora, epergne
Jared: **4** Leto **6** Sparks
grandson: **10** Methuselah
son: **5** Enoch
jargon: **4** cant **5** argot, idiom, lingo, slang **6** patois, speech **7** baloney, dialect **8** language, parlance, shoptalk **9** buzzwords **10** vernacular, vocabulary
suffix: **3** ese
see also baloney
jargonelle: **4** pear
Jarhead (2005 film)
cast: Jamie Foxx, Jake Gyllenhaal, Peter Sarsgaard
jarl: **9** chieftain
Jarlsberg: **6** cheese
Jarmusch: **3** Jim
Jaromir: **4** Jágr
Jaroslav: **5** Hasek **7** Seifert **9** Heyrovsky
jarrah: **4** tree
Jarre: **7** Maurice
Jarreau: **2** Al
Jarrell, Randall: **4** poet **6** writer
Jarrett: **4** Dale **5** Keith
Jarrett, Dale: **9** auto racer
milieu: **5** track
jarring: **5** bumpy, forte, harsh, noisy, rough, shock **6** jouncy, off-key **7** blaring, booming, grating, pealing, rackety, raucous, reboant, roaring **8** crashing, jangling, piercing, plangent, rumbling, sonorous, strident, turned up **9** big-voiced, clamorous, deafening, dissonant, unmusical **10** boisterous, discordant, resounding, stentorian, strepitous, thundering, uproarious, vociferous
Jarrott: **7** Charles
Jarry, Alfred: **6** French **10** playwright
__ Jar, The: **4** Bell
Jarvik: **6** Robert
Jascha: **7** Heifetz
jasmine: **4** vine **5** plant, shrub **6** flower, yellow
relative: ***see*** yellow color
jasmine __: **3** tea
Jasmine: **3** Guy
Jason: **3** Lee **4** Elam, hero, Kidd, Rick **5** Biggs, Gould **6** Hervey, Miller, Patric, Sehorn **7** Bateman, Connery, Gedrick, Robards, Statham **8** Argonaut **9** Alexander, Priestley
daughter: **7** Eriopis
father: **5** Aeson
ship: **4** Argo
son: **5** Argus, Medus, Thoas **6** Euneus, Medeus, Pheres **8** Deipylus, Mermerus, Tisander **9** Alcimedes, Alcimenes, Thessalus, Tisandrus
wife: **5** Medea
Jason __ Lee: **5** Scott
__ Jason Leigh: **8** Jennifer
jasper: **3** gem **4** rock **5** stone **7** pottery **8** ceramics **9** stoneware
ender: **4** ware
Jasper: **5** Johns
jass: **4** game **8** card game
Jassy in Romania: **4** Iasi
jaundice: **4** bias, mold, tint, warp **5** cloud, color, shade, shape, tinge, twist **9** influence, prejudice
jaundiced: **4** sour **6** sallow **7** partial **8** liverish, negative, partisan **9** distorted, resentful, skeptical **10** intolerant, prejudiced, suspicious, unfriendly
eye: **4** bias **6** enmity **7** bigotry **8** aversion **9** antipathy, prejudice **10** chauvinism, fanaticism, favoritism, narrowness, partiality
__ jaundiced eye upon: **5** cast a
jaunt: **3** hop, run **4** hike, ride, tour, trek, trip, turn, walk **5** drive, march, sally **6** cruise, frolic, junket, outing, picnic, ramble, safari, stroll, travel, voyage, wander **7** day trip, journey **9** adventure, excursion, gallivant **10** expedition
jaunty: **4** airy, bold, flip, pert **5** brash, cocky, natty, perky, sassy, sleek, swank **6** blithe, breezy, dapper, frisky, impish, lively, rakish, snazzy, spiffy, sporty, swanky **7** buoyant, dashing, raffish **8** animated, carefree, cheerful, debonair, flippant, gamesome, sporting, sportive **9** debonaire, sprightly, vivacious **10** debonnaire, frolicsome, rollicking, swaggering, unbothered
hat: **3** cap, tam **5** beret
java: **3** joe **5** mocha **6** coffee, jamoke
holder: **3** cup, mug, urn **7** samovar
inferior ~: **3** mud
locale: **4** café **6** bistro, eatery
type of ~: **5** decaf, latte **8** espresso
see also coffee
__ java: **5** mocha
Java: **3** sea **4** isle **6** island **8** language
alternative: ***see*** computer language
carriage: **4** sado **5** sadoo
city: **5** Bogor **8** Semarang
coin: **3** sen
folk art of ~: **5** batik **6** battik
locale: **4** Asia
neighbor: **4** Bali **6** Borneo
ruler: **4** raja
tree: **4** upas
volcano: **5** Kelut, Raung **6** Merapi, Semeru, Slamet
work: **6** applet
Java (1964 song)
artist: Al Hirt
Java __: **3** fig, man, Sea **7** sparrow
Javanese: **3** cat **5** felid **6** feline **8** language
Java Sea
island: **4** Laut
locale: **4** Bali
javelin: **3** gig **4** bolt, gaff, pike, pile **5** event, lance, shaft, spear, sport **7** assagai, assegai, harpoon **8** spontoon
cords: **6** amenta
Roman ~: **4** pila **5** pilum
javelin __: **5** throw
javelina: **7** peccary
__ Javelle: **5** eau de
Javier __ Cuellar: **7** Pérez de
jaw: **3** gab, say, yak, yap **4** bone, chat, chin, jowl, rail, rate, talk **5** chops, mouth, orate, scold, speak, utter **6** babble, berate, gossip, jabber, rail at, rattle, revile, yammer **7** censure, chatter, maxilla, prattle, upbraid **8** back talk, chitchat, mandible **9** criticize **10** chew the fat, tongue-lash, vituperate
combining form: **5** gnath- **6** gnatho-
drop one's ~: **4** gape, gawk **5** stare **6** goggle, marvel
ender: **4** bone **7** breaker **8** breaking

lower ~: 4 chin, jowl 6 muzzle
place: 3 mug 4 face, puss 6 kisser
starter: 4 lock
with dropped ~: 5 agape 6 aghast, amazed 7 floored, stunned 8 appalled 9 astounded, awestruck, stupefied, surprised 10 astonished, bewildered, dumbstruck, spellbound
__ jaw: 5 glass 7 lantern
Jawaharlal: 5 Nehru
daughter: 6 Indira
jawbone: 4 coax 6 rebuke 7 maxilla 8 mandible
source: 3 ass
jawbreaker: 5 candy
jawed
combining form: 8 -gnathous
tool: 4 vise 6 wrench
__-jawed: 4 iron 5 slack
Jaworski: 4 Leon
Jaws: 4 film 5 novel
author: Peter Benchley
boat: 4 Orca
cast: Richard Dreyfuss, Lorraine Gary, Roy Scheider, Robert Shaw
director: Steven Spielberg
dog: 6 Pippet
setting: 5 Amity
terror: 5 shark
__ Jaw, Saskatchewan: 5 Moose
Jaws of __: 4 Life
Jaws Theme (1975 song)
artist: John Williams
jay: 4 bird 6 letter
adjective: 5 avian
ender: 3 vee 4 bird, walk 6 hawker, walker 7 walking
follower: 3 kay
home: 4 nest 6 aviary
kin: 4 crow
starter: 3 dee, vee
__ jay: 4 blue
Jay: 4 John, Leno, Mohr, Ward 5 Gould, North, Ricky, Roach 8 Ferguson, Sandrich 9 McInerney 10 Livingston
ender: 3 cee
successor: 5 Conan
Jay and the Americans
leader: Jay Black
song: Cara Mia (1965)
Come a Little Bit Closer (1964)
Let's Lock the Door (1965)
Only in America (1963)
She Cried (1962)
This Magic Moment (1969)
jaybird, like a: 5 naked
Jay C. __: 7 Flippen
Jaye: 8 Davidson
Jaye P. __: 6 Morgan
__ Jay Friedman: 5 Bruce
__ Jay Gould: 7 Stephen
Jayhawker: 6 Kansan
__ Jay Hawkins: 8 Screamin'
__ Jay Lerner: 4 Alan
Jaymes partner: 7 Bartles
Jayne: 7 Kennedy, Meadows 9 Mansfield
jaywalk: 5 cross
jaywalker: 10 pedestrian
warn a ~: 4 beep, honk, toot 5 blare
Jay-Z: 7 rap star
jazz: 3 bop 4 jive, zest 5 bebop, blues, genre, music, swing 6 boogie, spirit 7 baloney 8 vivacity 9 Dixieland 10 excitement, liveliness
appreciate ~: 3 dig
bandleader: 4 Duke, Shaw 5 Basie 6 Dorsey, Herman 7 Goodman 9 Ellington 10 Count Basie
bassist: 6 Mingus 7 Blanton 9 Pettiford
clarinetist: 4 Shaw 6 Bechet, Herman 7 Goodman 8 Fountain
dance: 4 jive 5 bebop, stomp, swing 9 jitterbug
drummer: 4 Rich, Webb 5 Krupa, Roach 6 Blakey, Puente 7 Bellson
effect: 4 wail
ensemble: 4 band 5 combo 7 big band
fan: 3 cat 6 bopper, hepcat
flutist: 4 Laws, Mann
genre: 3 bop 4 scat 5 bebop, rebop, swing 6 boogie
guitarist: 4 Byrd, Paul 7 Les Paul 10 Montgomery
instrument: 3 axe, sax 4 horn 7 trumpet 8 clarinet 9 saxophone
Latin ~: 5 salsa
like some ~: 4 cool
nickname: 4 Duke 5 Count, Fatha, Trane 7 Satchmo
performance: 3 gig, jam, set
phrase: 4 lick, riff, vamp
pianist: 4 Monk 5 Basie, Blake, Evans, Hines, Hyman, Lewis, Tatum 6 Garner, Kenton, Morton, Simone, Waller 7 Allison, Brubeck, Hancock 8 Guaraldi, Marsalis 9 Ellington, Henderson, Strayhorn 10 McPartland
record label: 5 Verve
saxophonist: 4 Getz, Sims 5 Young 6 Barnet, Bechet, Beneke, Carter, Gordon, Herman, Kenny G, Parker 7 Coleman, Desmond, Hawkins, Rollins 8 Adderley, Coltrane, Marsalis, Mulligan
singing name: 4 Ella
trombonist: 3 Ory 6 Dorsey, Miller 9 Teagarden
trumpeter: 5 Davis, James 7 Nichols 8 Cheatham, Eldridge, Ferguson, Mangione, Marsalis 9 Armstrong, Gillespie 11 Beiderbecke
up: 4 hoke 7 enliven 8 decorate, emblazon, energize 9 embellish 10 supplement
vibraphonist: 5 Norvo 7 Hampton
see also baloney
jazz __: 4 band
jazz-__: 4 rock 6 fusion
__ jazz: 4 cool, free 6 modern
Jazz: 4 five
author: Toni Morrison
home: 4 Utah
org.: 3 NBA
rival: *see* NBA team
Jazz __: 3 Age
Jazzman (1974 song)
artist: Carole King
Jazzonia
author: Langston Hughes
Jazz Pizzicato
composer: Leroy Anderson
jazzy: 5 fancy, showy, zesty, zippy 6 active, flashy, lively, snazzy, tawdry 7 stylish, zestful 8 animated, spirited, striking 9 vivacious 10 flamboyant
street: 5 Beale
J.B.: 9 Priestley
j-bar: 3 tow 4 lift 6 ski tow 7 ski lift
__ J. Blige: 4 Mary
J.C.: 5 Powys, Snead 6 Penney 7 Dithers
__ J. Cannell: 7 Stephen
J. Carrol __: 5 Naish
__ J. Cobb: 3 Lee
__ J. Corbett: 5 James
JCS
mem.: 3 adm., CNO, gen.
part: 5 Joint, Staff 6 Chiefs
J.D.: 3 att. 4 atty., punk 5 tough 6 Cannon 8 hooligan, Salinger
forerunner: 3 LL.B.
part: 5 Juris 6 Doctor 8 juvenile 10 delinquent
-to-be's test: 4 LSAT
__ J. Dalton: 4 Lacy
jealous: 5 green 7 envious, envying, wishful 8 covetous, desirous, grudging 9 green-eyed, malicious, resentful 10 begrudging, possessive, protective, suspicious
one's cry: 5 me too
jealous mistress, Emerson's: 3 art
jealousy: 4 envy 9 suspicion 10 sour grapes
Jean: 3 Arp 4 Auel, Bach, Kerr, Rhys 5 Bodel, Borel, Fabre, Genet, Giono, Hagen, Marsh, Morel 6 Arthur, Dunant, Harlow, Ingres, Knight, Millet, Monnet, Parker, Perrin, Peters, Piaget, Racine, Renoir, Seberg, Toomer, Wyclef 7 Anouilh, Cocteau, Dausset, Fourier, Lafitte, Lamarck, Nicolet, Nidetch, Shepard, Simmons 8 Beliveau, Chrétien, Dubuffet, Foucault, Hersholt, Shepherd, Sibelius, Stafford 9 Fragonard, Froissart, Giraudoux, Negulesco, Shrimpton, Stapleton, Vander Pyl 10 de Brunhoff
in English: 4 John
see also French
Jean (1969 song)
artist: Oliver
Jean __ Getty: 4 Paul
Jean __ Marat: 4 Paul
Jean __ Pyl: 6 Vander
Jean-__ Aumont: 6 Pierre
Jean-__ Belmondo: 4 Paul
Jean-__ Duvalier: 6 Claude
Jean-__ Godard: 3 Luc
Jean-__ Killy: 6 Claude
Jean-__ Picard: 3 Luc
Jean-__ Rampal: 6 Pierre
Jean-__ Sartre: 4 Paul
Jean-__ Van Damme: 6 Claude
__ Jean: 6 Billie
Jean-Baptiste: 5 Lully
Jean-Claude: 5 Killy 8 Duvalier
Jeane: 5 Dixon
Jeanette: 5 Nolan 9 MacDonald
Jeanie With the Light Brown Hair
composer: Stephen Foster
Jean Jacques: 8 Rousseau
__ Jean King: 6 Billie
Jean-Luc: 6 Godard, Picard
Jeanmaire: 5 Renée
Jean-Marie: 4 Lehn 5 Le Pen
Jeanne: 3 ste. 4 Abel 5 Black, Crain 6 Lanvin, Moreau, Pruett, sainte
see also French
Jeanne __: 4 d'Arc
Jeannie: 5 Seely 6 Berlin
__ Jeannie: 6 Little
Jeannie C. __: 5 Riley
Jeannine: 5 Riley
Jeannot: 6 Szwarc
Jean Paul: 5 Getty, Marat
Jean-Paul: 6 Sartre 8 Belmondo, Gaultier
Jean-Pierre: 5 Léaud 6 Aumont, Rampal
jeans: 4 togs 5 cords, Levi's, pants 6 chinos, denims, slacks 8 trousers 9 corduroys, dungarees, Wranglers
cut of some ~: 4 slim 5 husky
iron-on: 5 patch 8 appliqué
like ~: 6 casual
material: 5 chino, denim 8 corduroy
measurement: 5 waist 6 inseam
name: 3 Lee 4 Levi 6 Gitano
partner: 3 tee 6 T-shirt
shortened ~: 7 cutoffs
starter: 4 blue
Jeb: 4 Bush 8 Magruder
J.E.B.: 6 Stuart
Jeckle: 4 toon 6 magpie
partner: 6 Heckle
Jed: 6 Harris 7 Bartlet 8 Clampett
daughter: 4 Elly 7 Elly May
nephew: 6 Jethro
Jeddah native: 5 Saudi
J. Edgar __: 6 Hoover
Jedi: 6 Kenobi, knight, Obi-Wan
ally: 4 Ewok
teacher: 4 Yoda
__-jeebies: 6 heebie
Jeep: 3 SUV 5 truck 7 vehicle
model: 6 Laredo, Sahara 8 Cherokee, Wagoneer, Wrangler
onetime ~ mfr.: 3 AMC
relative: 6 Humvee
jeepers: 3 wow 4 gosh, yipe 5 golly, yikes, yipes 6 oh gosh
Jeepers Creepers
composer: Johnny Mercer, Harry Warren
jeepney: 3 bus
jeer: 3 boo 4 gibe, hiss, hoot, jibe, mock, quip, razz, slam, slur, snub, twit 5 abuse, chaff, decry, fleer, libel, scoff, scorn, sneer, snipe, spurn, taunt, whoop 6 banter, defame, deride, dump on, heckle, hector, hiss at, hoot at, impugn, jibe at, malign, offend, rail at, rebuff, slight, vilify 7 affront, asperse, catcall, degrade, disdain, laugh at, mockery, poke fun, put down, rank out, sarcasm, slander, traduce 8 belittle, denounce, ridicule, vilipend 9 denigrate, discredit, disparage, humiliate, make fun of 10 calumniate, disrespect
at: 4 mock 5 scorn, taunt 8 ridicule
jeering: 7 mocking 8 derisive, scoffing, scornful, taunting 9 insulting, sarcastic 10 disdainful, ridiculing
Jeeves: 5 valet
author: P.G. Wodehouse

jeez: **4** dang, darn, drat, gosh, rats **5** golly
jefe: **5** chief **6** honcho, top dog **8** kingfish, superior **9** commander
Jeff: **4** Beck **5** Barry, Corey, Fahey, Lynne **6** Healey, Sluman **7** Bagwell, Bridges, Conaway, Daniels, Reardon **8** Chandler, Goldblum **9** Foxworthy
brother: **4** Beau
father: **5** Lloyd
friend: **4** Mutt
__ & Jeff: **4** Mutt
Jefferson: **5** Davis **6** Martha, Thomas
Jefferson Airplane
members: Slick, Kantner
song: Count on Me (1978)
Miracles (1975)
Somebody to Love (1967)
White Rabbit (1967)
Jefferson City: **4** city, town **7** capital
county: **4** Cole
locale: **8** Missouri
river: **8** Missouri
Jefferson in Paris (1995 film)
cast: James Earl Jones, Thandie Newton, Nick Nolte, Gwyneth Paltrow, Greta Scacchi
director: James Ivory
Jeffersons, The (CBS sitcom)
cast: Franklin Cover (Tom Willis)
Marla Gibbs (Florence Johnston)
Sherman Hemsley (George Jefferson)
Roxie Roker (Helen Willis)
Isabel Sanford (Louise Jefferson)
producer: **4** Lear
theme: Movin' On Up
Jefferson, Thomas: **9** president
belief: **5** deism
bill: **3** two
former occupation: **6** lawyer
hair: **3** red
home: **8** Virginia **10** Monticello
opponent: **5** Adams **8** Pinckney
predecessor: **5** Adams
sch. founded by ~: **3** U. Va.
V.P.: **4** Burr **7** Clinton
wife: **6** Martha
Jeffers, Robinson: **4** poet **6** writer
like ~'s stallion: **4** roan
Jeffrey: **4** Lynn **5** Jones **6** Archer, Hunter, Tambor **7** Osborne **10** Katzenberg
Jeffreys: **4** Anne
Jeffries: **6** Lionel
Jehan: **4** Shah
Jehoshaphat father: **3** Asa
Jehovah: **3** God **4** Lord
Jehovah's __: **7** Witness
jejune: **3** dry **4** arid, blah, dull, flat, naif, tame **5** banal, corny, empty, hokey, inane, naive, passé, silly, stale, trite, vapid **6** boring, callow, common, draggy, giggly, old hat **7** clichéd, fatuous, humdrum, insipid, kiddish, prosaic, puerile, tedious **8** bromidic, childish, immature, jevenile, juvenile, lifeless, ordinary, outdated, outmoded, tiresome **9** hackneyed, pointless, prosaical, senseless **10** pedestrian, spiritless, uninspired, unoriginal, wishy-washy
area: **6** desert
jejunum neighbor: **5** ileum
Jekyll and Hyde, like: **4** dual
Jekyll hangout: **3** lab
jell: **3** set **4** clot **5** occur **6** cohere, firm up, gelate, harden **7** congeal, stiffen, thicken **8** finalize, solidify, take form **9** coagulate, make sense, take shape **10** gelatinize
jelled: **3** set **5** stiff, thick
garnish: **5** aspic
Jellicle Ball musical: **4** Cats
Jellicoe: **3** Ann
jellied: **5** gummy, stiff, thick **6** gloppy **9** congealed, thickened **10** coagulated, gelatinous, solidified
appetizer: **9** macédoine
food: **3** eel **6** jujube
Jell-O: **7** dessert, gelatin
like freshly mixed ~: **5** unset
shaper: **4** mold
jelly: **3** jam **5** aspic, Kraft **6** Knott's, spread, Welch's **7** Polaner, stiffen **8** Smucker's **9** conserves, preserves
container: **3** jar, pot
dinner ~: **5** aspic
ender: **4** bean, fish, roll
flavor: **5** grape, guava **7** apricot **10** strawberry
lump of ~: **4** blob, glob **6** dollop
roll: **4** cake **10** confection
jelly __: **4** roll **5** donut
__ jelly: **5** royal
Jelly __ Morton: **4** Roll
jellybean: **5** candy
Jelly Belly: **5** candy
flavor: **4** pear **5** lemon, peach **6** banana, cherry **7** coconut, popcorn **8** cinnamon, jalapeño, licorice, root beer **9** blueberry, bubble gum, cream soda, lemon lime, margarita, pineapple, raspberry, tangerine **10** cantaloupe, cappuccino, grapefruit, grape jelly, green apple, piña colada, watermelon
jellyfish: **4** wimp **5** pansy, sissy **6** coward, craven, turkey **7** chicken, dastard, nebbish, quitter **8** poltroon, pushover, recreant, weakling **9** fraidy cat **10** pantywaist
part: **5** cnida **6** pileus
young ~: **5** polyp
jellylike: **5** shaky, thick **6** unfirm, wobbly **7** aquiver, viscous **10** gelatinous
Jellylorum: **3** cat
jelly roll: **4** cake
Jelly's __ Jam: **4** Last
Jellystone Park bear: **4** Yogi **6** Boo Boo
Jemima: **4** aunt, duck
Jemima Puddleduck
author: Beatrix Potter
Jemison, Mae: **9** astronaut
jemmy: **4** coat **6** jacket **8** overcoat
Jena: **4** city, town **6** battle, Malone
locale: **7** Germany
je ne __ quoi: **4** sais
Jenkins: **5** Allen **6** Fergie, Gordon, Tamara **8** Ferguson
Jenkins, Fergie: **7** pitcher
__ Jenks Bloomer: **6** Amelia
Jenna: **6** Elfman
Jenn-Air: **5** stove **6** fridge
alternative: *see* appliance brand
Jenner: **5** Bruce **6** Edward **10** decathlete
jennet: **3** ass **6** animal, donkey
Jenney: **7** William
Jennie: **5** Garth **6** Jerome
Jennie Gerhardt
author: Theodore Dreiser
Jennie Lee (1958 song)
artist: Jan & Dean
Jennifer: **4** Ehle, Grey, Lien, Salt **5** Beals, Grant, Jones, Lopez, Lynch, Paige, Tilly **6** Garner, Hudson, O'Neill, Warnes, Warren **7** Aniston **8** Bartlett, Capriati, Connelly, Holliday, Saunders
on WKRP: **4** Loni
Jennifer __ Hewitt: **4** Love
Jennifer __ Leigh: **5** Jason
Jennifer Lorn
author: Elinor Wylie
Jennilee: **8** Harrison
Jennings: **3** Ken **5** Peter **6** Hughie, Waylon
__ Jennings Bryan: **7** William
Jennings, Ken
forte: **6** trivia **8** Jeopardy!
Jennings, Peter: **6** anchor **10** journalist, newscaster
forte: **4** news
network: **3** ABC
jenny: **3** ass, jib **6** donkey
cry: **4** bray **6** heehaw
mate: **7** jackass
Jenny: **4** Lind **5** Craig, Jones **7** Agutter **8** McCarthy
Jennyanydots: **3** cat
Jenny, Jenny (1957 song)
artist: Little Richard
Jeno's: **5** pizza
alternative: **5** Tony's **6** Ellio's **7** Celeste, Totino's **8** DiGiorno **9** Tombstone **10** Freschetta
Jens: **4** Skou **6** Salome **8** Jacobsen
Jensen, J. Hans: **8** Nobelist **9** physicist
Jensen, Johannes: **6** Danish, writer **8** Nobelist
Jenufa: **5** opera
composer: Leos Janácek
jeopardize: **4** risk **5** peril, stake **6** chance, gamble, hazard, menace **7** imperil **8** endanger, threaten **10** compromise
jeopardous: **5** hairy, risky **7** parlous **9** dangerous, unhealthy
jeopardy: **4** risk **5** peril **6** danger, hazard, menace **7** trouble **8** exposure, unsafety **9** liability **10** insecurity
full of ~: **4** iffy **5** dicey, hairy, risky **6** chancy, daring, touchy, tricky, unsafe **7** fraught, parlous, unsound **8** perilous, ticklish **9** dangerous, daredevil, desperate, foolhardy, hazardous, uncertain **10** touch-and-go
in ~: **6** at risk **7** at stake **9** on the line **10** endangered
put in ~: **3** bet **4** dare, risk **5** brave, stake, wager **6** chance, gamble, hazard **7** venture **9** speculate **10** take a flyer
__ jeopardy: **6** double
Jeopardy!: **8** game show
announcer: **5** Pardo
clue: **6** answer
contestant: **5** asker
creator: Merv Griffin
host: Art Fleming, Alex Trebek
owner: **4** Sony
staple: **6** trivia
Jephtha
composer: George Frideric Handel
jerboa: **6** animal, mammal, rodent
relative: *see* rodent
jeremiad: **6** lamant, lament, tirade **8** diatribe, harangue **9** complaint, grievance, invective, philippic
Jeremiah: **5** Dixon **7** Johnson
brother: **6** Hanani
father: **7** Hilkiah
preceder: **6** Isaiah
Jeremiah Johnson (1972 film)
cast: Will Geer, Robert Redford
director: Sydney Pollack
Jeremiah Symphony
composer: Leonard Bernstein
Jeremy: **5** Brett, Clyde, Irons, Licht, Piven **6** Miller **7** Bentham
singing partner: **4** Chad
Jérez: **4** city, town
former name: **4** Xera **5** Xeres
locale: **6** Mexico **9** Zacatecas
Jergens: **5** Adele **6** lotion
alternative: **4** Keri **5** Curel, Nivea **6** Aveeno **7** Eucerin, Pacquin **9** Lubriderm
Jeri: **4** Ryan **8** Southern
Jericho: **6** battle
feature: **5** walls
rose of ~: **4** posy **5** bloom, plant **6** flower **7** blossom
Jerilyn: **5** Britz
Jeritza: **5** Maria
jerk: **3** cad, jar, jog, sap, tic, tug **4** boor, buck, bump, drip, dupe, heel, jolt, lout, nerd, pull, shmo, snap, whip, yank **5** brute, creep, dance, dweeb, idiot, loser, lurch, pluck, quake, shake, spasm, start, twerp, twirp, twist **6** bounce, hurtle, jiggle, jounce, quiver, recoil, shiver, snatch, thrash, thrust, turkey, twitch, wiggle, wrench, writhe **7** bumbler **8** preserve **9** lay hold of, schlemiel **10** nincompoop, noodlehead
away: **3** pry **4** tear **5** wrest **6** snatch, wrench **7** extract
companion: **5** clean
ender: **5** water
forward: **4** jump **5** heave, lunge, lurch, pitch
knee ~: **8** response
out: **3** tug **4** pick, pull, yank **5** pluck, tweak **6** uproot **7** extract **9** extirpate
up: **4** hike **5** boost, raise **7** elevate **8** increase
see also ninny
__ jerk: **4** knee, soda
__-jerker: **4** tear
jerkin: **4** coat, vest **6** jacket **7** doublet
Jerk, The (1979 film)
cast: Steve Martin, Bernadette Peters
director: Carl Reiner
jerkwater: **5** small **6** remote, two-bit **7** trivial **8** piddling **9** rinky-dink
jerky: **4** meat **5** bumpy **6** abrupt, fitful, uneven **7** fatuous **9** irregular, spasmodic **10** convulsive, nonuniform

like beef ~: **5** chewy, cured, spicy
motion: **3** bob
__-jerky: 5 herky
Jermaine: 7 Jackson
Jerne, Niels: 6 Danish **8** Nobelist
Jerome: 4 Kern **5** Geils, Hines, Karle, saint **6** Moross **7** Robbins, Weidman **8** Friedman
jerry __: 3 can
jerry-__: 5 build, built
Jerry: 4 Bock, Ford, Hall, Reed, Rees, Rice, Vale, Wald, West **5** Brown, Grote, Lewis, Lucas, Maren, mouse, Paris, Rubin **6** Belson, Butler, Garcia, Herman, Houser, Leiber, Orbach, Siegel, Zucker **7** Buckner, Colonna, Falwell, Maguire, Mathers, Stiller, Van Dyke, Wallace **8** Seinfeld, Springer **9** Goldsmith, Tarkanian **10** Schatzberg
Betty, to ~: 4 wife
daughter: 5 Susan
ex-partner: 4 Dean
friend: 6 Elaine
partner: 3 Ben
Tom and ~ ingredient: 3 egg, rum **4** milk **5** sugar **6** brandy **10** baking soda
Jerry __ Lewis: 3 Lee
__ Jerry: 5 Mungo
jerry-built: 5 cheap, junky **6** flimsy, shoddy, unfirm **7** rickety, unsound **8** slipshod **10** ramshackle, unthorough
structure: 3 hut **4** shed **5** shack **6** lean-to, shanty
Jerry Maguire (1996 film)
cast: Tom Cruise, Cuba Gooding Jr., Kelly Preston, Renée Zellweger
director: Cameron Crowe
jersey: 3 top **5** shirt **6** fabric **7** sweater **8** crew neck, pullover
fabric: 5 rayon **6** cotton
Jersey: 3 cow **4** bull, isle **6** bovine, cattle, island
see also New Jersey
Jersey __: 4 City, pine **5** Giant **6** Bounce
Jersey __ Walcott: 3 Joe
__ Jersey: 3 New
Jersey Girl (2004 film)
cast: Ben Affleck, Liv Tyler
Jerusalem: 4 city, town **7** capital
artichoke: 5 tuber
author: Selma Lagerlöf
hill: 4 Zion
locale: 6 Israel
town near ~: 3 Lod **4** Gaza **6** Bethel
Jerusalem Delivered: 4 epic, poem
author: Torquato Tasso
Jerzy: 6 Neyman **8** Kosinski
jess: 5 strap
Jess: 7 Willard
jessamine: 5 plant **6** flower
Jessamyn: 4 West
Jesse: 5 Helms, James, Lasky, Owens **6** Orosco, Powell **7** Jackson, Ventura **8** Bradford
son: 5 David, Eliab
Jesse (1980 song)
artist: Carly Simon
__ Jesse James: 5 Alias
Jessel, George: 2 MC **4** host **5** emcee
Jessi: 6 Colter
Jessica: 4 Alba, Biel **5** Lange, Tandy **6** Harper, Walter **7** Mitford, Simpson
__ Jessica Parker: 5 Sarah
Jessie: 4 Ames
Jessie __ Landis: 5 Royce
Jessye: 6 Norman
__ Jessy Raphael: 5 Sally
jest: 3 gag, kid, toy **4** gibe, jape, jibe, joke, josh, play, quip **5** caper, chaff, clown, crack, humor, laugh, prank, put on, sneer, spoof, sport, taunt, tease **6** banter, bon mot, japery **7** foolery, mockery **8** badinage, drollery, jocosity, nonsense, one-liner, raillery **9** crack wise, frivolity, kid around, wisecrack, witticism **10** crack jokes, joke around, pleasantry, rib-tickler, tomfoolery
in ~: 6 for fun
jester: 3 wag, wit **4** fool, mime, zany **5** clown, comic, cutup, joker, mimer **6** madcap **7** buffoon, pierrot **8** comedian, jokester **9** harlequin, prankster, Rigoletto
__ jester: 5 court
Jest 'Fore Christmas: 4 poem
author: Eugene Field
jesting: 3 fun **5** comic, droll, funny, humor, merry, sport, witty **6** banter, comedy, jocose, jocund, joking **7** comical, jocular, kidding, playful, roguish, waggish **8** badinage, humorous, laughing, raillery, spoofing, zaniness **9** facetious **10** frolicsome, rollicking
Jesuit: 9 clergyman **10** missionary
Jesus
brother: 5 James, Joses, Judas, Matty, Simon **6** Joseph
mother: 4 Mary
Jesús: 4 Alou
Jesus Christ Superstar: 7 musical
composer: Andrew Lloyd Webber, Tim Rice
Jesus to a Child (1996 song)
artist: George Michael
jet: 3 MiG, SST **4** ebon, gush, inky, pour, spew, spue, zoom **5** black, color, ebony, plane, raven, sable, sooty, spirt, spout, spurt, surge, turbo **6** airbus, geyser, squirt, stream, travel **8** aircraft, airliner, airplane, Concorde, fountain, midnight **9** transport **10** pitch-black, shoot forth
ender: 3 lag **4** foil, pack, port **5** liner **7** fighter
home: 6 hangar
hop a ~: 3 fly
mil. ~ locale: 3 AFB
relative: 4 inky, onyx **5** ebony, raven, sable, sooty
route: 4 lane **6** airway **7** air lane
starter: 3 fan, ram **4** prop, twin **5** pulse, scram
trail: 4 wake
unit: 4 Mach
water ~: 5 spirt, spout, spurt **6** geyser, spritz, squirt **8** fountain
jet __: 3 gun, lag, set **4** boat, wash **5** motor, pilot, plane **6** engine, setter, stream **7** fighter
jet-__: 3 hop **5** black
__ jet: 3 gas **4** jump **5** jumbo
Jet: 2 Li **5** NFLer
Jet (1974 song)
artist: Paul McCartney
Jet __: 3 Ski
__ Jet: 4 Lear
Jet Airliner (1977 song)
artist: Steve Miller Band
jet-black: 4 dark **5** ebony **9** lightless, unlighted
Jet Blue: 7 airline
alternative: *see* airline, U.S.
jeté: 4 jump, leap **8** movement
Jeter: 5 Derek **7** Michael
Jeter, Derek: 4 Yank **6** Yankee **9** shortstop
sport: 8 baseball
Jethro: 4 Tull **6** Bodine
cousin: 4 Elly **7** Elly May
son-in-law: 5 Moses
uncle: 3 Jed
__-jet printer: 3 ink
Jet Propulsion Lab org.: 4 NASA
Jets: 4 gang, team **6** eleven
foe: 6 Sharks
home: 7 New York
org.: 3 AFC, NFL
rival: *see* NFL team
sport: 8 football
jetsam: 5 trash **6** debris **7** garbage **8** discards **10** throwaways
Boston Harbor ~: 3 tea
jet set: 5 elite, haves **6** fliers, flyers **7** in-crowd, society **8** well-to-do **9** beau monde **10** glitterati, haute monde, socialites, upper crust
city: 4 Nice **6** Cannes
need: 4 visa
jet-setter: 7 tourist, visitor **8** gadabout, traveler **9** passenger, sightseer **10** vacationer
jetski: 10 watercraft
Jetsons, The (TV sitcom)
high school: Orbit
voice cast: Mel Blanc (Mr. Spacely)
Daws Butler (Elroy Jetson)
Don Messick (Astro)
George O'Hanlon (George Jetson)
Penny Singleton (Jane Jetson)
Jean Vander Pyl (Rosie the Robot)
Janet Waldo (Judy Jetson)
jet stream: 4 wind
Jett: 4 Joan, Rink
Jetta: 2 VW **3** car **4** auto **10** Volkswagen
Jett and the Blackhearts, Joan
song: Crimson and Clover (1982)
I Hate Myself for Loving You (1988)
I Love Rock 'n Roll (1982)
jettison: 4 cede, drop, dump, hurl, junk, sell, shed **5** chuck, ditch, eject, expel, forgo, heave, scrap, yield **6** forego, give up, reject, unload **7** abandon, cast off, deep-six, discard, forfeit, forsake, lighten **8** forswear, get rid of, hand over, part with, throw out **9** cast aside, dispose of, foreswear, surrender, throw away **10** relinquish
jettisoned cargo: 5 lagan, ligan
jetty: 4 dock, pier, quay, slip **5** berth, wharf **6** harbor **7** harbour, landing **9** anchorage **10** breakwater
support: 6 gabion
jeu __: 7 d'esprit
jeu de __: 4 mots
jeune __: 5 fille
jeunesse __: 5 dorée
Jeux d'eau
composer: Maurice Ravel
Jew: 9 Israelite
jewel: 3 gem **4** rock, ruby **5** angel, bijou, honey, pearl, prize, stone, topaz **6** amulet, baguet, bangle, bauble **7** darling, diamond, emerald, trinket **8** baguette, gemstone, ladylove, ornament, sapphire, sparkler, treasure **9** solitaire **10** birthstone
ender: 4 fish, weed
thief: 6 iceman
jewel __: 3 box **4** case **5** block
__ jewel: 5 crown
Jewel: 5 Akens
song: Foolish Games (1997)
Hands (1998)
You Were Meant for Me (1996)
Jewel __ Nile, The: 5 of the
jeweler: 6 artist **8** engraver, lapidary **9** craftsman **10** gemologist, horologist, watchmaker
measure: 2 kt. **5** carat, karat
tool: 3 dop **5** loupe
Jewell: 4 Geri **6** Isabel
Jewel of the East: 4 Bali
Jewel of the Nile, The (1985 film)
cast: Danny DeVito, Michael Douglas, Kathleen Turner
jewelry: 3 gem, ice, pin **4** band, ring **5** beads, bijou, bling, cameo, chain, charm, cross, crown, stone, tiara **6** anklet, armlet, bangle, bauble, bijoux, broach, brooch, choker, diadem, finery, locket, tiepin, tie tac **7** diamond, earring, pendant, tie tack, trinket **8** bracelet, diamonds, frippery, gemstone, necklace, ornament, scarfpin, sparkler, stickpin, treasure, wristlet **9** adornment, lavaliere, solitaire, valuables **10** bling-bling
box: 6 casket
box opener: 4 hasp **5** catch, latch
chain: 5 Zales
fake: 5 glass, paste
fastener: 5 clasp
holder: 3 box **4** case **5** chest **6** coffer
material: 5 amber
place for a ~ clasp: 4 nape, neck
wrist ~: 5 chain **6** bangle
__ jewelry: 4 junk **7** costume
jewels: 4 gems **6** bijoux **9** valuables
deck with ~: 5 begem
set, as ~: 3 fix **5** embed, imbed, inlay
Jewels
author: Danielle Steel
Jewels of Tessa Kent, The
author: Judith Krantz
Jewel Song: 4 aria
jewelweed: 6 balsam, flower **10** touch-me-not
Jewett: 8 Sara Orne
Jewish: 3 Sem. **6** Hebrew, Judaic **7** Hasidic, Semitic **9** Israelite **10** Ashkenazic
bread: 6 hallah

cabala work: 5 zohar
campus ~ organization: 6 Hillel
ceremonial palm branch: 5 lulab, lulav
holiday: 5 Purim 8 Passover 9 Yom Kippur
holiday dinner: 5 seder
holiday eve: 4 ereb, erev
homeland: 4 Sion, Zion
like some ~ food: 6 kasher, kosher
month: 2 Av 4 Adar, Elul, Iyar 5 Iyyar, Nisan, Sivan, Tevet 6 Kislev, Nissan, Shevat, Tammuz, Tishri 7 Heshvan
mystic: 6 Essene
prayer: 5 shema 6 Hallel
robot of ~ folklore: 5 golem
school: 5 heder 6 cheder 7 yeshiva
sect member: 5 Hasid
seven-week period: 4 omer
snack: 5 knish
teacher: 5 rabbi, rebbe
temple: 4 shul 5 schul 9 synagogue
youth org.: 4 YMHA, YWHA
Jewish __: 3 rye
Jewison: 6 Norman
Jew of Malta, The
author: Christopher Marlowe
jew's harp: 10 percussion
sound: 5 twang
Jex-Blake: 6 doctor, Sophia 9 physician
Jezebel: 4 vamp 5 hussy
deity: 4 Baal
father: 7 Ethbaal
hometown: 4 Tyre
husband: 4 Ahab
son: 7 Ahaziah
Jezebel (1938 film)
cast: George Brent, Bette Davis, Henry Fonda
Jezebel (1951 song)
artist: Frankie Laine
JFK: 3 Dem. 4 pres.
abbr.: 3 arr., ETA, ETD
data: 5 sched.
debater: 3 RMN
lander: 3 KLM, SST
locale: 3 NYC
predecessor: 3 DDE
regulator: 3 FAA
successor: 3 LBJ
to RFK: 3 bro
UN ambassador: 3 AES
see also airport, Kennedy
JFK (1991 film)
cast: Edward Asner, Kevin Bacon, Kevin Costner, Tommy Lee Jones, Jack Lemmon, Walter Matthau, Gary Oldman, Joe Pesci, Sissy Spacek, Donald Sutherland
director: Oliver Stone
__ J. Fox: 7 Michael
J. Fred __: 5 Coots, Muggs
jg., lt.: 3 off.
Jhabvala, Ruth Prawer: 6 writer 7 British
work: Amrita
JHS, part of: 3 sch. 4 high 6 junior, school
Jiang Qing
husband: 3 Mao
Jiangsu city: 4 Wuxi 5 Wuhsi, Wusih
jiao
ten: 4 yuan
jib: 3 arm 4 sail 6 canvas 8 foresail
racing ~: 5 Genoa, jenny
support: 4 boom, mast, pole, post, spar 6 mizzen, timber
jib __: 4 boom 5 crane
__ jib: 3 cap 5 Genoa, inner, miter 6 flying
jibaro: 5 music
jibe: 2 go 3 fit 4 mesh 5 agree, crack, fit in, match, scoff, tally 6 concur, square 7 comport, conform, put-down 8 coincide, dovetail, hit it off 9 harmonize 10 correspond, go together
at: 4 gibe, jeer, mock, slam 5 cavil, scoff, scorn, smirk, sneer, taunt 6 deride 7 nitpick, put down, quibble 8 belittle, ridicule 9 deprecate, disparage, find fault 10 look down on
jicama: 3 veg. 4 root 9 vegetable
Jicarilla: 5 tribe 6 Indian 7 Amerind
Jidda: 4 city, port, town
city near ~: 5 Mecca
from ~: 5 Saudi
water: 6 Red Sea
Jif
alternative: 6 Skippy 8 Peter Pan
jiff: 3 sec 5 trice 6 moment 7 instant
jiffy: 3 bit, sec 4 wink 5 flash, trice 6 breath, minute, moment, second 7 eyewink, instant 9 short time, twinkling 10 bat of an eye
in a ~: 3 PDQ 4 anon, ASAP, fast, soon 5 apace 6 presto 7 fleetly, hastily, quickly, rapidly, readily, swiftly 8 pell-mell, speedily 9 forthwith, hurriedly, instantly, like a shot, posthaste, right away
__ jiffy: 3 in a
Jiffy __: 3 Pop 4 Lube
jig: 3 bob 4 lure, ruse 5 dance, music
ender: 3 saw
ice-fishing ~: 5 tip up
sailor's ~: 8 hornpipe
jig __!, The: 4 is up
__ jig: 5 Irish
jigger: 3 tot 4 sail 5 glass 9 shot glass 10 manipulate
jiggerful: 3 nip 5 drink, snort
jiggery-__: 6 pokery
jiggle: 3 bob, jar, jog 4 jerk, rock, toss 5 nudge, shake 6 bobble, bounce, jounce, rattle, shimmy, teeter, twitch, wiggle 7 agitate, wriggle
jiggly: 5 shaky 6 uneven, wobbly 7 rickety 8 unstable, unsteady 9 teetering 10 precarious, unbalanced
Jiggs
wife: 6 Maggie
__ Jiggy Wit It: 6 Gettin
Jig of Forslin, The
author: Conrad Aiken
jigsaw: 4 tool 6 puzzle
part: 5 piece 8 fragment
jihad: 3 war 6 combat, strife 8 conflict
Jihan: 5 Sadat
Jilin: 4 city, port 8 province
locale: 5 China
Jill: 6 Sobule, St. John, Whelan 7 Ireland 8 Goodacre 9 Clayburgh 10 Eikenberry
Jillette: 4 Penn
Jillian: 3 Ann
Jillie: 4 Mack
jillions: 4 a lot, many, scad 6 oodles
jilt: 4 dump 5 ditch, leave, spurn 6 desert, reject 7 abandon, discard, forsake, stand up 8 forswear, run out on 9 cast aside, foreswear, leave flat, skip out on, throw over
jim-__: 5 dandy
Jim: 4 Dale, Fixx, Kaat, Lowe, Otto, Page, Ryun 5 Bowie, Brown, Croce, Davis, Kelly, Lange, McKay, Ringo, Seals 6 Backus, Bakker, Bishop, Bouton, Carrey, Henson, Hutton, Jordan, Langer, Lehrer, Nabors, Palmer, Parker, Reeves, Taylor, Thorpe, Varney 7 Bunning, Courier, Lonborg, McMahon, Messina, Metzler 8 Abrahams, Braddock, Caviezel, Garrison, Jarmusch, Morrison, Plunkett, Stafford 9 Broadbent, Weatherly
__ Jim: 4 Lord, Slim 5 Lucky 7 Diamond
__ Jima: 3 Iwo
__ Jim Brady: 7 Diamond
jim-dandy
see wonderful
Jimenez, Jose: Bill Dana
Jiménez, Juan: 4 poet 7 Spanish 8 Nobelist
Jimi: 7 Hendrix
jiminy: 3 gee, wow 4 gosh
Jiminy __: 7 Cricket
jimjams: 3 DTs 6 creeps
Jimmie: 4 Dodd, Foxx 5 Noone 6 Walker 7 Rodgers
jimmy: 3 pry 4 open 5 force, lever 7 crowbar, pry open 9 force open
card used to ~ spring locks: 4 loid
Jimmy: 3 Key, SUV 4 Baio, Dean, Page, Reed, Soul, Webb 5 Arias, Ellis, Hatlo, Hoffa, Jones, Lydon, Olsen, Smits 6 Carter, Castor, Dorsey, Fidler, Hughes, Kimmel, McHugh, Ruffin 7 Blanton, Breslin, Buffett, Charles, Clanton, Connors, Demaret, Durante, Rushing 8 McNichol, Piersall, Swaggart 10 McCracklin
daughter: 3 Amy
mfr.: 3 GMC
Rosalyn, to ~: 4 wife
successor: 3 Ron
Jimmy Carter Library site: 7 Atlanta
Jimmy Mack (1967 song)
artist: Martha & the Vandellas
Jimmy the __: 5 Greek
jimson weed: 6 datura
Jin: 7 dynasty
jingle: 4 ding, gong, ring, tune 5 clang, clink, ditty, verse 6 slogan, tinkle
give a ~: 4 call, dial 5 phone 6 ring up 9 telephone, touch base
writer: 5 adman
jingle __: 4 bell 5 shell
Jingle __: 5 Bells 6 Jangle
Jingle __ Rock: 4 Bell
Jingle Bells: 4 Noel 5 carol
preposition: 3 o'er
vehicle: 6 sleigh
jingles
where ~ are heard: 3 ads
jingo: 5 bigot 7 patriot 10 chauvinist
jingoism: 10 chauvinism, flag-waving, narrowness, patriotism
jingoistic: 7 hostile, warlike 8 militant 9 bellicose, combative 10 aggressive
jink: 4 spin, turn 5 pivot, twist, whirl 6 gyrate, rotate, swivel 9 pirouette
jinks, high: 5 caper, prank, spree 7 fooling, revelry 8 mischief 9 vandalism
jinni: 5 demon, genie 6 daemon, daimon
jinriksha: 4 cart, taxi 8 carriage
jinx: 3 hex 5 curse, Jonah, spell 6 hoodoo, whammy 7 bad luck, bedevil, bewitch, bugaboo, evil eye, sorcery
Jinx: 10 Falkenburg
jinxed: 7 hapless, unblest, unlucky 8 ill-fated, luckless 9 ill-omened, unblessed, unfavored 10 ill-starred
Jinx, Mr.: 3 cat 4 toon
jipijapa: 3 hat 5 plant
Jirásek, Alois: 5 Czech 6 writer 10 playwright
jird
relative: ***see*** rodent
'J' Is for Judgment
author: Sue Grafton
jitney: 3 bus 7 minibus, shuttle
relative: 3 cab 4 hack, taxi 7 taxicab
jitter: 5 quake, shake 6 fidget, quiver, shiver 7 shudder, tremble
jitterbug: 4 jive 5 dance
relative: 5 lindy
jitterbugger: 3 cat 6 hepcat
jitters: 4 fear 6 nerves, shakes 7 anxiety, fidgets, shivers, tension, willies 9 tightness 10 inquietude, uneasiness
jittery: 4 edgy 5 antsy, itchy, jumpy, nervy, shaky, tense, upset 6 jangly, on edge, uneasy 7 anxious, fearful, fidgety, keyed up, nervous, panicky, restive, spooked, uptight 8 agitated, cowardly, fluttery, restless, skittish, troubled 9 concerned, excitable, ill at ease, quivering, trembling, tremulous 10 frightened, high-strung
not ~: 4 calm, cool, even 5 quiet, sober, staid, tepid 6 placid, poised, remote, sedate, serene, steady, stolid 7 assured, offhand, relaxed, stoical 8 composed, detached, reserved, tranquil 9 apathetic, collected, easygoing, impassive, nerveless, unexcited, unruffled 10 nonchalant, phlegmatic, restrained, unagitated, untroubled
Jivaro: 5 tribe 8 language
jive: 3 kid 4 fool 5 dance, idiom, music 6 banter, delude 7 deceive, defraud, mislead 8 fast talk, ridicule 9 disinform, jitterbug, kid around, make fun of
talk: 5 argot, lingo, slang 6 patois 8 parlance 10 vernacular
see also baloney
Jive __: 4 Five 6 Talkin'
jiver: 3 cat 6 hepcat

Jive Talkin' (1975 song)
artist: Bee Gees
J.J.: 4 Cale 6 Abrams
J.K.: 7 Rowling
JKL on a phone: 4 five
J.M.: 6 Barrie
jo
see sweetheart
Jo: 5 March 8 Davidson, Stafford, Van Fleet 9 Mielziner
sister: 3 Amy, Meg 4 Beth
Jo __ Pflug: 3 Ann
Jo __ Worley: 4 Anne
__-Jo: 3 Flo
Joad: 2 Al 3 Tom 4 Noah 6 Ruthie
Joan: 4 Baez, Chen, Jett, Miró 5 Allen, Davis, Evans, Weber 6 Benoit, Cusack, Didion, Leslie, Lunden, Rivers, Van Ark 7 Bennett, Collins, Freeman, Hackett, Osborne 8 Blackman, Blondell, Crawford, Fontaine 9 Caulfield, Greenwood, Plowright, Severance 10 Sutherland
in Italian: 8 Giovanna
__ Joan: 5 Saint
__ Joan Hart: 7 Melissa
Joanie: 6 Somers
she played ~: 4 Erin
Jo Ann: 5 Pflug
Joanna: 4 font 5 Going, Kerns 6 Barnes, Lumley, Pacula, Pettet 7 Cassidy 8 typeface
Joanna (1983 song)
artist: Kool and the Gang
Joanne: 3 Dru 7 Whalley 8 Woodward
JoAnne: 6 Carner
Jo Anne: 6 Worley
Joan of Arc: 5 saint 6 martyr
city: 7 Orléans
Joan of Lorraine
author: Maxwell Anderson
Joanou: 4 Phil
Joan Van __: 3 Ark
Joaquin: 6 Miller 7 Phoenix
__ Joaquin Valley: 3 San
job: 2 do 3 act, aim, bag, bit, biz, gig, rut 4 case, deed, duty, feat, game, goal, keep, line, onus, part, post, role, slot, spot, task, toil, tour, work 5 berth, caper, chore, craft, crime, doing, drill, field, forte, fraud, grind, heist, labor, level, means, niche, place, quest, realm, score, shift, skill, stint, sweat, theft, thing, trade 6 action, affair, billet, career, charge, domain, drudge, effort, errand, holdup, income, living, matter, métier, milieu, office, outfit, racket, scheme, snatch, sphere, status, tenure 7 booking, break-in, calling, company, concern, con game, gesture, larceny, measure, mission, program, project, purpose, pursuit, rat race, robbery, routine, service, station, stickup, support, swindle, venture 8 activity, benefice, burglary, business, capacity, contract, covenant, dealings, drudgery, endeavor, exercise, exertion, function, homework, industry, lifework, measures, poaching, position, practice, province, thievery, vocation 9 adventure, bailiwick, condition, expertise, gruntwork, happening, life's work, objective, operation, procedure, salt mines, servitude, situation, specialty, workplace 10 assignment, commission, commitment, daily grind, department, discipline, employment, engagement, enterprise, initiative, line of work, livelihood, nine-to-five, obligation, occupation, plundering, profession, sustenance
action: 6 strike 8 slowdown
application datum: 3 SSN
ender: 6 holder, seeker, sharer
figuratively: 3 hat
second story ~: 5 heist, theft
job __: 3 lot 4 bank 5 order 6 action, market, seeker
job-__: 3 hop 4 hunt 6 hunter 7 hunting, sharing
__ job: 3 axe, bag, con, day, odd 4 desk, lube, nose, snow 5 cushy, on the 6 inside 7 hatchet
Job
follower: 6 Psalms
friend: 7 Eliphaz
lot: 3 woe 9 suffering
preceder: 6 Esther
Job __: 5 Corps
__ Job: 4 Get a
jobber: 4 hand, help 5 agent 6 broker, dealer, worker 7 laborer, migrant 8 handyman, merchant, salesman, supplier 9 consignor, dispenser, hired hand, middleman 10 freelancer, wholesaler
jobbery: 3 cut 4 loot, swag 5 booty, graft, gravy, honey 6 boodle, grease, payoff, payola, racket, velvet 7 plunder, rake-off 8 kickback, pickings, venality 9 hush money, shakedown 10 corruption
JoBeth: 8 Williams
jobholder: 4 hand 6 worker 7 employe, laborer, staffer 8 employee 9 hired hand 10 wage earner
job-hopper: 6 worker 8 employee
job-hunter: 6 seeker 7 hopeful 8 aspirant, prospect 9 applicant, candidate, contender 10 competitor, handshaker
bio: 4 vita 6 resume
jobless: 4 idle 9 out of work 10 unemployed
__ job on: 3 do a
Jobs: 5 Steve 6 Steven
company: 5 Apple
job safety org.: 4 OSHA
__-Jobson: 6 Hobson
job-training org.: 4 CETA
Jobyna: 7 Ralston
Jocasta
brother: 5 Creon
daughter: 6 Ismene 8 Antigone
husband: 5 Laius 7 Oedipus
son: 7 Oedipus
Jochebed
son: 5 Aaron, Moses
jock: 6 player 7 athlete 10 enthusiast
Jock: 5 Ewing 7 Mahoney
jockey: 3 Day 4 move, ride 5 Baeza, drive, guide, Krone, pilot, racer, rider, Sande, steer 6 Arcaro, direct, driver, handle, Pat Day, Pincay, strive 7 athlete, Cauthen, Cordero, finesse, Hartack 8 horseman, maneuver, navigate, scramble, Turcotte 9 Earl Sande, negotiate, Shoemaker 10 Julie Krone, manipulate
assistance for a ~: 5 boost, leg up
bench ~: 3 sub 5 scrub
disc ~: 6 deejay 9 announcer
for position: 3 pit, vie 5 rival 7 compete, contend 9 challenge
item: 4 crop, rein, tack
jockey __: 3 box, cap 4 club
__ jockey: 4 desk, disc, disk 5 bench, video
Jockeys: 6 boxers, briefs, shorts 9 underwear
rival: 4 BVDs 5 Hanes
Jockeys in the Rain
painter: Edgar Degas
jocko: 5 chimp
Jocko: 6 Conlan
jocose: 3 gay 4 camp, joky 5 comic, droll, flaky, funny, happy, jokey, jolly, merry, silly, witty 6 blithe, flakey, joking, jovial 7 amusing, comical, gleeful, jesting, joshing, playful, waggish 8 cheerful, farcical, humorous, prankish, roughish, sportive 9 facetious, laughable, ludicrous, whimsical 10 frolicsome
jocosity: 3 fun, wit 4 gags, glee 5 humor, jests, mirth 6 antics, banter, levity, whimsy 7 foolery, kidding, waggery 8 badinage, clowning, drollery, hilarity, raillery 9 flippancy, merriment 10 buffoonery, tomfoolery, wisecracks
jocular: 3 gay 4 camp, joky 5 comic, droll, flaky, funny, happy, jokey, jolly, merry, silly, witty 6 blithe, flakey, joking, jovial 7 amusing, comical, gleeful, jesting, joshing, playful, waggish 8 cheerful, farcical, humorous, prankish, roughish, sportive 9 facetious, laughable, ludicrous, whimsical 10 frolicsome
sounds: 4 ha-ha
suffix: 4 aroo, eroo
jocularity: 3 fun, wit 4 gags, glee 5 cheer, humor, jests, mirth 6 antics, banter, gaiety, gayety, levity, whimsy 7 delight, foolery, jollity, kidding, waggery 8 badinage, buoyance, buoyancy, clowning, drollery, gladness, hilarity, laughter, pleasure, raillery, sunshine 9 flippancy, happiness, joviality, merriment 10 buffoonery, tomfoolery, wisecracks
jocund: 3 gay 4 camp, joky 5 comic, droll, flaky, funny, happy, jokey, jolly, merry, silly, witty 6 blithe, cheery, flakey, genial, joking, jovial, lively 7 amusing, comical, festive, gleeful, jesting, joshing, playful, waggish 8 cheerful, farcical, humorous, prankish, roughish, sportive 9 convivial, facetious, laughable, ludicrous, whimsical 10 frolicsome
jocundity: 3 fun, wit 4 gags, glee 5 cheer, humor, jests, mirth 6 antics, banter, gaiety, gayety, levity, whimsy 7 delight, foolery, jollity, kidding, waggery 8 badinage, buoyance, buoyancy, clowning, drollery, gladness, hilarity, laughter, pleasure, raillery, sunshine 9 flippancy, happiness, joviality, merriment 10 buffoonery, tomfoolery, wisecracks
__ Jo Dean: 5 Sammy
Jodhpur: 4 city, town
locale: 5 India
jodhpurs: 5 boots, pants, shoes 8 breeches, footwear, knickers, trousers
Jodie: 6 Foster
Jodrell __ Observatory: 4 Bank
Jody: 6 Watley 8 Reynolds, Williams
joe: 4 java 5 latte, mocha 6 coffee, jamoke 8 beverage
joltless ~: 5 decaf, Sanka
like a sloppy ~: 5 spicy 6 spicey
relative: 5 latte
joe-__ weed: 3 pye
Joe: 3 Ely, May, Tex 4 Blow, Camp, Hill 5 Clark, Dante, Flynn, Jones, Lando, Louis, Orton, Penny, Perry, Pesci, Simon, South, Torre, Walsh 6 Cocker, Cronin, Doakes, Dowell, Friday, Greene, Morgan, Morton, Namath, Niekro, Sewell 7 Frazier, Jackson, Medwick, Montana, Palooka, Paterno, Piscopo, Schmidt, Shuster 8 DiMaggio, Johnston, Mantegna, McCarthy, McIntyre, Williams 9 Berlinger, Eszterhas, Garagiola, Henderson, McGinniss, McGinnity, Regalbuto 10 Campanella, Cartwright, Pantoliano
Joe __: 4 Blow 6 Doakes, Miller, Public 7 College, Six-pack
Joe __ Baker: 3 Don
__ Joe: 4 good, Holy, Poor 6 little, sloppy
__ Joe Black: 4 Meet
__ Joe Cartwright: 6 Little
Joe E. __: 4 Ross 5 Brown
__ Joe Greene: 4 Mean
Joel: 4 Coen, Grey 5 Billy, Zwick 6 Barlow, McCrea 8 Spingarn 10 Schumacher
follower: 4 Amos
preceder: 5 Hosea
Joel, Billy
song: Allentown (1982)
Big Shot (1979)
Don't Ask Me Why (1980)
Honesty (1979)
I Go to Extremes (1990)
An Innocent Man (1984)
It's Still Rock and Roll to Me (1980)
Just the Way You Are (1977)
The Longest Time (1984)
A Matter of Trust (1986)
Modern Woman (1986)
Movin' Out (1978)
My Life (1978)
Only the Good Die Young (1978)
Piano Man (1974)
The River of Dreams (1993)
She's Always a Woman (1978)
She's Got a Way (1981)
Tell Her About It (1983)
Uptown Girl (1983)
We Didn't Start the Fire (1989)
You May Be Right (1980)
You're Only Human (1985)
spouse: Christie Brinkley
Joel Mc__: 4 Crea
__ Joel Osment: 5 Haley
Joely: 6 Fisher 10 Richardson

__ **Joe McDonald:** **7** Country
Joe Miller offering: **4** joke **8** joke book
joe-pye: **4** weed
__ **Joe's:** **4** Papa **5** Eat at **6** Sloppy
__ **Joe Turner:** **3** Big
Joe Versus the Volcano (1990 film)
cast: Lloyd Bridges, Tom Hanks, Meg Ryan, Robert Stack
__ **Joe Walcott:** **6** Jersey
joey: **3** 'roo **5** money **6** animal **8** kangaroo
spot: **5** pouch
Joey: **3** Dee **5** Adams **6** Bishop, Powers **8** Lawrence, McIntyre **10** Heatherton
__ **Joey:** **3** Pal
__ **Joe Young:** **6** Mighty
Joffe: **6** Roland
Joffrey: **6** Robert
jog: **3** run **4** bend, bump, gait, jerk, lope, pace, prod, push, stir, trot, turn **5** nudge, press, shake **6** arouse, bounce, canter, jiggle, jostle, jounce, justle, prompt, remind, spring **7** agitate, refresh, work out **8** activate, exercise **9** stimulate **10** incitement
jogger: **4** shoe **6** runner **7** sneaker
brand: **4** Avia, Nike **6** Adidas, Reebok
memory ~: **4** list, note **8** reminder
wear: **6** sweats, T-shirt
woe: **4** ache **5** cramp
jogging __: **4** shoe, suit **5** pants
joggle: **3** bob **4** toss **5** shake **6** bobble, bounce, jostle, jounce, juggle, justle
Johan: **5** Bojer **8** Runeberg **10** Falkberget
Johann: **3** Eck **4** Fust, Kalb **6** Fichte, Goethe **7** Strauss **10** Pestalozzi **11** Deisenhofer
in English: **4** John
Johann __ Bach: **9** Sebastian
Johanna: **5** Spyri
johannes: **5** money
Johannes: **3** Rau **5** Stark **6** Brahms, Jensen, Kepler **7** Eckhart, Fibiger **9** Gutenberg
in English: **4** John
Johannesburg: **4** city, town
see also South Africa
Johansen: **5** David
Johansson: **8** Scarlett
john: **2** WC **3** can, lav, loo **5** privy **6** lounge, toilet **7** latrine **8** bathroom, lavatory, outhouse, rest room **10** powder room
starter: **4** demi
__**-john:** **5** cheap
John: **3** Doe, Dye, Gay, Hay, Jay, Pym, Rae, Ray, Woo **4** Agar, Amos, Beck, Cage, Dahl, Dall, Daly, Dean, Drew, Fenn, Ford, Glen, Hume, Hurt, Kerr, Knox, Lahr, Lone, Lund, Mott, Muir, Nash, Parr, Paul, pope, Reed, Ross, Shea, Tesh, Vane, Venn, Wain **5** Adams, Alden, Arden, Astin, Barth, Boles, Bosco, Brahm, Brown, Byner, Cabot, Candy, Clare, Davys, Deere, Derek, Dewey, Donne, Elton, Elway, Fiske, Fitch, Fleck, Gavin, Glenn, Gower, Gregg, Guare, Heard, Hicks, Hough, Jakes, James, Keats, Kerry, Korty, Litel, Locke, Loder, Lynch, Major, Marin, McKay, McVie, Megna, Mills, Nance, Oates, O'Hara, Payne, Pople, Prine, Raitt, Saxon, Sloan, Smith, Synge, Tommy, Tyler, Waite, Wayne **6** Badham, Banner, Braine, Buchan, Bunyan, Calvin, Carson, Carver, Cazale, Ciardi, Cleese, Cullum, Cusack, Dalton, Denver, Dryden, Duigan, Eccles, Eckert, Enders, Evelyn, Farrow, Fowles, Franco, Glover, Gorrie, Graunt, Harlan, Hawkes, Hersey, Hodiak, Hughes, Huston, Irving, Kander, Karlen, Landis, Larson, Lennon, Lupton, Madden, Mayall, McAdam, McCrae, McGraw, Milius, Milton, Musker, Napier, Olerud, Pankow, Ritter, Robert, Ruskin, Sayles, Schuck, Stamos, Strutt, Sutter, Sutton, Torrey, Turner, Updike, Vernon, Walker, Warner, Waters, Wesley, Wooden **7** Ashbery, Bardeen, Belushi, Boorman, Bubbles, Chapman, Cheever, Cleland, Fiedler, Fogerty, Gardner, Gielgud, Gilbert, Goodman, Grisham, Gunther, Hancock, Harvard, Hawkins, Heywood, Ireland, Kendrew, Knowles, le Carré, Lithgow, Macleod, Mahoney, Marston, McEnroe, Millais, Montagu, Munonye, Newbery, Newlove, Osborne, Patrick, Polanyi, pontiff, Russell, Skelton, Spencer, Stewart, Sturges, Sulston, Tyndall, Vianney, Webster, Whiting, Wyndham **8** Bartlett, Berryman, Betjeman, Boulting, Burgoyne, Cafferty, Coltrane, Crawford, Cromwell, Davidson, DeForest, DeLorean, Forsythe, Franklin, Garfield, Halliday, Hamilton, Harsanyi, Havlicek, Herschel, Houseman, Marshall, McIntire, McMartin, Newcombe, Northrop, Pershing, Phillips, Randolph, Rayleigh, Ringling, Roebling, Stockton, Suckling, Travolta, Turturro, Williams, Winthrop, Wycliffe, Zacherle **9** Barrymore, Burroughs, Carpenter, Carradine, Cleveland, Cockcroft, Constable, Cornforth, Dillinger, Entwistle, Harington, Hillerman, Macdonald, Malkovich, Masefield, McTiernan, Pemberton, Schneider, Sebastian, Singleton, Steinbeck **10** Barbirolli, Cassavetes, Chancellor, Chrysostom, Ehrlichman, Galsworthy, Guillermin, Schrieffer, Stallworth
follower: **4** Acts, Jude
in French: **4** Jean
in German: **4** Hans **6** Johann **8** Johannes
in Irish: **4** Sean **5** Shane
in Italian: **4** Gino **8** Giovanni
in Russian: **4** Ivan
in Scottish: **3** Ian **4** Iain
in Spanish: **4** Juan
in Welsh: **4** Evan
preceder: **4** Luke **5** Peter
Q. Public: **6** people
John __: **4** Bull **5** Henry
John __ Adams: **6** Quincy
John __ Astor: **5** Jacob
John __ Audubon: **5** James
John __ Body: **6** Brown's
John __ Booth: **6** Wilkes
John __ Carr: **7** Dickson
John __ Coley: **4** Ford
John __ Dulles: **6** Foster
John __ Garner: **5** Nance
John __ Hooker: **3** Lee
John __ II: **4** Paul
John __ Jones: **4** Paul
John __ Kellogg: **6** Harvey
John __ Keynes: **7** Maynard
John __ Law: **7** Phillip
John __ Lennon: **3** Ono
John __ Mellencamp: **6** Cougar
John __ Mill: **6** Stuart
John __ Neumann: **3** von
John __ Newman: **5** Henry
John __ Orr: **4** Boyd
John __ Passos: **3** Dos
John __ Sargent: **6** Singer
John __ Scotus: **4** Duns
John __ Sousa: **6** Philip
John __ Swayze: **7** Cameron
John __ Walton: **3** Boy
John __ Whittier: **9** Greenleaf
__ **John:** **6** Honest, Little
John Anderson My Jo: **4** poem
author: Robert Burns
John and Yoko son: **4** Sean
Johnathon: **7** Schaech
__ **John B:** **5** Sloop
John Barleycorn: **4** poem
author: Jack London
John Boyd __: **3** Orr
John Brown's Body
author: Stephen Vincent Benet
John Bull's Other Island
author: George Bernard Shaw
John C. __: **6** Reilly **7** Calhoun, Frémont **8** McGinley
John Cameron __: **6** Swayze
John Charles __: **7** Fremont
John Cougar __: **10** Mellencamp
John D. __: **9** MacDonald
John de __: **6** Lancie
John Dickson __: **4** Carr
John Doe: **9** anonymous
__ **John Doe:** **4** Meet
John Dory: **4** fish
John Dos __: **6** Passos
John, Elton: **3** Sir
collaborator: Taupin, Rice, Dee
musical: **4** Aida
song: Bennie and the Jets (1974)
Candle in the Wind (1987)
Can You Feel the Love Tonight (1994)
Crocodile Rock (1972)
Daniel (1973)
Don't Go Breaking My Heart (1976)
Don't Let the Sun Go... (1974)
Goodbye Yellow Brick Road (1973)
Honky Cat (1972)
I Don't Wanna Go On... (1988)
I Guess That's Why... (1983)
Island Girl (1975)
Little Jeannie (1980)
Lucy in the Sky With Diamonds (1974)
Mama Can't Buy You Love (1979)
Nikita (1986)
The One (1992)
Philadelphia Freedom (1975)
Rocket Man (1972)
Sad Songs (1984)
Someone Saved My Life Tonight (1975)
Sorry Seems to Be... (1976)
That's What Friends Are for (1985)
Your Song (1970)
John F. __: **7** Kennedy
John Ford __: **5** Coley
John Foster __: **6** Dulles
John G. __: **8** Avildsen
John Gabriel Borkman
author: Henrik Ibsen
John Greenleaf __: **8** Whittier
John Hancock: **9** signature
competitor: ***see*** insurance company
put one's ~ on: **3** ink **4** sign **7** endorse **9** formalize
John Hancock Building
architect: **3** Pei
John Harvey __: **7** Kellogg
John Henry: **9** signature
put one's ~ on: **3** ink **4** sign **7** endorse **9** formalize
John Henry __: **6** Newman
John Herschel __: **5** Glenn
John Jacob __: **5** Astor
John James __: **7** Audubon
John Kennedy __: **5** Toole
John le __: **5** Carré
John Lee __: **6** Hooker
__ **John Malkovich:** **5** Being
John Maynard __: **6** Keynes
John Mc__: **5** Enroe
__ **John, M.D.:** **7** Trapper
John Nance __: **6** Garner
Johnnie: **3** Ray **6** Taylor **8** Whitaker
Johnny: **3** Lee **4** Cash, Depp, Gill, Hart, Kemp, Mize, Nash, Otis, Sain **5** Bench, Burke, Evers, Green, Pesky **6** Carson, Horton, Mandel, Mathis, Mercer, Miller, Rivers, Rotten, Torrio, Unitas, Winter **7** Bristol, Desmond, Maestro, Preston **8** Burnette, Crawford, Paycheck **9** Appleseed, Sheffield, Tillotson
bandleader for ~: **3** Doc
in Italian: **6** Gianni
in Russian: **5** Vanya
Johnny __: **3** Reb **4** Cool **5** Angel, Eager, Suede **6** Apollo, collar, Guitar **7** Belinda, Holiday, Tremain
Johnny __ Meer: **6** Vander
Johnny __ Note: **3** One
Johnny-__-lately: **4** come
Johnny-__-spot: **5** on-the
Johnny-__-up: **4** jump
__ **Johnny!:** **5** Here's
Johnny Angel (1962 song)
artist: Shelley Fabares
Johnny B. __: **5** Goode
Johnny Belinda (1948 film)
cast: Lew Ayres, Agnes Moorehead, Jane Wyman
Johnny B. Goode (1958 song)
artist: Chuck Berry
johnnycake: **4** pone **5** bread
Johnny-come-lately: **7** upstart **8** newcomer **9** arriviste
__ **Johnny Comes Marching Home:** **4** When
Johnny Mnemonic (1995 film)
cast: Ice-T, Keanu Reeves

Johnny One Note
composer: Lorenz Hart, Richard Rodgers
Johnny-on-the-__: 4 spot
Johnny Reb org.: 3 CSA
Johnny Reno (1966 film)
cast: John Agar
Johnny's Theme
composer: Paul Anka
Johnny Vander __: 4 Meer
John of the Cross: 5 saint
John Paul: 4 pope 7 pontiff
John Paul __: 5 Jones, Young
John Paul II: 4 Pole, pope 7 pontiff
John Philip __: 5 Sousa
John Q (2002 film)
cast: Robert Duvall, Anne Heche, Denzel Washington, James Woods
John Q. __: 6 Public
John Quincy __: 5 Adams
John R. __: 6 Pierce 7 Coryell
John, Robert
song: The Lion Sleeps Tonight (1972)
Sad Eyes (1979)
John Ronald __ Tolkien: 5 Reuel
__ johns: 4 long
Johns: 5 Sammy 6 Glynis, Jasper 7 Hopkins
John's __ Wife: 5 Other
Johns Hopkins subj.: 4 anat.
__ John Silver: 4 Long
John Singer __: 7 Sargent
John Singleton __: 6 Copley
Johns, Jasper: 6 artist 7 painter
genre: 6 pop art
johns, long: 9 underwear
John Smith: 5 alias
Johnson: 3 Ben, Don, Jay, Kay, Osa, Tom, Uwe, Van 4 Arte, Brad, Chic, Jack, Marv, Rita 5 Betty, Celia, Magic, Rafer, Randy 6 Andrew, Betsey, Cherie, Earvin, Eyvind, Lamont, Lionel, Lyndon, Pamela, Philip, Samuel, Walter 7 Beverly, Russell 8 Lady Bird, Michelle, Nunnally 9 Lynn-Holly
Johnson & ~ competitor: 5 Curad
partner: 5 Olsen
Johnson, Andrew: 9 president
home: 9 Tennessee
predecessor: 7 Lincoln
successor: 5 Grant
wife: 5 Eliza
Johnson City: 4 city, town
locale: 5 Texas 9 Tennessee
Johnson, Don: 5 actor
film: Paradise (1991)
Sweet Hearts Dance (1988)
Tin Cup (1996)
song: Heartbeat (1986)
spouse: Melanie Griffith
TV: Miami Vice, Nash Bridges
Johnson, Earvin: 5 Magic
milieu: 5 court
org.: 3 NBA
sport: 10 basketball
Johnson, Eyvind: 6 writer 7 Swedish 8 Nobelist
Johnson, Jack: 5 boxer
milieu: 4 ring
Johnson, James Weldon: 6 writer
Johnson, Lady Bird
first name: 7 Claudia
middle name: 4 Alta
Johnson, Lionel: 4 poet 7 British
Johnson, Lyndon B.: 9 president
biographer: 4 Caro
cabinet member: 4 Barr, Boyd, Rusk, Wood 5 Clark, Cohen, Smith, Udall, Wirtz 6 Connor, Dillon, Fowler, Hodges, O'Brien, Watson, Weaver 7 Freeman, Gardner, Kennedy 8 Clifford, McNamara 9 Gronouski 10 Celebrezze, Katzenbach, Trowbridge
child: 4 Luci 5 Lynda
dog: 3 Her, Him
home: 5 Texas
middle name: 6 Baines
opponent: 9 Goldwater
predecessor: 7 Kennedy
successor: 5 Nixon
V.P.: 8 Humphrey
wife: 7 Claudia 8 Lady Bird
Johnson, Magic
first name: 6 Earvin
Johnson, Osa: 8 explorer
Johnson, Pamela: 6 writer 7 British
Johnson, Philip: 9 architect
Johnson, Rafer: 10 decathlete
Johnson, Randy: 3 ace 6 hurler 7 pitcher
nickname ~: 4 Unit 7 Big Unit
Johnson, Samuel: 6 writer 7 British
alma mater: Oxford
cat: 5 Hodge
friend: Boswell
work: The Idler 10 dictionary
Johnson, Uwe: 6 German, writer
Johnson, Walter: 6 hurler 7 pitcher, Senator
John's Other Wife: 9 radio show
Johnston: 3 Joe 4 city, town 7 Kristen
Johnstown: 4 city
disaster: 5 flood
locale: 4 Penn.
John Stuart __: 4 Mill
John the __: 7 Apostle, Baptist
John the Apostle: 5 saint
John the Baptist: 5 saint
parent: 9 Elizabeth, Zechariah
John van __: 5 Vleck
John von __: 7 Neumann
John Wilkes __: 5 Booth
Joi: 7 Lansing
Joie: 3 Lee
joie de vivre: 4 élan, zest 6 gaiety, gayety 8 pleasure
Joie de Vivre
author: Émile Zola
join: 3 mix, pin, tie, wed 4 abut, band, clip, fuse, glue, go to, knit, link, lock, mate, meet, melt, nail, pair, side, weld, yoke 5 affix, blend, clamp, clasp, enrol, enter, focus, graft, hitch, marry, merge, piece, reach, stick, tenon, tie up, touch, unify, unite, verge, weave 6 adhere, append, attach, border, bridge, cement, cleave, cohere, couple, enlist, enroll, fasten, gather, hook up, link up, mingle, sign on, sign up, solder, splice, team up 7 bracket, combine, connect, enter in, entwine, hitch on, intwine 8 assemble, border on, coalesce, neighbor, pair with, register, side with, take part 9 accompany, affiliate, enter into, integrate, interlace, interlink, socialize 10 amalgamate, assist with, fall in with, hook up with, synthesize, take part in, take up with, team up with
a jam session: 5 sit in
a jury: 3 sit
as hands: 4 grip 5 clasp
at the edge: 4 abut
at the seams: 3 sew 4 tack 5 baste 6 repair, stitch
forces: 4 pool 5 merge, unite 6 club up, gang up, league 9 cooperate 10 assist with
in: 4 help 6 accept, take on 7 partake, pitch in 8 deal with, take part 9 cooperate, partake of 10 contribute
(in): 4 chip 5 chime
the cast of: 5 act in
the enemy: 4 turn 6 defect, desert 7 forsake, pull out, sell out
the game: 6 ante up 8 shell out
the military: 5 serve 6 enlist, sign on, sign up 9 volunteer
the party: 4 be at 6 appear, attend, drop in, make it, show up 9 accompany
the rat race: 4 moil, slog, toil, work 5 labor, slave, sweat 6 drudge, hustle, strive 7 achieve, peg away 8 plug away 9 freelance, grind away, moonlight 10 buckle down
together: 3 fit, tie, wed 4 band, meld, pool 5 unite 6 fasten
up: 3 enl. 4 team 5 enrol, enter 6 enlist, enroll, sign on, sign up 10 rendezvous
up in space: 4 dock, link
up (with): 4 ally 5 align, aline 9 associate 10 go partners
with: 6 follow 7 go along 9 accompany
with heat: 4 bond, fuse, melt, weld 6 solder
wood: 4 nail 5 spike 6 fasten, hammer
joined: 3 wed 6 allied, linked, united 8 combined, in league 9 bracketed, connected, undivided 10 affiliated, associated
(with): 5 along 8 together
joiner: 3 and 4 link 5 clamp, miter, mixer 6 member, rabbet 7 artisan 8 vinculum 9 carpenter 10 journeyman, woodworker
cry: 5 ditto, me too
group: 4 club, frat 8 sorority 10 fraternity
joinery: 8 woodwork
joining: 4 link 5 union 7 meeting 8 assembly, marriage 9 confluent 10 contiguity, convergent
combining form: 3 gam- 4 gamo-
name meaning ~: 4 Levi
point: 4 link, seam 5 ridge 8 juncture 9 stitching 10 connection
joint: 3 bar, ell, pub, tee, tie 4 crux, dive, dump, home, jail, knee, link, mixt, node, seam, spot, stir 5 ankle, elbow, haunt, hinge, mixed, nexus, place, wrist 6 common, corner, mutual, prison, shared, splice, swivel, tavern, united, wedded 7 bracket, co-owned, domicil, grouped, hangout, knuckle, related, shelter 8 abutment, combined, communal, conjunct, coupling, domicile, junction, juncture, taphouse, vinculum 9 concerted, corporate, honky-tonk, nightclub, nightspot, speakeasy 10 agreed upon, collective, connection, restaurant
after-hours ~: 7 cabaret 9 nightclub, nightspot 10 supper club
arm ~: 5 elbow, wrist
beer ~: 3 bar, pub 6 saloon, tavern
blow the ~: 2 go 4 exit, quit 5 leave 6 bow out, cut out, decamp, depart, get out 7 abscond, bail out, pull out, push off 8 check out, hang it up, knock off, light out, pack it in, run out on, shove off, skip town 9 take a hike, walk out on 10 call it a day
carpentry ~: 5 bevel, miter
combining form: 5 arthr- 6 ancylo-, ankylo-, arthro- 7 anchylo-
filler: 5 grass
get one's nose out of ~: 6 resent
half a ~: 5 tenon 7 mortise
hip ~: 4 coxa
inspect the ~: 4 case, look 5 spy on 6 survey 7 examine 8 check out 10 scrutinize
leg ~: 4 knee 5 ankle
like some ~s: 6 creaky
metalworker's ~: 4 bond, weld 6 solder 8 juncture
miter ~ feature: 5 bevel
out of ~: 5 amiss 7 ominous, unhappy, unlucky 8 ill-timed
pelvic ~: 3 hip
plumber's ~: 3 ell, tee, wye
problem: 4 ache, gout 6 strain, twinge 8 soreness 9 arthritis, throbbing
sealer: 6 luting
sidewalk ~: 5 chink, crack 7 crevice
stem ~: 4 node 8 juncture, swelling
strengthener: 6 gusset
tenant: 3 con 5 felon 7 convict 8 prisoner
venture: 4 co-op
joint __: 3 bar, ill 5 issue, stock, stool 6 return 7 session, venture
joint __ insurance: 4 life
__ joint: 3 gin, hip, lap 4 clip, jook, juke 5 out of
Joint Chiefs off.: 3 adm., CNO, gen.
__-jointed: 5 loose 6 double
Join the __!: 4 club
jointly: 8 mutually, together 9 in concert 10 hand in hand
prefix: 3 col-, com-, con-
__-joint pliers: 4 slip
joints, like some: 5 stiff
joist: 4 beam 6 girder, rafter, timber
JoJo (1980 song)
artist: Boz Scaggs
jojoba: 3 oil 5 shrub
joke: 3 gag, kid, pun, rib, yak, yok, yuk 4 fool, jape, jest, josh, lark, play, quip, yock, yuck 5 antic, caper, chaff, clown, crack, cut up, farce, humor, laugh, prank, sally, spoof, tease 6 banter, bon mot, corker, gambol, gasser, japery

7 buffoon, caprice, mockery 8 drollery, escapade, nonsense, one-liner, raillery 9 crack wise, kid around, wisecrack, witticism 10 fool around, knock-knock, pleasantry, rib tickler
as a ~: 5 in fun 6 for fun, in jest 10 humorously
ender: 4 ster
enjoy a ~: 4 crow, grin, hoot, howl, roar, yuck 5 laugh, smile, snort, whoop 6 cackle, giggle, guffaw, scream, titter 7 chortle, chuckle, crack up, snicker, snigger
funny ~: 4 howl, riot 6 scream
knock-knock ~: 3 pun 8 wordplay
no ~: 4 ugly 5 heavy, tough 6 severe, urgent 7 arduous, crucial, serious, weighty 8 menacing, sobering, terrible 9 dangerous, difficult, laborious, momentous, strenuous 10 formidable
object of a ~: 4 butt, dupe 5 chump, patsy 7 fall guy
practical ~: 4 dido, hoax, jape, quiz 5 prank, sport, trick
react to a bad ~: 4 moan 5 groan, wince 6 flinch 7 grimace
response: 4 ha-ha 5 laugh 6 ha-ha-ha, I get it
response, informally: 4 laff
response to an online ~: 3 LOL
tell a ~: 5 amuse 6 regale
trite ~: 4 corn
writer: 6 gagman
__ joke: 6 inside 7 running
__-Joke: 5 Dial-a
joker: 3 sap, wag, wit 4 boob, card, clod, zany 5 chump, clown, cluck, comic, cutup, ninny, patsy, scamp 6 gagman, jester, kidder, person, scream, sucker, turkey 7 buffoon, farceur, fathead, gagster, half-wit, proviso, punster, saphead, wise guy 8 comedian, funnyman, humorist, numskull, obstacle, quipster, wild card, wiseacre 9 lamebrain, numbskull, prankster, provision
at times: 4 wild
see also ninny
Joker
foe: 5 Robin 6 Batman
Joker's Wild, The: game show
host: Jack Barry, Bill Cullen, Jim Peck
Joker, The (1973 song)
artist: Steve Miller Band
joke's __!, The: 4 on me 5 on you
jokester: 3 wag, wit 4 card 5 comic 6 jester 8 comedian, humorist, kibitzer, quipster
query: 5 get it
routine: 3 act
jokey: 5 funny, jolly 6 jovial 7 amusing, jocular 8 humorous 9 laughable
joking: 3 fun 5 humor, sport 6 banter, comedy, levity 7 jesting, jocular 8 badinage, raillery, zaniness 9 facetious 10 not serious
all ~ aside: 9 seriously, sincerely
__-joking: 4 half
jokingly: 5 in fun 6 in jest
in music: 7 giocoso
Jolene: 7 Blalock
Jolie: 5 Gabor 8 Angelina
daughter: 3 Eva 6 Zsa Zsa
Jolie, Angelina: 7 actress
father: Jon Voight
film: Alexander (2004)
The Bone Collector (1999)
Changeling (2008)
Girl, Interrupted (1999, AA)
Lara Croft: Tomb Raider (2001)
Life or Something Like It (2002)
A Mighty Heart (2007)
Mr. & Mrs. Smith (2005)
Original Sin (2001)
Pushing Tin (1999)
Wanted (2008)
spouse: Jonny Lee Miller, Billy Bob Thornton
Joliet: 4 city, town 5 Louis
locale: 8 Illinois
Joliet, Louis: 6 French 8 explorer
discovery: 4 Erie
Joliot-Curie: 5 Irène 8 Frédéric
Joliot-Curie, Frédéric: 6 French 7 chemist 8 Nobelist
Joliot-Curie, Irène: 6 French 7 chemist 8 Nobelist 9 physicist
jollies: 3 fun 5 kicks 7 thrills 8 pleasure 9 amusement 10 excitement
jollity: 3 fun 4 glee 5 mirth, revel, sport 6 gaiety, gayety 7 elation, gayness, revelry 8 buoyance, buoyancy, hilarity 9 festivity, jocundity, joviality, lightness, merriment
bit of ~: 5 laugh
jolly: 3 gay 4 boon, joky 5 funny, happy, jokey, merry, sunny 6 blithe, bouncy, bright, bubbly, cheery, chirpy, festal, genial, hearty, jocose, jocund, jovial, joyful, joyous 7 buoyant, chipper, festive, gleeful, jocular, joshing, lay it on, playful 8 carefree, cheerful, jubilant, laughing, mirthful, pleasant, sportive 9 convivial, enjoyable, full of fun, fun-loving, hilarious, sprightly, vivacious 10 frolicsome, rollicking
boat: 4 yawl
to the British: 4 very
Jolly __: 5 Roger 7 Rancher
Jolly __ Giant: 5 Green
...__ jolly good fellow: 4 he's a
jollying: 6 jovial 7 coaxing 8 cajolery 9 wheedling
Jolly Rancher: 5 candy
Jolly Roger: 4 flag
depiction: 5 skull 10 crossbones
Jolly Roger crewman: 4 Smee
Jolly Toper, The
painter: Frans Hals
Jolly Trio
painter: Frans Hals
Jolson, Al
contemporary: 6 Cantor, Jessel
real first name: 3 Asa
song: April Showers (1922)
California, Here I Come! (1924)
I'm Sitting on Top of the World (1926)
Let Me Sing and I'm Happy (1930)
Liza (1929)
My Mammy (1928)
Rock-a-Bye Your Baby With a Dixie Melody (1918)
Sonny Boy (1928)
Swanee (1920)
There's a Rainbow Round My Shoulder (1928)
Toot Toot Tootsie (1922)
spouse: Ruby Keeler
Jolson Story, The (1946 film)
cast: William Demarest, Evelyn Keyes, Larry Parks
jolt: 3 jar, zap 4 bang, blow, bump, daze, jerk, kick, push, rock, stun, toss 5 amaze, clash, crash, floor, punch, shake, shock, upset 6 impact, jostle, jounce, justle, rattle, recoil, trauma, wallop 7 astound, disturb, setback, shake up, stagger, startle 8 astonish, backlash, bang into, bowl over, bump into, disquiet, reversal, surprise, unstring, uppercut 9 bombshell, collision, galvanize 10 discompose, disconcert, earthquake, incitement
jolted: 5 agape 6 amazed 7 shocked, stunned 10 dumbstruck
Joltin' Joe: 8 DiMaggio
brother: 3 Dom 5 Vince
joltless joe: 5 decaf, Sanka
Jomo: 8 Kenyatta
Jon: 4 Agee, Hall, Lord, Seda 5 Amiel, Avnet, Brion, Cryer, Heder, Karon 6 Bauman, Lovitz, Peters, Secada, Tenney, Voight 7 Bon Jovi, Stewart, Vickers 8 Arbuckle, Walmsley 10 Turteltaub
Jon-__ Hexum: 4 Erik
Jonah: 4 jinx
father: 7 Amittai
follower: 5 Micah
preceder: 7 Obadiah
Jonas: 4 Salk 7 Savimbi
Jonas Brothers: Joe, Kevin, Nick
Jonathan: 4 Frid, Lynn 5 apple, Demme, Pryce, Swift 6 Frakes, Harris, Kaplan, Larson, Penner 7 Edwards, Winters 8 Lipnicki 9 Kellerman, Silverman
father: 4 Saul
relative: *see* apple
Jonathan Livingston Seagull
author: Richard Bach
Jon-Erik: 5 Hexum
Jones: 3 Joe, Tom 4 Amos, Bert, Davy, Dean, Etta, Indy, Jack, Oran 5 Allan, Bobby, Brian, Casey, Chuck, Cleon, Elvin, Grace, Inigo, Isham, James, Jenny, Jimmy, Leroi, Spike 6 Anissa, Deacon, Donell, George, Howard, Quincy 7 Barnaby, Carolyn, Grandpa, Indiana, January, Jeffrey, Rashida, Shirley 8 Jennifer, John Paul, Parnelli
__ Jones: 3 Dow, Tom 4 Davy 6 Carmen 7 Barnaby
Jones, Allan: 5 actor 6 singer
son: Jack
spouse: Irene Hervey
Jones, Barnaby
portrayer: Buddy Ebsen
Jones, Bobby: 6 golfer
Jonesboro: 4 city, town
locale: 8 Arkansas
Jones, Carolyn: 7 actress
spouse: Aaron Spelling
TV: The Addams Family
Jones, Casey vehicle: 5 train
Jones, Davy locker: 3 sea 5 ocean
Jones, Deacon
sport: 8 football
Jones' financial partner: 3 Dow
Jones, George: 6 singer
spouse: Tammy Wynette
Jones, Indiana
quest: 3 ark 5 Grail 9 Holy Grail
Jones, Jack
father: Allan
spouse: Jill St. John
Jones, James: 6 writer
work: From Here to Eternity
The Pistol
Some Came Running
The Thin Red Line
Viet Journal
Jones, James Earl: 5 actor
film: Coming to America (1988)
Conan the Barbarian (1982)
Convicts (1991)
Cry, the Beloved Country (1995)
Dr. Strangelove (1964)
Field of Dreams (1989)
Gardens of Stone (1987)
The Great White Hope (1970)
Jefferson in Paris (1995)
My Little Girl (1986)
A Piece of the Action (1977)
The River Niger (1976)
Sommersby (1993)
voice: The Empire Strikes Back (1980)
The Return of the Jedi (1983)
Star Wars (1977)
Jones, Jennifer: 7 actress
spouse: David O. Selznick
Jones, Parnelli: 5 racer 9 auto racer
milieu: 5 track
Jones, Quincy: 8 musician
record label: Qwest
spouse: Peggy Lipton
__ Jones's Diary: 7 Bridget
Jones, Shirley: 7 actress
film: Carousel (1956)
Elmer Gantry (1960, AA)
The Music Man (1962)
Oklahoma! (1955)
spouse: Jack Cassidy, Marty Ingels
TV: The Partridge Family
__ Jones's locker: 4 Davy
Jones, Tom
homeland: Wales
song: Delilah (1968)
Green, Green Grass of Home (1967)
I'll Never Fall in Love Again (1969)
It's Not Unusual (1965)
Love Me Tonight (1969)
She's a Lady (1971)
Thunderball (1966)
What's New Pussycat? (1965)
Without Love (1970)
Jones, Tommy Lee: 5 actor
film: Batman Forever (1995)
The Betsy (1978)
The Big Town (1987)
Blue Sky (1994)
The Client (1994)
Coal Miner's Daughter (1980)
Cobb (1994)
Double Jeopardy (1999)
Eyes of Laura Mars (1978)
The Fugitive (1993, AA)
The Hunted (2003)
JFK (1991)
Men in Black (1997)

The Missing (2003)
No Country for Old Men (2007)
Rules of Engagement (2000)
Space Cowboys (2000)
Stormy Monday (1988)
Under Siege (1992)
U.S. Marshals (1998)
Volcano (1997)

Jong, Erica: 6 writer
work: Any Woman's Blues
Fanny
Fear of Fifty
Fear of Flying
Half-Lives
How to Save Your Own Life
Loveroot
Parachutes and Kisses
Serenissima
Shylock's Daughter

___-jongg: 3 mah
Joni: 5 James **8** Mitchell
Jonny Quest dog: 6 Bandit
jonquil: 5 plant **6** flower
Jonson, Ben: 4 poet **6** writer **7** British **10** playwright
genre: 3 ode
work: The Alchemist
Epicene
Every Man in His Humour
Tale of a Tub
To Celia
Volpone

Jonze, Spike: 8 director
film: Being John Malkovich
spouse: Sofia Coppola

jook ___: 5 joint
___ & Joon: 5 Benny
Jooss, Kurt: 6 dancer **7** danseur
specialty: 6 ballet
Joplin: 4 city, town **5** Janis, Scott
locale: 8 Missouri
Joplin, Janis
nickname: Pearl
song: Me and Bobby McGee (1971)
Joplin, Scott: 8 composer
genre: 3 rag **7** ragtime
work: The Cascades
The Easy Winners
Elite Syncopations
The Entertainer
Euphonic Sounds
Maple Leaf Rag
Solace
Treemonisha

Jordan: 3 Jim **4** Neil **5** river **6** Knight, Marian, nation **7** Barbara, country, Michael, Montell, Richard, Stanley **8** Hamilton
ancient city: 5 Petra
ancient kingdom near ~: 5 Ammon
bovine: 6 Baladi
capital: 5 Amman
city: 5 Akaba, Amman, Aqaba, Irbid, Zarqa **7** Az-Zarqa
desert: 6 Syrian
former queen of ~: 4 Alia, Noor
group: 10 Arab League
lake: 7 Dead Sea
money: 4 fils **5** dinar
mountain: 4 Nebo **6** Gilead, Pisgah
neighbor: 4 Irak, Iraq **5** Syria **6** Israel **11** Saudi Arabia
once: 4 Moab
River locale: 6 Israel **7** Lebanon
river to the ~: 6 Yarmuk
sea: 4 Dead
where ~ is: 4 Asia **7** Mideast

Jordan ___: 5 curve **6** almond
___ Jordan: 3 Air
Jordana: 8 Brewster
Jordanian: 4 Arab
neighbor: 5 Saudi
Jordan, Michael
milieu: 5 court
org.: 3 NBA
sport: 10 basketball
Jor-El
son: 5 Kal-El **8** Superman
wife: 4 Lara
Jorge: 5 Adoum, Amado **7** Edwards, Guillén **8** Manrique
in English: 6 George
see also Spanish
Jorge ___ Borges: 4 Luis
___ Jorge: 3 Sao
Jorja: 3 Fox
jorum: 4 bowl **9** punchbowl
Jory: 6 Victor
Jo's Boys
author: Louisa May Alcott
Jose ___ Olazabal: 5 Maria
José: 4 Sert **5** Greco, Limón, Martí, Rizal, Silva **6** Donoso, Ferrer, Iturbi, Orozco, Rivera **7** Canseco, Jimenez **8** Carreras, Saramago **9** Echegaray, Feliciano **10** Capablanca, Ramos-Horta
see also Spanish
José ___ Duarte: 8 Napoleón
José ___ Martín: 5 de San
___ José: 3 San
Josef: 5 Krips **6** Sommer **7** Hofmann **9** Pilsudski, Skvorecky
in English: 6 Joseph
Josef ___ Sternberg: 3 von
Jose Maria: 6 Eguren **8** Arguedas, Olazabal **9** Gironella
José Napoleón ___: 6 Duarte
Joseph: 4 Kane, Papp **5** Alsop, Banks, Biden, Black, Haydn, Henry, Losey, Renan, Ruben, saint, Smith **6** Alioto, Bramah, Conrad, Cotten, Furphy, Heller, Kearns, Lister, Monier, Murray, Pevney, Stalin, Strick, Taylor, Wapner **7** Anthony, Barbera, Bologna, Bottoms, Brodsky, Fiennes, Glidden, Joachim, Rotblat, Sargent, Szigeti, Thomson, Wiseman **8** Califano, Erlanger, Lagrange, Pulitzer, Stiglitz, Wambaugh **9** Gay-Lussac, Goldstein, Priestley **10** Mankiewicz
brother: 3 Dan, Gad **4** Levi **5** Asher, Jesus, Judah **6** Reuben, Simeon **7** Zebulun **8** Benjamin, Issachar, Naphtali
father: 5 Jacob
in German: 5 Josef
in Italian: 8 Giuseppe
in Spanish: 4 José
mantle: 4 coat
mother: 6 Rachel
sister: 5 Dinah
son: 4 Igal **7** Ephraim **8** Manasseh
wife: 7 Asenath
___ Josepha Hale: 5 Sarah

Joseph and His Brothers
author: Thomas Mann
Joseph and the Amazing Technicolor Dreamcoat: 7 musical
composer: Andrew Lloyd Webber, Tim Rice
Joseph Ernest ___: 5 Renan
___ Joseph Haydn: 5 Franz
Josephine: 3 Tey **4** Hull **5** Baker, Miles
Joseph P. ___: 7 Kennedy
José Ramos-___: 5 Horta
___ Josey Wales, The: 6 Outlaw
josh: 3 guy, kid, rib **4** jest, jive, joke **5** chaff, tease **6** banter **8** ridicule
Josh: 5 Logan, Lucas **6** Brolin, Gibson, Mostel **7** Charles, Saviano **8** Billings, Hartnett
joshing: 5 jolly **6** banter, jovial **7** jocular **8** badinage, humorous, raillery **9** facetious, laughable
Joshua: 5 Logan **7** Jackson **8** Reynolds **9** Lederberg
composer: George Frideric Handel
father: 3 Nun
follower: 6 Judges
preceder: 11 Deuteronomy
tree: 5 yucca
Joshua Tree: 4 park
locale: 10 California
Josiah: 5 Royce, Spode **8** Wedgwood
Josip: 4 Broz
Joslyn: 5 Allyn
___ Jo Sperber: 6 Wendie
Josquin ___ Prez: 3 des
joss: 4 idol
burn a ~ stick: 5 cense
house: 6 temple
stick: 7 incense
Joss: 5 Addie, Stone **6** Whedon **7** Ackland
jostle: 3 jab, jar, jog, mob **4** bump, jolt, poke, push **5** elbow, knock, nudge, shake, shove **6** joggle, jounce, stir up, thrust **7** scuffle, squeeze **8** bang into, scramble
jot: 3 bit, dot, tad **4** atom, iota, mite, mote, spot, whit **5** grain, pinch, shred, spark, speck, straw, touch, trace, write **6** doodle, tittle, trifle **7** minimum, modicum, smidgen, smidgin **8** molecule, particle, smidgeon, take down **9** little bit, scintilla
down: 3 pen **4** note **5** write **6** record
jota: 5 dance
jot and ___: 6 tittle
jotting: 4 memo, note **8** notation, reminder **10** memorandum
joual: 7 dialect
Jouhaux: 4 Léon
Jouhaux, Léon: 6 French **8** Nobelist
joule fraction: 3 erg
Joule, James: 7 British **9** physicist
jounce: 3 bob, jar, jog **4** bump, jerk, jolt, rock **5** quake, shake **6** bobble, bounce, impact, jiggle, joggle, jostle, justle, rattle
jouncy: 5 bumpy, rocky, rough, stony **6** choppy, uneven **7** jarring **9** turbulent
jour: 3 day **5** jeudi, lundi, mardi **6** French, samedi **8** dimanche, mercredi, vendredi
bon ~: 7 welcome **8** greeting
carte du ~: 4 list, menu **10** bill of fare
early in the ~: 5 matin
time of ~: 4 nuit
Jourdan: 5 Louis
Jour de Fête (1949 film)
cast: Jacques Tati
journal: 3 log, mag **4** book **5** daily, diary, organ, paper, print **6** ledger, memoir, record, review **7** account, daybook, Filofax, gazette, logbook, tabloid, writing **8** magazine, register **9** chronicle, newspaper, recountal **10** chronology, periodical
ender: 3 ese
note: 4 item **5** entry **6** record
online ~: 4 blog
page: 3 day
ship's ~: 3 log **4** book **5** diary **6** record **7** account, daybook, logbook
trade ~: 5 organ **6** review **8** magazine **10** instrument, periodical
VIP: 2 ed. **6** editor **9** publisher
Journal: 5 paper **9** newspaper
locale: 8 Edmonton, Montreal
Journal ___ Plague Year: 5 of the
___ Journal: 4 Viet
journal bronze: 5 alloy
component: 3 tin **4** lead, zinc **6** copper
Journal-Bulletin: 5 paper **9** newspaper
locale: 10 Providence
Journal-Constitution: 5 paper **9** newspaper
locale: 7 Atlanta
journalism: 4 news **5** press **6** estate **7** writing **9** reportage, reporting
deg.: 2 MJ
___ journalism: 5 print, video **6** yellow
___ Journalism: 3 New
journalist: 5 press **6** author, scribe, writer **8** reporter, stringer **9** announcer, columnist, publicist, scrivener, wordsmith **10** ink slinger, newsperson
approach: 5 angle, pitch, slant, twist **7** opinion **9** viewpoint
credit: 6 byline
list: 6 five w's
need: 3 pad **4** copy **7** note pad
question: 3 how, who, why **4** what, when **5** where
starter: 5 photo
style: 5 gonzo
journalize: 3 log **5** write **6** record **8** take down
Journal of the Plague Year
author: Daniel Defoe
Journal Sentinel: 5 paper **9** newspaper
locale: 9 Milwaukee
journey: 2 go **3** fly, run **4** hike, lift, ride, roam, rove, tour, trek, trip **5** drive, jaunt, march, quest **6** cruise, flight, hegira, hejira, junket, outing, ramble, repair, safari, travel, voyage, wander **7** caravan, migrate, odyssey, passage, proceed, push off **8** long haul, movement, navigate, progress **9** adventure, excursion, globetrot, itinerary, migration, wandering, wayfaring **10** expedition, knock about, pilgrimage

begin a ~: 2 go 4 sail 5 leave, start 6 embark, set off, set out 7 emplane, entrain, jump off, set sail, ship out 8 go aboard, set forth 9 leave port, undertake
hero's ~: 5 quest 6 voyage 7 crusade, mission 9 adventure 10 expedition
in Latin: 4 iter
over: 5 cover, cross 8 traverse
segment: 3 leg 5 stage
Journey
author: Danielle Steel
song: Be Good to Yourself (1986)
Don't Stop Believin' (1981)
Only the Young (1985)
Open Arms (1982)
Separate Ways (1983)
Who's Crying Now (1981)
Journey __ a Dustless Room: 4 Into
Journey __ Fear: 4 Into
__ Journey: 4 Dark 5 Night
journeyer: 5 gypsy, rover 7 drifter, pilgrim, rambler, tourist, trekker, voyager 8 traveler, vagabond, wanderer, wayfarer 9 itinerant, passenger, sojourner, transient 10 adventurer
journeying: 6 errant 8 vagabond 9 itinerant, on the road, wayfaring
Journey Into a Dustless Room
author: Nelly Sachs
Journey Into Fear
author: Eric Ambler
journeyman: 6 joiner, master, worker 7 artisan 9 carpenter, craftsman
Journey of Natty __, The: 4 Gann
Journey to Jericho
author: Scott O'Dell
Journey to the Center of the Earth
author: Jules Verne
journeywork: 4 moil, toil 5 craft, labor, skill, trade 7 travail 8 drudgery
joust: 4 duel, spar, tilt 6 combat 7 compete 10 tournament
competitor: 6 knight 7 fighter, warrior 8 champion, defender, horseman
need: 5 armor, lance
ready to ~: 5 atilt
jousting: 5 atilt, sport
Jo Van __: 5 Fleet
Jove: 3 god 7 Jupiter
equivalent: 4 Zeus
__ Jovi: 3 Bon 6 Jon Bon
jovial: 3 gay 4 airy, glad, joky 5 happy, jokey, jolly, merry, sunny 6 blithe, bouncy, cheery, chirpy, genial, hearty, jocose, jocund, joyful, joyous, upbeat 7 affable, amiable, buoyant, chipper, cordial, festive, gleeful, jocular, joshing, larking, pleased, tickled 8 blissful, carefree, cheerful, ecstatic, euphoric, exultant, humorous, jollying, jubilant, laughing, mirthful, pleasant, sociable, thrilled 9 congenial, convivial, delighted, facetious, hilarious, overjoyed, rejoicing 10 delightful, frolicsome, rollicking, unbothered
joviality: 4 glee 5 mirth 6 frolic, gaiety, gayety 7 elation, jollity 8 airiness, hilarity 9 festivity, geniality, happiness, jocundity, merriment 10 good nature
Jovian: 7 emperor
planet: 6 Saturn, Uranus 7 Jupiter, Neptune
Jovovich: 5 Milla
Jowett: 8 Benjamin
jowl: 3 jaw 4 chop 5 cheek 6 dewlap, muzzle, wattle 8 mandible
cheek by ~: 4 near 5 close, dense, thick 6 beside, packed 7 crowded 8 abutting, adjacent, touching 9 congested, jam-packed 10 near-at-hand
joy: 3 fun 4 glee, kick 5 bliss, cheer, humor, mirth 6 frolic, gaiety, gayety 7 delight, ecstasy, elation, emotion, gayness, rapture, revelry, triumph 8 euphoria, felicity, gladness, hilarity, pleasure, radiance, radiancy 9 good humor, happiness, jubilance, lightness, merriment 10 ebullience, exultation, jubilation
bundle of ~: 3 tot 4 baby 6 infant 7 bambino, newborn, toddler 9 little one
causing ~: 8 cheering, gladsome, pleasant, pleasing
ender: 4 ride 5 stick
ending: 3 ful, ous
exclamation of ~: 2 ah 3 aah, yay, yea, yes, yow 4 evoe, whee, yeah 5 huzza 6 hoorah, hooray, hot dog, hurrah, hurray, huzzah, yippee 7 whoopee, whoopie 8 all right 10 hallelujah
fill with ~: 5 elate
jump for ~: 5 exult 9 celebrate
jumping for ~: 4 high 5 happy 6 elated 7 beaming, gleeful 8 ecstatic, euphoric, exultant, in heaven, jubilant 9 ebullient 10 flying high, triumphant
name meaning ~: 4 Gail 5 Alisa 6 Alissa
pride and ~: 8 treasure
sign of ~ maybe: 4 tear 8 teardrop
starter: 4 kill
wish ~ to: 4 fete 5 honor, toast 10 compliment, felicitate
with ~: 5 gaily, gayly 7 happily
joy __: 6 buzzer
Joy: 5 Behar 6 Robert 7 Adamson, Philbin 8 Leatrice 9 detergent
alternative: 4 Ajax, Dawn 7 Cascade 8 Sunlight 9 Palmolive 10 Electrasol
Joy __ Club, The: 4 Luck
Joy __ World: 5 to the
__ Joy: 4 Floy 5 Ode to 6 Almond
Joyce: 4 Cary, Ella 5 Hyser, James 6 DeWitt, Kilmer 8 Brothers, Randolph 9 Van Patten
Joyce __ Oates: 5 Carol
Joyce, James: 5 Irish 6 writer
homeland: 4 Eire, Erin
wife: 4 Nora
work: The Dubliners
Exiles
Finnegans Wake
A Portrait of the Artist as a Young Man
Ulysses
Joycelyn: 6 Elders
Joyeux __: 4 Noel
joyful: 3 gay 4 glad, high 5 blest, happy, jolly, merry, sunny 6 blithe, bright, cheery, elated, enrapt, festal, genial, golden, jovial, upbeat 7 beaming, blessed, excited, festive, gleeful, halcyon, pleased, radiant, tickled 8 blissful, cheerful, ecstatic, euphoric, exultant, grooving, jubilant, laughing, mirthful, thrilled 9 delighted, gratified, overjoyed, rapturous, rejoicing 10 enraptured, flying high, heartening, rollicking, triumphant
cry: 3 aah 4 whee 5 whoop
make ~: 7 beatify 8 enthrall 9 enrapture, transport
joyfulness: 4 glee 5 cheer 7 ecstasy 8 hilarity 9 festivity 10 enthusiasm
joyless: 3 low, sad 4 blue, cold, dark, glum, mopy 5 black, bleak, dusky, mopey, sorry, woful 6 bleary, broody, dismal, dreary, droopy, gloomy, morose, somber, woeful 7 doleful, in a funk, unhappy 8 dejected, desolate, downcast, mournful, troubled 9 bummed out, cheerless, depressed, heartsick, miserable, saddening, sorrowful, woebegone 10 chapfallen, depressing, dispirited, lugubrious, melancholy
Joy Luck Club, The
author: Amy Tan
Joyner-Kersee: 6 Jackie
__, Joy of Man's Desiring: 4 Jesu
Joy of Signing, The subj.: 3 ASL
joyous: 3 gay 4 glad 5 blest, happy, jolly, merry, sunny 6 blithe, bright, cheery, elated, festal, genial, golden, jovial, upbeat 7 blessed, excited, festive, gleeful, pleased, radiant, tickled 8 blissful, cheerful, ecstatic, euphoric, exultant, jubilant, mirthful, sporting, sportive, thrilled 9 delighted, gladdened, gratified, lightsome, overjoyed, rapturous, rejoicing, sprightly 10 enraptured, flying high, heartening, rollicking, triumphant
joyousness: 4 glee 5 cheer, mirth 6 gaiety, gayety 7 ecstasy 8 euphoria 10 exaltation, exultation
joyride: 4 spin 5 drive, jaunt
joystick, use a: 6 aviate
Joy to the World: 4 hymn
Joy to the World (1971 song)
artist: Three Dog Night
József, Attila: 4 poet 9 Hungarian
J.P.: 6 Morgan 8 Donleavy, Marquand
flee to a ~: 5 elope 6 run off 8 slip away
__ J. Pakula: 4 Alan
J. Paul: 5 Getty
JPEG
alternative: 3 gif, tif
__ J. Pollard: 7 Michael
jr.
eldest, maybe: 3 III
exam: 4 PSAT
grade officer: 5 lieut.
last yr.'s ~: 2 sr. 3 snr.
next year's ~: 4 soph.
J.R.: 5 Ewing
foe: 5 Cliff 6 Barnes
parent: 4 Jock 5 Ellie
J.R.R.: 7 Tolkien
part of ~: 5 Reuel
J.T.: 5 Walsh
J. Thaddeus __: 4 Toad
__ J. Travanti: 6 Daniel
Juan: 4 Gris, Ruiz 5 Benet, Perón, Rulfo 6 Boscán, Carlos 7 Jiménez 8 Cabrillo, Marichal, Montalvo
in English: 4 John
wife: 3 Eva 5 Evita 6 Isabel
see also Spanish
Juan __: 6 Carlos
__ Juan: 3 Don, San
Juana
see Spanish
__ Juana: 3 Tia
__ Juana Cruz: 3 Sor
__ Juan Capistrano: 3 San
Juan Carlos: 3 rey 4 king 7 Spanish
daughter: 5 Elena
Juan de Fuca __: 6 Strait
__ Juan DeMarco: 3 Don
Juan Fernándes: 7 islands
__ Juan Hill: 3 San
Juanita: 4 Hall 5 Kreps
see also Spanish
Juárez: 4 city, town 6 Benito
locale: 6 Mexico 9 Chihuahua
see also Spanish
juba: 5 dance
Juba: 5 river
locale: 6 Africa 7 Somalia 8 Ethiopia
Jubal: 5 Early
jubilance: 3 joy 4 glee 7 ecstasy, triumph 8 hilarity 10 exultation
express ~: 4 hoot, yell 5 cheer, shout, whoop 6 holler, hurrah, scream, shriek 7 exclaim
jubilant: 3 gay 4 glad 5 happy, jolly, merry, sunny 6 blithe, cheery, elated, jovial, joyful, joyous, upbeat 7 excited, festive, gleeful, pleased, tickled 8 blissful, cheerful, ecstatic, euphoric, exultant, grooving, laughing, mirthful, thrilled 9 delighted, gladdened, gratified, lightsome, overjoyed, rapturous, rejoicing 10 enraptured, flying high, heartening, triumphant
be ~: 5 exult 7 rejoice 9 celebrate
make ~: 5 elate 6 thrill, turn on 7 delight, gladden, hearten 9 inebriate 10 exhilarate, intoxicate
jubilate: 4 crow 5 exult, glory 7 delight, rejoice, triumph
jubilation: 3 joy 4 glee 7 ecstasy, elation, rapture, triumph 8 euphoria, felicity, pleasure, rhapsody 9 happiness 10 exaltation, exultation
jubilee: 2 do 4 bash, fete, gala 5 party 6 fiesta, revels 7 blowout, holiday, revelry, shindig, triumph 8 birthday, carnival, feast day, festival, jamboree, shivaree, wingding 9 festivity
diamond ~ number: 5 sixty
__ jubilee: 6 golden, silver 7 diamond
Jubilee: 7 musical
author: Margaret Walker
composer: Cole Porter
Judah: 6 Ben-Hur, ha-Levi
brother: 3 Dan, Gad 4 Levi 5 Asher 6 Joseph, Reuben, Simeon 7 Zebulun 8 Benjamin, Issachar, Naphtali

child: 4 Onan 5 Shela 6 Shelah
city in ~: 4 Enam, Lehi
king of ~: 3 Asa
parent: 4 Leah 5 Jacob
sister: 5 Dinah
Judaic: 6 Jewish
literature: 4 Tora 5 Torah
Judaism: 3 rel. 8 religion
see also Jewish
Judas: 7 traitor 8 betrayer, turncoat
brother: 5 Jesus
kiss: 9 duplicity
Judas ___: 4 tree 6 Priest
Judas, My Brother
author: Frank Yerby
Judd: 5 Naomi 6 Ashley, Hirsch, Nelson 7 Wynonna
Judd, Ashley: 7 actress
film: Crossing Over (2009)
De-Lovely (2004)
Double Jeopardy (1999)
Frida (2002)
High Crimes (2002)
Kiss the Girls (1997)
Ruby in Paradise (1993)
Simon Birch (1998)
mother: Naomi
sister: Wynonna
TV: Sisters

judder: 6 rattle, shimmy 7 vibrate
Jude: 3 Law 5 saint
follower: 10 Revelation
preceder: 4 John
___ Jude: 3 Hey
Judea: 8 Holy Land
king of ~: 5 Herod
Judean Plateau
locale: 6 Israel
Judeo-Spanish: 6 Ladino
Jude the Obscure
author: Thomas Hardy
character: 3 Sue 4 Anny, Donn 5 Sarah 6 Fawley 8 Arabella
judge: 3 say, try 4 cadi, call, deem, find, hold, make, rank, rate, rule, view 5 bench, check, count, court, gauge, guess, infer, jurat, rater, think, trier 6 assess, critic, decide, decree, deduce, hearer, jurist, reckon, regard, settle, size up, umpire 7 arbiter, believe, discern, examine, measure, mediate, referee 8 appraise, conclude, consider, estimate, evaluate, his Honor, keep tabs, look upon, moderate, penalize, sentence 9 arbitrate, ascertain, authority, criticize, determine, evaluator, inspector, interpose, moderator, preordain, pronounce 10 arbitrator, magistrate, negotiator
address: 3 hon. 9 honorable, Your Honor
as bad: 3 pan, rap 4 bash, damn, flay, slam 5 blame, blast, decry, knock, roast, trash 6 assail, berate, impugn, oppugn, rail at 7 censure, condemn, run down 8 belittle, denounce, talk down 9 criticize, cut to bits, disparage, excoriate, find fault, frown upon, skin alive 10 come down on, disapprove
bring before a ~: 3 try
chambers: 6 camera
come before a ~: 6 appear
concern: 5 guilt, trial 8 evidence
demand: 4 cite, fiat 5 edict, order, ukase 6 charge, decree, dictum, ruling 7 booking, mandate, precept 8 sentence 9 directive 10 injunction
expertise: 3 law
job: 4 case, suit 5 trial 7 lawsuit 9 probation 10 indictment, litigation
missing ~: 6 Crater
Muslim ~: 4 cadi, kadi, qadi, qaid
need: 4 gown, jury, robe 5 gavel
Old Testament ~: 3 Eli
order: 4 hold, stay 5 defer, delay, waive 6 arrest, detain, shelve 7 adjourn, suspend 8 postpone, prohibit, reprieve
seat: 4 banc 5 bench
sports ~: 3 ref, ump 6 umpire 7 referee
tell the ~: 3 sue 5 argue, plead 6 appeal 7 declare 8 petition
___ judge: 7 circuit
Judge: 4 Mike 8 Reinhold
Judge ___: 5 Dredd
judge advocate ___: 7 general
Judge Dredd
role: 4 Ilsa
Judge Not
author: Sholem Asch
Judges
follower: 4 Ruth
preceder: 6 Joshua
town in ~: 4 Lehi
Judge, The
author: Rebecca West
Judging ___: 3 Amy
Judging Amy (CBS drama)
cast: Amy Brenneman (Judge Amy Gray)
Tyne Daly (Maxine Gray)
judgment: 3 act, wit 4 tact, view, wits 5 grasp, guess, logic, savvy, sense, slant, stock, taste 6 acumen, belief, choice, decree, rating, reason, ruling, sanity, wisdom 7 feeling, finding, opinion, thought, verdict 8 analysis, capacity, critique, decision, estimate, position, prudence, sagacity, sapience, sentence 9 appraisal, awareness, deduction, induction, ingenuity, intellect, reasoning, sentiment, sharpness 10 assessment, astuteness, conclusion, discretion, estimation, evaluation, horse sense, perception, resolution, shrewdness
artistic ~: 5 taste
await ~: 4 pend 6 dangle 8 hang fire
breach of ~: 5 error, lapse
court ~: 4 fiat, writ 5 edict, order 6 decree, dictum, ruling 7 mandate, verdict 8 sanction 9 directive 10 injunction
exercise ~: 4 deem, hold, view 6 assess, decide, reckon, regard 7 presume, suppose, surmise
form ~: 3 fix 4 rule 6 choose, decide, settle 7 appoint 8 finalize, sentence 9 determine, establish, negotiate
pass ~: 4 jail, rule 5 assay 6 punish 7 censure, condemn, convict, put away 8 imprison, penalize, sentence
showing good ~: 4 wise 5 lucid, sober, sound 6 steady 7 logical, prudent 8 all there, balanced, moderate, rational, sensible, together 9 judicious, practical, pragmatic, realistic 10 discerning, fair-minded, reasonable, thoughtful
unfair ~: 5 frame 6 bum rap
use poor ~: 3 err 4 flub, goof, muff 5 botch 6 bungle, foul up, mess up, slip up 7 blunder, go wrong, louse up, snarl up, stumble 9 mishandle, mismanage
value ~: 4 idea, view 5 slant, stand 6 belief, notion 7 concept, feeling, opinion, outlook, thought 8 attitude, judgment, position 9 sentiment, viewpoint 10 assessment, conception, conviction, impression, persuasion, philosophy, standpoint
judgment ___: 4 call
___ judgment: 4 snap 5 value
Judgment ___: 3 Day 4 Book
___ Judgment: 4 Last 5 Day of, Final
Judgment at Nuremberg (1961 film)
cast: Montgomery Clift, Marlene Dietrich, Judy Garland, Burt Lancaster, Maximilian Schell, William Shatner, Spencer Tracy, Richard Widmark
director: Stanley Kramer
Judgment of Paris, The
composer: Thomas Arne
Judi: 5 Dench
___ judicata: 3 res
judicial: 5 legal, licit 6 lawful 8 forensic
action: 4 stay 6 appeal, decree, dictum
body: 5 court
garment: 4 gown, robe
inquiry: 6 assize
make a ~ decision: 4 find, rule 5 order 6 decide, decree, ordain 7 preside, resolve 8 sentence 9 prescribe, pronounce
opening: 4 oyes, oyez
system: 3 bar 5 bench, court
writ: 6 elegit
judiciary: 3 bar 5 bench 9 courtroom
judicious: 4 just, keen, sage, sane, wise 5 canny, clean, fussy, right, smart, sober, sound 6 astute, polite, shrewd, subtle, timely 7 careful, finicky, learned, logical, politic, prudent, sapient, tactful 8 cautious, discreet, exacting, finiking, finnicky, informed, moderate, rational, rigorous, sensible, skillful, thorough 9 advisable, assiduous, astucious, attentive, cognizant, courteous, expedient, observant, provident, sagacious, selective, sensitive 10 considered, diplomatic, discerning, farsighted, fastidious, meticulous, particular, perceptive, reasonable, scrupulous, seasonable, thoughtful, well-chosen
judiciousness: 4 care 5 sense 6 sanity, wisdom 8 maturity, prudence, sobriety 9 foresight 10 astuteness, horse sense, shrewdness
Judith: 4 Ivey 5 Crist, Guest, Light 6 Krantz, Viorst, Wright 7 Jamison, Leyster, Rossner 8 Anderson
composer: Thomas Arne
father: 5 Beeri
husband: 4 Esau
in German: 5 Jutta
judo: 5 sport 10 martial art
attire: 2 gi 4 belt
level: 3 dan
originator: 4 Kano
relative: 6 aikido, karate 7 jujitsu
studio: 4 dojo
teacher: 6 sensei
warm-up: 4 kata
Judson, E.Z.C.: 6 writer
pen name: Ned Buntline
subject: Cody
Judy: 5 Blume, Carne, Davis, Tyler 6 Canova, Geeson, Jetson, Rankin 7 Collins, Garland, Landers 8 Holliday
daughter: 4 Liza 5 Lorna
partner: 5 Punch
___: Judy Blue Eyes: 5 Suite
Judy's Turn to Cry (1963 song)
artist: Lesley Gore
jug: 3 pot 4 brig, ewer, jail, poky, wind 5 pokey 6 bottle, flagon, lockup, prison, vessel 7 hoosgow 8 hoosegow 9 container 10 receptacle
ancient ~: 4 olpe
chemist's ~: 6 carboy
contents: 5 cider 9 moonshine
cousin: 5 cruet 6 carafe 7 pitcher
handle: 3 ear
size: 5 quart 6 gallon
jug ___: 4 band, wine
jugal: 4 bone
locale: 5 cheek
jug band
instrument: 5 gazoo, kazoo 8 mirliton
juggernaut: 4 army 5 force
juggle: 3 fix, rig 5 alter 6 change, doctor, joggle 7 falsify, shuffle 10 keep in play, manipulate, tamper with
Juggler, The: 9 tarot card
jugglery: 6 dupery 8 trickery 9 chicanery, deception 10 hocus pocus
juggling: 3 art 5 skill
jughead
see ninny
Jughead: 4 teen 5 Jones
dog: 6 Hot Dog
Jug of Wine, A
poet: Omar Khayyám
___, Jugs & Speed: 6 Mother
jugular
locale: 4 neck
jugular ___: 4 vein
jugum: 4 yoke
juice: 4 fuel 5 clout, drink, fluid, power, vigor 6 energy, gossip, liquid, nectar, thrill 7 potable, potence, potency, scandal 8 beverage, solution, strength, vitality 9 influence, stimulate, subsidize 10 exuberance, percentage
bang ~: 5 nitro
combining form: 3 opo- 4 chyl- 5 chili-, chylo-
digestive ~: 4 bile
drink: 3 ade 5 cider
extract ~: 4 ream
fermented ~: 5 cider

flavor: **4** lime **5** apple, grape, lemon, prune **6** orange
holder: **3** can, cup **5** glass **6** bottle **7** tumbler
like some ~: **5** acerb, pulpy, tangy **6** acidic
make orange ~: **7** squeeze
meat ~: **5** gravy
moo ~: **4** milk
moo ~ container: **5** udder
out of ~: **4** dead **8** lifeless
partly fermented grape ~: **4** stum
seal in the ~: **4** sear
unfermented ~: **4** must
up: **5** liven **6** turn on, vivify **7** animate, enliven **8** activate, energize, vitalize **9** stimulate
__ juice: **3** moo
Juice: **6** Newton
juiced: **8** squeezed
up: **5** eager, wired **6** aflame **7** excited
juiceless: **3** dry **4** arid, sere **7** bone-dry, dried up, parched, wizened **8** withered **9** shriveled **10** dehydrated, desiccated
juicer: **6** gadget **9** appliance, extractor
refuse: **4** pulp **6** pomace **9** sarcocarp
juicy: **3** wet **4** rich **5** kicky, moist, spicy, undry, vivid **6** liquid, mellow, ribald, spicey **7** gossipy, piquant **8** colorful, dripping, exciting, luscious **9** saturated, succulent, with a kick **10** intriguing, scandalous
fruit: **4** pear **5** apple, berry, melon, peach **6** orange
like ~ turkeys: **6** basted
tidbit: **4** buzz, dirt, talk, word **5** rumor **6** gossip, report **7** hearsay, scandal
Juicy Fruit: **3** gum **10** chewing gum
alternative: *see* chewing gum
juillet: **4** July, mois **5** month **6** French
follower: **4** août
preceder: **4** juin
Juilliard
subject: **3** mus. **5** music
juin: **4** June, mois **5** month **6** French
follower: **7** juillet
preceder: **3** mai
jujitsu: **5** sport
relative: **4** judo **6** aikido, karate
juju: **4** mojo **5** charm **6** amulet, fetish
jujube: **4** date, tree **5** candy, fruit, snack
family: **9** buckthorn
juke: **4** fake, fool, ruse **5** dodge, feint
ender: **3** box
juke __: **5** joint
Jukebox __: **4** Baby
jukebox part: **4** slot
Jul.: **2** mo.
follower: **3** Aug.
preceder: **3** Jun.
Jule: **5** Styne
julep: **5** drink **8** beverage
__ julep: **4** mint
Jules: **4** bass **5** Verne **6** Bordet, Dassin **7** Feiffer, Mazarin, Munshin, Romains **8** Goncourt, Massenet, Michelet, Poincaré
see also French
Jules and Jim (1961 film)
cast: Jeanne Moreau, Oskar Werner
director: François Truffaut
Juli: **7** Inkster
Julia: **4** Raul **5** Child, Duffy **6** Ormond, Stiles **7** Marlowe, Migenes, Roberts, Sweeney **8** Phillips, Tutwiler
brother: **4** Eric
Julia (1977 film)
cast: Jane Fonda, Vanessa Redgrave, Jason Robards
Julia (NBC sitcom)
cast: Diahann Carroll (Julia Baker) Lloyd Nolan (Morton Chegley)
Julia __-Dreyfus: **5** Louis
Julia __ Howe: **4** Ward
Julian: **4** Bond **5** Roman **6** Barnes, Huxley, Lennon, Symons **7** emperor **9** Schwinger
to John: **3** son
Julian __: **4** Alps **8** calendar
Julianna: **9** Margulies
Julianne: **5** Moore **8** Phillips **9** Nicholson
Julia, Raul: **5** actor
film: The Addams Family (1991) Addams Family Values (1993) Compromising Positions (1985) The Gumball Rally (1976) Kiss of the Spider Woman (1985) Moon Over Parador (1988) Presumed Innocent (1990) Romero (1989) Tequila Sunrise (1988)
musical: **4** Nine
Julie: **4** Chen **5** Adams, Delpy, Krone, Moran **6** Bishop, Harris, Kavner, London, Newmar, Warner **7** Andrews, Hagerty, Walters **8** Christie
Julie __ Eisenhower: **5** Nixon
__ Julie: **4** Miss
Julie & Julia (2009 film)
cast: Amy Adams, Meryl Streep
director: Nora Ephron
Julien: **5** Green **8** Duvivier
julienne: **4** soup **5** broth **8** bouillon, consommé, potatoes
Juliet: **4** moon **5** lover, Mills **6** Prowse **7** Capulet
beloved: **5** Romeo
betrothed: **5** Paris
planet: **6** Uranus
__ Juliet: **5** Me and
Juliette: **3** Low **5** Lewis **7** Binoche
julio: **3** mes **4** July **5** month **7** Spanish
follower: **6** agosto
preceder: **5** junio
Julio: **5** Gallo **8** Cortázar, Iglesias
brother: **6** Ernest
see also Spanish
Julius: **4** pope **5** Boros, Rudel **6** Caesar, Erving, LaRosa **7** Axelrod, Dithers, Nyerere, pontiff **8** Dedekind **9** Rosenberg
__ Julius: **6** Orange
Julius Caesar: **4** play
author: William Shakespeare
character: **4** Cato **5** Casca, Cinna **6** Brutus, Cicero, Lucius, Portia, Strato **7** Cassius, Flavius, Messala, Publius **8** Marullus, Pindarus, Titinius **9** Calpurnia **10** Marc Antony
costume: **4** toga
director: Joseph L. Mankiewicz
quintet: **4** acts
setting: **4** Rome **6** Senate
__ Julius Caesar: **5** Caius, Gaius
July: **5** month **9** midsummer
birthstone: **4** ruby
clock setting: **3** DST
follower: **3** Aug. **6** August
preceder: **3** Jun. **4** June
sign: **3** Leo **4** Crab, Lion **6** Cancer
was named for him: **6** Caesar
July 15: **4** ides
July 7: **5** nones
Jumanji (1995 film)
cast: Kirsten Dunst, Bonnie Hunt, Robin Williams
jumble: **3** mix **4** hash, mess, muss, olio, pile, stew **5** chaos, mix up, snarl, upset **6** cookie, foul up, garble, huddle, jungle, litter, medley, mess up, muddle, tangle, tumble **7** clutter, confuse, derange, disturb, farrago, goulash, mélange, mistake, mixture, rummage, shuffle, snarl up **8** confound, disarray, dishevel, disorder, entangle, mishmash, pastiche, scramble, unsettle **9** confusion, dislocate, mare's nest, patchwork, potpourri **10** assortment, complicate, disarrange, hodgepodge, miscellany, salmagundi
jumbled: **5** messy, mussy **6** unneat, untidy **7** chaotic, in a mess, tangled **9** inside-out **10** disjointed, disorderly, incohesive, in disarray, out of order, topsy-turvy, upside-down
Jumblies, The: **4** poem
author: Edward Lear
vessel: **5** sieve
jumbo: **3** big **4** huge, size, vast **5** giant, great, large **6** mighty **7** hulking, immense, mammoth, massive, sizable, titanic **8** colossal, enormous, gigantic, king-size, oversize, sizeable, towering, whapping, whopping **9** cyclopean, Herculean, humongous, leviathan, overlarge **10** gargantuan, monumental, prodigious, stupendous, tremendous
jumbo __: **3** jet **4** eggs
__ jumbo: **5** mumbo
Jumbo: **7** musical
composer: Lorenz Hart, Richard Rodgers
jumbuck: **5** sheep
Jumna: **5** river
city on the ~: **4** Agra **5** Delhi
locale: **5** India
jump: **3** bob, hop **4** axel, buck, dive, flee, hike, jeté, leap, lutz, miss, move, omit, pass, rise, romp, skip, verb **5** avoid, boost, bound, dance, evade, frisk, lunge, lurch, spirt, spurt, start, surge, vault, wince **6** ambush, bounce, bypass, curvet, flinch, hurdle, hurtle, launch, plunge, pounce, prance, recoil, snatch, spring, twitch, upturn, waylay **7** abscond, bail out, gambado, hop over, saltate, skydive, startle, upsurge **8** capriole, increase, leapfrog, obstacle, pass over **9** advantage, barricade, head start, overshoot, parachute, saltation **10** go whole hog, hippety hop
all over: **4** flay **5** blame, chide, scold **6** attack, berate, lean on, rebuke **7** bawl out, chew out, go after, lay into, lecture, reprove, rip into, tell off, upbraid **8** admonish, lambaste **9** criticize, dress down, reprimand, tear apart **10** take to task
as a spark: **3** arc
at: **4** grab **5** catch **6** snatch
back: **5** wince
bail: **3** fly **6** run out **7** skip out **8** skip town **9** leave town **10** fly the coop
ender: **4** suit **6** master
for joy: **5** exult **7** rejoice **9** celebrate
get the ~ on: **4** best, lead **5** outdo **7** prevail, surpass **8** dominate, outstrip
high ~: **5** event **7** contest
horse ~: **6** curvet
in: **5** enter, start **6** butt in **7** burst in, get busy, pitch in **9** interject, interrupt
(in): **5** chime
into: **5** begin, enter, start **6** launch, set out, take up **7** kick off, lead off **8** commence, embark on, get going, initiate **9** undertake
long ~: **5** event **7** contest
make ~: **5** alarm, panic, scare, spook **7** disturb, startle **8** affright, frighten, surprise **9** galvanize, give a turn
off: **5** begin, start **6** alight, embark **7** detrain, get down **8** dismount
out of the way: **4** duck **5** avoid, dodge, elude, evade, parry, skirt **6** escape **8** sidestep
over: **3** hop **4** leap, skip **5** clear, vault **6** hurdle
rope: **3** toy **4** game, skip **7** pastime **9** amusement, diversion
skating ~: **4** axel, lutz
the gun: **4** rush **5** start **7** presume **10** anticipate
the line: **5** cut in
the track: **6** derail
up: **4** lift, rise **5** raise, stand **7** magnify
voltage ~: **5** surge
with a pole: **4** soar **5** bound, vault **6** hurdle, spring **8** overleap
jump __: **3** bid, cut, jet **4** bail, ball, rope, seat, shot
jump-__: **5** shift, start
__ jump: **3** ski **4** high, long, pole **5** broad, water **6** center, double, triple **7** gelände, quantum
Jump: **6** Gordon
Jump (song)
artist: Kris Kross, Van Halen
jumper: **3** 'roo **5** horse **6** equine, rabbit, romper **7** wallaby **8** kangaroo
Aussie ~: **3** 'roo **7** wallaby **8** kangaroo
Calaveras County ~: **4** frog
checkers ~: **4** king
for short: **4** para
need: **5** chute
starter: **5** smoke
jumper __: **3** ant **5** cable
__ jumper: **4** high, long **5** broad
__-jumper: **5** claim **6** puddle

jumper cable
connection: 5 anode 7 cathode
Jump (For My Love) (1984 song)
artist: Pointer Sisters
Jumpin' ___ Flash: 4 Jack
jumping: 4 busy, go-go 5 noisy 6 lively 7 hopping 8 tireless 9 vivacious
for joy: 4 high 5 happy 6 elated 7 beaming, gleeful 8 ecstatic, euphoric, exultant, in heaven, jubilant 9 ebullient 10 flying high, triumphant
out of a plane: 4 feat 5 stunt 7 exploit
the gun: 7 too soon 8 abortive, too early 9 overhasty, premature 10 half-cocked
to conclusions: 4 rash 5 hasty 8 careless, heedless, reckless 9 foolhardy, hotheaded, impetuous, imprudent, impulsive, overhasty 10 headstrong, incautious
jumping ___: 4 bean, jack 5 mouse
jumping-___ point: 3 off
___ jumping: 6 bungee
___ jumping bean: 7 Mexican
jumping-bean occupant: 4 worm
Jumpin' Jack Flash (1968 song)
artist: Rolling Stones
Jumpin' Jack flash, it's ___: 4 a gas
Jumpin', Jumpin' (2000 song)
artist: Destiny's Child
jump the ___: 3 gun
jump through ___: 5 hoops
___-jump-up: 6 Johnny
jumpy: 4 edgy 5 antsy, itchy, shaky, tense, upset, wired 6 fitful, jangly, on edge, scared, touchy, uneasy 7 alarmed, anxious, excited, fearful, fidgety, fretful, jittery, keyed up, nervous, panicky, restive, spooked, uptight 8 agitated, atremble, fluttery, fretsome, restless, skittish, timorous, troubled 9 concerned, excitable, ill at ease, quivering, trembling, tremulous, unrelaxed 10 disquieted, frightened, high-strung
in music: 4 stac. 8 staccato
Jun.: 2 mo.
follower: 3 Jul.
it ends in ~: 3 spr.
see also June
junco: 4 bird 8 snowbird
junction: 4 bond, link, lock, node, seam, weld 5 hinge, joint, tie-in, union 6 corner, hookup, splice 7 linking, meeting, mortice, mortise 8 coupling, crossing, dovetail 9 concourse 10 assemblage, attachment, confluence, connection, crossroads
electrical ~: 3 wye
of a ~ point: 5 nodal
road ~: 4 fork, turn 6 branch
junction ___: 3 box
___ Junction: 6 Tuxedo 9 Petticoat
Junction City: 4 city, town
locale: 6 Kansas
juncture: 4 bond, node, pass, seam, time, weld 5 hinge, joint, phase, point, stage, state, tie-in, union 6 crisis, hookup, moment, splice 7 dilemma, instant, linking, meeting, mortice, mortise 8 coupling, crossing, dovetail, occasion, quandary, zero hour 9 concourse, emergency 10 assemblage, attachment, concursion, confluence, crossroads, occurrence
at this ~: 3 now 4 here
leaf ~: 4 axil
picture frame ~: 5 bevel, miter, slant 8 diagonal
June: 5 Foray, Haver, Havoc, month, Valli 6 Carter 7 Allyson, Cleaver, Collyer 8 Lockhart
award: 6 degree
birthstone: 5 pearl
bug: 3 dor 4 dorr 6 beetle
dance: 4 prom
honoree: 3 dad 4 grad 5 Daddy 6 father
like ~: 5 sixth
sign: 4 Crab 5 Twins 6 Cancer, Gemini
to Ward: 4 wife
vow: 3 I do
June ___: 3 bug 5 bride 6 beetle
___ & June: 5 Henry
June 13: 4 ides
June 5: 5 nones
Juneau: 4 city, town 7 capital
locale: 6 Alaska
June Is Bustin' Out All Over
composer: Oscar Hammerstein, Richard Rodgers
June Moon: 4 play
author: George S. Kaufman, Ring Lardner
Jung: 4 Carl
rival: 5 Freud
topic: 3 ego 9 archetype
___ Jung: 6 Kim Dae
Jünger, Ernst: 6 German, writer
Jungfrau: 3 alp 4 peak 5 mount 8 mountain
locale: 4 Alps 6 Europe 11 Switzerland
jungle: 4 bush, heap, mass, maze 5 chaos, snarl, wilds 6 jumble, litter, region, sphere, tangle 7 clutter, society, thicket, tropics 8 disarray 9 confusion, labyrinth, mobocracy, wasteland 10 rain forest, wilderness
creature: 3 ape, boa 4 lion 5 hyena, rhino, tapir 6 hyaena
from the ~: 4 wild
home: 3 den 4 lair
knife: 4 bolo 7 machete
like a ~: 4 lush, rank, viny 9 overgrown
person: 4 Jane 6 Tarzan
sound: 3 cry, din 4 call, drum, howl, roar 5 blast, crash, growl, laugh 6 bellow, clamor, scream 7 trumpet
vine: 5 liana, liane
jungle ___: 3 gym
Jungle ___: 3 Jim 4 Book 5 Fever
Jungle Boogie (1974 song)
artist: Kool and the Gang
Jungle Book (1942 film)
cast: Sabu
director: Zoltan Korda
setting: 5 India
Jungle Books, The
author: Rudyard Kipling
character: 3 Kaa 5 Akela, Baloo, Hathi 6 Buldeo, Messua, Mowgli 8 Bagheera 9 Shere Khan
Jungle Fever (1991 film)
cast: Spike Lee, Annabella Sciorra, Wesley Snipes
director: Spike Lee
___ jungle out there!: 4 It's a
Jungle, The
author: Upton Sinclair
character: 3 Ona 5 Jonas 6 Connor, Jurgis, Marija, Rudkus
___ Jungle, The: 5 Naked 7 Asphalt
jung opposite: 3 alt
junio: 3 mes 4 June 5 month 7 Spanish
follower: 5 julio
preceder: 4 mayo
junior: 3 boy, lad, son 4 size, year 5 lower, minor, pupil, under, young 6 lesser, little, puisne 7 student, younger 8 juvenile 9 collegian, secondary, youngster
college degree: 2 AA, AS
dress size: 4 nine
officer: 5 cadet 7 soldier
sibling: 3 sis
junior ___: 4 high, miss, prom 7 college, varsity
Junior: 4 Seau 6 Walker 7 Gilliam 9 Girl Scout
watch ~: 3 sit
Junior (1994 film)
cast: Danny DeVito, Frank Langella, Arnold Schwarzenegger, Emma Thompson
director: Ivan Reitman
Junior ___: 6 League
Junior Bonner (1972 film)
cast: Ida Lupino, Steve McQueen, Robert Preston
director: Sam Peckinpah
junior high: 6 school
grade: 5 ninth 6 eighth 7 seventh
juniority: 9 childhood
Junior League wannabe: 3 deb
Junior's Farm (1974 song)
artist: Paul McCartney
juniper: 4 tree 5 savin, shrub 6 savine 9 evergreen
Biblical ~: 5 retem
product: 3 gin
relative: 7 cypress 8 sandarac 10 arborvitae
tar: 4 cade
Junípero: 5 Serra
junk: 3 rid 4 boat, dump, poor, toss 5 chaff, ditch, offal, scrap, stuff, trash, waste 6 debris, litter, no good, refuse, remove, shabby, shlock, shoddy, trashy 7 discard, garbage, rejects, rubbish, salvage, schlock, toss out, trinket 8 castoffs, discards, get rid of, inferior, jettison, leavings, narcotic, throw out, unusable 9 dispose of, houseboat, sweepings, throw away, worthless 10 second-rate
cyberspace ~ mail: 4 spam
drawer abbr.: 4 misc.
ender: 4 yard
food: 4 eats, nosh 5 snack, sweet 6 sweets 7 goodies, munchie
hunk of ~: 3 dud 5 lemon
mail: 3 ads 7 catalog
pile: 8 landfill
junk ___: 3 art, DNA 4 bond, call, food, mail 6 artist 7 jewelry
junker: 4 heap 5 crate, wreck 6 jalopy 10 rattletrap
junket: 3 hop 4 hike, ride, sail, tour, trek, trip, walk 5 drive, jaunt, sally, spree 6 airing, cruise, frolic, outing, picnic, stroll, travel, voyage 7 custard, journey, pudding, tapioca 9 excursion 10 blancmange, expedition
junkman: 6 carter
junky: 3 bad 5 cheap 6 shoddy, tawdry 7 devotee 8 slipshod 9 worthless 10 jerry-built
junkyard: 4 dump, heap 8 landfill
dog: 3 cur, mut 4 mutt 5 biter 7 mongrel 10 crossbreed
like a ~ dog: 3 bad 4 mean, ugly 5 dirty, mangy 7 lowdown, scruffy, vicious 8 churlish 9 dangerous 10 despicable, ill-natured
Juno: 3 dea 8 asteroid
brother: 5 Pluto 7 Jupiter, Neptune
epithet of ~: 6 Lucina, Moneta, Regina 7 Curitis 8 Lanuvina
equivalent: 4 Hera
husband: 7 Jupiter
messenger: 4 Iris
offered him a kingdom: 5 Paris
parent: 3 Ops 6 Saturn
sister: 5 Ceres, Vesta
son: 4 Mars 6 Vulcan
Juno (2007 film)
cast: Jason Bateman, Jennifer Garner, Ellen Page
Juno and the Paycock
author: Sean O'Casey
junta: 4 bloc, ring 5 cabal, party 7 council 9 coalition
act: 4 fiat 5 edict, order 6 decree, dictum, rulers 7 command, dictate, mandate 9 directive, manifesto 10 injunction
action: 4 coup 5 purge 6 revolt, stroke
junto: 4 band, gang, ring 5 cabal, party 6 circle, clique 7 coterie, faction 8 alliance 9 coalition
Jupiter: 3 deo, god 4 city, Jove, town
brother: 5 Pluto 7 Neptune
daughter: 3 Pax 5 Diana, Venus
domain: 3 sky
equivalent: 4 Zeus
locale: 7 Florida
moon: 2 Io 4 Leda 5 Carme, Elara, Metis, Thebe 6 Ananke, Europa, Sinope 7 Himalia 8 Adrastea, Amalthea, Callisto, Ganymede, Lysithea, Pasiphae
neighbor: 4 Mars 6 Saturn
parent: 3 Ops 6 Saturn
sister: 4 Juno 5 Ceres, Vesta
son: 4 Mars 6 Apollo 7 Bacchus, Mercury
wife: 4 Juno
Jupiter's ___: 4 Wife 5 Bones 7 Darling
Jupiter's-___: 5 beard
Jupiter's Bones
author: Faye Kellerman
Jupiter Symphony
composer: Wolfgang Amadeus Mozart
Jura: 5 range 9 mountains
locale: 5 Switz. 6 Europe, France
Jurado, Katy: 7 actress, Mexican
spouse: Ernest Borgnine

jural: 3 due 5 legal, legit, licit, valid 6 kosher, lawful 8 rightful 9 allowable, canonical, statutory, warranted 10 admissible, authorized, legitimate, sanctioned
Jurassic Park: 4 film 5 novel
  author: Michael Crichton
  beast: 4 T-rex 5 clone 6 raptor
  cast: Richard Attenborough, Laura Dern, Jeff Goldblum, Sam Neill
  composer: John Williams
  director: Steven Spielberg
  preserver: 5 amber, resin
  role: 5 Ellie
jurat: 5 judge 7 bailiff 10 magistrate
jure, de: 7 by right
Jürgen: 8 Prochnow
Jurgens: 4 Curt 6 lotion
  competitor: 5 Nivea
Jurgensen, Sonny: 2 QB
  sport: 8 football
juridical: 5 legal 6 lawful 8 forensic
___ juris: 3 sui
jurisdiction: 4 area, rule, sway, turf 5 field, orbit, power, range, reach, reign, scope 6 bounds, domain, empire, extent, limits, sphere 7 circuit, command, compass, control, purview 8 district, dominion, hegemony, province
  remove beyond legal ~: 5 eloin
jurisprudence: 3 law 10 due process
jurisprudent: 3 due 5 legal, legit, licit, valid 6 kosher, lawful, lawyer, legist, proper 7 condign 8 attorney, bona fide, mandated, official, rightful 9 allowable, barrister, canonical, counselor, solicitor, statutory, warranted 10 admissible, authorized, legal eagle, legitimate
jurist: 5 judge 6 lawyer 7 counsel, justice 8 attorney, defender, his Honor 9 barrister, counselor 10 magistrate
  Muslim ~: 5 mufti
juristic: 5 legal 8 forensic 9 polemical
___ juror: 5 grand, petit
jurors: 5 panel, peers 7 council
  place: 3 box 5 court 9 courtroom
Juror, The (1996 film)
  cast: Alec Baldwin, Anne Heche, Demi Moore
jury: 5 board, panel, peers 8 tribunal 9 veniremen
  award: 7 damages, penalty 9 indemnity 10 reparation
  complement: 5 dozen
  determination: 5 guilt
  grand ~ activity: 5 probe
  join a ~: 3 sit
  member: 4 peer 5 equal
jury ___: 3 box 4 room
jury-___: 3 rig 6 rigged
___ jury: 4 hung 5 grand, petit, petty, trial
___ Jury: 4 I, the
jury-rigged: 6 fill-in 7 interim, stopgap 9 contrived, expedient, impromptu, makeshift, temporary 10 improvised
jus: 5 gravy
jus ___: 7 gentium
just: 3 all, apt, but, due, fit 4 even, fair, meet, mere, only, wise 5 exact, legal, moral, newly, quite, right, sound, truly 6 actual, barely, cogent, decent, hardly, honest, kasher, kosher, lawful, merely, proper, purely, simply, square 7 by a nose, condign, correct, ethical, exactly, factual, fitting, freshly, merited, neutral, only now, precise, sincere, upright, utterly, veridic 8 accurate, actually, balanced, bona fide, deserved, entirely, faithful, flawless, narrowly, recently, reliable, rightful, squarely, straight, suitable, tolerant, unbiased, virtuous 9 authentic, befitting, equitable, errorless, faultless, honorable, impartial, judicious, objective, precisely, righteous, unbigoted, uncolored, uncorrupt, unslanted, veracious, veridical 10 aboveboard, absolutely, completely, definitely, dependable, evenhanded, fair-minded, felicitous, high-minded, legitimate, no more than, nothing but, principled, reasonable, scrupulous, upstanding
  about: 4 near 6 almost, nearly
  a little: 3 bit, nip, sip 4 bite, dash, dram, drop, shot 5 pinch, snort, taste 6 morsel, nibble, sample, tidbit, trifle 7 soupçon, swallow 8 mouthful, spoonful
  around the corner: 4 near 5 handy 7 close by 8 adjacent 10 accessible, convenient
  as: 4 then, when 5 while 6 during
  as soon: 6 gladly, rather 7 instead, mais oui 9 be my guest 10 by all means, preferably
  barely: 4 a bit 6 hardly 8 narrowly, scarcely
  beat: 4 edge 7 nose out 8 slip past
  before: 4 till, up to 5 until 6 down to 7 prior to
  bought: 3 new 5 fresh
  deserts: 3 due 5 merit 6 reward 7 payback 10 recompense
  exist: 4 loaf 7 go to pot 8 go to seed, languish, stagnate, vegetate
  get one's ~ deserts: 4 earn, rate 5 merit 10 have coming
  give ~ deserts: 5 spite 6 avenge 7 get even, hit back, pay back, requite, revenge 9 get back at, stick it to
  hired: 3 new, raw 5 green 9 untrained
  kidding: 5 in fun 7 as a lark 8 for a joke
  like: 4 as if 5 quasi 9 seemingly
  make it: 4 last 5 exist, get by 6 eke out, endure, hang on, manage 7 ride out, subsist, survive 8 scrape by 9 squeeze by, stay alive 10 stick it out
  miss sinking, as a putt: 3 lip
  more than ~ a little: 4 much, very 5 amply, quite 6 deeply, highly, hugely, unduly, vastly 7 greatly, largely, only too, rabidly 8 terribly 9 decidedly, extremely, seriously, unusually 10 enormously, incredibly, profoundly, remarkably, thoroughly, uncommonly
  now: 6 lately 8 latterly, recently
  once: 4 ever 5 at all
  only ~: 6 little 8 narrowly, scarcely
  out: 3 new 5 fresh 6 recent
  picked: 5 crisp, fresh
  punishment: 6 desert
  right: 4 to a T 5 ideal 6 to a tee 7 optimal, perfect, utopian 8 flawless 9 correctly, exemplary, faultless, nonpareil, on the nose, perfectly, precisely 10 accurately, consummate
  so: *see* of course
  the same: 3 yet 5 still 6 anyhow, anyway, even so 9 at any rate
  washed: 5 clean, fresh, snowy 8 dirtless, germfree, pristine, sanitary, spotless, unsoiled 9 laundered, sparkling, unsmudged, unspotted, unstained 10 immaculate
just ___: 3 now 4 a bit, a dab, a tad 5 about, folks 6 in case 7 deserts
just ___ on the map: 4 a dot
Just ___: 4 a sec, do it 5 a Girl, say no
Just ___ Before I Go: 5 a Song
Just ___ Look: 3 One
Just ___ Me: 4 Like, You 'N' 5 Shoot
Just ___ of Those Things: 3 One
Just ___, skip...: 4 a hop
Just ___ suspected!: 3 as I
Just ___ the guys: 5 one of
Just ___ thought!: 3 as I
Just a ___: 3 sec 6 Gigolo
Just Above My Head
  author: James Baldwin
Just a Little Bit Better (1965 song)
  artist: Herman's Hermits
Just a minute: 4 whoa 6 hang on, hold on, one sec
Just Another Day (1992 song)
  artist: Jon Secada
Just Ask Your Heart (1959 song)
  artist: Frankie Avalon
Just a Song Before I Go (1977 song)
  artist: Crosby, Stills & Nash
Just Between You and Me (song)
  artist: Chordettes, Lou Gramm
Just Do It company: 4 Nike
Just Dropped In (1968 song)
  artist: Kenny Rogers
juste-___: 6 milieu
___ juste: 3 mot
Just Got Paid (1988 song)
  artist: Johnny Kemp
justice: 5 judge, right 6 equity, jurist, virtue 7 redress 8 evenness, fairness, fair play, justness, morality 9 rectitude 10 due process, lawfulness, recompense
  bring to ~: 3 try 4 hear 9 prosecute 10 adjudicate
  do ~: 3 fix 4 mend 5 emend, right 6 remedy, repair, square 7 correct, realize, rectify, redress, requite, restore, succeed 9 make up for, vindicate 10 accomplish, take care of
  do ~ to: 9 vindicate
  hall of ~: 5 court
  it seasons ~: 5 mercy
justice ___ peace: 5 of the
___ justice: 5 chief, lit de 6 poetic
Justice Dept.
  div.: 3 FBI
  employee: 4 atty.
  head: 2 AG
___ justice for all: 3 and
justice of the ___: 5 peace
justifiable: 4 fair 5 legal, licit, right, sound, valid 6 lawful, proper 7 logical, tenable 8 deserved, rightful, suitable 9 allowable 10 legitimate, reasonable
justification: 4 call, plea 5 alibi, basis, title 6 excuse, reason 7 defense, grounds, pretext 8 apologia, argument, occasion 9 rationale
  means ~: 4 ends
justified: 3 due 5 legal 8 deserved
  not ~: 4 idle 5 empty, false, undue, wrong 6 unfair, wanton 7 extreme 8 baseless, needless 9 excessive, illogical, imaginary, overblown, unfounded, untenable 10 exorbitant, gratuitous, groundless, inordinate, undeserved, unprovoked
justifier: 9 apologist
justify: 5 gloze, merit, prove 6 defend, excuse, pardon, reason, uphold 7 bear out, confirm, explain, support, sustain, warrant 8 argue for, palliate, validate 9 recommend, vindicate, whitewash 10 legitimize, strengthen
___-justify: 4 cost
Justify My Love (1990 song)
  artist: Madonna
just in ___: 4 case
Justin: 4 Long 5 Henry
Justine: 7 Bateman
  author: de Sade, Lawrence Durrell
Just in Time
  composer: Betty Comden, Adolph Green, Jule Styne
Just kidding!: 3 not
Just like ___ and Bacall: 5 Bogie
Just Like Heaven (2005 film)
  cast: Mark Ruffalo, Reese Witherspoon
Just Like Jesse James (1989 song)
  artist: Cher
Just Like Paradise (1988 song)
  artist: David Lee Roth
(Just Like) Starting Over (1980 song)
  artist: John Lennon
justly: 5 right, truly 6 aright 8 by rights 10 virtuously
Just Married (2003 film)
  cast: Ashton Kutcher, Brittany Murphy
Just My Imagination (1971 song)
  artist: Temptations
justness: 6 equity 7 justice 8 meetness 9 rightness 10 lawfulness, moderation
___ just one of those things: 5 It was
Just One of Those Things
  composer: Cole Porter
Just Right: 6 cereal
  competitor: *see* cereal
Just say ___ drugs: 4 no to
Just Shoot Me (NBC sitcom)
  cast: Enrico Colantoni (Elliot DiMauro)
    Wendie Malick (Nina Van Horn)
    Laura San Giacomo (Maya Gallo)
    George Segal (Jack Gallo)
    David Spade (Dennis Finch)
  cat: Spartacus
  magazine: Blush

Just So Stories
author: Rudyard Kipling
__ just stand there: 4 Don't
Just Take My Heart (1992 song)
artist: Mr. Big
just the __: 4 same
Just the __, ma'am: 5 facts
Just the Two of Us (1981 song)
artist: Gr Washington Jr. Jr., Bill Withers
Just the Way You Are (1977 song)
artist: Billy Joel
Just this __...: 4 once
Just to Be Close to You (1976 song)
artist: Commodores
Just to See Her (1987 song)
artist: Smokey Robinson
Justus von __: 6 Liebig
Just Walking in the Rain (1956 song)
artist: Johnnie Ray
__ Just Want to Have Fun: 5 Girls
Justy: 3 car 4 auto 6 Subaru
Just You 'n' Me (1973 song)
artist: Chicago
Just you wait, __ 'iggins: 4 'enry
jut: 4 lean, poke 5 bulge 6 extend 7 poke out, project 8 overhang, protrude, stand out, stick out 10 projection
jute: 4 bast, rope 5 fiber
cousin: 4 hemp
fabric: 5 oakum 6 burlap
fiber resembling ~: 5 kenaf
product: 4 rope 5 twine 6 string 7 cordage
Jute invader: 5 Horsa
Jutland: 6 battle 9 peninsula
port: 6 Aarhus 7 Aalborg
resident: 4 Dane
jutting: 7 pendant, pendent, salient 9 obtrusive, prominent
piece: 8 abutment
Juvenal: 4 poet 5 Roman 8 satirist
see also Latin
juvenescent: 5 fresh, green, young 6 boyish, callow 7 budding, girlish, growing, newborn, puerile 8 childish, immature, teenaged 9 childlike, half-grown, unfledged 10 developing
juvenile: 3 boy, kid, lad, tot 4 baby, girl, teen 5 child, green, kiddy, minor, sprig, young, youth 6 boyish, callow, infant, jejune, junior, unripe, vernal 7 babyish, budding, girlish, kiddish, puerile, sapling, teenage, toddler 8 childish, half-pint, immature, nonvoter, teenager, underage, unweaned, youthful 9 childlike, frivolous, infantile, stripling, youngster 10 adolescent, nonserious
juvenile __: 10 delinquent
juvenility: 9 childhood 10 schooldays
juxtapose: 4 abut, meet 5 verge 6 adjoin 8 border on 9 lie beside
juxtaposed: 4 near 5 close 6 beside 8 abutting, adjacent, touching 9 adjoining, bordering, in contact 10 connecting, contiguous
juxtaposition: 7 abuttal, contact, joining, meeting 8 abutment, touching 9 adjacence, adjacency, adjoining, proximity 10 contiguity
place in ~: 6 appose
JVC: 2 TV 3 VCR 5 TV set 10 television
alternative: ***see*** electronics company
invention: 3 VHS
J. Walter __: 8 Thompson
J. William __: 9 Fulbright
__ J. Wilson: 6 Sheree

J
U

K: **3** vit. **4** elem. **6** letter **7** element, vitamin **9** potassium
19 for ~: **4** at. no.
followers: **3** LMN **4** LMNO **5** LMNOP
in phonetic alphabet: **4** Kilo
preceders: **3** HIJ **4** GHIJ **5** FGHIJ
rations: **4** chow
rations successor: **3** MRE
star: **8** Arcturus **9** Aldebaran
to 12: **4** elhi **5** grade
K __: **4** Mart **6** ration
K __ kind: **4** as in
K-__: **3** Tel
K. __: **3** of C., of P.
'K' __ Killer: **5** Is for
__-K: **3** pre
K2: **3** mtn. **4** peak **5** mount **8** mountain
locale: **4** Asia **7** Kashmir
K-6: **4** elem.
K-9 (1989 film)
cast: James Belushi, Mel Harris, Ed O'Neill
dog: **8** Jerry Lee
ka-__: **4** blam, boom **5** ching
Ka __, HI: **3** Lae
Kaaba
dedicatee: **5** Allah
pilgrim: **5** hadji
Kaat, Jim
sport: **8** baseball
Kabibble: **3** Ish
kabob: **9** brochette
ingredient: **4** lamb
skewer: **4** spit
kaboom: **3** pow **4** bang **5** blast, noise **6** whammo
kabuki: **5** drama **7** theater **8** Japanese
alternative: **3** noh
performer: **4** male
Kabul: **4** city, town **5** river **7** capital
locale: **4** Asia **11** Afghanistan
native: **6** Afghan **7** Afghani
River locale: **8** Pakistan
kachina: **4** doll
creator: **4** Hopi
Kadar: **3** Jan
Kádár: **5** János
Kaddish Symphony
composer: Leonard Bernstein
Kadeem: **8** Hardison
Kadett: **3** car **4** auto, Opel **10** automobile
Kadiddlehopper, Clem
portrayer: Red Skelton
Kael, Pauline: **6** critic
forte: **4** film **5** movie
Kaempfert, Bert: **9** conductor
kaffee
in German: **6** coffee
kaffee __: **6** klatch **7** klatsch
Kaffir: **6** Afghan **7** Afghani
kaffiyeh: **5** scarf **8** kerchief **9** headdress
cord: **4** agal
Kafkaesque: **5** weird
emotion: **5** angst
Kafka, Franz: **6** German, writer
birthplace: Prague
work: Amerika
The Castle
In the Penal Colony
The Metamorphosis
The Trial
kaftan: **4** robe
kin: **6** kimono
Kafue: **5** river
locale: **6** Zambia
Kahldun: **3** Ibn
Kahlil: **6** Gibran
Kahlo, Frida: **6** artist **7** Mexican, painter
spouse: Diego Rivera
work: The Broken Column
The Dream
My Birth
Kahn: **3** Gus **4** Otto **5** Louis **6** Albert **8** Madeline
Kahneman, Daniel: **8** Nobelist **9** economist
Kahn, Madeline: **7** actress
film: Blazing Saddles (1974)
City Heat (1984)
High Anxiety (1977)
Paper Moon (1973)
What's Up, Doc? (1972)
Young Frankenstein (1974)
Kahn's: **6** hot dog
alternative: **6** Armour **8** Ball Park **10** Oscar Mayer
Kahului: **4** city, town
locale: **4** Maui **6** Hawaii
kahuna: **3** VIP **7** big shot **9** dignitary
__ kahuna: **3** big
Kai: **7** Winding **8** Siegbahn
Kailas: **4** peak
dweller: **5** Shiva
locale: **9** Himalayas
Kailua: **4** city, town
locale: **4** Oahu **6** Hawaii
kaiser: **4** roll **5** ruler, title **6** gerent **7** monarch, Wilhelm
counterpart: **4** czar, king, tsar **7** emperor
Kaiser: **3** car **4** auto **5** Georg
Kaiser, Georg: **6** German **10** playwright
Kaiser Permanente: **3** HMO
Kai-shek: **6** Chiang
kaka: **6** parrot
kakapo: **6** parrot
kakemono: **6** scroll **8** painting
kaki: **4** tree **5** fruit **9** persimmon
Kal: **4** Penn
Kal __: **3** Kan
Kalahari: **6** desert
beast: **6** impala
lake north of the ~: **5** Ngami
like the ~: **3** dry **4** arid, bare, flat, sere **5** dusty **6** barren, desert **7** bone-dry, parched, thirsty **9** waterless
Kalamazoo: **4** city, town
athletes: **7** Broncos
locale: **8** Michigan
school: **3** WMU
Kalb: **6** Marvin **7** Bernard
kale: **6** greens, veggie **7** cabbage **8** borecole, colewort **9** vegetable
see also moolah
__ kale: **3** sea
Kaleidoscope
author: Danielle Steel
kaleidoscopic: **6** motley **7** protean, surreal **8** colorful, shifting
Kalember: **8** Patricia
Kalevala: **4** epic
Kalifornia (1993 film)
cast: David Duchovny, Juliette Lewis, Brad Pitt
kalimba: **5** mbira
origin: **6** Africa
Kaline: **2** Al **7** Mr. Tiger **10** outfielder
Kalispell: **4** city, town
locale: **7** Montana
Kal Kan
rival: **4** Alpo, Iams **6** Purina
Kallen: **5** Kitty
Kalmar: **4** Bert
Kama __: **5** Sutra
kamala: **4** tree
locale: **4** Asia
Kamali: **5** Norma
Kamchatka: **9** peninsula
locale: **4** Asia **7** Far East
kame: **5** mound, ridge
Kamehameha __: **3** Day
Kamehameha Highway
locale: **4** Oahu
Kamen: **4** Milt
Kamet: **8** mountain
locale: **9** Himalayas
kami: **3** god **6** spirit
Kami: **6** Cotler
Kaminska: **3** Ida
kampai: **5** salud, skoal, toast **6** cheers, prosit, salute **9** happy days
Kampala: **4** city, town **7** capital
former ~ kingpin: **3** Idi **4** Amin
locale: **6** Uganda
Kan.
neighbor: **2** Mo. **3** Col., Neb. **4** Colo., Nebr., Okla.
see also Kansas
__ Kan: **3** Kal
Kanab: **4** city, town
locale: **4** Utah
kanaka: **3** man **8** Hawaiian
Kanakaredes: **6** Melina
Kanaly: **5** Steve
Kanawha, city on the: **10** Charleston
Kanchenjunga: **4** peak **5** mount
locale: **4** Asia **5** Nepal **6** Sikkim
Kandel, Eric: **8** Nobelist
Kander, John: **8** composer
collaborator: Fred Ebb
musical: 70, Girls, 70
The Act
Cabaret
Chicago
A Family Affair
Flora, the Red Menace
The Happy Time
Kiss of the Spider Woman
The Rink
Steel Pier
Woman of the Year
Zorba
song: All I Care About
All That Jazz
But the World Goes 'Round
Cabaret
City Lights
Class
Coffee in a Cardboard Cup
Colored Lights
Dance With Me
Dressing Them Up
Everybody's Girl
First You Dream
The Happy Time
How Lucky Can You Get
I Don't Care Much
I Don't Remember You
Isn't This Better?
Life Is
Married
Marry Me
Maybe This Time
Me and My Baby
Mein Herr
Money
My Coloring Book
My Own Best Friend
My Own Space
New York, New York
Nowadays
Perfectly Marvelous
A Quiet Thing
Razzle Dazzle
Ring Them Bells
Roxie
Sara Lee
Sing Happy
Sometimes a Day Goes By
There Goes the Ball Game
We Can Make It
When You're Good to Mama
Where You Are
Wilkommen
Yes
Kandinsky: **6** Vasily **7** Wassily
Kandinsky, Vasily: **6** artist **7** painter
colleague: Paul Klee
homeland: **6** Russia
Kandy: **4** city **6** resort
locale: **8** Sri Lanka
Kandy-Kolored Tangerine...
author: Tom Wolfe
Kane: **3** Bob **5** Carol, Erica, Helen **6** Joseph
last memory: **4** sled **7** Rosebud
portrayer: **6** Welles
Xanadu to ~: **6** estate
__ Kane: **7** Citizen
Kane and __: **4** Abel
Kaneohe: **3** bay **4** city, town
locale: **4** Oahu **6** Hawaii
Kanga
creator: A.A. Milne
offspring: **3** Roo
kangaroo: **6** animal, hopper, jumper, mammal **9** marsupial
feature: **3** sac **5** pouch **6** pocket
female: **3** doe **5** flier, flyer
group: **5** troop
large ~: **4** euro
like a ~ court: **4** fake, mock, sham **5** bogus, false, hokey, phony **6** ersatz, parody, pseudo **8** so-called, spurious, travesty **9** pretended
male: **4** buck **6** boomer
relative: *see* marsupial
small ~: **5** tungo
young ~: **4** joey
kangaroo __: **3** rat **4** vine **5** court
Kangaroo
author: D.H. Lawrence
__ Kangaroo Down, Sport: **5** Tie Me
Kanin, Garson: **10** playwright
spouse: Ruth Gordon
work: Born Yesterday
kanji
alternative: **4** kana **6** romaji **8** hiragana, katakana

Kankakee: 4 city, town
locale: 8 Illinois
Kans.
see Kansas
Kansa: 5 tribe 6 Indian 7 Amerind
Kansan: 7 Bob Dole, Dorothy 8 Auntie Em 9 Alf Landon, Jayhawker, Jim Lehrer, Wyatt Earp 10 Mort Walker, Wizard of Oz
Kansas: 4 band 5 river, state
city: 4 Iola 5 Paola 6 Lenexa, Olathe, Salina, Topeka 7 Abilene, Emporia, Leawood, Liberal, Shawnee, Wichita 8 Lawrence 9 Dodge City, Fort Riley, Manhattan 10 Garden City, Hutchinson, Kansas City
city on the ~: 6 Topeka
conference: 9 Big Twelve
crop: 4 corn 5 wheat 7 sorghum 8 soybeans
Indian: 8 Kickapoo
like ~ in August: 5 corny
motto word: 5 astra 6 aspera
neighbor: 8 Colorado, Missouri, Nebraska, Oklahoma
pooch: 4 Toto
river: 5 Osage 6 Neosho
river to the ~: 10 Republican
song: Dust in the Wind (1978)
state animal: 7 buffalo
state bird: 10 meadowlark
state flower: 9 sunflower
state insect: 8 honeybee
state tree: 10 cottonwood
Kansas ___ steak: 4 City
Kansas City: 4 city, town
county: 4 Clay 6 Platte 7 Jackson
locale: 6 Kansas 8 Missouri
newspaper: 4 Star
pro team: 6 Chiefs, Royals
river: 8 Missouri
Kansas City (1959 song)
artist: Wilbert Harrison
Kansas-Nebraska ___: 3 Act
Kansas State University
athletes: 8 Wildcats
conference: 9 Big Twelve
locale: 9 Manhattan
Kant, Immanuel: 6 German 11 philosopher
Kantner: 4 Paul
Kantor: 4 Seth 6 Mickey 9 MacKinlay
Kantorovich, Leonid: 8 Nobelist 9 economist
Kanuri home: 4 Chad 5 Niger 6 Africa 7 Nigeria 8 Cameroon
kaolin: 4 clay 9 china clay, terra alba
kaon: 5 meson 8 particle
Kapell, William: 7 pianist
kaph: 6 Hebrew, letter
predecessor: 3 yod 4 yodh
successor: 5 lamed 6 lamedh
___ Kapital: 3 Das
Kapitän
command: 5 U-boat
Kapitsa: 5 Pyotr
Kaplan: 4 Gabe, peak 5 Hyman, mount 8 Jonathan, mountain
locale: 10 Antarctica
kapok: 4 fuzz, tree 5 ceiba, fiber 8 filament
Kapoor: 4 Anil
Kapor: 5 Mitch
kapow: 3 bam 4 boom, slam, wham
kappa: 5 Greek 6 letter
follower: 6 lambda
preceder: 4 iota
Kappelhoff, Doris: 3 Day
Kapture: 5 Mitzi
Kapuas: 5 river
locale: 6 Borneo
kaput: 4 beat, fini, over, shot, sunk, worn 5 broke 6 broken, done in, finito, no more, ruined, undone 7 all over, belly-up, damaged, defunct, done for, extinct, totaled, worn-out, wrecked 8 finished, obsolete, washed-up, wiped out 9 burned out, destroyed 10 beyond help, broken-down, demolished, dissipated, on the blink, on the fritz
go ~: 3 die 4 fail, flop, fold 6 fizzle 7 conk out 8 backfire 9 break down
not ~: 5 going 6 usable 7 running, working 8 operable, unbroken 9 operative
Kara: 9 DioGuardi
Kara ___: 3 Kum, Sea
Karachi: 4 city, port, town
language: 4 Urdu
locale: 8 Pakistan
river: 5 Indus
Karajan, Herbert von: 8 Austrian 9 conductor
Karakoram: 5 range
locale: 4 Asia 7 Kashmir 8 Cashmere
karakul: 3 fur 5 sheep
Kara Kum: 6 desert
Karamazov: 4 Ivan 5 Mitya 6 Alexey, Dmitri, Fyodor 7 Alyosha
Karan: 5 Donna
karanda: 4 tree 5 shrub
family: 7 dogbane
relative: 8 oleander 10 frangipani
___ karaoke: 5 laser
karaoke need: 4 mike
Karas, Anton instrument: zither
Kara Sea, river to the: 7 Yenisei
karate: 5 sport 10 martial art
attire: 2 gi 4 belt
belt: 5 black, brown, green, white
cousin: 4 judo 6 aikido
level: 3 dan
move: 4 chop, kick
origin: 5 Japan
studio: 4 dojo
target: 5 board
teacher: 6 sensei
warm-up: 4 kata
karate ___: 4 chop 6 sticks
Karate Kid, The (1984 film)
cast: Ralph Macchio, Pat Morita, Elisabeth Shue
Kareem: 3 Lew
alma mater: 4 UCLA
Kareem ___-Jabbar: 5 Abdul
Karel: 5 Capek, Reisz
Karen: 5 Akers, Allen, Black, Duffy 6 Blixen, Finlay, Horney, Morley, Sillas 7 Dotrice, Grassle 8 Silkwood 9 Carpenter, Valentine
___ Karenina: 4 Anna
Karim of the Khans: 3 Aga
Karin: 4 Enke
Karina: 7 Lombard
Karl: 4 Benz, Böhm, Marx, Rove 5 Barth, Bosch, Braun, Gauss, Kraus 6 Czerny, Eberth, Malden, Malone, Müller, Myrdal, Popper, Renner 7 Gutzkow, Jaspers, Pearson, Scheele, Shapiro, von Baer, Ziegler 8 Baedeker, Branting, Siegbahn, Wallenda 9 Gjellerup, Lagerfeld, Menninger, von Frisch
Karlfeldt, Erik: 4 poet 7 Swedish 8 Nobelist
Karloff, Boris: 5 actor
film: Bedlam (1946)
The Black Cat (1934)
The Black Room (1935)
The Body Snatcher (1945)
Bride of Frankenstein (1935)
The Climax (1944)
The Comedy of Terrors (1964)
Frankenstein (1931)
House of Rothschild (1934)
Isle of the Dead (1945)
The Lost Patrol (1934)
The Mummy (1932)
Night World (1932)
The Old Dark House (1932)
The Raven (1935)
The Secret Life of Walter Mitty (1947)
Son of Frankenstein (1939)
The Walking Dead (1936)
real last name: 5 Pratt
Karlovy Vary: 3 spa 5 Czech
Karlson: 4 Phil
Karl von ___: 4 Baer 6 Frisch
karma: 3 lot 4 fate, luck, vibe 5 vibes 6 kismat, kismet 7 destiny, fortune
___ Karma: 7 Instant
Karma Chameleon (1983 song)
artist: Culture Club
Karmann ___: 4 Ghia
Karnak
locale: 5 Egypt
neighbor: 5 Luxor
river: 4 Nile
Temple of ~ site: 6 Thebes
Karns: 6 Roscoe
Karo: 5 syrup
rival: 8 Log Cabin
Karok: 5 tribe
locale: 10 California
Karolyi, Bela: 5 coach
forte: 10 gymnastics
karoo: 7 plateau
Karpov, Anatoly
forte: 5 chess
Karras, Alex: 5 actor
film: Paper Lion (1968)
Victor/Victoria (1982)
spouse: Susan Clark
TV: Webster
Karrie: 4 Webb
Karsavina: 6 Tamara
Karsh: 6 Yousuf
karst: 9 limestone
kart: 5 racer
Karyn: 5 White 7 Allison
Kasbah
see Casbah
Kasdan: 4 Jake 8 Lawrence
Kasem, Casey: 6 deejay 10 disc jockey
kasha: 5 grain 6 groats 9 buckwheat
Kasha: 6 fabric
Kashi: 6 cereal
competitor: *see* cereal
Kashmir: 4 wool 7 sweater
cash: 5 rupee
deer: 6 hangul
feature: 4 vale
mountain: 6 Nunkun 7 Mustagh 9 Karakoram, Sia Kangri 10 Masherbrum
river: 5 Indus
Kashmir ___: 3 rug 4 goat
kashruth expert: 5 rabbi, rebbe
Kaskasia: 5 tribe
locale: 8 Illinois
Kaspar: 5 Wolff
Kasparov, Garry
forte: 5 chess
rival: 6 Karpov 8 Deep Blue
Kassebaum, Nancy: 6 Kansan
father: 3 Alf 6 Landon
formerly: 3 sen. 7 senator
Kassel: 4 city, town
locale: 7 Germany
river: 4 Eder 5 Fulda
Kastler, Alfred: 8 Nobelist 9 physicist
Kastner: 5 Peter
Katahdin: 4 peak 5 mount 8 mountain
locale: 5 Maine
katakana
alternative: 4 kana 5 kanji 6 romaji 8 hiragana
Katarina: 4 Witt
Katayev, Valentin: 6 writer 7 Russian 10 playwright
___-Kat Club: 3 Kit
Kate: 4 Bush, Moss, Reid 5 O'Mara, Smith 6 Chopin, Hudson, Linder, Wiggin 7 Capshaw, Fansler, Jackson, Millett, Mulgrew, Pierson, Winslet 8 Bosworth, Nelligan 9 Greenaway 10 Beckinsale
colleague: 6 Farrah, Jaclyn
companion: 5 Allie
to Petruchio: 4 wife
Kate & Allie (CBS sitcom)
cast: Jane Curtin (Allie Lowell)
Ari Meyers (Emma McArdle)
Susan Saint James (Kate McArdle)
Kate & Leopold (2001 film)
cast: Hugh Jackman, Meg Ryan, Liev Schreiber
___-Kate Olsen: 4 Mary
Katey: 5 Sagal
Katharine: 4 Ross 6 Graham 7 Cornell, Hepburn
Katharine ___ Bates: 3 Lee
Katharine ___ School: 5 Gibbs
Katherine: 5 Heigl 6 Dunham 7 Cornell, Helmond 9 Mansfield
in Irish: 7 Caitlin
Katherine ___ Porter: 4 Anne
Kathie ___ Gifford: 3 Lee
Kathleen: 5 Lloyd, Nolan, Noone, Raine 6 Battle, Kenyon, Norris, Turner 7 Freeman, Kinmont, Quinlan 8 Sullivan
Kathryn: 4 Erbe 5 Grant 6 Murray 7 Bigelow, Grayson, Harrold
Kathryn's dancing partner: 6 Arthur
Kathy: 5 Baker, Bates, Young 6 Garver, Kinney, Lennon, Linden, Mattea, Najimy 7 Ireland 9 Whitworth
Katie: 6 Couric, Holmes, Wagner
Katie Went to Haiti
composer: Cole Porter
Katina: 7 Paxinou
Katmai: 4 park, peak 5 mount 7 volcano 8 mountain
locale: 6 Alaska
Katmandu: 4 city, town 7 capital
like ~: 4 high 5 lofty 8 elevated
locale: 5 Nepal
Kato to the Green Hornet: 4 aide

Katrina and the Waves
song: Walking on Sunshine (1985)
Katrine: **4** loch
locale: **8** Scotland
Katt: **5** Nicky **7** William
Kattegat: **6** strait
locale: **8** North Sea
Katy: **6** Jurado
__-Katy: **3** K-K-K
katydid: **3** bug **6** insect
Katz: **4** Omri **7** Bernard
Katzenberg: **7** Jeffrey
katzenjammer: **6** clamor, uproar **7** anguish **8** distress, hangover **10** uneasiness
Katzenjammer Kids, The: **5** comic, strip
artist: Rudolph Dirks, Harold Knerr
cry: **3** ach
kid: **4** Hans **5** Fritz
Kauai: **4** isle **6** island
locale: **6** Hawaii
neighbor: **4** Oahu
Kaufman: **3** Bel **4** Andy **6** George, Philip
Kaufman, Andy sitcom: **4** Taxi
Kaufman, George S.: **6** writer **10** playwright
collaborator: **4** Hart **6** Ferber **7** Lardner, Ryskind **8** Connelly
middle name: Simon
nickname: The Great Collaborator
work: Animal Crackers
Beggar on Horseback
The Butter and Egg Man
The Cocoanuts
Dinner at Eight
Dulcy
I'd Rather Be Right
June Moon
The Man Who Came to Dinner
Of Thee I Sing
Once in a Lifetime
The Solid Gold Cadillac
Stage Door
You Can't Take It With You
kava: **5** booze, drink, shrub **7** alcohol, potable **8** beverage **10** intoxicant
relative: **5** cubeb **6** pepper
Kavafian: **3** Ani, Ida
Kavanaugh, Patrick: **4** poet **5** Irish
Kavi: **3** Raz
Kavir: **6** desert
Kavner, Julie: **7** actress
TV: Rhoda, The Simpsons, The Tracey Ullman Show
Kawabata: **8** Yasunari
Kawartha Lakes
locale: **7** Ontario
Kawasaki: **10** motorcycle
competitor: **6** Harley, Yamaha
kay: **6** letter
follower: **3** ell
preceder: **3** jay
Kay: **3** Yow **4** Lenz **5** Armen, Boyle, Kyser, Starr, Swift, Walsh **6** knight **7** Francis, Johnson, Kendall, Miniver **8** Corleone, Thompson
title for ~: **3** Sir
__ Kay: **4** Mary
kayak: **4** boat **5** canoe, skiff
cousin: **5** umiak **6** dugout **9** outrigger
locale: **6** Arctic, rapids
need: **3** oar
user: **5** Inuit, rower **6** Eskimo, Innuit, Inupik
__ Kay Ash: **4** Mary

Kaye: **4** Nora **5** Danny, Sammy **6** Stubby **7** Ballard
Kaye, Danny: **5** actor **8** comedian
film: Court Jester (1956)
Hans Christian Andersen (1952)
The Inspector General (1949)
The Kid From Brooklyn (1946)
Knock on Wood (1954)
On the Double (1961)
On the Riviera (1951)
The Secret Life of Walter Mitty (1947)
White Christmas (1954)
Wonder Man (1945)
Kaye Lani Rae __: **5** Rafko
Kaye, Sammy instrument: clarinet, sax
kayo: **3** hit **4** deck, stun **5** floor **6** defeat **7** flatten **8** knock out
__ Kay Place: **4** Mary
Kazakhstan: **6** nation **7** country
capital: **6** Astana
city: **6** Astana **7** Alma-Ata
desert: **7** Kara Kum **8** Kyzyl Kum
lake: **8** Balkhash
neighbor: **5** China **6** Russia **10** Kyrgyzstan, Uzbekistan
once: **3** SSR
range: **5** Altai
river: **4** Ural **5** Tobol
sea: **4** Aral
Kazan: **4** Elia **6** Lainie
republic: **5** Tatar
Kazan, Elia: **8** director
film: Baby Doll (1956)
East of Eden (1955)
A Face in the Crowd (1957)
Gentleman's Agreement (1947, AA)
The Last Tycoon (1976)
On the Waterfront (1954, AA)
Panic in the Streets (1950)
Splendor in the Grass (1961)
A Streetcar Named Desire (1951)
A Tree Grows in Brooklyn (1945)
Viva Zapata! (1952)
Kazantzakis, Nikos: **5** Greek **6** writer
work: The Last Temptation of Christ
Zorba the Greek
kazatsky: **5** dance **7** Russian
Kazbec: **5** mount **7** volcano
locale: **8** Caucasus
kazoo: **3** toy **4** wind, zobo
play a ~: **3** hum **4** buzz **5** drone
Kazurinsky: **3** Tim
KC and the Sunshine Band
song: Get Down Tonight (1975)
I'm Your Boogie Man (1977)
Keep It Comin' Love (1977)
Please Don't Go (1979)
Shake Your Booty (1976)
That's the Way (1975)
Yes I'm Ready (1979)
k.d.: **4** lang
__ K. Dick: **6** Philip
K-Doe: **5** Ernie
kea: **4** bird **6** parrot
__ Kea: **5** Mauna
Keach: **5** James, Stacy
Keach, James: **5** actor
brother: Stacy
spouse: Jane Seymour
Keach, Stacy: **5** actor
brother: James
TV: Caribe, Mike Hammer, Titus
Kean: **6** Edmund

Keane: **3** Bil
Keanu: **6** Reeves
Kearney: **4** city, town
locale: **8** Nebraska
__ Kearney: **4** Fort
Kearns: **6** Joseph
Kearny: **4** city, town
locale: **9** New Jersey
Keating: **5** Larry **7** Dominic
Keaton: **5** Diane **6** Buster **7** Michael
to Allen: **6** costar
Keaton, Buster: **5** actor **8** comedian
film: A Funny Thing Happened... (1966)
The General (1927)
It's a Mad Mad Mad Mad World (1963)
Sherlock, Jr. (1924)
Speak Easily (1932)
Steamboat Bill, Jr. (1928)
nickname: The Great Stone Face
Keaton, Diane: **7** actress
film: Annie Hall (1977, AA)
Baby Boom (1987)
Crimes of the Heart (1986)
The Family Stone (2005)
Father of the Bride (1991)
The First Wives Club (1996)
The Godfather (1972)
The Good Mother (1988)
Hanging Up (2000)
Interiors (1978)
The Little Drummer Girl (1984)
Looking for Mr. Goodbar (1977)
Love and Death (1975)
Mad Money (2008)
Manhattan (1979)
Manhattan Murder Mystery (1993)
The Other Sister (1999)
Play It Again, Sam (1972)
Reds (1981)
Shoot the Moon (1982)
Sleeper (1973)
Something's Gotta Give (2003)
Keaton, Elyse
child: **4** Alex **7** Mallory
Keaton, Michael: **5** actor
film: Batman (1989)
Batman Returns (1992)
Beetlejuice (1988)
Clean and Sober (1988)
The Dream Team (1989)
Gung Ho (1986)
Jack Frost (1998)
Jackie Brown (1997)
Mr. Mom (1983)
Night Shift (1982)
Out of Sight (1998)
Pacific Heights (1990)
The Paper (1994)
Speechless (1994)
Keats, John: **4** poet **7** British
contemporary: **5** Byron **7** Shelley
like some ~ works: **4** odic
Muse for ~: **5** Erato
work: Endymion
The Eve of St. Agnes
Hyperion
Isabella
Lamia
Meg Merrilies
Ode on a Grecian Urn
Ode on Indolence
Ode on Melancholy
Ode to a Nightingale
Ode to Autumn
Ode to Psyche
On First Looking Into Chapman's Homer
To Autumn
To Homer
To Sleep
When I Have Fears
kebab: **5** spear **6** skewer **9** brochette
bed: **5** pilaf, pilau, pilaw **6** pilaff
ingredient: **4** lamb, meat
__ kebab: **5** shish
kedge: **6** anchor
Kedrova, Lila Oscar: Zorba the Greek
Keds: **6** sneaks **8** sneakers
competitor: **4** Avia, Nike **6** Adidas, Reebok **8** Converse
Keebler: **6** cookie
brand: **5** Zesta
competitor: *see* cookie manufacturer
worker: **3** elf
Keefe: **3** Tim **9** Brasselle
keel: **3** yaw **4** cant, lean, list, reel, roll, sway, toss **5** heave, lurch, pitch, swing **6** careen, wallow **8** flounder
deck just above the ~: **5** orlop
ender: **4** boat, haul
extension: **4** skeg
on an even ~: **5** level **6** smooth, stable, steady
over: **3** tip **4** fall, list **5** faint, slump, swoon **6** go limp, topple **7** capsize, pass out **8** overturn
pole: **4** mast
keel __: **4** over
Keel: **6** Howard
keel, at right angles to: **5** abeam
keelbone, bird: **6** carina
Keeler: **4** Ruby **6** Willie
Keeler, Ruby: **6** dancer **7** actress
film: 42nd Street (1933)
Colleen (1936)
Dames (1934)
spouse: Al Jolson
style: **3** tap
Keeler, Willie: **10** outfielder
keelhaul: **6** punish, rebuke
Keel, Howard: **5** actor
film: Annie Get Your Gun (1950)
Calamity Jane (1953)
Day of the Triffids (1963)
Jupiter's Darling (1955)
Kiss Me Kate (1953)
Seven Brides for Seven Brothers (1954)
Show Boat (1951)
The War Wagon (1967)
TV: Dallas
keelson: **6** girder, timber
Keely: **5** Smith
keen: **3** mad **4** able, agog, avid, howl, moan, sour, wail, weep **5** acute, brisk, eager, edged, fresh, honed, itchy, mourn, quick, ready, sharp, smart, spicy, witty **6** ardent, astute, bright, fervid, gnarly, gung ho, intent, lament, lively, on edge, rah-rah, shrewd, spicey, strong, subtle **7** anxious, athirst, cunning, cutting, earnest, fervent, fired up, glowing, intense, pointed, pungent, thirsty, ululate, whetted, zealous **8** animated, deepfelt, desirous, enthused, incisive, lynx-eyed,

piercing, poignant, profound, spirited, vigilant, watchful **9** admirable, astucious, farseeing, judicious, observant, sagacious, sensitive, sharpened, sprightly, trenchant, wonderful **10** all fired up, discerning, insightful, inspirited, interested, longheaded, passionate, perceptive, raring to go, sharp-edged, solicitous, take it hard, thoughtful
be ~ on: **4** like, love **5** adore
make ~: **4** whet **5** pique, rally, rouse, strop **6** arouse, excite, kindle **7** sharpen
not ~: **4** dull, slow **5** blunt, dense **6** obtuse, stupid **7** witless **9** dimwitted
on: **6** fond of **7** stuck on, sweet on **9** partial to **10** in love with
perception: **3** wit **5** grasp **6** acuity, acumen, wisdom **7** insight **8** judgment, lucidity **9** acuteness, awareness **10** astuteness, brainpower, brilliance, cleverness, shrewdness
(to): **7** itching **9** hankering
see also wonderful
__ keen: **6** peachy
Keenan: **4** Wynn
father: **2** Ed
Keene: **7** Carolyn
sleuth: **4** Drew **5** Nancy
keen-edged: **5** sharp
Keenen __ Wayans: **5** Ivory
Keener, Catherine: **7** actress
film: Being John Malkovich (1999)
Capote (2005)
Death to Smoochy (2002)
Full Frontal (2002)
Living in Oblivion (1995)
The Real Blonde (1998)
The Soloist (2009)
keen-eyed: **4** wary **5** acute, alert, chary, sharp **6** bright, intent **7** careful, on guard, prudent **8** cautious, discreet, hawk-eyed, lynx-eyed, on the job, vigilant, watchful **9** eagle-eyed, observant, wide-awake **10** discerning, perceptive
keening: **6** lament **7** moaning, wailing **8** grieving, mourning, threnody
keenly: **4** hard **5** madly, sharp **6** avidly **7** acutely, eagerly **8** ardently, bitterly, doggedly, fiercely, intently, strongly, urgently **9** earnestly, intensely, painfully, zealously **10** rigorously
keenness: **3** wit **4** edge, wits, zeal, zest **5** ardor, depth, sense **6** acuity, acumen, smarts, thirst, vision, wisdom **7** cogency, cunning **8** foxiness, vivacity **9** assiduity, awareness, canniness, diligence, eagerness, intensity, poignancy, readiness, sharpness, smartness **10** astuteness, cleverness, cognizance, enthusiasm, perception
keen-witted: **5** alert, quick, smart **6** bright, clever **8** animated **9** sprightly
keep: **3** hog, own, run **4** feed, grip, have, hold, mind, save, tend **5** amass, cache, carry, grasp, hoard, lay by, lay up, put by, stack, stock, store, tower **6** detain, donjon, foster, garner, intern, living, manage, occupy, pickle, prison, retain, save up, shield, upkeep **7** aliment, care for, carry on, château, citadel, conduct, control, deposit, impound, nourish, nurture, observe, operate, possess, prevent, provide, put away, refrain, reserve, respect, shelter, support, sustain **8** adhere to, conserve, fastness, fortress, hang onto, hold on to, maintain, preserve, put aside, salt away, sanctify, withhold **9** carry over, celebrate, look after, ritualize, safeguard, solemnize, watch over **10** accumulate, administer, consecrate, livelihood, minister to, provide for, stronghold, sustenance
abreast of: **6** follow **7** monitor
account: **3** log **4** file, list **5** tally **6** record, report **7** archive, catalog, itemize, jot down, journal, monitor, put down, set down **8** mark down, register, tabulate **9** catalogue, chronicle, enumerate, inventory, write down
afloat: **4** swim **7** survive, sustain
after: **3** dun, nag **5** hound
after class: **6** detain
alert: **5** watch **6** beware **7** look out
a lid on: **4** curb **5** cover, limit **6** rein in, stifle **7** conceal, contain, control, cover up, repress **8** bottle up, hold back, restrain, restrict, suppress **9** constrain, stonewall, whitewash **10** keep secret
a low profile: **4** hide, lurk **6** hole up **7** conceal **9** take cover
an eye on: **4** boss, mark, mind, tend **5** guard, scout, study, watch **6** advert, attend, detect, direct, follow, manage, notice, patrol, police **7** babysit, discern, monitor, observe, oversee **8** chaperon, shepherd **9** look after, supervise **10** administer, ride herd on, scrutinize
apart: **7** isolate, seclude **8** separate
a promise: **4** meet **6** please **7** fulfill, gratify, perform, satisfy **8** make good, reassure **9** discharge
as a bird: **6** encage
a step ahead of: **5** one up, outdo
a stiff lower lip: **4** fume, mope, pout, sulk **5** brood, frown **6** glower
a stiff upper lip: **6** bear up, hang in **8** face up to
at: **7** stick to **8** continue, stay with **9** persist in **10** see through
at bay: **5** repel **6** rebuff **7** ward off **8** hold back
at it: **4** goon, plod **5** retry
away from: **4** duck, shun, skip, snub **5** avoid, ditch, dodge, elude, evade, parry, scorn, shirk **6** beware, escape, eschew, give up, ignore, refuse, reject, shrink **7** boycott, disdain, neglect, refrain **8** forswear, renounce, shake off, sidestep, swear off **9** ostracize
back: **5** check, dam up, delay, flunk **6** detain **7** forbear, reserve **8** withhold
busy: **5** tie up **6** employ, engage, occupy
castle ~: **6** donjon **7** dungeon
clear of: **4** shun **5** avoid, elude, skirt **6** rebuff **7** neglect, ward off
close: **3** hug, pet **5** clasp, touch **6** clutch, cradle, cuddle, enfold, nestle **7** embrace, snuggle
company: **3** woo **6** hobnob **7** consort **9** socialize
company with: **3** see **4** date **5** court
don't ~: **3** can **4** fire **5** let go, throw, yield **6** unhand **7** abandon, release, set free **8** cut loose **9** discharge, sacrifice, surrender **10** relinquish
don't ~ a secret: **3** air, gab **4** blab, leak, tell **5** blurt, let on, level, spill **6** clue in, fill in, gossip, impart, inform, notify, open up, relate, report, reveal, squeal, tattle, tip off, unveil **7** apprise, breathe, divulge, find out, give out, let in on, let know, let slip, mention, recount, spit out, whisper **8** acquaint, announce, disclose, give away **9** leave word, make known **10** keep posted, let be known
don't ~ straight: **4** bend, skew, warp **5** curve, slant **6** buckle, deform **7** contort, distort
down: **3** eat **5** abuse, bully, crush, force, grind **6** ingest, pick on, sadden, saddle, subdue **7** afflict, depress, oppress, put upon, smother **8** aggrieve, browbeat, domineer, maltreat, overload, suppress **9** overpower, overwhelm, persecute, subjugate, trample on, tyrannize
ender: **4** sake
expenses low: **4** save **5** skimp **6** scrape, scrimp **8** conserve, roll back **9** economize **10** cut corners
fail to ~: **4** lose **5** use up, waste **6** divest, mislay **7** forfeit **8** misplace, squander **9** dissipate **10** run through
fail to ~ up: **3** lag **4** drag, flag, poke **5** dally, tarry, trail **6** dawdle, falter, linger, loiter **7** fall off, slacken **8** hang back, lose time, straggle **9** inch along **10** dilly-dally, lose ground, move slowly
faithful to: **4** heed, obey **6** adhere, follow **7** abide by, conform, fulfill, observe, respect, stand by **8** carry out **9** discharge, stick with **10** comply with
fit: **3** jog, run **7** work out **8** exercise
from: **4** curb, fast, shun **5** avoid, evade, forgo, spurn **6** abjure, eschew, pass up, refuse, resist **7** abstain, back off, forbear, inhibit, refrain **8** abnegate, leave off, renounce, restrain, withhold **9** do without, interrupt
from falling: **5** brace, stake **6** hold up **7** shore up, support **8** buttress **9** reinforce, stabilize **10** strengthen
from happening: **4** foil **5** avert, avoid, block, deter **6** stifle, stymie, thwart **7** fend off, forfend, head off, hold off, prevent, ward off **8** hold back, obstruct, stave off **9** forestall, interrupt
from leaving: **4** hold **5** delay **6** detain, hold up, impede **7** set back **8** restrain, slow down **10** buttonhole
going: **5** run on **6** extend, hold on, push on **7** persist, subsist, sustain **8** continue, maintain, progress, protract **9** persevere **10** perpetuate
guard: **5** watch **6** defend, patrol, picket, police **7** protect
hanging: **5** tease, worry **6** entice, lead on **7** torment **8** interest **9** fascinate, frustrate, tantalize, titillate
house: **4** dust **6** settle **7** clean up
in: **6** ground, stifle **7** repress **9** constrain
in a steady state: **3** fix, set **4** prop **6** freeze, secure, steady **7** balance, support **8** maintain, preserve **9** stabilize
in custody: **4** hold, jail **6** arrest, detain, immure, intern, lock up, remand **7** confine, impound, put away **8** imprison, sentence
in line: **4** curb, stem **5** check, deter, leash, limit, sit on **6** forbid, stifle, tether **7** control, curtail, inhibit, repress, squelch **8** hold back, moderate, prohibit, restrain, restrict, straiten, suppress, tone down **9** constrain, crack down
in mind: **6** recall **7** bethink **8** remember **9** entertain, recognize, recollect
in play: **6** joggle, juggle **7** shuffle
in reserve: **5** put by, store **7** put away **8** put aside
inside: **6** garage **7** enclose
in sight: **3** dog, tag **4** tail **5** spy on, stalk, trail, watch **6** pursue, shadow **8** run after **9** accompany
in step: **4** obey **6** comply, follow **7** abide by, agree to, conform **10** toe the line
in stitches: **5** amuse **9** entertain
in stock: **4** have, save **5** carry, stock, store **6** handle **9** inventory
in the loop: **4** tell, warn **5** brief **6** advise, fill in, inform, notify, tip off **7** apprise, apprize **8** forewarn **9** enlighten
in touch: **4** meet **5** reach **6** roll in, show up **7** check in, contact **9** get hold of
it down: **4** mute **6** cool it **7** silence
it won't ~ you up: **5** decaf, Sanka
nothing back: **5** level
occupied: **4** hold **5** amuse, delay, tie up **6** divert, engage, hinder, impede **8** encumber, obstruct, slow down
on: **5** abide **6** endure, pursue, remain, resume **8** continue **9** persevere
one going: **3** aid **6** assist **8** tide over **9** help along **10** see through
one's distance: **4** shun, snub **5** evade, scorn, shirk, spurn **6** bypass, ignore, rebuff, slight **7** disdain, dismiss, neglect, tune out **8** brush off, shrug off **9** disregard, pay no mind **10** disrespect, leave alone
(oneself) away: **6** absent
one's fingers crossed: **4** hope,

wish 5 dream 6 aspire, expect 7 look for 10 anticipate
one's nose clean: 4 obey 6 behave 10 toe the line
one's nose to the grindstone: 4 moil, plod, toil, work 5 labor, sweat 6 drudge, strain, strive 8 work hard 9 plug along, pound away
one's shirt on: 4 bide, wait 5 abide 6 cool it, hold on 7 stand by, sweat it 8 sit tight
one who can't ~ a secret: 5 sieve
out: 3 ban, bar 4 tabu 5 debar 7 exclude, shut off
out of sight: 4 bury, hide, mask, palm, stow, veil 5 cache, cloak, couch, cover, shade, stash 6 harbor, lie low, pocket, screen, shield, shroud 7 blanket, conceal, cover up, envelop, harbour, obscure, seclude, secrete, shelter, shut off, shut out 8 disguise, ensconce, enshroud, stow away, suppress, withhold 9 adumbrate, dissemble, whitewash 10 camouflage
pace: 4 meet 5 rival 9 measure up
pace with: 3 tie 5 equal, match, rival 8 parallel
posted: 4 tell 5 ready 6 advise
quiet: 4 hide 5 quell, sit on 6 hush up, stifle 7 cover up, smother, squelch 8 suppress
repeating: 5 chant 6 intone
safe: 4 hide 5 guard 6 assure, back up, defend, foster, harbor, patrol, police, screen, secure, shield 7 fortify, protect, shelter, ward off 8 chaperon, fight for, preserve, shepherd 9 look after, safeguard, watch over 10 take care of
saying: 5 rub in 6 harp on 7 belabor
score: 3 add, sum 5 add up, count, sum up, tally, total, tot up 6 figure, number, record 7 compute 8 register 9 enumerate
secret: 4 hide, mask, veil 5 cache, cloak, couch, cover, sit on 6 hush up 7 conceal, cover up, obscure 8 disguise, suppress 10 camouflage
smiling: 5 amuse, cheer 6 divert, please, tickle 7 delight 9 entertain
starter: 3 bar 5 house
still: 3 gag 4 hush 5 choke, shush 6 muzzle, shut up, stifle 7 silence 8 pipe down
tabs: 5 gauge, judge 6 assess, figure, notice, reckon 7 account, compute, look out, measure 8 appraise, evaluate, watch out 9 calculate
the faith: 6 redeem 7 abide by, believe 8 adhere to, carry out
the wolf from the door: 4 work 7 peg away 9 grind away
time: 3 tap 4 clap
together: 3 mix, wed 4 ally, band, meet, pool 5 marry, unite 6 cleave, club up, hook up, mingle, pair up 7 partner 9 affiliate, associate, cooperate 10 close ranks, join forces
track of: 4 tend 5 track, watch 6 follow 7 monitor, oversee 9 check up on
under surveillance: 5 guard, watch 6 patrol, police 7 baby-sit, observe, protect 9 chaperone, safeguard
up: 8 continue, maintain, preserve, stay even
(up): 4 prop
up with: 3 tie 4 draw, meet 5 match, rival 9 break even
up with the times: 5 adapt 6 adjust, change, modify, revise 7 conform, remodel 8 accustom 10 assimilate, come around
waiting: 4 slow 5 delay, stall 6 detain, hang up, hinder, hold up, impede, retard 7 bog down, set back 8 postpone
within bounds: 4 curb 5 check, limit 6 temper 7 contain 8 moderate, regulate, restrain, restrict 9 constrict
keep __: 4 at it, back, down, it up, pace, time, up on 7 smiling
keep __ dark: 5 in the
keep __ of: 5 track
keep __ on: 4 tabs 5 an eye
keep __ out for: 5 an eye
keep __ profile: 4 a low
keep __ to the ground: 5 an ear
keep __ with: 7 company
Keep __ cards and letters coming!: 5 those
keep a __ eye open: 7 weather
keep a __ upper lip: 5 stiff
Keep A Knockin' (1957 song)
artist: Little Richard
keep an __: 5 eye on 6 eye out
keep an __ the ground: 5 ear to
keep a straight __: 4 face
Keep Coming Back (1991 song)
artist: Richard Marx
keeper: 4 host 5 guard, owner 6 jailer, warden 7 curator, steward 8 defender, guardian, overseer, watchdog 9 archivist, attendant, caretaker, custodian, protector 10 supervisor
peace ~: 7 bailiff, marshal, sheriff 9 policeman 10 law officer
starter: 3 bar, bee, inn, net, zoo 4 book, door, game, gate, goal, lock, shop, time 5 hotel, house, peace, score, store 6 greens, ground, saloon, wicket 7 grounds
Keeper of the Castle (1972 song)
artist: Four Tops
__ keepers: 7 finders
Keepers of the House, The
author: Shirley Ann Grau
keep in __: 4 mind
keeping: 4 care, egis 5 aegis, trust 6 accord, charge, saving 7 custody, harmony, holding 8 auspices, hoarding, tutelage, wardship 9 orthodoxy, oversight, patronage, retaining, storing up 10 conformity, husbanding, observance, preserving, protection
be in ~ with: 6 follow
in: 6 arrest 7 custody 9 detention, retention 10 constraint, detainment, immurement, internment, quarantine
in ~: 5 typic 7 typical 8 suitable 9 agreeable, agreeably 10 compatible
out: 7 boycott, embargo 9 exclusion, expulsion, interdict, ostracism
out of ~: 4 rude 5 crude, gross, inapt, undue 6 coarse, off-key, vulgar 7 lowbred, uncouth 8 immodest, improper, indecent, unseemly, untoward 9 inelegant, tasteless, unrefined 10 indecorous, indelicate, malapropos, suggestive, unbecoming, unsuitable
starter: 4 book, safe, time 5 house, peace, score, store
the faith: 6 upbeat 7 hopeful 8 aspiring, sanguine, trusting 9 confident, expectant 10 optimistic
Keeping Faith
author: Jimmy Carter
Keeping the Faith (2000 film)
cast: Anne Bancroft, Jenna Elfman, Edward Norton, Ben Stiller
keep in the __: 4 dark
keep-in-touch device: 5 pager
Keep It Comin' Love (1977 song)
artist: KC and the Sunshine Band
Keep it down!: 3 shh 4 hush 5 quiet
Keep It Together (1990 song)
artist: Madonna
keep one's __: 4 cool, head, word 5 eye on, peace, place 8 distance
keep one's __ above water: 4 head
keep one's __ clean: 4 nose
keep one's __ crossed: 7 fingers
keep one's __ dry: 6 powder
keep one's __ on: 5 shirt
keep one's __ up: 4 chin
keep one's eyes __: 4 open 6 peeled
Keep On, Keepin' On (1996 song)
artist: MC Lyte, Xscape
Keep On Loving You (1980 song)
artist: REO Speedwagon
Keep On Singing (1974 song)
artist: Helen Reddy
Keep on Truckin' (1973 song)
artist: Eddie Kendricks
keepsake: 5 favor, relic, token 7 memento 8 reminder, souvenir
holder: 5 attic 6 locket
keeps, for: 4 ever 6 always, grimly 7 for good, gravely, soberly 9 earnestly, eternally, seriously, sincerely 10 resolutely, unendingly
keep the __: 5 faith, peace
keep the __ from the door: 4 wolf
keep the __ rolling: 4 ball
Keep the Aspidistra Flying
author: George Orwell
Keep the Fire Burnin' (1982 song)
artist: REO Speedwagon
Keep Their Heads Ringin' (1995 song)
artist: Dr. Dre
Keep Ya Head Up (1993 song)
artist: Tupac
Keep your __ on!: 5 shirt
Keep your __ shut!: 3 yap 4 trap
Keep your __ the ball!: 5 eye on
Keeshan: 3 Bob
Keeshond: 3 dog 5 canid 6 canine
Keeslar: 4 Matt
Keesler: 3 AFB
Kefauver: 3 sen. 5 Estes 7 senator
home: 9 Tennessee
kefir: 5 drink 7 Russian 8 beverage
keg: 3 bbl., tub 4 cask 6 barrel, firkin 8 hogshead 9 container
adjunct: 3 tap
contents: 3 ale 4 beer 6 powder
cousin: 3 vat
party locale: 4 frat 10 fraternity
stopper: 4 bung, cork, plug
keg __: 5 party
__ keg: 6 powder
kegler: 6 bowler
Keighley: 7 William
Keillor: 8 Garrison
Keino, Kip: 6 Kenyan, runner 10 marathoner
Keio University
city: 5 Tokio, Tokyo
Keir: 6 Dullea
Keira: 9 Knightley
Keiser, Herman: 6 golfer
Keitel, Harvey: 5 actor
spouse: Lorraine Bracco
Keith: 4 Moon, Toby 5 Brian, David, Sweat 6 Coogan, Gordon, Haring, Reddin 7 Emerson, Jarrett 8 Lockhart, Richards 9 Carradine
Keith, Brian: 5 actor
TV: Family Affair
__ Keith Kellogg: 4 Will
Keizer: 4 city, town
locale: 6 Oregon
Keke: 6 Palmer
kelep: 3 ant
Kell: 6 George
Kellaway: 5 Cecil
Keller: 5 Helen 6 Marthe 7 Charlie 9 Gottfried
Keller, Gottfried: 4 poet 5 Swiss
Keller, Helen: 6 writer
portrayer: Patty Duke
work: Out of the Dark
Kellerman: 4 Faye 5 Sally 8 Jonathan
Kellerman, Faye: 6 writer
character: Decker, Lazarus, Rina
spouse: Jonathan
work: Blindman's Bluff
The Burnt House
Capital Crimes
Day of Atonement
False Prophet
The Forgotten
Grievous Sin
Jupiter's Bones
Milk and Honey
Moon Music
The Quality of Mercy
The Ritual Bath
Sacred and Profane
Sanctuary
Serpent's Tooth
Stalker
Stone Kiss
Street Dreams
Kellerman, Jonathan: 6 writer
character: Alex, Delaware
spouse: Faye
work: Bad Love
Billy Straight
Blood Test
Bones
Capital Crimes
The Clinic
A Cold Heart
Compulsion
The Conspiracy Club

Devil's Waltz
Evidence
Flesh and Blood
Gone
Monster
Obsession
Over the Edge
Rage
Silent Partner
Therapy
Time Bomb
True Detectives
Twisted
When the Bough Breaks
Kelley: 5 Barry, Kitty 6 David E., Sheila 8 DeForest, Florence
costar: 5 Nimoy 7 Shatner
Kelley, David E.
spouse: Michelle Pfeiffer
Kelley, Kitty
creation: 3 bio
Kellogg: 4 Lynn 5 Frank
brand: 4 Eggo
product: 6 cereal
Kellogg-___ Pact: 6 Briand
Kellogg, Frank: 8 Nobelist
Kellogg's cereal: 6 Smacks 7 All-Bran, Crispix, Hunny B's, Mueslix, Pokémon 8 Corn Pops, Special K 9 Just Right 10 Apple Jacks, Froot Loops, Mini-Wheats, Nutri-Grain, Smart Start
Kellogg's Frosted Flakes tiger: 4 Tony
kelly: 5 color, green
Kelly: 3 Jim, Ned 4 Gene, Jack, Reno, Ripa, Walt 5 Brian, Grace, Lynch, Moira, Nancy, Patsy, Price 6 Emmett, Harmon 7 LeBrock, Preston 8 McGillis 9 Ellsworth, Shipwreck 10 Rutherford
cohost: 5 Regis
Kelly, to Regis: 6 cohost
Kelly, Emmett: 4 hobo 5 clown
Kelly, Gene: 5 actor 6 dancer
film: An American in Paris (1951)
Anchors Aweigh (1945)
Brigadoon (1954)
The Cheyenne Social Club (1970)
Christmas Holiday (1944)
Cover Girl (1944)
DuBarry Was a Lady (1943)
For Me and My Gal (1942)
Gigot (1962)
Hello, Dolly! (1969)
Inherit the Wind (1960)
It's Always Fair Weather (1955)
Les Girls (1957)
Marjorie Morningstar (1958)
On the Town (1949)
The Pirate (1948)
Singin' in the Rain (1952)
Summer Stock (1950)
Take Me Out to the Ball Game (1949)
Kelly, Grace: 7 actress
film: The Bridges at Toko-Ri (1955)
The Country Girl (1954, AA)
Dial M for Murder (1954)
High Noon (1952)
High Society (1956)
Mogambo (1953)
Rear Window (1954)
The Swan (1956)
To Catch a Thief (1955)
spouse: Prince Rainier
Kelly, Jim: 2 QB
sport: 8 football
Kelly, R.
song: Bump 'n Grind (1994)
Down Low (1996)
Gotham City (1997)
I Believe I Can Fly (1996)
I Can't Sleep Baby (1996)
I'm Your Angel (1998)
Satisfy You (1999)
You Remind Me of Something (1995)
Kelly's Heroes (1970 film)
cast: Clint Eastwood, Carroll O'Connor, Don Rickles, Telly Savalas, Donald Sutherland
Kelly, Walt cartoon: 4 Pogo
kelp: 4 alga 5 algae 7 seaweed 10 health food
component: 5 algin, iodin 6 iodine
concoction: 4 agar 8 agar-agar
Kelp: 6 Julius
kelpie: 3 dog 5 canid 6 canine, spirit, sprite
kelpies herd them: 5 sheep
Kelsey: 5 Linda 7 Grammer
Kelton: 4 Pert
Kelvin: 5 scale 7 William
alternative: 7 Celsius 10 Fahrenheit
Kelvinator: 6 fridge
alternative: *see* appliance brand
Kelvin, William: 4 Lord 7 British 9 physicist
Kemal: 7 Atatürk
Kemble: 5 Fanny
Kemelman: 5 Harry
Kemi: 4 city, port, town
locale: 7 Finland
Kemo Sabe: 10 Lone Ranger
companion: 5 Tonto
trademark: 4 mask
Kemp: 4 Gary, Jack, Tara 6 Johnny
Kemper: 5 Ellie
Kemper ___: 4 Open 5 Arena
kempt: 4 neat, tidy, trim 6 spruce 7 orderly 9 shipshape 10 fastidious
not ~: 4 torn 5 messy, ratty, seedy 6 beat-up, grubby, ragged, shabby, shoddy, untidy 7 scruffy 8 slovenly, tattered 10 bedraggled, disheveled, threadbare
___-kempt: 3 ill
Kempton: 6 Murray
ken: 4 grip 5 grasp, range, reach, sight 6 fathom 7 eyeshot, purview 9 awareness, knowledge 10 cognizance, perception, understand
Ken: 4 doll, Olin, Wahl 5 Berry, Burns, Kesey, Starr 6 Curtis, Dryden, Howard, Hughes, Murray, Norton, Osmond 7 Annakin, Auletta, Daneyko, Follett, Griffey, Maynard, Russell, Stabler, Venturi 8 Jennings, Rosewall, Watanabe 9 Kercheval 10 Weatherwax
friend: 6 Barbie
Ken.
neighbor: 3 Ill., Ind., W. Va. 4 Tenn.
see also Kentucky
Kenai: 4 city, town
locale: 6 Alaska
Kenan & ___: 3 Kel
Kenaz
grandfather: 4 Esau
Kendal: 5 green 8 Felicity
Kendall: 3 Kay 5 Henry 6 Edward
kendo: 5 sport
practice ~: 5 fence
Kendrew, John: 7 chemist 8 Nobelist
Kendricks, Eddie
song: Boogie Down (1974)
Keep on Truckin' (1973)
Keneally, Thomas: 6 writer 10 Australian
work: American Scoundrel
Blood Red, Sister Rose
Bring Larks and Heroes
Flying Hero Class
Gossip From the Forest
The People's Train
The Playmaker
A River Town
Schindler's List
The Tyrant's Novel
Victim of the Aurora
Woman of the Inner Sea
Kenilworth: 5 novel
author: Walter Scott
character: 3 Amy 5 Giles, Janet 6 Blount, Dickie, Dudley, Edmund, Robert, Varney 7 Richard, Robsart, Wayland 10 Tressilian
Ken-L: 7 dog food
alternative: *see* pet food brand
Ken-L Ration: 7 dog food
alternative: 4 Alpo, Iams 5 Nutro 6 Kal Kan, Purina 8 Eukanuba
Kenmore: 9 appliance
alternative: *see* appliance brand
brand owner: 5 Sears
Kennebec: 5 river
city on the ~: 7 Augusta
locale: 5 Maine
Kennedy: 3 Joe, Ted, Tom 4 Burt, clan, John, Mimi, Rose 5 Bobby, Edgar, Ethel, Jayne, John F., Teddy 6 Arthur, Edward, George, Jackie, Joseph, Robert 7 Anthony, William 8 Caroline 10 Jacqueline
coin: 4 half
quote starter: 3 ask, ich
sister: 3 Pat 4 Jean 6 Eunice 8 Kathleen, Rosemary
Kennedy ___: 6 Center 7 Airport
___ Kennedy: 4 Cape
Kennedy Airport loc.: 3 NYC
Kennedy Center focus: 4 arts
Kennedy, John F.: 9 president
alma mater: 6 Choate 7 Harvard
biographer: 8 Sorensen
birthplace: 4 Mass. 9 Brookline
cabinet member: 3 Day 4 Rusk 5 Udall, Wirtz 6 Dillon, Hodges 7 Freeman 8 Goldberg, McNamara, Ribicoff
child: 8 Caroline
opponent: 5 Nixon
parent: 3 Joe 4 Rose 6 Joseph
sibling: 3 Pat, Ted 4 Jean 6 Eunice, Robert 8 Kathleen, Rosemary
V.P.: 7 Johnson
wife: 6 Jackie 10 Jacqueline
work: Profiles in Courage
The Strategy of Peace
Why England Slept
Kennedy Library architect: I.M. Pei
Kennedy, Ted: 3 sen. 6 Edward 7 senator
middle name: 5 Moore
Kennedy, William: 6 writer
work: The Ink Truck
Ironweed
Legs
kennel: 3 den 4 hole, lair, pack 5 pound 6 burrow 7 shelter 8 doghouse
cry: 3 arf, grr, yip 4 bark, woof, yelp, yowl 5 growl
feature: 3 pen, run 4 cage
resident: 3 dog, pet, pup 5 doggy, pooch, puppy, whelp 6 canine
kennel ___: 4 club
Kennelly-Heaviside ___: 5 layer
Kenner: 4 city, town 5 Chris
locale: 9 Louisiana
Kennesaw: 4 city, town
locale: 7 Georgia
Kenneth: 4 Koch, Mars, More 5 Anger, Arrow, Starr, Tynan 6 Wilson 7 Branagh, Grahame, Patchen, Rexroth, Roberts, Slessor
Kenny: 3 Tom 4 Ball, Tran 5 Baker, Nolan 6 Rogers 7 Loggins, Stabler 9 Elizabeth
___ Kenny: 6 Sister
Kenny G
genre: 4 jazz
instrument: alto sax 3 sax
last name: Gorelick
song: Songbird (1987)
keno: 4 game
kin: 5 lotto 7 lottery
play ~: 3 bet 5 wager 6 gamble
Kenobi: 6 Obi-Wan
Kenosha: 4 city, town
locale: 9 Wisconsin
Kensington ___ Stone: 4 Rune
Kensington and ___: 7 Chelsea
Kensit: 5 Patsy
Kent: 4 city, town 5 Clark, Hrbek, Smith 6 Arthur, county, McCord, Stacey 8 Rockwell
city: 5 Dover 7 Margate
colleague: 4 Lane 5 Olsen
locale: 4 Ohio 7 England 10 Washington
school: 3 KSU
Kent ___: 5 State
___ Kentaurus: 5 Rigel
Kentish ___: 4 fire
Kenton: 4 Erle, Stan
Kenton, Stan: 7 pianist
genre: 4 jazz
Kent, Rockwell: 6 artist 7 painter 11 illustrator
Kent, Stacey: 6 singer
genre: 4 jazz
Kent State University
conference: 3 MAC
locale: 4 Ohio
Kentucky: 5 river, state
city: 5 Berea, Eolia 7 Ashland, Fayette, Newburg, Paducah 8 Florence, Fort Knox, Radcliff, Richmond 9 Covington, Frankfort, Henderson, Lexington, Owensboro 10 Louisville
college: 5 Berea
conference: 3 SEC
county: 5 Boone
neighbor: 4 Ohio 7 Indiana 8 Illinois, Missouri, Virginia 9 Tennessee 12 West Virginia
pioneer: 5 Boone
state bird: 8 cardinal

state fish: 4 bass
state flower: 9 goldenrod
state fossil: 10 brachiopod
state mineral: 4 coal
state rock: 5 agate
statesman: 4 Clay
Kentucky ___: 5 Derby 7 colonel, warbler
Kentucky ___ Movie, The: 5 Fried
Kentucky Derby: 4 race
drink: 5 julep 9 mint julep
month: 3 May
Kentucky Derby winners:
2010 - Super Saver
2009 - Mine That Bird
2008 - Big Brown
2007 - Street Sense
2006 - Barbaro
2005 - Giacomo
2004 - Smarty Jones
2003 - Funny Cide
2002 - War Emblem
2001 - Monarchos
2000 - Fusaichi Pegasus
1999 - Charismatic
1998 - Real Quiet
1997 - Silver Charm
1996 - Grindstone
1995 - Thunder Gulch
1994 - Go For Gin
1993 - Sea Hero
1992 - Lil E. Tee
1991 - Strike the Gold
1990 - Unbridled
1989 - Sunday Silence
1988 - Winning Colors
1987 - Alysheba
1986 - Ferdinand
1985 - Spend A Buck
1984 - Swale
1983 - Sunny's Halo
1982 - Gato del Sol
1981 - Pleasant Colony
1980 - Genuine Risk
1979 - Spectacular Bid
1978 - Affirmed
1977 - Seattle Slew
1976 - Bold Forbes
1975 - Foolish Pleasure
1974 - Cannonade
1973 - Secretariat
1972 - Riva Ridge
1971 - Canonero II
1970 - Dust Commander
1969 - Majestic Prince
1968 - Forward Pass
1967 - Proud Clarion
1966 - Kauai King
1965 - Lucky Debonair
1964 - Northern Dancer
1963 - Chateaugay
1962 - Decidedly
1961 - Carry Back
1960 - Venetian Way
1959 - Tomy Lee
1958 - Tim Tam
1957 - Iron Liege
1956 - Needles
1955 - Swaps
1954 - Determine
1953 - Dark Star
1952 - Hill Gail
1951 - Count Turf
1950 - Middleground
1949 - Ponder
1948 - Citation
1947 - Jet Pilot
1946 - Assault
1945 - Hoop Jr.
1944 - Pensive
1943 - Count Fleet
1942 - Shut Out
1941 - Whirlaway
1940 - Gallahadion
1939 - Johnstown
1938 - Lawrin
1937 - War Admiral
1936 - Bold Venture
1935 - Omaha
1934 - Cavalcade
1933 - Brokers Tip
1932 - Burgoo King
1931 - Twenty Grand
1930 - Gallant Fox
1929 - Clyde Van Dusen
1928 - Reigh Count
1927 - Whiskery
1926 - Bubbling Over
1925 - Flying Ebony
1924 - Black Gold
1923 - Zev
1922 - Morvich
1921 - Behave Yourself
1920 - Paul Jones
1919 - Sir Barton
1918 - Exterminator
1917 - Omar Khayyam
1916 - George Smith
1915 - Regret
1914 - Old Rosebud
1913 - Donerail
1912 - Worth
1911 - Meridan
1910 - Donau
1909 - Wintergreen
1908 - Stone Street
1907 - Pink Star
1906 - Sir Huon
1905 - Agile
1904 - Elwood
1903 - Judge Himes
1902 - Alan-a-Dale
1901 - His Eminence
1900 - Lieut. Gibson
1899 - Manuel
1898 - Plaudit
1897 - Typhoon II
1896 - Ben Brush
1895 - Halma
1894 - Chant
1893 - Lookout
1892 - Azra
1891 - Kingman
1890 - Riley
1889 - Spokane
1888 - MacBeth II
1887 - Montrose
1886 - Ben Ali
1885 - Joe Cotton
1884 - Buchanan
1883 - Leonatus
1882 - Apollo
1881 - Hindoo
1880 - Fonso
1879 - Lord Murphy
1878 - Day Star
1877 - Baden Baden
1876 - Vagrant
1875 - Aristides
___ Kentucky Home: 5 My Old
Kentucky Rain (1970 song)
artist: Elvis Presley
Kentucky Woman (1967 song)
artist: Neil Diamond
Kenya: 6 nation 7 country
anthropologist: 6 Leakey
beast: 5 zebra
capital: 7 Nairobi
city: 4 Meru 5 Nyeri 6 Kisumu, Kitale, Nakuru 7 Eldoret, Mombasa, Nairobi 8 Machakos
half a ~ rebel group: 3 Mau
lake: 6 Rudolf 7 Turkana 8 Victoria
language: 3 Luo 5 Kamba, Masai, Nandi, Oromo 6 Kikuyu, Maasai 7 Swahili, Turkana
legislature: 5 Bunge
locale: 6 Africa
money: 4 cent 8 shilling
mountain: 5 Elgon
national park: 5 Tsavo
neighbor: 5 Sudan 6 Uganda 7 Somalia 8 Ethiopia, Tanzania
people: 3 Luo 5 Galla, Kamba, Masai, Nandi, Oromo 6 Dorobo, Kikuyu, Maasai, Somali 9 Wandorobo
river: 4 Tana 5 Tsana, Tsavo
runner: 5 Keino
Kenyatta: 4 Jomo
Kenyon, Kathleen: 4 Dame
Keogh
alternative: 3 IRA
Keogh ___: 4 plan 7 account
Keoghan: 4 Phil
Keokuk: 4 city
locale: 4 Iowa
kepi: 3 cap, hat, lid
feature: 5 visor, vizor
wearer: 5 poilu
Kepler, Johann: 6 German 10 astronomer
___-kept: 4 best, well
keratin: 7 protein
___ keratotomy: 6 radial
Kercheval: 3 Ken
kerchief: 5 curch, do-rag, scarf 6 hankie, madras 7 bandana, muffler 8 babushka, bandanna, covering, kaffiyeh, mantilla, neckwear 9 headcloth, headdress
bright ~: 6 Madras
starter: 4 hand
Kerensky successor: 5 Lenin
kerf: 3 cut 5 notch 6 groove
kerflooie: 6 broken, busted 10 broken-down, on the blink, on the fritz
Kerguelen: 7 islands
locale: 11 Indian Ocean
Keri: 6 lotion 7 Russell
alternative: 5 Curel, Nivea 6 Aveeno 7 Eucerin, Jergens, Pacquin 9 Lubriderm
Kerman: 4 city
locale: 4 Iran
kermes: 3 dye
kermis: 4 fair 8 carnival, festival
Kermit: 4 frog 6 Muppet 9 Roosevelt
colleague: 4 Bert 5 Ernie, Piggy
cousin: 4 toad
creator: Jim Henson
street: 6 Sesame
kernel: 3 hub, nub, nut 4 core, corn, crux, germ, gist, knub, meat, pith, seed 5 grain, heart 6 center, marrow 7 essence, keynote, nucleus, nutmeat 8 key point 9 substance
combining form: 5 caryo-, karyo-
holder: 3 cob, ear
kernite: 3 ore 7 mineral
yield: 5 boron
Kern, Jerome: 8 composer
collaborator: Buddy DeSylva, Dorothy Fields, Oscar Hammerstein, Otto Harbach, P.G. Wodehouse
contemporary: Harold Arlen, Irving Berlin, George Gershwin, Ira Gershwin, Cole Porter
musical: The Cat and the Fiddle
Criss Cross
Good Morning, Dearie
Have a Heart
Leave It to Jane
Love o' Mike
Miss 1917
Music in the Air
Oh, Boy!
Oh, Lady! Lady!
Roberta
Sally
Show Boat
Stepping Stones
Sunny
Sweet Adeline
Very Good Eddie
Very Warm for May
song: All the Things You Are
Bill
Can't Help Lovin' Dat Man
A Fine Romance
The Folks Who Live on the Hill
How'd You Like to Spoon With Me?
I'm Old Fashioned
I've Told Ev'ry Little Star
I Won't Dance
The Last Time I Saw Paris
Life Upon the Wicked Stage
Long Ago (And Far Away)
Look for the Silver Lining
Lovely to Look At
Make Believe
Ol' Man River
Pick Yourself Up
She Didn't Say Yes
Smoke Gets in Your Eyes
The Song Is You
Sunny
They Didn't Believe Me
Till the Clouds Roll By
The Way You Look Tonight
Who?
Why Do I Love You?
Why Was I Born?
You Are Love
You Couldn't Be Cuter
You Were Never Lovelier
Kerns: 6 Joanna
kerogen
yield: 3 oil
kerosene: 3 oil 7 coal oil, lantern
Kerouac, Jack: 6 writer
character: 3 Sal 8 Paradise
colleague: Gregory Corso, Allen Ginsberg, Gary Snyder, Philip Whalen
genre: Beat
hometown: Lowell
work: Big Sur
The Dharma Bums
Doctor Sax
On the Road
Satori in Paris
Visions of Cody
kerplunk: 6 splash

Kerr: 4 Jean, John 5 Anita, Smith 6 Graham, Philip, Walter 7 Deborah
Kerr, Deborah: 7 actress
  film: Bonjour Tristesse (1958)
    The Chalk Garden (1964)
    From Here to Eternity (1953)
    The Gypsy Moths (1969)
    Heaven Knows, Mr. Allison (1957)
    The Hucksters (1947)
    The Innocents (1961)
    The Journey (1959)
    The King and I (1956)
    King Solomon's Mines (1950)
    The Night of the Iguana (1964)
    Quo Vadis? (1951)
    Separate Tables (1958)
    The Sundowners (1960)
    Tea and Sympathy (1956)
  role: 4 Anna
Kerrey: 3 Bob, Jim, sen. 7 senator
Kerr, Graham: 4 chef 7 gourmet
Kerri: 5 Strug
Kerrigan, Nancy: 6 skater
Kerry: 3 cow, sen. 4 bull, John 6 bovine, Butler, cattle, Teresa 7 senator
Kerry Blue terrier: 3 dog 5 canid, pooch 6 canine
kersey: 4 wool 6 fabric
kerseymere: 4 wool 5 cloth 6 fabric 7 textile 8 material
kerseys: 5 pants
Kershner: 5 Irvin
Kert: 5 Larry
Kertész, Imre: 6 writer 8 Nobelist
Kerwin: 5 Brian, Lance 7 Mathews
Kesey, Ken: 6 writer
  work: Demon Box
    One Flew Over the Cuckoo's Nest
    Sometimes a Great Notion
Keshia __ Pulliam: 6 Knight
Kessel: 6 Barney
kestrel: 4 bird, hawk 6 falcon
ketch: 4 boat 5 yacht 8 sailboat
  Chesapeake Bay ~: 6 bugeye
  cousin: 4 yawl 6 galiot
  Levantine ~: 4 saic
Ketcham: 4 Hank
  creation: 6 Dennis
Ketchikan: 4 city, port, town
  locale: 6 Alaska
Ketchum: 3 Hal 4 city, town
  locale: 5 Idaho
ketchup: 5 Heinz, Hunt's, sauce 6 relish 8 Del Monte 9 condiment
  alternative: 4 mayo
  noise: 4 plop 5 plunk
ketone: 6 acetol
Kett: 4 Etta
Kettering: 4 city, town
  locale: 4 Ohio
Ketterle, Wolfgang: 8 Nobelist 9 physicist
kettle: 3 pan, pot, vat 6 boiler, teapot, vessel 7 caldron 8 cauldron 9 container
  ender: 4 drum
  handle: 4 bail
  insulter: 3 pot
  of fish: 3 fix, jam 4 mess, spot 5 snarl 6 fiasco, muddle, pickle, plight, scrape, tangle 7 dilemma, problem, screwup, trouble 8 bad scene 9 deep water, mare's nest
  output: 5 steam, vapor
  sound: 3 sss 4 ssss
  starter: 3 tea
Kettle: 2 Ma, Pa
kettledrum, Spanish: 6 atabal
Kevin: 5 Bacon, Brown, James, Kline, saint, Smith, Sorbo, Tighe 6 Conway, Curran, Dobson, Nealon, Pollak, Spacey 7 Costner 8 McCarthy, Mitchell 10 Williamson
Kevlar company: 6 Dupont
Kew
  locale: 6 London
Kew __: 7 Gardens
Kewpie: 3 toy 4 doll 5 prize
Kewpie Doll (1958 song)
  artist: Perry Como
key: 3 Alt, Del, End, Esc, Ins, Tab 4 A maj., A min., B maj., B min., clew, clue, C maj., C min., code, Ctrl, D maj., D min., E maj., E min., F maj., F min., G maj., G min., Home, isle, main, note, Pg Dn, Pg Up, West 5 A-flat, basic, B-flat, Break, C-flat, chief, D-flat, E-flat, Enter, F-flat, G-flat, islet, ivory, Largo, major, Pause, pitch, Shift, vital 6 A major, A minor, answer, A-sharp, B major, B minor, B-sharp, C major, C minor, C-sharp, Delete, D major, D minor, D-sharp, E major, E minor, E-sharp, F major, F minor, F-sharp, G major, G minor, G-sharp, Insert, island, legend, Page Up, staple, ticket 7 central, Control, crucial, pivotal, primary 8 A-flat maj., B-flat maj., Caps Lock, cardinal, critical, deciding, decisive, E-flat maj., linchpin, lynchpin, material, Page Down, password, solution 9 Backspace, coral reef, essential, important, operative, principal, right-hand, strategic 10 A-flat major, B-flat major, B-flat minor, E-flat major 11 C-sharp minor
  as data: 5 input
  bagpipe ~: 5 B-flat
  banjo ~ changer: 4 capo
  black ~: 5 A-flat, B-flat, D-flat, E-flat, G-flat 6 A-sharp, C-sharp, D-sharp, F-sharp, G-sharp
  calculator ~: 3 CLR, sin 4 sine
  car ~: 7 starter
  combining form: 5 clavi-, clavo-
  computer ~: 3 Alt, Del, Esc, Ins, Tab 4 Ctrl, Home, Pg Dn, Pg Up 5 Enter, Shift 6 Delete, Escape, Insert, Page Up 7 Control 8 Page Down
  ender: 3 pad, way 4 card, hole, note, word 5 board, noter, punch, stone 6 stroke
  find the ~ to: 5 crack, solve 6 decode, fathom, unlock 7 clear up, explain, hit upon, unravel, work out 8 decipher, get right, untangle 9 figure out, interpret, puzzle out 10 account for
  five-sharp ~: 6 B major
  Florida ~: 4 West 5 Largo 8 Biscayne
  four-sharp ~: 6 E major
  guitar ~ changer: 4 capo
  hit the + ~: 3 add
  in: 5 enter
  in ~: 7 musical, tuneful 9 melodious 10 euphonious, harmonious
  in French: 4 clef
  item: 6 answer
  it may have a ~: 4 door 5 diary
  it usually has a ~: 5 music
  lacking a ~: 6 atonal
  letter: 3 phi 4 beta 5 kappa
  locale: 3 Fla. 7 Florida
  material: 5 ebony, ivory
  musical ~: 4 A maj., A min., B maj., B min., C maj., C min., D maj., D min., E maj., E min., F maj., F min., G maj., G min. 5 A-flat, B-flat, C-flat, E-flat 6 A major, A minor, A-sharp, B major, B minor, C major, C minor, D major, D minor, E major, E minor, F major, F minor, G major, G minor 8 A-flat maj., B-flat maj., E-flat maj. 10 A-flat major, B-flat major, B-flat minor, E-flat major 11 C-sharp minor
  note: 5 tonic
  off ~: 4 flat 5 false, sharp
  on: 4 pick 6 choose, opt for, select 9 designate, single out
  on ~: 5 tonal 6 in tune 9 melodious 10 harmonious
  one-flat ~: 6 D minor, F major
  one-sharp ~: 6 E minor, G major
  partner: 4 lock
  personnel: 4 core 5 cadre
  player: 3 CEO, VIP 4 boss, czar 5 brass, mogul, wheel 6 honcho, leader, top dog, tycoon 7 big shot, magnate 8 big wheel, director, governor, higher-up, kingfish, top brass 9 commander, executive 10 head honcho, management
  point: 3 nub 4 crux, gist, meat, pith 5 drift, heart 6 kernel, marrow, thrust, upshot 7 essence 9 substance 10 bottom line
  position: 5 pivot
  starter: 3 off 4 pass, turn 5 latch
  three-sharp ~: 6 A major
  turn the ~: 4 lock 6 fasten, secure
  two-flat ~: 6 G minor
  two-sharp ~: 6 B minor, D major
  uncut ~: 5 blank
  under lock and ~: 4 held, safe 5 bound, caged 6 in jail, jailed, secure 7 captive, guarded, immured 8 confined, locked up 9 in custody, protected 10 imprisoned
  up: 4 spur 5 tense, upset 6 incite, kindle, thrill 7 actuate 9 stimulate
key __: 4 card, case, club, grip, in on, ring, word 5 chain
__ key: 6 church, master
__-key: 3 low, off 4 card 5 color
Key: 3 Ted 5 Jimmy
Key __: 4 deer, lime, West 5 Largo
Key __ pie: 4 lime
__ Key: 4 Duma
keyboard: 4 Moog 5 organ, piano, synth 6 spinet 7 celesta, celeste, cembalo, clavier, klavier, orphica, Pianola, upright, vocoder 8 calliope, melodeon, melodion, theremin, virginal 9 accordion, harmonium 10 clavichord, concertina, hurdy-gurdy, instrument, squeezebox
  sequence: 6 QWERTY
  slip: 4 typo 7 erratum, mistake 8 misprint 10 inaccuracy
  striker: 6 finger
  stroke: 3 tap
  use a ~: 4 type 5 enter 6 sign on 9 make music, typewrite
__ keyboard: 6 Dvorak, QWERTY
Keydets' sch.: 3 VMI
Keye: 4 Luke
keyed
  not ~: 6 atonal
  up: 4 agog, edgy 5 antsy, hyper, itchy, jumpy, tense 6 gung-ho, jangly, uneasy 7 anxious, excited, frantic, jittery, nervous, restive, uptight 8 agitated, feverish, fluttery, frenetic, frenzied, restless, skittish, troubled 9 concerned, excitable, ill at ease 10 high-strung
Keyes, Evelyn: 7 actress
  spouse: John Huston, Artie Shaw
__ Key, FL: 4 Boot, Duck, Long, Vaca 5 Conch, Craig, Crawl, Shark 6 Cudjoe, Fiesta, Grassy, Indian, Knight, No Name, Pigeon, Ramrod, Siesta, Wilson
keyhole: 4 slit, slot 7 opening 8 aperture
  glance: 4 peek, peep 6 gander 7 glimpse, look-see
keyhole __: 3 saw
Key Largo: 4 film, play, song
  artist: Bertie Higgins
  author: Maxwell Anderson
  cast: Lauren Bacall, Lionel Barrymore, Humphrey Bogart, Edward G. Robinson, Claire Trevor
  composer: Max Steiner
  director: John Huston
keyless: 6 atonal
Key lime __: 3 pie
Keynes subject: 4 econ. 9 economics
keynote: 3 nub 4 core, crux, germ, gist, knub, pith, root 5 basis, focus, heart, orate, speak, theme 6 center, kernel, marrow, speech 7 essence 8 linchpin, lynchpin, main idea, quiddity 9 substance
keynote __: 6 speech 7 address, speaker
__ keypad: 7 numeric
keypad place: 2 PC 3 ATM, Mac 8 computer
Keys: 6 Alicia
__ Keys: 7 Florida
__ Keys to Baldpate: 5 Seven
keystone: 5 basis, coign, quoin, wedge 6 coigne
  site: 4 arch
Keystone: 6 studio
  missile: 3 pie
  St.: 4 Penn. 5 Penna.
Keystone Kops
  boss: 7 Sennett
Keystone State
  see Pennsylvania
keystroke: 3 dah, dit
__ Key, The: 5 Glass, Third
Key to Midnight, The
  author: Dean Koontz
Key West: 4 city, port, town
  locale: 7 Florida

Key West Intermezzo (1996 song)
artist: John Cougar Mellencamp
KFC: 10 restaurant
order: 6 bucket
piece: 3 leg
rival: *see* restaurant chain
kg.: 2 wt. 3 amt. 4 meas.
__ K. Gandhi: 8 Mohandas
__ K. Gann: 6 Ernest
KGB
counterpart: 3 CIA
predecessor: 4 NKVD, OGPU
successor: 3 RIS
Khachaturian, Aram: 7 Russian 8 composer
work: Sabre Dance
khaddar: 6 fabric 8 material
Khafre
father: 6 Cheops
khaki: 3 tan 5 brown, color 6 fabric 7 uniform 9 yellowish
like ~: 3 tan 4 drab, dull 9 colorless
relative: *see* brown color
twill: 5 chino
khakis: 5 pants 6 slacks 8 trousers
Khambatta: 6 Persis
khamsin: 4 wind
khan: 5 ruler 6 gerent, hostel
concern: 6 empire
relative: 3 aga 4 agha
Khan: 3 Aga, Aly 4 Batu 5 Chaka, Kubla, Shere 6 Kublai, Tengri 7 Genghis
Khan, Aly
spouse: Rita Hayworth
Khan, Chaka
group: Rufus
song: I Feel for You (1984)
I'm Every Woman (1978)
Once You Get Started (1975)
Sweet Thing (1976)
Tell Me Something Good (1974)
Khan, Jasmine
grandfather: 3 Aga
Kharkov: 4 city, town
locale: 7 Ukraine
Khartoum: 4 city, town 7 capital
locale: 5 Sudan
river: 4 Nile
Khashoggi: 5 Adnan
Khayyám, Omar: 4 poet 7 Persian
Khigh: 6 Dheigh
Khirghiz range: 4 Alai
Khmer: 8 language 9 Cambodian
capital: 6 Angkor
Khmer __: 5 Rouge
Khomeini: 5 Irani
__ K. Howard: 7 William
Khrushchev: 6 Nikita
home: 4 USSR 6 Russia
Khrystyne: 4 Haje
Khuzistan capital: 5 Ahvaz, Ahwaz
Khyber __: 4 Pass 5 knife
Khyber Pass terminus: 5 Kabul 8 Peshawar
Kia: 3 car 4 auto 10 automobile
model: 3 Rio 6 Optima, Sedona, Sephia, Serona 7 Sorento, Spectra 8 Rio Cinco, Sportage
origin: 5 Korea
Kiam: 6 Victor
kiang: 6 donkey
origin: 5 Tibet 8 Mongolia
Kibbee: 3 Guy
kibble: 7 dog food
Kibble
alternative: *see* pet food brand
Kibbles: 7 dog food
kibbutz: 7 commune 10 collective
one born on a ~: 5 sabra
see also Israel
kibitz: 6 butt in, meddle 9 interpose
kibitzer: 3 wag, wit 4 card 5 clown, cutup 6 kidder 7 farceur 8 jokester, quipster
kibosh
put the ~ on: 3 ban, nix, zap 4 curb, halt, stop, veto 5 check, quash, quell 7 abolish, contain, put down, repress, squelch 8 cut short, suppress
see also baloney
kick: 3 fun, jar, joy, pep 4 bang, beef, bite, blow, boot, buck, buzz, carp, fuss, hoot, hurt, jolt, punt, quit, snap, tang, wail, zest, zing 5 force, gripe, power, punch, spark, spice, taste, verve, vigor, whine 6 give up, object, recoil, repine, thrill, twitch, wallop 7 abandon, grumble, potence, potency, protest, sparkle 8 backlash, complain, pleasure, pungency, reaction, stimulus, strength, vitality 9 complaint, enjoyment, intensity, make a fuss, sensation 10 excitement
around: 5 abuse 6 debate 7 discuss 8 cogitate, hash over, maltreat, mistreat, talk over, walk over 9 manhandle, speculate, sweat over 10 deliberate
back: 3 pay 4 loll 5 relax 7 rebound
dance with a ~: 5 conga
ender: 3 off 4 back 5 boxer, stand 6 boxing
get a ~ out of: 3 dig, use 4 like 5 enjoy, go for 6 relish 8 flip over, thrill to 9 delight in, get high on, indulge in
in: 3 pay 4 ante, open 6 ante up, donate, pony up, supply 7 present 10 contribute
in football: 4 punt
in the teeth: 4 slur 6 rebuff, rebuke 7 repulse 9 rejection
off: 4 open 5 begin, start 6 launch 7 lead off 8 commence, get going, initiate 9 enter upon, introduce, originate 10 inaugurate
oneself: 3 rue 6 lament, regret
out: 2 ax 3 axe, can 4 boot, oust 5 eject, evict, expel, roust 6 banish, bounce, deport, depose 7 dismiss 9 discharge
over the traces: 4 riot 5 rebel 6 mutiny, revolt
the habit: 4 quit, stop 5 cease 6 desist, lay off 8 renounce
up a fuss: 3 cry 4 yell 5 gripe, groan, shout, whine 6 holler, shriek, squawk, yammer 7 grumble, protest, screech 8 complain 9 bellyache, raise Cain
up one's heels: 4 lark, romp 5 caper, jaunt, revel 6 cavort, frolic, gambol, prance 7 carouse, rollick 9 celebrate, make merry, whoop it up
upstairs: 4 bump 5 boost, favor, raise 6 better, move up 7 advance, elevate, endorse, further, promote
with a ~: 3 hot 4 sour, tart 5 juicy, peppy, sharp, spicy, tangy, tasty, zesty 6 acidic, biting, lively, strong 7 acerbic, peppery, piquant, pungent 8 vinegary 9 flavorful, sparkling
kick __: 3 off, out 4 back, turn 5 about, plate, pleat, serve 6 around, boxing 8 upstairs
kick __ pants: 5 in the
kick __ the traces: 4 over
kick-__: 5 start
__ kick: 3 top 4 drop, free, frog, goal 5 place 6 onside
Kickapoo: 3 Fox 5 tribe 6 Indian 7 Amerind 8 language
kickback: 3 cut, oil, sop 4 gift 5 bribe, graft, share 6 boodle, grease, payoff, payola, rebate, refund, reward 7 jobbery, percent 8 reaction, response 9 hush money 10 commission, percentage
kick boxing: 5 sport
kicker: 4 snag 5 catch, hitch, point 7 proviso 8 obstacle 9 hindrance, provision 10 difficulty, impediment
asset: 3 toe
target: 4 shin
__-kicker: 5 place
kicking
alive and ~: 4 spry, well 5 sound
around: 5 about 9 somewhere
back: 6 at ease 7 content, relaxed 8 carefree
game: 6 soccer 8 football
kick in the __: 4 shin 5 pants
kickoff: 5 debut, onset, start 6 advent, opener, outset 7 opening 8 exordium 9 beginning, inception
get ready for ~: 5 tee up
prop: 3 tee
__ Kick Out of You: 5 I Get a
kick over the __: 6 traces
kicks: 3 fun 5 mirth 6 thrill 7 jollies 8 pleasure 10 excitement
__ kicks: 3 for
Kicks (1966 song)
artist: Paul Revere and the Raiders
kickshaw: 6 geegaw, gewgaw, tidbit, trifle 7 trinket 9 bagatelle
kick the __: 3 can 5 habit
kickup: 3 row 4 fuss 9 commotion
kick up __: 5 a fuss
kick up one's __: 5 heels
kicky: 3 fun 5 heady, juicy 7 amusing, zestful 8 electric, exciting 9 diverting, enjoyable, glamorous, thrilling
kid: 3 boy, cub, lad, rag, rib, son, tot 4 baby, fool, girl, jest, jive, joke, josh, lass, mock, razz, teen, tyke 5 chaff, child, minor, put on, roast, sonny, sprig, suede, tease, youth 6 animal, banter, bother, deride, infant, moppet, needle 7 leather, preteen, sapling 8 daughter, goatskin, half-pint, immature, juvenile, ridicule, teenager 9 little one, make fun of, offspring, poke fun at, stripling, youngster 10 adolescent
ammo: 3 BBs, pea
aunt's ~: 6 cousin
ball: 4 Nerf
block: 4 Lego
cereal: 3 Kix 4 Trix
colorer: 6 crayon
comment: 5 bleat
complaint: 5 mumps 7 measles
computer language: 4 Logo
cry: 5 Mommy
ender: 3 nap 4 skin
end of a ~ tune: 3 EIO 5 EIEIO
entertainer: 5 Raffi
game: 3 tag, war 5 jacks, t-ball 6 Cootie, go fish 7 old maid
in Spanish: 4 niña, niño
protest: 5 not me
query: 3 why
retort: 4 am so 5 am too, can so, did so
ride: 4 bike, pony 5 trike, wagon 6 go-cart, go-kart 7 scooter 8 tricycle 9 school bus
rotten ~: 3 imp 4 brat
sch.: 4 elem.
shooter: 5 BB gun
starter: 5 grand
stickum: 5 paste
taunt: 6 are not, did not
kid __: 5 glove, stuff 6 gloves 7 brother
kid-__: 3 vid
__ kid: 4 quiz, whiz
Kid: 3 Ory 6 Creole 7 Gavilan, Nichols
kid-brotherish: 5 pesky, pesty 7 irksome 8 annoying 9 maddening, provoking, vexatious 10 bothersome, irritating
Kid Brother, The (1927 film)
director: J.A. Howe, Ted Wilde
kidcom: 7 cartoon
Kidd: 5 Jason 7 Captain, Michael, William

kidder: 3 wag 5 joker, tease 8 kibitzer
Kidder: 6 Margot
role for ~: 4 Lane, Lois
kiddie: 3 tot
use the ~ pool: 4 wade 6 splash
kiddie __: 3 car, lit
kidding: 5 humor, sport 6 banter, japery 7 jesting 8 badinage, jocosity 9 facetious 10 jocoseness
just ~: 7 as a lark 8 for a joke
no ~: 6 honest, really
person who takes ~: 5 sport
wasn't ~: 7 meant it
__ kidding!: 5 You're
kiddingly: 5 in fun 6 in jest
Kiddio (1960 song)
artist: Brook Benton
kiddish: 6 jejune 7 babyish, puerile 8 childish, immature, juvenile 9 childlike, infantile
Kidd, Jason
milieu: 5 court
org.: 3 NBA
sport: 10 basketball
kiddo: 3 bro 4 dude 5 buddy 6 buster
kiddy: 3 tot 4 brat 5 bairn, child 6 moppet, nipper, squirt 7 bambino, preteen 8 juvenile, small fry 9 offspring, youngster
Kid From Brooklyn, The (1946 film)
cast: Danny Kaye, Virginia Mayo, Vera-Ellen
Kid Galahad (1937 film)
cast: Humphrey Bogart, Bette Davis, Edward G. Robinson
__ Kid in Town: 3 New
kid lit
doctor: 5 Seuss
inventor: 5 Swift 8 Tom Swift
sleuth: 4 Drew 5 Hardy
wizard: 5 Harry 6 Potter

Kidman: **3** Nic **6** Nicole
Kidman, Nicole: **7** actress
film: Australia (2008)
Batman Forever (1995)
Bewitched (2005)
Billy Bathgate (1991)
Birth (2004)
Cold Mountain (2003)
Days of Thunder (1990)
Dead Calm (1989)
Eyes Wide Shut (1999)
Far and Away (1992)
Fur (2006)
The Golden Compass (2007)
The Hours (2002, AA)
The Human Stain (2003)
The Interpreter (2005)
Malice (1993)
Moulin Rouge (2001)
The Others (2001)
The Peacemaker (1997)
Practical Magic (1998)
To Die For (1995)
spouse: Tom Cruise, Keith Urban
kidnap: **3** nab **4** grab **5** seize, steal **6** abduct, hijack, pirate, snatch, waylay **7** capture **8** carry off, grab away, highjack, shanghai **9** bundle off **10** spirit away
victim: **5** Helen
Kidnapped
author: Robert Louis Stevenson
kidnapper: **5** felon **6** captor **8** abductor, hijacker
kidnapping: **6** felony **7** capture, seizure
kidney: **3** cut **4** bean, cast, kind, make, mold, sort, type **5** brand, breed, organ **7** variety **9** character, chili bean
combining form: **4** reni-, reno- **5** nephr- **6** nephro-
enzyme: **5** renin
of a ~: **5** renal
-shaped nut: **6** cashew
kidney __: **4** bean
kidney bean: **6** legume, veggie **9** vegetable
__ kid on the block: **3** new
kids: **3** get **4** seed **5** heirs, issue, young **6** family, scions **7** progeny **8** children, small fry, young uns **9** offspring, posterity
like bored ~: **5** antsy, itchy **7** fidgety **8** restless **9** unsettled
not for ~: **5** adult
one with ~: **4** goat **5** billy, nanny **6** father, mother, parent
tend the ~: **3** sit
__ Kids: **3** Spy
Kids Are Alright, The
band: Who, The
Kids Are Alright, The (1979 film)
director: Jeff Stein
__ Kids on the Block: **3** New
kidstakes
see baloney
__ Kids, The: **4** Quiz
Kid, The
author: Conrad Aiken
Kid, The (1921 film)
cast: Charles Chaplin, Jackie Coogan, Edna Purviance
director: Charles Chaplin
__ Kid, The: **5** Cisco **6** Frisco, Karate
Kiefer: **10** Sutherland
to Donald: **3** son
Kieffer: **4** pear
Kiel: **4** city, port, town **5** canal **6** Martin **7** Richard
locale: **7** Germany
kielbasa: **4** meat **6** Polish **7** sausage
Kieran: **6** Culkin
Kierkegaard, Sören: **6** Danish **11** philosopher
Kiev: **4** city, town **7** capital
city near ~: **4** Lvov
locale: **7** Ukraine
river: **5** Dnepr **7** Dnieper
__ Kiev: **7** chicken
Kigali: **4** city, town **7** capital
locale: **6** Rwanda
Kiki: **3** Dee **6** Cuyler
kil.: **4** meas.
Kilauea: **7** volcano
city near ~: **4** Hilo
locale: **6** Hawaii
output: **4** lava
Kilborn: **5** Craig
Kilbride: **5** Percy
Kildare: **3** Jim **5** James **6** doctor
org.: **3** AMA
kilderkin: **4** cask
Kiley: **6** Steven **7** Richard
Kiley, Steven
colleague: **5** Welby
Kiley, Steven org.: **3** AMA
Kilgallen: **7** Dorothy
kilim: **3** rug **8** tapestry
Kilimanjaro: **4** peak **5** mount **8** mountain
like ~: **5** snowy, white
locale: **6** Africa **8** Tanzania
Kilkenny __: **4** cats
kill: **3** nix **4** halt, prey, slay, stop, veto **5** annul, douse, dowse, purge, quash, quell, shoot, spend **6** cancel, defeat, poison, reject, remove, repeal, revoke, scotch, squash, stifle **7** abolish, nullify, shut off, squelch, turn off, wipe out **8** prohibit, suppress **9** eighty-six, liquidate, overwhelm **10** do away with, extinguish, neutralize
as a bill: **4** veto
could ~ for: **4** want **5** covet, crave, fancy, yearn **6** desire **9** lust after
ender: **3** joy **4** deer
time: **4** idle, laze, loaf **5** stall **6** loiter, lounge
with kindness: **5** spoil **6** coddle, dote on, pamper **7** indulge **9** spoon-feed
kill __: **3** fee **4** shot, time
Killarney: **4** city
county: **5** Kerry
locale: **4** Eire, Erin **7** Ireland
Kill Bill Vol. 1 (2003 film)
cast: David Carradine, Daryl Hannah, Lucy Liu, Uma Thurman
director: Quentin Tarantino
killdeer: **4** bird **6** plover
Killebrew, Harmon: **4** Twin **7** slugger
Killeen: **4** city, town
locale: **5** Texas
killer: **5** doozy **6** doozie, slayer **8** assassin, criminal, enforcer **9** cutthroat
bug ~: **3** DDT
germ ~: **4** drug **10** antibiotic
having a ~ instinct: **5** cruel **6** brutal, savage **8** pitiless, ruthless **9** cutthroat, dog-eat-dog, ferocious, merciless
starter: **4** pain
whale: **3** orc **4** orca **7** grampus
killer __: **3** app, bee **4** bars, boat, cell **5** T cell, whale
killer-__: **6** diller
__-killer: **4** weed
killick: **6** anchor
killifish: **5** guppy
killing: **9** landslide
make a ~: **5** score **6** profit **7** prosper
killing __: **5** frost
__ killing: **4** twin
Killing 'em Softly (1982 film)
cast: Irene Cara, George Segal
Killing Fields, The (1984 film)
cast: John Malkovich, Haing S. Ngor, Sam Waterston
character: Dith Pran
director: Roland Joffe
Killing Me Softly With His Song (1973 song)
artist: Roberta Flack
Killing Time
author: Thomas Berger
killjoy: **5** cynic **6** downer **7** scoffer, skeptic, worrier **8** sourpuss **9** defeatist, gloomy Gus, pessimist, worrywart **10** complainer, wet blanket
Killy, Jean-Claude: **5** skier **6** French
Kilmer: **3** Val **5** Joyce
Kilmer, Joyce: **4** poet
work: Trees
Kilmer, Val: **5** actor
film: At First Sight (1998)
Batman Forever (1995)
The Doors (1991)
Heat (1995)
Pollock (2000)
The Saint (1997)
Thunderheart (1992)
Tombstone (1993)
Top Gun (1986)
Willow (1988)
spouse: Joanne Whalley
voice: The Prince of Egypt (1998)
kiln: **4** oast, oven **5** stove **7** furnace
operator: **5** firer
product: **5** brick
put in a ~: **3** dry
starter: **4** lime
use a ~: **4** bake, heat **6** season
kilocalories
1000 ~: **5** therm **6** therme
kiloelectron __: **4** volt
kilograms
1000 ~: **5** tonne
.454 ~: **5** pound
kilometers
1.609 ~: **4** mile
kilo, Turkish: **3** oka
kilowatt-hour fraction: **3** erg **5** joule
kilowatts: **3** pwr. **5** power
Kilroy __ here: **3** was
kilt: **5** skirt **7** filibeg **8** philibeg
cousin: **5** A-line
fold: **5** plait, pleat
material: **5** plaid
wearer: **4** clan, Gael, Scot **5** piper **8** bagpiper
kilter: **4** sync, trim **5** order
out of ~: **4** awry, shot **5** amiss, askew, atilt, kaput **6** aslant, broken, faulty, flawed **7** damaged **9** defective **10** on the blink, on the fritz, out of whack
kiltie: **4** shoe **8** footwear
Kim: **4** Andy **5** Darby, Novak, O'Hara, Wilde **6** Alexis, Carnes, Fields, Greist, Hunter, Philby **7** Delaney, Stanley **8** Basinger, Campbell, Cattrall
author: Rudyard Kipling
city in ~: **6** Lahore
Kim __ Jung: **3** Dae
__ Kim: **3** Lil'
Kim, Andy
song: Baby, I Love You (1969)
Rock Me Gently (1974)
Kimberly: **4** Beck **5** Elise **8** Williams
Kimberly-__: **5** Clark
Kimbrough: **7** Charles
kimchi country: **5** Korea
Kim Dae Jung: **6** Korean **8** Nobelist
Kim Il Sung opponent: **4** Rhee
Kimmel: **5** Jimmy
Kimmie: **8** Meissner
kimono: **4** robe **7** garment, wrapper **8** bathrobe, lingerie, negligee, peignoir **9** housecoat
accessory: **3** obi **4** inro
fabric: **4** silk
kin: **6** caftan, kaftan
wearer: **6** geisha
kin: **3** bro, rel., sib, sis **4** aunt, gong, sibs **5** aunts, blood, folks, stock, uncle **6** cousin, family, father, mother, people, sister **7** brother, grandma, grandpa, lineage, progeny, related, sibling, similar **8** brethren, relation, relative **9** connected, great-aunt, relations, relatives **10** great-uncle
ender: **4** folk
__ kin: **6** next of **7** kissing
-kin
kin: **3** -ule
Kin: **7** Hubbard
Kinabalu: **4** peak **5** mount **8** mountain
locale: **4** Asia **6** Borneo
kinase: **6** enzyme
kind: **3** big, ilk, lax **4** easy, form, good, mild, mold, nice, soft, sort, type, warm **5** brand, breed, civil, class, close, genre, genus, loose, model, order, style, sweet **6** benign, chummy, clubby, decent, family, genial, gentle, giving, humane, kidney, loving, manner, nature, polite, tender **7** affable, amiable, bracket, clement, cordial, fashion, gallant, heedful, helpful, lenient, liberal, mindful, pattern, quality, ruthful, sparing, species, tactful, variety **8** all heart, amicable, category, fatherly, flexible, friendly, generous, gracious, harmless, intimate, ladylike, laid-back, maternal, merciful, motherly, obliging, outgoing, parental, placable, sisterly, sociable, tolerant **9** assuasive, attentive, avuncular, brotherly, character, compliant, congenial, convivial, courteous, easygoing, favorable, forgiving, indulgent, sensitive, temperate, unselfish **10** altruistic, beneficent, benevo-

lent, bighearted, buddy-buddy, charitable, chivalrous, forbearing, hospitable, neighborly, permissive, solicitous, thoughtful, unexacting, unhardened
be ~: 4 care 10 have a heart
be so ~: 5 deign, lower, stoop 6 see fit 9 patronize 10 condescend
combining form: 4 phyl- 5 phylo-
deed: 3 aid 4 help 5 favor 7 service 8 courtesy
ender: 7 hearted
first of its ~: 3 new 5 novel 8 brand-new, original 10 avant-garde, futuristic, innovative, newfangled
in ~: 4 like, thus 8 likewise 9 similarly, tit-for-tat
in French: 3 bon
in Latin: 4 alma
make ~: 6 gentle, mellow, soften, temper 8 humanize
of: 4 a bit 5 quasi, sorta 6 fairly, in a way, pretty, rather, sort of 7 a little 8 slightly, somewhat 9 to a degree 10 moderately, more or less
of (prefix): 4 semi-
of (suffix): 3 -ish
of that ~: 4 such
one: 5 angel, donor, saint 6 backer, patron 7 sponsor 9 supporter 10 benefactor 11 underwriter
pay in ~: 6 avenge 7 get even, requite 9 get back at, retaliate
starter: 3 man 5 woman, women
that ~ of: 4 such 7 similar
two of a ~: 4 same 5 alike 9 identical 10 synonymous
wishes: 7 devoirs, regards 8 respects 9 greetings
Kind: 6 Roslyn 7 Richard
kinda: 5 sorta 6 rather, sort of
kindergarten: 5 class 6 school
break: 3 nap 4 rest 6 snooze
denizen: 3 boy, kid, tot 4 girl, tike, tyke 5 pupil 7 student
fare: 4 ABCs 6 letter 8 alphabet
game: 4 I spy
song opening: 3 ABC 4 ABCD 5 ABCDE
staple: 5 chalk, paste 6 crayon
wear: 5 smock
Kindergarten Cop (1990 film)
cast: Linda Hunt, Penelope Ann Miller, Pamela Reed, Arnold Schwarzenegger
director: Ivan Reitman
Kindertotenlieder
composer: Gustav Mahler
Kind & Generous (1998 song)
artist: Natalie Merchant
kindhearted: 3 big, lax 4 easy, good, mild, nice, soft, warm 5 great, loose, sweet 6 benign, gentle, humane, loving, tender 7 amiable, clement, cordial, lenient, ruthful, sparing 8 amicable, flexible, friendly, generous, gracious, laid-back, merciful, obliging, placable, tolerant 9 assuasive, compliant, congenial, courteous, easygoing, forgiving, indulgent, unselfish 10 altruistic, beneficent, benevolent, charitable, forbearing, hospitable, neighborly, permissive, solicitous, thoughtful, unexacting
soul: 5 softy, sport 6 softie
Kind Hearts and Coronets (1949 film)
cast: Alec Guinness, Valerie Hobson
kindle: 4 burn, fuel, lick, stir, wake, whet 5 cause, egg on, key up, light, liven, pique, raise, rally, rouse, spark, waken 6 arouse, awaken, bestir, excite, fire up, foment, ignite, incite, induce, turn on, whip up, work up 7 actuate, agitate, animate, enflame, inflame, inspire, provoke, quicken 8 activate, brighten, enspirit, inspirit, set afire, touch off 9 impassion, instigate, set alight, set fire to, stimulate 10 illuminate, intoxicate
kindliness: 4 pity 5 mercy 6 warmth 8 good deed, goodness, good turn 9 geniality 10 fellowship, good nature
kindling: 4 fuel, twig, wood 5 brush, fagot, twigs 6 firing, tinder 7 burning 8 arousing, firewood, igniting, lighting, shavings 9 awakening, driftwood, evocative, fomenting 10 combustion, quickening
kindly: 3 big, lax 4 easy, good, mild, nice, soft, warm 5 close, loose, moral, sweet 6 benign, chummy, clubby, decent, genial, gentle, humane, loving, please, polite, tender 7 affable, amiable, clement, cordial, gallant, heedful, helpful, lenient, mindful, ruthful, sparing, tactful 8 all heart, amicable, flexible, friendly, generous, gracious, intimate, laid-back, merciful, obliging, outgoing, placable, pleasant, sociable, tolerant 9 assuasive, compliant, congenial, convivial, courteous, easygoing, favorable, forgiving, indulgent, sensitive, unselfish 10 altruistic, beneficent, benevolent, buddy-buddy, charitable, forbearing, hospitable, neighborly, permissive, solicitous, thoughtful, unexacting, unhardened
__ kindly to: 4 take
kindness: 3 aid 4 hand, help, pity 5 favor, grace, heart, mercy 6 lenity, succor, virtue 7 amenity, charity, decency, service, thought 8 altruism, clemency, courtesy, good deed, goodness, good turn, good will, humanity, lenience, patience, sympathy 9 affection, tolerance 10 amiability, assistance, compassion, cordiality, generosity, indulgence, liberality, solicitude
kill with ~: 5 spoil 6 coddle, dote on, pamper 7 indulge 9 spoon-feed
Kind of a Drag (1967 song)
artist: Buckinghams
__ Kind of Fool Am I?: 4 What
__ Kind of Hero: 4 Some
__ Kind of Love: 6 Groovy
Kind of Magic, A
author: Edna Ferber
__ Kind of Wonderful: 4 Some
kindred: 4 akin, clan, like 5 alike, stock, tribe 6 agnate, allied, family 7 cognate, lineage, progeny, related, similar 8 parallel, relation 9 analogous, relatives 10 comparable, equivalent
kinds of, all: 4 gobs, lots, many, much, pile, tons 5 ample, heaps, loads, lotsa, no end, scads 6 barrel, galore, oodles, plenty 7 aplenty, copious 8 beaucoup, mountain, plethora 9 abundance, thousands
kine: 4 cows 5 herds 6 cattle 7 bovines, heifers 9 livestock
Kiner, Ralph: 6 Pirate 7 slugger 10 outfielder
kinetic: 7 dynamic 8 in motion 9 energetic
kinetic __: 3 art 6 energy
kinetics: 4 flow, flux 6 motion 8 movement
kinetoscope inventor: 6 Edison
kinfolk: 4 clan, kith, seed, sons 5 folks, heirs, issue 6 family, people 7 parents, progeny 8 ancestry, brethren, children, forbears 9 ancestors, daughters, offspring, posterity, relations, relatives
king: 3 bed, HRH, rex, sov. 4 boss, card, czar, dean, male, tsar, tzar 5 chief, doyen, mogul, Mr. Big, nabob, noble, royal, ruler, title 6 dynast, gerent, leader, top dog, tycoon, victor 7 big shot, his nibs, majesty, monarch, viceroy 8 big wheel, enthrone, inthrone, tetrarch 9 honor card, potentate, sovereign 10 chess piece, head honcho
address: 4 sire
beater: 3 ace
beater, in pinochle: 3 ten
Biblical ~: 3 Asa 4 Ahab, Reba, Saul 5 Abner, David, Herod 7 Solomon
Egyptian ~: 6 Ramses 7 Rameses
ender: 3 cup, dom, let, pin 4 bird, bolt, fish, ship, side, wood 5 craft, maker 6 fisher, making
fit for a ~: 5 regal, royal 9 luxurious
greedy ~: 5 Midas
home: 6 castle, palace
Hun ~: 4 Atli
in a Steve Martin tune: 3 Tut
Indian ~: 4 raja
in French: 3 roi
in Latin: 3 rex
in Spanish: 3 rey
Jack Kent's comic-strip ~: 4 Aroo
jungle ~: 4 lion
land of Anna's ~: 4 Siam
like the ~ of beasts: 5 noble
merry ~ of nursery rhymes: 4 Cole
move: 4 jump
mythical ~ of Calydon: 6 Oeneus
name meaning ~: 5 Elroy, Leroy
neighbor: 6 bishop
Norse mythical ~: 4 Atli
nursery-rhyme ~: 4 Cole
of beasts: 4 lion
of Phrygia: 5 Midas
of the hill: 5 on top
of the road: 4 hobo 5 tramp 7 vagrant 8 vagabond, wanderer
order: 3 act 4 fiat 5 edict, ukase 6 decree, dictum, ruling 7 dictate, mandate, precept 9 manifesto
place for a ~: 4 deck
Portuguese ~: 4 Joao, Luis 5 Pedro
Shakespearean ~: 4 Lear
Volsunga Saga ~: 4 Atli
king __: 4 clam, crab, post, rail 5 cobra
king __ hill: 5 of the
king-__: 4 size 5 sized
__ king: 3 à la
King: 2 B.B. 3 Don, Sky, Tut 4 Alan, Ben E., Fahd, peak, Saul 5 David, Floyd, Henry, Larry, Mabel, mount, Perry, ranch, Vidor 6 Albert, Carole, Claude, Evelyn, Oliver, Pee Wee 7 Morgana, Solomon, Stephen 8 Gillette, mountain 10 Billie Jean
had one: 5 dream
sport: 6 hockey 10 basketball
King __: 3 Rat, Tut 4 Aroo, Coal, John, Kong, Lear, Pest 5 Ralph 6 Cotton, Creole
King __ a Day: 3 for
King __ Bible: 5 James
King __ Road: 5 of the
King __ spaniel: 7 Charles
King __ Stomp: 6 Porter
King __, The: 4 and I
King __ tomb: 4 Tut's
King __ Version: 5 James
King __ War: 7 George's, Philip's
King __ York, A: 5 in New
King and I, The (1956 film): 7 musical
cast: Yul Brynner, Deborah Kerr, Rita Moreno
character: 4 Anna 5 Orton 6 Lun Tha, Tuptim 7 Mongkut
composer: Oscar Hammerstein, Richard Rodgers
director: Walter Lang
locale: 4 Siam
King Arthur
enchantress: 5 Le Fay 6 Morgan, Vivien
father: 5 Uther
foster brother: 3 Kay
island paradise: 6 Avalon
knight: 3 Kay, Tor 4 Bors, Eric 5 Ector, Floll, Lucan 6 Ewaine, Gareth, Gawain, Hector 7 Galahad, Geraint, Mordred, Tristan 8 Lancelot, Percival, Tristram 9 Launcelot
magician: 6 Merlin
palace site: 7 Camelot
queen: 9 Guinevere
quest: 9 Holy Grail
sister: 4 Anne 5 Le Fay 6 Morgan
sword: 9 Excalibur
King Arthur (2004 film)
cast: Keira Knightley, Clive Owen
King, B.B.: 8 bluesman 9 guitarist
first name: Riley
guitar: Lucille
King, Ben E.
song: Spanish Harlem (1961)
Stand by Me (1961)
Supernatural Thing (1975)
King, Billie Jean: 7 netster 9 tennis pro
milieu: 5 court
kingbird: 10 flycatcher
king can __ wrong, The: 4 do no
King, Carole
song: I Feel the Earth Move (1971)
It's Too Late (1971)
Jazzman (1974)

Nightingale (1975)
So Far Away (1971)
Sweet Seasons (1972)
King Charles __: 7 spaniel
King, Claude
song: Wolverton Mountain (1962)
King Coal
author: Upton Sinclair
king cobra: 5 snake 9 hamadryad
__ King Cole: 3 Nat, Old
King Cotton
composer: John Philip Sousa
__ king crab: 6 Alaska 7 Alaskan
King Creole (1958 film)
cast: Dolores Hart, Dean Jagger, Carolyn Jones, Elvis Presley
kingcup: 6 flower 7 cowslip
King David (1985 film)
cast: Richard Gere
kingdom: 4 land 5 realm 6 domain, empire, nation 7 country, dynasty 8 monarchy
ancient ~: 4 Cush, Edom, Elam, Kush, Moab 5 Ammon, Nubia, Ophir, Sheba 6 Epirus
Anglo-Saxon ~: 5 Essex
Asian ~: 5 Nepal 6 Bhutan
N. Sea ~: 4 Holl., Neth.
of a ~: 5 regal, royal 8 dynastic, imperial, majestic
onetime Asian ~: 4 Anam 5 Annam
Polynesian ~: 5 Tonga
subdivision: 6 phylum
kingdom __: 4 come
__ kingdom: 5 plant 6 animal 7 mineral
Kingdom __: 4 Hall
__ Kingdom: 4 Wild
Kingdom Come (2001 film)
cast: Vivica A. Fox, Whoopi Goldberg, LL Cool J, Jada Pinkett Smith
Kingdom of Heaven (2005 film)
cast: Orlando Bloom, Eva Green, Jeremy Irons
director: Ridley Scott
Kingdom, The
composer: Edward Elgar
Kingdom, The (2007 film)
cast: Chris Cooper, Jamie Foxx, Jennifer Garner
King, Evelyn
song: Shame (1978)
King Features
competitor: 3 NEA
kingfish: 4 amir, boss, czar, emir, exec, head, jefe, tsar, tzar 5 ameer, chief, emeer, ruler 6 honcho, leader, master, top dog 7 captain, headman, skipper 8 director, higher-up, top brass 9 big cheese, commander, executive, key player, top banana 10 mastermind
kingfisher: 4 bird 7 halcyon 10 kookaburra
coif: 5 crest
genus: 6 alcedo
relative: 4 tody 6 motmot
Kingfish, The: Huey Long
King for a Day (1986 song)
artist: Thompson Twins
King George __: 3 III
King George's __: 3 War
King in New York, A (1957 film)
cast: Charles Chaplin
director: Charles Chaplin
King James __: 5 Bible 7 Version
King John
author: William Shakespeare
kingklip catcher: 5 eeler
King Kong: 3 ape
author: Edgar Wallace
King Kong (1933 film)
cast: Robert Armstrong, Bruce Cabot, Fay Wray
character: 3 Ann 4 Carl 6 Darrow, Denham 9 Ann Darrow 10 Carl Denham
composer: Max Steiner
studio: 3 RKO
King Kong (1976 film)
cast: Jeff Bridges, Charles Grodin, Jessica Lange
King Kong (2005 film)
cast: Jack Black, Adrien Brody, Naomi Watts
King Lear: 4 play 7 tragedy
author: William Shakespeare
character: 5 Edgar, Regan 6 Edmund, Oswald 7 Goneril 8 Cordelia 10 Earl of Kent
Kurosawa's ~: 3 Ran
kinglike: 5 grand, noble, regal, royal 6 august, lordly 7 haughty 8 imperial, imposing, majestic 9 imperious 10 autocratic, commanding
kingliness: 7 dignity, majesty 8 eminence, grandeur, splendor
kingly: 5 noble, regal, royal 7 leonine, stately 8 despotic, imperial, majestic 9 imperious 10 autocratic, despotical, majestical
king mackerel: 4 fish 7 cavalla
Kingman: 4 city, Dave, town
locale: 7 Arizona
King Mark
wife: 6 Iseult, Isolde
King, Martin Luther: 8 Nobelist
title: 3 Rev. 8 Reverend
King Must Die, The
author: Mary Renault
king of __: 6 beasts
King of All Media: 5 Stern
King of Comedy, The (1983 film)
cast: Sandra Bernhard, Robert De Niro, Jerry Lewis
director: Martin Scorsese
King of Kings (1961 film)
cast: Jeffrey Hunter, Siobhan McKenna, Robert Ryan
director: Nicholas Ray
King of Marvin Gardens, The (1972 film)
cast: Ellen Burstyn, Bruce Dern, Jack Nicholson
King of Pain (1983 song)
artist: Police
King of Queens, The (CBS sitcom)
cast: Kevin James (Doug Heffernan)
Patton Oswalt (Spence Olchin)
Leah Remini (Carrie Heffernan)
Jerry Stiller (Arthur Spooner)
Gary Valentine (Danny Heffernan)
Victor Williams (Deacon Palmer)
king of the __: 4 hill 6 forest
King of the __: 4 Road
King of the Cowboys, The: 6 Rogers
King of the Hill (Fox sitcom)
setting: Arlen, Texas
voice cast: Mike Judge (Hank Hill)
Brittany Murphy (Luanne Platter)
Kathy Najimy (Peggy Hill)
King of the Road (1965 song)
artist: Roger Miller
King of Torts, The: Melvin Belli
King Olaf
composer: Edward Elgar
King Peak
locale: 5 Yukon 6 Canada
King Pest
author: Edgar Allan Poe
King Philip's __: 3 War
kingpin: 4 boss, czar, tsar 5 Mr. Big 7 headman 8 director 9 authority, commander, organizer
Kingpin (1996 film)
cast: Vanessa Angel, Woody Harrelson, Bill Murray, Randy Quaid
director: Bobby Farrelly, Peter Farrelly
King Ralph (1991 film)
cast: John Goodman, John Hurt, Peter O'Toole
King Ranch: 6 spread
locale: 5 Texas
unit: 4 acre
King Rat
author: James Clavell
king's __: 6 ransom 7 English
Kings: 3 six 4 five, team
follower: 10 Chronicles
home: 10 Los Angeles, Sacramento
milieu: 3 ice 4 rink
org.: 3 NBA, NHL
preceder: 6 Samuel
rival: *see* NBA team, hockey team
sport: 6 hockey 10 basketball
town near the Valley of the ~: 5 Luxor
Valley of the ~ locale: 5 Egypt
Kingsblood Royal
author: Sinclair Lewis
Kings Canyon: 4 park
locale: 10 California
Kingsfield profession: 3 law
King's Fifth, The
author: Scott O'Dell
kings, game of: 5 chess 8 checkers
King's Henchmen, The: 5 opera
composer: Deems Taylor
kingship: 4 rule, sway 5 crown, power, reign 6 regime, throne 7 command, royalty, scepter 8 dominion, monarchy 9 accession, authority, supremacy 10 ascendance, ascendancy, ascendence, ascendency, succession
king-size: 3 big 4 huge, vast 5 giant, great, jumbo, large 7 hulking, immense, mammoth, massive, sizable, titanic 8 colossal, enormous, gigantic, sizeable, towering, whapping, whopping 9 Herculean, humongous, overlarge 10 gargantuan, monumental, prodigious, stupendous, tremendous
Kingsley: 3 Ben 4 Amis 6 Sidney
Kingsley, Ben: 5 actor
film: Bugsy (1991)
Dave (1993)
Elegy (2008)
The Fifth Monkey (1990)
Gandhi (1982, AA)
House of Sand and Fog (2003)
Oliver Twist (2005)
Rules of Engagement (2000)
Schindler's List (1993)
Silas Marner (1985)
Sneakers (1992)
Species (1995)
Turtle Diary (1985)
Kingsmen
song: The Jolly Green Giant (1965)
Louie Louie (1963)
King Solomon's Mines: 4 film 5 novel
author: H. Rider Haggard
cast: Stewart Granger, Deborah Kerr
King Solomon's Ring
author: Konrad Lorenz
Kingsolver, Barbara: 6 writer
work: The Bean Trees
Pigs in Heaven
Prodigal Summer
Small Wonder
Kings Peak: 4 peak 5 mount 8 mountain
locale: 4 Utah 6 Uintas
Kings Row (1942 film)
cast: Robert Cummings, Ronald Reagan, Ann Sheridan
King's Stilts
author: Dr. Seuss
King, Stephen: 6 writer
enjoy ~: 4 read
genre: horror
home: Maine
like a ~ novel: 4 eery 5 eerie, scary, weird 6 creepy, spooky 7 bizarre, macabre, strange, uncanny 9 fantastic
pen name: Bachman
work: Bag of Bones
Blaze
Carrie
Cell
Christine
The Colorado Kid
Creepshow
Cujo
The Dark Half
The Dark Tower
The Dead Zone
Desperation
Dolores Claiborne
Dream Catcher
Duma Key
Faithful
Firestarter
The Green Mile
The Gunslinger
Insomnia
It
Lisey's Story
Misery
Needful Things
Night Shift
Pet Sematary
The Plant
Rage
Roadwork
Rose Madder
The Running Man
Salem's Lot
The Shining
The Stand
The Talisman
The Tommyknockers
Under the Dome
Ur
The Waste Lands
__ Kings, The: 5 Mambo

Kingston: **4** city, port, town **7** capital
athletes: **4** Rams
locale: **6** Canada **7** Jamaica, New York, Ontario
music: **3** ska
school: **3** URI **6** Queen's
Kingston Trio
song: M.T.A. (1959)
Reverend Mr. Black (1963)
Tom Dooley (1958)
King Sunny ___: **3** Adé
King, The: **5** Elvis, Gable **7** Presley
daughter: **4** Lisa
middle name: **4** Aron
portrayer: Yul Brynner
___ King, The: **3** Sun **4** Lion **5** March, Waltz **6** Fisher, Little
___-King, The: **3** Erl
King Tut's ___: **4** tomb
King William's ___: **3** War
Kinison, Sam: **5** comic **8** comedian
kink: **4** bend, coil, curl, flaw, flex, friz, knot, loop, pain, pang **5** cramp, crick, frizz, hitch, quirk, spasm, twist **6** curl up, defect, foible, glitch, tangle, twinge **7** sinuate **8** crotchet, soreness **9** stiffness **10** difficulty, impediment
kinkajou: **5** potto **6** animal, mammal
Kinko's
buyer: **5** FedEx
Kinks
song: All Day and All of the Night (1965)
Come Dancing (1983)
Lola (1970)
Tired of Waiting for You (1965)
You Really Got Me (1964)
kinky: **3** odd **4** wiry **5** curly, queer, weird **6** coiled, frizzy, matted **7** crimped, frizzly, knotted, oddball, tangled, twisted **8** peculiar **10** outlandish, unbalanced
Kinky: **8** Friedman
Kinmont: **8** Kathleen
___ Kinnan Rawlings: **8** Marjorie
Kinnear, Greg: **5** actor
film: As Good as It Gets (1997)
Auto Focus (2002)
Baby Mama (2008)
Bad News Bears (2005)
Dear God (1996)
Flash of Genius (2008)
Little Miss Sunshine (2006)
Mystery Men (1999)
Nurse Betty (2000)
Sabrina (1995)
Someone Like You (2001)
Stuck on You (2003)
We Were Soldiers (2002)
You've Got Mail (1998)
Kinnell, Galway: **4** poet
Kinney: **5** Kathy, Terry
kinnikinnick: **5** shrub, smoke **9** bearberry
berry color: **3** red
family: **5** heath
kino: **5** resin
kin's companion: **4** kith
Kinsella: **2** W.P. **6** Thomas
Kinsella, W.P.: **6** writer
work: Box Socials
The Iowa Baseball Confederacy
Magic Time
Shoeless Joe
Kinsey: **6** Alfred **8** Millhone
concern: **3** sex
creator: Sue Grafton

Kinshasa: **4** city, town **7** capital
locale: **5** Congo
locale, once: **5** Zaire
river: **5** Congo
kinship: **3** tie **5** blood **7** bearing, harmony **8** affinity, relation **9** belonging, community **10** connection, similarity
group: **4** clan **5** folks, tribe **6** family
Kinski: **5** Klaus **9** Nastassja
Kinski, Nastassja: **7** actress
film: Tess (1979)
kinsman: **3** son **4** aunt **5** child, enate, niece, uncle **6** affine, agnate, cousin, father, mother, nephew, parent, sister **7** brother, cognate **8** daughter, grandson, relation, relative **9** great-aunt **10** grandchild, great-uncle, stepfather, stepmother, stepsister
Kinsman Saga, The
author: Ben Bova
kinsperson: **6** sister **8** relation, relative
Kinston: **4** town
locale: **4** N. Car.
kinswoman: **4** aunt **5** enate, niece **6** affine, cousin, mother, sister **7** cognate, kinsman **8** relative **9** great-aunt
___ Kinte: **5** Kunta
kiosk: **5** booth, stall, stand **6** gazebo **9** bandstand, newsstand
buy: **3** mag **4** Elle, Time **8** magazine, Newsweek
Kiowa: **5** tribe **6** Indian **7** Amerind **8** language
kip: **3** bed **5** money
locale: **4** Laos
Kip: **5** Keino, Niven
Kipchoge: **5** Keino
Kipling, Rudyard: **4** poet **6** writer **7** British **8** Nobelist
bear: **5** Baloo
biographer: **4** Amis
birthplace: Bombay, India
elephant: **5** Hathi
setting: **5** India
villain: **5** cobra
work: Barrack-Room Ballads
Captains Courageous
Danny Deever
Fuzzy Wuzzy
Gunga Din
If
The Jungle Book
Just So Stories
Kim
The Light That Failed
Mandalay
The Man Who Would Be King
Recessional
kipper: **3** dry **4** cure, salt **5** smoke **6** salmon **7** herring **8** preserve
___ Kippur: **3** Yom
kir: **4** wine
ingredient: **6** cassis
Kirby: **4** Jack **5** Bruno, Grant **6** vacuum **7** Durward, Puckett
rival: **5** Miele, Oreck **6** Eureka, Hoover **10** Electrolux
Kirchhoff, Gustav: **6** German **9** physicist
Kirghiz: **8** language
city: **3** Osh
once: **3** SSR
range: **4** Alai
tent: **4** yurt

Kirghiz ___: **6** Steppe
___-kiri: **4** hara
Kiri: **8** Te Kanawa
Kiribati: **6** nation **7** country
capital: **6** Tarawa
money: **4** cent **6** dollar
kirigami: **3** art
origin: **5** Japan
kirk: **6** church, temple **8** Scottish
Kirk: **4** Alyn, Lisa **5** Tommy **6** Gibson **7** Cameron, captain, Douglas, Phyllis
Michael Douglas, to ~: **3** son
Kirk, Captain: **3** Jim **5** James
birthplace: **4** Iowa
crew: **4** Sulu **5** McCoy, Scott, Spock, Uhura **6** Chekov, Scotty
middle name: **8** Tiberius
Kirkland: **4** city, Lane, town **5** Sally **6** Gelsey
locale: **10** Washington
Kirkpatrick: **5** Jeane
Kirkstall Abbey
locale: **5** Leeds
Kirkuk: **4** city, town
locale: **4** Irak, Iraq
Kirkwood: **4** city, town
locale: **8** Missouri
Kirlian image: **4** aura
Kirman: **3** rug
kirsch: **5** drink **6** brandy **8** beverage
flavor: **6** cherry
kin: **6** cognac
Kirschner: **3** Don, Mia
Kirsten: **5** Dunst **8** Flagstad
Kirstie: **5** Alley
kirtle: **4** gown **5** dress, frock **7** garment
'K' Is for Killer
author: Sue Grafton
Kish
son: **4** Saul
kishka: **3** gut **5** derma
Kishwaukee, city on the: **6** De Kalb
Kiska
locale: **6** Alaska
Kislev: **5** month **6** Hebrew
predecessor: **7** Heshvan
successor: **5** Tevet
kismet: **3** lot **4** fate, luck **5** karma **7** destiny, fortune, portion **10** providence
Kismet: **7** musical
character: **4** Imam, Omar
melodist: **7** Borodin
setting: **4** Irak, Iraq
kiss: **3** pet **4** buss, love, neck, peck, skim **5** candy, graze, shave, smack, touch **6** cookie, smooch **8** osculate, pucker up **10** confection, osculation, salutation
and make up: **5** yield **6** accept, pardon **7** appease, forgive, let it go, let pass, patch up, placate, reunite **8** overlook, take back **9** acquiesce, reconcile **10** conciliate
babies: **3** run **4** gush **5** stump **6** hustle **8** campaign, politick
good-bye: **3** end, rid **4** drop, jilt, lose **5** eject, spend **6** reject **7** abandon, forsake **8** forswear **9** foreswear **10** relinquish
how dogs ~: **5** wetly
partner: **3** hug **4** ride, tell
Spanish words ~: **4** beso

target: **3** lip **5** cheek, mouth
the feet of: **5** adore, deify, honor **6** admire, dote on **7** glorify, idolize, worship **8** venerate **9** be stuck on, be sweet on **10** be mad about
kiss ___: **3** off **7** good-bye
___ kiss: **3** air
Kiss
members: Criss, Frehley, Simmons, Stanley
song: Beth (1976)
Forever (1990)
Kiss (1986 song)
artist: Prince
Kiss an Angel Good Mornin' (1971 song)
artist: Charley Pride
kiss and ___: **4** tell
kiss-and-___: **4** ride
Kiss and Say Goodbye (1976 song)
artist: Manhattans
Kiss Before Dying, A
author: Ira Levin
kisser: **3** mug, pan, yap **4** face, lips, puss **5** bazoo, mouth
baby ~: **3** pol **10** politician
kisses
love and ~: **7** devoirs, regards **9** greetings **10** best wishes, good wishes
symbols: **3** xes
___ Kisses: **8** Hershey's
Kisses on the Wind (1989 song)
artist: Neneh Cherry
Kisses Sweeter Than Wine (1957 song)
artist: Jimmie Rodgers
Kiss Hollywood Good-By
author: Anita Loos
Kissimmee: **4** city, town
locale: **7** Florida
kissing: **4** fond, warm **6** loving, tender **7** amorous **8** romantic **10** passionate
kissing ___: **3** kin **4** gate **6** bridge, cousin **7** gourami
Kissing a Fool (1988 song)
artist: George Michael
Kissinger, Henry: **8** Nobelist
Kissin' Time (1959 song)
artist: Bobby Rydell
Kiss, Kiss
author: Roald Dahl
Kiss Me Deadly
author: Mickey Spillane
Kiss Me Kate: **4** film **7** musical
cast: Kathryn Grayson, Howard Keel, Ann Miller
character: **4** Lane, Lois **5** Felix, Lilli **6** Virgil
composer: Cole Porter
Kiss me, my fool! sayer: **4** Bara
Kiss Me, Stupid (1964 film)
cast: Felicia Farr, Dean Martin, Kim Novak, Ray Walston
director: Billy Wilder
Kiss my grits!
role: **3** Flo
Kiss of the Spider Woman: **4** film **5** novel
author: Manuel Puig
cast: Sonia Braga, William Hurt, Raul Julia
Kiss on My List (1981 song)
artist: Hall and Oates

Kiss, The: **5** novel **8** painting **9** sculpture
artist: Gustav Klimt, Auguste Rodin
author: Danielle Steel
Kiss the Boys Goodbye
author: Clare Boothe Luce
Kiss the Girls (1997 film)
cast: Cary Elwes, Morgan Freeman, Tony Goldwyn, Ashley Judd
kissy-__: **4** face
__-Kist: **4** Star
Kistler: **5** Darci
kit: **3** fox, rig, set **4** gear, pack **5** stuff, tools **6** duffel, duffle, outfit, string, tackle **7** tool set **8** knapsack, supplies, utensils **9** apparatus, container, equipment **10** implements, provisions
and caboodle: **3** all, lot **6** entire
mother: **5** vixen
sewing ~: **4** etui **5** etwee
kit __: **3** bag, fox
__ kit: **4** mess, tool **5** press **6** sewing **8** first aid
Kit: **6** Carson **7** Marlowe
Kit-__ Club: **3** Cat, Kat
__-Kit: **6** Identi
Kitaen: **5** Tawny
kitbag: **4** pack **5** pouch **6** duffel, duffle **7** holdall **8** backpack, knapsack, rucksack **9** haversack
kitchen: **6** galley **7** canteen, cookery **8** scullery **9** cookhouse
appliance: **4** oven **5** mixer, range, stove **6** fridge, juicer **7** blender
attraction: **4** odor **5** aroma, scent, smell, whiff **9** fragrance, redolence
cloth: **5** towel
denizen of song: **5** Dinah
do a ~ chore: **4** chop, cube, dice, grat, mash, pare, peel, rice
doing ~ duty, to a GI: **4** on KP
employee: **4** chef, cook **5** baker
ender: **4** ette, ware
floor covering: **4** lino, tile **8** linoleum, oilcloth
gadget: **5** corer, parer, ricer, timer, whisk **6** baster, beater, canner, grater, masher, sifter
garment: **4** mitt **5** apron
helper: **4** tool **6** gadget **7** utensil **9** appliance
help in the ~: **3** dry, mop **4** wash, wipe **5** clean, clear **6** sponge
herb: **4** sage **5** basil, chive, thyme
kind of ~: **5** eat-in
like the ~ sink: **5** soapy, sudsy
meas.: **3** tbs., tsp. **4** tbsp.
pest: **5** roach **6** insect
portable ~: **7** canteen **10** chuck wagon
ruin, in the ~: **4** burn, char, sear **5** singe **6** scorch **9** carbonize
spice: **4** mace **5** clove, cumin
staple: **3** oil **4** oleo, salt **5** flour, sugar, yeast **9** margarine
staple, once: **4** lard **6** grease
tear-jerker: **5** onion
topper: **3** cap, lid **5** cover
utensil: **3** pan, pot, wok **5** knife, ladle, sieve **6** boiler, cooker
utensil brand: **3** Oxo **4** Ekco
wrap: **4** foil **5** Saran
kitchen __: **4** sink **5** match **6** garden, midden, police **7** cabinet
__ kitchen: **4** soup **7** country
Kitchen __, The: **4** Toto
__ Kitchen: **5** Hell's
KitchenAid: **9** appliance
alternative: ***see*** appliance brand
Kitchener: **4** city, earl, town
foe: **4** Boer
locale: **6** Canada **7** Ontario
Kitchen God's Wife, The
author: Amy Tan
kite: **3** toy **4** bird **5** glede **6** elanet, letter **9** plaything **10** bird of prey
cousin: **5** stilt
end: **4** tail
go fly a ~: **5** scram, split **6** beat it, begone **7** buzz off, get lost, take off **8** scramola **9** take a hike
nemesis: **4** tree
__ kite: **3** box
Kite, Tom: **6** golfer
kith: **7** kinfolk **8** kinfolks, kinsfolk
kith and __: **3** kin
kithara: **4** lyre **6** string
origin: **6** Greece
Kit Kat: **3** bar **5** candy **8** candy bar **9** chocolate
alternative: ***see*** candy brand
Kits, cats, sacks and ___...: **5** wives
kitschy: **5** gaudy, tacky **6** garish
Kitt: **6** Eartha
Kitt __ Observatory: **4** Peak
K.I.T.T.: **3** car **4** auto **10** automobile
kitten: **3** cat, pet **4** puss **5** felid, kitty, pussy **6** feline **8** pussycat
at times: **5** mewer **6** purrer
cry: **3** mew **4** meow, mewl **5** miaou, miaow, miaul
like a ~: **4** soft **5** furry, fuzzy **6** fluffy
Kitten __ Keys: **5** on the
kittenish: **6** frisky **9** fun-loving **10** coquettish, frolicsome
kittens: **5** young **6** litter
kittiwake: **4** bird, gull
kitty: **3** cat, pet, pot **4** fund, pool, puss, till **5** cache, felid, means, money, prize, purse, stake **6** feline, kitten **7** jackpot, savings **9** grimalkin, resources
command to ~: **4** scat, shoo
comment: **3** mew **4** meow **5** miaou, miaow, miaul
delighter: **6** catnip
feed the ~: **5** wager **6** chip in, kick in
retiree's ~: **3** IRA **7** nest egg, pension
start the ~: **3** bet **4** ante **5** stake, wager **8** shell out
Kitty: **3** cat **5** Wells **6** Kallen, Kelley **7** Dukakis **8** Carlisle **10** Carruthers
Kitty __: **4** Hawk **5** Foyle **6** Litter
kitty-corner: **8** diagonal
Kitty Foyle: **4** film **5** novel
author: Christopher Morley
cast: Dennis Morgan, Ginger Rogers
Kitty, Miss
establishment: **3** bar **6** saloon
friend: **4** Matt **6** Dillon
portrayer: Amanda Blake
Kivi, Aleksis: **6** writer **7** Finnish
Kiwanian
colleague: **4** Lion
kiwi: **4** bird **5** fruit **6** ratite **7** apteryx
kin: **3** emu, moa **4** emeu
language: **5** Maori
neighbor: **4** weka
Kix: **6** Brooks, cereal
competitor: ***see*** cereal
Kjellin: **3** Alf
KJV: **5** Bible
K-K-K-__: **4** Katy
Klaatu __ nikto: **6** barada
klaberjass: **4** game **8** card game
variant: **6** belote **7** belotte
Klagenfurt: **4** city **9** ski resort
locale: **7** Austria
Klamath Falls: **4** city, town
locale: **6** Oregon
Klammer, Franz: **5** skier
klatsch
in German: **6** gossip
__ klatsch: **6** coffee, kaffee
Klaus: **6** Kinski
in English: **8** Nicholas
Klaus __ Brandauer: **5** Maria
klaxon: **4** horn **5** alarm
Kleenex: **6** tissue
Klee, Paul: **5** Swiss **6** artist **7** painter
colleague: Jean (Hans) Arp
__ K. Le Guin: **6** Ursula
Kleiber, Erich: **8** Austrian **9** conductor
Klein: **2** A.M. **4** Anne **5** Chuck, Norma **6** bottle, Calvin, Robert **8** Lawrence
rival: **5** Beene, Blass
Klein, A.M.: **4** poet **8** Canadian
Klein, Chuck: **10** outfielder
__ kleine Nachtmusik: **4** Eine
Klein, Lawrence: **8** Nobelist **9** economist
Klein's Obsession: **5** scent **7** perfume
Kleiser: **6** Randal
Kleist, Heinrich von: **6** German, writer
Klem, Bill: **3** ump **6** umpire
Klemperer: **4** Otto **6** Werner
Klensch: **4** Elsa
beat: **5** style
kleptomaniac: **5** thief **10** shoplifter
kleptomaniacal: **8** thieving, thievish
Kliban: **7** Bernard
klieg __: **5** light
Klíma: **4** Ivan
Klíma, Ivan: **5** Czech **6** writer
Klimt, Gustav: **6** artist **7** painter **8** Austrian
Kline: **5** Franz, Kevin **7** Richard
Kline, Kevin: **5** actor
film: The Big Chill (1983)
Cry Freedom (1987)
Dave (1993)
De-Lovely (2004)
Fierce Creatures (1997)
A Fish Called Wanda (1988, AA)
Grand Canyon (1991)
The Ice Storm (1997)
In & Out (1997)
Life as a House (2001)
A Midsummer Night's Dream (1999)
The Pink Panther (2005)
The Pirates of Penzance (1983)
Silverado (1985)
Soapdish (1991)
Sophie's Choice (1982)
Wild Wild West (1999)
spouse: Phoebe Cates
Klinger: **3** Max **7** Maxwell
home: **4** Ohio **6** Toledo
portrayer: Jamie Farr
Klingon: **5** alien
Klinker: **5** dummy, Effie
Klink rank: **7** colonel
klipspringer: **8** antelope
relative: ***see*** antelope
KLM: **7** airline
destination: **3** Eur., JFK, Nor.
rival: ***see*** airline
Klondike: **5** river
locale: **5** Yukon
strike: **4** gold
Klondike Annie (1936 film)
cast: Mae West
Klone and I, The
author: Danielle Steel
kloof: **6** ravine
kludge: **3** fix **5** patch **6** repair
Klug, Aaron: **7** chemist **8** Nobelist
Klugman, Jack: **5** actor
film: 12 Angry Men (1957)
Goodbye, Columbus (1969)
role: **5** Oscar **7** Madison
spouse: Brett Somers
TV: The Odd Couple, Quincy, M.E.
Klum: **5** Heidi
Kluszewski, Ted: **7** slugger
Klute (1971 film)
cast: Jane Fonda, Donald Sutherland
director: Alan J. Pakula
klutz: **2** ox **3** oaf **4** dolt, gowk, lout **5** cluck, dunce, schmo **6** galoot, lubber, lummox, schmoe **7** botcher, bungler, dullard, fumbler, galloot, jackass, pinhead **8** bonehead, lunkhead, shlemiel, stumbler **9** blockhead, blunderer, harebrain, ignoramus, simpleton **10** bananahead, noodlehead
comment: **4** oh-oh, oops, uh-oh
klutzes: **4** oxes
klutzy: **5** gawky, inept, unapt **6** clumsy, gauche, oafish **7** awkward, gawkish, halting, unadept, unhandy **8** bumbling, bungling, cloddish, clownish, fumbling, lubberly, ungainly **9** all thumbs, graceless, ham-handed, inelegant, lumbering, maladroit, stumbling, unskilled **10** blundering, unskillful
km.: **4** lgth., meas.
knack: **3** art, way **4** bent, feel, gift, head, nose, turn **5** craft, flair, savvy, skill, touch, trick **6** genius, talent **7** ability, aptness, faculty, know-how, mastery, sleight **8** aptitude, capacity, facility, hang of it, instinct **9** dexterity, expertise, technique **10** adroitness, green thumb, propensity
ender: **5** wurst
get the ~ of: **5** grasp, learn **6** master, pick up **7** excel in **9** figure out
Knack
song: My Sharona (1979)
knaidel: **8** dumpling
knap ender: **4** sack, weed
knapsack: **3** bag, kit **4** pack, poke **5** pouch **6** duffel, duffle, kitbag **7** holdall **8** backpack, rucksack **9** haversack, saddlebag
part: **4** lash **5** strap
knar: **4** burl, knot, node **6** nodule
knave: **3** cad, cur, dog, rat **4** card, heel, jack, toad, worm **5** brute, cheat, churl, crook, fiend, louse,

Kl

phony, quack, rogue, scamp, shark, snake **6** bad boy, bad guy, bad hat, bad man, con man, phoney, rascal, varlet **7** bounder, cheater, dastard, lowlife, ruffian, sharper, sharpie, shyster, stinker, traitor, wastrel **8** betrayer, blighter, chiseler, deceiver, picaroon, recreant, scalawag, swindler **9** charlatan, hellhound, hypocrite, miscreant, pretender, reprobate, scallawag, scallywag, scoundrel, vulgarian **10** blackguard, dissembler, mountebank, ne'er-do-well, scapegrace
Knave of Hearts: 4 card
booty: 4 tart
crime: 5 theft
knavery: 4 hoax **5** blind, craft, guile, trick, wiles **7** con game, cunning, devilry, roguery **8** deviltry, evil ways, flimflam, mischief, trickery, villainy **9** chicanery, dirty pool, stratagem **10** artfulness, dishonesty, hanky-panky, subterfuge, wrongdoing
knavish: 3 low, sly **4** base, foxy, mean, wily **5** lying, nasty **6** artful, sneaky, tricky **7** corrupt, crooked, cunning, naughty, roguish, waggish **8** plotting, rascally, scheming **9** conniving, dastardly, deceitful, designing, dishonest, insidious, insincere, two-timing, unethical **10** mendacious, villainous
one: 5 rogue
knawel: 4 weed
knead: 3 mix, rub **4** mold, work **5** shape, twist **6** soften **7** massage **10** manipulate
kneaded: 4 mixt **5** mixed **7** blended
Knebel, Fletcher: 6 writer
work: Dark Horse
Night of Camp David
Seven Days in May
knee: 3 jab **4** genu **5** hinge, joint **7** patella
-ankle connector: 5 shank
be ~ deep in: 4 teem **5** swarm **6** abound, infest
bend the ~: 3 bow **7** bow down **9** genuflect, pay homage
bend the ~ to: 4 obey
combining form: 4 genu-
concealer: 4 midi **5** dress, skirt
counterpart: 5 elbow
ender: 3 cap, pad **4** hole **5** board
get down on one ~: 3 woo **7** propose
go on bended ~: 3 beg, sue **4** urge **5** crawl, plead **7** beseech, declare, entreat, implore **8** petition **9** importune **10** supplicate
jerk: 6 reflex **8** reaction, response
neighbor: 4 calf, shin **5** thigh, tibia
of the ~: 6 genual
put over one's ~: 3 tan **4** lick, whip **5** smack, spank **6** punish, thrash, wallop **8** chastise **10** paddywhack
saver: 3 rug **6** carpet, runner **9** carpeting
scrape, as the ~: 4 bark, skin **5** graze **6** abrade, scrape
knee __: 3 pad **4** bend, jerk, sock **5** brace, pants, socks
knee-__: 4 deep, high **7** slapper
__ knee: 5 trick
__ Knee: 7 Wounded
knee-ankle connector: 3 leg
__ knee bend: 4 deep
knee-bending dance: 5 limbo
knee bend, Nureyev's: 4 plie
kneecap: 4 bone **7** patella
__-kneed: 4 weak **5** knock
Knee-Deep in June: 4 poem
author: James Whitcomb Riley
knee-high: 4 flat, sock **5** short **6** midget **7** hosiery **8** sea-level **10** unelevated
kneehole: 4 desk
knee-jerk: 6 reflex **8** habitual, mindless, reaction **9** automatic, impulsive **10** mechanical, unthinking
kneel: 3 bow **4** bend **5** kotow, stoop **6** kowtow **7** bow down **8** bend down **9** genuflect, prostrate
kneeling
figure: 5 orans, orant **6** orante
site: 5 altar
kneeling __: 3 bus
knees
ask on one's ~: 5 plead
fall on one's ~: 7 bow down, worship **9** genuflect, pay homage, prostrate **10** pay tribute
move on one's hands and ~: 4 inch **5** crawl, creep, slink, sneak, steal **7** clamber, slither, wriggle
weak ~: 4 fear **8** cold feet, timidity **9** cowardice **10** faint heart
weak in the ~: 5 dazed, dizzy, faint, giddy, rocky, shaky, woozy **6** punchy, wobbly **7** reeling **8** unsteady
__ knees: 4 bee's
knee-slapper: 4 hoot, howl, joke **6** gasser, hot one, scream
knee-sock: 4 hose **7** hosiery
knell: 4 gong, peal, ring, toll **5** clang **7** pealing, ringing **9** genuflect
Knesset
language: 6 Hebrew
locale: 6 Israel
party: 5 Likud
knew homophone: 3 gnu, new
__ Knew Susie: 5 If You
__ Knew What They Wanted: 4 They
K'Nex
competitor: 4 Lego
Knick: 5 NBAer
Knickerbocker Holiday: 7 musical
author: Maxwell Anderson
composer: Kurt Weill
knickerbockers: 5 pants **8** trousers
Knickerbockers: 4 five, team
org.: 3 NBA
knickers: 5 pants **6** shorts **7** culotes, cut-offs, gauchos **8** bermudas, breeches, jodhpurs, trousers **9** plus fours
knickknack: 5 curio, dodad **6** bauble, doodad, geegaw, gewgaw, notion, trifle **7** bibelot, novelty, trinket, whatnot **8** furbelow, gimcrack, ornament **9** bagatelle, bric-a-brac, curiosity, miniature, objet d'art, plaything, showpiece
locale: 5 ledge, shelf **6** mantel, mantle **7** etagere **8** cupboard
Knicks: 4 five, team
home: 7 New York
loc.: 3 MSG
org.: 3 NBA
rival: *see* NBA team
sport: 10 basketball
Knievel: 4 Evel **6** Robbie **9** daredevil
knife: 4 bolo, dirk, shiv, slit, snee, stab, tool **5** blade, carve, parer, saber, sabre, slice, sword **6** cutlas, cutter, dagger, lancet, murder, pierce, scythe, sickle **7** bayonet, cleaver, cutlass, cutlery, machete, poniard, scalpel, sidearm, utensil **8** lacerate, puncture, scimitar, scimiter, spreader, stiletto **9** penetrate
African ~: 5 panga
brand of ~: 5 Xacto
eating peas with a ~: 7 faux pas
ender: 5 point
Eskimo ~: 3 ulu
game with a ~: 4 Clue
handle: 4 grip, haft
handle material: 5 nacre
Irish ~: 5 skean, skene
like a ~: 4 keen **5** edged, sharp
like an old ~: 4 dull
maker: 6 cutler
Nepalese ~: 5 kukri
part: 4 edge, hilt **5** blade **6** handle
Philippine ~: 4 bolo **6** barong
Scottish ~: 5 skean, skene
seen on TV: 5 Ginsu
starter: 3 pen **4** draw, jack **5** paper **6** pocket
use a ~: 3 cut, lop **4** chop, cube, dice, dock, gash, hack, maim, nick, pare, peel, scar, skin, slit, snip, stab, trim **5** carve, gouge, lance, mince, notch, prune, score, sever, shave, shred, slash, slice, wound **6** bisect, cleave, cut off, incise, injure, open up, scrape, sunder **7** cut away, cut back, cut down, dissect, scratch, whittle **8** lacerate, mutilate **9** split open
wielder's move: 3 cut, jab **4** stab **5** lunge, swing **6** plunge, pounce, spring, strike, thrust **8** fall upon
wound: 3 cut **4** gash, slit, stab **5** gouge, slash, slice **6** injury **7** scratch **8** incision **10** laceration
__ knife: 4 bolo, case, fish, moon **5** bowie, bread, steak **6** boning, butter, dinner, paring **7** butcher, carving, dessert, drawing, hunting, palette
knifelike: 4 keen **5** sharp **8** piercing
make ~: 4 file, hone, whet **5** grind, strop **7** sharpen
knight: 3 dub, Kay, sir **4** male, rank **5** piece, title **6** Gawain **7** fighter, Galahad, gallant, Geraint, Mordred, soldier, warrior **8** champion, defender, horseman, Lancelot, nobleman, Percival **9** Launcelot, protector **10** chess piece
address for a ~: 3 sir
attire: 4 mail **5** armor **6** helmet, tabard **8** gauntlet
attribute: 5 valor **6** daring, mettle **7** bravery, courage, heroism, prowess **8** boldness **9** derring-do, gallantry
award: 3 OBE
consort: 4 dame, lady
expedition: 5 quest
feat: 4 deed **7** exploit **9** adventure
fight: 4 duel, list, tilt **5** joust **6** charge, combat **7** contest, tourney **10** tournament
foe: 6 dragon
glove: 4 gage
King Arthur ~: 3 Kay, Tor **4** Bors, Eric **5** Ector, Floll, Lucan **6** Ewaine, Gareth, Gawain, Hector **7** Galahad, Geraint, Mordred, Tristan **8** Lancelot, Percival, Tristram **9** Launcelot
like a jousting ~: 5 atilt
lodging: 6 castle
name meaning ~: 5 Ryder **6** Ritter
neighbor: 6 bishop
noise: 5 clank
nose guard: 5 nasal
of the road: 4 hobo **5** tramp **7** drifter **8** vagabond, wanderer
protector, perhaps: 4 pawn
quest: 5 Grail **9** Holy Grail
rescuee: 6 damsel
sci-fi ~: 4 Jedi
-to-be: 4 page
weapon: 4 mace **5** lance, sword
white ~: 4 hero **5** model **7** paragon **8** champion, cynosure, exemplar
knight-__: 6 errant
__ knight: 4 Jedi **5** white
Knight: 3 Bob, car, Ted **4** auto, Eric, Jean **5** Bobby, Wayne **6** Gladys, Jordan, Philip, Willys **7** Shirley **9** Etheridge
Knight __: 5 Rider
__ Knight: 5 Black, First
Knight, Bobby: 5 coach
milieu: 5 court
org.: 4 NCAA
sport: 10 basketball
Knight, Death and the Devil
engraver: Albrecht Dürer
knighted, prepare to be: 5 kneel
Knight, Etheridge: 4 poet
Knight, Gladys
backup: 4 Pips
song: Best Thing That Ever Happened to Me (1974)
Every Beat of My Heart (1961)
If I Were Your Woman (1970)
I Heard It Through the Grapevine (1967)
I've Got to Use My Imagination (1973)
Midnight Train to Georgia (1973)
Neither One of Us (1973)
On and On (1974)
That's What Friends Are For (1985)
knighthood: 5 valor **7** bravery, courage **8** altruism, boldness, chivalry, courtesy, nobility
confer ~: 3 dub **7** entitle
initials: 3 OBE
Knight in Rusty Armour (1967 song)
artist: Peter and Gordon
knight in shining __: 5 armor
Knight, Jean
song: Mr. Big Stuff (1971)
Knightley: 5 Keira
knightly: 4 true **5** noble **7** gallant **9** honorable **10** chivalrous, high-minded
Knightly Quest, The
author: Tennessee Williams
Knight of the __: 4 Bath **6** Garter

KN

__ Knight Pulliam: 6 Keshia
Knight Rider (NBC adventure)
car: K.I.T.T.
cast: William Daniels (voice of K.I.T.T.)
David Hasselhoff (Michael Knight)
Edward Mulhare (Devon Miles)
Knights __: 7 Templar
Knights __ Round Table: 5 of the
Knightsbridge store: 7 Harrod's
knights of __: 4 yore
Knights of __: 5 Labor, Malta 7 Pythias 8 Columbus
Knights of the Range
author: Zane Grey
Knights, The
author: Aristophanes
Knight, Ted: 5 actor
film: Caddyshack (1980)
TV: The Mary Tyler Moore Show, Too Close for Comfort
knish: 5 snack
filling: 5 kasha 6 potato
kin: 8 turnover
place: 4 deli
knit: 4 heal, join, mend, purl 5 purse, unite, weave 6 furrow, pucker, splice, stitch 7 crochet, entwine, intwine 9 integrate, interlace, interlock 10 intertwine, interweave
ender: 4 wear
one's brow: 5 frown
partner: 4 purl
shoe: 6 bootee, bootie
together: 7 related 10 interwoven
__-knit: 4 hand 5 close, tight 6 double
knit one, __ two: 4 purl
knitter
material: 4 wool, yarn 5 Orlon 6 angora
need: 5 skein 6 needle
project: 5 scarf, socks 6 afghan 7 argyles, bootees, mittens, sweater
KNO3: 5 niter, nitre
knob: 3 nub 4 dial, knub, knur, lump, node, nurl 5 bulge, knurl 6 button, handle, nodule 8 swelling 10 projection, protrusion
combining form: 3 tyl- 4 tylo-
ornamental ~: 4 boss
shield ~: 4 umbo
starter: 4 door
stereo ~: 4 bass 6 treble, volume
violin ~: 3 peg
watch ~: 5 crown
knobby: 4 bony 5 boney, bumpy, lobed, lumpy, nodal, rough, warty 6 uneven 7 gnarled, knurled, nodular
item: 4 knee
knobcone __: 4 pine
knobkerrie: 4 club 6 weapon
knock: 3 dis, hit, pan, rap, tap 4 bang, bash, beat, blow, carp, clip, conk, cuff, drub, nick, ping, slam, slap, slur, swat, thud 5 abuse, clout, decry, flail, libel, pound, punch, roast, scoff, smack, swipe, thump, whack, whang 6 batter, beat up, bruise, buffet, defame, deride, hammer, impact, impugn, jostle, justle, oppugn, pommel, pummel, rattle, rebuff, strike, thrash, thwack, vilify, wallop 7 censure, condemn, lambast, protest, put-down, run down 8 badmouth, bang into, belittle, denounce, lambaste, minimize, talk down, throw mud 9 criticism, criticize, denigrate, deprecate, disparage, find fault, hammering, manhandle, reprehend 10 denunciate
about: 3 gad 4 maul, roam, rove, tour, trek 5 abuse, drift, range, tramp 6 bruise, damage, ramble, travel, wander 7 explore, journey, traipse 8 work over 9 bum around, gallivant, manhandle, run around
around: 4 beat, loaf, mall, maul, roam, rove, walk 5 pound 6 bang up, debate, ramble, travel 7 rough up 8 mistreat 9 manhandle
back: 4 gulp 5 drink 6 guzzle, imbibe
dead: 5 amaze, amuse 6 divert, regale 8 enthrall 9 entertain
down: 4 deck, earn, fell, rase, raze, ruin 5 abase, floor, level, smash, wreak, wreck 6 defame, demean, demote, lay low, reduce, topple 7 break up, destroy, flatten, unbuild 8 bulldoze, demolish, minimize, overturn 9 devastate, dismantle, prostrate, take apart
ender: 3 off, out 4 down 5 about, wurst
flat: 5 level
for a loop: 4 daze, jolt, stun, wham 5 amaze, floor
heavy ~: 4 slam, thud 5 clonk, clunk, thump, thunk
into: 3 hit, ram 4 bump
it off: 4 halt, quit, stop 5 cease 6 at ease, desist
loose: 4 bump 5 budge 8 dislodge, shake off 9 dislocate
off: 3 end, zap 4 make, quit, slay, stop 5 cease, relax, write 6 desist, make up, murder 8 leave off, simulate, subtract 10 call it a day
on, as a door: 3 rap 5 rap at
oneself out: 3 try 4 tire, toil 6 strive
one's socks off: 3 awe, wow 6 thrill
on the noggin: 3 bop 4 bonk
out: 2 KO 3 awe, wow 4 beat, drug, kayo, slay, stun, zonk 5 floor, punch, write 6 defeat 7 delight, fatigue, flatten, frazzle, impress, stupefy 8 abrogate, languish 9 eliminate, overpower
over: 3 rob, tip 5 level, spill, upend, upset 6 topple 7 astound 8 astonish, overturn, pull down
reply to a ~: 5 enter 6 come in
senseless: 4 kayo, stun 5 floor 6 lay out 9 overpower
something to ~ on: 4 wood
starter: 4 anti
stopper: 6 octane
together: 5 build 6 cobble 7 throw up 10 jerry-build
knock __: 3 off, out 4 back, cold, down, wood 5 about, it off, rummy 6 around
knock __ a loop: 3 for
knock __ of the box: 3 out
knock-__: 4 knee 5 kneed
knock-__-drag-out: 4 down
__-knock: 4 hard
Knock __!: 5 it off
Knock __ Times: 5 Three
Knock, __ shall be opened: 5 and it
knockabout: 5 sloop 8 sailboat
knockback: 7 refusal 8 turndown
Knockdown
author: Dick Francis
knock-down-drag-out: 5 melee, mixup 7 dustups
knocked out: 4 beat 5 all in, had it, spent, tired, weary 6 bushed, done in, drowsy, pooped, punchy, sleepy, zonked 7 drained 8 dog-tired, drooping, fatigued, flagging, out of gas 9 bone-tired, dead-tired, enervated, exhausted, overtired, prostrate
knocked over: 5 fazed, upset 7 shocked, shook up, spilled, toppled, unglued 8 agitated, capsized, dismayed, overcome, unstrung 9 bummed-out 10 disordered, freaked out, in disarray, overturned, psyched out, upside-down
knock for __: 5 a loop
knocking game: 3 gin 8 gin rummy
Knockin' on Heaven's Door (1973 song)
artist: Bob Dylan
Knock it off!: 3 shh 4 stop, whoa
knock-knock joke: 3 pun 8 wordplay
knockoff: 4 copy 5 clone, ditto 6 double 7 replica 8 likeness 9 duplicate, imitation
knock on __: 4 wood
Knock on __ Door: 3 Any
knock one's __ off: 5 socks
knockout: 5 smash 6 beauty, eraser, eyeful, looker, lovely
drink: 6 Mickey 10 Mickey Finn
gas: 5 ether
in boxing: 6 eraser
knocks, hard: 3 woe 7 bad luck, travail, trouble 9 adversity, mischance, tough luck 10 ill fortune, misfortune
knock the __ off: 5 socks
knock the __ out of: 3 tar
Knock Three Times (1970 song)
artist: Tony Orlando & Dawn
knockwurst: 4 meat 7 aliment, sausage
knoll: 4 hill, rise 5 mound, ridge 7 hillock, hummock 9 elevation 10 high ground, prominence
Knopf: 6 Alfred
Knossos site: 5 Crete 6 Candia
knot: 3 tie 4 bird, burl, hank, kink, link, loop, lump, mass, node, slip, snag, tuft 5 gnarl, hitch, nodus, skein, snarl, tie up, twist, unite 6 enigma, fasten, granny, nodule, puzzle, square, tangle 7 bowline, cat's-paw, chignon, dilemma, grannie 8 ligature 9 half hitch, interlace, intricacy, labyrinth, Turk's-head 10 clove hitch, complexity, get tangled, hawser bend, perplexity, sheepshank
cotton ~: 3 nep
detail: 4 loop 5 noose
ender: 4 hole, weed 5 grass
hair ~: 3 bun
like a ~: 5 nodal
rope ~: 4 loop 5 noose, snare
rug ~: 5 sehna
starter: 3 bow, top 4 slip
thread ~: 4 burl, node
tie the ~: 3 wed 4 mate 5 marry, unite 7 espouse 10 get hitched
tree ~: 4 burl, knar, knur 5 gnarl
untie the ~: 4 free, part 5 sever 6 loosen 7 break up, divorce, split up 8 separate 10 put asunder
up: 5 gnarl, snarl
__ knot: 6 granny, square 7 bowline, Gordian, Windsor
knots: 4 nodi
get rid of ~: 4 comb, undo 5 untie 6 loosen 8 untangle
in ~: 4 achy 5 tense 6 tied up
where ~ get tied: 5 altar 6 shrine 9 sanctuary
Knots Landing (CBS drama)
cast: William Devane (Gregory Sumner)
Kevin Dobson (Mack MacKenzie)
Julie Harris (Lilimae Clements)
Lisa Hartman (Ciji Dunne)
Michele Lee (Karen McKenzie)
Donna Mills (Abby Cunningham)
Ted Shackelford (Gary Ewing)
Nicolette Sheridan (Paige Matheson)
Joan Van Ark (Valene Ewing)
knotted: 5 kinky 6 matted 7 snarled, tangled, twisted 8 uncombed
Knott's: 5 jelly
alternative: 5 Kraft 6 Welch's 7 Polaner 8 Smucker's
Knott's __ Farm: 5 Berry
Knotts, Don: 5 actor
film: Gus (1976)
TV: The Andy Griffith Show, Three's Company
knotty: 4 hard, mazy 5 heavy, nodal, rough, tough 6 nodose, nodous, sticky, thorny, tricky 7 complex, prickly, tangled 8 baffling, involved, puzzling, worrying 9 difficult, elaborate, intricate 10 formidable, mystifying, perplexing
question: 6 riddle
wood: 4 pine 9 evergreen
knotty __: 4 pine 7 problem
knot-tying
org.: 3 BSA
place: 5 altar 6 chapel, church, shrine
words: 3 I do
knout: 4 lash, whip
know: 3 get, see, tie 4 bind, tell 5 grasp, learn, place, sense, taste 6 fathom, intuit, secure, tether 7 cognize, discern, realize 8 memorize, perceive 9 apprehend, recognize 10 appreciate, comprehend, experience, have in mind, understand
before you ~ it: 4 anon, soon 6 pronto
by heart: 4 cite 6 retain 8 memorize, remember
dying to ~: 4 nosy 5 nosey 6 prying, snoopy 7 curious 8 meddling 9 butting in, intrusive, obtrusive 10 meddlesome
for all we ~: 5 maybe 7 perhaps

8 feasibly, possibly, probably 9 perchance 10 imaginably
get to ~: 3 see 4 hear, meet, read 5 dig up, glean, grasp, greet, learn, reach, study 6 link up, master, peruse, pick up, take in, turn up 7 connect, contact, discern, find out, run into, uncover, unearth, welcome 8 approach, deal with, discover, pore over, smoke out 9 ascertain, catch on to, determine, encounter, forgather 10 experience, rendezvous, understand
how to: 3 can
in Scottish: 3 ken
instinctively: 4 feel 6 intuit 7 discern 10 have a hunch
in the ~: 3 hep, hip 4 onto, wise 5 aware, hep to, hip to, privy, savvy 6 astute, shrewd, versed, wise to, with it 7 knowing, learned, mindful 8 apprised, informed 9 astucious, cognizant
let ~: 3 air 4 tell 5 cue in 6 inform, tip off
let ~ indirectly: 4 hint 5 imply, let on 6 allude 7 suggest 8 intimate, lead up to 9 insinuate
old enough to ~ better: 5 adult, grown, of age 6 mature 7 grown-up
the language: 5 speak
the password: 5 enter, get in
want to ~: 3 ask 4 quiz, seek 5 grill, probe, query 7 canvass, consult, inquire
know-__: 3 all, how 5 it-all 7 nothing
__ know: 3 you 5 in the
Know __ enemy: 5 thine
__ Know: 3 I'll 4 All I 5 Do You
knowable: 4 bare 5 clear, lucid, naked, plain 6 patent 8 clear-cut, luminous, manifest, palpable, pellucid, revealed, unhidden, unmasked, unveiled 9 disclosed, learnable, uncloaked, unobscure 10 fathomable, ostensible, realizable
know-how: 3 art 5 craft, flair, knack, moxie, savvy, skill, trick 6 talent, wisdom 7 ability, command, faculty, finesse, mastery 8 aptitude, facility, hang of it, instinct 9 dexterity, expertise, technique 10 adroitness, capability, competence, efficiency, experience
has the ~: 3 can
knowing: 3 hep, hip 4 able, arch, in on, sage, wily, wise 5 aware, canny, quick, savvy, sharp, slick, smart 6 astute, brainy, bright, clever, expert, posted, shrewd, versed, wise to, with it 7 cunning, mindful, sapient, thought, tuned in, worldly 8 apprised, informed, profound, rational, sensible, sentient, skillful 9 astucious, brilliant, cognizant, competent, ingenious, inventive, plugged in, sagacious, sensitive 10 conversant, insightful, perceptive, reasonable
about: 4 onto 7 mindful 9 cognizant
combining form: 7 -gnostic 9 -gnostical
look: 4 leer, ogle 5 smirk, sneer
Knowing (2009 film)
cast: Rose Byrne, Nicolas Cage
knowingly: 9 purposely, wittingly 10 designedly
Knowing Me, Knowing You (1977 song)
artist: ABBA
__ know is what I read...: 4 all I
know-it-all: 5 cocky, maven, mavin 6 gascon, pedant, smarty 7 egghead, wise guy 8 braggart, cocksure, wiseacre 9 conceited 10 big-talking
knowledge: 3 ken, tip 4 dope, info, lore 5 facts, goods, grasp, light, sense 6 tipoff, wisdom 7 ability, insight, letters, reading, science, thought 8 learning, literacy, sapience 9 awareness, cognition, education, erudition, expertise, principle, schooling 10 experience, philosophy, refinement
anecdotal ~: 4 lore 5 myths, tales 6 fables 7 legends, sayings 10 traditions
basic ~: 4 ABCs
branch of ~: 5 ology
combining form: 5 -gnomy, -sophy 6 -gnosis
gain ~: 5 learn 6 absorb
having ~: 3 hep, hip 5 aware, privy 6 posted, wise to, with it 8 apprised, familiar, informed 9 au courant, cognizant, plugged in 10 acquainted, conversant
having private ~: 4 in on
impart ~: 4 show 5 brief, coach, drill, edify, guide, teach, train, tutor 6 advise, ground, inform, school 7 educate, explain, instill, lecture 8 instruct 9 catechize, enlighten, inculcate, interpret
mystical ~: 6 gnosis
seek ~: 3 ask 7 inquire
__ Knowledge: 6 Carnal
knowledgeable: 3 ace, hep, hip 4 sage, wise 5 aware, savvy, smart 6 au fait, brainy, bright, clever, expert, posted, versed, with it 7 abreast, erudite, learned, mindful, tuned in 8 apprised, educated, informed, literate 9 cognizant, plugged in, qualified, sagacious
about: 4 upon 6 versed 8 prepared 9 cognizant
one: 5 maven, mavin 6 oracle
Knowles: 4 John 6 Patric 7 Beyoncé
know like __: 5 a book
__ Know Me, Al: 3 You
__ Know Much: 4 Don't
known: 4 fact 5 noted 6 avowed, common, famous, public 7 popular 8 accepted, admitted, familiar, manifest, on the map 9 axiomatic, certified, published 10 celebrated, identified, proverbial, recognized, understood
also ~ as: 5 alias
become ~: 5 break 6 appear, emerge 7 come out, surface 9 transpire
by few: 4 deep 6 arcane, mystic, occult 8 esoteric, mystical 9 recondite 10 mysterious
let be ~: 4 blab, tell 6 tattle
make ~: 3 air, out, say 4 bare, leak, post, show, tell 5 admit, let on, speak, utter, voice 6 advise, convey, expose, herald, impart, let out, report, reveal, spread, unfold, unmask, unveil 7 declare, display, divulge, exhibit, lay bare, let slip, mention, narrate, uncover 8 advise of, announce, disclose, proclaim 9 advertise, circulate, introduce, propagate, publicize, ventilate 10 make public, promulgate
make one's position ~: 6 assert 7 declare, speak up 8 sound off, speak out 10 stand up for
once ~ as: 3 née 4 born 8 formerly 10 heretofore, previously
widely ~: 5 great, noted 6 fabled, famous 7 eminent, leading, popular, storied 8 immortal, renowned 9 acclaimed, legendary, memorable, notorious, prominent 10 celebrated, preeminent, publicized
__-known: 4 well
know-nothing: 3 sap 4 boob, dolt, dupe, fool, gull, jerk 5 chump, dummy, dunce, stupe 7 doubter, fathead, sceptic, skeptic 8 agnostic, bonehead, dumbbell, numskull 9 numbskull
Know Nothings: 5 party
__ known then...: 4 Had I
know one's __: 4 oats 5 place 6 onions
know one's __ mind: 3 own
__ knows: 3 God 6 heaven, nobody
__ Knows Best: 6 Father
__ Knows, Mr. Allison: 6 Heaven
__ Knows My Name: 6 Nobody
__ knows, The: 6 Shadow
know the __: 5 drill, ropes, score
Know what __?: 5 I mean
Knox: 4 Fort, John 9 Alexander
Knoxville: 4 city, town
athlete: 3 Vol 9 Volunteer
its HQ is in ~: 3 TVA
locale: 9 Tennessee
KNP part: 4 pawn 5 king's 7 knight's
knuckle: 5 joint
down: 4 work 5 begin, start 7 get busy 8 fire away, get going
down to: 6 have at 7 address, focus on 8 engage in, tear into 10 plug away at
ender: 4 ball, bone, head
sandwich: 4 fist 5 punch
under: 3 bow 4 obey 5 defer, kotow, stoop, yield 6 comply, give in, kowtow, submit 7 concede, consent, succumb, truckle 8 say uncle 9 surrender 10 capitulate
knuckle __: 4 down 5 under 8 sandwich
knuckle-__: 6 duster
__-knuckle: 4 bare 5 white
knuckleball: 4 toss 5 pitch, throw
knucklebone in the game of jacks: 3 dib
knucklehead: 3 ass, oaf, sap 4 boob, bozo, clod, dodo, dolt, dope, fool, simp 5 chump, clown, cluck, dummy, dunce, idiot, joker, klutz, ninny, patsy, schmo, stupe 6 dimwit, doofus, lummox, nitwit, schmoe, sucker, turkey 7 buffoon, dingbat, dullard, half-wit, jackass 8 dumbbell, numskull 9 birdbrain, lamebrain, numbskull, simpleton
knuckles
rap on the ~: 5 scold 6 punish 8 admonish
__ knuckles: 5 brass
Knud: 9 Rasmussen
knur: 4 knob, knot 5 gnarl
knurl: 4 knob, lump, node 5 ridge 8 swelling
knurled: 5 bumpy, lumpy 6 knobby, uneven 7 gnarled 9 irregular
Knut: 6 Hamsun
Knute Rockne, All American (1940 film)
cast: Donald Crisp, Pat O'Brien, Ronald Reagan
role: 4 Gipp 6 Gipper
Knute successor: 3 Ara
KO: 3 hit 4 deck, stun 5 crush, floor 6 defeat 7 flatten 8 knock out, vanquish
count: 3 ten
counter: 3 ref 7 referee
org.: 3 WBA
KOA: 10 campground
amenity: 6 hookup
vehicle: 2 RV
koala: 6 animal, Aussie 9 marsupial
company with a ~: 6 QANTAS
home: 9 Australia
like a ~: 5 furry
relative: ***see*** marsupial
koan: 5 poser 6 riddle 7 paradox, stumper 8 question 9 conundrum 10 puzzlement
discipline: 3 Zen
Kobe: 4 city, port, town 6 Bryant
locale: 5 Hondo, Japan 6 Honshu
Kobe __: 4 beef
Koblenz: 4 city, town
locale: 7 Germany
river: 5 Mosel 7 Moselle
Kobo: 3 Abe
kobold: 3 elf 5 gnome 6 goblin, sprite 7 gremlin
Kobuk Valley: 4 park
locale: 6 Alaska
Koch: 2 Ed 6 Howard, Robert 7 Kenneth
Kocher, Emil: 5 Swiss 8 Nobelist
Koch, Robert: 8 Nobelist
K-O connection: 3 LMN
Kodachrome (1973 song)
artist: Paul Simon
Kodak: 4 film 6 camera 10 photograph
alternative: ***see*** camera
__ Kodak: 7 Eastman
Kodály, Zoltán: 8 composer 9 Hungarian
Kodel: 6 fabric 8 material
__ Kodesh: 4 Aron
Kodes, Jan: 7 netster 9 tennis pro
milieu: 5 court
Kodiak: 4 bear, city, isle, town 5 ursid 6 island
locale: 6 Alaska
young ~: 3 cub
Koehler: 3 Ted
Koenig: 4 Mark 6 Walter
Koestler, Arthur: 6 writer
work: Darkness at Noon
Koffman: 3 Moe
Kofi: 5 Annan 7 Awoonor 8 Anyidoho
Kofu: 4 city, town
locale: 5 Japan 6 Honshu
KOH: 3 lye

Kohath
father: 4 Levi
Koh-i-__ Diamond: 4 noor
kohl: 5 paint 6 makeup, shadow 7 mascara 8 cosmetic, eyeliner 9 eye shadow 10 maquillage
site: 6 eyelid
Kohl: 6 Helmut
see also German
kohlrabi: 6 veggie 7 cabbage 9 vegetable
Kohn, Walter: 7 chemist 8 Nobelist
Kohoutek: 5 comet
koi: 4 carp, fish
Koichi: 6 Tanaka
Kojak (CBS drama)
cast: Kevin Dobson (Bobby Crocker)
Dan Frazer (Frank McNeil)
Telly Savalas (Lt. Theo Kojak)
employer: N.Y.P.D.
trademark: lollipop
Kojak, like: 4 bald
Kokomo: 4 city, town
locale: 7 Indiana
Kokomo (1988 song)
artist: Beach Boys
Koko Nor: 8 salt lake
locale: 5 China
Kokoschka: 5 Oskar
Ko-Ko weapon: 4 snee
Kol __: 5 Nidre
kola: 3 nut 4 tree
kolacky: 3 bun 6 pastry
kolinsky: 3 fur 4 mink
origin: 4 Asia
Kolkata: 4 city, town
locale: 5 India
Kollege of Musical Knowledge
leader: 5 Kyser
Kollwitz: 5 Käthe
Kollwitz, Kaethe: 6 artist 8 sculptor
Köln: 4 city, town 7 Cologne
locale: 7 Germany
river: 5 Rhein, Rhine
Koloski: 2 K.C.
__ Kommissar: 3 Der
Komodo __: 6 dragon, lizard
Komodo dragon: 6 animal 7 reptile
Komsomolsk-on-__: 4 Amur
Kon-__: 4 Tiki
Kona __: 5 coast 6 coffee
__ Kong: 4 Hong, King 6 Donkey
__ Kong, The: 5 Son of
Konica: 6 camera
alternative: ***see*** camera
Konrad: 5 Bloch 6 Lorenz 8 Adenauer
Konstantin: 9 Chernenko
Kon-Tiki: 4 raft
builder: 4 Thor 9 Heyerdahl
material: 5 balsa
Museum city: 4 Oslo
starting point: 4 Peru
Konwicki, Tadeusz: 6 Polish, writer
koodoo: 8 antelope
relative: ***see*** antelope
kook: 3 nut 4 zany 5 crank, flake, wacko 6 maniac, weirdo 7 dingbat, oddball 8 crackpot 9 character, eccentric, screwball
kookaburra: 4 bird 10 Australian
__ Kookie Byrnes: 3 Edd
Kookie, Kookie (1959 song)
artist: Edd Byrnes, Connie Stevens
kooky: 3 odd 4 daft, loco, zany 5 flaky, goofy, goosy, inane, weird 6 absurd, flakey 7 bizarre, bonkers, foolish, oddball 8 peculiar, reckless 9 eccentric 10 irrational
Kool __ Dee: 3 Moe
Kool-Aid flavor: 4 lime 5 grape, lemon 6 cherry, orange 9 lemon-lime, tangerine 10 strawberry
Kool and the Gang
song: Celebration (1980)
Cherish (1985)
Fresh (1985)
Get Down on It (1982)
Hollywood Swinging (1974)
Joanna (1983)
Jungle Boogie (1974)
Ladies Night (1979)
Misled (1985)
Stone Love (1987)
Too Hot (1980)
Victory (1986)
Koontz, Dean: 6 writer
like a ~ novel: 4 eery 5 eerie
work: After the Last Race
The Bad Place
Breathless
Brother Odd
City of Night
Cold Fire
The Darkest Evening of the Year
Darkfall
Dark Rivers of the Heart
Dead and Alive
Demon Seed
The Door to December
Dragonfly
Dragon Tears
The Eyes of Darkness
The Face of Fear
The Face
False Memory
Fear Nothing
Forever Odd
From the Corner of His Eye
The Funhouse
The Good Guy
Hideaway
The House of Thunder
The Husband
Icebound
Intensity
The Key to Midnight
Life Expectancy
Lightning
The Mask
Midnight
Mr. Murder
Night Chills
Nightmare Journey
Odd Hours
Odd Thomas
One Door Away From Heaven
Phantoms
Prison of Ice
Prodigal Son
Relentless
Santa's Twin
Seize the Night
The Servants of Twilight
Shadowfires
Shattered
Sole Survivor
Strangers
The Taking
Tick Tock
Twilight Eyes
Velocity
The Vision
The Voice of the Night
Watchers
Whispers
Winter Moon
Your Heart Belongs to Me
Koopmans, Tjalling: 8 Nobelist 9 economist
Kootenay: 5 river
locale: 5 Idaho 7 Montana
kopeck: 4 coin 5 money
100: 5 ruble 6 rouble
Kopell: 6 Bernie
koph: 6 Hebrew, letter
follower: 4 resh
preceder: 4 sadi 5 sadhe, tsade, tsadi
Kopit, Arthur: 10 playwright
Koppel, Ted: 6 anchor 10 journalist, newscaster
network: 3 ABC
show: 9 Nightline
Korah
father: 4 Esau
Koran: 8 holy book
alphabet: 5 Kufic
chapter: 4 sura 5 surah
deity: 5 Allah
honorific for ~ memorizers: 5 hafiz
language: 6 Arabic
reader: 4 imam 5 imaum
Korbut, Olga: 7 gymnast, Russian
Korda: 6 Zoltan 7 Michael 9 Alexander
Korda, Alexander: 8 director
spouse: Merle Oberon
Korea
alphabet: 6 Hangul
apricot: 4 ansu
automaker: 3 Kia 6 Daewoo
Buddhism of ~: 8 Mahayana
continent: 4 Asia
dish: 6 kimchi 7 kimchee
golfer: 3 Pak 7 Se Ri Pak
river: 4 Yalu
sea: 6 Yellow
seaport: 6 Inchon
soldier: 3 ROK
TV series set in ~: 4 MASH
see also North Korea, South Korea
Korean: 5 Asian 8 language
Korean War
flier: 3 MIG
grp.: 3 WAC
kor fraction: 4 epha 5 ephah
Korman, Harvey: 5 actor 8 comedian
film: Blazing Saddles (1974)
High Anxiety (1977)
TV: The Carol Burnett Show
Kornelia: 5 Ender
Korngold: 5 Erich
Korolyov: 6 Sergey
Korovin volcano
island: 4 Atka
koruna: 5 money
spender: 5 Czech
Kos: 4 isle 6 island
locale: 6 Turkey
Kosar, Bernie: 2 QB 11 quarterback
sport: 8 football
Koscina: 5 Sylva
Kosciusko: 4 peak 5 mount 8 mountain
locale: 9 Australia
kosher: 2 OK 4 good, just, okay, okeh, okey, pure, real 5 jural, legal, legit, licit, moral, sound, valid 6 lawful, proper 7 allowed, factual, genuine, logical 8 accepted, bona fide, rightful 9 allowable, authentic, befitting, by the book, permitted, veritable 10 acceptable, authorized, legitimate, sanctioned
expert: 5 rabbi, rebbe
it's not ~: 3 ham 4 pork 6 shrimp 7 lobster
not ~: 4 tref 5 trayf, treyf 6 pseudo 7 terefah
__ kosher: 5 glatt
Kosinski, Jerzy: 6 writer
birthplace: Lodz, Poland
work: Being There
Blind Date
Cockpit
The Painted Bird
Passion Play
Pinball
Steps
Kosovo peacekeeping org.: 4 NATO
Kossel, Albrecht: 6 German 7 chemist 8 Nobelist
Kostelanetz, André: 9 conductor
spouse: Lily Pons
Koster: 5 Henry 7 Palamas
Kosygin: 7 Aleksei
Kotch (1971 film)
cast: Felicia Farr, Walter Matthau
director: Jack Lemmon
Kotcheff: 3 Ted
Kotler: 4 Kami
koto: 6 string, zither 10 instrument
origin: 5 Japan
Kottke: 3 Leo
Kotto: 6 Yaphet
Koufax, Sandy: 5 lefty 6 Dodger, hurler 7 pitcher
stat: 3 ERA 4 wins 8 shutouts 10 strikeouts
Kournikova, Anna: 7 netster 9 tennis pro
milieu: 5 court
Koussevitzky, Serge: 9 conductor
Kovacs, Ernie
spouse: Edie Adams
Kovic: 3 Ron
portrayer: 6 Cruise
Kowalski: 6 Stella 7 Stanley
Kowloon: 4 city, port, town
locale: 8 Hong Kong
kowtow: 3 bow 4 fawn 5 bow to, cower, kneel, stoop, toady 6 cringe, grovel, submit 7 defer to, wheedle 9 be servile, prostrate, reverence
to: 3 woo 5 court, toady 6 stroke 7 adulate, flatter, truckle 8 bootlick, butter up, fawn over
kowtower: 5 toady 6 fawner, flunky, lackey, minion, stooge, yes-man 7 doormat, flunkey 8 courtier, groveler, hanger-on 9 flatterer, sycophant 10 bootlicker 13 apple-polisher
Kozlowski, Linda
spouse: Paul Hogan
KP
item: 4 spud 5 tater 6 potato
one on ~: 2 GI 7 private, recruit, soldier
tool: 5 parer 6 peeler
worker: 5 parer 6 peeler
K-P connection: 4 LMNO

__ K. Polk: 5 James
K-Q connection: 5 LMNOP
Kr: 4 elem. 7 element, krypton
  36 for ~: 4 at. no.
Kra: 7 isthmus
  locale: 6 Malaya
kraal: 7 village 9 enclosure
Krackel: 3 bar 5 candy 8 candy bar 9 chocolate
  alternative: ***see*** candy brand
kraft: 5 paper
krait: 3 asp 5 snake 6 animal 7 reptile, serpent
  relative: ***see*** snake
  weapon: 4 fang
Krakatoa: 4 isle 6 island 7 volcano
  output: 3 ash
Kraków: 4 city, town
  locale: 6 Poland
Krakowski: 4 Jane
Krall: 5 Diana
Kramden: 5 Alice, Ralph
  collection: 4 fare
  Norton, to ~: 3 pal
  vehicle: 3 bus
Kramer: 4 Jack 5 Cosmo 7 Stanley 9 Stepfanie
Kramer, Jack: 7 netster 9 tennis pro
  milieu: 5 court
Kramer vs. Kramer (1979 film)
  cast: Jane Alexander, Justin Henry, Dustin Hoffman, Meryl Streep
  director: Robert Benton
Kramnik, Vladimir forte: 5 chess
Kranepool: 2 Ed
Krantz, Judith: 6 writer
  work: Dazzle
    I'll Take Manhattan
    The Jewels of Tessa Kent
    Mistral's Daughter
    Princess Daisy
    Scruples
    Spring Collection
    Till We Meet Again
Krasicki, Ignacy: 4 poet 6 Polish
Krasna: 6 Norman
Krasner, Lee
  spouse: Jackson Pollock
Krasny: 4 Paul
krater: 4 bowl
  content: 4 wine 5 water
  user: 5 Greek, Roman
K-ration: 4 meal
Krauss: 6 Alison 7 Clemens
Krauss, Clemens: 9 conductor
Kravis: 5 Henry
Kravitz, Lenny
  song: It Ain't Over 'Til It's Over (1991)
  spouse: Lisa Bonet
Krazy __: 3 Kat 4 Glue
Krazy Kat: 5 comic, strip
  character: 6 Ignatz 11 Offissa Pupp
Krebs: 4 Hans 5 Edwin
Krebs cycle product: 3 ATP
Kreisler, Fritz: 8 Austrian 9 violinist
__ Kreme: 6 Krispy
Kremlin
  feature: 4 dome
  name: 5 Lenin 6 Stalin 8 Brezhnev 10 Khrushchev
Kremlin Colonel
  ingredient: 5 vodka
Kresge, S.S. today: 5 K Mart
Kreskin
  claim: 3 ESP
__ Kreskin, The: 7 Amazing
Kreuk: 7 Kristin
Kreutzer Sonata
  composer: Ludwig van Beethoven
kreuzer: 4 coin 5 money
Kriemhild
  brother: 7 Gunther
  husband: 9 Siegfried
Krige, Alice: 7 actress 12 South African
krill: 6 shrimp
Krimmler: 5 falls 9 waterfall
  locale: 7 Austria
__ Kringle: 4 Kris 5 Kriss
Krips, Josef: 8 Austrian 9 conductor
kris: 5 blade, knife
Kris: 6 Nelson 7 Kringle
Kris __: 5 Kross
Krishna: 3 god 4 shah 5 river 6 avatar
  avatar: 6 Vishnu
  beloved: 5 Radha
  devotee: 5 Hindu 6 Hindoo
  locale: 5 India
__ Krishna: 4 Hare
Kris Kross
  song: Jump (1992)
__ Krispies: 4 Rice 5 Cocoa
Krispy: 7 cracker
  alternative: ***see*** cracker
Krispy __: 5 Kreme
Kriss Kringle: 5 Santa
Kristen: 5 Marta 8 Johnston
Kristi: 9 Yamaguchi
  emulate ~: 5 skate
Kristin: 4 Otto 5 Davis, Kreuk
Kristin __ Thomas: 5 Scott
Kristofferson, Kris: 5 actor 6 singer
  film: Alice Doesn't Live Here Anymore (1974)
    Big Top Pee-wee (1988)
    Blade (1998)
    Blume in Love (1973)
    Cisco Pike (1972)
    Dance With Me (1998)
    Heaven's Gate (1980)
    Limbo (1999)
    Lone Star (1996)
    Semi-Tough (1977)
    A Star Is Born (1976)
  spouse: Rita Coolidge
Kristy: 7 Swanson 8 McNichol
Kroc: 3 Ray
Krock: 6 Arthur
Krofft: 3 Sid 5 Marty
Kroft: 5 Steve
__ Kröger: 5 Tonio
Krogh: 4 Egil 6 Schack
Krogh, Schack: 6 Danish 8 Nobelist
krona: 4 coin 5 money
  fractions: 5 aurar
krone: 4 coin 5 money
  word on a ~: 5 Norge
Krone, Julie: 6 jockey
  milieu: 5 track
Kropotkin: 5 Pyotr
__ Kross: 4 Kris
Krueger, Freddy street: 3 Elm
Kruger: 4 Alma, Otto, Paul 5 Diane
  ender: 4 rand
Kruger National Park
  terrain: 4 veld 5 veldt
Krugerrand: 4 coin 8 gold coin
Krull, Felix creator: Thomas Mann
krummkake: 6 cookie
Krupa, Gene: 7 drummer
  genre: 4 jazz
Krupp: 6 Alfred
  gun: 6 Bertha 9 Big Bertha
  home: 4 Ruhr 5 Essen
Krusty: 5 clown
Krylov, Ivan: 6 writer 7 Russian
krypton: 3 gas 7 element
  like ~: 5 inert
kryptonite: 4 rock
KS
  see Kansas
__ K. Smith: 6 Howard
KSU conference: 9 Big Twelve
kt.: 2 wt.
K.T.: 5 Oslin
Kuala Lumpur: 4 city, town 7 capital
  language: 5 Malay
  locale: 8 Malaysia
Kubek: 4 Tony
Kubelik: 3 Jan 6 Rafael
Kubelik, Jan: 5 Czech 9 violinist
Kubelik, Rafael: 5 Czech 9 conductor
Kublai: 4 Khan
Kubla Khan: 4 poem
  author: Samuel Taylor Coleridge
  locale: 4 Asia 6 Xanadu
  river: 4 Alph
Kubrick, Stanley: 8 director
  film: 2001: A Space Odyssey (1968)
    Barry Lyndon (1975)
    A Clockwork Orange (1971)
    Dr. Strangelove (1964)
    Eyes Wide Shut (1999)
    Full Metal Jacket (1987)
    The Killing (1956)
    Lolita (1962)
    Paths of Glory (1957)
    The Shining (1980)
    Spartacus (1960)
kuchen: 4 cake 6 German 7 dessert 10 coffeecake
Kuda __: 3 Bux
kudo: 6 praise 7 tribute 8 accolade 10 compliment
kudos: 5 éclat, glory, honor, raves 6 credit, esteem, homage, honors, praise, salute 7 acclaim, big hand, laurels, plaudit, tribute 8 accolade, applause, encomium, flattery, good word, plaudits 9 laudation, panegyric 10 exaltation, popularity, prominence
  heap ~ on: 4 laud 5 extol, honor 6 admire, extoll, praise, puff up, stroke 7 acclaim, applaud, approve, build up, commend, flatter, lionize 8 hand it to 10 compliment
Kudrow, Lisa: 7 actress
  film: Analyze That (2002)
    Analyze This (1999)
    Hanging Up (2000)
    Lucky Numbers (2000)
  TV: Friends
kudu: 6 animal, mammal 8 antelope
  relative: ***see*** antelope
kudzu: 4 vine
Kuhn: 4 Walt 5 Bowie 6 Maggie 7 Richard
Kukhoe
  locale: 10 South Korea
Kukla: 6 puppet
  creator: Burr Tillstrom
  friend: 4 Fran 5 Ollie 7 Allison
Kukla, Fran & Ollie (TV)
  cast: Fran Allison, Burr Tillstrom
kulak: 7 peasant, Russian
Kulik: 4 Buzz, Ilia
Kulik, Ilia: 6 skater 7 Russian
Kulp: 5 Nancy
Kulthum: 3 Umm
__ Kum: 4 Kara 5 Kyzyl
Kumin, Maxine: 6 writer
kumiss: 5 drink 8 beverage
kummel: 5 drink 8 beverage
kumquat: 4 tree 5 fruit, shrub 6 citrus
  cover: 4 rind
  relative: ***see*** citrus
  shape: 4 oval
Kun: 4 Béla
Kundera, Milan: 5 Czech 6 writer
  work: The Unbearable Lightness of Being
kundu: 4 drum
kung __ chicken: 3 pao
kung fu: 5 sport 10 martial art
  star: Bruce Lee
Kung Fu (ABC drama)
  cast: David Carradine (Caine)
Kung Fu-__: 3 Tse
kung-fu cousin: 6 karate
Kung Fu Fighting (1974 song)
  artist: Carl Douglas
Kung Fu Panda (2008 film)
  voice cast: Jack Black, Dustin Hoffman, Angelina Jolie
Kunis: 4 Mila
Kunitz, Stanley: 4 poet
Kunlun: 5 range 9 mountains
  locale: 4 Asia 5 China
Kunstler, William: 3 att. 4 atty. 8 attorney
  forte: 3 law
  org.: 3 ABA
Kunta Kinte
  portrayer: John Amos, LeVar Burton
Kunzel, Erich: 9 conductor
kunzite: 3 gem 7 mineral 8 gemstone
  color: 5 lilac
Kupcinet: 3 Irv
Kuralt: 7 Charles
Kurd: 5 Asian
Kurdi: 3 cow 4 bull 6 bovine, cattle
Kurdish: 8 language
  home: 4 Iran
Kure: 4 city, port, town
  locale: 5 Hondo, Japan 6 Honshu
Kurile Islands aborigine: 4 Ainu
Kurosawa, Akira: 8 director, Japanese
  film: Dersu Uzala (1975)
    Ikiru (1952)
    Kagemusha (1980)
    Ran (1985)
    Rashomon (1950)
    The Seven Samurai (1954)
    Stray Dog (1949)
    Throne of Blood (1957)
    Yojimbo (1961)
kurrajong: 4 tree 9 evergreen
  origin: 9 Australia
Kurt: 5 Adler, Alder, Jooss, Loder, Masur, Weill 6 Cobain, Thomas 7 Neumann, Russell 8 Vonnegut, Waldheim, Wüthrich
  wife: 5 Lotte
Kurtz: 5 Efrem 7 Swoosie
Kuryakin: 5 Illya
  partner: 4 Solo
Kurylenko: 4 Olga
Kurys: 5 Diane

Kush: 5 Nubia 7 kingdom 8 Ethiopia
father: 3 Ham
grandfather: 4 Noah
son: 6 Nimrod
__ Kush Mountains: 5 Hindu
Kushner: 4 Tony 6 Harold
Kutcher: 6 Ashton
Kutenai: 5 tribe
Kutuzov: 7 Mikhail
Kuvasz: 3 dog 5 canid 6 canine
Kuwait: 6 nation 7 country
capital: 10 Kuwait City
currency: 5 dinar
group: 10 Arab League
location: 6 Arabia
money: 4 fils 5 dinar
neighbor: 4 Irak, Iraq
nonvoter in ~: 5 woman
org.: 4 OPEC
ruler: 4 amir, emir 5 ameer, emeer
Kuwaiti: 4 Arab
neighbor: 5 Iraki, Iraqi, Saudi
Kuznets, Simon: 8 Nobelist 9 economist
kvass: 5 drink 8 beverage
ingredient: 3 rye 6 barley
relative: 4 beer 5 lager
kvetch: 3 nag 4 carp, crab 5 gripe, groan, shrew, whine 6 carper, grouse, whiner 7 grumble, needler 8 complain 9 bellyache, henpecker 10 complainer
be a ~: 4 carp, fuss, kick, moan, pule, sigh, wail 5 cavil, gripe, groan, whine 6 grouch, grouse, murmur, snivel, squawk, yammer 7 grumble, nitpick, quibble 8 complain 9 bellyache, criticize, make a fuss
phrase: 5 oy vey
Kwai: 5 river
Kwajalein: 5 atoll
Kwame: 7 Nkrumah
Kwan: 5 Nancy 8 Michelle
Kwan, Michelle: 6 skater
kwanza: 5 money
nation: 6 Angola
Kwanzaa: 8 festival
creator: Maulana Karenga
fifth day of ~: 3 Nia
principle: 5 faith, unity
seventh day of ~: 5 Imani
Kwik-E-Mart
owner: 3 Apu
__ kwon do: 3 tae
Ky.
neighbor: 3 Ill., Ind., W.Va. 4 Tenn., Virg.
see also Kentucky
Kyd, Thomas: 7 British 10 playwright
work: The Spanish Tragedy
Kyle: 4 Rote 8 Chandler 10 MacLachlan
Kylie: 7 Minogue
Kym: 4 Sims
Kyoga: 4 lake
locale: 6 Uganda
Kyongbok Palace
locale: 5 Seoul
kyoodle: 3 yap 4 bark, yelp
Kyoto: 4 city, town
carrier to ~: 3 ANA, JAL
coin: 3 sen, yen
locale: 5 Hondo, Japan 6 Honshu
port near ~: 4 Kobe
Kyra: 8 Sedgwick
Kyrgyz mountains: 4 Alai
Kyrgyzstan: 6 nation 7 country
capital: 7 Bishkek
city: 3 Osh 7 Bishkek
locale: 4 Asia
mountain: 8 Tian Shan, Tien Shan 9 Trans Alai
neighbor: 5 China 10 Kazakhstan, Tajikistan, Uzbekistan
Kyrie __: 7 eleison
Kyser: 3 Kay 10 bandleader
Kyu: 8 Sakamoto
Kyushu: 4 isle 6 island
city: 4 Oita, Saga 5 Beppu, Omuta 6 Kasuga, Kurume, Sasebo 8 Nagasaki 9 Kagoshima
locale: 5 Japan
volcano: 3 Aso 5 Unzen 6 Asosan
Kyzyl Kum: 6 desert
locale: 10 Kazakhstan, Uzbekistan

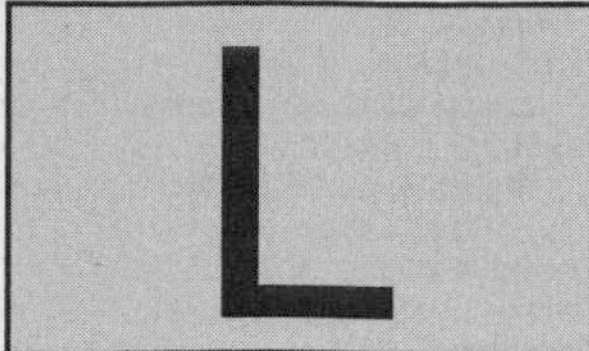

L: 6 letter
followers: 3 MNO **4** MNOP **5** MNOPQ
in phonetic alphabet: 4 Lima
preceders: 3 JKL **4** IJKL **5** HIJKL
L ___ Larry: 4 as in
L'___, c'est moi: 4 état
L'___ del Cairo: 3 Oca
L'___-midi d'un Faune: 5 après
L. ___ Baum: 5 Frank
L. ___ Hubbard: 3 Ron
___ L: 3 One **4** P and, S and
___ L.: 4 A.F. of
la: 4 note
à ~: 4 like **9** emulating **10** resembling
à ~ mode: 2 in **3** mod **4** chic, tony **5** faddy, toney **6** chi-chi, modish, trendy **7** current, in style, popular, stylish, voguish **8** up-to-date **9** in fashion **10** all the rage
preceder: 2 so **3** sol
la-___: 4 de-da, di-da
___-la: 3 tra **4** fa-la **5** tra-la **7** Shangri
La: 4 elem. **7** element **9** lanthanum
57 for ~: 4 at. no.
La ___: 3 Mer **5** Bamba, Valse **6** Boheme, Strada
La ___ aux Folles: 4 Cage
La ___, Bolivia: 3 Paz
La ___ Bonita: 4 Isla
La ___, CA: 4 Mesa **5** Jolla
La ___ del Destino: 5 Forza
La ___ des Nymphes: 5 Danse
La ___ en Rose: 3 Vie
La ___ Humaine: 4 Bête
La ___, IL: 5 Salle
La ___, IN: 5 Porte
La ___ Jackson: 4 Toya
La ___ Nikita: 5 Femme
La ___ nuova: 4 vita
La ___ opera house: 5 Scala
La ___ Pacifica: 4 Casa
La ___ Rose: 5 Vie en
La ___ tar pits: 4 Brea
La ___ Vita: 5 Dolce
La ___, WI: 6 Crosse
La, ___ to follow sew: 5 a note
La-___: 4 Z-Boy
La.
neighbor: 3 Ark., Tex. **4** Miss.
see also Louisiana
L.A.
to Bakersfield dir.: 3 NNW
to Reno direction: 3 NNW
to Seattle dir.: 3 NNW
see also Los Angeles
L.A. ___: 3 Law **5** Story
Laa-Laa: 9 Teletubby
La, a note to follow ___: 3 sew
lab
animal: 3 rat **5** mouse **9** guinea pig
assistant of film: 4 Igor
course: 3 bio. **4** chem., phys. **7** biology, physics, science **9** chemistry
culture: 4 agar **8** agar-agar
discovery: 4 cure, drug **5** serum
garment: 5 smock
glassware: 4 vial **5** ampul, flask, phial, pipet **6** aludel, ampule, beaker, retort **7** ampoule **9** Petri dish, Pitot tube
heater: 4 etna
liquid: 4 acid
project: 4 test **5** assay **6** retest
rat challenge: 4 maze
slide dye: 5 eosin **6** eosine
slide sighting: 5 ameba **6** amoeba, idatom **7** rotifer **10** animalcule, pamamecium
solution strength: 5 titer
unit: 2 cc, gr., mg. **3** mol **4** gram **9** milligram
weak, in a ~: 3 dil. **7** diluted
lab ___: 4 coat, test **5** class **7** session
Lab: 3 dog, pet **5** pooch **6** canine
La Bamba (1987 film)
cast: Esai Morales, Lou Diamond Phillips
La Bamba (song)
artist: Los Lobos, Ritchie Valens
Laban
daughter: 4 Leah **6** Rachel
father: 7 Bethuel
sister: 7 Rebekah
son-in-law: 5 Jacob
label: 3 dub, tab, tag **4** call, logo, mark, name, term **5** brand, class, decal, stamp, style, title **6** define, design, ticket **7** address, company, entitle, epithet, heading, insigne, intitle, specify, sticker, stick-on **8** bookmark, classify, describe, identify, insignia, nickname, subtitle **9** brand name, designate, trademark **10** stereotype
again: 5 retag
info: 3 UPC **4** size **5** waist **7** bar code **11** price inseam
___ label: 3 red **4** care **5** union
La Belle ___: 5 Paree **6** Helene
La Belle Dame sans Merci: 4 poem
author: John Keats
La Belle et la ___: 4 Bête
LaBelle, Patti
real name: Patricia Holt
song: Lady Marmalade (1975)
New Attitude (1985)
On My Own (1986)
LaBeouf: 4 Shia
La Bête Humaine
author: Émile Zola
labile: 7 mutable, protean **9** versatile **10** changeable
Labine: 4 Clem **6** Dodger, hurler **7** pitcher
labium: 3 lip
La Bohème: 5 opera
cafe: 5 Momus
character: 4 Mimi **6** Benoît **7** Colline, Musetta, Rodolfo **8** Marcello **9** Alcindoro, Schaunard
composer: Giacomo Puccini
highlight: 4 duet
musical based on ~: 4 Rent
setting: 5 Paris **6** France
labor: 3 act, job **4** grub, hack, hand, help, moil, plod, pull, push, task, tend, till, toil, wade, work **5** chore, drive, grind, pains, serve, slave, sweat **6** drudge, effort, energy, helper, strain, stress, strive, throes, toiler, worker **7** employe, hard hat, laborer, service, travail **8** activity, bear down, drudgery, employee, endeavor, exercise, exertion, hireling, industry, plug away, struggle **9** cultivate, diligence, grind away, gruntwork, moonlight, work force **10** apprentice, blue collar, daily grind, employment, instrument
forced ~: 7 slavery
group: 3 AFL, AFT, CIO, NEA, UAW, UFT **5** ILGWU, union **6** AFL-CIO **9** Teamsters
hard ~: 5 sweat **7** travail **8** drudgery, exertion
onetime ~ union: 3 IWW
opposite: 3 mgt. **4** mgmt. **10** management
requiring hard ~: 5 harsh, heavy **6** taxing, tiring **7** arduous, onerous **8** exacting, grinding, grueling, toilsome **9** demanding, difficult, herculean, laborious, strenuous **10** burdensome, exhausting, formidable, oppressive, overtaxing
saving device: 5 robot **7** machine
labor ___: 3 spy **5** force, union **6** market
labor ___ vincit: 5 omnia
___ labor: 3 big, day **4** hard **7** skilled
Labor
author: Émile Zola
laborare ___ orare: 3 est
Labor Day: 3 Mon.
kid: 5 Virgo
month: 3 Sep. **4** Sept
telethon org.: 3 MDA
Labor Dept. org.: 4 OSHA
labored: 4 hard **5** heavy, inept, stiff **6** clumsy, forced, stodgy, uphill **7** arduous, awkward, halting, operose, stilted, studied **8** affected, overdone, strained, toilsome **9** contrived, effortful, laborious, maladroit, ponderous, strenuous, unnatural **10** artificial
laborer: 4 hand, peon **5** grunt, labor, prole, slave **6** drudge, jobber, worker **7** employe **8** employee, farmhand, hireling **9** jobholder **10** working man
medieval ~: 4 esne **5** helot **6** vassal **7** bondman, chattel, villein
unskilled ~: 4 peon **6** drudge
___ laborer: 3 day
laboring: 4 busy **6** at work **7** working **8** employed, on the job
laborious: 4 hard **5** heavy, rough, stiff, tough **6** active, forced, no joke, sticky, thorny, trying, uphill, wicked **7** arduous, hard-won, labored, onerous, operose, painful, rough go, serious, tedious, wearing **8** diligent, grueling, sedulous, strained, tireless, tiresome, toilsome **9** assiduous, demanding, difficult, effortful, fatiguing, herculean, ponderous, strenuous, wearisome **10** burdensome, enervating, exhausting, formidable, oppressive, unflagging
task: 5 chore
laboriously: 4 hard **7** wearily **8** doggedly, in detail, steadily
labor of ___: 4 love
labor omnia ___: 6 vincit
Labour: 5 party
___ Labour's Lost: 5 Love's
La Boutique fantastique: 6 ballet
composer: Gioacchino Rossini
Labrador: 3 sea
Indian: 7 Naskapi
locale: 6 Canada
mountain: 8 Caubvick
zone: 3 AST
Labrador ___: 7 Current
Labrador Retriever: 3 dog, pet **5** canid, pooch **6** canine
La Brea ___ pits: 3 tar
___ Labs: 4 Bell
L'Absinthe
artist: Edgar Degas
laburnum: 5 plant **6** flower
labyrinth: 3 web **4** coil, knot, maze, mesh **5** skein, snarl **6** jungle, morass, puzzle, riddle, tangle **7** network, problem **9** catacombs, confusion, intricacy **10** complexity, perplexity
builder: 5 Minos **8** Daedalus
ender: 3 ine
locale: 3 ear **5** Crete **6** Candia
Labyrinth (1986 film)
cast: David Bowie, Jennifer Connelly
director: Jim Henson
dog: 6 Merlin
labyrinthine: 4 mazy **6** daedal, knotty **7** complex, winding **8** Daedalic, involved, mazelike, puzzling, tortuous
Labyrinth of Solitude, The
author: Octavio Paz
Labyrinth, The
author: Edwin Muir
lac: 5 resin
La Cage Aux Folles: 7 musical
character: 4 Zaza **5** Albin
composer: Jerry Herman
La Campagne de Rome
artist: Camille Corot
La Campanella: 5 étude
la casa, lady of: 6 señora
La Cava: 7 Gregory
lace: 3 add, hit, mix, net, tie **4** band, bind, cord, do up, mesh, plat, rope, trim **5** close, Cluny, filet, spike, strap, thong, twine **6** attach, border, edging, fabric, fasten, season, string, thread **7** Alençon, banding, crochet, entwine, fortify, intwine, netting, tatting **8** appliqué, filagree, filigree, openwork, ornament, shoelace, trimming **9** fillagree, interlace, punctuate **10** decoration, intertwine, interweave, shoestring, threadwork
apply ~: 4 edge, trim **5** adorn **6** bedeck **7** dress up **8** decorate, ornament, pretty up **9** embellish
collar: 4 ruff **5** ruche **6** bertha
ender: 4 wing
feature: 4 knot
for upholstery: 5 orris
French ~: 3 val
heavily: 4 lard
hole: 4 loop **6** eyelet
into: 4 slam **5** roast, scold **6** assail, oppugn, rave at, thwack **7** assault **9** haul off on **10** pounce upon, vituperate
(into): 4 sail, tear

like ~: 5 fancy 6 dainty, frilly 9 elaborate
make ~: 3 tat
something to ~: 5 punch
starter: 4 neck, shoe 5 inter
town: 5 Cluny 7 Alençon
up: 3 tie 4 bind 6 fasten 7 tighten
with liquor: 5 spike
work: 3 net 5 doily, frill, picot, ruche 6 doyley
yoke: 6 guimpe
lace __: 4 into
Lace (TV miniseries)
cast: Phoebe Cates (Elizabeth 'Lili' Lace)
__-laced: 6 strait
laced garment: 6 bodice, corset
lacer: 4 tier
lacerate: 3 cut, jag, rip 4 claw, gash, harm, hurt, maim, mall, maul, open, rend, stab, tear 5 knife, lance, score, slash, wound 6 injure, mangle 7 scratch, serrate, torment 8 mutilate, puncture
lacerated: 3 cut 4 hurt, rent, slit, torn 5 split 6 gashed, jagged, ragged 7 injured, slashed
laceration: 3 cut, rip 4 gash, hurt, slit, stab, tear 5 slash, slice, wound 6 injury, lesion, pierce 7 scratch 8 incision
laces
fix your ~: 5 retie
it has ~: 4 shoe 6 corset, girdle 7 sneaker
lacewing: 3 bug 6 insect
Lacey: 3 cop 7 Chabert
partner: 6 Cagney
La Chanson de la puce: 4 aria
__-la-Chapelle: 3 Aix
Lachesis: 4 Fate 8 asteroid
colleague: 6 Clotho 7 Atropos
mother: 6 Themis
La Chienne (1931 film)
director: Jean Renoir
Lachryma __: 7 Christi
lachrymal drop: 4 tear
lachrymose: 3 sad 5 teary, weepy, woful 6 crying, woeful 7 maudlin, sobbing, tearful 8 mournful 9 sniveling
become ~: 3 cry, sob 4 sigh, weep 6 boohoo 7 blubber 9 break down, cry a river, shed tears
lacing: 3 tie 4 cord 5 thong, twine 6 defeat, string 7 beating 8 shoelace 9 thrashing
__ la Cité: 5 île de
lack: 4 loss, miss, need, void, want 5 minus, stint 6 dearth, defect, haven't 7 absence, default, deficit, paucity, poverty, require 8 decrease, distress, exigence, exigency, exiguity, omission, run out of, scarcity, shortage, sparsity 9 depletion, fall short, indigence, necessity, privation, reduction, shortfall, shortness, shrinkage, shrinking 10 abridgment, deficiency, delinquent, have need of, inadequacy, meagerness, scantiness, slightness
circle ~: 3 end
ender: 6 luster
monokini ~: 3 bra
of enthusiasm: 6 apathy, tedium 7 boredom, languor 8 doldrums, monotony 9 lassitude, weariness
of faith: 8 distrust, mistrust, wariness 9 disbelief, misgiving, suspicion 10 skepticism
opposite: 3 own 4 have
prefix: 3 mis-
lackadaisical: 3 lax 4 dull, idle, lazy, limp, logy, poky, slow 5 hasty, inert, moony, slack 6 draggy, dreamy, remiss, sloppy, torpid 7 gradual, halting, impeded, lagging, languid, passive 8 careless, crawling, creeping, dawdling, dilatory, dragging, drawn-out, fainéant, hesitant, indolent, laidback, listless, plodding, romantic, slipshod, slothful, sluggish, toddling 9 apathetic, enervated, hit or miss, imprudent, incurious, leisurely, lethargic, negligent, prolonged, snaillike, unhurried, unmindful 10 abstracted, deliberate, energyless, incautious, languorous, nonchalant, protracted, spiritless, unthinking
lackadaisicalness: 5 sloth 6 torpor 8 laziness, lethargy 9 fainéance, indolence 10 stagnation
Lackaday!: 4 alas
__-Lackawanna Railroad: 4 Erie
lackey: 4 page, pawn, tool 5 gofer, groom, toady 6 fawner, flunky, gopher, helper, jackal, menial, minion, puppet, stooge, yes man 7 doormat, flunkey, footman, servant, steward 8 creature, factotum, groveler, hanger-on, henchman, kowtower 9 attendant, flatterer, stableboy, sycophant, underling 10 bootlicker, handshaker
lacking: 3 shy 4 gone, poor, sans, thin, weak 5 lousy, minus, out of, short 6 absent, bereft, devoid, except, faulty, feeble, flawed, free of, in need, meager, needed, skimpy 7 missing, needing, wanting, without 8 devoid of, impaired 9 defective, deficient, penniless, subnormal 10 deprived of, inadequate, incomplete, unfinished
combining form: 3 lyo- 4 lipo-
courage: 3 shy 4 weak 5 faint, timid 6 afraid, craven, scared, yellow 7 fearful, gutless, panicky 8 cowardly, recreant, timorous 9 dastardly, nerveless, spineless, tremulous 10 frightened
empathy: 4 mean 5 cruel, rigid, rough, stern, tough 6 bitter, brutal, severe, strict, unkind 7 austere, callous, harshly, hostile 8 despotic, grueling, indurate, pitiless, rocklike, ruthless, savagely, severely, stubborn, wearying 9 difficult, insensate, merciless, obstinate, stringent, unbending, unfeeling, unsparing, viciously 10 adamantine, inflexible, pitilessly, relentless, unmerciful, unpleasant
firmness: 4 soft 6 droopy, flabby, floppy, pliant 7 flaccid, pliable 8 drooping
force: 4 limp, weak 6 effete 8 weakened 9 enervated, powerless
nothing: 4 full 5 whole 6 entire 7 perfect 8 complete, thorough 9 inclusive 10 exhaustive
suffix: 4 -free, -less
value: 3 nil, zip 4 nada, none, zero 5 zilch 6 naught 7 nothing 8 goose egg
vegetation: 3 dry 4 arid 6 fallow 7 parched, sterile 8 deserted, desolate, infecund, lifeless 9 fruitless
vigor: 4 weak, worn 6 feeble 7 worn-out
volume: 4 bony, lank, lean, puny, slim, trim 5 gaunt, lanky, reedy, wispy 6 flimsy, meager, skimpy, skinny, slight, slinky, sparse 7 haggard, scrawny, slender 8 skeletal, twiglike, wisplike 9 emaciated, paper-thin, waferthin
wit: 4 dull 5 vapid 7 humdrum, prosaic, tedious
Lackland: 3 AFB
lackluster: 3 dim, dry 4 arid, blah, dead, drab, dull, flat, pale, zero 5 faded, ho-hum, mousy, muted, unfun, vapid 6 barren, boring, draggy, leaden, mousey, sickly, somber 7 nothing, obscure, prosaic, vanilla 8 laid-back, lifeless, unlively 9 colorless, prosaical, unsightly, washed-out
lacks: 5 hasn't
lackwit
see ninny
La classe de danse
painter: Edgar Degas
La Clemenza di Tito
composer: Wolfgang Amadeus Mozart
Lacombe, Lucien (1974 film)
director: Louis Malle
La Confession de Claude
author: Émile Zola
L.A. Confidential (1997 film)
cast: Kim Basinger, Russell Crowe, Kevin Spacey
laconic: 4 curt 5 brief, brusk, crisp, pithy, short, terse, tight 6 silent 7 brusque, compact, concise 8 succinct, taciturn 10 of few words, to the point
laconism: 3 mot, saw 4 quip 5 gnome, maxim, motto 6 saying 7 brevity, epigram 8 aphorism, apothegm 9 pithiness, terseness, witticsim 10 apophthegm
Lacoste, Rene: 7 netster 9 tennis pro
milieu: 5 court
La Cousine __: 5 Bette
lacquer: 4 coat 5 glaze, gloss, japan, layer 6 enamel, finish, veneer 7 coating, encrust, incrust, varnish 8 covering 10 lamination
black ~: 5 japan
component: 5 elemi, resin
lacquerware: 4 tole
Lacrima __: 7 Christi
lacrimal __: 3 sac 4 bone, duct 5 gland
lacrosse: 4 game 5 sport
area: 3 net 4 goal
position: 6 goalie
team: 3 ten
La Crosse: 4 city, town
locale: 4 Wisc. 9 Wisconsin
Lactaid: 7 antacid
alternative: *see* antacid
__ Lactea: 3 Via
lactic: 4 acid 5 milky
lacto-__-vegetarian: 3 ovo
lactose: 5 sugar
glucose, to ~: 6 isomer
__-lacto-vegetarian: 3 ovo
lacuna: 3 gap 4 gulf, hole 5 blank, break, lapse, pause, space 6 cavity, cesura, hiatus 7 caesura, interim, opening 8 interval, omission 10 interspace, interstice
La Curée
author: Émile Zola
lacy: 4 fine, open, thin 5 fancy, gauzy, meshy, sheer 6 dainty, frilly, ornate 7 elegant, netlike, weblike 8 delicate, filagree, filigree, finespun, gossamer, lacelike 9 filigreed, fillagree, patterned 10 diaphanous
Lacy: 6 Dalton
lad: 3 boy, cub, guy, kid, son 4 runt, tyke 5 bairn, buddy, child, minor, sprig, swain, youth 6 feller, fellow, junior 7 preteen 8 half-pint, juvenile, young man 9 schoolboy, stripling, youngster
date: 4 lass
in Spanish: 4 niño
Lad, __: 4 a Dog
Lada: 3 car 4 auto 7 Russian 10 automobile
model: 4 Niva 6 Samara
Lad: A Dog
author: Albert Terhune
dog: 5 Knave
La Dame __ Camélias: 3 aux
La Danse des Nymphes
artist: Camille Corot
Ladd: 4 Alan 5 Diane 6 Cheryl 8 Margaret
Ladd, Alan: 5 actor
film: The Badlanders (1958)
The Blue Dahlia (1946)
The Glass Key (1942)
O.S.S. (1946)
The Proud Rebel (1958)
Shane (1953)
This Gun for Hire (1942)
Ladd, Diane: 7 actress
daughter: Laura Dern
spouse: Bruce Dern
ladder: 3 run 5 scale 10 fire escape
component: 4 heel, rung, step
cousin: 5 stair
danger: 4 fall, slip 5 spill 6 topple
in Italian: 5 scala
use a ~: 4 go up 5 climb, mount, scale 6 ascend 7 clamber
__ ladder: 6 Jacob's
Ladder 49 (2004 film)
cast: Joaquin Phoenix, John Travolta
ladder-back: 5 chair
part: 4 slat
Ladder of Years
author: Anne Tyler
Ladders to Fire
author: Anaïs Nin
laddie: 3 boy, kid, son 4 male 5 child
lade: 3 tax 4 fill, load, pack 6 burden, fill up, infuse, lumber, pile on 8 overload

la-de-da
see la-di-da
laden: **4** full, rife **5** heavy, taxed **6** filled, jammed, loaded, packed **7** charged, crammed, crowded, fraught, replete, stuffed, teeming **8** brimming, burdened, hampered, weighted **9** oppressed **10** encumbered, loaded down
lader: **9** stevedore
la-di-da: **4** posh **6** snooty, snotty, too-too **7** foppish, genteel, mincing **8** affected, mannered, snobbish **9** conceited, high-toned, unnatural **10** artificial, hoity-toity, show-offish
__ ladies dancing...: **6** eleven
Ladies' Delight, The
author: Émile Zola
ladies' man: **3** cad **4** dude, rake, roué **8** lothario
Ladies Night (1979 song)
artist: Kool and the Gang
Ladies of the Canyon: **4** song
name: **5** Annie, Trina **8** Estrella
Ladies of the Canyon (1970 album)
artist: Joni Mitchell
lading: **4** haul, load **5** cargo, goods **6** burden, charge, weight **7** freight **8** boatload, cartload, shipment **9** truckload, wagonload
place: **4** dock, pier, port, quay **5** berth, jetty, wharf **7** landing
ladino: **5** horse **9** wild horse
ladle: **4** skim **5** scoop, spoon **6** dipper **7** dish out, utensil **8** spoon out
natural ~: **5** gourd
L.A. Doctors (CBS drama)
cast: Ken Olin (Dr. Roger Cattan)
Ladoga: **4** lake
locale: **6** Russia
La Dolce Vita (1960 film)
cast: Anouk Aimée, Anita Ekberg, Marcello Mastroianni
composer: Nino Rota
director: Federico Fellini
La donna è mobile: **4** aria
composer: Giuseppe Verdi
opera: **9** Rigoletto
__ la Douce: **4** Irma
lady: **3** gal, her, she **4** lass, wife **5** noble, title, woman **6** female, madame, matron, señora **7** duchess, grown-up, peeress, senhora, signora **8** baroness, countess **10** noblewoman
address for a ~: **4** ma'am **5** madam
alternative: **5** tiger
bow: **6** curtsy
ender: **3** bug **4** bird, fish, like, love, ship **6** beetle, finger
escort: **4** gent
fickle ~: **4** Luck
first ~: **3** Eve
in German: **4** frau
In Italian ~: **5** donna
in Portuguese ~: **4** dona
in Spanish: **3** sra. **4** dama, dona **6** Latina, señora
knight's ~: **4** dame
leading ~: **4** star **7** actress
malicious ~: **5** vixen
mate: **3** sir **4** lord
name meaning ~: **6** Martha
old ~ habitat: **4** shoe
painted ~: **3** bug **6** insect
palindromic ~: **3** Ada, Ava, Eve, Lil, Nan **4** Anna, ma'am **5** madam
starter: **4** fore, land **5** sales
that ~: **3** her, she **5** woman **6** female
title: **5** madam
wear: **4** flat, pump **5** frock, skirt **6** blouse, halter **7** camises, chemise **9** high heels, nightgown
young ~: **4** girl, lass, maid **5** missy **6** damsel, female **8** fräulein **9** stripling
see also woman
__ lady: **4** pink **5** first, young **6** dragon **7** leading, painted
Lady: **4** dame **5** title **7** duchess **8** baroness, countess **10** grande dame, noblewoman
author: Thomas Tryon
Lady (song)
artist: Commodores, D'Angelo, Kenny Rogers, Little River Band, Styx
Lady __: **3** Day **4** Jane, Love, Luck **6** Godiva **7** Madonna
Lady __ Dark: **5** in the
Lady __ Day: **4** for a
Lady __ Johnson: **4** Bird
Lady __ Lake, The: **5** in the, of the
Lady __ Memorial Trophy: **4** Byng
Lady __, The: **3** Eve **5** in Red
Lady __ the Blues: **5** Sings
Lady __ the Tramp: **3** and
Lady __ Tramp, The: **3** is a
__ Lady: **3** Our **4** Dark, Gray, Kind, Moon, Pink, That **5** A Lost, Disco, First, She's a **7** Chained, Dancing, Valiant
__ Lady, A: **4** Lost
Lady and the __: **5** Tramp
Lady Baltimore: **4** cake
Lady, Be Good!: **7** musical
composer: George Gershwin, Ira Gershwin
ladybird: **6** beetle, insect
Lady Bird: **7** Johnson
follower: **3** Pat
middle name: **4** Alta
preceder: **6** Jackie **10** Jacqueline
son-in-law: **4** Robb **6** Nugent
spouse: **6** Lyndon
ladybug: **6** beetle, insect
food: **5** aphid, aphis
Lady Byng Trophy org.: **3** NHL
Lady Chatterley's Lover
author: D.H. Lawrence
__ Lady Down: **4** Gray
Lady Eve, The (1941 film)
cast: Henry Fonda, Barbara Stanwyck
director: Preston Sturges
ladyfinger: **4** cake **6** cookie
Lady From Dubuque, The
author: Edward Albee
Lady From Shanghai, The (1948 film)
cast: Rita Hayworth, Everett Sloane, Orson Welles
director: Orson Welles
Lady From the Sea, The
author: Henrik Ibsen
Lady Godiva (1966 song)
artist: Peter and Gordon
Lady Gregory collaborator: **5** Yeats
Ladyhawke (1985 film)
cast: Matthew Broderick, Rutger Hauer, Leo McKern, Michelle Pfeiffer
lady-in-__: **7** waiting
Lady in __, The: **3** Red
Lady Inger of Osteraad
author: Henrik Ibsen
Lady in the Dark: **7** musical
author: Moss Hart
composer: Ira Gershwin, Kurt Weill
Lady in the Lake, The
author: Raymond Chandler
Lady Is a Tramp, The
composer: Lorenz Hart, Richard Rodgers
Lady Jane (1966 song)
artist: Rolling Stones
Lady Jane (1985 film)
cast: Helena Bonham Carter, Cary Elwes, John Wood
Lady Jane __: **4** Grey
Lady Jane Grey
author: Nicholas Rowe
Ladykillers, The (2004 film)
cast: Tom Hanks
Lady L (1965 film)
cast: Paul Newman, Sophia Loren
Lady Lazarus
author: Sylvia Plath
Lady Liberty's home: **3** USA **5** US of A **7** New York
ladylike: **4** kind, nice **5** civil **6** formal, gentle, polite, proper **7** correct, elegant, genteel, refined, womanly **8** cultured, decorous, feminine, gracious, polished, wellborn, well-bred **9** courteous, dignified, high-class **10** cultivated, well-spoken
ladylove
see sweetheart
Lady Love (1978 song)
artist: Lou Rawls
Lady Luck: **4** fate
like ~: **6** fickle
Lady Madonna (1968 song)
artist: Beatles
Lady Marmalade (song)
artist: Christina Aguilera, Patti LaBelle
Lady of __: **5** Spain
__ Lady of Fatima: **3** Our
__ Lady of Guadalupe: **3** Our
__ Lady of Lourdes: **3** Our
Lady of Shalott, The
author: Alfred Tennyson
Lady of Spain, I __ you: **5** adore
lady of the __: **5** house
Lady of the Lake: **5** Ellen **6** Vivien
Lady of the Lake, The
author: Walter Scott
character: **3** Dhu
Lady Oracle
author: Margaret Atwood
Lady or the Tiger?, The setting: **5** arena
Lady Remington
alternative: **4** Nair, Neet
lady's
slipper: **5** plant **6** flower
that ~: **4** hers
tresses: **5** plant **6** flower
lady's __: **3** man
Lady Schick
alternative: **4** Nair, Neet
Lady Sings the Blues (1972 film)
cast: Richard Pryor, Diana Ross, Billy Dee Williams
Lady's Not for Burning, The
author: Christopher Fry
lady's-slipper: **5** plant **6** flower
Lady's Yes, The
author: Elizabeth Barrett Browning
Lady Willpower (1968 song)
artist: Gary Puckett and the Union Gap
Lady Windermere's Fan
author: Oscar Wilde
Lae: **4** city, town
locale: **9** New Guinea
Laemmle: **4** Carl
Laertes: **4** Dane **5** Greek
father: **8** Polonius
friend: **6** Hamlet
sister: **7** Ophelia
son: **8** Odysseus
La Fanciulla __ West: **3** del
La Farge, Oliver: **6** writer
work: As Long as the Grass Shall Grow
The Enemy Gods
Laughing Boy
Raw Material
Lafayette: **3** car **4** auto, city, Nash, town
athletes: **8** Leopards
locale: **6** Easton **7** Indiana **8** Colorado **9** Louisiana **10** California
__ La Fayette: **3** Rue
Lafcadio: **5** Hearn
la femme: **4** elle
La Femme Nikita (1990 film)
director: Luc Besson
La Femme Nikita (USA action)
cast: Peta Wilson (Nikita Taylor)
Laffer __: **5** curve
Laffit: **6** Pincay
La Fille Perdue
author: Claude Anet
Lafitte: **4** Jean **6** pirate
see also French
Lafleur, Guy
milieu: **3** ice **4** rink **5** arena
org.: **3** NHL
La Follette: **6** Robert
La Fontaine, Henri: **8** Nobelist
model for ~: **4** Esop **5** Aesop
La Fontaine, Jean de: **6** French, writer
La Fortune des Rougons
author: Émile Zola
La Forza del Destino
composer: Giuseppe Verdi
role: **5** Carlo, Curra **6** Alvaro **7** Leonora **8** Don Carlo **9** Don Alvaro
setting: **5** Italy, Spain
__ la France!: **4** Vive
L'Africaine
role: **4** Inez
lag: **3** ebb **4** drag, fail, flag, idle, inch, laze, limp, loaf, plod, poke, slow, stay, tail, tool, wane **5** amble, dally, delay, mosey, stall, tarry, trail **6** dawdle, falter, hobble, linger, loiter, lounge, put off, retard, slouch, slow up, trudge **7** fall off, saunter, shuffle, slacken **8** decrease, diminish, hang back, interval, lollygag, lose time, relegate, straggle **9** inch along, lose speed, waste time **10** dillydally, lose ground
behind: **4** drag, flag **5** dally, delay, dog it, tarry, trail **6** dawdle, linger, loiter **7** draggle **8** drop back, hang back, straggle

9 poke along 10 fall behind
starter: 3 jet 4 gray, grey
__ lag: 3 jet 4 time
Lag __: 5 b'Omer
lagan: 7 flotsam
La Gare Saint-Lazare
artist: Claude Monet
Lagasse: 6 Emeril
L'Âge d'Or (1930 film)
director: Luis Buñuel
lager: 4 beer, brew 5 drink 7 pilsner 8 beverage
cousin: 3 ale
holder: 3 keg 4 cask 6 barrel
Lagerkvist, Pär: 6 writer 7 Swedish 8 Nobelist
work: Barabbas
The Dwarf
Guest of Reality
The Hangman
Pilgrim at Sea
The Sibyl
Lagerlöf, Selma: 6 writer 7 Swedish 8 Nobelist
work: The Further Adventures of Nils
Gosta Berlings Saga
Jerusalem
The Wonderful Adventures of Nils
laggard: 4 lazy, logy, poke, slow 5 idler, slack 6 loafer 7 dawdler, lounger, unready 8 dilatory, lingerer, loiterer, slowpoke 9 latecomer, lazybones, leisurely, lethargic, straggler
laggardly: 5 tardy 9 leisurely, reluctant
lagging: 4 late, lazy, poky, slow 6 behind, draggy, in back, losing 7 gradual, halting, impeded, languid, unready 8 dilatory, drawn-out, hesitant, listless, plodding, slothful, sluggish 9 leisurely, lethargic, prolonged, snaillike, unhurried 10 deliberate, protracted
La Gioconda: 5 opera
composer: Amilcare Ponchielli
highlight: 4 aria
name: 4 Lisa, Mona
role: 4 Enzo 5 Isepo, Laura, Zuane 6 Alvise 7 Barnaba, La Cieca
setting: 5 Italy 6 Venice
__ la giubba: 5 Vesti
lagniappe: 3 tip 4 gift, perk, plus 5 bonus, extra 6 reward, tipoff 7 douceur 8 gratuity
Lago: 4 Como 5 d'Orta, Garda 8 Maggiore, Titicaca 9 Maracaibo
lagomorph: 4 hare, pika 5 bunny 6 rabbit 10 jackrabbit
lagoon: 3 bay 4 gulf, lake, pond, pool 5 bayou, marsh, shoal 8 shallows
site: 4 reef 5 atoll 6 island
__ Lagoon, The: 4 Blue
Lagos: 4 city, port, town
locale: 7 Nigeria
La Grâce
author: Gabriel Marcel
Lagrange: 6 Joseph
La Guardia: 8 Fiorello
La Guardia Airport
locale: 3 NYC 6 Queens 7 New York
__ la guerre!: 4 C'est
laguna: 3 bay 5 inlet
Laguna: 3 car 4 auto, city, town 5 Chevy 6 Indian 7 Amerind, Renault 9 Chevrolet 10 automobile
locale: 10 California
Laguna Beach: 4 city, town
locale: 10 California
Laguna Hills: 4 city, town
locale: 10 California
Laguna Niguel: 4 city, town
locale: 10 California
lah-__: 5 di-dah
La Habra: 4 city, town
locale: 10 California
Lahaina
locale: 4 Maui 6 Hawaii
lah-di-dah: 4 posh 6 snooty, snotty, too-too 7 foppish, genteel, mincing 8 affected, mannered, snobbish 9 conceited, high-toned, unnatural 10 artificial, hoity-toity, show-offish
LaHood: 3 Ray
Lahore: 4 city, town
locale: 8 Pakistan
Lahr: 4 Bert, John
Lahr, Bert
role: 4 lion
Lahti, Christine: 7 actress
TV: Chicago Hope
laic: 7 secular 8 temporal 9 layperson 10 unordained
not ~: 8 clerical, priestly 9 religious
laics: 5 flock
laid
away: 4 kept 8 reserved, retained, set aside
low: 3 ill 5 unfit 7 invalid 9 unhealthy
off: 4 idle 10 unemployed
starter: 3 way
laid-__: 4 back
laid-back: 3 lax 4 calm, cool, easy, kind, mild, soft 5 loose, quiet, staid, stoic, type B 6 at ease, casual, gentle, kindly, low-key, mellow, placid, sedate, serene 7 amiable, at peace, clement, equable, languid, natural, offhand, pacific, relaxed, ruthful, sparing, stoical, unmoved 8 amicable, carefree, composed, fireside, flexible, informal, listless, merciful, peaceful, placable, sluggish, tolerant, tranquil 9 assuasive, collected, compliant, easygoing, forgiving, impassive, indulgent, leisurely, lethargic, quiescent, temperate, unexcited, unruffled 10 forbearing, lackluster, nonchalant, permissive, unaffected, unagitated, unbothered, unexacting, untroubled
not ~: 5 type B 10 aggressive
__ laid plans: 4 best
laid-up: 3 ill 4 abed, sick 5 in bed 6 ailing, infirm, sickly, unwell 7 unsound 8 confined, disabled, diseased 9 bedridden 10 indisposed
Laila: 3 Ali 6 Robins
Laine: 4 Cleo 7 Frankie
Laine, Frankie
real name: Frank LaVecchio
song: High Noon (1952)
I Believe (1953)
Jezebel (1951)
Love Is a Golden Ring (1957)
Moonlight Gambler (1956)
Mule Train (1949)
Laing: 2 R.D.
Lainie: 5 Kazan
lair: 3 den, pen 4 cave, hole, nest 5 earth, haunt 6 burrow, kennel, refuge 7 hideout, retreat, sanctum 8 cloister, hideaway 9 sanctuary 10 ivory tower
hawk's ~: 4 aery, eyry, nest 5 aerie, eyrie
Laird: 6 Cregar, Melvin
La Isla Bonita (1987 song)
artist: Madonna
laissez-faire: 9 free trade 10 neutrality
lait: 4 milk 6 French
__-lait: 4 sac-a
laity: 4 fold 5 flock 6 parish 10 worshipers
not ~: 6 clergy
place: 3 pew 4 nave
Laius
slayer of ~: 7 Oedipus
son: 7 Oedipus
wife: 7 Jocasta
Lajoie: 8 Napoleon
Lajoie, Nap: 6 Indian
La Jolla
campus: 4 UCSD
locale: 4 San Diego 10 California
lake: 4 loch, mere, pond, pool, tarn 5 basin, mouth 6 lagoon 8 millpond 9 reservoir
Africa: 4 Chad, Kivu, Tana 5 Assal, Mweru, Ngami, Nyasa, Tsana
Albania: 7 Scutari
Alberta: 6 Louise 9 Athabasca
Australia: 4 Eyre 7 Torrens
Banff: 6 Louise
bed mineral: 5 trona
Bern: 6 Brienz
boat: 5 canoe
Bolivia: 8 Titicaca
Botswana: 5 Ngami
bottom: 6 crater 7 benthos
Boulder Dam: 4 Mead
Buffalo: 4 Erie
California ~: 4 Mono 5 Tahoe 8 Lahontan 9 Salton Sea
Cambodia: 8 Tonle Sap
Cameroon: 4 Chad, Nios, Nyos
Canada: 4 Erie 5 Huron, Rainy 6 Louise, Simcoe 7 Nipigon, Ontario 8 Manitoba, Michigan, Superior, Winnipeg 9 Athabasca, Great Bear 10 Great Slave
Castel Gandolfo: 6 Albano
Chile: 4 Laja
China: 5 Tai Hu 7 Koko Nor 9 Qinghai Hu
Cleveland: 4 Erie
combining form: 4 limn- 5 limni-, limno-
Congo: 4 Kivu 5 Mweru 6 Albert, Mobuto 10 Tanganyika
Cornell: 6 Cayuga
denizen: 4 duck
desert ~: 6 mirage 8 illusion
dweller: 4 fish, swan 5 algae
Egypt: 6 Nasser
ender: 3 bed 4 side 5 front, shore
England: 8 Grasmere 10 Windermere
Estonia: 6 Peipus
Ethiopia: 4 Tana 5 Abaya, Tsana
feeder: 6 inflow
Finland: 4 Nasi 5 Enare, Inari 6 Saimaa
fish: 4 bass 5 trout
Florida: 10 Okeechobee
France: 6 Geneva
Geneva: 5 Leman
Guatemala: 6 Izabal, Yzabal 7 Atitlán
Hoover Dam: 4 Mead
Hungary: 7 Balaton
Iran: 5 Urmia
Ireland: 5 lough, Neagh
Israel: 7 Dead Sea
Italy: 4 Como, Orta 5 Garda 6 Albano, Averno, Lugano 8 Maggiore 9 Trasimeno
Japan: 3 Omi 4 Biwa
Jordan: 7 Dead Sea
Kazakhstan: 8 Balkhash
Kenya: 6 Rudolf 7 Turkana 8 Victoria
Lombardy: 4 Como
Maine: 9 Moosehead
maker: 3 dam
Manitoba: 8 Winnipeg
Michigan border ~: 5 Huron
Minnesota: 5 Rainy 6 Itasca
mountain ~: 4 pool, tarn 9 reservoir
Mozambique: 5 Nyasa 6 Malawi
Netherlands: 9 Zuider Zee 10 Ijsselmeer
Nevada: 4 Mead 5 Tahoe 8 Lahontan
New York: 5 Keuka 6 Cayuga, Oneida, Placid, Seneca 9 Champlain 10 Chautauqua
New Zealand: 5 Taupo
Niger: 4 Chad
Nigeria: 4 Chad
Ontario: 5 Rainy 6 Simcoe 7 Nipigon
Oregon: 6 Crater
Panama: 5 Gatún
Peru: 8 Titicaca
poetic ~: 4 mere
relative: 4 pond
Russia: 5 Onega 6 Ladoga, Peipus
Rwanda ~: 4 Kivu
Saginaw Bay ~: 5 Huron
saltwater ~: 4 Aral
Saskatchewan: 9 Athabasca
Scotland: 4 Ness 6 Lomond 8 Loch Ness 10 Loch Lomand
Scottish: 3 Awe 4 loch, Ness
Siberia: 6 Baikal
swamp ~: 5 kioga
Sweden: 5 Malar
Switzerland: 3 Zug 4 Biel 6 Bienne, Brienz
Switzerland ~: 4 Thun 6 Geneva, Lugano, Zurich 7 Lucerne 8 Maggiore 9 Neuchâtel
Tanzania: 5 Nyasa 6 Malawi 8 Victoria 10 Tanganyika
Toledo: 4 Erie
Turkey: 3 Van
Uganda: 5 Kioga, Kyoga 6 Albert, Mobuto 8 Victoria
Utah: 9 Great Salt
Venezuela: 9 Maracaibo
Vermont: 9 Champlain
Wisconsin: 9 Winnebago
world's deepest ~: 6 Baikal
Yugoslavia: 7 Scutari
Zambia: 5 Mweru 6 Kariba 9 Bangweulu
Zimbabwe: 6 Kariba

lake __: **6** effect
Lake: **4** Greg **5** Ricki **6** Arthur **8** Veronica
Lake __ City, AZ: **6** Havasu
Lake __, MN: **4** Elmo
Lake __ of Innisfree, The: **4** Isle
Lake __ Woods: **5** of the
__ Lake: **4** Loon **6** Crater
Lake Albert
  drainer: **4** Nile
  today: **6** Mobuto
__, Lake and Palmer: **7** Emerson
Lake Baikal
  river from ~: **4** Lena
  river to ~: **7** Selenga
Lake Chad
  river to ~: **5** Chari, Shari
Lake Champlain
  river to ~: **7** Ausuble
Lake Charles: **4** city, town
  locale: **9** Louisiana
__ Lake City: **4** Salt
Lake Erie: **6** battle
  city on ~: **6** Toledo **7** Buffalo **8** Sandusky **9** Cleveland
  river to ~: **6** Maumee **7** Detroit
Lake Forest: **4** city, town
  locale: **8** Illinois **10** California
Lake Geneva
  feeder: **5** Rhone
  spa town: **5** Evian
Lake Havasu City: **4** town
  locale: **7** Arizona
Lake House, The (2006 film)
  cast: Sandra Bullock, Keanu Reeves
Lake Huron
  bay: **7** Saginaw
  river to ~: **7** St. Marys
Lake Isle of Innisfree, The
  author: William Butler Yeats
Lakeland: **4** city, town
  locale: **7** Florida
Lake Louise, city near: **5** Banff
Lake Malawi: **5** Nyasa
Lake Mead
  city near: **5** Vegas **8** Las Vegas
  dam: **6** Hoover
Lake Michigan
  city: **4** Gary **6** Racine **7** Chicago, Hammond, Holland, Kenosha **8** Evanston, Green Bay, Waukegan **9** Milwaukee, Sheboygan
  river to ~: **5** Grand
Lake Mobuto formerly: **6** Albert
Lake Nasser
  dam: **5** Aswan
  site: **4** Nile
__ Lake, NM: **3** Ute
Lake Nyasa formerly: **6** Malawi
Lake of Brienz river: **3** Aar **4** Aare
Lake Ontario
  river to ~: **7** Genesee, Niagara
Lake Oswego: **4** city, town
  locale: **6** Oregon
Lake Placid: **3** spa **6** resort
  gear: **3** ski **4** skee
  locale: **7** New York
Lake Poet concern: **5** metre
Lakers: **4** five, team
  home: **10** Los Angeles
  org.: **3** NBA
  rival: *see* NBA team
  sport: **10** basketball
Lake Rudolf: **7** Turkana
__ Lakes: **5** Great, Land o' **6** Finger
Lakeshore Limited offerer: **6** Amtrak
lakeside: **5** shore
Lake Superior
  city: **6** Duluth
  island: **6** Royale
Lake Tahoe
  city near ~: **4** Reno
  tribe: **5** Washo
Lake Tanganyika explorer: **5** Speke
Lake Titicaca
  city near ~: **5** La Paz
  locale: **4** Peru **5** Andes **7** Bolivia
  people: **6** Aymara
Lake Tuz
  city near ~: **6** Angora, Ankara
Lake, Veronica: **7** actress
  film: The Blue Dahlia (1946)
    The Glass Key (1942)
    I Married a Witch (1942)
    So Proudly We Hail! (1943)
    Sullivan's Travels (1941)
    This Gun for Hire (1942)
Lake Victoria
  city on ~: **5** Jinja
  outlet: **4** Nile
  river to ~: **6** Kagera
Lake Wobegon __: **4** Days
Lakewood: **4** city, town
  locale: **4** Ohio **8** Colorado **9** New Jersey **10** California, Washington
Lake Worth: **4** city, town
  locale: **7** Florida
Lakhota: **5** Sioux, Teton **10** Crazy Horse
Lakmé: **5** opera
  composer: Léo Delibes
  highlight: **4** aria
  role: **4** Rose **5** Ellen, Hadji **6** Benson, Gérald **7** Mallika **8** Frédéric **10** Nilakantha
  setting: **5** India
Lakota: **5** Sioux, Teton, tribe **10** Crazy Horse
__ la la: **3** ooh, tra
__-La-La: **3** Sha
La La La (1969 song)
  artist: Bobby Sherman
la-la land, in: **5** spacy **6** asleep, spacey
La La Lucille: **7** musical
  composer: George Gershwin
La-La - Means I Love You (1968 song)
  artist: Delfonics
LaLanne: **4** Jack
  place: **3** spa
L.A. Law (NBC drama)
  business: **4** case **5** trial
  cast: Corbin Bernsen (Arnie Becker)
    Susan Dey (Grace Van Owen)
    Larry Drake (Benny Stulwicz)
    Richard Dysart (Leland McKenzie)
    Jill Eikenberry (Ann Kelsey)
    Michele Greene (Abby Perkins)
    Harry Hamlin (Michael Kuzak)
    Alan Rachins (Douglas Brackman)
    Susan Ruttan (Roxanne Melman)
    Jimmy Smits (Victor Sifuentes)
    Michael Tucker (Stuart Markowitz)
    Blair Underwood (Jonathan Rollins)
  figure: **2** DA **3** att. **4** atty. **8** attorney
__ la Liberté, A: **4** Nous
Lalique: **4** René
lall
  kin: **4** lisp
Lalla Rookh
  author: Thomas Moore
lallygag: **4** idle, laze, loaf, loll **6** dawdle, lounge **7** fritter, goof off **8** fool away, kill time **9** do nothing, lie around
Lalo: **7** Edouard **8** Schifrin
Lalo, Édouard
  work: Le Roi d'Ys
    Symphonie Espagnole
lam: **2** go **3** fly, run **4** bolt, flee **5** split **6** beat it, bug out, escape, flight **7** getaway, make off **9** scramming, skedaddle **10** hightail it, take flight
  one on the ~: **5** fleer **7** escapee
  on the ~: **4** free **5** loose **7** at large, escaped, fleeing
lama: **4** guru, monk **5** bonze **6** cleric, priest **9** religious
  land: **5** Tibet **6** Xizang **7** Sitsang
  melody: **5** chant **6** mantra **7** mantram
  reincarnate ~: **5** Tulku
...lama __ priest: **4** he's a
__ Lama: **5** Dalai
__ Lama Ding Dong: **4** Rama
__ la Mancha: **5** Man of
Lamarck: **4** Jean
La Mare au diable
  author: George Sand
Lamarr: **4** Hedy
La Marseillaise: **6** anthem
Lamas: **6** Carlos **7** Lorenzo **8** Fernando
Lamas, Carlos: **8** Nobelist
lamasery: **6** temple **8** cloister **9** monastery
Lamas, Fernando
  spouse: Arlene Dahl, Esther Williams
__ lama..., The: **4** one-l
lamb: **3** fur **4** dupe, meat, rack **5** chump, patsy, sheep **6** animal, sucker **7** darling, fall guy **8** easy mark, innocent, pushover, yearling **9** greenhorn **10** honeybunch
  bear a ~: **4** yean
  cry: **3** baa, maa **5** bleat
  dish: **4** chop, gyro, stew **5** cabob, gigot, kabab, kabob, kebab, kebob **6** cutlet, hot pot
  leg: **5** gigot
  like a ~: **5** ovine **6** lanose, woolly
  parent: **3** dam, eve, ram
  pet ~: **6** cosset
  place: **4** cote
  seasoning: **4** mint
__ lamb: **3** ewe **5** leg of **7** paschal
Lamb: **6** Willis **7** Charles **8** Caroline
Lamb __: **5** of God
lambada: **3** fad **4** step **5** dance
lambaste: **3** hit, pan **4** beat, flay, flog, lash, lick, pelt, slam, slap, trim, whip, zing **5** abuse, blast, cream, knock, pound, punch, roast, scold, slash, smear, smite, whack **6** assail, attack, batter, berate, cudgel, defeat, hammer, pummel, punish, rebuke, scathe, scorch, strike, thrash, thwack, wallop **7** blister, censure, clobber, lay into, overrun, rip into, scourge, shellac, smother, trounce, upbraid **8** bludgeon, denounce, lash into, shellack **9** castigate, criticize, dish it out, excoriate, lash out at, light into, reprimand **10** vituperate
Lamb, Charles: **4** Elia **6** writer **7** English **8** essayist
  genre: **5** essay
  work: A Chapter on Ears
    A Dissertation on Roast Pig
    Dream Children
    Mrs. Battle's Opinions of Whist
    The Supernatural Man
    Tales from Shakespeare
Lamb Chop: **6** puppet
  voice: **5** Lewis, Shari
lambda: **5** Greek **6** letter
  follower: **2** mu **4** mu nu
  preceder: **5** kappa
Lambeau: **5** Curly
lambency: **4** glow **5** light **6** luster **10** luminosity
lambent: **3** lit **5** agile, aglow, light, lucid, nitid, shiny **6** ablaze, bright, flashy **7** beaming, blazing, dancing, fulgent, glowing, playing, radiant, shining **8** dazzling, gleaming, luminous, lustrous **9** brilliant, sparkling **10** flickering
Lambert: **4** Jack **8** Constant
Lambert Field
  locale: **3** St. L. **7** St. Louis
Lambeth walk: **5** dance
lamblike: **4** meek, mild, naif, tame **5** naive **6** broken, docile, gentle, pliant, unwary **7** artless, pacific, passive, subdued, trained **8** dovelike, innocent, obedient, trusting **9** childlike, compliant, guileless, peaceable, tractable, unworldly **10** manageable, submissive
Lamborghini: **3** car **4** auto **7** Italian **10** automobile
  model: **5** Jalpa **6** Diablo **8** Countach **10** Murcielago
lambrusco: **3** red **4** wine
  origin: **5** Italy
lamb's
  in two shakes of a ~ tail: **3** now **4** anon, soon **6** at once, in a sec, pronto **7** hastily, quickly, rapidly, shortly **8** directly, promptly, right now, speedily **9** forthwith, in a minute, in a second, right away **10** this moment
  two shakes of a ~ tail: **4** jiff **5** jiffy, trice **6** moment
lamb's __: **4** wool
...lamb was __ go: **6** sure to
Lamb, Willis: **8** Nobelist **9** physicist
lame: **4** game, halt, poor, sore, thin, weak **5** stiff **6** faulty, feeble, flimsy **7** bruised, limping **8** hobbling, pathetic **9** faltering, indispose, sidelined **10** improbable, inadequate, pathetical, unsuitable
  duck: **5** goner
  ender: **5** brain
  name meaning ~: **6** Claude **7** Claudia
lame __: **4** duck
lamé: **6** fabric **8** material
lamebrain: **3** ass, nit, oaf, sap **4** boob, clod, dodo, dolt, dope, fool, simp, twit **5** chump, clown, cluck, dufus, dummy, dunce, joker, moron, ninny, patsy **6** dimwit,

doofus, lubber, lummox, nitwit, sucker, turkey 7 buffoon, dingbat, dullard, fathead, half-wit, jackass, lunatic, pinhead, saphead 8 bonehead, dumbbell, meathead, numskull 9 blockhead, numbskull, simpleton 10 dunderhead

lamebrained: 4 daft, dumb 5 batty, crazy, daffy, dippy, dizzy, dopey, goofy, inane, kooky, nutty, sappy, silly, vapid, wacky 6 absurd, insane, jejune, screwy, stupid, unwise 7 asinine, fatuous, foolish, idiotic, insipid, puerile, witless 8 mindless 9 airheaded, brainless, half-baked, laughable, ludicrous, pointless, senseless 10 boneheaded, ridiculous

Lamech
- **father:** 5 Enoch 10 Methuselah
- **son:** 4 Noah 5 Jabal, Jubal

lamed: 6 Hebrew, letter 7 injured
- **predecessor:** 4 kaph
- **successor:** 3 mem

lame-duck
- **held a ~ session:** 5 remet, resat

lamellar: 5 scaly

lament: 3 cry, rue, sob 4 alas, bawl, howl, hurt, keen, moan, mope, rain, sigh, sing, wail, weep, yell 5 bleed, brood, dirge, elegy, grief, groan, mourn, tears 6 bemoan, bewail, grieve, plaint, regret, repent, repine, sorrow 7 cry over, deplore, keening, moaning, requiem, sobbing, wailing, weep for, weeping 8 grieving, jeremiad, mourning, threnody 9 complaint, ululation 10 take it hard
- **poem of ~:** 5 dirge, elegy 6 monody 8 threnody
- **with:** 4 pity 7 ache for, feel for, weep for 8 bleed for 9 grieve for 10 sympathize

lamentable: 3 bad, low, sad 4 dire, grim, mean, poor 5 awful, dirty, lousy, woful 6 meager, rotten, rueful, tragic, woeful 7 doleful, hurting, piteous, pitiful, tearful 8 dolorous, God-awful, grievous, mournful, pathetic, stinking, tragical, wretched 9 miserable, plaintive, regretful, sorrowful, upsetting 10 afflictive, calamitous, deplorable, lugubrious, melancholy, pathetical
- **situation:** 6 bummer

lamentation: 3 rue, sob, woe 4 keen, moan, sigh, wail 5 dirge, elegy, grief, tears 6 lament, plaint, regret, sorrow 7 keening, moaning, requiem, sobbing, wailing, weeping 8 grieving, jeremiad, mourning, threnody 9 complaint, ululation

Lamentations
- **follower:** 7 Ezekiel
- **preceder:** 8 Jeremiah

lamenting: 6 sorrow 7 tearful 9 plaintive, querulous, sniveling

La Mer
- **composer:** Claude Debussy

la mer, land in: 3 île

La Mesa: 4 city, town
- **locale:** 10 California

Lamia
- **author:** John Keats

lamina: 3 ply 4 coat 5 layer, plate, scale, sheet 6 folium, veneer 7 overlay, stratum 8 membrane

laminate: 4 coat, face, foil 5 flake, layer, plate, split 6 veneer 7 foliate, overlay 8 separate, stratify 9 exfoliate, overlayer

laminated: 5 flaky 6 flakey 7 layered

lamination: 4 coat 5 layer 7 coating, lacquer

La Mirada: 4 city, town
- **locale:** 10 California

lammergeier: 4 bird

Lammermoor, Lucia di, like: 3 mad

__ la mode: 4 pie à

Lamont: 6 Dozier 7 Johnson 8 Cranston
- **portrayer:** 4 Alec

La Motta, Jake: 5 boxer

Lamour, Dorothy: 7 actress
- **costar:** Bing Crosby, Bob Hope

L'Amour, Louis: 6 writer
- **genre:** 7 western

lamp: 5 light 6 beacon 7 lantern
- **dweller:** 4 djin 5 djinn, genie 6 spirit
- **ender:** 4 post 5 black, light, shade, shell 7 lighter, working
- **fuel:** 3 oil 8 kerosene
- **gas:** 4 neon 5 argon
- **old-style:** 4 glim
- **part:** 4 base, blub, harp 5 shade 6 finial
- **part of an oil ~:** 4 wick
- **starter:** 4 head

__ lamp: 3 arc, oil, sun 4 heat, neon, pole 5 flood, floor, table 6 safety 7 halogen, Tiffany

...lamp __ my feet: 4 unto

__ Lamp: 4 Lava

lampblack: 4 soot 6 carbon

lamper __: 3 eel

lampoon: 4 jape, mock, rail, skit, twit 5 put on, roast, sneer, spoof, squib 6 debunk, parody, satire, send up 7 burlesk, laugh at, mockery, pasquil, takeoff 8 pastiche, ridicule, satirize, takedown, travesty 9 burlesque, invective, make fun of 10 caricature, pasquinade

lampoonery: 6 satire 7 burlesk, sarcasm 9 burlesque 10 vaudeville

lamppost-sign abbr.: 2 rd., st. 3 ave. 4 blvd.

lamprey: 3 eel 4 fish
- **kin:** 6 conger
- **lurer:** 5 eeler
- **trap:** 6 eelpot

LAN
- **part of ~:** 4 area 5 local 7 network
- **unit:** 2 PC

Lana: 4 Lang, Wood 6 Turner 8 Cantrell

lanai: 5 porch 6 piazza 7 veranda 8 verandah

Lanai: 4 isle 6 island
- **locale:** 6 Hawaii
- **neighbor:** 4 Maui

lanate: 5 fuzzy, wooly 6 fleecy, lanose, woolly

La Navarraise character: 5 Anita

Lancashire: 5 chair 6 county
- **city:** 7 Burnley
- **locale:** 7 England

Lancaster: 4 Burt, city, town 5 House
- **foe:** 4 York
- **locale:** 4 Ohio 5 Texas 10 California
- **symbol:** 4 rose 7 red rose

Lancaster, Burt: 5 actor
- **film:** Airport (1970)
  All My Sons (1948)
  Atlantic City (1981)
  Birdman of Alcatraz (1962)
  Brute Force (1947)
  The Cassandra Crossing (1977)
  A Child Is Waiting (1963)
  Come Back, Little Sheba (1952)
  Criss Cross (1949)
  The Devil's Disciple (1959)
  Elmer Gantry (1960, AA)
  Field of Dreams (1989)
  The Flame and the Arrow (1950)
  From Here to Eternity (1953)
  Gunfight at the O.K. Corral (1957)
  The Gypsy Moths (1969)
  The Island of Dr. Moreau (1977)
  Jim Thorpe - All-American (1951)
  Judgment at Nuremberg (1961)
  The Killers (1946)
  Lawman (1971)
  The Leopard (1963)
  Local Hero (1983)
  The Rainmaker (1956)
  Rocket Gibraltar (1988)
  The Rose Tattoo (1955)
  Run Silent, Run Deep (1958)
  Separate Tables (1958)
  Seven Days in May (1964)
  Sorry, Wrong Number (1948)
  Sweet Smell of Success (1957)
  Tough Guys (1986)
  The Train (1965)
  Trapeze (1956)
  Ulzana's Raid (1972)
  The Unforgiven (1960)
  Vera Cruz (1954)
  The Young Savages (1961)
  Zulu Dawn (1979)
- **role:** 5 Elmer, Moses 6 Gantry, Stroud, Thorpe

Lancaster County group: 5 Amish

lance: 4 open, slit, stab 5 spear, spike 6 empale, impale, incise, launch, pierce 7 cut open, harpoon, javelin, missile 8 lacerate 9 penetrate
- **carrying a ~:** 5 atilt
- **combining form:** 5 lonch- 6 loncho-
- **use a ~:** 4 tilt 5 joust

__-lance: 3 air 5 fer-de

Lance: 3 Ito 4 Bird 5 Major 6 Kerwin 7 Alworth, Parrish 9 Armstrong, Henriksen

Lancelot: 3 Sir 4 hero 6 knight
- **colleague:** 3 Kay
- **lover:** 6 Elaine
- **nephew:** 4 Bors
- **son:** 7 Galahad

Lancelot du __: 3 Lac

lancer: 4 ulan 5 uhlan 8 horseman 10 cavalryman, equestrian

__ lancer: 6 Bengal

Lancer: 3 car 4 auto 5 Dodge 10 automobile, Mitsubishi

lancet: 5 blade, knife 7 scalpel

lancet __: 4 arch 5 clock 6 window

Lanchester, Elsa: 7 actress
- **film:** Bride of Frankenstein (1935)
- **spouse:** Charles Laughton

lancinate: 4 stab 5 spear 6 impale, pierce

Lancome: 6 makeup
- **alternative:** ***see*** cosmetic brand

Lancs: 6 county
- **locale:** 7 England

land: 3 bag, get, sod, win 4 area, dirt, dock, farm, gain, grab, have, home, hook, loam, plot, soil, trap 5 acres, beach, berth, earth, field, fly in, grasp, light, manor, perch, pilot, put in, ranch, reach, realm, shore, snare, state, steer, tract 6 alight, arrive, come in, debark, estate, extent, ground, hop off, lumber, nation, obtain, old sod, parcel, quarry, realty, reel in, region, secure, settle, wind up 7 acquire, acreage, bring in, capture, country, expanse, get down, grounds, holding, kingdom, procure, purlieu, put down, set down, sit down, stretch, terrain, tillage 8 come down, dismount, district, freehold, get there, go ashore, homeland, mainland, make land, property, province, take down 9 bring down, continent, disembark, farmstead, lay hold of, territory, touch down 10 come ashore, drop anchor, real estate, splash down, terra firma
- **dot of ~:** 3 ait, cay, key 4 isle 5 atoll, islet 6 island
- **ender:** 4 fall, fill, form, lady, line, lord, mark, mass, side, slip, ward 5 owner, scape, slide, wards 6 holder, locked, lubber
- **expanse of ~:** 4 land, lots
- **high ~:** 4 mesa 5 butte, ridge 7 plateau 8 mountain
- **holding:** 3 lot 4 farm, park 5 manor, ranch 6 domain, estate 7 acreage 8 property 9 farmstead 10 plantation
- **in French:** 5 terre
- **in Italian:** 5 terra
- **in Latin:** 5 terra
- **in Spanish:** 6 tierra
- **in the ~ of Nod:** 3 out 6 asleep, dozing 7 napping 8 dreaming, snoozing 9 somnolent 10 slumbering
- **Inuit ~:** 7 Nunavut
- **low ~:** 3 bog, fen 5 marsh, swale, swamp 6 morass 8 quagmire
- **measure:** 3 are 4 acre 7 hectare
- **narrow ~:** 4 isth., spit 7 isthmus
- **native ~:** 3 sod 4 home 5 roots
- **never-never ~:** 6 heaven 8 paradise 9 Shangri-la
- **no man's ~:** 3 DMZ
- **not on ~:** 4 asea 5 at sea
- **of milk and honey:** 7 Arcadia, Erewhon 8 paradise 9 Shangri-la
- **on:** 5 reach
- **on ~:** 6 ashore
- **piece of ~:** 3 lot 4 acre, plot 5 field, patch, tract 6 parcel, spread
- **public ~:** 4 park
- **rich, as ~:** 6 arable 7 fertile 8 farmable, tillable 10 cultivable
- **starter:** 3 Ice, low, wet 4 crop, farm, flat, gang, head, high, home, main, Mary, moor, park, pine, Port, Saar, Scot, Thai, tide, wood 5 cloud, coast, Dixie, dream, fairy, Grace, grass, heart, march, marsh, range,

Rhine, scrub, south, swamp, Swazi, table, waste **6** border, bottom, father, forest, hinter, meadow, mother, screen, timber, wonder **7** fantasy, pasture **8** vacation
take by force, as ~: **5** annex
work the ~: **3** hoe **4** farm, plow **9** cultivate
land __: **4** crab, mass **5** agent, grant, of Nod **6** bridge, office, patent
land-__: **4** poor **7** grabber
land-__ business: **6** office
land-__ college: **5** grant
__ land: **4** la la **5** lotus **6** no man's
__-land: **5** crash
Land __: **4** of Oz **5** Dayak **6** O'Lakes
Land __!: **5** sakes
Land __ Midnight Sun: **5** of the
Land __ Rising Sun: **5** of the
__ Land: **3** Cop **4** Byrd, Holy, Love, Pure **5** Candy, Dixie
landau: **4** auto **8** carriage
Landau: **3** Lev **6** Martin
Landau, Lev: **8** Nobelist **9** physicist
Landau, Martin: **5** actor
film: Ed Wood (1994, AA)
North by Northwest (1959)
Tucker: The Man and His Dream (1988)
spouse: Barbara Bain
TV: Mission: Impossible, Space 1999
Landcruiser: **3** SUV **6** Toyota
landed: **3** lit **4** alit, rich **6** ashore
Land, Edwin: **8** inventor
company: **8** Polaroid
Landers: **3** Ann, Lew **4** Judy **6** Audrey
Landers, Ann: **4** twin **9** columnist
sister: **4** Abby **7** Abigail **8** Van Buren
landfill: **4** dump **5** depot **8** junk pile, junkyard
fodder: **4** junk **5** trash, waste **6** debris, litter, refuse, rubble, scraps **7** garbage **8** oddments **9** sweepings
Landi: **3** Sal **6** Elissa
landing: **4** dock, pier, port, quay, slip **5** floor, jetty, stage, wharf **6** harbor, runway **7** harbour, mooring **8** airfield, airstrip, platform **9** anchorage, touchdown **10** embankment, splashdown
place: **4** dock, pier, quay **5** field, levee, perch, stair, strip **7** airport **8** stairway
landing __: **4** gear **5** field, force, party
__ landing: **4** hard, soft **5** belly, crash **7** pancake
__ Landing: **5** Knots
Landing on the Sun, A
author: Michael Frayn
Landis: **4** John **6** Carole
Landis, John: **8** director
film: The Blues Brothers (1980)
Blues Brothers 2000 (1998)
Into the Night (1985)
The Kentucky Fried Movie (1977)
National Lampoon's Animal House (1978)
Spies Like Us (1985)
Three Amigos! (1986)
Trading Places (1983)
__ Land is Your Land: **4** This
landlady: **5** owner **6** lessor, porter **9** caretaker, concierge, custodian
ländler: **5** dance **8** Austrian
landlord: **3** saw **5** owner **6** leaser, lessor, squire **8** hotelier **9** innkeeper **10** freeholder, proprietor
concern: **4** rent **5** lease **6** tenant
notice: **5** to let **6** no pets, vacant **7** for rent **9** available
Landlord of New York: **5** Astor
Landlord, The (1970 film)
cast: Pearl Bailey, Beau Bridges, Diana Sands
landlubber's place: **6** ashore
landmark: **4** bend, hill, mark, sign, tree **5** blaze, cairn, event, guide, ruins, stage, stele, stone, trace **6** crisis, marker, museum **7** feature, remnant, vestige, waypost **8** fragment, memorial, milepost, monument, mountain, souvenir, specimen, survival **9** benchmark, milestone, watershed **10** promontory
Lando: **3** Joe **10** Calrissian
Land o' __!: **6** Goshen
Land o'__: **5** Lakes
land of __: **3** Nod
land of __ and honey: **4** milk
Land of __: **6** Beulah
Land of 1000 Dances (1966 song)
artist: Wilson Pickett
Land of Confusion (1986 song)
artist: Genesis
Land of Darkness, The
author: Émile Zola
Land of Mist, The
author: Arthur Conan Doyle
land of Nod, in the: **4** abed **6** asleep
Land of Smiles, The
composer: Franz Lehár
Land of the __ Sun: **6** Rising **8** Midnight
land of the free: **3** USA
Land of the Giants dog: **7** Chipper
Land of Unlikeness
author: Robert Lowell
Land O'Lakes: **4** city, town **6** butter
locale: **7** Florida
Landon: **3** Alf **7** Michael
__ Landon Kassebaum: **5** Nancy
Landon, Michael
TV: Bonanza, Highway to Heaven, Little House on the Prairie
land on one's __: **4** feet
Landor's Cottage
author: Edgar Allan Poe
Landover: **4** city, town
locale: **8** Maryland
landowner: **4** heir **5** owner **6** squire **7** heiress **9** bourgeois **10** capitalist
landowners: **6** gentry **8** nobility
Landowska, Wanda: **6** Polish **14** harpsichordist
Landry: **3** Ali, Tom
Landry, Tom: **5** coach
sport: **8** football
Land's __: **3** End
Land sakes!: **4** egad
landscape: **3** art **4** view **5** mural, scene, vista **6** ground, nature, sketch **7** outlook, picture, scenery, terrain **8** painting, panorama, prospect **10** photograph, topography
dip: **4** dale, glen **6** dingle, valley
do a ~: **5** paint
Landscape
author: Harold Pinter
landscaping
plant: **4** bush, rose **5** hedge, hosta, shrub
tool: **10** edger. mower
land's end: **6** border
Land's End: **4** cape
locale: **7** England **8** Cornwall
landslide: **3** win **4** rout **5** sweep **6** defeat **7** killing, triumph **8** conquest **9** advantage, avalanche, earthfall, grand slam, overthrow **10** clean sweep
result: **5** scree **6** debris **8** detritus
__ Land, The: **5** Waste **6** Secret
land with __: **5** a thud
lane: **3** way **4** path, road, walk **5** aisle, byway, track **6** airway, bypath, byroad, street **7** bikeway, footway, ingress, passage, pathway, walkway **8** air route, bike path, by-street, footpath, side road **10** passageway, side street
add a ~ to: **5** widen **7** broaden
button: **5** reset
conversion: **5** spare
for carpoolers: **3** HOV
in the fast ~: **3** lax **4** wild **5** loose **6** rakish, wanton **7** immoral **8** depraved, swinging, uncurbed **9** ambitious, debauched, dissolute **10** lascivious, profligate
marker: **4** cone
slow ~: **5** right
__ lane: **3** air, HOV, sea **4** fast, fire, land **6** lovers', memory **7** diamond, express, passing
Lane: **4** Abbe, Dick, Lois, Lola, Mark **5** Allen, Diane, Smith **6** Burton, Nathan **7** Charles, Christy **8** Kirkland, Rosemary **9** Priscilla
coworker: **4** Kent **5** Olsen
Lane, Abbe
spouse: Xavier Cugat
Lane, Diane: **7** actress
film: The Big Town (1987)
The Cotton Club (1984)
The Glass House (2001)
Hardball (2001)
Hollywoodland (2006)
Indian Summer (1993)
Jack (1996)
A Little Romance (1979)
Must Love Dogs (2005)
My Dog Skip (2000)
Nights in Rodanthe (2008)
The Perfect Storm (2000)
Rumble Fish (1983)
Streets of Fire (1984)
Under the Tuscan Sun (2003)
Unfaithful (2002)
Untraceable (2008)
A Walk on the Moon (1999)
__-lane highway: **4** four
Lane, Nathan: **5** actor
film: The Birdcage (1995)
Frankie and Johnny (1991)
Life With Mikey (1993)
Mouse Hunt (1997)
The Producers (2005)
film (voice): Stuart Little (1999)
__ Lane Theatre: **5** Drury
Lanfield: **6** Sidney
Lanford: **6** Wilson
lang: **2** k.d.
lang.: **3** Eng., Ger., Grk., Heb., Lat., Swe. **4** Hebr., Ital., Port., Russ., Span.
see also language
Lang: **4** Lana **5** Fritz **6** Andrew, Walter
Lang, Clubber
portrayer: **3** Mr. T
Langdon: **5** Harry **6** Sue Ane
Lange: **3** Jim, Ted **4** Hope **7** Jessica **8** Dorothea **9** Christian
Lange, Christian: **8** Nobelist
Lange, Hope: **7** actress
TV: The Ghost and Mrs. Muir
Lange, Jessica: **7** actress
film: All That Jazz (1979)
Blue Sky (1994, AA)
Cape Fear (1991)
Country (1984)
Cousin Bette (1998)
Crimes of the Heart (1986)
Everybody's All-American (1988)
Frances (1982)
King Kong (1976)
Losing Isaiah (1995)
Men Don't Leave (1990)
Music Box (1989)
Rob Roy (1995)
Sweet Dreams (1985)
Titus (1999)
Tootsie (1982, AA)
Langella, Frank: **5** actor
film: Cutthroat Island (1995)
Dave (1993)
Diary of a Mad Housewife (1970)
Frost/Nixon (2008)
Junior (1994)
Lolita (1997)
Superman Returns (2006)
Those Lips, Those Eyes (1980)
Langenkamp: **7** Heather
Langer: **2** A.J. **3** Jim **7** Susanne **8** Bernhard
Langer, Bernhard: **6** golfer
Langford: **7** Frances
l'anglaise, à: **6** boiled
Langley: **3** AFB **4** city, peak, town **5** mount **8** mountain
locale: **6** Canada **10** California
org.: **3** CIA
school: **3** TWU
Langmuir, Irving: **7** chemist **8** Nobelist
langoustine: **5** prawn
Langston: **6** Hughes
__ Lang Syne: **4** Auld
Langtry: **6** Lillie
language: **3** Ada, APL, Ebo, Ewe, Fon, Fox, Gbe, Ibo, Kwa, Lao, Oto, Sac, SQL, Tai, Twi, Ute, Yao **4** Ainu, Alef, cant, Cree, Crow, Eboe, Erse, Hopi, html, Icon, Igbo, Java, Lapp, LISP, Logo, Luba, Manx, Orca, Otoe, Pali, Perl, Sama, Sauk, Shan, Taal, talk, Thai, Tshi, Tupi, Urdu, word, Xosa, Yuma, Zulu, Zuni **5** Algol, argot, Aztec, Bantu, Basic, Caddo, Carib, Cecil, COBOL, Czech, Dayak, Dutch, Dylan, Greek, Haida, Hindi, Hmong, idiom, Iraki, Iraqi, Khmer, Kiowa, Koine, Latin, lingo, Maidu, Malay, Maori, Masai, Mayan, Norse, Osage, Oscan, Piute,

prose, Punic, SISAL, slang, Sotho, sound, style, Swazi, Tamil, Turki, Ugric, Uigur, Usbeg, Usbek, Uzbeg, Uzbek, voice, Welsh, Wolof, Xhosa, Yakut, Yaqui, Yurok 6 accent, Afghan, Arabic, Arawak, Aymara, Baltic, Basque, Berber, brogue, Celtic, Coptic, Creole, Dakota, Danish, Delphi, Eiffel, Erlang, French, Gaelic, German, Hebrew, Ibibio, jargon, Jivaro, Kechua, Kikuyu, Korean, Maasai, Manchu, Mbundu, Mixtec, Mohawk, Navaho, Navajo, Nepali, Oberon, Ojibwa, Oneida, Othman, Paiute, Papago, Pascal, Pashto, patois, Pawnee, Pequot, Polish, Prolog, Pushto, Pushtu, Quapaw, Romani, Romany, Sather, Scheme, Seneca, signal, Siouan, Slavic, Slovak, Snobol, Somali, speech, Tajiki, Telegu, Telugu, tongue, Tuscan, Uighur 7 Afghani, Aramaic, Arapaho, Ashanti, Bengali, Bisayan, Chinese, Chinook, dialect, diction, English, Finnish, Flemish, Fortran, Italian, Kechuan, Kirghiz, Kirundi, Kurdish, Latvian, lexicon, Malinke, Mohegan, Mohican, Montauk, Nahuatl, Ndebele, Ojibway, Ottoman, palaver, Persian, Punjabi, Quechua, Quichua, Rommany, Russian, Semitic, Serbian, Shawnee, Shilluk, Siamese, Slovene, Spanish, Swahili, Swedish, Tagalog, Tibetan, Tlingit, Turkish, Umbrian, Visayan, wording, Wyandot, Yiddish 8 Accadian, Akkadian, Albanian, Arapahoe, Armenian, Balinese, Cherokee, Cheyenne, Chippewa, Comanche, Croatian, Egyptian, Estonian, Etrurian, Etruscan, Filipino, Frankish, Hellenic, Japanese, Javanese, Kickapoo, locution, Mandarin, Nez Perce, Onondaga, parlance, Parthian, Phrygian, Quechuan, Romanian, Rumanian, Sanscrit, Sanskrit, Scythian, Slavonic, Thracian 9 Afrikaans, Bhutanese, Blackfoot, Bulgarian, Castilian, discourse, Esperanto, gibberish, Hungarian, Icelandic, Mongolian, Norwegian, Provençal, Roumanian, Sasquatch, Slovenian, Suquamish, Ukrainian, utterance, Winnebago, Wyandotte 10 Algonquian, dictionary, expression, Hindustani, Macedonian, Phoenician, Polynesian, Portuguese, Singhalese, Tarahumara, vernacular, Vietnamese, vocabulary

Afghanistan: 6 Pashto, Pushto, Pushtu
Africa: 7 Swahili
Alaska Indian: 5 Haida 7 Tlingit
Amazon: 4 Tupi
ancient ~: 3 Lat. 5 Assyr., Latin, Norse, Oscan, Punic 7 Aramaic 8 Assyrian, Etruscan, Frankish, Parthian, Phrygian, Thracian
Andes: 6 Kechua 7 Kechuan, Quechua, Quichua 8 Quechuan
Angola: 6 Mbundu
Antilles: 5 Carib
artificial ~: 9 Esperanto
Assyria: 8 Accadian, Akkadian
Austria: 6 German
Babylonia: 8 Accadian, Akkadian
Bangladesh: 7 Bengali
Benin: 3 Fon, Gbe
Bolivia: 6 Aymara
Borneo: 5 Dayak
Brazil: 10 Portuguese
Burundi: 7 Kirundi
Cambodia: 5 Khmer
Canada Indian: 4 Cree 5 Haida 6 Ojibwa 7 Ojibway, Tlingit 8 Chippewa
Central America: 7 Nahuatl
Chile: 6 Aymara
China: 4 Shan 5 Hmong, Uigur 6 Manchu, Uighur 7 Chinese 8 Mandarin 9 Cantonese
coarse ~: 5 abuse
Colorado Indian: 3 Ute 4 Yuma
combining form: 4 -glot
Connecticut Indian: 6 Pequot 7 Mohegan, Mohican
Djibouti: 6 Somali
Eastern Europe: 5 Turki, Usbeg, Usbek, Uzbeg, Uzbek 6 Slavic 7 Russian, Yiddish 8 Slavonic
Ecuador: 6 Jivaro
Egypt: 6 Coptic
Estonia: 6 Baltic
Ethiopia: 6 Somali
Finland: 4 Lapp
Gambia: 7 Malinke
Ghana: 3 Ewe, Gbe, Twi 4 Tshi 7 Ashanti
Great Basin Indian: 5 Piute 6 Paiute
Great Lakes Indian: 6 Ojibwa 7 Ojibway 8 Chippewa
Great Plains Indian: 3 Oto 4 Crow, Otoe 5 Caddo, Kiowa, Osage 6 Dakota, Pawnee, Quapaw, Siouan 7 Arapaho 8 Arapahoe, Cheyenne, Comanche, Kickapoo 9 Blackfoot
Guyana: 6 Arawak
Gypsy: 6 Romani, Romany 7 Rommany
Hungary: 5 Ugric
Inca: 6 Kechua 7 Kechuan, Quechua, Quichua 8 Quechuan
India: 4 Pali, Urdu 5 Hindi, Tamil 6 Telegu, Telugu 8 Sanscrit, Sanskrit 10 Hindustani
Iran: 6 Tajiki 7 Persian
Iraq: 6 Arabic
Ireland: 4 Erse 6 Celtic, Gaelic
Isle of Man: 4 Manx
Israel: 3 Heb. 4 Hebr. 6 Hebrew
Italy: 6 Tuscan 7 Umbrian
Japan: 4 Ainu
Kenya: 5 Masai 6 Kikuyu, Maasai
Laos: 3 Lao 5 Hmong
Louisiana: 6 Creole
Mexico: 5 Aztec, Mayan, Yaqui 6 Mixtec, Papago 7 Nahuatl, Spanish 10 Tarahumara
Middle East: 6 Arabic 7 Aramaic, Kurdish, Semitic
Netherlands: 5 Dutch
New York Indian: 6 Mohawk, Oneida, Seneca 7 Montauk 8 Onondaga 10 Algonquian
New Zealand: 5 Maori
Nigeria: 3 Ebo, Gbe, Ibo 4 Eboe, Igbo 6 Ibibio
North Africa: 6 Berber
Northwest Indian: 5 Yurok 7 Chinook 8 Nez Perce 9 Sasquatch, Suquamish
Pakistan: 4 Urdu
Peru: 6 Aymara, Jivaro 7 Spanish
Philippines: 4 Sama 7 Bisayan, Tagalog, Visayan 8 Filipino
Sarawak: 5 Dayak
Scotland: 4 Erse 6 Celtic, Gaelic
Senegal: 5 Wolof 7 Malinke
Siberia: 5 Yakut
sign ~: 3 ASL
South Africa: 4 Taal, Xosa, Zulu 5 Sotho, Swazi, Xhosa 7 Ndebele 9 Afrikaans
South America: 7 Spanish 10 Portuguese
Southeast Asia: 3 Tai, Yao 5 Malay
Southwest Indian: 4 Hopi, Zuni 5 Yaqui 6 Navaho, Navajo, Papago
Spain: 6 Basque 9 Castilian
Sri Lanka: 5 Tamil 10 Singhalese
Sudan: 7 Shilluk
suffix: 3 -ese
Suriname: 6 Arawak
Switzerland: 6 French, German 7 Italian
Tanzania: 5 Masai 6 Maasai
Thailand: 3 Lao 5 Hmong
Togo: 3 Ewe, Gbe
unit: 3 syl. 8 syllable
Vietnam: 5 Hmong
Wales: 5 Welsh 6 Celtic
Wisconsin Indian: 3 Fox, Sac 4 Sauk 9 Winnebago
written ~: 5 prose
Zaire: 4 Luba
Zimbabwe: 7 Ndebele

language __: 3 lab 4 arts

__ language: 4 body, sign 6 modern, mother

__-Language: 4 Sein

Language of Clothes, The
author: Alison Lurie

languid: 3 wan 4 blah, dopy, dull, easy, lazy, limp, logy, poky, slow, weak 5 dopey, faint, heavy, inert, moony, tardy, tepid, weary, wimpy 6 draggy, drowsy, feeble, infirm, leaden, otiose, pining, sickly, snoozy, supine, torpid 7 gradual, halting, impeded, lagging, nebbish, warmish, wimpish 8 comatose, crawling, creeping, dawdling, dilatory, dragging, drawn-out, drooping, fatigued, hesitant, inactive, indolent, laid-back, listless, plodding, slothful, sluggish, toddling 9 apathetic, enervated, impassive, leisurely, lethargic, prolonged, snaillike, unhurried 10 deliberate, energyless, languorous, phlegmatic, protracted, spiritless

languidly: 6 lazily, slowly 8 bit by bit 9 leisurely 10 indolently, listlessly

languidness: 5 sloth 6 apathy, phlegm, stupor, torpor 7 boredom, inertia, languor 8 doldrums, dullness, hebetude, laziness, lethargy, slowness 9 inanition, indolence, lassitude, unconcern 10 drowsiness, inactivity, sleepiness, stagnation

languish: 3 ail, ebb, rot, sag 4 fade, fail, flag, long, moon, mope, pine, sigh, wilt 5 brood, droop, faint, sleep, waste, yearn 6 desire, go soft, grieve, hanker, hunger, repine, sicken, snivel, sorrow, suffer, tucker, weaken, wither 7 conk out, decline, despond, dwindle, fatigue 8 get tired, knock out, listless, stagnate, vegetate 9 fizzle out, lie fallow, waste away 10 go to pieces

languishing: 4 limp, mopy, slow, weak 5 faint 6 ebbing, fading, feeble, pining, waning 7 failing, languid, longing, wistful 8 dejected, drawn-out, drooping, flagging, listless, lovelorn 9 declining 10 despairing, despondent, melancholy

languor: 5 ennui, sloth 6 acedia, stupor, torpor 7 fatigue, inertia, latency, laxness, slumber, vacuity 8 hebetude, idleness, inaction, laziness, lethargy, loginess, otiosity, weakness 9 faineance, inanition, indolence, inertness, lassitude, tiredness, torpidity, weariness 10 inactivity, stagnation

languorous: 4 lazy 6 torpid 7 languid 8 listless, sluggish 9 enervated, lethargic

Langway, Rod
milieu: 3 ice 4 rink 5 arena
org.: 3 NHL

Lani: 7 Guinier

Lanier: 3 Bob 6 Sidney, Willie

Lanier, Bob
milieu: 5 court
org.: 3 NBA
sport: 10 basketball

Lanier, Sidney: 4 poet
work: The Marshes of Glynn
The Song of the Chattahoochee
The Symphony
Tiger Lilies

lank: 4 bony, lean, long, slim, tall, thin, wiry 5 boney, eager, gaunt, gawky, rangy, spare, stilt, weedy 6 dainty, gangly, meager, skinny, slight, slinky, svelte, twiggy 7 angular, gawkish, gracile, scraggy, scrawny, slender, spidery, spindly, stringy, willowy 8 angulose, angulous, beanpole, gangling, rawboned 9 beanstalk, emaciated, spindling, sylphlike 10 attenuated, broomstick, extenuated

__ Lanka: 3 Sri

lanky: 4 bony, lean, long, slim, tall, thin, wiry 5 boney, eager, gaunt, rangy, spare, stilt, weedy 6 dainty, gangly, meager, skinny, slight, slinky, svelte, twiggy 7 angular, gracile, scraggy, scrawny, slender, spidery, spindly, stringy, willowy 8 angulose, angulous, beanpole, gangling, rawboned 9 beanstalk, spindling, sylphlike 10 attenuated, broomstick, extenuated

lanner: 4 bird 6 falcon 10 bird of prey

Lanny: 4 Ross 7 Wadkins

lanolin: 3 oil
source: 4 wool 6 fleece

Lanos: 3 car 4 auto 6 Daewoo 10 automobile

lanose: 5 wooly 6 lanate, woolly

Lansbury, Angela: 7 actress
Broadway role: 4 Mame
film: Bedknobs and Broomsticks (1971)
Blue Hawaii (1961)
Court Jester (1956)
The Manchurian Candidate (1962)
The Mirror Crack'd (1980)
National Velvet (1944)
The Picture of Dorian Gray (1945)
State of the Union (1948)
The World of Henry Orient (1964)
TV: Murder, She Wrote
Lansford: 6 Carney
Lansing: 3 Joi 4 city, town 6 Sherry
county: 5 Eaton 6 Ingham 7 Clinton
locale: 8 Illinois, Michigan
river: 5 Grand 8 Red Cedar
Lansing, Sherry
spouse: William Friedkin
Lansky: 5 Meyer
Lanson, Snooky
show: Your Hit Parade
song: It's Almost Tomorrow (1955)
Lantana: 4 city, town
locale: 7 Florida
lantern: 4 lamp 5 light, torch 6 beacon 7 gas lamp
part: 4 wick
lantern __: 3 jaw
__ lantern: 5 magic
__'-lantern: 5 jack-o
Lantern, The
author: Don Marquis
lanthanide: 6 cerium, erbium 7 holmium, terbium, thulium 8 europium, lutetium, samarium 9 neodymium, ytterbium 10 dysprosium, gadolinium, promethium
lanthanum: 5 metal 7 element
Lantz: 6 Walter
lanyard: 4 line, rope 6 hawser 7 cordage
Lanza, Mario: 5 tenor 6 singer
specialty: 5 opera
Lao: 3 She 8 language
neighbor: 3 Tai 4 Thai
Lao-__: 3 tse, tze, tzu
__ Lao: 6 Pathet
Laodice
brother: 5 Paris 6 Hector
parent: 5 Priam 6 Hecuba 7 Priamus
sister: 9 Cassandra
Laon: 4 city, town
locale: 6 France
Laos: 6 nation 7 country
bovine: 7 kouprey
capital: 9 Vientiane
language: 3 Lao 5 Hmong
locale: 4 Asia
money: 2 at 3 att, kip
neighbor: 5 China 7 Myanmar, Vietnam 8 Cambodia, Thailand
people: 4 Miao 5 Hmong
Laotian: 5 Asian
neighbor: 3 Tai 4 Thai
Lao-tzu: 4 sage 6 writer 7 Chinese 11 philosopher
way of ~: 3 Tao 6 Taoism
work: Tao Te Ching
lap: 3 leg, sip 4 fold, lave, lick, loop, purl, slap, turn, wash, wrap 5 bathe, cover, drink, orbit, plash, round, slosh, slurp, stage, swish 6 burble, circle, course, gurgle, ripple, splash, swathe 7 circuit, envelop, overlap, overlie, shingle, swaddle 8 distance, override 9 imbricate
dog: 3 pom 4 peke 6 Yorkie 7 Shih Tzu 9 Pekingese 10 Pomeranian
ender: 3 top 4 wing 5 board 6 streak
form a ~: 3 sit
in the ~ of luxury: 4 posh, rich 5 plush, ritzy, swank 6 swanky 7 upscale 8 affluent, pampered, princely 9 sumptuous, sybaritic
lose a ~: 4 rise 5 arise, get up, stand 7 stand up
of luxury: 5 means, money 6 riches, wealth 7 fortune 8 opulence 9 abundance, affluence 10 gravy train, prosperity
planetary ~: 4 year
starter: 3 dew, ear 4 ship
lap __: 3 dog 4 belt, link, robe
__ lap: 4 bell, pace
__ Lap: 4 Phar
LaPaglia: 7 Anthony
__ la Paix: 5 Rue de
La Palma: 4 isle 6 island
locale: 8 Canaries
La Paz: 4 city, town 7 capital
locale: 6 Mexico 7 Bolivia
see also Spanish
LAPD part: 3 Los 4 Dept. 6 Police 7 Angeles 10 Department
lapel: 4 flap 6 revere, revers
attachment: 4 mike 5 ID tag 9 carnation 10 microphone
attach to a ~: 5 pin on
La Petite Fadette
author: George Sand
lapidary: 6 etcher 7 jeweler 8 engraver 9 loupe user 10 gemologist
concern: 3 gem
measure: 5 carat
lapidify: 6 harden 7 petrify 9 fossilize
lapin: 3 fur 6 rabbit
lapis: 3 gem 5 azure 7 mineral, sky-blue 8 gemstone
lapis lazuli: 3 gem 4 blue 5 azure 7 mineral 8 gemstone
La Placa: 6 Alison
Laplace: 4 city, town 6 Pierre
locale: 9 Louisiana
Laplander: 4 Sami
__ la Plata: 5 Rio de
La Plata: 4 city, port, town
locale: 9 Argentina
La plume __ tante: 4 de ma
lap of __: 6 luxury
La Porte: 4 city, town
locale: 5 Texas 7 Indiana
Lapp: 4 Sami 5 nomad 8 language
neighbor: 4 Finn
lappet: 6 wattle
lapping: 4 purl 6 murmur
sound: 5 slurp 7 swallow
L'Après-midi d'un faune
composer: Claude Debussy
La Presse
locale: 8 Montreal
lapsang: 3 tea
lapse: 3 die, end, err, gap, sin 4 drop, fall, flub, gaff, goof, lull, pass, sink, slip, trip 5 cease, crime, error, fault, guilt, letup, pause, slide, space 6 boo-boo, breach, bungle, elapse, expire, foible, goof-up, hiatus, lacuna, miscue, recede, return, revert, run out, slip up, weaken 7 blooper, blunder, decline, default, descend, descent, failing, failure, frailty, misstep, mistake, neglect, offense, passage, regress, relapse, screw-up, subside 8 fall back, interval, omission, shortage, trespass, weakness 9 backslide, decadence, indecorum, oversight, recession, terminate, violation, worsening 10 aberration, apostatize, degenerate, devolution, infraction, negligence, nonpayment, recidivate, regression, retrograde
__-lapse: 4 time
lapsed: 3 ago 4 gone, lost, over, past 6 no more, run out 7 elapsed, expired 9 forgotten 10 terminated
lapses: 6 errata
lapsus: 4 slip 5 error 7 mistake 9 oversight
Laptev Sea
feeder: 4 Lena
locale: 6 Russia 7 Siberia
laptop: 2 PC 8 computer, notebook
lapwing: 4 bird 5 pewit 6 peewit
La Quinta: 4 city, town
locale: 10 California
lar: 6 gibbon 7 primate
Lar: 9 Lubovitch
Lara
author: Lord Byron
Lara __: Tomb Raider: 5 Croft
Lara Croft... (2001 film)
cast: Angelina Jolie, Noah Taylor, Jon Voight
director: Simon West
Lara Flynn __: 5 Boyle
Laraine: 3 Day 6 Newman
ex: 3 Leo
Laramie: 4 city, town 5 range
athletes: 7 Cowboys
locale: 3 Wyo. 4 Colo. 7 Wyoming 8 Colorado
__ Laramie: 4 Fort
Lara's Theme
composer: Maurice Jarre
larboard: 4 left, port
L'Arc en Ciel
artist: Erté
larcenist: 5 thief
larcenous: 7 crooked 8 thieving, thievish
larceny: 4 lift 5 crime, heist, pinch, steal, theft, touch 7 robbery 8 burglary, stealing, thievery, thieving 9 pilfering 10 purloining
__ larceny: 5 grand, petit, petty
larch: 4 tree 7 conifer 8 hardwood, tamarack
cousin: 4 pine
product: 4 cone
lard: 3 oil 6 enrich, grease 7 garnish 9 lubricate 10 shortening
get the ~ out: 5 defat
substitute: 4 oleo
larder: 5 store 6 pantry 8 cupboard
lardhead: 3 oaf 5 looby
Lardner, Ring: 6 writer 8 satirist
work: Gullible's Travels
Haircut
June Moon
The Love Nest and Other Stories
You Know Me, Al
lardy: 3 fat 4 oily 5 fatty 6 greasy 7 buttery 8 blubbery 9 fattening
lardy-__: 5 dardy
Laredo: 3 SUV 4 city, Jeep, town 5 Jaime
locale: 5 Texas
__ Laredo, Mexico: 5 Nuevo
__ la Renta: 7 Oscar de
La Repasseuse
painter: Edgar Degas
lares and __: 7 penates
large: 3 big 4 full, huge, size, tidy, vast, wide 5 ample, broad, bulky, giant, grand, great, gross, hefty, hulky, jumbo, plump, roomy, super 6 chubby, goodly, mighty, portly, robust 7 booming, copious, hulking, immense, liberal, mammoth, massive, sizable, stately, titanic 8 abundant, colossal, enormous, generous, gigantic, handsome, king-size, majestic, outsized, oversize, populous, sizeable, spacious, sweeping, thumping, towering, whapping, whopping 9 capacious, cavernous, corpulent, excessive, expansive, extensive, grandiose, Herculean, humongous, overgrown, plentiful, ponderous, prominent, well-known 10 commodious, embonpoint, exorbitant, family-size, gargantuan, majestical, monumental, overweight, prodigious, stupendous, tremendous, voluminous, well-padded
combining form: 3 meg- 4 macr-, magn-, maxi-, mega- 5 macro-, magni-, megal- 6 megalo-
name meaning ~: 5 Grant
large-__: 4 type 5 print, scale
__ large: 4 writ 5 by and 6 living
__ Large Array: 4 Very
large-bellied
see obese
large-hearted: 4 good, kind, mild, nice, soft 5 noble 6 benign, decent, genial, gentle, giving, humane, loving, tender 7 clement, lenient, liberal, pitying 8 generous, gracious, merciful
largely: 4 very 5 quite 6 mainly, mostly, widely 7 as a rule, broadly, chiefly, grandly, greatly, overall 8 lavishly 9 copiously, generally, in a big way, liberally, primarily 10 abundantly, far and wide, generously, imposingly, prodigally
largemouth: 4 bass, fish
largeness: 4 area, bulk, mass, room, size 5 range, reach, scope, space, width 6 extent, height, spread, volume 7 bigness, breadth, caliber, expanse 8 capacity, fullness, grandeur, hugeness, infinity, vastness 9 amplitude, immensity, magnitude
Largent, Steve
sport: 8 football
larger: 4 more 7 greater

get ~: 4 grow 5 build, swell, widen 6 dilate, expand 7 augment, broaden, develop, fill out, magnify 8 increase
on one side: 4 awry 5 askew 6 canted, uneven 7 crooked, unequal 8 cockeyed, lopsided, top-heavy 9 irregular 10 off-balance, unbalanced
part: 4 mass 8 majority
than: 5 above
than life: 4 epic 5 famed 6 famous, heroic 7 awesome 8 heroical, immortal, imposing, mythical, renowned, towering 9 legendary 10 celebrated, impressive
Larger Than Life (1999 song)
artist: Backstreet Boys
large-scale: 4 mass, vast, wide 5 broad, macro 6 cosmic 7 blown-up, diffuse, sizable 8 catholic, cosmical, expanded, extended, far-flung, sizeable, sweeping 9 extensive, wholesale
largesse: 3 aid 4 alms, boon, dole, gift, perk 5 bonus, grant 6 bounty, giving 7 charity, present, stipend, subsidy 8 bestowal, donation, free hand, generous, gratuity 9 emolument, endowment, sweetener 10 altruistic, benevolent, charitable, generosity, lavishness, liberality, thoughtful
largest: 3 max. 4 most 7 maximum
largo: 5 music, tempo 6 slowly
faster than ~: 5 lento
slower than ~: 5 grave
Largo: 3 key 4 city, town
locale: 7 Florida
___ Largo: 3 Key
lariat: 4 rope 5 lasso, reata, riata 6 tether 10 cow catcher
loop: 5 noose
larine: 8 gull-like
Larissa: 4 moon
planet: 7 Neptune
lark: 3 fun 4 bird, joke, play, whim 5 antic, caper, fling, frisk, prank, revel, spree 6 cavort, frolic, gambol, picnic 7 rollick, warbler 8 songbird 9 adventure, high jinks 10 shenanigan
as a ~: 5 in fun 10 humorously
ender: 4 spur
like a ~: 5 happy
starter: 3 sky, tit 4 wood 6 meadow
larking: 6 jovial
larkish: 8 sporting, sportive
larklike bird: 5 pipit
larkspur: 5 plant 6 annual, flower
Lark, The
author: Jean Anouilh
l'Arlésienne
composer: Georges Bizet
Laroche: 3 Guy
La Rochefoucauld: 8 François
La Ronde
author: Arthur Schnitzler
La Rondine
composer: Giacomo Puccini
LaRosa, Julius employer: Arthur Godfrey
Larouche: 6 Lyndon
La Rouchefoucauld, François de: 6 French, writer
Larrocha, Alicia de: 7 pianist, Spanish
Larroquette: 4 John
larrup: 3 hit, tan, tar 4 beat, flog, swat, whap, whip 5 pound, spank, whang, whomp 6 attack, thrash
Larry: 4 Bird, Bowa, Doby, Fine, Kert, King, Mize, Page 5 Adler, Brown, Drake, Gates, Groce, Hovis, Mahan, Niven, Parks, Verne 6 Blyden, Csonka, Gatlin, Graham, Hagman, Holmes, Peerce, Storch, Walker, Wilcox, Wilson 7 Gelbart, Mathews, Parrish 8 Linville, MacPhail, McMurtry
colleague: 3 Moe 5 Curly, Shemp
Larry ___ Melman: 3 Bud
Larry King Live
genre: 4 talk
network: 3 CNN
Larry, Moe and Curly: 4 trio 7 Stooges
Larry Sanders Show, The (HBO sitcom)
cast: Garry Shandling (Larry Sanders)
Jeffrey Tambor (Hank Kingsley)
Rip Torn (Artie)
Lars: 6 Hanson 7 Onsager, Porsena 10 Gustafsson
Larsen: 3 Don
Larsen ___ Shelf: 3 Ice
Larson: 4 Gary, Jack, John 8 Jonathan 9 Nicolette
play: 4 Rent
Larter: 3 Ali
LaRue: 4 Lash
larus: 4 gull
larva: 3 bug 4 grub, zoea 5 nymph, redia 6 insect, maggot 7 cutworm, tadpole 8 silkworm, wriggler
crustacean ~: 4 zoea
mayfly ~: 5 nymph
successor: 4 pupa 5 imago, pupae
larval: 6 masked 8 immature
laryngitic: 5 husky, raspy, rough 6 hoarse 7 throaty 8 croaking, gravelly
larynx: 8 voice box
affliction: 5 croup
opening: 7 glottis
Lary, Yale
sport: 8 football
Las ___: 5 Tunas, Vegas 6 Cruces, Palmas
Las ___, CO: 6 Animas
Las ___ night: 5 Vegas
lasagna: 5 pasta 7 noodles
alternative: *see* pasta
filling: 4 meat 6 cheese 7 ricotta
land of ~: 5 Italy
LaSalle: 4 Eriq
La Salle: 3 car 4 auto, city, town 10 automobile
locale: 6 Canada, Québec 7 Ontario
La Scala
highlight: 4 aria
home: 5 Milan
production: 5 opera
La Scala di ___: 4 Seta
Lascaux: 4 cave
locale: 6 France
lascivious: 4 blue, lewd 5 bawdy, crude, gross, nasty, randy 6 coarse, ribald, smutty, steamy, vulgar, wanton, X-rated 7 immoral, obscene, raunchy 8 indecent, off-color, unchaste, uncurbed 9 dissolute, libertine, offensive, salacious 10 licentious, profligate
Las Cruces: 4 city, town
athletes: 6 Aggies
locale: 9 New Mexico
school: 4 NMSU
la señorita: 4 ella
laser
cousin: 5 maser
crystal: 4 ruby
gas: 4 neon
output: 3 ray
part: 3 yag
radar: 5 lidar
sound: 3 zap
laser ___: 4 beam, disc, disk 7 printer, surgery
Laser: 3 car 4 auto 8 Plymouth 10 automobile
laser printer
alternative: 6 ink-jet
part: 4 drum
resolution: 3 dpi
lash: 3 hit, tie, wag 4 beat, bind, flay, flog, hurt, moor, whip 5 abuse, baste, pound, scold, smack, spank, strap, truss, whale 6 attack, batter, berate, buffet, cilium, hammer, pummel, punish, secure, strike, thrash 7 bawl out, belabor, blister, censure, chew out, lambast, scourge, tell off, tie down, upbraid, wear out 8 chastise, lambaste, ridicule, satirize, tear into 9 castigate, fulminate, horsewhip 10 flagellate, tongue-lash, vituperate
down a sail: 4 frap
holder: 3 lid 6 eyelid
out at: 3 hit 5 abuse, blast, chide, knock 6 assail, attack, berate, insult, rail at, rebuff, rebuke, revile, vilify 7 censure, lay into, put down, reprove, rip into, tell off 8 lambaste 9 criticize, light into, reprimand
starter: 3 eye 4 back, whip
lash ___: 3 out 4 line, rail
___-lash: 6 tongue
Lash: 5 LaRue
Lasher
author: Anne Rice
lashes
give twenty ~: 4 cane, drub, whip 5 flail 6 larrup 7 scourge 10 flagellate
___-lashing: 6 tongue
Lasker: 6 Albert 7 Emanuel
Lasker, Emanuel forte: 5 chess
Lasky: 5 Jesse 6 Victor
Lasorda: 5 Tommy 6 Dodger 7 manager
Las Palmas: 4 city, port, town
locale: 5 Spain
lass: 3 gal, kid 4 girl, maid, miss, Scot 5 bairn, missy, woman, youth 6 damsel, female, maiden 7 colleen 8 fraülein 9 debutante, young lady, youngster 10 young woman
counterpart: 3 lad
starter: 4 wind
Lasse: 9 Hallström
Lassen: 4 peak 5 mount 7 volcano 8 mountain
locale: 8 Cascades 10 California
Lasser, Louise
spouse: Woody Allen
lassie: 3 gal, kid 4 girl, maid, miss, Scot 5 bairn, missy, woman, youth 6 damsel, female, maiden 7 colleen 8 fraülein 9 debutante, young lady, youngster 10 young woman
Lassie: 3 dog 6 canine, collie
Lassie Come Home (1943 film)
cast: Donald Crisp, Roddy McDowall, May Whitty
lassitude: 5 ennui 6 apathy, stupor, torpor 7 boredom, fatigue, languor, laxness, malaise 8 doldrums, dullness, idleness, inaction, laziness, lethargy, weakness 9 disregard, tiredness, weariness 10 exhaustion, feebleness, inactivity, sleepiness
lasso: 4 rope, trap 5 catch, reata, riata 6 lariat, rope in
loop: 5 noose
wielder: 5 roper
last: 3 end, run 4 go on, hold, live, stay, wear 5 abide, exist, final, finis, go far, least, omega, stick 6 behind, ending, endure, finale, finish, hang on, hold up, latest, linger, lowest, newest, remain, utmost 7 closing, extreme, finally, meanest, parting, persist, subsist, supreme, survive, to sum up, weather 8 after all, at the end, continue, crowning, curtains, eventual, farthest, furthest, hindmost, in the end, previous, rearmost, remotest, swan song, terminal, trailing, ultimate 9 aftermost, antipodal, bitter end, climactic, finishing, in the rear, outermost, uttermost 10 brave it out, completion, concluding, conclusive, definitive, lattermost, most recent, stay around, stick it out, ultimately
of a series: 5 omega
last ___: 4 name, post, word 5 laugh, licks, straw 6 hurrah, minute, resort 7 quarter
last ___ not least: 3 but
last-___: 4 born 5 ditch
Last ___: 6 Supper
Last ___ Hero: 6 Action
Last ___ in Paris: 5 Tango
Last ___ I Saw Paris, The: 4 Time
Last ___ Man, The: 5 Angry
Last ___ Mohicans, The: 5 of the
Last ___ of Pompeii, The: 4 Days
Last ___ Red Hot Lovers: 5 of the
Last ___ Saw Paris, The: 5 Time I
Last ___ Show, The: 7 Picture
Last ___, The: 4 Leaf 6 Detail, Hurrah, Tycoon 7 Emperor
Last ___ to Brooklyn: 4 Exit
Last ___ to Clarksville: 5 Train
___ Last: 6 Safety
Last Action Hero (1993 film)
cast: F. Murray Abraham, Art Carney, Arnold Schwarzenegger
Last Act Is a Solo, The
author: Robert Anderson
Last Boy Scout, The (1991 film)
cast: Chelsea Field, Damon Wayans, Noble Willingham, Bruce Willis
Last Bus, The
author: Athol Fugard

last but not __: 5 least
Last Carousel, The
author: Nelson Algren
__ Last Case: 6 Trent's
Last Chance Gulch site: 6 Helena
Last Chance to Turn Around (1965 song)
artist: Gene Pitney
Last Dance (1978 song)
artist: Donna Summer
Last Date (1960 song)
artist: Floyd Cramer
Last Days
author: Joyce Carol Oates
Last Days of Pompeii: 4 book
author: Edward Bulwer-Lytton
character: 4 Ione 5 Burbo, Julia, Nydia 6 Diomed
Last Detail, The (1973 film)
cast: Jack Nicholson, Randy Quaid
director: Hal Ashby
last-ditch: 4 wild 5 final 6 all-out 7 do-or-die, frantic, gasping 8 frenzied
Last Emperor, The (1987 film)
cast: Joan Chen, John Lone, Peter O'Toole
director: Bernardo Bertolucci
role: 4 P'u Yi
Last Enchantment, The
author: Mary Stewart
Last Exit to Brooklyn
author: Hubert Selby Jr.
Last Frontier, The: 6 Alaska
last-in, __-out: 5 first
lasting: 3 old 6 stable 7 abiding, chronic, durable, endless, eternal, forever, undying 8 constant, enduring, lifelong, long-term, unending, unwaning 9 chronical, continual, deathless, incessant, indelible, long-lived, memorable, perennial, permanent, perpetual, unabating, unceasing 10 continuing, deep-rooted, inerasable, monumental, perdurable, persisting, unchanging
impression: 4 mark, scar 5 brand
starter: 4 ever
__-lasting: 4 long
lastingness: 4 time 6 length 9 longevity
Last Kiss (1999 song)
artist: Pearl Jam
last lamenting
Donne's ~ thing: 4 kiss
Last Leaf, The
author: O. Henry
lastly: 7 finally 10 ultimately
last-minute: 4 late 5 hasty 6 put off, recent 7 belated, cursory, hurried, offhand, overdue 8 careless, dilatory, slapdash, slipshod 9 haphazard 10 unpunctual
__ last minute: 5 at the
Last Night (song)
artist: Az Yet, Mar-Keys
__ Last Night ...: 5 About
Last of His Tribe subject: 4 Ishi
Last of Sheila, The (1973 film)
cast: Dyan Cannon, James Coburn, James Mason, Raquel Welch
Last of the Mohicans, The
author: James Fenimore Cooper
character: 4 Cora 5 Alice, David, Gamut, Magua, Munro, Natty, Uncas 6 Bumppo, Duncan 7 Hawkeye, Heyward 12 Chingachgook
Last of the Mohicans, The (1992 film)
cast: Daniel Day Lewis, Russell Means, Madeleine Stowe
Last of the Plainsmen, The
author: Zane Grey
Last of the Red Hot __: 5 Mamas
Last of the Red Hot Lovers: 4 film, play
author: Neil Simon
cast: Alan Arkin, Sally Kellerman, Paula Prentiss, Renee Taylor
director: Gene Saks
Last of the Vikings, The
author: Johan Bojer
character: 4 Lars
Last of the Wine, The
author: Mary Renault
character: 5 Lysis 7 Alexias
Last one __ rotten egg!: 4 in's a 5 in is a
L.A. Story (1991 film)
cast: Marilu Henner, Steve Martin, Victoria Tennant
Last Pad, The
author: William Inge
Last Picture Show: 4 film 5 novel
author: Larry McMurtry
cast: Timothy Bottoms, Jeff Bridges, Ellen Burstyn, Ben Johnson, Cloris Leachman, Cybill Shepherd
director: Peter Bogdanovich
setting: 5 Texas
last-place finisher: 5 loser
Last Puritan, The
author: George Santayana
La Strada (1954 film)
cast: Richard Basehart, Anthony Quinn
director: Federico Fellini
__ last resort: 3 as a
Last Resorts, The
author: Cleveland Amory
Last Samurai, The (2003 film)
cast: Tom Cruise
Last Seduction, The (1994 film)
cast: Linda Fiorentino, Bill Pullman, J.T. Walsh
director: John Dahl
Last Seen Wearing
author: Hillary Waugh
__ Lasts Forever: 7 Nothing
__ Last Stand: 7 Custer's
Last Supper, The: 5 mural
artist: Leonardo da Vinci
city: 5 Milan
cup: 5 Grail
Last Tango in Paris (1973 film)
cast: Marlon Brando, Maria Schneider
director: Bernardo Bertolucci
like: 6 X-rated
Last Temptation of Christ, The (1988 film)
cast: Willem Dafoe, Barbara Hershey, Harvey Keitel
director: Martin Scorsese
__ last theorem: 7 Fermat's
Last Time I Saw Paris, The
composer: Jerome Kern, Oscar Hammerstein
Last Time, The (1965 song)
artist: Rolling Stones
Last Trail, The
author: Zane Grey
Last Train to Clarksville (1966 song)
artist: Monkees
Last Tycoon: 4 film 5 novel
author: F. Scott Fitzgerald
cast: Tony Curtis, Robert De Niro, Robert Mitchum, Jeanne Moreau
character: 4 Pete 5 Brady, Stahr, Whyte, Wylie 6 Monroe 7 Cecilia
director: Elia Kazan
Last Wagon Train, The
author: Zane Grey
Last Waltz, The (1978 film)
cast: The Band, Bob Dylan, Neil Young
director: Martin Scorsese
last-word: 3 hip, mod, new, now 4 chic 5 faddy, smart 6 latest, modish, trendy, with-it 7 current, stylish 8 up-to-date 9 happening
Last Word in Lonesome __, The: 4 is Me
__ la suisse: 5 eggs à
Las Vegas: 4 city, town
area: 5 Strip
athletes: 6 Rebels 8 Wolf Pack
casino: 3 MGM, Rio 4 Aria, Wynn 5 Luxor 6 Bally's, Encore, Mirage, Sahara 7 Caesar's, Harrah's, Palazzo, Riviera 8 Bellagio, Flamingo, MGM Grand 9 Excalibur, Tropicana
county: 5 Clark
devotee: 5 gamer 7 gambler
employee: 6 dealer 7 pit boss 8 croupier
gas: 4 neon
locale: 3 Nev. 6 Nevada
lure: 4 keno, slot 5 poker 6 casino 8 baccarat, roulette
newspaper: 3 Sun
school: 4 UNLV
show: 5 revue 6 review
trade show: 6 Comdex
Las Vegas __: 5 night
__ Las Vegas: 4 Diva, Viva 7 Leaving
Laszlo: 4 Erno, Ilsa 6 Victor
Lat.: 4 lang.
see also Latin
Latakia
locale: 5 Syria
latch: 3 bar, dam 4 bolt, clog, cork, hasp, hook, lock, plug, seal, shut 5 block, catch, cinch, clamp, close, dam up 6 clog up, fasten, lock up, plug up, seal up, secure, stop up 7 close up, closure, padlock, seal off, shutter 8 blockade, button up, fastener, make fast, obstruct 9 fastening 10 hook and eye
door ~: 3 bar 4 bolt, hasp
draw the ~: 4 open 5 unbar
ender: 3 key 6 string
onto: 4 glom, grab 5 seize 6 absorb 7 acquire, possess, procure, receive
piece: 5 U-bolt
place: 4 door, exit, gate 5 entry 6 portal 7 postern 8 entrance
sound: 4 snap 5 clack, click
starter: 3 pot 6 throat
latch __: 4 hook, onto 6 needle
late: 3 new, old 4 once, past, slow 5 fresh, tardy 6 behind, bygone, former, held up, hung up, modern, put off, recent, stayed 7 belated, defunct, delayed, extinct, lagging, onetime, overdue, past due, quondam, tardily 8 advanced, deceased, departed, detained, dilatory, long gone, previous, sometime, untimely 9 erstwhile, nocturnal, not on time, postponed, preceding 10 after hours, behind time, delinquent, last-minute, unpunctual
be ~ for: 4 miss
ender: 5 comer
get ~: 6 darken
make ~: 4 keep 5 delay 6 detain, hang up, hinder, hold up, impede, retard 7 bog down, set back 8 slow down 10 buttonhole
not early or ~: 5 on cue 6 on time
of ~: 3 new 4 anew 5 newly 6 afresh 7 freshly, just now 8 hitherto, latterly, recently, until now 9 these days 10 not long ago
prefix: 3 neo-
state: 6 arrear 7 arrears
too little too ~: 6 paltry 9 deficient, half-baked, shortfall 10 inadequate
late __: 3 fee 4 pass, show 6 charge 7 bloomer
late-__: 5 night
Late __ Apley, The: 6 George
Late Child, The
author: Larry McMurtry
latecomer: 7 dallier, dawdler, laggard, parvenu, upstart 8 newcomer, slowpoke 9 arriviste
lateen: 4 sail
lateen-rigged
craft: 3 dau, dow 4 dhow
Late George Apley, The
author: J.P. Marquand
lately: 3 new 4 anew 5 newly 6 afresh 7 freshly, just now 8 hitherto, latterly, recently 9 these days 10 not long ago
Lately (song)
artist: Divine, Jodeci
latency: 5 sleep 6 torpor 7 languor, slumber 8 abeyance, dormancy 10 inactivity, quiescence, suspension
lateness: 4 stay 5 delay 6 holdup 8 deferral 10 suspension
late-news hour: 6 eleven
late-night
hangout: 3 bar, pub 4 dive 5 joint 6 lounge, saloon, tavern 7 barroom, gin mill, taproom 8 alehouse, grogshop, taphouse 9 roadhouse
host: 3 Jay 4 Dave, Leno 9 Letterman
hour: 3 one, two 4 four 5 one a.m., three, two a.m. 6 four a.m. 7 three a.m.
latent: 5 inert 6 covert, hidden, secret, torpid, unripe, unseen, veiled 7 abeyant, dormant, passive 8 implicit, inactive, inherent, possible, sleeping, untapped 9 concealed, intrinsic, invisible, out of view, potential, quiescent, unexposed 10 in abeyance, smoldering,

suppressed, underlying, undetected, unreactive, unrealized, unviewable
latent __: 4 heat
later: 4 anon, next, then **5** after **6** future, in a bit, in time, mañana, not now, not yet **7** by and by, ensuing, goodbye **8** au revoir, eventual, farewell, in a while **9** after a bit, afterward, following, posterior, proximate **10** afterwards, before long, downstream, sequential, subsequent, succeeding, thereafter
hold for ~: 5 sit on, table
not ~: 3 now **5** ahead, today **6** at once, before **7** earlier **8** directly, previous, right now, right off **9** forthwith, in advance, on the spot, preceding, right away **10** at this time, the present, this minute
not ~ than: 4 till, up to **5** until **7** through
prefix: 4 meta-, post- **5** infra-
see you ~: 3 bye **4** ciao, ta-ta **5** adieu, adios, aloha **6** bye-bye, shalom, so long **7** cheerio, goodbye **8** au revoir, farewell, sayonara, toodle-oo **10** hasta luego
sooner or ~: 3 yet **4** anon **5** after **6** at last, in a bit, in time **7** by and by, finally, later on, someday **8** in a while, in the end, sometime **9** afterward, hereafter **10** before long, eventually, inevitably
than: 5 after **6** behind
Later!: 3 bye **4** ciao, ta-ta **5** adieu, adios, aloha, I'm off, see ya **6** bye-bye, bye now, I'm gone, shalom, so long **7** cheerio, goodbye **8** au revoir, farewell, sayonara, toodle-oo
in French: 5 adieu
in Hawaiian: 5 aloha
in Italian: 4 ciao
in Latin: 3 ave **4** vale
in Spanish: 5 adios
lateral: 4 side **7** oblique, sideway **8** crabwise, edgeways, flanking, sidelong, sideward, sideways, sidewise, skirting **10** side-by-side
combining form: 5 pleur- **6** pleuro-
measurement: 4 span **5** girth, width **6** spread **7** breadth **9** broadness
starter: 3 tri, uni **5** multi
laterally: 6 beside **7** abreast, sideway **8** edgeways, edgewise, sidelong, sideways, sidewise
nautically: 5 abeam
__ later date: 3 at a
Late Show feature: 5 rerun
Late Show, The (1977 film)
cast: Art Carney, Bill Macy, Lily Tomlin
latest: 3 new **4** last, news, rage **5** faddy, final, fresh, vogue **6** gossip, latter, modern, modish, newest, skinny, trendy **7** current, in vogue **8** last word, ultimate, up-to-date **10** dernier cri
full of the ~: 5 newsy
the ~: 4 dope, news, poop, word **5** scoop, today **6** modern **7** current, just out, lowdown, release **8** bulletin, contempo, up-to-date **9** headlines, news flash **10** communiqué
thing: 4 mode, rage **5** trend **7** fashion
__ latest: 5 at the
__ Latest Flame: 3 His
__ late than never: 6 better
Late Walk, A
author: Robert Frost
latex: 5 paint **6** rubber
lath: 4 beam, slat **5** board, strip
lather: 4 beat, flap, foam, fuss, head, snit, soap, stew, suds, wash, whip **5** cream, fever, froth, scrub, spume, state, storm, sweat, tizzy, yeast **6** bustle, clamor, dither, frenzy, hassle, hoopla, hubbub, tumult **7** bubbles, fluster, turmoil, twitter **8** cleanser, perspire, soapsuds **9** agitation, commotion, confusion **10** hullabaloo, turbulence
in a ~: 5 het up, upset **6** pacing **7** worried **9** perturbed **10** distraught, distressed
source: 4 soap **7** shampoo
work into a ~: 5 rouse **6** arouse, foment, incite, stir up **7** agitate, inflame, provoke **9** instigate
lathery: 5 foamy, soapy, sudsy **6** bubbly, frothy **7** foaming **8** unrinsed
lathy: 4 long, tall, thin
__ Latifah: 5 Queen
Latin: 5 Cuban **8** Bolivian, language **9** Argentine, Brazilian, caballero, Dominican
case: 6 dative
dance: 5 conga, mambo, samba, tango **6** cha-cha
forerunner: 5 Oscan
words handle: 4 ansa
see also Spanish
Latin __: 4 Rite **5** cross **7** America, Quarter
__ Latin: 3 pig
Latina: 7 Chicana **8** señorita
see also Spanish
Latin America
see Central America, South America, Spanish
__ Latin from Manhattan: 5 She's a
Latino: 8 Hispanic
see also Spanish
Latinwords
year: 5 annum
Latin words
abbr.: 3 etc. **4** et al.
adverb: 3 hoc, quo
art: 3 ars
bear: 4 ursa **5** ursus
behold: 4 ecce
being: 4 esse
bird: 4 avis
birds: 4 aves
bones: 4 ossa
day: 4 diem
earth: 5 terra
eggs: 3 ova
eight: 4 octo
existence: 4 esse
god: 3 deo
goddess: 3 dea
gods: 3 dei
good: 4 bene
greeting: 3 ave
he loves: 4 amat
here: 3 hic
he was: 4 erat
I: 3 ego
I believe: 5 credo
I came: 4 veni
I conquered: 4 vici
I forbid: 4 veto
I love: 3 amo
in other words: 5 id est
in the same place: 4 ibid.
I saw: 4 vidi
it was: 4 erat
journey: 4 iter
kind: 4 alma
king: 3 rex
land: 5 terra
law: 3 lex
life: 4 esse
love: 4 amor
mass: 5 missa
monarch: 3 rex
moon: 4 luna
mouths: 3 ora
no: 3 non
one: 3 una
others: 4 alia
passage: 4 iter
phrase: 6 et alia, et alii, in esse
possessive: 3 sua
pray: 3 ora
prayer: 5 kyrie
pronoun: 3 sua **4** quis
road: 3 via **4** iter
room: 6 camera
route: 3 via
salutation: 3 ave **4** vale
she loves: 4 amat
sister: 5 soror
so: 3 sic
sun: 3 sol
that is: 5 id est
therefore: 4 ergo
thing: 3 res
this: 3 hic
thus: 3 sic **4** ergo
to be: 4 esse
uncommon: 4 rara
water: 4 aqua
way: 4 iter
wings: 4 alae
without: 4 sine
you love: 4 amas
latissimus __: 5 dorsi
latitude: 3 run **4** play, room, span **5** range, reach, scope, space, sweep, swing, width **6** extent, laxity, leeway, margin, spread **7** breadth, compass, freedom, liberty, license **8** free hand **9** elbowroom, situation **10** indulgence, liberality
segment: 3 arc **6** degree, minute, second
__ latitudes: 5 horse
latitudinarian: 4 easy, fair, just **7** lenient, liberal, neutral **8** amenable, balanced, catholic, straight, tolerant, unbiased **9** equitable, impartial
latitudinous: 5 broad
latke: 7 pancake
La Tosca
sculptor: Erté
La Toya: 7 Jackson
sister: 5 Janet
La Traviata: 5 opera
composer: Giuseppe Verdi
role: 5 Flora **6** Annina, Valery **7** Alfredo, Bervoix, Douphol, Gastone, Germont, Giorgio **8** Giuseppe, Violetta
song: 4 aria
latrine: 2 WC **3** can, loo **4** john **5** privy **6** lounge, toilet **8** bathroom, lavatory, men's room, outhouse, rest room, toilette **10** ladies' room, powder room
Latrobe: 4 city, town **8** Benjamin
locale: 4 Penn.
Latrobe, Benjamin: 9 architect
lats neighbors: 3 abs
Lattanzi: 4 Matt
latte: 6 coffee **8** espresso
place for a ~: 4 café **6** bistro
topping: 5 froth
latter: 5 final **6** latest, modern, recent, second **7** closing **8** eventual, hindmost, rearmost **9** following, posterior **10** concluding
Latter-__ Saint: 3 day
latter-day: 6 modern, recent
latterly: 8 recently
lattermost: 4 last **6** latest **8** ultimate
lattice: 3 net, web **4** grid, mesh **5** frame, grate, grill **6** screen **7** grating, network, tracery, trellis **8** filagree, filigree, fretwork, openwork **9** fillagree, structure
ender: 4 work
piece: 4 lath
latticework: 4 grid, mesh **5** arbor, frame, grill **6** screen **7** grating, trellis **8** openwork
La Tulipe __: 5 Noire
Latvia: 6 nation **7** country
capital: 4 Riga
legislature: 6 Saeima
money: 3 lat
neighbor: 4 Lith. **6** Russia **7** Belarus, Estonia **9** Lithuania
once: 3 SSR
region: 6 Baltic
river: 5 Dvina
Latvian: 4 Balt, Lett **5** Rigan **8** language
laud: 4 hail, hymn, sing **5** adore, bless, boost, cry up, ensky, exalt, extol, honor **6** admire, extoll, praise, puff up, revere, salute, stroke **7** acclaim, approve, beatify, build up, commend, flatter, glorify, hosanna, lionize, magnify, worship **8** encomium, eulogize, hand it to, venerate **9** celebrate, recommend **10** compliment, panegyrize
laudable: 4 fine, nice, okay **5** great, legit, moral, noble **6** of note, proper, worthy **7** ethical, stellar **8** all right, pleasant, pleasing, splendid, superior, terrific **9** admirable, agreeable, deserving, estimable, excellent, exemplary, praisable, reputable, wonderful **10** acceptable, beneficial, creditable
laudably: 4 ably, to a T, well **6** nicely **7** adeptly, capably **8** expertly, properly, suitably, worthily **9** admirably, fittingly, perfectly **10** skillfully, splendidly, swimmingly, thoroughly
laudanum: 4 drug **7** anodyne **8** narcotic
laudation: 5 honor, kudos **6** eulogy,

homage, praise, salute **7** acclaim, plaudit, tribute **8** accolade, encomium, flattery, good word **9** extolment, panegyric **10** compliment, exaltation
laudatory: 7 glowing **9** adulatory, approving, favorable, praiseful **10** eulogistic, flattering
__ laude: 3 cum
Lauder: 5 Estée, Harry **6** makeup
rival: 4 Coty **5** Arden, Arpel **6** Chanel
__ Lauderdale, FL: 4 Fort
Lauderhill: 4 city, town
locale: 7 Florida
Lauer: 4 Matt
laugh: 3 yak, yok, yuk **4** crow, grin, ha-ha, howl, jest, joke, roar, yock, yuck **5** burst, mirth, scoff, smile, snort, te-hee, whoop **6** cackle, giggle, guffaw, hahaha, haw-haw, heehee, scream, shriek, tee-hee, titter **7** break up, chortle, chuckle, crack up, snicker, snigger **8** fracture **9** convulsed, make merry, merriment **10** cachinnate
at: 4 hoot, jeer, mock **5** scoff, scorn, taunt **6** deride **7** lampoon, snicker, snigger **8** belittle, ridicule **9** make fun of
derisive ~: 3 hah, heh **4** he he, hoot **5** fleer, snort **6** cackle
getter: 3 wag, wit **4** card **5** clown, cutup **6** jester **7** buffoon, farceur **8** comedian, humorist, jokester, quipster
get the last ~: 7 triumph
hearty ~: 3 yuk **4** boff, ho ho, howl, roar **6** guffaw
make ~: 5 amuse, cheer **6** divert, regale, tickle **7** delight **9** entertain
off: 6 ignore **7** dismiss, forgive, neglect **8** overlook, ridicule, shrug off, sneeze at **9** disregard
starter: 5 horse
syllable: 3 har, hee
laugh __: 3 off **4** away, line, riot **5** track
laugh __ court: 5 out of
__ laugh: 4 last **5** belly, horse
laughable: 4 camp, joky, rich, riot **5** campy, comic, droll, funny, inane, jokey, nutty, silly, witty **6** absurd, har-har, jocose, scream, stupid **7** amusing, asinine, bizarre, comedic, comical, jocular, joshing, mocking, risible, unusual **8** derisive, derisory, farcical, gelastic, humorous, mirthful **9** diverting, eccentric, facetious, fantastic, hilarious, ludicrous, quizzical **10** ridiculous
Laughable Lyrics
author: Edward Lear
Laugh at Me (1965 song)
artist: Sonny and Cher
Laugh-In
bit: 4 skit
name: 3 Dan **4** Arte, Judy, Lily, Rick, Ruth **5** Rowan **6** Martin
laughing: 3 gay **5** happy, jolly, merry, riant, sunny **6** cheery, jovial, joyful **7** gleeful, jesting, roaring, smiling, yukking **8** cackling, cheerful, giggling, grooving, jubilant, mirthful **9** chuckling, guffawing, lightsome, tittering **10** flying high, snickering, sniggering
ender: 5 stock
matter: 3 fun, wit **4** gags **5** farce, humor, jests, jokes **6** comedy, gaiety, levity **8** drollery, raillery **10** wisecracks
no ~ matter: 3 bad, big **4** grim, ugly **5** grave, heavy, major, tough **6** urgent **7** serious, weighty **8** grievous, sobering, terrible **9** dangerous, important **10** formidable
laughing __: 3 gas **4** gull **5** hyena **6** matter **7** jackass
Laughing (1969 song)
artist: Guess Who
__ Laughing: 4 Exit **5** Enter
Laughing All the Way
author: Barbara Howar
Laughing Boy
author: Oliver La Farge
Laughing Cavalier
artist: Frans Hals
laughing jackass: 4 bird **10** kookaburra
Laughing Matter, The
author: William Saroyan
laughingstock: 3 ass **4** butt, dupe, fool, goat, joke **5** chump, sport **6** sucker **7** fall guy, mockery, schnook
make a ~ of: 8 ridicule
laugh in one's __: 6 sleeve
Laughlin: 3 AFB, Tom **6** Robert
Laughlin, Robert: 8 Nobelist **9** physicist
laughs: 3 fun **5** mirth **9** amusement, diversion, merriment **10** recreation
just for ~: 5 in fun **7** as a joke, as a lark **8** jokingly **10** humorously
Laugh's __, The: 4 on Me
__ laughs at probabilities: 4 Fate
laughter: 3 has, yuk **4** crow, glee, ha-ha, peal, roar, yuck **5** mirth, shout, snort, sound, sport **6** cackle, gaiety, giggle, guffaw, heehaw, shriek, titter **7** chortle, chuckle, crack-up, gesture, howling, snicker, snigger **8** giggling, hilarity **9** amusement, chuckling, jocundity, merriment, rejoicing
burst of ~: 4 gale, peal, roar
evoke: 5 amuse **6** tickle
exclamation: 4 ha-ha **5** te-hee **6** haw-haw, tee-hee
Laughter in the Rain (1974 song)
artist: Neil Sedaka
Laughter on the 23rd Floor
author: Neil Simon
Laughton, Charles: 5 actor
film: Advise & Consent (1962)
The Barretts of Wimpole Street (1934)
The Big Clock (1948)
The Canterville Ghost (1944)
The Hunchback of Notre Dame (1939)
It Started With Eve (1941)
Mutiny on the Bounty (1935)
The Night of the Hunter (1955)
The Private Life of Henry VIII (1933, AA)
Spartacus (1960)
Witness for the Prosecution (1957)
Young Bess (1953)
spouse: Elsa Lanchester
laugh up one's __: 6 sleeve
launch: 3 bow **4** boat, cast, fire, hurl, jump, open, toss **5** begin, drive, eject, fling, found, heave, lance, pitch, set up, shoot, sling, start, throw, usher **6** let fly, let rip, propel, send up, tackle **7** barrage, bombard, deliver, kick off, lead off, liftoff, pioneer, preface, project, rollout, send off, usher in **8** catapult, commence, dispatch, get going, initiate, put to sea, set about **9** discharge, enter upon, instigate, institute, introduce, originate, send forth, undertake, water taxi **10** embark upon, inaugurate
area: 3 pad
cancel a ~: 5 abort, scrub
deep-space ~: 5 probe
org.: 3 ESA, RKA **4** JAXA, NASA
launch __: 3 pad
__ launcher: 6 rocket **7** grenade
launching: 7 baptism, opening **10** conception
launching __: 3 pad
launder: 4 lave, wash **5** bathe, clean, rinse, scrub **7** cleanse, correct, deterge, rectify **8** legalize **9** disinfect
laundered: 5 clean, snowy **6** washed **8** dirtless, spotless, unsoiled **10** immaculate
launderer: 4 maid **5** valet **6** au pair **7** servant **8** domestic
laundering: 9 housework
Laundromat
fixture: 5 drier, dryer
like a ~: 6 coin-op
laundry: 4 wash **5** chore **7** washing **8** cleaning **9** housework
collection: 4 lint
cycle: 4 soak, spin **5** rinse **7** presoak
detergent: 3 All, Biz, Era, Fab, Yes **4** Bold, Dash, Gain, Surf, Tide, Wisk **5** Cheer, Dreft, Purex **6** Calgon, Dynamo, Oxydol **7** Octagon **9** Ivory Snow
do a ~ job: 3 dry **4** fold, iron, wash **5** wring
holder: 3 bin **6** basket, hamper
list: 6 agenda
loss, maybe: 4 sock
need: 4 soap **6** bleach **8** softener **9** detergent
problem: 5 grime, stain **6** grease
quantity: 4 load **6** bundle, hamper
worker: 6 ironer
laundry __: 4 list
__ laundry: 5 dirty
Lauper, Cyndi
song: All Through the Night (1984)
Change of Heart (1986)
Girls Just Want to Have Fun (1984)
The Goonies 'R' Good Enough (1985)
I Drove All Night (1989)
She Bop (1984)
Time After Time (1984)
True Colors (1986)
What's Going On (1987)
Laura: 4 Bush, Dern, Nyro, Tate **5** Baugh, Innes, Keene **6** Ashley, Hobson, Linney, Petrie, Prepon **7** Ingalls, Jackson **8** Branigan, Esquivel, Leighton **10** San Giacomo
to George W.: 4 wife
Laura (1944 film)
cast: Judith Anderson, Dana Andrews, Vincent Price, Gene Tierney, Clifton Webb
director: Otto Preminger
Laura Bush, __ Welch: 3 née
Laura Ingalls __: 6 Wilder
Laura Lee: 4 Hope
Laura Z. __: 6 Hobson
laureate: 4 poet **5** famed, noted **6** famous **7** honored, praised **8** immortal, renowned **9** acclaimed
__ laureate: 4 poet
laurel: 3 bay **4** tree **5** title **6** wreath **7** bay tree **9** evergreen **10** blue ribbon
tree: 3 bay **7** avocado, camphor **8** cinnamon **9** sassafras
wear the ~: 3 win **6** attain **7** achieve, conquer, edge out, succeed, triumph
wreathe with ~: 4 fete, hail, laud **5** award, crown, exalt, grace, honor **6** credit, praise, reward, salute **7** acclaim, adulate, applaud, commend, dignify, ennoble **8** decorate, eulogize **9** recognize **10** compliment
Laurel: 4 city, Stan, town
locale: 8 Maryland
Laurel and Hardy: 3 duo **4** pair, team
Laurel Canyon (2002 film)
cast: Christian Bale, Kate Beckinsale, Frances McDormand, Natascha McElhone
laurels: 4 fame, gold **5** award, badge, crown, glory, honor, kudos, prize **6** credit, honors, praise, renown, reward, trophy **7** acclaim, victory **8** accolade, gold star, prestige **10** decoration
Lauren: 4 Joey, Wood **5** Holly, Ralph, Tewes, Velez **6** Bacall, Chapin, Graham
rival: 4 Dior **5** Beene, Klein **6** Armani **7** Versace **9** St. Laurent
Laurence: 6 Binyon, Harvey, Sterne **7** Housman, Olivier **9** Fishburne **10** Luckinbill
Laurens: 10 van der Post
Laurentians: 5 range **9** mountains
locale: 6 Canada
__ Laurentiis: 6 Dino De
Laurents: 6 Arthur
Laurey's aunt: 5 Eller
Lauria: 3 Dan
Laurie: 4 Hugh **5** Piper **6** London **7** Metcalf
__ Laurie: 5 Annie
Lauritz: 8 Melchior
Lauryn: 4 Hill
Lausanne: 4 city, town
canton: 4 Vaud
Lautenberg: 3 Sen. **5** Frank **7** senator
Lauter: 2 Ed
lav
see lavatory
lava: 4 rock **5** magma **6** basalt, ejecta, pumice, scoria **7** mineral **8** obsidian, pahoehoe, rhyolite
from ~: 7 igneous
let out ~: 4 spew, spue **5** erupt
material: 3 ash **4** slag **6** basalt,

pumice, scoria **8** obsidian
move like ~: 4 flow, ooze **6** spread
Lava: 4 soap
alternative: *see* soap
Lava __: 4 Lamp
lavabo: 5 basin **8** washbowl
lavage: 7 washing
Lavagetto: 6 Cookie
Laval: 4 city, town
locale: 6 Canada, France, Quebec
Lava Lamp: 3 fad
lavalava: 5 pareo, pareu, skirt
lavaliere: 6 locket **7** jewelry
__-la-Vallée: 5 Marne
La Valse
composer: Maurice Ravel
Laval University
location: 6 Canada, Quebec
lavation: 4 bath, wash **8** ablution **9** cleansing
lavatory: 2 WC **3** can, loo **4** bath, john **5** privy **6** lounge, shower, toilet **7** latrine **8** bathroom, lavatory, men's room, outhouse, restroom, toilette, washroom **10** ladies' room, powder room
sign: 3 men **5** gents, in use, women **6** ladies **8** occupied **9** gentlemen
lave: 3 lap **4** wash **5** bathe, clean **6** shower, wash up **7** clean up, deterge, launder, scrub up, shampoo
lavender: 4 herb **5** color, mauve, plant, shrub **6** bluish, flower, purple **7** blueish
family: 4 mint
flower: 3 mum **4** lily **5** aster **6** orchid, thrift, violet **7** thistle **8** trillium, wistaria, wisteria **9** candytuft
relative: *see* purple color
__ lavender: 5 oil of
La vendetta: 4 aria
LaVerne: 7 Andrews
sister: 5 Patty **6** Maxene
Laverne & Shirley (ABC sitcom)
cast: Phil Foster (Frank De Fazio)
Betty Garrett (Edna Babish)
David L. Lander (Squiggy)
Penny Marshall (Laverne De Fazio)
Michael McKean (Lenny)
Eddie Mekka (Carmine Ragusa)
Cindy Williams (Shirley Feeney)
Laver, Rod: 7 netster **9** tennis pro
contemporary: 4 Ashe
milieu: 5 court
Lavi: 6 Dahlia
La Vida
author: Oscar Lewis
__ La Vida Loca: 5 Livin'
__ la vie: 4 c'est
La Vie en Rose
singer: Edith Piaf
Lavigne: 5 Avril
La Ville Noire
author: George Sand
Lavin, Linda
spouse: Ron Leibman
TV: Alice
lavish: 4 free, give, heap, lush, much, posh, pour, rain, rich, wild **5** ample, fancy, flush, grand, haute, plush, ritzy, showy, spend, swank, waste **6** bestow, costly, deluge, expend, flashy, frilly, glitzy, lordly, ornate, pamper, plenty, shower, swanky, wanton **7** copious, fritter, liberal, opulent, profuse, replete, riotous, scatter **8** abundant, effusive, generous, gorgeous, handsome, princely, prodigal, prolific, splendid, squander, wasteful **9** bountiful, decorated, dissipate, elaborate, excessive, expansive, expensive, exuberant, go through, luxuriant, luxurious, plentiful, profusive, sumptuous, unsparing, unstinted, unthrifty **10** first-class, immoderate, impressive, inordinate, munificent, openhanded, ornamented, profligate, run through, thriftless, thrust upon, unstinting
don't ~: 5 skimp
lavishly: 9 in a big way
lavishness: 6 bounty, excess, luxury **7** largess, surplus **8** largesse, richness **10** exuberance
__ la vista: 5 hasta
La vita nuova
author: Dante
Lavoisier, Antoine: 7 chemist
Lavoris: 9 mouthwash
alternative: 3 Act **4** Plax **5** Scope **6** Signal **9** Listerine **10** Fluorigard
law: 3 act **4** code, rule, tabu, writ **5** axiom, canon, edict, maxim, order, power, taboo, truth **6** assize, decree, police, ruling **7** command, dictate, formula, mandate, measure, precept, statute, theorem **8** covenant, exigence, exigency, standard **9** authority, criterion, enactment, ordinance, postulate, principle **10** due process, injunction, principium, profession, regulation
according to ~: 5 legal, licit
arm of the ~: 2 PD **6** police **7** marshal, sheriff
breach of ~: 5 crime, wrong **7** misdeed, offense **9** violation **10** misconduct, wrongdoing
break a ~: 3 sin **6** breach, offend **7** disobey, do wrong, infract, violate **8** encroach, infringe **9** disregard **10** transgress
brush with the ~: 4 bust **5** pinch, run-in **6** arrest, collar
by ~: 7 legally
church ~: 5 canon, dogma **7** precept **8** doctrine
combining form: 4 nomo-
deg.: 2 J.D **3** LL.B., LL.D, LL.M, S.J.D
ender: 3 man, men, yer **4** suit **5** giver, maker **6** making **7** breaker
enforcement grp.: 3 FOP, PBA
expert: 5 judge **6** legist **9** barrister
first-year ~ student: 4 one L
go to ~: 3 sue, try **6** accuse, appeal, indict, summon **7** arraign, contest, dispute **8** file suit, litigate **9** fight over, prosecute **10** put on trial
in French: 3 loi
in Italian: 5 legge
in Latin: 3 lex
in Spanish: 3 ley
lay down the ~: 4 rule **5** order, scold **6** decree, demand, direct, govern, insist **7** command, control, dictate, mandate **8** bulldoze, domineer, proclaim, regulate
make into ~: 4 pass **5** enact **9** institute, legislate
outside the ~: 4 tabu **5** taboo **6** banned **7** illegal, illicit **8** criminal, improper, unlawful, verboten, wrongful **9** felonious, forbidden **10** prohibited
partner: 5 order
pertaining to ~: 5 jural
starter: 5 scoff
to Mr. Bumble: 3 ass
unwritten ~: 4 lore **5** mores, usage **8** folkways, practice **9** tradition **10** convention
within the ~: 3 due **5** clean, legal, legit, licit, valid **6** kosher, proper **8** judicial, rightful **9** allowable, canonical, statutory **10** admissible, legitimate, prescribed, sanctioned
see also law terms, legal
law __: 5 clerk
law __ jungle: 5 of the
law-__: 4 hand **7** abiding
__ law: 4 blue, case **5** canon, civil, leash, lemon, Salic **6** Boyle's, common, Curie's, Hooke's, Joule's, public, shield, Snell's, sunset **7** Ampère's, blue-sky, Hubble's, martial, Mendel's, Pascal's
__-law: 5 son-in
Law: 4 Jude **5** Bonar
__ Law: 4 Corn, Ohm's **6** Burke's, Mosaic **7** Murphy's
law-abiding: 4 good **5** solid **6** honest **7** duteous, dutiful, orderly, upright **8** obedient, straight **9** compliant, righteous **10** upstanding
law and __: 5 order
LaWanda: 4 Page
lawbreaker: 4 . perp **5** felon **7** runaway **8** criminal, evildoer, internee, prisoner **9** desperado **10** delinquent
lawbreaking: 5 crime **6** breach, felony **7** misdeed, offense
lure into ~: 4 hook, trap **5** decoy, set up, trick **6** entice, entrap, reel in, suck in **8** inveigle
Lawes: 5 Henry
Lawford: 3 Pat **5** Peter **8** Patricia
Lawford, Peter: 5 actor
spouse: Patricia Kennedy
lawful: 3 due **4** fair, good, just **5** jural, legal, legit, licit, right, ruled, valid **6** judged, kasher, kosher, passed, proper, vested **7** allowed, condign, decreed, enacted, ordered, regular **8** bona fide, bone fide, enforced, enjoined, innocent, judicial, mandated, official, ordained, rightful **9** allowable, by the book, canonical, commanded, juridical, legalized, permitted, protected, statutory, warranted **10** aboveboard, admissible, authorized, legislated, legitimate, on the level, sanctioned
lawfully: 5 right, truly **6** justly **7** validly **10** rightfully, virtuously
lawfulness: 5 order, right **7** justice **8** justness, legality, validity **10** legitimacy
lawgiver: 5 Solon **7** senator **8** Congress **10** legislator
law is __, The: 4 a ass
Law, Jude
role: 5 Alfie
lawless: 3 bad **4** evil, wild **5** rowdy **6** fierce, savage, unruly **7** chaotic, illicit, radical, riotous, untamed, violent, warlike **8** anarchic, criminal, despotic, mutinous, reckless, recusant, unlawful, wrongful **9** barbarous, heterodox, insurgent, piratical, seditious, turbulent, tyrannous **10** anarchical, despotical, disordered, disorderly, infringing, nihilistic, rebellious, traitorous, ungoverned, unorthodox, unpeaceful
Lawless: 4 Lucy
role: 4 Xena
lawlessness: 4 riot **5** anomy, chaos, crime **6** anomie, felony, mutiny, piracy, racket, revolt **7** abandon, anarchy, bribery, license, mob rule, roguery **8** disorder, iniquity, nihilism, sedition, uprising, violence
lawmaker: 3 sen. **5** solon **7** senator **8** politico **9** statesman **10** legislator, politician
lawmaking body: 5 legis. **6** senate **8** Congress
lawman: 3 cop **4** Earp **6** deputy **7** sheriff **9** constable, Wyatt Earp **10** Matt Dillon
lawn: 3 sod **4** park, turf, yard **5** grass, green, sward **6** cotton, fabric, swarth **8** backyard **10** greensward
care brand: 5 Ortho
chemical: 4 lime **10** fertilizer
cover: 3 sod **5** grass **6** fescue, redtop, zoysia **7** festuca
do ~ work: 3 mow, sow **4** seed, weed
ender: 5 mower
equipment: 5 edger, mower
fix a ~: 3 sod **5** resod
game: 5 bocce, bocci, roque **6** boccia, boccie, tennis **7** croquet
item: 6 chaise
like some ~s: 5 soddy, weedy
mowing the ~: 4 task **5** chore
pest: 4 mole
weed: 6 arnica
work on the ~ again: 5 remow
lawn __: 5 chair, party **6** tennis **7** bowling
lawnmower
brand: 4 Toro **5** Deere
feature: 5 blade
path: 5 swath **6** swathe
Lawnmower Man, The (1992 film)
cast: Pierce Brosnan, Jeff Fahey
law of __: 5 sines
law of __ numbers: 5 large
law of diminishing __: 7 returns
law of the __: 4 mean **6** jungle
Law of the Lash (1947 film)
cast: Lash LaRue
Law & Order (NBC drama)
cast: George Dzundza (Det. Sgt. Max Greevey)
Angie Harmon (Abbie Carmichael)

LA

Steven Hill (Adam Schiff)
Christopher Noth (Det. Mike Logan)
Jerry Orbach (Det. Lennie Briscoe)
Sam Waterston (Jack McCoy)
character: 2 DA
Law & Order: Criminal Intent (NBC drama)
cast: Eric Bogosian (Daniel Ross)
Vincent D'Onofrio (Robert Goren)
Kathryn Erbe (Alexandra Eames)
Jeff Goldblum (Zach Nichols)
Chris Noth (Mike Logan)
Law & Order: Special Victims Unit (NBC drama)
cast: Dann Florek (Donald Cragen)
Mariska Hargitay (Olivia Benson)
Ice-T (Fin Tutuola)
Christopher Meloni (Elliot Stabler)
John Munch (Richard Belzer)
Lawrence: **2** D.H., T.E. **4** city, Joey, pope, town, Welk **5** Block, Carol, Klein, saint, Steve, Tracy, Vicki **6** Ernest, Eusden, Kasdan, Martin, Sharon, Taylor, Thomas **7** Durrell, pontiff, Sanders, Tibbett **8** Florence, Gertrude
athletes: **8** Jayhawks
city on the St. ~: **5** Laval, Sorel
locale: **6** Arabia, Kansas **7** Indiana
Lawrence, Carol
spouse: Robert Goulet
__ Lawrence College: **5** Sarah
Lawrence, D.H.: **6** writer **7** British
work: Birds, Beasts, and Flowers
Etruscan Places
Kangaroo
Lady Chatterley's Lover
The Lost Girl
Mornings in Mexico
Pansies
The Plumed Serpent
The Rainbow
Reflections on the Death of a Porcupine
Sea and Sardinia
Sons and Lovers
The Trespasser
Twilight in Italy
The White Peacock
Women in Love
Lawrence, Ernest: **8** Nobelist **9** physicist
Lawrence, Gertrude
Broadway role: **4** Anna
film bio: **4** Star
Lawrence of Arabia (1962 film)
cast: Sir Alec Guinness, Jack Hawkins, Arthur Kennedy, Peter O'Toole, Anthony Quayle, Anthony Quinn, Claude Rains, Omar Sharif
composer: Maurice Jarre
director: David Lean
locale: **5** Aqaba **6** desert
__ Lawrence Seaway: **5** Saint
Lawrence, Steve
spouse: Eydie Gorme
Lawrence, T.E.: **6** writer **7** British, soldier
work: Seven Pillars of Wisdom
Lawrence, Vicki
role: **4** Mama
song: The Night the Lights Went Out in Georgia (1973)
TV: The Carol Burnett Show, Mama's Family
Lawrenceville: **4** city, town
locale: **7** Georgia
lawrencium: **7** element
Laws of Our Fathers, The
author: Scott Turow
__-law student: **3** pre
lawsuit: **4** bill, case **5** cause, claim, fight, trial **6** action **7** contest, dispute **8** argument, replevin **9** assumpsit, court case **10** accusation, indictment, litigation
award: **5** costs **7** damages **10** reparation
beneficiary: **4** usee
cause: **4** tort **5** libel
law terms
against: **5** in rem
by word of mouth: **5** parol
country: **4** pais
eldest: **4** aine
hinder: **5** debar
husband: **3** vir
intermediate: **5** mesne
lease: **6** demise
legal: **5** licit **6** de jure
minor: **5** petit
negligence: **6** laches
not final: **4** nisi
prohibit: **5** estop
take: **5** seise
thing: **3** res
wife: **4** feme
wrongful act: **4** tort
Lawton: **5** Frank **6** Chiles
Law West of the Pecos, The: **4** Bean
lawyer: **3** att. **4** atty. **5** agent **6** arguer, jurist, legist **7** adviser, advisor, counsel, pleader, proctor **8** advocate, attorney, defender **9** ABA member, barrister, counselor, solicitor **10** counsellor, legal eagle, mouthpiece, procurator
concern: **4** case, jury **6** client
deg.: **3** LL.B., LL.D.
expel a ~: **6** disbar
group: **3** ABA, bar
hire a ~: **3** sue **5** plead, press **6** accuse, appeal, indict **7** contest **8** litigate, petition **9** fight over, prosecute
holding: **6** escrow
hurdle: **4** jury **7** bar exam
title: **3** esq. **7** esquire
__ lawyer: **5** trial
lax: **4** easy, idle, kind, lazy, limp, mild, soft **5** broad, hasty, inert, loose, relax, slack, vague **6** asleep, casual, draggy, flabby, gentle, kindly, remiss, sloppy, torpid **7** clement, dormant, flaccid, general, inexact, lenient, passive, ruthful, slacken, sparing **8** careless, derelict, dilatory, flexible, inactive, indolent, laid-back, merciful, overeasy, placable, slipshod, slothful, sluggish, tolerant, unstrict, yielding **9** assuasive, compliant, dissolute, easygoing, forgetful, forgiving, imprecise, imprudent, indulgent, leisurely, lethargic, negligent, oblivious, sedentary, shapeless, unheedful, unmindful **10** behindhand, delinquent, disengaged, forbearing, inaccurate, incautious, indefinite, licentious, neglectful, nonchalant, permissive, regardless, unexacting, unthinking
become ~: **6** go soft
not ~: **5** harsh, rigid, stern, tough **6** severe, strict **7** careful
LAX
airport NW of ~: **3** SFO
laxity: **5** sloth **7** freedom, license, neglect **8** latitude, laziness **9** disregard, looseness, oversight, slackness, unconcern **10** negligence, remissness, sloppiness
laxly: **9** any old way
laxness: **5** sloth **6** apathy **7** inertia, languor, neglect **8** idleness, laziness, lethargy **9** fainéance, indolence, lassitude, passivity, slackness, stolidity **10** negligence, remissness
Laxness, Halldór: **6** writer **8** Nobelist
lay: **3** bet, fix, put, set **4** cite, game, plan, rest, sink, site, tune **5** hatch, level, lodge, music, place, plant, quiet, stick, still, verse, wager **6** ballad, burden, charge, devise, gamble, hazard, impose, impute, instal, locate, melody, racket, saddle, set out, settle, spread **7** amateur, appease, arrange, ascribe, concoct, deposit, flatten, install, present, produce, profane, recline, secular, set down **8** contrive, encumber, inexpert, position, temporal **9** attribute, chalk up to, establish **10** put forward
a finger on: **5** touch
an egg: **4** bomb, bust, fail, flop, lose, slip, trip **5** flunk **6** blow it, falter **7** blunder, founder, go under, go wrong, misstep, stumble, wash out **8** fall flat, flounder **9** strike out
aside: **4** drop, save **5** defer, delay, shunt, table **6** ignore, put off, reject, shelve **7** abandon, discard, suspend **8** file away, renounce, salt away **9** disregard, pay no mind **10** pigeonhole, relinquish
at one's door: **3** tax **5** blame **6** accuse, charge, finger **7** censure **8** sentence **9** attribute, implicate **10** credit with
at one's feet: **4** give **5** offer **6** extend, tender **7** present, proffer, propose
away: **4** pile, save **5** amass, cache, hoard, set by, stash, store **6** garner, retain **7** deposit, reserve **8** set apart, set aside **9** economize, stockpile
back: **4** lull **5** relax, slack **6** relent **7** slacken **9** lighten up, lose speed
bare: **3** air **4** blab, leak, skin, tell **5** admit, strip **6** denude, expose, relate, reveal, show up, unfold, unmask, unveil **7** breathe, confess, divulge, exhibit, let slip, publish, uncloak, uncover **8** blurt out, disclose, unburden **9** broadcast, make known **10** make public
by: **4** keep, save, stow **5** amass, hoard, lay up, put by, stock **6** garner, load up **7** build up, procure, put away, store up **8** conserve, cumulate, hold on to, put aside, salt away, set apart, set aside **10** accumulate
by the heels: **3** bag **4** bust, grab, nail **5** catch, pinch, run in, seize **6** arrest, collar, detain, pick up, pull in, snap up, snatch **7** capture **9** apprehend
down: **3** set **4** drop **6** give up, impose, record **7** recline **8** turn over **9** prescribe, stipulate, surrender **10** relinquish
down the law: **4** rule **5** order, scold **6** decree, demand, direct, govern, insist **7** command, control, dictate, mandate **8** bulldoze, domineer, proclaim, regulate
ender: **3** man, men, off, out **4** away, back, over **5** about, woman, women **6** people, person
eyes on: **3** spy **4** espy, spot, view **5** stare
for: **4** lurk **5** prowl, sculk, set up, skulk **6** ambush, entrap, waylay **8** surprise
hold of: **3** get, nab **4** find, grab, grip, jerk, land, pull, snag, stop, take **5** catch, clasp, grasp, seize, twist, usurp, wrest **6** clinch, clutch, collar, locate, snatch **7** capture, grapple **8** come into
into: **4** whip **5** fight, fly at, set at, set on, smack **6** assail, attack, bang up, rebuke, thwack **7** assault, lambast, set upon **8** chastise, lambaste, let fly at **9** criticize, fustigate, haul off on, lash out at
it on: **4** fawn **5** boast, drool, jolly **6** cajole, overdo, pander, praise, slaver **7** blarney, flatter, talk big, wheedle **8** butter up, go too far, overplay, pile it on, softsoap **9** dish it out, embroider **10** exaggerate
low: **5** floor, level **7** flatten **9** knock down, overpower
off: **2** ax **3** axe, can, end **4** boot, drop, fire, halt, idle, oust, quit, sack, stop **5** cease, let be, let go, let up, spell **6** bounce, cool it, dehire, desist, give up **7** cashier, dismiss, drum out, release, suspend **8** get rid of, pink-slip, unemploy **9** discharge, stop doing, terminate **10** leave alone, take a break
on: **4** levy **5** apply **6** beetle **7** present **8** credit to **10** credit with
on the line: **4** risk
open: **4** tell **6** expose, unveil **7** uncover **8** endanger
out: **3** map, pay, zap **4** give, lend, plan, plot, show, stun **5** chart, put up, spend **6** assort, define, design, detail, expend, invest, sketch **7** arrange, diagram, display, exhibit, itemize, outline, program, specify **8** disburse, simplify **9** delineate **10** illustrate

over: 5 delay 8 postpone
siege to: 4 gird 5 beset, box in, hem in 6 attack, begird, circle 7 besiege, fence in 8 blockade, encircle, surround 9 beleaguer, close in on, encompass
starter: 3 way
the foundation: 5 begin, set up 6 launch 7 develop, kick off 8 commence 9 establish, institute, introduce, originate 10 inaugurate
the groundwork: 4 plan 5 draft, found, frame, set up, shape, start 6 create, draw up, launch 7 develop, provide 8 initiate 9 establish, formulate, institute, introduce, spearhead 10 anticipate, trailblaze
to: 6 attack
up: 4 harm, hurt, keep, save, shot 5 amass, hoard, lay in, store 6 garner, injure, obtain 7 confine, disable, put away, reserve 8 conserve, cumulate, preserve, salt away, set apart, set aside 9 indispose 10 accumulate, two-pointer
waste to: 4 raid, ruin, sack, undo 5 harry, smash, smite, wreck 6 ravage 7 consume, destroy, pillage, plunder, ransack 8 desolate, freeboot 9 depredate
: 3 low, off, out 4 away, back, down, into, it on, open, over 5 an egg, aside, waste

LA

lay __ land: 5 of the
lay __ on: 4 eyes
lay __ the law: 4 down
lay __ the line: 4 it on
lay __ thick: 4 it on
lay __ to: 5 claim, siege
lay-__: 3 ups
__-Lay: 5 Frito
layabout: 5 idler 6 truant 7 dawdler, lounger, shirker, slacker 10 ne'er-do-well
lay an __: 3 egg
lay at one's __: 4 door
layaway __: 4 plan
Lay Down (1970 song)
artist: Edwin Hawkins Singers, Melanie
Lay Down Sally (1978 song)
artist: Eric Clapton
lay down the __: 3 law
__ Lay Dying: 3 As I
layer: 3 bed, hen, ply 4 band, coat, film, leaf, seam, skin, slab, tier, vein 5 cover, crust, level, scale, sheet, strip 6 course, folium, lamina, pullet, streak, stripe, veneer 7 blanket, coating, lacquer, stratum 8 covering, laminate, snowfall 9 thickness 10 lamination, substratum
atmospheric ~: 5 ozone
combining form: 5 ptych- 6 ptycho-, strati-
outer ~: 4 bark, coat, hull, rind, skin 5 crust, shell 6 cortex 7 coating 8 covering 10 integument
starter: 4 mine 5 brick
thin ~: 4 film 5 sheet 6 lamina
layer __: 4 cake
__ layer: 5 cloud, ozone
layette
item: 6 bootee, bootie 9 crib sheet, stretchie
user: 4 babe, baby 6 infant 7 neonate, newborn
laying
it on the line: 4 free, open 5 bluff, blunt, frank, plain, vocal 6 abrupt, candid, direct, square 7 sincere, up-front 8 explicit, truthful 10 forthright, from the hip, point-blank, unreserved
laying on of hands: 8 blessing
lay it __ line: 5 on the
Lay it __!: 4 on me
lay it on __: 5 thick
Layla (1972 song)
artist: Eric Clapton
Lay Lady Lay (1969 song)
artist: Bob Dylan
layman: 7 amateur 8 civilian 9 nonexpert
__ lay me...: 4 Now I
Layne: 5 Bobby
layoff: 3 RIF 4 lull 6 hiatus, recess 7 cutback, interim 8 furlough, interval, stoppage 9 cessation, discharge, dismissal
on ~: 8 leisured 9 unengaged
Lay off!: 6 stop it
lay of the __: 4 land
Lay of the Last Minstrel, The
author: Walter Scott
lay one's __ on: 4 eyes 6 finger
lay one's __ on the table: 5 cards
layout: 3 map 4 plan, site 5 chart, draft, setup 6 design, format, scheme, spread 7 diagram, display, outline, purpose 8 proposal 9 blueprint, floor plan, formation, geography 10 ground plan
layover: 4 stay, stop 7 sojourn 8 stopover 9 overnight
layperson: 4 laic 6 laical, member, novice 7 amateur, recruit, secular 8 believer, follower, neophyte, outsider 9 proselyte 10 dilettante
lay to __: 4 rest
Lay Your Hands on Me (song)
artist: Bon Jovi, Thompson Twins
Lazar, Swifty: 5 agent
Lazarus: 4 Emma, Mell
Lazarus, Emma: 4 poet
work: By the Waters of Babylon
Dance to Death
The New Colossus
Lazarus Laughed
author: Eugene O'Neill
laze: 3 lag, lie 4 bask, idle, loaf, loll, rest 5 amble, dally, mosey, relax, spend, stall, tarry, while 6 dawdle, linger, loiter, lounge, trifle, veg out 7 fritter, goof off, hang out, saunter 8 fool away, kill time, lallygag, lollygag, straggle 9 bum around, do nothing, lie around, sit around 10 dillydally, hang around, take it easy, take it slow
Lazenby: 6 George
Lazer __: 3 Tag
lazily: 9 languidly
laziness: 5 sloth 6 acedia, apathy, laxity, torpor 7 inertia, languor, laxness 8 dullness, hebetude, idleness, lethargy, otiosity 9 fainéance, indolence, lassitude, passivity, slackness, stolidity, torpidity 10 dreaminess, drowsiness, inactivity, negligence, remissness, sleepiness, stagnation, torpidness
LaZonga: 3 Mme. 6 Madame
__ lazuli: 5 lapis
lazy: 3 lax 4 dull, idle, logy, slow 5 inert, slack, tardy, tired, weary 6 asleep, draggy, drowsy, loafer, otiose, remiss, sleepy, snoozy, supine, torpid 7 dormant, laggard, lagging, languid, loafing, out of it, passive, unready 8 careless, comatose, dallying, dilatory, feckless, flagging, inactive, indolent, lifeless, slothful, sluggish, trifling 9 apathetic, do-nothing, leisurely, lethargic, loitering, sedentary, shiftless, somnolent, unhurried 10 disengaged, languorous, neglectful, slow-moving
be ~: 4 idle, loaf, loll 5 drift, evade, shirk, stall 6 dawdle, loiter, lounge, piddle, slouch, sprawl 7 hang out 8 kill time, malinger, slack off, slow down, vegetate 9 bum around, goldbrick, sit around, waste time 10 dillydally, knock about, take it easy
ender: 5 bones
in a ~ way: 4 idly
one: 5 drone, idler, sloth, Susan 6 loafer
Susan: 4 tray 6 server
lazy __: 5 bones, Susan
Lazy
composer: Irving Berlin
lazybones: 4 poke 5 idler 6 loafer, slouch, truant 7 dawdler, goof-off, laggard 8 loiterer, slugabed, sluggard 9 do-nothing, goldbrick
bane: 3 job 4 work 5 labor 8 exertion
__ Lazy River: 3 Up a
Lazzeri, Tony: 6 Yankee
lb.: 2 wt. 4 meas.
fraction: 2 oz.
__ l Baltimore, The: 3 Hot
LBJ: 3 Dem. 4 pres.
Library site: 6 Austin
predecessor: 3 JFK
successor: 3 RMN
see also Lyndon B. Johnson
LCD
cousin: 3 CRT
part of ~: 5 least 6 common, liquid 7 crystal, display, divisor
l'chayim: 5 toast 6 Hebrew
ldr.: 3 CEO, gen. 4 cmdr., pres.
platoon ~: 3 NCO
team ~: 3 mgr.
see also leader
LDS center: 4 Utah
Le __: 3 Cid 4 Mans
Le __ d'Arthur: 5 Morte
Le __ de Lahore: 3 Roi
Le __ de Monte Cristo: 5 Comte
Le __ des cygnes: 3 lac
Le __ d'Or: 3 Coq
Le __ du printemps: 5 Sacre
Le __ d'Ys: 3 Roi
Le __ et le Noir: 5 Rouge
Le __ Field: 7 Bourget
Le __, France: 5 Havre
Le __ Goriot: 4 Père
Le __ Soleil: 3 Roi
Le __ Tho: 3 Duc
lea: 5 campo, field, grass, llano, sward, tract, veldt 6 meadow, pampas, swarth 7 pasture, savanna, verdure 8 farmland, savannah 9 grassland 10 meadowland
cry: 3 baa, maa, moo 5 bleat
lady: 3 cow, ewe
Lea: 7 Massari, Salonga 8 Thompson
Lea & __: 7 Perrins
leach: 4 ooze, seep 5 drain, empty 6 filter, strain 7 extract 8 filtrate, wash away 9 lixiviate, percolate
Leach: 5 Robin
Leachman, Cloris: 7 actress
film: The Beverly Hillbillies (1993)
Dillinger (1973)
High Anxiety (1977)
The Last Picture Show (1971, AA)
Young Frankenstein (1974)
TV: The Mary Tyler Moore Show, Phyllis
leachy: 6 porous, spongy 9 sievelike
Leacock: 6 Philip 7 Stephen
lead: 3 tip, top, win 4 clew, clue, draw, edge, head, helm, hero, hint, part, role, rule, sign, star, take, tend 5 actor, bring, cause, chair, excel, front, guide, leash, metal, model, outdo, pilot, point, proof, reach, spark, start, steer, usher 6 direct, escort, forego, govern, hot tip, induce, leader, manage, margin, player, prompt, squire, tether 7 actress, advance, command, conduce, conduct, control, convert, element, go ahead, go first, pioneer, plumbum, precede, presage, preside, prevail, primacy, surpass, top spot, vantage 8 antecede, dominate, evidence, foremost, headline, motivate, outstrip, persuade, premiere, priority, result in, shepherd 9 advantage, chaperone, come first, forefront, front rank, go ahead of, influence, introduce, plurality, principal, run things, spearhead, supervise, supremacy, title role, transcend 10 come before, contribute, first place, indication, mastermind, precedence, set the pace, show the way, suggestion, take charge, trail-blaze
alloy: 6 pewter 7 tinfoil 8 calamine, pot metal 9 type metal 10 gold bronze, soft solder, terne metal, Wood's metal
astray: 4 ruin 6 outwit 7 deprave, mislead 8 outsmart 9 misinform
away: 6 divert 8 distract 9 sidetrack
balloon: 3 dud 4 flop 6 fiasco 7 failure
by the nose: 4 rule, sway 6 induce 7 control 8 persuade 9 brainwash, influence, prevail on
combining form: 5 plumb- 6 plumbo-
down the aisle: 4 seat 5 guide, usher 6 escort, show in 7 conduct 9 accompany
get the ~ out: 3 hie 4 rush 5 hurry 6 hasten
hot ~: 3 tip
in: 5 usher

in the ~: **5** ahead, first, on top **7** in front, winning **8** jubilant, out front, unbeaten
into: **5** usher **9** introduce
into sin: **5** tempt **6** entice, entrap
off: **4** head, open **5** begin, start **6** launch, let rip **7** go ahead, go first, kick off **8** commence, get going, initiate **9** enter upon, introduce, originate **10** inaugurate
on: **3** toy **4** abet, bait, dupe, fool, lure **5** charm, decoy, flirt, shill, tease, tempt, trick **6** allure, delude, entice, entrap, invite, trifle **7** beguile, deceive, mislead **8** hoodwink, intrigue, inveigle **9** disinform, tantalize
ore: **6** galena **8** galanite **9** cerussite **10** vanadinite
pellets: **4** shot
pigment: **6** ceruse
remover: **6** eraser
role: **4** hero, star **7** heroine
sharer: **6** costar
slight ~: **4** edge **9** advantage, head start
source: **3** ore **6** galena **8** galenite **10** vanadinite
take the ~: **4** head, rule **5** exact, order, reign **6** direct, enjoin, govern, handle, manage **7** command, control, dictate, mandate, oversee **8** dominate, instruct **9** officiate, supervise
the way: **5** guide **7** conduct, pioneer, trigger, usher in **8** initiate **9** instigate
to: **4** make **5** cause, guide **6** induce **7** head for, provoke **8** engender, occasion, result in **10** bring about
to believe: **4** hint **5** imply, infer, let on **6** tip off **7** suggest **8** indicate, intimate **9** insinuate
to expect: **3** vow **4** bode, hint **5** augur, swear, vouch **6** assure, pledge, plight **7** betroth, declare, portend, presage, promise, warrant **8** forebode, foreshow, indicate **9** foretoken, guarantee, stipulate **10** foreshadow, take an oath
up to: **5** imply **6** hint at **7** suggest **8** intimate **9** insinuate
weight: **5** plumb
(with): **4** open
lead __: **3** off **4** foot, pipe, time, up to **5** story **6** pencil **7** balloon
lead __ altar: **5** to the
lead __ life: **5** a dog's
lead __ nose: **5** by the
lead __ the garden path: **4** down
lead-__ cinch: **4** pipe
lead-__ gas: **4** free
Lead __: **4** Me On
Lead __ into temptation...: **5** us not
lead a __ life: **4** dog's
lead by the __: **4** nose
lead down the __ path: **6** garden
leaded __: **3** gas **5** glass **7** crystal **8** gasoline
leaden: **4** dull, gray, grey, slow **5** bleak, drear, heavy, hefty, inert, livid **6** dismal, dreary, gloomy, taxing, torpid **7** languid, onerous, weighty **8** lifeless, listless, overcast, sluggish **9** ponderous **10** burdensome, lackluster, oppressive, spiritless
leader: **4** amir, boss, czar, dean, emir, exec, guru, head, king, lead, lion, pres., tsar, tzar **5** ameer, chair, chief, doyen, emeer, guide, nawab, pacer, pilot, ruler **6** gerent, herald, rector, top dog **7** captain, general, headman, magnate, manager, notable, officer, pioneer, skipper, viceroy **8** band boss, cynosure, director, eminence, governor, higher-up, kingfish, luminary, mistress, official, shepherd, superior **9** chieftain, commander, conductor, counselor, dignitary, downspout, executive, harbinger, key player, number one, organizer, precursor, president, principal, sovereign **10** controller, coryphaeus, counsellor, forerunner, legislator, mastermind, notability, pacesetter, politician, ringleader
combining form: **4** -agog **6** -agogue
starter: **4** band, fair, ring **5** cheer
suffix: **4** -arch
__ leader: **4** loss **5** civic, floor, squad
leaderless: **8** unguided
Leader of the Band (1981 song)
artist: Dan Fogelberg
Leader of the Pack (1964 song)
artist: Shangri-las
leaders: **5** brass
Leaders
author: Richard Nixon
leadership: **4** rule, sway **5** power, reign, skill **6** regime **7** command, conduct, control, primacy **8** capacity, guidance, hegemony, pilotage **9** authority, direction, executive, foresight, influence, supremacy **10** initiative
group: **5** cadre
position: **4** helm **5** front, reins, wheel **6** tiller
leadfooted: **5** gawky **6** clumsy, klutzy, oafish **7** awkward **8** ungainly **9** lumbering, maladroit
lead-in: **5** intro, segue **6** opener, prelim
leading: **3** big, top **4** arch, best, head, main, note, star **5** ahead, chief, first, front, grand, major, on top, prime **6** famous, master, ruling, senior, utmost **7** forward, highest, in front, initial, popular, premier, primary, stellar, supreme **8** cardinal, champion, dominant, foremost, greatest, headmost, superior **9** governing, inaugural, notorious, number one, paramount, preceding, principal, prominent, unrivaled, uppermost, well-known, worthiest **10** dominating, preeminent, unrivalled
lady: **4** star **7** actress, heroine
light: **4** rock **8** mainstay
man: **4** hero, star **5** actor
slightly: **5** one up
starter: **5** cheer
leading __: **3** man **4** edge, lady **5** light **8** question
leading-edge: **6** modern **7** current **8** advanced
Leading With My Chin
author: Jay Leno
Lead Me On (1979 song)
artist: Maxine Nightingale
leadoff: **5** onset, start **6** advent, outset **7** opening **8** exordium **9** beginning, inception
lead-off: **5** first **7** initial
lead-pipe __: **5** cinch
lead the __: **3** way
lead-tin alloy: **5** terne
lead to the __: **5** altar
leady: **4** dull **5** heavy **6** gloomy **8** listless, sluggish **10** spiritless
leaf: **2** pg. **3** pad **4** page, scan, skim **5** blade, bract, folio, frond, metal, organ, paper, petal, sheet, thumb, verso **6** browse, glance, needle, riffle **7** foliage, foliole
adjective: **5** erose
angle: **4** axil
area: **6** areola, areole
calyx ~: **5** sepal
collector: **5** raker
combining form: **5** phyll- **6** phyllo-
extra ~: **6** insert
fern ~: **5** bract, frond
gatherer: **5** raker
holder: **4** limb, stem **5** bough, shoot **6** branch **7** pedicel, pedicle **8** peduncle
in ~: **5** green
juncture: **4** axil
like an oak ~: **7** rounded
lucky ~: **6** clover **8** shamrock
opening: **4** pore **5** stoma
out: **3** bud **7** burgeon **10** burst forth
part: **3** rib **4** lobe, vein **5** pinna **6** midrib
plant ~: **6** earlet
point: **5** mucro
starter: **3** fly
starting point: **3** bud **4** node **8** juncture, swelling
through: **4** read, scan, skim **5** thumb **6** browse
turn over a new ~: **6** change, reform **7** redress, shape up
walking ~: **3** bug **4** fern **6** insect
leaf __: **7** lettuce
__ leaf: **3** bay, end, fig **4** drop, gold
__-leaf: **5** loose
__ Leaf: **4** A New **5** Maple
__-leaf binder: **5** loose
__-leaf clover: **4** four
__-leaf cluster: **3** oak
leafcutter __: **3** ant
leafless: **4** bare **5** naked
vine: **5** haoma
leaflet: **2** ad **4** bill **5** flier, flyer, tract **8** brochure, circular, handbill, pamphlet **10** literature
leaflike part: **5** bract
__ Leaf Rag: **5** Maple
Leafs: **3** six **4** team
home: **7** Toronto
milieu: **3** ice **4** rink
org.: **3** NHL
__-leaf table: **4** drop
__ Leaf, The: **4** Last
leafy: **5** green, shady **6** foliar, hidden, shaded, wooded **7** verdant **8** abundant **9** abounding **10** umbrageous
shelter: **5** arbor, bower **6** recess **7** pergola
league: **3** mob, soc. **4** ally, assn., band, bloc, club, crew, gang, gild, loop, pact, pool, rank, ring, tier, unit **5** bunch, class, grade, group, guild, level, order, party, union, unite **6** circle, concur, outfit, status, treaty **7** academy, circuit, combine, compact, company, conjoin, society **8** alliance, category, coadjute, congress, federate, grouping, sodality **9** anschluss, associate, coalition, cooperate **10** amalgamate, conference, consortium, federation, fellowship, join forces, membership, pigeonhole
baseball ~: **4** Amer., Natl. **8** American, National
in ~: **6** allied, joined, tied in, united **8** combined, hooked up **9** connected, in cahoots **10** affiliated, associated
in German ~: **4** bund
lowest minor ~: **6** class A
__ league: **3** big **4** bush **5** major, minor
__ League: **3** Ivy **4** Arab, Pony **5** Major **6** Delian, Junior, Little
__-league boots: **5** seven
League of __ Voters: **5** Women
League of Nations
home: **6** Geneva
successor: **5** The UN
League of Their Own, A (1992 film)
cast: Geena Davis, Tom Hanks, Jon Lovitz, Madonna, Garry Marshall, Lori Petty
director: Penny Marshall
League of Youth, The
author: Henrik Ibsen
__ leaguer: **3** big **4** bush **5** Texas
__-leaguer: **5** major, minor
__ Leaguer: **3** Ivy **6** Little
Leah: **6** Remini
daughter: **5** Dinah
father: **5** Laban
husband: **5** Jacob
son: **4** Levi **5** Judah **6** Reuben, Simeon **7** Zebulun **8** Issachar
Leahy: **7** Patrick
leak: **3** run **4** blab, drip, drop, flow, hole, loss, news, ooze, seep, tell **5** chink, crack, drain, drool, exude **6** escape, expose, filter, reveal, tattle, unmask, unveil **7** come out, crevice, divulge, dribble, exhibit, fissure, lay bare, let slip, opening, release, seep out, trickle, uncover **8** aperture, decrease, disclose, exposure, give away, puncture **9** discharge, make known, percolate **10** make public, revelation
apt to ~: **5** seepy
ender: **3** age **5** proof
sound: **4** hiss
stopper: **5** O-ring **6** gasket
tanker ~: **5** spill
leakage: **6** escape
Leakey: **4** Mary **5** Louis **7** Richard **14** anthropologist
Leakin' __: **4** Lena
leaking: **5** adrip
leakproof: **5** tight **6** sealed **8** airtight, hermetic
leaky: **5** holey **6** faulty, porous **7** seeping **8** dripping
device: **5** sieve **6** filter, screen **8** colander, strainer
tire sound: **4** ssss
lealty: **8** fidelity

lean: **3** fit, jut, sag, tip **4** bend, bony, cant, keel, lank, list, prop, rely, rest, slim, sway, tend, thin, tilt, trim, turn, veer, wiry **5** boney, droop, favor, gaunt, lanky, lithe, lurch, no-fat, pitch, rangy, slant, slope, spare, stoop, terse, trust, weedy **6** bank on, bear on, careen, dainty, depend, gangly, gnomic, meager, prefer, scanty, sinewy, skinny, slight, slinky, slouch, sparse, svelte, twiggy, wasted **7** angular, gracile, haggard, incline, recline, scraggy, scrawny, slender, spidery, stringy, willowy **8** angulose, angulous, bear upon, gangling, rawboned **9** efficient, emaciated, gravitate, lithesome, sylphlike

 backward: **4** arch, flex

 eater: **5** Sprat

 forward: **4** bend **7** bow down

 make ~: **5** defat

 not ~: **4** oily, rich **5** fatty, lardy, plump, stout **6** chubby, fleshy, portly **7** adipose **8** heavyset **9** corpulent

 on: **4** abut, hurt, push **5** bully, press, trust **6** coerce, menace, rebuke **7** squeeze **8** browbeat, chastise, pressure **9** criticize, shake down **10** intimidate

 (on): **4** rely, rest **5** hinge **6** depend

 one: **5** scrag **8** beanpole

 over: **3** bow, sag **4** bend, flex **5** droop, hunch, slump, stoop **6** hunker, slouch

 to one side: **4** cant, heel, list

 toward: **4** near, tend **5** favor, verge

lean ___ backward: **4** over

Lean ___: **4** on Me **7** Cuisine

lean and ___: **4** mean

Lean, David: **3** Sir **8** director

 film: Blithe Spirit (1945)
 The Bridge on the River Kwai (1957, AA)
 Brief Encounter (1945)
 Doctor Zhivago (1965)
 Great Expectations (1946)
 Lawrence of Arabia (1962, AA)
 A Passage to India (1984)
 Ryan's Daughter (1970)

Leander's love: **4** Hero

Leandro's love: **3** Ero

leaning: **4** bent, bias, tilt **5** alist, atilt, drift, slant, slope, taste, trend **6** aslant, liking, temper **7** mindset **8** aptitude, attitude, cup of tea, lopsided, penchant, tendency, velleity **9** appetence, inclining, incumbent, proneness, sentiment **10** partiality, preference, proclivity, propensity

Leaning ___ of Pisa: **5** Tower

leaning forward (ballet): **6** penché

Leaning on the Lamp Post (1966 song)

 artist: Herman's Hermits

Leaning Tower

 like the ~: **5** atilt **8** slanting

Leaning Tower, The

 author: Katherine Anne Porter

Leann: **6** Hunley

LeAnn: **5** Rimes

Lean on Me (1989 film)

 cast: Morgan Freeman, Robert Guillaume

Lean on Me (song)

 artist: Bill Withers, Club Nouveau

leant: **4** bent **6** canted, listed, tended, tilted **7** propped, slanted **8** inclined

lean-to: **3** hut **4** shed **5** annex, house, hovel, shack **6** shanty **7** cottage, shelter **8** addition, building

leap: **3** hop, pop **4** axel, jump, lick, Lutz, move, rise, rush, skip, soar **5** arise, bound, caper, clear, frisk, lunge, mount, start, surge, vault **6** ascend, bounce, cavort, hurdle, plunge, pounce, prance, rocket, spring **7** advance, saltate, upsurge, upswing **8** escalate, increase, jump over **9** skyrocket **10** escalation, go whole hog, hippety hop

 aboard: **6** jump on

 aside: **4** duck **5** avoid, dodge

 at: **5** go for **6** accept, fall on, relish

 ballet ~: **4** jeté **5** brisé, sauté **7** ciseaux, échappé **8** assemble, ballonné, cabriole, sissonne, sous-sous **9** entrechat, grand jeté, pas de chat **10** soubresaut

 dressage ~: **6** curvet

 ender: **4** frog

 fencing ~: **4** volt

 for joy: **4** crow **5** cheer, exult, glory **7** delight, triumph **9** celebrate

 over: **3** hop **5** clear **6** hurdle

 (over): **4** sail

 skater's ~: **4** axel, lutz

leap ___: **3** day **4** year **6** second

___ leap: **7** quantum

leapfrog: **4** game, jump, skip **5** vault **6** hurtle **7** advance

leap in the ___: **4** dark

leap of ___: **5** faith

Leap of Faith

 author: Danielle Steel

Leap of Faith (1992 film)

 cast: Lolita Davidovich, Steve Martin, Liam Neeson, Debra Winger

leaps and ___: **6** bounds

Lear: **4** poet **6** Edward, Evelyn, Norman

 daughter: **5** Regan **7** Goneril **8** Cordelia

 loyal companion: **4** Kent

Lear ___: **3** Jet

___ Lear: **4** King

Lear, Edward: **4** poet **7** British

 cat: **4** Foss

 elegant fowl: **3** owl

 specialty: limerick

 work: A Book of Nonsense
 Calico Pie
 The Jumblies
 Laughable Lyrics
 More Nonsense Songs
 Nonsense Songs
 The Owl and the Pussycat
 The Pobble Who Has No Toes

learn: **3** con, get, see **4** cram, hear, know, read, tell **5** dig up, enrol, glean, grasp, study **6** absorb, attain, detect, enroll, master, peruse, pick up, review, soak up, take in, tumble, turn up **7** catch on, discern, drink in, find out, major in, minor in, nose out, prepare, receive, train in, uncover, unearth **8** discover, memorize, pore over, remember, smoke out **9** ascertain, brush up on, catch on to, determine, establish, figure out, get word of, lucubrate **10** apprentice, get down pat, understand

 about: **6** hear of

 a lesson: **3** get **5** grasp **6** digest, soak up **7** drink in **9** apprehend **10** assimilate, comprehend, understand

 from: **3** use **4** gain **5** value **7** benefit, improve, realize

 (from): **6** profit

 how some ~: **6** by rote

 in a hurry: **4** cram

 one's part: **5** drill, study **6** go over **8** practice, rehearse

 one way to ~: **4** rote **7** routine **10** repetition

 quick to ~: **3** apt **4** able, keen **5** acute, adept, alert, canny, sharp, smart **6** astute, brainy, bright, clever, gifted, shrewd, with it **7** capable, erudite **8** well-read **9** brilliant, on the ball **10** discerning, insightful, precocious

 slowly: **5** glean

 something to ~: **6** lesson **7** precept, reading **8** exercise, homework, teaching **9** chalk talk **10** assignment, recitation

 the ropes: **5** adapt, train **6** master

 try to ~: **3** ask, dig **4** cram, heed, muse, plug, pump, quiz, read **5** probe, query, study, think, train **6** bone up, digest, go over, master, peruse, ponder, reason, review, survey, take up **7** analyze, consult, dissect, inquire, observe, reflect **8** check out, look into, meditate, mull over, polish up, pore over, practice, read up on, rehearse, research **9** grind away, pick apart, sweat over **10** crack a book, experiment

learned: **4** deep, sage **5** grave, sharp, smart, solid, sound **6** brainy, expert, posted, solemn, versed **7** bookish, erudite, sapient, skilled, studied **8** abstruse, academic, cultured, educated, esoteric, grounded, highbrow, lettered, literary, literate, pedantic, polymath, profound, skillful, studious, well-read **9** in the know, judicious, pansophic, recondite, scholarly **10** conversant, cultivated, omniscient, pedantical, scientific

 about: **4** up on **6** versed

 not ~: **6** innate, native **7** natural **9** intrinsic, intuitive

 one: **4** guru, sage **5** guide, solon **6** critic, expert, master, mentor, Nestor, pundit, savant **7** scholar, Solomon, teacher, thinker **9** abecedary, authority, professor **10** specialist

 something ~: **5** craft, skill, trade **7** know-how, mastery **9** expertise, technique

Learned: **4** Hand **7** Michael

learner: **3** cub **4** tiro, tyro **5** newie, pupil, tutee **6** intern, novice **7** interne, new hand, recruit, scholar, student, trainee **8** beginner, bookworm, disciple, initiate, neophyte **9** fledgling, greenhorn **10** apprentice, catechumen, tenderfoot

learning: **4** info, lore **5** study **6** wisdom **7** culture, letters, reading, science, tuition **8** literacy, research, training **9** education, erudition, knowledge, schooling **10** literature

 basics: **3** RRR **4** ABCs **7** three Rs

 branch of ~: **5** ology

 place: **3** sch. **4** acad., coll., inst., univ. **6** school **7** academy, college **9** institute **10** university

learning ___: **5** curve

Learning to Fly (1991 song)

 artist: Tom Petty

Leary: **5** Denis **7** Timothy

lease: **3** let **4** hire, loan, rent, take **6** engage, let out, occupy, sublet **7** charter, rent out **8** sublease **9** agreement, indenture, liability, residence

 ender: **4** back, hold **6** holder

 extend a ~: **5** relet, renew

 holder: **6** lessee, lessor, renter, tenant **8** landlady, landlord, occupant

 in law: **6** demise

___-Lease Act: **4** Lend

___ lease on life: **4** a new

leaser: **6** tenant **8** landlady, landlord

leash: **3** tie **4** bind, curb, lead, rein, rope, trio **5** chain, check, strap, tie up **6** bridle, fasten, fetter, hamper, hobble, secure, tether, triple **7** control **8** hold back, restrain, suppress **9** restraint **10** constraint

 on a ~: **5** in tow **10** restrained

leash ___: **3** law

least: **3** min. **4** last **5** basal, first, nadir, third **6** atomic, barest, bottom, fewest, gutter, lowest, minute, second **7** finical, meanest, minimal, minimum, poorest, tiniest, trivial **8** atomical, feeblest, littlest, minutest, niggling, piddling, short-end, smallest **9** molecular, narrowest, slightest **10** entry-level

 ender: **4** ways, wise

least ___: **5** of all

least ___ bound: **5** upper

least ___ denominator: **6** common

least ___ multiple: **6** common

___ least: **5** in the

least of ___: **3** all

leather: **3** elk, kid, Mor. **4** hide, roan, skin **5** mocha, suede **6** chammy, Levant, lizard, shammy, shamoy **7** chamois, cowhide, doeskin, Morocco, pigskin, rawhide **8** cordovan, deerskin, goatskin, shagreen **9** alligator, crocodile

 armor: **6** lorica

 dressing: **6** dubbin **7** dubbing

 ender: **4** back, ette, head, neck, wear, wood, work **6** jacket, worker

 fake ~: **5** vinyl

 go hellbent for ~: **6** careen, hasten, hurtle **7** rampage **8** stampede

 item: **4** belt, rein, weft, whip **5** knout, strap, strop, thong

 split ~: **5** skive

 to-be: **4** hide, pelt

 tool: **3** awl

 treat ~ again: **5** retan

 work with ~: **3** tan **4** cure, tool

leather-___: 6 lunged
___ leather: 5 glove 6 patent 7 morocco
Leather and Lace (1981 song)
artist: Don Henley, Stevie Nicks
leatherback: 6 animal, turtle 7 reptile
Leatherheads (2008 film)
cast: George Clooney, Renée Zellweger
director: George Clooney
leatherneck: 6 gyrene, Marine
org.: 4 USMC
Leather-Stocking Tales
author: James Fenimore Cooper
leatherwood: 4 titi
leathery: 4 hard 5 rough, tough 6 rugged, strong 7 durable 8 hardened, wrinkled 10 coriaceous
Leatrice: 3 Joy
leave: 2 go, OK 3 fly, let, vac. 4 drop, exit, flee, flit, jilt, move, okay, omit, park, part, quit, sail, stop, will 5 adieu, allot, allow, be off, ditch, elope, go off, go out, let be, R and R, sally, scram, spare, split, start 6 assent, beat it, be gone, bow out, bug out, cut out, decamp, defect, depart, desert, egress, embark, escape, forget, get out, go away, go home, maroon, move on, permit, pop off, repair, resign, retire, run off, secede, set off, set out, suffer, vacate, vanish 7 abandon, abscond, back out, bail out, bequest, consent, consign, drop off, drop out, entrust, forsake, freedom, go-ahead, go forth, goodbye, head out, holiday, intrust, liberty, license, make off, migrate, move out, neglect, parting, pull out, push off, retreat, ride off, ship out, skip out, slip out, step out, take off, time off, vamoose, walk out 8 abdicate, approval, bequeath, check out, clear out, come away, emigrate, evacuate, farewell, forswear, fugitate, furlough, hand down, hightail, light out, renounce, run along, sanction, separate, set forth, shove off, skip town, slip away, step down, vacation, withdraw 9 allowance, break away, break camp, clearance, departure, disappear, foreswear, skedaddle, stand down, surrender, take a hike, throw over 10 give notice, green light, hit the road, indulgence, permission, relinquish, sabbatical, say goodbye, shuffle off, withdrawal
alone: 5 let be 6 lay off, resist 7 neglect 10 deregulate
behind: 4 lose, pass 5 outdo 7 abandon 8 distance, overtake, shake off, throw off 9 transcend
compel to ~: 4 oust 5 eject, evict, exile, expel 6 banish, deport 8 drive off, drive out
empty: 6 vacate 7 move out
give ~: 2 OK 3 let 5 allow, grant 6 accede, free up, permit 7 approve, concede, endorse, license 8 sanction 9 authorize 10 say the word
hanging: 4 jilt, quit 5 ditch 6 cop out, desert, maroon, reject, strand 7 abandon, forsake, let down 8 abdicate
hastily: 3 hie, run 4 bolt, flee, skip 5 scram, split 6 bug out, decamp 7 take off, vamoose 8 shove off 9 bundle off
in: 4 stet
no part empty: 4 cram, pack, sate 5 crowd 6 occupy, top off 7 jampack, pervade, satiate 8 brim over, permeate
no stone unturned: 4 seek 5 scour 6 search, strive 7 persist, ransack, rummage 9 persevere
no trace of: 3 end 4 doom, raze, ruin, sack 5 blast, crush, level, total, wreck 6 blow up, ravage 7 butcher, despoil, destroy, flatten, pillage, scourge, scuttle, wipe out 8 bankrupt, bulldoze, clean out, decimate, demolish, lay waste 9 bring down, desecrate, devastate 10 annihilate, obliterate
obscurity: 6 emerge
of absence: 4 rest 5 break, leave, R and R 7 holiday, leisure, respite, time off 8 furlough, vacation 10 sabbatical
off: 3 end 4 halt, omit, quit, stop 5 cease 6 desist, give up 7 abstain, refrain 8 give over, keep from, surcease
on ~: 6 ashore
one's feet: 4 jump, leap 5 bound
one's seat: 5 arise, get up, stand 6 jump up
open-mouthed: 3 awe, wow 4 stun 5 amaze 8 surprise
out: 3 bar, cut 4 omit, skip, tabu 5 debar, elide, forgo 6 except, forego 7 exclude, scissor 8 overlook, pass over 9 cast aside, eliminate, gloss over
out in the cold: 4 shun, snub 6 ignore, rebuff, reject, slight 7 high-hat, neglect 8 overlook 9 ostracize
port: 4 sail 6 embark 7 set sail 8 go aboard, shove off
prepare to ~: 4 pack 8 get ready
secretly: 4 bolt, flee 5 elope 6 decamp, escape 7 abscond, run away 8 slip away, sneak off 9 steal away
take one's ~: 2 go 4 exit 5 split 6 beat it, depart, go away, move on, retire 7 make off, pull out, push off 8 blast off, hightail, light out, set forth, shove off, slip away, withdraw
the fold: 4 roam 6 depart, wander
the ground: 3 fly 4 soar 5 arise, climb, vault 6 ascend, rocket 7 balloon, take off 8 levitate
the nest: 8 take wing
the path: 3 err 4 rove, turn, veer 5 stray 6 swerve 7 deviate, diverge
the water: 7 surface
town: 4 move, relo 8 relocate
unceremoniously: 4 drop, dump, jilt 5 chuck, ditch 6 desert 7 abandon, forsake
undone: 4 omit 5 slack 8 overlook
wide-eyed: 3 awe, wow 4 stun 5 amaze
without escape: 4 trap, tree 6 corner
without paying: 5 stiff
leave ___: 3 off 5 alone
leave ___ dust: 5 in the
leave ___ enough alone: 4 well
leave-___: 6 taking
___ leave: 4 sick 5 shore 6 family, French
Leave ___ Beaver: 4 It to
Leave ___ Me!: 4 It to
Leave ___ that!: 4 it at
Leave ___ to Heaven: 3 Her
Leave!: 4 shoo 6 begone
leave in the ___: 4 dust
Leave It to Beaver (CBS/ABC sitcom)
cast: Frank Bank (Lumpy Rutherford)
Hugh Beaumont (Ward Cleaver)
Barbara Billingsley (June Cleaver)
Richard Deacon (Fred Rutherford)
Tony Dow (Wally Cleaver)
Jerry Mathers (Beaver Cleaver)
Ken Osmond (Eddie Haskell)
setting: Mayfield
Leave It to Me!: 7 musical
composer: Cole Porter
Leave me ___!: 5 alone
Leave Me Alone (1973 song)
artist: Helen Reddy
___ Leave Me Now: 5 If You
leaven: 4 barm, soda 5 yeast 7 lighten
leave no ___ unturned: 5 stone
Leavenworth: 4 city, Fort, town
locale: 6 Kansas
leave of ___: 7 absence
leaves: 6 fodder 7 foliage
gather ~: 4 rake 7 clean up
gatherer: 5 raker
like autumn ~: 3 dry 4 sere 7 parched 9 shriveled
like some ~: 5 lobed 6 lobate 7 lobated
lose ~: 4 shed 9 exfoliate
notched, as ~: 5 erose
one who ~: 4 goer
plant with two seed ~: 5 dicot 7 dicotyl
tea ~: 4 lees 5 dregs 8 sediment
___ Leaves: 6 Autumn
Leaves of Grass
author: Walt Whitman
leave-taking: 4 exit 5 adieu, adios, conge 6 congee 7 goodbye, parting 8 farewell
leave the ___ open: 4 door
leave to one's ___ devices: 3 own
leave well enough ___: 5 alone
leaving: 4 exit 6 exodus 8 outgoing 10 withdrawal
combining form: 4 lipo-
keep from ~: 5 delay 6 detain, hold up, impede 7 set back 8 slow down 10 buttonhole
out: 3 bar, but 5 minus 6 except 7 barring, besides, short of 8 omitting 9 apart from, aside from, excluding
___ Leaving Home: 4 She's
Leaving Las Vegas (1995 film)
cast: Nicolas Cage, Julian Sands, Elisabeth Shue
character: 4 Sera
director: Mike Figgis
Leaving on a Jet Plane (1969 song)
artist: Peter, Paul and Mary
leavings: 4 junk, orts, rest 5 ashes, chaff, dross, trash, truck, waste 6 litter, refuse 7 garbage, grounds, remains, remnant, residue, rubbish, rummage 8 detritus, leftover, oddments, remnants 9 remainder
Leb.
neighbor: 3 Isr., Syr.
Lebanese: 4 Arab 5 Asian
Lebanon: 4 city, town 6 nation 7 country
bovine: 6 Baladi
capital: 6 Beirut
city: 6 Beirut 7 Tripoli 8 Beyrouth
group: 10 Arab League
language: 6 Arabic
locale: 4 Asia 7 Mideast 9 Tennessee
money: 7 piaster, piastre
neighbor: 5 Syria 6 Israel
poet: 5 Accad, Adnan
port: 4 Tyre 5 Saida, Sayda, Sidon, Sydon, Zidon 6 Beirut 8 Beyrouth
tree: 5 cedar
writer: 6 Gibran
LeBaron: 3 car 4 auto 8 Chrysler 10 automobile
Leblanc: 7 Maurice, Nicolas
LeBlanc: 4 Matt
Le Bourget
alternative: ***see*** airport 4 Orly 8 de Gaulle
Lebowitz: 4 Fran
___ Lebowski, The: 3 Big
LeBrock, Kelly ex: Steven Seagal
Le Cain: 5 Errol
Le Car: 3 car 4 auto 7 Renault 10 automobile
le Carré, John: 6 writer 7 British
figure: 3 spy 5 agent
work: The Honourable Schoolboy
The Little Drummer Girl
The Looking-Glass War
A Perfect Spy
Smiley's people
The Spy Who Came in from the Cold
Tinker, Tailor, Soldier, Spy
Lech: 5 river 6 Walesa
city on the ~: 8 Augsburg
locale: 5 Tirol, Tyrol 7 Austria, Bavaria, Germany
leche
in English: 4 milk
seller: 6 bodega
Le Cid
author: Pierre Corneille
composer: Jules Massenet
Le Coq d'Or: 5 opera 6 ballet
composer: Nikolai Rimsky-Korsakov
Le Création du monde
composer: Darius Milhaud
lect.
giver: 4 prof.
Lecter: 8 Hannibal
like ~: 4 evil
lectern: 4 ambo, desk 5 ambon, stand, table 6 podium, pulpit 7 rostrum, support 8 platform
lector: 6 fellow, mentor, reader 7 academe, teacher 8 academic, educator, lecturer 9 pedagogue, preceptor, professor 10 instructor

Lectric __: 5 Shave
lecture: 3 rag, ser. 4 flay, rate, talk 5 chide, orate, pitch, scold, speak, spiel, spout, teach, tutor 6 berate, lesson, preach, punish, rank on, rebuke, recite, sermon, speech, tirade 7 address, censure, chiding, declaim, deliver, expound, monolog, oration, pep talk, prelect, reproof, reprove, soapbox, tell off 8 admonish, harangue, instruct, moralism, moralize, perorate, scolding 9 chalk talk, discourse, exprobate, going-over, hold forth, monologue, pound into, preaching, reprehend, reprimand, sermonize, talking-to 10 allocution, preachment, recitation, upbraiding, vocalizing
  follower: 5 Q and A
  give a ~: 4 talk 5 edify, orate, speak, spout, teach, tutor 6 advise, inform 7 address, declaim, deliver, educate, expound, instill 8 initiate, instruct 9 discourse, hold forth, inculcate, interpret, pound into, sermonize
  leader: 4 prof 7 speaker 9 professor
  place: 4 dais, hall 6 lyceum, podium 7 rostrum 10 auditorium
lecturer: 5 tutor 6 docent, fellow, lector, orator, reader, talker 7 academe, pedagog, speaker, teacher 8 academic, educator 9 abecedary, pedagogue, professor 10 instructor
lecturers: 5 profs 7 faculty 8 teachers 9 academics 10 professors
led
  being ~: 5 in tow
  easily ~: 4 meek, tame 5 mousy 6 docile 7 passive, pliable 8 amenable, obedient, yielding 9 compliant, tractable 10 submissive
  in: 5 began 6 guided 7 brought 8 escorted
  on: 5 lured 6 teased 7 deluded, enticed, tempted, tricked 8 beguiled, deceived 9 inveigled, misguided, toyed with 10 hoodwinked
  to: 6 caused 8 preceded 9 brought on 10 eventuated, resulted in
Leda: 4 moon
  daughter: 5 Helen 8 Timandra
  planet: 7 Jupiter
  son: 6 Castor, Pollux
Leda and the Swan
  author: William Butler Yeats
Le Déjeuner sur l'herbe
  artist: Édouard Manet
Leder: 4 Mimi
Lederberg, Joshua: 8 Nobelist
Lederer: 5 Eppir 7 Francis, William
lederhosen: 5 pants 6 shorts
Lederman, Leon: 8 Nobelist 9 physicist
ledge: 3 bar, rim 4 berm, edge, reef, sill 5 bench, berme, ridge, shelf 6 mantle 7 bracket 10 projection
  fireplace ~: 3 hob
  rocky ~: 3 tor 4 crag 5 arête, cliff 8 pinnacle 9 precipice 10 escarpment, prominence
  underwater ~: 3 bar 4 reef 5 atoll, ridge, shelf, shoal 7 sand bar
ledger: 5 books 7 account, daybook, journal 8 register
  abbr.: 3 amt., YTD
  check: 5 audit 10 inspection
  division: 4 acct. 7 account
  entry: 4 item, loss 5 asset, debit 6 credit
  expert: 3 CPA 7 auditor 10 accountant, bookkeeper
  put in the ~: 5 enter 7 set down
Ledger, Heath: 5 actor
  film: 10 Things I Hate About You (1999)
    Brokeback Mountain (2005)
    The Brothers Grimm (2005)
    The Dark Knight (2008, AA)
    The Four Feathers (2002)
    Monster's Ball (2001)
    The Patriot (2000)
Le Docteur miracle
  composer: Georges Bizet
LED part: 5 diode, light 8 emitting
Le Duc __: 3 Tho
Led Zeppelin
  members: Plant, Page, Jones, Bonham
  song: Stairway to Heaven (1970)
    Whole Lotta Love (1969)
lee: 4 dreg, side 5 cover 6 refuge 7 shelter 10 protection
  ender: 3 way 4 ward 5 board
  opposite: 5 stoss
lee __: 4 tide, wave 5 gauge, shore
Lee: 3 Ang, Ann, Reb 4 Anna, Fort, Joie, Lila, Sara, Stan, Yuan 5 Aaker, Alvin, Bruce, David, Elder, Grant, Jason, Peggy, Pinky, Smith, Spike, Tommy, Tracy 6 Albert, Bailey, Bowman, Brenda, Canada, Curtis, Dickey, Harper, Janzen, Johnny, Majors, Marvin, Remick, Sheryl, Tanith 7 Bernard, Brandon, Horsley, Iacocca, Krasner, Lorelei, Manfred, Michele, Robert E., Trevino 8 De Forest, Meredith, Michaels, Ritenour, Tsung-Dao, Van Cleef 9 Greenwood, Holdridge, Radziwill, Strasberg 10 Meriwether
  city on the ~: 4 Cork
  to Grant: 3 foe 5 enemy
Lee __: 5 Myles
__ Lee: 4 Aura, Fort, Sara 6 Jennie 7 Annabel, Stagger
Lee, Ang: 8 director
  film: Brokeback Mountain (2005, AA)
    Crouching Tiger, Hidden Dragon (2000)
    Hulk (2003)
    The Ice Storm (1997)
    Ride With the Devil (1999)
    Sense and Sensibility (1995)
    Taking Woodstock (2009)
Lee Ann: 6 Womack
Lee, Brenda
  nickname: Little Miss Dynamite
  real last name: Tarpley
  song: All Alone Am I (1962)
    As Usual (1963)
    Break It to Me Gently (1962)
    Coming On Strong (1966)
    Dum Dum (1961)
    Emotions (1961)
    Everybody Loves Me But You (1962)
    Fool #1 (1961)
    Heart in Hand (1962)
    I'm Sorry (1960)
    Is It True (1964)
    I Want to Be Wanted (1960)
    Losing You (1963)
    Rockin' Around the Christmas Tree (1960)
    Sweet Nothin's (1960)
    That's All You Gotta Do (1960)
    Too Many Rivers (1965)
    You Can Depend on Me (1961)
__ Lee Browne: 6 Roscoe
__ Lee Bunton: 4 Emma
leech: 3 bum 6 jackal, sponge 7 moocher, sponger 8 barnacle, deadbeat, freeload, hanger-on, parasite, scrounge 9 loan shark, scrounger, sycophant 10 freeloader
__ Lee Crosby: 5 Cathy
Lee, Curtis
  song: Pretty Little Angel Eyes (1961)
__ Lee Curtis: 5 Jamie
Leeds: 4 city, town 6 Andrea
  city near ~: 4 York
  locale: 7 England 9 Yorkshire
  river: 4 Aire
__ Lee Gifford: 6 Kathie
Lee, Harper work: To Kill a Mockingbird
__ Lee Hope: 5 Laura
Lee J. __: 4 Cobb
__ Lee Jones: 5 Tommy 6 Rickie
leek: 6 allium, veggie 9 vegetable
  relative: 5 chive, onion
Leek: 5 Sybil
__-leekie: 5 cock-a
Leelee: 8 Sobieski
__ Lee Lewis: 5 Jerry
Lee, Lorelei creator: Anita Loos
__ Lee Masters: 5 Edgar
Lee, Michele: 7 actress
  spouse: James Farentino
  TV: Knots Landing
__ Lee, NJ: 4 Fort
__ Lee Nolin: 4 Gena
Lee, Peggy
  film (voice): Lady and the Tramp
  real name: Norma Jean Egstrom
  song: Fever
    Fever (1958)
    Golden Earrings
    Is That All There Is (1969)
    Lover
    Manana
    Why Don't You Do Right
leer: 3 eye 4 look, ogle 5 smirk, sneer, stare 6 goggle, squint 7 eyeball 10 make eyes at
__ Lee Ralph: 6 Sheryl
__ Lee Ray: 4 Dixy
leerer: 5 ogler
leeriness: 5 doubt, qualm 8 wariness 9 chariness, misgiving, suspicion 10 skepticism
Lee, Robert E.: 3 gen. 7 general
  horse: 9 Traveller
  nation: 3 CSA
__ Lee Roth: 5 David
leery: 3 shy 4 cagy, wary 5 cagey, chary 6 unsure 7 careful, dubious, fearful, guarded, prudent 8 cautious, doubtful, doubting, overwary, skittish 9 skeptical, uncertain 10 suspicious, uneffusive
  be ~: 5 doubt 7 suspect 10 disbelieve
  one: 5 cynic 7 doubter, sceptic, scoffer, skeptic 8 nihilist 9 dissenter, pessimist
lees: 3 end 5 dregs 7 deposit, grounds, remnant 8 sediment 9 tea leaves
Leesburg: 4 city, town
  locale: 8 Virginia
Lee, Spike: 5 actor 8 director
  film: Clockers (1995)
    Crooklyn (1994)
    Do the Right Thing (1989)
    Get on the Bus (1996)
    He Got Game (1998)
    Inside Man (2006)
    Jungle Fever (1991)
    Malcolm X (1992)
    Miracle at St. Anna (2008)
    Mo' Better Blues (1990)
    The Original Kings of Comedy (2000)
    School Daze (1988)
    She Hate Me (2004)
    She's Gotta Have It (1986)
Lee's Summit: 4 city, town
  locale: 8 Missouri
Lee, Tommy
  spouse: Pamela Anderson, Heather Locklear
__ Lee, VA: 4 Fort
Leeward Island: 4 Saba 5 Nevis 7 Antigua, Barbuda, St. Kitts 8 Anguilla, Dominica, St. Martin 10 Guadeloupe, Montserrat, Saint Kitts
leeway: 4 play, room 5 range, scope, slack, space, swing 6 extent, margin 7 freedom 8 free hand, latitude 9 elbowroom, extra time, free space, tolerance 10 room to move, wiggle room
  having no ~: 4 snug 5 tight 6 narrow 7 cramped, crowded
Lee, Yuan: 7 chemist 8 Nobelist
Leeza: 7 Gibbons
Le Fanal
  author: Gabriel Marcel
Le Fifre
  artist: Édouard Manet
Leflore: 3 Ron
Le Freak (1978 song)
  artist: Chic
left: 4 gone, port 5 aport, extra, punch, split 6 extant, lonely, with us 7 gone out, liberal 8 departed, forsaken, larboard, liberals, marooned, portside, residual, sinister 9 abandoned, direction, remaining, sinistral, socialist 10 liberalism
  bank: 8 bohemian
  be ~: 6 remain 7 inherit, survive
  behind: 7 missing 9 abandoned, forgotten
  combining form: 3 lev- 4 levo- 5 laevo- 8 sinistro-
  ender: 3 ist 4 most, over, ward
  hang a ~: 4 turn
  in heraldry: 8 sinister
  in the time ~: 3 yet 4 till 5 still
  not ~: 5 right
  on a ship: 4 port 5 aport
  one ~ holding the bag: 4 dupe, goat 5 chump 6 sucker, victim 7 cat's-paw, fall guy 9 scapegoat

out: 7 missing, omitted
to a horse: 3 haw
to the ~: 4 levo 5 aside
to the imagination: 5 tacit 6 silent, unsaid 7 implied 8 implicit, inferred, unspoken, unstated, unvoiced, wordless 10 understood
to the ~, in French: 7 à gauche
what's ~: 3 net 4 orts, rest 6 excess, profit 7 balance, overage, remains, remnant, residue, surplus 8 leavings, take-home 9 remainder
left ___: 4 face, wing 5 brain, field, stage 7 fielder
left-___: 4 hand, laid 6 handed, hander
___ left: 4 eyes, quad 5 flush, hang a, stage
Left ___: 4 Bank
Left ___ of God, The: 4 Hand
___ Left: 3 New
Left Bank and Other Stories, The
author: Jean Rhys
Left Banke
song: Walk Away Renee (1966)
Left Bank river: 5 Seine
___ left field: 5 out in
left-handed: 6 clumsy 7 awkward, dubious, unadept 8 inexpert 9 equivocal, maladroit 10 unexplicit
compliment: 3 cut, dig 4 slam, snub 6 insult, slight, zinger 7 affront, offense, put-down
left-hand page: 5 verso
leftist: 6 Maoist 7 liberal, radical 8 ultraist 9 anarchist, communist, socialist 10 Bolshevist
Left Leg, The
author: T.F. Powys
left-of-___: 6 center
leftover: 3 odd, ort 4 dreg, orts 5 crumb, extra, scrap, spare, trash 6 debris, excess, legacy, scraps, unused 7 oddment, remnant, residue, surplus, uneaten 8 leavings, oddments, remnants, residual, survivor, unwanted 9 remainder, remaining, untouched, vestigial 10 unconsumed
leftovers: 4 hash, rest 5 waste 6 others 7 remnant, residue
dish: 4 hash, stew
fix ~: 3 zap 4 heat, nuke, warm 6 reheat, rewarm
Left Right Out of Your Heart (1958 song)
artist: Patti Page
Left Turn ___: 4 Only
lefty: 8 southpaw 9 portsider
Lefty: 5 Gomez, Grove 8 Frizzell
leg: 3 lap 4 limb, part, post, prop 5 brace, shank, stage, stump 6 column, member 7 portion, section, segment, stretch, support, upright 8 baluster 9 drumstick, extremity
an arm and a ~: 4 high 5 pricy, steep 6 costly, pricey 7 damages, ruinous 9 expensive 10 exorbitant
armor: 6 greave
bone: 4 shin 5 femur, tibia 6 fibula
bones: 6 femora, tibiae 7 fibulae
covering: 4 spat 6 gaiter, puttee 7 gambado
ender: 4 foot, horn, room, work 6 warmer
give a ~ up: 3 aid 4 help 5 boost, hoist 6 assist, succor 9 encourage
it: 3 run 4 hike, walk 7 hotfoot, vamoose
joint: 4 knee 5 ankle
lamb ~: 5 gigot
muscle: 4 quad 6 soleus 10 quadriceps
muscles: 5 solei
part: 4 calf, crus, knee, shin 5 ankle, shank, thigh
puller: 4 liar
pull one's ~: 3 guy, kid, rag, rib 4 fool, jest, joke, razz, twit 5 chaff, tease, trick 6 banter, take in 7 deceive, mislead
shake a ~: 3 fly, hie, rip, run, zip 4 dart, dash, flit, move, race, rush, stir, tear, zoom 5 hurry, scoot, speed 6 barrel, boogie, gallop, hasten, hustle, move it, rocket, scurry 7 floor it, hop to it, quicken, scamper, speed up 8 step on it 9 hotfoot it, skedaddle 10 get a move on, get hopping, hightail it
starter: 3 bow, dog 4 boot, fore, jack 5 black
up: 4 edge, hand, lift 5 boost 6 assist 9 advantage, headstart
leg ___: 7 warmers
leg-___: 4 pull 5 break 6 puller
___ leg: 4 gate, pant
legacy: 4 gift, will 6 devise, estate 7 bequest, product 8 heirloom, heritage, leftover 9 endowment, patrimony, throwback, tradition 10 birthright
recipient: 4 heir
revoke a ~: 5 adeem
sharer: 6 coheir
Legacy: 3 car 4 auto 6 Subaru 10 automobile
Legacy, The
author: Howard Fast, John Donne
legal: 3 due 4 fair, good, just 5 clean, jural, legit, licit, right, sound, valid 6 formal, kasher, kosher, lawful, proper, vested 7 allowed, decreed, granted 8 forensic, innocent, judicial, juristic, rightful, straight 9 allowable, canonical, chartered, juridical, justified, protected, statutory, warranted 10 aboveboard, admissible, authorized, legitimate, on the level, prescribed, sanctioned
action: 4 case, plea, suit 5 trial 6 appeal
adverb: 6 hereby, herein, hereof, hereon, hereto 8 hereunto, hereupon
adviser: 3 att. 4 atty. 6 jurist, lawyer 7 adviser, advisor, counsel 8 advocate, attorney 9 barrister, counselor, solicitor 10 mouthpiece
agreement: 6 escrow 8 contract
article: 6 clause 7 codicil, proviso 9 amendment
assistant: 4 para 5 clerk 10 amanuensis
bring ~ action: 3 sue 8 litigate
case statement: 5 facta
claim: 4 lien 5 droit 8 mortgage
concept: 6 intent, motive 8 volition
defense: 5 alibi
delay: 4 hold, stay, stop 5 waive 8 reprieve 9 deferment, remission 10 suspension
document: 4 deed, will, writ 5 brief, title
ender: 3 ese
force: 6 duress
joining: 6 merger 7 wedding, wedlock 8 contract, marriage, nuptials 9 matrimony
make ~: 2 OK 3 ink 4 sign 6 ratify 7 approve, certify, endorse, initial, witness 8 sanction, validate 9 authorize, establish, formalize, sign off on 10 constitute, legitimize
maturity: 8 majority
memo: 5 brief 8 abstract
not ~: 7 bootleg, illicit 8 criminal, improper, outlawed, unlawful, wrongful 9 felonious 10 contraband, prohibited, unlicensed
noun: 5 whoso
official: 2 DA 5 bench, judge 6 jurist, umpire 7 arbiter, referee 8 his Honor 9 moderator 10 arbitrator, magistrate, negotiator
phrase: 4 as to, in re 5 and/or, in rem
posting: 4 bail, bond 6 surety 7 warrant
record book: 5 liber
remove beyond ~ jurisdiction: 5 eloin
setting: 5 bench, court, venue 8 tribunal
starter: 4 para
start of a ~ conclusion: 5 I rest
substitute: 5 agent, proxy 6 deputy 7 stand-in 8 delegate 9 alternate, appointee, go-between, surrogate 10 lieutenant
tender: *see* moolah
under ~ age: 5 minor 8 juvenile 10 adolescent
unknown: 3 Doe, Roe
writ: 4 mise 6 elegit
see also law
legal ___: 3 age, aid, cap, fee, pad 5 eagle 6 tender 7 holiday
legal-___: 4 size
Legal ___ Society: 3 Aid
Legal Eagles (1986 film)
cast: Brian Dennehy, Daryl Hannah, Robert Redford, Debra Winger
director: Ivan Reitman
legality: 8 validity 10 lawfulness, legitimacy
legalize: 5 allow, enact 6 codify, decree, ordain, permit 7 approve, clean up, decrees, launder, license 8 regulate, sanction, validate 9 authorize, formulate, legislate 10 constitute, legitimate
legalized: 5 legit, licit 6 kosher, lawful 7 enacted 9 allowable 10 legitimate
Le Gallienne: 3 Eva
legally: 5 by law, right
Legally Blonde (2001 film)
cast: Selma Blair, Luke Wilson, Reese Witherspoon
dog: 7 Bruiser 9 Chihuahua
legan: 5 licit
legate: 5 agent, envoy 6 consul, deputy, nuncio 7 attaché, courier 8 bequeath, delegate, diplomat, emissary, minister 9 appointee 10 ambassador
legatee: 4 heir 5 owner 6 coheir 7 grantee, heiress, heritor 9 inheritor, recipient
legation: 5 staff 6 envoys 7 embassy, mission 9 committee, delegates 10 deputation, emissaries
legato: 6 smooth 7 flowing 8 smoothly
opposite: 4 stac. 8 staccato
symbol: 4 slur
legend: 3 key 4 code, head, lore, myth, saga, tale 5 fable, motto, story, table, title 6 cipher, device, mythos, record, rubric 7 account, caption, epitaph, fiction, heading, romance 8 epigraph, folklore, folktale 9 folk story, mythology, narrative, tradition, underline 10 fairy story
___ legend: 5 urban 6 living
Legend: 3 car 4 auto 5 Acura 10 automobile
___ Legend: 3 I Am
legendary: 5 famed, noted 6 fabled, famous, unreal 7 storied 8 fabulous, immortal, invented, mythical, renowned, romantic 9 imaginary, well-known 10 apocryphal, celebrated, improbable
Legend of Bagger Vance, The (2000 film)
cast: Matt Damon, Will Smith, Charlize Theron
director: Robert Redford
Legend of Sleepy Hollow, The
author: Washington Irving
Legend of Zorro, The (2005 film)
cast: Antonio Banderas, Catherine Zeta-Jones
legends: 4 lore 5 myths, tales 6 fables 8 folklore
Legends of Our Time
author: Elie Wiesel
leger ___: 4 line
Léger: 6 Aléxis 7 Fernand
legerdemain: 5 magic, trick 9 dexterity
expert: 5 magus 6 wizard 8 conjurer, magician, sorcerer
legerity: 7 agility 8 celerity, deftness 9 dexterity, quickness 10 nimbleness
___-legged: 4 duck, four 5 bandy, cross 7 feather, spindle
___-legged race: 5 three
legging: 7 gambado
leggings: 5 chaps, pants, spats 6 tights 7 gaiters, puttees 10 chaparajos
Leggo my ___!: 4 Eggo
L'eggs
rival: 5 Hanes
leggy: 4 tall 5 rangy 6 gangly 7 spindly, willowy 8 gangling
leghorn: 3 hat, hen 4 bird, fowl 7 chicken
relative: *see* chicken
Leghorn: 4 city, port, town
locale: 5 Italy

legibility: 4 ease 7 clarity 8 evenness, neatness

legible: 4 neat 5 clean, clear, lucid, plain, sharp 8 coherent, distinct, readable

legibly, write: 5 print

legion: 4 army, body, host, many, mass, rout 5 cloud, crowd, drove, flock, force, group, horde, ocean, swarm, troop 6 myriad, number, scores, sundry, throng 7 brigade, company, numbers, phalanx, various 8 division, multiple, numerous, populous 9 battalion, countless, multitude 10 numberless, voluminous

fraction: 6 cohort

__ legion: 7 foreign

legionary: 5 cadet 7 draftee, fighter, officer, private, recruit, soldier, trooper, veteran, warrior 8 commando 9 combatant, mercenary

Legion of __: 5 Honor, Merit

legions: 3 sea 4 army, host, lots, many, slew, tons 5 drove, horde, hosts, ocean, scads 6 clouds, crowds, droves, flocks, hoards, masses, myriad, scores, swarms 7 myriads, numbers, throngs 8 billions, millions, quantity, very many 9 battalion, multitude, profusion, trillions 10 multitudes

legislate: 4 make, pass 5 enact, order 6 codify, decree, oblige, ordain 8 legalize, regulate 9 establish, prescribe 10 constitute

legislated: 6 lawful

législateur group: 5 senat

legislation: 3 act, law 4 bill 6 ruling 7 charter, measure, passage, statute 9 enactment, lawmaking 10 regulation

nix, as ~: 4 kill, veto 5 quash 6 reject 8 override, throw out 9 shoot down

legislative: 8 enacting 9 decreeing, lawgiving, lawmaking, ordaining, synodical 10 senatorial

appendage: 5 rider 7 proviso 9 amendment

assemblies: 5 plena

body: 5 house 6 senate 7 council 10 parliament

disciplinarian: 4 whip

excess: 4 pork

matter: 3 act 4 bill 6 debate 7 cloture 10 filibuster

meeting: 4 sess. 7 session

ordinance: 3 law 4 rule 6 assize

legislator: 6 deputy, leader, member 7 senator 8 lawgiver, lawmaker 10 politician

legislature: 4 body, diet, parl. 5 house, taxer 6 plenum, senate 7 chamber, council 8 assembly, congress, politics 9 lawmakers 10 parliament

Austria: 9 Bundesrat

Canada: 6 Senate

Croatia: 5 Sabor

Denmark: 9 Folketing

Finland: 9 Eduskunta

France: 5 Senat 6 Senate

Germany: 9 Bundesrat, Bundestag

Greek: 5 Boule

Iceland: 7 Althing

India: 6 Sansad

Ireland: 4 Dail

Israel: 7 Knesset

Italy: 6 Senate

Japan: 4 Diet

Kenya: 5 Bunge

Latvia: 6 Saeima

Lichtenstein: 4 Diet

Lithuania: 6 Seimas

Mexico: 6 Senate

Norway: 8 Storting

Poland: 4 Sejm

Russia: 4 Duma

South Korea: 6 Kukhoe

Spain: 6 Cortes

Sweden: 7 Riksdag

Ukraine: 4 Rada

legist: 6 jurist, lawyer 7 counsel 8 attorney, defender 9 barrister, counselor, solicitor 10 counsellor

legit: 2 OK 4 fair, fine, good, nice, okay, okeh, okey, real, walk 5 frank, great, jural, legal, licit, moral, noble, sound, valid 6 honest, kasher, kosher, lawful, proper, square 7 allowed, ethical, factual, genuine, logical, upright 8 accepted, all right, bona fide, credible, laudable, pleasant, pleasing, rightful, splendid, straight, superior, truthful, verified 9 admirable, agreeable, allowable, authentic, by the book, excellent, legalized, permitted, reputable, veracious, veritable, wonderful 10 aboveboard, acceptable, authorized, beneficial, creditable, forthright, on the level, reasonable, sanctioned, scrupulous

not ~: 4 fake 5 bogus, phony, shady 6 phoney, pseudo

legitimacy: 5 force, right, truth 6 weight 7 grounds 8 legality, validity 9 authority, soundness 10 lawfulness

legitimate: 4 fair, good, just, real, sure, true 5 jural, legal, licit, right, sound, typic, usual, valid 6 cogent, honest, kasher, kosher, lawful, normal, proper 7 certain, correct, genuine, logical, natural, regular, typical 8 accepted, innocent, legalize, official, orthodox, probable, received, reliable, rightful, sensible, verified 9 allowable, authentic, canonical, customary, legalized, statutory, warranted 10 admissible, authorized, consistent, on the level, reasonable, sanctioned, true to type, verifiable

legitimately: 5 right, truly 6 indeed, in fact, really 7 de facto, in truth 8 actually, for a fact, honestly 9 assuredly, certainly, genuinely, in reality, precisely 10 positively

legitimize: 5 adopt 7 certify, entitle, intitle, justify, mandate 8 sanction, validate

legitimized: 5 legal, licit, valid 6 kosher, lawful 7 enacted 8 mandated, official 9 juridical, legalized, statutory 10 authorized, legislated, legitimate

legman: 5 gofer 6 gopher 8 reporter

job: 6 errand

__ legno: 3 col

Lego: 5 block

leg-of-mutton sleeve: 5 gigot

leg-puller: 3 wag 4 card, fool 5 clown, comic, cutup 6 jester, kidder 7 buffoon, farceur, gagster, wise guy 8 comedian, funnyman, humorist, wiseacre

Legrand: 6 Michel

Le Grand Orange: Rusty Staub

Legree: 5 Simon

LeGros: 5 James

leg rotation (ballet): 7 turnout

legs: 7 stamina 8 patience 9 longevity

creature with 14 ~: 6 isopod

go on hind ~: 4 ramp, rear

on its last ~: 4 weak 6 poorly 7 failing, not well 9 worsening

__ legs: 3 sea 4 crab, hind

Legs: 7 Diamond

author: William Kennedy

Legs (1984 song)

artist: ZZ Top

leg-smoothing product: 4 Nair, Neet

__-leg table: 4 gate

Le Guin: 6 Ursula

legume: 3 pea, soy 4 bean, miso, soya, tofu 5 vetch 6 acacia, cowpea, frijol, lentil, manioc, mimosa, peanut 7 cassava, haricot, mesquit, red bean, snow pea, soybean, wax bean 8 bean curd, bush bean, chickpea, fava bean, garbanzo, lima bean, mesquite, mung bean, navy bean, pink bean, pole bean, snap bean, sweet pea, yard-long 9 broad bean, cover crop, green bean, pinto bean, tonka bean, vegetable, white bean 10 adzuki bean, butter bean, kidney bean, string bean

holder: 3 pod 4 hull 6 jacket 8 seed case 10 integument

tree: 3 koa 5 carob 6 cassia, cercis, locust, padauk, padouk, redbud 7 araroba, mesquit 8 mesquite, tamarind 9 poinciana

__ leg up: 4 get a 5 give a

legwear: 5 socks 6 tights 7 hosiery 9 pantyhose, stockings

legwork: 6 search, survey 8 research

Lehár, Franz work: The Merry Widow

Le Havre: 4 city, port, town

city near ~: 4 Caen

locale: 6 France

Lehi

locale: 4 Utah

Lehigh: 5 river 6 school

athletes: 9 Engineers

locale: 4 Penn. 9 Bethlehem

Lehman: 3 Tom 5 Engel 6 Ernest

Lehmann: 5 Lotte 7 Michael

Lehmann, Lotte: 6 singer 7 soprano

specialty: 5 opera

Lehr: 3 Lew

Lehrer: 3 Jim, Tom

lei: 6 wreath 7 garland 9 neckpiece

land: 4 Maui, Oahu 5 Kauai 6 Hawaii

Leia: 8 princess

brother: 4 Luke

father: 5 Darth

rescuer: 3 Han

Leiber: 5 Fritz, Jerry

Leibman: 3 Ron

spouse: Linda Lavin, Jessica Walter

Leibnitz, Wilhelm von: 11 philosopher

Leibovitz: 5 Annie

Leibowitz, René: 9 conductor

Leica: 6 camera

alternative: *see* camera

Leicester: 4 city, earl, town 5 sheep 6 cheese

locale: 7 England

Leicestershire: 6 county

locale: 7 England

Leics: 6 county

locale: 7 England

Leiden: 4 city, town

locale: 7 Holland

Leie, city on the: 5 Ghent

Leif: 7 Ericson, Garrett 8 Erickson, Eriksson

father: 4 Eric

Leifer: 5 Carol

Leigh: 4 Hunt, Mike 5 Janet, Mitch 6 Vivien 7 Harline 9 McCloskey

__ Leigh Cook: 7 Rachael

Leigh, Janet: 7 actress

daughter: Jamie Lee Curtis

film: Angels in the Outfield (1951)
Bye Bye Birdie (1963)
The Fog (1980)
Houdini (1953)
Living It Up (1954)
The Manchurian Candidate (1962)
My Sister Eileen (1955)
The Naked Spur (1953)
One Is a Lonely Number (1972)
Psycho (1960)
Rogue Cop (1954)
Scaramouche (1952)
Touch of Evil (1958)
Walking My Baby Back Home (1953)
Who Was That Lady? (1960)

spouse: Tony Curtis

Leigh, Jennifer Jason: 7 actress

film: The Anniversary Party (2001)
Crooked Hearts (1991)
Dolores Claiborne (1995)
Fast Times at Ridgemont High (1982)
Grandview, U.S.A. (1984)
The Hudsucker Proxy (1994)
Road to Perdition (2002)
Single White Female (1992)

Leigh Taylor-__: 5 Young

Leighton: 5 Laura 8 Margaret

Leigh, Vivien: 7 actress

film: Gone With the Wind (1939, AA)
Ship of Fools (1965)
A Streetcar Named Desire (1951, AA)

role: 5 O'Hara 6 Stella 8 Scarlett

spouse: Laurence Olivier

Leila: 5 Hyams

author: Edward Bulwer-Lytton

__ Leilani: 5 Sweet

Leinsdorf, Erich: 9 conductor

Leinster: 6 Murray

Leipzig: 4 city, town

city near ~: 4 Gera 5 Halle 6 Dessau

locale: 7 Germany

river: 6 Parthe 7 Pleisse

see also German

Leisen: **8** Mitchell
leisure: **4** ease, rest, time **5** pause, quiet, range, scope **6** chance, luxury, recess, repose **7** freedom, holiday, liberty, respite, time off **8** free time, good life, vacation **9** spare time **10** recreation, relaxation, retirement, sabbatical
at ~: **4** free, idle **6** otiose
companion: **4** arts
ender: **4** wear
pursuit: **4** play **5** hobby **7** pastime
wear: **5** jeans **6** chinos, denims, slacks, T-shirt
leisure ___: **4** suit
Leisure: **5** David
leisure-class: **4** rich **5** flush **6** fat-cat, loaded, uptown **7** moneyed, opulent, upscale, wealthy, well-off **8** affluent, well-to-do **10** prosperous, well-heeled
leisured: **4** free, idle **7** jobless **8** inactive, on layoff **9** at liberty, on the dole **10** unemployed
leisurely: **3** lax **4** easy, free, idly, lazy, poky, slow **5** slack **6** calmly, casual, draggy, easily, gentle, lazily, pokily, slowly **7** delayed, gradual, halting, impeded, laggard, lagging, languid, relaxed, restful, tardily, unhasty **8** bit by bit, casually, crawling, creeping, dawdling, dilatory, dragging, drawn-out, hesitant, laid-back, plodding, slothful, sluggish, toddling, torpidly **9** gradually, haltingly, laggardly, languidly, lethargic, prolonged, slackened, snaillike, unhurried **10** composedly, crawlingly, creepingly, deliberate, dilatorily, inactively, indolently, listlessly, protracted, sluggishly
leisure-suit fabric: **4** poly **5** Orlon **6** Dacron **9** polyester
leitmotif: **3** air **4** idea **5** theme **6** melody, notion, strain **7** subject
Le Jazz ___: **3** Hot
Le Jet d'___: **3** Eau
___ Lejeune: **4** Camp
Lela: **6** Rochon
Leland: **7** Hayward **8** Hartwell, Stanford
Lélia
author: George Sand
L'Elisir d'Amore
composer: Gaetano Donizetti
Leloir, Luis F.: **7** chemist **8** Nobelist
Lely, Peter: **6** artist **7** painter
homeland: **7** Holland
Lem: **6** Barney **9** Stanislaw
LEM: **6** lander
Apollo 11 ~: **5** Eagle
locale: **4** moon
org.: **4** NASA
part of ~: **5** Lunar **6** Module **9** Excursion
LeMans: **3** car **4** auto **7** Pontiac **10** automobile
Le Mans: **4** city, race, town
locale: **6** France
___ Leman, Switzerland: **3** Lac
Le Marquis de Villemer
author: George Sand
Lema, Tony: **6** golfer
LeMat, Paul: **5** actor
film: American Graffiti (1973) Melvin and Howard (1980)
LeMay: **6** Curtis **7** general
milieu: **3** SAC **8** Air Force
Le menunier d'Angibault
author: George Sand
Lemieux, Mario
milieu: **3** ice **4** rink **5** arena
org.: **3** NHL
Lemme ___!: **4** at 'em
lemming: **6** animal, mammal, rodent
relative: ***see*** rodent
Lemmon: **4** Jack **5** Chris
Lemmon, Jack: **5** actor
film: Airport '77 (1977)
The Apartment (1960)
Avanti! (1972)
Bell, Book and Candle (1958)
Buddy Buddy (1981)
The China Syndrome (1979)
Cowboy (1958)
Dad (1989)
Days of Wine and Roses (1962)
The Fortune Cookie (1966)
The Front Page (1974)
Glengarry Glen Ross (1992)
Good Neighbor Sam (1964)
The Great Race (1965)
Grumpier Old Men (1995)
Grumpy Old Men (1993)
How to Murder Your Wife (1965)
Irma la Douce (1963)
It Should Happen to You (1954)
JFK (1991)
Kotch (1971)
Luv (1967)
Mass Appeal (1984)
Missing (1982)
Mister Roberts (1955, AA)
My Fellow Americans (1996)
My Sister Eileen (1955)
The Odd Couple (1968)
The Out-of-Towners (1970)
Out to Sea (1997)
Phffft! (1954)
The Prisoner of Second Avenue (1975)
Save the Tiger (1973, AA)
Short Cuts (1993)
Some Like It Hot (1959)
That's Life! (1986)
Under the Yum Yum Tree (1963)
The Wackiest Ship in the Army (1960)
spouse: Felicia Farr
Lemnos: **4** isle **6** island
locale: **5** Egean **6** Aegean
Le Moko: **4** Pepe
lemon: **3** car, dog, dud **4** auto, flop, tree **5** color, fruit **6** citrus, flavor, jalopy, turkey, yellow **7** clunker, failure **8** ice cream **10** automobile, hunk of junk, rattletrap
alternative: ***see*** ice cream flavor
bit of ~: **5** twist
candy: **4** drop
derivative: **6** citral
drink: **3** ade **5** juice
ender: **3** ade **5** grass
like ~ juice: **5** acerb **6** acidic
partner: **4** lime
relative: ***see*** citrus, yellow color
tree: **6** citron
lemon ___: **3** law, oil **4** drop **5** grass **6** yellow
lemon-___: **4** lime
Lemon: **3** Bob **10** Meadowlark
lemonade: **5** drink, juice **8** beverage
color: **4** pink
location: **5** stand
Lemonade Lucy: **5** Hayes
lemon balm: **4** herb
Lemon, Bob: **6** hurler, Indian **7** pitcher
LeMond: **4** Greg
___ le monde: **4** tout
Le Monde: **5** paper **6** French **9** newspaper
lemon drop: **5** candy
lemonlike fruit: **6** cedrat, citron
lemon meringue ___: **3** pie
Lemon Pipers
song: Green Tambourine (1967)
Lemon Tree (1962 song)
artist: Peter, Paul and Mary
lemony: **4** acid, sour, tart **5** tangy **6** citric
Lemuel: **8** Gulliver
lemur: **4** maki, vari **5** indri, loris, potto **6** animal, aye-aye, colugo, macaco, mammal, monkey **7** primate
relative: ***see*** primate
Len: **5** Barry **6** Berman, Cariou, Dawson **7** Dykstra, Wilkens **8** Deighton
Lena: **4** Olin **5** Horne, Nyman, river **6** Stolze
River locale: **4** Asia **6** Russia
River people: **5** Yakut
Le Nain: **5** Louis **7** Antoine, Mathieu
___ Lenape: **4** Leni **5** Lenni
Lenard: **4** Mark
Lena the ___: **5** Hyena
lend: **3** let **4** give, loan **5** allow, grant, share, stake, trust **6** afford, extend, impart, lay out, oblige, supply **7** advance, entrust, furnish, intrust, present, provide **10** contribute
a hand: **3** aid **4** abet, help **6** assist, step in **7** bail out, pitch in, sustain **9** cooperate
an ear: **4** heed **6** listen **7** hearken, hear out
one's name to: **4** back, sign **5** boost **7** endorse, indorse, promote, support, warrant **8** champion, stump for, vouch for **9** get behind, guarantee, recommend, subscribe **10** go to bat for, speak up for, stand up for
lend ___: **5** a hand, an ear
lend-___: **5** lease
lender: **3** FHA, SBA **4** bank, FNMA, GNMA **5** S and L **6** banker, loaner, usurer **7** Shylock **8** creditor **9** loan shark **10** pawnbroker
starter: **5** money
... ___ lender be: **4** nor a
lending ___: **7** library
lending, illegal: **5** usury
Lendl, Ivan: **7** netster **9** tennis pro
milieu: **5** court
rival: **6** Becker
Lend me your ___: **4** ears
Lenexa: **4** city, town
locale: **6** Kansas
L'Enfant: **6** Pierre
L'Enfer
poet: Clément Marot
length: **4** hank, size, span, term, time, unit, year **5** limit, orbit, piece, range, reach, realm, space, stage, sweep, width **6** course, degree, extent, height, milage, period, radius, season, strand, stride **7** breadth, compass, expanse, measure, mileage, portion, purview, section, segment, stretch **8** diameter, distance, duration, interval, longness, panorama, quantity, tallness **9** dimension, expansion, linearity, loftiness, longitude, magnitude, ranginess **10** elongation, remoteness
and width: **4** area, size **5** range, reach, scale, scope, space **6** extent, spread **7** compass **9** amplitude
arm's ~: **5** reach
at ~: **5** wordy **6** prolix **7** on and on **8** rambling **10** circuitous, discursive, long-winded
ender: **4** ways, wise
fashion ~: **4** maxi, mini
having only ~: **4** one-d
keep at arm's ~: **6** rebuff **7** neglect, ward off
of office: **4** span **6** period, tenure **8** duration, interval **9** occupancy
of time: **4** span, term **5** sweep **6** period
speak at ~: **3** jaw, yak **4** rant **5** orate, spout **6** expand, preach, rattle **7** address, amplify, declaim, descant, enlarge, lecture, maunder **8** harangue, perorate, sound off **9** discourse, elaborate, expatiate, explicate, hold forth, sermonize, speechify **10** dissertate
starter: **4** wave
times width: **4** area
unit: **2** cm., ft., in., km., mm., yd. **3** mil, rod **4** feet, foot, inch, mile, rood, span, yard **5** chain, cubit, meter **6** fathom, micron, parsec **7** furlong **8** angstrom **9** kilometer, light year **10** centimeter, millimeter
write at ~: **6** ramble **10** dissertate
___-length: **4** arm's, full **5** ankle, fixed, floor **7** feature
lengthen: **3** hem, pad **4** draw, grow **5** add to, reach, swell **6** beef up, dilate, expand, extend, let out, spread **7** amplify, augment, broaden, burgeon, distend, drag out, draw out, enlarge, inflate, proceed, prolong, spin out, stretch **8** bourgeon, continue, elongate, increase, protract **9** string out **10** prolongate
again: **5** rehem
lengthwise: **5** along **7** endways **8** vertical
lengthy: **4** long **5** gabby, windy, wordy **6** padded, prolix **7** diffuse, longish, tedious, unterse, verbose, voluble **8** dragging, drawn-out, elongate, extended, overlong, rambling, tiresome, very long **9** bombastic, elongated, extensive, garrulous, prolonged, talkative, wearisome **10** discursive, long-winded, loquacious, palaverous, protracted
Leni ___: **6** Lenape
leniency: **4** pity **5** grace, mercy **7** charity, quarter **8** clemency, easiness, humanity, kindness, mildness, patience, softness, sympathy **9** tolerance **10** compassion, gen-

erosity, gentleness, indulgence, moderation, tenderness
lenient: 3 lax 4 easy, kind, meek, mild, soft 5 light 6 benign, decent, gentle, humane, kindly, loving, tender 7 amiable, clement, letting, liberal, sparing 8 allowing, excusing, favoring, gracious, humoring, merciful, obliging, spoiling, tolerant, unstrict, yielding 9 assuasive, benignant, compliant, condoning, easygoing, emollient, forgiving, indulgent, pampering, pardoning, soft-shell 10 altruistic, benevolent, charitable, forbearing, permissive, unhardened
be ~: 5 spare 6 excuse, pardon 7 forgive 8 overlook
become ~: 5 yield 6 relent, soften 8 unfreeze
one: 5 softy 6 softie
Lenin: 3 Red 7 Marxist 8 Vladimir
land: 3 Rus. 4 USSR 6 Russia
police: 4 OGPU
predecessor: 4 czar, tsar
Leningrad: 4 city, port, town
locale: 6 Russia
river: 4 Neva
Leninism: 9 Communism, Socialism
Leninist: 3 Red 9 Communist
Lenin Peak: 4 peak 5 mount 8 mountain
locale: 4 Asia 10 Tajikistan
lenitive: 4 balm, soft 5 salve 6 lotion 7 anodyne, unguent 8 liniment, ointment, soothing 9 emollient
lenity: 4 pity 5 mercy 7 quarter 8 clemency, humanity, kindness, mildness, patience, softness, sympathy 10 compassion, generosity, gentleness, indulgence, moderation, toleration
Lenni __: 6 Lenape
Lennon: 4 John, Sean 5 Janet, Kathy, Peggy 6 Dianne, Julian
Lennon, John
middle name: 3 Ono 7 Winston
song: #9 Dream (1975)
Give Peace a Chance (1969)
Imagine (1971)
Instant Karma (1970)
(Just Like) Starting Over (1980)
Mind Games (1973)
Nobody Told Me (1984)
Power to the People (1971)
Stand By Me (1975)
Watching the Wheels (1981)
Whatever Gets You Thru the Night (1974)
Woman (1980)
spouse: Yoko Ono
Lennon, Julian
song: Too Late for Goodbyes (1985)
Valotte (1984)
stepmother: Yoko Ono
Lennon, Sean
mother: Yoko Ono
Lennox: 5 Annie, Lewis
alternative: 5 Rheem, Trane 7 Carrier, Fedders 9 Friedrich
Lennox, Annie
group: Eurythmics
song: Put a Little Love in Your Heart (1988)
Walking on Broken Glass (1992)
Lennoxville school: 7 Bishop's
Lenny: 5 Bruce, Moore, Welch 7 Dykstra, Kravitz, Wilkens
Lenny (1974 film)
cast: Dustin Hoffman, Valerie Perrine
director: Bob Fosse
leno: 5 weave 6 fabric 8 material
Leno, Jay: 4 host 5 emcee
predecessor: 4 Paar 5 Allen 6 Carson
prominent feature: 4 chin
successor: 6 O'Brian, O'Brien
to Letterman: 5 rival
Lenore
author: Edgar Allan Poe
Lenox: 4 city, town
alternative: 6 Mikasa 8 Wedgwood
locale: 4 Mass.
product: 5 china
Le Nozze di Figaro
composer: Wolfgang Amadeus Mozart
lens: 4 zoom 5 glass, loupe, optic 6 ocular 7 contact, fisheye, monocle 8 eyeglass, eyepiece, meniscus 9 magnifier, wide-angle
camera ~ scope: 5 field
cleaning aid: 6 eyecup
combining form: 4 phac-, phak- 5 phaco-, phako-
cover: 6 cornea
holder: 3 rim 5 frame
insect eye ~: 5 facet
jeweler's ~: 5 loupe
opening: 4 iris
setting: 5 f-stop
__ lens: 4 zoom 7 contact, fisheye
lenses
big name in ~: 4 Lomb 6 Bausch
like some ~: 6 convex 7 bulging, concave 9 outcurved
like some contact ~: 4 soft
Lent
follower: 6 Easter
observe ~: 4 fast 7 abstain
symbol: 3 ash
__ lente: 7 festina
Lenten: 6 frugal, meager 7 austere 8 rigorous
lenticular: 7 bulging, gibbose, gibbous
lentigo: 3 dot 4 spot 5 speck 7 freckle
lentil: 4 bean 6 legume, veggie 9 vegetable
dish: 3 dal 4 dahl, soup, stew 6 sambar
Lent Lily, The
author: A.E. Housman
lento: 4 slow 5 tempo 6 slowly
faster than ~: 6 adagio
slower than ~: 5 largo
Lenya, Lotte: 7 actress
spouse: Kurt Weill
Lenz, Kay
spouse: David Cassidy
Leo: 3 cat 4 Genn, lion, pope, sign 5 Esaki, saint, Sayer 6 Fender, Gorcey, Kottke, McKern, Popkin, Rosten 7 Carroll, Delibes, McCarey, pontiff, Szilard, Tolstoy 8 Carrillo, Durocher 9 Baekeland, Buscaglia, Nomellini, Rainwater
constituent: 4 star
month: 3 Aug., Jul. 4 July 6 August
predecessor: 4 Crab 6 Cancer
successor: 5 Virgo
see also lion
Leo __: 5 Minor
Léo: 7 Delibes
Leo G. __: 7 Carroll
Leominster: 4 city, town
locale: 4 Mass.
Leon: 4 Ames, Edel, Hess, Uris 5 Bakst, Errol 6 Cooper, Spinks 7 Alberti, Panetta, Redbone, Russell, Trotsky 8 Fleisher, Jaworski, Lederman
León: 4 city, town
locale: 6 Mexico 9 Nicaragua 10 Guanajuato
see also Spanish
__ León: 7 Ponce de
Léon: 5 Bakst 6 Daudet 7 Jouhaux 9 Bourgeois
see also French
Leona: 8 Helmsley, Mitchell
Leonard: 4 Buck 5 Cohen, Nimoy 6 Elmore, Maltin, Warren 7 Sheldon, Slatkin 9 Bernstein
in Russian: 6 Leonid
Leonardo: 7 da Vinci 8 DiCaprio
see also Italian
Leonard, Sugar Ray: 5 boxer
milieu: 4 ring
__ Leonard Wood: 4 Fort
Leonato to Beatrice: 4 aunt
Leoncavallo, Ruggiero: 8 composer
work: I Pagliacci
Serafita
Zaza
Leone: 3 car 4 auto 6 Sergio, Subaru 10 automobile
__ Leone: 6 Sierra
Leone, Sergio: 8 director
film: Fistful of Dollars (1964)
For a Few Dollars More (1966)
The Good, the Bad, and the Ugly (1966)
Once Upon a Time in America (1984)
Once Upon a Time in the West (1968)
Leonhard: 5 Euler
Leonid: 8 Andreyev, Brezhnev
see also Russian
Leonid __ shower: 6 meteor
leonine: 5 maned 6 feline, kingly, lordly, mighty 8 fearless 10 courageous
see also lion
Leoni, Téa: 7 actress
film: Deep Impact (1998)
The Family Man (2000)
Fun With Dick and Jane (2005)
Ghost Town (2008)
Hollywood Ending (2002)
Jurassic Park III (2001)
Spanglish (2004)
spouse: David Duchovny
TV: The Naked Truth
Leonore Overture
composer: Ludwig van Beethoven
Leonowens, Anna
where ~ taught: 4 Siam
Leontyne: 5 Price
leopard: 3 cat, fur 5 felid 6 animal, big cat, feline 7 panther
home: 3 zoo 4 Asia 6 Africa, jungle
relative: ***see*** feline
snow ~: 3 cat, fur 5 ounce
sound: 5 growl, snarl
spot: 7 rosette
leopard __: 4 frog, seal
__ leopard: 4 snow 7 clouded
Leopards: 9 Lafayette
Leopard, The
composer: Nino Rota
Leopold: 4 Aldo, Auer 7 Ruzicka 8 von Ranke 9 Stokowski
colleague: 4 Loeb
Leos: 7 Janácek
leotard: 6 tights 7 costume, garment
Lepanto: 4 gulf
Le Penseur
sculptor: Auguste Rodin
leper: 6 pariah 7 outcast
Le Père Goriot
author: Honoré de Balzac
Le Pew: 4 Pepe
lepidopterist
concern: 9 butterfly
gear: 3 net
Lepontine __: 4 Alps
__ Leppard: 3 Def
leprechaun: 3 elf, fay 4 pixy 5 elfin, fairy, gnome, nisse, pixie 6 sprite 7 brownie
country: 4 Eire, Erin 7 Ireland
cousin: 3 elf 5 gnome, troll
language: 6 Gaelic
like a ~: 3 wee 5 elfin 6 little, petite 7 puckish 10 diminutive
lepton: 4 muon 5 tauon 8 electron, particle
__ lepton: 3 tau
Lepus: 4 Hare
star in ~: 5 Arneb
Le Repos
artist: Camille Corot
Le rève: 4 aria
Lerner: 3 Max 4 Carl 7 Alan Jay, Michael
Lerner, Alan Jay: 8 lyricist
collaborator: Frederick Loewe
musical: Brigadoon
Camelot
Gigi
My Fair Lady
Paint Your Wagon
song: Almost Like Being in Love
Camelot
Get Me to the Church on Time
Gigi
The Heather on the Hill
I Could Have Danced All Night
If Ever I Would Leave You
I Remember It Well
I Talk to the Trees
I've Grown Accustomed to Her Face
The Night They Invented Champagne
On the Street Where You Live
The Rain in Spain
Thank Heaven for Little Girls
They Call the Wind Maria
With a Little Bit of Luck
Wouldn't It Be Loverly
__ le roi!: 4 A bas, Vive
LeRoi: 5 Jones
Le Roi __: 6 Soleil
Le Roi d'Ys
composer: Édouard Lalo
Le Roi Malgré __: 3 Lui
Le Rossignol: 6 ballet
composer: Igor Stravinsky
lerot: 6 rodent 8 dormouse

Le Rouge __ Noir: 4 et le
Leroux: 6 Gaston
Leroy: 3 Hal **6** Mervyn, Neiman **7** Grumman, Van Dyke **8** Anderson
__ Leroy: 4 Iola
LeRoy: 4 Baby **6** Mervyn, Neiman
Les: 4 Paul **5** Aspin, Brown, Crane **6** Baxter, Elgart **7** Nessman **8** Tremayne
Les __: 3 Miz **5** Girls
Les __ mousquetaires: 5 trois
Les __-Unis: 5 États
LeSabre: 3 car **4** auto **5** Buick **10** automobile
  rival: 3 LTD
Lesage, Alain: 6 French, writer
  work: Gil Blas
__-les-Bains: 3 Aix **5** Evian
Les Bergeries
  author: Claude Anet
Lesbos
  locale: 5 Egean **6** Aegean, Greece
__ Lescaut: 5 Manon
lèse __: 7 majesté, majesty
lèse majesty: 7 treason **8** betrayal, sedition **9** treachery **10** disrespect
Les États-__: 4 Unis
Les Girls (1957 film)
  cast: Mitzi Gaynor, Gene Kelly
  composer: Cole Porter
  director: George Cukor
Lesh: 4 Phil
LeShan: 3 Eda
lesion: 3 cut **4** gash, sore **5** wound **6** bruise, injury, scrape **7** scratch **8** abrasion **10** laceration
Lesley: 4 Gore **5** Stahl
Lesley Ann: 6 Warren
Lesley-Anne: 4 Down
Leslie: 4 Joan **5** Caron **6** Bethel, Howard, Uggams **7** Nielsen, Stephen **9** Charteris, Halliwell
Leslie __ Hope: 6 Townes
Les Maîtres Mosaïstes
  author: George Sand
Les Maîtres Sonneurs
  author: George Sand
Les Misérables
  author: Victor Hugo
  character: 4 Jean **5** Felix **6** Azelma, Javert, Marius **7** Cosette, Fantine, Valjean **8** Gavroche **9** Pontmercy, Tholomyès **10** Thénardier
  song: 5 Stars
Les Misérables (1998 film)
  cast: Claire Danes, Liam Neeson, Geoffrey Rush, Uma Thurman
Les Misérables author
  setting: 5 Paris, sewer **6** France
__-les-mois: 4 tous
Les Noces: 6 ballet
  composer: Igor Stravinsky
Les Nuits d'__: 3 Été
Le Soleil
  locale: 6 Quebec
Lesotho: 6 nation **7** country
  capital: 6 Maseru
  coin: 5 sente
  home: 6 Africa
  language: 4 Zulu
  locale: 6 Africa
  people: 5 Sotho **6** Basuto
  river: 6 Orange
Les pêcheurs de perles
  composer: Georges Bizet
Le Spectre de la Rose: 6 ballet
  composer: Carl Maria von Weber
Les Préludes
  composer: Franz Liszt
Les Rougon-Macquart
  author: Émile Zola
less: 5 fewer, lower, minor, minus **6** little **7** limited, reduced, shorter, smaller, wanting, without **8** inferior, slighter, take away **9** excepting, secondary, shortened **10** diminished
  important: 5 lower, minor **9** auxiliary, secondary **10** derivative, incidental, peripheral
  in music: 4 meno
  make ~: 5 allay **6** reduce **7** lighten **8** decrease
  make ~ narrow: 6 expand, spread **7** broaden, enlarge, thicken **9** spread out
  make ~ wild: 5 break **6** soften **7** harness **8** tone down
  more or ~: 4 near **5** quite, sorta **6** around, fairly, kind of, nearly, rather, sort of **8** slightly, somewhat, very well
  than: 5 below, lower, under **7** beneath **10** inferior to, unworthy of
less __: 4 than
__ Less Bell to Answer: 3 One
lessee: 5 liver **6** lodger, renter, roomer, tenant **7** boarder **8** occupant
  payment: 4 rent
lessen: 3 cut, ebb **4** bate, clip, crop, curb, drop, ease, fade, fall, pare, sink, slow, thin, wane **5** abate, allay, break, close, drain, erode, let up, limit, lower, relax, slack, taper **6** dampen, deduct, defuse, defuze, demean, dilute, impair, minify, modify, narrow, recede, reduce, shrink, soften, temper, weaken **7** abridge, assuage, curtail, cut back, cut down, decline, degrade, depress, detract, die down, drop off, dwindle, fall off, lighten, mollify, qualify, shorten, slacken, slack up, subside, tail off, thin out, whittle **8** amputate, contract, decrease, diminish, downsize, minimize, mitigate, moderate, palliate, peter out, roll back, slow down, taper off, tone down, trail off, truncate, wind down **9** alleviate, attenuate, cut down on, extenuate, scale down, soft-pedal **10** de-escalate, smooth over
lessened: 5 lower, short **7** cut back, reduced **9** decreased, pared down **10** diminished
lessening: 3 cut, ebb **4** drop, fall **5** letup **7** cutback, decline **8** decrease **9** abatement, reduction, remission **10** diminution
lesser: 3 low **4** bush, side **5** dinky, lower, minor, small, under **6** bottom, junior, nether, second **8** inferior, slighter, small-fry **9** secondary, small-time, subjacent **10** bush-league, second-rate, subsidiary, undersized
  prefix: 5 under-
lesser __: 3 ape
Lesser __: 3 Dog **4** Bear **5** panda
Lesser Antilles: 4 isls. **5** isles **7** islands
  island: 6 Tobago **8** Barbados, Leewards, Trinidad **9** Windwards
  native: 5 Carib
lesser of two __: 5 evils
Lesser Sundas: 5 isles **7** islands
  one of the ~: 4 Bali **5** Timor
Lessing: 5 Doris **8** Gotthold
Less is __: 4 more
lesson: 4 quiz, task, test **5** class, drill, model, moral, study **6** homily, notice, period, rebuke, sermon **7** censure, chiding, lecture, message, precept, reading, reproof, warning **8** coaching, exemplar, exercise, homework, practice, scolding, teaching, tutoring **9** chalk talk, class work, deterrent, education, reprimand, schooling **10** admonition, assignment, punishment, recitation, school work
  conduct a ~: 5 teach **7** lecture
  first-grade ~: 8 alphabet
  learn a ~: 3 get **5** grasp **6** absorb, digest, soak up **7** drink in **9** apprehend **10** assimilate, comprehend, understand
  story with a ~: 4 myth **5** fable **7** parable **8** allegory, apologue
  teach a ~ to: 6 punish
__ lesson: 6 object
Lesson From Aloes, A
  author: Athol Fugard
Lessons in Living
  author: Maya Angelou
Lesson, The
  author: Eugène Ionesco
__ Lesson, The: 5 Piano **7** Anatomy
lessor: 8 landlady, landlord
__ Less Ordinary: 5 A Life
Less Than Zero
  author: Bret Easton Ellis
Les Sylphides: 6 ballet
  composer: Frédéric Chopin
lest: 6 in case **7** perhaps **9** perchance
Lestat creator: Anne Rice
__ Lestat, The: 7 Vampire
Lester: 3 Tom **5** Flatt, Jerry, Ketty, Young **6** del Rey, Maddox **7** Pearson, Richard
Lester Pearson Award awarder: 3 NHL
Lestoil: 7 cleaner
  alternative: 5 Brite, Lysol **6** Top Job **7** Mr. Clean, Pine Sol **9** Fantastik, Step Saver
Les Trois Villes
  author: Émile Zola
Lest we lose our __: 5 Edens
let: 4 lend, rent **5** allow, brook, cause, grant, lease, leave, trust **6** accede, accept, do-over, enable, free up, leased, permit, suffer **7** approve, certify, charter, concede, endorse, indorse, license, rent out, warrant **8** accede to, assent to, sanction, stand for, sublease, tolerate **9** approve of, authorize, give leave, put up with **10** commission
  at: 5 sic on
  be: 5 leave, spare **6** lay off **10** leave alone
  be known: 3 air, say **4** blab, leak, tell, warn **5** level, speak, spill, state, utter, voice **6** advise, clue in, convey, detail, fill in, impart, inform, notify, relate, report, reveal, squeal, tip off, unveil **7** apprise, breathe, confess, declare, divulge, explain, express, give out, lay bare, mention, recount, uncover, whisper **8** acquaint, announce, disclose, instruct, proclaim **9** leave word, recognize, spit it out **10** keep posted
  bygones be bygones: 6 excuse, forget, pardon **7** forgive **8** overlook, play past
  down: 4 fail, mock, sink **5** lower **6** dismay **7** abandon, depress **9** depressed, fall short **10** disappoint, disenchant, dissatisfy
  ender: 4 down
  fall: 4 drop, shed **5** spill
  fall between the cracks: 4 omit **6** forget, ignore **7** neglect **9** disregard
  fly: 3 lob **4** cast, fire, hurl, send, toss **5** chuck, fling, heave, pitch, shoot, sling, throw **6** launch, let off, propel **7** fire off
  go: 2 ax **3** axe, can **4** axed, boot, drop, fire, free, miss, omit, oust, sack, weep **5** clear, fired, freed, loose, relax, spare, throw, untie, waive, yield **6** acquit, bounce, canned, excuse, lay off, let off, loosen, relent, sprang, spring, sprung, unhand, untied **7** abandon, cashier, dismiss, drum out, manumit, neglect, release, set free **8** cut loose, furlough, get rid of, liberate, overlook, pink-slip, released **9** discharge, disengage, dismissed, liberated, sacrifice, surrender, terminate, turn loose **10** discharged, relinquish
  go of: 4 dump, shed **5** ditch, spurn **6** give up, unload **7** abandon, discard, toss out **8** renounce **9** eighty-six, repudiate, throw away **10** relinquish
  happen: 6 permit **8** sanction, tolerate
  in: 5 admit, alter, greet **6** accept **7** accepts, altered, embrace, include, receive, welcome **8** accepted, admitted
  in on: 4 tell **5** ready **6** advise, inform, tip off **8** advise of
  it all hang out: 4 bare **6** reveal **7** divulge, lay bare **8** disclose **9** make known **10** make public
  it go: 6 excuse, pardon **7** forgive **8** laugh off, overlook
  it happen: 6 give in, give up **7** back off **9** acquiesce **10** capitulate
  it stand: 4 stet
  know: 4 tell **5** cue in **6** inform, tip off
  know indirectly: 4 hint **6** allude **7** suggest **8** intimate, lead up to **9** insinuate
  loose: 4 free, play, yell **5** shout, unpen, unpin, untie **6** bellow, unbind, untied **8** liberate
  off: 4 drop, emit, free **5** clear, spare **6** acquit, excuse, exempt,

let fly, pardon, wink at **7** absolve, dismiss, excused, forgive, release, relieve **9** allow to go, discharge, exonerate
off steam: 4 rage, vent, yell **7** release
on: 3 own, say **4** avow, fool, hint, tell **5** admit, allow, grant, imply, spill **6** fess up, reveal **7** admit to, concede, confess, divulge, pretend, suggest **8** disclose, give away, indicate **9** drop a hint, make known
oneself go: 5 unlax **6** rest up, unwind **7** lay back, sit back **8** loosen up, slack off **9** hang loose **10** settle back, take it easy
one's voice be heard: 6 assert, insist **7** declare **8** sound off **10** stand up for
out: 4 blab, free, loan, rent, vent **5** break, lease, loose, unpen, widen **6** exhale, expand, expose, loosen, reveal, unreel **7** divulge, release **8** disclose, lengthen, liberate **9** discharge, make known, open a seam
pass: 5 allow, spend **6** ignore, wink at **7** forgive, neglect **8** overlook **9** disregard
rip: 5 begin, start **6** launch **7** kick off, lead off, take off, usher in **8** commence, get going **10** inaugurate
slide: 4 omit **6** wink at **7** neglect **8** overlook
slip: 4 blab, leak, miss, tell **5** blurt, spill **6** betray, expose, forget, reveal, unmask, unveil **7** divulge, exhibit, lay bare, uncover **8** disclose **9** make known **10** make public
the cat out of the bag: 3 air **4** bare, leak, tell **5** admit, blurt, spill **6** betray, expose, gossip, reveal, squeal, tattle **7** divulge **8** disclose, give away **9** make known
the water out: 3 tap **4** vent **6** siphon **7** draw off
to ~: 4 free, open **5** empty **6** vacant **7** for rent, untaken **8** not in use, unfilled **9** available **10** tenantless, unoccupied
up: 3 ebb **4** ease, fall, lull, quit, stop, wane **5** abate, cease, eased, pause, relax, slack **6** abated, ceased, die out, ease up, go easy, lay off, lessen, paused, relent, relief **7** back off, die down, ease off, relaxed, release, relieve, respite, slacken, stopped, subside, tail off **8** decrease, diminish, intermit, level off, mitigate, moderate, slack off, slow down, tone down **9** backed off, lose speed, mitigated, moderated **10** diminished, slacked off, slowed down
use: 4 lend, loan, pool **5** allot, cut in, split, trust **6** assign, divide, extend, oblige **7** divvy up, provide **8** go in with
let __: 3 fly, off, out **4** down, in on, it go, slip **5** alone, loose
let __ a secret: 4 in on
let __ hang out: 5 it all
...let __ put asunder: 5 no man
Let __: 4 'Em In, It Be, Me In **5** Her In
Let __...: 5 me see
Let __ be said...: 5 it not
Let __ Cake: 5 'em Eat
Let __ do it: 6 George
Let __, Lover: 4 Me Go
Let __ Me: 4 It Be
Let __ Praise Famous Men: 5 Us Now
Let __ the One: 4 Me Be
Let __ There: 4 Me Be
Let a __ Be...: 5 Smile
L'état, c'est __: 3 moi
letdown: 4 balk **5** baulk **7** chagrin, sadness, setback, washout **10** anticlimax, bitter pill, melancholy
let-down: 7 unhappy
Let 'Em Eat Cake: 7 musical
composer: George Gershwin, Ira Gershwin
song: 4 Mine
Let 'Em In (1976 song)
artist: Paul McCartney
l'été, month of: 4 août, juin **7** juillet
Let 'er __!: 3 rip
Let George __: 4 do it
Lethal Weapon (1987 film)
cast: Gary Busey, Mel Gibson, Danny Glover
cat: 7 Burbank
director: Richard Donner
dog: 3 Sam
role: 5 Riggs **8** Murtaugh
lethargic: 3 lax **4** blah, dopy, dozy, dull, idle, lazy, limp, logy, poky, slow **5** dopey, heavy, inert, moony, slack, tardy, weary, wimpy **6** asleep, draggy, drowsy, otiose, sleepy, snoozy, stolid, supine, torpid **7** dormant, gradual, halting, impeded, laggard, lagging, languid, nebbish, out of it, passive, wimpish **8** comatose, crawling, creeping, dawdling, dilatory, dragging, drawn-out, hesitant, inactive, indolent, laid-back, lifeless, listless, plodding, slothful, sluggish, stretchy, toddling **9** apathetic, enervated, impassive, leisurely, lymphatic, prolonged, sedentary, snaillike, somnolent, stupefied, unhurried **10** deliberate, disengaged, languorous, phlegmatic, protracted, sleepyhead, slumberous, spiritless, unreactive
feeling: 5 ennui
one: 5 snail **7** dawdler
lethargy: 4 coma **5** sleep, sloth, sopor **6** apathy, phlegm, stupor, torpor **7** boredom, inertia, languor, laxness, slumber, vacuity **8** dullness, hebetude, idleness, inaction, laziness, loginess, slowness **9** disregard, inanition, indolence, inertness, lassitude, torpidity, unconcern, weariness **10** drowsiness, inactivity, sleepiness, supineness, torpidness
Lethe: 5 river
locale: 5 Hades
Let Her Cry (1995 song)
artist: Hootie and the Blowfish
Let Her In (1976 song)
artist: John Travolta
let it __ hang out: 3 all
Let It Be (1970 song) artist: Beatles
Let It Be Me (song)
artist: Betty Everett, Everly Brothers, Jerry Butler
Letitia: 9 Baldridge
Let Me Be the One (song)
artist: Carpenters, Exposé
Let Me Be There (1973 song)
artist: Olivia Newton-John
(Let Me Be Your) Teddy Bear (1957 song)
artist: Elvis Presley
Let Me Call You Sweetheart: 4 song **5** novel, waltz
author: Mary Higgins Clark
Let Me Entertain You
composer: Jule Styne, Stephen Sondheim
Let Me Go Lover (song)
artist: Joan Weber, Patti Page, Teresa Brewer
Let me in!: 6 open up
Let Me Ride rapper: 5 Dr. Dre
Let Me Sing and I'm Happy (1930 song)
artist: Al Jolson
composer: Irving Berlin
Let My Love Open the Door (1980 song)
artist: Pete Townshend
Leto: 5 Jared
daughter: 7 Artemis
parent: 5 Coeus **6** Phoebe
sister: 7 Asteria
son: 6 Apollo
symbol: 7 spindle
L'Étoile du Nord: 4 Minn. **9** Minnesota
let one's __ down: 4 hair
L'Étranger
author: Albert Camus
Let's __: 4 Do It, Ride **5** Dance **6** Groove **7** Pretend
Let's __ a Deal: 4 Make
Let's __ Again: 4 Do It **5** Twist
Let's __ an Old-Fashioned Walk: 4 Take
Let's __ Another Cup of Coffee: 4 Have
Let's __ in Love: 4 Fall
Let's __ it: 4 face
Let's __ It for the Boy: 4 Hear
Let's __ the Music and Dance: 4 Face
Let's __ the Whole Thing Off: 4 Call
Let's __ Together: 3 Get **4** Stay
Let's call __ day!: 3 it a
Let's Call the Whole Thing Off: 4 duet
composer: George Gershwin, Ira Gershwin
Let's Dance (song)
artist: Chris Montez, David Bowie
Let's do __!: 5 lunch
Let's Do It
composer: Cole Porter
Let's Do It Again (1975 film)
cast: Bill Cosby, Sidney Poitier, Jimmie Walker
director: Sidney Poitier
Let's Do It Again (1975 song)
artist: Staple Singers
Let's Face the Music and Dance
composer: Irving Berlin
Let's Fall in Love
composer: Harold Arlen, Ted Koehler
Let's Fall in Love (1967 song)
artist: Peaches and Herb
Let's Get Away From __: 5 It All
Let's Get It On (1973 song)
artist: Marvin Gaye
Let's Get Serious (1980 song)
artist: Jermaine Jackson
Let's Get Together (1961 song)
artist: Hayley Mills
Let's go!: 4 c'mon
Let's Go Crazy (1984 song)
artist: Prince
Let's Groove (1981 song)
artist: Earth, Wind & Fire
Let's Hang On (1965 song)
artist: Four Seasons
Let's Have Another Cup of Coffee
composer: Irving Berlin
Let's Hear It for the Boy (1984 song)
artist: Deniece Williams
Let's hear more...: 6 do tell
let sleeping dogs __: 3 lie
Let's Live for Today (1967 song)
artist: Grass Roots
Let's Lock the Door (1965 song)
artist: Jay and the Americans
Let's Make a Deal: 8 game show
choice: 3 box **7** curtain
host: Monty Hall
prize: 4 zonk
Let's Misbehave
composer: Cole Porter
Let's Pretend: 9 radio show
Let's Ride (1998 song)
artist: Master P, Montell Jordan, Silkk the Shocker
Let's see...: 3 hmm
Let's shake on it!: 4 deal
Let's Stay Together (1971 song)
artist: Al Green
Let's Take __ Around the Block: 5 a Walk
Let's Take an Old-Fashioned Walk
composer: Irving Berlin
Let's Twist Again (1961 song)
artist: Chubby Checker
Let's Wait Awhile (1987 song)
artist: Janet Jackson
Lett: 7 Latvian **8** European
neighbor: 4 Esth
letter: 2 ar, ef, el, em, en, ex, mu, nu, pi, xi **3** bee, cap, cee, chi, dee, ell, ess, eta, gee, jay, kay, phi, psi, rho, tau, tee, vee, wye, zee **4** beta, iota, kite, line, mail, memo, note, rune, sign, type, zeta **5** aitch, alpha, delta, gamma, kappa, omega, paper, print, prose, reply, sigma, theta **6** answer, billet, lambda, report, symbol, uncial **7** capital, double u, epistle, epsilon, initial, message, missive, omicron, receipt, upsilon, writing **8** alphabet, dispatch, junk mail, longhand **9** character, majuscule, minuscule
abbr.: 3 APO, att., FPO, RFD **4** attn.
closer: 4 seal
drop: 4 slot
ender: 3 box, man, men **4** Best, form, head, Love **5** press, Yours **7** Regards **9** Sincerely **10** Yours truly
first ~: 4 init. **7** initial
flourish: 5 serif
love ~ (French): 10 billet doux
starter: 4 dear, news

letter __: 3 box 4 drop 7 carrier
letter-__: 4 card, size 7 perfect, quality
__ letter: 3 air, day, fan 4 dead, form, hand, open 5 block, chain, cover, crank, to the 7 capital
__-letter: 3 red
__ Letter, Darling: 5 Take a
__-letter day: 3 red
lettered: 7 erudite, learned, refined 8 cultured, educated, literary, literate, polished 9 scholarly 10 cultivated, well-versed
Letter for __, A: 4 Evie
__-letter fraternity: 5 Greek
letterhead: 5 sheet 10 stationery
  abbr.: 3 inc.
  illustration: 4 logo
Letterman, David: 4 host 5 emcee
  first item on a ~ list: 3 ten
  genre: talk
  network: CBS
  rival: Conan O'Brien, Jay Leno
__ Letter Maria: 5 Take a
Lettermen: 4 trio
  members: Butala, Pike, Enegmann
  song: Come Back Silly Girl (1962)
    Hurt So Bad (1969)
    Theme from 'A Summer Place' (1965)
    The Way You Look Tonight (1961)
    When I Fall in Love (1961)
letter of __: 6 credit, intent
__ letter office: 4 dead
letter-perfect: 5 exact 7 precise 8 accurate, faithful, verbatim
letters: 5 print 6 script 7 writing 8 booklore, learning 9 erudition, knowledge 10 literature
__ letters: 4 call 5 man of
Letters
  author: Plato
Letters from Iwo Jima (2006 film)
  cast: Ken Watanabe
  director: Clint Eastwood
Letters From the Field
  author: Margaret Mead
__ Letters in the Sand: 4 Love
Letters to Father Flye
  author: James Agee
Letters to Olga
  author: Václav Havel
Letter, The (song)
  artist: Box Tops, Joe Cocker
__ Letter, The: 7 Scarlet
__-letter word: 4 four
let the __ out of the bag: 3 cat
__ Let the Dogs Out?: 3 Who
Let the Good Times Roll (1973 film)
  cast: Chuck Berry, Chubby Checker, Bo Diddley
Let the Little Girl Dance (1960 song)
  artist: Billy Bland
Let them eat __: 4 cake
let there be light in Latin: 7 fiat lux
Let the Sunshine In musical: 4 Hair
Letting Go
  author: Philip Roth
__ lettres: 6 belles
lettuce: 3 cos, oof 4 bibb, cash, gelt, jack, kail, kale, loot, peag, pelf 5 bills, bread, bucks, dough, funds, lucre, money, moola, mopus, pesos, rhino, sewan 6 dinero, do-re-mi, mammon, mazuma, moolah, seawan, silver, specie, veggie, wampum, wealth 7 cabbage, capital, dollars, ooftish, scratch, shekels 8 bankroll, cold cash, currency, hard cash, smackers 9 banknotes, frogskins, long green, simoleons, vegetable 10 greenbacks, green stuff
  cousin: 4 kail, kale
  layer: 3 bed
  like ~: 5 crisp, leafy
  sea ~: 4 ulva
  unit: 4 head, leaf
__ lettuce: 3 cos 4 Bibb, head, leaf, wild 6 Boston 7 iceberg, romaine
L'Etui de nacre
  author: Anatole France
letup: 4 halt, lull, rest, stop 5 break, lapse, pause, truce 6 easing, recess, relief 7 anodyne, interim, respite 8 interval, reprieve 9 abatement, cessation, lessening, reduction, remission 10 mitigation, slackening, suspension
  without ~: 4 a lot 5 no end, on end
Let us __: 4 pray
Let Us Now Praise Famous Men
  author: James Agee
let well enough __: 5 alone
Let your conscience be your __: 5 guide
Let Yourself Go
  composer: Irving Berlin
leukocyte carrier: 5 lymph
Leutnant Gustl
  author: Arthur Schnitzler
Leutze, Emanuel: 6 artist 7 painter
Lev: 6 Landau
Levant: 5 Oscar 7 leather, Mideast
levanter: 4 wind
Levantine: 7 Eastern, Mideast
  ancient ~ city: 5 Petra
  state: 5 Syria
  vessel: 4 saic
  weight: 4 rotl
Levant, Oscar: 7 pianist
  film: An American in Paris (1951)
    The Band Wagon (1953)
    Humoresque (1946)
LeVar: 6 Burton
levee: 3 dam 4 dike, dock, pier, quay, wall 5 wharf 7 sea wall 9 reception 10 breakwater, embankment
level: 3 aim, lay, mow, par, tie 4 akin, beam, calm, cast, down, drop, even, fell, flat, like, rank, rase, raze, roll, ruin, rung, same, step, tell, tier, trim, true, turn, zone 5 alike, equal, exact, floor, flush, focus, grade, layer, pitch, plain, plane, point, press, slant, stage, story, train, waste, wreck 6 common, degree, direct, equate, even up, ground, height, in line, lay low, league, on a par, planed, rating, rolled, smooth, spread, square, stable, status, steady, topple 7 abreast, address, aligned, balance, destroy, echelon, equable, even off, even out, flatten, incline, lined up, matched, on a line, planate, plateau, precise, regular, station, stratum, surface, trimmed, unbuild, uniform 8 altitude, balanced, bulldoze, category, constant, demolish, equalize, matching, parallel, polished, position, pull down, smoothen, standard, standing, straight, take down, tear down, unbroken, zero in on 9 bring down, come clean, devastate, dismantle, elevation, gradation, identical, knock down, knock over, nivellate, prostrate, recumbent, take apart 10 comparable, consistent, continuous, dependable, equivalent, horizontal, straighten, unchanging
  ender: 6 headed
  not ~: 5 atilt 6 aslope
  off: 3 ebb 4 ease, fall, wane 5 abate, let up 6 recede 7 decline, die down, dwindle, slacken, subside, tail off 8 decrease, moderate, taper off 10 de-escalate
  on the ~: 4 fair, open, true 5 clean, frank, legal, legit, licit, no lie, solid, sound, valid 6 candid, decent, honest, infelt, lawful, proven, square, trusty 7 earnest, ethical, factual, genuine, sincere, up-front, upright 8 bona fide, credible, like it is, out-front, reliable, straight, truthful 9 authentic, blameless, confirmed, guileless, heartfelt, honorable, reputable, rock-solid, veracious 10 aboveboard, dependable, documented, forthright, legitimate, principled, scrupulous, unarguable, upstanding
  top ~: 4 acme, peak, roof 6 apogee, heyday, summit 7 maximum 8 mountain, pinnacle
level __: 3 off
level __ field: 7 playing
__ level: 3 sea 5 on the 6 energy, ground 7 poverty, support
__-level: 3 low, mid, top 4 high 5 entry, split
levelheaded: 4 calm, cool, sane, wise 5 quiet, sober, solid, sound 6 low-key, mellow, placid, sedate, serene, steady, trusty 7 amiable, at peace, equable, pacific, prudent, relaxed, stoical, unmoved 8 all there, amicable, balanced, composed, discreet, laid-back, peaceful, rational, sensible, together, tranquil 9 collected, easy-going, impassive, judicious, practical, quiescent, realistic, temperate, unexcited, unruffled 10 cool-headed, dependable, farsighted, reasonable, unagitated, untroubled
levelheadedness: 5 sense 6 aplomb, sanity 8 presence
leveling: 6 razing 10 bulldozing, demolition
  device: 4 shim 5 wedge
Levene: 3 Sam
Levenson: 3 Sam
__ l'Évêque: 4 Pont
lever: 3 bar, pry 4 tool 5 crank, jimmy, raise 7 crowbar 9 force open
  ender: 3 age
  foot ~: 5 pedal 7 treadle
  November ~ puller: 5 voter
  organ ~: 4 stop 5 pedal
  piano ~: 5 pedal
  pull the ~: 3 opt 4 vote 5 elect 6 decide
Lever 2000: 4 soap
  alternative: ***see*** soap
leverage: 4 drag, edge, pull, rank 5 break, clout, power, ropes 6 grease, jump on, weight 7 hostage, suction 8 purchase 9 advantage, authority, influence 10 ascendance, ascendancy, ascendence, ascendency
leveraged __: 6 buyout
Lever Brothers brand: 3 Lux
leveret: 4 hare 6 animal
  coat: 5 lapin
Levert, Gerald
  song: Casanova (1987)
    Taking Everything (1999)
    Thinkin' Bout It (1998)
Levertov: 6 Denise
Lévesque: 4 René
Levi: 5 Carlo, Dolly, Primo, tribe 6 Eshkol, Morton, Stubbs 7 Strauss
  brother: 3 Dan, Gad 5 Asher, Judah 6 Joseph, Reuben, Simeon 7 Zebulun 8 Benjamin, Issachar, Naphtali
  parent: 4 Leah 5 Jacob
  sister: 5 Dinah
leviathan: 3 big 4 huge 5 giant, hippo, jumbo, rhino, titan, whale 6 beluga 7 mammoth, monster 8 behemoth, colossus, dinosaur, mastodon, Moby Dick 10 gargantuan
Leviathan
  author: Thomas Hobbes
levigate: 3 rub 4 file, mash, mill 5 crush, grate, grind, pound 6 powder 7 break up 9 pulverize
Le Villi
  composer: Giacomo Puccini
Levin: 3 Ira, Sid 4 Marc 5 Henry, Meyer
Levine: 3 Ted
Levine, James: 9 conductor
Levin, Ira: 6 writer
  work: The Boys From Brazil
    Critic's Choice
    Deathtrap
    General Seeger
    A Kiss Before Dying
    Rosemary's Baby
    Sliver
    Song of Rosemary
    The Stepford Wives
    This Perfect Day
Levinson, Barry: 8 director
  film: Avalon (1990)
    Bandits (2001)
    Bugsy (1991)
    Diner (1982)
    Disclosure (1994)
    Envy (2004)
    An Everlasting Piece (2000)
    Good Morning, Vietnam (1987)
    Liberty Heights (1999)
    Man of the Year (2006)
    The Natural (1984)
    Rain Man (1988, AA)
    Sleepers (1996)
    Sphere (1998)
    Tin Men (1987)
    Wag the Dog (1997)
    What Just Happened (2008)

Le Viol
artist: Edgar Degas
Levi's: 5 jeans, pants **8** trousers **9** dungarees
rival: 3 Lee **6** Gitano **8** Jordache
Lévi-Strauss: 6 Claude
levitate: 3 fly **4** hang, rise **5** arise, float, glide, hover **6** lift up **7** elevate, lighten
Leviticus: 4 book
follower: 7 Numbers
preceder: 6 Exodus
Levitt: 7 William
Levittown: 4 city
locale: 7 New York
levity: 3 wit **5** humor, mirth **6** joking **7** gayness **8** buoyance, buoyancy, hilarity, jocosity, zaniness **9** flippancy, frivolity, funniness, giddiness, lightness, merriment, silliness **10** fickleness, jocoseness, jocularity
__ Levu: 4 Viti **5** Vanua
levulose: 5 sugar
levy: 3 fee, put, set, tax **4** call, duty, fine, toll **5** asses, draft, exact, lay on, place, put on, raise, tithe, wrest, wring **6** assess, burden, call up, charge, custom, demand, enlist, excise, extort, gather, impose, impost, muster, summon, tariff, towage **7** collect, recruit **8** exaction, shanghai, usage fee **9** conscript, gathering **10** assessment, collection, imposition
impose a new ~ on: 5 retax
union ~: 7 charges **10** assessment
Levy: 4 Marv **6** Eugene
Levy, Marv: 5 coach
sport: 8 football
Lew: 4 Hoad, Lehr **5** Ayres, Grade **6** Archer **7** Landers, Wallace **8** Burdette **10** Dockstader
lewd: 4 base, blue, fast, foul, racy **5** bawdy, dirty, gross, loose, nasty **6** coarse, erotic, impure, rakish, ribald, risqué, smutty, vulgar, wanton, X-rated **7** immoral, lustful, naughty, obscene, sensual **8** immodest, improper, indecent, off-color, shameful, unchaste, uncurbed **9** libertine, low-minded, lubricous, salacious, shameless **10** in bad taste, indelicate, lascivious, licentious, lubricious, profligate, scandalous, scurrilous, suggestive
look: 4 leer, ogle **5** smirk
Lewes: 4 city, town
locale: 8 Delaware
Lewes, George Henry: 11 philosopher
Lewis: 2 Al, C.S. **3** Ted **4** Carl, Gary, Huey **5** Allen, Bobby, Dawnn, Donna, Jerry, Oscar, range, Shari, Stone **6** Arthur, Edward, Lennox, Ramsey, Seiler, Teague **7** Barbara, Carroll, Gilbert, Mumford, Padgett, Richard, Wyndham **8** Emmanuel, Geoffrey, Grizzard, Juliette, Sinclair **9** Charlotte, Milestone **10** Meriwether
in German: 6 Ludwig
in Italian: 8 Lodovico
in Spanish: 4 Luis
locale: 6 Canada **7** Montana
partner: 5 Clark
seat of ~ and Clark County: 6 Helena
Lewis and the News, Huey
song: Couple Days Off (1991)
Doing It All for My Baby (1987)
Do You Believe in Love (1982)
Heart and Soul (1983)
The Heart of Rock & Roll (1984)
Hip to Be Square (1986)
If This Is It (1984)
I Know What I Like (1987)
It Hit Me Like a Hammer (1991)
I Want a New Drug (1984)
Jacob's Ladder (1987)
Perfect World (1988)
The Power of Love (1985)
Stuck With You (1986)
Walking on a Thin Line (1984)
Lewis and the Playboys, Gary
song: Count Me In (1965)
Everybody Loves a Clown (1965)
This Diamond Ring (1965)
Lewis, Barbara
song: Baby, I'm Yours (1965)
Hello Stranger (1963)
Make Me Your Baby (1965)
Lewisburg
athletes: 5 Bison
school: 8 Bucknell
Lewis, Carl: 6 runner **8** sprinter **10** long jumper
event: 4 dash, race
Lewis, C.S.: 6 writer **7** British
work: The Allegory of Love
The Chronicles of Narnia
Out of the Silent Planet
The Screwtape Letters
Lewis, Edward: 8 Nobelist
Lewis grp., John L.: 3 UMW
Lewis, Jerry: 5 actor **8** comedian
film: Artists and Models (1955)
The Bellboy (1960)
Boeing Boeing (1965)
The Delicate Delinquent (1957)
The Disorderly Orderly (1964)
Don't Give Up the Ship (1959)
It'$ Only Money (1962)
The King of Comedy (1983)
The Ladies' Man (1961)
Living It Up (1954)
My Friend Irma (1949)
The Nutty Professor (1963)
Rock-a-Bye Baby (1958)
Sailor Beware (1951)
The Stooge (1953)
You're Never Too Young (1955)
Lewis, Jerry Lee
cousin: Jimmy Swaggart, Mickey Gilley
nickname: Killer
song: Breathless (1958)
Great Balls of Fire (1957)
High School Confidential (1958)
Whole Lot of Shakin' Going On (1957)
Lewis, Juliette: 7 actress
film: Cape Fear (1991)
Enough (2002)
The Evening Star (1996)
Husbands and Wives (1992)
Kalifornia (1993)
The Other Sister (1999)
Lewis, Lennox: 5 boxer
milieu: 4 ring
Lewis, Meriwether: 8 explorer
Lewis, Oscar: 6 writer
work: Children of Sanchez
Five Families
La Vida
Lewis, Ramsey: 7 pianist
genre: 4 jazz
song: The 'In' Crowd (1975)
Lewis, Sinclair: 6 writer **8** Nobelist
alma mater: 4 Yale
work: Ann Vickers
Arrowsmith
Babbitt
Cass Timberlane
Dodsworth
Elmer Gantry
The God-Seeker
Kingsblood Royal
Main Street
Lewiston: 4 city, town
locale: 5 Idaho, Maine
__ Lewis, WA: 4 Fort
Lex: 6 Barker, Luthor
Lex. __: 3 Ave.
lexicographer: 7 Webster **9** Partridge
concern: 4 word **8** meaning
creation: 3 def. **4** dict. **10** definition, dictionary
name: 4 Noah
lexicon: 3 OED **4** book, list **5** lexis, usage, vocab. **8** dict.. thes., glossary, language, wordbook, wordlist **9** thesaurus **10** cyclopedia, dictionary, vocabulary
Lexington: 2 Av. **4** city, town **6** avenue
athletes: 7 Keydets **8** Wildcats
county: 7 Fayette
locale: 8 Kentucky
school: 3 VMI
Lexington and Concord: 6 battle
lexis: 5 words **7** lexicon **8** glossary **9** thesaurus **10** dictionary, vocabulary
Lexus: 3 car **4** auto **10** automobile
ley: 6 pewter
Ley: 5 Willy
Leyden: 6 cheese
kin: ***see*** cheese
Leyden __: 3 jar
Leyte: 6 battle, island
neighbor: 5 Samar
LF: 3 pos.
L. Frank __: 4 Baum
LGA: 9 LaGuardia
locale: 3 NYC
lge., smaller than: 3 med.
lgth.: 2 ft., km., yd. **4** meas.
see also length
Lhasa: 4 city, town
leader: 4 lama **9** Dalai Lama
locale: 4 Asia **5** Tibet **6** Xizang **7** Sitsang **9** Himalayas
site: 6 Potala
Lhasa Apso: 3 dog, pet **5** canid, pooch **6** canine
Lhotse: 4 peak **5** mount **8** mountain
locale: 4 Asia **5** Nepal, Tibet
Li: 3 Jet **4** elem., Peng **7** element, lithium
3 for ~: 4 at. no.
liability: 3 due, IOU, tab **4** bill, bite, chit, debt, drag, duty, loan, onus, risk **5** blame, debit, guilt, lease, minus, owing, peril **6** arrear, burden, chance, damage, hurdle, pledge, red ink **7** account, bad news, baggage, balance, barrier **8** breakage, contract, drawback, exposure, handicap, jeopardy, mortgage, nuisance, obstacle, openness, tendency, weakness **9** arrearage, detriment, hindrance, millstone, proneness, remainder **10** commitment, compulsion, impediment, indebtment, likelihood, misfortune, obligation, subjection
opposite: 5 asset
liable: 3 apt **4** open, tied **5** bound, given, prone, wrong **6** at risk, guilty, likely **7** at fault, exposed, obliged, subject, tending, to blame **8** amenable, beatable, blamable, culpable, disposed, inclined, in danger, indebted, vincible **9** blameable, obligated, sensitive, subject to **10** answerable, assailable, attackable, chargeable, honor-bound, in the wrong, penetrable, vulnerable
be ~: 4 head, lead, mind, tend **5** do for, guard, nurse, see to, serve **6** manage **7** baby-sit, oversee, protect **8** see after, shepherd **9** look after, safeguard, supervise **10** administer, keep tabs on, minister to, ride herd on, take care of
become ~ for: 5 incur, run up **7** bring on, provoke
not ~: 4 free **5** clear **6** exempt **7** excused **8** absolved **10** off the hook, privileged
(to): 3 apt **4** open **5** given **6** likely
liaise: 4 link **7** contact **10** rendezvous
liaison: 2 in **3** tie **4** link **5** amour, fixer, fling **6** hookup **7** contact, romance **8** intrigue, relation **9** encounter, go-between, interface, interlude **10** connection, get a hold of, interceder
Liam: 6 Neeson **9** O'Flaherty **10** Cunningham
in English: 7 William
Liane: 6 Hansen
liang: 4 tael
Lianna (1983 film)
director: John Sayles
liar: 5 cheat, phony **6** fibber, phoney, rascal **7** deluder **8** deceiver, fabulist, palterer, perjurer **9** charlatan, con artist, falsifier, trickster **10** fabricator, tale teller
Liar (1971 song)
artist: Three Dog Night
__ Liar: 5 Billy
liard: 5 money
Liard: 5 river
locale: 5 Yukon **6** Canada
Liar, liar, __ on fire!: 5 pants
Liar Liar (1997 film)
cast: Jim Carrey, Swoosie Kurtz, Jennifer Tilly
liars __: 4 dice **5** poker
__ lib: 6 women's
libate: 4 pour **5** serve **6** decant **7** pour out
libation: 4 dram **5** drink, toast **6** bracer, liquid **7** draught, potable, tribute **8** apéritif, beverage, cocktail, highball, nightcap, offering, potation **9** sacrifice, sundowner **10** intoxicant
see also beverage, drink

Libation Bearers
  author: Aeschylus

Libby: 5 Frank 7 Willard

Libby, Frank: 7 chemist

Libby, Willard: 7 chemist 8 Nobelist

libel: 3 dig, lie 4 barb, gibe, jeer, jibe, mock, slam, slap, slur, snub, tort 5 abuse, decry, knock, scorn, smear, spurn, taunt, wrong 6 attack, defame, deride, dump on, heckle, impugn, insult, malign, offend, rebuff, revile, slight, vilify 7 affront, asperse, blacken, calumny, catcall, degrade, disdain, mockery, obloquy, offense, put down, rank out, scandal, slander, traduce 8 backbite, badmouth, belittle, contempt, denounce, derision, derogate, ridicule, tear down, throw mud, vilipend 9 aspersion, cheap shot, contumely, denigrate, discredit, disparage, humiliate 10 calumniate, defamation, disrespect, impugnment, imputation, opprobrium, villainize
  ending: 3 ous

libelous: 5 false 6 untrue 7 abusive 9 aspersive, injurious, invidious, malicious, traducing, vilifying 10 backbiting, calumnious, defamatory, derogatory, detractive, malevolent, pejorative, scandalous, scurrilous

Liberace: 3 Lee 7 pianist
  brother: 6 George

liberal: 3 big 4 free, kind, left, rich 5 ample, broad, large, loose, noble, no end 6 casual, galore, giving, lavish, plenty 7 aplenty, copious, general, leftist, lenient, profuse, radical 8 abundant, advanced, catholic, flexible, generous, handsome, merciful, princely, prodigal, rational, tolerant, ultraist, unbiased, wasteful 9 bounteous, bountiful, capacious, exuberant, indulgent, plentiful, receiving, receptive, reformist, soft-touch, unbigoted, unselfish, unsparing, unthrifty 10 altruistic, avant-garde, beneficent, benevolent, bighearted, charitable, dime a dozen, free-handed, high-minded, humanistic, interested, munificent, openhanded, permissive, reasonable, ungrudging, unorthodox, unstinting
  European ~: 5 Green
  lead-in: 3 neo

liberal __: 4 arts

Liberal: 4 city 9 town. party
  locale: 6 Kansas

liberalism: 4 left 8 left wing

liberality: 4 alms 6 bounty 7 bigness, breadth, charity, largess 8 free hand, kindness, largesse, latitude 10 generosity

liberalize: 4 ease, free, grow 5 relax, widen 6 expand, loosen, soften 7 broaden, develop, slacken

liberally: 4 much 7 largely 9 in a big way 10 handsomely

liberalness: 7 charity 8 altruism, humanity, kindness, sympathy 9 tolerance

liberals: 4 left

liberate: 3 rid, rob 4 free, lift, loot, save, take 5 let go, loose, steal, swipe, unmew, untie 6 acquit, detach, free up, let out, loosen, pilfer, ransom, redeem, rescue, unbind, unhand, unhook 7 absolve, bail out, deliver, manumit, release, set free, unchain 8 let loose 9 allow to go, discharge, extricate, unshackle 10 emancipate

liberated: 3 rid 4 free 5 loose, saved 6 untied 7 rescued, set free, unbound 8 set loose 9 unchained 10 unconfined, unfettered, unshackled

liberation: 7 freedom, liberty, release 8 delivery 9 acquittal, discharge, dismissal, salvation

liberator: 5 freer 6 savior 7 rescuer, saviour 8 redeemer

Liberia: 6 nation 7 country
  capital: 8 Monrovia
  flag has one: 4 star
  locale: 3 Afr. 6 Africa
  money: 4 cent 6 dollar
  neighbor: 6 Guinea 10 Ivory Coast
  people: 3 Gbe, Vei 5 Mende 6 Kpelle

Liberius: 4 pope 7 pontiff

Libertarians: 5 party

liberté, __, fraternité: 7 égalité

__ liberties: 5 civil

libertine: 4 lewd, rake, roué, wolf 5 flirt, lover, satyr 6 amoral, bad guy, wanton 7 Don Juan, gallant, playboy, swinger, villain 8 Casanova, hedonist, lothario, prodigal, rakehell, sybarite, uncurbed 9 dissolute, epicurean 10 lascivious, licentious, profligate, voluptuary
  no ~: 4 prig 5 prude 7 puritan 8 bluenose 9 nice Nelly 10 goody-goody

libertinism: 6 laxity 7 abandon, license 8 hedonism, wildness 9 looseness

liberty: 4 rest 5 leave, right, scope 6 choice, permit 7 freedom, holiday, leisure, license, release 8 autarchy, autonomy, decision, delivery, free time, furlough, immunity, latitude, sanction, suffrage, vacation 9 exemption, franchise, privilege 10 birthright, free speech, liberation, permission, relaxation
  at ~: 4 free 6 untied 8 leisured 9 out of work, unengaged 10 unattached, unemployed
  on ~: 6 ashore
  take the ~: 4 dare 6 impose 7 presume 8 be so bold 9 go so far as

Liberty: 5 apple
  relative: *see* apple

Liberty __: 4 Bell, bond, loan, ship 5 party 6 Island 7 Heights

__ Liberty: 4 Miss 5 Ode to, Radio, Sweet

Liberty Bell
  flaw: 5 crack

Liberty Bell, The
  composer: John Philip Sousa

Liberty Heights (1999 film)
  cast: Adrien Brody, Ben Foster, Orlando Jones, Bebe Neuwirth
  director: Barry Levinson

Liberty Mutual
  competitor: *see* insurance company

__ liberty, or...: 6 Give me

Liberty Tree, The
  author: Thomas Paine

__ liberum: 4 mare

libido: 2 id 4 Eros, lust

Libra: 4 sign 6 Scales 7 air sign, Balance
  author: Don DeLillo
  month: 3 Oct. 4 Sept. 7 October 9 September
  predecessor: 5 Virgo
  ruler of ~ in astrology: 5 Venus
  stone: 4 opal
  successor: 7 Scorpio

librairie unit: 5 livre

librarian degree: 3 BLS, MLS

library: 3 den 4 room 5 study 8 atheneum, book room 9 athenaeum
  desk: 6 carrel 7 carrell
  emulate a ~: 4 lend
  enjoy a ~: 4 read 6 browse
  feature: 5 globe 6 alcove, carrel 7 carrell
  ID: 4 ISBN
  no-no: 3 din 4 talk 5 noise 6 racket 7 chatter 9 commotion
  request: 5 quiet 7 silence 9 stillness
  section: 3 ref. 4 biog. 7 fiction 9 biography, reference 10 nonfiction
  sorter: 5 filer
  sound: 3 pst, shh 4 psst
  stamp: 5 dater
  transaction: 4 loan
  unit: 3 vol. 4 book, tome 5 shelf, stack 6 volume

library __: 4 card 5 paste, steps, table 7 binding, edition, science

__ library: 4 film 6 public 7 lending

librate: 4 rock 5 pivot, swing 6 seesaw, swivel 9 alternate, oscillate

__ libre: 4 Cuba, vers

librettist: 6 author, writer 9 dramatist, wordsmith 10 playwright

libretto: 4 book, text 5 story 6 script 7 writing 9 narrative
  feature: 4 aria

Libreville: 4 city, town 7 capital
  locale: 5 Gabon, Gabun

Libya: 6 nation 7 country
  capital: 7 Tripoli
  city: 4 Waha 6 Tobruk 7 Bengasi, Tripoli 8 Benghazi
  desert: 6 Sahara
  group: 4 OPEC 10 Arab League
  gulf: 5 Sidra
  it's n. of ~: 5 Medit.
  money: 5 dinar 6 dirham
  neighbor: 4 Chad 5 Egypt, Niger, Sudan 7 Algeria, Tunisia
  people: 6 Tuareg
  port: 7 Bengasi, Tripoli 8 Benghazi

Libyan: 6 desert

lice: 4 bugs 7 cooties, insects 9 parasites

Licence to Kill (1989 film)
  cast: Timothy Dalton, Robert Davi, Carey Lowell, Talisa Soto
  director: John Glen

license: 2 OK 3 let 4 okay, pass, room 5 allow, grant, leave, power, right, title 6 enable, excess, invest, laxity, patent, permit, ratify, suffer, ticket 7 abandon, anarchy, certify, charter, consent, empower, freedom, go-ahead, liberty, warrant 8 accredit, approval, audacity, boldness, delegate, disorder, gluttony, immunity, latitude, legalize, sanction, temerity, wildness 9 animalism, arrogance, authority, authorize, exemption, looseness, privilege, sauciness, slackness, tolerance 10 commission, debauchery, effrontery, green light, indulgence, permission, profligacy, relaxation, sensuality, sybaritism, unruliness, wantonness
  charge: 3 fee
  issuer: 3 DMV, FCC
  plate: 2 ID

license __: 3 fee 5 plate

__ license: 4 hack 6 poetic 7 driver's

licensed: 6 vested 8 official 9 qualified 10 privileged

licensed practical __: 5 nurse

license plate: 3 tag
  HQ: 3 DMV
  sticker: 5 decal

License to Wed (2007 film)
  cast: Mandy Moore, Robin Williams

licentious: 3 lax 4 fast, lewd, wild 5 loose, nasty 6 amoral, animal, impure, rakish, ribald, unruly, wanton 7 corrupt, Cyprian, fleshly, immoral, relaxed, satyric, unmoral 8 depraved, desirous, scabrous, swinging, uncurbed 9 abandoned, corrupted, dissolute, libertine, lickerish, reprobate, salacious 10 disorderly, libidinous, lubricious, profligate

lichee: 3 nut 4 tree

lichen: 4 moss 5 plant, usnea 6 fungus

lichenology: 7 science

Licht: 6 Jeremy

Lichtenfield: 3 Ted

Lichtenstein: 3 Roy 6 artist 8 sculptor

__ Licht Idylls: 4 Auld

Licia: 8 Albanese

licit: 2 OK 4 good, okay, okeh, okey 5 jural, legal, legan, legit, right, sound, valid 6 kasher, kosher, lawful, proper 7 allowed 8 judicial, mandated, rightful 9 allowable, by the book, legalized, permitted, statutory, warranted 10 aboveboard, acceptable, admissible, authorized, legitimate, on the level, sanctioned

lick: 3 bit, dab, hit, lap, rub, tan, top 4 beat, best, burn, calm, cast, dart, dash, down, drub, flog, hint, leap, play, rout, slap, trim, wash, whip, whup 5 blaze, brush, excel, flick, gloss, graze, outdo, quiet, shoot, smack, smear, solve, spank, speck, speed, sweep, swipe, taste, throw, tinge, touch, trace, waver, whiff, worst 6 caress, defeat, fondle, glance, hurdle, ignite, kindle, master, phrase, quiver, ripple, sample, soothe, strike, stroke, thrash, tongue, wallop 7 clobber, conquer, flicker, flutter, lambast, moisten, overrun, run

over, shellac, smother, surpass, tremble, trounce, vibrate 8 lambaste, move over, osculate, outstrip, overcome, pass over, play over, shellack, spoonful, surmount, vanquish 9 fluctuate, overwhelm, palpitate, vacillate 10 suggestion
and stick: 4 seal
into shape: 5 coach, groom 8 organize
not a ~: 3 nil 4 none, zero
one's chops: 5 savor 6 relish 10 anticipate
starter: 3 cow 4 boot
lick __ promise: 4 and a
lick __ shape: 4 into
__ lick: 3 hot 4 deer, salt
lickety-split: 3 PDQ 4 fast, soon 5 apace 6 presto 7 fleetly, hastily, quickly, rapidly, swiftly 8 in a flash, in a jiffy, in no time, pell-mell, promptly, speedily 9 forthwith, hurriedly, instantly, like a shot, posthaste
go ~: 3 hie, run 4 race 5 speed 6 hurtle
licking: 5 upset 6 defeat 7 beating, setback, tanning 8 drubbing, reversal, spanking, whipping 9 thrashing
__ licks: 4 last
lickspittle: 5 toady 6 fawner, flunky, jackal, lackey, sponge, yes man 7 flunkey, lacquey 8 adulator, hanger-on
licorice: 5 candy, plant 6 flavor
brand: 4 Nibs
flavoring: 5 anise 6 fennel
licorice __: 5 stick
licorice root: 4 herb
lid: 3 cap, hat, tam, top 4 kepi 5 cover 6 boater, bonnet, box top, fedora, helmet, Panama, topper 7 chapeau, closure, Stetson 8 covering, headgear, sombrero 9 stovepipe 10 upper limit
flip one's ~: 4 rage, rail, rant, rave 5 freak, go ape, go mad 7 bluster, carry on, explode, flare up, go crazy 8 freak out 9 go bananas 10 hit the roof
keep a ~ on: 3 gag 4 cork, curb, lull 5 cover, limit, quash, quell 6 muffle, rein in, stifle 7 conceal, contain, control, cover up, repress 8 bottle up, hold back, restrain, restrict, suppress 9 constrain, stonewall, whitewash
remove a ~: 5 uncap
starter: 3 eye
tighten a ~: 5 screw, twist
see also hat
Liddy: 4 Dole 6 Gordon 7 G. Gordon
radio nickname: 4 G-man
Lido
alternative: *see* cookie brand
Lido Shuffle (1977 song)
artist: Boz Scaggs
Lidwina: 5 saint
lie: 3 con, fib, sit 4 bull, dupe, fake, hoax, laze, loll, rest, sham, snow, tale, yarn 5 bluff, couch, exist, fudge, guile, libel, phony, place, put on, rumor, story 6 deceit, delude, dupery, extend, invent, lounge, malign, palter, phoney, remain, repose, reside, sprawl, spread, take in, turn in 7 beguile, calumny, concoct, deceive, distort, evasion, falsify, falsity, fiction, go to bed, mislead, obloquy, perjure, perjury, promote, recline, slander, snow job, untruth, whapper, whopper 8 forswear, go back on, misguide, misquote, misspeak, misstate, overdraw, simulate, softsoap 9 aspersion, deception, disinform, dissemble, falsehood, falseness, foreswear, four-flush, invention, mendacity, misinform, tall story 10 defamation, dishonesty, distortion, equivocate, exaggerate, imputation, inaccuracy, inveracity, stretch out, subterfuge
about: 4 laze 5 relax 6 lounge 7 traduce
adjacent to: 4 abut, join, meet 5 touch, verge 6 adjoin 8 border on, neighbor
against: 3 hug 6 cuddle, curl up, nestle, nuzzle 7 snuggle 8 ensconce, huddle up
along: 4 edge 5 flank, skirt, verge 6 border
around: 8 lallygag
beside: 9 juxtapose
dormant: 5 sleep 9 hibernate
down: 4 rest 5 relax 6 repose, rest up, turn in 7 recline 9 go to sleep
down on the job: 5 slack 7 slacken 8 slack off
down on the job, in Britain: 5 sculk, skulk
fallow: 3 rot 4 idle, rust 5 decay 7 decline 8 go to seed, languish, stagnate, vegetate
give the ~ to: 4 deny 5 rebut 6 differ, impugn, negate, refute 7 confute, counter, dispute, gainsay 8 disprove 9 overthrow
in store for: 4 look, wait 5 await 10 anticipate
in the sun: 4 bake, bask, laze, loll 5 relax 6 lounge 8 sunbathe 9 luxuriate
in wait: 4 lurk 5 sculk, skulk 6 waylay
low: 4 hide, wait 5 squat 6 hole up 9 take cover
spread out: 4 flop, loll 5 slump 6 lounge, slouch, sprawl 7 stretch
to: 4 halt 7 deceive, mislead 9 misinform
under oath: 7 falsify, perjure 8 forswear
lie __: 3 low 4 down 5 doggo
__ lie: 3 big 5 white
Lie: 6 Trygve
lie-abed: 5 idler 7 dawdler
__ liebe dich: 3 Ich
Liebestraum
composer: Franz Liszt
Liebfraumilch: 4 wine 9 white wine
origin: 7 Germany
Lieblich: 4 Amia
Liech.
neighbor of ~: 3 Aus. 4 Aust.
Liechtenstein: 6 nation 7 country
capital: 5 Vaduz
legislature: 4 Diet
locale: 3 Eur. 4 Alps 6 Europe
money: 5 franc
neighbor: 5 Switz. 7 Austria
lied: 4 hymn, song, tune 5 music
__ lied!: 3 So I
Liederkranz: 6 cheese
Lie Down in Darkness
author: William Styron
lie down on the __: 3 job
__ Lied von der Erde: 3 Das
lief: 6 gladly, rather 7 readily, willing 9 willingly
liege: 5 loyal 6 steady, vassal 7 devoted, staunch, subject 8 faithful 9 steadfast
Liège: 4 city, town
locale: 7 Belgium
river: 4 Maas 5 Meuse
town near ~: 3 Spa
lie in __: 4 wait
lien: 4 mtge. 5 claim 8 mortgage 10 attachment
Lien: 8 Jennifer
lienee: 6 debtor
lienor: 4 bank 8 claimant, creditor 9 mortgagee
lier: 7 sleeper 8 recliner
lies
see baloney
__ Lies: 4 Here, True 6 Little
__, lies, and videotape: 3 sex
__ Lies Beneath: 4 What
Lies My Father Told Me (1975 film)
director: Jan Kadar
lie through one's __: 5 teeth
Lie, Trygve home: 4 Oslo
lieu: 5 place, stead
in ~: 8 on behalf
in ~ of: 4 than 6 rather 10 rather than
stand in ~ of: 3 sub 5 alter 6 fill in 7 replace 10 substitute
lieut.: 3 off. 4 rank
right arm: 3 sgt.
sch.: 4 USMA
Lieut. __: 3 Col. 5 Comdr.
lieutenant: 4 aide, rank 5 looey, looie, louie, proxy 6 deputy, helper, second 7 officer 8 minister 9 man Friday
future ~: 5 cadet
subordinate: 3 NCO, PFC, pvt., sgt. 7 private 8 sergeant
superior: 3 col., gen., maj. 4 capt. 5 major 7 captain, colonel, general
trainer: 3 OCS
lieutenant __: 7 colonel, general
__ Lieutenant's Woman, The: 6 French
Liev: 9 Schreiber
lieve: 6 gladly 7 readily 9 willingly
__-lievio: 5 ring-a
Lifar, Serge: 6 dancer 7 danseur
life: 3 bio, zip 4 brio, dash, days, élan, soul, span, term, time, zest, zing 5 being, cycle, oomph, verve, vigor, world 6 bounce, breath, energy, esprit, growth, memoir, spirit 7 history, sparkle 8 activity, duration, lifetime, organism, survival, vitality, vivacity 9 animation, biography, élan vital, enjoyment, existence, happiness, longevity, sentience, viability 10 enthusiasm, excitement, exuberance, get up and go, human being, liveliness, metabolism
animal ~: 5 fauna
basis of ~: 6 carbon
big as ~: 5 plain 7 visible 8 apparent, manifest
breathe new ~ into: 6 revive 7 refresh 10 regenerate
breath of ~: 4 soul 5 anima 6 spirit 10 vital force
combining form: 3 bio-
ender: 4 boat, line, long, time, work 5 blood, guard, saver, style 6 saving
enhancer: 5 spice
family ~: 4 home 6 hearth 8 fireside
force: 2 qi 3 ch'i, Tao, vim 4 élan, fire, soul, will 5 prana, sense, spark, vigor 6 energy, esprit, spirit, warmth 7 essence, passion 8 presence, vitality 9 animation, élan vital, willpower
form: 5 being, human, plant 6 animal, mammal, person 8 creature, organism
former ~: 4 past
full of ~: 4 spry 5 lusty, peppy, zingy 7 healthy, zestful, zinging 8 spirited, youthful 9 energetic, vivacious
future ~: 7 rebirth 9 next world 10 afterworld
get extra ~ from: 5 reuse 7 recycle 8 pass down
give new ~ to: 7 refresh
give ~ to: 4 form 5 beget, breed, build, erect, forge, found, hatch, model, shape, spawn, start 6 author, create, design, devise, effect, father 7 compose, develop, dream up, fashion, imagine, produce, think up 8 conceive, engender, engineer, generate, occasion, organize 9 actualize, construct, establish, institute, originate 10 mastermind
good ~: 4 ease 6 luxury 7 comfort, leisure 9 affluence 10 bed of roses, prosperity
have ~: 2 be 4 go on, last, live 5 abide, exist 6 endure, remain 7 breathe, subsist, survive 8 continue
in French: 3 vie
in German: 5 leben
in Latin: 4 esse
in Spanish: 4 vida
larger than ~: 4 epic 5 famed 6 famous, heroic 7 awesome 8 heroical, immortal, imposing, mythical, renowned, towering 9 legendary 10 celebrated, impressive
love of ~: 2 go 3 pep, zip 4 brio, élan, zest 5 gusto, oomph, punch, spice, verve 6 ginger, relish, spirit 7 passion, sparkle 8 appetite, vitality 10 enthusiasm, exuberance, heartiness
name meaning ~: 3 Eve, Zoe
not on your ~: 4 nope 5 ixnay, never, no way 6 nowise 7 I refuse, not ever 8 at no time, forget it 9 by no means, fat chance, I think not 10 count me out, not a chance
of ~: 6 biotic 8 biotical
of the party: 3 wit 5 mixer 6 joiner
partner: 4 limb
plant ~: 5 flora 10 vegetation

prime of ~: 8 fullness, majority, maturity
rudimentary ~: 4 germ, seed 5 virus 6 embryo 7 microbe 8 pathogen 9 bacterium
saver: 4 hero 7 heroine
science: 3 bio. 4 biol., zool. 7 biology, zoology
sign of ~: 5 pulse 6 breath 9 heartbeat
staff of ~: 5 bread 7 aliment
starter: 3 low, mid 4 high, wild 5 after, night
story: 3 bio 4 biog. 6 memoir 7 memoirs 9 biography
time of one's ~: 4 ball 5 blast
true to ~: 9 realistic
walk of ~: 4 turf, work 5 field, orbit, realm 6 career, métier, milieu, sphere 7 calling, pursuit, purview, station 8 business, province, vocation 9 bailiwick, situation 10 livelihood, occupation, profession
you bet your ~: 4 amen, true 5 roger, uh-huh 6 agreed, indeed, just so, rather 7 exactly, granted, indeedy, mais oui, quite so, right on 8 for a fact 9 darn right, precisely, sure thing 10 by all means, definitely, that's right *see* of course
life __: 4 belt, buoy, form, peer, raft, span, vest 5 cycle, force, signs, story 6 jacket 7 science
life __ party: 5 of the
life-__: 4 size 6 giving
__ life: 3 for 4 dog's, good 5 big as, shelf, still 6 public 7 charmed
__ life!: 4 Get a
__-life: 4 half, real, true
...life __ know it: 4 as we
Life: 3 mag 5 Scout 6 cereal 8 Boy Scout, magazine
competitor: *see* cereal
founder: Henry Luce
rival: 4 Look
Life __ a dream: 5 is but
Life __ at Forty: 6 Begins
Life __ Beautiful: 5 Can Be
Life __ cabaret: 3 is a
Life __ Fast Lane: 5 in the
Life __ Father: 4 With
Life __ On: 4 Goes
__ Life: 3 Pop 4 A New, In My 5 All My, Big as, Still, That's
__ Life!: 5 That's
__ Life, A: 3 New 6 Double
Life among the Modocs
author: Joaquin Miller
life-and-death: 4 dire 5 acute, grave, heavy, major, vital 6 urgent 7 big-deal, crucial, pivotal, serious 8 critical, pressing 9 desperate, essential, important, paramount 10 imperative, portentous, touch-and-go
Life and Legend of Wyatt Earp, The (ABC western)
cast: Hugh O'Brian (Wyatt Earp)
Life and Times of Judge Roy Bean, The (1972 film)
cast: Ava Gardner, Paul Newman, Victoria Principal
director: John Huston
Life as a House (2001 film)
cast: Kevin Kline, Kristin Scott Thomas
Life Before Man
author: Margaret Atwood
lifeblood: 4 core 5 basis, heart 6 marrow 7 essence 9 substance
lifeboat
lowerer: 5 crane, davit 7 derrick
Lifeboat (1944 film)
cast: Tallulah Bankhead, William Bendix, Walter Slezak
director: Alfred Hitchcock
Lifebuoy: 4 soap
alternative: *see* soap
Life Can Be Beautiful: 9 radio show
Life Doesn't Frighten Me
author: Maya Angelou
Life for the Tsar, A
composer: Mikhail Glinka
Life Goes On (ABC drama)
cast: Christopher Burke (Corky Thatcher)
Patti LuPone (Libby Thatcher)
Kellie Martin (Becca Thatcher)
Bill Smitrovich (Drew Thatcher)
dog: 6 Arnold
lifeguard
at times: 5 saver
beat: 4 pool 5 beach
Life in London
author: Pierce Egan
Life in the Fast Lane (1977 song)
artist: Eagles
Life is a banquet lady: 4 Mame
Life Is Beautiful (1998 film)
cast: Roberto Benigni, Nicoletta Braschi
director: Roberto Benigni
__ Life Is It Anyway?: 5 Whose
Life Is Just __ of Cherries: 5 a Bowl
Life is like __ of chocolates: 4 a box
life jacket: 7 Mae West
stuffing: 5 kapok
lifeless: 3 dry 4 arid, bare, blah, cold, drab, dull, flat, late, lazy, slow, zero 5 brute, empty, faint, inert, prosy, spent, stiff, tepid, vapid, waste 6 asleep, barren, desert, draggy, glassy, hollow, jejune, leaden, static, torpid, wooden 7 defunct, extinct, insipid, nothing, out cold, pabulum, passive, prosaic, sterile, tedious 8 listless, slothful, sluggish, stagnant 9 colorless, exanimate, inanimate, inorganic, insensate, lethargic, ponderous, prosaical 10 glassy-eyed, insensible, insentient, lackluster, lusterless, mechanical, motionless, spiritless
combining form: 4 abio-
old-style: 5 amort
lifelike: 9 realistic
lifeline: 9 salvation
locale: 4 palm
lifelong: 3 old 7 lasting 8 constant, enduring 9 perennial, permanent 10 continuing, deep-rooted, inveterate, persistent
life of __: 5 Riley
Life of David Gale, The (2003 film)
cast: Laura Linney, Kevin Spacey, Kate Winslet
Life of Emile Zola, The (1937 film)
cast: Paul Muni
Life of Galileo, The
author: Bertolt Brecht
Life of Riley, The (NBC sitcom)
cast: William Bendix (Chester Riley)
John Brown (Digger O'Dell)
Marjorie Reynolds (Peg Riley)
dog: 3 Rex
life of the __: 5 party
Life of the Insects, The
author: Karel Capek
__ Life of Walter Mitty, The: 6 Secret
Life or Something Like It (2002 film)
cast: Edward Burns, Angelina Jolie, Tony Shalhoub
director: Stephen Herek
lifer: 3 con 5 felon 8 internee, jailbird, prisoner
lifesaver: 3 CPR, EMS, EMT 4 drug, hero 5 medic 6 doctor 7 surgeon, vaccine 10 antibiotic
at times: 3 net 6 airbag 9 safety net
Lifesavers: 5 candy
like ~: 5 toric
shapes: 4 tori
lifesaving
org.: 4 USCG
skill: 3 CPR
Life So Far
author: Betty Friedan
Lifestyles of the Rich and Famous
host: Robin Leach
lifetime: 3 age 4 days, span 5 years 6 career, course, period 9 endurance, existence
Lifetime
alternative: *see* cable channel
lifetimes
many ~: 3 eon 4 aeon
__ Life to Live: 3 One
Life With Father: 4 film, play
author: Clarence Day
cast: Irene Dunne, Edmund Gwenn, ZaSu Pitts, William Powell, Elizabeth Taylor
character: 4 Cora, Nora 5 Delia, Julie
Life With Mikey (1993 film)
cast: Michael J. Fox, Nathan Lane
Life With Mother
author: Clarence Day
lifework: 3 job 6 career 7 calling, mission, purpose, pursuit 8 business, interest, vocation 10 occupation, profession
Liffey: 5 river
city on the ~: 6 Dublin
locale: 4 Eire, Erin 7 Ireland
lift: 2 up 3 aid, cop, end, nip, rob, run 4 buoy, copy, crib, glom, hand, heft, help, hike, hook, loot, rear, ride, rise, soar, stop, take 5 annul, arise, boost, carry, cheer, climb, drive, erect, exalt, filch, goose, heave, heist, hoist, leg up, mount, pinch, put up, raise, relax, scoop, seize, steal, swipe 6 ascend, aspire, assist, buoy up, cancel, come up, draw up, haul up, hike up, jack up, jump up, move up, pick up, pilfer, pirate, pocket, recall, relief, remove, repeal, revoke, rip off, snitch, step up, succor, take up, thieve, uphold, uprear, vanish 7 advance, bring up, build up, comfort, console, dignify, elevate, enhance, improve, journey, larceny, lighten, passage, promote, purloin, ransack, rescind, reverse, rope tow, secours, support, upgrade, upheave, upraise 8 abstract, disperse, elevator, heighten, liberate, pick-me-up, pump iron, simulate 9 disappear, dismantle, dissipate, terminate, transport 10 ameliorate, assistance, exhilarate, pickpocket, plagiarize
a finger: 3 aid, try 4 help 6 assist 7 help out 10 contribute
easy to ~: 3 wee 4 puny, tiny 5 light, small 6 little, slight 8 feathery, portable 10 manageable, weightless
give a ~ to: 3 aid 4 cart 5 cheer, elate 6 assist, pick up 7 enliven 8 reassure
in America: 8 elevator
kind of ~: 4 tram
off: 6 ascend
ski ~: 4 J-bar, T-bar
starter: 3 air, eye, sea 4 boat, drag, fork, shop
up: 4 heft 5 elate, exalt, hoist 7 elevate 8 levitate 10 exhilarate
up one's voice: 5 chant, croon 6 intone, warble 7 belt out, perform 8 melodize, vocalize
user: 5 skier
weights: 8 exercise, pump iron
with effort: 4 heft 5 boost, heave, hoist
lift __: 3 off 4 bolt, pump 5 truck 6 bridge, ticket
__ lift: 3 air, ski 4 dead, J-bar, T-bar 5 chair
__-lift: 4 face
lift a __: 6 finger
Lift dat __: 4 bale
lifter: 4 jack 5 crane, thief, winch 6 pulley, tackle 7 derrick 8 windlass 10 dumbwaiter
mythical ~: 5 Atlas
starter: 4 shop 6 weight
wallet ~: 3 dip 10 pickpocket
lifting: 5 theft
device: 3 pry 5 crank, jimmy, lever 7 crowbar
starter: 4 face, shop 5 power 6 weight
__ lifting: 5 heavy
liftoff: 6 ascent, launch 8 blastoff 9 departure
ligament: 3 tie 4 link 8 ligature, vinculum
combining form: 4 desm- 5 desmo- 7 syndesm- 8 syndesmo-
ligand: 7 hormone 8 antibody
ligate: 3 tie 4 bind 5 tie up 6 tie off
ligation: 3 tie 4 link 8 ligature
ligature: 3 tie 4 band, bond, cord, knot, link, rope, yoke 5 nexus 7 bandage, binding 8 ligament 10 connection
Ligeia
author: Edgar Allan Poe
liger: 3 cat 5 felid 6 feline, hybrid
relative: *see* feline
light: 3 gay, ray, sit, sun, wee 4 airy, bulb, burn, cast, dawn, drop, easy, fair, fire, glow, high, lamp, land, mild, morn, pale, puny, rest, rich, sign, soft, spot, star, stop, thin,

tiny, weak, wiry **5** agile, aglow, angle, blaze, blond, clear, dizzy, downy, faded, faint, filmy, flame, flare, flash, flood, funny, gauzy, giddy, glare, gleam, glint, lithe, local, loose, merry, minor, model, perch, perky, petty, put on, roost, sandy, sheen, sheer, shine, shiny, slant, small, spark, start, sunny, taper, teeny, torch, vivid, white, witty **6** ablaze, alight, arrive, aspect, aurora, beacon, blithe, blonde, breezy, bright, candle, casual, cheery, chirpy, dainty, facile, fickle, flimsy, fluffy, frothy, frugal, gentle, glossy, ignite, illume, kindle, little, lively, lucent, luster, meager, minute, modest, nimble, pastel, porous, scanty, settle, simple, slight, smooth, sparse, spongy, teensy, turn on, upbeat, window **7** amusing, animate, buoyant, chipper, context, crumbly, daytime, deplane, descend, detrain, enflame, example, flighty, fly down, friable, get down, glimmer, glitter, glowing, inflame, insight, lambent, lantern, morning, paragon, radiant, set down, shining, sit down, slender, sparkle, sunbeam, sunrise, trivial, unheavy **8** animated, approach, attitude, bleached, brighten, carefree, cheerful, come down, daybreak, daylight, delicate, dismount, enkindle, ethereal, exemplar, feathery, finespun, flashing, floating, get there, gossamer, graceful, humorous, illumine, lambency, luminous, lustrous, moderate, pleasing, polished, portable, radiance, radiancy, splendor, standing, step down, sunshine, switch on, trifling, untaxing **9** awareness, brilliant, burnished, cloudless, condition, disembark, diverting, easygoing, education, emanation, floatable, frivolous, gossamery, hardly any, irradiate, knowledge, lithesome, minuscule, radiation, refulgent, set fire to, spotlight, sprightly, sylphlike, touch down, tow-headed, unclouded, viewpoint, whimsical **10** brightness, brilliance, brilliancy, digestible, effortless, effulgence, floodlight, fractional, illuminate, inadequate, incandesce, indistinct, low-calorie, luminosity, manageable, reflection, refulgence, restricted, settle down, shoestring, tissuelike, unexacting, unobscured, weightless

a fire under: **4** goad, spur, stir **5** rouse, spark **6** arouse, bestir, excite, fire up, incite, stir up, wake up, whip up, work up **7** animate, inflame, inspire, provoke, quicken **8** motivate **9** electrify, galvanize, stimulate

as a feather: **4** airy **6** aerial **8** gossamer

blinding ~: **5** glare **6** dazzle

bring to ~: **4** bare, find, show **5** admit, dig up **6** elicit, evince, expose, reveal, turn up, unmask, unveil **7** lay bare, uncover, unearth **8** disclose, discover **9** track down

circle of ~: **4** halo **6** corona **7** aureola, aureole

combining form: **4** luci-, phos-, phot- **5** lumin-, photo- **6** lumini-, lumino-

come to ~: **5** arise **6** arisen, emerge **7** surface

emit ~: **4** beam, glow **5** blaze, flare, flash, glare, gleam, glint, shine **6** dazzle **7** flicker, glimmer, glisten, glitter, radiate, reflect, shimmer, sparkle, twinkle **8** bedazzle, brighten, illumine **9** coruscate **10** illuminate, incandesce

ender: **4** face, foot, ship, some, wood **5** house, proof **6** headed, weight **7** hearted

film-set ~: **5** klieg

first ~: **4** dawn **5** sunup **7** genesis **8** daybreak, daylight

flash of ~: **5** blaze, gleam, spark

garish ~: **4** neon

give the green ~: **2** OK **4** okay **5** agree, allow, clear **6** accede, enable **7** endorse, indorse

green ~: **2** go, OK **3** yes **4** okay, word **5** leave **6** assent, permit, signal **7** go-ahead, license, mandate, warrant **8** approval, sanction **9** clearance **10** acceptance

guiding ~: **4** guru **6** beacon **8** cynosure, lodestar, polestar **10** apotheosis

high-tech ~: **5** laser

into: **4** flay, slam, wade **5** fight, fly at, roast, scold **6** assail, attack, hit out, oppugn **7** assault, lambast **8** lambaste **9** fustigate, haul off on, lash out at, reprimand

leading ~: **4** rock **6** pillar **8** mainstay

lower the ~: **5** bedim **6** darken

make ~ of: **3** rag **4** mock **5** scoff **6** deride, slight **7** neglect **8** minimize, overlook, palliate, play down, sneeze at **9** soft-pedal **10** understate

name meaning ~: **5** Lucia **6** Lucius

not ~: **4** dark **7** onerous

of heel: **4** fast **5** fleet, quick, rapid, swift **6** nimble, speedy, winged

on one's feet: **4** deft, spry **5** agile, fleet, lithe, quick **6** active, limber, lively, nimble, supple **7** lissome **8** graceful, spirited, vigorous **9** energetic, sprightly, vivacious

out: **3** hie, run **4** head, quit, race **5** leave **6** be gone, depart, escape **7** abscond, make off, push off, run away, take off **8** hightail **9** take a hike

pilot ~: **5** flame **6** gas jet

red ~: **4** flag **5** alert **6** signal **7** caution, warning

refractor: **5** prism **7** crystal, rainbow

regulator: **4** iris

science: **6** optics

see the ~: **5** get it **7** realize **10** understand

shaft: **3** ray **4** beam **7** sunbeam **8** moonbeam

shed ~ on: **4** show **5** solve **6** answer, unfold **7** clarify, explain, expound **8** illumine, simplify, spell out **9** bring home, elaborate, elucidate, interpret, make plain, translate **10** illuminate, illustrate

sky ~: **3** sun **4** moon, star **6** albedo, aurora

source: **3** sun **4** bulb, lamp, moon, star **5** flare, torch **6** candle **7** bonfire, lantern, oil lamp **8** campfire

starter: **3** day, fan, gas, pen, sky, sun, twi **4** back, dead, drop, fire, head, high, jack, lamp, lime, moon, rush, safe, side, spot, star, stop, tail, trap **5** earth, flash, flood **6** candle, search, street

switch: **6** dimmer

trip the ~ fantastic: **4** step **5** dance, party, rumba, tango, waltz **6** cha-cha, rhumba **7** cut a rug

unit: **3** lux **4** phot **5** lumen **10** foot-candle

up: **5** smoke **6** ignite **7** radiate, twinkle **8** brighten, illumine **9** irradiate **10** illuminate

upon: **4** find, spot **6** locate **8** discover **10** come across

vigil ~: **5** taper **6** shames **7** shammes **9** luminaria

warning ~: **5** flare **6** beacon, signal

light __: **3** box, pen **4** bulb, into, show **5** as air, cream, opera, table, verse **6** breeze **7** cruiser

light __ feather: **3** as a

light __ under: **5** a fire

light-__: **4** duty, rail, year **6** footed, handed

__ light: **3** arc, fog, hot, red **4** dome, grow **5** brake, first, green, idiot, klieg, night, pilot, white **6** hazard **7** leading, running, traffic

Light: **5** Allie, Enoch **6** Judith

Light-__ Harry Lee: **5** Horse

light a __ under: **4** fire

Light a Penny Candle
author: Maeve Binchy

light as a __: **7** feather

Light Brigade milieu: **6** Crimea, Russia

light-complexioned: **4** fair

lighted: **6** ablaze, aflame **8** luminous

light-emitting __: **5** diode

lighten: **4** buoy, ease, free, lift, take, thin **5** allay, break, cheer, elate, empty, flash, gleam, light, relax, shift, shine **6** bleach, buoy up, change, dilute, illume, leaven, lessen, perk up, put off, reduce, remove, revive, soften, unlade, unload, whiten **7** assuage, cheer up, comfort, cut down, gladden, hearten, inspire, mollify, pour out, relieve, tail off, upraise **8** brighten, decrease, jettison, levitate, mitigate, palliate, slack off, throw out, unburden **9** alleviate, attenuate, disburden, encourage, eradicate, extenuate, irradiate **10** ameliorate, facilitate, illuminate

up: **4** slow **5** relax **6** cool it, give in, relent, soften **7** back off, ease off, give way, lay back, slacken, subside **8** go easy on, moderate **9** mellow out **10** come around

lighter: **4** boat, fuse, fuze **5** barge, flint, fusee, fuzee, match, squib **6** tender **7** lucifer **8** ignition **9** detonator

brand: **3** Bic **5** Zippo

feature: **4** fuel, wick **5** flint **6** butane

starter: **4** high, lamp

lighter __: **5** fluid

lighter-__-air: **4** than

light-fingered: **3** sly **4** deft **5** agile **6** adroit, nimble **7** crooked **8** thieving, thievish

one: **4** yegg **5** crook, ganef, thief **6** bandit, rip-off, robber **7** brigand, burglar, filcher, footpad, heister, prowler, rustler, stealer **8** cutpurse, pilferer **9** purloiner **10** bushranger, cat burglar, highwayman, pickpocket, shoplifter

light-footed: **4** spry **5** agile, light, lithe, quick **6** nimble **9** lithesome, sprightly

Lightfoot, Gordon
homeland: Canada
song: Carefree Highway (1974)
If You Could Read My Mind (1971)
Rainy Day People (1975)
Sundown (1974)
The Wreck of the Edmund Fitzgerald (1976)

light-haired: **6** blonde

lightheaded: **4** gaga, hazy **5** dizzy, empty, faint, giddy, queer, rocky, silly, tired, woozy **6** fickle, punchy, swimmy **7** flighty, foolish, reeling, shallow **8** flippant, skittish, swimming, trifling, whirling **9** delirious, frivolous **10** changeable

lighthearted: **3** gay **4** glad **5** happy, jolly, light, merry, sunny **6** blithe, breezy, bright, jocund, jovial, joyful, joyous, lively, upbeat **7** buoyant, gleeful, jocular, playful **8** carefree, cheerful, feel-good, laid-back, sanguine, spirited, volatile **9** expansive, resilient, sprightly, vivacious **10** blithesome, frolicsome, insouciant, untroubled

lightheartedness: **4** glee **5** mirth **6** gaiety, gayety, levity **7** jollity **8** pleasure

Light-Horse Harry: **3** Lee

lighthouse: **5** tower **6** Pharos, signal **10** watchtower

feature: **4** beam, lamp **5** flare **6** beacon, signal **7** lantern

lighthouse __: **4** tube **5** clock

Lighthouse at the End of the World, The
author: Jules Verne

Light in August
author: William Faulkner

__ lighting: **3** rim **4** cove **5** panel, track **6** bounce, direct

lighting pro: **5** wirer

Light in the __, A: **5** Attic

Light in the Forest, The
author: Conrad Richter

__ Light in the Window: **4** Put a

lightless: **3** dim **4** dark, inky **5** black, dusky, unlit **6** gloomy, pitchy **7** shadowy, Stygian **8** jet black

lightly: 4 idly, skim 6 airily, easily, freely, gently, mildly, nimbly, simply, softly, subtly, thinly 7 agilely, faintly, quietly, timidly 8 breezily, casually, daintily, gingerly, slightly, smoothly, sparsely, tenderly 9 leniently, sparingly, tactfully, tenuously 10 carelessly, delicately, ethereally, flippantly, heedlessly, moderately, peacefully
light-minded: 5 giddy, petty, silly 6 callow 7 flyaway, shallow, vacuous 9 frivolous
Light My Fire (song)
artist: Doors, Jose Feliciano
lightness: 3 joy 4 glee 5 balon, grace, mirth 6 ballon, gaiety, gayety, levity 7 agility, elation, gayness, jollity 8 airiness, bouyancy, buoyance, buoyancy, deftness, delicacy, gladness, optimism, paleness, spryness 9 flippancy, frivolity 10 volatility
lightning: 4 bolt 5 chain, flash, forky, sheet, swift 6 forked, speedy 8 fireball
by-product: 5 ozone
go like ~: 3 hie, rip, run 4 race, rush 5 hurry 6 streak
like ~: 3 PDQ 4 fast 5 apace, fleet 6 presto 7 fleetly, hastily, quickly, rapidly, swiftly 8 in a flash, in a jiffy, in no time, pell-mell, speedily 9 forthwith, hurriedly, instantly, momentary, posthaste
white ~: 5 booze, hooch 6 hootch 9 moonshine
white ~ holder: 3 jug
lightning __: 3 bug, rod 5 chess
__ lightning: 4 ball 5 chain, sheet, white
Lightning: 3 six 4 team 5 novel
author: Danielle Steel, Dean Koontz
home: 5 Tampa 8 Tampa Bay
milieu: 3 ice 4 rink
org.: 3 NHL
rival: *see* hockey team
sport: 6 hockey
__ light of: 4 make
Light o' Love
author: Arthur Schnitzler
__ light on: 4 shed 5 throw
lights __: 3 out
__ Lights: 4 City 5 Party 6 Harbor
__ Lights, Big City: 6 Bright
Lights, camera, __!: 6 action
Light Sleeper (1992 film)
cast: Willem Dafoe, Dana Delany, Susan Sarandon
lightsome: 3 gay 4 airy, glad, spry 5 agile, giddy, happy, lithe, merry, silly 6 blithe, breezy, bright, cheery, fickle, fluffy, joyous, lissom, nimble, pliant, supple 7 buoyant, chipper, flighty, foolish, gleeful, lissome, playful, smiling 8 bodiless, carefree, cheerful, debonair, ethereal, feathery, flexible, floating, gossamer, graceful, jubilant, laughing, volatile 9 debonaire 10 debonnaire, flying high
Lights Out: 9 radio show
Lights out tune: 4 Taps
__ Light Special: 3 Red 4 Blue
Light That Failed: 4 film 5 novel
author: Rudyard Kipling
cast: Ronald Colman, Walter Huston, Ida Lupino
director: William Wellman
__ Light, The: 7 Guiding
__ Light Up My Life: 3 You
lightweight: 4 thin 5 petty 6 nobody, paltry, slight 7 failing, foolish, shallow, trivial 8 feathery, portable, trifling 9 jellyfish, nonentity, worthless
ligneous: 5 woody 6 wooden
lignite: 4 coal, fuel 7 mineral
Ligurian Sea
feeder: 4 Arno 6 Genova
locale: 5 Italy
port: 5 Genoa
likable: 4 good, nice 5 sweet 6 genial 7 amiable, lovable, popular, winning, winsome 8 charming, engaging, friendly, loveable, pleasant, pleasing 9 agreeable, appealing, enjoyable 10 attractive, personable, preferable, relishable
like: 3 à la, dig 4 akin, as if, love, same, such, want 5 adore, enjoy, equal, fancy, favor, gofor, level, prize, savor 6 accept, admire, akin to, care to, choose, desire, dote on, esteem, in kind, on a par, please, prefer, relish, revere, take to 7 approve, care for, cherish, close to, cognate, equal to, feast on, idolize, kindred, related, revel in, similar, stuck on, uniform, worship 8 dote upon, hold dear, matching, parallel, selfsame, treasure 9 analogous, care about, delight in, get high on, hanker for, identical, indulge in, rejoice in, similar to 10 appreciate, comparable, compatible, conforming, consistent, equivalent, homologous, resembling, synonymous, tantamount, true to type
prefix: 3 sym-, syn-
suffix: 3 -ine, -ish, -ose 4 -eous 5 -esque
like __: 3 mad 4 it is 5 a book, a shot, as not, crazy
like __ balloon: 5 a lead
like __ from the blue: 5 a bolt
like __ in a candy store: 4 a kid
like __ in a china shop: 5 a bull
like __ in a pod: 4 peas
like __ in a trap: 4 a rat
like __, like son: 6 father
like __ not: 4 it or
like __ of bricks: 4 a ton
like __ off a log: 7 falling
like __ of potatoes: 5 a sack
like __ of sunshine: 4 a ray
like __ on a log: 5 a bump
like __ out of hell: 4 a bat
like __ out of water: 5 a fish
like __ thumb: 5 a sore
like __ to the flame: 5 a moth
like-__: 6 minded
__ like: 4 feel, make
-like
kin: 3 -ish, -oid
Like __ love it!: 3 it I
Like __ not!: 4 it or
Like__!: 5 I care
like a __: 4 book, shot
like a __ afire: 5 house
like a __ a trap: 5 rat in
like a __ balloon: 4 lead
like a __ of bricks: 3 ton
like a __ on a log: 4 bump
like a __ out of water: 4 fish
__ like a baby: 3 cry
...like a big pizza pie, that's __: 5 amore
__ like a bird: 3 eat
likeable: 4 kind, nice, warm 6 decent, genial, kindly, mellow, polite 7 affable, amiable, cordial, helpful, winsome 8 amicable, charming, cheerful, friendly, gracious, inviting, obliging, pleasant, sociable 9 agreeable, congenial, courteous, simpatico 10 attractive, hospitable, neighborly, personable
like a bump on a __: 3 log
__ like a charm: 4 work
like a fish __ of water: 3 out
like a house __: 5 afire
like a lead __: 7 balloon
__ Like Alice: 5 A Town
__ Like a Man: 4 Walk
__ Like an Eagle: 3 Fly
Like a Prayer (1989 song)
artist: Madonna
like a rat in __: 5 a trap
Like a Rock (1986 song)
artist: Bob Seger
Like a Rolling Stone (1965 song)
artist: Bob Dylan
like a ton of __: 6 bricks
__ like a top: 4 spin 5 sleep
Like a Virgin (1984 song)
artist: Madonna
__ Like Being in Love: 6 Almost
liked: 3 big, hot 6 choice, culled, picked, trendy 7 elected, faddish, fancied, favored, in favor, in vogue, popular, selling, voguish 8 accepted, approved, embraced, endorsed, in demand, pleasing, selected 9 preferred 10 celebrated, fair-haired, handpicked, widespread
__-liked: 4 well
like falling off __: 4 a log
like father, like __: 3 son
__ like hotcakes: 4 sell
__ Like I: 5 A Girl
like it __: 5 or not
__ Like It: 5 As You
__ Like It Hot: 4 Some
__ like it is: 6 tell it
likelihood: 4 odds, prob. 5 trend 6 chance, toss-up 7 outlook, promise 8 long shot, prospect, tendency 9 direction, fair shake, liability 10 expectancy, fifty-fifty, good chance
likely: 3 apt 4 fair, true, wont 5 prone 6 adverb, doable, liable, odds-on, timely, viable 7 destine, earthly, hopeful, no doubt, seeming, subject, tending 8 apparent, assuring, credible, destined, disposed, expected, favorite, feasible, inclined, possible, probable, probably, rational, workable 9 assumably, doubtless, in favor of, inferable, plausible, potential, practical, promising, seemingly, thinkable 10 acceptable, achievable, attainable, believable, contingent, imaginable, in the cards, ostensible, presumable, presumably, prima facie, reasonable, supposable
likely story!, A: 3 hah 4 as if, I bet
__ Like Me: 4 Just 5 Black, Freak
__ Like Me Now: 4 How U
like-minded: 6 jibing, united 7 similar 8 agreeing, in accord 9 congenial, in harmony, unanimous 10 compatible, concurrent, harmonious, synchronal
like-mindedness: 5 amity, unity 6 accord, unison 7 concert, concord, harmony, oneness, rapport 8 sameness, sympathy 9 agreement, communion, consensus, unanimity 10 conformity, consonance, friendship, solidarity
liken: 6 equate 7 compare
likeness: 4 copy, form, icon, ikon 5 clone, ditto, eikon, guise, image, model, photo, study, xerox 6 carbon, double, ectype, effigy, parity, simile, sketch, statue 7 analogy, picture, profile, replica, thangka 8 affinity, equality, identity, knock-off, minature, portrait, sameness 9 agreement, depiction, duplicate, facsimile, imitation, lineation, photocopy, sculpture, semblance 10 appearance, carbon copy, comparison, conformity, dead ringer, photograph, reflection, silhouette, similarity, similitude, uniformity
combining form: 4 icon-, ikon- 5 eicon-, icono-, ikono-, -opsis 6 eicono-
likening: 6 simile 7 analogy 9 measuring, semblance 10 comparison
Like Niobe, __ tears: 3 all
__ Like Old Times: 5 Seems
liker: 7 admirer, fancier
__ Like the Wind: 4 Ride, She's
Like to Get to Know You (1968 song)
artist: Spanky and Our Gang
like two peas in __: 4 a pod
__ Like Us: 5 Spies 7 Thieves
like water __ duck's back: 4 off a
Like Water For Chocolate (1992 film)
director: Alfonso Arau
__ Like We Made It: 5 Looks
likewise: 2 so 3 too, yet 4 also, more, same 5 along, ditto 6 as well, either, in kind, withal 7 besides, further 8 moreover 9 similarly 10 in addition
not: 3 nor
...like you've __ ghost!: 5 seen a
liking: 4 bent, bias, love, mind, pref., will 5 fancy, shine, taste, tooth 6 desire, loving, palate, regard, relish 7 leaning, passion, stomach, valuing 8 affinity, appetite, devotion, fondness, penchant, pleasure, soft spot, sympathy, tendency, velleity, weakness 9 affection, appetence, proneness 10 attachment, attraction, favoritism, partiality, preference, propensity
combining form: 7 -philous
having a ~ for: 6 fond of 9 partial to
take a ~ (to): 6 cotton
Lil' __: 3 Kim
Lila: 6 McCann 7 Kedrova, Wallace

Li'l Abner: 5 strip 10 comic strip
animal: 5 Shmoo
cartoonist: Al Capp
son: 3 Abe
spouse: 8 Daisy Mae
surname: 5 Yokum
lilac: 5 color, mauve, plant, shrub 6 flower, purple 7 reddish
kin: 3 ash 5 olive 6 pikake, privet 7 jasmine 9 forsythia, jessamine
relative: *see* purple color
Lilac Bus, The
author: Maeve Binchy
Lilacs
author: Amy Lowell
Lil E. __: 3 Tee
Lili: 6 Damita, Taylor
Lili (1953 film)
cast: Leslie Caron, Mel Ferrer, Zsa Zsa Gabor
Lili __: 7 Marlene
__ Lili: 7 Darling
Lilia: 5 Skala
Lilienthal: 4 Otto
Lilies of the Field (1963 film)
cast: Sidney Poitier, Lilia Skala
character: 3 nun 5 Homer
Liliuokalani: 5 queen 8 Hawaiian
Liljekrans: 4 Olaf
Lil' Kim
real name: Kimberly Jones
song: It's All About the Benjamins (1997)
No Time (1996)
Not Tonight (1997)
Lille: 4 city, town
locale: 6 France
Lillehammer
city near ~: 4 Oslo
locale: 3 Nor. 4 Norw. 6 Norway
Lilli: 6 Palmer
Lillian: 4 Gish, Roth 5 Smith 7 Hellman 8 O'Donnell
Lillie: 3 Bea 7 Langtry 8 Beatrice
Lilliputian: 3 elf, wee 4 baby, mini, puny, tiny 5 bitty, dwarf, elfin, fairy, gnome, short, small, sylph, teeny, troll 6 atomic, bantam, little, midget, minute, pee-wee, petite, shorty, sprite, teensy 7 minikin, shortie 8 atomical, atomlike, half-pint, small fry 9 itsy-bitsy, itty-bitty, miniature, pint-sized, pipsqueak 10 diminutive, homunculus, leprechaun, teeny-weeny, vest-pocket
Lilly: 3 Bob, Eli 5 Daché
Lilongwe: 4 city, town 7 capital
locale: 6 Malawi
Lil' Red Riding Hood (1966 song)
artist: Sam the Sham
lilt: 4 tune 5 ditty, meter, swing 6 melody, rhythm 7 cadence, cadency
lilting: 6 dulcet, poetic 7 lyrical, melodic, musical, songful 8 pleasing, rhythmic 9 melodious, rhapsodic 10 euphonious, expressive, harmonious
syllables: 5 tra la
lily: 5 calla, plant 6 flower
African ~: 4 aloe
calla ~: 4 arum 5 aroid
corn ~ genus: 4 ixia
genus: 4 aloe
in French: 3 lis
kin: 4 irid, leek 5 camas, chive, onion, yucca 6 camass
maid of Astolat: 6 Elaine
part: 5 tepal
stone ~: 6 fossil
water ~: 3 pad 5 bloom, lotus 6 flower 7 blossom 9 perennial
lily __: 3 pad 4 pond
lily __ valley: 5 of the
lily-__: 7 livered
__ lily: 4 sego 5 calla, tiger, water
Lily: 4 Pons 5 St. Cyr 6 Tomlin 7 Munster
cohort: 4 Arte, Ruth
husband: 6 Herman
lily-livered: 5 timid 6 coward, craven, yellow 7 fearful 8 cowardly, unheroic 9 spineless
lily of the __: 6 valley
lily pad
lament: 5 croak
locale: 4 lake, pond
sitter: 4 frog
lily-trotter: 6 jacana
lily-white: 3 wan 4 pale, pure 6 chaste, pallid 8 innocent, spotless, unsoiled, untanned, virginal
lim.: 3 max., min.
lima: 4 bean 6 legume 10 butterbean
Lima: 4 city, town 7 capital
city near ~: 6 Callao
founder: Francisco Pizarro
locale: 4 Ohio, Peru
river: 5 Rímac
see also Spanish
__ Lima: 6 Rose of
limb: 3 arm, fin, gam, leg, pin 4 lobe, part, spur, stem, unit, wing 5 bough, spray, sprig, wheel 6 branch, member, pinion, spring, switch 7 process 8 offshoot 9 appendage, extension, extremity 10 projection
combining form: 3 mel-
feature: 4 leaf 7 foliage
go out on a ~: 5 guess 6 hazard 7 venture
holder: 4 bole 5 trunk
lower ~: 3 gam, leg
out on a ~: 5 risky, treed 9 foolhardy
thin ~: 4 twig, wand 5 sprig, stick
__ limb: 6 out on a
Limbaugh: 4 Rush
medium: 5 radio
limber: 4 deft, limp, spry, wiry 5 agile, lithe, loose 6 lissom, nimble, pliant, supple 7 elastic, lissome, plastic, pliable, springy, willowy 8 flexible, graceful 9 lithesome, resilient
up: 3 jog 5 train 6 tone up 7 work out 8 exercise
limbic: 8 marginal 9 on the edge 10 borderline
limbo: 5 dance, Hades 7 nowhere, Siberia 8 oblivion 9 left field
Limbo (1999 film)
cast: Kris Kristofferson, Vanessa Martinez, Mary Elizabeth Mastrantonio, David Strathairn
director: John Sayles
Limbo Rock (1962 song)
artist: Chubby Checker
Limburger: 6 cheese
feature: 4 odor 5 aroma, smell
relative: 6 Tilsit
limbus: 4 edge 6 border 8 boundary
lime: 4 bird, tree 5 color, fruit, green, oxide 6 alkali, citrus, flavor, linden, yellow 7 plaster 8 greenish
additive: 4 marl
bit of ~: 5 twist
drink: 3 ade 5 juice, sling 6 gimlet, rickey 9 margareta
ender: 3 ade 4 kiln 5 light, stone, water
relative: *see* citrus, green color, yellow color
starter: 4 bird 5 brook, quick
lime __: 6 rickey
__ lime: 3 Key
__-lime: 5 lemon
Lime: 5 Harry
limekiln: 4 oven
limelight: 5 light, stage 9 publicity, spotlight
in the ~: 3 big 5 large 6 famous, public 7 eminent, popular, splashy 8 familiar, infamous 9 acclaimed, important, prominent, well-known 10 celebrated, recognized
share the ~: 6 costar
Limelight (1952 film)
cast: Claire Bloom, Charles Chaplin
director: Charles Chaplin
limelike: 4 acid, sour, tart
__ lime pie: 3 Key
limequat: 4 tree 6 hybrid
limerick: 4 poem, rime 5 rhyme, verse
man: 4 Lear
opener: 5 there
writer: 4 poet 5 rimer
Limerick: 4 city, town
county north of ~: 5 Clare
land: 4 Eire, Erin 7 Ireland
town near ~: 5 Adare
limes, like: 4 acid, sour, tart
limestone: 4 malm, tufa 5 chalk 7 mineral
formation: 4 cave 6 cavern, grotto
metamorphosed ~: 6 marble
terrain: 5 karst
limit: 3 bar, cap, end, fix, max, rim, set, tie, top 4 brim, cork, curb, edge, side, term, tops 5 bound, bourn, brink, check, cramp, fence, hem in, orbit, quota, stint, tie up, verge 6 apogee, border, bounds, bourne, define, degree, demark, extent, fringe, height, hinder, length, lessen, margin, modify, narrow, period, radius, ration, reduce, utmost 7 abridge, barrier, ceiling, compass, confine, control, curtail, cut back, cut down, due date, extreme, inhibit, maximum, measure, minimum, prevent, purlieu, qualify, specify 8 capacity, confines, deadline, end point, frontier, handicap, precinct, restrain, restrict, straiten, ultimate 9 constrain, constrict, demarcate, last straw, outskirts, parameter, perimeter, periphery, prescribe, restraint, terminate 10 bottom line, boundaries, keep in line
beyond the ~: 5 rabid, ultra 6 far-out 7 bizarre, drastic, extreme, radical 9 excessive, fanatical 10 farfetched, immoderate, outlandish
exceed the ~: 3 fly, zip 4 race, rush, tear, whiz, zoom 5 speed 6 barrel, go fast, hurtle 8 hightail, step on it 10 lose no time
go the ~: 6 plunge, strive 7 persist
outer ~: 3 rim 4 edge 5 verge 6 apogee 8 boundary
over the ~: 4 long
reach a ~: 3 max 6 max out, top out
time ~: 6 curfew
to the ~: 4 A to Z 5 fully, plumb, sheer 6 in full, in toto, wholly 7 in depth, totally, utterly 8 entirely, whole hog 9 all the way, full blast, perfectly, to the hilt 10 absolutely, completely, thoroughly
upper ~: 3 cap, lid, max, top 7 ceiling, maximum 8 pinnacle
without ~: 6 all-out 7 flat-out 8 accurate, infinite 9 open-ended
__ limit: 4 term, time 5 speed 6 credit
Limit 10 __ or Less: 5 items
limitation: 3 bar, end 4 curb, snag, tabu 5 block, check, pinch, state, taboo 7 proviso 8 drawback, handicap 9 abatement, condition, hindrance, provision, restraint, stricture 10 constraint, discipline
limited: 3 set 4 less, mean, poor, slow, weak 5 bound, brief, fixed, local, scant, short, small, train 6 curbed, faulty, finite, little, meager, modest, narrow, paltry, scanty, scarce, select 7 bounded, checked, cramped, defined, insular, minimal, partial, precise, reduced, special, topical 8 confined, definite, exiguous, far apart, hampered, moderate, modified, one or two, orthodox, reserved, specific 9 confining, delimited, hardly any, parochial, qualified, sectarian, sectional 10 a handful of, compressed, contracted, controlled, diminished, inadequate, infrequent, measurable, particular, provincial, restrained, restricted, terminable
time: 4 span, term, tour 5 hitch, phase 6 period, tenure 7 stretch 8 duration, interval, semester, sentence
to: 6 at most
limited __: 7 edition, partner
limiting: 6 fixing 7 binding, curbing 9 confining
limitless: 3 big 4 vast 6 cosmic, eonian, untold 7 endless, immense, no end of, no end to 8 cosmical, infinite, spacious, unending, wide-open 9 boundless, countless, excessive, no-strings, unbounded, undefined 10 bottomless, indefinite, innumerous, numberless, unnumbered
limitlessly: 5 no end
limits: 4 ends 5 range 6 bounds 8 boundary 9 perimeter, periphery
free from ~: 5 uncap
off ~: 4 tabu 5 taboo 6 barred 8 outlawed 9 forbidden 10 prohibited
outer ~: 3 rim 5 ambit, ether, verge 6 aether
__ limits: 4 term

__-limits: 3 off
Limits of Interpretation, The
author: Umberto Eco
__ Limits, The: 5 Outer
Limmat, city on the: 6 Zurich
limn: 4 draw 5 paint 6 depict, sketch 7 outline, picture, portray 8 describe 9 delineate, interpret, represent 10 illustrate
limo
see limousine
Limoges: 4 city, town 5 china 9 porcelain
locale: 6 France
river: 6 Vienne
Limoges __: 4 ware
__ Limon, Costa Rica: 6 Puerto
limonite: 3 ore 7 mineral
Limón, José milieu: 5 dance
limousine: 3 car 4 auto 7 vehicle 10 automobile
capacity: 6 carful
feature: 2 TV 3 bar 5 TV set 9 chauffeur
passenger: 3 VIP
Russian ~: 3 Zil
what a ~ symbolizes: 6 status
limp: 3 lag, lax 4 halt, soft, weak 5 baggy, hitch, loose, loppy, slack, spent, tired, vapid 6 dodder, droopy, falter, feeble, flabby, flaggy, floppy, hobble, limber, pliant, sleazy, supple, totter, waddle, wilted 7 bending, flaccid, hanging, languid, plastic, pliable, relaxed, sagging, shuffle, wearied, worn out 8 dangling, drooping, flagging, flexible, lameness, listless, yielding 9 enervated, exhausted, lethargic 10 spiritless
along: 4 drag 6 schlep 7 shuffle 8 straggle
become ~: 4 wilt 5 swoon
go ~: 3 sag 5 droop, faint 6 weaken 7 crumple, pass out, shrivel 8 black out, keel over
limpet: 5 shell 7 mollusc, mollusk 8 conch kin, seashell
limpid: 4 pure, thin 5 clear, filmy, lucid, sheer 6 bright 7 obvious 8 definite, distinct, luculent, pellucid 10 see-through
Limpopo: 5 river
locale: 10 Mozambique
limp-watch
painter: Salvador Dali
Lin: 4 Biao, Maya, Piao 6 Yutang
Lina: 10 Wertmuller
linchpin: 3 key 7 keynote 8 mainstay
locale: 4 axle 5 shaft
Lincoln: 3 Abe, car 4 auto, city, Elmo, peak, town 5 mount, sheep 7 Abraham 8 mountain, Steffens 10 automobile
athlete: 10 Cornhusker
county: 9 Lancaster
locale: 3 Neb. 4 Nebr. 6 Canada 7 Ontario, Rockies 8 Colorado, Nebraska
model: 5 Capri 6 Zephyr 7 Aviator, Town Car 8 Premiere 9 Navigator 10 Versailles 11 Continental
what a ~ symbolizes: 4 rank 5 class 6 cachet, rating, status 7 footing, station 8 eminence, position, prestige, standing 10 importance, prominence
Lincoln __: 4 Logs
Lincoln, Abraham: 9 president
bill: 4 five
cabinet member: 5 Blair, Chase 6 Seward, Welles 7 Stanton
child: 3 Tad 6 Robert, Willie
coin: 4 cent 5 penny
feature: 5 beard
film portrayer: 5 Fonda 6 Massey
former occupation: 6 lawyer
home: 7 Indiana 8 Illinois, Kentucky
law partner: 7 Herndon
like ~: 4 tall
opponent: 4 Bell 7 Douglas 9 McClellan 12 Breckinridge
parent: 3 Tom 5 Nancy 6 Thomas
V.P.: 6 Hamlin 7 Johnson
wife: 4 Mary
Lincoln Center
attraction: 3 art, Met
__ Lincoln in Illinois: 3 Abe
Lincoln Log
competitor: 4 Lego
Lincoln Memorial
architect: 5 Bacon
muralist: 6 Guerin
scuptor: 6 French
Lincoln Navigator: 3 SUV
Lincoln Park Inn, The (1969 song)
artist: Bobby Bare
Lincoln Portrait, A
composer: Aaron Copland
Lincoln Red: 3 cow 4 bull 6 bovine, cattle
Lincolnshire: 6 county
locale: 7 England
Lincs: 6 county
locale: 7 England
Lind: 3 Bob 5 Jenny
Linda: 4 Dano, Eder, Gray, Hunt, Park, Purl 5 Blair, Evans, Lavin, Scott 6 Kelsey 7 Darnell, Thorson 8 Ellerbee, Hamilton, Ronstadt 9 Christian, Fratianne, Kozlowski, McCartney 10 Fiorentino
__ Linda, CA: 4 Loma 5 Yorba
Lindbergh: 4 Anne, Erik 7 Charles
Lindbergh, Charles: 7 aviator
linden: 4 teil, tree 8 basswood
Linden: 3 Hal 4 city, town 5 Kathy
locale: 9 New Jersey
Linder: 4 Kate
Lindfors: 6 Viveca
Lindgren: 6 Astrid
__ Lind Hayes: 5 Peter
Lind, Jenny: 6 singer 7 soprano, Swedish
specialty: 5 opera
Lindley: 5 Audra
Lindo: 6 Delroy
Lindros: 4 Eric
Lindsay: 3 Ted 4 Mark 5 Lohan 6 Crouse, Howard, Vachel, Wagner 8 Anderson, Margaret 9 Davenport
partner: 6 Crouse
Lindsay-Hogg: 7 Michael
Lindsay, Vachel: 4 poet
work: The Chinese Nightingale
The Congo
General William Booth Enters Into Heaven
The Ghost of the Buffaloes
In Praise of Johnny Appleseed
Rhymes to Be Traded for Bread
The Santa Fe Trail
Lindsey: 4 Mort 6 George 10 Buckingham
Lindstrom: 3 Pia
mother: 6 Ingrid 7 Bergman
Lindstrom, Phyllis
husband: 4 Lars
Lindt: 5 candy, Swiss 9 chocolate
lindy: 3 hop 5 dance
Lindy
contemporary: 6 Amelia
how ~ flew: 4 solo 5 alone
line: 3 arc, bar, job, pad, rim, row, way 4 axis, band, cord, dash, edge, face, file, mark, note, path, pipe, rank, rope, rule, scar, seam, tack, tape, text, tick, tier, vein, wire, work, yarn 5 bound, breed, cable, craft, goods, pitch, queue, ridge, route, skill, spiel, stock, track, trade, verge, wares 6 artery, border, career, column, come-on, crease, family, figure, furrow, groove, letter, method, métier, parade, patter, policy, series, streak, string, stripe, tackle, thread 7 calling, channel, contour, descent, encrust, incrust, lanyard, message, missive, passage, product, pursuit, tracing, wrinkle 8 ancestry, boundary, business, bus route, eremitic, heredity, ideology, insulate, pedigree, postcard, province, railroad, vocation 9 commodity, reinforce, threshold, vendibles 10 employment, occupation, procession, profession, sales pitch, silhouette, succession, trajectory
at the end of the ~: 4 last 8 farthest, rearmost, remotest
be in ~ for: 4 rate 5 merit 7 deserve 10 have coming
bottom ~: 3 net, sum 4 cost, crux 5 limit, point, tally, total 6 outlay, payoff, profit 7 essence, meaning, reality, revenue 8 key point, receipts 9 essential, main point 10 conclusion
curved ~: 3 arc
down the ~: 4 anon, soon, then 5 later 6 in a bit, in time 7 by and by, later on, someday 8 in a while, sometime 9 afterward, hereafter, presently 10 before long, eventually
draw a ~ through: 4 X out 6 delete 8 cross off, cross out
draw the ~: 3 bar, fix 4 halt, stop 5 check, limit 6 cut off, depart, step in 8 restrict 9 determine
drop a ~: 4 fish 5 write 10 correspond
end of the ~: 5 depot 7 station 8 terminal, terminus
feeder: 4 cuer 8 prompter
finish ~: 3 end 4 tape, wire
first in ~: 4 next 6 eldest 7 closest, nearest
get into ~: 4 heed 6 comply, follow, submit 7 conform, observe
get out of ~: 4 defy, riot, rise 5 act up 6 mutiny, oppose, resist, revolt, rise up 7 disobey, dissent, protest 9 make waves, misbehave
get the punch ~: 4 grin, howl, roar 5 laugh 6 giggle, guffaw 7 chortle, chuckle, crack up, snicker, snigger
graph ~: 4 axis 5 x-axis, y-axis, z-axis
help with a ~: 3 cue 6 prompt
in ~: 4 arow 5 level, ready 6 proper 7 abreast, waiting 8 eligible, orthodox, queued up, straight
in ~ (with): 5 along
jump the ~: 5 cut in 7 intrude 9 interpose
keep in ~: 3 pin 4 curb, stem 5 check, cramp, deter, leash, limit, sit on 6 bridle, enjoin, fetter, forbid, stifle, subdue, temper, tether 7 contain, control, curtail, harness, inhibit, repress, squelch 8 hold back, moderate, prohibit, restrain, restrict, slow down, straiten, suppress, tone down 9 constrain, crack down, hamstring 10 discourage
laying it on the ~: 4 free, open 5 bluff, blunt, frank, plain, vocal 6 abrupt, candid, direct, square 7 sincere, up-front 8 explicit, truthful 9 outspoken 10 forthright, from the hip, point-blank, unreserved
lay on the ~: 4 risk
like a straight ~: 4 one-d
map ~: 2 rd., rt. 3 hwy., riv., rte. 4 blvd., road 5 river, route 6 avenue 7 highway 9 boulevard 10 interstate
next in ~: 4 heir 7 heiress 9 inheritor, successor
oblique ~: 3 zig 4 bias, diag. 8 diagonal
of demarcation: 4 edge 5 verge 6 border, margin 8 boundary, frontier 9 perimeter, periphery 10 outer limit
of gab: 5 pitch 6 patter
of work: 3 job 10 occupation
on the ~: 6 at risk 7 sincere 9 veracious 10 in jeopardy
out of ~: 4 flip, pert, rude 5 askew, fresh, nervy, sassy, wrong 6 awless, brazen, cheeky, snippy, unruly, untrue 7 aweless, uncivil 8 aberrant, abnormal, flippant, impolite, insolent, snippety 10 prohibited, suspicious
part: 3 seg. 7 segment
sailor's ~: 5 brail 6 hawser 7 halyard
stand in ~: 4 wait 5 await 8 lose time, mark time
starter: 3 air, bee, bow, hem, hot, rat, red, set, sky, tag, tow 4 balk, bunt, date, dead, drag, hair, hard, head, land, life, main, neck, pipe, plot, roof, side, tape, tram, trot 5 blood, coast, drive, front, guide, ridge, shore, sight, touch, waist 6 border, center, strand, stream, timber 7 clothes
story ~: 4 plot
time ~: 4 plan 6 agenda 8 game plan, scenario, schedule, strategy 9 blueprint, framework 10 big picture
toe the ~: 4 heed, mind, obey 5 agree, bow to, defer, yield

6 accept, adhere, behave, bend to, comply, follow, fulfil, listen, submit 7 conform, consent, fulfill, observe, respect 8 carry out 10 keep in step
top of the ~: 4 A-one, best
unscripted ~: 5 ad-lib
up: 3 get 4 book, hire 5 align, array, enrol, order, queue, range 6 engage, enroll, obtain, secure 7 acquire, arrange, marshal, procure, program 8 organize 9 string out 10 straighten
(up): 3 set
walk the ~: 4 heed 6 listen, submit
weather ~: 5 front 6 isobar, isohel
line __: 3 art 5 dance, drive, score 7 drawing, officer, printer, segment, trimmer
line-__: 4 haul 6 hauler 7 casting
line-__ veto: 4 item
__ line: 3 bus, dew, gag, hot, red, tag, tie 4 base, belt, blue, chow, date, foul, goal, hard, main, plot, pure, snow, stag, time 5 bread, drop a, fault, front, laugh, leech, leger, on the, out of, party, plumb, power, punch, story, trunk, water, white 6 battle, border, bottom, credit, dotted, finish, firing, flight, ledger, picket, squall 7 contour, curtain, fishing, Maginot, morning, parting, poverty, product
__-line: 3 off, old 4 full 5 first, front
__ Line: 3 Hot 4 Main 5 Value
__ Line, A: 6 Chorus
lineage: 3 kin 4 clan, folk, race 5 birth, blood, breed, class, house, roots, stock, tribe 6 family, origin, stirps, strain 7 descent, kindred, progeny 8 ancestry, breeding, forbears, heredity, pedigree 9 forebears, genealogy, offspring, posterity 10 extraction, succession
lineal: 6 family, racial 8 familial, parental 9 ancestral 10 hereditary
not ~: 10 collateral
start: 5 matri, patri
lineament: 4 form, mark 5 shape 7 contour, feature, profile 10 silhouette
__, line and sinker: 4 hook
linear: 4 one-d 6 direct, in a row, narrow, unbent 7 unbowed 8 straight 9 arabesque 10 unswerving
extent: 4 span 5 orbit, range 6 course, length, radius 7 breadth, expanse, measure, purview, section, segment 8 diameter, distance, longness 9 longitude
lead-in: 5 recti
measure: 2 ft., km., mi., yd. 3 rod 4 foot, mile, yard 5 meter 7 furlong 9 kilometer
lineation: 5 shape 6 figure, sketch 7 profile 8 likeness, portrait 10 silhouette
line dance: 5 conga 8 bunny hop
lined up: 4 arow 5 level 6 in a row
__ Line Fever: 5 White
line-item __: 4 veto
lineman: 2 LG, LT, RG, RT 3 end 5 wirer 6 center, tackle 9 left guard 10 footballer, left tackle, right guard
__ Lineman: 7 Wichita
__ lineman for the county: 4 I am a
linen: 5 sheet, towel 6 damask, fabric, napery, napkin, sheets, towels 7 bedding, cambric, napkins 8 bed sheet 9 bed sheets, washcloth 10 pillowcase, washcloths
ancient ~: 6 byssus
buy: 9 white sale
dirty ~: 6 exposé, gossip 7 scandal
fabric: 4 lawn 5 toile 6 canvas, damask 7 cambric 8 chambray, marcella 10 seersucker
plant: 4 flax
shade: 3 tan 4 ecru 7 neutral
tape: 5 inkle
vestment: 3 alb 5 amice
linen __: 6 closet
__ linen: 3 bed 5 dirty, Irish, table
line of __: 4 fire 5 sight 6 battle, credit, vision
__ line of duty: 5 in the
__ Line of Fire: 5 In the
line one's __: 7 pockets
liner: 4 boat, QE II, ship 5 cover, craft, plane 6 makeup, vessel 7 mascara, steamer, vehicle 8 aircraft, airliner, airplane, cosmetic 9 eye pencil, eye shadow, steamship, transport 10 cruise ship, watercraft
level: 4 deck
location: 6 eyelid
ocean ~ name: 6 Cunard
place: 4 dock, mole, pier, port, quay, slip 5 berth, jetty, levee, wharf 6 harbor 7 landing 9 anchorage
starter: 3 air, eye, jet 4 head
liner __: 5 notes
__ liner: 5 cargo, ocean, party 6 helmet
__-liner: 3 day, one 4 hard 6 bottom
__ Line Railroad: 3 Soo
Liner She's a Lady, The: 4 poem
author: Rudyard Kipling
lines: 4 part 6 dialog, script 8 dialogue
combining form: 5 -stich
feed ~ to: 3 cue 6 prompt
forget one's ~: 4 flub, muff 5 choke, fluff 7 stumble
having ~: 4 rowy
having wavy ~: 6 gyrose
practice ~: 8 rehearse
read between the ~: 3 bet 5 glean, guess, infer, judge, wager, weigh 6 assume, call it, deduce, figure, gather, intuit, reckon, size up, take it, wonder 7 imagine, make out, presume, suppose, surmise, suspect 8 arrive at, conclude, construe 9 figure out, interpret, postulate, speculate 10 conjecture, have a hunch, understand
salesperson's ~: 4 puff, sell 5 offer, pitch, spiel 6 patter 9 promotion
Lines Composed a Few Miles Above Tintern Abbey
author: William Wordsworth
line-score letters: 3 RHE
Lines on the Mermaid Tavern: 4 poem
author: John Keats
lineup: 3 row 4 card, list, team 5 array, order, slate 6 agenda, roster 8 schedule 9 directory
entry: 4 name
pick from a ~: 2 ID 3 tag
remove from the ~: 5 bench
vertical ~: 4 heap, mass, pile 5 mound
lin. ft.: 4 meas.
ling: 4 fish 6 burbot
kin: 3 cod
__-ling: 5 ding-a, ting-a
lingcod: 4 fish
linger: 3 lag 4 bide, idle, last, laze, loaf, loll, mope, plod, poke, stay, stop, tool, wait 5 abide, amble, cling, crawl, dally, delay, drift, dwell, hover, mosey, stall, stand, stick, tarry, trail 6 dawdle, endure, falter, hang on, hobble, loiter, lumber, put off, putter, remain, slouch, stroll, totter, trapes, trifle, trudge 7 goof off, hang out, persist, saunter, shuffle, sojourn, stagger, survive, traipse 8 continue, hesitate, lollygag, lose time, straggle 9 sit around, vacillate, waste time 10 dillydally, fool around, hang around, stay a while, wait around
lingerer: 7 dawdler, laggard 8 slowpoke 9 straggler
lingerie: 3 bra, top 4 hose, robe, slip 5 pants, shift, stays, teddy 6 corset, girdle, jog bra, kimono, nighty, nylons, shimmy, undies 7 bikinis, chemise, drawers, nightie, pajamas, wrapper 8 bathrobe, bloomers, camisole, half-slip, skivvies 9 bedjacket, brassiere, hoop skirt, nightgown, pantyhose, petticoat, sleepwear, underwear 10 sleep shirt, undershirt
like some ~: 4 fine, lacy, soft 5 fancy, filmy, gauzy, sheer 6 dainty, frilly, smooth 7 elegant 8 delicate, gossamer 10 diaphanous, see-through
lingering: 8 dawdling, leftover, residual, tarrying 9 vestigial 10 continuing
__ Lingle Mungo: 3 Van
Ling-Ling: 5 panda
lingo: 4 cant, talk 5 argot, idiom, slang 6 jargon, patois, patter, speech, tongue 7 dialect 8 jive talk, language, Newspeak, parlance, pig Latin, shop talk 9 buzzwords 10 vernacular, vocabulary
lingua: 6 tongue
lingua __: 6 franca
__ linguae: 6 lapsus
lingual: 4 oral 6 spoken, verbal 7 sensory 9 sensorial
__-lingual: 5 audio
linguini: 5 pasta 7 noodles
alternative: *see* pasta
Chinese ~: 6 lo mein
topping: 5 sauce
linguist: 8 polyglot
linguistic: 8 semantic 10 semantical
comment: 5 rheme
group: 6 ethnos
root: 6 etymon
linguistics: 6 syntax 7 grammar 10 morphology
branch: 4 etym. 9 etymology
grp.: 3 MLA
__ Lingus: 3 Aer
liniment: 4 balm 5 cream, salve, slave 6 lotion 7 unction, unguent 8 dressing, lenitive, medicine, ointment 9 emollient 10 medication
apply, as ~: 5 rub on
target: 4 ache
lining: 6 facing, inside 7 backing 8 membrane
starter: 6 stream
stiff ~: 5 wigan
__ lining: 6 silver
link: 2 in 3 tie, wed 4 bind, bond, join, knot, lock, loop, part, ring, seam, span, unit, weld, yoke 5 annex, chain, group, hitch, joint, nexus, piece, segue, tag on, tie in, tie-up, unify, unite 6 adjoin, attach, bridge, cleave, cohere, copula, couple, enmesh, fasten, hook on, hookup, joiner, liaise, member, relate, slap on, splice, tack on 7 bracket, channel, combine, conjoin, connect, contact, coupler, element, hitch on, joining, liaison, network, rapport, section 8 catenate, coupling, division, dovetail, flambeau, identify, junction, ligament, ligation, ligature, meld with, plug into, relation, tag along, vinculum 9 associate, component, conjugate, correlate, fastening, integrate, interface, interlink, tie in with 10 attachment, connection, connective, team up with
ender: 3 age
firmly: 4 fuse, knit 5 weave 6 splice, stitch
missing ~: 6 apeman
site: 4 cuff
starter: 4 cuff, down
up: 4 dock, join, meet 5 unify, unite 6 plug in 9 get to know
with: 5 tie to
word ~: 6 hyphen
__ link: 3 lap 4 cuff 7 missing, sausage
Link: 4 Wray 5 Lyman
linkage: 5 logic, tie up 6 hookup
linked: 6 allied, joined, united 7 related 8 hooked up
__-link fence: 5 chain
linking: 6 hookup 8 junction, juncture 10 continuity
verb: 6 copula
word: 3 and
Linklater: 7 Richard
Linkletter: 3 Art 4 host 5 emcee
links: 5 wurst 6 course 7 sausage 10 golf course
see also golf
__ links: 4 golf 7 sausage
Lin, Maya: 9 architect
Linnaeus, Carolus: 5 Swede 8 botanist
Linn-Baker: 4 Mark
linnet: 4 bird 8 songbird
Linney, Laura: 7 actress
film: Absolute Power (1997)
Kinsey (2004)
The Nanny Diaries (2007)

Primal Fear (1996)
The Truman Show (1998)
You Can Count on Me (2000)
linoleum
alternative: 3 rug 4 tile 6 carpet
measurement: 4 area
oil: 4 tung
protector: 3 wax
linseed oil source: 4 flax
linsey: 6 fabric 8 material
linsey-__: 7 woolsey
lint: 4 dust, fuzz 5 fluff
collector: 4 trap 5 drier, dryer, navel, serge
lintel: 4 beam, jamb 8 crossbar 10 crosspiece
companion: 4 jamb
linty: 5 downy, fuzzy 6 fluffy, napped, woolly
Linus: 4 pope, Yale 7 Pauling, pontiff, Van Pelt
brother: 7 Orpheus
father: 6 Apollo
sister: 4 Lucy
son: 8 Calliope
Linville: 5 Larry
liny: 5 ruled 7 striped 8 streaked
Linz: 4 city, town
locale: 7 Austria
river: 6 Danube
Linzer __: 5 torte
Linz Symphony
composer: Wolfgang Amadeus Mozart
lion: 3 cat, Leo, VIP 4 hero, Nala 5 beast, felid, mogul, Mr. Big, Simba 6 animal, big cat, big gun, bigwig, feline, leader, mammal, roarer 7 big name, big shot, magnate 8 Clarence, luminary 9 big cheese, celebrity, dignitary
ant ~: 3 bug 6 insect
attack like a ~: 4 leap 6 pounce
beard the ~ in his den: 4 face 5 brave 8 confront
ender: 3 ess 4 fish 7 hearted
end of a ~ tail: 4 tuft
fare: 4 meat
greeting: 4 roar
home: 3 den, zoo 4 Asia, lair, veld 5 veldt 6 Africa
like a ~: 4 wild 5 maned, tawny
MGM ~: 3 Leo 4 logo
mountain ~: 4 puma 6 cougar 7 panther
mythical ~ home: 5 Nemea
name meaning ~: 3 Leo 4 Leon
Narnia ~: 5 Aslan
pack: 5 pride
prey: 5 zebra
pride: 4 mane
relative: *see* feline
to Tarzan: 5 simba
young: 3 cub 5 whelp
__ lion: 3 ant, sea 6 Nemean
Lion: 3 Leo 4 sign
month: 3 Aug., Jul. 4 July 6 August
predecessor: 4 Crab
successor: 6 Virgin
Lion __, The: 4 King
Lion __ Tonight, The: 6 Sleeps
__ Lion: 5 Paper
Lion and the Mouse, The
source: 4 Esop 5 Aesop
lion-eagle in heraldry: 7 griffin
Lionel: 4 Bart 6 Atwill, Richie 7 Hampton, Johnson, Stander 8 Jeffries, Trilling 9 Barrymore
lioness: 4 Elsa
Lioness and the Vixen, The: 5 fable
lionet: 3 cub
lionhearted: 4 bold, firm, game 5 brave, gutsy, manly, nervy, stout 6 awless, daring, gritty, heroic, plucky, spunky, sturdy, virile 7 aweless, defiant, doughty, gallant, leonine, staunch, valiant 8 fearless, heroical, intrepid, resolute, spirited, stalwart, unafraid, valorous 9 audacious, dauntless, dreadless, undaunted, unfearful 10 courageous
lionheartedness: 5 valor 6 daring 7 bravery, courage, heroism, prowess 8 boldness
Lion in Winter, The (1968 film)
cast: Katharine Hepburn, Peter O'Toole
lionize: 4 fete, laud, tout 5 exalt, honor 6 praise 7 acclaim, adulate, glorify, idolize, worship 8 eulogize, gush over, look up to 9 celebrate 10 aggrandize
Lionizing
author: Edgar Allan Poe
Lion King, The (1994 film)
role: 4 Nala, Scar 5 hyena, Simba, Timon 6 Mufasa
voice cast: Matthew Broderick, Whoopi Goldberg, Jeremy Irons, James Earl Jones, Moira Kelly, Nathan Lane, Cheech Marin, Jonathan Taylor Thomas
Lion of God, The: 3 Ali
lion's
share: 4 bulk, mass, most 7 big half, portion 8 majority
twist the ~ tail: 4 dare
lion's __: 3 den 5 share
Lions: 4 gulf, team 6 eleven 8 Columbia
colleagues: 4 Elks 5 Moose 7 Kiwanis
home: 7 Detroit
org.: 3 NFC, NFL
rival: *see* NFL team
sport: 8 football
Lions __: 4 Club
__ Lions: 7 Nittany
Lions and Shadows
author: Christopher Isherwood
Lions for Lambs (2007 film)
cast: Tom Cruise, Robert Redford, Meryl Streep
director: Robert Redford
Lion's Game, The
author: Nelson DeMille
Lion Sleeps Tonight, The (song)
artist: Robert John, Tokens
__ Lions, The: 5 Young
lion-tamer: 6 catman
need: 4 hoop, whip
place: 6 circus
prop: 5 chair
lion-to-lamb time: 5 March
Liotta, Ray: 5 actor
film: Cop Land (1997)
Corrina, Corrina (1994)
Crossing Over (2009)
Dominick and Eugene (1988)
Field of Dreams (1989)
GoodFellas (1990)
Hannibal (2001)
Heartbreakers (2001)
Identity (2003)
A Rumor of Angels (2002)
Unlawful Entry (1992)
lip: 3 rim 4 brim, edge, guff, sass, talk 5 brink, cheek, flare, mouth, reply, sauce, speak, spout, verge 6 border, flange, labium, margin 8 back talk, defiance, reaction, response, rudeness 9 freshness, impudence, insolence, sassiness, sauciness, smart talk 10 effrontery, embouchure
application: 4 balm 5 salve
balm target: 4 chap 5 crack
bite one's ~: 7 forbear, refrain, repress
button one's ~: 5 quiet 6 clam up, shut up 7 keep mum, let pass 8 play dumb 9 let it ride
combining form: 5 cheil-, chilo-, labio- 6 cheilo-
curl a ~: 4 mock, slam 5 flout, scoff, scorn, smirk, sneer 6 slight 7 grimace, put down, sniff at, snigger 8 ridicule 9 disparage 10 look down on
ender: 5 stick
give ~ to: 4 sass 8 get smart, mouth off, talk back 10 answer back
hang the ~: 4 mope, pout, sulk 5 brood
keep a stiff lower ~: 4 fume, mope, sulk 5 brood, frown 6 glower
keep a stiff upper ~: 6 bear up, hang in 8 face up to
ornament: 6 labret
service: 4 cant 7 mockery 8 pretense 9 hypocrisy, phoniness 10 pharisaism, pretension, sanctimony
shade: 3 red 4 pink, ruby 7 crimson
with a stiff upper ~: 5 stoic
lip __: 4 balm 5 gloss 6 reader 7 reading, service
lip-__: 4 read, sync 5 synch
__ lip: 3 fat
Liparis: 4 isls. 5 isles 7 islands
one of the ~: 9 Stromboli
lip-balm target: 5 crack
lipid: 3 fat, oil, wax 7 steroid
Lipinski, Tara: 6 skater
Lipizzaner: 5 horse, steed 6 equine
Lip My Reeds
composer: PDQ Bach
Lipnicki: 8 Jonathan
Li Po: 4 poet 7 Chinese
lipoid: 3 wax 5 fatty 8 lecithin
lipped: 7 labiate
__-lipped: 5 close, tight
Lippi: 5 Lippo 7 Filippo
Lippizaner: 5 horse, steed 6 equine
Lippmann: 6 Walter 7 Gabriel
Lippmann, Gabriel: 8 Nobelist 9 physicist
__ Lippo Lippi: 3 Fra
lip-puckering: 4 sour, tart 5 acerb
lippy: 4 pert 5 fresh, sassy 8 impudent
one: 4 snip
lips: 5 labia, mouth 6 kisser
bloodhound's ~: 5 flews
lock ~: 3 pet 4 kiss 6 smooch 8 osculate
of the ~: 6 labial
smack one's ~: 5 eat up, enjoy, gloat, savor 6 devour, relish 7 feast on
__ Lips Houlihan: 3 Hot
lip-smacking: 4 good, rich 5 spicy, sweet, tasty, yummy 6 delish, divine, mellow, savory 8 heavenly, luscious 9 ambrosial, delicious, flavorful, succulent, toothsome 10 appetizing, delectable
lipstick: 4 tree 5 paint 6 makeup 8 cosmetic
apply ~: 4 tint 5 color, paint 6 redden
holder: 3 bag 5 purse 6 clutch 7 handbag 8 reticule 10 pocketbook
like ~: 4 oily, waxy 8 lustrous
shade: 3 red 4 pink, puce 5 coral, peach 7 crimson
target: 5 mouth
type: 5 gloss
Lipstick on Your Collar (1959 song)
artist: Connie Francis
Liptauer: 6 cheese
Lipton: 3 tea 5 Peggy
alternative: 6 Nestea, Salada, Tetley 7 Bigelow, Red Rose 8 Twinings
brand: 4 Ragú
Lipton, Peggy
spouse: Quincy Jones
liq. measure: 2 pt., qt. 3 gal.
liquefied: 5 fluid 6 molten
liquefied natural __: 3 gas
liquefy: 3 run 4 melt, thaw 8 dissolve, fluidize, unfreeze 10 deliquesce
liqueur: 4 ouzo, port 5 booze, creme, drink 6 brandy, cognac, Kahlúa, kirsch, kümmel, pastis, Pernod 7 alcohol, cordial, curaçao, ratafia, sloe gin, spirits 8 apéritif, beverage, Drambuie, Tia Maria 9 alcoholic, aqua vitae, Cointreau, inebriant 10 chartreuse, intoxicant
anise ~: 4 ouzo 6 pastis, Pernod
cherry ~: 6 kirsch
coffee ~: 6 Kahlúa 8 Tia Maria
flavoring: 4 pear 5 anise, cacao 6 cherry, coffee, orange 8 licorice
German ~: 6 kümmel
Greek ~: 4 ouzo
licorice-flavored ~: 8 absinthe
orange ~: 9 Cointreau
orange peel ~: 7 curaçao
wine ~: 7 ratafia
liquid: 3 goo, sap, tea, wet 4 aqua, damp, flow, flux, free, goop, slop, soft, thin 5 broth, drink, fluid, juice, juicy, moist, pulpy, quick, ready, runny, sappy, swill, water 6 dulcet, elixir, fluent, mellow, melted, molten, moving, nectar, serous, smooth, thawed, usable, watery 7 aqueous, extract, flowing, fluidic, fusible, hydrous, melting, running, solvent, useable, viscose, viscous, wettish 8 ichorous, libation, luscious, meltable, moisture, solution 9 dissolved, secretion, splashing, succulent 10 marketable, negotiable, realizable
brush with ~: 5 baste 7 moisten

burn with ~: 5 scald
container: 4 ewer, tube, vial 5 phial 6 beaker, bottle, flagon 7 pitcher 8 test tube
foul ~: 3 mud 4 mire, muck, ooze, scum 5 slime 6 sludge
in physics: 5 state
measure: 2 oz., pt., qt. 3 gal., tsp. 4 fl. oz., gill, pint, tbsp. 5 liter, litre, ounce, quart 6 capful, gallon 8 teaspoon 10 tablespoon
refreshment: 5 drink, juice 8 beverage
science: 10 hydraulics
sweet ~: 5 sirup, syrup
viscous ~: 4 lard 5 pitch 6 grease 9 lubricant, petroleum
liquid __: 4 gold 5 asset 6 oxygen
Liquid __: 3 Sky 5 Paper, Plumr
liquidate: 3 pay 4 cash, do in, quit, sell, slay, vend 5 annul, honor, purge, repay, spend 6 cancel, cash in, divest, pay off, peddle, remove, rub out, settle, square, unload 7 abolish, cash out, convert, destroy, realize, satisfy, sell off, sell out, silence, wipe out 8 close out, dispatch, dissolve, exchange, get money, get rid of, vaporize 9 discharge, dispose of, eliminate, eradicate, finish off, polish off, reimburse, terminate 10 annihilate, auction off, do away with
liquid-crystal __: 7 display
Liquid Gold: 6 polish
alternative: 6 Behold, Endust, Pledge 10 Old English
Liquid Plumr
rival: 5 Drano
liquor: 3 alc., ale, gin, rum, rye 4 beer, grog, ouzo 5 booze, broth, drink, fluid, sauce, stock, vodka 6 brandy, cognac, elixir, mescal, poison, spirit, whisky 7 alcohol, aquavit, extract, potable, solvent, spirits, tequila, whiskey 8 infusion, schnapps, vermouth 9 aqua vitae, decoction, drinkable, firewater, hard stuff, inebriant, moonshine 10 intoxicant
add ~ to: 4 lace 5 spike 7 fortify
bottle: 5 fifth, flask 6 flagon
category: 5 blend
flavoring: 4 sloe
grp. for tough ~ laws: 4 MADD
Mideast ~: 4 arak, raki 5 rakee 6 arrack
over cracked ice: 4 mist
small ~ glass: 4 pony
spot of ~: 3 nip 4 dram
strength: 5 proof
__ liquor: 4 corn, malt
liquor-free: 3 dry
Liquor is quicker
poet: Ogden Nash
...liquor will __ contest quicker: 4 end a
lira: 5 money 6 string, violin
origin: 6 Greece
replacement: 4 euro
Lisa: 4 Kirk, Ling, Loeb 5 Bonet, McRee, Rinna 6 Kudrow, Loring 7 Hartman, Presley, Simpson 8 Birnbach, Eichhorn, Whelchel 9 Eilbacher 10 Stansfield
to Bart: 3 sis 6 sister
Lisa __ Presley: 5 Marie
__ Lisa: 4 Mona 5 I'm Not
Lisa Hartman __: 5 Black
Lisa Lisa and Cult Jam
song: All Cried Out (1986)
Head to Toe (1987)
Lost in Emotion (1987)
Lisa Marie dad: 5 Elvis
Lisbon: 4 city, port, town 7 capital
cape: 4 Roca
city near ~: 5 Evora
locale: 8 Portugal
river: 5 Tagus
Lisbon Antigua (1955 song)
artist: Nelson Riddle
Lise: 7 Meitner
Liselotte: 7 Neumann
Lisette: 5 Reese
'L' Is for Lawless
author: Sue Grafton
Lisi: 5 Virna
lisle: 6 fabric, thread
lisp: 8 sibilate 9 sibilance, sigmatism 10 assibilate, sibilation
kin: 4 lall
lisper's challenge: 3 ess
lissome: 4 wiry 5 agile, lithe, loose 6 limber, nimble, pliant, rubber, supple, svelte 7 bending, elastic, pliable, springy, willowy 8 bendable, flexible, graceful, moldable, stretchy 9 adaptable, lightsome, lithesome, malleable, resilient
quality: 5 grace
list: 3 sag, tab, tip 4 bill, heel, keel, lean, menu, name, note, poll, roll, sked, tilt 5 carte, enrol, index, lurch, slant, slate, slope, table, tally 6 agenda, careen, census, detail, docket, enroll, lineup, rattle, record, report, roster, series, ticket 7 archive, catalog, incline, invoice, itemize, lexicon, outline, recline, specify, tick off 8 calendar, classify, contents, glossary, heel over, keel over, manifest, register, schedule, syllabus, tabulate 9 catalogue, checklist, directory, enumerate, inventory, keep count, thesaurus, timetable, write down 10 cyclopedia, dictionary, memorandum, prospectus, tabulation, vocabulary
A ~: 5 elite
drop from a ~: 4 x out 6 delete 8 cross off, cross out
ender: 3 etc. 4 et al. 6 et alia, et alii
heading: 4 to do
item: 3 job 4 task 5 chore, entry 6 errand
preceder: 5 colon
separator: 5 comma
starter: 4 back 5 black, check
list __: 5 price 6 server
__ list: 4 to-do, want, wine, wish 5 check, dean's, price, short 7 laundry, mailing, waiting
List: 6 Eugene
__ List: 6 Emily's
listen: 4 hark, hear, heed, mind, obey 5 admit, adopt, audit, catch, watch 6 accept, attend, comply, harken, tune in 7 conform, consent, hearken, hear out, look out, monitor, observe, pay heed, receive, welcome 8 hear tell, overhear, pick up on 9 eavesdrop, entertain, lend an ear 10 get a load of, give heed to, take advice, take notice, toe the line
a lot to ~ to: 6 earful
don't ~: 7 disobey
in: 3 pry 4 hear 5 audit 9 eavesdrop
to: 3 bug 4 hear, heed, mind 6 advert, attend, follow, fulfil, notice, regard 7 abide by, fulfill, respect
(to): 3 bow 4 bend 5 agree, defer 6 adhere 8 carry out
unwilling to ~: 4 deaf 9 unhearing
willing to ~: 4 fair 6 mellow 8 amenable, flexible, open-door, outgoing, unbiased 9 impartial, objective, receptive, welcoming 10 accessible, hospitable, responsive
listeners: 5 crowd 7 gallery, hearers, turnout, viewers 8 assembly, audience 9 attendees, gathering, observers, onlookers, witnesses 10 assemblage, spectators
listening: 7 all ears, hearing 9 attentive
combining form: 4 acou- 5 acouo-
device: 3 bug, ear
Listening
author: Edward Albee
Listen People (1966 song)
artist: Herman's Hermits
Listen to the Music (1972 song)
artist: Doobie Brothers
Listen to What the Man Said (1975 song)
artist: Paul McCartney
Lister: 4 peak 5 mount 6 Joseph 8 mountain
locale: 10 Antarctica
Listerine: 9 mouthwash
alternative: 3 Act 4 Plax 5 Scope 6 Signal 7 Lavoris 10 Fluorigard
target: 4 germ
use ~: 6 gargle
List, Eugene: 7 pianist
listing: 3 log 4 sked 5 atilt 6 agenda, roster, tilted 7 program 8 schedule 9 timetable
listless: 4 blah, down, dull, limp, logy, mopy, slow 5 bored, faint, heavy, inert, leady, moony, mopey, musty, slack, weary 6 absent, anemic, dreamy, drowsy, leaden, mopish, sleepy, stupid, supine, torpid, vacant 7 anaemic, dormant, lagging, languid, neutral, out of it, passive 8 careless, downcast, heedless, indolent, laid-back, languish, lifeless, lukewarm, sluggish, stagnant 9 apathetic, easygoing, enervated, impassive, inanimate, lethargic, lymphatic 10 abstracted, energyless, insouciant, languorous, nonchalant, phlegmatic, regardless, spiritless, unreactive
become ~: 4 fade, flag, moon, mope, pine, sigh 5 brood, droop, yearn 6 grieve, repine, sicken 7 decline 8 languish, stagnate, vegetate 9 waste away
feeling: 5 ennui 6 apathy, tedium 7 boredom, languor 8 doldrums, monotony 9 lassitude, weariness 10 melancholy
listlessness: 5 blahs, ennui 6 apathy, phlegm, torpor 7 boredom, fatigue, inertia, languor 8 coolness, doldrums, dullness, laziness, lethargy 9 lassitude
showing ~: 4 mopy 5 mopey
List of Adrian Messenger, The (1963 film)
cast: Tony Curtis, George C. Scott, Dana Wynter
director: John Huston
Liston, Sonny: 5 boxer
milieu: 4 ring
Liszt, Franz: 7 pianist 8 composer
piece: 5 étude
work: Dante Symphony
Faust Symphony
Hungaria
Hungarian Rhapsodies
Les Préludes
Liebestraum
Mazeppa
Mephisto Waltz
Totentanz
lit: 5 afire, aglow, oiled, shiny, tipsy 6 ablaze, aflame, agleam, bright, flashy, got off, landed 7 beaming, blazing, burning, fired up, fulgent, glowing, ignited, kindled, lambent, perched, radiant, set down, settled, shining, torched 8 dazzling, gleaming, luminous, lustrous, turned on 9 brilliant, illumined, irrigated, set fire to, sparkling 10 came to rest, literature, touched off
on: 10 discovered
poorly ~: 3 dim 4 dark 5 murky 6 gloomy, somber 7 shadowy 9 tenebrous
softly ~: 5 aglow 7 lambent 9 refulgent
starter: 3 sun 4 back, moon, spot, star 5 flood
up: 5 aglow 6 beamed, glowed, smiled 7 beaming, glowing, grinned 8 grinning, spirited 10 brightened
lit-__: 4 crit
__ lit: 6 kiddie
__ Lit: 3 Eng. 7 English
Lita: 4 Ford, Grey
litany: 5 chant 6 prayer, tirade 7 account, catalog, recital 8 petition 9 catalogue 10 invocation, recitation, repetition
Lit.B.: 3 deg.
litchi: 3 nut 4 tree
relative: 4 akee 5 genip 6 longan, lungan 7 genipap 9 soapberry
lite: 5 lo-cal, lo-fat 6 low-cal
better than ~: 5 no-cal
make ~: 5 defat
product buyer: 6 dieter
Litel: 4 John
liter: 7 measure
about 3.8 ~s: 6 gallon
less than a ~: 5 quart
literacy: 8 learning 9 education, erudition, knowledge 10 articulacy, background, refinement
demonstrate ~: 4 read
volunteer: 5 coach, tutor
literal: 4 true 5 close, exact, plain, rigid 6 actual, simple, strict 7 prosaic 8 accurate, bona fide, faithful, truthful, unerring, verbatim 9 authentic, prosaical 10 unimagined

not ~: **8** symbolic **10** figurative, metaphoric
literally: 3 sic **5** truly **6** really, simply **7** exactly, plainly **8** actually, directly, strictly, verbatim **9** precisely **10** completely, faithfully, unerringly
literalness: 5 truth **7** honesty **8** accuracy, dullness, rigidity, slowness
literary: 6 formal **7** bookish, erudite, learned **8** lettered, well-read **9** classical, scholarly
adverb: 3 e'er **4** ne'er
category: 4 biog. **5** drama, essay, genre, novel, prose, sci-fi **6** poetry **7** fiction, romance **9** biography **10** non-fiction
composition: 4 opus **5** novel, piece **6** column, sketch **7** article, passage, romance **9** editorial
device: 5 irony, trope **6** pathos
drudge: 4 hack
form: 5 prose **6** poetry
medley: 5 cento
miscellany: 3 ana **5** varia
monogram: 3 LMA, PDJ, RLS, RWE, TSE
passage: 5 quote **9** quotation
pseudonym: 4 Elia, Saki
rep: 3 agt. **5** agent
sketch: 5 cameo
literary __: 4 lion
literate: 6 versed **7** erudite, learned **8** cultured, educated, lettered, schooled **9** scholarly **10** cultivated, instructed
literati: 5 elite, sages **7** pundits, savants **8** academes, scholars **9** aesthetes, highbrows, longhairs **10** illuminati, upper-crust
literatim: 7 exactly **8** verbatim **9** precisely
literature: 4 lore **5** books, drama, essay, novel, paper, poesy, prose, story, theme, tract **6** poetry, précis, report, thesis **7** article, comment, history, leaflet, letters, summary, writing **8** abstract, brochure, classics, critique, findings, learning, pamphlet, research, treatise, writings **9** biography, discourse, treatment **10** discussion, exposition
__-Lites: 3 Chi
Lith.: 3 SSR **4** once
lithe: 4 lean, slim, spry **5** agile, light **6** limber, lissom, nimble, pliant, slight, supple, svelte **7** lissome, pliable, sinuous, slender, willowy **8** flexible, graceful **9** lightsome
lithesome: 6 limber, supple **7** sinuous
Lithgow, John: 5 actor
film: Blow Out (1981)
Cliffhanger (1993)
Footloose (1984)
Terms of Endearment (1983)
The World According to Garp (1982)
film (voice): Shrek (2001)
TV: 3rd Rock from the Sun
lithic: 5 rocky, stony **6** stoney
-lithic starter: 3 neo **5** paleo
lithium: 5 metal **7** element
ore: 10 lepidolite
lithium-__ battery: 3 ion
litho-: 5 stone
lithograph: 5 plate, print **9** engraving
lithographer: 4 Ives **7** Currier
lithoid: 9 petrified, stonelike **10** adamantine
lithosphere: 5 crust, shell
Lithuania: 6 nation **7** country
capital: 5 Vilna **7** Vilnius
city: 5 Vilna **6** Kaunas **7** Vilnius
legislature: 6 Seimas
money: 5 litas
neighbor: 6 Latvia, Poland, Russia **7** Belarus
once: 3 SSR
region: 6 Baltic
Lithuanian: 4 Balt
neighbor: 4 Lett
litigant: 4 suer **5** party **6** suitor **7** accused, accuser **8** claimant, opponent **9** appellant, defendant, disputant, plaintiff **10** prosecutor
litigate: 3 sue **6** appeal **7** contest, dispute **8** file suit **9** fight over, go to court, prosecute
litigation: 4 case, feud, suit **5** cause, trial **6** action **7** dispute, lawsuit, process **10** contention
litigious: 9 bellicose, combative **10** disputable
be ~: 3 sue
litmus: 3 dye **7** pigment **8** colorant
color: 3 red **4** blue
it turns ~ blue: 3 alk. **4** base **6** alkali
it turns ~ red: 4 acid
source: 7 lichens
tester: 2 pH
use ~: 4 test **7** analyze **10** experiment
litmus __: 4 test **5** paper
__-Litovsk: 5 Brest
litter: 4 cubs, hash, junk, mess, muck, rash **5** brood, dirty, offal, strew, trash, waste, young **6** debris, family, jumble, jungle, mess up, muddle, refuse, school **7** clutter, confuse, derange, garbage, kittens, piglets, progeny, puppies, rubbish, rummage, scatter, shuffle **8** detritus, disarray, disorder, leavings, mishmash, scramble **9** confusion, make a mess, stretcher, sweepings **10** collateral, disarrange, hodgepodge, scattering, untidiness
ender: 3 bag, bug **4** mate
have a ~: 5 whelp
member: 3 pup **4** runt **5** puppy
pig ~: 6 farrow
__ litter: 3 cat
__ Litter: 5 Kitty
litterbug: 3 pig **4** slob, slop **6** sloven **8** polluter
unlike a ~: 4 neat, tidy, trim **6** dainty **7** orderly **8** well-kept **10** fastidious, methodical, systematic
littered: 5 messy **6** unneat, untidy **10** topsy-turvy
litter-free: 4 neat
little: 3 bit, dab, nip, set, tad, toy, wee **4** aper, baby, base, dash, hint, less, lick, mean, mini, puny, snub, spot, tiny, whit **5** bitty, brief, cheap, dinky, elfin, hasty, light, minor, petty, pinch, scant, short, small, speck, taste, teeny, touch, trace, weeny, young **6** atomic, bantam, barely, casual, hardly, infant, junior, meager, minute, narrow, paltry, peanut, peewee, petite, pocket, rarely, scanty, seldom, skimpy, slight, sparse, stubby, teensy, trifle, vulgar, wicked **7** babyish, bigoted, cramped, limited, modicum, not many, not much, selfish, shrimpy, slender, snippet, soupçon, stunted, trivial, wizened **8** atomical, atomlike, dwarfish, fleeting, fragment, immature, not often, not quite, only just, particle, pint-size, pittance, scarcely, somewhat, trifling **9** embryonic, hardly any, hidebound, illiberal, itsy-bitsy, itty-bitty, miniature, minuscule, parochial, pint-sized, shriveled, truncated, undersize **10** diminutive, hardly ever, negligible, provincial, shoestring, short-lived, teeny-weeny, undersized, vest-pocket
a ~: 3 any **4** some **6** kind of, little, rather **8** slightly, somewhat **10** moderately
bit: 3 dab, jot **4** iota, mite, spot **5** speck
boy: 3 imp **6** moppet **9** youngster
by little: 6 pokily **9** gradually, haltingly, languidly, leisurely, partially, piecemeal **10** crawlingly, creepingly, sluggishly
costing ~: 3 low **5** cheap **6** modest, on sale **7** cut-rate, reduced, slashed **8** for a song **9** half-price **10** economical, marked down, reasonable
darling: 3 tot **4** baby **5** angel, child **6** cherub, infant, moppet **7** neonate, newborn, toddler **8** cutie pie, dumpling, snookums **10** sweetie pie
devil: 3 imp **4** brat **5** scamp **6** urchin
do ~: 4 laze **5** slack **7** slacken
game: 4 plot, trap **5** cabal **6** racket, scheme **8** intrigue **9** coalition, collusion, treachery **10** complicity, connivance, conspiracy, disloyalty
give ~: 4 save **5** skimp **6** scrape, scrimp, slight **8** conserve, roll back, withhold **9** economize **10** cut corners
give a ~ extra: 6 slap on, tack on, toss in **8** increase
in a ~ while: 4 anon, soon **7** shortly **8** directly
in music: 4 poco
just a ~: 3 sip **4** bite, dash, dram, drop, shot **5** pinch, snort, taste **6** nibble **7** soupçon, swallow **8** spoonful
known: 3 new **4** dark **5** alien **6** exotic, hidden, humble, occult, remote, secret, unsung, untold **7** foreign, obscure, strange, unnamed, unnoted **8** nameless **9** anonymous, concealed, incognito, uncharted, unheard-of **10** mysterious, unexplored, unfamiliar, unrevealed
make ~ of: 5 gloss, gloze **6** lessen **8** discount, downplay, minimize, play down, pooh-pooh, shrug off, talk down **9** deprecate, underplay, whitewash **10** understate
more than: 4 mere
more than just a ~: 4 much **5** amply, quite **6** deeply, highly, hugely, unduly, vastly **7** greatly, largely, only too, rabidly **8** terribly **9** decidedly, extremely, seriously, unusually **10** enormously, incredibly, profoundly, remarkably, thoroughly, uncommonly
name meaning ~: 6 Vaughn **7** Vaughan
of ~ value: 4 mean, mere, poor, punk, puny **5** cheap, lousy, minor, petty, scant, small, sorry **6** crummy, feeble, humble, meager, measly, paltry, rotten, shoddy, sleazy, stingy **7** limited, pitiful, shallow, trivial **8** inferior, pathetic, picayune, piddling, trifling, wretched **9** fifth-rate, miserable, third-rate, worthless **10** fourth-rate, second-rate
one: 3 elf, kid, tot **4** babe, baby, tike, tyke **5** child, minor **6** infant, rug rat, sprite
people: 3 mob **4** fays, herd, imps **5** elves **6** dryads, dwarfs, gnomes, nymphs, pixies, public, rabble, sylphs, trolls **7** dwarves, fairies, midgets, sprites, squirts, workers **8** brownies, populace **9** hoi polloi
piggy: 3 toe **5** digit
prefix: 4 mini- **5** micro-
shaver: 3 boy, tot **4** tike, tyke **5** child
suffix: 3 -ino, -ule **4** -etta, -ette
think ~ of: 4 skip, snub **5** let go, scorn, spurn **6** forget, ignore, rebuff, slight **7** disdain, dismiss, let pass, neglect, tune out **8** discount, laugh off, let slide, pass over, shrug off **9** disregard, gloss over, pay no mind **10** brush aside
too ~: 3 shy **4** thin **5** short **6** meager, scanty, skimpy **7** wanting **9** deficient **10** inadequate
too ~ too late: 9 deficient, half-baked, shortfall **10** inadequate
while: 3 bit **4** jiff **5** jiffy
little __: 3 Joe, man, toe **4** slam **6** finger **7** theater
little __'ll do ya, A: 3 dab
little __ told me, A: 4 bird
little-__: 5 bitty
__ little: 4 not a
...little __ eat ivy...: 5 lambs
Little: 4 Rich **7** Cleavon
Little __: 3 Dog, Eva, Fox, Men **4** Bear, Em'ly, John, Lies, Lion, Lulu, Nemo, Star **5** Giant, Rhody, Tikes, Women **6** Caesar, Darlin', Dipper, Dorrit, Iodine, League **7** America, Anthony, Bighorn, Leaguer, Richard
Little __ and Big Halsy: 5 Fauss
Little __ and the Imperials: 7 Anthony
Little __ Annie: 6 Orphan **7** Orphant
Little __ Apples: 5 Green
Little __ Blue: 4 Girl
Little __ Book: 3 Red
Little __ Cartwright: 3 Joe
Little __ Coupe: 5 Deuce

Little __ Echo: 3 Sir
Little __ Fauntleroy: 4 Lord
Little __ Flowers: 4 Ida's
Little __ Jug: 5 Brown
Little __ Lies: 5 White
Little __ Man: 3 Big, Ole
Little __ Marker: 4 Miss
Little __ Mean a Lot: 6 Things
Little __ Music, A: 5 Night
Little __ of Horrors: 4 Shop
Little __ on the Prairie: 5 House
Little __ Pretty One: 5 Bitty
Little __ Riding Hood: 3 Red
Little __ Rooney: 5 Annie
Little __ Soap, A: 5 Bit of
Little __ Tate: 3 Man
Little __ Tear, A: 5 Bitty
Little __ That Could, The: 6 Engine
Little __, The: 3 Ark **4** King **5** Foxes, Giant **6** Prince, Sister **7** Colonel, Mermaid
__ Little: 6 Stuart **7** Chicken
__ Little Acre: 4 God's
__ Little Angel Eyes: 6 Pretty
Little Annie Rooney dog: 4 Zero
Little Anthony and the Imperials
 last name: Gourdine
 song: Goin' Out of My Head (1964)
  Hurt So Bad (1965)
  Shimmy, Shimmy, Ko-Ko-Bop (1960)
  Tears on My Pillow (1958)
Little Big Horn: 6 battle
Little Big Man: 4 film **5** novel
 author: Thomas Berger
 cast: Faye Dunaway, Dustin Hoffman
 director: Arthur Penn
little bird __ me, A: 4 told
Little Birds
 author: Anaïs Nin
__ Little Bit Better: 5 Just a
__ Little Bit Closer: 5 Come a
Little Bit Me, A Little Bit You, A (1967 song)
 artist: Monkees
__ Little Bit of Luck: 5 With a
Little Bit O' Soul (1967 song)
 artist: Music Explosion
Little Bitty Pretty One (song)
 artist: Clyde McPhatter, Thurston Harris
Little Bitty Tear, A (1962 song)
 artist: Burl Ives
Little Boy: 5 A-bomb
Little Boy __: 4 Blue
Little Brown __: 3 Jug
little by little, move: 4 edge, inch **5** creep, sidle
Little Caesar (1930 film)
 cast: Douglas Fairbanks Jr., Glenda Farrell, Edward G. Robinson
 director: Mervyn LeRoy
 role: 4 Rico
Little Colonel, The: 5 Reese
Little Darlings (1980 film)
 cast: Tatum O'Neal
Little Debbie
 competitor: ***see*** cookie manufacturer
Little Deuce __: 5 Coupe
Little Devil (1961 song)
 artist: Neil Sedaka
Little Diane (1962 song)
 artist: Dion
Little Dipper: 9 Ursa Minor
 star: 7 Polaris
__ Little Dividend: 7 Father's
Little Dorrit
 author: Charles Dickens
 character: 3 Amy, Tip **5** Casby, Doyce, Fanny, Flora **6** Arthur, Daniel, Merdle, Pancks
Little Drummer Boy
 syllable: 3 tum
Little Drummer Girl, The: 4 film **5** novel
 author: John le Carré
 cast: Diane Keaton, Klaus Kinski
 director: George Roy Hill
Little Engine
 verb: 3 can
Little Engine That __, The: 5 Could
Little Eva
 last name: Boyd
 song: The Loco-Motion (1962)
Little Eyolf
 author: Henrik Ibsen
__ little faith!: 4 Ye of
__ Little Fishes: 5 Three
__ Little Fool: 4 Poor
Little Foxes, The: 4 play
 author: Lillian Hellman
 character: 3 Cal, Leo **5** Addie, Oscar **6** Birdie, Horace, Regina
__ Little Foys, The: 5 Seven
Little Gidding
 author: T.S. Eliot
__ Little Girl: 3 Hey **6** Daddy's
Little Girl Blue
 composer: Lorenz Hart, Richard Rodgers
Little Green Apples (1968 song)
 artist: O.C. Smith
__ Little Helper: 7 Mothers
Little House on the Prairie (NBC drama)
 cast: Melissa Sue Anderson (Mary Ingalls)
  Richard Bull (Nels Oleson)
  Melissa Gilbert (Laura Ingalls)
  Karen Grassle (Caroline Ingalls)
  Michael Landon (Charles Ingalls)
 dog: 6 Bandit
__ Little Indians: 3 Ten
Little in Love, A (1981 song)
 artist: Cliff Richard
Little Iodine cartoonist: 5 Hatlo
__ Little Ironies: 5 Life's
Little Jack __: 6 Horner
Little Jeannie (1980 song)
 artist: Elton John
Little Joe: 10 Cartwright
 brother: 4 Adam, Hoss
Little Johnny Jones
 composer: George M. Cohan
little-known: 3 new **4** dark, deep, rare **6** arcane, hidden, mystic, occult, orphic, secret, unsung **7** cryptic, obscure, strange, unusual **8** abstruse, esoteric, mystical, nameless, shocking, singular, uncommon **9** recondite, unheard-of **10** mysterious, unrenowned
Little League coach, usually: 3 dad
Little Lies (1987 song)
 artist: Fleetwood Mac
Little Lord Fauntleroy dog: 6 Dougal
__ Little Love in Your Heart: 4 Put a
__ Little Luck: 5 With a
Little Man Tate (1991 film)
 cast: Jodie Foster, Dianne Wiest
 director: Jodie Foster
Little Men
 author: Louisa May Alcott
Little Mermaid, The
 author: Hans Christian Andersen
Little Mermaid, The (1989 film)
 character: Scuttle, Triton, Ursula **4** crab, Eric **5** Ariel **9** Sebastian
 director: Ron Clements, John Musker
 voice cast: René Auberjonois, Jodi Benson, Pat Carroll, Buddy Hackett, Kenneth Mars
Little Miss Muffet __ tuffet: 6 sat on a
Little Miss Sunshine (2006 film)
 cast: Alan Arkin, Abigail Breslin, Steve Carell, Toni Collette, Greg Kinnear
Little More Love, A (1978 song)
 artist: Olivia Newton-John
Little More Time on You, A (1998 song)
 artist: 'Nsync
Little Murders (1971 film)
 cast: Vincent Gardenia, Elliott Gould, Marcia Rodd
 director: Alan Arkin
littleneck: 4 clam **6** quahog **7** quahaug
Little Nemo: 5 strip **10** comic strip
 cartoonist: 5 McCay
 dog: 7 Slivers
Little Night Music, A: 7 musical
 composer: Stephen Sondheim
__ little of: 4 make **5** think
Little Old Lady, The (1964 song)
 artist: Jan & Dean
Little Ole Man (1967 song)
 artist: Bill Cosby
Little Order, A
 author: Evelyn Waugh
Little Orphan Annie: 5 strip **10** comic strip
 cartoonist: 4 Gray
 character: 3 Asp **6** Punjab **8** Warbucks
 dog: 5 Sandy
Little Orphant Annie: 4 poem
 author: James Whitcomb Riley
__ little piggy...: 4 this
Little Pigs building material: 5 straw **6** bricks, sticks
Little pitchers have big __!: 4 ears
Little Poison: 5 Waner
__ Little Prayer: 5 I Say a
Little Prince, The
 author: Antoine de Saint-Exupéry
Little Rascals
 dog: 4 Pete **5** Petey
 producer: 5 Roach
Little Red __ Hood: 6 Riding
Little Red Book
 author: Mao Zedong
Little Red Corvette (1983 song)
 artist: Prince
Little Red Hen, reply to: 4 not I
Littler, Gene: 6 golfer
Little, Rich: 4 aper
 emulate ~: 3 ape
Little Richard
 last name: Penniman
 song: Good Golly, Miss Molly (1958)
  Jenny, Jenny (1957)
  Keep A Knockin' (1957)
  Long Tall Sally (1956)
  Lucille (1957)
  Ooh! My Soul (1958)
  Rip It Up (1956)
  Slippin' and Slidin' (1956)
  Tutti-Frutti (1956)
__ Little Rich Girl: 4 Poor
Little River Band
 homeland: Australia
 song: Cool Change (1979)
  Help Is on Its Way (1977)
  Lady (1979)
  Lonesome Lover (1979)
  Man on Your Mind (1982)
  The Night Owls (1981)
  The Other Guy (1982)
  Reminiscing (1978)
  Take It Easy on Me (1981)
Little Rock: 4 city, town **7** capital
 county: 7 Pulaski
 locale: 3 Ark. **8** Arkansas
 river: 8 Arkansas
Little Romance, A (1979 film)
 cast: Diane Lane, Laurence Olivier
Little Shop of Horrors (1986 film)
 cast: Vincent Gardenia, Ellen Greene, Steve Martin, Rick Moranis
 character: 4 Luce, Orin, Snip **6** Audrey **7** Ronette
Little Shop of Horrors, The (1960 film)
 director: Roger Corman
Little Sir __: 4 Echo
Little Sister (1961 song)
 artist: Elvis Presley
Little Sister, The
 author: Raymond Chandler
__ Little Sixteen: 5 Sweet
Little Sparrow, The: 4 Piaf
littlest: 5 least **6** lowest, merest **7** minimal, minimum, modicum, nominal, tiniest **8** smallest **9** slightest
Little Star (1958 song)
 artist: Elegants
__ Little Teapot: 3 I'm a
__ Little Tenderness: 4 Try a
Little Things Mean __: 4 a Lot
__ Little Toaster, The: 5 Brave
Littleton: 4 city, town
 locale: 8 Colorado
__ Little We Know: 3 How
Little White __: 4 Lies
Little Women
 author: Louisa May Alcott
 character: 2 Jo **3** Amy, Meg **4** Beth, Demi **5** Bhaer, Daisy, Kirke, March **6** Carrol, Laurie, Marmee
Little Women (1994 film)
 cast: Trini Alvarado, Gabriel Byrne, Claire Danes, Winona Ryder, Susan Sarandon
__ Little Words: 5 Three
littoral: 5 beach, coast, sands, shore **6** marine, strand **7** coastal, seaside **8** maritime
 phenomenon: 4 tide
liturgical: 6 formal, ritual, solemn **10** ceremonial
 see also church
liturgy: 4 form, rite **6** ritual **7** formula, service, worship **8** ceremony, services **9** formality, sacrament **10** ceremonial, observance
Litvak: 7 Anatole
Liu: 4 Lucy

LIU
locale: 3 NYC
Liu Pang
dynasty: 3 Han
Liv: 5 Tyler 7 Ullmann
Broadway role for ~: 4 Mama
livable: 3 fit 4 cosy, cozy, homy, snug 5 cozey, cozie, homey 8 adequate, bearable, homelike, passable 9 endurable, habitable, tolerable 10 acceptable, worthwhile
live: 3 are, hot 4 bide, bunk, fare, feed, last, nest, real, stay 5 abide, alert, alive, crash, dwell, exist, get by, lodge, ready, roost, savor, vital, vivid 6 active, actual, belong, billet, endure, make it, occupy, remain, reside, settle, thrive 7 animate, breathe, burning, current, dynamic, organic, prevail, prosper, running, subsist, survive, topical, working 8 animated, continue, existent, flourish, get along, in person, pressing, vigorous 9 as we speak, breathing, conscious, energetic, explosive, make money, observant, operative, unsettled 10 draw breath, experience, performing, unimagined
at: 6 billet, occupy 7 inhabit
beneath one's station: 4 slum
can't ~ without: 4 need 5 crave 7 hurt for, require
ender: 4 long 5 stock
fit to ~ in: 9 habitable
high on the hog: 4 bask 5 revel 6 thrive 7 indulge, rollick 8 flourish
in: 6 occupy 7 inhabit 8 populate
it up: 4 riot 5 revel 8 roll in it 9 celebrate, luxuriate, make merry
on: 3 eat 6 endure 7 survive 8 continue
partner: 5 learn
place to ~: 4 home 5 abode 8 quarters
through: 4 bear, go on, last, stay 5 stand 6 endure, hang on, hold on, keep on, manage, suffer 7 carry on, hold out, make out, outlast, prevail, recover, ride out, survive, undergo, weather 8 overcome 9 persevere, put up with, withstand 10 keep afloat, sit through, stick it out, tough it out
up to: 5 honor 6 follow 8 practice
where most people ~: 4 Asia
wire: 4 doer, grig 6 dynamo 7 busy bee, hustler 8 fireball, go-getter 9 workhorse 10 powerhouse
with: 4 take 5 brook, stand 6 accept, suffer 8 overlook, stand for, tolerate 9 disregard
(with): 4 cope
words to ~ by: 5 adage, credo, creed, motto
live __: 3 oak 4 a lie, down, it up, up to, wire, with
live __ the fat of the land: 3 off
live-__: 6 action 7 forever
Live __: 3 Aid 5 or Die
live and __: 5 learn
live and __ live: 3 let
__ live and breathe!: 3 as I
Live and Let Die: 4 film, song 5 novel
artist: Paul McCartney
author: Ian Fleming
cast: Yaphet Kotto, Roger Moore, Jane Seymour
Live at Red Rocks
artist: John Tesh
__ Live by Night: 4 They
live by one's __: 4 wits
lived: 3 was 4 been
__-lived: 4 long 5 short
...lived happily __ after: 4 ever
lived-in: 8 occupied 9 inhabited
Live Free __: 5 or Die
Live Free or Die Hard (2007 film)
cast: Justin Long, Timothy Olyphant, Bruce Willis
Live from New York, __ Saturday Night!: 3 it's
live in __ paradise: 6 a fool's
live-in: 4 maid 6 au pair 7 servant
livelihood: 3 art, job 4 game, keep, slot, work 5 craft, grind, means, thing, trade 6 career, income, racket 7 aliment, rat race, support 8 business, vocation 9 resources 10 employment, nine-to-five, occupation, profession, sustenance, walk of life
liveliness: 3 fun, pep, vim, zip 4 brio, dash, élan, fire, glee, jazz, life, zeal, zest 5 ardor, mirth, spark, speed, spice, sport, verve, vigor 6 action, bounce, energy, esprit, fervor, gaiety, gayety, spirit, warmth 7 agility, revelry, sparkle 8 activity, airiness, alacrity, buoyance, buoyancy, vitality, vivacity 9 animation, élan vital 10 ebullience, exuberance, friskiness
livelong: 4 full 5 total, whole 6 entire
lively: 3 gay, yar 4 busy, go-go, keen, live, pert, racy, spry, yare 5 agile, alert, astir, brisk, fresh, happy, hyper, jazzy, light, merry, peart, peppy, perky, quick, salty, sassy, sharp, smart, vital, vivid, witty, zippy 6 active, at work, blithe, bouncy, breezy, bright, chirpy, dapper, feisty, festal, frisky, jaunty, jocund, madcap, nimble, snappy, speedy 7 animate, buoyant, buzzing, chipper, coltish, complex, dashing, driving, dynamic, festive, graphic, hyped-up, jumping, piquant, playful, rousing, vibrant, working, zestful 8 animated, bustling, cheerful, involved, skittish, sparking, spirited, sporting, sportive, stirring, swinging, vigorous 9 assiduous, convivial, energetic, enjoyable, exuberant, gamboling, graphical, sparkling, sprightly, vivacious, with a kick 10 blithesome, expressive, frolicsome, refreshing, rollicking
in music: 4 anim. 7 animato
name meaning ~: 6 Vivian, Vivien 8 Vivienne
__ lively!: 4 Step
Lively: 5 Blake
__ Lively Arts: 5 Seven
liven: 4 buoy, fire, goad, prod, zest 5 cheer, elate, pep up, rouse, spark, spice, waken 6 arouse, buck up, excite, kindle, perk up, pump up, spur on, stir up, turn on, vivify 7 animate, cheer up, gladden, hearten, inspire, juice up, quicken 8 activate, charge up, energize, vitalize 9 stimulate 10 brighten up, exhilarate, invigorate
__ live nephew...: 5 A real
live off the __ of the land: 3 fat
Live or Die
author: Anne Sexton
liver: 4 meat 5 gland, organ 6 lessee, lodger, native, renter, roomer, tenant 7 boarder, burgher, denizen, dweller, resider 8 occupant, resident 10 inhabitant
appetizer: 6 rumaki
combining form: 5 hepat- 6 hepato-
ender: 4 leaf, wort 5 wurst
nutrient: 4 iron
output: 4 bile
paste: 4 pâté
__ liver: 4 free, high 7 chopped
__-livered: 4 lily 7 chicken
liverish: 3 wan 4 glum, pale, rude, sour 5 nasty, sulky, surly, testy 6 bitter, cranky, dismal, gloomy, grumpy, morose, sallow, sickly, sullen, touchy, yellow 7 bilious, crabbed, grouchy 8 choleric, grumpish 9 depressed, irascible, irritable, jaundiced, saturnine, spleenful 10 melancholy
Livermore: 4 city, town
locale: 10 California
__ liver oil: 3 cod
Liverpool: 4 city, port, town
locale: 7 Britain, England
river: 6 Mersey
Liverpudlian: 4 Brit 6 Briton
liverwort
bud: 5 gemma
cousin: 4 moss
liverwurst: 4 meat 7 sausage
livery: 4 garb, suit 5 dress, get-up, habit 6 attire, outfit 7 apparel, clothes, costume, garment, raiment, regalia, threads, uniform 8 clothing, ensemble, garments 9 trappings 10 Sunday best
livery __: 3 cab 6 stable
Lives __ Bengal Lancer, The: 3 of a
__ Lives: 4 Men's 5 Three 7 Private
Livesey: 5 Roger
livestock: 4 cows, hogs, kine, pigs 5 goats, herds, sheep, stock 6 cattle, droves, flocks, horses, steers 7 animals
meal: 3 rye 4 feed 5 spelt 6 fodder
place: 4 barn 5 ranch 6 corral
show: 4 fair
live the __ life: 4 good
Live to Tell (1986 song)
artist: Madonna
__ Live With Me: 4 Come
Livia: 7 Soprano
author: Lawrence Durrell
livid: 3 wan 4 ashy, pale 5 angry, ashen, dusky, lurid, mirky, murky, pasty, waxen 6 gloomy, grisly, leaden, pallid, purple, raving 7 bruised, flaming, flushed, grayish, greyish, ranting 8 blanched, contused, in a pique, offended 9 bloodless, colorless 10 discolored, freaked out
be ~: 4 boil, burn, fume, rage, stew 5 froth 6 see red, seethe
see also angry
Livin' for the Weekend (1976 song)
artist: O'Jays
living: 3 job, way 4 born, keep, mode, salt, warm, work 5 alert, awake, brisk, in use, means, vital 6 active, actual, around, billet, career, extant, income, in esse, strong, with us 7 aliment, animate, current, dynamic, ongoing, organic, support, ticking 8 animated, existent, existing, vigorous 9 breathing, existence, lifestyle, operative 10 continuing, developing, occupation, persisting, subsisting, sustenance, unimagined
all ~ things: 5 world 6 nature 8 creation, universe
alone: 5 unwed 6 single 8 isolated, solitary 9 by oneself, on one's own, separated, unmarried 10 spouseless, unattached
combining form: 4 vivi-
daylights: 4 wits 5 sense
earn a ~: 4 fare, work 5 get by 6 make it 7 prosper, subsist, support, survive 8 get along 9 make money
high ~: 4 ease 5 style 6 luxury, wealth 7 comfort, leisure 8 elegance, hedonism, opulence, splendor 9 affluence 10 lavishness, prosperity
quarters: 4 home 5 abode, condo, house, place 7 lodging 9 apartment, dormitory
scratch out a ~: 3 eke 6 scrape
space: 4 area
thing: 5 being, human, plant 6 animal, mortal, person 8 creature, organism 10 human being, individual
living __: 3 end 4 room, wage 5 large 6 legend
__ living: 5 earn a
__-living: 4 free 5 clean
Living and Loving
author: Sophia Loren
Living Daylights, The: 4 film 5 novel
author: Ian Fleming
band: 3 A-ha
cast: Joe Don Baker, Maryam d'Abo, Timothy Dalton
director: John Glen
instrument: 5 cello
Living End, The suthor: 5 Elkin
Living Faith
author: Jimmy Carter
Living for the City (1973 song)
artist: Stevie Wonder
living fossil tree: 6 gingko, ginkgo
Living in America (1986 song)
artist: James Brown
living in the __: 4 past
Living on the Fault Line
author: Geoffrey Moore
Living Out Loud (1998 film)
cast: Danny DeVito, Holly Hunter, Queen Latifah
Living Reed, The
author: Pearl S. Buck
living room
appliance: 4 lamp 9 floor lamp
appliance of old: 5 radio
furniture: 4 sofa 5 chair 6 settee 8 armchair, end table, recliner 9 easy chair, sectional

Livingston: **3** Jay **4** city, town **5** Barry **7** Stanley

locale: **9** New Jersey

Livingstone: **4** Mark, Mary **5** David

Livingstone, David: **4** Scot **8** explorer

Livingstone, Mary

spouse: Jack Benny

Livin' La Vida Loca (1999 song)

artist: Ricky Martin

Livin' on a Prayer (1987 song)

artist: Bon Jovi

___ Livin' to Do, A: **5** Lot of

Livonia: **4** city, town

locale: **8** Michigan

Livorno: **4** city, port, town

island south of ~: **4** Elba

locale: **5** Italy **6** Italia

livre: **4** coin **5** money

Livy: **5** Roman **6** writer **9** historian

contemporary: **4** Ovid

see also Latin

Liwung

city on the: **7** Jakarta **8** Djakarta

lixiviate: **5** leach **6** filter, strain **7** extract **8** wash away **9** percolate

lixivium: **3** lye

Liz: **5** Phair, Smith **6** Taylor **9** Claiborne

ex: **4** Dick **5** Eddie, Larry, Nicky

role for ~: **4** Cleo

Liza: **6** Snyder **8** Minnelli

half-sister: **4** Luft **5** Lorna

mother: **4** Judy

Liza (1929 song)

artist: Al Jolson

composer: George Gershwin, Gus Kahn, Ira Gershwin

Lizabeth: **5** Scott

___ Liza Jane: **3** Li'l

lizard: **3** eft **4** newt, uran **5** agama, anole, gecko, skink, teiid **6** agamid, animal, goanna, iguana, moloch **7** iguanid, leather, monitor, reptile, saurian **8** dinosaur **9** alligator, chameleon, crocodile

Australia: **6** goanna, moloch

color-changing ~: **5** agama, anole **9** chameleon

combining form: **4** saur- **5** -saura, sauro-

Hawaiian ~ fish: **4** ulae

like a ~: **5** scaly **8** lamellar, squamose, squamous

lounge ~: **5** idler **8** parasite

Mexico: **3** uta **6** iguana

monitor ~: **4** uran **6** goanna

___ lizard: **6** lounge

___ lizards!: **6** Leapin'

Lizette: **5** Reese

___ lizzie: **3** tin

Lizzie Borden took ___: **4** an ax **5** an axe

Lizzie McGuire Movie, The (2003 film) cast: Hilary Duff

___ L. Jackson: **6** Samuel

Ljubljana: **4** city, town **7** capital

locale: **8** Slovenia

LL ___ J: **4** Cool

L.L.: **4** Bean

llama: **6** animal, mammal

herder, once: **5** Incan

milieu: **4** Peru **5** Andes

relative: **5** camel **6** alpaca, vicuña **7** guanaco **8** Bactrian **9** dromedary

Llanelly: **4** city, port, town

locale: **5** Wales

llano: **3** lea, ley **5** plain, veldt **7** prairie **9** grassland

LL.B.: **3** deg.

holder: **3** att. **4** atty.

offerer: **4** univ.

org.: **3** ABA

LLC

kin: **3** inc.

LL Cool J: **6** rapper

real name: James Todd Smith

song: Around the Way Girl (1991)

Doin It (1996)

Father (1998)

Going Back to Cali (1988)

Hey Lover (1995)

I'm That Kind of Guy (1989)

I Need Love (1987)

Loungin (1996)

Mama Said Knock You Out (1991)

This Is for the Lover in You (1996)

LL.D.: **3** deg.

Llewellyn: **7** Richard

Lloyd: **5** Bacon, Emily, Frank, Nolan, Price, Waner **6** Harold, Haynes **7** Bentsen, Bochner, Bridges **8** Kathleen

Lloyd, Christopher: **5** actor

film: The Addams Family (1991)

Addams Family Values (1993)

Back to the Future (1985)

The Dream Team (1989)

Eight Men Out (1988)

Goin' South (1978)

Who Framed Roger Rabbit (1988)

___ Lloyd Garrison: **7** William

___ Lloyd George: **5** David

Lloyd, Harold: **5** actor **8** comedian

film: The Freshman (1925)

Girl Shy (1924)

Hot Water (1924)

Movie Crazy (1932)

Safety Last (1923)

Speedy (1928)

Why Worry? (1923)

Lloyd Webber, Andrew: **3** Sir **7** British **8** composer

musical: Aspects of Love

Cats

Evita

Jesus Christ Superstar

Joseph and the Amazing Technicolor Dreamcoat

The Phantom of the Opera

Starlight Express

Sunset Boulevard

The Woman in White

___ Lloyd Wright: **5** Frank

lmt.: **3** max., min.

ln.: **2** rd.

kin: **2** av., st. **3** ave. **4** blvd.

LNG vehicle: **2** RV

lo

partner: **6** behold

lo ___: **4** mein

lo-___: **3** cal, res

___ Loa: **5** Mauna

load: **3** arm, jam, lot, tax **4** care, cram, fill, glut, haul, heap, lade, mass, onus, pack, pile, scad, stow **5** cargo, flood, goods, stack, store, stuff, swamp, trial **6** armful, bundle, burden, cumber, eyeful, hamper, heap up, infuse, lading, lumber, misery, parcel, pile on, saddle, weight **7** freight, install, oppress, surfeit **8** contents, encumber, irritant, pile it on, pressure, quantity, shipment, truckful **9** albatross, hindrance, millstone, profusion, put aboard, weigh down **10** affliction, commission, dead weight, freightage, infliction, overburden, oversupply

carrier: **3** rig, van **4** semi **5** truck, wagon **6** big rig **7** flatbed **10** freight car

ender: **4** star **5** stone **6** master

get a ~ of: **3** eye, see, spy **4** look, peek, peep, peer, view **5** watch **6** behold, glance, listen, look at, notice, regard **7** glimpse, observe, witness **10** sneak a look

heavy ~: **6** burden, weight

off one's mind: **6** relief

reduce a ~: **7** lighten

share the ~: **4** ease, help **6** assist, join in **7** pitch in, relieve **9** cooperate, lend a hand **10** see through

starter: **3** arm, bus, car, off, pay, van **4** boat, cart, case, down, free, ship, work **5** plane, train, truck, wagon

take a ~ off: **3** sit **5** relax **6** unload **7** lighten

up: **4** fill, heap, pile **5** amass, cache, hoard, lay by, stock, store **6** gather, supply **9** replenish, stockpile **10** accumulate

___ load: **4** case, dead, work **8** front-end

___-load: **3** off **4** back **5** carbo, front

loaded: **4** full, rich, rife **5** armed, drunk, flush, laden, tight, tipsy **6** aboard, deluxe, monied, packed, soused **7** charged, crowded, moneyed, replete, stuffed, teeming, wealthy, well-off **8** affluent, brimming, cram-full, in clover, perilous, well-to-do **9** chock-full, jam-packed, well-fixed **10** in the dough, in the money, precarious, privileged, propertied, prosperous, wall-to-wall, well-heeled

down: **10** encumbered

question: **4** bait, ruse **6** ambush, come-on, device **8** maneuver **9** booby trap, deception **10** enticement, subterfuge

loaded ___: **8** question

___ loaded: **5** bases

loaded for ___: **4** bear

loader: **9** stevedore

starter: **4** free **6** breech, muzzle

___ loader: **3** top **5** front

loading

apparatus: **5** crane, hoist, sling **7** derrick

area: **4** dock, pier, quay **5** wharf

loading ___: **4** coil, dock

___-loading: **5** carbo

___ load of: **4** get a

loads: **4** a lot, a ton, lots, many, much, tons **5** horde **6** flocks, hoards, myriad, oodles, plenty, scores **7** numbers **9** multitude, quite a few

load the ___: **4** dice

loaf: **3** bun, lag, veg **4** cake, cube, idle, laze, loll, lump, rest **5** amble, block, bread, dally, dogit, dough, dream, drift, evade, mosey, relax, shirk, stall, tarry, twist **6** dawdle, linger, loiter, lounge, piddle, repose, slouch **7** hang out, saunter **8** kill time, lallygag, lollygag, malinger, pass time, slack off, slow down, straggle, vegetate **9** bum around, goldbrick, hang loose, sit around, waste time **10** dillydally, fool around, knock about, take it easy

bakery ~: **3** rye **5** white **10** whole wheat

in Britain: **5** sculk, skulk

part: **4** half, heel **5** slice

loaf ___: **3** pan **5** bread **6** around

___ loaf: **4** meat

___-loaf: **5** sugar

___ Loaf Aday: **4** Meat

loafer: **3** bum **4** lazy, shoe **5** drone, idler **6** rascal, slip-on, slouch, truant, waster **7** goof-off, laggard, lounger, shirker, slacker, sponger, wastrel **8** deadbeat, footgear, footwear, loiterer, parasite, sluggard, wanderer **9** do-nothing, goldbrick, lazybones, miscreant **10** malingerer, ne'er-do-well

___ loafer: **5** penny

loafers: **5** flats, shoes **8** footwear

wearing ~: **4** shod

loafing: **4** idle, lazy **9** loitering **10** unemployed

___ loaf is...: **5** Half a

___ Loaf Mountain: **5** Sugar

loam: **4** clay, dirt, land, soil **5** earth, loess **7** topsoil

loamy: **6** arable **7** fertile, friable

soil: **5** loess

loan: **3** mtg. **4** debt, lend, mtge. **5** allow, lease, stake, touch, trust **6** credit, let out, let use **7** advance, floater, imprest **8** mortgage **9** extension, liability

abbr.: **3** APR

arranger: **4** bank **6** banker

assist with a ~: **6** cosign

clear a ~: **5** repay **7** pay back, satisfy **8** make good, settle up, square up **9** liquidate, reimburse **10** compensate

fed. ~ agcy.: **3** FCA, FHA, SBA **4** FNMA, GNMA

fee: **3** int. **6** points **8** interest

get a ~: **3** owe **6** borrow

get a ~ on: **4** hock, pawn **6** pledge

home ~: **3** mtg. **4** mtge. **8** mortgage

home ~ org.: **3** FHA **4** FNMA, GNMA **5** S and L

shark: **5** leech **6** lender, usurer **7** Shylock

shark's crime: **5** usury

try for a ~: **5** hit up

variable-interest ~: **3** ARM

loan ___: **4** word **5** shark

___ loan: **4** bank **6** bridge

loaner: **6** lender, usurer **8** creditor

loath: **4** hate **5** abhor **6** afraid, averse, remiss **7** against, counter, opposed, uneager **8** hesitant **9** reluctant, resisting, unwilling **10** indisposed, uninclined, unobliging

not ~: **3** hot **4** agog, avid, game,

keen **5** eager **6** gung-ho, hungry, intent **7** burning, excited, pleased, willing **8** amenable, animated, cheerful, disposed, inclined, unforced **9** agreeable, ambitious, compliant, in the mood, psyched up **10** consenting, raring to go
to: 3 con **8** opposing **10** at odds with
loathe: 4 hate **5** abhor, spurn **6** detest, refuse, reject, revolt **7** decline, despise, dislike **8** can't take, execrate **9** abominate, can't stand, disrelish, repudiate
old-style: 5 spise
loathing: 4 hate **5** odium **6** enmity, hatred, nausea, phobia **7** disgust, dislike **8** aversion, contempt, distaste **9** antipathy, repulsion, revulsion **10** abhorrence, repugnance
look of ~: 5 frown, glare, scowl **6** glower **7** grimace
loathly: 5 skyly **6** slowly **9** haltingly **10** hesitantly
loathsome: 4 base, evil, vile **5** awful, pesky, pesty, slimy **6** creepy, filthy, rancid, sleazy, uncool **7** noisome, satanic **8** God-awful, shocking **9** invidious, obnoxious, repellent, repugnant, repulsive, satanical **10** virtueless
one: 3 cad, cur, rat **4** heel, toad, worm **5** skunk, snake, sneak, swine **6** wretch **7** stinker **9** scoundrel **10** blackguard
see also awful
lob: 3 arc **4** flip, hurl, shot, toss **5** chuck, fling, pitch, sling, throw **6** let fly
ender: 4 worm **5** lolly
path: 3 arc, bow **5** curve **8** crescent, half-moon
lobbies, high-ceiling: 5 atria
lobby: 3 NRA **4** bill, drum, hall, hype, plug, push, sell, spot, sway, urge **5** alter, boost, foyer, pitch, porch, press, thump **6** affect, atrium, induce, lounge, modify, sell on, splash **7** advance, build up, doorway, faction, further, gateway, hallway, ingress, passage, promote, request, solicit **8** anteroom, arm-twist, campaign, corridor, persuade, politick, soft-sell, soft-soap **9** billboard, influence, sweet-talk, vestibule **10** passageway
ender: 3 ist
furnishing: 4 seat, sofa **5** couch, divan **6** settee **7** seating
org.: 4 assn.
lobbyist: 5 urger
lobe: 4 flap, limb **6** earlap **10** projection
adornment: 4 hoop, stud **7** earring
locale: 3 ear **4** lung **5** brain
__ lobe: 3 ear **7** frontal
lobed: 6 convex, knobby **7** rounded
Lo Bianco: 4 Tony
loblolly: 4 pine, tree
lobo: 4 wolf **10** timber wolf
Lobo
song: Don't Expect Me to Be Your Friend (1973)
I'd Love You to Want Me (1972)
Me and You and a Dog Named Boo (1971)
Lobo (NBC sitcom)
cast: Claude Akins (Sheriff Elroy Lobo)
__ Lobo: 3 Rio
__ Lobos: 3 Los
lobscouse: 4 stew
lobster: 6 entrée **7** seafood
abdomen: 5 pleon
catcher: 3 pot **4** trap
eater's wear: 3 bib
eggs: 3 roe **5** coral
extremity: 4 claw **5** chela
feeler: 4 palp **6** palpus
feelers: 5 palpi
female ~: 3 hen
home: 5 shell
on some menus: 4 surf
pot, perhaps: 5 lagan, ligan
sauce ingredient: 3 egg
lobster __: 3 pot **6** bisque **7** Newburg
lobster __ Diavolo: 3 Fra
__ lobster: 5 Maine
__ Lobster: 3 Red
loc.: 3 pos.
loc. __: 3 cit.
__ Loc: 4 Tone
loca: 5 sites **6** places
L'Oca __ Cairo: 3 del
local: 4 home **5** civic, towny, union **6** narrow, native, parish, townee, townie **7** barroom, endemic, limited, topical **8** confined, district, indigene, regional, resident, townsman **9** endemical, home-grown, in the area, milk train, municipal, parochial, sectional, small-town **10** indigenous, inhabitant, provincial, restricted, trade union
area: 4 hood, turf **8** environs, vicinity
booster: 6 jaycee
color: 8 ambiance, ambience **9** character **10** atmosphere, background
combining form: 3 top- **4** topo-
government unit: 2 tp. **3** twp. **8** township
group: 5 union
not a ~: 3 exp. **7** express
opposite: 7 express
local __: 4 time **5** color
local __ network: 4 area
lo-cal: 4 diet, lite **5** light
Local Color
author: Truman Capote
locale: 4 area, belt, hole, home, site, spot, turf, zone **5** haunt, place, scene, situs, stage, tract, venue **6** domain, milieu, region, sector, sphere **7** habitat, quarter, setting, theater, theatre **8** district, position, vicinity **9** bailiwick, situation, territory **10** where it's at
localism: 4 burr **5** drawl, idiom, slang, twang **6** accent, brogue, custom, patois **7** dialect **8** practice **9** tradition **10** observance
locality: 4 area, belt, hole, home, site, spot, turf, zone **5** haunt, locus, place, scene, stage, tract, venue **6** domain, region, sector, sphere **7** quarter, section, theater, theatre **8** district, location, position, vicinity **9** bailiwick, community, situation, territory
localize: 6 finger **8** home in on, identify, pinpoint, zero in on **9** get a fix on
localized: 7 endemic **8** regional **9** parochial **10** indigenous
locally: 6 nearby **7** close-by **10** around here
Locarno __: 4 Pact
locate: 3 fix, lay, put, set **4** base, find, hook, park, plot, read, seat, site, spot **5** dig in, dig up, dwell, get at, lodge, pitch, place, squat, stand **6** detect, orient, reside, settle, strike, turn up **7** deposit, dispose, hit upon, inhabit, pin down, situate, station, uncover, unearth **8** come upon, discover, ensconce, meet with, pick up on, pinpoint, position, smell out, smoke out, sniff out, trip over, zero in on **9** determine, establish, ferret out, get a fix on, get hold of, light upon, search out, stumble on, track down **10** come across, happen upon
as data: 6 access
located: 3 set **5** based **6** placed, posted **8** situated **9** occupying, stationed **10** positioned
as ~: 6 in situ
centrally ~: 4 amid **5** among **6** amidst, mongst **7** amongst
location: 4 area, hold, part, post, seat, site, spot, turf **5** place, point, scene, space, stead, tract, venue, where **6** region **7** address, quarter, section, setting, station **8** bearings, district, position **9** situation
starter: 4 echo
locations, add new: 6 expand
locator, position: 6 cursor
loch: 4 lake
eerie ~: 4 Ness
Loch: 4 Ness **5** Leven **6** Lomond **7** Katrine
locale: 8 Scotland
Loch __ monster: 4 Ness
loci: 4 hubs **5** areas, sites, spots **6** places, points, venues **9** positions **10** situations
lock: 3 bar, dam, fix, hug **4** bolt, bond, clog, cork, curl, grip, hair, hasp, hook, join, link, mesh, plug, seal, shut **5** block, catch, cinch, clamp, clasp, close, dam up, grasp, latch, press, tress, unite **6** button, clench, clinch, clog up, clutch, engage, fasten, plug up, seal up, secure, stop up, strand **7** close up, closure, embrace, enclose, entwine, fixture, grapple, inclose, intwine, ringlet, seal off, shutter **8** blockade, button up, deadbolt, encircle, fastener, junction, make fast, obstruct, vinculum **9** certainty, fastening **10** connection
away: 5 store
companion: 3 key
ender: 3 age, jaw, nut, out, set **4** step **5** smith **6** keeper, master
horns: 4 spar **5** argue, clash **6** debate **7** compete, contend, quarrel, wrangle **8** conflict, struggle **9** have words, square off
in: 6 ensure **7** enclose, inclose **8** imprison
lips: 4 kiss, neck **6** smooch **8** osculate
maker: 4 Yale
of hair: 4 coil, curl, hair **5** tress **7** ringlet
out: 3 bar **7** exclude, occlude, shut off **9** foreclose
part: 4 bolt, hasp **5** catch
place: 4 door, exit, gate **5** hatch **6** portal, window **7** postern **8** entrance, entryway
put a ~ on: 6 ensure, secure **9** safeguard
starter: 3 elf, gun, hem, oar, pad, row, shy, war, wed **4** anti, dead, fire, fore, grid, head, love, pick **5** flint, match, wrist **6** hammer
stock and barrel: 6 in toto, wholly
under ~ and key: 4 held, safe **5** bound, caged **6** in jail, jailed, secure **7** captive, guarded **8** confined **9** in custody, protected **10** imprisoned
up: 3 tie **4** bind, cage, hold, jail **5** close, embar, tie up **6** assure, closet, detain, encage, ensure, immure, intern, secure **7** acquire, confine, interne, possess, put away **8** imprison, prohibit, restrain **10** monopolize
lock __: 3 out **5** horns
lock, __ and barrel: 5 stock
__ lock: 3 air **4** time **5** shift, vapor
__-Locka, FL: 3 Opa
lockbox: 4 safe **5** vault **6** coffer **9** strongbox **10** repository
__-lock brakes: 4 anti
Locke: 4 John **5** Alain **6** Sondra
locked: 5 tight **6** closed, secure
in: 3 set **5** rigid **9** immovable, obstinate, unbending **10** unyielding
starter: 4 land
up: 6 jailed **7** captive
Locke, John: 7 British **11** philosopher
work: An Essay Concerning Human Understanding
Two Treatises on Government
locker: 5 chest, trunk **6** closet **7** cabinet **8** wardrobe
locale: 3 gym, spa **4** mall **5** depot **10** bus station, health club
photo: 5 pin-up
starter: 4 foot
locker __: 4 room
locker room
supply: 4 talc **6** towels
Locke, Sondra: 7 actress
film: Any Which Way You Can (1980)
Bronco Billy (1980)
Every Which Way But Loose (1978)
The Gauntlet (1977)
Impulse (1990)
The Outlaw Josey Wales (1976)
Sudden Impact (1983)
locket: 5 bijou **6** bauble **7** jewelry, pendant **8** necklace **9** lavaliere
item: 5 cameo
place: 4 neck
shape: 5 heart
Lockhart: 4 Anne, Gene, June **5** Keith
Lockhart, June: 7 actress
TV: Lassie, Lost in Space, Petticoat Junction
Lockhart, Keith: 9 conductor
Lockheed
product: 3 jet **5** plane **8** airplane

Lockheed __-Star: 3 Tri
Lockhorns, The
cartoonist: 5 Hoest
lock-in: 10 commitment
Locklear, Heather
spouse: Tommy Lee, Richie Sambora
TV: Dynasty, Melrose Place, T.J. Hooker
lockout: 8 stoppage 9 exclusion
Lockport: 4 city, town
locale: 7 New York
Lockridge: 7 Frances, Richard
locks: 4 hair
locale: 5 canal
starter: 5 dread
__ Locks: 3 Soo
Locksley Hall
author: Alfred Tennyson
Locksmith
painter: Paul Klee
locksmithing: 5 trade
lock, stock and barrel: 3 all
__ Lock the Door: 4 Let's
lockup: 3 can, jug, pen 4 brig, coop, jail, poky, stir 5 clink, pokey 6 cooler, donjon, prison 7 dungeon, hoosgow, slammer 8 big house, hoosegow 9 calaboose 10 guardhouse, paddy wagon
Lockwood: 4 Gary 8 Margaret
Lockwood, Gary
spouse: Stefanie Powers
loco: 4 amok, bats, daft 5 amuck, batty, buggy, daffy, dotty, goofy, kooky, nutty, wacky 6 cuckoo, kookie, whacky 7 bananas, bonkers 8 cockeyed, crackers 10 off the beam
ender: 4 weed
not ~: 4 sane
loco __: 4 weed
__ loco: 5 plumb
Loco-__, The: 6 Motion
Loco, Antonio music: 3 rap
locomotion: 6 action, motion, moving, travel 8 mobility, movement 9 traveling 10 mobileness
organ of ~: 3 pad, paw 4 foot, hoof
loco-motion: 5 dance
Loco-Motion, The (song)
artist: Grand Funk, Kylie Minogue, Little Eva
locomotive: 6 barney, diesel, dinkey, engine 9 iron horse
part: 3 cab, cam
slangily: 3 pig
small ~: 5 dolly
sound: 4 chug 5 chuff
steam ~: 6 Big Boy
__ locomotive: 3 cog 5 steam
locoweed, like: 5 toxic
loc. primo __: 3 cit.
locum __: 6 tenens
locus: 4 site, spot 5 place, point 7 station 8 position 9 situation
locus in __: 3 quo
locust: 3 bug 4 tree 6 acacia, cicada, insect 8 hardwood
bean: 5 carob
family: 6 legume
group: 5 swarm
relative: *see* legume tree
locust __: 4 bean
locution: 4 talk, word 5 idiom 6 accent 7 dialect, diction, wording 8 language, phrasing 10 expression, inflection
Lod: 4 city, town
locale: 6 Israel
lode: 3 ore 4 mine, seam, vein 5 store 6 pocket 7 bonanza, pay dirt 8 gold mine
ender: 4 star 5 stone
__ lode: 6 mother 8 Comstock
loden: 4 coat 5 green 6 fabric, jacket
Loder: 4 John, Kurt
lodestar: 4 sign 5 guide, model 6 beacon, signal 7 pointer, Polaris 8 cynosure
lodestone: 7 mineral 9 magnetite
lodge: 3 den, fix, hut, inn, lay, set 4 bunk, camp, club, digs, home, lair, live, nest, park, rent, room, root, stay, stop, stow 5 abide, abode, board, bower, cabin, catch, couch, crash, dwell, embed, haunt, hotel, house, imbed, infix, motel, perch, place, plant, put up, roost, shack, squat, stick, villa 6 belong, bestow, billet, burrow, canton, chalet, harbor, hole up, hostel, instal, locate, remain, reside, resort, settle, shanty, take in, tavern 7 auberge, coterie, cottage, domicil, engrain, harbour, hospice, implant, ingrain, install, quarter, retreat, shelter, sojourn, station 8 domicile, dwelling, entrench, hostelry, log cabin, quarters, stay over, stopover 9 dormitory, entertain, gatehouse, roadhouse 10 come to rest, guesthouse
a complaint: 3 sue 4 cite 5 blame 6 accuse, allege, charge, impute, indict 7 arraign 8 denounce 9 prosecute
builder: 6 beaver
in: 5 dwell 6 occupy, reside 7 inhabit
income: 4 dues
letters: 4 BPOE, IOOF
member: 3 Elk 4 Lion 5 Mason, Moose
Navajo ~: 5 hogan
ski ~: 6 A-frame, chalet
visitor: 5 skier
__ lodge: 5 motor
__-Lodge: 5 Econo
lodgepole __: 4 pine
lodger: 5 guest, liver 6 lessee, renter, roomer, tenant 7 boarder 8 occupant, resident 10 vacationer
meals: 5 board
lodging: 3 inn 4 camp, dorm, flat, home, port, roof, room 5 abode, B and B, botel, cabin, cover, hotel, motel, place 6 billet, boatel, castle, harbor, hostel, palace, resort 7 address, domicil, habitat, harbour, shelter 8 chambers, domicile, dwelling, quarters 9 apartment, dormitory, residence 10 habitation, pied-à-terre, protection
military ~: 6 billet, casern 7 caserne
provide ~: 4 bunk 5 board, house, put up 6 billet, harbor 7 quarter, shelter 8 domicile
lodgment: 3 inn, pad 4 digs, home, room 5 B and B, cabin, condo, hotel, house, motel, store 6 billet, hostel, tavern 7 bivouac, cottage, deposit, domicil 8 chambers, domicile, dwelling, foothold, quarters 9 apartment, beachhead, residence
Lodi: 4 city, town 5 apple
locale: 9 New Jersey 10 California
relative: *see* apple
Lodovico: 7 Ariosto
Lódz: 4 city, town
locale: 6 Poland
resident: 4 Pole
Loeb: 4 Lisa
__ l'oeil: 6 trompe
loess: 4 clay, loam, marl, soil 5 earth
Loesser, Frank: 8 composer
musical: Guys and Dolls
How to Succeed in Business Without Really Trying
The Most Happy Fella
Where's Charley
song: Baby It's Cold Outside
A Bushel and a Peck
Heart and Soul
I Believe in You
Luck Be a Lady
On a Slow Boat to China
Once in Love With Amy
Standing on the Corner
Two Sleepy People
Loew: 6 Marcus
Loewe, Frederick: 8 composer
collaborator: Alan Jay Lerner
musical: Brigadoon
Camelot
Gigi
My Fair Lady
Paint Your Wagon
song: Almost Like Being in Love
Camelot
Get Me to the Church on Time
Gigi
The Heather on the Hill
I Could Have Danced All Night
If Ever I Would Leave You
I Remember It Well
I Talk to the Trees
I've Grown Accustomed to Her Face
The Night They Invented Champagne
On the Street Where You Live
The Rain in Spain
Thank Heaven for Little Girls
They Call the Wind Maria
With a Little Bit of Luck
Wouldn't It Be Loverly
Loewi, Otto: 8 Nobelist
lo-fat: 4 diet, lite
Lofgren: 4 Nils
loft: 5 attic 6 dormer, garret, haymow, studio 7 atelier, storage 8 top floor 9 apartment
contents: 3 hay 4 bale, feed 5 easel, straw 6 artist, fodder
invite to one's ~: 5 ask up
pigeon ~: 6 aviary
singers: 5 choir 6 chorus 8 ensemble
__ loft: 5 choir
Lofthouse
competitor: *see* cookie manufacturer
loftier than: 4 high, over 5 above 7 on top of 8 overhead, superior
loftiest: 3 top 6 apical 9 uppermost
loftiness: 5 pride 6 height, hubris, hybris, length 8 altitude, eminence, grandeur, nobility 9 arrogance, elevation, greatness 10 exaltation
Lofting: 4 Hugh
lofty: 3 big 4 airy, high, tall 5 grand, great, noble, proud, royal, skyey, steep 6 aerial, Andean, august, high up, lifted, lordly, raised, snooty, superb 7 eminent, exalted, gallant, haughty, sky-high, skyward, soaring, spiring, stately, sublime, utopian 8 arrogant, cavalier, elevated, empyreal, empyrean, generous, high-rise, immodest, imposing, insolent, majestic, rarefied, renowned, striking, superior, towering, uplifted 9 ambitious, arresting, dignified, grandiose, high-flown, idealized, sovereign, visionary 10 benevolent, chivalrous, commanding, disdainful, high-minded, majestical, monumental
area: 4 peak, rise 5 cliff 6 atrium, height, summit 8 eminence, mountain 9 elevation, precipice 10 prominence
goal: 5 ideal 6 vision
set a ~ goal: 4 hope, wish 5 dream 6 aspire
log: 4 bole, book, cast, wood 5 chart, diary, enter, trunk 6 lumber, record, timber 7 account, daybook, Filofax, journal, listing, put down 8 register 10 journalize
a few z's: 3 nap 4 doze, rest 5 sleep 6 catnap, drowse, nod off, snooze 7 drop off, slumber 10 fall asleep
bump on a ~: 3 nub 4 knub, knur, node
cabin: 3 hut 5 abode, shack 7 retreat 8 dwelling
ender: 3 jam 4 book, roll, wood 6 normal 7 rolling
in: 6 sign on 8 register
like falling off a ~: 4 easy 6 facile, simple 7 a picnic, no sweat 8 no bother 9 no problem, no trouble 10 child's play, effortless, elementary
notation: 4 item 5 entry 6 record
off: 7 card out, sign out 8 shut down 10 disconnect
on: 6 card in, sign in 7 connect
splitter's aid: 3 ram 5 chock, wedge
stack: 4 rick
starter: 3 ana, dia, epi, pro 4 back, mono 5 water
transport: 5 chute, flume 6 sluice 7 channel
tread a floating ~: 4 birl
log __: 3 off, out 5 cabin
__ log: 3 gas, saw 4 yule
Logan: 4 city, Ella, Josh, peak, town 5 mount 6 Joshua 8 mountain
Airport symbol: 3 BOS
athletes: 6 Aggies
info: 3 arr., ETD
locale: 4 Utah 5 Yukon 6 Boston, Canada
school: 3 USU 9 Utah State
loganberry: 5 fruit
logania: 4 bush 5 shrub
Logan's Run (1976 film)
android: 3 Rem
cast: Jenny Agutter, Michael York
__ logarithm: 6 Briggs, common 7 natural
logarithm base: 4 root 5 radix

Log Cabin: **5** syrup
rival: **4** Karo
loge: **7** gallery **9** mezzanine
logged starter: **4** back **5** water
logger: **9** lumberman **10** lumberjack, Paul Bunyan
commodity: **4** pulp
contest: **5** roleo
ender: **4** head
leaving: **5** stump
small-scale ~: **5** gyppo
tool: **3** axe, saw **4** rope **5** wedge, winch **7** skidder **8** cant hook, chain saw
loggerhead: **4** dolt **6** animal, turtle **7** reptile
loggerheads, at: **7** opposed **10** quarreling
loggia: **6** arcade **7** balcony, gallery
Loggia: **6** Robert
logging
do ~: **3** axe, hew, saw **4** fell **5** saw up **7** saw down **8** chainsaw, clear-cut
Loggins: **4** Dave **5** Kenny
partner: **7** Messina
Loggins, Dave
song: Please Come to Boston (1974)
Loggins, Kenny
song: Danger Zone (1986)
Don't Fight It (1982)
Footloose (1984)
Heart to Heart (1982)
I'm Alright (1980)
I'm Free (1984)
Meet Me Half Way (1987)
Nobody's Fool (1988)
This Is It (1979)
Whenever I Call You 'Friend' (1978)
logic: **5** sense **6** reason, sanity, thesis **7** linkage, thought **9** coherence, deduction, dialectic, good sense, induction, inference, rationale, reasoning, syllogism **10** connection, philosophy
apply ~: **3** see **4** muse **5** guess, infer, judge, study, think, weigh **6** assume, deduce, gather, ideate, ponder, reason, reckon **7** analyze, examine, presume, reflect, sort out, surmise, suspect **8** appraise, cogitate, conceive, conclude, consider, estimate, evaluate, mull over, perceive, ruminate, theorize **9** cerebrate, determine, figure out, speculate **10** conjecture, deliberate
for action: **6** excuse, motive, reason **7** big idea, grounds, purpose **9** rationale, reasoning **10** motivation
__ logic: **5** fuzzy
logical: **4** fair, sane, wise **5** clear, legit, lucid, right, solid, sound, valid, water **6** cogent, kasher, kosher, likely, subtle **7** germane, holding, natural, obvious, telling, tenable **8** analytic, coherent, luculent, methodic, probable, rational, relevant, sensible, thinking **9** congruent, deducible, judicious, necessary, pertinent, plausible, pragmatic **10** analytical, compelling, consequent, consistent, convincing, defensible, discerning, legitimate, methodical, perceptive, persuasive, reasonable, scientific, systematic, thoughtful
not ~: **5** ditsy, ditzy
premise: **5** given, lemma
proposition: **5** axiom **6** if-then
starter: **3** eco, neo **4** ideo **5** neuro, patho, socio
logician: **7** casuist, sophist **8** reasoner
abbr.: **3** QED
transition: **4** ergo, then, thus **5** hence **9** therefore
loginess: **5** sloth **6** apathy, stupor, torpor **7** inertia, languor **8** dullness, lethargy **9** indolence
logjam: **5** tie-up **6** backup, pileup **7** impasse, traffic **8** blockage, deadlock, gridlock, obstacle **10** bottleneck, congestion, parking lot
logo: **2** TM **3** tag **4** mark, sign **5** brand, label **6** device, emblem, symbol **9** trademark
ender: **4** gram, type **5** graph
logophile love: **3** wds. **5** words
logophobe fear: **5** words
logrolling, engage in: **4** birl
logs
haul ~: **4** skid
saw ~: **3** nap **5** crash, sleep, snore, snort **6** nod off, retire, snooze, turn in **7** drop off, sack out, slumber, snuffle, zonk out **8** take a nap **9** cop some z's, hit the hay **10** hit the sack
sawing ~: **3** out **4** abed **6** asleep **8** snoozing **9** sacked out
__ Logs: **7** Lincoln
logwood: **4** tree
logy: **4** dull, idle, lazy **5** heavy, inert, thick **6** drowsy, sleepy, torpid **7** dormant, laggard, languid, passive **8** comatose, fainéant, inactive, indolent, listless, slothful, sluggish **9** apathetic, enervated, lethargic, stupefied **10** phlegmatic, slow-moving, unreactive
-logy cousin: **3** -ism
Lohan: **3** Ali **7** Lindsay
Lohengrin: **5** opera
bird: **4** swan
composer: Richard Wagner
role: **4** Elsa **5** Henry **6** Ortrud **9** Frederick, Gottfried
setting: **7** Antwerp, Belgium
loi: **3** law **6** French
it might pass une ~: **5** senat
loin: **4** meat, side **6** haunch
cut: **5** T-bone
ender: **5** cloth
leg and ~: **6** haunch
muscle: **5** psoas
muscles: **5** psoae, psoai
starter: **3** sir **6** tender
loincloth, Hindu: **5** dhoti, dhuti **6** dhooti **7** dhootie
Loire: **5** river
city on the ~: **5** Blois, Tours **6** Nantes **7** Orleans
locale: **6** France
river to the ~: **4** Cher **6** Allier
__-Loire: **5** Haute
Loir-et-__: **4** Cher
Loire Valley
city: **6** Le Mans
region: **5** Anjou
Lois: **4** Lane **6** Chiles **7** Maxwell
Lois & Clark (ABC sci-fi)
cast: Dean Cain (Clark Kent/Superman)
Teri Hatcher (Lois Lane)
John Shea (Lex Luthor)
Lane Smith (Perry White)
loiter: **3** lag **4** away, drag, flag, halt, idle, laze, loaf, loll, poke, slow, stay, wait **5** amble, dally, delay, hover, mosey, pause, stall, tarry, trail **6** dabble, dawdle, diddle, linger, lounge, put off, ramble, slough, stroll **7** fritter, hang out, saunter, shamble, shuffle, slacken, traipse **8** hang back, kill time, lollygag, lose time, pass time, straggle **9** lose speed, poke along, waste time **10** dillydally, hang around, mess around, wait around
loiterer: **5** idler **6** loafer, slouch, truant **7** dawdler, goof-off, laggard **8** slowpoke, sluggard **9** do-nothing, goldbrick, lazybones
loitering: **4** free, idle, lazy, slow **5** slack **7** loafing **8** indolent, slothful
loiteringly: **6** pokily **8** bit by bit **9** gradually, haltingly, languidly, leisurely **10** crawlingly, creepingly, sluggishly
Loki: **9** trickster
daughter: **3** Hel
son: **4** Nare **6** Fenrir
Lola: **4** Lane **6** Falana, Montez **8** Albright
Lola (1970 song)
artist: Kinks
Lolita: **4** Haze **10** Davidovich
author: Vladimir Nabokov
Lolita (1962 film)
cast: Sue Lyon, James Mason, Peter Sellers, Shelley Winters
director: Stanley Kubrick
Lolita (1997 film)
cast: Melanie Griffith, Jeremy Irons, Frank Langella
director: Adrian Lyne
loll: **3** lie, sag **4** bask, drop, flap, flop, idle, laze, loaf, rest **5** droop, relax, slump **6** dangle, dawdle, linger, loiter, lounge, repose, slouch, sprawl, wallow **7** goof off, recline **8** kick back, lallygag **9** hang loose **10** hang around, wait around
lollapalooza: **3** pip **4** lulu, oner **5** beaut, dandy, dilly, doozy
lolling: **6** at ease
lollipop: **5** candy, treat **9** sweetmeat
eat a ~: **4** lick
flavor: **5** grape, lemon **6** cherry, orange
Lollipop (1958 song)
artist: Chordettes
__ Lollipop: **5** My Boy
Lollipop, Good Ship: **5** plane **8** airplane
Lollipops and __: **5** Roses
Lollobrigida: **4** Gina
lollop: **3** bob **4** leap **5** bound **6** lounge
lolly: **5** candy, sweet **6** bonbon **9** sweetmeat **10** confection
ender: **3** gag, pop
starter: **3** lob
lollygag: **3** lag **4** idle, laze, loaf **5** amble, dally, mosey, stall, tarry **6** linger, loiter, trifle **7** goof off, saunter **8** straggle **9** waste time **10** dillydally
Lolly Willowes
author: Sylvia Warner
Lom: **7** Herbert
Loma __, CA: **5** Linda
__ Loma, CA: **4** Alta, Mira
Loman, Willy
emulate ~: **4** sell
goal: **4** sale
son: **4** Biff **5** Happy
__ Loma Orchestra: **4** Casa
Lombard: **5** Alain **6** Carole, Karina, street
Lombard, Carole: **7** actress
spouse: Clark Gable, William Powell
Lombardi, Vince: **5** coach
sport: **8** football
Lombardo: **3** Guy **6** Carmen
Lombardy
capital: **5** Milan
city: **4** Enna, Lodi **5** Milan, Monza **6** Milano **7** Brescia
lake: **4** Como
locale: **5** Italy
Lomb partner: **6** Bausch
Lomé: **4** city, town **7** capital
locale: **4** Togo
lo-mein cooker: **3** wok
Lomita: **4** city, town
locale: **10** California
Lomond: **4** lake, Loch
locale: **8** Scotland
Lompoc: **4** city, town
locale: **10** California
Lon: **3** Nol **6** Chaney, Hinkle
__-Lon: **3** Ban
Lonborg, Jim: **6** hurler **7** pitcher
London: **3** Roy **4** city, Jack, port, town **5** Julie **6** Laurie **7** capital
art gallery: **4** Tate
botanical gardens: **3** Kew
district: **3** Kew **4** Soho **6** Barnet, Ealing
doctors' street: **6** Harley
emporium: **7** Harrod's
forecast: **3** fog **4** mist, rain
hotel: **5** Savoy
landmark: **5** tower **6** Big Ben
like ~ in 1666: **5** afire
locale: **2** UK **3** Eng., Ont. **6** Canada **7** England, Ontario
one of a ~ pair: **5** Magog
park: **4** Hyde
prison: **7** Newgate
river: **6** Thames
street: **5** Fleet
Tower of ~ once: **4** gaol **6** prison
see also England
London __: **3** Fog **5** broil **6** Bridge
London Bridge
locale: **4** Ariz. **7** Arizona
Londonderry: **4** city, port, town
college: **5** Magee
locale: **7** Ireland
Londonderry __: **3** Air
Londoner: **4** Brit **6** Briton
London Fields
author: Kingsley Amis
character: **5** Enola
London, Jack: **5** alias **6** writer
work: The Call of the Wild
The Iron Heel
John Barleycorn
Martin Eden
The Sea Wolf

Tales of Adventure
The Valley of the Moon
White Fang
London, Julie: **6** singer **7** actress
song: Cry Me a River (1955)
spouse: Bobby Troup, Jack Webb
TV: Emergency
London Suite
author: Neil Simon
lone: **3** odd, one **4** only, sole, solo, stag **6** single, unique **7** onliest **8** deserted, forsaken, isolated, secluded, separate, singular, solitary **9** abandoned, by oneself, separated **10** friendless, individual, one and only, unattended, unescorted, unexampled
ender: **4** some
lone __: **4** wolf
Lone: **4** John
Lone __: **5** Canoe, Eagle
Lone __ State: **4** Star
Lone __, The: **6** Ranger
Lone Canoe
author: David Mamet
Lone Eagle
author: Danielle Steel
loneliest number, The: **3** one
loneliness: **5** gloom, grief **6** misery **7** anguish, despair, sadness **8** distress, solitude **9** bleakness, dejection, emptiness, heartache, isolation **10** depression, desolation, gloominess, heartbreak, melancholy
lonely: **4** down, left **5** apart, bleak, empty, quiet **6** remote, secret, single **7** forlorn, obscure, outcast, private, removed, retired **8** deserted, desolate, forsaken, homeless, isolated, rejected, secluded, solitary, unsocial **9** abandoned, by oneself, destitute, estranged, reclusive, renounced, withdrawn **10** friendless, unattended
combining form: **4** erem- **5** eremo-
Lonely __, The: **4** Bull
Lonely Blue Boy (1960 song)
artist: Conway Twitty
Lonely Boy (song)
artist: Andrew Gold, Donny Osmond, Paul Anka
Lonely Bull, The (1962 song)
artist: Herb Alpert and the Tijuana Brass
Lonely Days (1970 song)
artist: Bee Gees
Lonely Guy, The (1984 film)
cast: Charles Grodin, Judith Ivey, Steve Martin
Lonely Lady, The
author: Harold Robbins
Lonely Night (1976 song)
artist: Captain & Tennille
Lonely Ol' Night (1985 song)
artist: John Cougar Mellencamp
Lonely People (1975 song)
artist: America
Lonely Silver Rain, The
author: John D. MacDonald
Lonely Street (1959 song)
artist: Andy Williams
Lonely Teardrops (1958 song)
artist: Jackie Wilson
loner: **3** shy **6** hermit, single **7** eremite, isolato, recluse **8** homebody, maverick, singular **9** anchorite, introvert, reclusive, singleton **10** stay-at-home, wallflower
Lone Ranger and Tonto: **3** duo **4** pair
Lone Ranger, The (TV western): **5** oater
attire: **4** mask
cast: Clayton Moore (The Lone Ranger)
Jay Silverheels (Tonto)
foe: **4** Bart **9** Black Bart
horse: **5** Scout **6** Silver
real name: John Reid
lonesome: **6** dreary, gloomy, lonely, remote **7** forlorn **8** deserted, desolate, homesick, isolated, secluded, solitary **9** cheerless **10** friendless
Lonesome Dove
author: Larry McMurtry
Lonesome George: **5** Gobel
lonesomeness: **8** solitude **9** isolation, seclusion **10** desolation, loneliness, withdrawal
Lonesome Town (1958 song)
artist: Ricky Nelson
Lone Star Ranger, The
author: Zane Grey
Lone Star State: **5** Texas
Lone Star Trail, The: **5** oater
Lonette: **5** McKee
long: **4** ache, itch, miss, pine, tall, want, wish, yowl **5** covet, crave, gabby, lanky, lathy, rangy, wordy, yearn **6** aspire, desire, gangly, hanker, hunger, prolix, thirst **7** diffuse, dream of, lengthy, spun-out, stringy, unterse, verbose, voluble **8** dragging, drawn-out, extended, gangling, languish, rambling, unending **9** bombastic, elongated, extensive, garrulous, outspread, talkative **10** discursive, long-winded, loquacious, palaverous, protracted
ago: **4** once, past, yore **5** of old **6** erenow **8** formerly **9** in the past **10** previously
as ~ as: **5** since, while **6** whilst **7** because **9** providing
be ~: **3** lag **4** idle, last, plod, poke **5** dally, delay, hover, mosey, tarry **6** dawdle, linger, loiter, putter **7** goof off **8** hesitate, lose time **9** sit around, vacillate **10** dillydally, hang around
before ~: **4** anon, soon, then **5** after, later **6** in a bit, in time **7** by and by, later on, someday **8** hereupon, in a while, sometime **9** afterward, hereafter, presently, thereupon **10** eventually, in good time
combining form: **3** mec- **4** macr-, meco- **5** macro- **7** dolicho-
ender: **3** bow **4** boat, hair, hand, head, horn, neck, some, spur, time, wise **5** house, shore **6** haired, headed
ere ~: **8** hereupon **10** in good time
for: **4** love, miss, need, seek **5** covet, crave **6** desire
(for): **4** ache, burn, hope, itch, pant, pine, sigh, wish **5** spoil, yearn **6** hanker, starve, thirst
gone: **3** ago **4** late, over, past, yore **6** former **7** old-time, one-time **8** finished, obsolete **9** forgotten, out-of-date, preceding **10** historical, out of style
green: *see* moolah
haul: **4** hadj, hike, trek, trip **5** fight, march, tramp **6** battle **7** journey, odyssey **8** struggle **10** expedition, pilgrimage
in for the ~ haul: **6** stable **7** abiding, durable **8** enduring **9** permanent, unabating
in Hawaiian: **3** loa
in the ~ run: **7** finally, overall **8** after all **10** eventually, ultimately
in the tooth: **3** old **4** aged **5** aging, hoary **6** ageing **7** ancient, elderly, wizened **8** grizzled **9** geriatric, getting on, senescent, up in years
jump: **5** event **7** contest
look: **4** gaze **5** stare
look too ~: **4** ogle **5** stare
not ~: **5** brief, pithy, short, terse **6** stubby **7** briefly, concise, cursory, hurried, laconic, summary **8** abridged, sawed-off, succinct **9** condensed, truncated **10** boiled down, short-lived
not ~ ago: **5** newly **6** lately **8** latterly, recently **9** yesterday
not by a ~ shot: **4** uh-uh **5** ixnay, no how **7** I refuse **8** forget it **9** fat chance, I think not **10** count me out, not a chance, thumbs down
of ~ standing: **3** old **5** early, hoary **6** age-old, senior **7** ancient, lasting, vintage **8** enduring **9** perennial, venerable **10** immemorial
row to hoe: **5** grind **6** burden
shot: **3** bet **4** risk **5** fluke, flyer, wager **6** chance, gamble, toss-up **7** venture **9** adventure, dark horse
so ~: **3** bye **4** ciao, ta-ta **5** adieu, adios, aloha, later, peace, see ya **6** bye-bye, shalom, sholom **7** cheerio, goodbye **8** au revoir, farewell, sayonara, toodle-oo
starter: **3** day, end, ere, pro **4** foot, head, hour, life, live, side, year **5** night **6** decade **7** century
suit: **5** forte
take too ~: **5** run on
the ~ and short of it: **4** core, crux, gist, pith **5** heart **6** kernel
time: **3** age, eon **4** aeon **5** years **7** century, decades
(to): **6** aspire
trip: **4** trek **7** journey, sojourn **10** pilgrimage
very ~ term: **6** eonian
very ~ time: **3** age, eon **4** aeon, ages **7** century
walk: **4** hike, trek **5** jaunt **6** ramble **7** journey **10** expedition
way: **3** far **6** far cry, far off
way around: **6** bypass, detour
wear a ~ face: **4** ache, fret, idle, moon, mope, pine, pout, sulk **5** brood, droop, gripe, scowl **6** grieve, grouse, lament **8** be silent **9** lose heart
wearing a ~ face: **3** low, sad **4** blue, dark, dour, down, glum, grim, mopy **5** moody, mopey, sulky, surly **6** crabby, dismal, gloomy, morose, sullen **8** dejected, downcast **9** bummed-out, depressed **10** despondent, dispirited, melancholy
long __: **3** ago, run, ton **4** face, haul, iron, jump, shot, suit **5** green, johns
long __ no see: **4** time
long __ of the law: **3** arm
long __ to hoe: **3** row
long __ tooth: **5** in the
long-__: **3** day, run **4** haul, term, time **5** faced, lived, range **6** acting, limbed, winded **7** lasting, sighted
long-__ memory: **4** term
long-__-out: **5** drawn
long-__ rose: **7** stemmed
long.
opposite: **3** lat.
__ long: **6** before
__ long...: **5** Art is
Long: **3** Nia **4** Huey, isle **6** island, Justin, Shorty **7** Richard, Shelley
successor on Cheers: **5** Alley
Long __: **5** Beach, March **6** Branch, Island
Long __ and Far Away: **3** Ago
Long __ Home, The: **4** Road, Walk **6** Voyage
Long __ Journey into Night: **4** Day's
Long __ Line, The: **4** Gray
Long __ Sally: **4** Tall
Long __ Silver: **4** John
Long __ Sound: **6** Island
Long __ Summer, The: **3** Hot
Long __, The: **3** Run **5** March **6** Riders **7** Goodbye
Long __ wave...: **5** may it
__ Longa: **4** Alba
long and the __ of it, the: **5** short
Long and Winding Road, The (1970 song)
artist: Beatles
long-answer exam: **5** essay
long-armed entity: **3** law
__ longa, vita brevis: **3** ars
Long Beach: **4** city, port, town
locale: **7** New York **10** California
Longboat __: **3** Key
longbow
ammo: **5** arrow
sound: **5** twang
user: **6** archer **9** Robin Hood
wood: **3** yew
Long Branch, New Jersey
artist: Winslow Homer
Long Cool Woman (1972 song)
artist: Hollies
Long Day's Journey Into Night
author: Eugene O'Neill
Long Day Wanes, The
author: Anthony Burgess
long-delayed: **4** slow
long-distance
cost: **4** toll
long-drawn-out: **4** slow **5** windy, wordy **6** boring, prolix **7** lengthy, tedious, verbose
long-eared beast: **3** ass **4** hare **5** burro **6** basset
longer: **4** more **8** expanded, extended **9** augmented **10** additional

make ~: **3** pad **5** add to **6** extend, let out **7** augment, drag out, draw out, prolong, spin out, stretch **8** continue, elongate, increase, lengthen, protract **9** string out
no ~ hungry: **5** sated **6** gorged **7** glutted, stuffed **8** satiated **9** surfeited
no ~ in use: **3** out **4** gone **5** dated, dusty, moldy, musty, passé, stale **6** old-hat **7** archaic, outworn **8** outdated, outmoded, timeworn **9** discarded, moth-eaten, out-of-date **10** antiquated, superseded
no ~ qualified: **5** stale **10** out of shape
no ~ used: **3** obs., old, out **5** dated, passé **6** bygone, old hat, square **7** archaic, outworn **8** obsolete, outdated, outmoded, timeworn **10** antiquated, out of style
of ~ standing: **5** elder, older **6** senior

__ longer: **3** any
Longer (1980 song)
artist: Dan Fogelberg
Longest __, The: **3** Day **4** Time, Walk, Yard
long-established: **3** old
Longest Day, The: **4** film **5** novel
author: Cornelius Ryan
cast: Eddie Albert, Paul Anka, Richard Burton, Red Buttons, Sean Connery, Mel Ferrer, Henry Fonda, Peter Lawford, Roddy McDowall, Sal Mineo, Robert Mitchum, Robert Ryan, Rod Steiger, John Wayne
extras: **3** GIs
setting: **4** Caen, WWII **6** France
singer: Paul Anka
Longest Time, The (1984 song)
artist: Billy Joel
Longest Walk, The (1955 song)
artist: Jaye P. Morgan
Longest Yard, The (1974 film)
cast: Eddie Albert, Burt Reynolds
Longest Yard, The (2005 film)
cast: Chris Rock, Adam Sandler
Longet: **8** Claudine
longevity: **4** legs, life, span **6** tenure **8** duration **9** endurance **10** durability
long-faced: **3** sad **4** mopy **5** mopey **7** hangdog, unhappy **8** lowering **9** woebegone
one: **5** moper
Longfellow: **5** Deeds
Longfellow, Henry Wadsworth: **4** poet
bell town: **4** Atri
character: **5** Alden **9** Priscilla
work: Azrael
Ballads and Other Poems
The Children's Hour
The Courtship of Miles Standish
Evangeline
The Golden Legend
Hiawatha
Hyperion
O Ship of State
Paul Revere's Ride
The Song of Hiawatha
Tales of a Wayside Inn
The Village Blacksmith
Voices of the Night
The Wreck of the Hesperus
Longfellow Serenade (1974 song)
artist: Neil Diamond
Long Goodbye, The
author: Raymond Chandler
longhair: **3** cat **5** brain, felid, hippy **6** feline, genius, hippie **7** beatnik, bookish, egghead, erudite, esthete, scholar **8** aesthete, cerebral, highbrow **9** professor, scholarly
long-haired: **6** shaggy **7** hirsute, unshorn
longhairs: **8** academes, literati, scholars **9** aesthetes, highbrows **10** illuminati
longhand: **5** diary **6** letter, scrawl, script **7** writing **8** scribble **9** autograph, signature **10** penmanship
__ Long Has This Been Going On?: **3** How
longheaded: **4** keen, wise **6** astute, shrewd **7** prudent **8** cautious, discreet, watchful **9** astucious, farseeing
longhorn: **5** steer **6** cattle, cheese
__ longhorn: **5** Texas
Longhorn
rival: **5** Aggie
long-horned __: **6** beetle
Long Hot Summer, The (1958 film)
cast: Tony Franciosa, Paul Newman, Joanne Woodward
director: Martin Ritt
Longines: **5** watch **10** wristwatch
alternative: *see* wristwatch
longing: **3** yen **4** avid, hope, itch, need, urge, want, will, wish **5** eager, itchy **6** ardent, desire, hunger, hungry, pining, thirst **7** anxious, athirst, craving, wishful, wistful **8** ambition, appetite, coveting, cupidity, desirous, ravenous, yearning **9** appetence, eagerness, hankering, hungering **10** aspiration
feeling: **4** ache, pang **5** throb **6** regret **7** craving **9** hankering
one ~: **5** piner
sound: **3** sob **4** sigh
longingly, look: **4** gaze
long in the __: **5** tooth
Long Island: **3** snd. **5** sound
airport: **5** Islip **9** MacArthur
campus: **6** C.W. Post **7** Adelphi, Hofstra
newspaper: **7** Newsday
town: **5** Islip, Upton **6** Elmont **7** Merrick, Montauk, Seaford, Wantagh **8** Bellmore, Freeport **10** Massapequa
Long Island Sound
city: **3** Rye **6** Darien **8** Stamford
river to ~: **10** Housatonic
Long Island University
athletes: **10** Blackbirds
locale: **7** New York **8** Brooklyn
longitude: **6** length
line of ~: **8** meridian
unit: **6** degree, minute, second
zero ~ setting: **3** GMT, GST
Long John Silver: **6** pirate
long jumper: **5** Lewis **6** Beamon
long-lasting: **3** old **5** solid, sound **6** aeonic, eonian, rugged, strong, sturdy **7** durable **8** enduring, lifelong, well-made **9** permanent, well-built
longleaf: **4** pine **7** conifer **9** evergreen
Long-Legged Fly
author: William Butler Yeats
__ Long Legs: **5** Daddy
longlegs, daddy: **3** bug **6** insect
long-limbed: **4** tall **5** leggy, rangy **6** gangly **7** willowy **8** gangling
long-lived: **3** old **7** durable, lasting **8** enduring **10** inveterate
Long, Long __: **3** Ago
long, long way to run, A: **3** far
Long March
leader: **3** Mao **10** Mao Tse-Tung
site: **5** China
Long March, The
author: William Styron
Longmont: **4** city, town
locale: **8** Colorado
long-neck __: **4** clam
Long, Nia: **7** actress
film: The Best Man (1999)
The Boiler Room (2000)
Boyz N the Hood (1991)
In Too Deep (1999)
__ Longoria Parker: **3** Eva
long-playing __: **6** record
Long Road Home, The
author: Danielle Steel
long row __: **5** to hoe
__ long run: **5** in the
long-running combining form: **5** -athon
Long Run, The (1979 song)
artist: Eagles
long-serving: **7** veteran **8** seasoned **9** exercised, practiced
Long, Shelley: **7** actress
film: The Brady Bunch Movie (1995)
Caveman (1981)
Hello Again (1987)
Irreconcilable Differences (1984)
The Money Pit (1986)
Night Shift (1982)
Outrageous Fortune (1987)
Troop Beverly Hills (1989)
TV: Cheers
longshoreman: **5** lader **9** stevedore
device: **5** davit
org.: **3** ILA
longshot: **8** underdog
__ long shot: **3** by a
Longshot
author: Dick Francis
longstanding: **6** rooted **7** chronic, lasting **9** chronical
long-stemmed __: **4** rose
Longstocking: **5** Pippi
long-suffering: **4** meek, mild **5** stoic **7** passive, patient, stoical **8** patience, resigned, tolerant **9** forgiving
one: **3** Job **5** saint
Long Tall Glasses (1975 song)
artist: Leo Sayer
Long Tall Sally (1956 song)
artist: Little Richard, Pat Boone
long-term: **6** stable **7** chronic, lasting **8** enduring **9** perennial, permanent, perpetual **10** continuing, unchanging
longtime: **7** veteran **10** deep-seated
__ long time: **5** last a
Long time __!: **5** no see
Long Train Runnin' (1973 song)
artist: Doobie Brothers
__ longue: **6** chaise
Long Voyage Home, The
author: Eugene O'Neill
Long Walk Home, The (1990 film)
cast: Whoopi Goldberg, Sissy Spacek
__ long way: **3** go a
__ Long Way to Tipperary: **4** It's a
long-winded: **4** long **5** gabby, talky, windy, wordy **6** chatty, prolix **7** diffuse, lengthy, unterse, verbose, voluble **8** rambling **9** bombastic, garrulous, ponderous, redundant, talkative **10** big-mouthed, euphuistic, loquacious, palaverous
one: **4** bore, drag, pain, pest, pill **6** gasbag **8** nuisance
__ long, with many..., The: **6** road is
Loni: **8** Anderson
Lonigan: **5** Studs
Lonnie: **4** Mack **7** Donegan
loo: **2** WC **3** can, lav **4** bath, game, john **5** privy **6** lounge, toilet **7** latrine **8** bathroom, card game, lavatory, men's room, outhouse, rest room, toilette **10** ladies' room, powder room
looby: **3** lug **4** boor, hick, lout, rube, yo-yo **5** booby, churl, klutz, ninny, yahoo, yokel **6** duffer **7** bumbler, bumpkin, bungler, fumbler, hayseed **8** lardhead, lunkhead **9** blunderer, ding-a-ling, schlemiel **10** stumblebum
see also ninny
loofah: **6** sponge
looie: **7** officer
subordinate: **3** NCO, PFC, pvt., sgt. **4** corp. **5** sarge **7** private **8** corporal, sergeant
superior: **3** col, gen., maj. **4** capt. **5** lt. col., major **7** captain, colonel, general
look: **3** air, eye, mug, see, spy **4** case, cast, face, gape, gawk, gaze, heed, hope, hunt, leer, mark, mien, mind, mode, note, ogle, peek, peep, peer, read, scan, seek, show, spot, tend, view **5** await, flash, focus, front, guise, scout, shape, sight, slant, sound, stare, study, trend, watch **6** admire, appear, aspect, attend, behold, beware, browse, divine, effect, expect, format, gander, glance, glower, goggle, manner, notice, regard, review, search, squint, survey, swivel, visage **7** bearing, count on, display, evil eye, exhibit, express, fashion, front on, glimpse, inspect, marking, observe, present, seeming, viewing **8** demeanor, evidence, forecast, foretell, give onto, indicate, manifest, noticing, once-over, pore over, presence, reckon on, resemble, scrutiny, seem to be, strike as **9** attention, beholding, count upon, make clear, regarding, semblance **10** anticipate, appearance, complexion, expression, get a load of, inspection, rubberneck, scrutinize
after: **3** run **4** keep, mind, tend **5** guard, nurse, see to, serve,

watch **6** advert, attend, defend, tend to **7** baby-sit, care for, oversee, protect, provide, sit with **8** keep safe, maintain, shepherd **9** accompany, safeguard, supervise **10** take care of
ahead: **4** plan
alike: **5** match
amused: **10** be gracious
angry ~: **5** frown, glare, scowl, snarl, sneer
another ~: **6** review
around: **6** browse
as if: **4** seem **6** appear
askance: **6** squint
at: **3** eye, see **4** case, ogle, view **5** assay, gauge, probe, scout, try on, watch **6** advert, assess, behold, peruse, regard, size up, survey, verify **7** confirm, examine, focus on, inspect, observe, qualify **8** appraise, check out, consider, evaluate, follow up **9** flirt with **10** get a load of, scrutinize
at again: **5** resee **6** review
awestruck: **4** gape, gawk, gaze **5** stare **6** goggle, marvel
back: **4** muse **5** brood **6** ponder, recall, regret, review **7** reflect **8** dredge up, mull over, remember, ruminate **9** recollect, reminisce
brief ~: **4** peek, peep
closely: **3** eye, fix, spy **4** bore, gape, gawk, gaze, leer, ogle, peer **5** focus, rivet, stare, watch **6** appear, goggle, marvel **7** eyeball, inspect, ransack **10** get a load of, rubberneck, scrutinize
coldly upon: **4** snub
cross-eyed: **6** squint
daggers: **4** rage **5** glare, scowl, sneer **6** glower **8** threaten
dejected: **4** mope, pout
down on: **5** abhor, scorn, scout, sneer, spurn **6** jibe at **7** contemn, despise, disdain, sneer at, sniff at **9** patronize **10** depreciate, disapprove
everywhere: **4** comb, hunt, rake, seek, sift, sort **5** flush, probe, scour, sweep **6** forage, search **7** examine, inspect, ransack, rummage **9** ferret out, track down
favorably (on): **5** smile
fixed ~: **4** gaze **5** stare
for: **3** spy **4** hope, hunt, seek, shop, wait **5** await, watch **6** expect, forage, search **7** count on, prepare, require, scout up **8** scout out **9** cast about, count upon **10** anticipate
forbidding ~: **5** frown, glare **6** glower
forward to: **4** wait **5** await **6** expect **8** envision, see ahead, watch for
good ~: **6** eyeful
good on: **3** fit **4** suit **6** become **7** flatter **10** go together
happy: **4** beam, glow, grin **5** smile
hard: **4** gape, gawk, gaze **5** focus, glare, rivet, stare **7** eyeball
have a ~ at: **4** scan, view **5** study **6** browse, peruse, regard, survey **7** observe **8** pore over
healthy ~: **4** glow **7** sparkle **9** freshness
high and low: **4** hunt, seek **5** scour **6** search **7** ransack, rummage
impolite ~: **4** leer, ogle **5** smirk, sneer, stare
in Latin: **4** ecce
in on: **4** call **5** visit, watch
insulting ~: **4** gibe **5** smirk **7** snigger
intense ~: **3** eye **4** gaze, leer, peer **5** glare, stare
into: **3** dig **4** sift **5** audit, check, delve, probe, study **7** enquire, examine, explore, inquire, inspect, ransack **8** check out, follow up, prospect, research, see about **9** delve into **10** scrutinize
(into): **2** go **5** delve
in your eye: **3** ray **4** beam **5** gleam, glint, spark **6** glance **7** glimmer, glisten, sparkle, twinkle
knowing ~: **4** ogle **5** smirk, sneer
lewd ~: **4** ogle **5** smirk
like: **4** seem **5** mimic **6** appear **7** smack of **8** resemble
listlessly: **4** moon
long ~: **5** stare
lovely to ~ at: **6** comely, pretty **8** gorgeous, handsome **9** beautiful **10** attractive, enchanting
of loathing: **5** frown, glare **6** glower **7** grimace
on: **4** deem, view **5** judge, treat **6** regard **7** witness **8** consider, perceive **9** think of as
out: **3** peg, spy **4** mind, spot **5** scope **6** beware, be wary, listen, notice, size up **7** heads up, hearken, watch it **8** keep tabs, pick up on **9** be careful, be on guard, have a care
out on to: **5** front
over: **4** case, pore, read, scan **5** check **6** peruse, survey **7** examine, inspect, monitor, proctor **8** appraise, check out, evaluate, look into **10** run through, scrutinize, zip through
quick ~: **4** peek, peep **6** aperçu
right through: **3** cut **4** shun, snub **5** spurn **6** ignore, insult, rebuff, slight **7** disdain, put down, tune out **8** brush off **9** blackball, disregard, humiliate, ostracize
second ~: **6** replay, review
smug ~: **4** grin, leer **5** smirk, sneer **6** simper
sneak a ~: **3** pry, see, spy **4** peek, peep, peer **5** snoop **6** glance **7** glimpse **10** get a load of
sullen: **4** lour, pout, sulk **5** scowl
take another ~: **5** audit, check, resee, weigh **6** assess, go over, rehash, review, survey **7** analyze, examine, inspect, revisit **8** appraise, critique, evaluate, reassess **9** reexamine, think over **10** reconsider, reevaluate, run through, scrutinize
take a quick ~: **4** leaf, scan, skim **5** check **6** browse, riffle, size up, survey **7** monitor **10** glance over, run through
the joint over: **4** case
the other way: **6** ignore **7** neglect **8** overlook
to: **2** do **5** avail, trust **6** accept, assume, attend, bank on, rely on, resort **7** believe, consult, count on **8** depend on **9** count upon, make use of **10** fall back on
too long: **4** ogle **5** stare
toward: **4** face **7** eyeball **8** confront **9** front onto
unauthorized ~: **4** peep
up: **4** find, gain, mend, scan, seek **5** refer, visit **6** peruse **7** advance, confirm, go to see, hunt for, improve, seek out **8** come upon, discover, progress, research **9** come along, get better, reference, search for, track down **10** ameliorate, convalesce, recuperate
upon: **3** eye, see **4** deem, gaze, take, view **5** count, judge, opine, think, treat **6** reckon, regard, survey **8** consider **9** think of as
up to: **5** adore, defer, honor, rever **6** admire, esteem, revere **7** idolize, lionize, respect, worship **8** venerate **9** reverence
well on: **4** suit **7** enhance, flatter
look __: **3** for, out **4** in on, into, over, upon, up to **5** after, alive, sharp
look __ at: **7** daggers
look __ on: **4** down
look __ to: **7** forward
look __ you leap: **6** before
look-__: **3** see **5** alike
__ look: **3** new **5** dirty
...look __ like Christmas: **4** a lot
Look __!: **4** at me **5** alive
Look __ dancing!: **4** Ma I'm
Look __ hands!: **4** Ma no
Look __, I'm as helpless...: **4** at me
Look __, I'm Sandra Dee: **4** at Me
Look __ in Anger: **4** Back
Look __ Talking: **4** Who's
Look __ this way...: **4** at it
Look __ ye leap: **3** Ere
look-alike: **4** copy, twin **5** clone, match **6** double, ectype, ringer **7** picture, replica, stand-in **9** duplicate, facsimile, identical **10** carbon copy, dead ringer, similarity
maybe: **4** fake, lure **5** decoy
look and __: **3** see
Look at __ Sandra Dee: **4** Me I'm
Look at me!: **4** ta-da **5** ta-dah
Look Away (1988 song)
artist: Chicago
__ Look Back: **4** Don't
Look Back in Anger
author: John Osborne
character: **5** Cliff **6** Alison, Helena **7** Redfern
look before you __: **4** leap
look down one's __ at: **4** nose
looker: **3** fox **4** dish, doll, hunk **5** belle, ogler, peach **6** Apollo, beauty, eyeful, vision **7** goddess, picture, stunner, witness **8** knockout, observer, passerby **9** sightseer, spectator **10** eyewitness
looker-on: **7** witness **9** spectator **10** eyewitness
Look for the Silver Lining
composer: Buddy DeSylva, Jerome Kern
Look Homeward, Angel
author: Thomas Wolfe
character: **3** Ben **4** Gant, Luke **5** Eliza, Laura, Steve **6** Eugene, Oliver
Lookin' __ Back Door: **5** Out My
Lookin' at Me (1998 song)
artist: Mase, Puff Daddy
Lookin' for Love (1980 song)
artist: Johnny Lee
looking __: **5** glass
__-looking: **4** good **7** forward
Looking __ Goodbar: **5** for Mr.
__ looking at you, kid: **5** Here's
Looking Back (1958 song)
artist: Nat King Cole
looking backward in heraldry: **9** regardant
Looking for a New Love (1987 song)
artist: Jody Watley
Looking for Mr. Goodbar: **4** film **5** novel
author: Judith Rossner
cast: Richard Gere, Diane Keaton, Tuesday Weld
Looking Glass
song: Brandy (1972)
Looking Glass girl: **5** Alice
Looking-Glass War, The
author: John le Carré
Looking Through the Eyes of Love (1965 song)
artist: Gene Pitney
Looking Through Your Eyes (1998 song)
artist: LeAnn Rimes
Lookinland: **4** Mike
Look in My Eyes Pretty Woman (1975 song)
artist: Tony Orlando & Dawn
Lookin' Out My Back Door (1970 song)
artist: Creedence Clearwater Revival
...look into the __ of time...: **5** seeds
__ Look Into You Eyes: **5** When I
Look Look
author: Michael Frayn
Look, Ma, no __!: **5** hands
Look Ma! toothpaste: **5** Crest
__, Look Me Over: **3** Hey
__ look now: **4** Don't
Look of Love, The (1968 song)
artist: Sergio Mendes & Brasil '66
lookout: **3** spy, tip **4** case, hawk, post, view, ward **5** guard, scene, scout, tower, vigil, watch **6** anchor, beacon, cupola, patrol, picket, sentry **7** citadel, spotter, station, watcher **8** eagle eye, panorama, sentinel **9** belvedere, crow's nest, vigilance **10** gatekeeper, observance, watchtower, weather eye
be a ~: **3** aid **4** abet, help **6** assist **7** collude
on the ~: **4** wary **5** alert **7** wakeful **8** cautious, keen-eyed, vigilant, watchful **9** wide-awake
Look out __!: **5** below
looks: **6** visage
good: **4** plus **5** class **7** glamour **8** elegance **9** advantage **10** loveliness
__ looks: **4** good

look-see: **4** peek, peep, view **5** recon **6** glance **7** glimpse **10** inspection
Looks Like We Made It (1977 song)
artist: Barry Manilow
Look, up in the ___!: **3** sky
Look What They've Done to My Song Ma (1970 song)
artist: New Seekers
Look What You Done for Me (1972 song)
artist: Al Green
Look Who's Talking (1989 film)
cast: Kirstie Alley, Olympia Dukakis, John Travolta
loom: **4** hulk, near, rise **5** hover, tower **6** appear, emerge, fade in, gather, impend, impose, menace **7** overtop, portend **8** dominate, hang over, overhang, stand out, threaten **9** take shape **10** overshadow
made on a ~: **4** wove **5** woven
over: **8** dominate **10** tower above
(over): **5** tower
part: **4** slay, sley **5** dobby, easer **6** heddle, sleigh
starter: **4** heir **5** broad
up: **5** arise **6** appear, emerge **7** surface **8** approach, threaten
use a ~: **4** knit, spin **5** weave **9** fabricate
looming: **4** near, nigh **8** imminent, lowering, menacing, oncoming, towering, upcoming **9** impending, in the wind
loon: **4** bird, fool, zany **5** diver **6** maniac **7** jackass **8** crackpot **9** harebrain
move like a ~: **3** fly **4** dive **5** swoop **6** plunge **7** plummet **9** sweep down
relative: **5** grebe
Looney Tunes character: **3** Taz **4** Bugs, Fudd, Pepe **5** Daffy, Elmer, Le Pew, Porky, Wile E. **6** Coyote, Tweety **8** Porky Pig **9** Bugs Bunny, Daffy Duck, Elmer Fudd, Pepe Le Pew, Sylvester **10** Road Runner
Loon Lake
author: E.L. Doctorow
loop: **3** arc, bow, lap **4** arch, bend, coil, curl, flex, gird, hank, hoop, kink, knot, link, purl, ring, roll, turn, wind **5** crook, curve, noose, picot, twine, twirl, twist, whorl **6** circle, eyelet, girdle, league, spiral, wreath **7** circuit, compass, scallop, scollop, sinuate **8** encircle **9** encompass, enwreathe, sinuosity **10** wind around
anatomical ~: **4** ansa
embroidery ~: **5** picot
ender: **4** hole
keep in the ~: **4** tell, warn **5** brief **6** advise, fill in, inform, notify, tip off **7** apprise, apprize **8** forewarn **9** enlighten
knock for a ~: **3** awe, wow **4** faze, jolt, stun, wham **5** amaze, floor
needlework ~: **5** bride
rope ~: **5** bight, noose, snare
loop-___-loop: **3** the
___ loop: **3** toe **5** in the
Loop
initials: **3** CTA
locale: **7** Chicago
trains: **3** els
looped: **5** round **6** coiled **9** connected **10** continuous
looper: **3** bug, fly **6** insect, pop fly
loophole: **3** out **6** device, escape, outlet, way out
looping: **5** curly **6** coiled **7** winding
___ Loops: **5** Froot
loopy: **4** daft, gaga **5** dotty **7** offbeat **9** befuddled, eccentric **10** off-the-wall
not ~: **4** sane **6** normal **8** all there, balanced, rational, together
Loos, Anita: **6** writer
work: But Gentlemen Marry Brunettes
Gentlemen Prefer Blondes
Gigi
A Girl Like I
Kiss Hollywood Goodby
The Talmadge Girls
This Brunette Prefers Work
The Women
loose: **3** lax **4** ease, easy, emit, fast, free, kind, limp, mild, soft, undo, wide **5** apart, baggy, let go, light, relax, roomy, slack, unbar, unfix, unpin, untie, vague **6** at ease, casual, detach, flabby, gentle, kindly, let out, limber, lissom, rakish, redeem, remiss, sloppy, unbind, unbolt, undone, unhand, unhook, unlace, unlash, unlock, unsnap, untied, unwind, wabbly, wanton, wobbly **7** asunder, at large, break up, clement, corrupt, deliver, diffuse, disjoin, ease off, escaped, flaccid, general, hanging, immoral, liberal, lissome, manumit, movable, naughty, powdery, relaxed, release, ruthful, set free, slacken, sparing, unbound, uncaged, unchain, unclasp, unhitch, unlatch, unleash, unscrew, unstick, unstrap, untwine **8** careless, detached, flexible, floating, heedless, informal, laid-back, liberate, loosened, merciful, mitigate, moveable, on the lam, placable, rambling, released, separate, slipshod, slovenly, swinging, tolerant, unbolted, unbuckle, unbutton, unchaste, uncurbed, unfasten, unfetter, unhinged, unhooked, unlocked, unpinned, unstrict, work free **9** abandoned, alleviate, assuasive, compliant, corrupted, debauched, discharge, disengage, dissolute, easygoing, extricate, forgiving, haphazard, imprecise, imprudent, indulgent, liberated, negligent, slackened, unclasped, unheedful, unlatched, unleashed, unplanned, unscrewed, unsecured, untighten, work loose **10** disconnect, disjointed, dissipated, emancipate, forbearing, ill-defined, ill-fitting, immoderate, indefinite, licentious, nonchalant, on the prowl, permissive, profligate, unattached, unbuttoned, unconfined, unexacting, unfastened, unfettered, unpackaged, unrigorous, unshackled, unspecific
at ~ ends: **6** adrift **8** dallying, drifting, wavering **9** uncertain, unsettled
break ~: **4** bail, flee **6** escape, run off **7** get away
cut ~: **4** free **5** let go, revel, untie **6** escape, unbind, untied **7** abandon, manumit, release, run wild **9** disengage
end: **6** detail, nicety **7** minutia **9** punctilio
fast and ~: **4** rash, wild **5** hasty **6** amoral, unruly, unwise **7** corrupt, immoral **8** careless, feckless, headlong, heedless, reckless **9** corrupted, foolhardy, imprudent, negligent **10** incautious, indiscreet
hang ~: **3** sag **4** flap, flop, idle, loaf, rest **5** droop, relax **6** dangle, lounge
hanging ~: **6** at ease **7** relaxed **8** carefree, composed, tranquil
in Britain: **5** lowse
knock ~: **4** bump **5** budge **8** dislodge, shake off **9** dislocate
let ~: **4** free, play, yell **5** shout, unpen, unpin, untie **6** bellow, unbind, untied **8** liberate
on the ~: **4** fled, free **5** flown **6** untied **7** at large, escaped, runaway **8** scot-free **10** unconfined
partner: **4** fast
set ~: **6** untied **9** liberated
starter: **4** foot
tie up ~ ends: **6** finish, wind up, wrap up **8** complete, finalize
loose ___: **4** ends **6** cannon
loose ___ goose: **3** as a
loose-___: **4** leaf **6** footed, limbed
___ loose: **3** cut, let **4** hang, stay, turn **5** break, on the
Loose ___ sink ships: **4** lips
___ Loose: **6** Bustin'
loose as a ___: **5** goose
loose-fitting: **4** wide **5** baggy **6** droopy, floppy **7** sagging **9** shapeless
loose-leaf: **6** binder
divider: **3** tab
loose-limbed: **4** spry **5** agile, lithe **6** limber, nimble, supple **7** lissome
loose-lipped: **5** gabby, talky, windy, wordy **6** blabby, chatty, mouthy, prolix **7** gossipy, verbose, voluble **8** effusive **9** expansive, garrulous, talkative **10** bigmouthed, long-winded, loquacious
loosen: **4** ease, free, thaw, undo **5** let go, ravel, relax, slack, unbar, unfix, unpeg, unpin, untie, unzip **6** detach, ease up, let out, unbind, unbolt, unfold, unhook, unlace, unlash, unlock, unsnap, unwind **7** break up, deliver, disjoin, ease off, get soft, manumit, release, set free, slacken, tear off, unchain, uncinch, unclasp, unhitch, unlatch, unleash, unravel, unscrew, unstick, unstrap **8** liberate, mitigate, separate, unbuckle, unbutton, unfasten, work free **9** alleviate, discharge, disengage, extricate, unshackle, untighten **10** disconnect, emancipate, liberalize
forcibly: **3** pry **4** tear **5** wrest **6** wrench
one's grip: **4** free **6** unhand **7** release, set free **9** disengage
one's hold: **4** free **5** untie **6** let off **7** release, set free **9** disengage
up: **5** relax **6** relent, unwind **8** calm down **10** take a break, take it easy
looseness: **4** give, vice **6** laxity **7** abandon, license, neglect **8** disorder, venality, wildness **10** corruption
combining form: **3** lyo-
loosestrife tree: **5** henna
loosey-goosey: **6** at ease
loot: **3** rob **4** haul, lift, raid, sack, take **5** boost, booty, graft, prize, rifle, steal, swipe **6** bounty, bundle, harrow, invade, maraud, prizes, ravage, rip off, snatch, snitch, spoils, thieve, wealth **7** despoil, jobbery, pillage, plunder, ransack, relieve, salvage, seizure, stick up **8** embezzle, freeboot, hot goods, liberate, pickings **9** depredate **10** burglarize
hidden ~: **5** cache, hoard, stash **8** treasure
see also moolah
Loot
author: Joe Orton
looter: **6** pirate, robber, vandal **7** brigand **10** freebooter, highwayman
looting: **5** theft **6** rapine **8** thievery
lop: **3** cut, top **4** chop, crop, pare, trim **5** droop, prune, sever, shear, slice **6** cut off, detach, excise, spring **7** chop off, exscind, scissor, shorten, tear off, trim off **8** hang down, shear off, slice off, truncate **9** eliminate
ender: **5** sided
lop ___: **3** off
lop-___: **5** eared
Lopat: **2** Ed **5** Eddie **6** hurler **7** pitcher
lope: **3** jog, run **4** skip, trip, trot **6** canter
Lope: **6** de Vega
loper: **8** sprinter
Lopes: **5** Davey **6** Fernao
Lopes, Davey
sport: **8** baseball
Lopez: **2** Al **5** Nancy, Trini **6** George **8** Jennifer
Lopez, Jennifer: **6** singer **7** actress
film: Angel Eyes (2001)
The Cell (2000)
Enough (2002)
Gigli (2003)
Jack (1996)
Maid in Manhattan (2002)
Monster-in-Law (2005)
Out of Sight (1998)
Selena (1997)
Shall We Dance? (2004)
An Unfinished Life (2005)
U Turn (1997)
The Wedding Planner (2001)
nickname: J. Lo
song: Ain't It Funny (2003)
All I Have (2003)
If You Had My Love (1999)
Waiting for Tonight (1999)
Lopez, Nancy: **6** golfer
___ Lopez opening: **3** Ruy
Lopez, Trini
homeland: Trinidad
song: If I Had a Hammer (1963)

Lopez, Vincent: 10 bandleader
theme: 4 Nola
loppy: 4 limp 6 droopy, floppy 7 sagging
lopsided: 3 wry 4 awry 5 askew, atilt 6 canted, skewed, squint, uneven, warped 7 crooked, leaning, tilting, unequal 8 cockeyed, top-heavy, unsteady 9 egg-shaped, irregular 10 ill-matched, off-balance, out of shape, unbalanced
win: 4 rout 5 upset 7 debacle, shut out 8 disaster, drubbing, walkover 9 trouncing
loquacious: 4 glib, long 5 gabby, talky, windy, wordy 6 chatty, fluent, prolix 7 diffuse, gossipy, lengthy, unterse, verbose, voluble, yacking, yakking 8 babbling, rambling 9 bombastic, expansive, garrulous, jabbering, redundant, talkative 10 bigmouthed, chattering, discursive, long-winded, motormouth, palaverous
far from ~: 4 curt 5 brief, crisp, pithy, short, terse 7 brusque, concise, laconic 8 succinct, taciturn
loquacity: 4 guff 6 babble, hot air, jabber 7 blabber, blather, blether, chatter, palaver, yakking 8 bigmouth, idle talk, verbiage 9 eloquence, garrulity, gift of gab, wordiness
loquat: 4 tree 5 fruit 9 evergreen
Lorain: 4 city, town
locale: 4 Ohio
___ l'orange: 5 duck à
loran part: 3 nav. 4 long 5 range 10 navigation
Lorax, The
author: Dr. Seuss
lord: 4 boss, duke, earl, male, peer 5 baron, mogul, noble, ruler, title 6 gerent, honcho, master 7 marquis 8 marquess, nobleman, viscount 9 blueblood 10 aristocrat
feudal ~: 5 liege, mesne, thane, thegn
holding: 4 fief, land 5 manor 6 estate
In Turkish: 3 aga 4 agha
it over: 5 gloat 7 swagger 9 trample on, tyrannize
lady: 4 dame
mate: 4 dame, lady
servant: 4 page, serf
starter: 3 war 4 land, slum
Lord: 3 God, Jon 4 Jack 5 Jahve, Jahwe, title, Yahve, Yahwe 6 Jahveh, Jahweh, Yahveh, Yahweh 7 Holy One, Jehovah 8 Immanuel, Marjorie, Most High
& Taylor rival: 4 Saks
Lord ___: 3 Jim 7 Krishna
Lord ___ Duck: 5 Love a
Lord ___ Flies: 5 of the
Lord ___ Rings, The: 5 of the
Lord ___ shepherd, The: 4 is my
Lord Baltimore: 4 cake
___ Lord Fauntleroy: 6 Little
Lord-High-Everything-___: 4 Else
Lord, is ___?: 3 it I
Lord Jim: 4 film 5 novel
author: Joseph Conrad
cast: Curt Jurgens, James Mason, Peter O'Toole, Eli Wallach
character: 4 Dain 5 Stein, Waris 6 Marlow
director: Richard Brooks
Lord knows ___ tried!: 3 I've
lordly: 4 high, posh 5 grand, lofty, noble, proud, regal, ritzy, royal, swank 6 august, formal, lavish 7 exalted, haughty, leonine, stately 8 arrogant, baronial, cavalier, despotic, imperial, imposing, kinglike, majestic, princely, snobbish, splendid 9 arbitrary, dignified, grandiose, imperious, luxurious, masterful, sumptuous 10 commanding, despotical, high-handed, impressive, majestical, peremptory
Lord of the Flies
author: William Golding
Lord of the Rings, The
author: J.R.R. Tolkien
character: 3 elf, ent, orc, Sam 5 Bilbo, dwarf, Frodo, Smaug, troll 6 dragon, hobbit, Sauron, wizard 7 Baggins, Gandalf
locale: 9 Mount Doom 11 Middle Earth
Lord of the Rings - The Fellowship... (2001 film)
cast: Ian McKellen, Viggo Mortensen, Liv Tyler, Elijah Wood
director: Peter Jackson
Lord of the Rings: The Two Towers, The (2002 film)
cast: Sean Astin, Cate Blanchett, Ian McKellen, Viggo Mortensen, Liv Tyler, Elijah Wood
director: Peter Jackson
lords: 6 gentry 7 peerage, royalty 8 nobility 10 bluebloods, patricians, upper class, upper crust
Lords: 5 Traci
Lord's ___: 6 Prayer
___ lords a-leaping...: 3 ten
lordship: 5 title 9 honorific
Lords of Flatbush, The (1974 film)
cast: Sylvester Stallone, Henry Winkler
Lord's Prayer: 5 Pater
pronoun: 3 thy
Lord Weary's Castle
author: Robert Lowell
Lordy!: 4 egad 5 egads
lore: 4 myth, saws 5 myths, sagas, tales 6 adages, fables, legend 7 beliefs, customs, legends, sayings 8 doctrine, learning, teaching 9 erudition, knowledge, mythology, tradition 10 fairy story, literature, refinement, traditions
starter: 4 book, folk
Lorelei: 3 Lee 5 lurer, siren
emulate ~: 5 tempt
poet: Heinrich Heine
river of the ~: 5 Rhine
Lorelei (1976 song)
artist: Styx
Loren: 4 Dean 5 Donna 6 Sophia
Loren, Sophia: 7 actress
birthplace: 4 Rome
film: Aida (1953)
Arabesque (1966)
The Cassandra Crossing (1977)
A Countess From Hong Kong (1967)
El Cid (1961)
The Fall of the Roman Empire (1964)
Grumpier Old Men (1995)
Houseboat (1958)
Operation Crossbow (1965)
That Kind of Woman (1959)
Two Women (1961, AA)
spouse: Carlo Ponti
Lorentz, Hendrik: 8 Nobelist 9 physicist
Lorenz: 4 Hart 6 Konrad
Lorenz, Konrad: 6 writer 8 Austrian, Nobelist
work: King Solomon's Ring
On Agression
Lorenzo: 5 lamas 8 de' Medici, Ghiberti
see also Spanish
Lorenzo's Oil (1992 film)
cast: Nick Nolte, Susan Sarandon, Peter Ustinov
Loretta: 4 Lynn, Swit 5 Young 6 Devine
sister: 7 Crystal
lorgnette: 7 glasses 10 eyeglasses, spectacles
part: 4 lens
Lori: 5 Petty 6 Singer 8 Loughlin
Lorin: 6 Maazel 9 Hollander
Loring: 4 Lisa 6 Gloria
Loring, Gloria
song: Friends and Lovers (1986)
spouse: Alan Thicke
TV: Days of Our Lives
lorn: 6 bereft 7 in a funk 8 derelict, deserted, desolate, forsaken, lovesick 9 abandoned
starter: 3 for 4 love
Lorna: 4 Luft 5 Doone
half-sister: 4 Liza
Lorna Doone: 5 cooky, novel 6 cookie
alternative: ***see*** cookie brand
author: R.D. Blackmore
character: 3 Fry, Tom 4 Alan, Ridd 5 Ensor 6 Carver, Faggus, Jeremy, Reuben 7 Brandir 8 Stickles 9 Huckaback
setting: 6 Exmoor 7 England
Lorne: 6 Greene, Marion 8 Michaels
Lorn port, Firth of: 4 Oban
loro: 4 fish 6 parrot 10 parrot fish
Lorraine: 4 Gary 6 Bracco 9 Hansberry
city: 5 Nancy
neighbor: 6 Alsace
___ Lorraine: 5 Sweet 6 quiche
Lorre: 5 Peter
role: Mr. Moto
Lorrie: 6 Morgan
lorry: 3 rig, van 4 semi 5 truck, U-Haul 6 wheels 7 vehicle 9 transport
Lorus: 5 watch 10 wristwatch
alternative: ***see*** wristwatch
lory: 4 bird 6 parrot
Los ___: 5 Altos, Gatos, Lobos 6 Alamos 7 Angeles
Los ___, CA: 5 Altos, Gatos
Los ___, NM: 6 Alamos
Los ___ Rio: 3 Del
Los Alamos: 4 city, town
locale: 9 New Mexico
Los Altos: 4 city, town
locale: 10 California
Los Angeles: 4 city, port, town
City of ~: 5 train
college athlete: 5 Bruin 6 Trojan 10 Golden Bear
East ~: 6 barrio
forecast: 4 haze, smog
locale: 10 California
newspaper: 4 News 5 Times
pro athlete: 4 King 5 Laker 6 Dodger 7 Clipper
school: 3 USC 4 UCLA
suburb: 5 Azusa 6 Bel Air, Encino, Orange
thoroughfare: 4 Pico 6 Sunset
zone: 3 PDT, PST
Los Del Rio
homeland: Spain
song: Macarena (1996)
lose: 3 rid 4 bomb, bust, drop, duck, fail, flop, miss, oust, shed, slip, trip 5 avoid, dodge, drain, elude, evade, flunk, shake, spill, use up, waste, yield 6 baffle, blow it, divest, escape, expend, falter, forget, give up, go down, mislay, outrun, pass up 7 blunder, decline, default, exhaust, forfeit, founder, get beat, go under, go wrong, misstep, stumble, succumb, wash out 8 confound, displace, fall flat, flounder, get rid of, lay an egg, misplace, misspend, shake off, slip away, squander, throw off, unburden 9 disorient, dissipate, fall short, get licked, miss out on, sacrifice, strike out, surrender, take a dive, throw away 10 be defeated, capitulate, disinherit, dispossess, gamble away, get clear of, relinquish, run through
a lap: 4 rise 5 arise, get up 7 stand up
altitude: 4 drop, fall 7 descend
as a lead: 4 blow
balance: 4 fall, reel, slip, trip 5 lurch, slide 6 sprawl, teeter, topple, totter, tumble, wobble 7 stagger, stumble 10 go headlong
color: 4 fade, pale 5 bleed 6 blanch 8 etiolate
consciousness: 5 faint, swoon 6 go limp 7 crumple, pass out 8 black out, keel over
energy: 3 sag, tax 4 flag, fold, tire 5 droop, weary 6 weaken 7 exhaust, give out, overtax, poop out 8 collapse, enervate, overwork, wear down
faith: 7 despair 10 give up hope
focus: 5 blear, cloud, muddy
freshness: 4 wilt 5 droop, go bad, spoil 6 wither 7 shrivel
ground: 3 lag 5 slide 7 regress 8 fall back
heart: 4 mope 5 quail 6 give up 7 despair, despond 10 give up hope
intensity: 3 ebb 4 cool, fade, flag, slow, wane 5 abate, let up 6 ease up, lessen, recede, soften, weaken 7 decline, die down, dwindle, slacken, subside, tail off 8 blow over, decrease, diminish, moderate, taper off
interest: 3 nod 4 pale, pall, tire 5 weary
it: 4 boil, flip, rage, snap 5 crack, freak, go ape, panic 6 blow up, get mad, go nuts, go wild 7 explode, flip out 8 freak out,

have a fit 9 go bananas, go berserk
leaves: 9 exfoliate
luster: 4 fade, pale 7 tarnish
no time: 3 hie, run 4 race, rush 5 hurry, speed 6 hasten 10 get hopping
one's shirt: 4 fold 6 go bust
one's way: 3 err 5 drift 6 ramble 7 digress, diverge, meander 9 wander off
on purpose: 4 diet, slim 5 throw 6 reduce 8 slim down
out: 4 bomb, fail, flop, fold 6 blow it, give up, pass up 7 forfeit 8 fall flat 9 fall short 10 be defeated, capitulate
out on: 4 fail, flub, miss, muff 6 fumble, ignore, pass up 7 default, misfire 8 overlook, pass over 9 fall short
sight of: 4 miss 6 forget, ignore 7 neglect 8 overlook, pass over
speed: 3 lag 4 slow 5 brake, check, choke, delay, let up, relax, stall, unlax 6 ease up, go easy, loiter, reduce, unwind, weaken 7 bog down, lay back, sit back 8 moderate, slack off, slow down, wind down 9 soft-pedal 10 decelerate, settle back, simmer down
(to): 3 bow
traction: 4 skid, slip 5 coast, skate, slide 7 slither
value: 4 sink 5 lower 6 reduce 7 decline, deflate 8 decrease 10 depreciate
weight: 4 diet 6 reduce 8 slim down
lose __: 3 out 4 face, time 5 out on 7 sight of
lose __ of: 5 track
lose-lose situation: 5 no-win
lose one's __: 4 head 5 shirt 6 tongue
lose one's __ to: 5 heart
__, Lose or Draw: 3 Win
loser: 3 dud 4 flop, jerk, nerd, wimp 5 creep, dweeb, moron, patsy 6 lummox, misfit 7 also-ran, failure, has-been 8 deadbeat, underdog 9 nonwinner 10 ne'er-do-well
be a sore ~: 4 sulk
cry: 5 I give, uncle 6 enough
election ~: 3 out
of 1588: 6 Armada
of 1917: 4 tsar
storied ~: 4 hare
__ loser: 4 born, sore
__ Loser: 3 I'm a
__ Loses a Tail: 6 Eeyore
Los Gatos: 4 city, town
locale: 10 California
losing: 6 behind 7 lagging 8 trailing
streak: 5 slide, slump 9 downslide
Losing __: 3 You 6 Ground, Isaiah
Losing Isaiah (1995 film)
cast: Halle Berry, Cuba Gooding Jr., Jessica Lange
Losing My Religion (1991 song)
artist: R.E.M.
Losing You (1963 song)
artist: Brenda Lee
Los Lobos
song: La Bamba (1987)
loss: 3 dud 4 bomb, bust, cost, debt, flop, harm, hurt, lack, leak, miss, ruin 5 debit, minus, trial, waste 6 damage, defeat, fiasco, injury, losing, mishap, red ink, turkey 7 bad luck, blunder, debacle, deficit, failure, misstep, setback, stumble, trouble, undoing, washout 8 accident, breakage, calamity, casualty, decrease, disaster, downfall, fatality, wreckage 9 cataclysm, depletion, detriment, privation, sacrifice, shrinkage 10 deficiency, forfeiture, impairment, misfortune, nonsuccess
at a ~: 4 asea, beat 5 at sea, blank, stuck 7 baffled, puzzled, stumped 8 confused, overcome 9 mystified, perplexed 10 bewildered, confounded, nonplussed, tongue-tied
at a ~ for words: 5 dazed 7 shocked, stunned 9 awestruck 10 bowled over, nonplussed, speechless
business ~: 4 bath 8 reversal
feel a ~: 4 miss 5 mourn
leader: 5 promo 6 come-on 7 gimmick 9 promotion
of face: 5 odium, shame 6 stigma 7 chagrin, scandal 8 disgrace, dishonor, ignominy, ridicule 9 abashment, disrepute, ill repute 10 opprobrium
take a ~: 3 eat 7 devalue 8 give up on, write off
loss __: 6 leader
__ loss: 3 at a 7 capital
__ loss for words: 3 at a
Loss of Breath
author: Edgar Allan Poe
Loss of Roses, A
author: William Inge
__-loss order: 4 stop
lost: 4 asea, gone, past, rapt 5 at sea, minus, spent, stray 6 adrift, astray, bygone, doomed, dreamy, hidden, in a fog, lapsed, missed, musing, ruined, unsure, wasted 7 bemused, extinct, faraway, mislaid, missing, misused, puzzled, strange, wayward, wrecked 8 absorbed, cast away, clueless, consumed, distrait, dreaming, finished, hopeless, misspent, obscured, off-track, perished, vanished, wiped out 9 abandoned, destroyed, engrossed, entranced, flummoxed, forfeited, forgotten, frittered, misplaced, off-course, perplexed, wandering 10 abstracted, bewildered, demolished, devastated, dissipated, distracted, eradicated, gone astray, spellbound, squandered
cause: 5 goner
face: 5 shame, stain, taint 8 disgrace, dishonor 9 disrepute
get ~: 2 go 5 scram, stray 6 beat it, begone, bug off, wander 7 push off 8 withdraw 10 go fly a kite
(in): 4 deep
in thought: 4 rapt 5 moony, taken 6 intent 7 bemused, gripped 8 absorbed, immersed, involved 9 engrossed, oblivious 10 fascinated
not ~: 6 extant
partner: 5 found
word on a ~ sign: 6 reward
lost __: 5 cause
__ lost!: 3 Get
Lost __: 5 in You 7 Command, Horizon, In Love
Lost __, A: 4 Lady
Lost __ Harem: 3 in a
Lost __ Stars: 5 in the
lost and __: 5 found
Lost Angel, The
author: Mary Higgins Clark
Lost Dutchman: 4 mine
Lost Generation coiner: 5 Stein
Lost Girl, The
author: D.H. Lawrence
Lost Horizon: 4 film 5 novel
author: James Hilton
cast: Ronald Colman, Edward Everett Horton, Sam Jaffe, Margo, Jane Wyatt
character: 4 lama
director: Frank Capra
setting: 4 Asia 5 Tibet
Lost in America (1985 film)
cast: Albert Brooks, Julie Hagerty, Garry Marshall
director: Albert Brooks
Lost in Emotion (1987 song)
artist: Lisa Lisa and Cult Jam
__ Lost in His Arms: 4 I Got
Lost in Love (1980 song)
artist: Air Supply
Lost in Space (1998 film)
cast: Heather Graham, William Hurt, Matt LeBlanc, Gary Oldman, Mimi Rogers
Lost in Space (CBS sci-fi)
cast: Angela Cartwright (Penny Robinson)
Mark Goddard (Don West)
Jonathan Harris (Zachary Smith)
Marta Kristen (Judy Robinson)
June Lockhart (Maureen Robinson)
Billy Mumy (Will Robinson)
Guy Williams (John Robinson)
character: 5 robot
Lost in the Funhouse
author: John Barth
Lost in the Stars: 4 play 7 musical
author: Maxwell Anderson
composer: Kurt Weill
Lost in Translation (2003 film)
cast: Scarlett Johansson, Bill Murray
Lost in Yonkers: 4 film, play
author: Neil Simon
cast: Richard Dreyfuss, Mercedes Ruehl
role: 3 Jay 4 Arty, Gert 5 Bella, Louie
Lost in You (song)
artist: Garth Brooks, Rod Stewart
Lost in Your Eyes (1989 song)
artist: Debbie Gibson
Lost Lady, A
author: Willa Cather
Lost Pueblo
author: Zane Grey
__ Lost Souls: 3 Two
__ Lost, The: 5 Love I
Lost Weekend, The (1945 film)
cast: Ray Milland, Jane Wyman
character: 3 Bim, Don 4 Wick 5 Helen 6 Birnam, Gloria 9 Don Birnam
director: Billy Wilder
Lost Without Your Love (1976 song)
artist: Bread
Lost World of the Kalahari, The
author: Laurens Van der Post
Lost World, The
author: Arthur Conan Doyle, Michael Crichton
beast: 4 T-Rex
Lost Zoo, The
author: Countee Cullen
lot: 3 cut, hap, mob, ton 4 area, doom, fate, gang, heap, load, lump, mass, mess, mete, mold, much, pack, part, pile, plat, plot, raft, slew, sort, yard 5 array, batch, block, bunch, field, group, karma, ocean, order, patch, quota, reams, share, slice, stack, stamp, store, tract, whole 6 armful, boodle, bundle, chance, kismat, kismet, number, oodles, parcel, passel, plenty, plight, ration, scores, stacks 7 acreage, destiny, fortune, grounds, numbers, portion, species, tragedy 8 frontage, homesite, movie set, property, quantity 9 abundance, aggregate, allotment, great deal, multitude, plenitude, profusion 10 assortment, collection, percentage, real estate
a ~: 3 oft, ton 4 gobs, many, much, scad, tons 5 heaps, loads, no end, often, piles, rafts, scads 6 highly, myriad, oceans, oodles, plenty, vastly 7 barrels, buckets, bunches, but good, greatly 8 beaucoup, jillions, very much, zillions 9 great deal, immensely, like crazy, many a time, quite a bit, regularly 10 ever so much
a ~ of: 4 many 6 divers, myriad, umteen, untold 7 copious, profuse, umpteen 8 abundant, manifold, numerous, umpsteen 9 bountiful, countless, quite a few
a ~ of fun: 4 howl, kick
bad ~: 7 rotters 8 stinkers, villains 10 no-goodniks, scoundrels
filler: 4 cars 5 autos
measure: 4 acre, area
not a ~: 3 few 4 some 7 handful 10 infrequent, sprinkling
starter: 4 feed, sand, wood
the ~: 3 all 5 whole 9 aggregate 10 everything
throw one's ~ in with: 3 wed 4 join 5 marry 6 go with, hook up
use a ~: 4 park
__ lot: 3 job, odd 4 back, not a 5 round 7 parking
Lot: 5 river
brother: 5 Iscah 6 Milcah
father: 5 Haran
River locale: 6 France
son: 4 Moab 7 Ben-Ammi
uncle: 7 Abraham
__ Lot: 6 Salem's
lothario: 4 rake, roué, wolf 5 lover, Romeo 7 Don Juan 8 Casanova, lover boy 9 ladies' man, libertine
lotion: 4 balm, Keri, wash 5 cream, Curel, Nivea, salve 6 Aveeno, bay rum 7 Eucerin, Jergens, Pacquin,

soother, unguent 8 cosmetic, lenitive, liniment, medicine, ointment, sunblock 9 demulcent, emollient, Lubriderm, sunscreen 10 aftershave, medication, palliative
apply, as ~: 5 rub in, rub on, smear
ingredient: 4 aloe
__ lotion: 8 calamine
Loti, Pierre: 6 French, writer
work: Matelot
__ lot like: 5 look a
lots: 4 a ton, gobs, heap, many, mint, much, peck, scad, slew, tons, wads 5 acres, a heap, heaps, loads, mucho, piles, scads, slews 6 a bunch, flocks, hoards, oceans, oodles, plenty, raffle, scores, stacks, worlds 7 aplenty, barrels, legions, numbers 8 good deal, mountain, numerous 9 great deal, multitude, truckload
draw ~: 4 pick 6 choose, decide, select 9 determine
of: 4 many, much 6 divers, myriad, umteen, untold 7 copious, profuse, umpteen 8 abundant, manifold, numerous, umpsteen 9 bountiful, countless, quite a few
Lots, Feast of: 5 Purim
book: 6 Esther
Lott: 5 Trent 6 Ronnie
Lotta Love (1978 song)
artist: Nicolette Larson
Lotte: 5 Lenya 7 Lehmann
lottery: 5 Lotto 6 chance, raffle 7 drawing 8 gambling 10 sweepstake
equipment: 6 hopper
org., once: 3 SSS
Lottery, The
author: Shirley Jackson
Lottery Winner, The
author: Mary Higgins Clark
lotto: 4 game
kin: 4 keno 5 beano, bingo
Lott, Ronnie
sport: 8 football
lotus: 3 pad 5 plant 6 flower 9 water lily
lotus __: 4 land
lotus-__: 5 eater
__ lotus: 4 blue 5 white 6 Indian, sacred
Lotus-Eaters, The
author: Alfred Tennyson
Lou: 4 Bega, Reed 5 Adler, Brock, Dobbs, Gramm, Grant, Groza, Holtz, Rawls 6 Gehrig, Harris, Hoover, Jacobi 7 Antonio, Breslow, Gossett 8 Boudreau, Christie, Costello, Ferrigno, Novikoff, Piniella 10 Carnesecca
Lou __ Hoover: 5 Henry
Lou __ Phillips: 7 Diamond
louche: 4 iffy 5 fishy, shady 6 shifty 7 corrupt, crooked, devious, dubious, suspect 8 doubtful, slippery 9 dishonest, unethical 10 fly-by-night, suspicious
loud: 4 deep, rude 5 aroar, boomy, brash, crass, crude, forte, gaudy, gross, noisy, pushy, rowdy, showy, vivid, vocal 6 ablare, brassy, brazen, coarse, flashy, garish, strong, tawdry, vulgar 7 blaring, blatant, booming, boorish, chintzy, hooting, intense, loutish, lowbred, raucous, ringing, roaring, uncouth 8 crashing, emphatic, piercing, powerful, resonant, sonorous, strident, turned up, vehement 9 clamorous, deafening, obnoxious, obtrusive, offensive, tasteless 10 blustering, boisterous, clangorous, flamboyant, resounding, stentorian, thundering, uproarious, vociferant, vociferous
be too ~: 6 deafen
ender: 5 mouth 7 speaker
in music: 5 forte
not ~: 3 low 4 soft, weak 5 muted, quiet 6 feeble, hushed 7 muffled 9 whispered
sound: 3 bam, din, pop, pow 4 bang, boom, slam, thud, wham, yell 5 blare, blast, crack, noise, thump, whang 6 kaboom, report
very ~ in music: 3 fff
__ loud: 3 out
loud and __: 5 clear
louder
gradually ~ in music: 4 cres. 5 cresc. 9 crescendo
make ~: 3 amp 5 amp up
Lou Diamond __: 8 Phillips
loudly: 5 forte 8 viva voce
loudmouth: 5 raver 6 magpie 7 boaster, windbag 8 blowhard, braggart
loudmouthed: 5 noisy, rowdy 7 uncouth 9 talkative
loudness: 3 vol. 6 volume 9 amplitude, intensity, magnitude
unit: 2 db 3 bel 4 phon, sone 7 decibel
Loudon: 7 Dorothy 10 Wainwright
loudspeaker: 4 horn 8 bullhorn, intercom, PA system
loud-voiced: 10 vociferant
Louella: 7 Parsons
contemporary: 5 Hedda
successor: 3 Liz 4 Rona
Louganis, Greg: 5 diver
lough: 4 lake, mere, pond, tarn 5 basin 9 reservoir
Loughlin: 4 Lori
Lou Grant (CBS drama)
cast: Mason Adams (Charlie Hume)
Daryl Anderson (Dennis 'Animal' Price)
Edward Asner (Lou Grant)
Linda Kelsey (Billie Newman)
Nancy Marchand (Margaret Pynchon)
Robert Walden (Joe Rossi)
dog: 6 Barney
paper: 4 Trib 7 Tribune
producer: MTM
setting: 10 California, Los Angeles
Louie: 4 duck 8 Anderson
brother: 4 Huey 5 Dewey
Donald Duck, to ~: 4 unca
Louie Louie (1963 song)
artist: Kingsmen
louis __: 3 d'or
Louis: 3 Joe, Nye, roi 4 Néel 5 David, Dudek, Hémon, Horst, Malle, Mayer, Nizer, Prima, Wirth 6 Aragon, Joliet, L'Amour, Leakey, Le Nain 7 Agassiz, Bellson, Braille, Calhern, Gossett, Hayward, Ignarro, Jolliet, Jourdan, Lumière, Pasteur, Renault, Simpson, Teicher, Tiffany 8 Brandeis, Couperus, Daguerre, MacNeice, Rukeyser, Sullivan, Zukofsky 9 Armstrong, Bromfield, Chevrolet, de Broglie, Fréchette 10 Untermeyer
in German: 6 Ludwig
in Italian: 5 Luigi 8 Lodovico
see also French
Louis __: 3 XIV 4 heel 5 Seize 6 Le Nain, Quinze, Treize
Louisa __ Alcott: 3 May
Louis B. __: 5 Mayer
Louis-Dreyfus: 5 Julia
role: 6 Elaine
Louise: 4 Labé, lake, Tina 5 Anita, Bogan, Brown, Gluck, opera, Suggs 6 Brooks, Brough, Lasser 7 Beavers, Dresser, Erdrich 8 Fletcher, Mandrell 10 Allbritton
composer: Gustave Charpentier
in French: 6 Eloise
locale: 6 Canada 7 Alberta
soprano: 4 Irma
__ & Louise: 6 Thelma
__-Louise Parker: 4 Mary
Louisiana: 5 state
city: 5 Houma 6 Gretna, Harvey, Kenner, Monroe, Ruston 7 Laplace, Marrero, Slidell, Sulphur 8 Metairie 9 Chalmette, Lafayette, New Iberia, Opelousas, Terrytown 10 Alexandria, Baton Rouge, New Orleans, Shreveport
cuisine: 5 Cajun 6 Creole
Indian: 5 Caddo 7 Atakapa, Washita 8 Ouachita
neighbor: 5 Texas 8 Arkansas
nickname: 10 Bayou State
once: 3 ter. 4 terr. 9 territory
parish: 6 Acadia
politician: 4 Long 8 Huey Long
port: 10 Baton Rouge, New Orleans
region: 5 bayou
school: 3 LSU, LTU 6 Tulane 9 Grambling
state beverage: 4 milk
state bird: 7 pelican
state crustacean: 8 crawfish
state flower: 8 magnolia
state freshwater fish: 10 white perch
state gemstone: 5 agate
state insect: 8 honeybee
state mammal: 9 black bear
state reptile: 9 alligator
state wildflower: 4 iris
Louisiana Purchase: 7 musical
composer: Irving Berlin
part: 3 Ark., Kan., Neb., Wyo. 4 Colo., Iowa, Minn., Miss., Mont., N. Dak., Nebr., Okla., S. Dak. 6 Kansas 7 Montana, Wyoming 8 Arkansas, Colorado, Missouri, Nebraska, Oklahoma 9 Minnesota
Louisiana State
conference: 3 SEC
locale: 10 Baton Rouge
Louisiana Tech
athletes: 8 Bulldogs
conference: 3 WAC
locale: 6 Ruston
Louis IX: 5 saint
Louis, Joe: 5 boxer
foe: 4 Baer, Conn, Farr, Mann, Nova 5 Godoy, McCoy, Musto, Roper, Simon 6 Burman, Pastor 7 Al McCoy, Charles, Dorazio, Galento, Lou Nova, Walcott 8 Abe Simon 9 Billy Conn, Bob Pastor, Buddy Baer, Jack Roper, Mauriello, Red Burman, Schmeling, Tommy Farr, Tony Musto
milieu: 4 ring
Louis Quatorze: 3 roi 5 style
see also French
__ Louis Stevenson: 6 Robert
Louisville: 4 city, town
annual event: 5 Derby
athletes: 9 Cardinals
county: 9 Jefferson
locale: 3 Ken. 8 Kentucky
river: 4 Ohio
Louis XIV: 3 roi
see also French
Louis XVI: 3 roi
wife: 5 Marie
lounge: 3 bar, bum, lag, lie, pub, sit, tap 4 bask, club, dive, idle, laze, loaf, loll, rest, sofa, spot 5 couch, divan, lobby, relax 6 bistro, dawdle, loiter, lollop, parlor, repose, saloon, slouch, sprawl, tavern 7 barroom, club car, goof off, recline, saunter, seating, taproom 8 club room, drinkery, hideaway, kill time, lallygag, lie about, pass time, rest area, restroom, taphouse 9 goldbrick, greenroom, hang loose, mezzanine, reception, waste time 10 hang around, public room, take it easy
chair: 6 chaise
cocktail ~: 3 bar 6 lounge, saloon
ender: 4 wear
entertainment: 4 band 5 combo
lizard: 5 idler 8 parasite
lounge __: 5 chair 6 lizard
__ lounge: 6 chaise
lounger: 4 robe 5 drone 6 loafer 7 dawdler, laggard
loungewear: 6 caftan, kaftan 7 pajamas
Loungin (1996 song)
artist: LL Cool J
lounging: 5 lying 6 at ease 7 relaxed, resting 8 reposing 9 incumbent
loup-__: 5 garou
loupe: 4 lens 6 ocular, viewer 7 monocle 8 eyeglass, eyepiece 9 magnifier
user: 7 jeweler 8 engraver, lapidary 9 craftsman 10 gemologist, horologist, watchmaker
lour: 5 frown, scowl 6 gloomy
Lourdes
author: Émile Zola
city near ~: 3 Pau
__ Lou Retton: 4 Mary
louse: 3 bug, bum, cad, nit 4 heel 5 aphid, aphis, cooty, knave, scamp, sneak, swine 6 bad guy, cootie, insect, isopod 7 crumbum, screw up, spoiler, stinker 8 parasite 9 miscreant, no-goodnik
egg: 3 nit

up: 3 err, mar 4 goof, ruin 5 botch, cross, spite, wreck 6 boggle, bungle, foozle, fumble, mess up, muddle 7 butcher 9 mismanage
__ Louse: 3 To a
louse-up
see error
lousy: 3 low 4 base, grim, mean, punk, sick, thin, vile, weak 5 awful, cheap, dirty, woful 6 faulty, feeble, horrid, no good, odious, rotten, shoddy, skimpy, stinky, two-bit, woeful 7 harmful, ill-done, lacking, vicious 8 disliked, God-awful, slovenly 9 third-rate, unpopular, unwelcome 10 fourth-rate, inadequate, outrageous, second-rate
be ~: 5 stink
with: 4 gobs, lots, rife, tons 5 heaps, piles, scads 6 oodles, untold 7 no end of, profuse, teeming, umpteen 8 numerous 9 plentiful 10 numberless
(with): 7 replete 8 abundant
see also awful
lout: 2 ox 3 ape, cad, lug, oaf 4 boor, bozo, clod, jerk 5 brute, chump, churl, klutz, looby, rowdy, swine, yahoo 6 duffer, galoot, lubber, lummox, wampus 7 boggler, botcher, bumbler, bumpkin, bungler, fumbler, galloot, palooka 9 blunderer, harebrain, vulgarian 10 clodhopper, stumblebum
in Britain: 3 yob
loutish: 4 loud, rude 5 crude, dense, gawky, gross, gruff, rough 6 clumsy, coarse, oafish, ornery, rustic, vulgar 7 bearish, bestial, boorish, doltish, gawkish, ill-bred, raffish, swinish, uncouth 8 barbaric, bungling, churlish, cloddish, clownish, impolite 9 graceless, ungallant, unrefined 10 indecorous, uncultured, uneducated, ungracious, unmannerly, unpolished
louver: 4 slat, slit, vent 6 outlet 7 opening 8 aperture
l'Ouverture country: 5 Haiti
Louvre: 5 musée 6 museum
annex architect: 3 Pei 5 I.M. Pei
display: 3 art 4 Nike, oils 8 Mona Lisa
locale: 5 Paris 6 France
lovable: 5 sweet 6 cuddly, genial 7 amiable, angelic, darling, snuggly, winning, winsome 8 adorable, alluring, charming, engaging, fetching, friendly, pleasing, precious 9 agreeable, angelical, appealing, covetable, desirable, endearing, ravishing 10 attractive, bewitching, cuddlesome, delightful, enchanting, entrancing
make ~: 6 endear
lovage: 4 herb
kin: 7 parsley
love: 3 hug, woo 4 beau, dear, Eros, feel, kiss, like, lust, zero 5 adore, amity, amour, ardor, court, deify, enjoy, fancy, flame, go for, honey, lover, prize, spark, swain 6 admire, caress, cosset, cuddle, dote on, esteem, fervor, fiancé, gone on, liking, prefer, regard, relish, revere, soothe, suitor, virtue 7 care for, cherish, cling to, darling, dear one, embrace, emotion, fall for, fiancée, idolize, long for, passion, rapture, regards, revel in, romance, worship 8 devotion, dote upon, fidelity, fondness, hold dear, paramour, soft spot, treasure, venerate, yearning 9 adoration, affection, betrothed, boyfriend, care about, delight in, enjoyment, hankering, inamorata, inamorato, luxuriate, sentiment, valentine 10 admiration, allegiance, attachment, bridegroom, friendship, girlfriend, high regard, honeybunch, partiality, sweetheart, sweetie pie, tenderness
and kisses: 7 devoirs 9 greetings 10 best wishes, good wishes
avenger of unrequited ~: 7 Anteros, Anterus
ender: 4 bird, lock, lorn, seat, sick
feast: 5 agape
fill with ~: 6 enamor, endear
god: 4 Amor, Eros 5 Cupid 8 amoretto
Greek ~ goddess: 9 Aphrodite
handles: 3 fat 4 flab
Hindu god of: 4 Kama
in ~: 4 gaga 5 crazy 7 amorous, far gone, hugging, smitten 8 enamored 10 dreamy-eyed
in French: 5 amour
in Italian: 5 amore
in Latin: 4 amor
in ~ old-style: 4 smit
in Spanish: 4 amor
in ~ with: 6 keen on
letter: 10 billet doux
Norse ~ goddess: 5 Freya
of life: 2 go 3 pep, zip 4 élan 5 gusto, oomph, punch, spice, verve 6 ginger, relish, spirit 7 passion, sparkle 8 appetite, vitality 10 enthusiasm, exuberance, heartiness
old-style: 5 leman
play at ~: 3 toy 4 vamp 5 flirt, tease 6 trifle 8 coquette
puppy ~: 5 ardor, crush 8 devotion, fondness 9 affection 10 admiration, attachment 11 infatuation
Roman ~ goddess: 5 Venus
seat: 4 sofa 5 couch 7 seating 9 furniture
starter: 4 lady, true
story: 5 novel 7 romance
symbol: 5 heart
to cynics: 5 blind
too much: 4 dote 6 obsess
what ~ may mean: 4 zero
where ~ means nothing: 6 tennis
love __: 3 bug, set 4 game, knot, nest, seat, vine 5 apple, beads, feast, match 6 potion
love-__ relationship: 4 hate
__ love: 5 puppy, tough
__ love!: 4 I'm in
Love: 4 Mike 5 Davis 6 Bessie 7 Darlene 8 Courtney
Love __: 4 Land, Me Do, Zone 5 Bites, Child, Grows, Hurts, Power, Shack, Story, Train, You So 6 Affair, Stinks
Love __ Andy Hardy: 5 Finds
Love __ Around: 5 Is All
Love __ Battlefield: 3 Is a
Love __ Elevator: 4 in an
Love __ Find a Way: 4 Will
Love __ Hurtin' Thing: 3 is a
Love __ In: 6 Walked
Love __ in the Sand: 7 Letters
Love __ leave it!: 4 it or
Love __ Leave Me: 4 Me or
Love __ Madly: 3 Her
Love __ Many Splendored Thing: 3 Is a
Love __ neighbor: 3 thy
Love __ Number Nine: 6 Potion
Love __ of J. Alfred Prufrock, The: 4 Song
Love __ Rocks: 5 on the
Love __ Rooftop: 3 on a
Love __, The: 3 Bug 4 Boat 5 I Lost 6 Parade
Love __ the Air: 4 Is in
Love __ the Ruins: 5 Among
Love __ Two-Way Street: 3 on a
Love __ you need: 5 is all
__ Love: 3 Bad, Big, Mad, Our 4 Baby, Be My, Cool, Hula, Is It, Lady, More, Real, So in, True, Your 5 April, Crazy, First, I Feel, I Need, Irish, Puppy, Sea of, Stone, Sweet, We Got, Young 6 Secret, Stoned 7 Burning, Endless, Muskrat, Without
Love Actually (2003 film)
cast: Hugh Grant, Keira Knightley, Liam Neeson, Alan Rickman, Emma Thompson
__ Love a Duck: 4 Lord
Love Affair (1994 film)
cast: Warren Beatty, Annette Bening, Katharine Hepburn, Garry Shandling
__ Love Again: 4 I'm in
Love Among the Cannibals
author: Wright Morris
Love and Affection (1990 song)
artist: Nelson
Love and Basketball (2000 film)
cast: Omar Epps, Dennis Haysbert, Sanaa Lathan, Alfre Woodard
Love and Death (1975 film)
cast: Woody Allen, Diane Keaton
director: Woody Allen
Love and Friendship
author: Alison Lurie
Love and Marriage (1955 song)
artist: Dinah Shore, Frank Sinatra
composer: Jimmy Van Heusen, Sammy Cahn
love apple: 5 fruit 6 tomato
love at first __: 5 sight
Love at First Bite (1979 film)
cast: Richard Benjamin, George Hamilton, Susan Saint James
director: Stan Dragoti
love-beads wearer: 5 hippy 6 hippie 8 longhair
__ Love Belongs..., The: 4 One I
lovebird: 3 pet 5 cooer 10 sweetheart
Love Bites (1988 song)
artist: Def Leppard
Love Boat, The (ABC sitcom)
cast: Fred Grandy (Yeoman-Purser Gopher Smith)
Bernie Kopell (Dr. Adam Bricker)
Ted Lange (Bartender Isaac Washington)
Gavin MacLeod (Capt. Merrill Stubing)
Lauren Tewes (Cruise Director Julie McCoy)
locale: 5 at sea, liner 6 cruise
stop: 3 POC 10 port of call
Love Boat: The Next Wave
captain: 5 Urich
Love Bug: 2 VW 3 car 6 Herbie 10 automobile, Volkswagen
Love Bug, The (1969 film)
cast: Buddy Hackett, Dean Jones, Michele Lee
__ Love Call: 6 Indian
Love Came to Me (1962 song)
artist: Dion
Love Can Build a Bridge (1990 song) artist: Judds
Love Child (1968 song)
artist: Supremes
love conquers __: 3 all
Love, Courtney
band: 4 Hole
spouse: Kurt Cobain
Lovecraft, H.P.: 6 writer
like ~ stories: 4 eery 5 eerie
loved: 4 dear 5 sweet 7 darling 8 precious
one: 3 pet 4 dear, idol, love 7 darling 10 sweetheart
Loved him, __ her: 5 hated
Loved One, The
author: Evelyn Waugh
__ Loved You: 3 If I
Love for Sale
composer: Cole Porter
Love for Three Oranges, The
composer: Sergei Prokofiev
Love Grows (1970 song)
artist: Edison Lighthouse
Love Hangover (1976 song)
artist: Diana Ross
__ Love Has Gone: 5 Where
Love Her __: 5 Madly
__ Love Her: 4 And I
__ Love Hewitt: 8 Jennifer
Love III, Davis: 6 golfer
Love I Lost, The (1973 song)
artist: Harold Melvin and the Blue Notes
__ Love I'm After: 3 It's
love-in: 7 protest
Love in __: 5 a Taxi, Bloom
Love in a Cold Climate
author: Nancy Mitford
Love in a Life
author: Robert Browning
Love in an Elevator (1989 song)
artist: Aerosmith
Love in the Afternoon (1957 film)
cast: Maurice Chevalier, Gary Cooper, Audrey Hepburn
director: Billy Wilder
Love in the Ruins
author: Walker Percy
Love Is (1993 song)
artist: Brian McKnight, Vanessa Williams
Love Is a __-Splendored Thing: 4 Many
Love Is a Battlefield (1983 song)
artist: Pat Benatar
Love Is a Golden Ring (1957 song)
artist: Frankie Laine
Love Is a Hurtin' Thing (1966 song)
artist: Lou Rawls

Love Is All Around (1968 song)
artist: Troggs
Love Is a Many Splendored Thing: 4 film, song
artist: Four Aces
cast: William Holden, Jennifer Jones
Love Is a Wonderful Thing (1991 song)
artist: Michael Bolton
Love Is Blue (1968 song)
artist: Paul Mauriat
Love Is Eternal
author: Irving Stone
Love Is Forever (1986 song)
artist: Billy Ocean
Love Is Here and Now You're Gone (1967 song)
artist: Supremes
Love Is Here to Stay
composer: George Gershwin, Ira Gershwin
Love Is in Control (1982 song)
artist: Donna Summer
Love Is Like an Itching in My Heart (1966 song)
artist: Supremes
Love is not __: 4 a toy
Love Is Not All: 4 poem
author: Edna St. Vincent Millay
Love Is Strange (1967 song)
artist: Peaches and Herb
Love Is Stronger Than Pride
artist: Sade
Love Is Sweeping the Country
composer: George Gershwin, Ira Gershwin
Lovejoy: 5 Frank
Lovelace: 3 Ada 7 Richard
Lovelace, Richard: 4 poet 7 English
work: To Althea from Prison
To Lucasta, Going to the Wars
Loveland: 4 city, town
locale: 8 Colorado
loveless: 3 icy 4 cold, cool 5 hated 6 frigid 7 loathed 8 despised, detested, disliked, unwanted
Loveless: 5 Patty
love-letter letters: 4 SWAK
Love Letters (song)
artist: Elvis Presley, Ketty Lester
Love Letters in the Sand (song)
artist: Pat Boone
composer: J. Fred Coots
love-lies-bleeding: 5 plant 6 flower
Loveliest of Trees
author: A.E. Housman
loveliness: 5 charm, grace 6 allure, beauty, glamor 7 glamour 8 elegance, radiance 9 good looks
Lovell, James: 9 astronaut
portrayer: Tom Hanks
lovely
see wonderful
Lovely __, meter maid...: 4 Rita
__ lovely as a tree: 5 A poem
Lovely Day for Creve Coeur, A
author: Tennessee Williams
__ Lovely Day Today: 4 It's a
Lovely to Look At
composer: Dorothy Fields, Jerome Kern
Love Machine (1975 song)
artist: Miracles
Love Me (song)
artist: Elvis Presley, Mase
__ Love Me: 5 Do You, If You
Love Me Do (1964 song)
artist: Beatles
Love Me for a Reason (1974 song)
artist: Osmonds
Love Me or Leave Me
artist: Ruth Etting
Love Me Tender
artist: Elvis Presley
Love Me Tonight (1932 film)
cast: Maurice Chevalier, Myrna Loy, Jeanette MacDonald
director: Rouben Mamoulian
music: Lorenz Hart, Richard Rodgers
tune: 4 Mimi
Love Me Tonight (1969 song)
artist: Tom Jones
Love Me With All Your Heart (1964 song)
artist: Ray Charles Singers
Love Nest and Other Stories, The
author: Ring Lardner
__ love, not war: 4 make
Love of Four Colonels, The
author: Peter Ustinov
Love of Life (CBS): 4 soap 9 soap opera
__ Love of the Game: 3 For
Love on a Dark Street
author: Irwin Shaw
Love on a Rooftop (ABC sitcom)
cast: Judy Carne (Julie Willis) Peter Deuel (David Willis)
Love on the Rocks (1980 song)
artist: Neil Diamond
Love or Let Me Be Lonely (1970 song)
artist: Friends of Distinction
__ love or money: 3 for
love-potion effect: 5 spell
Love Potion Number Nine (1964 song)
artist: Searchers
Love Power (1987 song)
artist: Dionne Warwick, Jeffrey Osborne
lover
boy: 4 rake, roué 5 flirt, Romeo, swain, wooer 7 Don Juan, gallant, playboy, swinger 8 Casanova, hedonist, lothario, prodigal, sybarite 9 libertine
combining form: 4 -phil 5 -phile
forsake a ~: 4 dump, jilt 5 ditch, leave 6 desert 7 abandon 8 run out on 9 cast aside, throw over
lucre ~: 7 Scrooge 8 tightwad 9 skinflint 10 cheapskate, pinchpenny
opposite: 5 hater
Roxane ~: 6 Cyrano
see also sweetheart
Lover __ Back: 4 Come
__ Lover: 3 Hey 4 Be My, Easy 5 Dream
Loverboy (1984 song)
artist: Billy Ocean
Lovergirl (1985 song)
artist: Teena Marie
Lover in Me, The (1988 song)
artist: Sheena Easton
Loveroot
author: Erica Jong
Lover Please (1962 song)
artist: Clyde McPhatter
lovers' __: 4 knot, lane
Lovers and Idol
sculptor: Erté
Lovers and Other Strangers (1970 film)
cast: Bea Arthur, Bonnie Bedelia, Anne Meara, Gig Young
director: Cy Howard
Lover's Concerto, A (1965 song)
artist: Toys
Lover's Question, A (1958 song)
artist: Clyde McPhatter
Lovers Who Wander (1962 song)
artist: Dion
Lover, The
author: Harold Pinter
L'Overture: 9 Toussaint
Love's __ Lost: 7 Labour's
Love's Alchemy
author: John Donne
__ Loves Angela: 5 Aaron
Love's Been a Little Bit Hard on Me (1982 song)
artist: Juice Newton
Love's Comedy
author: Henrik Ibsen
loveseat: 6 settee
lovesick: 4 gaga, lorn 6 doting
Love's Labour's Lost
author: William Shakespeare
__ Loves Mambo: 4 Papa
__ loves me...: 3 She
Loves Me Like a Rock (1973 song)
artist: Paul Simon
Loves Music, Loves to Dance
author: Mary Higgins Clark
Love Sneakin' Up on You (1994 song)
artist: Bonnie Raitt
__ Loves of Dobie Gillis, The: 4 Many
Loves of Harry Dancer, The
author: Lawrence Sanders
Love Somebody (1984 song)
artist: Rick Springfield
Love Song (song)
artist: Anne Murray, Cure, Tesla
__ Love Song: 5 Pagan
Love Song of J. Alfred Prufrock, The: 4 poem
author: T.S. Eliot
Love Songs
author: Lawrence Sanders, Sara Teasdale
__ Love Songs: 5 Silly
Love So Right (1976 song)
artist: Bee Gees
Love Story: 4 film 5 novel
author: Erich Segal
cast: Ali MacGraw, Ray Milland, Ryan O'Neal
composer: Francis Lai
Love Story (1971 song)
artist: Andy Williams
__ loves ya, baby?: 3 Who
__ Loves You: 3 She
Love Takes Time (song)
artist: Mariah Carey, Orleans
__ Love, The: 4 Man I, One I 5 Art of, Way of, Way to
Love the One You're With (1970 song)
artist: Stephen Stills
Love the World __: 4 Away
Love thy neighbor: 5 adage, credo, motto
Love to Love You Baby (1975 song)
artist: Donna Summer
Love Touch (1986 song)
artist: Rod Stewart
Love Train (1973 song)
artist: O'Jays
Lovett, Lyle ex: Julia Roberts
Love Walked In
composer: George Gershwin, Ira Gershwin
Love Will Conquer All (1986 song)
artist: Lionel Richie
Love Will Find a Way (1978 song)
artist: Pablo Cruise
Love Will Keep Us Together (1975 song)
artist: Captain & Tennille
Love Will Lead You Back (1990 song)
artist: Taylor Dayne
Love Will Never Do (1990 song)
artist: Janet Jackson
Love Will Save the Day (1988 song)
artist: Whitney Houston
Love Will Turn You Around (1982 song)
artist: Kenny Rogers
Lovey Childs
author: John O'Hara
lovey-dovey: 5 mushy 6 tender 7 amorous, mawkish 8 romantic
__ Love You: 3 P.S. I 5 Baby I
__ Love You in My Dreams: 3 I'll
Love You Inside Out (1979 song)
artist: Bee Gees
Love You Save, The (1970 song)
artist: Jackson 5
__ Love You So: 4 And I
Love Zone (1986 song)
artist: Billy Ocean
loving: 3 cup 4 dear, fond, font, kind, warm 5 close, loyal, sweet 6 ardent, caring, doting, filial, kindly, liking, tender 7 adoring, amatory, amiable, amorous, anxious, bound up, cordial, devoted, earnest, fervent, kissing, lenient, valuing, zealous 8 admiring, attached, enamored, faithful, friendly, generous, intimate, parental, reverent, romantic 9 amatorial, attentive, concerned, unselfish 10 benevolent, delightful, expressive, idolatrous, infatuated, passionate, respecting, solicitous, thoughtful, warmhearted, worshipful
combining form: 4 phil- 5 philo- 6 -philic
touch: 3 hug, pat, pet 6 caress, cuddle, stroke 7 embrace
loving __: 3 cup
Loving: 4 soap 9 soap opera
loving cup: 5 award 6 trophy
feature: 3 ear 4 base 6 plaque
__ Loving, The: 5 Art of
Lovin' Spoonful
lead singer: John Sebastian
song: Darling Be Home Soon (1967)
Daydream (1966)
Did You Ever Have to Make Up Your Mind? (1966)
Do You Believe in Magic (1965)
Nashville Cats (1966)
Rain on the Roof (1966)
Six O'Clock (1967)
Summer in the City (1966)
You Didn't Have to Be So Nice (1965)

Lovin' You (1975 song)
artist: Minnie Riperton
Lovitz: **3** Jon
low: **3** ill, moo **4** base, bass, deep, evil, gear, mean, mopy, poor, sick, soft, vile, weak **5** bated, cheap, crass, crude, faint, fed up, gross, lousy, mangy, mopey, muted, nasty, piano, quiet, scant, seamy, short, slump, squat, under **6** abject, ailing, coarse, common, crumby, feeble, gloomy, humble, hushed, lesser, mangey, meager, menial, modest, nether, on sale, paltry, poorly, scurvy, shoddy, sickly, sleazy, sneaky, sordid, sparse, sunken, unfair, unwell, vulgar, yellow **7** bargain, beastly, beneath, bestial, crushed, cut-rate, ignoble, ill-bred, knavish, muffled, nominal, reduced, servile, shallow, sinking, slashed, squalid, squatty, stunted, subdued, uncouth **8** baseborn, crouched, dampened, deadened, degraded, depleted, depraved, guttural, indecent, inferior, marginal, moderate, murmured, plebeian, stricken, subsided, trifling, uncostly, unworthy **9** dastardly, deficient, execrable, in the pits, malicious, prostrate, toned down, unethical, whispered **10** despicable, down and out, economical, inadequate, indelicate, indisposed, lamentable, marked down, reasonable, rock-bottom, scurrilous, spiritless, turned down, unbecoming, unelevated, virtueless
as ~ as it gets: **5** worst
below ~: **3** dry **5** empty, spent **6** devoid **8** depleted **9** exhausted
blow: **4** foul **6** insult **9** cheap shot
bring ~: **4** bust, ruin **5** abase, crush **6** defeat, demean, demote, humble, reduce, weaken **7** conquer, deflate, degrade **8** bankrupt, pull down, vanquish **9** humiliate, knock down, overpower, pauperize, subjugate **10** impoverish
ender: **3** boy **4** ball, born, bred, brow, down, land, life **5** lands **6** lander
go ~: **5** slump
high and ~: **7** all over **9** all around **10** everywhere
hold ~: **4** hate **5** abhor **6** detest, loathe **7** despise, dislike **8** execrate **9** abominate
in French: **3** bas
keep a ~ profile: **4** hide, lurk **6** hole up **9** take cover
keep expenses ~: **4** save **6** scrape, scrimp **8** conserve, roll back **9** economize **10** cut corners
laid ~: **3** ill **5** unfit **7** invalid **9** unhealthy
lay ~: **5** floor, level **7** flatten
lie ~: **4** hide, wait **5** squat **6** hole up **9** take cover
look high and ~: **4** hunt, seek **5** scour **6** search **7** ransack, rummage
on: **7** needing, short of
on ~: **9** simmering
one: **3** cad **5** snake
point: **5** abysm, floor, nadir **6** bottom, trough
spirits: **4** funk **5** blues, gloom **8** glumness **10** depression, melancholy
voice: **3** hum **4** alto, bass, deep **5** basso **6** breath, mumble, murmur, mutter **7** whisper
see also gloomy
low __: **4** beam, blow, gear, road, tide **6** comedy **7** hurdles
low-__: **3** cal, end, fat, key, res **4** ball, carb, cost, down, rate, rise, tech, test **5** count, grade, level, lying, power **6** budget, income, minded, priced
low-__ diet: **4** carb
low-__ district: **4** rent
low-__ mark: **5** water
__ low: **3** lay, lie
Low: **4** Seth **8** Juliette
lowball: **4** game **8** card game
lowborn: **4** mean, poor **6** humble, simple **7** obscure **8** plebeian, untitled
lowboy: **5** chest **6** bureau **9** furniture
lowbred: **4** loud **5** crass, crude **6** brassy, brazen, coarse, common, vulgar **7** boorish **8** churlish, ignorant, impolite, unseemly **9** rough-hewn **10** boisterous, indecorous, unbecoming, unladylike, unpolished
lowbrow: **5** crass, yahoo **8** barbaric **9** barbarian, barbarous **10** uneducated
love: **6** kitsch
low-cal: **4** diet, lite **5** light
low-class: **4** non-U
low-cost: **5** cheap **6** on sale **7** bargain, cut-rate **8** moderate **9** half-price **10** economical, reasonable
Low Countries
locale: **3** Eur., Lux. **4** Belg., Neth. **6** Europe **7** Belgium, Holland **10** Luxembourg **11** Netherlands
lowdown: **4** base, dirt, dope, info, mean, news, poop **5** facts, rumor, scoop, truth **6** notice, skinny **7** account **8** the goods **9** real story
get the ~: **5** learn
give the ~: **3** cue **4** leak, talk, tell, warn **5** brief, spill, steer **6** advise, impart, let out, reveal, tip off **7** caution, confide, divulge, give out, lay bare **8** disclose
low-down: **4** mean, ugly **5** nasty **6** shabby, sordid, unjust, wicked **8** degraded, wretched **10** undeserved
Lowdown (1976 song)
artist: Boz Scaggs
Lowe: **3** Jim, Rob **4** Chad, Nick **5** Chris **6** Edmund
Lowe, Chad: **5** actir
spouse: Hilary Swank
Lowell: **3** Amy **4** city, town **5** Carey **6** Robert **7** Sherman
locale: **4** Mass.
Lowell, Amy: **4** poet
work: A Dome of Many-Coloured Glass
Lilacs
Patterns
Sword Blades and Poppy Seed
What's O'Clock
Lowell, Carey
spouse: Richard Gere
Lowell, James Russell: **4** poet **6** editor, writer
work: The Biglow Papers
The Vision of Sir Launfal
Lowell, Robert: **4** poet
work: Day by Day
The Dolphin
Land of Unlikeness
Lord Weary's Castle
The Mills of the Kavanaughs
The Old Glory
Lowenbrau: **4** beer
alternative: *see* beer
low-end: **5** cheap **7** chintzy **9** downscale
lower: **3** cut, dim, dip, ebb, sag **4** clip, curb, down, drop, fall, less, mute, pare, sink, sulk **5** abase, abate, berth, couch, decry, deign, demit, droop, frown, glare, minor, prune, relax, scowl, shave, slash, stoop, under **6** bemean, debase, demean, demote, ground, humble, junior, lessen, lesser, modify, nether, reduce, second, shrink, soften, weaken **7** beneath, curtail, cut back, cut down, decline, deflate, degrade, depress, descend, detract, detrude, devalue, dwindle, fall off, let down, reduced, set down, smaller, subside, tail off **8** belittle, cast down, close out, decrease, diminish, discount, disgrace, downsize, inferior, lessened, mark down, minimize, moderate, modulate, peter out, pull down, push down, roll back, submerge, take down, tone down, write off **9** bring down, curtailed, decreased, devaluate, downgrade, humiliate, pared down, scale down, secondary, subjacent **10** bush-league, condescend, deescalate, depreciate, diminished, underneath, undervalue
class: **4** herd, scum **5** dregs **6** masses, rabble **8** riffraff **9** commoners, hoi polloi, peasantry **10** underworld
ender: **4** case, most
get ~: **4** drop, wane **6** lessen, recede **7** decline, dwindle, retreat, subside, tail off **8** decrease, diminish, fall back, slack off
in esteem: **5** shame **6** defile, demean, vilify **7** cheapen, degrade, deprave, devalue, profane, put down, vitiate **8** disgrace, dishonor, take down **9** humiliate, shoot down, undermine **10** adulterate
keep a stiff ~ lip: **4** fume, mope, sulk **5** brood, frown **6** glower
oneself: **5** deign, kneel, stoop **6** see fit **9** patronize **10** condescend
prefix: **3** sub- **5** infra-
than: **5** neath, under **7** beneath **10** underneath
lower __: **5** berth, class, house
Lower __ Side: **4** East
Lower California: **4** Baja
lowercase: **5** small **9** minuscule
lower-class: **4** base **6** coarse, common, humble, vulgar **8** baseborn, plebeian **9** unrefined **10** uncultured
__ Lowered the Boom: **6** Clancy
lowering: **3** cut, dim, dip, low **4** dark, dour, drop, fall, glum, gray, grey, grim **5** angry, black, bleak, dusky, mirky, murky, surly **6** cloudy, dismal, dreary, gloomy, sullen **7** cutback, decline, descent, looming, ominous **8** brooding, darkened, darkling, frowning, menacing, minatory, overcast, scowling, sinister **9** impending, long-faced, pitch-dark, tenebrous, unsmiling **10** chapfallen, lugubrious, melancholy
lowermost: **6** bottom
Lowe, Rob: **5** actor
brother: **4** Chad
TV: The West Wing
lowery: **4** dark **6** gloomy
lowest: **4** last **5** basal, least, nadir **6** bottom **7** minimal, minimum **8** littlest
lowest form of wit: **3** pun
low-fat: **4** diet, lite, skim **5** light
low-grade: **3** low **4** poor **6** common **8** inferior **10** second-rate
low-key: **4** calm, cool, soft **5** muted, quiet, sober, staid, stoic **6** at ease, folksy, mellow, placid, sedate, serene, subtle **7** amiable, at peace, equable, muffled, pacific, relaxed, stoical, subdued, unmoved **8** amicable, carefree, composed, fireside, laid-back, moderate, peaceful, softened, soft-sell, tranquil **9** collected, easygoing, impassive, quiescent, temperate, toned down, unexcited, unruffled **10** nonchalant, played down, restrained, unagitated, untroubled
lowland: **3** bog **4** flat, mesa, moor **5** campo, heath, marsh, plain, swale, swamp **6** meadow, morass, pampas, steppe, tundra, valley **7** plateau, prairie **8** savannah **9** champaign
South African ~: **4** vlei
Low-Lands
author: Thomas Pynchon
lowlands hazard: **5** flood
lowlife: **3** cad, cur **4** heel, punk, scum, toad **5** creep, knave, rogue, scamp, slime, swine, yahoo **6** bad guy **7** villain **9** miscreant, reprobate, scoundrel
hang out with ~s: **4** slum
lowliness: **7** modesty **8** humility, meekness
lowly: **4** base, mean, meek, mild, poor **5** plain **6** common, docile, gentle, humble, menial, modest, simple **7** average, dutiful, ignoble, mundane, obscure, prosaic, servile **8** baseborn, cast down, everyday, inferior, ordinary, plebeian, retiring **9** prosaical **10** obsequious, submissive, unassuming
low-lying area: **3** bog, fen **4** dale, vale **5** swale, swamp **6** hollow, valley **8** wetlands
low-minded: **4** foul, lewd, rank **5** bawdy, crass, crude, dirty, gross, lurid **6** coarse, filthy, ribald, smutty, sordid, vulgar **7** ignoble, immoral,

obscene, raunchy, uncouth **8** depraved, improper, indecent, unseemly **9** dissolute, offensive, revolting **10** disgusting
lowness: 5 depth **7** crudity
low-pH: 6 acidic
compound: 4 acid
low-pitched: 4 bass, deep **5** quiet
__-low poker: 4 high
low-power period: 6 dim-out
low-pressure: 6 breezy, casual **8** informal
low-priced: 5 cheap **7** bargain, cut-rate, good buy, nominal **8** moderate **10** economical, reasonable
__ low profile: 5 keep a
low-quality: 3 off **4** poor **5** cheap **6** cheapo **8** el cheapo, inferior
low-ranking: 4 poor **5** minor, small **6** humble, modest **7** nominal **8** marginal **9** secondary **10** bush-league, negligible
Lowry: 3 AFB **7** Malcolm
low-spirited: 3 sad **4** blue, glum **5** woful **6** gloomy, morose, somber, woeful **7** doleful, joyless, unhappy **8** dejected, downcast, troubled **9** bummed out, cheerless, heart-sick, miserable, saturnine, sorrowful, woebegone **10** chapfallen, dispirited, melancholy
__ Low, Sweet Chariot: 5 Swing
low-toned: 4 bass, deep
low-water __: 4 mark
lox: 4 fish, nova **6** salmon **9** appetizer
companion: 5 bagel
like ~: 5 salty
LOX: 4 fuel **10** propellant
user: 6 rocket
__ Loxy: 4 Foxy
loyal: 4 fast, firm, good, true **5** liege, sound, stout **6** ardent, loving, steady, trusty **7** devoted, dutiful, staunch **8** attached, constant, faithful, reliable, resolute, true-blue, yeomanly **9** allegiant, believing, dedicated, fraternal, patriotic, steadfast, unfailing **10** dependable, inviolable, unswerving, unwavering
be ~: 6 adhere, cleave **8** hold fast
be ~ to: 4 heed, mind, obey **6** follow **7** observe
not ~: 6 fickle **9** faithless, mercurial **10** capricious, changeable, coquettish, inconstant, unfaithful, unreliable
Loyale: 3 car **4** auto **6** Subaru **10** automobile
loyalist: 4 Tory **7** diehard, patriot **8** adherent, partisan
Loyal Order of __: 5 Moose
loyalty: 3 tie **4** bond, duty, zeal **5** ardor, faith, honor, troth, truth **6** fealty, homage **7** honesty, probity, support **8** devotion, fidelity, trueness **9** adherence, belonging, constancy, fixedness, integrity, obedience, sincerity **10** allegiance, attachment, dedication, patriotism, resolution, singleness, subjection, submission, trustiness
expect ~ from: 4 rely **5** trust **6** bank on, look to **7** count on, entrust **8** delegate, depend on, gamble on, rely upon **9** patronize
model of ~: 4 Enid
Loy, Myrna: 7 actress
costar: 4 Asta **6** Powell
film: The Bachelor and the Bobby-Soxer (1947)
Belles on Their Toes (1952)
The Best Years of Our Lives (1946)
Cheaper by the Dozen (1950)
A Connecticut Yankee (1931)
From the Terrace (1960)
The Great Ziegfeld (1936)
Love Me Tonight (1932)
Manhattan Melodrama (1934)
Mr. Blandings Builds His Dream House (1948)
The Red Pony (1949)
Test Pilot (1938)
The Thin Man (1934)
Too Hot to Handle (1938)
Topaze (1933)
Loyola: 6 school
athletes: 8 Ramblers
locale: 7 Chicago **8** Illinois
lozenge: 4 pill **6** cachou, pastil, tablet, troche **8** pastille **9** cough drop
LP: 4 disc, disk **5** album, vinyl **7** platter
feature: 4 hole **5** track **6** groove
holder: 5 liner **6** sleeve
make an ~: 5 press
needle: 6 stylus
needles: 5 styli
player: 4 hi-fi **5** phono **6** stereo
problem: 4 skip
speed: 3 rpm
spinner: 2 DJ **6** deejay **10** disk jockey
successor: 2 CD
surface: 4 side **5** A-side, B-side, side A, side B
type: 4 mono **6** stereo
L-P center: 3 MNO
LPGA
concern: 4 golf
member: 5 woman
LPN: 5 nurse
boss: 2 dr., MD
colleague: 2 RN
field: 3 med.
place: 2 ER, OR **3** ICU **4** hosp.
specialty: 3 TLC
L-Q filler: 4 MNOP
Lr: 10 lawrencium
__-L-Ration: 3 Ken
L. Ron: 7 Hubbard
LSAT
cousin: 3 GRE
creator: 3 ETS
__ L. Shirer: 7 William
LST part: 4 Ship, Tank **7** Landing
__ L. Sullivan: 4 John
LSU org: 3 SEC **4** NCAA
lt.: 3 off.
employer: 3 USA, USN **4** USCG, USMC
subordinate: 3 NCO, PFC, pvt., sgt.
superior: 3 cap., col, gen., maj. **4** capt.
trainer: 3 OCS, OTS **4** ROTC, USMA
Lt. __: 3 Col., Com., Gen., Gov. **5** Comdr.
lt. col.: 3 off.
subordinate: 3 maj., NCO, PFC, pvt., sgt. **7** cap.. capt.
superior: 3 gen.
ltd.
kin: 3 inc.
LTD: 3 car **4** auto, Ford **10** automobile
LTJG
part: 2 lt. **5** grade, lieut. **6** junior
subordinate: 3 CPO, ens.
ltr.: 4 init.
addendum: 2 p.s. **3** pps
handler: 2 PO **4** USPS
lt. yr.: 4 meas.
Lu: 4 elem. **7** element **8** lutetium
71 for ~: 4 at. no.
Luana: 6 Anders
Luanda: 4 city, town **7** capital
locale: 3 Ang. **6** Angola
tongue: 5 Bantu
Luang Prabang land: 4 Laos
luau: 4 meal **5** feast **6** spread **7** banquet, blowout
entertainment: 3 uke **4** hula **7** ukulele
fare: 3 pig, poi **4** taro **6** lau lau **8** mahimahi, roast pig
locale: 4 Maui, Oahu **5** Kauai **6** Hawaii **7** Waikiki **8** Honolulu
neckwear: 3 lei
oven: 3 imu
lubber
place: 6 ashore
starter: 4 land
see also ninny
lubberly: 4 dull **5** gawky, inept, thick **6** clumsy, klutzy, obtuse, stolid, stupid **7** awkward, gawkish **8** bungling, ungainly **9** maladroit **10** blundering
Lubbock: 4 city, town
athletes: 10 Red Raiders
locale: 5 Texas
school: 3 TTU **9** Texas Tech
lube
see lubricate
lube __: 3 job
__ Lube: 5 Jiffy
Lubec: 4 city, town
locale: 5 Maine
Lübeck: 4 city, port, town
locale: 7 Germany
Lubin: 6 Arthur
Lubitsch, Ernst: 8 director
film: Cluny Brown (1946)
Design for Living (1933)
Heaven Can Wait (1943)
The Merry Widow (1934)
Ninotchka (1939)
One Hour With You (1932)
The Shop Around the Corner (1940)
That Uncertain Feeling (1941)
To Be or Not to Be (1942)
Trouble in Paradise (1932)
Lublin: 4 city, town
locale: 6 Poland
Lubovitch: 3 Lar
lubricant: 3 oil, wax **5** salve **6** grease **7** coating **8** silicone
organic ~: 4 tear **5** sebum
textile ~: 5 olein **6** oleine
lubricate: 3 oil, wax **4** lard **5** bribe, cream, slick, smear **6** anoint, grease, smooth, tallow **9** embrocate
again: 5 reoil
lubricated: 4 oily **5** slick **6** greasy, smooth **8** slippery, unctuous
lubricious: 4 lewd, oily **6** greasy **8** slippery, uncurbed **10** capricious, licentious
lubricity: 4 lust, porn, smut, vice **7** abandon **8** impurity, lewdness, oiliness, ribaldry, salacity, waxiness **10** corruption
lubricous: 3 hot, icy **4** lewd, oily, waxy **5** crude, dirty, gross, oiled, randy, sleek, slick, soapy **6** coarse, filthy, glassy, glossy, greasy, impure, risqué, vulgar, wanton **7** buttery, goatish, immoral **8** prurient, slippery, slithery, unchaste, unctuous
Lubriderm: 6 lotion
alternative: 4 Keri **5** Curel, Nivea **6** Aveeno **7** Eucerin, Jergens, Pacquin
Luc: 6 Besson
Luca __ Robbia: 5 Della
Lucan: 4 poet **5** Roman
Lucania: 4 peak **5** mount **8** mountain
locale: 5 Yukon **6** Canada
Lucas: 4 Josh **5** Jerry **6** George, Robert, Tanner
Lucas, George: 8 director
film: American Graffiti (1973)
Star Wars (1977)
Star Wars Episode II: Attack of the Clones (2002)
Star Wars Episode III: Revenge of the Sith (2005)
Star Wars Episode I: The Phantom Menace (1999)
Star Wars Episode IV: A New Hope (1977)
Lucas, Jerry
milieu: 5 court
org.: 3 NBA
sport: 10 basketball
Lucci, Susan
role: 5 Erica
Luce: 5 Clare, Henry
colleague: 6 Hadden
publication: 4 Life, Time **7** Fortune
Luce, Clare Boothe: 6 writer
work: Child of the Morning
Kiss the Boys Goodbye
Margin for Error
Slam the Door Softly
Stuffed Shirts
The Women
lucent: 5 clear, light, nitid **7** beaming, radiant, shining **8** luminous, lustrous **9** brilliant
lucerne: 7 alfalfa
Lucerne: 4 lake
locale: 11 Switzerland
river: 5 Reuss
__-Luc Godard: 4 Jean
Luchino: 8 Visconti
Lucia: 4 Popp **5** saint
__ Lucia: 5 Santa
Lucia di Lammermoor: 5 opera
character: 5 Alisa **6** Arturo, Ashton, Enrico **7** Bucklaw, Edgardo **8** Normanno, Raimondo
composer: Gaetano Donizetti
setting: 8 Scotland
Luciano: 5 Lucky **9** Pavarotti
lucid: 4 cool, pure, sane **5** clear, gauzy, plain, right, sheer, sober, sound, vivid **6** bright, glassy, limpid, normal, simple **7** beaming, evident, graphic, lambent, legible,

logical, obvious, radiant, shining **8** all there, clear-cut, coherent, distinct, explicit, gleaming, knowable, luculent, luminous, lustrous, rational, readable, sensible, together, vitreous **9** brilliant, effulgent, graphical, graspable, refulgent, unblurred, unobscure **10** articulate, diaphanous, fathomable, reasonable
prefix for ~: **3** pel
lucidity: **3** wit **4** wits **6** reason, sanity **7** clarity
Lucie: **5** Arnaz
brother or dad: **4** Desi
lucifer: **5** match **7** lighter
Lucifer: **3** cat **5** angel, Devil, rebel, Satan, Yokum **6** Diablo **7** evil one **9** archangel, Beelzebub
forte: **4** evil
son: **5** Abner
Lucile: **6** Watson
Lucille: **4** Ball **6** Bremer **8** Fletcher
Lucille (song)
artist: Kenny Rogers, Little Richard
__ Lucille: **4** La-La
Lucinda: **6** Childs
Lucine: **5** Amara
Lucite: **5** resin **9** Plexiglas
Lucius: **4** pope **7** pontiff
luck: **3** hap, win **4** fate, lady, weal **5** break, fluke, karma, smile **6** chance, hazard, health, kismat, kismet, profit, stroke, toss-up, wealth **7** destiny, fortune, godsend, portion, success, triumph, victory **8** accident, big break, blessing, fortuity, occasion, windfall **9** advantage **10** fifty-fifty, in the cards, occurrence, prosperity
as ~ would have it: **8** by chance
bad ~: **4** blow, jinx, loss, pity **6** downer, hoodoo, mishap **7** reverse, setback, tragedy, undoing **8** distress **9** adversity, mischance **10** hard knocks, ill fortune, infelicity, misfortune
bad ~ old-style: **5** unhap
bring bad ~: **3** hex **4** jinx **5** curse
down on one's ~: **4** flat, poor **5** broke, needy **6** bad off, hard up, in need, in want **7** lacking, pinched **8** dirt poor, indigent, strapped **9** dead broke, desperate, destitute, flat broke, insolvent, moneyless, penniless **10** stone-broke, straitened
hard ~: **7** setback, trouble **8** bad break, calamity **9** adversity, mischance, suffering
Irish ~: **4** cess
out: **3** win **5** score **6** make it, thrive **7** prevail, prosper, triumph **8** flourish, get ahead, go places, make good
press one's ~: **4** dare, risk **6** gamble **8** chance it
starter: **3** pot
stretch of good ~: **3** run
luck __ draw: **5** of the
luck __ Irish: **5** of the
__ luck: **5** out of, tough
__ luck!: **5** Lotsa
__ luck?: **3** Any
Luck __ Lady: **3** Be a
__ Luck: **3** Bad, Pot **4** Lady, Pure **7** Sailor's
Luck and Pluck
author: Horatio Alger
__ luck charm: **4** good
__ Luck Club, The: **3** Joy
luckily: **7** happily **8** by chance
Luckinbill, Laurence
spouse: Lucie Arnaz
luckless: **4** poor **5** curst, hexed, sorry, woful **6** cursed, doomed, jinxed, woeful **7** accurst, hapless, ruinous, unblest, unhappy **8** accursed, ill-fated, wretched **9** ill-omened, unblessed, unfavored **10** disastrous, ill-starred
Luckman, Sid: **2** QB
sport: **8** football
Lucknow: **4** city, town
locale: **5** India
Luck of Roaring Camp, The
author: Bret Harte
luck of the __: **4** draw **5** Irish
Luck of the Draw (1991 song)
artist: Bonnie Raitt
lucky: **3** hot **4** well **5** blest, happy **6** benign, chance, golden, timely **7** blessed, charmed, favored, hopeful, on a roll, well-off **8** enviable **9** fortunate, on a streak, opportune, promising **10** auspicious, beneficial, felicitous, fortuitous, propitious, prosperous, successful, triumphant
be ~: **3** win **8** hit it big
break: **4** boon **5** fluke **6** chance **7** godsend **8** blessing, fortuity, windfall
if you're ~: **6** at best
leaf: **6** clover **8** shamrock
number: **5** seven
strike: **5** trove **10** mother lode
lucky __: **5** stiff
Lucky: **6** Vanous **7** Luciano
Lucky __: **3** Jim **4** Star
Lucky Charms: **6** cereal
competitor: ***see*** cereal
Lucky Day
author: Mary Higgins Clark
Lucky Jim
author: Kingsley Amis
Lucky Numbers (2000 film)
cast: Lisa Kudrow, Ed O'Neill, Tim Roth, John Travolta
director: Nora Ephron
Lucky Spot, The
author: Beth Henley
Lucky Star (1984 song)
artist: Madonna
__-Luc Picard: **4** Jean
lucrative: **4** good **5** sweet **6** paying **7** fatness, gainful **8** fruitful, well-paid **10** high-income, in the black, productive, profitable, successful, worthwhile
lucre
lover: **5** miser **7** Scrooge **8** tightwad **9** skinflint **10** cheapskate, pinchpenny
see also moolah
__ lucre: **6** filthy
Lucretia: **4** Mott
Lucretius: **4** poet **5** Roman **11** philosopher
work: On the Nature of Things
Lucrezia: **4** Bori **6** Borgia
Lucrezia Borgia
composer: Gaetano Donizetti
Lucrezia Floriani
author: George Sand
lucubrate: **3** dig **4** cram, toil **5** grind, learn, study, write **8** pore over **9** grind away
lucubration: **4** opus **5** essay, grind, paper, study, tract **6** thesis **7** writing **8** exegesis, headwork, treatise
luculent: **5** clear, lucid, sound **6** cogent, limpid **7** graphic, logical **8** manifest, rational **9** graphical, plausible **10** compelling, convincing, persuasive, reasonable
Lucy: **3** Liu **4** Ball **5** Ewing, Hayes, Stone **7** hominid, Lawless, Ricardo, Van Pelt
author: William Wordsworth
brother: **5** Linus
friend: **4** Fred **5** Ethel
husband: **4** Desi
role: **4** Mame **7** Ricardo
telecast: **5** rerun
to Desi: **6** costar
Lucy __ Montgomery: **4** Maud
__ Lucy: **5** Here's, I Love
Lucy Gayheart
author: Willa Cather
Lucy Gray
author: William Wordsworth
Lucy in the Sky With Diamonds (song)
artist: Beatles, Elton John
Lucy Show, The (CBS sitcom)
cast: Lucille Ball (Lucy Carmichael)
Gale Gordon (Theodore Mooney)
Vivian Vance (Vivian Bagley)
Ludden, Allen
spouse: Betty White
ludicrous: **3** mad, odd **4** rich, zany **5** antic, comic, crazy, droll, funny, goony, inane, silly **6** absurd, har-har, insane, stupid **7** bizarre, burlesk, comical, fatuous, foolish, jocular, risible **8** cockeyed, farcical, gelastic, humorous **9** burlesque, facetious, fantastic, grotesque, laughable, senseless **10** impossible, outlandish, ridiculous, unfeasible
ludicrousness: **5** folly **6** antics **7** foolery, inanity **8** jocosity, nonsense **9** absurdity, silliness, stupidity
Ludlum, Robert: **6** writer
work: The Apocalypse Watch
The Aquitaine Progression
The Bourne Identity
The Bourne Supremacy
The Bourne Ultimatum
The Cassandra Compact
The Cry of the Halidon
The Gemini Contenders
The Hades Factor
The Holcroft Covenant
The Icarus Agenda
The Janson Directive
The Matarese Circle
The Matarese Countdown
The Matlock Paper
The Osterman Weekend
The Paris Option
The Parsifal Mosaic
The Prometheus Deception
The Rhinemann Exchange
The Road to Gandolfo
The Road to Omaha
The Scarlatti Inheritance
The Scorpio Illusion
The Sigma Protocol
Trevayne
Ludovico: **7** Ariosto
Ludwig: **4** Emil **5** Tieck **6** Donath, Edward, Minkus, Quidde **8** von Drake **9** Beethoven, Bemelmans, Feuerbach
in English: **5** Lewis, Louis
Ludwig __ Beethoven: **3** van
Ludwig __ van der Rohe: **4** Mies
__ luego!: **5** Hasta
Luft: **3** Sid **5** Lorna
Luftwaffe foe: **3** RAF
lug: **2** ox **3** ape, oaf, tow, tug **4** bear, cart, drag, haul, lout, pack, pull, take, tote, yank **5** bring, brute, carry, ferry, heave, looby, shlep **6** convey, galoot, lubber **7** galloot, schlepp **8** transfer **9** blockhead, drag along, transport
lug __: **3** nut **6** wrench
__-lug: **5** chug-a
Lugano: **4** lake
locale: **5** Italy **11** Switzerland
Lugar, Richard: **3** sen. **7** senator
luge: **4** sled **5** sport
Luger: **3** gun **5** Georg **6** German, pistol **7** handgun
luggage: **3** bag **4** case, gear **5** stuff, trunk **6** duffel, duffle, things, valise **7** baggage, carry-on, tote bag **8** suitcase **9** duffel bag, duffle bag
attachment: **5** ID tag **8** claim tag
collect, as ~: **5** claim
load ~: **4** pack
lugger: **4** boat, ship **5** toter
lug-nut protector: **6** hubcap
Lugosi, Bela: **5** actor
film: Abbott and Costello Meet Frankenstein (1948)
The Black Cat (1934)
The Body Snatcher (1945)
The Death Kiss (1933)
Dracula (1931)
Frankenstein Meets the Wolf Man (1943)
Island of Lost Souls (1933)
Mark of the Vampire (1935)
Ninotchka (1939)
The Raven (1935)
Son of Frankenstein (1939)
White Zombie (1932)
role: **4** Ygor
lugubrious: **3** sad **4** dark **5** black, bleak, drear, moody **6** dismal, dreary, gloomy, morose, rueful, somber **7** doleful, elegiac, forlorn, joyless **8** dolorous, funereal, lowering, mournful **9** cheerless, depressed, elegiacal, saddening, saturnine, sorrowful, woebegone **10** depressing, lamentable, melancholy
__ lui: **4** chez
Luigi: **4** Alva **7** Capuana, Galvani **10** Pirandello
see also Italian
Luis: **5** Firpo, Tiant **6** Buñuel, Puenzo, Valdez **7** Alvarez, Mandoki **8** Aparicio
in English: **5** Lewis, Louis
see also Spanish
Luisa: **10** Tetrazzini

Luisa Miller
composer: Giuseppe Verdi
__ Luis Borges: 5 Jorge
__ Luis, Brazil: 3 Sao
Luise: 6 Rainer
__ Luis Obispo, CA: 3 San
__ Luis Potosí: 3 San
Luka (1987 song)
artist: Suzanne Vega
Lukas: 4 Foss, Haas, Paul
Luke: 4 Duke, Keye 5 Perry, Robin, saint 6 Halpin 7 Appling 9 Skywalker
book by ~: 4 Acts
colleague: 7 Han Solo
foe: 5 Darth
follower: 4 John
mentor: 4 Yoda 6 Obi Wan
preceder: 4 Mark
sister: 4 Leia
town in ~ 7: 4 Nain
Luke Havergal
author: Edward Arlington Robinson
lukewarm: 4 cold, cool, mild, so-so 5 tepid, unhot 6 chilly 8 hesitant, listless 9 apathetic, uncertain, undecided 10 indecisive, irresolute, nonchalant, phlegmatic, unagitated, unresolved, wishy-washy
Luleå: 4 city, port 7 seaport
locale: 6 Sweden
lull: 3 ebb, gap 4 balm, calm, cool, fall, hush, rest, stop, wane 5 abate, allay, break, cease, comma, lapse, letup, pause, quell, quiet, still, truce 6 becalm, hiatus, layoff, pacify, recess, settle, soothe, stroke, subdue, temper 7 compose, cool off, die down, dwindle, ease off, lay back, mollify, qualify, respite, silence, slacken, subside, time-out 8 abeyance, breather, calm down, calmness, chill out, decrease, diminish, downtime, interval, moderate, reprieve, slowdown 9 interlude, put a lid on, quiet down, soft-pedal, stillness, untrouble 10 quiescence, take it easy
lullaby: 4 song 5 ditty, music 8 berceuse 10 cradlesong
Irish ~ start: 5 too-ra
word: 4 hush
Lullaby of Broadway
composer: Al Dubin, Harry Warren
Lully, Raymond: 11 philosopher
lulu: 3 pip 4 oner 5 beaut, dilly, doozy 6 corker, doozer 7 whapper, whopper 9 humdinger 10 ripsnorter
Lulu: 5 opera 6 singer
composer: Alban Berg
song: To Sir with Love (1967)
spouse: Maurice Gibb
__ Lulu: 6 Little
__ Lulu Bett: 4 Miss
Lulu's Back in Town
composer: Al Dubin, Harry Warren
Lum and Abner: 9 radio show
setting: 5 store
lumbago: 4 ache
lumbar: 4 back 8 vertebra
lumbar __: 6 plexus
lumber: 3 log, tax 4 hulk, lade, land, load, lump, plod, roll, slog, walk, wood 5 barge, board, clump, plank, stump, weigh, woods 6 boards, burden, charge, cumber, linger, planks, saddle, timber, trudge, waddle 7 galumph, shamble, shuffle, trundle 8 encumber 10 impose upon
ender: 4 jack, yard
flaw: 4 bend, knot, warp 5 curve 6 buckle
measure: 4 bd. ft. 5 lin. ft. 9 board foot 10 linear foot
process ~: 3 cut, saw
processed, as ~: 4 sawn
source: 3 ash, oak 4 pine 5 maple
worker: 5 sawer
lumbering: 3 oxy 5 gawky, unapt 6 clumsy, klutzy, oafish 7 awkward, gawkish, hulking, lumpish 8 bumbling, bungling, clunking, ungainly, unwieldy 9 all thumbs, graceless, maladroit, ponderous, stumbling, unskilled, unwieldly 10 lead-footed, unskillful
lumberjack: 5 axman 6 axeman, Bunyan, logger 8 woodsman 10 Paul Bunyan
cap: 5 toque
commodity: 3 log 4 wood 6 lumber, timber
competition: 5 roleo
leaving: 5 stump 7 sawdust 9 woodchips
need: 3 axe, saw 4 boot, rope 5 wedge, winch 7 skidder 8 cant hook, chainsaw
shirt pattern: 5 plaid
Lumberton: 4 city, town
locale: 4 N. Car.
lumberyard buy: 4 beam 5 board, joist, plank 6 girder, rafter 7 plywood
Lumet, Sidney: 8 director
film: 12 Angry Men (1957)
The Anderson Tapes (1972)
Daniel (1983)
The Deadly Affair (1967)
Deathtrap (1982)
Dog Day Afternoon (1975)
Fail-Safe (1964)
Family Business (1989)
Garbo Talks (1984)
The Group (1966)
The Hill (1965)
Long Day's Journey Into Night (1962)
Murder on the Orient Express (1974)
Network (1976)
The Pawnbroker (1965)
Prince of the City (1981)
Running on Empty (1988)
Serpico (1973)
That Kind of Woman (1959)
The Verdict (1982)
spouse: Rita Gam, Gloria Vanderbilt
__ lumière: 5 son et
Lumière: 5 Louis
Lumina: 3 car 4 auto 5 Chevy 9 Chevrolet 10 automobile
luminaria: 5 light 6 candle
luminary: 3 sun, VIP 4 hero, idol, lion, name, star 5 celeb 6 leader, worthy 7 big name, notable 8 eminence, somebody 9 celebrity, dignitary, personage, superstar
luminesce: 4 glow 5 gleam, shine 7 flicker, glimmer, glisten, glitter, radiate, shimmer
luminescence: 4 glow, tint 5 gleam, light, sheen, shine 7 insight, shimmer 8 lambency, radiance, radiancy, splendor
luminescent: 6 bright, lucent 7 glowing, lambent, radiant, shining 8 luminous 9 effulgent
luminosity: 4 glow, tint 5 gleam, light, sheen, shine 7 insight, shimmer 8 lambency, radiance, radiancy, splendor
unit: 6 candle 7 candela
luminous: 3 lit 5 aglow, clear, light, lucid, shiny, vivid 6 ablaze, bright, flashy, lucent 7 beaming, blazing, crystal, evident, fulgent, glowing, lambent, lighted, obvious, radiant, shining 8 dazzling, gleaming, knowable, lustrous 9 brilliant, effulgent, graspable, inspiring, refulgent, sparkling, unobscure 10 fathomable
luminousness: 4 glow 6 luster 8 lambency, radiance 10 effulgence, refulgence
Lumley: 6 Joanna
lummox: 2 ox 3 ape 4 boor, bozo, goon, lout 5 beast, brute, klutz, looby, loser, ninny, yahoo, yokel 6 big ape 7 bruiser, bumpkin, hayseed 8 lunkhead 9 blunderer 10 clodhopper
cry: 4 oops, uh-oh
like a ~: 5 dense, inept 6 clumsy, gauche 7 awkward 8 bumbling, bungling, cloddish, fumbling 9 all thumbs, graceless, maladroit
see also ninny
lump: 3 bit, dab, gob, lot, mix, nub, pat, wad 4 ball, bear, blob, bulk, bump, cake, chip, clod, clot, glob, heap, hunk, knob, knot, knub, loaf, mass, much, node, nurl, part, peck, pile, slab, spot, take 5 abide, amass, batch, block, brook, bulge, bunch, chunk, clump, crumb, gnarl, group, knurl, piece, scrap, solid, stand, tumor, wedge 6 digest, dollop, endure, gobbet, growth, lumber, morsel, nodule, nugget, suffer 7 cluster, handful, portion, section, stomach, swallow 8 mountain, swelling, tolerate 9 aggregate, put up with, withstand 10 protrusion, tumescence
of jelly: 4 blob 6 dollop
together: 4 join 5 batch, bunch, group 6 bundle 7 bunch up, combine
lump __: 3 sum
lumper: 7 laborer 10 day laborer
lump in one's __: 6 throat
lumpish: 4 dopy, dull, slow 5 dense, dopey, heavy 6 bovine, clumsy, obtuse, stolid, stupid 7 awkward 8 backward, sluggish, ungainly 9 lumbering, ponderous 10 phlegmatic
lump of __: 5 sugar
lumps: 10 punishment
some ~: 5 sugar
__ Lumpur: 5 Kuala
lumpy: 5 bumpy, nubby 6 chunky, knobby, uneven 7 gnarled, knurled 8 unsmooth 9 irregular 10 nonuniform
not ~: 4 even 6 creamy, smooth 7 uniform, velvety
luna __: 4 moth
Luna: 4 moon 7 Barbara, goddess
Luna (1979 film)
cast: Jill Clayburgh
director: Bernardo Bertolucci
__ Luna: 3 Eva
Luna, Barbara
spouse: Doug McClure
lunacy: 5 folly, mania 6 idiocy 7 fatuity, inanity, madness 8 insanity 9 absurdity, asininity, craziness, imbalance, silliness
lunar
craft: 3 LEM 5 probe, rover 6 lander
crater: 5 Tycho
depression: 6 crater
gap between solar and ~ year: 5 epact
phase: 3 new 4 full 7 gibbous 8 crescent
phenomenon: 4 halo, tide 6 corona 7 eclipse
plain: 3 sea 4 mare
valley: 4 rill 5 rille
see also moon
lunar __: 3 day 4 year 5 cycle, month, orbit, rover 6 module 7 eclipse, orbiter
lunar excursion __: 6 module
__ Lunas, NM: 3 Los
Lunatic Villas
author: Marian Engel
lunch: 3 eat 4 bite, meal 6 spread 9 grab a bite
at ~: 3 out 5 not in
before ~: 4 morn 7 morning 8 forenoon
choice: 3 BLT, ham, sub 4 hero, Spam, to go, tuna 5 pizza, salad 6 cheese 7 bologna 8 sandwich, tuna fish 9 roast beef, submarine
ender: 3 eon 4 meat, room, time
have ~: 3 eat 4 dine, meet
out to ~: 4 gaga 7 unaware 8 confused 9 forgetful
reading: 4 menu
stop: 4 cafe, deli 5 diner 6 eatery 9 mall court 10 restaurant
time: 3 one 4 hour, noon 5 one p.m. 6 midday, twelve
lunch __: 4 hour 7 counter
__ lunch: 3 box 4 free 5 out to, power
luncheon: 4 meal 5 party 6 affair, social 8 function 9 blue plate, gathering
ender: 4 ette
luncheon __: 4 meat
luncheonette: 4 café 5 diner 6 eatery 10 restaurant
Luncheon on the Grass
artist: Édouard Manet
Lunch Poems
author: Frank O'Hara
lunchroom: 4 café 5 diner, grill 6 eatery 7 canteen 9 cafeteria 10 restaurant
lure: 5 aroma
__ Lunch, The: 5 Naked
Lund: 4 Ilsa, John

Lunden: **4** Joan
Lundgren: **5** Dolph
lundi: **4** jour **6** French, Monday
follower: **5** mardi
preceder: **8** dimanche
lune: **4** moon **5** leash **8** crescent, half-moon
lung: **5** organ **8** breather
combining form: **5** pneum-, pulmo-
ender: **4** fish, worm, wort
fish ~: **4** gill
like a ~: **5** lobar, lobed
__-Lung: **4** Aqua
lunge: **3** cut, hit, jab **4** dart, dash, dive, jump, leap, pass, poke, push, rush, stab **5** bound, burst, drive, forge, lurch, pitch, reach, surge, swing, swipe **6** charge, hurtle, plunge, pounce, spring, strike, thrust **7** set upon **8** fall upon
(at): **3** run
lungful: **3** air
lungi: **5** scarf **6** sarong, turban **9** loincloth
lungs, use: **6** exhale, inhale **7** breathe
lunker: **4** bass
lunkhead
see ninny
__ lunn: **5** sally
Lunt, Alfred: **5** actor
spouse: Lynn Fontanne
Lunts milieu: **5** stage **8** Broadway
Luo home: **5** Kenya **6** Africa
Lupe: **5** Velez
Lupin: **6** Arsene
lupine: **5** plant **6** fierce, flower, savage **7** wolfish **8** ravening, ravenous, wolflike **9** ferocious, predatory, rapacious **10** wildflower
animal: **4** wolf
Lupino, Ida: **7** actress **8** director
spouse: Howard Duff
LuPone: **5** Patti
role: **5** Evita
Lupton: **4** John
Lupus: **5** Peter
lurch: **3** yaw **4** cant, duck, jerk, jump, keel, lean, list, reel, rock, roll, slip, snap, sway, tilt, toss, trip **5** dodge, heave, lunge, pitch, slide, swing, weave **6** bumble, careen, falter, plunge, seesaw, swerve, teeter, totter, wabble, wallow, wobble **7** blunder, stagger, stammer, stumble **8** flounder
forward, nautically: **5** scend
leave in the ~: **4** jilt, quit **5** ditch **6** cop out, desert, reject, strand **7** abandon, forsake, let down **8** abdicate
lure: **3** fly, jig **4** bait, coax, draw, hook, plug, pull, trap, wile **5** bribe, charm, decoy, shill, snare, spoon, tempt, trick **6** beckon, cajole, carrot, come-on, entice, entrap, induce, invite, lead on, magnet, pull in, rope in, suck in **7** attract, beguile, bewitch, capture, con game, enchant, ensnare, gimmick, insnare, mislead, spinner **8** appeal to, flypaper, interest, inveigle, persuade **9** appetence, captivate, fascinate, incentive, magnetism, mousetrap, siren song, sweetener **10** attractant, attraction, camouflage, enticement, inducement, invitation, temptation
fishing ~: **3** fly, jig **4** plug **5** spoon, troll **6** dry fly
into wrongdoing: **4** hook, trap **5** decoy, set up, snare, trick **6** entice, lead on, reel in, suck in **7** beguile, ensnare **8** entangle, inveigle
Lurene: **6** Tuttle
lurer: **5** siren **7** enticer, Lorelei **9** temptress
Luria, Salvador: **8** Nobelist **9** biologist
lurid: **4** gory, grim, pale, racy **5** ashen, fiery, livid, vivid **6** bloody, dismal, grisly, pallid, risqué, sultry **7** flaming, flaring, ghastly, graphic, hideous, intense, macaber, macabre, violent **8** gruesome, horrible, shocking, sinister **9** appalling, frightful, graphical, low-minded **10** horrifying, scandalous
Lurie, Alison: **6** writer
work: Foreign Affairs
Imaginary Friends
The Language of Clothes
Love and Friendship
Only Children
The War Between the Tates
lurk: **4** hide, slip, wait **5** creep, prowl, sculk, shirk, skulk, slide, slink, snake, sneak, snoop, steal **6** crouch, lay for, waylay **7** gumshoe, slither **9** lie in wait **10** hang around, nose around
lurker's plan: **4** trap **6** ambush
lurking: **5** snaky **6** unseen **9** potential **10** underlying, undetected
Lusaka: **4** city, town **7** capital
locale: **6** Zambia
luscious: **4** good, rich **5** juicy, sapid, sweet, tasty, yummy **6** choice, creamy, delish, liquid, mellow, savory, toothy **7** opulent **8** heavenly **9** ambrosial, delicious, exquisite, flavorful, luxuriant, luxurious, nectarous, palatable, succulent, sumptuous, toothsome **10** appetizing, delectable, flavorsome
lush: **3** sot **4** posh, rank, rich, wild, wino **5** cushy, dense, grand, green, plush, ritzy, souse, toper **6** barfly, bibber, creamy, deluxe, lavish, tender **7** fertile, guzzler, opulent, profuse, riotous, teeming, tippler, tosspot, verdant **8** abundant, heavenly, palatial, prodigal, prolific, tropical **9** exuberant, luxuriant, luxurious, overgrown, plentiful, succulent, sumptuous
lushness: **8** elegance **9** abundance, profusion
Lusitania: **4** boat, ship **5** liner
sinker: **5** U-boat
lust: **3** sin, yen **4** ache, itch, love, need, sigh, urge, vice, want **5** covet, crave, greed, yearn **6** desire, fervor, hanker, libido, thirst **7** avidity, craving, passion **8** appetite, cupidity, salacity **9** appetence, esurience, lubricity
for: **4** want **5** covet, crave **6** desire
(for): **3** die **4** ache, itch, long, pant, pine, sigh, wish **5** yearn **6** hunger, thirst
luster: **4** glow **5** glaze, gleam, glint, gloss, light, sheen, shine **6** dazzle, finish, polish, renown **7** burnish, glitter, shimmer, sparkle, varnish **8** lambency, radiance, radiancy, splendor **9** afterglow **10** brightness, brilliance, brilliancy, effulgence, refulgence
ender: **4** ware
lose ~: **4** fade **7** tarnish
starter: **4** lack
lusterless: **3** dim, dun **4** dark, drab, dull, flat, pale **5** dingy, dirty, dusty, faded, grimy, matte, muddy **6** gritty, opaque **7** unwaxed **8** lifeless
Lust for Life: **4** film **5** novel
author: Irving Stone
cast: James Donald, Kirk Douglas, Anthony Quinn
director: Vincente Minnelli
lustful: **4** avid, lewd **5** randy **6** greedy, wanton **7** craving, goatish, hoggish, immoral, piggish, sensual, wolfish **8** covetous, desirous, prurient, ravening, unchaste, uncurbed **9** abandoned, dissolute, rapacious, salacious, voracious **10** avaricious, gluttonous, hot-blooded, insatiable, lascivious, licentious, passionate, profligate, unvirtuous
lustiness: **5** vigor **7** stamina **8** vitality
lustrous: **3** lit **4** waxy **5** aglow, glacé, light, lucid, nitid, shiny, silky, sleek, waxen **6** ablaze, bright, flashy, glassy, glazed, glossy, lucent, pearly, satiny, silver, smooth **7** beaming, blazing, fulgent, glowing, lambent, radiant, shining **8** dazzling, gleaming, glinting, glorious, luminous, nacreous, polished, splendid **9** brilliant, burnished, effulgent, refulgent, sparkling **10** glistening, iridescent, shimmering
fabric: **4** lamé, silk **5** ramee, ramie, satin
Lustrous __ of sun: **3** orb
lusty: **4** hale, iron, wiry **5** beefy, burly, hardy, hefty, hunky, husky, stout, tough, vital **6** brawny, earthy, hearty, mighty, potent, robust, rugged, sinewy, steely, stocky, strong, sturdy, virile **7** doughty, dynamic, healthy **8** athletic, forceful, indurate, muscular, powerful, puissant, spirited, stalwart, vigorous **9** Atlantean, energetic, Herculean, strapping, strenuous, well-built **10** able-bodied, full of life, hot-blooded, red-blooded
Lut: **6** desert
locale: **4** Iran
lute: **3** oud, saz, uti **4** biwa, pipa, ruan **5** cobza **6** buzuki, string **7** bandore, kantele, mandola, pandora, samisen, tambura, theorbo **8** bousouki, bouzouki, surbahar **9** balalaika
Arab: **3** oud
cousin: **4** lyre, viol **5** rebab, rebec **6** guitar, rebeck
feature: **4** fret
Hindu: **5** sarod, sitar
lutefisk: **3** cod **8** fish dish
tenderizer: **3** lye
Lute Song
author: Sidney Howard
lutetium: **7** element **9** rare earth
Luth.: **4** Prot.
school: **3** sem.
Luther: **5** Adler **6** Ingram, Martin **7** Burbank **8** Campbell, Vandross
__ Luther King: **6** Martin
Luther, Martin: **6** German **8** reformer
foe: **3** Eck
postings: **6** theses
work: Ninety-Five Theses
Luthor: **3** Lex
like: **4** evil
to Superman: **3** foe **5** enemy
Lutuli, Albert: **8** Nobelist
Lutz: **4** leap
alternative: **4** axel
where to do a ~: **3** ice **4** rink
luv: **3** hon **4** dear **5** honey **7** darling **10** sweetheart
Luv (1967 film)
cast: Peter Falk, Jack Lemmon, Elaine May
character: **4** Milt **5** Ellen
Luvs: **6** diaper
alternative: **7** Drypers, Huggies, Pampers
__ lux: **4** fiat
Lux: **4** soap
alternative: *see* soap
Lux __ Theatre: **5** Radio
luxe: **4** fine, posh, rich **5** class, plush **6** classy **7** elegant, opulent **8** elegance, fineness, opulence, opulency, poshness, richness, splendid, splendor **9** high-class, plushness, sumptuous
Luxembourg: **4** city, town **5** duchy **6** nation **7** capital, country
capital: **10** Luxembourg
locale: **3** Eur. **6** Europe
money: **5** franc
neighbor: **3** Ger. **4** Belg. **6** France **7** Belgium, Germany
Nobelist in Medicine: **6** Claude
org.: **4** NATO
Luxor: **4** city, town **6** casino
city near ~: **4** Qena **5** Aswan **6** Assuan **7** Assouan
locale: **5** Egypt, Vegas **8** Las Vegas
river: **4** Nile
luxuriance: **6** wealth **9** fecundity, fertility **10** exuberance
luxuriant: **4** lush, rank, rich, wild **5** ample, dense, fancy, plush **6** deluxe, fecund, florid, lavish, ornate **7** copious, fertile, flowery, opulent, profuse, rampant, riotous, teeming **8** abundant, fruitful, generous, luscious, palatial, prodigal, prolific, thriving **9** bountiful, elaborate, excessive, exuberant, plenteous, plentiful, profusive, sumptuous **10** flamboyant, productive
luxuriate: **4** bask, grow, love, riot, roll **5** bloom, eat up, enjoy, feast, revel **6** abound, overdo, relish, roll in, thrive, wallow, wanton **7** burgeon, delight, indulge, prosper, rollick, run riot **8** abound in, bourgeon, flourish, increase, live it up **9** delight in, feast upon **10** take it easy
in: **4** like **5** adore, enjoy, revel, savor **6** relish, wallow **7** indulge **10** appreciate

luxurious: **4** easy, lush, posh, rich **5** fancy, grand, haute, plush, ritzy, showy, silky, swank, swell **6** costly, deluxe, flashy, frilly, glitzy, lavish, lordly, ornate, plushy, swanky **7** elegant, opulent, stately, upscale **8** affluent, gorgeous, imposing, luscious, majestic, palatial, pampered, princely, prodigal, splendid **9** decorated, elaborate, epicurean, expensive, grandiose, indulgent, sumptuous, sybaritic **10** gratifying, hedonistic, immoderate, impressive, majestical, ornamented
  hardly ~: **4** mean **5** dingy, mangy, ratty, seedy **6** beat-up, crummy, shabby, shoddy, sleazy, sordid **7** run-down, sagging, scruffy, squalid **8** decaying, decrepit
luxury: **4** ease, posh **5** bliss, frill, ritzy, style, treat **6** rarity, wealth **7** amenity, comfort, delight, leisure **8** delicacy, elegance, good life, grandeur, hedonism, noblesse, opulence, opulency, richness, splendor **9** affluence, enjoyment, well-being **10** high living, indulgence, lavishness, prosperity
  in the lap of ~: **4** posh, rich **5** plush, ritzy, swank **6** swanky **7** upscale **8** affluent, pampered, princely **9** sumptuous, sybaritic
  lap of ~: **5** means, money **6** riches, wealth **7** fortune **8** opulence **9** abundance, affluence **10** gravy train, prosperity
LU
luxury __: **3** car, tax
__ luxury: **5** lap of
Luyendyk, Arie: **9** auto racer
  milieu: **5** track
Luzinski: **4** Greg
Luzon: **4** isle **6** island
  bay: **5** Subic
  neighbor: **5** Samar
  peninsula: **6** Bataan
  people: **5** Bikol
  port: **6** Aparri
  river: **5** Pasig
  volcano: **4** Taal **5** Mayon **7** Bulusan **8** Pinatubo
Lvov: **4** city, town
  locale: **7** Ukraine
Lwoff, André: **8** Nobelist
lwyr.: **3** att. **4** atty.
lycée: **6** French, school **7** academy **9** institute
  kin: **5** école
lyceum: **4** hall **6** school **7** academy, gallery, theater, theatre **9** gymnasium, institute **10** auditorium
Lycia
  city of ancient ~: **4** Myra
Lycidas
  author: John Milton
Lycra
  cousin: **5** nylon
Lydgate, John: **4** poet
Lydia: **5** Child, Lunch **7** Cornell
  capital of ~: **6** Sardis
  poet: **4** Cato
Lydian __: **4** mode
Lydia, the Tattooed Lady
  composer: Harold Arlen, Yip Harburg
Lydie Breeze
  author: John Guare
Lydon: **5** James, Jimmy
lye: **3** KOH **4** NaOH **6** alkali, potash **7** caustic **8** lixivium
Lyin' Eyes (1975 song)
  artist: Eagles
lying: **3** sin **4** sham **5** false, trick, wrong **6** deceit, dupery, shifty, tricky, untrue **7** crooked, fibbing, knavish, perjury **8** delusive, delusory, guileful, lounging, two-faced **9** deceitful, deception, deceptive, dishonest, incumbent, insincere, inventing, mendacity, pretended, two-timing **10** committing, dishonesty, falsifying, mendacious, misleading, misstating, perfidious, unreliable, untruthful
  down: **5** level, prone **6** face up, supine **8** face down **9** prostrate, recumbent **10** horizontal
  still: **4** idle **5** inert **7** dormant
  stop ~: **5** sit up
__-lying: **3** low
lying down
  in heraldry: **7** dormant **8** couchant
Lyle: **5** Sandy **6** Alzado, Lovett, Sparky, Talbot **7** Bettger **8** Waggoner
Lyle, Sandy: **6** golfer
Lyman: **4** Link **6** Arthur **7** Beecher, Dorothy
Lymon and the Teenagers, Frankie
  song: Goody Goody (1957)
    I Want You to Be My Girl (1956)
    Why Do Fools Fall in Love (1956)
lymph __: **4** node **5** gland
lymphatic: **8** listless, sluggish **9** lethargic
lymph-gland location: **6** armpit
Lyn: **4** Dawn
__ Lyn Bauer: **5** Jaime
Lynch: **4** John **5** David, Kelly **8** Jennifer
Lynchburg: **4** city, town
  locale: **8** Virginia
Lynch, David: **8** director
  film: Blue Velvet (1986)
    The Elephant Man (1980)
    Eraserhead (1978)
    Mulholland Dr. (2001)
    The Straight Story (1999)
    Wild at Heart (1990)
Lynda: **6** Carter **7** Johnson
Lynda __ George: **3** Day
Lynda Bird's sister: **4** Luci
Lynda Johnson __: **4** Robb
Lynde: **4** Paul
Lyndon: **5** Barré **7** Johnson **8** Larouche
  daughter: **4** Luci **5** Lynda
__ Lyndon: **5** Barry
Lyne, Adrian: **8** director
  film: Fatal Attraction (1987)
    Flashdance (1983)
    Indecent Proposal (1993)
    Lolita (1997)
    Unfaithful (2002)
Lynen, Feodor: **8** Nobelist
Lynley: **5** Carol
Lynn: **4** Bari, city, Fred, town, Vera **5** Diana, Janet, Sherr, Swann **6** Carlin, Cheryl **7** Barbara, Jeffrey, Kellogg, Loretta **8** Anderson, Fontanne, Jonathan, Redgrave, Reynolds
  locale: **4** Mass.
Lynne: **4** Jeff **6** Shelby
__ Lynne: **4** East
Lynne, Jeff rock band: **3** ELO
__ Lynn Gorney: **5** Karen
Lynn-Holly: **7** Johnson
Lynn, Loretta: **6** singer
  father: **5** miner
  sister: Crystal Gayle
Lynnwood: **4** city, town
  locale: **10** Washington
Lynwood: **4** city, town
  locale: **10** California, Los Angeles
lynx: **3** cat **5** felid **6** animal, bobcat, feline, mammal
  relative: ***see*** feline
Lynx: **3** car **4** auto, Merc **7** Mercury **10** automobile
lynx-eyed: **4** keen **5** acute, aware, sharp **9** all-seeing, intuitive, observant **10** discerning, insightful, perceptive
Lynyrd Skynyrd
  lead singer: Ronnie Van Zant
  song: Free Bird (1975)
    Saturday Night Special (1975)
    Sweet Home Alabama (1974)
    What's Your Name (1978)
Lyon: **3** Ben, Sue **4** city, town
  locale: **6** France
  river: **5** Rhone, Saône
  see also French
lyonnaise ingredient: **5** onion
Lyons: **4** city, town **7** Douglas, Jeffrey
  river: **5** Rhone, Saône
  town north of ~: **5** Cluny
  see also French
Lyra
  neighbor: **6** Cygnus
  star in ~: **4** Vega
lyre: **5** crwth, kerar **6** bagana, kissar, string **7** cithara, kithara, obukano
  cousin: **4** harp
  ender: **4** bird
  goddess with a ~: **5** Erato
  Hebrew ~: **4** asor
__ lyre: **6** Aeolic **7** Aeolian
lyric: **4** song **5** verse, vocal, words **6** choral, melody, poetic **7** melodic, musical, songful, tuneful **8** poetical, songlike **9** melodious **10** coloratura
  poet: **5** odist
  work: **3** lai, ode **4** poem **5** epode **6** arioso
lyrical: **4** odic **6** choral, dulcet, in tune, poetic **7** chiming, lilting, melodic, musical, songful, soulful, tuneful **8** blending, operatic, pleasing, poetical, rhythmic, songlike, sonorous **9** agreeable, emotional, melodious, rhapsodic, symphonic, well-tuned **10** euphonious, expressive, harmonious, orchestral, passionate
Lyrical Ballads
  author: William Wordsworth
lyricism: **4** brio, fire **5** ardor **6** warmth **7** ecstasy, emotion, passion, rapture **8** rhapsody **9** intensity
lyricist: **4** poet **9** songsmith **10** songwriter
lyrics: **5** words
  feature: **5** meter, rhyme **7** cadence, measure
  forgo the ~: **3** hum **7** whistle
lyrist: **4** poet **7** Orpheus **8** composer, musician
lysine: **9** amino acid
Lysithea: **4** moon
  planet: **7** Jupiter
Lysol: **7** cleaner
  alternative: **5** Brite, Tilex **6** Top Job **7** Lestoil, Mr. Clean, Pine Sol **9** Fantastik, Step Saver
  target: **5** staph **6** mildew
lyssa: **6** rabies

M

m
to Einstein: 4 mass
m.: 4 lgth., meas.
M: 4 size 6 letter 8 thousand
followers: 3 NOP 4 NOPQ 5 NOPQR
in phonetic alphabet: 4 Mike
portrayer: Judi Dench, Bernard Lee
preceders: 3 JKL 4 IJKL 5 HIJKL
M (1931 film)
cast: Peter Lorre
director: Fritz Lang
M __ Mary: 4 as in
M __ the million things...: 5 is for
M. __ Walsh: 5 Emmet
__ M?: 3 N or
'M' __ Malice: 5 Is for
M-1 inventor: 6 Garand
ma: 6 parent
see also mother
Ma: 4 Bell, Yo-Yo 6 Barker, Rainey
Ma __: 7 Perkins
Ma __ Amie: 5 Belle
Ma! (He's Making Eyes __): 4 at Me
Má __: 5 Vlast
MA
region: 4 N. Eng.
zone: 3 EDT, EST
see also Massachusetts
M.A.: 3 deg. 6 degree
part of ~: 4 arts 6 master
pursuer's test: 3 GRE
maa: 5 bleat
sounder: 4 goat 5 nanny 6 nannie
Maalox: 7 antacid
alternative: *see* antacid
__, ma'am: 3 Yes
ma'am companion: 3 sir
Ma and Pa operation: 5 store
__ Maarten: 4 Sint
Maas: 5 river
city on the ~: 5 Liege, Sedan 6 Verdun 9 Rotterdam
locale: 6 France 7 Belgium, Holland 11 Netherlands
Maasai home: 5 Kenya 6 Africa 8 Tanzania
Maastricht: 4 city, town
locale: 7 Holland 11 Netherlands
Maazel, Lorin: 9 conductor
Mab: 5 Queen 6 sprite
mate: 6 Oberon
Mabel: 4 King 6 Mercer 7 Normand
__ & Mabel: 4 Mack
Ma Belle __: 4 Amie
__ Mable: 4 Dere
Mabley: 4 Moms
mac: 3 bub 5 buddy 6 buster, jacket 7 slicker 8 raincoat, rainwear 10 protection
starter: 3 tar
wearer: 4 Brit 6 Briton
Mac: 5 Davis, Hyman 6 Bernie 8 computer 9 McAnnally
alternative: *see* computer
producer: 5 Apple
what ~ means: 5 son of
__ Mac: 3 Big 7 Freddie
MAC
school: 3 NIU 4 Ohio 5 Akron, Miami 6 Toledo 7 Buffalo 8 Marshall 9 Ball State, Kent State
macabre: 4 eery, gory, grim, sick 5 eerie, lurid, scary, weird 6 creepy, grisly, morbid, spooky 7 fearful, ghastly, ghostly, hideous 8 ghoulish, gruesome, horrible 9 frightful, monstrous
being: 5 ghoul
master of the ~: 3 Poe
__ Macabre: 5 Danse
macadam
ingredient: 3 tar
layer: 5 paver
put down ~: 4 pave
macadamia: 3 nut 4 tree
macadamize: 4 pave
MacAllen: 4 city, town
locale: 5 Texas
Macao: 4 city, port, town
coin: 3 avo
neighbor: 5 China
macaque: 5 jocko 6 animal, rhesus 7 primate 10 Barbary ape
relative: *see* primate
macarena: 5 dance
Macarena (1996 song)
artist: Los Del Rio
macaroni: 3 fop 4 dude, ziti 5 pasta, penne, zitti 6 elbows, noodle 7 lasagna, lasagne, noodles, pastina, ravioli 8 bucatini, couscous, farfalle, linguine, linguini, rigatoni 9 agnolotti, angelhair, cavatelli, manicotti, spaghetti 10 cannelloni, fettuccini, jack-a-dandy, tortellini, vermicelli
salad ingredient: 4 mayo
macaroni __: 5 salad
macaroon: 6 cookie
MacArthur: 4 Park 5 James 7 Charles, Douglas
onetime ~ command: 5 Korea
word in a ~ quote: 5 shall 6 return
MacArthur (1977 film)
cast: Gregory Peck
MacArthur, Charles
spouse: Helen Hayes
MacArthur, James: 5 actor
mother: Helen Hayes
TV: Hawaii Five-O
MacArthur Park (song)
artist: Richard Harris, Donna Summer
composer: Jimmy Webb
Macau
see Macao
Macaulay: 4 Rose 6 Culkin, Thomas
Macaulay, Rose: 4 Dame 6 writer 7 British
work: Crewe Train
The Shadow Flies
Told by an Idiot
The Towers of Trezibond
Macavity: 3 cat
macaw: 3 ara 4 bird 5 arara
Macbeth: 4 Lady, play, Scot 5 opera
composer: Giuseppe Verdi
Macbeth (1948 film)
cast: Jeanette Nolan, Dan O'Herlihy, Orson Welles
director: Orson Welles
Macbeth (play)
author: William Shakespeare
recipe ingredient: 3 dog 4 frog, newt
role: 4 Ross 5 Angus, Witch 6 Banquo, Duncan, Hecate, Lennox, Seyton, Siward 7 Fleance, Macbeth, Macduff, Malcolm 8 Menteith 9 Caithness, Donalbain
trio: 4 hags 7 witches
MacBride, Sean: 8 Nobelist
__ Maccabaeus: 5 Judas
__ Maccabeus: 5 Judah
Macchio: 5 Ralph
MacCorkindale: 5 Simon
MacDiarmid, Alan: 7 chemist 8 Nobelist
Macdonald: 4 John, Norm, Ross 5 Carey
MacDonald: 4 Ross 8 Jeanette
__ MacDonald: 3 Old
MacDonald, Jeanette: 7 actress
film: Bitter Sweet (1940)
The Cat and the Fiddle (1934)
Love Me Tonight (1932)
The Love Parade (1929)
Maytime (1937)
The Merry Widow (1934)
One Hour With You (1932)
Rose Marie (1936)
San Francisco (1936)
partner: Nelson Eddy
MacDonald, John D.: 6 writer
work: Condominium
The Deep Blue Good-by
The Dreadful Lemon Sky
Free Fall in Crimson
The Green Ripper
The Lonely Silver Rain
Nightmare in Pink
Macdonald, Ross: 6 writer
work: The Blue Hammer
The Moving Target
Sleeping Beauty
The Underground Man
MacDowell, Andie: 7 actress
film: Four Weddings and a Funeral (1994)
Green Card (1990)
Greystoke... (1984)
Groundhog Day (1993)
Just the Ticket (1999)
Michael (1996)
The Muse (1999)
The Object of Beauty (1991)
sex, lies, and videotape (1989)
Shadrach (1998)
Short Cuts (1993)
Macduff: 4 Scot
command to ~: 5 lay on
mace: 4 club 5 baton, spice, staff 6 cudgel 9 truncheon
bearer: 4 aril 6 beadle
macédoine: 5 salad 9 appetizer
Macedonia: 6 nation 7 country
ancient capital of ~: 6 Edessa
ancient ~ city: 5 Pella
bovine: 4 Busa
capital: 6 Skopje
city: 6 Bitola, Tetovo
mountain: 5 Korab
neighbor: 6 Greece 7 Albania 8 Bulgaria 10 Yugoslavia
Macedonian: 8 language
macerate: 3 ret 4 mash 6 squash
macfarlane: 4 coat 6 jacket 8 overcoat
MacGibbon: 7 Harriet
MacGraw, Ali: 7 actress
film: The Getaway (1972)
Goodbye, Columbus (1969)
Love Story (1970)
spouse: Robert Evans, Steve McQueen
MacGregor: 4 clan, Mary, Scot 5 Byron
MacGregor, Mary
song: Torn Between Two Lovers (1967)
MacGyver (ABC adventure)
cast: Richard Dean Anderson (MacGyver)
Mach: 5 Ernst
3 rival: 4 Atra
it travels at ~ 1: 5 sound
__-mâché: 5 paper 6 papier
Mach, Ernst: 8 Austrian 9 physicist
machete: 5 knife, panga 6 tarpon
kin: 4 bolo
origin: 8 Portugal
Machiavelli: 7 Niccolò
Machiavellian: 3 sly 6 amoral, artful, clever, crafty, shrewd 7 cunning, devious 9 deceitful, deceptive
machinate: 4 plot 5 hatch 6 scheme, wangle 7 collude, connive, finagle 8 conspire, contrive, engineer, intrigue, maneuver 9 play games 10 manipulate
machination: 4 plan, plot, ploy, ruse, trap 5 cabal, dodge, trick 6 device, scheme 8 artifice, intrigue, maneuver 9 dirty work, stratagem
machine: 4 tool 5 gizmo, motor, robot, setup, thing, zombi 6 agency, device, engine, gadget, system, widget, zombie 7 iron man, vehicle 8 computer 9 apparatus, appliance, automaton, implement, mechanism 10 automobile, instrument
insides of a ~: 5 works 9 mechanism
part: 3 cam, cog 4 gear
pattern: 3 die
machine __: 3 gun 4 shop, tool
__ machine: 4 copy, slot, time 5 money 6 adding, flying, rowing, sewing, simple, voting 7 copying, pinball, talking, vending, virtual, washing
machine-gun bunker: 4 nest
machinery: 3 rig 4 gear, tool 5 gears, means, motor, organ, plant, works 6 agency, engine, gadget, medium, system, tackle 7 vehicle 8 materiel, workings 9 apparatus, equipment, mechanism, structure 10 implements
adapt, as ~: 5 refit
lubricant: 6 ben oil
maintain the ~: 5 reoil
machine-shop
fixture: 3 jig 5 lathe 6 jigsaw
wear: 5 apron
__ Machine, The: 4 Time
macho: 4 male 5 manly, tough 6 brawny, strong, studly, virile 8 intrepid 9 assertive, masculine, two-fisted 10 aggressive, dominating
guy: 4 hunk 5 he-man
no ~ man: 4 wimp 5 sissy
not ~: 4 weak 5 timid, wimpy 6 trepid 7 fearful, wimpish

Macho Man (1978 song)
artist: Village People
Machree, Mother home: 4 Eire, Erin 7 Ireland
Machu Picchu
locale: 4 Peru
resident: 4 Inca 5 Incan
MacInnes: 5 Colin, Helen
Mack: 3 Ted 5 Craig, Helen, truck 6 Connie, Jillie, Lonnie, Marion 7 Sennett
__ Mack: 5 Jimmy
Mackenzie: 5 Astin, range, river 8 Phillips 9 Alexander
locale: 6 Canada
river to the ~: 5 Liard
MacKenzie: 6 Gisele 7 Compton
MacKenzie, Gisele: 6 singer
homeland: Canada
Mackenzie's Hundred
author: Frank Yerby
mackerel: 4 cero, fish, peto 5 wahoo
relative: 6 bonito
mackerel __: 3 sky
__ mackerel: 4 holy
Mackie: 3 Bob
Mackinac __: 6 Bridge, Island
Mackinac Island
locale: 5 Huron 8 Michigan
Mackinaw __: 4 coat
MacKinlay: 6 Kantor
mackintosh: 4 coat 6 jacket 7 topcoat 8 raincoat 10 protection
Mack & Mabel
character: 4 Ella, Iris 7 Normand, Sennett
composer: Jerry Herman
Mack, Ted: 4 host 5 emcee
Mack the Knife (1959 song)
artist: Bobby Darin
name: 4 Lucy 5 Lenya, Lotte, Polly
MacLachlan: 4 Kyle
MacLaine, Shirley: 7 actress
brother: Warren Beatty
film: The Apartment (1960)
Around the World in Eighty Days (1956)
Ask Any Girl (1959)
Being There (1979)
Bewitched (2005)
Bruno (2000)
Can-Can (1960)
Career (1959)
Desperate Characters (1971)
The Evening Star (1996)
Gambit (1966)
Guarding Tess (1994)
In Her Shoes (2005)
Irma la Douce (1963)
Madame Sousatzka (1988)
Mrs. Winterbourne (1996)
Postcards From the Edge (1990)
Rumor Has It (2005)
Some Came Running (1959)
Steel Magnolias (1989)
Sweet Charity (1969)
Terms of Endearment (1983, AA)
The Trouble With Harry (1955)
The Turning Point (1977)
Two for the Seesaw (1962)
Two Mules for Sister Sara (1970)
What a Way to Go! (1964)
Woman Times Seven (1967)
The Yellow Rolls-Royce (1964)
MacLane: 6 Barton
MacLean: 4 city, town 8 Alistair
locale: 8 Virginia
MacLeish, Archibald: 4 poet 6 writer
work: Conquistador
Songs for a Summer Day
Tower of Ivory
MacLeod: 5 Gavin
Macleod, John: 8 Nobelist
MacMahon: 5 Aline
Macmillan, Harold: 2 P.M. 7 British
predecessor: 4 Eden
successor: 11 Douglas-Home
MacMinnville: 4 city, town
locale: 6 Oregon
MacMurray, Fred: 5 actor
film: Above Suspicion (1943)
The Absent-Minded Professor (1961)
Alice Adams (1935)
The Apartment (1960)
The Caine Mutiny (1954)
Double Indemnity (1944)
The Egg and I (1947)
The Gilded Lily (1935)
Honeymoon in Bali (1939)
The Shaggy Dog (1959)
Sing, You Sinners (1938)
Son of Flubber (1963)
Take a Letter, Darling (1942)
Too Many Husbands (1940)
spouse: June Haver
TV: My Three Sons
Macnee: 7 Patrick
costar: 4 Rigg 7 Thorson
TV role: 5 Steed
MacNeice, Louis: 4 poet 5 Irish
work: Autumn Sequel
Blind Fireworks
Eighty-Five Poems
Solstices
MacNeil, Robert: 7 newsman
partner: 6 Lehrer
MacNelly, Jeff comic strip: 4 Shoe
MacNicol: Peter: 5 actor
TV: Ally McBeal
Macomb: 4 city, town
locale: 8 Illinois
Macon: 4 city, town
locale: 7 Georgia
Mâcon: 4 city, town, wine 5 white
locale: 6 France
river: 5 Saône
MacPhail: 3 Lee 4 Andy 5 Larry
Macpherson: 4 Elle
MacPherson __: 5 strut
Macquarie: 5 river
locale: 9 Australia
MacRae: 6 Gordon, Sheila 8 Meredith
MacRae, Gordon
spouse: Sheila MacRae
macramé: 5 craft
material: 5 twine
Macready: 6 George
macro: 10 large-scale
macrocosm: 5 world 6 nature 8 universe
macroeconomic stat: 3 GNP
macromolecular letters: 3 DNA
macrophysics: 7 science
macroscopic: 7 visible
macroseism: 10 earthquake
macula
locale: 3 eye
maculate: 5 dirty, grimy, sooty, stain, sully 6 defile, filthy, fouled, grubby, grungy, impure, soiled 7 debased, defiled, dirtied, smudged, spotted, stained, sullied, tainted 8 befouled, begrimed, polluted, slovenly, vitiated 9 blackened, corrupted, tarnished 10 besmirched, unsanitary
Macy: 2 R.H. 4 Bill 7 Rowland 8 William H.
Macy, Bill: 5 actor
TV: Maude
Macy's: 5 store
rival: 4 Saks 7 Gimbel's
Macy, William H.: 5 actor
film: A Civil Action (1998)
The Deal (2008)
Fargo (1996)
Focus (2001)
Happy, Texas (1999)
Mr. Holland's Opus (1995)
Panic (2000)
Pleasantville (1998)
State and Main (2000)
Wild Hogs (2007)
mad: 4 avid, daft, keen, loco, wild 5 angry, batty, crazy, goony, kooky, loony, manic, nutty, rabid, wacky 6 absurd, crazed, cuckoo, insane, kookie, looney, raving, unsafe, whacky 7 bananas, berserk, excited, foolish, frantic, in a rage, in a snit, rampage, ranting, teed off, unsound, violent, zealous 8 agitated, crackers, frenetic, frenzied, maniacal, provoked, unhinged, unstable, wild-eyed 9 fanatical, far gone on, foolhardy, illogical, imprudent, irritated, ludicrous, possessed, senseless 10 distraught, freaked out, infatuated, irrational, outrageous
about: 7 sweet on 10 enamored of, in love with
at: 9 angry with, cross with, upset with
be ~: 4 burn, fume, rage, rave, stew 6 blow up, see red, seethe
be ~ about: 4 love, rave 5 adore 6 admire
ender: 3 cap 4 wort 5 house
get ~: 3 ire, irk 4 rile 5 anger, peeve, upset 6 blow up, enrage, rear up 10 hit the roof
hopping ~: 4 sore 5 angry, cross, huffy, irate 6 ireful 7 furious 9 irritated
like ~: 6 wildly 8 fiercely 9 furiously, violently 10 vehemently, vigorously
one: 6 maniac
rush: 5 furor, hurry, panic 6 bustle, plunge, scurry 7 ferment, scamper, turmoil 8 outburst, stampede
see also angry
mad __: 4 dash 5 money
mad __ hatter: 3 as a
mad __ hornet: 3 as a
mad __ March hare: 3 as a
mad __ wet hen: 3 as a
__ mad: 4 like 7 hopping
Mad: 3 mag 8 magazine
feature: 6 parody, satire
Mad __: 3 Max 4 Love
Mad __ and Glory: 3 Dog
Mad __ You: 5 About
Mad About You (1986 song)
artist: Belinda Carlisle
Mad About You (NBC sitcom)
cast: Helen Hunt (Jamie Buchman)
Paul Reiser (Paul Buchman)
cousin: 3 Ira
dog: 6 Murray
Madách: 4 Imre
Madagascar: 4 isle 6 island, nation 7 country
beast: 4 vari 5 fossa
locale: 3 Afr. 6 Africa
money: 5 franc
primate: 5 indri, lemur 6 aye-aye
tree: 6 balata
Madagascar (2005 film)
voice cast: Jada Pinkett Smith, Chris Rock, David Schwimmer, Ben Stiller
Madalyn: 5 O'Hair
madam: 5 title, woman 6 female
mate: 3 sir
Madama Butterfly piece: 4 aria
madame: 3 gal, she 4 lady, marm 5 woman 6 female
Madame: 5 title
see also French
Madame __: 3 Nhu 4 Rosa 5 Curie 6 Bovary 7 de Staël, LaZonga
Madame Bovary: 5 novel
author: Gustave Flaubert
character: 4 Emma, Léon 5 Binet 6 Berthe 7 Heloise
Madame Butterfly: 5 opera 6 geisha
composer: Giacomo Puccini
role: 4 Goro, Kate 6 Suzuki 8 Yamadori 9 Cio-Cio-San, Pinkerton, Sharpless
setting: 5 Japan 8 Nagasaki
Madame Curie (1943 film)
cast: Greer Garson, Walter Pidgeon
director: Mervyn LeRoy
Madame Sousatzka (1988 film)
cast: Shirley MacLaine
Madame X (1966 film)
cast: Lana Turner
Madam, I'm __: 4 Adam
Madamina: 4 aria
Madam, Will You Talk?
author: Mary Stewart
Mad Anthony: 5 Wayne
mad as __ hen: 4 a wet
mad as a __: 6 hatter, hornet
mad as a __ hare: 5 March
madcap: 4 rash, wild, zany 5 antic, brash, clown, crazy, goony, hasty 6 jester, lively, stupid 7 foolish 8 heedless, reckless 9 daredevil, foolhardy, frivolous, hotheaded, imprudent, impulsive, uncareful 10 ill-advised, incautious, nonserious
Mädchen: 5 Amick
MADD concern: 3 DUI, DWI
madden: 3 ire, irk, vex 4 rile 5 anger, annoy, craze, haunt, peeve, upset 6 bother, enrage, frenzy, pester 7 derange, enflame, incense, inflame, outrage, possess, provoke, shatter, steam up, unhinge 8 distract, irritate 9 infuriate, unbalance 10 drive crazy, exasperate
Madden: 4 John
maddened: 3 hot 4 ired, sore 5 angry, cross, huffy, irate, livid, riled, wroth 6 fuming, ireful, raging, raving, red-hot 7 furious, ranting,

violent **8** choleric, wrathful **9** indignant, resentful, splenetic
maddening: 5 pesky, pesty
__ madder: 4 rose, wild
madder family shrub: 5 ixora **6** coffee **8** cinchona, gardenia **9** bouvardia
Mad Dog and Glory (1993 film)
cast: Robert De Niro, Bill Murray, Uma Thurman
Maddow: 6 Rachel
Maddox: 5 Garry **6** Lester
Maddox and the Rhythmasters, Johnny
song: The Crazy Otto (1955)
Maddux, Greg: 3 ace **6** hurler **7** pitcher
sport: 8 baseball
made: 7 devised **8** invented **9** concocted, contrived **10** fabricated
first: 5 newer
in French: 4 fait
in heaven: 7 perfect, utopian **9** exemplary, nonpareil
just ~: 3 new **5** fresh
not ~ up: 6 actual
of (suffix): 3 -ine
starter: 3 man **4** hand, home
made __ shade: 5 in the
__-made: 3 man **4** self, well **5** ready, union **6** custom, tailor
Made (2001 film)
cast: Peter Falk, Jon Favreau, Famke Janssen, Vince Vaughn
Made for Each Other (1971 film)
cast: Joseph Bologna, Paul Sorvino, Renee Taylor
Made in __: 3 USA
made in the __: 3 USA **5** shade
Madeira: 4 isle, wine **5** river, white **6** island
origin: 8 Portugal
port: 7 Funchal
River locale: 6 Brazil
madeleine: 4 cake **6** pastry
Madeleine: 5 Stowe **6** L'Engle **7** Carroll **8** Albright **9** de Scudéry
author: Ludwig Bemelmans
see also French
Madeleine Férat
author: Émile Zola
Madeline: 4 Kahn
Madeline (1998 film)
cast: Ben Daniels, Nigel Hawthorne, Hatty Jones, Frances McDormand
__ Madelon Claudet, The: 5 Sin of
__-made man: 4 self
__ made me do it!, The: 5 devil
__ Made Me Love You: 3 You
__-made millionaire: 4 self
mademoiselle: 4 girl, lass, maid, miss **5** title, youth **6** damsel, lassie, maiden **7** colleen **8** fraülein
see also French
Mademoiselle: 3 mag **8** magazine
rival: 4 Elle **5** Vogue **7** Glamour
Mademoiselle Merquem
author: George Sand
Madera: 4 city, town
locale: 6 Mexico **9** Chihuahua **10** California
made-to-__: 5 order **7** measure
made-up: 5 false **6** unreal, untrue **7** assumed **8** mythical, specious **9** fictional, imaginary, unnatural **10** fabricated, fictitious
story: 7 fiction

Madge: 5 Blake, Evans **7** Bellamy **8** Sinclair
madhouse: 3 zoo **5** chaos **6** bedlam, uproar **7** turmoil **8** shambles **9** mobocracy
Madhya Pradesh, capital of: 6 Bhopal
Madigan (1968 film)
cast: Henry Fonda, Harry Guardino, Richard Widmark
__ Madigan: 6 Elvira
Madigan, Amy: 7 actress
film: Field of Dreams (1989)
Love Letters (1983)
Places in the Heart (1984)
Pollock (2000)
Uncle Buck (1989)
With Friends Like These... (1999)
spouse: Ed Harris
Madison: 2 av. **3** ave., Guy **4** city, town **5** James, Oscar **6** avenue, Dolley
athletes: 7 Badgers
county: 4 Dane
locale: 3 Ala. **4** Wisc. **7** Alabama **9** Wisconsin
Madison Avenue
magazine: 6 Ad Week
output: 3 ads
payment: 5 ad fee
worker: 5 adman
Madison County structure: 6 bridge
Madison, Guy: 5 actor
TV: The Adventures of Wild Bill Hickok
Madison, James: 9 president
alma mater: 9 Princeton
home: 8 Virginia **10** Montpelier
opponent: 7 Clinton **8** Pinckney
V.P.: 5 Gerry **7** Clinton
wife: 6 Dolley
Madison, Oscar: 4 slob
creator: Neil Simon
like ~: 5 messy
portrayer: 7 Klugman, Matthau
roommate: Felix Unger
unlike ~: 4 neat
Madison Square Garden: 5 arena
Madlock, Bill
sport: 8 baseball
madly: 4 a lot, hard **6** keenly, rashly, wildly **7** crazily, hastily, quickly, rabidly, rapidly **8** absurdly, ardently, fiercely, insanely, speedily, stormily, urgently **9** devotedly, excitedly, extremely, fervently, foolishly, furiously, hurriedly, intensely, like crazy, viciously, violently **10** dementedly, frenziedly, recklessly
__ Madly Deeply: 5 Truly
Madlyn: 4 Rhue
__ Mad Mad Mad Mad World: 4 It's a
Madman at My Door
author: Hillary Waugh
Mad Max (1979 film)
cast: Mel Gibson
Mad Money (2008 film)
cast: Ted Danson, Katie Holmes, Diane Keaton, Queen Latifah
madness: 4 rage **5** folly, mania **6** lunacy **8** nonsense
__ Madness: 5 A Fine, March
mado: 4 fish
Madonna
documentary: Truth or Dare

film: Desperately Seeking Susan (1985)
Dick Tracy (1990)
Evita (1996)
A League of Their Own (1992)
The Next Best Thing (2000)
last name: Ciccone
role: 3 Eva **5** Evita, Perón
song: Angel (1985)
Beautiful Stranger (1999)
Borderline (1984)
Causing a Commotion (1987)
Cherish (1989)
Crazy for You (1985)
Deeper and Deeper (1992)
Don't Cry for Me Argentina (1997)
Dress You Up (1985)
Erotica (1992)
Express Yourself (1989)
Frozen (1998)
Hanky Panky (1990)
Holiday (1983)
I'll Remember (1994)
Justify My Love (1990)
Keep It Together (1990)
La Isla Bonita (1987)
Like a Prayer (1989)
Like a Virgin (1984)
Live to Tell (1986)
Lucky Star (1984)
Material Girl (1985)
Oh Father (1989)
Open Your Heart (1986)
Papa Don't Preach (1986)
The Power of Good-Bye (1998)
Rain (1993)
Ray of Light (1998)
Rescue Me (1991)
Secret (1994)
Take a Bow (1994)
This Used to Be My Playground (1992)
True Blue (1986)
Vogue (1990)
Who's That Girl (1987)
You'll See (1995)
You Must Love Me (1996)
spouse: Sean Penn, Guy Ritchie
work: Sex
__ Madonna: 4 Lady **7** Sistine
Madonna and __: 5 Child
Madonna With Rosary
artist: Guido Reni
Madonna With Saints
artist: Fra Lippi
__ Madox Brown: 4 Ford
madras: 5 scarf **6** fabric **8** kerchief
Madras: 4 city, port, town
language: 4 Urdu
locale: 5 India
madre: 6 mother **7** Spanish
baby: 4 nene
brother: 3 tío
sister: 3 tía
__ Madre: 6 Sierra
Madrid: 4 city, town **7** capital
airline to ~: 6 Iberia
city NW of ~: 4 Leon
locale: 5 Spain **6** España, Europe, Iberia
museum: 5 Prado **7** El Prado
neighbor: 5 Avila
river: 10 Manzanares
Madrid-to-Avila dir.: 3 WNW
madrigal: 3 lay **4** fala, song **5** music

madrilène: 4 soup
Madsen: 7 Michael **8** Virginia
Mad Trapper, The
author: Rudy Wiebe
Mad TV bit: 4 skit
Madura: 4 isle **6** island
locale: 4 Java **9** Indonesia
Madwoman of Chaillot, The
role: 4 Irma
Mae: 4 West **5** Busch, Marsh **6** Clarke, Murray **7** Jemison, Whitman
__ Mae: 5 Daisy **6** Fannie, Ginnie, Sallie
__ Mae Brown: 4 Rita
maelstrom: 4 eddy, vort **5** furor, hoo-ha, swirl **6** hoo-hah, hubbub, tumult, uproar, vortex **7** turmoil **8** sea swirl, shambles **9** whirlpool
Maelzel's Chess-Player
author: Edgar Allan Poe
__ Mae Morse: 4 Ella
maenad: 8 baccanal
maestro: 5 adept **6** master **9** conductor
need: 5 baton, score **9** orchestra
Maestro, Johnny: 6 singer
group: Brooklyn Bridge, Crests
Maeterlinck, Maurice: 4 poet **6** writer **8** Nobelist
Maeve: 6 Binchy
Mafia: 3 mob **9** gangsters **10** Cosa Nostra, underworld
leader: 3 don **4** capo **9** godfather
mag: 4 zine **7** fanzine, journal **10** periodical
see also magazine
mag __: 4 card, tape **5** wheel
mag.
edition: 3 iss., vol.
sales: 4 circ.
magazine: 3 rag **4** case, pulp **5** cache, daily, depot, ebony, issue, organ, print, shell, store **6** armory, digest, glossy, review, weekly **7** arsenal, gazette, journal, monthly **8** biweekly, circular **9** bimonthly, quarterly, warehouse **10** depository, periodical, repository, semiweekly, storehouse
Army ~: 4 Yank
business ~: 3 Inc. **6** Forbes **7** Fortune
category: 4 men's **6** women's
cheap ~: 4 pulp
computer: 4 Byte
contents: 4 ammo
current-events: 4 Time **6** US News **8** Newsweek
exec: 2 ed. **6** editor
extra: 6 insert
feature: 3 ads **4** item **5** essay **7** columns, letters **9** crossword
German ~: 5 Stern
glossy ~: 5 slick
ID: 4 ISSN
like some ~s: 5 illus., newsy, pulpy
look: 6 format
onetime: 4 Life, Look **5** Sport
online ~: 5 Slate
part: 2 pg. **4** page **5** cover
satire ~: 3 Mad
science ~: 4 Omni
science fiction ~: 6 Analog
section: 4 roto

space: 6 linage 7 lineage
stand: 4 rack 5 kiosk
starter: 4 news
title word: 6 Digest
women's ~: 4 Elle, Self 5 Cosmo, Vogue 6 Allure 7 Glamour
Magaziner: 3 Ira
magazines: 5 media, press
Magda: 5 Gabor
sister: 3 Eva 6 Zsa Zsa
Magdalene: 4 Mary
Magdalene College student: 6 Cantab
Magdeburg: 4 city, town
locale: 7 Germany
river: 4 Elbe
mage: 6 wizard 8 sorcerer
like a ~: 4 wise
Magee: 7 Patrick
Magellan: 5 probe 6 strait 10 space probe
destination: 5 Venus
org.: 4 NASA
Magellan, Ferdinand: 8 explorer 10 Portuguese
Magellania
author: Jules Verne
Magen __: 5 David
magenta: 3 red 5 color 6 purple, purply 7 crimson 8 purplish
relative: *see* red color
Maggie: 3 nag 4 Kuhn 5 Grace, Smith 7 Simpson
author: Stephen Crane
Maggie May (1971 song)
artist: Rod Stewart
Maggio: 6 Angelo
maggiore: 5 major 7 Italian
Maggiore: 4 Lago, lake
locale: 5 Italy 11 Switzerland
maggot: 3 bug 5 larva 6 insect 9 scoundrel
magi
member: 6 Gaspar
Magi: 4 trio 7 wise men
carrier: 5 camel
emulate the ~: 5 adore
guide: 4 star
member: 6 Caspar, Casper 8 Melchior 9 Balthazar
offering: 4 gift, gold 5 myrrh 12 frankincense
magic: 3 hex 4 tabu 5 charm, spell, taboo, vodun 6 hoodoo, occult, tricks, voodoo 7 charism, conjury, sorcery 8 black art, charisma, illusion, wizardry 9 bewitched, conjuring, enchanted, occultism, voodooism, witchlike 10 bewitching, divination, enchanting, entrancing, hocus-pocus, mysterious, necromancy, witchcraft
act: 5 trick 6 escape
black ~: 5 vodun 7 sorcery 9 diabolism 10 necromancy, witchcraft
charm: 4 mojo 6 fetich, fetish
do ~: 3 hex 6 invoke 7 conjure
potion: 7 arcanum
power: 4 mojo 5 spell
say ~ words: 6 incant
spirit: 5 fairy, genie
West Indies ~: 3 obi 5 obeah
white ~: 5 wicca
word: 4 poof 5 hocus, pocus, voilà 6 chango, please, presto 10 hocus-pocus 11 abracadabra
magic __: 4 wand 6 bullet, carpet, number, potion, square 7 lantern
__ magic: 5 black, white
Magic: 4 five 7 Johnson
home: 3 Fla. 7 Florida, Orlando
org.: 3 NBA
rival: *see* NBA team
where the ~ plays: 5 Orena
Magic (song)
artist: Olivia Newton-John, Pilot
Magic __: 3 Bus, Man 4 Chef, Time, Town 6 Marker
Magic __, The: 3 Box 5 Flute 6 Barrel
__ Magic: 3 It's 4 Blue 5 Night
__ magica: 3 ars
magical: 3 fey 5 runic, weird 6 mystic, occult 7 uncanny 8 mystical, wizardly 9 enchanted 10 bewitching, enchanting, entrancing, miraculous, mysterious
symbol: 5 sigil
Magical Mystery Tour
artist: Beatles
Magic Barrel, The
author: Bernard Malamud
Magic Bus (1968 song)
artist: Who, The
Magic Carpet Ride (1968 song)
artist: Steppenwolf
Magic Chef
alternative: *see* appliance brand
Magic Flute, The: 5 opera
composer: Wolfgang Amadeus Mozart
role: 6 Pamina, Tamino 8 Papagena, Papageno, Sarastro
setting: 5 Egypt 7 Memphis
Magic Hour
author: Susan Isaacs
magician: 3 wiz 5 magus 6 Merlin, wizard 7 charmer, diviner, warlock 8 conjurer, conjuror, sorcerer 9 enchanter
assistant: 7 famulus
need: 3 hat, saw 4 deck, wand 5 cards 6 rabbit, top hat
see also magic
__ Magic Moment: 4 This
Magic Moments (1958 song)
artist: Perry Como
Magic Mountain, The
author: Thomas Mann
character: 3 Leo 4 Hans 5 Albin, Berta 6 Hofrat, Naphta 7 Behrens, Castorp, Clavdia, Joachim, Marusja
Magic Mountain, The author
setting: 4 Alps 7 Germany
Magic Theater
painter: Paul Klee
Magic Time
author: W.P. Kinsella
__ Magic Woman: 5 Black
Maginot: 4 line 5 André
magisterial: 6 lordly 8 dogmatic 10 dogmatical
Magister Ludi
author: Hermann Hesse
magistrate: 5 judge, jurat 6 jurist 7 bailiff, officer 8 his Honor, official
ancient ~: 4 doge 5 edile, ephor 6 aedile, archon 8 triumvir
attendant: 6 lictor
Maglie, Sal: 6 hurler 7 pitcher 9 the Barber
magma: 4 lava, rock 7 mineral
magna __ laude: 3 cum
Magna: 3 car 4 auto, city, town 10 automobile, Mitsubishi
locale: 4 Utah
Magna __: 5 Carta 6 Charta
Magnani, Anna Oscar: The Rose Tattoo
magnanimity: 6 lenity 7 charity 8 kindness, nobility 9 tolerance
magnanimous: 3 big 4 free, kind 5 lofty, noble 6 decent, gentle, humane, kindly, tender 7 clement, gallant, lenient, liberal, sparing 8 all heart, generous, gracious, handsome, merciful, tolerant 9 bountiful, forgiving, unselfish 10 altruistic, benevolent, bighearted, charitable
magnate: 3 VIP 4 czar, lion, tsar, tzar 5 baron, mogul, nabob, nawab 6 bigwig, leader, tycoon 7 notable 9 financier, plutocrat 10 capitalist
Magnavox: 2 TV 3 VCR 5 TV set 10 television
alternative: *see* electronics company
magnesium: 5 metal 7 element
silicate: 4 talc
magnet: 4 lure
__ magnet: 3 bar 5 field
Magnet and Steel (1978 song)
artist: Walter Egan
magnetic: 8 alluring, charming, hypnotic, inviting 9 arresting, glamorous 10 attractive, bewitching, entrancing
alloy: 6 alnico
element: 4 iron 6 cobalt
unit: 3 ESU 5 gamma, gauss, henry, tesla, weber 7 oersted
magnetic __: 4 pole 5 field, storm
magnetic resonance __: 4 scan 7 imaging
magnetism: 4 lure, pull 5 charm, power 6 allure, appeal, glamor 7 charism, glamour 8 charisma, mystique 9 appetence, hypnotism, influence 10 attraction
__ magnetism: 6 animal
magnetite: 3 ore 7 mineral
magnetize: 4 draw 7 attract 9 captivate, electrify, hypnotize
Magnificat: 4 hymn, song
magnificence: 4 pomp 5 glory 7 majesty 8 elegance, grandeur, nobility, splendor
magnificent: 5 proud, regal, royal 6 august, lavish, lordly, mighty, ornate, solemn, swanky 7 exalted, opulent, radiant, stately 8 imposing, majestic, palatial, princely, towering, wondrous 9 arresting, luxurious, sumptuous, thrilling, wonderful 10 majestical
see also wonderful
Magnificent Ambersons, The: 4 film 5 novel
author: Booth Tarkington
director: Orson Welles
Magnificent Obsession (1954 film)
cast: Rock Hudson, Barbara Rush, Jane Wyman
director: Douglas Sirk
Magnificent Seven, The (1960 film)
cast: Charles Bronson, Yul Brynner, Horst Buchholz, James Coburn, Steve McQueen, Robert Vaughn, Eli Wallach
magnifico: 8 nobleman, splendid
magnifier: 4 lens 5 loupe
__ Magnifique: 4 C'est
magnify: 3 pad, wax 4 grow, hike, laud 5 add to, bless, boost, color, ensky, exalt, honor, raise, run up, swell 6 blow up, deepen, dilate, expand, extend, jack up, jump up, overdo, play up, puff up, revere, step up 7 advance, amplify, augment, build up, develop, elevate, enhance, enlarge, ennoble, glorify, inflate, promote, pyramid, worship 8 escalate, eulogize, heighten, increase, multiply, overplay, overrate, redouble 9 aggravate, embellish, embroider, intensify, overstate, recommend 10 aggrandize, exaggerate, overstress
magnifying __: 5 glass
magniloquence: 7 bombast 8 rhetoric
magniloquent: 5 lofty, tumid 7 fustian, orotund, pompous, stilted, verbose 9 bombastic, grandiose, overblown
magniloquize: 5 orate
Magnitogorsk river: 4 Ural
magnitude: 4 bulk, note, size 5 range, reach 6 amount, extent, import, length, moment, volume, weight 7 bigness, breadth, compass, expanse 8 capacity, eminence, enormity, grandeur, hugeness, loudness, strength, vastness 9 amplitude, greatness, immensity, intensity, largeness 10 dimensions, importance, proportion
magnolia: 4 tree 5 plant, shrub 6 flower
tree: 5 yulan 7 champac 8 champaca
Magnolia (1999 film)
cast: Tom Cruise, Julianne Moore, Jason Robards
__ Magnolias: 5 Steel
Magnolia St.: 4 Miss.
__-Magnon: 3 Cro
magnum: 3 gun 6 bottle 9 container
opus: 4 tome, work 7 classic 8 monument
magnum __: 4 opus
Magnum: 3 car 4 auto 5 Dodge 6 Thomas 10 automobile
Magnum Force (1973 film)
cast: Clint Eastwood, Hal Holbrook
Magnum, P.I. (CBS drama)
cast: John Hillerman (Jonathan Higgins)
Roger E. Mosley (T.C.)
Tom Selleck (Thomas Magnum)
dog: 4 Zeus 6 Apollo
setting: Oahu, Hawaii
Magnus: 4 Edie 8 Albertus
Magnuson: 3 Ann
Magog
ally: 3 Gog
father: 7 Japheth
grandfather: 4 Noah

Magoo: 5 myope 6 Quincy
dog: 6 Bowser
nephew: 5 Waldo
__ Magoos: 5 Blues
magpie: 3 daw 4 bird 6 yakker 7 babbler, windbag 9 loud-mouth 10 chatterbox
Magritte, René: 6 artist 7 Belgian, painter
contemporary: 4 Dali
Magruder: 3 Jeb
maguey: 6 cactus
Maguire: 3 AFB 5 Jerry, Molly, Tobey
Maguire, Jerry: 3 rep 5 agent
Maguire, Tobey: 5 actor
film: Cider House Rules (1999)
Pleasantville (1998)
Ride With the Devil (1999)
Spider-Man (2002)
Wonder Boys (2000)
magus: 4 sage 6 wizard 7 diviner, prophet 8 conjurer, conjuror, magician
__ Magus: 5 Simon
Magus, The: 5 novel
author: John Fowles
setting: 6 Greece
Magwitch: 4 Abel
Magyar tongue: 5 Ugric
mah-__: 4 jong 5 jongg
Mahabharata: 4 epic, poem
__ Mahal: 3 Taj
Mahalia: 7 Jackson
mahalo __ loa: 3 nui
maharajah: 5 ruler, title 6 gerent, Indian
maharani: 4 lady 5 noble, ruler, title 6 gerent
cover: 4 sari 5 saree
Maharis: 6 George
maharishi: 5 title 6 cleric
mahatma: 4 sage 6 cleric
garment: 5 dhoti, dhuti 6 dhooti 7 dhootie
Mahatma: 5 title 6 Gandhi
Mahayana
school: 3 Zen 4 Chan
teacher: 4 lama
Maher: 4 Bill
Ma, he's making eyes __: 4 at me
Mahican: 6 Indian 7 Amerind
mahimahi: 6 dorado 7 dolphin
mah-jongg: 4 game
counter: 4 tile
tile: 3 bam 4 soap, wind 5 crack
Mahler, Gustav: 8 Austrian, composer
wife: 4 Alma
work: Das Lied von der Erde
Kindertotenlieder
Resurrection Symphony
Symphony of a Thousand
Mahlon
mother: 5 Naomi
mahogany: 4 tree, wood 5 brown 7 reddish 8 hardwood
relative: *see* brown color
tree: 4 neem 5 lauan 6 acajou, carapa, sapele 7 avodire 8 andiroba, crabwood
mahoganylike tree: 4 agba
Mahogany Row denizen: 4 exec 9 executive
Mahogany Theme (1975 song)
artist: Diana Ross
Mahoney: 4 Jock, John 5 Jerry
mahout master: 5 saheb, sahib
Mahre, Phil: 5 skier
Mahwah: 4 city, town
locale: 9 New Jersey
mai: 3 May 4 mois 5 month 6 French
follower: 4 juin
preceder: 5 avril
mai __: 3 tai
Mai: 10 Zetterling
Maia: 4 star 6 Pleiad
father: 5 Atlas
son: 6 Hermes
maid: 4 girl, lass, miss 5 bonne, Hazel, woman 6 damsel, duster, female, lassie 7 abigail, colleen, servant 8 domestic, fraülein 9 launderer, soubrette, young lady
at times: 6 ironer
British ~: 4 char
ender: 7 servant
India ~: 4 ayah
in French: 5 bonne, fille
starter: 3 bar 4 bond, hand, milk 5 dairy, house, nurse 6 brides 7 chamber
target: 4 dust
__ maid: 3 old 5 lady's, meter 6 live-in
Maid __: 6 Marian
__ Maid: 3 Old 6 Minute
maiden: 4 girl, lass, miss 5 first, woman, youth 6 damsel, female, lassie 7 colleen, initial 8 earliest, fraülein, señorita 9 inaugural 10 demoiselle, initiatory
lack: 3 win
name indicator: 3 née
starter: 4 hand
yon ~: 3 her, she
maiden __: 4 name 6 voyage
maidenhair: 4 fern, tree, vine 6 gingko, ginkgo
maidenly: 4 pure 6 chaste
M'aidez!: 3 SOS 4 help 5 alarm, alert
maid-in-__: 7 waiting
Maid in Manhattan (2002 film)
cast: Ralph Fiennes, Jennifer Lopez, Natasha Richardson
maid of __: 5 honor
Maid of __: 5 Salem 7 Orléans
Maid of Athens, __ we part: 3 ere
Maid of Orleans, The
author: Friedrich von Schiller
Maid of the Mist: 4 boat
maids: 4 help
__ Maids All in a Row: 6 Pretty
__ maids a-milking...: 5 Eight
Maids, The
author: Jean Genet
Maidstone county: 4 Kent
Maid to Order (1987 film)
cast: Beverly D'Angelo, Valerie Perrine, Ally Sheedy
Maigret: 4 Insp. 9 Inspector
see also French
mail: 4 post, send 5 armor, metal, remit 6 direct, letter, parcel, shield 7 arrival, express, forward, package 8 dispatch, postcard, transfer, transmit
accompaniment: 3 SAE 4 SASE
agcy.: 4 USPS
Army ~ addr.: 3 APO, FPO
beat: 3 rte. 5 route
check one's ~ maybe: 5 log in, log on
drop: 2 PO 3 APO, box, FPO, GPO 5 PO box
ender: 3 bag, box, man, men 4 room
for free: 5 frank
holder: 3 bag, box 4 slot 5 chute, pouch
junk ~: 3 ads 4 spam 6 letter 7 catalog
motto word: 3 nor 4 rain, snow 5 sleet
need: 5 stamp 7 zip code 8 envelope
piece of ~: 3 ltr. 4 card 6 letter 8 postcard 10 postal card
prepare to ~: 4 seal 5 stamp
railroad ~ place: 3 RPO
starter: 3 air 4 gray, grey 5 black, green
mail __: 3 car 4 boat, call, drop, flag, room 5 order 7 carrier
__ mail: 3 air, fan 4 bulk, dead, hate, junk 5 chain, snail, voice 6 direct
__ Mail: 5 Night 7 Express 8 Priority
mailed __: 4 fist
Mailer, Norman: 6 writer
work: An American Dream
The Armies of the Night
The Big Empty
The Castle in the Forest
The Deer Park
The Executioner's Song
The Naked and the Dead
On God
The Presidential Papers
The Spooky Art
Tough Guys Don't Dance
mailing: 8 delivery
including ~ cost: 3 ppd. 7 prepaid
mailing __: 4 list
mailing-list unit: 4 name
maillot: 5 shirt 6 tights 7 costume 8 pullover
mail-order
benefit, perhaps: 5 no tax
charge: 3 COD 5 S and H
company: 4 K-Tel 6 L.L. Bean
Mail Order Bride (1964 film)
cast: Keir Dullea, Buddy Ebsen, Warren Oates
mailroom
gizmo: 5 dater
stamp: 3 rcd. 8 received
work in the ~: 4 sort
maim: 4 harm, hurt, ruin 5 crush, wound 6 batter, damage, deface, impair, injure, mangle 8 lacerate 9 hamstring, indispose
maimed: 4 hurt 7 injured
Maimonides: 5 Moses 6 Jewish 7 Spanish 11 philosopher
main: 3 key, sea 4 arch, duct, head, pipe, prin., star 5 basic, briny, chief, first, grand, major, ocean, prime, sheer, trunk, utter, vital 6 ruling, staple, utmost 7 capital, central, conduit, crucial, gas line, leading, premier, primary, special, stellar, supreme 8 cardinal, critical, dominant, favorite, foremost 9 essential, governing, paramount, principal, prominent, uppermost, water line, water pipe 10 overriding, preeminent, prevailing
bounding ~: 3 sea 5 ocean
ender: 3 top 4 land, line, mast, sail, stay 5 frame, sheet 6 lander, spring, stream
event: 4 bout, duel 5 fight, match, round 7 contest, feature 8 showcase 9 headliner, highlight 10 engagement
focus: 4 gist 5 tenor, topic
give the ~ idea: 9 summarize
idea: 3 nub 4 core, crux, gist, knub, pith 5 focus, motif, point 7 essence, keynote, outline 10 bottom line
in the ~: 7 as a rule, usually 9 routinely
on the ~: 4 asea 5 at sea
part: 4 body, bulk
partner: 5 might
main __: 4 drag, line 6 course
__ main: 3 gas 5 in the, water
Main: 2 st. 5 river 6 street 8 Marjorie
city on the ~: 9 Frankfurt
River locale: 7 Germany
Main __: 6 Street
__ Main: 7 Spanish
Maine: 4 boat, ship 5 state 8 Down East 10 battleship
animal: 5 moose 7 caribou
bay: 5 Casco 9 Penobscot
city: 4 Saco 5 Lubec, Orono 6 Auburn, Bangor, Calais 7 Augusta, Caribou, Sanford 8 Lewiston, Portland 9 Biddeford, Brunswick
Indian: 6 Abnaki 7 Abenaki 8 Malecite, Wabanaki 9 Penobscot
lake: 9 Moosehead
like a ~ woods: 5 piney
merchant: 6 L.L. Bean
motto: 6 Dirigo
mountain: 8 Katahdin
national park: 6 Acadia
neighbor: 6 Canada, Quebec
river: 4 Saco
senator: 5 Snowe
state animal: 5 moose
state bird: 9 chickadee
state cat: 7 coon cat
state fish: 6 salmon
state gemstone: 10 tourmaline
state insect: 8 honeybee
state tree: 4 pine 9 white pine
Tom's of ~: 10 toothpaste
University of ~ locale: 5 Orono
where the ~ blew up: 4 Cuba 6 Havana
Maine __ cat: 4 coon
Maine-et-__: 5 Loire
Maines: 7 Natalie
Maine-to-Florida route: 5 US one
Main Event, The (1979 film)
cast: Ryan O'Neal, Barbra Streisand
mainframe: 3 CPU 8 computer
mainland __: 5 China 7 Chinese
Mainline: 3 car 4 auto, Ford 10 automobile
mainly: 6 mostly 7 at large, chiefly, largely, overall, usually 8 above all, all in all 9 generally, in general, most of all, primarily 10 especially, on the whole
mainsail neighbor: 3 jib
mainspring: 4 root 6 motive, origin
mainstay: 4 prop, rock 5 brace 6 anchor, pillar, staple 7 bastion, bulwark, sponsor, support 8 backbone, buttress, linchpin, lynchpin, strength, upholder 9 supporter, sustainer

mainstream: **4** mode **5** usual **6** center, middle **7** average, popular **8** mediocre, moderate
in the ~: **7** current
not ~: **5** outré
out of the ~: **5** apart
Main Street
author: Sinclair Lewis
character: **3** Bea, Guy, Sam **4** Erik, Hugh, Vida **5** Carol
maintain: **3** say **4** aver, avow, bear, have, hold, keep, save, tend **5** amass, argue, cache, claim, hoard, put by, reach, state, store, swear, vouch **6** affirm, allege, assert, attest, defend, garner, hold to, insist, keep up, manage, occupy, pursue, resist, retain, save up, uphold **7** believe, care for, carry on, contend, declare, finance, nurture, persist, possess, profess, prolong, protect, protest, provide, purport, put away, reserve, stand by, support, sustain **8** conserve, continue, go on with, hang onto, hold onto, preserve, put aside **9** keep going, look after, persevere, predicate, stabilize, vindicate **10** accumulate, asseverate, perpetuate, take care of
barely ~: **6** eke out
maintainable: **7** tenable
maintenance: **4** care, keep **6** living, upkeep **7** alimony, repairs, running, service, support **10** livelihood
worker: **5** super **8** handyman
maintenance-__: **4** free
maintop: **8** platform
Mainz: **4** city, town
locale: **7** Germany
river: **5** Rhine
Mairzy __: **5** Doats
maison: **5** house **6** French
division: **5** salle
entrance: **5** porte
floor in a ~: **5** étage
__ maison: **3** à la
mais oui
see of course
mai tai: **5** drink **8** beverage, cocktail
ingredient: **3** rum **7** curaçao **10** fruit juice
maître __: **6** d'hôtel
maître d' offering: **4** menu
maize: **4** corn **5** color **6** yellow
genus: **3** zea
relative: *see* yellow color
Spanish ~ grinding stone: **4** mano
maj.: **4** rank
employer: **3** USA **4** USMC
subordinate: **3** NCO, PFC, pvt., sgt. **4** capt. **5** lieut.
superior: **3** col., gen. **5** lt. col.
Maj. __: **3** Gen.
__ Maj.: **3** Sgt.
__ Maja, The: **5** Naked
Majel: **7** Barrett
__ majesté: **4** lèse
majestic: **4** epic **5** grand, large, lofty, noble, proud, regal, royal **6** august, epical, kingly, lordly, mighty, solemn, superb **7** awesome, elegant, exalted, stately, sublime **8** empyreal, empyrean, glorious, imperial, imposing, kinglike, palatial, splendid **9** dignified, luxurious, sovereign **10** impressive, monumental, statuesque
majesty: **4** king **5** glory, state **7** dignity, monarch **8** grandeur, nobility, splendor **9** sovereign **10** kingliness
lese ~: **7** treason **8** betrayal, sedition **9** treachery
__ majesty: **3** her, his **4** lese, leze, your
Majesty: **5** title
__ Majesty's Secret Service: **5** On Her
__ majeure: **5** force
majolica glaze: **3** tin
major: **3** key, top **4** arch, main, more, rank, star, ugly **5** chief, grave, vital **6** Hoople, larger, needed, senior, utmost **7** crucial, greater, leading, pivotal, primary, serious, sizable, special, weighty **8** critical, dominant, greatest, Houlihan, required, sizeable **9** big-league, governing, important, mandatory, necessary, principal, specialty, uttermost **10** overriding, preeminent
college ~: **3** art, bio, mus. **4** biol., chem., econ, educ., hist, math, phys. **5** drama, music **6** acting, anthro, cinema, French, phys. ed. **7** biology, English, geology, history, physics., poli sci **9** chemistry, economics, education
command: **6** at ease
ender: **4** ette
grad-school ~: **3** law **7** finance **8** medicine **9** dentistry, economics
in music: **3** dur **8** maggiore
not ~: **5** minor
portion: **4** bulk
major __: **3** key **5** scale **6** league **7** general, medical
major-__: **4** domo **7** leaguer
__ major: **4** drum
Major: **4** John **5** Bowes, Lance **6** Harris **7** Barbara
Major __: **3** Dad **6** League **7** Barbara, Prophet
__ Major: **4** Ursa **5** Canis **6** Syrtis
Major and the Minor, The (1942 film)
cast: Rita Johnson, Ray Milland, Ginger Rogers
director: Billy Wilder
Major Barbara
author: George Bernard Shaw
Majorca: **4** isle **6** island
neighbor: **5** Ibiza, Iviza
port: **5** Palma
see also Spanish
Major Dad (CBS sitcom)
cast: Gerald McRaney (Maj. John MacGillis)
Shanna Reed (Polly MacGillis)
major-domo: **6** butler **10** manservant
majorette
gait: **5** strut
motion: **5** twirl
twirler: **5** baton
__ majorette: **4** drum
Majorino: **4** Tina
__ Majoris: **5** Canis, Ursae
majority: **4** body, bulk, mass, most, vote **5** prime **7** manhood **8** best part, maturity **9** adulthood, plurality, womanhood **10** lion's share
attain ~: **6** mature
majority __: **4** rule **6** leader
majority __, a: **5** of one
__ majority: **6** silent, simple
Majority __, A: **5** of One
__ Majority, The: **5** Moral
Major, John: **2** P.M. **4** Tory **7** British
predecessor: **8** Thatcher
successor: **5** Blair
major league
see baseball
major-league: **3** big **5** great
Major League: **4** Amer., Natl. **8** American, National
Major League (1989 film)
cast: Tom Berenger, Corbin Bernsen, Charlie Sheen
major leaguer: **3** pro
major-leaguers: **7** big boys
Majors, Lee
spouse: Farrah Fawcett
TV: The Big Valley, The Fall Guy, The Six Million Dollar Man
Majuro: **4** city, town
locale: **9** Marshalls
majuscule: **6** letter **7** capital
Makarov: **4** Oleg
Makarova: **7** Natalia
make: **3** fix, get, net, set **4** brew, cook, earn, form, gain, mint, mold, name, sort, verb, wage **5** build, cause, clear, craft, draft, drive, elect, enact, erect, force, forge, frame, gauge, gross, hatch, impel, judge, press, put up, reach, ready, shape, spawn **6** attain, coerce, come to, compel, cook up, create, deduce, derive, draw up, finger, invent, kidney, lead to, oblige, ordain, parent, put out, reckon, spoils, take in, whip up **7** achieve, add up to, advance, appoint, bring in, compose, dragoon, dream up, fashion, prepare, produce, proffer, quality, realize, receive, turn out, variety **8** amount to, assemble, compound, comprise, conclude, delegate, engender, estimate, generate, knock off, nominate, pull down **9** brand name, calculate, constrain, construct, designate, establish, fabricate, formulate, legislate, originate, recognize, structure **10** bring about, bring forth, constitute, pressurize, synthesize
a break: **7** go south
a face: **3** mug **5** scowl, smirk, wince
a faux pas: **3** err **4** flub, goof, muff, slip, trip **5** botch, lapse, stray **6** boo-boo, bungle, foul up, fumble, mess up, slip up **7** blunder, go wrong, louse up, misstep, stumble **8** go astray
a fuss: **4** beef, carp, kick, mind, moan, rail, rant, sigh, wail, weep, yell **5** cavil, demur, gripe, groan, growl, mourn, whine **6** grouch, grouse, holler, mutter, repine, squawk, squeal, yammer **7** grumble, protest, quarrel, trouble, whimper **8** complain, sound off **9** bellyache, find fault, give a darn
a gaffe: **6** slip up **7** blunder
a getaway: **3** run **4** bolt, flee, flit, skip **5** elude, evade **6** decamp, escape **7** abscond **8** jump bail, shake off **9** cut and run, disappear, skedaddle **10** hightail it
a gift: **5** grant, offer **6** bestow, confer **8** bequeath **10** contribute
a hash of: **4** flub, goof, muff **5** botch, gum up **6** bungle, foul up, goof up, mess up **7** louse up
a hit: **7** succeed, triumph
a hole: **4** bore **5** gouge **6** burrow, dredge **8** excavate **9** hollow out
a judicial decision: **4** find **5** order **6** decide, decree, ordain **7** preside, resolve **8** sentence **9** prescribe, pronounce
a long face: **4** mope, sulk **5** brood
amends: **3** pay **5** atone, repay **6** redeem, reform, refund **7** appease, expiate, redress, requite **8** atone for **9** apologize, indemnify **10** compensate, recompense
a mess of: **4** muff **6** ball up, bungle, foul up, muddle **7** butcher, screw up **9** mishandle, mismanage
an entreaty: **3** beg **4** seek, urge **5** plead, probe, query **6** appeal **7** beseech, implore, inquire, request **8** call upon, petition
as if: **3** act **4** pose **5** feign **7** pretend **8** simulate
a stand: **4** dare, defy **5** claim, fight, query, rally **6** accost, object, take on, threat **7** contest, dispute, protest, vie with **8** confront, denounce, face down, question **9** challenge, discredit, stimulate, vindicate **10** contradict, controvert, insist upon
back: **6** regain
barely ~: **6** eke out
believe: **3** lie **4** fool, play, pose **5** dream, enact, feign **7** act as if, act like, imagine, playact, pretend **8** simulate **9** fantasize
book: **3** bet **4** punt **5** stake, wager **6** gamble **8** give odds, take bets **9** speculate
clear: **4** look, show **5** state **6** decode, define, detail, evince, refine **7** exhibit, explain **8** decipher, describe, simplify **9** bring home, emphasize, explicate, expound on, get across, put across, translate **10** illuminate, illustrate
do: **3** eke **4** cope **5** adapt, get by **6** eke out, manage **7** survive **8** get along, scrape by
do with: **3** use
ecstatic: **5** liven **6** lift up, please, thrill **7** delight, elevate, gladden, hearten, satisfy **9** enrapture **10** exhilarate
effervescent: **7** freshen **9** oxygenate, ventilate
eligible: **6** enable, permit **7** empower, qualify **8** christen **9** authorize, designate, privilege **10** legitimize

ender: **4** over **5** shift **6** weight
enemies: **5** anger **6** fire up, madden **7** incense, inflame, provoke **8** irritate **9** displease, infuriate **10** exasperate
equivalent: **5** level **7** balance
exuberant: **4** gush, rave, send **5** psych **6** excite, fire up, thrill, work up **7** impress **8** interest **9** electrify **10** bubble over, effervesce, get excited
eyes at: **3** eye **4** ogle **5** stare, tease **7** eyeball **8** coquette
fast: **3** fix, peg, tie **4** bind, lock, moor, nail **5** hitch, latch, rivet, truss
feasible: **3** let **6** permit **7** empower, license, qualify **9** authorize
feeble: **6** weaken **8** enervate **9** attenuate **10** devitalize
filthy: **4** foul, soil **5** dirty, spoil, stain, sully, taint **6** befoul, defile **7** corrupt, vitiate **9** desecrate **10** adulterate
final: **5** close **6** clinch **8** finalize **10** consummate
finer: **6** better **7** enhance, improve, sweeten **9** embellish **10** supplement
firewood: **3** cut **4** chop
firm: **3** pin, tie **4** bind, bond, gird, lock, nail, root, weld **5** brace, build, plant, rivet, shore, steel **6** anchor, cement, enroot, fasten, harden, secure, tone up **7** bolster, build up, fortify, implant, shore up, stiffen, tighten, toughen **8** buttress, entrench, nail down, rigidify, solidify **9** reinforce, stabilize **10** straighten
fit: **4** suit **5** adapt, alter, amend **6** adjust, recast, remold, revamp, revise, tailor **7** correct, reshape **8** fine-tune, renovate
flat: **4** even **8** straight
for: **7** advance, promote **8** go toward **10** facilitate, head toward
friends: **7** connect
fun of: **3** kid, rag, rib **4** bait, gibe, jape, jeer, jibe, jive, mock, razz, twit **5** fleer, mimic, rag on, taunt, tease **6** banter, deride, go like **7** lampoon, laugh at, run down, scoff at **8** ridicule
furious: **6** enrage
fuzzy: **4** blur, roil, veil **5** bedim, befog **7** obscure
gape: **3** awe **4** daze, rock, stun **5** floor **6** bemuse, boggle, dazzle, thrill **7** astound, nonplus **8** astonish, blow away, bowl over, confound, transfix **9** dumbfound, take aback **10** strike dumb
gentle: **6** mellow, soften **8** civilize
gloomy: **6** dampen, deject, sadden, shadow **7** depress, obscure **8** dispirit **9** bring down **10** demoralize, discourage, dishearten
glow: **5** shine **6** polish **7** burnish, cheer up, light up **8** illumine **10** illuminate
godlike: **5** adore, exalt, extol **7** elevate, glorify, worship **8** sanctify, venerate **10** consecrate
good: **3** pay, win **5** atone, pay up, repay **6** arrive, do well, fulfil, hack it, pan out, pay for, recoup, redeem, refund, settle, thrive **7** deliver, fulfill, luck out, pay back, prevail, prosper, realize, recover, rectify, satisfy, succeed, triumph, work out **8** atone for, flourish, get ahead, go places, hit it big, square up **9** indemnify, reimburse **10** accomplish, do all right, make amends, recompense
goo-goo eyes at: **5** flirt **8** check out
greater: **3** pad **4** feed, hike **5** add to, boost, swell, widen **6** beef up, expand, extend, jack up **7** amplify, build up, develop, enhance, enlarge, inflate, magnify, scale up **8** heighten, increase, lengthen **9** intensify **10** aggrandize, strengthen, supplement
happy: **5** cheer, elate, liven **6** lift up, please, thrill, turn on **7** beatify, content, delight, gladden, gratify, hearten, lighten, overjoy, satisfy, sweeten **8** brighten, enthrall **9** enrapture, inebriate, make happy, transport **10** exhilarate, intoxicate
harmonious: **9** reconcile
haste: **8** hightail **10** burn rubber, get hopping
hazy: **5** bedim, befog, blear, cloud, muddy, smear **7** becloud, obscure **9** adumbrate
heads or tails of: **3** see **6** fathom, follow, pick up **9** figure out **10** comprehend, understand
headway: **4** gain
help to ~ up: **6** pacify, soothe **7** appease, assuage, mediate, mollify, patch up, placate, reunite, satisfy, sweeten, win over **9** arbitrate, intervene, reconcile **10** compromise, conciliate
higher: **4** hike **5** boost, raise **7** elevate **8** increase
hit the ceiling: **5** anger **6** madden, offend **7** incense **9** infuriate
hostile: **10** antagonize
ill: **5** repel, upset **6** infect, offend, revolt **7** afflict
into law: **4** pass **9** institute, legislate
it: **3** win **4** come, live **5** pop up, reach **6** arrive, attend, do well, pan out, thrive **7** luck out, prevail, prosper, qualify, succeed, triumph, weather, work out **8** flourish, get ahead, get there, go places **10** do all right
jump: **5** alarm, panic, scare, spook **7** disturb, startle **8** affright, frighten, surprise **9** galvanize, give a turn
just ~ it: **4** last **5** exist **6** endure, hang on, manage **7** ride out, survive **8** scrape by **9** stay alive **10** stick it out
keen: **5** pique, rally, rouse, strop **6** arouse, excite, kindle **7** sharpen
kind: **6** gentle, mellow, soften, temper
kiss and ~ up: **5** yield **6** accept, pardon **7** appease, let it go, let pass, patch up, placate, reunite **8** overlook, take back **9** acquiesce
knifelike: **4** file, hone, whet **5** grind, strop
known: **3** air, say **4** bare, leak, post, show, tell **5** admit, let on, speak, utter, voice **6** advise, convey, expose, herald, impart, let out, report, reveal, spread, unfold, unmask, unveil **7** declare, display, divulge, exhibit, lay bare, let slip, mention, narrate, uncover **8** advise of, announce, disclose, proclaim **9** advertise, circulate, introduce, propagate, publicize, ventilate **10** make public, promulgate
late: **4** keep **5** delay **6** hang up, hinder, hold up, impede, retard **7** bog down, set back **8** slow down **10** buttonhole
laugh: **5** cheer **6** divert, regale, tickle **7** delight **9** entertain
legal: **2** OK **3** ink **6** ratify **7** approve, certify, endorse, initial, witness **8** legalize, sanction **9** authorize, establish, formalize, sign off on **10** constitute, legitimize
less: **5** allay **6** reduce
less narrow: **6** expand, spread **7** broaden, enlarge, thicken **9** spread out
less wild: **5** break **6** soften **7** harness **8** tone down
light of: **3** rag **4** mock **5** gloze, scoff **6** deride, lessen, slight **7** neglect **8** discount, downplay, minimize, overlook, palliate, play down, pooh-pooh, shrug off, sneeze at, talk down **9** deprecate, soft-pedal, underplay, whitewash **10** understate
like: **3** ape **4** copy, echo **5** mimic **6** mirror **7** imitate
longer: **3** pad **5** add to **6** extend, let out **7** augment, drag out, draw out, prolong, spin out, stretch **8** continue, increase, protract **9** string out
merry: **4** play, romp **5** amuse, exult, laugh, party, revel **6** cavort, frolic **7** carouse, rejoice, satisfy **8** live it up **9** celebrate, entertain, have a ball
more inclusive: **6** expand, spread **7** augment, broaden, enlarge
much of: **4** tout **5** exalt **6** praise, stress **7** amplify, magnify **9** emphasize **10** compliment
naked: **4** bare **5** strip **7** disrobe, uncover, undress
neat: **4** tidy **5** clean, fix up, order **6** spruce **7** freshen, shape up **8** organize, spruce up **9** smarten up **10** straighten
nervous: **5** spook **6** rattle, unglue **7** fluster **8** unsettle **10** discompose, disconcert, intimidate
not ~ the grade: **4** bomb, flop, fold **7** lose out **8** fall flat **9** fall short
null: **6** cancel, repeal **7** rescind, reverse **8** set aside **9** supersede **10** invalidate
obligatory: **5** exact, force, order **6** charge, compel, decree, demand, enjoin **7** command, dictate, inflict **9** establish, institute, prescribe, stipulate **10** promulgate
off: **2** go **3** fly, run **4** bolt, flee, skip **5** lam it, leave, scoot, scram, split **6** beat it, be gone, cut out, decamp, depart, escape **7** abscond, bail out, go south, run away, scamper, skip out, vamoose **8** clear out, fugitate, light out, run for it, skip town, withdraw **9** cut and run, skedaddle **10** hightail it
off with: **3** rob **5** filch, steal, swipe **6** abduct, kidnap, pilfer, snatch **7** ransack
one: **3** wed **5** merge
one's flesh crawl: **5** chill, panic, scare, spook **7** horrify, petrify, terrify **8** frighten **9** terrorize
one's head swim: **5** amaze **6** dazzle **7** impress
one's own: **5** adopt **7** espouse
one's position known: **6** assert **7** declare **8** sound off **10** stand up for
orderly: **5** clean **6** neaten **8** spruce up **10** straighten
out: **2** go **3** see, win **4** cope, espy, fare, find, hint, read, spot, tell **5** get by, get on, grasp, imply, infer, sight, solve **6** deduce, descry, detect, do with, endure, fathom, follow, hack it, impute, manage, notice, reason, thrive **7** achieve, discern, observe, prevail, profess, prosper, succeed, suggest, survive, triumph **8** decipher, flourish, get ahead, get along, go places, hit it big, identify, intimate, make good, perceive, scrape by **9** insinuate, recognize **10** comprehend, do all right, understand
over: **4** redo **5** alter **6** change, reform, revamp **7** correct, remodel, reshape **8** transfer **9** transform **10** redecorate, reorganize
plain: **4** show **6** evince **7** clarify, exhibit, speak up **8** manifest, simplify, speak out **9** bring home, elucidate, explicate **10** illustrate
public: **3** air **4** bare, leak **5** break, speak **6** expose, report, reveal, spread, unmask, unveil **7** divulge, exhibit, lay bare, let slip, uncover **8** announce, disclose, proclaim **9** broadcast
quake: **5** alarm, panic **6** rattle **7** horrify, petrify, shake up, startle, terrify **8** frighten **10** intimidate
readable: **5** crack **7** decrypt **8** decipher **9** interpret, translate
ready: **3** set **4** prep **5** equip, groom, prime, train **7** arrange **8** mobilize **9** condition
ringlets: **4** coil **5** swirl, twine, twirl, twist
room for: **3** add **5** admit **6** append, insert **9** interject

sense: 4 jell 5 add up, fit in 6 cohere, figure, relate, square 7 conform, connect 8 dovetail 9 hold water 10 correspond
sure: 5 check 6 affirm, verify 7 confirm, see to it 9 ascertain, guarantee
the best of: 5 get by 6 manage 8 tolerate 9 put up with, reconcile
the cut: 6 hack it
the grade: 3 win 4 pass 5 ace it, cut it, score 6 arrive, hack it, pan out, thrive 7 luck out, prevail, prosper, qualify, satisfy, succeed, triumph, work out 8 flourish, get ahead, go places 9 measure up 10 pass muster
the rounds: 3 mix 4 walk 5 watch 6 hobnob, mingle, police 7 inspect
the scene: 4 come, show 5 enter, reach, visit 6 appear, arrive, attend, emerge, stop by 7 turn out
too much of: 8 overrate 9 overstate 10 exaggerate
tracks: 3 hie, run 4 bolt, flee, race, rush, tear 5 hurry, scoot, scram, spank 6 depart, hasten 7 vamoose 8 fugitate 10 accelerate, get hopping
unclear: 3 dim, fog 4 blur, roil, veil 5 bedim, befog 6 darken 7 confuse, mystify, obscure 8 bewilder, confound 9 obfuscate
understandable: 7 clarify, clear up 9 elucidate, explicate, get across 10 illuminate, illustrate
unfit: 4 lame, maim, ruin 5 lay up, wreck 6 injure 8 sabotage 9 hamstring
uniform: 4 even, sand 5 level, plane
untidy: 6 jumble, mess up, ruffle, rumple, tangle, tousle 7 clutter, crumple, disturb, rummage, wrinkle 8 dishevel 10 disarrange
up: 3 fix, mix 4 coin, fill, form, meet 5 ad-lib, atone, blend, frame, hatch, ready 6 cook up, create, devise, draw up, inhere, invent, mingle, settle, soothe, whip up, wing it 7 combine, compose, concoct, fashion, imagine, prepare, redress, trump up 8 beautify, complete, compound, comprise, conceive, contrive, knock off 9 fabricate, formulate, improvise, originate, play by ear, reconcile, replenish 10 compensate, constitute, make amends, recompense, shake hands
(up): 5 dream, think
up for: 5 atone, cover, right 6 offset, recoup, redeem, refund 7 balance, expiate, rectify, redress 8 outweigh 9 apologize, do justice, reimburse 10 compensate, recompense
up-to-date: 5 fix up, refit 6 extend, resume 7 freshen, furbish, remodel, restore 8 overhaul, renovate, spruce up 9 modernize, refurbish 10 revitalize
usable: 3 fit 5 alter 6 adjust, change, modify, revise, tailor 7 remodel 8 regulate
usable again: 5 renew 9 refurbish
use of: 5 avail, exert, wield 6 employ, look to, resort 7 utilize 10 fall back on
vague: 3 fog 4 daze, mist 5 befog, blear, cloud, muddy, smear 6 smudge 7 becloud, obscure
vapid: 6 benumb, dampen, muffle, stifle 7 repress, silence 8 diminish, suppress
vertical: 5 plumb
visible: 5 flare, flash, shine 6 ignite, illume, kindle, turn on 7 inflame, lighten 8 brighten, enkindle, illumine 9 highlight, set fire to, set on fire, spotlight 10 illuminate
waves: 4 stir 5 rebel, shake, upset 6 revolt 7 trouble 9 instigate 10 complicate, exasperate
wavy: 4 curl 5 frizz, swirl
whole: 4 cure, heal, mend 5 right, treat 6 remedy, repair 7 correct, relieve, restore 8 medicate
make __: 3 for, hay, off, out, way 4 as if, book, eyes, fast, good, like, nice, over, sure, time, with 5 a face, a go of, a mint, a stab, fun of, haste, ready, up for, use of, waves 6 amends, public, tracks 7 believe, whoopee
make __ buck: 5 a fast
make __ dash: 4 a mad
make __ for: 5 a case, a play, it hot
make __ for it: 4 a run
make __ for oneself: 5 a name
make __ in: 5 a dent
make __ like a bandit: 3 out
make __ meet: 4 ends
make __ of: 3 a go, fun, use 4 much 5 a fool, a mess, a note, a show, light 6 little
make __ of faith: 5 a leap
make __ of it: 3 a go
make __ of the tongue: 5 a slip
make __ on: 4 book 5 a move
make __ out of: 4 a man
make __ with: 3 off 4 a hit, away 6 points 7 friends
make-__: 4 work 5 ahead, peace, ready 7 believe
Make __!: 4 it so
Make __ double!: 3 it a
Make __ for Daddy: 4 Room
Make __ Happy: 7 Someone
Make __ Music: 4 Mine
Make-__ Foundation: 5 a-Wish
make a __: 4 face, go of 5 stink
make a __ for: 4 case, play
make a __ for oneself: 4 name
make a __ it: 4 go of
make a __ of: 4 show 5 point
make a __ on: 4 move
make a __ out of: 6 monkey
make a day __: 4 of it
__ Make a Deal: 4 Let's
make a go __: 4 of it
Make a Move on Me (1982 song)
artist: Olivia Newton-John
make-and-__: 5 break
Make and Break
author: Michael Frayn
make a run __: 5 for it
Makeba, Miriam
homeland: South Africa
song: Pata Pata (1967)
make-believe: 4 fake, mock, sham 5 bogus, false, phony, put-on 6 ersatz, fakery, forged, phoney, pseudo, unreal 7 assumed, charade, fantasy, feigned, pretend 8 imagined, pretense, spurious 9 fairy-tale, fictional, imaginary, imitation, pretended, simulated, synthetic, unnatural, unreality 10 artificial, fabricated, fictitious, fraudulent
Make Believe
composer: Oscar Hammerstein, Jerome Kern
Make Believe (1969 song)
artist: Tony Orlando & Dawn
__ Make Believe: 4 Only
make both ends __: 4 meet
make-do: 9 makeshift, temporary 10 pro tempore
make it __: 6 snappy
Make it __ for my baby...: 3 one
Make It Happen (1992 song)
artist: Mariah Carey
Make It Hot (1998 song)
artist: Missy Elliott, Nicole
Make it snappy!: 4 ASAP, stat
Make It With You (1970 song)
artist: Bread
Make like __ and leave: 5 a tree
Make Me Lose Control (1988 song)
artist: Eric Carmen
__ Make Me Over: 4 Don't
Make Me Smile (1970 song)
artist: Chicago
Make my day!: 4 dare
make no __ about: 5 bones
make one's __: 3 way 4 case, mark
make one's __ water: 5 mouth
make oneself __: 6 scarce
make-or-__: 5 break
make out __ bandit: 5 like a
__ Makepeace Thackeray: 7 William
maker: 5 cause 6 framer, wright 7 creator 8 designer, inventer, inventor, producer 9 architect, artificer, craftsman 10 fabricator
starter: 3 car, hay, ice, law, map 4 auto, book, chip, deal, film, home, king, myth, news, odds, pace, play, rain, shoe, tool, wine 5 dress, glass, match, merry, money, movie, noise, paper, peace, print, taste, watch 6 boiler, coffee, policy, speech, violin 7 cabinet, trouble
suffix: 3 -ist
__ maker: 3 tea 6 coffee
Maker: 3 God 7 Creator 8 Almighty
makeshift: 4 rude, temp 5 crude, rough 6 coarse, refuge, shoddy 7 interim, stopgap 8 homemade, slapdash 9 expedient, hit-or-miss, inelegant, patchwork, primitive, temporary, unrefined 10 amateurish, improvised, jury-rigged, last resort, pro tempore, substitute, unpolished, unreliable
make short __ of: 4 work
...makes Jack __ boy: 5 a dull
Make Someone Happy
composer: Betty Comden, Adolph Green, Jule Styne
__ Makes Sammy Run?: 4 What
__ makes two of us!: 4 That
__ makes waste: 5 haste
make the __: 5 grade, scene 6 rounds
make the __ fly: 3 fur 4 dust
make the __ of: 4 most
Make thee __ of greatness: 5 a name
make the fur __: 3 fly
make the most __: 4 of it
Make the World Go Away (1965 song)
artist: Eddy Arnold
makeup: 4 Avon, body, mold 5 Almay, blush, gloss, humor, liner, paint, rouge, stamp 6 design, format, nature, powder, Revlon, shadow, stripe, temper 7 anatomy, Lancome, Mary Kay, mascara, pancake, texture 8 Clinique, cosmetic, eyeliner, lipstick 9 character, cosmetics, Cover Girl, eye shadow, formation, Max Factor, mentality, structure 10 complexion, foundation, maquillage, Maybelline 11 Estée Lauder, Merle Norman
apply ~: 3 dab
eye ~: 4 kohl 5 liner
fuss with ~: 5 primp
take a ~ exam: 5 resit
makeup __: 4 exam
__ makeup: 4 cake 7 Pan-Cake
make up one's __: 4 mind
__ Make Waves: 4 Don't
Make yourself __: 6 at home
Make Yourself Comfortable (1954 song)
artist: Sarah Vaughan
Makin' __: 7 Whoopee
making: 8 creation
not ~ it: 7 failing
starter: 3 law, map 4 book, film, home, king, myth, play, rain, rate, shoe, snow, wine 5 glass, match, merry, money, movie, peace, print 6 speech, violin 7 cabinet
__ making eyes at me: 5 Ma he's
Making Love out of Nothing at All (1983 song)
artist: Air Supply
Making Mr. Right (1987 film)
cast: Glenne Headly, Ann Magnuson, John Malkovich
director: Susan Seidelman
Making of an American, The
author: Jacob Riis
Making of the President, The
author: Theodore H. White
makings: 8 capacity 9 potential
Making Tracks
author: Alan Ayckbourn
Makin' Whoopee
composer: Walter Donaldson, Gus Kahn
mako: 4 fish 5 shark
Maksim: 5 Gorki, Gorky
Makua home: 6 Africa 8 Tanzania 10 Mozambique
mal
opposite: 4 bien
mal __: 5 de mer
mal-: 3 bad, ill
mala __: 4 fide
Mala: 6 Powers
Malabar Coast district: 3 Goa
Malacca: 3 str. 4 cane 6 strait
Malachi: 6 Throne
preceder: 9 Zechariah

malachite: **3** ore **7** mineral
maladroit: **5** gawky, inapt, inept, unapt **6** clumsy, gauche, klutzy, oafish, wooden **7** awkward, gawkish, halting, labored, unadept, unhandy **8** bumbling, bungling, cloddish, fumbling, inexpert, lubberly, tactless, ungainly **9** all thumbs, graceless, impolitic, lumbering, stumbling, unskilled, untactful **10** blundering, leadfooted, left-handed, unbecoming, ungraceful, unskillful
malady: **3** bug, ill **7** ailment, disease, illness, trouble **8** disorder, sickness, syndrome **9** complaint, condition, infirmity **10** affliction, unwellness
  childhood ~: **5** colic, croup, mumps **7** measles **10** chicken pox
  suffix: **4** -itis
mala fide: **8** bad faith
Malaga: **4** wine
  origin: **5** Spain
Málaga: **4** city, port, town
  locale: **5** Spain
malagueña: **5** dance
malaise: **3** woe **4** pain **5** angst, gloom **6** unease **7** anxiety, despair, fidgets, illness **8** debility, disquiet, distress, doldrums, ill-being, sickness, weakness **9** infirmity, lassitude **10** depression, discomfort, enervation, feebleness, infirmness, inquietude, melancholy, sickliness, uneasiness, unwellness, woefulness
Malamud, Bernard: **6** writer
  work: The Assistant
    The Fixer
    Idiots First
    The Magic Barrel
    The Natural
    The Tenants
malamute: **3** dog, pet **5** pooch **6** canine
  burden: **4** sled
  command to a ~: **4** mush
__ malamute: **7** Alaskan
__ Malaprop: **3** Mrs.
malapropism: **6** misuse **8** wordplay
malapropos: **5** badly, inapt, unapt, wrong **8** improper, unseemly, untimely
malar: **4** bone **9** cheekbone
malaria symptom: **4** ague
malarkey
  see baloney
Malawi: **4** lake **6** nation **7** country
  city: **5** Zomba **8** Lilongwe
  Lake locale: **8** Tanzania **10** Mozambique
  money: **6** kwacha **7** tambala
  neighbor: **6** Zambia **8** Tanzania **10** Mozambique
  people: **3** Yao **4** Cewa **5** Bemba, Chewa, Makua, Ngoni, Nguni **6** Nyanja
Malay: **8** language **10** Indonesian
  address: **4** tuan
  boat: **4** prao, prau, proa **5** prahu
  bovine: **4** gaur **5** gayal **6** mithan **7** banteng, banting
  cuckoo: **4** koel
  dagger: **4** kris **6** crease, creese
  gecko: **5** tokay
  island: **5** Timor
  isthmus: **3** Kra
  mammal: **5** tapir
  native: **4** Moro
  primate: **3** lar **7** siamang
  prince: **4** raja
  region: **6** Indies
  reptile: **5** krait
  sea: **7** Andaman
  sultanate: **6** Brunei
  tree: **5** areca, mahua, mahwa, mohwa, mowra **6** mowrah **8** jelutong
__-Malayan: **4** Indo
Malay Archipelago: **4** isls. **5** isles **7** islands
  island: **4** Java **5** Luzon **6** Borneo, Sundas **7** Celebes, Sumatra **8** Mindanao, Sulawesi **9** Indonesia, New Guinea **10** East Indies
Malaysia: **6** nation **7** country
  bay: **6** Brunei
  capital: **11** Kuala Lumpur
  city: **4** Ipoh **6** Penang
  export: **3** tin **5** copra **8** copperah
  money: **3** sen
  neighbor: **6** Brunei **8** Thailand **9** Indonesia, Singapore
  port: **6** Penang **10** George Town
  river: **5** Perak
  sarong: **4** kain
  state: **5** Johor, Kedah, Perak, Sabah **6** Melaka, Pahang, Penang, Perlis **7** Sarawak **8** Kelantan, Selangor
Malcolm: **4** Gets **5** Lowry, Young **6** Forbes **7** McLaren, Sargent **8** Bradbury, McDowell **9** Baldridge **10** Muggeridge
  author: James Purdy
Malcolm __ Middle: **5** in the
Malcolm-Jamal: **6** Warner
Malcolm X (1992 film)
  cast: Angela Bassett, Albert Hall, Denzel Washington
  director: Spike Lee
malcontent: **4** crab **5** grump, rebel **6** griper, grouch, moaner **7** crybaby, heretic **8** agitator, maverick, renegade **9** anarchist, dissenter, insurgent, protester **10** iconoclast
Malcontent, The
  author: John Marston
mal de __: **3** mer **4** tête **5** dents
mal de mer: **6** nausea
Malden: **4** city, Karl, town
  locale: **4** Mass.
Malden, Karl: **5** actor
  film: Baby Doll (1956)
    Cheyenne Autumn (1964)
    The Cincinnati Kid (1965)
    Fear Strikes Out (1957)
    The Great Impostor (1961)
    Gypsy (1962)
    Murderers' Row (1966)
    Nevada Smith (1966)
    Nuts (1987)
    One-Eyed Jacks (1961)
    On the Waterfront (1954)
    Patton (1970)
    A Streetcar Named Desire (1951, AA)
  TV: Skag, The Streets of San Francisco
Maldives: **4** isls. **5** isles **6** atolls, islets, nation **7** country, islands
  capital: **4** Male
  coin: **4** lari **5** laree
mal du __: **4** pays
male: **2** he, Mr., pa **3** boy, cob, dad, guy, him, man, pop, ram, sir, son **4** bass, boar, buck, bull, chap, colt, czar, gent, hero, hunk, papa, sire, stag, stud, tsar, tzar **5** bloke, calif, capon, daddy, drake, drone, groom, kalif, macho, manly, pappy, Romeo, steer, swain, tenor, uncle, youth **6** butler, caliph, father, feller, fellow, gender, kaliph, khalif, laddie, mister, nephew, potent, spouse, tomcat, virile **7** brother, danseur, husband, rooster **8** bachelor, baritone, barytone, cardinal, paternal, stallion **9** boyfriend, chevalier, gentleman, masculine
  combining form: **4** andr- **5** andro-, -andry **7** -androus
  vain ~: **4** dude **5** dandy **9** pretty boy
male __: **7** bonding
__ male: **5** alpha
Malé: **4** city, town **7** capital
  locale: **8** Maldives
Male and Female
  author: Margaret Mead
Male Animal, The
  author: James Thurber
Malebranche, Nicolas de: **6** French **11** philosopher
malediction: **4** jinx, oath **5** curse **6** tirade, whammy **8** anathema **9** damnation, profanity
malefaction: **3** sin **4** evil, harm, vice **5** guilt **7** misdeed
malefactor: **5** felon, scamp **6** bad guy **7** villain **9** miscreant **10** delinquent, holy terror
malefic: **4** evil **6** malign **7** baneful, harmful, ominous, satanic **8** sinister **9** satanical
maleficent: **4** base, evil, foul **6** malign, wicked **7** harmful, hurtful **8** diabolic, fiendish **9** injurious **10** diabolical, villainous
males and females, for: **4** coed **6** unisex
malevolence: **4** evil **5** spite, venom, wrong **6** animus, malice, rancor **8** acrimony
malevolent: **3** ill **4** cold, evil, mean, ugly **5** catty, cruel, nasty, surly **6** chilly, malign, ornery, wanton, wicked **7** baleful, hateful, hellish, hostile, satanic, vicious, waspish **8** infernal, inimical, libelous, sinister, spiteful, vengeful, venomous, virulent **9** bellicose, malicious, poisonous, rancorous, satanical **10** derogatory, evil-minded, ill-natured, pugnacious, virtueless
  one: **5** hater
__ Male War Bride: **5** I Was a
malfeasance: **5** abuse, fault, guilt **7** offense **9** improbity
malformed: **6** skewed, warped **7** crooked, twisted **8** abnormal **9** contorted, distorted, grotesque, irregular, misshapen, shapeless
Malfoy: **5** Draco
malfunction: **3** bug **4** fail, flaw, slip **5** act up, crash, fault **6** defect, glitch **7** failure, gremlin, trouble **9** breakdown
malfunctioning: **6** faulty
__ malgre lui: **5** Le roi
Mali: **6** nation **7** country
  capital: **6** Bamako
  city: **3** Gao **5** Mopti, Ségou **6** Bamako **7** Sikasso
  desert: **6** Sahara
  locale: **3** Afr. **6** Africa
  money: **5** franc
  neighbor: **5** Niger **6** Guinea **7** Algeria, Senegal **10** Ivory Coast, Mauritania
  people: **4** Fula **5** Dogon **6** Fulani, Senufo, Tuareg **7** Bambara, Malinka, Malinke, Songhai **8** Mandingo, Mandinka
  river: **5** Niger
Malibu: **3** car **4** auto **5** beach, Chevy **9** Chevrolet **10** automobile
  athletes: **5** Waves
  locale: **10** California
  school: **10** Pepperdine
  sight: **4** surf
malic: **4** acid
malice: **3** ill **4** bile, evil, hate **5** odium, spite, venom **6** animus, enmity, grudge, hatred, rancor, spleen **7** cruelty, ill will, umbrage **8** acrimony, bad blood, contempt, meanness **9** animosity, antipathy, hostility, mordacity, nastiness **10** abhorrence, backbiting, bitterness, resentment, unkindness
  bear ~ toward: **4** hate **7** dislike
Malice
  author: Danielle Steel
Malice (1993 film)
  cast: Alec Baldwin, Nicole Kidman, Bebe Neuwirth, Bill Pullman
malicious: **3** ill, low **4** evil, mean **5** catty, nasty, petty, snide, surly **6** bitter, cussed, ornery, sneaky, uncool, unkind, wanton, wicked **7** baleful, beastly, cutting, envious, harmful, hateful, hostile, hurtful, jealous, vicious **8** fiendish, inimical, libelous, spiteful, vengeful, venomous, virulent **9** bellicose, green-eyed, injurious, poisonous, rancorous, resentful, splenetic **10** bad-natured, derogatory, evil-minded, ill-natured, malevolent, pernicious, pugnacious, unfriendly, vindictive, virtueless
  intent: **6** enmity, hatred, malice, rancor **7** cruelty, ill will **8** acrimony **9** animosity, hostility, vengeance
  one: **5** viper, vixen
  tale: **6** canard
Malick: **6** Wendie **8** Terrence
malign: **3** dis, hit, lie, rap **4** evil, gibe, harm, jeer, jibe, mock, slam, slur, snub, soil **5** abuse, curse, decry, libel, roast, scorn, smear, spurn, stain, sully, taint, taunt, toxic, wrong **6** accuse, assail, befoul, defame, defile, deride, dump on, heckle, impugn, injure, insult, nocent, offend, rebuff, revile, slight, vilify, wicked **7** adverse, affront, asperse, baleful, baneful, blacken, degrade, detract, disdain, harmful, hateful, hostile, hurtful, inhuman, malefic, put down, rank out, rip into, ruinous, run down, slander,

tarnish, traduce, vicious **8** backbite, badmouth, belittle, besmirch, damaging, denounce, derogate, inhumane, inimical, mudsling, negative, ridicule, sinister, spiteful, tear down, throw mud, vilipend, virulent **9** bespatter, dangerous, denigrate, deprecate, discredit, disparage, humiliate, injurious, rancorous **10** blackguard, calamitous, calumniate, disastrous, disrespect, maleficent, malevolent, pernicious, speak ill of, villainize, vituperate
maligner: 6 critic **8** vilifier **9** detractor
maligning: 5 abuse **9** invidious **10** defamatory, derogatory, detraction, muckraking
malignity: 4 evil **6** animus, rancor **9** animosity
malinger: 4 idle, loaf **5** shirk, slack **7** goof off, pretend **8** slack off **9** goldbrick
in Britain: 5 sculk, skulk
malingerer: 5 shirk **6** loafer, truant **7** shirker, slacker **10** ne'er-do-well
Malinowski, Bronislaw: 6 Polish **14** anthropologist
malkin: 3 cat, mop **4** hare
Malkovich, John: 5 actor
film: Burn After Reading (2008)
Changeling (2008)
Con Air (1997)
Dangerous Liaisons (1988)
Eleni (1985)
Empire of the Sun (1987)
The Glass Menagerie (1987)
In the Line of Fire (1993)
The Killing Fields (1984)
Making Mr. Right (1987)
Man in the Iron Mask (1998)
The Object of Beauty (1991)
Of Mice and Men (1992)
Places in the Heart (1984)
Shadow of the Vampire (2000)
spouse: Glenne Headly
mall: 4 mart, walk **5** plaza **6** arcade, market **9** boulevard, esplanade, promenade
binge: 5 spree
feature: 3 map **4** sale, shop **5** kiosk, store **6** arcade, atrium, cinema **8** boutique **9** food court
forerunner: 5 agora
frequenter: 4 teen **7** shopper
hit the ~: 4 shop **5** spend
shopping ~: 4 mart **5** plaza **6** market
__ mall: 5 strip
__ Mall: 4 Pall
mallard: 4 bird, duck, fowl
flock: 4 sute
relative: ***see*** duck
Mallarmé, Stéphane: 4 poet **6** French
malleable: 4 soft **5** fluid **6** clayey, lissom, pliant, supple **7** clayish, ductile, lissome, plastic, pliable **8** flexible, formable, moldable, obedient, tractile, workable, yielding **9** adaptable, compliant, formative, tractable **10** governable, manageable, submissive
Malle, Louis: 8 director
film: Atlantic City (1981)
Au Revoir, Les Enfants (1987)
God's Country (1985)
Lacombe, Lucien (1974)
The Lovers (1958)
Pretty Baby (1978)
The Silent World (1956)
The Thief of Paris (1967)
spouse: Candice Bergen
mallet: 4 club, tool **5** gavel **6** hammer
doctor's ~: 6 plexor
game: 4 polo **5** roque **7** croquet
target: 4 gong
malleus: 4 bone
locale: 3 ear
Mallon: 3 Meg **4** Mary
Mallon, Meg: 6 golfer
Mallorca: 4 isla, isle **6** island
see also Majorca, Spanish
Mallory: 6 George
mallow: 5 plant **6** flower
family shrub: 4 ocra, okra, okro **5** urena **8** abutilon
genus: 5 malva
starter: 5 marsh
tree: 8 hibiscus
Malmö: 4 city, port, town
city near ~: 4 Lund
locale: 6 Sweden
malmsey: 4 wine
origin: 6 Greece **8** Portugal
malnourished: 6 skinny **7** starved **8** starving
malodor: 4 reek **5** smell, stink **6** stench **9** fetidness
malodorous: 3 bad, off **4** foul, gamy, high, olid, rank, vile **5** fetid, fusty, gamey, musty, nasty, stale **6** foetid, frowsy, frowzy, rancid, rotten, smelly, stinky, strong **7** decayed, noisome, noxious, reeking, tainted **8** mephitic, overripe, stinking **9** offensive
Malone: 3 Sam **4** Jena, Karl **5** Moses **7** Dorothy
Malone Dies
author: Samuel Beckett
Malone, Dorothy: 7 actress
TV: Peyton Place
Malone, Karl
milieu: 5 court
org.: 3 NBA
sport: 10 basketball
Malone, Moses
milieu: 5 court
org.: 3 NBA
sport: 10 basketball
Malory: 6 Thomas
malpractice: 5 abuse **7** misdeed, offense **9** improbity, violation
Malraux: 5 André
malt
beverage: 3 ale **4** beer, suds **5** lager, stout **6** porter **7** brewage
dryer: 4 oast
ender: 3 ase, ose
fermenting ~ infusion: 4 wort
liquor yeast: 4 barm
vinegar: 6 alegar
malt __: 4 shop **5** sugar **6** liquor, whisky
Malta: 4 isle **6** island, nation **7** country
capital: 8 Valletta
locale: 3 Eur. **5** Medit. **6** Europe
money: 4 cent, lira, lire, tari **6** sequin
neighbor: 6 Sicily
Maltbie: 5 Roger
Maltby: 7 Richard
malted: 8 beverage
malted __: 4 milk
Maltese: 3 cat, dog **5** canid, felid **6** canine, feline
remark: 3 mew **4** meow **5** miaou, miaow, miaul
Maltese __: 3 cat, dog **5** cross
Maltese __, The: 5 Bippy **6** Falcon
Maltese Falcon, The: 4 film **5** novel
author: Dashiell Hammett
cast: Mary Astor, Humphrey Bogart, Ward Bond, Elisha Cook Jr., Sydney Greenstreet, Peter Lorre
character: 3 Iva, Sam **4** Cook, Joel, Rhea **5** Cairo, Effie, Floyd, Miles, Spade **6** Archer, Brigid, Casper, Gutman, Jacobi, Perine, Wilmer **7** Kemidov, Thursby **8** Sam Spade **9** Iva Archer, Joel Cairo **10** Rhea Gutman, Wilmer Cook
director: John Huston
Malthus, Thomas: 7 British **9** economist
Maltin: 7 Leonard
maltose: 5 sugar
maltreat: 4 beat, harm, hurt, mall, maul **5** abuse, wrong **6** ill-use, injure, misuse **7** corrupt, oppress, outrage, rough up **8** aggrieve, keep down **9** manhandle, persecute **10** excruciate, kick around
maltreatment: 5 abuse **6** misuse **8** inequity
malt-shop
freebie: 5 straw
order: 4 soda **5** float
malvasia: 5 grape
relative: ***see*** wine
__ Malvinas: 5 Islas
mama: 3 dam **4** mate **6** mother, parent **8** baby talk
Mama: 4 Cass **8** Michelle
warning: 4 don't, no-no
Mama (1960 song)
artist: Connie Francis
Mama (CBS sitcom)
cast: Judson Laire (Lars Hansen)
Rosemary Rice (Katrin Hansen)
Dick Van Patten (Nels Hansen)
Peggy Wood (Marta Hansen)
dog: 6 Willie
mama and __: 4 papa
Mama Can't Buy You Love (1979 song)
artist: Elton John
__ Mama Don't Dance: 4 Your
Mama from the Train (1956 song)
artist: Patti Page
Mama Said (1961 song)
artist: Shirelles
Mama Said Knock You Out (1991 song)
artist: LL Cool J
mama's boy: 4 wimp **5** sissy **7** milksop **8** weakling **10** namby-pamby
Mama's Family (NBC sitcom)
cast: Ken Berry (Vinton Harper)
Vicki Lawrence (Mama Harper)
Dorothy Lyman (Naomi Harper)
Mama's Pearl (1971 song)
artist: Jackson 5
Mamas & the Papas
members: 6 Elliot **7** Doherty, Elliott **8** Phillips
song: California Dreamin' (1966)
Creeque Alley (1967)
Dedicated to the One I Love (1967)
I Saw Her Again (1966)
Monday, Monday (1966)
Twelve Thirty (1967)
Words of Love (1966)
Mama Told Me (1970 song)
artist: Three Dog Night
mamba: 5 snake **6** animal **7** reptile
relative: ***see*** snake
mambo: 5 dance
relative: 5 rumba **6** cha-cha, rhumba
Mambo Italiano (1954 song)
artist: Rosemary Clooney
Mame: 7 musical
composer: Jerry Herman
to Patrick: 4 aunt
Mame (1966 song)
artist: Herb Alpert and the Tijuana Brass
__ Mame: 6 Auntie
Ma mère, je la vois: 4 duet
Mamet, David: 6 writer **8** director **9** dramatist **10** playwright
film: Edmond (2005)
Heist (2001)
House of Games (1987)
Redbelt (2008)
The Spanish Prisoner (1998)
Spartan (2004)
State and Main (2000)
The Winslow Boy (1999)
spouse: Lindsay Crouse
TV: The Unit
work: American Buffalo
Faustus
Glengarry Glen Ross
Lakeboat
Lone Canoe
Romance
Mamie: 8 Van Doren **10** Eisenhower
predecessor: 4 Bess
spouse: 3 Ike
successor: 6 Jackie **10** Jacqueline
Mamie Eisenhower, __ Doud: 3 née
Mamma __!: 3 Mia
mammal: 2 ai **3** ape, bat, cat, cow, dog, elk, fox, gnu, kob, man, pig, yak **4** anoa, bear, boar, cavy, deer, goat, guib, hare, ibex, kudu, lion, lynx, mink, mole, mule, orca, oryx, paca, peba, pika, puku, puma, saki, seal, titi, topi, unau, vole, wolf, zebu **5** addax, apara, bison, bongo, camel, chimp, chiru, civet, coati, dhole, drill, eland, genet, goral, hippo, horse, human, hyena, hyrax, jocko, koala, korin, lemur, llama, loris, magot, moose, mouse, nyala, okapi, orang, oribi, otary, otter, panda, potto, ratel, rhino, sable, saiga, serow, sheep, shrew, skunk, sloth, stoat, tapir, tiger, whale, zebra **6** agouti, alpaca, animal, aye-aye, baboon, badger, Bandar, beaver, bobcat, canine, chammy, cougar, coyote, dassie, desman, dik-dik, dugong, duiker, ermine, feline, ferret, galago, gelada, gerbil, gibbon, gopher, grivet, guenon, howler, hyaena, impala, jackal, jaguar, jerboa, koodoo, langur, lechwe, macaco, marmot, marten, monkey, nilgai,

ocelot, peludo, possum, rabbit, racoon, rhebok, rhesus, shammy, shamoy, tanrec, tenrec, uakari, vervet, vicuña, walrus, wapiti, weasel **7** blaubok, blesbok, buffalo, chamois, cheetah, colobus, defassa, dolphin, echidna, gazelle, gemsbok, gerenuk, giraffe, gorilla, grysbok, guanaco, guereza, hamster, hoolock, lemming, leopard, macaque, manatee, meerkat, muskrat, narwhal, nylghai, nylghau, opossum, panther, peccary, polecat, primate, raccoon, rorqual, sapajou, sassaby, sea lion, siamang, tamarin, tarsier, tatuasu, wallaby, warthog **8** aardvark, aardwolf, anteater, antelope, blesbuck, bontebok, bush baby, bushbuck, capuchin, capybara, chipmunk, dormouse, elephant, gemsbuck, hedgehog, kangaroo, kinkajou, mandrill, mangabey, marmoset, mongoose, pangolin, platypus, porpoise, reedbuck, reindeer, ruminant, squirrel, steenbok, steinbok, talapoin, wallaroo **9** armadillo, bandicoot, blackbuck, dromedary, guinea pig, marsupial, orangutan, porcupine, pronghorn, razorback, sitatunga, springbok, waterbuck, wolverine **10** Barbary ape, chimpanzee, coatimundi, hartebeest, orangutang, prairie dog, rhinoceros, wildebeest
aquatic ~: **4** seal **5** hippo, otary, otter **6** desman, dugong
arboreal ~: **5** koala, lemur, sloth
characteristic: **4** hair
largest ~: **5** whale
Mamma Mia (1976 song)
artist: ABBA
Mamma Mia! (2008 film)
cast: Pierce Brosnan, Colin Firth, Amanda Seyfried
director: Meryl Streep
mammee: **4** tree
mammon
see moolah
mammoth: **3** big **4** huge, vast **5** bulky, giant, great, jumbo, large **6** animal **7** hulking, immense, massive, monster, sizable, titanic **8** colossal, colossus, elephant, enormous, gigantic, king-size, oversize, sizeable, towering, whapping, whopping **9** Herculean, humongous, leviathan, monstrous, overlarge **10** behemothic, formidable, gargantuan, monumental, prodigious, stupendous, tremendous
feature: **4** tusk **5** trunk
period: **6** ice age
__ mammoth: **6** woolly
Mammoth Cave: **4** Park
locale: **3** Ken. **8** Kentucky
Mammoth Hunters, The
author: Jean Auel
character: **4** Ayla
period: **6** Ice Age
Mamoulian: **6** Rouben
man: **2** he **3** dad, guy, him, wow **4** chap, gent, male, stag **5** adult, fella, human, señor, staff **6** animal, butler, feller, fellow, mensch, mister, mortal, person, senhor, spouse, suitor **7** checker, fortify, grown-up, operate **8** monsieur, naked ape **9** earthling, game piece, human race **10** chess piece, human being, individual
combining form: **5** homin- **6** homini-
ender: **3** age **4** hole, hunt, kind, made, rope, trap, ward, wise **5** drake, drill, power, wards **6** handle **7** servant
Friday: **4** aide, asst. **9** assistant
Lady's ~: **4** earl, lord, peer
starter: **3** air, bag, bar, bat, bow, bus, cab, cow, foe, gag, gun, ice, law, lay, mad, pen, pit, rag, rod, sea, tax **4** alms, base, bats, bell, bird, boat, bogy, bond, cave, club, desk, door, dray, fire, flag, foot, fore, free, frog, glee, good, head, jazz, line, mail, Manx, milk, news, oars, pack, plow, post, reed, sand, ship, show, side, snow, swag, wing, wire, wood, work, yard **5** alder, bails, bands, barge, blues, bogey, bonds, brake, chain, chair, chess, clans, coach, corps, dairy, Dutch, earth, freed, fresh, fugle, funny, games, gowns, handy, helms, herds, horse, house, hunts, Irish, lands, leads, liege, lines, marks, money, motor, noble, Norse, North, pitch, place, press, radio, ranch, rifle, sales, Scots, sound, spear, stock, stunt, swing, towns, track, train, watch, water, wheel, woods **6** anchor, boogie, bushel, camera, cattle, church, clergy, crafts, drafts, fellow, fields, fisher, French, gentle, grooms, guards, guilds, letter, livery, middle, minute, muscle, oyster, patrol, plains, police, repair, rounds, safety, school, select, spokes, sports, states, steers, strong, switch, swords, trades, tribes, vestry, wheels, yachts
traveling ~: **5** nomad
man __: **4** lock **5** of God, power **6** Friday
man __ cloth: **5** of the
man __ hour: **5** of the
man __ house: **5** of the
man __ moon: **5** in the
man __ mouse: **3** or a
man __ street: **5** in the, on the
man __ town: **5** about
man __ world: **5** of the
man __ year: **5** of the
man-__: **3** day **4** hour, made, trap, year **5** child, of-war, sized **6** at-arms
__ man: **3** bad, con, day, end, old, rim, to a, yes **4** beat, best, cave, idea, iron, Java, mass, ring, slot, Solo, wild **5** as one, inner, lady's, party, point, sixth, sound, straw, stunt, third **6** detail, family, holdup, ladies', Peking **7** advance, company, hatchet, leading, miracle
__-man: **3** ape, yes
Man: **3** Ray **4** isle **6** island
locale: **7** England
Man __ All Seasons, A: **3** for
Man __ Dog: **5** Bites
Man __ Gray Flannel Suit, The: **5** in the
Man __ Iron Mask, The: **5** in the
Man __ Knew Too Much, The: **3** Who
Man __ Mancha: **4** of La
Man __ social animal: **3** is a
Man __, The: **5** I Love
Man __ Thousand Faces: **3** of a
Man __ Would Be King, The: **3** Who
Man-__: **4** o'War
Man.: **4** prov.
neighbor: **3** Ont. **4** N. Dak., Sask.
see also Manitoba
__ Man: **3** Ape, Big, I'm a, Tin **4** Dead, Rain, Repo, Soul **5** Gypsy, Handy, Macho, Magic, No One, Piano, Son of **6** Poetry, Rocket, Wonder **7** Nowhere, Ramblin
__-Man: **3** Pac **6** Spider
man, a __, a canal..., A: **4** plan
man about __: **4** town
manacle: **4** bind, bond, cuff, iron **5** chain **6** fetter, pinion **7** enchain **8** bracelet, handcuff, restrain
place for a ~: **5** wrist
manacled: **7** in irons
manacles: **5** irons **6** chains **8** shackles, trammels **9** bracelets, handcuffs
manacode: **4** bird
Manadalay river: **9** Irrawaddy
Man Against the Sky, The
author: E.A. Robinson
manage: **3** con, ply, run, use **4** boss, cope, fare, head, keep, lead, rule, tend **5** get by, guide, pilot, shift, steer, swing **6** afford, bear up, direct, eke out, endure, govern, hack it, handle, make do, wangle **7** achieve, captain, care for, carry on, command, conduct, control, make out, operate, oversee, preside, pull off, subsist, succeed, survive, swing it **8** bring off, carry out, contrive, deal with, dispense, dominate, engineer, get along, hold down, maintain, minister, regulate, scrape by, take over, transact **9** influence, negotiate, officiate, play games, supervise, watch over **10** accomplish, administer, manipulate, mastermind, run the show
just ~: **5** get by
without: **5** spare
__-manage: **5** floor, stage
manageable: **4** easy, meek, ruly, soft, tame **5** light **6** broken, docile, pliant, simple, wieldy **7** subdued, trained **8** lamblike, obedient, portable, untaxing **9** compliant, malleable, tractable **10** governable, submissive
managed-care option: **3** HMO
management: **4** care, head **5** board, brass, execs, power, suits, usage **6** bosses, charge, policy, regime **7** command, conduct, control, running **8** guidance, handling, top brass, upstairs **9** authority, direction, directors, employers, executive, operation, overseers, oversight, treatment **10** executives, government
combining form: **4** -nomy
group: **5** board
level: **4** tier
opposite: **5** labor
prefix for ~: **5** micro
__ management: **4** risk **5** yield **6** crisis, middle
manager: **4** boss, exec, head, host, suit **5** chief, coach, hirer **6** gerent, leader, top dog, warden **7** curator, foreman, headman, officer **8** director, employer, governor, higher-up, official, overseer, superior, watchdog **9** custodian, executive, organizer, straw boss **10** mastermind, proprietor, supervisor
spot: **6** dugout, office
__ manager: **4** city, town **5** floor, house, stage **6** credit, middle
managing __: **6** editor **8** director
Managua: **4** city, lake, town **7** capital
locale: **9** Nicaragua
see also Spanish
__ man a horse he can ride: **5** Give a
mañana: **5** later **7** Spanish
marking: **5** tilde
opposite: **4** ayer
__ mañana!: **5** Hasta
Man and a Woman, A (1966 film)
cast: Anouk Aimée
composer: Francis Lai
__ Man and Little Boy: **3** Fat
Man and Superman
author: George Bernard Shaw
character: **3** Ana, Ann **5** Rhoda **6** Hector
__ Man and the Sea, The: **3** Old
Manannan
father: **3** Ler, Lir
__ Man Answers: **3** If a
Manassas: **4** city, town **6** battle
locale: **8** Virginia
man-at-__: **4** arms
manatee: **5** siren **6** animal, mammal
kin: **6** dugong
Manaus: **4** city, port, town
locale: **6** Brazil
__-man band: **3** one
Manche capital: **4** St. Lô
Manchester: **4** city, town **7** Melissa, William
city near ~: **5** Leeds
locale: **7** England
Manchester, Melissa
song: Don't Cry Out Loud (1979) Midnight Blue (1975) You Should Hear How She Talks About You (1982)
Manchild in the Promised Land
author: Claude Brown
Manchu: **8** language
Manchurian Candidate, The (1962 film)
cast: Laurence Harvey, Angela Lansbury, Janet Leigh, Frank Sinatra
Manchurian Candidate, The (2004 film)
cast: Liev Schreiber, Meryl Streep, Denzel Washington
director: Jonathan Demme
Manchuria river: **4** Amur, Liao, Yalu
Mancini: **3** Ray **5** Henry
Mancini, Henry: **8** composer **9** conductor
film score: Breakfast at Tiffany's Charade

Days of Wine and Roses
The Great Race
Hatari!
The Pink Panther
Victor/Victoria
Wait Until Dark
song: Charade (1964)
Days of Wine and Roses (1963)
Moon River (1961)
Mr. Lucky (1960)
The Pink Panther Theme (1964)
Man Crazy
author: Joyce Carol Oates
mandala: **4** icon, ikon **5** eikon
Mandala
author: Pearl S. Buck
Mandalay: **4** city, poem, town
author: Rudyard Kipling
locale: **5** Burma **7** Myanmar
Mandan: **6** Indian, Robert **7** Amerind
mandarin: **4** fowl, tree **5** fruit **6** citrus **7** scholar
relative: *see* citrus, duck
mandarin __: **4** duck **6** collar, orange
Mandarin: **5** Kuoyu **8** language
Mandarins, The
author: Simone de Beauvoir
mandate: **2** OK **3** law **4** fiat, must, okay, word, writ **5** bylaw, edict, order **6** behest, charge, decree, dictum, firman **7** bidding, command, dictate, go-ahead, precept, warrant **8** sanction **9** directive, ordinance, territory **10** blank check, commission, green light, imperative, injunction, legitimize
mandated: **5** licit **6** lawful
mandatory: **5** major, vital **6** forced, needed **7** binding, crucial, needful, pivotal, primary **8** required **9** de rigueur, essential, important, necessary, requisite **10** compelling, compulsory, imperative, obligatory, peremptory
Mandel: **5** Howie **6** Johnny
Mandela: **6** Nelson, Winnie
Mandela, Nelson: **8** Nobelist
land: **3** RSA **11** South Africa
Mandeville, Bernard: **7** British **8** satirist
Mandeville, John: **3** Sir
mandible: **3** jaw **4** bone, jowl **7** jawbone
mandilion: **5** cloak
Mandingo home: **4** Mali **6** Africa, Gambia, Guinea **10** Ivory Coast
Mandlikova, Hana: **7** netster **9** tennis pro
milieu: **5** court
Mandoki: **4** Luis
mandolin: **6** string
ancestor: **4** lute
part: **3** peg
play a ~: **5** strum
Mandrell: **6** Irlene, Louise **7** Barbara
Mandrells: **4** trio
mandrill: **5** jocko **6** animal **7** primate
relative: *see* primate
Mandy: **5** Moore **8** Patinkin
Mandy (1974 song)
artist: Barry Manilow
mane: **3** mop **4** hair, ruff
clip a horse's ~: **5** roach
like some ~s: **5** tawny
owner: **4** lion, mare **5** horse **6** equine
site: **4** nape
Maneater (1982 song)
artist: Hall and Oates
Manet, Édouard: **6** artist, French **7** painter
medium: **3** oil
maneuver: **3** act, fix, ply, rig **4** move, plan, play, plot, ploy, ruse, scam, step, trap, urge, wile, work **5** angle, dodge, drill, pilot, shift, steer, trick **6** action, design, device, gambit, handle, jockey, scheme, tactic, wangle **7** finagle, finesse, gimmick, operate, sleight **8** artifice, conspire, contrive, engineer, intrigue, inveigle, movement, navigate **9** imposture, machinate, negotiate, operation, play games, stratagem **10** manipulate, reposition, subterfuge
in basketball: **4** pass **5** block, press, steal **7** dribble, rebound
in boxing: **3** bob **5** feint **6** clinch
in fencing: **5** feint, lunge, parry **6** remise, thrust **7** riposte
in football: **4** rush, snap **5** blitz, block, sneak **6** end run **7** handoff, reverse **8** drop kick, pitch-out
maneuverable: **3** yar **4** yare
maneuvering: **7** tactics **9** diplomacy
maneuvers: **5** drill **8** war games **9** exercises **10** inspection
__ Man Flint: **3** Our
Man for All Seasons, A (1966 film)
cast: Wendy Hiller, Leo McKern, Paul Scofield, Robert Shaw, Orson Welles, Susannah York
man for all seasons, The: **4** More
__ man for himself!: **5** Every
Man For Himself
author: Erich Fromm
Manfred: **3** Lee **4** Mann, poem **5** Eigen
author: Lord Byron
Manfred __ Richthofen: **3** von
Manfred Overture
composer: Robert Schumann
Manfred Symphony
composer: Peter Tchaikovsky
Man From U.N.C.L.E., The (NBC adventure)
cast: Leo G. Carroll (Alexander Waverly)
David McCallum (Illya Kuryakin)
Robert Vaughn (Napoleon Solo)
foe: THRUSH
manganese: **5** metal **7** element
alloy: **5** Monel **7** Everdur
Mangano: **7** Silvana
mangel-wurzel: **4** beet
manger: **3** bin **4** crib **6** trough
locale: **4** barn
scene: **6** crèche
visitors: **4** Magi
Mangia!: **3** eat **5** dig in
Mangione, Chuck: **9** trumpeter
genre: **4** jazz
instrument: flugelhorn
song: Feels So Good (1978)
mangle: **3** cut, mar **4** claw, hack, iron, maim, mall, maul, rend, ruin, tear **5** crush, press, slash, spoil, wound, wreck **6** damage, deface, deform, hackle, heckle, impair, injure **7** contort, destroy, distort **8** lacerate, mutilate
use a ~: **4** iron
mango: **4** tree **5** fruit
relative: **5** sumac **6** cashew, fustet, mastic, sumach **9** pistachio
mangrove: **4** tree **5** shrub
__-Manguean: **3** Oto
mangy: **3** low **4** mean **5** dirty, seedy **6** filthy, ragtag, shabby, shoddy, sleazy, sordid **7** rundown, scruffy, squalid **8** decrepit, tattered **9** motheaten, ungroomed
manhandle: **3** paw **4** mawl **5** abuse, knock, paw at **6** bang up **7** rough up **8** ill-treat, maltreat, mistreat **10** kick around, knock about
manhandling: **5** abuse
Manhattan: **4** city, isle, NY NY, town **5** drink **6** island **8** beverage, cocktail
athletes: **8** Wildcats
district: **4** Soho **6** Harlem **7** Tribeca
eatery: **6** Lutèce, Sardi's **7** Elaine's
ender: **3** -ite
ingredient: **3** rye **7** bitters, whiskey **8** vermouth
island off ~: **5** Ellis
locale: **3** Kan., NYC **4** Kans. **6** Kansas **7** New York
school: **3** KSU, NYU **6** Hunter
subway: **3** BMT, IRT
Manhattan (1979 film)
cast: Woody Allen, Mariel Hemingway, Diane Keaton, Meryl Streep
director: Woody Allen
dog: **7** Waffles
Manhattan (song)
composer: Lorenz Hart, Richard Rodgers
Manhattan __: **5** Beach **6** Island **7** Project
Manhattan __ chowder: **4** clam
Manhattan Beach: **4** city, town **5** march
composer: John Philip Sousa
locale: **10** California
Manhattan Mary
artist: Erté
Manhattan Melodrama (1934 film)
cast: Clark Gable, Myrna Loy, William Powell
Manhattan Murder Mystery (1993 film)
cast: Alan Alda, Woody Allen, Anjelica Huston, Diane Keaton
director: Woody Allen
Manhattan Project
event: **5** A-test
participant: **4** Urey
result: **5** A-bomb
Manhattan Transfer: **5** novel **7** singers
author: John Dos Passos
character: **3** Gus **4** Herf, Stan **5** Ellen, Emery, Emile, Susie **6** Cecily
song: Boy from New York City (1981)
Operator (1975)
Twilight Zone (1980)
Manheim: **6** Camryn
manhood: **8** majority, maturity
manhunt: **3** APB **7** dragnet
mania: **3** bug, fad **4** rage, to-do, zeal **5** craze, thing **6** fetich, fetish, frenzy, hang-up, lunacy, uproar **7** craving, madness, passion **8** delirium, disorder, fixation, idée fixe, insanity **9** commotion, craziness, obsession **10** aberration, compulsion, enthusiasm, hullabaloo, partiality
maniac: **3** fan, nut **4** kook **5** crank, fiend, flake **7** fanatic **8** crackpot **9** screwball **10** enthusiast
Maniac (1983 song)
artist: Michael Sembello
maniacal: **3** mad **4** wild **5** crazy, nutty, rabid **6** crazed, freaky, raving **7** berserk, demonic, excited, frantic, hog-wild, violent **8** daemonic, frenetic, frenzied, wild-eyed **9** demonical **10** flipped out, freaked out
manic: **3** mad **4** wild **5** crazy, hyper, nutty, rabid, wired **6** crazed, freaky, raving **7** berserk, demonic, excited, frantic, hog-wild **8** agitated, daemonic, frenzied, in a tizzy, wild-eyed **9** demonical, fanatical, wrought-up **10** flipped out, freaked out, off-the-wall
manicotti: **5** pasta **7** noodles
alternative: *see* pasta
manicurist: **5** filer
concern: **4** nail
item: **4** file **5** emery **6** enamel
manifest: **4** bold, easy, give, list, look, open, show **5** clear, gross, known, occur, overt, plain, prove, shown, vivid **6** attest, cogent, embody, evince, imbody, in view, marked, patent, public, reveal, unfold **7** declare, display, evident, exhibit, exposed, express, for sure, glaring, obvious, reflect, signify, visible **8** apparent, clear-cut, distinct, evidence, explicit, indicate, knowable, luculent, palpable, proclaim, register, revealed, tangible, unhidden, unveiled **9** axiomatic, barefaced, big as life, bring home, disclosed, graspable, make plain, personify, touchable, unobscure **10** illustrate, noticeable, observable, ostensible, spelled out, undeniable, unshrouded
be ~: **6** appear
Manifest __: **7** Destiny
manifestation: **4** form, mark, show, sign **5** token **7** display, symptom **8** epiphany, instance, presence **9** testimony
manifestly: **6** surely **7** plainly **8** markedly **9** evidently, expressly **10** apparently
manifestness: **7** clarity
manifesto: **5** edict **6** firman **8** platform **9** statement
manifold: **4** many **6** a lot of, divers, gobs of, lots of, myriad, sundry, umteen, untold, varied **7** a host of, a slew of, complex, copious, diverse, heaps of, no end of, piles of, profuse, scads of, umpteen, various **8** a bunch of, abundant, an army of, assorted, frequent, iterated, multiple, multiply, numerous, oodles of, scores of, umpsteen **9** a

passel of, bountiful, countless, different, multifold, multiform, quite a few **10** unnumbered, zillions of
__ manifold: 6 intake **7** exhaust
manikin: 5 model **6** puppet **10** homunculus
manila: 5 paper
Manila: 3 bay **4** city, port, town **7** capital
hemp: 5 abaca
locale: 5 Luzon **11** Philippines
river: 5 Pasig
Manila __: 3 Bay **4** hemp, rope **5** paper
Manila Bay: 6 battle
city: 6 Cavite
Man I Love, The
composer: George Gershwin, Ira Gershwin
Manilow, Barry
instrument: 5 piano
song: Can't Smile Without You (1978)
Copacabana (1978)
Could It Be Magic (1975)
Even Now (1978)
I Made It Throught the Rain (1980)
It's a Miracle (1975)
I Write the Songs (1975)
Looks Like We Made It (1977)
Mandy (1974)
The Old Songs (1981)
Read 'Em and Weep (1983)
Ready to Take a Chance Again (1978)
Ships (1979)
Somewhere in the Night (1979)
This One's for You (1976)
Tryin' to Get the Feeling Again (1976)
Weekend in New England (1976)
When I Wanted You (1980)
Man in a Slouch Hat
painter: Frans Hals
Man in Black, The: Johnny Cash
Man in Full, A
author: Tom Wolfe
__ Man in Havana: 3 Our
Man in Lower Ten, The
author: Mary Roberts Rinehart
man in the __: 4 moon **6** street
Man in the Gray Flannel Suit, The: 4 film **5** novel
author: Sloan Wilson
cast: Jennifer Jones, Fredric March, Gregory Peck
character: 4 Rath, Saul **5** Ogden
Man in the Iron Mask (1998 film)
cast: Gérard Depardieu, Leonardo DiCaprio, Jeremy Irons, John Malkovich
Man in the Iron Mask, The
author: Alexandre Dumas
Man in the Mirror (1988 song)
artist: Michael Jackson
Man in The Shower
cartoonist: 4 Arno
maniple: 5 fanon, orale **10** canonicals
manipulate: 3 fix, ply, rig, use **4** feel, hoke, play, work **5** knead, shape, steer, touch, wield **6** direct, employ, finger, handle, jigger, jockey, juggle, manage, tamper **7** control, exploit, finagle, finesse, massage, operate **8** contrive, engineer, maneuver **9** influence, machinate, play games
manipulated one: 4 pawn **5** patsy
manipulation: 8 intrigue **9** treatment
manipulative one: 4 user **5** toyer
Manipur, capital of: 6 Imphal
__ Man is Hard to Find: 5 A Good
Manitoba: 4 lake **8** province
city: 6 Birtle, The Pas **7** Brandon **8** Flin Flon, Winnipeg
Indian: 4 Cree **9** Saulteaux
lake: 8 Winnipeg
locale: 6 Canada
school: 7 Brandon
Manitoulin Islands lake: 5 Huron
Manitowoc: 4 city, town
locale: 9 Wisconsin
__ man jack: 5 every
Mankato: 4 city, town
locale: 9 Minnesota
Mankiewicz: 3 Tom **5** Frank **6** Herman, Joseph
mankind: 5 Earth, world **6** people **9** human race
Mankind in the Making
author: H.G. Wells
Man Lay Dead, A
author: Ngaio Marsh
__ Manley Hopkins: 6 Gerard
__ Man Loves a Woman: 5 When a
manly: 4 bold, male **5** brave, macho **6** virile **9** masculine **10** courageous
not ~: 5 sissy
man-made: 8 cultured **9** synthetic **10** artificial
Mann: 3 Ron **5** Aimee, Barry, Carol **6** Daniel, Herbie, Horace, Thomas **7** Anthony, Delbert, Manfred, Michael **8** Heinrich
manna: 7 aliment **8** blessing, windfall
book: 6 Exodus
from heaven: 4 boon **7** godsend **8** windfall
Mormon ~: 4 sego
Mann, Carol: 6 golfer
mannequin: 5 dummy, model
part: 3 arm, leg **4** head
topper: 3 wig
manner: 3 air, way **4** cast, form, kind, look, mien, mode, sort, tone, type, vein, wise, wont **5** brand, breed, class, means, style, usage **6** aspect, custom, method, system **7** bearing, conduct, fashion, process, variety **8** approach, attitude, behavior, category, demeanor, practice, presence **9** procedure, technique **10** appearance, deportment
affected ~: 4 airs
all ~ of: 4 many **6** sundry **7** various
assume the ~ of: 2 do **3** ape **7** emulate, imitate
dignity of ~: 5 poise
in a ~: 4 as if **8** as it were **9** so to speak
in the ~ of: 3 à la **4** like
in the same ~: 8 likewise
in this ~: 2 so **6** like so
in what ~: 3 how
of a ~: 5 modal
of walking: 4 pace, step
to the ~ born: 5 noble **7** genteel **9** patrician
__ manner: 7 bedside
__ manner born: 5 to the
mannered: 5 artsy, campy, posed, put-on, stiff **6** chichi, la-de-da, la-di-da, poised **7** stilted **8** affected, lah-di-dah **9** unnatural **10** artificial, theatrical
__-mannered: 3 ill **4** mild, well
Mannerhouse
author: Thomas Wolfe
mannerism: 3 air, tic, way **4** mien, pose **5** habit, quirk, trait **6** foible, manner **7** oddness **10** pretension
mannerless: 8 impolite
one: 3 cad, oaf **4** boor
mannerly: 4 good **5** civil **6** decent, polite, proper, social, urbane **7** genteel, refined **8** charming, decorous, gracious, polished, well-bred **9** civilized, courteous **10** respectful
__ manner of speaking: 3 in a
manners: 5 couth, mores **6** polish **7** conduct, culture, decorum, p's and q's **8** behavior, breeding, civility, courtesy, folkways, protocol, urbanity **9** etiquette, politesse, propriety **10** civilities, deportment, politeness, refinement
mind one's ~: 6 behave
__ manners: 3 bad **5** table
Manners: 5 David
Manners, Miss subject: 4 tact
Mannheim: 4 city, town
locale: 7 Germany
Mann, Herbie: 7 flutist **8** flautist, musician
genre: 4 jazz
song: Hijack (1975)
Superman (1979)
Manning: 3 Eli **6** Archie, Peyton **8** Adelaide, Frederic
mannish: 9 masculine
Mannix (CBS drama)
cast: Joseph Campanella (Lou Wickersham)
Mike Connors (Joe Mannix)
Gail Fisher (Peggy Fair)
Mann, Manfred
homeland: South Africa
real name: Michael Lubowitz
song: Blinded by the Light (1976)
Do Wah Diddy Diddy (1964)
Mighty Quinn (1968)
Sha La La (1964)
Mann, Thomas: 6 German, writer **8** essayist, Nobelist
work: Buddenbrooks
Confessions of Felix Krull
Death in Venice
Joseph and His Brothers
The Magic Mountain
Tonio Kroger
Mannucci: 4 Aldo
Manny: 4 Mota **6** Trillo **7** Ramirez
man-o'-__ bird: 3 war
Manoah
son: 6 Samson
man of __: 3 God **5** straw **7** letters
man-of-__: 3 war
Man of __: 4 Aran, Iron **5** Steel
Man of a Thousand Faces, The: Lon Chaney
Man of Destiny, The
author: George Bernard Shaw
Manoff: 5 Dinah
Man of God, A
author: Gabriel Marcel
Man of Iron (1980 film)
director: Andrzej Wajda
Man of La Mancha
star: Richard Kiley
Man of Marble (1977 film)
director: Andrzej Wajda
__ man of means...: 3 I'm a
Man of Steel
see Superman
man of the __: 4 hour, year **5** cloth, house, world
Man of the Crowd, A
author: Edgar Allan Poe
Man of the Forest, The
author: Zane Grey
Man of the House (2005 film)
cast: Cedric the Entertainer, Tommy Lee Jones
Man of the Year magazine: 4 Time
man-of-war: 4 boat **7** flattop, frigate, gunboat **9** destroyer **10** battleship
__, ma! No hands!: 4 Look
Manolete: 6 torero **7** matador **8** toreador **11** bullfighter
foe: 4 bull, toro
see also Spanish
Manon: 5 opera
composer: Jules Massenet
piece: 4 aria
role: 7 Lescaut **9** des Grieux
setting: 5 Paris **6** Amiens, France **7** Le Havre
Man on Fire (2004 film)
cast: Dakota Fanning, Christopher Walken, Denzel Washington
Manon Lescaut: 5 opera
author: Abbé Prévost
composer: Giacomo Puccini
man on the __: 6 street
Man on the Flying Trapeze, The (1935 film)
cast: W.C. Fields
Man on the Moon (1993 song)
artist: R.E.M.
Man on the Moon (1999 film)
cast: Jim Carrey, Danny DeVito, Courtney Love
director: Milos Forman
man-on-the-moon org.: 4 NASA
manor: 4 home, land **5** abode **6** castle, estate, palace **7** mansion **9** residence **10** plantation
house: 7 chateau
master: 3 esq. **4** lord **7** esquire
worker: 4 serf
manorial court: 4 leet
__ man out: 3 odd
man-o'-war: 4 bird
Man O'War: 5 horse **9** racehorse
only horse to beat ~: 5 Upset
__ Man, Poor Man: 4 Rich
manpower: 9 personnel
...__ man put asunder: 5 let no
Man Ray: 6 artist **7** painter
art: 4 Dada
Manrique, Jorge: 4 poet **7** Spanish
man's
best friend: 3 dog
no ~ land: 3 DMZ
that ~: 3 his
man's __ friend: 4 best
mansard: 4 roof **5** attic **6** garret
part: 4 eave
__ Man's Curve: 4 Dead
manse: 7 rectory **8** vicarage **9** parsonage
manservant: 5 valet **6** butler **7** steward **9** major-domo

__ Manse, The: 3 Old
__ Man's Family: 3 One
Mansfield: 4 city, town 5 Jayne 9 Katherine
locale: 4 Ohio 5 Texas
Mansfield, Jayne
film: Will Success Spoil Rock Hunter? (1957)
Mansfield, Katherine: 6 writer
work: Bliss
A Dill Pickle
The Dove's Nest
The Garden Party
Mansfield Park
author: Jane Austen
Mansfield, Peter
work: 8 Arabs, The
man's home is __ castle, A: 3 His
__-man show: 3 one
mansion: 4 hall, home, seat 5 abode, house, manor, villa 6 castle, estate, palace 7 chateau, domicil, housing 8 building, domicile, dwelling, hacienda 9 residence 10 habitation
and grounds: 6 estate
like a ~: 5 roomy
opposite: 3 hut 5 hovel
__ Mansion: 6 Gracie
__ Mansions: 5 Green
man-size: 3 big
Manson: 7 Marilyn, Shirley
manta: 3 ray 4 fish 5 cloak, shawl 8 devil ray 9 devilfish
kin: 5 skate
manta __: 3 ray
Manta: 3 bay, car 4 auto, Opel
__ Man Tate: 6 Little
manteau: 4 cape 5 cloak
Mantegna: 3 Joe 6 Andrea
mantel: 5 shelf
ender: 4 tree 5 piece, shelf
Man That Got Away, The
composer: Harold Arlen, Ira Gershwin
Man That Was Used Up, The
author: Edgar Allan Poe
Man, The: 4 Stan 6 Musial
__ Man, The: 4 Best, Next, Thin, Wolf 5 Candy, Great, Green, Music, Omega, Quiet, Squaw, Stunt, Tenth, Third, Wrong 6 Wicker 7 Running
mantic: 9 prophetic
mantilla: 4 cape, veil 5 scarf, shawl, throw 8 covering, kerchief 9 headcloth
mantis: 3 bug 6 insect, prayer
__ mantis: 7 praying
M.A.N.T.I.S. (Fox sci-fi)
cast: Carl Lumbly (Dr. Miles Hawkins)
Roger Rees (John Stonebrake)
Mantissa
author: John Fowles
mantle: 4 cape, pall, rock, veil, wrap 5 capot, cloak, cover, ledge, shelf 6 capote, dolman, redden, screen 7 chlamys 8 covering
layer between Earth's crust and ~: 4 moho
Mantle: 5 Burns 6 Mickey
Mantle, Mickey: 4 Yank 6 Yankee 7 slugger 10 outfielder
number: 5 seven
mantlet: 4 cape 5 cloak
man-to-man __: 4 talk 7 defense
Mantooth: 8 Randolph
Mantovani, Annunzio: 9 conductor
mantra: 2 om 3 aum 5 chant
beads: 4 mala
__ Man Triathlon: 4 Iron
mantua: 4 robe
Mäntyranta: 4 Eero
Manua: 4 isls. 5 isles 7 islands
locale: 5 Samoa
manual: 4 book, text 5 bible, guide, how-to 6 primer 8 cookbook, handbook, physical, textbook, workbook 9 guidebook 10 compendium
arts workroom: 4 shop
skill: 5 craft
training system: 5 sloid, slojd, sloyd
worker: 5 prole 7 laborer
manually: 6 by hand
Manuel: 5 Rojas 6 Gálvez 7 de Falla, Noriega, Padilla 8 Bandeira
see also Spanish
manufacture: 4 form, make, mill, mold, tool, work 5 build, forge, frame, hatch 6 cook up, create, devise, invent, output, prefab, put out 7 concoct, fashion, produce, think up, trump up, turn out 8 assemble, assembly, contrive 9 construct, fabricate
manufactured: 5 false 9 synthetic
manufacturer: 5 maker
claim: 3 new 8 improved
come-on: 6 coupon, rebate
tag: 5 label
manufacturing: 6 making, output 7 casting, tooling 8 assembly 9 producing 10 production
plant: 4 mill
manumission: 7 freedom, release
manumit: 4 free 5 let go, loose 6 loosen, redeem 7 release, set free 8 liberate, set loose, unfetter 9 discharge, turn loose, unshackle 10 emancipate
manuscript: 5 draft 6 record, script 7 galleys, writing
ancient ~: 5 codex
correct a ~: 4 edit 5 emend
enclosure: 3 SAE 4 SASE
marking: 6 obelus
markings: 5 obeli
notation: 4 stet
page: 5 folio
polisher: 6 editor
manuscripts, unsolicited: 5 slush
Manush: 6 Heinie
Manute: 3 Bol
Manutius: 5 Aldus
__ Man Walking: 4 Dead
Man Who Came to Dinner, The: 4 play
author: Moss Hart, George S. Kaufman
Man Who Cried I AM, The
author: John Williams
Man Who Died Twice, The
author: E.A. Robinson
Man Who Fell to Earth, The (1976 film)
cast: David Bowie, Candy Clark, Rip Torn
director: Nicolas Roeg
Man Who Had Three Arms, The
author: Edward Albee
Man Who Knew Too Much, The (1956 film)
cast: Doris Day, James Stewart
composer: Bernard Herrmann
director: Alfred Hitchcock
Man Who Loved Cat Dancing, The (1973 film): 5 oater
cast: George Hamilton, Sarah Miles, Burt Reynolds
Man Who Loved Children, The
author: Christina Stead
Man Who Mistook His Wife For __, The: 4 a Hat
Man Who Owned Broadway, The: 5 Cohan
Man Who Shot Liberty Valance, The (1962 film): 5 oater
cast: Lee Marvin, Vera Miles, Jeanette Nolan, James Stewart, John Wayne
director: John Ford
Man Who Shot Liberty Valance, The (1962 song)
artist: Gene Pitney
Man Who Wasn't There, The (2001 film)
cast: James Gandolfini, Frances McDormand, Billy Bob Thornton
director: Joel Coen
Man Who Would Be King, The: 4 film 10 short story
author: Rudyard Kipling
cast: Michael Caine, Sean Connery, Christopher Plummer
director: John Huston
__ Man With a Horn: 5 Young
Man Without a Country, The
author: Edward Everett Hale
character: Philip Nolan
Man Without a Face, The (1993 film)
cast: Mel Gibson
director: Mel Gibson
__ man with seven...: 5 I met a
Man with the Blue Guitar, The
author: Wallace Stevens
Man With the Golden Arm, The: 4 film 5 novel
author: Nelson Algren
cast: Kim Novak, Eleanor Parker, Frank Sinatra
director: Otto Preminger
Man With the Golden Gun, The: 4 film 5 novel
author: Ian Fleming
cast: Maud Adams, Britt Ekland, Christopher Lee, Roger Moore
Man With the Hoe, The: 4 poem
author: Edwin Markham
Man With Two Brains, The (1983 film)
cast: Steve Martin, Kathleen Turner, David Warner
cat: 6 Jarvis
director: Carl Reiner
Manx: 3 cat 5 felid 6 feline 8 language
cat's lack: 4 tail
language: 4 Erse 6 Gaelic
many: 4 a lot, gobs, lots, much, rife, tons 5 heaps, horde, loads, piles, scads 6 a lot of, divers, dozens, legion, lots of, myriad, oodles, plenty, scores, sundry, throng, umteen, untold, varied 7 copious, jillion, legions, no end of, numbers, profuse, several, teeming, umpteen, various 8 abundant, frequent, jillions, manifold, millions, multiple, numerous, umpsteen, zillions 9 abundance, bountiful, countless, legions of, multitude, plentiful, quite a few, thousands, uncounted 10 bezillions, innumerous, numberless
a good ~: 8 numerous
a time: 3 oft 4 a lot, much 5 often 9 quite a bit, regularly, routinely 10 frequently, habitually, repeatedly
combining form: 4 mult-, poly- 5 multi-, pluri-
ender: 4 fold
eras: 3 age 4 ages 6 period 8 long time
find how ~: 5 count
in Greek: 6 polloi
in Spanish: 5 mucha, mucho
not ~: 3 few 4 a few 5 light 6 little
too ~: 9 excessive
with ~ irons in the fire: 6 hectic
many __: 5 a time 6 thanks
many __ ago: 5 moons, years
many __ returns: 5 happy
Many __ Day: 4 a New
Many __ has to fall...: 5 a tear
Many __ of Dobie Gillis, The: 5 Loves
many a __: 4 time
Many a New Day
composer: Oscar Hammerstein, Richard Rodgers
__ many cooks...: 3 Too
__ Many Girls: 3 Too
many happy __: 7 returns
__ Many Husbands: 3 Too
__ many irons in the fire: 3 too
Many Loves of Dobie Gillis, The (CBS sitcom)
cast: Warren Beatty (Milton Armitage)
Bob Denver (Maynard G. Krebs)
Dwayne Hickman (Dobie Gillis)
Sheila James (Zelda Gilroy)
Tuesday Weld (Thalia Menninger)
many moons __: 3 ago
many-sided: 9 versatile
many splendored thing, A: 4 love
Many Tears Ago (1960 song)
artist: Connie Francis
__ many words: 4 in so
Manzanares
city on the ~: 6 Madrid
Manzarek: 3 Ray
mao-__: 3 tai
Mao: 6 Zedong 7 Tse-tung
colleague: 4 Chou, Deng, Zhou
opponent: 6 Chiang
Mao __: 4 suit 6 jacket
Mao II
author: Don DeLillo
Maoist: 3 Red 7 leftist 9 Communist
Maori: 8 language 10 Polynesian
bird the ~ once hunted: 3 moa
greeting: 5 hongi
war dance: 4 haka
map: 4 plan, plat, plot 5 atlas, chart, draft, frame, globe, graph, trace 6 design, layout, sketch, survey 7 diagram, drawing, outline, picture 9 formulate, visual aid 10 projection
abbr.: 2 av., st. 3 alt., Atl., ave., hwy., isl., lat., mtn., mts., Pac., str., ter. 4 elev., N. Lat., terr.

be all over the ~: 5 stray 6 ramble 7 meander
blue spot on a ~: 4 lake
city ~: 4 plat
direction: 3 ENE, ESE, NNE, NNW, SSE, SSW, WNW, WSW 4 east, west 5 north, south 9 northeast, northwest, southeast, southwest
dot: 4 town 5 islet 6 island
ender: 5 maker 6 making
feature: 4 grid 5 inset, scale 6 legend
former ~ abbr.: 4 USSR
line: 2 rt. 3 riv., rte. 4 road 5 river, route 6 avenue, border, street
on the ~: 5 known
out: 4 plan, plot 5 frame 6 depict, devise, sketch 7 pioneer, program, project 9 formulate
put on the ~: 9 publicize
science: 9 geography 10 topography
starter: 4 road 5 photo
wipe off the ~: 4 rase, raze, ruin, sack, undo 5 blast, crush, level, smash, total, trash, waste, wreck 6 defeat, ravage, uproot 7 despoil, destroy, flatten, shatter, torpedo 8 bulldoze, decimate, demolish, desolate, spoliate 9 depredate, devastate, eradicate, extirpate, overwhelm, pulverize, take apart 10 annihilate, obliterate

map __: 3 out
__ map: 3 bit 4 road 6 relief 7 contour, genetic, weather
Ma Perkins: 9 radio show
__ Mapes Dodge: 4 Mary
maple: 4 tree, wood 8 hardwood 10 bowling pin
extract: 3 sap
genus: 4 acer
like a ~ leaf: 5 erose
like ~ seeds: 4 alar 5 alary
of ~ trees: 6 aceric
seed: 6 samara
maple __: 5 honey, sugar, syrup
__ maple: 3 red 5 sugar
Maple Leaf: 4 coin
Maple Leaf __: 3 Rag
Maple Leafs: 3 six 4 team
home: 7 Toronto
milieu: 3 ice 4 rink
org.: 3 NHL
rival: *see* hockey team
sport: 6 hockey
target: 3 net
Maples, Marla
spouse: Donald Trump
maple walnut: 8 ice cream
alternative: *see* ice cream flavor
Mapocho, city on the: 8 Santiago
Map of the World, A (1999 film)
cast: Julianne Moore, David Strathairn, Sigourney Weaver
__ mapping: 4 gene
MapQuest
request: 3 rte.
Maputo: 4 city, port, town 7 capital
locale: 10 Mozambique
maquillage: 4 kohl 6 makeup
mar: 4 bend, blot, dent, ding, harm, hurt, nick, ruin, scar, soil, warp 5 abuse, botch, break, score, scuff, spoil, stain, sully, taint, wreck 6 bang up, befoul, blight, bruise, damage, deface, foul up, impair, injure, mangle, mess up 7 blemish, despoil, detract, louse up, scratch, tarnish, vitiate 8 discolor 9 vandalize 10 adulterate
Mar __ Plata: 3 del
Mar.: 2 mo.
follower: 3 Apr.
honoree: 5 St. Pat
it starts in ~: 3 DST, spr.
preceder: 3 Feb.
see also March
Mara: 3 Tim 5 Adele 6 Corday, Wilson 10 Wellington
marabou: 4 bird 5 stork
Maracaibo: 4 city, gulf, Lago, lake, port, town
locale: 9 Venezuela
Maracot Deep, The
author: Arthur Conan Doyle
Maranville: 6 Rabbit
marasca: 5 fruit 6 cherry
relative: 4 Bing 7 morello, oxheart
maraschino cherry: 7 marasca
Marat: 5 Safin 8 Jean Paul
see also French
marathon: 4 race 5 event 10 protracted
award: 6 anadem, laurel
city: 6 Boston
contender: 5 racer 6 runner
handout: 5 water
terminus: 4 tape
unit: 4 mile
Marathon: 6 battle
marathoner: 6 Benoit, Bikila 7 athlete, Shorter
bane: 5 cramp
breaking point: 4 wall
load-up: 4 carb
ordeal: 4 hill
Marathon Man (1976 film)
cast: William Devane, Dustin Hoffman, Laurence Olivier, Roy Scheider
Marat/Sade
author: Peter Weiss
maraud: 4 loot, raid, sack 5 foray, harry 6 harass, invade, ravage 7 despoil, pillage, plunder, ransack 8 freeboot, spoliate 9 depredate 10 encroach on
marauder: 3 Hun 5 thief 6 bandit, outlaw, pirate, robber 7 brigand, corsair, rustler 8 rapparee 9 buccaneer 10 freebooter, highwayman
Marauder: 3 car 4 auto 7 Mercury 10 automobile
marauding: 9 predatory, rapacious
Maravich, Pete
milieu: 5 court
org.: 3 NBA
sport: 10 basketball
marble: 4 cake, rock 5 agate 6 camlet, sphere, statue, streak 7 mineral
Belgian ~: 5 rance
big blue ~: 5 Earth
block: 4 slab
Greek ~ island: 5 Paros
Italian ~ city: 5 Massa
marking: 4 vein
playing ~: 3 mib, mig, taw 4 migg 5 agate, aggie, dobie, immie 6 miggle, peewee 7 cat's-eye, steelie
marble __: 4 cake
__ marble: 7 cat's-eye
Marble __, The: 4 Faun
Marble, Alice: 7 netster 9 tennis pro
milieu: 5 court
marbled: 7 mottled 8 brindled
Marble Faun, The
author: William Faulkner, Nathaniel Hawthorne
Marblehead: 4 city, town
locale: 4 Mass.
marbles: 3 wit 4 game, mind, wits 6 reason
having all one's ~: 4 sane 5 lucid 8 sensible
__ Marbles: 5 Elgin
marc: 5 drink 6 brandy 8 beverage
Marc: 5 Levin, Price 6 Antony, Singer 7 Anthony, Chagall, McClure, Summers 8 Allegret, Connelly 10 Blitzstein
beloved: 4 Cleo
Marcal
alternative: 5 Scott 7 Charmin 8 Northern, Soft Weve 10 Cottonelle, White Cloud
marcando: 8 accented
Marceau: 6 Marcel, Sophie
role: 3 Bip
marcel: 4 coif 6 hairdo 8 coiffure
Marcel: 4 Aymé 5 Carné 6 Dionne, Ophuls, Pagnol, Proust 7 Duchamp, Gabriel, Marceau
see also French
Marcel, Gabriel: 6 French, writer
work: Being and Having
La Grâce
Le Fanal
A Man of God
The Mystery of Being
Marcello: 8 Malpighi 11 Mastroianni
Marcels
song: Blue Moon (1961)
Heartaches (1961)
march: 4 gait, hike, move, pace, slog, trek, walk 5 drill, jaunt, music, stalk, strut, tramp, tread, troop 6 course, file by, foot it, parade, stride, trudge 7 advance, journey, proceed, protest, step out 8 long haul, neighbor, progress 9 go forward, promenade 10 forge ahead, procession
against: 3 war 5 fight 6 battle
day's ~: 5 étape
ender: 4 halt, land, pane
line of ~: 9 direction
off: 6 decamp
on the ~: 6 moving 9 advancing
starter: 7 counter
steal a ~ on: 5 one-up
__ march: 5 grand, on the 6 forced 7 freedom, wedding
March: 2 Jo 3 Amy, Hal, Meg 4 Alex, Beth, Jane 5 month 7 Fredric
17th color: 5 green
birthstone: 10 aquamarine
date: 4 ides 5 nones
follower: 3 Apr. 5 April
honoree: 5 St. Pat
like a ~ day: 5 gusty
like a ~ hare: 3 mad 4 daft
one of the ~ sisters: 2 Jo 3 Amy, Meg 4 Beth
preceder: 3 Feb. 8 February
sign: 3 Ram 4 Fish 5 Aries 6 Pisces
March __ said: 4 on he
__ March: 4 Long
March 15: 4 ides
March 7: 5 nones
Marchand: 5 Nancy
march-command word: 3 hep, hup
__ marché: 3 bon, pas
Marche __: 5 Slave 7 Funèbre
Marche Funèbre
composer: Georges Bizet
marché, pas: 4 step
marchers, univ.: 4 ROTC
marchesa: 4 rank 5 title
marchese: 4 rank 5 title
Marche Slave
composer: Peter Tchaikovsky
Marchetti, Gino
sport: 8 football
March, Fredric: 5 actor
film: Anthony Adverse (1936)
The Barretts of Wimpole Street (1934)
Bedtime Story (1941)
The Best Years of Our Lives (1946, AA)
The Bridges at Toko-Ri (1955)
The Buccaneer (1938)
Death of a Salesman (1951)
Death Takes a Holiday (1934)
Design for Living (1933)
The Desperate Hours (1955)
Dr. Jekyll and Mr. Hyde (1932, AA)
Inherit the Wind (1960)
Les Miserables (1935)
The Man in the Gray Flannel Suit (1956)
Seven Days in May (1964)
A Star Is Born (1937)
marching: 5 drill
give ~ orders: 4 sack
order: 3 hup, hut 4 halt
syllable: 3 hut
marching __: 6 orders
Marching __ war: 4 as to
Marching Along
author: John Philip Sousa
Marching as __: 5 to war
marching band
hat: 5 shako
instrument: 4 drum, fife, tuba 5 flute 8 clarinet
Marching Man
author: Sherwood Anderson
marchioness: 4 lady, peer, rank 5 noble, title
March King, The: John Philip Sousa
March, Little Peggy
song: I Will Follow Him (1963)
March Madness org.: 4 NCAA
March of __: 5 Dimes
March of Time, The: 9 radio show
marchpane: 5 candy
march-past: 9 cavalcade
March to Quebec
author: Kenneth Roberts
__ marcia: 4 alla
Marcia: 4 Rodd 5 Cross 7 Wallace 9 Strassman
Marcia __ Harden: 3 Gay
Marciano, Rocky: 5 boxer
milieu: 4 ring
Marco: 4 Polo
see also Italian
Marconi, Guglielmo: 8 Nobelist 9 physicist, scientist
invention: 5 radio

Marco Polo Sings a Solo
author: John Guare
Marcos: 6 Imelda **9** Ferdinand
__ Marcos, TX: 3 San
Marcovicci: 6 Andrea
Marcus: 4 Loew, pope **5** Allen, Welby **6** Garvey **7** pontiff, Rudolph **8** Aurelius
__ Marcus: 6 Neiman
Marcus Aurelius: 5 Roman, Stoic **6** Caesar **11** philosopher
physician of ~: 5 Galen
see also Latin
Marcuse, Herbert: 6 writer **11** philosopher, sociologist
work: Eros and Civilization
One-Dimensional Man
Marcus Welby M.D. (ABC drama)
cast: James Brolin (Dr. Steven Kiley)
Elena Verdugo (Consuelo Lopez)
Robert Young (Dr. Marcus Welby)
Marcy: 4 peak **5** mount **6** Carsey, Walker **7** William **8** mountain
locale: 7 New York **11** Adirondacks
mardi: 6 French **7** Tuesday
follower: 8 mercredi
preceder: 5 lundi
Mardi Gras: 3 Tue. **4** gala, Tues. **7** Tuesday **8** carnival **10** masquerade
city: 3 Rio **4** Nice
event: 6 parade
follower: 4 Lent
organizers: 5 krewe
VIP: 3 Rex
wear: 6 domino **7** costume
mare: 3 dam, she **5** filly, horse, mount, steed **6** animal, equine
go by shanks' ~: 4 slog, walk **5** leg it, march **6** foot it, hoof it, trudge
offspring: 4 colt, foal **5** filly
sound: 5 neigh **6** whinny
starter: 5 night
mare __: 7 nostrum
__ mare: 6 shanks'
Mare: 10 Winningham
Maren: 5 Jerry
Marengo: 5 horse, steed **6** battle
Maresca: 5 Ernie
Mares eat __: 4 oats
mare's-nest: 3 zoo **4** fake, hoax, mess, sham **5** fraud, snafu **6** dupery, foul-up, jumble, muddle **8** delusion **9** deception, imbroglio
mare's-tail: 5 cloud **6** cirrus
Margaret: 3 Cho, Rey **4** Ladd, Mead **5** Colin, Court, saint, Smith **6** Atwood, Avison, Dumont, Farrar, Fuller, Hillis, O'Brien, Sanger, Truman, Walker **7** Drabble, Lindsay, Whiting **8** Hamilton, Leighton, Lockwood, Mitchell, Sullavan, Thatcher **10** Rutherford
dad's monogram: 3 HST
in French: 7 Margaux
in German: 8 Gretchen
mother: 4 Bess
nickname: 3 Meg, Peg **5** Marge, Peggy
Margaret __ Smith: 5 Chase
Margaret __ Thatcher: 5 Hilda
Margaret Bourke-__: 5 White
margarine: 4 oleo **6** Parkay, Shedd's, spread **7** Promise **8** Imperial
fat: 5 olein **6** oleine
serving: 3 pat
margarita: 5 drink **8** beverage, cocktail
ingredient: 4 salt **7** tequila **9** lime juice, triple sec **10** lemon juice
Margaritaville (1977 song)
artist: Jimmy Buffett
Margate: 4 city, town
locale: 4 Kent **7** England, Florida
Margaux: 9 Hemingway
grandfather: 6 Ernest
in English: 8 Margaret
sister: 6 Mariel
Marge: 7 Simpson **8** Champion
Margery: 3 Daw
margin: 3 hem, lip, rim **4** brim, edge, lead, play, room, side **5** bound, brink, extra, limit, scope, shore, skirt, space, verge **6** border, fringe, leeway **7** selvage, surplus **8** boundary, latitude, selvedge **9** allowance, extremity, perimeter, periphery
for error: 4 room **5** range, slack, space **6** leeway **8** latitude **9** elbowroom **10** room to move
make a larger ~: 6 indent
narrow ~: 4 hair, inch, neck, nose
not on the ~: 5 set in
margin __: 4 call
margin __ error: 3 for
__ margin: 6 profit
marginal: 3 low **4** side **5** minor, small **6** limbic, slight **7** minimal, outside **9** on the edge **10** borderline, low-ranking, negligible, peripheral
notation: 4 dele, stet
marginalia: 5 notes **7** doodles
marginally: 8 slightly
margin for __: 5 error
Margin for Error
author: Clare Boothe Luce
margin of __: 6 safety
Margo: 7 actress **8** Channing
spouse: Eddie Albert
Margolin: 5 Janet **6** Stuart
Margot: 6 Kidder **7** Fonteyn
role for ~: 4 Lois
margrave: 5 title
__-Margret: 3 Ann
Margrethe II: 4 Dane **5** queen
marguerite: 5 daisy, plant **6** flower
Marguerite: 5 Duras **9** Yourcenar
see also French
Maria: 5 Bueno, McKee **6** Agnesi, Bombal, Callas, Montez, Schell **7** Jeritza, Muldaur, Pitillo, Shriver **8** von Trapp **9** Edgeworth, Tallchief **10** Montessori
author: Jorge Isaacs
husband: 6 Arnold
in the song: 4 wind
to Ted: 5 niece
see also Spanish
Maria __: 5 Elena **7** Theresa
Maria __ Alonso: 8 Conchita
Maria __ Trapp: 3 Von
__ Maria: 3 Ave, Tia **5** Black, Santa
__ Maria Alberghetti: 4 Anna
__ Maria Brandauer: 5 Klaus
mariachi
gig: 6 fiesta
wear: 6 sarape, serape
Maria Conchita __: 6 Alonso
Mariah: 5 Carey
__ Maria Horsford: 4 Anna
Marian: 5 Engel, Marsh **6** Jordan, Mercer **8** Anderson **10** McPartland
the Librarian's last name: 5 Paroo
__ Marian: 4 Maid
Mariana
author: Alfred Tennyson
Mariana __: 6 Trench **7** Islands
Marianas: 4 isls. **5** isles **7** islands
island: 4 Guam, Rota **5** Pagan **6** Guguan, Saipan, Tinian **7** Agrihan, Aguijan
port: 4 Apra
Mariana Trench, like the: 4 deep
Marianne: 5 Moore **9** Faithfull **10** Sägebrecht
author: George Sand
Marianne (1957 song)
artist: Hilltoppers, Terry Gilkyson and the Easy Riders
__ Marianne: 4 C'mon
__ Maria Olazabal: 4 Jose
__ Maria Remarque: 5 Erich
__ Maria Rilke: 6 Rainer
Marías, Julián: 6 writer **7** Spanish **11** philosopher
Marichal, Juan: 5 Giant **7** pitcher
__-marie: 4 bain
Marie: 3 Ste. **4** Rose **5** Curie, Teena **6** Dionne, Osmond, sainte, Wilson **7** Corelli, Tempest **8** Dressler **9** de Médicis **10** Antoinette, LaChapelle
brother: 5 Donny
in English: 4 Mary
see also French
Marie __: 6 Claire
Marie __ Land: 4 Byrd
__ Marie: 4 Rose, Tina **5** Teena
Marie Antoinette: 5 queen, reine **6** French
Marie Byrd Land, toward: 5 south
__ Marie Cox: 3 Ana
Marie de France: 4 poet **6** French
Mariel: 4 city, port, town **9** Hemingway
grandpa: 6 Ernest
locale: 4 Cuba
Marienbad: 3 spa **4** city, town
locale: Czech Republic
__ Marie Presley: 4 Lisa
__ Marie Saint: 3 Eva
Marietta: 4 city, town
locale: 7 Georgia
Mariette: 7 Hartley
marigold: 5 plant **6** annual, flower
Marilu: 6 Henner
Marilyn: 5 Horne, McCoo **6** French, Manson, Martin, Miller, Monroe **7** Bergman, Maxwell, Munster
real first name: 5 Norma
Marilyn __ Savant: 3 Vos
marimba: 7 kalimba **10** percussion
Marin: 4 John **6** Cheech
marina: 4 dock **5** wharf **6** harbor **7** harbour
hoist: 5 davit
place: 4 cove **5** inlet
sight: 4 mast, spar **5** yacht **8** boat. slip
Marina: 6 Sirtis
marinade: 5 steep **6** pickle
Marina del __, CA: 3 Rey
marinara: 5 sauce
alternative: 5 pesto
ingredient: 6 garlic, tomato
Marinaro: 2 Ed
marinate: 4 soak **5** souse, steep
Marin, Cheech: 5 actor **8** comedian
film: Paulie (1998)
Tin Cup (1996)
Up in Smoke (1978)
Yellowbeard (1983)
partner: Tommy Chong
TV: Nash Bridges
marine: 4 naut. **5** naval **7** aquatic, coastal, deep-sea, oceanic, pelagic, soldier **8** littoral, maritime, natatory, nautical **9** salt-water, seafaring **10** oceangoing
life: 4 alga, fish **5** algae **7** seaweed
starter: 3 sub **4** aqua **5** ultra
see also ocean, sea
marine __: 7 biology
Marine: 6 gyrene
officer: 3 col., gen., maj. **4** capt. **5** lieut., lt. col., major **7** captain, colonel, general **10** lieutenant
poster words: 4 a few
response: 5 no sir **6** yes sir
Marine __: 5 Corps
mariner: 3 gob, tar **4** mate, salt, swab, swob **6** sailor, sea dog, seaman **7** captain, jack tar, yachtie **8** deckhand, helmsman, seafarer, shipmate **9** navigator **10** bluejacket
aid: 4 buoy **6** beacon **10** lighthouse
ancient ~: 4 Eric, Leif, Noah **7** Ericson **8** Columbus
danger: 4 reef **5** rocks
heading: 3 ENE, ESE, NNE, NNW, SSE, SSW, WNW, WSW
see also sailor
Mariners: 3 ten **4** team
home: 7 Seattle
org.: 3 ALW, MLB
rival: *see* baseball team
sport: 8 baseball
Marines: 5 Corps **8** military
join the ~: 6 enlist
stay in the ~: 4 reup
__ Marino: 3 San
Marino, Dan: 2 QB **11** quarterback
sport: 8 football
Mario: 3 Pei **4** Puzo **5** Cuomo, Lanza, Zampi **6** Molina **7** Andrade, Lemieux, Soldati **8** Andretti **9** Benedetti, Monicelli **10** Van Peebles
see also Italian
Mario __ Llosa: 6 Vargas
Mario __ Peebles: 3 Van
Marion: 4 Mack, Ross **5** Barry, Lorne, Marty **6** Davies, Motley **7** Donovan, Francis **9** Cotillard
marionette: 4 doll **6** puppet
Mario Vargas __: 5 Llosa
Maris: 3 Ada **5** Roger
__ Maris: 6 Stella
Marisa: 5 Pavan, Tomei **8** Berenson
Mariska: 8 Hargitay
mother: 5 Jayne
Maris, Roger
sport: 8 baseball
marital: 6 bridal, wedded **7** nuptial, spousal **8** conjugal **9** connubial
rites: 7 wedding **9** matrimony
maritime: 3 nav. **4** naut. **5** naval

MA

6 marine 7 aquatic, coastal, deep-sea, oceanic, pelagic 8 littoral, maritime, nautical, seagoing 9 saltwater, seafaring 10 oceangoing
clandestine ~ org.: 3 ONI
convoy: 6 armada
outpost: 3 NAS
pal: 5 matey
rescue org.: 4 USCG
saint: 4 Elmo
see also navy, ocean, sea
Maritime __: 4 Alps
__ Maritime: 5 Seine
Maritime Provinces
locale: 6 Canada
__-Maritimes: 5 Alpes
Marius the Epicurean
author: Walter Pater
Marjoe: 7 Gortner
marjoram: 4 herb
__ marjoram: 3 pot 4 wild 5 sweet
Marjorie: 4 Lord, Main 8 Reynolds
Marjorie __ Rawlings: 6 Kinnan
Marjorie Merriweather __: 4 Post
Marjorie Morningstar: 4 film 5 novel
author: Herman Wouk
cast: Gene Kelly, Claire Trevor, Natalie Wood, Ed Wynn
character: 3 Guy 4 Eden, Noel
composer: Max Steiner
mark: 2 ID 3 add, aim, bar, bit, con, cue, cut, dab, dot, eye, IOU, jot, log, mar, nip, opt, peg, pit, rub, rut, sap, say, see, tab, tag, tip 4 atom, aura, band, blob, blot, blur, boob, butt, call, cash, chip, cite, claw, clew, clue, coin, dash, data, daub, dent, draw, dupe, edit, etch, fame, feel, file, find, flaw, fool, form, foul, gain, gash, goal, goat, gull, heed, hint, hurt, iota, kind, lamb, lead, line, list, logo, look, make, mean, mind, mint, mite, name, nick, note, omen, pawn, pick, pink, plan, plot, prey, rank, rate, scab, scan, scar, seal, seam, show, sign, slit, soil, sort, spot, stub, tack, take, tear, tend, tick, tier, tint, tool, view, vote, welt, whit, wisp 5 affix, augur, badge, blaze, brand, carve, catch, chart, cheat, check, chump, claim, class, count, crest, cross, dirty, dough, draft, éclat, elect, enter, fleck, gauge, gouge, grade, grain, graph, graze, guard, guide, honor, image, imply, index, judge, label, money, notch, odium, patsy, point, prick, print, proof, quirk, refer, ridge, savor, score, scout, sense, shade, shame, shape, slash, smear, speck, stain, stamp, sully, taint, tally, tilde, tinge, token, total, touch, trace, track, trail, trait, value, vouch, watch, weigh, worth, wound, write 6 accent, advert, affect, append, aspect, assess, assign, assort, attend, attest, augury, bang up, batter, beacon, bedaub, behold, blotch, boo-boo, bruise, cachet, center, change, choose, course, crater, crease, credit, crud up, damage, dapple, darken, debase, decide, deface, defect, defile, define, denote, depict, descry, design, detail, detect, dimple, emblem, evince, figure, finger, flavor, follow, groove, herald, hunted, incise, injure, intend, intent, lackey, lay out, lesion, listen, locate, martyr, mottle, nature, notice, oddity, opt for, pepper, pigeon, pimple, play up, pledge, puppet, rating, record, regard, schook, scrape, scrawl, screen, select, signal, size up, sketch, smirch, smudge, status, stigma, stooge, streak, stress, stripe, stroke, sucker, survey, symbol, take in, target, ticket, tip-off, victim, wretch 7 abide by, acclaim, archive, auspice, begrime, besmear, betoken, blacken, blemish, catalog, certify, chalk up, comment, confirm, connote, contour, discern, doormat, earmark, earnest, endorse, engrave, exhibit, explain, express, extract, eyeball, fall guy, feature, freckle, glimpse, hearken, implant, impress, imprint, ingrain, initial, inkling, insigne, instill, itemize, jot down, jotting, license, look out, make out, meaning, measure, mention, monitor, nebbish, observe, outline, pick out, pin down, pointer, point to, point up, portend, portent, presage, put down, quality, recount, refer to, reflect, reserve, scratch, set down, signify, smidgen, snippet, sort out, spatter, specify, speckle, splotch, stipple, suggest, symptom, tarnish, tracing, unknown, vestige, witness 8 abrasion, adhere to, allocate, allude to, annotate, appraise, attest to, besmirch, black eye, boundary, bull's-eye, check off, check out, classify, colophon, currency, delegate, describe, diagnose, discolor, disgrace, dishonor, document, eminence, estimate, evaluate, evidence, flyspeck, home in on, identify, ideogram, impurity, indicate, inscribe, insignia, intimate, lacerate, maculate, milepost, particle, perceive, pinpoint, point out, position, pushover, register, reminder, scribble, see after, set aside, squiggle, stake out, stand for, standing, sure sign, swelling, take down, take heed, tincture, zero in on 9 adumbrate, appraisal, apprehend, assertion, attribute, authorize, bespatter, bespeckle, born loser, brand name, calibrate, catalogue, celebrate, character, chronicle, condition, contusion, criterion, delineate, designate, determine, disfigure, disrepute, emphasize, engraving, enumerate, footprint, greatness, harbinger, highlight, indicator, influence, insinuate, intention, interpret, italicize, keep score, lend an ear, lineament, look after, objective, parameter, pay heed to, precursor, punctuate, recognize, reinforce, represent, scapegoat, schlemiel, scintilla, semicolon, signifier, single out, soft touch, solemnize, symbolize, touch upon, underline, valuation, write down, yardstick 10 accentuate, annotation, apostrophe, assessment, beauty spot, blame-taker, categorize, coat of arms, denotation, depression, evaluation, foreshadow, get a load of, illustrate, impression, imputation, indication, intimation, keep tabs on, laceration, predispose, prognostic, reputation, stigmatize, take care of, traumatize, underscore
black ~: 4 slur, smut 5 stain 6 stigma
black-and-blue ~: 4 hurt 6 boo-boo, bruise
diacritical ~: 4 shwa 5 breve, hacek, schwa, tilde 6 macron, obelus, umlaut
down: 3 cut 4 note 5 enter, lower, price, retag, slash, tally, write 6 notate, record, reduce 7 devalue 8 close out, decrease, discount 9 devaluate, keep score
easy ~: 3 sap 4 butt, dupe, goat, lamb, simp, tool 5 chump, patsy, setup 6 pigeon, sucker, victim 8 pushover
fraction: 7 pfennig
high-water ~: 4 acme, apex, peak 5 crest 6 apogee, summit, zenith 8 pinnacle
hunter ~: 4 game 6 quarry
leave a ~: 4 scar
make one's ~: 7 prosper
miss the ~: 3 err 4 fail
off: 4 drop 7 delimit 8 cross out, graduate 10 measure out
off the ~: 4 awry 5 amiss, wrong 6 afield, astray, errant, faulty 7 inexact 8 mistaken 9 erroneous, imprecise 10 inaccurate
on the ~: 3 apt 4 true 5 right 7 correct 8 accurate
out: 4 pace, plan 6 define
punctuation ~: 4 dash 5 colon, comma, paren. 6 hyphen
replacement: 4 euro
starter: 3 ear, pug, sea 4 book, foot, hall, land, mint, post, tide 5 bench, birth, metal, press, trade, water 7 chatter
time: 4 drag, idle, tick, wait
up: 4 edit, hike 5 boost, price, raise 8 increase
see also grade
mark __: 3 off 4 down, time
__ mark: 4 hash 5 bench, black, check, ditto, quote 6 accent, beauty, maker's
Mark: 4 Lane, Roth 5 Clark, Damon, Grace, saint, Shera, Spitz, Twain, Wills 6 Antony, Hamill, Harmon, Lenard, McEwen, O'Meara, Robson, Rothko, Rydell, Strand 7 Dinning, Fidrych, Goddard, Goodson, Lindsay, McGwire, Messier, Ruffalo, Russell, Stevens 8 Hatfield, Morrison, Sandrich, Van Doren, Wahlberg 9 Linn-Baker
follower: 4 Luke
preceder: 7 Matthew
to Tristan: 5 uncle
Mark __-Baker: 4 Linn
Markandaya, Kamala: 6 Indian, writer
work: Nectar in a Sieve
markdown: 4 sale 7 bargain 8 discount 9 abatement, reduction
marked: 3 x'ed 5 clear, sharp 6 patent, signal, strong 7 decided, evident, intense, notable, salient, special, telling, visible 8 apparent, definite, distinct, manifest, striking 9 arresting, prominent 10 noticeable, pronounced
be ~ at: 4 cost
down: 3 low 5 cheap 6 on sale 7 reduced 8 a good buy, uncostly 9 half-price 10 economical
markedly: 5 extra 6 vastly 7 clearly, greatly, notably 8 patently, severely, signally, terribly 9 decidedly, evidently, extremely, obviously 10 distinctly, especially, incredibly, manifestly, noticeably, remarkably, strikingly
marker: 3 IOU, pen, tab, tag 4 buoy, chit, cone, debt 5 arrow, chalk, pylon, stela, stele 6 ticket 7 felt-tip, waypost 8 landmark, monument
__ marker: 4 felt 7 genetic
__ Marker: 5 Magic
markers
having ~ out: 6 in debt
one with ~: 4 ower
market: 4 co-op, deli, fair, hawk, mall, mart, sell, shop, souk, vend 5 bazar, booth, stall, store, trade 6 bazaar, bourse, outlet, peddle, retail 7 grocery 8 business, emporium, exchange 9 advertise, dime store, drugstore, move goods, wholesale 10 chain store, Wall Street
abroad: 6 export
aid: 4 cart
collapse: 5 crash
corner the ~: 5 buy up, sew up 7 possess
downturn: 5 slide
employee: 3 arb 5 clerk 6 bagger, broker 7 cashier
ender: 5 place
flood the ~: 4 glut
free ~: 10 capitalism
in the ~: 7 looking, seeking, wanting
just on the ~: 3 new
letters: 3 IPO, OTC 4 AMEX, NYSE 6 NASDAQ
Mideast ~: 3 suk, suq 4 souk 5 bazar 6 bazaar
offering: 5 stock
off the ~: 4 sold
on the ~: 7 for sale 9 available, up for sale
order: 3 buy 4 sell
play the ~: 5 trade 6 invest 7 venture 9 speculate
price: 4 cost 5 quote, value 9 quotation
put on the ~: 5 offer
segment: 5 niche
starter: 4 down 5 green
upturn: 5 rally 6 uptick 8 recovery 10 turnaround
visit the ~: 4 shop 6 browse
market __: 5 maker, order, price, share, value 6 basket
__ market: 3 job 4 bear, bull, call, curb, flea, gray, grey, open, spot 5 black, labor, money, on the, stock, white 6 buyer's 7 farmers', futures, seller's

___-market: 4 down, mass, test 5 after
___ Market: 6 Boston, Common
marketability: 5 value
marketable: 3 hot 6 liquid 7 popular, salable 8 bankable, in demand, saleable, sellable, vendible 10 commercial
marketer: 6 dealer, seller
___-market fund: 5 money
marketing
  budget item: 2 ad
  device: 5 tie in
  online ~: 5 e-tail
  starter: 4 tele
  target: 5 buyer
___ marketing: 4 mass 5 viral 6 direct
___-market paperback: 4 mass
marketplace: 5 bazar, plaza 6 bazaar
  ancient ~: 5 agora, Forum
___-market price: 4 fair
Markevich, Igor: 7 Russian 9 conductor
Markey: 4 Enid, Gene
Markham: 4 city, peak, town 5 Beryl, Edwin, Monte, mount 7 Pigmeat 8 mountain
  locale: 6 Canada 7 Ontario 10 Antarctica
Markham, Beryl: 5 pilot
Markham, Edwin: 4 poet
  subject: 4 hoer
Markham, Pigmeat
  song: Here Comes the Judge (1968)
Markie: 4 Post
___ Markie: 3 Biz
marking: 4 look 5 brand 7 pattern
marking ___: 3 pen
Mark Mc___: 4 Ewen
Markova, Alicia: 6 dancer 7 British 8 danseuse 9 ballerina
Marks and Spencer: 4 shop 5 store
marksman: 4 shot 7 deadeye
  order: 3 aim 4 fire 5 ready
Mark Trail dog: 4 Andy
Mark Twain National Forest, site of: 6 Ozarks
Mark Twain Prize
  winners: 2010 - Tina Fey
    2009 - Bill Cosby
    2008 - George Carlin
    2007 - Billy Crystal
    2006 - Neil Simon
    2005 - Steve Martin
    2004 - Lorne Michaels
    2003 - Lily Tomlin
    2002 - Bob Newhart
    2001 - Whoopi Goldberg
    2000 - Jonathan Winters
    1999 - Carl Reiner
    1998 - Richard Pryor
Mark Twain Suite
  composer: Ferde Grofé
markup: 6 profit
  basis: 4 cost
  sans ~: 6 at cost
Mark Van ___: 5 Doren
Marky Mark and the Funky Bunch
  song: Good Vibrations (1991)
    Wildside (1991)
marl: 4 clay 5 earth, loess
Marla: 5 Gibbs 6 Maples
Marlee: 6 Matlin
Marlene: 5 Hagge 8 Dietrich
___ Marlene: 4 Lili
Marley: 3 Bob 5 Jacob, Ziggy
  genre: 6 reggae
Marley & Me (2008 film)
  cast: Jennifer Aniston, Owen Wilson
marlin: 4 fish
___ marlin: 4 blue
Marlin: 3 AMC, car 4 auto 7 Perkins, Rambler 9 Fitzwater 10 automobile
marline: 5 twine
Marlins: 4 nine, team
  home: 3 Fla. 5 Miami 7 Florida
  org.: 3 MLB, NLE
  rival: *see* baseball team
  sport: 8 baseball
Marlo: 6 Thomas
  spouse: 4 Phil
Marlon: 6 Brando 7 Jackson
Marlow Chronicles, The
  author: Lawrence Sanders
Marlowe: 4 Hugh 6 Philip
  contemporary: 3 Kid, Kyd
Marlowe, Christopher: 4 poet 7 British 10 playwright
  work: Come live with me...
    Hero and Leander
    The Jew of Malta
    Tamburlaine the Great
    The Tragical History of Dr. Faustus
marm: 6 madame
Marmaduke: 3 dog, pet
marmalade: 3 cat 6 spread 9 conserves, preserves
  ingredient: 4 peel, rind 6 orange
  kin: 5 jelly
___ Marmalade: 4 Lady
Marmara: 3 sea
  locale: 6 Turkey
  Sea of ~ port: 5 Izmit
Marmion
  author: Walter Scott
marmoset: 5 jocko 6 animal 7 primate, tamarin
  fare: 6 insect
  relative: *see* primate
marmot: 6 animal, mammal, rodent
  relative: *see* rodent
Marne: 5 river 6 battle
  locale: 6 France
___-Marne: 5 Haute
Marner: 5 Silas
Marnie (1964 film)
  cast: Sean Connery, Tippi Hedren
  composer: Bernard Herrmann
  director: Alfred Hitchcock
___ Marnier: 5 Grand
maroon: 3 red 5 beach, color, leave 6 desert, enisle, strand 7 abandon, crimson, forsake, isolate 8 forswear 9 foreswear 10 cast ashore
  relative: *see* red color
marooned: 4 left 5 alone 7 aground 8 castaway, forsaken, stranded 9 foundered 10 high and dry
Marot, Clément: 4 poet 6 French
Marouf, baritone in: 3 Ali
Marple, Miss: 4 Jane
Marquand: 2 J.P. 7 Richard
Marquand, J.P.: 6 writer
  sleuth: Mr. Moto
  work: The Late George Apley
    Wickford Point
Marquard, Rube: 6 hurler 7 pitcher
___ marqué: 3 sou
marquee: 6 awning, canopy
  light: 4 neon
  share the ~: 6 costar
Marquesas: 4 isls. 5 isles 7 islands
  island: 4 Eïao, Ua Pu 6 Hatutu, Hiva Oa, Ua Huka 7 Tahuata 8 Fatu Hiva, Nuku Hiva
marquess: 4 peer 5 noble, title
Marquette: 4 city, Père, town
  locale: 8 Michigan 9 Milwaukee, Wisconsin
Márquez, Gabriel García: 6 writer 8 Nobelist 9 Colombian
  work: One Hundred Years of Solitude
Marquina, Eduardo: 6 writer 7 Spanish
marquis: 4 lord, male, peer, rank 5 noble, title 8 nobleman
  rank above ~: 4 duke
  rank below ~: 4 earl
Marquis: 3 car, Don 4 auto 6 Childs 7 Mercury 10 automobile
Marquis de ___: 4 Sade 9 Lafayette
Marquis, Don: 6 writer 8 humorist
  work: Archy and Mehitabel
    The Lantern
    The Sun Dial
marquise: 3 gem
marquisette: 5 gauze 6 fabric
Marquis of Queensberry ___: 5 rules
Marrakesh: 4 city, town
  locale: 7 Morocco
  section: 6 casbah
Marrakesh Express (1969 song)
  artist: Crosby, Stills & Nash
marred: 4 hurt 6 broken, faulty, flawed 7 injured, unsound 8 fallible 9 defective, imperfect
marriage: 4 bond, rite 5 match, union 6 mating, merger 7 wedding, wedlock 8 alliance, contract, espousal, monogamy, nuptials, polygamy 9 matrimony, sacrament
  absence of ~ laws: 5 agamy
  before ~: 3 née
  combining form: 4 -gamy 6 -gamous
  document: 3 lic. 7 license
  it's given in ~: 4 hand
  notice: 4 bans 5 banns
  of ~: 7 marital
  offer ~: 7 propose
  perform a ~: 5 unite
  place: 5 altar 6 chapel
  relative by ~: 5 in-law 6 affine
  seek in ~: 3 woo
  symbol: 4 ring
  vows: 5 troth
  vow word: 5 worse 6 better, poorer, richer
marriageable one: 4 miss
Marriage at ___: 4 Cana
Marriage Italian Style (1964 film)
  cast: Sophia Loren
Marriage of Figaro, The: 5 opera
  composer: Wolfgang Amadeus Mozart
  role: 6 Curzio 7 Antonio, Bartolo, Basilio, Susanna 8 Almaviva 9 Don Curzio 10 Don Basilio, Marcellina
  setting: 5 Spain 7 Seville
Marriage Play
  author: Edward Albee
married
  get ~: 3 wed
  name meaning ~: 6 Beulah
  not ~: 5 unwed 6 single
  one: 4 wife 5 bride, groom 6 spouse 7 husband
Married to the Mob (1988 film)
  cast: Alec Baldwin, Joan Cusack, Matthew Modine, Michelle Pfeiffer, Mercedes Ruehl, Dean Stockwell
  director: Jonathan Demme
  dog: 5 Lucky
Married...With Children (Fox sitcom)
  cast: Christina Applegate (Kelly Bundy)
    David Faustino (Bud Bundy)
    Ed O'Neill (Al Bundy)
    Katey Sagal (Peg Bundy)
  dog: Buck
Marriner, Neville: 7 British 9 conductor
marring: 6 defect 8 graffiti
Marriott: 5 hotel
  alternative: *see* hotel
marrons glacés: 7 dessert 9 chestnuts
marrow: 4 core, gist, meat, pith, root, soul 5 cream, heart, point, quick 6 kernel, middle 7 essence, keynote 8 interior, key point 9 innermost, lifeblood, substance
  combining form: 4 myel- 5 myelo-
___ marrow: 4 bone
Marrow, Tracy
  stage name: 4 Ice-T
marry: 3 tie, wed 4 bond, join, mate, take, wive, yoke 5 blend, catch, merge, unify, unite 6 splice 7 combine, espouse 10 get hitched, settle down, tie the knot
  again: 5 rewed
  on the run: 5 elope
  persuade to ~: 3 win
  promise to ~: 5 troth
___ Marry a Millionaire: 5 How to
Marryat, Frederick: 6 writer 7 British
  work: Frank Mildmay, or the Naval Officer
    Masterman Ready
    Mr. Midshipman Easy
    Peter Simple
Marryin' ___: 3 Sam
marrying man: 2 JP 6 parson, priest
Marrying Man, The (1991 film)
  cast: Alec Baldwin, Kim Basinger, Elisabeth Shue
  director: Jerry Rees
mars: 4 mois 5 March, month 6 French
  follower: 5 avril
  preceder: 7 février
Mars: 3 bar, deo, god, orb 4 Ares, Mick 5 candy 6 planet 7 Kenneth 8 candy bar 9 chocolate 10 candy maker
  alternative: *see* candy brand
  combining form: 4 areo-
  equivalent: 4 Ares
  explorer: 5 probe, Rover
  Explorer: 5 robot
  feature: 5 canal 6 crater, icecap
  from ~: 5 alien
  moon of ~: 6 Deimos, Phobos
  neighbor: 5 Earth 7 Jupiter
  opposite: 3 Pax
  parent: 4 Juno 7 Jupiter
  Pathfinder org.: 4 NASA
  sister: 7 Bellona
  son: 5 Remus 7 Romulus

__ marsala: 4 veal 7 chicken
Marsala: 4 port, wine
origin: 5 Italy 6 Sicily
Marsalis: 5 Ellis 6 Wynton 8 Branford
Marsalis, Branford: 11 saxophonist
genre: 4 jazz
Marsalis, Ellis: 7 pianist
genre: 4 jazz
Marsalis, Wynton: 9 trumpeter
genre: 4 jazz
Mars Attacks! (1996 film)
cast: Annette Bening, Pierce Brosnan, Glenn Close, Jack Nicholson
director: Tim Burton
dog: 5 Rusty
Marsden: 5 Gerry, James
Marseille: 4 city, port, town
city near ~: 4 Lyon 5 Lyons
locale: 6 France
Marseilles: 4 city, port, town
city near ~: 3 Aix 5 Nîmes
locale: 6 France
marsh: 3 bog, fen 4 mire, sink 5 bayou, swale, swamp 6 lagoon, morass, slough 7 estuary, lowland, wetland 8 quagmire 9 backwater, everglade, swampland 10 everglades
bird: 4 rail, sora 5 crake, egret, heron, snipe 8 water hen
combining form: 4 helo- 6 paludi-
dweller: 4 frog
elder: 3 iva
ender: 4 land 5 lands 6 mallow
like a ~: 5 boggy, fenny, rushy, sedgy 6 swampy
plant: 4 reed, rush 5 ament, calla, sedge 6 catkin 8 arum lily
marsh __: 3 gas
__ marsh: 4 salt
Marsh: 3 Mae 4 Jean 5 Ngaio 6 Marian 8 Reginald
Marsha: 4 Hunt 5 Mason 6 Norman 8 Warfield
marshal: 5 align, aline, array, group, order, rally, usher 6 deploy, draw up, gather, lawman, line up, muster 7 arrange, bailiff, collect, compile, convoke, dispose, officer, round up, sheriff 8 assemble, mobilize, muster up, official, organize 9 fire chief
force: 5 posse
__ marshal: 3 air, sky 4 fire 5 field, grand 7 provost
Marshal __: 4 Tito
Marshall: 2 E.G. 4 city, John, town 5 Field, Frank, Garry, Penny, Peter 6 Brenda, George 7 Herbert, McLuhan 8 Thurgood 9 Nirenberg
locale: 5 Texas
Marshall __: 4 Plan 7 Islands
__ Marshall, Counselor at Law: 4 Owen
Marshall, E.G.: 5 actor
TV: The Defenders
Marshall, Garry: 8 director
film: Beaches (1988)
Dear Eleanor (2009)
The Flamingo Kid (1984)
Frankie and Johnny (1991)
Georgia Rule (2007)
A League of Their Own (1992)
Lost in America (1985)
Nothing in Common (1986)
The Other Sister (1999)
Overboard (1987)
Pretty Woman (1990)
The Princess Diaries (2001)
Raising Helen (2004)
Runaway Bride (1999)
Marshall, George C.: 7 general 8 Nobelist
Marshall Islands
capital: 6 Majuro
island: 6 Bikini 8 Eniwetok
Marshall, Penny: 7 actress 8 director
film: Awakenings (1990)
Big (1988)
A League of Their Own (1992)
The Preacher's Wife (1996)
Renaissance Man (1994)
spouse: Rob Reiner
TV: Laverne and Shirley, The Odd Couple
Marshall Plan agcy.: 3 ECA
Marshalls: 4 isls. 5 isles 7 islands
Marshall University
locale: 10 Huntington
Marshes of Glynn, The: 4 poem
author: Sidney Lanier
marshland: 4 mire, quag 5 swamp, waste 8 quagmire
marshmallow: 5 plant, snack
chocolate ~ snack: 5 s'more
holder: 4 twig
like a ~: 4 soft
Marsh, Ngaio: 6 writer
sleuth: Roderick Alleyn
work: Artists in Crime
Black as He's Painted
Hand in Glove
A Man Lay Dead
Night at the Vulcan
Photo Finish
marshy: 5 boggy, fenny, muddy 6 swampy, watery
Marsilius of Padua: 11 philosopher
Marston __: 4 Moor
Marston, John: 6 writer 7 British
work: The Dutch Courtezan
The Malcontent
marsupial: 3 'roo 4 euro, tait 5 bilbi, bilby, koala 6 animal, numbat, wombat 7 bettong, dasyure, opossum, wallaby 8 kangaroo, wallaroo 9 bandicoot, phalanger
place for a young ~: 5 pouch
marsupium: 3 sac 5 pouch
mart: 4 co-op, deli, fair, mall, shop, souk 5 bazar, booth, stall, store 6 bazaar, market, outlet 8 boutique, business, emporium, exchange, showroom 9 dime store, drugstore 10 chain store
__-Mart: 3 Wal
Marta: 7 Kristen
Martel: 7 Charles
marten: 3 fur 5 pekan, tayra 6 animal, fisher, weasel
relative: *see* weasel
__ marten: 4 pine
martes: 3 día 7 Spanish, Tuesday
follower: 9 miércoles
preceder: 5 lunes
Martha: 4 Hyer, Raye 5 opera, saint, Scott 6 Graham, Grimes, Reeves 7 Stewart, Vickers 8 Coolidge, Plimpton 9 Jefferson 10 Washington
to George: 4 wife
Martha's Vineyard: 4 isle 6 island
Martha & the Vandellas
last name: Reeves
song: Dancing in the Street (1964)
Heat Wave (1963)
Honey Chile (1967)
I'm Ready for Love (1966)
Jimmy Mack (1967)
Nowhere to Run (1965)
Quicksand (1963)
Marthe: 6 Keller
Martí: 4 José
martial: 7 hawkish, hostile, warlike 8 fighting, military, ructious 9 bellicose, combative, soldierly 10 aggressive, pugnacious
court ~: 5 trial
god: 4 Ares, Mars
martial __: 3 law 4 arts
__-martial: 5 court
Martial: 4 poet 5 Roman 6 writer
martial art: 4 judo 5 kendo, taebo, wushu 6 aikido, karate, kung fu, t'ai chi 7 jujitsu 9 tae kwon do
attire: 2 gi 4 belt 9 black belt
blow: 4 chop
exercise: 4 kata
expert: 5 ninja 6 judoka, sansei
legend: 3 Lee 8 Bruce Lee
school: 4 dojo
Martian: 2 ET 5 alien
craft, maybe: 3 UFO
invasion report: 4 hoax
Martian Chronicles, The
author: Ray Bradbury
Martí, José: 4 poet 5 Cuban 6 writer
martin: 4 bird 8 boundary
Martin: 3 Don 4 Amis, Beck, Dean, Dick, Eden, Kiel, Mary, Moon, Mull, Nexo, Perl, pope, Ritt, Ross, Ryle, Tony 5 Billy, Brest, Buber, Denny, Gabel, Ricky, Sheen, Short, Steve 6 Archer, Balsam, Behaim, Kellie, Landau, Luther, Milner, Pepper, Walser 7 Darnell, Gregory, Marilyn, Melcher, pontiff, Rodbell 8 Agronsky, Clouseau, de Porres, Lawrence, Scorsese, Strother, Van Buren 9 Frobisher, Heidegger
partner: 5 Aston, Rowan
Martin (1978 film)
director: George A. Romero
Martin __ King: 6 Luther
Martin __ Smith: 4 Cruz
__ Martin: 4 Remy 5 Aston
__ Martín: 3 San
Martina: 6 Hingis 7 McBride
Chris, to ~: 5 rival
__, Martin and John: 7 Abraham
Martin Chuzzlewit
author: Charles Dickens
Martindale, Wink: 2 MC 5 emcee
song: Deck of Cards (1959)
TV: Gambit, Tic Tac Dough
Martin, Dean: 5 actor 6 singer
film: Ada (1961)
Airport (1970)
The Ambushers (1968)
Artists and Models (1955)
Bandolero! (1968)
Bells Are Ringing (1960)
Kiss Me, Stupid (1964)
Living It Up (1954)
Murderers' Row (1966)
My Friend Irma (1949)
Ocean's Eleven (1960)
Rio Bravo (1959)
Robin and the Seven Hoods (1964)
The Silencers (1966)
Some Came Running (1959)
The Sons of Katie Elder (1965)
The Stooge (1953)
Who Was That Lady? (1960)
The Wrecking Crew (1969)
The Young Lions (1958)
You're Never Too Young (1955)
film role: Matt Helm
movie partner: Jerry Lewis
real name: Dino Crocetti
song: Everybody Loves Somebody (1964)
In the Chapel in the Moonlight (1967)
Memories Are Made of This (1955)
Return to Me (1958)
Send Me the Pillow You Dream On (1965)
That's Amore (1953)
Volare (1958)
You're Nobody Till Somebody Loves You (1965)
specialty: 5 roast
Martin du Gard, Roger: 6 French, writer
work: The Postman
Martin Eden
author: Jack London
Martinelli: 4 Elsa
martinet: 4 ogre 6 ramrod, tyrant 8 stickler 10 taskmaster
Martinez: 4 city, Tino, town 5 Edgar, Pedro
locale: 7 Georgia 10 California
Martinez, Edgar
sport: 8 baseball
Martínez Ruiz, José: 6 writer 7 Spanish
Martínez Sierra, Gregorio: 6 writer 7 Spanish
work: Cradle Song
martini: 5 drink 8 beverage, cocktail
impact: 4 kick
ingredient: 3 gin 5 olive, vodka 8 vermouth
maker: 6 barman 9 bartender
preference: 3 dry
with an onion: 6 Gibson
__ martini: 3 gin
Martini and __: 5 Rossi
Martinique: 3 île 4 isle 6 banana, island
money: 4 euro 5 franc
poet: 7 Césaire
volcano: 5 Pelee
writer: 8 Glissant
see also French
Martin Luther __: 4 King
Martino: 2 Al
Martin of Tours: 5 saint
Martin, Ricky
song: Livin' La Vida Loca (1999)
She's All I Ever Had (1999)
TV: General Hospital
Martinson, Harry: 6 writer 8 Nobelist
Martins, Peter: 6 dancer 7 danseur
specialty: 6 ballet
Martin, Steve: 5 actor 8 comedian
birthplace: 4 Waco 5 Texas
film: All of Me (1984)
Bowfinger (1999)
Cheaper by the Dozen (2003)
Dead Men Don't Wear Plaid (1982)

Dirty Rotten Scoundrels (1988)
Father of the Bride (1991)
Grand Canyon (1991)
The Jerk (1979)
L.A. Story (1991)
Leap of Faith (1992)
Little Shop of Horrors (1986)
The Lonely Guy (1984)
The Man With Two Brains (1983)
My Blue Heaven (1990)
Novocaine (2001)
The Out-of-Towners (1999)
Parenthood (1989)
Pennies From Heaven (1981)
The Pink Panther (2006)
Planes, Trains & Automobiles (1987)
Roxanne (1987)
Sgt. Bilko (1996)
Shopgirl (2005)
A Simple Twist of Faith (1994)
The Spanish Prisoner (1998)
Three Amigos! (1986)
song: King Tut (1978)
spouse: Victoria Tennant
Martin, Tony
real name: Alvin Morris
song: Walk Hand in Hand (1956)
spouse: Cyd Charisse, Alice Faye
Marton: 3 Eva **6** Andrew
Marty: 5 Balin **6** Ingels, Marion **7** Feldman, Melcher, Riessen, Robbins
author: Paddy Chayefsky
Marty (1955 film)
cast: Betsy Blair, Ernest Borgnine
director: Delbert Mann
Marv: 4 Levy **6** Albert **7** Johnson **11** Throneberry
marvel: 3 awe **4** gape, whiz **5** stare **6** genius, goggle, puzzle, wonder **7** miracle, portent, prodigy, stunner **8** surprise **9** amazement, curiosity, sensation, spectacle **10** phenomenon
Marvelettes
song: Beechwood 4-5789 (1962)
Don's Mess with Bill (1966)
Playboy (1962)
Please Mr. Postman (1961)
Marvell, Andrew: 4 poet **7** British
work: To His Coy Mistress
marvelous
see wonderful
Marvelous!: 3 ooh
__ Marvelous for Words: 3 Too
Marvin: 3 Lee **4** Gaye, Kalb **6** Hagler, Miller **8** Hamlisch **9** Rainwater
Marvin dog: 5 Bitsy
Marvin, Lee: 5 actor
film: Attack! (1956)
The Big Red One (1980)
Cat Ballou (1965, AA)
The Comancheros (1961)
The Dirty Dozen (1967)
Donovan's Reef (1963)
Emperor of the North (1973)
Gorky Park (1983)
Hell in the Pacific (1968)
The Iceman Cometh (1973)
The Man Who Shot Liberty Valance (1962)
Paint Your Wagon (1969)
Point Blank (1967)
Prime Cut (1972)
The Professionals (1966)
Seven Men From Now (1956)
marvy
see wonderful
Marx: 3 red **4** Karl **5** Chico, Gummo, Harpo, Zeppo **7** Groucho, Richard
ender: 3 ism, ist
instrument: 4 harp **5** piano
Marx __: 8 Brothers
Marx, Arthur: 5 Harpo
instrument: 4 harp
Marx, Groucho: 3 wit **4** host **5** emcee
brother: 5 Chico, Gummo, Harpo, Zeppo
cap: 5 beret
glance from ~: 4 leer
specialty: 5 ad-lib
Marxism: 9 Communism, Socialism
Marxist: 9 Communist, Socialist
Marx, Karl: 6 German, writer **9** socialist **11** philosopher
collaborator: 6 Engels
exhortation: 5 unite
work: Das Kapital
Marx, Richard
song: Angelia (1989)
Children of the Night (1990)
Don't Mean Nothing (1987)
Endless Summers Nights (1988)
Hazard (1992)
Hold On to the Nights (1988)
Keep Coming Back (1991)
Now and Forever (1994)
Right Here Waiting (1989)
Satisfied (1989)
Should've Known Better (1987)
Take This Heart (1992)
Too Late to Say Goodbye (1990)
Mary: 3 Ure **4** Hart **5** Astor, Brian, Frann, Gross, O'Hara, Quant, saint, Tudor, Wells **6** Boland, Crosby, Decker, Garden, Hopkin, Leakey, Mallon, Martin, Norton, Stuart, Wilson **7** Cassatt, Lincoln, Matalin, McGrory, Poppins, Renault, Shelley, Stewart, Travers, Woronov **8** McCarthy, McFadden, Pickford **9** MacGregor, Magdalene, McCormack, McDonnell, McDonough
author: Sholem Asch
boss at WJM: 3 Lou
follower: 4 lamb
friend: 5 Rhoda
in French: 5 Marie
in Irish: 5 Moira
in Scottish: 5 Moira
to Abe: 4 wife
Mary __: 3 Kay **5** Janes
Mary __ a little lamb: 3 had
Mary __ Ash: 3 Kay
Mary __, Backstage Wife: 5 Noble
Mary __ Carpenter: 6 Chapin
Mary __ Clark: 7 Higgins
Mary __ Dodge: 5 Mapes
Mary __ Eddy: 5 Baker
Mary __ Hurt: 4 Beth
Mary __ Lincoln: 4 Todd
Mary __ Masterson: 6 Stuart
Mary __ Mobley: 3 Ann
Mary __ Moore: 5 Tyler
Mary __ Place: 3 Kay
Mary __ Retton: 3 Lou
Mary __ Rinehart: 7 Roberts
Mary, __ of Scots: 5 Queen
Mary-__ Olsen: 4 Kate
Mary-__ Parker: 6 Louise
__ Mary: 4 Hail **5** Proud, Sweet **6** Bloody, Virgin **7** Typhoid
Maryam: 4 d'Abo
Mary Ann: 6 Mobley
Mary Baker __: 4 Eddy
Mary Beth: 4 Hurt
Mary Chapin __: 9 Carpenter
Mary Had a Little Lamb
author: Sarah Hale
Mary Hartman, Mary Hartman (TV sitcom)
cast: Dody Goodman (Martha Shumway)
Louise Lasser (Mary Hartman)
Greg Mullavey (Tom Hartman)
Mary Kay Place (Loretta Haggers)
setting: Fernwood, Ohio
Mary Higgins __: 5 Clark
Mary J. __: 5 Blige, Latis
Mary Janes: 5 shoes **8** footwear
Mary Jane's Last Dance (1994 song)
artist: Tom Petty
Mary-Kate: 5 Olsen
sister: 6 Ashley
Mary Kay: 3 Ash **5** Place **6** makeup
alternative: *see* cosmetic brand
Maryland: 5 state
athlete: 4 Terp **8** Terrapin
bay: 10 Chesapeake
capital: 9 Annapolis
city: 5 Bowie, Essex, Olney **6** Arnold, Bel Air, Carney, Elkton, Laurel, Severn, Towson **7** Arbutus, Chillum, Clinton, Crofton, Dundalk, Odenton, Potomac, Waldorf, Wheaton **8** Aberdeen, Bethesda, Columbia, Edgewood, Elkridge, Fairland, Glenmont, Landover, Lochearn, Oxon Hill, Suitland, White Oak, Woodlawn **9** Annapolis, Aspen Hill, Baltimore, Fort Meade, Frederick, Greenbelt, Parkville, Perry Hall, Rockville, Salisbury, South Gate, St. Charles **10** Chevy Chase, Colesville, Cumberland, Eldersburg, Germantown, Glassmanor, Glen Burnie, Hagerstown, Montgomery, Pikesville, Silver Hill
conference: 3 ACC
fort: 5 Meade
Indian: 9 Nanticoke
mountains: 8 Catoctin
neighbor: 8 Delaware, Virginia
once: 6 colony
port: 9 Baltimore
school: 4 Navy, USNA
state beverage: 4 milk
state bird: 6 oriole
state boat: 8 skipjack
state crustacean: 8 blue crab
state fish: 8 rockfish
state sport: 8 jousting
state tree: 3 oak **8** white oak
zone: 3 EDT, EST
Mary Lincoln, __ Todd: 3 née
Mary Lou: 6 Retton
__ Mary Lou: 5 Hello
Mary-Louise: 6 Parker
Mary Magdalene: 5 saint
Mary Mapes __: 5 Dodge
Mary McLeod __: 7 Bethune
Mary Montagu: 4 Lady
Mary Noble, Backstage Wife: 9 radio show
Mary of __: 4 Teck
Mary of Scotland
author: Maxwell Anderson
__ Mary pass: 4 Hail
Mary Poppins: 4 film **5** novel
author: P.L. Travers
cast: Julie Andrews, Glynis Johns, Dick Van Dyke
song: Chim Chim Cheree
Mary, Queen of Scots (1971 film)
cast: Glenda Jackson, Patrick McGoohan, Vanessa Redgrave
Mary Queen of Scots' son: 5 James
Mary Roberts __: 8 Rinehart
Mary's a Grand Old Name
composer: George M. Cohan
Mary Stuart __: 9 Masterson
Mary Todd __: 7 Lincoln
Mary Tyler Moore Show, The (CBS sitcom)
cast: Edward Asner (Lou Grant)
Georgia Engel (Georgette Baxter)
Valerie Harper (Rhoda Morgenstern)
Ted Knight (Ted Baxter)
Cloris Leachman (Phyllis Lindstrom)
Gavin MacLeod (Murray Slaughter)
Mary Tyler Moore (Mary Richards)
Betty White (Sue Ann Nivens)
Lou Grant ex: Edie
setting: 9 Minnesota **11** Minneapolis
spinoff: Rhoda, Phyllis
station: WJM
marzipan: 5 candy
base: 6 almond
Masai: 8 language
home: 5 Kenya **6** Africa **8** Tanzania
Masaoka Shiki: 4 poet **8** Japanese
specialty: haiku
masc.: 6 gender
not ~: 3 fem. **4** neut.
Mascagni, Pietro: 7 Italian **8** composer
work: Amica
Cavalleria Rusticana
Iris
Isabeau
Nero
Parisina
Pinotta
Silvano
Zanetto
mascara: 4 kohl **5** liner **6** makeup
applicator: 4 wand
apply ~: 6 darken
site: 4 brow, lash **7** eyebrow, eyelash
mascarpone: 6 cheese
masculine: 4 male **5** macho, manly **6** gender, virile **7** mannish
principle: 4 yang **6** animus
masculinity: 8 machismo, maleness, virility **9** manliness
Masefield, John: 4 poet **7** British
work: Dauber
The Everlasting Mercy
Reynard the Fox
Salt-Water Ballads
The Tragedy of Nan

Masekela, Hugh: 9 trumpeter
homeland: South Africa
song: Grazing in the Grass (1968)
Maserati: 7 Ernesto
Maseru: 4 city, town **7** capital
locale: 7 Lesotho
mash: 3 pap **4** beat, pulp, wort **5** cream, crush, grind, pound, press, purée, smash, sqush **6** bruise, pestle, soften, squash, squish, squush **7** scrunch, squeeze, squoosh **8** levigate, macerate **9** pulverize
partner: 7 bangers
preceder: 4 mish
__ mash: 4 sour
__ Mash: 7 Monster
MASH (1970 film)
cast: Robert Duvall, Elliott Gould, Sally Kellerman, Tom Skerritt, Donald Sutherland
director: Robert Altman
MASH (CBS sitcom)
cast: Alan Alda (Capt. Hawkeye Pierce)
Gary Burghoff (Cpl. Walter 'Radar' O'Reilly)
Mike Farrell (Capt. B.J. Hunnicutt)
Jamie Farr (Cpl. Maxwell Klinger)
Larry Linville (Maj. Frank Burns)
Harry Morgan (Col. Sherman Potter)
Wayne Rogers (Capt. Trapper John McIntyre)
McLean Stevenson (Lt. Col. Henry Blake)
David Ogden Stiers (Maj. Charles Winchester)
Loretta Swit (Maj. Margaret 'Hot Lips' Houlihan)
cook: 4 Igor
drink: 4 Ne-Hi **7** martini
extra: 2 GI, MP **5** medic, nurse
hangout: Rosie's
Hawkeye's home: Maine
meal: 4 mess, Spam
nurse: 4 Able
protocol: 6 triage
Radar's drink: Nehi
Radar's home: Iowa
remove to a ~ maybe: 4 evac
setting: Korea
shelter: 4 tent
soldier: 3 ROK
vehicle: 4 jeep **7** chopper
mashed potato: 5 dance
Mashed Potato Time (1962 song)
artist: Dee Dee Sharp
masher: 4 roué **5** flirt, ogler **6** pestle
comeuppance: 4 slap
expression: 4 leer
Mashhad: 4 city, town
locale: 4 Iran
mashie: 4 club, iron **8** golf club
mask: 3 air **4** hide, hood, loup, pose, veil, wrap **5** beard, blind, cache, cloak, couch, cover, front, guise, shade, visor, vizor **6** aspect, domino, facade, screen, veneer **7** conceal, cover up, obscure, posture, pretext, secrete, shut off, shut out **8** disguise, pretense **9** dissemble, false face, semblance **10** appearance, camouflage, false front
part: 4 slit **7** eyehole
starter: 4 face
the smell of: 6 purify **7** freshen, sweeten **8** sanitize **9** deodorize
wearer: 5 Robin, Zorro **6** Batman **10** Lone Ranger
__ mask: 3 gas, ski **4** face, swim **6** oxygen
Mask (1985 film)
cast: Cher, Sam Elliott, Eric Stoltz
director: Peter Bogdanovich
masked: 6 covert, hidden, larval, secret, unseen **7** furtive, larvate, private **8** hush-hush **9** incognito, unexposed **10** undercover, under wraps
critter: 4 coon **7** raccoon
man: 6 bandit
masked __: 4 ball
Masked Ball, A aria: 5 Eri tu
Masked Man companion: 5 Tonto
masking __: 4 tape
Mask of Dimitrios, The
author: Eric Ambler
Mask of Zorro, The (1998 film)
cast: Antonio Banderas, Anthony Hopkins, Catherine Zeta-Jones
role: 5 Elena
Mask, The
author: Dean Koontz
Mask, The (1994 film)
cast: Jim Carrey, Cameron Diaz
mason: 7 builder **10** bricklayer
device: 3 hod **4** shim **6** trowel
helper: 6 hodman
starter: 4 free **5** stone
Mason: 3 A.E.W. **4** city, Dave, town **5** Adams, James, Perry, Reese, Weems **6** Daniel, Jackie, Marsha, Pamela **7** Barbara **8** Williams
locale: 4 Ohio
partner: 4 Legg
Mason __: 3 jar
Mason-__ line: 5 Dixon
Mason, A.E.W.: 6 writer **7** British
work: The Four Feathers
Mason, Barbara
song: Yes, I'm Ready (1965)
Mason City: 4 town
locale: 4 Iowa
Mason-Dixon
below the ~ line: 5 south
Masonic doorkeeper: 5 tiler
Mason, James: 5 actor
film: 20,000 Leagues Under the Sea (1954)
The Desert Fox (1951)
The Desert Rats (1953)
The Fall of the Roman Empire (1964)
ffolkes (1980)
Georgy Girl (1966)
Journey to the Center of the Earth (1959)
Julius Caesar (1953)
The Last of Sheila (1973)
Lolita (1962)
Lord Jim (1965)
Madame Bovary (1949)
North by Northwest (1959)
Odd Man Out (1947)
The Pumpkin Eater (1964)
The Seventh Veil (1945)
The Shooting Party (1984)
A Star Is Born (1954)
A Touch of Larceny (1959)
The Verdict (1982)
role: 4 Nemo **5** Maine
Mason jar topper: 3 lid
Mason, Marsha: 7 actress
film: Cinderella Liberty (1973)
The Goodbye Girl (1977)
Heartbreak Ridge (1986)
Max Dugan Returns (1983)
Only When I Laugh (1981)
spouse: Neil Simon
Mason, Perry: 3 att. **4** atty. **6** lawyer **8** attorney
assistant: 4 Paul **5** Della, Drake **6** Street **9** Paul Drake
creator: Erle Stanley Gardner
job for ~: 4 case
opponent: 6 Berger
profession: 3 law
masonry: 5 trade
face with ~: 5 revet
starter: 4 free **5** stone
stone: 6 ashlar, ashler
__ masqué: 3 bal
Masque of Alfred, The
composer: Thomas Arne
masquerade: 3 act **4** pose **5** cloak, front, guise, put on, revel **6** domino, dupery, facade, fake it **7** costume, cover-up, mummery, posture, pretend, pretext **8** carnival, disguise, pretense **9** deception, dissemble, festivity, imposture, Mardi Gras **10** camouflage, impression
wear: 3 wig **6** domino
Masquerade (1988 film)
cast: Kim Cattrall, Rob Lowe, Meg Tilly
__ Masquerade: 4 This
masquerader: 8 baccanal, imposter, impostor
mass: 3 gob, lot, mob, wad **4** blob, body, bulk, cake, clot, glob, heap, heft, herd, host, hunk, knot, load, lump, pile, rite, ruck, size **5** batch, block, bunch, chunk, clump, crowd, flock, group, hoard, horde, mound, press, shock, stack, swarm, total, troop **6** gather, gobbet, huddle, jungle, legion, matter, number, rabble, throng, volume, weight **7** cluster, collect, pyramid **8** assemble, majority, mountain, quantity **9** aggregate, amplitude, bulkiness, congeries, gathering, great deal, heaviness, immensity, largeness, multitude, plurality, profusion, stockpile, wholesale **10** accumulate, collection, concretion, cumulation, large-scale, lion's share
combining form: 5 cumul- **6** cumuli-, cumulo-
unit: 3 mol **4** gram, kilo **8** kilogram
mass __: 5 media **7** meeting, transit
mass-__: 6 market **7** produce
__ mass: 3 air **4** high, land **7** nuptial
Mass
composer: J.S. Bach, Leonard Bernstein
exclamation ~: 4 amen **7** hosanna **10** hallelujah
like ~ music: 6 choral
part of the ~: 5 canon
place: 5 abbey, altar **6** chapel, church **9** cathedral
plate: 5 paten
seating: 3 pew
vestment: 3 alb **5** orale
see also Latin
Mass __: 4 book, card **6** Appeal
Mass.
neighbor: 3 Atl. **4** Conn.
see also Massachusetts
__ Mass: 3 Low **4** High **7** Requiem
Massachusetts: 5 state
bay: 8 Buzzard's
cape: 3 Ann, Cod
capital: 6 Boston
city: 4 Lynn **5** Lenox, Salem, Truro **6** Agawam, Boston, Dedham, Lowell, Malden, Milton, Newton, Quincy, Revere, Saugus, Woburn **7** Amherst, Belmont, Beverly, Chelsea, Danvers, Everett, Gardner, Holyoke, Ipswich, Medford, Melrose, Methuen, Milford, Needham, Norwood, Peabody, Reading, Taunton, Waltham **8** Brockton, Chicopee, Franklin, Lawrence, Randolph, Stoneham, Weymouth **9** Arlington, Attleboro, Braintree, Brookline, Cambridge, Fall River, Fitchburg, Haverhill, Lexington, Wakefield, Watertown, Wellesley, Westfield, Worcester **10** Barnstable, Burlington, Framingham, Gloucester, Leominster, Marblehead, New Bedford, Pittsfield, Somerville, Wilmington, Winchester
Indian: 7 Nipmuck **9** Wampanoag
neighbor: 7 New York, Vermont
nickname: 8 Bay State
port: 9 Nantucket **10** New Bedford
school: 3 MIT **5** Regis, Tufts **6** Babson **7** Amherst, Harvard **9** Holy Cross, Radcliffe
start of ~ motto: 4 Ense
state bean: 8 navy bean
state bird: 9 chickadee
state building rock: 7 granite
state cat: 5 tabby
state fish: 3 cod
state flower: 9 mayflower
state game bird: 10 wild turkey
state gem: 9 rhodonite
state horse: 6 Morgan
state insect: 7 ladybug
state marine mammal: 10 right whale
state muffin: 10 corn muffin
state shell: 7 Neptune
state tree: 3 elm
Massachusetts __: 3 Bay **6** ballot
Massachusetts __ Company: 3 Bay
__ Massacre: 6 Boston
massage: 3 rub **4** edit **5** knead, touch **7** back rub, rolfing, rubbing, rub down, shiatsu **9** stimulate **10** manipulate
milieu: 3 spa **6** day spa **9** health spa
need: 3 oil **5** towel **6** hot oil
needing a ~: 4 achy **5** tense
target: 4 ache, kink
__ massage: 7 Swedish
Massapequa: 4 city, town
locale: 7 New York
Mass Appeal (1984 film)
cast: Charles Durning, Jack Lemmon
massé: 4 shot
Massen: 3 Osa

Massena: 4 city, town
locale: 7 New York
Massenet, Jules: 6 French 8 composer
genre: 5 opera
work: Eve
Le Cid
Manon
Narcisse
Phèdre
Thaïs
Werther 4 Roma 5 Sapho
6 Amadis, Ariane, Le Mage
masses: 3 mob 4 raff 5 crowd, reams 6 cattle, people, plenty, public, rabble, scores 7 legions 8 populace, riffraff 9 hoi polloi, multitude 10 lower class
one of the ~: 4 pleb 8 plebeian
masseur
see massage
masseuse employer: 6 day spa
Massey: 5 Ilona 7 Raymond
Massey, Raymond: 5 actor
film: Abe Lincoln in Illinois (1940)
Arsenic and Old Lace (1944)
Drums (1938)
East of Eden (1955)
The Great Impostor (1961)
The Naked and the Dead (1958)
Possessed (1947)
The Scarlet Pimpernel (1935)
Seven Angry Men (1955)
Stairway to Heaven (1946)
Things to Come (1936)
TV: Dr. Kildare
__ Massif: 6 Vinson
Massillon: 4 city, town
locale: 4 Ohio
Mass in B Minor
composer: J.S. Bach
Massine, Léonide: 6 dancer 7 danseur
specialty: 6 ballet
Massinger, Philip: 7 British 10 playwright
work: A New Way to Pay Old Debts
massive: 3 big 4 huge, vast 5 beefy, bulky, giant, grand, great, gross, heavy, hefty, jumbo, large, thick 6 mighty 7 hulking, immense, mammoth, sizable, stately, titanic, weighty 8 colossal, enormous, gigantic, imposing, king-size, oversize, sizeable, towering, unwieldy, whapping, whopping 9 extensive, fantastic, Herculean, humongous, monstrous, overlarge, ponderous, unwieldly, walloping, whalelike 10 cumbersome, gargantuan, impressive, monumental, overweight, prodigious, stupendous, tremendous, voluminous
massiveness: 4 bulk 8 enormity 9 immensity
Masson, Paul: 7 vintner 9 winemaker
mass transit: 3 bus 5 train 6 subway
problem: 5 delay
mast: 4 boom, pole, post, spar 5 mizen, stick, tower 6 mizzen, timber 7 spanker 8 flagpole
attachment: 4 gaff
bracket: 4 bibb
ender: 4 head
rope: 3 tye
starter: 3 top 4 main 5 mizen, royal 6 mizzen 7 foretop
support: 4 stay
__-mast: 4 half
master: 3 ace, win 4 cram, guru, head, lick, lord, sage, whiz 5 adept, chief, grasp, learn, maven, mavin, owner, prime, ruler, study, swami, swamy, tutor 6 artist, bone up, defeat, expert, genius, old pro, pick up, pundit, reduce, savant, top dog, victor, wizard 7 artisan, artiste, captain, conquer, excel in, leading, maestro, major in, old hand, pedagog, skipper, supreme, teacher 8 champion, director, employer, foremost, governor, graduate, kingfish, original, overcome, overlord, overseer, virtuoso 9 abecedary, authority, chieftain, commander, conqueror, pedagogue, preceptor, principal, sovereign 10 commandant, comprehend, controller, instructor, journeyman, past master, subjugator, supervisor, taskmaster, understand
ender: 3 dom, ful 4 mind, ship, work 5 piece 6 singer
in Arabic: 5 saheb, sahib
of ceremonies: 4 host 5 emcee
starter: 3 pay, spy 4 band, brew, bush, head, jump, load, lock, over, post, ring, ship, task, yard 5 choir, drill, grand, house, scout, toast, whore 6 harbor, school 7 concert, harbour, quarter, station
master __: 3 key 4 bath, file, plan 5 class 6 stroke 7 bedroom, builder
__ master: 3 old 4 past, task 5 wagon 6 harbor
Master __ Game: 5 of the
master-at-__: 4 arms
Master Blaster (1980 song)
artist: Stevie Wonder
Master Blaster, The: Joe Weider
Master Builder, The
author: Henrik Ibsen
character: 4 Kaia, Knut 5 Aline, Fosli, Hilda 6 Brovik, Wangel 7 Halvard, Solness
MasterCard
use: 3 owe 6 charge
Master Class
subject: 6 Callas
masterful: 3 ace 4 able, deft, fine 5 adept, slick 6 adroit, au fait, clever, expert, habile, lordly, nimble, virile 7 capable, cunning, dynamic, skilled, trained 8 dextrous, forceful, graceful, resolute, seasoned, skillful, talented 9 competent, dexterous, efficient, excellent, exquisite, first-rate, practiced, virtuosic 10 aggressive, consummate, proficient
Masterman Ready
author: Frederick Marryat
Master Melvin: 3 Ott
mastermind: 3 ace 4 lead, plan, whiz 5 brain 6 brains, create, design, devise, direct, genius, invent, leader, manage 7 builder, creator, develop, dream up, egghead, execute, manager, planner, prodigy, thinker, think up 8 conceive, designer, director, Einstein, engineer, highbrow, kingfish, virtuoso 9 architect, commander, fashioner, organizer, originate, tactician 10 originator, strategist
Master Mosaic Workers, The
author: George Sand
Master of __: 4 Arts 7 Science
Master of Ballantrae, The
author: Robert Louis Stevenson
Master of the Game
author: Sidney Sheldon
Master of the World, The
author: Jules Verne
masterpiece: 3 gem 4 work 5 jewel, pearl 7 classic 8 treasure 9 specialty, work of art
Masterpiece (song)
artist: Atlantic Starr, Temptations
Masterpiece Theatre
network: 3 PBS
Master Pipers, The
author: George Sand
master's: 6 degree
paper: 6 thesis
Masters, Edgar Lee: 4 poet 6 writer
work: Spoon River Anthology
Masters golf champ:
2010 - Phil Mickelson
2009 - Angel Cabrera
2008 - Trevor Immelman
2007 - Zach Johnson
2006 - Phil Mickelson
2005 - Tiger Woods
2004 - Phil Mickelson
2003 - Mike Weir
2002 - Tiger Woods
2001 - Tiger Woods
2000 - Vijay Singh
1999 - Jose Maria Olazabal
1998 - Mark O'Meara
1997 - Tiger Woods
1996 - Nick Faldo
1995 - Ben Crenshaw
1994 - Jose Maria Olazabal
1993 - Bernhard Langer
1992 - Fred Couples
1991 - Ian Woosnam
1990 - Nick Faldo
1989 - Nick Faldo
1988 - Sandy Lyle
1987 - Larry Mize
1986 - Jack Nicklaus
1985 - Bernhard Langer
1984 - Ben Crenshaw
1983 - Seve Ballesteros
1982 - Craig Stadler
1981 - Tom Watson
1980 - Seve Ballesteros
1979 - Fuzzy Zoeller
1978 - Gary Player
1977 - Tom Watson
1976 - Ray Floyd
1975 - Jack Nicklaus
1974 - Gary Player
1973 - Tommy Aaron
1972 - Jack Nicklaus
1971 - Charles Coody
1970 - Billy Casper
1969 - George Archer
1968 - Bob Goalby
1967 - Gay Brewer
1966 - Jack Nicklaus
1965 - Jack Nicklaus
1964 - Arnold Palmer
1963 - Jack Nicklaus
1962 - Arnold Palmer
1961 - Gary Player
1960 - Arnold Palmer
1959 - Art Wall
1958 - Arnold Palmer
1957 - Doug Ford
1956 - Jack Burke
1955 - Cary Middlecoff
1954 - Sam Snead
1953 - Ben Hogan
1952 - Sam Snead
1951 - Ben Hogan
1950 - Jimmy Demaret
1949 - Sam Snead
1948 - Claude Harmon
1947 - Jimmy Demaret
1946 - Herman Keiser
1943-1945 - NOT PLAYED
1942 - Byron Nelson
1941 - Craig Wood
1940 - Jimmy Demaret
1939 - Ralph Guldahl
1938 - Henry Picard
1937 - Byron Nelson
1936 - Horton Smith
1935 - Gene Sarazen
1934 - Horton Smith
Masterson: 3 Bat, Sky 5 Peter
colleague: 4 Earp
prop: 4 cane
Masterson, Mrs. Sky: 5 Sarah
Masters org.: 3 PGA
masterstroke: 4 coup
__ Master's Voice: 3 His
mastery: 3 art 4 grip 5 grasp, knack, power, reach, skill, touch 7 ability, command, control, finesse, know-how, prowess 8 artistry, deftness, hang of it 9 adeptness, dexterity, dominance, expertise 10 adroitness, ascendance, ascendancy, ascendence, ascendency, attainment, expertness, virtuosity
masthead listing: 3 eds. 5 staff 6 editor
mastic: 4 tree 5 resin
relative: 5 mango, sumac 6 cashew, fustet, sumach 9 pistachio
masticate: 3 eat 4 bite, chaw, chew, gnaw 5 graze, munch 6 chew on, crunch, gnaw on, nibble 7 munch on 8 crunch on, nibble on
mastiff: 3 dog 5 canid, pooch 6 canine
__ mastiff: 4 bull
mastodon: 6 animal 9 leviathan
mastoid __: 4 bone
Mastrantonio, Mary Elizabeth: 7 actress
film: The Abyss (1989)
Class Action (1991)
The Color of Money (1986)
Limbo (1999)
Robin Hood: Prince of Thieves (1991)
Scarface (1983)
White Sands (1992)
Mastroianni, Marcello: 8 director
costar: 5 Loren
film: Big Deal on Madonna Street (1958)
Dark Eyes (1987)
Divorce-Italian Style (1962)
La Dolce Vita (1960)
Yesterday, Today and Tomorrow (1964)
masts, change: 5 rerig

Masur, Kurt: **9** conductor
mat: **3** pad **4** yapa **5** doily **6** darken, tangle, tatami **7** cushion, zabuton **9** interlace
Buddhist sitting ~: **7** zabuton
go to the ~ for: **4** back **5** stake, vouch **7** endorse, promote, sponsor, support, warrant **8** champion **9** get behind **10** underwrite
Japan ~: **6** tatami
Japanese: **6** tatami
place ~: **5** doily **6** doyley
South American ~: **4** yapa
starter: **4** bath, door
victory: **3** pin
__ mat: **7** welcome
Mata __: **4** Hari
matador: **6** torero **8** toreador
cape color: **4** rojo
foe: **4** bull, toro **6** el toro
maneuver: **4** pase **5** faena
procession: **5** paseo
wear: **4** capa **6** bolero
Matador: **3** car **4** auto **5** Dodge **10** automobile
Mata Hari: **3** spy
Mata Hari (1932 film)
cast: Lionel Barrymore, Greta Garbo, Ramon Novarro
Matalin, Mary
spouse: James Carville
Matamoros: **4** city, port, town
locale: **6** Mexico **8** Coahuila **10** Tamaulipas
see also Spanish
Matanzas: **4** city, town
locale: **4** Cuba
Matarese Circle, The
author: Robert Ludlum
Matarese Countdown, The
author: Robert Ludlum
match: **2** go **3** fit, pit, tie, vie **4** boot, bout, duel, even, game, gybe, jibe, mate, meet, pair, peer, race, sort, suit, twin **5** agree, equal, event, fight, fusee, fuzee, rival, tie up, union, vesta **6** beseem, couple, double, equate, mating, ringer, square, take on **7** compeer, conform, contest, lighter, lucifer, pairing, reflect, replica, rivalry **8** arsonist, coincide, dovetail, equalize, espousal, marriage, opponent, parallel, rank with, resemble **9** companion, correlate, duplicate, harmonize, look alike, matrimony **10** competitor, complement, coordinate, correspond, dead ringer, engagement, go together, keep up with, tournament
be a ~ for: **5** equal, rival
division: **3** set
don't ~: **5** clash **6** differ **8** disagree
end: **2** KO **3** TKO **4** kayo
ender: **3** box **4** book, lock, wood **5** board, maker, stick **6** making
make a ~: **3** wed
partner: **3** mix
prepare for a ~: **4** spar
put another ~ to: **5** relit
put a ~ to: **5** light **6** ignite, kindle, set off **8** enkindle
start a ~: **5** serve
up: **4** pair, test **5** unite
wrestling ~: **5** fight, round **6** tussle **7** contest **9** encounter
match __: **4** play **5** plate, point
__ match: **4** book, love, slow, test **5** paper **6** rubber, safety **7** kitchen, lucifer
__-match: **5** cross
matched: **5** equal, level **6** in sync **7** coequal
group: **3** set **4** pair, suit, team **5** suite
Match Game, The: **8** game show
host: Gene Rayburn
matching: **4** even, like, same, twin **5** level **6** on a par, paired **7** similar **8** parallel **9** analogous, duplicate, identical **10** comparable, equivalent, reciprocal
not ~: **3** odd
piece: **4** mate
matchless: **3** ace **4** best, only, rare, sole **5** alone, prime **6** superb, unique **7** optimum, perfect, supreme **8** peerless, splendid, superior **9** excellent, exquisite, nonpareil, topflight, unequaled, unmatched, unrivaled, virtuosic **10** consummate, inimitable, preeminent, unequalled, unexampled, unrivalled
matchmaker: **4** Amor, Eros **5** Cupid **9** go-between
Matchmaker, The
author: Thornton Wilder
matchsticks game: **3** nim
mate: **3** bro, pal, wed **4** ally, chum, join, papa, peer, twin, wife **5** bride, buddy, crony, groom, hubby, marry, match, pater, unite **6** cohort, defeat, double, frater, friend, helper, missis, missus, mister, splice, spouse **7** coequal, comrade, consort, mariner, partner **8** alter ego, confrere, coworker, deckhand, familiar, helpmate, intimate, playmate, roommate, sidekick **9** assistant, associate, classmate, colleague, companion, duplicate **10** bridegroom, complement, coordinate, schoolmate, tie the knot
starter: **3** bed **4** bunk, case, cell, crew, help, mess, play, room, seat, ship, team **5** check, class, house, stale, table **6** litter, school
__ mate: **4** soul **5** chief, first, third **6** second **7** running
maté: **8** beverage
__ maté: **5** yerba
__ Mate: **5** Paper
Maté: **7** Rudolph
mateless: **3** odd **8** unpaired **10** unattached
matelot: **3** gob, tar **4** salt **6** sailor **7** jack tar
Matelot
author: Pierre Loti
matelote: **4** stew **8** fish stew
__ Mateo, CA: **3** San
mater: **5** mumsy
__ mater: **3** pia **4** alma, dura
__ Mater: **6** Stabat
materia __: **6** medica
material: **3** key **4** bolt, data, felt, fuel, gear, real, text **5** ad rem, cloth, facts, frisé, goods, lisse, notes, solid, stock, stuff, thing, wares **6** actual, fabric, matter, ratiné, supply **7** apropos, earthly, element, fleshly, germane, telling, textile, worldly, worsted **8** apposite, concrete, jacquard, physical, relevant, tangible, temporal **9** commodity, component, corporeal, essential, grosgrain, important, momentous, pertinent, substance, touchable **10** applicable, ingredient, phenomenal, unimagined
building ~: **4** wood **5** adobe, brick, steel **6** cement, stucco
foil ~: **8** aluminum
foundation ~: **8** concrete
golf-course ~: **4** lawn, turf **5** grass, sward
goods: **9** resources
introductory ~: **6** basics
jacket ~: **7** leather
organic ~: **5** mulch **7** compost **10** fertilizer
outfield ~: **4** turf **5** grass
raw ~: **3** ore
sample: **4** snip **6** swatch
suffix: **3** -ine
see also fabric
__ material: **3** raw
Material Girl (1985 song)
artist: Madonna
materialistic: **6** greedy **7** mundane, profane, secular, worldly **8** banausic, temporal
materialization: **8** fruition
materialize: **3** pop **4** come, form, show **5** bob up, occur, reify **6** appear, embody, emerge, evolve, happen, imbody, turn up, unfold **7** develop, realize, surface **8** coalesce, manifest, take form **9** actualize, come about, take place, take shape
materials: **5** goods, order **8** supplies
matériel: **4** ammo, arms, guns **6** outfit, tackle **7** cannons, weapons **8** ordnance, weaponry **9** armaments, artillery, firepower, machinery, munitions **10** ammunition
issue ~: **3** arm
maternal: **4** kind, warm **6** caring, gentle, tender **7** devoted **8** motherly, parental **10** protective
kin: **5** enate
__ maternelle: **5** école
maternity: **10** motherhood, parenthood
ward stat: **2** wt. **3** hgt. **4** lgth. **6** height, length, weight
maternity __: **4** ward **5** leave
mates: **4** pair
former ~: **4** exes
matey: **3** pal **4** Brit
matgrass: **4** nard
__ math: **3** new **5** fuzzy
mathematical: **9** algebraic, numerical
relation: **8** equation, fraction
mathematician: **4** Omar, Venn **5** Euler, Gauss **6** Kepler, Napier, Newton, Pascal **7** Doppler, Laplace, Ptolemy **8** Lagrange **9** Whitehead **10** Archimedes, Pythagoras
Austrian ~: **7** Doppler
British ~: **6** Newton **7** Russell **9** Whitehead
Egyptian ~: **7** Ptolemy
French ~: **6** Pascal **7** Laplace **8** Lagrange
German ~: **5** Gauss **6** Kepler
Greek ~: **10** Pythagoras
letters: **3** QED
Persian ~: **4** Omar
Scottish ~: **6** Napier
starter: **4** meta
Swiss ~: **5** Euler
mathematics: **3** alg. **4** calc., geom., trig **5** arith. **7** algebra, geodesy **8** calculus, geometry **10** arithmetic
abbr.: **3** div., exp., GCD, iff, LCD, lim., pct., QED **5** recip.
concept: **2** pi **3** set **5** limit, ratio **10** reciprocal
do ~: **3** add **5** graph **6** divide **8** multiply, subtract **9** calculate
expression: **4** is to
rule: **3** law **5** axiom **9** postulate
work: **4** area **5** proof
__ mathematics: **6** higher
Mather: **6** Cotton **8** Increase
Mathers: **5** Jerry
Matheson: **3** Tim **7** Richard
Mathew: **5** Brady
Mathews: **5** Eddie, Larry **6** Kerwin
Mathews, Eddie: **5** Brave
Mathewson, Christy: **5** Giant **6** hurler **7** pitcher
Mathias, Bob: **10** decathlete
Mathilde: **8** asteroid
Mathis: **6** Johnny **8** Samantha
Mathis, Johnny
song: Call Me (1958)
A Certain Smile (1958)
Chances Are (1957)
Come to Me (1958)
Gina (1962)
It's Not for Me to Say (1957)
Misty (1959)
Too Much, Too Little, Too Late (1978)
The Twelfth of Never (1957)
What Will Mary Say (1963)
Wonderful! Wonderful! (1957)
Mathison, Melissa
spouse: Harrison Ford
matin: **6** French **7** morning
opposite: **4** soir
matinal period: **4** morn **7** morning
Matineau, Harriet: **6** writer **7** British
matinée: **4** show **9** reception
time: **3** aft. **9** afternoon
matinée __: **4** idol
mating: **5** match **8** marriage
game: **5** chess
Mating Game, The (1959 film)
cast: Tony Randall, Debbie Reynolds
matins: **4** hour **7** worship
Matinson, Harry: **6** writer **7** Swedish
work: Cape Farewell
The Road
Matisse: **4** font **5** Henri **8** typeface
Matisse, Henri: **6** artist **7** painter
homeland: **6** France
medium for ~: **3** oil
piece: **3** art **8** painting
matjes __: **7** herring
Matlin, Marlee Oscar: Children of a Lesser God
Matlock: **3** Ben
job: **3** att. **4** atty. **6** lawyer **8** attorney
matter: **4** case
org.: **3** ABA
profession: **3** law

Matlock (NBC/ABC drama)
cast: Andy Griffith (Ben Matlock)
setting: Atlanta, Georgia
Matlock Paper, The
author: Robert Ludlum
Mato __: **6** Grosso
matriarch: **5** elder **6** female, granny, senior **7** grannie **10** forebearer
matriarchal: **6** lineal
kin: **5** enate
matriculate: **4** join **5** begin, enrol, enter, learn **6** enroll, record, sign up **8** register
matrimonial: **6** bridal, wedded **7** marital, nuptial, spousal **8** conjugal **9** connubial
hopeful: **5** swain, wooer
matrimony: **5** match, union **7** wedding, wedlock **8** alliance, marriage, nuptials **9** sacrament
commit ~: **3** wed **5** marry
__ Matrimony: **4** Holy
matrix: **4** cast, grid, mold **5** array **6** origin, source
Matrix: **3** car **4** auto **6** Toyota **10** automobile
__-matrix printer: **3** dot
Matrix Reloaded, The (2003 film)
cast: Laurence Fishburne, Carrie-Anne Moss, Keanu Reeves
Matrix, The (1999 film)
cast: Laurence Fishburne, Carrie-Anne Moss, Keanu Reeves
character: **3** Neo
matron: **3** Mrs. **4** dame, lady, wife **5** woman **6** female **10** noblewoman
matron of __: **5** honor
Mats: **8** Wilander
Matson: **5** Ollie
Matt: **4** Helm **5** Damon, Lauer, Stone **6** Biondi, Dillon, Drudge, Frewer **7** Houston, Keeslar, LeBlanc **8** Groening, Lattanzi
matte: **4** dull, flat **10** lusterless
matte __: **4** shot
Mattea: **5** Kathy
matted: **5** kinky **7** knotted, rumpled, snarled, tangled, tousled, twisted **8** uncombed
matter: **3** job **4** body, mass, text, to-do **5** being, count, issue, sense, stuff, thing, topic, weigh, worry **6** affair, affect, cut ice, entity, regard **7** content, episode, problem, project, purport, reality, trouble **8** argument, business, elements, incident, interest, material, question, sediment **9** grievance, situation, substance **10** difficulty, phenomenon, protoplasm
as a ~ of fact: **5** truly **6** really **7** in truth **8** actually **9** in reality
at hand: **3** job **5** theme, topic **7** subject
bit of ~: **4** atom
combining form: **3** hyl- **4** hylo-
foreign ~: **5** taint
gray ~: **4** head, mind **5** brain **9** mentality
heart of the ~: **3** nub **4** crux, gist, knub **5** nexus, point
in the ~ of: **4** as to **5** about, as for
laughing ~: **3** fun, wit **4** gags **5** farce, jests, jokes **6** comedy, gaiety, levity **8** drollery, raillery **10** wisecracks
no ~: **6** drop it **8** forget it **9** never mind
no laughing ~: **3** bad, big **4** grim, ugly **5** grave, heavy, major, tough **6** urgent **7** weighty **8** grievous, sobering, terrible **9** dangerous, important **10** formidable
no ~ what: **5** still **6** anyhow, anyway **9** at any rate **10** in any event, regardless
science of ~: **7** physics
starter: **4** anti
state of ~: **3** gas **5** solid **6** liquid
to, old-style: **4** reck
use the gray ~: **5** think **6** ideate, reason
worthless ~: **5** dregs **6** debris, refuse **7** rubbish
__ matter: **3** end **4** back, dark, gray, grey **5** front, white
Matterhorn: **3** alp, mtn. **4** peak **5** mount **8** mountain
echo: **5** yodel, yodle
locale: **4** Alps **6** Europe **11** Switzerland
matter of __: **3** law **4** fact **6** course, record
matter-of-course: **5** usual
matter-of-fact: **3** dry **4** calm, cool **5** blunt, brusk, frank, plain, prosy, stoic **6** abrupt, candid, direct, honest, stolid **7** brusque, factual, prosaic, stoical **8** accurate, impolite, sensible, tactless **9** objective, outspoken, practical, pragmatic, prosaical, realistic **10** indelicate
__ matter of fact: **3** as a
Matter of Fact
columnist: **5** Alsop
matter-of-factly: **6** simply
Matter of Trust, A (1986 song)
artist: Billy Joel
matters: **6** doings **7** affairs **8** dealings
Matthau, Walter: **5** actor
film: The Bad News Bears (1976)
Buddy Buddy (1981)
Cactus Flower (1969)
California Suite (1978)
Charade (1963)
Charley Varrick (1973)
A Face in the Crowd (1957)
Fail-Safe (1964)
The Fortune Cookie (1966, AA)
The Front Page (1974)
The Grass Harp (1996)
Grumpier Old Men (1995)
Grumpy Old Men (1993)
A Guide for the Married Man (1967)
Hanging Up (2000)
Hello, Dolly! (1969)
Hopscotch (1980)
House Calls (1978)
JFK (1991)
Kotch (1971)
Mirage (1965)
A New Leaf (1971)
The Odd Couple (1968)
Out to Sea (1997)
Plaza Suite (1971)
The Sunshine Boys (1975)
The Taking of Pelham One Two Three (1974)
Matthew: **3** Fox **5** Perry, saint **6** Arnold, Garber, Modine, Wilder **8** Flinders **9** Broderick
follower: **4** Mark
original name: **4** Levi
Matthews: **5** Chris
Matthews Band, Dave
song: Crash into Me (1997)
Matthiessen, Peter: **6** writer
work: At Play in the Fields of the Lord
Blue Meridian
The Cloud Forest
Far Tortuga
Men's Lives
Sand Rivers
The Snow Leopard
Under the Mountain Wall
Matt Houston (ABC adventure)
cast: Pamela Hensley (C.J. Parsons)
Lee Horsley (Matt Houston)
Mattingly: **3** Don
mattock: **4** tool
use a ~: **3** dig
mattress: **3** bed, pad **5** futon
brand: **5** Sealy, Serta **7** Simmons
category: **4** firm, hard **9** extra-firm, super-firm
covering: **3** pad **5** sheet
filling: **3** air **5** kapok
in England: **4** lilo
on the ~: **4** abed **8** sleeping
part: **4** coil **6** spring **7** ticking
problem: **4** lump
support: **4** slat **9** box spring
__ mattress: **3** air
Matty: **4** Alou
brother: **5** Jesus **6** Felipe
maturate: **4** grow **5** ripen **7** develop
maturation: **6** growth **9** evolution, expansion, gestation
mature: **3** age, big, old **4** aged, form, grow, ripe **5** adult, bloom, grown, of age, owing, ready, ripen **6** arrive, evolve, flower, grow up, mellow, season, trusty, unfold, unpaid **7** advance, blossom, come due, develop, fill out, grown-up, payable, perfect, ripened, settled, shoot up, vintage **8** complete, cultured, full-size, incubate, mellowed, mushroom, progress, seasoned **9** come of age, culminate, developed, full-blown, full-grown **10** fully grown, precocious, settle down
into: **6** become
not ~: **5** green, young
Mature, Victor: **5** actor
film: Million Dollar Mermaid (1952)
My Darling Clementine (1946)
My Gal Sal (1942)
Samson and Delilah (1949)
Maturin, Charles Robert: **5** Irish **6** writer
work: Melmoth the Wanderer
maturing agent: **4** ager
maturity: **5** prime **6** wisdom **7** manhood **8** fruition, fullness, majority, ripeness **9** adulthood, readiness, stability, womanhood **10** completion, experience, perfection
Matute, Ana María: **6** writer **7** Spanish
matzo __: **4** ball, brei, meal **6** farfel
matzo ball __: **4** soup
matzoh: **5** bread
lack: **5** yeast **9** leavening
meal with ~: **5** seder
Mauch: **4** Gene **5** Billy, Bobby
Maud: **5** Adams
author: Alfred Tennyson
Maude (CBS sitcom)
cast: Bea Arthur (Maude Findlay)
Conrad Bain (Arthur Harman)
Adrienne Barbeau (Carol Findlay)
Bill Macy (Walter Findlay)
Rue McClanahan (Vivian Harman)
producer: Norman Lear
__ + Maude: **5** Micki
__ Maud Land: **5** Queen
maudlin: **4** weak **5** gooey, gushy, mushy, sappy, soppy, teary, weepy **6** sirupy, slushy, syrupy **7** cloying, insipid, mawkish, tearful **8** bathetic, cornball, romantic, schmalzy, shmaltzy **9** schmaltzy, sniveling **10** lachrymose
Maud Martha
author: Gwendolyn Brooks
__ Maud Montgomery: **4** Lucy
Maud Muller
author: John Greenleaf Whittier
Maugham, W. Somerset: **6** writer **7** British
work: Cakes and Ale
The Circle
The Constant Wife
The Hero
Miss Thompson
The Moon and Sixpence
Of Human Bondage
Our Betters
Rain
The Razor's Edge
Maui: **4** isle **6** island
locale: **6** Hawaii
neighbor: **5** Lanai
maul: **3** hit, paw **4** bash, beat, claw, drub, hurt, maim **5** abuse, paste, pound **6** bang up, batter, beat up, bruise, injure, mangle, misuse, pummel, savage, thrash **7** rough up, trample, trounce **8** bludgeon, ill-treat, lacerate, maltreat, mistreat, work over **9** mishandle **10** knock about, take care of
ender: **5** stick
Mauldin: **4** Bill
mauling: **5** abuse
Maumee: **5** river
locale: **4** Ohio **7** Indiana
Mauna __: **3** Kea, Loa
Mauna Loa: **7** volcano
locale: **4** Hilo **6** Hawaii
maunder: **3** yak **4** roam, rove **5** run on, stray **6** babble, mumble, ramble, wander **7** chatter **8** ramble on
maundering: **10** incoherent
maundy money: **4** alms
Maupassant, Guy de: **6** French, writer
work: The Necklace
The Umbrella
Maupin: **9** Armistead
Mauprat
author: George Sand
Maura: **7** Tierney **8** Jacobson
Maureen: **5** O'Hara **8** Connolly, McGovern **9** McCormick, O'Sullivan, Stapleton
daughter: **3** Mia
Mauriac, François: **6** French, writer **8** Nobelist

work: Asmodée
The Desert of Love
Genitrix
God and Mammon
Vipers' Tangle
A Woman of the Pharisees
Mauriat and His Orchestra, Paul
homeland: France
song: Love Is Blue (1968)
Maurice: **4** Gibb **5** Evans, Jarre, Ravel, saint, Scève **6** Allais, Barrès, Béjart, Sendak **7** Leblanc, Richard, Utrillo, Wilkins **8** Williams **9** Chevalier
see also French
Mauritania: **6** nation **7** country
bovine: **5** Maure
capital: **10** Nouakchott
desert: **6** Sahara
group: **10** Arab League
neighbor: **4** Mali **7** Algeria, Senegal
people: **4** Fula **6** Fulani
Mauritanian: **4** Arab
Mauritius: **4** isle **6** island, nation **7** country
bird, once: **4** dodo
capital: **9** Port Louis
money: **4** cent **5** rupee
Maurois, André: **6** French, writer **10** biographer
work: Ariel
Disraeli
The Family Circle
Mape
Prometheus
The Silence of Colonel Bramble
The Titans
Maury: **5** Wills **6** Povich
mauve: **4** plum **5** color, lilac **6** bluish, purple, violet **7** blueish **8** lavender
relative: ***see*** purple color
mauve __: **6** decade
Mauve Gloves & Madmen, Clutter & Vine
author: Tom Wolfe
Mav: **5** NBAer
maven: **3** pro **4** buff, guru, whiz **6** expert, master **8** virtuoso **9** authority, know-it-all **10** specialist
maverick: **4** calf **5** leppy, loner, rebel, stray **7** heretic, oddball, radical **8** newcomer, renegade, ultraist **9** dissenter, protester **10** iconoclast, malcontent
Maverick: **3** car **4** auto, Bart, Bret, Ford **10** automobile
Maverick (1994 film)
cast: Jodie Foster, James Garner, Mel Gibson
director: Richard Donner
Maverick (ABC western)
cast: James Garner (Bret Maverick)
Jack Kelly (Bart Maverick)
Maverick Queen, The
author: Zane Grey
Mavericks: **4** five
home: **5** Texas **6** Dallas
org.: **3** NBA
rival: ***see*** NBA team
mavin
see maven
mavis: **4** bird **6** thrush **8** songbird **10** song thrush
Mavis: **7** Gallant
Má Vlast
composer: Bedrich Smetana

Mavs
see Mavericks
maw: **4** craw, crop, hole **5** chops, mouth **6** gullet, throat **7** gizzard, stomach
partner: **3** paw
mawkish: **5** corny, gooey, gushy, hokey, mushy, sappy, soppy, teary **6** drippy, feeble, sickly, sirupy, sloppy, syrupy **7** cloying, gushing, maudlin **8** bathetic, schmalzy, shmaltzy **9** emotional, schmaltzy **10** lovey-dovey, saccharine
mawkishness: **4** corn, glop, mush **5** slush **6** bathos
mawl: **9** manhandle
__ Mawr: **4** Bryn
max: **4** most **5** limit **8** ultimate **10** upper limit
out: **4** peak
to the ~: **6** all-out
max __: **3** out
max.: **3** lim., lmt.
factor: **3** GCD
opposite: **3** min.
__ max: **5** to the
Max: **3** Aub **4** Baer, Born, Euwe, Gail **5** Brand, Bruch, Ernst, Jacob, Peter, Roach, Weber **6** Baucus, Factor, Frisch, Lerner, Morath, Ophuls, Perutz, Planck, Rudolf **7** Eastman, Klinger, Shulman, Steiner, Theiler, von Laue **8** Beckmann, Beerbohm, Delbrück, Pomeranc, Schuster, von Sydow **9** Fleischer, Schmeling **10** Bialystock, Liebermann
author: Howard Fast
Max __ Returns: **5** Dugan
__ Max: **3** Mad
Max and the White Phagocytes
author: Henry Miller
Max Dugan Returns (1983 film)
cast: Marsha Mason, Jason Robards, Donald Sutherland
director: Herbert Ross
Maxene: **7** Andrews
sister: **5** Patty **7** LaVerne
Max Factor: **6** makeup
alternative: ***see*** cosmetic brand
maxi: **4** coat **5** skirt **9** extra-long
make a ~: **5** rehem
terminus: **5** ankle
Maxie: **10** Rosenbloom
Maxie (1985 film)
cast: Glenn Close, Ruth Gordon
maxilla: **3** jaw **4** bone **7** jawbone
maxim: **3** law, saw **4** rule **5** adage, axiom, moral, motto, truth **6** belief, byword, dictum, phrase, saying, truism **7** precept, proverb **8** aphorism, laconism **9** catchword, platitude, principle
like a ~: **5** pithy
Maxim: **5** Gorki, Gorky
Maxim __: **3** gun
Maxima: **3** car **4** auto **6** Nissan **10** automobile
maximal: **6** utmost **7** maximum, topmost
maximally: **6** at best, at most
Maximilian: **6** Schell
maximum: **3** cap, nth, top, ult. **4** apex, full, most, peak **5** crest, limit **6** all-out, apogee, climax, height, record, summit, utmost, zenith **7** biggest, ceiling, highest, largest, optimum, outside, supreme, topmost **8** greatest, pinnacle, ultimate **9** uttermost **10** upper limit
number: **5** quota
reach a ~: **4** peak
Maximus, Circus: **5** arena
Maximus Poems, The
author: Charles Olson
Maxine: **5** Kumin
Max, Peter
genre: **6** pop art
maxwell: **4** unit
Maxwell: **3** AFB, car **4** auto, Elsa, Lois **5** Gavin, Shane, Smart **7** Marilyn **8** Anderson **9** Bodenheim, Caulfield
contemporary: **3** Reo
Don Adams' ~: **5** Smart
nanny: **4** Fran
Maxwell House: **6** coffee
alternative: **5** Sanka, Yuban **7** Folgers, Melitta, Nescafé, Savarin **9** Hills Bros.
Maxwell, James Clerk: **8** Scottish **9** physicist
may: **5** might
be that as it ~: **6** anyhow, anyway, even so **7** however
come what ~: **6** surely **7** somehow **10** in any event
ender: **3** day, fly, hap, pop **4** pole, weed **6** flower
May: **3** Joe **4** cape, Phil **5** Brian, Britt, month **6** Elaine, McAvoy, Robson, Sarton, Whitty **7** Swenson
birthstone: **5** agate **7** emerald
ender: **4** pole
event, familiarly: **4** Indy
follower: **3** Jun. **4** June
honoree: **3** mom **6** mother
in French: **3** Mai
in Spanish: **4** mayo
preceder: **3** Apr. **5** April
sign: **4** Bull **5** Twins **6** Gemini, Taurus
May __: **3** Day **4** wine **5** apple, queen **6** beetle
May __ to You: **5** I Sing
May __ you?: **5** I help
__ May: **3** If I **4** Cape **6** Maggie
May 13: **4** ides
May 7: **5** nones
May 8, 1945: **5** V-E Day
Maya: **3** Lin **6** Indian **7** Amerind, Angelou, Yucatec
ancient ~ city: **5** Tikal, Uxmal
archeological site: **5** Copan
farmland: **5** milpa
food staple: **5** maize
predecessor: **5** Olmec
sacrificial pool: **6** cenote
tree: **6** balche
Mayakovsky, Vladimir: **4** poet **7** Russian
__ May Alcott: **6** Louisa
Mayall: **4** John
Mayan: **3** Mam **8** language
maybe: **6** I'll see **7** perhaps, we'll see **8** possibly **9** perchance **10** God willing, imaginably
Maybe
author: Lillian Hellman
composer: George Gershwin, Ira Gershwin
Maybe __ ragged and funny...: **4** we're

Maybe I'm Amazed (1977 song)
artist: Paul McCartney
Maybe It Was Memphis (1991 song)
artist: Pam Tillis
Maybelle: **6** Carter
Maybellene (song)
artist: Chuck Berry, Johnny Rivers
Maybelline: **6** makeup
alternative: ***see*** cosmetic brand
__ May Be Right: **3** You
Mayberry
see Andy Griffith Show
Mayberry __: **3** RFD
maybes: **3** ifs
__-may-care: **5** devil
__ May Clampett: **4** Elly
Mayday: **3** SOS **4** help **5** alarm, alert **6** signal **7** warning
author: Nelson DeMille
May-Day
author: Ralph Waldo Emerson
May Day dance: **6** morris
May, Elaine: **7** actress **8** director
film: California Suite (1978)
The Heartbreak Kid (1972)
Ishtar (1987)
Luv (1967)
A New Leaf (1971)
Small Time Crooks (2000)
partner: Mike Nichols
__ Mayer: **5** Oscar
Mayfield, Curtis
leader of: The Impressions
song: Freddie's Dead (1972)
Superfly (1972)
Mayflower: **4** ship **5** mover
competitor: **6** Allied, Global
passenger: **5** Alden **8** Standish, Winthrop
mayfly: **3** bug, dun **6** insect
larva: **5** nymph
mayhem: **4** mess **5** chaos, havoc **6** bedlam, fracas, tumult, unrest, uproar **7** anarchy, battery, ferment, rioting, trouble, turmoil **8** disarray, disorder, upheaval, violence **9** commotion, confusion, mobocracy
May I help you?: **3** yes
May I interrupt?: **4** ahem
Mayim: **6** Bialik
__ May Lester: **5** Ellie
__ may look at a king: **4** A cat
Maynard: **3** Don, Ken **7** Jackson **8** Ferguson
Maynard G. __: **5** Krebs
Maynard, Ken
film: **5** oater
__ Maynard Keynes: **4** John
__ May, NJ: **4** Cape
mayo: **3** mes **5** month **7** Spanish
follower: **5** junio
preceder: **5** abril
see also mayonnaise
Mayo: **4** city, town **6** Archie, county **7** Charles, Whitman, William **8** Virginia
locale: **6** Canada **7** Ireland
neighbor: **5** Sligo
__ May Oliver: **4** Edna
mayonnaise: **8** dressing
cover: **3** lid
garlic-flavored ~: **5** aioli
holder: **3** jar
serving: **4** glob

MA

mayor: 8 Hizzoner, official
bailiwick: 4 city
name meaning ~: 7 Schultz
__ mayor: 4 lord
Mayor
author: Edward Koch
Mayor of Casterbridge, The
author: Thomas Hardy
Ma, Yo-Yo: 7 cellist, Chinese
birthplace: 5 Paris
maypop: 5 fruit, plant **6** flower
Mayron: 7 Melanie
Mays, Willie: 5 Giant **10** outfielder
Maytag
alternative: *see* appliance brand
dog: 6 Newton
mayten: 4 tree
May the __ be with you: 5 Force
Maytime (1937 film)
cast: Nelson Eddy, Jeanette MacDonald
__ May Wong: 4 Anna
Mazama lake, Mount: 6 Crater
Mazar: 4 Debi
Mazatlán: 4 city, port, town
locale: 6 Mexico **7** Sinaloa
see also Spanish
Mazda: 3 car **4** auto **10** automobile
competitor: 5 Isuzu
model: 3 MPV **5** Miata **7** Protege, Tribute **8** Millenia
maze: 3 web **5** snarl **6** jungle, morass, riddle, tangle **7** complex, network, red tape **9** catacombs, confusion, imbroglio, labyrinth **10** perplexity
part: 4 wall
runner: 6 lab rat
word: 5 Enter, Start
Mazel __!: 3 tov
Mazeppa
composer: Franz Liszt
Mazeroski, Bill: 6 Pirate
Mazes and Monsters
author: Rona Jaffe
Mazo __ Roche: 4 de la
Mazola: 3 oil **10** cooking oil
alternative: 6 Crisco, Wesson **7** Puritan
mazuma
see moolah
mazurka: 5 dance, music
Mazursky: 4 Paul
mazy: 6 knotty **7** winding **8** tortuous
MBA: 3 deg. **6** degree
course: 4 econ. **9** economics
Mbabane: 4 city, town **7** capital
locale: 9 Swaziland
__ M. Barrie: 5 James
Mbeki org.: 3 ANC
M. Butterfly star: 4 Wong
M.C.: 4 host **6** Hammer
need: 4 mike **10** microphone
McAdoo, Bob
org.: 3 NBA
sport: 10 basketball
__ M. Cain: 5 James
McAnuff: 3 Des
McArdle, Andrea
role: 5 Annie
McAuliffe: 7 Christa
McAvoy: 3 May **5** James
McBain: 2 Ed **5** Diane
McBeal: 4 Ally
McBride: 3 Chi
McCabe & Mrs. Miller (1971 film)
cast: Warren Beatty, Julie Christie
director: Robert Altman
McCaffrey: 4 Anne
McCain: 4 John **5** Cindy
McCall: 2 C.W. **5** Mitzi
McCall, C.W.
song: Convoy (1975)
McCallum, David: 5 actor
spouse: Jill Ireland
TV: The Man From U.N.C.L.E., NCIS
McCambridge, Mercedes
film: All the King's Men (1949, AA)
McCann: 4 Lila **5** Chuck, Peter
McCarey: 3 Leo
McCarthy: 3 Joe **4** Mary **5** Jenny, Kevin, Peter **6** Andrew, Eugene
partner: 6 Bergen
trunkmate: 5 Snerd **7** Klinker
McCarthy, Andrew: 5 actor
film: Heaven Help Us (1985)
I'm Losing You (1999)
Pretty in Pink (1987)
St. Elmo's Fire (1985)
McCarthy, Mary: 6 writer
work: Cannibals and Missionaries
A Charmed Life
The Company She Keeps
The Group
The Groves of Academe
Memories of a Catholic Girlhood
The Oasis
McCartney: 4 Paul **5** Jesse, Linda **6** Stella
McCartney, Paul: 3 Sir
album: 3 Ram
colleague: George Harrison, John Lennon, Ringo Starr
instrument: bass guitar
real first name: James
song: Another Day (1971)
Band on the Run (1974)
Coming Up (1980)
Ebony and Ivory (1982)
Getting Closer (1979)
The Girl Is Mine (1982)
Goodnight Tonight (1979)
Helen Wheels (1973)
Hi, Hi, Hi (1972)
Jet (1974)
Junior's Farm (1974)
Let 'Em In (1976)
Listen to What the Man Said (1975)
Live and Let Die (1973)
Maybe I'm Amazed (1977)
My Love (1973)
No More Lonely Nights (1984)
Sally G (1974)
Say Say Say (1983)
Silly Love Songs (1976)
So Bad (1984)
Spies Like Us (1985)
Take It Away (1982)
Uncle Albert/Admiral Halsey (1971)
With a Little Luck (1978)
spouse: Linda Eastman, Heather Mills
McCarver: 3 Tim
McCay: 6 Winsor
McClain: 6 Charly
McClanahan: 3 Rue
McClellan: 6 George
adversary: 3 Lee
colleague: 5 Meade
McClintock, Barbara: 8 Nobelist
McCloskey: 5 Leigh
McCloud (NBC drama)
cast: J.D. Cannon (Peter Clifford)
Terry Carter (Joe Broadhurst)
Dennis Weaver (Sam McCloud)
hometown: 4 Taos
McClure: 2 S.S. **4** Doug, Marc
McClure, Doug: 5 actor
spouse: Barbara Luna
TV: The Virginian
McClurg: 4 Edie
McConaughey, Matthew: 5 actor
film: Amistad (1997)
Boys on the Side (1995)
Contact (1997)
Ed TV (1999)
Failure to Launch (2006)
Fool's Gold (2008)
Ghosts of Girlfriends Past (2009)
How to Lose a Guy in Ten Days (2003)
A Time to Kill (1996)
Tropic Thunder (2008)
U-571 (2000)
The Wedding Planner (2001)
McCoo, Marilyn
spouse: Billy Davis Jr.
McCord: 4 Kent
McCormack: 4 Eric, Mary
McCormack, John: 5 tenor
McCormick: 5 Cyrus, Myron **7** Maureen
McCourt, Frank: 6 writer
work: Angela's Ashes
Brotherhood
'Tis
McCovey, Willie: 5 Giant **7** slugger
McCowen: 4 Alec
McCoy: 3 Van **4** Amos, Neal **6** Elijah **7** Charlie
Hatfield, to a ~: 3 foe **5** enemy
the real ~: 5 legit
__ McCoy: 4 real
McCoys: 4 clan
song: Fever (1965)
Hang on Sloopy (1965)
McCoy, Van
song: The Hustle (1975)
__ McCoy, WI: 4 Fort
McCrae: 4 Gwen, John **6** George
McCrary, Tex
spouse: Jinx Falkenburg
McCrea: 4 Joel
McCready: 5 Mindy
McCullers, Carson: 6 writer
work: The Ballad of the Sad Cafe
Clock without Hands
The Heart is a Lonely Hunter
The Member of the Wedding
Reflections in a Golden Eye
The Square Root of Wonderful
McCullough: 5 David **7** Colleen
McCullough, Colleen: 6 writer **10** Australian
MCCX halved: 3 DCV
work: An Indecent Obsession
The Thorn Birds
McDaniel: 3 Mel **6** Hattie, Xavier
McDaniel, Hattie Oscar: Gone With the Wind
McDermott: 5 Dylan
McDonald's
freebie: 5 straw **6** catsup, napkin **7** ketchup
rival: *see* restaurant chain
McDonnell: 4 Mary
McDonough: 4 Mary
McDormand, Frances: 7 actress
film: Almost Famous (2000)
Blood Simple (1984)
Burn After Reading (2008)
Darkman (1990)
Fargo (1996, AA)
Laurel Canyon (2002)
Madeline (1998)
The Man Who Wasn't There (2001)
Mississippi Burning (1988)
Miss Pettigrew Lives for a Day (2008)
North Country (2005)
Talk of Angels (1998)
Wonder Boys (2000)
McDowall, Roddy: 5 actor
film: How Green Was My Valley (1941)
Inside Daisy Clover (1965)
Lassie Come Home (1943)
The Legend of Hell House (1973)
The Longest Day (1962)
Lord Love a Duck (1966)
My Friend Flicka (1943)
Planet of the Apes (1968)
The Poseidon Adventure (1972)
McDowell: 6 Ronnie **7** Malcolm
McDowell, Malcolm: 5 actor
film: Bopha! (1993)
A Clockwork Orange (1971)
Cross Creek (1983)
O Lucky Man! (1973)
Star Trek Generations (1994)
Sunset (1988)
Time After Time (1979)
spouse: Mary Steenburgen
McElhone: 8 Natascha
McElligot's Pool
author: Dr. Seuss
McEnroe, John: 7 netster **9** tennis pro
doubles partner: 5 Stich
milieu: 5 court
rival: 4 Borg **5** Lendl
spouse: Tatum O'Neal
McEntire: 4 Reba
McEveety: 7 Vincent
McEwan: 3 Ian
McEwen: 4 Mark
McFadden: 4 Mary **5** Gates **6** Daniel
McFarland: 6 Spanky
McFerrin, Bobby
sing like ~: 4 scat
song: Don't Worry Be Happy (1988)
McFly
portrayer: 3 Fox
McGavin: 6 Darren
McGee: 5 Molly **6** Fibber, Willie
McGee, Fibber
medium: 5 radio
mess: 6 closet
McGillis, Kelly: 7 actress
film: The Accused (1988)
At First Sight (1998)
The Babe (1992)
Reuben, Reuben (1983)
Top Gun (1986)
Witness (1985)
McGill University
location: 6 Canada, Quebec **8** Montreal
McGinley: 3 Ted **7** Phyllis
McGinnis: 6 George
McGinnity: 3 Joe

McGoohan, Patrick: 5 actor
TV: The Prisoner, Secret Agent
McGovern: 6 George 7 Maureen 9 Elizabeth
McGovern, Elizabeth: 7 actress
film: Bedroom Window (1987)
Once Upon a Time in America (1984)
Racing With the Moon (1984)
Ragtime (1981)
She's Having a Baby (1988)
McGovern, George home: 4 S. Dak.
McGovern, Maureen
song: The Morning After (1973)
McGraw: 3 Tim, Tug 4 John, Phil 5 James 7 Charles
McGraw-__: 4 Hill
McGraw, Tim
father: Tug
song: Indian Outlaw (1994)
It's Your Love (1997)
Please Remember Me (1999)
spouse: Faith Hill
McGregor: 4 Ewan
McGrew: 3 Dan
lady: 3 Lou
McGriff, Fred
sport: 8 baseball
McGuire: 2 Al 3 Don 5 Barry 7 Dorothy, Phyllis 9 Christine
McGuire, Barry
member: New Christy Minstrels
song: Eve of Destruction (1965)
McGuire Sisters: 4 trio
members: Phyllis, Christine, Dorothy
song: Delilah Jones (1956)
He (1955)
It May Sound Silly (1955)
May You Always (1959)
Picnic (1956)
Rhythm 'N' Blues (1955)
Sincerely (1955)
Something's Gotta Give (1955)
Sugartime (1958)
McGwire, Mark: 7 slugger
rival: 9 Sammy Sosa
sport: 8 baseball
stat for ~: 3 RBI 5 homer
McHale's Navy (ABC sitcom)
cast: Ernest Borgnine (Lt. Cmdr. Quinton McHale)
Tim Conway (Ens. Charles Parker)
Joe Flynn (Capt. Wallace Binghamton)
catchphrase: 5 why me
M.C. Hammer: 6 rapper
real name: Stanley Burrell
song: 2 Legit 2 Quit (1991)
Addams Groove (1991)
Have You Seen Her (1990)
Pray (1990)
U Can't Touch This (1990)
McHenry: 4 Fort
McHugh: 5 Frank, Jimmy
McInerney: 3 Jay
McIntire: 3 Tim 4 John
McIntosh: 5 apple
relative: *see* apple
McIntyre: 3 Hal, Joe 4 Joey
McKay: 3 Jim 4 John 6 Claude 7 Gardner
McKean, Michael: 5 actor
film: Best in Show (2000)
The Brady Bunch Movie (1995)
Planes, Trains & Automobiles (1987)
This Is Spinal Tap (1984)
TV: Laverne & Shirley
McKechnie: 4 Bill
McKee: 5 Maria 7 Lonette
competitor: *see* cookie manufacturer
McKellen, Ian: 3 Sir 5 actor
film: The Ballad of Little Jo (1993)
Gods and Monsters (1998)
The Lord of the Rings... (2001)
Priest of Love (1981)
Richard III (1995)
Six Degrees of Separation (1993)
Thank You All Very Much (1969)
X-Men (2000)
McKenna: 7 Siobhan 8 Virginia
McKennitt, Loreena instrument: harp
McKenzie, Scott
song: San Francisco (1967)
McKeon: 4 Doug 5 Nancy 6 Philip
McKern: 3 Leo
McKim: 7 Charles
McKinley: 2 mt. 3 Ida, mtn. 4 peak 5 mount 7 William 8 mountain
locale: 6 Alaska
McKinley, William: 9 president
assassin: 8 Czolgosz
birthplace: 4 Ohio 5 Niles
former occupation: 6 lawyer
opponent: 5 Bryan
supporter: 5 Hanna
V.P.: 6 Hobart 9 Roosevelt
wife: 3 Ida
McKinney, Ruth work: My Sister Eileen
McKinney, Tamara: 5 skier
McKuen: 3 Rod
McLachlan, Sarah
homeland: Canada
song: Adia (1998)
Angel (1998)
Building a Mystery (1997)
I Will Remember You (1999)
Sweet Surrender (1998)
McLaglen: 6 Andrew, Victor
McLain: 5 Denny
McLean: 3 Don 9 Stevenson
McLean, Don
song: American Pie (1971)
Castles in the Air (1972)
Crying (1981)
Vincent (1972)
McLean, Va. org.: 3 CIA
__ McLeod Bethune: 4 Mary
McLintock! (1963 film)
cast: Maureen O'Hara, John Wayne
McLuhan, Marshall: 6 critic, writer 8 Canadian
work: The Gutenberg Galaxy
The Mechanical Bride
The Medium is the Massage
Understanding Media
McMahon: 2 Ed 3 Jim 6 Horace
word: 5 Here's 6 Johnny
McManus: 6 George
McMartin: 4 John
McMillan: 5 Edwin, Terry 6 Donald
McMillan and Wife (NBC drama)
cast: Rock Hudson (Stewart McMillan)
Susan Saint James (Sally McMillan)
Nancy Walker (Mildred)
McMillan, Edwin: 7 chemist 8 Nobelist
McMurdo: 5 Sound
locale: 10 Antarctica
McMurtry, Larry: 6 writer
work: All My Friends Are Going to Be Strangers
Anything for Billy
Boone's Lick
Buffalo Girls
By Sorrow's River
Cadillac Jack
Dead Man's Walk
Duane's Depressed
The Evening Star
Folly and Glory
Horseman Pass By
The Last Picture Show
The Late Child
Lonesome Dove
Loop Group
Panhandle Cowboy
Paradise
Rhino Ranch
Rodeo
Sin Killer
Somebody's Darling
Some Can Whistle
Streets of Laredo
Telegraph Days
Terms of Endearment
Texasville
The Wandering Hill
Whatever Happened to Jacy Farrow?
When the Light Goes
McNair: 4 Fort 7 Barbara
McNally: 4 Dave 7 Stephen 8 Terrence
partner: 4 Rand
McNally's Alibi
author: Lawrence Sanders
McNally's Caper
author: Lawrence Sanders
McNally's Chance
author: Lawrence Sanders
McNally's Dilemma
author: Lawrence Sanders
McNally's Folly
author: Lawrence Sanders
McNally's Gamble
author: Lawrence Sanders
McNally's Luck
author: Lawrence Sanders
McNally's Puzzle
author: Lawrence Sanders
McNally's Risk
author: Lawrence Sanders
McNally's Secret
author: Lawrence Sanders
McNally's Trial
author: Lawrence Sanders
McNamara: 5 Robin 6 Robert
McNaughton: 3 Ian
__ McNeill Whistler: 5 James
McNichol: 5 Jimmy 6 Kristy
McNichol, Kristy: 7 actress
TV: Empty Nest, Family
__ McNutt: 4 Boob
__ M. Cohan: 6 George
McPartland, Marian: 7 pianist
genre: 4 jazz
McPhatter, Clyde
group: Dominoes, Drifters
song: Little Bitty Pretty One (1962)
Lover Please (1962)
A Lover's Question (1958)
Treasure of Love (1956)
__ McPhee: 5 Nanny
McPherson: 5 Aimee
__ McPherson, GA: 4 Fort
McQ (1974 film)
cast: Eddie Albert, Colleen Dewhurst, Diana Muldaur, John Wayne
McQueen: 5 Steve 9 Butterfly
McQueen, Steve: 5 actor
film: Baby The Rain Must Fall (1965)
Bullitt (1968)
The Cincinnati Kid (1965)
The Getaway (1972)
The Great Escape (1963)
Hell Is for Heroes (1962)
Junior Bonner (1972)
Le Mans (1971)
Love With the Proper Stranger (1963)
The Magnificent Seven (1960)
Nevada Smith (1966)
On Any Sunday (1971)
Papillon (1973)
The Reivers (1969)
The Sand Pebbles (1966)
Soldier in the Rain (1963)
The Thomas Crown Affair (1968)
The Towering Inferno (1974)
spouse: Ali MacGraw
TV: Wanted: Dead or Alive
McRae: 6 Carmen
McRaney, Gerald
spouse: Delta Burke
McRee: 4 Lisa
McShane: 3 Ian
McSorley's Bar
artist: John Sloan
McTeague
author: Frank Norris
McTiernan, John: 8 director
film: Die Hard (1988)
The Hunt for Red October (1990)
Last Action Hero (1993)
Medicine Man (1992)
Predator (1987)
Rollerball (2002)
The Thomas Crown Affair (1999)
McVie: 4 John 9 Christine
McVie, Christine
homeland: England
member: Fleetwood Mac
song: Got a Hold of Me (1984)
McWhirter: 4 Ross 6 Norris
Md: 4 elem. 7 element 11 mendelevium
101 for ~: 4 at. no.
M.D.: 2 dr., GP 3 deg., doc 6 degree, doctor 9 physician
assistant: 2 RN
employer: 3 HMO
needle: 4 hypo
order: 2 Rx 4 stat
org.: 3 ACP, AMA
place: 2 ER, OR 4 hosp.
publication: 4 JAMA
reference: 3 PDR
request: 3 ECG, EEG, EKG, MRI, NMR 4 X-ray
specialty: 3 ENT
see also doctor, physician
Md. neighbor: 3 Del., W.Va. 4 Virg.
see also Maryland

mdse.: 3 gds., stk.
bars: 3 UPC
bill: 3 inv.
outlet: 3 mkt.
second-quality ~: 4 impf. 5 irreg.
MDT part: 3 Mtn., Std. 4 Time 8 Mountain, Standard
MDX: 3 SUV 5 Acura
me: 4 pron., self 7 pronoun
ah ~: 4 alas, sigh
belonging to ~: 4 mine
between you and ~: 7 sub rosa 8 in secret, secretly 9 entre nous, privately
count ~ out: 4 uh-uh 10 not a chance
dear ~: 7 my stars 10 I do declare, my goodness
excuse ~: 4 ahem, oops 5 sorry 6 whoops
in French: 3 moi
in German: 3 mir
it wasn't ~: 4 not I
not ~: 3 you
suits ~: 2 OK 3 yes 4 fine, okay 5 swell 8 very well
too: 5 ditto
me __: 6 decade
me-__: 3 too 5 tooer
__ me!: 5 Woe is 6 Search
__ me?: 3 Why
__, me?: 3 Who
Me __ Shadow: 5 and My
Me __, The: 6 decade
Me, __ I call myself: 5 a name
Me, __ & Irene: 6 Myself
Me.
neighbor: 3 Que.
region: 4 N. Eng.
see also Maine
__ Me: 3 Ask, Sue, Use 4 Call, Dang, Dare, Help, Hold, Kiss, Love, Play, Rock, Tell 5 All of, Bad to, Touch 6 Rescue 7 Release
M.E.: 3 deg.
awarder: 3 MIT
part of ~: 3 Eng. 4 Engr., Mech. 8 Engineer 10 Mechanical
__, M.E.: 6 Quincy
mea culpa: 5 sorry 7 apology, I'm sorry, my fault
mead: 5 drink 6 meadow 8 beverage
ingredient: 5 honey
Mead: 4 lake 8 Margaret
locale: 5 Samoa
Meade: 5 James 6 George
__ Meade: 4 Fort
Mead Johnson cereal: 6 Pablum
Mead, Margaret: 6 writer 14 anthropologist
work: Blackberry Winter
Coming of Age in Samoa
Growing Up in New Guinea
Letters From the Field
Male and Female
meadow: 3 fld., lea, ley, sod 4 mead, park 5 field, grass, heath, plain, range, sward, veldt 6 steppe, swarth 7 bottoms, lowland, pasture, prairie, verdure 9 grassland
ender: 4 land, lark 5 lands, sweet
grazer: 3 cow, ewe 5 sheep
munch in the ~: 5 graze
remark: 3 baa, maa, moo 5 bleat
rolling ~: 4 down
Meadowlands Arena team: 4 Nets
Meadowlark: 5 Lemon
meadowlark cousin: 4 wren
Meadows: 3 Tim 5 Jayne 6 Audrey
Meadows, Jayne
spouse: Steve Allen
meager: 3 low 4 bare, bony, lank, lean, poor, puny, slim, thin 5 boney, gaunt, lanky, light, scant, short, small, spare 6 flimsy, gangly, humble, Lenten, little, measly, paltry, scanty, scrimp, shabby, skimpy, skinny, slight, sparse, stingy 7 angular, lacking, limited, scraggy, scrawny, scrimpy, slender, stinted, trivial, wanting 8 angulose, angulous, beggarly, exiguous, gangling, pathetic, rawboned, underfed 9 deficient, emaciated, miserable 10 inadequate, infrequent, lamentable, pathetical, unfruitful
not ~: 8 generous 9 plentiful
meagerness: 4 lack, want 6 dearth 7 paucity, poverty 8 exiguity, scarcity, sparsity 10 deficiency, inadequacy
meal: 3 tea 4 chow, dish, eats, fare, feed, food, grub, luau, mess 5 board, feast, flour, lunch, plate, snack, table 6 brunch, buffet, din-din, dinner, entrée, farina, picnic, powder, repast, spread, supper 7 aliment, banquet, cookout, dessert, fish fry, high tea, potluck, special 8 barbecue, carryout, clambake, luncheon, munchies, prix fixe, TV dinner, victuals 9 blue plate, breakfast, collation, refection
afternoon ~: 5 lunch
Army ~: 4 chow, hash, mess 7 K-ration
baby's ~: 6 din-din
ender: 4 time, worm
enjoy your ~ in French: 10 bon appétit
evening ~: 6 dinner, repast, supper 9 collation
fix a ~: 4 cook 6 whip up
for the humbled: 4 crow
gluttonous ~: 5 gorge
ground ~: 5 flour
have a ~: 3 eat, sup 4 dine 5 feast
horse ~: 4 feed 6 fodder
ingredient: 3 oat 4 corn
in need of a ~: 5 unfed 6 hungry
light ~: 4 bite 5 salad, snack 9 collation
Mexican ~: 6 flauta
morning ~: 9 breakfast
oater ~: 4 chow, grub 7 vittles
outdoor ~: 6 picnic 8 barbecue
part: 5 drink 6 entrée 7 dessert 9 appetizer
prayer: 5 grace
starter: 3 oat 4 corn, fish, inch 5 piece, salad
sumptuous ~: 5 feast 7 banquet
unappetizing ~: 4 slop 5 gruel
meal __: 6 ticket
__ meal: 4 bone, corn, fish 5 matzo 6 matzah, matzoh, square
__ Me Along: 4 Take
meals: 4 fare 5 board
meals on __: 6 wheels
mealy: 3 dry 4 oaty, pale, soft 6 floury, sallow 7 crumbly, powdery 8 granular
ender: 3 bug
mealy-__: 7 mouthed
mealybug: 6 insect
mean: 2 av. 3 aim, avg., bad, low, par 4 base, cold, cool, evil, hard, norm, plan, poor, rude, sour, ugly, vile 5 augur, catty, cheap, close, dirty, harsh, imply, lousy, lowly, mangy, nasty, petty, rough, seedy, snide, spell, surly, testy, tight, tough 6 animal, aspire, attest, brutal, chilly, convey, denote, entail, fierce, herald, hint at, humble, intend, little, mangey, measly, medial, median, mesial, middle, modest, narrow, odious, ogrish, ornery, paltry, ragged, remote, rotten, savage, shabby, sleazy, sneaky, sordid, stingy, tawdry, unfair, unkind, wanton, wicked 7 add up to, average, balance, beastly, bestial, betoken, callous, connote, crabbed, drive at, halfway, hateful, hostile, hurtful, ignoble, inhuman, knavish, limited, lowborn, lowdown, miserly, ogreish, peevish, pitiful, point to, portend, presage, propose, purport, run-down, scruffy, selfish, servile, signify, squalid, suggest, thrifty, trivial, vicious, waspish 8 allude to, barbaric, beggarly, churlish, contrary, degraded, fiendish, foreshow, foretell, indicate, inferior, inhumane, inimical, intimate, midpoint, moderate, ordinary, pitiless, plebeian, ruthless, sadistic, spell out, spiteful, standard, stand for, ungiving, vengeful, venomous, wretched 9 adumbrate, bellicose, cutthroat, dangerous, dastardly, determine, ferocious, fractious, hard-nosed, malicious, merciless, miserable, monstrous, obnoxious, penurious, represent, sarcastic, shameless, symbolize, truculent, unpitying, vexatious, withdrawn 10 anticipate, catchpenny, despicable, diabolical, evil-minded, foreshadow, have in mind, ill-natured, lamentable, malevolent, oppressive, pugnacious, scurrilous, ungenerous, vindictive
ender: 4 time 5 while
kid: 3 imp 4 brat
lean and ~: 4 wiry
look: 5 scowl, sneer
not ~: 4 nice
one: 3 cur 4 ogre 5 brute, fiend 6 despot
partner: 4 lean
something: 6 matter
take to ~: 4 draw, make 5 glean, guess, infer, think 6 assume, decode, deduce, derive, gather 7 imagine, surmise 8 conclude, construe 10 understand
(to): 3 aim 4 hope
words: 5 venom
mean __: 4 well
__ mean: 6 golden
Mean __ Greene: 3 Joe
Me and Bobby McGee (1971 song)
artist: Janis Joplin
meander: 3 gad 4 coil, roam, rove, turn, walk, wind 5 amble, drift, range, slink, snake, stray, twine, twist, weave 6 browse, change, cruise, ramble, stroll, trapes, wander, zigzag 7 saunter, sinuate, slither, traipse 8 straggle 9 bat around, gallivant
meanderer: 5 rover 8 wanderer, wayfarer
meandering: 5 snaky, twiny, windy 6 errant, zigzag 7 crooked, erratic, sinuous, winding 8 indirect, tortuous 9 difficult, irregular 10 circuitous, convoluted, serpentine
Me and Juliet: 7 musical
composer: Oscar Hammerstein, Richard Rodgers
Me and Julio... (1972 song)
artist: Paul Simon
Me and Mrs. Jones (1972 song)
artist: Billy Paul
Me and My __: 6 Shadow
__ Me and My Gal: 3 For
Me and My Shadow
composer: Billy Rose
meandrous: 5 snaky 7 sinuous
Me and You and a Dog Named Boo (1971 song)
artist: Lobo
Meaney, Colm: 5 actor
TV: Star Trek: Deep Space Nine, Star Trek: The Next Generation
Mean Girls (2004 film)
cast: Tina Fey, Lindsay Lohan, Rachel McAdams
Mean Green: 10 North Texas
meanie: 4 ogre 5 fiend
meaning: 3 aim, use 4 gist, goal, pith 5 drift, heart, point, sense, tenor, value, worth 6 effect, import, intent, nuance, object, spirit, thrust, upshot 7 bearing, content, context, essence, message, purport, purpose 8 overtone 9 intention, substance 10 bottom line, definition, denotation
business: 7 serious 8 resolute 9 tenacious
different ~: 5 twist
fraught with ~: 4 deep 8 profound
give the ~ of: 6 define 7 explain 8 spell out 9 interpret
having a secret ~: 5 runic
__-meaning: 4 well
meaningful: 3 big 4 deep, rich 5 meaty, pithy, valid, vital 6 cogent 7 earnest, pointed, serious, weighty 8 eloquent, pregnant, telltale 9 important, momentous 10 expressive, portentous, suggestive, worthwhile
meaningless: 4 idle, vain, void 5 empty, inane, silly, vague, vapid 6 absurd, futile, hollow 7 aimless, shallow, trivial, useless 8 nugatory, trifling 9 pointless, senseless, valueless, worthless
Mean Joe: 6 Greene
meanness: 4 evil 5 spite 6 malice 8 asperity 9 hostility
means: 3 job, way 4 dint, mode, path, road, step, tool 5 agent, dough, funds, kitty, money, organ, power, purse, route, stake, thing 6 agency, assets, avenue, budget, bundle, engine, estate, income, living, manner, medium, method, riches, system, tactic, wealth 7 backing, capital, channel,

fortune, ingress, measure, nest egg, process, revenue, savings, support, tactics, vehicle **8** approach, bankroll, finances, holdings, property, reserves **9** affluence, apparatus, equipment, expedient, implement, machinery, mechanism, resources, substance, technique **10** capability, expediency, instrument, livelihood, pocketbook, securities
by all ~: *see* of course **2** da, ja, OK, sí **3** oui **4** okay, okeh, okey **5** good-o, quite, right, roger, uh-huh **6** agreed, gladly, good-oh, indeed, just so, rather, righto, yowzah **7** exactly, go ahead, indeedy, mais oui, quite so, ten-four **8** all right, as you say, for a fact, thumbs up, very well **9** be my guest, darn right, decidedly, precisely, sure thing, you said it **10** definitely, far and away, sure enough, that's right
by any ~: **5** at all
by no ~: **3** nah, naw, nay, nix, non **4** nein, nope, nyet, uh-uh **5** I won't, ixnay, never, no way **6** hardly, noways, nowise **7** I refuse **8** forget it, I will not, negative, negatory **9** fat chance, I think not **10** count me out, not a chance, thumbs down
by ~ of: **3** via **5** using **6** hereby **7** through
by what ~: **3** how
have the ~ for: **6** afford
having the ~: **4** able **6** able to
justifiers: **4** ends
man of ~: **5** nabob **6** fat cat **9** moneybags, plutocrat
of getting there: **4** belt, lane, path, pike, road, ship **5** guide, route, trail **6** access, artery, avenue, detour, street **7** channel, freeway, highway, parkway, passage, roadway, thruway, viaduct **8** short cut, turnpike **9** boulevard, itinerary **10** expressway, throughway
of independent ~: **4** rich **5** flush **6** loaded **7** moneyed, opulent, upscale, wealthy, well-off **8** affluent, thriving, well-to-do **10** in the money, privileged, prosperous, successful, well-heeled
partner: **4** ways
ways and ~: **7** capital, revenue
means __ end: **4** to an
__ means: **4** by no **5** by all, by any
meanspirited: **5** harsh, nasty, petty **10** ungenerous
Mean Streets (1973 film)
cast: Robert De Niro, Harvey Keitel
director: Martin Scorsese
__ means war!: **4** This
meant: **6** wilful **7** planned, sincere, willful **8** destined, intended **9** voluntary **10** deliberate, preplanned, purposeful, volitional
mean-tempered: **4** evil, sour, ugly **5** catty, cruel, nasty, surly **6** chilly, malign, ornery, wanton, wicked **7** baleful, hateful, hostile, satanic, vicious, waspish **8** inimical, spiteful, vengeful, venomous **9** bellicose, malicious, rancorous **10** derogatory, ill-natured, pugnacious
meantime: **5** while **7** interim
in the ~: **4** till **5** until **6** for now
meanwhile: **4** till **5** until **6** for now
Meanwhile, back at the __...: **5** ranch
Mean Woman Blues (1963 song)
artist: Roy Orbison
Meany: **6** George
Meara, Anne
spouse: Jerry Stiller
Meara, Anne spouse
son: Ben Stiller
__ Me a River: **3** Cry
Mears, Rick: **9** auto racer
milieu: **5** track
meas.: **2** cc., cm., ft., in., kg., km., lb., mg., mi., mm., oz., pt., qt., yd. **3** deg., fth., gal., qty., tsp. **4** cu. ft., cu. in., cu. yd., fath., fl. oz., sq. ft., sq. yd., tbsp.
area ~: **4** sq. ft., sq. mi., sq. yd.
heat ~: **3** deg.
length ~: **2** cm., ft., km., mi., mm., yd. **3** fth. **4** fath.
liquid ~: **2** oz., pt., qt. **3** gal., tsp. **4** fl. oz., tbsp.
volume ~: **2** cc. **4** cu. ft., cu. in., cu. yd.
weight: **2** kg., lb., mg., oz.
see also measure
__ measles: **6** German
measles, like: **5** viral
measly: **4** mean, mere, poor, puny **5** petty **6** humble, meager, paltry, scanty, skimpy, stingy **7** miserly, pitiful **8** beggarly, niggling, pathetic, picayune, piddling, trifling **9** miserable **10** pathetical
measurable: **6** finite **7** bounded, limited **9** weighable **10** calculable, terminable
measure: **3** act, bar, eye, fit, law, peg **4** beat, bill, dose, mark, mete, move, norm, pace, rank, rate, read, rime, rule, span, step, time **5** bylaw, check, gauge, grade, judge, limit, means, meter, plumb, quota, ratio, reach, rhyme, scale, scope, share, sound, swing, tempo, weigh, width **6** action, amount, assess, bounds, course, degree, effort, extent, figure, length, method, ration, reckon, resort, rhythm, size up, strain, stress, survey, tailor **7** cadence, cadency, compute, dope out, pace off, portion, process, statute, stopgap **8** appraise, estimate, evaluate, keep tabs, proposal, quantify, quantity, regulate, resource, standard **9** allotment, benchmark, calculate, calibrate, criterion, determine, dimension, enactment, expedient, immensity, procedure, restraint, stratagem, yardstick **10** proceeding, proportion, resolution, touchstone
area ~: **4** acre, sq. ft., sq. mi., sq. yd. **7** hectare **10** square foot, square mile, square yard
combining form: **5** -meter, metro-
heat ~: **3** deg. **6** degree
in music: **3** bar
lateral ~: **4** span **5** girth **6** spread **7** breadth **9** broadness
length ~: **2** cm., ft., km., mi., mm., yd. **3** fth., rod **4** fath., foot, inch, mile, yard **5** meter **6** fathom **8** kilogram **9** kilometer **10** centimeter, millimeter
liquid ~: **2** oz., pt., qt. **3** gal., tsp. **4** fl. oz., pint, tbsp. **5** ounce, quart **8** teaspoon **10** fluid ounce, tablespoon
starter: **7** counter
volume ~: **2** cc. **4** cu. ft., cu. in., cu. yd. **9** cubic foot, cubic inch, cubic yard
weight ~: **2** kg., lb., mg., oz. **3** ton **5** ounce, pound **8** kilogram **9** milligram
__ measure: **4** tape **6** beyond
measured: **5** paced **7** regular, stately **8** moderate
amount: **4** dose **6** dosage
combining form: **6** -metric
Measure for Measure: **4** play
author: William Shakespeare
character: **5** Lucio **6** Angelo **7** Escalus, Mariana **8** Isabella
measureless: **3** big **4** vast **6** cosmic, untold **7** endless **8** cosmical, infinite **9** limitless, unlimited
measurement: **4** area, mass, size **5** depth, width **6** amount, degree, extent, height, length, survey, volume, weight **7** density **8** altitude, analysis, capacity, distance, quantity **9** amplitude, appraisal, dimension, frequency, magnitude, thickness, valuation
combining form: **5** -metry
see also measure
measurements: **4** data **7** figures **10** statistics
measurers' org.: **4** ANSI
measures: **6** action
take ~: **3** act
Measure twice, cut __: **4** once
measuring: **8** checking, likening **9** analyzing, balancing **10** comparison, estimation
device: **4** dial, rule **5** gauge, ruler, sizer, spoon
science: **7** metrics
measuring __: **3** cup **5** spoon
meat: **3** ham, nub, nut **4** beef, chop, chow, core, crux, duck, fare, fish, food, fowl, gist, goat, grub, knub, lamb, loin, pâté, pith, pork, ribs, Spam, veal **5** bacon, brawn, chops, flank, frank, goose, heart, jerky, liver, point, roast, sense, shank, sheep, steak, T-bone, Treet, tripe, wings, wurst **6** banger, burger, collop, cutlet, entrée, fillet, hot dog, kernel, marrow, muscle, mutton, ragout, rib eye, saddle, salami, thrust, turkey, upshot, vittle, wiener **7** aliment, biltong, bologna, brisket, charqui, chicken, chorizo, cold cut, edibles, essence, giblets, nucleus, pemican, poultry, purport, rissole, roulade, sausage, sirloin, terrine, venison, victual **8** baked ham, barbecue, braciola, chili dog, cold cuts, foie gras, key point, kielbasa, lamb chop, linguiça, noisette, pastrami, pemmican, pork chop, pot-au-feu, pot roast, quenelle, rib roast, rib steak, salt pork, scrapple, shoulder, teriyaki, top round **9** andouille, beefsteak, bratwurst, carbonado, club steak, croquette, cube steak, drumstick, foodstuff, forcemeat, fricassee, galantine, hamburger, liver pâté, lunchmeat, medallion, nutriment, pork roast, provender, roast duck, rump steak, short ribs, spareribs, substance **10** beefburger, blade steak, boudin noir, comestible, corned beef, Cornish hen, cracklings, deviled ham, flank steak, headcheese, knockwurst, liverwurst, main course, mortadella, prosciutto, provisions, roast goose, round steak, scaloppine, scaloppini, shank steak, shell steak, shish kebab, skirt steak, sustenance, tenderloin
accompaniment: **6** potato **9** vegetable
alternative: **4** tofu **8** bean curd
avoider: **5** vegan **10** vegetarian
breakfast ~: **3** ham **5** bacon
canned ~: **4** Spam
cured ~: **5** jerky
cut: **4** chop, loin **5** flank, shank, T-bone **6** fillet
dark ~: **3** leg **5** thigh **9** drumstick
deli ~: **3** ham **6** salami **7** bologna **8** pastrami **10** corned beef
dish: **4** stew
dried ~: **5** jerky
ender: **4** ball, head, loaf **6** packer **7** packing
exotic ~: **3** emu **4** emeu
GI ~: **4** Spam
grade: **5** prime **6** choice
in Spanish: **5** carne
jelly: **5** aspic
juices: **5** gravy
made without milk or ~: **5** parve **6** pareve
moisten ~: **5** baste
on a stick: **5** cabob, kabab, kabob, kebab, kebob
pie: **5** pasty
red ~: **4** beef **5** steak
seller: **7** butcher
site: **6** locker
slice of ~: **6** collop
starter: **3** nut **4** crab **5** force, lunch, mince, sweet
strong, as ~: **4** gamy **5** gamey
treat ~: **4** corn, cure **5** smoke
trim ~: **5** defat
meat __: **3** tea **4** hook, loaf **7** grinder
__ meat: **3** red **4** dark **5** white
Meat __ Aday: **4** Loaf
meat-and-potatoes: **5** vital **7** radical
concoction: **4** hash
__ meatball: **7** Swedish
Meatballs (1979 film)
cast: Bill Murray
director: Ivan Reitman
setting: **4** camp
meathead: **3** ass, nit, oaf, sap **4** boob, clod, dolt, fool **5** chump, clown, cluck, dummy, dunce, joker, looby, ninny, patsy **6** dimwit, lubber, lummox, nitwit, sucker, turkey **7** buffoon, dingbat, dullard, half-wit, jackass **8** dumbbell, numskull **9** birdbrain, lamebrain, numbskull, simpleton **10** nincompoop
Meathead: **4** Mike **6** Stivic
father-in-law: **6** Archie

mother-in-law: 5 Edith
wife: 6 Gloria
Meat Loaf
real name: Marvin Lee Aday
song: I'd Do Anything for Your Love (1993)
I'd Lie for You (1995)
Paradise by the Dashboard Light (1978)
Rock and Roll Dreams Come Through (1994)
Two Out of Three Ain't Bad (1978)
meatus site: 3 ear
meaty: 4 rich 5 beefy, pithy 7 weighty 8 profound 10 meaningful
__ Me Back to Old Virginny: 5 Carry
__ Me Badd: 5 Color
__ Me Be the One: 3 Let
__ Me Be There: 3 Let
__ Me By: 4 Pass
__ Me Call You Sweetheart: 3 Let
Mecca: 3 hub 4 city, town 10 attraction
locale: 5 Hejaz, Hijaz 6 Hedjaz 11 Saudi Arabia
pilgrim: 5 hadji
pilgrimage to ~: 3 haj 4 hadj, hajj
port: 5 Jedda, Jidda
resident: 5 Saudi
shrine: 4 Kaba 5 Kaaba, Kabah 6 Kaabah
Mecham: 4 Evan
mechanic: 8 repairer 10 technician
concern: 6 engine
device: 5 dolly, U-bolt
job: 4 lube 6 tuneup
specialty ~: 3 car 4 auto 10 automobile
mechanical: 4 cold 5 fixed, stiff 6 useful 7 cursory, regular, routine 8 habitual, knee-jerk, lifeless 9 automated, automatic, technical, unfeeling 10 industrial
man: 5 droid, robot 7 android
person: 5 droid
procedure: 4 rote
mechanical __: 3 man 4 bank 6 pencil 7 drawing
Mechanical Bride, The
author: Marshall McLuhan
mechanics: 7 science
study: 6 forces, motion
mechanic's __: 4 lien
__ mechanics: 4 body, soil, wave 5 fluid 6 matrix 7 quantum
mechanism: 4 mode, tool 5 gears, means, motor, thing, works 6 agency, device, engine, gadget, medium, method, system 7 gimmick, innards, machine, process, vehicle 8 black box, workings 9 apparatus, appliance, doohickey, machinery, operation, procedure 10 components, instrument
__ mechanism: 6 coping, escape 7 defense, trigger
mechanized: 9 automated, automatic 10 electrical, industrial
mecum, vade: 5 bible, guide 8 handbook
med __: 6 school
med.
bigger than ~: 2 XL 3 lge.
conglomerate: 3 HMO
degree: 2 MD 3 DMD 4 M.Sc.D.
facility: 4 hosp.
staffer: 2 RN 3 LPN
test: 3 ECG, EEG, EKG, MRI
__ Med: 4 Club
medal: 3 DCM, DFC, DSM, DSO 4 gold 5 award, badge, honor, prize, title 6 bronze, reward, ribbon, trophy 9 Navy Cross 10 Bronze Star, decoration, Silver Star
attachment: 5 clasp
British ~: 3 DCM, DSO
bronze ~: 3 DSC
give a ~ to: 4 cite 5 honor 8 decorate
grounds for a ~: 5 valor
material: 4 gold 6 bronze, silver
shape: 4 star
winner: 4 best, hero
__ medal: 4 gold 6 bronze, silver
medalist: 6 victor, winner 8 champion
gold ~: 4 hero 5 first 6 winner 8 champion
Medalist: 3 car 4 auto 7 Mercury 10 automobile
medallion: 4 meat, seal 5 badge, prize
Medal of __: 5 Honor 7 Freedom
meddle: 3 pry, spy 4 nose, poke 5 mix in, snoop 6 butt in, horn in, impose, kibitz, tamper, worm in 7 barge in, break in, chime in, enquire, inquire, intrude, obtrude 8 encroach, infringe, trespass 9 interfere, interpose, intervene
don't ~: 5 let be 10 deregulate
ender: 4 some
meddler: 5 snoop, yenta 6 gossip 8 busybody, intruder, quidnunc
meddlesome: 4 busy, nosy 5 nosey, pushy 6 prying, snoopy 7 curious 8 busybody, snooping 9 intrusive, kibitzing, obtrusive, officious
in Britain: 5 nebby
meddling: 4 nosy 5 nosey 7 curious 9 intrusive, obtrusive, officious 10 snoopiness
Medea
author: Euripides
brother: 8 Apsyrtus
character: 5 Creon, Jason 6 Aegeus, Glauce
father: 6 Aeetes, Hecate, Hekate
husband: 5 Jason 6 Aegeus
sailed on it: 4 Argo
sister: 5 Aeaea, Circe, Kirke 9 Chalciope
son: 5 Argus 8 Tisander 9 Alcimenes
__ Me Deadly: 4 Kiss
Médée
author: Pierre Corneille
Medeiros: 5 Glenn
Medellín: 4 city, town
locale: 8 Colombia
Medford: 3 Don 4 city, town
locale: 4 Mass. 6 Oregon
school: 5 Tufts
Medgar: 5 Evers
media: 4 news, oils 5 cable, press, radio 7 dailies 9 magazines 10 newspapers, publishing, television
barrage: 4 hype 5 blitz
center: 7 library
initials: 3 ABC, CBS, NBC
messages: 3 ads
monitor: 3 FCC
one of the news ~: 2 TV 5 print, radio 10 television
prefix: 5 multi
room: 3 den
star: 5 celeb 9 celebrity
workers' union: 5 AFTRA
media __: 5 blitz, event, hound, mogul 6 center
__ media: 3 new, via 4 mass, news 5 mixed
Media
today: 4 Iran
medial: 4 mean 6 center
median: 3 avg., par 4 mean, norm 6 middle 7 average, central, halfway 8 midpoint, standard
median __: 5 plane, point, strip
mediate: 5 judge 6 settle, step in, umpire 7 referee, resolve 8 moderate, trade off 9 arbitrate, intercede, interpose, intervene, make a deal, make peace, negotiate, reconcile, take a hand 10 adjudicate, conciliate, propitiate
Mediate, Rocco: 6 golfer
mediation: 9 agreement
agcy.: 4 NLRB
mediator: 5 fixer 6 broker, umpire 7 arbiter, referee 9 appointee, go-between, moderator 10 arbitrator, interceder, negotiator, peacemaker
goal: 5 peace 6 accord 8 contract 9 agreement 10 settlement
medic: 3 doc, EMT 6 aidman, doctor, healer, intern 7 interne 8 corpsman 9 lifesaver, physician
starter: 4 para
medical: 6 iatric 8 curative, iatrical
British ~ journal: 6 Lancet
British ~ org.: 3 NHS
center: 4 hosp. 6 clinic 8 hospital 9 infirmary 10 dispensary
charge: 3 fee
deg.: 2 MD 3 DDS, DMD
discovery: 4 cure 9 treatment
meas.: 2 cc.
org.: 3 AMA
prefix: 4 neur- 5 iatro-, neuro-
research agcy.: 3 CDC, NIH
school subject: 4 anat. 7 anatomy
specialty: 3 ENT
suffix: 4 -itis, -osis 5 -iatry
test: 3 ECG, EEG, EKG, MRI, NMR 4 X-ray
tool: 5 laser 6 lancet
worker: 2 dr., MD, RN 3 LPN 5 nurse 6 doctor, extern, intern 7 interne 8 resident 9 physician
__ medical: 5 major
Medical Center (CBS drama)
cast: James Daly (Dr. Paul Lochner)
Chad Everett (Dr. Joe Gannon)
Medicare org.: 3 SSA
medicaster: 5 quack
medicate: 4 drug 5 treat 6 doctor
medicated: 10 antiseptic
medication: 4 balm, cure, dose, drug, pill 5 salve, serum, tonic 6 elixir, lotion, physic, potion, remedy, tablet 7 capsule, vaccine 8 antidote, liniment, ointment, sedative, tincture 9 antitoxin, injection, treatment 10 antibiotic
amount: 4 dose 6 dosage
Medici in-law: 4 Este
medicinal: 4 herb 6 iatric 8 curative, iatrical, remedial, sanative
application: 5 salve
in taste: 6 bitter
medium: 4 pill 5 serum 6 caplet 7 vaccine
paper: 6 charta
plant: 3 rue 4 aloe, sage 5 jalap, senna, sumac, urena 6 arnica, cassia, croton, ipecac, sumach
plant derivative: 5 aloin
tea: 5 tansy
medicine: 4 balm, cure, dose, drug, pill 5 salve, serum, tonic 6 elixir, lotion, physic, potion, remedy, tablet 7 capsule, science, therapy, vaccine 8 antidote, liniment, ointment, sedative, tincture 9 antitoxin, injection, treatment 10 antibiotic, profession
agency: 3 FDA
chest item: 4 Q-tip 5 floss, gauze 6 iodine 9 boric acid, mouthwash 10 toothpaste
combining form: 5 iatro-, -iatry 7 -iatrics
dispenser: 5 doser
folk ~: 4 lore
give ~ to: 4 dose
holder: 4 vial 5 ampul, phial 6 ampule 7 ampoule
like some ~: 3 OTC
man: 6 healer, shaman
measure: 6 capful
open, as a ~ bottle: 5 uncap
patent ~: 6 elixir 7 panacea
sugarcoated ~: 6 dragée
medicine __: 3 man 4 ball, show
__ medicine: 4 folk 5 cough 6 family, patent, sports 7 nuclear
Medicine Hat: 4 city, town
locale: 6 Canada 7 Alberta
Medicine Man (1992 film)
cast: Lorraine Bracco, Sean Connery
medico: 3 doc 6 doctor, healer 9 physician
medieval: 6 feudal, Gothic 7 buisine 10 antiquated
entertainer: 4 poet 8 minstrel
laborer: 5 helot 6 vassal 7 bondman, chattel, villein
trade union: 4 club
Medina: 4 city, town
locale: 4 Ohio 5 Hejaz, Hijaz 6 Hedjaz 11 Saudi Arabia
resident: 4 Arab 5 Saudi
mediocre: 4 blah, dull, fair, poor, so-so 5 cheap 6 decent 7 average, humdrum, vanilla 8 inferior, middling, moderate, ordinary, passable, standard 9 colorless, tolerable, unnotable 10 fairly good, mainstream, pedestrian, second-rate, uninspired
meditate: 4 mull, muse, pore 5 study, think, weigh 6 ponder 7 reflect 8 cogitate, consider, mull over, ruminate, turn over 9 think over 10 deliberate, introspect, puzzle over
meditation: 6 revery 7 reverie, thought 9 deduction 10 cogitation
aid: 5 chant
breakthrough in ~: 6 satori

ME

exercise: 4 yoga
room: 5 zendo
sound: 2 om
meditative: 6 broody 7 pensive, wistful 8 ruminant, studious
one: 5 muser
sect: 3 Zen
Mediterranean: 3 sea
arm of the ~: 6 Aegean, Ionian
country: 3 Alg., Isr., Leb., Mor., Syr. 5 Egypt, Italy, Libya, Spain, Syria 6 France, Greece, Israel, Turkey 7 Algeria, Lebanon, Morocco, Tunisia
eastern ~: 6 Levant
fish: 5 porgy 6 nonnat 7 anchovy 8 gilthead
gulf: 5 Gabès, Lions, Sidra
island: 3 Sar. 4 Elba 5 Capri, Corfu, Crete, Egadi, Ibiza, Iviza, Malta 6 Candia, Cyprus, Sicily 7 Corsica 8 Sardinia
locale: 3 Afr., Eur. 4 Asia 6 Africa, Europe
port: 4 Gaza, Oran, Yafo 5 Haifa, Jaffa, Tunis 6 Beirut, Naples 8 Beyrouth 10 Marseilles
resort: 4 Nice 7 Antibes
river to the ~: 4 Ebro, Nile 5 Rhone, Tiber 6 Seyhan 7 Orontes
ship: 5 xebec, zebec 6 caique, zebeck 7 chebeck
shrub: 5 caper 8 rosemary
staple: 5 olive
tree: 4 cork 5 carob 6 mastic
wind: 6 solano 7 sirocco 8 levanter
Mediterranean __: 3 Sea 7 climate
__ Méditerranée: 3 Mer
medium: 3 art, par 4 fair, form, mode, norm, seer, size, so-so, tool 5 agent, dance, drama, means, music, organ, sibyl 6 agency, avenue, factor, median, milieu, normal, speech 7 average, channel, habitat, neutral, prophet, psychic, setting, vehicle, writing 8 ambience, middling, moderate, ordinary, painting, passable, standard 9 machinery, mechanism, sculpture, temperate, tolerable, unextreme 10 instrument
device: 5 Ouija, tarot 7 crystal 10 Ouija board
in music: 5 mezzo
skill: 3 ESP
__ medium: 4 mass 7 culture
medium-dry: 3 sec
Medium is the Massage, The
author: Marshall McLuhan
medlar: 4 tree 5 apple 9 crab apple
family: 4 rose
relative: *see* apple
medley: 3 mix 4 brew, hash, olio, stew 5 combo 6 jumble 7 farrago, mélange, mixture, variety 8 mishmash, mixed bag, pastiche 9 composite, diversity, patchwork, potpourri 10 assortment, collection, cumulation, hodgepodge, miscellany, salmagundi
play a ~: 5 segue
medley __: 5 relay
Medley: 4 Bill
__ Me Do: 4 Love
Médoc: 3 red, vin 4 wine 6 claret 7 red wine
origin: 6 France
__-me-down: 4 hand
medregal: 4 fish
__-med student: 3 pre
Medusa
bearer: 4 egis 5 aegis
home: 3 sea 5 ocean
parent: 4 Ceto 7 Phorcys
sister: 6 Stheno 7 Euryale
slayer of ~: 7 Perseus
son: 7 Pegasus 8 Chrysaor
tress: 5 snake
Medwick, Joe: 8 Cardinal 10 outfielder
meed: 6 ration, reward
meek: 3 shy 4 mild, soft, tame, weak, zero 5 lowly, mousy, quiet, timid 6 demure, docile, gentle, humble, modest, mousey, serene 7 lenient, passive, patient, servile, slavish, subdued 8 lamblike, obedient, peaceful, resigned, retiring, tolerant, yielding 9 compliant, diffident, flinching, spineless, tractable 10 forbearing, manageable, obsequious, spiritless, submissive, unassuming
inheritance: 5 Earth
one: 4 lamb 5 sheep
meek as __: 5 a lamb
Meek comic-strip partner: 3 Eek
Meeker: 5 Howie, Ralph
meekness: 7 modesty 8 humility 9 lowliness, timidness 10 diffidence, submission
__ Me Entertain You: 3 Let
meeny preceder: 4 eeny
meerkat: 8 mongoose
milieu: 3 Afr. 6 Africa, desert
meerschaum: 4 pipe 7 mineral
Meese: 2 Ed 5 Edwin
meet: 3 apt, fit, see, sit, tie 4 abut, face, find, good, join, just, race, tilt 5 event, flock, focus, front, greet, match, merge, moral, rally, reach, right, rival, touch, unite 6 accost, adjoin, answer, border, caucus, comply, confab, engage, fulfil, gather, handle, huddle, link up, make up, muster, powwow, proper, redeem, rise to, timely 7 collide, condign, conform, connect, contact, contest, convene, do lunch, fitting, fulfill, qualify, receive, run into, satisfy, session, tourney, welcome 8 adhere to, apposite, approach, assemble, bump into, carry out, chance on, coincide, come up to, confront, converge, cope with, deal with, deserved, face up to, happen on, keep pace, suitable 9 discharge, encounter, expedient, forgather, get to know, intersect, juxtapose, measure up, opportune, road rally, run across, stand up to 10 applicable, chance upon, come across, comply with, congregate, convention, engagement, experience, get a hold of, hook up with, keep up with, rendezvous, tournament
again: 5 resee, resit
a raise: 3 see 4 call
halfway: 7 mediate 9 arbitrate, negotiate, reconcile 10 compromise, conciliate
head on: 4 face 8 confront, cope with, deal with
make ends ~: 3 eke 4 live, save 5 skimp, stint 6 eke out 7 subsist
one's enemy: 4 face 6 attack, line up, take on 7 assault 9 fight with
participant: 5 racer 6 runner 8 sprinter
requirements: 2 do 4 pass, suit 5 serve 7 fulfill, qualify, satisfy
segment: 3 run 4 race 5 event 6 sprint
starter: 4 help
with: 3 see 4 spot 5 taste 6 endure, fall on, locate, suffer 7 receive, run into, undergo 8 come upon, fall upon 9 encounter 10 experience
meet __: 7 halfway
__ meet: 4 swap 5 track
...meet __ coming...: 5 a body
Meet __ Black: 3 Joe
Meet __ Doe: 4 John
Meet __ St. Louis: 4 Me in
Meet Corliss Archer: 9 radio show
meeting: 4 conf., conv., date, sess., talk 5 forum, Q and A, rally, tryst 6 caucus, confab, huddle, parley, powwow 7 contact, hearing, joining, reunion, session, turnout 8 assembly, audience, conclave, congress, crossing, junction, juncture, showdown 9 concourse, confluent, encounter, gathering, reception, symposium 10 cattle call, conference, confluence, contiguity, convention, convergent, discussion, engagement, rendezvous
attend a ~: 3 sit
call a ~: 6 gather, muster, summon 7 convene, convoke, marshal 8 assemble
ender: 5 house
have another ~ with: 5 resee
hold a ~: 3 sit 4 call 5 rally 6 confer, gather, muster, summon 7 conduct, convene, convoke 8 assemble 10 congregate
in a ~: 4 busy
nautical ~: 3 gam
never ~: 8 parallel
of the minds: 6 accord 7 concord, harmony 9 agreement, consensus
outline: 6 agenda
place: 3 hub 5 forum, haunt
plan: 6 agenda
run the ~: 5 chair 7 preside
secret ~: 5 tryst 10 rendezvous
the quota: 8 adequate 10 acceptable, sufficient
unpleasant ~: 5 run-in
__ meeting: 4 camp, mass, tent, town 6 prayer, summit
__-meeting: 4 go-to
meeting of the __: 5 minds
Meet Joe Black (1998 film)
cast: Claire Forlani, Anthony Hopkins, Brad Pitt
director: Martin Brest
Meet John Doe (1941 film)
cast: Gary Cooper, Barbara Stanwyck
composer: Dimitri Tiomkin
director: Frank Capra
Meet Me Half Way (1987 song)
artist: Kenny Loggins
Meet Me in St. Louis (1944 film)
cast: Mary Astor, Judy Garland, Margaret O'Brien
director: Vincente Minnelli
meetness: 8 justness 9 propriety
meet one's __: 5 match
__ Meets Girl: 3 Boy
Meet the Fockers (2004 film)
cast: Robert De Niro, Dustin Hoffman, Teri Polo, Ben Stiller, Barbra Streisand
Meet the Parents (2000 film)
cast: Blythe Danner, Robert De Niro, Teri Polo, Ben Stiller
cat: 6 Mr. Jinx
Meet the Press (NBC news)
host: Tom Brokaw, Ned Brooks, David Gregory, Marvin Kalb, Bill Monroe, Roger Mudd, Martha Rountree, Tim Russert, Lawrence Spivak, Garrick Utley, Chris Wallace
Mefistofele: 5 opera
composer: Arrigo Boito
role: 5 Elena, Faust, Marta 6 Wagner 10 Margherita
setting: 6 Greece, Heaven 7 Germany
Meg: 4 Ryan 5 Tilly 6 Foster, Mallon 8 Wolitzer
daughter: 4 Demi
sister: 2 Jo 3 Amy 4 Beth
mega: 4 huge, much
megacorporation: 5 giant, trust 9 syndicate
megalomaniac's craving: 5 power
megalopolis: 4 city
Megan: 3 Fox 7 Follows
megaphone
inventor: 6 Edison
like a ~: 5 conic 7 conical
megastar: 4 idol
megatherian: 3 big
__ Me Gently: 4 Rock
megilla: 4 tale
Meg Merrilies
author: John Keats
Megna: 4 John
__ Me Go, Lover: 3 Let
megrim: 8 headache
__ Me Half Way: 4 Meet
Mehitabel: 3 cat
friend: 5 Archy, roach 9 cockroach
Mehta: 3 Ved 5 Zubin
successor: 5 Masur
Mehta, Ved: 6 Indian, writer
Mehta, Zubin: 6 Indian 9 conductor
__ Meigs: 4 Fort
__ mein: 4 chow
__ me in!: 3 Let 4 Deal 5 Count
Mein Gott!: 3 ach
Mein Herr Marquis: 4 aria
Meins: 3 Gus
__ Me in St. Louis: 4 Meet
__ Me in the Morning: 5 Touch
Meir, Golda: 2 P.M. 7 Israeli
predecessor: 6 Eshkol
successor: 5 Rabin
__ Me Irresponsible: 4 Call
Meisner: 5 Randy
__ Meistersinger: 3 Die
Meitner, Lise: 9 physicist, scientist
__ Me Kangaroo Down, Sport: 3 Tie
__ Me Kate: 4 Kiss
Mekka: 5 Eddie
Mekong: 5 Delta, river
locale: 4 Laos 5 China 7 Myanmar, Vietnam 8 Thailand

ME

Mel: **3** Ott **4** Hein **5** Allen, Blanc, Tormé **6** Brooks, Carter, Ferrer, Gibson, Harris, Renfro, Stuart, Tillis **8** McDaniel
Melancholia
engraver: Albrecht Dürer
melancholy: **3** low, woe **4** funk, mood, mopy, pall **5** blahs, blues, dolor, ennui, funky, gloom, grief, moony, mopey **6** droopy, gloomy, misery, sorrow, tedium **7** anguish, boredom, despair, dim view, dismals, doleful, elegiac, emotion, letdown, malaise, pensive, sadness, wistful **8** blue funk, dolorous, glumness, lowering, mournful, saddened, the blues **9** dejection, heartache, pessimism, plaintive **10** deplorable, depression, desolation, despairing, heavy heart, in the dumps, lamentable, loneliness, woefulness
in music: **5** mesto
mood: **4** funk
with ~: **5** sadly
see also gloomy
__ Melancholy: **5** Ode on
Melanesian: **6** Fijian
mélange: **3** mix **4** hash, olio, stew **5** combo **6** jumble, medley **7** farrago, goulash, mixture, variety **8** mishmash, mixed bag, pastiche **9** admixture, pasticcio, patchwork, potpourri **10** assortment, hodgepodge, miscellany, salmagundi
Melanie: **6** Mayron **8** Griffith
last name: Safka
song: Brand New Key (1971)
Lay Down (1970)
spouse: **7** Antonio
to Pittypat: **5** niece
Melba: **5** Moore **6** Nellie
Melba __: **5** sauce, toast
__ Melba: **5** peach, pêche
Melba, Nellie: **4** Dame, diva **6** singer **7** soprano **10** Australian
specialty: **5** opera
melba toast: **5** bread
Melbourne: **4** city, port, town
locale: **7** Florida **9** Australia
river: **5** Yarra
Melcher: **5** Marty **6** Martin
Melchior: **5** magus **7** Lauritz
and others: **4** Magi
colleague: **6** Caspar **9** Balthazar
like ~: **4** wise
Melchior, Lauritz: **5** tenor **6** singer
specialty: **5** opera
meld: **3** mix **4** fuse, link **5** blend, immix, merge, unify **6** mingle **7** connect **8** conflate **9** commingle, integrate **10** amalgamate
melded: **4** mixt **5** fused, mixed **6** merged **7** blended **9** composite
melding: **5** union
melee: **3** ado, row **4** fray, to-do **5** brawl, broil, brush, clash, fight, set-to, storm **6** affray, barney, fracas, ruckus, rumpus, tussle, uproar **7** ruction, scuffle **8** brouhaha, rowdydow, scramble, skirmish **9** brannigan, scrimmage **10** donnybrook, free-for-all, hullabaloo
Melendez: **4** Bill

meliad: **5** nymph
__ Me Like a Rock: **5** Loves
Melina: **8** Mercouri
Melinda: **6** Dillon
meliorate: **5** fix up **6** better, enrich, polish, reform **7** enhance, improve, shape up, sharpen, upgrade **8** spruce up
Melisande
artist: Erté
Melissa: **6** Hayden **7** Gilbert **8** Mathison **9** Etheridge **10** Manchester
Melissa __ Anderson: **3** Sue
Melissa Joan __: **4** Hart
Melitta: **6** coffee
alternative: **5** Sanka, Yuban **7** Folgers, Nescafé, Savarin **9** Hills Bros.
__-mell: **4** pell
Mell: **7** Lazarus
Mellencamp, John Cougar
song: Authority Song (1984)
Check It Out (1988)
Cherry Bomb (1987)
Crumblin' Down (1983)
Get a Leg Up (1991)
Hand to Hold on to (1982)
Hurts So Good (1982)
Jack and Diane (1982)
Key West Intermezzo (1996)
Lonely Ol' Night (1985)
Paper in Fire (1987)
Pink Houses (1983)
Pop Singer (1989)
R.O.C.K. in the U.S.A. (1986)
Small Town (1985)
Wild Night (1994)
mellifluous: **4** rich, soft **5** lyric, round, sweet **6** dulcet, honied, liquid, smooth **7** flowing, melodic, tuneful **8** euphonic **9** melodious **10** euphonical
Mello __: **5** Yello
Mellon: **6** Andrew
Mellonta Tauta
author: Edgar Allan Poe
mellow: **3** age **4** aged, calm, cool, mild, open, rich, ripe, soft **5** juicy, quiet, relax, ripen, staid, stoic, sweet, tasty, tipsy **6** at ease, casual, docile, gentle, go soft, liquid, low-key, mature, placid, relent, season, sedate, serene, smooth, soften, subdue, toothy **7** amiable, at peace, cordial, develop, equable, mollify, musical, offhand, pacific, relaxed, ripened, stoical, subdued, unmoved **8** amicable, carefree, composed, humanize, informal, laid-back, likeable, luscious, peaceful, resonant, seasoned, tranquil **9** collected, congenial, easy-going, impassive, melodious, quiescent, succulent, temperate, unexcited, unruffled **10** come around, full-bodied, nonchalant, settle down, unagitated, unhardened, untroubled
out: **9** lighten up
mellow __: **3** out
mellowed: **6** mature
Mellow Yellow (1966 song)
artist: Donovan
Mello Yello: **3** pop **4** soda **9** soft drink
alternative: ***see*** soft drink

Melmac native: **3** Alf
Melmoth the Wanderer
author: Charles Robert Maturin
melodeon: **5** organ **8** keyboard **10** instrument
part: **4** reed
melodic: **4** soft **5** clear, lyric, sweet, tonal **6** ariose, arioso, dulcet, in tune, mellow, poetic **7** lilting, lyrical, musical, silvery, tuneful **8** poetical, resonant, sonorous **9** agreeable, well-tuned **10** euphonious, harmonious
not ~: **6** atonal
phrase: **4** riff
subject: **4** tema
Melodie d'Amour (1957 song)
artist: Ames Brothers
__ Melodies: **6** Merrie
melodious: **4** soft **5** clear, in key, lyric, on key, sweet, tonal **6** ariose, arioso, dulcet, in tune, mellow, poetic **7** lilting, lyrical, musical, silvery, tuneful **8** poetical, resonant, sonorous **9** agreeable, well-tuned **10** euphonious, harmonious
melodiousness: **7** harmony **8** lyricism
melodist: **6** singer
melodize: **4** sing
melodrama: **4** play **5** genre **7** romance **10** excitement, production
role: **4** hero **6** damsel **7** villain
melodramatic: **5** hammy, hokey, lurid, soapy, stagy, sudsy, teary **6** stagey **8** affected **10** theatrical
cry: **3** oho **4** alas **5** never
get ~: **3** act **5** emote **7** carry on, overact
one: **3** ham
melodramatize: **5** emote
melody: **3** air, lay **4** aria, lilt, pean, raga, riff, song, tema, tune **5** canto, chant, dirge, ditty, lyric, music, paean, sound, theme **6** chorus, strain **7** descant, discant, euphony, harmony, refrain **8** diapason **9** leitmotif
partner: **5** lyric **6** lyrics
recurring ~: **5** motif, thema
Melody: **8** Anderson **9** Patterson
Melody of Love (1955 song)
artist: David Carroll, Four Aces, Billy Vaughan
Melody Ranch: **9** radio show
host: Gene Autry
melon: **4** pepo, pink **5** color, fruit, gourd **6** casaba **7** cassaba, Persian **8** Crenshaw, honeydew, windfall **9** cantaloup **10** cantaloupe
like a ~: **5** juicy
relative: **4** nude **6** damask, salmon **7** apricot **8** flamingo **9** carnation
starter: **4** musk **5** water
throwaway: **4** rind
__ melon: **6** casaba
melonlike fruit: **5** papaw
__ Me Loose: **4** Turn
Melos: **4** isle **6** island
Melpomene: **4** Muse
colleague: ***see*** Muse
parent: **4** Zeus **9** Mnemosyne
Melrose: **4** city, town
locale: **4** Mass.
Melrose Park: **4** city, town
locale: **8** Illinois

Melrose Place (Fox drama)
cast: Thomas Calabro (Michael Mancini)
Rob Estes (Kyle McBride)
Heather Locklear (Amanda Woodward)
Grant Show (Jake Hanson)
Andrew Shue (Billy Campbell)
Courtney Thorne-Smith (Alison Parker)
Jack Wagner (Peter Burns)
Mel's Diner waitress: **3** Flo **4** Vera **5** Alice
melt: **3** run **4** fade, fuse, join, thaw, warm **5** deice, touch, yield **6** ablate, disarm, give in, relent, render, scorch, soften, vanish, warm up **7** diffuse, liquefy, liquify **8** disperse, dissolve, evanesce, fluidize, unfreeze **9** blend into, disappear **10** deliquesce
away: **3** die **4** fade, thaw **9** dissipate
down: **4** heat **6** render
ender: **3** age **4** down
into: **5** merge
starter: **4** snow
together: **4** weld **5** blend
__ melt: **4** tuna **5** patty
meltdown: **9** emergency
site: **4** core **7** reactor
melted: **6** fusile, liquid, molten
melting __: **3** pot **5** point
Melton: **3** Sid
Melvil: **5** Dewey
Melville: **6** Cooper, Herman **9** Shavelson
Melville, Herman: **6** writer
captain: **4** Ahab
setting: **3** sea **5** ocean
work: Benito Cereno
Billy Budd
Moby-Dick
Omoo
Typée
Melvin: **5** Belli, Frank, Laird **6** Calvin, Harold **8** Schwartz
Melvin and Howard (1980 film)
cast: Paul LeMat, Jason Robards, Mary Steenburgen
director: Jonathan Demme
Melvin and the Blue Notes, Harold
song: Bad Luck (1975)
If You Don't Know Me by Now (1972)
The Love I Lost (1973)
Wake Up Everybody (1975)
Melvyn: **7** Douglas
mem: **6** Hebrew, letter
predecessor: **5** lamed **6** lamedh
successor: **3** nun
__ Me Madam: **4** Call
member: **3** arm, leg, toe **4** beam, foot, hand, limb, link, part, unit, wing **5** bough, digit, organ, shoot **6** branch, finger, joiner **7** chapter, element, segment **8** division **9** affiliate, appendage, associate, component, extremity, layperson **10** legislator
member __: **4** firm
__ member: **7** charter
Member of the Wedding, The
author: Carson McCullers
Members __: **4** Only
membership: **4** body, club, roll **6** league, roster **7** company,

ME

fellows, society 9 personnel
fee: 4 dues
have a ~ card: 6 belong
membrane: 3 web 4 film, skin, wall 5 palea, sheet 6 intima, lamina, lining, septum, sheath, tissue 10 integument
combining form: 5 chori- 6 chorio-, hymeno-
memento: 5 favor, relic, token 6 trophy 7 vestige 8 keepsake, reminder, souvenir
Memento Mori
author: Muriel Spark
M. Emmet __: 5 Walsh
Memnoch the Devil
author: Anne Rice
memo: 4 list, note 5 aviso 6 advice, letter, notice, record, report 7 jotting, message, missive, tickler 8 dispatch, notation, register, reminder 9 directive
abbr.: 3 FYI 4 ASAP, attn.
high-tech ~: 3 fax 5 e-mail
legal ~: 5 brief 8 abstract
starter: 4 in re
memoir: 3 bio 4 life 5 diary, story 6 record 7 account, journal 9 biography, chronicle, life story, narrative, recountal
__-mémoire: 4 aide
memoirs: 3 bio 9 life story
Memoirs of a Fox-Hunting Man
author: Siegfried Sassoon
memorabilia: 3 ana 6 trivia 9 souvenirs
memorable: 5 great, noted, vivid 6 famous, signal 7 crucial, lasting, notable, special, unusual 8 critical, decisive, enduring, eventful, glorious, haunting, historic, striking 9 bodacious, deathless, important, indelible, momentous, red-letter, top-drawer 10 celebrated, monumental, noteworthy, remarkable
memorandum: 4 list, note 5 aviso 6 advice, letter, notice, record, report 7 jotting, message, missive, tickler 8 dispatch, notation, register, reminder 9 directive
maker: 5 noter
Memorandum, The
author: Václav Havel
__ Memorandum, The: 7 Quiller
memorial: 4 carn 5 cairn, stela, stele 6 column, pillar, plaque, record, statue, tablet 7 obelisk, tribute 8 landmark, monolith, monument 10 dedicatory
__ Memorial: 7 Lincoln 9 Jefferson
Memorial Day race: 4 Indy
Memorial University
location: 6 Canada 7 St. John's
memories
awaken ~: 6 remind
Memories Are Made of This (1955 song)
artist: Dean Martin, Gale Storm
Memories of __: 3 Eld
Memories of a Catholic Girlhood
author: Mary McCarthy
Memories of Another Day
author: Harold Robbins
Memories of Me (1988 film)
cast: Billy Crystal, Alan King
director: Henry Winkler
Memories of Midnight
author: Sidney Sheldon
Memories of You
composer: Eubie Blake, Andy Razaf
memorization process: 4 rote
memorize: 4 know 5 learn 6 retain 8 remember
memorized, have: 4 know
memory: 4 game 6 recall 8 card game, mind's eye 9 anamnesis, awareness, flashback, retention 10 cognizance, impression, retrospect
book: 5 album
combining form: 4 mnem- 5 mnemo-
commit to ~: 4 etch 5 learn
computer ~: 3 ram 4 core 5 EPROM
fetch from ~: 6 call up, recall
flub: 5 lapse
from ~: 6 by rote
jogger: 4 list, note 8 reminder
jog the ~: 4 prod 5 tweak 6 remind
Muse: 5 Mneme
refresh one's ~ in Britain: 5 rub up
site: 6 cortex
trace: 6 engram
unit: 3 bit 4 byte
memory __: 4 bank, lane
__ memory: 4 rote
Memory musical: 4 Cats
memory of God, name meaning: 7 Zachary
Memory of Trees, The (1995 song)
artist: Enya
Memphis: 4 city, font, town 8 typeface
athletes: 6 Tigers
county: 6 Shelby
god: 4 Ptah
locale: 4 Tenn. 5 Egypt 9 Tennessee
pro team: 9 Grizzlies
river: 4 Nile 11 Mississippi
street: 5 Beale
Memphis (song)
artist: Lonnie Mack, Johnny Rivers
Me, Myself, __: 4 and I
Me, Myself & Irene (2000 film)
cast: Jim Carrey, Renée Zellweger
director: Bobby Farrelly, Peter Farrelly
men: 3 he's 6 Messrs.
and women: 4 folk 6 masses, people, public, voters 7 society 8 citizens 9 hoi polloi, personnel
for ~ and women: 4 coed 6 unisex
for ~ only: 4 stag
in blue: 6 police
of ~: 4 masc. 9 masculine
org. for a few good ~: 4 USMC
Men __ From Mars...: 3 Are
Men __ Leave: 4 Don't
__ Men: 3 Tin, Two 4 Mojo, Safe 5 I Hate, King's, Metal 6 Little, Public, Simple 7 Diamond, Mystery
Mena: 6 Suvari
menace: 4 loom, risk, thug 5 bully, daunt, peril, scare 6 danger, hazard, impend, lean on, threat 7 imperil, portend, terrify, torment 8 browbeat, domineer, endanger, frighten, jeopardy, threaten 9 strong-arm, terrorize 10 intimidate, jeopardize, scare stiff
Menachem: 5 Begin
menacing: 4 ugly 5 scary 6 fierce, stormy 7 baleful, harmful, looming, ominous, parlous, serious 8 alarming, coercion, lowering, minatory, perilous, sinister 9 dangerous, frightful, impending 10 forbidding, formidable, pugnacious
be vaguely ~: 4 loom
look: 5 scowl
sound: 3 grr
menad: 9 bacchante
ménage: 9 household
menagerie: 3 zoo
member: 5 beast 6 animal
__ Menagerie, The: 5 Glass
Menahem: 5 Golan
Mena, Juan de: 4 poet 7 Spanish
__ Men and a Baby: 5 Three
Menander: 5 Greek 10 playwright
Men at Arms
author: Evelyn Waugh
__ Men Can't Jump: 5 White
Mencken, H.L.: 6 writer 8 satirist
work: A Book of Burlesques
Damn: A Book of Calumny
In Defense of Women
Newspaper Days
Prejudices
mend: 3 fix, sew 4 cure, darn, gain, heal, knit, vamp 5 fix up, patch, piece, renew, resew, right 6 doctor, reform, repair, revamp, revise, stitch, tape up 7 correct, get well, improve, patch up, rebound, recover, rectify, redress, restore, retouch, service 8 overhaul, renovate 9 get better, refurbish 10 convalesce, recuperate
on the ~: 6 better 7 healing 9 improving 10 recovering
mend __: 6 fences
__ mend: 5 on the
mendacious: 5 false, lying, wrong 6 shifty, tricky, untrue 7 crooked, devious, fibbing 8 delusive, guileful, perjured, spurious 9 deceitful, deceptive, dishonest, erroneous, insincere, paltering 10 ungrounded, untruthful
mendacity: 3 fib, lie 4 tale 5 lying 6 dupery 7 falsity, untruth, whapper, whopper 9 deception, falsehood 10 dishonesty
Mendeleev, Dmitri: 7 chemist, Russian
mendelevium: 7 element
Mendel, Gregor: 8 botanist 9 biologist, scientist
Mendelssohn: 5 Felix, Moses
Mendelssohn, Felix: 6 German 8 composer
work: Hebrides Overture
Italian Symphony
A Midsummer Night's Dream
Ruy Blas Overture
Scottish Symphony
Songs Without Words
St. Paul
Trumpet Overture
Mendelssohn, Moses: 11 philosopher
mender: 6 healer
target: 4 hole
Mendes: 3 Eva, Sam 6 Sérgio
Mendes & Brasil '66, Sérgio
song: The Fool on the Hill (1968)
The Look of Love (1968)
Never Gonna Let You Go (1983)
Scarborough Fair (1968)
Mendes, Sam Oscar: American Beauty
mendicant: 5 faker, fakir, faqir, friar 6 beggar, faquir, pauper 7 have-not
desire: 4 alms
home: 6 friary
mendicate: 3 beg 9 impetrate
__-mending: 5 fence
Mending Wall: 4 poem
author: Robert Frost
Mendocino: 4 cape
locale: 10 California
Men Don't Leave (1990 film)
cast: Joan Cusack, Jessica Lange
__ Men Don't Wear Plaid: 4 Dead
Me neither!: 4 Nor I
Menelaus
brother: 9 Agamemnon
daughter: 8 Hermione
parent: 6 Aerope, Atreus
wife: 5 Helen
mene, mene, __, upharsin: 5 tekel
Menen, Aubrey: 6 writer 7 British
menhaden: 4 fish, pogy
cousin: 4 shad
menial: 3 low 4 base 5 lowly, slave 6 abject, drudge, flunky, humble, lackey, nobody 7 fawning, flunkey, ignoble, lacquey, servant, servile, slavish 9 degrading, demeaning, groveling, low-status, nonentity 10 obsequious
worker: 4 peon, serf 6 drudge
__ Me Nice: 5 Treat
__ men in a tub: 5 three
Men in Black (1997 film)
cast: Linda Fiorentino, Tommy Lee Jones, Will Smith, Rip Torn
cat: 5 Orion
director: Barry Sonnenfeld
menace: 2 ET 5 alien
Men in Black (1997 song)
artist: Will Smith
Men in My Little Girl's Life, The (1966 song)
artist: Mike Douglas
meniscus: 4 lens 8 crescent
Menjou: 7 Adolphe
Menken: 4 Adah
Men Like Gods
author: H.G. Wells
Menlo Park: 4 city, town
initials: 3 TAE
locale: 9 New Jersey 10 California
name: 4 Alva 6 Edison, Thomas
Mennen
rival: 5 Arrid
Menninger: 4 Karl
Mennonites: 4 sect 5 Amish
meno: 4 less
meno __: 5 mosso
Men of Honor (2000 film)
cast: Robert De Niro, Cuba Gooding Jr., Charlize Theron
__ Me No Flowers: 4 Send
Menomonee, city on the: 9 Milwaukee
Menomonee Falls: 4 city, town
locale: 9 Wisconsin
__ Men on a Horse: 5 Three
__ me no questions...: 3 Ask
__-me-not: 5 touch 6 forget

Menotti, Gian Carlo
work: Amahl and the Night Visitors
___ Men Out: 5 Eight
mens ___: 3 rea
mens ___ in corpore sano: 4 sana
Mensa: 4 club
like a ~ member: 5 smart
member: 5 brain 6 genius
qualifier: 6 IQ test
mensch: 3 man 7 good egg
mense: 8 civility 9 propriety 10 discretion
Men's Lives
author: Peter Matthiessen
men's org.: 4 YMCA, YMHA
mens sana in corpore ___: 4 sano
...___ men's souls: 3 try
Mentadent: 10 toothpaste
alternative: *see* toothpaste
mental: 7 psychic 8 cerebral, rational, thinking 9 reasoning 10 subjective, subliminal, telepathic
ability: 3 ken 4 wits 6 brains, reason 9 knowledge
discipline: 4 will, yoga
faculties: 4 mind 5 sense 6 brains, reason, wisdom 8 judgment, lucidity, sagacity, sapience 9 intellect 10 perception
giant: 3 ace 4 whiz 5 brain 6 genius 7 egghead, prodigy, thinker 8 Einstein, highbrow, virtuoso 10 mastermind
health: 6 sanity
impression: 5 image 6 memory, vision
invention: 7 figment
picture: 4 idea 5 image 6 memory, vision 7 concept
state: 4 mood 6 esprit, fettle 7 emotion 8 attitude
mental ___: 3 age 5 giant, image 6 health
mentalist asset: 3 ESP
mentality: 2 IQ 3 wit 4 head, mind, wits 5 brain 6 acumen, brains, makeup, reason, smarts 7 mindset, outlook 8 attitude 9 character, intellect 10 brainpower, gray matter
___ mentality: 4 herd 5 siege
mentally: 8 inwardly
Men, The (1950 film)
cast: Marlon Brando, Teresa Wright
menthol, with: 5 minty
mention: 3 say 4 cite, name, note, plug, tell 5 infer, quote, refer, state, touch, voice 6 adduce, advert, broach, hint at, impart, notice, recite, remark, report, reveal 7 bring up, comment, discuss, divulge, itemize, observe, recount, refer to, speak of, specify, suggest, touch on, tribute 8 acquaint, allude to, allusion, citation, disclose, footnote, intimate, point out, throw out 9 enumerate, make known, recognize, reference, statement, touch upon 10 speak about
again: 5 resay
favorable ~: 4 plug, puff
not to ~: 3 and 4 also, plus 7 besides 8 as well as
___ mention: 5 not to
mentioned: 6 spoken
heretofore ~: 5 above
starter: 5 afore
those not ~: 6 others
mentioning: 9 reference
keep ~: 5 rub in
not worth ~: 5 minor, petty 7 trivial 8 trifling 9 small-time 10 incidental
mentis, compos: 4 sane 5 lucid, right, sound
mentor: 4 guru, sage 5 coach, guide, tutor 6 lector, pundit 7 adviser, advisor, teacher, trainer 8 educator 9 abecedary, counselor 10 connection, instructor
charge: 7 protégé, student, trainee
Mentor: 4 city, town
father: 8 Heracles
locale: 4 Ohio
Mentos
alternative: 5 Certs 6 Binaca, Tic Tac 7 Altoids, Clorets, Dentyne
menu: 4 diet, fare, list 5 carte, table 6 dishes 7 cuisine 10 bill of fare, gastronomy
kind of ~: 5 pop up
lighten one's ~: 4 diet
phrase: 3 à la 5 au jus 6 du jour
selection: 4 soup 5 order, salad 6 course, entrée 7 dessert
symbol: 4 icon
menudo: 4 soup
ingredient: 5 tripe
Menuhin, Yehudi: 9 violinist
contemporary: 5 Stern
Men With Guns (1998 film)
director: John Sayles
Menzies: 7 Heather
___ Me On: 4 Lead
___ Me or Leave Me: 4 Love
___ me out!: 4 Hear
___ Me Out to the Ball Game: 4 Take
meow: 9 caterwaul
___ meow: 4 cat's
Meow ___: 3 Mix
Mephistopheles: 5 Devil, Satan 7 Lucifer
forte: 4 evil
Mephistophelian: 3 bad 4 evil 5 cruel 6 wicked 7 demonic, hellish, satanic 8 daemonic, demoniac, devilish, diabolic, fiendish, infernal 9 demonical, nefarious, satanical 10 diabolical, maleficent, unhallowed
Mephisto Waltz
composer: Franz Liszt
Mephisto Waltz, The (1971 film)
cast: Alan Alda, Jacqueline Bisset
mephitic: 4 foul, rank 5 fetid, reeky 6 foetid, smelly, stinky 7 noisome, noxious, odorous, reeking 8 stinking 10 malodorous
mephitis: 3 gas 6 stench
___ mer: 5 mal de
Merc
rival: 5 Chevy, COMEX
mercantile: 8 economic 10 commercial
mercantilism: 5 trade
Mercator: 8 Gerardus 9 Gerhardus
Mercator, Gerhardus: 7 Flemish 12 cartographer
creation: 3 map 5 atlas
Merce: 10 Cunningham
Merced: 4 city, town
locale: 10 California
Mercedario: 4 peak 5 mount 8 mountain
locale: 9 Argentina
Mercedes: 5 Ruehl 11 McCambridge
Mercedes-Benz: 3 car 4 auto 6 German 10 automobile
category: 6 A class, E class
competitor: 3 BMW 4 Audi 5 Lexus 8 Infiniti
mercenary: 5 ninja, venal 6 grabby, greedy, rotten, sordid, stingy 7 corrupt, fighter, selfish, soldier, warrior 8 bribable, covetous, grasping, hireling, ungiving 9 legionary, unethical, warmonger 10 adventurer, avaricious, commercial
job: 6 combat
Mercer: 5 Mabel 6 Johnny, Marian 9 Ellington
Mercer Island: 4 city, town
locale: 10 Washington
Mercer University's home: 5 Macon
merchandise: 4 line, sell, vend 5 goods, stock, trade, wares 6 deal in, job lot, lading, market, retail 7 freight, produce, product, promote, seconds, staples 9 advertise, publicize, traffic in, wholesale
group: 3 lot
ID: 3 SKU, UPC
outlet: 3 mkt. 4 shop 5 store 6 market 8 boutique
piece of ~: 4 ware
shrinkage: 5 theft
warning: 4 as is
Merchandise ___: 4 Mart
merchandiser: 6 broker, dealer, jobber, seller, trader, vender, vendor 8 marketer, retailer 10 wholesaler
___ merchandiser: 4 mass
merchant: 6 broker, dealer, grocer, jobber, seller, trader, vender, vendor 7 shipper 8 exporter, operator, retailer 9 consigner 10 franchisee, shopkeeper, trafficker, wholesaler
guild: 5 hansa, hanse
help the ~: 3 buy
name meaning ~: 7 Kaufman
ship: 6 argosy, carack, trader 7 carrack, clipper, galleon 8 schooner 9 freighter 10 brigantine, tea clipper
wholesale ~: 6 jobber
merchant ___: 4 bank, flag, ship 5 guild 6 marine, prince, seaman, vessel
Merchant: 6 Ismail, Vivien 7 Natalie
Merchant, Natalie
song: Carnival (1995)
Jealousy (1996)
Kind & Generous (1998)
Wonder (1996)
Merchant of Venice, The: 4 play
author: William Shakespeare
character: 5 Gobbo, Tubal 6 Portia 7 Antonio, Jessica, Lorenzo, Nerissa, Shylock 8 Bassanio, Gratiano
merchantry: 5 trade
___ Merchants, The: 5 Dream
merci: 6 French, thanks 7 gracias, spasibo 8 thank you
___ Mercies: 6 Tender
merciful: 3 lax 4 easy, good, kind, mild, soft 5 loose 6 benign, decent, gentle, humane, kindly, tender 7 clement, lenient, liberal, pitying, ruthful, sparing 8 all heart, empathic, flexible, generous, gracious, laid-back, placable, tolerant 9 assuasive, compliant, easygoing, forgiving, indulgent, pardoning 10 altruistic, beneficent, benevolent, charitable, forbearing, permissive, unexacting
be ~: 5 spare 6 relent 10 have a heart
mercifulness: 4 pity 5 grace 6 lenity, pardon 7 charity, quarter, release 8 clemency, kindness, lenience, leniency 9 tolerance 10 compassion, gentleness
merciless: 4 grim, hard, iron, mean 5 cruel, harsh, nasty, stony, tough 6 animal, brutal, fierce, savage, severe, stoney, unkind, wanton 7 beastly, callous, hurtful, onerous, vicious 8 barbaric, fiendish, inhumane, pitiless, ruthless, sadistic, vengeful 9 barbarian, barbarous, cutthroat, dog-eat-dog, ferocious, heartless, inclement, monstrous, truculent, unfeeling, unpitying, unsparing 10 implacable, inexorable, ironfisted, relentless, unmerciful, unyielding, vindictive
mercilessly: 4 hard
mercilessness: 7 cruelty 8 hardness
Merck
competitor: 5 Glaxo, Lilly 6 Pfizer
Merckx: 4 Eddy
Mercouri: 6 Melina
Mercredi: 6 French 9 Wednesday
follower: 5 Jeudi
preceder: 5 Mardi
Mercure
composer: Erik Satie
mercurial: 4 yo-yo 5 fluid, moody, quick 6 fickle, mobile, uneven 7 erratic, flighty, mutable, protean 8 shifting, ticklish, unstable, unsteady, variable, volatile, wavering 9 excitable, impulsive, uncertain, up-and-down, vagarious 10 capricious, changeable, inconstant
mercury: 5 azoth, metal 6 liquid 7 element
alloy: 7 amalgam
ore: 8 cinnabar
mercury-___ lamp: 5 vapor
Mercury: 3 car, deo, god, orb 4 auto, Ford 7 Freddie 10 automobile
astronaut: 5 Glenn 6 Cooper 7 Grissom, Schirra, Shepard, Slayton 9 Carpenter, John Glenn 10 Gus Grissom
equivalent: 6 Hermes
father: 7 Jupiter
follower: 6 Gemini
model: 4 Lynx 5 Capri, Comet, Milan, sable, Topaz 6 Bobcat, Cougar, Meteor, Tracer, Zephyr 7 Cougars, Mariner, Marquis, Monarch, Montego, Voyager 8 Marauder, Medalist, Monterey, Mystique, Park Lane, Villager 9 Montclair 10 Colony Park 11 Mountaineer
neighbor: 5 Venus
org.: 4 NASA

Mercury __: 4 dime 6 Rising
Mercury News: 5 paper 9 newspaper
locale: 7 San Jose
Mercury Rising (1998 film)
cast: Alec Baldwin, Bruce Willis
Mercury Theatre
name: Orson Welles
Mercutio
friend: 5 Romeo
mercy: 4 pity 5 grace 6 lenity, pardon 7 charity, quarter 8 blessing, clemency, humanity, kindness, lenience, leniency, mildness, sympathy 9 tolerance 10 compassion, generosity, gentleness, kindliness, tenderness
show ~: 4 pity 5 spare 6 relent 10 sympathize
Mercy!: 4 oh my 5 lordy
Mercy Mercy Me (song)
artist: Marvin Gaye, Robert Palmer
Mercy, Mercy, Mercy (1967 song)
artist: Buckinghams
...mercy on such __: 4 as we
mere: 4 just, lake, pond, pool, pure, very 5 lough, scant, sheer, small, utter 6 measly, paltry, simple, simply, slight 8 trifling 9 unadorned 10 negligible
combining form: 4 psil- 5 psilo-
mère: 6 French, mother
brother: 5 oncle
partner: 4 père
Meredith: 3 Don, Lee 6 Baxter, George, MacRae, Vieira 7 Burgess, Willson
Meredith __-Birney: 6 Baxter
Meredith, Burgess: 5 actor
spouse: Paulette Goddard
TV: Batman
Meredith, George: 6 writer 7 British
work: The Egoist
The Ordeal of Richard Feverel
Rhoda Fleming
merely: 3 but 4 just, only 6 purely, simply, solely 10 nothing but
merengue: 5 dance 7 Haitian 9 Dominican
merest: 7 minimum 8 littlest 9 narrowest
bit: 4 wisp
meretricious: 4 sham 5 bogus, gaudy, phony, showy, tacky 6 flashy, garish, phoney, tawdry, tinsel, trashy, untrue 7 chintzy, glaring 8 spurious 9 insincere
merganser: 4 bird, duck, fowl, smew
relative: *see* duck
merge: 3 mix, wed 4 band, fuse, join, meet, meld, pool, sign 5 blend, focus, immix, marry, tie in, unify, unite 6 cement, cohere, commix, embody, gather, imbody, mingle, team up 7 combine, network 8 assemble, coalesce, converge, cumulate, federate, intermix, road sign 9 commingle, integrate, syndicate 10 amalgamate, centralize, join forces, synthesize
(into): 4 melt
merger: 3 LBO 4 deal 5 union 6 buyout 8 marriage, takeover
merging: 7 joining 8 blending 10 convergent
__ Me, Rhonda: 4 Help
Meriden: 4 city, town
locale: 4 Conn.
meridian: 4 acme, apex, noon, peak 5 crest 6 apogee, summit, zenith 8 high noon, pinnacle
__ meridian: 5 prime
Meridian: 4 city, town
author: Alice Walker
locale: 4 Miss. 5 Idaho 10 Washington
__ meridiem: 4 ante, post
meridiem, ante: 7 morning
Mérimée, Prosper: 6 French, writer
work: Carmen
meringue: 6 pastry 7 dessert
ingredient: 3 egg 8 egg white
it's not in ~: 4 yolk 7 egg yolk
like ~: 4 eggy 6 beaten
make ~: 4 whip
__ meringue pie: 5 lemon
merino: 5 sheep 6 fabric
relative: *see* sheep
merit: 4 earn, rate 5 honor, title, value, worth 6 beauty, credit, reward, status, virtue 7 benefit, deserve, dignity, justify, quality, stature, warrant 8 goodness 9 advantage 10 excellence, have coming, worthiness
artistic ~: 5 vertu, virtu
award: 5 badge, bonus
merit __: 3 pay 5 badge, raise 6 system
merit badge
holder: 4 sash
org.: 3 BSA
merited: 3 due 4 just 5 right 8 deserved, rightful
meritorious: 5 moral, noble 6 worthy 8 laudable, virtuous 9 admirable, deserving, estimable, excellent, exemplary, righteous
meritoriously: 4 well
Meriwether: 3 Lee 5 Lewis
Merkel: 3 Una 6 Angela
merl: 4 bird 9 blackbird
Merl: 6 Reagle
merle: 4 bird, gray, grey 6 bluish 7 blueish 9 blackbird
relative: *see* gray color
Merle: 6 Miller, Oberon 7 Haggard
Merle Norman: 6 makeup
alternative: *see* cosmetic brand
merlin: 4 bird
Merlin: 5 Olsen 6 wizard 8 conjurer, conjuror
Merlot: 4 wine 5 grape
relative: *see* wine
mermaid: 6 biform
feature: 4 tail
habitat: 3 sea 5 ocean
Mermaids (1990 film)
cast: Cher, Bob Hoskins, Winona Ryder
__ Mermaid, The: 6 Little
Merman, Ethel: 6 singer
role: 4 Reno 5 Annie, Mesta, Perle 10 Perle Mesta
spouse: Ernest Borgnine
mero: 4 fish 7 grouper
Merope: 4 star 6 Pleiad
father: 5 Atlas
husband: 8 Sisyphus
Merops: 4 seer
Merriam: 3 Eve
Merrick: 4 city, town 5 David
author: Anne Rice
locale: 7 New York
merrie __ England: 4 olde
Merrie Melodies name: 4 Bugs, Fudd, Pepe 5 Daffy, Elmer, Porky 6 Tweety 9 Sylvester
Merrifield, Robert: 7 chemist 8 Nobelist
Merrilee: 4 Rush
Merrill: 4 Dina, Gary 5 James, Stump 6 Robert 7 Charles
partner: 5 Beane, Lynch, Smith 6 Fenner, Pierce
Merrill, Dina: 7 actress
spouse: Cliff Robertson
Merrill, James: 6 writer
work: Divine Comedies
Merrill, Robert: 6 singer 8 baritone, barytone
specialty: 5 opera
Merrillville: 4 city, town
locale: 7 Indiana
merrily: 5 gaily, gayly
Merrily we __ along: 4 roll
Merrimac: 4 boat, ship 8 ironclad
Merrimack: 4 city, town 5 river
city on the ~: 6 Lowell, Nashua 7 Concord
Merriman, Nan: 5 mezzo 6 singer
specialty: 5 opera
merriment: 3 fun, joy 4 glee 5 cheer, laugh, mirth, sport 6 frolic, gaiety, gayety, laughs, levity 7 gayness, jollity, revelry, triumph 8 felicity, hilarity, jocosity, laughter, pleasure 9 amusement, enjoyment, festivity, happiness, jocundity, joviality 10 buffoonery, exultation, jocularity, risibility
Merritt Island: 4 city, town
locale: 7 Florida
Merrivale, Henry: 3 Sir
__ Merriweather Post: 8 Marjorie
merry: 3 fun, gay 4 glad 5 happy, jolly, light, sunny, tipsy 6 blithe, bright, cheery, festal, genial, jocose, jocund, jovial, joyful, joyous, lively, upbeat 7 amusing, chipper, festive, gleeful, jesting, jocular, playful, pleased, rocking, romping, tickled 8 blissful, carefree, cheerful, ecstatic, euphoric, exultant, giggling, grooving, humorous, jubilant, laughing, mirthful, sporting, sportive, thrilled 9 convivial, delighted, enjoyable, fun-loving, hilarious, lightsome, overjoyed, rejoicing, vivacious 10 flying high, frolicsome, optimistic, rollicking, skylarking, uproarious
ender: 5 maker 6 making 7 thought
in music: 7 festoso
make ~: 4 play, romp 5 amuse, exult, laugh, party, revel 6 cavort, frolic 7 carouse, rejoice, satisfy 8 live it up 9 celebrate, entertain, have a ball
Merry __, The: 5 Widow
merry-andrew: 5 clown 7 buffoon 9 harlequin
Merry Christmas preceder: 6 ho ho ho
Merry Company
artist: Jan Steen
merry-go-round: 4 ride 5 spree
Merry Madcap: 4 Baer 7 Max Baer
merrymaker: 9 wassailer
merrymaking: 3 fun, joy 4 glee, play 5 cheer, mirth, revel, sport 6 fiesta, frolic, gaiety, gayety, laughs, levity 7 jollity, revelry 8 festival, hilarity, laughter 9 amusement, enjoyment, festivity, happiness, joviality
__ Merry Oldsmobile: 4 In My
Merry Widow, The: 8 operetta
composer: Franz Lehár
role: 4 Zeta 5 Hanna 6 Danilo 7 Glawari
Merry Wives of Windsor, The: 4 play 6 comedy
author: William Shakespeare
role: 3 Nym 4 Ford, Hugh, Page 5 Caius, Evans, Robin 6 Fenton, Pistol, Simple 7 Quickly, Shallow, Slender 8 Anne Page, Bardolph, Falstaff 9 Hugh Evans
Mersey: 5 river
city on the ~: 9 Liverpool
locale: 7 England
Merton: 6 Miller, Robert, Thomas
Merton, Robert: 8 Nobelist 9 economist
Merton, Thomas: 6 writer
work: Mystics and Zen Masters
The Seven Storey Mountain
Mertz: 4 Fred 5 Ethel
Merv: 7 Griffin
Mervyn: 5 LeRoy
Meryl: 6 Streep
mes: 4 mayo 5 abril, enero, julio, junio, marzo, month 6 agosto 7 febrero, octubre, Spanish 9 diciembre, noviembre 10 septiembre
mesa: 4 hill 5 table 7 flattop, lowland, plateau 9 tableland 10 prominence
dweller: 4 Hopi
Mesa: 4 city, town
county: 8 Maricopa
locale: 7 Arizona
Mesa __: 5 Falls, Verde
Mesabi: 5 Range
product: 3 ore 4 iron
workplace: 4 mine
__ Mesa, CA: 5 Costa
Mesa Verde: 4 park
locale: 8 Colorado
sight: 4 ruin
mescal: 4 bean 5 drink 6 cactus 8 beverage
source: 5 agave
mesh: 2 go 3 net, web 4 gybe, jibe, lace, lock, rete 5 agree, catch, gauze, snarl, toils 6 belong, cobweb, engage, fabric, screen, splice, tangle 7 combine, conjoin, connect, ensnare, insnare, lattice, netting, network, weaving 8 coincide, dovetail, entangle 9 harmonize, integrate, interlink, interlock, labyrinth, screening 10 coordinate, interspace, intertwine, interweave
ender: 4 work
fabric: 3 net 4 leno 7 fishnet, netting, tiffany 8 tarlatan
__ Me, Shape Me: 4 Bend
Meshed: 4 city, town
locale: 4 Iran
meshlike: 4 lacy 5 netty
fabric: 5 gauze, tulle
meshy: 7 netlike
__ Me Sing and I'm Happy: 3 Let
Mesmer: 5 Franz
mesmeric: 8 hypnotic

Mesmeric Revelation
author: Edgar Allan Poe
mesmerism: 5 spell 8 hypnosis
mesmerize: 4 grip 5 charm 7 catch up, control, enchant, enthral, inthral 8 enthrall, entrance, inthrall, transfix 9 captivate, fascinate, hypnotize, spellbind
mesmerized: 4 rapt 5 under 6 enrapt 9 bewitched 10 fascinated
mesmerizing: 8 magnetic 9 soporific 10 magnetical
__ Me Softly: 7 Killing
meson: 4 kaon, pion 5 boson 8 particle
place: 4 atom
mesophyte: 5 plant
Mesopotamia
ancient city of ~: 4 Kish 6 Edessa
kingdom: 4 Elam
neighbor: 6 Arabia
region: 5 Sumer
today: 4 Irak, Iraq
Mesozoic: 3 Era
mesquite: 4 tree 5 shrub 6 legume
family: 6 legume
relative: *see* legume tree
treat with ~: 5 smoke
__ mesquite: 5 honey
Mesquite: 4 city, town
locale: 5 Texas
mess: 3 fix, jam, lot 4 food, hash, meal, much, muck, muff, soil, spot 5 botch, chaos, mix-up, sapfu, sight, snafu, snarl, wreck 6 bedlam, fiasco, fright, huddle, jumble, litter, mayhem, muddle, pickle, pigpen, pigsty, plight, scrape, strait, tangle, tinker, tumult, unrest, uproar 7 anarchy, clutter, dilemma, eyesore, farrago, ferment, piggery, problem, screwup, trouble, turmoil 8 bad scene, disarray, dishevel, disorder, mishmash, shambles, upheaval 9 confusion, deep water, dirtiness, mare's nest, mobocracy, profusion 10 difficulty, dining hall, dining room, hodgepodge, miscellany, untidiness
around: 3 toy 4 play 5 dally 6 dabble, dawdle, doodle, fiddle, loiter, potter, putter, tinker, trifle 7 goof off 8 fool with
ender: 3 age 4 mate
gooey ~: 4 glop
in a ~: 7 trapped 10 on the ropes
make a ~: 4 slop 6 litter
make a ~ of: 4 muff 6 ball up, bungle, foul up, muddle 7 butcher 9 mishandle, mismanage
sergeant: 4 cook
unholy ~: 5 havoc 7 debacle 8 collapse, disaster
up: 3 err, mar 4 blow, flub, goof, harm, hurt, muff, muss, ruin, soil 5 botch, dirty, misdo, smear, snarl, spoil, upset 6 blight, bobble, boggle, bollix, bungle, damage, foozle, fumble, jumble, litter, misuse, ruffle, tousle 7 clutter, disrupt, disturb 8 dishevel, disorder, mistreat, mutilate 9 mishandle, mismanage 10 complicate, disarrange, disconcert
(up): 3 gum, mix 4 foul, goof 5 louse 6 bollix
with: 6 pester 7 disturb
(with): 6 fiddle, monkey, tamper, tinker
working in a ~: 4 on KP
mess __: 3 kit 4 call, gear, hall 6 around
message: 3 fax 4 info, line, mail, memo, news, note, wire, word 5 moral, point, sense, telex, theme 6 earful, import, lesson, letter, notice, report 7 epistle, meaning, missive, purport, tidings 8 bulletin, dispatch, telegram 9 directive, radiogram 10 communiqué, memorandum
bearer: 4 aide, page 5 e-mail
combining form: 4 -gram
conceal a ~: 6 encode
concealed: 4 code 6 cipher 10 cryptogram
get the ~: 3 see 4 hear 8 perceive
holder: 5 in-box, pager 6 bottle, letter 8 postcard 9 enveloper
mangle a ~: 6 garble
return a ~: 5 reply
send a ~ to: 4 wire
__ message: 4 text, veto 5 send a
Message from Nam
author: Danielle Steel
Message in a Bottle (1999 film)
cast: Kevin Costner, Paul Newman, Robin Wright
Message in the Bottle, The
author: Walker Percy
Message received: 5 Roger
Message, The
author: John Donne
Message to Michael (1966 song)
artist: Dionne Warwick
messed up: 7 tousled 8 slovenly
messenger: 5 agent, envoy, gofer 6 bearer, gopher, herald, runner 7 carrier, courier, prophet 8 delegate, emissary 9 errand boy, go-between, harbinger, precursor, town crier 10 ambassador, connection, dispatcher, forerunner, missionary
divine ~: 5 angel
Greek ~ of the gods: 4 Iris
name meaning ~: 6 Angela, Angelo
vehicle: 4 bike
messenger __: 3 RNA
Messerschmitt: 5 Willy
mess hall: 10 dining room
amenity: 4 tray
meal: 4 chow, hash
staff: 2 KP
messiah: 5 Mahdi 6 savior 7 saviour 8 redeemer 9 deliverer
Messiah: 8 oratorio
composer: George Frideric Handel
piece: 4 aria
Messick: 3 Don 4 Dale
Messier: 4 Mark
Messina: 3 Jim 4 city, port, town
locale: 5 Italy 6 Sicily
partner: 7 Loggins
Messing, Debra: 7 actress
TV: Ned and Stacey, Will & Grace
__ Mess with Bill: 4 Don't
messy: 4 ugly, wild 5 dirty, dowdy, grimy, tacky, upset 6 blowsy, blowzy, grubby, grungy, sloppy, unneat, untidy 7 awkward, blotchy, blowsed, blowzed, chaotic, jumbled, muddled, rumpled, scruffy, tousled, unclean, unkempt, unswept 8 careless, confused, littered, slapdash, slipshod, slovenly 9 cluttered, difficult, inside-out, ungroomed 10 bothersome, disheveled, disordered, disorderly, disturbing, in disarray, topsy-turvy
one: 4 slob
place: 3 sty 6 pigsty
Mesta: 5 Perle
__ Me, Stupid: 4 Kiss
met: 6 solved 7 reached
hail-fellow well ~: 7 mingler 9 extrovert 10 socializer
not ~: 3 due
seldom ~ with: 6 scarce
Met: 4 NLer 10 opera house
Hall-of-Famer: 6 Seaver
performance: 4 aria, solo 5 opera
singer: 4 alto, bass, diva 5 basso, mezzo, tenor
__ metabolism: 5 basal
metabolism chemical: 3 ADP, ATP
metacarpus: 4 bone
locale: 5 wrist
Metairie: 4 city, town
locale: 9 Louisiana
metal: 3 ore, tin 4 foil, gold, iron, lead, leaf, mail, vein, zinc 5 alloy, brass, ingot, plate, steel 6 cerium, cesium, cobalt, copper, curium, indium, nickel, ormolu, osmium, radium, silver, sodium, solder 7 caesium, casting, fermium, gallium, hafnium, iridium, lithium, mercury, mineral, niobium, rhenium, rhodium, terbium, thorium, uranium, wolfram, yttrium 8 chromium, electrum, francium, hardware, platinum, polonium, rubidium, samarium, scandium, tantalum, thallium, titanium, tungsten, vanadium 9 conductor, lanthanum, magnesium, manganese, neptunium, palladium, plutonium, potassium, rare earth, ruthenium, strontium, tellurium, zirconium 10 gadolinium, molybdenum
bar: 5 ingot
blend: 5 alloy
cloth: 4 lamé
coat with ~: 5 plate
cylinder: 6 gabion
deposit: 3 ore 4 lode, mine
ender: 4 mark, work 6 worker
fastener: 4 bolt, brad, nail 5 rivet, screw, U-bolt
filings: 5 swarf
framework: 5 grate
fuse ~: 4 weld 6 solder
heavy ~: 4 iron, lead 5 armor, brass, music
in heraldry: 8 tincture
mold: 3 pig
mold opening: 5 sprue
precious ~: 4 gold 6 silver 8 platinum
problem: 4 rust 9 corrosion
rare earth ~: 6 cerium, cesium, erbium 7 caesium, holmium, terbium, thulium, yttrium 8 europium, lutetium, samarium, scandium 9 neodymium, ytterbium 10 dysprosium, gadolinium, promethium 12 praseodymium
receptacle: 3 can, pan, pot, tin
refine ~: 5 smelt
refuse: 4 slag 5 dross
shaper: 5 swage
sound: 4 ding, ping, tick 5 clack, clang, clank, click, clink
starter: 3 gun
thin ~: 4 foil 7 coating
treat ~: 6 anneal
worker: 5 smith 7 smelter 8 tinsmith 9 goldsmith
write on ~: 4 etch
yarn: 5 lurex
__ metal: 4 base 5 heavy, sheet
Metalious, Grace: 6 writer
work: Peyton Place
__ Metal Jacket: 4 Full
metallurgy: 7 science
study: 4 ores 6 alloys, metals
metalware: 4 tole
metalworker's
joint: 4 bond 6 solder 8 juncture
metamorphic rock: 5 slate 6 gneiss, schist 9 quartzite
metamorphose: 4 turn 5 alter 6 change, evolve, mutate 7 convert 8 innovate 9 transform, transmute
Metamorphoses
author: Ovid
metamorphosis: 6 change 8 mutation
stage: 4 pupa 5 larva
Metamorphosis, The
author: Franz Kafka
__ me tangere: 4 noli
metaphor: 5 image, trope 6 symbol 7 analogy 8 allegory 10 comparison, similitude
__ metaphor: 5 mixed
metaphysical: 4 deep 6 mystic 7 psychic 8 abstract, abstruse, esoteric, mystical, numinous, profound 9 recondite, spiritual
beings: 5 entia
metaphysics: 10 philosophy
unit: 5 monad
Metaphysics of Morals
author: Immanuel Kant
Me Tarzan, you __!: 4 Jane
metatarsus: 4 bone
locale: 5 ankle
metate, use a: 5 grind
Metcalf: 6 Laurie
Metchnikoff, Elie: 7 Russian 8 Nobelist 9 zoologist
mete: 3 lot 4 deal, dole, give 5 allot, allow, share 6 assign, divide, parcel, ration 7 give out, hand out, measure, portion 8 allocate, boundary, disburse, dispense 9 apportion 10 distribute
out: 5 allot, divvy, issue, share, split 6 assign, ration 7 divvy up, inflict, portion 8 allocate, disburse, dispense, sentence 9 apportion 10 administer, distribute
(out): 4 deal, dish, dole 6 parcel, ration
mete __: 3 out
__ Me Tender: 4 Love
meteor: 6 bolide
impact site: 6 crater
path: 3 arc

shower: 6 Lyrids 7 Cygnids, Leonids 8 Perseids
suffix: 3 -ite
meteor __: 5 swarm 6 shower
Meteor
author: Karel Capek
meteoric: 5 brief, fleet, rapid, swift 6 speedy, sudden 8 dazzling, flashing, fleeting 9 ephemeral, momentary, overnight, transient
meteorology: 7 climate, science, weather
event: 4 tide 5 storm 6 aurora, shower 7 cyclone, tornado, typhoon 8 blizzard 9 hurricane
govt. ~ agcy.: 3 NWS
info: 4 temp 8 forecast
line: 6 isobar, isohel
prefix: 3 aer- 4 aero-, atmo-
region: 5 front, ridge 9 cold front, warm front
unit: 6 degree 9 degree day
zone: 5 clime
meter: 4 beat, feet, lilt, rime 5 gauge, rhyme, swing, tempo 6 rhythm 7 cadence, cadency, measure 9 indicator
cubic ~: 5 stere
fraction: 6 micron
gas ~: 9 indicator
marker: 6 needle
reader: 5 cabby 6 cabbie, gasman
reading: 4 fare
relative: 4 yard
starter: 3 odo, ohm 4 alti, kilo, nano, taxi, volt, watt 5 audio, centi, milli, penta, radio, tacho 6 alkali 7 alcohol
two-foot ~: 6 dipody
user: 4 poet
Welsh ~: 6 cywydd
meter __: 4 maid
__ meter: 3 gas 5 light, water 7 parking, postage
meter-candle: 3 lux
metered vehicle: 3 cab
meter maid, Beatles': 4 Rita
meters
1000 ~: 4 one K
10,000 ~: 4 ten K
1000 square ~: 6 decare
100 square ~: 7 hectare
meth.: 3 sys. 4 syst.
Meth.: 4 Prot.
methane: 6 alkane
liquid ~: 3 LNG
Metheny: 3 Pat
__ Me the Pillow You Dream On: 4 Send
__ Me the Simple Life: 4 Give
__ Me the Way: 4 Show
method: 3 sys., way 4 form, line, mode, plan, syst., tack, wise 5 means, style, trick, usage 6 avenue, course, custom, manner, recipe, schema, scheme, system 7 fashion, formula, measure, process, program, purpose, routine, science, tactics, wrinkle 8 approach, hang of it, practice, strategy 9 expedient, mechanism, procedure, technique, treatment 10 expediency
by what ~: 3 how
methodical: 4 neat, nice, tidy 5 exact, fixed, sound 6 cogent, formal 7 careful, logical, ordered, orderly, planned, precise, regular, tenable 8 accurate, analytic, coherent, habitual, rational, sensible 9 by the book, efficient, organized, pragmatic 10 analytical, consistent, deliberate, economical, meticulous, scrupulous, structured, systematic
methodize: 5 array, order 7 arrange 8 regulate
methodology: 4 mode 6 system
Methuselah: 7 measure, oldster
father: 5 Enoch
fraction: 5 quart 6 magnum 8 jereboam
grandfather: 5 Jared
grandson: 4 Noah
like ~: 3 old 4 aged
son: 6 Lamech
__ Methuselah: 5 old as
meticulous: 4 nice 5 exact, fussy 6 minute, strict 7 careful, correct, finicky, heedful, precise, prudent 8 accurate, cautious, detailed, exacting, finiking, finnicky, methodic, rigorous, thorough, whole-hog 9 assiduous, attentive, exquisite, judicious, observant 10 deliberate, fastidious, particular, scrupulous, soup-to-nuts
meticulously: 8 in detail
meticulousness: 4 care 5 rigor 8 accuracy 9 precision
métier: 3 job 4 area, line, work 5 field, forte, place, trade 6 career 7 calling 8 business, vocation 9 specialty 10 occupation, profession, walk of life
__ me timbers: 6 shiver
Metis: 4 moon
planet: 7 Jupiter
Met Life
competitor: *see* insurance company
__ Me Tonight: 4 Love, Rock 5 Teach
metonymy: 5 trope
Me too!: 5 ditto, so am I, so do I
__ Me to the Church on Time: 3 Get
__ Me to the Moon: 3 Fly
metric
area measure: 3 are 6 decare 7 hectare
prefix: 3 exa- 4 atto-, deci-, deka-, giga-, kilo-, mega-, nano-, peta-, pico-, tera- 5 centi-, femto-, hecto-, micro-, milli-, yocto-, yotta-, zepto-, zetta-
volume measure: 2 cL., dL., hL., kL. 3 daL. 5 liter, stere 9 dekaliter, kiloliter 10 centiliter, hectoliter, milliliter
weight: 2 cg., dg., hg., kg. 3 dag., mcg., ton 4 gram, kilo 5 tonne 8 decigram, dekagram, kilogram 9 centigram, hectogram, microgram, milligram
metric __: 3 ton 6 system
metrical: 6 poetic 8 poetical
foot: 4 iamb 6 dactyl 7 anapest, spondee, trochee
unit: 4 mora
writing: 4 poem 5 poesy, verse
metro: 4 city 6 subway 8 railroad
alternative: 3 bus, cab
area: 3 urb 4 city
ending: 4 plex 5 polis
part of the ~: 5 exurb
Metro: 3 car, Geo 4 auto 10 automobile
Metroliner company: 6 Amtrak
metronome setting: 5 tempo
__ Metropole: 4 Café
metropolis: 4 burg, city, town 7 capital
Metropolis (1926 film)
director: Fritz Lang
metropolitan: 4 city 5 civic, urban 6 bishop, public 9 municipal
Metropolitan: 3 car 4 auto, Nash 10 automobile
Metropolitan __: 4 Life 5 Opera
Mets: 4 nine, team
former home: 4 Shea
home: 6 Queens 7 New York 9 Citi Field
org.: 3 MLB, NLE
rival: *see* baseball team
sport: 8 baseball
mettle: 4 grit, guts 5 heart, moxie, nerve, pluck, spine, spunk, valor 6 morale, spirit, starch 7 bravery, courage, prowess, resolve, stamina 8 audacity, backbone, boldness, gameness 9 character, endurance, fortitude, gallantry 10 confidence, feistiness, resolution
man of ~: 4 hero
mettlesome: 4 bold, game 5 brave, gutsy 6 gritty, heroic, plucky, spunky 7 valiant 8 fearless, heroical, intrepid, spirited 9 dauntless, undaunted, unfearing 10 courageous, undismayed
Metuchen: 4 city, town
locale: 9 New Jersey
Metz: 4 city, town
city near ~: 5 Nancy
locale: 6 France
river: 5 Mosel 7 Moselle
Metzengerstein
author: Edgar Allan Poe
meum et __: 4 tuum
__-me-up: 4 pick
__ me up, Scotty!: 4 Beam
Meursault: 4 wine 5 white
origin: 6 France
Meurthe, city on the: 5 Nancy
Meuse: 4 Maas 5 river
city on the ~: 5 Liege, Namur, Ornes, Sedan 6 Verdun 9 Rotterdam
locale: 6 France 7 Belgium
river to the ~: 3 Lek 4 Waal 6 Sambre
mew: 3 cry 4 bird, gull 7 seabird, seagull 8 hideaway
Mewati: 3 cow 4 bull 6 bovine, cattle
__ Me Why: 4 Tell
__ me with a spoon!: 3 Gag
mewl: 3 cry, sob 4 bawl, pule, wail, weep, yowl 5 whine 6 boohoo, snivel 7 blubber, whimper 9 shed tears
mews: 5 alley
Mex.
locale: 5 N. Amer.
neighbor: 3 Cal, Tex. 4 Ariz.
org.: 3 OAS 4 NATO
see also Mexico
__-Mex: 3 Tex
Mexicali: 4 city, town
locale: 4 Baja 6 Mexico
see also Spanish
Mexicali Rose: 5 oater 7 western
Mexican __: 3 War
Mexican __ bean: 7 jumping
Mexican __ dance: 3 hat
Mexican Spitfire (1939 film)
cast: Lupe Velez
Mexico: 4 gulf 6 nation 7 country
agreement with ~: 5 NAFTA
appetizer: 5 nacho 6 fajita
author: James A. Michener
basket grass: 5 otate
bay: 9 Magdalena
bean: 6 frijol 7 frijole
beer: 6 Corona 8 Dos Equis
bird: 5 potoo
blanket: 6 sarape, serape
city: 4 Apan, Ario, Isla, Kino, León, Muná, Nava, Peto, Ruiz, Tala, Tula, Umán, Xico 5 Acala, Acuña, Ahome, Alamo, Ameca, Canoa, Clara, Ébano, Jalpa, Jamay, Jérez, La Paz, Lerdo, Lerma, Mitla, Motul, Oluta, Palau, Silao, Taxco, Teapa, Tekax, Tepic, Tetla, Ticul, Tlapa, Yaquí 6 Acatic, Ajijic, Aldama, Amozoc, Apaxco, Atempa, Atenco, Atoyac, Autlán, Bochil, Cabada, Cancún, Carmen, Celaya, Chalco, Chemax, Cherán, Chiapa, Chilac, Cocula, Colima, Contla, Cotija, Coyuca, Fortín, García, Guzmán, Iguala, Ixtapa, Izamal, Izúcar, Jacona, Jalapa, Juárez, La Doce, La Joya, La Mira, La Poza, Libres, Loreto, Madera, Madero, Marfil, Meoqui, Mérida, México, Oaxaca, Ozumba, Pánuco, Perote, Poanas, Puebla, Romita, Sayula, Serdán, Tamuín, Tecate, Tecpan, Tepeji, Tixtla, Tlaxco, Toluca, Tonalá, Tuxpam, Tuxpan, Tuxtla, Vindho, Zacapú, Zamora 7 Camargo, Cozumel, Durango, Hidalgo, Linares, Nogales, Tampico, Tijuana, Tizimín 8 Acapulco, Altamira, Alvarado, Cárdenas, Ensenada, Mexicali, Río Bravo, Veracruz, Zaragoza 9 Chihuahua, Guadalupe, Matamoros, Monterrey, Salamanca, San Felipe
condiment: 5 salsa
corn flour: 4 masa
cowboy: 6 charro
critic: 3 Paz
dance: 5 raspa
desert: 7 Sonoran 10 Chihuahuan
essayist: 5 Reyes
explorer: 6 Cortés
export: 4 opal
feline: 6 ocelot
figurine mineral: 4 onyx
fish: 7 garlopa 8 anableps
fruit: 7 chayote 8 eggfruit 9 sapodilla, tomatillo
gulf: 8 Campeche
Gulf of ~ port: 6 Biloxi
hut: 5 jacal
Indian: 3 Mam 4 Maya, Pima, Seri 5 Aztec, Mayan, Nahua, Olmec, Otomi, Yaqui 6 Papago, Toltec 7 Huastec, Mazatec, Yucatec, Zapotec 8 Tarascan 10 Tarahumara

land unit: 6 fanega
language: 4 Maya 5 Aztec, Mayan, Otomi, Yaqui 6 Papago 7 Nahuatl, Spanish 10 Tarahumara
legislature: 6 Senate
meal: 6 flauta
money: 4 peso, tlac 5 tlaco 7 centavo
neighbor: 3 USA 6 Belize 9 Guatemala
Nobelist in Chemistry: 6 Molina
Nobelist in Literature: 3 Paz
Nobelist in Peace: 6 Robles
org.: 3 OAS
painter: 5 Kahlo 6 Rivera 10 Frida Kahlo
pastry: 6 churro
poet: 3 Paz 4 Cruz 5 Nervo, Reyes
political party: 3 PRI
port: 7 Guaymas, Tampico 8 Acapulco, Vera Cruz
prepare ~ beans: 5 refry
promenade: 5 paseo
raccoon: 5 coati
region: 4 Baja
reptile: 3 uta 6 iguana 9 coachwhip
resort: 6 Cancún 7 Cozumel 8 Acapulco
revolutionary: Pancho Villa
river: 5 Yaqui 6 Pánuco 7 Conchos 8 Rio Bravo
rodent: 7 rice rat
sauce: 4 mole
shrub: 6 jojoba 7 goldcup, guayule 8 ocotillo
state of ~: 6 Colima, Oaxaca, Puebla, Sonora 7 Chiapas, Durango, Hidalgo, Jalisco, Morelos, Nayarit, Sinaloa, Tabasco, Yucatán 8 Campeche, Coahuila, Guerrero, Tlaxcala, Veracruz 9 Chihuahua, Michoacán, Nuevo León, Querétaro, Zacatecas
tree: 5 cirio 6 boojum, sapota
volcano: 4 Popo 6 Colima, Toluca 7 Orizaba
weasel: 5 tayra
writer: 5 Rulfo, Yañez 6 Azuela, Guzmán 7 Fuentes
see also Spanish
Mexico City: 4 town 7 capital
newspaper: 5 El Sol
town near ~: 5 Taxco
Meyer: 3 Ray 4 Dina, Russ 5 Levin 6 Debbie, Lansky 8 Nicholas
Meyerbeer, Giacomo: 6 German 8 composer
Meyer, Conrad Ferdinand: 5 Swiss 6 writer
Meyerhof, Otto: 8 Nobelist
Meyers: 3 Ann, Ari
Meyers, Ann
milieu: 5 court
org.: 3 NBA
sport: 10 basketball
Meynell, Alice Thompson: 6 writer 7 British
...__ me your ears: 4 lend
mezz.
alternative: 4 orch.
mezza __: 4 voce
mezza-mezza: 4 so-so
mezzanine: 4 loge, tier 5 floor 6 lounge 7 gallery
mezzo: 4 half 6 medium, middle
mezzo __: 5 forte, piano
mezzo-__: 7 relievo, soprano
mezzo-soprano: 5 Horne, Stade, voice 6 singer 7 Stevens 8 Merriman, Troyanos
mezzotint: 7 engrave, etching 9 engraving
MFA: 3 deg.
__ M for Murder: 4 Dial
mfr.: 4 bldr.
bill: 3 inv.
mg.: 2 wt. 4 meas.
Mg: 4 elem. 7 element 9 magnesium
12 for ~: 4 at. no.
MGM: 6 studio
competitor: *see* movie studio
creation: 4 film 5 movie 7 musical
former ~ head: 4 Loew 5 Mayer
former rival: 3 RKO
mascot: 3 Leo 4 lion
motto word: 3 Ars 5 Artis 6 Gratia
offering: 5 movie
part: 5 Mayer, Metro 7 Goldwyn
sound effect: 4 roar
workplace: 3 lot 10 soundstage
MGM __ Hotel: 5 Grand
MGM Grand
locale: 5 Vegas 8 Las Vegas
mgmt.: 5 admin.
VIP: 3 CEO, CFO, COO 4 pres.
mgr.: 3 ldr. 4 exec., supt. 5 admin., supvr.
mi: 4 note
follower: 2 fa
preceder: 2 re
mi.: 4 meas.
about .62 ~: 2 km. 3 kil.
about 6 billion ~: 4 lt. yr.
Mi __ es su...: 4 casa
__ Mi: 4 Do Re
MI
see Michigan
Mia: 4 Hamm, Sara 6 Farrow 9 Kirschner
sister: 4 Tisa
__ Mia: 4 Cara 5 Mamma
Miami: 4 city, port, town 5 river 6 Indian 7 Amerind
athlete: 4 Cane 7 RedHawk 9 Hurricane
author: Joan Didion
city on the ~: 6 Dayton
conference: 3 MAC 7 Big East
county: 4 Dade 9 Miami-Dade
golf tournament: 5 Doral
locale: 4 Ohio 7 Florida
newspaper: 6 Herald
pro team: 4 Heat 7 Marlins 8 Dolphins
River locale: 4 Ohio
zone: 3 EDT, EST
Miami __: 4 Vice 5 Beach
Miami-__ County: 4 Dade
__ Miami: 3 CSI
Miami Beach: 4 city, town
locale: 7 Florida
Miami of __: 4 Ohio
Miami University
athletes: 8 RedHawks
locale: 4 Ohio 6 Oxford
Miami Vice (NBC drama)
cast: Don Johnson (Det. Sonny Crockett)
Philip Michael Thomas (Det. Ricardo Tubbs)
theme artist: Jan Hammer
miaow sayer: 3 cat 5 tabby
miasma: 5 vapor 9 effluvium
miasmal: 7 noxious
miasmic: 4 fumy 5 gassy 7 odorous 10 pernicious
Miata: 3 car 4 auto 5 Mazda 10 automobile
mib: 5 aggie 6 marble
relative: 5 immie
mica: 4 rock 7 biotite, mineral 9 isinglass, muscovite
Micah
follower: 5 Nahum
preceder: 5 Jonah
son: 4 Ahaz
Micah Clarke
author: Arthur Conan Doyle
Micawber: 7 Wilkins
mice to cats: 4 prey
Mich.
co.: 2 GM
neighbor: 3 Ind., Ont. 4 Ohio, Wisc.
see also Michigan
Michael: 4 Cole, Dorn, Dunn, Gore, Kidd, Mann, Paré, York 5 angel, Apted, Arlen, Biehn, Brown, Caine, Chang, Frayn, Gross, Innes, Jeter, Korda, Moore, Nouri, O'Shea, Ovitz, Palin, Parks, saint, Sarne, Sheen, Smith, Stipe 6 Ansara, Bishop, Bolton, Callan, Cimino, Conrad, Curtiz, Damian, Eisner, Gambon, George, Gordon, Jordan, Keaton, Landon, Lerner, Madsen, McKean, Murphy, Phelps, Powell, Rennie, Rooker, Spence, Spinks, Tucker, Warren, Winner 7 Collins, De Bakey, Douglas, Drayton, Dukakis, Faraday, Jackson, Learned, Lehmann, Murphey, Ontkean, Radford, Ritchie, Wilding 8 Anderson, Corleone, Crawford, Crichton, Dudikoff, McDonald, Moriarty, Redgrave, Richards, Sarrazin, Schenker, Sembello 9 Feinstein, Hutchence, Montaigne, Rosenbaum 10 Caton-Jones, Harrington
author: William Wordsworth
in French: 6 Michel
in Italian: 7 Michele
in Russian: 7 Mikhail
in Spanish: 6 Miguel
sister: 5 Janet 6 La Toya
Michael (1961 song)
artist: Highwaymen
Michael (1996 film)
cast: William Hurt, Andie MacDowell, John Travolta
director: Nora Ephron
dog: 6 Sparky
Michael __-Jones: 5 Caton
Michael __ Thomas: 6 Tilson
Michael Clarke __: 6 Duncan
Michael Clayton (2007 film)
cast: George Clooney, Tilda Swinton
Michael Collins (1996 film)
cast: Liam Neeson, Aidan Quinn, Stephen Rea, Julia Roberts
Michael, George
homeland: England
member of: Wham!
song: Careless Whisper (1984)
A Different Corner (1986)
The Edge of Heaven (1987)
Everything She Wants (1985)
Faith (1987)
Fastlove (1996)
Father Figure (1988)
Freedom (1985)
Heaven Help Me (1989)
I Knew You Were Waiting (1987)
I'm Your Man (1985)
Jesus to a Child (1996)
Kissing a Fool (1988)
Monkey (1988)
One More Try (1988)
Praying for Time (1990)
Too Funky (1992)
Wake Me Up Before You Go-Go (1984)
__ Michael Glaser: 4 Paul
__ Michael Hall: 7 Anthony
Michael J. __: 3 Fox 7 Pollard
Michaelmas __: 3 Day 5 daisy
Michaelmas daisy: 5 aster, plant 6 flower
Michael, Row Your Boat __: 6 Ashore
Michaels: 2 Al 3 Lee 4 Bret 5 Lorne 7 Barbara
Michael Strogoff
author: Jules Verne
Michael Tilson __: 6 Thomas
__-Michael Vincent: 3 Jan
Michaux, Henri: 4 poet 6 French
Michel: 5 Butor 6 Fokine 7 Hartmut, Legrand, Piccoli
in English: 7 Michael
Michelangelo: 6 artist 7 Italian, painter 8 sculptor
sculpture: 5 Pietà
work: 4 arte
see also Italian
Michele: 3 Lee 6 Greene
Michel, Hartmut: 7 chemist 8 Nobelist
Michelin: 4 tire 5 André
rival: 6 Dunlop 7 General, Pirelli 8 Goodrich, Goodyear 9 Firestone 11 Bridgestone
Michelle: 3 Wie 4 Kwan, Mama, Yeoh 7 Johnson 8 Monaghan, Pfeiffer, Phillips, Williams
__ Michelle Gellar: 5 Sarah
Michelob: 4 beer
alternative: *see* beer
Michelson, Albert: 8 Nobelist 9 physicist, scientist
Michener, James A.: 6 writer
work: Alaska
Centennial
Chesapeake
The Covenant
Hawaii
Iberia
Poland
The Source
Space
Tales of the South Pacific
Texas
Mi chiamano Mimi: 4 aria
Michigan: 4 game, lake 5 rummy, state 6 avenue 8 card game
bay: 7 Saginaw
canals: 3 Soo
capital: 7 Lansing
city: 4 Novi, Troy 5 Flint, Niles 6 Adrian, Burton, Canton,

Monroe, Okemos, Paw Paw, Taylor, Walker, Warren **7** Bay City, Clinton, Detroit, Holland, Inkster, Jackson, Lansing, Livonia, Midland, Oak Park, Pontiac, Portage, Redford, Romulus, Saginaw, Trenton, Wyoming **8** Ann Arbor, Dearborn, Ferndale, Harrison, Kentwood, Muskegon, Royal Oak, Westland **9** Allen Park, Hazel Park, Kalamazoo, Marquette, Port Huron, Roseville, Southgate, Waterford, Wyandotte, Ypsilanti **10** Bloomfield, Eastpointe, Garden City, Southfield
college: 4 Alma
conference: 6 Big Ten
Indian: 5 Miami **10** Potawatomi
lake: 4 Erie **5** Black, Huron **6** Beaver, Turtle **8** Houghton, Superior
national park: 10 Isle Royale
neighbor: 3 Ind., Ont., Wis. **4** Minn., Ohio, Wisc. **6** Canada **7** Indiana, Ontario **9** Minnesota, Wisconsin
port: 7 Detroit, Saginaw **8** Green Bay
state bird: 5 robin
state fish: 10 brook trout
state tree: 9 white pine
Michigan __: 4 roll **5** rummy
Michigan City: 4 town
locale: 7 Indiana
Michigan rummy: 4 game **8** card game
Michigan State
athletes: 8 Spartans
conference: 6 Big Ten
Mick: 4 Mars **6** Jagger **9** Fleetwood
Mickelson, Phil: 6 golfer
Mickey: 4 Owen **5** drink, mouse **6** Dolenz, Gilley, Mantle, Rivers, Rooney, Rourke, Wright **8** beverage, Cochrane, Hargitay, Spillane
Mickey __: 4 Finn **5** Mouse
Mickey Finn: 5 drink **8** beverage
Mickey Mouse Club, The
leader: 4 Dodd
member: 5 Cubby, Karen **6** Cheryl, Doreen **7** Annette, Darlene
Mickey Mouse nephew: 5 Morty **6** Ferdie
Mickey's Monkey (1963 song)
artist: Miracles
Mickiewicz, Adam: 4 poet **6** Polish
Micki + Maude (1984 film)
cast: Amy Irving, Dudley Moore, Ann Reinking
director: Blake Edwards
__ Micklin Silver: 4 Joan
Micky: 6 Dolenz
Micmac: 5 tribe **6** Indian **7** Amerind
micraner: 3 ant
micro: 2 PC **8** computer
microbe: 3 bug **4** germ **5** virus **6** amoeba **8** bacillus, pathogen **9** bacterium
microbes: 8 bacteria
microbiology: 7 science
microbrewery product: 3 ale **4** beer
microchip giant: 5 Intel
microfilm: 5 fiche
micromanager concern: 6 detail
Micronesia: 4 isls. **5** isles **7** islands
island: 3 Yap **4** Guam, Truk **5** Nauru, Palau **6** Tuvalu **8** Gilberts, Kiribati, Marianas **9** Carolines, Marshalls
micronutrient: 4 iron, zinc **9** magnesium
microorganism: 3 bug **4** germ, alga **6** aerobe, amoeba, fungus **7** microbe
microorganisms: 8 bacteria
microphone, hidden: 3 bug
microphysics: 7 science
microprocessor
maker: 5 Intel
speed unit: 3 MHz **9** megahertz
microscope
accessory: 5 slide
adjust a ~: 5 focus
part: 4 lens
__ microscope: 3 ion
microscopic: 3 wee **4** baby, puny, tiny **5** bitty, least, small, teeny **6** atomic, bantam, little, minute, peewee, petite, teensy **7** trivial **8** atomical, atomlike **9** invisible, itsy-bitsy, itty-bitty, miniature, minuscule, pint-sized **10** diminutive, teeny-weeny, vest-pocket
amount: 5 trace
Microsoft
CEO: Steve Ballmer
founder: Paul Allen, Bill Gates
product: 3 DOS **4** Bing, Word, Xbox, Zune **5** Basic, Excel, MSN TV, Visio **6** Access, Office **7** Outlook, Windows
rival: 3 IBM **5** Apple
__ Microsystems: 3 Sun
microwave: 3 fix, zap **4** cook, oven, warm
brand: 5 Amana
device: 5 maser, timer
no-no: 4 foil
one way to ~: 5 on low
use a ~: 3 zap **4** bake, cook, warm
mid: 5 among, cadet **6** center, mongst **7** amongst, central, halfway
mid-__: 3 cap **4** rise, size **5** level
mid-__ car: 4 size
mid.: 3 ctr.
'mid: 5 'twixt
Mid-__ Sunday: 4 Lent
midafternoon: 5 three **7** three p.m.
midair, float in: 9 hover. hang
Mid-American Conference
school: 3 NIU **4** Ohio **5** Akron, Miami **6** Toledo **7** Buffalo **8** Marshall **9** Ball State, Kent State
Midas: 4 king **8** Phrygian
father: 7 Gordius
mother: 6 Cybebe, Cybele
son: 8 Anchurus **9** Lityerses
Midas __: 5 touch
midday: 4 noon **6** twelve **10** eight bells
middie: 7 student
counterpart: 5 cadet
sch.: 4 USNA
middle: 3 hub, tum **4** core, mean **5** heart, inner, mezzo, thick, tummy, waist **6** center, inside, marrow, median **7** abdomen, average, between, central, halfway **10** mainstream
combining form: 3 mes- **4** meso- **5** centr- **6** centri-, centro-
ender: 3 man, men **4** brow, most **6** weight
in the ~: 5 'tween **6** inside **9** undecided
in the ~ of: 4 amid **5** among **6** atween, during, mongst **7** amongst, between
of nowhere: 5 limbo, wilds
person: 5 agent **6** broker, jobber **8** mediator **9** go-between
middle __: 3 age, ear **4** name **5** class **6** finger, ground, school **7** manager
middle-__: 4 aged **6** income
middle-__-road: 5 of-the
Middle __: 4 Ages, East, West **7** Eastern, English
Middle-Aged Man on the Flying Trapeze, The
author: James Thurber
Middle Ages
of the ~: 8 medieval **9** mediaeval
Middlecoff, Cary: 6 golfer
Middle Earth
inhabitant: 3 Ent, orc **6** hobbit
Middle East
see Mideast
middleman: 3 rep **5** agent **6** broker, jobber **8** reseller **9** appointee, go-between, negotiant **10** interceder
Middlemarch
author: George Eliot
character: 3 Ben, Ned **4** Dodo, Fred, Rigg, Tyke **5** Caleb, Celia, Garth, Letty, Vincy **6** Cranch, Selina
Middle of the Night
author: Paddy Chayefsky
middle-of-the-road: 7 average, neutral **8** centrist, moderate
Middle of the Road (1984 song)
artist: Pretenders
middle-school grade: 5 ninth **6** eighth **7** seventh
Middlesex: 6 county
locale: 7 England
Middleton, Thomas: 7 British **10** playwright
work: The Changeling
The Roaring Girl
A Trick to Catch the Old One
Middletown
author: Robert Lynd
middling: 2 OK **4** fair, okay, okeh, okey, so-so **6** decent, medium, modest **7** average **8** adequate, all right, inferior, mediocre, moderate, ordinary, passable **9** tolerable, unnotable **10** fairly good
fair to ~: 4 so-so **8** mediocre, moderate **9** tolerable
grade: 3 cee **5** C plus
middy: 5 shirt **6** blouse, sailor **7** jack tar
opponent: 5 cadet
middy __: 6 blouse
Mideast: 6 Levant
airline: 4 El Al
airport: 3 Lod
ancient ~ nomads: 5 Alani
ancient ~ region: 4 Moab **5** Sumer
bay: 6 Abukir
bovine: 6 Baladi, Jaulan
bread: 4 pita
capital: 4 Aden, Doha, Sana **5** Amman, Cairo, Sanaa **6** Bagdad, Beirut, Manama, Muscat, Riyadh, Tehran **7** Baghdad, Teheran **8** Abu Dhabi, Beyrouth, Damascus **9** Jerusalem **10** Kuwait City
coffee cup: 6 finjan
cup holder: 4 zarf, zurf
dam: 5 Aswan
desert: 5 Negeb, Negev, Sinai
dish: 5 pilaf, pilau, pilaw **6** pilaff
dough: 4 filo
emirate: 5 Dibai, Dubai, Katar, Qatar **6** Kuwait
export: 3 oil
federation: 3 UAE
fiddle: 5 rebab
former ~ alliance: 3 UAR
garment: 3 aba **4** abba
grp.: 3 PLO
gulf: 4 Aden, Oman, Suez **5** Akaba, Aqaba, Sidra **7** Arabian, Persian
headgear: 3 fez
head of state: 4 amir, emir **5** ameer, emeer
inn: 5 serai
instrument: 3 oud
language: 5 Farsi **6** Arabic, Hebrew **7** Aramaic, Kurdish, Semitic
liquor: 4 arak, raki **5** rakee **6** arrack
market: 3 suk, suq **4** souk **5** bazar **6** bazaar
messiah: 5 Mahdi
missile: 4 Scud
money: 4 rial **5** dinar **6** shekel, talent
name: 3 Ali
nation: 3 Isr., Leb., Syr. **4** Irak, Iran, Iraq, Oman **5** Egypt, Katar, Qatar, Yemen **6** Israel, Jordan, Kuwait **7** Lebanon
native: 4 Arab, Kurd **5** Adeni, Iraki, Irani, Iraqi, Omani, sabra, Saudi **6** Qatari, Semite, Yemeni **7** Israeli, Kuwaiti **8** Lebanese **9** Jordanian
palace area: 5 haram, harem, harim **6** hareem
pilgrimage: 3 haj **4** hadj, hajj
port: 4 Aden
porter: 5 hamal **6** hammal
region: 4 Gaza **5** Sinai **6** Arabia
religion: 5 Baha'I, Islam **7** Judaism
ruler: 3 aga **4** agha, amir, emir **5** ameer, emeer
shrub: 5 retem
title: 3 aga **4** agha, imam **5** imaum, rebbe
weapon: 3 Uzi
weight: 4 rotl
midevening: 5 eight, seven **7** eight p.m., seven p.m.
midge: 3 bug **4** gnat, pest **6** insect
midget: 4 baby, runt, tiny **5** gnome, small, teeny, weeny **6** bantam, pocket, teensy **8** knee-high **9** miniature, undersize **10** diminutive, homunculus
midi: 5 skirt **10** calf-length
__-midi: 5 après
Midianite king: 4 Reba
midiron: 4 club
Midkiff: 4 Dale
Midland: 4 city, town
locale: 5 Texas **8** Michigan

Midler, Bette: 6 singer 7 actress
film: Beaches (1988)
Big Business (1988)
Down and Out in Beverly Hills (1986)
Drowning Mona (2000)
The First Wives Club (1996)
For the Boys (1991)
Outrageous Fortune (1987)
The Rose (1979)
Ruthless People (1986)
nickname: 5 Miss M
song: Boogie Woogie Bugle Boy (1973)
Do You Want to Dance? (1973)
From a Distance (1990)
The Rose (1980)
Wind Beneath My Wings (1989)
midmonth day: 4 ides
midmorning: 3 ten 4 nine 5 ten a.m. 6 nine a.m.
midnight: 3 jet 5 night
after ~: 4 late 7 morning
approach ~: 5 laten
burn the ~ oil: 4 cram 5 study
follower: 3 one 5 one a.m.
on some clocks: 3 XII
opposite: 4 noon
midnight __: 3 sun 5 snack
Midnight
author: Dean Koontz
Midnight __: 6 Cowboy
Midnight __ to Georgia: 5 Train
__ Midnight: 5 After, Round
Midnight at the Oasis (1974 song)
artist: Maria Muldaur
Midnight Blue (song)
artist: Lou Gramm, Melissa Manchester
Midnight Choo Choo
destination: 6 Alabam'
Midnight Confessions (1968 song)
artist: Grass Roots
Midnight Cowboy (1969 film)
cast: Dustin Hoffman, Sylvia Miles, Jon Voight
like: 6 X-rated
role: 3 Joe 4 Buck 5 Ratso, Rizzo 7 Joe Buck 10 Ratso Rizzo
Midnight in the Garden of Good and Evil (1997 film)
cast: John Cusack, Kevin Spacey
director: Clint Eastwood
Midnight Rider (1975 song)
artist: Allman Brothers Band
Midnight Run (1988 film)
cast: Robert De Niro, Charles Grodin, Yaphet Kotto
director: Martin Brest
Midnight's Children
author: Salman Rushdie
Midnight Special (1965 song)
artist: Johnny Rivers
Midnight Sun dweller: 4 Lapp
Midnight Train to Georgia (1973 song)
artist: Gladys Knight and the Pips
midocean
in ~: 4 asea 5 at sea
Midori: 3 Ito 7 liqueur 8 Japanese, musician 9 violinist
midpoint: 2 av. 3 avg. 4 mean 5 midst 6 center, median, middle 7 average
midpt.: 3 ctr.
__ Midrash: 4 Beth
midsection: 3 gut, tum 4 core 5 belly, tummy, waist 6 center 7 abdomen
midshipman: 6 sailor 7 jack tar
counterpart: 5 cadet
Midshipmen: 4 Navy, USNA
midshipwoman: 6 sailor
mid-size __: 3 car
midst: 3 hub 4 core 5 heart, thick 6 center, depths, middle 7 halfway, nucleus 8 interior, presence
in the ~ of: 5 among, 'twixt 6 during, mongst 7 amongst, between
in the ~ of (prefix): 5 inter-
midsummer: 4 July
Midsummer __: 3 Day, Eve 5 Night
Midsummer Night's Dream, A: 4 play 6 comedy
author: William Shakespeare
character: 4 Nick, Puck, Snug 5 Egeus, Flute, Peter, Snout 6 Bottom, Helena, Hermia, Oberon, Quince 7 Theseus, Titania 8 Lysander 9 Demetrius, Hippolyta 10 Nick Bottom, Starveling
Midsummer Night's Dream, A (1999 film)
cast: Rupert Everett, Kevin Kline, Michelle Pfeiffer, Stanley Tucci
Midsummer Night's Sex Comedy, A (1982 film)
cast: Woody Allen, Mia Farrow, José Ferrer, Julie Hagerty, Tony Roberts, Mary Steenburgen
director: Woody Allen
midterm: 4 exam, test
midway: 7 between, en route 8 moderate
attraction: 4 ride
prize: 4 doll 6 kewpie 8 goldfish 10 kewpie doll
Midway: 4 isle 6 battle, island 7 airport
alternative: *see* airport 5 O'Hare
like the Battle of ~: 5 naval
loc.: 3 Chi. 7 Chicago
Midwest
city: 5 Omaha 7 Chicago, St. Louis, Wichita 9 Des Moines
crop: 4 corn 5 grain, wheat
Indian: 3 Ute 5 Osage
sight: 4 silo
state: 3 Ill., Ind., Kan., Neb. 4 Iowa, N. Dak., Nebr., S. Dak. 6 Kansas 7 Indiana 8 Illinois, Missouri, Nebraska
zone: 3 CDT, CST
Midwinter's Tale, A
author: Andrew Greeley
midyear: 4 exam, test
Mielziner: 2 Jo
mien: 3 air, set 4 aura, cast, look, pose 5 front, guise 6 aspect, manner 7 bearing, conduct, posture 8 attitude, carriage, demeanor, features, presence 9 mannerism 10 appearance, deportment, expression
Mies van der Rohe, Ludwig: 9 architect
miff: 3 irk, vex 4 hurt, roil, tiff 5 anger, annoy, peeve, pique, upset 6 bother, nettle, offend, put out, tee off 7 perturb, provoke, tick off 8 aggrieve, irritate 9 displease
miffed: 4 hurt, sore 5 angry 9 indignant, resentful
easily ~: 5 pouty 6 touchy
more than ~: 3 mad 5 het up, livid 7 furious
Mifune: 7 Toshiro
MiG: 3 jet
weapon: 3 AAM
might: 3 may, vim 4 beef, dint, sway, thew 5 brawn, clout, could, force, power, steam, thews, vigor 6 energy, muscle 7 ability, command, control, fitness, muscles, potence, potency, prowess, stamina 8 capacity, strength, violence, vitality 9 authority, beefiness, endurance, fortitude, hardiness, huskiness, intensity, puissance, stoutness, strong arm, toughness 10 brawniness, brute force, capability, competence, robustness, ruggedness, sturdiness
partner: 4 main
symbol of ~: 4 fist
with all one's ~: 4 hard 5 amain
__ Might Be Giants: 4 They
Might I interrupt?: 4 ahem
mightily: 7 greatly 8 forcibly, strongly 9 arduously, intensely 10 forcefully, incredibly, powerfully, vigorously
mighty: 3 big 4 hale, huge, iron, vast, wiry 5 beefy, burly, hardy, hefty, hunky, husky, jumbo, large, lusty, nervy, stout, tough 6 brawny, hearty, heroic, potent, robust, rugged, sinewy, steely, stocky, strong, sturdy, virile 7 doughty, immense, leonine, massive, titanic, violent 8 athletic, colossal, enormous, forceful, gigantic, heroical, imposing, indurate, majestic, muscular, powerful, puissant, renowned, stalwart, towering, vigorous, whapping, whopping 9 Atlantean, herculean, strapping, unusually, well-built 10 able-bodied, formidable, impressive, majestical, monumental, omnipotent, prodigious, red-blooded, stupendous, tremendous
high and ~: 5 lofty 7 haughty, pompous 8 arrogant, dogmatic, snobbish 10 dogmatical
partner: 4 high
mighty __ oak: 4 as an
Mighty __: 5 Mouse, Quinn
Mighty __ a Rose: 3 Lak'
Mighty __, The: 5 Ducks 6 Barnum 7 Orinoco
Mighty __ Young: 3 Joe
Mighty Aphrodite (1995 film)
cast: F. Murray Abraham, Woody Allen, Claire Bloom, Helena Bonham Carter, Olympia Dukakis, Mira Sorvino
director: Woody Allen
Mighty Dog
rival: 4 Alpo, Iams 6 Purina 10 Ken-L-Ration
Mighty Duck
rival: *see* hockey team
Mighty Ducks: 3 six 4 team
home: 7 Anaheim
milieu: 3 ice 4 rink
org.: 3 NHL
sport: 6 hockey
Mighty Joe Young: 3 ape 7 gorilla
Mighty Joe Young (1949 film)
cast: Robert Armstrong, Terry Moore
Mighty Joe Young (1998 film)
cast: Regina King, Bill Paxton, David Paymer, Charlize Theron
Mighty Lak' a Rose
composer: Ethelbert Nevin
Mighty Morphin Power Rangers: The Movie villain: 4 Ooze
Mighty Mouse: 4 hero, toon
garb: 4 cape
Mighty Orinoco, The
author: Jules Verne
Mighty Quinn (1968 song)
artist: Manfred Mann
composer: Bob Dylan
__ mignon: 5 filet
mignonette: 5 plant 6 flower
migraine: 4 ache 8 headache
so to speak: 4 vise
migrant: 4 hobo 5 gypsy, mover, nomad, tramp 6 jobber, mobile, moving, roving 7 drifter, nomadic, ranging 8 changing, drifting, stranger, traveler, vagabond 9 itinerant, on the move, temporary, transient, unsettled, wandering
worker: 7 laborer
worker's org.: 3 UFW
migrate: 2 go 4 move, roam, rove, trek 5 drift, leave, range 6 depart, travel, wander 7 journey, scatter 8 emigrate, relocate
migration: 4 trek 6 hejira 7 journey 8 movement 9 departure
plant ~: 6 ecesis
migratory: 5 gypsy 6 mobile, moving, roving 7 nomadic, ranging 8 drifting, seasonal 9 itinerant, on the move, peregrine, temporary, transient, traveling, unsettled, wandering
animal: 4 loon, tern 5 goose, vireo, whale 6 locust
mammal: 5 whale
Miguel: 6 Barnet, Ferrer, Mihura 7 Unamuno 8 Asturias 9 Cervantes
__ Miguel, Azores: 3 Sao
Mihura, Miguel: 7 Spanish 10 playwright
mikado: 5 ruler 6 gerent 8 Japanese
Mikado, The: 8 operetta
character: 4 Ko-Ko 6 Mikado, Peep-Bo, Yum-Yum 7 Katisha, Pooh-Bah 8 Nanki-Poo, Pish-Tush 9 Pitti-Sing
composer: W.S. Gilbert, Arthur Sullivan
sash: 3 obi
trio: 5 maids
Mikan, George
milieu: 5 court
org.: 3 NBA
sport: 10 basketball
Mikasa
competitor: 5 Lenox
mike: 3 bug
adjunct: 3 amp
place for a ~: 5 lapel
problem: 4 echo
user: 2 DJ, MC 5 emcee 6 deejay
mike __: 6 fright
__ mike: 4 body 5 lapel
Mike: 4 Fink, Love, Post, Reno, Todd, Weir 5 Aulby, Bossy, Ditka, Judge, Myers, Royko, Tyson

6 Brewer, Figgis, Hodges, Newell, Piazza 7 Connors, Douglas, Farrell, Nesmith, Nichols, Schmidt, Stoller, Wallace 8 Oldfield 10 Lookinland
in Russian: 5 Misha
Mike and ___: 3 Ike
___ Mike Tyson: 4 Iron
Mikhail: 3 Tal 4 tsar 6 Glinka 7 Bakunin, Kutuzov, Romanov 8 Bulgakov, Saltykov 9 Botvinnik, Gorbachev, Sholokhov 10 Zoshchenko
spouse: 5 Raisa
successor: 5 Boris
see also Russian
Mikita, Stan
milieu: 3 ice 4 rink 5 arena
org.: 3 NHL
Mikrokosmos
composer: Béla Bartók
mil: 5 money
1/1000 of a ~: 5 grand
mil.: 3 GIs
address: 3 APO, FPO
aide: 3 GSO
award: 3 DFC, DSC, DSM
boat: 3 LST
branch: 3 USN, WAC 4 RCAF, USAF, USMC
British ~ branch: 3 RNR
college: 3 VMI
concern: 3 def.
former ~ auxiliary: 3 WAF
group: 2 tp. 3 div., reg., trp.
offender: 4 AWOL
plane: 4 STOL, VTOL
post: 2 HQ 3 AFB, NAS
rank: 2 BG 3 cdr., CNO, Col., cpl., CPO, ens., gen., maj., NCO, PFC, pvt., SFC, sgt. 4 capt., cmdr., genl., m.sgt., serg., SSgt. 5 lieut., lt. col., lt. gen.
sign up for ~ service: 3 enl.
spy org.: 3 ONI
staff officer: 4 adjt.
training place: 3 OCS, OTC, OTS 4 ROTC
see also military
Mila: 5 Kunis
Mila 18
author: Leon Uris
Milagro Beanfield War, The (1988 film)
cast: Ruben Blades, Sonia Braga
director: Robert Redford
Milan: 4 city, town 7 Kundera
attraction: 7 La Scala
city near ~: 4 Lodi 5 Parma
ender: 3 ese
locale: 5 Italy
Milano: 3 car 4 auto, city, town 6 Alyssa 9 Alfa Romeo 10 automobile
alternative: *see* cookie brand
locale: 5 Italy 6 Italia
Milburn: 5 Stone
mild: 3 lax 4 blah, calm, cool, dull, easy, fair, fine, flat, kind, meek, soft, tame, warm, weak 5 balmy, bland, clear, ho-hum, light, loose, lowly, quiet, sunny, sweet, tepid, vapid, wimpy 6 benign, breezy, docile, genial, gentle, humane, irenic, kindly, mellow, placid, polite, serene, simple, smooth, tender 7 amiable, clement, equable, insipid, lenient, patient, ruthful, sparing, subdued, vanilla, warmish, wimpish 8 flexible, irenical, laid-back, lamblike, lukewarm, merciful, moderate, not so hot, obliging, peaceful, placable, pleasant, reserved, soothing, tolerant, tranquil 9 assuasive, compliant, easygoing, forgiving, indulgent, innocuous, peaceable, tasteless, temperate, unextreme 10 forbearing, permissive, restrained, springlike, submissive, unagitated, unassuming, unexacting, unhardened
mildew: 4 mold 5 ergot, mould, plant, spoil 6 blight, fungus, go sour
mildew-fighting product: 5 Tilex
mildewy: 4 damp, dank 5 fusty, musty, trite
mild-mannered: 4 meek, mild, tame 8 ladylike, pleasant
mildness: 5 mercy 6 lenity 8 lenience 9 balminess 10 moderation
Mildred: 6 Bailey, Pierce 7 Natwick
Mildred Pierce: 4 film 5 novel
author: James M. Cain
cast: Eve Arden, Ann Blyth, Jack Carson, Joan Crawford
composer: Max Steiner
director: Michael Curtiz
mile
a ~ a minute: 5 sixty
ender: 3 age 4 post 5 stone
equivalent: 4 miss 5 a miss
off by a ~: 5 wrong
___ mile: 3 air, sea 6 square 7 country, miracle, statute 8 nautical
___-mile: 3 ton 4 half
mileage: 3 use 4 wear 6 length
get extra ~ from: 5 reuse 7 recycle
get ~ out of: 3 use 7 exploit
Mile High ___: 6 Center 7 Stadium
Mile High Center architect: 3 Pei
mile-high city: 5 Kabul 6 Denver
___ Mile in My Shoes: 5 Walk a
___ Mile Island: 5 Three
___-mile limit: 5 three 6 twelve
milepost: 8 landmark, occasion
miler: 3 Coe 4 Ryun 5 Ovett, racer 6 runner 7 Jim Ryun 9 Bannister 10 Steve Ovett
concern: 4 pace
miles: 3 far
about three ~: 6 league
away: 4 afar
per hour: 4 rate
Miles: 4 Vera 5 Buddy, Davis, Sarah 6 Sylvia 8 Franklin, Standish 9 Josephine
Miles, Josephine: 4 poet
___ Miles Minter: 4 Mary
___ Miles of Bad Road: 5 Forty
milestone: 5 event 7 waypost 8 landmark, occasion 9 happening
Milestone: 5 Lewis
___ Mile, The: 4 Last 5 Green
Miley: 5 Cyrus
Milford: 4 city, town
locale: 4 Conn.
Milhaud, Darius: 6 French 8 composer
work: The Creation of the World
milieu: 3 job 4 area, nabe 5 place, scene, world 6 locale, medium, sphere 7 climate, element, purlieu, setting 8 ambience 10 atmosphere, background, walk of life
___ militaire: 5 école
militancy: 5 fight 6 hatred
militant: 5 pushy 7 fanatic, hawkish, hostile, radical, scrappy, warlike 8 activist, fighting, partisan, ructious, up in arms 9 assertive, bellicose, combative, embattled, protester, truculent 10 aggressive, jingoistic, pugnacious
god: 4 Ares, Mars
militaristic: 7 warlike 8 fighting
militarize: 3 arm 8 embattle
military: 4 army, navy 6 troops 7 Marines, martial, service, warlike 8 air force 9 combative, soldierly 10 aggressive
acronym: 5 NORAD 6 DEFCON
action: 3 war 7 warfare
address: 3 APO, FPO, sir
advisory grp.: 3 NSC
aircraft: 5 AWACS 6 Apache
alliance: 3 OAS 4 NATO
ammo: 4 ordn. 8 ordnance
assignment: 6 KP duty, patrol
assistant: 3 ADC 6 yeoman 8 adjutant
backup org.: 4 USAR, USNR
base: 4 post 8 garrison
bed: 3 cot
careerist: 5 lifer
cash: 5 scrip
coat: 5 tunic 9 pea jacket 10 flak jacket
command: 4 fire, halt 5 march 6 at ease
commando: 4 SEAL
council: 5 junta
decoration: 5 medal
defense: 5 stand
education facility: 3 OCS, OTC, OTS 4 acad., ROTC 7 academy
elite ~ group: 5 A-team
encampment: 5 étape
encounter: 6 action, battle 8 skirmish
flag: 6 colors, ensign
formation: 5 wedge
former ~ grp.: 3 WAF
fortification: 5 redan
group: 2 tp. 3 rgt., trp. 4 regt., unit 5 cadre, force, squad, troop 6 legion, patrol 7 brigade 8 regiment 9 battalion
hat: 5 beret, busby, shako
installation: 4 silo
instrument: 4 drum 5 bugle
join the ~: 6 enlist, sign up 9 volunteer
make a ~ stopover: 6 encamp
mission, in Britain: 5 recce, recco
mix-up: 5 snafu
musician: 6 bugler
neckwear: 6 dogtag
no-show: 8 deserter
not ~: 5 civvy 8 civilian
offender: 4 AWOL
org.: 3 SAC, USN 4 USAF
person: 7 soldier
physician: 5 medic
prison: 4 brig
quarters: 4 base, tent 6 armory, billet 7 bivouac 8 barracks
rank: 2 BG 3 cdr., CNO, col., cpl., CPO, ens., gen., maj., NCO, PFC, pvt., SFC, sgt. 4 capt., cmdr., genl., m.sgt., serg., SSgt. 5 lieut., lt. col., lt. gen., major 6 airman, ensign, seaman 7 captain, colonel, general, private 8 corporal, sergeant 10 lieutenant
response: 5 no sir 6 yes sir
rookie: 3 rct. 7 recruit
salute: 5 salvo
stay in the ~: 4 reup
stint: 4 tour 5 hitch
store: 2 PX
student: 4 pleb 5 cadet, middy, plebe 6 middie
tactic: 5 recon, siege 6 attack
takeover: 4 coup
tune: 4 Taps 5 march
uniform: 3 ODs 4 camo 6 khakis
vacation: 5 leave 8 furlough
vehicle: 3 LCT, LST 4 jeep, tank 6 amtrac, camion 7 amtrack
VIPs: 5 brass
woman: 3 WAC 4 WAAC, Wave
see also army, navy
military ___: 3 law 4 pace 5 brush, march 6 police, school 7 academy, attaché, science
military-industrial ___: 7 complex
Military Symphony
composer: Joseph Haydn
militate: 4 tell 5 weigh
Milius: 4 John
milk: 3 tap, use 4 pump, skim 5 bleed, cream, dairy, drain, press, white, wring 6 elicit, extort, fleece 7 defraud, deplete, draw off, draw out, exhaust, exploit, extract, formula, squeeze 8 beverage, moo juice 9 siphon off 10 buttermilk, one-percent, two-percent
acid in ~: 5 color, oleic, white 6 lactic
alternative: 3 tea 5 cream 6 coffee
amount: 2 pt., qt. 3 gal. 4 pint 5 quart 6 gallon
buying ~: 6 errand
combining form: 4 lact- 5 lacti-, lacto- 6 galact- 7 galacto-
component: 3 fat 4 whey 6 casein
cry over spilled ~: 5 whine 6 regret
drinker: 3 boy, cat 4 girl 9 youngster
ender: 3 man, men, sop 4 fish, maid, weed
fermented ~ drink: 5 kefir 6 kumiss
go bad, as ~: 4 sour 6 curdle
grader: 4 USDA
holder: 4 pail 5 udder 6 bottle, bucket, carton
in French: 4 lait
in Italian: 5 latte
in prescriptions: 3 lac
in Spanish: 5 leche
land of ~ and honey: 6 utopia 7 Arcadia, Erewhon 8 paradise 9 Shangri-la
like a ~ shake: 5 foamy
like some ~: 5 spilt 6 low-fat
like supermarket ~: 5 dated
made without ~ or meat: 5 parve 6 pareve
of ~: 6 lactic 7 lacteal
produce skim ~: 5 defat

product: 4 curd 6 yogurt 7 yoghurt 8 ice cream, yoghourt
rating: 6 grade A
relative: *see* white color
sans ~: 5 black
source: 3 cow, ewe 4 goat 5 dairy, udder 6 Jersey
starter: 6 butter
milk __: 3 bar, cow, run 5 float, glass, gravy, shake, sugar, tooth, train 6 powder
__ milk: 3 ice 4 skim, soya 5 whole 6 malted
Milk (2008 film)
cast: Josh Brolin, Emile Hirsch, Sean Penn
director: Gus Van Sant
Milk-__: 4 Bone
__ Milk?: 3 Got
Milk and Honey
author: Faye Kellerman
milk-cap collectible: 3 pog
Milk Duds: 5 candy
alternative: *see* candy brand
milking: 5 chore
need: 5 stool
time: 4 dawn 5 sunup 8 daybreak
milking __: 5 stool
milk shake: 7 dessert 8 beverage
alternative: 5 bombe 6 frappe 10 peach Melba
ingredient: 8 ice cream
milksop: 4 wimp 6 coward 8 mama's boy, recreant
lack: 5 nerve, spine
unlike a ~: 5 brave, macho, manly
Milk Train Doesn't Stop Here Anymore, The
author: Tennessee Williams
milkwood: 4 tree
__ Milk Wood: 5 Under
milky: 5 white 6 chalky, lactic, opaque, pearly 7 clouded, lacteal, opaline, whitish 9 alabaster, albescent 10 opalescent
relative: *see* white color
Milky Way: 3 bar 5 candy 6 galaxy 8 candy bar 9 chocolate, Via Lactea
alternative: *see* candy brand
unit: 4 star
mill: 4 shop 5 churn, crush, flour, grind, money, plant, pound, press, works 7 factory, foundry 8 levigate 9 granulate, pulverize, sweatshop
around: 6 dither 9 circulate
(around): 4 move
ender: 3 age, dam, run 4 pond, race, work 5 board, stone 6 stream, wright
gin ~: 3 pub 6 tavern 7 barroom 8 taphouse
input: 4 iron
lumber ~ worker: 5 sawer
output: 5 steel
paper ~ commodity: 4 pulp
primitive ~: 5 quern
starter: 3 saw 4 wind 5 grist, tread
to a cent: 5 tenth
use a ~: 5 grind
__ mill: 3 gin 5 flour, grist, paper, puppy, rumor, steel, water 6 degree, pepper 7 diploma
Mill __ Floss, The: 5 on the
__ Mill: 7 Sutter's
Milla: 8 Jovovich
Milland, Ray: 5 actor
film: Alias Nick Beal (1943)
Beau Geste (1939)
The Big Clock (1948)
Dial M for Murder (1954)
The Doctor Takes a Wife (1940)
The Lost Weekend (1945, AA)
Love Story (1970)
The Major and the Minor (1942)
Reap the Wild Wind (1942)
The Uninvited (1944)
A Woman of Distinction (1950)
Millard: 8 Fillmore
Millay, Edna St. Vincent: 4 poet
work: The Buck in the Snow
A Few Figs From Thistles
The Harp Weaver and Other Poems
Renascence and Other Poems
Millbrae: 4 city, town
locale: 10 California
milled: 7 powdery
mille-feuilles: 6 pastry 7 dessert
Millenia: 3 car 4 auto 5 Mazda 10 automobile
millennia: 4 ages
many ~: 3 eon 4 aeon
millennium
part: 2 yr. 3 cen. 4 year 6 decade 7 century
Millennium Falcon: 4 ship 10 spacecraft
pilot: 3 Han 4 Solo 7 Han Solo
Miller: 3 Ann, Ned 4 beer 5 David, Glenn, Henry, Jason, Merle, Mitch, Roger, Steve, Wiley 6 Arthur, Barney, Cheryl, Dennis, George, Jeremy, Johnny, Marvin, Merton 7 Christa, Huggins, Joaquin, Marilyn, Shannon 9 Stephanie
alternative: *see* beer
Miller __: 4 Lite
__ Miller: 3 Joe 5 Daisy, Luisa, Molly
Miller, Arthur: 10 playwright
spouse: Marilyn Monroe
work: After the Fall
All My Sons
The Crucible
Death of a Salesman
Incident at Vichy
The Misfits
A View from the Bridge
Miller Band, Steve
song: Abracadabra (1982)
Fly Like an Eagle (1977)
Jet Airliner (1977)
The Joker (1973)
Rock'n Me (1976)
Swingtown (1977)
Take the Money and Run (1976)
Miller, Glenn: 10 trombonist
protégé: 6 Eberle
Miller, Henry: 6 writer
work: The Air-Conditioned Nightmare
The Colossus of Maroussi
The Cosmological Eye
Max and the White Phagocytes
Tropic of Cancer
Tropic of Capricorn
Miller, Joaquin: 4 poet 6 writer
work: Columbus
Kit Carson's Ride
Life among the Modocs
Songs of the Sierras
Miller, Joe material: 4 corn, joke
Miller, Johnny: 6 golfer
Miller, Merton: 8 Nobelist 9 economist
Miller, Mitch
song: The Children's Marching Song (1959)
The Yellow Rose of Texas (1955)
Miller of Angibault, The
author: George Sand
Miller, Penelope Ann: 7 actress
film: Big Top Pee-wee (1988)
Carlito's Way (1993)
The Freshman (1990)
Kindergarten Cop (1990)
Other People's Money (1991)
The Shadow (1994)
Miller, Roger
song: Chug-A-Lug (1964)
Dang Me (1964)
Do-Wacka-Do (1965)
Engine Engine #9 (1965)
England Swings (1965)
King of the Road (1965)
Miller, Wiley: 10 cartoonist
millet: 5 grain 6 cereal
Indian ~: 5 doura, durra 6 dourah
Millett: 4 Kate
Millhone: 6 Kinsey
Milli __: 7 Vanilli
Millie: 3 dog, pet 4 aunt 5 Small 7 Jackson, Perkins, spaniel
Millie's Book
author: Barbara Bush
Milligan: 5 Spike
Millikan, Robert: 8 Nobelist 9 physicist
milliliters, 237: 3 cup
milliner: 6 hatter
millinery item: 3 hat 5 toque, tuque 6 cloche, hatpin
Millinery Shop, The
artist: Edgar Degas
million
combining form: 3 meg- 4 mega-
ender: 4 aire
one in a ~: 4 rare
prefix: 4 mega-
worth a ~: 4 rich
million __, a: 5 to one
__ million: 6 one in a
millionaire: 9 moneybags, plutocrat
home: 5 manor 6 estate
maker: 5 lotto
prefix for ~: 5 multi
toy: 5 yacht
Millionairess, The: 4 film, play
author: George Bernard Shaw
cast: Sophia Loren, Peter Sellers, Alastair Sim
Millionaire, The (CBS drama)
boss: Tipton
cast: Marvin Miller (Michael Anthony)
Million Dollar Baby (2004 film)
cast: Clint Eastwood, Morgan Freeman, Hilary Swank
director: Clint Eastwood
Million Dollar Legs (1932 film)
cast: W.C. Fields, Jack Oakie
__ Million Dollar Man, The: 3 Six
Million Dollar Mermaid (1952 film)
cast: Victor Mature, Walter Pidgeon, Esther Williams
__ Million Frenchmen: 5 Fifty
millions: 4 many, mint 6 flocks, hoards, scores 7 legions
__ Millions: 3 Kid 5 Marco
million-selling: 4 gold
Million to One, A (song)
artist: Jimmy Charles, Donny Osmond
__ Million Years B.C.: 3 One
Milli Vanilli
members: Pilatus, Morvan
song: All or Nothing (1990)
Baby Don't Forget My Number (1989)
Blame It on the Rain (1989)
Girl I'm Gonna Miss You (1989)
Girl You Know It's True (1989)
Mill, James: 8 Scottish 11 philosopher
Mill, John Stuart: 7 British 11 philosopher
Mill on the Floss, The
author: George Eliot
character: 4 Kenn 5 Deane, Glegg, Jakin, Moggs, Sophy, Wakem
dog: 3 Yap
millpond: 4 lake, pool
Mills: 4 Enos, Erie, John 5 Alley, Donna, Frank 6 Hayley, Juliet, Robert 9 Stephanie
__ Mills: 7 General
Mills, Erie: 6 singer 7 soprano
specialty: 5 opera
Mills, Hayley: 7 actress
father: 4 John
film: The Family Way (1966)
The Parent Trap (1961)
Pollyanna (1960)
That Darn Cat! (1965)
__ Mills, MD: 6 Owings
Mills of the Kavanaughs, The
author: Robert Lowell
mills, ten: 4 cent
millstone: 4 buhr, load, onus, task 6 burden, weight 9 albatross, hindrance, liability 10 difficulty, impediment
bar: 4 rynd
product: 5 grist
Milne, A.A.: 6 writer 7 British
character: 3 Owl, Roo 4 Pooh 5 Kanga 6 Eeyore
first name: 4 Alan
work: Eeyore Has a Birthday
Eeyore Loses a Tail
Hello, Eeyore!
The House at Pooh Corner
Mr. Pim Passes By
Now We Are Six
Pooh Goes Visiting
Santa Roo and Pooh Box
Tigger Comes to the Forest
When We Were Very Young
Winnie the Pooh
Milner, Martin: 5 actor
TV: Adam 12, Route 66
Milnes, Sherrill: 6 singer 8 baritone, barytone
specialty: 5 opera
milo: 5 grain 7 sorghum
Milo: 5 O'Shea
Milos: 6 Forman
Milosz, Czeslaw: 6 Polish, writer 8 Nobelist
Milpitas: 4 city, town
locale: 10 California
Milquetoast: 4 meek, wimp 5 sissy, timid, vapid 6 Caspar 8 mama's boy, recreant, weakling 9 jellyfish
like a ~: 4 meek 5 timid
unlike a ~: 5 bossy, manly

Milsap, Ronnie
song: (There's) No Gettin' Over Me (1981)
Milstein: **5** César **6** Nathan
Milstein, Nathan: **7** Russian **9** violinist
teacher: **4** Auer
Milt: **5** Gross **6** Caniff, Pappas **7** Jackson
Miltie, Uncle: **5** Berle
contemporary: **3** Sid
Milton: **4** Ager, John **5** Berle, Obote **6** Caniff, Delugg **7** Hershey **8** Friedman **10** Eisenhower
Milton, John: **4** poet **6** writer **7** British
nutbrown brew: **3** ale
work: Areopagitica
Comus
Il Penseroso
Lycidas
On His Blindness
Paradise Lost
Paradise Regained
Samson Agonistes
Milwaukee: **4** city, town
beverage: **4** beer
locale: **3** Wis. **4** Wisc. **9** Wisconsin
pro team: **5** Bucks **7** Brewers
river: **9** Menomonee
school: **9** Marquette
Milwaukie: **4** city, town
locale: **6** Oregon
Mimas: **4** moon
planet: **6** Saturn
mime: **3** ape **4** aper, mock **5** clown, farce **6** acting, jester, parrot, player **7** copycat, gesture, pierrot **9** performer
like a ~: **3** mum **6** silent
prefix with ~: **5** panto
mimeo: **4** copy, dupe **6** ectype, run off **9** duplicate, facsimile, reproduce
mimeograph: **4** copy **6** ectype, run off **7** replica **9** reproduce
inventor: **6** Edison
mimer: **3** ape **4** aper **6** jester **7** copycat
mimetic: **9** imitative
Mimi: **5** Leder **6** Rogers **7** Benzell, Kennedy
composer: Lorenz Hart, Richard Rodgers
see also French
mimic: **3** ape **4** aper, copy, echo, mock **5** actor, ditto, mynah **6** assume, echoer, follow, mirror, mummer, parody, parrot, player **7** act like, burlesk, copycat, emulate, imitate, portray, pretend, take off **8** comedian, imitator, imposter, impostor, look like, make like, resemble, ridicule, simulate, thespian **9** burlesque, make fun of, pantomime **10** caricature
natural ~: **4** mina, myna **5** minah, mynah
mimicking: **9** emulative
mimicry: **5** apery **6** acting **7** mockery **9** imitation
Mimieux: **6** Yvette
mimosa: **4** tree **5** drink, plant, shrub **6** flower, legume **8** beverage, cocktail
family shrub: **6** acacia
ingredient: **2** OJ **9** champagne
relative: **6** acacia
min.: **3** lim., lmt. **4** inst. **5** least
division: **3** sec. **4** msec., nsec.
many ~: **3** hrs.
Min: **4** Gump
mina: **4** bird **5** money
minaret: **5** tower
call from a ~: **4** azan
minatory: **7** ominous **8** lowering, menacing
mince: **3** cut, pie **4** chop, cube, dice, hack, hash, pose **5** grate, grind, shred, spare, strut **6** prance, sashay, soften, weaken **7** crumble, posture **8** mitigate, palliate, tone down **9** euphemize, gloss over, pulverize, put on airs, whitewash
ender: **4** meat
words: **10** equivocate
mince ___: **3** pie
minced oath: **4** darn, drat, rats
mincemeat: **3** pie **7** dessert
ingredient: **4** suet
make ~ of: **5** smash **7** trounce
mincing: **4** nice **5** fussy, sissy **6** dainty, la-de-da, la-di-da, too-too **7** finicky, prudish **8** affected, delicate, finiking, finnicky, lah-di-dah, precious **9** insincere, squeamish, unnatural **10** artificial, effeminate, fastidious
not ~ words: **5** blunt, frank **6** candid **10** forthright, from the hip, unreserved
mind: **3** wit **4** care, head, heed, keep, look, mark, nous, obey, soul, tend, view, wits **5** bow to, brain, guard, see to, sense, watch **6** accept, advert, animus, attend, behave, bend to, beware, be wary, brains, comply, ensure, follow, fulfil, genius, liking, listen, noggin, noodle, object, psyche, reason, recall, regard, remark, resent, tend to, wisdom **7** abide by, agree to, baby-sit, care for, defer to, fulfill, look out, marbles, observe, opinion, oversee, respect **8** adhere to, attend to, carry out, cerebrum, complain, listen to, object to, remember, take heed, thoughts, watch out **9** attention, conform to, consent to, frown upon, give a damn, give a darn, give a hoot, intellect, look after, make a fuss, mentality, pay heed to, recollect, supervise, watch over **10** brainpower, disapprove, gray matter, ride herd on, toe the line
bear in ~: **4** heed **6** recall **7** bethink **8** remember **9** entertain, recognize, recollect **10** reckon with
be of one ~: **5** agree
blow one's ~: **3** awe **5** amaze
bring to ~: **5** evoke, think **6** recall, review **7** suggest **8** remember **9** recollect, visualize
change of ~: **5** U-turn
change one's ~: **4** bend **6** relent **7** retract **9** vacillate
combining form: **3** noo- **5** menti-, phren-, psych- **6** phreni-, phreno-, psycho-
come back to ~: **5** recur
come to ~: **4** dawn **5** arise, occur **6** strike
dismiss from one's ~: **6** forget
don't ~: **7** disobey
ender: **5** scape
fix in one's ~: **3** con **4** etch **5** learn
frame of ~: **4** mood, vein **5** frame, humor, state **6** spirit, temper **7** feeling, outlook, posture **8** attitude **9** mentality
give a piece of one's ~: **7** lecture, tell off **8** admonish
have in ~: **4** know, mean, plan **5** think **6** intend **7** propose
healthy ~: **6** sanity
improve a ~: **5** learn, teach
in philosophy: **4** nous
load off one's ~: **6** relief
make up one's ~: **5** elect **6** choose, decide **7** resolve **9** determine
name meaning ~: **4** Hugh
never ~: **8** forget it, no matter **10** don't bother
of a ~ (to): **3** apt **5** prone **8** disposed, prepared
of one ~: **6** united **9** unanimous **10** harmonious, like-minded
of sound ~: **4** able, sane **5** lucid **8** rational, sensible **10** reasonable
of the ~: **5** inner **6** mental
one's manners: **6** behave
one's p's and q's: **10** toe the line
one-track ~: **5** mania **6** hang-up **8** fixation, idée fixe **9** monomania, obsession
pay no ~ to: **6** ignore **7** neglect, tune out **8** file away, lay aside, overlook **9** disregard
peace of ~: **4** ease **8** security, serenity
picture: **5** image
presence of ~: **5** poise **6** aplomb **8** calmness **9** composure, sangfroid, stability
prey on one's ~: **6** plague
put one's ~ to rest: **4** buoy **5** cheer **7** cheer up, comfort, console, hearten, satisfy **8** inspirit, reassure
rational ~: **3** ego
science of ~: **10** psychology
sound ~: **6** reason
strength of ~: **4** will **5** spine **7** resolve **8** backbone, decision, firmness **9** fortitude, will power **10** resolution
trip: **6** revery **7** reverie **8** daydream
mind ___: **4** game **6** bender, reader **7** reading
mind-___: **3** set **7** blowing
___ mind: **5** of one
___ mind!: **5** Never
___ mind?: **5** Do you
Mindanao: **3** sea **4** isle **6** island
city: **6** Butuan
gulf: **5** Davao
native: **4** Aeta, Moro
neighbor: **5** Leyte
volcano: **3** Apo
Mind at the End of Its Tether
author: H.G. Wells
Mindbend
author: Robin Cook
mind-bender: **5** poser **6** enigma, puzzle **7** mystery, problem, stumper
mind-blowing: **6** moving **7** awesome **8** fabulous, imposing **9** memorable, thrilling
mind-changing mark: **4** stet
___-minded: **3** air, ear, eye, low **4** even, evil, fair, high, like, open, weak **5** broad, civic, close, noble, right, small, tough **6** absent, closed, feeble, narrow, single
Minderbinder: **4** Milo
mindful: **3** hep, hip **4** cagy, kind, wary, wise **5** alert, aware, cagey, chary, savvy **6** kindly, polite, versed, wise to, with it **7** alive to, careful, gallant, heedful, knowing, tactful, tuned in **8** apprised, cautious, gracious, informed, obliging, on the job, sensible, vigilant, watchful **9** attentive, cognizant, conscious, in the know, observant, on the ball, plugged in, regardful, sensitive, unselfish **10** on one's toes, solicitous, thoughtful
be ~: **7** observe
of: **4** onto
mindfulness: **9** chariness **10** discretion, weather eye
Mind Games (1973 song)
artist: John Lennon
___ Minding the Mint?: **4** Who's
mindless: **4** dopy, rash **5** blind, dense, dopey, inane, moony, silly **6** obtuse, simple, wanton **7** asinine, doltish, fatuous, foolish, out of it, unaware, witless **8** careless, headless, heedless, knee-jerk, reckless **9** automatic, dim-witted, forgetful, negligent, nitwitted, oblivious, senseless, spaced-out, unheedful **10** gratuitous, irrational, neglectful, regardless, unthinking
Mind Murders, The
author: Janwillem van de Wetering
mind one's ___ Q's: **5** P's and
Mindoro: **4** isle **6** island
neighbor: **5** Panay
mind reader: **4** seer **9** mentalist
gift: **3** ESP
mind-reading: **9** telepathy
minds
meeting of ~: **6** accord **7** concord, harmony **9** agreement, consensus
of two ~: **4** torn **8** wavering **9** undecided **10** ambivalent, indecisive, on the fence
mind's
heat: **4** zeal **6** fervor **7** avidity, passion
mind's ___: **3** eye
mind-set: **4** mood **6** belief **7** leaning, outlook **8** attitude, tendency **9** mentality, prejudice **10** standpoint
mind's eye: **5** image **6** memory
view: **7** concept **10** appearance, envisaging, impression, perception, projection
Mindspring: **3** ISP
Mindy: **4** Cohn **8** McCready
friend: **4** Mork
portrayer: 3 Pam
mine: **3** dig, pan, pit **4** bomb, bore, fund, lode, vein **5** cache, delve, dig up, fount, hoard, shaft, stock, store **6** burrow, dig for, quarry, source, supply, tunnel, wealth **7** bonanza, deposit, extract, pronoun, reserve **8** excavate, fountain, treasury **9** abundance, booby trap, explo-

sive 10 excavation, mother lode, wellspring
car: 4 tram
detector: 5 sonar
ender: 5 field, layer, shaft 6 worker 7 sweeper
entrance: 4 adit
excavation: 5 stope
find: 3 ore 4 coal, gold, lode, seam, vein 6 silver 7 diamond
gold ~: 4 lode 5 cache, stock, store 6 source, supply, wealth 7 bonanza, cash cow, deposit, fortune, reserve 8 windfall 10 mother lode
in French: 4 à moi
in Latin: 4 meum
in part: 4 ours
like ~: 4 poss. 10 possessive
machine: 6 dredge
mishap: 6 cave-in
nail: 4 spad
not ~: 3 his 4 hers, your 5 thine, yours
passage: 3 pit 5 shaft, winze 6 airway
timber: 5 brace, sprag, stull
vapor: 4 damp
work a ~: 3 dig 8 prospect
yours and ~: 3 our 4 ours
__ mine: 4 coal, gold, salt
__-mine: 5 strip
Mine
composer: George Gershwin, Ira Gershwin
Mine __ dog, though he had bit me...: 6 enemy's
__ Mine: 3 He's, I Me, Not 4 She's 5 Enemy
__, Mine and Ours: 5 Yours
Mine eyes have __...: 4 seen
minelayer: 4 boat
Mineo: 3 Sal
miner: 9 excavator, sourdough 10 forty-niner, prospector
name meaning ~: 7 Collier
need: 5 claim 7 lantern
org.: 3 UMW
tool: 3 gad 4 pick
__ miner: 4 coal
Miner: 3 Jan 5 Steve
mineral: 3 oil, ore 4 coal, jade, lava, mica, opal, rock, ruby, talc, trap, tuff 5 agate, beryl, chalk, chert, emery, flint, geode, lapis, magma, metal, niter, ocher, ochre, shale, slate, stone, topaz, trass, wacke 6 basalt, blende, gabbro, galena, garnet, gneiss, gypsum, halite, iolite, marble, natron, oolite, ophite, pyrite, quartz, rutile, schist, scoria, silica, spinel, zircon 7 azurite, bauxite, biotite, breccia, citrine, diamond, emerald, granite, hyalite, kernite, lignite, olivine, realgar, sylvite, thorite, zincite, zoisite 8 asbestos, cinnabar, corundum, cryolite, dolerite, dolomite, feldspar, fluorite, graphite, hematite, ilmenite, limonite, mudstone, obsidian, plumbago, porphyry, resource, rhyolite, rock salt, sapphire, siderite, smaltite, stannite, stibnite, taconite 9 alabaster, amazonite, argentite, celestite, columbite, graywacke, insensate, limestone, lodestone, magnetite, malachite, millerite, niccolite, pipestone, quartzite, sandstone, scheelite, soapstone, sylvanite, turquoise, uraninite, willemite, wulfenite 10 chalcedony, chrysolite, hornblende, insentient, iron pyrite, lepidolite, meerschaum, polybasite, rose quartz, serpentine, sphalerite, tourmaline, travertine, vanadinite
abrasive ~: 6 garnet 8 corundum
blue ~: 5 lapis 6 iolite 8 fluorite, sapphire 9 turquoise 10 tourmaline
clear ~: 6 zircon 10 tourmaline
combining form: 4 -lite, -lyte 5 oryct- 6 orycto-
commonest ~: 6 quartz
deposit: 4 lode, seam, vein 5 scale
green ~: 4 jade 5 prase 7 olivine 8 fluorite 9 malachite 10 hornblende, serpentine, tourmaline
igneous ~: 6 basalt, gabbro 7 granite, olivine 8 dolerite, feldspar, rhyolite 10 hornblende
metamorphic ~: 5 slate 6 gneiss, schist 9 soapstone
nutrient: 4 iron, zinc 9 magnesium
ornamental stonework ~: 7 zoisite
partner: 3 vit. 7 vitamin
red ~: 4 ruby, sard 6 garnet, rutile, spinel 7 sardine, sardius 8 cinnabar, porphyry 10 rose quartz
residue: 4 calx
Roman ~: 5 murra 6 murrha
sedimentary ~: 5 shale 8 dolomite, mudstone 9 limestone, sandstone
silica ~: 4 mica 6 quartz
soft ~: 4 talc 8 graphite 9 soapstone
suffix: 3 -ite 4 -lite
translucent ~: 4 mica, opal 9 alabaster
volcanic ~: 4 lava, tuff 6 basalt, scoria 8 porphyry
white ~: 5 chalk 6 gypsum 9 alabaster 10 meerschaum
worthless ~: 6 gangue
yellow ~: 5 topaz 8 fluorite
mineral __: 3 oil 5 water 6 spring
__ minérale: 3 eau
mineralize: 7 petrify
mineralogy: 7 science
miner's __: 4 dial, inch 7 lettuce
Miners: 4 UTEP
__ Miner's Daughter: 4 Coal
Minerva: 3 dea 5 Roman 7 goddess
equivalent: 6 Athena, Athene
father: 7 Jupiter
symbol: 3 owl
mines
look for ~: 5 sweep
salt ~: 4 work 6 office
minestrone: 4 soup
follower, maybe: 5 pasta
minesweeper: 4 boat
fictional ~: 5 Caine
__ Mine, The: 5 Boy Is
miney
follower: 3 moe
preceder: 5 meeny
Ming: 3 Yao
Ming __: 4 vase 7 Dynasty
Minghella, Anthony Oscar: The English Patient
mingle: 3 mix 4 fuse, join, meld, pool 5 admix, alloy, blend, cross, immix, merge, tie in, unite 6 hobnob, make up 7 combine, consort, hang out, network 8 intermix 9 associate, circulate, interlace, socialize 10 assimilate, fraternize, interbreed, interweave
unlikely to ~: 3 shy
mingling with: 4 amid 5 among 6 amidst, mongst 7 amongst
Mingo: 6 Norman
portrayer: Ed Ames
__ Ming Pei: 4 Ieoh
Ming the Merciless
daughter: 4 Aura
Mingus, Charles: 7 bassist
genre: 4 jazz
__ Minh: 4 Viet 5 Ho Chi
Minho: 5 river
locale: 5 Spain 6 Iberia 8 Portugal
mini: 2 PC 4 tiny 5 skirt, small, teeny 6 little, teensy 8 computer
change a ~: 5 rehem
opposite: 4 maxi
smaller than ~: 5 micro
mini-: 4 tiny 5 teeny 6 teensy
Mini-__: 3 Vac
mini-album: 2 EP
miniature: 3 toy, wee 4 baby, puny, tiny 5 bitty, dwarf, eensy, model, pigmy, pygmy, small, teeny, weeny 6 atomic, bantam, little, midget, minute, peewee, petite, pocket, teensy 7 replica 8 atomical, atomlike, nicknack 9 facsimile, itsy-bitsy, itty-bitty, minuscule, pint-sized, undersize 10 diminutive, homunculus, knickknack, scaled-down, teeny-weeny, vest-pocket
suffix: 3 -ino, -ita, -ito, -ock 4 -ella, -ette
miniature __: 4 golf
miniature-golf shot: 4 putt
minibike
kin: 5 moped
minibus: 6 jitney
minicomputer, '70s: 3 Vax
Minicoy: 4 isle 6 island
locale: 5 India
minify: 6 lessen
minikin: 3 wee 4 tiny 5 small, teeny 6 little, teensy
alternative: *see* point size
minim: 4 note 7 modicum 8 half note, molecule, particle
minimal: 5 basic, least, scant, token 6 barest, lowest, minute, scanty 7 limited, nominal 8 littlest, marginal, smallest 9 essential, narrowest, slightest
amount: 3 bit, tad 4 hoot, iota
exert ~ effort: 5 glide, slide 6 cruise
minimize: 3 pan 4 pare 5 dwarf, gloze, knock, lower, prune 6 lessen, reduce, shrink, weaken 7 cheapen, curtail, detract, put down, run down, shorten 8 belittle, decrease, derogate, diminish, discount, downplay, palliate, play down, pooh-pooh, shrug off, talk down 9 attenuate, deprecate, disparage, extenuate, knock down, poor-mouth, soft-pedal, underplay, underrate, whitewash 10 abbreviate, understate
minimizing: 8 critical, scornful, spiteful 9 slighting 10 belittling, derogatory, detracting, disdainful, pejorative
minimum: 3 dab, jot 4 hair, iota, tiny, whit 5 basal, grain, least, limit, point, spark, speck, teeny 6 barest, bottom, lowest, merest, shadow, teensy 7 modicum, smidgen, smidgin, soupçon, tiniest 8 littlest, pittance, smallest, smidgeon 9 bare-bones, narrowest, scintilla, slightest
number: 5 quota 6 quorum
minimum __: 4 wage
__ minimum: 3 at a 4 bare
__ mining: 4 coal 5 strip
minion: 4 pawn, tool 5 toady 6 flunky, jackal, lackey, yes man 7 flunkey, lacquey, servant 8 follower, kowtower, truckler 9 sycophant, underling 10 handshaker
miniseries
landmark ~: 5 Roots
maybe: 4 epic
minister: 3 rev. 4 abbé, aide, dean, give, heal, help, tend 5 abbot, agent, do for, envoy, nurse, padre, rabbi, rebbe, serve, treat, vicar 6 bishop, clergy, cleric, consul, curate, deacon, deputy, doctor, father, foster, legate, manage, parson, pastor, priest, rector, succor, supply, wait on 7 prelate, premier, sit with 8 chaplain, delegate, diplomat, official, preacher, reverend, shepherd, wait upon 9 assistant, confesser, confessor, secretary 10 ambassador, archbishop, evangelist, lieutenant, missionary, take care of
assistant: 6 deacon
home: 5 manse
school: 3 sem. 8 seminary
to: 4 keep, tend 5 nurse, serve, treat 6 attend, wait on 8 wait upon
(to): 5 cater
minister __ portfolio: 7 without
__ minister: 5 prime 7 foreign
ministerial: 8 clerical 9 religious
Minister's Wooing, The
author: Harriet Beecher Stowe
ministration: 3 aid 4 care, help 6 relief, solace, succor 7 service
ministry: 5 abbey 6 clergy 9 rabbinate
former TV ~: 3 PTL
miniver: 3 fur 4 vair
Miniver: 3 Kay
Mr. ~: 4 Clem
__ Miniver: 3 Mrs.
Miniver Cheevy
author: E.A. Robinson
Mini-Wheats: 6 cereal
competitor: *see* cereal
mink: 3 fur 4 wrap 6 animal, mammal, weasel 8 kolinsky
home: 5 ranch
relative: *see* weasel
Minn.
neighbor: 2 N.D. 3 Man., Ont., Wis. 4 N. Dak., S. Dak., Wisc.
see also Minnesota

Minneapolis: 4 city, town
county: 8 Hennepin
exurb: 5 Edina
locale: 9 Minnesota
river: 11 Mississippi
suburb: 5 Anoka, Eagan, Edina, Osseo
town near ~: 5 Osseo
Minneapolis-to-Fargo highway: 5 US ten
Minnelli: 4 Liza 8 Vincente
Minnelli, Liza: 6 singer 7 actress
film: Arthur (1981)
Cabaret (1972, AA)
New York, New York (1977)
The Sterile Cuckoo (1969)
Tell Me That You Love Me, Junie Moon (1970)
mother: Judy Garland
sister: Lorna Luft
spouse: Peter Allen, Jack Haley Jr.
Minnelli, Vincente: 8 director
film: An American in Paris (1951)
The Bad and the Beautiful (1952)
The Band Wagon (1953)
Bells Are Ringing (1960)
Brigadoon (1954)
Cabin in the Sky (1943)
The Clock (1945)
The Courtship of Eddie's Father (1963)
Designing Woman (1957)
Father of the Bride (1950)
Father's Little Dividend (1951)
Gigi (1958, AA)
Home From the Hill (1960)
Lust for Life (1956)
Madame Bovary (1949)
Meet Me in St. Louis (1944)
On a Clear Day You Can See Forever (1970)
The Pirate (1948)
The Sandpiper (1965)
Some Came Running (1959)
Tea and Sympathy (1956)
Ziegfeld Follies (1946)
spouse: Judy Garland
Minnesota: 5 river, state
capital: 6 St. Paul
city: 5 Eagan, Edina, Osseo 6 Austin, Blaine, Duluth, Savage, St. Paul, Winona 7 Andover, Crystal, Fridley, Hibbing, Mankato, New Hope, Oakdale, St. Cloud, Wabasha 8 Champlin, Moorhead, Owatonna, Plymouth, Shakopee, Woodbury 9 Albert Lea, Faribault, Lakeville, Maplewood, Richfield, Rochester, Roseville, Shoreview 10 Burnsville, Chanhassen, Coon Rapids, Maple Grove, Minnetonka, Sauk Centre
clinic: 4 Mayo
conference: 6 Big Ten
county: 5 Anoka 6 Dakota, Isanti, Itasca, McLeod, Meeker, Sibley, Wadena, Waseca, Winona 7 Le Sueur, Olmsted, Red Lake 8 Chippewa, Hennepin, Nicollet 9 Otter Tail
lake: 5 Rainy 6 Itasca
national park: 9 Voyageurs
neighbor: 4 Iowa 6 Canada 7 Ontario 8 Manitoba, Michigan 9 Wisconsin
port: 6 Duluth
pro team: 5 Twins 7 Vikings 12 Timberwolves
state beverage: 4 milk
state bird: 4 loon
state fish: 7 walleye
state gemstone: 5 agate
state grain: 8 wild rice
state mineral: 6 galena
state muffin: 9 blueberry
state mushroom: 5 morel
state tree: 10 Norway pine
University of ~ athlete: 6 Gopher
Minnesota __: 4 Fats
Minnesota Fats
game: 4 pool
need: 3 cue
shot: 5 carom, massé 6 carrom
Minnie: 4 Marx 5 mouse, Pearl 6 Driver 8 Riperton
Minnie Mouse dog: 4 Fifi
Minnie the Moocher
artist: Cab Calloway
minnow: 4 bait, dace, fish 5 danio
alternative: 4 worm
eater: 4 tern
kin: 4 carp, chub 5 bream
Miño: 5 river
locale: 5 Spain 6 Iberia 8 Portugal
Minoan
capital: 7 Cnossus, Gnossus, Knossos
island: 5 Crete 6 Candia
Minogue: 5 Kylie
Minolta: 6 camera
alternative: *see* camera
minor: 3 boy, kid, lad 4 baby, girl, less, side, teen, ward 5 child, dinky, light, lower, petty, small, youth 6 infant, junior, lesser, little, paltry, slight, two-bit 7 smaller, trivial, younger 8 inferior, juvenile, marginal, picayune, piddling, small-fry, teenager, trifling, underage 9 accessory, ancillary, dependent, little one, schoolboy, secondary, small-time, stripling, youngster 10 adolescent, bush-league, incidental, low-ranking, negligible, peripheral, schoolgirl, second-rate, subsidiary
falling-out: 4 spat 5 scrap 8 squabble
flaw: 4 nick
in law: 5 petit
in music: 4 moll
no longer a ~: 5 adult
not ~: 5 major 7 crucial, serious
weakness: 6 foible
minor __: 3 key 5 party, scale 6 league
minor-__: 7 leaguer
Minor __: 7 Prophet
__ Minor: 3 Leo 4 Asia, Ursa 5 Canis, Friar
Minorca: 4 isle 6 island
port: 5 Mahon
__ Minoris: 5 Canis, Ursae
minority: 5 youth 9 childhood
minority __: 5 group 6 leader
Minority Report (2002 film)
cast: Tom Cruise, Max von Sydow
director: Steven Spielberg
minor-league: 4 bush 5 dinky, small 6 lesser 9 secondary
club: 8 farm team
roundball org.: 3 CBA
Minor Prophet: 4 Amos, Joel 5 Hosea, Micah, Nahum 6 Haggai 7 Malachi, Obadiah 8 Habakkuk 9 Zechariah, Zephaniah
Minos
daughter: 7 Ariadne, Euryale, Phaedra
home: 5 Crete 6 Candia
parent: 4 Zeus 6 Europa
wife: 8 Pasiphae
Minot: 4 city, town 6 George
locale: 4 N. Dak.
Minotaur
home: 4 maze 5 Crete 6 Candia
slayer of ~: 7 Theseus
Minsk: 4 city, town 7 capital
locale: 7 Belarus
minster: 6 church 9 cathedral
minstrel: 4 bard, scop 6 singer 10 troubadour
instrument: 4 lute
name meaning ~: 6 Harper
poem: 3 lay
minstrel show: 5 revue 6 review
figure: 6 endman
instrument: 5 banjo
mint: 3 new, pot, wad 4 coin, heap, herb, lots, make, pile 5 candy, forge, fresh, issue, shape, stamp, whole 6 boodle, bundle, intact, invent, myriad, packet, unused, virgin 7 fortune, like new 8 billions, brand-new, millions, original, unmarred 9 high grade, undamaged
ender: 3 age 4 mark
family plant: 4 chia, sage 5 thyme 6 betony, catnip, henbit, hyssop 8 lavender, rosemary
jelly: 5 aspic
jelly accompaniment: 4 lamb
not ~: 4 used
output: 4 cent, coin, dime 5 money 6 nickel 7 quarter 10 half-dollar
starter: 3 cat 5 horse, spear 6 pepper
mint __: 3 tea 5 julep
Mintaka: 4 star
constellation: 5 Orion
Mint Condition
song: Breakin' My Heart (1992)
mint julep: 5 drink 8 beverage
minty: 5 tangy 7 piquant
minuet: 5 dance, music, piece
movement: 4 trio
Minuet __: 3 in G
minus: 4 lack, less, loss, lost, sans 6 absent, except, hurdle 7 barrier, deficit, lacking, missing, needing, wanting, without 8 drawback, handicap, negative, obstacle, take away, weakness, weak spot 9 detriment, hindrance, liability 10 deficiency, impediment, leaving out
entry: 5 debit
toppings: 5 plain
minus __: 4 sign
minuscule: 3 wee 4 itsy, puny, tiny 5 bitty, light, small, teeny, weeny 6 atomic, bantam, letter, little, paltry, peewee, petite, teensy 7 trivial 8 atomical, atomlike, picayune, piddling, trifling 9 itsy-bitsy, itty-bitty, pint-sized 10 teeny-weeny, vest-pocket
minute: 3 sec, wee 4 baby, full, jiff, nice, puny, tick, tiny, wink 5 bitty, close, flash, jiffy, least, light, shake, small, teeny, weeny 6 atomic, bantam, breath, little, moment, paltry, peewee, petite, pocket, second, slight, teensy 7 careful, instant, precise, slender, trivial 8 atomical, atomlike, critical, detailed, exiguous, picayune, piddling, thorough, trifling 9 invisible, itsy-bitsy, itty-bitty, pint-sized, twinkling, undersize, very small 10 diminutive, exhaustive, meticulous, negligible, scrupulous, teeny-weeny, unviewable, vest-pocket
a mile a ~: 5 sixty
any ~ now: 4 anon, soon 7 shortly
fraction: 3 sec. 6 second
hands, essentially: 5 radii
in a ~: 4 soon 9 presently
in a New York ~: 9 instantly, posthaste, right away
New York ~: 5 trice
quantity: 4 drib
this ~: 3 now 4 stat 5 today 6 at once 8 promptly, right now, right off 9 at present, forthwith, instantly, presently, right away 10 here and now
minute __: 4 hand 5 steak
__ minute: 3 any, in a 4 last 5 mile a, wait a
Minute __: 4 Maid, Rice 5 Waltz
Minute Maid product: 2 OJ
Minuteman: 4 ICBM 7 missile
Minutemen: 5 U Mass
Redcoats, to ~: 5 enemy
Minute Rice
alternative: 7 Success 8 Carolina 9 Uncle Ben's
minutes: 3 log 4 acta 6 record
boxer's three ~: 5 round
every 60 ~: 5 horal
fifty ~ past: 5 ten of, ten to
in a few ~: 4 anon, soon 5 later 7 erelong, shortly 8 directly 9 presently 10 before long
keep ~: 4 note 6 record
keeper: 5 noter 9 secretary
one who keeps ~: 5 noter
sixty ~: 4 hour
__ Minutes More: 4 Five
minutest: 5 least
__ Minutes With Andy Rooney, A: 3 Few
Minute Waltz
composer: Frédéric Chopin
__-minute warning: 3 two
minutiae: 6 trivia 7 details, trifles 8 niceties
expert: 4 wonk
minx: 4 miss, snip, vamp 5 flirt, hussy 8 coquette
like a ~: 4 pert 5 saucy
__ Mio: 4 O Dio 5 O Sole
Miocene: 5 Epoch
Mir
in English: 5 peace
milieu: 5 space
Mira: 4 Nair, star 6 pulsar 7 Sorvino 8 red giant
Mirabel: 4 city, town
locale: 6 Canada, Québec
Mirabella: 5 Grace
mirabile __: 5 dictu

__ mirabiles: 4 anni
__ mirabilis: 5 annus
miracle: 6 marvel, rarity, wonder 7 prodigy, stunner 8 surprise 9 sensation 10 phenomenon
combining form: 8 thaumato-
food: 5 manna
Islam ~: 5 miraj
subject of a Biblical ~: 6 loaves
miracle __: 3 man 4 drug, mile, play
Miracle (1991 song)
artist: Whitney Houston
Miracle __: 4 Mile, Whip
Miracle __, The: 6 Worker
Miracle-__: 3 Gro
__ Miracle: 4 It's a
Miracle at Indian River
author: Alden Nowlan
Miracle Mile (1988 film)
cast: John Agar
Miracle of the Rose
author: Jean Genet
Miracle on 34th Street (1947 film)
boss: 4 Macy
cast: Edmund Gwenn, Maureen O'Hara, John Payne, Natalie Wood
Miracles
lead singer: Smokey Robinson
song: Baby, Baby Don't Cry (1969)
Do It Baby (1974)
Going to a Go-Go (1966)
If You Can Want (1968)
I Second That Emotion (1967)
Love Machine (1975)
Mickey's Monkey (1963)
My Girl Has Gone (1965)
Ooo Baby Baby (1965)
Shop Around (1960)
The Tears of a Clown (1970)
The Tracks of My Tears (1965)
Yester Lover (1968)
You've Really Got A Hold on Me (1963)
Miracles (1975 song)
artist: Jefferson Starship
Miracle Whip maker: 5 Kraft
Miracle Worker, The (1962 film)
cast: Anne Bancroft, Patty Duke
role: Helen Keller, Annie Sullivan
miraculous: 7 amazing, awesome, magical, strange, uncanny 8 fabulous, numinous, wondrous 9 marvelous, thrilling, wonderful
Miraculous Mandarin, The: 6 ballet
composer: Béla Bartók
Mirada: 3 car 4 auto 5 Dodge 10 automobile
mirage: 6 fantom, vision 7 fantasm, fantasy, phantom 8 delusion, illusion, phantasm
perhaps: 5 oasis
site: 6 desert
Mirage: 3 car 4 auto 10 automobile, Mitsubishi
locale: 5 Vegas
Mirage (1967 song)
artist: Tommy James and the Shondells
__ Mirage, CA: 6 Rancho
Miramar: 4 city, town
locale: 7 Florida
Miramax: 6 studio
competitor: *see* movie studio
creation: 4 film 5 movie
Miranda: 3 Isa 4 moon, Otto 6 Carmen 10 Richardson
planet: 6 Uranus
__ Mir Bist du Schön: 3 Bei
mire: 3 bog, fen, mud 4 dirt, muck, ooze, quag, sink 5 delay, marsh, slime, slush, snare, swamp 6 detain, enmesh, entrap, immesh, inmesh, morass 7 bog down, embroil, ensnare, insnare, involve, set back 8 entangle 9 catch up in, implicate, marshland, quicksand, swampland
down: 5 embog
drag through the ~: 5 sully
in a ~: 5 stuck
move in ~: 5 slosh
starter: 4 quag
Miriam: 6 Makeba 7 Hopkins
brother: 5 Aaron, Moses
father: 5 Amram
Mirisch: 6 Walter
mirky: 7 obscure
Miró, Joan: 6 artist 7 painter, Spanish
contemporary: Salvador Dalí, Josep Lluís Sert
Mirren: 5 Helen
Mirren, Helen: 4 Dame
film: Calendar Girls (2003) The Queen (2006, AA)
mirror: 3 ape 4 copy, echo, mock, show 5 glass, image, mimic, shine 6 follow, typify 7 act like, emulate, imitate, reflect 8 make like, resemble, simulate 9 personify, reflector, represent, symbolize 10 illustrate
backing: 4 foil, tain
element: 6 indium 7 silicon
fogger: 5 steam
image: 4 refl. 10 reflection
like a ~: 6 glassy, smooth
stand before a ~: 5 preen, prink
mirror __: 5 image
Mirror Crack'd, The (1980 film)
cast: Rock Hudson, Angela Lansbury, Kim Novak, Elizabeth Taylor
Mirror Has Two Faces, The (1996 film)
cast: Lauren Bacall, Jeff Bridges, Mimi Rogers, Barbra Streisand
director: Barbra Streisand
Mirror Image
author: Danielle Steel
Mirror, Mirror (1982 song)
artist: Diana Ross
mirrors, smoke and: 6 deceit
mirth: 3 fun, joy 4 glee 5 cheer, kicks, laugh, sport 6 frolic, gaiety, gayety, laughs, levity 7 gayness, jollity, revelry 8 felicity, gladness, hilarity, laughter, pleasure 9 amusement, festivity, frivolity, happiness, jocundity, joviality, lightness, merriment, rejoicing 10 jocularity, joyousness, liveliness, recreation, regalement, risibility
mirthful: 3 gay 4 glad 5 funny, happy, jolly, merry, riant, sunny 6 blithe, cheery, jovial, joyous, upbeat 7 buoyant, chipper, festive, gleeful, playful, pleased, tickled 8 ecstatic, euphoric, exultant, giggling, grooving, jubilant, laughing, thrilled 9 convivial, delighted, laughable, overjoyed, rejoicing
sound: 4 ha-ha
mirthless: 6 gloomy 7 unhappy 10 melancholy
MIRV: 4 ICBM 7 missile
miry: 5 boggy, mucky, muddy, slimy 6 swampy
not ~: 5 solid
terrain: 3 bog, fen 4 quag 5 swamp
mis-: 3 bad, ill 4 lack
misadd: 3 err
misadventure: 3 woe 4 loss, slip 5 folly 6 mishap 7 bad luck, blunder, debacle, failure, reverse, setback, tragedy 8 accident, bad break, calamity, casualty, disaster 9 adversity, cataclysm, mischance
misanthrope: 5 cynic, hater, loner 6 hermit 7 doubter, recluse, sceptic, skeptic 9 pessimist
Misanthrope, The
author: Molière
misanthropic: 6 crabby, hating 7 cynical, recluse 8 eremitic, reserved, solitary 9 reclusive, sarcastic
misapplication: 5 abuse 6 misuse 7 mistake
misapply: 5 abuse, waste 6 misuse
misapprehend: 3 err 4 miss 7 blunder, confuse, misread, mistake 8 misjudge
misapprehension: 7 fallacy, mistake 8 delusion, illusion
misappropriate: 3 rob 4 crib, grab 5 abuse, filch, steal, usurp 6 misuse, pocket, thieve 7 plunder, swindle 8 embezzle, misapply, misspend, peculate 9 defalcate
misappropriation: 5 abuse, theft 7 larceny
misarrange: 6 muddle
misbegotten: 5 inept 7 illegal, illicit, natural 8 baseborn, spurious, unlawful
misbehave: 3 err, sin 5 act up, be bad, cut up 6 offend 7 carry on, deviate, do wrong, go wrong 8 go astray, trespass 10 fool around, misconduct, roughhouse, transgress
__ Misbehave: 4 Let's
misbehaver: 3 imp 4 brat
__ Misbehaves: 5 Julia
__ Misbehavin': 4 Ain't
misbehaving: 3 bad 4 wild 6 errant
child: 3 imp 4 brat, tike, tyke
misbehavior: 5 guilt 7 misdeed 8 acting up, mischief, misdoing, rudeness
misbelief: 5 error 8 delusion, illusion
misbeliever: 7 sceptic, skeptic
misc.: 3 var.
miscalculate: 3 err 4 goof, slip, trip 5 mix up 6 mess up, slip up 7 blunder, misread, mistake, stumble 8 get wrong, miscount, misjudge, overlook, overrate 9 overvalue, underrate
miscalculated: 5 wrong
miscalculation: 5 boner, error 7 mistake 8 surprise
miscellaneous: 3 NOC, odd 4 many, mixt 5 mixed 6 divers, motley, sundry, varied 7 diverse, jumbled, mingled, oddball, various 8 assorted, multiple, unsorted 9 different, disparate, divergent, unmatched
miscellany: 3 mix 4 hash, mess, olio, stew 5 combo 6 jumble, medley 7 farrago, mélange, mixture, variety 8 mishmash, mixed bag, pastiche 9 anthology, diversity, patchwork, potpourri 10 assortment, collection, cumulation, hodgepodge, salmagundi
literary ~: 3 ana 5 varia
Mischa: 4 Auer 5 Elman
mischance: 4 pity 5 fluke 6 mishap 7 bad luck, reverse, tragedy, undoing 8 hard luck 9 adversity 10 hard knocks, misfortune
mischief: 3 gag 4 evil, harm, hurt 5 antic, caper, prank 6 damage, injury 7 devilry, hot foot, knavery, outrage, roguery, trouble 8 deviltry, sabotage 9 devilment, high jinks, rascality, vandalism 10 dirty trick, friskiness, impishness, misconduct, tomfoolery, wrongdoing
fond of ~: 3 sly
get into ~: 5 act up, cut up 8 go astray 9 misbehave 10 fool around, roughhouse
maker: 3 imp 4 pixy, punk 5 demon, pixie 6 daemon, daimon 7 hellion
mischief __: 5 night
mischief-maker: 3 elf 5 rogue, scamp 6 rascal, vandal 7 gremlin 9 scoundrel
mischieviously: 5 in fun
mischievous: 3 bad, sly 4 arch, evil, foxy 5 apish, elfin, rowdy 6 artful, elfish, elvish, impish, tricky, vexing, wicked 7 coltish, harmful, hurtful, irksome, jocular, knavish, naughty, nocuous, playful, puckish, teasing, vicious, wayward 8 damaging, devilish, prankish, rascally, sinister, spiteful, sporting, sportive 9 injurious, insidious, malicious, vexatious
be ~: 5 act up 9 misbehave
child: 3 imp 4 tike, tyke 6 gamine, urchin
one: 3 elf 5 rogue, scamp
mischievousness: 7 devilry 8 deviltry
misconceive: 7 mistake 8 misjudge
misconception: 5 error, fault 7 fallacy, mistake 8 delusion, illusion
misconduct: 3 sin 4 evil 5 fault, guilt 7 misdeed, offense 8 mischief, misdoing, rudeness 9 improbity, misbehave, vandalism, veniality
misconstrue: 4 skew 7 distort, misread, mistake 8 get wrong, misjudge
misconstrued: 5 wrong 8 mistaken
miscount: 5 error
miscreancy: 8 iniquity
miscreant: 3 cad, cur, rat 4 evil, fink, heel, scum, worm 5 bully, churl, felon, hater, knave, louse, rogue, rowdy, scamp, sneak 6 loafer, outlaw, rascal, wicked, wretch 7 caitiff, convict, corrupt, culprit, hoodlum, immoral, lowlife, outcast, ruffian, vicious, villain 8 criminal, depraved, evildoer, infamous, jailbird, perverse, picaroon, rakehell, rascally, scalawag 9 heretical,

nefarious, racketeer, reprobate, scallawag, scallywag, scoundrel, vulgarian, wrongdoer **10** blackguard, black sheep, bootlegger, degenerate, delinquent, holy terror, iniquitous, malefactor, pickpocket, villainous
miscue: **3** err **5** boner, error, fault, fluff, lapse **6** fumble, slip-up **7** misstep **9** oversight
remover: **6** eraser
misdeal: **3** err
misdeed: **3** sin **4** no-no, slip **5** crime, error, fault, wrong **6** slip-up **7** offense **8** trespass, villainy **9** dirty pool, veniality, violation **10** illegality, misconduct, peccadillo, wrongdoing
misdemeanor: **3** sin **5** crime, fault, wrong **6** delict, miscue, slip-up **7** offense **8** trespass, villainy **9** dirty deed, dirty pool, violation
misdirect: **8** throw off **9** misinform **10** lead astray
misdirected: **5** led on **6** astray
misdo: **3** err **4** muff **5** botch **6** blow it, bungle, foul up, mess up **7** go wrong
misdoing: **5** wrong **7** outrage **10** misconduct
mise en __: **5** scène
misemploy: **5** abuse, waste **6** misuse
misemployment: **5** abuse
miser: **5** churl **6** cheapo **7** hoarder, Scrooge **8** el cheapo, muckworm, tightwad **9** skinflint **10** cheapskate, pinchpenny
like a ~: **6** stingy **7** chintzy
motivation: **5** greed
no ~: **5** donor, giver
stash: **5** hoard
miserable: **3** ill, low, sad **4** blue, down, glum, hurt, mean, sick, vile **5** awful, lousy, moody, needy, sorry **6** abject, ailing, broody, gloomy, humble, in pain, meager, measly, morose, pained, paltry, racked, rueful, scanty, scurvy, shabby, sickly, somber, sordid **7** forlorn, hapless, hurting, in a funk, injured, joyless, piteous, pitiful, ruthful, squalid, unhappy, wounded **8** beggarly, dejected, desolate, dolorous, downcast, dreadful, God-awful, hopeless, indigent, mournful, pathetic, pitiable, strained, tortured, troubled **9** afflicted, bummed out, cheerless, depressed, destitute, destroyed, heartsick, penniless, sorrowful, suffering, thankless, third-rate, tormented, woebegone, worthless **10** chapfallen, despairing, despondent, dispirited, distressed, melancholy, pathetical
feeling: **5** agony
see also awful
__ Misérables: **3** Les
Miserere: **5** psalm
miserliness: **7** avarice
miserly: **4** mean **5** cheap, close, tight **6** greedy, measly, shabby, skimpy, stingy **7** ignoble, selfish **8** churlish, covetous, grasping, ungiving **9** illiberal, penurious, skinflint **10** avaricious, cheapskate, inadequate, skinflinty, ungenerous
misery: **3** ill, woe **4** ache, bane, hell, load, need, pain, pang, want **5** agony, blues, curse, dolor, gloom, grief, throe, trial, worry **6** burden, ordeal, penury, sorrow, stitch, twinge **7** anguish, anxiety, bad news, despair, hurting, passion, poverty, problem, sadness, squalor, torment, torture, travail, trouble **8** calamity, disaster, distress, hardship, headache, the blues **9** adversity, dejection, heartache, indigence, privation, suffering **10** affliction, bitter pill, depression, desolation, difficulty, discomfort, heartbreak, heavy heart, infelicity, loneliness, melancholy, misfortune, oppression, sordidness, woefulness
cause of ~: **4** bane
Misery: **4** film **5** novel
author: Stephen King
cast: Kathy Bates, James Caan, Frances Sternhagen
character: **5** Annie
director: Rob Reiner
misfeasance: **5** abuse
misfield: **6** fumble
misfigured: **5** wrong
misfire: **4** miss **6** fizzle, glitch **7** lose out **8** fall flat
misfit: **4** geek, nerd **5** dweeb, loser **6** wretch **7** oddball
high-school ~: **4** nerd **7** egghead
Misfits, The (1961 film)
author: Arthur Miller
cast: Montgomery Clift, Clark Gable, Marilyn Monroe
director: John Huston
dog: Tom Dooley
'M' Is for Malice
author: Sue Grafton
misfortunate: **7** unhappy
misfortune: **3** ill, woe **4** blow, harm, loss, pity **5** cross, trial **6** crunch, misery, sorrow **7** bad luck, bad news, debacle, failure, reverse, setback, tragedy, trouble, undoing **8** accident, bad break, calamity, casualty, disaster, distress, hard luck, hardship **9** adversity, cataclysm, liability, mischance, suffering, tough luck **10** affliction, difficulty, hard knocks
cause of ~: **3** hex **4** jinx **5** curse **6** hoodoo
misgiving: **8** bad vibes **9** nonbelief
misgivings: **4** care, fear, pang **5** doubt, qualm, worry **6** regret, unease **7** anxiety, scruple **8** distrust, mistrust, question, wariness **9** leeriness, suspicion **10** foreboding, hesitation, insecurity, skepticism
have ~ about: **3** rue
more than ~: **5** dread
misguess: **3** err
misguide: **3** lie **6** delude **7** mislead **9** disinform, misinform
misguided: **5** led on, wrong **6** misled, unwise **7** deluded, foolish **8** confused, deceived, faked-out, mistaken **9** erroneous, impolitic, imprudent, misplaced **10** ill-advised, indiscreet
act: **5** folly
Misha: **7** Dichter
mishandle: **3** err **4** blow, flub, goof, harm, mall, maul, muff **5** abuse, botch, gum up **6** blow it, bungle, foozle, foul up, fumble, goof up, mess up, misuse **7** blunder **8** aggrieve, mistreat, overlook
mishandled: **5** wrong
mishandling: **5** abuse
mishap: **3** dud **4** blow, bomb, bust, flop, harm, loss, pity **5** event, hitch, snafu **6** defeat, fiasco, glitch, turkey **7** blunder, debacle, misstep, reverse, setback, stumble, tragedy, trouble, washout **8** accident, bad break, calamity, casualty, disaster, downfall, hard luck, hardship **9** adversity, breakdown, cataclysm, mischance, tough luck **10** visitation
razor ~: **3** cut
Mishawaka: **4** city, town
locale: **7** Indiana
mishearing: **6** otosis
Mishima, Yukio: **6** writer **8** Japanese
work: The Sailor Who Fell from Grace with the Sea
The Sound of Waves
The Temple of the Golden Pavilion
mishmash: **3** mix **4** hash, mess, muss, olio, stew **5** mix-up, snarl **6** jumble, litter, medley **7** farrago, goulash, mélange, mixture, variety **8** pastiche, scramble **9** pasticcio, patchwork, potpourri **10** assortment, hodgepodge, miscellany, salmagundi
Mishnah: **4** laws **6** Jewish
authority: **5** rabbi, rebbe
misimpression: **8** illusion
misinform: **3** lie **5** lie to **7** cover up, deceive, mislead **8** misguide, misstate **9** misdirect, mousetrap **10** lead astray, put on an act, steer wrong
misinformed: **6** lied to **8** mistaken **9** misguided
misinstruct: **3** lie
misinterpret: **4** skew **6** garble **7** distort, mistake
misinterpretation: **5** error
misjudge: **3** err **4** slip **7** mistake, presume **8** be misled, overrate, prejudge **9** dogmatize, underrate **10** presuppose
misjudgment: **5** error **7** mistake
Miskito: **6** Indian **7** Amerind
Miskolc: **4** city, town
locale: **7** Hungary
mislaid: **4** lost **7** missing
mislay: **4** lose, miss **8** misplace
mislead: **3** con, lie **4** bait, bilk, dupe, fool, gull, hoax, hose, jive, lure, nick, rook, scam, sell, sham, snow **5** bluff, cheat, cozen, lie to, put on, shaft, tempt, trick **6** betray, delude, entice, outwit, rip off, rope in, suck in, take in **7** beguile, confuse, deceive, defraud, ensnare, insnare, pretend, sell out, two-time **8** confound, hoodwink, inveigle, misguide, outsmart, throw off **9** disinform, four-flush, misinform, victimize
misleading: **4** sham **5** false, lying, wrong **6** tricky, unreal, untrue **7** devious, evasive **8** deluding, delusive, delusory, puzzling, specious, spurious **9** ambiguous, beguiling, confusing, deceitful, deceiving, deception, deceptive, dishonest, equivocal **10** fallacious, fictitious, inexplicit, unexplicit, ungrounded
move: **4** ruse
one: **4** liar
Misled (1985 song)
artist: Kool and the Gang
mismanage: **3** err **4** flub, goof, harm, muff **5** abuse, botch, gum up **6** blow it, bungle, foozle, foul up, fumble, goof up, mess up, misuse **7** blunder, louse up **8** overlook
mismatch: **6** differ **8** contrast **9** disparity
mismatched: **6** unlike **7** unalike, unequal **9** different **10** dissimilar
miso: **4** soup **6** legume
ingredient: **3** soy
misogynist: **5** hater
mispickel: **3** ore
misplace: **4** lose, miss **6** mislay **7** misfile
misplaced: **4** lost **7** missing **9** misguided
misplay: **3** err **4** muff **5** error
misprint: **4** typo **5** error **7** erratum, mistake
misprints: **6** errata
misquote: **3** lie **4** skew, warp **5** slant, twist **6** garble **7** distort, falsify, stretch, trump up **8** miscolor **9** embellish, embroider, overstate **10** equivocate, exaggerate
Misr
natives call it ~: **5** Egypt
Misreadings
author: Umberto Eco
misreckon: **3** err
misrender: **4** skew **5** color
misreport: **4** skew **10** exaggerate
misrepresent: **3** con, lie **4** hoke, skew, snow, warp **5** belie, color, fudge, slant, twist, wrong **6** garble, palter **7** cover up, distort, falsify, mislead, stretch, trump up **8** disguise, miscolor, simulate **9** embellish, embroider, overstate
misrepresentation: **3** fib, lie **4** hoax, ruse, sham **5** feint, fraud **6** deceit, humbug **7** falsity, slander, snow job, swindle **8** artifice, pretense **9** imposture **10** subterfuge
miss: **3** deb, err **4** fail, flub, girl, jump, lack, lass, long, lose, loss, maid, minx, muff, need, omit, skip, slip, trip, verb, want, wish **5** botch, crave, error, fault, fluff, forgo, let go, mourn, title, woman, yearn **6** blow it, damsel, desire, falter, female, forego, forget, fumble, gamine, ignore, lassie, maiden, mislay, pass up, regret, tomboy **7** blunder, colleen, default, failure, let slip, long for, misfire, misstep, mistake, neglect, pine for, require **8** fraülein, misjudge, misplace, omission, overlook, pass over **9** debutante, disregard, fall short, go without, lose out on, overshoot, oversight **10** bobbysoxer, schoolgirl, undershoot
any ~: **3** her, she
hit or ~: **6** random **10** undesigned

in French: 4 Mlle.
in Japanese: 3 san
in Spanish: 4 srta. 8 señorita
partner: 3 hit
the boat: 4 fail 7 lose out
miss __: 4 a cue 5 out on
miss __ good..., A: 4 is as
miss __ mile: 3 by a
miss __ on: 3 out
__ miss: 4 near 5 hit or 6 junior
Miss __: 3 USA, You 5 Julie, Peach, Piggy 6 Saigon 7 America, Liberty, Manners 8 Universe
Miss __ at the Cirque Fernando: 4 Lola
Miss __ Bett: 4 Lulu
Miss __ Disposes: 3 Pym
Miss __ Regrets: 4 Otis
Miss __ Thompson: 5 Sadie
Miss __ USA: 4 Teen
Miss.
city on the ~: 3 St. L.
neighbor: 3 Ala., Ark., Tex. 4 Tenn.
see also Mississippi
__ Miss: 3 Old, Ole
missa __: 7 cantata
miss a __: 3 cue
Missa Hilarious
composer: PDQ Bach
Miss America
author: Howard Stern
former ~ host: 3 Ely 5 Parks 6 Ron Ely 9 Bert Parks
wear: 4 sash 5 tiara 8 swimsuit
Missa Solemnis
composer: Ludwig van Beethoven
__ Miss Brooks: 3 Our
miss by __: 5 a mile
Miss Congeniality (2000 film)
cast: Benjamin Bratt, Sandra Bullock, Michael Caine, William Shatner
__ Miss Daisy: 7 Driving
missed: 4 lost 5 unhit
Miss Firecracker (1989 film)
cast: Holly Hunter, Tim Robbins, Mary Steenburgen
Miss Firecracker Contest, The
author: Beth Henley
misshape: 4 warp 6 deform 7 contort
misshapen: 9 grotesque, malformed
missile: 2 MX 3 bat, SAM 4 ammo, bolt, bomb, dart, ICBM, MIRV, Nike, nuke, Scud, shot, Thor 5 arrow, lance, spear, Titan 6 bullet, pellet, rocket, weapon 9 cartridge, explosive 10 ammunition, projectile, trajectile
housing: 4 silo
of yore: 5 arrow, spear, stone
part: 4 cone
path: 3 arc 4 traj. 10 trajectory
treaty acronym: 4 SALT 5 START
type: 8 air-to-air
warning grp.: 5 NORAD
missile __: 3 gap
__ missile: 6 cruise, guided
__-missile: 4 anti
__ Missile Crisis: 5 Cuban
missing: 4 away, AWOL, gone, lost 5 minus, out of, short 6 absent, astray, bereft 7 at large, lacking, left out, mislaid, needing, omitted, removed, wanting 8 vanished 9 elsewhere, misplaced 10 left behind
go ~: 6 vanish 9 disappear
link: 6 apeman
not ~ a trick: 8 watchful 9 observant
nothing: 4 full 6 entire 8 complete, thorough 10 exhaustive, unabridged
part: 4 hole 6 lacuna
something ~: 4 lack
missing __: 4 link
Missing (1982 film)
cast: Jack Lemmon, Sissy Spacek
director: Costa-Gavras
setting: 5 Chile
__ missing something?: 3 am I
Missing, The (2003 film)
cast: Cate Blanchett, Tommy Lee Jones, Evan Rachel Wood
director: Ron Howard
Missing You (song)
artist: Ray Peterson, Diana Ross, John Waite
mission: 3 aim, end, job 4 duty, goal, task, work 5 quest, trust 6 affair, charge, church, errand, object, sortie 7 calling, embassy, purpose, pursuit 8 business, function, legation, lifework, vocation 9 objective, operation 10 assignment, commission, profession
military ~: 5 recon
military ~ in Britain: 5 recce, recco
scrap a ~: 5 abort
starter: 5 trans
mission __: 7 control
__ mission: 3 on a 6 rescue
Mission __, CA: 5 Viejo
missionary: 6 clergy, herald, jesuit, pastor 7 apostle, teacher 8 minister, preacher, promoter 9 converter, messenger
book: 5 Bible
Missionary __: 5 Ridge
Mission Bend: 4 city, town
locale: 5 Texas
Mission Control concern: 6 G force
Mission Impossible (1996 film)
cast: Emmanuelle Béart, Tom Cruise, Emilio Estevez, Vanessa Redgrave, Ving Rhames, Jon Voight
director: Brian De Palma
Mission Impossible (CBS drama)
cast: Barbara Bain (Cinnamon Carter)
Lynda Day George (Lisa Casey)
Peter Graves (Jim Phelps)
Steven Hill (Dan Briggs)
Martin Landau (Rollin Hand)
Peter Lupus (Willy Armitage)
Greg Morris (Barney Collier)
Leonard Nimoy (Paris)
Mission Impossible II (2000 film)
cast: Tom Cruise, Thandie Newton, Ving Rhames, Dougray Scott
director: John Woo
Mission: Impossible org.: 3 IMF
Mission to __: 4 Mars
Mission Viejo: 4 city, town
locale: 10 California
town near ~: 6 El Toro
missis: 4 mate, wife 5 bride, woman 6 female, spouse 9 other half
miss is as good as __, A: 5 a mile
Mississauga: 4 city, town
locale: 6 Canada 7 Ontario
Mississippi: 3 riv. 5 river, state
capital: 7 Jackson
city: 5 Pearl 6 Biloxi, Tupelo 7 Clinton, Jackson, Natchez 8 Columbus, Gulfport, Meridian 9 Southaven, Vicksburg 10 Clarksdale, Greenville, Pascagoula, Southhaven, Starkville
conference: 3 SEC
neighbor: 3 Ala., Ark. 4 Tenn. 7 Alabama 8 Arkansas 9 Louisiana, Tennessee
river: 5 Yazoo
state beverage: 4 milk
state flower: 8 magnolia
state game bird: 8 wood duck
state insect: 8 honeybee
state shell: 6 oyster
state tree: 8 magnolia
Mississippi __: 3 Mud 5 Blues, Delta
Mississippi Burning (1988 film)
cast: Willem Dafoe, Gene Hackman, Frances McDormand
Mississippi River
city on the ~: 6 Keokuk, St. Paul 7 Memphis, St. Louis 10 Baton Rouge
explorer: 6 Joliet 7 Jolliet, La Salle
feature: 4 silt 5 bayou, delta
flatboat: 3 ark
river to the ~: 3 Red 4 Iowa, Ohio 5 White, Yazoo 7 St. Croix 8 Arkansas, Big Muddy, Illinois 9 Minnesota, Wisconsin
source: 6 Itasca
state: 3 Ill, Ken., Wis. 4 Iowa, Minn., Tenn., Wisc. 8 Illinois, Kentucky, Missouri 9 Louisiana, Minnesota, Tennessee, Wisconsin
vessel: 3 ark, str. 7 steamer 8 flatboat
Mississippi State
athletes: 8 Bulldogs
conference: 3 SEC
locale: 10 Starkville
Mississippi Suite
composer: Ferde Grofé
missive: 3 ltr. 4 line, memo, note, word 6 letter, report 7 epistle, message 8 dispatch 10 memorandum
Miss Julie
author: August Strindberg
composer: Ned Rorem
Miss Kitty
friend: 4 Matt
Miss Liberty: 7 musical
composer: Irving Berlin
Miss Lonelyhearts
author: Nathanael West
Miss Lulu Bett
author: Zona Gale
Miss Mama __: 5 Aimee
__ Miss Marker: 6 Little
Miss Me Blind (1984 song)
artist: Culture Club
Miss Otis Regrets
composer: Cole Porter
Missoula: 4 city, town
athletes: 9 Grizzlies
locale: 4 Mont. 7 Montana
Missouri: 3 riv 5 river, state 6 Indian 7 Amerind 10 battleship
capital: Jefferson City
city: 3 St. L. 5 Lamar, Rolla, St. Joe 6 Affton, Arnold, Belton, Joplin 7 Ballwin, Branson, Liberty, O'Fallon, Raytown, Sedalia, St. Louis 8 Columbia, Ferguson, Hannibal, Kirkwood, Oakville, St. Joseph, St. Peters, Wildwood 9 Gladstone, Grandview, Hazelwood, Mehlville, St. Charles 10 Florissant, Kansas City, Lee's Summit
conference: 9 Big Twelve
motto word: 4 esto
mountain range: 6 Ozarks
neighbor: 3 Ark., Ill., Kan., Ken., Neb. 4 Iowa, Nebr:, Okla., Tenn. 6 Kansas 8 Arkansas, Illinois, Kentucky, Nebraska, Oklahoma 9 Tennessee
plateau: 5 Ozark
port: 7 St. Louis
state animal: 4 mule
state aquatic animal: 10 paddlefish
state bird: 8 bluebird
state fish: 7 catfish
state fossil: 7 crinoid
state insect: 8 honeybee
state mineral: 6 galena
state musical instrument: 6 fiddle
state rock: 9 mozarkite
state tree: 7 dogwood
__ Missouri: 3 USS
Missouri River
city: 5 Omaha 6 Pierre 8 Bismarck, St. Joseph 9 Sioux City 10 Great Falls
city on the ~: 5 Omaha 6 Pierre 8 Bismarck 10 Kansas City
river to the ~: 5 Osage 6 Kansas 8 Cheyenne, Niobrara
tribe: 3 Oto 4 Otoe
Miss Peach: 5 comic 10 comic strip
artist: Mell Lazarus
character: 3 Ira
misspeak: 3 err, lie
misspell: 3 err
misspend: 4 lose 5 waste 8 squander 9 dissipate
misspent: 4 idle, lost 5 blown 6 wasted 8 prodigal 10 dissipated, misapplied, profitless, squandered, thrown away
Miss Piggy: 3 sow 6 Muppet
friend: 6 Kermit
pronoun: 3 moi
Miss Pym Disposes
author: Josephine Tey
Miss Saigon setting: 3 Nam 7 Vietnam
misstate: 3 lie 4 skew 5 twist 6 invent 7 falsify 9 misinform
misstatement: 3 lie 5 error, gaffe 7 blooper, mistake 8 pretense
misstep: 3 dud, err 4 bomb, bust, flop, lose, loss, slip, trip 5 boner, error, fluff, flunk, gaffe, guilt, lapse 6 blow it, boo-boo, bungle, defeat, falter, fiasco, miscue, slip-up, turkey 7 blunder, debacle, failure, faux pas, founder, go under, go wrong, mistake, stumble, washout 8 downfall, fall flat, flounder, lay an

egg 9 indecorum, strike out
miss the __: 4 boat
Miss Thompson
author: W. Somerset Maugham
Miss Universe
wear: 5 tiara
missus: 4 mate, wife 5 woman 6 female, spouse 9 other half
missy: 4 girl, lass 5 woman
Missy: 4 Gold 7 Elliott, Francis
Miss You (1978 song)
artist: Rolling Stones
Miss You Like Crazy (1989 song)
artist: Natalie Cole
Miss You Much (1989 song)
artist: Janet Jackson
mist: 3 dew, dim, fog 4 blur, film, haze, mirk, murk, rain, smog, soup 5 befog, blear, brume, cloud, spray, steam, vapor 6 mizzle, shower 7 drizzle, moisten, obscure, steam up 8 moisture, sprinkle 9 overcloud
__ mist: 3 sea 6 Scotch
__ Mist: 5 Irish
mistake: 3 err 4 fail, flub, goof, miss, omit, slip, trip, typo 5 boner, botch, error, fault, fluff, gaffe, lapse, mix-up, snafu, snarl 6 barney, bobble, boo-boo, bungle, goof-up, gotcha, howler, jumble, lapsus, muddle, slip-up, tangle 7 blooper, blunder, confuse, erratum, faux pas, misread, misstep, neglect 8 confound, delusion, get wrong, illusion, miscount, misjudge, misprint, omission, overlook, solecism 9 confusion, false move, false step, oversight 10 aberration, inaccuracy
by ~: 7 in error 8 unawares
exclamation: 4 oh-oh, oops, uh-oh 6 whoops
indicated a ~: 3 x'ed
make a ~: 3 err 4 goof, miss, slip
no ~: 5 truly 6 surely 7 flat out 8 in spades 9 certainly, decidedly, downright 10 absolutely, definitely, distinctly, positively
remover: 6 eraser
mistaken: 5 duped, false, wrong 6 all wet, erring, faulty, fooled, misled, unreal, untrue, way off 7 at fault, deluded, off-base, tricked, unsound 8 confused, deceived 9 erroneous, illogical, incorrect, misguided, unadvised, unfounded 10 confounded, fallacious, ill-advised, inaccurate, misjudging, ungrounded, unreliable
__ mistaken: 5 sadly
mistakenly: 5 amiss, wrong 9 foolishly
mistakes: 6 errata
mister: 2 he 3 guy, man, sir 4 chap, gent, male, mate 5 bloke, hubby 6 feller, fellow, spouse 7 grown-up, husband
in French: 8 monsieur
in German: 4 herr
in India: 3 sri 4 shri 5 saheb, sahib
in Spanish: 5 señor
Mister __: 7 Roberts, Sandman
Mister Ed (CBS sitcom)
cast: Connie Hines (Carol Post)
Alan Young (Wilbur Post)
title character: 5 horse
Mister Roberts (1955 film)
cast: James Cagney, Henry Fonda, Jack Lemmon, William Powell
director: John Ford, Mervyn LeRoy
Mister Sandman (1954 song)
artist: Four Aces
mistimed: 3 off 5 wrong
mistletoe: 5 plant, shrub
month: 3 Dec. 8 December
ritual: 4 kiss
unit: 5 sprig
__ misto: 6 fritto
mistral: 4 wind
Mistral: 8 Frédéric, Gabriela
Mistral's Daughter
author: Judith Krantz
mistranscription: 4 typo
mistreat: 3 rip 4 bash, harm, mall, maul 5 abuse, trash, wound, wrong 6 dump on, ill-use, injure, mess up, misuse 7 corrupt, outrage, rough up, shake up, torment, torture 8 aggrieve, backbite, maltreat 9 brutalize, manhandle, mishandle 10 excruciate, kick around, push around, roughhouse
mistreatment: 5 abuse 6 misuse 8 inequity
__, Mistress of the Dark: 6 Elvira
mistrust: 4 fear 5 doubt, query 6 beware, wonder 7 dispute, suspect 8 bad vibes, discount, disfavor, distrust, question, wariness 9 challenge, chariness, disbelief, discredit, misgiving, nonbelief, smell a rat, suspicion 10 disbelieve, foreboding, skepticism
mistrustful: 4 wary 5 chary 6 unsure 7 dubious, guarded 8 cautious, doubting, hesitant 9 skeptical, uncertain 10 suspicious
misty: 3 dim, wet 4 damp, dark, dewy, hazy 5 foggy, fuzzy, mirky, moist, murky, soupy, undry, vague 6 bleary, cloudy, opaque, steamy 7 blurred, clouded, obscure, unclear, wettish 8 closed in, nebulous, overcast, shrouded, socked in, vaporous 9 drizzling 10 indistinct
become ~: 5 fog up
get ~: 3 sob 4 weep 7 blubber 9 shed tears
Misty (1959 song)
artist: Johnny Mathis
misty-eyed: 5 teary
__ Misty for Me: 4 Play
misunderstand: 4 miss 7 confuse, misread, mistake 8 confound, get wrong, misapply, misjudge 9 take amiss
misunderstanding: 3 row 4 feud, fuss, rift, spat, tiff 5 break, clash, error, fight, mix-up, run-in, set-to, words 6 blowup, breach 7 discord, mistake, quarrel, rupture 8 argument, bad vibes, conflict, delusion, mistaken, sour note, squabble, variance 9 confusion
misuse: 4 harm, mall, maul 5 abuse, spend, waste 6 injury, mess up, play on, punish, trifle 7 corrupt, exploit, outrage, profane 8 aggrieve, ill-treat, maltreat, misapply, mistreat, play upon, solecism, squander 9 brutalize, desecrate, go through, misemploy, mishandle, mismanage, pollution 10 gamble away, run through
misused: 4 lost 7 injured
mit: 4 with 6 German
in French: 4 avec
in Spanish: 3 con
MIT: 3 sch. 4 coll. 6 school 7 college
business school: 5 Sloan
degree: 2 EE, IE, ME 3 BME
grad: 3 eng. 4 engr.
part: 4 inst., Mass., Tech.
stat: 3 GPA
Mitch: 5 Leigh, Ryder 6 Miller 7 Gaylord, Pileggi
Mitchell: 3 Don, Guy 4 diva, Eric, Joni, peak 5 Abbie, Ayres, Bobby, Brian, Kevin, Leona, mount, Peter, Radha, Sasha 6 Andrea, Arthur, Leisen, Thomas, Yvonne 7 Cameron 8 Margaret, mountain
locale: 4 N. Car.
Mitchell, Andrea
spouse: Alan Greenspan
Mitchell, Arthur: 6 dancer 7 danseur
specialty: 6 ballet
Mitchell, Guy
song: Heartaches by the Numbers (1959)
Rock-A-Billy (1957)
Singing the Blues (1956)
Mitchell, John Leslie: 6 writer 8 Scottish
Mitchell, Joni
homeland: Canada
song: Big Yellow Taxi (1975)
Help Me (1974)
Mitchell, Margaret: 6 writer
heroine: 5 O'Hara
mansion: 4 Tara
work: Gone With the Wind
Mitchison, Naomi: 6 writer 7 British
Mitchum: 6 Robert 9 deodorant
alternative: *see* deodorant
Mitchum, Robert: 5 actor
film: Bandido (1956)
Big Steal (1949)
Blood on the Moon (1948)
Cape Fear (1962)
Crossfire (1947)
El Dorado (1967)
The Enemy Below (1957)
The Friends of Eddie Coyle (1973)
Going Home (1971)
The Grass Is Greener (1960)
Heaven Knows, Mr. Allison (1957)
Holiday Affair (1949)
Home From the Hill (1960)
The Last Tycoon (1976)
The Longest Day (1962)
The Night of the Hunter (1955)
Not as a Stranger (1955)
Out of the Past (1947)
Pursued (1947)
The Racket (1951)
The Red Pony (1949)
Ryan's Daughter (1970)
Secret Ceremony (1968)
The Story of G.I. Joe (1945)
The Sundowners (1960)
Thunder Road (1958)
Till the End of Time (1946)
Two for the Seesaw (1962)
What a Way to Go! (1964)
mite: 3 bit, bug, dot, jot, tad 4 atom, iota, pest, snip, tick, whit 5 child, crumb, grain, pinch, scrap, speck 6 acarid, acarus, insect, tittle 7 granule, modicum, smidgen, smidgin 8 arachnid, molecule, particle, pittance, smidgeon 9 scintilla
a ~: 8 slightly, somewhat
combining form: 4 acar- 5 acari-, acaro-
__ mite: 4 dust
miter: 3 cut, hat 5 bevel 6 joiner
wearer: 4 Pope 6 bishop
miter __: 3 box, saw
Mitford, Jessica: 6 writer
work: The American Way of Death
Daughters and Rebels
A Fine Old Conflict
Mitford, Nancy: 6 writer 7 British
concept: 4 non-U
work: The Blessing
Love in a Cold Climate
The Pursuit of Love
mitigate: 4 calm, cool, dull, ease, help 5 abate, allay, blunt, check, let up, loose, mince, quell, quiet, relax, remit 6 lessen, loosen, modify, pacify, quench, reduce, remedy, smooth, soften, solace, soothe, subdue, temper, weaken 7 appease, assuage, comfort, commute, lighten, mollify, placate, qualify, relieve 8 diminish, moderate, palliate, tone down 9 alleviate, attenuate, extenuate, reconcile 10 ameliorate
mitigation: 4 balm, ease 5 letup 6 easing, relief 7 anodyne 8 easement 9 abatement
Mitla Pass
author: Leon Uris
mitosis
undergo ~: 6 divide
Mitropoulos, Dimitri: 5 Greek 9 conductor
Mitsou
author: Colette
Mitsubishi: 3 car 4 auto 10 automobile
model: 3 FTO 4 Colt, Expo 5 Magna, Sigma 6 Cordia, Galant, Lancer, Mirage, Precis, Raider, Tredia 7 Eclipse, Montero, Starion 8 Diamante 9 Evolution, Outlander
mitt: 3 paw 4 hand 5 glove 6 holder
__ mitt: 4 oven 8 catcher's
mitten
lack: 7 fingers
part: 4 palm 5 thumb
Mitterrand, François: 6 French 9 president
mitts on, get one's: 5 seize
Mitty: 6 Walter
Mitty, Mrs.: 3 nag
Mitzi: 6 Gaynor, McCall 7 Kapture
__ mitzvah: 3 bar, bas, bat 4 bath
Miuccia: 5 Prada
mix: 4 beat, fuse, join, lace, lump, meld, soup, stew, stir, whip 5 alloy, blend, combo, cross, dough, knead, merge, union, unite 6 batter, commix, hobnob, hybrid, infuse, jumble, make up, medley, mingle, mosaic, muddle, tangle, work in 7 amalgam, combine, conjoin, consort, goulash, grab bag, hang out, mélange, shake up,

suffuse, variety **8** coalesce, compound, get along, mishmash, solution, table-hop **9** admixture, aggregate, associate, commingle, composite, diversify, hybridize, integrate, interlace, potpourri, socialize **10** adulterate, amalgamate, assortment, concoction, confection, fraternize, hodgepodge, homogenize, infiltrate, interbreed, interweave, miscellany, salmagundi
ending: **5** ology
in: **6** meddle **8** dissolve **9** intercede, interfere, interlard, intervene
it up: **4** spat **5** argue, clash, fight **6** battle, go at it, tussle **7** quarrel, scuffle
up: **4** goof, mess **5** addle, botch, churn, dizzy, throw, upset **6** garble, hassle, jumble, muddle, puzzle, tangle **7** confuse, disrupt, disturb, fluster, mistake, perplex, shuffle, trouble **8** befuddle, bewilder, confound, disorder, distract, entangle, scramble **9** confusion, dislocate, disorient **10** complicate, disarrange, disconcert, disorderly
mix ___: **4** it up
mix-___: **3** ups
___ mix: **4** cake **5** trail
___-mix: **5** ready
Mix: **3** Ron, Tom
___ Mix: **4** Meow
___ Mix-a-Lot: **3** Sir
mix-and-___: **5** match
mixed: **5** fused, joint **6** melded, merged, motley, united, varied **7** alloyed, blended, diverse, infused, kneaded, mingled, unalike, various **8** assorted, combined, multiple **9** aggregate, composite, crossbred, different, interbred **10** compounded, hybridized, transfused
bag: **4** misc., olio, stew **6** medley **7** mélange, variety **9** diversity, potpourri **10** assortment, hodgepodge, miscellany, salmagundi
breed: **3** mut **4** mule, mutt **7** mongrel
up: **6** addled **7** tangled **8** pell-mell **10** disorderly, topsy-turvy, upside-down
mixed ___: **3** bag **4** nuts **5** drink, grill, media **6** number **7** company, doubles
Mixed Blessings
author: Danielle Steel
Mixed Company
author: Irwin Shaw
Mixed Emotions (1989 song)
artist: Rolling Stones
mixer: **2** do **4** cola, soda **5** dance, whisk **6** beater, joiner, social **7** blender, mingler, seltzer **8** club soda **9** eggbeater, extrovert, ginger ale **10** socializer, tonic water
alternative: **5** whisk
bar ~: **4** cola, soda **5** tonic, water **7** bitters, seltzer **8** club soda **9** ginger ale **10** tonic water
maker: **5** Oster
without a ~: **4** neat **8** straight
___ mixer: **6** cement
mixing ___: **4** bowl
mixing bowl: **6** krater
mixologist: **6** barman **9** bartender
cube: **4** rock
measure: **4** shot
Mix, Tom
film: **5** oater **7** western
horse: **4** Tony
mixture: **4** hash, olio, soup, stew **5** alloy, batch, blend, combo, cross, dough, union **6** batter, fusion, hybrid, jumble, medley, mosaic, potion **7** amalgam, collage, combine, farrago, goulash, grab bag, mélange, mongrel, variety **8** compound, mishmash, pastiche, solution **9** composite, potpourri **10** assortment, concoction, confection, hodgepodge, miscellany, salmagundi, sprinkling
flour ~: **6** batter
mix-up: **3** row **4** fray, mess, riot **5** brawl, chaos, fight, snafu, twist **6** battle, fracas, jumble, muddle, rumpus, tangle, tussle, uproar **7** mistake, problem, turmoil **8** disorder, mishmash, shambles, skirmish **9** commotion, confusion, imbroglio, scrimmage **10** donnybrook, free-for-all
Miyoshi: **5** Umeki
___ Miz: **3** Les
Mize: **5** Larry **6** Johnny
Mize, Larry: **6** golfer
Mizner: **6** Wilson
mizzen: **4** mast, sail
mizzen-royal: **4** mast
mizzle: **4** mist
___ M. Kennedy: **6** Edward
mkt.: **3** OTC **4** AMEX, NYSE **6** NASDAQ
MLB
award: **3** MVP
league: **4** Amer., Natl.
part: **5** Major **6** League **8** Baseball
stat: **3** ABs, avg., ERA, HRs **4** RBIs
team: **4** Cubs, Mets, Nats, Rays, Reds **5** Twins **6** Angels, Astros, Braves, Giants, Padres, Red Sox, Royals, Tigers **7** Brewers, Dodgers, Indians, Marlins, Orioles, Pirates, Rangers, Rockies, Yankees **8** Blue Jays, Mariners, Phillies, White Sox **9** Athletics, Cardinals, Nationals
see also baseball
M'Liss
author: Bret Harte
MLK
title: **3** Rev.
see also Martin Luther King
mlle.: **2** Ms.
Mlle.
canonized ~: **3** Ste.
in Spanish: **4** Srta.
married ~: **3** Mme.
mm.: **4** meas.
Mme.
daughter: **4** mlle.
in Spanish: **3** Sra.
in the US: **3** Mrs.
Mme. Tussaud's ___ Museum: **3** Wax
MMMBop (1997 song)
artist: Hanson
M&M's: **5** candy, snack **9** chocolate
Mn: **4** elem. **7** element **9** manganese
25 for ~: **4** at. no.
MN
see Minnesota
MNA holder: **5** nurse
Mneme: **4** Muse
mnemonic: **3** cue, tip **4** hint, prod, sign **6** prompt, signal **8** reminder **10** indication
mnemonic ___: **6** device
Mnemosyne: **5** giant, Titan
daughter: **4** Clio, Muse **5** Erato **6** Thalia, Urania **7** Euterpe **8** Calliope **9** Melpomene **10** Polyhymnia **11** Terpsichore
lover: **4** Zeus
parent: **4** Gaea **6** Uranus
mngr.: **4** exec.
MNO on a phone: **3** six
mo
half a ~: **4** jiff **5** jiffy
mo.: **3** Apr., Aug., Dec., Feb., Jan., Jul., Jun., Mar., Nov., Oct. **4** Sept.
30-day ~: **3** Apr., Jun., Nov., Sep.
autumn ~: **3** Dec., Nov., Oct. **4** Sept.
equinox ~: **3** Mar., Sep.
first ~: **3** Jan.
fraction: **2** wk.
last ~: **3** Dec., ult.
spring ~: **3** Apr., Jun., Mar.
summer ~: **3** Aug., Jul., Jun. **4** Sept.
valentine ~: **3** Feb.
winter ~: **3** Dec., Feb., Jan., Mar.
see also month
___-mo: **3** slo
Mo: **4** elem. **7** element **10** molybdenum
42 for ~: **4** at. no.
Mo' ___: **5** Money
Mo' ___ Blues: **6** Better
Mo.
city: **3** St. L. **5** St. Joe
neighbor: **3** Ark., Ill., Kan., Ken., Neb. **4** Iowa, Tenn.
president from ~: **3** HST
see also Missouri
___ Mo: **4** Ko Ko
M.O.
part: **5** modus **8** operandi
moa: **4** bird
relative: **4** kiwi
Moab: **4** city, town **7** kingdom
father: **3** Lot
locale: **4** Utah
today: **6** Jordan
moan: **3** cry, sob **4** beef, carp, howl, keen, sigh, wail, weep **5** gripe, groan, growl, mourn, sound, whine **6** bewail, grieve, grouch, grouse, lament, murmur, mutter, plaint, regret, repine, sorrow, yammer **7** deplore, grumble, whimper **8** complain, vocalize **9** bellyache, complaint, make a fuss
about: **6** bewail
moan and ___: **5** groan
moaner: **4** wimp **5** sissy **6** critic, griper, grouch, whiner **7** crybaby **8** grumbler **10** bellyacher, complainer, malcontent
moat: **4** foss **5** ditch, fosse **6** trench, trough **7** barrier
place: **6** castle
mob: **3** jam, lot, set **4** army, body, clan, crew, fill, gang, herd, host, mass, pack, ring, riot **5** cabal, crowd, crush, drove, flock, horde, Mafia, posse, press, swarm, troop **6** attack, cattle, circle, clique, hustle, jostle, justle, league, masses, people, public, rabble, throng **7** company, coterie, overrun, set upon **8** canaille, populace, riffraff, surround **9** gangsters, gathering, multitude, syndicate **10** assemblage, converge on, Cosa Nostra, underworld
boss: **3** don **4** capo **9** godfather
ender: **3** cap **4** ster
member: **4** thug **7** hoodlum
rule: **7** anarchy **8** disorder, nihilism
scene: **4** riot
mob ___: **4** rule **5** scene
Moberg, Vilhelm: **6** writer **7** Swedish
Mo' Better Blues (1990 film)
cast: Spike Lee, Wesley Snipes, Denzel Washington
director: Spike Lee
Mobil: **3** oil **8** gasoline
partner: **5** Exxon
rival: **4** Arco, Gulf, Hess **5** Amoco, Getty, Shell **7** Chevron
mobile: **3** art **5** fluid **6** motile, moving **7** migrant, movable, mutable, nomadic, ranging **8** moveable, portable, restless, unstable **9** adaptable, itinerant, mercurial, migratory, motorized, sculpture, traveling, unsettled, versatile **10** changeable
home: **4** tent, tipi **5** tepee **6** camper, teepee
sculptor: **6** Calder
starter: **3** air, art, Bat, ski **4** auto, book, snow **5** blood
mobile ___: **4** home, unit **5** phone
Mobile: **3** bay **4** city, town **5** river
locale: **3** Ala. **7** Alabama
newspaper: **8** Register
Mobile Bay: **6** battle
mobileness: **10** locomotion
mobility: **6** motion **8** movement **10** locomotion
___ mobility: **6** upward
mobilize: **5** impel, raise, rally, ready **6** call up, enlist, gather, gear up, get set, muster, propel, summon **7** actuate, harness, marshal, prepare, recruit **8** activate, assemble, embattle, get ready, organize **9** make ready **10** call to arms, coordinate
again: **5** rearm
Möbius ___: **4** band **5** strip
Möbius strips have one: **4** side
Mobley, Mary Ann
spouse: Gary Collins
mobocracy: **4** mess, riot **5** chaos, havoc, snarl **6** bedlam, jungle, mayhem, muddle, uproar **7** anarchy, discord, entropy, turmoil **8** disarray, disorder, madhouse, shambles **9** confusion **10** unruliness
mobs
like some: **4** ugly
mobster: **4** hood **6** gunsel, outlaw **7** hoodlum **8** criminal, gangster, hooligan **9** racketeer
lady: **4** moll **7** gun moll
weapon: **3** gat

Mobuto: **4** lake
locale: **5** Zaire **6** Uganda
Mobutu __ Seko: **4** Sese
Moby-Dick: **4** film **5** novel, whale **9** leviathan
author: Herman Melville
cast: Richard Basehart, Friedrich Ledebur, Gregory Peck
character: **3** Pip **4** Ahab **5** Flask, Peleg, Perth, Stubb **6** Bildad, Daggoo, Elijah, Fleece, Mapple **7** Ishmael **8** Dough-Boy, Fedallah, Queequeg, Starbuck, Tashtego **10** Bulkington
Crossed Harpoons, in ~: **3** inn
director: John Huston
setting: **3** sea **5** ocean
ship: **6** Pequod
moccasin: **3** pac **4** shoe **5** snake **6** animal **7** reptile **8** footgear, footwear
defense: **4** fang **5** venom
relative: ***see*** snake
water ~: **7** serpent
__ moccasin: **5** water
Mocedades
song: Eres Tu (1974)
mocha: **3** joe, mud **4** brew, java **5** brown, color, drink **6** coffee **7** leather **8** beverage, goatskin, ice cream
relative: ***see*** brown color, ice cream flavor
mocha __: **4** java
Mocha: **4** city, port, town **7** seaport
land: **5** Yemen
Mochrie: **5** Colin
mock: **3** ape, kid, rag, rib **4** bait, copy, defy, dupe, fake, faux, gibe, hoke, hoot, jape, jeer, jibe, jive, mime, sham, slam, slur, snub, twit **5** abuse, belie, bogus, chaff, decry, ditto, dummy, faked, false, feign, fleer, flout, hokey, libel, mimic, phony, put on, quasi, rally, roast, scoff, scorn, sneer, spoof, sport, spurn, taunt, tease **6** banter, defame, deride, dump on, ersatz, forged, heckle, hoot at, impugn, insult, jeer at, jibe at, malign, mirror, needle, offend, parody, phoney, pseudo, rebuff, send up, slight, thwart, unreal, vilify **7** affront, asperse, degrade, disdain, feigned, imitate, lampoon, laugh at, let down, profane, put down, rank out, slander, traduce **8** belittle, denounce, ridicule, satirize, simulate, sneeze at, so-called, spurious, travesty, vilipend **9** challenge, denigrate, discredit, disparage, frustrate, humiliate, imitation, make fun of, poke fun at, pretended, simulated, synthetic **10** artificial, calumniate, caricature, disappoint, disrespect, factitious, fraudulent, substitute
mock __ soup: **6** turtle
mock-__: **3** ups **6** heroic
mock apple __: **3** pie
Mocker Mocked, The
artist: Paul Klee
mockery: **3** dig **4** barb, gibe, jeer, jest, jibe, joke, quip, sham, slam, slap, slur, snub **5** abuse, farce, libel, put-on, scorn, spoof, sport, taunt **6** insult, parody, rebuff, satire, send-up, slight **7** affront, burlesk, calumny, catcall, disdain, fooling, lampoon, mimicry, obloquy, offense, put-down, sarcasm, slander, takeoff **8** contempt, derision, pretense, ridicule, scoffing, travesty **9** aspersion, burlesque, cheap shot, contumely, hypocrisy, imitation, sacrilege **10** caricature, defamation, disrespect, lip service, opprobrium
mocking: **3** wry **6** japery **7** cynical, jeering, satiric **8** derisive, sardonic **9** laughable, quizzical, sarcastic, satirical, vitriolic **10** irreverent
ender: **4** bird
mockingbird: **4** aper **5** mimic
relative: **8** thrasher
Mockingbird (song)
artist: Inez Foxx, Carly Simon, James Taylor
mock turtle: **4** soup
mock-up: **5** model **9** prototype
mod: **2** in **3** hip, neo **4** chic, tony **5** faddy, toney, vogue **6** chi-chi, trendy **7** current, in style, popular, stylish, voguish **8** last word **9** in fashion **10** all the rage
ender: **3** ule **4** ular
Mod __, The: **5** Squad
mode: **3** fad, way **4** chic, form, look, rage, rule, vein, wise **5** craze, decor, means, state, style, trend, usage, vogue **6** course, custom, living, manner, medium, method, status, system **7** fashion, process **8** approach, channels, last word, practice **9** mechanism, procedure, situation, technique **10** convention, dernier cri, mainstream
à la ~: **4** chic, tony **5** faddy, toney **6** chi-chi, modish, trendy **7** current, in style, popular, stylish, voguish **8** up-to-date **9** in fashion **10** all the rage
in the ~ of: **3** à la
__ mode: **3** à la **5** major, minor **6** Aeolic, church, Dorian, Ionian, Lydian **7** Aeolian
__ Mode: **7** Depeche
model: **3** kit, sit **4** base, cast, form, hero, Iman, kind, lead, mold, norm, nude, pose, rule, type, wear **5** carve, clone, dummy, frame, gauge, ideal, image, light, poser, saint, shape, sport, style, Tiegs, typic **6** create, design, effigy, lesson, mock-up, parade, relief, sample, sculpt, sitter, statue, symbol, Twiggy **7** classic, display, epitome, example, fashion, manikin, nonsuch, paragon, paste-up, pattern, perfect, portray, replica, show off, subject, typical, version, whittle **8** assemble, exemplar, figurine, flawless, game plan, likeness, lodestar, mannikin, nonesuch, original, paradigm, specimen, standard **9** archetype, beau ideal, blueprint, classical, cover girl, criterion, duplicate, exemplary, facsimile, faultless, mannequin, miniature, nonpareil, precedent, prototype, sculpture, statuette, Tyra Banks **10** archetypal, embodiment, touchstone
asset: **5** poise, smile **6** allure
binder: **4** glue
combining form: **3** typ- **4** typo-
display ~: **4** demo
earth ~: **3** map, orb **6** sphere
male ~: **4** hunk **5** he-man
material: **4** clay, wood **5** balsa
need: **3** rep **5** agent **6** agency
oneself on: **6** follow **7** imitate
role ~: **4** hero, idol **5** ideal, model
very thin ~: **4** waif
__ model: **4** role **5** floor, scale
Model __: **5** A Ford, B Ford, T Ford
Model A: **3** car **4** auto, Ford **10** automobile
Model B: **3** car **4** auto, Ford **10** automobile
Model T: **3** car **4** auto, Ford **10** automobile
contemporary: **3** Reo
model-train brand: **4** Tyco **6** Lionel
modem
high-speed ~ connection: **3** DSL
message: **3** fax **5** e-mail
name: **5** Hayes
speed unit: **3** bps **4** baud
use a ~: **6** dial in
__ modem: **3** fax
Modena: **3** car **4** auto, city, town **7** Ferrari **10** automobile
locale: **5** Italy
mode of life combining form: **6** -biosis
moderate: **3** ebb, low **4** bate, calm, cool, curb, ease, even, fair, fall, lull, mean, mild, mute, sane, slow, soft, so-so, wane, warm **5** abate, allay, break, chair, cheap, check, judge, let up, light, lower, quell, quiet, relax, sober, tepid **6** dampen, defuse, defuze, gentle, lessen, low-key, medium, midway, modest, modify, obtund, pacify, reduce, relent, soften, subdue, temper, umpire, weaken **7** appease, assuage, average, bargain, control, cut-rate, decline, die down, ease off, equable, limited, low-cost, mediate, mollify, neutral, pacific, preside, qualify, referee, relieve, slacken, subside, tail off, warmish **8** balanced, bearable, cautious, decrease, diminish, level off, measured, mediocre, middling, mitigate, modulate, ordinary, palliate, passable, play down, pleasant, regulate, reserved, restrain, restrict, tolerant, tone down **9** abstinent, alleviate, constrain, extenuate, impartial, judicious, lighten up, low-priced, make peace, negotiate, peaceable, retrocede, soft-pedal, temperate, tolerable, unextreme, unslanted **10** abstemious, considered, controlled, deliberate, economical, keep in line, mainstream, reasonable, restrained, smooth over, unagitated, unhardened, well-chosen
moderately: **4** some, so-so **5** quite **6** enough, fairly, gently, kind of, pretty, rather, sort of **7** a little, lightly **8** passably, slightly, somewhat **9** gradually, quite a bit, to a degree, tolerably
moderating: **10** abstemious
moderation: **5** poise **6** lenity, reason **7** balance **8** calmness, coolness, eschewal, fairness, justness, lenience, mildness, patience, sobriety **9** abatement, composure, frugality, restraint **10** abstinence, temperance
without ~: **6** arrant
moderato: **5** tempo
faster than ~: **7** allegro
slower than ~: **7** andante
moderator: **4** host **5** fixer, judge **6** umpire **8** mediator **10** negotiator
milieu: **5** forum
modern: **3** new, now **4** late **5** fresh, in use, novel, today, young **6** extant, hi-tech, latest, latter, recent, timely, with-it **7** current, new-wave, present, stylish, topical, updated **8** contempo, last word, neoteric, up-to-date **9** latter-day **10** avant-garde, newfangled, present-day
not ~: **3** old **5** olden
prefix: **3** neo-
starter: **5** ultra
modern __: **3** art, cut **4** jazz **5** dance
__-modern: **4** post
__ Modern: **6** Danish
moderne, not: **6** ancien
Modern Fables
author: George Ade
modernism: **10** innovation
modernist: **3** neo
modernistic: **3** new **5** novel **6** recent **8** up-to-date
modernize: **4** redo **5** renew **6** remake, revamp, revive, update **7** improve, refresh, remodel, restore, restyle **8** innovate, overhaul, renovate **9** refurbish **10** regenerate, rejuvenate, streamline
Modern Maturity
today: **4** AARP
Modern Painters
author: John Ruskin
Modern Problems (1981 film)
cast: Nell Carter, Chevy Chase, Mary Kay Place
Modern Times (1936 film)
cast: Charles Chaplin, Paulette Goddard
director: Charles Chaplin
tune: **5** Smile
Modern Utopia, A
author: H.G. Wells
Modern Woman (1986 song)
artist: Billy Joel
modest: **3** coy, low, shy **4** bare, fair, mean, meek, nice, poor, pure, so-so **5** cheap, light, lowly, moral, plain, quiet, small, spare, timid **6** chaste, demure, folksy, humble, proper, seemly, simple, slight **7** average, bashful, ignoble, limited **8** blushing, discreet, middling, ordinary, reserved, reticent, retiring, spotless, uncostly, virginal **9** diffident, temperate, unadorned, unextreme **10** economical, low-ranking, reasonable, unaffected, unassuming, uneffusive
not ~: **6** brassy
overly ~ one: **5** prude
Modest: **10** Mussorgsky

Modesto: 4 city, town
locale: 10 California
winery: 5 Gallo
Modest Proposal, A
author: Jonathan Swift
modesty: 5 shame 6 purity, virtue 7 coyness, decency, prudery, reserve, shyness 8 chastity, delicacy, humility, meekness, timidity 9 lowliness, propriety, reticence, timidness 10 demureness, diffidence, humbleness, simplicity
modesty __: 5 panel
modicum: 3 bit, jot 4 atom, dash, drop, inch, iota, mite, mote, whit 5 crumb, grain, minim, ounce, pinch, scrap, shred, speck, tinge, touch 6 little, smidge, trifle 7 minimum 8 fraction, fragment, littlest, molecule, particle, pittance 9 scintilla
modicum of __: 5 sense
modifiable: 9 adaptable
modification: 5 shift 6 change 7 variant 8 revision 9 variation
make ~ to: 4 edit 5 adapt, alter, amend, emend
without ~: 4 as is
modified: 7 limited, variant 9 qualified
combining form: 2 ne- 3 neo-
it's often ~: 4 noun
modified American __: 4 plan
modifier: 3 adj., adv. 6 adverb 9 adjective
modify: 3 fit 4 curb, redo, suit, turn, vary 5 abate, act on, adapt, alter, amend, limit, lobby, lower, relax, remit, reset, shape, tweak 6 adjust, affect, become, change, divert, doctor, lessen, mutate, recast, reduce, reform, repair, revise, rework, soften, tailor, temper 7 act upon, convert, correct, mollify, permute, qualify, remodel, reshape, restyle, slacken, touch up 8 decrease, mitigate, moderate, modulate, readjust, restrict, tone down 9 condition, customize, diversify, refashion, transform, transmute 10 reorganize, shift gears, switch over
Modigliani, Amedeo: 6 artist 7 Italian, painter
Modigliani, Franco: 8 Nobelist 9 economist
Modine, Matthew: 5 actor
film: Birdy (1984)
Bye Bye, Love (1995)
Cutthroat Island (1995)
Fluke (1995)
Full Metal Jacket (1987)
Gross Anatomy (1989)
Married to the Mob (1988)
Pacific Heights (1990)
The Real Blonde (1998)
Streamers (1983)
modish: 2 in 3 hip, new, now 4 chic, posh, tony 5 faddy, fresh, funky, smart, swank, swell, toney, vogue 6 chi-chi, classy, latest, snappy, trendy, with-it 7 current, dashing, elegant, in style, in-thing, in vogue, popular, stylish, voguish 8 last word, up-to-date 9 exclusive, happening, in fashion 10 all the rage
modishness: 4 chic 5 style, vogue
modiste: 10 dressmaker
Mod Squad, The (1999 film)
cast: Claire Danes, Omar Epps, Dennis Farina, Giovanni Ribisi
Mod Squad, The (ABC drama)
cast: Tige Andrews (Capt. Adam Greer)
Michael Cole (Pete Cochran)
Peggy Lipton (Julie Barnes)
Clarence Williams III (Linc Hayes)
Modugno, Domenico
song: Volaré (1958)
modulate: 4 pace, tune, vary 5 lower, relax, speak 6 adjust, change, modify, reduce, soften, switch, temper 7 balance, inflect, qualify 8 fine-tune, moderate, regulate, tone down 9 harmonize
modulation: 4 tone 5 pitch, sound 6 accent, change 7 cadence, cadency 8 delivery 10 inflection
modulator, prefix with: 5 neuro-
module: 4 unit
__ module: 4 load 5 lunar 7 command, service
modus __: 7 vivendi
modus operandi: 3 way 4 line 5 means 6 method, recipe 7 process 9 procedure, technique
Moe: 4 Berg 5 Bandy, Tommy 6 Howard, Stooge
brother: 5 Curly, Shemp
partner: 3 Joe 5 Larry 8 Curly Joe
__ Moe Dee: 4 Kool
Moesha (UPN sitcom)
cast: Brandy (Moesha Mitchell)
Moet: 4 wine 6 French
Moe, Tommy: 5 skier
Moffat: 6 Donald
Moffo, Anna: 6 singer 7 soprano
specialty: 4 aria 5 opera
Mogadishu: 4 city, town 7 capital
locale: 7 Somalia
model from ~: 4 Iman
Mogador: 6 fabric 8 material
Mogambo (1953 film)
cast: Clark Gable, Ava Gardner, Grace Kelly
director: John Ford
Mogen __: 5 David
Mogg: 4 Phil
moggy: 3 cat
mogul: 3 VIP 4 bump, czar, king, lord, tsar, tzar 5 baron, nabob, nawab, ruler, titan, wheel 6 bigwig, fat cat, gerent, prince, tycoon 7 big shot, magnate, notable 8 big wheel, top brass 9 big cheese, executive, potentate
home: 6 estate
lover: 5 skier
Mogul: 3 Era
capital of India: 4 Agra 5 Delhi
ruler: 5 nawab
mohair: 6 fabric 7 grogram 8 material, sanglier
source: 4 goat 6 angora
Mohammed
birthplace of ~: 5 Mecca
daughter: 6 Fatima
religion: 5 Islam
son-in-law: 3 Ali
wife: 6 Ayesha
Mohammed __ Pahlevi: 4 Reza
Mohandas: 6 Gandhi
Mohave: 5 tribe 6 desert, Indian 7 Amerind
Mohawk: 4 coif 5 river, tribe 6 hairdo, Indian 7 Amerind, haircut 8 coiffure, language 9 hairstyle
ally: 6 Cayuga, Oneida, Seneca 8 Onondaga 9 Tuscarora
city on the ~: 5 Utica
craft: 5 canoe
River locale: 7 New York
sporter: 3 Mr. T
sporting a ~: 5 shorn
Valley city: 6 Elmira
Valley tribe: 6 Oneida
Mohegan: 6 Indian 7 Amerind 8 language
Mohican: 5 tribe 6 Indian 7 Amerind
Mohs scale minerals:
1 - Talc
2 - Gypsum
3 - Calcite
4 - Fluorite
5 - Apatite
6 - Orthoclase
7 - Quartz
8 - Topaz
9 - Corundum
10 - Diamond
__ moi: 4 chez
__-moi: 7 excusez
moiety: 4 half, part 7 portion, section, segment
moil: 4 plod, toil, work 5 churn, labor, slave, sweat 6 drudge, strain, strive 8 drudgery, hard work, work hard 9 grunt work, plug along, pound away
__ moi, le déluge: 5 Après
moiling: 9 turbulent
__ Moines, IA: 3 Des
Moira: 5 Kelly 7 Shearer
in English: 4 Mary
moiré: 6 fabric 8 material
mois: 3 mai 4 août, juin, mars 5 avril, month 6 French 7 février, janvier, juillet, octobre 8 décembre, novembre 9 septembre
douze ~: 5 année
Moises: 4 Alou
uncle: 5 Jesus, Matty
Moissan, Henri: 7 chemist 8 Nobelist
moist: 3 wet 4 damp, dank, dewy 5 humid, juicy, misty, muggy, rainy, soggy, teary, undry 6 basted, clammy, drippy, hygric, liquid, oozing, steamy, sweaty, watery 7 bedewed, drizzly, tearful, wettish 8 dampened, dripping 9 drizzling, succulent
adapted to a ~ habitat: 5 mesic
combining form: 5 hygro-
ender: 3 ure
moisten: 3 dip, sog, sop, wet 4 damp, lick, mist, soak, wash 5 baste, bathe, bedew, rinse, spray, steam, steep, water 6 dampen, drench, humify, quench, rain on, shower, soften, splash, squirt 8 humidify, irrigate, saturate, splatter, sprinkle, waterlog 10 moisturize
again: 5 rewet
with water: 4 soak 5 bathe, douse, flush 6 drench, shower 7 immerse
moist-eyed: 5 teary
moisture: 3 dew, fog, wet 4 damp, mist, rain, tear 5 sweat, tears, vapor, water 6 liquid 7 drizzle, wetness 8 dampness, dankness, humidity, teardrop 9 mugginess, sogginess
exude ~: 5 sweat
lacking ~: 3 dry 4 arid, sere 7 parched 8 droughty 10 dehydrated
lose ~: 4 seep 6 dry out
remove ~: 3 dry 5 defog
remover: 5 drier, dryer
requiring little ~: 5 xeric
moistureless: 3 dry 4 arid, sere
moisturize: 8 humidify
moisturizer: 4 balm 5 cream, salve 6 lotion 7 unguent 8 cosmetic, ointment 9 emollient
skin ~: 4 aloe 6 lotion
Mojave: 5 tribe 6 desert, Indian 7 Amerind
like the ~: 3 dry 4 arid
plant: 5 agave 6 cactus, cholla
mojo: 4 doll, juju 5 charm, spell 6 amulet 8 talisman
moke: 3 ass 5 horse 6 equine 7 jackass
Mol: 8 Gretchen
molar: 5 tooth 7 grinder
hole: 6 cavity
malady: 4 ache
material: 4 pulp 6 enamel
molars
use the ~: 4 chew 5 grind
molasses
like ~: 4 poky, slow
move like ~: 3 lag 4 ooze
product: 3 rum 5 taffy, toffy 6 toffee
__ molasses: 6 slow as
mold: 3 die, lot, pat, pig, rot 4 bend, cast, form, kind, last, make, must, plan, plot, rust, sort, turn, type 5 build, class, ergot, forge, frame, image, knead, model, plant, shape, stamp, train 6 beetle, cavity, design, devise, dry rot, fungus, kidney, makeup, matrix, mildew, nature, sculpt 7 fashion, ferment, pattern, whittle 8 assemble, jaundice 9 character, construct, container, influence, sculpture 10 depression, impression
filler: 5 Jell-O 7 gelatin
like ~: 6 fungal
mold __: 5 spore
moldable: 4 soft 6 lissom 7 lissome, plastic 8 flexible 9 formative, malleable
Moldau: 5 river
city on the ~: 6 Prague
Moldavia once: 3 SSR
molder: 3 rot 4 turn 5 decay, spoil 7 crumble 9 decompose
moldering: 6 rotten
molding: 4 cyma, edge, ogee, trim 5 ledge, ogive, ovolo
combining form: 6 -plasty
profile: 3 ess
__ molding: 5 crown
moldings: 4 tori 5 ovoli
Moldova: 6 nation 7 country
capital: 8 Chisinau
neighbor: 7 Romania, Ukraine
moldy: 3 bad 4 rank 5 fusty, musty 6 frowsy, frowzy, rancid, rotten 7 odorous 8 inedible, obsolete, out-

moded **9** hackneyed **10** antiquated
get ~: 3 rot
mole: 3 spy **4** pier **5** agent, plant **6** animal, mammal, naevus, rodent **8** burrower, hot sauce **9** birthmark **10** breakwater
combining form: 5 talpi-
cousin: 5 shrew
ender: 4 hill, skin
mole __: 3 rat
molecular
component: 4 atom
variation: 6 isomer
molecular biologist, Japanese: 6 Susumu
molecular biology: 7 science
study: 3 DNA, RNA **4** gene **8** genetics
molecule: 3 bit, jot **4** iota, mite, mote, spot, unit **5** grain, minim, ounce, speck **7** modicum **8** fragment, particle
part: 4 atom
molehill: 5 mound
make a mountain of a ~: 7 magnify **10** exaggerate
Mole People, The (1956 film)
cast: John Agar
moles: 4 nevi **5** naevi
moleskin: 6 fabric **8** material
color: 5 taupe
moleskins: 5 pants **8** trousers
molest: 3 paw **4** harm **5** abuse, harry **6** bother **7** disturb
molestation: 5 abuse
Molière: 6 French **10** playwright
character: 5 Elise
work: The Misanthrope
The School for Wives
Molina: 5 Mario **6** Alfred
Molina, Alfred: 5 actor
film: Dudley Do-Right (1999)
Frida (2002)
The Hoax (2007)
The Imposters (1998)
Not Without My Daughter (1991)
Prick Up Your Ears (1987)
Spider-Man 2 (2004)
Molina, Mario: 7 chemist **8** Nobelist
Molinaro: 2 Al
Moline: 4 city, town
locale: 8 Illinois
manufacturer: 5 Deere
Molitor, Paul
sport: 8 baseball
moll: 5 minor
man: 6 gunsel **7** hoodlum
__ moll: 3 gun
Moll: 7 Richard
Moll Flanders
author: Daniel Defoe
mollification: 7 anodyne **9** abatement
mollifier: 5 salve
mollify: 4 calm, cool, ease, lull **5** abate, allay, blunt, fix up, humor, quell, quiet, salve, slake **6** defuse, defuze, lessen, mellow, modify, pacify, reduce, smooth, soften, soothe, temper **7** appease, assuage, compose, cushion, lighten, placate, relieve, satisfy, sweeten **8** decrease, diminish, mitigate, moderate, palliate **9** alleviate, untrouble **10** ameliorate, conciliate, propitiate, smooth over
mollifying: 6 irenic **8** irenical **9** demulcent
Molloy
author: Samuel Beckett
mollusk: 4 clam, slug **5** conch, snail, squid, whelk **6** chiton, limpet, oyster, quahog **7** bivalve, geoduck, octopus, quahaug, scallop **8** escargot, nautilus **9** gastropod **10** cuttlefish
part: 5 valve
ridge on a ~ shell: 5 varix
shell lining: 5 nacre
tongue: 6 radula
molly: 3 pet
ender: 6 coddle
Molly: 4 Berg, Sims, Yard **5** Ivins, Picon **6** Malone **7** Pitcher **8** Ringwald
Molly __: 7 Maguire
mollycoddle: 4 baby **5** nurse, spoil **6** dote on, pamper **7** cater to, indulge **8** dote upon **9** spoon-feed
mollycoddling: 4 easy **7** lenient
Molly Maguire: 5 miner
Molnár, Ferenc: 6 writer **9** Hungarian **10** playwright
work: The Devil
Liliom
The Red Mill
The Swan
moloch: 6 animal **7** reptile
Molokai: 4 isle **6** island
neighbor: 4 Maui, Oahu **5** Kauai, Lanai, Nihoa **6** Hawaii, Niihau **9** Kahoolawe
Molonglo, city on the: 8 Canberra
Molopo: 5 river
locale: 3 Afr. **6** Africa **8** Botswana
Molotov cocktail: 4 bomb
Molson: 4 beer
alternative: *see* beer
molt: 4 peel, shed **6** slough **7** cast off, peel off **8** exuviate **9** exfoliate **10** desquamate
molten: 5 fluid **6** fusile, liquid, melted **9** liquefied
material: 4 lava **5** magma
metal channel: 6 ingate
work ~ glass: 4 blow
molting: 7 ecdysis
molto: 4 much, very **9** extremely
opposite: 4 poco
Moluccas: 4 isls. **5** isles **7** islands
island: 3 Aru **4** Aroe, Arru, Buru, Leti **5** Ambon, Babar, Banda, Ceram, Wetar **6** Serang, Tidore **7** Morotai, Ternate **8** Tanimbar **9** Halmahera
__ moly: 4 holy
molybdenite: 3 ore **7** mineral
molybdenum: 5 metal **7** element
alloy: 9 Vitallium
ore: 9 wulfenite
mom: 6 mother, parent **8** relative
admonition: 6 be good, be nice
brother: 3 unc, unk **5** uncle
expectant ~ visitor: 5 stork
like a ~ at a wedding: 5 weepy
mom's ~: 4 gran, nana **6** granny **7** grannie
month: 3 May
on ~'s side: 5 enate
partner: 3 dad, pop **5** daddy **6** father
sister: 4 aunt **5** aunty **6** auntie
__ mom: 3 den **6** soccer
__ Mom: 6 Serial
MOMA
artist: 4 Dali, Klee
exhibit: 4 Dada **5** op art
locale: 3 NYC **4** NY NY **9** Manhattan
part of ~: 3 Art **6** Modern, Museum
mom and __ store: 3 pop
Mombasa: 4 city, isle, port, town **6** island
locale: 5 Kenya
moment: 3 bit, sec, use **4** hour, jiff, note, pith, tick, time, wink **5** flash, jiffy, point, stage, trice, value, while, worth **6** import, minute, second, weight **7** concern, eyewink, gravity, instant **8** juncture, occasion **9** magnitude, substance, twinkling **10** importance, time period
a ~ ago: 4 just **10** just before
at that ~: 4 then
at this ~: 3 now **5** as yet, today **8** promptly, right now, right off **9** forthwith, presently, right away **10** here and now, this minute
ending: 3 ous
for the ~: 8 meantime **9** meanwhile
in a ~: 4 anon, soon **8** directly **9** presently
of truth: 4 D-day, test **8** showdown, zero hour
on the spur of the ~: 5 ad-lib **6** rashly **7** brashly, hastily **8** abruptly, headlong, pell-mell, suddenly **9** headfirst
spare: 7 leisure
vital ~: 4 D-day **6** crisis **8** juncture **9** crossroad, emergency
__ moment: 3 in a **6** senior
momentarily: 3 now **4** anon, nigh, soon **6** awhile, in a sec **7** briefly **8** right now **9** instantly
momentary: 5 brief, hasty, quick, short **6** flying **7** cursory, passing, regular, summary, trivial **8** flashing, fleeting, flitting, fugitive, meteoric, shifting, temporal, volatile **9** dreamlike, ephemeral, impulsive, spasmodic, temporary, transient, vanishing **10** evanescent, short-lived, transitory, unenduring
Momentary __ of Reason, A: 5 Lapse
__ Moment in Time: 3 One
__ momento!: 3 Uno
moment of __: 5 truth
momentous: 3 big **5** grave, heavy, vital **6** signal, solemn, urgent **7** crucial, epochal, fateful, notable, pivotal, serious, special, weighty **8** critical, decisive, eventful, historic, material, pregnant **9** front-page, high-level, important, memorable **10** impressive, meaningful, portentous
momentousness: 6 import, weight **9** magnitude
__ Moments: 5 Magic
__ moment's notice: 3 at a, on a
Moments to Remember (1955 song)
artist: Four Lads
__ moment too soon!: 4 Not a
momentum: 4 pace, push **5** drive, force, power, speed, tempo **6** energy, thrust **7** impetus, impulse **8** progress, strength **10** propulsion
component: 5 speed **8** velocity
forward ~: 4 birr
gather ~: 5 speed **10** accelerate
__ Momma From the Train: 5 Throw
momma's partner: 5 poppa
Mommie Dearest: 4 book, film
author: Christina Crawford
cast: Howard da Silva, Faye Dunaway, Steve Forrest, Diana Scarwid
Mommsen, Theodor: 6 writer **8** Nobelist
mommy: 6 mother, parent **8** relative
see also mom
mommy __: 5 track
__ Mommy Kissing...: 4 I Saw
Momo
author: Michael Ende
Mo Money Mo Problems (1997 song)
artist: Mase, Notorious B.I.G., Puff Daddy
Moms: 6 Mabley
momus: 3 nag **5** shrew
Momus
mother: 3 Nyx
mon __: 3 ami **4** cher
mon-: 3 one, uni-
Mon __: 5 Oncle
Mon __!: 4 Dieu
Mon.: 3 day
follower: 3 Tue. **4** Tues.
preceder: 3 Sun.
to Tues.: 4 yest.
Mona: 6 Barrie **7** Freeman, Simpson, Van Duyn **10** Washbourne
Mona __: 4 Lisa, Yoko
Monaco: 3 car **4** auto, city, town **5** Dodge **6** nation **7** country **10** automobile
capital: 11 Monaco-Ville
city: 10 Monte Carlo
city near ~: 4 Nice
locale: 3 Eur. **6** Europe
money: 5 franc
neighbor: 6 France
monad: 3 one **4** unit **6** amoeba, single **9** protozoan
Monaghan: 8 Michelle
Mona Lisa: 8 painting
attribute: 5 smile
home: 5 Paris **6** France, Louvre
painter: Leonardo da Vinci
Mona Lisa (1950 song)
artist: Nat King Cole
composer: Ray Evans, Jay Livingston
Mona Lisa Smile (2003 film)
cast: Kirsten Dunst, Julia Roberts, Julia Stiles
monarch: 4 amir, czar, emir, king, raja, shah, tsar, tzar **5** ameer, crown, emeer, queen, rajah, royal, ruler **6** despot, gerent, prince, sultan **7** emperor, empress, majesty, viceroy **8** autocrat, princess **9** butterfly, potentate, sovereign
become a ~: 6 accede
future ~: 5 larva **6** prince **8** princess
hazard: 4 nets
in French: 3 roi **5** reine
in Latin: 3 rex
in Spanish: 3 rey **5** reina
letters: 3 HRH

Monarch: 3 car 4 auto 7 Mercury 10 automobile
monarchal: 8 imperial 9 sovereign
monarchical: 5 royal
...monarch of __ survey: 4 all I
monarchy: 5 realm, reign 6 nation 7 kingdom 8 kingship
monarque: 3 roi
monastery: 5 abbey, house 6 friary, priory, temple 7 convent 8 cloister, lamasery
  chamber: 4 cell
  dweller: 6 oblate
  figure: 4 abbé, monk 5 abbot, friar, prior
  layperson: 6 oblate
  office: 6 abbacy
  Tibetan ~: 5 gompa
  title: 3 dom, fra
Monastery of __: 4 Iona
monastic: 4 abbé, monk 5 friar 6 Essene 7 recluse 8 clerical 9 reclusive, religious
monaural, not: 6 stereo
monazite: 3 ore
Mondale: 5 Fritz 6 Walter 7 Eleanor
Monday __ quarterback: 7 morning
__ Monday: 4 blue 6 Easter, Shrove
Monday feeling: 5 blahs
Monday, Monday (1966 song)
  artist: Mamas & the Papas
Monday Night Football
  network: ABC
monde: 5 world 6 French
  beau ~: 5 elite 7 society
  haute ~: 6 gentry, jet set 7 society, who's who 10 upper class, upper crust
  starter: 4 demi
__ monde: 4 beau, haut
__ mondes: 5 beaux
__-mondi: 5 coati
Mondial: 3 car 4 auto 7 Ferrari 10 automobile
Mon dieu!: 4 oh no
mondo: 3 big 4 huge 5 great
Mondo Cane theme: 4 More
Mondrian, Piet: 6 artist 7 painter
  homeland: 7 Holland 11 Netherlands
Monel: 5 alloy
Moneta, Ernesto: 7 Italian 8 Nobelist
monetary: 4 cash 6 fiscal 7 capital 8 economic 9 budgetary, financial, pecuniary 10 commercial
  award: 5 prize, purse
  gain: 5 lucre
  punishment: 4 fine
  value: 5 worth
monetary __: 4 gain, unit
Monet, Claude: 6 artist, French 7 painter
  contemporary: Edgar Degas
  setting: 5 Rouen
money: 2 as, at, xu 3 ban, bit, bob, cob, ecu, fen, kip, lat, lek, leu, lev, ley, mil, oof, ore, pay, pie, pul, pya, sen, sol, sou, tip, wad, won, yen 4 anna, baht, bill, birr, buck, cash, cedi, cent, chon, coin, dime, doit, dong, duit, euro, fils, fund, gelt, gold, inti, jack, jeon, joey, kail, kale, kobo, kran, kyat, lira, loot, mark, merk, mill, mina, obol, para, peag, pelf, peso, pice, pile, pony, pula, quid, rand, real, rial, riel, roll, tael, taka, tala, wage, yuan 5 agora, angel, asper, belga, bills, bread, broad, bucks, butut, check, chips, coins, colon, conto, crown, daric, dimes, dinar, dough, ducat, eagle, eyrir, franc, funds, girsh, gravy, groat, grosz, gursh, kopec, kopek, krona, krone, kroon, kurus, leone, liard, libra, litas, livre, louis, lucre, means, mohur, mongo, moola, naira, ngwee, noble, paisa, pengo, penni, penny, pesos, plack, pound, purse, qirsh, qursh, riyal, ruble, rupee, sceat, scudi, scudo, semis, sewan, soldo, sucre, sycee, taler, thebe, tical, uncia, unite, zaire, zloty 6 assets, aureus, balboa, bawbee, bezant, boodle, bundle, change, condor, copeck, dalasi, decime, dinero, dirham, doblon, dollar, do-re-mi, drachm, escudo, filler, florin, forint, ghirsh, gilder, gourde, guinea, gulden, heller, income, kopeck, korona, koruna, kwacha, lepton, likuta, makuta, mammon, markka, mazuma, monkey, moolah, nickel, peseta, pesewa, poisha, qindar, qintar, quezal, qurush, riches, rouble, salary, seawan, sequin, shekel, silver, specie, stater, stiver, talent, tanner, tender, tester, teston, thaler, tipoff, tugrik, wampum, wealth 7 afghani, austral, bolivar, cabbage, capital, carolus, centavo, centime, centimo, coinage, cordoba, cruzado, denarii, dollars, drachma, guarani, guilder, halalas, jacobus, lempira, lettuce, milreis, moidore, nickels, payment, pennies, pfennig, piaster, piastre, pistole, quarter, quetzal, revenue, rughrik, sceatta, scratch, sextans, shekels, support, tambala, testoon, tukhrik, unicorn 8 banknote, bankroll, big bucks, cold cash, cruzeiro, currency, denarius, doubloon, ducatoon, farthing, finances, florence, groschen, hard cash, johannes, kreutzer, louis d'or, maravedi, millieme, napoleon, new pence, new penny, picayune, property, quarters, receipts, services, sesterce, shilling, sixpence, stotinka, treasure, tuppence, twopence 9 affluence, banknotes, boliviano, centesimo, didrachma, dupondius, greenback, half-crown, halfpenny, long green, pistareen, principal, resources, rix-dollar, rose-noble, schilling, sestertia, sestertii, simoleons, sovereign 10 gold stater, greenbacks, half dollar, half-guinea, sestertium, threepence, tripondius
  back: 6 rebate, refund
  broker: 6 banker, lender
  color of ~: 5 green
  dirty ~: 4 pelf 5 lucre
  earn ~: 4 live, work
  emergency ~: 5 scrip
  ender: 3 bag, man, men 4 wort 5 maker 6 lender, making 7 changer, grubber
  finish in the ~: 3 win 4 show 5 place
  front ~: 4 loan 7 advance
  funny ~: 4 slug
  get ~: 6 redeem 9 liquidate
  get ~ for: 4 sell 6 cash in, redeem
  give ~: 4 lend, loan 6 donate 7 advance
  give ~ for: 3 buy, pay 6 lay out
  hunger: 5 greed
  hush ~: 5 bribe, graft 6 payoff 7 jobbery 8 kickback 9 blackmail
  in the ~: 4 rich 5 flush 6 loaded, monied 7 wealthy, well-off 8 affluent, well-to-do 9 well-fixed 10 privileged, propertied, prosperous, well-heeled
  in the bank: 4 acct. 5 asset 7 deposit, savings
  like funny ~: 5 bogus 11 counterfeit
  lot of ~: 3 wad 4 mint, pile 5 stack 8 bankroll
  make ~: 3 pay 4 coin, earn, live, mint 6 profit 7 prosper
  make ~ the old- fashioned way: 6 earn it
  management: 7 finance
  manager: 6 banker, broker
  medium: 4 coin 5 paper
  minimal ~: 4 cent, song
  of ~: 6 fiscal 8 monetary
  old ~: 4 rich 5 elite
  on the ~: 5 exact, right 7 correct, exactly, perfect, precise 8 accurate, very well 10 absolutely
  owed: 4 debt 6 arrear 7 arrears
  paper ~: 4 bill, note 8 currency 9 greenback
  place: 3 ATM 4 bank, belt, safe, till 5 chest, purse, S and L 6 coffer, wallet 8 register, treasury 9 piggy bank 10 pocketbook
  pocket ~: 4 cash, ones, tens 5 bills, coins, dimes, fives 6 change 7 coinage, nickels, pennies, singles 8 quarters, twenties
  pool: 4 fund 5 kitty
  press for ~: 3 dun
  provide ~ at interest: 4 loan
  put (down) ~: 5 plunk
  put ~ (on): 4 bank, rely 6 depend
  put up ~: 3 bet 4 ante, back, fund 5 wager 6 invest 7 finance, sponsor 9 speculate
  rainy-day ~: 4 fund
  recipient: 5 payee
  save ~: 6 scrimp 9 economize
  send ~: 3 pay 5 remit
  set aside: 6 escrow
  slangily: *see* moolah
  solicit ~: 5 hit up 7 squeeze
  source: 4 loan
  waste ~: 6 lavish 8 squander
  without ~: 4 poor 5 broke, needy, short 6 bad off, hard up, ill off, in need, in want 7 pinched 8 badly off, bankrupt, beggarly, deprived, indigent, strapped 9 destitute, insolvent, penniless, penurious 10 down and out, pauperized, straitened
  see also coin
money __: 3 box 4 belt, fund, tree 5 order, plant, shell 6 cowrie, market, player, supply 7 machine
money-__ fund: 6 market
__ money: 3 big, hot, key, mad, old, pin 4 cash, easy, even, hush, play, seed, side, soft 5 blood, found, front, funny, in the, on the, paper, prize, ready, smart 6 pocket 7 earnest, folding
Money
  author: Martin Amis, Émile Zola
Money (1973 song)
  artist: Pink Floyd
Money __ everything!: 4 isn't
Money __ Nothing: 3 for
Money __ object!: 4 is no
moneybag: 5 purse
moneybags: 5 nabob 6 fat cat 9 financier, plutocrat 10 capitalist, man of means
moneychanger, name meaning: 8 Wechsler
moneyed: 4 rich 5 flush 6 fat-cat, loaded, uptown 7 opulent, upscale, wealthy, well-off 8 affluent, in clover, well-to-do 9 well-fixed 10 in the dough, privileged, propertied, prosperous, upper-class, well-heeled
  class: 6 jet set
Money, Eddie
  song: Baby Hold On (1978)
    Endless Nights (1987)
    I'll Get By (1992)
    I Wanna Go Back (1987)
    Peace in Our Time (1989)
    Take Me Home Tonight (1986)
    Think I'm in Love (1982)
    Two Tickets to Paradise (1978)
    Walk on Water (1988)
Money for Nothing (1985 song)
  artist: Dire Straits
moneygrubber: 5 miser, piker 10 cheapskate
moneygrubbing: 5 cheap, crass 6 greedy, stingy 7 sparing 9 mercenary
Money Honey (1976 song)
  artist: Bay City Rollers
Money isn't everything: 5 adage
...money is the __ of...: 4 root
moneylender: 4 bank 6 banker, factor, loaner, usurer 7 Shylock 8 creditor
moneyless: 4 poor 5 broke, needy 6 bad off, hard up, ill off, in need, in want 7 pinched 8 badly off, bankrupt, beggarly, deprived, indigent, strapped 9 destitute, insolvent, penniless, penurious 10 down and out, pauperized, straitened
  in Britain: 5 skint
Moneyline
  network: 3 CNN
moneymaker: 6 earner 7 bonanza, cash cow, success 8 gold mine
moneymaking: 4 good 5 going 6 paying 7 gainful 8 economic, thriving 9 lucrative 10 profitable, worthwhile
money-market __: 4 fund
Money, Money, Money
  artist: ABBA
__ money on: 3 put
money order: 5 draft
  recipient: 5 payee
  sender: 6 drawee
Money Pit, The (1986 film)
  cast: Tom Hanks, Shelley Long, Maureen Stapleton
Moneytalks
  artist: AC/DC
__ Money, The: 3 Big

monger: 6 seller 7 peddler 8 merchant
starter: 3 war 4 fish, iron, news, word 5 rumor, scare 6 gossip, phrase 7 fashion, scandal
Mongibello: 4 Etna 5 Aetna 7 volcano
Mongkut, King
domain: 4 Siam
nanny: 4 Anna
portrayer: Yul Brynner
mongo: 5 money
Mongol: 3 Hun 5 Asian, Tatar 6 empire
dynasty: 4 Yuan
locale: 4 Asia
monk: 4 lama
ruler: 4 khan
tent: 4 yurt
tribe: 5 horde
Mongolia: 6 nation 7 country
bovine: 5 Sanhe
city: 6 Hohhot 9 Ulan Bator
equine: 5 kiang 8 chigetai 9 dziggetai
language family: 6 Altaic
like ~: 3 dry 4 arid
locale: 4 Asia
money: 5 mongo 6 tugrik 7 rughrik, tukhrik
much of ~: 4 Gobi 6 desert
neighbor: 5 China 6 Russia
people: 3 Lai
range: 5 Altai
sheep: 5 argal 6 argali
__ Mongolia: 5 Inner, Outer
Mongolian __ pot: 3 hot
mongoose: 6 animal, mammal
foe: 5 cobra
Mongoose, The: Archie Moore
mongrel: 3 cur, dog, mut 4 mutt 5 cross, feist, hound, scrub, stray 6 hybrid 7 mixture 10 crossbreed, mixed breed
Monica: 5 saint, Seles 6 Potter
brother on Friends: 4 Ross
in French: 7 Monique
__ Monica, CA: 5 Santa
monied class: 5 haves
monies
see money
moniker: 4 name 5 alias, title 6 handle 8 nickname 9 sobriquet
Monique
see French
Mo'Nique
film: Precious... (2009, AA)
monitor: 2 TV 3 CRT, VDT 4 scan 5 audit, check, guide, see to, track, TV set 6 censor, follow, listen, lizard, record, survey 7 auditor, control, observe, oversee, proctor, scanner 8 look over, overseer, regulate, terminal, watchdog 9 check up on, eavesdrop, informant, inspector, supervise 10 flat-screen, gatekeeper, supervisor
lizard: 4 uran 6 goanna
Monitor: 4 ship 6 vessel 8 ironclad
feature: 6 turret
Moniz, Antonio: 8 Nobelist 10 Portuguese
monja: 3 nun
monk: 3 Fra 4 abbé, lama 5 abbot, friar, prior 6 hermit, priest, sensei 7 ascetic, bhikshu, brother, eremite, recluse 8 cenobite, monastic, rinpoche, solitary, Trappist 9 anchorite, religious 10 monastical
Asian ~: 4 lama 5 bonze, sadhu 7 bhikshu 9 bhikshuni
French ~: 5 frère
garb: 4 cowl, hood 5 frock, habit 7 mandyas
group: 5 skete
habitat: 4 cell 5 abbey 6 friary
like a ~: 6 hooded
monotone: 5 chant
of yore: 6 Essene
superior: 5 abbot
title: 3 dom, fra
Monk: 10 Thelonious
Monk (USA drama)
cast: Jason Gray-Stanford (Randy Disher)
Traylor Howard (Natalie Teeger)
Ted Levine (Leland Stottlemeyer)
Bitty Schram (Sharona Fleming)
Tony Shalhoub (Adrian Monk)
Monkees
film: Head (1968)
song: Daydream Believer (1967)
I'm a Believer (1966)
Last Train to Clarksville (1966)
A Little Bit Me, A Little Bit You (1967)
Pleasant Valley Sunday (1967)
She (1967)
Steppin' Stone (1966)
That Was Then, This Is Now (1986)
Valleri (1968)
Words (1967)
Monkees, The (NBC sitcom)
cast: Micky Dolenz
Davy Jones
Mike Nesmith
Peter Tork
monkey: 4 saki, titi 5 dance, jocko, lemur, money, scamp 6 animal, baboon, Bandar, fiddle, gelada, grivet, guenon, howler, langur, rascal, rhesus, simian, tamper, tinker, trifle, uakari, vervet 7 colobus, guereza, hoolock, macaque, primate, sapajou, tamarin 8 capuchin, imitator, mandrill, mangabey, marmoset, mess with, talapoin 9 obsession 10 anthropoid, fool around, jackanapes
African ~: 6 grivet, guenon
around: 6 cavort 7 fribble, goof off
Asian ~: 6 Bandar, langur, rhesus
business: 6 antics, deceit 7 foolery 8 falderal, falderol, mischief
Capuchin ~: 3 sai
combining form: 6 pithec- 7 pitheco-
ender: 5 shine 6 shines
food: 6 banana
home: 3 zoo
make a ~ of: 6 outwit 8 outsmart 9 embarrass, humiliate
pot: 4 tree
puzzle: 4 tree
relative: *see* primate
South American ~: 3 sai 4 titi 6 howler
suit: 3 tux 4 tuck 5 tails 6 tuxedo
throw a ~ wrench into: 5 block 6 hamper, hinder 7 disrupt 8 obstruct, sabotage 9 frustrate, undermine
(with): 4 fool 6 fiddle, tamper, trifle
wrench: 4 snag 5 block, crimp, hitch, snarl 7 barrier, problem, setback 8 handicap, obstacle 10 impediment
monkey __: 4 bars, suit 6 wrench
__ monkey: 3 owl 6 grease, howler, rhesus, spider
Monkey (1988 song)
artist: George Michael
Monkey __, monkey do: 3 see
monkey bread: 5 fruit
tree: 6 baobab
Monkey Business (1931 film)
cast: Chico Marx, Groucho Marx, Harpo Marx, Zeppo Marx, Thelma Todd
__ monkey out of: 5 make a
Monkey's __, The: 3 Paw
__ Monkeys: 6 Twelve
monkeyshine: 3 gag 4 dido, jape, joke 5 antic, caper, prank, trick 6 frolic 7 foolery 8 escapade, jocosity 10 hanky-panky, tomfoolery
Monkey, the: 5 dance
Monkey Trial
defendant: 6 Scopes
lawyer: 5 Bryan 6 Darrow
locale: 6 Dayton 9 Tennessee
Monkey Trouble (1994 film)
cast: Thora Birch, Harvey Keitel, Mimi Rogers
monkfish: 5 lotte
monkish: 8 clerical
monklike: 5 pious
monkshood: 5 plant 6 flower
Monk, Thelonious: 7 pianist
genre: 3 bop 4 jazz
__ Monmouth, NJ: 4 Fort
mono
not ~: 6 stereo
monocle: 4 lens 5 glass, loupe
mono- cousin: 3 uni
monocratic: 8 absolute 9 arbitrary
monody: 5 dirge
monogamist: 4 wife 6 spouse 7 husband
monogamy: 8 marriage 9 matrimony
monogrammed item: 5 shirt, towel
monogram unit: 4 init. 6 letter 7 initial
monograph: 5 paper 6 thesis 8 treatise 9 discourse 10 exposition
monokini
lack: 3 bra
monolith: 5 pylon, tower 6 column 8 memorial, monument
monolithic: 7 uniform
monologist: 5 comic 6 diseur 8 comedian
seating: 5 stool
monologue: 4 talk 6 sermon, speech 7 address, descant, discant, lecture, stand-up 8 harangue 9 discourse, soliloquy 10 recitation, vocalizing
material: 3 gag 4 joke, news, quip 8 one-liner
Monologue
author: Harold Pinter
monomania: 4 zeal 6 fervor 8 fixation 9 obsession 10 fanaticism
Mon Oncle (1958 film)
cast: Jacques Tati
director: Jacques Tati
Monongahela: 5 river
city on the ~: 10 Pittsburgh
monopolist's trait: 5 greed
monopolize: 3 hog, own 4 have, hold 5 buy up, sew up, sit on 6 absorb, corner, devour, engage, lock up, occupy, patent, take up 7 acquire, consume, control, engross, exclude, possess 8 dominate, take over 9 copyright, syndicate
monopoly: 4 pool 5 trust 6 cartel, corner, patent 7 holding 8 business 9 copyright, oligopoly, ownership, syndicate 10 consortium
get a ~ on: 5 sew up 6 corner
Monopoly: 4 game 9 board game
collection: 4 rent
company: 6 Hasbro
need: 4 dice 5 board, deeds, money 6 hotels, houses
pieces: 8 moneybag 11 wheelbarrow
player: 6 banker
Monopoly pieces:
battleship
cannon
dog
iron
race car
shoe
thimble
top hat
Monopoly railroads:
B and O
Pennsylvania
Reading
Short Line
Monopoly squares (misc.):
Chance
Community Chest
Free Parking
Go to Jail
Income Tax
Jail
Luxury Tax
Monopoly streets:
Atlantic Avenue
Baltic Avenue
Boardwalk
Connecticut Avenue
Illinois Avenue
Indiana Avenue
Kentucky Avenue
Marvin Gardens
Mediterranean Avenue
New York Avenue
North Carolina Avenue
Oriental Avenue
Pacific Avenue
Park Place
Pennsylvania Avenue
States Avenue
St. Charles Place
St. James Place
Tennessee Avenue
Ventnor Avenue
Vermont Avenue
Virginia Avenue
Monopoly utilities:
Electric Company
Water Works
monosaccharide: 5 sugar 6 aldose
suffix: 3 ose
monotone: 5 drone
in a ~: 6 evenly

Monotones
song: Book of Love (1958)
monotonous: 3 dry 4 blah, dull, flat, tame 5 bland, ho-hum, plain, unfun 6 boring, dreary, smooth, stodgy 7 droning, humdrum, prosaic, tedious, uniform 8 banausic, constant, dragging, plodding, singsong, tiresome, toneless, unlively, unvaried, wearying 9 colorless, incessant, ponderous, prosaical, recurrent, soporific, treadmill, unchanged, unvarying, wearisome 10 enervating, invariable
monotony: 3 rut 5 ennui 6 tedium 7 boredom, dryness, humdrum, routine 8 drabness, dullness, evenness, flatness, sameness 9 levelness 10 continuity, dreariness, equability, insipidity, uniformity
Monroe: 4 Bill, city, Earl, fort, town 5 James 6 Vaughn 7 Harriet, Marilyn
coll.: 3 NLU
locale: 8 Michigan 9 Louisiana
Monroe, Earl
milieu: 5 court
org.: 3 NBA
sport: 10 basketball
Monroe, James: 9 president
home: 7 Oak Hill 8 Virginia
opponent: 4 King
predecessor: 7 Madison
successor: 5 Adams
V.P.: 8 Tompkins
wife: 9 Elizabeth
Monroe, Marilyn: 7 actress
contemporary: 6 Bardot 9 Mansfield
film: The Asphalt Jungle (1950)
Bus Stop (1956)
Gentlemen Prefer Blondes (1953)
How to Marry a Millionaire (1953)
Let's Make Love (1960)
The Misfits (1961)
Niagara (1953)
The Seven Year Itch (1955)
Some Like It Hot (1959)
spouse: Joe DiMaggio, Arthur Miller
__ Monroe, VA: 4 Fort
Monrovia: 4 city, town 7 capital
locale: 7 Liberia 10 California
Mons: 4 city, town
locale: 7 Belgium
monsieur: 3 man 5 title 6 French
in German: 4 herr
in Italian: 6 signor
in Spanish: 5 señor
Monsieur Verdoux (1947 film)
cast: Charles Chaplin, Martha Raye
director: Charles Chaplin
monsignor: 5 title 6 cleric, priest
monsoon: 4 rain, wind 5 storm 8 downpour 9 hurricane 10 inundation
monster: 3 big 4 huge, ogre 5 beast, brute, demon, devil, fiend, freak, ghoul, giant, whale 6 bad guy, daemon, daimon, dragon, horror, mutant, savage 7 chimera, hellion, mammoth, villain, werwolf 8 behemoth, bogeyman, chimaera, colossus, gargoyle, gigantic, werewolf 9 archfiend, barbarian, hellhound, leviathan
combining form: 5 terat- 6 terato-
green-eyed ~: 4 envy
home: 4 loch 8 Loch Ness
of myth: 5 harpy, hydra, lamia 6 dragon, gorgon, Medusa
__ monster: 4 Gila 8 Loch Ness
Monster
artist: R.E.M.
author: Jonathan Kellerman
Monster (2003 film)
cast: Bruce Dern, Christina Ricci, Charlize Theron
Monster __ Closet: 5 in the
__ Monster: 6 Cookie
Monster-in-Law (2005 film)
cast: Jane Fonda, Jennifer Lopez
Monster Mash (1962 song)
artist: Bobby Pickett
Monster's Ball (2001 film)
cast: Halle Berry, Peter Boyle, Heath Ledger, Billy Bob Thornton
Monsters, Inc. (2001 film)
voice cast: Steve Buscemi, Billy Crystal, John Goodman
Monsters vs. Aliens (2009 film)
voice cast: Hugh Laurie, Seth Rogen, Reese Witherspoon
monstrosity: 4 ogre 5 sight 6 fright
monstrous: 4 evil, foul, huge, mean, ugly, vast, vile 5 awful, cruel, enorm, giant, great, gross, harsh, nasty 6 animal, brutal, fierce, morbid, odious, savage, unkind, wanton 7 beastly, callous, fearful, heinous, hellish, hideous, hurtful, immense, inhuman, macaber, macabre, mammoth, massive, obscene, ominous, satanic, titanic, ungodly, vicious 8 aberrant, barbaric, colossal, diabolic, dreadful, enormous, fiendish, flagrant, freakish, gigantic, grievous, gruesome, horrible, infamous, infernal, inhumane, pitiless, ruthless, sadistic, shocking, teratoid, terrible, terrific, towering, vengeful, whapping, whopping, wretched 9 appalling, atrocious, barbarous, cutthroat, desperate, egregious, execrable, fantastic, ferocious, frightful, grandiose, grotesque, loathsome, merciless, nefarious, offensive, repellant, revolting, satanical, truculent, unnatural, unpitying, unsightly 10 detestable, diabolical, disgusting, gargantuan, horrendous, horrifying, impressive, monumental, outrageous, petrifying, prodigious, scandalous, stupendous, tremendous, unmerciful, unpleasant, villainous, vindictive, virtueless
Mont: 4 alpe 5 Blanc 6 Cervin
Mont-__-Michel: 5 Saint
Mont.
neighbor: 3 Alb., Ida., Wyo. 4 Alta., N. Dak., Sask., S. Dak.
see also Montana
Montadale: 5 sheep
montagne: 6 French 8 mountain
opposite: 3 val
Montagu: 4 John 6 Ashley
Montague: 5 Romeo
Montagu, Mary Wortley: 6 writer 7 British
work: Turkish Letters
Montaigne, Michel de: 6 French, writer 8 essayist
work: 5 essai
Montalban, Ricardo: 5 actor
film: Star Trek II: The Wrath of Khan (1982)
TV: Fantasy Island
Montale, Eugenio: 4 poet 6 writer 7 Italian 8 Nobelist
Montana: 3 Bob, Joe, van 5 state 6 Big Sky 7 Pontiac
capital: 6 Helena
city: 5 Butte 6 Helena 7 Bozeman 8 Billings, Missoula 9 Kalispell, Silver Bow 10 Great Falls
Indian: 4 Cree, Crow 7 Kutenai 8 Cheyenne 10 Assiniboin
motto word: 3 oro 5 plata
mountain: 5 Lewis 7 Granite, Purcell
national park: 7 Glacier
neighbor: 5 Idaho 6 Canada 7 Alberta, Wyoming
state bird: 10 meadowlark
state flower: 10 bitterroot
__ Montana: 6 Hannah
Montana, Joe: 2 QB 11 quarterback
sport: 8 football
Montand, Yves
spouse: Simone Signoret
Montauk: 4 city, town 5 tribe 6 Indian 8 language
locale: 7 New York
Montauk __, NY: 5 Point
Mont Blanc: 3 alp 4 alpe, peak 5 mount 8 mountain
covering: 4 snow 5 neige
locale: 4 Alps 5 Italy 6 Europe, France
neighbor: 5 Aosta
Montclair: 3 car 4 auto, city, town 7 Mercury 10 automobile
locale: 9 New Jersey 10 California
monte: 4 game, scam 8 card game
Monte: 5 Irvin 7 Hellman, Markham
Monte __: 4 Rosa 5 Albán, Carlo, Corno, Walsh 6 Cristo 7 Cassino
Monte __ sandwich: 6 Cristo
__ Monte: 3 Del
Montebello: 4 city, town
locale: 10 California
Monte Carlo: 3 car 4 auto, city, town 5 Chevy 9 Chevrolet 10 automobile
action: 3 bet
game: 6 écarté 8 baccarat, roulette 9 blackjack
locale: 6 Monaco
Monte Corno: 4 peak 5 mount 8 mountain
locale: 5 Italy 6 Europe 8 Apenines
Montego: 3 car 4 auto 7 Mercury 10 automobile
Montego Bay: 4 city, port, town
locale: 7 Jamaica
Montego Bay (1970 song)
artist: Bobby Bloom
Montel: 8 Williams
colleague: 5 Oprah
Montemezzi: 5 Italo
Montenegro, Hugo
song: The Good, the Bad, and the Ugly (1968)
Monterey: 3 bay, car 4 auto, city, town 7 Mercury 10 automobile
locale: 10 California
Monterey __: 3 Bay, Pop 4 Jack
Monterey Jack: 6 cheese
montero: 3 cap, hat 8 headgear
feature: 6 earlap
Montero: 3 SUV 10 Mitsubishi
Monte Rosa: 3 alp 4 peak 5 mount 8 mountain
locale: 4 Alps 6 Europe 11 Switzerland
Monterrey: 4 city, town
locale: 6 Mexico 9 Nuevo León
see also Spanish
Montesquieu: 6 French, writer 11 philosopher
Montessori, Maria: 7 Italian, teacher 8 educator
Monteux, Pierre: 6 French 9 conductor
Monteverdi, Claudio: 7 Italian 8 composer
work: 5 Orfeo 6 l'Orfeo
Montevideo: 4 city, port, town 7 capital
estuary: 5 Plata
locale: 3 Uru. 7 Uruguay
see also Spanish
Montez: 4 Lola 5 Chris, Maria
Montezuma: 5 Aztec 7 emperor
Montgomerie: 5 Colin
Montgomery: 3 Wes 4 city, town, Ward 5 Clift 6 George, Robert 7 Anthony, Belinda, Bernard 8 Douglass 9 Elizabeth
locale: 3 Ala. 7 Alabama 8 Maryland
milieu: 3 ETO
river: 7 Alabama
sch.: 3 ASU
Montgomery __: 4 Ward
Montgomery, Elizabeth
spouse: Gig Young
__ Montgomery Flagg: 5 James
Montgomery, George: 5 actor
spouse: Dinah Shore
Montgomery, Lucy Maud: 6 writer 8 Canadian
work: Anne of Green Gables
Montgomery, Wes: 9 guitarist
genre: 4 jazz
month: 3 Apr., Aug., Dec., Feb., Jan., Jul., Jun., Mar., May, Nov., Oct., Sep. 4 July, June, moon, Sept., time 5 April, March 6 August 7 January, October, Ramadan 8 December, February, November 9 September
autumn ~: 3 Dec., Nov., Oct., Sep. 4 Sept. 7 October 8 December, November 9 September
combining form: 3 men- 4 meno-
fraction: 2 wk. 4 week
French ~: 3 mai 4 août, juin, mars 5 avril 7 février, janvier, juillet, octobre 8 décembre, novembre 9 septembre
German ~: 3 Mai 4 Juli, Juni, März 5 April 6 August, Januar 7 Februar, Oktober 8 Dezember, November 9 September
Hebrew ~: 2 Av 4 Adar, Elul, Iyar 5 Iyyar, Nisan, Sivan, Tevet 6 Kislev, Nissan, Shevat, Tammuz, Tishri 7 Heshvan
Islamic ~: 4 Magh, Rabi 5 Rajab, Safar 6 Jumada, Sha'ban 7 Ramadan, Shawwal 8 Muharram

Italian ~: **5** marzo **6** agosto, aprile, giugno, lùglio, màggio **7** gennaio, ottobre **8** dicèmbre, febbraio, novèmbre **9** settèmbre
last ~: **3** ult. **6** ultimo
Spanish ~: **3** mes **4** mayo **5** abril, enero, julio, junio, marzo **6** agosto **7** febrero, octubre **9** diciembre, noviembre **10** septiembre
spring ~: **3** Apr., Mar., May **4** June **5** April **8** March. Jun.
summer ~: **3** Aug., Jul., Jun., Sep. **4** July, June, Sept. **6** August **9** September
winter ~: **3** Dec., Feb., Jan., Mar. **5** March **7** January **8** December, February
Month in the Country, A
author: Ivan Turgenev
monthly: **5** paper **6** mensal **8** magazine, periodic **10** periodical
in Latin: **9** per mensum
month of ___: **7** Sundays
months
every twelve ~: **6** yearly
twelve ~: **4** year
Monticello: **6** estate
locale: **8** Virginia
owner: **9** Jefferson
Montilla: **4** wine **7** Spanish
Montmartre
locale: **5** Paris **6** France
Montoya, Carlos: **7** Spanish **9** guitarist
Montpelier: **4** city, town
county: **10** Washington
locale: **7** Vermont
river: **8** Winooski
Montpellier: **4** city, town
locale: **6** France
neighbor of ~: **5** Nîmes
Montrachet: **4** wine **5** white **6** French
Montréal: **4** city, port, town
locale: **3** Que. **6** Canada, Québec
newspaper: **7** Gazette, Journal **8** La Presse
pro team: **5** Expos **9** Canadiens
river: **10** St. Lawrence
school: **6** McGill **9** Concordia
suburb: **5** Laval
subway: **5** Metro
see also French
Montrose: **4** Scot **6** Ronnie
Mont-Saint-___: **6** Michel
Montserrat: **4** isle **6** island
Monty: **4** Hall **7** Woolley
colleague: **3** Ike **4** Omar
Monty Python's The Meaning of Life (1983 film)
cast: Graham Chapman, John Cleese, Terry Gilliam, Eric Idle, Terry Jones, Michael Palin
director: Terry Jones
___ Monty's Double: **4** I Was
monument: **4** carn, slab, tomb, tope **5** cairn, henge, pylon, relic, stela, stele, stone, tower **6** column, ledger, marker, pillar, record, shrine, statue, tablet **7** obelisk, tribute **8** cenotaph, landmark, memorial, monolith **10** magnum opus
monumental: **3** big **4** epic, huge, vast **5** giant, grand, great, jumbo, large, lofty **6** mighty, mortal **7** awesome, classic, Homeric, hulking, immense, lasting, mammoth, massive, sizable, stately, titanic **8** colossal, enduring, enormous, gigantic, historic, immortal, imposing, king-size, majestic, oversize, sizeable, towering, whapping, whopping **9** fantastic, grandiose, Herculean, humongous, important, memorable, monstrous, overlarge **10** gargantuan, impressive, majestical, prodigious, stupendous, tremendous
Mony Mony (song)
artist: Billy Idol, Tommy James and the Shondells
Monza: **3** car **4** auto, city, town **5** Chevy **9** Chevrolet **10** automobile
locale: **5** Italy
moo: **5** bleat
juice: **4** milk
relative: **3** baa, maa **4** oink
moo ___: **5** juice
moo ___ gai pan: **3** goo
moo ___ pork: **3** shu
mooch: **3** beg, bum **5** cadge, sneak **6** borrow, sponge **7** solicit, sponger **8** freeload, scrounge **9** impetrate, panhandle
from: **5** hit up **7** squeeze
moocher: **3** bum **5** leech **6** sponge **7** sponger **8** deadbeat, parasite **9** do-nothing
mood: **3** air **4** aura, feel, huff, stew, tone, vein **5** humor, pique, state, tenor **6** desire, esprit, morale, nature, spirit, temper **7** climate, feeling, mind-set **8** ambiance, ambience, attitude **9** character, semblance **10** atmosphere
bad ~: **3** pet **4** funk, huff, rage, snit, sulk, tiff **6** temper **9** surliness **10** grumpiness
dejected ~: **4** funk **5** blues, dumps **8** doldrums **10** depression, melancholy
in a bad ~: **3** mad **4** sore, sour **5** cross, huffy, irate, riled, upset **6** crabby, grumpy, morose **8** grumpish
in a good ~: **4** glad **5** happy, merry **6** cheery, elated
in the ~: **7** willing
not in the ~: **9** unwilling
rings: **3** fad **5** craze
mood ___: **4** ring **5** music
Mood ___: **6** Indigo
___ Mood: **5** In the
Moodie, Susanna: **6** writer **8** Canadian
work: Roughing It in the Bush
moodiness: **8** glumness
moody: **3** low, sad **4** blue, dour, down, glum, mopy **5** angry, cross, huffy, mopey, sulky, testy **6** crabby, cranky, crusty, dismal, fickle, fitful, gloomy, grumpy, moping, mopish, morbid, morose, piqued, sullen, touchy **7** crabbed, doleful, erratic, flighty, grouchy, in a huff, peevish, pensive **8** brooding, downcast, grumpish, offended, petulant, snappish **9** crotchety, depressed, impulsive, irascible, irritable, mercurial, miserable, saturnine, splenetic **10** capricious, changeable, ill-humored, lugubrious, melancholy, out of sorts
be ~: **4** mope, pout, sulk **5** brood
Moody: **3** Ron **6** Dwight
Moody Blues
song: Gemini Dream (1981)
Go Now! (1965)
I'm Just a Singer (1973)
Nights in White Satin (1972)
The Voice (1981)
Your Wildest Dreams (1986)
Moody, Helen Wills: **7** netster **9** tennis pro
milieu: **5** court
Moody River (1961 song)
artist: Pat Boone
Moody's: **5** rater
best rating: **3** Aaa
rival: **5** Fitch, S and P **6** A.M. Best
Moog: **6** Robert **8** keyboard **10** instrument
familiarly: **5** synth
moo goo ___ pan: **3** gai
Mookie: **6** Wilson
moolah: **3** oof, wad **4** cash, gelt, jack, kail, kale, loot, peag, pelf **5** bills, bread, bucks, dough, funds, green, lucre, money, mopus, pesos, rhino, sewan **6** dinero, do-re-mi, mammon, mazuma, seawan, silver, specie, wampum, wealth **7** cabbage, capital, dollars, lettuce, ooftish, scratch, shekels **8** bankroll, cold cash, currency, hard cash, smackers **9** banknotes, frogskins, long green, simoleons **10** greenbacks, green stuff
moon: **2** Io **3** orb, Pan **4** idle, Leda, Luna, mope, pine, Puck, Rhea, sulk **5** Ariel, Atlas, Carme, Dione, dream, Elara, Janus, Metis, Mimas, month, Naiad, Thebe, Titan, yearn **6** Ananke, Bianca, Charon, Deimos, Europa, Helene, Juliet, Nereid, Oberon, Phobos, Phoebe, Portia, Sinope, Tethys, Triton **7** Belinda, Caliban, Calypso, Despina, Galatea, Himalia, Iapetus, Larissa, Miranda, Ophelia, Pandora, Proteus, Sycorax, Telesto, Titania, Umbriel **8** Adrastea, Amalthea, Callisto, Cordelia, crescent, Cressida, daydream, Ganymede, Hyperion, languish, Lysithea, Pasiphae, Rosalind, Thalassa **9** Desdemona, Enceladus, fantasize, satellite, waste time **10** Epimetheus, Prometheus, woolgather
combining form: **4** luni- **5** selen- **6** seleni-, seleno-
crater: **5** Tycho
ender: **3** eye, lit, set **4** beam, calf, eyed, fish, rise, seed, walk, wort **5** blind, child, light, quake, scape, shine, stone **6** flower, shiner, struck **8** children, lighting, stricken
feature: **3** sea **4** mare **5** rille **6** corona, crater
goddess: **4** Luna **5** Diana
greet the ~: **3** bay **4** howl **7** ululate
hider: **5** cloud
in Italian: **4** luna
in Latin: **4** luna
Jupiter ~: **2** Io **4** Leda **5** Carme, Elara, Metis, Thebe **6** Ananke, Europa, Sinope **7** Himalia **8** Adrastea, Amalthea, Callisto, Ganymede, Lysithea, Pasiphae
man on the ~: **4** Bean, Duke **5** Irwin, Scott, Young **6** Aldrin, Cernan, Conrad **7** Schmitt, Shepard **8** Alan Bean, Mitchell **9** Armstrong, John Young **10** Buzz Aldrin, David Scott, James Irwin
Mars ~: **6** Deimos, Phobos
Neptune ~: **5** Naiad **6** Nereid, Triton **7** Despina, Galatea, Larissa, Proteus **8** Thalassa
of the ~: **5** lunar
once in a blue ~: **6** rarely, seldom
over the ~: **6** elated
phase: **3** new **4** full **7** gibbous **8** crescent
Pluto ~: **6** Charon
project: **6** Apollo
pull: **4** tide
ring: **4** halo
Saturn ~: **3** Pan **4** Rhea **5** Atlas, Dione, Janus, Mimas, Titan **6** Helene, Phoebe, Tethys **7** Calypso, Iapetus, Pandora, Telesto **8** Hyperion **9** Enceladus **10** Epimetheus, Prometheus
shoot for the ~: **6** aspire, gamble
starter: **5** honey
track: **5** orbit
Uranus ~: **4** Puck **5** Ariel **6** Bianca, Juliet, Oberon, Portia **7** Belinda, Caliban, Miranda, Ophelia, Sycorax, Titania, Umbriel **8** Cordelia, Cressida, Rosalind **9** Desdemona
USSR ~ probe: **5** Lunik
vehicle: **3** LEM **5** Rover **6** lander
moon ___: **3** dog **4** shot
moon-___: **4** eyed **5** faced
___ moon: **3** new, old **4** blue, full **7** harvest
___-moon: **4** half
Moon: **5** Keith **6** Martin, Warren **7** Mullins
Moon ___: **5** River
Moon ___ Miami: **4** Over
Moon ___ Parador: **4** Over
Moon ___ Zappa: **4** Unit
___ Moon: **4** Blue **5** Paper
___ Moon and Empty Arms: **4** Full
Moon and Sixpence, The: **5** novel
author: W. Somerset Maugham
character: **3** Amy, Ata **4** Dirk **7** Blanche
moonbeam: **3** ray
mooneye: **4** fish
moonfish: **4** opah
Moon for the Misbegotten, A: **4** play **5** drama
author: Eugene O'Neill
character: **4** Mike, Phil **5** Josie **6** Harder, Tyrone
___ Moon Frye: **6** Soleil
Moon Is ___, The: **4** Blue
Moon, Keith: **5** Stone **7** drummer
Moon Lady
author: Amy Tan
moonless: **4** dark
planet: **5** Venus **7** Mercury
moonlight: **4** work **5** labor **10** occupation

Moonlight __: **3** Bay **6** Sonata **7** Gambler
Moonlight and Valentino (1995 film)
cast: Whoopi Goldberg, Elizabeth Perkins, Kathleen Turner
Moonlight Becomes You: **4** song **5** novel
author: Mary Higgins Clark
composer: Johnny Burke, Jimmy Van Heusen
Moonlight Feels Right (1976 song)
artist: Starbuck
Moonlight Gambler (1956 song)
artist: Frankie Laine
Moonlighting (ABC sitcom)
cast: Allyce Beasley (Agnes Dipesto)
Cybill Shepherd (Maddie Hayes)
Bruce Willis (David Addison)
Moonlight Sonata
composer: Ludwig van Beethoven
moonlit: **6** bright
Moon Mullins: **5** strip **10** comic strip
artist: Frank Willard
character: **4** Kayo **5** Mamie **6** Willie
Moon Music
author: Faye Kellerman
Moon Over Parador (1988 film)
cast: Sonia Braga, Richard Dreyfuss, Raul Julia, Jonathan Winters
Moonraker: **4** film **5** novel
author: Ian Fleming
cast: Lois Chiles, Richard Kiel, Roger Moore
villain: **4** Jaws
__ Moon Rising: **3** Bad
Moon River: **4** song **5** waltz
composer: Henry Mancini, Johnny Mercer
Moon's a Balloon, The
author: David Niven
__ moons ago: **4** many
Moon Shadow (1971 song)
artist: Cat Stevens
moonshine: **5** booze, drink, hooch **6** hootch, liquor, whisky **7** alcohol, baloney, spirits, whiskey **8** beverage **9** inebriant
container: **3** jug
ingredient: **4** corn, mash
machine: **5** still
quantity: **6** jugful
see also baloney
moonstone: **4** opal
Moonstone, The
author: Wilkie Collins
__ Moon Street: **4** Half
moonstruck: **4** rapt **7** bananas **8** ravished
Moonstruck (1987 film)
cast: Danny Aiello, Nicolas Cage, Cher, Olympia Dukakis, Vincent Gardenia
director: Norman Jewison
Moon Unit: **5** Zappa
to Dweezil: **3** sis
moonwalk: **5** dance
moonwalker: **9** astronaut
Moon, Warren: **2** QB **11** quarterback
sport: **8** football
moonwort: **4** fern
moony: **6** dreamy **7** languid, passive **8** listless, mindless **9** lethargic **10** melancholy
moor: **3** fix, tie **4** dock, down, fell, lash, wold **5** berth, chain, heath, hitch, plain, swamp, tie up, waste **6** anchor, fasten, secure, steppe, tether, tundra **7** lowland, peat bog, savanna **8** make fast, savannah **9** wasteland
ender: **3** age, hen **4** fowl, land
plant: **4** nard **5** gorse
Moor: **5** Azeem **6** Berber **7** Othello
betrayer: **4** Iago
see also Moorish
__ Moor: **7** Marston
Moore: **2** G.E. **3** Bob **4** Alvy, Demi, diva, poet **5** Brian, Dinty, Garry, Grace, Henry, Lenny, Mandy, Melba, Robin, Roger, Terry **6** Archie, Chanté, Dudley, George, Hannah, Kieron, Robert, Thomas, Victor **7** Clayton, Clement, Colleen, Dorothy, Douglas, Michael **8** Julianne, Marianne, Stanford **9** Constance
Moore, Archie: **5** boxer
milieu: **4** ring
Moore, Brian: **6** writer **8** Canadian
Moore, Clement: **4** poet
character: **5** Santa
first word: **4** 'Twas
moored: **10** stationary
not ~: **6** adrift
Moore, Demi: **7** actress
film: About Last Night... (1986)
Blame It on Rio (1984)
Disclosure (1994)
A Few Good Men (1992)
Ghost (1990)
G.I. Jane (1997)
Indecent Proposal (1993)
The Juror (1996)
Mr. Brooks (2007)
St. Elmo's Fire (1985)
spouse: Bruce Willis
Moore, Dudley: **5** actor
film: 10 (1979)
Arthur (1981)
Bedazzled (1967)
Foul Play (1978)
Micki + Maude (1984)
spouse: Tuesday Weld
Moore, George: **5** Irish **6** writer
work: Aphrodite in Aulis
Héloise and Abélard
Moore, Grace: **6** singer **7** soprano
specialty: **5** opera
Moore, Hannah: **6** writer **7** British
work: Percy
Moorehead: **4** Alan **5** Agnes
Moorehead, Alan: **6** writer **10** Australian
work: Gallipoli
No Room in the Ark
Moore, Henry: **6** artist **7** British **8** sculptor
Moore, Julianne: **7** actress
film: Assassins (1995)
The Big Lebowski (1998)
Boogie Nights (1997)
Cookie's Fortune (1999)
Far From Heaven (2002)
The Forgotten (2004)
Freedomland (2006)
Hannibal (2001)
The Hours (2002)
The Lost World: Jurassic Park (1997)
Magnolia (1999)
A Map of the World (1999)
Next (2007)
Nine Months (1995)
The Shipping News (2001)
Short Cuts (1993)
Vanya on 42nd Street (1994)
Moore, Marianne: **4** poet
Moore, Mary Tyler: **7** actress
film: Change of Habit (1969)
Ordinary People (1980)
Thoroughly Modern Millie (1967)
spouse: Grant Tinker
TV: The Dick Van Dyke Show
Moore, Michael: **8** director
film: Bowling for Columbine (2002)
Canadian Bacon (1995)
Capitalism: A Love Story (2009)
Fahrenheit 9/11 (2004)
Roger and Me (1989)
Sicko (2007)
Moore, Roger: **5** actor
film: The Cannonball Run (1981)
ffolkes (1980)
For Your Eyes Only (1981)
Live and Let Die (1973)
The Man With the Golden Gun (1974)
Moonraker (1979)
Octopussy (1983)
The Spy Who Loved Me (1977)
A View to a Kill (1985)
TV: The Saint
Moore, Stanford: **7** chemist **8** Nobelist
Moore, Terry: **7** actress
spouse: Howard Hughes
Moore, Thomas: **4** poet **5** Irish
work: Lalla Rookh
Moorhead: **4** city, town
locale: **9** Minnesota
mooring: **6** harbor **7** harbour, landing **9** anchorage
line: **6** hawser
place: **4** cove, dock, pier **5** berth, inlet, layby, wharf
post: **4** bitt **7** bollard
mooring __: **4** buoy, mast
Moorish: **5** style
drum: **6** atabal
faith: **5** Islam
money: **8** maravedi
Moorpark: **4** city, town
locale: **10** California
moose: **6** animal, cervid, mammal **10** Bullwinkle
ender: **4** bird, wood
feature: **6** antler
female: **3** cow
genus: **5** alces
male: **4** bull
relative: ***see*** deer
young: **4** calf
Moosehead: **3** ale **4** beer, lake
locale: **5** Maine
Moose Jaw: **4** city, town
locale: **4** Sask. **6** Canada
moosemilk: **5** drink **8** beverage, cocktail
ingredient: **3** rum **4** milk **7** whiskey
__ Moose Party: **4** Bull
moot: **4** open **7** at issue, dubious, suspect **8** academic, arguable, doubtful, forensic **9** debatable, uncertain, undecided, unsettled **10** disputable, irrelevant, unresolved
moot __: **4** hall **5** court, point
__ moo, there...: **5** Here a
mop: **3** rub **4** dust, hair, mane, swab, swob, wash, wipe **5** clean, scrub, shock, sweep **6** duster, soak up, sponge, tangle, thatch **7** tresses
like a ~: **6** shaggy, unruly
starter: **4** roll
the floor with: **4** rout **6** defeat
up: **4** swab, swob, whip **5** clean **6** absorb, finish **9** finish off
__ mop: **3** dry, wet **4** dust
__-mop: **4** damp
__ Mop: **3** Rag
mope: **4** ache, fret, idle, moon, pine, pout, stew, sulk **5** bleed, brood, chafe, droop, grump, piner, sweat, yearn **6** grieve, lament, linger, pouter, regret, repine, sulker **7** brooder, despair, grumble **8** languish, sourpuss **9** gloomy Gus, lose heart, waste time **10** take it hard
moped: **4** bike **9** motorbike
kin: **5** cycle **10** motorcycle
user: **5** rider
mopes: **5** gloom **7** sadness **8** glumness
mopey: **3** low, sad **4** blue, down, glum **5** moody, sulky **6** broody, sullen **7** forlorn, hangdog, joyless **8** dejected, downcast, listless **9** cheerless, depressed, long-faced, woebegone **10** despondent, dispirited, melancholy, out of sorts
Mop & Glo: **7** cleaner
alternative: **5** Brite, Lysol **6** Top Job **7** Lestoil, Mr. Clean, Pine Sol **9** Fantastik, Step Saver
mopish: **5** moody **6** broody, gloomy **8** dejected, listless
__ M-O-P-P...: **4** R-A-G-G
moppet: **3** kid, tot **4** tike, tyke **5** child, kiddy, youth **6** cherub **9** youngster
mopping: **5** chore **9** housework
Mopsus: **4** seer **8** Argonaut
father: **6** Apollo
mop the __ with: **5** floor
mor: **3** god **4** Eros **5** Cupid **6** cherub **7** love god
Moraes, Dom: **4** poet **6** Indian **10** journalist
moral: **3** saw **4** fine, good, just, meet, nice, okay, pure, rule **5** adage, axiom, clean, gnome, great, legit, maxim, motto, noble, point, right **6** chaste, decent, dictum, honest, kasher, kindly, kosher, lesson, modest, proper, saying, seemly, square, truism, worthy **7** correct, dutiful, epigram, ethical, message, precept, proverb, saintly, upright **8** all right, aphorism, decorous, elevated, laudable, pleasant, pleasing, splendid, straight, superior, true-blue, truthful, virtuous **9** admirable, agreeable, blameless, courteous, excellent, exemplary, high-toned, honorable, religious, reputable, righteous, wholesome, wonderful **10** aboveboard, acceptable, apophthegm, beneficial, creditable, folk wisdom, goody-goody, high-minded, inculcable, principled, scrupulous, upstanding
error: **3** sin **5** lapse
fiber: **4** grit, guts, will **5** pluck, spine, spunk, valor **6** mettle, spirit **7** bravery, courage **8** back-

MO

bone, firmness, tenacity **9** fortitude, toughness **10** resolution
principle: **5** ethic, honor **6** ethics
sense: **8** superego **10** conscience, small voice
tale with a ~: **5** fable **7** apology **8** apologue
morale: **5** heart **6** esprit, mettle, spirit **7** outlook, resolve **8** attitude, optimism **9** character **10** confidence
Morales, Esai: **5** actor
film: Bad Boys (1983)
La Bamba (1987)
My Family/Mi Familia (1995)
The Wonderful Ice Cream Suit (1999)
TV: N.Y.P.D. Blue
Moralia
author: Plutarch
moralist: **4** Cato, Esop **5** Aesop
moralistic: **8** virtuous
morality: **4** good **5** honor, mores, right **6** ethics, ideals, purity, virtue **7** conduct, decency, honesty, justice, probity **8** chastity, goodness **9** integrity, principle, rectitude, rightness, standards **10** gentleness, good habits, honestness, principles, worthiness
morality __: **4** play
moralization: **6** homily
moralize: **6** preach **7** lecture **9** exprobate
morally: **9** honorably **10** virtuously
morals: **5** ethic, mores **6** ideals, values **7** customs **8** behavior, policies, scruples, standard **9** standards **10** principles
Moran: **4** Bugs, Erin **5** Julie
contemporary: **6** Capone
Moranis, Rick: **5** actor
film: Honey, I Blew Up the Kid (1992)
Honey, I Shrunk the Kids (1989)
Little Shop of Horrors (1986)
My Blue Heaven (1990)
Parenthood (1989)
Spaceballs (1987)
Streets of Fire (1984)
__ Morant: **7** Breaker
Morante, Elsa: **4** poet **6** writer **7** Italian
morass: **3** bog, fen, web **4** maze, mire **5** marsh, snarl, swamp **6** tangle **7** lowland **8** quagmire **9** labyrinth
Morath: **3** Max **4** Inge
Morath, Max: **7** pianist
moratorium: **5** pause, truce **7** respite **9** white flag
Moravia: **6** Albert
old capital of ~: **4** Brno
Moravia, Albert: **6** writer **7** Italian
pen name of: Alberto Pincherle
work: The Fancy Dress Party
Two Women
Moravian: **4** Slav **5** Czech
moray: **3** eel **4** fish
catcher: **5** eeler **6** eelpot
home: **3** sea **5** ocean **6** eelery
kin: **6** conger
like a ~: **4** eely
young ~: **5** elver
Moray Firth
locale: **8** North Sea, Scotland
morbid: **4** dark, grim, sick **5** moody **6** gloomy, grisly, horrid, sickly, somber **7** ghastly, hideous, macaber, macabre, unsound **8** aberrant, abnormal, brooding, ghoulish, gruesome **9** depressed, frightful, monstrous, saturnine, unhealthy, unnatural **10** despondent, melancholy
mordancy: **6** malice, rancor **8** acerbity, acrimony **10** bitterness
mordant: **4** acid **5** acerb **6** biting, ireful, severe **7** caustic, cutting, pungent, satiric **8** derisive, incisive, sardonic, scornful **9** sarcastic, satirical, trenchant
Mordecai: **7** Richler **10** Anielewicz
cousin: **6** Esther
mordent
relative: **5** trill
more: **3** and, new, too, yet **4** also, else, over **5** extra, fresh, major, other, spare, wider **6** as well, better, beyond, encore, higher, larger, longer **7** another, besides, farther, further, greater, heavier **8** enhanced, expanded, extended, likewise **9** along with, augmented, exceeding, increased **10** additional, in addition
combining form: **4** pleo-, plio **5** pleio-
ender: **4** over
excellent: **5** finer **6** enrich, fitter **7** enhance, greater, surpass, upgrade **8** improved, souped up, stronger, superior, worthier **9** healthier, sharpened **10** preferable
in music: **3** piu
in Spanish: **3** más
make ~ inclusive: **6** expand, spread **7** augment, broaden, enlarge
no ~: **4** once, stop **5** kaput **6** lapsed
no ~ than: **4** just, mere, only **6** at most, merely
nothing ~ than: **4** just **6** merely, simply, solely, wholly **7** totally, utterly **8** entirely
often than not: **6** simply **7** as a rule, usually **8** commonly, normally **9** naturally **10** ordinarily
once ~: **4** anew, over **5** again **6** afresh, de novo, encore
one or ~: **3** any
or less: **4** near **5** quite, sorta **6** approx., around, fairly, kind of, nearly, rather, sort of **8** slightly, somewhat
prefix: **5** super-
provide ~: **6** refill **9** replenish
recent: **6** latter **9** following
starter: **3** any **4** ever **5** never **7** further
than: **4** over **5** above **6** beyond **7** besides **9** upwards of
than a few: **4** gobs, lots, much, tons **5** heaps, piles, scads **6** oodles, plenty, scores **7** copious, umpteen **8** abundant, numerous **9** bountiful, multitude, thousands
than a little: **4** much **5** amply, quite **6** deeply, highly, hugely, unduly, vastly **7** greatly, largely, only too, rabidly **8** terribly **9** decidedly, extremely, seriously, unusually **10** enormously, incredibly, profoundly, remarkably, thoroughly, uncommonly
than enough: **5** ample, spare, undue **6** excess, galore, oodles
than one: **3** plu. **4** plur., some **5** group **6** plural
to minimalists: **4** less
what's ~: **3** and **4** also, plus **7** besides
more __ meets the eye: **4** than
__ more: **6** less is
More: **6** Thomas **7** Kenneth
More (song)
artist: Perry Como, Kai Winding
More __ Feeling: **5** Than a
More __ You Know: **4** Than
More __ You, The: **4** I See
More!: **6** encore
Moreau, Jeanne: **7** actress
spouse: William Friedkin
More deadly than __ dog's tooth: **4** a mad
More Die of Heartbreak
author: Saul Bellow
moreen: **6** fabric **8** material
morel: **6** fungus **8** mushroom
Morel, Jean: **6** French **9** conductor
Morella
author: Edgar Allan Poe
morello: **4** tree **6** cherry
relative: **4** Bing **7** marasca, oxheart
Morelos: **5** state **7** Mexican
city: **7** Cuautla, Jojutla, Temixco **8** Apatlaco, Jiutepec, Yautepec **9** Zacatepec **10** Cuernavaca
More Love (1980 song)
artist: Kim Carnes
__ More Night: **3** One
More Nonsense Songs
author: Edward Lear
Moreno, Rita: **7** actress
film: The Four Seasons (1981)
The King and I (1956)
Popi (1969)
West Side Story (1961, AA)
Moreno Valley: **4** city, town
locale: **10** California
Morenz: **5** Howie
more or __: **4** less
moreover: **3** and, too, yet **4** also **5** again **6** as well, to boot **7** besides, further **8** likewise **10** in addition
More powerful __ locomotive: **5** than a
mores: **5** ethos **6** ethics, morals, values **7** culture, customs, manners **8** folkways, morality, niceties **9** ethnology, propriety, tradition
more than __ the eye: **5** meets
More Than a Feeling (1976 song)
artist: Boston
More Than Ever (1991 song)
artist: Nelson
More Than I Can Say (1980 song)
artist: Leo Sayer
more than one way to skin __: **4** a cat
More Than That (2001 song)
artist: Backstreet Boys
More Than Words Can Say (1990 song)
artist: Alias
More, Thomas: **3** Sir **5** saint **6** writer **7** British **8** essayist, humanist **9** statesman
work: Utopia
__ more time!: **3** One
Morey: **9** Amsterdam
Morgan: **2** J.P. **3** Gil, Joe, Rex **4** Earp, Jane, Russ **5** Debbi, Frank, Harry, Helen, Henry, horse, Jaye P., Le Fay, Tracy **6** Dennis, Lorrie, Thomas **7** Charles, Freeman **8** Brittany **9** Fairchild
brother: **5** Wyatt **6** Virgil
marking: **4** star
Morgan __: **7** Stanley
Morgana: **4** King
__ Morgana: **4** Fata
Morgan, Charles: **6** writer **7** British **10** playwright
Morgan, Gil: **6** golfer
Morgan, Harry: **5** actor
TV: Dragnet, MASH
Morgan Hill: **4** city, town
locale: **10** California
Morgan, Jane
song: Fascination (1957)
Morgan Le __: **3** Fay
Morgan's Passing
author: Anne Tyler
Morgan, Thomas: **8** Nobelist
Morgantown: **4** city
locale: **3** W. Va.
school: **3** WVU
Morgenstern: **3** Ida **5** Rhoda
Morgenthau: **5** Henry
Moriarty: **5** Cathy **7** Michael
moribund: **8** stagnant
Mörike, Eduard: **4** poet **6** German
Morini, Erika: **8** Austrian **9** violinist
Mori Ōgai: **6** writer **8** Japanese
work: The Abe Family
The Wild Geese
Morissette, Alanis
homeland: Canada
song: Hand in My Pocket (1995)
Head over Feet (1997)
Ironic (1996)
Thank U (1998)
Uninvited (1998)
You Learn (1996)
You Oughta Know (1995)
Morita: **3** Pat **4** Akio
Moritat (1956 song)
artist: Dick Hyman
__ Moritz: **5** Saint
Mork: **2** ET **5** alien
spaceship: **3** egg
Mork & Mindy (ABC sitcom)
cast: Pam Dawber (Mindy McConnell)
Ralph James (Orson)
Conrad Janis (Frederick McConnell)
Tom Poston (Mr. Bickley)
Robin Williams (Mork)
Jonathan Winters (Mearth)
Mork's home: Ork
Mork's word: nanu
setting: Boulder, Colorado
Morley: **5** Karen, Safer **6** Robert **9** Callaghan
Morley, Christopher: **6** writer
founder of: Saturday Review
work: Kitty Foyle
Parnassus on Wheels
Morlocks' prey: **4** Eloi
Mormon
Book of ~ book: **4** Alma, Enos, Omni **5** Ether, Jacob, Jarom, Nephi **6** Moroni, Mosiah **7** Helaman

Mormons: 3 LDS
manna: 4 sego
official: 5 elder
predecessor: 3 Ute
state: 4 Utah
morn
opposite: 3 eve
see also morning
Mornay: 5 sauce
Mornay, Rebecca De: 7 actress
__ Morne National Park: 4 Gros
morning: 2 a.m. 4 dawn 5 early, light, prime, sunup 6 aurora, morrow 7 sunrise 8 cockcrow, daybreak, daylight, forenoon 9 dayspring 10 break of day, first blush
activity: 5 shave
and afternoon: 6 all day
beverage: 3 tea 5 latte 6 coffee
draw toward ~: 5 laten
early ~: 3 one, two 4 dawn, five, four 5 one a.m., sunup, three, two a.m. 6 five a.m., four a.m. 7 sunrise, three a.m. 8 wee hours
every ~: 5 daily 7 diurnal, regular, routine 9 quotidian
follower: 3 aft. 4 noon 9 afternoon
good ~ in French: 7 bon jour
good ~ in German: 8 guten tag
good ~ in Japanese: 5 ohayo
good ~ in Spanish: 10 buenos días
greet the ~: 4 rise, wake 5 arise, awake, get up, waken 6 awaken
hour: 3 six, ten 4 nine 5 eight, seven, six a.m., ten a.m. 6 eleven, nine a.m. 7 eight a.m., seven a.m. 8 eleven a.m.
like ~ air: 5 brisk
like grass in the ~: 3 wet 4 damp, dewy 5 moist
meal: 6 brunch 9 breakfast
mist: 3 fog 4 haze
moisture: 3 dew
poem: 6 aubade
prayer: 5 matin
prefix for ~: 3 mid
service: 5 terce
sound: 5 alarm
morning __: 4 coat, line, star 5 glory
__ morning: 4 good
Morning __, The: 5 After, Watch
__ Morning: 7 Chelsea
Morning After, The (1973 song)
artist: Maureen McGovern
__ Morning, America: 4 Good
Morning Edition
network: 3 NPR
morning glory: 5 plant 6 flower
dried ~ root: 5 jalap
Morning Glory (1933 film)
cast: Douglas Fairbanks Jr., Katharine Hepburn, Adolphe Menjou
flower: 5 calla
Morning Has Broken (1972 song)
artist: Cat Stevens
Morning News: 5 paper 9 newspaper
locale: 6 Dallas
Morning Noon and Night
author: Sidney Sheldon
__ morning quarterback: 6 Monday
__ Morning Rain: 5 Early
Morning Side of the Mountain (1974 song)
artist: Donny and Marie Osmond
Mornings in Mexico
author: D.H. Lawrence
__ Morning Starshine: 4 Good
Morning Train (1981 song)
artist: Sheena Easton
__ Morning, Vietnam: 4 Good
Morning Watch, The
author: James Agee
Moro: 4 Aldo 5 César 7 Malayan 8 Filipino
morocco __: 7 leather
Morocco: 6 nation 7 country
capital: 5 Rabat
city: 3 Fez 4 Ujda 5 Oujda, Rabat 6 Agadir, Meknes 7 Tangier 8 Tangiers 9 Marrakesh 10 Casablanca
desert: 6 Sahara
group: 10 Arab League
money: 6 dirham
mount: 5 camel
mountain: 5 Atlas 7 Toubkal
neighbor: 5 Spain 7 Algeria 14 Gibraltar. Medit.
people: 4 Riff 5 Shilh
port: 4 Safi 5 Rabat, Saffi 6 Agadir 7 Tangier 8 Tangiers 10 Casablanca
region: 3 Rif 4 Ifni
writer: 10 Ben Jelloun
Moro, César: 4 poet 8 Peruvian
Moroder: 7 Giorgio
Moroni: 4 city, town 5 angel 7 capital
locale: 7 Comoros
morose: 3 low, sad 4 blue, dark, dour, down, glum, grim, sick, sour, ugly 5 brusk, cross, gruff, harsh, moody, sulky, surly, testy, woful 6 broody, crabby, cranky, gloomy, moping, sickly, somber, sullen, woeful 7 brusque, crabbed, doleful, grouchy, joyless, peevish, unhappy 8 choleric, churlish, dejected, downcast, frowning, liverish, mournful, perverse, snappish, taciturn, troubled 9 bummed out, cheerless, depressed, heartsick, irritable, miserable, saturnine, sorrowful, splenetic, woebegone 10 chapfallen, despondent, dispirited, ill-humored, lugubrious, melancholy
be ~: 4 sulk
Moross: 6 Jerome
morph: 6 change
into: 6 become
starter: 4 ecto, endo, meso
morpheme: 4 word
Morpheus
father: 6 Hypnos
morphology: 7 grammar, science 9 structure
Morphy, Paul game: 5 chess
Morricone, Ennio: 7 Italian 8 composer
morris: 5 dance
Morris: 3 cat, Jan, pet 4 Greg, Phil, West 5 Anita, Cohen, Errol, Wayne 6 Albert, Howard, Willie, Wright 7 Chester, Garrett, Stoloff, William 9 Carnovsky
Morris __: 5 chair
Morris, Jack: 6 hurler 7 pitcher
Morris, Jan: 6 writer 7 British 10 journalist
Morrison: 3 Jim, Van 4 Jane, Mark, Toni 5 Waite
Morrison, Jim: 4 Door
Morrison, Toni: 6 writer 8 Nobelist
work: Beloved
The Bluest Eye
Jazz
Paradise
Song of Solomon
Sula
Tar Baby
Morrison, Van
homeland: Ireland
song: Blue Money (1971)
Brown Eyed Girl (1967)
Come Running (1970)
Domino (1970)
Wild Night (1971)
Morristown: 4 city
locale: 9 New Jersey
Morris, William: 4 poet 6 agency, artist 7 British, printer 8 designer 9 architect
employee: 3 rep 5 agent
Morris, Wright: 6 writer
work: Love Among the Cannibals
The Works of Love
Morro Bay: 4 city, town
locale: 10 California
Morro Castle site: 4 Cuba 6 Havana
morrow: 4 morn 7 morning
Morrow: 3 Rob, Vic
Morrow, Vic: 5 actor
TV: Combat
Morse: 5 Barry, David, Wayne 6 Robert, Samuel
invention: 4 code 9 telegraph
Morse __: 4 code
Morse code
code unit: 3 dah, dit, dot 4 dash
e, in ~: 3 dit, dot
message: 3 SOS
send ~: 3 tap
sound: 5 click
t, in ~: 3 dah 4 dash
Morse, David: 5 actor
film: Crazy in Alabama (1999)
The Green Mile (1999)
The Indian Runner (1991)
The Negotiator (1998)
Personal Foul (1987)
Proof of Life (2000)
morsel: 3 bit, ort 4 atom, bite, drop, hunk, iota, lump, nosh, part, snip 5 chunk, crumb, grain, piece, scrap, slice, snack, taste, treat 6 nibble, sample, tidbit 7 portion, soupçon 8 delicacy, fraction, fragment, mouthful, particle, spoonful
Morse, Robert: 5 actor
film: A Guide for the Married Man (1967)
How to Succeed in Business Without Really Trying (1967)
The Loved Ones (1965)
Mort: 4 Sahl 6 Walker 7 Drucker, Lindsey
mortadella: 4 meat 7 Italian, sausage
mortal: 3 man 4 body, soul 5 alive, being, great, human, woman 6 finite, person 7 animate, earthly, passing 8 creature, temporal 9 earthborn, earthling, ephemeral, transient 10 evanescent, individual, inexpiable
mortal __: 3 sin
Mortal Fear
author: Robin Cook, Greg Iles
mortar: 3 gun 5 grout 6 cannon, cement
mixer: 3 rab
support: 5 bipod
trough: 3 hod
mortarboard: 3 cap
Morte d'Arthur: 4 poem
author: Alfred Tennyson
Mortensen: 5 Viggo
mortgage: 3 IOU 4 debt, lien, loan 6 credit, red ink 9 liability
bearer: 4 ower 6 lienee
datum: 3 APR 4 rate 7 payment
get a ~: 3 owe 6 borrow
grant a ~: 4 lend, loan
issuer: 3 FHA 4 bank, FNMA, GNMA 5 S and L 6 lienor
option: 4 refi
second ~ to brokers: 4 refi
__ mortgage: 5 first 6 second 7 balloon, reverse
mortgaged: 6 in debt 8 indebted
Morticia: 6 Addams
cousin: 3 Itt
husband: 5 Gomez
to Fester: 5 niece
mortification: 8 distress 9 abashment
mortified: 5 stern 6 aghast 7 abashed 8 sheepish
mortify: 4 deny 5 abash, appal, shame 6 appall, humble, rankle 7 chagrin, chasten, deflate 8 belittle, confound, disgrace, ridicule, take down 9 discomfit, embarrass, humiliate 10 disgruntle, put to shame
mortifying: 8 shameful
Mortimer: 5 Adler, Snerd 8 Penelope
voice of ~: 5 Edgar
Mortimer, Penelope: 6 writer 7 British
work: The Pumpkin Eater
mortise: 6 fasten 8 junction, juncture
partner: 5 tenon
Morton: 3 Joe 4 Levi, salt 5 Gould 6 Downey 7 Da Costa, Feldman, Janklow, William
Morton Grove: 4 city, town
locale: 8 Illinois
Morton, Jelly Roll: 7 pianist
genre: 4 jazz
__ Morton Stanley: 5 Henry
mos.
3 ~: 3 qtr.
every 12 ~: 4 yrly.
Mos __: 3 Def
mosaic: 3 mix 4 tile 5 inlay 6 inlaid 7 mixture 8 speckled
detail: 5 inset
Mosaic __: 3 Law
mosaic gold: 5 alloy
component: 4 zinc 6 copper
Moscato d'__: 4 Asti
Mosconi, Willie
game: 4 pool
prop: 3 cue 4 rack 5 chalk 6 bridge
Moscow: 4 city, town 7 capital
athletes: 7 Vandals
city near ~: 4 Orel 5 Gorki, Kirov
department store: 3 GUM
locale: 5 Idaho 6 Russia
school: 3 Ida. 5 Idaho
Moscow mule: 5 drink 8 beverage, cocktail

ingredient: 5 vodka 9 lime juice 10 ginger beer
Moscow on the Hudson (1984 film)
cast: Maria Conchita Alonso, Alejandro Rey, Robin Williams
Mose: 7 Allison
Mosè
composer: Gioacchino Rossini
Mosel: 3 Tad 5 river
city on the ~: 7 Coblenz, Koblenz
locale: 7 Germany
Moselle: 4 wine 5 river, white
city on the ~: 4 Metz 5 Trier 6 Épinal, Treves
locale: 6 France
river to the ~: 4 Saar
Moses: 4 Gunn 5 Edwin 6 Malone
attire: 4 robe
author: Sholem Asch
book of ~: 3 Lev. 4 Deut., Exod. 6 Exodus 7 Genesis, Numbers. 9 Leviticus
books of ~: 4 Tora 5 Torah
brother: 5 Aaron
father-in-law: 6 Jethro
grandson: 8 Jonathan, Rehabiah
mountain: 4 Nebo 5 Sinai 6 Pisgah
parent: 5 Amram 8 Jochebed
sister: 6 Miriam
son: 7 Eliezer, Gershom
spy: 5 Caleb
uncle: 6 Hebron
where baby ~ was found: 6 rushes
wife: 8 Zipporah
__ Moses: 4 Amos, holy 5 Law of 7 Grandma
Moses, Grandma: 4 Anna 6 artist 7 painter
Moses und __: 4 Aron
mosey: 2 go 3 lag 4 idle, laze, loaf, move, poke 5 amble, dally, drift, stall, tarry 6 dawdle, linger, loiter, sashay, stroll 7 saunter 8 lollygag, straggle 9 waste time 10 dillydally
mosh: 9 slam-dance
mosh __: 3 pit
Moshe: 5 Dayan 7 Sharett
Moslem
see Muslim
Mosque of __: 4 Omar
mosquito: 3 bug 4 fern, pest 5 biter, culex 6 insect
barrier: 3 net
combining form: 5 culic- 6 culici-
genus: 5 aedes
like a ~ bite: 5 itchy
sound: 4 buzz 5 whine
young: 5 nymph
mosquito __: 3 net 4 bite 7 netting
Mosquito Coast, The: 4 film 5 novel
author: Paul Theroux
cast: Harrison Ford, Helen Mirren, River Phoenix
character: 5 Allie
director: Peter Weir
mosquito-like insect: 5 midge
moss: 5 color, plant, pyxie 6 lichen 8 sphagnum 9 bryophyte
combining form: 3 bry- 4 bryo-, musc- 5 musci-, -musco
ender: 4 back 5 grown 6 bunker
science: 8 bryology
source: 4 peat
undersea: 6 obelia
__ moss: 3 bog, sea, sun 4 peat
Moss: 4 Hart, Kate 6 Arnold 8 Stirling 10 Carrie-Anne
mossback: 4 fogy 5 fogey 7 diehard
Mössbauer, Rudolf: 6 German 8 Nobelist 9 physicist
Mosses From an Old __: 5 Manse
moss-grown: 8 out of use
mosslike: 5 peaty
plant: 5 sedum, usnea
__ mosso: 4 meno
mosspink: 5 plant 6 flower
mossy: 9 overgrown 10 antiquated
most: 3 max, too 4 best, bulk, much, nigh, very 6 all but, almost, nearly, utmost 7 biggest, greatly, highest, largest, maximum 8 about all, greatest, majority, ultimate, well-nigh 9 extremely, nearly all, plurality 10 lion's share
in Spanish: 3 más
opposite: 5 least
starter: 3 aft, end, top 4 head, hind, left 5 after, inner, lower, outer, right, stern, upper, utter 6 bottom, hinder, hither, middle 7 eastern, farther, further, western
most __ list: 6 wanted
most-__-nation: 7 favored
Most: 5 Donny
Most __ Fella, The: 5 Happy
mostaccioli: 5 pasta
alternative: *see* pasta
Most Beautiful Girl in the World, The
composer: Lorenz Hart, Richard Rodgers
Most Beautiful Girl in the World, The (1994 song)
artist: Prince
Most Beautiful Girl, The (1973 song)
artist: Charlie Rich
Mostel: 4 Josh, Zero
Mostel, Zero: 5 actor
film: The Front (1976) The Producers (1968)
most-favored-__: 6 nation
__ Most Foul: 6 Murder
Most Happy __, The: 5 Fella
Most Happy Fella, The: 7 musical
composer: Frank Loesser
__ Most Likely, The: 4 Girl
mostly: 5 often 6 mainly 7 as a rule, chiefly, largely, overall, usually 8 above all 9 generally, primarily, regularly 10 frequently, on the whole
Most of It, The
author: Robert Frost
__ Most Unusual Day: 4 It's a
Most Valuable Player: 5 award
most wanted __: 4 list
Most Wanted
agcy.: 3 FBI
subject: 5 felon
Mosul: 4 city, town
locale: 4 Irak, Iraq
mot: 4 word 6 French
bon ~: 3 pun 4 jest, joke, quip 6 remark, zinger 7 epigram 8 laconism, repartee, wordplay 9 wisecrack, witticism 10 pleasantry
polite ~: 5 merci
mot __: 5 juste
__ mot: 3 bon
Mota, Manny
sport: 8 baseball
mote: 3 bit, dot, jot 4 atom, iota, whit 5 crumb, fleck, grain 7 modicum 8 flyspeck, molecule, particle 9 scintilla
motel: 3 inn 5 court, lodge 7 Days Inn, lodging 8 lodgment, rest stop, stopover 9 Ramada Inn 10 Comfort Inn, Econo Lodge, Hampton Inn, Holiday Inn, motor court, motor lodge, Quality Inn, Red Roof Inn, Travelodge 11 Best Western
amenity: 2 AC 4 pool 5 Bible, sauna
approver: 3 AAA
freebie: 3 ice 4 soap 7 shampoo 9 sewing kit
offering: 2 rm. 4 room
on wheels: 2 RV
sign: 6 no pets 7 vacancy
__ Motel: 5 Roach
Motel 6
alternative: *see* motel
motes: 4 dust
moth: 2 lo 3 bug 5 egger 6 bogong, insect 8 bombycid
detractor: 5 cedar
ender: 4 ball 5 proof
lure: 5 flame
stage: 4 pupa 5 pupae
__ moth: 4 luna 5 gypsy
mothball: 5 store 6 shelve 8 preserve
mothballed: 4 idle
moth-eaten: 3 old 4 worn 5 holey, mangy, musty, ratty, tatty, trite 6 mangey, ragged, shabby 8 obsolete, outdated, outmoded 9 hackneyed, out-of-date 10 threadbare
mother: 3 mom, nun, she 4 mama 5 mamma, mommy, woman 6 female, mommie, origin, parent, source 7 creator, kinsman 8 ancestor, forebear, relative 9 kinswoman, religious 10 progenitor
combining form: 4 matr- 5 matri-, matro-
country: 8 homeland
directive: 3 eat 4 don't
ender: 4 land, wort 5 board
in French: 4 mère
in Italian: 7 madonna
in Spanish: 5 madre
kin: 5 enate
person without a ~: 3 Eve 4 Adam
sibling: 4 aunt 5 uncle
starter: 3 god 4 step 5 birth, grand, house
Whistler's ~ wear: 5 shawl
mother __: 3 hen 4 lode, ship 5 earth 6 figure, tongue 7 country
mother __ bride: 5 of the
mother-__: 5 in-law
__ mother: 3 den 4 room 5 birth, earth, queen 6 foster
Mother __: 5 Goose, of God, o' Mine 6 Teresa 7 Hubbard
Mother __ All, The: 4 of Us
Mother __ Tights: 4 Wore
Mother, __ I?: 3 may
__ Mother: 4 Holy
Mother and Child Reunion (1972 song)
artist: Paul Simon
Mother Courage and Her Children
author: Bertolt Brecht
Mother Goose dwelling: 4 shoe
Mother Goose Suite
composer: Maurice Ravel
motherhood: 9 maternity
motherhouse: 6 temple
mother-in-__: 3 law
Mother, Jugs & Speed (1976 film)
cast: Bill Cosby, Harvey Keitel, Raquel Welch
motherly: 4 kind 8 maternal, parental 10 protective
mother-of-__: 5 pearl
mother of all living, The: 3 Eve
Mother of Cities, The: 4 Kiev
mother-of-pearl: 5 nacre
mother of the __: 5 bride
Mother of Us All, The
composer: Virgil Thomson
mother's __: 6 helper
Mother's __: 3 Day
Mothers and Sons
author: Isabel Allende
__ Mother Should Know: 4 Your
Mother's Little Helper (1966 song)
artist: Rolling Stones
Mothers of Invention
leader: 5 Zappa
mothers' org.: 4 MADD
__ Mothers' Son: 5 Every
mother superior: 6 cleric
counterpart: 5 abbot
Mother Teresa: 3 nun 8 Albanian, Nobelist
__ Mother, The: 4 Good
motherwort: 5 plant 6 flower
__ Moths, The: 5 Gypsy
Moth, The
author: James M. Cain
motif: 5 theme, topic 6 design, symbol 7 pattern, subject 9 arabesque
music ~: 4 riff, tema
motile: 6 mobile, moving
motility: 6 motion 8 movement
motion: 3 nod 4 flow, flux, move, sign, step, wave 5 drift 6 action, beckon, change, signal, stream, travel 7 advance, gesture, passage, transit 8 activity, dynamics, high sign, kinetics, mobility, motility, movement, progress, proposal, question, stirring 9 agitation, full swing 10 resolution, suggestion
be in ~: 4 move
circular ~: 4 gyre, spin 5 twist 8 gyration
combining form: 3 cin-, kin- 4 cino-, kine-, kino-
in ~: 5 about, afoot, astir 6 moving 7 kinetic 8 on the fly, stirring, underway 9 on the move
make a ~: 5 offer 7 propose
not in ~: 5 inert 6 at rest
picture: 3 pic 4 cine, film, show 5 flick, movie 6 talkie
pictures: 6 cinema
put in ~: 3 set 4 open, spur 5 begin, impel, shake, spark, start 6 arouse, launch 7 trigger 8 activate, mobilize, touch off 9 originate 10 lead the way
rate of ~: 5 speed 8 velocity
rotary ~: 5 twirl
science: 7 physics 8 kinetics 9 mechanics
sudden ~: 4 dart 5 slash, start

motion __: 7 picture
__ motion: 4 fast, lost, slow, stop 5 law of, set in
Motion, Andrew: 4 poet
__-motion cinematography: 4 stop
motionless: 3 put 4 calm, dead, firm, idle, numb 5 at bay, fixed, inert, quiet, still 6 at rest, frozen, halted, rooted, stable, static, torpid 7 stalled, unmoved 8 becalmed, immobile, inactive, lifeless, stagnant, unmoving 9 immovable, inanimate, paralyzed, petrified, quiescent, sedentary, unmovable 10 stock-still, unreactive
become ~: 6 freeze
not ~: 5 astir 6 moving
motion picture prefix: 4 cine-
__-Motion, The: 4 Loco
motivate: 4 draw, fire, goad, lead, move, prod, push, spur, stir, sway, urge, whet 5 bring, cause, drive, egg on, goose, hop up, impel, prime, rouse, spark, tempt 6 arouse, bestir, buck up, excite, incite, induce, prompt, propel, stir up 7 actuate, dispose, hearten, incline, inspire, provoke, quicken, suggest, trigger 8 embolden, energize, enspirit, imbolden, inspirit, persuade, psyche up, set astir, touch off 9 enhearten, galvanize, impassion, instigate, stimulate 10 predispose
hard to ~: 4 lazy
motivated: 5 can-do 8 sedulous, studious 9 assiduous
motivation: 4 goad, spur, urge 5 angle, cause, drive 6 reason, spirit 7 gimmick, impetus, impulse, purpose 8 catalyst, interest, occasion 9 impulsion, incentive, rationale 10 excitement
lack of ~: 5 ennui
motive: 3 aim, end 4 idea, root, sake, spur 5 basis, cause, drive, point 6 intent, object, origin, reason, spring 7 grounds, impulse, inspire, purpose 8 occasion, thinking 9 incentive, intention, rationale 10 incitement, inducement, mainspring
a question of ~: 3 why
having a ~: 6 causal
questioner: 5 cynic 7 doubter, skeptic
secret ~: 5 angle
__ motive: 6 profit 8 ulterior
motiveless: 6 wanton
mot juste, like a: 3 apt 7 apropos
motley: 4 mixt, pied 5 mixed 6 unlike, varied 7 dappled, mottled, rainbow, various 8 assorted, speckled 9 disparate, harlequin, multihued 10 dissimilar, multicolor, variegated
Motley: 6 Marion 7 Willard
Mötley __: 4 Crüe
Motley, Willard: 6 writer
__ moto: 3 con
__ motocross: 7 bicycle
Moto, Mr.
portrayer: Peter Lorre
motor: 4 ride, V-six 5 drive, V-four 6 engine, travel, V-eight 7 machine, turbine 8 outboard 9 machinery, mechanism, take a ride, take a trip, tool along 10 go for a ride
along: 5 scoot
court: 5 motel 8 rest stop
ender: 3 bus, car, man, men, way 4 bike, boat 5 cycle
gun a ~: 3 rev
home: 2 RV
part: 3 cam
sound: 3 hum 4 ping, whir 5 vroom, whirr 6 varoom
trip: 4 spin
motor __: 3 inn, oil 4 home, pool 5 coach, court, lodge, mouth 6 neuron 7 scooter, vehicle
motor __ law: 5 voter
motor-__: 5 mouth
Motor __: 5 Trend
motorbike: 5 moped
motorboat trail: 4 wake
motorcade: 7 pageant 10 procession
Motor City: 7 Detroit
motorcycle: 3 hog 4 bike 7 vehicle
hero: 4 Evel 7 Knievel
maker: 5 Honda 6 Harley, Suzuki, Yamaha 8 Kawasaki
race: 6 enduro
sound: 5 vroom 6 varoom
motoring: 7 en route
motorist: 6 driver, honker
choice: 3 rte. 5 route
crime: 3 DUI, DWI 8 speeding
diversion: 6 detour
invitation: 5 hop in
maneuver: 5 U-turn
org.: 3 AAA
motorized: 5 power 6 mobile 8 electric 9 automated, automatic 10 electrical
motorless craft: 6 glider
motormouth: 6 gabber 10 chatterbox
motor-oil measurement: 5 quart
Motorola: 5 pager, phone 9 cell phone
alternative: 5 Nokia 6 Nextel 8 Ericsson
cell phone: 4 RAZR
__ Motors: 7 General
Motown: 5 label
founder: Berry Gordy
group: 4 Pips 8 Four Tops, Jacksons, Miracles, Supremes 9 Vandellas 11 Temptations
megastar: 4 Gaye, Ross 9 Diana Ross 10 Marvin Gaye
music: 4 soul
purchaser: 3 MCA
see also Detroit
Motown __: 5 sound
Motownphilly (1991 song)
artist: Boyz II Men
Motown Song, The (1991 song)
artist: Rod Stewart, Temptations
Motrin: 9 analgesic 10 painkiller
alternative: ***see*** pain reliever brand
__ mots: 5 jeu de
Mott: 4 John 6 Nevill 8 Lucretia
Mottelson, Ben: 8 Nobelist 9 physicist
Mott, John: 8 Nobelist
mottle: 5 fleck, stain 6 dapple 7 spatter
mottled: 6 motley 7 blotchy, dappled, flecked, marbled, spotted 8 brindled, freckled, speckled, splotchy, streaked
garment: 4 camo
mottling: 6 blotch
Mott, Nevill: 8 Nobelist 9 physicist
motto: 3 cry, saw 5 adage, axiom, maxim, moral 6 byword, dictum, legend, phrase, saying, slogan, truism, war cry 7 epigram, precept, proverb 8 aphorism, apothegm, epigraph, laconism 9 battle cry, catchword, platitude, watchword 10 apophthegm, shibboleth
Harvard ~: 7 Veritas
moue: 3 mug 4 pout 7 grimace
Moulin Rouge (2001 film)
cast: Jim Broadbent, Nicole Kidman, John Leguizamo, Ewan McGregor
director: Baz Luhrmann
mound: 4 bank, dune, heap, hill, hump, mass, pile, rise 5 drift, knoll, ridge, shock, stack 6 barrow 7 anthill, hayrick, hillock, hummock, rampart, tumulus 8 haystack, molehill, mountain 10 embankment, prominence
of earth: 4 berm 5 berme
see also pitcher
Mounds: 3 bar 5 candy 8 candy bar 9 chocolate
alternative: ***see*** candy brand
mount: 3 fit, set, wax 4 go up, grow, hoss, leap, lift, mare, peak, pony, rise, show, zoom 5 bronc, build, camel, climb, frame, get on, hop on, horse, pacer, raise, scale, set up, stage, stand, steed, surge, swell, tower, vault 6 ascend, bronco, cayuse, deepen, dobbin, equine, instal, pile up, shinny 7 augment, broncho, charger, clamber, cow pony, enlarge, get up on, install, mustang, palfrey, produce, shinney 8 bangtail, elephant, escalate, heighten, increase, multiply, position, stallion, straddle 9 clamber up, intensify, skyrocket 10 accumulate, strengthen
up: 4 grow, ride, rise 5 total 6 accrue 7 balloon 8 increase
up to: 5 total
mountain: 3 alp, Api, ton, tor 4 Anne, Batu, Bear, Bona, Cook, crag, dome, glob, Guna, heap, Hood, hump, Jaja, King, lots, lump, Mana, mass, Meru, Mohl, much, Muir, peak, pile, Rysy, Sill, Solo, Toro, Wade, Yale, Zupo 5 Adams, Aneto, Astor, bluff, Borah, Bross, Cachi, Chani, cliff, Coman, Cusco, Cuzco, Eiger, Elgon, Eolus, Evans, Falla, Galan, Gughe, Horeb, Kabru, Kamet, Kekes, Korab, Laudo, Logan, Marcy, Minto, Negro, Press, Pular, Quela, range, ridge, Shear, Shinn, Sinai, stack, Teide, Tyree, Walsh 6 Alaska, Ampato, Antero, Ararat, Bonete, Castor, Cho Oyu, Denali, Ecrins, Elbert, Elbrus, Elbruz, Erebus, Estats, Gilead, Harney, height, Hermon, Hunter, Juncal, Kangto, Kaplan, Katmai, Kungur, Lassen, Lhotse, Lister, Makalu, Musala, myriad, Nunkun, Nuptse, Oxford, Pisgah, Pissis, Posets, Robson, Rogers, Sabine, Sajama, Shasta, Sidley, sierra, Snezka, Steele, Trisul, Wexler, Wilson 7 Aragats, Augusta, Belford, Bernina, Cameron, Epperly, Everest, Foraker, Gardner, Granite, Harvard, Huandoy, Hubbard, Illampu, Langley, Lincoln, Lucania, Lysaght, Manaslu, Markham, Odishaw, Olympus, Ostenso, Palermo, Palomar, Pyramid, Rainier, Russell, Sanford, San Juan, Sellery, Shavano, Sherman, St. Elias, Toubkal, Triglov, Trikora, Trisuli, Tyndall, volcano, Wheeler, Whitney 8 Anapurna, Ancohuma, Baruntse, Ben Nevis, Caubvick, Chamlang, Changtzu, Columbia, Coropuna, Democrat, Dunagiri, El Condor, El Muerto, eminence, Famatina, Illimani, Jungfrau, Katahdin, landmark, McKinley, Mitchell, obstacle, Pauhunri, Polleras, Sneffels, Solimana, St. Helens, Tent Peak, Tortolas, Wrangell, Yerupaja 9 abundance, Aconcagua, Ama Dablam, Annapurna, Antofalla, Badrinath, Bierstadt, Blackburn, Broad Peak, Churchill, Condoriri, El Capitan, elevation, Huascarán, Incahuasi, Istoro Nal, Kanjut Sar, Kings Peak, Kosciusko, Lenin Peak, Marmolejo, Mont Blanc, Monte Rosa, Nanda Devi, Nepal Peak, Pikes Peak, precipice, Princeton, profusion, Pumasillo, Rakaposhi, Ras Dashan, Salcantay, Sia Kangri, Tirich Mir, Tupungato, Vancouver 10 Alverstone, Amne Machin, Chimborazo, Chomo Lhari, Dhaulagiri, Gasherbrum, high ground, Himalchuli, Kula Kangri, Masherbrum, Matterhorn, Mercedario, Minya Konka, Monte Corno, Muztagh Ata, Nacimiento, Parinacota, prominence, Tres Cruces, Williamson
basin: 3 cwm 6 cirque
Biblical ~: 4 Nebo 5 Horeb, Sinai 6 Ararat, Carmel, Pisgah
chain: 5 range, ridge
combining form: 3 ore-, oro- 4 oreo-
crest: 5 arête, ridge
curve: 3 ess
debris: 5 scree
deity: 5 nymph, oread
ending: 3 eer, ous, top 4 side
feature: 4 crag 5 ridge
home: 4 aery, eyry 5 aerie, cabin, eyrie 6 chalet
in Greek: 4 oros
lake: 4 pool, tarn 9 reservoir
like ~ roads: 5 curvy 6 curvey
make a ~ of a molehill: 7 magnify
pass: 3 col, gap
range: 4 ghat 5 chain, ghaut
road abbr.: 3 alt. 4 elev.
round ~ peak: 4 dome
route: 3 col, gap 4 ghat, pass 5 ghaut, notch 6 defile
sacred to Buddhism: 4 Omei
science: 7 orology
song: 5 yodel, yodle
sound: 4 echo
top: 4 acme, apex 5 crest 6 summit

transport: **4** mule **5** burro
wind: **5** foehn **9** katabatic
mountain __: **3** dew, man **4** bike, goat, lion **5** chain, range
__-mountain: **4** cat-o'
__ Mountain Boys: **5** Green
mountain climber
see mountaineer
__ Mountain Daisy: **3** To a
mountain dew: **5** drink, hooch **6** hootch, whisky **7** whiskey **8** beverage **9** moonshine
maker: **5** still
Mountain Dew: **3** pop **4** soda **9** soft drink
alternative: *see* soft drink
mountaineer
activity: **5** climb **6** ascent
foothold: **4** crag
gear: **5** belay, ice ax, piton
goal: **4** acme **6** summit
wear: **5** parka
Mountaineer: **3** SUV **7** Mercury
Mountain Greenery
composer: Lorenz Hart, Richard Rodgers
Mountain Hawks: **6** Lehigh
__ Mountain High: **5** Rocky
__ Mountain Landis: **7** Kenesaw
mountain lion: **3** cat **5** felid **6** feline
relative: *see* feline
Mountain of Love (1964 song)
artist: Johnny Rivers
mountainous: **3** big **4** huge **5** hilly, large, rocky, steep **6** alpine, craggy, rugged **7** cragged, mammoth, massive **8** whapping, whopping
mountain ranges (Africa):
Atlas (Morocco/Algeria/Tunisia)
Mitumba (Congo)
mountain ranges (Antarctica):
Admiralty Range
Edsel Ford Range
Queen Maud Range
mountain ranges (Asia):
Ala Dagh (Turkey)
Alai (Kyrgyzstan)
Altai (Russia)
Anadir (Russia/Siberia)
Cardamom (India)
Elburz (Iran)
Ghats (India)
Himalayas (India/Tibet)
Hindu Kush (Afghanistan)
Karakoram/Mustagh (Kashmir)
Kolyma (Russia/Siberia)
Kunlun (China)
Nan Ling (China)
Owen Stanley (New Guinea)
Pontic (Turkey)
Sayan (Russia)
Stanovoi (Asia)
Taurus (Turkey)
Tien Shan/Tian Shan (China/Kyrgyzstan)
Trans Alai (Kyrgyzstan/Tajikistan)
Urals (Russia)
Zagros (Iran/Turkey/Iraq)
mountain ranges (Australia/New Zealand):
Alps (Australia)
Darling Range (Australia)
Flinders (Australia)
James Range (Australia)
Southern Alps (New Zealand)
mountain ranges (Europe):
Alps
Apennines (Italy)
Athos (Greece)
Balkan
Bernese Alps (Switzerland)
Cadore (Italy)
Carnic Alps (Austria/Italy)
Carpathian
Caucasus (Russia/Georgia/Azerbaijan)
Cevennes (France)
Cottian Alps (France/Italy)
Dolomites (Italy)
Erz (Germany/Czech Republic)
Harz (Germany)
Jura (France/Switzerland)
Kjölen (Norway/Sweden)
Pennine Alps (Switzerland/Italy)
Pindus (Greece)
Pyrenees (Spain/France)
Rhodope (Bulgaria)
Rhon (Germany)
Savoy Alps (France)
St. Gotthard (Switzerland)
Sudeten (Czech Republic)
Tatra (Slovakia/Poland)
Transylvanian Alps (Romania)
Urals (Russia)
mountain ranges (North America):
Adirondacks (New York)
Aleutians (Alaska)
Alleghenies (U.S.)
Appalachians (U.S./Canada)
Baird (Alaska)
Bighorn (Wyoming)
Black (North Carolina)
Blue Ridge (U.S.)
Brooks (Alaska)
Cariboo (Canada)
Cascades (U.S./Canada)
Catoctin (Virginia/Maryland)
Green (Vermont)
Laramie (Colorado/Wyoming)
Lasal (Utah)
Laurentians (Canada)
Lewis (Montana/Canada)
Mackenzie (Canada)
Mogollon (New Mexico)
Ozarks (Missouri/Arkansas/Oklahoma)
Panamint (California)
Poconos (Pennsylvania)
Purcell (Montana/Canada)
Rockies (U.S./Canada)
San Bernardino (California)
Sangre de Cristo (Colorado/New Mexico)
San Juan (Colorado/New Mexico)
Sawatch (Colorado)
Selkirk (Canada)
Sierra Madres (Wyoming/Colorado)
Sierra Nevadas (California)
St. Elias (Canada)
Tetons (Wyoming/Idaho)
Torngat (Canada)
Uinta (Utah)
Wasatch (Utah/Idaho)
White (New Hampshire)
mountain ranges (South America):
Andes
Serra do Mar (Brazil)
mountains: **4** lots **5** loads, scads **6** plenty **8** outdoors **9** highlands
mountains (Africa):
Batu (Ethiopia)
Elgon (Kenya/Uganda)
Gughe (Ethiopia)
Guna (Ethiopia)
Kilimanjaro (Tanzania)
Meru (Tanzania)
Ras Dashan (Ethiopia)
Toubkal (Morocco)
mountains (Antarctica):
Anne
Astor
Coman
Epperly
Erebus
Falla
Gardner
Kaplan
Lister
Lysaght
Markham
Minto
Mohl
Odishaw
Ostenso
Press
Sabine
Sellery
Shear
Shinn
Sidley
Tyree
Vinson Massif
Wade
Wexler
mountains (Asia):
Ama Dablam (Nepal, Himalayas)
Amne Machin (China)
Annapurna (Nepal, Himalayas)
Api (Nepal (Himalayas)
Ararat (Turkey)
Asia Alung Gangri (Tibet, Himalayas)
Badrinath (India, Himalayas)
Baltoro Kangri (Kashmir, Himalayas)
Baruntse (Nepal, Himalayas)
Broad Peak (Pakistan/China)
Chamlang (Nepal, Himalayas)
Changtzu (Tibet, Himalayas)
Chomo Lhari (Tibet/Bhutan, Himalayas)
Cho Oyu (Nepal/Tibet, Himalayas)
Dhaulagiri (Nepal, Himalayas)
Disteghil Sar (Pakistan)
Dunagiri (India, Himalayas)
Everest (Nepal/Tibet, Himalayas)
Fuji (Japan)
Gasherbrum (Pakistan/China)
Gauri Sankar (Nepal/Tibet, Himalayas)
Gilead (Jordan)
Gurla Mandhata (Tibet, Himalayas)
Gyachung Kang (Nepal, Himalayas)
Haramosh Peak (Pakistan)
Hermon (Syria)
Himalchuli (Nepal, Himalayas)
Ismail Samani Peak (Tajikistan)
Istoro Nal (Pakistan)
Jaja (New Guinea)
Jongsong Peak (Nepal, Himalayas)
K2/Godwin Austen (Pakistan/China)
Kabru (Nepal, Himalayas)
Kamet (India/Tibet, Himalayas)
Kanchenjunga (India/Nepal, Himalayas)
Kangto (Tibet, Himalayas)
Kanjut Sar (Pakistan)
Kula Kangri (Bhutan, Himalayas)
Kungur (China)
Lenin Peak (Tajikistan)
Lhotse (Nepal/Tibet, Himalayas)
Makalu (Nepal/Tibet, Himalayas)
Mana (India, Himalayas)
Manaslu (Nepal, Himalayas)
Masherbrum (Kashmir)
Minya Konka (China)
Muztagh Ata (China)
Namcha Barwa (Tibet, Himalayas)
Nanda Devi (India, Himalayas)
Nanga Parbat (Pakistan, Himalayas)
Nebo (Jordan)
Nepal Peak (Nepal, Himalayas)
Nunkun (Kashmir, Himalayas)
Nuptse (Nepal, Himalayas)
Oyama (Japan)
Pauhunri (India/Tibet, Himalayas)
Pisgah (Jordan)
Pyramid (Nepal, Himalayas)
Rakaposhi (Pakistan)
Sia Kangri (Kashmir, Himalayas)
Skyang Kangri (Kashmir, Himalayas)
Tabor (Israel)
Tent Peak (Nepal, Himalayas)
Tirich Mir (Pakistan)
Trikora (New Guinea)
Trisuli (India, Himalayas)
Trisul (India, Himalayas)
Ulugh Muztagh (Tibet)
mountains (Australia/New Zealand):
Cook (New Zealand)
Kosciusko (Australia)
Ossa (Tasmania)
mountains (Europe):
Aneto (Spain, Pyrenees)
Aragats (Armenia)
Ben Nevis (Scotland)
Bernina (Italy/Switzerland, Alps)
Castor (Switzerland, Alps)
Ecrins (France, Alps)
Eiger (Switzerland, Alps)
Elbrus (Russia, Caucasus)
Estats (Spain, Pyrenees)
Etna/Aetna (Sicily)
Ida (Crete)
Jungfrau (Switzerland, Alps)
Kekes (Hungary)
Korab (Macedonia/Albania)
Matterhorn (Switzerland, Alps)
Mont Blanc (France/Italy, Alps)
Monte Corno (Italy, Apenines)
Monte Rosa (Switzerland, Alps)
Musala (Bulgaria)
Narodnaya (Russia, Urals)
Oeta (Greece)
Olympus (Greece)
Ossa (Greece)
Posets (Spain, Pyrenees)
Rysy (Poland)
Snezka (Czech Republic)
Teide (Spain)
Triglov (Croatia)
Zupo (Switzerland, Alps)
mountains (North America):
Adams (Washington, Cascades)
Alverstone (Alaska)
Antero (Colorado, Sawatch/Rockies)
Augusta (Alaska)
Bear (Alaska)
Belford (Colorado, Rockies)
Bierstadt (Colorado, Rockies)

Blackburn (Alaska)
Bona (Alaska)
Borah (Idaho)
Bross (Colorado, Rockies)
Cameron (Colorado, Rockies)
Caubvick (Newfoundland and Labrador)
Churchill (Alaska)
Columbia (Alberta)
Columbia (Colorado, Rockies)
Democrat (Colorado, Rockies)
Elbert (Colorado, Rockies)
El Capitan (California, Sierra Nevadas)
Eolus (Colorado, Rockies)
Evans (Colorado, Rockies)
Fairweather (Alaska)
Foraker (Alaska)
Granite (California, Sierra Nevadas)
Granite (Montana)
Harney (South Dakota, Black Hills)
Harvard (Colorado, Sawatch/Rockies)
Hood (Oregon, Cascades)
Hubbard (Alaska)
Hunter (Alaska)
Katahdin (Maine, Appalachians)
Katmai (Alaska)
Kings Peak (Utah, Uintas)
King (Yukon)
Langley (California, Sierra Nevadas)
Lassen (California, Cascades)
Lincoln (Colorado, Rockies)
Logan (Yukon)
Lucania (Yukon)
Marcy (New York, Adirondacks)
Mauna Kea (Hawaii)
Mauna Loa (Hawaii)
McKinley/Denali (Alaska)
Mitchell (North Carolina, Appalachians)
Muir (California, Sierra Nevadas)
Oxford (Colorado, Rockies)
Palomar (California)
Pikes Peak (Colorado, Rockies)
Princeton (Colorado, Sawatch/Rockies)
Rainier (Washington, Cascades)
Robson (British Columbia, Rockies)
Rogers (Virginia, Appalachians)
Rushmore (South Dakota, Black Hills)
Russell (California, Sierra Nevadas)
Sanford (Alaska)
Shasta (California, Cascades)
Shavano (Colorado, Sawatch/Rockies)
Sherman (Colorado, Rockies)
Sill (California, Sierra Nevadas)
Sneffels (Colorado, Rockies)
Steele (Yukon)
St. Elias (Alaska, Canada)
St. Helens (Washington, Cascades)
Tyndall (California, Sierra Nevadas)
Vancouver (Alaska)
Walsh (Yukon)
Wheeler (New Mexico)
Whitney (California, Sierra Nevadas)
Williamson (California, Sierra Nevadas)
Wilson (California)
Wilson (Colorado, Rockies)
Wrangell (Alaska)
Yale (Colorado, Sawatch/Rockies)

mountains (South America):
Aconcagua (Argentina, Andes)
Ampato (Peru, Andes)
Ancohuma (Bolivia, Andes)
Antofalla (Argentina, Andes)
Bonete (Argentina/Chile, Andes)
Cachi (Argentina, Andes)
Chañi (Argentina, Andes)
Chimborazo (Ecuador, Andes)
Condoriri (Bolivia, Andes)
Coropuna (Peru, Andes)
Cuzco (Peru, Andes)
El Condor (Argentina, Andes)
El Libertador (Argentina, Andes)
El Muerto (Argentina/Chile, Andes)
Famatina (Argentina, Andes)
Galan (Argentina, Andes)
Huandoy (Peru, Andes)
Huascarán (Peru, Andes)
Illampu (Bolivia, Andes)
Illimani (Bolivia, Andes)
Incahuasi (Argentina/Chile, Andes)
Juncal (Argentina/Chile, Andes)
Laudo (Argentina, Andes)
Llullaillaco (Argentina/Chile, Andes)
Marmolejo (Argentina/Chile, Andes)
Mercedario (Argentina/Chile, Andes)
Nacimiento (Argentina, Andes)
Negro (Argentina, Andes)
Ojos del Salado (Argentina/Chile, Andes)
Palermo (Argentina, Andes)
Parinacota (Bolivia/Chile, Andes)
Pissis (Argentina, Andes)
Polleras (Argentina, Andes)
Pular (Chile, Andes)
Pumasillo (Peru, Andes)
Quela (Argentina, Andes)
Sajama (Bolivia, Andes)
Salcantay (Peru, Andes)
San Juan (Argentina/Chile, Andes)
Solimana (Peru, Andes)
Solo (Argentina, Andes)
Toro (Argentina/Chile, Andes)
Tortolas (Argentina/Chile, Andes)
Tres Cruces (Argentina/Chile, Andes)
Tupungato (Argentina/Chile, Andes)
Yerupaja (Peru, Andes)

__ Mountain, The: 5 Magic
Mountain Time state: 3 Ida., Neb., Tex., Wyo. **4** Ariz., Colo., Mont., N. Dak., Nebr., N. Mex, S. Dak., Utah **5** Idaho, Texas **7** Arizona, Montana, Wyoming **8** Colorado, Nebraska **9** New Mexico
mountaintop: 4 acme, apex, peak **6** summit
Mountain View: 4 city, town
  locale: 10 California
Mountbatten: 5 Louis
mountebank: 4 fake, sham **5** faker, fraud, knave, phony, quack, rogue **6** bad guy, phoney **8** huckster, imposter, impostor, swindler **9** charlatan, scoundrel
Mount Everest pioneer: 6 Norgay **7** Hillary
Mount Hamilton observatory: 4 Lick
Mount Holyoke grad: 5 woman **6** alumna
Mounties: 4 RCMP
mounting: 4 rise **5** frame **7** setting
Mountolive
  author: Lawrence Durrell
Mount Pleasant: 4 city, town
  athletes: 9 Chippewas
  locale: 8 Michigan **9** Wisconsin
  school: 3 CMU
Mount Prospect: 4 city, town
  locale: 8 Illinois
Mount Saint Helens
  emulate ~: 4 spew, spue **5** erupt
  output: 3 ash **4** lava
Mount St. __: 5 Elias **6** Helens
Mount Vernon: 4 city, town **6** estate
  locale: 7 New York **8** Virginia **10** Washington
mourn: 3 cry, rue, sob **4** ache, fret, keen, miss, moan, pine, sigh, wail, weep **5** bleed **6** bemoan, bewail, cry for, grieve, lament, regret, sorrow **7** agonize, carry on, deplore **10** take it hard
Mourners Below
  author: James Purdy
mournful: 3 sad **5** bleak, funky, sorry, woful **6** dreary, morose, somber, tragic, triste, woeful **7** doleful, elegiac, joyless, pitiful, tearful, unhappy, wistful **8** dolorous, grievous, tragical **9** heartsick, miserable, plaintive, regretful, saddening, sniveling, sorrowful, woebegone **10** deplorable, depressing, lachrymose, lamentable, lugubrious, melancholy
  poem: 5 dirge, elegy
  sound: 4 sigh, wail, yowl **5** dirge, groan, knell
mournfulness: 5 blues, grief **7** sadness
mourning: 3 woe **5** crape, grief **6** lament, sorrow **7** keening, sadness, wailing, weeping **8** grieving
  cloak: 3 bug **6** insect
mourning __: 4 dove, iris **5** cloak **7** warbler
Mourning, Alonzo
  milieu: 5 court
  org.: 3 NBA
  sport: 10 basketball
Mourning Becomes Electra
  author: Eugene O'Neill
  character: 3 Ira **4** Adam, Ames, Amos, Emma, Ezra, Orin, Seth **5** Abner, Brant, Hazel, Niles, Silva **6** Louisa, Mannon, Minnie
mouse: 4 pest, welt **5** dance, Dixie, Jerry, murid, Pixie **6** animal, coward, Ignatz, mammal, Mickey, Minnie, murine, rodent, shiner, vermin **7** quitter **8** black eye, squeaker
  appendage: 4 tail
  catcher: 3 cat **4** trap **6** feline
  cat with a ~ perhaps: 5 toyer
  clicker: 6 button
  combining form: 3 -mys
  ender: 4 trap
  female: 3 doe
  field ~: 4 vole
  like a ~: 4 meek **5** timid
  male: 4 buck
  move like a ~: 4 dart **5** scoot
  relative: *see* rodent
  spotter reaction: 3 eek
  target: 4 icon
  to an owl: 4 prey **6** quarry
  use a ~: 4 drag **5** click
  young: 3 pup **6** kitten
mouse __ the clock, The: 5 ran up
__ mouse: 5 field, house
__ Mouse: 3 To a **6** Ignatz, Mickey, Mighty, Minnie
mouse!, A: 3 eek
__ Mouse Detective, The: 5 Great
mouselike animal: 4 vole **5** shrew **6** jerboa **7** lemming
Mouse of hockey: 6 Mikita
mouser: 3 cat **4** puss **5** felid **6** feline
mouse ran up the __, The: 5 clock
mouse-tail: 5 plant
Mouse That Roared, The (1959 film)
  cast: Jean Seberg, Peter Sellers
mousetrap: 4 lure **5** tempt **7** pitfall **9** misinform **10** enticement
  bait: 6 cheese
Mousetrap, The: 4 play **5** drama
  author: Agatha Christie
  character: 4 Wren **5** Giles **6** Mollie
mousiness: 9 timidness **10** diffidence
Mouskouri: 4 Nana
mousquetaires, number of: 5 trois
moussaka: 5 Greek **6** entrée
  drink with ~: 4 ouzo
  ingredient: 4 lamb **5** onion **6** cheese, tomato **8** cinnamon, eggplant
mousse: 5 aspic **7** dessert, pudding **8** hair foam
  alternative: 3 gel
mousy: 3 shy **4** drab, dull, gray, grey, meek **5** plain, timid **6** docile **7** bashful, fearful **8** obedient, timorous **9** colorless, compliant, easily led **10** lackluster, unassuming, uneffusive
mouth: 3 gas, jaw, lip, maw, mug, rim, yap **4** beak, guff, jaws, lips, puss, sass, trap **5** bazoo, cheek, chops, delta, firth, frith, inlet, sauce, speak, utter **6** cavity, crater, hot air, intone, kisser, parrot, recess **7** estuary, opening, orifice **8** aperture, back talk, entrance, rudeness **9** impudence, insolence, sauciness **10** embouchure
  away from the ~: 6 aboral
  be down in the ~: 4 mope, sulk
  big ~: 7 tattler **10** taleteller, tattletale
  combining form: 3 ori-, oro- **5** bucco-, -stoma, -stome **6** stomat- **7** stomato-
  down in the ~: 3 low, sad **4** blue, glum, mopy **5** moody, mopey **6** abject, morose **7** daunted, joyless, unhappy **8** dejected **9** depressed, miserable **10** dispirited
  ender: 4 part, wash **5** piece **7** breeder **8** watering
  foam at the ~: 4 rage **6** seethe
  foaming at the ~: 4 wild **5** manic, rabid, upset **6** raging **7** frantic, unglued **8** agitated, frenzied, maniacal, unstrung, vehement **9** bummed-out, fanatical **10** freaked out, hysterical

from the horse's ~: 6 direct
gaping ~: 3 maw
have a big ~: 6 tattle
horse's ~: 6 expert, origin, source 9 authority 10 originator
hush one's ~: 6 shut up
it's down in the ~: 5 uvula
locale: 4 head 5 river
make one's ~ water: 5 tempt 9 tantalize
off: 3 dis, yap 4 sass 7 observe 8 get fresh, get smart, talk back 9 give lip to
of the ~: 4 oral
open one's ~: 4 talk 5 speak
part: 3 jaw, lip 4 roof
run off at the ~: 3 yak 4 blab 6 babble, jabber 7 blather, blether
shoot off one's ~: 4 brag 5 spout 7 bluster
starter: 3 bad, big 4 frog, loud, poor 5 snake 6 cotton 7 blabber
toward the ~: 4 orad
with ~ shut: 3 mum
word of ~: 5 parol 7 hearsay
mouth __: 3 off 4 harp 5 organ
__ mouth: 4 poor 5 motor
__-mouth: 3 bad
__-mouthed: 4 foul, full, open 5 close, mealy, tight
mouthed combining form: 7 -stomous
mouthful: 3 gob 4 bite, gulp, swig 5 scrap, taste 6 morsel, tidbit 8 spoonful
mouthlike opening: 5 stoma
mouthpiece: 3 att., rep 4 atty., reed 5 agent 6 fipple, lawyer, puppet 7 counsel 8 attorney 9 counselor 10 figurehead
mouths in Latin: 3 ora
mouth-to-mouth: 4 oral
mouthwash: 3 Act 4 Plax 5 Scope 6 Signal 7 Lavoris 9 Listerine 10 Fluorigard
approving org.: 3 ADA
like some ~: 5 minty
use ~: 5 rinse 6 gargle
mouth-watering: 5 sapid, tasty, yummy 6 savory 8 inviting, luscious, tempting 9 palatable, succulent
mouthy: 8 impudent 9 talkative 10 rhetorical
movable: 5 loose 6 mobile 8 floating, haulable, on wheels, portable 10 adjustable, detachable, unattached
movable __: 4 type 5 feast
Movado: 5 watch 10 wristwatch
alternative: *see* wristwatch
move: 2 go 3 act, fly, run 4 cart, deed, drag, flow, haul, jump, leap, ploy, push, relo, send, ship, slip, step, stir, sway, trot, turn, urge, walk 5 budge, carry, cause, climb, crawl, drift, drive, glide, hurry, impel, leave, march, offer, prime, reach, rouse, scram, shake, shift, shove, touch 6 action, affect, bestir, betake, bustle, change, convey, depart, excite, incite, induce, jockey, motion, prompt, propel, reason, thrill, travel, uproot, work up 7 actuate, advance, agitate, cart off, disturb, get busy, give way, head out, hop to it, impress, inspire, measure, migrate, proceed, propose, provoke, pull out, quicken, skip out, suggest, take off 8 cart away, displace, get going, interest, maneuver, motivate, persuade, position, relocate, resettle, run along, transfer, traverse, withdraw 9 galvanize, influence, recommend, shake a leg, stratagem, transport, transpose 10 get hopping, get started, put forward, reposition, shuffle off, take action, transplant
along: 2 go 4 ride 5 scoot, slide
around: 3 gad 4 mill, ring, roam, rove, stir 5 drift, shift 6 mingle, wander 9 circulate 10 reposition
awkwardly: 6 gangle
back: 6 return
bad ~: 4 trip 5 boner, error, folly 7 misstep, mistake 9 indecorum
be reluctant to ~: 8 hang back
blithely: 4 skip
clever ~: 4 coup, ruse 6 device
close: 6 cuddle, nestle 7 snuggle
deceptive ~: 4 deke 5 feint
don't ~: 4 stay 5 stall 6 freeze
down: 4 drop, fall, sink 5 slide 7 descend
erratically: 3 zag, zig 4 dart, flit
forward: 4 gain 8 progress
get a ~ on: 2 go 3 fly, hie, rip, run, zip 4 dart, dash, flit, race, rush, stir, tear, zoom 5 hurry, scoot, spank, speed 6 barrel, gallop, hasten, hustle, rocket, scurry 7 floor it, hop to it, quicken, scamper, speed up 8 step on it 9 hotfoot it, shake a leg, skedaddle 10 hightail it
get ready to ~: 4 pack
goods: 4 hawk, push, sell, vend 5 pitch, trade 6 barter, handle, hustle, market, peddle, retail, unload 7 auction, promote, traffic 9 wholesale
hard to ~: 6 leaden
hither and thither: 3 gad 4 roam 6 ramble, wander 7 meander, traipse 8 ambulate, nomadize 9 bum around, gallivant, globetrot
in: 5 enter
in on: 5 usurp
into: 10 infiltrate
laterally: 3 zag 4 edge, skew 5 sidle
lazily: 5 amble, mosey 7 shuffle
make a ~: 3 act
make a wrong ~: 3 err
nautically: 5 heave
not inclined to ~: 4 lazy
on: 4 pass 5 leave 6 depart 7 advance, proceed 8 progress 9 go forward
one on the ~: 4 goer 5 nomad
on one's hands and knees: 4 inch 5 crawl, creep, slink, sneak, steal 7 clamber, slither, wriggle
on the ~: 4 at it, busy 5 afoot, astir 6 active, at work 7 engaged, migrant, working 8 employed, in motion, occupied, underway 9 advancing, migratory, traveling, wayfaring 10 proceeding
out: 2 go 4 exit 5 leave 6 set off, vacate 7 ride off 8 set forth
over: 4 lick 5 shift, slide
room to ~: 4 give, play 6 leeway 8 latitude
rudely: 4 push 5 elbow, shove 6 jostle
secretly: 4 lurk 5 prowl, sculk, sidle, skulk, slink, sneak, steal
slightly: 4 stir 5 budge
slowly: 3 lag 4 drag, ease, inch, nose, poke 5 crawl, creep, mosey 9 limp along
smoothly: 4 flow, sail 5 coast, glide, slide
softly: 3 pad 6 tiptoe
suddenly: 4 dart, jerk, jump, leap 5 lunge, lurch, shoot, swoop
(to): 3 try 7 attempt
to action: 6 arouse
to and fro: 3 wag 4 rock, sway, wave 5 swing 9 oscillate
to Realtors: 4 relo
to tears: 3 get 4 move 6 affect
toward: 4 near, tend 6 go up to 7 head for 8 approach 9 gravitate
(toward): 4 come, head, tend
unsteadily: 3 yaw 4 reel 6 teeter, totter
up: 4 bump, lift, rise, soar 5 arise, climb, raise, surge 6 ascend 7 advance, elevate, promote, surface, upgrade 8 escalate
up and down: 3 bob
up in the world: 6 make it 7 prosper, succeed 8 get ahead
wildly: 6 careen, career
wrong ~: 4 slip 5 boner, error, fluff, gaffe, lapse 6 bungle, miscue, slipup 7 blunder, faux pas, misdeed, misstep, mistake
move __: 3 out 4 away, in on
move __ and earth: 6 heaven
__ move: 5 false, on the 6 career
Move!: 4 C'mon 6 Let's go
Moveable Feast, A
author: Ernest Hemingway
moved: 4 gone
be ~: 3 cry, sob 5 react
move heaven and __: 5 earth
movement: 4 flow, flux, play, tide 5 cause, shift, steps, trend 6 action, change, course, flight, motion, signal, stroke, travel, unrest 7 advance, crusade, gesture, journey, process, transit 8 activity, campaign, exercise, kinetics, maneuver, mobility, motility, progress, stirring, transfer, velocity 9 agitation, animation, migration 10 locomotion, procession, regression, transferal, transition
freedom of ~: 4 room 5 range, scope 6 leeway 8 latitude 9 elbowroom
in music: 4 moto
lack of ~: 6 stasis
last ~: 6 finale
of ~: 6 gestic 8 gestical
unexpected ~: 3 jab 4 dash, dive, jump, leap, poke 5 bound, burst, lurch, pitch, surge, swing, swipe 6 charge, plunge, pounce, spring, strike, thrust
upward ~: 4 rise
see also move
__ movement: 4 mass 5 labor
__ move on: 4 get a 5 make a
mover: 3 VIP 5 lader 6 Allied, dynamo, Global 7 migrant, van line 8 go-getter 9 Mayflower
and shaker: 4 doer 5 mogul
burden: 3 box 5 piano 9 furniture
device: 5 dolly 6 bungee, caster
earth ~: 3 hoe 6 dredge
prime ~: 5 cause 9 architect
starter: 5 earth
vehicle: 3 van 5 truck, U-Haul
__ mover: 5 prime 6 people
mover and __: 6 shaker
movie: 3 pic 4 cine, film, show 5 flick 6 cinema, silent, talkie 7 feature, picture, theater, theatre 9 photoplay, spectacle, videotape 10 production, screenplay
ad photo: 5 still
be in a ~: 3 act
board member: 5 rater
combining form: 4 cine-
ender: 3 dom 4 goer 5 going, maker 6 making
lot locale: 3 set 6 studio 10 soundstage
promo: 4 clip 7 trailer
rating org.: 4 MPAA
studio: 3 Fox, MGM 6 Disney 7 Miramax, New Line 8 Columbia 9 Paramount, Universal 10 Dreamworks, Warner Bros.
theater suffix: 4 plex
union: 3 SAG
movie __: 5 house 7 theater, theatre
__ movie: 4 home 7 drive-in
__ Movie: 5 Scary 6 Silent
moviegoer: 6 viewer 9 spectator
moviegoers: 5 crowd 8 audience
Moviegoer, The
author: Walker Percy
Movie Movie (1978 film)
cast: George C. Scott, Trish Van Devere, Eli Wallach
movies: 3 pix 6 cinema
like some ~: 4 gory 6 G-rated, R-rated 8 animated
like vampire ~: 5 lurid 6 bloody
sound at the ~: 3 shh
Movin' __: 3 Out 4 on Up
moving: 5 about, astir 6 active, liquid, mobile, motile, onward, tender 7 dynamic, migrant, onwards, piteous, pitiful, sensual, soulful 8 dramatic, eloquent, exciting, gripping, in motion, pathetic, poignant, touching, underway 9 emotional, impelling, inspiring, migratory 10 convincing, emigration, expressive, impressive, locomotion, on the march, pathetical, persuasive
combining form: 4 plan- 5 -grade, plano- 6 kineto- 7 -kinetic
get ~: 3 hie, run 4 roll, stir 5 speed 6 bestir 7 speed up 8 hightail, run along
not ~: 5 inert, still 6 at rest
picture: 4 film 5 flick
vehicle: 5 truck, U-Haul
see also mover
moving __: 3 van 6 target 7 average, picture
__-moving: 4 fast, slow
Moving right __...: 5 along

Moving Target, The
author: Ross Macdonald
Movin' Out (1978 song)
artist: Billy Joel
mow: 3 cut **4** clip, crop, reap, trim **5** level, prune, shave, shear **6** scythe **7** hayloft
again: 5 recut
down: 4 rase, raze **6** defeat **9** eradicate
starter: 3 hay
mow __: 4 down
Mowat, Farley: 6 writer **8** Canadian
work: The Desperate People
People of the Deer
The Snow Walker
Mowbray: 4 Alan
mowed area: 5 swath **6** swathe
mower: 4 tool
place: 4 shed **6** garage
starter: 4 lawn
__ mower: 4 hand, lawn **5** power
Mowgli
friend: 5 Akela, Baloo
rearer: 4 wolf
mowing: 5 chore
place: 4 lawn **5** grass
the lawn: 4 task
Mowing
author: Robert Frost
__-mown: 3 new
moxie: 3 pep **4** grit, guts, will, zest **5** brass, drive, heart, nerve, pluck, skill, spine, spunk, valor, verve, vigor **6** daring, energy, mettle, spirit **7** courage, know-how, stamina **8** audacity, chutzpah, gumption, tenacity **9** endurance, fortitude, gutsiness **10** durability, feistiness, get-up-and-go, initiative
having ~: 4 game **5** brash, gutsy, nervy **6** brassy, daring, gritty, plucky, spunky **9** audacious **10** courageous
Moyers: 4 Bill
Moyet: 6 Alison
Moynihan: 3 Pat
Mozambique: 6 nation **7** country
bay: 7 Delagoa
bovine: 5 Nguni **7** Mashona
capital: 6 Maputo
city: 4 Sena **5** Beira **6** Maputo
lake: 5 Nyasa **6** Malawi
nation off ~: 7 Comoros
neighbor: 6 Malawi, Zambia **8** Tanzania, Zimbabwe **9** Swaziland
people: 3 Yao **4** Cewa **5** Chewa, Makua, Shona **6** Nyanja **7** Makonde, Mashona
__ Mozart: 6 Mostly
Mozart, Wolfgang Amadeus: 8 Austrian, composer
contemporary: 5 Haydn
father: 7 Leopold
genre: 5 opera **6** sonata **8** concerto, symphony
work: Così fan tutte
Don Giovanni
Eine Kleine Nachtmusik
Haffner Symphony
Idomeneo
Jupiter Symphony
La Clemenza di Tito
Linz Symphony
The Magic Flute
The Marriage of Figaro
Paris Symphony
Prague Symphony
Serenade in D
Zaide
mozzarella: 6 cheese **7** Italian
MP
part: 3 Mil., Pol. **6** Police **8** Military
quest: 4 AWOL
task: 6 arrest
MPAA employee: 5 rater
MPG
monitor: 3 EPA
part of ~: 3 gal., per **5** miles **6** gallon
MPH part: 3 per **4** hour **5** miles
MPV: 3 van **5** Mazda
Mr.: 3 man **4** male **5** title
Mr. __: 3 Big, Lee, Mom **4** Blue, Cool, Jaws, Moto **5** Bones, Clean, Fixit, Jones, Lucky, Right, Wrong **6** Lonely **7** America, Peepers, Sandman
Mr. __ Goes to Town: 5 Deeds
Mr. __ Goes to Washington: 5 Smith
Mr. __ Guy: 4 Nice
Mr. __ Jeans: 5 Green
Mr. __ Neighborhood: 6 Rogers'
Mr. __ Passes By: 3 Pim
Mr. __ Stuff: 3 Big
Mr. __, Tracer of Lost Persons: 4 Keen
MR __: 4 scan **6** imager **7** scanner
Mr. 3000 (2004 film)
cast: Angela Bassett, Bernie Mac
Mr. and __: 3 Mrs.
Mr. Beluncle
author: V.S. Pritchett
Mr. Belvedere (ABC sitcom)
cast: Ilene Graff (Marsha Owens)
Christopher Hewitt (Lynn Belvedere)
George Owens (Bob Uecker)
Mr. Big: 3 VIP **4** lion **5** mogul
Mr. Big Stuff (1971 song)
artist: Jean Knight
Mr. Blandings Builds His Dream House (1948 film)
cast: Melvyn Douglas, Cary Grant, Myrna Loy
Mr. Blue (1959 song)
artist: Fleetwoods
Mr. Bojangles (1971 song)
artist: Nitty Gritty Dirt Band
Mr. Brooks (2007 film)
cast: Dane Cook, Demi Moore
director: Kevin Costner
Mr. Burden
author: Hilaire Belloc
__, Mr. Chips: 7 Goodbye
Mr. Clean
alternative: 5 Brite, Lysol **6** Top Job **7** Lestoil, Pine Sol **9** Fantastik, Step Saver
Mr. Deeds Goes to Town (1936 film)
cast: Jean Arthur, George Bancroft, Gary Cooper
director: Frank Capra
MRE consumer: 2 GI **7** soldier
Mr. Flood's Party: 4 poem
author: E.A. Robinson
Mr. Goodbar: 5 candy **8** candy bar **9** chocolate
alternative: *see* candy brand
Mr. Guitar: 6 Atkins
Mr. Holland's Opus (1995 film)
cast: Richard Dreyfuss, Olympia Dukakis, Glenne Headly, William H. Macy, Jay Thomas, Alicia Witt
Mr. Hulot's Holiday (1954 film)
cast: Jacques Tati
MRI: 6 imager **7** scanner
Mr. Keen, Tracer of Lost Persons: 9 radio show
Mr. Lee (1957 song)
artist: Bobbettes
__ Mr. Lincoln: 5 Young
Mr. Lincoln's Army
author: Bruce Catton
Mr. Lonely (1964 song)
artist: Bobby Vinton
Mr. Lucky (1960 song)
artist: Henry Mancini
Mr. Midshipman Easy
author: Frederick Marryat
Mr. Mom (1983 film)
cast: Teri Garr, Ann Jillian, Michael Keaton, Martin Mull
Mr. & Mrs. Bridge (1990 film)
cast: Blythe Danner, Paul Newman, Joanne Woodward
Mr. & Mrs. Smith (2005 film)
cast: Angelina Jolie, Brad Pitt, Vince Vaughn
Mr. Murder
author: Dean Koontz
Mr. Nice __: 3 Guy
Mr. Norris Changes Trains
author: Christopher Isherwood
Mrozek, Slawomir: 6 Polish, writer
Mr. Palomar
author: Italo Calvino
Mr. Peepers (NBC sitcom)
cast: Wally Cox (Robinson Peepers)
Mr. Perrin and Mr. Traill
author: Hugh Walpole
__ Mr. Postman: 6 Please
Mr. Potato Head
piece: 3 ear
Mr. President: 7 musical
composer: Irving Berlin
Mr. Republican: 4 Taft
__ Mr. Right: 6 Making
Mr. Roboto (1983 song)
artist: Styx
Mrs.: 4 wife **5** title, woman **6** female
in French: 3 Mme.
in German: 4 frau
in Japanese: 3 san
in Spanish: 3 Sra.
new ~: 5 bride
Mrs. __: 6 Grundy **7** Miniver
Mrs. __ Goes to Paris: 5 'Arris
__ Mrs.: 5 Mr. and
Mr. Sammler's Planet
author: Saul Bellow
Mr. Sandman (1954 song)
artist: Chordettes
Mr. Saturday Night (1992 film)
cast: Billy Crystal, Helen Hunt, David Paymer, Julie Warner
director: Billy Crystal
Mrs. Battle's Opinions of Whist
author: Charles Lamb (Elia)
Mrs. Brown You've Got a Lovely Daughter (1965 song)
artist: Herman's Hermits
Mrs. Butterworth's: 5 syrup
alternative: 8 Log Cabin
__ Mrs. Carrolls, The: 3 Two
Mrs. Dalloway: 5 novel
author: Virginia Woolf
character: 5 Doris, Rezia, Walsh **8** Clarissa
Mrs. Doubtfire (1993 film)
cast: Pierce Brosnan, Sally Field, Robin Williams
director: Chris Columbus
Mrs. Fields
competitor: *see* cookie manufacturer
__ Mrs. Jones: 5 Me and
Mr. Skeffington (1944 film)
cast: Bette Davis, Claude Rains
__ Mrs. Leslie: 5 About
__ & Mrs. Miller: 6 McCabe
Mrs. Miniver (1942 film)
cast: Greer Garson, Walter Pidgeon, May Whitty, Teresa Wright
character: 3 Kay **4** Clem
director: William Wyler
studio: 3 MGM
Mr. Smith Goes to Washington (1939 film)
cast: Jean Arthur, Claude Rains, James Stewart
composer: Dimitri Tiomkin
director: Frank Capra
Mrs. Robinson (1968 song)
artist: Simon and Garfunkel
Mrs. Warren's Profession
author: George Bernard Shaw
Mrs. Winterbourne (1996 film)
cast: Brendan Fraser, Ricki Lake, Shirley MacLaine
Mr. Tambourine Man (1965 song)
artist: Byrds
Mr. Television: 5 Berle
Mr. T group: 5 A-Team
Mr Weston's Good Wine
author: T.F. Powys
__ Mr. Wizard: 5 Watch
Mr. Wrong (1996 film)
cast: Joan Cusack, Ellen DeGeneres, Bill Pullman, Dean Stockwell
ms.
enclosure: 3 SAE
reader: 2 ed.
Ms.: 5 title, woman **6** female
founder: Gloria Steinem
rival: 4 Elle
MS
see Mississippi
MS-__: 3 DOS
M.Sc.D.: 3 deg.
M. Scott: 4 Peck
MS-DOS popularizer: 3 IBM
MS. Found in a Bottle
author: Edgar Allan Poe
MSG part: 4 mono **6** sodium **9** glutamate
M.Sgt.: 3 NCO
subordinate: 3 SFC
MSN: 3 ISP
MSNBC: 7 channel
rival: 3 CNN **4** CNBC
MSN holder: 5 nurse
M.S., part of: 3 sci. **6** master **7** science
MST part: 3 Mtn., Std. **4** Time **8** Mountain, Standard
MSU
conference: 6 Big Sky, Big Ten
locale: 7 Bozeman **11** East Lansing
athlete: 6 Bobcat **7** Spartan

mt.: 3 hgt.
see also mountain
MT
see Montana
M.T.A. (1959 song)
artist: Kingston Trio
mtg.: 4 appt., sess.
mtge.
lender: 3 FHA 4 FNMA, GNMA 5 S and L
obligation: 3 pmt 4 payt.
see also mortgage
Mt. St. __: 6 Helens
MTV: 7 channel
alternative: *see* cable channel
employee: 2 VJ 6 veejay
music: 3 rap
offering: 4 trax 5 video
part of ~: 4 tele 5 music 6 vision
prize: 3 Ava
viewer: 4 teen
mu: 5 Greek 6 letter
follower: 2 nu
preceder: 6 lambda
Mubarak: 4 Arab 5 Hosni 8 Egyptian 9 president
capital: 5 Cairo
predecessor: 5 Sadat
much: 3 far, lot, oft 4 a lot, gobs, lots, lump, many, mega, mess, most, peck, pile, tons, very 5 ample, heaps, loads, lotsa, no end, often, scads 6 barrel, excess, galore, highly, hugely, lavish, lots of, nearly, oodles, plenty, vastly, volume 7 aplenty, awfully, copious, endless, greatly, notably, profuse, sizable 8 abundant, beaucoup, generous, mountain, plethora, sizeable, terribly, very many 9 abundance, copiously, extremely, immensely, in a big way, liberally, many a time, plenteous, plentiful, profusely, quite a bit, regularly, thousands 10 abundantly, a great deal, all kinds of, enormously, frequently, oversupply, repeatedly, voluminous
a bit ~: 10 untempered
as: 5 while 6 though
as ~ as: 4 up to
be too ~: 4 cloy
combining form: 4 poly-
ever so ~: 4 many 6 highly 7 greatly
give too ~: 4 cloy, glut 5 gorge 7 surfeit
in music: 5 molto
make ~ of: 4 tout 5 exalt 6 praise, stress 7 amplify, magnify 9 emphasize 10 compliment
make too ~ of: 8 overrate 9 overstate 10 exaggerate
not ~: 4 a bit, a dab 5 light 6 hardly, little 8 somewhat
obliged: 5 danke, merci 6 grazie, thanks 7 gracias, spasibo 8 beholden, grateful, indebted, thank you
prefix: 4 poly-
so ~ in music: 5 tanto
the same: 4 like 5 alike 7 similar
too ~: 5 ultra, undue 6 de trop, excess, overly 8 annoying, tiresome, to a fault 9 excessive, overblown 10 inordinate, outrageous, stupendous, unbearable, untempered
too ~ in French: 6 de trop
too ~ of a good thing: 4 glut 5 flood 7 surfeit, surplus 8 overload 10 indulgence, oversupply
used: 4 flat 5 banal, corny, stale, stock, tired 6 common, jejune 7 clichéd, insipid, worn-out 8 bathetic, bromidic, cornball, ordinary, shopworn, timeworn, well-worn 9 hackneyed, motheaten, played out 10 pedestrian, uninspired, unoriginal, warmed-over
very ~: 3 far 4 a lot, well 5 badly, by far, no end 6 highly, indeed 7 greatly 10 incredibly
__ much: 4 very 6 pretty
__ Much!: 5 No Not
muchacho: 3 boy 4 niño
__, muchachos: 5 Adios
Much Ado About Nothing: 4 film, play
author: William Shakespeare
cast: Kenneth Branagh, Michael Keaton, Keanu Reeves, Emma Thompson, Denzel Washington
director: Kenneth Branagh
role: 4 Hero 6 Ursula, Verges 7 Claudio, Conrade, Leonato 8 Beatrice, Don Pedro
much-heard: 5 banal
__ Much Heaven: 3 Too
mucho: 4 lots, very 5 lotsa 6 highly 7 but good, Spanish
__ Mucho: 6 Bésame
__ much of: 4 make 5 think
much-wanted: 3 hot 7 popular 8 in demand
mucilage: 3 gum 4 glue 5 paste 6 cement 8 adhesive, fixative
mucilaginous: 5 gooey, gummy 7 viscose, viscous 8 adhesive
muck: 3 goo, mud 4 crud, dirt, glop, gunk, mess, mire, ooze, soil 5 filth, grime, slime, snarl 6 litter, muddle, refuse
about: 6 tamper, tinker
ender: 4 rake, worm 5 raker 6 raking
move in ~: 5 slosh
up: 4 harm, soil 5 botch, spoil 7 disrupt, screw up 10 complicate
muck-a-muck: 3 VIP 7 big shot
__-muck-a-muck: 4 high
muckraker: 6 critic 8 vilifier
muckraking: 7 slander 9 aspersion, disesteem, maligning, traducing 10 backbiting, defamation, derogation, detraction, revilement, scurrility
muckworm: 3 bug 5 churl, miser 6 cheapo, insect 7 hoarder, Scrooge 8 el cheapo, tightwad 9 skinflint 10 cheapskate, pinchpenny
mucky: 4 miry, oozy 5 grimy, muddy, muggy, slimy, soggy 6 sticky
make ~: 5 sully
mud: 4 dirt, mire, muck, ooze, slop, soil 5 earth, mocha, slime, swamp 6 coffee, gossip, jamoke 7 earthen, scandal, slander
clear as ~: 5 mirky, murky, vague 9 equivocal 10 unexplicit
dauber: 4 wasp
ender: 3 bug 4 fish, flow, sill 5 guard, puppy, slide, stone 7 skipper, slinger 8 slinging
like ~: 4 oozy 5 slimy
lover: 3 hog, pig 5 swine
move through ~: 4 slog 5 slosh
product: 3 pie 4 pack
propel ~: 5 sling
sink in ~: 4 mire
throw ~ at: 4 slam, slur 5 knock, libel, smear, sully, taint, wrong 6 defame, malign, vilify 7 asperse, blacken, run down, slander, tarnish, traduce 8 backbite, badmouth, besmirch, dishonor 9 denigrate, discredit, disparage 10 calumniate, stigmatize, vituperate
mud __: 3 eel, hen, pie 4 bath, room 5 slide 6 puddle
Mudd: 5 Roger
mudder: 5 horse 9 racehorse
muddied: 5 dirty, grimy 6 opaque, turbid 10 bedraggled
muddle: 3 fog, mix 4 daze, hash, haze, mess, muck, muss, stir 5 addle, befog, boner, botch, chaos, cloud, mix up, snafu, snarl, upset 6 baffle, bumble, bungle, foul up, fuddle, jumble, litter, plight, rattle, tangle 7 bedevil, blunder, clutter, confuse, dilemma, disrupt, disturb, fluster, louse up, mistake, nonplus, perplex, screwup, shuffle, snarl up, stupefy 8 befuddle, bewilder, confound, disarray, disorder, entangle, flounder, quagmire, quandary, scramble, shambles 9 adumbrate, confusion, disorient, inebriate, mare's nest, mobocracy, patchwork 10 complexity, complicate, intoxicate, misarrange
through: 4 cope 5 get by 6 manage 7 make out, press on
muddle __: 7 through
muddled: 4 asea, hazy 5 at sea, dizzy, messy, mussy, upset, wooly, woozy 6 turbid, woolly 7 out of it 8 pell-mell 9 equivocal, inside-out 10 disjointed, disorderly, incohesive, topsy-turvy, unexplicit
muddleheaded: 4 asea, daft, loco 5 at sea, balmy, dense, dotty, flaky, inane, kooky, wacky 6 absurd 7 asinine, bonkers, doltish, foolish, witless 9 brainless, half-baked
muddy: 3 dim, fog 4 blur, damp, dull, hazy, miry, oozy, roil, soil 5 boggy, caked, dirty, fuzzy, grimy, gummy, gunky, mirky, mucky, murky, roily, silty, slimy, soggy, taint, thick, undry, vague 6 bemire, cloudy, crud up, filthy, grubby, marshy, opaque, sloppy, slushy, sodden, soiled, swampy, turbid 7 bemired, confuse, obscure, unclean, unclear, wettish 8 abstruse, besmirch, confused, darkened, roiled up, unwashed 9 obfuscate, uncertain, unfocused 10 lusterless
not ~: 5 clear
spot: 3 sty 6 pigpen, pigsty
Muddy: 6 Waters
__ Muddy: 3 Big
Muddy Water (1966 song)
artist: Johnny Rivers
mudguard: 6 fender
Mud Hens home: 6 Toledo
__ mud in your eye!: 5 Here's
mudpack: 6 facial
mudpuppy: 9 amphibian 10 salamander
mudslide: 9 earthfall
mudsling: 5 smear 6 malign, vilify 7 slander 9 denigrate 10 villainize
mudstone: 7 mineral
Mueller-Stahl: 5 Armin
muenster: 6 cheese
Mueslix: 6 cereal
competitor: *see* cereal
muezzin's call: 4 azan
Mufasa: 4 lion
muff: 3 err 4 blow, boot, fail, flub, mess, miss, slip, wrap 5 boner, botch, fluff, misdo, snafu 6 bobble, boggle, bumble, bungle, foozle, foul up, fumble, mess up, slip up 7 blunder, failure, lose out, misplay, screw up, stumble 9 gaucherie, mishandle, mismanage
starter: 3 ear
muffed grounder: 5 error
Muffet, emulate: 3 eat, sit
muffin: 3 gem 5 bread
starter: 4 raga
__ muffin: 4 bran, corn 7 English
Muffin Man's lane: 5 Drury
muffle: 3 gag 4 damp, dull, hush, mute, wrap 5 drown, quiet, still 6 dampen, deaden, muzzle, obtund, soften, stifle, subdue 7 cushion, envelop, quieten, repress, silence, smother, squelch 8 bundle up, decrease, suppress, tone down
up: 4 wrap 6 swathe 7 envelop, swaddle
muffled: 3 low 4 dull, mute, weak 5 faint, muted, piano, quiet 6 hollow, low-key 8 deadened, hushed up
muffler: 4 mute 5 scarf, throw 8 kerchief
car ~ in Britain: 8 silencer
support: 4 nape 5 U-bolt
mufti: 6 civies 7 civvies, clothes
mug: 3 cup, rob 4 face, gull, look, moue, phiz, pose, puss, toby 5 mouth, stein 6 ambush, attack, beat up, kisser, prey on, seidel, visage 7 assault, grimace, tankard 8 features, overplay, schooner 9 coffee cup, make a face, steal from, strong-arm 10 expression
filler: 3 ale 4 beer, java, suds 6 coffee
shot subject: 4 perp 7 suspect
mug __: 4 shot
Mugabe: 6 Robert
mugger: 4 thug 5 rowdy, thief 6 outlaw, robber 7 brigand 8 attacker 9 assailant
deterrent: 4 mace
__-mugger: 6 hugger
Muggeridge, Malcolm: 6 writer 7 British
mugginess: 8 humidity, moisture
mugging: 5 theft 6 attack, holdup 7 offense, robbery 8 thievery
Muggs, J. Fred: 5 chimp 10 chimpanzee
show: 5 Today

muggy: 3 wet 4 damp, dank 5 close, humid, moist, mucky, soggy, undry 6 clammy, steamy, sticky, stuffy, sultry 7 wettish 10 oppressive
Muhammad: 3 Ali 5 Iqbal 6 Elijah
  birthplace: 5 Mecca
  book: 5 Koran, Quran
  cat: 6 Muezza
  daughter: 5 Laila 6 Fatima
  faith: 5 Islam
  horse: 7 Alborak
  journey: 5 Hijra 6 Hijrah, Hegira
  wife: 5 Aisha
Muir: 4 John, peak 5 Edwin, Gavin, mount 7 glacier 8 mountain
  locale: 10 California
Muir __ National Monument: 5 Woods
Muir, Edwin: 4 poet 8 Scottish
  work: The Labyrinth
Muir, John: 6 writer 10 naturalist
mujer: 5 woman 7 Spanish
  husband: 6 hombre
__ Mujeres, Mexico: 4 Isla
mukluk: 4 boot 5 kamik
  wearer: 3 Esk. 5 Inuit 6 Eskimo, Innuit, Inupik
Mulan (1998 film)
  voice cast: Eddie Murphy, Lea Salonga, B.D. Wong
mulberry: 4 tree 5 color, fruit 6 banian, banyan, fustic, purple 7 grayish
  bark: 4 tapa
  relative: *see* purple color
  tree: 3 fig 4 upas 5 ficus, ramon 6 antiar, fustic 10 breadfruit
Mulberry Bush, The
  author: Angus Wilson
mulch: 4 till 5 humus 7 compost 9 fertilize
mulct: 4 fine, gull 5 cheat 6 amerce, extort, fleece, punish 7 defraud, swindle 8 penalize 10 amercement, forfeiture
Muldaur: 5 Diana, Maria
Muldaur, Maria
  song: I'm a Woman (1975) Midnight at the Oasis (1974)
Mulder: 3 Fox 5 agent
  org.: 3 FBI
  partner: 6 Scully
Muldoon: 3 cop 7 Francis
  partner: 5 Toody
Muldowney, Shirley: 6 Cha Cha 9 auto racer
  milieu: 5 track
mule: 3 Sal 4 sail, shoe 5 scuff 6 animal, brayer, equine, hybrid, mammal 7 Francis, holdout 8 footgear, footwear 10 crossbreed, mixed breed
  blanket: 5 manta
  burden: 4 plow
  command to a ~: 3 gee, haw
  cousin: 5 burro
  emulate a ~: 4 balk, bray 5 baulk
  father: 3 ass 6 donkey
  foot: 4 hoof
  its mascot is a ~: 4 Army
  mother: 4 mare
  of song: 3 Sal
mule __: 4 deer 5 chest, train 7 skinner
__ mule: 4 pack 5 white 6 Moscow
Mule __ Blues: 7 Skinner
Mule Bone
  author: Langston Hughes, Zora Neale Hurston
__ Mules for Sister Sara: 3 Two
muleta: 4 cape
  color: 3 red
Mule Train
  artist: Frankie Laine
Mulgrew: 4 Kate
Mulhare: 6 Edward
Mulholland Dr. (2001 film)
  cast: Ann Miller, Justin Theroux, Naomi Watts
  director: David Lynch
Mulholland Falls (1996 film)
  cast: Nick Nolte
muliebral: 6 female 8 feminine
mulish: 5 balky, rigid 6 ornery, wilful 7 decided, hard-set, piggish, wayward, willful 8 contrary, indocile, obdurate, perverse, stubborn 9 hard-nosed, impliable, ironjawed, obstinate, pigheaded, tenacious, unbending 10 hardbitten, headstrong, inflexible, refractory, unyielding
Mulk __ Anand: 3 Raj
mull: 4 muse 5 study, weigh 6 figure, ponder, review 7 revolve, sweeten 8 chaw over, chew over, cogitate, consider, headland, meditate, pore over, question, ruminate, turn over 9 brood over, reflect on, sweat over, think over 10 deliberate, meditate on
  over: 4 muse, roll 5 study, think, weigh 6 ponder, puzzle 7 focus on, reflect, revolve, sleep on 8 cogitate, consider, look back, meditate, ruminate, turn over 9 reflect on 10 cogitate on, deliberate, reconsider, think about
Mull: 6 Martin
mullah
  text: 5 Koran, Quran
  tongue: 6 Arabic
Mullavey: 4 Greg
mullein: 5 plant 6 flower
__ Muller: 4 Maud
Müller: 4 Paul 7 Hermann 9 Alexander
mullet: 4 fish
mulligan: 4 soup, stew
Mulligan: 5 Gerry 6 Robert 7 Richard
Mulligan, Gerry: 11 saxophonist
  genre: 4 jazz
Mulligan, Richard: 5 actor
  TV: Empty Nest, Soap
mulligatawny: 4 soup
  ingredient: 5 curry
Mullins: 4 Moon 5 Shawn 9 Priscilla
Mullis, Kary: 7 chemist 8 Nobelist
mulloway: 4 fish
Mulroney: 5 Brian 6 Dermot
Mulroney, Brian: 2 P.M. 8 Canadian
  predecessor: 6 Turner
  successor: 8 Campbell
multi-
  kin: 4 poly-
multicolor: 6 motley 7 dappled
multicolored: 4 pied 5 plaid 6 motley, veined 7 dappled, flecked, marbled, mottled, piebald, rainbow, spotted, striped 8 speckled, streaked 9 checkered, harlequin, prismatic
multiculturalism: 9 diversity
multifaceted: 9 versatile
multifarious: 4 many, mixt 5 mixed 6 legion, motley, sundry, varied 7 diverse, various 8 assorted, manifold, numerous, populous 9 different
multiflora: 4 rose
multiform: 7 unalike 8 manifold 9 different
multihued: 6 motley 7 dappled
multilingual: 8 polyglot
multiloquent: 9 talkative 10 loquacious
multimedia format: 5 CD/ROM
multinational: 9 universal, worldwide
multiple: 4 many, mixt 5 mixed 6 legion, sundry, varied 7 diverse, various 8 assorted, manifold, numerous 9 different
multiple-__: 6 choice
Multiple __ Service: 7 Listing
multiple-choice
  not ~: 5 essay
  option: 4 true 5 false, guess
  word: 3 any
multiplex: 5 movie 6 cinema 7 theater, theatre
multiplication: 6 growth
  symbol: 3 dot
multiplication __: 4 sign 5 table
multiplicity: 3 lot, ton 4 heap, host, pile, slew 5 bunch, ocean, stack 7 variety 9 abundance, great deal
multiply: 3 add 4 cube, grow, rise 5 boost, breed, build, mount, raise, spawn 6 double, expand, extend, repeat, spread, square 7 augment, build up, burgeon, compute, enlarge, magnify, produce, prosper 8 bourgeon, compound, generate, heighten, increase, manifold 9 calculate, propagate, reinforce, reproduce 10 accumulate, aggrandize, strengthen
multitude: 3 jam, lot, mob, sea 4 army, heap, herd, host, lots, many, mass, raff, slew 5 bunch, crowd, crush, drove, flock, horde, loads, ocean, press, stack, swarm, troop 6 legion, masses, myriad, number, oodles, people, public, rabble, scores, throng 7 legions, numbers, turnout 8 assembly, infinity, populace, quantity 9 battalion, concourse, profusion 10 confluence
multitudes: 4 lots 6 scores 7 legions
multitudinous: 4 many, rife 5 heaps 6 a lot of, divers, gobs of, legion, lots of, myriad, umteen, untold 7 a host of, a slew of, copious, heaps of, no end of, piles of, profuse, scads of, teeming, umpteen, various 8 a bunch of, abundant, an army of, infinite, manifold, numerous, oodles of, scores of, umpsteen 9 abounding, a passel of, bountiful, countless, quite a few, uncounted 10 zillions of
mum: 4 beer, mute 5 mater, plant, quiet 6 flower, silent 7 aphonic 8 hushed up, nonvocal, taciturn, wordless 9 clammed up, secretive, soundless, voiceless 10 pantomimic, speechless, tongue-tied, unspeaking
  half of a ~: 3 pom
  maybe: 4 word
  move a ~: 5 repot
  not ~: 7 talking
  one: 4 mime 5 mimer
Mumbai: 4 city, town 6 Bombay
  locale: 5 India
mumble: 3 hum 4 slur, talk 5 speak, utter, voice 6 babble, murmur, mutter, ramble, rumble 7 grumble, maunder, stammer, stutter, whisper 8 vocalize 9 undertone, verbalize
mumbletypeg: 4 game
  need: 5 knife
mumbo jumbo
  see baloney
Mumford (1999 film)
  cast: Hope Davis, Jason Lee, Alfre Woodard
Mumford, Lewis: 6 writer
  work: The Culture of Cities Myth and Machine The Urban Prospect
mummer: 5 actor, clown, mimic 6 player 7 pierrot
mummery: 10 masquerade
mummy: 3 Tut 7 King Tut
Mummy, The
  author: Anne Rice
Mummy, The (1932 film)
  cast: Boris Karloff
Mummy, The (1999 film)
  cast: Brendan Fraser, Rachel Weisz
mumps: 9 parotitis
Mum's __ word!: 3 the
mumsy: 5 mater
mumu
  see muumuu
Mumy: 5 Billy
munch: 3 eat 4 bite, chew, gnaw, nosh 5 champ, chomp, crush, grind, snack 6 crunch, nibble 7 scrunch 9 masticate
  on: 9 grab a bite
Munchausen: 4 liar 5 baron
  like ~'s tales: 4 tall
Münch, Charles: 6 French 9 conductor
Munch, Edvard: 6 artist 7 painter 9 Norwegian
  home: 4 Oslo
München: 4 city, town 5 stadt 6 Munich
  locale: 7 Germany
munchies: 4 nosh 5 snack 6 hunger 7 craving
Munchkin
  kin: 3 elf
  official: 5 mayor
Muncie: 4 city, town
  athletes: 9 Cardinals
  locale: 3 Ind. 7 Indiana
  school: 3 BSU 9 Ball State
mundane: 5 banal, ho-hum, lowly, vapid 6 normal 7 earthly, humdrum, insipid, profane, prosaic, routine, workday, worldly 8 day-to-day, everyday, ordinary, temporal, workaday 9 prosaical 10 pedestrian
Mundelein: 4 city, town
  locale: 8 Illinois
__ mundi: 4 anno
__-mundi: 5 coati
mung: 3 urd 4 bean 6 legume
Mungo: 4 Park

Mungojerrie: **3** cat
Mungo Jerry
song: In the Summertime (1970)
muni: **4** bond
Munich: **4** city, town
locale: **7** Germany
river: **4** Isar
Munich (2005 film)
cast: Eric Bana, Daniel Craig, Geoffrey Rush
director: Steven Spielberg
municipal: **4** city, town **5** civic, civil, local, urban **6** public **9** community
see also city
municipal __: **4** bond **5** court
municipality: **4** city, town **6** hamlet **7** borough, village **8** township **10** metropolis
munificent: **3** big **4** free **5** ample **6** giving, lavish **7** liberal, profuse **8** generous, handsome, prodigal **9** bounteous, bountiful, unsparing **10** altruistic, free-handed, open-handed, ungrudging
Muni, Paul: **5** actor
film: The Good Earth (1937)
I Am a Fugitive From a Chain Gang (1932)
Juarez (1939)
The Last Angry Man (1959)
The Life of Emile Zola (1937)
Scarface (1932)
The Story of Louis Pasteur (1936, AA)
munition: **3** arm **8** accouter
munitions: **4** ammo, arms, guns **5** bombs **7** cannons, weapons **8** equipage, grenades, materiel, ordnance, weaponry **9** armaments, artillery, firepower, torpedoes **10** explosives
place: **4** dump **6** armory **8** magazine
Munro: **2** H.H. **5** Alice, Janet
Munro, Alice: **6** writer **8** Canadian
Munro, H.H.: **4** Saki **6** writer **8** Scottish
Munshin: **5** Jules
Munson: **3** Ona **7** Thurman
Munster: **4** city, Lily, town **5** Eddie **6** Herman **7** Marilyn
county: **5** Clare
locale: **7** Indiana
Münster: **4** city, port, town
locale: **7** Germany
Munsters, The (CBS sitcom)
cast: Yvonne DeCarlo (Lily Munster)
Fred Gwynne (Herman Munster)
Al Lewis (Grandpa)
Butch Patrick (Eddie Munster)
Pat Priest (Marilyn Munster)
pet: Spot, Igor
muon: **6** lepton **8** particle
Muppet: **3** Sam **4** Bert, Elmo **5** Ernie, Gonzo, Oscar, Piggy, Rizzo, Rowlf **6** Animal, Fozzie, Kermit, Rosita **7** Statler, Waldorf **9** Miss Piggy
Muppet Christmas Carol, The (1992 film)
cast: Michael Caine, Fozzie Bear, Kermit the Frog, Miss Piggy
Muppet Movie, The (1979 film)
cast: Fozzie Bear, Kermit the Frog, Miss Piggy
Muppets From Space (1999 film)
cast: Gonzo, Kermit the Frog, Miss Piggy, Jeffrey Tambor
Muppets Take Manhattan, The (1984 film)
cast: Fozzie Bear, Gonzo, Kermit the Frog, Miss Piggy
director: Frank Oz
Murad, Ferid: **8** Nobelist
mural: **3** art **5** décor, secco **6** fresco **8** painting **9** landscape
place: **4** wall
starter: **5** inter, intra
Murano: **3** SUV **6** Nissan
Murasaki Shikibu: **6** writer **8** Japanese
work: The Tale of Genji
Murcia: **4** city, town
locale: **5** Spain
Murcielago: **3** car **4** auto **10** automobile **11** Lamborghini
Murder, __ Wrote: **3** She
Murder at 1600 (1997 film)
cast: Alan Alda, Diane Lane, Wesley Snipes
Murder by Death (1976 film)
cast: Eileen Brennan, James Coco, Peter Falk, Alec Guinness, Elsa Lanchester, David Niven, Peter Sellers, Maggie Smith
dog: **5** Myron
Murder by Numbers (2002 film)
cast: Sandra Bullock, Ben Chaplin, Ryan Gosling
Murderers' Row (1966 film)
cast: Ann-Margret, Karl Malden, Dean Martin
Murder in the Cathedral
author: T.S. Eliot
Murder Most __: **4** Foul
Murder Must Advertise
author: Dorothy Sayers
Murder of Roger Ackroyd, The
author: Agatha Christie
Murder on the Orient Express: **4** film **5** novel
author: Agatha Christie
cast: Lauren Bacall, Martin Balsam, Ingrid Bergman, Jacqueline Bisset, Sean Connery, Albert Finney, John Gielgud, Wendy Hiller, Anthony Perkins, Vanessa Redgrave, Richard Widmark, Michael York
director: Sidney Lumet
murderous: **4** fell **5** cruel **6** brutal, savage **7** arduous, hellish, ruinous, vicious, violent **8** criminal, ruthless **9** dangerous, difficult, ferocious, harrowing, rapacious, strenuous **10** exhausting, malevolent
Murder, She Wrote (CBS drama)
cast: Tom Bosley (Amos Tupper)
Angela Lansbury (Jessica Fletcher)
William Windom (Dr. Seth Hazlitt)
setting: Cabot Cove, Maine
Murders in the Rue Morgue, The
author: Edgar Allan Poe
beast: **3** ape
Murdoch: **4** Iris **6** Rupert
Murdoch, Iris: **5** Irish **6** writer
work: An Accidental Man
The Bell
Henry and Cato
The Sandcastle
The Sea, the Sea
A Severed Head
Under the Net
The Unicorn
An Unofficial Rose
Murdoch University home: **5** Perth
Murfreesboro: **4** city, town
athletes: **11** Blue Raiders
locale: **9** Tennessee
school: **4** MTSU
muriatic __: **4** acid
murid: **5** mouse
Muriel: **5** Spark **8** Humphrey, Rukeyser
Muriel's Wedding (1994 film)
cast: Toni Collette, Rachel Griffiths
murine: **5** mouse **6** animal, mammal, rodent
relative: *see* rodent
murk: **3** fog **4** dark, haze, mist **5** gloom **8** darkness
murky: **3** dim **4** dark, drab, dull, gray, grey, grim, hazy **5** black, dingy, dusky, faded, foggy, fuzzy, livid, misty, muddy, muted, smoky, thick, vague **6** cloudy, dismal, dreary, gloomy, ill-lit, opaque, somber, turbid **7** cryptic, obscure, shadowy, unclear **8** darkened, lowering, nebulous, overcast, puzzling, roiled up **9** ambiguous, cheerless, cryptical, enigmatic, tenebrous, unlighted **10** caliginous, clear as mud, depressing, indistinct, perplexing, tenebrific
make ~: **5** cloud
Murmansk: **4** city, port, town
locale: **6** Russia
murmur: **3** coo, hum, pur **4** buzz, moan, purl, purr, sigh, wash **5** drone, sough, sound, speak, voice, whine **6** babble, breath, burble, gurgle, intone, mumble, mutter, ripple, rumble, rustle, tinkle **7** buzzing, grumble, humming, lapping, trickle, whisper **8** susurrus, vocalize **9** undertone, verbalize
murmured: **3** low **4** soft **5** bated, faint, muted, piano, quiet **6** hushed **7** muffled, subdued **8** dampened, deadened **9** toned down **10** turned down
Murphey, Michael
song: What's Forever For (1982)
Wildfire (1975)
Murphy: **3** bed, Ben **4** Dale **5** Audie, Brown, Eddie **6** Calvin, George, Walter **7** Cillian, Michael, William **8** Brittany
author: Samuel Beckett
bed's place: **6** closet
Murphy __: **3** bed **5** Brown
__ Murphy: **6** Father
Murphy, Audie: **4** hero **5** actor **7** soldier
film: To Hell and Back (1955)
Murphy Brown (CBS sitcom)
cast: Candice Bergen (Murphy Brown)
Faith Ford (Corky Sherwood)
Charles Kimbrough (Jim Dial)
Joe Regalbuto (Frank Fontana)
housekeeper: **5** Eldin
program: F.Y.I.
setting: **10** Washington
son: **5** Avery
tavern owner: **4** Phil
Murphy, Eddie: **5** actor **8** comedian
film: 48HRS. (1982)
Beverly Hills Cop (1984)
Bowfinger (1999)
Coming to America (1988)
Daddy Day Care (2003)
The Distinguished Gentleman (1992)
Doctor Dolittle (1998)
Dreamgirls (2006)
The Haunted Mansion (2003)
I Spy (2002)
Life (1999)
Meet Dave (2008)
Norbit (2007)
The Nutty Professor (1996)
Showtime (2002)
Trading Places (1983)
film (voice): Mulan (1998)
Shrek (2001)
TV: Saturday Night Live
Murphy, Rose Mary
spouse: **4** Abie
Murphy's __: **3** Law, War **7** Romance
Murphy's Law word: **5** wrong
Murphy's Romance (1985 film)
cast: Sally Field, James Garner
director: Martin Ritt
Murphy, Walter
song: A Fifth of Beethoven (1976)
Murray: **3** Don, Jan, Ken, Mae **4** Anne, Bill, city, Head, town **5** river **6** Arthur, Butler, Joseph **7** Kempton **8** Gell-Mann, Hamilton, Leinster
locale: **4** Utah
River locale: **9** Australia
Murray __: **4** the K
Murray, Anne
homeland: Canada
song: Broken Hearted Me (1979)
Danny's Song (1973)
Daydream Believer (1980)
I Just Fall in Love Again (1979)
Love Song (1974)
Snowbird (1970)
You Needed Me (1978)
You Won't See Me (1974)
Murray, Arthur
lesson: **4** step **5** tango
Murray, Bill: **5** actor **8** comedian
film: Caddyshack (1980)
Charlie's Angels (2000)
Ed Wood (1994)
Ghostbusters (1984)
Groundhog Day (1993)
Kingpin (1996)
The Life Aquatic With Steve Zissou (2004)
Lost in Translation (2003)
Mad Dog and Glory (1993)
Meatballs (1979)
Quick Change (1990)
Rushmore (1998)
Scrooged (1988)
Stripes (1981)
Tootsie (1982)
What About Bob? (1991)
TV: Saturday Night Live
Murray, J.A.H. lexicon: **3** OED
murre: **4** bird **9** guillemot
emulate a ~: **4** dive
genus: **4** uria
Murrow, Edward R.: **10** journalist
forte: **4** news
network: CBS

mus.
adaptation: 3 arr.
detached, in ~: 4 stac.
ensemble: 4 orch.
slower, in ~: 3 rit. 4 rall.
strongly accented, in ~: 3 sfz.
see also music
Musante: 4 Tony
TV series: 4 Toma
Musberger: 5 Brent
Muscadet: 4 wine 5 white
origin: 6 France
muscadine: 5 fruit, grape
relative: *see* wine
muscat: 4 wine
Muscat: 4 city, town 5 grape 7 capital
locale: 4 Oman
native: 4 Arab
muscatel: 3 red 4 wine 5 grape
relative: *see* wine
Muscatine: 4 city, town
locale: 4 Iowa
muscle: 3 vim 4 beef, dint, meat, push, thew, work 5 brawn, clout, flesh, force, might, power, sinew, steam, thews, vigor 6 energy, flexor, tendon, tissue 7 fitness, potence, potency, stamina 8 strength, vitality 9 beefiness, endurance, fortitude, hardiness, huskiness, influence, puissance, stoutness, toughness 10 brawniness, brute force, horsepower, mightiness, robustness, ruggedness, sturdiness
arm ~: 6 biceps
back ~: 3 lat
belly ~: 2 ab 6 rectus
cell: 5 fiber, stria
chest ~: 3 pec
combining form: 2 my- 3 myo-
contract a ~: 4 flex
contraction chemical: 3 ATP
ender: 3 man, men 5 bound
hip ~: 5 psoas
hired ~: 4 goon 7 torpedo
in: 5 usurp 8 trespass 9 insinuate, interpose, intervene
(in): 5 barge
injury: 4 pull, tear
in on: 6 invade
lacking ~: 4 puny, weak 6 flabby
leg ~: 4 quad 6 rectus, soleus, vastus 9 hamstring
loss of ~ coordination: 5 ataxy 6 ataxia
move a ~: 4 stir
pain: 4 ache, kink, knot, pang 5 cramp, crick, spasm 6 twinge
protein: 5 actin
quality: 4 tone 5 tonus
science: 7 myology
shoulder ~: 4 delt
show some ~: 5 exert
soother: 3 spa 6 hot tub 7 Jacuzzi
straight ~: 6 rectus
treat a ~ pull: 5 chill
weakness: 5 atony 6 atonia
muscle __: 3 car 5 beach, fiber, shirt
Muscle __, AL: 6 Shoals
Muscle Beach Party (1964 film)
cast: Frankie Avalon, Annette Funicello, Buddy Hackett
muscleman, mythical: 5 Atlas
Muscles (1982 song)
artist: Diana Ross
muscovado: 5 sugar
muscovite: 4 mica
muscular: 3 fit 4 buff, hale, iron, wiry 5 beefy, burly, hardy, hefty, hunky, husky, lusty, nervy, stout, thewy, tough 6 brawny, hearty, mighty, potent, robust, rugged, sinewy, steely, stocky, strong, sturdy, virile 7 doughty, healthy, hulking 8 athletic, forceful, indurate, powerful, puissant, pumped up, stalwart, vigorous 9 Atlantean, herculean, strapping, well-built 10 able-bodied, red-blooded
not ~: 4 puny, weak 6 flabby
one: 5 he-man
muscularity: 5 power, thews
musculature: 8 physique
muse: 4 mull 5 dream, study, think, weigh 6 ponder, puzzle, trance 7 reflect, revolve 8 chew over, cogitate, consider, look back, meditate, mull over, ruminate, turn over 9 cerebrate, percolate, speculate, think over 10 brown study, deliberate, introspect, puzzle over
Muse:
Calliope (epic poetry)
Clio (history)
Erato (lyric poetry)
Euterpe (music)
Melpomene (tragedy)
Polyhymnia (sacred music)
Terpsichore (dance)
Thalia (comedy)
Urania (astronomy)
complement: 4 nine
domain: 4 arts
gift from a ~: 4 idea
instrument: 4 lyre
parent: 4 Zeus 9 Mnemosyne
musée: 6 Louvre
Musée des Beaux Arts
author: W.H. Auden
Museo del __: 5 Prado
muser: 8 ponderer, theorist 9 meditator
Muses are Heard, The
author: Truman Capote
Muse, The (1999 film)
cast: Jeff Bridges, Albert Brooks, Andie MacDowell, Sharon Stone
director: Albert Brooks
musette: 4 wind 7 bagpipe 10 instrument
origin: 6 France
museum: 4 hall 7 archive, gallery 8 building, landmark, treasury 10 exhibition, foundation, repository, storehouse
add-on: 4 wing
employee: 5 guard 7 curator 8 restorer
funder: 3 NEA
guide: 6 docent
piece: 3 art, urn 4 bust 5 relic, torso 6 fossil
regular: 4 goer
room: 6 atrium
vessel: 7 samovar
worker's deg.: 3 MFA
museum __: 5 piece
__ museum: 3 wax
__ Museum: 7 British
mush: 4 glop, pulp, samp 5 slush 6 batter 8 porridge
ender: 4 room
musher conveyance: 4 sled
mushroom: 3 cep 4 boom, cepe 5 burst, enoki, morel, plant, swell 6 agaric, blewit, blow up, button, expand, fungus, mature, spread, spring, sprout, thrive 7 amanita, blewitt, blueleg, bluette, burgeon, explode, shoot up, truffle 8 bourgeon, flourish, increase, shiitake, spring up 9 shaggy cap 10 champignon, shaggymane
cloud maker: 5 A-bomb, A-test, H-bomb, N-test
combining form: 3 myc- 4 myco- 6 -mycete
like some ~s: 6 edible
part: 5 stipe, theca 6 pileus
source: 5 spore
mushroom __: 5 cloud
mushy: 4 soft 5 corny, pulpy, sappy, soggy, soppy, sweet, weepy 6 sirupy, sloppy, slushy, spongy, sugary, syrupy, tender 7 maudlin, mawkish, squashy, squishy 8 bathetic, effusive, romantic, schmalzy, shmaltzy, yielding 9 emotional, pastelike, schmaltzy, semisolid 10 lovey-dovey, saccharine, semiliquid
Musial, Stan: 8 Cardinal 10 outfielder
music: 3 air, art, bop, jig, lay, pop, rag, rap, ska 4 aria, duet, folk, hymn, jazz, lied, opus, raga, reel, rock, scat, song, soul, trio, tune 5 bebop, blues, C and W, canon, carol, chant, dirge, ditty, etude, fugue, galop, gavot, gigue, largo, march, motet, octet, opera, pavan, pavin, piece, polka, R and B, rondo, rumba, salsa, samba, score, sound, suite, swing, tango, waltz 6 adagio, anthem, ballad, bolero, chorus, doo-wop, gospel, medium, melody, minuet, pavane, reggae, rhumba, sonata, strain 7 andante, arietta, ariette, big band, calypso, cantata, caprice, chamber, chanson, chorale, country, euphony, foxtrot, gavotte, harmony, klezmer, lullaby, mazurka, octette, prelude, ragtime, refrain, scherzo, singing, skiffle, toccata, two-step 8 acid rock, acoustic, canticle, canzonet, cavatina, concerto, fantasia, folk rock, hard rock, hornpipe, mazourka, nocturne, operetta, oratorio, overture, punk rock, rhapsody, serenade, serenata, soft rock, symphony 9 a cappella, bluegrass, bossa nova, capriccio, classical, Dixieland, honky-tonk, pastorale, plainsong, polonaise 10 acoustical, heavy metal, trumpeting
copyright org.: 3 BMI 5 ASCAP
enhancer: 3 amp
genre: 7 gangsta
holder: 5 stand
knack for ~: 3 ear
like modern ~: 6 atonal
media: 3 CDs
player: 4 iPod
sheet ~ abbr.: 3 arr.
music __: 3 box 4 hall, roll 5 drama, stand, video
music __ spheres: 5 of the
__ music: 3 rap 4 chin, folk, mood, part, soul 5 house, sheet, swing 6 choral, gospel 7 chamber, country, klezmer, program
Music __ charms...: 4 hath
__ Music: 4 Moon 5 I Hear, I Love, Night, Water
musical: 4 play, show 5 in key, lyric, revue, sweet, tonal 6 ariose, choral, dulcet, mellow, poetic, review 7 lilting, lyrical, melodic, recital, silvery, songful, tuneful 8 pleasing, poetical, rhythmic 9 agreeable, melodious 10 euphonious, harmonious, production
accompaniment: 6 backup
beginning: 4 vamp 5 intro 8 overture
Broadway: 3 Big 4 Cats, Coco, Hair, Mame, Nine, Rent 5 Annie, Dolly!, Evita, Gypsy, Hello, Zorba 6 Barnum, Can-Can, Grease, I Do! I Do!, Kismet, Les Miz, Oliver!, Pippin, Purlie, Wiz, The 7 Allegro, Cabaret, Camelot, Chicago, Company, Follies, Pal Joey, Passion, Ragtime, Titanic, Whoopee 8 Applause, Big River, Carousel, Fiorello!, Godspell, Oklahoma!, Peter Pan, Show Boat, Two by Two 9 Brigadoon, Funny Girl, Girl Crazy, No Strings, On the Town, Pipe Dream 10 Dreamgirls, Kiss Me Kate, Lady Be Good!, Miss Saigon, My Fair Lady, Shenandoah 11 A Chorus Line, Crazy For You, Damn Yankees, King and I, The, Leave It to Me, Lion King, The, Me and Juliet, Music Man, The, No No Nanette, Of Thee I Sing, Sweeney Todd
direction: 3 rit., sfz. 4 a due, anim., stac. 5 assai, dolce, forte, grave, largo, lento, piano, secco, tacet, tutti 6 adagio, al fine, arioso, da capo, legato, presto, rubato, subito, vivace 7 agitato, allegro, amoroso, andante, animato, con brio, con moto, marcato, tremolo, vibrato, volante 8 con amore, con anima, grazioso, maestoso, moderato, parlando, semplice, spiccato 9 alla breve, andantino, cantabile, crescendo, glissando, larghetto, non troppo, pizzicato, sforzando, sostenuto 10 allegretto, fortissimo, pianissimo, ritardando, scherzando
epilogue: 4 coda
Greek ~ note: 4 nete
group: 4 band, trio 5 combo, nonet, octet 6 sestet, sextet 7 nonette, octette, quartet, quintet 8 sextette
hall: 5 odeon, odeum
halls: 4 odea
instrument: 3 sax, uke 4 fife, gong, harp, horn, lute, lyre, Moog, oboe, tuba, viol 5 banjo, bongo, bugle, cello, flute, kazoo, organ, piano, viola 6 chimes, cornet, fiddle, guitar, tam-tam, tom-tom, violin, zither 7 alto sax, bagpipe, bassoon, celesta,

cymbals, helicon, maracas, marimba, musette, ocarina, panpipe, piccolo, saxhorn, trumpet, ukulele **8** altohorn, autoharp, bass drum, bass viol, calliope, castanet, clarinet, dulcimer, mandolin, melodeon, recorder, theremin, triangle, trombone **9** accordion, alpenhorn, balalaika, euphonium, harmonica, harmonium, saxophone, vibraharp **10** clavichord, concertina, contrabass, flugelhorn, hurdy-gurdy, kettledrum, sousaphone, squeezebox, tambourine, vibraphone **11** harpsichord
interval: **4** step **5** fifth, ninth, sixth, third **6** fourth, octave **7** seventh, tritone **8** half-step
key: **4** A maj., A min., B maj., B min., C maj., C min., D maj., D min., E maj., E min., F maj., F min., G maj., G min. **5** A-flat, B-flat, E-flat **6** A major, A minor, B major, B minor, C major, C minor, D major, D minor, E major, E minor, F major, F minor, G major, G minor **8** A-flat maj., B-flat maj., E-flat maj. **10** A-flat major, B-flat major, B-flat minor, E-flat major **11** C-sharp minor
liability: **5** no ear **6** tin ear
measure: **3** bar
motif: **4** riff
notation: **3** tie **4** clef, flat, neum, rest, slur **5** C clef, F clef, G clef, neume, segno, sharp **6** accent, ottava **7** mordent, natural **8** alto clef, bass clef **9** signature
note: **2** do, fa, la, mi, re, so, ti **3** sol
notes: **5** chord, triad
phrase: **5** tra la
sample: **4** demo
sound: **4** note, tone **5** trill
staff letters: **4** FACE **5** EGBDF
style: **5** sound
syllables: **5** solfa
talent: **3** ear
tempo: **4** time
theme: **4** tema
toy: **5** gazoo, kazoo **8** mirliton
transition: **5** segue **6** bridge
musical __: **3** saw **6** chairs, comedy
musical chairs: **4** game
quest: **4** seat
musicale: **3** gig **4** show **6** accord, unison **7** concert, harmony, recital **9** agreement, festivity **10** jam session
Music and Lyrics (2007 film)
cast: Drew Barrymore, Hugh Grant
Music Box (1989 film)
cast: Frederic Forrest, Jessica Lange
Music Box Dancer (1979 song)
artist: Frank Mills
Music Box Revue
composer: Irving Berlin
Music for Airports
composer: Brian Eno
Music for Chameleons
author: Truman Capote
Music for the Millions
author: David Ewen
musician: **4** diva **5** fifer, piper **6** artist, bugler, harper, lutist, lyrist, oboist, player, singer **7** artiste, bassist, cellist, drummer, flutist, harpist, pianist, soloist, violist **8** banjoist, composer, flautist, lyricist, organist, virtuoso, vocalist **9** conductor, cornetist, guitarist, performer, violinist **10** trombonist
job: **3** gig
street ~: **6** busker
musicians: **4** band, orch. **8** ensemble **9** orchestra
Music in the Air
composer: Oscar Hammerstein, Jerome Kern
Music Man, The (1962 film)
cast: Buddy Hackett, Ron Howard, Shirley Jones, Robert Preston
character: **3** Hix **4** Alma, Hill, Maud **5** Ewart, Jacey, Paroo, Shinn **6** Dunlop, Harold, Marian, Oliver **7** Alma Hix, Eulalie, Squires **9** Oliver Hix **10** Harold Hill, Maud Dunlop
composer: Meredith Willson
director: Morton Da Costa
setting: **4** Iowa **9** River City
Music of My Heart (1999 song)
artist: Gloria Estefan, 'Nsync
music of the __: **7** spheres
Music of the Heart (1999 film)
cast: Angela Bassett, Gloria Estefan, Aidan Quinn, Meryl Streep
director: Wes Craven
Music of the Night, The: **4** aria
Musigny: **3** red **4** wine
origin: **6** France
Musil, Robert: **6** writer **8** Austrian
musing: **4** lost **6** revery **7** pensive, reverie, thought, wistful **10** reflection, thoughtful
musk: **4** odor
ender: **3** rat **4** oxen, root **5** melon
source: **5** civet
muskeg: **3** fen **5** swamp
Muskegon: **4** city, town
locale: **8** Michigan
muskellunge: **4** fish, pike
musket: **3** arm, gun **5** fusil, rifle **6** jingal, weapon **7** firearm **9** flintlock
ball: **4** slug
ender: **3** eer
musketeer: **7** soldier
Musketeers
motto word: **3** all, one
one of the ~: **5** Athos **6** Aramis **7** Porthos **9** d'Artagnan
school: **6** Xavier
__ Musketeers, The: **4** Four **5** Three
Muskie, Edmund: **3** sen. **7** senator
state: **5** Maine
muskmelon: **4** pepo **5** fruit **6** casaba **7** cassaba
Muskogee: **4** city, town **6** Indian **7** Amerind
locale: **8** Oklahoma
muskox: **5** bovid **6** bovine
relative: *see* bovine
muskrat: **6** animal, mammal, rodent
relative: *see* rodent
Muskrat Love (1976 song)
artist: Captain & Tennille
Muskrat Ramble
composer: Kid Ory
Muslim: **3** Era
Almighty: **5** Allah
ascetic: **4** Sufi **5** faker, fakir, faqir **6** faquir
bridge to paradise: **5** sirat
call from a ~: **4** azan
cap: **3** taj
edict: **5** irade
festival: **6** Bairam
garment: **4** izar **5** burqa, burka, ihram, jibba **6** burkha, chadar, chador, jubbah **7** bourkha, chaddar, chuddar
high-ranking ~ woman: **5** begum
holy book: **5** Koran, Quran
holy man: **4** imam **5** imaum, mulla **6** mullah
holy place: **5** Mecca **6** Medina
household: **5** haram, harem, harim **6** hareem
judge: **4** cadi, kadi, qadi, qaid **5** mufti
law: **5** sunna
messiah: **5** Mahdi
miracle: **5** miraj
month: **4** Rabi **5** Rajab, Safar **6** Jumada, Shaban **7** Ramadan, Shawwal **8** Muharram **9** Dhu al-Qa'da **10** Dhu al-Hijja
nymph: **5** houri
of a ~ sect: **5** Sufic
people: **5** Kazak **6** Kazakh
physician: **5** hakim
pilgrimage: **3** haj **4** hadj, hajj
pilgrimage center: **4** Kufa
ritual: **4** raka
ruler: **3** aga **4** agha, amir, emir **5** ameer, calif, emeer, kalif, mogul **6** caliph, kaliph, khalif
saint: **3** pir
scholar: **4** imam **5** imaum
scholars: **5** ulama, ulema
sect: **5** Sunni **6** Shi'ite
shrine: **4** Kaba **5** Kaaba, Kabah **6** Kaabah
soldier: **5** ghazi
student: **5** softa
temple: **6** mosque
title: **5** sayid
weight: **4** rotl
world: **5** Islam
__ Muslim: **5** Black
muslin: **4** mull **6** fabric **8** material
musophobe
fear: **4** mice
muss: **4** hash, mess **6** jumble, mess up, muddle, ruck up, ruffle, rumple, tangle, tousle, touzle **7** clutter, crumple, disturb, rummage, wrinkle **8** disarray, dishevel, mishmash **9** bedraggle **10** disarrange, untidiness
up: **4** soil **6** ruffle, rumple, tousle, touzle **7** derange **8** disarray, dishevel, scramble
mussed: **7** tousled, unkempt
mussel: **4** unio **5** naiad, shell **6** cockle **8** seashell
cousin: **4** clam **6** oyster
prepare ~s: **5** steam
Musset, Alfred de: **4** poet **6** French **10** playwright
Mussolini: **6** Benito
son-in-law: **5** Ciano
Mussorgsky, Modest: **7** Russian **8** composer
work: Boris Godunov
Edipo
A Night on Bald Mountain
Pictures at an Exhibition
mussy: **5** dirty **6** sloppy, unneat, untidy **7** chaotic, jumbled, muddled, rumpled, tousled, unkempt **8** slovenly, wrinkled **9** cluttered **10** disarrayed, disheveled, disordered, disorderly, in disarray, out of order, out of place, topsy-turvy
not ~: **4** neat, tidy
must: **4** duty, need **5** has to, ought, vital **6** devoir, have to, need to, should **9** condition, essential, moldiness, necessary, necessity, obsession, requisite **10** commitment, imperative, obligation, sine qua non
must-__: **3** see **4** have, read
mustache
application: **3** wax
get rid of a ~: **5** shave
site: **3** lip
teen ~: **4** wisp
mustache __: **3** cup, wax
__ mustache: **6** walrus, Zapata **9** handlebar
mustang: **4** pony **5** horse, mount **6** animal, equine
Mustang: **3** car **4** auto, Ford **10** automobile
competitor: **6** Camaro
Mustangs: **3** SMU
Mustang Sally (1966 song)
artist: Wilson Pickett
mustard: **4** herb, seed **5** color, Dijon, spice **6** yellow **7** French's, Gulden's **9** condiment **10** Grey Poupon
alternative: **4** mayo **6** catsup
cut the ~: **6** hack it **7** succeed
family plant: **4** cole, kail, kale **5** cress
like some ~: **4** mild
relative: *see* yellow color
mustard __: **3** oil **7** plaster
__ mustard: **5** brown, Dijon
Mustard, Colonel game: **4** Clue
__-mustard dressing: **5** honey
Mustard, Mr., like: **4** mean
__ Must Be Crazy, The: **4** Gods
musteline mammal: **4** mink
muster: **4** bevy, bloc, crew, gang, levy, meet, roll **5** array, bunch, crowd, draft, enrol, enter, group, raise, rally, troop **6** call up, enlist, enroll, gather, roster, sign up, summon, throng, troupe **7** collect, compile, convene, convoke, marshal, pluck up, produce, recruit, roundup, send for **8** assemble, assembly, mobilize, roll call **9** coalition, forgather, gathering **10** congregate
out: **9** allow to go, discharge
pass ~: **4** suit **6** hack it **7** qualify, satisfy
up: **6** gather, summon **7** collect, marshal
muster __: **3** out **4** roll
__ muster: **4** pass
__ Must Fall: **5** Night
__ must go on, The: **4** show
Must Love Dogs (2005 film)
cast: John Cusack, Diane Lane
Must've been something __: **4** I ate

musty: **3** old **4** dank, dull, rank, sour **5** banal, fusty, hoary, moldy, passé, stale, tired, trite **6** frowsy, frowzy, old hat, rancid, smelly, spoilt, stuffy **7** airless, clichéd, decayed, mildewy, noisome, odorous, spoiled **8** decrepit, listless, mildewed, obsolete, outdated, outmoded, overripe **9** apathetic, crumbling, hackneyed, moth-eaten, old-school, out-of-date **10** antiquated, malodorous, threadbare
make less ~: **6** air out **9** ventilate
mut
see mutt
mutability: **4** flux
mutable: **5** fluid **6** fickle, labile, mobile, uneven **7** erratic, protean, varying **8** changing, shifting, unstable, unsteady, variable, wavering **9** mercurial, uncertain, unsettled **10** capricious, changeable, inconstant
mutant: **5** freak **7** monster
mutate: **4** turn, vary **5** alter, morph **6** change, evolve, modify **9** transform
mutation: **5** freak **6** change, mutant **7** anomaly **9** deviation, variation **10** alteration
gene ~: **6** allele
starter: **5** trans
subject: **4** gene
Mutation
author: Robin Cook
mute: **3** mum **4** hush **5** lower, quiet, tacit **6** dampen, damper, deaden, muffle, reduce, silent, soften, subdue **7** muffled, silence **8** moderate, nonvocal, reticent, silenced, taciturn, tone down, turn down, unvoiced, wordless **9** noiseless, soft-pedal, unsounded, voiceless **10** speechless, tongue-tied, unspeaking
effect: **4** wawa
in music: **7** sordino **8** sourdine
performer: **4** mime **5** mimer
muted: **3** dim, low **4** dark, soft **5** dusky, faded, faint, fuzzy, mirky, murky, piano, quiet **6** bleary, blurry, gentle, hollow, low-key, pastel, silent **7** muffled, shadowy, subdued **8** murmured, nonvocal **9** noiseless, whispered **10** indistinct, lackluster, restrained, unspeaking
muteness: **7** secrecy, silence
Muti: **8** Riccardo
mutineer: **5** rebel **7** traitor **8** renegade **9** insurgent
mutinous: **6** unruly **7** defiant, lawless, radical **8** factious, renegade **9** insurgent **10** rebellious, unpeaceful
mutiny: **4** riot, rise **5** rebel **6** resist, revolt, rise up **7** disobey, treason **8** defiance, outbreak, uprising **9** overthrow **10** resistance, revolution
__ Mutiny: **5** Sepoy
Mutiny on the Bounty: **4** book
author: James Norman Hall, Charles Nordhoff
character: **4** Byam **5** Bligh, Peggy, Roger **6** Tehani **7** Maimiti **8** Fletcher, Hitihiti **9** Christian, Roger Byam
Mutiny on the Bounty (1935 film)
cast: Clark Gable, Charles Laughton
Mutiny on the Bounty (1962 film)
cast: Marlon Brando, Richard Harris, Trevor Howard
music: Bronislau Kaper
__ Mutiny, The: **5** Caine
Muti, Riccardo: **7** Italian **9** conductor
mutt: **3** cur, dog **5** canid, feist, hound, pooch, scrub **6** canine **7** jackass, mongrel **10** mixed breed
see also canine, dog
Mutt and Jeff: **3** duo **4** pair
mutter: **4** bark, moan **5** croak, gripe, groan, growl, grunt, snarl, speak, utter, voice **6** grouch, grouse, jabber, mumble, murmur, rumble **7** grumble, sputter, whisper **8** complain **9** make a fuss, undertone
Mutter, Anne-Sophie: **6** German **9** violinist
mutton: **4** lamb, meat
dish: **6** hot pot
ender: **4** fish, head **5** chops **6** headed
__-mutton: **4** leg-o' **5** leg-of
muttonbird: **3** oii
muttonfish: **4** sama
muttonhead
see ninny
muttonheaded
see foolish
Mutts: **5** comic **10** comic strip
cat: **5** Mooch
dog: **4** Earl **6** Woofie
mutual: **5** joint **6** common, shared **7** grouped, related **8** communal, conjoint, requited, returned **9** bilateral, concerted, dependant, dependent **10** agreed upon, associated, collective, reciprocal
prefix: **5** inter-
__ Mutual Friend: **3** Our
mutual fund
acct.: **3** IRA **5** Keogh **7** Roth IRA **8** Roth plan
charge: **4** load
fund price: **3** NAV
type: **4** bond, muni, REIT **5** stock **6** growth, income
mutuality: **10** dependence
mutually: **7** en masse, jointly **8** as a group, together **9** in concert **10** conjointly
Mutual of Omaha
competitor: *see* insurance company
__-mutuel: **4** pari
muumuu: **5** dress **8** Hawaiian
accessory: **3** lei
like a ~: **5** loose
Muy __!: **4** bien
muzzle: **3** gag, jaw **4** curb, hush, jowl, stop **5** check, quiet, snout, still **6** bridle, censor, muffle, rein in, shut up, stifle **7** prevent, repress, silence **8** restrain, suppress, throttle **9** keep still
muzzled: **4** tame **10** unspeaking
muzzleloader: **3** gun **5** rifle **6** weapon **7** firearm
muzzy: **4** dull, hazy **7** blurred **8** confused **9** equivocal **10** unexplicit
MVP part: **4** Most **6** Player **8** Valuable
MX: **4** ICBM **7** missile
my
in Italian: **3** mia, mio
oh ~: **6** dear me, oh dear **7** heavens **8** goodness, well well
My __: **3** All, Boy, Dad, Guy, Lai, Man, Sin, Way **5** Mammy **7** Antonia, Sharona
My __!: **3** eye **4** hero **5** stars **7** heavens
My __ Adored You: **4** Eyes
My __ Amour: **6** Cherie
My __ and Only: **3** One
My __ and Welcome to It: **5** World
My __ Angel: **7** Special
My __ are sealed!: **4** lips
My __ Belongs to Daddy: **5** Heart
My __ Chickadee: **6** Little
My __ Clementine: **7** Darling
My __ Dads: **3** Two
My __ Duchess: **4** Last
My __ Eileen: **6** Sister
My __ Fat Greek Wedding: **3** Big
My __ Flame: **3** Old
My __ Flicka: **6** Friend
My __ Foot: **4** Left
My __ Friend's Wedding: **4** Best
My __ Godfrey: **3** Man
My __ Heaven: **4** Blue
My __ in the Highlands: **6** Heart's
My __ Irish Rose: **4** Wild
My __ Irma: **6** Friend
My __ Is Aram: **4** Name
My __ is as a lusty winter...: **3** age
My __ Is Asher Lev: **4** Name
My __ Lady: **4** Fair
My __ Leaps Up: **5** Heart
My __ Lollipop: **3** Boy
My __ Lord: **5** Sweet
My __ Margie: **6** Little
My __ of Town: **4** Kind
My __ perfume: **3** Sin
My __ Private Idaho: **3** Own
My __ Runneth Over: **3** Cup
My __ Sal: **3** Gal
My __ Sons: **5** Three
My __ Star: **5** Lucky
My __ Stood Still: **5** Heart
My __, the doctor: **3** son
My __ Town: **4** Home **6** Little
My __ Trigger: **3** Pal
My __ True: **5** Aim Is
My __ Valentine: **5** Funny
My __, Vietnam: **3** Lai
My __ Vinny: **6** Cousin
My __ Will Go On: **5** Heart
My __ Years in a Quandary: **3** Ten
My-__: **5** T-Fine
My All (1998 song)
artist: Mariah Carey
Myanmar: **5** Burma **6** nation **7** country
bay: **6** Bengal
bovine: **5** takin
capital: **6** Yangon **7** Rangoon
city: **6** Yangon **7** Rangoon **8** Mandalay
export: **4** teak
garment of ~: **5** lungi **6** lungee, lungyi
gulf: **8** Martaban
locale: **4** Asia
money: **3** pya **4** kyat
native: **4** Nosu, Shan **6** Burman
neighbor: **4** Laos **5** China, India **8** Thailand **10** Bangladesh
Nobelist in Peace: **6** Suu Kyi
robber: **6** dacoit, dakoit
__ my Annabel Lee: **4** I and
My Antonia: **5** novel
author: Willa Cather
character: **3** Jan, Leo **4** Anna, Lena, Nina, Otto **5** Cuzak, Lucie, Marek, Pavel, Yulka
__ my backyard!: **5** Not in
My Beautiful Laundrette (1985 film)
cast: Daniel Day Lewis, Saeed Jaffrey, Roshan Seth
director: Stephen Frears
My Best Friend's Wedding (1997 film)
cast: Cameron Diaz, Rupert Everett, Dermot Mulroney, Julia Roberts
My Big Fat Greek Wedding (2002 film)
cast: Michael Constantine, Lainie Kazan, Nia Vardalos
director: Joel Zwick
__ my big mouth!: **5** Me and
My Blue Heaven (1990 film)
cast: Joan Cusack, Steve Martin, Rick Moranis
My bologna __ first name...: **4** has a
My Bonnie __ over...: **4** lies
My Boy (1975 song)
artist: Elvis Presley
My Boyfriend's Back (1963 song)
artist: Angels
My Boy Lollipop (1964 song)
artist: Millie Small
My Brilliant Career (1979 film)
cast: Judy Davis, Sam Neill
...__ my brother: **3** he's
__ my brother's keeper?: **3** Am I
My Buddy
composer: Walter Donaldson, Gus Kahn
__ my case: **5** I rest
Mycenaean: **3** Era **5** Greek
My Cherie Amour (1969 song)
artist: Stevie Wonder
__ My Children: **3** All
mycology: **7** science
study: **6** fungus
__ My Co-Pilot: **5** God Is
My country __ of thee...: **3** 'tis
My Country
author: Abba Eban
My Cousin in Milwaukee
composer: George Gershwin, Ira Gershwin
My Cousin Vinny (1992 film)
cast: Fred Gwynne, Ralph Macchio, Joe Pesci, Marisa Tomei
__ my cup of tea: **3** not
My Cup Runneth Over (1967 song)
artist: Ed Ames
musical: **6** I Do! I Do!
My Dad (1962 song)
artist: Paul Petersen
...my dainty __! I shall miss thee: **5** Ariel
My dame has lost her __: **4** shoe
My Days
author: Eleanor Roosevelt
My Ding-a-Ling (1972 song)
artist: Chuck Berry
My dog has __: **5** fleas
My Dog Skip (2000 film)
cast: Kevin Bacon, Diane Lane, Luke Wilson

__ my drift?: 3 Get
__ my dust!: 3 Eat
My Empty Arms (1961 song)
artist: Jackie Wilson
__ **Myer:** 4 Fort
Myers: 3 Ned 4 Mike 6 Dee Dee 7 Russell
__**-Myers:** 7 Bristol
Myers, Mike: 5 actor 8 comedian
film: Austin Powers in Goldmember (2002)
Austin Powers: International Man of Mystery (1997)
Austin Powers: The Spy Who Shagged Me (1999)
The Cat in the Hat (2003)
Wayne's World (1992)
film (voice): Shrek (2001)
Myerson: 4 Alan, Bess
__ **My Ex's Live in Texas:** 3 All
My eye!: 5 no way 8 forget it
__ **My Eye:** 7 Earache
My Eyes Adored You (1975 song)
artist: Frankie Valli
My Fair Lady
composer: Alan Jay Lerner, Frederick Loewe
My Fair Lady (1964 film): 7 musical
cast: Jeremy Brett, Gladys Cooper, Rex Harrison, Audrey Hepburn, Stanley Holloway, Wilfrid Hyde-White
director: George Cukor
role: 5 Eliza, Henry 6 Alfred, Zoltan 7 Higgins 8 Karpathy 9 Doolittle, Pickering
setting: 5 Ascot 6 London 7 England
My Family (1995 film)
cast: Esai Morales, Edward James Olmos, Jimmy Smits
My father moved through dooms of love: 4 poem
author: e.e. cummings
__ **My Father Told Me:** 4 Lies
My fault!: 5 sorry 7 so sorry 8 mea culpa 9 forgive me
My Favorite __: 4 Year 7 Martian
My Favorite Martian (CBS sitcom)
cast: Bill Bixby (Tim O'Hara)
Ray Walston (Martin)
My Favorite Things
composer: Oscar Hammerstein, Richard Rodgers
My Favorite Year (1982 film)
cast: Joseph Bologna, Selma Diamond, Lainie Kazan, Mark Linn-Baker, Bill Macy, Peter O'Toole
My Fellow Americans (1996 film)
cast: Dan Aykroyd, Lauren Bacall, James Garner, Jack Lemmon
__ **My Fire:** 5 Light
My First Mister (2001 film)
cast: Albert Brooks, Carol Kane, Leelee Sobieski
director: Christine Lahti
My Friend __: 4 Irma 6 Flicka
My Friend Flicka
author: Mary O'Hara
My Funny Valentine
composer: Lorenz Hart, Richard Rodgers
__ **My Gal:** 5 Me and
My Gal Sunday
author: Mary Higgins Clark
My Game
author: Bobby Orr
My Girl (1965 song)
artist: Temptations
My Girl (1991 film)
cast: Dan Aykroyd, Anna Chlumsky, Macaulay Culkin, Jamie Lee Curtis
My Girl Has Gone (1965 song)
artist: Miracles
__**, My God, to Thee:** 6 Nearer
My goodness!: 3 gee, wow 4 egad, gosh 5 egads
My Guy (1974 song)
artist: Mary Wells
My Happiness (1958 song)
artist: Connie Francis
__ **My Heart:** 4 Peg o' 7 Un-Break, Unchain
My Heart and I
author: Elizabeth Barrett Browning
My Heart Belongs to Daddy
composer: Cole Porter
My Heart Belongs to Me (1977 song)
artist: Barbra Streisand
My Heart Belongs to Only You (1964 song)
artist: Bobby Vinton
My Heart Can't Tell You No (1989 song)
artist: Rod Stewart
My Heart Has a Mind of Its Own (1960 song)
artist: Connie Francis
__ **My Heart in San Francisco:** 5 I Left
My Heart Leaps Up: 4 poem
author: William Wordsworth
My Heart Reminds Me (1957 song)
artist: Kay Starr
My Heart's in the Highlands: 4 poem 5 novel
author: William Saroyan
poet: Robert Burns
My heart skipped __: 5 a beat
My Heart Stood Still
composer: Lorenz Hart, Richard Rodgers
My Heart Will Go On (1998 song)
artist: Celine Dion
My Hometown (1985 song)
artist: Bruce Springsteen
My Home Town (1960 song)
artist: Paul Anka
My Kind of Town
composer: Sammy Cahn, Jimmy Van Heusen
My kingdom for a __!: 5 horse
Mykonos: 4 isle 6 island
locale: 6 Aegean, Greece
neighbor: 5 Delos
__ **my lamp beside...:** 5 I lift
Mylanta: 7 antacid
alternative: *see* antacid
My Last Duchess: 4 poem
author: Robert Browning
My Left Foot (1989 film)
cast: Daniel Day Lewis, Brenda Fricker
Myles: 7 Alannah 8 Standish
My life __ open book!: 4 is an
My Life
autobiographer: Golda Meir
My Life (1978 song)
artist: Billy Joel
My Life as __: 4 a Dog
My Life as a Man
author: Philip Roth
My Life in Court
author: Louis Nizer
My Life on Trial
author: Melvin Belli
__ **My Line?:** 5 What's
__ **my lips...:** 4 Read
My lips __ sealed: 3 are
My lips are __: 6 sealed
My Little Chickadee (1940 film)
cast: W.C. Fields, Mae West
My Little Margie (CBS/NBC sitcom)
cast: Charles Farrell (Vern Albright)
Gale Storm (Margie Albright)
My Little Town (1975 song)
artist: Simon and Garfunkel
My Lost Youth: 4 poem
author: Henry Wadsworth Longfellow
My Love (song)
artist: Petula Clark, Paul McCartney, Lionel Richie
__ **My Love:** 5 Never, Sleep 7 Justify
__**, My Love:** 6 Angelo
My Love Is Like a Red, Red Rose: 4 poem
author: Robert Burns
My Love Is Your Love (1999 song)
artist: Whitney Houston
My Lovin' (1992 song)
artist: En Vogue
My mama done __ me: 3 tol'
My Mammy (1928 song)
artist: Al Jolson
My man!: 3 bro
My Man Godfrey (1936 film)
cast: Mischa Auer, Carole Lombard, William Powell
__ **my Maypo!:** 5 I Want
My Melody of Love (1974 song)
artist: Bobby Vinton
My Mortal Enemy
author: Willa Cather
My Mother the Car (NBC sitcom)
car: Porter
cast: Ann Sothern (The Car)
Jerry Van Dyke (Dave Crabtree)
__ **my MTV!:** 5 I Want
My, my!: 3 tsk 6 do tell, tsk tsk
mynah: 3 pet 4 bird 5 mimic 6 talker
My Name Is Aram
author: William Saroyan
My Name Is Asher Lev
author: Chaim Potok
Mynheer: 3 sir 5 Dutch, title 6 mister
MYOB
part of ~: 3 own 4 mind, your 8 business
My Old __: 5 Flame
My Old Kentucky Home
composer: Stephen Foster
myology: 7 science
study: 7 muscles
My One and Only
composer: George Gershwin, Ira Gershwin
My One and Only (2009 film)
cast: Kevin Bacon, Chris Noth, Renée Zellweger
myopic: 6 biased 11 nearsighted
mammal: 5 rhino
myoporum: 5 shrub
My Own Private Idaho (1991 film)
cast: River Phoenix, Keanu Reeves, James Russo
director: Gus Van Sant
My Pal Trigger: 5 oater
__ **My Party:** 3 It's
My People
author: Abba Eban
My pleasure!: 6 glad to
My Prayer (1956 song)
artist: Platters
My Prerogative (1988 song)
artist: Bobby Brown
Myra: 4 Hess
Myra Breckinridge (1970 film)
author: Gore Vidal
cast: John Huston, Rex Reed, Raquel Welch, Mae West
Myrdal: 4 Alva 6 Gunnar
__ **My Regards to Broadway:** 4 Give
myriad: 3 ton 4 a lot, army, gobs, heap, host, many, mint, slew 5 flood, horde, loads, swarm 6 a lot of, divers, gobs of, legion, lots of, oodles, scores, stacks, umteen, untold 7 a host of, a slew of, copious, endless, heaping, heaps of, legions, no end of, numbers, piles of, profuse, scads of, umpteen 8 a bunch of, abundant, an army of, infinite, manifold, mountain, numerous, oodles of, prodigal, scores of, umpsteen, variable 9 abundance, a passel of, bountiful, countless, multitude, quite a few, thousands, uncounted 10 innumerous, numberless, unnumbered, zillions of
myrmecology study: 4 ants
Myrna: 3 Loy
role for ~: 4 Nora
Myron: 5 Cohen 7 Scholes 9 McCormick
Myrt and Marge: 9 radio show
myrtle: 5 green, plant, shrub 6 bluish, flower 7 blueish
family shrub: 6 feijoa
relative: *see* green color
tree: 5 guava 7 cajeput 10 eucalyptus
Myrtle Beach: 4 city, town
locale: 4 S. Car.
My Saber Is Bent
author: Jack Paar
__ **My Sarong:** 6 Pardon
__ **Myself:** 5 All by
My Several Worlds
author: Pearl S. Buck
__ **My Shadow:** 5 Me and
My Sharona (1979 song)
artist: Knack
Myshkin, Prince: 5 Idiot
My Sin: 7 perfume
My Sister __: 3 Sam 6 Eileen
My Sister Eileen
author: Ruth McKinney
My Sister's Keeper (2009 film)
cast: Alec Baldwin, Abigail Breslin, Cameron Diaz
__ **My Sons:** 3 All
mysophobe fear: 4 dirt
__ **my soul!:** 5 Bless
__ **My Souvenirs:** 5 Among
My Special Angel (song)
artist: Bobby Helms, Vogues
My Stepmother Is an Alien (1988 film)
cast: Dan Aykroyd, Kim Basinger
mysteries: 6 arcana
Mysteries of Marseilles
author: Émile Zola

Mysteries of Paris, The
author: Eugène Sue
Mysteries of Udolpho, The
author: Ann Radcliffe
Mysteries of Winterthurn
author: Joyce Carol Oates
mysterious: **4** dark, deep, eery **5** eerie, magic, queer, weird **6** arcane, hidden, occult, secret, spooky, veiled **7** cryptic, curious, elusive, elusory, magical, obscure, strange, uncanny, unknown **8** abstruse, baffling, esoteric, mystical, oracular, profound, puzzling, romantic **9** cryptical, difficult, enigmatic, insoluble, recondite, secretive, spiritual **10** unknowable
Mysterious Affair at Styles, The
author: Agatha Christie
Mysterious Island, The
author: Jules Verne
character: **3** Neb **4** Jack **5** Brown **6** Ayrton, Gideon **7** Harding, Herbert, Spilett **8** Pencroft **9** Nemo. Cyrus
Mysterious Rider, The
author: Zane Grey
mystery: **5** genre, novel, story, vexer **6** enigma, puzzle, riddle, secret **7** arcanum, chiller, grabber, problem, romance, secrecy **8** question, subtlety, thriller, whodunit **9** conundrum **10** closed book, puzzlement
element: **4** clew, clue
man: **3** Mr X
not a ~: **5** known
writers' award: **5** Edgar
mystery __: **4** play
Mystery __ X, The: **4** of Mr.
Mystery!
host: **4** Rigg
Mystery Men (1999 film)
cast: Hank Azaria, Claire Forlani, Janeane Garofalo, Greg Kinnear
Mystery of Being, The
author: Gabriel Marcel
Mystery of Cloomber, The
author: Arthur Conan Doyle
Mystery of Edwin Drood, The
author: Charles Dickens
character: **3** Bud **4** Rosa **6** Helena, Jasper **7** Durdles, Neville, Rosa Bud **8** Datchery, Landless **9** Grewgious **10** Crisparkle
Mystery of Marie Roget, The
author: Edgar Allan Poe
mystic: **4** seer, yogi **5** faker, fakir, faqir, swami, swamy, yogin **6** arcane, faquir, hidden, occult, secret **7** magical, psychic **8** abstruse, anagogic, esoteric, numinous **9** enigmatic, recondite, spiritual, visionary **10** anagogical, enshrouded, paranormal
Hindu ~: **4** yogi **5** faker, fakir, faqir, swami, swamy, yogin **6** faquir
Mystic: **4** city, town
locale: **4** Conn.
mystical: **5** runic **6** arcane, hidden, occult, secret **7** magical **8** abstruse, anagogic, esoteric, numinous, oracular, profound **9** recondite, spiritual, visionary **10** anagogical, mysterious, paranormal, unknowable
emanation: **4** aura
force: **5** karma **6** kismet
knowledge: **6** gnosis
society: **4** cult
mysticism: **6** cabala, kabala **7** cabbala, kabbala **8** dzogchen
Mystic Pizza (1988 film)
cast: Annabeth Gish, Julia Roberts, Lili Taylor
Mystic River (2003 film)
cast: Kevin Bacon, Lawrence Fishburne, Sean Penn, Tim Robbins
director: Clint Eastwood
Mystics and Zen Masters
author: Thomas Merton
Mystification
author: Edgar Allan Poe
mystified: **5** at sea **7** at a loss, bemused, puzzled, stumped **8** clueless, confused **9** buffaloed, flummoxed, in the dark, perplexed **10** bewildered
mystify: **4** beat **5** befog, elude, floor, stump, throw **6** baffle, bemuse, boggle, escape, puzzle **7** becloud, buffalo, confuse, nonplus, perplex **8** bewilder, confound **9** bamboozle
mystifying: **4** dark **6** knotty **7** strange, uncanny **8** puzzling **9** difficult, insoluble
mystique: **4** aura **6** glamor **7** charism, glamour **8** charisma **9** character, magnetism
Mystique: **3** car **4** auto **7** Mercury **10** automobile
My Sweet Lord (1970 song)
artist: George Harrison
My-T-__: **4** Fine
My Ten Years in a Quandary
author: Robert Benchley
myth: **4** lore, tale **5** fable, story **6** legend, mythos **7** fantasy, fiction **8** allegory, delusion, folktale, illusion, nonsense, religion **9** falsehood, half-truth, invention **10** fairy story
__ myth: **5** urban
Myth and Machine
author: Lewis Mumford
My Theodosia
author: Anya Seton
mythical: **5** false **6** fabled, made-up, unreal **7** storied **8** fabulous, invented **9** fairy-tale, imaginary, legendary, visionary **10** fabricated, fictitious
Myth of Sisyphus, The
author: Albert Camus
mythology: **4** lore **5** myths **6** legend **8** religion **9** tradition
branch of ~: **5** Greek, Norse, Roman
mythomaniac: **4** liar
mythos: **6** legend **9** tradition
My Three Sons (ABC/CBS sitcom)
cast: Tina Cole (Katie Douglas)
Tim Considine (Mike Douglas)
William Demarest (Charlie O'Casey)
William Frawley (Michael 'Bub' O'Casey)
Beverly Garland (Barbara Douglas)
Don Grady (Robbie Douglas)
Barry Livingston (Ernie Douglas)
Stanley Livingston (Chip Douglas)
Fred MacMurray (Steve Douglas)
dog: Tramp
myths: **4** lore **7** legends
__-my-thumb: **4** hop-o'
__ My Time: **5** Bidin'
__ My Turn: **3** It's
My Two Dads (NBC sitcom)
cast: Greg Evigan (Joey Harris)
Paul Reiser (Michael Taylor)
__ my type: **3** not
__ Myung Moon: **3** Sun
My Way (1969 song)
artist: Frank Sinatra
__ My Way: **4** I'm on **5** Going
My Wide World
author: Jim McKay
My Wild Irish __: **4** Rose
__ my wits' end!: **4** I'm at
__ my word!: **4** Upon
My word!: **4** egad, I say **5** egads
__ my words!: **4** Mark
My World Is Empty Without You (1966 song)
artist: Supremes

N

9
figure above ~: 5 paren.
to 5: 5 shift
9 A.M. service: 5 terce
9 Lives: 7 cat food
alternative: *see* pet food brand
__ 9 'til 5: 4 open
9 to 5 (1980 song)
artist: Dolly Parton
19th __: 4 hole
19th Amendment beneficiary: 5 woman
94th __ Squadron: 4 Aero
96 Tears (1966 song)
artist: Question Mark and the Mysterians
98°
song: Because of You (1998)
The Hardest Thing (1999)
I Do (Cherish You) (1999)
Invisible Man (1997)
98.6 (1967 song)
artist: Keith
99: 5 agent
99 beautiful names, one with: 5 Allah
99 Luftballons (1984 song)
artist: Nena
99 and 44/100% __: 4 pure
911
like a ~ call: 4 emer.
__ 911: 6 Rescue
1914-1918 conflict: 3 WWI
1917
leader until ~: 4 czar, tsar, tzar
1929 event: 5 crash
1930s
agcy.: 3 WPA
migrant worker: 4 Okie
org.: 3 CCC
1940s conflict: 4 WWII
1941 (1979 film)
cast: Dan Aykroyd, Ned Beatty, John Belushi
director: Steven Spielberg
1979 (1996 song)
artist: Smashing Pumpkins
1984: 5 novel
author: George Orwell
character: 5 Julia, Smith 6 O'Brien 7 Winston
setting: 7 Oceania
1999 (1983 song)
artist: Prince
9000 automaker: 4 Saab
90125 band: 3 Yes
N: 2 nu 3 dir. 4 elem. 5 point 6 letter 7 element 8 nitrogen 9 direction
7 for ~: 4 at. no.
followers: 3 OPQ 4 OPQR 5 OPQRS
in phonetic alphabet: 8 November
not quite ~: 3 NNW
preceders: 3 KLM 4 JKLM 5 IJKLM
star: 3 sun
N __?: 3 or M
N __ Nancy: 4 as in
N-__: 4 bomb 5 shell
'N __: 4 Sync
'N'__ Noose: 5 Is for
Na: 4 elem. 6 sodium 7 element
11 for ~: 4 at. no.
N.A.: 4 cont.
nation: 3 Can., Mex., USA
part of ~: 4 Amer.
NAACP
concern: 6 rights
part: 4 Assn., Natl. 5 Assoc. 6 People 7 Colored
NAA member: 5 flyer, pilot 7 aviator
nab: 3 bag, cop, get, net 4 bust, grab, jail, nail, snag, take, trap 5 catch, pinch, run in, seize, snare, swipe 6 arrest, collar, corner, detain, kidnap, obtain, pick up, pull in, rip off, snap up, snatch 7 capture, ensnare, insnare 8 grab away, surprise 9 apprehend, lay hold of 10 bring to bay
Nabisco: 6 cookie
brand: 4 Oreo, Ritz 5 Nilla 6 Newton
competitor: *see* cookie manufacturer
__ Nabisco: 3 RJR
nabob: 3 VIP 4 czar, king 5 mogul 6 bigwig, fat cat, tycoon 7 big shot, magnate 8 big wheel, somebody 9 big cheese, dignitary, moneybags, plutocrat 10 man of means
residence: 6 estate 7 mansion
Nabokov, Vladimir: 6 writer 7 Russian
work: Ada
Lolita
Pnin
Nabors: 3 Jim
role: 4 Pyle 5 Gomer
Nabucco
composer: Giuseppe Verdi
nachos: 5 chips, snack 9 appetizer
dip: 5 salsa
like ~: 5 crisp, spicy 6 spicey
make ~: 5 broil
__ Nacht: 4 Gute 6 Stille
__ Nacht in Venedig: 4 Eine
nación: 6 España, Méjico
NaCl: 4 salt 9 table salt
remove ~: 6 desalt 10 desalinate, desalinize
Nacogdoches: 4 city, town
locale: 5 Texas
nacre
source: 7 abalone
nacreous: 6 pearly 8 lustrous 10 iridescent
nacre source: 5 conch 6 oyster
nada: 3 nil, nix, zip 4 none, zero 5 squat, zilch, zippo 6 bubkes, bupkis, naught, nought 7 nothing 8 goose egg
in French: 4 rien
Nadab
father: 5 Aaron
Nadal: 6 Rafael
Nada the Lily
author: H. Rider Haggard
Nadelman: 4 Elie
Nader: 5 Ralph
Nader's __: 7 Raiders
Nadia: 8 Comaneci 9 Boulanger
predecessor: 4 Olga
Nadia's Theme (1976 song)
artist: Perry Botkin, Barry De Vorzon
Nadine: 8 Gordimer
Nadine (1987 film)
cast: Kim Basinger, Jeff Bridges, Rip Torn
nadir: 4 foot, zero 5 depth, floor, least, worst 6 bathos, bottom, depths, low ebb 7 the pits 8 low point 10 rock bottom
Nadja (1994 film)
cast: Suzy Amis, Peter Fonda
nae: 2 no 8 Scottish
naevus: 4 mole
N. Afr. country: 3 Alg., Mor., Tun. 4 Egyp.
NAFTA
forerunner: 4 GATT
opponent: 5 Perot
part: 4 Amer., Free 5 North, Trade 8 American 9 Agreement
signatory: 3 USA 6 Canada, Mexico
topic: 6 tariff
nag: 3 bug, dog, dun, vex 4 bait, carp, coax, fret, fuss, goad, harp, pest, plug, prod, ride 5 annoy, cavil, chide, gripe, groan, harry, horse, hound, momus, nudge, press, scold, shrew, worry 6 badger, berate, bother, carp at, carper, chivvy, critic, equine, harass, harper, harp on, hassle, heckle, hector, Maggie, needle, noodge, peck at, pester, pick at, plague, virago, work on 7 annoyer, henpeck, needler, nitpick, provoke, torment, upbraid 8 browbeat, harangue, harridan, irritate 9 aggravate, find fault, henpecker, importune, keep after, Xanthippe 10 complainer, complain to, tongue-lash
Nagai Kafu: 6 writer 8 Japanese
Nagaland, capital of: 6 Kohima
Nagano: 4 city, town
locale: 5 Japan
volcano near ~: 5 Asama
Nagano Olympics
network: 3 CBS
Nagasaki: 4 city, port, town
locale: 5 Japan 6 Kiushu, Kyushu
Nagel: 6 Conrad
nagging: 5 pesky, pesty 7 carping 8 captious, critical, haunting 9 annoyance, demanding, vexatious
feeling: 6 déjà vu
naggy: 8 shrewish
__ Nagila: 4 Hava
Nagori: 3 cow 4 bull 6 bovine, cattle
Nagoya: 4 city, town
locale: 5 Japan
Naguib: 7 Mahfous, Mahfouz
Nagurski, Bronko
sport: 8 football
Nagy: 4 Imre
nah: 2 no 3 naw, nay, nix, non 4 nein, nope, nyet, uh-uh 5 I won't, ixnay, never, no how, no way 6 no deal, noways, nowise, unh-unh 7 I refuse 8 forget it, I will not, negative, negatory 9 by no means, fat chance, I think not 10 count me out, not a chance, thumbs down
Nahath
grandfather: 4 Esau
NaHCO3: 6 bicarb
Nahua: 5 Aztec 6 Toltec
Nahuatl: 8 language
language: 5 Aztec
Nahum: 4 Tate
follower: 8 Habakkuk
preceder: 5 Micah
naiad: 5 nymph 10 water nymph
Naiad: 4 moon
planet: 7 Neptune
naif: 4 babe, tiro, tyro 7 ingenue, new hand 8 innocent 9 credulous, greenhorn 10 unaffected
__-naïf: 4 faux
nail: 3 bag, fix, get, nab, pin 4 brad, claw, grab, join, snag, sock, spad, tack, take, trap 5 catch, pinch, place, pound, seize, spike, whack 6 arrest, attach, clinch, collar, detain, expose, fasten, hammer, pull in, secure, snatch, tackle, unguis 7 capture, pin down 8 fastener, transfix 9 apprehend, recognize 10 tenterhook
biting: 4 vice
combining form: 4 helo- 5 onych-, ungui- 6 onycho-
container: 3 box, keg
down: 3 fix 5 sew up 6 assure, batten, clinch, define, ensure, firm up, recall, settle 7 resolve 8 finalize 9 determine, formalize
drive a ~ aslant: 3 toe
ender: 5 brush
groomer: 4 file 5 emery 8 scissors
like some ~ polish: 5 clear
locale: 3 toe 6 finger
polish: 5 Cutex, paint 6 enamel
relative: 4 tack 5 screw, spike
starter: 3 hob, toe 4 door, hang, tree 5 thumb 6 finger
tooth and ~: 5 madly 6 wildly 8 fiercely, savagely 9 violently
nail __: 3 set 4 down, file 6 enamel, polish
nailed: 4 firm 5 exact, tight 6 secure, stable 8 immobile 10 definitive
nail-polish color: 3 red 4 pink
nails
bite one's ~: 5 worry 7 agonize
hard as ~: 5 rigid, tough 6 steely, strong 9 unbending
__ nails: 5 bed of 6 hard as
Naina predecessor: 5 Raisa
Naipaul, V.S.: 6 writer 8 essayist, Nobelist 10 West Indian
Nair: 4 Mira 10 depilatory
alternative: 4 Neet 5 razor
Nairn: 6 county
locale: 8 Scotland
Nairobi: 4 city, town 7 capital
locale: 5 Kenya
Nairobi __, The: 4 Trio
nais: 5 nymph
Naismith: 5 James
naître
form of: 3 née
in English: 4 born
naive: 4 easy, open 5 fresh, green, plain 6 callow, candid, honest, jejune, simple, stupid, trusty, unwary, unwise 7 artless, genuine, natural, sincere, unjaded 8 clueless, dewy-eyed, foolable, gullable, gullible, ignorant, innocent, lamblike, trustful, trusting, unartful, untaught, unversed, wide-eyed

9 backwater, childlike, confiding, credulous, deludable, guileless, ingenuous, unfledged, unguarded, unknowing, unworldly 10 deceivable, falling for, sophomoric, unaffected, uninformed, unschooled, unseasoned
be ~: 6 accept 7 believe, fall for, swallow
not ~: 4 foxy, wily 5 cagey, canny, slick, smart 6 artful, astute, crafty, shrewd 7 cunning, furtive 8 guileful
one: 4 babe, lamb 8 innocent
naiveté: 6 candor 8 openness 9 credulity, frankness, greenness, ignorance, innocence 10 simplicity
Najimy: 5 Kathy
naked: 3 raw 4 bald, bare, nude, open, pure 5 frank, overt, plain, sheer, stark 6 patent, peeled, simple, unclad 7 blatant, denuded, evident, exposed, obvious 8 disrobed, divested, glabrous, helpless, in the raw, knowable, leafless, palpable, revealed, starkers, stripped, undraped, unveiled, wide-open 9 au naturel, in the buff, unadorned, unattired, unclothed, uncovered, undressed, unobscure 10 unshielded, vulnerable
ape: 3 man 5 being, human 6 mortal
combining form: 4 gymn-, nudi- 5 gymno-
make ~: 4 bare 5 strip 6 denude 7 disrobe, uncover, undress
naked __: 3 eye 5 truth
naked __ jaybird: 3 as a
__-naked: 4 buck 5 stark
Naked __: 4 City, Eyes 5 Lunch
Naked __, The: 3 Ape, God, Gun, Sun 4 City, Face, Kiss, Maja, Prey, Spur 5 Truth 6 Jungle
Naked and the Dead, The
author: Norman Mailer
Naked Ape, The
author: Desmond Morris
Naked City (ABC drama)
cast: Horace McMahon (Lt. Mike Parker)
Naked Face, The
author: Sidney Sheldon
Naked God, The
author: Howard Fast
Naked Gun, The (1988 film)
cast: George Kennedy, Ricardo Montalban, Leslie Nielsen, Priscilla Presley
director: David Zucker
Naked Jungle, The (1954 film)
cast: Charlton Heston
menace: 4 ants
Naked Lunch
author: William S. Burroughs
Naked Maja
artist: Francisco de Goya
Naked Sun, The
author: Isaac Asimov
Naked Truth, The (ABC/NBC sitcom)
cast: Téa Leoni (Nora Wilde)
Nala: 4 lion
Naldi: 4 Nita
__ Nam: 4 Viet
Namath: 3 Joe 9 Joe Willie
alma mater: 4 Bama 7 Alabama
once: 3 Jet, Ram
namaycush: 4 fish 5 trout
namby-pamby: 4 soft, weak 5 sissy, timid 8 mama's boy 9 spineless
name: 3 dub, peg, rep, set, tab, tag, tap 4 call, cite, fame, flag, list, make, pick, sign, star, term, word 5 alias, brand, celeb, elect, honor, label, nomen, place, style, title 6 anoint, assign, choose, credit, define, denote, eponym, finger, handle, indict, renown, report, repute, select 7 agnomen, appoint, baptize, big star, declare, entitle, epithet, heading, imprint, intitle, mention, moniker, pin down, point to, propose, qualify, refer to, speak of, specify 8 christen, classify, cognomen, delegate, deputize, eminence, identify, luminary, monicker, nominate, prenomen, snitch on, somebody, subtitle 9 autograph, celebrity, designate, enumerate, headliner, personage, pseudonym, recognize, signature, single out, sobriquet, stipulate, superstar 10 commission, denominate, nom de plume, prominence, reputation
combining form: 4 -onym 7 onomato-
ender: 3 tag 4 sake, tape 5 plate
fake ~: 5 alias 6 anonym 10 nom de plume
in French: 3 nom
in Spanish: 6 nombre
names: 3 rat 4 bare, blab, leak
starter: 3 pen 4 nick
name __: 3 day 4 tape 5 brand, names 7 dropper
name __ game: 5 of the
name-__: 4 drop 6 caller 7 calling, dropper
__ name: 3 big, day, pen, pet 4 code, font, last 5 birth, brand, first, given, trade 6 common, domain, family, maiden, middle, proper, street
Name (1995 song)
artist: Goo Goo Dolls
Name __ Rose, The: 5 of the
Name __, The: 4 Game
Name __ Tune: 4 That
__ Name: 5 I Got a, Say My
Name Above the Title, The
author: Frank Capra
named: 6 cleped, yclept 7 nominal, ycleped 9 preferred
commonly ~: 8 so-called
derived from a person: 6 eponym
originally ~: 3 née
__ Named Charlie Brown: 4 A Boy
name-dropper: 4 snob 5 snoot 7 elitist 8 braggart
__ Named Sue: 4 A Boy
__ name for oneself: 5 make a
Name Game, The (1965 song)
artist: Shirley Ellis
nameless: 6 unsung 7 obscure, unfamed, unknown 8 untitled 9 anonymous, incognito, unheard-of 10 unrenowned
namely: 3 viz. 4 scil. 5 id est, to wit 6 such as 8 scilicet 9 expressly, videlicet 10 especially
__ name of: 5 in the
name of God, name meaning: 6 Samuel
name of the __: 4 game
__ Name of the Father: 5 In the
Name of the Game, The (NBC drama)
cast: Gene Barry (Glenn Howard) Tony Franciosa (Jeff Dillon) Susan Saint James (Peggy Maxwell) Robert Stack (Dan Farrell)
Name of the Rose, The: 4 film 5 novel
author: Umberto Eco
cast: F. Murray Abraham, Sean Connery, Christian Slater
setting: Italy
nameplates, make: 6 emboss
namer: 3 rat 4 fink 6 parent 7 tattler 8 informer 9 informant 10 tattletale
names
inability to recognize ~: 6 anomia
name ~: 3 rat 4 bare, blab, leak
__ names: 4 call, name
namesake: 6 eponym, junior
names - English/French:
Henry - Henri
John - Jean
names - English/German:
Frank - Franz
John - Hans
names - English/Irish:
Jane - Shana
John - Sean
Mary - Moira
names - English/Italian:
Donald - Aldo
Ellen - Elena
Guy - Guido
Helen - Elena
Hugh - Ugo
Louis - Luigi
Paul - Paolo
names - English/Russian:
Ann - Nina
Elijah - Ilya
George - Yuri
Irene - Irina
Jacob - Yakov
John - Ivan
Mike - Misha
Paul - Pavel
Peter - Pyotr
names - English/Scottish:
Jane - Sheena
Jane - Shona
John - Iain
John - Ian
Mary - Moira
names - English/Spanish:
Ellen - Elena
Helen - Elena
James - Diego
James - Iago
James - Jaime
John - Juan
Joseph - José
Lewis - Luis
Louis - Luis
Paul - Pablo
Peter - Pedro
Thomas - Tomás
names - French/English:
Alain - Alan
André - Andrew
Henri - Henry
Jean - John
Marie - Mary
names - German/English:
Franz - Frank
Hans - John
names - Irish/English:
Moira - Mary
Sean - John
Shana - Jane
Shane - John
names - Italian/English:
Aldo - Donald
Guido - Guy
Luigi - Louis
Paolo - Paul
Ugo - Hugh
names, meaning of:
Ada - noble
Adele - noble
Adler - eagle
Agatha - good
Alice - noble
Alissa - joy
Alma - kind
Amos - burden
Amy - beloved
Anne - grace
Ava - water
Barry - spear
Basil - royal
Baum - tree
Beck - baker
Bjorn - bear
Bonnie - good
Bruno - brown
Caleb - dog
Calvin - bald
Carmen - song
Casey - brave
Cecil - blind
Charles - man
Claude - lame
Cora - girl
Cosmo - order
Craig - rock
Cyril - lord, ruler
Daniel - the Lord is my judge
Dean - valley
Deborah - bee
Dora - gift
Drew - trusty
Dyker - mason
Earl - noble
Edna - birth
Eli - height
Ella - all
Elmo - helmet
Elroy - king
Eric - ruler
Erna - eagle
Ethel - noble
Eve - life
Ezra - help
Felix - happy
Gail - joy
Grant - great, large
Guy - woods
Haas - hare
Helga - holy
Hiram - noble
Horst - wood
Hoyt - glee
Hugh - heart, mind
Ida - happy
Jemima - dove
Jonah - dove
Jonas - dove

Jonathan - God gave
Kay - rejoice
Klein - small
Leah - weary
Leila - night
Leon - lion
Leroy - king
Linus - flax
Lloyd - gray
Lucia - light
Martha - lady
Nadia - hope
Nathan - gift
Noah - rest
Nora - honor
Olga - holy
Paul - small
Peter - rock
Rachel - lamb
Roth - red
Roy - red
Russell - red
Samuel - name of God
Stanley - stone field
Stella - star
Tara - hill
Thomas - twin
Tristan - sad
Ursula - bear
Vera - faith, truth
Vogel - bird
Weiss - white
Yves - yew
Zoe - life
names - Russian/English:
Ilya - Elijah
Irina - Irene
Ivan - John
Misha - Mike
Nina - Ann
Pavel - Paul
Pyotr - Peter
Yakov - Jacob
Yuri - George
names - Scottish/English:
Iain - John
Ian - John
Moira - Mary
Sheena - Jane
Shona - Jane
names - Spanish/English:
Diego - James
Iago - James
Jaime - James
José - Joseph
Juan - John
Pablo - Paul
Pedro - Peter
Tomás - Thomas
Names, The
author: Don DeLillo
nametag site: 5 lapel **6** pocket
nametags, like some: 6 clip-on
Name That Tune: game show
clue: note
Namib: 6 desert
locale: 6 Africa
Namibia: 6 nation **7** country
bay: 6 Walvis **7** Walfish
bovine: 6 Ovambo
capital: 8 Windhoek
desert: 8 Kalahari
money: 4 cent
native: 4 Nama **5** Bantu **6** Herero
neighbor: 3 Ang., Bot., RSA, Zam. **6** Angola, Zambia **8** Botswana
once: 3 SWA
Namouna
composer: Édouard Lalo
Nampa: 4 city, town
locale: 5 Idaho
nan: 5 bread
Nan: 4 Grey **7** Bobbsey **8** Merriman
sibling: 4 Bert **7** Flossie, Freddie
nana: 4 gran **6** granny **7** grandma, grannie **8** babushka **9** governess, nursemaid
husband: 5 gramp **6** grampa
son: 5 uncle
Nana: 3 dog **7** Visitor **9** Mouskouri
author: Émile Zola
portrayer: Anna Sten
__ Na Na: 3 Sha
Na Na Hey Hey... band: 5 Steam
Nanaimo: 4 city, town
locale: 6 Canada
__ Nance Garner: 4 John
Nancy: 4 Ames, city, Drew, Kulp, Kwan, town **5** Allen, Astor, comic, Davis, Kelly, Lopez, Olson, strip **6** McKeon, Pelosi, Savoca, Travis, Walker, Wilson **7** Mitford, Sinatra **8** Dussault, Kerrigan, Marchand, Schuster **10** Cartwright, comic strip
character: 4 Irma, Ritz **5** Rollo **6** Fritzi, Sluggo
dog: 7 Poochie
locale: 6 France
river: 7 Meurthe
Nancy __ Kassebaum: 6 Landon
__ 'n' Andy: 4 Amos
Nanette: 6 Fabray, Newman
__, Nanette: 4 No No
nankeen: 4 lily **6** fabric, yellow **8** brownish
Nanking
now: 7 Nanjing
Treaty of ~ port: 4 Amoy
Nanki-Poo's beloved: 6 Yum Yum
nanna: 6 granny **7** grannie
nanny: 4 goat **6** au pair **7** watcher **9** governess, nursemaid
a ~ pushes it: 4 pram
Asian ~: 4 amah, ayah
concern: 3 tot **5** child
cry: 3 maa
ender: 5 berry
mate: 5 billy
offspring: 3 kid
nanny __: 3 tax **4** goat, plum
Nanny Diaries, The (2007 film)
cast: Paul Giamatti, Scarlett Johansson, Laura Linney
Nanny McPhee (2006 film)
cast: Colin Firth, Angela Lansbury, Emma Thompson
Nanny, The (CBS sitcom)
cast: Fran Drescher (Fran Fine) Maxwell Shaughnessy (Maxwell Sheffield)
Renée Taylor (Sylvia Fine)
dog: Chester
nano-: 4 tiny **5** teeny **6** teensy
Nanon
author: George Sand
Nanook
home: 4 iglu **5** igloo
vehicle: 4 sled **5** kayak
Nanook of the North (1922 film)
director: Robert Flaherty
Nanook of the North sequel: 5 Moana
Nansen: 8 Fridtjof
Nantes: 4 city, port, town
locale: 6 France
river: 5 Loire
Nanticoke: 4 city, town **6** Indian **7** Amerind
locale: 6 Canada **7** Ontario
Nantucket: 4 isle, port **6** island
locale: 3 Atl. **8** Atlantic
TV sitcom set on ~: 5 Wings
NaOH: 3 lye **4** base **6** alkali
Naomi: 4 Judd, Wolf **5** Watts **8** Campbell **9** Mitchison
colleague: 4 Elle, Tyra **5** Cindy **7** Claudia
daughter: 6 Ashley **7** Wynonna
daughter-in-law: 4 Ruth **5** Orpah
husband: 9 Elimelech
son: 6 Mahlon **7** Chilion
naos: 5 cella **6** temple
nap: 3 nod **4** down, doze, fuzz, game, pile, rest, shag, woof, yawn **5** fiber, fluff, relax, sleep **6** drowse, nod off, siesta, snooze, turn in **7** doze off, drop off, respite, shuteye, slumber, surface, texture, time-out **8** card game, dog ender, down time **9** go to sleep **10** fall asleep, forty winks
end a ~: 4 rise, stir, wake **5** arise, awake, get up, waken **6** awaken, bestir, wake up
ender: 4 time
inducer: 4 bore
sound: 3 zzz **5** snore
starter: 3 cat, dog, kid
unit: 4 wink
Nap: 6 Lajoie
Napa: 4 city, town **6** valley
locale: 10 California
product: 4 wine **5** pinot
winery: 5 Gallo
Napalm & Silly Putty
author: George Carlin
N/A, part of: 3 not **4** appl. **10** applicable
nape: 4 neck **5** nucha, scrag **6** scruff
coverer: 6 collar
knot: 3 bun
Naperville: 4 city, town
locale: 8 Illinois
napery: 5 linen
Naphtali
parent: 5 Jacob **6** Bilhah
sibling: 3 Dan, Gad **4** Levi **5** Asher, Dinah, Judah **6** Joseph, Reuben, Simeon **7** Zebulun **8** Benjamin, Issachar
napier: 5 grass
Napier: 4 Alan, John **7** Charles
Napier's __: 4 rods **5** bones
napkin: 3 bib **5** doily, linen **6** doyley
in Britain: 9 serviette
material: 6 damask
place: 3 lap **5** table
napkin __: 4 ring
Naples: 3 bay **4** city, port, town
city near ~: 5 Gaeta **6** Amalfi
island near ~: 5 Capri **6** Ischia
lake near ~: 6 Averno
locale: 5 Italy **7** Florida
napoleon: 4 coin, game **5** money **6** pastry **7** dessert **8** card game
cousin: 6 éclair
locale: 6 bakery
Napoleon: 4 Solo **5** exile **6** Lajoie **9** Bonaparte
emblem: 5 eagle
horse: 7 Marengo
island: 4 Elba **7** Corsica **8** St. Helena
marshal: 3 Ney
river ~ navigated: 4 Nile
sister: 5 Elisa
victory site: 4 Jena, Lodi, Yafo **5** Jaffa **6** Lützen, Wagram **7** Bautzen, Marengo **8** Borodino, Smolensk **10** Austerlitz
word in a ~ palindrome: 3 ere, saw, was **4** able, Elba
see also French
Napoleon (1927 film)
director: Abel Gance
__ Napoléon: 4 Code
__ Napoleon Duarte: 4 José
Napoleonic __: 3 Era **4** Code, Wars
__ Napoleon, The: 5 Age of
Napoli: 4 city, town
locale: 5 Italy **6** Italia
napped: 5 downy, fuzzy **6** fluffy
fabric: 5 baize **7** flannel
napping: 5 adoze **6** asleep, at rest **7** dormant **9** sacked out, somnolent, unmindful
caught ~: 6 dozing, spacey **7** in a daze, out of it, unaware **8** heedless **9** negligent, unmindful, unwitting **10** out to lunch
place: 4 sofa **8** recliner
quit ~: 4 rise, wake **5** arise, awake, get up, waken **6** awaken
nappy: 4 soft **5** curly, downy, furry, fuzzy, plush **6** diaper, fleecy, fluffy, shaggy **7** squishy, velvety **8** cushiony
Napster opponent: 4 RIAA
Nara: 4 city, town
locale: 5 Hondo, Japan **6** Honshu
Naranjos: 4 city, town
locale: 6 Mexico **8** Veracruz
NARAS award: 6 Grammy
part of: 3 Nat. **4** Acad., Arts, Natl., Scis. **7** Academy **8** National, Sciences **9** Recording
Narayan, R.K.: 6 Indian, writer
narc: 3 cop **4** G-man **6** buster, shamus **9** detective, policeman
activity: 4 bust, raid **5** pinch **6** arrest, collar **7** seizure
find: 4 kilo, perp **5** drugs
org.: 3 DEA
Narcisse
author: George Sand
composer: Jules Massenet
narcissism: 3 ego **5** pride **6** egoism, vanity **7** conceit, egotism, hauteur **8** self-love, snobbery **9** immodesty, vainglory **10** pretension
narcissist: 4 snob **6** egoist **9** introvert **10** self-seeker, self-server
narcissistic: 4 smug, vain **5** cocky, proud **6** snobby, stuffy **7** fustian, haughty, pompous, selfish, stuck-up **8** arrogant, boastful, snobbish **9** big-headed, conceited, egotistic
narcissus: 5 plant **6** flower
Narcissus
like ~: 4 vain
love: 3 ego **4** Echo, self **5** image
parent: 6 Selene **7** Liriope **8** Endymion **9** Cephissus
play ~: 5 preen

NA

nard: **5** plant **8** ointment
nardus: **5** grass **8** matgrass
nares: **8** nostrils
naris: **7** nostril
nark: **3** rat **4** fink **6** canary, snitch, weasel **7** stoolie, tattler, traitor **8** informer, squealer, turncoat **10** tattletale
Narnia
  creator: C.S. Lewis
  lion: **5** Aslan
Narragansett: **3** bay
narrate: **4** tell, yarn **5** state **6** depict, detail, recite, relate, repeat, report, unfold **7** portray, recount **8** describe, rehearse, set forth **9** chronicle, hold forth, make known
narrated: **4** oral **5** vocal **6** spoken, verbal **9** unwritten, vocalized
narration: **4** news, tale, yarn **5** story **6** report **7** account, reading, recital **8** anecdote **9** chronicle, recountal, voice-over **10** commentary, confession, expression, recitation, recounting
narrative: **4** acct., book, epic, plot, saga, tale, yarn **5** novel, story **6** legend, memoir, report **7** account, article, fiction, history, recital, romance, version **8** anecdote, libretto, thriller, whodunit **9** chronicle, potboiler, recountal, statement **10** recounting, short story
  French ~ poem: **3** lai
  poem: **4** idyl **5** idyll
  song: **6** ballad
Narrative of A. Gordon Pym
  author: Edgar Allan Poe
narrow: **3** set **4** fine, mean, slim, thin **5** close, fixed, limit, local, scant, small, taper, tight **6** biased, lessen, linear, little, recede, reduce, shrink **7** abridge, bigoted, compact, cramped, curtail, insular, limited, partial, pinched, shallow, shorten, slender, thin out, tighten **8** compress, condense, contract, decrease, dogmatic, hemmed in, isolated, obdurate, orthodox, restrict, shrunken, tapering, taper off **9** confining, exclusive, hidebound, illiberal, parochial, sectarian **10** abbreviate, attenuated, compressed, contracted, dogmatical, inflexible, intolerant, prejudiced, provincial, restricted, threadlike
  band: **4** rein **5** leash, strap
  board: **4** lath
  boat: **5** canoe, kayak, skiff **9** outrigger
  combining form: **4** sten- **5** steno-
  conduit: **4** tube
  connector: **4** neck
  ender: **4** back, cast **7** casting
  get ~: **5** taper
  land: **4** spit
  make less ~: **5** widen **6** expand, spread **7** broaden, enlarge, thicken **9** spread out
  margin: **4** hair, neck, nose
  not ~: **4** wide **5** broad, roomy **8** spacious **9** capacious, expansive, extensive **10** commodious
  off the straight and ~: **4** awry, lost **5** amiss **6** adrift, afield, astray **7** missing, roaming **9** wandering
  opening: **4** slit, slot **5** chink **6** cranny
  passage: **4** lane **5** alley, fiord, fjord, inlet
  route: **4** pass **6** strait
  shelf: **5** ledge
  shoe: **3** AAA **4** AAAA, ten A
  the gap: **4** near **5** close **6** gain on **7** catch up, close in **8** approach, overtake **9** close in on
  valley: **5** combe, coomb **6** coombe
  waterway: **5** sound **7** channel
  window opening: **6** louver, louvre
narrow ___: **5** gauge **6** escape, margin
narrow-___: **6** fisted, minded
narrowest: **5** least **6** lowest, merest **7** minimal, minimum, tiniest **8** smallest **9** slightest
narrow horizontal
  in heraldry: **5** label **6** fillet
narrowly: **4** just **6** almost, barely, nearly **7** by a hair, by a nose, closely **8** only just, scarcely **10** by a whisker
narrow-minded: **5** petty, rabid, rigid, small **6** biased, little, narrow, stuffy **7** bigoted, insular, prudish, selfish, shallow **8** dogmatic **9** hidebound, illiberal, parochial, sectarian **10** dogmatical
  one: **5** bigot
narrowness: **4** bias **8** jingoism **9** prejudice **10** chauvinism, fanaticism
Narrow Rooms
  author: James Purdy
narrows: **4** neck **6** strait **7** channel
narrow-waisted stinger: **4** wasp
narthex: **8** anteroom
  neighbor: **4** apse, nave
Narvik: **4** city, port, town
  locale: **6** Norway
narwhal: **6** animal **8** cetacean
  feature: **4** tusk
  nosh: **5** krill
  relative: *see* cetacean
nary: **3** not **4** none, zero **5** never **6** not any
  a soul: **4** none **5** no one
nary ___: **4** a one **5** a clue, a soul
NASA
  1960 ~ launch: **5** Tiros
  acronym: **3** ELV, EVA, LEM
  affirmative: **3** A-OK **5** A-okay
  chimp: **4** Enos
  concern: **7** shuttle
  countdown word: **3** one, six, ten, two **4** five, four, nine **5** eight, minus, seven, three **7** liftoff **8** ignition
  counterpart: **3** ESA
  creation: **5** robot
  decision: **4** no-go
  destination: **3** Mir **4** Mars, moon **5** orbit
  event: **6** launch
  gasket: **5** O-ring
  name: **3** Gus **4** Alan, Buzz, Deke, Neil, Ride **5** Glenn **6** Aldrin **7** Grissom, Shepard, Slayton **9** Armstrong
  normal gravity, to ~: **4** one G
  number: **5** niner
  outfit: **5** G-suit
  part: **3** Nat. **4** Natl. **5** Admin., Space **8** National
  project: **6** Apollo, Aurora, Gemini **7** Mercury
  spacewalk: **3** EVA
  vehicle: **3** LEM **5** Agena, Atlas **6** Skylab **7** orbiter
nasal: **6** rhinal, twangy **9** adenoidal
  bone: **5** vomer
  divider: **6** septum
  input: **4** odor **5** aroma, scent, smell, whiff **9** fragrance
  of the ~ cavity: **5** naric
  opening: **5** naris **7** nostril
  openings: **5** nares
  passage: **5** sinus
  sound: **5** snore, snort, twang, whine
nasal ___: **5** spray
nasally offensive: **4** olid, rank **6** stinky
NASCAR
  broadcaster: **4** ESPN
  event: **4** race
  Hall of Fame designer: **5** I.M. Pei
  part: **3** Car **4** Assn., Auto **5** Assoc., Stock **6** Racing
  sponsor: **3** STP
nascence: **5** birth **7** genesis, infancy **9** childhood
nascent: **5** early **6** infant **7** initial **9** beginning, inceptive
Nascimento, Edson Arantes do: **4** Pelé
NASDAQ: **3** mkt.
  how ~ stocks trade: **3** OTC
  offering: **3** IPO, stk. **4** shrs. **5** stock
  orgs.: **3** cos.
  rival: **4** AMEX, NYSE
  transaction: **5** trade
Nash: **3** car **4** auto, John, poet **5** Ogden, Steve **6** Graham, Johnny **7** Bridges, Charles **8** Clarence **10** automobile
  colleague: **5** Young **6** Crosby, Stills
  competitor: **6** De Soto
Nash Bridges (CBS drama)
  cast: Don Johnson (Insp. Nash Bridges)
    Cheech Marin (Insp. Joe Dominguez)
  employer: SFPD
Nashe, Thomas: **7** English **8** satirist **10** playwright
Nash, John: **8** Nobelist **9** economist
Nash, Johnny
  song: Hold Me Tight (1968)
    I Can See Clearly Now (1972)
    Stir It Up (1973)
Nash, Ogden: **4** poet **6** writer
  one-L priest: **4** lama
  two-L beast: **5** llama
  work: Bed Riddance
    Everyone But Thee and Me
Nashua: **4** city, town **5** horse **9** racehorse
  locale: New Hampshire
Nashville: **4** city, town
  athletes: **9** Predators **10** Commodores
  county: **8** Davidson
  locale: **9** Tennessee
  music hall: **4** Opry
  river: **10** Cumberland
  school: **3** TSU **4** Fisk **10** Vanderbilt
Nashville (1975 film)
  cast: Karen Black, Ronee Blakley, Keith Carradine, Geraldine Chaplin, Henry Gibson, Lily Tomlin
  director: Robert Altman
  song: **6** I'm Easy
Nashville ___: **4** Cats **7** warbler
Nashville Cats (1966 song)
  artist: Lovin' Spoonful
Nashville-to-Chicago dir.: **3** NNW
nasolacrimal ___: **4** duct
NAS org.: **3** USN
Nassau: **4** city, port, town **7** capital
  locale: **7** Bahamas
Nasser: **4** lake **5** Gamal
  locale: **5** Egypt
  org.: **3** UAR
  successor: **5** Sadat
Nast: **5** Condé **6** Thomas
  symbol: **6** donkey **8** elephant
  target: **5** Tweed
Nastase, Ilie: **7** netster **9** tennis pro
  milieu: **5** court
Nastassja: **6** Kinski
nastiness: **5** spite, venom **6** enmity, malice, rancor **7** cruelty, ill will **8** acrimony, bad blood **9** animosity, hostility **10** resentment
Nast, Thomas: **10** cartoonist
nasturtium: **5** bloom, plant **6** flower **7** blossom
nasty: **3** bad, low **4** acid, cold, cool, evil, foul, icky, lewd, mean, rank, ugly, vile **5** awful, catty, cruel, dance, dirty, gross, harsh, lousy, rough, snide, surly, yucky **6** animal, bad guy, bitter, bratty, brutal, chilly, coarse, crabby, fierce, filthy, grubby, horrid, odious, ornery, putrid, rancid, remote, ribald, rotten, savage, severe, smutty, snappy, sneaky, sordid, sticky, unkind, vulgar, wanton, wicked **7** abusive, beastly, brutish, callous, cutting, glacial, hateful, heinous, hellish, hostile, hurtful, immoral, knavish, lowdown, noisome, noxious, obscene, painful, profane, raunchy, squalid, unclean, vicious **8** abrasive, annoying, barbaric, contrary, critical, diabolic, fiendish, horrible, immodest, improper, indecent, inhumane, inimical, liverish, pitiless, polluted, ruthless, sadistic, shameful, sinister, spiteful, stinking, unsavory, unseemly, vengeful **9** abhorrent, bellicose, cutthroat, dangerous, ferocious, inclement, loathsome, malicious, merciless, monstrous, obnoxious, offensive, poisonous, repellent, repugnant, repulsive, revolting, sarcastic, truculent, withdrawn **10** despicable, diabolical, disgusting, ill-humored, ill-natured, indecorous, indelicate, iniquitous, malevolent, malodorous, pugnacious, scurrilous, unfriendly, unpleasant, villainous, vindictive
  comment: **3** heh, mud **7** put-down
  habit: **4** vice
  look: **4** leer **5** sneer
  mood: **4** snit **5** pique
  one: **3** cur **4** ogre **5** meany **6** meanie

Nasty (1986 song)
artist: Janet Jackson
Nasty on the courts: 4 Ilie
nasus: 4 nose
part of a ~: 5 nares, naris
Nat: 4 Cole **5** Hiken **6** Holman, Turner **7** Currier, Hentoff **9** Fleischer
Nat __ Cole: 4 King
Natal: 4 city, town
locale: 6 Brazil
native: 4 Zulu
seaport: 6 Durban
Natalia: 8 Ginzburg, Makarova
see also Italian
Natalie: 4 Cole, Wood **6** Maines **7** Portman, Schafer **8** Merchant **9** Imbruglia
father: 3 Nat
in Russian: 7 Natasha
played her: 5 Maria
natality: 5 birth
natal starter: 3 neo
Natascha: 8 McElhone
Natasha: 6 Lyonne **10** Henstridge, Richardson
aunt: 4 Lynn
husband: 4 Liam
in English: 7 Natalie
mother: 7 Vanessa
partner: 5 Boris
see also Russian
Natasha __ Wagner: 7 Gregson
natatorium: 4 pool
natatory: 6 marine **7** aquatic, oceanic
natch
see of course
Natchez: 4 city, town
locale: 4 Miss.
Natchez __: 5 Trace
Nate: 4 Dogg **6** Parker **8** Thurmond **9** Archibald
Nathalie: 8 Sarraute
Nathan: 4 Hale, Lane **5** Juran **8** Alterman, Milstein **9** Söderblom
Nathanael: 4 West **5** saint
Nathaniel: 7 Currier **9** Hawthorne
nation: 4 land, race **5** realm, state, tribe, union **6** domain, empire, people, public **7** country, kingdom, society **8** dominion, monarchy, republic **9** democracy, territory
ender: 4 wide
nation-__: 5 state
Nation: 5 Carry
__ Nation: 5 Alien **6** Rhythm
national: 6 ethnic, public, racial **7** citizen, federal **8** domestic, interior, internal, societal **10** interstate
song: 6 anthem
spirit: 5 ethos
starter: 5 inter, multi
symbol: 4 flag **8** standard
national __: 4 bank, debt, park **6** forest **7** holiday
National
alternative: *see* car rental
National __: 5 Guard **6** League, Velvet
National __ Award: 4 Book
National __ Foundation: 7 Science
National __ of Sciences: 7 Academy
National __ of Standards: 6 Bureau
National __ Radio: 6 Public
National __ Relations Act: 5 Labor
National __ Scholarship: 5 Merit
National __ Service: 4 Park **7** Weather
National Assembly
locale: 6 France
National Do __ Call Registry: 3 Not
National Enquirer
rival: 4 Star
National Forest: 4 Gila, Inyo, Pike **5** Boise, Delta, Dixie, Huron, Modoc, Ocala, Ozark, Routt, Tahoe, Teton, Tonto, Twain, Uinta, Wayne **6** Apache, Ashley, Carson, Cibola, Custer, De Soto, Helena, Kaibab, Lassen, Marion, Ochoco, Oconee, Oglala, Ottawa, Pawnee, Pisgah, Plumas, Sabine, Salmon, Shasta, Sierra, Sumter, Umpqua, Winema **7** Angeles, Arapaho, Bighorn, Bridger, Caribou, Challis, Chugach, Conecuh, Fremont, Hoosier, Houston, Klamath, Lincoln, Malheur, Nicolet, Olympic, Osceola, Payette, Pinchot, San Juan, Santa Fe, Sequoia, Shawnee, Siuslaw, Targhee, Tongass, Trinity, Wasatch **8** Angelina, Bankhead, Cherokee, Chippewa, Coconino, Colville, Croatoan, Crockett, Eldorado, Fishlake, Flathead, Gallatin, Hiawatha, Humboldt, Kootenai, Manistee, Nez Perce, Okanogan, Ouachita, Prescott, Sawtooth, Shoshone, Superior, Tombigee, Tuskegee, Uwharrie **9** Allegheny, Bienville, Deschutes, Kisatchie, Roosevelt, Talladega, Wenatchee
National Gallery __: 5 of Art
National Geographic insert: 3 map
__ National Guard: 3 Air
National Guard building: 6 armory
nationalism: 8 jingoism **10** chauvinism, flag-waving, patriotism
nationalist: 5 jingo **7** patriot **8** jingoist **9** flag-waver
org.: 3 IRA
Nationalist __: 5 China
nationality: 4 race **6** origin, people **7** country, society
indicator: 6 ensign
suffix: 3 -ese, -ish
__ nationality: 4 dual
National Labor Relations __: 3 Act
National Lampoon's Animal House (1978 film)
attire: toga
cast: Kevin Bacon, John Belushi, Stephen Furst, Tom Hulce, Tim Matheson, Peter Riegert, Donald Sutherland, John Vernon
college: 5 Faber
director: John Landis
role: 4 D-Day, Doug, Greg, Katy **5** Bluto, Mandy, Otter, Pinto **6** Wormer **8** Flounder
National Lampoon's Christmas Vacation (1989 film)
cast: Chevy Chase, Beverly D'Angelo, Randy Quaid
National Lampoon's Vacation (1983 film)
cast: Chevy Chase, Beverly D'Angelo, Anthony Michael Hall
director: Harold Ramis
National League
city: 3 Atl., Chi., NYC, St. L. **4** Milw. **5** Miami, Phila. **6** Denver **7** Atlanta, Chicago, Houston, New York, Phoenix, St. Louis **8** San Diego **9** Milwaukee **10** Cincinnati, Los Angeles, Pittsburgh, Washington **12** Philadelphia, San Francisco
division: 4 East, West
former stadium: 4 Shea
player: 3 Cub, Met, Nat, Red **4** Card **5** Astro, Brave, Giant, NY Met, Padre, Rocky **6** Brewer, Dodger, Marlin, Pirate **7** Phillie **8** Cardinal, National **11** Diamondback
National Park: 4 Zion **5** Banff **6** Acadia, Arches, Denali, Katmai **7** Big Bend, Glacier, Olympic, Redwood, Saguaro, Sequoia **8** Badlands, Biscayne, Wind Cave, Yosemite **9** Haleakala, Lake Clark, Mesa Verde, Voyageurs **10** Crater Lake, Everglades, Glacier Bay, Grand Teton, Great Basin, Hot Springs, Isle Royale, Joshua Tree **11** Yellowstone
__ national product: 3 net **5** gross
National Public __: 5 Radio
Nationalrat
locale: 7 Austria
National Security __: 6 Agency **7** Council
National Treasure (2004 film)
cast: Nicolas Cage, Diane Kruger, Christopher Plummer, Jon Voight
National Velvet (1944 film)
cast: Angela Lansbury, Mickey Rooney, Elizabeth Taylor
highlight: race
National Weather Service agency: 4 NOAA
Nation, Carry: 3 dry
like ~: 5 sober
weapon: 3 axe
__ nation indivisible...: 3 one
__ Nations: 3 Six **4** Five **6** United
nations, allied: 4 bloc
__ Nations Day: 6 United
Nationwide
competitor: *see* insurance company
native: 4 real, wild **5** liver, local, voter **6** ethnic, inborn, inbred, innate, vulgar **7** ancient, built-in, citizen, denizen, endemic, natural, radical, resider **8** domestic, indigene, inherent, original, primeval, regional, resident **9** aborigine, belonging, endemical, homegrown, indweller, inherited, intrinsic, primaeval, primitive **10** aboriginal, autochthon, indigenous, inhabitant, unacquired
(suffix): 3 ese, ite, ote
native __: 3 son
native-__: 4 born
Native __: 3 Son
Native American: 3 Fox, Han, Kaw, Oto, Sac, Ute **4** Cree, Crow, Cuna, Erie, Eyak, Hopi, Inca, Iowa, Maya, Otoe, Pima, Pomo, Sauk, Seri, Tama, Taos, Tewa, Tiwa, Tupi, Yana, Yuma, Zuni **5** Ahtna, Asian, brave, Brulé, Caddo, Carib, Creek, Haida, Huron, Kansa, Kaska, Kiowa, Lenca, Lipan, Maidu, Makah, Miami, Miwok, Modoc, Omaha, Osage, Otomi, Piute, Ponca, Sioux, Taino, Teton, Unami, Washo, Wintu, Yaqui **6** Abnaki, Ahtena, Apache, Arawak, Aymara, Cayuga, Cayuse, Dakota, Feller, Galibi, Indian, Jivaro, Kechua, Laguna, Lakota, Lengua, Lumbee, Mandan, Micmac, Mohave, Mohawk, Mojave, Munsee, Navaho, Navajo, Nootka, Oglala, Ojibwa, Oneida, Ottawa, Paiute, Papago, Patwin, Pawnee, Pequot, Plains, Pueblo, Quapaw, Salish, Santee, Seneca, Tanana, Toltec, Wintun, Yahgan, Yakima, Yokuts **7** Abenaki, Arapaho, Arikara, Atakapa, Bannock, Chibcha, Chilcat, Chilkat, Chinook, Choctaw, Chumash, Guarani, Huastec, Kechuan, Klamath, Koyukon, Kutchin, Kutenai, Lakhota, Mahican, Mazatec, Miskito, Mohegan, Mohican, Naskapi, Nipmuck, Ojibway, Quechua, Quichua, San Blas, Shawnee, Takelma, Tanaina, Tlingit, Washita, Wichita, Wyandot, Yankton, Yavapai, Yucatec, Zapotec **8** Arapahoe, Cahuilla, Caingang, Cherokee, Cheyenne, Chippewa, Comanche, Delaware, Hunkpapa, Illinois, Iroquois, Kickapoo, Kwakiutl, Malecite, Maricopa, Mikasuki, Missouri, Muskogee, Nez Percé, Onondaga, Ouachita, Puyallup, Quechuan, Sahaptin, Seminole, Squamish, Tarascan, Wabanaki, Wahpeton **9** Blackfoot, Chickasaw, Havasupai, Jicarilla, Karankawa, Menominee, Mescalero, Nanticoke, Penobscot, Saulteaux, Suquamish, Tehuelche, Tiger Lily, Tsimshian, Tuscarora, Wahpekute, Wampanoag, Winnebago, Wyandotte **10** Adirondack, Araucanian, Assiniboin, Athabaskan, Bellabella, Bellacoola, Chiricahua, Miniconjou, Potawatomi, Tarahumara
corn: 5 maize
group: 5 tribe
see also Indian
natives: 10 population
Native Son: 5 novel
author: Richard Wright
character: 6 Bigger, Thomas
nativity: 5 birth **6** origin
figures: 4 Magi
scene: 6 crèche
Nat King __: 4 Cole
natl.: 3 fed. **9** govt.-owned
NATO: 4 pact **8** alliance
cousin: 3 OAS
former ~ commander: 3 DDE **4** Haig
member: 3 Can., Eng., Ger., Lux., Mex., Nor., USA **4** Belg., Holl., Icel., Neth., Norw., Port. **5** Italy, Spain **6** Canada, France, Greece, Latvia, Norway, Poland, Turkey **7** Albania, Belgium, Croatia, Denmark, Estonia, Germany, Hungary, Iceland, Romania **8** Bulgaria, Portugal,

Slovakia, Slovenia **9** Lithuania **10** Luxembourg
part: 3 Atl., Org. **5** North **6** Treaty **8** Atlantic
Natta, Giulio: 7 chemist **8** Nobelist
natter: 3 gab, yak **4** chat **7** chatter, grumble
nattering nabobs coiner: 5 Agnew
natterjack: 4 toad **9** amphibian
nattiness: 4 chic **5** style, swank, vogue
natty: 4 chic, neat **5** dandy, sharp, sleek, smart, swank **6** dapper, dressy, jaunty, rakish, snazzy, spiffy, sporty, spruce, swanky **7** duded up, groomed, stylish, voguish **9** decked out, gussied up
Natty's dog: 6 Hector
natural: 3 raw, tan **4** Afro, easy, homy, naif, open, pure, real, true, wild **5** crude, frank, homey, naive, plain, typic, usual **6** candid, direct, earthy, folksy, inborn, innate, native, normal, simple **7** artless, genuine, logical, organic, outdoor, radical, regular, sincere, typical, up-front **8** everyday, familiar, habitual, inherent, laid-back, ordinary, physical, unartful, unforced **9** childlike, customary, guileless, hairstyle, ingenuous, intrinsic, intuitive, primitive, realistic, unfeigned, universal, unlabored, unrefined, unstudied **10** forthright, indigenous, legitimate, reasonable, unacquired, unaffected, unbleached
ability: 4 gift **5** flair, knack **6** genius **8** instinct **9** endowment
casino ~: 5 seven **6** eleven
combining form: 7 physico-
fiber: 4 jute, wool
history museum display: 4 T-rex
mimic: 4 mina, myna **5** minah, mynah
resource: 3 gas, oil, ore **5** water
toxin: 5 venin **6** venene, venine
undergo ~ selection: 6 evolve
world: 8 creation, universe
natural __: 3 gas, law **7** history, science
natural-__: 4 born
Natural __: 4 High **5** Woman
Natural __, A: 3 Man **5** Woman
Natural Blonde
author: Liz Smith
natural food additive: 4 herb
natural gas
constituent: 6 ethane **8** dimethyl
Natural High (1973 song)
artist: Bloodstone
natural historian: 3 Ray **4** Baer **6** Buffon, Cuvier, Darwin, Gesner **7** Agassiz, Lamarck, Wallace
British ~: 3 Ray **6** Darwin **7** Wallace
French ~: 6 Buffon, Cuvier **7** Lamarck
German ~: 4 Baer
Swiss ~: 6 Gesner
natural history: 7 science
study: 6 nature **9** organisms
Natural History
author: Pliny
naturalist study: 5 flora
naturally: 6 easily, freely, openly, simply **7** by birth, readily **8** by nature, candidly, casually, commonly, normally **9** artlessly, be my guest, genuinely, precisely, typically **10** habitually, informally, innocently, ordinarily
exist ~: 6 inhere
see also of course
__ Naturally: 3 Act
Natural Man, A (1971 song)
artist: Lou Rawls
naturalness: 4 ease **7** naiveté
Natural, The: 4 film **5** novel
author: Bernard Malamud
cast: Kim Basinger, Glenn Close, Robert Duvall, Robert Redford
director: Barry Levinson
role: Roy Hobbs
Natural Woman, A (1967 song)
artist: Aretha Franklin
nature: 3 ilk, way **4** cast, kind, mold, mood, self, sort, type, vein **5** being, color, earth, fiber, heart, humor, order, state, style, world **6** aspect, cosmos, entity, forest, makeup, stripe, temper, traits **7** essence, meaning, outlook, quality, scenery, species **8** creation, features, outdoors, seascape, universe **9** character, framework, landscape, macrocosm, structure **10** attributes, complexion
building block of ~: 4 atom
by ~: 5 per se **8** normally **10** inherently
combining form: 3 eco- **5** physi- **6** physio-
good ~: 6 gaiety, warmth **9** geniality, joviality, pleasance, sunniness **10** affability, amiability, cheeriness, cordiality, kindliness
imitator: 3 art
of the ~ of (suffix): 3 -ine
prefix: 3 eco-
preserve: 4 park **9** sanctuary
second ~: 5 habit
spirit of Africa: 4 ngai
walk: 4 hike **5** trail
nature __: 4 walk **5** study, trail
__ nature: 3 ill **4** good **5** human **6** second
Nature
author: Ralph Waldo Emerson
network: 3 PBS
Nature __: 3 Boy
nature concentrated: 3 art
__-natured: 3 ill **4** good
naturel, au: 3 raw **4** bare, nude **5** naked **9** in the buff, unattired
nature-loving: 6 rustic **7** outdoor
__ Nature of Things: 5 On the
...nature's copy's not __: 6 eterne
nature-walk snack: 7 berries
Natwick: 7 Mildred
Naugahyde: 6 fabric
coating: 5 vinyl
Naugatuck: 4 city, town
locale: 4 Conn.
naught: 3 nil, zip **4** nada, none, zero **5** squat, zilch **6** bubkes, bupkes, cipher **7** nothing **8** goose egg
bring to ~: 4 undo **5** annul **6** cancel, negate **7** abolish, destroy, nullify, reverse **8** abrogate, demolish **10** invalidate, neutralize
come to ~: 4 bomb, bust, fail, flop, sink **6** fizzle **7** founder **8** backfire, fall flat, flounder **10** run aground
for ~: 4 idle, vain **6** futile, otiose **7** inutile, useless **8** bootless, hopeless **9** fruitless, pointless, worthless **10** unavailing
naughtiness: 5 prank **7** knavery, roguery, trouble **8** deviltry, mischief **9** high jinks, rascality, vandalism **10** misconduct, wrongdoing
Naughton: 4 Greg **5** David, James, Keira **6** Amanda
naughts-and-crosses: 9 tic-tac-toe
nonwinner: 3 OOX, OXO, OXX, XOO, XOX, XXO
winner: 3 OOO, XXX
naughty: 3 bad **4** blue, lewd, racy **5** bawdy, dirty, loose, rough, rowdy, wrong **6** erotic, errant, feisty, impish, ornery, ribald, risqué, steamy, unruly, vulgar, wanton, wicked, wilful **7** defiant, knavish, obscene, playful, raunchy, teasing, wayward, willful **8** annoying, contrary, improper, off-color, perverse, rascally, stubborn **9** fractious **10** headstrong, indecorous, rebellious, refractory
one: 3 cad, cur, imp **4** brat **5** churl, knave, louse, rogue, scamp **6** rascal **7** bounder, stinker **8** blighter, picaroon, scalawag, spalpeen **9** miscreant, prankster, reprobate, scoundrel **10** blackguard, holy terror, ne'er-do-well
Naughty __ of Shady Lane, The: 4 Lady
Naughty by Nature
song: Feel Me Flow (1995)
Hip Hop Hooray (1993)
Jamboree (1999)
O.P.P. (1991)
Naughty Lady of Shady Lane, The (1954 song)
artist: Ames Brothers
Naughty, naughty!: 3 tsk, tut **6** tsk tsk, tut-tut
Nauru money: 4 cent **6** dollar
Nausea
author: Jean-Paul Sartre
__ Nautica: 5 Pyxis
nautical: 5 naval **6** marine **7** aquatic, deep-sea, oceanic, pelagic **8** maritime, sailorly, seagoing, yachting **9** seafaring, thalassic **10** oceangoing
adjective: 3 yar **4** yare
adverb: 3 aft **4** alee, alow **6** astern
AFB's ~ counterpart: 3 NAS
art: 5 navig. **10** navigation
assent: 3 aye
boom: 5 sprit
chain: 3 tye
CIA's ~ cousin: 3 ONI
diary: 3 log
direction: 3 aft, EbN, EbS, ENE, ESE, NbE, NbW, NNE, NNW, SbE, SbW, SSE, SSW, WbN, WbS, WNW, WSW **4** alee, fore **5** abeam, aport **6** astern
distance: 6 league
exclamation: 4 ahoy **5** avast, heave **7** heave ho
gear: 3 rig
greeting: 4 ahoy
group: 4 crew **5** hands **7** sailors
law enforcers: 4 USCG
line: 6 inhaul
measure: 2 kn., kt. **4** knot **6** fathom, league
nose: 4 prow
pole: 4 spar **5** sprit
quarters: 5 berth, cabin
rope: 3 tye **4** vang **6** cablet, earing, hawser
signal: 4 bell
starter: 4 aero **5** astro
see also naval, Navy
nautical __: 3 day **4** mile
nautilus: 5 shell **8** seashell
Nautilus
branch: 3 USN **4** Navy
captain: 4 Nemo
locale: 3 gym, spa
use a ~: 4 lift, tone **5** train **6** tone up **7** work out **8** exercise
user's muscle: 2 ab **3** pec **4** delt, quad **9** hamstring
Navajo: 5 tribe **6** Indian **7** Amerind **8** language
hello: 6 yateeh
kin: 6 Apache
lodge: 5 hogan
silver: 6 concha
naval: 6 marine **7** aquatic, deep-sea, oceanic, pelagic **8** maritime, nautical, sailorly, seagoing, yachting **9** seafaring, thalassic **10** oceangoing
alert: 3 SOS
arena: 3 sea **5** ocean
barrage: 5 salvo **6** volley **7** barrage **9** broadside, cannonade, fusillade
cadet: 3 mid **5** middy **6** middie
call: 4 ahoy **5** avast
force: 5 fleet **6** argosy, armada **8** flotilla
German WWII ~ base: 5 Emden
guide: 6 beacon **10** lighthouse, watchtower
inits.: 3 HMS, USN, USS
officer: 6 gunner
on ~ maneuvers: 4 asea **5** at sea
rank: 2 lt. **3** cdr., com., CPO, ens., yeo. **4** cmdr., lt. jg., RAdm., VAdm. **5** lieut. **6** ensign, yeoman **7** admiral, captain **9** commander
response: 3 aye **6** aye aye **9** aye aye sir
second-in-command: 4 exec
tracking system: 5 loran
US ~ base, familiarly: 5 Gitmo
vessel: 4 boat **6** PT boat **10** battleship
see also nautical, Navy
naval __: 5 brass **7** academy
Naval Academy
freshman: 4 pleb **5** plebe
mascot: 4 goat
Navarre
see Spanish
Navarro: 4 Dave, Fats
nave: 3 hub
bisector: 5 aisle
neighbor: 4 apse
seat: 3 pew
navel: 5 innie, outie **8** omphalos **9** umbilicus **11** belly button
combining form: 6 omphal- **7** omphalo-
ender: 4 wort
filler: 4 lint

___ **Navidad!: 5** Feliz
navigable: 4 open **5** clear **8** passable **9** unblocked
navigate: 4 plot, sail **5** cross, guide, pilot, steer **6** aviate, cruise, direct, jockey, paddle, voyage **7** captain, journey, operate, ride out **8** maneuver
on snow: 3 ski **4** skee
tricky to ~: 5 reefy
navigation: 6 flying, travel **7** boating, sailing **8** cruising, piloting, shipping, steering, voyaging, yachting **9** seafaring, traveling
aid: 3 map, oar **5** chart, racon
device: 4 gyro **5** loran, radar, sonar
hazard: 3 fog **4** berb, reef **5** shoal
navigational: 5 naval **8** maritime, nautical
navigator: 5 flyer, pilot **7** mariner **8** helmsman, traveler
concern: 5 route **6** course **7** heading
heading: 3 EbS, ENE, ESE, NbE, NbW, NNE, NNW, SbE, SbW, SSE, SSW, WbN, WbS, WNW, WSW **9** SbE EbN EbN
Navigator: 3 SUV **4** Linc **7** Lincoln
Navigator Islands: 5 Samoa
Navratilova, Martina: 5 Czech **7** netster **9** tennis pro
milieu: 5 court
rival: 4 Graf **5** Evert
navy: 4 bean, blue **5** color, fleet **6** armada **8** dark blue, flotilla, military
relative: ***see*** blue color
navy ___: 4 bean, blue, yard
Navy: 4 USNA
athletes: 10 Midshipmen
CIA: 3 ONI
diver: 4 Seal
join the ~: 6 enlist, sign on
lawyer TV show: 3 JAG
locale: 8 Maryland **9** Annapolis
man: 3 gob
policemen: 2 SP
position: 4 rank
rank: 2 lt. **3** cdr., com., CPO, ens., yeo. **4** cmdr., lt. jg., RAdm., VAdm. **5** lieut., lt. com. **6** ensign, yeoman **7** admiral, captain **9** commander
reply: 3 aye **5** no sir **6** aye aye
rival: 4 Army
signal pennant: 6 cornet
stay in the ~: 4 reup
VIP: 3 Adm., CNO **4** RAdm., VAdm.
see also nautical, naval
Navy ___: 4 Blue **5** Blues, Cross, Seals
___ **Navy: 3** Old **5** In the **7** McHale's
navy bean: 6 legume
Navy Cross: 5 medal
___**-navy store: 4** army
naw: 2 no **3** nah, nay, nix, non **4** nein, nope, nyet, uh-uh **5** I won't, ixnay, never, no how, no way, nuh-uh **6** no deal, noways, nowise **7** I refuse **8** forget it, I will not, negative, negatory **9** by no means, fat chance, I think not **10** count me out, not a chance, thumbs down
nawab: 3 VIP **4** czar, king **5** baron, chief, mogul, ruler **6** bigwig, fat cat, leader, tycoon **7** big shot, magnate **8** big wheel, somebody **9** big cheese, dignitary, moneybags, plutocrat **10** man of means
Naxos: 4 isle **6** island
locale: 6 Greece
nay: 2 no **3** nah, naw, nix, non **4** nein, nope, nyet, uh-uh, veto, vote **5** I won't, ixnay, never, no how, noway **6** indeed, no deal, noways, nowise **7** I refuse **8** forget it, I will not, negative, negatory, to be sure **9** by no means, fat chance, I think not **10** count me out, not a chance, thumbs down
ender: 3 say **4** said **5** sayer **6** saying
not ~: 2 ay **3** aye, yea
sayer: 4 anti
Naya: 5 water
alternative: 5 Evian **7** Perrier **8** Aquafina **9** Arrowhead
naysay: 6 negate, refute **7** confute, dispute **8** disagree, disprove **9** disaffirm, discredit **10** contradict, contravene
naysayer: 4 anti **5** cynic **6** censor, denier
perhaps: 5 voter
naysaying: 8 negative
Nazarenes: 4 sect
Nazarene, The
author: Sholem Asch
Nazareth: 4 band, city, town
locale: 6 Israel
mountain near ~: 5 Tabor
song: Love Hurts (1976)
Nazimova: 4 Alla
Nb: 4 elem. **7** element, niobium
41 for ~: 4 at. no.
N.B.: 4 prov.
part of ~: 4 bene, nota
see also New Brunswick
NBA: 6 cagers, league.
arena: 5 court **6** Garden
broadcaster: 4 ESPN
former ~ venue: 4 Omni
like most ~ players: 4 tall
locale: 3 Atl., Chi. **4** Milw., Utah **5** Miami, Phila. **6** Boston, Dallas, Denver **7** Atlanta, Chicago, Detroit, Houston, Memphis, New York, Oakland, Orlando, Phoenix, Seattle, Toronto **8** Portland **9** Cleveland, Milwaukee **10** Los Angeles, New Orleans, Sacramento, San Antonio, Washington **11** Minneapolis **12** Indianapolis, Philadelphia **14** Salt Lake locale
official: 3 ref **7** referee
part: 3 Nat. **4** Assn., Natl. **5** Assoc. **10** Basketball
period: 3 qtr. **7** quarter
position: 3 fwd. **5** guard **6** center **7** forward
score: 2 pt. **5** point **9** field goal, free throw
shot: 5 lay-up
statistic: 6 assist
team: 4 Heat, Jazz, Nets, Suns **5** Bucks, Bulls, Celts, Hawks, Kings, Magic, Spurs **6** Knicks, Lakers, Pacers, Sixers **7** Celtics, Hornets, Nuggets, Pistons, Raptors, Rockets, Thunder, Wizards **8** Clippers, Warriors **9** Cavaliers, Grizzlies, Mavericks **12** Timberwolves, Trail Blazers
tiebreaker: 2 OT
see also basketball
NBAer: 3 pro **5** cager
___ **'N Bake: 5** Shake
NBC: 7 network
former ~ owner: 3 RCA
HQ: 3 NYC
overseer: 3 FCC
part of ~: 3 Nat **4** Natl.
peacock: 4 logo
rival: 3 ABC, CBS, Fox, PBS **5** The CW
show: 3 SNL **5** Today
___ **'n Boots: 4** Puss
N.C.
city: 3 Ral.
neighbor: 4 S. Car., Tenn.
water off ~: 3 Atl.
zone: 3 EDT, EST
see also North Carolina
NC-17: 6 rating
issuer: 4 MPAA
NCAA
division: 3 ACC
part of ~: 4 assn.
regional: 4 East, West
rival: 3 NIT
tiebreaker: 2 OT
NCIS (CBS drama)
cast: Rocky Carroll (Leon Vance)
Cote de Pablo (Ziva David)
Mark Harmon (Leroy Gibbs)
David McCallum (Donald 'Ducky' Mallard)
Sean Murray (Timothy McGee)
Pauley Perrette (Abby Sciuto)
Michael Weatherly (Anthony DiNozzo)
NCO: 2 DI, G.I. **3** cpl., CPO, SFC, sgt. **4** MSgt., serg., SSgt., TSgt. **5** sarge **6** noncom, sgt. maj. **8** corporal
part of ~: 3 com., non, off.
store: 2 PX
subordinate: 3 PFC
superior: 2 lt.
NCR
product: 3 ATM **4** till
Nd: 4 elem. **7** element **9** neodymium
60 for ~: 4 at. no.
ND
neighbor: 3 Man. **4** Minn.
see also North Dakota
Ndegeocello: 7 Meshell
___ **'n dip: 4** chip
N'Djamena: 4 city, town **7** capital
locale: 4 Chad
Ndola: 4 city, town
locale: 6 Zambia
___ **'n Dri: 4** Wash
NDU conference: 7 Big East
Ne: 4 elem., neon **7** element
10 for ~: 4 at. no.
NE: 3 dir.
see also Nebraska
NEA: 5 union
be eligible for the ~: 5 teach
beneficiary: 3 PBS
chapter: 3 lcl. **5** local
concern: 7 three R's
member: 4 tchr. **7** teacher
part of ~: 3 Nat. **4** Arts, Assn., Educ., Natl. **8** National **9** Endowment
rival: 3 AFT, UFT
Neagle: 4 Anna
Neal: 5 Conan, Curly, Elise, Hefti, McCoy **6** Gabler **7** Jiminez **8** Patricia
Neale: 6 Fraser, Greasy
Neale, Greasy: 5 coach
sport: 8 football
___ **Neale Hurston: 4** Zora
Neal, Patricia: 7 actress
film: Breakfast at Tiffany's (1961)
The Day the Earth Stood Still (1951)
Hud (1963, AA)
The Subject Was Roses (1968)
spouse: Roald Dahl
Neame: 6 Ronald
Neanderthal: 3 man **7** caveman
neap: 4 tide
neaped: 8 grounded
Neapolitan: 5 pizza **7** Italian **8** ice cream
alternative: ***see*** ice cream flavor
flavor: 7 vanilla **9** chocolate **10** strawberry
near: 4 akin, dear, loom, nigh **5** aside, cheap, close, handy, quasi, ready, tight **6** almost, around, at hand, beside, hard by, impend, stingy **7** abreast, advance, close by, close to, handy to, looming, up close, verge on **8** abutting, adjacent, approach, imminent, intimate, next door, proximal, relative, touching **9** adjoining, affecting, alongside, belly up to, bordering, close in on, hereabout, immediate, impending, in the area, in the wind, penurious, proximate, sneak up on **10** accessible, adjacent to, contiguous, convenient, converge on, get close to, in the cards, juxtaposed, near-at-hand, side-by-side, skinflinty, ungenerous
combining form: 4 peri-, pros- **5** juxta-, plesi- **6** plesio-
ender: 7 sighted
in German: 4 nahe
prefix: 3 epi- **4** para-
suffix: 3 -ish
near ___: 4 beer, miss **6** at hand
near-___: 4 term **5** point
Near: 5 Holly
Near ___: 3 You **4** East
near and ___: 3 far
nearby: 4 nigh **5** about, aside, close, handy, ready **6** around, at hand, at heel **7** locally, present **8** adjacent, imminent, next-door **9** adjoining, bordering, immediate, impending, proximate **10** contiguous, convenient, time-saving
objects ~: 5 these
place ~: 6 appose
resident: 8 neighbor
wait ~: 5 hover **6** linger, loiter, remain
Near East
see Mideast
nearer
get ~: 6 gain on
prefix: 3 cis-
Nearer, My ___, to Thee: 3 God
nearest: 4 next **6** direct **9** proximate
one: 4 this
Nearest the Pole
author: Robert Peary

nearing: **7** close to **8** imminent, oncoming, upcoming **9** impending, in the wind **10** in the cards
the hour: **5** ten of, ten to
Near Island: **4** Attu **6** Agattu **7** Semichi
nearly: **4** most, much, nigh **5** about, circa, round **6** all but, almost, toward **7** halfway, roughly, towards **8** as good as, in effect, narrowly, not quite **9** in essence, just about, upwards of, virtually **10** more or less
near miss: **6** escape **9** close call
exclamation: **4** whew
nearness: **8** presence, vicinity **9** adjacency, immediacy, proximity
Nearness __, The: **5** of You
nearsighted: **4** owly **6** myopic
one: **5** myope
__ near!, The: **5** end is
Near You was his theme: **5** Berle
__ 'n' Easy: **4** Nice
neat: **4** deft, pure, tidy, trim **5** clean, kempt, natty, smart, swept **6** adroit, dainty, dapper, deftly, pretty, shrewd, spruce **7** adeptly, finicky, groomed, handily, iceless, in place, legible, nattily, ordered, orderly, precise, shapely, slickly, smartly, stylish, unmixed **8** adroitly, clean-cut, cleverly, expertly, graceful, methodic, skillful, spotless, straight, well-kept **9** admirable, dexterous, effective, efficient, organized, practiced, shipshape, spruced up, unblended, wonderful **10** fastidious, immaculate, methodical, nicely done, remarkable, skillfully, straight up, systematic
ender: **3** nik **4** ness
in England: **4** trig
make ~: **4** tidy **5** clean, fix up, order **6** spruce, tidy up **7** freshen, shape up **8** organize, spruce up **9** smarten up **10** straighten
stiffly ~: **4** prim **7** stilted **8** starched
see also wonderful
neat __ pin: **3** as a
neaten: **4** tidy, trim, wash **5** brush, clean, fix up, groom, order **6** spruce, tidy up **7** clean up **8** spruce up **9** smarten up **10** straighten
neath: **5** below, under
opposite: **3** o'er
neatness: **4** trim **5** order **8** symmetry **10** legibility
neatnik bane: **4** dirt, dust, slob
neato: **3** rad **4** cool, keen, phat **5** marvy, nifty, super, swell **6** far out, groovy, peachy
neat's-__ oil: **4** foot
neb: **4** beak, bill **5** point **8** penpoint
nebbish: **4** drip, nerd, wimp **5** dweeb, patsy, twerp, twirp **7** languid, milksop **9** jellyfish, lethargic
Nebraska: **5** state
airport code: **3** OMA
capital: **7** Lincoln
city: **4** Elko **5** Omaha, Wahoo **7** Fremont, Kearney, Lincoln, Norfolk **8** Bellevue, Columbus, Hastings
conference: **9** Big Twelve
county: **4** Otoe **5** Sioux **6** Pawnee, Platte
Indian: **5** Omaha, Ponca **9** Winnebago **10** Miniconjou
institution: **8** Boys Town
like ~: **6** inland
mil. group headquartered in ~: **3** SAC
neighbor: **3** Kan., Wyo. **4** Colo., Iowa, Kans., S. Dak. **6** Kansas **7** Wyoming **8** Colorado, Missouri
river: **4** Loup **6** Platte
school: **9** Creighton
state beverage: **4** milk
state bird: **10** meadowlark
state fish: **7** catfish
state flower: **9** goldenrod
state fossil: **7** mammoth
state insect: **8** honeybee
state river: **6** Platte
state rock: **5** agate
state soft drink: **7** Kool-Aid
state tree: **10** cottonwood
student: **6** Husker **10** Cornhusker
__-Nebraska Act: **6** Kansas
__ Nebula: **4** Crab, Ring **5** Orion
nebulous: **3** dim **4** dark, hazy **5** foggy, mirky, misty, murky, vague **6** arcane, cloudy **7** cryptic, obscure, shadowy, tenuous, unclear **8** abstruse, confused, puzzling, unformed **9** ambiguous, amorphous, confusing, cryptical, enigmatic, imprecise, shapeless, uncertain **10** indefinite, indistinct, perplexing, unspecific
NEC: **2** TV **5** TV set **10** television
alternative: ***see*** electronics company
necessaries: **4** food **6** viands **7** aliment, rations **8** victuals **9** nutriment, provender **10** provisions, sustenance
necessarily: **8** perforce
necessary: **3** req. **4** must, reqd. **5** basic, fated, major, vital **6** needed, staple, urgent **7** binding, crucial, logical, needful, pivotal, primary **8** decisive, integral, pressing, required **9** de rigueur, essential, expedient, important, mandatory, paramount, requisite, specified, strategic **10** compelling, compulsory, imperative, inevitable, inexorable, obligatory, undeniable, underlying
amount: **5** quota **7** minimum
find ~: **4** need **6** have to
part: **3** cog
necessitate: **3** ask **4** make, need, take **5** force, impel **6** compel, demand, entail, oblige **7** behoove, call for, involve, require **9** constrain
__ necessities: **4** bare
necessitude: **4** need **7** urgency **8** exigency **9** privation
necessity: **4** call, lack, must, need **5** cause, pinch **6** demand, duress **7** essence, poverty, urgency **8** exigence, exigency, pressure **9** condition, emergency, essential, requisite, vital part **10** compulsion, constraint, imperative, obligation, sine qua non
neck: **4** kiss, nape **5** scrag, spoon **6** giblet, scruff, smooch, strait, throat **7** channel, isthmus, narrows, snuggle **8** osculate, pitch woo **10** bill and coo
and neck: **4** even, tied **5** close, tight **10** nose to nose
annoyance: **4** kink, pain **5** crick, spasm **6** twinge **9** stiffness
back of the ~: **4** nape **5** nucha, nuque
break one's ~: **4** toil **5** slave, sweat **6** hustle, strain, strive **8** bear down, struggle
combining form: **3** der- **4** dero- **7** trachei- **8** tracheio-
cover: **3** boa **5** dicky, scarf **6** collar, dickey, dickie **7** muffler
crew ~: **7** sweater
ender: **3** tie **4** band, lace, line, wear **5** piece
feather: **6** hackle, heckle **7** hatchel
feature: **6** dewlap **10** Adam's apple
front of the ~: **4** gula
hair: **7** hackles
jewelry: **5** chain **6** choker, pearls, shells
of land: **4** isth. **7** isthmus
of the ~: **5** napal
of the woods: **4** area **6** locale, region, sphere **7** quarter **8** locality, location, purlieus, vicinity **9** territory
pain in the ~: **4** ache, kink, pest, pill **5** crick, trial **6** bother, hassle, noodge, nudnik, odious **8** headache, irritant **9** annoyance
save one's ~: **4** free, save **5** spare **6** let off, pardon, rescue **7** bail out, manumit, release, set free, unchain **8** liberate **9** extricate, unshackle
starter: **3** wry **4** long **5** break, crook, goose, rough **6** bottle, little, rubber, turtle **7** leather
stick one's ~ out: **4** gawk, risk **5** crane **6** gamble **7** venture **9** speculate
neck __ woods: **5** of the
__ neck: **4** crew
__-neck: **3** ewe
Neckar: **5** river
city on the ~: **9** Stuttgart **10** Heidelberg
__-necked: **3** low **4** bull, high, ring **5** stiff
neckerchief: **5** scarf **8** bandanna
necklace: **5** beads **6** choker, string **7** jewelry **8** ornament
flowery ~: **3** lei
Hawaiian ~ shell: **4** puka
make a ~: **4** link
part: **4** bead **5** charm, clasp **6** amulet, locket
place for a ~ clasp: **4** nape
Necklace, The
author: Guy de Maupassant
neckline shape: **3** vee
neckpiece: **3** boa, lei **5** scarf
neckwear: **3** boa, lei, tie **4** bola, bolo **5** ascot **6** bowtie, clip-on, cravat, dogtag **7** bandana, bola tie, bolo tie, foulard, paisley **8** bandanna, kerchief **10** four-in-hand
like some ~: **4** loud **6** clip-on
necromancer: **4** mage **5** magus, witch **6** wizard **7** warlock **8** conjurer, magician, sorcerer
necromancy: **5** magic **7** conjury, sorcery **8** black art, wizardry **9** occultism **10** black magic, divination, witchcraft
nectar: **3** sap **5** drink, fluid, juice **6** elixir, liquid **7** extract **8** beverage
amber ~: **4** beer, brew, suds **5** lager **7** brewski
collector: **3** bee **4** hive
ender: **3** ine
finally: **5** honey
Hindu ~: **6** amrita **7** amreeta
source: **4** pear **5** apple, bloom, peach **6** flower **7** blossom
nectared: **5** sweet **7** honeyed
Nectar in a Sieve
author: Kamala Markandaya
nectarine: **4** tree **5** fruit
relative: **5** peach
__ Nectaris: **4** Mare
nectarous: **5** sapid, sweet, tasty, yummy **6** divine, savory **8** heavenly, luscious **9** ambrosial, delicious, flavorful, palatable, succulent, toothsome **10** appetizing, delectable, delightful
Ned: **4** Land **5** Rorem, Uncle **6** Beatty, Miller, Romero, Sparks **8** Buntline, Flanders **10** Washington
Ned and Stacey (Fox sitcom)
cast: Thomas Haden Church (Ned Dorsey)
Debra Messing (Stacey Colbert)
neddy: **5** horse **6** donkey **7** jackass
Ned's __ Dustbin: **6** Atomic
née: **4** born **8** formerly **10** christened, heretofore, previously
need: **3** use, yen **4** call, duty, food, itch, lack, lust, miss, must, take, want **5** covet, crave, ought **6** dearth, demand, desire, devoir, hanker, hunger, misery, penury, thirst **7** absence, beggary, call for, craving, hope for, hurt for, long for, longing, paucity, pine for, poverty, require, urgency, wish for **8** distress, exigence, exigency, go hungry, must have, occasion, poorness, shortage, sparsity, weakness, yearn for **9** appetence, be without, cry out for, do without, emergency, emptiness, essential, extremity, indigence, necessity, privation, requisite, shortfall **10** compulsion, deficiency, difficulty, have use for, inadequacy, obligation
needed: **5** major, vital **7** crucial, lacking, pivotal, primary **8** required **9** essential, important, mandatory, necessary
as ~ on prescriptions: **3** p.r.n.
something ~: **4** lack **9** necessity
__ needed: **6** sorely
__ Needed Me: **3** You
needful: **8** required **9** essential, mandatory, necessary, requisite
needfulness: **8** exigency **9** necessity
Needful Things
author: Stephen King
Needham: **3** Hal **4** city, town
locale: **4** Mass.
neediness: **4** want **6** penury **7** beggary
needing: **3** shy **4** sans **5** low on, minus, short **7** lacking, missing, without **8** bereft of **10** deprived of

N
E

immediate attention: **4** dire **5** acute **7** crucial, exigent, serious **8** critical, pressing **9** desperate, important **10** compelling, imperative
__ Need Is a Miracle: **4** All I
__ Need Is the Girl: **4** All I
needle: **3** bug, egg, irk, nag, rib, vex **4** bait, barb, goad, hypo, leaf, mock, prod, razz, ride, rile, spur, twit **5** annoy, peeve, pique, prick, spite, sting, taunt, tease, worry **6** badger, bother, darner, harass, heckle, hector, nettle, noodge, pester, pick on, plague, ruffle, stylus **7** bedevil, disturb, henpeck, perturb, pointer, provoke, syringe, unnerve **8** distress, irritate, pinnacle, question, ridicule, splinter **9** aggravate, injection, instigate, poke fun at
bug: **4** nepa
case: **4** etui **5** etwee
combining form: **3** acu-
ender: **4** fish, work **5** craft, point
feature: **3** eye **4** hole **5** point
locale: **6** groove
phonograph: **6** stylus
ply a ~: **3** sew **4** darn **5** baste **6** stitch **9** embroider
point: **3** ENE, ESE, NNE, NNW, SSE, SSW, WNW, WSW **4** east, west **5** north, south
producer: **4** pine
whelk: **5** shell **8** seashell
worker: **6** tailor **8** clothier **9** couturier **10** dressmaker
__ needle: **4** pine **6** sewing **7** crochet, darning
needle and __: **6** thread
needlefish: **3** gar **7** garpike
needlelike: **4** thin **5** sharp **7** acerose, pointed
needlepoint: **5** craft
need: **4** mesh **6** thread
needler: **3** nag **5** scold, shrew **6** kvetch, virago **8** fishwife **9** termagant
Needles and Pins (1964 song)
artist: Searchers
needles
on pins and ~: **4** edgy **5** antsy, itchy, jumpy, tense **6** sweaty, uneasy **7** anxious, jittery, keyed up, nervous, restive, uptight, worried **8** agitated, restless, skittish, troubled **9** concerned, excitable, ill at ease **10** high-strung
needless: **5** extra, minor, undue **6** wanton **7** trivial, useless **8** optional, overmuch, picayune, trifling, unwanted, wasteful **9** causeless, excessive, pointless, redundant, undesired **10** expendable, gratuitous, groundless, inordinate, undeserved, unrequired
to say: ***see*** of course **7** clearly **9** obviously
needlework: **6** crewel **10** embroidery
do ~: **3** sew **4** knit, purl **6** stitch
needs: **5** hasn't
like some ~: **5** unmet
__ need-to-know basis: **3** on a
needy: **4** flat, poor **5** broke, short, sorry **6** bad off, hard up, ill off, in want **7** pinched **8** badly off, bankrupt, beggarly, deprived, dirt poor, indigent, strapped **9** dead broke, dependant, dependent, destitute, insolvent, miserable, moneyless, on welfare, penniless, penurious **10** down and out, down at heel, pauperized, straitened
help for the ~: **7** charity
__ Need You: **5** I Don't, When I
Need You Tonight (1987 song)
artist: INXS
Neel, Alice: **6** artist **7** painter
Néel, Louis: **8** Nobelist **9** physicist
Neenah: **4** city, town
locale: **9** Wisconsin
ne'er-do-well: **3** bum, cad, cur **5** drone, idler, knave, loser, rogue, scamp **6** bad hat, loafer, rascal **7** goof-off, shirker, wastrel **8** derelict, fainéant, layabout, picaroon, scalawag, sluggard **9** do-nothing, goldbrick, no-account, reprobate, scallawag, scallywag, scoundrel **10** blackguard, malingerer, scapegrace
Neeson, Liam: **5** actor
film: Before and After (1996)
Darkman (1990)
The Dead Pool (1988)
The Good Mother (1988)
Gun Shy (2000)
Husbands and Wives (1992)
Kinsey (2004)
Leap of Faith (1992)
Les Misérables (1998)
Michael Collins (1996)
Nell (1994)
Rob Roy (1995)
Schindler's List (1993)
Seraphim Falls (2007)
Shining Through (1992)
Star Wars Episode 1 - The Phantom Menace (1999)
Suspect (1987)
Taken (2008)
spouse: Natasha Richardson
Neet
alternative: **4** Nair **5** razor
nefarious: **3** bad **4** base, evil, foul, rank, vile **5** gross **6** odious, rotten, wicked **7** corrupt, crooked, glaring, heinous, hellish, immoral, satanic, vicious **8** criminal, depraved, devilish, diabolic, dreadful, fiendish, flagrant, horrible, infamous, infernal, perverse, shameful, unlawful **9** atrocious, egregious, execrable, miscreant, monstrous, satanical, unhealthy **10** abominable, degenerate, detestable, diabolical, flagitious, iniquitous, outrageous, pernicious, villainous, virtueless
Nefertiti
god: **4** Aten, Aton
river: **4** Nile
to Tut: **4** aunt
Neff: **10** Hildegarde
Nefud: **6** desert
locale: **6** Arabia **7** Mideast
neg.: **3** chg.
maker: **3** SLR
not ~: **3** aff., pos.
see also negative
negate: **3** nix **4** deny, undo, veto, void **5** annul, belie, erase, quash, rebut **6** cancel, impugn, naysay, offset, oppose, refute, repeal, revoke **7** abolish, confute, dispute, gainsay, nullify, put down, redress, rescind, retract, reverse, vitiate **8** abrogate, disagree, disallow, disprove **9** cancel out, disaffirm, discredit, frustrate **10** annihilate, contradict, contravene, controvert, counteract, disconfirm, invalidate, neutralize, prove wrong
negation: **4** veto **6** denial **7** inverse, refusal, reverse **9** disavowal, rejection **10** antithesis, disclaimer, gainsaying, opposition
negative: **3** nah, naw, nay, nix, non, not **4** anti, nein, nope, nyet, uh-uh **5** balky, I won't, ixnay, minus, never, no how, no way, toxic **6** gloomy, malign, no deal, noways, nowise **7** adverse, baleful, baneful, cynical, denying, I refuse, redress, ruinous **8** contrary, damaging, downbeat, forget it, I will not, nugatory, opposing **9** by no means, dangerous, fat chance, impugning, injurious, I think not, jaundiced, naysaying, rejecting, resistive, unhealthy, unhopeful, unwilling **10** calamitous, count me out, disastrous, dissenting, gainsaying, not a chance, pejorative, photograph, thumbs down
contraction: **4** ain't, can't, don't, isn't, won't **5** aren't, didn't, shan't **6** mustn't **7** couldn't, wouldn't **8** shouldn't
emotion: **4** hate, rage **5** anger, odium, pique, scorn, spite, wrath **6** animus, enmity, malice, rancor **7** disgust, ill will, offense, outrage, umbrage **8** acrimony, loathing, vexation **9** animosity, antipathy, petulance, revulsion **10** abhorrence, repugnance
in French: **3** non
in German: **4** nein
in Scottish: **3** nae
make a positive from a ~: **5** print
nonstandard ~: **4** ain't **5** t'isn't
polite ~: **5** no sir
prefix: **3** dis-, non-
slangy ~: **3** nah, naw **4** nope **5** ixnay, no how, no way
suffix: **4** -less
toward: **6** down on **8** averse to **9** hostile to
vote: **2** no **3** nay
__ negative: **6** double
negatively charged atom: **5** anion
negatory: **3** nah, naw, nay, nix, non **4** nein, nope, nyet, uh-uh **5** I won't, ixnay, never, no how, no way **6** no deal, noways, nowise **7** I refuse **8** forget it, I will not **9** by no means, fat chance, I think not **10** count me out, not a chance, thumbs down
Negev: **6** desert
like the ~: **3** dry **4** arid **7** parched **8** rainless **9** waterless
locale: **6** Israel
neglect: **4** fail, miss, omit, shun, skip, snub **5** defer, delay, evade, lapse, leave, let go, scorn, shirk, slack, spurn **6** bypass, disuse, forget, ignore, laxity, pass by, rebuff, slight **7** default, disdain, dismiss, laxness, let pass, mistake, slacken, suspend, tune out **8** brush off, coolness, discount, laugh off, let slide, omission, overleap, overlook, pass over, postpone, shrug off **9** disregard, gloss over, looseness, oversight, pay no mind, slackness, unconcern **10** brush aside, disrespect, leave alone, negligence, remissness
sign of ~: **3** rot **4** dust **6** cobweb
state of ~: **5** limbo
neglected: **4** wild **5** rusty, seedy **6** shabby **7** run-down, unkempt **8** derelict, deserted, slipshod, untended **9** abandoned, unnoticed
as a garden: **5** weedy
be ~: **8** languish, stagnate, vegetate
neglectful: **3** lax **4** lazy **5** slack **6** otiose, remiss **8** careless, dallying, derelict, heedless, indolent, mindless, omissive, slothful, uncaring **9** apathetic, forgetful, negligent, shiftless, unheedful, unmindful **10** delinquent, incautious, regardless
negligee: **7** nightie **9** nightgown
like a ~: **4** lacy **10** diaphanous
negligence: **5** fault, lapse **6** laxity **8** laziness **9** disregard, injustice
in law: **6** laches
negligent: **3** lax **4** slow **5** hasty, loose, slack **6** otiose, remiss, sloppy **7** cursory, offhand, unaware **8** careless, dallying, derelict, heedless, indolent, mindless, off-guard, reckless, slapdash, slipshod, slothful, slovenly **9** apathetic, forgetful, imprudent, shiftless, unheedful, unmindful **10** behindhand, delinquent, incautious, neglectful, nonchalant, regardless, unthinking, unthorough
negligently: **5** laxly **7** hastily **8** absently, sloppily **10** carelessly
negligible: **4** mere, poor, slim, tiny **5** minor, petty, small, teeny **6** little, minute, remote, slight, teensy **7** outside, slender, trivial **8** exiguous, marginal, trifling
amount: **4** crop, drab, drib **7** smidgen
negotiable: **4** open **6** liquid **8** flexible
negotiant: **5** agent **6** broker **8** emissary **9** go-between, middleman
negotiate: **4** deal, swap, swop, talk **5** agree, clear, swing, vault **6** adjust, confer, debate, dicker, haggle, handle, jockey, manage, parley, settle, step in **7** achieve, arrange, bargain, consult, discuss, get over, get past, mediate, network, referee, work out **8** contract, cut a deal, engineer, maneuver, moderate, surmount, transact, traverse **9** arbitrate, get around, hammer out, intercede, intervene, make a deal, make peace **10** adjudicate, compromise, horse trade
unwilling to ~: **4** firm, iron **5** rigid **6** flinty, intent, steely **7** adamant, diehard **8** hardened, hard-line, hellbent, obdurate, resolute, stubborn **9** immovable, immutable, obstinate, steadfast **10** inflexible
negotiation: **6** debate, treaty **7** bargain, meeting **9** agreement,

diplomacy, mediation 10 bargaining, discussion
conclude a ~: 5 agree 6 settle
point of ~: 6 demand
stage: 4 snag 5 offer 10 settlement
negotiator: 3 rep 5 agent, fixer, judge 6 broker, umpire 8 delegate, diplomat, mediator 9 go-between, moderator 10 interceder
asset: 4 tact 8 delicacy 9 diplomacy
Negotiator, The (1998 film)
cast: Samuel L. Jackson, Kevin Spacey
Negri: 4 Pola
Negro: 4 peak 5 mount, river 8 mountain
locale: 5 Andes 6 Brazil 8 Colombia 9 Argentina
__ Negro: 3 Rio
negroni: 5 drink 8 beverage, cocktail
ingredient: 3 gin 7 bitters 8 vermouth
Negulesco: 4 Jean
negus: 5 drink 8 beverage
ingredient: 4 wine
Nehemiah: 7 Persoff
follower: 6 Esther
preceder: 4 Ezra
Neher, Erwin: 8 Nobelist
Nehi: 3 pop 4 soda 9 soft drink
alternative: *see* soft drink
drinker: 5 Radar
flavor: 5 grape, peach 6 cherry, orange
Nehru: 10 Jawaharlal
daughter: 6 Indira
see also India
neigh
cousin: 4 bray 6 whinny
homophone: 3 nay, née
sayer: 4 mare 5 filly, horse 6 equine
neighbor: 4 abut, join 5 march, touch, verge 6 adjoin, border, friend 7 connect 8 surround
__ neighbor and weigh: 4 as in
neighborhood: 3 vic. 4 area, slum, turf, ward, zone 5 block, local, place, range, tract 6 ghetto, locale, milieu, parish, region, street, suburb 7 quarter, section 8 confines, district, environs, locality, location, precinct, presence, purlieus, vicinity 9 community, territory
hangout: 5 stoop 8 malt shop
Hispanic ~: 6 barrio
in the ~: 4 near 5 close, local 6 around, nearby, nearly 7 close by, locally
in the ~ of: 4 near 5 about, anear 6 almost, around 7 close to
rundown ~: 4 slum 5 slurb
sign: 4 lost 7 lost dog 8 yard sale
upscale ~: 5 exurb
neighboring: 4 near, next, nigh 5 close 6 at hand, beside, nearby 8 adjacent, imminent 9 impending, proximate 10 convenient
neighborliness: 5 amity 6 comity 8 goodwill 10 cordiality, friendship
neighborly: 4 kind 5 civil, close 6 chummy, clubby, genial, kindly, polite, social 7 affable, amiable, cordial, helpful 8 amicable, friendly, gracious, intimate, obliging, outgoing, sociable 9 brotherly, convivial 10 benevolent, buddy-buddy, hospitable, solicitous
__ Neighbor Policy: 4 Good
Neighbors
author: Thomas Berger
Neighbors (1981 film)
cast: Dan Aykroyd, John Belushi, Cathy Moriarty
__ Neighbor Sam: 4 Good
neighbors
friends and ~: 4 kith
__ Neighbor's Wife: 3 Thy
Neil: 5 Simon, Vince, Young 6 Harris, Jordan, Sedaka 7 Diamond, Sheehan 8 Hamilton 9 Armstrong
Neil __ Harris: 7 Patrick
Neill: 3 Sam 4 Noel
Neill, Sam: 5 actor
film: Bicentennial Man (1999)
Country Life (1995)
A Cry in the Dark (1988)
Dead Calm (1989)
The Horse Whisperer (1998)
Jurassic Park (1993)
My Brilliant Career (1979)
The Piano (1993)
Restoration (1995)
Neilson: 5 James
Neiman: 5 Leroy
Neiman __: 6 Marcus
nein: 2 no 3 nah, naw, nay, nix, non 4 nope, nyet, uh-uh 5 I won't, ixnay, never, no how, noway 6 no deal, noways, nowise 7 I refuse 8 forget it, I will not, negative, negatory 9 by no means, fat chance, I think not 10 count me out, not a chance, thumbs down
in French: 3 non
in Latin: 3 non
in Russian: 4 nyet
in Scottish: 3 nae
opposite: 2 ja
Neisse: 5 river
locale: 6 Poland 7 Germany
__-Neisse Line: 4 Oder
neither __ nor fowl: 4 fish
neither __ nor there: 4 here
Neither __ of Us: 3 One
Neither One of Us (1973 song)
artist: Gladys Knight and the Pips
neither partner: 3 nor
Neither snow, __ rain,...: 3 nor
Nejd
locale: 6 Arabia
native: 5 Saudi
Nekrasov: 6 Viktor 7 Nikolay
Nel Blu Dipinto Di Blu (Volaré) (1958 song)
artist: Domenico Modugno
Nell: 4 Gwyn 5 Trent 6 Carter 8 Campbell
Nell (1994 film)
cast: Jodie Foster, Liam Neeson, Natasha Richardson
director: Michael Apted
__ Nell: 3 Our
Nellie: 3 Bly, Fox 4 Ross 5 Melba 7 Forbush
man: 5 Emile
nosy ~: 5 prier, pryer
Nellie __ Ross: 6 Tayloe
__ Nellie: 7 nervous
__, Nellie!: 4 Whoa
Nelligan, Kate: 7 actress
film: Eleni (1985)
Nellis: 3 AFB
Nelly: 5 Sachs
nice ~: 4 prig 5 prude 7 puritan 8 bluenose 10 goody-goody
nelson: 4 hold
__ nelson: 4 full, half 7 quarter
Nelson: 2 Ed 3 duo, Fox 4 Eddy, Gene, Judd, Kris 5 Barry, Byron, David, Ozzie, Ralph, Ricky, river, Sandy 6 Algren, Burton, Craig T., Riddle, Willie 7 Demille, Harriet, Horatio, Mandela 9 Doubleday
River locale: 6 Canada 8 Manitoba
song: After the Rain (1990)
Love and Affection (1990)
More Than Ever (1991)
Nelson, Byron: 6 golfer
Nelson, Craig T.: 5 actor
TV: Coach
Nelson, Harriet
spouse: Ozzie Nelson
Nelson, Judd: 5 actor
film: The Breakfast Club (1985)
St. Elmo's Fire (1985)
TV: Suddenly Susan
Nelson, Ozzie
spouse: Harriet Nelson
__ Nelson Reilly: 7 Charles
Nelson, Ricky
brother: 5 David
film: Rio Bravo (1959)
The Wackiest Ship in the Army (1960)
parent: 5 Ozzie 7 Harriet
song: Be-Bop Baby (1957)
Believe What You Say (1958)
Everlovin' (1961)
Fools Rush In (1963)
For You (1964)
Garden Party (1972)
Hello Mary Lou (1961)
I Got a Feeling (1958)
I'm Walking (1957)
It's Late (1959)
It's Up to You (1962)
Just a Little Too Much (1959)
Lonesome Town (1958)
Never Be Anyone Else But You (1959)
Poor Little Fool (1958)
Stood Up (1957)
String Along (1963)
Sweeter Than You (1959)
Teen Age Idol (1962)
A Teenager's Romance (1957)
Travelin' Man (1961)
A Wonder Like You (1961)
TV: The Adventures of Ozzie and Harriet
Nelson, Tony servant: 5 genie 7 Jeannie
Nelson, Willie
cause: 7 Farm Aid
film: Barbarosa (1982)
The Electric Horseman (1979)
Honeysuckle Rose (1980)
Thief (1981)
song: Always on My Mind (1982)
Blue Eyes Crying in the Rain (1975)
Good Hearted Woman (1976)
On the Road Again (1980)
To All the Girls I've Loved Before (1984)
Nels to Marta: 3 son
Nemean __: 4 lion 5 Games
Nemec: 5 Corin, Corky
Nemerov, Howard: 4 poet
work: Inside the Onion
nemesis: 3 foe 4 bane, ruin 5 enemy, rival 8 opponent 9 ill-wisher 10 infliction
Nemesis: 8 asteroid
lover: 4 Zeus
parent: 6 Erebus
play ~: 6 avenge
Nen: 4 Robb
nene: 4 bird, fowl 5 goose
home: 6 Hawaii
relative: 5 brant 7 graylag 9 snow goose
Neneh: 6 Cherry
Nennius: 5 Welsh 6 writer 9 historian
Nen, Robb
sport: 8 baseball
neo: 3 mod 8 newcomer 9 modernist 10 revivalist
neo-: 3 new 4 late
opposite: 5 paleo-
neoclassical: 5 style
architect: 4 Adam
neodymium: 7 element
Neolithic: 7 ancient
chisel: 4 celt
monument: 5 henge
neologism: 5 slang 7 coinage, new word 8 buzzword
neon: 3 gas 4 bulb 7 element 8 inert gas, noble gas
tetra: 3 pet 4 fish
neon __: 4 lamp 5 tetra
Neon: 3 car 4 auto 5 Dodge 8 Plymouth
neonate: 4 babe, baby 5 child 6 infant 7 newborn
garment: 6 bootee, bootie
neon tetra: 4 fish
Neon Wilderness, The
author: Nelson Algren
neophyte: 4 colt, tiro, tyro 5 newie, pupil 6 greeny, newbie, novice, rookie 7 convert, entrant, learner, new hand, recruit, trainee 8 beginner, newcomer 9 fledgling, greenhorn, layperson 10 apprentice, catechumen, tenderfoot
Neopolitan poet: 10 Sannazzaro
neoteric: 5 fresh, novel 6 modern, recent 8 up-to-date
nep: 4 knot
Nepal: 6 nation 7 country
capital: 8 Katmandu 9 Kathmandu
ender: 3 ese
knife: 5 kukri
locale: 4 Asia
money: 4 pice 5 paisa, rupee
mountain: 3 Api 5 Kabru 6 Cho Oyu, Lhotse, Makalu, Nuptse 7 Everest, Manaslu, Pyramid 8 Anapurna, Baruntse, Chamlang, Tent Peak 9 Ama Dablam, Annapurna, Nepal Peak 10 Dhaulagiri, Himalchuli
neighbor: 5 China, India
people: 6 Lepcha
soldier: 6 Gurkha
Nepali: 8 language
Nepean: 4 city, town
locale: 6 Canada 7 Ontario
nepenthe: 7 anodyne 8 narcotic 9 analgesic 10 palliative
Nephalion

father: 5 Minos
nephew: 4 male 7 kinsman 8 relative
sister: 5 niece
starter: 5 grand
Nephew, The
author: James Purdy
nephric: 5 renal
nephrite: 3 gem 4 jade 8 gemstone
Nephthys
sister: 4 Isis
ne plus ultra: 3 top 4 acme, A-one, apex, best, peak, tops 5 crest, crown, elite, first, ideal, model, prime 6 apogee, choice, far-out, finest, select, superb, unique, zenith 7 highest, maximum, optimal, optimum, paragon, perfect, stellar, sublime, supreme 8 choicest, exemplar, five-star, foremost, four-star, greatest, high spot, lodestar, nonesuch, paradigm, peerless, pinnacle, superior, topnotch, ultimate, very good 9 beau ideal, Endsville, excellent, exemplary, first-rate, high point, matchless, nonpareil, top-flight, unequaled, unrivaled 10 consummate, first-class, inimitable, out of sight, phenomenal, preeminent, touchstone, unrivalled
nepotism: 8 inequity 9 injustice 10 corruption, favoritism, partiality, unfairness
Neptune: 3 deo, god, orb 6 planet, sea god
brother: 5 Pluto 7 Jupiter
Celtic ~: 3 Ler, Lir
daughter: 7 Minerva
discoverer: Johann Galle
domain: 3 sea 5 ocean
equivalent: 8 Poseidon
moon: 5 Naiad 6 Nereid, Triton 7 Despina, Galatea, Larissa, Proteus 8 Thalassa
neighbor: 5 Pluto 6 Uranus
parent: 3 Ops 6 Saturn
sister: 4 Juno 5 Ceres, Vesta
wife: 7 Salacia
Neptune's Daughter (1949 film)
cast: Esther Williams
neptunium: 5 metal 7 element
Ner
grandson: 4 Saul
son: 5 Abner
nerd: 3 sap 4 clod, dork, drip, geek, jerk, wimp, wonk, wuss 5 dufus, dweeb, loser, schmo, sissy, twerp, twirp, weeny 6 doofus, schmoe, square, techie, tekkie 7 egghead, nebbish, oddball 8 bookworm, goofball
like a ~: 5 unhip 6 square
no ~: 4 BMOC, jock 7 hipster
Nerd, The
author: Larry Shue
nerdy: 5 sissy, unhip 6 square, uncool 8 dweebish 9 unpopular
Nereid: 4 Ione, moon 5 nymph 6 Thetis 7 Cydippe, Galatea 8 Arethusa, Psamathe, sea nymph 10 Amphitrite
planet: 7 Neptune
Nereus: 8 asteroid
daughter: 7 Galatea
mother: 4 Gaea
Nerf: 3 orb 4 ball
like a ~: 4 soft 6 spongy 7 squishy

Neri, Philip: 5 saint
Nernst, Walther: 7 chemist 8 Nobelist 9 physicist
Nero: 5 Peter, Roman, Wolfe 6 Caesar, Franco
city: 4 Rome
composer: Pietro Mascagni
friend: 4 Otho
instrument: 5 piano
mother: 9 Agrippina
outfit for ~: 4 toga
predecessor: 8 Claudius
successor: 5 Galba
tutor: 6 Seneca
see also Latin
neroli: 3 oil
Nero, Peter instrument: piano
nerts: 4 dang, darn, drat, oath, phoo 6 darn it, phooey
Neruda, Jan: 4 poet 5 Czech
Neruda, Pablo: 4 poet 6 writer 7 Chilean 8 Nobelist
nerve: 4 face, gall, grit, guts, will 5 brass, cheek, crust, heart, moxie, pluck, sauce, spunk, steel, valor 6 daring, hubris, hutzpa, hybris, mettle, spirit, starch 7 bravery, chutzpa, courage, hauteur, hutzpah, prowess, sciatic 8 audacity, backbone, boldness, chutzpah, coolness, firmness, gameness, gumption, rudeness, strength, temerity, tenacity 9 arrogance, assurance, brashness, fortitude, gallantry, impudence, insolence 10 brazenness, confidence, effrontery, resolution
cell: 5 fiber
cells: 4 glia
center: 3 hub 4 seat 5 focus
combining form: 4 neur- 5 neuro-
deprive of one's ~: 5 unman
have the ~: 4 dare, defy 7 venture 9 challenge, speculate
like some ~ cells: 6 apolar
lose one's ~: 5 blink, choke 6 freeze 7 back out 10 chicken out
network: 4 rete
networks: 5 retia
part of a ~ cell: 4 axon 5 axone
nerve __: 3 net 4 cell, cord, root 5 block, fiber, trunk 6 center 7 impulse
__ nerve: 4 hit a 5 mixed, optic, ulnar, vagus 6 facial, sacral, spinal 7 cranial, sciatic
__ nerve!: 4 Some, What
Nerve
author: Dick Francis
nerveless: 4 calm, cool, weak 5 timid 6 afraid, feeble 7 fearful 8 composed, cowardly, intrepid, tranquil 9 collected, enervated, impassive, petrified, spineless 10 controlled, unagitated
nerve-racking: 5 hairy, jumpy, tense 7 anxious 9 stressful
nerves: 4 glia 6 strain, stress 7 anxiety, fidgets, ganglia, jitters, tension 8 hysteria 9 imbalance, tenseness, tightness 10 irritation, uneasiness
bundle of ~: 4 edgy 5 antsy, itchy, jumpy, tense 6 on edge, uneasy 7 anxious, jittery, keyed up, nervous, restive, uptight 8 agitated, restless, skittish, troubled 9 concerned, excitable, ill at ease 10 high-strung
cranial ~: 4 vagi
get on one's ~: 3 bug, get, ire, irk, jar, vex 4 fret, goad, miff, rile, weed 5 anger, annoy, chafe, grate, peeve, pique, shrub, spite, upset 6 bother, burn up, harass, needle, noodge, offend, pester, pother, put out, rankle, ruffle 7 bramble, disturb, incense, prickle, provoke 8 irritate 9 aggravate, displease 10 discompose, exasperate
__ nerves: 5 war of
nerves of __: 5 steel
Nervo, Amado Ruiz de: 4 poet 7 Mexican
nervous: 3 shy 4 edgy, taut, weak 5 antsy, fazed, fussy, itchy, jumpy, shaky, tense, timid, upset, wired 6 afraid, gun-shy, jangly, on edge, pacing, queasy, queazy, scared, sweaty, trepid, uneasy 7 abashed, alarmed, anxious, chicken, daunted, dithery, excited, fearful, fidgety, jittery, keyed up, panicky, restive, ruffled, spooked, twitchy, uptight, worried 8 agitated, cowardly, fearsome, fluttery, hesitant, restless, skittish, snappish, timorous, troubled, unstrung, volatile 9 concerned, disturbed, emotional, excitable, flustered, ill at ease, irritable, petrified, querulous, sensitive, shrinking, terrified, tremulous 10 distressed, frightened, high-strung, hysterical, solicitous
make ~: 5 spook 6 rattle, unglue 7 fluster 8 psych out, unsettle 10 discompose, disconcert, intimidate
nervous __: 5 Nelly 6 Nellie, system
nervously, react: 4 jump 5 start, wince
nervousness: 5 alarm, qualm, tizzy, worry 6 creeps, shakes, stress 7 anxiety, dithers, fidgets, jimjams, jitters, quivers, tension, willies 8 disquiet, timidity 9 agitation, cold sweat, jumpiness
__ nervous system: 7 central
nervy: 4 bold, flip, game, pert, rude, wise 5 brash, brave, cocky, crass, crude, fresh, gutsy, pushy, sassy, saucy, smart, stout 6 awless, brassy, brawny, brazen, cheeky, daring, gritty, heroic, mighty, on edge, plucky, sinewy, snippy, spunky, strong 7 anxious, aweless, boorish, defiant, doughty, forward, gallant, impavid, jittery, selfish, staunch, uncivil, valiant 8 cocksure, familiar, fearless, flippant, forceful, heedless, heroical, impolite, impudent, insolent, intrepid, muscular, powerful, resolute, restless, skittish, snippety, spirited, stalwart, tactless, unafraid, valorous, vigorous 9 audacious, bumptious, dauntless, dreadless, excitable, out of line, tenacious, undaunted, unfearful 10 courageous, undismayed, ungracious, unthinking
Nesbitt: 8 Cathleen
Nescafé: 6 coffee
alternative: 5 Sanka, Yuban 7 Folgers, Melitta, Savarin 9 Hills Bros.
nescient: 7 unaware 8 ignorant, innocent
Nesmith: 4 Mike 6 Monkee
colleague: 4 Tork 5 Jones 6 Dolenz
ness: 6 suffix 8 headland 10 promontory
Ness: 3 Fed 4 lake, Loch, T-man 5 Eliot
locale: 8 Scotland
to Capone: 3 foe 5 enemy
Nessen: 3 Ron
Nessie's home: 4 loch
Nessman: 3 Les 7 newsman
employer: 4 WKRP
Nessun dorma: 4 aria
Nessus: 7 centaur
nest: 3 den 4 aery, coop, eyry, hive, home, lair, live, stay 5 aerie, covey, dwell, embed, eyrie, haunt, haven, imbed, lodge, nidus, perch, roost 6 asylum, colony, hotbed, refuge, reside 7 anthill, beehive, cluster, habitat, hangout, hideout, retreat, shelter, sojourn 8 cloister, hideaway, settle in, snuggery, vespiary 9 formicary
bird with a cup-shaped ~: 5 vireo
crow's ~: 7 lookout, station
eagle's ~: 4 aery, eyry 5 aerie, eyrie
egg: 3 IRA 5 cache, funds, means, store 7 reserve, savings 9 resources
feather one's ~: 4 save 6 make it, thrive 7 advance, develop, make out, prosper, succeed 8 flourish, go places, grow rich, hit it big, make good, progress
hornet's ~: 3 ado, fix 4 hive, mess, stir 5 furor 6 clamor, pickle, plight, rumpus, scrape, tumult, uproar 7 travail, trouble, turmoil 8 quagmire, quandary
insect ~: 5 nidus
leave the ~: 3 fly 8 take wing
like a ~: 4 cozy, snug 5 comfy, homey
locale: 4 limb, tree 5 hedge
mare's ~: 3 zoo 4 fake, hoax, mess, sham 5 fraud, snafu 6 foul-up, jumble, muddle 8 delusion 9 deception
noise: 5 cheep, tweet
of an insect ~: 5 nidal
paper ~ builder: 4 wasp
rob a ~: 5 poach
sound: 3 coo 4 peep 5 cheep, chirp, tweet
(within): 3 sit
nest __: 3 egg
__ nest: 4 love, rat's 5 bird's 7 hornet's
__-nest: 5 crow's, mare's
__ Nest: 4 Love 5 Empty
n'est-ce pas?: 3 yes 4 okay 5 right
Nestea: 9 soft drink
alternative: 6 Lipton, Salada, Tetley 7 Bigelow, Red Rose

8 Twinings
__ nester: 5 empty
nestle: 3 hug 4 seat, snug 6 burrow, cozy up, cradle, cuddle, curl up, huddle, nuzzle 7 snuggle 8 ensconce, huddle up, settle in 9 keep close 10 settle down
Nestlé: 5 candy 9 chocolate
product: 4 Alpo, Baci, Quik 5 Wonka 6 Chunky, Crunch 7 Buitoni, Goobers, Oh Henry, Sno-Caps 8 Baby Ruth, Friskies, Perugina, PowerBar 9 Bit-O-Honey, Carnation, Mighty Dog, Raisinets, Stouffer's 10 Coffee-Mate, Fancy Feast, Juicy Juice
nestled: 4 cosy, cozy 5 cozey, cozie 8 tucked in
nestling: 4 baby, bird 5 owlet 6 eaglet 9 fledgling
call: 5 chirp, tweet
nestlings: 5 brood
nest of __: 7 drawers
nest of robins..., A poem: 5 Trees
Nest of Simple Folk, A
author: Sean O'Faolain
Nestor: 4 sage
daughter: 8 Pisidice 9 Polycaste
like ~: 4 sage, wise 9 sagacious
parent: 6 Neleus 7 Chloris
son: 6 Aretus 7 Perseus 10 Antilochus, Stratichus
wife: 8 Anaxibia, Eurydice
__-nest soup: 5 bird's
__ nest syndrome: 5 empty
net: 3 bag, get, nab, web 4 earn, hook, lace, make, mesh, trap, veil 5 catch, clear, cloth, crisp, final, snare, snood, yield 6 collar, enmesh, entrap, fabric, garner, immesh, inmesh, profit, return, screen 7 bring in, capture, ensnare, insnare, lattice, realize, revenue 8 entangle, lacework, openwork, pull down, receipts, residual, take home 9 bring home, end up with, profiting, remaining 10 after taxes, bottom line, conclusive
alternative: 4 gaff
combining form: 5 dicty- 6 dictyo-
ender: 4 back, ball, work 6 keeper
fabric: 4 lace 5 tulle
feat: 5 spike
fish ~: 5 seine, trawl
game: 6 hockey, tennis 8 Ping Pong 9 badminton 10 volleyball
holder: 3 rim
org.: 4 USTA
plus expenses: 5 gross
starter: 4 drag, fish, gill
work without a ~: 4 dare, defy, risk 6 hazard 9 take a risk
worth: 6 estate
see also basketball
net __: 3 pay, ton 4 gain, line, loss 5 worth 6 assets, income, profit
net __ value: 5 asset
__ net: 4 hair 6 neural, safety 9 butterfly
Net: 3 Web
access the ~: 5 log on 6 dial up
address: 3 URL, www
connector: 5 modem
giant: 3 AOL
surfer: 4 user
Netanya: 4 city, town
locale: 6 Israel
Netanyahu, Benjamin: 4 Bibi 7 Israeli
alma mater: 3 MIT
predecessor: 5 Peres
successor: 5 Barak
Netflix
mailing: 3 DVD
Neth.
locale: 3 Eur.
neighbor: 3 Ger. 4 Belg.
org.: 4 NATO
see also Netherlands
nether: 3 low 5 lower, under 6 lesser 7 Stygian 8 infernal 10 underneath
ender: 5 world
region: 4 hell 5 Hades, Sheol 7 inferno 10 underworld
nether __: 5 world
__ Netherland: 3 New
Netherlands: 6 nation 7 country
airline: 3 KLM
astronomer: 4 Oort 6 Sitter 7 Huygens
beer: 6 Amstel
botanist: 5 Vries
bovine: 8 Holstein
capital: 7 Den Haag 8 The Hague 9 Amsterdam
cheese: 4 Brie, Edam 5 Gouda 6 Leyden
city: 3 Ede 4 Edam 5 Breda, Delft, Emmen, Gouda, Venlo, Zeist 6 Arnhem, Beilen, Leiden, Leyden, Venloo 7 Den Haag, Haarlem, Tilburg, Utrecht 8 The Hague 9 Amsterdam, Rotterdam 10 Maastricht
colonist: 4 Boer
conductor: 7 De Waart
explorer: 6 Tasman 7 Barents
export: 4 bulb, Edam 5 Gouda, tulip 6 cheese
farmer: 4 Boer
fishing boat: 6 dogger
former colony: 5 Timor
lake: 9 Zuider Zee 10 Ijsselmeer
language: 5 Dutch
Meuse in ~: 4 Maas
money: 4 cent, doit, duit, euro 6 florin, gilder, gulden, stiver 7 guilder 8 ducatoon 9 rix-dollar
neighbor: 7 Belgium, Germany
Nobelist in Chemistry: 5 Debye 7 Crutzen 8 van't Hoff
Nobelist in Economics: 8 Koopmans 9 Tinbergen
Nobelist in Medicine: 7 Eijkman 9 Einthoven
Nobelist in Peace: 5 Asser
Nobelist in Physics: 5 Hooft 6 Zeeman 7 Lorentz, Veltman, Zernike 10 van der Meer 11 van der Waals
org.: 4 NATO
painter: 4 Hals, Lely 5 Steen 7 van Gogh, Vermeer 8 Mondrian, Ter Borch 9 de Kooning, Rembrandt
philosopher: 7 Spinoza
physicist: 7 Huygens 11 van der Waals
port: 5 Delft 8 Flushing 9 Amsterdam, Rotterdam 10 Vlissingen
river: 3 Lek 4 Maas, Rijn, Waal 5 Issel, Yssel 6 Ijssel
royal house: 6 Orange
scientist: 5 Vries 6 Sitter 7 Huygens 11 van der Waals
shoe: 5 sabot
South African: 4 Boer
waterway: 3 zee
writer: 7 Erasmus, Spinoza 8 Couperus
see also Dutch, Holland
Netherlands Antilles
money: 4 cent 6 gilder, gulden 7 guilder
one of the ~: 4 Saba 7 Bonaire, Curaçao
nethermost point: 5 nadir 6 bottom
netherworld: 4 hell 5 Hades, Sheol 7 inferno
net judge call: 3 let
netkeeper: 6 goalie
netlike: 4 fine, lacy 5 meshy 6 dainty, frilly 8 delicate, gossamer
cap: 5 snood
fabric: 4 lace
Nets: 4 five, team
home: 9 New Jersey
org.: 3 NBA
rival: *see* NBA team
sport: 10 basketball
Netscape purchaser: 3 AOL
netster: 4 Ashe, Borg, Hoad, King, Wade 5 Budge, Bueno, Chang, Court, Evert, Kodes, Laver, Lendl, Moody, Riggs, Seles, Smith, Vilas 6 Agassi, Austin, Casals, Fraser, Gibson, Hingis, Kramer, Marble, Rafter, Segura, Stolle, Tilden 7 Connors, Emerson, Lacoste, Lew Hoad, McEnroe, Nastase, Ralston, Roddick, Sampras, Trabert 8 Capriati, Connolly, Don Budge, Gonzales, Newcombe, Rod Laver, Rosewall, Williams 9 Bjorn Borg, Davenport, Goolagong, Ivan Lendl, Stan Smith, tennis pro 10 Arthur Ashe, Bill Tilden, Bobby Riggs, Chris Evert, Fred Stolle, Jack Kramer, Kournikova, Mandlikova, Maria Bueno 11 Navratilova
Nets to Catch the Wind
author: Elinor Wylie
netsuke container: 4 inro
__-netter: 4 gill
Net, The (1995 film)
cast: Sandra Bullock, Dennis Miller
netting: 3 web 4 lace, mesh 6 fabric
like ~: 5 meshy
nettle: 3 bug, get, ire, irk, jar, vex 4 fret, goad, miff, rile, weed 5 anger, annoy, chafe, grate, peeve, pique, shrub, spite, tease, upset, worry 6 bother, burn up, harass, needle, noodge, offend, pester, pother, put out, rankle, ruffle 7 bramble, disturb, incense, prickle, provoke 8 irritate 9 aggravate, displease 10 discompose, exasperate
family shrub: 5 pilea, ramee, ramie
nettled: 5 huffy, irate, upset 9 irritated
Nettles, Graig
sport: 8 baseball
nettlesome: 5 pesky, pesty 6 thorny 7 prickly 8 annoying, worrying 10 in one's hair
Nettleton: 4 Lois
network: 3 net, sys., tie, web 4 bond, grid, link, maze, mesh, syst., talk 5 merge, nexus 6 hookup, medium, mingle, plexus, scheme, system 7 complex, lattice, society 8 interact 9 broadcast, circuitry, labyrinth, negotiate, structure
electrical ~: 4 grid
English ~: 3 BBC
link: 5 modem
transmission: 4 feed
TV ~: 3 ABC, CBS, Fox, PBS 5 The CW
__ network: 4 star 6 neural, old-boy 7 old-girl
Network (1976 film)
cast: Faye Dunaway, Robert Duvall, Peter Finch, William Holden, Beatrice Straight
director: Sidney Lumet
network: 3 UBS
networks
TV ~: 5 media
net worth
component: 5 asset
Neuchâtel: 4 lake
locale: Switzerland
Neufchâtel: 6 cheese
Neuharth: 2 Al
Neuilly-__-Seine: 3 sur
Neuman, Alfred E.
mag: 3 Mad
Neumann: 4 Kurt 5 Lotta
neural: 7 sensory 9 sensorial
network: 4 rete
tissue: 4 glia
transmitter: 4 axon 5 axone
neural __: 3 net
neurological: 7 sensory 9 sensorial
exam.: 3 EEG
__ neuron: 5 motor
neuron appendage: 4 axon 5 axone
neurotransmitter: 4 dopa
Neuss: 4 city, town
locale: 7 Germany
neuter: 4 geld, spay 5 alter 6 gender
not ~: 3 fem. 4 masc. 8 feminine 9 masculine
neutral: 3 tan 4 cool, drab, ecru, gray, grey, just 5 aloof, beige, cream, ivory, white 6 medium 7 subdued 8 clinical, detached, listless, moderate, peaceful, unbiased 9 impartial, objective, unaligned, undecided, unslanted 10 achromatic, disengaged, evenhanded, fair-minded, impersonal, nonaligned, nonchalant, on the fence, pacifistic, poker-faced, unagitated, uninvolved
color: 3 tan 4 ecru, gray, grey 5 beige, flesh, taupe
ethically ~: 6 amoral
run in ~: 3 rev 4 idle 5 coast
zone: 3 DMZ 6 buffer
neutral __: 4 zone 6 corner
__-neutral: 6 gender
neutrality: 8 coolness 9 aloofness, unconcern 10 detachment, equanimity
neutralize: 4 undo 5 annul, block, check, unarm 6 cancel, defeat,

NE

negate, offset, oppose, scotch 7 balance, nullify, redress 8 abrogate, overcome 9 frustrate 10 antagonize, compensate, counteract, invalidate
neutralizer
poison ~: 8 antidote
neutrino: 8 particle
neutron: 8 particle
neutron __: 4 star 5 dance 6 number
__ neutron: 4 slow 7 thermal
Neutron Dance (1984 song)
artist: Pointer Sisters
Neuwirth, Bebe: 7 actress
TV: Cheers
Neva: 5 river
locale: 6 Russia
Nevada: 5 state
author: Zane Grey
capital: 10 Carson City
casino: 5 Luxor, Sands 6 Sahara 7 Harrah's 8 MGM Grand
city: 3 Ely 4 Elko, Reno 5 Vegas 6 Sparks 7 Pahrump 8 Las Vegas, Paradise 9 Henderson, Sun Valley 10 Carson City, Winchester
conference: 3 WAC
county: 3 Nye 4 Elko 6 Washoe
desert: 11 Death Valley
Indian: 5 Piute, Washo 6 Paiute
lake: 4 Mead 5 Tahoe 8 Lahontan
national park: 10 Great Basin
neighbor: 4 Utah 5 Idaho 6 Oregon 7 Arizona 10 California
peak: 3 Ely 5 Mt. Ely
state bird: 8 bluebird
state flower: 9 sagebrush
state metal: 6 silver
state precious gemstone: 8 fire opal
state rock: 9 sandstone
state semi-precious gemstone: 9 turquoise
University of ~ site: 4 Reno
waterfall: 6 Ribbon
Nevada __: 5 Smith
__ Nevada: 6 Sierra
Nevada Smith (1966 film)
cast: Brian Keith, Karl Malden, Steve McQueen
__ ne va plus: 4 rien
névé: 4 firn, snow
Neve: 8 Campbell
never: 2 no 3 nah, naw, nay, nix, non 4 nary, ne'er, nein, nope, nyet, uh-uh 5 I won't, ixnay, no how, no way 6 no deal, noways, nowise 7 I refuse, not ever 8 at no time, forget it, I will not, negative, negatory, not at all 9 by no means, fat chance, I think not, nevermore 10 count me out, impossible, not a chance, thumbs down
almost ~: 6 rarely, seldom 8 not often 10 hardly ever, now and then
before seen: 3 new 6 all-new
ender: 4 more
meeting: 8 parallel
mind: 6 skip it 8 forget it, no matter 10 don't bother
still: 5 antsy, hyper, jumpy 6 on edge 7 fidgety, jittery 8 restless
used, in coin-collecting: 3 unc.
never __ die: 3 say
never-__: 6 ending
__ never: 5 now or
Never (1985 song)
artist: Heart
Never __: 3 Lie 4 Ever 5 Again 6 Enough
Never __ Diet: 3 Say
Never __ moment!: 5 a dull
Never __ Never Again: 3 Say
Never __ Say Goodbye: 3 Can
Never Again
author: Flora Nwapa
Never Be Anyone Else But You (1959 song)
artist: Ricky Nelson
Never Been Kissed (1999 film)
cast: David Arquette, Drew Barrymore, Molly Shannon
__ Never Been to Me: 3 I've
Never Been to Spain (1972 song)
artist: Three Dog Night
__ never believe me...: 5 They'd
Never Bet the Devil Your Head
author: Edgar Allan Poe
Never Call Retreat
author: Bruce Catton
Never Can Say Goodbye (song)
artist: Gloria Gaynor, Jackson 5
Never Come Morning
author: Nelson Algren
never-ending: 4 vast 6 eonian, eterne, steady 7 abiding, chronic, eternal, nonstop, undying 8 constant, enduring, immortal, infinite, timeless, unbroken 9 boundless, ceaseless, chronical, continual, countless, deathless, incessant, limitless, perennial, permanent, perpetual, unceasing, unlimited
Neverending Story, The
author: Michael Ende
Never Enough
author: Harold Robbins
never-failing: 4 sure 6 steady 7 constant 9 steadfast
__ Never Get Rich: 5 You'll
Never Give a Sucker an Even Break (1941 film)
cast: Leon Errol, W.C. Fields
Never Gonna Give You Up (1988 song)
artist: Rick Astley
Never Gonna Let You Go (1983 song)
artist: Sérgio Mendes & Brasil '66
__ never heard them at all...: 3 No I
Never Knew Lonely (1990 song)
artist: Vince Gill
Never Knew Love Like This Before (1980 song)
artist: Stephanie Mills
__ Never Know: 5 You'll
Never Leave Me
author: Harold Robbins
Never Love a Stranger
author: Harold Robbins
...never met __ I didn't like: 4 a man
never missing __: 5 a beat
Nevermore! bird: 5 raven
Never My Love (song)
artist: Association, The, Blue Swede
Never, Never Gonna Give Ya Up (1973 song)
artist: Barry White
never-never land: 6 heaven, utopia 8 paradise 9 fairyland, Shangri-la
Never on Sunday (1960 film)
cast: Melina Mercouri
setting: 6 Greece
Nevers: 4 city, town 5 Ernie
locale: 6 France
Never Say __: 3 Die 4 Diet
Never Say Never Again (1983 film)
cast: Kim Basinger, Klaus Maria Brandauer, Barbara Carrera, Sean Connery, Max von Sydow
director: Irvin Kershner
__ Never Seen Those Eyes: 5 Mama's
Nevers, Ernie
sport: 8 football
__ Never Smile Again: 3 I'll
Never Tear Us Apart (1988 song)
artist: INXS
nevertheless: 3 but, tho, yet 5 altho, still 6 anyway, even so, though 7 howbeit, however 8 after all, although
__ never too late...: 3 it's
__ Never Walk Alone: 5 You'll
__ never work!: 4 It'll
nevi: 5 moles 10 birthmarks
Nevil: 5 Shute 6 Robbie
Nevill: 4 Mott
Neville: 3 Art 5 Aaron, Brand, Cyril 7 Charles 8 Marriner 11 Chamberlain
Neville, Aaron
song: Don't Know Much (1989) Everybody Plays the Fool (1991) Tell It Like It Is (1966)
Nevin: 9 Ethelbert
Nevins, Allan: 6 writer 9 historian
Nevis
partner: 7 St. Kitts
Nev. neighbor: 3 Cal., Ida., Ore. 4 Ariz., Oreg. 5 Calif.
see also Nevada
Nevsky: 9 Alexander
Nevsky Cathedral
locale: 5 Sofia 6 Sofiya 8 Bulgaria
nevus: 4 mole 9 birthmark
new: 3 mod, now, raw 4 dewy, late, mint, more 5 added, faddy, fresh, green, novel, other, sweet, young 6 afresh, clever, just in, latest, modern, modish, of late, recent, red-hot, unique, unlike, unused, virgin 7 altered, current, just out, revived, strange, topical, unknown, untried, unusual, updated 8 advanced, creative, directly, improved, inspired, original, restored, singular, spanking, untapped, up-to-date, virginal, youthful 9 au courant, different, increased, ingenious, inventive, unhandled, unheard-of, unskilled, unspoiled, untouched, untrained, untrodden 10 additional, dissimilar, innovative, redesigned, refreshing, starting up, unfamiliar, unseasoned
breathe ~ life into: 6 revive 7 refresh 10 regenerate
combining form: 2 ne- 3 neo-, nov- 4 ceno-, novo-
ender: 4 born 5 comer, found, speak 6 sprint
face a ~ day: 4 rise, wake 5 awake, waken 6 awaken
growth: 4 twig, wand 5 shoot
hand: 4 babe, lamb, naif, tiro, tyro 6 intern, novice 7 learner, recruit 8 beginner, freshman, neophyte 9 fledgling 10 tenderfoot
homophone of ~: 3 gnu 4 knew
in French: 7 nouveau 8 nouvelle
in German: 3 neu 4 neue
in Spanish: 5 nueva, nuevo
like ~: 4 mint 5 fresh 9 unspoiled
like a ~ coin: 5 shiny 6 agleam, bright 8 gleaming
like ~ to a coin collector: 3 unc.
make ~: 3 fix 4 heal 6 repair 7 refresh, restore
open to ~ ideas: 7 pliable 8 amenable, tolerant 9 acceptive, sensitive 10 hospitable, responsive
person: 4 baby, tiro, tyro 5 hiree 7 recruit 8 beginner 9 greenhorn
phrase: 7 coinage 9 neologism
turn over a ~ leaf: 6 change, reform 7 redress, shape up
version: 6 change, update 7 redraft, rewrite 8 overhaul, revision 9 amendment, redaction 10 adjustment, alteration, correction, emendation
wave: 5 novel 6 exotic, modern 7 radical 8 vanguard 9 inventive 10 avant-garde, innovative, pioneering
wrinkle: 6 change 7 novelty 9 departure 10 innovation
new __: 4 look, math, moon, town, wave, year 5 blood, media, order
new __ in old bottles: 4 wine
new __ order: 5 world
new-__: 4 mown
__ new?: 5 What's
__-new: 4 span 5 brand
New __: 3 Age 4 Ager, Deal, Left, Look, Test., York 5 Delhi, Haven, Right, Spain, Style, World 6 Dealer, France, Guinea, Hebrew, Jersey, London, Mexico, Sweden, Yorker 7 Balance, Edition, England, Orleans 9 Amsterdam, Caledonia, Hampshire
New __, A: 4 Leaf, Life
New __ City: 4 York
New __ clam chowder: 7 England
New __, CT: 5 Haven 6 Canaan
New __ Day: 5 Year's
New __ Eve: 5 Year's
New __, India: 5 Delhi
New __ in Town: 3 Kid
New __, LA: 6 Iberia
New __ Mets: 4 York
New __ minute: 4 York
New __ on the Block: 4 Kids
New __ Pay Old Debts, A: 5 Way to
New __ steak: 4 York
New __ Symphony: 5 World
New __ Wales: 5 South
New Age
glow: 4 aura
philosophy: 6 holism
pianist: 4 Tesh
syllable: 2 om
New Albany: 4 city, town
locale: 7 Indiana
Newark: 3 bay 4 city, port, town
athletes: 8 Blue Hens

county: 5 Essex
locale: 3 Cal., Del. 4 Ohio 5 Calif. 8 Delaware 9 New Jersey 10 California
newspaper: 10 Star-Ledger
New Attitude (1985 song)
artist: Patti LaBelle
New Balance
competitor: 4 Avia, Keds 6 Adidas, Reebok 8 Converse
__ new ball game: 5 whole
New Bedford: 4 city, port, town
locale: 4 Mass.
New Berlin: 4 city, town
locale: 9 Wisconsin
New Bern: 4 city, town
locale: 4 N. Car.
Newbery: 4 John 5 Award, medal
newbie: 4 tiro, tyro 6 novice 8 beginner, neophyte 9 greenhorn
newborn: 4 babe, baby 5 child, young 6 infant, recent 7 neonate
bed: 4 crib 6 cradle
New Britain: 4 city, town
locale: 4 Conn.
New Brunswick: 4 city, town 8 province
city: 6 St. John 7 Cap-Pelé, Moncton 9 Miramichi, Port Elgin
Indian: 8 Malecite
locale: 6 Canada 9 New Jersey
neighbor: 5 Maine
school: 7 Rutgers
__ Newburg: 7 lobster
Newburgh: 4 city, town
locale: 7 New York
New Caledonia: 4 isle 6 island
bird: 4 kagu
capital: 6 Nouméa
Newcastle: 4 city, port, town
locale: 7 England 9 Australia
product: 4 coal
New Castle: 4 city, town
locale: 7 Indiana 8 Delaware
Newcastle-under-__: 4 Lyme
Newcastle-upon-__: 4 Tyne
New Centurions, The (1972 film)
cast: Jane Alexander, Stacy Keach, George C. Scott
New Colossus, The
author: Emma Lazarus
Newcombe: 3 Don 4 John
Newcombe, John: 7 netster 9 tennis pro
milieu: 5 court
rival: 4 Ashe
newcomer: 3 neo 4 colt, tiro, tyro 5 alien 6 blow-in, novice, rookie 7 entrant, recruit, settler 8 beginner, maverick, neophyte, outsider, stranger 9 foreigner, greenhorn, immigrant, latecomer 10 apprentice, tenderfoot
academy ~: 4 pleb 5 frosh, plebe
__ New Day: 5 Many a
New Day Has Come, A (2002 song)
artist: Celine Dion
New Deal agcy.: 3 AAA, CCC, FHA, FSA, NRA, NYA, PWA, REA, RFC, SSA, TVA, WPA 4 FDIC, NLRB
New Deal for Christmas, A show: 5 Annie
New Delhi: 4 city, town 7 capital
locale: 5 India
New Diplomacy, The
author: Abba Eban
New Edition
song: Cool It Now (1984)
Hit Me Off (1996)
If It Isn't Love (1988)
I'm Still in Love with You (1996)
Mr. Telephone Man (1985)
newel: 4 post 9 stairpost
Newell: 4 Mike
new-employee offering (abbr.): 3 OJT
New England
campus: 3 MIT, UNH, URI 4 Yale 5 Brown, Tufts, U Mass 7 Amherst, Harvard 9 Dartmouth
cape: 3 Ann, Cod
fish: 5 scrod 6 schrod
native: 4 Yank 6 Mainer 9 Bay Stater, Nutmegger, Vermonter
port: 6 Boston 10 New Bedford
pro team: 6 Bruins, Red Sox 7 Celtics 8 Patriots
soda fountain: 3 spa
state: 4 Conn., Mass. 5 Maine 7 Vermont
New England Suite
composer: Ferde Grofé
newest: 4 last 6 latest 8 up-to-date
wrinkle: 3 fad 4 rage 5 style, trend, vogue 7 fashion 10 dernier cri
Newf.: 3 isl. 4 prov.
newfangled: 5 fresh, novel 6 modern, recent 7 in vogue, popular, strange 8 gimmicky, up-to-date 10 innovative
Newfoundland: 3 dog 4 isle, prov. 5 canid 6 canine, island 8 province
airport: 6 Gander
city: 6 Brigus 7 Botwood, St. John's 10 Mount Pearl
explorer: 7 Gilbert
fisherman: 6 banker
hrs.: 3 AST
mountain: 8 Caubvick
school: 8 Memorial
New Glasgow: 4 city, town
locale: 6 Canada 10 Nova Scotia
New Guinea: 4 isle 6 island
bay: 6 Sarera
bird: 7 mudlark 8 manacode 9 bowerbird, cassowary
city: 3 Lae
gulf: 5 Papua
island off ~: 4 Biak
islands near ~: 3 Aru 4 Aroe, Arru
mountain: 4 Jaja 7 Trikora
reptile: 6 taipan
sea: 5 Coral 7 Arafura 8 Bismarck
snake: 6 taipan
strait off ~: 6 Torres
territory: 5 Papua
to Indonesians: 5 Irian
New Hampshire: 3 hen 4 fowl 5 state 7 chicken, poultry
capital: 7 Concord
city: 5 Derry, Dover, Keene, Salem 6 Exeter, Hudson, Nashua 7 Concord, Laconia 9 Merrimack, Rochester 10 Manchester, Portsmouth
mountain: 5 White
neighbor: 5 Maine 6 Canada, Quebec 7 Vermont
school: 9 Dartmouth
state amphibian: 4 newt
state bird: 5 finch
state flower: 5 lilac
state game fish: 10 brook trout
state insect: 7 ladybug
state mineral: 5 beryl
state rock: 7 granite
state sport: 6 skiing
state tree: 10 white birch
__ New Hampshire, The: 5 Hotel
New Harmony
founder: Robert Owen
Newhart (CBS sitcom)
cast: Julia Duffy (Stephanie Vanderkellen)
Mary Frann (Joanna Loudon)
Bob Newhart (Dick Loudon)
Tom Poston (George Utley)
producer: MTM
setting: 3 inn 7 Vermont 9 Stratford
Newhart, Bob: 5 actor 8 comedian
film: Catch-22 (1970)
Cold Turkey (1971)
TV: The Bob Newhart Show, Newhart
Newhaven: 4 port
locale: 6 Sussex 7 England
New Haven: 4 city, town
locale: 4 Conn.
neighbor: 6 Hamden
school: 4 Yale 5 Yale U
student: 3 Eli 5 Yalie 7 Bulldog
tree: 3 elm
New Hebrides: 5 isles 7 islands
see also Vanuatu
New Hope: 4 city, town
locale: 4 Penn. 9 Minnesota
Newhouse: 2 S.I.
Newhouser, Hal: 5 Tiger 6 hurler 7 pitcher
New Iberia: 4 city, town
locale: 9 Louisiana
newie: 4 tiro, tyro 5 plebe 6 novice, rookie 7 learner, recruit, trainee 8 beginner, initiate, neophyte 9 fledgling, greenhorn 10 apprentice, tenderfoot
New Jack City (1991 film)
cast: Ice-T, Wesley Snipes
New Jersey: 5 state
bay: 6 Newark 8 Delaware
cape: 3 May
capital: 7 Trenton
city: 4 Lodi 5 Brick, Ewing, Union, Wayne 6 Camden, Edison, Iselin, Kearny, Leonia, Linden, Mahwah, Newark, Nutley, Orange, Rahway, Summit 7 Bayonne, Cape May, Clifton, Fort Dix, Fort Lee, Hoboken, Paramus, Passaic, Roselle, Teaneck, Tenafly, Trenton 8 Carteret, Cranbury, Cranford, Fair Lawn, Freehold, Garfield, Hamilton, Hillside, Lakewood, Metuchen, Millburn, Paterson, Somerset, Vineland 9 Bridgeton, Elizabeth, Englewood, Irvington, Maplewood, Millville, Montclair, Old Bridge, Princeton, Ridgewood, Toms River, Union City, Westfield 10 Belleville, Bloomfield, Cherry Hill, East Orange, Hackensack, Jersey City, Livingston, Long Branch, Parsippany, Pennsauken, Perth Amboy, Plainfield, Sayreville, West Orange
ender: 3 ite
fort: 3 Dix
mountains: 6 Ramapo
neighbor: 4 Penn. 5 Penna. 7 New York 8 Delaware
pro team: 4 Nets 6 Devils
river: 7 Passaic, Raritan
school: 4 Drew 7 Rutgers 9 Princeton, Seton Hall
state bird: 9 goldfinch
state fish: 10 brook trout
state flower: 6 violet
state insect: 8 honeybee
state mammal: 5 horse
state shell: 5 whelk
state tree: 6 red oak
New Kid in Town (1976 song)
artist: Eagles
New Kids on the Block
hometown: Boston
members: McIntyre, Wahlberg, Wood, Knight
song: Cover Girl (1989)
Didn't I (Blow Your Mind) (1989)
Hangin' Tough (1989)
I'll Be Loving You (1989)
Please Don't Go Girl (1988)
Step by Step (1990)
This One's for the Children (1989)
Tonight (1990)
You Got It (1989)
New Leaf, A (1971 film)
cast: Walter Matthau, Elaine May
director: Elaine May
__ new lease on life: 4 get a
New Left org.: 3 SDS
Newley, Anthony
spouse: Joan Collins
New Life, A (1988 film)
cast: Alan Alda, Ann-Margret, Veronica Hamel, Hal Linden
director: Alan Alda
New Life, The
author: Dante
New Line: 6 studio
competitor: *see* movie studio
creation: 4 film 5 movie
New London: 4 city, town
locale: 4 Conn.
river: 6 Thames
sch.: 5 USCGA
New Look designer: 4 Dior
Newlove, John: 4 poet 8 Canadian
newly: 4 anew, just 6 afresh, lately, of late 7 freshly 8 recently
arrived: 6 just in
ender: 3 wed
produced: 5 fresh 6 recent 7 just out 8 just made
newlywed: 5 bride, groom 10 bridegroom
promise: 3 I do
Newlywed Game, The: 8 game show
host: Bob Eubanks
newlyweds: 6 couple 7 twosome
New Machiavelli, The
author: H.G. Wells
Newman: 4 Paul 5 Barry, Edwin, Jerry, Randy 6 Alfred, Claire, Thomas 7 Laraine, Nanette
__ Newman, M.D.: 7 Captain
Newman, Paul: 5 actor
film: Absence of Malice (1981)
Blaze (1989)
Butch Cassidy and the Sun-

dance Kid (1969)
Cat on a Hot Tin Roof (1958)
The Color of Money (1986, AA)
Cool Hand Luke (1967)
Exodus (1960)
Fat Man and Little Boy (1989)
Fort Apache, The Bronx (1981)
The Glass Menagerie (1987)
Harper (1966)
Hombre (1967)
Hud (1963)
The Hudsucker Proxy (1994)
The Hustler (1961)
The Life and Times of Judge Roy Bean (1972)
The Long Hot Summer (1958)
Message in a Bottle (1999)
Mr. & Mrs. Bridge (1990)
Nobody's Fool (1994)
Paris Blues (1961)
Pocket Money (1972)
The Prize (1963)
Rachel, Rachel (1968)
The Rack (1956)
Road to Perdition (2002)
Slap Shot (1977)
Somebody Up There Likes Me (1956)
The Sting (1973)
Sweet Bird of Youth (1962)
Torn Curtain (1966)
The Towering Inferno (1974)
Twilight (1998)
The Verdict (1982)
What a Way to Go! (1964)
Winning (1969)
WUSA (1970)
The Young Philadelphians (1959)
spouse: Joanne Woodward
Newman, Randy
song: Short People (1977)
Newman's Own: 10 pasta sauce
alternative: 4 Ragú **5** Prego **6** Prince **8** Classico
Newmar: 5 Julie
Newmarket: 4 city, town
locale: 6 Canada **7** Ontario
New Men, The
author: C.P. Snow
New Mexico: 5 state
capital: 7 Santa Fe
city: 4 Taos **5** Hobbs **6** Clovis, Gallup **7** Roswell, Santa Fe **8** Carlsbad **9** Las Cruces, Los Alamos, Rio Rancho **10** Alamogordo, Farmington
county: 3 Lea **4** Eddy, Luna, Mora, Quay, Taos **5** Otero **6** Cibola
desert: 10 Chihuahuan
Indian: 3 Sia, Ute **4** Piro, Tano, Taos, Tewa, Tiwa, Zuni **6** Laguna, Navaho, Navajo, Pueblo **9** Jicarilla, Mescalero **10** Chiricahua
lake: 3 Ute
mountain: 7 San Juan, Wheeler **8** Mogollon
neighbor: 4 Utah **5** Texas **6** Mexico **7** Arizona **8** Colorado, Oklahoma
pueblo: 5 Acoma
state bird: 10 roadrunner
state flower: 5 yucca
state gem: 9 turquoise
state mammal: 9 black bear
state tree: 5 piñon
New Mexico State
athletes: 6 Aggies
locale: 9 Las Cruces
Newnan: 4 city, town
locale: 7 Georgia
newness: 7 novelty **10** innovation
New Orleans: 3 spt. **4** city, port, town **6** battle **7** seaport
athletes: 9 Green Wave
city near ~: 5 Houma **6** Kenner
City of ~: 5 train
cuisine: 6 creole
locale: 9 Louisiana
music: 4 jazz
pro team: 6 Saints
sandwich: 5 po boy
school: 6 Loyola, Tulane
New Orleans (1960 song)
artist: Gary U.S. Bonds
Newport: 3 car **4** auto, city, town **8** Chrysler **10** automobile
locale: 5 Wales
New Port ___, FL: 6 Richey
Newport Beach: 4 city, town
locale: 10 California
Newport News: 4 city, town
locale: 8 Virginia
___ New, Pussycat?: 5 What's
New Republic: 3 mag **8** magazine
founder: Herbert Croly
piece: 5 essay
New Rochelle: 4 city, town
athletes: 5 Gaels
locale: 7 New York
school: 4 Iona
news: 3 tip **4** copy, data, dope, info, leak, word **5** cable, media, paper, rumor, scoop, story, telex **6** expose, latest, report, tip-off **7** account, hearsay, lowdown, message, release, scandal, tidings **8** bulletin, dispatch, telecast, telegram **9** broadcast, discovery, eyeopener, headlines, narration, statement **10** communiqué, disclosure, journalism, revelation
bad ~: 4 blow **5** rogue, worry **6** downer, misery, sorrow **7** problem, trouble **9** liability, reckoning, scoundrel **10** misfortune, unpleasant
break the ~: 3 air **4** leak, tell **6** advise, clue in, inform, report, reveal, tip off **7** let slip **8** announce, disclose **9** make known **10** make public
center: 6 agency, bureau
clip: 5 video
ender: 3 boy, man, men **4** cast, girl, reel, room **5** break, maker, paper, print, stand, woman, women **6** caster, letter, monger, people, person, weekly, worthy **8** magazine **9** gathering
exclusive: 5 scoop
flash: 6 notice **8** bulletin, dispatch **10** communiqué, revelation
fresh ~: 4 poop **6** latest
govt. ~ source: 4 USIA
hour: 3 six **4** five, noon **5** seven, six p.m. **6** eleven, five p.m. **7** seven p.m.
in the ~: 3 now **5** fresh **6** recent, trendy **7** current, ongoing, popular, topical **9** happening, immediate **10** in progress, widespread
Italian ~ agency: 4 ANSA
item: 4 clip, obit **5** event, flash, squib, story **9** sound bite
10 communiqué
like a ~ bulletin: 6 just in
like bad ~: 4 glum, grim **5** bleak **6** gloomy **7** ghastly, serious, unhappy **9** cheerless **10** lamentable
like the evening ~: 4 on TV
magazine: 4 Time
maker: 4 star **5** celeb **9** celebrity
medium: 5 daily, press, print, radio
noncommercial ~ source: 3 NPR, PBS
org.: 3 UPI **4** USIA **7** Reuters
perspective: 5 slant
reaction to bad ~: 4 oh no
receive, as ~: 4 hear **5** catch, learn **6** pick up **7** find out **8** discover **9** get wind of
reporter of yore: 5 crier
Russian ~ agency: 4 Tass **8** ITAR-Tass
source: 3 CNN **4** leak **5** MSNBC, paper, radio **6** herald
summary: 5 recap **6** review **8** synopsis
top ~ story: 4 lead **6** leader **8** headline
news ___: 3 peg **4** case, clip **5** flash, media, story
___ news: 3 bad **4** good, hard, soft, spot
___ news?: 3 Any
News: 5 paper
locale: 7 Buffalo, Detroit, Halifax, New York **9** Anchorage **10** Los Angeles
___ News: 4 Good, Nick
___ News Bears, The: 3 Bad
newsboy cry: 5 extra
newscaster: 6 anchor **8** reporter **9** announcer
colonial ~: 5 crier
newscast segment: 5 recap **6** sports
news conference
attendees: 5 media, press
Newsday: 5 paper **9** newspaper
locale: 7 New York **10** Long Island
New Seekers
song: I'd Like to Teach the World to Sing (1971)
Look What They've Done to My Song, Ma (1970)
New Sensation (1988 song)
artist: INXS
newsgroup
problem: 4 spam
protocol: 4 nntp
system: 6 Usenet
newshawk: 8 reporter
goal: 5 scoop
novice ~: 3 cub
pursuit: 5 story
query: 3 how, who, why **4** what, when **5** where
newsmen: 5 press **7** editors, scribes
News-Miner: 5 paper **9** newspaper
locale: 9 Fairbanks
Newsom, Bobo
sport: 8 baseball
Newsome: 5 Ozzie
New South Wales: 5 state **10** Australian
capital: 6 Sydney
city: 6 Sydney **9** Newcastle **10** Wollongong
newspaper: 3 rag **5** daily, extra, organ, press, print, sheet, trade **6** medium, review, weekly **7** gazette, journal, tabloid **8** biweekly **10** periodical
bygone New York ~: 3 Sun **5** World **6** Herald **7** Journal, Tribune **8** American, Telegram
edition: 5 final
employee: 2 ed. **6** critic, editor, writer **8** pressman, reporter
ender: 3 man **5** woman
feature: 3 ads, col. **4** item, obit, Op-Ed, roto **5** piece **6** byline, column, comics **7** funnies, section
filler: 5 squib
holder: 5 twine
Italian ~: 6 Avanti
old ~ machine: 3 TTY **8** teletype
post: 4 beat, desk
Russian ~: 6 Pravda **8** Izvestia
section: 4 desk **5** metro **6** insert, sports
space: 6 linage **7** lineage
special edition: 5 extra
stand: 5 kiosk
third-rate ~: 3 rag
typography: 5 agate, print
Newspaper Days
author: H.L. Mencken
newspaperman: 6 editor, scribe **8** reporter **10** ink slinger, journalist
newspapers: 5 media, press
newspapers (Canada):
Calgary - Herald, Sun
Edmonton - Journal, Sun
Halifax - News, Herald
Montreal - Gazette, Journal, La Presse
Ottawa - Citizen, Le Droit, Sun
Quebec - Le Soleil
Toronto - Globe and Mail, Star, Sun
Vancouver - Province, Sun
Winnipeg - Free Press
newspapers (U.S.):
Albuquerque - Journal, Tribune
Anchorage - News
Atlanta - Journal-Constitution
Baltimore - Sun
Boise - Idaho Statesman
Boston - Globe, Herald
Buffalo - News
Charlotte - Observer
Chicago - Sun-Times, Tribune
Cincinnati - Enquirer, Post
Cleveland - Plain Dealer
Columbus - Dispatch
Dallas - Morning News
Denver - Post
Des Moines - Register
Detroit - Free Press, News
Fairbanks - News-Miner
Fresno - Bee
Ft. Lauderdale - Sun-Sentinel
Ft. Worth - Star-Telegram
Hartford - Courant
Honolulu - Advertiser, Star-Bulletin
Houston - Chronicle
Indianapolis - Star
Jacksonville - Florida Times-Union
Kansas City - Star
Las Vegas - Review-Journal, Sun
Little Rock - Democrat-Gazette
Long Island - Newsday

Los Angeles - News, Times
Louisville - Courier Journal
Memphis - Commercial Appeal
Miami - Herald
Milwaukee - Journal Sentinel
Minneapolis/St. Paul - Pioneer Press, Star Tribune
Mobile - Register
Nashville - Tennesseean
Newark - Star-Ledger
New Orleans - Times-Picayune
New York - News, Post, Times
Norfolk - Virginian-Pilot
Oakland - Tribune
Omaha- World-Herald
Orlando - Sentinel
Philadelphia - Inquirer, News
Phoenix - Arizona Republic
Pittsburgh - Post-Gazette, Tribune-Review
Portland - Oregonian
Providence - Journal-Bulletin
Richmond - Times-Dispatch
Sacramento - Bee
Salt Lake City - Deseret News, Tribune
San Diego - Union-Tribune
San Francisco - Chronicle
San Jose - Mercury News
Santa Ana - Orange County Register
Seattle - Times
St. Louis - Post-Dispatch
St. Petersburg - Times
Tampa - Tribune
Toledo - Blade
Tombstone - Epitaph
Tulsa - World
Washington, D.C. - Post, Times

Newspeak: 5 lingo 10 propaganda
newsprint material: 4 pulp
newsreel: 7 feature
name: 5 Pathé
newsstand: 5 kiosk
Newsweek: 3 mag 8 magazine
items: 3 ads
rival: 4 Time
newsy: 7 gossipy, topical 9 au courant
newt: 3 eft 6 triton 7 axolotl 9 amphibian 10 salamander
__ newt: 5 eye of
Newt: 8 Gingrich
New Tenant, The
author: Eugène Ionesco
New Testament
book: 3 Col., Eph., Gal., Heb., Rev., Rom., Tim. 4 Acts, Hebr., John, Jude, Luke, Mark, Matt., Thes. 5 James, Peter, Thess., Titus 6 Romans 7 Hebrews, Matthew, Timothy 8 Philemon 9 Ephesians, Galatians 10 Colossians, Revelation 11 Corinthians, Philippians 13 Thessalonians
sages: 4 Magi
villain: 5 Herod
see also Bible
Newton: 4 city, Huey, town 5 Isaac, Juice, Minow, Wayne 6 Robert 7 Thandie
contemporary: 6 Halley
__ Newton: 3 Fig
newton cousin: 3 erg 4 dyne 5 joule
Newton, Isaac: 3 Sir 9 physicist, scientist
Newton-John, Olivia
grandfather: Max Born
song: Have You Never Been Mellow (1975)
Heart Attack (1982)
Hopelessly Devoted to You (1978)
I Can't Help It (1980)
If Not for You (1971)
If You Love Me (1974)
I Honestly Love You (1974)
Let Me Be There (1973)
A Little More Love (1978)
Magic (1980)
Make a Move on Me (1982)
Physical (1981)
Please Mr. Please (1975)
Suddenly (1980)
Summer Nights (1978)
Twist of Fate (1983)
Xanadu (1980)
You're the One That I Want (1978)
Newton, Juice
song: Angel of the Morning (1981)
Break It to Me Gently (1982)
Love's Been a Little Bit Hard on Me (1982)
Queen of Hearts (1981)
The Sweetest Thing (1981)
Newton's __ of motion: 3 law
Newton, Wayne
song: Daddy Don't You Walk So Fast (1972)
Danke Schoen (1963)
New Vaudeville Band
song: Winchester Cathedral (1966)
new-wave prefix: 3 neo
New Wave rock group: 4 Devo
__ New Window: 5 Open a
new wine in __ bottles: 3 old
New Woman
rival: 4 Self
new world __: 5 order
New World: 4 Amer. 7 America
__ New World: 5 Brave
__ New World, A: 5 Whole
New World Symphony
composer: Antonín Dvorák
New Year
lunar ~: 3 Tet
noise: 4 toot
resolution: 4 diet
word: 4 auld, lang, syne
New Year's __: 3 Day, Eve
New Year's game: 4 Bowl
New York: 4 city, port, town 5 state
canal: 4 Erie
capital: 6 Albany
city: 3 Rye 4 Rome, Troy 5 Coram, Depew, Islip, Nyack, Olean, Owego, Utica 6 Albany, Armonk, Attica, Auburn, Cohoes, Elmira, Elmont, Ithaca, Selden 7 Baldwin, Buffalo, Commack, Massena, Medford, Merrick, Montauk, New City, New York, Oneonta, Penn Yan, Shirley, Yonkers 8 Bay Shore, Brighton, Copiague, Deer Park, Dix Hills, Freeport, Glen Cove, Harrison, Holbrook, Kingston, Lockport, Newburgh, Ossining, Syracuse 9 Amsterdam, Brentwood, Great Neck, Hauppauge, Hempstead, Jamestown, Levittown, Long Beach, Oceanside, Peekskill, Plainview, Rochester, Rotterdam, Sag Harbor, Smithtown, Tonawanda, Uniondale, Watertown, West Islip 10 Binghamton, Centereach, East Meadow, Garden City, Hicksville, Huntington, Lackawanna, Massapequa, Middletown, Ronkonkoma, West Seneca
college: 4 Iona, Pace 5 Mercy, Siena, Touro 6 C.W. Post, Hunter, Marist, Vassar 7 Adelphi, Colgate, Cornell, Fordham, Hofstra, St. John's 8 Columbia 9 West Point 10 Saint John's
county: 4 Erie 5 Bronx, Tioga, Yates 6 Albany, Cayuga, Nassau, Oneida, Otsego, Seneca, Ulster 7 Genesee, Ontario, Steuben, Suffolk 8 Saratoga
in a ~ minute: 4 fast 6 at once 9 instantly, posthaste, right away
Indian: 4 Erie 6 Cayuga, Mohawk, Oneida, Seneca 7 Mahican, Mohican 8 Onondaga 9 Tuscarora
island: 4 Fire 5 Coney, Ellis 6 Rikers, Staten 9 Manhattan
lake: 5 Keuka 6 Cayuga, Oneida, Otsego, Seneca 9 Champlain 10 Chautauqua, Lake Placid
minute: 5 trice
motto: 9 Excelsior
mountain: 5 Marcy
neighbor: 6 Canada, Quebec 7 Ontario, Vermont 9 New Jersey
pro team: 4 Jets, Mets 5 Bills 6 Giants, Knicks 7 Rangers, Yankees 9 Islanders
river: 4 East 5 Tioga 6 Harlem, Hudson, Mohawk
state beverage: 4 milk
state bird: 8 bluebird
state fish: 10 brook trout
state flower: 4 rose
state fruit: 5 apple
state gem: 6 garnet
state insect: 7 ladybug
state mammal: 6 beaver
state motto: 9 Excelsior
state muffin: 5 apple
state shell: 7 scallop
state tree: 10 sugar maple
waterfall: 7 Niagara
New York __: 3 Bay, cut 4 City, Post 5 steak, strip, Times 6 minute
New York __ Exchange: 5 Stock
New York __ of Mind: 5 State
__ New York: 3 Old 7 Greater
New York Bay
island: 4 Long 5 Ellis 6 Staten 7 Liberty 9 Manhattan
river to ~: 6 Hudson
New York City: 3 spt. 4 port 6 Gotham 7 seaport 8 Big Apple
area: 4 Soho 6 Bowery, Harlem 7 Chelsea, Tribeca
avenue: 4 Park 5 Fifth 7 Madison 9 Lexington
baseballer: 3 Met 4 Yank 6 Yankee
borough: 5 Bronx 6 Queens 8 Brooklyn 9 Manhattan
cager: 5 Knick
county: 5 Bronx, Kings 6 Queens 7 New York 8 Richmond
footballer: 3 Jet 5 Giant
former ballpark: 4 Shea
hotel: 5 Plaza
newspaper: 4 News, Post 5 Times
restaurant: 6 Sardi's 7 Elaine's
river: 4 East 6 Harlem, Hudson
store: 4 Saks 5 Macy's
street: 4 Wall 8 Broadway
suburb: 3 Rye 5 Nyack
New York Cosmos
org.: 4 NASL
star: 4 Pelé
New York cut: 5 steak
New York Enquirer boss: 4 Kane
New Yorker: 3 car 4 auto 8 Chrysler
New Yorkers, The: 7 musical
composer: Cole Porter
New Yorker, The: 3 mag
cartoonist: 3 Rea 4 Arno 5 Chast, Steig 6 Addams 7 Thurber
editor: 5 Brown, Shawn
founder: Jane Grant, Harold Ross
mascot: 6 Tilley 7 Eustace
__ New York in June...: 5 I like
New York Liberty
org.: 4 WNBA
New York Life
competitor: **see** insurance company
__ New York minute: 3 in a
New York, New York (1977 film)
cast: Robert De Niro, Liza Minnelli
director: Martin Scorsese
New York's __: 6 Finest
New York Times
onetime ~ publisher: 4 Ochs
New York World journalist: 3 Bly
New Zealand: 4 isls. 5 isles 6 nation 7 country, islands
aborigine: 5 Maori
bird: 3 kea, moa, oii, tui 4 huia, kaka, kiwi, weka 6 kakapo, takahe 8 notornis
capital: 10 Wellington
city: 6 Nelson 7 Dunedin, Manukau 8 Auckland, Hamilton 10 Wellington
evergreen: 5 kauri
explorer: 6 Tasman
export: 4 lamb, wool
fish: 3 ihi 4 hiku 6 hapuku, inanga 7 whapuku 8 hiwi hiwi
island: 4 Niue 5 North, South 9 Antipodes
lake: 5 Taupo
language: 5 Maori
money: 4 cent 6 dollar
mountain: 4 Cook
nation north of ~: 4 Fiji
native: 4 kiwi 5 Maori
parrot: 3 kea 4 kaka 6 kakapo
playwright: 8 Sargeson
poet: 6 Adcock, Baxter, Curnow
river: 6 Clutha
sea: 4 Ross 6 Tasman
sheep: 10 Corriedale
shrub: 4 hebe, karo 7 geebung 8 myoporum
soldier: 5 Anzac
soprano: 4 Alda 8 te Kanawa
tree: 4 hebe, karo, rimu 5 kauri, mapau 6 kapuka, kowhai, tarata

volcano: 7 Ruapehu
waterfall: 6 Helena
writer: 5 Frame, Marsh 8 Ihimaera, Sargeson 9 Mansfield
Nexö, Martin Andersen: 6 Danish, writer
work: Pelle the Conqueror
next: 4 then 5 close, later 6 behind, beside, hard by, on deck, second 7 closest, ensuing, nearest 8 abutting, adjacent, coming up, touching 9 adjoining, after that, afterward, alongside, following, proximate, thereupon 10 back-to-back, consequent, sequential, subsequent, succeeding, successive, thereafter
be ~ to: 4 abut 6 adjoin, appose 8 neighbor
come ~: 5 ensue 6 follow 7 succeed
coming ~: 3 fol. 5 after 9 following
door: 4 near 5 close 6 at hand, nearby 8 abutting, adjacent, touching 9 adjoining, bordering, immediate, in contact 10 contiguous, convenient, juxtaposed
get ~ to: 3 woo 7 flatter, promote 8 butter up 9 cultivate, shine up to 10 curry favor
go ~: 7 succeed 9 come after
in baseball: 6 on deck
in line: 4 heir 5 first 7 heiress, legatee 9 inheritor
to: 4 with 6 at hand, beside 8 abutting, adjacent 9 alongside
to nothing: 5 least, scant 6 meager
world: 6 heaven 7 Elysium 8 paradise 9 hereafter
next-__ neighbor: 4 door
__ next?: 4 Who's
Next
song: I Still Love You (1998) Too Close (1998)
Next (2007 film)
cast: Jessica Biel, Nicolas Cage, Julianne Moore
Next Best Thing, The (2000 film)
cast: Benjamin Bratt, Rupert Everett, Madonna
__ next door: 3 boy 4 girl
Next Door to an Angel (1962 song)
artist: Neil Sedaka
Nextel
alternative: 5 Nokia 7 T-Mobile 8 Ericsson, Motorola
next in __: 4 line
next of __: 3 kin
Next Time I Fall, The (1986 song)
artist: Peter Cetera, Amy Grant
__ Next Time, The: 4 Fire
next-to-last
item: 6 penult
nexus: 3 tie 4 link, yoke 5 focus, joint 6 center 7 network 8 ligature, vinculum 10 connection
Neyman: 5 Jerzy
__-nez: 5 pince
__-Nez: 4 Gris
Nez Percé: 5 tribe 6 Indian 7 Amerind 8 language
NFC
division: 4 East, West
team: 4 Bucs, Rams 5 Bears, Lions, Skins, Vikes 6 Eagles, Giants, Niners, Saints 7 Cowboys, Falcons, Packers, Vikings 8 Panthers, Redskins, Seahawks 9 Cardinals 10 Buccaneers
NFL
broadcaster: 4 ESPN
city: 5 Miami, Tampa 6 Dallas, Denver 7 Atlanta, Buffalo, Chicago, Detroit, New York, Oakland, Seattle, St. Louis 8 Green Bay, San Diego 9 Baltimore, Cleveland 10 Cincinnati, Kansas City, New Orleans, Pittsburgh, Washington 12 Indianapolis, Jacksonville, Philadelphia, San Francisco
conference: 4 East, West
div.: 3 AFC, NFC
exec: 2 GM
honor: 6 All-Pro
official: 3 ref 5 zebra 7 referee
part: 4 Natl. 6 League 8 Football, National
period: 2 OT 3 qtr. 7 quarter 8 overtime
player: 2 FB, LG, LH, LT, QB, RB, RG, RT 3 end, pro, RFB, RHB 4 back 5 guard 6 center, tackle 8 fullback, halfback
score: 2 FG, pt., TD 5 point 9 field goal, touchdown
squad: 3 def., off. 7 defense, offense
team: 4 Jets, Rams 5 Bears, Bills, Colts, Lions 6 Browns, Chiefs, Eagles, eleven, Giants, Niners, Ravens, Saints, Sharks, Texans, Titans 7 Bengals, Broncos, Cowboys, Falcons, Jaguars, Packers, Raiders, Vikings 8 Chargers, Dolphins, Panthers, Patriots, Redskins, Seahawks, Steelers 9 Cardinals 10 Buccaneers
see also football
Nfld.: 3 isl. 4 prov.
see also Newfoundland
Ngaio: 5 Marsh
Ngo __ Diem: 4 Dinh
Ngor, Haing S. Oscar: The Killing Fields
Nguyen Van __: 5 Thieu
NH
neighbor: 3 Que. 4 Mass.
region: 4 N. Eng.
see also New Hampshire
NH2, compound with: 5 amide
NH3, derived from: 6 ammono
Nha Trang: 4 city, town
locale: 7 Vietnam
NHL
city: 5 Tampa 6 Boston, Dallas, Ottawa 7 Buffalo, Calgary, Chicago, Detroit, New York, Phoenix, San Jose, St. Louis, Toronto 8 Columbus, Edmonton, Montreal 9 Nashville, Vancouver 10 Los Angeles, Pittsburgh, Washington 12 Philadelphia
fake-out: 4 deke
Hall-of-Famer: 3 Orr 4 Howe, Hull, Park 5 Bossy 6 Dionne, Mikita, Parent, Plante, Potvin 7 Federko, Gilbert, Gillies, Gretzky, Lafleur, Langway, Lemieux, Richard, Sawchuk, Worsley 8 Bathgate, Bobby Orr, Brad Park, Esposito, Trottier 9 Bobby Hull, Geoffrion, Mike Bossy 10 Gordie Howe, Guy Lafleur, Rod Gilbert, Stan Mikita
player: 2 LW, RW 3 pro 6 center, goalie, iceman, skater 8 left wing 9 right wing
player at times: 4 icer
stat: 3 pts. 5 goals 6 points 7 assists.
team: 3 six 4 Caps, Habs, Wild 5 Blues, Isles, Kings, Leafs, Stars 6 Bruins, Devils, Flames, Flyers, Oilers, Sabres, Sharks 7 Canucks, Coyotes, Rangers 8 Capitals, Panthers, Penguins, Red Wings, Senators 9 Avalanche, Canadiens, Islanders, Lightning, Predators, Thrashers 10 Blackhawks, Hurricanes, Maple Leafs
tiebreaker: 2 OT 8 overtime
venue: 3 ice 4 rink
see also hockey
Ni: 4 elem. 6 nickel 7 element
28 for ~: 4 at. no.
Nia: 4 Long 7 Peeples 8 Vardalos
niacin: 4 acid 7 vitamin 8 B vitamin
niagara: 7 cascade, torrent 9 waterfall
Niagara: 5 falls, grape, green, river 9 waterfall
fort: 4 Erie
relative: 8 Cabernet
see also wine
Niagara (1953 film)
cast: Joseph Cotten, Marilyn Monroe
Niagara Falls: 4 city, town
craft: 6 barrel
like ~: 3 wet 5 aroar, misty
locale: 6 Canada 7 New York, Ontario
Niamey: 4 city, town 7 capital
locale: 5 Niger
nib: 3 pen, tip 4 beak, bill 5 point, tinge 8 penpoint
nibble: 3 eat, nip 4 bite, chew, crop, gnaw, nosh, peck 5 crumb, eat at, graze, munch, snack, taste 6 morsel, nosh on, pick at, tidbit 7 consume, soupçon 8 spoonful 9 grab a bite, masticate
__ Nibelungen: 3 Die
Nibelungenlied: 4 epic, saga
Nibelung hoard: 4 gold
niblick: 4 club, iron 8 golf club
__ niblick: 6 mashie
Niblo: 4 Fred
__ nibs: 3 her, his
nibs, his: 4 king
nicad __: 7 battery
Nicaragua: 6 nation 7 country
capital: 7 Managua
city: 4 León 6 Estelí, Masaya 7 Managua
from ~: 6 Latino
Indian: 7 Miskito
money: 7 cordoba
neighbor: 8 Honduras 9 Costa Rica
org.: 3 OAS
poet: 5 Darío 8 Cardinal
rebel: 6 Contra
volcano: 6 Masaya 9 Momotombo
see also Spanish
Niccolò: 8 Paganini
NiCd __: 7 battery
nice: 4 cosy, cozy, fair, homy, kind, okey, prim, tidy, trim, warm 5 cozey, cozie, exact, fussy, homey, nifty, picky, right, sweet, tasty 6 dainty, dead-on, decent, deluxe, genial, gentle, kindly, minute, modest, polite, pretty, savory, seemly, smooth, social, subtle, toothy 7 affable, amiable, amusing, careful, cordial, correct, ethical, genteel, helpful, likable, mincing, precise, refined, upscale, welcome, winning, winsome 8 becoming, charming, cheerful, clean-cut, cultured, decorous, delicate, esthetic, faithful, flawless, friendly, generous, graceful, gracious, humorous, inviting, ladylike, likeable, obliging, polished, tasteful, ticklish, virtuous, well-bred, wondrous 9 befitting, civilized, courteous, delicious, faultless, favorable, simpatico, succulent, wonderful 10 attractive, charitable, cultivated, delightful, fastidious, methodical, meticulous, particular, personable, satisfying, scrupulous
insincerely ~: 4 oily 6 greasy, smarmy 7 servile 8 unctuous 10 obsequious
make ~: 3 pat 6 caress, soothe 7 appease
Nelly: 4 prig 7 puritan 8 bluenose 10 goody-goody
no ~ guy: 4 ogre 5 meany 6 meanie
see also wonderful
nice __: 5 as pie, nelly
__ nice: 4 make
Nice: 4 city, town
locale: 6 France
port near ~: 7 Antibes
Nice __: 5 'n' Easy
Nice __!: 5 catch, going
Nice __ With You: 4 to Be
__ Nice Clambake: 5 A Real
__ nice day!: 5 Have a
Nice guys finish __: 4 last
nicely: 4 well 8 worthily
Nice 'N' __: 4 Easy
Nicene __: 5 Creed 7 Council
Nicene Council concern: 6 heresy
__ nice place to visit...: 4 It's a
Nice & Slow (1998 song)
artist: Usher
niceties: 5 mores 7 decency, decorum, details, nuances 8 courtesy, minutiae, protocol 9 etiquette, fine print, gentility, politesse, propriety, punctilio 10 convention, politeness, refinement, seemliness
Nice to Be With You (1972 song)
artist: Gallery
__ Nice to Have a Man...: 5 It's So
nicety: 5 point 6 detail, nuance 8 ceremony, quiddity, subtlety 9 fine point, punctilio 10 refinement
Nice Work if You Can Get It
composer: George Gershwin, Ira Gershwin
niche: 3 bay, job 4 hole, nest, nook, room, slot 5 cubby, place 6 alcove, corner, cranny, hollow, recess 7 calling, opening 8 position, vocation 9 cubbyhole, specialty 10 pigeonhole
Nichelle: 7 Nichols
Nicholas: 3 Ray 4 Gage, Paul, pope,

Rowe, tsar **5** Brady, Meyer, saint **6** Biddle, Denise, Fayard, Harold **7** Boileau, Brendon, Pileggi, pontiff, Webster **9** Colasanto
in German: **5** Klaus
in Italian: **6** Nicola
Nicholas Nickleby
author: Charles Dickens
character: **3** Peg **4** Bray, Kate, Knag, Pyke **5** Celia, Edwin, Fanny, Gride, Noggs, Ralph, Smike **7** Matilda, Squeers
Nicholas Nickleby (play)
cast: Roger Rees
Nichols: **3** Kid, Red **4** Anne, Mike **5** Peter **8** Nichelle
Nichols, Anne hero: **4** Abie
Nichols, Mike: **8** director
collaborator: Elaine May
film: Biloxi Blues (1988)
the Birdcage (1995)
Carnal Knowledge (1971)
Catch-22 (1970)
Charlie Wilson's War (2007)
Closer (2004)
The Graduate (1967, AA)
Heartburn (1986)
Postcards From the Edge (1990)
Primary Colors (1998)
Regarding Henry (1991)
Silkwood (1983)
What Planet Are You From? (2000)
Who's Afraid of Virginia Woolf? (1966)
Wolf (1994)
Working Girl (1988)
spouse: Diane Sawyer
Nicholson, Jack: **5** actor
film: About Schmidt (2002)
Anger Management (2003)
As Good as It Gets (1997, AA)
Batman (1989)
The Border (1982)
The Bucket List (2007)
Carnal Knowledge (1971)
Chinatown (1974)
The Departed (2006)
Easy Rider (1969)
A Few Good Men (1992)
Five Easy Pieces (1970)
Goin' South (1978)
Heartburn (1986)
Hoffa (1992)
Ironweed (1987)
The King of Marvin Gardens (1972)
The Last Detail (1973)
Mars Attacks! (1996)
One Flew Over the Cuckoo's Nest (1975, AA)
The Pledge (2001)
Prizzi's Honor (1985)
Reds (1981)
The Shining (1980)
The Shooting (1967)
Something's Gotta Give (2003)
Terms of Endearment (1983, AA)
The Two Jakes (1990)
The Witches of Eastwick (1987)
Wolf (1994)
Nichols, Peter: **7** English **10** playwright
Nichols, Red: **9** trumpeter
genre: **4** jazz
nicht __: **4** wahr
nick: **3** con, cut, jag, mar **4** bilk, chip, dent, ding, dupe, gaol, hurt, jail, mark, rook, scar, slit, snip **5** cheat, gouge, knock, notch, score, swipe, trick, wound **6** damage, delude, fleece, incise, injury, take in **7** defraud, mislead, scratch, swindle, two-time **8** flimflam, hoodwink, puncture, sucker in **9** bamboozle, victimize
cause: **5** razor
ender: **4** name
in the ~ of time: **6** barely **9** opportune **10** felicitous
Nick: **4** Lowe **5** Adams, Faldo, Nolte, Price, Stahl **6** Gilder, Lachey, Searcy **7** Ashford, Charles, Clooney **10** Buoniconti, Cassavetes
dog: **4** Asta
wife: **4** Nora
__ Nick: **3** Old **5** Saint
Nick at Nite staple: **5** rerun
nickel: **4** cash, coin **5** bread, dough, metal, money **6** change **7** element
alloy: **5** Invar, Monel **6** alnico **7** Elinvar, Inconel, Mumetal, nitinol
bad ~: **4** slug
ender: **5** odeon
like a new ~: **5** shiny **6** bright
ore: **9** millerite, niccolite
word on a ~: **3** God **4** five, unum **5** cents, trust **7** liberty **8** pluribus
nickel-__ battery: **7** cadmium
__ nickel: **4** plug **7** plugged
__-nickel: **6** double
nickel-and-__: **4** dime
nickelodeon
heroine: **6** damsel
opening: **4** slot
Nickelodeon (1976 film)
cast: Ryan O'Neal, Tatum O'Neal, Burt Reynolds
director: Peter Bogdanovich
nicker: **5** neigh
Nicklaus, Jack: **6** golfer **10** Golden Bear
alma mater: **3** OSU
rival: **6** Palmer, Player
Nickleby portrayer: **4** Rees
nickname: **3** dub, tag **5** alias, label **6** handle **7** agnomen, entitle, epithet, intitle, moniker **8** cognomen, monicker **9** sobriquet **10** diminutive
in Spanish: **4** mote
Nick News (Nickelodeon) host: Linda Ellerbee
nick of __: **4** time
Nick of Time (1989 album)
artist: Bonnie Raitt
Nickolas: **7** Ashford
Nicks, Stevie
member: Fleetwood Mac
song: Edge of Seventeen (1982)
I Can't Wait (1986)
If Anyone Falls (1983)
Leather and Lace (1981)
Rooms on Fire (1989)
Stand Back (1983)
Stop Draggin' My Heart Around (1981)
Talk to Me (1985)
Nicol: **10** Williamson
Nicola: **5** Sacco
Nicolai: **4** Otto
Nicolaou: **3** Ted
Nicolas: **4** Cage, Roeg **6** Appert **7** Leblanc, Poussin, Sarkozy
aunt: **5** Talia
see also French
Nicolás: **7** Guillén
Nicolaus: **10** Copernicus
Nicolay: **5** Basov
Nicole: **6** Eggert, Kidman
__ Nicole Carson: **4** Lisa
Nicolet: **4** Jean
Nicolette: **6** Larson **8** Sheridan
Nicollette: **8** Sheridan
Nicolo: **5** Amati
Nicolson: **5** Adela
Nicosia: **4** city, town **7** capital
locale: **6** Cyprus
nicotinic __: **4** acid
nictate: **4** wink **5** blink
nictitate: **4** wink **5** blink
__ Nidal: **3** Abu
Nidetch: **4** Jean
nidge: **6** quiver
__ Nidre: **3** Kol
nidus: **4** nest **6** hotbed
builder: **4** wasp **6** insect, spider
Niebuhr: **8** Reinhold
niece: **3** kin **5** woman **7** kinsman **8** relative **9** kinswoman
maybe: **4** heir **9** inheritor
starter: **5** grand
Niekro: **3** Joe **4** Phil
Niels: **4** Bohr **5** Jerne **6** Finsen
Nielsen: **4** Asta, Rick **5** rater **6** Arthur, Leslie **8** Brigitte
family need: **2** TV **5** TV set **10** television
letters: **3** ABC, CBS, Fox, NBC
Nielsen __: **6** rating
Nielsen, Brigitte: **7** actress
spouse: Sylvester Stallone
Nielsen, Leslie: **5** actor
film: Airplane! (1980)
Forbidden Planet (1956)
The Naked Gun (1988)
The Poseidon Adventure (1972)
Spy Hard (1996)
Nietzsche, Friedrich: **4** poet **6** German **11** philosopher
concept: **10** Ubermensch
work: Beyond Good and Evil
Thus Spake Zarathustra
nifty: **4** chic, cool, good, keen, neat, nice **5** dandy, great, marvy, neato, quick, sharp, smart, super, swell **6** adroit, clever, dapper, far-out, groovy, peachy, spruce **7** corking, stylish, voguish **8** pleasing, terrific **9** agreeable, enjoyable, excellent, ingenious, marvelous **10** out of sight, peachy-keen
Nigel: **5** Bruce, Green **6** Havers **7** Patrick **9** Davenport, Hawthorne
Niger: **5** river **6** nation **7** country
bovine: **4** Kuri
capital: **6** Niamey
city: **6** Agadez, Maradi, Niamey, Tahoua, Zinder
city on the ~: **8** Timbuktu
delta resident: **3** Ijo
lake: **4** Chad
language of ~: **5** Hausa
money: **5** franc
neighbor: **4** Chad, Mali **5** Benin, Libya **7** Algeria, Nigeria
people: **3** Ebo, Ibo **4** Eboe, Igbo **5** Hausa **6** Haussa, Kanuri, Tuareg **7** Songhai
River locale: **4** Mali **6** Guinea **7** Nigeria
river to the ~: **5** Benue
Nigeria: **6** nation **7** country
bovine: **4** Kuri
capital: **5** Abuja
city: **3** Aba, Ede, Ife, Ila, Oyo **4** Kano **5** Abuja, Lagos, Zaria **6** Ibadan, Ilesha, Ilorin, Kaduna **9** Benin City
district: **5** Benin
former ~ region: **6** Biafra
lake: **4** Chad
language: **3** Ebo, Gbe, Ibo **4** Eboe, Igbo **6** Ibibio
locale: **6** Africa
money: **4** kobo **5** naira
neighbor: **4** Chad **5** Benin, Niger **8** Cameroon
Nobelist in Literature: **7** Soyinka
org.: **4** OPEC
people: **3** Ebo, Edo, Ibo, Ijo, Tiv **4** Bini, Eboe, Efik, Ekoi, Fula, Igbo, Ijaw, Yedo **5** Gbari, Gwari, Hausa, Yeddo **6** Fulani, Haussa, Ibibio, Kanuri, Yoruba
singer: **4** Sade
writer: **5** Aluko, Amadi, Nwapa, Okara **6** Achebe **7** Ekwensi, Equiano, Munonye, Soyinka
niggle: **4** carp **5** argue, cavil, gripe **6** bicker, dabble, tinker **7** nitpick, quibble **8** pettifog, squabble **9** criticize **10** play around, split hairs
niggling: **4** puny **5** least, petty **6** measly **7** trivial **8** piddling, trifling
nigh: **4** most, near, soon **5** anear, close **6** almost, at hand, hard by, nearby, nearly **7** close by, looming **8** adjacent, imminent **9** bordering, impending, in the wind, presently, proximate, virtually **10** convenient
__-nigh: **4** well
night: **4** dark **5** gloom **6** sunset **7** bedtime, evening, sundown **8** darkness, eventide, twilight, wee hours **9** after dark, nocturnal, pitch dark **10** after hours
and day: **7** nonstop **9** endlessly **10** unendingly
attire: **3** PJs **4** gown, robe **6** kimono **7** jammies, pajamas **8** lingerie, negligee
before: **3** eve
biter: **6** bedbug
combining form: **4** noct-, nyct- **5** nocti-, nycti-, nycto-
dance all ~: **5** party, revel **9** celebrate, make merry
display: **6** aurora
duty: **5** vigil
ender: **3** cap, jar **4** club, fall, glow, gown, hawk, life, long, mare, spot, time, wear **5** dress, rider, scape, shade, shift, shirt, stand, stick **7** clothes
end of the ~: **4** dawn **5** sunup **7** sunrise
flyer: **3** bat, owl **4** moth
hunter: **5** civet
in French: **4** nuit
in German: **5** nacht
in Spanish: **5** noche
light: **4** neon, star
name meaning ~: **5** Leila

opening ~: 5 debut 8 premiere
place to spend the ~: 3 bed, inn, pad 4 room 5 B and B, hotel, motel 6 hostel 8 motor inn 10 motor lodge
preceder: 4 dusk 6 sunset 7 sundown 8 twilight
prepare to spend the ~: 6 encamp
Roman goddess of ~: 3 Nox
shade: 4 ebon 5 sable
sound: 3 ZZZ 5 snore
spot: 3 bar, bed 4 bunk, café, dive, spot 5 boîte, disco, joint, venue 6 bistro, casino, tavern 7 cabaret 8 hideaway 9 honky-tonk, roadhouse, speakeasy 10 restaurant, supper club
starter: 3 mid, twi 4 fort, over, week
they're counted at ~: 5 sheep
three-dog ~: 3 raw 6 chilly, frigid, wintry 7 wintery 8 freezing
to poets: 3 e'en
watchman: 5 guard 6 sentry 7 lookout
night __: 3 key, owl 5 court, light, shift, stick, table, watch 6 school 7 crawler
__ night: 4 bank, good 5 first 6 school 7 amateur, opening
__-night: 3 all 4 late 5 fly-by 6 nighty
Night
author: Elie Wiesel
Night (1960 song)
artist: Jackie Wilson
Night __: 5 Court, Fever, Magic, Moves, Music, Train 6 and Day 7 Gallery, Journey, Passage
Night __ a Thousand Eyes, The: 3 Has
Night __ Lane: 5 Train
__ Night: 3 One 4 Last, Prom, Wild 5 Such a 6 Fright, Ladies, Lonely, Silent, Starry 7 Opening, Twelfth
Night and Day
composer: Cole Porter
Night and Day (1946 film): 7 musical
cast: Cary Grant, Alexis Smith
Night at the Museum (2006 film)
cast: Mickey Rooney, Ben Stiller, Dick Van Dyke, Robin Williams
Night at the Opera, A (1935 film)
cast: Kitty Carlisle, Margaret Dumont, Allan Jones, Chico Marx, Groucho Marx, Harpo Marx
role: 4 Otis, Rosa 6 Baroni 7 Tomasso 8 Claypool, Fiorello 9 Driftwood
song: 5 Alone 8 Cosi Cosa
Night at the Vulcan
author: Ngaio Marsh
Night Awakens, The
author: Mary Higgins Clark
nightcap: 4 game 5 drink 8 libation
Night Chills
author: Dean Koontz
nightclothes: 3 PJs 4 gown, robe 6 kimono 7 jammies, pajamas 8 lingerie, negligee
nightclub: 3 bar 4 café, dive, spot 5 boîte, disco, joint, venue 6 bistro, casino 7 cabaret 8 hideaway 9 honky-tonk, roadhouse, speakeasy 10 restaurant
charge: 5 cover
New York ~: 4 Copa
number: 4 song 6 ballad
production: 3 act 5 revue 6 review
worker: 2 MC 5 B-girl, comic, emcee 6 singer, waiter 8 comedian, waitress 9 bartender
Night Court (NBC sitcom)
cast: Harry Anderson (Judge Harry Stone)
Selma Diamond (Selma Hacker)
John Larroquette (Dan Fielding)
Richard Moll (Bailiff Bull Shannon)
Markie Post (Christine Sullivan)
Marsha Warfield (Bailiff Roz Russell)
nightcrawler: 4 bait, worm
__-night doubleheader: 3 twi
__-nighter: 3 all
__ Nighter: 5 First
nightfall: 4 dark, dusk 6 curfew, sunset 7 day's end, evening, sundown 8 darkness, eventide, gloaming, moonrise, twilight 10 crepuscule
Night Fever (1978 song)
artist: Bee Gees
Night Flight
author: Antoine de Saint-Exupéry
Night Gallery (NBC sci-fi) host: Rod Serling
nightgown: 8 lingerie 10 sleep shirt
Night Has a Thousand Eyes, The (1962 song)
artist: Bobby Vee
nighthawk: 4 bird
nightie: 8 lingerie
Night in Casablanca, A (1946 film)
cast: Chico Marx, Groucho Marx, Harpo Marx
nightingale: 4 bird 6 bulbul, singer
Nightingale: 5 nurse 6 Maxine 8 Florence
prop: 4 lamp
Nightingale (1975 song)
artist: Carole King
Nightingale, Maxine
song: Lead Me On (1979)
Right Back Where We Started From (1976)
__ Night in the Tropics: 3 One
__ Night, Irene: 4 Good
nightjar: 4 bird 10 goatsucker
__ Night, Ladies: 4 Good
Nightline (ABC news)
anchor: Ted Koppel
__ Night Long: 3 All
nightly: 9 after dark, nocturnal
Night Magic
author: Thomas Tryon
Night Mail
author: W.H. Auden
nightmare: 4 bane, hell 5 dream, trial 6 blight, ordeal, plague, vision 7 bugbear, incubus 8 bad dream, calamity, disaster, illusion 9 detriment, ruination
Nightmare Abbey
author: Thomas Peacock
Nightmare in Pink
author: John D. MacDonald
Nightmare Journey
author: Dean Koontz
Nightmare on Elm Street, A (1984 film)
cast: Ronee Blakley, Heather Langenkamp, John Saxon
director: Wes Craven
nightmarish: 4 dire 5 awful, scary, weird 6 creepy, horrid 7 ghastly, surreal 8 alarming, dreadful, horrible 9 frightful, harrowing, unearthly 10 terrifying
'Night, Mother: 4 film, play
author: Marsha Norman
cast: Anne Bancroft, Sissy Spacek
Night Moves (1975 film)
cast: Susan Clark, Gene Hackman, Jennifer Warren
director: Arthur Penn
Night Moves (1977 song)
artist: Bob Seger
Night Music
author: Clifford Odets
__ Night Music, A: 6 Little
Night of Camp David
author: Fletcher Knebel
Night of the Grizzly, The (1966 film)
cast: Jack Elam, Ron Ely, Martha Hyer
Night of the Hunter, The (1955 film)
cast: Lillian Gish, Robert Mitchum, Shelley Winters
director: Charles Laughton
screenwriter: 4 Agee
Night of the Iguana, The: 4 film, play
author: Tennessee Williams
cast: Richard Burton, Ava Gardner, Deborah Kerr
director: John Huston
Night of the Living Dead (1968 film)
director: George A. Romero
Night of the Moonbow
author: Thomas Tryon
Night on Bald Mountain, A
composer: Modest Mussorgsky
Night on Earth (1991 film)
cast: Giancarlo Esposito, Gena Rowlands, Winona Ryder
Night Over Taos
author: Maxwell Anderson
__ Nights: 6 Boogie, Summer 7 Endless
Nights Are Forever Without You (1976 song)
artist: England Dan and John Ford Coley
nightshade: 4 weed 5 plant 6 datura
__ nightshade: 6 deadly
Nightshift (1985 song)
artist: Commodores
Night Shift
author: Stephen King
Night Shift (1982 film)
cast: Michael Keaton, Shelley Long, Henry Winkler
director: Ron Howard
nightshirt, British: 4 sark
Nights in Rodanthe (2008 film)
cast: Diane Lane
director: Richard Gere
Nights in White Satin (1972 song)
artist: Moody Blues
Nights on Broadway (1975 song)
artist: Bee Gees
nightspot: 3 bar 4 café, dive, spot 5 boîte, disco, joint, venue 6 bistro, casino 7 cabaret 8 hideaway, piano bar, taphouse 9 honky-tonk, roadhouse, speakeasy 10 restaurant, supper club
nightstick: 4 club 5 baton 6 cudgel 8 bludgeon 9 billy club, truncheon
__ Night, Sweetheart: 4 Good
Night the Lights Went Out in Georgia, The (1973 song)
artist: Vicki Lawrence
Night They Drove Old Dixie Down, The (1971 song)
artist: Joan Baez
Night They Invented Champagne, The
composer: Alan Jay Lerner, Frederick Loewe
musical: 4 Gigi
Night They Raided Minsky's, The (1968 film)
cast: Britt Ekland, Jason Robards, Norman Wisdom
director: William Friedkin
nighttime: 3 eve 7 evening 8 eventide, twilight, wee hours 9 after dark 10 after hours
to a poet: 3 e'en
Night Train: 4 Lane
Nightwatch (1998 film)
cast: Patricia Arquette, Josh Brolin, Ewan McGregor, Nick Nolte
nightwear: 3 PJs 7 jammies, pajamas
Nightwood
author: Djuna Barnes
NIH
department: 3 HHS
part: 3 Nat. 4 Inst., Natl. 6 Health 8 National 10 Institutes
nihilism: 6 denial 7 anarchy, atheism, mob rule 8 disorder 9 disbelief, nonbelief, rejection, terrorism 10 skepticism
nihilist: 5 rebel 7 radical, sceptic, skeptic 8 ultraist
nihilistic: 7 lawless, radical
nihility: 4 hole, void, zero 5 abyss 6 vacuum 7 vacuity
Nijinsky, Vaslav: 6 dancer 7 danseur
specialty: 5 dance 6 ballet
Nik: 7 Kershaw
Nike: 6 sneaks 7 missile 8 sneakers
endorser: 5 Tiger, Woods 7 athlete
parent: 4 Ares, Styx 6 Pallas
rival: 4 Avia, Keds, Puma 6 Adidas, Etonic, Reebok
swoosh: 4 logo
Niki: 5 Lauda
Nikita: 10 Khrushchev
see also Russian
Nikita (1986 song)
artist: Elton John
Nikki: 3 Cox 7 Blonsky 8 Giovanni
Nikola: 5 Tesla
Nikolaas: 9 Tinbergen
Nikolai: 5 Gogol 8 Berdyaev
see also Russian
Nikolai __-Korsakov: 6 Rimsky
Nikolaidi: 5 Elena
Nikolaus: 4 Otto
Nikolay: 7 Semenov 8 Karamzin, Nekrasov 10 Zabolotsky
Nikon: 3 SLR 6 camera
rival: *see* camera
nil: 3 nix, zip 4 nada, none, zero 5 aught, ought, zilch, zippo 6 bubkes, bupkis, cipher, naught, nought 7 nothing 8 goose egg 9 valueless

in Spanish: 4 nada
nil __ bonum: 4 nisi
Nile: 4 blue 5 green, river 6 battle 8 greenish
alternative: *see* blue color, green color
ancient ~ city: 4 Sais 5 Meroe, Tanis 6 Thebes
ancient ~ kingdom: 5 Nubia
annual ~ event: 5 flood
city on the ~: 4 Giza 5 Aswan, Asyut, Cairo, Luxor, Tanta 6 Assiut, Assuan 7 Assouan 10 Alexandria
dam: 5 Aswan
denizen: 4 croc, ibis
desert bordering the ~: 6 Sahara
feature: 4 bank 5 delta
feeder: 6 Atbara
gift: 4 silt
island: 6 Philae
locale: 5 Egypt, Sudan 6 Africa
obstruction: 4 sudd
people: 5 Dinka
queen: 4 Cleo
relative: 5 Alice
reptile: 3 asp
symbol of life: 4 ankh
Nile __: 4 blue 5 green
__ Nile: 4 Blue 5 White
Niles: 4 city, town
locale: 4 Ohio 8 Illinois
Nilla
alternative: *see* cookie brand
__-nilly: 5 willy
Nils: 5 Dalén 6 Asther 7 Lofgren
Nilsson: 3 Ulf 5 Harry 6 Birgit
song: Coconut (1972)
Everybody's Talkin' (1969)
Without You (1972)
Nilsson, Birgit: 6 singer 7 soprano, Swedish
specialty: 5 opera
nim: 4 game
__ 'n' image: 4 spit
nimbi: 5 auras, halos 6 clouds, haloes
nimble: 4 deft, pert, spry 5 adept, agile, alert, brisk, canny, fleet, handy, light, lithe, quick, sharp, slick, smart, swift 6 active, adroit, au fait, clever, dapper, expert, limber, lissom, lively, speedy 7 capable, lissome, skilled, trained 8 dextrous, graceful, masterly, seasoned, skillful 9 competent, dexterous, efficient, lightsome, lithesome, masterful, sprightly 10 proficient
nimbleness: 4 ease 5 skill 7 agility 8 deftness, legerity 9 adeptness, dexterity, handiness, quickness 10 adroitness
nimbostratus: 5 cloud
nimbus: 4 aura, halo 5 cloud 7 aureola, aureole 8 gloriole
product: 4 rain, snow
NIMBY
part of ~: 3 not 4 back, yard
Nimes
neighbor: 5 Arles
Nîmes: 4 city, town
locale: 6 France
neighbor: 4 Alès
nimiety: 4 glut 6 excess 7 surfeit, surplus 8 plethora 9 profusion 10 oversupply
niminy-__: 6 piminy
Nimitz: 7 Chester
org.: 3 USN
__ Nimitz: 3 USS
Nimoy, Leonard: 5 actor 8 director
film: 3 Men and a Baby (1987)
The Good Mother (1988)
Funny About Love (1990)
Invasion of the Body Snatchers (1978)
Star Trek (2009)
Star Trek III: The Search for Spock (1984)
Star Trek II: The Wrath of Khan (1982)
Star Trek IV: The Voyage Home (1986)
Star Trek-The Motion Picture (1979)
Star Trek VI: The Undiscovered Country (1991)
role: 5 Paris, Spock
TV: Mission: Impossible, Star Trek
Nimrod: 6 hunter
father: 4 Cush, Kush
grandfather: 4 Noah
Nim's Island (2008 film)
cast: Abigail Breslin, Jodie Foster
Nimzowitsch: 4 Aron
Nina: 4 Foch 5 Ricci 6 Simone 7 Persson
in English: 3 Ann
Niña: 4 boat, ship
companion: 5 Pinta 10 Santa Maria
Nin, Anaïs: 6 French, writer 7 diarist
work: Cities of the Interior
Collages
The Delta of Venus
The Diary of Anaïs Nin
Glass Bell
Ladders to Fire
Little Birds
Solar Barque
A Spy in the House of Love
Under a Glass Bell
Winter of Artifice
niña's parent: 5 madre, padre
nincompoop
see ninny
nine: 5 digit 6 ennead, number
cloud ~: 6 heaven 7 rapture 8 paradise
combining form: 3 non- 4 nona- 5 ennea-
ender: 3 pin 4 bark, teen
group of ~: 5 nonet 6 ennead
inches: 4 span
in French: 4 neuf
in German: 4 neun
in Italian: 4 nove
in Japanese: 3 kyu
in Portuguese: 4 nove
in Spanish: 5 nueve
on cloud ~: 4 glad, high 5 happy, merry 6 blithe, cheery, elated, jovial, joyful, joyous, upbeat 7 gleeful, pleased, tickled 8 blissful, cheerful, ecstatic, euphoric, exultant, jubilant, mirthful, thrilled 9 delighted, overjoyed, rapturous, rejoicing, rhapsodic
one of ~: 4 Clio, Muse 5 Erato 6 inning, Thalia, Urania 7 Euterpe 8 Calliope 9 Melpomene 10 Polyhymnia 11 Terpsichore
put on cloud ~: 5 cheer, elate, exult 6 buck up, perk up, uplift 7 cheer up, delight, gladden, hearten 8 inspirit 10 exhilarate
to Mohs: 8 corundum
whole ~ yards: 3 all 4 a to z 5 whole 8 entirety 10 everything
nine __: 4 ball, iron
nine __ wonder: 4 days'
__ nine: 4 back 5 cloud, front
Nine, __ big fat hen: 4 ten a
nine-digit number: 3 SSN, Zip
nine-headed monster: 5 hydra
Nine Inch Nails
member: Trent Reznor
song: The Day the World Went Away (1999)
nine-iron, use a: 4 loft
Nine Lives: 7 cat food
alternative: *see* pet food brand
Nine Lives cat: 6 Morris
Nine Months (1995 film)
cast: Tom Arnold, Joan Cusack, Jeff Goldblum, Hugh Grant, Julianne Moore
director: Chris Columbus
ninepins: 4 game 5 sport 7 bowling
__-niner: 5 forty
__ nines: 5 to the
nine-sided
figure: 7 nonagon 8 enneagon
Nine Tailors, The
author: Dorothy Sayers
__-nine-tails: 4 cat-o'
nineteenth __: 4 hole
__ Nineties, The: 3 Gay 7 Naughty
nine-to-five: 3 job 4 toil, work 5 grind 8 position, vocation 10 livelihood
Nine to Five (1980 film)
cast: Dabney Coleman, Jane Fonda, Dolly Parton, Lily Tomlin
nine-to-fiver: 6 worker 8 employee 10 blue collar, wage earner
cry: 4 TGIF
Ninette: 8 De Valois
ninety-__ wonder: 3 day
Ninety-Eight: 3 car 4 auto, Olds 10 automobile, Oldsmobile
Ninety-Five Theses
author: Martin Luther
Nineveh: 4 city
locale: 4 Irak, Iraq 7 Assyria
river: 6 Tigris
Nine Women
author: Shirley Ann Grau
__ Nine Yards, The: 5 Whole
Ninja Turtles: 7 quartet
home: 5 sewer
meal: 5 pizza
ninny: 3 ass, nit, oaf, sap 4 boob, clod, ditz, dodo, dolt, dope, fool, gowk, jerk, simp 5 chump, clown, cluck, dummy, dunce, goose, joker, patsy, stupe 6 dimwit, lubber, lummox, nitwit, sucker, turkey 7 buffoon, bumbler, dingbat, dullard, fathead, half-wit, jackass, pinhead, saphead 8 bonehead, dumbbell, meathead, numskull 9 birdbrain, blockhead, harebrain, lamebrain, numbskull, simpleton 10 dunderhead, nincompoop
in French: 3 ane
niño: 3 boy, lad, tot 7 Spanish
Nino: 4 Rota 5 Tempo 9 Benvenuti
ninon: 5 voile 6 fabric 7 chiffon
Ninotchka (1939 film)
cast: Ina Claire, Melvyn Douglas, Greta Garbo, Bela Lugosi
director: Ernst Lubitsch
Nintendo: 4 game 9 video game
competitor: 4 Sega
fanatic: 5 gamer
hero: 5 Mario
predecessor: 5 Atari
Niobe: 5 crier 6 weeper
brother: 6 Pelops 7 Broteas
father: 8 Tantalus
husband: 7 Amphion
like ~: 5 teary, weepy 10 lachrymose
lover: 4 Zeus
son: 5 Argus 7 Amyclas
niobium: 5 metal 7 element
ore: 9 columbite
nip: 3 sip, tip 4 bite, clip, dash, dram, drop, lift, shot, slug, snap, snip, spot, stop, tang 5 catch, check, chill, nab at, pinch, snort, taste, tweak 6 arrest, nibble, thieve, thwart, tip-off 7 soupçon, squeeze, swallow 8 compress, cut short, piquancy, pungency, spoonful 9 briskness, crispness, frustrate, jiggerful, sharpness 10 frostiness
and tuck: 5 close, tight
in sports: 4 edge 6 defeat 7 nose out
in the air: 4 bite, cold 5 chill
in the bud: 4 foil, halt, stem, stop 5 avert, quash 6 arrest, put out, scotch 7 obviate, prevent, put down, squelch 8 preclude, stamp out 9 forestall 10 extinguish, put an end to
more than a ~: 4 swig
partner: 4 tuck
nipa: 4 palm 6 thatch
palm: 4 atap
nipper: 3 dog 4 baby 5 child, kiddy
nose ~: 9 Jack Frost
Nipper company: 3 RCA
Nippon: 5 Japan
nippy: 3 icy 4 cold, cool 5 brisk, chill, crisp, polar 6 arctic, biting, chilly, frigid, frosty, frozen, wintry 7 glacial, numbing, shivery, wintery 8 freezing
__ Nips: 6 Cheese
Nipsey: 7 Russell
Nirvana: 4 Eden 5 bliss 6 heaven 7 Elysium, rapture
attainer: 5 arhat
members: Cobain, Novoselic, Grohl
seeker: 5 Hindu 6 Hindoo
song: About a Girl (1994)
Come As You Are (1992)
Smells Like Teen Spirit (1991)
Nisan: 5 month 6 Hebrew
follower: 4 Iyar 5 Iyyar
preceder: 4 Adar
Nisei's parent: 5 Issei
'N' Is for Noose
author: Sue Grafton
Nissan: 3 car 4 auto 10 automobile
competitor: 5 Mazda
formerly: 6 Datsun
model: 5 Quest 6 Altima, Axxess, Maxima, Murano, Pulsar, Sentra, Stanza, Xterra 8 Frontier 10 Pathfinder
nisse: 3 elf 5 pixie 6 sprite 7 brownie

10 leprechaun
nit: 3 bug, oaf 4 boob, dodo, dolt, fool, jerk 5 cluck, dunce, louse, ninny 6 dimwit, insect 7 airhead, buffoon, dullard, halfwit, jackass, pinhead 8 bonehead, dumbbell, lunkhead, meathead 9 birdbrain, blockhead, ignoramus, lamebrain, numbskull, simpleton 10 dunderhead, nincompoop
ender: 3 wit 4 pick, rite 6 picker
NIT
rival: 4 NCAA
Nita: 5 Naldi 6 Talbot
Nite and Day (1988 song)
artist: Al B. Sure
niter: 7 mineral
nitid: 5 shiny 6 bright, glossy, lucent 7 lambent, radiant, shining 8 lustrous 9 effulgent, refulgent
nitpick: 3 nag 4 carp, fuss 5 cavil, whine 6 jibe at, niggle 7 quibble 8 pettifog 9 criticize, find fault 10 split hairs
nitpicker: 3 nag 4 prig 6 critic 8 stickler 10 fussbudget
nit-picking: 4 prim 5 fussy, petty 7 finicky 8 captious, critical, exacting, finiking, pedantic 9 criticism 10 pedantical
nitrate: 4 film, salt 5 ester
potassium ~: 5 niter
nitric __: 4 acid
nitrite: 4 salt 5 ester
NIT rival
tiebreaker: 2 OT 8 overtime
nitro: 4 soup 9 explosive
nitrogen: 3 gas 5 azote 7 element
based dye: 3 azo
combining form: 3 azo-
compound: 5 amide, amine, azide, azole
it's mostly ~: 3 air
liquid ~ container: 5 Dewar
__ nitrogen: 5 heavy
__-nitrogen cycle: 6 carbon
nitrous __: 5 oxide
Nitschke, Ray
sport: 8 football
Nittany Lions school: 3 PSU 9 Penn State
Nitti nabber: 4 Ness, T-man
nitty-gritty: 3 nub 4 core, crux, gist, knub, pith 5 heart, point, sense, truth 6 detail 7 essence, meaning
Nitty Gritty Dirt Band
song: An American Dream (1980) Mr. Bojangles (1971)
Nitty Gritty, The (1963 song)
artist: Shirley Ellis
nitwit
see ninny
nitwitted: 5 silly 6 simple 8 mindless
NIU conference: 3 MAC
Niva: 3 car 4 auto, Lada 7 Russian 10 automobile
Nivea: 6 lotion
rival: 4 Keri 5 Curel 6 Aveeno 7 Eucerin, Jergens, Pacquin 9 Lubriderm
nivellate: 5 level
Niven: 3 Kip 5 Busch, David, Larry
Niven, David: 5 actor
film: 55 Days at Peking (1963)
Around the World in Eighty Days (1956)
Ask Any Girl (1959)
Bachelor Mother (1939)
The Best of Enemies (1961)
The Bishop's Wife (1947)
Bonjour Tristesse (1958)
Casino Royale (1967)
Court Martial (1955)
Dodsworth (1936)
Enchantment (1948)
The Guns of Navarone (1961)
The King's Thief (1955)
Murder by Death (1976)
The Pink Panther (1964)
Please Don't Eat the Daisies (1960)
The Sea Wolves (1980)
Separate Tables (1958, AA)
Soldiers Three (1951)
Spitfire (1942)
Stairway to Heaven (1946)
Tonight's the Night (1954)
Where the Spies Are (1965)
Wuthering Heights (1939)
niveous: 5 snowy, white 9 alabaster
nix: 2 no 3 ban, bar, nah, naw, nay, nil, non 4 deny, kill, nada, nein, nope, nyet, stop, uh-uh, veto, void, zero 5 annul, debar, I won't, never, no how, no way, quash, spurn, zilch 6 abjure, cancel, cool it, diddly, forbid, negate, no deal, noways, nowise, rebuff, refuse, reject, repeal, sprite 7 abolish, decline, I refuse, nothing, nullify, refusal, rule out, silence, squelch 8 abrogate, disallow, forget it, I will not, negative, negatory, overrule, prohibit, suppress, turn down 9 by no means, eighty-six, fat chance, I think not, proscribe, rejection, strike out 10 count me out, invalidate, not a chance, put an end to, thumbs down
nixie: 3 elf 6 goblin, sprite
Nixon: 5 Agnes
Nixon (1995 film)
cast: Joan Allen, Powers Boothe, Ed Harris, Anthony Hopkins, Bob Hoskins, E.G. Marshall, David Paymer, David Hyde Pierce, Paul Sorvino, Mary Steenburgen, James Woods
director: Oliver Stone
Nixon in China: 5 opera
composer: John Adams
role: 3 Mao
Nixon, Richard: 9 president
alma mater: 4 Duke 8 Whittier
birthplace: 10 California, Yorba Linda
cabinet member: 4 Butz, Dent, Lynn 5 Finch, Laird, Saxbe, Simon, Stans, Volpe 6 Blount, Hickel, Morton, Rogers, Romney, Shultz 8 Connally 9 Kissinger
child: 5 Julie 6 Tricia
former occupation: 6 lawyer
middle name: 7 Milhous
opponent: 3 JFK 7 Kennedy, Wallace 8 Humphrey, McGovern
parent: 5 Frank 6 Hannah
V.P.: 4 Ford 5 Agnew
wife: 3 Pat 6 Thelma
work: In the Arena 7 Leaders 9 Real Peace, Six Crises 10 Real War, The
Nizer, Louis: 3 att. 4 atty. 6 lawyer 8 attorney
N.J.
neighbor: 3 Del. 4 Penn. 5 Penna.
ocean: 3 Atl.
see also New Jersey
NJ base: 5 Ft. Dix
Nkrumah: 5 Kwame
NL
award: 3 MVP
city: 3 Atl., Chi., NYC, St. L. 4 Milw. 5 Miami, Phila. 6 Denver 7 Atlanta, Chicago, Houston, New York, Phoenix, St. Louis 8 San Diego 9 Milwaukee 10 Cincinnati, Los Angeles, Pittsburgh, Washington 12 Philadelphia, San Francisco
division: 4 East, West
part of ~: 3 Nat. 4 Natl. 6 League 8 National
player: 3 Buc, Cub, Met, Nat, Red 4 Card 5 Astro, Brave, D-back, Giant, NY Met, Padre, Rocky 6 Brewer, Dodger, Marlin, Pirate 7 Phillie 8 Cardinal, National 11 Diamondback
stat: 3 HRs 4 RBIs
see also baseball, National League
NLC team: 4 Cubs, Reds 6 Astros 7 Brewers, Pirates 9 Cardinals
NLE team: 4 Mets, Nats 6 Braves 7 Marlins 8 Phillies 9 Nationals
NLRB
part of ~: 3 Lab., Nat, Rel. 4 Natl. 5 Board, Labor 8 National 9 Relations
NLU locale: 6 Monroe
NLW team: 6 Giants, Padres 7 Dodgers 13 Rockies. D-backs
NM
see New Mexico
N. Mex.
see New Mexico
NNE: 3 dir.
opposite: 3 SSW
NNP, part of: 3 Nat., Net 4 Natl., Prod. 7 Product 8 National
NNW: 3 dir.
opposite: 3 SSE
no: 3 nah, naw, nay, nix 4 nein, nope, nyet, uh-uh, veto, vote 5 I won't, ixnay, never 6 denial, rebuff 7 denials, dissent, I refuse, refusal 8 forget it, turndown 9 rejection 10 count me out, refutation, thumbs down
big thing: 3 pip 4 blip 6 trifle 7 trivial 10 immaterial
contest: 4 plea 9 hands down
don't take ~ for an answer: 6 insist 7 persist, protest 8 speak out 9 stand firm
doubt: *see* of course 5 truly 6 likely 8 probably
end: 4 a lot, much 6 vastly 7 liberal 8 very many, very much 9 eternally, extremely, immensely, in a big way 10 a great deal
ender: 5 siree
end of: 4 many 6 divers, myriad, umteen, untold 7 copious, profuse, umpteen 8 abundant, manifold, numerous, umpsteen 9 bountiful, countless, limitless, quite a few, unlimited
fooling: 5 truly 6 honest, really, solemn 7 serious, sincere 8 honestly 9 precisely, sincerely
get ~ place fast: 4 flag, idle, limp, plod, poke 5 delay, tarry 6 dabble, dawdle, diddle 7 fall off, fritter, slacken 8 hang back 9 inch along, poke along, waste time 10 dillydally, lose ground, mess around, wait around
give ~ ground: 5 force, order, press 6 demand 8 pressure 9 stand firm
good: 4 evil, junk 5 lousy 7 of no use, useless 10 virtueless
great shakes: 4 so-so 8 mediocre, ordinary
holds barred: 8 absolute, straight 9 limitless
ifs ands or buts: 7 exactly 10 absolutely, definitely, positively
in French: 3 non
in German: 4 nein
in Latin: 3 non
in music: 3 non
in Portuguese: 3 nao
in Russian: 4 nyet
in Scottish: 3 nae
in ~ time: 3 PDQ 4 anon, fast, soon 5 apace 6 presto 7 fleetly, hastily, quickly, rapidly, readily, swiftly 8 pell-mell, speedily 9 forthwith, hurriedly, instantly, like a shot, posthaste
it waits for ~ man: 4 tide, time
joke: 4 ugly 5 heavy, tough 6 severe, urgent 7 arduous, crucial, weighty 8 menacing, sobering, terrible 9 dangerous, difficult, laborious, momentous, strenuous 10 formidable
leave ~ stone unturned: 4 seek 5 scour 6 search, strive 7 persist, ransack, rummage 9 persevere
leave ~ vestige of: 3 mar 4 doom, raze, sack 5 crush, level, total, wreck 6 blow up, ravage 7 butcher, destroy, flatten, pillage, wipe out 8 bankrupt, bulldoze, clean out, decimate, demolish 9 bring down, desecrate, devastate 10 annihilate, obliterate
longer used: 3 obs., old, out 4 gone 5 dated, dusty, moldy, musty, passé, stale 6 bygone, old hat, square 7 archaic, outworn 8 obsolete, outdated, outmoded, timeworn 9 discarded, moth-eaten, out-of-date 10 antiquated, out of style, superseded
matter: 6 drop it 8 forget it 9 never mind
matter what: 5 still 6 anyhow, anyway 9 at any rate 10 in any event, regardless
mistake: 5 truly 6 surely 7 flat out 8 in spades 9 certainly, decidedly, downright 10 absolutely, definitely, distinctly, positively
more: 4 once, stop 5 kaput 6 lapsed
more than: 4 just, mere, only 6 at most
of ~ importance: 4 moot 7 trivial,

useless **9** worthless
of ~ use: 4 vain **6** futile, hollow **7** inutile, worn-out **8** bootless, hopeless, pathetic **9** pointless, worthless **10** not working, profitless, unavailing, unworkable
one: 4 none **6** nobody **7** pronoun **9** nary a soul
on ~ occasion: 7 not ever **8** not at all **9** nevermore
pay ~ attention to: 6 forget, ignore **7** disobey, neglect, tune out **8** file away, lay aside, overlook, sneeze at **9** disregard
picnic: 4 hard **5** bumpy, harsh, rough, tough **6** brutal, rugged, severe, taxing, thorny, trying, woolly **7** arduous, painful, serious **8** terrible **9** strenuous **10** formidable, unpleasant
problem: 4 easy, snap **5** cinch **6** simple **8** workable **10** attainable, effortless, obtainable
say ~ to: 3 nix **4** deny, shun, veto **5** spurn **6** bounce, forbid, pass on, rebuff, refuse, reject, resist **7** decline, disdain, dismiss, exclude, protest **8** disallow, override, overrule, turn down **9** blackball, cast aside, repudiate
show: 4 AWOL **8** absentee
strings: 8 optional **9** boundless, limitless, unlimited
sweat: 4 easy, snap **6** simple **8** duck soup **9** easy as pie **10** child's play, effortless
take ~ note of: 6 ignore **7** neglect **8** brush off, skip over **9** disregard
to ~ avail: 4 vain **6** futile, in vain, otiose, vainly **8** bootless, hopeless **9** fruitless, pointless, uselessly **10** for nothing
unable to say ~: 4 meek **5** timid **6** docile **7** lenient, servile, slavish **8** lamblike, yielding **9** spineless **10** obsequious, submissive
vote ~: 6 oppose
voter: 4 anti **8** opponent
no __: 3 end, one, use, way **4** ball, bill, dice, fair, sale, soap **5** doubt, sweat **6** longer, matter **7** contest
no __ attached: 7 strings
no __ at the inn: 4 room
no __ barred: 5 holds
no __ feat: 4 mean
no __ intended: 3 pun
no __ land: 4 man's
no __ lost: 4 love
no __, no return: 7 deposit
no __ roses: 5 bed of
no __ shakes: 5 great
no __ sight: 5 end in
no __ than: 6 sooner
no __ to: 6 thanks
no __ ways about it: 3 two
no-__: 3 cal, hit, win **4** good, iron, load, lose, name, show **5** hoper, see-um, stick, trump **6** frills, hitter **7** account, brainer, goodnik
no-__ clause: 5 trade
no-__ contract: 3 cut
no-__ fund: 4 load
no-__ insurance: 5 fault
no-__ stock: 3 par
no-__-um: 3 see
no-__ zone: 3 fly
no.: 3 amt., fig., qty.
kind of ~: 3 neg., pos.
see also number
No: 2 Dr. **4** elem., lake **5** drama **6** doctor **7** element **8** nobelium
102 for ~: 4 at. no.
Dr. ~ first name: 6 Julius
lake locale: 5 Sudan **6** Africa
No __: 3 más, MSG **4** Exit **5** U-Turn
No __!: 3 way **4** dice, joke, prob **5** can do, siree, sweat **6** foolin' **7** fooling, kidding, problem
No __, ands, or buts!: 3 ifs
No __ an island: 5 man is
No __ Bob!: 5 siree
No __ for Sergeants: 4 Time
No __ for the weary: 4 rest
No __ Land: 4 Man's
No __ Love: 5 Other **7** Greater
No __ luck!: 4 such
No __, no gain: 4 pain
No __, no glory!: 4 guts
No __ on Red: 4 Turn
No __ Out: 3 Way
No __ talk to...: 5 one to
No __ Tears: 4 More
No __ Traffic: 4 Thru
No, __ Much!: 3 Not
No-__: 3 Doz
__ No. 5: 5 Mambo **6** Chanel
NOAA
department: 8 Commerce
part: 3 Nat. **4** Natl. **5** Admin. **7** Oceanic **8** National
no-account: 5 idler **8** unusable, unworthy **9** worthless **10** ne'er-do-well
Noachian: 3 old **7** ancient
Noah: 4 Wyle **5** Beery **7** Webster, Yannick **8** Emmerich
count: 3 two
craft: 3 ark
father: 6 Lamech
grandson: 3 Lud, Put **4** Aram, Cush, Elam, Kush **5** Egypt, Gomer, Madai, Magog, Tiras, Tubal **6** Asshur, Canaan, Nimrod
landing place: 6 Ararat
passengers: 5 pairs **6** beasts **7** animals
son: 3 Ham **4** Shem **7** Japheth
Noam: 7 Chomsky
__ No Angels: 4 We're
nob: 4 bean, gent **6** aristo, noodle
starter: 3 hob
Nob __: 4 Hill
Nobel, Alfred: 7 chemist, Swedish
invention: 3 TNT
nobelium: 7 element
Nobel Prize: 5 award
city: 4 Oslo **9** Stockholm
Nobel Prizes - Chemistry:
2009 - Venkatraman Ramakrishnan, Thomas Steitz, Ada Yonath
2008 - Osamu Shimomura, Martin Chalfie, Roger Tsien
2007 - Gerhard Ertl
2006 - Roger Kornberg
2005 - Yves Chauvin, Robert Grubbs, Richard Schrock
2004 - Aaron Ciechanover, Avram Hershko, Irwin Rose
2003 - Peter Agre, Roderick MacKinnon
2002 - John Fenn, Koichi Tanaka, Kurt Wüthrich
2001 - William S. Knowles, Ryoji Noyori, Barry Sharpless
2000 - Alan Heeger, Alan MacDiarmid, Hideki Shirakawa
1999 - Ahmed Zewail
1998 - Walter Kohn, John Pople
1997 - Paul Boyer, John Walker, Jens Skou
1996 - Robert Curl, Harold Kroto, Richard Smalley
1995 - Paul Crutzen, Mario Molina, Sherwood Rowland
1994 - George Olah
1993 - Kary Mullis, Michael Smith
1992 - Rudolph Marcus
1991 - Richard Ernst
1990 - Elias Corey
1989 - Sidney Altman, Thomas Cech
1988 - Johann Deisenhofer, Robert Huber, Hartmut Michel
1987 - Donald Cram, Jean-Marie Lehn, Charles Pedersen
1986 - Dudley Herschbach, Yuan Lee, John Polanyi
1985 - Herbert Hauptman, Jerome Karle
1984 - Robert Merrifield
1983 - Henry Taube
1982 - Aaron Klug
1981 - Kenichi Fukui, Roald Hoffmann
1980 - Paul Berg, Walter Gilbert, Frederick Sanger
1979 - Herbert Brown, Georg Wittig
1978 - Peter Mitchell
1977 - Ilya Prigogine
1976 - William Lipscomb
1975 - John Cornforth, Vladimir Prelog
1974 - Paul Flory
1973 - Ernst Fischer, Geoffrey Wilkinson
1972 - Christian Anfinsen, Stanford Moore, William Stein
1971 - Gerhard Herzberg
1970 - Luis F. Leloir
1969 - Derek Barton, Odd Hassel
1968 - Lars Onsager
1967 - Manfred Eigen, Ronald Norrish, George Porter
1966 - Robert Mulliken
1965 - Robert Woodward
1964 - Dorothy Hodgkin
1963 - Karl Ziegler, Giulio Natta
1962 - Max Perutz, John Kendrew
1961 - Melvin Calvin
1960 - Willard Libby
1959 - Jaroslav Heyrovsky
1958 - Frederick Sanger
1957 - Alexander Todd
1956 - Cyril Hinshelwood, Nikolay Semenov
1955 - Vincent du Vigneaud
1954 - Linus Pauling
1953 - Hermann Staudinger
1952 - Archer Martin, Richard Synge
1951 - Edwin McMillan, Glenn Seaborg
1950 - Otto Diels, Kurt Alder
1949 - William Giauque
1948 - Arne Tiselius
1947 - Robert Robinson
1946 - James Sumner, John Northrop, Wendell Stanley
1945 - Artturi Virtanen
1944 - Otto Hahn
1943 - George de Hevesy
1942 - NO AWARD
1941 - NO AWARD
1940 - NO AWARD
1939 - Adolf Butenandt, Leopold Ruzicka
1938 - Richard Kuhn
1937 - Walter Haworth, Paul Karrer
1936 - Peter Debye
1935 - Frédéric Joliot-Curie, Irène Joliot-Curie
1934 - Harold Urey
1933 - NO AWARD
1932 - Irving Langmuir
1931 - Carl Bosch, Friedrich Bergius
1930 - Hans Fischer
1929 - Arthur Harden, Hans von Euler-Chelpin
1928 - Adolf Windaus
1927 - Heinrich Wieland
1926 - Theodor Svedberg
1925 - Richard Zsigmondy
1924 - NO AWARD
1923 - Fritz Pregl
1922 - Francis Aston
1921 - Frederick Soddy
1920 - Walther Nernst
1919 - NO AWARD
1918 - Fritz Haber
1917 - NO AWARD
1916 - NO AWARD
1915 - Richard Willstötter
1914 - Theodore Richards
1913 - Alfred Werner
1912 - Victor Grignard, Paul Sabatier
1911 - Marie Curie
1910 - Otto Wallach
1909 - Wilhelm Ostwald
1908 - Ernest Rutherford
1907 - Eduard Buchner
1906 - Henri Moissan
1905 - Adolf von Baeyer
1904 - William Ramsay
1903 - Svante Arrhenius
1902 - Hermann Fischer
1901 - Jacobus van't Hoff
Nobel Prizes - Economics:
2009 - Elinor Ostrom, Oliver Williamson
2008 - Paul Krugman
2007 - Leonid Hurwicz, Eric Maskin, Roger Myerson
2006 - Edmund Phelps
2005 - Robert Aumann, Thomas Schelling
2004 - Finn Kydland, Edward Prescott
2003 - Robert Engle, Clive Granger
2002 - Daniel Kahneman, Vernon Smith
2001 - George Akerlof, Michael Spence, Joseph Stiglitz
2000 - James Heckman, Daniel McFadden
1999 - Robert Mundell
1998 - Amartya Sen
1997 - Robert Merton, Myron Scholes
1996 - James Mirrlees, William

Vickrey
1995 - Robert Lucas
1994 - John Harsanyi, John Nash, Reinhard Selten
1993 - Robert Fogel, Douglass North
1992 - Gary Becker
1991 - Ronald Coase
1990 - Harry Markowitz, Merton Miller, William Sharpe
1989 - Trygve Haavelmo
1988 - Maurice Allais
1987 - Robert Solow
1986 - James Buchanan
1985 - Franco Modigliani
1984 - Richard Stone
1983 - Gerard Debreu
1982 - George Stigler
1981 - James Tobin
1980 - Lawrence Klein
1979 - Theodore Schultz, Arthur Lewis
1978 - Herbert Simon
1977 - Bertil Ohlin, James Meade
1976 - Milton Friedman
1975 - Leonid Kantorovich, Tjalling Koopmans
1974 - Gunnar Myrdal, Friedrich von Hayek
1973 - Wassily Leontief
1972 - John Hicks, Kenneth Arrow
1971 - Simon Kuznets
1970 - Paul Samuelson
1969 - Ragnar Frisch, Jan Tinbergen

Nobel Prizes - Literature:

2009 - Herta Müller
2008 - J.M.G. Le Clezio
2007 - Doris Lessing
2006 - Orhan Pamuk
2005 - Harold Pinter
2004 - Elfriede Jelinek
2003 - J.M. Coetzee
2002 - Imre Kertész
2001 - V.S. Naipaul
2000 - Gao Xingjian
1999 - Günter Grass
1998 - José Saramago
1997 - Dario Fo
1996 - Wislawa Szymborska
1995 - Seamus Heaney
1994 - Kenzaburo Oe
1993 - Toni Morrison
1992 - Derek Walcott
1991 - Nadine Gordimer
1990 - Octavio Paz
1989 - Camilo Cela
1988 - Naguib Mahfouz
1987 - Joseph Brodsky
1986 - Wole Soyinka
1985 - Claude Simon
1984 - Jaroslav Seifert
1983 - William Golding
1982 - Gabriel García Márquez
1981 - Elias Canetti
1980 - Czeslaw Milosz
1979 - Odysseus Elytis
1978 - Isaac Bashevis Singer
1977 - Vicente Aleixandre
1976 - Saul Bellow
1975 - Eugenio Montale
1974 - Eyvind Johnson, Harry Martinson
1973 - Patrick White
1972 - Heinrich Böll
1971 - Pablo Neruda
1970 - Aleksandr Solzhenitsyn
1969 - Samuel Beckett
1968 - Yasunari Kawabata
1967 - Miguel Asturias
1966 - Shmuel Agnon, Nelly Sachs
1965 - Mikhail Sholokhov
1964 - Jean-Paul Sartre
1963 - Giorgos Seferis
1962 - John Steinbeck
1961 - Ivo Andric
1960 - St.-John Perse
1959 - Salvatore Quasimodo
1958 - Boris Pasternak
1957 - Albert Camus
1956 - Juan Ramón Jiménez
1955 - Halldór Laxness
1954 - Ernest Hemingway
1953 - Winston Churchill
1952 - François Mauriac
1951 - Pär Lagerkvist
1950 - Bertrand Russell
1949 - William Faulkner
1948 - T.S. Eliot
1947 - André Gide
1946 - Hermann Hesse
1945 - Gabriela Mistral
1944 - Johannes Jensen
1943 - NO AWARD
1942 - NO AWARD
1941 - NO AWARD
1940 - NO AWARD
1939 - Frans Sillanpöö
1938 - Pearl S. Buck
1937 - Roger du Gard
1936 - Eugene O'Neill
1935 - NO AWARD
1934 - Luigi Pirandello
1933 - Ivan Bunin
1932 - John Galsworthy
1931 - Erik Karlfeldt
1930 - Sinclair Lewis
1929 - Thomas Mann
1928 - Sigrid Undset
1927 - Henri Bergson
1926 - Grazia Deledda
1925 - George Bernard Shaw
1924 - Wladyslaw Reymont
1923 - William Butler Yeats
1922 - Jacinto Benavente
1921 - Anatole France
1920 - Knut Hamsun
1919 - Carl Spitteler
1918 - NO AWARD
1917 - Karl Gjellerup, Henrik Pontoppidan
1916 - Verner von Heidenstam
1915 - Romain Rolland
1914 - NO AWARD
1913 - Rabindranath Tagore
1912 - Gerhart Hauptmann
1911 - Maurice Maeterlinck
1910 - Paul Heyse
1909 - Selma Lagerlöf
1908 - Rudolf Eucken
1907 - Rudyard Kipling
1906 - Giosuè Carducci
1905 - Henryk Sienkiewicz
1904 - Frédéric Mistral, José Echegaray
1903 - Bjornstjerne Bjornson
1902 - Theodor Mommsen
1901 - Sully Prudhomme

Nobel Prizes - Medicine:

2009 - Elizabeth Blackburn, Carol Greider, Jack Szostak
2008 - Harald zur Hausen, Francoise Barre-Sinoussi, Luc Montagnier
2007 - Mario Capecchi, Martin Evans, Oliver Smithies
2006 - Andrew Fire, Craig Mello
2005 - Barry Marshall, J. Robin Warren
2004 - Richard Axel, Linda Buck
2003 - Paul Lauterbur, Peter Mansfield
2002 - Sydney Brenner, Robert Horvitz, John Sulston
2001 - Leland Hartwell, Tim Hunt, Paul Nurse
2000 - Arvid Carlsson, Paul Greengard, Eric Kandel
1999 - Günter Blobel
1998 - Robert Furchgott, Louis Ignarro, Ferid Murad
1997 - Stanley B. Prusiner
1996 - Peter Doherty, Rolf Zinkernagel
1995 - Edward Lewis, Christiane Nüsslein-Volhard, Eric Wieschaus
1994 - Alfred Gilman, Martin Rodbell
1993 - Richard Roberts, Phillip Sharp
1992 - Edmond Fischer, Edwin Krebs
1991 - Erwin Neher, Bert Sakmann
1990 - Joseph Murray, Donnall Thomas
1989 - Michael Bishop, Harold Varmus
1988 - James Black, Gertrude Elion, George Hitchings
1987 - Susumu Tonegawa
1986 - Stanley Cohen, Rita Levi-Montalcini
1985 - Michael Brown, Joseph Goldstein
1984 - Niels Jerne, Georges Köhler, César Milstein
1983 - Barbara McClintock
1982 - Sune Bergström, Bengt Samuelsson, John Vane
1981 - Roger Sperry, David Hubel, Torsten Wiesel
1980 - Baruj Benacerraf, Jean Dausset, George Snell
1979 - Allan Cormack, Godfrey Hounsfield
1978 - Werner Arber, Daniel Nathans, Hamilton Smith
1977 - Roger Guillemin, Andrew Schally, Rosalyn Yalow
1976 - Baruch Blumberg, Carleton Gajdusek
1975 - David Baltimore, Renato Dulbecco, Howard Temin
1974 - Albert Claude, Christian de Duve, George Palade
1973 - Karl von Frisch, Konrad Lorenz, Nikolaas Tinbergen
1972 - Gerald Edelman, Rodney Porter
1971 - Earl Sutherland
1970 - Bernard Katz, Ulf von Euler, Julius Axelrod
1969 - Max Delbrück, Alfred Hershey, Salvador Luria
1968 - Robert Holley, Gobind Khorana, Marshall Nirenberg
1967 - Ragnar Granit, Haldan Hartline, George Wald
1966 - Peyton Rous, Charles Huggins
1965 - François Jacob, André Lwoff, Jacques Monod
1964 - Konrad Bloch, Feodor Lynen
1963 - John Eccles, Alan Hodgkin, Andrew Huxley
1962 - Francis Crick, James Watson, Maurice Wilkins
1961 - Georg von Békésy
1960 - Frank Burnet, Peter Medawar
1959 - Severo Ochoa, Arthur Kornberg
1958 - George Beadle, Edward Tatum, Joshua Lederberg
1957 - Daniel Bovet
1956 - André Cournand, Werner Forssmann, Dickinson Richards
1955 - Axel Theorell
1954 - John Enders, Thomas Weller, Frederick Robbins
1953 - Hans Krebs, Fritz Lipmann
1952 - Selman Waksman
1951 - Max Theiler
1950 - Edward Kendall, Tadeus Reichstein, Philip Hench
1949 - Walter Hess, Antonio Moniz
1948 - Paul Müller
1947 - Carl Cori, Gerty Cori, Bernardo Houssay
1946 - Hermann Muller
1945 - Alexander Fleming, Ernst Chain, Howard Florey
1944 - Joseph Erlanger, Herbert Gasser
1943 - Henrik Dam, Edward Doisy
1942 - NO AWARD
1941 - NO AWARD
1940 - NO AWARD
1939 - Gerhard Domagk
1938 - Corneille Heymans
1937 - Albert von Szent-Györgyi
1936 - Henry Dale, Otto Loewi
1935 - Hans Spemann
1934 - George Whipple, George Minot, William Murphy
1933 - Thomas Morgan
1932 - Charles Sherrington, Edgar Adrian
1931 - Otto Warburg
1930 - Karl Landsteiner
1929 - Christiaan Eijkman, Frederick Hopkins
1928 - Charles Nicolle
1927 - Julius Wagner-Jauregg
1926 - Johannes Fibiger
1925 - NO AWARD
1924 - Willem Einthoven
1923 - Frederick Banting, John Macleod
1922 - Archibald Hill, Otto Meyerhof
1921 - NO AWARD
1920 - Schack Krogh
1919 - Jules Bordet
1918 - NO AWARD
1917 - NO AWARD
1916 - NO AWARD
1915 - NO AWARD
1914 - Robert Bárány
1913 - Charles Richet
1912 - Alexis Carrel
1911 - Allvar Gullstrand
1910 - Albrecht Kossel
1909 - Emil Kocher
1908 - Elie Metchnikoff, Paul Ehrlich

1907 - Charles Laveran
1906 - Camillo Golgi, Santiago Ramón y Cajal
1905 - Robert Koch
1904 - Ivan Pavlov
1903 - Niels Finsen
1902 - Ronald Ross
1901 - Emil von Behring

Nobel Prizes - Peace:

2009 - Barack Obama
2008 - Martti Ahtisaari
2007 - Al Gore, Intergovernmental Panel on Climate Change
2006 - Muhammad Yunus, Grameen Bank
2005 - International Atomic Energy Agency, Mohamed ElBaradei
2004 - Wangari Maathai
2003 - Shirin Ebadi
2002 - Jimmy Carter
2001 - United Nations, Kofi Annan
2000 - Kim Dae Jung
1999 - Doctors Without Borders
1998 - John Hume, David Trimble
1997 - International Campaign to Ban Landmines (ICBL), Jody Williams
1996 - Carlos Belo, José Ramos-Horta
1995 - Joseph Rotblat, Pugwash Conferences on Science and World Affairs
1994 - Yasser Arafat, Shimon Peres, Yitzhak Rabin
1993 - Nelson Mandela, F.W. de Klerk
1992 - Rigoberta Tum
1991 - Aung San Suu Kyi
1990 - Mikhail Gorbachev
1989 - Dalai Lama
1988 - United Nations Peacekeeping Forces
1987 - Oscar Arias Sanchez
1986 - Elie Wiesel
1985 - International Physicians for the Prevention of Nuclear War Inc.
1984 - Desmond Tutu
1983 - Lech Walesa
1982 - Alva Myrdal, Alfonso García Robles
1981 - Office of the United Nations High Commissioner for Refugees
1980 - Adolfo Pérez Esquivel
1979 - Mother Teresa
1978 - Anwar Sadat, Menachem Begin
1977 - Amnesty International
1976 - Betty Williams, Mairead Corrigan
1975 - Andrei Sakharov
1974 - Sean MacBride, Eisaku Sato
1973 - Henry Kissinger, Le Duc Tho
1972 - NO AWARD
1971 - Willy Brandt
1970 - Norman Borlaug
1969 - International Labor Organization (ILO)
1968 - René Cassin
1967 - NO AWARD
1966 - NO AWARD
1965 - UNICEF
1964 - Martin Luther King
1963 - International Committee of the Red Cross, League of Red Cross Societies
1962 - Linus Pauling
1961 - Dag Hammarskjöld
1960 - Albert Lutuli
1959 - Philip Noel-Baker
1958 - Georges Pire
1957 - Lester Pearson
1956 - NO AWARD
1955 - NO AWARD
1954 - Office of the United Nations High Commissioner for Refugees
1953 - George Marshall
1952 - Albert Schweitzer
1951 - Léon Jouhaux
1950 - Ralph Bunche
1949 - John Boyd Orr
1948 - NO AWARD
1947 - Friends Service Council, American Friends Service Committee
1946 - Emily Balch, John Mott
1945 - Cordell Hull
1944 - International Committee of the Red Cross
1943 - NO AWARD
1942 - NO AWARD
1941 - NO AWARD
1940 - NO AWARD
1939 - NO AWARD
1938 - Nansen International Office for Refugees
1937 - Edgar Cecil
1936 - Carlos Lamas
1935 - Carl von Ossietzky
1934 - Arthur Henderson
1933 - Norman Angell
1932 - NO AWARD
1931 - Jane Addams, Murray Butler
1930 - Nathan Söderblom
1929 - Frank Kellogg
1928 - NO AWARD
1927 - Ferdinand Buisson, Ludwig Quidde
1926 - Aristide Briand, Gustav Stresemann
1925 - Austen Chamberlain, Charles Dawes
1924 - NO AWARD
1923 - NO AWARD
1922 - Fridtjof Nansen
1921 - Karl Branting, Christian Lange
1920 - Léon Bourgeois
1919 - Woodrow Wilson
1918 - NO AWARD
1917 - International Committee of the Red Cross
1916 - NO AWARD
1915 - NO AWARD
1914 - NO AWARD
1913 - Henri La Fontaine
1912 - Elihu Root
1911 - Tobias Asser, Alfred Fried
1910 - Permanent International Peace Bureau
1909 - Auguste Beernaert, Paul Balluet, Paul d'Estournelles de Constant
1908 - Klas Arnoldson, Fredrik Bajer
1907 - Ernesto Moneta, Louis Renault
1906 - Theodore Roosevelt
1905 - Bertha von Suttner
1904 - Institute of International Law
1903 - William Cremer
1902 - Élie Ducommun, Charles Gobat
1901 - Jean Dunant, Frédéric Passy

Nobel Prizes - Physics:

2009 - Charles Kao, Willard Boyle, George Smith
2008 - Makoto Kobayashi, Toshihide Maskawa, Yoichiro Nambu
2007 - Albert Fert, Peter Grunberg
2006 - John Mather, George Smoot
2005 - Roy Glauber, John Hall, Theodor Hansch
2004 - David Gross, H. David Politzer, Frank Wilczek
2003 - Alexei Abrikosov, Vitaly Ginzburg, Anthony Leggett
2002 - Raymond Davis, Masatoshi Koshiba, Riccardo Giacconi
2001 - Eric Cornell, Wolfgang Ketterle, Carl Wieman
2000 - Zhores Alferov, Herbert Kroemer, Jack Kilby
1999 - Gerardus 't Hooft, Martinus Veltman
1998 - Robert Laughlin, Horst Störmer, Daniel Tsui
1997 - Steven Chu, Claude Cohen-Tannoudji, William Phillips
1996 - David Lee, Douglas Osheroff, Robert Richardson
1995 - Martin Perl, Frederick Reines
1994 - Bertram Brockhouse, Clifford Shull
1993 - Russell Hulse, Joseph Taylor
1992 - Georges Charpak
1991 - Pierre-Gilles de Gennes
1990 - Jerome Friedman, Henry Kendall, Richard Taylor
1989 - Norman Ramsey, Hans Dehmelt, Wolfgang Paul
1988 - Leon Lederman, Melvin Schwartz, Jack Steinberger
1987 - Georg Bednorz, Alexander Müller
1986 - Ernst Ruska, Gerd Binnig, Heinrich Rohrer
1985 - Klaus von Klitzing
1984 - Carlo Rubbia, Simon van der Meer
1983 - Subramanyan Chandrasekhar, William Fowler
1982 - Kenneth Wilson
1981 - Nicolaas Bloembergen, Arthur Schawlow, Kai Siegbahn
1980 - James Cronin, Val Fitch
1979 - Sheldon Glashow, Abdus Salam, Steven Weinberg
1978 - Pyotr Kapitsa, Arno Penzias, Robert Wilson
1977 - Philip Anderson, Nevill Mott, John van Vleck
1976 - Burton Richter, Samuel Ting
1975 - Aage Bohr, Ben Mottelson, Leo Rainwater
1974 - Martin Ryle, Antony Hewish
1973 - Leo Esaki, Ivar Giaever, Brian Josephson
1972 - John Bardeen, Leon Cooper, John Schrieffer
1971 - Dennis Gabor
1970 - Hannes Alfvén, Louis Néel
1969 - Murray Gell-Mann
1968 - Luis Alvarez
1967 - Hans Bethe
1966 - Alfred Kastler
1965 - Sin-Itiro Tomonaga, Julian Schwinger, Richard Feynman
1964 - Charles Townes, Nicolay Basov, Aleksandr Prokhorov
1963 - Eugene Wigner, Maria Goeppert-Mayer, J. Hans Jensen
1962 - Lev Landau
1961 - Robert Hofstadter, Rudolf Mössbauer
1960 - Donald Glaser
1959 - Emilio Segrè, Owen Chamberlain
1958 - Pavel Cherenkov, Ilja Frank, Igor Tamm
1957 - Chen Ning Yang, Tsung-Dao Lee
1956 - William Shockley, John Bardeen, Walter Brattain
1955 - Willis Lamb, Polykarp Kusch
1954 - Max Born, Walther Bothe
1953 - Frits Zernike
1952 - Felix Bloch, Edward Purcell
1951 - John Cockcroft, Ernest Walton
1950 - Cecil Powell
1949 - Hideki Yukawa
1948 - Patrick Blackett
1947 - Edward Appleton
1946 - Percy Bridgman
1945 - Wolfgang Pauli
1944 - Isidor Rabi
1943 - Otto Stern
1942 - NO AWARD
1941 - NO AWARD
1940 - NO AWARD
1939 - Ernest Lawrence
1938 - Enrico Fermi
1937 - Clinton Davisson, George Thomson
1936 - Victor Hess, Carl Anderson
1935 - James Chadwick
1934 - NO AWARD
1933 - Erwin Schrödinger, Paul Dirac
1932 - Werner Heisenberg
1931 - NO AWARD
1930 - Chandrasekhara Raman
1929 - Louis de Broglie
1928 - Owen Richardson
1927 - Arthur Compton, Charles Wilson
1926 - Jean Perrin
1925 - James Franck, Gustav Hertz
1924 - Karl Siegbahn
1923 - Robert Millikan
1922 - Niels Bohr
1921 - Albert Einstein
1920 - Charles Guillaume
1919 - Johannes Stark
1918 - Max Planck
1917 - Charles Barkla
1916 - NO AWARD
1915 - William Bragg
1914 - Max von Laue
1913 - Heike Kamerlingh-Onnes
1912 - Nils Dalén
1911 - Wilhelm Wien
1910 - Johannes van der Waals
1909 - Guglielmo Marconi, Carl

Braun
1908 - Gabriel Lippmann
1907 - Albert Michelson
1906 - Joseph Thomson
1905 - Philipp von Lenard
1904 - John Strutt
1903 - Antoine Becquerel, Pierre Curie, Marie Curie
1902 - Hendrik Lorentz, Pieter Zeeman
1901 - Wilhelm Röntgen

No bid: 4 pass 5 I pass
Nobile, Umberto: 7 Italian 8 explorer
airship: 5 Norge
nobility: 4 rank, soul 5 elite, glory, honor, lords 6 gentry, virtue 7 culture, dignity, majesty, peerage, royalty 8 elegance, eminence, grandeur 9 elevation, gallantry, greatness, integrity, loftiness, sublimity 10 bluebloods, excellence, generosity, knighthood, patricians, upper class, upper crust
name meaning ~: 8 Adelaide
__ nobis pacem: 4 dona
noble: 3 big 4 dame, duke, earl, fine, high, king, lady, lord, nice, okay, peer, raja, rani 5 baron, count, elite, grand, great, legit, lofty, money, moral, proud, queen, rajah, regal, royal 6 august, benign, gentle, heroic, humane, kingly, knight, lordly, prince, proper, superb, titled, worthy 7 baronet, courtly, czarina, duchess, eminent, emperor, empress, ethical, exalted, gallant, genteel, liberal, marquis, peeress, queenly, refined, royalty, stately, sublime, supreme, tsarina, tzarina, upright, valiant 8 all right, archduke, baroness, baronial, countess, elevated, empyreal, empyrean, generous, glorious, gracious, heroical, highborn, highbred, imperial, imposing, kinglike, knightly, laudable, maharaja, maharani, majestic, marquess, pleasant, pleasing, princely, princess, splendid, superior, tolerant, virtuous, viscount, wellborn, well-bred 9 admirable, agreeable, blue blood, bounteous, brilliant, chevalier, dignified, excellent, gentleman, grandiose, honorable, maharajah, patrician, reputable, unselfish, venerable, wonderful 10 acceptable, aristocrat, beneficent, beneficial, benevolent, bighearted, charitable, creditable, cultivated, highminded, impressive, majestical, preeminent, remarkable, upper-class
action: 4 deed, feat 5 geste 6 lesson
domain: 6 barony 7 dukedom, earldom
gas: 4 neon 5 argon, radon, xenon 6 helium 7 krypton
like a ~: 5 ducal, regal, royal 8 baronial, knightly
name meaning ~: 3 Ada 4 Earl 5 Adela, Adele, Alice, Ethel, Hiram 7 Patrick 8 Patricia
noble __: 3 gas
Noble: 5 James 7 Chelsea 10 Willingham
__ Noble, Backstage Wife: 4 Mary
Noble House
author: James Clavell
nobles: 5 class 6 estate 7 peerage
noblesse: 6 luxury 7 culture, hauteur 8 breeding, elegance 9 gentility 10 refinement
noblesse __: 6 oblige
noblest __ of them all, The: 5 Roman
noblewoman: 4 dame, lady 6 matron 7 dowager, peeress 8 baroness 9 blueblood 10 aristocrat
nobody: 4 none, wimp, zero 6 menial, squirt 7 parvenu, upstart 8 not a soul 9 nonentity
in Latin: 4 nemo
nobody __ business: 5 else's
Nobody But You
composer: George Gershwin
Nobody Does It Better (song)
artist: Nate Dogg, Carly Simon
Nobody doesn't like __ Lee: 4 Sara
Nobody I Know (1964 song)
artist: Peter and Gordon
Nobody Knows My Name
author: James Baldwin
Nobody Knows the Trouble __: 5 I Seen
nobody's fool: 4 keen 5 sharp 8 lynx-eyed 10 discerning
Nobody's Fool (1988 song)
artist: Kenny Loggins
Nobody's Fool (1994 film)
cast: Melanie Griffith, Paul Newman, Jessica Tandy, Bruce Willis
Nobody Told Me (1984 song)
artist: John Lennon
__ no bones about: 4 make
__ No Business...: 6 There's
no-cal: 4 diet 8 dietetic
nocent: 6 malign 7 baleful, baneful, harmful, hurtful 8 damaging 9 dangerous, injurious, unhealthy 10 pernicious
No chance!: 5 never 8 forget it
__ noches: 6 buenas
__ no circumstances: 5 under
No Clouds of Glory
author: Marian Engel
No Country for Old Men (2007 film)
cast: Javier Bardem, Josh Brolin, Tommy Lee Jones
director: Joel and Ethan Coen
nocturnal: 4 late 5 night 7 nightly 9 after dark
animal: 3 bat, owl 4 paca, vari 5 cimex, gecko, krait, lemur 6 aye-aye
not ~: 7 diurnal
sound: 3 ZZZ 4 hoot 5 snore
nocturne: 5 music, piece
nocuous: 5 toxic 7 baneful, harmful, hurtful, noisome 9 injurious, poisonous
nod: 3 bow, dip, nap, wag 4 beck, bend, doze, duck, rest, sign 5 agree, droop, greet, sleep, slump 6 assent, beckon, concur, curtsy, drowse, motion, salute, signal 7 approve, consent, doze off, drop off, gesture, go-ahead, respond 8 drift off, greeting, indicate, sanction 9 acquiesce, recognize 10 acceptance, fall asleep, permission
ender: 3 ule 4 ular
give the ~: 2 OK 3 cue 4 okay 5 admit, adopt, allow, go for 6 accept, assent, comply, concur 7 consent, endorse, include, indorse, sign off, welcome 8 sanction, stand for 9 recognize
off: 3 nap 4 doze 5 sleep 6 drowse, snooze
to: 5 greet 7 welcome
Nod: 9 dreamland
in the land of ~: 3 out 6 asleep, dozing 7 napping 8 dreaming, snoozing 9 somnolent 10 slumbering
land west of ~: 4 Eden
partner: 6 Wynken 7 Blynken
resident: 4 Cain
visit ~: 3 nap 4 doze, rest 6 catnap, drowse, repose, retire, snooze, turn in 7 drop off, shuteye, slumber 8 take a nap 9 hibernate, hit the hay 10 hit the sack
nodal: 6 knobby, knotty 8 knotlike
nodding: 6 asleep, sleepy 9 soporific
noddy: 4 bird, tern
node: 3 bud 4 bump, burl, knar, knob, knot, lump, nurl 5 bulge, joint, knurl, stage 6 growth, vertex 8 junction, juncture, swelling 10 connection, focal point
__ node: 5 lymph
no deposit, no __: 6 return
No Diggity (1996 song)
artist: Blackstreet, Dr. Dre
No doubt in my mind!: 6 I'm sure
nodular: 5 bumpy 6 knobby, knotty
nodule: 3 bud 4 bump, burl, knar, knob, knot, lump 5 bulge 6 growth 8 swelling
nodus: 4 knot
Noel: 4 song, Xmas, yule 5 Black, carol, Neill 7 Buckner 8 Harrison, Yuletide 9 Christmas, Gallagher
see also Christmas
Noël: 4 Père 6 Coward
Noel-Baker, Philip: 7 British 8 Nobelist
__ no evil: 3 see 4 hear 5 speak
No Excuses
rival: 6 Gitano
No Exit
author: Jean-Paul Sartre
no-fat: 4 lean
no-fly __: 4 zone
NO follower: 3 PQR 4 PQRS 5 PQRST
__ no fool like...: 6 There's
no-frills: 5 plain 7 vanilla
Nofziger: 3 Lyn
nog: 5 drink, quaff 8 beverage, cocktail
ingredient: 3 egg, rum 4 milk 6 brandy
Nogales: 4 city, town
locale: 6 Mexico, Sonora 7 Arizona 8 Veracruz
see also Spanish
noggin: 4 bean, dome, head, mind, pate 5 gourd 6 noodle, sconce 7 cranium 9 braincase
hit on the ~: 3 bop 4 bonk, conk
Noggin
alternative: *see* cable channel
no-good: 5 awful 6 crumby 8 unusable, unworthy 9 worthless 10 despicable
__ no good: 4 up to
__ No Good: 5 You're
no-goodnik: 3 bum, cad, rat 4 heel 5 baddy, crook, louse, rogue, scamp, viper 6 baddie, bad egg 10 ne'er-do-well
no-goodniks: 6 bad lot
no great __: 6 shakes
No Greater Love
author: Danielle Steel
Noguchi: 5 Isamu 6 Thomas
Noguchi, Isamu: 6 artist 8 sculptor
No guts, no __!: 5 glory
Noh: 5 drama 8 Japanese
prop: 3 fan
__, no hands!: 6 Look ma
Nohant
author: George Sand
no-hat: 10 bareheaded
No Highway
author: Nevil Shute
no-hitter line score, maybe: 3 OOO
no-holds-barred: 6 all-out
__ No Hooks: 3 Use
__ no ice: 3 cut
__ no idea!: 4 I had
no ifs, __, or buts: 4 ands
noir: 3 bet 5 black 6 French
opposite: 5 blanc, rouge
__ noir: 4 café, film
noire
bête ~: 8 anathema
noise: 3 din, row, yak 4 bang, boom, buzz, fuss, peal, ring, roar, shot, talk, thud 5 blare, blast, clang, crack, crash, drone, hoo-ha, sound 6 babble, bedlam, bellow, clamor, fracas, hubbub, jabber, jangle, outcry, racket, rumors, squawk, tumult, uproar 7 buzzing, chatter, clangor, clatter, discord, fanfare, hearsay, yelling 8 babbling, disquiet, drumming, eruption, shouting 9 cacophony, commotion, explosion, fireworks, stridency 10 clattering, detonation, dissonance, hullabaloo, turbulence
about: 5 bruit, rumor 6 gossip
dull ~: 4 thud 5 clonk, clunk, thunk
ender: 5 maker
grating ~: 6 squeak, squeal
loud ~: 3 bam, din, pop, pow 4 bang, thud, wham, yell 5 alarm, blare, siren, whang 6 kaboom, report, scream
overwhelm with ~: 6 deafen 8 drown out
urban ~: 4 beep, toot 5 blare, blast
__ noise: 5 white
noiseless: 4 mute 5 muted, quiet, still 6 hushed, silent 8 stealthy, wordless 9 inaudible, soundless, voiceless 10 speechless
noiselessness: 4 calm 5 peace, quiet, still 7 silence
Noiseless Patient Spider, A: 4 poem
author: Walt Whitman
Noises Off: 4 film, play 5 farce
author: Michael Frayn
cast: Carol Burnett, Michael Caine, Denholm Elliott, Julie Hagerty, Marilu Henner, Christopher Reeve, John Ritter, Nicollette Sheridan
director: Peter Bogdanovich

noisette: **4** loin, meat, rose **6** fillet
noisome: **3** bad **4** foul, rank, ugly, vile **5** fetid, funky, musty, nasty **6** deadly, foetid, frowsy, frowzy, horrid, rancid, rotten, smelly, stinky, strong **7** baneful, harmful, hurtful, nocuous, noxious, odorous, reeking **8** mephitic, stinking **9** dangerous, injurious, loathsome, offensive, poisonous, repugnant, repulsive, revolting, unhealthy **10** disgusting, insalutary, malodorous
noisy: **4** loud, wild **5** aroar, forte, harsh, rowdy, vocal **7** bawling, blaring, booming, gabbing, grating, hooting, jarring, jumping, pealing, rackety, raucous, reboant, riotous, roaring, wailing, yelling **8** babbling, blasting, clanging, crashing, piercing, plangent, rumbling, shouting, sonorous, strident, turned up, whooping **9** bellowing, big-voiced, clamorous, deafening, dissonant, hollering, jabbering, loudmouth, screaming, shrieking, turbulent **10** boisterous, chattering, clangorous, clattering, discordant, disorderly, ear-popping, resounding, rip-roaring, screeching, stentorian, strepitous, stridulous, thundering, tumultuous, uproarious, vociferant, vociferous
bird: **3** pie **5** goose, macaw
disturbance: **5** brawl, melee **6** fracas
not ~: **4** calm, mute **5** quiet, still **6** at rest, hushed, placid, serene, silent **8** peaceful **9** soundless
Nokia: **5** phone **9** cell phone
alternative: **6** Nextel **8** Ericsson, Motorola
__ no kick...: **4** I get
No kidding!: **3** gee, wow **4** gosh **6** do tell, honest, really
Nolan: **4** Ryan **5** Kathy, Kenny, Lloyd **6** Philip **8** Jeanette, Kathleen
Nolan, Kenny
song: I Like Dreamin' (1976)
Nolan, Philip fate: **5** exile
Nolde: **4** Emil
no-lead: **3** gas **6** petrol **7** premium, regular **8** gasoline
nolens volens: **10** willy-nilly
noli me tangere: **10** touch me not
Nolin: **7** Gena Lee
Noll, Chuck: **5** coach
sport: **8** football
team: **8** Steelers
no-load __: **4** fund
nolo contendere: **4** plea
no love __: **4** lost
Nolte, Nick: **5** actor
film: 48HRS. (1982)
Affliction (1998)
Cannery Row (1982)
Cape Fear (1991)
The Deep (1977)
Down and Out in Beverly Hills (1986)
The Golden Bowl (2001)
Jefferson in Paris (1995)
Lorenzo's Oil (1992)
Nightwatch (1998)
North Dallas Forty (1979)
The Prince of Tides (1991)
Teachers (1984)
Under Fire (1983)
U Turn (1997)
Who'll Stop the Rain (1978)
nomad: **3** vag **4** hobo, Lapp **5** gypsy, rover **6** Berber, roamer **7** Bedouin, drifter, migrant, pilgrim, rambler **8** gadabout, traveler, vagabond, wanderer, wayfarer **9** itinerant
be a ~: **3** gad **4** roam, rove **6** ramble, wander **7** migrate **9** itinerate
home: **4** tent
Nomad: **3** car **4** auto **5** Chevy **9** Chevrolet **10** automobile
nomadic: **5** gypsy **6** mobile, roving **7** migrant, roaming, vagrant **8** drifting, pastoral, vagabond **9** itinerant, migratory, traveling, wandering, wayfaring
No man __ island: **4** is an
No Man __ Own: **5** of Her
...no man has __ before: **4** gone
No man is __ to his valet: **5** a hero
No man is an island
author: John Donne
no man's __: **4** land
No Man's Land
author: Harold Pinter
No más boxer: **5** Duran
nom de __: **5** plume **6** guerre
nom de plume: **4** name **5** alias, title **6** anonym **7** pen name **8** cognomen **9** false name, pseudonym
__ nome: **4** Caro
Nome: **4** city, port, town
home: **4** iglu **5** igloo **6** Alaska
native: **5** Inuit **6** Eskimo
no mean __: **4** feat
Nomellini: **3** Leo
nomen: **4** name **5** title
nomenclature: **4** name, term **8** glossary, taxonomy
No Mercy
song: Please Don't Go (1997)
Where Do You Go (1996)
nominal: **3** low **5** cheap, given, named, quasi, small, token **6** formal, puppet, stated **7** alleged, minimal, seeming, titular, trivial **8** apparent, honorary, so-called, supposed, symbolic, trifling **9** low-priced, pretended, professed, purported, suggested **10** in name only, ostensible, self-styled
lacking ~ value: **5** no par
nominate: **3** tab, tap **4** call, make, name, pick, term **5** draft, elect, put up, slate **6** assign, choose, decide, select, submit, tender **7** appoint, elevate, empower, present, propose, purpose, specify, suggest **8** delegate, handpick, settle on **9** designate, recommend **10** commission, settle upon
nomination: **6** choice, naming **8** election, proposal **9** selection **10** assignment, delegation
nominee: **6** runner **7** hopeful **8** prospect **9** appointee, candidate, contender **10** contestant
nominees: **5** field, slate
Nomo, Hideo
sport: **8** baseball
nomologist
forte: **3** law
No more!: **4** stop **5** uncle **6** cool it, enough, quit it, stop it
No More Lonely Nights (1984 song)
artist: Paul McCartney
No more Mr. __ Guy!: **4** Nice
__ No More, My Lady: **4** Weep
No More Tears (1979 song)
artist: Barbra Streisand, Donna Summer
No More Vietnams
author: Richard Nixon
__ No Mountain High Enough: **4** Ain't
non: **3** nah, naw, nay, nix, not **4** nein, nope, nyet, uh-uh **5** I won't, ixnay, never, no how, noway **6** no deal, noways, nowise **7** I refuse **8** forget it, I will not, negative, negatory **9** by no means, fat chance, I think not **10** count me out, not a chance, thumbs down
in German: **4** nein
in Russian: **4** nyet
in Scottish: **3** nae
persona ~ grata: **3** bum **5** tramp **6** pariah **7** outcast **8** derelict **9** miscreant, reprobate
sine qua ~: **4** must, need **9** condition, essential, necessity, requisite
non __ mentis: **6** compos
non-__ employee: **6** exempt
Nona: **4** Gaye **7** Hendryx
nonabrasive: **4** mild **6** benign, genial, gentle, mellow, placid, serene **7** tactful **8** harmless, laid back, pleasant, tranquil **9** easygoing
nonacceptance: **4** veto **6** denial, rebuff **7** refusal **8** turndown **9** disavowal, rejection **10** gainsaying, refutation
nonage: **5** youth **8** minority **10** immaturity
nonalcoholic beer brand: **6** O'Doul's
nonaligned: **7** neutral
nonattendance: **7** absence
nonbelief: **5** doubt, qualm **7** atheism **8** cynicism, distrust, mistrust, nihilism, wariness **9** chariness, misgiving, suspicion **10** skepticism
nonbeliever: **5** cynic, pagan **7** atheist, heathen, infidel
nonbelieving: **7** cynical, godless, mocking **8** doubtful **9** skeptical **10** suspicious
nonbelligerent: **6** irenic, placid, serene **7** neutral, pacific **8** amicable, friendly, peaceful, tranquil **9** peaceable **10** harmonious, pacifistic
noncarbonated: **4** flat **5** still
drink: **7** iced tea
nonce: **7** present **9** time being
nonchalance: **4** ease **5** poise, skill **6** aplomb, laxity **7** fluency **8** calmness, facility **9** composure, dexterity **10** adroitness, facileness, nimbleness
nonchalant: **3** lax **4** airy, calm, cool **5** aloof, blasé, happy, hasty, loose, staid, stoic **6** at ease, casual, low-key, mellow, placid, remiss, sedate, serene, sloppy, smooth **7** at peace, neutral, offhand, relaxed, stoical **8** carefree, careless, composed, detached, laid back, listless, lukewarm, slipshod, tranquil, uncaring **9** apathetic, collected, easygoing, impassive, imprudent, incurious, negligent, temperate, unexcited, unfeeling, unheedful, unmindful, unruffled, unworried **10** incautious, insouciant, unagitated, unthinking, untroubled
nonchooser: **6** beggar
noncitizen: **5** alien
non-civilian: **4** navy **7** soldier **8** military
nonclergy: **5** laity
nonclerical: **3** lay **4** laic **6** laical
noncom: **3** cpl., CPO, CWO, NCO, SFC, sgt. **4** MSgt., serg., SSgt., TSgt. **5** sarge
sch. for a ~: **3** OCS, OTS
superior: **5** looey, looie, louie
noncombatant: **7** neutral **8** pacifist
noncommercial news source: **3** NPR, PBS
noncommissioned __: **7** officer
noncommittal: **3** coy, mum **4** mute, wary **5** blank, vague **7** careful, evasive, guarded, neutral, politic, prudent, tactful **8** cautious, discreet, reserved **9** ambiguous, equivocal, judicious, tentative **10** wishy-washy
be ~: **4** duck **5** evade, fudge, hedge, stall **6** waffle **7** shuffle **8** flip-flop, hesitate **9** hem and haw, pussyfoot, stonewall, vacillate **10** equivocate
response: **4** I see **5** maybe **7** perhaps **8** possibly, probably **9** it could be, it might be
noncompliance: **5** break, lapse **6** breach, schism **7** discord, refusal **9** violation **10** infraction
noncompliant: **5** rowdy **6** unruly **7** chaotic, lawless **8** anarchic, mutinous, refusing **9** divergent, irregular, objecting, truculent **10** anarchical, disorderly, dissenting, rebellious
non compos __: **6** mentis
noncompulsory: **8** optional
nonconcrete: **8** abstract **9** imaginary **10** intangible
nonconforming: **6** atypic **8** atypical, contrary **10** unorthodox
nonconformism: **6** heresy, revolt, schism, strife **7** discord, dissent, protest **8** conflict, disunity **9** rebellion **10** heterodoxy, resistance
nonconformist: **5** flake, hippy, rebel **6** defier, hippie, weirdo **7** beatnik, dropout, heretic, lawless, liberal, oddball, offbeat, radical, swinger **8** bohemian, maverick, original **9** dissenter, dissident, eccentric, heretical, heterodox, protester **10** unorthodox
nonconformity: **6** breach, denial, heresy **7** dissent **8** negation **9** exception, objection, rebellion, rejection, violation
nonconsent: **4** veto **6** rebuff **7** refusal **8** turndown **9** rejection

10 thumbs down
nondescript: **4** blah, dull **5** mousy, plain **6** common, mousey **7** insipid, prosaic **8** mediocre, ordinary, uncommon **9** colorless, prosaical
nondiscriminatory: **4** fair, just, open **8** unbiased
nondrinker: **3** dry **10** teetotaler
nondurable: **5** shaky **6** flimsy **7** brittle, crumbly, fragile **9** frangible
none: **3** nil, zip **4** nada, nary, zero **5** aught, ought, zilch **6** naught, nobody, not any, not one, nought **7** not a bit, nothing, pronoun **8** goose egg, not a soul **9** nary a soul, not a thing
bar ~: **3** all **8** everyone
combining form: **5** nulli-
ender: **4** such
in French: **4** rien
in law: **3** nul
in Scottish: **4** naen
in Spanish: **4** nada
of the above: **5** other
omitting ~: **4** full **5** fully **6** entire, wholly **7** totally **8** complete, entirely, everyone **9** everybody **10** completely, everything
second to ~: **4** A-one, best, tops **5** first, prime **8** peerless **9** unequaled **10** preeminent
none __ above: **5** of the
__ none: **3** bar
__-none: **5** all-or
non-earthling: **2** ET **5** alien
None But the Lonely Heart: **4** film, play
author: Clifford Odets
character: **3** Ada
nonecclesiastic: **4** laic **6** laical
nonemployment: **6** disuse
nonentity: **4** wimp, zero **6** cipher, menial, nobody, squirt **7** parvenu, upstart **10** figurehead
none of __ business: **4** your
none of the above: **5** other
nones: **4** date, hour
plus eight: **4** ides
nonessential: **4** side **5** extra, petty, spare, undue **6** luxury **7** trivial **8** deadwood, needless **9** excessive
nonesuch: **5** ideal, model **7** paragon
nonet: **4** nine **5** choir, Muses **6** ennead **8** ensemble, ninesome
none the __: **5** wiser
none the __ for wear: **5** worse
nonetheless: **3** tho, yet **6** anyway, even so, though **7** however
non-ethical: **6** amoral
No news is __ news!: **4** good
non-exchange mkt.: **3** OTC
nonexclusive: **4** open **7** generic **8** exoteric **9** generical
nonexistent: **3** nil **4** dead, gone, lost, null, void **5** blank, empty, false, vague **6** absent, dreamy, fantom, unreal **7** defunct, extinct, fancied, missing, phantom, shadowy, tenuous **8** baseless, departed, ethereal, fanciful, illusive, illusory, imagined, mythical, vaporous **9** dreamlike, fictional, imaginary, legendary
nonexpert: **6** layman
nonfeasance: **6** laxity **8** leniency
nonfiction: **4** real **5** prose, story
category: **4** biog. **7** history **9** biography
nonflowering plant: **4** fern, moss
nonforthcoming: **3** coy **6** demure **7** evasive **9** diffident **10** coquettish
nonfunctional: **6** barren, no good, otiose **7** useless **9** valueless, worthless
nongamblers play for it: **3** fun **5** kicks, sport **9** enjoyment
nongermane: **5** inapt, unapt, unfit **9** ill-suited **10** inapposite, irrelevant, out of order, out of place
Nongogo
author: Athol Fugard
__ non grata: **7** persona
nongregarious: **3** coy, shy **4** meek **5** timid **6** demure **7** bashful, private **8** detached, reserved, reticent, retiring, sheepish, solitary **9** reclusive, secretive, shrinking, withdrawn **10** antisocial, unsociable
nonharmonious sound: **4** bang **5** blare, crash, noise **6** jangle, squawk **7** clangor **9** cacophony, commotion, explosion, stridency **10** clattering, dissonance
noninclusion: **4** skip **5** lapse **8** omission
nonindulgent: **5** sober, staid, stoic **7** ascetic, austere, stoical **8** reserved, sensible **9** abstinent, temperate **10** abstaining, abstemious, controlled, restrained
nonirritating: **4** mild, safe, soft **6** benign, gentle **8** harmless
nonitalicized: **5** roman
nonliable: **4** free **6** exempt **8** excluded
nonmaterial: **9** spiritual
nonmetal: **4** neon **5** argon, boron, xenon **6** carbon, helium, iodine, oxygen, sulfur **7** bromine, krypton, silicon, sulphur **8** chlorine, fluorine, hydrogen, nitrogen **10** phosphorus
nonmilitary: **8** civilian
nonministerial: **3** lay **4** laic **6** laical
non-motorized vehicle: **4** bike, luge, sled **5** trike, wagon
non-Muslim: **6** giaour
nonnative: **5** alien **7** foreign
nonnegotiable, it's: **4** must
non-nocturnal: **7** diurnal
no-no: **4** don't, rule, tabu **5** taboo **7** misdeed **9** profanity
nonobligatory: **8** elective, optional **9** voluntary
nonobservance: **4** foul **5** wrong **6** breach, laxity **7** neglect, offense **9** disregard, violation **10** infraction, remissness
No, No, Nanette
composer: Irving Caesar, Otto Harbach, Vincent Youmans
No, No, No (1997 song)
artist: Destiny's Child, Wyclef Jean
No-No Nonette
composer: PDQ Bach
no-nonsense: **4** firm, hard **5** bossy, cruel, picky, rigid, sober, staid, stern, tough **6** severe, solemn, somber, strict **7** austere, deadpan, earnest, serious, sincere, Spartan **8** despotic, exacting, hard-line, rigorous **9** demanding, draconian, humorless, stringent, unamusing, unbending, unsparing **10** despotical, inflexible, iron-fisted, oppressive, point-blank, tyrannical, unhumorous
nonordained: **3** lay **4** laic **6** laical
No No Song (1975 song)
artist: Ringo Starr
No, Not Much! (1956 song)
artist: Four Lads
non-oyster months, like: **5** r-less
nonpareil: **3** gem **4** A-one, best, oner, sole **5** candy, ideal, model, prime **6** unique **7** in front, paragon, supreme **8** champion, peerless, treasure **9** just right, matchless, unequaled, unmatched, unrivaled, worthiest **10** inimitable, phenomenon, unbeatable, unequalled, unexampled, unrivalled
alternative: *see* point size
nonpartisan: **4** even, fair, just **5** equal **7** neutral **8** detached, moderate, unbiased **9** equitable, impartial, objective, on one's own, unbigoted, uncolored **10** evenhanded, on the fence
nonpastoral: **3** lay **4** laic **6** laical **7** secular **8** temporal
nonpayment: **5** lapse **7** default, failure **10** bankruptcy, insolvency
result: **4** repo
nonperformer: **3** dud **5** lemon **7** failure
nonphysical: **8** ethereal **9** ineffable, spiritual, unearthly **10** intangible
Non più andrai: **4** aria
nonplus: **3** get **4** balk, daze, faze, stun **5** addle, baulk, floor, stimy, stump, stymy, throw **6** baffle, bemuse, boggle, dismay, flurry, fuddle, muddle, puzzle, rattle, stymie, thwart, unglue **7** astound, buffalo, confuse, fluster, mystify, perplex, stagger **8** astonish, bewilder, confound, paralyse, paralyze, surprise **9** discomfit, dumbfound, embarrass, frustrate, take aback **10** demoralize, disconcert
nonplussed: **4** asea **5** at sea, blank **7** at a loss, puzzled **10** distraught
nonpoisonous: **4** safe **6** edible **8** harmless **9** innocuous
non-Polynesian: **5** haole
nonporous: **4** firm **5** solid, tight **6** sealed **8** hermetic **10** impervious
nonprescription: **3** OTC
nonproductive: **4** arid, drab, idle **5** dusty **6** barren, fallow **7** dormant, humdrum, sterile **8** blighted, inactive **10** lackluster, unanimated, unfruitful
nonprofessional: **3** lay **6** layman **7** amateur, dabbler **9** layperson
nonproliferation treaty: **4** SALT **6** SALT II
non-pro sports org.: **3** AAU **4** NCAA
nonpublic: **5** inner **6** covert, hidden, secret **7** private **8** hush-hush, isolated, personal **9** concealed, reclusive, secretive **10** restricted, tucked away, undercover, under wraps
nonreactive: **5** inert **9** impassive, insensate
non-realist: **7** dreamer, ostrich **8** escapist, idealist **9** fantasist **10** daydreamer
nonreligious: **3** lay **4** laic **6** laical **7** secular, worldly
nonresident professional: **6** extern
nonresistant: **7** passive **8** resigned, yielding
non-returnable: **9** throwaway **10** disposable
non-rural: **4** city **5** civic, urban **9** municipal
nonsense: **3** fun, pap **4** jest, joke, myth **5** farce, folly **7** baloney, fatuity, fooling **8** babbling **9** absurdity, craziness, frivolity, giddiness, goofiness, silliness, stupidity
partner: **5** stuff
talk ~: **4** jive **5** prate **6** babble, footle, gabble, ramble, wander **7** blather, blether
see also baloney
Nonsense!: **3** bah, rot, tut **4** pooh **5** pshaw **6** phooey **7** baloney
Nonsense Songs
author: Edward Lear
nonsensical: **3** mad **4** idle, wild **5** crazy, daffy, flaky, goofy, inane, kooky, nutty, silly, wacky **6** absurd, flakey, kookie, screwy, whacky **7** asinine, fatuous, foolish **8** cockeyed **9** laughable, ludicrous, pointless
nonserious: **4** flip **5** giddy, inane, silly **6** madcap **7** puerile, shallow, trivial **8** childish, juvenile **9** facetious, frivolous, whimsical
nonsocial one: **4** geek, nerd **5** dweeb, loner
nonspecialist: **6** layman **10** generalist
nonspecific adjective: **3** any, few **4** some **9** whichever
nonspiritual: **7** earthly, fleshly, mundane, secular, worldly **8** material, physical, tangible, temporal **9** corporeal
nonspoken tongue: **3** ASL
non-staff: **9** freelance
nonstandard: **3** var. **7** variant **8** aberrant
nonstop: **6** direct, steady **7** endless, express, through **8** constant, enduring, straight, unbroken, unending **9** ceaseless, incessant, perennial, perpetual **10** continuous, relentless
non-studio film: **5** indie
nonsuccess: **3** dud **4** bomb, bust, flop, loss **6** defeat, fiasco, turkey **7** failure, washout **8** collapse, disaster
nonsupporter: **3** foe **4** anti **8** opponent
non-surfing surfer: **5** ho-dad
non-swimmer: **5** wader
nonsymmetrical: **6** uneven **7** unequal **8** lopsided **10** unbalanced
nontaxable: **6** exempt
nontoxic: **4** safe **6** edible, gentle **8** harmless **9** innoxious
nontransparent: **6** opaque, turbid
non-U: **5** inapt **7** uncouth **8** low-class **9** bourgeois **10** uncultured
nonuniform: **5** bumpy, jerky, lumpy, rough **6** jagged, patchy, random, wobbly, zigzag **7** crooked, erratic **8** aberrant, shifting, sporadic, unsteady **9** divergent, haphazard, hit-or-miss, irregular **10** inconstant

nonuse result: 4 dust, rust
nonvarsity player: 5 scrub
nonverbal feedback: 3 nod 5 vibes
nonviolent: 5 quiet 6 irenic 7 orderly, passive 8 irenical, pacifist, peaceful 9 peaceable
  demonstration: 5 lie in, sit-in
nonvocal: 3 mum 4 mute 5 muted, quiet 6 silent 7 aphonic 8 wordless 9 soundless 10 speechless, tongue-tied
nonvoter: 3 tot 4 baby 5 child, minor 6 infant 8 juvenile
  before 1920: 5 woman
nonwinner: 4 flop 5 loser 7 also-ran
nonwoven fabric: 4 felt
noodge: 3 bug, irk, nag, rag, vex 4 goad, pest 5 annoy, beset, harry, hound, shrew, taunt 6 badger, bother, critic, harass, hassle, heckle, hector, nagger, needle, nettle, pester, plague, rattle, ruffle, virago 7 bedevil, disturb, henpeck, torment 8 irritate 9 beleaguer, Xanthippe 10 complainer
noodle: 3 nob, nut 4 bean, head, mind 5 pasta, skull 6 noggin, sconce 7 cranium 9 braincase
  around: 4 muse 5 think 6 ponder, reason 7 reflect 8 cogitate, conceive, mull over, ruminate 9 cerebrate, speculate 10 brainstorm
  like a wet ~: 4 limp 5 saggy 6 droopy, flabby 7 flaccid
  use one's ~: 5 think 6 deduce, ideate, reason 7 analyze 8 cogitate 9 cerebrate, figure out
noodlehead
  see ninny
noodleheaded
  see foolish
noodles: 4 ziti 5 pasta 6 ditali, elbows, lo mein, rigati, shells 7 fusilli, gnocchi, lasagna, ravioli, rotelle 8 farfalle, linguini, macaroni, rigatoni 9 manicotti, spaghetti 10 cannelloni, fettuccini, tagliarini, tortellini, vermicelli
  Japanese ~: 5 ramen 6 larmen
__ noodles: 3 egg
nook: 3 bay, den 4 hole 5 coign, cubby, niche, place, quoin 6 alcove, cavity, coigne, corner, cranny, recess 7 crevice, cubicle, dinette, hideout, opening, retreat 8 hideaway 9 cubbyhole, inglenook 10 pigeonhole
  shady ~: 5 bower
  starter: 5 ingle
nook and __: 6 cranny
noon: 4 apex 6 midday, twelve, zenith 8 meridian
  before ~: 7 morning
  ender: 3 day 4 tide, time
  in French: 4 midi
  meal: 5 lunch
  on some clocks: 3 XII
  starter: 4 fore 5 after
__ Noon: 4 High
Noonan: 3 Tom 4 Fred 5 Chris, Peggy
Noone: 5 Peter 6 Jimmie 8 Kathleen
Noon Wine
  author: Katherine Anne Porter
__-noor Diamond: 4 Koh-i
No Ordinary Love (1992 song)
  artist: Sade
noose: 4 loop, trap 5 snare 8 slipknot
__ no pain: 4 feel 7 feeling
No pain, no __: 4 gain
nopal: 5 fruit 6 cactus
no-par __: 5 stock
No Particular Place to Go (1964 song)
  artist: Chuck Berry
nope: 3 nah, naw, nay, nix, non 4 nein, nyet, uh-uh 5 I won't, ixnay, never, no how, no way 6 no deal, noways, nowise, unh-unh 7 I refuse 8 forget it, I will not, negative, negatory 9 by no means, fat chance, I think not 10 count me out, not a chance, thumbs down
  opposite: 3 yep, yup
__ no place like home: 6 There's
__-no-prisoners: 4 take
No problem!: 4 easy, sure 5 a snap, can do, it's OK 6 glad to, OK by me 7 happy to
  see also of course
__ no questions...: 5 Ask me
nor: 6 and not 9 connector 10 connective
  partner: 7 neither
Nor.
  neighbor: 3 Den, Fin., Swe. 4 Swed.
  see also Norway
...nor a __ be: 6 lender
Nora: 4 Dunn 5 Bayes 6 Ephron 7 Charles
  dog: 4 Asta
  partner: 4 Nick
  portrayer: Myrna Loy
NORAD resident: 4 ICBM
Norah: 5 Jones, Lofts
  father: 4 Ravi
Norbert: 10 Burgmüller
Norcross: 4 city, town
  locale: 7 Georgia
nord
  opposite: 3 sud
Nord
  capital of ~: 5 Lille
Norden: 5 Tommy
Nordenskjöld: 4 Nils 5 Adolf
Nordheim: 4 Arne
Nordhoff, Charles: 6 writer
  partner: 4 Hall
  work: Mutiny on the Bounty
Nordic: 5 Arian, Aryan
  alternative: 6 Alpine
  enthusiast: 5 skier
  name: 4 Erik, Leif
Nordstrom: 5 Elmer
  competitor: 4 Saks 5 Macy's
nor'easter: 4 wind
Noreen: 8 Corcoran
Norelco: 5 razor
  alternative: 5 Braun 9 Remington
Norfolk: 4 city, isle, port, town 6 county, island
  locale: 7 England 8 Nebraska, Virginia
  sch.: 3 ODU
Norgay, Tenzing: 6 Nepali 7 climber
Norge: 9 appliance
  alternative: *see* appliance brand
__ nor hair: 4 hide
noria: 5 wheel 10 water wheel
Noriega: 6 Manuel
No Right __: 5 on Red
Nor iron bars __: 5 a cage
Noritake
  competitor: 5 Lenox 6 Mikasa 8 Wedgwood
norm: 3 avg., par, std. 4 mean, rule, type 5 gauge, model, scale, usual 6 median, medium 7 average, measure, pattern 8 standard 9 barometer, benchmark, criterion, prototype, yardstick 10 touchstone
  departure from the ~: 8 variance 9 deviation, disparity, variation 10 aberration, divergence
Norm: 4 Cash 6 Crosby, Ullman 9 Macdonald
  occupation on Cheers: 3 CPA
  wife on Cheers: 4 Vera
Norm __ Brocklin: 3 Van
Norma: 4 font 5 Klein, opera 6 Kamali 7 Desmond, Shearer 8 Talmadge, typeface
  composer: Vincenzo Bellini
  neighbor: 5 Lupus
  piece: 4 aria
Norma __: 3 Rae 4 Ashe
normal: 3 par, reg., std. 4 sane 5 lucid, right, stock, typic, usual 6 common, medium, wonted 7 average, general, mundane, natural, regular, routine, typical 8 accepted, everyday, habitual, ordinary, orthodox, rational, standard 9 customary, prevalent 10 accustomed, legitimate, prevailing, uneventful
  back to ~: 4 fine 5 cured 6 aright, healed, itself, mended 8 all right
  not ~: 3 odd 5 flaky, outré, weird 6 way-out 7 bizarre, deviant, strange, unusual 8 aberrant, atypical, peculiar, uncommon 9 anomalous, eccentric, grotesque, irregular
  starter: 3 log
normal __: 5 curve
Normal: 4 city, town
  campus: 3 ISU
  locale: 8 Illinois
normalize: 8 regulate 10 stereotype
normally: 7 as a rule, as usual, usually 8 by nature 9 in general, most often 10 by and large
Norman: 4 city, diva, Fell, Greg, Lear, René, town 5 Merle, Mingo, Stone, Tokar 6 Angell, Foster, Jessye, Krasna, Mailer, Marsha, McLeod, Norell, Panama, Ramsey, Taurog, Thomas, Wisdom 7 Borlaug, Cousins, Douglas, Jewison 8 Rockwell 9 Bel Geddes, Dello Joio, Greenbaum, Podhoretz
  athletes: 7 Sooners
  city: 4 Caen
  crown tax: 4 geld
  enemy: 5 Saxon
  locale: 4 Okla. 8 Oklahoma
  neighbor: 6 Breton
  poet: 4 Wace
Norman __ Geddes: 3 Bel
Norman __ Joio: 5 Dello
Norman __ Peale: 7 Vincent
Norman Conquest tapestry: 6 Bayeux
Normand: 5 Mabel
__ Normandes: 4 Iles
Normandy
  beach: 4 Gold, Juno, Utah 5 Omaha, Sword
  event: 4 D-Day
  river: 4 Orne
  town: 4 Caen, St. Lô 5 Rouen
  see also French
Norman, Greg: 5 Shark 6 golfer
  spouse: Chris Evert
Norman, Jessye: 4 diva 6 singer 7 soprano
  specialty: 4 aria 5 opera
Norman Vincent: 5 Peale
Norma Rae (1979 film)
  cast: Beau Bridges, Sally Field, Ron Leibman
  director: Martin Ritt
  focus: 5 union
  setting: 3 Ala. 7 Alabama, factory
norms
  lack of ~: 5 anomy 6 anomie
Norm Van __: 8 Brocklin
No Room in the Ark
  author: Alan Moorehead
__ nor reason: 5 rhyme
Norris: 5 Chuck, Frank 6 Church 8 Kathleen 9 McWhirter
Norris Division org.: 3 NHL
Norris, Frank: 6 writer
  work: McTeague
    The Octopus
    The Pit
Norrish, Ronald: 7 chemist 8 Nobelist
Norristown: 4 city
  locale: 4 Penn.
Norse: 7 Vikings 8 language
  ender: 3 man, men
  epic: 4 edda, saga
  giant: 4 Ymer, Ymir 5 Jotun
  god: 4 Frey, Loki, Odin, Thor 5 Aegir, Njord, Othin 6 Balder 7 Forseti
  goddess: 3 Hel, Urd, Vor 4 Norn 5 Freya, Frigg
  gods: 5 Aesir, Vanir
  mariner: 4 Eric
  mythical king: 4 Atli
  of old ~ poetry: 5 eddic
  Olympus: 6 Asgard
  royal name: 4 Olaf, Olav
  symbol: 4 rune
  toast: 5 skoal
north: 2 pt. 5 point 6 Arctic, boreal 9 direction
  combining form: 4 arct- 5 arcto-
  ender: 3 ern 4 ward, west 5 bound, wards 6 lander, wester 7 eastern, western 8 easterly, eastward, westerly, westward
  of: 4 over 5 above 6 beyond 8 more than
__ north: 4 true
North: 3 Jay, sea 5 Ollie, Union 6 Oliver, Sheree 8 Douglass 9 Frederick
  ender: 3 man, men 4 east, land 5 ridge
North __: 3 Sea 4 Pole, Star 7 America
North __ Forty: 6 Dallas
North __, NE: 6 Platte
North __-Westphalia: 5 Rhine
North __ Zone: 6 Frigid
North Africa
  antelope: 5 addax
  fortress: 6 Casbah, Kasbah
  language: 6 Berber
  mountains: 5 Atlas
  official: 3 dey 5 pacha, pasha
  port: 4 Oran

NO

saint: 7 Cyprian 9 Augustine
stew: 8 couscous
wind: 6 ghibli
North African: 6 Berber
North America
capital: 6 Ottawa 10 Mexico City, Washington
desert: 6 Mohave 7 Sonoran 10 Chihuahuan 11 Death Valley
explorer: 5 Cabot 6 Balboa, Hudson 8 Columbus, Vespucci
Northampton: 4 city, town
locale: 4 Mass.
Northamptonshire: 6 county
locale: 7 England
river: 4 Ouse
North and South
author: John Jakes
Northanger __: 5 Abbey
Northanger Abbey
author: Jane Austen
Northants: 6 county
locale: 7 England
North Atlantic
fish: 3 cod
island: 6 Azores 7 Faeroes, Iceland, Ireland 9 Greenland 10 West Indies
sighting: 4 berg, floe
north by __: 4 east, west
North by Northwest (1959 film)
cast: Leo G. Carroll, Cary Grant, Martin Landau, James Mason, Eva Marie Saint
composer: Bernard Herrmann
director: Alfred Hitchcock
North Carolina: 5 state
capital: 7 Raleigh
city: 4 Apex, Cary 6 Durham, Monroe, Shelby, Wilson 7 Concord, Hickory, Kinston, New Bern, Raleigh, Sanford 8 Asheboro, Gastonia, Havelock, Matthews 9 Asheville, Charlotte, Fort Bragg, Goldsboro, High Point, Lexington, Lumberton, Salisbury 10 Burlington, Chapel Hill, Greensboro, Greenville, Kannapolis, Rocky Mount, Wilmington
conference: 3 ACC
county: 3 Lee 4 Ashe, Eden, Hoke 5 Avery, Selma, Surry 6 Bertie, Yancey 7 Pamlico
fort: 5 Bragg
Indian: 6 Lumbee 8 Cherokee
island off ~: 7 Roanoke
mountain: 5 Black 8 Mitchell
neighbor: 7 Georgia 8 Virginia 9 Tennessee
river: 3 Eno
school: 4 Duke, Elon 10 Wake Forest
start of ~ motto: 4 esse
state beverage: 4 milk
state bird: 8 cardinal
state dog: 10 Plott hound
state flower: 7 dogwood
state insect: 8 honeybee
state mammal: 8 squirrel
state precious stone: 7 emerald
state reptile: 9 box turtle
state rock: 7 granite
state tree: 4 pine
North Carolina State
athletes: 8 Wolfpack
conference: 3 ACC
locale: 7 Raleigh
North Cascades: 4 park
locale: 10 Washington
North Dakota: 5 state
capital: 8 Bismarck
city: 5 Fargo, Minot, Rolla, Rugby 8 Bismarck 10 Grand Forks
Indian: 6 Mandan
neighbor: 6 Canada 7 Montana 8 Manitoba 9 Minnesota
state beverage: 4 milk
state bird: 10 meadowlark
state fish: 4 pike
state tree: 3 elm
North Dallas Forty (1979 film)
cast: Mac Davis, Charles Durning, Nick Nolte
North, Douglass: 8 Nobelist 9 economist
northeaster: 4 wind
Northeastern: 6 school
athletes: 7 Huskies
locale: 6 Boston
neighbor: 3 MIT
Northeasterner: 4 Yank 6 Yankee
norther: 4 wind
northerly: 4 wind
more ~: 5 upper
northern: 6 boreal
northern __: 6 lights
Northern: 10 paper towel
alternative: 5 Scott 6 Marcal 7 Charmin 8 Soft Weve 10 Cottonelle, White Cloud
constellation: 4 Lyra
lights: 6 aurora
Northern __: 3 Spy
Northerner: 4 Yank 6 Yankee
Northern Exposure (CBS drama)
animal: 4 bear 5 moose
cast: Rob Morrow (Dr. Joel Fleischman)
Janine Turner (Maggie O'Connell)
radio station: 4 KBHR
setting: 6 Alaska, Cicely
Northern Illinois: 6 school
athletes: 7 Huskies
conference: 3 MAC
locale: 6 De Kalb
Northern Ireland
capital: 7 Belfast
city: 5 Larne, Newry 6 Antrim, Lurgan 7 Belfast, Lisburn
Northern Spy: 5 apple
relative: *see* apple
Northern Territory city: 6 Darwin
north forty unit: 4 acre
__ North Frederick: 3 Ten
North Frigid __: 4 Zone
North Korea: 6 nation 7 country
capital: 9 Pyongyang
city: 5 Nampo 7 Hamhung 8 Chongjin 9 Pyongyang
money: 3 won 4 chon
neighbor: 5 China 6 Russia
north-of-the-border
see Canada
North, Oliver rank: 3 Col.
North Olmsted: 4 city, town
locale: 4 Ohio
North Pacific __: 5 Ocean 7 Current
North Platte: 4 city, town 5 river
city on the ~: 6 Casper
locale: 8 Nebraska
North Pole
denizen: 3 elf 5 Santa
explorer: 5 Peary 6 Nansen, Nobile
near the ~: 6 Arctic
North Sea
hazard: 4 berg, floe 7 iceberg, ice floe
inlet: 5 fiord, fjord
island: 7 Frisian, Orkneys
port: 5 Emden
river to the ~: 3 Dee, Ems 4 Elbe, Maas, Oder, Odra, Tees, Tyne, Yser 5 Meuse, Rhine, Tweed, Weser 6 Thames 7 Schelde, Scheldt
__ Northside 777: 4 Call
North Slope
garment: 5 parka
quest: 3 oil
state: 6 Alaska
North Temperate __: 4 Zone
North Texas
athletes: 9 Mean Green
locale: 6 Denton
North to the Future state: 6 Alaska
Northumberland: 6 county
city: 5 Blyth 7 Berwick
locale: 7 England
neighbor: 4 Scot
river: 4 Tyne
Northwest: 7 airline
former rival: 3 TWA 5 Pan Am 7 Braniff, Eastern
rival: 5 Delta 6 United 8 American 11 Continental
northwester: 4 wind
Northwestern: 10 university
athletes: 8 Wildcats
capital: 5 Boise, Salem 6 Helena 7 Olympia
conference: 6 Big Ten
locale: 8 Evanston, Illinois
sound: 5 Puget
state: 5 Idaho 6 Oregon 7 Montana 10 Washington
Northwest Passage
author: Kenneth Roberts
explorer: 5 Parry 6 Baffin 7 Gilbert 8 Franklin 9 Frobisher
locale: 6 Canada
Northwest Territories
city: 6 Inuvik 8 Hay River
__ North Whitehead: 6 Alfred
North Woods state: 4 Minn. 9 Minnesota
Norton: 2 Ed 3 Ken 4 Mary 5 André, Simon, sound 6 Edward, Trixie 7 Charles
Norton, Charles: 6 writer
Norton, Ed: Art Carney
to Kramden: 3 pal
wear: 3 hat 4 vest
wife: 6 Trixie
workplace: 5 sewer
Norton, Edward: 5 actor
film: American History X (1998)
Death to Smoochy (2002)
The Illusionist (2006)
The Incredible Hulk (2008)
The Italian Job (2003)
Keeping the Faith (2000)
Pride and Glory (2008)
Primal Fear (1996)
Red Dragon (2002)
Rounders (1998)
The Score (2001)
Norton, Ken: 5 boxer
foe: 3 Ali
milieu: 4 ring
Norton-Taylor: 4 Judy
Norval the Great
author: Dr. Seuss
Norville: 7 Deborah
Norvo: 3 Red
Norwalk: 4 city, town
locale: 4 Conn. 10 California
Norway: 6 nation 7 country
bay: 5 fiord, fjord
capital: 4 Oslo
cheese: 9 Jarlsberg
city: 4 Oslo, Voss 6 Bergen, Narvik, Tromsö 9 Stavanger, Trondheim 10 Hammerfest
explorer: 6 Nansen 7 Ericson 8 Amundsen 9 Heyerdahl
figure skater: 5 Henie
in Norway: 5 Norge
king: 4 Karl, Olaf, Olav 5 Oscar 6 Haakon, Harald
legislature: 8 Storting
locale: 3 Eur. 5 Scand. 6 Europe
money: 3 öre 5 krone
mountain: 6 Kjölen
native: 4 Lapp
neighbor: 6 Russia, Sweden 7 Finland
Nobelist in Chemistry: 6 Hassel
Nobelist in Economics: 6 Frisch 8 Haavelmo
Nobelist in Literature: 6 Hamsun, Undset 8 Bjornson
Nobelist in Peace: 5 Lange 6 Nansen
org.: 4 NATO
painter: 5 Munch
patron saint: 4 Olaf, Olav
playwright: 5 Ibsen
rug: 3 rya
sea monster: 7 krakens
sea near ~: 7 Barents
soprano: 8 Flagstad
toast: 5 skoal
violinist: 4 Bull 7 Ole Bull
writer: 4 Duun 5 Bojer 6 Hamsun, Sandel 10 Falkberget
Norway __: 3 rat 4 pine 5 maple 6 spruce
Norwegian: 3 sea 8 language
to Norwegians: 5 Norsk
Norwegian elkhound: 3 dog 5 canid 6 canine
Norwegian Forest: 3 cat 5 felid 6 feline
Norwegian Wood group: 7 Beatles
instrument: 5 sitar
nor'wester: 4 wind
Norwich: 4 city, town 7 terrier
locale: 7 England, Norfolk
nos.: 4 data 6 digits 7 figures 10 statistics
No Sad Songs for Me (1950 film)
director: Rudolph Maté
No Scrubs (1999 song)
artist: TLC
nose: 3 pry 4 beak, gift, odor, root, seek 5 aroma, flair, knack, organ, scent, snoot, snout 6 butt in, meddle, schnoz, talent 7 bouquet, edge out, intrude, schnozz, smeller 8 instinct 9 fragrance, interfere, proboscis, schnozzle 10 schnozzola
around: 4 lurk 5 prowl, skulk, slink, sneak, snoop 7 slither
bone: 5 vomer

by a ~: 4 just 6 barely 8 narrowly
combining form: 3 nas- 4 nasi-, naso-, rhin- 5 rhino-
ender: 3 bag, gay 4 band, dive 5 bleed, piece
follow one's ~: 3 gad 4 roam, rove 6 ramble, wander 7 meander, traipse 9 gallivant, itinerate
get one's ~ out of joint: 6 resent
hurt a ~: 5 tweak
in French: 3 nez
in Latin: 5 nasus
keep one's ~ clean: 6 behave 10 toe the line
keep one's ~ to the grindstone: 4 moil, plod, toil, work 5 labor, sweat 6 drudge, strain, strive 8 work hard 9 plug along, pound away
long ~: 5 trunk
nautical ~: 4 prow
noise: 5 achoo, snore, snort 6 ahchoo, hachoo 7 kerchoo
nose to ~: 4 even 5 equal, level
offend the ~: 4 reek 5 smell, stink
of the ~: 5 nasal
on the ~: 4 to a T 5 exact, right, sharp 6 just so, prompt, to a tee 7 correct, exactly 8 accurate, for a fact, promptly, very well 9 befitting, just right, perfectly, precisely 10 absolutely, applicable, positively
opening: 6 meatus
out: 4 beat, edge 5 learn, trail 6 defeat 8 discover, squeak by
part of the ~: 5 naris 6 septum 7 nostril
parts of the ~: 5 nares, septa
perceive with the ~: 5 smell, sniff, whiff
poke one's ~ in: 3 pry 5 snoop 6 meddle 7 intrude 9 eavesdrop, interfere
snowman's ~: 6 carrot
starter: 4 blue, cone, hook, tube 6 shovel 7 bladder
stick one's ~ in: 3 pry 5 snoop 6 meddle 7 obtrude 9 interfere
stimulus: 4 odor 5 aroma, scent, smell, whiff 7 perfume 9 fragrance
thumb one's ~ at: 4 defy, mock 5 flout
turn up one's ~: 5 sneer, spurn 7 disdain 10 look down on
under one's ~: 4 near 5 close 6 nearby, openly 7 visible
nose ___: 3 bag, job, out 4 clip, cone, dive, ring 5 about, drops, guard 6 around
___ nose: 3 by a, pug 5 on the, Roman
No seats available: 3 SRO
nosebag
don the ~: 3 eat, sup 4 dine
fill: 4 feed, oats 6 fodder
___-nosed: 3 pug 4 hard, snub
___-nosed dolphin: 6 bottle
nosedive: 3 dip 4 drop, fall 5 slump, swoop 6 plunge 7 decline, descend, descent, plummet 8 tailspin 9 worsening
no-see-um: 3 bug 4 gnat, pest 6 insect
nosegay: 4 posy 7 bouquet
holder: 4 vase
nose-in-air type: 4 snob 5 snoot
nosepiece: 5 armor
noser: 4 gale, wind 5 snoop 6 squall
noses
count ~: 4 poll 6 reckon 9 enumerate
like some ~: 5 Roman, runny, shiny
nosey
see nosy
Nosey Parker
see Nosy Parker
Nosferatu garb: 4 cape
nosh: 3 eat 4 bite, grub 5 munch, snack 6 ingest, morsel, munchy, nibble 7 consume, munchie 8 junk food 9 collation, grab a bite
party ~: 3 dip, nut 4 chip 6 canapé
noshable: 5 tasty, yummy 6 savory 9 delicious
no-show: 6 absent 8 absentee
military ~: 4 AWOL 8 deserter
no sooner ___: 4 than
nosophobe fear: 7 disease
nostalgic: 5 retro 6 quaint 7 wistful 8 haunting, romantic 9 regretful
clothes style: 5 retro
feel ~ for: 4 miss
one: 5 piner
record label: 5 Rhino
song: 4 oldy 5 oldie
sound: 4 sigh
time: 4 yore 10 yesteryear
nostoc: 4 alga
___ no stone unturned: 5 leave
___ Nostra: 4 Cosa
Nostradamus: 4 seer 7 diviner, prophet
nostril: 5 naris
parrot's ~: 4 cere
nostrils: 5 nares
assault the ~: 4 reek 5 smell, stink
No Strings: 7 musical
composer: Richard Rodgers
No Strings Attached
artist: 'Nsync
Nostromo
author: Joseph Conrad
nostrum: 4 cure 6 elixir, potion 7 arcanum, cure-all, panacea
peddler: 5 quack 9 charlatan
___ nostrum: 4 mare
___ No Sunshine: 4 Ain't
No sweat!: 4 easy 6 simple
nosy: 4 busy 6 prying, snoopy 7 curious, peering 8 meddling, snooping 9 butting in, inquiring, intrusive, obtrusive 10 meddlesome
be ~: 3 ask, pry 5 snoop 6 butt in
one: 5 prier, pryer, yenta
Nosy Parker: 5 prier, pryer, snoop, yenta 7 meddler 8 busybody, quidnunc
be a ~: 3 pry 5 snoop 6 butt in, meddle 7 intrude, obtrude
not: 4 nary 6 untrue 8 negative
in French: 3 pas
in music: 3 non
in Scottish: 3 nae
(prefix): 3 dis-, non-
not ___: 3 bad 4 a lot, a one 5 so bad
not ___ a finger: 4 lift
not ___ a hair: 4 turn
not ___ a sou: 5 worth
not ___ a trick: 4 miss
not ___ bad: 3 too 4 half
not ___ eye in the house: 4 a dry
not ___ from Adam: 4 know
not ___ heads or tails of: 4 make
not ___ in the world: 5 a care
not ___ least: 5 in the
not ___ long shot: 3 by a
not ___ of tea: 5 my cup
not ___ red cent: 3 one
not ___ trick: 5 miss a
not-___-profit: 3 for
___-not: 4 have, what
...not ___ a mouse: 4 even
...not ___ do: 3 as I
Not ___!: 5 again, at all 6 on a bet
Not ___ can help it!: 3 if I
Not ___ many words: 4 in so
Not ___ million years!: 3 in a
Not ___ Stranger: 3 as a
nota ___: 4 bene
not a ___: 3 lot, one 4 soul 6 little
not a ___ in the sky: 5 cloud
not a ___ in the world: 4 care
not a ___ too soon: 6 moment
notability: 4 fame 6 leader 8 eminence, luminary 9 celebrity 10 importance
notable: 3 VIP 4 idol, star 5 celeb, famed, great, mogul 6 big gun, bigwig, famous, figure, leader, marked, signal 7 big name, big shot, eminent, magnate, salient 8 big wheel, historic, luminary, renowned, somebody, uncommon 9 big cheese, celebrity, dignitary, honorable, important, memorable, momentous, personage, prominent, well-known 10 celebrated, impressive, pronounced, remarkable, successful
notably: 4 much 6 rarely, vastly 7 greatly 8 markedly 9 extremely 10 especially, thoroughly
Not a chance!: 4 nope 8 forget it
...not always what they ___: 4 seem
___ not amused: 5 We are
notarize: 2 OK 4 okay, sign 6 enseal 7 approve, endorse, indorse
notary ___: 6 public
notary need: 4 seal 5 stamp
not as ___: 5 a rule
notate: 5 tally 6 record 8 mark down
notation: 5 entry 6 record 7 jotting 10 memorandum
musical ~: 5 segno 6 ottava
not by ___ shot: 5 a long
not care ___: 4 a fig, a rap 5 a hang
notch: 3 cut 4 chip, dent, kerf, mark, nick, pink, slot, step 5 gouge, score, stage 6 degree, groove, hollow, incise, indent, ravine, valley 7 chalk up, cut into
arrow ~: 4 nock
ender: 4 back
parapet ~: 6 crenel 8 crenelle
starter: 3 top
notch ___: 4 baby
___ notch: 3 up a
___-notch: 3 top
notched: 5 jaggy 6 jagged, ragged, uneven 7 incised 8 serrated
as leaves: 5 erose
bar: 5 ratch 7 ratchet
___ Not Dressing: 4 We're
note: 2 do, fa, la, mi, re, so, ti 3 IOU, key, see, sol, tag 4 cite, fame, line, list, look, mark, memo, sign, tone, vein 5 A-flat, B-flat, breve, D-flat, E-flat, G-flat, gloss, high C, input, minim, sound, token, watch, worth 6 A-sharp, C-sharp, detect, D-sharp, F-sharp, G-sharp, letter, moment, quaver, record, regard, remark, report, symbol, take in, ticket 7 comment, crochet, discern, jot down, jotting, leading, mention, message, middle C, missive, observe, refer to, set down, witness 8 annotate, eminence, interest, mark down, perceive, point out, register, remark on, reminder, take down 9 greatness, magnitude, recognize, reference, semibreve, touch upon, write down 10 annotation, importance, memorandum, prominence, remark upon, semiquaver, understand
bad ~: 4 clam
bank ~: 4 bill
double whole ~: 5 breve
drop a ~: 5 write 10 correspond, epistolize
eighth ~ in music: 6 quaver
ender: 3 pad 4 book 5 paper 6 worthy
explanatory ~: 5 gloss 7 comment
extended ~ in music: 5 longa
federal promissory ~ for short: 5 T-bill, T-bond
from the boss: 5 see me
Greek musical ~: 4 nete
Guido's ~: 3 é la
half ~: 5 minim
high ~: 3 alt, cee, é la
hit a sour ~: 5 clash 6 jangle, rattle
hitting the right ~: 5 on key
holder: 5 payee 8 creditor
journal ~: 4 item 5 entry 6 record
key ~: 5 tonic
make a ~ of: 3 jot 5 write 7 jot down 8 take down 9 write down
notation: 4 flat 5 sharp 7 natural
of ~: 8 laudable, renowned 9 important
office ~: 7 message, missive, tickler 8 reminder 9 directive
online ~: 5 e-mail
person of ~: 3 VIP 4 name, star 7 notable 8 luminary, somebody 9 celebrity, dignitary
piano ~: 5 A-flat, B-flat, D-flat, E-flat, G-flat 6 A-sharp, C-sharp, D-sharp, F-sharp, G-sharp
promissory ~: 3 IOU 4 chit
quarter ~: 8 crotchet
scale ~: 2 do, fa, la, mi, re, so, ti, ut 3 sol
signer: 4 ower 6 debtor
soprano's ~: 5 high C
sour ~: 5 clash 6 jangle, off-key 7 discord 9 cacophony 10 disharmony
starter: 3 end, key 4 foot, wood
strike a ~: 6 recall 8 remember, summon up 10 call to mind
take no ~ of: 4 snub 6 ignore 7 neglect 8 brush off, skip over 9 disregard
take ~ of: 3 see 4 heed 6 advert 9 recognize 10 reckon with
whole ~: 9 semibreve
___ note: 4 bank, blue, half 5 grace
___-note: 4 half 5 whole 6 eighth 7 quarter

__ **Note:** **6** Post-It, Sticky
notebook: **2** PC **3** pad **6** binder, laptop, tablet **8** computer **10** scratch pad
contents: **4** leaf **5** paper
Notebook, The (2004 film)
cast: James Garner, Ryan Gosling, Rachel McAdams, Gena Rowlands
noted: **5** famed, grand, great, known **6** fabled, famous **7** big-name, big-time, eminent, exalted, honored **8** esteemed, glorious, laureate, renowned **9** acclaimed, legendary, memorable, prominent, respected, well-known **10** celebrated, preeminent
__ **Not Enough:** **6** Once Is
notepad: **4** book **5** paper **6** tablet
notes: **8** material **10** marginalia
compare ~: **4** meet, talk **6** confer, huddle, parley, powwow **7** consult, discuss **8** converse **9** interface, touch base **10** brainstorm, chew the fat, deliberate
place for ~: **3** pad **5** staff
played together: **5** chord
__ **notes:** **5** liner **7** compare
Notes __ Scandal: **3** on a
Notes __ the Underground: **4** From
__ **Notes:** **6** Cliffs
__ **Note Samba:** **3** One
Notes From a Sea Diary
author: Nelson Algren
Notes From the Underground
author: Fyodor Dostoyevsky
Notes of a Native Son
author: James Baldwin
Notes on a Cowardly Lion subject: **4** Lahr
__ **note to follow sew:** **3** La a
noteworthy: **4** high **5** great, lofty, noted **6** famous, signal **7** eminent, notable, unusual **8** renowned, singular, striking, superior, uncommon **9** arresting, important, memorable, prominent **10** celebrated
not-for-__: **6** profit
__ **Not for Burning, The:** **5** Lady's
__ **Not for Me:** **3** But
__ **Not for Me to Say:** **3** It's
Not from where __!: **4** I sit
not give __: **5** a darn, a hoot
Not Gon' Cry (1996 song)
artist: Mary J. Blige
not guilty: **4** plea
not half __: **3** bad
nothing: **3** nil, nix, zip **4** nada, none, zero **5** aught, ought, squat, zilch, zippo **6** bubkes, bupkes, bupkis, cipher, naught, nought **7** trinket **8** goose egg, lifeless **10** lackluster
better than ~: **4** fair, so-so **6** decent **8** adequate, bearable, mediocre, passable **9** tolerable **10** acceptable
but: **3** all **4** just, mere, only **6** merely, purely, simply, solely
come to ~: **4** fail, flop, wane **6** fizzle, lessen, run dry, run out **7** dwindle, founder, misfire, run down, subside, tail off, thin out **8** collapse, peter out, taper off **9** evaporate
containing ~: **4** bare, void **5** empty **6** barren, hollow, vacant **7** vacated **9** evacuated
do ~: **3** veg **4** idle, laze, loll **5** sit by, slack **6** rest up **7** slacken
do ~ about: **5** sit on **6** stifle **7** squelch **8** suppress, withhold
doing: **2** no **3** nah, naw, nay, nix, non **4** nein, nope, nyet, uh-uh **5** I won't, ixnay, never, no how, no way **6** no deal, noways, nowise, rebuff **7** I refuse **8** forget it, I will not, negative, negatory **9** by no means, fat chance, I think not, rejection **10** count me out, not a chance, thumbs down
doing ~: **4** idle, lazy **5** inert **6** otiose, torpid **7** dormant, jobless, loafing, out of it, resting **8** inactive, indolent, slothful, sluggish, stagnant **9** lethargic, loitering, out of work, sedentary, shiftless **10** motionless, on the shelf, stationary
flat: **6** minute, moment, second
for ~: **4** free, vain **6** futile, gratis, vainly **7** as a gift, useless **8** futilely **9** on the cuff, to no avail, uselessly **10** gratuitous, on the house
good for ~: **3** bad **5** sorry **6** abject, dismal, rotten **7** pitiful **8** wretched **9** miserable, worthless **10** deplorable, despicable, detestable
gripe about ~: **3** nag **4** carp **5** whine **6** bicker, grouse **7** nitpick, quibble **8** pettifog **9** find fault, make a fuss
have ~ to do with: **4** shun **5** avoid **6** eschew
hiding ~: **4** bare, open **5** frank, overt, plain **7** exposed, obvious **8** wide-open
if ~ changes: **6** as it is
in ~ flat: **3** PDQ **4** anon, fast **5** apace **6** presto **7** fleetly, hastily, quickly, rapidly, swiftly **8** pell-mell, promptly, speedily **9** forthwith, hurriedly, instantly, like a shot, posthaste
in French: **4** rien
in Spanish: **4** nada
in tennis: **4** love
keep ~ back: **5** level
missing ~: **4** full **6** entire **8** complete, thorough **10** exhaustive, unabridged
more than: **4** just, mere **6** merely, simply, solely, wholly **7** totally, utterly **8** entirely
much: **4** mild, so-so
one with ~ to say: **4** mime **5** mimer
opposite: **3** all **10** everything
plenty of ~: **3** OOO **4** OOOO **5** OOOOO
saying ~: **3** mum **4** mute **5** quiet **6** silent **7** aphonic **8** nonvocal, taciturn, wordless **9** secretive, soundless, voiceless **10** pantomimic, speechless, tongue-tied
special: **5** plain, usual **7** average, routine, typical **8** ordinary, standard
to it: **4** easy **6** simple **7** a picnic **9** a pushover **10** child's play
to write home about: **4** fair **7** average **8** mediocre, middling, ordinary, passable **9** tolerable
where love means ~: **6** tennis
with ~ on: **3** raw **4** bare, nude **5** naked **6** unclad **7** unrobed **8** disrobed, in the raw, starkers, stripped, undraped **9** au naturel, in the buff, unadorned, unattired, unclothed, uncovered, undressed
nothing __: **4** much **5** at all
__-nothing: **4** know **5** all-or
Nothing __!: **4** to it **5** doing
Nothing __?: **4** else
__ **Nothing:** **4** Fear **5** All or, I Have
__ **Nothing at All:** **5** All or
Nothing but blue skies do __: **4** I see
Nothing But Heartaches (1965 song)
artist: Supremes
Nothing but net: **5** swish
Nothing but the __: **4** best
Nothing can stop __!: **5** me now
Nothing Compares 2 U (1990 song)
artist: Sinéad O'Connor
Nothing doing!: **2** no **3** nah, naw, nay, nix, non **4** nein, nope, nyet, uh-uh **5** I won't, ixnay, never, no how, no way **6** no deal, noways, nowise, rebuff **7** I refuse **8** forget it, I will not, negative, negatory **9** by no means, fat chance, I think not, rejection **10** count me out, not a chance, thumbs down
Nothing From Nothing (1964 song)
artist: Billy Preston
Nothing Gold Can Stay: **4** poem
author: Robert Frost
Nothing in Common (1986 film)
cast: Jackie Gleason, Tom Hanks, Eva Marie Saint, Sela Ward
director: Garry Marshall
Nothing Lasts Forever
author: Sidney Sheldon
nothingness: **4** void **5** limbo **6** vacuum
__ **nothing of:** **5** think, to say
Nothing runs like a __: **5** Deere
__ **nothings:** **5** sweet
__-Nothings: **4** Know
Nothing's Gonna Stop Us Now (1987 song)
artist: Starship
nothing to __ at: **6** sneeze
Nothin' Yet (1967 song)
artist: Blues Magoos
notice: **3** att., eye, see, spy **4** attn., call, data, dope, espy, find, heed, info, look, mark, memo, poop, sign, spot, view, wind, word **5** sense, watch **6** advert, attend, behold, caveat, credit, descry, detect, espial, lesson, regard, remark, report, take in, ticket, tipoff **7** account, caution, discern, handout, look out, lowdown, make out, mention, message, observe, pay heed, receipt, release, warning **8** advisory, bulletin, discover, interest, keep tabs, listen to, perceive, reminder **9** attention, give ear to, news flash, recognize **10** admonition, communiqué, get a load of, memorandum
at short ~: **7** quickly **9** summarily
don't ~: **4** miss **6** forget, ignore, pass up **7** tune out **8** overlook, pass over
favorable ~: **4** rave
give ~: **4** quit, warn **5** leave **6** be gone, resign
in French: **4** avis
put on ~: **4** warn **5** alert **6** inform, remind, signal, tip off **7** caution **8** admonish, forewarn, threaten
put up a ~: **4** post
take ~: **5** sit up, watch **6** listen
take ~ of: **3** see **4** heed, mark **6** regard
__ **notice:** **4** give, take **5** put on, short **7** advance
noticeable: **5** plain **6** marked, signal **7** evident, glaring, obvious, outward, salient, visible **8** apparent, distinct, flagrant, manifest, palpable, striking **9** arresting, obtrusive, prominent
noticeably: **4** very **5** extra, plain, quite **6** rather **8** markedly
__ **notice of:** **4** take
notices, old-style: **5** seest
Not if __ help it!: **4** I can
notification: **4** info **5** alert **6** report, signal **7** heads-up, message, warning
notify: **4** call, post, tell, warn **5** alert, phone, prime, write **6** advise, fill in, inform, report, tip off **7** apprise, apprize, caution **8** advise of, instruct **9** telephone, touch base **10** send word to
No Time (1970 song)
artist: Guess Who
No Time (1996 song)
artist: Lil' Kim, Puff Daddy
No Time for Sergeants (1958 film)
cast: Nick Adams, Andy Griffith, Don Knotts
dog: **7** Old Blue
Not interested!: **3** nah **4** nope
not in the __: **5** least
notion: **4** idea, view, whim **5** guess, hunch, image, stand, thing **6** belief, intent, reason, vagary **7** caprice, concept, feeling, inkling, opinion, surmise, thought **8** nicknack **9** intention, leitmotif, suspicion **10** conception, impression, knick-knack, suggestion
case: **4** etui **5** etwee
combining form: **4** ideo-
false ~: **4** myth **7** fantasy **8** delusion, illusion
form a ~: **5** think **6** ideate
in French: **4** idée
odd ~: **4** whim **5** fancy **6** vagary **7** caprice **8** crotchet
preconceived ~: **4** bias, tilt **5** slant **7** bigotry, leaning **9** prejudice **10** partiality
notional: **6** unreal **8** academic **9** imaginary **10** capricious
not know from __: **4** Adam
not lift a __: **6** finger
not make __ or tails of: **5** heads
not miss __: **5** a beat **6** a trick
not my __: **4** type
not my __ of tea: **3** cup
not on __ life: **4** your
Not on a bet!: **4** uh-uh **8** forget it
not one __ cent: **3** red
...not one __ for tribute: **4** cent
Not One Minute More (1959 song)

artist: Della Reese
Not on your life!: 3 nay 4 as if, nope 5 never, no sir 8 forget it
notoriety: 4 fame 6 infamy, renown, repute 7 obloquy, réclame 8 dishonor 9 celebrity, disrepute, ill repute, publicity, spotlight 10 reputation
notorious: 3 bad 4 evil, foul 5 shady 6 arrant, famous 7 leading 8 infamous, shameful 9 egregious, well-known 10 outrageous, villainous
Notorious (1946 film)
cast: Ingrid Bergman, Cary Grant, Claude Rains
director: Alfred Hitchcock
setting: 3 Rio 6 Brazil
Notorious (1986 song)
artist: Duran Duran
Notorious B.I.G.
song: Been Around the World (1998)
Big Poppa (1995)
Can't You See (1995)
Hypnotize (1997)
It's All About the Benjamins (1997)
Juicy (1994)
Mo Money Mo Problems (1997)
One More Chance (1995)
Victory (1998)
Notre Dame: 6 school 9 cathedral
abbr.: 3 UND
conference: 7 Big East
former ~ name: 3 Ara 5 Knute
locale: 5 Paris 6 France 7 Indiana
river: 5 Seine
service: 5 messe
sight: 3 île
team: 5 Irish
see also French
not so ___: 3 bad, far, hot 4 fast
not so bad: 2 OK 4 fair, okay, so-so 8 adequate, passable
Not so fast!: 4 stop 6 hold it
Not So Stories
author: Saki
___ Not Spock: 3 I Am
___ Not Taken, The: 4 Road
___ notte: 5 buona
not the ___ of it: 4 half
___ Not the Cat: 5 Touch
___ Not There: 4 She's
Nottingham: 4 city, town
locale: 7 England
river: 5 Trent
Notting Hill (1999 film)
cast: Hugh Grant, Julia Roberts
not to ___: 5 worry 7 mention
Not to Keep
author: Robert Frost
Not Tonight (1997 song)
artist: Da Brat, Lil' Kim, Missy Elliott
not too ___: 3 bad 6 shabby
___ not to reason why...: 4 ours 6 theirs
Not to worry!: 5 it's OK
Notts: 6 county
locale: 7 England
not turn ___: 5 a hair
___ Not Unusual: 3 It's
No Turn ___: 5 on Red
Notus
mother: 3 Eos
___ not what your country...: 3 Ask
Not with ___ but...: 5 a bang
Not With My Wife You Don't! (1966 film)
cast: Tony Curtis, Virna Lisi, Carroll O'Connor, George C. Scott
Not Without My Daughter (1991 film)
cast: Sally Field, Alfred Molina
notwithstanding: 3 but, tho, yet 5 altho, aside, still 6 albeit, anyhow, anyway, though 7 despite, however 8 after all, although 9 at any rate, in any case, in spite of 10 in any event, regardless
no two ___ about it: 4 ways
not worth ___: 4 a fig, a sou 5 a cent
not worth ___ cent: 4 a red
not worth ___ of beans: 5 a hill
not worth his ___: 4 salt
no two ways ___ it: 5 about
Not Yet the Dodo
author: Noël Coward
Not you ___!: 5 again
NO U-___: 4 TURN
Nouakchott: 4 city, port, town 7 capital
locale: 10 Mauritania
nougat: 5 candy 6 bonbon 9 sweetmeat
nought: 3 nil, zip 4 nada, zero 5 squat, zilch 6 bubkes, bupkes, bupkis, cipher 7 nothing 8 goose egg
bring to ~: 4 do in, raze, ruin, undo 5 total 7 destroy, wipe out 8 bulldoze, demolish 9 devastate 10 annihilate, obliterate
starter: 5 dread
noughts-and-crosses: 9 tic-tac-toe
nonwinner: 3 OOX, OXO, OXX, XOO, XOX, XXO
winner: 3 OOO, XXX
see also tic-tac-toe
noun: 4 word 6 object 7 subject
in French: 3 nom
starter: 3 pro
suffix: 3 -acy, -ade, -age, -ana, -ant, -ard, -ary, -ase, -ate, -cle, -dom, -een, -eer, -ent, -eon, -ery, -ese, -ess, -eum, -eur, -ian, -ice, -ics, -ier, -ile, -ine, -ion, -ism, -ist, -ite, -ity, -ium, -kin, -let, -mas, -nik, -oid, -ola, -oon, -ory, -ose, -ton, -tor, -ude, -ure 4 -aire, -ance, -ancy, -ator, -cade, -ella, -elle, ence, -ency, -enne, -eroo, -ette, -etum, -euse, -goer, -hood, -iana, -itis, -kins, -ling, -ment, -mony, -ness, -osis, -plex, -ship, -some, -ster, -tain, -tion, -tory, -trix, -tude 5 -acity, -arian, -arium, -aster, -athon, -ation, -ician, -ition, -maker, -ology, -orial, -scape, -shire 6 -making, -mobile 7 -ability, -escence, -faction, -fulness, -ibility, -ization, -manship, -meister 8 -fication
___ noun: 6 common, proper
nouns, like some foreign: 3 fem. 4 masc., neut. 6 neuter 8 feminine 9 masculine
Nouri: 7 Michael
nourish: 4 feed, fuel, keep, rear 5 breed, raise 6 foster 7 bring up, care for, nurture, support, sustain 9 cultivate 10 strengthen
nourished: 3 fed
was ~: 3 ate
was ~ by: 5 fed on
nourishing: 4 rich 6 alible, edible 7 healthy 9 wholesome 10 alimentary
nourishing, name meaning: 4 Alma
nourishment: 4 chow, diet, eats, food, fuel, grub, meat 5 bread 6 intake, viands 7 aliment, vittles 8 victuals 9 provender 10 provisions
combining form: 5 troph- 6 tropho-
divine ~: 5 manna
needing ~: 5 unfed 6 hungry 9 famishedd
take ~: 3 eat, sup 4 dine, nosh 5 feast, graze 6 ingest 7 consume, partake 9 have a bite 10 gormandize
nous: 5 brain 6 reason 9 intellect, mentality, reasoning
entre ~: 7 sub rosa 8 in secret, secretly 9 between us, privately
___ no use!: 3 It's
___ no use for: 4 have
nouveau ___: 5 riche 6 pauvre
___ Nouveau: 3 Art 4 Club
nouveau riche: 7 parvenu, upstart 9 arriviste
nouvelle ___: 5 vague 7 cuisine
Nov.: 2 mo.
event: 4 elec.
follower: 3 Dec.
predecessor: 3 Oct.
see also November
nova: 3 lox 6 salmon
bossa ~: 5 dance, music
Nova: 3 car 4 auto 5 Chevy 9 Chevrolet
network: 3 PBS
subject: 3 sci. 7 science
Nova ___: 6 Scotia 7 Express
___ Nova: 3 Ars
Nova Express
author: William S. Burroughs
Novak: 3 Eva, Kim 6 Robert
colleague: 5 Evans
Novak, Kim: 7 actress
film: Bell, Book and Candle (1958)
Kiss Me, Stupid (1964)
The Man With the Golden Arm (1955)
The Mirror Crack'd (1980)
Pal Joey (1957)
Picnic (1955)
Vertigo (1958)
Novarro: 5 Ramon
Nova Scotia
bay: 5 Fundy
cape: 5 Canso
capital: 7 Halifax
city: 5 Truro 6 Argyle, Pictou 7 Baddeck, Halifax 8 New Minas 9 Dartmouth, Sackville 10 Cape Breton, New Glasgow
hrs.: 3 AST
Indian: 6 Micmac
locale: 6 Canada
once: 6 Acadia
school: 6 Acadia 9 Dalhousie
Nova Scotia ___: 3 lox 6 salmon
Novato: 4 city, town
locale: 10 California
nove: 4 nine 7 Italian
follower: 5 dieci
preceder: 4 otto
novel: 3 new 4 book, saga, tale 5 fresh, genre, prose, story 6 clever, modern, recent, unique 7 fiction, mystery, new wave, offbeat, romance, strange, unusual, Western, writing 8 brand-new, creative, inspired, neoteric, original, thriller, uncommon, whodunit 9 adventure, different, ingenious, inventive, love story, narrative, paperback, potboiler, unheard-of 10 avant-garde, bestseller, futuristic, innovative, literature, newfangled, pocket book, refreshing, roman à clef, unexplored, unfamiliar
ender: 3 ist 4 ette
___ novel: 4 dime, saga 6 Gothic 7 graphic
novelist: 6 author, writer 9 wordsmith
concern: 4 plot 9 story line
Novell, home of: 4 Utah 5 Provo
Novello: 3 Don 4 Ivor
novelty: 3 fad 5 curio, gismo, gizmo 6 change, dingus, doodad, gadget, trifle 7 newness, trinket 8 nicknack, original 9 departure, doohickey, freshness, invention 10 innovation, knickknack, new wrinkle, uniqueness
novelty ___: 3 act
November: 5 month
birthstone: 5 topaz
form: 6 ballot
honoree: 3 vet 7 veteran
lever puller: 5 voter
lineup: 5 slate
sign: 6 Archer 7 Scorpio 8 Scorpion
victors: 3 ins
November 13: 4 ides
November 5: 5 nones
November Rain (1992 song)
artist: Guns N' Roses
November Woods
composer: Arnold Bax
novembre: 4 mois 5 month 6 French
follower: 8 décembre
preceder: 7 octobre
Novgorod: 4 city, town
locale: 6 Russia
Novi ___: 3 Sad
novice: 3 cub 4 tiro, tyro 5 newie, pupil 6 greeny, intern, newbie, rookie 7 amateur, convert, dabbler, entrant, interne, learner, new hand, recruit, student, trainee 8 beginner, freshman, green one, neophyte, newcomer, putterer 9 fledgling, greenhorn, layperson, religious 10 apprentice, catechumen, dilettante, tenderfoot
academy ~: 4 pleb 5 frosh, plebe
Novikoff: 3 Lou
Novi Sad: 4 city, town
locale: 6 Serbia
novitiate: 4 tiro, tyro 7 convert, recruit 8 beginner 10 apprentice, catechumen
novo
de ~: 4 anew 5 again 6 afresh 10 from the top
novocaine
give ~: 4 numb 6 benumb, deaden, inject

target: **5** nerve
Novocaine (2001 film)
cast: Helena Bonham Carter, Laura Dern, Steve Martin
Novotna: 4 Jana
Novus __ seclorum: 4 ordo
now: 2 in **3** new, PDQ, yet **4** anon, ASAP, chic, stat **5** as yet, faddy, today, vogue **6** at once, modern, modish, pronto, timely, trendy, with it **7** current, in vogue, popular, present, stylish **8** promptly, right off, up-to-date **9** at present, currently, forthwith, on the spot, presently, right away **10** at this time, the present, this minute
and forever: 7 eternal **8** immortal, timeless, unending **9** perpetual
and then: 6 rarely, seldom **7** at times **9** sometimes **10** on occasion
any minute ~: 4 anon, soon **7** shortly
before ~: 3 ago **7** already **8** hitherto
between then and ~: 5 since, so far
by ~: 3 yet **5** so far **7** already **10** beforehand, heretofore, previously
for ~: 8 meantime **9** meanwhile
from Jan. 1 to ~: 3 YTD **5** so far
from ~ on: 5 hence **8** evermore **9** hereafter **10** henceforth
happening ~: 4 live **7** current, running
here and ~: 5 today **6** at once **7** quickly **8** promptly, right off **9** at present, forthwith, presently, right away **10** at this time, this minute
hours from ~: 5 after **6** in time **7** by and by **8** in a while **9** afterward **10** thereafter
how ~: 4 ciao **5** aloha, hello **6** shalom **7** bon jour **8** greeting
not ~: 4 anon, then **5** after, later **6** in a bit, in time **7** by and by **8** in a while **9** afterward **10** eventually, thereafter
only ~: 4 just **6** lately **8** latterly, recently
partner: 4 here, then
right ~: 3 PDQ **4** anon, ASAP, stat **5** as yet, today **6** at once, pronto **7** quickly, swiftly **8** promptly **9** at present, forthwith, instantly, on the spot, presently **10** at this time, the present, this minute
starter: 3 ere
until ~: 3 ago, yet **4** once, till **5** as yet, so far, still **6** before, hereto, of late, to date **7** earlier, prior to, thus far **8** formerly, hereunto, hitherto **9** preceding, to this day **10** before this, heretofore, previously, to this time
__ now: 4 as of, just, up to **5** until
__ now!: 3 Act
Now __ here!: 3 see
Now __ me...: 4 I lay
Now __ seen everything!: 3 I've
Now __ theater near you!: 3 at a
Now __ this!: 4 hear
Now __ time for all...: 5 is the
Now __ you!: 4 I ask
__ Now: 3 'Til **4** Even **5** See It
NOW
cause: 3 ERA
part of ~: 3 Org. **4** Natl. **5** Women
NOW __: 7 account
nowadays: 6 lately **9** presently
Nowadays musical: 7 Chicago
now and __: 4 then **5** again
Now and Forever (1994 song)
artist: Richard Marx
__ now and then: 5 every
No way!: 3 nah **4** as if, uh-uh **5** never **6** can't be
No way, __!: 4 José
__ No Way: 4 Ain't
No Way Out (1987 film)
cast: Kevin Costner, Gene Hackman, Sean Young
__ No Way to Treat a Lady: 4 Ain't
__ now, brown cow: 3 How
Now hear __!: 4 this
nowhere: 4 dull **5** ho-hum, limbo **6** boring, uncool **7** humdrum **8** tiresome **10** dullsville
come out of ~: 5 bob up, pop up
going ~: 6 adrift, in a rut **9** pointless
middle of ~: 5 limbo, wilds **6** remote
near: 4 afar **6** remote
to be found: 4 away, AWOL, gone, lost **6** absent **7** far away, missing **8** vanished
__ nowhere: 3 get **5** out of
Nowhere
author: Thomas Berger
Nowhere __: 3 Man **5** to Run
Nowhere Man (1966 song)
artist: Beatles
Nowhere to Run (1965 song)
artist: Martha & the Vandellas
Now I __ me...: 3 lay
Now I get it!: 3 aha, oho
no-win: 4 grim, vain **5** bleak **6** futile **7** useless **8** hopeless **9** desperate, fruitless, pointless, senseless **10** impossible, irremedial
situation: 3 tie **4** bind **7** dilemma **8** dead heat, deadlock, quandary, standoff **9** stalemate
nowise: 3 nah, naw, nay, nix, non **4** nein, nope, nyet, uh-uh **5** I won't, ixnay, never **7** I refuse **8** forget it, I will not, negative, negatory **9** fat chance, I think not **10** count me out, not a chance, thumbs down
Now It Can Be __: 4 Told
Now I understand!: 3 Aha
Now I've __ everything!: 4 seen
Nowlan: 4 Phil **5** Alden
Nowlan, Alden: 6 writer **8** Canadian
work: Between Tears and Laughter
Bread, Wine and Salt
I'm a Stranger Here Myself
Miracle at Indian River
now more __ ever: 4 than
__ Now My Love?: 4 What
__ no wonder!: 3 It's
now or __: 5 never
__ Now or Never: 3 It's
__ Now Praise Famous Men: 5 Let Us
Now see __!: 4 here
Now that __ there: 6 April's
Now, Voyager (1942 film)
cast: Bette Davis, Paul Henreid, Claude Rains
composer: Max Steiner
Now We Are Six
author: A.A. Milne
Now you __...: 5 see it
Now You Know
author: Michael Frayn
noxious: 4 foul, rank, vile **5** fetid, nasty, toxic **6** foetid, lethal, rancid, rotten, sickly, smelly, stinky **7** baneful, harmful, hurtful, miasmal, noisome, odorous, reeking **8** inimical, mephitic, stinking **9** injurious, pestilent, poisonous, unhealthy **10** insanitary, malodorous, pernicious
plant: 4 weed **9** stinkweed
vapor: 4 fume
Noyce: 6 Robert **7** Phillip
Noyes, Alfred: 4 poet **6** writer **7** British
work: The Barrel-Organ
Drake
The Highwayman
The Torch-Bearers
Noyori, Ryoji: 7 chemist **8** Nobelist
nozzle: 3 tap **5** spout **6** outlet
output: 4 mist **5** spray, water
Np: 4 elem. **7** element **9** neptunium
93 for ~: 4 at. no.
__-n-Pepa: 4 Salt
NPR part: 3 Nat. **4** Natl. **5** Radio **6** Public **8** National
NPS
department: 8 Interior
part: 3 Nat. **4** Natl., Park **7** Service **8** National
NRA: 5 lobby
part: 3 Nat. **4** Assn., Natl. **5** Admin., Assoc., Rifle **8** National, Recovery
program: 3 CCC
symbol: 5 eagle
NRC
part: 3 Reg. **4** Comm. **7** Nuclear **10** Regulatory
predecessor: 3 AEC
N-R connection: 3 OPQ
__-'n'-roll: 4 rock
NSA: 3 org.
part: 3 Nat., Sec. **4** Agcy., Natl. **6** Agency **8** National, Security
worker: 3 spy
NSC
org. that advises the ~: 3 CIA
part: 3 Nat., Sec. **4** Natl. **7** Council **8** National, Security
N-S connection: 4 OPQR
NSF part: 3 Nat., not, Sci. **4** Natl. **5** funds **7** Science **8** National **10** Foundation, sufficient
NSX: 3 car **4** auto **5** Acura **10** automobile
automaker: 5 Acura
'N Sync
hometown: Orlando
members: Kirkpatrick, Chasez, Fatone, Timberlake, Bass
song: I Want You Back (1998)
A Little More Time on You (1998)
Music of My Heart (1999)
N.T.
book: 3 Col., Eph., Gal., Heb., Rev., Rom., Tim. **4** Hebr., Matt., Thes. **5** Thess.
letter: 5 Epist.
passage: 3 ver.
see also Bible, New Testament
N-T connection: 5 OPQRS
nth: 3 ult. **6** utmost **7** extreme, highest, maximum **8** ultimate
degree: 3 max **4** hilt **6** utmost **7** extreme **8** ultimate
to the ~ degree: 6 in full, in toto, wholly **7** utterly **9** all the way, extremely, to the hilt **10** altogether, thoroughly
nth __: 5 power **6** degree
__ N the Hood: 4 Boyz
NTSB
part of ~: 3 Nat. **4** Natl. **5** Board, Trans. **6** Safety
__-'n'-turf: 4 surf
nu: 5 Greek **6** letter
follower: 2 xi
preceder: 2 mu
nuance: 5 sense, shade, tinge, trace **6** nicety **7** meaning, shading **8** delicacy, overtone, quiddity, subtlety **9** fine point, punctilio **10** refinement
nub: 4 core, crux, gist, knob, lump, meat, root **5** focus, heart, piece, point, stump **6** center, kernel **7** essence, keynote, nucleus, purport **8** key point **9** main point, substance **10** protrusion
nubbin: 5 stump
nubby: 5 bumpy, rough **6** coarse **7** bristly, grating, scruffy, stubbly **8** abrasive
nubia: 5 scarf
Nubia
ancient city: 5 Meroe
ancient kingdom: 4 Cush, Kush
Nubian: 6 desert
locale: 5 Sudan **6** Africa
Nubian __: 4 goat **6** Desert
Nubira: 3 car **4** auto **6** Daewoo **10** automobile
__ Nubium: 4 Mare
nucha: 4 nape **6** scruff
site: 4 neck
nuclear: 6 atomic **7** central
1979 ~ accident site: 3 TMI
element used in ~ reactors: 5 boron
energy source: 4 atom
energy watchdog: 3 AEC, NRC
experiment: 5 A-test, H-test, N-test
reaction: 6 fusion **7** fission
reactor part: 4 core, pile
tryout: 5 A-test
weapon: 4 ICBM, MIRV **5** A-bomb, H-bomb, N-bomb
nuclear __: 3 age **4** fuel **5** power **6** energy, family, fusion, isomer, weapon **7** fission, physics, reactor
Nuclear __-Ban Treaty: 4 Test
nuclear physics: 7 science
study: 5 atoms
nucleic: 4 acid
compound: 3 DNA, RNA
starter: 4 ribo
nucleotide, DNA: 3 ATP
nucleus: 3 hub, nub **4** core, germ, knub, meat, pith, seed **5** basis, cadre, heart, midst, spark **6** center, embryo, kernel, origin **7** essence
nuclide: 6 isomer **7** isotope
nude: 3 raw **4** bare, pink **5** brown, model, naked **6** unclad **7** exposed, grayish **8** brownish, disrobed, in the raw, starkers, undraped **9** au

naturel, in the buff, unattired, unclothed, uncovered, undressed, yellowish **10** unshielded
relative: *see* brown color
nudge: 3 jab, jog **4** bump, poke, prod, push, wake **5** brush, elbow, punch, shove, tease, touch, waken **6** badger, bother, jiggle, jostle, justle, pester, prompt, thrust **8** shoulder
nudnik: 4 pest, pill, twit **5** twerp, twirp
Nueces: 5 river
locale: 5 Texas
nueve: 4 nine **7** Spanish
follower: 4 diez
preceder: 4 ocho
__ nuevo: 3 año
__ nuff!: 3 Sho'
nugatory: 4 vain **6** futile **7** invalid, trivial **8** negative, trifling
Nugent: 3 Ted **7** Elliott
nugget: 4 hunk, lump, plum **5** chunk, clump **8** valuable
material: 4 gold **6** silver
Nugget: 5 cager
Nuggets: 4 five, team
home: 6 Denver
org.: 3 NBA
rival: *see* NBA team
sport: 10 basketball
__ Nui: 4 Rapa
nuisance: 4 bane, bore, drag, pain, pest, pill **5** trial **6** bother, gadfly, hassle, plague **7** trouble **8** headache, irritant, vexation **9** annoyance, liability
winged ~: 3 fly **4** gnat **5** midge
__ nuit!: 5 Bonne
__ Nuits: 3 Les
nuke: 3 fix, zap **4** cook **5** blast
Nukualofa: 4 city, town **7** capital
locale: 5 Tonga
null: 4 vain, void, zero **5** blank, empty **6** futile **7** inutile, invalid, useless, vacuous **8** goose egg **9** senseless, valueless, worthless **10** groundless, unavailing
make ~: 5 quash **6** cancel, repeal, revoke **7** rescind, reverse **8** override, overrule, set aside **9** repudiate, supersede **10** invalidate
__-null: 5 aleph
null and __: 4 void
nullification: 6 recall **8** negation
nullify: 3 nix **4** kill, undo, void **5** erase, quash **6** cancel, defeat, negate, offset, recall, recant, repeal, revoke, scotch, vacate **7** abolish, balance, destroy, rescind, reverse **8** abrogate, override, overrule, overturn **9** frustrate, repudiate **10** invalidate, neutralize
nullity: 4 zero **10** invalidity
num.: 3 amt., qty.
Numa
wife: 6 Egeria
Numan: 4 Gary
numb: 4 stun **5** dazed, inert, shock, stiff **6** asleep, deaden, freeze, frozen, tingly, torpid **7** petrify, sedated, stupefy **8** deadened, hardened, paralyse, paralyze, tuned out **9** apathetic, insensate, senseless, unfeeling **10** anesthetic, impervious, insentient, motionless
ender: 4 fish **5** skull
perhaps: 3 ice
numbat: 9 marsupial
relative: *see* marsupial
tidbit: 3 ant
number: 3 add, amt., lot, one, qty., six, sum, ten, two **4** five, four, mass, nine, page, poll, song, sort, tell, tune, zero **5** count, digit, ditty, eight, gauge, seven, tally, three, total, tot up, troop **6** amount, cipher, figure, legion, reckon, volume **7** add up to, compute, include, itemize, species, tick off **8** amount to, classify, quantity **9** aggregate, calculate, character, enumerate, multitude, specialty
additional ~: 6 encore
a ~ of: 4 some **7** several
a ~ of times: 5 often **9** regularly **10** frequently, repeatedly
back ~: 7 vintage **8** obsolete, outdated, outmoded **9** out-of-date **10** antiquated
base of a ~ system: 5 radix
combining form: 7 arithmo-
countdown ~: 3 one, six, ten, two **4** five, four, nine, zero **5** eight, seven, three
cruncher: 3 CPA **4** acct. **7** analyst
do a ~: 4 sing **5** croon **6** warble **7** perform **8** vocalize
do a ~ on: 3 con **4** bilk, dupe, gull, rook **5** cheat, shaft **6** defame, delude, take in **7** deceive, defraud, swindle **8** flimflam
five-digit ~: 3 Zip
French ~: 2 un **3** dix, six **4** cent, cinq, deux, huit, neuf, onze, sept, zero **5** douze, mille, seize, trois, vingt **6** quatre, quinze, treize, trente **8** quarante, quatorze, soixante **9** cinquante
German ~: 3 elf **4** acht, drei, eins, fünf, neun, null, vier, zehn, zwei **5** sechs, zwölf **6** sieben **7** achtzig, fünfzig, hundert, neunzig, sechzig, siebzig, tausend, vierzig, zwanzig
goodly ~: 4 gobs, lots, tons **5** heaps, horde, piles, scads **6** divers, legion, myriad, oodles, plenty, scores, throng, untold **7** jillion, no end of, umpteen **8** numerous **9** abundance, countless, multitude, thousands, uncounted **10** numberless
indefinite ~: 3 any, few **4** many, some
irrational ~: 4 surd
Italian ~: 3 due, sei, tre, uno **4** nove, otto, zero **5** cento, dieci, mille, sette, venti **6** cinque, dodici, sedici, trenta, undici **7** novanta, ottanta, quattro, tredici **8** diciotto, quaranta, quindici, sessanta **9** cinquanta
large ~: 3 lot, ton **4** host, load, lots, many, raft, scad, slew, tons **5** crowd, loads, scads, spate **6** googol, scores **9** multitude
lucky ~: 5 seven
next to a plus sign: 6 addend
nightclub ~: 4 song **6** ballad
nine-digit ~: 3 Zip
one: 3 ace, top **4** best, tops **5** champ, chief, first, great, prime **6** leader, select, top dog, winner **7** leading, primary **8** champion, favorite, foremost, stunning **9** governing **10** celebrated, overriding, preeminent
out for ~ one: 6 greedy **7** hoggish, selfish **8** egoistic **9** egotistic **10** egocentric, egoistical
small ~: 3 few **7** handful, not many **10** scattering, smattering
Spanish ~: 3 dos, mil, uno **4** cero, cien, diez, doce, ocho, once, seis, tres **5** cinco, nueve, siete, trece **6** quarto, quince, veinte **7** catorce, noventa, ochenta, sesenta, setenta, treinta **8** cuarenta **9** cincuenta
system: 5 octal **6** binary
target: 5 quota
two: 4 veep, vice **6** veepee
number __: 3 one **4** line, sign **6** please
__ number: 4 back, call, mach, mass **5** index, lucky, magic, mixed, prime, whole, wrong **6** atomic, beyond, octane, random **7** ordinal
Number 23, The (2007 film)
cast: Jim Carrey, Virginia Madsen
__ number can play: 3 any
numbered composition: 4 opus
numbering: 5 count, tally **9** reckoning
computer ~ system: 5 octal **6** binary
numberless: 4 many **6** legion, myriad, untold **8** prodigal **9** countless, limitless, unlimited
__ number on: 3 do a
__ number one!: 4 We're
Number One Son
father: Charlie Chan
portrayer: Keye Luke
numbers: 3 lot, mob, sea **4** heap, herd, host, lots, many, mass, math, slew **5** bunch, crowd, crush, drove, horde, loads, ocean, swarm, troop **6** legion, myriad, oodles, scores, throng **8** quantity **9** multitude, profusion **10** regulation
by the ~: 5 exact **6** proper **7** exactly **8** methodic, properly **9** stringent
change the ~: 5 fudge
combine ~: 3 add, sum, tot **5** count, sum up, tally, total, tot up **6** figure **7** compute, count up **9** calculate
exist in great ~: 4 teem **5** swarm **6** abound, thrive **8** flourish, overflow
game: 4 keno **5** beano, bingo, lotto **6** sudoku **7** lottery
in great ~: 6 galore **9** profusely
like our ~: 6 Arabic
numbers __: 4 game **6** racket
__ numbers: 5 by the
Numbers
follower: 4 Deut. **11** Deuteronomy
preceder: 3 Lev. **5** Levit. **9** Leviticus
Number Two Son
portrayer: Victor Sen Yung
numbing: 3 icy, raw **4** cold **5** chill, nippy, polar **6** arctic, biting, chilly, frigid, frosty, frozen, wintry **7** shivery, wintery **8** freezing, narcotic, piercing **9** soporific **10** anesthetic
numbskull
see ninny
numbskulled: 4 dull, slow **5** dopey **6** obtuse **9** dim-witted **10** dull-witted, half-witted, slow-witted
numen: 5 deity
numeral: 5 digit **6** figure, symbol **9** character
clock ~: 3 III, VII, XII **4** IIII, VIII
__ numeral: 5 Roman **6** Arabic **7** ordinal
numerals, like our: 6 Arabic
Numerals, The
painter: Erté
numerate: 4 tell **5** count, tally **9** keep score
numerical
base: 5 radix
correspondence: 5 ratio
fact: 4 stat **5** datum **9** statistic
goal: 5 quota
prefix: 3 ter-, tri-, uni- **4** hexa-, mono-, octa-, octo- **5** hepta-, penta-, septi-, tetra- **6** quadri-
suffix: 3 -eth **4** -teen
numeric starter: 5 alpha
numero uno: 4 boss **5** first **8** champion **10** celebrated
place: 5 on top
numerous: 4 lots, many, rife **5** lotsa, thick **6** a lot of, divers, gobs of, legion, lots of, myriad, umteen, untold **7** a host of, a slew of, copious, heaps of, no end of, piles of, profuse, scads of, several, teeming, umpteen, various **8** a bunch of, abundant, an army of, frequent, iterated, manifold, multiple, oodles of, prodigal, scores of, umpsteen **9** a good many, a passel of, bountiful, countless, prevalent, quite a few **10** zillions of
be ~: 4 teem **5** swarm **6** abound
combining form: 4 myri- **5** myrio-
numinous: 4 holy **6** mystic, sacred **8** mystical **10** miraculous
numismatic grade: 3 unc. **4** fine
nummulite: 6 fossil
numskull
see ninny
nun: 6 abbess, Hebrew, letter, mother, sister **7** recluse **8** prioress **9** anchoress, Carmelite, Poor Clare, postulant, religious **10** conventual
Albanian-born ~: 6 Teresa
group: 6 clergy
home: 4 cell **5** abbey **7** convent
predecessor: 3 mem
Spanish ~: 5 monja
successor: 6 samech, samekh
wear: 4 coif, veil **5** habit **6** wimple
nun __: 4 buoy
Nunavut
city: 7 Iqaluit
native: 5 Inuit
nuncio: 5 envoy **6** legate **8** delegate, emissary
nuncupative: 4 oral
__ Núñez de Balboa: 5 Vasco
Nunn: 3 Sam **6** Trevor
Nunnally: 7 Johnson
nunnery: 5 abbey **7** convent **8** cloister
Nun's Story, The (1959 film)
cast: Peter Finch, Audrey Hepburn

NU

___ **Nun, The: 6** Flying
nuptial: 6 bridal, wedded **7** marital, spousal **9** connubial
  party member: 5 bride, groom, usher **7** best man **8** newlywed **10** ring bearer
  phrase: 3 I do
  starter: 3 pre
nuptial ___: 4 mass
nuptials: 7 wedding **8** espousal, marriage **9** matrimony
  site: 5 altar
Nuremberg: 4 city, town
  city near ~: 5 Furth **6** Coburg
  locale: 7 Germany
Nureyev, Rudolf: 6 dancer **7** danseur
  specialty: 6 ballet
Nurmi, Paavo: 6 runner **7** Finnish **10** Flying Finn
Nürnberg: 4 city, town **5** stadt
  locale: 7 Germany
nurse: 2 RN **3** LPN, sip **4** baby, heal, tend **5** carer, serve, shark, train, treat **6** attend, Barton, coddle, foster, pamper, tend to, wait on **7** bring up, care for, nurture, sit with, support, sustain **8** attend to, Houlihan, minister, wait upon **9** governess, look after **10** minister to, take care of
  a drink: 3 sip **5** sip at
  Asian ~: 4 amah, ayah
  deg.: 3 BSN, MNA, MSN
  ender: 4 maid
  helper: 4 aide
  name: 5 Clara
  org.: 3 ANA
  portion: 3 CCs **4** dose **5** ampul **6** ampule **7** ampoule
  specialty: 3 TLC
  subject: 4 anat. **7** anatomy
___ **nurse: 5** scrub
Nurse Betty (2000 film)
  cast: Morgan Freeman, Greg Kinnear, Chris Rock, Renée Zellweger
nursemaid: 4 nana **5** nanny **6** au pair, nannie **9** governess
  Asian ~: 4 amah, ayah
nursery: 4 room **6** hotbed
  color: 4 blue, pink
  complaint: 5 colic
  cry: 3 mom **4** dada, mama **5** mamma
  do a ~ chore: 5 repot
  item: 4 crib, wipe **6** cradle, diaper **8** bassinet
  noise: 3 wah **6** gurgle
  playmate: 3 tot **4** baby **6** infant, sister **7** brother **9** youngster
  purchase: 4 peat, seed, soil **5** plant
  worker: 5 nanny **6** nannie
nursery ___: 5 rhyme **6** school
___ **nursery: 3** day
nursery rhyme
  crooked gate of ~: 5 stile
  flower: 4 posy
  food: 4 whey **5** curds, pease
  home of ~: 4 shoe
  merry king of ~: 4 Cole
  start: 6 baa baa
  trio: 4 mice
nursery school: 4 pre-K
  attendee: 3 tot
  item: 4 clay
  ritual: 3 nap
nurse's ___: 4 aide
nurture: 4 back, feed, keep, rear, tend **5** boost, breed, groom, nurse, raise, teach, train **6** cradle, foster, regale, school, uplift **7** advance, aliment, bring up, care for, develop, educate, forward, further, nourish, promote, support, sustain **8** advocate, incubate, instruct, maintain **9** cultivate, encourage, stimulate **10** strengthen, take care of
nut: 3 fan **4** bean, buff, cola, kola, kook, meat, seed, zany **5** acorn, betel, crank, fiend, freak, fruit, funds, pecan, piñon **6** addict, almond, budget, cashew, cobnut, kernel, lichee, litchi, maniac, noodle, peanut, pignut, pinyon, quinoa, souari, walnut, zealot **7** admirer, booster, buckeye, caltrop, coconut, devotee, fanatic, filbert, groupie, hickory, leechee, lunatic, pignoli **8** adherent, beechnut, betelnut, chestnut, fastener, follower, hazelnut, pignolia, shagbark **9** butternut, candlenut, ding-a-ling, macadamia, pistachio **10** aficionado, chinquapin, enthusiast
  astringent ~: 8 betelnut
  bitter ~: 6 pignut
  brittle-shelled ~: 6 lichee, litchi
  cake: 5 torte
  candy: 6 comfit, confit
  candy ~: 6 almond
  case: 3 bur **4** hull, kook **5** crank, shell
  Chinese ~: 6 lichee, litchi **7** leechee
  combining form: 4 nuci- **5** caryo-, karyo-
  ender: 4 gall, meat, pick **5** hatch, shell **7** cracker
  greenish ~: 9 pistachio
  hard-shelled ~: 7 coconut, hickory **8** shagbark **9** macadamia
  holder: 4 bolt
  oily ~: 6 souari **9** butternut, candlenut
  part: 4 meat **6** kernel
  piñon ~: 7 pignoli **8** pignolia
  prickly ~: 8 chestnut **10** chinquapin
  source: 4 tree
  starter: 3 cob, pea, pig **4** gall, lock **5** beech, betel, bread, chest, cocoa, dough, earth, hazel, thumb **6** bitter, butter, candle, ground **7** bladder
  sugarcoated ~: 6 dragée
  tough ~ to crack: 5 poser **6** enigma **7** mystery, stumper, toughie
  tree: 4 kola, pili **5** beech, hazel, pecan **6** acajou, almond, cashew, lichee, litchi **7** buckeye, filbert, leechee **9** macadamia, pistachio
___ **nut: 3** hex, lug **4** cola, kola, lock, pine, wing **5** betel **6** Brazil, cashew, lichee, litchi
Nut
  daughter: 4 Isis
  son: 6 Osiris
___**-Nut: 5** Beech
nutbrown: 5 hazel
___ **Nut Cheerios: 5** Honey
nutcracker: 4 bird
  suite: 4 nest
Nutcracker ___: 5 Suite
Nutcracker, The: 6 ballet
  composer: Peter Tchaikovsky
  role: 5 Clara, fairy
nuthatch: 4 bird
  home: 4 nest
Nuthin' But a 'G' Thang (1993 song)
  artist: Dr. Dre, Snoop Doggy Dogg
Nutley: 4 city, town
  locale: 9 New Jersey
nutmeat: 6 kernel
nutmeg: 4 tree **5** spice **9** seasoning
  cousin: 4 mace
  cover: 4 aril
  drink topped with ~: 4 flip
NutRageous: 3 bar **5** candy **8** candy bar **9** chocolate
  alternative: ***see*** candy brand
Nutri-___: 5 Grain
nutria: 3 fur **5** coypu **6** rodent
nutrient
  add a ~ to: 6 enrich
  combining form: 5 troph- **6** tropho-
  mineral ~: 4 iron, zinc
nutrient-___: 5 dense
Nutri-Grain: 6 cereal
  competitor: ***see*** cereal
nutriment: 4 diet, food, meat **6** viands **7** aliment, victual **8** victuals
nutrition: 4 diet, food **10** sustenance
  lacking ~: 5 unfed
  stat: 3 RDA
  supplement: 5 yeast
  watchdog: 3 FDA
nutritional: 10 alimentary
nutritious: 4 rich **7** healthy **9** healthful, wholesome **10** alimentary
  snack: 4 gorp **8** trail mix
nutritive: 6 edible **7** dietary **9** palatable, wholesome **10** alimentary, comestible
  acid: 5 folic
  mineral: 4 iron, zinc
Nutro: 7 dog food
  alternative: ***see*** pet food brand
nuts
  and bolts: 3 nub **4** knub, pith **6** detail **7** reality
  open ~: 5 crack
  sans ~: 5 plain
  soup to ~: 4 A to Z **6** all-out **7** in-depth **8** complete, sweeping, thorough **9** extensive **10** exhaustive, meticulous
___ **nuts: 5** mixed
Nuts (1987 film)
  cast: Richard Dreyfuss, Karl Malden, Maureen Stapleton, Barbra Streisand, Eli Wallach
  director: Martin Ritt
Nuts!: 4 darn, rats **6** darn it, phooey
___ **Nuts: 4** Beer **5** Grape
nuts-and-bolts: 9 practical
nuts-and-honey confection: 5 halva **6** halvah **7** halavah
nutshell
  contents: 4 meat
  in a ~: 5 short, terse **8** succinct
  put in a ~: 4 trim **5** sum up **6** digest **7** abridge, shorten **8** simplify **9** summarize
Nuttin' for Christmas (1955 song)
  artist: Barry Gordon, Art Mooney, Ricky Zahnd and the Blue Jeaners
___ **nut to crack: 4** hard **5** tough
Nutty Professor, The (1963 film)
  cast: Jerry Lewis, Stella Stevens
  director: Jerry Lewis
Nutty Professor, The (1996 film)
  cast: James Coburn, Eddie Murphy, Jada Pinkett
Nuyen: 6 France
nuzzle: 6 cuddle, nestle **7** embrace, snuggle
NV
  see Nevada
NW: 3 dir.
  state: 3 Ida., Ore. **4** Oreg., Wash.
Nwapa, Flora: 6 writer **8** Nigerian
  work: Efuru
    Idu
    Never Again
    One Is Enough
___ **'N Wash: 5** Spray
NWT
  locale: 3 Can.
  native: 3 Esk.
  part of ~: 3 Ter. **4** Terr., West **5** North
NY
  college: 3 LIU, RIT, RPI, SBU
  neighbor: 3 Ont., Que. **4** Conn., Mass., Penn. **5** Penna.
  setting: 3 EDT, EST
  see also New York
Nyack: 4 city, town
  locale: 7 New York
Nyasa: 4 lake
  locale: 8 Tanzania **10** Mozambique
Nyby: 9 Christian
NYC: 3 spt. **8** Big Apple
  airport: 3 EWR, JFK, LGA
  art center: 4 MOMA
  borough: 3 Man., Qns. **4** Manh. **5** Bklyn.
  clock setting: 3 EDT, EST
  commuter line: 4 LIRR
  dance co.: 3 ABT
  division: 3 bor.
  dwelling: 3 apt.
  HQ: 5 The UN
  like some ~ plays: 3 OOB
  opera house: 3 Met
  part: 3 bor., Man., New, Qns. **4** City, Manh., York **5** Bklyn.
  PBS affiliate: 4 WNET
  race track: 4 Big A
  radio station: 3 WOR
  sports venue: 3 MSG
  subway: 3 BMT, IND, IRT **6** A Train
  transit org.: 3 MTA
  see also New York City
NY Central: 2 RR
nyctophobe fear: 8 darkness
Nye: 4 Bill **5** Louis **6** Carrie
Nye, Bill subject: 3 sci. **7** science
Nye, Carrie
  spouse: Dick Cavett
NYer: 9 Gothamite
Nyeri: 4 city, town

locale: 5 Kenya
nyet: 2 no 3 nah, naw, nay, nix, non 4 nein, nope, uh-uh, veto 5 I won't, ixnay, never, no how, no way 6 no deal, noways, nowise 7 I refuse 8 forget it, I will not, negative, negatory 9 by no means, fat chance, I think not 10 count me out, not a chance, thumbs down
in French: 3 non
in Latin: 3 non
in Scottish: 3 nae
Nykvist: 4 Sven
NYLIC
competitor: *see* insurance company
nylon: 4 hose 5 fiber 6 fabric 7 hosiery 8 stocking
fabric: 5 satin, tulle 6 gloria, jersey, tricot, velvet 7 chiffon, organza, taffeta 8 Milanese 9 grenadine, sailcloth
fiber: 6 Antron
like ~: 5 sheer
ruin a ~: 3 jag 4 snag
shade: 4 nude 5 flesh, taupe
Nyman: 4 Lena 7 Michael
nymph: 3 Soe 4 Ceto, Echo, Hora, Ione, Lara, Loxo, Neda, Nyse, Opis, Sose, Urea 5 dryad, naiad, oread, Siren 6 Creusa, Danais, Egeria, meliad, nereid, Oenone, Phoebe, sprite, Syrinx 7 Calypso, Daphnis, hydriad, oceanid 8 Arethusa, Harmonia, Hesperia
aquatic ~: 4 nais 5 naiad
chaser: 5 satyr
mountain ~: 5 oread
Muslim ~: 5 houri
sea ~: 4 Ione 5 siren 6 nereid
tree ~: 5 dryad
__ nymph: 3 sea 4 wood 5 water
Nymphéas
artist: Claude Monet
NYPD
call: 3 APB
part of ~: 4 Dept.
rank: 4 insp.
NYPD Blue (ABC drama)
cast: Amy Brenneman (Off. Janice Licalsi)
David Caruso (Det. John Kelly)
Kim Delaney (Det. Diane Russell)
Dennis Franz (Det. Andy Sipowicz)
Sharon Lawrence (Sylvia Costas)
Esai Morales (Lt. Tony Rodriguez)
Rick Schroder (Det. Danny Sorenson)
Jimmy Smits (Det. Bobby Simone)
creator: Steven Bochco
Nyquil
alternative: *see* cold remedy
maker: 5 Vicks
Nyro, Laura: 6 singer 8 composer
song: And When I Die
Blowing Away
Eli's Coming
Stoned Soul Picnic
Stoney End
Sweet Blindness
Wedding Bell Blues
NYSE: 3 mkt.
abbr.: 3 IPO, pfd., rts., shr. 4 util.
alternative: 3 OTC 4 AMEX 6 NASDAQ
buy: 3 stk. 5 stock
listing: 2 co. 3 GTE, ITT 4 corp.
membership: 4 seat
number: 5 quote
regulator: 3 SEC
street: 4 Wall
worker: 3 arb 6 trader
Nystrom: 3 Bob 4 Eric 5 Bobby
Nytol: 8 sleep aid
alternative: 6 Compoz, Unisom 7 Sominex
NYU: 3 sch. 4 coll.
locale: 9 Manhattan
part of ~: 4 Univ.
Nyx
brother: 6 Erebus
daughter: 4 Eris 6 Hemera 7 Hespera, Nemesis
father: 5 Chaos
husband: 5 Chaos
son: 4 Eros 5 Momus 6 Erebus, Hypnos, Somnus
N.Z.
see New Zealand

1
prior to yr. ~: 3 BCE
scale where talc = ~: 4 Mohs
1/1
since: 3 YTD
1%: 4 milk
100%: 6 all-out
$100
bill: 5 C-note, C-spot
100-__ dash: 4 yard 5 meter
100-lb. unit: 3 cwt
100% Pure Love (1994 song)
artist: Crystal Waters
101 Dalmatians (1996 film)
cast: Glenn Close, Jeff Daniels, Joan Plowright, Joely Richardson
dog: 5 Pongo 7 Perdita
101-digit number: 6 googol
112
hometown: Atlanta
song: All Cried Out (1997)
Anywhere (1999)
Cupid (1997)
I'll Be Missing You (1997)
Love Me (1998)
Only You (1996)
1-2-3
software company: 5 Lotus
1-2-3 (song)
artist: Gloria Estefan, Len Barry
144
objects: 3 gro. 5 gross
180
do a ~: 7 retreat 9 back-pedal
180-degree
maneuver: 5 U-turn
turn: 3 uey
1000: 1 M 4 thou
kilocalories: 5 therm 6 therme
kilograms: 5 tonne
meters: 4 one K
pounds: 3 kip
square meters: 6 decare
yards: 4 one K
1,001 __: 4 uses
1024 bytes: 4 one K
__-1138: 3 THX
1, 2, 3, 4 (1996 song)
artist: Coolio
10001: 3 NYC 4 NY NY
100,000
BTUs: 5 therm 6 therme
rupees: 4 lakh
O: 4 elem., type 5 vowel 6 letter, oxygen 7 element 9 blood type
8 for ~: 4 at. no.
code word for ~: 4 oboe 5 Oscar
followers: 3 PQR 4 PQRS 5 PQRST
in phonetic alphabet: 5 Oscar
meaning of ~ in XOXOX: 3 hug
one ~ , maybe: 3 tac, tic, toe
preceders: 3 ens, LMN 4 KLMN 5 JLKMN
star: 7 blue sun
O (2001 film)
cast: Josh Hartnett, Martin Sheen, Julia Stiles
O __: 5 Henry 6 Canada
O __ All Ye Faithful: 4 Come
O __ babbino caro: 3 mio
O __ can you see...: 3 say
O __ Mio: 3 Dio 4 Sole
O __ odd: 4 as in
O __ of State: 4 Ship
O __! O mores!: 7 tempora
O, __ fortune's fool!: 3 I am
O, __ me the lass...: 3 gie
O-__: 4 ring, Zone 5 Cedar
'O' __ Outlaw: 5 Is for
__-O: 3 Day 4 Jell 6 double
oaf
see ninny
oafish: 3 dim 5 dense, gawky, unapt 6 clumsy, gauche, klutzy 7 awkward, bearish, bestial, boorish, gawkish, loutish, uncouth 8 bumbling, bungling, churlish, cloddish, fumbling, impolite, ungainly 9 all thumbs, difficult, graceless, lumbering, maladroit, stumbling, unskilled 10 unskillful
Oahu: 4 isle 6 island
city: 4 Aiea 6 Kailua 8 Honolulu
cookout: 4 luau
goose: 4 nene
greeting: 5 aloha
island near ~: 5 Kauai
locale: 6 Hawaii
souvenir: 3 lei
oak: 4 tree, wood 5 roble 7 quercus 8 hardwood 9 shade tree
evergreen ~: 4 holm, ilex
flower: 5 ament 6 catkin
leaf wearer: 3 maj. 5 lt. col., major
like an ~ leaf: 5 erose, lobed 7 rounded
live ~: 6 encina
nut: 5 acorn
oak __ cluster: 4 leaf
Oak __: 4 Park 5 Ridge
Oak __ Boys, The: 5 Ridge
__ Oak: 5 Royal 7 Charter
__ Oaken Bucket, The: 3 Old
Oakes: 5 Randi
Oakie: 4 Jack
Oakland: 4 city, port, town 5 Simon
county: 7 Alameda
locale: 10 California
newspaper: 7 Tribune
team: 5 A's, The 7 Raiders 9 Athletics
oak leaf __: 7 cluster
Oakley, Annie: 4 pass 7 deadeye
emulate ~: 3 aim 5 shoot
Oak Park: 4 city, town
locale: 8 Illinois, Michigan
Oak Ridge: 4 city, town
agcy.: 3 AEC
locale: 7 Florida 9 Tennessee
Oak Ridge Boys
album: Fancy Free (1982)
song: Bobbie Sue (1982)
Elvira (1981)
__ Oaks, CA: 7 Sherman 8 Thousand
oakum: 4 rope 5 fiber
source: 4 jute
oar: 3 row 5 rower, scull 6 paddle, propel 7 paddler
ender: 4 fish, lock
fulcrum: 5 thole
stroke: 4 pull
wood: 3 ash
oarlock: 5 thole
oars
boat with ~: 4 dory
both ~ in water: 4 sane
rest on one's ~: 4 idle 8 intermit
oarsmen: 4 crew 6 rowers
OAS: 8 alliance
birthplace: 6 Bogotá 8 Colombia
member: 3 Arg., Can., Col., Mex., Pan., Uru., USA 4 Cuba, Peru 5 Chile, Haiti 6 Belize, Brazil, Canada, Guyana, Mexico, Panama 7 Bahamas, Bolivia, Ecuador, Grenada, Jamaica, Uruguay 8 Barbados, Colombia, Dominica, Honduras, Paraguay, Suriname 9 Argentina, Costa Rica, Guatemala, Nicaragua, Venezuela 10 El Salvador, Saint Lucia
part of ~: 3 Org. 4 Amer. 6 States 8 American
predecessor: 3 PAU
oasis: 5 haven 6 asylum, refuge 7 retreat, sanctum 9 sanctuary
of a sort: 3 bar, pub 6 lounge, saloon, tavern 7 taproom
urban ~: 4 park 6 common 8 preserve 10 playground
view: 4 palm, sand, well
Oasis, The
author: Mary McCarthy
oast: 4 kiln, oven 7 furnace
oat: 5 grain 6 cereal
eater of song: 3 doe 4 mare
ender: 4 cake, meal
genus: 5 avena
part: 3 awn 5 groat
Oat Bran: 6 cereal
competitor: *see* cereal
oatcake: 5 bread
oater: 5 flick 7 western 9 shoot-'em-up 10 horse opera
affirmative: 3 yep, yup
ammo: 6 blanks
character: 5 posse 6 cowboy, outlaw 7 marshal, sheriff
command: 4 draw, whoa 7 giddyap
locale: 4 fort, mesa 5 cañon, ranch 6 canyon
meal: 4 chow, grub 7 vittles
name: 4 Duke, Hoot, Lash 5 Gabby
prop: 3 gun 4 Colt 5 rifle 10 six-shooter
salutation: 3 how 5 howdy
sound: 4 bray, clop 5 neigh 6 whinny
Oates: 4 John 6 Warren
partner: 4 Hall
Oates, Joyce Carol: 6 writer
work: American Appetites
Angel of Light
Bellefleur
Black Girl / White Girl
Crossing the Border
Expensive People
The Falls
Foxfire
A Garden of Earthly Delights
Last Days
Man Crazy
My Sister, My Love
Mysteries of Winterthurn
Solstice
Them
Unholy Loves
oath: 3 I do, vow 4 damn, darn, drat, gawd, heck, word 5 curse 6 avowal, dang it, pledge 7 promise 8 averment, cussword 9 assertion, assurance, expletive, guarantee, profanity, swearword 10 adjuration, avouchment, engagement
British ~: 3 cor, gor 5 blimy 6 blimey
French: 8 zut alors 9 sacre bleu
lie under ~: 7 falsify, perjure 8 forswear
mild ~: 3 gad 4 dang, darn, drat, gosh, heck, jeez 5 by gum, nerts, nertz 6 by gosh, cripes
old ~: 3 fie 4 egad 5 egads 6 by Jove, jiminy 10 ods bodkins
say under ~: 6 attest, depone, depose 7 witness 8 attest to
take an ~: 5 swear 7 promise, warrant
taker's need: 5 Bible
__ oath: 5 under
oath of __: 6 office
oatmeal: 5 gruel 6 cereal, cookie 8 flummery
clot: 4 lump
like cooked ~: 4 soft 5 mushy, soggy 7 squishy
porridge: 6 burgoo
oats: 4 feed 5 grain 6 cereal, fodder, groats, silage
feeling one's ~: 5 happy, jolly, merry 6 frisky, impish, lively 7 coltish, naughty, playful, puckish, teasing, waggish 8 mirthful, prankish, skittish, sportive 9 fun-loving, lightsome, sprightly, vivacious, whimsical 10 frolicsome, rollicking
sow wild ~: 3 err, sin 5 act up, be bad, cut up, stray 7 carry on, do wrong, go wrong 8 go astray 9 misbehave 10 fool around
__ oats: 4 wild 6 rolled
__ Oats: 6 Quaker
oats and nuts cereal: 7 granola
OAU, part of: 3 Afr., Org. 5 Unity 7 African
Oaxaca: 4 city, town 5 state 7 Mexican
language: 6 Mixtec
ruins site near ~: 5 Mitla
see also Spanish
ob-__: 3 gyn
Ob: 5 river
feeder: 6 Irtysh
locale: 6 Russia
OB: 2 MD 6 doctor 9 physician
Obadiah: 4 book 7 prophet
follower: 5 Jonah
preceder: 4 Amos
Obama, Barack: 9 president
alma mater: 7 Harvard 8 Columbia
birthplace: 6 Hawaii 8 Honolulu
cabinet member: 3 Chu 5 Gates, Locke, Solis 6 Duncan, Holder, LaHood 7 Clinton, Donovan, Salazar, Vilsack 8 Geithner, Sebelius, Shinseki 9 Gary Locke, Ray LaHood, Steven Chu 10 Arne Duncan, Eric Holder, Hilda Solis, Napolitano
child: 5 Malia, Sasha
home: 7 Chicago 8 Illinois
middle name: 7 Hussein
mother: 3 Ann

opponent: 6 McCain
veep: 5 Biden
wife: 8 Michelle
obdt. __: 4 serv.
obdurate: 4 firm, iron 5 balky, rigid, stony, tough 6 flinty, mulish, narrow, ornery, severe, stoney, wilful 7 adamant, hard-set, wayward, willful 8 contrary, hardened, indocile, indurate, perverse, pitiless, stubborn 9 immovable, impliable, obstinate, tenacious, unbending, unfeeling 10 hard-bitten, headstrong, inexorable, inflexible, persistent, relentless, unyielding
OBE: 5 award 6 honour
awarder: 4 Brit., Gr. Br. 5 the U.K.
obeah: 5 charm 6 fetich, fetish, voodoo
Obed
parent: 4 Boaz, Ruth
obedience: 7 loyalty 9 deference, servitude 10 allegiance, compliance, conformity, observance, submission
class command: 3 beg, sit 4 heel, stay
obedient: 4 easy, good, meek, ruly, tame, true 5 mousy 6 broken, docile, filial, mousey, pliant 7 duteous, dutiful, orderly, passive, servile, subdued, subject, trained, willing 8 faithful, flexible, lamblike, obliging, resigned, yielding 9 adaptable, agreeable, assenting, compliant, malleable, prostrate, tractable 10 governable, law-abiding, manageable, respectful, submissive
one: 5 robot, sheep 6 heeder
obeisance: 6 homage, praise 7 respect 9 deference, reverence 10 admiration
pay ~: 3 bow 5 kneel 6 kowtow, salaam 9 genuflect, prostrate
obeisant: 4 oily 7 fawning, servile, slavish 8 toadyish, unctuous 9 adulatory 10 obsequious
obelisk: 5 pylon, tower 6 column, dagger, pillar 8 memorial, monument, pinnacle
Oberammergau: 4 city, town
locale: 7 Germany
Oberlin
locale: 4 Ohio
Oberon: 4 moon 5 Merle 6 sprite
planet: 6 Uranus
Oberto
composer: Giuseppe Verdi
obese: 5 beefy, fubsy, heavy, plump, pudgy, pursy, stout, thick, tubby 6 chubby, fleshy, portly, pyknic, rotund, stocky, zaftig, zoftig 7 adipose, paunchy, weighty 8 roly-poly, thickset 9 corpulent 10 abdominous, overweight, well-padded
obey: 4 heed, mind 5 act on, bow to 6 accept, bend to, comply, follow, fulfil, listen, submit 7 abide by, act upon, agree to, defer to, fulfill, observe, respect, stick to 8 adhere to, carry out, listen to 9 conform to, consent to, prostrate, truckle to 10 comply with, keep in step, toe the line
refuse to ~: 4 balk 5 baulk, rebel 6 mutiny, resist
the clock: 4 rise, wake 5 arise, awake, get up, waken 6 awaken
obfuscate: 3 dim, fog 4 hide 5 bedim, befog, cloud, muddy 6 darken 7 becloud 8 disguise 9 adumbrate, blindfold 10 camouflage, overshadow
obfuscated: 3 dim 4 hazy 5 foggy, fuzzy, misty, muddy, murky, muzzy, smoky, vague 6 addled, bleary, blurry, cloudy, in a fog, opaque 7 blurred, clouded, muddled, obscure, shadowy, unclear 8 confused, nebulous 9 befuddled, imprecise, uncertain 10 bewildered, indistinct
obi: 4 band, belt, sash 8 Japanese
companion: 4 inro 6 kimono
fabric: 4 silk 5 satin
wearer: 6 geisha
Obie: 5 award, prize 6 reward, trophy
contender: 4 play 5 actor
obiter dictum: 6 remark 7 comment 9 assertion, statement, utterance 10 observance
Obi-Wan: 4 hero 6 Kenobi
AKA ~: 3 Ben
foe: 5 Darth, Vader
portrayer: Alec Guinness
object: 3 aim, end 4 care, goal, item, kick, mind, noun 5 demur, drift, point, thing 6 entity, intent, motive, reason, target 7 article, dissent, meaning, mission, protest, purport, purpose, reality 8 function 9 commodity, frown upon, give a darn, intention, something 10 disapprove, make a stand
of a joke: 4 dupe, gull 5 chump, patsy 7 fall guy
of ridicule: 4 butt 5 sport 6 effigy
of worship: 3 god 4 icon, idol, ikon 5 deity, eikon
to: 4 mind 5 fight 6 oppose, resent 7 contest, deplore, dislike, quarrel
ultimate ~: 5 be-all 6 end-all
objection: 3 but 4 beef, fuss 5 cavil, demur, qualm, query 6 outcry, plaint 7 dissent, quarrel 8 question 9 challenge, complaint, criticism, grievance
vocal ~: 2 no 3 nah, naw, nay, nix, non 4 nein, nope, nyet, uh-uh, veto 5 I won't, ixnay, never, no how, no way 6 indeed, no deal, nowise 7 I refuse, opposed 8 forget it, I will not, negative, negatory, to be sure 9 by no means, fat chance, I think not 10 count me out, not a chance, thumbs down
objectionable: 4 foul, grim, poor, ugly 5 awful, lousy, nasty, woful 6 crumby, crummy, dismal, horrid, odious, rotten, woeful 7 accurst, baleful, baneful, beastly, doleful, ghastly 8 accursed, annoying, dreadful, God-awful, grievous, horrible, inferior, shameful, stinking, terrible, unsavory, wretched 9 abhorrent, appalling, atrocious, defective, execrable, frightful, insidious, loathsome, miserable, offensive, repugnant, repulsive, revolting, unwelcome 10 abominable, despicable, detestable, disastrous, horrendous
__ objections?: 3 Any
objective: 3 aim, end, job 4 case, fair, goal, just, mark, open, sake 5 cause, equal, point, quest 6 design, honest, intent, square, target 7 mission, purport, purpose, resolve 8 ambition, balanced, detached, function, physical, rational, tangible, unbiased 9 corporeal, direction, equitable, impartial, uncolored, unslanted 10 aspiration, even-handed, ground zero, impersonal, reasonable, scientific
not ~: 6 biased, skewed 7 bigoted 8 partisan 10 intolerant, subjective
ultimate ~: 3 aim, end 4 goal 5 be-all 6 end-all, payoff, reason, target 7 mission, outcome, purpose 8 terminus 10 aspiration, conclusion
objective __: 4 case, lens
objectless: 5 fluky, stray 6 casual, chance, random 7 aimless, oddball, unaimed 8 isolated, sporadic 9 haphazard, hit-or-miss, unplanned 10 accidental, fortuitous, incidental, unintended
Object of Beauty, The (1991 film)
cast: Lolita Davidovich, Andie MacDowell, John Malkovich
Object of My Affection, The (1998 film)
cast: Alan Alda, Jennifer Aniston, Nigel Hawthorne
objector: 5 NIMBY, rebel 7 fanatic, leftist, liberal, radical 8 maverick, militant, nihilist, pacifist, reformer, renegade 9 anarchist, extremist, firebrand, insurgent 10 immoderate, left-winger
objects: 5 stuff 6 things
inability to name ~: 6 anomia
nearby ~: 5 these
remote ~: 5 those
objet __: 4 d'art 6 trouvé
objet d'art: 5 curio 7 trinket 8 nick-nack 9 curiosity 10 knickknack
objets d'art: 5 vertu, virtu
objurgate: 4 rail, ream 5 abuse, baste, blame, chide, scold 6 berate, jump on, preach 7 bawl out, censure, chew out, lecture, tell off, upbraid 8 chastise, denounce, lace into, lambaste, sail into, tear into 9 castigate, dress down, excoriate, find fault, light into 10 take to task, tongue-lash, vituperate
objurgation: 5 abuse 6 earful, rebuke 7 censure, chiding, reproof 8 hard time, reproach, scolding 9 reprimand, talking-to 10 bawling-out, chewing-out, telling-off, upbraiding
oblation: 4 alms, gift 7 charity, worship 8 donation, libation, offering 9 sacrifice
obligate: 4 bind 5 force 6 adjure, hold to 7 promise, require
obligated: 5 bound 6 in hock, liable 8 beholden, indebted 10 answerable, honor-bound
be ~: 4 must 6 have to
obligation: 3 job, tie 4 bond, call, debt, duty, must, need, onus, task 5 score, trust 6 charge, red ink 7 arrears, promise 8 contract, pressure, protocol 9 gratitude, liability, necessity 10 allegiance, commission, commitment, compulsion, engagement
be under ~: 3 owe 5 incur 6 borrow, charge 9 run up a tab
charge an ~: 5 debit
fulfill an ~: 5 pay up, repay 6 square 7 satisfy 10 remunerate
under an ~: 5 bound 6 in debt, liable 8 beholden, grateful, indebted, thankful 10 answerable, honor-bound
word of ~: 4 must 5 ought
obligatory: 6 forced 7 binding 8 required 9 mandatory, necessary, requisite 10 compulsory, imperative, inevitable, peremptory
in French: 9 de rigueur
make ~: 5 exact, force, order 6 charge, compel, decree, demand, enjoin, impose 7 command, dictate, inflict 9 establish, institute, prescribe, stipulate 10 promulgate
oblige: 4 bind, lend, make, push 5 favor, force, serve, spoil, stoop 6 compel 7 cater to, gratify, require 9 constrain, legislate
obliged: 5 bound 6 in hock, liable 8 beholden, grateful, impelled, indebted 10 honor-bound
be ~: 3 owe 4 must 5 thank 6 have to 10 appreciate
much ~: 5 danke, merci 6 grazie, thanks 7 gracias, spasibo 8 beholden, grateful, indebted, thankful, thank you
not ~: 4 free 6 exempt, let off 7 excused 8 released 10 off the hook
obliging: 4 easy, good, kind, mild, nice 5 civil, suave 6 aidful, benign, decent, kindly, polite, urbane 7 affable, amiable, gallant, heedful, helpful, lenient, mindful, tactful 8 flexible, gracious, obedient, pleasant 9 agreeable, attentive, compliant, sensitive, unselfish 10 charitable, hospitable, neighborly, thoughtful
oblique: 4 skew 5 askew, bevel 6 aslant, biased, skewed, tilted, zigzag 7 devious, evasive, lateral 8 diagonal, indirect, slanting 9 equivocal, underhand 10 roundabout, unexplicit
cut: 5 bevel, miter
direction: 4 bias, skew 5 slant
line: 3 zig 4 bias, cant, diag. 8 diagonal
obliquely: 6 askant, aslant 7 asquint, athwart, sideway 8 sideways, sidewise 9 slantways, slantwise 10 diagonally
obliqueness: 4 bias 5 slant, slope
obliterate: 4 rase, raze, ruin, wipe, x out 5 crush, erase 6 defeat, delete, efface, remove, rub off, rub out 7 abolish, expunge, pluck up, wipe out 8 demolish, stamp out 9 eradicate, sponge out 10 annihilate, extinguish
obliterated: 4 gone, lost 5 ended 7 extinct 8 finished, vanished,

wiped out **9** destroyed **10** demolished, devastated, eradicated
oblivion: 5 limbo
river of ~: 5 Lethe
oblivious: 3 lax **4** deaf, rapt **5** blind **7** unaware **8** careless, heedless, mindless **9** forgetful, unmindful **10** unthinking
be ~ to: 4 miss **6** forget, ignore **7** neglect, tune out **8** brush off, discount, laugh off, lay aside, overlook, pass over, pooh-pooh, shrug off **9** disregard
oblong: 4 oval, rect. **5** ovate **9** rectangle **10** elliptical
Oblong Box, The
author: Edgar Allan Poe
obloquy: 3 dig, lie **4** barb, gibe, jibe, slam, slap, slur, snub **5** abuse, blame, libel, odium, scorn, taunt **6** infamy, insult, rebuff, slight **7** affront, calumny, catcall, censure, disdain, mockery, offense, put-down, slander **8** contempt, derision, disgrace, dishonor, ridicule **9** aspersion, cheap shot, contumely, disrepute, ill repute, invective, notoriety **10** backbiting, defamation, disrespect, impugnment, opprobrium, reflection
obnoxious: 4 loud, mean, rude, ugly, vile **5** nasty, pesky, pesty, pushy **6** odious **7** hateful **8** annoying, horrible, sinister, terrible **9** execrable, loathsome, offensive, repellant, repellent, repugnant, unpopular, unwelcome **10** abominable, detestable, disgusting, in one's hair, unpleasant
find ~: 4 hate **6** detest, loathe **7** despise **8** execrate **9** abominate
one: 4 jerk, pest **5** creep, schmo, skunk **6** schmoe
oboe: 3 cor **4** reed, wind **7** arghool, hautboy **8** woodwind **10** double-reed
ancestor: 5 shawm
like an ~: 5 reedy
oboe __: 6 d'amore, d'amour
obol: 4 coin **5** money
place: 5 agora
Oboler: 4 Arch
Obote foe: 4 Amin
O'Brian: 4 Hugh **7** Patrick
O'Brian, Hugh: 5 actor
TV: The Life and Legend of Wyatt Earp
O'Brien: 3 Dan, Pat **4** Edna **5** Conan, Flann **6** Edmond, George **8** Margaret
successor: 4 Leno
O'Brien, Edmond: 5 actor
film: The Barefoot Contessa (1954, AA)
The Bigamist (1953)
D.O.A. (1950)
A Double Life (1947)
Fantastic Voyage (1966)
The Killers (1946)
Rio Conchos (1964)
White Heat (1949)
The Wild Bunch (1969)
Obringa today: 3 Aar **4** Aare
O Brother, Where Art Thou? (2000 film)
cast: George Clooney, Holly Hunter, John Turturro
director: Joel Coen
obscene: 3 raw **4** blue, lewd **5** bawdy, dirty, nasty **6** coarse, ribald, risqué, smutty, vulgar **7** naughty, profane **8** indecent, shameful **9** low-minded, monstrous, revolting **10** indelicate, lascivious, scurrilous, suggestive
obscenity: 8 lewdness, ribaldry **9** indecency, profanity
obscuration: 5 shade **6** shadow **7** eclipse
obscure: 3 dim, fog **4** blur, dark, deep, hazy, hide, mask, mist, veil **5** bedim, befog, blear, cache, cloak, cloud, couch, cover, faint, foggy, fuzzy, lowly, mirky, misty, muddy, murky, runic, shade, thick, vague **6** arcane, cloudy, darken, gloomy, hidden, ill-lit, lonely, occult, opaque, remote, screen, secret, shadow, somber, unseen, unsung **7** becloud, conceal, confuse, cryptic, dubious, eclipse, lowborn, secrete, unclear, unfamed, unknown **8** abstruse, darkened, disguise, esoteric, nameless, nebulous, oracular, puzzling, ulterior **9** adumbrate, blindfold, confusing, cryptical, difficult, enigmatic, hard to see, illegible, insoluble, recondite, tenebrous, unheard-of **10** camouflage, extinguish, indistinct, keep secret, lackluster, mysterious, perplexing, unfamiliar, unreadable, unrenowned
obscured: 3 dim **4** hazy, lost **5** blind, foggy **6** covert, hidden, secret, unseen **7** furtive, private **8** hush-hush, ulterior **9** invisible **10** undercover, under wraps, unviewable
Obscure Destinies
author: Willa Cather
obscurity: 4 dark, haze **5** gloom, shade **6** shadow **8** darkness **9** ambiguity
leave ~: 6 arrive, emerge **7** succeed
obsequious: 4 meek, oily **5** lowly **6** menial **7** fawning **8** unctuous **9** adulatory, groveling **10** complacent
be ~: 4 fawn **5** kotow **6** grovel, kowtow **8** fawn over
observable: 4 open **5** clear, overt, plain **6** in view, patent, public **7** evident, exposed, obvious, outward, visible **8** apparent, clear-cut, explicit, manifest, palpable, sensible, tangible, unhidden, unveiled **10** unshrouded
observance: 4 form, heed, rite, rule, wont **6** custom, regard, remark, ritual **7** heeding, keeping, liturgy, lookout, service **8** ceremony, fidelity, honoring, localism, practice, religion **9** acquittal, adherence, awareness, discharge, formality, obedience, tradition **10** compliance, conformity
observant: 4 keen, live **5** alert, alive, awake, aware, fussy, quick, sharp **6** bright, wise to, with it **7** careful, finicky, heedful, mindful, prudent, tactful, wakeful **8** cautious, deducing, exacting, finiking, finnicky, keen-eyed, lynx-eyed, rigorous, sentient, thorough, vigilant, watchful **9** assiduous, attentive, au courant, cognizant, designing, detecting, eagle-eyed, judicious, on the ball, receptive, regardful, searching, sensitive, sharp-eyed, surveying, wide-awake **10** discerning, fastidious, interested, meticulous, on one's toes, particular, perceptive, reflective, responsive, scrupulous, sensible of, thoughtful
one: 4 eyer, seer **5** noter **7** watcher
observation: 3 mot **4** heed, look, view **5** check, crack, probe, sight, study **6** espial, regard, remark, review, saying **7** comment, finding, lookout, mention, opinion, thought **8** comeback, mouthful, noticing, once-over, research, scrutiny, watching **9** attention, cognition, detection, knowledge, statement, utterance, wisecrack **10** empiricism
observation __: 3 car **4** deck, post
observatory: 7 lookout
structure: 4 dome **6** cupola
__ Observatory: 4 Lick **5** Naval **6** Lowell, Yerkes **7** Arecibo, Palomar
observe: 3 say, see, spy **4** espy, find, heed, hold, keep, look, mark, mind, note, obey, read, spot, view **5** adopt, audit, bow to, catch, guard, honor, input, opine, scout, sense, sight, spy on, state, study, watch **6** accept, advert, behold, bend to, comply, detect, follow, fulfil, listen, look at, notice, peek at, regard, remark, revere, survey, take in **7** abide by, agree to, comment, conform, declare, defer to, discern, examine, eyeball, fulfill, inspect, make out, mention, monitor, pay heed, perform, respect, satisfy, sit in on, witness **8** adhere to, carry out, discover, eagle-eye, mouth off, perceive, pick up on, practice, remember, venerate **9** celebrate, consent to, recognize, solemnize, wisecrack **10** commentate, comply with, eyewitness, get a load of, scrutinize, toe the line
observer: 3 spy **4** eyer, seer **5** noter, spier **6** looker, viewer **7** student, witness **8** beholder, onlooker **9** spectator **10** eyewitness
Observer: 5 paper **9** newspaper
locale: 9 Charlotte
__ Observer: 4 Mars
observers: 5 crowd **8** audience **10** attendance
observing: 4 live **5** alert, alive, awake, aware **6** wilful, with it **7** mindful, studied, willful **8** rational, sensible, sentient **9** attentive, au courant, cognizant, conscious, reasoning, regardful, sensitive **10** acquainted, calculated, conversant, deliberate, discerning, perceiving, perceptive, percipient, purposeful, reasonable, reflective, responsive
obsess: 5 haunt **6** absorb, fixate, plague, rankle **7** bedevil, consume, engross **8** dominate **9** infatuate, preoccupy
obsessed: 4 held, into **5** beset, rabid **6** dogged, driven, hooked, hung up, seized, tied up **7** fixated, gripped, haunted, plagued, touched, zealous **8** consumed, fiendish, hell-bent, troubled, turned on **9** bedeviled, bewitched, dominated, engrossed, fanatical, possessed, taken over, tormented **10** captivated, controlled, infatuated
by: 4 into **9** far gone on
obsession: 3 bug **4** case, must **5** craze, crush, fancy, mania, thing **6** desire, fantom, fetich, fetish, hang-up, monkey, phobia **7** complex, passion, phantom **8** delusion, fixation, idée fixe, neurosis **9** addiction, ax to grind, monomania **10** attraction, compulsion, enthusiasm
in French: 8 idée fixe
Obsession: 5 scent **7** perfume
obsessive: 8 haunting **9** fanatical **10** compulsive
fan: 3 nut **4** nerd
obsidian: 4 lava, rock **7** mineral
obsolescence: 3 age **6** disuse
__ obsolescence: 7 built-in, planned
obsolescent: 3 out **5** dated, passé, stale **6** old-hat **8** outmoded
obsolete: 3 old, out **4** dead, gone, past **5** dated, dusty, fusty, kaput, moldy, musty, passé, stale **6** bygone, fossil, old-hat **7** ancient, antique, archaic, disused, done for, extinct, fogyish, outworn **8** dinosaur, outdated, outmoded, out of use, timeworn, unusable **9** discarded, moth-eaten, old-school, out-of-date **10** antiquated, back-number, out of style, superseded
become ~: 3 die, end **4** pass **5** cease, lapse **6** expire **7** decline **9** terminate
diction: 8 archaism **10** archaicism
obstacle: 3 bar, rub **4** bump, clog, dike, jump, snag, wall **5** block, catch, check, crimp, hitch, joker, minus, snarl **6** hang-up, hazard, hurdle, kicker, logjam **7** barrier, problem, setback, trammel **8** blockade, drawback, handicap, hardship, mountain, weakness **9** booby trap, deterrent, detriment, hindrance, impedance, liability **10** bottleneck, difficulty, impediment
teamwork ~: 3 ego
obstacle __: 4 race **6** course
obstetric adjective: 5 fetal **6** foetal
obstinacy: 8 defiance, firmness, rigidity, tenacity **10** fanaticism
obstinate: 3 set **4** firm, hard **5** balky, fusty, rigid, stiff, stout, tough **6** dogged, mulish, ornery, sullen, wilful **7** adamant, defiant, hard-set, piggish, restive, wayward, willful **8** contrary, dogmatic, factious, hardened, indocile, indurate, like iron, locked in, obdurate, perverse, resolved, stubborn **9** convinced, crotchety, dead set on, difficult, fanatical, immovable, impliable, insistent, pigheaded, steadfast, tenacious, unbending **10** determined, dogmatical, hard-bitten, headstrong, inexorable, inflexible, persistent, rebellious, refractory,

relentless, self-willed, unamenable, unyielding
be ~: 4 balk, don't 5 baulk 6 refuse
one: 3 ass 4 mule

obstreperous: 4 loud, wild 5 noisy, rowdy 6 brassy, ornery, unruly 7 defiant, naughty 9 crotchety, unbridled 10 rebellious

obstruct: 3 bar, dam, jam, tie 4 bolt, clog, cork, curb, halt, lock, plug, seal, shut, stay, stop 5 block, check, choke, close, cramp, cross, dam up, delay, deter, latch, stall, stimy, stymy, tie up 6 arrest, clog up, cut off, forbid, foul up, hamper, hang up, hinder, hold up, impede, lock up, oppose, plug up, retard, seal up, secure, stop up, stymie, thwart 7 congest, inhibit, occlude, prevent, sandbag, seal off, shut off, shut out, shutter, trammel 8 blockade, button up, encumber, prohibit, restrain, restrict, sabotage, slow down, throttle 9 barricade, foreclose, forestall, frustrate, hamstring, intercept, interfere, interrupt, stonewall, terminate, weigh down 10 discourage, monkey with

obstructed: 5 blind, tight 10 impassable

obstruction: 3 bar, dam, jam 4 clog, dike, lock, plug, snag, stop, wall 5 block, check, limit 6 arrest, hamper, holdup, hurdle 7 barrier, trammel, trouble 8 blockade, blockage, blocking, gridlock, mountain, obstacle, stoppage 9 barricade, booby trap, checkmate, hindrance, restraint, roadblock 10 resistance

obstructive: 7 counter, opposed 8 opposing

obtain: 3 buy, cop, get, nab, win 4 earn, find, gain, grab, have, land, reap, save, snag, take 5 annex, fetch, get at, glean, go get, hoard, lay up, order, reach, seize, stand 6 accept, access, attain, come by, corral, derive, drum up, effect, elicit, enlist, gather, line up, occupy, pick up, pocket, secure, wangle 7 achieve, acquire, capture, chalk up, collect, compass, conquer, extract, inherit, persist, possess, preempt, prevail, procure, realize, receive, recover, recruit, salvage, scare up 8 come into, gobble up, invest in, purchase, retrieve, scrape up 9 get hold of 10 accomplish, fall heir to, get hands on
again: 4 find 6 ransom, recoup, redeem, regain, retake 7 get back, reclaim, recover, win back 8 reoccupy, retrieve, take back 9 bring back, reacquire, recapture, repossess
as support: 5 draft 6 enlist, muster 7 recruit 8 mobilize
as vengeance: 5 exact, force 6 demand, direct 7 call for, command, inflict
by force: 3 pry 5 bully, exact, gouge, wrest, wring 6 coerce, extort, wrench 7 squeeze 9 blackmail, shake down
by fraud: 3 con 4 bilk, rook, scam 5 cheat, grift 6 fleece
in Dogpatch: 3 git
the services of: 3 use 4 book, hire 5 enrol 6 employ, engage, enlist, enroll, line up, secure, sign up, take on 7 appoint, charter, recruit, reserve 8 contract 10 commission

obtainable: 4 open 5 on tap, ready 6 at hand, on deck 7 in stock, no sweat, to be had 8 gettable, possible 9 available, derivable, no problem, ready to go, securable 10 accessible, attainable, up for grabs

obtrude: 3 pry 6 butt in, impose, insert, meddle 7 barge in, break in, pry into, push out 8 butt into, horn into, nose into, stick out, trespass 9 break into, interfere, intervene

obtrusive: 4 loud, nosy 5 nosey, pushy 6 prying 7 blatant, bulging, forward, glaring, jutting, obvious, salient, visible 8 meddling 9 bumptious, horning in, intrusive, officious, prominent 10 meddlesome, noticeable, projecting, protruding

obtund: 4 dull 5 blunt, slake 6 deaden, muffle, soften 8 moderate, tone down

obtuse: 3 dim 4 dopy, dull 5 blunt, crass, dense, dopey, thick 6 bovine, opaque, stolid, stupid 7 doltish, foolish, lumpish, rounded, witless 8 ignorant, lubberly, mindless 9 dim-witted
not ~: 4 keen 5 acute, canny, quick, sharp, smart 6 astute, clever, shrewd 8 vigilant 9 intuitive, sagacious 10 discerning, insightful, perceptive

obverse: 5 front 8 flip-side, opposite

obviate: 5 avert, block, deter 6 remove 7 counter, forfend, prevent, rule out, ward off 8 forefend, preclude, prohibit, stave off 9 forestall 10 anticipate, counteract, do away with

obvious: 4 easy, open 5 clear, gross, lucid, naked, overt, plain, vivid 6 bright, cogent, in view, limpid, marked, patent, public 7 blatant, evident, exposed, express, glaring, logical, outward, precise, salient, visible 8 apparent, clear-cut, definite, distinct, explicit, flagrant, luminous, manifest, palpable, tangible, unhidden, unsubtle, unveiled 9 axiomatic, barefaced, graspable, obtrusive, prominent 10 accessible, conclusive, in evidence, noticeable, observable, pronounced, spelled out, unarguable, undeniable, unshrouded, well-marked

obviously: 5 by far 6 openly 7 clearly 10 far and away
see also of course

O.C.: 5 Smith

Ocala: 4 city, town
locale: 7 Florida

O Canada: 6 anthem

O Captain! My Captain!: 4 poem
author: Walt Whitman

ocarina: 4 wind 10 instrument

Ocasek, Ric
group: The Cars
spouse: Paulina Porizkova

O'Casey, Sean: 5 Irish 10 playwright
home: 4 Eire, Erin
work: Juno and the Paycock
The Plough and the Stars
Purple Dust
Within the Gates 4 play 5 drama

__ o' cat: 3 one, two 4 four 5 three

Occam's __: 5 razor

occasion: 3 use 4 call, case, luck, need, room, shot, time 5 basis, cause, event, evoke, nonce, state, thing 6 affair, chance, create, demand, effect, elicit, excuse, induce, lead to, moment, motive, prompt, reason 7 episode, grounds, inspire, opening, produce, provoke, warrant 8 engender, goings-on, incident, instance, juncture, milepost 9 happening, milestone, originate 10 antecedent, bring about, foundation, give rise to, inducement, make happen, motivation
grand ~: 4 ball, bash, fete, gala, prom 5 anniv., feast, party 6 affair, dinner, fiesta 7 blowout, jubilee, pageant, shindig 8 birthday, festival, function, wingding
have ~ for: 3 use 4 need, want 6 desire 7 require
on ~: 7 at times 8 sometime 9 sometimes 10 now and then
on any ~: 4 ever 6 always 10 at all times, invariably
on no ~: 5 never 7 not ever 8 not at all 9 nevermore
on that ~: 4 then, when 9 thereupon

occasional: 3 few, odd 4 rare 5 stray 6 casual, fitful, random, scarce, seldom, sparse 7 oddball, special, unusual 8 especial, far apart, off and on, periodic, specific, sporadic, uncommon 9 desultory, irregular 10 incidental, infrequent, sporadical, unfrequent

occasionally: 6 hardly, rarely, seldom 7 at times 8 at random, off and on, on and off, scarcely, sometime 9 sometimes 10 hardly ever, now and then

Occident: 4 West

occipital: 4 bone
locale: 4 head 5 skull 7 cranium
point: 5 inion

occipital __: 4 bone, lobe

occlude: 3 dam 4 clog, plug, seal, shut, stop 5 block, choke, close, dam up 6 hinder, impede, stop up 7 congest, lock out, prevent, shut out, stopper 8 close off, obstruct, throttle

occluded __: 5 front

occlusion: 4 clog 8 blockage, stoppage 9 exclusion, impedance

occult: 4 dark, deep, eery 5 eerie, magic, weird 6 arcane, hidden, mystic, orphic, secret, unseen, veiled 7 magical, obscure, psychic, unknown 8 abstruse, esoteric, hermetic, mystical, oracular, profound 9 concealed, invisible, prophetic, recondite, unearthly 10 cabalistic, mysterious, unknowable, unrevealed, witchcraft
philosophy: 6 cabala, kabala 7 cabbala, kabbala
sign: 5 sigil

occultism: 5 magic 6 cabala, kabala 7 cabbala, kabbala 10 necromancy

Occult, The
author: Colin Wilson

occupancy: 3 use 4 deed, term 5 title 6 tenure 7 control, holding, tenancy 8 presence 9 ownership, residence, retention 10 habitation, possession, settlement

__-occupancy vehicle: 4 high

occupant: 5 liver 6 holder, lessee, lodger, renter, tenant 7 denizen, dweller, resider 8 occupier, resident 9 addressee, incumbent, possessor 10 inhabitant
agreement: 5 lease 8 contract, sublease

occupation: 3 job 4 line, slot, work 5 clerk, craft, field, pilot, place, trade 6 career, doctor, lawyer, living, métier, racket, tenure 7 calling, capture, control, painter, plumber, pursuit, seizure, station, teacher, tenancy 8 activity, business, conquest, entering, function, invasion, lifework, position, takeover, vocation 9 avocation, carpenter, ownership, residence, specialty 10 department, employment, livelihood, profession, walk of life 11 moonlighter
outmoded ~: 6 iceman 9 town crier 11 lamp lighter
suffix: 3 -eer, -eur, -ier, -ist 4 -euse, -ster 5 -arian
tame ~: 5 McJob

occupational __: 6 hazard 7 therapy

occupied: 4 busy, full 5 in use, taken 6 active, intent, leased, rented, tied up 7 engaged, lived-in, peopled, settled, working 8 employed, utilized 9 engrossed, inhabited, on the move, populated
keep ~: 4 hold 5 delay, tie up 6 divert, engage, hinder, impede 8 encumber, obstruct, slow down
not ~: 4 open 5 empty 6 lonely, vacant 7 vacated 8 deserted, desolate 9 abandoned, available
with: 4 into, up to 7 taken by 8 obsessed, turned on 10 involved in

__-occupied: 5 owner

occupy: 3 man, own, sit, use 4 fill, hold, keep, live, stay 5 amuse, dwell, seize, sit at, spend, stand, tie up 6 absorb, attend, divert, employ, engage, invade, live at, live in, obtain, people, remain, reside, take up, tenant 7 capture, conquer, engross, immerse, inhabit, involve, overrun, pervade, possess, utilize 8 ensconce, garrison, interest, keep busy, maintain, permeate, populate, take over 9 entertain, establish, preoccupy 10 monopolize
an abandoned building: 5 squat
temporarily: 3 let 4 rent 5 lease
time and space: 2 be 4 last, live 5 exist 7 breathe 8 continue

occur: 2 be, go 3 hit 4 come, dawn, fall, jell, show 5 arise, break, ensue, exist, pop up 6 appear, befall, betide, chance, crop up, dawn on, happen, result, strike, turn up 7 come off, develop, turn out 8 come to be, come true, mani-

fest **9** come about, eventuate, intervene, take place, transpire **10** come to mind, come to pass
again: **6** repeat **7** iterate
subsequently: **5** ensue **6** follow, result **9** arise from, eventuate, transpire
to: **4** dawn **6** befall, strike
with: **9** accompany
occurrence: **3** hap **4** case, luck, show **5** event, scene, state, thing **6** affair **7** episode **8** accident, exigence, exigency, incident, instance, juncture **9** adventure, condition, emergency, existence, happening, incidence, situation **10** experience
occurring: **5** afoot **7** going on, ongoing **8** underway **9** happening **10** in progress
occurs, as it: **4** live
ocean: **3** Atl., lot, Pac., sea, ton **4** blue, deep, gobs, heap, host, main, pile, slew, tide, tons **5** briny, drink, heaps, water **6** Arctic, Indian, legion, seaway **7** numbers, Pacific, zillion **8** Atlantic, high seas, plethora **9** abundance, Antarctic, multitude, profusion, salt water, seven seas
across an ~: **6** abroad **7** far away, foreign, oversea **8** overseas
area: **4** deep **5** abyss **7** benthos
compound: **4** NaCl, salt
craft: **3** str. **4** boat, ship **5** liner **6** vessel **7** steamer
cross the ~: **4** sail **5** pilot **6** cruise, voyage **7** captain, journey **8** navigate
dweller: **3** cod **4** alga, fish, hake, mako, mola, opah, salp **5** algae, porgy, salpa, squid
edge: **4** sand **5** beach, coast, shore **8** littoral, seacoast **10** waterfront
Egyptian god of the ~: **4** Nunu
ender: **4** aria **5** front, going, ology
enjoy the ~: **4** surf, swim, wade **5** bathe **7** hang ten
explorer: **5** Beebe **8** Cousteau
flier: **4** tern
floor fissure: **4** vent
Greek god of the ~: **8** Poseidon
hail: **4** ahoy
in Tibetan: **5** Dalai
like an ~: **4** deep, wavy **7** aqueous
liner name: **6** Cunard
motion: **4** tide, wave **5** swell
on the ~: **4** asea **5** asail, at sea **7** en route
on the ~ floor: **5** below
pollution: **5** slick
re ~ depths: **5** hadal
rescuer: **4** USCG **10** Coast Guard
ring in the ~: **5** atoll
route: **4** lane **7** passage, sea lane
sound: **4** boom, roar, roll **5** crash
spot in the ~: **3** isl. **4** isle **5** islet **6** island
spray: **4** foam, surf, wave **5** froth, spume **8** breakers **9** spindrift
treat ~ water: **6** desalt **10** desalinate, desalinize
ocean __: **5** liner
Ocean __: **5** Spray
__ Ocean: **6** Arctic, German, Indian **7** Pacific, Western **9** Antarctic
Ocean, Billy
homeland: Trinidad
song: Caribbean Queen (1984)
The Colour of Love (1988)
Get Outta My Dreams... (1988)
Love Is Forever (1986)
Loverboy (1984)
Love Zone (1986)
Suddenly (1985)
There'll Be Sad Songs (1986)
When the Going Gets Tough... (1985)
oceangoing: **5** naval **6** marine **7** pelagic **8** maritime, nautical
Oceania: **4** isls. **5** isles **7** islands
republic: **4** Fiji **9** Australia
oceanic: **4** huge, vast **5** large, naval **6** marine **7** aquatic, immense **8** maritime, natatory, nautical
oceanid: **6** Nereid
Oceanid: **4** Asia **5** nymph
oceanographic: **5** naval **6** marine **8** maritime, nautical
oceanography: **7** science
oceans: **4** a lot, gobs, lots, slew, tons **5** heaps, loads, piles, scads **9** Seven Seas
Ocean's Eleven (1960 film)
cast: Joey Bishop, Richard Conte, Sammy Davis Jr., Angie Dickinson, Peter Lawford, Dean Martin, Cesar Romero, Frank Sinatra
Ocean's Eleven (2001 film)
cast: George Clooney, Matt Damon, Andy García, Brad Pitt, Carl Reiner, Julia Roberts
Oceanus: **5** giant, Titan
daughter: **4** Asia **5** Argia, Metis
parent: **4** Gaea **6** Uranus
wife: **6** Tethys
ocelot: **3** cat **5** felid **6** animal, big cat, feline **7** wildcat
relative: *see* feline
ocher: **3** sil **5** brown, color **6** yellow **7** mineral, reddish **8** orangish **9** earth tone
Egyptian source of ~: **6** Dakhla
relative: *see* yellow color
ochlophobe fear: **6** crowds
ocho: **5** eight **7** Spanish
follower: **5** nueve
preceder: **5** siete
Ocho __, Jamaica: **4** Rios
Ochoa, Severo: **8** Nobelist
ochre
see ocher
Ochs: **4** Phil **6** Adolph
Ockham's __: **5** razor
__ O'Clock High: **6** Twelve
__ O'Clock Jump: **3** One
... o'clock scholar: **4** a ten
__ o'clock shadow: **4** five
Ocmulgee
city on the ~: **5** Macon
O Come, All Ye Faithful: **4** noel **5** carol
O come, let us __ Him: **5** adore
O'Connell: **5** Helen **6** Arthur
O'Connor: **3** Des, Pat, Una **5** Edwin, Frank, Renee **6** Donald, Sinéad **7** Carroll, Glynnis **8** Flannery
successor: **5** Alito
O'Connor, Carroll: **5** actor
TV: All in the Family, Archie Bunker's Place, In the Heat of the Night
O'Connor, Flannery: **6** writer
work: Everything That Rises Must Converge
A Good Man is Hard to Find
The Violent Bear It Away
Wise Blood
O'Connor, Sinéad
homeland: Ireland, Eire, Erin
song: Nothing Compares 2 U (1990)
OCS
candidate: **3** NCO
grad: **2** lt. **5** lieut.
Oct.: **2** mo.
follower: **3** Nov.
it ends in ~: **3** DST
preceder: **3** Sep. **4** Sept.
see also October
octa-: **5** eight
half of ~: **5** tetra-
minus one: **5** septi-
octagon: **5** shape
word: **4** Stop
Octagon: **9** detergent
alternative: *see* detergent
__-octane: **4** high
octave: **6** eighth
plus one: **5** ninth
Octavia: **6** Butler
husband: **4** Nero
Octavian: **5** Roman
see also Latin
Octavio: **3** Paz
octet: **5** combo, group **8** ensemble **9** vocalists
fraction: **6** eighth
in Spanish: **4** ocho
plus one: **5** nonet
October: **5** month
announcement: **5** Nobel
birthstone: **4** opal
observance: **5** UN Day
position of ~: **5** tenth
sign: **5** Libra **6** Scales **7** Balance, Scorpio **8** Scorpion
where Thanksgiving is in ~: **6** Canada
October 13: **4** ides
October 1964
author: David Halberstam
October 7: **5** nones
October Revolution name: **5** Lenin
October Sky (1999 film)
cast: Chris Cooper, Laura Dern, Jake Gyllenhaal
octobre: **4** mois **5** month **6** French
follower: **8** novembre
preceder: **9** septembre
octogenarian
milestone: **6** eighty
Octoot
composer: PDQ Bach
octopus
defense: **3** ink
female ~: **3** hen
home: **3** sea **5** ocean
octet: **4** arms, legs **9** tentacles
Octopussy: **4** film **5** novel
author: Ian Fleming
cast: Maud Adams, Louis Jourdan, Roger Moore
director: John Glen
Octopus, The
author: Frank Norris
ocular: **4** lens **6** visual **7** sensory **9** sensorial
device: **6** eyecup
layer: **4** uvea
socket: **6** eyepit
oculist: **9** eye doctor
ocupado: **5** in use **7** Spanish
OD
wearer: **2** GI **7** private, recruit, soldier
oda
locale: **5** haram, harem, harim **6** hareem
Oda __ Brown: **3** Mae
odalisque: **5** haram, harem, harim **6** hareem
O'Day: **4** Alan **5** Anita
odd: **3** one **4** eery, lone, rare, sole **5** alien, eerie, flaky, fluky, freak, funny, kinky, kooky, queer, spare, wacky, weird, wiggy **6** atypic, chance, cranky, exotic, far-out, flakey, flukey, freaky, kookie, quaint, quirky, random, single, spacey, sundry, uneven, unique, varied, way-out, whacky **7** bizarre, curious, deviant, erratic, offbeat, strange, surplus, unalike, uncanny, unequal, unusual, various **8** aberrant, abnormal, atypical, freakish, leftover, mateless, peculiar, periodic, seasonal, singular, solitary, sporadic, uncommon, unpaired **9** anomalous, crotchety, different, divergent, eccentric, fantastic, grotesque, irregular, ludicrous, off-center, quizzical, remaining, unheard-of, unmatched, unnatural, whimsical **10** avant-garde, fortuitous, incidental, occasional, off-the-wall, outlandish, remarkable, sporadical, unexpected, unfamiliar, unorthodox
ender: **4** ball, ment **6** jobber
job: **4** task **5** chore **6** errand
not ~: **4** even **6** normal **7** regular **8** matching **10** true to type
notion: **4** whim **5** fancy **6** vagary **7** caprice **8** crotchet
one: **4** kook **5** crank, flake **6** codger, weirdo **9** character, eccentric **10** individual
one out: **8** newcomer, outsider, stranger
odd __: **3** job, lot **5** trick
odd __ out: **3** man
Odd __: **4** John **6** Fellow
oddball: **4** geek, kook, nerd, rare **5** crazy, flake, flaky, fluky, freak, funny, kinky, kooky, queer, weird **6** atypic, chance, far-out, flakey, flukey, freaky, kookie, misfit, quaint, random, sundry, unique, weirdo **7** anomaly, bizarre, curious, deviant, erratic, offbeat, strange, uncanny, unusual **8** abnormal, atypical, freakish, maverick, original, peculiar, rara avis, singular, solitary, uncommon **9** character, different, eccentric, fantastic, irregular **10** avant-garde, fortuitous, individual, occasional, off-the-wall, outlandish
Odd Couple, The: **4** film, play
author: Neil Simon
cast: Jack Lemmon, Walter Matthau
director: Gene Saks
game: **5** poker
role: **3** Roy **5** Felix, Oscar, Speed, Unger **6** Cecily, Murray, Pigeon, Vinnie **7** Madison **9** Gwendolyn

Odd Couple, The (ABC sitcom)
cast: Jack Klugman (Oscar Madison)
Tony Randall (Felix Unger)
oddity: 3 tic **5** quirk, trait, twist **6** foible, rarity **7** anomaly, paradox **8** original, rara avis **9** curiosity, exception **10** aberration, phenomenon
carnival ~: 4 geek **5** freak
Oddjob: 7 villain
creator: Ian Fleming
Odd John
author: Olaf Stapledon
odd man __: 3 out
oddment: 3 bit **5** scrap **6** snatch **7** remnant, snippet **8** fragment, leftover **9** remainder
oddments: 5 trash **6** excess, scraps **7** remnant, rummage **8** leavings **9** remainder
odd-numbered page: 5 recto
odd or __: 4 even
odds: 4 edge **5** ratio **6** chance **7** chances **8** handicap, ten to one, two to one **9** advantage, allowance **10** likelihood
and ends: 4 bits, misc., olio, rest **5** melee, scrap, trash **6** debris, job lot, jumble, litter, medley, scraps, things **7** mélange, remnant, rubbish, rummage **8** et cetera, leavings, leftover, remnants, snatches, snippets **9** fragments, leftovers, potpourri, remainder **10** miscellany
at ~: 7 opposed **8** battling, clashing, opposing **9** differing, on the outs **10** in conflict, poles apart
at ~ with: 3 con **7** loath to **8** averse to, opposing **9** counter to, hostile to
be at ~: 4 feud **5** clash **8** conflict
ender: 5 maker, to one
give ~: 3 bet, fix, lay **5** wager **6** gamble **8** make book, take bets **9** speculate
set at ~: 6 divide **7** break up, disrupt, quarrel **8** alienate, disunite, estrange **9** disaffect
taker: 6 better, bettor, player **7** gambler, wagerer **8** gamester
take the ~: 3 bet **5** wager **6** gamble
Odds ___...: 3 are
Odds Against
author: Dick Francis
odds and __: 4 ends
odds-on: 6 liable, likely **8** expected, favorite, probable **9** promising, seemingly **10** in the cards
ode: 4 hymn, poem, rime **5** rhyme, verse **7** canzona, canzone, writing **8** canticle **9** epinicion
like an ~: 5 lyric **6** poetic
Old French ~: 3 lai
subject: 3 urn
__ ode: 7 Sapphic
Ode __ Grecian Urn: 3 on a
Ode __ Nightingale: 3 to a
Ode __ West Wind: 5 to the
Ode: Intimations of Immortality
author: William Wordsworth
Odense: 4 city, font, port, town **8** typeface
island: 3 Fyn
locale: 7 Denmark
odeon: 7 theater, theatre **9** music hall, playhouse
Ode on a Grecian Urn
author: John Keats
Ode on Indolence
author: John Keats
Ode on Melancholy
author: John Keats
Oder: 5 river
locale: 6 Poland **7** Germany
river to the ~: 5 Warta **6** Neisse
Oder-__ Line: 6 Neisse
Odes
author: Horace
Odessa: 4 city, port, town **6** Turner
locale: 5 Texas **7** Ukraine **8** Black Sea
river: 6 Dnestr **8** Dniester
__ Odessa: 6 Little
Odessa File, The (1974 film)
cast: Derek Jacobi, Maria Schell, Maximilian Schell, Jon Voight
director: Ronald Neame
Ode to a Nightingale
author: John Keats
Ode to Autumn
author: John Keats
Ode to Billy Joe (1967 song)
artist: Bobbie Gentry
Ode to Duty
author: William Wordsworth
Ode to Liberty
author: Percy Bysshe Shelley
Ode to Psyche
author: John Keats
Ode to the Confederate Dead
author: Allen Tate
Ode to the West Wind
author: Percy Bysshe Shelley
Odets, Clifford: 10 playwright
spouse: Luise Rainer
work: Awake and Sing!
The Big Knife
Clash by Night
The Country Girl
The Flowering Peach
Golden Boy
Night Music
None But the Lonely Heart
Paradise Lost
Sweet Smell of Success
Till the Day I Die
The Time Is Ripe
Waiting for Lefty
odeum: 7 theater, theatre **9** music hall, playhouse
odic: 7 lyrical **8** Horatian, Pindaric
Odi et __: 3 Amo
Odilon: 5 Redon
Odin: 3 god **5** Norse, Wotan
home: 6 Asgard
horse: 8 Sleipner, Sleipnir
son: 3 Tyr **5** Baldr **6** Balder
wife: 5 Frigg
O Dio Mio (1960 song)
artist: Annette Funicello
odious: 4 base, foul, grim, mean, poor, ugly, vile **5** awful, lousy, nasty, woful **6** crumby, crummy, dismal, horrid, ornery, rotten, woeful **7** accurst, baleful, baneful, beastly, doleful, ghastly, hateful, heinous, hideous **8** accursed, annoying, dreadful, God-awful, grievous, horrible, infamous, inferior, shameful, shocking, stinking, terrible, wretched **9** abhorrent, appalling, atrocious, defective, execrable, frightful, insidious, invidious, loathsome, miserable, monstrous, nefarious, obnoxious, offensive, repellant, repellent, repugnant, repulsive, revolting **10** abominable, despicable, detestable, disastrous, disgusting, forbidding, horrendous, outrageous, unpleasant
one: 3 cad, cur, rat **4** heel, toad, worm **5** knave, rogue, scamp, skunk, snake, sneak, swine **6** wretch **7** stinker **9** scoundrel **10** blackguard
odist: 4 bard, poet, scop **6** rhymer **8** minstrel **9** poetaster, rhymester, versifier
Muse: 5 Erato
odium: 4 blot, hate, slur, spot **5** blame, brand, shame, stain **6** animus, enmity, hatred, infamy, malice, rancor, stigma **7** censure, disgust, dislike, ill will, obloquy **8** acrimony, aversion, black eye, contempt, disfavor, disgrace, dishonor, ignominy, loathing **9** animosity, antipathy, discredit, disrepute, ill repute, repulsion, revulsion **10** abhorrence, opprobrium, repugnance
odometer: 5 gauge
abbr.: 3 mph
new ~ reading: 4 OOOO **5** OOOOO
rig an ~: 5 reset
unit: 4 mile
O'Donnell: 5 Cathy, Chris, Rosie **7** Lillian
O'Donnell, Chris: 5 actor
film: Batman Forever (1995)
Batman & Robin (1997)
Circle of Friends (1995)
Cookie's Fortune (1999)
Scent of a Woman (1992)
School Ties (1992)
The Three Musketeers (1993)
odontophobe fear: 7 dentist
odor: 3 air **4** musk, nose, reek, tang **5** aroma, savor, scent, smell, stink, whiff **6** breath, flavor, repute, stench **7** bouquet, essence, perfume **8** pungency, tincture **9** effluvium, emanation, fragrance, redolence **10** exhalation, reputation
detector: 4 nose
foul ~: 4 reek **5** smell, stink **6** stench **9** effluvium
give off an ~: 4 reek **5** stink
having a bad ~: 4 foul, rank **5** fetid, musty, reeky **6** putrid, rancid, rotten, smelly, stinky, strong **7** noisome, reeking **8** mephitic, stinking
offensive ~: 5 fetor, stink **6** foetor
slight ~: 4 hint **5** sniff, trace, whiff **6** breath **9** suspicion
Odor __: 6 Eaters
Odor of Sanctity, An
author: Frank Yerby
odorous: 4 dank, foul, gamy, rank **5** fetid, gamey, moldy, musty, reeky, sharp, spicy **6** foetid, rotten, skunky, smelly, spicey, stinky, strong **7** miasmic, noisome, noxious, pungent, reeking, scented, squalid **8** aromatic, fragrant, mephitic, redolent, stagnant, stinking, unsavory **9** offensive, olfactory **10** effluvious
starter: 3 mal
__ O. Douglas: 7 William
Ods bodkins!: 4 egad **5** egads **6** zounds
ODU
locale: 7 Norfolk **8** Virginia
Odysseus: 4 hero **6** Elytis **7** warrior
advisor: 6 Athena, Athene
dog: 5 Argus
emulate ~: 4 roam, rove **5** drift, range, stray **6** travel, wander **7** journey, meander **9** gallivant
home: 6 Greece, Ithaca
lover: 5 Aeaea, Circe, Kirke **6** Evippe **7** Calypso **9** Callidice
parent: 7 Laertes **8** Anticlea, Sisyphus
son: 5 Romus **6** Agrius **7** Latinus, Romanus **8** Euryalus **9** Acusilaus, Telegonus **10** Polypoetes, Telemachus
wife: 8 Penelope
odyssey: 4 trek, trip, hijra **6** hegira, hijrah **7** journey **8** long haul
Odyssey: 3 van **5** Honda
Odyssey, The: 4 epic, epos, poem **6** epopee
author: Homer
character: 4 Irus, Maro, Zeus **5** Arete, Circe, Helen, Kirke, Medon, siren **6** Athena, Athene, Hermes, Mentor, Nestor, Noëmon, Scylla **7** Calypso, Elpenor, Eumaeus, Laertes, Phemius **8** Alcinous, Antinous, Eurynome, Melantho, Menelaus, Nausicaä, Odysseus, Peiraeus, Penelope, Poseidon, Tiresias **9** Charybdis, Eurycleia **10** Eurylochus, Eurymachus, Melanthius, Philoetius, Polyphemus, Telemachus
herb: 4 moly
peak: 4 Ossa
__ Odyssey, The: 6 Talbot
__ Oe: 5 Aloha
OED: 4 dict. **10** dictionary
ender: 3 zed
info: 3 def., wds. **5** words
unit: 3 vol. **6** volume
Oedipus
daughter: 6 Ismene **8** Antigone
parent: 5 Laius **7** Jocasta
son: 8 Eteocles **9** Polynices
victim of ~: 5 Laius
wife: 7 Jocasta
Oedipus __: 3 Rex, Tex **7** complex
Oedipus at Colonus
author: Sophocles
Oedipus Rex
author: Sophocles
Oedipus Tex
composer: PDQ Bach
oeil-de-__: 5 boeuf
oenochoe: 3 jug **4** ewer **6** vessel **7** pitcher **9** container
oenology topic: 4 Napa, wine **5** aroma
oenomel: 5 drink **8** beverage
ingredient: 4 wine **5** honey
Oenone: 5 nymph
author: Alfred Tennyson
husband: 5 Paris
o'er: 4 thru **7** finish'd
opposite: 5 neath
o'er __ and dale: 4 hill

Oersted, Hans: **6** Danish **9** physicist
Oerter: **2** Al
forte: **4** shot **7** shot put
oeuf: **3** egg **6** French
layer: **5** poule
oeuvre: **4** opus, work **5** canon **6** corpus **10** opera omnia
of __: **4** late, note **5** a kind, a sort, sorts **6** choice, course
of __ proportions: **4** epic
of __ words: **3** few
__ of: **3** all, off **4** back, fond, hear, kind, sort **5** ahead, aware, by way, on top, short, think **6** become, inside **7** apropos, because, dispose, outside, upwards
__-of: **7** unheard
Of __ and Men: **4** Mice
Of __ and the River: **4** Time
Of __ Bondage: **5** Human
Of __ I Sing: **4** Thee
__ of 1812: **3** War
__ of '42: **6** Summer
__ of '76: **6** Spirit
of a __: **4** kind, sort **5** piece
__ of Abraham: **6** Plains
__ of absence: **5** leave
__ of a chance: **5** ghost
__ of a Clown: **5** Tears
__ of a different color: **5** horse
__ of admissions: **4** dean
__ of a Doubt: **6** Shadow
__ of a Drag: **4** Kind
__ of Adrian Messenger, The: **4** List
__ of a feather: **5** birds
__ of affairs: **5** state
__ of Africa: **3** Out
__ of Age in Samoa: **6** Coming
__ of Ages: **4** Rock
__ of a gun: **3** son
__ of a kind: **3** one
__ of Alcatraz: **7** Birdman
__ of ale: **4** yard
__ of all: **5** least
__ of Allegiance: **6** Pledge
__ of All Fears, The: **3** Sum
__ of All Flesh, The: **3** Way
__-of-all-trades: **4** jack
__ of America: **3** Men **4** Bank **5** Voice
__ of Amontillado, The: **4** Cask
__ of a Nation, The: **5** Birth
__ of an era, the: **3** end
__ of Angels: **4** City, Rage
__ of an idea: **4** germ
__ of Anxiety, The: **3** Age
O'Faolain, Sean: **5** Irish **6** writer
work: A Nest of Simple Folk The Talking Trees
__ of appeals: **5** court
__ of approval: **4** seal **5** stamp
__ of a Preacher Man: **3** Son
__ of Aquarius: **3** Age
__ of Aquitaine: **7** Eleanor
__ of Arabia: **8** Lawrence
__ of Araby, The: **5** Sheik
__ of Aragon: **9** Catherine
__ of Arc: **4** Joan
__ of arms: **4** coat
__ of art: **4** work
__ of a Salesman: **5** Death
__ of Assisi: **5** Clara, Clare **7** Francis
__ of assistance: **4** writ
__ of a sudden: **3** all
__ of Athens: **5** Timon
__ of Atonement: **3** Day
__ of attack: **4** plan **5** angle
__ of attainder: **4** bill
__ of attorney: **5** power
__ of August, The: **4** Guns **6** Whales
__ of averages: **3** law
__ of Avila: **6** Teresa **7** Theresa
__ of Avon: **4** Bard
__ of a Wayside Inn: **5** Tales
__ of a Woman: **5** Scent
__ of Babel: **5** Tower
__ of Baghdad, The: **5** Thief
__ of baloney: **4** full
__ of Base: **3** Ace
__ of beans: **4** full, hill
__ of beasts: **4** king
__ of beef: **4** side **5** baron, round
__ of Bernadette, The: **4** Song
__ of Bethlehem: **4** Star
__ of Biscay: **3** Bay
__ of bounds: **3** out
__ of breath: **3** out
__ of burden: **5** beast
__ of business: **5** order, piece
__ of cake: **5** piece
__ of call: **4** port
__ of Cancer: **6** Tropic
__ of Capricorn: **6** Tropic
__ of cards: **4** deck **5** house
__-of-center: **4** left **5** right
__ of ceremonies: **6** master
__ of certiorari: **4** writ
__ of chance: **4** game
__ of character: **3** out
__ of civilization: **6** cradle
__ of claims: **5** court
__ of clay: **4** feet
__ of Cleves: **4** Anne
__ of command: **5** chain
__ of commission: **3** out
__ of Concord: **4** Sage
__ of Confusion: **4** Ball, Land, Year
__ of Congress: **7** Library
__ of consciousness: **6** stream
__ of contention: **4** bone
__ of Corinth: **4** Gulf **7** Isthmus
of course: **2** ay **3** aye, yea, yep, yes **4** fine, I see, okay, sure, yeah **5** natch, oh yes **6** surely, you bet **7** for sure **8** be glad to **9** assuredly, certainly, doubtless, naturally, you betcha **10** absolutely, by all means, definitely, for certain, positively
__ of Court: **4** Inns
__ of credit: **4** line **6** letter
__ of Damocles: **5** sword
__ of Darkness: **4** Edge **5** Color, Heart **6** Prince
__ of date: **3** out
__ of David: **4** Star
__ of dawn: **5** crack
__ of day: **4** time **5** break
__ of Day: **5** Break
__ of defeat: **5** agony
__ of departure: **5** point
__ of Divorcement: **5** A Bill
__ of Dog: **6** Beware
__ of do or die: **5** a case
__-of-doors: **3** out
__ of Dover: **6** Strait
__ of drawers: **4** nest **5** chest
__ of Dreams: **5** Field
__ of duty: **4** tour
__ of Earl: **4** Duke
__ of Eden: **4** East **6** Garden
__ of education: **5** board
__ of eight: **5** piece
__ of Elea: **4** Zeno
__ of elections: **5** board
__ of Enchantment: **4** Land
__ of Endearment: **5** Terms
__ of Engineers: **5** Corps
__ of entry: **4** bill, port
__ of errors: **6** comedy
__ of ethics: **4** code
off: **3** bad, far, out **4** afar, away, awry, gone, over, poor, rank, slim, slow, sour **5** apart, aside, askew, atilt, flaky, not on, small **6** absent, astray, behind, flakey, murder, rancid, remote, rotten, slight, spoilt, untrue **7** gone bad, inexact, outside, removed, slender, spoiled, strange, tainted **8** canceled, inferior, not right, sluggish **9** divergent, elsewhere, imprecise, incorrect, on one's way, out of here, out of sync, postponed, to one side, vanishing **10** decomposed, low-quality, malodorous, not working, on vacation
ender: **3** key, set **4** beat, hand, load, side **5** print, shoot, shore, sides, stage **6** handed, screen, spring **7** setting **8** scouring
in Italian: **3** via
off __: **4** year **5** and on, guard
off __ good start: **3** to a
off __ tangent: **3** on a
off-__: **3** air, key **4** base, duty, hour, line, load, mike, peak, ramp, site **5** board, brand, glide, price, white **6** budget, camera, campus, center, island, limits, screen, season **7** putting
off-__ betting: **5** track
off-__ pitch: **5** speed
off-__ vehicle: **4** road
off.
aide: **4** asst.
assistant: **4** secy.
church ~: **4** msgr.
city ~: **3** ald.
main ~: **5** hdqrs.
military ~: **2** lt. **3** col., cpl., gen., maj., sgt. **4** MSgt., SSgt., TSgt. **5** lieut., lt. gen.
naval ~: **3** CPO **4** bo's'n, cmdr., lt. jg., RAdm., VAdm. **5** lieut.
police ~: **3** sgt. **4** capt. **5** lieut.
see also office, officer, official
__ off: **3** bad, beg, bug, buy, cry, cut, fob, get, lay, let, log, lop, mid, nod, pay, pop, put, rip, run, set, tap, tee, top **4** back, blow, buzz, call, cast, come, dash, doze, drop, dust, ease, face, fair, fall, fend, fire, give, hand, haul, head, hold, kick, kiss, lead, lift, make, pack, palm, pass, peel, pick, pull, push, rake, reel, ring, rope, seal, sell, send, show, shut, sign, spin, step, stop, tail, take, tear, tell, tick, toss, turn, ward, wear, whip, wipe, work **5** a ways, blast, break, bring, brown, brush, carry, choke, clear, dusts, fight, first, hit it, knock, laugh, leave, level, mouth, on and, right, round, shake, shove, shrug, slack, smart, sound, split, spout, stand, stave, swear, taper, throw, touch, write **6** better, change, polish, square, switch
__-off: **3** far, ill, rip, tip **4** bake, cook, face, goof, spin, well **5** angle, fence, sawed, trade
Off __ Comet: **3** on a
Off __ into the wild...: **4** we go
Off __, on...: **5** again
__-Off: **4** Bake, Easy
__ of fact: **5** point **6** matter
__ of faculty: **4** dean
__ off after: **4** take
__ of faith: **3** act **4** leap **6** breach **7** article
__ of Faith: **4** Leap **6** Breach
offal: **4** junk **5** swill, trash, waste **6** debris, litter, refuse **7** carrion, garbage, rubbish
__ of Fame: **4** Hall
off and __: **7** running
__ of fare: **4** bill
__ of fate: **5** quirk, twist
off-balance: **6** uneven **7** unequal **8** lopsided **9** irregular
off-base: **6** all wet, errant, risqué **7** inexact **8** aberrant, abnormal, improper
offbeat: **3** odd **4** eery, luny **5** alien, eerie, fresh, funky, loony, loopy, novel, outré, weird **6** atypic, far out, freaky, looney, quaint, quirky, unique, unlike, way-out **7** bizarre, deviant, oddball, strange, unalike, unusual **8** aberrant, atypical, bohemian, freakish, peculiar, uncommon **9** anomalous, different, divergent, eccentric, fantastic, irregular, quizzical, unheard-of **10** unorthodox
off-Broadway trophy: **4** Obie
off-center: **3** odd **4** awry, side **5** askew, atilt, wacky **6** whacky **7** strange **9** eccentric, irregular
off-color: **4** blue, lewd, racy, rank **5** bawdy, dirty, salty, shady, spicy **6** coarse, earthy, ribald, risqué, sickly, smutty, spicey, vulgar **7** naughty **8** indecent **9** offensive, tasteless **10** indelicate, lascivious, suggestive
__-off coupon: **5** cents
off-course: **4** awry, lost, wide **6** errant
go ~: **3** yaw **4** veer **7** deviate
off-duty: **4** free, idle, open **7** resting **8** inactive, released **9** at leisure, at liberty, available **10** disengaged, unoccupied
outfit: **5** mufti **7** civvies
Offenbach, Jacques: **6** French **8** composer
work: Orpheus in the Underworld Tales of Hoffmann
offend: **3** jar, sin, vex **4** fret, gall, gibe, hurt, jeer, jibe, miff, mock, pain, rile, slam, slur, snub, zing **5** abuse, anger, annoy, chafe, decry, libel, pique, repel, scorn, shock, spite, spurn, sting, taunt, upset, wound, wrong **6** defame, deride, dump on, heckle, impugn, insult, malign, nettle, rebuff, revolt, sicken, slight, vilify **7** affront, asperse, degrade, disdain, disgust, disturb, fend off, hold off, horrify, outrage, provoke, put down, rank out, repulse, slander, tick off, traduce, turn off **8** aggrieve, alienate, belittle, denounce, distress, drive off, gross out, irritate, ridicule, trespass, vilipend **9** denigrate, discredit, disoblige, disparage, displease, humiliate, misbehave **10** antagonize, calumniate, disgruntle, disrespect, exasperate, transgress

the eye: 5 clash
the nose: 4 reek 5 smell, stink
unlikely to ~: 4 kind, nice, warm 5 homey 6 decent, genial, gentle, kindly, modest, polite, proper, seemly 7 affable, amiable, amusing, cordial, correct, genteel, helpful, likable, refined, winsome 8 charming, cheerful, cultured, decorous, friendly, generous, gracious, ladylike, obliging, pleasant, pleasing, tasteful, very good, virtuous, well-bred 9 admirable, agreeable, befitting, courteous, exemplary, simpatico 10 attractive, meticulous, personable, scrupulous

offended: 4 hurt, sore 5 huffy, livid, moody 7 injured
be ~ by: 4 mind 6 resent
easily ~: 5 huffy, miffy 6 touchy 7 bristly
easily ~ one: 4 prig 5 prude 7 Puritan

offender: 4 perp 5 felon 6 bad guy 7 runaway, villain 8 criminal, internee, prisoner 10 delinquent
mil. ~: 4 AWOL 6 absent

offense: 3 cut, dig, hit, ire, sin 4 barb, foul, gibe, harm, hurt, jibe, quip, slam, slap, slur, snub, tort 5 abuse, anger, blitz, crime, fault, guilt, lapse, libel, pique, scorn, taunt, wrath, wrong 6 attack, breach, felony, injury, insult, rebuff, slight, zinger 7 affront, assault, battery, calumny, catcall, disdain, flare-up, misdeed, mockery, mugging, obloquy, outrage, put-down, slander, umbrage 8 contempt, derision, ridicule, trespass 9 annoyance, aspersion, cheap shot, contumely, indignity, injustice, offensive, onslaught, veniality, violation 10 aggression, blitzkrieg, defamation, disrespect, illegality, infraction, irritation, misconduct, opprobrium, peccadillo, resentment, wrongdoing
beat the ~: 5 parry, repel 6 defeat, rebuff, resist 7 hold off, repulse 8 push back, turn back 9 force back, keep at bay, withstand
deprive of ~: 5 unarm 6 disarm
Inquisition ~: 6 heresy
serious ~: 4 tort 5 arson, crime, heist, theft 6 felony, holdup, murder 7 assault, robbery, treason 8 burglary, delictum 10 kidnapping
show ~: 4 mind, slap 6 resent

offensive: 4 base, evil, foul, grim, loud, poor, push, raid, rude, ugly, vile 5 awful, blitz, gross, lousy, nasty, onset, pushy, sally, seamy, woful 6 attack, biting, crumby, crummy, dismal, horrid, odious, rancid, risqué, rotten, sortie, vulgar, woeful 7 abusive, accurst, assault, baleful, baneful, beastly, cutting, doleful, ghastly, hateful, heinous, hideous, noisome, odorous, offense, squalid, uncivil 8 accursed, annoying, campaign, dreadful, God-awful, grievous, horrible, inferior, insolent, invasion, off-color, shameful, shocking, stinking, terrible, unsavory, wretched 9 abhorrent, appalling, atrocious, defective, execrable, frightful, insidious, insulting, invidious, loathsome, low-minded, miserable, monstrous, obnoxious, onslaught, repellant, repellent, repugnant, repulsive, revolting, sarcastic, unsightly 10 abominable, aggression, aggressive, derogatory, despicable, detestable, disastrous, disgusting, forbidding, horrendous, impossible, indelicate, irritating, lascivious, malodorous, outrageous, scandalous, scurrilous, unbecoming, unmannerly, unpleasant
starter: 7 counter
take the ~: 4 lead 6 attack 7 aggress

offensive __: 3 end 4 line 6 tackle

__ offensive: 3 Tet 5 peace

offer: 3 bid 4 cite, give, hand, move, pass, pose, show 5 bring, grant, pitch, press, yield 6 afford, donate, extend, feeler, hand in, submit, tender 7 furnish, hold out, present, produce, proffer, propose, provide, request, suggest 8 endeavor, overture, proposal, put forth 9 hold forth, introduce, sacrifice, volunteer 10 administer, invitation, make a pitch, put forward
an opinion: 3 say 5 guide, opine 7 comment, counsel, observe, suggest, suppose, surmise 8 point out 9 recommend
assurance: 4 aver, avow 6 attest
evidence: 5 quote 6 attest 8 attest to
for a price: 4 hawk, sell, vend 5 put up 6 market, peddle
starter: 7 counter
temporarily: 4 lend, loan 7 advance
up: 4 cede, give 5 endow, grant 6 bestow, devote, donate, impart, render, tender 7 let have, proffer 8 fork over, heap upon, immolate, renounce, shell out 9 sacrifice, surrender 10 contribute, relinquish

__ offer: 5 final 6 tender

offering: 3 bid 4 alms, gift 5 tithe 7 charity, present, release, tribute, worship 8 donation, gratuity, libation, oblation 9 atonement, sacrifice

__ offering: 5 burnt, peace

of few __: 5 words

__ of few words: 4 a man

off-guard: 5 aback, short 6 unwary 7 napping 8 careless, reckless, sleeping 9 negligent 10 by surprise, unthinking
catch ~: 5 shock 8 surprise
put ~: 6 disarm 10 disconcert

offhand: 4 cool, curt, glib, rude 5 ad-lib, aloof, brusk 6 abrupt, breezy, casual, chance, mellow 7 brusque, cursory 8 careless, cavalier, laid-back, slapdash 9 arbitrary, easygoing, extempore, haphazard, impromptu, impulsive, negligent, throwaway, unguarded, unheedful, unstudied, whipped up 10 improvised, nonchalant, unagitated, uncritical, unprepared, unprompted, willy-nilly
do ~: 5 ad-lib 6 wing it 7 dash off 9 improvise
in Latin: 9 brevi manu

office: 3 job 4 duty, part, post, role, room, shop, work 5 place, suite, trust 6 agency, branch, bureau, center, charge 7 factory, foundry, station 8 benefice, building, business, capacity, facility, function, position, province, vocation 9 personnel, salt mines, situation, workplace 10 commission, department, profession
acronym: 4 ASAP
asst.: 4 secy.
away from the ~: 3 out 5 not in 9 elsewhere
break time: 5 ten a.m.
building area: 6 atrium
communication: 4 memo 5 e-mail
connection: 3 LAN 5 modem
copy of yore: 5 mimeo 6 carbon 10 mimeograph
crew: 5 staff 9 employees
do an ~ job: 4 file, sort, type 5 index 6 docket, record 7 arrange, catalog 8 classify, register 10 pigeonhole
dupe: 2 cc. 4 copy
ender: 6 holder
expense: 4 rent 5 lease 8 overhead
freebie: 4 perk, plus 5 bonus 7 benefit 8 dividend 10 perquisite
front ~: 5 board 8 official 9 directors 10 executives, management
furniture: 4 desk, sofa 5 couch, divan, table 6 lounge, settee 7 rolltop 9 davenport, secretary, sectional 10 escritoire
hold ~: 5 serve 6 act for 7 serve as 8 speak for 9 represent 10 administer
home ~: 3 den 5 study 7 station
length of ~: 4 span, term 6 period, tenure 8 duration, interval 9 occupancy
note: 4 memo 7 message, missive, tickler 8 reminder 9 directive
phone: 3 ext. 9 extension
plant: 4 fern
put in ~: 4 seat, vote 5 elect 6 enseat
remove from ~: 4 oust 5 purge 6 depose
return to ~: 6 recall 7 reelect 9 bring back, reinstate
rooms: 5 suite
seek ~: 3 run 5 stump 7 contend 8 politick
seeker: 3 pol 9 candidate 10 politician
skills stat.: 3 wpm
stamp: 4 null, paid, recd. 7 invalid 9 cancelled
suffix: 3 -dom 4 -ship
supply: 2 PC 3 fax 4 pads, pens 5 dater, paper, Xerox 6 copier 7 erasers, pencils 8 computer
symbol of ~: 4 mace
wear: 3 tie 4 suit 6 outfit 7 uniform 8 ensemble
withdraw from ~: 4 quit 5 demit, leave
worker: 4 asst., boss, page, temp 5 clerk, filer, gofer, steno 6 gopher 7 manager 9 assistant

office __: 3 boy 4 girl, park 5 block, hours, plaza 6 seeker

__ office: 3 box 4 back, home, land, loan, post 5 assay, front 6 patent, ticket

Office __: 3 Max 5 Depot

__ Office: 4 Holy, Oval

__-office business: 4 land

officeholder: 2 in 8 minister, official 10 politician

officer: 3 arm, cop 4 head 5 agent, badge, chief 6 captor, deputy, leader, mounty, shamus, warden 7 captain, manager, marshal, sheriff, soldier 8 director, sergeant 9 appointee, detective, dignitary, executive, policeman, president 10 bureaucrat, lieutenant, magistrate
antidrug ~: 4 narc, nark
career ~: 5 lifer
church ~: 5 elder, prior
Church of England ~: 6 beadle
command: 4 halt
company ~: 2 VP 3 CEO, CFO, COO 4 pres., secy. 5 treas. 9 president, secretary, treasurer
corrections ~: 6 jailer, warden 7 turnkey
financial: 2 tr. 3 CFO 5 treas. 9 treasurer
junior ~: 5 cadet 7 soldier
mil. ~: 2 lt. 3 cdr. 4 adjt., SSgt.
military ~: 2 lt. 3 adm., col., ens., gen., maj., sgt. 4 capt., mate 5 bosun, lieut., lt. col., major 6 ensign, gunner 7 admiral, captain, colonel, general 8 sergeant
Ottoman ~: 3 aga 4 agha 5 vizir
peace ~: 3 cop 6 lawman 7 marshal, sheriff
petty ~: 3 yeo. 4 rank 5 bosun 6 sailor, yeoman
police ~: 3 cop, law 4 bear, fuzz, heat, narc, nark 5 badge, bobby 6 copper, patrol 7 officer 8 bluecoat, gendarme 9 constable, detective
presiding ~: 4 head 5 chief 6 leader, top dog, warden 7 manager 8 director, governor 9 executive, president 10 supervisor
undercover ~ at times: 4 bait, lure 5 shill 6 come-on

__ officer: 4 deck, flag, line, loan 5 field, first, peace, petty, staff, third 6 flight, health, police, public, second, truant

Officer and a Gentleman, An (1982 film)
cast: Richard Gere, Louis Gossett Jr., Debra Winger
character: 4 Emil
setting: 3 OCS

__, Officer Krupke: 3 Gee

officers: 5 brass, staff

Officers and Gentlemen
author: Evelyn Waugh

offices: 4 help 7 service 10 assistance

Office, The (NBC sitcom)
cast: Steve Carell (Michael Scott) Jenna Fischer (Pam Beesly)

Ellie Kemper (Erin Hannon)
John Krasinski (Jim Halpert)
B.J. Novak (Ryan Howard)
Rainn Wilson (Dwight Schrute)
official: 3 CEO, ref 4 boss, exec, OKed, true 5 agent, brass, mayor, valid 6 formal, gerent, lawful, leader, top dog 7 big shot, cleared, correct, manager, marshal, prefect, premier, referee, regular 8 approved, bona fide, director, endorsed, governor, higher-up, licensed, minister, orthodox, rightful, standard, top brass, verified 9 canonical, certified, dignitary, executive, incumbent, president, secretary, treasurer 10 accredited, authorized, bureaucrat, chancellor, conclusive, ex cathedra, legitimate, magistrate, panjandrum, recognized, sanctioned, unarguable, unmistaken
church ~: 5 vicar 6 cleric, deacon, lector, warden 8 minister 9 monsignor
college ~: 4 dean 6 bursar 9 registrar
ender: 3 dom
government ~: 5 envoy 6 legate 8 delegate, diplomat, emissary, minister 10 ambassador
Muslim ~: 3 aga 4 agha, amir, emir 5 ameer, emeer
proceedings: 4 acta
sports ~: 3 ref, ump 5 judge, timer, zebra 6 umpire 7 referee 8 linesman
officiate: 3 run, sit 4 boss 5 chair, emcee, serve 6 direct, govern, handle, manage, umpire 7 command, conduct, oversee, preside, referee
officious: 4 busy, rude 5 bossy, pushy 7 forward 8 impudent, meddling 9 intrusive, obtrusive, pragmatic 10 meddlesome
offing: 6 coming, future 7 by and by 8 imminent 9 impending, potential
be in the ~: 4 loom 6 impend 8 approach, threaten
in the ~: 4 near 6 coming 7 pending 8 imminent
__ of fire: 4 ball, line, zone 5 field 7 baptism
__ of Fire: 4 Ball, Face, Ring 7 Streets
offish: 3 icy 4 cold, cool 5 aloof 6 chilly, frigid, remote 7 distant, glacial, haughty 8 detached, reserved 9 withdrawn 10 antisocial, unfriendly, unsociable
__ of fish: 6 kettle
__ off it!: 4 Come
off-key: 4 flat, sour 5 harsh, sharp 7 deviant, grating, jarring 8 abnormal, jangling, strident 9 anomalous, dissonant, divergent, irregular, out of tune, unmusical, unnatural 10 discordant
__ of Flanders: 4 A Dog
off-limits: 4 tabu 5 taboo 9 forbidden
activity: 4 no-no, tabu 5 taboo
off-load: 4 dump 6 unlade
__ of Flubber: 3 Son
__ of Flying: 4 Fear
off on a __: 7 tangent
Off on a Comet
author: Jules Verne
off one's __: 4 feed 5 guard, hands
__ off one's back, the: 5 shirt
__ off one's feet: 5 sweep
__ of Fools: 4 Ship 5 Chain, Feast
__ of force: 4 line 5 field
__ of fortune: 5 wheel 7 soldier
__ of Four, The: 4 Gang, Sign
off-peak time: 4 lull 5 letup 6 hiatus 8 breather
off-putting: 4 dour, grim, ugly, vile 5 nasty, stern 6 odious, severe, strict 7 hateful, hideous, hostile, noisome, ominous, squalid 8 daunting, menacing, shocking, sinister 9 abhorrent, execrable, loathsome, offensive, repellent, repugnant, repulsive, revolting, unsightly 10 abominable, detestable, disgusting, forbidding, unfriendly, unpleasant
not ~: 4 nice
off-ramp: 4 exit 6 egress
__ of Frankenstein: 3 Son 5 Bride
__ of Freedom: 5 Medal
__ of Friends: 6 Circle 7 Society
off-road vehicle: 3 ATV 4 jeep
offset: 4 undo 5 cover, hedge, repay, stamp 6 cancel, negate, redeem 7 balance, counter, imprint, nullify, recover, redress 8 allow for, equalize, outweigh 9 cancel out, make up for, reimburse 10 compensate, counteract, invalidate, neutralize, recompense
offshoot: 3 arm 4 cion, limb, spur, twig 5 scion 6 branch, colony, result, sprout 7 adjunct, faction, product 9 affiliate, appendage, by-product, outgrowth 10 derivative, descendant
offshore: 4 asea, wind 5 alien, at sea. 7 foreign, oversea 8 overseas
activity: 5 scuba 6 diving
lodging: 5 botel 6 boatel
structure: 3 rig 6 oil rig
offspring: 3 cub, kid, pup, son 4 baby, cion, desc., heir, kids, seed 5 brood, child, issue, kiddy, puppy, scion, spawn, young 6 family, litter 7 bambino, kinfolk, lineage, progeny 8 children, daughter, kinfolks, kinsfolk 9 posterity, successor 10 descendant, generation
of ~: 6 filial
offstage area: 4 wing
__ off steam: 3 let 4 blow
off-target: 4 wide 6 errant
off the __: 3 bat 4 cuff, face, hook, rack, wall 5 books, shelf, track 6 ground, record
off the __ end: 4 deep
off the __ of one's head: 3 top
off the __ path: 6 beaten
__ off the bat: 5 right
Off the Court
author: Arthur Ashe
off-the-cuff: 5 ad-lib 6 casual, improv, vamped 8 informal 9 extempore, impromptu, whipped up 10 unscripted
__ off the handle: 3 fly
__ off the hog: 4 high
__ off the old block: 5 a chip
off-the-rack: 3 RTW
off-the-wall: 3 odd 4 daft, zany 5 batty, dotty, flaky, loopy, manic, nutty, outré, wacky 6 absurd, flakey, insane, way-out, whacky 7 bizarre, comical, oddball 8 peculiar 9 eccentric, illogical 10 irrational, outlandish
Off the Wall (1980 song)
artist: Michael Jackson
__ Off to See the Wizard: 4 We're
__ of Fugue, The: 3 Art
__ of fun: 5 loads 6 barrel
off-white: 4 bone 5 pearl 6 pearly
__ off with: 3 run 4 make, walk
__ of gab: 4 gift
__ of Galilee: 3 Man, Sea
__ of gas: 3 out
__ of Gibraltar: 4 Rock
__ of Gilead: 4 balm
__ of Glory: 5 Blaze, Paths
__ of God: 3 act, man, Son 4 A Man, City, John, Lamb, Word 5 Agnes, house 6 Church, Mother
__ of gold: 3 pot 5 heart
__ of Good Feeling: 3 Era
__ of Good Hope: 4 Cape
__ of goods: 4 bill
...__ of good will: 5 to men
__ of grace: 4 days, year 5 state
__ of gratitude: 4 debt
__ of gravity: 3 law 6 center
__ of Green Gables: 4 Anne
__ of habit: 5 force 6 change
__ of Hammurabi: 4 Code
__ of hand: 3 out 4 note 7 sleight
__ of hands: 4 show
__ of Hazzard, The: 5 Dukes
__ of health: 4 bill 5 board
__ of heart: 6 change
__ of Heaven: 4 Days, rose 5 Gates, Queen
__ of Hercules: 6 labors 7 Pillars
__ of Hiawatha, The: 4 Song
__ of Hoffmann: 5 Tales
__ of Honey, A: 5 Taste
__ of honor: 4 debt, maid, word 5 court, field, guard, guest, point 6 matron
__ of Honor: 3 Men 4 Word 5 Guard, Medal 6 Legion
__ of hope: 3 ray
__ of Hormuz: 6 Strait
Of Human Bondage: 5 novel
author: W. Somerset Maugham
character: 5 Carey, Fanny, Norah 6 Louisa, Nesbit 7 Mildred
__ of human kindness: 4 milk
__ of humor: 5 sense
__ of Id, The: 6 Wizard
__ of Independence: 3 War
__ of industry: 4 czar 7 captain
__ of influence: 6 sphere
__ of iniquity: 3 den
__ of Innocence, The: 3 Age, End
__ of intent: 6 letter
__ of Iron: 3 Man 5 Cross
__-O-Fish: 5 Filet
__ of it?: 4 What
__ of itself: 5 in and
__ of ivy: 5 halls
__ of Iwo Jima: 5 Sands
__ of Japan: 3 Sea
__ of joint: 3 out
__ of Judah: 4 Lion
__ of July: 6 Fourth
__ of justice: 6 scales
__ of Kilimanjaro, The: 5 Snows
__ of kin: 4 next
__ of knowledge: 4 tree
__ of lading: 4 bill
O'Flaherty, Liam: 5 Irish 6 writer
work: The Informer
__ of La Mancha: 3 Man
__ of lamb: 3 leg 4 rack
__ of Lambeth: 4 Liza
__ of Langerhans: 5 islet 6 island, islets 7 islands
__ of Laredo: 7 Streets
__ of laughs: 6 barrel
__ of Laura Mars: 4 Eyes
__ of law: 5 court 6 matter, school
__ of least resistance: 4 path
__ of Lebanon: 6 cedars
__ of Lepanto: 4 Gulf
__ of letters: 3 man 5 woman
__ of Liberty: 4 Sons 6 Statue
__ of life: 4 fact, full, tree, walk 5 prime, slice, staff, wheel 6 elixir 7 quality
__ of Life: 4 Jaws, Love
__ of Light: 3 Ray 4 City 5 Angel
__ of Lights: 5 Feast
__ of Lima: 4 Rose
__ of limitations: 7 statute
__ of line: 3 out
__ of little faith: 3 O ye
__ of living: 4 cost
__ of Living Dangerously, The: 4 Year
__ of Livin' to Do: 4 A Lot
__ of London: 5 Tower 6 Lloyd's
__ of Lords: 5 House
__ of Lots: 5 Feast
__ of love: 5 labor 6 tunnel
__ of Love: 3 Sea 4 Book, Game 5 Glory, Power, Price, Words 6 Chains, Chapel, Cradle, Melody, Priest, Vision 7 Aspects
Of Love and Shadows
author: Isabel Allende
__ of Love, The: 3 Art, Way 4 Look 5 Place, Power, Works 6 Tunnel
__ of Loving, The: 3 Art
__ of luck: 3 out
__ of luxury, the: 3 lap
__ of Macedon: 6 Philip
__ of Magellan: 6 Strait
__ of magnesia: 4 milk
__ of magnitude: 5 order
__ of mail: 4 coat
__ of Malacca: 6 Strait
__ of Malta, The: 3 Jew
__ of Man: 3 Son 4 Isle
__ of manners: 6 comedy
__ of Man, The: 4 Tree 6 Ascent, Rights
__ of many colors: 5 a coat
__ of March: 4 Ides
__ of Marmara: 3 Sea
__ of Me: 3 All
__ of means by no means...: 4 a man
__ of measure: 4 unit
__ of Melos: 5 Venus
__ of Merit: 6 Legion
__ of Mexico: 4 Gulf
Of Mice and Men
author: John Steinbeck
character: 4 Slim 5 Candy, Small 6 Crooks, Curley, George, Lennie, Milton
Of Mice and Men (1992 film)
cast: Alexis Arquette, Sherilyn Fenn, John Malkovich, Gary Sinise
__ of milk: 4 pint 5 quart 6 gallon

__ of milk and honey: 4 land
__ of Miss Jean Brodie, The: 5 Prime
__ of mistaken identity: 5 a case
__ of Money, The: 5 Color
__ of Monte Cristo, The: 3 Son 5 Count
__ of Montreal: 4 Bank
__ of Mormon: 4 Book
__ of Moses: 3 Law
__ of motion: 3 law
__ of mouth: 4 word
__ of Music, The: 5 Sound
__-of-mutton: 3 leg
__ of Myself: 4 Song
__ of nails: 3 bed
__ of Nantes: 5 Edict
__ of Napoleon, The: 3 Age
__ of Nations, The: 6 League, Wealth
__ of nature: 5 freak 7 balance
__ of Naval Operations: 5 Chief
__ of Navarone, The: 4 Guns
__ of nerves: 3 war 6 bundle
__ of New Orleans, The: 4 City 5 Flame 6 Battle
__ of newt: 3 eye
__ of Night, The: 4 Edge
__ of Nod: 4 land
__ of no return: 5 point
__ of nowhere: 3 out
__ of office: 4 oath
__ of Okhotsk: 3 Sea
__ of Olay: 3 Oil
__ of Old Smokey: 5 On Top
__ of Omaha: 6 Mutual
__ of Oman: 4 Gulf
__ of one's brow: 5 sweat
__ of oneself: 4 give
__ of one's existence: 4 bane
__ of one's eye: 5 apple
__ of one's heart: 7 cockles
__ of one's life: 4 time
__ of One's Own: 5 A Room
__ of Opportunity: 4 Land
__ of Orange: 7 William
__ of order: 3 out 5 point, rules
__ of Orléans: 4 Maid
...__ of others: 5 a host
__ of Otranto: 6 Strait
__ of Our Discontent, The: 6 Winter
__ of Our Lives: 4 Days
__ of Ours: 3 One
__ of Our Teeth, The: 4 Skin
__ of Oz: 4 Land 6 Wizard
__ of pace: 6 change
__ of palm: 5 heart
__ of Panama: 4 Gulf 7 Isthmus
__ of pants: 4 pair
__ of paradise: 4 bird 6 grains
__ of Paris: 6 Treaty 7 plaster
__ of parsimony: 3 law
__ of particulars: 4 bill
__ of passage: 4 bird, rite
__ of Passage, The: 6 Plains
__ of Pauline, The: 6 Perils
__ of payments: 7 balance
__ of peace: 4 bird, kiss, pipe
__ of Peace: 6 Prince
__-of-pearl: 6 mother
__ of Penzance, The: 7 Pirates
__ of phase: 3 out
__ of Philadelphia: 7 Streets
__ of Philosophy: 6 Doctor
__ of Picardy: 5 Roses
__ of Pigs: 3 Bay
__ of Pines: 4 Isle
__ of play: 3 out
__ of plenty: 4 horn
__ of plumb: 3 out
__ of pocket: 3 out
__ of Pooh, The: 3 Tao
__ of possibility: 5 realm
__ of pottage: 4 mess
__ of power: 7 balance
__ of Power: 5 Tower
__ of prayer: 5 house
__ of prevention: 5 ounce
__ of prey: 4 bird 5 beast
__ of print: 3 out
__ of promise: 6 breach
__ of proof: 6 burden
__ of purchase: 5 point, proof
__ of Pythias: 7 Knights
__ of Queensberry rules: 7 Marquis
__ of Queens, The: 4 King
__ of Rain, A: 6 Hatful
__ of Ranchipur, The: 5 Rains
__ of Reading Gaol, The: 6 Ballad
__ of Reason: 3 Age
__ of Rebellion: 3 War
__ of reckoning: 3 day
__ of Red Chief, The: 6 Ransom
__ of reference: 5 frame
__ of relativity: 6 theory
__ of Representatives: 5 House
__ of rest: 3 day
__ of Riga: 4 Gulf
__ of right: 4 writ
__ of Rights: 4 Bill
__ of Riley, the: 4 life
__ of Roaring Camp, The: 4 Luck
__ of robins...: 5 A nest
__ of Rome: 6 Church
__ of Rome, The: 5 Pines
__ of roses: 3 bed 5 attar
__ of safety: 6 factor, margin
__ of Saint Agnes: 5 Feast
__ of Saint James's: 5 Court
__ of Saint Lawrence: 4 Gulf
__ of sale: 4 bill 5 point
__ of Salisbury: 4 Earl, John
__ of Samothrace: 4 Nike 7 Victory
__ of Sandwich: 4 Earl
__ of San Francisco, The: 7 Streets
__ of San Luis Rey, The: 6 Bridge
__ of Saros: 4 Gulf
__ of schedule: 5 ahead
__ of Science: 6 Master 8 Bachelor
__ of Scone: 5 Stone
__ of scrimmage: 4 line
__ of season: 3 out
__ of Seven Gables, The: 5 House
__ of Seville, The: 6 Barber
__ of Shalott, The: 4 Lady
__ of Sharon: 4 rose
__ of Sheba: 5 Queen
__ of Sheila, The: 4 Last
__ of Shoals: 5 Isles
__ of shock: 5 state
__ of Siam: 4 Gulf
__ of Sidra: 4 Gulf
__ of siege: 5 state
__ of Siena: 9 Catherine
__ of Sighs: 6 Bridge
__ of sight: 3 out 4 line
__ of significance: 5 level
__ of Silas Lapham, The: 4 Rise
__ of silence: 4 code, cone 5 tower
__ of Silence, The: 6 Sounds
__ of skill: 4 game
__ of Skye: 4 Isle
__ of Sleepy Hollow, The: 6 Legend
__ of sole: 5 filet
__ of Solomon: 4 Odes, Song 6 Wisdom
__ of sorts: 3 out
__ of South Africa: 5 Union
__ of Spain: 4 Lady
__-of-Spain: 4 Port
__ of Species, The: 6 Origin
__ of speech: 4 part 6 figure 7 freedom
__ of Spring, The: 4 Rite
__ of square: 3 out
__ of staff: 5 chief
__ of St. Agnes, The: 3 Eve
__ of star-cross'd lovers: 5 a pair
__ of state: 3 out 4 head, ship 5 chief 7 council
__ of State: 5 O Ship
__ of steel: 6 nerves
__ of Steel: 3 Abs, Man
__ of step: 3 out
__ of Steve, The: 3 Tao
__ of St. James's: 5 Court
__ of St. Louis: 6 Spirit
__ of St. Mark, The: 3 Eve
__ of St. Mary's, The: 5 Bells
__ of stock: 3 out
__ of Stone: 5 Heart 6 Hearts 7 Gardens
__ of straw: 3 man
__ of strength: 4 test 5 tower
__ of students: 4 dean
__ of style: 3 out 5 go out
__ of sublimation: 4 heat
__ of Suez: 4 Gulf 7 Isthmus
__ of sugar: 4 lump
__ of Sulu, The: 6 Sultan
__ of Summer, The: 4 Boys
__ of summons: 4 writ
__ of Sundays: 5 month
__ of sunlight: 3 ray
__ of supervisors: 5 board
__ of Swat: 6 Sultan
__ of symmetry: 4 axis 6 center
__ of sync: 3 out
oft: 4 a lot, much 7 usually 8 commonly 9 generally, regularly 10 frequently, habitually, repeatedly
ender: 5 times
__ of Tabernacles: 5 Feast
__ of Tarsus: 4 Saul
__ of tartar: 5 cream
__ of tea: 3 cup 4 spot
__ of tears: 4 vale
often: 4 a lot, much 6 hourly, mostly 7 usually 9 generally, many a time, quite a bit, regularly 10 frequently, repeatedly
ender: 5 times
often __: 5 as not
__ of Terror: 5 Reign, Tales
__ of Texas..., The: 4 eyes
of the __: 7 essence
of the __ dye: 7 deepest
__ of the Aar: 5 Gorge
__ of the above: 4 none
__ of the absurd: 7 theater, theatre
__ of the action: 5 piece
__ of the American Revolution: 4 Sons 9 Daughters
__ of the Americas: 3 Ave. 6 Avenue
__ of the Ancient Mariner, The: 4 Rime
__ of the Apes: 6 Planet
__ of the Apostles: 4 Acts
__ of the Army: 7 General
__ of the art: 5 state
__ of the arts: 6 patron
__ of the Ball: 5 Belle
__ of the band: 6 leader
__ of the Baskervilles, The: 5 Hound
__ of the Bay, The: 4 Dock
__ of the beast: 4 mark
__ of the big-time spenders: 4 last
of the blackest __: 3 dye
__ of the blue: 3 out
__ of the Blues, The: 5 Birth
__ of the Brave: 4 Home
__ of the bride: 6 father, mother
__ of the Bulge: 6 Battle
__ of the Cat: 4 Year
__ of the Cat People, The: 5 Curse
__ of the Cave Bear, The: 4 Clan
__ of the Census: 6 Bureau
__ of the Century: 4 Sale
__ of the Circus: 4 A Son
__ of the city: 7 freedom
__ of the City: 4 Edge 6 Prince
__ of the Class: 4 Head
__ of the clear blue sky: 3 out
__ of the cloth: 3 man
__ of the community: 6 pillar
__ of the County: 6 Coward
__ of the Covenant: 3 Ark
__ of the crime: 5 scene
__ of the crop: 5 cream
__ of the cross: 3 way 4 sign
...__ of the Crowd, the: 5 Smell
__ of the day: 4 word 5 catch, order 7 officer
__ of the Day, The: 7 Remains
__ of the Deal, The: 3 Art
__ of the deck: 7 officer
of the deepest __: 3 dye
__ of the Desert: 4 Sons 5 Simon
__ of the dog: 4 hair
__ of the Dolls: 6 Valley
__ of the doubt: 7 benefit
__ of the draw: 4 luck
__ of the d'Urbervilles: 4 Tess
...__ of thee: 3 'tis
__ of the earth: 4 ends, salt
Of Thee I Sing: 7 musical
author: George S. Kaufman
composer: George Gershwin, Ira Gershwin
__ of the evening: 5 shank
__ of the Field: 6 Lilies
__ of the Fisherman, The: 5 Shoes
__ of the flame: 6 keeper
__ of the Fleet: 7 Admiral
__ of the Flies, The: 4 Lord
__ of the forest: 4 king
__ of the Fugue, The: 3 Art
__ of the future: 4 wave
__ of the game: 4 name
__ of the Game: 4 Name 5 Rules 6 Master
__ of the Garter: 5 Order
__ of the gods: 4 food 6 nectar
__ of the Golden West: 4 Girl
__ of the Greasepaint..., The: 4 Roar
__ of the guard: 6 yeoman
__ of the Heart: 5 Music 6 Affair, Crimes
__ of the Hesperus, The: 5 Wreck
__ of the hill: 4 king
__ of the Hop: 5 Queen
__ of the hour: 3 man

__ of the Hours: 5 Dance
__ of the house: 3 man 4 lady 5 woman
__ of the House of Usher, The: 4 Fall
__ of the iceberg: 3 tip
__ of the Iguana, The: 5 Night
__ of the Irish: 4 luck
__ of Their Lives, The: 4 Time
__ of Their Own, A: 6 League
__ of the Islands: 4 Song 7 Outcast
__ of the Jackal, The: 3 Day
__ of the Jedi: 6 Return
__ of the jungle: 3 law 4 king
__ of the Jungle: 5 Ramar 6 George
__ of the King: 6 Idylls
__ of the Kings: 6 Valley
__ of the Lake, The: 4 Lady
__ of the Lambs, The: 7 Silence
__ of the land: 3 fat, law, lay
__ of the Last Minstrel, The: 3 Lay
__ of the Light Brigade: 6 Charge
__ of the line: 3 end 4 ship
__-of-the-line: 3 top 6 bottom
__ of the litter: 4 pick
__ of the Lock, The: 4 Rape
__ of the Locust, The: 3 Day
__ of the Lonesome Pine, The: 5 Trail
__ of the Loom: 5 Fruit
__ of the Lost Ark: 7 Raiders
__ of the Magi, The: 4 Gift
__ of the mark: 4 wide
__ of the matter: 5 heart
__ of the Midnight Sun: 4 Land
__-of-the-mill: 3 run
__ of the minds: 7 meeting
__-of-the-mine: 3 run
__ of the Mohicans, The: 4 Last
__ of the moment: 4 heat, spur
__ of the month: 6 flavor
__ of the Moon: 4 Dark 5 A Tour 7 Craters
__ of the morning: 3 top 5 pride
__ of the Morning: 5 Angel, Child
__ of the Native, The: 6 Return
__ of the Needle: 3 Eye
__ of the Nibelung, The: 4 Ring
__ of the Night: 4 Dark, Heat 5 Heart 6 Armies, Middle, Rhythm, Voices
__ of the Night, The: 5 Music, Voice 6 Armies
__ of the Nile: 5 Queen
__ of the Nile, The: 5 Jewel
__ of the Nineties: 5 Belle
__ of the North: 5 Spawn 6 Nanook 7 Emperor
__ of the Opera, The: 7 Phantom
__ of the Pack: 6 Leader
__-of-the-pants: 4 seat
__ of the party: 4 life
__ of the past: 3 out
__ of the peace: 6 breach 7 justice
__ of the People, An: 5 Enemy
__ of the Perverse, The: 3 Imp
__ of the Phoenix: 6 Flight
__ of the Pioneers: 4 Sons
__ of the Plague Year: 7 Journal
__ of the Plainsmen, The: 4 Last
__ of the Potomac: 4 Army
__ of the President, The: 6 Making
__ of the press: 7 freedom
__ of the pudding: 5 proof
__ of the Purple Sage: 6 Riders
__ of the question: 3 out
__ of the realm: 4 coin, peer
__ of the Red Death, The: 6 Masque
__ of the Red Hot Lovers: 4 Last
__ of the Red Hot Mamas: 4 Last
__ of the Rings, The: 4 Lord
__ of the Rising Sun: 4 Land 5 House
__ of the road: 4 rule
__-of-the-road: 6 middle
__ of the Road: 3 End 4 King 5 Kings 6 Middle
__ of the Roses: 4 Wars
__ of the Rose, The: 4 Name
__ of the Round Table: 7 Knights
__ of the running: 3 out
__ of the Sad Cafe, The: 6 Ballad
__ of the Screw, The: 4 Turn
__ of the Sea: 7 Chicken
__ of the Season: 4 Time
__ of These Days: 4 Some
__ of these days, Alice...: 3 One
__ of the Seven Gables, The: 5 House
__ of the sexes: 6 battle
__ of the Sheik: 3 Son
__ of the Shrew, The: 6 Taming
__ of the Sixth Happiness, The: 3 Inn
__ of the Snark, The: 7 Hunting
__ of the South: 4 Song
__ of the South Pacific: 5 Tales
__ of the spheres: 5 music
__ of the Spider Woman: 4 Kiss
__ of the State: 5 Enemy
__ of the Sun: 4 Dark, East 6 Empire, Island, Valley
__ of the Thousand Days: 4 Anne
__ of the Tiger: 3 Eye
__ of the time: 3 all 4 much, some
__ of the Titans: 5 Clash
__ of the tongue: 4 slip
__ of the Toreadors: 5 Waltz
__ of the Town, The: 4 Talk 5 Woman
__ of the trade: 5 tools 6 tricks
__ of the Turtle, The: 5 Voice
__ of the Union: 5 State
__ of the Unknown Soldier: 4 Tomb
__ of the valley: 4 lily
__ of the Vampire: 4 Mark 6 Shadow
__ of the Vanities, The: 7 Bonfire
__ of the walk: 4 cock
__ of the way: 3 out
__ of the Wedding, The: 6 Member
__ of the West: 3 Man 4 Code 6 Hearts
__ of the Western World: 7 Playboy
__ of the Wild, The: 4 Call
__ of the Wind: 6 Colors
__ of the woods: 3 out 4 neck
__ of the Woods: 4 Lake
__ of the woodwork: 3 out
__ of the world: 3 man, map, way 5 on top, state, woman
__ of the World: 3 Top 4 A Map
__ of the Worlds, The: 3 War
__ of the World, The: 3 End 4 Edge 6 Center, Master
__ of the Yankees, The: 5 Pride
__ of the Year: 3 Man 5 Woman 6 Rookie
__ of the zodiac: 4 sign
__ of thieves: 3 den 4 a den 5 a nest
__ of things to come, the: 5 shape
__ of This Earth: 3 Not
__ of this world: 3 out
__ of thorns: 5 crown
__ of thought: 6 school
__ of thousands: 5 a cast
__ of thumb: 4 rule
__ of thunder: 4 clap
__ of Thunder: 4 Days
__ of Tides, The: 6 Prince
__ of time: 5 ahead, sands
Of Time and the River
author: Thomas Wolfe
character: 3 Abe, Ann 4 Gant, Joel 5 Eliza 6 Elinor, Esther, Eugene, Oliver 10 Eugene Gant
__ of Times, The: 4 Best
__ of Time, The: 4 Care 5 March, Sands
__ of Titus: 4 Arch
__ of Tomorrow, The: 5 World
__ of touch: 3 out
__-of-town: 3 out
__-of-Towners, The: 3 Out
__ of trade: 5 board 7 balance
__ of traitors!: 5 A nest
__ of Tralee: 4 Rose
__ of Tranquillity: 3 Sea
__ of tricks: 3 bag
__ of Tripoli: 6 shores
__ of Triumph: 4 Arch
...__ of troubles: 4 a sea
__ of Troy: 5 Helen
__ of trustees: 5 board
__ of truth: 6 moment
ofttimes: 4 much 7 as a rule 9 generally, quite a bit, regularly 10 frequently, habitually, ordinarily, repeatedly
__ of Turin: 6 Shroud
__ of turn: 3 out
__ of Two Cities: 5 A Tale
__ of two evils: 6 lesser
__ of Us All, The: 6 Mother
__ of Usher: 5 House
__ of vantage: 5 coign
__ of venue: 6 change
__ of Venus, The: 5 Delta
__ of view: 5 angle, field, point
__ of vision: 4 line 5 field
__ of vitriol: 3 oil
__ of voice: 4 tone
__ of Wakefield, The: 5 Vicar
__ of Wales: 6 Prince
__ of war: 3 act, law, tug 4 ship 5 sloop, state 6 honors 7 council, theater, theatre
__-of-war: 3 man
__ of War, The: 3 Art 4 Dogs 5 Winds
__ of wax: 4 ball
__ of Wax: 5 House
__ of way: 5 right
__ of Wellington: 4 Duke
__ of whack: 3 out
__ of Wheat: 5 Cream
__ of whole cloth: 3 out
__ of Wight: 4 Isle
__ of wind: 3 bag
__ of Wine and Roses: 4 Days
__ of wintergreen: 3 oil
__ of wisdom: 5 pearl
__ of woe: 4 tale
__ of Women Voters: 6 League
__ of wonder: 5 sense
__ of work: 3 out 5 a lick, piece
__ of worms: 3 can
__ of Worms: 4 Diet
__ of worship: 5 house
__ of Wrath, The: 6 Grapes
__ of yore: 4 days 7 knights
__ of You: 3 All 4 I Beg 7 Because
__ of your beeswax!: 4 None
__ of your business!: 4 None
__ of Your Life: 5 Times
__ of Your Life, The: 4 Time
__ of Your Smile, The: 6 Shadow
__ of You, The: 6 Wonder
__ of Zorro, The: 4 Mark, Mask, Sign
Ogden: 4 city, Nash, town
locale: 4 Utah
__ Ogden Stiers: 5 David
ogee: 4 arch 5 curve
shape: 3 ess
ogive: 3 rib 4 arch 7 molding
Ogives
composer: Erik Satie
Oglala: 5 tribe 6 Indian 7 Amerind
ogle: 3 eye 4 gaup, gawk, gawp, leer, look 5 stare 6 gaze at, goggle, leer at, look at 7 stare at 8 check out 9 flirt with 10 give the eye, make eyes at, rubberneck, scrutinize
ogler: 4 eyer, rake, wolf 5 flirt 6 masher, starer
OGPU, like the: 3 Sov. 6 Soviet 7 Russian
O'Grady: 4 Gail, Lani 5 Rosie 7 Desmond
ogre: 5 brute, demon, devil, fiend, giant, meany, Shrek, troll 6 bad guy, daemon, daimon, meanie, tyrant 7 bugbear, Grendel, monster 8 bogeyman, gargoyle, martinet 9 archfiend, barbarian
ogreish: 4 mean 9 irascible
ogress: 5 harpy, scold, shrew, vixen 6 beldam, virago 8 fishwife, harridan 9 henpecker, termagant, Xanthippe
oh: 3 cry 4 I see
boy: 3 wow 4 whee 5 great, zowie
dear: 4 alas, darn, egad, gosh, heck, my my, pooh 5 alack, egads, fudge, lordy 6 dash it 7 heavens, woe is me 8 goodness
in German: 3 ach
so: 4 very 5 quite 9 extremely 10 remarkably
Oh: 8 Sadaharu
Oh __ can you see...: 3 say
Oh __ Day: 5 Happy
Oh __ Young: 4 Very
Oh! __: 5 Carol 7 Susanna
Oh! __ danced...: 5 how we
Oh, __!: 3 Boy, God, Kay, woe 4 dear, Mama
Oh, __ a Beautiful Mornin': 4 What
Oh, __ Beautiful Mornin': 5 What a
Oh, __ Golden Slippers: 3 Dem
Oh, __ in England...: 4 to be
Oh, __ Woman: 6 Pretty
Oh.
neighbor: 3 Ind., Ken. 4 Penn.
see also Ohio
O'Hair: 7 atheist, Madalyn
O'Hanlon: 6 George 8 Virginia
O'Hara: 3 Kim 4 John, Mary 5 Frank 7 Maureen 8 Scarlett 9 Catherine
estate: 4 Tara
O'Hara, Frank: 4 poet 10 playwright
O'Hara, John: 6 writer
work: Appointment in Samarra
Butterfield 8
Elizabeth Appleton
The Ewings
From the Terrace
Lovey Childs
Pal Joey
A Rage to Live
Ten North Frederick

O'Hara, Mary: 6 writer
work: The Green Grass of Wyoming
My Friend Flicka
O'Hara, Maureen: 7 actress
film: The Black Swan (1942)
How Green Was My Valley (1941)
The Long Gray Line (1955)
McLintock! (1963)
Miracle on 34th Street (1947)
Only the Lonely (1991)
The Parent Trap (1961)
The Quiet Man (1952)
Rio Grande (1950)
O'Hara's Choice
author: Leon Uris
O'Hare: 7 airport
departure: 6 flight
info: 3 arr., ETA, ETD
locale: 3 Chi. 7 Chicago
on luggage tags: 3 ORD
Oh, Boy! (1957 song)
artist: Buddy Holly and the Crickets
Oh, But __: 3 I Do
Oh! Carol (1959 song)
artist: Neil Sedaka
Oh, come on now!: 6 really
O Henry, __ thine eyes!: 3 ope
O. Henry: 5 alias 6 Porter
O'Herlihy: 3 Dan
Oh Father (1989 song)
artist: Madonna
Oh Girl (song)
artist: Chi-Lites, Paul Young
Oh, give __ home: 3 me a
Oh, God! (1977 film)
cast: George Burns, John Denver, Teri Garr, Paul Sorvino
director: Carl Reiner
Oh, Heavenly Dog dog: 5 Benji
Oh Henry: 3 bar 5 candy 8 candy bar 9 chocolate
alternative: *see* candy brand
Oh, How __ to Get Up...: 5 I Hate
Oh, How I Hate to Get Up...
composer: Irving Berlin
O'Higgins: 8 Bernardo
Ohio: 5 river, state
capital: 8 Columbus
city: 3 Ada 4 Avon, Kent, Lima, Stow, Troy 5 Akron, Berea, Green, Mason, Miami, Niles, Parma, Piqua, Solon, Xenia 6 Athens, Canton, Dayton, Dublin, Elyria, Euclid, Hudson, Lorain, Marion, Medina, Mentor, Newark, Oxford, Sidney, Toledo, Warren 7 Ashland, Findlay, Gahanna, Norwood, Wooster 8 Alliance, Boardman, Columbus, Delaware, Eastlake, Fairborn, Hamilton, Hilliard, Lakewood, Sandusky, Trotwood, Westlake 9 Ashtabula, Barberton, Brook Park, Brunswick, Cleveland, Fairfield, Grove City, Kettering, Lancaster, Mansfield, Massillon, Riverside, Whitehall 10 Austintown, Cincinnati, Middletown, Portsmouth, Rocky River, Willoughby, Youngstown, Zanesville
city on the ~: 10 Cincinnati, Pittsburgh
college: 5 Hiram 6 Ashland, Denison, Kenyon, Oberlin, Wooster, Xavier 9 Kent State
conference: 3 MAC
county: 4 Erie 6 Scioto 7 Wyandot
Indian: 4 Erie
neighbor: 7 Indiana, Ontario 8 Kentucky, Michigan
political name: 4 Taft
river to the ~: 5 Miami 6 Scioto, Wabash 8 Kentucky 9 Tennessee 10 Cumberland
state bird: 8 cardinal
state flower: 9 carnation
state fossil: 9 trilobite
state gemstone: 5 flint
state insect: 7 ladybug
state reptile: 5 racer
state tree: 7 buckeye
Ohio Express
song: Chewy Chewy (1968)
Yummy Yummy Yummy (1968)
Ohio State
athletes: 8 Buckeyes
conference: 6 Big Ten
locale: 8 Columbus
Ohio University
athletes: 7 Bobcats
locale: 6 Athens
Oh, Kay!: 7 musical
composer: George Gershwin, Ira Gershwin
Oh, Lady Be Good
composer: George Gershwin, Ira Gershwin
Ohlin, Bertil: 8 Nobelist 9 economist
Oh Lonesome Me (1958 song)
artist: Don Gibson
Oh, Look __ Now: 4 at Me
ohm ender: 5 meter
Ohm, Georg: 6 German 9 physicist
Ohm's __: 3 law
Oh, my __ back!: 6 aching
Oh My My (1974 song)
artist: Ringo Starr
Oh! My Pa-Pa (1953 song)
artist: Eddie Fisher
Ohno: 5 Apolo
Oh no!: 4 darn, drat, rats, yipe 5 yikes, yipes
Oh No (1981 song)
artist: Commodores
Oh, no! Not __!: 5 again
Oholibamah
husband: 4 Esau
__-o-Honey: 3 Bit
Oh, Pretty Woman (1964 song)
artist: Roy Orbison
Ohre: 4 Eger 5 river
locale: 7 Germany
Oh Say Can You Say
author: Dr. Seuss
Oh sure!: 4 As if, I bet
Oh! Susanna: 4 song 6 sitcom
composer: Stephen Foster
instrument: 5 banjo
Oh, Susanna
star: Gale Storm
Oh, the Places You'll Go!
author: Dr. Seuss
Oh, the Thinks You Can Think!
author: Dr. Seuss
Oh to __ England: 4 be in
Oh Very Young (1974 song)
artist: Cat Stevens
Oh! What __ Was Mary: 4 a Pal
Oh, What a Beautiful Mornin': 5 waltz
composer: Oscar Hammerstein, Richard Rodgers
Oh What a Paradise It Seems
author: John Cheever
Oh, what a relief __!: 4 it is
Oh what fun __ to...: 4 it is
...oh where can __?: 4 he be
Oh yeah? response: 6 sez who
Oh, You Beautiful __: 4 Doll
-oid
relative: 3 -ish 4 -like
oil: 3 lub. 4 coal, corn, fuel, lard, lube, tung 5 crude, fluid, lipid, slick, tempt 6 anoint, buy off, canola, canvas, castor, grease, lipide, pomade 7 coconut, lanolin, lantern, picture, unguent, wheedle 8 cocoanut, cod-liver, flattery, kerosene, kerosine, kickback, lanoline, painting 9 black gold, lubricant, lubricate, petroleum, safflower 10 cottonseed, fossil fuel
additive: 3 STP
alternative: 3 gas
aromatic ~: 5 anise 6 bay rum
banana ~: *see* baloney
baron: 5 sheik 6 shaikh, sheikh
boil in ~: 3 fry 5 sauté
burn the midnight ~: 4 cram 5 learn, study
-can letters: 3 SAE
cartel: 4 OPEC
combining form: 3 ole- 4 eleo-, olei-, oleo- 5 elaeo-, elaio-, petro-
company: 3 Oxy 4 Arco, Esso, Gulf, Hess 5 Amoco, Exxon, Getty, Mobil 6 Texaco 7 Chevron
container: 4 lamp 5 cruse 6 barrel
cooking ~: 4 corn 6 canola
cosmetic ~: 6 jojoba
ender: 3 can 4 bird, skin 5 cloth, paper, stone
exporter: 4 Iran, Iraq 5 Katar, Qatar 6 Arabia, Brunei, Kuwait 7 Nigeria 9 Venezuela
flow like an ~ well: 4 gush
holy ~: 6 chrism 7 chrisom
man, perhaps: 5 Texan
name in ~ filters: 4 Fram
need ~: 5 creak, grate 6 squeak, squeal
oil-field ~: 5 crude
painting: 3 art 6 canvas 7 picture 8 portrait 9 still life
part of an ~ lamp: 4 wick 7 chimney
perfume ~: 4 atar, otto 5 athar, attar, nerol, ottar
pour ~ on: 4 calm, ease 5 allay, salve 6 defuse, pacify, smooth, soften, soothe, stroke 7 appease, assuage, mollify, placate, relieve, sweeten 8 calm down 9 alleviate, untrouble 10 conciliate, smooth over
problem: 5 slick, spill
prospect for ~: 5 drill 7 wildcat
rose-scented ~: 5 nerol 6 neroli
sacramental ~: 6 chrism 7 chrisom
source: 3 cod, soy 4 corn, fish, palm, soya, well 5 copra, olive, shale 6 sesame 8 copperah
unit: 2 qt. 3 bbl. 5 quart 6 barrel
varnish ~: 4 tung
well: 6 gusher
oil __: 3 can, pan 4 cake, lamp, meal, palm, sand, well 5 color, field, paint, patch, shale, slick, spill 6 beetle, burner, tanker 7 derrick, gilding, varnish
__ oil: 4 bone, coal, corn, fuel, holy, lamp, lard, oleo, palm, rock, rose, soya, tall, tung 5 anise, crude, lemon, maize, motor, olive, salad, shale, snake 6 banana, castor, diesel, neroli, peanut, sesame, strike, suntan 7 camphor, coconut, linseed, mineral, soybean
Oil __ Boyd: 3 Can
Oil!
author: Upton Sinclair
__ Oil: 4 Gulf 5 Ewing, Mobil
oil and vinegar: 8 dressing
Oil Capital of the World: 5 Tulsa
oilcloth: 4 lino 6 fabric 8 linoleum
oiled: 4 waxy 5 slick, tipsy 6 greasy 8 slippery 9 lubricous
oiler: 4 boat, ship 6 tanker 7 garment
Oilers: 3 six 4 team
home: 8 Edmonton
milieu: 3 ice 4 rink
org.: 3 NHL
rival: *see* hockey team
sport: 6 hockey
oil of __: 4 cade 5 anise 6 cloves 7 vitriol
Oil of __: 4 Olay
oils: 3 art 5 media, paint
oilskin: 4 coat 6 fabric, jacket 7 slicker 8 raincoat
oilstone, use an: 4 hone, whet 7 sharpen
oily: 4 glib, rich, waxy 5 fatty, lardy, sleek, slick, suave 6 creamy, greasy, smarmy, smooth 7 adipose, buttery, coaxing, fawning, fulsome, gushing, servile 8 cajoling, polished, slippery, unctuous 9 adulatory, lubricous, wheedling 10 flattering, lubricious, obsequious
liquid: 5 olein 6 oleine
oinker: 3 hog, pig, sow 5 swine
home: 3 pen, sty 6 pigpen, pigsty
ointment: 4 aloe, balm, nard, ungt. 5 cream, salve 6 balsam, Ben-Gay, cerate, lotion 7 unction, unguent 8 dressing, lenitive, liniment, medicine 9 demulcent, emollient 10 medication
apply ~: 5 rub on
bit of ~: 3 dab
fly in the ~: 3 rub 4 flaw, kink, snag 5 catch, hitch, snafu 6 defect, kicker 7 problem 8 drawback
holder: 4 tube
Oise: 5 river
locale: 6 France 7 Belgium
river to the ~: 5 Aisne
oiseau: 4 bird 6 French
feature: 3 bec 4 aile
'O' Is for Outlaw
author: Sue Grafton
Oistrakh, David: 7 Russian 9 violinist
O.J.: 5 juice 7 Simpson
Ojai: 4 city, town
locale: 10 California
O'Jays
hometown: Canton
song: Back Stabbers (1972)
For the Love of Money (1974)
I Love Music (1975)
Livin' for the Weekend (1976)

Love Train (1973)
Put Your Hands Together (1974)
Use Ta Be My Girl (1978)
Ojibwa: 5 tribe 6 Indian 7 Amerind 8 language
language akin to ~: 4 Cree
OK
see okay, Oklahoma
O.K. __: 6 Corral
Oka: 5 river
city on the ~: 4 Orel
locale: 6 Russia
okay: 3 nod 4 fair, good, jake, nice, pass, safe, sign, so-so 5 admit, adopt, allow, go for, great, leave, legit, licit, moral, noble, say-so, valid, yield 6 accede, accept, aright, assent, comply, decent, enable, kosher, not bad, pass on, permit, proper, ratify, signal 7 agree to, approve, certify, confirm, consent, correct, endorse, ethical, go along, include, indorse, in order, license, mandate, popular, up to par, welcome 8 accredit, accurate, adequate, all right, approval, approved, assent to, as you say, blessing, laudable, middling, notarize, not great, of course, passable, pleasant, pleasing, sanction, say yes to, splendid, stand for, suitable, superior, thumbs up, validate, very well 9 admirable, agreeable, agreement, allowable, authorize, certified, clearance, consent to, excellent, permitted, put up with, recognize, reputable, sign off on, tolerable, undamaged, wonderful 10 acceptable, acceptance, admissible, beneficial, concur with, creditable, give the nod, green light, permission, personable, reasonable, unmistaken
in French: 3 oui
in Spanish: 2 sí
see also of course
O.K. Corral name: Billy Clanton, Ike Clanton, Morgan Earp, Virgil Earp, Wyatt Earp, Doc Holliday
Okeechobee: 4 lake
locale: 7 Florida
O'Keefe: 5 Danny 6 Dennis
O'Keeffe, Georgia: 6 artist 7 painter
spouse: Alfred Stieglitz
Okefenokee: 5 swamp
okey-__: 4 doke 5 dokey
okey-dokey
see okay
Okhotsk: 3 sea 7 current
feeder: 4 Amur
islands: 6 Kurile 8 Sakhalin
locale: 6 Russia
Okinawa: 4 isle 6 island
town: 4 Nago, Naha
Okla.
campus: 3 OSU
football rival: 3 Neb. 4 Nebr.
neighbor: 3 Ark., Kan., Tex. 4 Kans., N. Mex.
once: 3 ter. 4 terr.
Oklahoma: 5 state
Air Force base: 5 Vance
capital: Oklahoma City
city: 3 Ada 4 Enid 5 Altus, Moore, Tulsa, Yukon 6 Duncan, Edmond, El Reno, Lawton, Norman 7 Ardmore, Bethany, Del City, Guthrie, Shawnee 8 Fort Sill, Muskogee 9 Ponca City 10 Stillwater
conference: 9 Big Twelve
fort: 4 Sill
Indian: 3 Kaw, Oto, Sac 4 Otoe, Sauk 5 Caddo, Erick, Kansa, Osage, Ponca, Sayre 6 Pawnee, Quapaw 7 Arapaho, Choctaw, Wichita 8 Arapahoe, Cherokee, Cheyenne, Comanche, Kickapoo, Muskogee, Seminole 9 Chickasaw 10 Chiricahua
neighbor: 5 Texas 6 Kansas 8 Arkansas, Colorado, Missouri 9 New Mexico
pro team: 7 Thunder
range: 6 Ozarks
state animal: 7 buffalo
state beverage: 4 milk
state bird: 10 flycatcher
state fish: 4 bass
state flower: 9 mistletoe
state furbearing animal: 7 raccoon
state game bird: 10 wild turkey
state insect: 8 honeybee
state musical instrument: 6 fiddle
state percussion instrument: 4 drum
state rock: 10 rose quartz
state tree: 6 redbud
Oklahoma __, The: 3 Kid
Oklahoma! (1955 film): 7 musical
cast: Eddie Albert, Gloria Grahame, Shirley Jones, Gordon MacRae, Rod Steiger, James Whitmore
character: 3 Fry, Ike, Jud 4 Cord, Elam, Fred, Slim, Will 5 Curly, Eller 6 Carnes, Gertie, Laurey, Parker 8 Ado Annie, Ali Hakim 9 Aunt Eller
composer: Oscar Hammerstein, Richard Rodgers
producer: 4 Todd
prop: 3 hay 4 bale 6 surrey
Oklahoma City
pro team: 7 Thunder
Oklahoma Crude (1973 film)
cast: Faye Dunaway, John Mills, George C. Scott
Oklahoma State
athletes: 7 Cowboys
conference: 9 Big Twelve
locale: 10 Stillwater
okra: 5 shrub 6 veggie 9 vegetable
dish: 5 gumbo
family: 6 mallow
relative: 5 urena 8 abutilon
Oksana: 5 Baiul
see also Russian
Oktoberfest
need: 3 keg 4 beer, bier, brew, suds, tent 5 lager, stein 7 brewski
tune: 5 polka
Ol' __ River: 3 Man
Ola: 7 Ullsten, Winslow
Olaf: 4 Bull 5 saint 9 Stapledon
Olaf Liljekrans
author: Henrik Ibsen
Olaf's Saga
author: Snorri Sturluson
Olah, George: 7 chemist 8 Nobelist
Olajuwon: 5 Akeem 6 Hakeem
milieu: 5 court
org.: 3 NBA
sport: 10 basketball
__ O'Lakes: 4 Land
Olan: 5 Soule
Oland, Warner: 5 actor
role: Charlie Chan
__-o'-lantern: 4 jack
Olathe: 4 city, town
locale: 6 Kansas
Olay
competitor: 5 Nivea 7 Jergens
__ Olay: 5 Oil of
Olazabal, Jose Maria: 6 golfer
Olbermann: 5 Keith
__ ol' boy: 4 good
old: 4 aged, done, gray, grey, late, once, past, used, worn 5 dated, early, hoary, musty, passé, rusty, stale, tired 6 bygone, démodé, former, fossil, infirm, mature, of yore, rancid, remote, senior 7 ancient, antique, archaic, decayed, elderly, lasting, matured, onetime, quondam, run-down, veteran, vintage, wizened, worn-out 8 decrepit, enduring, familiar, grizzled, hardened, inactive, lifelong, longtime, obsolete, original, outdated, outmoded, out of use, overripe, previous, primeval, seasoned, skillful, sometime, timeworn, well-used 9 crumbling, enfeebled, erstwhile, geriatric, getting on, hackneyed, long-lived, moth-eaten, out-of-date, perennial, perpetual, primaeval, primitive, twice-told, venerable, vestigial 10 aboriginal, antiquated, backnumber, gray-haired, immemorial, inveterate, primordial, threadbare, time-tested, unoriginal
combining form: 4 pale- 5 palae-, paleo-
ender: 4 ster
old __: 3 boy, hat, man 4 Adam, chap, fogy, girl, gold, hand, maid, moon, rose, shoe, tale 5 flame, fogey, guard, money 6 fellow, master, school 7 country
old __ hills: 5 as the
old __ tale: 5 wives'
old-__: 4 line, time 5 timer
old-__ network: 3 boy 4 girl
__-old: 3 age
Old __: 3 Sod, Vic 4 Days, Maid, Miss, Navy, Nick, Stoa, Test., West 5 Delhi, Glory, Spice, World 6 Bailey, Gringo, Yeller 7 Hickory, Scratch
Old __ and the Sea, The: 3 Man
Old __ at Home: 5 Folks
Old __ Bucket, The: 5 Oaken
Old __ Cod: 4 Cape
Old __ Cole: 4 King
Old __, CT: 4 Lyme
Old __ Moon: 5 Devil
Old __, The: 4 Maid 5 Glory, Manse, Songs
Old __ Tray: 3 Dog
__ old age: 4 ripe
old as the __: 5 hills
Old Bailey: 5 bench, court 8 tribunal
Old Black Joe
composer: Stephen Foster
__ Old Black Magic: 4 That
Old Blue __: 4 Eyes
old-boy __: 7 network
__ old boy: 4 good
Old Cape Cod (1957 song)
artist: Patti Page
__, old chap...: 4 I say
old college __, the: 3 try
__ Old Cowhand: 4 I'm an
Old Curiosity Shop, The
author: Charles Dickens
character: 3 Jem, Kit 4 Abel, Davy, Matt, Nell 5 Isaac, Quilp, Sally, Trent 6 Betsey 7 Melissa
Old Days (1975 song)
artist: Chicago
__ old days, the: 4 good
Old Devil __: 4 Moon
Old Devils, The
author: Kingsley Amis
Old Dog Tray
composer: Stephen Foster
Old Dominion: 8 Virginia
__ olde England: 6 merrie
Old El __: 4 Paso
olden: 6 bygone, former 7 ancient, archaic 8 outmoded 10 antiquated, immemorial
days: 4 past, yore 7 history 9 antiquity
in ~ days: 3 ago 4 once, then 6 before 7 earlier, long ago 8 back then, back when, formerly 9 at one time, in the past 10 heretofore, previously
not ~: 3 now 5 fresh, today 6 modern, recent 7 current, just out 8 contempo, up-to-date 10 avant-garde, newfangled, present-day
Oldenbourg, Zoé: 6 French, writer
work: The World Is Not Enough
Old English: 5 Saxon 6 polish
alternative: 6 Behold, Endust, Pledge 10 Liquid Gold
conger: 3 ele
festival: 6 lammas
laborer: 4 esne
letter: 3 edh, eth, wen 4 wynn
money: 3 ora 4 orae
writer: 7 Aelfric
older: 5 elder, first, prior 6 former, senior 7 earlier 9 first-born, preceding
grow ~: 3 age 4 grow 6 mature 7 develop
older but __: 5 wiser
Oldest Living Confederate Widow Tells All
author: Allan Gurganus
Old Faithful: 6 geyser
Old Familiar Faces
poet: Elia
old-fashioned: 3 odd, out 4 dead 5 corny, dated, dowdy, drink, fusty, hoary, moldy, mossy, musty, passé 6 bygone, démodé, quaint, square, stuffy 7 antique, archaic, vintage 8 beverage, cocktail, medieval, obsolete, outdated, outmoded 9 mediaeval, not with it, out-of-date, unstylish 10 antiquated, out of style
get the ~ way: 4 earn
ingredient: 7 bitters, whiskey
one: 4 fogy, marm 5 fogey 6 square
Old Fashioned Love Song, An (1971 song)
artist: Three Dog Night

Oldfield, Barney: 5 racer 9 auto racer
milieu: 5 track
Oldfield, Mike
homeland: England
song: Tubular Bells (1974)
Old Folks at Home
composer: Stephen Foster
river: 6 Swanee
Old Fuss and Feathers: 5 Scott
__ Old Gang of Mine: 4 That
old-girl __: 7 network
Old Glory: 4 flag
Old Glory, The
author: Robert Lowell
old gold: 6 yellow
relative: *see* yellow color
Old Gray __, The: 4 Mare
Old Gringo (1989 film)
cast: Jane Fonda, Gregory Peck, Jimmy Smits
Old Gringo, The
author: Carlos Fuentes
Old Harry: 5 Satan
old-hat: 3 out 5 dowdy, passé 8 obsolete, outdated, outmoded, timeworn 9 out-of-date 10 antiquated
__ Old House: 4 This
oldie: 4 song, tune 6 melody
often: 5 goody 6 goodie
__ oldie: 5 moldy 6 golden
Old Ironsides: 4 boat, ship
author: Oliver Wendell Holmes
Old King __: 4 Cole
old-line: 7 diehard, fogyish 8 mossback
Old Lyme: 4 city, town
locale: 4 Conn.
Old MacDonald
animal: 3 cat, cow, dog, pig 5 horse
refrain: 5 EIEIO
Old MacDonald had __...: 5 a farm
old maid: 4 game 8 card game
__ old man: 5 grand
Old Man and the Sea, The: 4 film 5 novel
author: Ernest Hemingway
cast: Spencer Tracy
character: 7 Manolin 8 Santiago
composer: Dimitri Tiomkin
director: John Sturges
fish: 6 marlin
Old Man Down the Road, The (1985 song)
artist: John Fogerty
Oldman, Gary: 5 actor
film: Air Force One (1997)
Bram Stoker's Dracula (1992)
The Fifth Element (1997)
Immortal Beloved (1994)
JFK (1991)
Lost in Space (1998)
Sid and Nancy (1986)
State of Grace (1990)
True Romance (1993)
film (voice): Quest for Camelot (1998)
spouse: Uma Thurman
Old Manse, The
author: Nathaniel Hawthorne
Old Man's Winter Night, An
poet: Robert Frost
Old Man, Woman and Flower
painter: Max Ernst
__ Old Men: 6 Grumpy
Old Mortality
author: Katherine Anne Porter
oldness: 3 age 5 years 6 dotage 8 lifespan 10 senescence
Old New York
author: Edith Wharton
Old Nick: 5 Satan
Old North __: 6 Church
Old Oaken Bucket, The
artist: Grandma Moses
old one in German: 4 alte
__ Old Party: 5 Grand
Old Patagonian Express, The
author: Paul Theroux
Olds: 3 car 4 auto, city, town 6 Ransom 10 automobile
locale: 6 Canada 7 Alberta
middle name: 3 Eli
old ~: 3 Reo
see also Oldsmobile
old-school: 5 fusty, musty 7 fogyish 8 obsolete
Old Scratch: 5 Devil, Satan
specialty: 4 evil
old sledge: 4 game 8 card game
alias: 5 pitch 7 seven-up 11 high-low-jack
Oldsmobile: 3 car 4 auto
like an ~ of song: 5 merry
model: 5 Alero, Ciera, Delta, Omega 6 Aurora, Calais, Fiesta, Royale 7 Achieva, Bravada, Cutlass, Delmont, Firenza, Holiday, Jetfire, Jetstar 8 Intrigue, Starfire, Toronado 9 Celebrity, Futuramic 10 Silhouette 11 Eighty-Eight, Ninety-Eight
Old Smokey topper: 4 snow
Old Sod, from the: 5 Irish
old soft __, the: 4 shoe
Old Songs, The (1981 song)
artist: Barry Manilow
old-style: 4 late 5 areek, prior 6 bygone, former, whilom 7 earlier, one-time, quondam 8 previous 9 erstwhile, foregoing, preceding
Old Swimmin' Hole, The: 4 poem
author: James Whitcomb Riley
Old Testament
book: 3 Bar., Ezr., Gen., Hab., Hos., Isa., Jer., Job, Lam., Lev., Mac., Mic., Nah., Neh., Num., Psa. 4 Amos, Deut., Eccl., Exod., Ezek., Ezra, Joel, Macc., Obad., Prov., Ruth, Zech. 5 Hosea, Jonah, Kings, Levit., Micah, Nahum 6 Daniel, Eccles., Esther, Exodus, Haggai, Isaiah, Joshua, Judges, Psalms, Samuel 7 Ezekiel, Genesis, Malachi, Numbers, Obadiah 8 Habakkuk, Jeremiah, Nehemiah, Proverbs 9 Leviticus, Zechariah, Zephaniah 10 Chronicles 11 Deuteronomy
city: 4 Lehi 5 Babel, Sodom
judge: 3 Eli
kingdom: 4 Aram, Edom 5 Sheba
mountain: 4 Nebo 5 Sinai
patriarch: 4 Enos 5 Isaac 7 Abraham
tower: 5 Babel
verb: 5 begat, beget, smite
see also Bible
old-time: 4 past 5 passé 6 bygone, former, quaint 7 quondam 8 outmoded, previous 9 erstwhile, graybeard
old-timer: 3 vet 6 senior 7 veteran
Old Time Rock & Roll (1989 song)
artist: Bob Seger
Old Times
author: Harold Pinter
Old Time Saloon, The
author: George Ade
Oldtown Folks
author: Harriet Beecher Stowe
Old Uncle __: 3 Ned
Olduvai Gorge
locale: 6 Africa 8 Tanzania
Old Vic city: 6 London
Old West
conveyance: 3 nag 4 mare, pony 5 bronc, horse, mount, stage, wagon 6 bronco, cayuse, equine 7 gelding, mustang 8 stallion 10 stagecoach
walk in the ~: 4 poke 5 amble, drift, mosey
warrior: 6 Apache, Paiute
weapon of the ~: 4 Colt 5 rifle
oldwife: 4 fish
old wives' __: 4 tale
Old Wives' Tale, The
author: George Peele
character: 5 Delia
Old Yeller (1957 film)
cast: Tommy Kirk, Dorothy McGuire, Fess Parker
Ole: 4 Bull 5 Olsen 7 Rölvaag
Ole __: 4 Miss
Olé!: 3 cry, rah
accompaniment: 4 clap
oleaceous tree: 3 ash 5 olive
oleaginous: 4 oily 5 lardy, slick 6 greasy 8 slippery, unctuous 9 lubricous
Olean: 4 city, town
locale: 7 New York
oleander: 5 plant, shrub 6 flower
relative: 7 dogbane, karanda 10 frangipani
oleaster: 4 tree 5 shrub
oleate: 5 ester
__ ole boy: 4 good
Ole Buttermilk __: 3 Sky
olecranon: 4 bone, ulna
locale: 3 arm 7 forearm
Oleg: 7 Cassini
__ Ole Man: 6 Little
Ole Miss student: 5 Rebel
olent: 7 scented 8 aromatic, fragrant
oleo: 6 spread 9 margarine
holder: 3 tub
in Britain: 5 marge
serving: 3 pat
__ Ole Opry: 5 Grand
oleoresin: 5 elemi
Olerud, John
sport: 8 baseball
Olesha, Yury: 6 writer 7 Russian
Olestra
lack: 3 fat
org. that approved ~: 3 FDA
Oleta: 5 Adams
olfactory: 7 odorous, sensory 9 sensorial
organ: 4 nose 5 snoot, snout 7 schnozz 9 proboscis 10 schnozzola
stimulus: 4 odor, reek 5 aroma, smell, stink
Olga: 5 James 6 Korbut 9 Baclanova
sister in Chekhov: 5 Irina
olid: 4 rank 5 fetid 6 foetid, smelly, stinky 10 malodorous
oligarch: 5 ruler 6 gerent
oligarchic group: 4 bloc, ring 5 junta 7 council 9 coalition
Oligocene preceder: 6 Eocene
Olimpiade
composer: Thomas Arne
Olin: 3 Ken 4 Lena 5 Dutra
Olin, Ken: 5 actor
spouse: Patricia Wettig
Olin, Lena: 7 actress
film: Chocolat (2000)
Enemies, A Love Story (1989)
Havana (1990)
Polish Wedding (1998)
The Unbearable Lightness of Being (1988)
olio: 5 blend 6 jumble, medley 7 collage, mélange 8 mishmash, mixed bag, pastiche 9 pasticcio, patchwork, potpourri 10 assortment, crazy quilt, hodgepodge, miscellany, salmagundi
Oliphant: 3 Pat
Oliva, Tony
sport: 8 baseball
olive: 3 tan 4 tree 5 color, fruit, green 6 veggie 8 brownish 9 evergreen, vegetable, yellowish
branch: 5 truce 7 amnesty 9 armistice, cease-fire 10 moratorium
drab: 4 garb 5 dress, khaki 6 attire 7 uniform
family shrub: 5 lilac 7 jasmine 9 forsythia, jessamine
genus: 4 olea
product: 3 oil
relative: *see* green color
tree cousin: 3 ash
olive __: 3 oil 4 drab 5 drabs, green 6 branch
__ olive: 5 black
Olive: 3 Oyl 9 Schreiner
Olive Oyl's parent: 4 Cole, Nana
Oliver: 3 cat 4 Reed 5 Evans, Hardy, North, Perry, Platt, Sacks, Stone, Susan, Twist 7 Edna May, La Farge 8 Cromwell 9 Goldsmith
partner: 4 Stan
song: Good Morning Starshine (1969)
Jean (1969)
Oliver __ Holmes: 7 Wendell
Oliver __ Perry: 6 Hazard
Oliver! (1968 film)
cast: Ron Moody, Oliver Reed, Shani Wallis
director: Carol Reed
Oliver & Company
cat: 6 Oliver
dog: 4 Rita, Tito 6 DeSoto, Dodger, Roscoe 7 Francis 8 Einstein
Oliver's Story
author: Erich Segal
Oliver Twist
author: Charles Dickens
character: 4 Bill, Fang, Jack, Mann, Noah, Rose, Toby 5 Bates, Fagin, Harry, Monks, Nancy, Sally, Sikes 6 Bedwin, Bumble, Corney, Dodger, Edward, Maylie 7 Charley, Crackit, Dawkins, Grimwig,

Leeford **8** Brownlow, Claypole, Losberne **9** Charlotte **10** Sowerberry
dog: 8 Bull's-eye
Oliver Wendell __: 6 Holmes
Olivia: 4 d'Abo **6** Hussey **10** Newton-John **11** de Havilland
Olivier: 8 Laurence, Messiaen
emulate ~: 3 act
Olivier, Laurence: 3 Sir **4** Lord **5** actor
film: As You Like It (1936)
The Beggar's Opera (1953)
The Betsy (1978)
The Bounty (1984)
Dance of Death (1968)
The Demi-Paradise (1943)
The Devil's Disciple (1959)
The Entertainer (1960)
Hamlet (1948, AA)
Henry V (1945)
A Little Romance (1979)
Marathon Man (1976)
Othello (1965)
Pride and Prejudice (1940)
Rebecca (1940)
Richard III (1955)
Sleuth (1972)
Spartacus (1960)
That Hamilton Woman (1941)
Three Sisters (1970)
Wuthering Heights (1939)
spouse: Vivien Leigh, Joan Plowright
olivine: 7 mineral **10** chrysolite
transparent green ~ gem: 7 peridot
olla podrida: 4 olio, stew **5** blend **6** jumble, medley **7** collage, farrago, mélange **8** mishmash, mixed bag, pastiche **9** pasticcio, patchwork, potpourri **10** assortment, crazy quilt, hodgepodge, miscellany, salmagundi
Ollie: 5 Hardy, North **6** Matson
friend: 4 Fran, Stan **5** Kukla
Olly olly __ free!: 4 oxen
olm: 9 amphibian **10** salamander
Ol' Man __: 4 Mose
Ol' Man River
composer: Oscar Hammerstein, Jerome Kern
Olmec descendant: 4 Maya
Olmert: 4 Ehud
Olmos, Edward James: 5 actor
film: The Ballad of Gregorio Cortez (1983)
Blade Runner (1982)
My Family/Mi Familia (1995)
Selena (1997)
Stand and Deliver (1987)
Triumph of the Spirit (1989)
Wolfen (1981)
The Wonderful Ice Cream Suit (1999)
Zoot Suit (1981)
spouse: Lorraine Bracco
TV: Battlestar Galactica, Miami Vice
Olmsted, Frederick: 9 architect
Olof: 5 Palme
ology: 7 science
olor: 4 swan
olpe: 3 jug **4** ewer **6** carafe, flagon, vessel **9** container
Olsen: 3 Mrs., Ole **5** Jimmy, Susan **6** Ashley, Merlin, Tillie **8** Mary-Kate
coworker: 4 Kent, Lane **5** White
Olsen, Merlin
sport: 8 football
Olson: 4 Lute **5** Nancy **7** Charles
Olson, Charles: 4 poet
work: The Maximus Poems
Olson, Charles work: The Maximus Poems
Olson, Lute: 5 coach
milieu: 5 court
org.: 3 NBA
sport: 10 basketball
Olympia: 4 city, nude, town **5** Snowe **7** Dukakis
artist: Édouard Manet
county: 8 Thurston
locale: 10 Washington
rival: *see* beer
Olympia (1936 film)
director: Leni Riefenstahl
Olympian: 4 Ares, Hera, Zeus **5** Greek **6** Apollo
matchmaker: 4 Eros
troublemaker: 4 Eris
what an ~ breathed: 6 aether
Olympic: 4 park
locale: 10 Washington
Olympic __: 5 Games **7** Village
Olympics
ceremony song: 6 anthem
chant: 3 USA **6** USA USA
event: 4 dash, épée, race **5** event, relay **6** boxing, discus, hammer **7** fencing, javelin, shot put **8** marathon
first ~ site: 4 Elis
gear: 4 disc, disk, épée, shot **5** saber, scull **7** javelin
Jr. ~ sponsor: 3 AAU
L.A. ~ boycotter: 4 USSR
perfection: 3 ten
quest: 4 gold **5** medal
race unit: 5 meter
regulatory gp.: 3 IOC
site: 5 venue
symbol: 5 flame, torch
__ Olympics: 6 Junior, Summer, Winter **7** Special
Olympics sites (Summer):
2016 - Rio de Janeiro, Brazil
2012 - London, England
2008 - Beijing, China
2004 - Athens, Greece
2000 - Sydney, Australia
1996 - Atlanta, Georgia
1992 - Barcelona, Spain
1988 - Seoul, South Korea
1984 - Los Angeles, USA
1980 - Moscow, USSR
1976 - Montreal, Canada
1972 - Munich, West Germany
1968 - Mexico City, Mexico
1964 - Tokyo, Japan
1960 - Rome, Italy
1956 - Melbourne, Australia
1952 - Helsinki, Finland
1948 - London, England
1936 - Berlin, Germany
1932 - Los Angeles, USA
1928 - Amsterdam, Holland
1924 - Paris, France
1920 - Antwerp, Belgium
1912 - Stockholm, Sweden
1908 - London, England
1904 - St. Louis, USA
1900 - Paris, France
1896 - Athens, Greece
Olympics sites (Winter):
2014 - Sochi, Russia
2010 - Vancouver, Canada
2006 - Turin, Italy
2002 - Salt Lake City, USA
1998 - Nagano, Japan
1994 - Lillehammer, Norway
1992 - Albertville, France
1988 - Calgary, Canada
1984 - Sarajevo, Yugoslavia
1980 - Lake Placid, USA
1976 - Innsbruck, Austria
1972 - Sapporo, Japan
1968 - Grenoble, France
1964 - Innsbruck, Austria
1960 - Squaw Valley, USA
1956 - Cortina d'Ampezzo, Italy
1952 - Oslo, Norway
1948 - St. Moritz, Switzerland
1936 - Garmisch, Germany
1932 - Lake Placid, USA
1928 - St. Moritz, Switzerland
1924 - Chamonix, France
Olympics stars (Summer)
1912: 6 Thorpe
1920: 5 Nurmi
1924: 5 Nurmi
1932: 6 Crabbe
1936: 5 Owens
1948: 7 Mathias
1952: 7 Mathias, Zátopek **8** Richards
1956: 6 Fraser, Oerter **8** Richards
1960: 6 Bikila, Fraser, Oerter **7** Johnson, Rudolph
1964: 4 Tyus **5** Hayes **6** Bikila, Brumel, Fraser, Oerter
1968: 4 Tyus **5** Keino **6** Beamon, Oerter, Toomey **7** Fosbury, Seagren
1972: 5 Gould, Spitz **6** Korbut **7** Shorter
1976: 5 Ender **6** Jenner **8** Comaneci
1980: 3 Coe **5** Ovett
1984: 3 Coe **5** Lewis **6** Benoit, Retton **7** Ashford **8** Louganis
1988: 4 Otto **5** Bubka, Evans, Flo-Jo, Lewis **6** Biondi **8** Louganis
1992: 5 Evans, Lewis **6** Devers
1996: 5 Dyken, Lewis **6** Devers
2004: 6 Holmes, Phelps
2008: 4 Bolt **6** Phelps
Olympics stars (Winter)
1928: 5 Henie
1932: 5 Henie
1936: 5 Henie
1948: 6 Button
1952: 6 Button
1956: 8 Albright
1960: 5 Heiss
1968: 5 Killy **7** Fleming
1976: 6 Hamill **7** Klammer
1980: 4 Enke **6** Heiden **7** Cousins
1984: 4 Enke, Witt **5** Mahre **8** Hamilton
1988: 4 Witt **5** Tomba **7** Boitano
1992: 5 Blair, Tomba **9** Yamaguchi
1994: 3 Moe **5** Baiul, Blair
1998: 5 Kulik **6** Street **8** Lipinski
2002: 6 Hughes
2006: 6 Pärson
2010: 4 Vonn
Olympus: 4 peak **5** mount **6** camera **8** mountain
alternative: *see* camera
locale: 6 Europe, Greece
neighbor: 4 Ossa
resident: 3 god
sight from ~: 5 Egean **6** Aegean
see also Olympian
Olyphant: 7 Timothy
om: 6 mantra **7** mantram
Omaha: 4 city, town **5** tribe **6** Indian **7** Amerind
athletes: 8 Bluejays
county: 7 Douglas
home: 4 tipi **5** tepee **6** teepee
institution: 8 Boys Town
locale: 3 Neb. **4** Nebr. **8** Nebraska
river: 8 Missouri
school: 9 Creighton
Oman: 4 gulf **6** nation **7** country **9** sultanate
capital: 6 Muscat
coin: 5 baisa, baiza
group: 10 Arab League
locale: 6 Arabia
money: 4 rial
neighbor: 3 UAE **5** Saudi, Yemen
resident: 4 Arab
title: 4 amir, emir **5** ameer, emeer
Omani: 4 Arab
Omar: 4 Epps **6** Sharif **7** Bradley, Gooding, Khayyám **8** Torrijos
grandfather: 4 Esau
Omar Khayyám: 4 poet **7** Persian **9** tentmaker **10** astronomer
work: Rubáiyát
Omarr: 6 Sydney
omber: 4 game **8** card game
alias: 6 hombre
variety: 9 quadrille
ombrophobe fear: 4 rain
ombu: 4 tree
'ome: 4 'ouse
O'Meara, Mark: 6 golfer
omega: 3 end **4** last **5** Greek **6** ending, letter
counterpart: 3 zee
in physics: 3 ohm
opposite: 5 alpha
preceder: 3 psi
Omega: 3 car **4** auto, Olds, Opel **5** watch **10** automobile, Oldsmobile, wristwatch
alternative: *see* wristwatch
omega-3 __ acid: 5 fatty
O Mein __: 4 Papa
omelet: 8 frittata
cooker: 3 pan **5** grill **7** skillet
ingredient: 3 egg, ham **4** yolk **5** onion **6** cheese
__ omelet: 6 Denver **7** Spanish, western
omen: 4 sign **5** augur, token **6** augury, herald, signal, threat **7** auspice, bad sign, portent, presage, promise, warning **8** black cat, foreshow **9** foretoken, harbinger, indicator, predictor **10** foreboding, indication, prediction
be an ~ of: 4 bode, mean **5** augur **6** herald **7** betoken, point to, portend, presage, promise, signify **8** foreshow, foretell, indicate, prophesy **9** foretoken **10** foreshadow
good ~: 7 promise
interpreter: 4 seer **5** augur **6** auspex, shaman
Omen, The (2006 film)
cast: Mia Farrow, Liev Schreiber, Julia Stiles

Omerta
author: Mario Puzo
omicron: **5** Greek **6** letter
follower: **2** pi
preceder: **2** xi
Omigosh!: **4** egad, yipe **5** egads, yikes, yipes
ominous: **4** dark, dire, grim, ugly **5** black, grave **6** creepy, dismal, doomed, gloomy, spooky **7** baleful, baneful, fateful, fearful, hostile, malefic, unlucky, warning **8** ill-fated, lowering, menacing, minatory, perilous, sinister **9** dangerous, frightful, ill-boding, impending, monstrous, prophetic **10** forbidding, foreboding, out of joint, portentous
sound: **4** toll **5** knell
O mio babbino __: **4** caro
omission: **3** gap **4** lack, miss, skip, slip **5** blank, break, error, lapse, space **6** hiatus, lacuna **7** absence, default, elision, mistake, neglect **9** disregard, exception, exclusion, oversight
omit: **3** cut **4** drop, edit, jump, miss, shun, skip **5** avoid, elide, leave, let go **6** bypass, cut out, delete, except, forget, go past, ignore, pass up, slight **7** discard, dismiss, exclude, forbear, mistake, neglect, scissor **8** count out, leave off, leave out, let slide, overlook, pass over, preclude **9** disregard, eliminate, gloss over
in fast-food lingo: **4** hold
prefix: **3** for-
omitted: **6** absent **7** missing **9** forgotten
omitting: **3** bar **4** save **6** except **9** except for
none: **3** all **4** full **5** fully **6** entire, wholly **7** totally **8** complete, entirely, everyone **9** everybody **10** completely, everything
not ~: **4** incl., with **9** including
__ omnes: **6** exeunt
omni
ender: **3** bus **4** vore **6** potent
Omni: **3** car **4** auto **5** arena, Dodge, hotel **10** automobile
alternative: *see* automobile, hotel
omnia __ amor: **6** vincit
__ omnia vincit: **5** labor
omnibus: **4** book, tome, work **6** volume **10** compendium, cyclopedia
omnifarious: **5** mixed **6** divers, sundry, unlike, varied **7** diverse, unalike, various **8** assorted, distinct, manifold **9** different, disparate **10** dissimilar
omnipotent: **6** divine, mighty **7** godlike **8** almighty, powerful
omnipresent: **6** divine **8** almighty **9** pervasive, universal, worldwide
omniscient: **4** wise **6** divine **7** all-wise, learned **8** almighty **9** all-seeing **10** all-knowing, infallible
omnium-gatherum: **4** olio **6** medley **7** grab bag, mélange, mixture **8** mishmash, pastiche **9** pasticcio, potpourri **10** hodgepodge, miscellany
omnivore: **4** bear, goat **6** eat-all
omnivorous: **8** ravenous **9** insatiate, voracious **10** gluttonous
Omoo: **5** novel **7** romance
author: Herman Melville
dog: **9** Boatswain
__-o'-mountain: **3** cat
omphalos: **5** navel **9** umbilicus
omphaloskepsis
find: **4** lint
focus: **5** navel
Omri
son: **4** Ahab
Omsk: **4** city, port, town
locale: **6** Russia
river: **6** Irtysh
__-o'-mutton: **3** leg
__ o' My Heart: **3** Peg
O, my luve is like __...: **4** a red
__-o'-my-thumb: **3** hop
on: **3** lit **4** as of, atop, near, over, upon **5** about, above, along, forth **6** aboard, airing **7** ahead of, close to, forward **8** adjacent, covering, touching **9** astraddle, supported
prefix: **3** epi-
on __: **3** end, ice, tap, top **4** call, deck, duty, edge, file, fire, hand, high, hold, line, spec, time, view **5** a dare, a diet, a lark, and on, a roll, a tear, a whim, draft, earth, order, paper, sight, the go, top of, trial **6** a leash, a spree, demand, report, stream, strike, target, tiptoe **7** balance, purpose, request, standby
on __ and a prayer: **5** a wing
on __ and needles: **4** pins
on __ ear: **3** its
on __ fours: **3** all
on __ knee: **6** bended
on __ of: **3** top **4** pain **6** behalf **7** account
on __ of the world: **3** top
on __-to-know basis: **5** a need
on __ with: **4** a par
on-__: **3** air, dit **4** line, mike, peak, ramp, seam, site **5** board, glide, stage **6** camera, limits, record, screen, season, stream
on-__ catalog: **4** line
__ on: **3** big, egg, get, has, hit, lay, let, log, mid, pin, put, rat, run, sit, spy, try **4** bear, dote, down, draw, fall, goof, hand, hang, harp, have, hold, jump, lead, lean, lock, look, move, pick, play, push, rely, sail, sign, sold, spur, step, take, trod, turn, wait, work **5** and so, bring, build, carry, catch, check, count, dwell, early, key in, let in, on and, pitch, stand, sweet, touch, trade **6** chance, figure, freeze, switch **7** bargain, reflect
__-on: **3** add **4** come, dead, head, odds, slip **5** blush, brush **6** goings, hanger
On __: **5** My Own **7** Liberty, Nothing
On __ Blindness: **3** His
On __ Boat to China: **5** a Slow
On __ Majesty's Secret Service: **3** Her
On __ of Old Smokey: **3** Top
On __ Pond: **6** Golden
On __ Toes: **4** Your
On __ Zebra: **6** Beyond
__ On: **4** Hold, Rave, Rock **5** Dream, Float, Get It
__ on 34th Street: **7** Miracle
on a __: **4** dare, lark, roll, tear, whim **5** hunch, spree **6** string **7** rampage
on a __ basis: **5** trial
on a __ budget: **5** tight
on a __ errand: **5** fool's
on a __-name basis: **5** first
on a __ notice: **7** moment's
on a __ of one to ten: **5** scale
on a __ platter: **6** silver
on a __-to-know basis: **4** need
Ona: **6** Munson
On a __ Day...: **5** Clear
__ on a bet!: **3** not
On a Clear Day You Can See Forever (1970 film)
cast: Larry Blyden, Yves Montand, Bob Newhart, Barbra Streisand
director: Vincente Minnelli
__ on a dime: **4** stop
__ on a Feeling: **6** Hooked
on a first-__ basis: **4** name
on a fool's __: **6** errand
on-again, off-again: **6** spotty **8** periodic, sporadic **9** spasmodic **10** sporadical
onager: **3** ass **6** donkey, equine **7** jackass
relative: *see* equine
On Aggression
author: Konrad Lorenz
__ on a Grecian Urn: **3** Ode
__ on a Happy Face: **3** Put
__ on a high note: **3** end
__ on a Hot Tin Roof: **3** Cat
__ on air: **4** walk **7** walking
on-air personality: **2** DJ **6** deejay
__ on airs: **3** put
__ on a Jet Plane: **7** Leaving
__ on a limb: **3** out
on all __: **5** fours
__ on a Match: **5** Three
on a moment's __: **6** notice
on an __: **7** average, impulse, upswing
on an __ keel: **4** even
on an __ of mercy: **6** errand
__ on an act: **3** put
on-and-off: **6** random, spotty **7** erratic **8** periodic **9** irregular, spasmodic
device: **3** tap **5** valve **6** faucet, spigot, switch **7** hydrant
On and On (song)
artist: Stephen Bishop, Gladys Knight and the Pips
on a need-to-__ basis: **4** know
on an even __: **4** keel
__ on a Rooftop: **4** Love
on a scale of __ to ten: **3** one
on a silver __: **7** platter
Onassis: **3** Ari **8** Cristina **9** Aristotle, Christina **10** Jacqueline
__ on a String: **3** Man **6** Puppet
__ on a tangent: **3** off
__ on a true story: **5** based
...__ on a tuffet...: **3** sat
...on a wing __ prayer: **4** and a
__ on a Wire: **4** Bird
__-on baggage: **5** carry
__ on Bald Mountain, A: **5** Night
__ on balls: **4** base
on bended __: **4** knee
On Bended Knee (1994 song)
artist: Boyz II Men
On Beyond Zebra
author: Dr. Seuss
On Boxing
author: Joyce Carol Oates
On Broadway (song)
artist: George Benson, Drifters
__ On By: **4** Walk
once: **3** old **4** erst, late, past **6** before, bygone, erenow, whilom **7** ages ago, already, earlier, long ago, quondam, time was, way back **8** as soon as, back then, back when, formerly, sometime, until now, years ago **9** a while ago, erstwhile, in the past **10** back in time, heretofore, previously
once __: **4** a day **5** a week, a year
once __ a time: **4** upon
once __ blue moon: **3** in a
once __ lightly: **4** over
once __ twice shy: **6** bitten
once __ while: **3** in a
once-__: **4** over
once-__-lightly: **4** over
__ once: **5** all at
Once __ a Mattress: **4** Upon
Once __ a midnight...: **4** upon
Once __ a time...: **4** upon
Once __ Enough: **5** Is Not
Once __ Lifetime: **3** in a
Once __ Pacific: **5** by the
once and __ all: **3** for
Once and __ King, The: **6** Future
Once and Future King, The
author: T.H. White
Once a Thief (1950 film)
cast: June Havoc
once-a-year: **6** annual **8** periodic
Once by the Pacific
author: Robert Frost
once in __ moon: **5** a blue
once in a __: **5** while
Once in a Lifetime
author: Moss Hart, George S. Kaufman, Danielle Steel
__ once in a while: **5** every
Once in Love With __: **3** Amy
__ Once in My Life: **3** For **4** Just
once more: **4** anew **5** again
Once more unto the __: **6** breach
once, not even: **4** ne'er **5** never
once over __: **7** lightly
once-over: **4** look **6** gander, regard **10** inspection
give the ~: **3** eye **4** ogle, peek, scan, skim **7** inspect **8** check out
once upon __: **5** a time
Once Upon a Crime (1992 film)
cast: James Belushi, John Candy, Cybill Shepherd, Sean Young
director: Eugene Levy
Once Upon a Mattress prop: **3** pea
once upon a time: **3** ago
Once Upon a Time in America (1984 film)
cast: Robert De Niro, Elizabeth McGovern, Tuesday Weld, James Woods
director: Sergio Leone
Once Upon a Time in the West (1968 film)
cast: Charles Bronson, Claudia Cardinale, Henry Fonda, Jason Robards
director: Sergio Leone
__ once was a man...: **5** There
Once You Get Started (1975 song)
artist: Chaka Khan
oncle: **5** uncle **6** French
brother: **4** père
wife: **5** tante
__ Oncle: **3** Mon

oncoming: **5** ahead **7** looming, nearing **8** expected, imminent **9** advancing, impending, onrushing
__ on Criticism, An: **5** Essay
__ on deaf ears: **4** fall
__ on delivery: **4** cash **7** collect
__ On Down the Road: **4** Ease
one: **3** ace, odd **4** buck, folk, lone, only, sole, unit **5** monad, whole **6** dollar, number, person, single, unique, united **7** pronoun, unified, wee hour **8** separate, singular, solitary, somebody, together **9** connected, undivided **10** dollar bill, individual
  and only: **4** lone, sole
  at least ~: **3** any **4** some
  combining form: **3** mon-, uni- **4** heno-, mono-
  ender: **4** self
  in French: **2** un **3** une
  in German: **3** ein **4** eins
  in Italian: **3** uno
  in Japanese: **4** ichi
  in Latin: **3** una
  in Scottish: **3** ane
  in Spanish: **3** una, uno
  starter: **3** any **4** some **5** every
  to Mohs: **4** talc
one __: **4** o' cat **5** to ten **7** another
one __ at a time: **3** day **4** step **5** thing
one __ customer: **3** to a
one __ fits all: **4** size
one __ kind: **3** of a
one __ million: **3** in a
one __ or the other: **3** way
one __ other: **5** or the
one __ the books: **3** for
one __ the road: **3** for
one __ time: **3** at a
one __ two..., A: **4** and a
one-__: **4** a-cat, many, shot, spot, star, step, time **5** acter, liner, piece, sided, track **6** bagger, eighty, handed, reeler, suiter **7** worlder
one-__ band: **3** man
one-__ bandit: **5** armed
one-__ chance: **5** in-ten
one-__ deal: **4** shot
one-__ hit: **4** base
one-__ mind: **5** track
one-__ play: **3** act
one-__ punch: **3** two
one-__ shopping: **4** stop
one-__ show: **3** man **5** woman
one-__ street: **3** way
one-__ town: **5** horse
__ one: **3** big, day **4** cold, fast, long, not a, tall **5** admit, loved, nary a, young **6** number, square
__-one: **4** many **5** all-in, ten-to
One (song)
  artist: Backstreet Boys, Bee Gees, Elton John, Three Dog Night, U2
One __ Apple: **3** Bad
One __ at a Time: **3** Day
One __ a Time: **5** Day at
One __ Baby: **5** for My
One __ Bell to Answer: **4** Less
One __ Beyond: **4** Step
One __ Chance: **4** More
One __ Day: **4** Fine **5** Sweet
One __ Family: **4** Man's
One __ in the Tropics: **5** Night
One __ in Time: **6** Moment
One __ Jump: **6** O'Clock
One __ land...: **4** if by
One __ Mind: **5** Track
One __ Move: **5** False
One __ My Baby: **3** for
One __ Night: **4** More **6** Lonely, Summer
One __ of Venus: **5** Touch
One __ or two?: **4** lump
One __ Over the Cuckoo's Nest: **4** Flew
One __ Photo: **4** Hour
One __, The: **5** I Love
One __ the Heart: **4** From
One __ to Live: **4** Life
One, __, Three: **3** Two
One-__ Jacks: **4** Eyed
One-__ vitamins: **4** a-Day
__ One: **3** Act **4** Bank, Holy, Wild **5** Fiber, One on
one-a-__: **3** cat
one-acter: **4** play
O'Neal: **4** Ryan, Shaq **5** Tatum **7** Patrick **9** Shaquille
O'Neal, Ryan: **5** actor
  film: Barry Lyndon (1975)
    Chances Are (1989)
    The Driver (1978)
    Irreconcilable Differences (1984)
    Love Story (1970)
    Nickelodeon (1976)
    Paper Moon (1973)
    So Fine (1981)
    What's Up, Doc? (1972)
    Wild Rovers (1971)
    Zero Effect (1998)
  TV: Peyton Place
O'Neal, Shaquille
  milieu: **5** court
  org.: **3** NBA
  sport: **10** basketball
O'Neal, Tatum: **7** actress
  film: The Bad News Bears (1976)
    Nickelodeon (1976)
    Paper Moon (1973, AA)
  spouse: John McEnroe
one and __: **3** all **4** only
one and a half, combining form: **6** sesqui-
one-armed bandit feature: **4** bell, slot **6** wheels
__ on Ears, A: **7** Chapter
On earth __ is in heaven: **4** as it
one at __: **5** a time
One Bad Apple (1971 song)
  artist: Osmonds
one-base __: **3** hit
One Basket
  author: Edna Ferber
One Big Happy dog: **5** Rowdy
one-billionth (prefix): **4** nano-
one by one, taken: **4** each **6** apiece
one-celled organism: **4** alga **5** ameba **6** amoeba
one-D: **6** linear
one day __ time: **3** at a
One Day at a Time (CBS sitcom)
  cast: Valerie Bertinelli (Barbara Cooper)
    Bonnie Franklin (Ann Romano)
    Pat Harrington Jr. (Dwayne Schneider)
    Mackenzie Phillips (Julie Cooper)
One Day of the Year, The
  author: Alan Seymour
one-dimensional: **6** linear
One-Dimensional Man
  author: Herbert Marcuse
One Door Away From Heaven
  author: Dean Koontz
one-eighty: **3** uey **5** U-turn **8** reversal **9** inversion, turnabout
__ one-eighty: **3** do a
One-Eyed Jacks (1961 film)
  cast: Marlon Brando, Ben Johnson, Katy Jurado, Karl Malden, Slim Pickens
  director: Marlon Brando
One Fine Day (1963 song)
  artist: Chiffons
One Flew Over the Cuckoo's Nest: **4** film **5** novel
  author: Ken Kesey
  cast: Brad Dourif, Louise Fletcher, Jack Nicholson
  director: Milos Forman
One for My Baby
  artist: Lena Horne
  composer: Harold Arlen, Johnny Mercer
one-for-one deal: **4** swap, swop **5** trade **6** change
one for the __: **4** road **5** books
..._ one for the Gipper: **3** win
Oneg __: **7** Shabbat
Onega: **3** bay **4** lake **5** river
  locale: **6** Russia
One Generation After
  author: Elie Wiesel
__ on eggs: **4** walk
...one giant __ for mankind: **4** leap
Onegin: **6** Eugene
One Good Woman (1988 song)
  artist: Peter Cetera
__ one hand: **5** on the
One Happy Island: **5** Aruba
One Heartbeat (1987 song)
  artist: Smokey Robinson
one-horse __: **4** town
one-horse carriage: **3** gig **5** buggy, sulky
one-hoss shay owner: **6** deacon
One Hour Photo (2002 film)
  cast: Robin Williams
One Human Minute
  author: Stanislaw Lem
One Hundred Poems of Kabir
  author: Rabindranath Tagore
One Hundred Years of Solitude
  author: Gabriel García Márquez
Oneida: **4** lake **5** tribe **6** Indian **7** Amerind **8** language **9** Iroquoian
  ally: **6** Cayuga, Mohawk, Seneca **8** Onondaga **9** Tuscarora
  cousin: **4** Erie
  locale: **7** New York
One I Gave My Heart to, The (1997 song)
  artist: Aaliyah
O'Neill: **2** Ed **3** Tip **4** Oona **6** Eugene **8** Jennifer
O'Neill, Ed: **5** actor
  TV: Married...With Children
O'Neill, Eugene: **6** writer **8** Nobelist
  daughter: **4** Oona
  forte: **4** play **5** drama
  work: Ah, Wilderness!
    All God's Chillun Got Wings
    Anna Christie
    Beyond the Horizon
    Bound East for Cardiff
    Days Without End
    Desire Under the Elms
    The Emperor Jones
    The Great God Brown
    The Hairy Ape
    The Haunted
    Homecoming
    Hughie
    The Hunted
    The Iceman Cometh
    Ile
    In the Zone
    Lazarus Laughed
    Long Day's Journey Into Night
    The Long Voyage Home
    Marco Millions
    A Moon for the Misbegotten
    The Moon of the Caribbees
    Mourning Becomes Electra
    The Rope
    Strange Interlude
    A Touch of the Poet
O'Neill, Oona
  spouse: Charles Chaplin
One I Love, The (1987 song)
  artist: R.E.M.
one-in-a-million: **4** rare **6** choice, superb, unique **7** special, unusual **8** peerless, singular, uncommon **9** a cut above, matchless, priceless **10** at a premium, hard to find, inimitable, invaluable, phenomenal, remarkable
One in a Million (1957 song)
  artist: Platters
oneiromancy: **10** divination
  subject: **5** dream **6** vision **9** nightmare
oneiromancy subject: **5** dream
One Is Enough
  author: Flora Nwapa
One L
  author: Scott Turow
One Less Bell to Answer (1970 song)
  artist: Fifth Dimension
One Life to Live (ABC soap opera)
  cast: Erika Slezak (Viki Lord)
    Robin Strasser (Dorian Lord)
  creator: Agnes Nixon
one-liner: **3** gag **4** jest, joke, quip **9** sound bite, witticism
  response: **4** ha-ha
one-liners, quick with: **5** witty
One-L lama
  poet: Ogden Nash
One Lonely Night (1985 song)
  artist: REO Speedwagon
one-man __: **4** band, show
One man's __...: **4** meat
One man's __ is another man's Persian: **4** Mede
One Man's Family: **9** radio show
One Man's San Francisco
  author: Herb Caen
One Man Woman... (1974 song)
  artist: Paul Anka
One Million Years B.C. (1966 film)
  cast: Raquel Welch
One Mint Julep (1961 song)
  artist: Ray Charles
One Minute Man (2001 song)
  artist: Missy Elliott
One Moment in Time (1988 song)
  artist: Whitney Houston
One More Chance (1995 song)
  artist: Notorious B.I.G.
One More Night (1985 song)
  artist: Phil Collins
One More Try (song)
  artist: George Michael, Timmy -T-

__ on empty: 7 running
One must __ live: 5 eat to
oneness: 5 unity, whole 7 harmony 8 sameness 9 unanimity 10 solidarity
One never knows, __?: 5 do one
One Night (1958 song)
artist: Elvis Presley
One Night at McCool's (2001 film)
cast: Matt Dillon, John Goodman, Paul Reiser, Liv Tyler
One Note __: 5 Samba
__ One Note: 6 Johnny
one o' __: 3 cat
one of __: 5 a kind
One of __: 4 Ours
One of __ days...: 5 these
one-of-a-kind: 6 unique 10 unexampled
One of a Kind (1973 song)
artist: Spinners
One of Ours
author: Willa Cather
One of These Nights (1975 song)
artist: Eagles
__ One of Those Things: 4 Just
One of Us (1995 song)
artist: Joan Osborne
__ One of Us: 7 Neither
one old __: 3 cat
__ one on: 3 tie
one-on-one
participant: 5 tutee, tutor 6 dueler
One on One (1977 film)
cast: Robby Benson, Annette O'Toole
One on One (1983 song)
artist: Hall and Oates
Oneonta: 4 city, town
locale: 7 New York
one or the __: 5 other
one-percent
alternative: 4 skim
oner: 4 lulu 5 beaut, dilly, doozy 8 rara avis, rare bird, standout 9 humdinger, nonpareil
onerous: 4 hard 5 grave, harsh, heavy, hefty, rough, tough 6 leaden, severe, taxing, thorny, tiring, trying, uphill 7 arduous, galling, irksome, painful, weighty 8 crushing, exacting, grievous, grinding, grueling, pressing, tiresome, toilsome 9 demanding, difficult, excessive, herculean, laborious, merciless, ponderous, strenuous, vexatious 10 burdensome, cumbersome, enervating, exhausting, formidable, oppressive, overtaxing
make ~: 3 tax
not ~: 4 easy 5 light
ones
column next to ~: 4 tens
the ~ here: 5 these
the ~ there: 5 those
unnamed ~: 4 they
__ one's act together: 3 get
__ one's all: 4 give
__ one's arm: 5 twist
__ one's back on: 4 turn
__ one's belt: 5 under 7 tighten
__ one's blessings: 5 count
__ one's bluff: 4 call
__ one's brain: 4 pick, rack
__ one's breath: 4 save 5 catch, under, waste
__ one's breath away: 4 take
__ one's bridges: 4 burn
__ one's cap for: 3 set
__ one's cards on the table: 3 lay, put
__ one's cards right: 4 play
__ one's case: 4 make
__ one's chin up: 4 keep
__ one's chops: 4 bust, lick
__ one's clock: 5 clean
__ one's cool: 4 blow, keep
__ one's door: 5 lay at
__ one's ducks in a row: 3 get
__ one's dues: 3 pay
__ one's ear: 4 bend
__ one's ears: 4 up to
__ one's elbows: 4 up to
__ oneself: 5 all by 6 beside, forget
oneself, by: 9 alone. solo
__ oneself go: 3 let
__ oneself of: 5 avail
__ oneself scarce: 4 make
__ oneself thin: 6 spread
__ oneself to: 4 help
__ oneself together: 4 pull
__ one's eye: 5 catch
__ one's eye on: 4 have
__ one's eyes: 4 open
__ one's eyes on: 3 lay, set 5 feast
__ one's eyes open: 4 keep, with
__ one's eyes out: 3 cry
__ one's eyes over: 3 run
__ one's eyes peeled: 4 keep
__ one's eyes to: 4 shut
__ one's eyeteeth on: 3 cut
__ one's face: 4 show 5 egg on, stuff
__ one's feathers: 6 ruffle
__ one's feed: 3 off
__ one's feet: 4 drag 5 lay at
__ one's finger on: 3 lay, put
__ one's fingers: 5 cross
__ one's fingers crossed: 4 have, keep
__ one's foot down: 3 put
__ one's foot in it: 3 put
__ one's foot in the door: 3 get
__ One's for You: 4 This
__ one's goat: 3 get
__ one's goose: 4 cook
__ one's ground: 4 hold 5 stand
__ one's guard: 3 off
__ one's guts: 5 spill
__ one's hackles up: 3 get
__ one's hair: 4 curl, tear 5 get in
__ one's hair down: 3 let
__ one's hair out: 4 tear
__ one's hand: 3 tip, try 4 show 5 force
__ one's hands: 3 off 5 sit on
__ one's hands of: 3 rub 4 wash
__ one's hand to: 4 turn
__ one's hash: 6 settle
__ one's hat: 5 under
__ one's hat in the ring: 5 throw
__ one's hat off to: 4 take
__ one's head: 4 go to, hide, keep, lose, over, turn 5 shake
__ one's head above water: 4 keep
__ one's head off: 4 snap
__ one's heart: 4 from 5 break, cross, steal
__ one's heart on: 3 set
__ one's heart out: 3 cry, eat
__ one's heart set on: 4 have
__ one's heart to: 4 lose
__ one's heels: 4 cool, drag, show 5 nip at
__ one's hide: 3 tan
__ one's high horse: 5 get on 6 get off
__ one's horses: 4 hold
one-shot __: 4 deal
__ one's house in order: 3 put, set
one-sided: 6 biased, uneven, unfair, unjust 7 partial, unequal 8 partisan 9 arbitrary 10 ill-matched, prejudiced, unbalanced
one-sidedness: 4 bias 5 slant 9 prejudice
one size __ all: 4 fits
__ one's leave: 4 take
__ one's leg: 4 pull
__ one's legs: 7 stretch
one's level __: 4 best
__ one's lid: 4 flip
__ one's lip: 4 bite, curl 6 button
__ one's lips: 4 pass 5 smack
__ one's loins: 4 gird
__ one's losses: 3 cut
__ one's lot with: 4 cast
__ one's luck: 3 try 4 push
__ one's lucky stars: 5 thank
One small __ for a man...: 4 step
__ one's mark: 4 make
__ one's match: 4 meet
__ one's mind: 4 blow, slip 5 cross 6 change
__ one's mouth water: 4 make
__ one's muscles: 4 flex
__ one's neck: 4 up to 5 break
__ one's neck out: 5 stick
__ one's nerves: 5 get on
__ one's nest: 7 feather
__ one's nose: 5 under 6 follow
__ one's nose at: 5 thumb
__ one's nose clean: 4 keep
__ one's nose in: 3 rub
__ one's nose into: 4 poke
__ one's number: 3 get 4 have
__ one's oar in: 3 put
__ one's oats: 4 feel, know 7 feeling
__ one's old tricks: 4 up to
__ one's onions: 4 know
__ one's own: 4 hold
__ one's own business: 4 mind
one's own, combining form: 7 proprio-
__ one's own heart: 5 after
__ one's own horn: 4 blow, toot
__ one's own mind: 4 know
__ one's own ticket: 5 write
__ one's palm: 5 cross 6 grease
__ one's part: 4 take
__ one's path: 5 cross
__ one's peace: 4 hold, keep
__ one's place: 4 keep, know
__ one's pockets: 4 line
one-spot: 3 ace 4 bill, buck 6 dollar, single 9 greenback
__ one's powder dry: 4 keep
__ one's praises: 4 sing
__ one's punches: 4 pull
__ one's sails: 4 trim
__ one's salt: 5 worth
One's-Self I Sing: 4 poem
author: Walt Whitman
__ one's shirt: 4 lose
__ one's shirt on: 4 keep
__ one's shoes: 4 fill
__ one's shoulder: 5 cry on
__ one's sights on: 3 set
__ one's socks off: 5 knock
__ one's soul: 4 bare
__ one's spleen: 4 vent
__ one's spurs: 4 earn
__ one's stack: 4 blow
__ one's step: 5 watch
__ one's stride: 3 hit
__ one's stuff: 5 strut
__ one's style: 5 cramp
__ one's teeth: 4 bare, grit, show
__ one's teeth into: 3 get 4 sink
__ one's teeth on: 3 cut
one step __ time: 3 at a
one-step: 5 dance
One Step Up (1988 song)
artist: Bruce Springsteen
__ Ones, The: 5 Loved 7 Defiant
__ one's thumb: 5 under
__ one's thumbs: 7 twiddle
__ one's thunder: 5 steal
__ one's time: 4 bide, take
__ one's tongue: 4 bite, hold, lose
__ one's top: 4 blow
__ one's tracks: 5 cover
__ one straight: 3 set
one-striper: 3 ens., PFC
__ one's troth: 6 plight
__ one's wagon: 3 fix
__ one's Waterloo: 4 meet
__ one's way: 3 pay 4 come, make, pick, wend
__ one's way clear: 3 see
__ one's ways: 5 set in
One Sweet Day (1995 song)
artist: Boyz II Men, Mariah Carey
__ one's weight: 4 pull
__ one's weight around: 5 throw
__ one's wheels: 4 spin
__ one's whistle: 3 wet
__ one's wig: 4 flip
__ one's wild oats: 3 sow
__ one's wing: 5 under
__ one's word: 4 keep
__ one's words: 3 eat 5 weigh
__ one's wounds: 4 lick
one that got __, the: 4 away
One That You Love, The (1981 song)
artist: Air Supply
__ One, The: 4 Wild
one thing __ time: 3 at a
One Thing Leads to Another (1983 song)
artist: Fixx
one-time: 3 old 4 late, past 5 prior 6 bygone, former, whilom 7 earlier, quondam 8 previous 9 erstwhile, preceding
one to __: 3 ten
one to __ on: 4 grow
__ one to grow on: 3 and
One Touch of Venus: 7 musical
composer: Ogden Nash, Kurt Weill
Venus in ~: 3 Ava
one-track: 4 mono
mind: 5 mania 6 hang-up 8 fixation, idée fixe 9 monomania, obsession
One-Trick __: 4 Pony
One True Thing (1998 film)
cast: William Hurt, Meryl Streep, Renée Zellweger
one-two: 3 hit, jab 4 belt, biff, blow, clip, cuff, slam, slug, sock 5 clout, punch, smack, smash, whomp

6 wallop 8 haymaker, uppercut 10 roundhouse
One, Two, Three (1961 film)
cast: Horst Buchholz, James Cagney, Arlene Francis, Pamela Tiffin
director: Billy Wilder
one-up: 3 top 4 best 5 outdo, trump
On Everything
author: Hilaire Belloc
one way __ other: 5 or the
one-way __: 6 street
one way or the __: 5 other
one-way symbol: 5 arrow
one-wheel vehicle: 6 barrow 8 unicycle
One Who Really Loves You, The (1962 song)
artist: Mary Wells
One with Nineveh and __: 4 Tyre
__-on favorite: 4 odds
__ on Film: 4 Agee
__ on fire: 3 set
__ on Fire: 5 Rooms, Souls 6 Hearts
__ on first?: 4 Who's
On First Looking Into Chapman's Homer
author: John Keats
on foot (French): 5 à pied
__ on for size: 3 try
On Glory's Course
author: James Purdy
ongoing: 6 extant, living, with us 7 current, growing 8 evolving, marching, underway 9 advancing, open-ended, unfolding 10 continuing, continuous, developing, in progress, successful, unfinished
On Golden Pond (1981 film)
bird: 4 loon
cast: Dabney Coleman, Henry Fonda, Jane Fonda, Katharine Hepburn
director: Mark Rydell
__ on, Harvest Moon: 5 Shine
__ on Heaven's Door: 7 Knockin'
__ on her fingers...: 5 Rings
On Her Majesty's Secret Service: 4 film 5 novel
author: Ian Fleming
cast: George Lazenby, Diana Rigg
On His Blindness
author: John Milton
__ on horseback: 3 man
__ on Horseback: 6 Beggar, Sailor
ONI
grp.: 3 USN
part of ~: 3 Nav., Off. 5 Naval 6 Office
__ on Ice: 4 Soul
__ on Indolence: 3 Ode
__-o'-nine-tails: 3 cat
onion: 4 bulb 6 allium, veggie 7 shallot 9 condiment, vegetable
cousin: 4 leek 5 chive 6 garlic
cover: 4 skin
ender: 4 skin
martini with an ~: 6 Gibson
outgrowth: 6 bulbel, bulbil 7 bulblet
product: 4 ring
onion __: 4 dome, roll 5 rings 6 powder
__ onion: 3 sea 5 green, pearl 7 Bermuda, Spanish, Vidalia
onions
partner: 5 liver
prepare ~: 4 chop, dice 5 mince, sauté
react to ~: 3 cry 4 weep
onionskin: 5 paper
__ onion soup: 6 French
__ on it: 4 step 5 sleep
__ on it!: 3 Sit
on its __: 3 ear
__-on label: 5 stick
On Liberty
author: John Stuart Mill
onliest: 4 lone 6 unique 8 solitary
online
back ~: 5 fixed
bookseller: 6 Amazon
browse ~ without posting: 4 lurk
choice: 3 AOL
convenience: 4 link 5 e-mail 6 hookup 7 network 9 interface 10 attachment
conversation: 2 IM 4 chat
diary: 4 blog
discussion: 4 chat
info: 3 FAQ
investing service: 6 E-Trade
journal: 4 blog
magazine: 5 Slate
marketing: 5 e-tail
marketplace: 4 eBay
need: 5 modem
one ~: 4 user
publication: 4 e-mag 5 e-book, e-zine
response to an ~ joke: 3 LOL
site: 5 forum 9 newsgroup
VIP: 5 sysop
onlooker: 4 eyer, seer 6 viewer 7 watcher, witness 8 beholder, observer 9 bystander, sightseer, spectator 10 eyewitness
onlookers: 7 gallery 8 audience 10 attendance
only: 3 all, but, one 4 just, lone, sole 6 at most, barely, hardly, merely, purely, simply, single, solely, unique, wholly 7 totally, utterly 8 entirely, isolated, peerless, separate, singular, solitary, uniquely 9 matchless, unequaled, unrivaled 10 nothing but, unrivalled
only __ in town, the: 4 game
__-only: 4 eyes
Only __: 3 You 5 a Curl, a Rose 7 Sixteen
__ only a bird...: 4 She's
Only a Curl
author: Elizabeth Barrett Browning
only animal that blushes: 3 man
__ Only a Paper Moon: 3 It's
__ only as directed: 3 use
Only Children
author: Alison Lurie
...only God can make __: 5 a tree
__ Only Had a Brain: 3 If I
only have __ for: 4 eyes
__ Only Have Love: 4 If We
Only in America (1963 song)
artist: Jay and the Americans
Only in My Dreams (1987 song)
artist: Debbie Gibson
__ Only Just Begun: 4 We've
__ Only Live Once: 3 You
__ Only Live Twice: 3 You
Only Love Can Break a Heart (1962 song)
artist: Gene Pitney
__-only memory: 4 read
__ Only Money: 3 It's
__ Only Old Once!: 5 You're
Only Sixteen (1976 song)
artist: Dr. Hook
Only the Good Die Young (1978 song)
artist: Billy Joel
Only the Lonely (1991 film)
cast: James Belushi, John Candy, Maureen O'Hara, Ally Sheedy
director: Chris Columbus
Only the Lonely (song)
artist: Motels, Roy Orbison
Only the Strong Survive (1969 song)
artist: Jerry Butler
Only Time (2000 song)
artist: Enya
Only Wanna Be With You (1995 song)
artist: Hootie and the Blowfish
...only with __ eyes: 5 thine
Only Yesterday (1975 song)
artist: Carpenters
Only You (1994 film)
cast: Robert Downey Jr., Bonnie Hunt, Marisa Tomei, Billy Zane
Only You (song)
artist: Franck Pourcel's French Fiddles, Hilltoppers, Platters, Ringo Starr
Only you can prevent __ fires: 6 forest
__ on Man, An: 5 Essay
__ on me: 5 Lay it
__ on Me: 4 Call, Lean, Take 5 Count
__ on Melancholy: 3 Ode
On Moonlight __: 3 Bay
__ on My Mind: 6 Always, Gentle 7 Georgia
On My Own
author: Eleanor Roosevelt
On My Own (1986 song)
artist: Patti LaBelle, Michael McDonald
__ on My Pillow: 5 Tears
__ on My Shoulder: 5 Angel
On My Word of Honor (1957 song)
artist: Platters
on no __: 7 account
On Nothing
author: Hilaire Belloc
Ono: 4 Yoko
__ Ono Band: 7 Plastic
__ on of hands: 6 laying
onomastician's concern: 4 name
onomatopoeic: 6 echoic 9 imitative
word: 3 bam, pow 4 wham
Onondaga: 5 tribe 6 Indian 7 Amerind 8 language
ally: 6 Cayuga, Mohawk, Oneida, Seneca 9 Tuscarora
enemy: 4 Erie
on one's __: 3 ear, own, way 4 feet, mind, part, toes 5 guard, hands, knees 6 mettle, uppers
on one's __ account: 3 own
on one's __ horse: 4 high
on one's __ initiative: 3 own
on one's __ legs: 4 last
__ on one's back: 4 flat
__ on one's escutcheon: 5 a blot
__ on one's face: 3 egg
__ on one's feet: 4 land
__ on one's hands: 3 sit 4 time
on one's high __: 5 horse
__ on one's high horse: 3 get
on one's last __: 4 legs
__ on one's luck: 4 down
__ on one's nerves: 3 get
__ on one's oars: 4 rest
on one's own __: 7 account
__ on one's own two feet: 5 stand
__ on one's shoulder: 3 cry 4 chip
__ on one's toes: 4 step 5 tread
on or __: 5 about
Onorati: 5 Peter
On Our Own (1989 song)
artist: Bobby Brown
__ on over: 4 come
Ono, Yoko: 8 musician
spouse: John Lennon
on-paper: 8 unproved
__ on parle français: 3 ici
__-on part: 4 walk
__-on patch: 4 iron
on pins and __: 7 needles
__ on Pop: 3 Hop
on-ramp sign: 5 merge
onrush: 4 flow, wave 5 flood, onset, river, sally, surge, swash 6 deluge, stream 7 cascade, torrent 8 stampede 9 avalanche, onslaught, upwelling 10 outpouring
emotional ~: 5 throe
onrushing: 7 looming, nearing 8 imminent, oncoming, upcoming 9 advancing, impending
__ on rye: 3 ham 4 tuna
Onsager, Lars: 7 chemist 8 Nobelist
On Seeing the Elgin Marbles: 4 poem
author: John Keats
__-on sentence: 3 run
onset: 4 dawn, rise 5 birth, get-go, start, storm 6 advent, attack, charge, day one, onrush, source 7 assault, dawning, genesis, kickoff, leadoff, opening 8 exordium, outbreak 9 beginning, first sign, inception, offensive, onslaught 10 aggression, incipience, initiation
__-on shoes: 4 slip
onshore __: 4 wind
on short __: 6 notice
onside __: 4 kick
onslaught: 4 raid, rush 5 blitz, onset, sally, storm 6 attack, battle, charge, inroad, onrush, sortie, thrust 7 assault, barrage, battery, offense 8 invasion, violence 9 broadside, incursion, offensive 10 aggression
__ on Sloopy: 4 Hang
__ on Solitude: 3 Ode
on speaking __: 5 terms
onstage
prop: 5 phone, stool
walk ~: 5 enter
__ on strong: 4 come
__ on Sunday: 5 Never
Ont.: 4 prov.
neighbor: 3 Man., Que. 4 Minn.
__ on tap: 4 beer
Ontario: 4 city, lake, town 8 province
capital: 7 Toronto
city: 4 Ajax 5 Elgin 6 Aurora, Barrie, Dundas, Guelph, Kanata, London, Milton, Nepean, Oshawa, Ottawa, Sarnia,

Scugog, Whitby 7 Caledon, Chatham, Grimsby, La Salle, Lincoln, Markham, Orillia, Sudbury, Timmins, Toronto, Vaughan, Welland, Windsor 8 Ancaster, Bradford, Brampton, Cornwall, Fort Erie, Georgina, Hamilton, Kingston, North Bay, Oakville, St. Thomas, Waterloo 9 Brantford, Cambridge, Haldimand, Innisfail, Kitchener, Nanticoke, Newmarket, Owen Sound, Pickering, Stratford, Woodstock 10 Belleville, Brockville, Burlington, Clarington, Cumberland, Gloucester, Thunder Bay, Whitchurch
Indian: 4 Cree 5 Huron 9 Saulteaux
lake: 5 Rainy 6 Simcoe 7 Nipigon
locale: 6 Canada 10 California
neighbor: 4 Erie
river: 5 Trent
school: 4 York 5 Brock, Trent 6 Queen's 7 Ryerson 8 Carleton, Lakehead, McMaster
waterfall: 7 Niagara
__-on-Thames: 6 Henley
on the __: 3 dot, fly, job, lam, run, sly, way 4 ball, beam, cuff, dole, edge, hoof, hook, line, mend, move, nose, outs, rack, road, side, spot, take, town, wane, wing 5 alert, blink, brain, cheap, fence, fritz, house, level, loose, march, money, prowl, rocks, ropes, scene, shelf, skids, table, whole 6 button, carpet, double, inside, market, record, square, street 7 surface
on the __ chance: 3 off
on the __ foot: 5 right, wrong
on the __ hand: 3 one 5 other
on the __ of: 4 edge, part 5 heels, order
on the __ of a dilemma: 5 horns
on the __ of it: 4 face
on the __ of one's tongue: 3 tip
on the __ of the moment: 4 spur
on the __ vive: 3 qui
on the __ wavelength: 4 same
On the __: 4 Road
On the __ hand...: 5 other
__ on the back: 3 pat 4 a pat
__ on the barrelhead: 4 cash
On the Beach: 4 film 5 novel
author: Nevil Shute
cast: Fred Astaire, Ava Gardner, Gregory Peck
director: Stanley Kramer
__ on the block: 3 put
__ on the Bounty: 6 Mutiny
__ on the cake: 5 icing
__ on the cob: 4 corn
__ on the dog: 3 put
On the double!: 4 ASAP, stat 6 move it
__ on the draw: 5 quick
__ on the escutcheon: 4 blot
on the face __: 4 of it
__ on the feedbag: 3 put
on-the-fence: 9 undecided 10 irresolute
__-on-the-floor: 4 four
__ on the Floss, The: 4 Mill
__ on the Flying Trapeze, The: 3 Man
__ on the Fourth of July: 4 Born
On the Frontier
author: W.H. Auden
__ on the gas: 4 step
On the Good __ Lollipop: 4 Ship
__ on the ground floor: 5 get in, got in
__ on the hand may be...: 5 A kiss
__ on the Hill, The: 4 Fool 5 House 7 Heather
__ on the hog: 4 high
on the horns of a __: 7 dilemma
__ on the Hudson: 6 Castle, Moscow
On the Idle Hill of Summer
author: A.E. Housman
__ on the Keys: 6 Kitten
on-the-level: 5 legit 6 square 7 serious
__ on the line: 5 lay it
__ on the market: 4 drug
__ on the money: 5 right
__ on the Mount: 6 Sermon
On the Nature of Things
author: Lucretius
__ on the Nile: 5 Death
on the off __: 6 chance
on the one __: 4 hand
__ on the Orient Express: 6 Murder
on the other __: 4 hand
on the qui __: 4 vive
On the Radio (1980 song)
artist: Donna Summer
__ on the Range: 4 Home
On the Rebound (1961 song)
artist: Floyd Cramer
__ on the Rhine: 5 Watch
on the right __: 4 foot
__ on the ritz: 3 put
__ on the Ritz: 6 Puttin'
On the Road: 5 novel
author: Jack Kerouac
character: 3 Sal 4 Dean, Inez 8 Paradise
On the Road Again (1980 song)
artist: Willie Nelson
__ on the Rocks: 4 Love
__ on the Roof: 4 Rain 7 Fiddler
__ on the Run: 3 Fox 4 Band, Nuns
__ on the Side: 4 Boys
on-the-spot: 6 snappy 7 instant, present
TV report: 4 nemo
__-on-the-spot: 6 Johnny
on the spur of the __: 6 moment
__ on the stick: 3 get
__ On The Storm: 6 Riders
__ on the street: 3 man
On the Street Where You Live: 4 song 5 novel
artist: Vic Damone, Andy Williams
author: Mary Higgins Clark
composer: Alan Jay Lerner, Frederick Loewe
On the Third Day band: 3 ELO
on the tip of one's __: 6 tongue
On the Town (1949 film)
cast: Betty Garrett, Gene Kelly, Ann Miller, Jules Munshin, Frank Sinatra, Vera-Ellen
director: Stanley Donen, Gene Kelly
__ on the trail: 3 hot
On the Waterfront (1954 film)
cast: Marlon Brando, Lee J. Cobb, Karl Malden, Eva Marie Saint, Rod Steiger
director: Elia Kazan
__ on the Wild Side: 4 Walk 5 A Walk
__ on the Wind: 6 Kisses 7 Written
__ on the wrist: 4 slap
on the wrong __: 4 foot
__ on thick: 5 lay it
__ on thin ice: 7 skating
on this side prefix: 3 cis-
__-on tie: 4 clip
__ on Tight: 4 Hold
Ontkean, Michael: 5 actor
TV: The Rookies
onto: 3 hep 4 upon, wise 5 aware 7 aware of 8 informed 9 in the know, mindful of
__ on to: 4 glom, hang 5 latch 6 freeze
ontologist's concern: 5 being 7 essence, reality 9 existence
on top __ world: 5 of the
On Top of Old __: 6 Smokey
__-on-Trent: 5 Stoke
__ on Truckin': 4 Keep
onus: 3 job 4 duty, load, slur, task 5 blame, fault, guilt 6 burden, charge, weight 7 incubus 9 liability, millstone 10 dead weight, imposition, obligation, oppression
__ on Venice: 3 Ode
__ on Walkin': 4 Keep
onward: 5 ahead, along, forth, going, hence 6 beyond, moving 7 forward, in front
move ~: 2 go 4 pass 5 impel, shlep 6 schlep 7 advance, schlepp 8 progress 9 go forward
__ on water: 4 walk
On Wenlock Edge
author: A.E. Housman
__ on wheels: 5 meals
__ on wood: 5 knock
__ on words: 4 play
__ on you!: 5 Shame
__ on You: 4 High 5 Crush, Stuck
On Your __: 4 Toes
__ on your life!: 3 Not
On your mark! follower: 6 get set
__ on Your Mind: 3 Man 5 What's
On Your Toes: 7 musical
composer: Lorenz Hart, Richard Rodgers
onyx: 3 gem 5 black 6 marble 8 gemstone 10 chalcedony
decoration: 5 cameo
relative: 3 jet 4 inky 5 ebony, raven, sable, sooty
slipper: 5 shell 8 seashell
starter: 4 sard
white ~ gem: 8 sardonyx
Onyx
song: Slam (1993)
__-oo: 6 toodle
OO __: 5 gauge
oodles: 3 lot, ton 4 a lot, lots, many, much, peck, pile, raft, tons, wads 5 heaps, loads, scads 6 hoards, myriad, oceans, plenty, scores 7 numbers 8 jillions 9 a whole lot, multitude, truckload
of: 5 lotsa 6 divers, myriad, umteen, untold 7 copious, profuse, umpteen 8 abundant, manifold, numerous, umpsteen 9 bountiful, countless, quite a few
ooh: 3 wow 4 gosh 5 golly
ooh __: 4 la la
ooh and __: 3 aah
Ooh Baby Baby (1978 song)
artist: Linda Ronstadt
O-o-h Child (1970 song)
artist: Five Stairsteps
Ooh! My Soul (1958 song)
artist: Little Richard
ooid: 4 oval 5 ovate 9 egg-shaped
oology subject: 4 eggs
oolong: 3 tea 8 beverage
Oom __: 4 Paul
oom-pah instrument: 4 tuba
oomph: 2 go 3 pep, vim, zip 4 dash, élan, life, zeal, zest, zing 5 ardor, flair, verve, vigor 6 energy, fervor, pizazz, spirit 7 pizzazz 8 vitality 9 animation, sex appeal 10 enthusiasm, get up and go
Oona: 6 O'Neill 7 Chaplin
father: 6 Eugene
Ooo Baby Baby (1965 song)
artist: Miracles
Oola's boyfriend: Alley Oop
__-oop: 5 alley
oopak: 3 tea 8 black tea
Oop, Alley kingdom: 3 Moo
oops: 5 sorry 6 pardon 8 excuse me, pardon me
Oops!: 4 oh oh, uh-oh 6 oh dear
oospore: 3 egg
ooze: 3 goo, mud 4 drip, drop, emit, flow, glop, gook, guck, gunk, leak, mire, muck, seep, silt, weep, well 5 bleed, drain, exude, fluid, issue, leach, slime, spirt, spurt, sweat 6 effuse, escape, filter, sludge, strain 7 dribble, exudate, seep out, trickle 8 alluvium, overflow, perspire 9 discharge, exudation, percolate
oozing: 5 moist, seepy, undry 9 emanation
oozy: 4 damp, ropy 5 gooey, gunky, mucky, muddy, ropey, slimy, undry 6 drippy, sludgy 7 squishy, wettish 8 swampish
op __: 3 art
op. __: 3 cit.
__ op: 5 photo
__-op: 3 pre 4 coin, post
Opa-__, FL: 5 Locka
opah: 4 fish 8 moonfish
opal: 3 gem 7 girasol, hyalite, mineral 8 gemstone, girasole
ender: 3 ine
like an ~: 5 milky 6 porous
month: 3 Oct. 7 October
__ opal: 4 fire
opalescence: 4 glow 5 gleam, sheen 6 luster 7 shimmer 8 lambency 10 brilliance, effulgence, refulgence
opalescent: 5 milky 6 pearly 7 whitish 10 iridescent
opaline: 7 whitish
opaque: 3 dim 4 dark, dull, hazy 5 milky, mirky, misty, muddy, murky, thick 6 cloudy, obtuse, turbid 7 muddied, obscure, unclear 8 abstruse, darkened 9 adumbrate, difficult, tenebrous 10 lusterless
combining form: 5 glauc- 6 glauco-
op art pattern: 5 moiré
Opatoshu: 5 David
O patria mia: 4 aria
opera: 4 Aïda
op. cit.: 8 notation
cousin: 4 ibid.
part of ~: 5 opere 6 citato

OPEC: 4 bloc, pact 6 cartel
concern: 3 oil
delegate: 5 Iraki, Irani, Iraqi
former member: 5 Gabon 9 Indonesia
headquarters: 6 Vienna
leader: 4 amir, emir 5 ameer, emeer
member: 3 UAE 4 Arab, Irak, Iran, Iraq 5 Katar, Libya, Qatar 6 Angola, Kuwait 7 Algeria, Ecuador, Nigeria 9 Venezuela 11 Saudi Arabia
part: 3 Org. 9 Countries, Exporting, Petroleum
unit: 3 bbl. 4 drum 6 barrel
vessel: 5 oiler
Op-Ed __: 4 page
Op-Ed piece: 5 essay 6 column 7 article
Opel: 3 car 4 auto 10 automobile
like an ~: 6 German
model: 2 GT 5 Astra, Corsa, Manta, Omega, Tigra 6 Kadett, Vectra 7 Calibra
open: 3 gap, pop, tap 4 airy, ajar, bare, fair, free, gape, lacy, lead, moot, naif, rent, slit, tear, undo, vent, wide 5 agape, begin, burst, clear, crack, force, frank, jimmy, known, lance, naive, naked, on tap, overt, plain, split, start, unbar, unbox, uncap, unhid, unpeg, unpin, untie, unzip 6 broach, bust in, candid, direct, expand, free up, gaping, honest, in view, kick in, launch, let out, liable, mellow, on deck, patent, pierce, public, reveal, ring in, spread, trusty, turn on, unbolt, uncork, unfold, unfurl, unlock, unroll, unseal, unshut, unstop, unwrap, usable, vacant 7 artless, at issue, blatant, break in, cleared, convene, dubious, evident, exposed, glaring, kick off, lead off, natural, obvious, outside, outward, plenary, release, rolling, rupture, sincere, suspect, to be had, unblock, unclose, uncover, unlatch, untaken, up-front, useable, vacated, visible, yawning 8 amenable, apparent, break out, clear-cut, commence, disclose, doubtful, exoteric, explicit, extended, flagrant, flexible, get going, initiate, innocent, lacerate, manifest, outdoors, outgoing, passable, puncture, revealed, spacious, truthful, unartful, unbarred, unbiased, unbolted, unbuckle, unburden, unclosed, uncorked, unfasten, unfolded, unfurled, unhidden, unlidded, unlocked, unsealed, unveiled 9 agreeable, ambiguous, available, barefaced, come apart, debatable, dehiscent, disclosed, downright, dubitable, enter upon, equivocal, expansive, extensive, guileless, impartial, ingenuous, institute, navigable, objective, operative, originate, outspoken, penetrate, perforate, permitted, receptive, set up shop, spread out, unblocked, uncertain, uncovered, uncrowded, undecided, unguarded, unimpeded, unsettled, unstopped, ventilate, veracious, welcoming 10 aboveboard, accessible, come undone, flat-footed, forthright, free-spoken, from the hip, hospitable, inaugurate, in question, observable, obtainable, on the level, point-blank, responsive, tournament, unfastened, unhindered, unobstruct, unoccupied, unreserved, unresolved, unreticent, unshrouded, up for grabs, up in the air, ventilated
air: 6 nature 7 outside
and shut: 5 clear, plain, vivid 6 cogent, patent, simple 7 evident, express, obvious 8 apparent, distinct, explicit, manifest, palpable 9 graspable 10 spelled out
be ~: 4 tell 5 level 9 come clean
bring into the ~: 3 air 4 vent 7 freshen, publish 9 make known, talk about, ventilate
combining form: 6 phaner- 7 phanero-
cut ~: 4 slit, torn 5 lance
don't ~: 4 pass, shut 5 close, stick
door: 6 access, entrée
doors for: 3 aid 4 ease, help 6 assist 10 facilitate
ender: 4 work 6 handed 7 hearted
force ~: 3 pry 4 bust, rift 5 burst, crack, force, jimmy, lever 7 crowbar
for consideration: 4 iffy 8 doubtful, not final 9 dependent, provisory, tentative, uncertain, undecided, unsettled 10 contingent, indefinite
in the ~: 5 overt, unhid 7 outdoor, visible 8 apparent 10 aboveboard
lay ~: 4 tell 6 expose, unveil 7 uncover 8 endanger
not ~: 3 sly 4 shut 6 closed
one's eyes: 4 wake 5 awake, edify, waken 6 awaken
one's mouth: 4 blab, talk 5 speak
out: 5 widen 6 expand, spread 7 broaden
sesame: 6 ticket 8 password 10 hocus-pocus
space: 5 glade 8 clearing, headroom 9 clearance, elbowroom
tear ~: 5 unrip
the door for: 5 let go, let in, usher 6 accept, let out
the eyes of: 5 edify 7 educate 8 disabuse, illumine
to attack: 9 unguarded 10 undefended, vulnerable
to new ideas: 7 pliable 8 amenable, tolerant 9 acceptive, sensitive 10 hospitable, responsive
up: 4 stab, tell, thaw 5 admit, bloom, shoot, slash, unbar, widen, wound 6 broach 7 broaden, pioneer, profess, release, uncover 8 unfreeze 9 originate, spread out 10 accelerate
wide: 4 gape, yawn 5 agape
wide ~: 5 agape 6 gaping 7 yawning 9 unlimited 10 undefended, vulnerable
with ~ arms: 6 warmly 8 friendly 9 cordially 10 graciously
with eyes ~: 4 wary 5 awake, leery 10 suspicious
wrench ~: 3 rip 4 rive, tear 5 smash, split 6 sunder
open __: 3 air, bar, sea 4 arms, book, call, door, shop 5 house, space, stock, union 6 letter, quotes, season, secret, sesame
open __ of worms: 4 a can
open-__: 3 air, end, pit 4 eyed 5 ended, faced, shelf, sided 6 hearth, letter, minded 7 hearted, mouthed
open-__ policy: 4 door
open-__ sandwich: 5 faced
__ open: 3 lay
__-open: 4 wide
Open: 4 sign
Open __: 4 wide
open 9 __ 5: 3 'til
open-air: 7 outdoor, outside 8 alfresco 10 out-of-doors
open-and-shut __: 4 case
Open Arms (1982 song)
artist: Journey
Open Boat, The
author: Stephen Crane
Open Conspiracy, The
author: H.G. Wells
open-door: 6 public 9 available 10 accessible, responsive
Open Door Policy proponent: 3 Hay
opened: 4 ajar 7 abroach
just ~: 3 new 8 brand-new
open-ended: 5 broad 7 ongoing 8 optional 9 undefined
opener: 5 intro, start 6 lead-in 7 release
__ opener: 3 can, eye 4 door
__ openers: 3 for
open-eyed: 5 alert 6 astare 7 wakeful 8 vigilant, watchful
openhanded: 6 giving, lavish 7 liberal, profuse 8 generous 9 unselfish 10 altruistic, munificent
move: 4 cuff, slap, swat 5 smack, spank, whack
open-hearted: 4 kind, open, warm 5 frank 6 candid, giving, honest, humane, kindly 7 liberal, sincere 10 benevolent, forthright
Open House
author: Theodore Roethke
opening: 3 cut, gap, maw 4 dawn, door, exit, hole, leak, nook, pore, rent, rift, room, slit, slot, tear, time, vent, view, void 5 break, chink, cleft, crack, debut, first, hatch, intro, mouth, niche, onset, Part I, proem, space, split, spout, start 6 breach, cavity, cranny, eyelet, lacuna, lead-in, opener, outlet, outset, pocket, portal, recess, refuge, source, window 7 crevice, fissure, ingress, initial, keyhole, kickoff, leadoff, orifice, passage, premier, rupture, vacancy, vacuity 8 aperture, big break, occasion, original, overture, preamble, premiere, puncture 9 beginning, inception, launching, threshold 10 initiation, initiatory, interspace, interstice, passageway
grand ~: 5 debut 7 kickoff 8 premiere
have an ~ for: 4 need
jacket ~: 4 slit
staff ~: 3 job 4 slot 7 vacancy 8 position
word: 5 hello 7 welcome 8 greeting 10 salutation
words: 5 intro 6 prolog 7 prelude 8 foreword, preamble, prologue
opening __: 3 day 5 night
__ opening: 5 grand
__-opening: 3 eye
opening-night
attendee: 6 critic 8 reviewer
memento: 4 stub 6 ticket
openly: 5 fully 6 simply 7 frankly, naively, plainly, readily 8 brazenly, candidly, directly, honestly, in public, publicly, straight, wantonly 9 artlessly, blatantly, naturally, willingly 10 aboveboard, face-to-face, flagrantly, in full view, point-blank
oppose ~: 4 defy 5 cross, decry
open-minded: 8 amenable, catholic, tolerant, unbiased 9 impartial, receptive, unslanted 10 hospitable
open-mouthed: 4 agog 5 agape, agasp, in awe 6 amazed, gaping 7 shocked 8 startled 9 astounded, awestruck
leave ~: 3 awe, wow 4 stun 5 amaze 8 surprise
stand ~: 4 gape, gawk, ogle 5 stare 6 goggle
openness: 4 risk 6 candor 7 honesty, naiveté 8 veracity 9 liability, sincerity
open one's __: 4 eyes
Open Range (2003 film)
cast: Annette Bening, Kevin Costner, Robert Duvall
open-sandwich topper: 5 gravy
open sesame sayer: 3 Ali 4 Baba
Open thine eyes __: 6 eterne
open weave fabric: 4 leno, mesh 5 gauze, scrim
Open wide!: 5 say ah
response: 3 aah
Open Window, The
author: Saki
openwork: 3 net 4 lace, mesh 5 grill 6 grille 7 lattice
do ~: 3 tat
Open Your Heart (1986 song)
artist: Madonna
opera: 3 art 4 play, song 5 drama, genre, music, piece 9 singspiel
American ~ role: 4 Bess 5 Amahl, Porgy
box: 4 loge
cheer: 5 brava, bravo
comic ~: 6 bouffe
comic ~ singer: 5 buffo
division: 3 act 5 scene
extra, for short: 4 supe
horse ~: 5 drama, oater 7 western
house: 5 odeon, odeum 7 theater, theatre 10 auditorium
house section: 3 row 4 loge, tier
NYC ~ house: 3 Met
omnia: 4 body 5 whole 6 corpus, oeuvre 8 entirety 10 collection
opener: 4 Act I 6 act one
passage: 4 aria 5 scena 6 arioso
performer: 4 bass, diva 5 basso, mezzo, tenor 6 chorus, etoile 7 soprano 8 baritone 10 coloratura
perform in an ~: 4 sing 6 intone 7 belt out 8 vocalize
prince: 4 Igor

princess: 4 Aïda 8 Turandot
prop: 5 lance, spear
set in Egypt: 4 Aïda
slave: 4 Aïda
soap ~: 5 drama, story 6 series 9 imbroglio
opera __: 3 hat 5 buffa, glass, house, seria 6 bouffe 7 glasses
__ opera: 4 soap 5 comic, grand, horse, light, space
opéra __: 6 bouffe 7 comique
operable: 4 live 5 going 6 usable 7 running, working 10 functional
operand, having one: 5 unary
operandi
modus ~: 3 way 5 means 6 method, recipe 7 process 9 procedure, technique
Opera of Operas
composer: Thomas Arne
opera omnia: 4 body 5 whole 6 corpus, oeuvre 8 entirety 10 body of work, collection
__ operas: 5 Savoy
operate: 2 do, go 3 hum, man, ply, run, use 4 hold, keep, play, roll, tick, work 5 drive, pilot, steer, treat, wield 6 behave, direct, employ, handle, manage 7 conduct, perform 8 engineer, exercise, function, maneuver, navigate, transact 10 manipulate
__-operated: 3 gas 4 coin
operatic: 5 vocal 7 lyrical 10 theatrical
operating: 5 alive, in use 6 active 7 engaged, rolling, running, working 10 performing
computer ~ system: 4 Unix 5 Linux, MSDOS 7 Windows
not ~: 3 off
operating __: 4 room 6 income, system
__ operating system: 4 disk
operation: 3 job, use 5 doing, force, usage 6 action, affair, effort, system 7 mission, process, project, running, surgery, working 8 activity, campaign, exercise, function, maneuver, practice 9 execution, mechanism, procedure, treatment 10 dissection, employment, enterprise, management
in ~: 5 going 6 moving 7 engaged, running 9 operative
loc.: 2 ER, OR
police ~: 4 raid 5 front, sting
sting ~: 3 con 4 trap 5 bunco, setup
__ operation: 6 covert
Operation Dumbo Drop elephant: 3 Tai
Operation Overlord
when ~ began: 4 D-day
Operation Petticoat (1959 film)
cast: Tony Curtis, Cary Grant, Dina Merrill
director: Blake Edwards
operations
base of ~: 7 station
like some ~: 6 covert 8 hush-hush 10 undercover, under wraps
operative: 3 key, spy 4 aide, live, open 5 agent, alive, ninja, spook, valid 6 living, shamus, usable, worker 7 crucial, helpful, in force, running, staffer, useable, working 8 workable 9 detective, effective, important 10 accessible, functional, prevailing
operator: 4 doer, user 5 wheel 6 con man, driver, robber 7 employe 8 big wheel, employee, merchant, swindler
__-operator: 5 owner
Operator (1975 song)
artist: Manhattan Transfer
__ Operator: 6 Smooth
opere __: 6 citato
operetta: 5 music
composer: 5 Lehár 7 Gilbert 8 Sullivan
operose: 4 hard 6 boring, taxing, uphill 7 arduous, labored, tedious 8 tiresome, toilsome 9 difficult, laborious, strenuous
Ophelia: 4 Dane, moon
brother: 7 Laertes
love: 6 Hamlet
planet: 6 Uranus
ophidian: 3 asp 5 adder, krait, snake 6 animal, uraeus 7 reptile
ophidiophobe fear: 6 snakes
ophiology: 7 science
study: 6 snakes
ophthalmic: 5 optic 6 ocular, visual 7 sensory 9 sensorial
ophthalmo-
relative: 5 oculo-
ophthalmologist: 9 eye doctor
concern: 4 iris 6 cornea, retina
need: 6 eyecup
Ophuls: 3 Max 6 Marcel
opiate: 4 drug 6 codeia 7 anodyne, codeine 8 narcotic, sedative 9 soporific 10 anesthetic
Opie: 4 Alan 6 Taylor
aunt: 3 Bee
father: 4 Andy
portrayer: Ron Howard
opine: 3 say 4 aver 5 guess, voice 6 ideate 7 comment, observe, suggest, suppose, surmise 8 look upon
opinion: 3 say 4 idea, mind, side, take, view 5 guess, input, say-so, slant, stand, voice 6 advice, belief, notion, regard, theory, thesis 7 comment, feeling, surmise, theorem, thought, verdict 8 analysis, attitude, estimate, judgment, position, reaction 9 criticism, editorial, postulate, sentiment, suspicion, utterance, viewpoint 10 assessment, assumption, conception, conclusion, conjecture, contention, conviction, estimation, evaluation, hypothesis, impression, persuasion, reflection, standpoint
be of the ~: 4 feel 5 think 6 reckon 7 believe
difference of ~: 4 rift, spat, tiff 5 break, clash 7 dispute, quarrel 8 argument, squabble, variance
give an ~: 3 say 5 argue, speak, state, voice 6 assert, remark 7 chime in, observe 8 maintain, propound
good ~: 6 esteem, regard 7 respect 8 approval, prestige 10 reputation
have another ~: 4 vary 6 differ 7 deviate, dissent, diverge 8 disagree
high ~: 6 regard 7 respect 9 reverence 10 admiration
in French: 4 avis
offer an ~: 5 guide 6 advise 7 counsel, suggest 8 point out 9 recommend
of the same ~: 3 one 5 joint 6 agreed, united 8 in accord 9 concerted, unanimous, undivided 10 like-minded
piece: 4 Op-Ed 5 essay, tract 6 thesis 8 critique
public ~ gauge: 4 poll 6 survey 9 straw poll
seek the ~ of: 3 ask 4 talk 5 refer 6 call in, confer, huddle, parlay, powwow, turn to 7 consult 9 negotiate, touch base 10 brainstorm
unorthodox ~: 6 heresy 7 dissent 9 blasphemy, sacrilege
__ opinion: 6 public 8 matter of
opinionated: 5 bossy, cocky, vocal 6 biased 7 adamant, bigoted 8 cocksure, dogmatic, hard-line, indocile, locked in, obdurate, one-sided, positive, stubborn, vehement 9 arbitrary, assertive, conceited, obstinate, officious, pigheaded, pragmatic 10 dogmatical
O Pioneers!: 5 novel
author: Willa Cather
character: 3 Lou 4 Carl, Emil, Ivar 5 Marie, Nelse, Oscar, Sadie, Signa 6 Stella
opium: 4 drug 7 anodyne 8 hypnotic, laudanum, narcotic, nepenthe, sedative 9 calmative, soporific 10 painkiller, palliative
Opium: 5 scent 9 fragrance
Opium __: 3 War
Oporto: 4 city, port, town
city near ~: 6 Lisbon
locale: 6 Europe 8 Portugal
river: 5 Douro
opossum: 5 yapok 6 animal 9 marsupial
female: 4 jill
male: 4 jack
relative: *see* marsupial
young: 4 joey
opp.: 3 ant. 8 opposite
O.P.P. (1991 song)
artist: Naughty by Nature
Oppenheimer, J. Robert: 9 physicist
opponent: 3 con, foe 4 anti 5 enemy, match, rival 6 bandit, bidder, player 7 nemesis 8 litigant 9 adversary, assailant, candidate, dark horse, disputant, ill-wisher 10 antagonist, challenger, competitor, contestant
opportune: 3 apt, fit, pat 4 good, meet, ripe 5 happy, lucky, right 6 golden, proper, timely 7 apropos, fitting, helpful, hopeful 8 suitable 9 expedient, favorable, fortunate, well-timed 10 auspicious, convenient, felicitous, fortuitous, propitious, prosperous, seasonable, time-saving
time: 4 shot 6 chance 8 occasion
opportunist: 3 cad 4 user 5 cheat, knave, rogue 6 rascal 9 cardsharp, charlatan, scoundrel 10 blackguard, black sheep, scapegrace
opportunistic: 7 selfish, worldly 8 ulterior 10 exploitive
opportunity: 2 go 3 way 4 luck, risk, room, shot, time, turn 5 break, crack, means, scope, start, whack 6 chance, excuse 7 leisure, liberty, opening, vacancy 8 good luck, occasion 9 elbowroom, fair shake, privilege 10 good chance
at the first ~: 4 anon, soon 7 shortly 8 directly, promptly 9 forthwith, presently, right away 10 before long
__ opportunity: 5 equal, photo 6 golden
opposable digit: 5 thumb
oppose: 3 bar, pit, vie 4 buck, defy, deny, stem 5 argue, check, cross, fight, flout, rebel, rebut, rival 6 assail, attack, battle, combat, debate, hinder, ignore, impugn, negate, rebuff, rebuke, refute, resist, revolt, take on, thwart 7 assault, compare, contest, counter, dispute, frown at, gainsay, play off, prevent, protest, reverse, vie with, violate 8 confront, contrast, disagree, face down, obstruct, question 9 disregard, frown upon, stand up to, take issue, withstand 10 antagonize, contradict, contravene, controvert, counteract, disapprove, neutralize, set against, take a stand
opposed: 4 agin, anti, loth 5 loath, polar 6 at odds, averse 7 adverse, against, counter, denying, hostile, warring 8 battling, clashing, contrary, crossing, indocile, inimical, rivaling 9 combating, defending, defensive, disputing, objecting, repelling, unwilling, up against 10 antithetic, antonymous, facing down, gainsaying, protesting
be ~: 4 mind 5 demur, rebel 6 object 7 dispute
diametrically ~: 5 polar 7 counter 8 contrary 9 antipodal 10 antipodean
to: 4 agin 6 gainst, versus 7 against, athwart
opposer: 3 foe 4 anti 5 enemy, rival 9 adversary, ill-wisher 10 antagonist
opposing: 3 con 4 anti 5 rival 6 at odds, averse, head-on, versus 7 against, counter, denying, hostile, loath to, warring 8 averse to, battling, clashing, contrary, crossing, disputed, inimical, negative, rivaling 9 combating, counter to, defending, defensive, disputing, hostile to, objecting, repelling, up against 10 antonymous, at odds with, facing down, gainsaying, protesting
prefix: 4 anti- 6 contra-
vote: 3 nay
opposite: 5 other, polar 6 contra, facing, gainst, unlike 7 abreast, adverse, against, antonym, counter, diverse, inverse, obverse, reverse, unalike, vis-à-vis 8 antipode, contrary, converse, flip-side, fronting, inimical, reversed 9 antipodal, crossways, crosswise, different, differing, inversion, other side, vice versa 10 antipodean, antithesis, antithetic, dissimilar, face-to-face

prefix: **3** dis- **4** anti- **7** counter-, enantio-
opposite __: **3** sex **6** number
oppositely: **9** in reverse, inversely, vice versa **10** conversely
Opposite of Fate, The
author: Amy Tan
Opposite of Sex, The (1998 film)
cast: Lisa Kudrow, Lyle Lovett, Christina Ricci
director: Don Roos
Opposites Attract (1990 song)
artist: Paula Abdul
opposition: **3** foe **4** flak **5** enemy, fight, flack, rival **6** combat, rebuff **7** defense, dissent, rivalry, warfare **8** aversion, conflict, defiance, friction, negation **9** adversary, antipathy, hostility, other side, rebellion **10** antagonism, antithesis, comparison, competitor, contention, difference, filibuster
check out the ~: **5** recon, scout
in direct ~: **6** head-on **10** face-to-face, unmediated
in ~ to: **3** con **4** anti **7** against, athwart
__ opposition: **5** loyal
oppositionist: **3** foe **4** anti
oppress: **3** tax **4** load, rack, ride, rule **5** abuse, bully, crush, force, grind, harry, hound, press, tread, weary, worry, wrong **6** burden, harass, pick on, plague, prey on, punish, sadden, saddle, subdue **7** afflict, depress, dragoon, put upon, smother, squeeze, squelch, torment, torture, trample **8** aggrieve, beat down, browbeat, dispirit, distress, domineer, encumber, handicap, keep down, maltreat, overload, suppress **9** despotize, overpower, overwhelm, persecute, subjugate, terrorize, trample on, tyrannize, weigh down **10** dishearten
oppressed: **5** laden **9** aggrieved **10** despairing
oppression: **4** onus, yoke **5** abuse, force, wrong **6** injury, misery, stress **7** control, cruelty, fascism, torment, tyranny **8** coercion, hardship, iron hand, severity, subduing **9** autocracy, brutality, despotism, extortion, harshness, injustice, suffering **10** difficulty, domination
oppressive: **4** firm, hard, mean **5** bleak, bossy, close, cruel, harsh, heavy, hefty, muggy, picky, rigid, rough, stern, stiff, tough **6** brutal, dismal, gloomy, leaden, severe, somber, steamy, sticky, strict, stuffy, sultry, taxing, thorny, torrid, trying, unjust, uphill **7** airless, arduous, austere, exigent, inhuman, onerous, Spartan, unhappy, weighty **8** despotic, exacting, exigeant, grievous, grinding, grueling, hard-line, overcast, rigorous, stifling, tiresome, toilsome **9** cheerless, confining, demanding, draconian, imperious, laborious, ponderous, saddening, strenuous, stringent, unbending, unsparing **10** burdensome, cumbersome, depressing, despotical, enervating, formidable, inflexible, iron-fisted, no-nonsense, tenebrific, tyrannical
not ~: **4** easy, mild **5** light, loose **6** gentle **8** moderate **9** easygoing **10** unexacting
oppressor: **4** tsar **5** bully **6** despot, tyrant **8** dictator **10** inquisitor
opprobriate: **4** slam **5** decry **6** vilify **7** asperse, censure, condemn, run down **8** badmouth, denounce, derogate **9** criticize, disparage **10** calumniate
opprobrious: **4** evil, ugly, vile **7** abusive, damning **8** damaging, reviling, shameful **9** malicious, maligning, nefarious, offensive, vitriolic **10** censorious, scurrilous
opprobrium: **3** dig **4** barb, evil, gibe, jibe, slam, slap, slur, snub **5** abuse, libel, odium, scorn, shame, taunt **6** infamy, insult, rebuff, slight **7** affront, calumny, catcall, disdain, mockery, obloquy, offense, put-down, slander **8** contempt, derision, disgrace, dishonor, ignominy, ridicule **9** aspersion, cheap shot, contumely, criticism, disrepute, ill repute, indignity **10** defamation, disrespect
oppugn: **3** pan **5** blast, knock **6** assail, attack **7** confute, put down, rip into **8** lace into, tear into **9** blaspheme, criticize, light into **10** controvert, prove wrong
oppugnant: **3** icy **5** nasty, stony **6** averse, bitter, chilly **7** adverse, hateful, hostile, opposed, scrappy **8** clashing, contrary, inimical, militant, opposing, venomous, virulent **9** bellicose, vitriolic **10** antagonist, pugnacious, unfriendly
Oprah: **7** Winfrey
emulate ~: **4** diet, host **6** reduce
former rival: **4** Phil **5** Rosie
production company: **5** Harpo
stock-in-trade: **4** chat, talk **8** dialogue **9** interview **10** discussion
Opry
greeting: **5** howdy
instrument: **5** banjo **6** guitar
locale: **9** Nashville, Tennessee
Ops: **7** goddess
brother: **6** Saturn
daughter: **4** Juno **5** Ceres, Vesta **8** Euryclea
equivalent: **4** Rhea
husband: **6** Saturn
son: **5** Pluto **7** Jupiter, Neptune
opt: **4** cull, mark, pick, take, vote, will **5** elect **6** choose, decide, prefer, select **9** single out
for: **2** go **4** pick, take **5** elect, favor, key on **6** choose, prefer, select **7** pick out **8** decide on **9** single out **10** settle upon
out: **4** quit **5** leave, rebel **7** abandon, retreat **8** abdicate, renounce **9** disengage **10** relinquish
opt __: **3** for, out
optic: **5** nerve **6** visual **7** sensory **9** sensorial
cover: **6** eyelid
optic __: **4** disk **5** nerve
__ optic: **5** fiber
optical: **6** visual
device: **4** lens **5** loupe **7** monocle **8** eyeglass, eyepiece **9** magnifier **10** spectacles
illusion: **6** mirage
organ: **3** eye
optical __: **4** disc, disk
optician product: **4** lens **6** frames **7** glasses **8** contacts **10** spectacles
optics: **6** vision **7** science
adjective: **5** focal
device: **5** prism
study: **5** light
verb in ~: **4** lase
__ optics: **5** fiber
Optima: **3** car, Kia **4** auto, font **8** typeface
optimal: **4** best **5** first, ideal **6** superb **7** in front **9** just right
optimally: **6** at best, at most
optimism: **4** hope **5** cheer, trust **6** morale **7** elation **8** buoyance, buoyancy, calmness, easiness, idealism, sureness **9** assurance, certainty, good cheer, happiness, lightness **10** brightness, confidence, enthusiasm, positivism
optimist: **4** bull **5** hoper **7** dreamer **8** idealist, romantic **9** Pollyanna
Wall Street ~: **4** bull
optimistic: **3** gay **4** high, rosy, sure **5** happy, jolly, merry, perky, sunny **6** blithe, bright, cheery, elated, hoping, joyful, upbeat **7** buoyant, certain, hopeful, radiant, roseate, utopian **8** carefree, cheerful, cheering, grooving, jubilant, laughing, positive, sanguine, trusting **9** believing, confident, convinced, expectant, overjoyed, promising, satisfied, sprightly **10** flying high, heartening, inspirited
about: **6** high on
be ~: **4** hope, wish **5** dream **6** aspire, expect **7** believe, look for **8** daydream **10** anticipate
phrase: **4** I can **5** I hope
optimistically: **6** at best
Optimist's Daughter, The
author: Eudora Welty
optimum: **4** A-one, best, peak **5** first, ideal **6** all-out, choice **7** capital, highest, maximum, perfect **8** choicest, flawless, gilt-edge, greatest, peerless **9** excellent, matchless, solid gold **10** world-class
option: **5** add-on, spare, voice **6** choice, voting **7** refusal **8** druthers, election, flip side, free will, recourse, volition **9** privilege, selection **10** discretion, first claim, preference, supplement
__ option: **3** put **4** call **5** stock
optional: **3** req. **5** extra, minor **8** elective, needless, possible, unforced, unneeded **9** allowable, open-ended, redundant, voluntary **10** additional
options list: **4** menu
optometría concern: **3** ojo
optométrie concern: **4** oeil
optometrist: **7** oculist **9** eye doctor
concern: **4** iris, lens **5** pupil **6** cornea, frames, retina **7** glasses
opulence: **4** luxe **6** luxury, plenty, riches, wealth **7** comfort, fortune **8** grandeur **9** abundance, affluence **10** prosperity
opulent: **4** lush, luxe, posh, rich **5** fancy, flush, grand, plush, ritzy, showy, swank **6** deluxe, flashy, frilly, glitzy, lavish, ornate **7** copious, elegant, moneyed, profuse, riotous, stately, wealthy, well-off **8** affluent, luscious, palatial, well-to-do **9** decorated, elaborate, exuberant, luxuriant, luxurious, plentiful, profusive, sumptuous **10** ornamented, prosperous, well-heeled
opuntia: **5** plant **6** cactus
opus: **4** tome, work **5** piece **6** oeuvre **7** product, writing **8** creation, symphony **9** great work **10** production
magnum ~: **4** tome, work **7** classic **8** monument **9** specialty
opus __: **3** Dei
or: **4** else **9** connector, otherwise
in music: **5** ossia
or __: **4** else
__-or: **6** either
...or __ Memorex?: **4** is it
...or __ to be...: **3** not
OR
workers: **3** Drs., MDs., RNs
see also Oregon
ora __ nobis: **3** pro
oracle: **4** sage, seer **5** augur, sibyl **6** answer, augury, vision **7** adviser, diviner, fortune, prophet **8** prophecy **9** divinator **10** divination, forecaster, prediction, revelation, soothsayer
site: **6** Delphi, Phocis
words: **4** I see
oracular: **4** wise **5** vague, vatic **6** arcane, occult, secret **7** cryptic, obscure, vatical **8** Delphian, divining, mystical **9** ambiguous, cryptical, presaging, prescient, prophetic, sibylline, vaticinal **10** auspicious, cabalistic, mysterious, portending, portentous, predicting, unknowable
oral: **4** exam, said, test, told **5** vocal **6** buccal, phonic, spoken, verbal, voiced **7** lingual, related, sounded, uttered **8** narrated, phonetic, viva-voce **9** outspoken, recounted, unwritten, vocalized **10** articulate, verbalized
cavity: **5** mouth
communication: **4** talk **6** debate, homily, sermon, speech **7** address, lecture **8** dialogue, rhetoric **9** discourse **10** discussion
history: **4** lore, myth **5** sagas, tales **7** beliefs, customs, legends, sayings **8** folklore **10** traditions
oral __: **4** exam **7** history, hygiene, surgeon, vaccine
orale: **4** cape **5** fanon **7** maniple
wearer: **4** Pope **6** bishop **7** pontiff, prelate
orally: **5** aloud, parol **8** viva voce
Oral Roberts University
locale: **5** Tulsa **8** Oklahoma
oral surgeon deg.: **3** DDS
Oran: **4** city, port, town **5** Jones
locale: **7** Algeria
orang: **3** ape **6** animal, simian **7** primate
relative: ***see*** primate
orange: **4** soda, tree **5** coral, fruit, Jaffa, Osage, peach **6** carrot,

citrus, flavor, salmon, tangor, titian 7 apricot, Seville 8 bergamot, Valencia 9 cantaloup, tangerine 10 cantaloupe
brownish ~: 10 terra cotta
coating: 4 rust
color: 5 flame, henna 7 pumpkin, saffron 8 hyacinth 9 tangerine 10 terra cotta
container: 3 box 4 case 5 crate 6 carton
derivative: 6 citral
drink: 3 ade 5 Crush, Fanta
ender: 3 ade 4 root, wood
feature: 5 navel
flower: 5 poppy, tulip 6 cosmos 7 day lily 8 hawkweed, marigold 9 calendula 10 nasturtium, wallflower
gem: 4 sard 5 balas 7 sardine, sardius
like ~ juice: 5 tangy
like ~ traffic markers: 5 conic 7 conical
make ~ juice: 4 bore, ream
part: 4 peel, pulp, rind, skin
pekoe: 3 tea 4 brew 5 drink
reddish ~: 5 flame, henna 8 hyacinth 9 tangerine
relative: *see* citrus
seed: 3 pip
seedless ~: 5 navel
vegetable: 3 yam
yellowish ~: 7 saffron
zircon: 6 ligure
orange __: 5 juice, pekoe
__ orange: 5 blood, Jaffa, navel, Osage 6 temple 7 Seville
Orange: 4 city, town 5 river
locale: 5 Texas 9 New Jersey 10 California
River locale: 7 Lesotho
river to the ~: 4 Vaal
William of ~ foe: 6 De Witt
Orange __: 4 Bowl 6 Julius
Orange __ State: 4 Free
__ Orange: 4 Fort 5 Agent
orangeade: 5 drink 8 beverage
orange-and-black bird: 6 oriole
orange-and-white rental: 5 U-Haul
orange-billed bird: 5 mynah
orange blossom: 5 drink 8 beverage, cocktail
derivative: 5 nerol 6 neroli
ingredient: 3 gin
Orange Blossom Special: 5 train
Orange Bowl
locale: 5 Miami 7 Florida
org.: 4 NCAA
Orange County Register: 5 paper 9 newspaper
locale: 8 Santa Ana 10 California
Orange Free __: 5 State
__ or Angel: 5 Devil
__ Orange, NJ: 4 East
orange pekoe: 8 beverage
__ Orange Pips, The: 4 Five
orange-red
flower: 9 safflower
mineral: 4 sard 7 sardine, sardius
orange-roof eatery: 4 HoJo
oranges, apples and: 6 unlike 9 different
Oranges & Lemons
artist: XTC
orange-yellow: 5 amber
orangish: 5 ocher, ochre, poppy 6 crocus 7 saffron
orangutan: 3 ape 5 biped 6 animal 7 primate
relative: *see* primate
Orani: 8 Algerian
Oranjestad: 4 city, town
locale: 5 Aruba
orant: 4 icon, ikon 5 eikon
ora pro nobis: 9 pray for us
orate: 3 jaw, say 4 rant, talk 5 Bryan, speak, spout 6 preach 7 address, declaim, expound, lecture 8 bloviate, harangue, homilize, sound off 9 discourse, hold forth, sermonize, speechify
oration: 4 talk 5 eloge, pitch, spiel 6 eulogy, homily, sermon, speech 7 address, lecture, pep talk, soapbox 8 harangue, rhetoric 9 chalk talk, discourse, panegyric, utterance 10 apostrophe, recitation, vocalizing
give an ~: 4 talk 5 speak, spout 7 declaim 9 hold forth
orator: 4 Cato, Clay 6 Cicero, rhetor 7 reciter, speaker 8 lecturer, Pericles, preacher 9 declaimer, Isocrates 10 Protagoras, sermonizer
contest: 6 debate 8 polemics
device: 5 irony
perch: 4 dais 6 podium 7 rostrum 8 platform
Orator: 4 font 8 typeface
oratorio: 5 music, piece
composer: 4 Bach 5 Haydn 6 Handel 7 Vivaldi
melody: 4 aria
singers: 5 choir 6 chorus
Orators, The
author: W.H. Auden
oratory: 4 rhet. 6 chapel, speech 7 diction 8 rhetoric, sacellum 9 elocution, eloquence 10 vocalizing
orb: 3 eye, sph., sun 4 ball, moon 5 globe, world 6 planet, sphere 8 baby blue, baseball 10 basketball
edible ~: 3 pea
Orbach, Jerry: 5 actor
film: Dirty Dancing (1987)
Prince of the City (1981)
TV: Law & Order
orbed: 5 round 7 circled, rounded 8 circular 9 encircled, spherical
Orbison, Roy: 5 tenor 6 singer
song: Blue Angel (1960)
Blue Bayou (1963)
Crying (1961)
Dream Baby (1962)
Falling (1963)
Goodnight (1965)
In Dreams (1963)
It's Over (1964)
Leah (1962)
Mean Woman Blues (1963)
Oh, Pretty Woman (1964)
Only the Lonely (1960)
Pretty Paper (1963)
Running Scared (1961)
You Got It (1989)
orbit: 3 lap, way 4 path, turn 5 ambit, curve, field, limit, range, reach, realm, round, scope, sweep, track, wheel 6 bounds, circle, course, domain, length, radius, sphere, travel 7 circuit, compass, ellipse, expanse, purview, revolve 8 confines, dominion, encircle, province, rotation 9 influence 10 boundaries, revolution, trajectory
lose ~: 5 decay
period: 4 year
point: 4 apse 5 apsis 6 apogee 7 perigee
segment: 3 arc 5 curve
shape: 4 oval
transmission station: 6 Comsat
__ orbit: 5 lunar, polar
Orbit: 3 gum 10 chewing gum
alternative: *see* chewing gum
orbiter: 4 moon 6 planet 8 asteroid 9 satellite
solar ~: 4 Mars 5 comet, Earth, Pluto, Venus 6 Saturn, Uranus 7 Jupiter, Mercury
__ Orbiter: 5 Lunar
Orbiter org.: 4 NASA
orbiting: 7 in space
__-or-break: 4 make
__-or-bust: 4 boom
orc: 5 whale 7 grampus 8 cetacean
relative: *see* cetacean
orca: 5 Shamu, Willy 8 predator
orch.
section: 3 str. 4 perc.
union: 3 AFM
work: 3 sym.
see also orchestra
orchard: 5 grove, stand
device: 6 fogger
former ~ spray: 4 Alar
pest: 5 borer
product: 3 nut 4 pear, tree 5 apple, fruit, peach 6 cherry
tend an ~: 3 lop, mow, top 4 clip, crop, snip, trim 5 prune, shear
unit: 6 bushel
__ orchard: 5 apple, peach 6 cherry
__ Orchard, The: 6 Cherry
orchestra: 4 band 8 ensemble, symphony
arrange for an ~: 5 score
be in an ~: 4 play
cheer for an ~: 5 bravo
funding org.: 3 NEA
locale: 3 pit 4 row B, row C
member: 3 sax 4 bass, drum, gong, harp, horn, oboe, reed, tuba, wind 5 cello, flute, piano, viola 6 cymbal, violin 7 bassoon, piccolo, timpani 8 clarinet 9 saxophone 10 French horn 11 English horn
movement: 4 trio 5 largo, rondo 6 adagio 7 allegro
output: 5 music
practice: 3 reh. 9 rehearsal
section: 3 str. 5 brass 7 strings 8 woodwind 10 percussion
VIP: 3 ldr. 7 maestro, soloist 9 conductor
work: 5 fugue, music, rondo, score, suite 6 sonata 7 cantata, chorale, scherzo, toccata 8 concerto, nocturne, oratorio, overture, symphony 9 pastorale
orchestra __: 3 pit
__ orchestra: 7 chamber 8 symphony
orchestrate: 5 score, set up, stage 6 direct, manage 7 arrange, control 8 organize 9 harmonize 10 manipulate
orchid: 5 plant 6 bluish, flower, purple 7 blueish, calypso, reddish 8 cattleya 9 swamp pink
product: 5 salep
relative: *see* purple color
orchidlike flower: 4 iris
__ or Consequences: 5 Truth
Orcus: 4 hell 5 abyss, Hades, limbo 7 inferno 9 perdition 10 lower world, underworld
__ or cut bait: 4 fish
Orczy, Emmuska: 6 writer 7 English
work: The Scarlet Pimpernel
Ord: 4 Fort
ORD: 5 O'Hare
abbr.: 3 arr., ETA
locale: 3 Chi. 15 Chicago. Illinois
ordain: 3 fix, run, set 4 make, rule, will 5 bless, enact, frock 6 anoint, decree, enjoin, instal, invest 7 command, destine, dictate, install, instate 8 delegate, legalize 9 legislate, prescribe, pronounce 10 commission, consecrate, constitute
ordained: 5 fated 6 doomed, lawful 7 assured, certain, decided, decreed 8 destined, mandated 9 impending, statutory 10 determined, inevitable, inexorable, prescribed
one: 4 abbé 5 abbot, padre, rabbi, vicar 6 clergy, cleric, deacon, parson, pastor, priest 8 chaplain, minister, preacher
__ or Dare: 5 Truth
ordeal: 4 hell, test 5 agony, cross, curse, trial 6 misery, trauma 7 anguish, torment, torture, trouble 8 calamity, crucible, distress, irritant 9 martyrdom, nightmare, suffering 10 affliction, difficulty, infliction, visitation
Ordeal of Gilbert Pinfold, The
author: Evelyn Waugh
order: 3 bid, buy, law, lot, set, sys. 4 book, calm, cite, club, fiat, file, form, gild, kind, rank, rule, sect, sort, syst., tell, tidy, tier, trim, type, warn, wish, word 5 align, aline, array, caste, class, edict, enact, force, genre, genus, goods, group, guild, index, peace, queue, range, ready, say-so, setup, ukase 6 adjure, amount, assign, behest, charge, codify, decree, degree, demand, dictum, direct, divide, engage, enjoin, impose, insist, kilter, league, lineup, nature, neaten, obtain, rating, ruling, secure, series, settle, stripe, summon, system 7 arrange, bidding, booking, catalog, command, dictate, dispose, harmony, mandate, marshal, pattern, precept, request, require, reserve, routine, society, sort out, species, station, variety 8 classify, graduate, instruct, neatness, organize, priority, purchase, quantity, regiment, regulate, sentence, sequence, shipment, sodality, sorority, subclass, symmetry, tabulate, tidiness 9 authorize, catalogue, direction, directive, gradation, hierarchy, legislate, materials, methodize, ordinance, prescribe, propriety, structure

10 categorize, discipline, distribute, fraternity, injunction, lawfulness, permission, pigeonhole, procession, regularity, regulation, sisterhood, succession, uniformity
absence of ~: 4 mess, riot 5 chaos, havoc, snarl 6 bedlam, mayhem, tumult, uproar 7 anarchy, clutter, discord, turmoil 8 disarray, shambles 9 confusion 10 unruliness
around: 4 boss 9 trample on, tyrannize 10 lord it over
be out of ~: 5 act up 9 misbehave
blank: 4 form 6 coupon
change the ~: 5 mix up 6 jumble, muddle 7 shuffle 8 disarray, scramble 9 rearrange 10 disarrange
combining form: 3 tax- 4 taxi-, taxo-, -taxy 5 -taxis
court ~: 4 rise, stay, writ 5 paper 7 all rise
for dinner: 3 eat, get 4 have 5 enjoy 7 procure
handle an ~: 4 fill, lade, load, pack 6 make up, supply 7 process, satisfy
in ~: 2 OK 4 neat, okay, okeh, okey, tidy 5 clean, ready 6 aright, proper, spruce, usable 7 orderly, regular, useable 8 prepared, straight
in short ~: 4 anon, fast, soon
in the ~ given (abbr.): 4 resp.
in ~ (to): 4 so as
king ~: 3 act 4 fiat 5 ukase 6 decree, dictum, ruling 7 dictate, mandate, precept 9 manifesto
make to ~: 6 tailor
member: 4 lama, monk 5 abbot, friar 6 priest, sensei 7 ascetic, bhikshu, brother 8 cenobite, monastic, rinpoche 9 religious
name meaning ~: 5 Cosmo
of business: 6 agenda 7 program 8 schedule
on the ~ of: 4 like 5 about 9 similar to 10 resembling
out of ~: 4 down 5 amiss, mussy, unapt, wrong 6 blooey, blooie, broken, busted, faulty 7 haywire, jumbled 8 improper 9 defective, disrepair, irregular 10 broken-down, nongermane, on the fritz
partner: 3 law
pecking ~: 4 rank 5 class, order, place 6 regime
put in ~: 4 sort, tidy 6 assort, settle 7 correct 8 organize, regulate, untangle
taker: 6 garçon, server, waiter
to go: 4 fire, mail, oust, post, send, ship 5 eat in, expel, route 6 assign, banish, deport, direct, put out 7 cast out, consign, turn out 8 dispatch, displace, drive out, transfer 9 dismissal, ostracize, transport 10 expatriate
written ~: 3 req.
order __: 5 blank
__ order: 3 gag, job, new 4 back, mail, open, tall, work 5 a tall, court, money, short 7 batting, pecking, working
__-order: 6 custom
Order __ Garter: 5 of the
__ & Order: 3 Law
__-order cook: 5 short
__-order drill: 5 close
ordered: 4 bade, neat, tidy 6 lawful 7 regular 8 methodic 10 methodical
ordering: 5 array 6 system 8 sequence 9 placement
orderliness: 3 law 4 calm, form 5 order, peace 7 harmony 8 neatness, symmetry, tidiness 10 discipline, uniformity
orderly: 4 aide, calm, good, neat, tidy, trim 5 clean, crisp, kempt, quiet 6 docile, formal, spruce 7 in shape, regular, uniform 8 coherent, decorous, methodic, obedient, readable, straight, thorough, to rights, tranquil, well-kept 9 attendant, organized, peaceable, regulated, shipshape 10 controlled, fastidious, law-abiding, methodical, neat as a pin, nonviolent, submissive, systematic
British army ~: 6 batman
make ~: 4 tidy 5 clean 6 neaten 8 spruce up 10 straighten
thinking: 5 logic, sense 6 reason, sanity, thesis 9 coherence, deduction, dialectic, good sense, induction, inference, rationale, reasoning, syllogism 10 philosophy
__ order of: 5 on the
Order of __: 5 Lenin, Merit
__ Order of Moose: 5 Loyal
Order of the __: 6 Garter
orders
follow ~: 4 heed, mind, obey 5 act on, bow to 6 accept, bend to, listen, submit 7 abide by, agree to, defer to, observe, stick to 8 adhere to, carry out 9 conform to, consent to, truckle to 10 comply with, keep in step, toe the line
give ~: 4 boss, head, lead, rule, tell 5 steer 6 advise, charge, direct, enjoin, govern, manage 7 command, dictate, oversee, preside 8 dominate 9 officiate, prescribe, supervise 10 administer, mastermind, ride herd on, run the show
holy ~: 9 sacrament
not following ~: 5 rogue 10 rebellious
prone to giving ~: 5 bossy, pushy 8 arrogant, despotic 9 imperious 10 commanding, ironhanded, oppressive, peremptory, tyrannical
__ ordinaire: 3 vin
ordinal: 2 no. 6 number
imprecise ~: 3 nth
suffix: 3 -eth
ordinal __: 6 number
ordinance: 3 act, law 4 code, fiat, rule 5 bylaw, canon, edict, order, ukase 6 assize, decree, dictum, ruling 7 command, mandate, precept, statute 9 direction, directive, enactment, prescript 10 regulation
ordinarily: 6 simply 7 as a rule, usually 8 commonly, normally 9 generally, in general, most often, naturally, regularly 10 by and large, frequently
ordinary: 4 dull, fair, mean, so-so 5 banal, daily, lowly, plain, prosy, stock, trite, typic, usual 6 cleric, common, humble, jejune, medium, modest, normal, public, simple, vulgar, wonted 7 average, general, generic, humdrum, ignoble, insipid, mundane, natural, popular, prosaic, regular, routine, typical, vanilla 8 everyday, familiar, frequent, habitual, homespun, inferior, mediocre, middling, moderate, orthodox, plebeian, standard, workaday 9 customary, generical, household, prosaical, quotidian, tolerable, unnotable 10 accustomed, dullsville, fairly good, pedestrian, prevailing, second-rate, uneventful, uninspired, white-bread, widespread
out of the ~: 3 odd 4 rare 5 novel, queer, weird 7 bizarre, curious, oddball, special, strange, unusual 8 striking, uncommon 9 different
Ordinary Life, An
author: Karel Capek
__ Ordinary Man: 4 I'm an
Ordinary People (1980 film)
cast: Judd Hirsch, Timothy Hutton, Mary Tyler Moore, Donald Sutherland
director: Robert Redford
Ordinary World (1993 song)
artist: Duran Duran
ordination: 9 induction 10 delegation
ordnance: 4 arms 6 cannon 7 weapons 8 armament, materiel, weaponry 9 artillery, munitions
__ Ordo Seclorum: 5 Novus
ore: 4 lode, rock 5 borax, metal, money, prill, stone 6 barite, blende, galena, pyrite, raddle, reddle, ruddle, rutile 7 azurite, barytes, bauxite, bonanza, bornite, cuprite, kernite, mineral, pay dirt, realgar, sylvite, thorite, zincite 8 autunite, cinnabar, dolomite, galenite, goethite, hematite, ilmenite, limonite, monazite, siderite, smaltite, stannite, stibnite, taconite 9 argentite, carnotite, celestite, cerussite, columbite, covellite, magnetite, malachite, millerite, mispickel, niccolite, proustite, scheelite, sylvanite, tantalite, uraninite, willemite, wulfenite 10 calaverite, carnallite, chalcocite, garnierite, lepidolite, mother lode, polybasite, pyrolusite, sphalerite, vanadinite, yellowcake
aluminum ~: 7 bauxite
analyze ~: 5 assay
antimony ~: 8 stibnite
arsenic ~: 7 realgar
boron ~: 7 kernite
carrier: 4 scow, tram 5 barge
cobalt ~: 8 smaltite
copper ~: 7 azurite 9 malachite
diggers' org.: 3 UMW
gold ~: 9 sylvanite
iron ~: 8 hematite, limonite, siderite, taconite 9 magnetite
lead ~: 6 galena 9 cerussite 10 vanadinite
lithium ~: 10 lepidolite
mixture: 4 flux
molybdenum ~: 9 wulfenite
nickel ~: 9 millerite, niccolite
niobium ~: 9 columbite
potassium ~: 7 sylvite
process ~: 5 smelt 6 reduce, refine
science: 10 metallurgy
seeker: 5 miner 6 digger 7 collier
silver ~: 9 argentite, sylvanite 10 polybasite
source: 4 lode, mine, seam, vein
splinter: 5 spall
strontium ~: 9 celestite
suffix: 3 -ite
tin ~: 8 stannite
titanium ~: 8 ilmenite
tungsten ~: 9 scheelite
zinc ~: 7 zincite 9 willemite 10 sphalerite
öre: 4 coin
word on an ~: 5 Norge
Ore-__: 3 Ida
Ore.
campus: 3 OSU
neighbor: 3 Cal., Ida., Nev. 4 Wash. 5 Calif.
zone: 3 PDT, PST
see also Oregon
oread: 4 Echo 5 nymph 6 Daphne
Oreck: 3 vac 6 vacuum
rival: 5 Kirby 6 Eureka, Hoover 10 Electrolux
orectic: 7 athirst 8 desirous
Oreg.
see Oregon
oregano: 4 herb 9 seasoning
Oregon: 5 state, trail
campus: 3 OSU
capital: 5 Salem
city: 4 Bend 5 Aloha, Salem 6 Albany, Eugene, Keizer, Tigard 7 Ashland, Gresham, Medford 8 Altamont, Portland, Roseburg, Tualatin, West Linn, Woodburn 9 Beaverton, Corvallis, Hillsboro, Milwaukie 10 Grants Pass, Lake Oswego
conference: 6 Pac-Ten
county: 4 Coos 5 Wasco 7 Clatsop, Klamath
Indian: 5 Modoc 6 Cayuse 7 Klamath, Takelma 8 Sahaptin
lake: 6 Crater
mountain: 4 Hood
national park: 10 Crater Lake
native: 6 Beaver
neighbor: 3 Cal., Ida., Nev. 4 Wash. 5 Idaho 6 Nevada 10 California, Washington
river: 5 Rogue
start of ~ motto: 4 Alis
state animal: 6 beaver
state beverage: 4 milk
state bird: 10 meadowlark
state flower: 5 grape
state gemstone: 8 sunstone
state nut: 8 hazelnut
state rock: 5 geode
state tree: 10 Douglas fir
University of ~ locale: 6 Eugene
zone: 3 PDT, PST
Oregon __: 5 Trail
Oregonian: 5 paper 9 newspaper
locale: 8 Portland
Oregon State
athletes: 7 Beavers
conference: 6 Pac-Ten
locale: 9 Corvallis

Oregon Trail
river: 5 Snake 6 Kansas, Platte 7 Elkhorn, Laramie 8 Columbia, Missouri
Oregon Trail city: 5 Boise
Oregon Trail, The
author: Francis Parkman
O'Reilly: 4 Bill 5 Radar
Orel: 4 city, town 9 Hershiser
locale: 6 Russia
river: 3 Oka
or else, in music: 5 ossia
Orem: 4 city, town
locale: 4 Utah
Orenburg: 4 city, town
locale: 6 Russia
river: 4 Ural
Oreo: 5 cooky, treat 6 cookie
alternative: ***see*** cookie brand
component: 5 cream, creme, wafer
Oresteia
author: Aeschylus
Orestes
author: Euripides
father: 9 Agamemnon
lover: 7 Erigone
nurse of ~: 7 Arsinoe
sister: 7 Electra 9 Iphigenia
wife: 8 Hermione
__ or even: 3 odd
__-or-famine: 5 feast
Orfeo: 5 opera
composer: Luigi Rossi
Orfeo ed Euridice
role: 4 Amor
Orff: 4 Carl
__-or-flight: 5 fight
__ or foe?: 6 friend
org.: 2 co., gp. 3 CIA, grp., NSA, soc. 4 agcy., assn., corp. 5 assoc., group
part: 3 div. 4 dept.
.org
alternative: 3 com, edu, gov, net
organ: 3 ear, eye 4 gill, leaf, lung, nose, skin, tool, wing 5 agent, brain, chela, forum, gland, heart, liver, means, paper, voice 6 agency, feeler, kidney, medium, member, review, spinet, spleen, stamen, tongue 7 antenna, channel, gizzard, journal, pincers, stomach, vehicle 8 body part, magazine, pinchers, tentacle 9 flagellum, machinery, newspaper, spinneret 10 instrument, periodical
ender: 3 ism
insect sense ~: 4 palp 6 palpus 7 antenna
largest ~: 4 skin
lever: 4 stop 5 pedal
lining: 6 intima
meat: 5 liver, tripe 6 kidney
mouth ~: 9 harmonica
olfactory ~: 5 snoot, snout 7 schnozz 9 proboscis 10 schnozzola
opening: 5 hilum
part: 3 key 4 pipe, stop 5 pedal
rudimentary ~: 6 anlage
stop: 4 oboe 5 quint
organ __: 7 grinder
__ organ: 5 chord, house, mouth, sense, vital 6 barrel
__ Organa: 4 Leia
organdy: 6 fabric 8 material
organic: 4 live 5 basal, basic, vital 6 biotic, bodily, innate, living 7 animate, natural, plasmic, radical 8 anatomic, biotical, cellular, inherent, integral 9 elemental, essential, innermost 10 anatomical, biological, structural
compound: 4 enol 5 aldol, amide, amine, azole, ester, imide, imine, tolan 6 acetal, ethene, hexane, isomer, ketone 9 acetaldol
compound suffix: 3 -ene, -ine
dye: 3 azo 6 kermes
material: 5 guano, humus, mulch 7 compost 10 fertilizer
not ~: 9 inanimate, insensate 10 insentient
radical: 4 amyl
unit: 3 egg 4 cell, germ 5 spore
organism: 4 body, life 5 being, plant, whole 6 animal, entity, person 8 creature 9 structure
body of an ~: 4 soma
combining form: 3 bio-, -zoa 4 -zoon
infectious ~: 3 bug 4 germ 5 virus 7 microbe
modified by environment: 4 ecad
of a blue-green ~: 5 algal
simple ~: 5 monad 6 amoeba, diatom 7 rotifer 8 plankton 10 paramecium
organization: 2 co., gp. 3 grp., set 4 band, body, clan, club, crew, firm, form, gild, team 5 group, guild, house, lodge, order, party, setup, staff, trust, union 6 agency, cartel, circle, clique, design, format, layout, league, make-up, outfit, system, troupe 7 brigade, combine, company, concern, concord, conduct, coterie, harmony, machine, network, pattern, society 8 alliance, assembly, business, disposal, grouping, industry, movement, planning, sodality, sorority, symmetry 9 coalition, formation, framework, institute, structure, syndicate
part: 3 div. 4 dept. 8 division 10 department
organization __: 5 chart
organizational div.: 4 dept.
Organization, The (1971 film)
cast: Barbara McNair, Sidney Poitier
organize: 3 run 4 form, plan, sort 5 array, found, frame, group, mount, order, rally, ready, set up, stage 6 codify, create, embody, format, get set, imbody, line up, tidy up 7 arrange, catalog, compile, compose, conduct, dispose, marshal 8 classify, engineer, get going, mobilize, regulate, schedule 9 catalogue, correlate, establish, formulate 10 coordinate, pigeonhole
organized: 4 neat, tidy 5 ready 6 social 7 orderly, regular 8 coherent, methodic 9 efficient 10 methodical, systematic
get ~: 4 plan, plot 5 chart, frame, set up 6 lay out, map out 7 outline, prepare, project, propose, work out 8 engineer, rough out, schedule, think out 9 formulate 10 mastermind
group: 4 team 7 machine 9 task force
organized __: 5 crime, labor
organizer: 4 boss, head 5 chair, chief, super 6 honcho, leader, regent, tycoon 7 curator, founder, kingpin, manager 8 director, governor, overseer 9 commander, executive, principal 10 mastermind, supervisor
organ of __: 5 Corti
organs: 6 vitals
__ Organum: 5 Novum
organza: 5 cloth 6 fabric 8 material
like ~: 4 fine, thin 5 filmy, gauzy, light, sheer 8 delicate, gossamer 10 diaphanous, see-through
Oriani, Alfredo: 4 poet 7 Italian 10 playwright
oribi: 6 animal 8 antelope
relative: ***see*** antelope
oriel: 6 recess, window 9 bay window
like an ~: 5 paned
orient: 3 set 4 turn 5 adapt, align, aline 6 adjust, direct, locate, relate 7 conform 8 accustom 9 determine, orientate
Orient: 4 Asia, east 5 Henry 7 Far East
Orient __: 7 Express
Oriental: 7 Eastern
Oriental __: 3 rug
orientation: 3 fix 8 bearings, location, position 9 direction, placement
orienteer need: 3 map 5 atlas, chart 7 compass
Orient Express: 5 coach, train 9 transport
stop: 5 Paris 6 Calais 8 Istanbul
unit: 3 car
orifice: 4 hole, pore, vent 5 mouth 6 outlet 7 opening
leaf ~: 5 stoma
orig.
not an ~: 4 dupl., imit. 5 repro.
origami: 3 art 8 Japanese
feature: 4 bend, fold 6 crease 7 fluting
need: 5 paper, sheet
origin: 3 egg 4 base, dawn, font, germ, head, rise, root, seed, well 5 agent, basis, birth, blood, cause, fount, git-go, roots, start, stock 6 author, cradle, day one, family, father, matrix, mother, motive, outset, parent, source, spring 7 creator, dawning, descent, genesis, lineage, nucleus 8 ancestor, ancestry, creation, fountain, heritage, nativity, pedigree, producer 9 beginning, causation, emergence, etymology, generator, inception, parentage, principle, square one, threshold 10 antecedent, beginnings, conception, derivation, envisaging, extraction, foundation, incipience, initiation, mainspring, progenitor, provenance, wellspring
combining form: 4 -geny
original: 3 new, old 4 card, mint, real 5 early, first, fresh, model, novel, prime, valid, witty 6 clever, infant, master, native, oddity, quaint, single, virgin, weirdo 7 anomaly, coinage, fertile, genuine, initial, novelty, oddball, opening, paragon, pattern, pioneer, primary, radical, seminal, untried, unusual 8 creation, creative, earliest, exemplar, inspired, paradigm, primeval, pristine, singular, starting, uncommon, virginal 9 aborigine, archetype, authentic, beginning, character, demiurgic, eccentric, embryonic, firsthand, formative, inceptive, ingenious, inspiring, inventive, precursor, primaeval, primitive, prototype, realistic, underived 10 archetypal, avant-garde, commencing, conceiving, elementary, forerunner, generative, innovative, primordial, productive, refreshing, unfamiliar
at the ~ place: 6 in situ
combining form: 4 arch- 5 arche-, archi-
in ~ form: 5 uncut
not ~: 5 deriv. 6 copied 8 borrowed, rehashed 9 imitative 10 derivative
production: 5 debut 7 opening 8 premiere 10 first night
strategy: 5 plan A
original __: 3 sin
Original Amateur Hour, The host: Major Bowes, Ted Mack
originality: 6 daring 7 newness, novelty 8 boldness 9 freshness, ingenuity 10 uniqueness
Original Kings of Comedy, The (2000 film)
cast: Cedric the Entertainer, Steve Harvey, D.L. Hughley, Bernie Mac
director: Spike Lee
originally: 5 first 7 at first, by birth 8 by origin, formerly 9 basically, initially, primarily
Original Sin (2001 film)
cast: Pedro Armendariz, Antonio Banderas, Angelina Jolie
originate: 4 coin, come, dawn, flow, form, make, open, rise, stem 5 arise, begin, build, cause, found, hatch, issue, pop up, set up, spark, spawn, start 6 create, derive, design, emerge, evolve, invent, launch, make up, open up, parent, spring 7 compose, concoct, descend, develop, emanate, kick off, lead off, pioneer, proceed, produce, think up, usher in 8 come from, commence, conceive, discover, engineer, generate, get going, initiate, innovate, occasion 9 enter upon, establish, formulate, germinate, grow out of, institute, introduce 10 bring about, come up with, inaugurate, mastermind
(from): 4 hail 6 derive, result
origination: 4 dawn 6 origin, source 8 creation 9 causation
originator: 5 cause 6 father, parent, source 7 creator, founder 8 designer, inventer, inventor 9 architect, artificer, fashioner 10 forebearer, forerunner, mastermind
Origin, The
author: Irving Stone
Orillia: 4 city, town
locale: 6 Canada 7 Ontario

Orinda: **4** city, town
locale: **10** California
O-ring: **4** seal **6** gasket
Orinoco: **3** río **5** river
feeder: **4** Meta **6** Caroni
locale: **6** Brazil **8** Colombia **9** Venezuela
tributary: **3** Aro **5** Apure
Orinoco Flow
artist: Enya
oriole: **4** bird **8** songbird
Oriole: **6** Ripken **9** Cal Ripken
Hall-of-Famer: **6** Palmer, Ripken **8** Robinson **9** Cal Ripken
Orioles: **3** ten **4** team
home: **9** Baltimore
org.: **3** ALE, MLB
rival: *see* baseball team
sport: **8** baseball
Orion: **3** cat **5** giant **6** hunter, nebula
dog of ~: **6** Sirius **10** Canis Major, Canis Minor
has one: **4** belt
lover: **3** Eos
parent: **4** Gaea **7** Euryale **8** Poseidon
star in ~: **5** Rigel **10** Betelgeuse
orison: **4** plea **5** grace **6** appeal, litany, prayer, rosary **7** service, worship **8** devotion, entreaty, petition, rogation **10** invocation
ending: **4** amen
Orissa language: **5** Oriya
Orkan, bit of: **4** nanu **5** bleem **7** shazbot
Orkhon: **5** river
River locale: **8** Mongolia
Orkin: **4** Ruth
target: **3** ant, bug **4** pest **6** insect
Orkney Islands
ancient ~ dweller: **4** Pict
locale: **8** Scotland
Orlando: **4** city, Tony, town **5** Bloom **6** Cepeda
attraction: **5** Epcot
author: Virginia Woolf
character: **5** Sasha
composer: George Frideric Handel
locale: **7** Florida
newspaper: **8** Sentinel
pro team: **5** Magic
school: **3** UCF
stadium: **5** Orena
Orlando Furioso: **4** epic, poem
author: Lodovico Ariosto
Orlando, Tony
song: Candida (1970)
He Don't Love You (1975)
Knock Three Times (1970)
Look in My Eyes Pretty Woman (1975)
Say, Has Anybody Seen My Sweet Gypsy Rose (1973)
Steppin' Out (1974)
Tie a Yellow Ribbon Round the Ole Oak Tree (1973)
__ or later: **6** sooner
Orleans: **6** battle
song: Dance With Me (1975)
Love Takes Time (1979)
Still the One (1976)
__ Orleans: **3** New
Orléans: **4** city, town
city southeast of ~: **6** Nevers
department: **6** Loiret
locale: **6** France
river: **5** Loire
__ or less: **4** more
orlo: **6** plinth
Orlon: **5** fiber **6** fabric **8** material
Orlons
song: Don't Hang Up (1962)
South Street (1963)
The Wah Watusi (1962)
orlop: **4** deck
__ or lose...: **5** Use it
Orly: **4** city, town **7** airport
locale: **6** France
Ormandy, Eugene: **9** conductor
__ or miss: **3** hit
ormolu: **5** alloy, metal
component: **4** zinc **6** copper
Ormond, Julia: **7** actress
film: First Knight (1995)
Sabrina (1995)
Smilla's Sense of Snow (1997)
ornament: **3** art, gem **4** deck, gild, lace, ring, trim **5** adorn, array, beads, bijou, dodad, dress, fix up, frill, grace, honor, jewel, pride, primp, prink **6** anklet, bangle, bauble, bedaub, bedeck, design, doodad, emboss, enrich, finial, flower, geegaw, gewgaw, polish **7** bedizen, corsage, dress up, encrust, festoon, flatter, garnish, incrust, jewelry, smarten, trinket **8** accouter, accoutre, beautify, bracelet, brighten, decorate, emblazon, figurine, froufrou, furbelow, necklace, nicknack, prettify, spruce up, trapping, trimming, wristlet **9** accessory, adornment, embellish, embroider **10** decoration, knickknack
Christmas ~: **4** ball, cane, tree **5** angel
head ~: **5** crown, tiara **6** wreath **7** coronet
roof ~: **3** epi **6** finial
showy ~: **4** gaud **6** bauble, geegaw, gewgaw
__ ornament: **4** hood
ornamental: **5** fancy, plant, showy, shrub **6** azalea, dressy, frilly **7** for show **8** delicate, justicia **9** beautiful, elaborate, enhancing, exquisite **10** decorative
band: **4** sash **6** armlet, frieze
plant: **5** pilea **6** azalea, coleus
ornamentation: **4** trim **5** decor, frill **9** arabesque
ornamented: **5** fancy, showy **6** flashy, florid, frilly, glitzy, inlaid, lavish **7** baroque, flowery, opulent **9** decorated, elaborate, garnished, luxurious, sumptuous
not ~: **4** bare **5** basic, naked, plain, stark **6** modest, severe, simple **7** austere, natural, Spartan, vanilla **9** unadorned
ornate: **4** busy, fine, lacy, rich **5** fancy, fussy, gaudy, plush, showy **6** chichi, dressy, flashy, florid, frilly, gilded, glitzy, lavish, rococo, tawdry **7** aureate, baroque, elegant, flowery, for show, opulent, splashy **8** dazzling, overdone, splendid **9** bejeweled, brilliant, elaborate, high-flown, luxuriant, luxurious, sumptuous, tasteless **10** convoluted, flamboyant, rhetorical
not ~: **5** plain, stark **6** chaste
Orne
city on the ~: **4** Caen
__ Orne Jewett: **5** Sarah
ornery: **4** cold, cool, mean **5** aloof, balky, cross, huffy, nasty, rigid, sharp, surly, testy **6** chilly, crabby, cranky, crusty, feisty, grumpy, mulish, odious, remote, snappy, sullen, touchy, unruly, wilful **7** adverse, bearish, bilious, defiant, fretful, glacial, grouchy, hateful, hostile, loutish, naughty, peevish, restive, waspish, wayward, willful **8** choleric, churlish, contrary, fretsome, growling, grumpish, inimical, obdurate, perverse, snappish, snarling, spiteful, stubborn **9** bellicose, crotchety, fractious, irascible, irritable, malicious, obstinate, pigheaded, sarcastic, splenetic, truculent, withdrawn **10** hard-bitten, headstrong, ill-natured, inflexible, malevolent, out of sorts, pugnacious, rebellious
mood: **3** pet **4** huff, snit, stew **5** pique **6** temper **9** surliness
one: **4** cuss, mule **10** curmudgeon
Ornette: **7** Coleman
__ or never: **3** now
ornithological: **5** avian
ornithologist: **6** birder
ornithology: **7** science
study: **5** birds
ornithophobe fear: **4** fowl **5** birds
__ or no: **7** whether
__ or none: **3** all
__ or not...: **4** to be **5** Ready
__ or nothing: **3** all **6** double
__ Oro: **5** Rio de
orology: **7** science
study: **9** mountains
Orono: **4** city, town
athletes: **10** Black Bears
locale: **5** Maine
Orosco, Jesse
sport: **8** baseball
__ or other: **7** somehow
orotund: **4** deep, full **5** round, tumid **6** strong **7** booming, fustian, hyped up, pompous **8** globular, powerful, resonant, sonorous **9** bombastic, grandiose, overblown
O'Rourke: **2** P.J. **3** sgt. **6** Morgan **7** Heather **8** sergeant
Oro Valley: **4** city, town
locale: **7** Arizona
Oroville: **3** dam
oro y __: **5** plata
Orozco: **4** José
Orpah
mother-in-law: **5** Naomi
or partner: **6** either
orphan: **4** waif, ward **5** Annie **9** foundling **10** ragamuffin
ender: **3** age
herd ~: **4** dogy **5** dogey, stray **6** doggie
__ Orphan Annie: **6** Little
Orphan, The
author: Thomas Otway, David Rabe
Orphée
artist: Camille Corot
Orpheus: **4** poet **6** ballet **8** Argonaut
brother: **5** Linus
composer: Igor Stravinsky
instrument: **4** lyre
parent: **7** Oeagrus **8** Calliope
wife: **8** Eurydice
__ Orpheus: **5** Black
Orpheus Descending
author: Tennessee Williams
Orpheus in the Underworld
composer: Jacques Offenbach
orphic: **6** occult **8** esoteric, profound **9** recondite
Orr: **5** Bobby, James **8** Benjamin
Orr, Bobby
emulate ~: **5** skate
milieu: **3** ice **4** rink **5** arena **6** hockey
org.: **3** NHL
Orrie's Story
author: Thomas Berger
Orrin: **5** Hatch **6** Tucker
orris: **5** braid
ender: **4** root
root extract: **5** irone
Orr, John Boyd: **7** British **8** Nobelist
__ or shine: **4** rain
__ or shut...: **5** put up
Orsk: **4** city, town
locale: **6** Russia
river: **4** Ural
__ or Something Like It: **4** Life
Orson: **4** Bean **5** Orkan **6** Welles
ex: **4** Rita
__ or swim: **4** sink
ort: **5** crumb, scrap **7** leaving, remnant **8** leftover
__ or tails: **5** heads
__ or take: **4** give
Ortega y Gasset, José: **6** writer **7** Spanish **8** essayist
orth-
kin: **4** rect-
__ or the other: **3** one
__ or the Tiger?, The: **4** Lady
__-orthicon tube: **5** image
orthoclase to Mohs: **3** six
orthodontist
concern: **4** bite
deg.: **3** DDS, DMD
org.: **3** ADA
orthodox: **4** good, true **5** pious, right, sound, typic, usual **6** common, devout, in line, narrow, normal, proper, square, wonted **7** correct, diehard, limited, regular, routine, typical **8** accepted, approved, dogmatic, everyday, habitual, hardline, official, ordinary, rightful, standard, straight **9** by the book, canonical, customary, doctrinal, religious **10** accustomed, conformist, dogmatical, legitimate, prevailing, recognized, sanctioned
opener: **3** neo
orthodoxy: **4** tune **7** harmony, keeping **8** likeness, religion, symmetry **9** agreement, coherence, congruity, obedience **10** allegiance, compliance, conformity, consonance, exactitude, observance, similarity, submission
orthopedist tool: **4** X-ray **10** radiograph
Ortiz: **3** Ana
ortolan: **4** bird
Orton, Joe: **7** British **10** playwright
work: Loot
What the Butler Saw
Or to take __ against a sea...: **4** arms

__ **or treat:** **5** trick
orts: **4** rest **5** waste **7** residue
Orvieto: **4** wine **5** white
  origin: **5** Italy
Orville: **5** Moody **6** Wright **11** Redenbacher
Orwell, George: **5** alias **6** writer **7** British
  alma mater: **4** Eton
  birthplace: **5** India
  real name: Eric Blair
  work: 1984
    Animal Farm
    Down and Out in Paris and London
    Keep the Aspidistra Flying
    Shooting an Elephant
__ **or When:** **5** Where
__ **Ory:** **5** Comte
Ory, Kid: **10** trombonist
  genre: **4** jazz
oryx: **6** animal **8** antelope
  relative: ***see*** antelope
orzo: **5** pasta
  alternative: ***see*** pasta
Os: **4** elem. **6** osmium **7** element
  76 for ~: **4** at. no.
OS/2 company: **3** IBM
Osa: **6** Massen **7** Johnson
Osage: **5** river, tribe **6** Indian, orange **7** Amerind **8** language
  River locale: **6** Kansas **8** Missouri
Osaka: **4** city, port, town
  city near ~: **4** Nara **5** Kioto, Kyoto, Sakai
  locale: **5** Japan **6** Honshu
Osaka Bay, port on: **4** Kobe
Osbert: **7** Sitwell
Osborne: **4** Joan, John **7** Jeffrey
Osborne, Joan
  song: One of Us (1995)
Osborne, John: **7** British **10** playwright
  work: Look Back in Anger
Osbourne, Ozzy
  group: Black Sabbath
  homeland: England
  song: Close My Eyes Forever (1989)
Oscar: **4** slob **5** Arias, award, Lewis, Mayer, Wilde **6** grouch, Levant, Muppet, statue, trophy **7** Handlin, Homolka, Madison **8** de la Hoya, Hijuelos, Peterson **9** de la Renta, Pettiford, Robertson, statuette **10** Charleston
  colleague: **4** Bert **5** Ernie, Piggy **6** Kermit **7** Big Bird
  cousin: **4** Emmy, Obie, Tony
  French ~: **5** César
  night rental: **4** gown **7** costume
  nominee: **4** star **5** actor **8** director
  org.: **5** AMPAS
Oscar __ Hoya: **4** de la
Oscar __ Renta: **4** de la
Oscar __ Sanchez: **5** Arias
Oscar Mayer: **5** frank **6** hot dog, wiener
  alternative: **5** Kahn's **6** Armour **8** Ball Park
Oscar winners (Actor):
  2009 - Jeff Bridges
  2008 - Sean Penn
  2007 - Daniel Day-Lewis
  2006 - Forest Whitaker
  2005 - Philip Seymour Hoffman
  2004 - Jamie Foxx
  2003 - Sean Penn
  2002 - Adrien Brody
  2001 - Denzel Washington
  2000 - Russell Crowe
  1999 - Kevin Spacey
  1998 - Roberto Benigni
  1997 - Jack Nicholson
  1996 - Geoffrey Rush
  1995 - Nicolas Cage
  1994 - Tom Hanks
  1993 - Tom Hanks
  1992 - Al Pacino
  1991 - Anthony Hopkins
  1990 - Jeremy Irons
  1989 - Daniel Day-Lewis
  1988 - Dustin Hoffman
  1987 - Michael Douglas
  1986 - Paul Newman
  1985 - William Hurt
  1984 - F. Murray Abraham
  1983 - Robert Duvall
  1982 - Ben Kingsley
  1981 - Henry Fonda
  1980 - Robert De Niro
  1979 - Dustin Hoffman
  1978 - Jon Voight
  1977 - Richard Dreyfuss
  1976 - Peter Finch
  1975 - Jack Nicholson
  1974 - Art Carney
  1973 - Jack Lemmon
  1972 - Marlon Brando
  1971 - Gene Hackman
  1970 - George C. Scott
  1969 - John Wayne
  1968 - Cliff Robertson
  1967 - Rod Steiger
  1966 - Paul Scofield
  1965 - Lee Marvin
  1964 - Rex Harrison
  1963 - Sidney Poitier
  1962 - Gregory Peck
  1961 - Maximilian Schell
  1960 - Burt Lancaster
  1959 - Charlton Heston
  1958 - David Niven
  1957 - Alec Guinness
  1956 - Yul Brynner
  1955 - Ernest Borgnine
  1954 - Marlon Brando
  1953 - William Holden
  1952 - Gary Cooper
  1951 - Humphrey Bogart
  1950 - José Ferrer
  1949 - Broderick Crawford
  1948 - Laurence Olivier
  1947 - Ronald Colman
  1946 - Fredric March
  1945 - Ray Milland
  1944 - Bing Crosby
  1943 - Paul Lukas
  1942 - James Cagney
  1941 - Gary Cooper
  1940 - James Stewart
  1939 - Robert Donat
  1938 - Spencer Tracy
  1937 - Spencer Tracy
  1936 - Paul Muni
  1935 - Victor McLaglen
  1934 - Clark Gable
  1932/33 - Charles Laughton
  1931/32 - Fredric March
  1931/32 - Wallace Beery
  1930/31 - Lionel Barrymore
  1929/30 - George Arliss
  1928/29 - Warner Baxter
  1927/28 - Emil Jannings
Oscar winners (Actress):
  2009 - Sandra Bullock
  2008 - Kate Winslet
  2007 - Marion Cotillard
  2006 - Helen Mirren
  2005 - Reese Witherspoon
  2004 - Hilary Swank
  2003 - Charlize Theron
  2002 - Nicole Kidman
  2001 - Halle Berry
  2000 - Julia Roberts
  1999 - Hilary Swank
  1998 - Gwyneth Paltrow
  1997 - Helen Hunt
  1996 - Frances McDormand
  1995 - Susan Sarandon
  1994 - Jessica Lange
  1993 - Holly Hunter
  1992 - Emma Thompson
  1991 - Jodie Foster
  1990 - Kathy Bates
  1989 - Jessica Tandy
  1988 - Jodie Foster
  1987 - Cher
  1986 - Marlee Matlin
  1985 - Geraldine Page
  1984 - Sally Field
  1983 - Shirley MacLaine
  1982 - Meryl Streep
  1981 - Katharine Hepburn
  1980 - Sissy Spacek
  1979 - Sally Field
  1978 - Jane Fonda
  1977 - Diane Keaton
  1976 - Faye Dunaway
  1975 - Louise Fletcher
  1974 - Ellen Burstyn
  1973 - Glenda Jackson
  1972 - Liza Minnelli
  1971 - Jane Fonda
  1970 - Glenda Jackson
  1969 - Maggie Smith
  1968 - Barbra Streisand, Katharine Hepburn
  1967 - Katharine Hepburn
  1966 - Elizabeth Taylor
  1965 - Julie Christie
  1964 - Julie Andrews
  1963 - Patricia Neal
  1962 - Anne Bancroft
  1961 - Sophia Loren
  1960 - Elizabeth Taylor
  1959 - Simone Signoret
  1958 - Susan Hayward
  1957 - Joanne Woodward
  1956 - Ingrid Bergman
  1955 - Anna Magnani
  1954 - Grace Kelly
  1953 - Audrey Hepburn
  1952 - Shirley Booth
  1951 - Vivien Leigh
  1950 - Judy Holliday
  1949 - Olivia de Havilland
  1948 - Jane Wyman
  1947 - Loretta Young
  1946 - Olivia de Havilland
  1945 - Joan Crawford
  1944 - Ingrid Bergman
  1943 - Jennifer Jones
  1942 - Greer Garson
  1941 - Joan Fontaine
  1940 - Ginger Rogers
  1939 - Vivien Leigh
  1938 - Bette Davis
  1937 - Luise Rainer
  1936 - Luise Rainer
  1935 - Bette Davis
  1934 - Claudette Colbert
  1932/33 - Katharine Hepburn
  1931/32 - Helen Hayes
  1930/31 - Marie Dressler
  1929/30 - Norma Shearer
  1928/29 - Mary Pickford
  1927/28 - Janet Gaynor
Oscar winners (Animated Feature):
  2009 - Up
  2008 - WALL-E
  2007 - Ratatouille
  2006 - Happy Feet
  2005 - Wallace & Gromit: The Curse of the Were-Rabbit
  2004 - The Incredibles
  2003 - Finding Nemo
  2002 - Spirited Away
  2001 - Shrek
Oscar winners (Director):
  2009 - Kathryn Bigelow
  2008 - Danny Boyle
  2007 - Joel & Ethan Coen
  2006 - Martin Scorsese
  2005 - Ang Lee
  2004 - Clint Eastwood
  2003 - Peter Jackson
  2002 - Roman Polanski
  2001 - Ron Howard
  2000 - Steven Soderbergh
  1999 - Sam Mendes
  1998 - Steven Spielberg
  1997 - James Cameron
  1996 - Anthony Minghella
  1995 - Mel Gibson
  1994 - Robert Zemeckis
  1993 - Steven Spielberg
  1992 - Clint Eastwood
  1991 - Jonathan Demme
  1990 - Kevin Costner
  1989 - Oliver Stone
  1988 - Barry Levinson
  1987 - Bernardo Bertolucci
  1986 - Oliver Stone
  1985 - Sydney Pollack
  1984 - Milos Forman
  1983 - James L. Brooks
  1982 - Richard Attenborough
  1981 - Warren Beatty
  1980 - Robert Redford
  1979 - Robert Benton
  1978 - Michael Cimino
  1977 - Woody Allen
  1976 - John G. Avildsen
  1975 - Milos Forman
  1974 - Francis Ford Coppola
  1973 - George Roy Hill
  1972 - Bob Fosse
  1971 - William Friedkin
  1970 - Franklin Schaffner
  1969 - John Schlesinger
  1968 - Carol Reed
  1967 - Mike Nichols
  1966 - Fred Zinnemann
  1965 - Robert Wise
  1964 - George Cukor
  1963 - Tony Richardson
  1962 - David Lean
  1961 - Robert Wise, Jerome Robbins
  1960 - Billy Wilder
  1959 - William Wyler
  1958 - Vincente Minnelli
  1957 - David Lean
  1956 - George Stevens
  1955 - Delbert Mann
  1954 - Elia Kazan
  1953 - Fred Zinnemann

1952 - John Ford
1951 - George Stevens
1950 - Joseph L. Mankiewicz
1949 - Joseph L. Mankiewicz
1948 - John Huston
1947 - Elia Kazan
1946 - William Wyler
1945 - Billy Wilder
1944 - Leo McCarey
1943 - Michael Curtiz
1942 - William Wyler
1941 - John Ford
1940 - John Ford
1939 - Victor Fleming
1938 - Frank Capra
1937 - Leo McCarey
1936 - Frank Capra
1935 - John Ford
1934 - Frank Capra
1932/33 - Frank Lloyd
1931/32 - Frank Borzage
1930/31 - Norman Taurog
1929/30 - Lewis Milestone
1928/29 - Frank Lloyd
1927/28 - Frank Borzage
1927/28 - Lewis Milestone

Oscar winners (Picture):
2009 - The Hurt Locker
2008 - Slumdog Millionaire
2007 - No Country for Old Men
2006 - The Departed
2005 - Crash
2004 - Million Dollar Baby
2003 - The Lord of the Rings: The Return of the King
2002 - Chicago
2001 - A Beautiful Mind
2000 - Gladiator
1999 - American Beauty
1998 - Shakespeare in Love
1997 - Titanic
1996 - The English Patient
1995 - Braveheart
1994 - Forrest Gump
1993 - Schindler's List
1992 - Unforgiven
1991 - The Silence of the Lambs
1990 - Dances With Wolves
1989 - Driving Miss Daisy
1988 - Rain Man
1987 - The Last Emperor
1986 - Platoon
1985 - Out of Africa
1984 - Amadeus
1983 - Terms of Endearment
1982 - Gandhi
1981 - Chariots of Fire
1980 - Ordinary People
1979 - Kramer vs. Kramer
1978 - The Deer Hunter
1977 - Annie Hall
1976 - Rocky
1975 - One Flew Over the Cuckoo's Nest
1974 - The Godfather Part II
1973 - The Sting
1972 - The Godfather
1971 - The French Connection
1970 - Patton
1969 - Midnight Cowboy
1968 - Oliver!
1967 - In the Heat of the Night
1966 - A Man for All Seasons
1965 - The Sound of Music
1964 - My Fair Lady
1963 - Tom Jones
1962 - Lawrence of Arabia
1961 - West Side Story
1960 - The Apartment
1959 - Ben-Hur
1958 - Gigi
1957 - The Bridge on the River Kwai
1956 - Around the World in 80 Days
1955 - Marty
1954 - On the Waterfront
1953 - From Here to Eternity
1952 - The Greatest Show on Earth
1951 - An American in Paris
1950 - All About Eve
1949 - All the King's Men
1948 - Hamlet
1947 - Gentleman's Agreement
1946 - The Best Years of Our Lives
1945 - The Lost Weekend
1944 - Going My Way
1943 - Casablanca
1942 - Mrs. Miniver
1941 - How Green Was My Valley
1940 - Rebecca
1939 - Gone With the Wind
1938 - You Can't Take It With You
1937 - The Life of Emile Zola
1936 - The Great Ziegfeld
1935 - Mutiny on the Bounty
1934 - It Happened One Night
1932/33 - Cavalcade
1931/32 - Grand Hotel
1930/31 - Cimarron
1929/30 - All Quiet on the Western Front
1928/29 - Broadway Melody
1927/28 - Wings

Oscar winners (Supp. Actor):
2009 - Christoph Waltz
2008 - Heath Ledger
2007 - Javier Bardem
2006 - Alan Arkin
2005 - George Clooney
2004 - Morgan Freeman
2003 - Tim Robbins
2002 - Chris Cooper
2001 - Jim Broadbent
2000 - Benicio Del Toro
1999 - Michael Caine
1998 - James Coburn
1997 - Robin Williams
1996 - Cuba Gooding Jr.
1995 - Kevin Spacey
1994 - Martin Landau
1993 - Tommy Lee Jones
1992 - Gene Hackman
1991 - Jack Palance
1990 - Joe Pesci
1989 - Denzel Washington
1988 - Kevin Kline
1987 - Sean Connery
1986 - Michael Caine
1985 - Don Ameche
1984 - Haing S. Ngor
1983 - Jack Nicholson
1982 - Louis Gossett Jr.
1981 - John Gielgud
1980 - Timothy Hutton
1979 - Melvyn Douglas
1978 - Christopher Walken
1977 - Jason Robards
1976 - Jason Robards
1975 - George Burns
1974 - Robert De Niro
1973 - John Houseman
1972 - Joel Grey
1971 - Ben Johnson
1970 - John Mills
1969 - Gig Young
1968 - Jack Albertson
1967 - George Kennedy
1966 - Walter Matthau
1965 - Martin Balsam
1964 - Peter Ustinov
1963 - Melvyn Douglas
1962 - Ed Begley
1961 - George Chakiris
1960 - Peter Ustinov
1959 - Hugh Griffith
1958 - Burl Ives
1957 - Red Buttons
1956 - Anthony Quinn
1955 - Jack Lemmon
1954 - Edmond O'Brien
1953 - Frank Sinatra
1952 - Anthony Quinn
1951 - Karl Malden
1950 - George Sanders
1949 - Dean Jagger
1948 - Walter Huston
1947 - Edmund Gwenn
1946 - Harold Russell
1945 - James Dunn
1944 - Barry Fitzgerald
1943 - Charles Coburn
1942 - Van Heflin
1941 - Donald Crisp
1940 - Walter Brennan
1939 - Thomas Mitchell
1938 - Walter Brennan
1937 - Joseph Schildkraut
1936 - Walter Brennan

Oscar winners (Supp. Actress):
2009 - Mo'Nique
2008 - Penélope Cruz
2007 - Tilda Swinton
2006 - Jennifer Hudson
2005 - Rachel Weisz
2004 - Cate Blanchett
2003 - Renée Zellweger
2002 - Catherine Zeta-Jones
2001 - Jennifer Connelly
2000 - Marcia Gay Harden
1999 - Angelina Jolie
1998 - Judi Dench
1997 - Kim Basinger
1996 - Juliette Binoche
1995 - Mira Sorvino
1994 - Dianne Wiest
1993 - Anna Paquin
1992 - Marisa Tomei
1991 - Mercedes Ruehl
1990 - Whoopi Goldberg
1989 - Brenda Fricker
1988 - Geena Davis
1987 - Olympia Dukakis
1986 - Dianne Wiest
1985 - Anjelica Huston
1984 - Peggy Ashcroft
1983 - Linda Hunt
1982 - Jessica Lange
1981 - Maureen Stapleton
1980 - Mary Steenburgen
1979 - Meryl Streep
1978 - Maggie Smith
1977 - Vanessa Redgrave
1976 - Beatrice Straight
1975 - Lee Grant
1974 - Ingrid Bergman
1973 - Tatum O'Neal
1972 - Eileen Heckart
1971 - Cloris Leachman
1970 - Helen Hayes
1969 - Goldie Hawn
1968 - Ruth Gordon
1967 - Estelle Parsons
1966 - Sandy Dennis
1965 - Shelley Winters
1964 - Lila Kedrova
1963 - Margaret Rutherford
1962 - Patty Duke
1961 - Rita Moreno
1960 - Shirley Jones
1959 - Shelley Winters
1958 - Wendy Hiller
1957 - Miyoshi Umeki
1956 - Dorothy Malone
1955 - Jo Van Fleet
1954 - Eva Marie Saint
1953 - Donna Reed
1952 - Gloria Grahame
1951 - Kim Hunter
1950 - Josephine Hull
1949 - Mercedes McCambridge
1948 - Claire Trevor
1947 - Celeste Holm
1946 - Anne Baxter
1945 - Anne Revere
1944 - Ethel Barrymore
1943 - Katina Paxinou
1942 - Teresa Wright
1941 - Mary Astor
1940 - Jane Darwell
1939 - Hattie McDaniel
1938 - Fay Bainter
1937 - Alice Brady
1936 - Gale Sondergaard

oscillate: **3** bob, wag **4** beat, rock, spin, sway, turn, vary, wave **5** pivot, pulse, shake, swing, waver **6** change, dangle, quiver, seesaw, switch, swivel, teeter, totter, wabble, waggle, wobble, zigzag **7** librate, pulsate, tremble, vibrate **8** fishtail, hesitate **9** alternate, come and go, fluctuate, vacillate **10** ebb and flow, equivocate
oscillation: **4** beat, vibe **6** motion **9** vibration **10** hesitation
oscine: **4** crow, lark **6** bulbul, shrike **8** trembler, tremblor **9** bowerbird **10** honeyeater
oscitate: **4** gape, yawn
osculate: **4** buss, kiss, lick, neck, peck **5** touch **6** smooch
osculation: **4** buss, kiss, peck **5** smack **6** smooch
-ose: **4** like **5** sugar
__ O. Selznick: **5** David
Osgood: **7** Charles, Conklin
OSHA
department: **5** Labor
part: **5** Admin. **6** Health, Safety
__-o'-shanter: **3** tam
O'Shea: **4** Milo **6** Tessie **7** Michael
O Ship of State
author: Henry Wadsworth Longfellow
Oshkosh: **4** city, town
locale: **9** Wisconsin
OshKosh __: **5** B'Gosh
osier: **4** tree **6** willow
Osiris: **3** god **8** Egyptian
brother: **3** Set
parent: **3** Geb, Nut
sister: **4** Isis
slayer of ~: **3** Set
son: **5** Horus **6** Anubis
wife: **4** Isis
Oskar: **6** Werner **9** Kokoschka, Schindler

Oslin: **2** K.T.
Oslo: **4** city, port, town **7** capital
locale: **6** Norway
sight: **5** fiord, fjord
Osman: **4** amir, emir **5** ameer, emeer
Osment, Haley Joel: **5** actor
film: AI: Artificial Intelligence (2001)
Forrest Gump (1994)
Pay It Forward (2000)
The Sixth Sense (1999)
osmics: **7** science
study: **5** smell
osmium: **5** metal **7** element
alloy: **7** platina
Osmond: **3** Ken **4** Alan **5** Donny, Marie
Osmond, Donny
song: Are You Lonesome Tonight (1973)
Go Away Little Girl (1971)
Hey Girl (1971)
Lonely Boy (1972)
A Million to One (1973)
My Love Is a Fire (1990)
Puppy Love (1972)
Sacred Emotion (1989)
Soldier of Love (1989)
Sweet and Innocent (1971)
Too Young (1972)
The Twelfth of Never (1973)
Why (1972)
Osmond, Donny and Marie
song: I'm Leaving It Up to You (1974)
Morning Side of the Mountain (1974)
Osmond, Marie
song: Paper Roses (1973)
Osmonds
home: **4** Utah **5** Ogden
members: Alan, Wayne, Merrill, Jay, Donny
song: Crazy Horses (1972)
Double Lovin' (1971)
Down by the Lazy River (1972)
Hold Her Tight (1972)
Love Me for a Reason (1974)
One Bad Apple (1971)
Yo-Yo (1971)
osmose: **4** seep **5** drain, sop up **6** absorb, draw in, filter, gather, ingest, soak up, suck up, take in **7** drink in, swallow **10** assimilate
osmunda: **4** fern
O sole __: **3** mio
osprey: **4** bird **8** fish hawk
cousin: **3** ern **4** erne
O.S.S. (1946 film)
cast: Alan Ladd
Ossa: **2** mt. **3** mtn. **4** peak **8** mountain
locale: **6** Greece **8** Tasmania
osseous: **4** bony **5** boney
ossia: **2** or **6** or else **9** otherwise
Ossie: **5** Davis
wife: **4** Ruby
ossified: **3** set **5** rigid, stiff **6** frozen **8** hardened **9** hidebound, petrified, unpliable **10** inflexible
ossify: **6** freeze, harden **7** petrify, stiffen **8** indurate, rigidify **9** fossilize, stabilize
Ossining: **4** city, town
locale: **7** New York
osso __: **4** buco
OSS successor: **3** CIA
osteal: **4** bony **5** boney
Ostend: **4** port
locale: **7** Belgium
ostensible: **5** quasi **6** avowed, likely **7** alleged, nominal, outward, reputed, seeming **8** apparent, illusive, illusory, knowable, manifest, palpable, probable, so-called, specious, supposed **9** pretended, professed, purported
ostensibly: **7** for show **8** to the eye **9** doubtless, evidently, outwardly, seemingly **10** apparently
ostentation: **4** fuss, pomp, ritz, show **5** array, flash, glitz, shine **6** parade, vanity **7** bravado, display, swagger **8** boasting, bragging, pretense, vaunting **9** flaunting, pageantry, showiness, spectacle, vainglory **10** pretension
ostentatious: **3** gay **4** arty, loud, tony, vain **5** crass, fancy, fussy, gaudy, grand, proud, ritzy, showy, stagy, swank, toney **6** chichi, classy, flashy, garish, glitzy, ornate, solemn, stagey, swanky, tinsel, uptown, vulgar **7** blatant, dashing, opulent, pompous, splashy **8** affected, boastful, flaunted, glittery, pedantic, snobbish, specious **9** egotistic, grandiose, luxurious, tasteless **10** pedantical
be ~: **5** boast, strut **6** flaunt, parade **7** show off, trot out
Osterizer
use an ~: **3** mix **5** blend, puree
Osterman Weekend, The
author: Robert Ludlum
Österreich, capital of: **4** Wien
Osterwald: **4** Bibi
Ostia: **4** port **7** seaport
neighbor: **4** Roma
river: **5** Tiber
see also Latin
ostracism: **5** exile **6** rebuke **9** dismissal, exclusion, expulsion, isolation **10** punishment
ostracize: **3** ban, bar, cut **4** drop, oust, shun, snub, tabu **5** avoid, exile, expel, scorn **6** banish, deport, reject **7** boycott, cast out, censure, exclude, expulse, isolate, seclude, shut off, shut out **8** displace, relegate, throw out **9** blackball, blacklist, order to go **10** expatriate
ostracized: **5** rogue **9** unpopular **10** friendless
ostrich: **4** bird, fern **5** biped **8** escapist
cousin: **3** emu, moa **4** emeu, rhea
OSU
conference: **6** Big Ten, Pac-Ten **9** Big Twelve
part of ~: **3** Ore. **4** Ohio, Okla., Oreg., Univ. **6** Oregon **8** Oklahoma
see also Ohio State, Oklahoma State, Oregon State
O'Sullivan: **7** Gilbert, Maureen
O'Sullivan, Gilbert
homeland: Ireland
song: Alone Again (Naturally) (1972)
Clair (1972)
O'Sullivan, Maureen: **7** actress
daughter: Mia Farrow
film: The Big Clock (1948)
A Connecticut Yankee (1931)
David Copperfield (1935)
A Day at the Races (1937)
Hannah and Her Sisters (1986)
The Tall T (1957)
Tarzan and His Mate (1934)
Tarzan Escapes (1936)
Tarzan Finds a Son! (1939)
Tarzan, the Ape Man (1932)
The Thin Man (1934)
A Yank at Oxford (1938)
role: **4** Jane
Oswald: **4** Gerd **8** Spengler
Oswalt: **6** Patton
Oswego: **4** lake
locale: **6** Oregon
tea: **5** plant **6** flower
O.T.
book: **3** Bar., Ezr., Gen., Hab., Hos., Isa., Jer., Job, Lam., Lev., Mac., Mic., Nah., Neh., Num., Psa. **4** Deut., Eccl., Exod., Ezek., Macc., Obad., Prov., Zech. **5** Levit. **6** Eccles.
passage: **3** ver.
see also Bible, Old Testament
Ota: **4** city, town
locale: **5** Japan
Otaheite __: **5** apple **6** orange
O Tannenbaum: **5** carol
subject: **3** fir **4** tree
Otaru: **4** city, town
locale: **5** Japan
otary: **4** seal **9** eared seal
OTB
activity: **5** wager **6** exacta **8** perfecta, quinella, trifecta
part of: **3** off **5** track **7** betting
posting: **4** odds **7** winners
OTC
buy: **5** stock
part: **4** over **7** counter
source: **4** phar. **5** pharm.
Otello: **5** opera
composer: Giuseppe Verdi
librettist: Arrigo Boito
role: **4** Iago
song: **4** aria
O tempora! O __!: **5** mores
O-T filler: **4** PQRS
O the Chimneys
author: Nelly Sachs
Othello: **4** Moor, play **7** tragedy
author: William Shakespeare
character: **4** Iago **6** Bianca, Cassio, Emilia **7** Michael, Montano, Othello **8** Gratiano, Lodovico, Roderigo **9** Brabantio, Desdemona
Othello (1952 film)
cast: Orson Welles
director: Orson Welles
Othello (1995 film)
cast: Kenneth Branagh, Laurence Fishburne
__ o' the mornin': **3** top
other: **3** new **4** else, more **5** added, extra, fresh, spare **6** unlike **7** another, distant, diverse, farther, further, unalike, unequal, variant **8** distinct, opposite, separate **9** alternate, auxiliary, different, disparate, divergent, unrelated **10** additional, dissimilar, substitute
combining form: **3** all- **4** allo- **5** heter- **6** hetero-
ender: **4** wise **5** world **7** worldly
in Spanish: **4** otra, otro
people: **4** them
other __: **4** half, than
other __ of the coin, the: **4** side
other __ to fry: **4** fish
__ other: **4** each **5** every
Other Boleyn Girl, The (2008 film)
cast: Eric Bana, Scarlett Johansson, Natalie Portman
other fish __: **5** to fry
__ other hand: **5** on the
otherness: **8** contrast, variance **9** departure, deviation, disparity, diversity, variation **10** aberration, difference, dissonance, divergence
Other People's Money
author: Jerome Weidman
Other People's Money (1991 film)
cast: Danny DeVito, Piper Laurie, Penelope Ann Miller, Gregory Peck
others: **4** alii, rest, them, they **6** extras **7** the rest **9** leftovers, outsiders
and ~: **6** et alia, et alii
how ~ see us: **5** image **9** depiction **10** appearance, conception, impression, perception, projection
in Durango: **5** otras, otros
in Spanish: **5** otras, otros
not ~: **2** us **5** these **6** myself
others': **5** their
__ others...: **6** Do unto
...others __!: **5** see us
Other Side of Midnight, The
author: Sidney Sheldon
Other Side of the Rainbow, The
author: Mel Tormé
Other Sister, The (1999 film)
cast: Diane Keaton, Juliette Lewis, Tom Skerritt
director: Garry Marshall
Others, The (2001 film)
cast: Fionnula Flanagan, Nicole Kidman
Other, The
author: Thomas Tryon
Other Voices, Other Rooms
author: Truman Capote
other white meat, the: **4** pork
__ Other Wife: **5** John's
otherwise: **4** else **5** if not **6** or else, or then **7** besides, unalike **9** different **10** contrarily
called: **3** AKA **5** alias
in music: **5** ossia
literally: **5** alias
show ~: **4** deny **5** belie, quash, rebut **6** negate, refute **7** confute, dispute **8** confound, disprove, overturn **9** discredit, shoot down **10** contradict, disconfirm, prove false, prove wrong
otherworldly: **3** fey **4** eery **5** eerie **7** magical, utopian **8** mystical **9** spiritual, visionary
__-o'-the-wisp: **4** will
otic: **5** aural **8** auditory **9** auricular
otiose: **4** idle, lazy **6** futile **7** languid, useless **8** dallying, inactive, indolent, slothful **9** apathetic, at leisure, do-nothing, for naught, lethargic, negligent, pointless, shiftless, to no avail, unhurried **10** neglectful, unavailing
otiosity: **5** sloth **6** acedia, torpor **7** inertia, languor **8** idleness, lazi-

ness **9** faineance, indolence, torpidity **10** stagnation
Otis: 4 Amos, Miss **5** Carré **6** Elisha, Johnny **7** Redding, Skinner **8** Birdsong, Chandler, Williams **9** Armstrong
friend: 4 Milo
Otis, Amos
sport: 8 baseball
__ Otis Regrets: 4 Miss
__ Otis Skinner: 8 Cornelia
otitis site: 3 ear
Oto: 5 tribe **6** Indian, Siouan **7** Amerind **8** language
prey: 5 bison
Otoe: 5 tribe **6** Indian, Siouan **7** Amerind
otolaryngology: 3 ENT
focus: 3 ear **4** nose **6** throat
otologist concern: 3 ear
O'Toole: 5 Peter **7** Annette
O'Toole, Peter: 5 actor
film: Becket (1964)
Creator (1985)
The Dark Angel (1991)
How to Steal a Million (1966)
The Last Emperor (1987)
Lawrence of Arabia (1962)
The Lion in Winter (1968)
Lord Jim (1965)
Murphy's War (1971)
My Favorite Year (1982)
The Ruling Class (1972)
The Stunt Man (1980)
Venus (2006)
Zulu Dawn (1979)
otra __: 3 vez
Otranto: 3 str. **6** strait
OTS grad: 2 lt. **5** lieut.
Ott: 2 Ed **3** Mel
ottava __: 4 rima
Ottawa: 4 city, town **5** river **6** Indian **7** Amerind, capital
locale: 3 Ont. **6** Canada **7** Ontario
network: 3 CBC
newspaper: 3 Sun **7** Citizen, Le Droit
pro team: 8 Senators
River locale: 6 Quebec **7** Ontario
school: 8 Carleton
otter: 3 fur **6** animal, mammal, weasel
milieu: 3 sea, zoo **5** ocean, river, water
relative: *see* weasel
secretion: 4 musk
__ otter: 3 sea
Ott, Mel: 5 Giant **7** slugger **10** outfielder
otto: 5 eight **7** Italian
follower: 4 nove
preceder: 5 sette
Otto: 3 dog, Jim **4** Hahn, Kahn **5** Diels, Loewi, Stern **6** Graham, Kruger, Soglow **7** bulldog, Harbach, Kristin, Miranda, Nicolai, Wallach, Warburg **8** Bismarck, Meyerhof, Nikolaus **9** Klemperer, Preminger **10** Lilienthal
see also German
Otto __ Bismarck: 3 von
Otto, Kristin: 6 German **7** swimmer
ottoman: 4 seat **5** divan, stool **6** fabric **7** hassock **8** footrest **9** footstool
occupy an ~: 3 sit **5** perch **6** hunker
relative: 4 pouf
Ottoman: 4 Turk **7** Osmanli **8** language
court: 5 porte
inn: 6 imaret
peasant: 4 raya
sultan: 5 selim
title: 3 aga, bey **4** agha **5** calif, kalif, pacha, pasha, vizir **6** caliph, kaliph, khalif, vizier
Ottoman __: 6 Empire
Ottone
composer: George Frideric Handel
Ottorino: 8 Respighi
Ottumwa: 4 city, town
locale: 4 Iowa
Ouagadougou: 4 city, town **7** capital
locale: Burkina Faso
oubliette: 5 vault **6** prison **7** dungeon
ouch: 3 cry, yow **4** hurt, yipe **9** that hurts
Ouche
city on the ~: 5 Dijon
Oue, Eiji: 9 conductor
ought: 4 duty, have, must, need, zero **6** should
to: 6 should **7** had best **9** had better
__ Oughta Be in Pictures: 3 You
__ Oughta Know: 3 You
oui: 3 yes **6** French
mais ~: 8 very well
opposite: 3 non
__ oui!: 4 Mais
oui-dire: 4 buzz, news, talk, word **5** noise, rumor **6** gossip, report, tattle **7** hearsay, scandal **9** grapevine
Ouija: 4 game **5** board
word: 3 yes
Ouimet, Francis: 6 golfer
Oulu: 4 city, town **5** river
locale: 7 Finland
ounce: 3 bit, cat **4** unit **5** felid, grain, shred **6** feline **7** modicum **8** molecule, particle
cousin: 4 gram
fraction: 4 dram **5** pound
of whiskey: 3 nip **4** shot, slug **5** drink
__ ounce: 5 fluid
ounces
16 ~: 5 pound
4 fluid ~: 4 gill
8 fluid ~: 3 cup
ouphe: 3 elf **5** fairy, gnome, nixie, pixie **6** goblin, kobold **7** brownie, gremlin **9** hobgoblin
our: 4 poss., pron. **7** pronoun **10** possessive
ender: 4 self **6** selves
in French: 3 nos **5** notre
not ~: 5 their
Our __: 4 Gang, Lady, Love, Time, Town **5** House **6** Father
Our __ Brooks: 4 Miss
Our __ Friend: 6 Mutual
Our __ in Havana: 3 Man
Our __ of Guadalupe: 4 Lady
Our __ Sunday: 3 Gal
Our __ Will Come: 3 Day
Our Betters
author: W. Somerset Maugham
Our Day Will Come (song)
artist: Frankie Valli, Ruby and the Romantics
Our Father who __ heaven: 5 art in
Our Gal Sunday: 9 radio show
Our Gang
affirmative: 4 otay
author: Philip Roth
dog: 4 Pete **5** Petey
kid: 6 Rascal
member: 5 Butch, Darla, Porky, Waldo **6** Chubby, Farina, Froggy, Spanky **7** Alfalfa, Wheezer **9** Buckwheat
producer: 5 Roach
teacher: 8 Crabtree
Our Hearts Were Young and Gay
author: Cornelia Otis Skinner
__, Our Help in Ages Past: 4 O God
Our House (song)
artist: Crosby, Stills & Nash, Madness
composer: Graham Nash
Our Lady of Guadalupe: 5 saint
Our Lady of Lourdes: 5 saint
Our Lady of the Flowers
author: Jean Genet
Our Love (1978 song)
artist: Natalie Cole
Our Man Flint (1966 film)
cast: Lee J. Cobb, James Coburn
dog: 6 Caesar
org.: 5 Z.O.W.I.E.
Our Man in Havana: 4 book, film
author: Graham Greene
Our Man in Havana (1959 film)
cast: Alec Guinness, Burl Ives, Ernie Kovacs, Maureen O'Hara
director: Carol Reed
Our Miss Brooks (CBS sitcom)
cast: Eve Arden (Connie Brooks) Richard Crenna (Walter Denton) Gale Gordon (Osgood Conklin) Robert Rockwell (Philip Boynton)
cat: 7 Minerva
Our Mutual Friend
author: Charles Dickens
Our National Parks
author: John Muir
__ Our Part: 4 We Do
ours: 4 poss., pron. **7** pronoun **10** possessive
__ Ours: 5 One of
ourselves
between ~: 8 in secret **9** entre nous, privately
in Spanish: 3 nos
not ~: 6 others
Our Town: 4 play
author: Thornton Wilder
character: 3 Joe **4** Webb **5** Emily, Gibbs, Howie, Simon, Wally **6** George **7** Crowell, Newsome, Rebecca, Stimson
'ouse: 3 'ome
Ouse: 5 river
locale: 7 England
river to the ~: 3 Cam **4** Aire
ousel: 4 bird **6** dipper
emulate an ~: 4 dive
Ouspenskaya: 5 Maria
oust: 3 axe, can **4** boot, drop, fire, lose, sack **5** eject, evict, exile, expel, let go, purge **6** banish, bounce, depose, divest, lay off, remove, topple, unseat **7** boot out, cashier, cast out, deprive, dismiss, drum out, exclude, expulse, kick out, pack off, release, replace, subvert, turn out **8** dethrone, dislodge, displace, drive out, force out, furlough, get rid of, pink-slip, relegate, supplant, throw out **9** blackball, bundle off, chase away, discharge, drive away, eliminate, order to go, ostracize, overthrow, terminate, transport **10** disinherit, dispossess
ouster: 4 boot, coup **5** purge **9** exclusion, expulsion **10** deposition
out: 3 off **4** away, cold, dead, exit, gone, plea **5** alibi, dated, ended, forth, not in, passé **6** absent, asleep, démodé, deport, doused, old hat, used up **7** all gone, archaic, at an end, expired, forward, not home, on a date, pretext, without **8** finished, obsolete, on strike **9** elsewhere, exhausted, make known, not at home, unpopular **10** antiquated, impossible, not working, unfeasible
out __: 4 loud, of it **5** front, of gas, to sea
out __ blue: 5 of the
out __ clear blue sky: 5 of the
out __ cold: 5 in the
out __ elbows: 5 at the
out __ heels: 5 at the
out __ light: 5 like a
out __ limb: 3 on a
out __ question: 5 of the
out __ running: 5 of the
out __ under: 4 from
out __ way: 5 of the
out __ woods: 5 of the
out __ woodwork: 5 of the
out-__: 3 box **5** front, group **6** basket **7** country, migrate
__ out: 3 act, ask, bow, bug, buy, cop, cut, dig, eke, fan, far, get, ice, lay, let, log, map, max, opt, pan, pay, pig, put, rub, run, see, set, sit, tog, try, veg, win **4** back, bail, bawl, bear, beat, blot, blow, burn, call, camp, cash, cast, chew, clip, come, conk, cool, dish, dope, draw, drop, drum, ease, edge, fake, fall, farm, feel, fill, find, fish, flat, give, hand, hang, hash, help, hide, hike, hold, iron, kick, lash, lock, look, lose, luck, make, mete, move, nose, pass, pick, play, poop, pull, rack, read, ream, ride, roll, rule, sack, sell, send, ship, shut, sign, sing, sort, spin, step, stop, take, talk, tear, trot, tune, turn, walk, wash, wear, weed, wink, wipe, work **5** black, bleep, bliss, block, break, bring, carry, check, chill, churn, clean, clear, close, count, crank, cross, cut it, flunk, freak, fresh, gross, knock, peter, phase, prove, psych, punch, round, scope, shell, smoke, sound, speak, spell, stake, stand, stick, storm, swear, sweat, tease, throw, watch, write **6** bottom, figure, follow, freeze, inside, lights, mellow, muster, strike, thrash, weasel **7** chicken, filling, infield, stretch
__ out!: 3 Far, Yer
__ out?: 4 In or
__-out: 3 all, far, way **4** comb, cook, fade, flat, iris, sold, time, worn **5** diner, flame, force, in-and **6** bombed, washed

Out!: **4** call, scat, shoo **5** leave, scram
Out, __ spot!: **6** damned
__ Out: **4** Blow, Wipe **5** Movin', No Way **6** Lights **7** School's, Steppin'
__ out a living: **3** eke
__ out all the stops: **4** pull
out-and-out: **4** pure, rank **5** gross, plumb, right, sheer, stark, total, utter **6** arrant, wholly **8** absolute, complete, flagrant, outright, positive, profound, straight, thorough **9** downright, full-dress, intensive **10** consummate, exhaustive
Outa-Space (1972 song)
  artist: Billy Preston
out at the __: **5** heels, plate **6** elbows
outback: **4** bush **5** wilds **8** frontier **9** backwater **10** wilderness
  denizen: **3** emu, 'roo **4** emeu **5** dingo **8** kangaroo
  mineral: **4** opal
  native: **6** Aussie
  youngster: **4** joey
  see also Australia
Outback: **3** SUV **6** Subaru
outboard: **5** motor **6** engine
outbreak: **3** fit **4** gush, riot, wave **5** blast, brawl, burst, flash, onset, storm, surge **6** attack, blowup, émeute, mutiny, plague, tumult, volley **7** flare-up **8** disorder, epidemic, eruption, paroxysm, uprising **9** commotion, explosion, irruption, rebellion **10** disruption, epidemical, revolution
Outbreak: **4** film **5** novel
  author: Robin Cook
  cast: Morgan Freeman, Dustin Hoffman, Rene Russo, Kevin Spacey
outbuilding: **4** barn, shed **6** lean-to
outburst: **3** cry, fit **4** gush, gust, rage, riot **5** blast, blaze, flare, flash, round, sally, salvo, scene, shout, spasm, spirt, spurt, storm, surge **6** access, attack, fantod, flurry, frenzy, temper, tirade **7** flare-up, tantrum, torrent **8** eruption, paroxysm, upheaval **9** discharge, explosion, hysterics **10** conniption
outcast: **3** bum **4** hobo, nerd **5** exile, gypsy, rogue, tramp **6** abject, lonely, pariah, rascal, wretch **7** refugee, vagrant **8** castaway, deportee, derelict, forsaken, fugitive, vagabond **9** abandoned, miscreant, reprobate **10** expatriate
Outcasts of Poker Flat, The
  author: Bret Harte
outclass: **3** top **4** beat **5** excel, one-up **6** defeat, exceed **7** surpass **10** put to shame, tower above
outcome: **3** end **4** fate **5** fruit, score **6** effect, ending, payoff, result, sequel, upshot, windup **7** payback, product **8** decision, reaction **9** aftermath, end result **10** conclusion, resolution
  favorable ~: **3** win **7** success, victory
  guarantee the ~: **3** fix, peg, rig **5** frame, set up **6** buy off, cement, doctor **8** nail down **9** formalize, plan ahead, preordain **10** manipulate, prearrange, tamper with
outcropping: **4** crag **5** ledge, shelf
outcry: **4** call, flak, howl, roar, yell **5** flack, hoo-ha, noise, shout, stink, storm, whoop **6** clamor, racket, scream, tumult, uproar **7** ferment, protest **9** commotion, complaint, objection **10** hubba-hubba, hullabaloo
outcurved: **6** arched, convex **7** bulging, rounded
Out, damned __!: **4** spot
outdated: **3** obs., old **4** dull **5** corny, dated, dowdy, dusty, fusty, hokey, musty, passé, stale, tired, trite, vapid **6** common, démodé, jejune, old-hat, square **7** antique, archaic, cliché d, fatuous, fogyish, has-been, humdrum, prosaic, vintage **8** bromidic, obsolete **9** hackneyed, moth-eaten, prosaical **10** antiquated, back-number, uninspired, unoriginal
  not ~: **3** new, now **5** faddy, novel **6** latest, modern, modish, recent, red-hot **7** current, revived, topical **8** advanced, brand-new **9** au courant **10** innovative, newfangled, redesigned
outdistance: **3** top **4** beat, pass **6** defeat, exceed **7** succeed, surpass **8** overtake, throw off
outdistanced, be: **4** lose
outdistancing: **7** ahead of
outdo: **3** cap, top **4** beat, best, bury, cook, down, lead, lick, pass, snow **5** break, cream, excel, one-up, trash, trump **6** better, defeat, exceed, show up **7** eclipse, get past, surpass **8** bulldoze, overcome, overtake, shake off **9** rise above, transcend **10** put to shame, shoot ahead
outdoor: **6** casual, garden, rustic **7** hilltop, natural, open-air **8** alfresco, exterior, informal **9** healthful, in the open
  area: **4** camp, deck, yard **5** patio **7** terrace
outdoors: **4** open, yard **5** hills, woods **6** garden, nature **7** country **8** alfresco, fresh air **9** mountains
  ender: **3** man, men **5** woman, women
  not ~: **6** inside **7** indoors
__ outdoors, the: **5** great
outdoorsy type: **5** hiker
outen: **10** extinguish
outer: **3** ext. **4** over **5** alien, ectal **6** beyond, remote **7** exposed, surface **8** exoteric, exterior, external **9** extrinsic **10** extraneous, peripheral
  combining form: **2** ex- **3** ect-, epi-, exo- **4** ecto-
  ender: **4** most, wear
  garment: **3** fur **4** coat, robe **5** cloak, parka, stole **6** jacket **8** overcoat
  layer: **4** bark, coat, hull, husk, rind, skin **5** crust, shell **6** cortex **7** coating **8** covering **10** integument
  limit: **3** rim **4** edge **5** ambit, ether, verge **6** aether, apogee **8** boundary **9** periphery
  not ~: **5** inner **6** middle, within **7** central
  space: **3** sky **6** vacuum
  visitor from ~ space: **5** alien, comet **6** meteor
outer __: **3** ear **5** space
Outer __, NC: **5** Banks
Outer Limits, The genre: sci-fi
outermost: **4** last **7** extreme
outer space: **3** sky **6** vacuum
  prefix: **5** astro-
  wear: **5** G-suit
outerwear: **3** fur **4** coat, robe **5** cloak, parka, stole **6** anorak, jacket **8** overcoat, raincoat
  material: **5** loden
  woolen ~: **5** cloak, ruana, shawl
outfield
  boundary: **5** fence
  hit: **3** fly **5** bloop
  make ~ repairs: **5** resod
  material: **3** sod **4** turf **5** grass
outfielder: **2** CF, LF, RF **7** athlete
  call: **6** I got it
  Hall of Fame ~: **3** Ott **4** Bell, Cobb, Doby, Mays, Rice, Ruth **5** Aaron, Brock, Combs, Flick, Gwynn, Irvin, Kiner, Klein, Roush, Waner, Wheat **6** Cuyler, Goslin, Kaline, Keeler, Mantle, Mel Ott, Musial, Snider, Ty Cobb, Wilson **7** Ashburn, Averill, Jackson, Jim Rice, Medwick, Puckett, Sam Rice, Speaker, Stearns **8** Al Kaline, Babe Ruth, Clemente, DiMaggio, Edd Roush, Lou Brock, Robinson, Stargell, Williams, Winfield **9** Hank Aaron, Henderson, Larry Doby, Slaughter, Tony Gwynn, Zack Wheat **10** Chuck Klein, Duke Snider, Earle Combs, Elmer Flick, Hack Wilson, Henry Aaron, Joe Medwick, Kiki Cuyler, Monte Irvin, Ralph Kiner, Stan Musial, Willie Mays **11** Yastrzemski
  pride: **3** arm
outfit: **3** arm, kit, rig, set, tie, tog **4** band, clan, club, crew, deck, duds, firm, gang, garb, gear, pack, ring, suit, team, togs, unit **5** array, cater, corps, drape, dress, equip, getup, group, guise, hands, house, party, rig up, squad, stock, troop **6** attire, clique, clothe, gear up, league, livery, purvey, supply, tackle, troupe **7** apparel, appoint, bedrape, brigade, clothes, company, concern, costume, coterie, furnish, garment, in-group, platoon, prepare, provide, rigging, society **8** accouter, accoutre, business, clothing, ensemble, equipage, garments, materiel, supplies, wardrobe **9** apparatus, caparison, provision, trappings **10** enterprise, Sunday best
outfits: **7** apparel, clothes **8** clothing, wardrobe
outfitted: **4** clad **8** equipped, supplied **10** accoutered
outfitter: **3** EMS, REI **6** L.L. Bean, tailor **7** Cabela's **8** clothier **9** couturier **10** dressmaker
outflank: **3** fox **4** foil **6** defeat, thwart **9** frustrate, overreach **10** circumvent
outflow: **3** ebb **5** issue, sally **6** efflux **9** effluence, emanation
  opposite: **6** intake
outflux: **3** ebb
__ out for: **3** cut
outfox: **3** top **4** fool, have **5** outdo **6** outwit **8** outsmart
out from __: **5** under
out-front: **4** open **5** bluff, blunt, frank, plain **6** candid, direct, honest, square **7** artless, genuine, sincere **8** straight, truthful **9** guileless, ingenuous, unguarded, veracious **10** aboveboard, flat-footed, forthright, foursquare, free-spoken, from the hip, on the level, point-blank, unaffected, unreserved
outgas: **4** vent
outgo: **7** expense, payment, produce **8** expenses, spending
outgoing: **4** easy, kind, open, past, warm **5** civil, close **6** chummy, clubby, former, genial, kindly **7** affable, amiable, cordial, leaving **8** amicable, friendly, informal, intimate, retiring, sociable **9** convivial, departing, expansive, extrovert **10** benevolent, buddy-buddy, gregarious, neighborly, personable, solicitous, unreserved
  not ~: **3** coy, shy **4** meek **5** mousy, quiet, timid **6** demure, modest, silent **7** bashful, fearful, nervous, prudish **8** backward, hesitant, reserved, reticent, retiring **9** diffident, shrinking, unassured, withdrawn **10** unassuming, uneffusive, unsociable
  one: **5** mixer **7** mingler
... __ outgrabe: **5** raths
outgrowth: **5** bulge **6** branch, effect, result, upshot **7** outcome, product, spin-off **8** offshoot **9** by-product **10** derivative
outgushing: **5** flood, spate, surge **6** deluge **7** cascade, freshet, torrent **8** downpour, drencher, overflow **9** avalanche **10** inundation
outhaul: **4** line, rope **5** cable **6** hawser **7** lanyard
outhit: **3** tan **4** beat, best, drub, edge, lick, whip **5** cream, crush, skunk, swamp, trash, upset **6** defeat, thrash **7** mow down, shellac, trounce **8** demolish **9** plow under, steamroll
outie: **5** navel
out in __ field: **4** left
outing: **3** run **4** date, hike, ride, spin, tour, trek, trip, turn **5** drive, jaunt, sally, spree **6** junket, picnic **7** journey, weekend **8** vacation **9** excursion **10** expedition, roundabout
out in the __: **4** cold
Outland character: **4** Opus
outlander: **5** alien **7** incomer **8** outsider, stranger **9** foreigner
outlandish: **3** odd **4** eery, wild, zany **5** alien, campy, droll, eerie, kinky, outré, queer, ultra, weird **6** clumsy, exotic, far-out, gauche, quaint **7** awkward, bizarre, boorish, curious, erratic, foreign, oddball, strange, uncouth, unusual **8** barbaric, freakish, peculiar, singular **9** barbarous, eccentric, fantastic, graceless, grotesque, ludicrous, tasteless, unheard-of, unnatural, whimsical **10** incredible, ridiculous
  not ~: **3** fit **4** sane, wise **5** sober,

sound **6** normal **7** logical, prudent **8** moderate, rational, sensible **9** practical, pragmatic, realistic **10** reasonable

outlast: **6** endure, hang on, remain **7** survive

outlaw: **3** ban, bar, con **4** damn, hood, stop, tabu, thug, veto **5** crook, ex-con, felon, rogue, taboo, thief **6** bad guy, bad man, bandit, banish, forbid, mugger, pariah, robber **7** brigand, burglar, condemn, drifter, embargo, exclude, hoodlum, mobster, prevent **8** criminal, disallow, fugitive, gangster, hooligan, jailbird, marauder, prohibit, renegade, tough guy **9** buccaneer, desperado, interdict, miscreant, proscribe, racketeer **10** delinquent, gunslinger

outlawed: **4** tabu **5** taboo **6** banned **7** illegal, illicit **8** criminal, improper, unlawful, verboten, wrongful **9** felonious, off-limits **10** prohibited

blast: **5** N-test

Outlaw Josey Wales, The (1976 film): **5** oater **7** western **10** horse opera

cast: Clint Eastwood, Chief Dan George, Sondra Locke

director: Clint Eastwood

Outlaw, The (1943 film)

cast: Jane Russell

character: **3** Rio

director: Howard Hughes

studio: **3** RKO

outlay: **3** tab **4** bite, cost, tune **5** price, spend **6** amount, charge, damage, expend, upkeep **7** expense, payment, setback **8** expenses, overhead, price tag, spending **10** bottom line, investment

outlays, after: **3** net

outlet: **4** duct, exit, mart, pore, shop, vent **5** crack, drain, spout, store **6** avenue, egress, escape, market, nozzle, refuge **7** channel, opening, orifice **8** aperture, emporium, loophole, retailer, showroom **9** mill store

danger: **5** shock

insert: **4** plug

OK in any ~: **4** AC/DC

output: **5** power **7** voltage

outlet __: **4** mall

__ outlet: **7** factory

outline: **3** map **4** edge, form, limn, list, plan, plot **5** brief, chart, draft, frame, paint, shape, sum up, trace **6** aperçu, define, depict, design, figure, précis, report, résumé, scheme, sketch, survey **7** contour, diagram, drawing, profile, program, rundown, sketchy, summary, tracing **8** abstract, describe, proposal, scenario, skeleton, synopsis **9** adumbrate, bare facts, blueprint, delineate, depiction, floor plan, framework, perimeter, rough idea, summarize, synopsize **10** figuration, impression, rough draft, silhouette

make an ~: **5** trace

sharply: **4** etch **6** incise **8** inscribe

Outline of History

author: H.G. Wells

outlive: **6** linger, remain **7** survive

outlook: **4** view **5** angle, scape, scene, sight, slant, state, vista **6** aspect, morale, nature, school, spirit, vision **7** chances, headset, mind-set **8** attitude, forecast, panorama, position, prospect, size of it **9** direction, landscape, mentality, prospects, viewpoint **10** likelihood, philosophy, standpoint

positive ~: **4** hope **5** trust **6** morale **7** elation **8** buoyancy, calmness, easiness, idealism, optimism **9** assurance, certainty, good cheer, happiness, lightness **10** brightness, confidence, enthusiasm

__ out loud: **5** think

outlying: **3** far **4** afar **6** far-off, remote **7** distant, faraway, removed **8** external, far-flung **9** backwoods **10** peripheral, provincial

area: **4** burb **5** exurb **6** suburb

outmaneuver: **4** undo **5** one-up **6** defeat **9** get around

outmatch: **4** beat **6** defeat **7** surpass

outmode: **7** replace **8** archaize, displace, supplant **9** antiquate, supersede

outmoded: **3** obs., old **4** dead, dull **5** corny, dated, dowdy, hokey, moldy, musty, olden, passé, stale, tacky, tired, trite, vapid **6** bygone, common, effete, jejune, old-hat **7** antique, archaic, clichéd, disused, extinct, fatuous, has-been, humdrum, old-time, prosaic, vintage **8** bromidic, obsolete, unusable **9** hackneyed, moth-eaten, prosaical, unstylish **10** antiquated, back-number, uninspired, unoriginal

title: **3** Mrs.

outmost: **4** last **5** outer **7** extreme **8** farthest, furthest

out of __: **3** gas **4** date, hand, hock, line, luck, play, step, sync, trim, turn, work **5** joint, phase, plumb, print, sight, sorts, stock, style, synch, whack **6** bounds, breath, kilter, pocket, season, square **7** nowhere

out of __ cloth: **5** whole

out of __ way: **5** harm's

out of __ world: **4** this

out-of-__: **4** date, sync, town **5** court, doors, print, round, state **6** pocket, towner

Out of Africa: **4** book, film

author: Isak Dinesen

cast: Robert Redford, Meryl Streep

character: **4** Bror **5** Karen **6** Blixen

director: Sydney Pollack

__ out of bed: **4** fall

out-of-bounds: **4** foul **6** vulgar **9** offensive, priceless **10** indelicate, scandalous

serve: **5** fault

Out of Control

author: G. Gordon Liddy

__ out of court: **5** laugh

out-of-date: **3** obs., old **4** past **5** dowdy, dusty, fusty, hoary, musty, passé, stale, tacky, tired **6** bygone, démodé, old-hat, square **7** antique, archaic, fogyish, has-been, vintage **8** obsolete, timeworn **9** hackneyed, moth-eaten **10** antiquated, back-number

__ out of gas: **3** run

__ out of house and home: **3** eat

__ out of it: **4** snap

out of line: **4** pert **5** saucy **6** risqué **8** impudent **10** disorderly, disruptive, irreverent

__ out of mind: **4** time

Out of Mulberry Street

author: Jacob Riis

Out of my dreams and __ your arms...: **4** into

__ Out of My Head: **4** Goin'

__ Out of My Life: **4** She's

__ out of one's hand: **3** eat

out-of-place: **5** inapt, messy, mussy **6** untidy **10** disjointed, disordered

out of sight: **4** neat **6** costly **9** expensive, priceless

Out of Sight (1998 film)

cast: George Clooney, Jennifer Lopez, Ving Rhames

out of sorts: **5** angry, cross, huffy, moody, surly, testy, vexed **6** crabby, cranky, grumpy, morose, ornery, sullen **7** annoyed, fretful, grouchy, peevish, waspish **8** churlish, petulant **9** crotchety, irascible, irritable **10** ill-humored

out of style: **5** dated, hoary, passé, tacky, tired **6** démodé, square **7** vintage

out of the __: **3** way **4** blue **5** woods **7** running

out of the __ blue sky: **5** clear

Out of the Blue (song)

artist: ELO, Debbie Gibson

__ out of the box: **5** knock

Out of the Cellar

artist: Ratt

Out of the Cradle...: **4** poem

author: Walt Whitman

Out of the Dark

author: Helen Keller

Out of the Deeps

author: John Wyndham

Out of the frying pan, __ the fire: **4** into

Out of the Inkwell clown: **4** Koko

out-of-the-ordinary: **4** rare **8** singular, uncommon **9** arresting

Out of the Silent Planet

author: C.S. Lewis

out-of-the-way: **3** far **5** apart, aside **6** far-off, lonely, remote, secret **7** distant, private, removed, strange **8** desolate, far-flung, isolated, secluded, solitary, uncommon **9** reclusive, sheltered **10** cloistered, unexplored

not ~: **5** usual

out of this __: **5** world

Out of Time

artist: R.E.M.

Out of Time (2003 film)

cast: Eva Mendes, Denzel Washington

Out of Touch (1984 song)

artist: Hall and Oates

out-of-towner: **5** guest **6** caller **7** company, invitee, tourist, visitor **8** stranger, underdog **9** foreigner, sightseer, transient

Out-of-Towners, The (1970 film)

cast: Sandy Dennis, Jack Lemmon, Anne Meara

Out-of-Towners, The (1999 film)

cast: John Cleese, Goldie Hawn, Steve Martin

out-of-uniform garb: **5** mufti **7** civvies

__ out of water: **4** fish

out-of-whack: **10** disorderly

out of whole __: **5** cloth

out on __: **5** a limb

__ out on: **3** run **4** lose, miss, walk

__ out one's welcome: **4** wear

outpace: **3** cap, top **4** beat, best, pass **6** better, exceed **7** eclipse, surpass **8** go beyond **10** put to shame

outpatient facility: **6** clinic **8** hospital **9** infirmary **10** dispensary

outperform: **4** beat **5** trump **6** defeat **7** surpass **10** tower above

outplay: **4** beat, best **5** upset **6** defeat

outpost: **4** base, camp, fort **5** scout **6** branch, colony **9** outskirts **10** settlement

maritime ~: **3** NAS

outpour: **4** flow, gush, spew **5** spate, spirt, spout, spurt, surge **6** stream **8** eruption **9** discharge

outpouring: **4** flow, gush, wave **5** flood, river, sally, spate, spirt, spurt, surge **6** deluge, efflux, onrush, stream **7** cascade, torrent **9** effluence

output: **4** crop, gain, take, work **5** yield **6** amount, profit **7** harvest, product **10** production

outrage: **3** ire **4** evil, fury **5** abuse, anger, appal, crime, shock, storm, wrath, wrong **6** appall, burn up, fire up, injury, insult, madden, misuse, offend **7** affront, disgust, incense, offense, scandal **8** aggrieve, atrocity, enormity, maltreat, mischief, misdoing, mistreat **9** barbarism, evildoing, infuriate, injustice **10** inhumanity, resentment, scandalize, wrongdoing

cry of ~: **4** well **6** I never

outraged: **3** hot, mad **4** ired, sore **5** angry, cross, huffy, irate, livid, riled, upset, wroth **6** fuming, ireful, peeved, raging, raving, red-hot **7** furious, ranting **8** choleric, wrathful **9** disgusted, indignant, resentful, splenetic

outrageous: **3** mad **4** wild **5** crazy, gross, lousy, steep **6** brazen, odious, unholy, wanton, wicked **7** beastly, corrupt, extreme, glaring, heinous, ignoble, inhuman, rampant, too much, ungodly **8** barbaric, criminal, depraved, enormous, fabulous, flagrant, grievous, horrible, infamous, shameful, shocking **9** atrocious, barbarous, desperate, egregious, excessive, monstrous, nefarious, notorious, offensive, shameless, unnatural **10** detestable, disgusting, exorbitant, impossible, indelicate, inordinate, scandalous

Outrageous Fortune (1987 film)

cast: Peter Coyote, Shelley Long, Bette Midler

outrageously: **3** too **4** much, very **5** quite, truly **6** hugely, really, unduly, vastly **7** only too **8** terribly **9** decidedly, downright, extremely, seriously **10** incredibly, sure-enough

outrank: **7** precede, surpass **8** antecede
outranking: **7** ahead of
outré: **5** queer, weird **7** bizarre, extreme, offbeat, strange, unusual **8** freakish, shocking **9** eccentric **10** off-the-wall, outlandish
outrider: **3** spy **5** scout, watch **7** lookout, spotter
outrigger: **4** boat, prao, prau, proa **5** canoe, craft, prahu **6** vessel
outright: **4** flat, pure, rank **5** fully, gross, sheer, stark, total, utter **6** arrant, direct, entire **7** perfect **8** absolute, by itself, complete, positive, specific, straight, thorough **9** instantly, wholesale **10** consummate, undeniable, unmediated
__ Outright, The: **4** Gift
outrival: **4** beat, best **6** defeat **9** transcend
outrun: **4** beat, lose **5** elude **6** exceed **7** surpass **8** throw off
outrush: **4** gale, gust, puff, wind **5** blast, burst, draft, sally **7** flare-up **8** eruption **9** irruption
outs
ins and ~: **4** ways **5** bends, turns **6** curves, habits, traits, twists **7** customs, details **8** patterns, windings
on the ~: **5** at war, in bad **6** at odds **7** feuding **10** quarreling
six ~: **6** inning
__ outs: **5** on the
outscore: **3** win **4** beat, best **6** defeat
outset: **4** dawn, rise **5** birth, git-go, start **6** advent, origin **7** genesis, kickoff, leadoff, opening **8** exordium **9** beginning, inception, threshold **10** conception, incipience
at the ~: **5** first **9** in advance, initially **10** beforehand
outshine: **3** cap, top **4** beat, best, pass **5** excel **6** better, exceed, show up **7** eclipse, surpass **8** dominate **9** transcend **10** overshadow, put to shame, tower above
outside: **3** far, off **4** away, face, husk, open, over, skin, slim **5** alien, faint, front, shell, small **6** beyond, facade, remote, sheath, slight, veneer **7** distant, extreme, farther, foreign, maximum, open-air, seeming, slender, surface, topside, without **8** alfresco, covering, exoteric, exterior, external, farthest, furthest, marginal, unlikely **9** apart from, periphery **10** appearance, extraneous, integument, negligible
at the ~: **9** maximally
not ~: **6** indoor, within **7** indoors
of: **3** bar **4** save **6** except **7** besides **9** other than
prefix: **4** ecto- **5** extra-
the law: **4** tabu **5** taboo **6** banned **7** illegal, illicit **8** criminal, improper, unlawful, verboten, wrongful **9** felonious, forbidden **10** prohibited
outside __: **4** shot **6** chance
outsider: **5** alien **7** floater, incomer, refugee **8** intruder, newcomer, stranger **9** foreigner, layperson, odd man out, odd one out **10** interloper
Outsider in Amsterdam
author: Janwillem van de Wetering
outsiders: **6** others
Outsiders
song: Time Won't Let Me (1966)
Outsider, The
author: Colin Wilson
outsize: **3** big **4** huge **5** giant, large **7** hulking, immense **10** overweight
outskirts: **3** rim **4** edge **5** exurb, limit **6** border, fringe, sticks, suburb **7** exurbia, purlieu **8** boundary, environs, purlieus, suburbia, vicinity **9** periphery
outsmart: **3** cap, con, fox, top **4** beat, dupe, gull, have, hoax, undo **5** cheat, goose, trick, worst **6** baffle, defeat, end-run, take in **7** confuse, deceive, defraud, finagle, mislead, swindle **8** bewilder, hoodwink **9** bamboozle, get around, overreach **10** circumvent, lead astray
outspoken: **4** bold, free, open, oral **5** bluff, blunt, brusk, frank, plain, vocal **6** abrupt, brassy, candid, direct, square **7** artless, brusque, sincere, up-front **8** explicit, impolite, strident, tactless, truthful **9** ingenuous **10** forthright, foursquare, from the hip, indelicate, point-blank, unreserved, unreticent
outspread: **3** big **4** long, wide **5** broad **6** expand
outstanding: **3** bad, due, wow **4** main, open, star, tops **5** chief, major, owing, primo **6** banner, famous, marked, signal, unpaid **7** eminent, exalted, leading, mostest, notable, ongoing, overdue, payable, pending, salient, special, unusual **8** dominant, especial, greatest, historic, renowned, singular, towering, wondrous **9** arresting, important, memorable, momentous, number one, principal, prominent, remaining, unsettled, well-known, wonderful **10** world-class
amount: **4** debt **6** arrear **7** arrears
be ~: **4** star **5** excel, shine
person: **4** oner, star **5** adept, great **7** notable **9** superstar
see also wonderful
outstep: **3** cap, top **4** beat, best, lead, lick **5** excel **6** better, exceed **7** eclipse, surpass **8** go beyond **10** put to shame
outstretch: **5** widen **6** spread
outstretched: **4** flat, long, wide
outstrip: **3** cap, top **4** beat, lead, lick, pass, race, zoom **5** break, excel **6** better, exceed **7** eclipse, get past, surpass **8** antecede, overtake **9** transcend **10** put to shame, tower above
outstripping: **6** beyond **7** ahead of, beating **10** superior to, surpassing
Outta here!: **4** scat, shoo **5** scram
__ out the clock: **3** run
__ out the red carpet: **4** roll
out to __: **3** sea **5** lunch
__ out to pasture: **3** put
__ out to sea: **3** put
Out to Sea (1997 film)
cast: Dyan Cannon, Jack Lemmon, Walter Matthau, Donald O'Connor, Brent Spiner, Elaine Stritch
outvote: **4** rule **5** upset **8** dominate, override, overturn
outward: **4** open, over **5** forth, outer **7** evident, obvious, surface, visible **8** apparent, exoteric, exterior, external, to the eye **10** from within, noticeable, observable, ostensible
appearance: **4** face, look, mask, mien, pose **5** cloak, cover, front, guise, shape **6** aspect, facade, manner, veneer **7** bearing **8** demeanor, disguise, exterior **9** semblance **10** camouflage, false front, impression, masquerade
curved ~: **6** convex
extend ~: **3** jut **4** lean, poke **5** bulge **7** project **8** overhang, protrude
flow: **3** ebb **4** tide **6** efflux **9** abatement, discharge, recession
prefix: **5** extro-
project ~: **3** jut **5** bloat, bulge, swell **6** expand **7** balloon, distend **8** protrude
turn ~: **5** flare, splay
outward-__: **5** bound
outwardly: **8** to the eye **9** seemingly **10** officially
outweigh: **3** top **5** excel **6** exceed, offset, redeem, set off **7** balance, eclipse, prevail, surpass **8** atone for, overcome, override, overrule **9** make up for, transcend **10** compensate, overshadow
__ Out West: **3** Way
outwit: **3** cap, con, fox, get, top **4** beat, dupe, foil, gull, have, hoax **5** cheat, elude, goose, stump, trick, trump, worst **6** baffle, defeat, end-run, take in, thwart **7** confuse, conquer, deceive, defraud, finagle, mislead, swindle **8** bewilder, hoodwink **9** bamboozle, frustrate, get around, overreach **10** circumvent, lead astray
tough to ~: **3** hip, sly **4** foxy, keen, wily, wise **5** acute, canny, quick, ready, savvy, sharp, smart **6** astute, brainy, bright, clever, crafty, shrewd **7** cunning, knowing **8** sensible **9** astucious, farseeing, judicious, on the ball, realistic, sagacious **10** discerning, insightful, perceptive, thoughtful
__ Out With My Baby: **7** Steppin'
outworn: **3** old **5** dated, passé, stale **6** old hat **8** obsolete
outwrestle: **3** pin **6** pinion **8** hold down **10** immobilize
ouzel: **4** bird **6** dipper
emulate a ~: **4** dive
ouzo: **5** drink **8** beverage
flavoring: **5** anise
ova: **3** roe **4** eggs **6** caviar **7** caviare
oval: **4** ooid **5** round, shape **6** oblong **7** rounded **8** elliptic, roundish **9** cartouche, egg-shaped, ellipsoid, racetrack **10** elliptical, racecourse
Oval __: **6** Office
Oval Portrait, The
author: Edgar Allan Poe
ovate: **9** egg-shaped **10** elliptical
ovation: **4** hand **5** salvo **6** bravos, praise **7** acclaim, big hand, tribute, welcome **8** applause, cheering, clapping, plaudits **9** standing O
give an ~: **4** clap **5** cheer, honor **6** praise **7** acclaim, applaud
Ovation: **7** channel
alternative: *see* cable channel
oven: **4** kiln, lehr, oast **5** stove **7** broiler, tandoor **8** limekiln **9** brickkiln, microwave **10** rotisserie
accessory: **4** mitt **5** glove
emanation: **5** aroma, smell
ender: **4** bird, ware **5** proof
gadget: **5** timer
like an ~: **3** hot **4** warm **6** heated, sultry, sweaty, toasty, torrid **7** blazing, boiling, burning, summery, sweltry **8** broiling, parching, roasting, scalding, sizzling, steaming, tropical **9** scorching **10** blistering, sweltering
name: **5** Amana
use the ~: **4** bake, heat **5** broil, roast
oven __: **4** mitt
__ oven: **5** Dutch **7** toaster **10** convection
Oven Bird, The
author: Robert Frost
ovenware: **5** Pyrex
over: **3** off, too **4** anew, atop, done, gone, more, past **5** above, again, aloft, ended, extra, kaput, outer **6** across, afresh, beyond, bygone, closed, finito, lapsed, on high, unduly, unused, upward **7** at an end, on top of, outside, outward, settled, surplus, through **8** apparent, covering, done with, finished, in excess, in heaven, in the sky, once more, superior, upstairs **9** completed, concluded, excessive, extremely, immensely, instead of, remaining, upwards of **10** from the top, higher than, in addition, in excess of, rather than, straight up, terminated
ender: **3** age **4** much **6** master
in German: **4** über
not ~: **5** below, under **8** less than
prefix: **3** epi-, sur- **5** hyper-, super-
starter: **3** all, cut, lay, pop **4** hang, hold, hung, left, make, more, pull, push, roll, slip, stop, take, turn, walk, wing **5** carry, cross, flash, sleep, spill, voice **6** change, strike, switch
over __: **4** easy, with **5** again
__ over: **3** all, get, lay, put, run **4** blow, boil, bowl, come, give, hand, hold, keel, look, make, pass, pick, pore, roll, stop, talk, tide, turn, walk, work **5** carry, check, cross, gloss, scoot, sleep, stand, throw, watch **6** bowled
__-over: **3** cab, fly **4** once **5** going, voice **6** warmed
Over __: **4** Easy **5** There
over a __: **6** barrel
overabundance: **4** glut **6** excess **7** nimiety, satiety, surfeit, surplus, too much **8** plethora **9** plenitude, profusion
overact: **5** emote **7** ham it up
overacted: **5** hammy, stagy **6** stagey **10** histrionic, theatrical
overactive: **5** hyper **7** fidgety **8** fluttery, frenetic, frenzied, restless **10** high-strung

overage: **4** rest **6** excess **7** surplus **8** plethora
overall: **5** gross, total **6** global, mainly, mostly **7** blanket, general, largely **8** complete, long-term, sweeping, thorough, umbrella **9** inclusive, in general, long-range, primarily, wholesale **10** everywhere, on the whole, throughout
total: **3** all, sum **5** gross, whole **8** entirety, receipts **9** aggregate
overalls: **5** pants **8** trousers **10** protection
material: **5** denim
part: **3** bib
over and __: **3** out **4** done **5** above
Over and Over (1965 song)
artist: Dave Clark Five
__ over a new leaf: **4** turn
overanxious: **5** antsy, tense **7** nervous
overawe: **3** cow **5** daunt, deter **10** discourage, intimidate
__ over backward: **4** bend, fall, lean
overbalance: **3** tip **4** fall, roll **5** spill, upend, upset **6** go down, teeter, topple, totter **7** capsize
overbalanced: **6** uneven **7** unequal **8** lopsided
overbear: **5** bully **10** lord it over
overbearing: **4** hard **5** bossy, cocky, lofty, proud, pushy **6** lordly, severe, uppity **7** haughty, pompous **8** arrogant, assuming, cavalier, despotic, dogmatic, dominant, imperial, insolent, superior **9** bumptious, egotistic, imperious, officious, sovereign **10** despotical, dogmatical, peremptory, tyrannical
not ~: **3** shy **4** meek, mild, soft, tame, weak **5** lowly, quiet, timid **6** docile, gentle, humble, modest **7** lenient, passive, patient, subdued **8** lamblike, peaceful, retiring, tolerant, yielding **10** manageable, submissive, unassuming
one: **4** czar, tsar **5** bully **6** despot, tyrant **7** monarch **8** autocrat, dictator, martinet **9** oppressor
__ Over Beethoven: **4** Roll
overblown: **3** big **4** tall **5** tumid, undue, windy **6** turgid **7** flowery, fulsome, hyped up, orotund, pompous, profuse, stilted, too much, verbose **8** inflated **9** bombastic, excessive **10** immoderate, oratorical, rhetorical
praise: **4** hype, plug, puff **5** promo **7** puffery **9** publicity
overboard: **9** excessive **10** exorbitant
goods thrown ~: **5** lagan, ligan
throw ~: **4** dump, junk **5** chuck, ditch, heave, scrap **6** unload **7** abandon, cast off, deep-six, discard, lighten **8** jettison
__ overboard!: **3** Man
Overboard (1987 film)
cast: Goldie Hawn, Kurt Russell
overbold: **6** brassy, brazen **7** blatant **8** impudent **9** daredevil
__ Over Broadway: **6** Angels **7** Bullets
overburden: **3** tax **4** load, tire **5** abuse, swamp **6** overdo **7** congest, oppress **9** weigh down
overcast: **4** dark, dull, gray, grey, hazy **5** dusky, foggy, mirky, misty, murky **6** cloudy, dismal, dreary, gloomy, leaden, shadow, somber **7** clouded, sunless **8** darkened, lowering **9** adumbrate **10** oppressive
overcharge: **4** bilk, soak **5** bleed, cheat, gouge, sting **6** fleece, rip off
for tickets: **5** scalp
overcloud: **3** dim **4** mist **7** obscure
overcoat: **5** capot, jemmy **6** capote, duffle, duster, jacket, raglan, ulster **7** kuletuk **8** benjamin **9** balmacaan, Inverness **10** fearnought, macfarlane
fabric: **9** cothamore
Japanese straw ~: **4** mino
Overcoat, The
author: Nikolai Gogol
overcome: **3** awe, win **4** beat, best, down, lick, rush, stun **5** crush, drown, outdo, quash, quell, seize, shock, still, unarm, upset, whelm, worst **6** beaten, buried, defeat, hurdle, master, reduce, subdue **7** conquer, prevail, rebound, recover, shocked, stunned, succeed, survive, swamped, triumph, trounce, weather **8** affected, convince, defeated, gang up on, outweigh, suppress, surmount, vanquish **9** blown-away, conquered, get around, prostrate, rise above, subjugate **10** neutralize, speechless
adversity: **3** win **4** beat, cope **6** attain, manage **7** achieve, conquer, make out, prevail, pull off, realize, succeed, triumph **8** struggle **9** withstand **10** accomplish
illness: **6** revive **7** get well, rebound, recover, shape up **9** get better **10** bounce back, come around, recuperate, turn around
with fear: **3** cow **4** faze **5** bully, daunt **6** dismay, menace **7** terrify, unnerve **8** paralyze **10** demoralize, intimidate, scare stiff
overconfident: **4** rash, smug **5** brash, cocky, pushy **8** careless, cocksure, heedless, impudent, reckless **9** bumptious, foolhardy, hubristic, presuming
overcook: **4** burn, char **7** blacken
overcritical: **7** carping, finicky **8** captious, caviling, contrary, exacting **9** demanding **10** censorious, nitpicking
overcrowd: **3** jam **4** cram, pack **5** jam in, stuff, swamp **6** cram in, pack in **7** congest, squeeze, stuff in **9** squeeze in
overcrowded: **4** full **5** awash, close, dense, thick **6** jammed, packed **7** crammed, stuffed, teeming **8** brimming, bursting **9** chock-full, jam-packed
overcurious: **4** nosy **5** nosey **6** prying, snoopy **8** snooping **9** butting in, intrusive, obtrusive **10** meddlesome
overdecorated: **4** busy
overdo: **4** hype, puff **6** pile on, stress **7** amplify, belabor, fatigue, lay it on, magnify, run riot, stretch, talk big **8** pressure, wear down **9** embroider, luxuriate **10** exaggerate
it: **4** brag, fawn **5** boast **6** pander **7** lay it on, talk big **8** go too far
overdone: **4** arty **5** artsy, burnt, campy, hammy, sappy, showy, stagy, tough **6** garish, ornate, stagey **7** fulsome, labored **8** affected, wasteful **9** contrived, excessive
overdraft letters: **3** NSF
overdramatic: **5** stagy **6** stagey **10** theatrical
overdramatize: **4** gush **5** emote **7** carry on, ham it up
overdub: **3** add **7** include **9** interject
unit: **5** track
overdue: **3** due **4** late, ripe **5** owing, tardy **6** behind, held up, hung up, unpaid **7** belated, delayed, payable **8** detained **9** unsettled **10** behindhand, behind time, delinquent
payment: **6** arrear **7** arrears
overeager: **5** antsy, itchy **7** anxious, zealous **9** impatient
overeagerness: **4** fire, zeal **6** fervor **9** intensity, vehemence **10** fanaticism
overeasy: **3** lax **7** lenient
overeat: **5** gorge, stuff **6** pig out **7** engorge **10** gormandize
overeater: **3** pig **7** glutton **8** gourmand
overelaborate: **4** busy, lacy **5** fancy, fussy, showy **6** flashy, frilly, gilded, glitzy, ornate, rococo **7** baroque, flowery, opulent, splashy **9** tasteless **10** convoluted, flamboyant
overemotional: **5** gooey, gushy, hammy, mushy, sappy, soppy, stagy, teary, weepy **6** slushy, syrupy **7** cloying, insipid, maudlin, mawkish, tearful **8** bathetic, cornball **9** schmaltzy, sniveling **10** lachrymose, theatrical
over-enthuse: **4** gush, rave **5** drool, emote **6** effuse
overenthusiastic: **4** wild **5** rabid, ultra **6** crazed **7** berserk, violent, zealous **8** frenzied, obsessed, wild-eyed **9** delirious, fanatical **10** hysterical
overestimate: **3** err **6** puff up **7** inflate, mistake **8** misjudge
overexcited: **5** irate, manic **8** maniacal
overexert: **3** tax **4** ache, push, tire, toil **5** drive, labor, sweat **6** strain, stress **7** fatigue, peg away **8** go all out
overexertion result: **4** ache
overextend: **3** tax **5** force, press **6** burden, strain, stress **7** stretch
overfamiliar: **5** banal, corny, stale, tired, trite **6** common **7** clichéd, worn-out **8** bathetic, bromidic, shopworn **9** hackneyed **10** pedestrian, unoriginal
overfeed: **4** glut, sate **6** fatten **7** surfeit
overfill: **4** clog, cloy, cram, glut, sate **5** spill, stuff **7** congest, satiate, surfeit **8** saturate
__ over fist: **4** hand
overflow: **4** brim, gush, ooze, slop, teem **5** cover, drown, flood, issue, slosh, spate, spill, spirt, spout, spurt, surge, swamp **6** abound, deluge, engulf, excess, ingulf, irrupt **7** cascade, pour out, surfeit, surplus, torrent **8** cataract, inundate, plethora, submerge **9** overcrowd **10** congestion, inundation, redundancy
point: **3** lip, rim **4** brim, edge **5** brink, limit, verge **6** margin **9** periphery
overflowing: **4** full, rife **5** awash, flush, laden, thick **6** filled, jammed, loaded, packed **7** copious, crammed, crowded, profuse, replete, stuffed, teeming **8** abundant, effusive, generous **9** chock-full, luxuriant, plentiful
overfly: **3** spy **5** recon
overfond of, be: **4** baby **5** spoil **6** coddle, cosset, dote on, pamper **7** idolize, indulge **8** dote upon
overfull: **5** awash **6** jammed, loaded **7** crammed, crowded, fraught, replete, stuffed **8** brimming
overgenerous: **6** lavish, wanton **8** prodigal, wasteful **9** excessive **10** immoderate, profligate
overgrow: **6** sprawl, spread **7** overrun **8** multiply, mushroom
overgrown: **4** lush, rank, wild **5** large, mossy, reedy, seedy, weedy **6** jungly
tend to an ~ plant: **5** repot
overhang: **3** jut **4** eave, loom, poke **5** bulge, cliff **6** beetle, canopy, dangle, extend, impend **7** project **8** endanger, protrude, stand out, stick out, threaten **10** projection, tower above
overhanging: **7** pendant, pendent **8** lowering, towering
overhasty: **4** rash **9** imprudent, premature **10** ill-advised
overhaul: **3** fix **4** mend, redo **5** check, debug, patch, refit, renew **6** doctor, repair, revamp, revise **7** examine, improve, inspect, ransack, rebuild, restore, retread, service **8** renovate, revision **9** modernize, reexamine, refurbish **10** fiddle with, reorganize
overhead: **4** atop, cost, over, rent, roof **5** above, aloft, upper **6** aerial, burden, on high, outlay, upkeep, upward **7** expense, hanging, skyward, up above, upwards **8** expenses, in the sky **9** insurance, utilities
overhead-__ engine: **3** cam
overhear: **6** listen **9** eavesdrop, intercept
overheat: **4** burn, char **5** singe **6** scorch
__ over heels: **4** head
Over here!: **3** hey, pst **4** psst **6** hey you, yoo-hoo
Over hill, over ___: **4** dale
overindulge: **4** baby, dote, glut, sate, tope **5** binge, gorge, spoil, stuff **6** coddle, dote on, pamper, pig out **7** cater to, satiate, surfeit **8** dote upon **10** gormandize
overindulged: **4** soft **8** pampered **10** namby-pamby
overindulgence: **3** jag **4** bash, orgy, tear **5** binge, fling, spree **6** excess

7 blowout, license, nimiety, revelry, splurge, surfeit 8 carousal 9 bacchanal, decadence 10 immoderacy, saturnalia
overindulgent: 3 lax 4 fond, soft 6 lavish, wanton 8 prodigal 9 excessive 10 immoderate, profligate
one: 5 doter
overindulgently: 3 too 4 very 6 too-too
overinquisitive: 4 nosy 5 nosey
be ~: 3 pry 4 nose, peer
one: 5 yenta 6 gossip 7 meddler 8 busybody, quidnunc
overjoy: 5 elate 6 please, ravish
overjoyed: 4 glad 5 happy, merry 6 blithe, cheery, elated, jovial, upbeat, wallow 7 charmed, gleeful, pleased, tickled 8 blissful, cheerful, ecstatic, euphoric, exultant, jubilant, mirthful, ravished, thrilled 9 delighted, delirious, gladdened, rapturous, rejoicing, rhapsodic 10 flying high
be ~: 4 crow 5 cheer, exult, glory, revel 7 delight, rejoice, triumph 8 jubilate 9 celebrate, make merry 10 effervesce
overkill: 6 excess 7 surfeit 8 plethora
Overkill (1983 song)
artist: Men at Work
Overland __: 5 Trail
Overland Park: 4 city, town
locale: 6 Kansas
org.: 4 NCAA
overlap: 3 lap 4 flap 7 project, shingle, stagger, stretch 8 go beyond, overhang, protrude 9 imbricate
overlarge: 4 huge, vast 5 giant, great, jumbo 7 hulking, immense, mammoth, massive, sizable, titanic 8 colossal, enormous, gigantic, king-size, sizeable, towering, whapping, whopping 9 Herculean, humongous 10 gargantuan, monumental, prodigious, stupendous, tremendous
overlay: 4 coat, gild, wash 5 cover, glaze, plate, sheet, smear 6 lamina, rest on, spread, veneer 7 blanket, encrust, incrust, plaster 8 laminate
thin metal ~: 4 wash 7 coating
overleap: 4 jump, miss, omit, skip 5 scorn, shirk, vault 6 bypass, hurdle, ignore, spring 7 neglect 8 shrug off 9 disregard, pay no mind 10 brush aside
overlie: 3 lap 5 cover 7 envelop
__ over lightly: 4 once
overload: 3 tax 4 glut, lade 5 swamp 6 burden, deluge, excess, strain 7 congest, oppress 8 encumber, keep down 9 weigh down
protector: 4 fuse
overloaded: 4 busy 6 hectic, snowed 7 popping, swamped
overlong: 7 lengthy 8 dragging 10 protracted
overlook: 4 face, look, miss, omit, pass, skip, view 5 cliff, front, let go, waive 6 excuse, forget, ignore, pardon, pass by, regard, slight, slip up, survey, wink at 7 blink at, condone, forgive, front on, let pass, lookout, mistake, neglect, rule out, stomach, tune out 8 bear with, discount, laugh off, leave out, let slide, live with, play past, prospect, shrug off, stand for 9 check up on, disregard, look out on, mishandle, mismanage, pay no mind, put up with, supervise, whitewash
overlord: 4 czar, tsar, tzar 5 ruler 6 gerent, master 7 viceroy 8 autocrat
overly: 3 too 4 over 6 too-too, unduly 7 too much 8 overmuch 9 extremely 10 improperly
__ over matter: 4 mind
__ Over Miami: 4 Moon
overmodest: 3 coy 4 prim 7 prudish
overmuch: 3 too 4 over 5 undue 6 overly, unduly 8 needless, to a fault 9 excessive, extremely 10 inordinate
overnice: 6 prissy 7 prudish 8 pedantic, precious 10 pedantical
overnight: 4 tour, trip 6 travel 7 layover 8 meteoric 9 temporary
duds: 3 PJs 7 jammies, pajamas
gear: 6 kitbag
send ~: 4 rush 5 FedEx 6 hasten 7 speed up 8 expedite 10 accelerate, lose no time
stay ~: 4 rest 5 crash, sleep 6 repose, turn in 7 sack out, saw wood, shuteye, slumber, zonk out 9 hit the hay 10 hit the sack
stop: 4 camp 5 hotel, motel 6 hostel 8 campsite, motor inn 10 motor lodge
temperature, usually: 3 low
overnighters: 7 baggage, luggage 8 carry-ons 9 suitcases
over one's __: 4 head
__ over oneself: 4 fall
over-ornament: 4 gild
overpack: 3 jam, ram 4 cram, tamp 5 crowd, crush, stuff 6 squash 7 squeeze
overpamper: 4 baby 5 humor, spoil 6 coddle, dote on 7 cater to, indulge 9 spoon-feed
__ Over Parador: 4 Moon
overparticular
see picky
overpass: 6 bridge 7 viaduct 8 crossing, traverse
abbr.: 3 max
overpermissive: 3 lax 4 easy, soft 5 loose, slack 6 casual 7 lenient 8 tolerant, yielding
overplay: 3 mug 5 ham up 7 ham it up, labor at, magnify, show off, stretch 8 maximize 9 dramatize 10 accentuate, exaggerate
overpower: 3 awe, get 4 beat, bury, drub, rout, stun 5 break, cream, crush, drown, quell, seize, smash, swamp, total, trash, upset, waste 6 defeat, lay low, obsess, reduce, subdue 7 clobber, conquer, oppress, put away, shut off, stagger, take out, torpedo, trounce 8 bear down, beat down, blow away, bulldoze, keep down, knock out, shellack, suppress, vanquish 9 fascinate, prostrate, subjugate 10 immobilize, take care of
overpowering: 4 hale, iron, wiry 5 beefy, burly, hardy, hefty, hunky, husky, lusty, stout, tough 6 brawny, hearty, mighty, potent, robust, rugged, sinewy, steely, stocky, strong, sturdy, virile 7 awesome, doughty, onerous 8 athletic, forceful, indurate, muscular, powerful, puissant, stalwart, vigorous 9 Atlantean, Herculean, strapping, well-built 10 able-bodied, red-blooded
overpraise: 4 puff 6 fawn on, puff up 7 blarney, flatter
overprecise: 4 nice, prim 5 fussy, stiff 6 choosy, demure, formal, prissy, proper, stuffy 7 genteel, prudish, stilted, uptight 8 decorous, priggish, starched 9 bluenosed, squeamish 10 fastidious, fuddy-duddy, goody-goody, nit-picking, particular
overpriced: 4 dear, high, rich 5 steep 9 expensive 10 at a premium
overprofusion: 4 glut 6 excess 7 nimiety, surfeit, surplus 8 plethora
overproud: 4 smug 7 pompous, stuck-up 8 arrogant, egoistic, priggish, puffed-up, snobbish, superior 9 conceited 10 big-talking, complacent
overrate: 6 exceed 7 build up, magnify 8 misjudge 10 exaggerate
overreach: 4 undo 6 outwit 8 outflank, outsmart 10 circumvent
overreact: 5 panic 6 lose it 8 freeze up, have a fit, stampede 9 come apart, run scared 10 chicken out, go to pieces
overrefined: 6 prissy 7 finicky 8 precious 10 fastidious
overregulate: 6 corset 9 hamstring
override: 3 lap 4 rule, veto 5 alter, annul, quash, upset 6 cancel, recall, repeal, revoke, thwart 7 nullify, outvote, rescind, reverse, trample 8 disallow, dominate, outweigh, set aside 9 disregard, influence, supersede 10 invalidate
overriding: 4 main 5 chief, final, focal, major, prime 6 ruling 7 central, pivotal, primary, supreme 8 cardinal, dominant, ultimate 9 number one, paramount, principal, uppermost
overripe: 3 bad, old 4 soft 5 musty 6 rotten 7 decayed 10 malodorous
overrule: 3 nix 4 veto 5 alter, annul, quash, upset 6 cancel, ignore, recall, repeal, revoke, thwart 7 nullify, prevail, rescind, reverse, trample 8 disallow, dominate, hold sway, outweigh, overturn, set aside 9 disregard, influence, supersede 10 invalidate
overrun: 3 mob, top 4 beat, drub, lick, raid, rife, rout, teem, trim, whip, wild 5 beset, choke, foray, seize, spill, surge, swamp, swarm, worst 6 defeat, deluge, engulf, exceed, infest, ingulf, inroad, invade, occupy, ravage, thrash 7 clobber, lambast, surpass, surplus 8 go beyond, inundate, lambaste, massacre 9 intrude on
__ overrun: 4 cost
oversatisfy: 4 cloy, glut, jade, pall, sate 5 gorge, stuff, weary 7 satiate, surfeit
overseas: 5 alien 6 abroad 7 far away, foreign 8 offshore
overseasoned: 5 salty
oversee: 3 eye, run 4 boss, head, herd, mind, tend 5 watch 6 direct, govern, manage, survey 7 baby-sit, captain, command, conduct, control, inspect, monitor, preside, skipper 8 chaperon, regulate, shepherd 9 chaperone, check up on, look after, officiate, supervise 10 administer, ride herd on, run the show, sit on top of
overseer: 3 mgr. 4 boss, head, mgmt., supt. 5 chief 6 bishop, gerent, keeper, master, top dog, warden 7 manager, monitor, pit boss 8 director, guardian, higher-up, watchdog 9 custodian, executive, inspector, organizer, straw boss 10 head honcho, management, supervisor
oversensitive: 5 huffy, wired 6 touchy 7 prickly, waspish
oversentimental: 5 sappy, soppy, soupy
one: 5 softy 6 softie
oversentimentality: 4 mush 5 slush 8 schmaltz 9 mushiness
overset: 3 tip 4 tilt, undo 5 spill, upend 6 careen, invert, renege, revert, revoke, switch, topple 7 capsize, counter, retract, reverse 8 flip-flop 9 about-face, back-pedal, volte-face 10 turn around
overshadow: 3 dim 4 haze, loom 5 bedim, cloud, dwarf, excel 6 darken, show up 7 becloud, eclipse, surpass 8 dominate, outshine, outweigh 9 adumbrate, obfuscate, transcend 10 put to shame, tower above
overshoe: 4 boot 5 wader 6 galosh, golosh, rubber 7 galoshe, hip boot
overshoot: 4 jump, miss 6 go past
oversight: 4 egis, miss, skip, slip 5 aegis, error, fault, lapse, watch 6 boo-boo, charge, lapsus, laxity, miscue, slip-up 7 blunder, conduct, control, custody, default, failure, keeping, mistake, neglect 8 handling, omission, tutelage 9 disregard 10 management
oversize: 3 big 4 huge, vast 5 baggy, giant, great, jumbo, large 7 hulking, immense, mammoth, massive, titanic 8 colossal, enormous, gigantic, towering, whapping, whopping 9 Herculean, humongous 10 gargantuan, monumental, prodigious, stupendous, tremendous
oversoon: 8 untimely 9 premature
overspend: 4 lose 5 drain, use up, waste 6 burn up, lavish, misuse 7 deplete, fribble, splurge 8 squander 9 throw away 10 gamble away, run through, trifle away
__ over spilled milk: 3 cry
overspread: 4 fill, teem 5 choke, cover, swamp, swarm 6 engulf, extend, infest, invade 7 pervade, suffuse 8 inundate, permeate 9 percolate
overstate: 5 color, fudge 6 blow up 7 inflate, magnify, stretch 8 misquote 9 dramatize, embellish, embroider 10 exaggerate
overstatement: 4 tale 8 tall tale

OV

overstep: 6 exceed 7 surpass 8 go beyond, trespass
overstock: 4 cram, glut, load 5 extra, flood 6 excess 7 congest, surplus 8 saturate 9 remainder
overstrain: 3 sap, tax 4 bush, tire 5 drain, weary 7 burn out, exhaust, fatigue, give out, go stale, poop out, wear out 8 enervate 9 prostrate
overstress: 4 hype 6 hype up, play up, puff up, step up 7 magnify, promote 8 escalate, overplay 9 aggravate, intensify 10 exaggerate
overstretch: 6 strain
overstrung: 4 edgy, taut 5 drawn, hyper, jumpy, tense, wired 6 on edge 7 anxious, excited, fidgety, fretful, jittery, keyed up, nervous, uptight, wound up 8 agitated, fluttery, in a tizzy, unnerved 9 unsettled, up the wall
overstuff: 3 jam 4 cram, fill 5 bloat
overstuffed: 5 tumid 7 bloated
oversupply: 4 glut, load, much, sate 5 flood 6 excess 7 nimiety, satiate, surfeit, surplus 8 plethora 9 profusion
oversweet: 6 sirupy, syrupy 10 saccharine
overt: 4 open 5 clear, naked, plain 6 patent, public 7 evident, glaring, obvious, visible 8 apparent, definite, manifest, unhidden, unsubtle, unveiled 9 in the open 10 aboveboard, observable, plain to see, unshrouded
overtake: 3 lap 4 beat, pass, trap 5 catch, outdo, reach 6 befall, engulf, gain on, ingulf, pursue 7 get past, run down 8 come upon, outstrip
overtask: 3 tax 6 strain 9 weigh down
overtax: 4 jade, tire 5 abuse 6 strain 9 weigh down
overtaxing: 4 hard 5 harsh, heavy 6 tiring, trying 7 arduous, galling, onerous, weighty 8 crushing, exacting, grievous, grinding, grueling, pressing, toilsome 9 demanding, difficult, excessive, herculean, laborious, ponderous, strenuous 10 burdensome, enervating, exhausting, formidable, oppressive
over the __: 3 top 4 edge, hill, hump, line 7 counter, transom
over-the-__: 3 air 4 road
Over the __-dark sea: 4 wine
__ Over, The: 6 Party's
__ over the coals: 4 haul, rake
over-the-counter: 5 goods, stock, store, wares 8 supplies
Over the Edge
author: Jonathan Kellerman
Over the Hedge (2006 film)
voice cast: Steve Carell, Garry Shandling, William Shatner, Wanda Sykes, Bruce Willis
Over the Rainbow: 4 song
composer: Harold Arlen, Yip Harburg
ending: 5 can't I
Over There: 4 song
composer: George M. Cohan
era: 3 WWI
__ Over the River Kwai, The: 6 Bridge
__ over the traces: 4 kick
overthrow: 3 err, zap 4 beat, fall, oust, rout, tilt, undo 5 purge, quash, rebel, smash, upend, upset 6 defeat, depose, everse, mutiny, ravage, refute, revolt, topple, unseat 7 abolish, conquer, reverse, subvert 8 conquest, dethrone, suppress, vanquish 9 abolition, bring down, landslide, prostrate 10 deposition, invalidate, put an end to, revolution
overtime situation: 3 tie
overtire: 4 bore, bush, flag, jade 5 drain 6 strain, stress 7 conk out, exhaust, fatigue, poop out 8 enervate, wear down 9 tucker out
overtired: 4 beat, shot, worn 5 all in, drawn, fed up, had it, jaded, spent, stale, taxed, trite, weary 6 bushed, done in, pooped, punchy, used up, zonked 7 clichéd, drained, haggard, worn out 8 drooping, fatigued, flagging, out of gas, wiped out, wrung out 9 burned out, enervated, exhausted, hackneyed, played out, prostrate 10 knocked out
overtone: 4 hint, tone 5 sense, tinge 6 flavor, nuance 7 meaning 8 innuendo 9 inference 10 intimation, suggestion
overtrusting: 4 easy, naif 5 green, naive 6 simple, unwary, unwise 7 artless 8 gullible, innocent, lamblike, wide-eyed 9 childlike, confiding, credulous, guileless, ingenuous, unguarded, unworldly 10 unschooled, unseasoned
overture: 3 bid 4 pass 5 intro, music, offer 6 feeler, prolog, tender 7 advance, opening, preface, prelude 8 approach, foreword, prologue, proposal 9 intrusion 10 invitation
follower: 4 Act I 6 act one
make an ~ to: 3 ask 8 approach
__ Overture: 5 Cuban 6 Tragic 7 Leonore, Manfred
__ Overtures: 7 Pacific
overturn: 3 tip 4 roll, undo, void 5 annul, rebel, rebut, smash, spill, upend, upset 6 invert, repeal, revolt, topple, tumble 7 abolish, capsize, confute, nullify, rescind, reverse, shake up, subvert 8 set aside, vanquish 9 bring down, knock down, prostrate 10 invalidate, prove wrong
overturned: 5 spilt, upset 7 spilled, toppled 8 capsized 10 in disarray, upside-down
overused: 4 worn 5 stale, stock, trite 7 worn-out 9 played out 10 threadbare
phrase: 6 cliché
overventuresome: 4 rash, wild 5 brash, hasty 6 daring, madcap, unwary, unwise 8 feckless, headlong, heedless, mindless, pell-mell, reckless 9 audacious, breakneck, daredevil, foolhardy, hotheaded, imprudent, unadvised, uncareful 10 ill-advised, incautious
overview: 6 digest, survey 7 outline 8 panorama 10 compendium
give an ~: 5 sum up 6 digest 7 outline 8 condense 9 synopsize
overwary: 5 chary, leery 9 skeptical 10 suspicious
overweening: 4 vain 6 lordly 8 egoistic 9 egotistic
overweight: 4 huge 5 ample, beefy, bulky, fubsy, gross, heavy, hefty, large, obese, plump, pudgy, pursy, stout 6 chubby, fleshy, portly, pyknic, rotund, stocky, zaftig, zoftig 7 adipose, massive, outsize, overfed, paunchy, weighty 8 roly-poly 9 corpulent 10 abdominous, well-padded
overwhelm: 3 awe, win, wow 4 beat, bury, do in, drub, lick, rout, sink, slay, snow, stun, whip 5 amaze, crush, drown, flood, floor, seize, shock, swamp, total, upset, wreck 6 boggle, dazzle, defeat, deluge, engulf, ingulf, puzzle, ravage, thrash 7 astound, confuse, conquer, destroy, disturb, oppress, shatter, smother, stagger, stupefy, triumph, trounce 8 astonish, bedazzle, bewilder, confound, inundate, keep down, submerge, surprise, vanquish 9 devastate, downgrade, dumbfound, fascinate, prostrate, snow under 10 demoralize
with noise: 5 drown 6 deafen 8 drown out
with work: 5 swamp 6 deluge 9 snow under
overwhelmed: 5 agape, cowed 6 aghast, amazed, beaten, buried 7 abashed, daunted, shocked, stunned, swamped 8 affected, appalled, defeated, dismayed 9 astounded, awestruck, blown-away, conquered, prostrate 10 astonished, bewildered, bowled over, overthrown, speechless
overwhelming: 6 solemn 7 awesome 8 imposing 9 thrilling 10 prodigious
victory: 4 rout 5 upset 6 defeat 7 beating, debacle, laugher, pasting, shutout, washout 8 conquest, disaster, drubbing, stampede 9 thrashing, trouncing
__ over with: 3 all
overwork: 3 tax 4 jade, tire 5 weary 6 strain 7 belabor, exhaust
overworked: 4 worn 5 tired, trite, weary 7 harried, worn-out 9 elaborate, hackneyed, pressured
phrase: 6 cliché, saying 7 bromide 8 chestnut 9 platitude
overwrought: 3 hot, mad 4 edgy, high, ired, sore 5 crazy, cross, huffy, hyper, irate, livid, manic, riled, showy, spent, tense, tired, upset, vexed, wired, wroth 6 fuming, ireful, on edge, ornate, peeved, raging, raving, red-hot, rococo, uneasy 7 anxious, enraged, excited, fired up, frantic, furious, keyed-up, labored, nervous, ranting, stirred, uptight, worried, wound-up 8 affected, agitated, choleric, feverish, frenetic, frenzied, in a state, incensed, inflamed, maddened, outraged, unstrung, worked-up, wrathful 9 emotional, excitable, indignant, irritated, resentful, splenetic, steamed up, strung-out 10 freaked out, infuriated
Over You (1968 song)
artist: Gary Puckett and the Union Gap
overzealous: 5 pushy 9 obtrusive, officious
Oveta __ Hobby: 4 Culp
Ovett, Steve: 6 runner
rival: 3 Coe
Ovid: 4 poet 5 Roman
work: The Art of Love Metamorphoses
see also Latin
Oviedo: 4 city, town
locale: 5 Spain 7 Florida
oviform: 4 ooid 6 oblong 9 egg-shaped, ellipsoid 10 elliptical
ovine: 8 sheepish
creature: 3 ewe, ram 4 lamb 5 sheep
product: 4 wool 6 fleece
sound: 3 baa, maa 5 bleat
Ovitz: 7 Michael
ovo-__-vegetarian: 5 lacto
ovoid: 4 eggy 8 elliptic 9 egg-shaped 10 elliptical
ovule: 3 egg 4 seed 6 embryo
ovum: 3 egg 4 cell, seed
owe: 5 incur 6 borrow, charge 7 run a tab 9 attribute
owed: 3 due 7 payable 8 indebted
money ~: 4 debt, levy 6 arrear 7 arrears
one ~ money: 5 payee 8 creditor
Owego's county: 5 Tioga
Owen: 3 Don 5 Clive, Davis, Randy, Spike, Steve 6 Bieber, Mickey, Robert, Wilson, Wister 7 Wilfred 8 Reginald 10 Richardson
Owens: 4 Buck, Gary 5 Jesse 6 George
Owens __: 7 Corning
Owensboro: 4 city, town
locale: 8 Kentucky
Owens, Jesse: 6 runner 8 sprinter
Owen, Wilfred: 4 poet 7 British
work: Dulce et Decorum Est
ower: 6 debtor 8 deadbeat
document: 3 IOU 4 chit, note 6 marker
owing: 3 due 6 in debt, mature, unpaid 7 overdue, payable 8 beholden 9 liability, unsettled
to: 7 because 9 because of, imputable 10 by reason of, by virtue of
owl: 4 bird 6 hooter, raptor
hangout: 4 barn
like an ~: 4 wise
like some ~s: 5 eared
mouse, to an ~: 4 prey 6 quarry
sound: 3 hoo, who 4 hoot, whoo
__ owl: 4 barn, hoot 5 night, pygmy, snowy, tawny 6 horned 7 screech, spotted
Owl and the Pussycat, The
author: Edward Lear
Owl and the Pussycat, The (1970 film)
cast: Robert Klein, George Segal, Barbra Streisand
Owl's Clover
author: Wallace Stevens
Owls school: 4 Rice 6 Temple
Owl went, where the: 5 to sea
owly: 7 big-eyed 10 starry-eyed

own: 3 buy, run 4 avow, have, hold, keep 5 admit, allow, boast, enjoy, grant, let on 6 assert, fess up, occupy, pay for, proper, retain 7 concede, confess, control, declare, inherit, possess, private, reserve 8 personal 9 come clean, intrinsic, recognize 10 fall heir to, individual, monopolize, particular, respective
all you ~: 5 means 6 assets, estate, wealth
doesn't ~: 5 hasn't, rents
do on one's ~: 5 offer 6 enlist, sign up 7 pitch in, proffer, recruit, stand up, venture 9 undertake, volunteer 10 put forward
hold one's ~: 4 cope 5 get by 6 manage 7 make out
make one's ~: 5 co-opt 6 borrow 7 espouse
of one's ~ accord: 6 at will, freely, gladly 7 happily, readily 8 by choice 9 agreeably, voluntary, willingly
on one's ~: 4 free, solo 5 alone, unwed 6 single 9 unmarried
place of one's ~: 4 home, slot 5 niche
up: 3 own 4 avow 5 admit 7 concede, confess, profess 9 come clean
ownable property: 4 farm, home, land 5 acres, field, manor, ranch, tract 6 estate, parcel, realty 7 acreage, grounds, holding 9 farmstead 10 real estate
owned: 3 had 4 kept
apartment: 4 co-op 5 condo
be ~ by: 8 belong to
previously ~: 4 used, worn 10 hand-me-down, secondhand
___-owned: 3 pre
owner: 4 heir, host 5 buyer 6 dealer, holder, keeper, master, squire 7 heiress, legatee, partner 8 investor, landlady, landlord 9 possessor, purchaser 10 proprietor
property ~: 6 lienee, squire 8 landlord 10 freeholder
starter: 4 home, land 5 share, stock, store
ownerless: 5 stray 6 no one's 7 cast off 8 derelict 9 abandoned, discarded
Owner of a Lonely Heart (1983 song)
artist: Yes
ownership: 4 deed 5 claim, slice, title 6 buying, patent, tenure 7 control, holding, tenancy 8 dominion, monopoly, property 9 enjoyment, occupancy 10 occupation, possession, purchasing
proof of ~: 4 deed 5 paper, title 8 document
owns, old-style: 4 hath
___ Own, The: 6 Devil's
ox: 3 lug, oaf, yak 4 anoa, Babe, bozo, clod, dolt, gaur, lout, male, urus, zebu 5 bovid, gayal, klutz, looby, steer 6 animal, bovine, duffer, galoot, lubber, lummox, mammal, mithan 7 banteng, banting, boggler, botcher, bumbler, bungler, fumbler, galloot, kouprey 9 blunderer, harebrain 10 clodhopper, stumblebum
Asian ~: 3 yak 4 anoa, zebu 5 gayal
attachment: 4 yoke
big ~: 3 oaf 4 bozo 6 lummox
Celebes ~: 4 anoa
prehistoric ~: 7 aurochs
team: 4 span
wild ~: 4 gaur, urus
___ ox: 4 musk
oxalate: 4 salt 5 ester
oxalis: 5 plant 6 flower 10 wood sorrel
oxblood: 3 red 5 color
Ox-Bow Incident, The: 5 novel, oater
author: Walter van Tilburg Clark
character: 3 Art, Gil 4 Rose 5 Canby, Croft, Mapes
Oxbridge school: 4 Eton
Oxenberg, Catherine
spouse: Robert Evans
oxeye: 4 bird, posy 5 bloom, daisy, plant 6 flower 7 blossom 9 perennial, sunflower
oxford: 4 shoe 5 cloth 6 fabric 8 footwear
part: 4 heel, sole 5 upper 6 insole
Oxford: 4 city, peak, town 5 mount, sheep 8 mountain
athletes: 6 Rebels 7 Ole Miss 8 RedHawks
college: 3 New 5 Jesus, Oriel 6 Exeter, Merton, Wadham 7 Balliol, Linacre, Lincoln, St. Anne's, St. Cross, St. Hugh's, St. John's, Trinity 8 All Souls, Hertford, Magdalen, Nuffield, Pembroke, St. Hilda's, St. Peter's 9 Brasenose, Mansfield, St. Antony's, Worcester 11 Summerville
locale: 4 Miss., Ohio 7 England, Rockies 8 Colorado
river: 6 Thames
teacher: 3 don
Oxfordshire: 4 Oxon 6 county
city: 7 Banbury
locale: 7 England
oxheart: 6 cherry
relative: 4 Bing 7 marasca, morello
oxhide strap: 4 riem
oxidation: 4 film, rust 6 patina 7 coating, tarnish 9 corrosion
oxide: 4 calx, rust 5 water 6 patina, patine 7 tarnish 8 corundum 9 quicklime
component: 5 metal
iron ~: 4 rust 9 corrosion
___ oxide ointment: 4 zinc
oxidize: 4 rust 7 corrode, tarnish
oxidizing ___: 5 agent
...ox is ___: 5 gored
Oxnard: 4 city, town
locale: 10 California
Oxon: 6 county
locale: 7 England
Oxon Hill: 4 city, town
locale: 8 Maryland
Oxonian: 4 Brit 6 Briton 7 student
rival: 6 Cantab
oxpecker: 4 bird
oxtail: 4 soup
oxy: 9 lumbering
Oxydol: 9 detergent
alternative: see detergent
oxygen: 3 air 5 ozone 7 element
add ~ to: 6 aerate
lack of ~: 6 anoxia
producer: 4 leaf, tree 5 plant
user: 6 aerobe
oxygenate: 3 air 6 aerate, purify
Oy ___!: 3 vay, vey
Oy!: 4 alas, oh no
Oye Como Va (1971 song)
artist: Santana
oyez: 6 hear ye
Oyl: 5 Olive 6 Castor
oyster: 5 color, shell, white 7 grayish 8 seashell
combining form: 5 ostre- 6 ostrei-, ostreo-
home: 3 bed 5 culch 6 cultch
lift, as an ~: 4 tong
open, as an ~: 5 shuck
product: 5 pearl
relative: see white color
young ~: 4 spat 5 culch 6 cultch
oyster ___: 3 bed 4 fork 7 cracker
___ oyster: 4 seed 5 pearl
Oyster ___: 3 Bay
oystercatcher: 4 bird
___ Oyster Cult: 4 Blue
oysters ___ season: 3 R in
oz.: 2 wt. 3 qty. 4 meas.
fraction of an ~: 3 pwt., tsp. 4 tbsp.
multiple: 2 lb., pt. 3 gal.
sixteen ~: 2 lb. 5 one lb.
Oz: 4 Amos 5 Frank, Scott
actor: 4 Lahr 5 Burke, Haley 6 Bolger, Morgan 7 Garland 8 Hamilton
associate: 6 Henson
creator: L. Frank Baum
role: 4 lion, Toto 5 witch 7 Dorothy
Oz, Amos: 6 writer 7 Israeli
work: A Perfect Peace
Ozark parent: 3 maw, paw
Ozarks: 5 range
locale: 8 Arkansas, Missouri, Oklahoma
Ozawa, Seiji: 8 Japanese 9 conductor
contemporary: 5 Mehta
Oz, Frank: 8 director 9 puppeteer
film: Bowfinger (1999)
The Dark Crystal (1982)
Dirty Rotten Scoundrels (1988)
The Indian in the Cupboard (1995)
In & Out (1997)
Little Shop of Horrors (1986)
The Muppets Take Manhattan (1984)
The Score (2001)
What About Bob? (1991)
TV: The Muppet Show
ozone: 3 air, gas 5 layer 6 oxygen 8 fresh air
alert prompter: 3 fog 4 haze, murk, smog 5 brume, vapor 9 fogginess
enemy: 3 CFC 5 Freon
ozone ___: 4 hole 5 layer
O-Zone
author: Paul Theroux
Ozymandias: 4 poem 6 sonnet
author: Percy Bysshe Shelley
Ozzie: 5 Smith 6 Nelson 7 Newsome
Ozzie son: 4 Rick 5 David, Ricky
Ozzy: 8 Osbourne

P

p ___ puzzle: 4 as in
P: 3 rho, vit. 4 elem. 6 letter 7 element, vitamin 10 phosphorus
15 for ~: 4 at. no.
followers: 3 QRS 4 QRST 5 QRSTU
in phonetic alphabet: 4 Papa
preceders: 3 MNO 4 LMNO 5 KLMNO
vitamin ~: 5 rutin
P ___: 4 and L
P. ___: 5 Diddy
___ P: 4 A and
___ P.: 3 K. of
'P' ___ Peril: 5 Is for
pa: 3 dad, pop 4 male 5 daddy, pappy 6 father, parent
pa's ~: 5 gramp 6 gramps
Pa: 4 elem. 7 element 11 proactinium
91 for ~: 4 at. no.
Pa.
see Pennsylvania
PA
see Pennsylvania
PA ___: 6 system
Paar, Jack: 2 MC 4 host 5 emcee
follower: 4 Leno
preceder: 5 Allen
Paavo: 5 Nurmi 8 Haavikko
PABA, part of: 4 acid, para 5 amino
Pablo: 6 Casals, Cruise, Neruda 7 Picasso
in English: 4 Paul
___ Pablo, CA: 3 San
Pablo Cruise
song: Cool Love (1981)
Don't Want to Live Without It (1978)
I Want You Tonight (1979)
Love Will Find a Way (1978)
Whatcha Gonna Do? (1977)
Pablum: 6 cereal
eater: 3 tot 4 baby 6 infant
Pabst: 2 G.W. 4 beer
alternative: *see* beer
pac: 4 boot, shoe 8 footwear, moccasin
Pac-___: 3 Man
Pac-___ Conference: 3 Ten
Pac.
see Pacific
PAC
contributor: 6 fat cat 8 politico 10 politician
donee: 3 rep., sen. 7 senator
Pac-10
overseer: 4 NCAA
school: 3 ASU, Ore., OSU, UCB, USC, WSU 4 Ariz., UCLA, Wash. 6 Oregon 7 Arizona 8 Stanford 10 Washington 11 Oregon State
paca: 4 cavy 6 animal, mammal, rodent
relative: *see* rodent
pace: 3 jog, run 4 gait, lope, rate, step, time, trot, walk 5 amble, march, speed, stalk, tempo, tread 6 canter, gallop, patrol, stride 7 mark out, measure 8 ambulate, footstep, galopade, momentum, rapidity, velocity 9 gallopade, swiftness
ender: 5 maker 6 setter 7 setting
fast ~: 4 clip
keep ~: 4 meet 5 equal, rival
keep ~ with: 3 tie 5 equal, match, rival 8 parallel
off: 7 measure
pick up the ~: 3 fly, hie, run 4 dash, race, tear 5 hurry, speed
set the ~: 4 lead
snail's ~: 3 lag 4 slow 5 crawl
starter: 4 foot
pace ___: 3 car, lap
___ pace: 4 keep 6 snail's
paced: 6 steady 7 metered, regular, uniform 8 constant, measured 9 modulated, regulated 10 rhythmical
Pacem in ___: 6 terris
pacer: 5 horse, mount, steed 6 equine, leader 7 trotter 9 racehorse 10 forerunner
burden: 5 sulky
Pacer: 3 AMC, car 4 auto 5 Edsel
Pacers: 4 five, team
former org.: 3 ABA
home: 7 Indiana
org.: 3 NBA
rival: *see* NBA team
sport: 10 basketball
pacesetter: 6 leader
pachinko: 4 game
pachisi: 4 game 9 board game
form of ~: 4 ludo
pachyderm: 5 hippo, rhino 6 animal, mammal 8 elephant 10 rhinoceros
tooth: 4 tusk
pacific: 4 calm, cool 5 quiet 6 gentle, irenic, low-key, mellow, placid, sedate, serene 7 amiable, at peace, equable, relaxed, restful, stoical, unmoved 8 amicable, composed, irenical, laid-back, lamblike, moderate, peaceful, tranquil 9 collected, easygoing, impassive, quiescent, temperate, unexcited, unruffled 10 unagitated, untroubled
Pacific: 5 ocean
archipelago: 4 Fiji, Riau 5 Malay
atoll: 6 Bikini, Tarawa 8 Funafuti 9 Eniewetok
bay: 5 Manta 8 Monterey
bird: 5 goony 6 gooney
fish: 5 sargo 6 beshow, bigeye, salmon, tomcod 7 cabezon, corbina, corvina, halibut, herring, nibbler, opaleye, pomfret, ronquil, sand dab, wolf-eel 8 baysmelt, flathead, mahimahi, palometa, topsmelt, tubenose 9 greenling, surfperch, tubesnout
former ~ alliance: 5 SEATO
fruit: 7 coconut 9 pineapple
goatfish: 5 Moana
goose: 4 nene
greeting: 5 aloha
gulf: 5 Davao, Papua, Penas 6 Alaska 7 Fonseca 8 Papagayo 9 Guayaquil 10 California
island: 4 Guam, Java, Wake 5 Nauru, Timor 6 Borneo, Easter, Honshu 7 Rapa Nui, Sumatra 8 Hokkaido, Sakhalin 9 New Guinea
islands: 4 Cook, Fiji, Truk 5 Banda, Bonin, Kuril, Palau, Samoa 6 Futuna, Midway, Ryukyu 7 Mariana, Marshal, Oceania, Society, Solomon 8 Friendly, Gilberts, Hawaiian, Moluccas, Sandwich, South Sea 9 Galapagos, Marquesas, Melanesia, Polynesia 10 Micronesia, New Zealand 11 Philippines
islands flower: 5 lehua 6 orchid 8 hibiscus
islands palm: 4 nipa 7 coconut
river to the ~: 5 Lempa, Santa 6 Bio-Bio 7 Klamath 8 Columbia
salmon: 4 chum, coho 5 cohoe
sea: 4 Sulu 5 Banda, Coral 6 Tasman, Yellow 7 Celebes 10 South China
South ~ capital: 4 Apia, Suva 5 Agana 6 Majuro, Manila, Nouméa, Tarawa 7 Honiara, Papeete 8 Funafuti, Pago Pago, Port-Vila 9 Nuku'alofa
Pacific ___: 3 cod, rim 4 high, time 5 Ocean, Plate
___ Pacific: 5 South, Union
___-Pacific: 4 Indo 7 Georgia
Pacifica: 3 SUV 4 city, town 8 Chrysler
locale: 10 California
Pacific Coast
fruit: 5 salal 9 manzanita
range: 5 Andes 11 Sierra Madre
state: 3 Cal., Ore. 4 Wash. 5 Calif. 6 Oregon 10 California, Washington
Pacific Coast explorer: 6 Balboa 9 Vancouver
Pacific Heights (1990 film)
cast: Melanie Griffith, Michael Keaton, Matthew Modine
Pacific Overtures: 7 musical
composer: Stephen Sondheim
Pacific Princess: 4 boat, ship 5 liner
pacifier: 3 sop
in Britain: 5 dummy
pacifist: 4 dove 7 radical 8 ultraist 10 nonviolent
pacifists' protest: 5 march, sit-in, vigil
pacify: 4 calm, ease, lull, tame 5 allay, quell, quiet, slake 6 defuse, defuze, soothe, stroke, subdue, temper 7 appease, assuage, compose, mollify, placate, relieve, satisfy, sweeten 8 mitigate, moderate 9 alleviate, quiet down, reconcile, soft-pedal, untrouble 10 ameliorate, conciliate, propitiate, smooth over
pacing: 5 upset 6 uneasy 7 anxious, fearful, in a stew, nervous, uptight, worried 9 attentive, concerned, disturbed, exercised, in a lather, perturbed 10 distraught, distressed
Pacino, Al: 5 actor
film: ... And Justice for All (1979)
Any Given Sunday (1999)
Author! Author! (1982)
Carlito's Way (1993)
City Hall (1996)
The Devil's Advocate (1997)
Dick Tracy (1990)
Dog Day Afternoon (1975)
Donnie Brasco (1997)
Frankie and Johnny (1991)
Glengarry Glen Ross (1992)
The Godfather (1972)
Heat (1995)
The Insider (1999)
Insomnia (2002)
The Panic in Needle Park (1971)
The Recruit (2003)
Scarecrow (1973)
Scarface (1983)
Scent of a Woman (1992, AA)
Sea of Love (1989)
Serpico (1973)
Simone (2002)
___ Pacis: 3 Ara
pack: 3 box, jam, kit, lot, lug, mob, ram, set 4 bale, band, bevy, case, cram, crew, deck, fill, gang, haul, heap, herd, lade, load, pile, plug, stow, take, tamp, tote, wrap 5 batch, bunch, carry, crate, crowd, drove, ferry, flock, group, horde, press, stack, stuff, swarm, troop, wedge 6 bundle, clique, decamp, encase, gear up, incase, kennel, kitbag, outfit, parcel, rabble, throng 7 cluster, company, congest, coterie, put away, squeeze 8 get ready, knapsack, rucksack, shoulder 9 haversack, overcrowd, piggyback, transport
again: 5 rebag
a heater: 4 tote 5 carry
animal: 3 ass 4 mule 5 burro, horse, llama 6 donkey
away: 3 eat 4 stow 5 store 6 ingest
Cub Scout ~ leader: 5 Akela
ender: 3 age 4 sack 5 horse 6 saddle
extra: 5 joker
it in: 3 eat, end 4 halt, quit 5 cease, close 6 finish, wind up, wrap up 7 adjourn, break up 8 conclude 9 terminate
leading the ~: 5 on top 7 winning
member: 4 wolf 5 hyena 6 hyaena
rat: 5 saver 6 animal, mammal, rodent, storer 7 amasser, hoarder 8 gatherer 9 collector
scavenger: 5 hyena 6 jackal
starter: 3 day, mud 4 back
toter: 5 hiker 6 camper 7 student 8 traveler 10 hitchhiker
pack ___: 3 ice, off, rat 4 away, date, it in, mule 6 animal
___ pack: 3 hot, ice 4 cold, disk, film, wolf 5 power 6 bubble, shrink, vacuum 7 blister
___-pack: 3 jam, six
___ Pack: 3 Rat 4 Brat
package: 3 box, can, tin 4 bale, mail, wrap 5 box up, crate 6 bundle, carton, encase, incase, parcel 7 arrival 9 container 10 assortment
CARE ~: 3 aid
deliverer: 3 UPS 4 USPS 5 FedEx
letters: 3 COD, ppd
of paper: 4 ream
open a ~: 4 undo 6 unwrap
secure a ~: 3 tie 4 tape
send a ~: 4 mail, ship
wrapped ~: 4 gift 7 present
wrapper: 4 cord, tape 5 paper, twine 6 ribbon
package ___: 4 deal, plan, tour 5 store

package store buy: 3 ale, gin, keg, rum, rye 4 beer, wine 5 vodka 6 brandy, liquor, whisky 7 spirits, whiskey
packaging material: 5 paper 9 cellulose, newspaper, Styrofoam 10 bubble wrap
Packard: 3 car 4 auto 5 David, Vance
competitor: 6 De Soto
Packard __: 4 Bell
__-Packard: 7 Hewlett
packed: 4 full, rife 5 awash, close, dense, laden, thick, tight 6 loaded, mobbed 7 brimful, compact, crowded, replete, stuffed, teeming 8 arranged, brimfull, brimming, swarming, thronged 9 chock-full, condensed, congested, to the roof 10 compressed, gridlocked, wall-to-wall
packer
pistol ~: 4 thug 6 bandit, gunman, hit man, outlaw, robber 7 marshal, mobster, sheriff 9 desperado
starter: 4 back, meat
Packer: 3 Ann
Packers: 4 team 6 eleven
div.: 3 NFC
home: 3 Wis. 4 Wisc. 8 Green Bay
org.: 3 NFL
rival: *see* NFL team
sport: 8 football
packet: 3 box 4 boat 5 ferry, pouch 6 bundle, carton, folder, parcel 8 envelope 9 container
nursery ~: 4 seed
packhorse: 6 equine
packing: 5 armed
a pistol: 5 armed
a wallop: 5 harsh 6 potent, strong 8 powerful
container: 3 box 4 case 5 crate
send ~: 2 ax 3 axe, can, rid 4 boot, drop, fire, oust, sack 5 eject, evict, exile, expel, let go 6 banish, bounce, depose, lay off 7 cashier, dismiss, drum out, release, turn out 8 chase out, furlough, get rid of, pink-slip 9 discharge, terminate
slip: 3 inv. 7 invoice
some weight: 5 heavy, hefty
__ Packin' Mama: 6 Pistol
packsack: 5 kyack 6 duffel, duffle
Pac-Man: 4 game 9 video game
blue ghost, in ~: 4 Inky
emulate ~: 3 eat 6 devour
home: 6 arcade
morsel: 3 dot
Paco
see Spanish
Pacquin: 6 lotion
alternative: 4 Keri 5 Curel, Nivea 6 Aveeno 7 Eucerin, Jergens 9 Lubriderm
pact: 4 bond, deal, SALT 5 SEATO 6 accord, league, pledge, treaty 7 bargain, charter, concord, entente, promise, tontine 8 alliance, contract, covenant, protocol 9 agreement, concordat 10 compromise, engagement, settlement
defunct ~: 5 SEATO
name: 6 Briand 7 Kellogg
party to a ~: 4 ally
since 1949: 4 NATO
tariff ~: 5 NAFTA
tenant's ~: 5 lease
US-USSR ~: 4 SALT
__ Pact: 6 Warsaw 7 Locarno
Pac-Ten: 6 league 10 conference
rival: 3 ACC, SEC 6 Big Ten 7 Big East
Pacula: 6 Joanna
pad: 3 mat, wad 4 digs, flat, foot, home, leaf, line, spot, trot, walk 5 abode, creep, fudge, house, paper, place, sneak, stuff, tread 6 bulk up, expand, extend, patter, tablet 7 amplify, augment, bolster, cushion, domicil, enlarge, fill out, habitat, housing, inflate, magnify, protect, shelter, shuffle, wadding, zabuton 8 domicile, dressing, dwelling, flesh out, lengthen, lodgment, mattress, notebook, stuffing 9 apartment, fingertip, upholster 10 exaggerate, supplement
brake ~: 4 shoe
combining form: 3 tyl- 4 tylo-
ender: 4 lock
engraver's ~: 6 dabber
freshen a stamp ~: 5 reink
hair ~: 3 rat
memo ~: 6 tablet
shoe ~: 6 insole
starter: 3 key 4 foot 6 sketch 7 scratch
tumbler's ~: 3 mat
__ pad: 4 knee, lily, soap 5 brake, crash, legal, stamp, steno 6 launch, yellow 7 heating, scratch
__ P. Adams: 8 Franklin
Padang: 4 city, port, town
locale: 9 Indonesia
padded: 4 soft 5 comfy, cushy 9 cushioned, redundant
padding: 5 straw 6 buffer, cotton, excess 7 bombast, cushion, filling, wadding 8 stuffing 9 Styrofoam 10 bubble wrap, protection
excess ~: 3 fat 4 flab
paddle: 3 oar, tan 4 flog, pull, swim, wade 5 canoe, spank 6 cudgel, dabble, punish, racket, splash, thrash 7 flipper 8 navigate
dog ~: 4 swim
ender: 4 ball, boat, fish 5 board
pin: 5 thole
wheeler site: 4 lake 5 river
paddle __: 5 wheel 6 tennis 7 wheeler
paddleball: 4 game
paddler: 3 oar 6 rafter 7 oarsman 8 canoeist
milieu: 4 lake, pond 5 creek, river 6 stream
org: 3 ACA
paddlewheeler: 4 boat, ship 5 craft 6 vessel
paddock: 3 pen 6 corral
adjunct: 4 hasp
occupant: 4 colt, foal, mare 5 filly, horse 6 bronco, equine 8 stallion
papa: 4 sire
paddy
crop: 4 rice
wagon: 6 lockup 7 vehicle
Paddy: 9 Chayefsky
paddywhack: 5 spank
Paderewski, Ignace: 6 Polish 7 pianist
Padgett: 5 Lewis
__ Padilla Jr.: 6 Manuel
padlock: 5 latch 6 secure 7 closure
partner: 4 hasp
Padova: 4 city, town
locale: 5 Italy
Padraic: 5 Colum
padre: 4 abbé 5 friar 6 cleric, curate, father, parson, pastor, priest, rector 7 brother 8 chaplain, minister, preacher, reverend, sky pilot 9 clergyman, pulpiteer, sermonist 10 sermonizer
brother: 3 tio
daughter: 4 hija 5 chica 8 muchacha
sister: 3 tia
son: 4 hijo 5 chico 8 muchacho
wife: 5 madre 6 esposa
Padre: 4 NLer
Padre Island
locale: 5 Texas
Padres: 4 nine, team
div.: 3 NLW
home: 8 San Diego
org.: 3 MLB
rival: *see* baseball team
sport: 8 baseball
pads, work with: 5 scour
Padua: 4 city, town
locale: 5 Italy
town near ~: 4 Este
Paducah: 4 city, town
locale: 3 Ken. 8 Kentucky
paean: 4 hymn, poem, song, tune 5 psalm 6 anthem, homage, melody 7 hosanna 8 alleluia, encomium 9 extolment, panegyric 10 hallelujah
paella: 6 entrée 7 Spanish
cooker: 4 olla
ingredient: 4 rice 7 chicken, mussels, saffron, sausage
__ Paese: 3 Bel
pagan: 7 atheist, heathen, infidel 8 agnostic, hedonist, idolator 9 pantheist 10 idolatrous, polytheist, unbeliever
ender: 3 ism
practice: 5 wicca 10 witchcraft
prefix with: 3 neo
Paganini
composer: Franz Lehár
Paganini, Niccolò instrument: 6 violin
page: 4 aide, beep, call, leaf, Op-Ed 5 check, folio, gofer, recto, sheet, usher, verso 6 gopher, lackey, number, summon 7 bellhop, call for, equerry, lacquey, send for, servant 8 announce, document 9 attendant
book ~: 4 leaf 5 recto, verso
cal. ~: 2 mo.
calendar ~: 5 month
calendario ~: 3 mes
commentators ~: 4 Op-Ed
fold: 6 dog-ear
home ~ address: 3 URL
job: 6 errand
last ~: 6 ending
like left-hand ~ numbers: 4 even
like right-hand ~ numbers: 3 odd
manuscript ~: 5 folio
type of ~ edge: 6 deckel, deckle 7 deckled
web ~ access: 4 link
__ page: 3 web 4 home, Op-Ed 5 front, title
Page: 2 P.K. 3 Jim 4 Alan 5 Ellen, Jimmy, Patti, Tommy 6 Hannah 7 Anthony, LaWanda 9 Geraldine
pageant: 4 gala, play, show 5 sight 6 parade, ritual 7 display 8 splendor 9 festivity, motorcade, spectacle 10 exhibition, procession
prop: 5 tiara 7 bouquet
winner: 5 queen 6 beauty
pageantry: 4 pomp, show 7 glitter 8 heraldry
page-bottom info: 6 footer
pageboy: 4 coif 6 hairdo 8 coiffure 9 hairstyle
relative: 3 bob
__ Page Farrell: 5 Front
Page, Geraldine: 7 actress
spouse: Rip Torn
Page, Patti: 6 singer
song: Allegheny Moon (1956)
Another Time, Another Place (1958)
Belonging to Someone (1958)
Go On with the Wedding (1956)
Hush, Hush, Sweet Charlotte (1965)
Let Me Go, Lover! (1954)
Mama from the Train (1956)
Old Cape Cod (1957)
A Poor Man's Roses (1957)
pager: 6 beeper
signal: 4 beep 9 vibration
pages, turn: 4 flip, scan, skim 9 speedread
Paget: 5 Debra
page-turner: 8 good book, good read
Pagliacci: 5 opera
Canio in ~: 5 tenor
role: 5 Beppe, Canio, Nedda, Tonio 6 Silvio
setting: 5 Italy 8 Calabria, Montalto
__ Pagliaccio: 4 Ridi
pagoda: 6 shrine, temple
Chinese ~: 3 taa
feature: 4 gong 6 statue 7 incense
land: 5 China
Pago Pago: 4 city, port, town
locale: 5 Samoa
__-pah: 3 oom
Pahlavi: 4 Reza 5 Irani
realm, once: 4 Iran
title: 4 shah
pahoehoe: 4 lava
Pahrump: 4 city, town
locale: 6 Nevada
paid
get ~: 4 earn, work
marker: 5 stamp
notice: 2 ad
performer: 3 pro
something ~: 5 visit 9 attention 10 compliment
starter: 4 post
to be ~: 3 due
work: 3 job 4 post 6 employ 8 position
__-paid: 4 well
Paige: 5 Janis, Turco 7 Satchel 8 Jennifer
Paige, Satchel: 6 hurler 7 pitcher
real first name: 5 Leroy

pail: 6 bailer, bucket, vessel 7 scuttle 9 container 10 receptacle
pain: 3 ail, irk, vex, woe 4 ache, bore, burn, drag, gall, harm, hurt, kink, pang, pest, pill, rack, rile, tire 5 agony, catch, cramp, crick, grief, gripe, smart, spasm, sting, throb, throe, trial, upset, worry, wound 6 aching, bother, effort, grieve, harass, harrow, injure, injury, misery, offend, rankle, sadden, sorrow, stitch, strain, trauma, twinge, twitch 7 anguish, anxiety, malaise, sadness, torment, torture, travail, trouble 8 aggrieve, distress, irritate, nuisance, soreness, vexation 9 annoyance, heartache, suffering 10 bitterness, difficulty, discomfort, imposition, tenderness
be a ~: 3 nag 4 bore, carp 5 tease 6 bother, yammer 8 complain
cause ~: 4 hurt 6 injure 10 discomfort
combining form: 3 alg- 4 algo-, -algy, noci- 5 -algia 6 -odynia
draw back, as in ~: 5 wince 6 cringe, flinch
exclamation of ~: 2 ow 3 oof, yow 4 ouch, yeow, yipe 5 yipes
express ~: 3 cry, sob 4 howl, mewl, wail, weep 5 whine 6 scream 7 whimper
feeling no ~: 4 numb 5 tipsy
in ~: 4 hurt 6 aching 7 hurting, unhappy 9 miserable, sorrowful
in the neck: 4 ache, bore, kink, pest, pill 5 crick, trial 6 bother, hassle 8 headache, irritant 9 annoyance
in the side: 5 thorn
reliever: 5 Advil, Aleve, salve 6 Ben-Gay, Motrin, opiate 7 anodyne, aspirin, Ecotrin, hot pack, Tylenol 8 Bufferin, cold pack, narcotic, ointment, sedative 9 analgesic 10 anesthetic
Pain and the Great One, The
author: Judy Blume
Paine ___: 6 Webber
Paine, Thomas: 5 deist 6 writer 7 British, radical 8 essayist
work: The Age of Reason
Common Sense
The Rights of Man
painful: 3 bad, raw, sad 4 achy, dire, hard, sore 5 nasty 6 aching, bitter, sticky, tender, tragic, trying 7 arduous, burning, hurting, onerous, tedious 8 dolorous, grievous, inflamed, piercing, stinging, terrible, tragical 9 agonizing, difficult, harrowing, irritated, laborious, sensitive, sorrowful, throbbing, vexatious 10 unpleasant
be ~: 4 ache, burn, itch 5 smart, throb
make less ~: 6 soothe 7 relieve
painless: 4 easy, snap 5 cinch, cushy 6 breeze, picnic, simple 8 duck soup, pushover 9 innocuous 10 child's play, effortless, unexacting
pains: 3 TLC 4 care, toil 5 labor 6 effort 7 trouble 8 exertion, struggle
partner: 5 aches
take ~: 6 bother 7 trouble
___ pains: 7 growing
painstaking: 5 exact, fussy 6 minute 7 careful, earnest, finicky, precise, prudent 8 cautious, diligent, exacting, finiking, finnicky, methodic, rigorous, sedulous, thorough 9 assiduous, attentive, by the book, judicious, laborious, observant 10 fastidious, meticulous, particular, scrupulous
paint: 3 dye, oil 4 coat, daub, draw, kohl, limn, oils, tint, wash 5 color, cover, horse, latex, pinto, rouge, stain 6 depict, enamel, equine, makeup, poster, redden, veneer 7 acrylic, blusher, encrust, gouache, impasto, incrust, outline, pigment, portray, stipple, tempera, touch up, varnish 8 colorant, cosmetic, decorate, emulsion, lipstick 9 adumbrate, delineate, represent, whitewash 10 illustrate, watercolor
additive: 5 drier, water 7 thinner 10 turpentine
apply ~: 4 coat, roll 5 brush, spray
base: 5 latex
container: 3 can 4 tube
crudely: 4 daub 5 smear
ender: 5 brush
fluorescent ~: 6 Day-Glo
glossy ~: 6 enamel
remove ~: 5 strip
splotch: 4 blob
starter: 3 war 6 finger, grease
surface: 4 coat 5 layer
the town red: 5 party, revel 6 barhop 7 carouse, roister 8 cut loose, let loose, live it up 9 celebrate, make merry, raise Cain, whoop it up
paintbrush
devil's ~: 5 plant 6 flower
material: 4 foam 5 nylon 8 bristles
paint-drier ingredient: 5 rosin
painted
freshly ~: 3 wet
lady: 3 bug 6 insect 9 butterfly
metal: 4 tole
Painted ___, The: 4 Bird, Mesa, Veil
Painted Bird, The
author: Jerzy Kosinski
Painted Desert feature: 4 mesa, rock, sand
painter: 3 Arp 4 Dali, Dufy, Goya, Gris, Hals, Kent, Klee, Lely, Miró, Reni, Sert, Wood 5 Bosch, Corot, Degas, Dürer, Ensor, Ernst, Homer, Johns, Kahlo, Klimt, Léger, Manet, Monet, Moses, Munch, Peale, Shahn, Sloan, Steen, Wyeth 6 artist, Benton, Braque, Copley, Eakins, Giotto, Hassam, Hopper, Ingres, Inness, Leutze, Man Ray, Renoir, Rivera, Rothko, Rubens, Seurat, Stuart, Tanguy, Tissot, Titian 7 Bonheur, Bruegel, Cassatt, Cézanne, Chagall, da Vinci, Duchamp, El Greco, Gauguin, Hogarth, Holbein, Matisse, O'Keeffe, Picasso, Pisarro, Pollock, Raphael, Sargent, Tiepolo, Utrillo, van Dyck, van Eyck, van Gogh, Vermeer 8 Angelico, Dubuffet, Magritte, Mondrian, Reynolds, Rockwell, Ter Borch, Whistler 9 Constable, de Kooning, Delacroix, Kandinsky, Rembrandt, Remington, Velázquez 10 Botticelli, Modigliani, Tintoretto 12 Gainsborough, Michelangelo
abstract ~: 6 Cubist
Abstractionist ~: 4 Klee 8 Mondrian 9 Kandinsky
American ~: 4 Kent, Wood 5 Homer, Johns, Moses, Peale, Shahn, Sloan, Wyeth 6 Benton, Copley, Eakins, Hassam, Hopper, Inness, Leutze, Man Ray, Rothko, Stuart 7 Cassatt, O'Keeffe, Pollock, Sargent 8 Rockwell, Whistler 9 Remington
Austrian ~: 5 Klimt 7 Schiele
Baroque ~: 6 Rubens 9 Velázquez
Belgian ~: 5 Ensor 8 Magritte
British ~: 7 Hogarth 8 Reynolds 9 Constable 12 Gainsborough
coverall: 5 smock
Cubist ~: 6 Braque
Dada ~: 6 Man Ray 7 Duchamp, Hans Arp, Jean Arp
deg.: 3 MFA
Dutch ~: 4 Hals, Lely 5 Steen 7 van Gogh, Vermeer 8 Mondrian, Ter Borch 9 de Kooning, Rembrandt
Fauvist ~: 4 Dufy 7 Matisse
Flemish ~: 5 Bosch 6 Rubens 7 Bruegel, van Dyck, van Eyck
French ~: 3 Arp 4 Dufy 5 Corot, Degas, Léger, Manet, Monet 6 Braque, Ingres, Renoir, Seurat, Tanguy, Tissot 7 Bonheur, Cézanne, Duchamp, Gauguin, Matisse, Utrillo 8 Dubuffet 9 Delacroix
from Iowa: 4 Wood
German ~: 5 Dürer, Ernst 7 Holbein
Impressionist ~: 5 Monet 6 Renoir 7 Cassatt, Utrillo
Italian ~: 4 Reni 6 Giotto, Titian 7 da Vinci, Raphael, Tiepolo 8 Angelico 10 Botticelli, Modigliani, Tintoretto 12 Michelangelo
Japanese ~: 6 Sesshu
Mexican ~: 5 Kahlo 6 Rivera
mishap: 4 glob, spot 5 smear, stain 7 splotch
Norwegian ~: 5 Munch
Renaissance ~: 5 Dürer 6 Titian 7 Raphael 8 Angelico 10 Botticelli
Russian ~: 7 Chagall 9 Kandinsky
Spanish ~: 4 Dali, Goya, Gris, Miró, Sert 7 El Greco, Picasso, Pisarro 9 Velázquez
stand: 5 easel
surface: 4 wood 5 gesso, metal, paper 6 canvas
Surrealist ~: 4 Dali 6 Tanguy
Swiss ~: 4 Klee
tool: 5 brush 6 airgun, ladder, roller 7 palette
Western ~: 9 Remington
___ painter: 5 house
painting: 3 art, oil 4 work 5 mural 6 canvas, fresco 7 acrylic, picture 8 portrait, seascape 9 aquarelle, landscape, still life, work of art 10 watercolor
combining form: 6 -chromy
family name: 5 Peale
holder: 3 mat 4 nail 5 frame
illusional ~: 5 op art
medium: 3 oil 6 pastel 7 acrylic 10 watercolor
oil ~: 3 art 6 canvas 7 picture 8 portrait 9 still life
on dry plaster: 5 secco
rock ~ symbol: 5 glyph
round ~: 5 tondo
Sistine Chapel ~: 6 fresco
subject: 3 jug 4 nude, vase 5 model 6 nature 7 flowers, pitcher
work on an old ~: 7 restore
___ painting: 3 oil
Paint It, Black (1966 song)
artist: Rolling Stones
Paint the Sky with Stars (1997 album)
artist: Enya
Paint Your Wagon: 7 musical
composer: Alan Jay Lerner, Frederick Loewe
Paint Your Wagon (1969 film)
cast: Clint Eastwood, Lee Marvin, Harve Presnell, Jean Seberg, Ray Walston
character: 5 Elisa
director: Joshua Logan
pair: 3 duo, two 4 duad, duet, dyad, join, span, team, yoke 5 brace, match, mates, twain, twins 6 couple, hook up 7 doublet, match up, twosome
au ~: 4 amah 5 nanny 6 nannie 8 domestic 9 nursemaid
connector: 2 no 3 and, nor
matched ~: 4 team
one of a ~: 4 half, mate, twin
paired: 4 dual 6 double, duplex, dyadic 8 matching
combining form: 4 dipl- 5 diplo-
pair of ___: 5 pants, socks 6 slacks 7 glasses 8 trousers
pairs skating: 5 event, sport
___ pais: 5 mal du, vin de
paisa: 5 money
100: 5 rupee
paisano: 3 pal 4 chum 5 amigo, buddy 6 cohort 8 sidekick 9 colleague
paisley: 3 tie 5 print, scarf 6 fabric 7 pattern 8 neckwear
Paisley: 4 city, town
locale: 8 Scotland
Paiute: 5 tribe 6 Indian 7 Amerind 8 language
pajama ___: 5 party
Pajama Game, The (1957 film): 7 musical
cast: Doris Day, Carol Haney, John Raitt
character: 3 Mae, Sid 4 Babe 5 Mabel 6 Brenda, Gladys, Hasler
composer: Richard Adler, Jerry Ross
director: George Abbott, Stanley Donen
pajamas: 3 PJ's 7 jammies 8 lingerie, sleepers 9 nightwear 10 loungewear
alternative: 7 nightie 9 nightgown
coverer: 4 robe 8 bathrobe
material: 4 silk 5 nylon 6 cotton 7 flannel
part: 3 top 7 bottoms

__ pajamas: 4 cat's
Pakistan: 6 nation 7 country
bovine: 6 Channi, Dhanni, Lohani 7 Sahiwal
capital: 9 Islamabad
city: 6 Lahore 7 Karachi 9 Islamabad
crocodile: 6 gavial
desert: 4 Tahr, Thar, Tuhr
garment: 4 sari 5 lungi, saree 6 lungee, lungyi
language: 4 Urdu
location: 4 Asia
money: 4 anna, pice 5 paisa, rupee
mountain: 9 Broad Peak, Istoro Nal, Kanjut Sar, Rakaposhi, Tirich Mir 10 Gasherbrum
neighbor: 4 Iran 5 China, India 11 Afghanistan
Nobelist in Physics: 5 Salam
port: 7 Karachi
province: 4 Sind
region: 5 Tirah
river: 5 Indus
symbol on flag: 4 lune
Pak, Se Ri: 6 golfer, Korean
Pakula: 5 Alan J.
pal: 3 bro, cuz 4 ally, chum, mate, pard 5 amiga, amigo, buddy, crony 6 cohort, frater, friend 7 brother, compeer, comrade, homeboy, pardner, partner 8 alter ego, confrere, homegirl, intimate, roommate, sidekick, soulmate 9 associate, colleague, companion, confidant, good buddy 10 bosom buddy, compatriot, wellwisher
in French: 3 ami 4 amie
in Spanish: 5 amiga, amigo 9 compañera, compañero
__ pal: 3 gal, pen
Pal: 6 George
palace: 4 hall, home 5 manor 6 castle 7 alcazar, chateau, lodging, mansion 8 dwelling 9 residence
dweller: 4 king 5 queen, royal 6 prince 7 monarch 8 princess
French ~: 6 Elysée
ice ~: 4 rink 5 arena
in Florence: 5 Pitti
Mideast ~ area: 5 haram, harem, harim 6 hareem
palace __: 4 coup 5 guard
__ palace: 3 ice
__ Palace: 3 Cow 5 White 7 Caesar's, Crystal
paladin: 8 advocate, champion, defender, guardian 9 paraclete
Paladin
portrayer: Richard Boone
palaestra: 5 arena
Palais des Nations home: 6 Geneva
Palamas, Koster: 4 poet 5 Greek
Palance: 4 Jack 5 Holly
Palance, Jack: 5 actor
film: Bagdad Cafe (1988)
City Slickers (1991, AA)
Contempt (1963)
Monte Walsh (1970)
Shane (1953)
Sudden Fear (1952)
palatable: 4 fair, good 5 sapid, tasty, yummy 6 divine, edible, savory, toothy 8 luscious, pleasant, pleasing, tempting 9 agreeable, ambrosial, delicious, enjoyable, flavorful, nectarous, nutritive, toothsome 10 acceptable, appetizing, attractive, delectable, delightful, flavorsome
palate: 5 taste 6 liking
of the soft ~: 5 velar
part of the soft ~: 5 uvula
soft ~: 5 velum
palatial: 4 lush, posh, rich 5 grand, plush, regal, ritzy, swank 6 deluxe, swanky 7 opulent, stately 8 imposing, majestic, splendid 9 luxuriant, luxurious, sumptuous 10 impressive, majestical
dwelling: 5 manor 6 castle, estate 7 chateau
palatine: 4 bone, cape
locale: 5 mouth
Palatine: 4 hill
locale: 4 Rome
Palatino: 4 font 8 typeface
Palau: 4 isls. 5 isles 7 islands
capital: 5 Koror
palaver: 3 gab, rap, yak 4 chat, talk 5 clack, prate 6 confer, gibber, gossip, huddle, jargon, parley, powwow 7 blather, blether, chatter, coaxing 8 babbling, cajolery, chitchat, claptrap, converse, flattery, language, nonsense, soft soap 9 gibberish, loquacity, small talk, sweet talk, table talk 10 conference
palaverous: 4 long 5 gabby, windy, wordy 6 prolix 7 diffuse, lengthy, verbose, voluble 8 rambling 9 bombastic, garrulous, talkative 10 discursive, long-winded, loquacious
Palazzo Pubblico site: 5 Siena
pale: 3 dim, wan 4 ashy, fade, gray, grey, post, soft, weak 5 ashen, bourn, faded, faint, light, livid, lurid, mealy, pasty, stake, stave, waxen, white 6 anemic, blanch, bounds, chalky, doughy, flaxen, pallid, pastel, peaked, picket, sallow, sickly, silver, watery, whiten 7 anaemic, ghastly, grayish, greyish, haggard, tail off, whitish 8 blanched, bleached, decrease, diminish, liverish, untanned 9 albescent, bloodless, colorless, ghostlike, lily-white, washed out 10 exsanguine, indistinct, lackluster, lusterless, white-faced
beyond the ~: 4 tabu 5 taboo 8 improper, unseemly 9 forbidden, impolitic, out of line
color: 4 tint 6 pastel
combining form: 7 palladi-
ender: 4 face
not ~: 4 rosy 5 ruddy 8 red-faced
turn ~: 6 blanch
pale __: 3 ale
pale __ ghost: 3 as a
pale-__ ginger ale: 3 dry
__ Paleface: 5 Son of
Paleface, The (1948 film)
cast: Bob Hope, Jane Russell
Pale Horse, Pale Rider
author: Katherine Anne Porter
Pale Horse, The
author: Agatha Christie
Paleocene follower: 6 Eocene
Paleolithic: 8 Stone-age
paleontologist: 9 scientist
find: 5 bones 6 fossil 8 artefact, artifact, skeleton
paleontology: 7 science
branch of ~: 9 ichnology
paleo- opposite: 3 neo-
Paleozoic: 3 Era
Pale Rider (1985 film)
cast: Clint Eastwood, Michael Moriarty, Carrie Snodgress
director: Clint Eastwood
Palermo: 4 city, peak, port, town 5 mount 8 mountain
locale: 5 Andes, Italy 9 Argentina
party: 5 festa
spa near ~: 4 Enna
Palestine
ancient ~ city: 3 Dan 6 Bethel
ancient district: 6 Gilead
ancient dweller: 6 Essene
ancient region: 6 Bashan, Judaea
area: 4 Gaza
group: 10 Arab League
Nobelist in Peace: 6 Arafat
peak in ancient ~: 4 Nebo
region near ancient ~: 4 Edom
region of ancient ~: 5 Judea 6 Judaea
seaport: 5 Haifa
Palestrina: 8 Giovanni
paletot: 4 cape, coat 6 jacket
palette
partner: 5 brush, easel, knife
pigment: 5 ocher, ochre, umber
shape: 4 oval
user: 6 artist 7 painter
Paley: 5 Grace 7 William
Paley, William
company: 3 CBS
palfrey: 5 horse, mount, steed 6 equine 7 charger 8 warhorse
Pali: 8 language
relative: 8 Sanskrit
Palillo: 3 Ron
Palin: 5 Sarah 7 Michael
home: 6 Alaska
palindromic
address: 3 dad, mom, pop 4 ma'am 5 madam
animal: 3 ewe
bird: 3 tit
city: 3 Ada, Ede
computer language: 3 Ada
constellation: 3 Ara
emperor: 4 Otto
exclamation: 3 aha, hah, oho, tut, wow
Indian: 3 Oto
name: 3 Ada, Ava, Bob, Eve, Lil, Nan 4 Anna, Otto 6 Hannah
periodical: 4 Elle
pop group: 3 Aha 4 ABBA
potentate: 3 aga
principle: 5 tenet
time: 4 noon
verb: 3 tat
paling: 4 rail 5 fence, stake, stave 6 picket 7 railing
palisade: 4 post, wall 5 fence 6 picket 7 defense 9 barricade, precipice
Palisades Park (1962 song)
artist: Freddy Cannon
Pal Joey (1940 musical)
composer: Lorenz Hart, Richard Rodgers
Pal Joey (1957 film): 4 play 7 musical
author: John O'Hara
cast: Rita Hayworth, Kim Novak, Frank Sinatra
character: 3 Max 4 Vera 5 Agnes, Linda 6 Ernest, Gladys
pall: 4 bore, cloy, haze, jade, tire, veil 5 gloom, weary 6 mantle, shadow, shroud 7 dimness, satiate, surfeit 8 peter out 10 black cloud, depression, desolation, melancholy
cast a ~ over: 6 dampen, rain on
Pall __: 4 Mall
palladium: 5 metal 7 element
alloy: 7 platina 9 white gold
Palladium portrayal: 6 Athena, Athene
Pallas: 8 asteroid
daughter: 4 Nike
father: 6 Triton 8 Heracles
Pallas __: 6 Athena, Athene
pallet: 3 bed 4 skid 8 mattress, platform
palliate: 4 cure, ease, help 5 abate, allay, gloze, mince, quiet, salve, slake 6 hush up, lessen, remedy, smooth, soften, soothe, temper 7 assuage, justify, lighten, mollify, relieve, varnish 8 minimize, mitigate, moderate 9 alleviate, extenuate, gloss over, underplay, whitewash
palliative: 4 balm 5 salve 6 lotion, relief 7 anodyne 9 demulcent 10 corrective
pallid: 3 wan 4 ashy, pale, soft 5 ashen, livid, lurid, pasty, waxen, white 6 anemic, chalky, doughy, peaked, sallow, sickly 7 ghastly, grayish, greyish 8 untanned 9 albescent, bloodless, innocuous, lily-white
pallor: 6 anemia 7 anaemia, wanness 8 grayness, paleness
palm: 4 nipa, sago, tree 5 areca, assai, honor 6 pilfer, raffia, raphia, rattan, thenar 7 babassu, conceal, coquito, secrete, success, triumph, victory 8 carnauba, cocoanut, fishtail, ivory-nut, piassava, umbrella 9 coco-de-mer 10 decoration
Asian ~: 4 nipa 5 areca, betel
basketry ~: 4 nipa
betel ~: 5 areca
Brazilian ~: 5 assai
cat's ~: 3 pad
Central American ~: 6 cohune
ceremonial ~ branch: 5 lulab, lulav
East Indian ~: 4 nipa
examine a ~: 4 read
fermented ~ sap: 4 arak 6 arrack
genus: 5 areca
grease a ~: 5 bribe, get to 6 buy off, pay off, suborn 7 corrupt 9 lubricate
itching ~: 5 greed
leaf: 3 fan 5 frond
nipa ~: 4 atap
nut: 5 betel
off: 3 fob 5 foist 7 pass off

of the ~: 5 volar
of the hand: 4 vola
Pacific ~: 4 nipa
product: 4 date 5 copra 6 thatch 7 coconut 8 copperah
reader: 4 seer 7 psychic
thatch: 4 atap, nipa
tropical ~: 4 nipa 5 betel
trunk: 6 caudex
palm __: 3 off, oil 4 chat, crab, leaf, wine 5 civet, sugar 6 reader 7 cabbage, warbler
__ palm: 4 date, sago 5 royal 6 potted
Palm __: 5 Beach 6 Sunday 7 Springs
Palma: 4 city, port, town 7 Ricardo 8 asteroid
locale: 5 Spain
see also Spanish
Palma, Ricardo: 6 writer 8 Peruvian
work: Tradiciones Peruanas
__ Palmas: 3 Las
Palm Beach: 4 city, town
diversion: 4 golf, polo
locale: 7 Florida
residence: 5 condo 6 estate
Palm Beach Story, The (1942 film)
cast: Claudette Colbert, Joel McCrea, Rudy Vallee
director: Preston Sturges
Palm Desert: 4 city, town
locale: 10 California
Palme __: 3 d'Or
Palmeiro, Rafael
sport: 8 baseball
Palmer: 3 Jim 4 Keke 5 Arnie, Betsy, Lilli, Vance 6 Arnold, Robert
Palmer, Arnold: 6 golfer
followers: 4 army
Palmer, George Herbert: 11 philosopher
Palmer, Jim: 6 hurler, Oriole 7 pitcher
Palmer, Lilli: 7 actress
spouse: Rex Harrison
Palmer, Robert
song: Addicted to Love (1986)
Bad Case of Loving You (1979)
Early in the Morning (1988)
Every Kinda People (1978)
I Didn't Mean to Turn You On (1986)
Mercy Mercy Me (1991)
Simply Irresistible (1988)
Palmer, Vance: 4 poet 6 writer 10 Australian, playwright
work: The Passage
Palminteri: 5 Chazz
palmlike conifer: 5 cycad
Palmolive: 4 soap
alternative: *see* soap
palm reader phrase: 4 I see
palms-down call: 4 safe
Palm Springs: 4 city, town
former ~ mayor: 4 Bono
locale: 10 California
neighbor: 5 Indio
Palm Sunday
cry: 3 hosanna
mount: 3 ass
period: 4 Lent
palmy: 4 rosy 7 booming, halcyon 8 glorious, thriving 9 bounteous 10 prosperous, successful
Palo Alto: 4 city, town
college near ~: 5 Menlo
locale: 10 California
Palomar: 4 peak 5 mount 8 mountain
locale: 10 California
palomino: 5 horse 6 equine
pride: 4 mane
palooka: 3 oaf, pug 4 lout 5 boxer 6 galoot 8 pugilist
Palooka: 3 Joe
bride: 3 Ann
palpable: 5 clear, naked, plain, solid, stark, vivid 6 cogent, patent 7 blatant, evident, express, obvious, visible 8 apparent, concrete, definite, distinct, explicit, knowable, manifest, tangible 9 barefaced, graspable, touchable 10 detectable, noticeable, observable, ostensible, spelled out
palpate: 4 feel 5 touch
palpitate: 4 beat, pant 5 pound, pulse, shake, throb 6 quiver, shiver 7 flutter, pitapat, pulsate, tremble
palsy-walsy: 5 close, thick 6 chummy 8 familiar
palter: 3 lie 5 waver 6 higgle, trifle
paltering: 5 lying 10 mendacious
Paltrow, Gwyneth: 7 actress
film: Bounce (2000)
Emma (1996)
Great Expectations (1998)
Jefferson in Paris (1995)
A Perfect Murder (1998)
The Royal Tenenbaums (2001)
Se7en (1995)
Shakespeare in Love (1998, AA)
Sliding Doors (1998)
The Talented Mr. Ripley (1999)
mother: Blythe Danner
paltry: 3 low 4 mean, mere, poor, puny 5 minor, petty, scant, small, sorry 6 feeble, humble, little, meager, measly, minute, shabby, shoddy, sleazy, slight, stingy, yeasty 7 limited, pitiful, shallow, trivial 8 beggarly, exiguous, pathetic, picayune, piddling, trifling, wretched 9 miserable, worthless 10 pathetical
paludal: 3 low, wet 6 marshy, swampy 8 low-lying
Pam: 4 Gems 5 Ewing, Grier 6 Dawber, Tillis 7 Shriver
__-pamby: 5 namby
Pamela: 4 Reed 5 Mason 6 Tiffin 7 Britton, Hensley, Johnson 8 Anderson, Harriman
author: Samuel Richardson
Pamela __ Anderson: 3 Lee
Pamela __ Martin: 3 Sue
pampas: 3 lea, ley 5 plain, veldt 7 lowland, prairie 9 grassland
bird: 4 rhea
cousin: 5 llano
cow catcher: 4 bola
rider: 6 gaucho
pamper: 3 pet 4 baby 5 favor, humor, nurse, spoil 6 coddle, cosher, cosset, dandle, dote on, lavish, please 7 cater to, gratify, indulge 8 dote upon, give in to 9 spoon-feed
Pampers: 6 diaper
alternative: 4 Luvs 7 Drypers, Huggies
pamphlet: 5 flier, flyer, tract 6 folder 7 booklet, handout, leaflet, writing 8 brochure, bulletin, circular 9 broadside, throwaway 10 literature
Pamplona: 4 city, town
hazard: 4 bull, toro
locale: 5 Spain
pan: 3 pot, rap, wok 4 flay, mine, scan, sift, slam, zoom 5 decry, knock, scale, scoff, smear, sweep, track 6 boiler, defame, demean, deride, follow, kettle, kisser, oppugn, review, swivel, vessel, vilify 7 degrade, griddle, lambast, put-down, roaster, skillet, slander, utensil 8 badmouth, belittle, features, lambaste, minimize, saucepan, talk down 9 container, criticize, disparage, find fault, pick apart
baking ~: 3 tin 5 sheet
ender: 3 fry 4 cake, pipe 5 dowdy 6 handle 7 handler 8 handling
expand in the ~: 4 rise
for gold: 8 prospect
frying ~: 6 spider, vessel 7 skillet
opposite: 4 rave
out: 2 go 3 win 5 click, prove, solve 6 go over, happen, make it, result, thrive 7 prevail, prosper, resolve, succeed, triumph 8 flourish, get ahead, go places, make good 9 culminate, eventuate 10 come to pass
starter: 4 dead, dish, dust, hard 5 brain, patty, sauce
stir-fry ~: 3 wok
__ pan: 3 oil, pie 4 cake, drip, loaf, salt, tube 5 Bundt 6 frying, muffin, vacuum
Pan: 3 god 4 moon 5 deity, Peter, satyr 6 Hermes
daughter: 4 Lynx
father: 4 Zeus 6 Hermes
lover: 3 Aex 4 Echo 7 Eupheme
mother: 8 Penelope
planet: 6 Saturn
son: 6 Crotus 7 Aegipan
Pan-__ makeup: 4 Cake
__-Pan: 3 Tai
panacea: 4 cure 6 elixir, potion, remedy 7 arcanum, cure-all, nostrum 10 catholicon
panache: 4 brio, dash, élan, snap, zest 5 éclat, flair, plume, spunk, style, verve 7 sparkle
having ~: 4 chic, posh, tony 5 ritzy, sharp, swank, swish, toney 6 classy, dapper, dressy, modish, snappy, spruce, swanky 7 dashing, elegant, in vogue, stylish 9 exclusive, glamorous
lacking ~: 4 blah 6 boring
__ Pan Alley: 3 Tin
Pan Am: 7 airline
Panama: 3 hat 4 gulf 5 canal 6 nation, Norman 7 country, isthmus
capital: 10 Panama City
gulf: 7 San Blas
hat: 8 jipijapa
Indian: 4 Cuna 7 San Blas
lake: 5 Gatún
money: 6 balboa 9 centesimo
neighbor: 8 Colombia 9 Costa Rica
org.: 3 OAS
pest: 5 aedes 8 mosquito
port: 6 Balboa 9 Cristobal
see also Spanish
Panama (1984 song)
artist: Van Halen
Panama __: 3 hat 5 Canal 6 Hattie
Panama Canal
dam: 5 Gatún
island near the ~: 4 Naos
ocean: 7 Pacific 8 Atlantic
terminus: 5 Colón
Panama City: 4 city, town 7 capital
locale: 6 Panama 7 Florida
Panama Deception, The (1992 film)
director: Barbara Trent
Panama Hattie: 4 film 7 musical
cast: Bebes Daniels, Ethel Merman
composer: Cole Porter
Pan American __: 5 Games, Union
Pan-American __: 7 Highway
Pan American Union successor: 3 OAS
Panasonic: 2 TV 3 VCR 5 TV set 10 television
alternative: *see* electronics company
panatela: 5 cigar
Panay: 4 isle 6 island
city: 6 Iloilo
native: 3 Ati
pan-broil: 3 fry
pancake: 5 bread, crash 6 blintz, makeup 7 blintze 8 flapjack
breakfast: 7 benefit
deli ~: 5 latke
Hanukkah ~: 5 latke
ingredient: 3 egg 4 milk 5 flour
mix: 6 batter
order: 5 stack
palace: 4 IHOP
Russian ~: 5 blini, bliny
thin ~: 5 blini, bliny, crape, crepe
topper: 5 sirup, syrup
pancake __: 7 landing
Pan-Cake __: 6 makeup
Panchen __: 4 Lama
Panchen Lama: 4 monk 6 cleric
Pancho: 5 Villa 6 Segura 8 Gonzales
see also Spanish
__ Pan collar: 5 Peter
pancreas: 5 gland
enzyme: 6 lipase
hormone: 7 insulin
neighbor: 5 liver
panda: 6 animal, mammal 8 Ling-Ling
female: 3 sow
food: 6 bamboo
habitat: 5 China
male: 4 boar
young: 3 cub
__ panda: 3 red 5 giant
pandect: 5 brief 6 digest 7 summary 8 synopsis 10 abridgment, compendium
pandemic: 4 rife 7 rampant 8 catching 9 extensive, worldwide 10 widespread
pandemonium: 3 din 4 riot, stir 5 babel, chaos, havoc, noise 6 bedlam, clamor, hubbub, mayhem, racket, ruckus, rumpus, tumult, uproar 7 anarchy, turmoil 8 madhouse 9 commotion, confusion, craziness, hue and cry 10 hurly-burly, turbulence
pander: 6 cajole, please 7 cater to, gratify, indulge, lay it on, satisfy

8 give in to, play up to, soften up, suck up to
P and L
column heading: 3 YTD
Pandora: 4 moon
author: Anne Rice
daughter: 6 Pyrrha
husband: 9 Epimethus
lover: 4 Zeus
planet: 6 Saturn
what ~ unleashed: 4 ills
Pandora's __: 3 box
pandowdy: 7 dessert
__ pandowdy: 5 apple
pane: 5 glass, sheet 9 partition
adhesive: 5 putty
holder: 4 sash
piece: 5 shard, sherd
starter: 5 march 6 window 7 counter
panegyric: 4 pean 5 eloge, honor, kudos, paean 6 eulogy, homage, praise, salute 7 acclaim, oration, plaudit, tribute 8 accolade, encomium, flattery 9 extolment, laudation 10 compliment, exaltation
panegyrical: 7 glowing 9 laudatory
panegyrize: 4 hail, laud 5 bless, exalt, extol, honor 6 extoll, praise, salute 7 acclaim, applaud, commend, flatter, glorify 8 eulogize, sanctify
panel: 4 gore, jury, wall 5 board, sheet 6 jurors 7 council, divider, inquest 8 bulkhead, trustees, wainscot 9 committee, grand jury, partition
dress ~: 4 gore 5 inset
focus: 5 issue, topic
member: 5 judge, juror
triptych ~: 5 volet
panel __: 3 saw 5 house, truck
__ panel: 5 solar 7 control, modesty
Panetta: 4 Leon
org.: 3 CIA
pang: 4 ache, hurt, kink, pain, stab 5 cramp, gripe, qualm, shame, spasm, sting, throb, throe 6 injury, misery, regret, stitch, twinge, wrench 8 distress 9 misgiving
Pangborn: 8 Franklin
pangolin: 6 animal, mammal
snack: 3 ant
pangs of conscience: 7 remorse
panhandle: 3 beg 5 cadge, mooch 7 solicit 8 freeload, scrounge 9 impetrate
state with a ~: 3 Fla., Ida., Tex., W. Va. 4 Okla. 5 Idaho, Texas 6 Alaska 7 Florida 8 Oklahoma
Panhandle Cowboy
author: Larry McMurtry
panhandler: 3 bum 5 tramp 6 beggar 10 ragamuffin
request: 4 alms 5 coins, money
panic: 4 fear, flap, funk, rush 5 alarm, crash, dread, scare, slump 6 dismay, frenzy, fright, lose it, scream, terror 7 mad rush, unnerve 8 cold feet, downturn, freeze up, frighten, have a fit, hysteria, stampede 9 come apart, confusion, go berserk, overreact, run scared, trepidity 10 chicken out, depression, go to pieces
button: 5 alarm
in a ~: 6 scared 7 alarmed 9 terrified 10 frightened
PC ~ button: 3 ESC
panic __: 6 attack, button
__ panic: 3 in a
Panic (2000 film)
cast: Neve Campbell, William H. Macy, Donald Sutherland, Tracey Ullman
panic button, push the: 5 alarm, alert
Panic in Needle Park, The (1971 film)
cast: Al Pacino
panicky: 5 jumpy, timid 6 afraid, scared, trepid 7 abashed, alarmed, anxious, chicken, daunted, fearful, jittery, nervous, spooked 8 cowardly, fearsome, hesitant, timorous 9 petrified, terrified, tremulous 10 frightened
Panic Room (2002 film)
cast: Jodie Foster, Jared Leto, Forest Whitaker, Dwight Yoakam
panic-stricken: 6 afraid, scared 9 terrified 10 frightened
panjandrum: 7 pooh-bah 8 official
__-panky: 5 hanky
panned, it's often: 4 gold, play 5 movie
panner: 6 critic 9 sourdough 10 prospector
pannier: 6 basket, dosser
panophobe fear: 3 all 10 everything
panoply: 4 pomp 5 armor, array 6 parade 9 trappings
panorama: 4 view 5 gamut, scape, scene, sweep, vista 6 length 7 diorama, display, lookout, outlook, picture, scenery, tableau 8 overview, prospect 9 landscape
panoramic: 3 big 4 wide 5 broad 6 scenic
panoramic __: 4 view
Panova, Vera: 6 writer 7 Russian
panpipe: 4 wind 6 syrinx
Pansies
author: D.H. Lawrence
pansophic: 4 sage, wise 7 learned
pansy: 5 plant, viola 6 flower 10 heart's-ease
combining form: 4 viol-
Pansy: 5 Yokum
pant: 4 blow, gasp, gulp, huff, puff, sigh 5 chuff, crave, heave, snort, yearn 6 breath, desire, wheeze 7 breathe 9 palpitate
ender: 4 suit
(for): 4 ache, burn, itch, long, lust, pine, wish 5 yearn 6 hunger, thirst
Pantagruel: 5 giant
Pantene: 7 shampoo
alternative: 4 Flex, Pert 5 Prell, Suave, Wella 7 Finesse
pantheist: 5 pagan
pantheon: 6 temple
member: 3 god
panther: 3 cat 4 puma 5 felid 6 animal, cougar, feline 7 leopard, wildcat 9 catamount
literary ~: 4 pard
perch: 4 tree
relative: *see* feline
Panther: 5 Falls, NHLer 10 footballer
__ Panther: 3 Joe 4 Gray 5 Black
Panthers: 3 six 4 team 6 eleven
div.: 3 NFC
home: 5 Miami 7 Florida 8 Carolina
milieu: 3 ice 4 rink
org.: 3 NFL, NHL
rival: *see* hockey team, NFL team
sport: 6 hockey 8 football
__ Panther, The: 4 Pink
panting: 7 excited, gasping, gulping, heaving 10 breathless
Pantoliano: 3 Joe
pantologist: 4 sage
pantomime: 3 ape, mum 5 mimic 6 act out 7 charade, gesture
actor: 4 Tati
dance: 4 hula
pantothenic __: 4 acid
pantry: 5 store 6 larder 8 cupboard
boat ~: 5 cuddy
feature: 3 bin, can, jar, tin 4 food 5 flour, shelf, sugar 6 closet 8 canister
keep in the ~: 5 store
old ~ supply: 4 lard
stock the ~: 5 lay in
pants: 5 chaps, cords, ducks, jeans, Levi's, trews 6 breeks, briefs, Capris, chinos, denims, khakis, shorts, slacks, tweeds 7 bikinis, drawers, gauchos, kerseys, panties, peg tops, shalwar, shulwar 8 bermudas, bloomers, breeches, britches, culottes, flannels, jodhpurs, knickers, leggings, overalls, trousers 9 blue jeans, corduroys, dungarees, moleskins, plus fours 10 hiphuggers, lederhosen 12 pedal-pushers
adjust ~: 5 rehem
alternative: 5 skirt
and jacket: 4 suit 6 outfit 8 ensemble
beat the ~ off: 5 cream, crush, tromp 7 trounce
British ~: 6 breeks
calf-length ~: 6 Capris
cuff in Britain: 6 turnup
cut: 4 full, slim 5 husky 7 regular
feature: 3 hem 4 cuff, seam 5 pleat 6 crease
India ~: 7 shalwar, shulwar
inhabitants: 4 ants
material: 4 duck, wool 5 denim, nylon, tweed, twill 6 cotton 8 corduroy 9 polyester
measure: 4 hips 5 waist 6 inseam, length
part: 3 leg 4 knee, seat
riding ~: 8 jodhpurs
Scottish ~: 5 trews
slangily: 4 slax
smarty ~: 4 snob 8 wiseacre
starter: 5 sweat
unit: 4 pair
pants __: 4 suit
__ pants: 3 hot, ski 4 knee 5 Capri, harem
__-pants: 5 fancy 6 smarty
pantyhose: 8 lingerie
brand: 5 Hanes, Leggs
color: 3 tan 4 ecru 5 beige, black, flesh, taupe
part: 3 leg 4 foot
ruin one's ~: 3 jag, run 4 snag
pantywaist: 5 sissy 6 coward 7 chicken 9 jellyfish 10 scaredy-cat
Pan With Us
author: Robert Frost
__ Panza: 6 Sancho
panzer: 4 tank
Paolo: 7 Uccello 8 Veronese
in English: 4 Paul
see also Italian
pap: 8 baby food
see also baloney
papa: 3 dad, pop 4 dada, male, mate, pops, sire 5 daddy, pappy, pater 6 father, parent 8 baby talk
paddock ~: 4 sire
partner: 4 mama 5 mamma
Papa __: 3 Doc 4 Bear, Joe's
__ Pa-pa: 4 Oh! My
Papa Bear: 5 Halas
__ Papa Bell: 4 Cool
Papa Doc country: 5 Haiti
Papa Don't Preach (1986 song)
artist: Madonna
papal: 3 fig 4 tree 6 popish 8 clerical, pontific 10 pontifical
bull: 6 decree
cape: 5 fanon
diplomat: 6 legate, nuncio
document: 4 bull
envoy: 6 nuncio
hat: 5 miter
headdress: 5 tiara
letter: 5 brief
name: *see* popes
seal: 5 bulla
vestment: 5 orale
papal __: 4 bull 5 cross
Papa Loves Mambo (1954 song)
artist: Perry Como
paparazzo
creation: 3 pic 4 snap 5 photo 8 snapshot 10 photograph
need: 6 camera, tripod
quarry: 5 celeb 9 celebrity
papas __: 6 fritas
Papas: 5 Irene
Papa's Got a Brand New Bag (1965 song)
artist: James Brown
papaw: 4 tree 5 fruit 9 fruit tree
Papa Was a Rollin' Stone (1972 song)
artist: Temptations
papaya: 4 tree 5 fruit, shrub
Papeete: 4 city, port, town
location: 6 Tahiti
paper: 3 pad, rag 4 bond, deed, leaf, news, pass, will, writ 5 daily, essay, organ, press, sheet, stock, study, theme 6 letter, manila, poster, record, report, thesis, ticket, tissue, vellum, weekly 7 diploma, gazette, journal, monthly, notepad, papyrus, summons, tabloid, voucher, warrant, writing 8 contract, document, gift wrap, subpoena, treatise 9 affidavit, cardboard, monograph, onionskin 10 assignment, court order, exposition, instrument, periodical, stationery
bureaucrat's ~: 4 form
business owner's ~: 4 deed 5 lease, title 7 charter 8 contract
chem-lab ~: 6 litmus
chief: 6 editor
commit to ~: 3 jot, pen 4 note 5 write 6 record 8 scribble 9 chronicle

corrugated ~ feature: 5 ridge
covering: 5 emery
decorative ~: 5 crape, crepe 6 tissue 8 giftwrap
deliverer's way: 5 route
doll: 6 cutout
ender: 3 boy 4 back, clip, girl, work 5 board, bound, knife, maker 6 hanger, making, weight 7 hanging
holder: 3 pad 4 clip 6 binder
legal ~: 4 deed, will 5 lease, title 7 charter 8 contract 9 agreement
medical ~: 5 chart
mill commodity: 4 pulp, wood
money: 4 bill 8 currency
nest builder: 4 wasp
ower's ~: 3 IOU 4 note 8 mortgage
part of a ~ towel roll: 4 tube
party ~: 5 crape, crepe
piece of ~: 4 leaf, slip 5 sheet
quantity of ~: 4 ream 5 quire, sheaf
research ~: 6 thesis 8 treatise 9 monograph
school ~: 5 essay, theme 6 thesis
size: 4 demy, post, pott 5 atlas, crown, folio, legal, royal, sexto 6 medium, octavo, quarto 8 elephant, foolscap, imperial, twelvemo, twentymo, vigesimo 9 duodecimo, sixteenmo 10 octodecimo, super-royal
starter: 3 end, fly, oil, tar 4 news, sand, wall 5 waste
strong brown ~: 5 kraft
trail: 5 proof 6 record 7 red tape
wrapping ~: 5 kraft 6 tissue 8 giftwrap
paper __: 3 bag 4 clip, doll, mill, tape 5 chase, knife, match, money, tiger, towel, trail 6 cutter, profit
paper-__: 4 thin 5 mâché 6 pusher
__ paper: 3 end, fax, rag, wax 4 bond, copy, rice, test 5 crepe, funny, graph, trade, waxed, white 6 carbon, litmus, Manila, tissue
Paper __: 4 Doll, Lace, Lion, Mate, Moon 5 Roses
paperback: 4 book 5 novel
ID: 4 ISBN
publisher: 4 Avon, Dell 6 Bantam
__ paperback: 5 trade
Paperback Writer (1966 song)
artist: Beatles
Paper Chase, The: 4 film 5 novel
author: John Jay Osborn, Hal Porter
cast: Timothy Bottoms, John Houseman, Lindsay Wagner
student: 4 one-L
subject: 3 law
paper doll: 3 toy
dress part: 3 tab 4 slot
Paper in Fire (1987 song)
artist: John Cougar Mellencamp
Paper Lion (1968 film)
cast: Alan Alda, Lauren Hutton, Alex Karras
PaperMate: 3 pen
alternative: 3 Bic 5 Pilot 7 Uni-Ball
Paper Moon (1973 film)
cast: Madeline Kahn, Ryan O'Neal, Tatum O'Neal
kid: 5 Addie
Paper Roses (song)
artist: Anita Bryant, Marie Osmond
papers: 2 ID 4 visa 7 dossier 8 passport
funny ~: 6 comics
mark ~: 5 grade
pup without ~: 3 mut 4 mutt
walking ~: 5 the ax
__ papers: 7 walking, working
__ Papers, The: 6 Aspern, Biglow, Rachel
Paper, The (1994 film)
cast: Glenn Close, Robert Duvall, Michael Keaton, Jason Robards, Marisa Tomei
director: Ron Howard
paper towel brand: 4 Viva 5 Scott 6 Bounty, Brawny
paperwork: 4 form 5 forms 7 red tape
insurance ~: 5 claim
processor: 5 clerk
papier-__: 5 mâché
papillon: 3 dog 5 canid 6 canine
Papillon (1973 film)
cast: Dustin Hoffman, Steve McQueen
papoose: 4 baby 6 infant 7 newborn
Papp: 6 Joseph
Pappas: 3 Ike 4 Milt
pappy: 2 pa 3 dad, pop 4 male, papa, soft 6 father, old man, parent
Pappy: 9 Boyington
paprika: 5 spice 9 condiment
Papua New Guinea: 4 isls. 5 isles 6 nation 7 country, islands
capital: Port Moresby
city: 3 Lae
coin: 4 toea
currency: 4 kina
neighbor: 9 Indonesia
noted ~ raft: 3 Ra I 4 Ra II
papyrus: 4 reed 5 paper, sedge
port: 4 daru
volcano: 5 Manam 6 Bagana, Rabaul, Ulawun 7 Langila
papyrus: 6 scroll
papyrus-swamp lake: 5 kioga
Paquin, Anna: 7 actress
film: Finding Forrester (2000) The Piano (1993, AA) A Walk on the Moon (1999)
par: 3 avg., std. 4 mean, norm 5 level, usual 6 median, medium, normal, parity 7 average, balance 8 equality, sameness, standard
beater: 5 eagle 6 birdie
below ~: 3 ill, off 4 poor 5 unfit 6 ailing, sickly 7 lacking, rundown, wanting 9 imperfect 10 inadequate, indisposed
for the course: 4 norm 5 typic, usual 7 typical 8 expected
neither under nor over ~: 4 even
on a ~: 4 akin, even, like, same, such, tied 5 alike, equal, level 7 cognate, similar 8 matching, parallel 9 analogous, consonant 10 comparable, equivalent, homogenous, tantamount
one over ~: 5 bogey
one under ~: 6 birdie
two under ~: 5 eagle
up to ~: 2 OK 4 hale, okay, well 7 healthy 8 all right 10 acceptable
par __: 5 avion, value
par __ the course: 3 for
__ par: 4 up to
para: 4 aide 5 money
para-: 2 by 4 near, past
parable: 4 tale 5 fable, story 8 allegory
feature: 5 moral 6 lesson
parabola: 3 arc 5 curve 9 sinuosity
make a ~: 3 arc
peak: 6 apogee
Paracelsus
author: Robert Browning
parachute: 4 drop, jump 6 drogue
material: 5 nylon
part: 4 cord 6 canopy
strap: 5 riser
parachute __: 4 jump
__ parachute: 6 golden
Parachutes and Kisses
author: Erica Jong
parachuting: 5 sport
parachutist: 6 bailer, jumper
paraclete: 7 paladin 8 advocate, champion, defender
parade: 3 air 4 brag, line, show, walk 5 array, boast, march, model, sight, strut, swash, troop, vaunt 6 column, flaunt, prance, review, series, stream 7 cortege, display, exhibit, fanfare, pageant, panoply, show off, swagger, trot out 8 autocade, brandish 9 cavalcade, festivity, promenade, spectacle 10 procession, wave around
Chinese ~ feature: 6 dragon
command: 4 halt
day: 6 Easter, Fourth 10 July Fourth 12 Thanksgiving
feature: 4 band 5 float, march 8 confetti 9 majorette
sponsor: 5 Macy's
stopper: 4 rain
__ parade: 3 hit
Parade: 6 ballet
composer: Erik Satie
__ Parade: 6 Easter
__ Parade, The: 3 Big 4 Love
paradigm: 4 type 5 guide, ideal, model 7 example, paragon, pattern 8 exemplar, original, standard 9 archetype, beau ideal, criterion, prototype 10 touchstone
paradigmatic: 5 ideal, model 7 typical
paradise: 4 Eden 5 bliss 6 heaven, utopia 7 Arcadia, ecstasy, Elysium, nirvana, rapture 8 empyrean, Valhalla 9 cloud nine, next world, Shangri-la
Arthurian ~: 6 Avalon
bird of ~ feature: 5 plume
Celtic ~: 6 Avalon
dweller: 3 god 5 angel, houri 7 goddess 8 Valkyrie 9 archangel
evictee: 3 Eve 4 Adam
fool's ~: 7 fantasy, reverie 8 delusion
Muslim bridge to ~: 5 sirat
opposite: 4 hell 10 underworld
Paradise: 3 Sal 4 city, town
author: Larry McMurtry
Bird of ~ constellation: 4 Apus
locale: 6 Nevada 10 California
Paradise (1988 song)
artist: Sade
Paradise (1991 film)
cast: Thora Birch, Melanie Griffith, Don Johnson, Elijah Wood
Paradise __: 4 Lost
__ Paradise: 3 Sal 6 Almost
Paradise by the Dashboard Light (1978 song)
artist: Meat Loaf
Paradise is where __: 3 I am
Paradise Lost: 4 epic, poem
author: John Milton, Clifford Odets
character: 3 Eve, Sin 4 Adam 5 Ariel, Satan, Uriel 6 Abdiel, Belial, Mammon, Moloch 7 Gabriel, Michael, Raphael 8 Mulciber 9 Beelzebub
Paradise of exiles: 5 Italy
Paradise Regained
author: John Milton
__-Paradise, The: 4 Demi
paradisical: 6 divine 8 beatific, heavenly
Paradiso
author: Dante
__ Paradiso: 4 Gran 5 Hotel 6 Cinema
paradox: 4 koan 6 enigma, oddity, puzzle, riddle 7 anomaly, mystery
__ paradox: 4 liar 5 Zeno's
paradoxical: 5 polar 6 ironic, unlike 7 adverse, counter, reverse 8 clashing, contrary, opposite 9 different 10 antithetic
paraffin: 3 wax
paraffin-based: 5 waxen
paragon: 3 gem 4 hero 5 angel, ideal, light, model 7 epitome, example, pattern 8 cynosure, exemplar, original, paradigm, standard, treasure, ultimate 9 archetype, beau ideal, criterion, nonpareil, prototype 10 apotheosis
paragraph: 4 text 6 clause 7 passage
start a ~: 6 indent
unit: 8 sentence
Paraguay: 5 river 6 nation 7 country
capital: 8 Asunción
from ~: 6 Latino
Indian: 6 Lengua 7 Guarani
money: 7 centimo, guarani
neighbor: 6 Brazil 7 Bolivia 9 Argentina
see also Spanish
parakeet: 3 pet 4 bird 6 budgie 10 budgerigar, budgerygah
home: 4 cage
seat: 5 perch
treat: 4 seed 8 bird seed
Parallax View, The (1974 film)
cast: Warren Beatty, Paula Prentiss
parallel: 3 tie 4 akin, echo, even, like, such 5 agree, alike, equal, level, match 6 allied, analog, equate, on a par 7 aligned, analogy, cognate, compare, imitate, kindred, related, similar 8 matching, relative, resemble 9 alongside, analogous, collimate, collocate, correlate 10 comparable, coordinate, equivalent, resembling, side-by-side, similarity
draw a ~: 6 equate 7 compare
make ~: 5 align, aline
parallel __: 4 bars
Parallel Lives
author: Plutarch
parallelogram: 5 rhomb 6 square 7 rhombus 9 rectangle

paralyze: **4** daze, halt, lame, numb, stun **5** daunt, scare, shock **6** arrest, bemuse, benumb, freeze, weaken **7** destroy, nonplus, petrify, stupefy, terrify **8** shut down, transfix **9** indispose **10** immobilize
paralyzed: **6** torpid **9** enervated, powerless **10** motionless
Paramaribo: **4** city, port, town **7** capital
locale: **8** Suriname
paramecium: **9** protozoan
like a ~: **6** apodal **7** apodous
paramedic
job: **3** aid **4** help **6** rescue **10** resusitate
letters: **3** EMT
org.: **3** EMS
skill: **3** CPR
parameters: **5** range, scope **6** bounds, limits **8** boundary, criteria **10** guidelines
set ~: **5** limit **6** define **7** delimit
paramnesia: **6** déjà vu
paramount: **3** big, top **4** best, main, star, tops **5** chief, first, prime, vital **6** urgent, utmost **7** capital, central, in front, leading, premier, primary, supreme, topmost **8** cardinal, crowning, dominant, foremost, headmost, powerful, superior, towering, ultimate **9** governing, high-level, immediate, important, necessary, prevalent, principal, sovereign, topflight, unequaled, uppermost **10** overriding, preeminent
Paramount: **6** studio
competitor: ***see*** movie studio
creation: **4** film **5** flick, movie
workplace: **3** lot, set **10** soundstage
paramour
see sweetheart
Paramus: **4** city, town
locale: **9** New Jersey
paranormal: **4** eery **5** eerie **6** mystic **7** psychic **8** mystical
ability: **3** ESP
parapet: **4** wall **7** bastion, defense, rampart **10** battlement
fortification: **5** redan
notch: **6** crenel **8** crenelle
paraphernalia: **3** rig **4** gear **5** goods, items, means, stuff, thing **6** outfit, tackle, things **7** baggage, effects, luggage, regalia **8** material **9** apparatus, equipment, machinery, trappings
paraphrase: **5** quote **6** digest, rehash, render, reword **7** reading, restate, version **8** rephrase **9** interpret, translate
paraprofessional: **4** aide **6** helper **9** assistant, secretary
parapsychology: **3** psi **9** telepathy
pioneer: **5** Rhine
subject: **3** ESP **10** sixth sense
parasite: **4** flea, lice **5** drone, idler, leech, louse, toady **6** cadger, jackal, loafer, sponge **7** moocher, shirker, slacker, sponger **8** deadbeat, hanger-on **9** goldbrick, scrounger, sycophant **10** freeloader
animal ~: **4** flea, lice, mite, tick **5** ameba, louse
need: **4** host
plant ~: **5** aphid, aphis **9** mistletoe
worm: **4** nema
Parasite, The
author: Arthur Conan Doyle
parasol: **8** sunshade, umbrella
paratrooper: **7** soldier
gear: **5** chute **9** parachute
__ paratus: **6** semper
parboil: **4** cook **5** scald **6** blanch, simmer
parcel: **3** cut, lot, pak. **4** area, bale, deal, give, land, load, mail, mete, pack, part, plat, plot, sort **5** allot, chunk, group, piece, share, slice, split, tract **6** bundle, carton, divide, packet, ration **7** acreage, arrival, carve up, divvy up, dole out, package, portion, section, segment, split up **8** allocate, delegate, division, freehold, property **9** apportion, house site, partition **10** distribute
auction ~: **3** lot
land ~: **3** lot **4** acre
marking: **3** COD, ppd **4** rush **7** fragile
protector: **4** tape **5** paper, twine **9** cellulose, Stryofoam **10** bubble wrap
send a ~: **4** mail, ship
service: **3** UPS **4** USPS **5** FedEx
parcel __: **4** post
Parcells, Bill: **5** coach
nickname: **4** Tuna
sport: **8** football
parch: **3** dry **4** burn, sear **5** dry up, toast **6** dry out, scorch, wither **7** shrivel, torrefy, torrify **9** anhydrate, dehydrate, desiccate, exsiccate
parched: **3** dry **4** arid, sere **5** stale, unwet **6** barren, torrid **7** athirst, dried up, thirsty **8** dried out, droughty, scorched, withered **9** juiceless, shriveled, waterless **10** dehydrated
Parcheesi: **4** game **9** board game
feature: **3** die **4** dice **5** board
parching: **3** hot **6** sultry, torrid **8** stifling
parchment __: **5** paper
pard: **3** cat, pal **6** cowboy **7** cowpoke, panther, pardner, partner
pardalis, felis: **6** ocelot
pardner: **3** pal **6** cowboy **7** cowpoke
Pardo: **3** Don
pardon: **4** free, pity **5** clear, grace, mercy, remit, spare **6** accept, acquit, assoil, excuse, let off, spring **7** absolve, amnesty, commute, forgive, justify, release **8** clemency, overlook, reprieve, write off **9** acquittal, discharge, exculpate, exonerate, indemnity, remission, salvation **10** absolution
beg ~: **9** apologize
pardonable: **6** venial **9** excusable **10** defensible, forgivable, remittable, vindicable
pardoning: **7** lenient **8** merciful **9** forgiving
Pardon me!: **4** ahem **5** sorry
Pardon my __: **6** French
Pardon My English: **7** musical
composer: George Gershwin, Ira Gershwin
Pardonnez-__: **3** moi
pare: **3** cut, lop **4** clip, crop, dock, flay, peel, skin, slow, trim **5** carve, lower, prune, shave, slash **6** cut off, lessen, reduce, scrape **7** abridge, curtail, cut away, cut back, shorten, whittle **8** decrease, diminish, downsize, minimize, truncate **9** cut back on, scale down **10** abbreviate
Paré: **7** Michael **8** Ambroise
__ Paree: **3** Gay
parent: **3** dad, mom **4** make, mama, papa, rear **5** cause, mamma, pappy **6** author, chider, father, mother, origin, source **7** kinsman, produce **8** ancestor, begetter, guardian, relative **9** architect, originate **10** forerunner, originator, progenitor
admonition: **3** eat **4** don't, quit, stop **6** behave
backwoods ~: **2** ma, pa **3** maw, paw **5** mammy, pappy
barnyard ~: **3** cow, dam, ewe, hen, ram, sow **4** boar, bull, duck, mare, sire **5** billy, drake, goose, nanny **6** gander **7** rooster **8** stallion
British ~: **5** mater, pater
cub ~: **4** bear, lion **5** panda, tiger **7** lioness, tigress
ender: **3** age
female ~: **2** ma **3** mom **4** mama **5** momma, mommy **6** mother
gen-Xer ~: **6** boomer
in French: **4** mère, père
in Spanish: **5** madre, padre
male ~: **2** pa **3** dad **4** dada, papa, sire **5** daddy, poppa **6** father
mule ~: **3** ass **4** mare
new ~: **5** namer
org.: **3** PTA **4** MADD
quadruped ~: **3** dam **4** sire
responsibility: **3** son, tot **4** baby, teen **5** child, minor **6** infant **8** daughter, teen-ager **9** youngster
restriction: **6** curfew
starter: **3** god **4** step **5** grand, trans
parentage: **4** line **5** stock **6** origin **7** lineage **9** genealogy **10** extraction
parental: **4** fond, kind, warm **6** benign, caring, gentle, lineal, loving, tender **7** devoted **8** fatherly, maternal, motherly, paternal, watchful **9** indulgent **10** benevolent, comforting, forbearing, protective, supportive
parental __: **5** leave
Parent, Bernie
milieu: **3** ice **4** rink **5** arena
org.: **3** NHL
parenthesis shape: **3** arc
parenthetical: **4** side **10** qualifying
parenthood: **9** maternity, paternity
Parenthood (1989 film)
cast: Tom Hulce, Steve Martin, Rick Moranis, Martha Plimpton, Jason Robards, Mary Steenburgen, Dianne Wiest
director: Ron Howard
parentless child: **6** orphan **9** foundling
parents: **5** folks
Parent Trap, The (1961 film)
cast: Brian Keith, Hayley Mills, Maureen O'Hara
dog: **9** Andromeda
kid: **4** twin
Parent Trap, The (1998 film)
cast: Lindsay Lohan, Dennis Quaid, Natasha Richardson
parer: **4** tool **6** cutter, device, gadget, peeler
user: **4** chef, cook
Paretsky,Sara: **6** writer
pareu: **4** wrap **5** skirt **8** lavalava
par excellence: **3** ace **4** A-one, best, only, rare, tops **5** alone, great **6** single, superb, unique **7** in front, optimum, perfect, supreme **8** flawless, peerless, splendid, superior **9** faultless, matchless, nonpareil, solid-gold, topflight, unequaled, unmatched, unrivaled, virtuosic **10** consummate, inimitable, preeminent, unexampled, unrivalled, world-class
parfait: **7** dessert **8** ice cream
alternative: **6** gelati, gelato, sundae **7** spumone, spumoni, tortoni
par for the __: **6** course
pari __: **5** passu
pari-__: **6** mutuel
pariah: **5** exile, Jonah **6** outlaw, wretch **7** outcast **8** anathema
campus ~: **4** nerd, wonk **5** dweeb **7** egghead
social ~: **4** bore, jerk **5** creep
treat like a ~: **3** cut **4** shun **5** avoid **6** slight **9** blackball
__ paribus: **7** ceteris
parietal: **4** bone
locale: **5** skull **7** cranium **9** braincase
parietal __: **4** lobe
Parigi, o cara: **4** duet
Parillaud: **4** Anne
pari-mutuel
listing: **4** odds
transaction: **3** bet **5** wager
pari passu: **6** evenly, fairly
Paris: **4** city, Mica, town **5** Jerry **6** Trojan **7** capital, musical
abductee: **5** Helen
airport: **4** Orly **8** de Gaulle
attraction: **4** arch **5** musée **6** cancan, Louvre **8** Left Bank **11** Eiffel Tower
brother: **6** Hector, Pammon **7** Helenus, Polites, Troilus
city near ~: **5** Lille, Melun **6** Amiens, Sèvres
composer: Cole Porter
cop: **4** flic
designer: **4** Dior
home: **4** Troy
hotel: **4** Ritz
locale: **5** Texas **6** France
lover: **5** Helen **6** Oenone
money: **3** sou **4** euro **5** franc
palace: **6** Elysée
paper: **7** Le Monde
parent: **5** Priam **6** Hecuba **7** Priamus
plaster of ~: **6** gypsum
river: **5** Seine

ruffian: **6** apache
sister: **6** Creusa, Iliona **7** Laodice **8** Polyxena **9** Cassandra
subway: **5** Metro
to Romeo: **5** rival
to Ulysses: **3** foe **5** enemy
victim: **8** Achilles
see also French

Paris ___: **5** Blues, daisy, green, Trout
___ Paris: **5** I Love **6** Forget
parish: **4** fold, ward **5** flock, laity, local **6** church **8** brethren, district **9** community, territory **10** worshipers
donation: **5** tithe
hall shout: **5** bingo
Louisiana ~: **6** Acadia
official: **4** abbé **5** padre, vicar **6** beadle, curate, father
Parish: **5** Peggy **6** Robert
parishioner: **4** laic **5** laity **9** layperson
Parish, Robert: **5** cager
milieu: **5** court
org.: **3** NBA
sport: **10** basketball
___ parisienne: **3** à la
Parisienne: **3** mme. **4** mlle. **5** femme **6** madame
Parisina
author: Lord Byron
composer: Pietro Mascagni
Paris in the Twentieth Century
author: Jules Verne
Paris Option, The
author: Robert Ludlum
Paris Symphony
composer: Wolfgang Amadeus Mozart
Paris Trout (1991 film)
cast: Ed Harris, Barbara Hershey, Dennis Hopper
parity: **3** par **7** balance, isonomy **8** equality, likeness, sameness **9** congruity **10** similarity, uniformity
park: **3** put, set, sit **4** lawn, stop **5** field, green, grove, leave, lodge, oasis, place, plaza, woods **6** common, curb it, estate, forest, locate, meadow, pull in, settle, square **7** commons, deposit, grounds, reserve, stadium, station **8** preserve, pull over, woodland **9** sanctuary **10** playground
activity: **4** hike, walk **6** picnic **7** camping, cookout
alcove: **5** arbor
amusement ~ ride: **5** flume **7** coaster **8** carousel **9** bumper car
animal ~: **3** zoo
carefully: **4** ease
ender: **3** way **4** land
feature: **5** bench, grass, shade, slide, swing, trail **6** gazebo, seesaw **8** fountain
in the ball ~: **4** near **5** about, close **7** roughly
Kenya ~: **5** Tsavo
London ~: **4** Hyde
municipal ~: **6** square
national ~: **4** Zion **5** Banff **6** Acadia, Arches, Denali, Katmai **7** Big Bend, Glacier, Olympic, Redwood, reserve, Saguaro, Sequoia **8** Badlands, Biscayne, preserve, Wind Cave, Yosemite **9** Haleakala, Lake Clark, Mesa Verde, sanctuary, Voyageurs **10** Crater Lake, Everglades, Glacier Bay, Grand Teton, Great Basin, Hot Springs, Isle Royale, Joshua Tree **11** Yellowstone
one way to ~: **6** back in, head-in
South Africa ~: **6** Kruger
visitor: **5** hiker, nanny **6** camper **7** tourist **8** stroller **9** sightseer
___ park: **4** ball, game **5** theme **7** trailer
___-park: **6** double
Park: **4** Brad **5** Linda, Mungo
in Monopoly: **5** Place
___ Park: **3** Oak **4** Echo, Hyde **5** Estes, Gorky **7** Battery, Central
parka: **4** coat **6** anorak, jacket **7** skiwear **9** outerwear **10** protection
feature: **4** hood **6** lining, pocket, zipper
lining: **4** down **10** Thinsulate
wearer: **5** hiker **6** Eskimo
park-and-___: **4** ride
Park Avenue: **3** car **4** auto **5** Buick **10** automobile
Parkay: **9** margarine
alternative: **6** Shedd's **7** Promise **8** Imperial
Park, Brad: **8** puckster
milieu: **3** ice **4** rink **5** arena
org.: **3** NHL
___ Park, CA: **5** Buena, Menlo
Park Chung ___: **3** Hee
Park City
author: Ann Beattie
___ Park, CO: **5** Estes
parked: **7** garaged **10** not running, stationary
Parker: **3** Ace, Jim, Ray, Tom, wit **4** Alan, city, Dave, Fess, Jean, Nate, Suzy, town, Trey **5** Cecil, Posey **6** Bonnie, Graham **7** Charlie, Dorothy, Eleanor, Gilbert, Jameson **9** Stevenson **10** Mary-Louise
end: **3** nib
fluid: **3** ink
locale: **8** Colorado
Nosy ~: **5** prier, pryer, snoop
partner: **6** Barrow
___ Parker: **4** Nosy **5** Nosey
Parker-Bowles: **7** Camilla
Parker, Charlie: **11** saxophonist
genre: **3** bop **4** jazz
instrument: **3** sax **4** alto
nickname: **4** Bird
Parker, Dorothy: **3** wit **6** writer
work: After Such Pleasures
Enough Rope
Here Lies
Parker, Fess: **5** actor
film: Davy Crockett... (1955)
Old Yeller (1957)
song: Ballad of Davy Crockett (1955)
TV: Daniel Boone
Parker, Gilbert: **6** writer **8** Canadian
work: The Seats of the Mighty
Parker House: **4** roll **5** hotel
Parker Jr., Ray
song: Ghostbusters (1984)
I Still Can't Get Over Loving You (1983)
Jack and Jill (1978)
Jamie (1984)
The Other Woman (1982)
A Woman Needs Love (1981)
You Can't Change That (1979)
Parker Lewis Can't Lose (Fox sitcom)
cast: Corin Nemec (Parker Lewis)
Parker, Mary-Louise: **7** actress
film: Boys on the Side (1995)
Fried Green Tomatoes (1991)
Let the Devil Wear Black (2000)
Parker, Sarah Jessica: **7** actress
film: Dudley Do-Right (1999)
Ed Wood (1994)
Honeymoon in Vegas (1992)
Somewhere Tomorrow (1983)
State and Main (2000)
role: **6** Carrie
spouse: Matthew Broderick
TV: Sex and the City
___ Park, IL: **3** Oak
parking
airport ~: **5** apron
attendant: **5** valet
garage section: **5** level
lights: **6** dimmer
lot sight: **3** bus, car, van **4** auto **5** truck **7** minibus, vehicle **10** automobile
lot sign: **4** Exit, Full **5** Enter
mishap: **4** dent **7** scratch
place: **3** lot **6** garage, street
railroad ~ space: **4** yard
scofflaw stopper: **4** boot **6** ticket
parking ___: **3** lot **5** brake, meter, space, strip
___ parking: **5** valet **8** parallel
parking in ___: **4** rear
___ Parkington: **3** Mrs.
Parkins, Barbara: **7** actress
TV: Peyton Place
Parkinson: **4** Dian
Parkinson's ___: **3** law
Park Lane: **3** car **4** auto **7** Mercury
Parkman, Francis: **6** writer **9** historian
work: The Oregon Trail
Park, Mungo: **4** Scot **8** explorer
Park Near Lucerne
artist: Paul Klee
___ Park, NJ: **5** Menlo **6** Asbury
___ Park, NY: **4** Hyde, Rego **6** Tuxedo
Park Place neighbor: **6** Chance
Park Ridge: **4** city, town
locale: **8** Illinois
Parks: **4** Bert, Rosa **5** Larry **6** Gordon **7** Michael, Van Dyke
Parks, Bert successor: **3** Ely
Parks, Larry: **5** actor
film: The Jolson Story (1946)
spouse: Betty Garrett
parkway: **4** pike, road **5** route **6** avenue, street **8** turnpike **9** boulevard
parlance: **4** cant, talk **5** argot, idiom, lingo **6** jargon, patois, speech, tongue **7** wording **8** language, verbiage **10** vernacular
parlay: **3** bet **5** wager
parley: **3** gab, rap, yak **4** chat, talk **5** speak **6** caucus, confer, dialog, huddle, powwow, speech **7** commune, meeting, palaver, schmoos **8** chitchat, colloquy, converse, dialogue, schmoose, schmooze **9** discourse, gathering, negotiate, touch base **10** chew the rag, conference, deliberate, discussion, round table
Parley: **4** Baer
parliament: **5** house
czar's ~: **4** Duma
Ireland ~: **4** Dail
Japan ~: **4** Diet
Poland ~: **4** Sejm
Parliament
first female in ~: **5** Astor
member: **4** lord, peer
VIP: **2** P.M.
___ Parliament: **4** Long, Rump **5** Act of
parliamentary
activity: **6** debate
phrase: **5** I move **7** I second
program: **6** agenda
vote: **3** aye, nay
parlor: **5** salon **6** lounge **8** anteroom **10** living room
beauty ~: **5** salon **9** hair salon
beauty ~ item: **3** net **4** clip **5** drier, dryer, razor **6** curler, roller **7** hairpin **8** bobby pin, scissors
beauty ~ treatment: **3** cut, set **4** perm, trim **5** rinse **6** dye job, facial **8** manicure, pedicure **9** permanent
piece: **4** lamp, sofa **5** chair, couch, divan **6** settee **8** armchair, loveseat, recliner **9** easy chair, floor lamp
parlor ___: **3** car **4** game
___ parlor: **3** sun **6** beauty
parlous: **5** hairy, risky **6** chancy, unsafe, wicked **7** unsound, vicious **8** menacing, perilous, unstable **9** dangerous, desperate, harrowing, hazardous, unhealthy **10** jeopardous, touch-and-go, vulnerable
Parma: **4** city, town
locale: **4** Ohio **5** Italy
Parmenides: **5** Greek **11** philosopher
home: **4** Elea
specialty: **7** Eleatic
Parmesan ___: **6** cheese
___ parmigiana: **4** veal
Parnassus: **4** peak **5** mount **8** mountain
town near ~: **6** Delphi
Parnassus on Wheels
author: Christopher Morley
Parnell: **5** Emory **6** Thomas
___ Parnell: **6** Lee Roy
Parnelli: **5** Jones
Parnell, Thomas: **4** poet **5** Irish
parochial: **5** local, petty **6** biased, little, narrow **7** bigoted, insular, limited, topical **8** regional **9** hidebound, localized, sectarian, small-town **10** prejudiced, provincial
parochial ___: **6** school
parody: **3** ape **4** copy, mock, skit **5** farce, genre, mimic, put-on, revue, roast, spoof **6** deride, review, satire, send-up **7** burlesk, imitate, lampoon, mockery, portray, takeoff **8** ridicule, satirize, travesty **9** burlesque, imitation **10** caricature, impression
parol: **6** orally, verbal **8** verbally **9** utterance
parole: **4** free, word **7** freedom, promise **8** password **9** discharge
parolee: **5** ex-con **8** jailbird

paronomasia: 3 pun 8 wordplay
Paros: 5 Greek 6 island
neighbor of ~: 5 Naxos
parotitis: 5 mumps
paroxysm: 3 fit 4 rage 5 furor, spasm, throe 6 frenzy, tumult 7 seizure, tantrum 8 eruption, outbreak, outburst 9 hysterics 10 convulsion
parquet __: 4 tile
parquetry: 5 inlay 10 decoration
installer: 5 tiler
wood: 3 oak
parr: 4 fish 6 salmon
Parr: 4 John 9 Catherine
Parra, Nicanor: 4 poet 7 Chilean
parrier equipment: 4 épée
Parris: 4 isle 6 island
Parrish: 5 Lance, Larry
Parris Island: 4 city, town
grp.: 4 USMC
locale: 4 S. Car.
parrot: 3 ape, kea, pet 4 aper, bird, copy, echo, kaka, lory, mime 5 macaw, mimic, mouth, quote, resay 6 conure, echoer, kakapo, recite, repeat 7 copycat, imitate 8 feed back, imitator, lorikeet, lovebird 9 reiterate
Australian ~: 4 lory
cry: 3 awk 5 hello
emulate a ~: 3 ape 4 copy 5 mimic
ender: 4 fish
genus: 3 ara
home: 4 cage 6 aviary, jungle 7 tropics
kin: 8 cockatoo, parakeet, paraquet, paroquet, parroket 9 cockateel, cockatiel, parrakeet, parroquet
monk ~: 4 loro
name: 5 Polly
New Zealand ~: 3 kea 4 kaka 6 kakapo
nostril: 4 cere
seat: 5 perch
parrotfish: 4 loro
parry: 4 duck, shun 5 avert, avoid, block, dodge, elude, evade, fence, rebut, repel, shirk 6 refute 7 confute, counter, deflect, fend off, hold off, repulse, ward off 8 sidestep, stave off 9 forestall, hold at bay, turn aside 10 anticipate, circumvent
alternative: 5 lunge
response: 7 riposte
Parry, William: 8 explorer
Parsees: 4 sect
Parseghian: 3 Ara
parse, something to: 6 clause 8 sentence
Parsifal: 5 opera
character: 6 Kundry 7 Titurel 8 Amfortas, Klingsor 9 Gurnemanz
composer: Richard Wagner
quest: 5 Grail 9 Holy Grail
setting: 5 Spain 8 Pyrenees
Parsifal Mosaic, The
author: Robert Ludlum
parsimonious: 4 mean 5 close, tight 6 frugal, greedy, saving, skimpy, stingy 7 chintzy, miserly, scrimpy, selfish, sparing, thrifty 8 tightwad 9 illiberal, penurious 10 avaricious, skinflinty
be ~: 3 eke 4 mete, save 5 skimp, stint 8 begrudge, keep back 9 economize
one: 5 miser 7 Scrooge 8 tightwad 9 skinflint 10 cheapskate, pinchpenny
parsimony: 6 thrift 9 frugality 10 stinginess
Parsippany: 4 city, town
locale: 9 New Jersey
parsley: 4 herb
piece: 5 sprig
relative: 4 dill 5 anise, cumin 6 fennel, lovage
with ~: 5 garni
Parsley, __, Rosemary and Thyme: 4 Sage
parsnip: 4 root 6 veggie 7 taproot 9 vegetable
parson: 5 padre, vicar 6 cleric, curate, father, pastor, priest, rector 8 chaplain, minister, preacher, reverend 9 churchman, clergyman
bird: 3 tui
ender: 3 age
expletive: 4 amen
home: 5 manse 8 vicarage
parsonage: 5 manse 8 vicarage
Parsons: 4 Alan, Gram 7 Estelle, Louella
Parsons __: 5 table
Parsons, Estelle Oscar: Bonnie and Clyde
Parsons Project, Alan
song: Don't Answer Me (1984) Eye in the Sky (1982) Games People Play (1981)
Parsons School of __: 6 Design
part: 2 go 3 any, bit, cut, job, leg, lot 4 chip, duty, fork, hero, hunk, item, lead, limb, link, lump, role, side, sift, some, task, tear, unit, yawn 5 cameo, chunk, divvy, extra, leave, lines, piece, quota, scrap, sever, share, shred, slice, split, voice 6 aspect, behalf, branch, cleave, cut off, detach, detail, divide, factor, member, moiety, morsel, office, parcel, ration, region, sample, sector, spread, sunder, unlink, walk-on 7 break up, concern, deviate, disjoin, ease out, element, excerpt, faction, fitting, helping, portion, pull out, push off, quarter, radiate, scatter, section, segment, ship out, split up, take off, villain 8 break off, disunite, division, fraction, fragment, function, interest, location, province, separate, shove off, specimen, splinter, uncouple, withdraw 9 allotment, bifurcate, character, component, cut and run, dismantle, partition, take a hike 10 antagonist, disconnect, ingredient, proportion
combining form: 4 -mere, -plex
starter: 3 ram 7 counter
part __: 4 with
part-__: 4 time 5 timer
__ part: 3 bit 4 act a, real, take 5 spare, voice 6 walk-on
partake: 3 eat, sip 4 have 5 eat of, quaff, savor, share, taste, touch 6 accept, devour, ingest, join in, sample 7 consume, receive, share in 8 deal with 9 enter into
of: 3 use
part and __: 6 parcel
Parthe: 5 river
city on the ~: 7 Leipsic, Leipzig
Parthenon
goddess: 6 Athena, Athene, Pallas
site: 6 Athens, Greece
style: 5 Doric
Parthenope: 5 siren
lover: 6 Apollo 8 Heracles
partial: 3 cut 5 gonzo 6 biased, fond of, narrow, unfair, unjust 7 bigoted, colored, halfway, limited, reduced, sketchy 8 abridged, disposed, one-sided 9 arbitrary, condensed, curtailed, jaundiced, qualified, shortened 10 diminished, expurgated, fractional, incomplete, prejudiced, unbalanced, unfinished
be ~ to: 4 like 5 favor 6 prefer
prefix: 4 demi-, hemi-, semi-
refund: 6 rebate
to: 6 keen on
partial __: 3 sum 4 tone 5 score 6 vacuum
partiality: 4 bias, love 5 fancy, mania, slant, taste 6 liking, relish 7 leaning 8 affinity, druthers, fondness, nepotism, penchant, tendency, velleity, weakness 9 appetence, injustice, prejudice, sentiment 10 attachment, fanaticism, favoritism, friendship, indulgence, proclivity, propensity
partially: 6 partly 7 halfway 8 somewhat 9 by degrees, piecemeal
participant: 5 actor, party 6 helper, member, player, sharer 7 entrant, partner 8 follower 9 associate, attendant, colleague
participate: 3 aid 4 play 5 enter, get in, share 6 accept, attend, chip in, join in, take on 7 compete, pitch in 8 deal with, engage in 9 cooperate, enter into, lend a hand
as a visitor: 5 audit, sit in
chance to ~: 4 turn 5 break
participation: 5 voice 8 interest
__ participle: 4 past 7 perfect, present
participle suffix: 3 ing
particle: 3 bit, dot, jot, ray 4 atom, drop, hoot, iota, mite, mote, seed, spot, whit 5 crumb, fleck, grain, minim, ounce, piece, scrap, shred, speck, trace 6 little, morsel, stitch, trifle 7 dribble, granule, modicum, smidgen, smidgin 8 fragment, molecule, smidgeon 10 smithereen
burning ~: 4 coal 5 ember, spark
charged ~: 3 ion 5 anion 6 cation, kation
dirt ~: 4 grit, mote 5 speck
ender: 5 board
hypothetical ~: 5 axion
subatomic ~: 2 xi 4 kaon, muon, pion 5 axion, boson, gluon, meson, quark, tauon 6 baryon, hadron, K meson, lepton, photon, proton 7 fermion, hyperon, neutron, nucleon, pi meson, tachyon 8 deuteron, electron, graviton, neutrino, positron
parti-colored: 6 calico, dapple 7 dappled
particular: 3 own 4 fact, item, nice, prim, sole, spec 5 exact, fussy, picky, point, thing 6 choosy, dainty, detail, prissy, proper, regard, single, strict, unique 7 careful, certain, choosey, element, express, feature, finicky, limited, precise, prudent, respect, several, special, topical 8 accurate, cautious, critical, definite, distinct, especial, exacting, finiking, finnicky, personal, rigorous, separate, singular, specific, thorough 9 assiduous, attentive, demanding, exclusive, judicious, observant, punctilio, selective, squeamish 10 fastidious, individual, meticulous, respective, scrupulous
particularize: 4 list 6 denote, detail, relate 7 specify, spec out 8 describe 9 stipulate
particularly: 5 extra 6 mostly, singly 7 notably 8 markedly 9 decidedly, expressly, specially, unusually
particulars: 5 terms 7 details
particulate matter: 3 ash 4 dust, grit, smut, soot
parting: 4 last 5 adieu, final, going, leave 6 schism 7 breakup, fission, goodbye, split-up 8 division, farewell 9 departure 10 crossroads, divergence, separation, withdrawal
shot: 5 taunt 6 retort, zinger
words: 3 bye 4 ciao, ta-ta, vale 5 adieu, adios, aloha, later, peace, see ya 6 bye-bye, shalom, sholom, so long 7 cheerio, good-bye 8 farewell, sayonara 10 hasta luego
parting __: 4 line, shot
parting __ ways: 5 of the
Parting __ we know of heaven: 5 is all
Parting is such sweet __: 6 sorrow
parting of the __: 4 ways
parti pris: 9 prejudice
partisan: 3 fan 4 ally 5 blind 6 backer, biased, rooter, unfair, unjust, votary 7 admirer, booster, colored, devotee, diehard, fanatic, slanted, zealous 8 adherent, exponent, follower, guerilla, loyalist, militant, one-sided 9 arbitrary, factional, guerrilla, jaundiced, proponent, satellite, sectarian, supporter 10 enthusiast, prejudiced, unbalanced
be ~: 4 root, side
Partita __ Minor: 3 in E
partition: 4 pane, wall 5 cut up, panel, sever, share, split 6 divide, screen 7 barrier, divider, divvy up, portion, rope off, section, split up, wall off 8 division, fence off, separate 9 apportion, parcel out, subdivide 10 distribute, separation
biological ~: 6 septum
court ~: 3 net
Japanese ~: 6 fusuma
ship ~: 8 bulkhead
partly: 5 quasi 7 halfway 8 slightly, somewhat 9 partially, to a degree 10 to an extent, up to a point
partner: 3 pal 4 ally, chum, date, mate, wife 5 buddy, crony, owner, unite 6 cohort, co-mate, friend, helper, spouse 7 coequal, comrade, consort, husband 8 coworker, helpmate, playmate,

sidekick, teammate **9** accessory, affiliate, assistant, associate, colleague, companion **10** accomplice
__ partner: 6 silent
partnerless: 4 stag **5** alone **8** solitary
partners, go: 5 unite **6** hook up, team up **9** affiliate **10** join up with
partnership: 3 tie **4** bond, firm, link **5** house, joint, match, nexus, union **6** cahoot, cartel, hookup, league **7** cahoots, combine, company, liaison **8** affinity, alliance, business, coupling, relation **9** ownership **10** connection
word: 3 and, son
Partnership for Peace org.: 4 NATO
part of __: 6 speech
Parton, Dolly: 6 singer
song: 9 to 5 (1980)
Here You Come Again (1977)
Islands in the Stream (1983)
I Will Always Love You (1974)
Real Love (1985)
Two Doors Down (1978)
theme park: Dollywood
__ partout: 5 passe
partridge: 4 bird, fowl **5** quail **6** chukar, grouse **8** pheasant **9** francolin
family: 5 covey
relative: *see* fowl
...partridge __ pear tree: 3 in a
Partridge, Eric: 6 writer **7** British
concern: 5 slang
Partridge Family
lead singer: David Cassidy
song: Doesn't Somebody Want to Be Wanted (1971)
I'll Meet You Halfway (1971)
I Think I Love You (1970)
I Woke Up in Love This Morning (1971)
Partridge Family, The (ABC sitcom)
cast: Danny Bonaduce (Danny Partridge)
David Cassidy (Keith Partridge)
Susan Dey (Laurie Partridge)
Shirley Jones (Shirley Partridge)
dog: 6 Simone
...__ partridge in a pear tree: 4 and a
parts
auto ~ brand: 4 Fram, NAPA
it had three ~: 4 Gaul
remove vital ~: 3 gut **4** sack **5** rifle **6** ravage **7** destroy, pillage, plunder, ransack **8** clean out, decimate
sum of the ~: 5 whole
unknown: 5 about **6** around **9** scattered, somewhere
__ parts: 4 auto
Part-Time Lover (1985 song)
artist: Stevie Wonder
parturition: 5 birth
party: 2 do **3** bee, GOP, set, tea **4** ball, band, bash, bloc, body, crew, fest, fete, gala, luau, prom, rave, ring, side, team, unit **5** actor, agent, blast, cabal, dance, feast, group, junta, junto, revel, salon, spree, squad, treat, troop, Whigs **6** affair, dinner, fiesta, league, outfit, person, regale, social, soiree, troupe **7** banquet, blowout, carry on, combine, company, coterie, faction, jubilee, Liberal, potluck, revelry, shindig **8** barbecue, function, jamboree, litigant, luncheon, visitors, wingding **9** amusement, Bull Moose, celebrate, coalition, coming-out, defendant, diversion, festivity, gathering, have a ball, make merry, plaintiff, reception, whoop it up **10** contractor, Democratic, detachment, electorate, have a blast, individual, persuasion
19th-century ~: 4 Whig
bachelor ~: 4 stag
be a ~ to: 4 abet, plot **8** conspire
big shot: 4 whip **9** candidate
birthday ~ item: 4 cake, gift **6** candle **7** present
British political ~: 6 Labour
cheese: 4 Brie, Edam **5** Gouda
costume ~: 10 masquerade
debutante's ~: 4 ball
dinner ~: 5 feast **7** banquet
drink: 4 beer, wine **5** punch **9** champagne
elephant ~: 3 GOP
evening ~: 4 ball **6** soiree
food: 3 dip **4** cake, nuts, pâté **5** chips, salsa, tarts **6** caviar, olives, pastry **7** canapés, cashews, Cheetos, peanuts, popcorn **8** brownies, crackers, crudités, pretzels **10** macadamias
frat ~: 4 stag **5** mixer
give a ~ for: 4 fete **5** honor **7** lionize **9** celebrate, entertain
hearty: 5 revel **9** have a ball, whoop it up
injured ~: 6 sucker, victim **9** scapegoat
Israeli political ~: 5 Likud, Mapam
join the ~: 4 be at **6** appear, attend, drop in, make it, show up **9** accompany
leader's goal: 5 unity
life of the ~: 3 wag, wit **4** card **5** mixer **6** joiner
line: 8 platform
memento: 5 favor
old-fashioned ~: 3 bee **6** social **7** potluck
Palermo ~: 5 festa
paper: 5 crape, crepe
pick: 5 slate **9** candidate
Polynesian ~: 4 luau
pooper: 4 bore, drip **10** wet blanket
quilting ~: 3 bee
search ~: 5 posse
site: 5 yacht **8** ballroom **9** frat house
staple: 3 keg
supply a ~: 5 cater
throw a ~: 4 host **6** regale **7** splurge **9** celebrate, entertain
thrower: 4 host **6** cohost
thrower plea: 4 RSVP
to: 4 in on
wedding ~ member: 5 bride, groom, usher **7** best man **10** bridesmaid, flower girl, ring bearer **11** maid of honor
wedding ~ members: 6 family **7** kinfolk
wild ~: 4 bash **5** blast **6** bustup **7** blowout **8** wingding
party __: 3 man **4** girl, line, whip **6** animal, pooper
__ party: 3 hen, keg, tea, war **4** frat, lawn **5** block, Green, house, major, minor, third **6** bridal, garden, pajama, search **7** costume, slumber
Party __: 4 Doll, Girl, Wire **6** Lights
__ Party: 5 Beach, House, It's My **6** Pajama
Party Doll (1957 song)
artist: Buddy Knox with the Rhythm Orchids, Steve Lawrence
partygoer: 5 guest **7** invitee **8** attendee
Party Lights (1962 song)
artist: Claudine Clark
Partyman (1989 song)
artist: Prince
Party of Five (Fox drama)
cast: Neve Campbell (Julia Salinger)
Lacey Chabert (Claudia Salinger)
Matthew Fox (Charlie Salinger)
Jennifer Love Hewitt (Sarah Reeves)
Jacob Smith (Owen Salinger)
Scott Wolf (Bailey Salinger)
Party's Over, The
composer: Jule Styne
Parvati: 7 goddess
consort: 4 Siva **5** Shiva
devotee: 5 Hindu **6** Hindoo
parvenu: 5 yahoo **6** nobody **7** upstart, wannabe **9** arriviste, latecomer, nonentity, vulgarian
pas: 4 step **9** dance step
de deux: 5 dance
faux ~: 4 slip **5** boner, error, gaffe, wrong **6** bêtise, boo-boo, howler, slip-up **7** blooper, blunder, misstep, mistake **8** indecoru **9** gaucherie
make a faux ~: 3 err **4** flub, goof, muff, slip, trip **5** botch, lapse, stray **6** boo-boo, bungle, foul up, fumble, mess up, slip up **7** blunder, go wrong, louse up, misstep, stumble **8** go astray
seul: 5 dance
pas __: 4 allé, d'âne, seul
__ pas: 4 faux
__ pas?: 6 n'est-ce
__ pasa?: 3 Qué
__ Pasa: 8 El Condor
Pasadena: 4 city, town
happening: 6 parade
locale: 5 Texas **10** California
parade flower: 4 rose
Pascagoula: 4 city, town
locale: 4 Miss.
Pascal: 8 language
alternative: *see* computer language
predecessor: 5 Algol
Pascal, Blaise: 6 French, writer **11** philosopher
work: Pensées
Pasch: 5 Pesah **6** Easter, Pesach **8** Passover
season: 6 spring
paschal __: 4 lamb
Pasdar: 6 Adrian
pas de __: 4 chat, côté, deux **5** trois **6** basque, cheval, quatre **7** bourrée
Pas de Deux
artist: Erté
pas-de-deux sequence: 6 adagio
Pas de 'Duke' choreographer: 5 Ailey
pas du __: 4 tout
pase: 8 veronica
paseo: 4 walk **6** avenue, stroll **9** boulevard, promenade
Paseo: 3 car **4** auto **6** Toyota
pasha: 5 ruler **6** gerent
Tunis ~: 3 dey
__ Pasha: 3 Ali **5** Enver
Pasiphae: 4 moon
daughter: 7 Ariadne, Phaedra
father: 6 Helios
husband: 5 Minos
planet: 7 Jupiter
sister: 5 Aeaea, Circe, Kirke
paso __: 5 doble
Paso __, CA: 6 Robles
__ Paso: 5 Old El
paso doble: 5 dance
Pasolini, Pier Paolo: 7 Italian **8** director
__ Pasquale: 3 Don
pasquinade: 7 lampoon **10** caricature
pass: 2 go, OK **3** bye, gap **4** comp, fade, fare, flow, go by, jump, okay, skip, visa **5** adopt, badge, bandy, enact, excel, fly by, gorge, lapse, lunge, offer, outdo, paper, pinch, reach, serve, shoot, spend, stage, state **6** accept, aerial, befall, crisis, defile, elapse, exceed, hack it, perish, permit, plight, ratify, ravine, roll on, strait, ticket, vote in **7** advance, approve, decline, excrete, freebee, freebie, glide by, go ahead, let have, license, proceed, promote, qualify, refrain, refusal, run over, sneak by, succeed, suffice, surpass **8** blow over, exigence, exigency, free ride, furlough, go beyond, graduate, hand over, juncture, outshine, outstrip, overlook, overtake, overture, sanction, surmount, transfer, transmit **9** admission, emergency, get around, legislate, rejection, situation, transcend, transpire **10** free ticket, transferal
a bill: 5 adopt, enact
allow to ~: 5 let by
along: 4 send **5** relay
as: 7 imitate **9** represent
as time: 5 spend, while
bring to ~: 5 cause **6** ask for **7** achieve **10** effectuate
by: 2 go **3** fly **4** tick **5** spurn **6** elapse, ignore, reject, roll on **7** neglect **8** overlook **9** disregard
catcher: 3 end
come to ~: 2 be **4** fall **5** break, ensue, occur **6** befall, betide, happen, pan out, turn up **9** eventuate, intervene, take place, transpire
easily: 3 ace
ender: 3 ade, age, ion, ive, key **4** book, port, word
for: 8 look like, resemble
free ~: 4 comp **6** ticket
gambler's ~: 5 no bet
in baseball: 4 walk

in football: **4** bomb **6** aerial, looper, spiral **7** lateral
judgment: **4** jail, rule **6** punish **7** censure, condemn, convict, put away **8** imprison, penalize, sentence
let ~: **5** allow **6** wink at **7** forgive, neglect **8** overlook **9** disregard
matador ~: **5** faena
mountain ~: **3** col, gap **4** ghat **5** ghaut, notch **6** defile
mountain ~ info: **4** elev. **8** altitude **9** elevation
muster: **4** suit **6** hack it **7** qualify, satisfy
not ~: **4** fail **5** flunk
off: **5** foist **7** palm off
on: **4** skip, veto, will **5** forgo, refer, relay, spurn **6** convey, forego, hand in, impart, perish, rebuff, reject, report **7** dismiss, exclude, kick off **8** disallow, hand down, relegate, transfer, transmit, turn down, turn over **9** blackball, cast aside, repudiate
out: **4** deal, give, zonk **5** faint, issue, sleep, swoon **6** assign, go limp, ration **7** divvy up **8** black out, disburse, dispense, fall over, keel over **10** distribute
over: **4** jump, lick, miss, omit, skip, snub, span **5** clear, cross, elide **6** except, forget, ignore **7** exclude, lose out, neglect **8** discount, go across, leave out, overlook **9** disregard
pretty ~: **4** mess, spot **5** pinch **6** crisis, pickle **7** trouble **8** hot water, quandary **10** difficulty **11** predicament
quietly: **5** creep, slink, steal **6** tiptoe **7** slither
slowly: **3** lag **4** drag
starter: **3** sur **4** over **5** under
take a ~ at: **3** try **7** attempt
the buck: **5** blame, refer **6** accuse
the hat: **3** beg **7** collect, solicit **9** fundraise
the time idly: **4** bask, laze, loaf **6** trifle **8** vegetate
the word: **4** tell **6** inform
through: **4** seep, sift **6** filter **8** permeate, traverse **9** negotiate, penetrate, percolate
tournament ~: **3** bye
up: **4** lose, miss, omit, shun, skip, snub **5** forgo, spurn, waive **6** forego, ignore, rebuff, refuse, reject **7** abstain, decline, dismiss, lose out, refrain **8** brush off, forswear, keep from **9** foreswear
__ pass: **4** late
Pass __: **4** it on, Me By
__ Pass: **3** Ute **5** Mitla **6** Donner, Khyber **7** Brenner
passable: **2** OK **4** fair, okay, open, so-so, tidy **6** decent, medium **7** average, livable **8** adequate, all right, drivable, liveable, mediocre, middling, moderate, traveled, very well **9** navigable, tolerable, unblocked, unnotable **10** acceptable, accessible, admissible, fairly good
passably: **8** very well
passacaglia: **5** dance
passage: **3** run, way **4** duct, exit, fare, flow, hall, lane, lift, line, path, road, text, trek, trip, visa, walk **5** aisle, alley, canal, lapse, lobby, piece, quote, route, shaft, verse **6** access, artery, avenue, clause, course, motion, strait, street, ticket, travel, tunnel, voyage **7** channel, conduit, excerpt, extract, freedom, hallway, ingress, journey, opening, section, transit, warrant **8** alleyway, citation, corridor, crossing, entrance, sentence **9** concourse, enactment, paragraph, quotation, transport, vestibule **10** acceptance, admittance, recitation, transition
air ~: **4** duct, flue, vent **7** chimney
brain ~: **4** iter
drainage ~: **5** ditch **6** trench
elevator ~: **5** shaft
ender: **3** way **4** work
horizontal ~: **4** adit **6** tunnel
literary ~: **5** quote **8** citation **9** quotation
mine ~: **4** adit **5** shaft **6** tunnel
monk's ~: **4** slip **5** slype
musical ~: **4** coda
nasal ~: **5** sinus
right of ~: **6** access
theater ~: **5** aisle
to the sea: **3** ria **5** creek, inlet, river **6** stream **9** tributary
trolley ~: **4** fare **5** token
underground ~: **4** cave, pipe **5** drain, sewer **6** cavern, grotto **7** conduit, culvert **8** lava tube
water ~: **4** duct, hose, pipe **8** aqueduct
white-water ~: **5** chute, rapid
Passage of Arms, A
author: Eric Ambler
Passage, The
author: Vance Palmer
Passage to India, A: **5** novel
author: E.M. Forster
character: **4** Aziz **5** Adela, Cecil **6** Stella
director: David Lean
subject: **3** Raj
passageway: **3** gap **4** door, duct, exit, gate, hall, lane, path **5** aisle, alley, canal, lobby, shaft, track, trail **6** access, arcade, strait, tunnel **7** channel, ingress, opening **8** corridor, entrance **9** concourse, vestibule
covered ~: **4** stoa **6** arcade, bridge **7** gallery
vertical ~: **3** rod **4** axis, beam, pole, post **5** pylon, stalk **6** column, pillar
Passaic: **4** city, town
locale: **9** New Jersey
Passamaquoddy __: **3** Bay
passant
en ~: **7** by the by **8** by the way **9** in passing
en ~ capture: **4** pawn
Passat: **2** VW **3** car **4** auto **10** automobile, Volkswagen
passbook
holder: **5** saver
information: **7** account, balance, deposit **8** interest **10** withdrawal
passe-__: **7** partout
passé: **3** old, out **4** dull **5** corny, dated, dowdy, fusty, hoary, hokey, musty, stale, trite, vapid **6** bygone, common, démodé, jejune, old hat **7** ancient, antique, archaic, clichéd, disused, extinct, fatuous, fogyish, has-been, humdrum, old-time, outworn, prosaic **8** bromidic, movement, obsolete, outdated, outmoded, out of use, timeworn, unusable **9** forgotten, hackneyed, moss-grown, out of date, prosaical **10** antiquated, gone to seed, out of style, superseded, uninspired, unoriginal
passel: **3** lot, ton **4** lots, many, raft, slew **5** batch, bunch, crowd, group, horde **6** divers, myriad, umteen, untold **7** copious, profuse, umpteen **8** abundant, manifold, numerous **9** bountiful, countless, quite a few
passenger: **4** fare, ride **5** rider **7** arrival, voyager **8** commuter, traveler, wayfarer **9** journeyer **10** hitchhiker
limo ~: **3** VIP
payment: **4** fare, pass **5** token **6** ticket
rail company: **6** Amtrak **9** Via Canada
ship: **5** ferry, liner **7** steamer **9** freighter **10** cruise ship
taxi ~: **4** fare
vehicle: **3** bus, car, van **4** auto, boat, ship **5** ferry, train, truck **6** jitney
Passenger 57 (1992 film)
cast: Tom Sizemore, Wesley Snipes
passengers: **7** traffic
disgorge ~: **6** let off, unload **7** deplane, detrain
where ~ wait: **5** depot, lobby **6** lounge **7** bus stop **8** sidewalk, terminal
passe-partout: **3** key
Passepartout to Phileas Fogg: **5** valet
passer
baton ~ race: **5** relay
forged-check ~: **5** kiter
rush the ~: **5** blitz
touchdown ~: **11** quarterback
__ passer: **4** buck
Passer: **4** Ivan
passerby: **6** looker **10** pedestrian
passerine: **4** bird **5** finch, pitta, vireo **6** becard, drongo, oriole **7** bunting, manakin, swallow **8** leafbird, lyrebird, ovenbird, starling **9** broadbill, currawong, sharpbill **10** tailorbird
__ Passes: **5** Pippa
passes, informally: **3** tix
__ pass GO: **5** Do not
__ passim: **3** sic
passing: **3** end **5** brief, short **6** demise, mortal, slight **7** cursory **8** fleeting, fugitive, temporal **9** ephemeral, momentary, temporary, transient **10** evanescent, pro tempore, short-lived, transition, transitory, unenduring
fancy: **3** fad **4** rage, urge, whim **5** craze, mania, quirk **6** notion, vagary **7** caprice, impulse **8** crotchet
grade: **3** cee
in ~: **7** by the by **8** by the way
through: **7** migrant, nomadic **9** migratory
passing __: **4** lane, shot **5** fancy
passion: **3** yen **4** élan, fire, fury, heat, itch, love, rage, urge, will, zeal, zest **5** amour, anger, ardor, craze, crush, drive, fancy, fever, flame, gusto, mania, storm, wrath **6** desire, fervor, frenzy, liking, misery, spirit, temper, thirst, warmth **7** beloved, craving, ecstasy, emotion, feeling, impulse, rapture, romance **8** ambition, appetite, delirium, devotion, fervency, fondness, interest, lyricism, rabidity, violence, weakness **9** adoration, affection, appetence, intensity, life force, obsession, sensation, sentiment, suffering, transport, vehemence **10** attachment, dedication, enthusiasm
ender: **3** ate **4** less, tide **5** fruit **6** flower
feel ~ for: **4** love, want **5** adore **6** desire **7** idolize
goddess of ~: **5** Venus **9** Aphrodite
god of ~: **4** Amor, Eros
infuse with ~: **4** vamp **5** charm, flirt **6** enamor **7** beguile, enchant **8** entrance **9** transport
without ~: **5** icily **6** calmly, coldly, coolly
passion __: **4** play
Passion: **7** musical
composer: Stephen Sondheim
Passion (1980 song)
artist: Rod Stewart
Passion __: **4** Fish, Play, Week **6** Sunday
Passion According to St. John
composer: J.S. Bach
Passion According to St. Matthew
composer: J.S. Bach
passionate: **3** hot **4** avid, deep, keen, warm, wild **5** eager, fiery, heavy **6** ardent, devout, fervid, fierce, gung-ho, hearty, heated, loving, red-hot, steamy, stormy, strong, sultry, torrid, urgent **7** amatory, amorous, aroused, blazing, burning, earnest, excited, fervent, flaming, furious, glowing, hugging, intense, kissing, lyrical, violent, zealous **8** desirous, eloquent, forceful, frenzied, headlong, inflamed, romantic, spirited, stirring, turned-on, vehement, wild-eyed **9** amatorial, emotional, excitable, exuberant, heartfelt, hotheaded, impetuous, impulsive, inspiring, thrilling **10** compulsive, expressive, hot-blooded
Passion Fish (1992 film)
cast: Mary McDonnell, David Strathairn, Alfre Woodard
director: John Sayles
passionflower fruit: **10** granadilla
passionfruit: **6** maypop
passionless: **3** icy **4** cold, cool **6** frigid **7** ice-cold
Passion of Anna, The (1969 film)
cast: Bibi Andersson, Liv Ullmann, Max von Sydow
director: Ingmar Bergman
Passion of Molly T, The
author: Lawrence Sanders

Passion Play
author: Jerzy Kosinski
passive: **3** lax **4** idle, lazy, logy, meek **5** inert, moony, slack, voice **6** asleep, docile, draggy, frigid, latent, static, stolid, torpid **7** dormant, servile **8** enduring, inactive, indolent, lamblike, lifeless, listless, obedient, resigned, slothful, sluggish, stagnant, yielding **9** apathetic, compliant, lethargic, quiescent, receptive, sedentary, tractable **10** disengaged, nonviolent, phlegmatic, submissive, unreactive
be ~: **5** sit by **6** ignore, submit **7** tune out **8** vegetate
protest: **5** sit-in
restraint: **6** airbag
passiveness: **8** laziness, lethargy, meekness **10** compliance, submission
passivity: **7** laxness
__ Passos: **3** Dos **7** John Dos
Passover: **5** Pasch
beverage: **4** wine
bread: **5** matzo **6** matzah, matzoh
meal: **5** seder
prayer: **6** Hallel
time from ~ to Shavuoth: **4** omer
passport: **2** ID **6** entrée, ID card, papers, permit, ticket
automobile ~: **6** carnet
department: **5** State
entry: **5** stamp
requirement: **5** photo **7** picture **8** snapshot **10** photograph
stamp: **4** visa
Passport: **3** SUV **5** Honda
pass the __: **3** hat **4** buck, time **5** torch
password: **3** key **4** word **6** parole, signal **9** watchword **10** open sesame
enter one's ~: **5** log in
know the ~: **5** enter, get in **6** access
preceder: **6** user ID
Password: **8** game show
host: Allen Ludden
past: **3** ago, eld, old **4** done, gone, late, lost, once, over, time, yore **5** ended, prior **6** beyond, bygone, former, gone by, lapsed, recent **7** defunct, earlier, elapsed, history, long ago, old-time, one-time, quondam, through **8** anterior, back then, back when, finished, foregone, long gone, obsolete, old times, outgoing, previous, years ago **9** antiquity, erstwhile, foregoing, forgotten, olden days, out-of-date, preceding, yesterday **10** historical, out of style, yesteryear
behavior: **4** file **6** record **7** dossier
brush ~: **5** graze, touch
dig into the ~: **6** recall **8** remember
due: **4** late **5** tardy **6** behind, unpaid
edge ~: **4** inch **5** sidle, skirt
events: **6** annals **7** account, history **9** chronicle, olden days, posterity, recountal
from ages ~: **3** old **5** early, hoary, of old, olden **7** ancient **8** primeval **9** primitive, venerable **10** primordial
from years ~: **3** old **6** bygone **7** archaic **8** outmoded
get ~: **3** ace **4** beat **5** clear, outdo, score, steer **6** detour **7** resolve **8** maneuver, outstrip, overtake **9** negotiate
go ~: **4** omit, skip **6** exceed **9** overshoot
graze ~: **5** brush, touch
in the ~: **3** ago, ere **4** once, then **6** before, erenow **7** long ago **8** formerly **9** at one time, a while ago **10** heretofore, previously
it flows ~ the Winter Palace: **4** Neva
it may be ~: **5** tense
its prime: **3** old **5** moldy, passé, stale **7** has-been
master: **4** guru **5** adept **6** expert, old pro
object from the ~: **4** idol **5** mummy, relic, stele **6** fossil, scroll **7** antique **8** artifact
play ~: **6** forget, ignore **8** overlook
prefix: **4** para- **6** preter-
recent ~: **7** just now **8** last week, last year **9** last month, yesterday **10** not long ago
slip ~: **4** edge
story of the ~: **4** epic, myth, saga, tale **6** legend
the deadline: **4** late
past __: **3** due **5** tense **6** master **7** perfect
pasta: **4** carb, orzo, ziti **5** carbo, penne, tubes, zitti **6** ditali, elbows, noodle, rigati, shells **7** fusilli, gnocchi, lasagna, lasagne, noodles, pastina, ravioli, rotelle, spirals **8** bucatini, couscous, farfalle, linguine, linguini, macaroni, rigatoni **9** agnolotti, alphabets, angelhair, cavatelli, manicotti, spaghetti **10** cannelloni, conchiglie, fettuccine, fettuccini, tagliarini, tortellini, vermicelli
alternative: **4** rice **6** potato **8** potatoes
bow tie ~: **8** farfalle
flat ~: **6** noodle **7** lasagna, lasagne **8** linguine, linguini **10** fettuccini
granular ~: **4** orzo **8** couscous
half-moon ~: **9** agnolotti
in brand names: **4** Roni
Japan ~: **4** udon
Japanese ~: **5** ramen **6** larmen
long ~: **9** angelhair, spaghetti **10** vermicelli
maker's need: **5** flour
maker's wheat: **5** durum
on a Chinese menu: **4** mein
order: **7** al dente
pellet-sized ~: **6** farfel
ricelike ~: **4** orzo
ring-shaped ~: **10** tortellini
shape: **5** elbow, shell **6** bowtie
shell ~: **9** cavatelli
square pocket ~: **7** ravioli
tiny piece of ~: **7** pastina
topping: **5** herbs, pesto, sauce **6** cheese **8** marinara, Parmesan **9** meatballs
tube ~: **4** ziti **5** penne, zitti **9** manicotti **10** cannelloni
pasta __: **5** sauce **6** fazool
pasta al __: **5** dente
pasta sauce: **4** Ragú **5** Prego **6** Prince **8** Classico **10** Newman's Own **11** Aunt Millie's
paste: **2** KO **3** fix, gem, goo, gum **4** bash, belt, bond, glue, mall, maul, pulp, rout, slug, sock, tack, verb, whup **5** affix, pound, stick **6** adhere, batter, cement, fasten, thrash, thwack, wallop **7** clobber, stickum, trounce **8** adhesive, fixative, mucilage
artist's ~: **5** gesso
edible ~: **5** guava **6** tomato
ender: **5** board
fruit used for ~: **5** guava
liver ~: **4** pâté
soybean ~: **4** miso, tofu
starter: **5** tooth
__ paste: **6** tomato **7** library
pastel: **4** pale, soft **5** light, muted **8** delicate
artist's ~: **5** chalk
color: **4** aqua, pink **5** lilac **8** baby-blue, lavender
Pasternak, Boris: **4** poet **6** writer **7** Russian **8** Nobelist
heroine: **4** Lara
work: Doctor Zhivago Safe Conduct
paste-up: **5** model
pasteurized: **4** pure **7** sterile
not ~: **3** raw
product: **4** milk **5** honey
pasteurizing
plant: **5** dairy **8** creamery
Pasteur, Louis: **7** chemist
Oscar-winner as ~: **4** Muni
pasticcio: **4** olio **6** medley **7** mélange **8** mishmash **9** potpourri **10** hodgepodge, miscellany, salmagundi
pastiche: **4** olio **6** jumble, medley **7** collage, lampoon, mélange **8** mishmash **9** patchwork, potpourri, synthesis, work of art **10** assortment, collection, cumulation, hodgepodge, miscellany, salmagundi
pastille: **6** troche **7** lozenge
pastime: **3** fun **4** game, play **5** hobby, sport **6** escape **7** pursuit **8** activity, interest, jump rope **9** amusement, avocation, diversion **10** recreation, relaxation
__ past is prologue: **5** What's
pastor: **4** abbé **5** padre, vicar **6** cleric, father, parson, priest, rector **8** chaplain, minister, preacher, reverend, shepherd **10** missionary
flock: **5** laity **8** faithful **9** laypeople
pastoral: **4** calm, idyl **5** idyll, rural **6** rustic, serene, silvan, simple, sylvan **7** bucolic, country, eclogue, idyllic, nomadic **8** agrarian, Arcadian, clerical, farmlike, tranquil **9** bucolical, episcopal **10** provincial
deity: **3** Pan **4** faun **8** Silvanus
far from ~: **5** urban **8** citified
poem: **4** idyl **5** idyll **7** eclogue
spot: **3** lea, ley **5** field, glade **6** meadow
pastoral __: **5** staff **6** letter, prayer
pastorale: **5** music
Pastorale d'__: **3** Été
Pastorals
author: Alexander Pope
Pastoral Symphony
composer: Ludwig van Beethoven
pastorate: **6** clergy
__ Pastore: **4** Il re
pastrami: **4** meat
partner: **3** rye
seller: **4** deli
pastry: **4** flan, puff, tart **5** donut, scone, torte, twist **6** churro, cornet, Danish, éclair, kuchen, phyllo, quiche **7** baklava, bear paw, beignet, cannoli, cruller, crumpet, fritter, pirogen, popover, rissole, strudel, timbale **8** bear claw, clafouti, crescent, doughnut, meringue, napoleon, roly-poly, rugalach, turnover **9** cream puff, croustade, madeleine, petit four, schnecken, sweet roll **10** baba au rhum, coffee roll, confection, feuilletée, frangipane, sopaipilla
cheese ~: **6** Danish
chef, at times: **4** icer
custard-filled ~: **6** éclair
filler: **3** jam **5** creme, fruit, jelly **7** custard
Mexican ~: **6** churro
pro: **4** chef, cook **5** baker
prune ~ filling: **6** lekvar
Queen of Hearts' ~: **4** tart
seller: **4** café **5** diner **6** bakery, eatery **10** coffee shop
tissue-thin ~: **4** filo
pastry __: **4** chef
__ pastry: **4** puff **6** Danish **7** toaster
pasturage: **3** hay **4** feed **7** verdure
pasture: **3** lea, ley, sod **5** field, grass, range, veldt **6** meadow **7** prairie, verdure **9** grassland
crop: **5** grass **6** clover, forage **7** alfalfa
divider: **5** fence **8** barb-wire **10** barbed wire
entry: **4** gate **5** stile
grass: **5** grama **6** fescue, redtop **7** festuca
grazer: **3** cow, ewe, ram **4** bull, calf, colt, foal, goat, mare, mule, pony **5** burro, filly, horse, llama, sheep **6** donkey **8** stallion
in poetry: **3** lea **4** mead
lands: **5** acres
plaint: **3** baa, maa, moo **5** bleat, neigh **6** hee-haw **7** whinney
pasty: **3** wan **4** ashy, dull, pale **5** ashen, gluey, livid, waxen, white **6** anemic, clayey, doughy, pallid, sallow, sickly **7** anaemic, clayish, greyish, meat pie **9** bloodless, unhealthy **10** exsanguine
pasty-__: **5** faced
P.A. system component: **3** amp
pat: **3** apt, dab, pet, rub, set, tap **4** daub, glib, lump, mold **5** flick, shape, slick, touch **6** caress, dollop, facile, fondle, smooth, soothe, stroke, tickle, timely **7** apropos, exactly, fitting **8** apposite, suitable **9** contrived, opportune, perfectly, precisely, rehearsed **10** flawlessly, stationary, understood
an infant: **4** burp
down: **4** tamp **5** frisk
dry: **4** blot
gently: **3** dab
get down ~: **4** know **5** learn **6** master **8** memorize

oneself on the back: 4 brag 5 boast, gloat 7 swagger
on the back: 4 hail, kudo, laud 5 exalt, extol, honor, kudos 6 credit, extoll, homage, praise, salute 7 acclaim, applaud, commend, flatter, glorify, plaudit, tribute 8 accolade, approval, encomium, flattery, good word 9 laudation, panegyric, patronize 10 compliment, exaltation, panegyrize
stand ~: 4 stay 6 endure, remain, resist 7 persist
pat ___: 4 down, hand
pat-___: 5 a-cake
___ pat: 5 stand
Pat: 3 Day 4 Cash, host 5 Boone, emcee, Nixon, Riley, Sajak 6 Conroy, Cooper, Corley, Hingle, Morita, O'Brien, Priest 7 Benatar, Buttram, Carroll, Crowley, Garrett, Lawford, Metheny, O'Connor, Paulsen 8 Buchanan, Moynihan, Oliphant, Sullivan 9 Robertson, Schroeder, Summerall
Pat ___ Mike: 3 and
pataca fraction: 3 avo
Patagonia
cowboy: 6 gaucho
locale: 9 Argentina
plain: 5 pampa 6 pampas
steer stopper: 4 bola
Pat and Mike (1952 film)
cast: Katharine Hepburn, Spencer Tracy
director: George Cukor
Pata Pata (1967 song)
artist: Miriam Makeba
Patapsco
city on the ~: 9 Baltimore
patch: 3 bed, fix, lot, sew 4 area, blob, blot, darn, mend, plot, spot, vamp 5 clump, cover, field, piece, resew, scrap, spell, strip, tract 6 cobble, doctor, emblem, garden, ground, iron-on, repair, stitch 7 cover up, insigne, restore, retread, stretch, touch up 8 appliqué, insignia, overhaul
berry ~ hazard: 4 bear 5 briar, brier, thorn 7 prickle
ender: 4 work
item in a ~: 3 pea 5 melon 10 watermelon
pavement: 5 retar
place for a ~: 4 knee
site: 3 jag, rip 4 hole, tear 5 split
starter: 5 cross
things up: 6 soothe 7 mollify, placate 9 reconcile 10 conciliate
up: 7 retouch
___ patch: 5 rough 6 iron-on
Patch: 3 Dan
Patch Adams (1998 film)
cast: Philip Seymour Hoffman, Robin Williams
patched: 3 old 4 worn 6 ragged 7 worn out
Patches (song)
artist: Clarence Carter, Dickey Lee
patching compound: 5 putty
___ Patch Kids: 7 Cabbage
Patch of Blue, A (1965 film)
cast: Elizabeth Hartman, Sidney Poitier, Shelley Winters
patchwork: 4 hash, olio 5 quilt 6 calico, jumble, medley, muddle, tangle 7 grab bag, mélange 8 disorder, mishmash, pastiche 9 checkered, confusion, makeshift, potpourri 10 hodgepodge, improvised, miscellany, salmagundi
product: 5 quilt
Patchwork Planet
author: Anne Tyler
patchy: 4 pied 6 fitful, random, spotty, uneven 7 erratic, sketchy, varying 8 speckled, variable 9 imperfect, irregular, piecemeal 10 nonuniform
pate: 4 head 5 crown 6 noggin
topper: 3 wig 4 fall, hair 6 toupee 7 tresses 9 hairpiece
pâté: 4 meat 5 paste 6 spread 9 appetizer
base: 4 foie 5 liver
Patek: 7 Freddie
Patek Philippe
competitor: *see* wristwatch
Patel: 3 Dev
patella: 4 bone 7 kneecap
locale: 4 knee
neighbor: 5 femur, tibia 6 fibula
paten: 5 plate
patent: 4 open 5 clear, gross, naked, overt, plain, stark 6 in view, marked, permit, public 7 blatant, evident, exposed, glaring, license, obvious, visible 8 apparent, clear-cut, distinct, explicit, flagrant, knowable, manifest, monopoly, palpable, registry, unhidden, unsubtle, unveiled 9 franchise, ownership 10 concession, monopolize, observable, undeniable, unshrouded
kin: 9 copyright, trademark
medicine: 5 tonic 6 elixir, remedy 7 panacea 8 snake oil
office: 3 PTO
subject: 6 device, gadget 9 discovery, invention
patent ___: 6 office 7 leather
patently: 8 markedly
true: 9 axiomatic
pater: 3 dad, pop 4 papa, pops 5 daddy, poppa 6 father 9 family man
daughter: 5 filia
partner: 5 mater
son: 6 filius
paternal: 4 male 6 agnate 8 fatherly, parental 10 protective
paternity: 6 source 10 fatherhood
paternity ___: 5 leave
Paterno, Joe: 5 coach
sport: 8 football
Paterson: 4 city, town
author: William Carlos Williams
locale: 9 New Jersey
Pater, Walter: 6 writer 7 British 8 essayist
path: 3 way 4 lane, line, road, slog, tack, walk 5 aisle, alley, byway, means, orbit, route, steps, track, trail 6 access, avenue, course 7 bikeway, footway, ingress, passage, walkway 8 approach, shortcut 9 concourse, direction, esplanade, itinerary
alternative ~: 5 shunt 6 detour
ball's ~: 3 arc
beaten ~: 3 rut 5 track, trail
bike ~: 4 lane
bridal ~: 5 aisle
bridle ~: 5 trail
car's ~: 4 lane, pike, road 5 alley 6 avenue, street 7 highway 8 turnpike 9 boulevard 10 expressway
Chinese ~: 3 Tao
circular ~: 3 arc 5 orbit
dirt ~: 5 track, trail
ender: 3 way 6 finder
flight ~: 6 airway, ascent 8 jet route
go off the beaten ~: 4 rove 5 stray 6 wander 7 explore
hiking ~: 5 trace, track, trail
in a glacier's ~: 5 stoss
lawnmower ~: 5 swath 6 swathe
lead up the garden ~: 7 deceive 8 misguide
lob ~: 3 bow 5 curve 8 crescent, half-moon
moon ~: 3 arc 5 orbit
off the ~: 4 lost 6 astray
off the beaten ~: 6 afield, remote
perplexing ~: 4 maze 9 labyrinth
planetary ~: 3 arc 4 oval 5 orbit
raised ~: 4 berm, dike 5 berme, levee 8 causeway 10 embankment
river ~: 4 flow 6 course 7 channel
satellite ~: 3 arc 5 orbit
scythe ~: 5 swath 6 swathe
sprinter's ~: 4 lane
starter: 3 tow, war 4 foot, tele 5 osteo
to success: 5 rungs 6 ladder
user: 5 hiker 6 walker 7 tourist 9 sightseer
wilderness ~: 5 trace, track, trail
___ path: 4 bike 5 glide 6 beaten, bridle, flight 7 bicycle, optical
Pathet ___: 3 Lao
pathetic: 3 sad 4 lame, poor, puny, weak 5 sorry, woful 6 crumby, crummy, feeble, meager, measly, moving, paltry, tragic, woeful 7 piteous, pitiful, tearful, useless 8 pitiable, poignant, touching, tragical, unusable, wretched 9 affecting, miserable, plaintive, sniveling, third-rate, worthless 10 deplorable, inadequate, lamentable
Pathétique Sonata
composer: Ludwig van Beethoven
Pathétique Symphony
composer: Peter Tchaikovsky
pathfinder: 5 guide, scout 7 pioneer 8 explorer 10 discoverer
Pathfinder: 3 SUV 5 probe 6 Nissan
destination: 4 Mars
launcher: 4 NASA
Pathfinder, The
author: James Fenimore Cooper
character: 5 Mabel, McNab, Natty 6 Bumppo, Jasper
path of ___ resistance: 5 least
Path of Dalliance
author: Auberon Waugh
pathogen: 4 germ 5 staph, toxin 7 microbe 9 bacterium
pathophobe fear: 7 disease
pathos: 4 pity 5 drama 7 emotion, feeling, sadness 8 sympathy 9 poignancy, sentiment 10 compassion, desolation, heavy heart
sign of ~: 4 sigh, tear
Paths of Glory (1957 film)
cast: Kirk Douglas, Ralph Meeker, Adolphe Menjou
director: Stanley Kubrick
Path to Rome, The
author: Hilaire Belloc
pathway: 4 lane, path, road, walk 5 alley, trace, track, trail 6 artery, avenue 7 channel, ingress 8 crossing
blood ~: 4 vein 6 artery 9 capillary
sloped ~: 4 ramp
supermarket ~: 5 aisle
winding ~: 4 maze 9 labyrinth
patience: 4 game, legs 5 poise 6 lenity, starch 8 calmness, card game, kindness, lenience, stoicism 9 diligence, endurance, fortitude, restraint, tolerance 10 equanimity, even temper, indulgence, moderation
cultivate ~: 4 wait 7 refrain 8 restrain
in America: 9 solitaire
lost one's ~: 5 had it 6 blew up 8 exploded 9 blew a fuse 10 came down on
out of ~: 5 fed up 6 fuming
strain one's ~: 3 irk, try 5 weary 7 provoke
patience ___ saint: 3 of a
Patience
composer: W.S. Gilbert, Arthur Sullivan
Patience (1989 song)
artist: Guns N' Roses
Patience of a Saint
author: Andrew Greeley
Patience & Prudence
song: Tonight You Belong to Me (1956)
patient: 4 calm, case, meek, mild 5 stoic, type B 6 client, dogged, gentle, inmate, serene, shut-in, steady 7 stoical, subject 8 enduring, examinee, resigned, resolute, sufferer, tolerant, untiring 9 easygoing, forgiving, unruffled 10 forbearing, outpatient, unflagging
attendant: 2 RN 4 aide 5 nurse 6 doctor, medico 7 orderly 9 physician
be ~: 3 sit 4 wait 5 await 6 endure, hang on 7 refrain, stand by
pediatrician ~: 3 kid, tot 4 baby 5 child, minor 6 infant 9 youngster
place: 6 clinic 8 hospital 9 ambulance
response: 2 ow 3 aah, yow 4 ouch 6 aaargh
vet ~: 3 cat, cow, cur, dog, ewe, hog, pet, pig, pup, ram, sow 4 bull, calf, colt, foal, goat, lamb, mare, mutt, pony 5 horse, hound, kitty, pooch, puppy, pussy, sheep, tabby 6 animal, canine, feline, kitten, parrot 7 mongrel 8 stallion
patient-care group: 3 HMO
Patientia: 8 asteroid
___ Patient, The: 7 English
patina: 4 film, rust 5 glaze, oxide, sheen, shine 6 finish 7 coating
Patinkin, Mandy: 5 actor
film: The Adventures of Elmo in Grouchland (1999)

Daniel (1983)
Impromptu (1991)
Maxie (1985)
The Princess Bride (1987)
Squanto: A Warrior's Tale (1994)
Yentl (1983)
TV: Chicago Hope
patio: 4 yard 5 court 9 courtyard, peristyle
appliance: 5 grill 6 hot tub 7 hibachi
block: 5 paver
cousin: 4 deck 5 lanai
enclosed ~: 5 court 6 atrium 9 courtyard
furniture: 5 chair, swing, table 6 chaise, glider 8 umbrella
on the ~: 7 outside 8 al fresco, outdoors
server: 4 cart
site: 4 lawn, yard
patisserie: 6 bakery
offering: 4 tart 5 tarte 6 éclair, gateau, pastry 9 cream puff
Pátmos: 4 isle 6 island
locale: 6 Greece
Patna: 4 city, town
locale: 5 India
river: 6 Ganges
state: 5 Behar, Bihar
patois: 4 cant, talk 5 argot, gumbo, idiom, lingo, slang 6 jargon, patter, tongue 7 dialect 8 language, localism, parlance 9 academese 10 vernacular
Paton, Alan: 6 writer 12 South African
work: Cry, the Beloved Country
pat on the __: 4 back
__ Patri: 6 Gloria
__ patriae: 4 amor
patriarch: 4 male, rank 5 elder, title 6 bishop, cleric, father, senior 9 graybeard 10 forebearer
deputy: 6 exarch
patriarchal: 6 lineal 9 ancestral
Patric: 5 Jason 7 Knowles
Patricia: 4 Neal 5 Ellis, Nixon 6 Heaton, Wettig 8 Arquette, Clarkson, Cornwell, Kalember 9 Highsmith, Schroeder 10 Richardson
patrician: 4 peer 5 baron, noble, royal 6 aristo 8 highborn, nobleman, well-born, well-bred 9 blue blood, gentleman 10 aristocrat, upper-class, upper-crust
opposite: 4 pleb 5 slave 6 common, humble 7 plebian 8 commoner 10 lower-class
patricians: 5 lords 6 gentry 7 peerage 8 nobility 10 upper class 11 aristocracy
Patrick: 4 Gail, John 5 Butch, Duffy, Ewing, Henry, Leahy, Magee, Nigel, O'Neal, saint, White 6 Dennis, Macnee, O'Brian, Rafter, Robert, Swayze 7 Cassidy, Dempsey, Stewart 8 Blackett, McGoohan 9 Kavanaugh
in Irish: 7 Padraic, Padraig
Patrick, Saint
land: 4 Eire, Erin 7 Ireland
service: 4 Mass
Patrick's Day, Saint
color: 5 green
dance: 3 jig
month: 5 March
musician: 5 piper
patrimony: 6 estate, legacy 7 bequest
patriot: 4 hawk 5 jingo 8 jingoist, loyalist 9 flag-waver
ender: 3 ism
Patriot Day's month: 5 April
Patriot Games (1992 film)
cast: Anne Archer, Harrison Ford
character: 4 Ryan
org.: 3 IRA
patriotic: 4 true 5 loyal 7 hawkish 9 right-wing 10 flag-waving, jingoistic
organization: 3 DAR, SAR
song: 6 anthem
symbol: 4 flag
Patriotic Gore
author: Edmund Wilson
patriotism: 7 loyalty 8 jingoism
Patriot missile: 3 ABM
target: 4 Scud
Patriots: 4 team 6 eleven
home: 6 Boston 10 New England
org.: 3 AFC, NFL
rival: *see* NFL team
sport: 8 football
Patriot, The (2000 film)
cast: Chris Cooper, Mel Gibson, Heath Ledger, Joely Richardson
patrol: 3 spy 4 beat, pace, walk 5 guard, scout, watch 6 cruise, defend, detail, picket, police, rounds 7 inspect, lookout, protect 8 sentinel, squadron 9 keep watch, safeguard 10 detachment
boat: 5 aviso
ender: 3 man, men 5 woman, women
one on ~: 3 cop 6 sentry 7 lookout, officer 9 policeman 11 policewoman
what a ~ car might get: 3 APB
patrol __: 3 car 4 boat 5 wagon
__ patrol: 5 shore 7 highway
__ Patrol: 3 Rat
patrolman: 3 cop 4 fuzz 6 Smokey 7 trooper
__ Patrol, The: 4 Dawn, Lost
patron: 4 user 5 angel, buyer, donor, urger 6 backer, client, friend, helper, vendee, votary 7 admirer, booster, grantor, habitué, shopper, sponsor 8 champion, customer, financer 9 guarantor, proponent, purchaser, supporter 10 benefactor, frequenter, well-wisher
diner ~: 5 eater
ender: 3 age, ess
patron __: 5 saint
patronage: 3 aid 4 egis, help 5 aegis, grant, trade 6 buying, custom 7 backing, funding, keeping, subsidy, support, traffic 8 auspices, business, commerce, cronyism, regulars, shopping 9 clientele, financing, following, promotion 10 assistance, pork barrel, protection
political ~: 4 pork
patronize: 3 use 4 back, fund 5 buy at, deign, favor, stoop, trust 6 foster, shop at 7 buy from, promote, sponsor, stoop to, support 8 deal with, frequent, purchase 9 cultivate, hang out at, shine up to, trade with 10 condescend, look down on, talk down to
a restaurant: 3 eat 4 dine 5 order
patronizing: 5 lofty 6 lordly, snobby, snooty 7 haughty, high-hat 8 snobbish, superior
patron of the __: 4 arts
patrons: 8 habitués, regulars 9 clientele, following
soup-kitchen ~: 4 poor 5 needy 8 homeless
patron saints
accountants: Matthew
actors: Genesius
airline passengers: Joseph of Cupertino
Americas: Rose of Lima
anesthetists: Rene Goupil
animals: Francis of Assisi
archers: Sebastian
architects: Barbara, Thomas
arthritis: James the Greater
astronauts: Joseph of Cupertino
astronomers: Dominic
aviators: Our Lady of Loreto, Therese of Lisieux
bachelors: Casimir of Poland
bad weather: Medard, Scholastica
bakers: Elizabeth of Hungary, Nicholas of Myra
bankers: Matthew
barbers: Cosmas, Damian, Louis IX, Martin de Porres
basket makers: Anthony the Abbot
bee keepers: Ambrose
beggars: Giles
bellringers: Agatha
blackbirds: Kevin
blacksmiths: Dunstan
blood banks: Januarius
bodily ills: Our Lady of Lourdes
bookbinders: Peter Celestine
booksellers: John of God
boys: John Bosco
brewers: Augustine
bricklayers: Stephen
brides: Nicholas of Myra
butchers: Anthony the Abbot
charities: Vincent de Paul
Chile: James the Greater
civil servants: Thomas More
comedians: Vitus
computer users: Isidore of Seville
contemplatives: John of the Cross
cooks: Lawrence, Martha
cows: Perpetua
dancers: Vitus
dentists: Apollonia
disasters: Genevieve
dogs: Hubert, Roch
domestic animals: Antony
doves: David
drought relief: Godeberta, Herbert
earaches: Polycarp
ecologists: Francis of Assisi
embroiderers: Clare
England: George
epidemics: Godeberta
farmers: Isidore the Farmer
fear of rats and mice: Gertrude
fear of snakes: Patrick
firefighters: Florian
fire prevention: Lawrence
fishermen: Andrew, Peter
florists: Rose of Lima, Therese of Lisieux
flyers: Michael
foreign missions: Francis Xavier
France: Denis, Denys
gardeners: Adelard
glassworkers: Luke
goldsmiths: Dunstan
gout: Maurice
hairdressers: Martin de Porres
headaches: Denis, Denys, Teresa of Avila
horsemen: Martin of Tours
hospitals: John of God
housewives: Anne, Martha
Hungary: Elizabeth of Hungary
hunters: Eustachius, Hubert
in-law problems: Elizabeth Ann Seton
innkeepers: Amand
Ireland: Brigid, Patrick
Italy: Catherine of Siena
jewelers: Eligius
judges: John of Capistrano
jury members: John of Capistrano
knee problems: Roch
lambs: John the Baptist
lawyers: Mark
learning: Thomas Aquinas
librarians: Jerome
lions: Mark
longevity: Peter
lost articles: Anthony of Padua
lost causes: Jude
lost keys: Zita
lovers: Valentine
maids: Zita
marble workers: Clement
marriages: Edward the Confessor
married women: Monica
medical technicians: Albertus Magnus
metalworkers: Eligius
Mexico: Our Lady of Guadalupe
mothers: Anne
music: Cecilia, Gregory
Naples: Januarius
orators: John Chrysostom
painters: Luke
paratroopers: Michael
Paris: Genevieve
pawnbrokers: Nicholas of Myra
pharmacists: Cosmas, Damian
Philippines: Rose of Lima
physicians: Cosmas, Damian, Luke
plasterers: Bartholomew
poets: David
Poland: Florian
poor: Giles
postal workers: Gabriel the Archangel
pregnant women: Margaret
priests: John Vianney
prisoners: Dismas
racial harmony: Martin de Porres
radio: Gabriel the Archangel
resolving of schisms: Cyril, Methodius
rheumatism: James the Greater
sailors: Elmo
Scandinavia: Ansgar
schools: Thomas Aquinas
scientists: Albertus Magnus
sculptors: Claude
Serbia: Sava
servants: Martha
shepherds: Bernadette

PA

shoemakers: Crispin
silversmiths: Andronicus
sinners: Mary Magdalene
skaters: Lidwina
skiers: Bernard
snake bite victims: Hilary, Paul
soldiers: Ignatius, Joan of Arc, Martin of Tours
stonemasons: Stephen
students: Benedict
swordsmiths: Maurice
tax collectors: Matthew
taxi drivers: Fiacre
teenagers: Aloysius
television: Clare
theater: Genesius
thunderstorms: Barbara
travelers: Anthony of Padua, Christopher
undertakers: Joseph of Arimathea
volcanoes: Januarius
volunteers: Vincent de Paul
Wales: David
weavers: Maurice
winegrowers: Vincent of Saragossa
writers: Francis de Sales, John the Apostle
young girls: Agnes
patronymic: 4 name 7 surname 8 cognomen
patroons: 6 gentry
Pats
see Patriots
patsy: 4 butt, dupe, foil, goat, gull, lamb, mark, pawn, prey, tool 5 ninny 6 hunted, pigeon, puppet, stooge, target, victim 7 cat's-paw, doormat, fall guy, nebbish 8 easy mark, pushover 9 born loser, scapegoat, schlemiel
see also ninny
Patsy: 5 Cline, Kelly 6 Kensit
patten: 4 boot, shoe 8 footwear
patter: 3 gab, pad, tap, yak 4 beat, blab, cant, drum, jive, line, pelt, rain, talk 5 argot, lingo, pitch, prate, sound, spiel, spout 6 babble, jabber, jargon, patois, rustle, tattoo 7 chatter, pitapat, prattle, rat-a-tat 8 fast talk, hard sell 9 yakety-yak 10 chew the rag, vernacular
glib ~: 4 jive, line 5 pitch, spiel 6 come-on
prideful ~: 4 brag 5 boast
provider: 4 host 5 emcee 6 deejay, vee-jay 10 disc jockey
__-patter: 6 pitter
pattern: 3 rut 4 form, kind, mold, norm, plan, type 5 array, guide, model, motif, order, shape, style 6 custom, design, figure, follow, format, rhythm, sample, scheme, symbol, system 7 emulate, example, fashion, imitate, paragon, stencil, templet, variety 8 exemplar, markings, original, paradigm, specimen, standard, template 9 archetype, prototype 10 decoration, impression, stereotype, touchstone
behavior ~: 5 habit, type A, type B 8 syndrome
fabric ~: 4 dots 5 plaid, print 6 checks 9 polka dots 13 stripes. Argyle
holding ~: 5 delay
intricate ~: 4 maze 9 labyrinth
machine ~: 3 die
oneself after: 4 copy 5 model 6 follow 7 imitate
repetitive ~: 3 rut 5 cycle 6 series 7 routine
rhythmic ~ for a poet: 5 meter
Scottish ~: 5 plaid
speech ~: 6 accent, stress
statistical ~: 5 trend
transfer: 5 rub-on 6 iron-on
wavelike ~: 5 moiré
wood ~: 5 grain
__ pattern: 4 test 5 dress 7 holding
Patterns
author: Amy Lowell
Patterson: 5 Floyd, James 6 Melody
Patterson, Floyd: 5 boxer
milieu: 4 ring
Patti: 4 Page 5 Davis, Smith 6 Austin, Hansen, LuPone 7 Adelina, LaBelle
Patti, Adelina: 6 singer 7 soprano
specialty: 5 opera
Patton: 4 Will 6 George, Oswalt
Patton (1970 film)
cast: Karl Malden, George C. Scott
Patton, George: 7 general
dog: 6 Willie
superior: 3 DDE
vehicle: 4 tank
Patton, Will: 5 actor
film: Entrapment (1999)
Remember the Titans (2000)
Tollbooth (1994)
patty-__: 4 cake
Patty: 4 Berg, Duke 5 Smyth 6 Hearst 7 Andrews, Sheehan 8 Loveless
Patty Duke Show, The dog: 5 Tiger
pattypan: 6 squash, veggie 9 vegetable
paucis verbis: 7 briefly
paucity: 4 lack, need, want 6 dearth, famine 7 absence, fewness, poverty 8 exiguity, scarcity, shortage, sparsity 10 deficiency, inadequacy, meagerness, scantiness, sparseness
Paul: 3 Fix, Les 4 Anka, Berg, Ford, John, Klee, Leni, Muni, pope, Rudd, Sand, tsar 5 Billy, Boyer, Brown, Burke, Celan, Davis, Dirac, Drake, Dukas, Evans, Flory, Fusco, Green, Hayne, Heyse, Hogan, LeMat, Lukas, Lynde, Nurse, saint, Silas, Simon, Waner, Wylie, Young 6 Adrian, Almond, Annett, Auster, Bartel, Bogart, Bowles, Bunyan, Dooley, Dunbar, Éluard, Erdman, Harvey, Horgan, Karrer, Krasny, Kruger, Masson, Müller, Newman, Powell, Reiser, Revere, Valéry 7 apostle, Azinger, Balluet, Bourget, Carrack, Cézanne, Claudel, Creston, Crutzen, Czinner, Desmond, Douglas, Ehrlich, Gallico, Gauguin, Henreid, Hornung, Kantner, Mauriat, Molitor, pontiff, Reubens, Robeson, Shaffer, Sorvino, Stookey, Theroux, Tillich, Wendkos 8 Benedict, Brickman, Brinegar, Giamatti, Mazursky, Nicholas, Petersen, Sabatier, Schrader, Scofield, Verlaine, Warfield, Whiteman, Williams, Winchell, Winfield, Wolfgang 9 Alexandra, Greengard, Hindemith, McCartney, Morrissey, Prudhomme, Samuelson, Schneider, Verhoeven 10 Hindenburg
companion: 5 Demas, Silas, Titus 7 Artemas 8 Crescens
Paul __ Glaser: 7 Michael
Paul __ Hindenburg: 3 von
__ Paul: 3 Oom 4 Tall
Paula: 4 Cole, Zahn 5 Abdul 6 Devicq 8 Prentiss 10 Poundstone
author: Isabel Allende
__ Paula: 3 Hey
__, Paul and Mary: 5 Peter
Paul and Mary Ford, Les
song: Hummingbird (1955)
Paul and Paula
song: Hey Paula (1963)
Young Lovers (1963)
__-Paul Belmondo: 4 Jean
Paul, Billy
song: Me and Mrs. Jones (1972)
Paulette: 7 Goddard
Pauley, Jane
spouse: Garry Trudeau
__ Paul Getty: 4 Jean
__ Paul II: 4 John
Paulina: 9 Porizkova
Pauline: 4 Kael 7 Collins
adventure: 5 peril
author: Robert Browning
Pauling, Linus: 7 chemist 8 Nobelist
school: 7 Caltech
Pauli, Wolfgang: 8 Nobelist 9 physicist
__ Paul Jones: 4 John
__ Paul Kruger: 3 Oom
Paul, Les: 9 guitarist
tune: 4 Nola
__ Paul Marat: 4 Jean
Paul Michael __: 6 Glaser
__ Paulo: 3 Sao
Paul Pry: 7 meddler 8 quidnunc 9 buttinsky
Paul Revere's Ride
author: Henry Wadsworth Longfellow
__ Paul Rubens: 5 Peter
__-Paul Sartre: 4 Jean
Paul's Case
author: Willa Cather
Paulsen: 3 Pat 4 Axel 6 Albert
Pauly: 5 Shore
paunch: 3 gut 5 belly, bulge, tummy 7 abdomen, stomach 8 potbelly 9 bay window, beer belly, spare tire
paunchy: 5 beefy, fubsy, obese, plump, pudgy, pursy, stout 6 chubby, fleshy, portly, pyknic, rotund, stocky, zaftig, zoftig 7 adipose 8 roly-poly 9 corpulent 10 abdominous, overweight
pauper: 6 beggar 7 have-not 8 bankrupt, indigent 9 mendicant 10 supplicant
pauperism: 7 beggary 10 bankruptcy
pauperize: 5 break 6 reduce 8 straiten 10 impoverish
pauperized: 5 broke, needy 6 bad off, hard up, in need, in want 7 pinched 8 bankrupt, beggarly, homeless, indigent, strapped 9 destitute, insolvent, moneyless, penniless, penurious 10 down and out, straitened
pause: 3 gap 4 halt, hush, lull, rest, stay, stop, wait 5 break, cease, comma, delay, hitch, hover, lapse, letup, stand, tarry, truce, waver 6 boggle, breath, cesura, desist, freeze, hiatus, lacuna, loiter, recess 7 caesura, interim, leisure, reflect, respite, scruple, take ten, time out 8 abeyance, breather, call time, downtime, hesitate, intermit, interval, reprieve, take five 9 cessation, hesitancy, interlude, stalemate, vacillate 10 deliberate, hesitation, moratorium, standstill, suspension, take a break, think twice
Biblical ~: 5 selah
continue without ~: 5 segue 9 keep going
give ~: 3 cow 4 faze 5 alarm, daunt, deter, shake, worry 6 bemuse, dismay 7 overawe, unnerve 8 bewilder, dispirit, frighten 10 demoralize, discourage, dishearten, intimidate
indicator: 5 colon, comma 6 period 9 semi-colon
in music: 7 fermata
speaker's ~: 2 er, uh, um 3 hmm
that refreshes: 3 nap 6 catnap, siesta, snooze
Pavan: 6 Marisa
pavane: 5 dance, music
accompaniment: 4 lute
Pavarotti, Luciano: 5 tenor 6 singer 7 Italian
milieu: 5 opera
piece: 4 aria
pave: 3 tar 4 tile 7 encrust, incrust, surface 8 blacktop 9 resurface 10 macadamize
anew: 5 retar, retop 9 resurface
the way: 4 ease 5 ready, usher 6 enable, get set, smooth 9 introduce 10 facilitate
Pavel: 9 Cherenkov
pavement: 4 road 6 street 7 highway 8 concrete, shoulder, sidewalk
pound the ~: 4 walk 7 job-hunt
Pavese, Cesare: 4 poet 7 Italian
work: The House on the Hill
pavid: 5 timid 6 afraid, scared 7 fearful, quaking, shaking 9 terrified, trembling 10 frightened
pavilion: 4 tent 6 canopy, gazebo 7 pergola 9 bandshell
__ Pavilions, The: 3 Far
Pavin, Corey: 6 golfer
paving
flaw: 3 rut 4 bump 5 crack 7 pothole
hexagonal ~ stone: 5 favus
hexagonal ~ stones: 4 favi
job: 4 road 6 street 7 highway 8 shoulder, sidewalk
letters: 3 SLO 4 stop 6 detour 7 one-lane 10 lane closed
material: 3 tar 5 rebar 6 cement, gravel 7 asphalt 8 concrete
stone: 4 sett 5 favus 6 cobble
Pavlova, Anna: 6 dancer 8 danseuse
specialty: 6 ballet
Pavlov, Ivan: 7 Russian 8 Nobelist

Pavo: **7** Peacock **13** constellation
neighbor of: **3** Ara
paw: **3** pad, pes **4** foot, hand, hoof, maul, mitt **5** touch **6** claw at, molest **8** forefoot **9** manhandle
bottom: **3** pad **4** palm
starter: **4** cat's **5** south
pawl: **3** bar **5** catch **6** detent
pawn: **4** bond, dupe, gage, hock, mark, tool **5** agent, patsy, token **6** flunky, hunted, lackey, minion, pigeon, pledge, puppet, stooge, sucker, victim **7** cat's-paw, earnest, flunkey, forfeit, hostage, lacquey **8** borrow on, creature, guaranty, henchman, mortgage **9** assurance, guarantee, underling **10** chesspiece, collateral, instrument
ender: **4** shop **6** broker
pawnbroker: **6** lender
Pawnbroker, The (1965 film)
cast: Brock Peters, Rod Steiger
director: Sidney Lumet
pawned: **6** in hock
Pawnee: **5** Caddo, tribe **6** Indian **7** Amerind **8** language
cousin: **4** Erie
home: **4** tipi **5** tepee **6** teepee
Indian: **7** Arikara
pawpaw: **4** tree **5** fruit
family: **6** annona
relative: **7** soursop
Paw Paw: **4** city, town
locale: **8** Michigan
Pax
counterpart: **5** Irene
father: **7** Jupiter
Pax ___: **6** Romana
Paxinou, Katina: **7** actress
film: For Whom the Bell Tolls (1943, AA)
Paxton, Bill: **5** actor
film: Apollo 13 (1995)
The Evening Star (1996)
Mighty Joe Young (1998)
One False Move (1992)
A Simple Plan (1998)
Titanic (1997)
Trespass (1992)
Twister (1996)
Weird Science (1985)
TV: Big Love
pay: **3** fee **4** give, hire, wage **5** atone, bacon, bread, clear, fruit, money, put up, remit, spend, wages, yield **6** adjust, answer, ante up, chip in, defray, expend, fork up, income, kick in, lay out, pony up, profit, rebuke, refund, render, reward, salary, settle **7** bring in, cough up, dish out, fork out, redress, requite, revenue, satisfy, stipend, sweeten **8** be a sport, disburse, earnings, fork over, hand over, kick back, make good, pittance, proceeds, settle up, shell out, square up, take-home **9** allowance, discharge, emolument, indemnify, indemnity, liquidate, make money, plunk down, reimburse, retaliate **10** commission, compensate, emoluments, honorarium, make amends, perquisite, recompense, remunerate, reparation, take care of, underwrite
a call: **3** see **5** visit **6** drop by **10** come around
a premium for: **6** ensure, insure
as a bill: **4** foot
attention: **4** hark, hear, mark, mind, note **5** study, watch **6** harken, listen, notice, regard **7** hearken, look out, observe, respect
attention to: **3** sue, woo **4** tend **5** charm, court, flirt, spark **6** listen **9** visit with
back: **3** fix **5** repay **6** avenge, punish, refund, render, return **7** get even, revenge **8** make good, square up **9** indemnify, reimburse, retaliate **10** recompense
blackmail: **6** ransom
by mail: **5** remit
court to: **3** sue, woo **5** flirt, spark **6** call on
deduction: **3** tax **4** FICA
dirt: **3** ore **4** lode
ender: **3** day, off, ola, out **4** back, load, roll **5** check **6** master
extra ~: **5** bonus **8** overtime
for: **3** buy, own **4** fund, take **5** atone, treat **6** afford, defray **7** finance, redress, support **8** answer to, make good, purchase, shell out **10** recompense
for services: **4** hire, rent **6** employ, engage **7** charter **8** contract
for the use of: **4** hire, rent **5** lease **6** engage **7** charter **8** sublease
heed: **6** attend, beware, listen, notice **7** hearken, observe, respect **8** watch out
hell to ~: **7** censure, penalty **10** punishment
hike: **5** raise **8** increase
hit ~ dirt: **5** score **7** succeed **8** get lucky
homage: **3** bow **4** hail **5** kneel **6** attend, curtsy, revere, salaam, salute **7** curtsey **9** genuflect, prostrate
increase: **4** COLA **5** raise
in kind: **6** avenge **7** get even, requite **9** get back at, retaliate
into the pot: **4** pool **6** ante up, chip in **7** cough up **10** contribute
it doesn't ~: **5** crime
no attention to: **4** snub **6** ignore, slight **7** disobey, neglect, tune out **8** overlook, sneeze at **9** disregard
obeisance: **6** kowtow **9** genuflect
off: **5** bribe **6** grease, redeem, settle, square **7** benefit, satisfy, succeed **8** square up **9** discharge, liquidate
part of: **6** defray
period: **4** week **5** month
promise to ~: **3** IOU **4** debt **9** debenture
the initiation fee: **4** join
the penalty: **5** atone **6** do time
tribute: **5** exalt, extol, honor **6** praise **7** glorify **8** eulogize
TV: *see* cable, cable channel, movie channel
two weeks with ~: **7** benefit **8** vacation
up: **4** ante **5** spend **6** settle, square **7** satisfy **8** make good **10** remunerate
with plastic: **3** owe **6** charge
pay ___: **3** off, out **4** dirt **5** phone, raise **6** in full, period
pay ___ the nose: **7** through
pay-___-go: **5** as-you
pay-___-view: **3** per
___ pay: **3** net **4** base, sick **5** merit
payable: **3** due **4** owed **5** owing **6** mature, unpaid **7** overdue **9** unsettled
to: **9** in favor of
when ~: **5** as due
payback: **6** rebate, return **7** outcome, revenge **8** reprisal
paycheck
amount: **3** net **5** gross
get a ~: **4** earn, work
letters: **3** hrs., YTD **4** FICA
plus: **5** bonus **8** overtime
remainder: **4** stub
Paycheck: **6** Johnny
Paycheck (2003 film)
cast: Ben Affleck, Aaron Eckhart, Uma Thurman
director: John Woo
Paycock partner: **4** Juno
PayDay: **3** bar **5** candy **8** candy bar **9** chocolate
alternative: *see* candy brand
payee: **6** winner **8** creditor, receiver **9** recipient
April ~: **3** IRS
check ~: **6** bearer
item: **3** pot **4** cash **5** check, kitty **6** refund **7** voucher **10** money order
payer: **5** buyer, loser **8** remitter
dues ~: **3** mem. **6** member
fee ~: **6** client, patron **7** patient **8** customer
mortgage ~: **4** ower **5** buyer
rent ~: **6** lessee, tenant
starter: **3** tax
paying: **9** lucrative **10** profitable, successful, worthwhile
attention: **5** alert, aware **7** mindful
guest: **5** liver **6** lodger, patron **7** boarder
interest: **5** owing **6** in debt
leave without ~: **5** stiff
no mind: **3** lax **4** lazy **6** sleepy **8** uncaring **9** apathetic
stop ~ attention: **4** moon **5** dream, drift **8** daydream **9** fantasize **10** woolgather
Pay It Forward (2000 film)
cast: Helen Hunt, Haley Joel Osment, Kevin Spacey
director: Mimi Leder
payload: **5** cargo **7** freight
paymaster: **7** cashier
payment: **3** fee, sum **4** wage **5** money, outgo, price, terms, wages **6** amends, charge, outlay, payoff, ransom, refund, reward **7** alimony, annuity, expense, pension, premium, redress, subsidy, support **8** defrayal, requital **9** discharge, emolument **10** honorarium, recompense, remittance, reparation, settlement
acknowledgment: **7** receipt
banque ~: **5** rente
club ~: **4** dues
demand ~: **3** dun, sue
details: **5** terms
down ~: **7** advance, deposit
freelance ~: **3** fee
homeowner's ~: **8** mortgage
hound for ~: **3** dun **9** keep after
insurance ~: **7** premium
Madison Avenue ~: **5** ad fee
mail ~: **5** remit
means: **4** cash **5** check **10** money order
monthly ~: **3** gas **4** rent **5** water **8** electric **9** utilities
overdue ~: **7** arrears
poker ~: **4** ante
rider's ~: **4** fare
time ~: **4** loan
unlawful ~: **3** sop **5** bribe, graft **8** kickback **9** blackmail
yearly ~: **3** tax **4** dues
___ payment: **4** down, stop
Paymer: **5** David
Payne: **4** John **5** Freda **7** Stewart
___ Payne: **5** Major
Payne, Freda
song: Band of Gold (1970)
Bring the Boys Home (1971)
pay no ___: **4** mind
payoff: **3** end, sop **5** bribe, graft, prize **6** climax, grease, income, ransom, result, reward, sequel, upshot **7** outcome, payment, rake-off, revenue **8** clincher, earnings, high spot, kickback, venality **9** hush money, punch line **10** adjustment, bottom line, conclusion, corruption, percentage, settlement
political ~: **4** pork **5** graft **10** pork barrel
payola: **3** sop **5** bribe, graft, lucre **7** jobbery, rake-off **8** kickback, venality **10** corruption
pay one's ___: **3** way **4** dues
payout ratio: **4** odds
PayPal
owner: **4** eBay
pay-per-___: **4** view
pay phone
feature: **4** slot
word: **6** insert **7** deposit
payroll: **7** expense
addition: **5** hiree
deduction: **3** tax **4** FICA
ID: **3** SSN
ones on the ~: **5** staff
on the ~: **7** working **8** employed
put on the ~: **4** hire **6** employ, engage
Pays, Amanda: **7** actress
spouse: Corbin Bernsen
pay the ___: **5** piper
pay through the ___: **4** nose
Payton, Walter: **4** back
sport: **8** football
Paz, Octavio: **4** poet **6** critic, writer **7** Mexican **8** Nobelist
work: The Labyrinth of Solitude
Pb: **4** elem., lead **7** element
82 for ~: **4** at. no.
PBA
area: **4** lane **5** alley
member: **3** cop **6** bowler, kegler
members: **6** police
PBJ
alternative: **3** BLT
PbS: **6** galena **8** galenite
PBS: **7** network
affiliate: **3** NPR

affiliate in NYC: 4 WNET
benefactor: 3 NEA
funding: 5 grant
no-no: 2 ad
onetime ~ kids' show: 5 Rebop
program: 3 POV
rival: 3 ABC, CBS, Fox, NBC 5 The CW
science program: 4 Nova
supplier: 3 BBC
talk host: 4 Rose
PBX number: 3 ext. 9 extension
PC: 2 AT, XT 3 CPU 4 mini 5 clone, micro 6 laptop 8 computer, notebook
alternative: *see* computer
ancestor: 5 Eniac
attacker: 5 virus
capacity: 3 meg, MHz, RAM
chip maker: 5 Intel
clicker: 5 mouse
command: 4 copy, edit, move, save, sort 5 erase
communication: 5 e-mail
component: 3 CPU, RAM, ROM
connector: 3 USB
cooler: 3 fan
data-exchange standard: 3 FTP
data medium: 2 CD 3 DVD 6 floppy
device: 3 DVD 5 CD-ROM, modem, mouse 6 floppy 7 printer 8 CD burner, keyboard, touchpad 9 hard drive 10 flash drive
early ~: 2 AT, XT
enthusiast: 4 user 6 hacker
flasher: 6 cursor
food: 4 byte, data 5 bytes
hookup: 3 LAN
image: 4 icon 6 bit map 7 graphic
image file format: 4 jpeg
innards: 3 ROM
insert: 2 CD 3 DVD 4 disk 6 floppy
key: 3 Alt, Del, End, Esc, Ins, tab 4 Ctrl, Home, Pg Dn, Pg Up 5 arrow, Break, Enter, Pause, Shift 6 Delete, Escape, Insert, Page Up 7 Control, Num Lock 8 Caps Lock, Page Down 9 backslash, Backspace
maker: 2 HP 3 IBM 4 Acer, Dell, Sony 6 Lenovo 7 Gateway, Toshiba
menu selection: 4 Help
monitor: 3 LCD
operating system: 3 DOS 5 MS/DOS 7 Windows
panic button: 3 ESC
port: 3 USB 6 serial 8 parallel
portable ~: 6 laptop 8 notebook
reseller: 3 OEM
scanning ability: 3 OCR
screen: 3 CRT
screen image: 4 icon 7 graphic
timesaver: 5 macro
World rival: 4 Byte
see also computer
P.C.: 4 Wren
PC-based learning: 3 CAI
PCB regulator: 3 EPA
__ P. Chase: 6 Salmon
PCV __: 5 valve
Pd: 4 elem. 7 element 9 palladium
46 for ~: 4 at. no.
PD
broadcast: 3 APB
employee: 4 insp.
member: 3 cop
rank: 2 lt. 3 det., sgt. 4 capt. 5 lieut.
see also police
P.D.: 5 James
PDQ: 3 now 4 ASAP, fast, stat 5 apace 6 at once, in a sec, presto, pronto 7 fleetly, hastily, quickly, rapidly, swiftly 8 in a flash, in a jiffy, in no time, pell-mell, promptly, right now, right off, speedily 9 forthwith, hurriedly, instantly, like a shot, posthaste, right away
P.D.Q.: 4 Bach
PDR
user: 2 GP, MD
pe: 6 Hebrew, letter
predecer: 4 ayin
successor: 4 sadi 5 sadhe, tsade, tsadi
P.E.: 3 gym
pea: 6 legume, veggie 8 spheroid 9 vegetable
container: 3 pod 4 hull
ender: 3 hen, nut 4 cock, fowl, king 7 shooter
soup: 3 fog
starter: 3 cow 5 chick
sweet ~: 5 plant 6 flower
pea __: 4 coal, coat, crab, soup 5 aphid, green 6 jacket 7 shooter
__ pea: 4 snap, snow 5 green, sugar, sweet
__ Pea: 4 Swee'
Peabo: 6 Bryson
peabody: 5 dance
peabrain
see ninny
peace: 4 calm, ease, hush, rest 5 amity, order, quiet, truce, unity 6 accord, repose, shalom, sholom, solace, treaty 7 concord, harmony, silence 8 calmness, quietude, serenity, solitude 9 agreement, armistice, stillness, unanimity 10 equanimity, friendship, placidness, relaxation
break the ~: 4 riot
ender: 4 time 5 maker 6 keeper
gesture: 3 vee 5 V sign
goddess: 3 Pax 5 Irene
in Russian: 3 mir
keeper: 7 bailiff, officer, sheriff
make ~: 6 settle, soothe 7 mediate 8 moderate 9 negotiate, reconcile 10 conciliate, smooth over
name meaning ~: 5 Irene 6 Salome 7 Solomon
offering: 10 reparation
officer: 3 cop 6 lawman 7 marshal, sheriff 9 policeman 11 policewoman
of mind: 4 ease 8 security, serenity
symbol: 4 dove 11 olive branch
temporary ~: 5 truce 9 ceasefire
peace __: 4 pipe, sign 6 treaty
Peace __: 5 Corps, Train
Peace!: 3 pax 6 shalom, sholom
peaceable: 4 calm, mild 5 quiet, still 6 gentle, irenic, serene 7 amiable, orderly, restful 8 amicable, dovelike, friendly, lamblike, moderate, peaceful, resigned, tranquil 10 nonviolent
__ Peace a Chance: 4 Give
peace and __: 5 quiet
Peace Corps counterpart: 5 VISTA
peaceful: 4 calm, cool, easy, even, meek, mild 5 quiet, still 6 gentle, irenic, low-key, mellow, placid, sedate, serene, smooth 7 amiable, content, easeful, equable, halcyon, neutral, pacific, relaxed, restful, stoical, unmoved 8 amicable, carefree, composed, friendly, irenical, laid-back, tranquil 9 collected, easygoing, impassive, quiescent, temperate, unexcited, unruffled 10 harmonious, nonchalant, nonviolent, pacifistic, rippleless, unagitated, untroubled
name meaning ~ friend: 7 Winfred 8 Winifred
period: 4 lull 5 truce 9 ceasefire
protest: 4 be-in 5 march, sit-in, vigil 6 love-in
Peaceful (1973 song)
artist: Helen Reddy
peacefulness: 4 hush 5 order, quiet 7 comfort 8 serenity
Peace Garden: 4 park
locale: North Dakota
Peace in Our Time (1989 song)
artist: Eddie Money
Peacekeeper: 4 ICBM
peacekeeper, international: 4 NATO
peacemaker: 8 diplomat, mediator 9 go-between 10 ambassador, arbitrator, interceder, negotiator
peacenik: 4 dove
peace of __: 4 mind
Peace Train (1971 song)
artist: Cat Stevens
peach: 3 gem, pie, pip 4 tree 5 cling, color, drupe, fruit, honey, prize 6 flavor, looker, orange, yellow 7 delight, pinkish 8 ice cream 9 freestone 10 clingstone
butter: 3 jam 9 preserves
center: 3 pit 5 stone
dessert: 3 pie 7 cobbler 8 ice cream
family: 4 rose
fuzzless ~: 9 nectarine
pulp: 5 flesh
skin: 4 fuzz
peach __: 4 moth 5 Melba 6 brandy
__ Peach: 4 Miss
peaches and __: 5 cream
Peaches and Herb
song: Close Your Eyes (1967)
For Your Love (1967)
Let's Fall in Love (1967)
Love Is Strange (1967)
Reunited (1979)
Shake Your Groove Thing (1979)
peach Melba: 7 dessert
alternative: 5 bombe 6 frappe 7 parfait
ingredient: 8 ice cream 9 raspberry
Peachum: 5 Polly
peachy
see wonderful
peacoat: 6 jacket
peacock: 3 fop 4 bird, blue, cyan, fowl, male, teal 5 azure, strut 6 indigo 7 swagger 8 greenish, pheasant 10 jack-a-dandy
act like a ~: 5 preen, strut
blue: 4 paon
feather spot: 3 eye
feature: 3 eye, fan 5 plume
like a ~: 4 vain 5 proud, showy
NBC ~: 4 logo
network: 3 NBC
relative: *see* fowl
peacock __: 4 blue
Peacock constellation: 4 Pavo
Peacock, Thomas: 4 poet 6 writer 7 British
work: Crotchet Castle
Headlong Hall
Nightmare Abbey
Peacock Throne country: 4 Iran
peag: 5 sewan 6 seawan, wampum
pea-green boat passenger: 3 owl 8 pussycat
peahen: 4 bird, fowl 6 female
relative: *see* fowl
peak: 3 alp, tip, top 4 acme, apex, best, brow, crag, head, pink, roof, time 5 crest, crown, mount, prime, spire 6 apogee, climax, height, heyday, heydey, max out, summit, tipoff, tiptop, top out, vertex, zenith 7 maximum, optimum, volcano 8 aiguille, high spot, meridian, mountain, pinnacle 9 crescendo, culminate, highlight, high point 10 prominence
at the ~: 4 atop 5 on top
covering: 4 snow
place: 5 graph 9 mountains
round mountain ~: 4 dome
scale a ~: 5 climb 6 ascend
tall ~: 5 spire 6 needle 8 pinnacle
time: 6 season
see also mountain
__ peak: 6 widow's
__ Peak: 5 Borah, Lenin, Pikes
peaked: 3 ill, wan 4 pale, sick, thin 5 ashen, drawn, sharp, spiky, white 6 pallid, pointy, sallow, sickly 7 bilious, haggard, run-down, starved 9 emaciated, unhealthy
roof: 6 A-frame, chalet
Peak Freans: 6 cookie
competitor: *see* cookie manufacturer
__ Peak Observatory: 4 Kitt
__ Peak or bust!: 5 Pikes
__ Peaks: 4 Twin
peal: 4 bong, clap, gong, ring, roar, roll, toll 5 blast, chime, clang, crack, crash, knell, noise 6 clamor, rumble 7 resound, ringing, ring out, thunder 8 laughter, resonate
mournful ~: 4 toll 5 knell
of laughter: 4 gale
Peale: 7 Charles 9 Rembrandt
peanut: 4 seed 5 snack 6 goober
brittle: 5 candy, sweet 10 confection
butter: 6 spread
butter brand: 3 Jif 6 Skippy 8 Peter Pan
butter companion: 5 jelly
product: 3 oil
shell: 4 husk
type of ~ butter: 6 chunky, creamy
peanut __: 3 oil 6 butter 7 brittle, gallery
peanut brittle: 5 candy

peanuts: 8 pittance 10 slave wages
Peanuts: 10 comic strip
character: Charlie Brown, Franklin, Linus, Lucy, Marcie, Peppermint Patty, Pig Pen, Rerun, Sally, Schroeder, Snoopy, Woodstock
creator: Charles Schulz
exclamation: 4 Rats 9 Good grief
lack: 6 adults
pea-picking machine: 5 viner
pear: 4 pome, tree 5 fruit, shape
family: 4 rose
fermented ~: 5 perry
prickly ~: 5 nopal, sabra 6 cactus
relative: 4 plum 5 apple, peach 6 almond, cherry, medlar, quince 7 apricot 8 hawthorn
thrips: 3 bug 4 pest 6 insect
type of ~: 4 Bosc 5 Anjou 6 Comice, Seckel 7 Kieffer 8 Bartlett, Bergamot
pearl: 3 gem 4 gray, grey 5 color, prize 8 off-white, treasure
Japanese ~ diver: 3 ama
month: 4 June
name meaning ~: 8 Margaret
seeker: 5 diver
source: 3 sea 4 grit, sand 6 oyster
pearl __: 4 blue, gray, grey 5 diver, onion 6 barley
__ pearl: 4 seed 8 cultured
Pearl: 4 Buck 5 river 6 Bailey, Minnie
city on the ~: 7 Jackson 8 Hong Kong
Pearl __: 3 Jam 6 Harbor
Pearl Drops: 10 toothpaste
alternative: *see* toothpaste
Pearl Fishers, The: 5 opera
composer: Georges Bizet
Pearl Harbor: 4 port
code word: 4 Tora
locale: 4 Oahu 6 Hawaii
Pearl Harbor (2001 film)
cast: Ben Affleck, Kate Beckinsale, Cuba Gooding Jr., Josh Hartnett, Jon Voight
Pearl Jam
hometown: Seattle
lead singer: Eddie Vedder
song: Better Man (1994)
I Got Id (1995)
Last Kiss (1999)
Tremor Christ (1994)
Pearl Mosque
locale: 4 Agra 5 India
Pearl S. __: 4 Buck
pearls before __: 5 swine
Pearl, The
author: John Steinbeck
pearly: 5 milky, white 6 silver 7 frosted, opaline, whitish 8 lustrous, nacreous, off-white 10 iridescent, opalescent
pearly __: 5 white
Pearly __: 5 Gates
pear-shaped: 5 round
fruit: 3 fig
gem: 5 boule
instrument: 4 lute 5 rebec 6 cither, guitar, rebeck
sound: 2 oh
vessel: 6 aludel
Pearson: 4 Drew 6 Lester
Pearson, Lester: 2 P.M. 8 Canadian, Nobelist
predecessor: 11 Diefenbaker
successor: 7 Trudeau
Pears, Peter: 5 tenor 6 singer 7 British
milieu: 5 opera
piece: 4 aria
Peary, Robert: 8 explorer
of interest to ~: 5 polar 6 arctic
peasant: 4 boor, hind, peon, pleb, serf 5 churl, yahoo, yokel 6 rustic, worker 7 bumpkin 8 commoner, plebeian 9 vulgarian 10 clodhopper
commune: 5 artel
dress: 6 bodice, dirndl
Egyptian ~: 6 fellah
girl: 5 wench
of India: 4 ryot
Ottoman ~: 4 raya
Russian ~: 5 mujik
peasantry: 3 mob 4 herd 5 crowd, plebs 6 masses, proles, rabble 8 canaille, riffraff 9 hoi polloi, multitude 10 lower class
Peasants' Revolt
leader: 8 Wat Tyler
peashooter: 3 toy
__-pea soup: 5 split
pea-souper: 3 fog
peat: 4 fuel, moss 8 sphagnum
source: 3 bog 4 moor 5 swamp
peat __: 3 bog, pot 4 moss
peau de soie: 6 fabric 7 textile 8 material
pebble: 4 rock 5 stone
Pebble Beach
event: 5 pro-am
game: 4 golf
peg: 3 tee
warning: 4 fore
Pebbles: 10 Flintstone
parent: 4 Fred 5 Wilma
pet: 4 Dino
__ Pebbles, The: 4 Sand
pebbly: 5 rocky 8 gravelly
pecan: 3 nut, pie 4 tree 7 hickory
candy: 7 praline
pecan __: 3 pie 5 patty
Pecan Sandies: 6 cookie
peccability: 5 guilt
peccadillo: 3 sin 7 misdeed, offense 9 veniality
peccant: 6 erring
peccary: 3 hog, pig 5 swine 6 animal, mammal
peccatophobe fear: 3 sin 7 sinning
pêche __: 5 Melba
__ pêcheurs de perles: 3 Les
peck: 3 jab, rap, tap 4 gobs, heap, kiss, lots, lump, much, pile 5 slews 6 nibble, oodles, plenty, strike 8 osculate 10 osculation
at: 3 nag 4 carp 6 harp on 9 criticize
hunt and ~: 4 type
starter: 3 hen
Peck, Annie Smith: 8 explorer
__ Peck Dam: 4 Fort
Peck, Gregory: 5 actor
film: Arabesque (1966)
The Big Country (1958)
The Bravados (1958)
Cape Fear (1962)
Captain Horatio Hornblower (1951)
Captain Newman, M.D. (1963)
Designing Woman (1957)
Duel in the Sun (1946)
Gentleman's Agreement (1947)
The Guns of Navarone (1961)
How the West Was Won (1962)
The Keys of the Kingdom (1944)
MacArthur (1977)
The Macomber Affair (1947)
The Man in the Gray Flannel Suit (1956)
Mirage (1965)
Moby Dick (1956)
Night People (1954)
Old Gringo (1989)
On the Beach (1959)
Other People's Money (1991)
Pork Chop Hill (1959)
Roman Holiday (1953)
The Sea Wolves (1980)
The Snows of Kilimanjaro (1952)
Spellbound (1945)
To Kill a Mockingbird (1962, AA)
Twelve O'Clock High (1949)
The Valley of Decision (1945)
The Yearling (1946)
Yellow Sky (1948)
film, with The: 4 Omen
role: 4 Ahab
pecking order: 4 rank 5 class, order, place 6 regime
Peckinpah, Sam: 8 director
film: The Ballad of Cable Hogue (1970)
Cross of Iron (1977)
The Getaway (1972)
Junior Bonner (1972)
Ride the High Country (1962)
Straw Dogs (1971)
The Wild Bunch (1969)
peckish: 5 unfed 7 starved 8 edacious, esurient, famished, ravenous 9 voracious
Peck of Gold, A
author: Robert Frost
Peck's __ Boy: 3 Bad
pecks, four: 6 bushel
Pecksniff: 4 Seth
pecorino: 6 cheese
Pecos: 5 river
locale: 5 Texas 9 New Mexico
Pecos __: 4 Bill
pecs: 7 muscles
relative: 3 abs 6 glutes
show off the ~: 4 flex
pectin, react to: 3 gel 4 jell
pectoral __: 3 fin
peculate: 5 steal 6 pilfer 8 embezzle
peculation: 5 theft 9 pilfering
peculator: 5 thief 8 pilferer 9 embezzler
peculiar: 3 odd 4 eery 5 eerie, flaky, funny, kinky, kooky, queer, wacky, weird 6 atypic, creepy, flakey, freaky, kookie, quaint, quirky, unique, way-out, whacky 7 bizarre, curious, deviant, erratic, oddball, offbeat, special, strange, touched, unalike, unusual 8 aberrant, abnormal, atypical, freakish, personal, separate, singular, specific, uncommon 9 anomalous, different, divergent, eccentric, fantastic, intrinsic, irregular, quizzical, whimsical 10 individual, off-the-wall, outlandish, suspicious, unfamiliar, unorthodox
combining form: 4 idio-
peculiarity: 3 tic 4 kink, mark, sign 5 quirk, trait, twist 6 foible, manner, oddity 7 anomaly, earmark, feature, quality, schtick 8 crotchet, property 9 attribute, mannerism, queerness
peculiarly: 5 oddly 9 strangely, unusually 10 especially
Peculiar Treasure, A
author: Edna Ferber
pecuniary: 6 fiscal 8 economic, monetary 9 financial 10 commercial
sum: 5 money
pecunious: 4 rich 5 flush 6 loaded 7 wealthy 8 affluent 9 properous, well-fixed 10 in the money
Ped __: 4 Xing
pedagogic: 7 bookish, donnish 8 academic, didactic, pedantic, tutorial 9 scholarly 10 didactical, pedantical
pedagogue: 6 lector, master 7 teacher, trainer 8 lecturer 9 abecedary, professor 10 instructor
org.: 3 AFT, NEA
pedagogy: 8 teaching, training 9 education
pedal: 4 bike 5 cycle
car ~: 3 gas 5 brake 6 clutch
extremity: 3 toe 4 foot
foot ~: 5 lever
piano ~: 6 damper
pusher: 4 foot 5 biker
pushers: 5 pants 6 Capris
put the ~ to the metal: 3 rev, zip 4 zoom 5 speed 6 barrel
pedal __: 4 boat 7 pushers
__ pedal: 3 gas 5 brake
__-pedal: 4 back, soft
pedaling, ride without: 5 coast
pedal to the __: 5 metal
pedant: 9 nitpicker
pedantic: 3 dry 4 arid, dull 5 fussy 6 stodgy 7 bookish, donnish, erudite, learned, pompous, stilted 8 abstruse, academic, affected, didactic, overnice, priggish 9 pedagogic, ponderous, recondite 10 didactical, nit-picking, scholastic
peddle: 4 hawk, push, sell, vend 5 trade 6 market, monger, unload 7 solicit 9 dispose of, liquidate 10 auction off
peddler: 5 crier 6 hawker, seller, vender, vendor
goal: 4 sale, sell
Pedernales: 5 river
locale: 5 Texas
pedestal: 4 foot, post, rest 6 column, podium
bowl: 5 tazza
figure: 4 bust, idol 9 sculpture
part: 4 base, dado 5 socle
put on a ~: 5 adore, exalt, extol 6 esteem, extoll, praise 7 adulate, ennoble, glorify, idolize, worship 8 canonize, idealize, venerate
pedestrian: 3 dim 4 blah, dull, flat, so-so 5 banal, hiker, ho-hum, inane, trite, unfun 6 ambler, boring, common, dreary, footer, jejune, stodgy, walker 7 humdrum, mundane, prosaic 8 banausic, everyday, mediocre, ordinary, passerby, plebeian, plodding,

stroller **9** hackneyed, jaywalker, prosaical
haven: 4 curb **6** island
help for a ~: 3 arm **4** lift, ride
pediatrician: 2 MD **6** doctor **9** physician
patient: 3 kid, tot **4** baby **5** child, minor **6** infant **7** toddler **9** youngster
pedicle: 4 stem **5** stalk
pedicurist
coat: 6 enamel
target: 3 toe **4** nail **7** cuticle, toenail
pedigree: 4 line **5** birth, blood, breed, class, roots, stock **6** origin, strain **7** descent, lineage **8** ancestry, heritage, purebred **9** genealogy **10** derivation, extraction, family tree
org.: 3 AKC
pedigreed: 8 pure-bred
pediment: 5 gable **8** triangle
pedometer
new ~ reading: 3 OOO
reading: 5 miles **8** distance
Pedro: 6 Cabral **7** Salinas **8** Calderón, card game, Guerrero, Martinez **9** Almodóvar **10** Armendariz
in English: 5 Peter
see also Spanish
__ Pedro: 3 San
Peds: 7 hosiery
peduncle: 4 stem **5** scape, stalk
Pee __ King: 3 Wee
Pee __ Reese: 3 Wee
Pee-__ Herman: 3 Wee
Pee Dee: 5 river
locale: 4 N. Car., S. Car.
peek: 3 eye, pry, see, spy **4** gaze, look, peep, peer, view **5** snoop **6** behold, gander, glance, squint **7** eyeshot, glimpse, look-see, observe **10** get a load of, sneak a look
at the cards: 5 cheat
peek-__: 4 a-boo
Peek __: 6 Freans
Peek-a-boo: 4 game
Peek-a-boo, __ you!: 4 I see
Peekskill: 4 city, town
locale: 7 New York
peel: 4 bark, flay, hull, husk, molt, pare, rind, skin **5** cover, flake, shave, shell, shuck, strip **6** cortex, denude, scrape **7** coating, disrobe, epicarp, exocarp, surface, undress **8** covering, flake off, get out of, unclothe **9** exfoliate **10** delaminate, desquamate
fruit ~: 4 rind, skin, zest
in a drink: 5 twist
off: 4 molt **5** flake, strip
precursor: 4 burn **7** blister, sunburn
rubber: 3 rev **4** zoom **5** speed **10** accelerate
something to ~: 4 pear, spud **5** apple, fruit, peach **6** potato
peel __: 3 off
Peel: 4 Emma **6** Robert
partner: 5 Steed
peel-and-__: 5 stick
peeled: 4 bare **5** naked
keep one's eyes ~: 5 watch **8** watch out **9** be careful
with eyes ~: 7 mindful **8** vigilant, watchful
peeler: 4 tool **5** parer **6** gadget
spud ~: 2 GI, KP **7** private, recruit
peeling: 4 rind, skin **10** integument
potatoes, perhaps: 4 on KP
tool: 5 parer
Peel me a grape lady: 3 Mae **4** West
__-peen hammer: 4 ball
peep: 3 coo, pry, see, spy **4** call, gaze, look, peek, peer, pipe **5** cheep, chirp, snoop, tweet **6** appear, emerge, gander, glance, squint **7** chirrup, glimpse, look-see, twitter **8** bird call **10** get a load of, sneak a look
ender: 4 hole
out: 6 emerge, sprout **9** germinate
show: 5 raree
Peep at Polynesian Life, A: 5 Typée
peeper: 3 eye, spy **4** frog **9** amphibian
farm ~: 5 chick
plaint: 5 croak
protector: 3 lid **4** lash **6** eyelid **7** eyelash
spring ~: 4 frog, hyla **9** amphibian
peephole: 4 slit **5** Judas **6** eyelet
peeping __: 3 Tom
Peeples, Nia
song: Street of Dreams (1991)
peer: 3 pry, see, spy **4** gape, gawk, gaze, look, lord, mate, peek, peep, scan, view **5** baron, equal, juror, match, noble, rival, snoop, stare, watch **6** appear, emerge, fellow, squint **7** coequal, compeer, examine, eyeball, glimpse, inspect, ransack **8** nobleman **9** associate, classmate, patrician **10** aristocrat, get a load of, rubberneck, scrutinize, sneak a look
ender: 3 age, ess
group: 4 jury
recognition: 5 honor
sheik's ~: 4 amir, emir **5** ameer, emeer
social ~: 5 equal
without ~: 5 alone **6** unique **7** perfect **9** unequaled, unmatched
peer __: 5 group **6** review
peer __ realm: 5 of the
Peer __: 4 Gynt
peerage: 5 lords **8** nobility **10** upper class, upper crust
member: 4 dame, duke, earl, lady, lord **5** baron, noble **7** duchess, marquis **8** baroness, countess, viscount **11** marchioness
Peer and the __, The: 4 Peri
Peerce: 3 Jan **5** Larry
Peerce, Jan: 5 tenor **6** singer
milieu: 5 opera
peeress: 4 dame, lady **5** noble **7** duchess **8** countess **10** noblewoman **11** marchioness
Peer Gynt
author: Henrik Ibsen
character: 3 Ase **4** Aase, Huhu, Kari **5** Aslak, Brosë, troll **6** Anitra, Ingrid **7** Solveig **8** Mads Moën **9** Troll King
composer: Edvard Grieg
peering: 4 nosy **5** nosey **6** snoopy **7** curious **9** quizzical
peerless: 3 ace **4** A-one, best, only, rare, tops **5** alone, great **6** single, superb, unique **7** in front, optimum, perfect, supreme **8** flawless, splendid, superior **9** excellent, faultless, matchless, nonpareil, solid-gold, topflight, unequaled, unmatched, unrivaled, virtuosic **10** consummate, inimitable, preeminent, unexampled, unrivalled, world-class
peer of the __: 5 realm
Peet: 6 Amanda
Peete: 6 Calvin
peeve: 3 bug, get, irk, vex **4** burn, fret, gall, miff, rile, roil **5** anger, annoy, get to, grate, gripe, pique, spite, steam, upset **6** bother, bum out, hector, madden, needle, nettle, put out, rankle, ruffle, tee off, work up **7** disturb, enflame, incense, perturb, provoke, tick off, trouble **8** distress, irritate **9** aggravate, annoyance, displease **10** exasperate
pet ~: 7 bugbear **9** hot button
__ peeve: 3 pet
peeved: 3 hot, mad **4** ired, sore **5** angry, cross, huffy, irate, livid, riled, upset, wroth **6** fuming, in a pet **7** in a stew **8** choleric, in a pique **9** aggrieved, indignant, resentful
peevish: 4 mean, sour, ugly **5** cross, huffy, moody, spiky, sulky, surly, techy, testy, upset **6** crabby, cranky, crusty, cussed, grumpy, ireful, morose, ornery, snappy, sullen, tetchy, touchy **7** bearish, carping, crabbed, fretful, grouchy, huffish, prickly, waspish, whining **8** captious, childish, choleric, churlish, critical, fretsome, grousing, growling, grumpish, petulant, snappish **9** crotchety, excitable, fractious, irascible, irritable, querulous, splenetic **10** ill-natured, out of sorts
mood: 4 huff, snit
peevishness: 4 bile **6** spleen, temper **8** asperity
pee-wee: 4 baby, puny, runt, tiny **5** bitty, teeny **6** atomic, bantam, little, minute, petite, pocket, teensy **7** stunted **8** half-pint **9** itsy-bitsy, itty-bitty, miniature, pint-sized, undersize **10** diminutive, homunculus, teeny-weeny, vest-pocket
Pee-wee __: 6 Herman
Pee Wee __: 4 King **5** Reese
Pee Wee's Big Adventure dog: 5 Speck
peewit: 4 bird
peg: 3 fix, pin, see, tee **4** cast, hurl, name, rank, rate, sort, type **5** dowel, fling, pitch, place, point, throw **6** assess, fasten, select, verify **7** look out, measure, specify **8** identify, indicate, make fast, work away **9** designate, recognize **10** categorize, clothespin
away: 4 toil, work **6** strain
driver's ~: 3 tee
ender: 5 board
quoits ~: 3 hob
replacer: 4 hook, nail **5** screw
take down a ~: 5 abase, lower, shame **6** demean, demote, humble, reduce **7** degrade, mortify **8** belittle **9** downgrade
wooden ~: 5 dowel
__-peg: 6 mumbly
Peg: 5 Bundy **7** Bracken
Peg __ Heart: 3 o' My
Pegasus: 5 horse, steed **6** equine
father: 8 Poseidon
feature: 5 wings
mother: 6 Medusa
neighbor: 6 Cygnus **8** Aquarius
Pegeen: 10 Fitzgerald
Peggy: 3 Dow, Lee, Rea **4** Cass, Ryan, Wood **5** Rosen **6** Lennon, Lipton, Parish **7** Cummins, Fleming **8** Ashcroft **10** Guggenheim
Peggy __: 3 Sue
Peggy __ Garner: 3 Ann
Peggy from Paris
author: George Ade
Peggy Sue (1957 song)
artist: Buddy Holly and the Crickets
Peggy Sue Got Married (1986 film)
cast: Nicolas Cage, Catherine Hicks, Kathleen Turner
director: Francis Ford Coppola
__ peg in a round hole: 6 square
Pegler: 9 Westbrook
Peg o' My __: 5 Heart
Peg Woffington
author: Charles Reade
peh: 6 Hebrew, letter
follower: 4 sadi **5** sadhe, tsade, tsadi
preceder: 4 ayin
Pei: 2 I.M. **4** Ieoh **5** Mario
__-Pei: 4 Shar
PEI: 4 prov. **8** province
clock setting: 3 AST
locale: 6 Canada
part of ~: 3 Edw. **6** Edward, Island, Prince
peignoir: 6 kimono **8** negligee
Peignot: 4 font **8** typeface
Pei, I.M.: 7 Chinese **9** architect
Peirce, Charles Sanders: 6 writer **11** philosopher
specialty: 10 pragmatism
pejorative: 8 debasing, derisive, libelous, negative, scornful **9** degrading, demeaning, slighting **10** derogatory, detraction, minimizing
pekan: 6 fisher, marten
peke: 3 dog, pet, toy **5** canid **6** canine, lap dog, toy dog
alternative: 3 pom **6** poodle
pekin: 4 silk **6** fabric **7** textile **8** material
Peking: 4 city, town **7** capital
ender: 3 ese
locale: 5 China
Peking __: 3 man **4** duck
Pekingese: 3 dog, pet, toy **5** canid **6** canine, lap dog, toy dog
__-Pekka Salonen: 3 Esa
pekoe: 3 tea **4** brew **5** drink **8** beverage
__ pekoe: 6 orange
pelage: 3 fur **4** coat, hair, wool **6** fleece
pelagic: 5 naval **6** marine **8** maritime, nautical
Pélé
first name: 5 Edson
sport: 6 soccer

Pelee: **7** volcano
flow: **4** lava
locale: **9** Caribbean **10** Martinique
Peleg
father: **4** Eber
son: **3** Reu
pelerine: **4** cape
pelf
see moolah
Pelham
author: Edward Bulwer-Lytton
pelican: **4** bird
feature: **5** pouch
relative: **6** gannet
Pelican Brief, The (1993 film)
cast: Tony Goldwyn, John Heard, Julia Roberts, Sam Shepard, Denzel Washington
Pelion base: **4** Ossa
pelisse: **4** cape **5** cloak
pell-__: **4** mell
Pell: **9** Claiborne
pellet: **2** BB **4** ammo, pill, shot **7** granule, missile
rifle ~: **2** BB
shooter: **5** BB gun **6** airgun
Pelle the Conqueror
author: Martin Andersen Nexö
pellets: **3** BBs
ice ~: **4** hail **5** sleet
lead ~: **4** ammo, shot
pistol ~: **4** ammo
Pelli, Cesar: **9** architect
pell-mell: **3** PDQ **4** rash **5** apace, hasty **6** abrupt, presto, rashly **7** blindly, chaotic, fleetly, hastily, hurried, mixed up, muddled, quickly, rapidly, swiftly, tangled **8** abruptly, careless, confused, headlong, in a flash, in a jiffy, in no time, reckless, slapdash, speedily **9** forthwith, haphazard, hurriedly, instantly, like a shot, posthaste, scrambled, uncareful **10** at full tilt, carelessly, disordered, disorderly, heedlessly, recklessly, topsy-turvy, willy-nilly
go ~: **3** hie, run, zip **4** bolt, leap, race, rush, tear, whiz, zoom **5** hurry, lunge, speed **6** charge, gallop, hurtle **8** scramble
pellucid: **4** pure **5** clear, lucid, sheer **6** limpid **8** knowable **9** unobscure **10** diaphanous
pelon: **4** bald **8** hairless
Peloponnesian
city: **5** Argos **7** Amalias
region: **4** Elis **6** Achaea
valley: **5** Nemea
Peloponnesian __: **3** War
Peloponnesus: **5** Morea
Pelosi: **5** Nancy
pelota: **5** sport **7** jai alai
basket: **5** cesta
pelt: **3** fur, hie, hit, run **4** beat, coat, hair, hide, hurl, race, rain, rush, skin, wool **5** hurry, pound, speed, stone, throw **6** assail, batter, beetle, ermine, fleece, hammer, patter, pepper, pummel, shower, strike, thrash, wallop **7** bombard, krimmer, lambast **8** fur piece, lambaste **9** epidermis
beaver ~: **3** plu **4** plew
pelvic
bones: **4** ilia **5** sacra
joint: **3** hip
of the ~ region: **5** ileal
prefix: **5** sacro-
pelvis: **4** bone **7** hip bone
combining form: **4** pyel- **5** pyelo-
of the ~: **5** iliac
Pemberton: **4** John
pemmican: **4** food, meat **6** staple
Pemmican language: **4** Cree
pen: **3** Bic, box, nib, she, sty **4** bird, cage, coop, fold, jail, lair, poky, reed, stir, swan **5** draft, fence, Flair, hedge, hem in, hutch, pokey, quill, write **6** author, cooler, coop up, corral, encage, female, indite, intern, lockup, marker, pigsty, prison, shut in, stylus **7** close in, compose, confine, enclose, felt-tip, fence in, hoosgow, impound, inclose, interne, jot down, paddock, piggery, put down, shelter, slammer, Uni-Ball **8** big house, hoosegow, inscribe **9** autograph, ball point, calaboose, enclosure, handwrite, PaperMate **10** put on paper, stylograph
brand: **3** Bic **5** Flair **7** Uni-Ball **9** PaperMate
chicken ~: **4** coop
dweller: **3** hen, hog, pig, sow **4** boar, fowl **5** swine **6** rabbit **7** chicken **9** livestock
ender: **5** knife, light **6** holder
fluid: **3** ink
fountain ~: **3** pen
have a ~ pal: **5** write **10** correspond
holding ~: **9** detention
livestock ~: **6** corral
mate: **3** cob
name: **5** alias **6** anonym **9** pseudonym **10** nom de plume
old-fashioned ~: **5** plume, quill
one in a ~: **5** felon **7** convict **8** criminal
point: **3** nib
problem: **4** leak
sheep ~: **4** fold
starter: **3** pig **4** bull, play
young: **6** cygnet
pen __: **3** pal **4** name **5** point
__ pen: **3** sea **4** felt **5** fiber, light **6** poison **7** felt-tip
Peña: **4** Tony **9** Alejandro, Elizabeth
penal: **8** punitive **9** punishing **10** corrective, inflictive
institution: **3** can, jug, pen **4** gaol, jail, stir **5** clink **6** cooler, lockup, prison **7** slammer **8** bastille, big house, hoosegow **9** calaboose
penal __: **4** code **6** colony
penalize: **4** dock, fine **5** judge, mulct **6** amerce, punish **7** condemn, correct **8** chastise, handicap, sentence, slap with **9** castigate **10** discipline
penalties, like some: **5** stiff
penalty: **3** rap **4** cost, fine, toll **5** price **6** diktat, ticket **7** damages, forfeit **8** handicap, sanction, sentence **9** hell to pay **10** discipline, forfeiture, infliction, punishment
caller: **3** ref **7** referee
non-payer's ~: **4** repo
pay the ~: **5** atone **6** do time
speeder's ~: **4** fine **6** ticket
penalty __: **3** box **4** kick
penance: **9** atonement, expiation, hair shirt, sacrament **10** contrition, punishment, reparation
do ~: **5** atone **7** expiate
Penang: **4** city, isle, port, town **6** island
locale: **8** Malaysia
Penates partners: **5** Lares
pence: **6** copper
starter: **3** six, two **4** half **5** three
__ pence: **6** Peter's
penchant: **4** bent, bias, gift, wont **5** fancy, habit, taste **6** liking, relish **7** faculty, leaning **8** affinity, appetite, druthers, fondness, tendency, velleity, weakness **9** appetence, proneness, sentiment **10** partiality, proclivity, propensity
pencil: **3** jot **5** write **8** scribble
blue ~: **4** edit, trim, void **5** amend **6** censor, revise **7** abridge, shorten **10** censorship
end: **5** point **6** eraser
eye ~: **5** liner
filler: **4** lead **8** graphite
holder: **3** ear **4** hand **6** finger
in: **7** program **8** schedule
maker: **5** Faber
partner: **3** pad **5** paper **6** tablet
pusher: **5** clerk
wax ~: **6** crayon
wood: **5** cedar
worn-down ~: **3** nub **4** knub, stub
pencil __: **3** box **4** case **6** pusher
__ pencil: **4** lead **5** light **6** grease **7** eyebrow, styptic
__-pencil: **3** red **4** blue
pencil-and-paper game: **5** Jotto
pencil box item: **5** ruler **6** eraser **7** compass
pend: **4** hang **5** await **6** dangle **7** suspend **8** hang fire
__ pend.: **3** pat.
pendant: **4** drop **6** locket **7** jewelry **8** lavalier
place: **4** neck **6** throat
Pendennis
author: William Makepeace Thackeray
pendent: **7** hanging, jutting **8** dangling **9** suspended, undecided **10** protruding
Pendergrass, Teddy: **6** singer
song: Close the Door (1978)
pending: **5** until **7** hanging, on board **8** awaiting, imminent **9** in the wind, undecided, unsettled **10** continuing, in the works, unresolved, up in the air
in law: **4** nisi
Pendleton: **4** camp **5** Terry **6** Austin
Pendragon: **5** Uther
son: **6** Arthur
pendulous: **6** droopy **7** hanging, sagging **8** dangling, drooping, swinging
pendulum
direction: **3** fro
move like a ~: **5** swing **9** oscillate
path: **3** arc
Penelope: **8** Gilliatt, Mortimer, Spheeris
husband: **8** Odysseus
son: **3** Pan **6** Italus **9** Acusilaus **10** Telemachus
Penelope __ Miller: **3** Ann
Penélope: **4** Cruz
Pénélope
composer: Gabriel Fauré
penetrable: **6** liable **8** vincible **9** absorbent, permeable
penetrate: **3** jab, see **4** bore, gore, open, ream, seep, soak, stab **5** crack, drill, enter, grasp, knife, lance, plumb, prick, probe, spear, stick **6** access, affect, empale, fathom, filter, impale, invade, pierce, sink in, soak in, thrust, tunnel **7** break in, discern, ingress, pervade, suffuse, unravel **8** decipher, encroach, filter in, permeate, puncture, saturate, transfix, trespass **9** ferret out, figure out, go through, percolate, perforate **10** comprehend, eat through, encroach on, infiltrate, see through, understand
slowly: **4** leak, ooze, seep **6** filter
penetrating: **4** cold, keen **5** acute, crisp, quick, sharp, witty **6** astute, biting, cogent, shrewd, shrill, subtle **7** cutting, pointed, pungent **8** carrying, clear-cut, critical, incisive, piercing, poignant, profound, stinging **9** astucious, observant, pervasive, sagacious, searching, trenchant **10** discerning, perceptive
beam: **4** X-ray **5** laser
penetration: **5** depth **6** wisdom **7** insight **8** infusion, keenness
penguin: **4** bird
kind of ~: **4** king **6** Adelie **7** emperor
locale: **3** zoo **9** Antarctic, South Pole **10** Antarctica
Outland ~: **4** Opus
Penguin: **3** Cey **6** iceman
foe: **6** Batman
Penguin Island
author: Anatole France
Penguins: **3** six **4** team
home: **10** Pittsburgh
milieu: **3** ice **4** rink
org.: **3** NHL
rival: *see* hockey team
song: Earth Angel (1954)
sport: **6** hockey
__ Penh: **4** Pnom **5** Phnom
penicillin: **4** drug **10** antibiotic
source: **4** mold
target: **4** germ **5** strep **8** bacteria **9** infection
penicillium: **6** fungus
Penick, Harvey: **6** golfer
peninsula
Adriatic ~: **6** Istria
Alaskan ~: **5** Kenai
Asian ~: **5** Malay **6** Arabia
Canadian ~: **5** Gaspé **6** Avalon, Ungava **7** Boothia **8** Labrador **10** Nova Scotia
European ~: **5** Italy **6** Iberia
Greek ~: **5** Morea
Indian ~: **6** Deccan
Luzon ~: **6** Bataan
Mexican ~: **4** Baja
Mideast ~: **4** Aden **5** Sinai **6** Arabia
Philippine ~: **6** Bataan
Québec ~: **5** Gaspé
small ~: **4** spit
two-nation ~: **6** Iberia
Ukraine ~: **6** Crimea
world's largest ~: **6** Arabia

___ Peninsula: 4 Door, Eyre, Kola 5 Eyre's, Gaspé, Kenai, Lower, Malay, Sinai, Upper 6 Balkan, Seward 7 Iberian 8 Delmarva
Peniston, CeCe
hometown: Dayton
song: Finally (1991)
Keep on Walkin' (1992)
We Got a Love Thing (1992)
penitence: 5 shame 6 regret, sorrow 7 remorse 9 attrition, hair shirt 10 contrition, ruefulness
penitent: 5 sorry 6 abject, rueful, shamed 7 ashamed, humbled 8 contrite 9 regretful 10 apologetic, remorseful
be ~: 3 rue 4 weep 5 atone 6 regret
penitential period: 4 Lent
penitentiary: 3 can, jug, pen 4 gaol, jail, poky, stir 5 clink, joint, pokey 6 cooler, inside, lockup, prison 7 bastile, hoosgow, slammer 8 bastille, big house, hoosegow 9 calaboose
penmanship: 6 script 7 writing 8 longhand
Penn: 3 Kal 4 Sean 6 Arthur 7 William 8 Jillette
Penn ___: 3 Ave., Sta. 5 State 6 Relays 7 Station
Penn ___, NY: 3 Yan
Penn.
see Pennsylvania
penna: 5 plume 7 feather
pennant: 4 flag, jack 6 banner, burgee, colors, cornet, emblem, ensign 7 bunting 8 screamer, standard, streamer 9 banderole 10 decoration
penne: 5 pasta
alternative: *see* pasta
Penney
rival: 5 Kmart, Sears 6 Target 7 Walmart
Penney, J.C. middle name: 4 Cash
Pennies From Heaven (1981 film)
cast: Steve Martin, Bernadette Peters, Christopher Walken
penniless: 4 flat, poor 5 broke, needy 6 bad off, hard up, ill off, in need, in want, ruined 7 lacking, pinched 8 badly off, bankrupt, beggarly, deprived, dirt poor, indigent, stranded, strapped 9 dead broke, destitute, flat broke, insolvent, miserable, moneyless, penurious, tapped out 10 cleaned out, down-and-out, pauperized, straitened
in Britain: 5 skint
Pennines: 4 Alps 5 range
locale: 5 Italy 6 Europe 11 Switzerland
Pennock: 4 Herb
pennon: 4 flag 6 banner
Penn, Sean: 5 actor
film: At Close Range (1986)
Bad Boys (1983)
Before Night Falls (2000)
Carlito's Way (1993)
Colors (1988)
Dead Man Walking (1995)
Fast Times at Ridgemont High (1982)
The Game (1997)
I Am Sam (2001)
The Indian Runner (1991)
The Interpreter (2005)
Milk (2008, AA)
Mystic River (2003, AA)
The Pledge (2001)
Racing With the Moon (1984)
State of Grace (1990)
Sweet and Lowdown (1999)
The Thin Red Line (1998)
U Turn (1997)
spouse: Madonna, Robin Wright
Penn State: 3 PSU
conference: 6 Big Ten
Penn Station: 5 depot 8 terminal
carrier: 4 LIRR 6 Amtrak
posting: 4 sked 8 schedule
Pennsylvania: 5 state 6 avenue
capital: 10 Harrisburg
city: 4 Erie, Plum, Ross, York 5 Sayre 6 Donora, Easton, Radnor, Shaler 7 Altoona, Baldwin, Chester, Latrobe, Lebanon, Reading 8 Hazleton, Scranton 9 Allentown, Bethlehem, Johnstown, Lancaster, Levittown, New Castle, Penn Hills, Pottstown 10 Bethel Park, Drexel Hill, Harrisburg, Norristown, Pittsburgh
county: 3 Elk 4 Erie, York 5 Berks, Bucks, Tioga 6 McKean 7 Dauphin, Wyoming 10 Schuylkill
Indian: 9 Nanticoke
league: 3 Ivy
mountains: 7 Poconos
neighbor: 4 Ohio 7 New York 8 Delaware, Maryland 9 New Jersey
people: 5 Amish
port: 4 Erie
school: 5 Thiel 6 Drexel, Lehigh, Temple 8 Bucknell, Duquesne 9 Lafayette, Penn State, Villanova
state bird: 6 grouse
state dog: 9 Great Dane
state fish: 10 brook trout
state flower: 6 laurel
state fossil: 9 trilobite
state tree: 7 hemlock
Pennsylvania ___: 5 Dutch, Polka
Pennsylvania Dutch: 4 sect 5 Amish, style
barn symbol: 3 hex 7 hex sign
___ Penn Warren: 6 Robert
penny: 4 cent, coin 5 money 6 copper
ante: 4 game 5 poker 8 card game
bad ~: 4 slug
black: 5 stamp
down to one's last ~: 5 broke 6 busted 8 strapped
dreadful: 5 novel
ender: 4 wise, wort 5 cress, royal, worth 6 weight 7 whistle
like a new ~: 5 shiny
onetime ~ depiction: 5 wheat
pretty ~: 4 dear, high 5 bucks, pricy, steep 6 bundle, costly, pricey 8 big bucks, precious 9 expensive, priceless 10 exorbitant, high-priced, overpriced
starter: 3 six, two 4 half, true 5 catch, pinch, three
word on a ~: 3 God, one 4 cent, unum 5 trust 6 States, United 7 America, liberty 8 pluribus
penny ___: 4 ante, post 5 stock 6 arcade, loafer 7 pincher, whistle
penny-___: 4 wise
Penny: 3 Joe 6 Sydney 8 Marshall 9 Singleton
to Sky King: 5 niece
Penny ___: 4 Lane 5 Lover
___ Penny: 4 Will 5 Henny
penny-a-___: 5 liner
penny-ante: 5 petty 8 picayune, trifling
pennycress: 4 weed
...___ penny earned: 3 is a
Penny Lover (1984 song)
artist: Lionel Richie
___ Penny Opera: 5 Three
penny pincher: 5 miser, piker 6 cheapo 7 Scrooge 8 el cheapo, tightwad 9 skinflint 10 cheapskate
penny-pinching: 4 mean 5 cheap, tight 6 greedy, skimpy, stingy 7 miserly, selfish, thrifty 8 grasping 9 penurious, provident 10 avaricious, skinflinty
penny-wise: 6 frugal, stingy 8 ungiving 10 economical
Penny wise, pound foolish: 5 adage
Penobscot: 3 bay 5 river 6 Indian 7 Amerind
city on the ~: 5 Orono 6 Bangor
river locale: 5 Maine
Penrod
author: Booth Tarkington
friend: 3 Sam
Pensacola: 3 bay 4 city, port, town
initials at ~: 3 NAS
locale: 7 Florida
Pensées
author: Blaise Pascal
pen-shaped instrument: 6 stylus
pension: 5 grant, hotel 6 reward 7 annuity, payment, premium, stipend, subsidy, support 9 allowance
federal ~: 3 SSA
plan: 3 IRA 5 ERISA, Keogh
pensive: 3 sad 5 grave, moody, sober 6 dreamy, musing 7 serious, wistful 8 absorbed, thinking 9 pondering 10 abstracted, meditative, melancholy, reflective, ruminating, thoughtful
sound: 3 hmm
pent: 5 caged 6 shut in 7 boxed in, encaged, immured 8 closed in, confined, cooped up, fenced in, hedged in, hemmed in, interned, walled in 9 corralled 10 cloistered, imprisoned
penta-: 4 five
pentacle: 4 star
pentad: 7 quintet 9 quintette
Pentagon
bigwigs: 5 brass
org.: 3 DoD
VIP: 3 gen. 7 general
pentameter
iambic ~: 4 rime 5 meter, rhyme
unit: 4 foot, iamb
___ pentameter: 6 iambic
pentane derivative: 4 amyl
Pentateuch: 4 Tora 5 Torah
author: Moses
book: 6 Exodus 7 Genesis, Numbers 9 Leviticus 11 Deuteronomy
pentathlon: 5 sport
modern ~ event: 4 épée
Pentax: 6 camera
alternative: *see* camera
Pente: 4 game 9 board game
Pentecost: 5 feast 7 Holy Day
penthouse: 5 suite 9 apartment
feature: 4 view
in the ~: 4 atop
like a ~: 4 posh 5 plush, swank 6 swanky 9 expensive, luxurious
of a sort: 4 aery, eyry 5 aerie, eyrie
Pentimento
author: Lillian Hellman
Pentium: 4 chip
manufacturer: 5 Intel
unit: 3 GHz, MHz
pent-up: 6 curbed, shut in 7 bridled, checked, stifled 8 confined, held back, reined in 9 bottled-up, inhibited, repressed, smothered 10 restrained, restricted, suppressed
penultimate: 10 next-to-last
penumbra: 5 shade 6 shadow
penurious: 4 mean, near, poor 5 broke, cheap, close, needy, tight 6 bad off, greedy, hard up, ill off, in need, in want, skimpy, stingy 7 miserly, pinched, selfish 8 badly off, bankrupt, beggarly, deprived, grasping, indigent, strapped 9 destitute, flat broke, insolvent, moneyless, penniless 10 avaricious, down and out, economical, pauperized, skinflinty, straitened
state: 4 need 7 poverty
penuriousness: 5 greed 7 avarice
penury: 4 need, ruin, want 6 misery 7 beggary, poverty 9 indigence, privation 10 insolvency
Penzance: 4 port
locale: 7 England
Penzias, Arno: 8 Nobelist 9 physicist
peon: 4 esne, hand, serf 5 slave 6 drudge, thrall 7 laborer, peasant 9 field hand
peonage: 4 yoke 7 slavery 9 servitude
peony: 5 plant, shrub 6 flower
people: 3 kin, mob 4 cats, clan, folk, herd, race, they 5 crowd, folks, plebs, tribe 6 bodies, family, humans, masses, nation, occupy, public, rabble 7 kinfolk, mankind, mortals, persons, society 8 citizens, humanity, kinfolks, kinsfolk, populace, riffraff 9 bourgeois, citizenry, hoi polloi, human race, multitude, plebeians, residents, vox populi 10 population
additional ~: 6 others
beautiful ~: 5 elite 6 jet set 7 society 8 nobility 10 blue bloods, upper crust
combining form: 3 dem- 4 demo- 5 ethno-
common ~: 4 herd 5 plebs 6 masses, rabble 8 plebians, riffraff 9 hoi polloi
full of ~: 5 dense 7 crowded 8 populous
let ~ know: 3 air 4 tell, vent 7 publish 8 proclaim 9 broadcast, publicize
many ~: 3 mob 4 gang, mass 5 crowd, crush, troop 9 multitude

values of a ~: **5** ethos
where most ~ live: **4** Asia
working ~: **5** labor **9** employees
people __: **5** mover **6** person
__ people: **3** lay **4** boat **6** little
People: **3** mag **4** song **8** magazine
composer: Bob Merrill, Jule Styne
person: **4** star **5** celeb **6** editor **9** celebrity
People (1964 song)
artist: Barbra Streisand
People __ Strange: **3** Are
__ People: **3** Cat **4** Show, Used **5** Night, Plain, Short, We the **6** Chosen, Listen, Lonely **7** Smiley's, Village
People Are Funny: **8** game show
host: Art Linkletter
peopled: **7** settled **8** occupied **9** colonized
__ People Eater, The: **6** Purple
__ people go: **5** Let my
People Got to Be Free (1968 song)
artist: Rascals
People of the Deer
author: Farley Mowat
__ People Play: **5** Games
people's
minding other ~ business: **4** nosy **5** nosey **6** prying, snoopy **7** gossipy
People's Choice, The
author: Herbert Agar
dog: **4** Cleo
People's Court, The
judge: Joseph Wapner
People's Liberation __: **4** Army
__ People's Money: **5** Other
People Will Say We're in Love
composer: Oscar Hammerstein, Richard Rodgers
People, Yes, The: **4** poem
author: Carl Sandburg
Peoria: **4** city, town
athletes: **6** Braves
city near ~: **5** Pekin
locale: **7** Arizona **8** Illinois
school: **7** Bradley
pep: **2** go **3** vim, zip **4** kick, push, snap, zest, zing **5** drive, gusto, moxie, oomph, punch, spice, verve, vigor **6** bounce, energy, spirit, starch **8** buoyance, buoyancy, vitality, vivacity **9** animation **10** exuberance, friskiness, get up and go, liveliness
full of ~: **4** spry **5** agile, alive, vital **6** lively **7** playful, zestful
give a ~ talk: **4** urge **6** charge, exhort **7** cheer on, enliven **8** admonish, motivate **9** encourage
lack of ~: **6** anemia, apathy **7** anaemia **8** lethargy
lose ~: **4** flag, tire **5** weary **7** exhaust **8** slow down
rally shout: **3** rah, yay, yea **6** go team
up: **4** wake **5** cheer, liven, waken **6** turn on, vivify **7** animate, enliven, quicken **8** activate, energize, vitalize **9** encourage, stimulate **10** exhilarate, invigorate
pep __: **4** talk **5** rally
Pep: **6** Willie
Pep Boy: **3** Moe **4** Jack **5** Manny
Pepcid: **7** antacid
alternative: *see* antacid
Pepe: **5** Le Pew **6** Le Moko
Pepe Le __: **4** Moko
Pepe Le Pew defense: **4** odor
Pepin the __: **5** Short
pepita: **5** snack
pepo: **5** gourd, melon **6** squash, veggie **7** pumpkin **8** cucumber **9** cantaloup, muskmelon, vegetable **10** cantaloupe, watermelon
Peppard, George: **5** actor
film: Breakfast at Tiffany's (1961) How the West Was Won (1962)
spouse: Elizabeth Ashley
TV: The A-Team
pepper: **3** dot **4** pelt, spot **5** betel, cover, spice, throw **6** flavor, season, veggie **7** spice up **8** jalapeño, sprinkle **9** condiment, punctuate, seasoning, vegetable
companion: **4** salt
dispenser: **4** mill **6** shaker
ender: **3** box, oni **4** corn, mint **5** grass
family shrub: **4** kava **5** cubeb
hot ~: **3** aji **5** chile, chili **6** chilli **7** cayenne, tabasco
kind of ~: **3** hot, red **4** bell **5** black, chile, green, sweet, white **6** cherry **7** cayenne, stuffed, tabasco
picker: **5** Peter
pot: **4** stew
pot ingredient: **4** meat, okra **5** tripe
rings: **9** appetizer
use a ~ mill: **5** grind **6** season
pepper __: **3** pot, rat **4** game, mill, tree **5** steak
pepper-__: **5** upper
__ pepper: **3** red
Pepper: **2** Dr. **3** Art, Sgt. **6** Martin
pepper-and-__: **4** salt
Pepperdine: **6** school **10** university
athletes: **5** Waves
locale: **6** Malibu **10** California
Pepper-Hot Baby (1955 song)
artist: Jaye P. Morgan
Pepperidge __: **4** Farm
peppermint: **4** herb **5** candy, sweet
candy: **5** patty, stick **6** pattie
peppermint __: **3** oil **5** stick
Peppermint Patty to Marcie: **3** sir
Peppermint Twist (1961 song)
artist: Joey Dee and the Starliters
pepperoni: **7** cold cut, sausage
place: **5** pizza **8** pizzeria
peppershrike: **5** vireo
pepperwort: **4** fern
peppery: **3** hot **4** gray, grey, sour **5** cross, fiery, sharp, spicy, testy **6** cranky, red-hot, snappy, spicey, touchy **7** piquant, pungent, zestful **8** choleric, snappish, spirited, stinging **9** irascible, irritable, trenchant, with a kick
Pepper Young's Family: **9** radio show
peppy: **4** spry **5** alert, brisk, perky, vital, zesty, zippy **6** active, bright, bubbly, feisty, frisky, lively **7** dashing, dynamic, piquant, rocking, romping, vibrant, zestful **8** animated, grooving, skittish, spirited, vigorous **9** energetic, sparkling, sprightly, vivacious
Pepsi: **3** pop **4** cola, soda **9** soft drink
competitor: **4** Coke **8** Diet Rite, Dr. Pepper
__ Pepsi: **4** Diet
pepsin: **6** enzyme
Pepsodent: **10** toothpaste
alternative: *see* toothpaste
peptide hormone: **5** kinin
Pepto-Bismol: **7** antacid
alternative: *see* antacid
Pep, Willie: **5** boxer
milieu: **4** ring
Pepys, Samuel: **6** writer **7** British, diarist
destination: **3** bed
Pequod: **4** boat, ship **6** whaler
captain: **4** Ahab
Pequot: **6** Indian **7** Amerind **8** language
per: **3** via **4** a pop, each **5** a head, every **6** apiece **7** for each, through
ender: **4** cent **5** force **6** chance, sister
per __: **4** cent, diem **5** annum **6** capita, centum
perambulate: **4** rove, step, walk **5** amble, leg it, mosey **6** foot it, ramble, stroll **7** saunter **8** traverse, walk over
Per ardua ad __: **5** astra
percale: **6** fabric **8** material, sheeting
per capita: **4** each **6** apiece
__ Percé: **3** Nez
perceivable: **7** obvious, visible **8** apparent, palpable
perceive: **3** get, see **4** feel, find, know, mark, note, spot, tell, view **5** catch, grasp, sense, sight, smell, think **6** behold, deduce, descry, divine, fathom, intuit, look on, notice, regard, remark, take in **7** cognize, discern, make out, observe, realize, receive **8** discover **9** apprehend, recognize **10** appreciate, comprehend, understand
ability to ~: **5** sight **7** empathy, insight **8** sympathy **9** intuition
fail to ~: **4** miss
with the nose: **5** sniff, whiff
perceiver: **4** eyer **6** viewer **7** witness **9** spectator
perceiving: **8** sentient **9** conscious, intuitive, sensitive **10** insightful
percent: **5** ratio **8** fraction **10** proportion
ender: **3** age, ile
fifty ~: **4** half **6** moiety
hundred ~: **3** all **5** fully **6** in full, in toto, purely, wholly **7** cap-à-pie, totally, utterly **8** entirely, from A to Z **9** all the way, every inch, to the hilt **10** absolutely, completely, thoroughly, to the limit
ten ~: **5** tithe
percentage: **3** cut, lot **4** bite, gain, rate **5** bonus, chunk, juice, piece, quota, ratio, share, slice, split **6** payoff, profit **7** benefit, portion **8** discount, interest, kickback **9** advantage, allowance, brokerage **10** commission
percenter, ten: **5** agent
__-Per-Cent Solution, The: **5** Seven
perceptible: **4** real **5** clear, plain, vivid **6** cogent, visual **7** audible, evident, express, obvious, outward, sensory, visible **8** apparent, distinct, explicit, manifest, palpable, tangible **9** graspable, sensorial **10** noticeable, spelled out
perception: **3** ear, eye, ken, wit **4** grip, idea, plan, tact, wits **5** grasp, image, sense, sight **6** acumen, vision **7** concept, culture, feeling, hearing, insight, picture, thought **8** epiphany, eyesight, judgment, keenness **9** awareness, discovery, foresight, intuition, sensation **10** cognizance, horse sense, impression
extrasensory ~: **3** ESP **9** telepathy
keen ~: **5** grasp **6** acuity, acumen, wisdom **7** insight **8** judgment, lucidity **9** acuteness, awareness **10** astuteness, brainpower, brilliance, cleverness, shrewdness
__ perception: **5** depth
__-perception: **4** self
perceptive: **4** keen, wise **5** acute, alert, aware, quick, ready, sharp **6** astute, shrewd, subtle, wise to **7** knowing, logical, tactful, tuned in **8** keen-eyed, lynx-eyed **9** astucious, cognizant, conscious, intuitive, judicious, observant, sagacious, sensitive **10** conversant, discerning, farsighted, insightful, responsive
perch: **3** sit **4** aery, eyry, fish, land, nest, pole, post, seat, stay **5** aerie, eyrie, light, lodge, roost, squat, stool **6** alight, branch, remain, settle **7** balance, seafood, sojourn **9** touch down
find a ~: **4** land **5** light **6** settle
high ~: **4** aery, eyry **5** aerie, eyrie
returned to the ~: **3** lit **4** alit **7** settled
__-percha: **5** gutta
perchance: **4** lest **5** maybe **6** in case, mayhap **7** perhaps **8** feasibly, possibly, probably
Percheron: **5** horse **6** animal, equine
repast: **3** hay **4** oats **5** grass **6** forage
perciatelli: **5** pasta
alternative: *see* pasta
percipience: **3** wit **6** acumen
percipient: **5** aware, sharp **9** conscious, intuitive, observant **10** discerning
Percival: **6** Lowell
percolate: **4** drip, leak, ooze, seep, soak, weep **5** bleed, drain, exude, froth, leach, sweat **6** bubble, filter, ramble, strain **7** pervade, trickle **8** filter in, filtrate, permeate **9** lixiviate, penetrate, transfuse **10** impregnate, infiltrate
percussion: **5** crash **6** impact **9** collision, explosion
instrument: **3** riq, zil **4** bell, drum, gong, harp, trap **5** mbira, spoon, vibes **6** cabasa, caxixi, chimes, chimta, claves, cymbal, densho, ipu ipu, kenong, piatti, rattle, tam-tam **7** balafon, bonnang, cymbals, kalimba, maracas, marimba, mokugyo, sanh sua, shekere, sistrum **8** amadinda, angklung, carillon, ceng ceng, chocalho, clappers, gankogui, hyoshigi, Jew's harp, pandéiro,

triangle **9** castanets, vibraharp **10** vibraphone
percussion __: 3 cap **4** lock **7** flaking, welding
Percy: 5 Adlon, Faith, Henry **6** Sledge, Walker **7** Shelley **8** Bridgman, Kilbride **9** Rodrigues
author: Hannah Moore
Percy __ Shelley: 6 Bysshe
Percy, Walker: 6 writer
work: Love in the Ruins
The Message in the Bottle
The Moviegoer
The Thanatos Syndrome
per diem: 4 a day **5** daily **7** diurnal **9** circadian, quotidian
Perdita's partner: 5 Pongo
perdition: 4 fall, hell, ruin **5** Hades **8** downfall **9** damnation
consign to ~: 4 damn **5** curse **9** imprecate
perdu: 6 hidden **9** concealed, invisible, unnoticed **10** out of sight, unviewable
père: 6 cleric, father, French
Père __: 4 Noël **6** Goriot
peregrinate: 4 hike, roam, rove, trek, walk **5** jaunt, march **6** ramble, travel, wander **7** journey, meander, wayfare **8** ambulate, traverse, walk over **9** itinerate **10** travel over
peregrination: 4 hike, tour, trek, trip, walk **5** jaunt **6** ramble, travel **7** journey **9** excursion
peregrine: 4 bird **5** alien **6** falcon **7** foreign **9** migrating, traveling, wandering
cover a ~'s eyes: 4 hood, seel
peregrine __: 6 falcon
Peregrine Pickle
author: Tobias Smollett
peremptorily: 9 summarily
peremptory: 4 curt, firm, rude **5** bossy, final **6** lordly **7** binding **8** absolute, decisive, despotic, dogmatic **9** arbitrary, assertive, imperious, insistent, mandatory **10** aggressive, autocratic, commanding, despotical, dogmatical, high-handed, imperative, obligatory, tyrannical
peremptory __: 4 plea
perennial: 3 old **5** plant **6** flower, steady, yearly **7** abiding, chronic, endless, eternal, lasting, nonstop, undying **8** constant, enduring, immortal, lifelong, long-term, timeless, unending, unwaning **9** ceaseless, chronical, continual, incessant, permanent, perpetual, recurrent, sustained, unabating, unceasing, unfailing **10** continuing, inveterate, persistent, unchanging
garden ~: 4 iris, lily, rose **5** aster, daisy, peony, phlox **7** daylily **9** coreopsis, oneflower **10** delphinium
Peres, Shimon: 2 P.M. **7** Israeli **8** Nobelist
predecessor: 5 Rabin **6** Shamir
successor: 6 Shamir **9** Netanyahu
Peretti: 4 Elsa
Peretz: 4 Amir
Perez: 4 Tony **5** Prado, Rosie **7** Vincent
__ Pérez de Cuellar: 6 Javier
Pérez Galdós, Benito: 6 writer **7** Spanish **10** playwright
Perez, Tony: 3 Red
perfect: 3 A-OK, ten **4** best, hone, pure, tops **5** clean, crown, exact, ideal, model, right, sheer, sound, total, utter, whole **6** better, dead-on, entire, evolve, finish, intact, mature, polish, refine, revise, smooth, strict **7** achieve, correct, develop, improve, optimum, precise, realize, supreme, to a turn, touch up, utopian **8** absolute, accurate, complete, flawless, outright, peerless, polish up, round off, round out, suitable, textbook, thorough, unbroken, unerring, unharmed, unmarred, wondrous **9** faultless, foolproof, just right, matchless, unalloyed, undamaged, unrivaled, unspoiled, untouched, virtuosic, wonderful **10** accomplish, complement, consummate, immaculate, impeccable, infallible, inimitable, on the money, unimpaired, unrivalled
4.0 is a ~ one: 3 GPA
at NASA: 3 AOK **5** a-okay
condition: 4 mint **7** like new
example: 7 epitome
game: 7 shutout **8** no-hitter
game spoiler: 3 hit **4** walk
in a ~ world: 7 ideally
it can be ~: 5 tense
not ~: 6 faulty, flawed **7** lacking **8** mediocre **10** incomplete
pair: 5 match
place: 4 Eden **6** heaven, Utopia **8** Paradise
rating: 3 ten
serve: 3 ace
see also wonderful
perfect __: 4 game **5** pitch
__ perfect: 4 past **6** future **7** present
__-perfect: 6 letter
Perfect (1985 film)
cast: Jamie Lee Curtis, John Travolta
Perfect __, A: 5 Peace, World **6** Couple, Murder
Perfect __, The: 3 Spy **5** Storm
perfecta: 3 bet **5** wager
kin: 6 exacta
Perfect Day for Bananafish, A
author: J.D. Salinger
perfection: 4 pink **5** ideal, prime, worth **6** purity **7** quality **8** fruition, maturity, ripeness **9** evolution, exactness, integrity, precision, sublimity, supremacy, wholeness **10** completion, excellence
standard of ~: 5 ideal
perfectionist: 5 type A **8** stickler
perfectly: 3 pat **4** to a T, well **5** fully, quite, right **6** dead-on, wholly **7** rightly, to a turn, totally, utterly **8** entirely, laudably, superbly, very well, worthily **9** correctly, just right, on the nose, supremely **10** absolutely, altogether, completely, flawlessly, impeccably, thoroughly, to the limit
Perfect Murder, A (1998 film)
cast: Michael Douglas, Viggo Mortensen, Gwyneth Paltrow
perfecto: 5 cigar
Perfect Peace, A
author: Amos Oz
Perfect Recall
author: Ann Beattie
Perfect Sleeper maker: 5 Serta
Perfect Spy, A
author: John le Carré
Perfect Storm, The (2000 film)
cast: George Clooney, Diane Lane, Mark Wahlberg
setting: 3 sea
Perfect Strangers (ABC sitcom)
cast: Mark Linn-Baker (Larry Appleton)
Bronson Pinchot (Balki Bartokomous)
setting: Chicago, Illinois
Perfect World (1988 song)
artist: Huey Lewis and the News
Perfect World, A (1993 film)
cast: Kevin Costner, Laura Dern, Clint Eastwood
director: Clint Eastwood
perfidious: 4 evil **5** false, lying **6** untrue **7** corrupt **8** disloyal, recreant **9** dishonest, faithless, insidious, insincere, two-timing **10** inconstant, traitorous
perfidy: 7 falsity, treason **8** bad faith, betrayal **9** dirty work, duplicity, treachery **10** disloyalty, untrueness, wickedness
perforate: 3 cut, pit **4** bore, open, stab **5** drill, prick, punch **6** pierce, riddle **8** puncture **9** honeycomb, penetrate
perforation: 4 hole **7** opening **8** puncture
perform: 2 do **3** act **4** sing **5** dance, emote, enact, serve, stage **6** acquit, commit, comply, effect, finish, fulfil, recite, render **7** achieve, execute, fulfill, ham it up, observe, operate, playact, produce, pull off, realize, satisfy **8** appear as, bring off, carry out, complete, function, generate, practice, transact **9** discharge, dramatize, implement, interpret **10** accomplish, effectuate
alone: 4 solo
a marriage: 3 wed **5** unite
in an opera: 4 sing **6** intone **7** belt out **8** vocalize
well: 5 excel, shine **7** surpass
with a baton: 5 twirl **7** conduct
without words: 4 mime **7** gesture **9** pantomime
performance: 3 act, gig **4** play, rite, show, work **5** dance, doing, drama, event, opera, revue, stunt **6** acting, action, ballet, record, rescue, review **7** burlesk, concert, matinee, pageant, pursuit, recital, special **8** ceremony, exercise, practice **9** burlesque, discharge, enactment, execution, operation, portrayal, rehearsal, rendition, spectacle, stage show, technique **10** recitation
acknowledge a ~: 4 clap **5** cheer **7** applaud
added ~: 6 encore
date: 7 booking
diva's ~: 4 aria **5** opera
extemporaneous ~: 6 improv
first ~: 7 opening **8** premiere
for charity: 7 benefit
jazz ~: 3 gig, set
mount a ~: 5 put on, stage
prepare for a ~: 8 practice, rehearse
short ~: 4 skit
virtuoso ~: 5 éclat
__ performance: 6 repeat **7** command
performed: 7 wrought
performer: 4 mime **5** actor, comic **6** artist, player **7** actress, trouper **8** comedian, musician, thespian, virtuoso
bit-part ~: 5 extra
carnival ~: 4 geek
circus ~: 3 dog **4** flea, pony, seal **5** clown, horse **7** acrobat, juggler **8** elephant **9** lion tamer
coffeehouse ~: 4 poet
extra: 6 encore
gesturing ~: 4 mime **5** clown, mimer, mimic
improv ~: 5 comic **8** comedian
kabuki ~: 4 male
monologue ~: 6 diseur
nightclub ~: 5 comic **6** singer **8** comedian
operatic ~: 4 alto, bass **5** basso, mezzo, tenor **7** soprano
paid ~: 3 pro
platform: 5 stage
rodeo ~: 5 roper **6** cowboy **7** cowgirl **8** cow belle **9** bullrider
solo ~: 4 diva **6** skater **7** danseur **9** ballerina, ice skater **10** prima donna
stunt ~: 5 clown **7** acrobat, juggler
symphony ~: 9 conductor, orchestra
top ~: 3 ace **4** star **9** headliner
union: 3 SAG **5** AFTRA
performing __: 4 arts, seal
perfume: 4 atar, balm, odor, otto **5** aroma, athar, attar, cense, ottar, scent, smell **6** sachet **7** bouquet, cologne, essence, incense **9** fragrance, rose water
amount: 3 dab **6** squirt
apply ~: 3 dab **5** spray
base: 4 atar, musk, otto **5** athar, attar, civet, orris, ottar
holder: 4 vial **5** phial **6** bottle, flacon
ingredient: 4 atar, musk, otto **5** athar, attar, civet, ester, myrrh, nerol, orris, ottar **6** acetal, citral, ionone
Japanese ~ source: 5 rasse
measure: 4 dram **5** ounce
name: 5 Estée **6** Chanel, Lanvin
oil: 6 neroli
scent: 4 lily, musk **7** jasmine **8** gardenia
solvent: 5 aldol **9** acetaldol
source: 5 civet, petal **6** flower
test spot: 5 wrist
__ perfumed sea: 4 o'er a
perfumy: 5 sweet **8** fragrant
perfunctory: 3 lax **4** cool **5** hasty, quick, stock, token **6** casual, remiss, sloppy, wooden **7** cursory, hurried, offhand, routine, sketchy, summary **8** careless, listless, lukewarm, slapdash, slipshod **9** apathetic, automatic, imprudent, negligent, unmindful **10** incautious, mechanical, nonchalant, uncritical, unthinking

pergola: **5** arbor, bower **8** pavilion **9** colonnade
perhaps: **4** lest **5** maybe **8** feasibly, possibly, probably **9** perchance **10** imaginably
peri: **3** fay **5** fairy **6** sprite
ending: **5** scope
Peri: **6** Gilpin
perianth: **5** calyx **7** corolla
part: **5** sepal
periapt: **5** charm **6** amulet, scarab **8** talisman
pericarp: **4** aril **5** shell
Pericles: **5** Greek **6** orator
author: William Shakespeare
foe: **5** Cleon
peridot: **3** gem **8** gemstone
color: **5** green
month: **6** August
perigee's opposite: **6** apogee
__ Pérignon: **3** Dom
peril: **4** risk **5** stake **6** danger, hazard, menace, threat **7** pitfall **8** endanger, exposure, jeopardy, unsafety **9** adventure, liability **10** insecurity, jeopardize
in ~: **6** at risk **7** at stake, exposed
perilous: **5** dicey, grave, hairy, risky, rocky, shaky, tight **6** chancy, loaded, touchy, unsafe, wicked **7** ominous, parlous, unsound **8** delicate, dynamite, menacing, slippery, ticklish **9** dangerous, hazardous, on thin ice, uncertain, unhealthy **10** precarious, touch and go
__ Perilous: **5** Siege
perilousness: **4** risk **6** danger **7** gravity
Perils of Pauline, The: **6** serial
perimeter: **3** hem, rim **4** edge, side **5** ambit, limit, skirt, verge **6** border, bounds, circle, fringe, limits, margin **7** circuit, compass, outline **8** boundary, confines **9** periphery **10** boundaries
period: **3** age, day, dot, end, eon, era, run **4** aeon, halt, span, stop, term, time **5** close, cycle, epoch, limit, phase, point, shift, space, spell, stage, while **6** course, length, lesson, season, spread, streak **7** session, stretch **8** duration, interval, lifetime **9** cessation **10** conclusion, generation
brief ~: **5** spell
busy ~: **4** rush
calendar ~: **3** day **4** week, year **5** month
census ~: **6** decade
cooling-off ~: **4** stay **5** delay, grace, truce
galactic time ~: **3** age
geologic ~: **3** age, era **5** epoch
historical ~: **3** age, era **5** epoch **6** decade **7** century
of decline: **3** ebb **5** slump **9** downswing **10** depression
off-peak ~: **4** lull **5** letup **6** hiatus **8** breather
of inactivity: **4** calm, lull **6** hiatus, layoff, recess, stasis **7** respite, time-out **8** downtime **9** interlude
of office: **4** term
of stability: **3** pax **5** peace
of time: **3** age, day, eon **4** aeon, hour, week **5** month, space **6** minute, moment, second **7** century **9** chilicosm **10** nanosecond
orbital ~: **4** year
pay ~: **4** week **5** month
probationary ~: **5** trial
prolonged ~ of trouble: **5** siege
prosperous ~: **4** boom **7** upswing
quiet ~: **4** lull
school ~: **4** term **8** semester
sports ~: **4** half **5** round **6** inning **7** chukker, quarter
work ~: **3** day **4** week **5** shift
period __: **5** piece
__ period: **3** pay **5** grace
periodic: **3** odd **4** eral **5** daily **6** annual, cyclic, hourly, random, spotty, weekly, yearly **7** epochal, erratic, monthly, regular, routine **8** cyclical, frequent, on-and-off, repeated, seasonal, sporadic **9** alternate, irregular, recurrent, recurring, spasmodic **10** occasional, sporadical
periodic __: **5** table
periodical: **3** mag, rag **4** zine **5** daily, organ, paper, press, print, slick **6** review, weekly **7** journal, monthly **8** magazine **9** newspaper, quarterly
for short: **3** mag **4** zine
palindromic ~: **4** Elle
www. ~: **5** e-zine
periodically: **7** at times **9** sometimes **10** now and then
periodicals: **5** media
periodicity: **6** rhythm **10** regularity
periodic table
category: **3** gas **5** metal
datum: **4** at. no., at. wt.
member: **7** element
table suffix: **3** -ium
Periodic Table, The
author: Primo Levi
periodontist
concern: **3** gum
degree: **3** DDS
org.: **3** ADA
plea: **5** floss
peripatetic: **5** rover **6** mobile, roving **7** migrant, nomadic, roaming, vagrant **8** ambulant, gadabout, vagabond **9** itinerant, migratory, traveling, wandering, wayfaring
one: **4** goer **5** nomad, rover **8** gadabout, wanderer
peripheral: **5** add-on, minor, outer **7** surface **8** exterior, external, marginal, outlying **9** component, extrinsic, secondary **10** extraneous
peripheral __: **6** vision
periphery: **3** hem, rim **4** brim, edge, side **5** limit, skirt, verge **6** border, fringe, limits, margin **7** outside, surface **8** boundary, confines **9** outskirts, perimeter **10** boundaries
periphrastic: **5** wordy **6** prolix **7** verbose **8** rambling **10** long-winded
periscope part: **4** tube **5** prism **6** mirror
peristyle: **5** patio **6** arcade, atrium **8** cloister **9** courtyard
periwinkle: **4** blue **5** plant, shell, vinca **6** flower **8** seashell
perjure oneself: **3** lie **7** falsify **8** forswear **9** foreswear
perjurer: **4** liar
confession: **5** I lied
perjury: **3** lie **5** lying
perk: **3** tip **4** brew, plus **5** bonus, extra, gravy **6** tipoff **7** benefit, largess, premium **8** dividend, gratuity, largesse **9** advantage, lagniappe
up: **4** gain **5** cheer, elate, extra, liven, rally, renew **6** revive, reward **7** elevate, enliven, improve, inspire, lighten, recover, refresh **8** brighten, interest, reassure **9** stimulate, take heart **10** convalesce, exhilarate, invigorate **16** recuperate. vivify
worker's ~: **4** ESOP **5** bonus **7** holiday **8** vacation
Perkins: **4** Carl, Tony **6** Marlin, Millie **7** Anthony, Frances **9** Elizabeth
Perkins, Anthony: **5** actor
film: Catch-22 (1970)
Fear Strikes Out (1957)
ffolkes (1980)
The Fool Killer (1965)
Friendly Persuasion (1956)
Green Mansions (1959)
The Matchmaker (1958)
Pretty Poison (1968)
Psycho (1960)
WUSA (1970)
role: **5** Bates **6** Norman
Perkins, Carl
song: Blue Suede Shoes (1956)
Perkins, Maxwell: **6** editor
perky: **4** busy, cute, pert, spry **5** alert, astir, brisk, happy, light, peppy, sunny **6** active, at work, bouncy, bright, bubbly, cheery, jaunty, lively **7** buoyant, chipper, dynamic, rocking, working **8** animated, bubbling, bustling, cheerful, grooving, spirited, tireless, untiring **9** assiduous, energetic, sprightly, vivacious
Perle: **5** Mesta
Perlman: **3** Ron **4** Rhea **6** Itzhak
Perlman, Itzhak: **7** Israeli **9** violinist
Perlman, Rhea: **7** actress
spouse: Danny DeVito
perm: **4** curl, wave
follow-up: **3** set **4** trim
part of a ~ kit: **6** curler
permafrost: **3** ice
permanence: **6** fixity **9** constancy, endurance, existence, fixedness, stability **10** durability
permanent: **4** coif, firm **5** fixed **6** hairdo, rooted, stable, static **7** abiding, lasting, settled, undying **8** coiffure, constant, definite, enduring, immortal, ironclad, lifelong, long-term, standing, unfading, unwaning **9** continual, immutable, indelible, perennial, perpetual, steadfast **10** changeless, inerasable, inveterate, stationary, unchanging, undecaying
be ~: **4** last, stay **6** endure
make ~: **3** fix, set **6** lock in
marker: **3** pen
place: **5** salon **10** beauty shop
result: **4** curl, wave
permanent __: **4** wave **5** press
permanently: **5** in pen **6** always **7** forever, for good **8** evermore, for keeps **9** for always **10** for all time
Permanent Midnight (1998 film)
cast: Maria Bello, Elizabeth Hurley, Ben Stiller, Owen Wilson
permanent-press feature: **5** pleat **6** crease
permeable: **4** thin **6** porous **8** bibulous, pervious **9** absorbent **10** penetrable, spongelike
permeate: **4** fill, seep, soak **5** imbue, steep **6** charge, drench, embrue, filter, imbrue, infuse, invade, occupy **7** pervade, suffuse **8** filter in, saturate **9** go through, penetrate, percolate **10** impregnate, infiltrate
permed: **4** wavy **5** curly **6** frizzy **7** frizzly
per mensum: **7** monthly
permissible: **2** OK **4** good, okay **5** legal, legit, licit **6** kasher, kosher, lawful, proper **8** all right, approved, bearable, endorsed **9** allowable, permitted, tolerable, tolerated
permission: **2** OK **3** nod **4** okay **5** leave, order, right, the OK **6** assent, permit **7** consent, freedom, go-ahead, liberty, license, warrant **8** approval, blessing, sanction **9** admission, agreement, authority **10** acceptance, concession
give ~: **3** let **5** agree, allow, grant, yield **6** accede, enable, permit **7** approve, certify, concede, empower, endorse, entitle, license **8** sanction **9** acquiesce, authorize
refuse ~: **3** nix **4** veto **6** forbid
word of ~: *see* of course
written ~: **4** pass
permissive: **3** lax **4** easy, free, kind, mild, soft **5** loose, slack **6** gentle, kindly **7** clement, lenient, liberal, ruthful, sparing **8** allowing, flexible, laid-back, merciful, placable, tolerant, unstrict **9** agreeable, approving, assuasive, compliant, easygoing, forgiving, indulgent **10** forbearing, unexacting, unhardened
word: **3** may, yes
permissiveness: **6** laxity, lenity **8** lenience **9** tolerance
permit: **2** OK **3** let **4** bear, have, okay, pass, visa **5** agree, allow, bless, brook, grant, humor, leave, say OK, yield **6** accede, accept, enable, endure, patent, say yes, suffer, ticket, wink at **7** approve, consent, empower, endorse, entitle, go-ahead, indorse, indulge, intitle, liberty, license, qualify, receive, warrant **8** accede to, assent to, legalize, passport, sanction, stand for, thumbs-up, tolerate, variance **9** acquiesce, approve of, authorize, franchise, give leave, let happen, put up with, sign off on **10** green light, permission
travel ~: **4** visa **6** carnet **8** passport
Permit Me Voyage
author: James Agee
permitted: **2** OK **4** able, okay, open **5** legit, licit **6** kosher, lawful, proper **8** rightful **9** by the book **10** admissible

permutable: 6 in flux 8 changing, shifting 10 changeable
permutation: 5 shift 6 change 8 mutation
permute: 4 vary 5 alter, shift 6 change, modify
Pernell: 7 Roberts
pernicious: 3 bad 4 evil 5 fatal, toxic 6 deadly, lethal, malign, nocent, wicked 7 baleful, baneful, harmful, hurtful, miasmic, nocuous, noxious, ruinous 8 damaging, sinister, venomous, virulent 9 dangerous, injurious, malicious, nefarious, pestilent, poisonous 10 calamitous, evil-minded
Pernod: 5 drink 7 liqueur 8 beverage
ingredient: 5 anise
Perón: 3 Eva 4 Juan 5 Evita 6 Isabel
perorate: 4 rant 6 preach 7 declaim, descant, discant, lecture 8 bloviate, harangue 9 discourse, expatiate, hold forth, sermonize, speechify
Perot: 4 Ross 5 H. Ross
__ peroxide: 7 benzoyl
peroxide user: 6 blonde
perp: 5 felon 7 accused, suspect 8 criminal 9 wrongdoer 10 lawbreaker
catcher: 3 cop 6 police 9 detective, policeman
pick up a ~: 3 nab 4 bust 5 catch, pinch 6 arrest, collar 7 capture
perpendicular: 5 erect, on end, plumb, sheer, steep 7 upright 8 standing, straight, vertical
almost ~: 5 sheer, steep
off the ~: 5 alist 7 leaning, tilting 9 at an angle
to the keel: 5 abeam
perpetrate: 2 do 3 act 5 enact, wreak 6 commit, effect 7 execute, pull off 8 carry out 9 force upon, succeed in
perpetrator: 5 felon, thief 6 robber 8 criminal
__ perpetua: 4 esto
perpetual: 3 old 4 same 6 eterne, steady 7 abiding, endless, eternal, lasting, nonstop, undying 8 constant, enduring, immortal, infinite, long-term, repeated, standing, timeless, unbroken, unending, unwaning 9 ceaseless, continual, immutable, incessant, perennial, permanent, recurrent, recurring, repeating, unceasing, unfailing 10 continuous, invariable, unchanging, without end
perpetual __: 5 check 6 motion
perpetually: 4 ever 6 always 7 forever 8 evermore 9 for always
Perpetual Peace
author: Immanuel Kant
perpetuate: 6 secure 7 prolong, support, sustain 8 continue, maintain, preserve 9 keep going
perpetuity: 8 duration, sequence 9 constancy, continuum, extension, stability 10 continuity
in ~: 6 always 7 forever 9 eternally
perplex: 4 balk, faze 5 addle, amaze, baulk, cloud, floor, mix up, snarl, stump 6 baffle, bemuse, boggle, fuddle, muddle, puzzle, rattle, stymie 7 astound, buffalo, confuse, fluster, mystify, nonplus, perturb, stagger, trouble 8 astonish, befuddle, bewilder, confound, encumber, entangle, surprise 9 discomfit, dumbfound 10 discompose, disconcert
perplexed: 4 asea, lost 5 at sea 6 in a fog 7 at a loss, in a daze, puzzled 9 flummoxed 10 bewildered
perplexing: 4 hard 5 funny, mirky, murky, tough, vague 6 arcane, knotty, thorny, tricky 7 complex, cryptic, obscure, strange, unclear 8 abstruse, nebulous, puzzling 9 confusing, cryptical, difficult, enigmatic, intricate 10 indistinct, unsettling
perplexity: 4 knot, maze 5 worry 6 enigma, strait 8 quandary 9 amazement, confusion, labyrinth 10 difficulty
state of ~: 3 fog 4 daze
perquisite: 3 pay, tip 5 bonus, extra, gravy, right 6 tipoff 7 benefit, premium, revenue 8 dividend, gratuity 9 lagniappe, privilege
Perrault, Charles: 6 French, writer
Perreau: 4 Gigi
Perrier
alternative: 4 Naya 5 Evian 8 Aquafina 9 Arrowhead
Perrine, Valerie: 7 actress
film: The Electric Horseman (1979)
The Last American Hero (1973)
Lenny (1974)
Maid to Order (1987)
Superman (1978)
W.C. Fields and Me (1976)
Superman role: 3 Eve
__ & Perrins: 3 Lea
Perry: 3 Joe 4 Como, King, Luke 5 Ellis, Frank, Mason, Steve, White 6 Botkin, Oliver 7 Gaylord, Matthew 10 Antoinette
victory site: 4 Erie
Perry, Gaylord: 6 hurler 7 pitcher
Perry Mason
creator: Erle Stanley Gardner
Perry Mason (CBS drama)
cast: Raymond Burr (Perry Mason)
Barbara Hale (Della Street)
William Hopper (Paul Drake)
William Talman (Hamilton Burger)
feature: 5 trial 6 murder 9 courtroom
Persa daughter: 5 Aeaea, Circe, Kirke
perscrutation: 5 probe
persecute: 3 dog, rag 4 bait, ride 5 abuse, bully, grind, harry, hound, spite, tease, worry, wrong 6 badger, harass, hector, pester, pick on, plague, pursue 7 afflict, oppress, torment, torture 8 aggrieve, ill-treat, keep down, maltreat 9 beleaguer, tyrannize, victimize
persecutor: 3 foe 5 bully, enemy
Persephone
equivalent: 10 Proserpina
husband: 5 Hades, Pluto
parent: 4 Zeus 7 Demeter
Persepolis
locale: 4 Iran
Perseus
father: 4 Zeus
mother: 5 Danae
neighbor of ~: 5 Aries
star in ~: 5 Algol
victim of ~: 6 Medusa
wife: 9 Andromeda
perseverance: 4 cool, grit, guts, zeal 5 drive, moxie, pluck, spunk 7 stamina 8 backbone, hard work, patience, sedulity, tenacity 9 constancy, diligence, endurance, stability
persevere: 4 go on, hold, plod 5 abide, retry 6 endure, hang in, hold on, insist, keep on, pursue, remain, resist 7 carry on, go for it, persist, press on, proceed, survive 8 continue, go on with, keep at it, maintain, plug away, work hard 9 hang tough, keep going, stand firm 10 go for broke
persevering: 4 at it 6 dogged 7 patient 8 diligent, hellbent, resolute, sedulous, stubborn, tireless, untiring 9 laborious, steadfast, tenacious
Pershing: 4 John 9 Black Jack
colleague: 4 Foch
Pershing II: 4 ICBM 7 missile
Persia
ancient city: 4 Susa
ancient native: 4 Mede
astronomer: 4 Omar 7 Khayyám
bird: 6 bulbul
lamb: 3 fur
language: 5 Farsi, Parsi 7 Avestan 8 Parthian
mathematician: 4 Omar 7 Khayyám
money: 5 daric
mythology angel: 3 Mah
poet: 4 Omar, Sa'di 5 Hafez, Hafiz 7 Khayyám
queen: 6 Esther
religion: 5 Baha'i
ruler: 4 Shah 6 satrap
siren: 5 houri
sprite: 4 peri
tiger: 4 sher
title: 5 sophy
today: 4 Iran
Persian: 3 cat 4 Gulf 5 felid, Irani 6 feline 8 language
remark: 3 mew 4 meow, purr 5 miaou, miaow, miaul
rug: 5 kilim 6 Kirman
Persian __: 3 cat, rug 4 Gulf
Persian Boy, The
author: Mary Renault
Persian Gulf
ancient kingdom: 4 Elam
capital: 4 Doha
city: 5 Basra, Busra 6 Busrah
country: 5 Katar, Qatar 6 Kuwait
federation: 3 UAE
island: 7 Bahrain, Bahrein
port: 5 Dibai, Dubai
region: 4 Hasa
strait: 5 Ormuz 6 Hormuz
vessel: 5 oiler 6 tanker
Persians, The
author: Aeschylus
persiflage: 4 talk 6 banter 7 ribbing 8 badinage, raillery, repartee, wordplay
persimmon: 4 tree 5 fruit
family: 5 ebony
Japanese ~: 4 kaki
Persis: 9 Khambatta
persist: 2 go 4 go on, hold, last 5 abide, recur, stick 6 endure, hang it, hold on, insist, linger, obtain, pursue, remain, resist 7 carry on, survive 8 continue, go on with, maintain, plug away 9 hang tough, keep going, persevere, stand firm 10 go the limit, tough it out
persistence: 7 purpose 8 patience, tenacity 10 resolution
Persistence of Memory: 8 painting
artist: Salvador Dali
persistent: 4 firm 5 fixed, pushy 6 dogged, steady, wilful 7 abiding, chronic, endless, undying, willful 8 constant, diligent, enduring, frequent, habitual, haunting, hellbent, lifelong, obdurate, repeated, resolute, sedulous, stubborn, tireless, untiring, unwaning 9 assiduous, chronical, continual, incessant, insistent, obstinate, perennial, steadfast, tenacious, unabating, unfailing 10 consistent, determined, inveterate, undeterred, unflagging, unwearying
persisting: 6 living 7 lasting 8 unwaning 9 continual 10 inveterate
Persky: 4 Bill
persnickety: 5 fussy, picky 6 choosy, dainty, prissy 7 choosey, finicky, mincing, precise 8 exacting, finiking, finnicky, snobbish 9 selective 10 fastidious, nitpicking
Persoff: 8 Nehemiah
person: 3 gal, guy, man 4 body, self, sort, soul 5 being, human, joker, party, woman 6 feller, mortal 7 grown-up 8 customer, organism, somebody, specimen 9 character, earthling, personage 10 human being, individual, living soul
artificial ~: 5 droid, robot
beautiful ~: 6 vision
boat ~: 7 refugee
busy ~: 4 doer 6 dynamo
charitable ~: 5 donor
cleaning ~: 4 maid 7 janitor, servant
clumsy ~: 3 oaf 4 clod 5 klutz 7 bumbler
combining form: 6 prosop- 7 prosopo-
contemptible ~: 3 cad 4 jerk, worm 9 no-good-nik, sleazebag
crafty ~: 3 fox 8 slyboots
delivery ~: 6 driver 7 mailman 9 messenger
different ~: 5 other 7 another
displaced ~: 5 exile 6 émigré 7 outcast, refugee 8 emigrant
enlisted ~: 7 private, recruit, soldier
experienced ~: 3 pro 6 old pro 7 old hand, veteran
famous ~: 4 star 5 celeb 6 phenom 7 notable 8 luminary 9 celebrity, dignitary, headliner 10 phenomenon
funny ~: 3 wag 4 card, riot, zany 5 comic 6 scream
gifted ~: 3 wiz 6 genius 10 precocious

gullible ~: 3 sap 4 butt, dupe, tool 5 chump, patsy 6 pigeon, sucker, victim 7 fall guy 8 pushover
haughty ~: 4 snob 5 snoot
head ~: 4 boss 5 chief 7 foreman, manager 8 official
important ~: 3 VIP 4 czar, lion, name, star, tsar 5 mogul, mover, nabob, titan 6 shaker, tycoon 7 magnate, notable 8 luminary, somebody 9 celebrity, dignitary, plutocrat
in custody: 4 ward 5 felon 6 orphan 8 detainee
learned ~: 4 prof, sage 5 brain 7 scholar 9 professor
little ~: 3 elf 5 dwarf, faery, fairy, troll 6 faerie, midget 10 leprechaun
mean ~: 4 ogre 5 brute, bully
messy ~: 4 slob 5 frump
middle ~: 5 agent 6 broker, jobber 8 mediator 9 go-between
named derived from a ~: 6 eponym
new ~: 4 baby 5 hiree 6 novice 7 recruit 9 greenhorn 10 tenderfoot
newspaper ~: 6 editor 8 reporter 10 journalist
odd ~: 4 kook 5 crank, flake 6 weirdo 7 oddball 9 character, eccentric 10 individual
outgoing ~: 5 mixer 9 extrovert
per ~: 4 a pop, each 6 apiece
PR ~: 5 flack 8 promoter
repair ~: 5 fixer 8 mechanic 9 carpenter, craftsman
retired ~: 6 senior
rich ~: 6 fat cat 9 financier, moneybags
right-hand ~: 4 aide, asst. 6 helper 8 henchman, mainstay 9 assistant, gal Friday, man Friday 10 girl Friday
second ~: 3 you
starter: 3 lay 4 news, wait 5 chair, sales 6 anchor, spokes 8 business
surly ~: 4 crab 5 churl, crank 6 grouch 10 curmudgeon
swell ~: 5 brick, honey, peach 7 sweetie 10 sweetheart
tiresome ~: 4 bore, pain, pest, pill
unfashionable ~: 4 geek, wonk 7 egghead
watch ~: 5 guard, scout 6 sentry 7 lookout
young ~: 3 boy, imp, kid, lad, son 4 babe, baby, brat, cion, teen, ward 5 bairn, child, minor, scion, youth 6 cherub, infant, moppet, nipper, squirt 7 bambino, neonate, newborn, preteen, sapling 8 daughter, juvenile, small fry, teenager 9 offspring, stripling 10 adolescent, descendant

persona
cast ~: 4 role 9 character
Halloween ~: 5 ghost, ghoul, haunt, spook, witch 7 vampire
opposite: 5 anima
public ~: 5 image 6 facade

persona __ grata: 3 non
personable: 2 OK 4 nice, okay, warm 7 affable, amiable, cordial, likable, winning 8 all heart, all right, amicable, charming, friendly, likeable, outgoing, pleasant, pleasing, sociable 9 agreeable, easygoing 10 gregarious
personae, dramatis: 4 cast
personage: 3 VIP 4 name, soul 5 brass, celeb 6 bigwig, figure, person, top dog, worthy 7 big shot, hotshot, notable 8 eminence, luminary, somebody 9 celebrity, character, dignitary, superstar 10 individual
personal: 3 own 5 inner, privy 6 bodily, direct, inward, proper, secret 7 private, special 8 intimate, peculiar, ulterior 9 exclusive, innermost, nonpublic 10 individual, particular, respective, subjective
ad letters: 3 SWF, SWM
advisor: 4 guru 6 lawyer 7 teacher, trainer 8 attorney 9 counselor
asset: 4 pull 5 charm, magic 6 allure, appeal, glamor 7 charism, glamour 8 charisma, mystique, presence 9 magnetism
atmosphere: 4 aura 5 vibes 8 charisma
attendant: 4 aide 5 valet 9 chauffeur, secretary
combining form: 4 idio-
effects: 5 stuff 6 things 8 property
get too ~: 3 spy 5 snoop, stare 6 butt in, horn in, meddle 7 intrude, obtrude, wiretap 8 question 9 interfere
history: 3 bio 6 memoir, résumé 7 autobio, memoirs, profile 9 biography
interest: 5 share 10 investment
viewpoint: 4 bias 5 slant 7 opinion

personal __: 4 best, care, foul 5 space, staff 7 effects, pronoun, trainer
Personal Best (1982 film)
cast: Scott Glenn, Mariel Hemingway
Personal Finance
rival: 5 Money
Personal Injuries
author: Scott Turow
personality: 3 VIP, way 4 name, self, star 5 brass, celeb, charm 6 bigwig, figure, makeup, nature, psyche, temper, top dog, traits, worthy 7 big shot, charism, hotshot, notable 8 charisma, dynamism, eminence, identity, luminary, presence, selfhood, somebody 9 celebrity, dignitary, magnetism, mentality, superstar
asset: 4 tact 5 charm, poise
kind of ~: 5 type A, type B
part: 2 id 3 ego 5 anima 7 persona 8 superego

__ personality: 5 split
Personality
composer: Johnny Burke, Jimmy Van Heusen
Personality (1959 song)
artist: Lloyd Price
personalize: 7 initial 8 monogram
Personal Witness
author: Abba Eban
persona non __: 5 grata
personate: 7 imitate
personify: 6 embody, imbody, mirror, typify 7 express 8 manifest, stand for 9 exemplify, incarnate, represent, symbolize 10 illustrate
personnel: 4 crew 5 cadre, corps, staff, troop 6 office, troops 7 faculty, helpers, members, workers 8 manpower 9 employees, work force 10 associates
datum: 3 age, sex
enlisted ~: 3 GIs 6 grunts 8 privates, recruits, soldiers
hire ~: 3 man 5 reman, staff 6 take on
key ~: 4 core
slot: 3 job 4 post 8 position
Person, place, and Thing
author: Karl Shapiro
person, place or __: 5 thing
Persons and Places
author: George Santayana
__ Person Singular: 6 Absurd
Person to Person (CBS) host: Edward R. Murrow
perspective: 4 view 5 angle, scene, slant, vista 6 aspect 7 context, horizon, mindset, outlook 8 attitude, overview, panorama, prospect 9 landscape, viewpoint
perspicacious: 4 keen, wise 5 acute, alert, canny, quick, savvy, sharp, smart 6 astute, clever, shrewd 7 politic 8 incisive, luminous, rational 9 astucious, observant, sagacious
perspicacity: 3 wit 4 wits 6 acumen, wisdom 7 insight 8 judgment, keenness
perspicuous: 5 clear, lucid 6 limpid 7 graphic, logical 8 apparent, clear-cut, luminous 9 graphical
perspiration: 5 sweat 6 egesta 8 moisture
perspire: 4 drip, glow, ooze 5 egest, exude, sweat 6 lather 7 excrete, secrete, swelter
perspiring: 3 hot 4 warm 6 sweaty 10 overheated
Persson: 4 Nina
persuadable: 4 meek 6 docile 8 amenable 9 receptive, tractable 10 indecisive
persuade: 3 con, get, win, woo 4 bend, coax, draw, hook, lead, lure, move, push, sell, sway, talk, turn, urge 5 budge, impel, lobby, tempt 6 advise, affect, assure, cajole, compel, enlist, entice, exhort, incite, induce, prompt, reason 7 convert, counsel, impress, incline, involve, satisfy, wheedle, win over 8 blandish, convince, inveigle, motivate, talk into, wear down 9 argue into, brainwash, influence, instigate, prevail on
more than ~: 5 force 6 compel 8 armtwist, pressure
to marry: 3 win, woo 5 court
persuasion: 4 cult, sect, type, urge, view 5 creed, faith, party, tenet 6 advice, belief, church, school 7 coaxing, faction, opinion, snow job 8 cajolery, hard sell, pressure, religion, soft soap 9 dialectic, incentive, sentiment, sweet talk, wheedling 10 conviction, enticement
Persuasion
author: Jane Austen
persuasive: 5 slick 6 cogent, moving, potent, smooth, strong 7 logical, telling, weighty 8 alluring, credible, eloquent, enticing, forceful, inviting, luculent, powerful 9 dialectic, disarming, effective, effectual, impelling, plausible 10 believable, convincing
pert: 4 bold, cute, flip, rude, spry 5 brash, brisk, fresh, lippy, nervy, perky, sassy, saucy, smart 6 awless, brazen, breezy, bright, cheeky, dapper, jaunty, lively, nimble, snappy, snippy 7 aweless, chipper, forward, uncivil 8 animated, cheerful, flippant, impolite, impudent, insolent, snippety, spirited 9 audacious, out of line, sprightly, vivacious 10 ungracious
female: 4 minx 5 hussy
Pert: 6 Kelton 7 shampoo
competitor: 4 Flex 5 Prell, Suave, Wella 7 Finesse, Pantene
pertain: 5 apply, refer, touch 6 affect, bear on, belong, regard, relate 7 concern, connect, touch on 8 bear upon, belong to 9 touch upon
pertaining: 4 as to 8 relative 9 pertinent 10 concerning, in regard to
Perth: 4 city, town
locale: 9 Australia
river: 3 Tay
Perth Amboy: 4 city, town
locale: 9 New Jersey
pertinacious: 5 rigid 6 dogged, mulish, ornery, wilful 7 adamant, staunch, willful 8 contrary, obdurate, resolute, stalwart, stubborn, untiring 9 obstinate, pigheaded, steadfast, unbending 10 determined, headstrong, inflexible, persistent, unyielding
pertinent: 3 apt 5 ad rem, valid 6 cogent, proper, timely 7 apropos, fitting, germane, logical, on point, on topic, pointed, related, salient 8 apposite, material, relative, relevant, suitable, verified 9 competent, connected 10 admissible, applicable, felicitous, pertaining, to the point
be ~: 5 apply, refer 6 bear on, regard, relate 7 concern, touch on
pertness: 5 sauce 9 flippancy, impudence, insolence
perturb: 3 ail, bug, get, irk, vex 4 faze, miff 5 alarm, anger, annoy, harry, peeve, shake, upset, worry 6 affect, bother, dismay, flurry, needle, pester, put out, rattle, ruffle 7 agitate, chagrin, confuse, disturb, fluster, perplex, provoke, shake up, trouble, unnerve 8 bewilder, confound, disquiet, exercise, irritate, unsettle, unstring 9 discomfit 10 discomfort, discompose, disconcert, disgruntle
perturbed: 5 het up, upset 6 on edge, pacing, uneasy 7 shook up, worried 8 in a tizzy, restless 9 con-

cerned, in a lather, unsettled **10** distraught, distressed, up in the air

Peru: 6 nation **7** country
ancient culture: 4 Inca **5** Nazca
beast: 5 llama **6** alpaca, vicuña
brandy: 5 pisco
capital: 4 Lima
cereal: 6 quinoa
city: 5 Cusco, Cuzco, Piura, Tacna **8** Arequipa, Trujillo
desert: 7 Sechura
explorer: 7 Pizarro
lake: 8 Titicaca
language: 6 Aymara, Jivaro, Kechua **7** Spanish
money: 3 sol **4** inti
mountain: 5 Cusco, Cuzco **6** Ampato **7** Huandoy **8** Coropuna, Solimana, Yerupaja **9** Huascarán, Pumasillo, Salcantay
mountains: 5 Andes
native: 4 Inca **6** Aymara, Jivaro, Kechua **7** Kechuan, Quechua, Quichua **8** Quechuan
neighbor: 5 Chile **6** Brazil **7** Bolivia, Ecuador **8** Colombia
org.: 3 OAS
poet: 4 Moro **6** Eguren
port: 5 Paita **6** Callao
river: 5 Purus **6** Amazon, Javari
saint: 10 Rose of Lima
tanager: 4 yeni
volcano: 7 El Misti
wind: 4 puna
writer: 5 Palma **7** Alegría **8** Arguedas
see also Spanish

Perugia: 4 city, town
locale: 5 Italy
town near ~: 6 Assisi

Perugina: 5 candy **9** chocolate
peruke: 3 wig **6** toupee
perusal: 5 study **6** review, survey **7** reading **8** scrutiny **10** inspection
peruse: 3 con **4** pore, read, scan, skim **5** learn, study **6** browse, look up **7** analyze, examine, inspect **8** check out, look over, pore over **10** glance over, scrutinize
pervade: 4 fill **5** imbue, steep **6** charge, extend, infuse, occupy, riddle, spread **7** suffuse **8** permeate, saturate **9** penetrate, percolate **10** overspread
pervasive: 4 rife **6** common **7** all over, general **8** infested, profound **9** extensive, prevalent, universal **10** ubiquitous, widespread
quality: 4 aura, odor **5** aroma, vibes **10** atmosphere, vibrations

perverse: 3 wry **5** balky, rigid, surly, wrong **6** dogged, morose, mulish, ornery, sullen, unruly, wanton, wilful **7** corrupt, naughty, vicious, wayward, willful **8** contrary, factious, indocile, obdurate, sadistic, sinister, stubborn, untoward **9** fractious, miscreant, nefarious, obstinate, pigheaded, unhealthy, unnatural **10** headstrong, ill-natured, inflexible, rebellious, refractory, self-willed
___-per-view: 3 pay

pervious: 6 porous **9** permeable, pregnable **10** vulnerable
pesante: 7 heavily
Pescadores: 4 isls. **5** isles **7** islands
locale: 6 Taiwan

Pesci, Joe: 5 actor
film: Betsy's Wedding (1990)
Casino (1995)
GoodFellas (1990, AA)
Home Alone (1990)
JFK (1991)
Lethal Weapon 2 (1989)
Lethal Weapon 3 (1992)
Lethal Weapon 4 (1998)
My Cousin Vinny (1992)
Raging Bull (1980)

Pescow: 5 Donna
peseta: 5 money
word: 6 España

pesky: 7 irksome, nagging **8** annoying, worrying **9** loathsome, maddening, obnoxious, provoking, unwelcome, vexatious **10** bothersome, in one's hair, irritating, nettlesome
insect: 3 ant, fly **4** flea, gnat, wasp **5** midge **6** hornet **8** mosquito
plant: 4 weed

Pesky: 6 Johnny
peso: 5 money
ancestor: 4 tlac **5** tlaco
repository: 5 banco

pesos: 6 dinero
see also moolah

pessimism: 5 gloom **7** despair, sadness **8** cynicism, dark side, distrust, glumness **9** dejection **10** depression, gloominess, melancholy
pessimist: 5 cynic **6** downer **7** killjoy, sceptic, scoffer, skeptic, worrier **8** sourpuss **9** defeatist, gloomy Gus, worrywart **10** complainer, wet blanket
pessimistic: 3 sad **4** dark, glum, grim **5** bleak **6** gloomy, morbid, morose, sullen **7** bearish, cynical, worried **8** dejected, downbeat, hopeless, negative, resigned, troubled **9** depressed
investor: 4 bear
phrase: 5 I can't

pest: 3 ant, bug, fly, nag **4** bane, bore, drag, drip, flea, gnat, mite, pain, pill, slug, tick, wasp, weed **5** creep, mouse, roach, tease, trial, twerp, twirp, worry **6** bother, gadfly, hornet, insect, noodge, nudnik, plague, teaser, weevil **7** annoyer, heckler, no-see-um, scourge, termite **8** harasser, headache, horse fly, housefly, irritant, mosquito, nuisance, vexation **9** annoyance, buttinsky, cockroach, tormentor **10** irritation
closet ~: 4 moth
control: 3 cat **4** D Con, Raid **7** swatter **8** fumigant
cornfield ~: 4 coon, crow, deer **7** raccoon
ender: 4 hole
garden ~: 4 lice, mole, slug **5** aphid, aphis, borer, louse **6** earwig
hotel ~: 6 bedbug
household ~: 3 ant, fly **5** mouse, roach **6** insect, rodent **7** termite **8** mosquito
picnic ~: 3 ant
tiny ~: 3 ant **4** flea, gnat, mite **5** midge
winged ~: 3 fly **4** gnat, wasp **6** hornet **8** mosquito

pester: 3 bug, dog, dun, irk, nag, rag, vex **4** ride, wear **5** annoy, devil, get to, harry, hound, nag at, nudge, stalk, tease, worry **6** badger, bother, harass, hassle, heckle, hector, insist, madden, needle, nettle, noodge, pick at, plague, pother, put out, rankle, remind, work on **7** afflict, bedevil, bombard, disturb, henpeck, perturb, provoke, torment, trouble **8** disquiet, distress, irritate, mess with **9** aggravate, importune, persecute **10** drive crazy
pesthole: 3 sty **7** fleabag
pesticide: 5 spray
banned ~: 3 DDT

pestiferous: 8 annoying **9** vexatious **10** bothersome
pestilence: 6 plague **7** scourge **9** contagion
pestilential: 5 toxic **7** baneful, harmful, noisome, noxious, ruinous **9** dangerous, injurious **10** contagious, infectious, pernicious
pestle: 4 mash **5** grind, pound **6** masher **7** grinder, pounder **9** pulverize **10** pulverizer
pesto: 5 sauce
ingredient: 5 basil
partner: 5 pasta
seasoning: 6 garlic

pet: 3 cat, dog, hug, pat **4** huff, kiss, neck, pony, tiff **5** bunny, Corgi, pique, puppy, spoil, spoon, sweet, touch **6** adored, canary, caress, cosset, cuddle, dandle, feline, ferret, fondle, kitten, pamper, parrot, rabbit, smooch, stroke, sweets, tickle, toucan, turtle **7** favored, hamster, special, sweetie **8** canoodle, favorite, foul mood, goldfish, housecat, loved one, parakeet, sweetums **9** best-liked, cherished, guinea pig, inamorata, keep close, preferred **10** fair-haired, sweetheart, sweetie pie
big-eared ~: 5 bunny, burro, hound **6** basset, donkey, rabbit **9** dachshund
chatty ~: 4 mina, myna **5** minah, mynah **6** parrot
common ~ name: 4 Fido, Spot **5** Rover **6** Fluffy
cuddly ~: 5 bunny, puppy **6** kitten
exotic ~: 3 boa **6** iguana
food brand: 4 Alpo, Iams, Ken-L **5** Amore, Nutro, Rival **6** Figaro, Purina **7** Kibbles, Whiskas **8** Eukanuba, Friskies **9** Nine Lives **10** Chef's Blend, Fancy Feast
house ~: 3 cat, dog **4** bird, fish, myna **5** bunny, kitty, mouse, mynah, puppy **6** canary, ferret, kitten, parrot, rabbit, toucan, turtle **7** hamster **8** goldfish, parakeet
in a ~: 4 sore **5** irate, irked, testy, upset **6** peeved **7** annoyed, grouchy, sulking **8** snappish **9** irritated
lover org.: 4 SPCA
name: 3 hon **4** dear, name **5** deary, honey **6** dearie, sweets **7** darling, sweetie **8** nickname, sweetums **10** endearment, sweetie-pie
of nursery rhyme: 4 lamb
owner's need: 4 cage **5** leash **6** collar **8** aquarium
pampered ~: 6 lap dog
peeve: 7 bugbear **9** bête noire, hot button
problem: 5 mange, worms **8** parasite
project: 3 job **7** venture **10** enterprise
protection org.: 5 ASPCA
shop buy: 3 pup **4** bird, bone, cage, fish **5** bunny, leash, mouse, puppy, snake **6** canary, collar, gerbil, kitten, parrot, rabbit, turtle **7** hamster **8** parakeet **9** cat litter, doggy chew, guinea pig
small ~: 3 pup **5** bunny, mouse, puppy **6** gerbil, kitten, lap dog, turtle **7** hamster **9** guinea pig
see also sweetheart

pet ___: 4 name **5** peeve **6** sitter
___ pet: 3 in a
Pet ___: 4 Rock
Pet ___ Boys: 4 Shop
___ Pet: 4 Chia
PET ___: 4 scan
Peta: 6 Wilson
PETA cousin: 5 ASPCA
petal: 4 leaf
base: 5 sepal
oil: 4 atar, otto **5** athar, attar, ottar

Petaluma: 4 city, town
locale: 10 California

petcock: 3 tap **6** faucet
___ pete: 6 sneaky
Pete: 4 Best, Rose **6** Hamill, Reiser, Seeger, Wilson **7** Rozelle, Sampras **8** Fountain, Maravich **9** Townshend **10** Incaviglia
___ peter: 4 blue
Peter: 3 Max, Pan **4** Arno, Cook, Falk, Funt, Gunn, Hall, Hunt, Lely, Nero, pope, Tork, Tosh, tsar, Weir, Wolf **5** Adler, Allen, Boyle, Breck, Brook, Brown, Davis, Debye, Deuel, Finch, Fonda, Guber, Hyams, Lorre, Lupus, Medak, Noone, Osnos, Pears, Roget, saint, Sasdy, Sykes, Weiss, Yates **6** Bonerz, Cetera, Coyote, Duchin, Faiman, Gordon, Graves, Handke, Hertel, Horton, Markle, McCann, O'Toole, Rabbit, Serkin, Straub, Weller, Werner, Wimsey, Yarrow **7** Abelard, apostle, Behrens, Cushing, DeLuise, Doherty, Drucker, Gabriel, Gennaro, Godfrey, Hammond, Jackson, Kastner, Lawford, Martins, Medawar, Nichols, Onorati, pontiff, Riegert, Scolari, Sellers, Shaffer, Strauss, Ustinov, Watkins **8** Abrahams, Benchley, Farrelly, Frampton, Goldmark, Jennings, MacNicol, Marshall, McCarthy,

Mitchell, Newbrook, Quennell, Strastny 9 Celestine, Gallagher, Glenville, Greenaway, Masterson, Sarsgaard, Tewksbury, Ueberroth 10 Cottontail, Stuyvesant
partner: 4 Mary
successor of ~: 4 pope
Peter __ collar: 3 Pan
Peter __ Fabergé: 4 Carl
Peter __ Hayes: 4 Lind
Peter __ Rubens: 4 Paul
__ Peter: 5 Simon
Peter and Gordon
members: Asher, Waller
song: I Go to Pieces (1965)
Lady Godiva (1966)
Nobody I Know (1964)
True Love Ways (1965)
Woman (1966)
A World Without Love (1964)
Peter and the Wolf
animal: 3 cat 4 bird, duck, wolf
bird: 5 flute, Sasha
character: 5 Sonia
composer: Sergei Prokofiev
duck: 4 oboe
__ Peter Blatty: 7 William
__ Peter Dunne: 6 Finley
Peter Grimes: 5 opera
composer: Benjamin Britten
song: 4 aria
Peter Gunn (1959 song)
artist: Ray Anthony
Peter Gunn (NBC/ABC drama)
cast: Lola Albright (Edie Hart)
Craig Stevens (Peter Gunn)
hangout: Mother's
Peter Gunn guitarist: 4 Eddy
Peter Lind __: 5 Hayes
peterman: 4 yegg
Peter O'__: 5 Toole
peter out: 3 die, ebb 4 burn, conk, curb, drop, fade, fail, flag, give, pall, slow, stop, tire, wane 5 abate, droop, lower 6 lessen, reduce, run dry, shrink, weaken 7 curtail, cut down, decline, dwindle, fall off, fatigue, run down, subside, tail off 8 decrease, diminish, get tired, slack off, slow down, taper off 9 evaporate, grow weary
Peter Pan
alternative: 3 Jif 6 Skippy
author: James M. Barrie
beast: 4 croc
character: 5 Wendy
collar kin: 4 Eton
dog: 4 Nana
friends' nickname: 4 Tink
pirate: 4 Smee
Peter Pan __: 6 collar
Peter Paul __: 6 Rubens
Peter, Paul and Mary
members: Yarrow, Stookey, Travers
song: Blowin' in the Wind (1963)
Don't Think Twice, It's All Right (1963)
I Dig Rock and Roll Music (1967)
If I Had a Hammer (1962)
Leaving on a Jet Plane (1969)
Lemon Tree (1962)
Puff (The Magic Dragon) (1963)
Peter, Peter, pumpkin __: 5 eater
Peter Piper picked __...: 5 a peck
Peter Quince at the Clavier: 4 poem
author: Wallace Stevens
Peter Rabbit and __ of Beatrix Potter: 5 Tales
Peter Rabbit sibling: 5 Mopsy 6 Flopsy 10 Cottontail
Peters: 3 Jon 4 Jean 5 Brock 7 Roberta 10 Bernadette
Peter's __: 5 pence 7 Friends
Petersburg: 4 city, town
locale: 8 Virginia
Petersen: 4 Paul 8 Wolfgang
Petersen, Paul
song: My Dad (1962)
Petersen, Wolfgang: 8 director
film: Air Force One (1997)
Das Boot (1981)
Enemy Mine (1985)
In the Line of Fire (1993)
The NeverEnding Story (1984)
Outbreak (1995)
The Perfect Storm (2000)
Poseidon (2006)
Troy (2004)
Peter's Friends (1992 film)
cast: Kenneth Branagh, Rita Rudner, Emma Thompson
director: Kenneth Branagh
petersham: 4 coat 6 jacket
Peter Simple
author: Frederick Marryat
Peters, Jean: 7 actress
spouse: Howard Hughes
Peters, Jon
spouse: Lesley Ann Warren
Peterson: 3 Ray 5 Oscar
Peterson, Oscar: 7 pianist 8 Canadian
genre: 4 jazz
Peters, Roberta: 6 singer 7 soprano
milieu: 5 opera
piece: 4 aria
peter starter: 4 salt
Peter the Great: 4 czar, tsar 7 Russian
__ Pete's Sake: 3 For
petiole: 5 stipe
petit: 5 minor, small
petit __: 3 feu 4 four, jury 5 juror, point 6 beurre 7 larceny
petit chou
see sweetheart
petite: 3 wee 4 baby, puny, size, tiny 5 bitty, dwarf, elfin, short, small, teeny 6 atomic, bantam, dainty, little, minute, peewee, teensy 8 atomical, atomlike, delicate 9 dress size, itsy-bitsy, itty-bitty, miniature, pint-sized, undersize 10 diminutive, teeny-weeny, vest-pocket
__ Petite: 4 Reet
Petite Suite
composer: Béla Bartók
petit four: 4 cake 6 cookie, pastry 10 confection
petition: 3 ask, beg, sue 4 case, plea, pray, seek, suit, urge 5 apply, claim, plead, press 6 appeal, demand, invite, invoke, litany, orison, prayer 7 beseech, entreat, implore, request, solicit 8 entreaty, press for, put in for, question 10 invitation, round robin, supplicate
petits __: 4 pois
Petr: 5 Korda
Petrarch: 4 poet 7 Italian, scholar
beloved: 5 Laura
opus: 6 sonnet
petrel: 4 bird 5 cahow 10 shearwater
lair: 4 aery, eyry 5 aerie, eyrie
relative: 6 fulmar
__ petrel: 6 stormy
petri __: 4 dish
Petri: 4 Elio
petri dish contents: 4 agar 7 culture 8 agar-agar, bacteria
Petrie: 3 Ann, Rob 5 Laura 6 Daniel, Donald 7 Ritchie 8 Flinders
Petrie, Laura
husband: 3 Rob
portrayer: Mary Tyler Moore
petrified: 5 rocky, stiff, timid 6 afraid, frozen, scared, trepid 7 anxious, chicken, fearful, lithoid, nervous, panicky 8 cowardly, fearsome, hesitant, timorous 9 lithoidal, nerveless, unpliable 10 frightened, motionless, spellbound
sap: 5 amber
stand ~: 6 freeze
Petrified Forest: 4 park 8 monument
locale: 7 Arizona
Petrified Forest, The (1936 film)
cast: Humphrey Bogart, Bette Davis, Leslie Howard
petrify: 3 set 4 numb, stun 5 alarm, amaze, appal, chill, scare, spook 6 appall, benumb, dismay, harden, ossify 7 astound, horrify, stiffen, stupefy, terrify 8 astonish, frighten, indurate, lapidify, paralyse, paralyze, transfix 9 dumbfound, fossilize, terrorize 10 immobilize, mineralize, scare stiff
petrifying: 5 scary 8 terrible 9 appalling
Pet Rocks: 3 fad 5 craze
petrographer specimen: 4 rock 5 stone 7 mineral
petrol: 3 gas 4 fuel 8 gasoline
measure: 5 litre
petroleum: 3 oil 8 crude oil, resource
byproduct: 3 tar 6 alkane, benzol, butene, ethane 8 dimethyl
exporter: 4 Iran, Iraq, OPEC 5 Libya 6 Mexico 7 Nigeria 8 Colombia 9 Venezuela 11 Saudi Arabia
measure: 3 bbl. 6 barrel
source: 4 well 5 shale 8 oil shale
petroleum __: 5 jelly
petrology: 7 science
study: 5 rocks
Petrosian, Tigran
forte: 5 chess
Petrouchka: 6 ballet
composer: 10 Stravinsky
Petrovic, Drazen: 5 cager
milieu: 5 court
org.: 3 NBA
sport: 10 basketball
Petruchio: 5 lover, tamer
emulate ~: 4 tame
intended: 4 Kate
Petrushka
composer: Igor Stravinsky
Pet Sematary: 4 book 5 novel
author: Stephen King
cat: 6 Church
Pet Shop Boys
homeland: England
members: Tennant, Lowe
song: Always on My Mind (1988)
It's a Sin (1987)
Opportunities (1986)
West End Girls (1986)
What Have I Done to Deserve This? (1987)
Pettet: 6 Joanna
petticoat: 4 slip 8 lingerie 10 underskirt
antebellum ~: 4 hoop
Petticoat Junction (CBS sitcom)
cast: Bea Benaderet (Kate Bradley)
Edgar Buchanan (Joe Carson)
Frank Cady (Sam Drucker)
pettifog: 3 con 4 fool, jive, snow 5 cavil, trick 6 bicker, delude, niggle 7 deceive, nitpick, quibble 8 flimflam, hoodwink 9 bamboozle, disinform 10 split hairs
pettifogger: 6 lawyer 7 shyster 8 quibbler 10 fussbudget
Pettiford, Oscar: 7 bassist
genre: 4 jazz
petting zoo attraction: 3 boa 4 calf, colt, deer, pony 5 horse
Pettit, Bob: 5 cager
milieu: 5 court
org.: 3 NBA
sport: 10 basketball
Pettitte: 4 Andy
__ Pet Tricks: 6 Stupid
petty: 4 mean, puny, vain 5 catty, cheap, light, minor, small 6 little, measly, paltry, shabby, slight, stingy, two-bit, unfair, yeasty 7 shallow, trivial 8 niggling, picayune, piddling, spiteful, trifling 9 frivolous, malicious, parochial, penny-ante, secondary, valueless 10 negligible, nitpicking
be ~: 4 carp 5 cavil 7 nitpick, quibble
criminal: 4 punk 10 pickpocket, shoplifter
criminal, in Britain: 4 spiv
officer: 4 bo's'n 5 bosun 6 yeoman
quarrel: 4 fuss, huff, spat, tiff 5 set-to
sum: 7 peanuts
petty __: 4 cash, jury 5 juror, theft 7 larceny, officer
Petty: 3 Tom 4 Lori 7 Richard
Petty and the Heartbreakers, Tom
song: Change of Heart (1983)
Don't Come Around Here No More (1985)
Don't Do Me Like That (1979)
Free Fallin' (1989)
I Won't Back Down (1989)
Jammin' Me (1987)
Learning to Fly (1991)
Mary Jane's Last Dance (1994)
Refugee (1980)
Runnin' Down a Dream (1989)
Stop Draggin' My Heart Around (1981)
The Waiting (1981)
You Don't Know How It Feels (1994)
You Got Lucky (1982)
__ petty officer: 5 chief
Petty, Richard: 9 auto racer
milieu: 5 track
org.: 6 NASCAR
petulance: 5 anger 6 spleen, temper 9 surliness
show ~: 4 pout

petulant: **5** cross, huffy, irate, moody, sulky, testy, waspy, whiny **6** crabby, cranky, grumpy, ireful, snappy, sullen, touchy, whiney **7** crabbed, fretful, grouchy, peevish, pouting, prickly, waspish, whining **8** captious, fretsome, grumpish, snappish **9** fractious, grumbling, impatient, irascible, irritable, querulous, splenetic **10** ill-humored, ill-natured, out of sorts, ungracious
mood: **4** fret, huff, pout, snit, sulk
petunia: **5** plant **6** flower
Petunia Pig: **3** sow **4** toon
friend: **5** Porky
peut-__: **4** être
Pevney: **6** Joseph
pew: **4** seat **5** bench
book: **6** hymnal
escort to a ~: **4** seat **5** usher
locale: **4** nave **6** church
separator: **5** aisle
use a ~: **3** sit
pewee: **4** bird **6** phoebe **10** flycatcher
pewit: **4** bird **6** phoebe, plover **7** lapwing
pewter: **3** ley **5** alloy
component: **3** tin **4** lead
peyote: **6** cactus
Peyton: **7** Manning
Peyton Place: **4** book **5** novel
author: Grace Metalious
street in ~: **3** Elm
Peyton Place (1957 film)
cast: Hope Lange, Lloyd Nolan, Lana Turner
Peyton Place (ABC drama): **4** soap **9** soap opera
cast: Mia Farrow (Allison Mackenzie)
Dorothy Malone (Constance Mackenzie)
Ed Nelson (Dr. Michael Rossi)
Ryan O'Neal (Rodney Harrington)
Barbara Parkins (Betty Anderson)
PEZ: **4** nosh **5** candy, snack
PFC: **2** GI
address: **3** APO
boss: **3** sgt. **5** sarge
hangout: **2** PX **3** USO
rank above ~: **3** cpl.
see also private
Pfeiffer: **5** Dedee **8** Michelle
Pfeiffer, Michelle: **7** actress
film: The Age of Innocence (1993)
Batman Returns (1992)
Cheri (2009)
Dangerous Liaisons (1988)
Deep End of the Ocean (1999)
The Fabulous Baker Boys (1989)
Frankie and Johnny (1991)
Hairspray (2007)
I Am Sam (2001)
Into the Night (1985)
Ladyhawke (1985)
Married to the Mob (1988)
A Midsummer Night's Dream (1999)
The Russia House (1990)
Scarface (1983)
Stardust (2007)
Sweet Liberty (1986)
Tequila Sunrise (1988)
To Gillian on Her 37th Birthday (1996)
Up Close & Personal (1996)
What Lies Beneath (2000)
White Oleander (2002)
The Witches of Eastwick (1987)
Wolf (1994)
film (voice): The Prince of Egypt (1998)
spouse: David E. Kelley
pfennig: **4** coin **5** money
multiple: **4** mark
pfft, go: **4** fail **6** vanish **7** conk out **8** collapse **9** disappear
Pfizer
competitor: **5** Lilly, Merck
Pflug, Jo Ann: **7** actress
spouse: Chuck Woolery
pfui: **4** drat, rats, yuck **6** darn it
PG: **6** rating
issuer: **4** MPAA
P.G.: **9** Wodehouse
PG-13: **6** rating
issuer: **4** MPAA
PGA
event: **5** Doral, pro-am
member: **3** pro **6** golfer
part: **4** Assn., Golf **5** Assoc.
pH: **4** meas. **7** measure
high ~ substance: **3** alk. **4** base **8** alkaline
low ~ substance: **4** acid
tester: **6** litmus
Phaedra
author: Seneca
parent: **5** Minos **8** Pasiphae
sister: **7** Ariadne
phaeton: **3** car **4** auto **5** coach **7** vehicle **8** carriage **10** automobile
Phair: **3** Liz
phalanger: **9** marsupial
relative: *see* marsupial
phalanx: **4** bone **6** legion **7** brigade, platoon **8** division, regiment **9** battalion
phalarope: **4** bird
phantasm: **5** ghost, haunt, shade, spook **6** mirage, spirit, wraith **7** eidolon, phantom, specter **8** delusion, presence **10** apparition
phantasmagorical: **4** eery **5** eerie **6** unreal **7** ghostly **9** imaginary
phantasmal: **7** eidolic
phantasy: **6** revery **7** fantasy, reverie **8** daydream
phantom: **4** soul **5** ghost, haunt, shade, shape, spook **6** mirage, shadow, spirit, vision, wraith **7** bugbear, chimera, eidolon, specter **8** chimaera, delusion, illusive, illusory, revenant, spectral **9** obsession, unearthly **10** apparition, fictitious
Phantom: **3** car **4** auto **10** Rolls-Royce
Phantom Menace, The planet: **5** Naboo
Phantom of the Opera, The: **7** musical
author: Gaston Leroux
composer: Andrew Lloyd Webber
instrument: **5** organ
prop: **4** mask
role: **5** Raoul
setting: **5** Paris
Phantom Regiment, The
composer: Leroy Anderson
Phantoms
author: Dean Koontz
Phantom, The: **10** comic strip
character: **4** Sala
horse: **4** Hero
Pharaoh: **3** Tut **4** king **5** ruler, title **6** Cheops, gerent, Ramses, red ant **7** Rameses **8** Egyptian, Thutmose **9** Akhenaton, Amenhotep **10** Hatshepsut **11** Tutankhamen
amulet: **4** ankh
city: **6** Amarna, Thebes **7** Memphis
deity: **3** Set **4** Amon, Aten, Aton, Bast, Isis, Ptah, Seth **5** Horus **6** Amen-Ra, Amon-Ra, Osiris **7** Sekhmet
fabric: **5** linen
headdress: **6** uraeus
perhaps: **5** mummy
river: **4** Nile
Pharaoh __: **3** ant
pharisaism: **10** lip service
Pharisees: **4** sect
pharmaceutical: **4** drug **6** remedy **8** medicine **10** medication
giant: **5** Lilly, Merck **6** Pfizer
watchdog: **3** FDA
pharmacist: **8** druggist **10** apothecary
concern: **4** dose **6** dosage **7** formula **8** medicine **10** medication
container: **4** vial **5** phial **7** capsule
in Britain: **7** chemist
measure: **4** dram **5** minim
pharmacology: **7** science
study: **5** drugs **9** medicines
pharmacy: **5** store **7** chemist, science **9** drug store **10** apothecary, dispensary
Pharos: **6** beacon **10** lighthouse
pharynx: **6** gullet
neighbor: **5** uvula
prefix for ~: **4** naso
phase: **4** side, step, term **5** angle, cycle, facet, point, slant, stage, state **6** aspect, degree, period **7** chapter, feature, process **8** juncture, position **9** condition **10** appearance
moon ~: **3** new **4** full **7** gibbous **8** crescent
out: **6** remove **8** obsolete, withdraw **9** eliminate
phaser setting: **4** stun
phat
see wonderful
Ph.D.: **3** deg. **6** degree, doctor **8** graduate **9** doctorate
at times: **4** prof
exam: **5** orals
submission: **6** thesis
test for ~ entrants: **3** GRE
pheasant: **4** bird, fowl
Asian ~: **8** tragopan
brood: **3** nid **4** nide
dish: **5** salmi **6** salmis
female ~: **3** hen
relative: *see* fowl
young ~: **5** poult
Phèdre
author: Jean Racine
composer: Jules Massenet
Phelps: **4** Babe **6** Digger **7** Michael
phenol compound: **5** ester
phenom: **4** name, star **5** celeb **7** big name **9** celebrity, headliner
phenomenal
see wonderful
phenomenon: **4** fact **5** event, thing **6** marvel, matter, oddity, rarity, wonder **7** anomaly, miracle, prodigy, reality **8** incident **9** actuality, curiosity, happening, nonpareil, sensation, spectacle **10** appearance
Phenomenon (1996 film)
cast: Robert Duvall, Kyra Sedgwick, John Travolta, Forest Whitaker
dog: **6** Attila
phi: **5** Greek **6** letter
follower: **3** chi
preceder: **7** upsilon
Phi __: **4** Bete
phial: **6** bottle
Phi Beta Kappa concern: **3** GPA
Phil: **3** May **4** Fish, Lesh, Mogg, Ochs **5** Gramm, Mahre, Simms **6** Everly, Foster, Harris, Joanou, Lynott, McGraw, Morris, Niekro, Nowlan **7** Collins, Donahue, Hartman, Jackson, Karlson, Keoghan, Rizzuto, Silvers, Spector **8** Esposito **9** Esterhaus, Mickelson
Dr. ~: **6** McGraw
Philadelphia: **4** city, town
athletes: **4** Owls **7** Dragons, Quakers
city near ~: **6** Camden, Easton
clock setting: **3** EDT, EST
locale: **4** Penn.
newspaper: **4** News **8** Inquirer
pro team: **6** Eagles, Flyers, Sixers **8** Phillies
river: **8** Delaware **10** Schuylkill
school: **4** Penn **6** Drexel, Temple
transit system: **5** SEPTA
Philadelphia (1993 film)
cast: Tom Hanks, Jason Robards, Mary Steenburgen, Denzel Washington
director: Jonathan Demme
Philadelphia Freedom (1975 song)
artist: Elton John
__ Philadelphians, The: **5** Young
Philadelphia Story, The: **4** film, play
author: Philip Barry
cast: Cary Grant, Katharine Hepburn, James Stewart
director: George Cukor
Philae: **4** isle **6** island
her temple was at ~: **4** Isis
Philanderer, The
author: George Bernard Shaw
philanthropic: **4** good, kind **6** giving, humane, kindly **7** liberal **8** generous, gracious, selfless **9** bountiful, unselfish, unsparing **10** altruistic, beneficent, benevolent, charitable, free-handed, munificent, unstinting
be ~: **4** fund, give **6** do good, donate **10** contribute
philanthropist: **5** donor **6** patron **7** donator **10** benefactor
no ~: **5** miser **9** skinflint **10** pinchpenny
philanthropy: **7** largess **8** donation, kindness, largesse
philatelist concern: **5** stamp
abbr.: **4** perf.
need: **5** album, hinge

Philbin, Regis: **2** MC **4** host **5** emcee
partner: Kathie Lee Gifford, Kelly Ripa
Philby, Kim: **3** spy **4** mole
philemaphobe fear: **7** kissing
Philemon: **4** book
follower: **7** Hebrews
preceder: **5** Titus
philharmonic: **9** orchestra
philibeg: **4** kilt **5** skirt
Philip: **3** Ahn **4** Dorn, Hale, Neri, pope, Roth **5** Barry, Bosco, Dunne, Glass, Hench **6** Abbott, Bailey, Knight, Larkin, McKeon, Sidney **7** Freneau, Johnson, Kaufman, Leacock, Marlowe, pontiff **8** Anderson **9** Massinger, Noel-Baker
in Spanish: **6** Felipe
Philip ___: **4** Neri
Philip ___-Baker: **4** Noel
Philip K. ___: **4** Dick
Philip Michael ___: **6** Thomas
Philip of ___: **7** Macedon
Philippe: **5** Pinel **6** Noiret **7** Gaubert **8** Soupault **9** Desportes
see also French
___ Philippe: **5** Patek
Philippi: **4** city, town **6** battle
locale: **6** Greece **9** Macedonia
Philippians
follower: **10** Colossians
preceder: **9** Ephesians
philippic: **6** screed, tirade **8** diatribe, harangue, jeremiad **9** invective
Philippines: **4** isls. **5** isles **6** nation **7** country, islands
banana: **4** Saba
bay: **5** Subic **6** Manila
bivalve: **5** capiz
bovine: **7** carabao, tamarao, tamarau, timarau
capital: **6** Manila
city: **4** Cebu, Oton **5** Davao **6** Bacoor, Baguio, Iloilo, Manila **7** Bacolod
deer: **6** sambar, sambur **7** sambhar, sambhur
fish: **9** martinico
guerrilla: **3** huk
gulf: **5** Davao, Panay
island: **4** Cebu **5** Bohol, Leyte, Luzon, Panay, Samar **6** Negros **7** Mindoro **8** Mindanao, Visayans
islands near ~: **8** Marianas **9** Carolines
knife: **4** bolo **6** barong
language: **4** Moro, Sama **7** Bisayan, Tagalog, Visayan **8** Filipino
mahogany: **5** lauan
money: **4** peso **7** centavo
Muslim: **4** Moro
native: **3** Ati **4** Aeta **6** Igorot
palm: **4** nipa
peak: **3** Apo, Iba **8** Mount Apo
peninsula: **6** Bataan
plant: **5** abaca
port: **3** Iba **4** Cebu **5** Davao **6** Aparri, Iloilo, Manila
primate: **7** tarsier
river: **5** Pasig
sea: **4** Sulu **7** Celebes, Sibuyan **10** Philippine
seashell: **5** capiz
stew: **5** adobo
tree: **3** tua **4** acle, ipil, pili **5** almon, lauan **6** amugis
volcano: **3** Apo **4** Taal **5** Mayon **7** Bulusan, Canlaon **8** Pinatubo
writer: **5** Rizal
___ Philip Randolph: **3** Asa
Philips: **3** Emo
Philips, Ambrose: **4** poet
Philip Seymour ___: **7** Hoffman
___ Philip Sousa: **4** John
Philip the ___: **4** Fair
philistine: **4** boor **5** yahoo **9** barbarian, bourgeois
Philistine
ancient city-kingdom: **4** Gaza
city: **4** Gath
god: **4** Baal **5** Dagon
Phillies: **4** nine, team
org.: **3** MLB, NLE
rival: ***see*** baseball team
sport: **8** baseball
Phillip: **5** Noyce, Sharp
Phillippe, Ryan
spouse: Reese Witherspoon
Phillips: **3** Sam **4** John, Kyra, Loud, Sian **5** Ethan, Julia, screw, Stone **6** Chynna, Esther **7** William **8** Julianne, Michelle **9** Mackenzie
Phillips ___: **4** head
Phillips ___ Academy: **6** Exeter
___ Phillips: **6** Wilson
Phillips, Chynna
spouse: William Baldwin
Phillips, Julianne
spouse: Bruce Springsteen
Phillips, Lou Diamond: **5** actor
film: The Big Hit (1998)
La Bamba (1987)
Stand and Deliver (1987)
Young Guns (1988)
Phillips, Michelle: **6** singer
once: **4** Mama
spouse: Dennis Hopper
Phillips University, home of: **4** Enid
Phillips, William: **8** Nobelist **9** physicist
Phillpotts: **4** Eden
Philly
Hall-of-Famer: **7** Ashburn, Carlton, Roberts, Schmidt
philodendron: **5** aroid
family: **4** arum
philosopher: **4** Hook, Hume, Kant, Mach, Marx, Mead, Mill, Reid, Ryle, sage, Weil **5** Adler, Bacon, Bayle, Bruno, Buber, Camus, Cohen, Comte, Croce, Dewey, Digby, Fiske, Hegel, Hu Shi, James, Jones, Lewes, Locke, Lully, Moore, Paley, Perry, Plato, Renan, Royce, Smith, Sorel, Taine, Wolff **6** Alcott, Anselm, Besant, Cicero, Colden, Eucken, Fichte, Harris, Herder, Hobbes, Langer, Lao-tse, Lao-tzu, Littré, Ockham, Origen, Palmer, Pascal, Peirce, Popper, pundit, Sartre, Seneca, Thales **7** Abelard, Aquinas, Beattie, Bentham, Bergson, Bradley, Calkins, Diderot, Driesch, Edwards, Emerson, Erastus, Erigena, Haeckel, Haldane, Herbart, Husserl, Jaspers, Marcuse, Mencius, Proclus, Russell, scholar, Spencer, Spinoza, Steiner, Stewart, Tillich, Tolstoy, Unamuno **8** Alembert, Apuleius, Averroës, Avicenna, Berdyaev, Berkeley, Boethius, Cassirer, Diogenes, Epicurus, highbrow, Leibnitz, Longinus, Maritain, Plotinus, Plutarch, Rousseau, Schlegel, Socrates, Spengler, Voltaire **9** Aristotle, Augustine, Cleanthes, Condorcet, Confucius, Descartes, Epictetus, Feuerbach, Heidegger, Helvétius, Jefferson, Kropotkin, Lucretius, Nietzsche, Plekhanov, Santayana, Schelling, Whitehead **10** Anaxagoras, Bonhoeffer, Democritus, Empedocles, Heraclitus, Maimonides, Mandeville, Parmenides, Parrington, Protagoras, Pythagoras, Saint-Simon, Schweitzer, Xenophanes, Zeno of Elea **11** Anaximander, Antisthenes, Kierkegaard, Malebranche, Mendelssohn, Montesquieu
Austrian ~: **4** Mach **5** Buber **7** Steiner
British ~: **4** Hume, Mill, Ryle **5** Bacon, Digby, Lewes, Locke, Moore, Paley **6** Anselm, Besant, Hobbes, Ockham, Popper **7** Bentham, Bradley, Russell, Spencer, Stewart **9** Stapledon, Whitehead
Chinese ~: **4** Mo Ti **5** Hu Shi **6** Lao-tse, Lao-tzu **7** Mencius **9** Confucius
Danish ~: **11** Kierkegaard
Dutch ~: **7** Spinoza **10** Mandeville
French ~: **4** Weil **5** Bayle, Camus, Comte, Renan, Sorel, Taine **6** Littré, Pascal, Sartre **7** Abelard, Bergson, Diderot **8** Alembert, Maritain, Rousseau, Voltaire **9** Condorcet, Descartes, Helvétius **10** Saint-Simon, Schweitzer **11** Malebranche, Montesquieu
German ~: **4** Kant, Marx **5** Hegel, Wolff **6** Eucken, Fichte, Herder **7** Driesch, Haeckel, Herbart, Husserl, Jaspers, Marcuse **8** Cassirer, Leibnitz, Schlegel, Spengler **9** Feuerbach, Heidegger, Nietzsche, Schelling **10** Bonhoeffer **11** Mendelssohn
Greek ~: **5** Plato **6** Origen, Thales **7** Proclus **8** Diogenes, Epicurus, Longinus, Plotinus, Plutarch, Socrates **9** Aristotle, Cleanthes, Epictetus **10** Anaxagoras, Democritus, Empedocles, Heraclitus, Parmenides, Protagoras, Pythagoras, Xenophanes, Zeno of Elea **11** Anaximander, Antisthenes
Irish ~: **6** Colden **7** Erigena, Murdoch **8** Berkeley
Italian ~: **5** Bruno, Croce **7** Aquinas
Jewish ~: **10** Maimonides
Marxist ~: **4** Hook
North African ~: **9** Augustine
Persian ~: **8** Avicenna
Quaker ~: **5** Jones
Roman ~: **6** Cicero, Seneca **8** Apuleius, Boethius, Plotinus **9** Lucretius
Russian ~: **7** Tolstoy **8** Berdyaev **9** Kropotkin, Plekhanov
Scottish ~: **4** Mill, Reid **5** Smith **7** Beattie, Haldane
Spanish ~: **5** Lully **6** Marías **7** Unamuno
Spanish-Muslim ~: **8** Averroës
stoic ~: **4** Zeno
Swedish ~: **10** Swedenborg
Swiss ~: **7** Erastus
philosopher's ___: **5** stone
philosophical: **4** calm, cool, deep, wise **6** serene **7** erudite, learned, logical, patient, stoical, unmoved **8** abstract, composed, profound, rational, resigned, tranquil **9** impassive, judicious, sagacious, unruffled
philosophize: **6** reason
philosophy: **3** art, ism **4** idea, view **5** credo, creed, logic **6** reason, system, theory, wisdom **7** beliefs, outlook, thought **8** doctrine, ideology, ontology, thinking **9** knowledge, rationale, reasoning, viewpoint **10** hypothesis
mind, in ~: **4** nous
moral ~: **6** ethics
New Age ~: **6** holism
occult ~: **6** cabala, kabala **7** cabbala, kabbala
things, in ~: **5** entia
Philosophy of Composition, The
author: Edgar Allan Poe
Philosophy of Furniture
author: Edgar Allan Poe
Philosophy of Right, The man: **5** Hegel
Phil Silvers Show, The (CBS sitcom)
cast: Phil Silvers (M.Sgt. Ernie Bilko)
setting: Kansas
philter: **6** potion **10** love potion
Phineas: **6** Barnum
Phineas Finn
author: Anthony Trollope
Phineas Redux
author: Anthony Trollope
Phineus: **4** seer
brother: **6** Cadmus
father: **8** Poseidon
sister: **6** Europa
phiz: **3** mug, pan **4** face, puss **6** kisser
phlegm: **7** inertia **8** lethargy **9** lassitude
phlegmatic: **4** calm, cool, logy, slow **5** aloof, stoic **6** bovine, poised, steady, stolid **7** equable, languid, lumpish, passive, stoical **8** listless, lukewarm, sluggish, together **9** apathetic, collected, impassive, lethargic, temperate, unexcited, unruffled **10** unagitated
phloem
locale: **4** tree, wood
phlox: **5** plant **6** flower **9** perennial
Phnom Penh: **4** city, town **7** capital
locale: **8** Cambodia
phobia: **4** fear **5** dread, thing **6** hang-up, hatred, horror, terror **7** anxiety **8** aversion, loathing, neurosis **9** obsession
phobic: **6** scared **7** fearful
Phobos: **3** god **4** moon **5** deity
brother: **6** Deimos
parent: **4** Ares **9** Aphrodite
planet: **4** Mars
sister: **8** Harmonia

phoebe: 4 bird 5 pewee
Phoebe: 4 moon, Snow 5 Cates, giant, nymph, Titan 6 Amazon, Gordon
  daughter: 4 Leto
  planet: 6 Saturn
Phoenicia: 7 country
  city: 4 Tyre, Yafo 5 Jaffa, Saida, Sayda, Sidon, Zidon 6 Byblos
  deity: 4 Baal 7 Astarte
phoenix: 4 bird
  origin: 4 pyre 5 ashes
Phoenix: 3 car 4 auto, city, Rain, town 5 Dodge, River 6 Summer 7 Joaquin, Pontiac 10 automobile
  brother: 6 Cadmus
  city near ~: 4 Mesa 5 Tempe
  county: 8 Maricopa
  locale: 7 Arizona
  pro team: 4 Suns 6 D-Backs 7 Coyotes
  river: 4 Salt
  sister: 6 Europa
Phoenix, Joaquin: 5 actor
  film: Clay Pigeons (1998)
    Gladiator (2000)
    Quills (2000)
    Return to Paradise (1998)
    To Die For (1995)
    Walk the Line (2005)
Phoenix, River: 5 actor
  film: Dogfight (1991)
    The Mosquito Coast (1986)
    My Own Private Idaho (1991)
    Running on Empty (1988)
    Stand by Me (1986)
Phoenix-to-Boise dir.: 3 NNW
Phoenix-to-Seattle dir.: 3 NNW
phone: 4 buzz, call, horn, ring 6 blower, call up, dial up, notify, ring up 7 contact, headset 8 receiver 9 extension, telephone, touch base 10 get a hold of
  2, on a ~: 3 ABC
  3, on a ~: 3 DEF
  4, on a ~: 3 GHI
  5, on a ~: 3 JKL
  6 on a ~: 3 MNO
  7 on a ~: 3 PRS
  8, on a ~: 3 TUV
  9, on a ~: 3 WXY
  ABC, on a ~: 3 two
  bug: 3 tap 4 mike
  bulk-rate ~ line: 4 WATS
  button: 4 hold, star
  call beginning: 5 hello
  cord shape: 4 coil
  DEF, on a ~: 5 three
  feature: 4 dial 6 button, cradle 8 receiver
  GHI, on a ~: 4 four
  grab the ~: 6 answer
  hold the ~: 4 wait 6 cool it 7 stand by 8 mark time, sit tight
  hook-up: 4 jack
  JKL, on a ~: 4 five
  line: 4 cord 5 trunk
  London ~ booth: 5 kiosk
  mind the ~: 3 man
  MNO, on a ~: 3 six
  office ~ line: 3 ext. 9 extension
  onstage ~: 4 prop
  PQRS, on a ~: 5 seven
  PRS, on a ~: 5 seven
  put the ~ down: 6 hang up
  signal: 4 busy 8 dial tone
  starter: 3 ear 4 head, mega, tele, xylo 5 micro, radio
  system: 3 PBX
  temporary ~ hookup: 5 patch
  transmission: 3 fax
  TUV, on a ~: 5 eight
  WXY, on a ~: 4 nine
  WXYZ, on a ~: 4 nine
  see also telephone
phone __: 3 tag 4 book, call, card 5 booth
__ phone: 3 pay 4 cell 6 mobile 8 cellular
phone book
  home, in the ~: 3 res
  listing: 2 ad 4 name 6 number
  put in the ~: 4 list
Phone Booth (2003 film)
  cast: Colin Farrell, Kiefer Sutherland, Forest Whitaker
phone-line attachment: 3 fax 5 modem
phonemes, sequence of: 5 morph
phonetic: 4 oral 5 vocal 6 spoken
  alphabet: 3 IPA
  notation method: 5 romic
  punctuation creator: Victor Borge
  symbol: 5 schwa
phonetic alphabet:
  A - Alpha
  B - Bravo
  C - Charlie
  D - Delta
  E - Echo
  F - Foxtrot
  G - Golf
  H - Hotel
  I - India
  J - Juliet
  K - Kilo
  L - Lima
  M - Mike
  N - November
  O - Oscar
  P - Papa
  Q - Quebec
  R - Romeo
  S - Sierra
  T - Tango
  U - Uniform
  V - Victor
  W - Whiskey
  X - X-ray
  Y - Yankee
  Z - Zulu
phonetics
  smooth, in ~: 4 lene
  weak, in ~: 5 lenis
phonic: 4 oral 5 vocal 6 spoken 7 sensory 8 acoustic 9 sensorial 10 acoustical
  starter: 6 stereo
phoniness: 3 act 4 sham 6 facade 8 quackery 9 hypocrisy 10 lip service
phonograph: 4 hi-fi 6 stereo 8 Victrola
  inventor: 6 Edison
  inventor's monogram: 3 TAE
  needle: 6 stylus
  needles: 5 styli
  part: 3 arm 7 tonearm 9 turntable
  record: 2 LP 4 disc, disk 5 album
phony: 3 lie 4 fake, imit., liar, mock, sham 5 bogus, faker, false, fraud, hokey, knave, put-on, quack, spoof, trick 6 bad guy, ersatz, forged, poseur, pseudo, unreal 7 assumed, feigned, forgery, plastic 8 affected, imitator, imposter, impostor, simulate, spurious 9 charlatan, contrived, deceptive, hypocrite, imitation, imposture, insincere, pretended, pretender, simulated, synthetic, unnatural 10 artificial, fabricated, fallacious, fictitious, fraudulent, mountebank, suspicious
  front: 6 facade
  handle: 5 alias 9 pseudonym 10 nom de plume
  not ~: 4 real 5 legit 7 genuine, sincere 9 heartfelt
  up: 4 hoke 5 feign, forge 6 tamper 7 distort, falsify
phony-__: 7 baloney
phony as a __-dollar bill: 5 three
phooey: 2 aw 3 bah, fie 4 dang, darn, drat, nuts, pooh, rats 5 nerts, nertz 6 dang it, darn it, drat it, durn it
phosphate: 4 salt
phosphoresce: 4 glow 5 shine 7 shimmer
phosphorescence: 4 glow 5 light, shine 7 shimmer
phosphorus: 7 element
photo: 2 ID 3 pic 4 snap 5 print, shoot 6 candid, glossy 7 picture 8 likeness, snapshot 10 photograph
  document: 6 ID card 7 license 8 passport
  ender: 3 map, mat 4 copy, play, stat 5 drama 6 copier, setter 10 journalist
  enlargement: 6 blowup
  finish: 5 gloss, matte 9 semi-gloss
  finish margin: 4 nose 5 a nose
  frame a ~: 3 mat 5 remat
  holder: 5 frame
  locker ~: 5 pin-up
  magazine of yore: 4 Life, Look
  movie-ad ~: 5 still
  physician's ~: 4 X-ray
  session: 5 shoot
  snapper: 3 SLR 6 camera
  starter: 4 tele
  take a ~ of: 4 snap 5 shoot
  tint: 5 sepia
  transparency: 5 slide
  trim a ~: 4 crop
photo __: 2 ID 3 IDs, lab, ops 5 essay, shoot 6 layout
photocopier: 6 imager
  ancestor: 5 mimeo
  company: 4 Mita 5 Canon, Xerox
  input: 8 original
photocopy: 4 copy, dupe, stat 5 clone, ditto, image, repro, Xerox 6 double, ectype 7 replica 8 knock-off, likeness 9 duplicate, facsimile, imitation, reproduce
photoelectric
  cell component: 6 cesium 7 caesium
photoelectric __: 4 cell
Photo Finish
  author: Ngaio Marsh
photograph: 3 pic 4 copy, film, shot, snap, x-ray 5 image, Kodak, pin-up, print, shoot, slide 6 blowup, poster, record 7 capture, close-up, picture, portray 8 likeness, negative, Polaroid, portrait, positive, snapshot 9 landscape, microfilm, reproduce
Photograph (1973 song)
  artist: Ringo Starr
photographer: 4 Capa 5 Adams, Arbus, Brady, Karsh, press 6 Abbott, Avedon 9 Stieglitz 11 Bourke-White, Eisenstaedt
  choice: 3 SLR 7 instant
  concern: 4 blur 5 glare, light 9 film speed
  need: 4 film, lens 6 camera, filter, tripod
  output: 3 pix 4 snap 5 print, proof, slide 6 blowup 7 picture 8 negative, snapshot
  pose for a ~: 3 sit
  ratio: 5 f-stop
  word: 5 smile 6 cheese
photographic: 5 exact, vivid 6 visual 8 accurate, detailed, faithful 9 cinematic, realistic
photography
  powder: 6 amidol
  primary color in ~: 4 cyan 6 yellow 7 magenta
__ photography: 5 flash 6 aerial 7 digital, instant, Kirlian
photogravure process: 4 roto
photo-lab print: 5 proof
photon: 8 particle
  stream: 4 x-ray
photophobe fear: 5 light
photoplay: 4 cine, film 5 flick, movie 6 cinema, script
Photostat: 4 copy 5 repro 6 ectype 9 duplicate, facsimile
Phouma, Souvanna country: 4 Laos
phrase: 3 put 4 term, word 5 couch, frame, idiom, maxim, motto, voice 6 byword, cliché, remark, saying, slogan, truism 7 diction, express, proverb, wording 8 aphorism, subtitle 9 catchword, formulate, platitude, utterance, verbalize, watchword 10 expression, shibboleth
  descriptive ~: 3 tag 5 label
phraseology: 6 syntax 7 grammar 8 language, locution, parlance, verbiage
phrasing: 5 style, usage 7 diction 8 locution, verbiage
Phrygia: 7 country, kingdom
  king: 5 Midas
  locale: 6 turkey 9 Asia Minor
Phyfe: 6 Duncan
Phylicia: 6 Rashad
Phyllis: 4 Kirk 6 Coates, Diller, George 7 McGuire, Whitney 8 McGinley, Schlafly
phyllo: 6 pastry
phylum subdivision: 5 class
phys ed: 3 gym
physical: 4 exam, real 5 solid 6 actual, bodily, manual 7 natural, somatic, worldly 8 concrete, corporal, existent, material, sensible, tangible, temporal, visceral 9 corporeal, incarnate, objective, touchable 10 phenomenal, unimagined
  activity: 4 game, work 5 sport 7 workout 8 exercise, training
  arrangement: 6 design, layout
  boundary: 3 lip, rim 4 edge 5 limit 6 margin

condition: 6 fettle, health
setting: 4 site 6 locale 8 locality
starter: 4 meta
strength: 4 main 5 might, thews
world: 6 matter 8 universe
physical ___: 4 exam 7 science, therapy
Physical (1981 song)
artist: Olivia Newton-John
physical science: 7 geology, physics 9 astronomy, chemistry
physician: 2 GP, MD 3 doc 5 bones, medic, quack 6 doctor, extern, healer, intern, medico 7 interne, surgeon 8 sawbones 10 specialist
advice: 4 rest 5 relax
ancient Greek ~: 5 Galen
Canada ~: 5 Osler
clinic ~: 4 Mayo
Danish ~: 6 Finsen
group: 3 HMO 6 clinic
military ~: 5 medic
Muslim ~: 5 hakim
org.: 3 AMA
photo: 4 X-ray 7 CAT scan
request: 5 say ah 8 open wide
turned wordsmith: 5 Roget
see also doctor
Physician, ___ thyself: 4 heal
physicist: 3 Ohm 4 Bohr, Born, Hess, Rabi 5 Boyle, Bragg, Dewar, Dirac, Esaki, Fermi, Fitch, Gamow, Henry, Hertz, Hooke, Joule, Pauli, Raman, Ruska, Stern, Tesla, Volta 6 Ampère, Binnig, Franck, Kelvin, Nernst, Newton, Perrin, Planck, Rohrer, Stokes, Yukawa 7 Compton, Coulomb, Crookes, Doppler, Faraday, Fourier, Fresnel, Goddard, Huygens, Marconi, Maxwell, Meitner, Oersted, Piccard, Réaumur, Thomson, Tyndall 8 Ångström, Avogadro, Blackett, Chadwick, Einstein, Foucault, Friedman, Millikan, Rayleigh, Roentgen, Sakharov, Van Allen 9 Arrhenius, Cavendish, Eddington, Gay-Lussac, Kirchhoff, Michelson 10 Archimedes, Fahrenheit, Fraunhofer, Heisenberg, Rutherford, Torricelli 11 Joliot-Curie, Oppenheimer, van der Waals
Austrian ~: 5 Pauli 7 Doppler, Meitner
British ~: 5 Boyle, Bragg, Dirac, Hooke, Joule 6 Kelvin, Newton, Stokes 7 Crookes, Faraday, Thomson, Tyndall 8 Blackett, Chadwick, Rayleigh 9 Cavendish, Eddington 10 Rutherford
Danish ~: 4 Bohr 7 Oersted
Dutch ~: 7 Huygens 11 van der Waals
French ~: 6 Ampère, Franck, Perrin 7 Coulomb, Fourier, Fresnel, Réaumur 8 Foucault 9 Gay-Lussac 11 Joliot-Curie
German ~: 3 Ohm 4 Born 5 Hertz, Ruska, Stern 6 Binnig, Nernst, Planck 8 Einstein, Roentgen 9 Kirchhoff 10 Fahrenheit, Fraunhofer, Heisenberg
Greek ~: 10 Archimedes
Indian ~: 5 Raman
Italian ~: 5 Fermi, Volta 7 Marconi 8 Avogadro 10 Torricelli
Japanese ~: 5 Esaki 6 Yukawa
particle: 3 ion
Scottish ~: 5 Dewar 7 Maxwell
Soviet ~: 8 Sakharov
Swedish ~: 8 Ångström 9 Arrhenius
Swiss ~: 6 Rohrer 7 Piccard
physics: 7 science
branch of: 6 optics 9 acoustics, mechanics
calculation: 4 mass 8 velocity
degree: 3 Ph.D., Sc.D.
F, in ~: 5 farad
particle: 3 ion 4 atom, beta, kaon, muon, pion 5 alpha, boson, charm, gluon, meson, quark 6 baryon, lepton, photon, proton 7 neutron, pi meson 8 electron, molecule, neutrino
research center: 4 CERN
starter: 3 geo 4 meta 5 astro
state: 3 gas 5 solid 6 liquid
study: 5 chaos 6 energy, matter, motion
unit: 3 erg, ion, rad 4 atom, dyne 8 molecule, particle
workplace: 3 lab 10 laboratory
___ physics: 7 nuclear
physiognomy: 3 mug 4 face, look, puss 6 kisser
physique: 3 bod 4 body, form 5 build, frame, shape 6 figure
phytology: 6 botany
pi: 5 Greek, ratio 6 letter
preceder: 7 omicron
successor: 3 rho
___, p.i.: 6 Magnum
P.I.: 3 tec 4 dick, tail 6 shadow, shamus, sleuth 7 gumshoe 9 detective 10 private eye
job: 4 case
see also detective, private eye
pia ___: 5 mater
Pia: 6 Zadora 9 Lindstrom
Piaf, Edith: 6 French, singer 9 chanteuse
Piaget, Jean: 5 Swiss 6 writer 8 educator 12 psychologist
pianissimo: 4 soft
pianist: 2 Ax 4 Hess, List, Monk, Nero, Tesh, Wild 5 Arrau, Basie, Blake, Borge, Bülow, Corea, Gould, Hines, Hyman, Lewis, Short, Tatum, Watts 6 Bolcom, Cortot, Duchin, Garner, Gilels, Iturbi, Kapell, Kenton, Levant, Morath, Morton, Serkin, Simone, Waller 7 Allison, Brendel, Brubeck, Cliburn, Connick, Dichter, Fischer, Hancock, Hofmann, Istomin, Teicher 8 Ferrante, Graffman, Guaraldi, Helfgott, Horowitz, Larrocha, Liberace, Marsalis, Peterson, Schnabel, Shearing, Williams 9 Ashkenazy, Ellington, Feinstein, Henderson, Hollander, Strayhorn 10 McPartland, Paderewski, Rubinstein
Austrian ~: 7 Brendel 8 Schnabel
British ~: 4 Hess 8 Helfgott
Canadian ~: 5 Gould 8 Peterson
Chilean ~: 5 Arrau
Danish ~: 5 Borge
German ~: 5 Bülow
Grammy-winning ~: 4 Nero
jazz ~: 4 Monk 5 Blake, Hines, Hyman, Lewis, Tatum 6 Garner, Kenton, Morton, Simone, Waller 7 Allison, Brubeck, Hancock 8 Guaraldi, Marsalis 9 Ellington, Henderson, Strayhorn 10 McPartland
New Age ~: 4 Tesh
Polish ~: 7 Hofmann 10 Paderewski, Rubinstein
Russian ~: 6 Gilels 9 Ashkenazy
Spanish ~: 6 Iturbi 8 Larrocha
Swiss ~: 6 Cortot 7 Fischer
Pianist, The (2002 film)
cast: Adrien Brody
director: Roman Polanski
piano: 3 low 4 soft 5 bated, faint, grand, muted, quiet 6 hushed, spinet 7 Baldwin, ivories, muffled, subdued, upright 8 dampened, deadened, keyboard, murmured, Steinway, virginal 9 baby grand, toned down, whispered
easiest ~ scale: 6 C major
ender: 5 forte
exercise: 5 étude, scale
fix a ~: 4 tune
four-handed ~ piece: 4 duet
hammer material: 4 felt
instructor's degree: 3 BME
key: 4 note
key material: 5 ebony, ivory
like a frontier ~: 5 tinny
note: 5 A-flat, B-flat, C-flat, D-flat, E-flat, F-flat, G-flat 6 A-sharp, B-sharp, C-sharp, D-sharp, E-sharp, F-sharp, G-sharp 7 middle C
opposite: 5 forte
output: 5 music
part: 3 key, leg 5 pedal 6 hammer
pedal: 6 damper
piece: 3 rag 4 duet, solo 5 étude 8 rhapsody 9 arabesque
seat: 5 bench, stool
size: 5 grand 6 spinet 7 upright 9 baby grand
tuner's tool: 5 wrest
piano ___: 3 bar 4 roll, solo, wire 5 bench, stool, tuner
___ piano: 5 grand, mezzo 6 spinet 7 console, upright
Piano Man (1974 song)
artist: Billy Joel
Piano, The (1993 film)
cast: Holly Hunter, Harvey Keitel, Sam Neill, Anna Paquin
director: Jane Campion
heroine: 3 Ada
piazza: 5 court, lanai, porch 7 balcony, veranda 8 verandah
Piazza: 3 Ben 4 Mike
del Campo site: 5 Siena
Piazza, Mike
sport: 8 baseball
pic: 4 film, snap 5 flick, movie, photo 6 cinema 8 snapshot 10 photograph
ender: 4 king
pica: 4 font, type
alternative: *see* point size
fraction: 5 point
widths: 3 ems
Pica: 4 font 8 typeface
Picabo: 6 Street
picador
opponent: 4 bull, toro
weapon: 5 lance
Picard: 5 Henry 7 Jean-Luc
Picard, Henry: 6 golfer
Picardo, Robert: 5 actor
picaresque: 6 rakish 7 raffish, roguish 8 rascally
picaroon: 5 knave, rogue, scamp 6 bad hat, pirate, rascal, rotter 7 brigand, so and so 8 scalawag 9 buccaneer, miscreant, reprobate, scallawag, scallywag, scoundrel 10 blackguard, ne'er-do-well
Picasso, Pablo: 6 artist 7 painter, Spanish 8 sculptor
cap: 5 beret
contemporary: 4 Miró 6 Braque
daughter: 6 Paloma
sister: 4 Lola
specialty: 6 cubism
picayune: 4 puny 5 dinky, minor, money, petty, small 6 measly, minute, paltry, trifle, two-bit 7 trivial 8 piddling, trifling 9 penny-ante, rinky-dink
Piccadilly ___: 6 Circus
Piccadilly statue: 4 Eros
piccalilli: 6 relish
___ piccata: 4 veal
___ Picchu: 5 Machu
piccolo: 4 wind 10 instrument
relative: 4 fife 5 flute
Piccolo: 5 Brian
Pichel: 6 Irving
pick: 3 opt, tag 4 best, cull, name, pull, sort, take, tool 5 adopt, cream, elect, elite, glean, key on, pluck, prize 6 accept, choice, choose, finger, gather, opt for, prefer, select, vote in, winnow 7 excerpt, fix upon, harvest, jerk out 8 decide on, draw lots, nominate, plectrum, settle on 9 designate, selection, single out 10 decide upon, preference, settle upon
apart: 3 pan 5 probe, roast, study, trash 6 assess, review 7 analyze, examine, run down 8 evaluate 9 criticize, cut to bits, find fault 10 scrutinize
at: 3 nag 4 carp 5 cavil 6 badger, nibble, pester 7 quibble 9 criticize, find fault
bone to ~: 4 feud, spat, tiff 5 gripe 7 dispute, quarrel 8 argument, conflict, squabble 9 exception 10 contention, difference
ender: 3 axe 4 lock 6 pocket
from a lineup: 2 ID 3 tag 6 finger 8 identify
on: 3 nag, rib 4 bait 5 blame, bully, tease, upset 6 badger, bother, harass, hassle, hector, needle 7 henpeck, oppress, torment 8 distress, keep down 9 aggravate, persecute, victimize
one with a ~: 5 miner 7 convict 9 guitarist
out: 4 cull, spot 5 elect, glean 6 choose, gather, opt for, screen, select 7 discern, excerpt 8 decide on, identify, settle on
party ~: 5 slate 7 nominee 9 candidate
starter: 3 nit, nut 4 hand 5 tooth 6 finger
the brains of: 4 pump, quiz 7 consult 8 question

through: 4 cull, sift 5 glean 6 screen 7 examine
top ~: 4 fave 5 A-list 8 favorite
up: 3 buy, get, nab, win 4 book, bust, earn, gain, have, hear, lift, take 5 cheer, glean, grasp, hoist, learn, raise, rally, run in, scoop, score, seize, sense 6 arrest, collar, detain, detect, gather, handle, invite, master, obtain, pull in, resume, secure, take in 7 acquire, call for, capture, collect, enliven, improve, procure, realize, rebound, receive, recover, rectify, restart, stop for 8 continue, go on with, increase, invest in, purchase, reassure 9 apprehend, extradite, get better, get word of, reinforce 10 gain ground, invigorate, recommence, recuperate
up a lease: 5 renew
up a perp: 3 nab 4 bust 5 catch 6 arrest, collar 7 capture
up a stitch: 3 tat 4 knit 7 crochet
up furtively: 4 palm 5 filch, steal
up on: 3 see 4 note 6 listen, notice, remark 7 observe
up the pace: 3 hie, run, zip 4 race, zoom 5 hurry, speed
up the tab: 3 pay 4 fund 5 spend, treat 6 defray 7 finance 9 subsidize
use a ~: 5 strum
pick-__: 4 me-up
__ pick: 3 ice, toe
Pick __, any...: 5 a card
pickaback: 9 astraddle
pick and __: 6 choose, shovel
pickaxe: 4 hack
cousin: 3 adz 4 adze
picked: 6 chosen, select
it may be ~: 4 bone, lock
just ~: 4 ripe 5 crisp, fresh
Pickens: 4 Fort, Slim
picker-__: 5 upper
__ picker: 3 rag 6 cherry, cotton
__-picker: 3 nit
picker starter: 3 nit
picker-upper
see pick-me-up
picket: 4 pale 5 fence, guard, scout, stake, stave, watch 6 paling, patrol, sentry, strike, tether 7 boycott, lookout, protest, striker, upright, walk out 8 blockade, palisade, sentinel 9 keep guard, protester, stanchion
picket __: 4 boat, line 5 fence
Picket Fences (CBS drama)
cast: Kathy Baker (Jill Brock) Fyvush Finkel (Douglas Wambaugh) Tom Skerritt (Jimmy Brock) Ray Walston (Judge Henry Bone)
setting: Rome, Wisconsin
picket line crosser: 4 scab
Pickett: 5 Bobby 6 Wilson
Pickett, Bobby
song: Monster Mash (1962)
Pickett, Wilson
song: Don't Knock My Love (1971) Don't Let the Green Grass Fool You (1971) Engine Number 9 (1970) Funky Broadway (1967) In the Midnight Hour (1921) Land of 1000 Dances (1966) Mustang Sally (1966) She's Lookin' Good (1968)
Pickford, Mary: 7 actress
Oscar film: Coquette
spouse: Douglas Fairbanks Sr., Buddy Rogers
pickings: 4 loot 5 prize 6 spoils 7 jobbery, plunder
easy ~: 6 breeze 8 kid stuff, pushover 10 child's play
slim ~: 3 few 6 little
pickle: 3 can, fix, jam 4 bind, cure, hole, keep, mess, salt, snag, spot 5 pinch, souse, state, steep 6 corner, plight, scrape, veggie 7 dilemma, gherkin, problem, trouble 8 hot water, marinade, preserve, quagmire, quandary 9 deep water, inebriate, tight spot, vegetable 10 difficulty, intoxicate
brand: 5 Heinz 6 Vlasic
container: 3 jar 6 barrel
flavoring: 4 dill 5 cumin, sugar 6 garlic
ingredient: 4 alum
measure: 3 jar 5 quart
piece: 5 slice, spear
solution: 5 brine
source: 4 cuke 8 cucumber
type: 4 dill 6 garlic 7 gherkin
__ pickle: 3 in a 4 dill
pickled: 4 high 5 tight, tipsy 6 stewed 7 smashed 9 plastered
flower bud: 5 caper
pepper measure: 4 peck
veggie: 4 beet, cuke 8 cucumber
pickled __: 5 beets 7 herring
pickled __ feet: 4 pigs'
pickled-pepper picker: 5 Peter, Piper
Pickles: 5 comic 10 comic strip
cat: 6 Muffin
dog: 6 Roscoe
pick-me-up: 4 lift 5 boost, snack, tonic 6 bracer, elixir 7 revival 8 stimulus 9 energizer, eyeopener, stimulant 10 invigorant
pickpocket: 3 dip 4 lift 5 Fagin, taker, thief 6 robber 8 cutpurse 9 miscreant
pickup: 5 tonic, truck
enclosure: 3 cab
for ~: 4 to go
garbage ~ place: 4 curb
pick-up-sticks game: 3 nim
Pick up the Pieces (1974 song)
artist: AWB
Pickwick Papers
author: Charles Dickens
character: 4 Fogg, Pott 5 Emily 6 Buzfuz, Rachel, Wardle, Weller, Winkle 8 Arabella, Isabella
picky: 4 nice 5 bossy, fussy, rigid 6 choosy, prissy 7 carping, choosey, finicky, precise 8 critical, exacting, finiking, finnicky, rigorous 9 demanding, difficult, selective, stringent 10 fastidious, inflexible, particular
Pick Yourself Up
composer: Dorothy Fields, Jerome Kern
picnic: 3 eat 4 easy, lark, meal, snap 5 cinch, cushy, jaunt 6 breeze, junket, outing, simple 7 cookout, fish fry 8 barbecue, clambake, duck soup, kid stuff, painless, walkover 9 excursion, no problem, no trouble, sure thing 10 child's play, effortless, recreation
days: 6 summer
drink: 3 ade, pop 4 beer, soda, wine 6 ice tea 7 iced tea, Kool-Aid 8 lemonade
fare: 4 cola, slaw, soda 5 chips, salad 8 sandwich
gear: 6 basket, cooler, hamper
go to a family ~: 5 reune
no ~: 4 hard 5 bumpy, harsh, rough, tough 6 brutal, severe, taxing, thorny, trying, woolly 7 arduous, complex, painful, serious 8 terrible 9 difficult, strenuous 10 formidable, unpleasant
pest: 3 ant, bug, fly 4 gnat 6 insect 8 mosquito
spoiler: 4 rain 6 clouds 7 drizzle 8 overcast
spot: 4 deck, park, yard 5 patio 7 grounds
Picnic: 4 film, play
author: William Inge
cast: William Holden, Kim Novak, Rosalind Russell
character: 3 Flo, Hal 4 Alan, Irma, Owen 5 Madge, Potts 6 Millie
director: Joshua Logan
Picnic (1956 song)
artist: McGuire Sisters
Pico de __: 5 Aneto
Picon: 5 Molly
__-Picone: 4 Evan
Pico Rivera: 4 city, town
locale: 10 California
picot: 4 lace, trim 6 edging, ribbon
Pict: 4 Celt 5 tribe
foe: 5 Roman
pictograph: 5 glyph 8 artifact
computer ~: 4 icon 8 emoticon
picture: 3 art, map, oil, see 4 film, icon, ikon, limn, plot, show, view 5 eikon, fancy, flick, illus., image, movie, photo, print, proof, scape, scene, tanka 6 canvas, depict, effigy, ideate, looker, lovely, recite, render, scheme, sketch 7 cartoon, diagram, drawing, etching, gouache, imagine, portray, recount, replica, tableau, thangka, tintype 8 daydream, describe, envisage, envision, likeness, painting, panorama, portrait, seascape, snapshot 9 blueprint, delineate, engraving, fantasize, landscape, look-alike, portrayal, represent, situation, spectacle, statement, visualize 10 conceive of, dead ringer, embodiment, illustrate, perception, photograph, reflection, watercolor, woolgather
barracks ~: 5 pin-up
be the very ~ of: 8 look like, resemble
big ~: 4 plan 5 mural, whole 6 blowup, fresco 8 time line
book: 5 album
enter the ~: 5 arise 6 appear 7 develop
eye-fooling ~: 5 op art
frame juncture: 5 bevel, miter, slant 8 diagonal
get the ~: 3 see 5 sense 7 catch on, realize 8 perceive 9 visualize
holder: 3 mat 4 nail, tack 5 frame
iron-on ~: 5 decal, patch
medical ~: 4 X-ray 7 CAT scan
mental ~: 4 idea 5 image 6 memory, vision 7 concept
motion ~: 3 pic 4 cine, film, show 5 flick, movie 6 cinema, silent, talkie
mount a ~: 4 hang
postcard ~ often: 5 vista
religious ~: 4 icon, ikon 5 eikon, tanka 7 thangka
take a ~: 4 snap 5 shoot
taker: 3 SLR 6 camera 7 tourist 9 sightseer
within a picture: 5 inset
picture __: 4 book, card, show, tube 6 window
__ picture: 3 big 4 word 5 flash 6 motion, moving 7 talking
Picture of Dorian Gray, The: 5 novel
author: Oscar Wilde
character: 4 Alan, Vane 5 Basil, Sibyl
Pictures at an Exhibition
composer: Modest Mussorgsky
__ Picture Show, The: 4 Last
picturesque: 5 vivid 6 quaint, rustic, scenic 7 graphic 8 artistic, charming, colorful, romantic, scenical, striking 9 arresting, beautiful, graphical 10 artistical
Picturing Will
author: Ann Beattie
piddle around: 4 loaf 5 delay 6 putter
piddling: 4 puny 5 least, minor, petty, small 6 meager, measly, minute, paltry, skimpy, slight, yeasty 7 shallow, trivial 8 beggarly, niggling, picayune, trifling 9 worthless
Pidgeon: 6 Walter
pidgin __: 7 English
pie: 4 bird, tart 5 money, pizza 6 quiche 7 cobbler, dessert
Canadian ~: 5 rappe 6 rappie
chart: 5 graph
chart line: 6 radius
chart lines: 5 radii
cooling place: 4 rack, sill 5 ledge 6 fridge, window
crust: 5 shell
crust ingredient: 4 lard 6 Crisco
cutie ~: 4 doll
easy as ~: 4 snap 6 simple 7 no sweat
eat humble ~: 6 grovel 9 apologize
ender: 4 bald
filling: 3 mud 4 lime 5 apple, fruit, lemon, mince, peach, pecan 6 cherry 7 chiffon, custard, pumpkin, rhubarb, spinach 10 strawberry
finish a ~ crust: 5 crimp, flute
in apple ~ order: 4 neat, tidy, trim 9 shipshape
in the sky: 5 dream 7 fantasy
like ~ crust: 5 flaky 6 flakey
maker's device: 3 tin 5 corer, parer 6 peeler
meat ~: 5 pasty 8 empanada, turnover

piece of the ~: 3 cut 5 share
serving: 5 piece, slice, wedge
shepherd's ~ ingredient: 4 meat, spud 6 potato
small ~: 4 tart
starter: 3 pot 4 pork
store: 6 bakery 10 patisserie
sweetie ~: 3 hon 4 doll, love 5 cutey, cutie, deary 6 dearie
pie ___: 3 bed, pan, tin 5 chart, graph, plant, plate
pie ___ mode: 3 à la
___ pie: 3 mud 5 cutie 6 easy as, humble 7 shoo-fly, sweetie 8 deep-dish 9 shepherd's
___-pie: 4 cap-à
Pie: 7 Traynor
___ Pie: 6 Eskimo, Tweety
piebald: 4 pony 5 horse, pinto 6 dapple, equine 7 dappled 8 brindled
marking: 4 spot 6 dapple
piece: 3 bit, cut, gat, gun, rod, sew 4 bite, chip, clip, coin, half, hank, hunk, item, join, link, lump, mend, opus, part, slab, song, tune, unit 5 chunk, music, opera, patch, queen, quilt, quota, scrap, shard, share, sherd, shred, slice, snack 6 bishop, column, dollop, factor, gobbet, heater, knight, length, morsel, parcel, pistol, rasher, roscoe, sample, sketch, sliver, snatch, statue 7 article, element, example, extract, firearm, fitting, flinder, passage, portion, remnant, section, segment, writing 8 assemble, chessman, clipping, division, fraction, fragment, instance, interest, nocturne, oratorio, particle, specimen, symphony 9 allotment, component, editorial, sound bite 10 percentage, recitation, smithereen
ender: 4 meal, work 6 worker
playing ~: 3 man 4 king, pawn, tile 5 queen 6 bishop, knight
starter: 3 ear, eye 4 hair, nose, show, time 5 cross, mouth 6 center, mantel, master 7 chimney
together: 4 mend 5 patch, quilt, solve 8 assemble 9 figure out
piece ___ action: 5 of the
___ piece: 3 far, of a, set 4 Op-Ed, puff 5 think 6 museum, period
pièce de résistance: 4 dish 8 ultimate 9 specialty
piecemeal: 6 patchy, slowly, spotty 7 gradual 8 bit by bit, fitfully, one by one 9 by degrees, gradually, partially 10 fractional, one at a time, step by step
gather ~: 5 glean 7 collect 8 scrounge
piece of ___: 4 cake, work 5 eight
piece of cake: 4 easy 5 can do 6 no prob, simple 7 no sweat 8 kid stuff 9 no problem 10 child's play
Piece of My Mind, A
author: Edmund Wilson
Piece of the Action, A (1977 film)
cast: Bill Cosby, James Earl Jones, Sidney Poitier
director: Sidney Poitier
pieces
bits and ~: 6 scraps
break into ~: 5 smash, stave 6 shiver 7 shatter 8 splinter
chop into small ~: 4 cube, dice 5 mince
fly to ~: 5 burst 7 explode
go to ~: 3 rot 5 decay, panic 7 crumble 8 collapse 9 break down 10 degenerate, tumble down
in ~: 6 broken 7 smashed 8 crumbled 9 shattered 10 fragmented
pick to ~: 3 pan 9 criticize, excoriate, find fault
Pieces of April (1972 song)
artist: Three Dog Night
Pieces of Eight band: 4 Styx
___-piece suit: 3 two 5 three
pieceworker: 6 jobber 8 handyman
pied: 6 calico, motley, patchy 7 dappled, spotted 8 brindled 10 variegated
changement de ~: 4 leap
pied-à-terre: 3 pad 4 flat 7 lodging 9 apartment, residence
pied-billed bird: 5 grebe
Piedmont
city: 4 Asti 5 Turin 6 Torino
Pied Piper
author: Nevil Shute
city: 6 Hamlin 7 Hamelin
emulate the ~: 3 rid
follower: 3 rat
Pied Piper of Hamelin, The
author: Robert Browning
___ Piedras, PR: 3 Rio
Piegan: 5 tribe
pie in the ___: 3 sky
___-pie order: 5 apple
pier: 4 anta, dock, mole, pile, port, post, quay, slip, walk 5 berth, jetty, levee, pylon, wharf 6 column, harbor, piling, pillar 7 harbour, landing, support, upright 8 buttress, pilaster 9 anchorage 10 breakwater
architectural ~: 4 anta 6 column, pillar
foundation: 4 pile 6 piling
glass: 6 mirror
support: 6 gabion
Pier: 6 Angeli
pierce: 3 cut 4 bore, gore, open, slit, stab 5 drill, enter, knife, lance, prick, punch, slash, slice, spear, spike, stick, wound 6 broach, empale, impale, riddle, thrust 8 puncture, transfix 9 penetrate, perforate, stick into 10 cut through, laceration, run through
Pierce: 3 car 4 auto, Egan, Webb 7 Brosnan, Hawkeye, Mildred 8 Franklin
on M*A*S*H: 4 Alda
Pierce Arrow contemporary: 3 Reo
pierced
object: 3 ear, lip 4 lobe, nose 6 eyelid
Pierce, David Hyde: 5 actor
role: 5 Niles
TV: Frasier
Pierce, Franklin: 9 president
alma mater: 7 Bowdoin
former occupation: 6 lawyer
home: 7 Concord
opponent: 5 Scott
veep: 4 King
wife: 4 Jane
piercing: 3 raw 4 cold, high, keen, loud, stab 5 acute, forte, noisy, sharp, witty 6 biting, bitter, fierce, shrewd, shrill, treble 7 blaring, blatant, booming, glacial, intense, jarring, numbing, painful, pealing, probing, pungent, rackety, raucous, reboant, roaring 8 crashing, freezing, incisive, plangent, poignant, rumbling, sonorous, stabbing, strident, turned up 9 agonizing, big-voiced, clamorous, deafening, exquisite, knifelike, searching 10 boisterous, resounding, stentorian, strepitous, thundering, uproarious, vociferant, vociferous
tool: 3 awl 5 auger, borer 6 needle
Pierre: 4 city, Loti, town 5 Bayle, Curie 6 Boulez, Boulle, Cardin, Laclos 7 Bonnard, Fresnay, L'Enfant, Monteux, Reverdy, Trudeau 8 Gringore, Proudhon, Salinger 9 Beauchamp, Berthelot, Corneille 10 Beauregard
in English: 5 Peter
locale: 4 S. Dak.
river: 8 Missouri
see also French
Pierre-Auguste: 6 Renoir
___-Pierre Aumont: 4 Jean
Pierre de ___: 6 Fermat 7 Laplace
___-Pierre Rampal: 4 Jean
pierrot: 4 fool, mime 5 clown 6 jester, mummer 7 buffoon, farceur 9 harlequin
Piers ___: 7 Plowman
Piersall, Jimmy
sport: 8 baseball
Pierson: 4 Kate
Piet: 8 Mondrian
Pieta: 6 statue 9 sculpture
Pieter: 6 Zeeman 7 Bruegel
Pietermaritzburg: 4 city, town 7 capital
locale: 5 Natal
pietistic: 5 godly, pious 7 devoted 9 dedicated, religious 10 goody-goody
pietoso: 8 tenderly
Pietro: 7 Aretino 8 Mascagni
piety: 4 zeal 5 faith 7 respect 8 devotion, fidelity, holiness, religion, sanctity 9 godliness, reverence 10 devoutness, veneration
false ~: 4 cant, show 6 facade 9 hypocrisy
piffle
see baloney
pig: 3 hog, sow 4 boar, gilt, Kele, mold 5 Bazna, Duroc, Hezuo, piggy, shoat, shote, shott, swine, Welsh 6 farrow, Jinhua, mammal, Minzhu, Mukota, oinker, piggie, piglet, porker, rooter, sloven 7 glutton, grunter, Iberian, Lacombe, Meishan, Mong Cai, peccary, Suffolk 8 Hereford, Landrace, Pietrain, Potbelly, squealer, Tamworth 9 barbarian, Berkshire, chowhound, Hampshire, litterbug, overeater, razorback, Yorkshire
Animal Farm ~: 8 Napoleon, Old Major, Snowball, Squealer
calling shout: 5 sooey
cartoon ~: 5 Porky 7 Hampton, Petunia
combining form: 3 hyo- 7 -choerus
digs: 3 pen, sty
ender: 3 nut, pen 4 skin, tail, weed 6 headed
food: 4 mast, slop 5 swill
guinea ~: 3 pet 4 cavy 6 animal, mammal, rodent 7 subject
hair: 7 bristle
hoof: 5 cloot 7 dewclaw
jungle ~: 4 boar 5 tapir
kiddie-lit ~: 6 Wilbur
Latin turndown: 5 ixnay
litter: 6 farrow
movie ~: 4 Babe
noise: 4 oink 5 grunt
out: 3 eat 5 binge, gorge 7 indulge, overeat
product: 3 ham 4 pork 5 bacon 7 chitlin, sausage 8 chitling
Scottish ~: 5 grice 7 grumphy 8 grumphie
thief of rhyme: 3 Tom
TV ~: 6 Arnold
young: 4 gilt 5 shoat, shote, shott 6 farrow
pig ___: 3 out 4 iron 5 Latin
pig ___ blanket: 3 in a
pig ___ poke: 3 in a
pigeon: 3 sap 4 bird, butt, dupe, fool, gull, pawn, prey 5 chump, cooer, patsy, squab 6 culver, hunted, sucker, target, victim 7 fall guy, schnook 8 easy mark, pushover 9 soft touch
clay ~: 6 target
ender: 4 hole
home: 4 cote, loft
relative: 4 dove
sound: 3 coo
stool ~: 3 rat 4 fink, tool 5 namer 7 tattler, traitor 8 informer, turncoat 9 informant 10 tattletale
walk like a ~: 3 bob
pigeon-___: 4 toed 7 hearted, livered
___ pigeon: 4 clay, rock, wood 5 stool 6 homing 7 carrier
Pigeon Feathers
author: John Updike
Pigeon Forge: 4 city, town
locale: 9 Tennessee
pigeonhole: 4 file, nook, rank, rate, slot, sort, tier, type 5 defer, group, niche, order, table 6 assort, league, put off, recess, shelve 7 arrange, catalog, cubicle, suspend 8 category, classify, file away, lay aside, organize, postpone, set apart, set aside 9 catalogue 10 categorize
locale: 4 desk
piggery: 3 pen, sty
piggish: 5 balky 6 greedy, mulish, wilful 7 adamant, hoggish, lustful, willful 8 contrary, edacious, ravenous, stubborn 9 impliable, insatiate, obstinate, unbending, voracious 10 gluttonous, headstrong, implacable, inflexible
piggy: 3 pig, toe 5 swine 6 greedy, piglet 8 slovenly 9 voracious 10 gluttonous
ender: 4 back
fourth ~ portion: 4 none
little ~: 3 toe 5 digit
third ~ portion: 9 roast beef
where the first ~ went: 6 market
where the second ~ stayed: 4 home

__ Piggy: 4 Miss
piggyback __: 4 ride
piggy bank
deposit: 4 coin, dime 5 penny 6 nickel 7 quarter
opening: 4 slot
pigheaded: 5 balky, dense, rigid 6 mulish, ornery, stupid, wilful 7 adamant, froward, hard-set, willful 8 contrary, dogmatic, indocile, perverse, stubborn 9 impliable, insistent, obstinate, unbending 10 dogmatical, hard-bitten, headstrong, implacable, inflexible, refractory, self-willed, unyielding
pig in a __: 4 poke 7 blanket
__ pig in a poke: 4 buy a
Piglet
creator: A.A. Milne
pal: 3 Owl 4 Pooh 6 Eeyore
Pigmeat: 7 Markham
pigment: 3 dye 4 tint, woad 5 color, paint, stain, tinct, tinge 6 litmus 8 colorant, dyestuff, tincture
combining form: 5 chrom- 6 chromo-
containing iron: 4 heme
earth ~: 5 ocher, ochre, umber 6 bister, bistre, sienna
lacking ~: 5 white 6 albino 8 pink-eyed
natural ~: 4 bice, lake 6 ceruse
pignoli: 3 nut
pignut: 4 tree 7 hickory
pigpen: 3 sty 4 dump, mess 5 hovel 7 rathole
__ Pigs: 5 Bay of
__ pig's eye!: 3 In a
__ pigs fly!: 4 When
Pigs in Heaven
author: Barbara Kingsolver
pigskin: 4 ball 7 leather 8 football
carry the ~: 3 run 4 rush
give up the ~: 4 punt
prop: 3 tee
pigtail: 5 braid, plait, queue
pika: 4 cony 5 coney 6 animal, mammal
pike: 4 fish, road 5 route 7 highway, javelin, parkway 8 autobahn, toll-gate, toll road 10 expressway, interstate
come down the ~: 6 appear, emerge
ender: 5 staff
starter: 4 turn
piker: 8 tightwad 9 skinflint 10 cheapskate
Pikes Peak: 4 peak 5 mount 8 mountain
locale: 7 Rockies 8 Colorado
Pike, Zebulon: 8 explorer
pilaf: 4 dish
base: 4 rice
partner: 5 kebab
__ pilaf: 4 rice
pilar: 5 hairy 7 hirsute
pilaster: 4 anta, pier 5 pylon 6 column, pillar
__ Pilate: 7 Pontius
Pilatus: 3 Alp
pilchard: 4 fish 7 sardine
pile: 3 gob, lot, nap, wad 4 bank, down, heap, load, lump, mass, mint, much, pack, peck, pier, post, raft, rush, shag 5 amass, batch, bunch, chunk, crowd, crush, drift, flock, hoard, money, mound, ocean, plush, press, shock, stack, store 6 boodle, bundle, fleece, gather, heap up, jumble, load up, oodles, pillar, riches, wealth 7 collect, fortune, javelin, lay away, pyramid, upright 8 mountain, quantity, treasure 9 aggregate, congeries, great deal, profusion, stanchion, stockpile 10 accumulate, assemblage, assortment, collection, cumulation
of hay: 4 rick 5 stack
of stones: 4 carn 5 cairn
rubbish ~: 4 dump 7 ash heap 8 junkyard, landfill
starter: 4 wood 5 stock
up: 5 amass, hoard, mount, score, stack 6 gather, rake in 7 collide 8 hold on to, salt away 9 stash away 10 accumulate
pile __: 6 driver
__ pile: 4 sand 5 slush 6 atomic
pile-driver head: 3 tup
Pileggi: 5 Mitch 8 Nicholas
pileous: 5 hairy 7 hirsute
piles: 4 a lot, lots 5 reams
of: 4 many 6 divers, myriad, plenty, umteen, untold 7 copious, profuse, umpteen 8 abundant, manifold, numerous, umpsteen 9 bountiful, countless, quite a few
put in ~: 4 sort 6 assort 8 classify
pile-up: 5 crash, smash, wreck 6 logjam 8 accident 9 collision, rear-ender
pilfer: 3 cop, rob 4 crib, glom, hook, lift, palm, take 5 boost, filch, heist, pinch, snare, steal, swipe 6 finger, pirate, pocket, rip off, snatch, thieve 7 purloin, ransack 8 embezzle, liberate, scrounge 10 run off with
pilferage: 5 heist, theft 8 burglary, thievery
pilferer: 5 crook, thief 6 robber 7 burglar 9 purloiner
pilgrim: 5 hadji, rover 7 pioneer, rambler, tourist 8 traveler, wanderer, wayfarer 9 journeyer
destination: 4 Puri 5 Kaaba, Mecca, stupa 6 Ganges, shrine, temple 7 Kailash, Lourdes 8 Bodh-gaya 9 Jerusalem
Pilgrim
memorable ~: 5 Alden 9 Priscilla
pronoun: 4 thee, thou
pilgrimage: 3 haj 4 hadj, hajj, trek, trip 5 quest 6 hejira 7 crusade, journey, sojourn 8 long haul
Pilgrim at Sea
author: Pär Lagerkvist
Pilgrim's Progress: 8 allegory
author: John Bunyan
character: 4 Pope 5 Pagan 7 Hopeful, Pliable, Sincere 8 Watchful
pill: 4 bore, dose, drag, pain, pest 5 bolus, creep, trial 6 caplet, nudnik, pellet, remedy, tablet, troche 7 capsule, lozenge, placebo 8 medicine, nuisance 10 medication
allotment: 4 dose 6 dosage
bitter ~: 4 blow 6 misery 7 letdown, setback 8 comedown
bug: 6 isopod
ender: 3 box
large ~: 5 bolus
pillage: 3 gut, rob 4 loot, raid, ruin, sack 5 booty, harry, rifle, spoil, steal, strip, waste 6 devour, harrow, invade, maraud, prey on, ravage, spoils 7 despoil, destroy, plunder, predate, ransack 8 desolate, freeboot, lay waste, spoliate, trespass 9 depredate, desecrate, devastate
pillager: 6 pirate, raider, vandal, Viking 7 brigand 10 freebooter
pillar: 4 beam, pier, pile, post, prop, rock 5 pylon, shaft, tower 6 column, piling 7 obelisk, support, upright 8 mainstay, memorial, monument, pilaster 9 reinforce, stanchion
ancient ~: 5 pylon, stele 6 column
combining form: 4 clon-, styl- 5 clono-, stylo-
engraved ~: 5 stele
go from ~ to post: 4 roam, rove 5 drift 6 ramble, wander
memorial ~ of India: 5 minah
of heaven, to Pindar: 4 Etna 5 Aetna
Pillars of __: 5 Islam
Pillars of Society
author: Henrik Ibsen
__ Pillars of Wisdom: 5 Seven
__ pillar to post: 4 from
pillbox: 3 hat
pillow: 4 seat 7 beanbag, bedding, cushion, protect
candy: 4 mint
casing: 4 tick
cover: 4 sham, slip 5 linen
plump the ~: 5 fluff
stuffing: 4 down, foam 5 hulls, kapok 6 cotton 7 batting 9 buckwheat
pillow __: 4 sham, talk
Pillow Talk (1959 film)
cast: Doris Day, Rock Hudson, Tony Randall
Pillow Talk (1973 song)
artist: Sylvia
pilose: 5 hairy 6 haired, shaggy 7 hirsute
pilot: 3 ace, fly 4 land, lead, sail, take 5 flier, flyer, guide, steer, trial 6 airman, aviate, direct, fly boy, govern, jockey, leader, manage 7 aviator, birdman, captain, conduct, control, operate, war hero 8 aeronaut, coxswain, helmsman, maneuver, navigate 9 navigator, sky jockey
affirmative: 3 A-OK 5 roger
aid: 4 gyro 5 LORAN, radar 9 gyroscope
assignment: 6 flight
bomber ~ concern: 4 flak 5 flack 7 missile
button: 5 eject
concern: 3 ice 4 drag 5 birds, geese, icing 8 altitude 9 wind shear 10 visibility
control: 4 helm 5 stick 6 tiller
expert ~: 3 ace
guidepost: 5 pylon
insignia: 5 wings
light: 3 jet 5 flame 6 gas jet
maneuver: 4 bank, dive 5 climb
milestone: 4 solo
military ~ award: 3 DFC
org.: 3 ADF, FAA, NAA
place: 3 jet 4 helm, port, ship 5 plane 6 hangar, tiller 7 airport, cockpit 8 jetliner
plane without a ~: 5 drone
shuttle ~ wear: 5 G-suit
sky ~: 5 padre
starter: 4 auto
the shuttle: 5 orbit
UFO ~: 2 ET 5 alien
pilot __: 5 light
__ pilot: 3 sky 4 bush, test
Pilot: 3 pen, SUV 5 Honda
alternative: 3 Bic 7 Uni-Ball 9 PaperMate
pilotage: 10 leadership
pilous: 5 hairy 7 hirsute
pilsner: 4 beer, brew, suds 5 lager
Piltdown man: 4 hoax
pilum: 5 lance, spear 6 weapon
pilus: 4 hair
Pima: 5 tribe 6 Indian 7 Amerind
Pima __: 6 cotton
pimento: 3 red 5 spice
color kin: 4 rose, ruby, rust, wine 5 brick, coral, grape, poppy 6 cerise, cherry, claret, garnet, maroon 7 carmine, crimson, fuchsia, magenta, scarlet, sultana, vermeil 8 cardinal, geranium 9 cranberry, vermilion 10 strawberry
pimiento: 5 spice
holder: 5 olive
__-piminy: 6 niminy
Pimlico
event: 4 race 9 horse race
racer: 5 filly, horse
sound: 5 neigh 7 whinney
transaction: 3 bet 5 wager
Pim, Mr. creator: A.A. Milne
__ Pimpernel, The: 7 Scarlet
pimple: 3 zit 7 blemish
__ pimples: 5 goose
pin: 3 fix, peg, rod, tag 4 bind, join, limb, nail, tack 5 affix, badge, clasp, spike, stick 6 attach, broach, brooch, fasten, hatpin, secure, skewer 7 jewelry, sticker 8 hold down, restrain 9 thumbtack 10 immobilize, keep in line, outwrestle
a crime on: 5 frame, set up 6 accuse
bowling ~: 5 maple
down: 4 bind, nail, name 5 force, point, press 6 locate, select 7 specify 8 home in on, indicate, restrict, zero in on 9 determine
ender: 4 ball, head, hole, tail, worm 5 point, prick, wheel 6 stripe 7 cushion, feather
hard to ~ down: 4 eely 5 dodgy, vague 7 evasive 8 slippery
holder: 4 etui 5 etwee 7 cushion
metalworker's ~: 5 rivet
neat as a ~: 4 tidy, trim 7 orderly 9 shipshape
place for a ~: 5 lapel
rowboat ~: 5 thole
starter: 3 hat, ten 4 duck, hair, king, nine, push 5 crank, stick 6 candle 7 clothes 8 thorough
wooden ~: 3 peg 4 nogg 5 dowel

pin __: 3 oak 4 curl, down 5 money
__ pin: 4 head 5 bobby, lapel 6 cotter, firing, safety 7 rolling
piña colada: 5 drink 8 beverage, cocktail
ingredient: 3 rum 9 grenadine, pineapple
pinafore: 5 apron, dress
Pinafore: 4 boat, ship
__ Pinafore: 3 HMS
piñata occasion: 6 fiesta
Pinatubo: 7 volcano
emulate ~: 5 erupt
locale: 4 Asia 5 Luzon 11 Philippines
output: 3 ash 4 lava
pinball: 4 game
foul: 4 tilt
palace: 6 arcade
pinball __: 7 machine
Pinball
author: Jerzy Kosinski
Pinball Wizard (1969 song)
artist: Who
Pincay, Laffit: 6 jockey
milieu: 5 track 9 racetrack
pince-nez: 7 glasses 10 eyeglasses
part: 4 lens
pincer: 4 claw 5 chela
pinch: 3 bit, cop, jot, nab, nip, rob 4 bust, crib, dash, hurt, iota, lift, mite, nail, pass, spot, take, whit 5 cramp, crumb, filch, purse, run in, seize, spare, speck, steal, swipe, theft, tinge, trace, tweak 6 arrest, collar, crisis, detain, little, pickle, pilfer, plight, pocket, pucker, pull in, rip off, scrape, snatch, strait, thieve, trifle, twinge 7 capture, jailing, larceny, modicum, purloin, ransack, smidgen, smidgin, soupçon, squeeze, tighten 8 compress, exigence, exigency, quagmire, smidgeon, thievery 9 apprehend, deep water, emergency, necessity, tight spot, tough spot, vellicate 10 difficulty, limitation, run off with
a pooch: 6 dognap, petnap
ender: 5 penny
hitter: 3 sub 9 surrogate 10 substitute
pennies: 3 eke 4 save 5 skimp 6 scrape, scrimp
reaction: 2 ow 3 yow 4 ouch, yeow
pinch __: 3 hit 6 hitter, of salt, runner 7 pennies
__ pinch: 3 in a
Pinchas: 8 Zukerman
pinched: 4 poor, thin, worn 5 broke, needy, ran in 6 bad off, hard up, ill off, in need, in want, narrow 7 starved, worn-out 8 badly off, bankrupt, beggarly, indigent, starving, strapped 9 destitute, insolvent, moneyless, penniless, penurious 10 down and out, pauperized, straitened
__ pincher: 5 penny
pinchers: 6 pliers 7 forceps
pinch-hit: 3 sub 5 cover 6 act for, fill in 7 stand-in 8 cover for 10 substitute
Pinchot: 7 Bronson, Gifford
pinchpenny: 5 miser 6 stingy 8 tightwad, ungiving 9 skinflint
pin curls: 4 coif 6 hairdo 8 coiffure
Pindar: 4 poet 5 Greek
work: 3 ode
pine: 4 ache, fret, long, moon, mope, sigh, tree, want, wish, wood 5 brood, mourn, yearn 6 desire, grieve, hanker 7 conifer, dream of, long for 8 languish, loblolly, longleaf 9 evergreen, ponderosa
Australian ~: 5 bunya
cone projection: 4 umbo
ender: 5 apple
extract: 5 furan, resin, rosin 10 turpentine
New Zealand ~: 5 kauri
nut: 5 piñon
product: 3 nut, tar 4 cone 6 needle
red ~: 4 rimu
relative: 3 fir 4 mugo 5 larch, mugho 6 spruce 7 hemlock 8 tamarack
sauce made with ~ nuts: 5 pesto
Tasmanian ~: 4 huon
pine __: 3 nut, tar 4 cone 6 barren, marten, needle
__ pine: 5 mugho 6 knotty, Scotch, Torrey
Pine: 5 Chris
Pine __: 5 Bluff 7 Barrens
pineal __: 3 eye 5 gland
pineapple: 5 fruit 7 grenade 8 ice cream 9 explosive 11 hand grenade
alternative: *see* ice cream flavor
name: 4 Dole
source: 4 Maui 5 Lanai 6 Hawaii
pineapple __-down cake: 6 upside
Pineapple Island, The: 5 Lanai
Pine Bluff: 4 city, town
locale: 8 Arkansas
Piñero (2001 film)
cast: Benjamin Bratt, Giancarlo Esposito, Talisa Soto
Pinero, Arthur Wing: 5 actor 7 British 8 essayist 10 playwright
__ Pines: 6 Torrey
Pines of Rome, The
composer: Ottorino Respighi
Pine Sol: 7 cleaner
competitor: 5 Brite, Lysol 6 Top Job 7 Lestoil, Mr. Clean 9 Fantastik, Step Saver
Pine Tree State: 5 Maine
ping: 5 knock, sound, whine 6 signal
Ping Pong: 4 game 5 sport
need: 3 net 4 ball 5 table 6 paddle
pinhead
see ninny
pinhole: 7 opening 8 aperture
Piniella: 3 Lou
pining: 3 sad 6 dreamy, morose 7 languid 10 melancholy
pinion: 4 bind, gear, limb, wing 5 plume, tie up 6 fetter, hogtie 7 feather, manacle, shackle, tie down 8 handcuff, restrain
partner: 4 rack
pink: 3 cut, hue 4 acme, peak, rose, rosy 5 bloom, blush, coral, notch, plant, prime, ruddy 6 ablush, flower, heyday, heydey, redden, salmon 7 flushed, fuchsia, roseate, scallop, scollop 8 blushing, cold duck 9 carnation 10 good health, perfection
and white flower: 8 dianthus 9 carnation
city of India: 6 Jaipur
color: 4 rose 5 coral, flesh, melon 6 damask, salmon 7 apricot 8 flamingo 9 carnation
flower: 4 lily 5 aster, lotus, peony, phlox, poppy 6 cosmos, lupine, mallow, mimosa, spirea, thrift 7 arbutus, begonia, dog rose, dogwood, freesia, rambler, spiraea, tea rose 8 arethusa, asphodel, camellia, geranium, hawthorn, larkspur, moss rose, oleander, tamarisk, wild rose 9 amaryllis, candytuft, corydalis, eglantine, hollyhock, hydrangea, mayflower, snowberry, water lily 10 bitterroot, cornflower, damask rose, delphinium, poinsettia, sweetbriar, sweetbrier
in the ~: 3 fit 4 hale, well 5 hardy, sound 6 robust 7 healthy 8 vigorous
not in the ~: 3 ill 4 sick 6 ailing 9 unhealthy
swamp ~: 5 plant 6 flower
tickle ~: 5 charm 6 please 9 titillate
tickled ~: 4 glad 5 happy 9 overjoyed
turn ~: 5 blush, flush 6 redden 7 sunburn
yellowish ~: 5 coral, peach 6 salmon 7 apricot
pink __: 3 gin, tea 4 lady, slip
__ pink: 5 in the 6 tickle
Pink __: 4 Lady 5 Floyd, Marsh 6 Houses
Pink Cadillac (1988 song)
artist: Natalie Cole
Pink Cadillac (1989 film)
cast: Clint Eastwood, Bernadette Peters
director: Buddy Van Horn
Pinkerton: 5 Allan
logo: 3 eye
Pinkett, Jada
spouse: Will Smith
pink-eyed one: 3 rat 6 albino
Pink Floyd
homeland: England
members: Gilmour, Waters, Wright, Mason
song: Another Brick in the Wall (1980)
Money (1973)
__ Pinkham's Medicine: 5 Lydia
Pink Houses (1983 song)
artist: John Cougar Mellencamp
pinkie: 5 digit 6 finger
pinking __: 4 iron 6 shears
Pink Lady: 5 drink 8 beverage, cocktail
ingredient: 3 gin 4 lime 5 lemon 6 brandy
Pink Marsh
author: George Ade
pinko: 4 left 7 leftist, radical
Pink Panther, The (1964 film)
cast: Capucine, David Niven, Peter Sellers
composer: Henry Mancini
director: Blake Edwards
Pink Panther, The (2006 film)
cast: Kevin Kline, Beyoncé Knowles, Steve Martin
pink-slip: 3 axe, can 4 boot, drop, fire, oust, sack 5 let go 6 bounce, lay off 7 cashier, dismiss, drum out, release 8 furlough, get rid of 9 discharge, terminate
pinky: 5 digit 6 finger
Pinky: 3 Lee
pinna: 3 fin 4 wing 7 auricle, feather, flipper
locale: 3 ear
pinnace: 4 boat 8 sailboat
pinnacle: 3 top, tor 4 acme, apex, crag, peak 5 crest, crown, ridge, spire, tower 6 apogee, belfry, climax, flèche, height, heyday, heydey, needle, summit, vertex, zenith 7 maximum, obelisk, steeple 8 high spot, meridian 9 bell tower, campanile, crescendo 10 prominence
combining form: 5 apico-
glacial ice ~: 5 serac
pinned: 8 held down
Pinocchio: 4 liar
author: Carlo Collodi
cat: 6 Figaro
goldfish: 4 Cleo
polygraph: 4 nose
undoing: 3 lie
whale: 7 Monstro
Pinochet: 7 Augusto
pinochle: 4 game 8 card game
card: 3 ten 4 jack, nine
holding: 4 meld
lowest ~ card: 4 nine
term: 5 trick
__ pinochle: 7 auction
piñon: 3 nut 4 tree 7 pine nut
Pinot: 3 vin 4 wine 5 grape 7 red wine 8 Burgundy 9 white wine
relative: *see* wine
Pinot __: 4 Noir 5 Blanc
Pinotta
composer: Pietro Mascagni
__ pin, pick...: 4 See a
pinpoint: 3 dot, set 4 find, mark, spot 5 place, speck 6 define, denote, detect, finger, home in, locate 8 diagnose, home in on, identify, indicate, localize, smell out, zero in on 9 determine, get a fix on, recognize
PIN prompter: 3 ATM
pins and needles, on: 4 edgy 5 antsy, itchy, jumpy, tense 6 uneasy 7 anxious, jittery, keyed up, nervous, restive, uptight, worried 8 agitated, restless, skittish, troubled 9 concerned, excitable, ill at ease 10 high-strung, sweating it
pinsetter
company: 3 AMF 9 Brunswick
place: 4 lane 5 alley
Pinsk: 4 city, town
locale: 7 Belarus
river: 6 Pripet
Pinson, Vada
sport: 8 baseball
pint: 3 ale 4 unit
enjoy a ~: 5 drink
fraction: 3 cup 4 gill 5 ounce
one-half ~: 3 cup
one-quarter ~: 4 gill
place for a ~: 3 bar, pub 6 tavern 8 alehouse
starter: 6 cuckoo
two ~s: 5 quart

pint-___: 4 size 5 sized
___-pint: 4 half
Pinta: 4 boat, ship 7 caravel
  companion: 4 Niña 10 Santa Maria
pintail: 4 duck, fowl
  relative: *see* duck
Pintauro: 5 Danny
Pinter, Harold: 7 British 10 playwright
  work: The Birthday Party
    The Caretaker
    The Collection
    The Dumb Waiter
    The Homecoming
    Landscape
    The Lover
    Monologue
    No Man's Land
    Old Times
    The Room
    Silence
    A Slight Ache
pin the ___ on the donkey: 4 tail
pinto: 4 bean 5 horse, paint, Scout 6 equine 9 chili bean
Pinto: 3 car 4 auto, Ford 6 Freida 10 automobile
pint-sized: 3 wee 4 baby, puny, tiny 5 bitty, short, small, teeny 6 atomic, bantam, little, minute, peewee, petite, teensy 7 stunted 8 atomical, atomlike 9 itsy-bitsy, itty-bitty, miniature 10 diminutive, teeny-weeny, vest-pocket
pin-up: 3 art 5 photo 6 poster 10 photograph
pinwheel: 3 toy
  sound: 4 whir 5 whirr
piny: 5 spicy 8 fragrant 10 coniferous
Pinza, Ezio: 4 bass 5 basso 6 singer
  specialty: 5 opera
pion: 5 boson, meson 8 particle
pioneer: 4 lead 5 early, first, found, guide, start 6 create, invent, launch, leader, map out, open up 7 develop, explore, founder, go first, initial, pilgrim, settler 8 colonist, discover, explorer, initiate, inventer, inventor, original, squatter 9 developer, establish, immigrant, inaugural, inceptive, innovator, institute, introduce, originate, spearhead 10 avant-garde, lead the way, pathfinder, show the way, trailblaze
  place: 3 hut 5 cabin, shack 9 homestead
  transport: 4 mule 5 horse, wagon 9 buckboard, Conestoga 10 wagon train
Pioneer: 3 car 4 auto 5 Dodge, probe
pioneering: 7 new wave 8 advanced 10 avant-garde
Pioneer Press: 5 paper 9 newspaper
  locale: 6 St. Paul
Pioneers, The
  author: James Fenimore Cooper
pious: 4 holy 5 godly 6 devout, sacred 7 angelic, devoted, saintly 8 clerical, orthodox, priestly, reverent, seraphic, virtuous 9 angelical, born-again, prayerful, religious, righteous 10 goody-goody, seraphical, worshipful
  ending: 4 amen
pip: 3 dot 4 lulu, seed 5 beaut, dandy, dilly, doozy, peach, prize 6 beauty, corker 9 humdinger
  domino ~: 3 ace
pipe: 3 cob 4 duct, flue, hose, line, main, peep, play, sing, toot, tube, vent, wind 5 cheep, chirp, drain, sewer, speak, spout, trill, tweet 6 convey, regard, siphon, squeak, syphon, warble 7 bring in, conduit, corncob, twitter, whistle 8 aqueduct, bird call, cylinder, transmit 9 water main 10 meerschaum
  Asian ~: 5 hooka
  clay ~: 6 dudeen
  clean a ~: 4 ream
  cleaner: 3 lye 5 Drano, snake
  collar: 6 flange
  curved ~: 4 trap
  cutter: 3 saw
  down: 3 shh 4 hush 5 shush 6 shut up 7 be quiet, silence 9 keep still
  dream: 5 fancy 6 revery, vision 7 chimera, fantasy, reverie 8 chimaera, delusion
  ender: 4 line 5 stone
  enjoy a ~: 4 puff 5 smoke
  feature: 5 valve
  hole: 5 crack, drain
  Indian ~: 5 plant 6 flower
  joint: 3 ell, wye
  material: 3 cob, PVC 4 clay 5 briar, brier 6 copper 7 corncob, plastic 10 meerschaum
  opening: 6 intake
  part: 4 bowl, stem 5 shank
  problem: 4 drip, leak
  put down ~: 3 lay
  rainwater ~: 5 spout
  residue: 6 dottel, dottle
  sealer: 5 putty
  short ~: 4 spud
  starter: 3 bag, pan 4 blow, horn, tail, wind 5 drain, stand, stove
  stove ~: 3 hat 6 top hat
  tobacco ~: 3 cob 4 clay 5 briar, brier 7 corncob 10 meerschaum
  up: 3 say 5 speak, utter
  water ~: 4 main 5 hooka 6 hookah 7 conduit 8 aqueduct
pipe ___: 4 down, rack 5 dream, organ
___ pipe: 3 Pan 4 flue 5 peace, pitch, water 7 corncob, exhaust
___-pipe cactus: 5 organ
___-pipe cinch: 4 lead
Pipe Dream: 7 musical
  composer: Oscar Hammerstein, Richard Rodgers
pipeline: 4 main, pipe 7 channel, conduit 8 aqueduct
piper: 4 Scot 6 tooter 8 flautist 10 Highlander
  mythical ~: 3 Pan
  starter: 3 bag 4 sand
  the ~'s son: 3 Tom
Piper: 6 Laurie
pipette: 4 tube 5 pipet 7 lab tube 9 glassware
  unit: 2 cc.
piping: 3 hot 4 high, trim 5 reedy 6 shrill
pipistrelle: 3 bat
pipit: 4 bird 7 titlark 8 songbird
  relative: 4 lark
Pippa: 5 Scott
Pippa Passes: 4 poem
  author: Robert Browning
Pippen, Scottie: 5 cager
  milieu: 5 court
  org.: 3 NBA
  sport: 10 basketball
Pippig: 3 Uta
Pippin: 5 apple
  relative: *see* apple
pips
  piece with ~: 6 domino
  with the ~ showing: 6 face-up
pipsqueak: 4 runt 5 scrub, twerp, twirp, weeny
Piqua: 4 city, town
  locale: 4 Ohio
piquancy: 3 nip 4 bite, tang, zest 5 spice, taste 10 bitterness
piquant: 3 hot 4 racy, sour, tart 5 juicy, minty, peppy, salty, sharp, spicy, tangy, tasty, zesty, zingy 6 biting, lively, red-hot, savory, spicey, strong 7 peppery, pungent, zestful 8 poignant, spirited, stinging 9 flavorful, sparkling, trenchant
  flavor: 3 zip 4 bite, tang, zest, zing
  not ~: 4 blah, mild
pique: 3 get, ire, irk, pet, vex 4 fret, gall, goad, huff, hurt, miff, rile, roil, snit, spur, step, stir, tiff, whet 5 anger, annoy, goose, grate, peeve, prick, rouse, sting, upset, wound 6 arouse, dander, excite, fire up, hatred, kindle, needle, nettle, offend, pother, put out, rancor, ruffle 7 affront, dudgeon, enflame, incense, offense, provoke, quicken, umbrage 8 interest, intrigue, irritate, slow burn, vexation 9 aggravate, annoyance, displease, galvanize, stimulate 10 conniption, exasperate, irritation, resentment
  fit of ~: 3 ire 4 huff, pout, snit
piqué: 6 fabric 8 material
piqued: 3 hot, mad 4 hurt, ired, sore 5 angry, huffy, irate, livid, moody, upset 6 galled, put out 7 excited 8 steaming 9 indignant, irritated, resentful
Piraeus: 4 city, port, town
  locale: 6 Greece
Pirandello, Luigi: 6 writer 7 Italian 8 Nobelist 10 playwright
  work: Six Characters in Search of an Author
piranha: 4 fish 6 caribe
Piranha
  author: Harold Robbins
pirate: 4 copy, lift, raid 5 forge, steal, thief, usurp 6 bandit, borrow, kidnap, looter, pilfer, ravage, robber, sailor, vandal 7 brigand, corsair, jack tar, sea wolf, smuggle 8 freeboot, marauder, picaroon, rapparee, sea rover, simulate, spurious 9 buccaneer, depredate, reproduce 10 freebooter
  drink: 3 rum 4 grog
  feature: 5 patch 6 peg leg 8 eye-patch
  fictional ~: 4 Hook, Smee
  flag: 10 Jolly Roger
  flag emblem: 5 skull 10 crossbones
  haul: 4 loot, pelf, swag 5 booty 7 plunder 8 treasure
  noted ~: 4 Kidd 5 Teach 6 Morgan 7 Lafitte 10 Blackbeard
  pet: 6 parrot
  ship: 5 rover, xebec, zebec 6 zebeck 7 corsair 8 sea rover
  shout: 6 yo-ho-ho
  trunk: 5 chest
Pirate
  author: Harold Robbins
  Hall-of-Famer: 5 Kiner, Waner 6 Wagner 7 Averill, Vaughan 8 Clemente, Stargell 9 Mazeroski, Paul Waner 10 Lloyd Waner, Ralph Kiner
Pirate Jenny
  composer: Kurt Weill
Pirates: 4 nine, team 9 Seton Hall
  home: 3 PGH 10 Pittsburgh
  org.: 3 MLB, NLC
  rival: *see* baseball team
  sport: 8 baseball
Pirates of Penzance, The: 8 operetta
  character: 4 Kate, Ruth 5 Edith, Mabel 6 Isabel
  composer: W.S. Gilbert, Arthur Sullivan
Pirates of Penzance, The (1983 film)
  cast: Kevin Kline, Angela Lansbury, Linda Ronstadt
Pirate, The (1948 film)
  cast: Judy Garland, Gene Kelly
  director: Vincente Minnelli
piratical: 7 lawless 8 thieving 9 predatory
Pirelli product: 4 tire
pirogi cousin: 5 knish
pirogue: 4 boat 5 canoe, skiff
  need: 4 pole
  waters: 5 bayou
pirouette: 4 jink, spin, turn 5 pivot, twirl, wheel, whirl 6 gyrate, rotate, swivel 7 revolve 8 gyration
Pisa: 4 city, town
  attraction: 5 tower
  city near ~: 5 Lucca
  locale: 5 Italy 6 Italia
  river: 4 Arno
Pisarro, Camille: 6 artist 7 painter, Spanish 8 sculptor
piscator: 6 angler 9 fisherman
Pisces: 4 fish, sign
  follower: 5 Aries
  month: 3 Feb., Mar. 5 March 8 February
  preceder: 8 Aquarius
  unit: 4 star
piscivore, flying: 3 ern 4 erne
Piscopo, Joe: 8 comedian
'P' Is for Peril
  author: Sue Grafton
Pisgah: 4 peak 5 mount 8 mountain
  locale: 4 Asia 6 Jordan
  summit: 4 Nebo
pismire: 3 ant, bug 5 emmet 6 insect
pismo ___: 4 clam
Pismo Beach: 4 city, town
  locale: 10 California
pistachio: 3 nut 4 tree 5 color, green 8 ice cream
  alternative: *see* green color, ice cream flavor
  family: 6 cashew
piste: 6 ski run 8 ski trail
pistil part: 5 ovary, style 6 stigma
pistol: 3 gat, gun, rod 4 Colt 5 piece 6 heater, roscoe 7 firearm,

handgun **8** revolver **9** derringer, humdinger **10** six-shooter
ammo: 4 slug **6** bullet
German ~: 5 Luger
handle: 5 stock
packer: 6 gunman, outlaw, robber **7** marshal, sheriff **9** desperado **10** bank robber, gunfighter
packing a ~: 5 armed **8** carrying
point a ~: 3 aim **4** warn **8** threaten
starter ~ ammo: 5 blank
water ~: 3 toy **8** squirter
__ pistol: 3 air, cap **5** water
Pistol Packin' __: 4 Mama
pistol-packing: 5 armed
pistols: 8 weaponry
Pistol, The
author: James Jones
piston
location: 3 cyl. **6** engine **8** cylinder
sealer: 6 gasket
Pistons: 4 five, team
home: 7 Detroit
org.: 3 NBA
rival: *see* NBA team
sport: 10 basketball
Piston, Walter: 8 composer
pit: 3 vie **4** dent, gulf, hole, mine, seed, tomb, well **5** abyss, chasm, ditch, fossa, gouge, match, shaft, stone, vault **6** cavity, crater, dimple, dugout, hollow, oppose, quarry, riddle, take on, trench, tunnel **7** foxhole, play off, pothole, vie with **9** perforate **10** depression, excavation, set against
boss: 8 overseer
bottomless ~: 5 abysm, abyss, chasm
ceremonial ~: 4 kiva
cherry ~: 5 stone
ender: 4 cher, fall
grape ~: 6 acinus
luau cooking ~: 3 imu
make a ~ stop: 5 gas up
starter: 3 arm **4** cess, cock, flea, sand
pit __: 4 boss, bull, stop **5** viper
__ pit: 4 coal, mosh **5** snake
pita: 5 bread
sandwich: 4 gyro
Pit and the Pendulum, The
author: Edgar Allan Poe
pitapat: 5 throb **6** patter **9** palpitate
go: 4 beat **5** pound **7** flutter **9** palpitate
pit bull: 3 dog **5** canid **6** canine
sound: 3 arf, yap **4** bark, gnar, yelp **5** gnarr, growl
Pitcairn: 4 isle **6** island
pitch: 2 ad **3** bid, dip, key, lob, peg, tar, yaw **4** buck, cant, cast, dive, fall, fire, flip, game, hurl, keel, lean, line, puff, rate, reel, rock, roll, sell, talk, tilt, tone, toss, trip **5** angle, chuck, drive, erect, fling, grade, heave, level, lobby, lunge, lurch, offer, plant, point, put up, raise, resin, set up, slant, sling, slope, slump, sound, speak, spiel, state, throw **6** billow, careen, degree, height, launch, let fly, locate, patter, plunge, scheme, seesaw, settle, slider, speech, submit, thrash, timbre, topple, tumble, wallow, welter **7** asphalt, deliver, incline, lecture, oration, present, proffer, project, promote, stagger, station **8** beanball, card game, change-up, fastball, flounder, forkball, gradient, heel over, proposal, spitball, splitter **9** advertise, curveball, frequency, promotion, publicity, publicize, sales talk, screwball, steepness **10** commercial, inflection, modulation, suggestion, turpentine
advertising ~: 5 try it
a tent: 4 camp **6** encamp **7** bivouac, rough it
baseball ~: 5 fader **6** sinker, slider **8** change-up, forkball, spitball, splitter **9** curve ball
detector: 3 ear
ender: 4 fork **6** blende
hay: 4 fork
in: 3 aid **4** give, help, join, pool **5** set to **6** assist, donate, fall to, go to it, pony up, tackle, tee off **7** get busy, hop to it **8** get going **9** cooperate, lend a hand, subscribe, undertake, volunteer **10** buckle down, contribute
indicator: 4 clef
into: 5 fly at **6** tackle
lacking ~: 6 atonal
make a ~: 3 bid **5** lobby, offer **6** submit **7** present, proffer, propose **9** advertise
of voice ~: 5 tonal
sales ~: 2 ad **4** line **5** spiel **8** hard sell, soft sell **10** commercial
slow ~: 3 lob
source: 3 tar **4** pine
water: 4 bail
woo: 3 hug **4** kiss, neck **5** spoon **6** caress
pitch __: 3 woo **4** pipe, shot **5** a tent
pitch-__: 4 dark **5** black
__-pitch: 3 slo
pitch-black: 3 jet **4** dark, inky **5** sable, unlit **8** lowering **9** unlighted
pitchblende: 3 ore **7** mineral **9** uraninite
pitch-dark: 4 inky **5** black, sable, unlit **8** lowering **9** unlighted
pitched
it may be ~: 3 woo **4** tent
steeply ~: 6 gabled
too high: 5 sharp
too low: 4 flat
pitcher: 3 jug **4** ewer **5** adman **6** carafe, hurler, seller, vender, vendor, vessel **7** amphora, athlete, creamer **8** decanter, sales rep **9** gravy boat **10** advertiser
asset: 3 arm
bag: 5 rosin
big-mouthed ~: 3 jug **4** ewer
coup: 4 save **7** shutout **8** no-hitter
dread: 3 hit **4** walk **5** homer
error: 4 balk
face the ~: 3 bat
facing the ~: 5 at bat
feature: 3 ear, lip **5** spout **6** handle
goal: 3 out, win **4** save **8** no-hitter
Greek wine ~: 4 olpe **7** amphora
Hall of Fame ~: 4 Dean, Ford, Hoyt, Ryan, Wynn **5** Gomez, Grove, Lemon, Paige, Perry, Rixey, Rusie, Spahn, Vance, Young **6** Bender, Feller, Gibson, Hunter, Koufax, Niekro, Palmer, Seaver, Sutter, Sutton **7** Bunning, Carlton, Cy Young, Fingers, Gossage, Hubbell, Jenkins, Johnson, Roberts, Ruffing, Waddell, Wilhelm **8** Bob Lemon, Drysdale, Marichal, Marquard **9** Alexander, Amos Rusie, Bob Feller, Bob Gibson, Dizzy Dean, Don Sutton, Early Wynn, Eckersley, Eppa Rixey, Jim Hunter, Jim Palmer, Mathewson, Newhouser, Nolan Ryan, Radbourne, Tom Seaver **10** Dazzy Vance, Jim Bunning, Lefty Gomez, Lefty Grove, Phil Niekro, Red Ruffing, Whitey Ford
mate: 5 basin
relief ~: 6 closer
Roman wine ~: 4 olpe **7** amphora
spot for a ~: 4 slab **5** mound
stat: 3 ERA **5** saves **8** shutouts **10** strikeouts
target: 4 mitt **5** plate
Pitcher: 5 Molly
pitchfork part: 4 tine **5** prong, tooth
pitchman: 6 barker
aide: 5 shill
payoff: 4 sale
__-pitch softball: 3 slo
piteous: 3 sad **5** woful **6** moving, woeful **7** doleful **8** grievous, pathetic, poignant, touching, wretched **9** affective, miserable, plaintive, sorrowful **10** deplorable, lamentable, pathetical
pitfall: 3 web **4** flaw, risk, snag, trap **5** catch, peril, setup, snare **6** danger, hazard **8** drawback **9** booby trap, mousetrap, quicksand
pith: 4 core, crux, gist, meat **5** focus, heart, point, tenor **6** center, kernel, marrow, moment, thrust, upshot **7** essence, keynote, meaning, nucleus, purport **8** solidity **9** innermost, main point, substance **10** focal point, importance
helmet: 3 hat **4** topi **5** topee
Pithecanthropus: 6 apeman
relative: 3 ape
pithecologist study: 3 ape
pithless: 4 puny **5** frail, wimpy **6** anemic, atonic, effete, feeble, flabby, flimsy **7** anaemic, fragile, wimpish **8** delicate, helpless **9** faltering, powerless, spineless **10** vulnerable
pithy: 4 curt, soft **5** brief, crisp, meaty, short, terse **6** cogent, gnomic **7** compact, concise, laconic, pointed, summary **8** succinct, vigorous **9** axiomatic, forceable, trenchant **10** meaningful, to the point
saying: 3 mot, saw **5** adage, gnome, motto **7** epigram **9** witticism
pitiable: 3 sad **5** woful **6** abject, tragic, woeful **7** forlorn **8** pathetic, tragical, wretched **9** miserable **10** deplorable
pitiful: 3 sad **4** mean, poor, vile **5** small, sorry, woful **6** abject, dismal, humble, measly, moving, paltry, scurvy, shabby, tragic, woeful **7** doleful, forlorn **8** beggarly, grievous, mournful, pathetic, poignant, touching, tragical, wretched **9** affecting, miserable, suffering, worthless **10** deplorable, despicable, inadequate, in bad shape, lamentable, pathetical
pitiless: 4 cold, hard, mean **5** cruel, harsh, nasty, stiff, stony **6** animal, brutal, fierce, savage, severe, stoney, unkind, wanton **7** austere, beastly, callous, hurtful, inhuman, vicious **8** barbaric, fiendish, inhumane, obdurate, ruthless, sadistic, vengeful **9** barbarous, cutthroat, dog-eat-dog, ferocious, heartless, impliable, inclement, merciless, monstrous, truculent, unfeeling **10** implacable, inexorable, insensible, relentless, unmerciful, vindictive
Pitman: 5 Isaac
pupil: 5 steno **9** secretary
topic: 9 shorthand
Pitney __: 5 Bowes
Pitney, Gene
song: I'm Gonna Be Strong (1964)
It Hurts to Be in Love (1964)
Last Chance to Turn Around (1965)
Looking Through the Eyes of Love (1965)
Mecca (1963)
Only Love Can Break a Heart (1962)
She's a Heartbreaker (1968)
(The Man Who Shot) Liberty Valance (1962)
Town Without Pity (1961)
Twenty Four Hours from Tulsa (1963)
pitons: 6 spikes
use ~: 5 climb **6** ascend
pits
in the ~: 3 low **6** broody **7** way down **8** dejected, wretched **9** depressed, miserable **10** despairing, despondent
remove ~: 6 deseed
tar ~ locale: 6 La Brea
the ~: 5 awful, nadir, worst **10** rock bottom
pit stop item: 3 air, gas, gum, oil, pop **4** fuel, soda, tire **5** candy, chips, juice, snack **6** diesel **8** fast food, gasoline
Pitt: 4 Brad, Dirk
pitta: 4 bird
pittance: 3 bit, sou **4** mite **5** crumb, scrap **6** little **7** driblet, minimum, modicum, peanuts **10** slave wages
__ pittance: 4 mere
Pitt, Brad: 5 actor
film: Babel (2006)
Burn After Reading (2007)
Cool World (1992)
The Curious Case of Benjamin Button (2008)
The Devil's Own (1997)
Interview With the Vampire: The Vampire Chronicles (1994)
Johnny Suede (1991)
Kalifornia (1993)
Meet Joe Black (1998)
Mr. & Mrs. Smith (2005)
Ocean's Eleven (2001)
A River Runs Through It (1992)
Se7en (1995)

Snatch (2000)
Troy (2004)
Twelve Monkeys (1995)
spouse: Jennifer Aniston
pitter-__: 6 patter
Pit, The: 5 novel
author: Frank Norris
__ Pit, The: 5 Money, Snake
Pitts: 4 ZaSu
Pittsburgh: 4 city, town
city north of ~: 4 Erie
conference: 7 Big East
county: 9 Allegheny
locale: 4 Penn.
product: 4 coal 5 steel
pro team: 7 Pirates 8 Panthers, Penguins, Steelers
river: 4 Ohio 9 Allegheny 11 Monongahela
school: 8 Duquesne
Pittsfield: 4 city, town
locale: 4 Mass.
__ Pittypat: 4 Aunt
pituitary: 5 gland
output: 4 ACTH 7 hormone
pity: 4 ruth 5 crime, mercy, shame, spare 6 lenity, mishap, pardon, pathos, relent, sorrow, warmth 7 ache for, bad luck, charity, comfort, console, empathy, feel for, forgive, quarter, weep for 8 bleed for, clemency, go easy on, goodness, kindness, lenience, sympathy 9 grieve for, mischance 10 compassion, grieve with, kindliness, misfortune, ruefulness, sympathize, tenderness
exclamation of ~: 4 alas 5 alack 8 lackaday
feel ~: 3 cry 4 ache, weep
have ~: 6 excuse, relent, soften 7 forgive
without ~: 4 hard 5 cruel 8 ruthless 10 relentless
Pity This Busy Monster...: 4 poem
author: e.e. cummings
piu: 4 more
Pius: 4 pope 7 pontiff
pivot: 4 axis, axle, jink, slew, slue, spin, turn, veer 5 hinge, round, swing, twirl, wheel, whirl 6 center, circle, depend, hang on, rely on, rotate, slough, swivel, teeter 7 fulcrum, librate, revolve 9 oscillate, pirouette
ballet ~: 3 toe
pivotal: 3 key 5 focal, major, polar, vital 6 needed, ruling 7 central, crucial, primary 8 cardinal, critical, decisive, pregnant, required 9 essential, important, mandatory, momentous, necessary, principal 10 overriding, portentous
factor: 5 hinge 7 fulcrum
point: 3 toe 4 crux
pix: 5 films, snaps 6 flicks, movies, photos 9 snapshots
pixel: 3 dot
term: 6 low-res 7 graphic, high-res 8 graphics
pixie: 3 elf, imp 5 fairy, gnome, nisse, troll 6 goblin, sprite 7 brownie 10 leprechaun
Pixie: 4 toon 5 mouse
pixyish: 3 fey 5 elfin 6 impish
Pizarro, Francisco: 7 Spanish 8 explorer 9 conqueror
capital: 4 Lima
conquest: 4 Peru 5 Incas
quest: 3 oro 4 gold 8 treasure
pizazz: 3 vim, zip 4 brio, dash, élan, zest, zing 5 class, flair, flash, oomph, punch, style, verve, vigor 6 energy 8 vitality, vivacity
lacking ~: 4 blah, drab, flat
Piz Bernina: 3 Alp
pizza: 3 pie 8 fast food
base: 5 crust
frozen ~: 5 Jeno's, Tony's 6 Ellio's 7 Celeste, Totino's 8 DiGiorno 9 Tombstone 10 Freschetta
go for ~: 6 eat out
order: 4 to-go
portion: 5 sixth, slice 6 eighth
slices per ~ often: 3 six 5 eight
topping: 3 ham 5 bacon, olive, onion, sauce 6 cheese, pepper 7 anchovy, sausage 8 eggplant, meat ball, mushroom 9 pepperoni, pineapple 10 black olive, green olive
pizza __: 3 box, pie 4 oven 5 dough 6 parlor
__ Pizza: 6 Mystic
Pizza Hut
rival: ***see*** restaurant chain
pizzazz
see pizazz
pizzeria: 10 restaurant
appliance: 4 oven
pizzicato: 4 note 7 plucked
P.J.: 7 O'Rourke
PJs: 7 pajamas 9 Dr. Dentons, nightwear, sleepwear 10 bedclothes
pkg.
see package
P.L.: 7 Travers
placable: 3 lax 4 easy, kind, mild, soft 5 loose 6 gentle, kindly 7 clement, ruthful, sparing 8 flexible, laid-back, merciful, tolerant 9 assuasive, compliant, easygoing, forgiving, indulgent 10 forbearing, permissive, unexacting
placard: 4 bill, sign 6 poster 9 broadside
placate: 4 calm 6 pacify, soothe 7 appease, assuage, compose, mollify, satisfy, sweeten 8 mitigate 9 reconcile, untrouble 10 conciliate, propitiate
place: 3 fix, job, lay, lie, pad, peg, put, set 4 area, city, duty, home, know, levy, lieu, nail, name, nook, park, post, rank, role, room, seat, site, slot, spot, stow, town, zone 5 abode, berth, house, joint, locus, lodge, niche, plant, posit, scene, stand, stead, stick, store, venue, where 6 assign, corner, hamlet, insert, instal, locale, locate, métier, milieu, office, reckon, region, settle, status, street, suburb 7 appoint, arrange, country, deposit, domicil, habitat, hangout, install, lay down, lodging, quarter, section, set down, situate, station, village 8 classify, diagnose, district, domicile, dwelling, function, identify, locality, location, lodgings, pinpoint, position, property, province, quarters, remember, standing, vicinity 9 apartment, bailiwick, community, designate, determine, recognize, recollect, residence, situation 10 categorize, commission, employment, occupation
combining form: 3 top- 4 loco-, topo- 5 -orium
on a pedestal: 5 adore 7 idolize, worship 8 idealize
starter: 3 any, dis, mis, out 4 fire, show, some, work 5 birth, every 6 common, market
place __: 3 mat 4 a bet, an ad, card, kick 7 setting
__ place: 4 high, take, ten's 5 run in, unit's 7 decimal, polling
Place: 4 Etta 7 Mary Kay
Place __ Arts: 3 des
__ Place: 6 Peyton 7 Melrose
__ Place, A: 6 Far-Off, Summer
Place de l'Opera
artist: Erté
__ Place I Hang My Hat Is Home: 3 Any
place in the __: 3 sun
Place in the Sun, A (1951 film)
cast: Montgomery Clift, Elizabeth Taylor, Shelley Winters
Place in the Sun, A (1966 song)
artist: Stevie Wonder
place-kicker: 7 athlete 10 footballer
pride: 3 toe
prop: 3 tee
Place, Mary Kay: 7 actress
TV: Mary Hartman, Mary Hartman
placement: 4 form 8 sequence 9 situation
Placentia: 4 city, town
locale: 10 California
Place of Love, The
author: Karl Shapiro
places: 4 loca, loci
go ~: 3 win 4 rise 6 hack it, make it, pan out, thrive 7 advance, luck out, make out, prevail, prosper, succeed, triumph, work out 8 flourish, get ahead, get along, hit it big, make good 10 do all right
trade ~: 4 swap 5 shift
__ Places: 7 Far-Away, Trading
Places in the Heart (1984 film)
cast: Lindsay Crouse, Sally Field, Danny Glover, Ed Harris, Amy Madigan, John Malkovich
__ Places You'll Go!: 5 Oh the
placid: 4 calm, cool, even, mild, tame 5 quiet, staid, still, stoic 6 at ease, gentle, low-key, mellow, sedate, serene 7 amiable, at peace, easeful, equable, pacific, relaxed, restful, stoical, unmoved 8 amicable, carefree, composed, in repose, laid-back, peaceful, reserved, tranquil 9 collected, easygoing, impassive, quiescent, temperate, unexcited, unruffled, unworried 10 complacent, nonchalant, unagitated, untroubled
placidity: 4 calm 5 peace, quiet 8 calmness, serenity 9 composure 10 equanimity, sedateness
__ Placid, NY: 4 Lake
plack: 5 money
plage: 5 beach
plagiarism: 5 fraud, theft 6 piracy 8 cribbing, stealing, thievery 9 borrowing
plagiarist: 6 copier 7 usurper 8 imitator
plagiarize: 3 rob 4 copy, crib, lift 5 steal, usurp 6 borrow 8 arrogate 10 infringe on
plague: 3 ail, bug, dog, dun, irk, nag, pox, rag, try, vex 4 bane, gall, pest, ride, roil 5 annoy, curse, grind, harry, haunt, hound, press, tease, worry 6 badger, blight, bother, gnaw at, harass, hassle, heckle, hector, needle, noodge, obsess, pester, pursue, rankle 7 afflict, disease, disturb, oppress, scourge, torment, trouble 8 aggrieve, calamity, disaster, distress, epidemic, nuisance, outbreak 9 beleaguer, contagion, detriment, importune, infection, nightmare, persecute, ruination 10 affliction, discompose, epidemical, pestilence
unit: 6 locust
__ Plague: 5 Black
plagued: 5 beset 8 besieged, obsessed
Plague Dogs, The (1982 film)
director: Martin Rosen
Plague, The: 5 novel
author: Albert Camus
setting: 4 Oran
plaid: 6 fabric, tartan 9 checkered 10 Black Watch
fabric: 6 Madras, tartan
garment: 4 kilt
plain: 3 dry 4 bare, dull, easy, moor, naif, open, pure 5 basic, blunt, clean, clear, field, frank, heath, level, llano, lowly, lucid, mousy, naive, naked, overt, pampa, sober, stark, usual, vivid 6 candid, cogent, direct, folksy, honest, humble, in view, meadow, modest, mousey, pampas, patent, public, rustic, severe, simple, smooth, steppe, tundra, valley 7 audible, austere, clearly, evident, exposed, express, flat-out, insipid, legible, literal, lowland, natural, obvious, prairie, regular, sincere, Spartan, unfussy, vanilla, visible 8 apparent, clear-cut, definite, distinct, everyday, explicit, flatland, homespun, informal, knowable, manifest, moorland, no-frills, ordinary, out-front, palpable, readable, straight, unhidden, unsubtle, unveiled 9 big as life, downright, graspable, grassland, ingenuous, outspoken, tasteless, unadorned, unsightly 10 elementary, explicitly, forthright, from the hip, manifestly, monotonous, noticeable, noticeably, observable, spelled out, unaffected, unassuming, unshrouded, well-marked
African ~: 4 veld 5 veldt
alluvial ~: 5 delta
Asian ~: 6 steppe 7 steppes
combining form: 4 pedi- 5 pedio-
elevated ~: 4 mesa 5 butte 7 plateau 9 altiplano
ender: 4 song 5 chant 6 spoken

in ~ view: 5 overt 7 obvious, visible 8 apparent
Latin American ~: 5 campo, llano 6 pampas 7 el campo
lunar ~: 3 sea 4 mare
make ~: 4 show 6 evince 7 clarify, exhibit, speak up 8 manifest, simplify, speak out 9 bring home, elucidate, explicate 10 illustrate
name meaning ~: 6 Sharon
not ~: 4 lacy 5 fancy, fussy 6 frilly, ornate, rococo 7 ruffled 9 elaborate
starter: 5 flood
upland ~: 4 moor, wold
plain __: 5 as day, to see
__, Plain and Tall: 5 Sarah
plain as __: 3 day
Plain Dealer: 5 paper 9 newspaper
locale: 9 Cleveland
Plain Dealer, The
author: William Wycherley
plain-dealing: 6 honest 7 upfront 8 straight
__ Plaines, IL: 3 Des
Plainfield: 4 city, town
locale: 9 New Jersey
plainly: 5 by far 6 easily
Plain People: 5 Amish
Plains: 4 city, town
Amerind: 3 Ute 4 Cree, Crow 5 Teton 6 Apache, Dakota, Lakota 7 Lakhota
animal: 4 deer 5 bison, steer 6 coyote 7 buffalo 8 antelope 10 prairie dog
locale: 4 Iowa 7 Georgia
__ Plains: 5 Great
__ Plains Drifter: 4 High
Plainsman, The (1936 film)
cast: Jean Arthur, Gary Cooper
character: 3 Del
director: Cecil B. DeMille
Plains of __: 7 Abraham
Plains of Passage, The: 5 novel
author: Jean Auel
plainsong: 5 chant, music 9 Gregorian
notation: 4 neum 5 neume
plainspoken: 5 bluff, blunt, brusk, frank, vocal 6 abrupt, candid, direct, honest 7 brusque, sincere, upfront 8 impolite, tactless, truthful 9 outspoken 10 forthright, foursquare, indelicate
plaint: 4 beef, moan 5 elegy, gripe, groan, whine 6 grouse, lament, squawk 9 grievance, objection
cat's ~: 3 mew 4 meow 5 miaou, miaow, miaul
coyote's ~: 4 howl
farm ~: 3 baa, low, moo 5 bleat, neigh, quack 6 gobble, squawk 7 whinney
peeper's ~: 5 croak
pound ~: 3 arf, yip 4 bark, woof, yelp
Shakespearean ~: 4 alas 8 lackaday
Yiddish ~: 2 oy
plaintiff: 4 suer 5 party 8 litigant
plaintive: 3 sad 5 sorry, woful 6 woeful 7 doleful, hangdog, piteous, wistful 8 dolorous, grievous, mournful, pathetic 9 lamenting, querulous, sorrowful, woebegone 10 lamentable, melancholy, pathetical
cry: 5 whine
poem: 5 elegy
sound: 4 sigh
plain-vanilla: 5 basic 6 simple 7 humdrum, prosaic
__ plaisir: 4 avec
plait: 4 coif, fold 5 braid, queue, tress, weave 6 hairdo, splice 7 cornrow, entwine, intwine, pigtail 8 coiffure 9 interlace 10 intertwine, interweave
s'il vous ~: 6 kindly, please
plan: 3 aim, lay, map, way 4 brew, idea, mean, mold, plot, spec 5 chart, draft, frame, hatch, setup, shape 6 agenda, cook up, design, devise, format, gambit, ideate, intend, intent, layout, map out, method, scheme, sketch, system 7 agendum, concoct, diagram, drawing, mark out, outline, pattern, prepare, program, project, propose, purpose, tactics, thought, work out 8 ambition, approach, block out, conceive, conspire, contrive, engineer, envisage, figure on, intrigue, maneuver, organize, proposal, reckon on, rough out, scenario, schedule, strategy, syllabus, think out, time line 9 blueprint, calculate, expedient, formulate, framework, intention, itinerary, look ahead, procedure, provision, visual aid 10 aspiration, bargain for, big picture, enterprise, mastermind, perception, prospectus, rough draft, strategize, suggestion
ahead: 3 fix 5 set up 6 budget 7 arrange, project 8 schedule
fiscal ~: 6 budget
floor ~: 5 chart 6 design, layout, sketch 7 diagram, drawing, outline 9 blueprint
food ~: 4 diet 7 regimen
game ~: 4 idea, ruse 5 model 6 design, scheme 8 scenario, strategy, time line 9 blueprint
ground ~: 3 map 5 chart, draft 6 design, layout, scheme, sketch, survey 7 diagram, program, rundown 8 proposal, scenario 9 blueprint, framework, rough idea 10 rough draft
in Britain: 4 rede
lurker's ~: 4 trap
on: 6 expect, reckon 7 wait for 9 calculate 10 anticipate
retirement ~: 3 IRA 5 Keogh
travel ~: 9 itinerary
__ plan: 4 game 5 floor 6 battle, flight, master 7 layaway, pension
Plan 9 From Outer Space
director: Ed Wood
role: 4 Eros
__ Plan, A: 6 Simple
__ plan, a canal...: 1 a 4 A man
planate: 4 flat 5 level 6 planar, smooth
planchette
board with a: 5 Ouija
Planck, Max: 8 Nobelist 9 physicist, scientist
contemporary: 4 Bohr
plane: 3 jet, MiG, SST 4 bird, even, face, flat, prop, STOL, tool, tree, trim, VTOL 5 AWACS, craft, facet, level, liner, shave 6 Airbus, bomber, degree, ramjet, smooth, sphere, steppe 7 flatten, footing, pontoon, prairie, propjet, regular, stratum, surface, uniform, vehicle 8 aircraft, Concorde, flatland, jetliner, turbojet 9 transport, turboprop 10 crop duster, horizontal, twin-engine
alternative: 3 bus, car 4 auto, boat, ship 5 liner, train 9 freighter 10 cruise ship
area: 4 hold 5 cabin 7 cockpit
booster: 4 jato
bring the ~ in: 4 land 9 touch down
builders' org.: 3 UAW
crew: 5 pilot 6 airman 7 copilot, steward 9 navigator 10 stewardess
crystal ~: 4 face
datum: 3 arr., ETA
engine: 3 jet 6 fanjet 9 turboprop
European ~: 6 Airbus
fast ~: 3 jet, SST 8 Concorde
former Air France ~: 3 SST
gemstone ~: 5 facet
German ~: 5 Stuka
go by ~: 3 fly 6 aviate
grab a ~: 6 hijack 8 highjack
inspection agency: 3 FAA
jumping out of a ~: 4 feat 7 exploit
leave the ~: 4 jump 5 eject 7 deplane 9 parachute
left the ~: 3 lit 4 alit
light ~: 6 Cessna, glider
load: 5 cargo 7 baggage 10 passengers
locale: 3 sky 5 apron 6 hangar, runway 8 airstrip
military ~: 4 STOL, VTOL 5 AWACS
on a high ~: 5 lofty, noble
onetime enemy ~: 3 MIG
part: 3 fin 4 flap, tail, wing 5 aisle, cabin, strut 6 engine, galley 7 cockpit 8 bulkhead, fuselage
pontoon ~: 5 hydro
remote-controlled ~: 5 drone
reservation: 4 seat 6 flight
route: 6 airway
seating choice: 5 aisle 6 window 8 bulkhead
Soviet ~: 3 MiG
spotter: 5 LORAN, radar
spray: 6 deicer
stabilizer: 3 fin
starter: 2 bi 3 air, sea, tri, war 4 aero, aqua, jack, mono, sail 5 float
take a ~: 3 fly 6 aviate, travel
unidentified ~: 5 bogey, bogie
__ plane: 3 jet 5 fault 6 astral
Planes, Trains & Automobiles (1987 film)
cast: John Candy, Steve Martin, Michael McKean
planet: 3 orb 4 Mars 5 Earth, globe, Pluto, Venus, world 6 Saturn, sphere, Uranus 7 Jupiter, Mercury, Neptune, orbiter
circuit: 4 year
course: 3 arc 5 orbit
dwarf ~: 4 Eris 5 Ceres, Pluto
ender: 3 oid
fictional ~: 3 Ork 6 Vulcan
Jovian: 6 Saturn, Uranus 7 Jupiter, Neptune
red ~: 4 Mars
reflecting power: 6 albedo
shadow: 5 umbra
planetarium: 6 orrery
planetarium, Chicago: 5 Adler
Planet of the Apes
author: Pierre Boulle
Planet of the Apes (1968 film)
cast: Charlton Heston, Kim Hunter, Roddy McDowall
Planet of the Apes (2001 film)
cast: Helena Bonham Carter, Michael Clarke Duncan, Tim Roth, Mark Wahlberg
director: Tim Burton
role: 4 Nova
savage: 5 human
setting: 5 Earth 6 future
Planets, The
composer: Gustav Holst
plangent: 5 forte, noisy 7 blaring, booming, jarring, pealing, rackety, raucous, reboant, roaring 8 crashing, piercing, rumbling, sonorous, strident, turned up 9 big-voiced, clamorous, deafening 10 boisterous, resounding, stentorian, strepitous, thundering, uproarious, vociferous
planimeter measurement: 4 area
plank: 5 board 6 timber 8 platform
material: 4 wood
ship ~: 3 sny 4 wale
slopes ~: 3 ski 4 skee
starter: 4 gang
Plank: 5 Eddie
__, Plank, Plunk: 5 Plink
planks: 4 wood 6 lumber
plankton: 4 brit 5 algae
component: 4 alga 6 diatom 9 protozoan
strainer: 6 baleen
planned: 5 meant 6 wilful 7 studied, willful 8 intended, prepared 9 strategic, voluntary 10 deliberate, methodical, preplanned, purposeful, volitional
as ~: 5 slick 7 perfect 10 swimmingly
planner: 6 framer 8 designer, engineer 9 architect, developer, fashioner, tactician 10 mastermind, strategist
urban ~: 5 zoner
Plano: 4 city, town
locale: 5 Texas
plan of __: 6 attack
plant: 3 fix, lay, pot, put, set, sow, spy 4 alga, bury, bush, cane, chia, farm, grow, herb, mill, mold, mole, moss, reed, seat, seed, shop, slip, till, tree, vine, weed, yard 5 embed, found, grass, imbed, lodge, pitch, place, put in, raise, shoot, shrub, stick, stock, works 6 anchor, annual, clover, croton, enroot, flower, fungus, hybrid, insert, instal, instil, set out, sprout, tamper 7 climber, creeper, cutting, deposit, factory, foundry, install, instill, potherb, seaweed, station 8 biennial, cultivar, cyclamen, engender, ensconce, entrench, organism, seedling 9 accessory,

equipment, establish, inculcate, machinery, perennial, toadstool, vegetable **10** accomplice, ornamental, transplant, vegetation
again: **5** resow
anchor: **4** bulb, root **7** rhizome, taproot
aquatic ~: **4** alga, iris **5** lotus, sedge **6** elodea **7** cattail, papyrus **9** water lily
aromatic ~: **4** herb, nard **5** spice **9** evergreen
century ~: **4** aloe **5** agave, plant **6** flower
climbing ~: **3** ivy, pea **4** rose, vine **5** grape, liana, liane **8** clematis, sweet pea
combining form: **4** phyt- **5** -phyte, phyto-
desert ~: **5** agave, sotol, yucca **6** cactus
disease: **4** rust **6** blight
dwarfed ~: **6** bonsai
dye-yielding ~: **4** anil **5** henna
fiber ~: **4** jute **5** agave, istle, ixtle
fit to ~: **4** rich **5** loamy **6** arable **7** fertile
flowering ~: **5** dicot **7** dicotyl
flowerless ~: **4** fern, moss
fluid: **3** sap **5** latex, resin
forage ~ of Asia: **3** urd
future ~: **4** bulb, seed **7** cutting, rhizome
gum-yielding ~: **4** guar
landscaping ~: **4** bush **5** shrub **9** perennial
life: **5** flora **10** vegetation
locale: **3** bed **6** garden **7** nursery **8** orangery **9** herbarium, terrarium **10** greenhouse
manufacturing ~: **4** mill **5** works **7** factory
marsh ~: **4** reed, rush **5** ament, calla, sedge **7** cattail **8** arum lily
medicinal ~: **4** aloe, herb **5** jalap **6** arnica, croton, ipecac
microscopic ~: **4** alga **6** diatom
moor ~: **5** gorse **7** heather
part: **5** ovule, petal, sepal **6** anther, pistil, stamen
pasteurizing ~: **5** dairy **8** creamery
pest: **4** lice **5** aphid, aphis, louse **6** fungus
Polynesian ~: **2** ti **5** lehua **6** orchid
pore: **5** stoma
power ~: **5** hydro
protection: **5** mulch, straw
salad ~: **3** udo **5** cress **6** borage, carrot, celery, tomato **7** lettuce **8** cucumber **10** watercress
science: **6** botany
seed: **5** spore
shade-loving ~: **5** hosta **9** impatiens
stalk: **4** stem **5** stipe
starter: **3** egg **5** house
sticker: **3** bur **5** briar, brier, spine, thorn **7** prickle
succulent ~: **4** aloe **5** sedum **6** cactus
surveillant's ~: **3** bug **4** mike **7** wiretap
terrarium ~: **4** fern, moss
tissue: **5** xylem **6** cambia
unwanted ~: **4** weed
__ plant: **5** power
Plant: **6** Robert
plantain: **4** weed **6** banana
lily: **5** hosta
pudding: **6** foofoo
plantation: **4** farm **5** manor **6** estate, spread **8** hacienda
drink: **5** julep **9** mint julep
fictional ~: **4** Tara
Plante, Jacques: **8** puckster
milieu: **3** ice **4** rink **5** arena
org.: **3** NHL
planter: **6** grower
planter's punch: **5** drink **8** beverage, cocktail
ingredient: **3** rum **7** bitters **9** grenadine, lime juice **10** lemon juice
planting
area: **3** bed **4** park **5** field **6** garden, meadow **7** orchard
backyard ~: **5** shrub
fall ~: **4** bulb, corm
garden ~: **3** row
lawn ~: **4** bush, tree **5** grass, shrub
medium: **4** dirt, loam, peat, soil **5** earth
tool: **3** hoe **4** rake **5** spade **6** dibble, shovel
plants: **5** flora **10** vegetation
regional ~ and animals: **5** biota
Plant, The
author: Stephen King
plant-to-be: **4** seed
plaque: **5** award **8** memorial
plash: **3** lap **5** froth, slosh **6** ripple, splash **7** spatter
plasma __: **3** TVs
plasm starter: **4** ecto, endo, meta **5** proto
plaster: **4** cast, coat, daub, lime, sock **5** cover, grout, smear **6** bedaub, cement, gypsum, smudge, stucco **7** encrust, incrust, overlay, spackle **8** dressing **10** intoxicate
art: **5** mural, secco **6** fresco
coat with ~: **5** parge
mold: **4** cast
of Paris: **5** gesso **6** gypsum
overhead: **4** ceil
support: **4** lath
plaster __: **4** cast
__ plaster: **7** mustard
plastered: **4** high **5** drunk, tight, tipsy **10** inebriated
plastic: **4** limp, soft **5** false, phony **6** clayey, credit, ersatz, giving, limber, phoney, pliant, pseudo, supple **7** clayish, ductile, elastic, pliable **8** flexible, formable, workable, yielding **9** insincere, malleable, resilient, shapeable, synthetic, tractable **10** artificial, substitute
building block: **4** Lego
clear ~: **5** Saran **6** Lucite
component: **4** urea **5** resin
hose ~: **3** PVC
pay with ~: **3** owe **6** charge
shiny ~: **5** vinyl
substitute: **4** cash **5** money
plastic __: **4** wrap **7** surgery
Plastic __: **4** Wood
Plastic __ Band: **3** Ono
plastron: **5** armor
plat: **3** lot, map **4** lace, plot **5** tract **6** parcel **10** interweave
make a new ~: **5** remap
portion: **4** acre
__ plata: **4** oro y
plat du __: **4** jour
plate: **4** coat, disc, dish, disk, meal, slab, tray **5** metal, scale, sheet **6** lamina, saucer, silver **7** anodize, encrust, helping, incrust, overlay, platter, serving, woodcut **8** choppers, dentures, laminate, trencher **10** escutcheon, lithograph
armadillo ~: **5** scute **6** scutum
armor ~: **4** tace **5** tasse
blue ~ special: **4** meal **8** luncheon
boundary hazard: **5** quake **6** tremor **7** temblor **8** slippage **10** earthquake
church ~: **5** paten
combining form: **4** plac- **5** elasm-, placo- **6** elasmo-
cross the ~: **5** score
dental ~: **5** lower, upper
fashion ~: **3** fop **4** dude **5** dandy **7** coxcomb
fish ~: **5** scale
flue ~: **6** damper
home ~: **4** base
insect ~: **5** notum
license ~: **2** ID **3** tag
scraping: **3** ort **5** scrap
starter: **4** book, name **6** boiler, breast, copper
thin ~: **6** lamina
tin ~: **4** tain
plate __: **4** mark **5** armor, glass, proof **6** girder
__ plate: **3** end, hot, pie, tin **4** gold, home, kick, soup **5** armor, salad **6** boiler, dinner, silver, switch, vanity **7** fashion, license
plateau: **4** mesa, puna **5** butte, level, stage, table **6** upland **7** lowland **8** highland **9** elevation, tableland **10** high ground
Scandinavian ~: **5** fjeld
South African ~: **6** karroo
__ Plateau: **5** Ozark **7** Iranian
__-plated: **4** gold **5** armor **6** chrome, silver
platen: **6** roller **8** cylinder
__ plate special: **4** blue
platform: **4** dais, shoe, walk **5** plank, stage, stand, stump **6** podium, policy, pulpit, tenets **7** balcony, landing, lectern, program, rostrum, soapbox, support, terrace **8** scaffold **9** elevation, manifesto, party line **10** objectives
by the water: **4** dock, pier, quay, slip **5** berth, jetty
Chinese sleeping ~: **4** kang
emcee ~: **6** podium **7** rostrum **8** platform
floating ~: **4** raft **5** barge
gas-pump ~: **6** island
nautical ~: **7** maintop
raised ~: **4** dais **5** altar, riser, stage **6** podium
synagogue ~: **4** bema
theater ~: **5** stage
warehouse ~: **4** skid
platform __: **3** bed **4** shoe **6** diving, tennis
platforms: **5** podia
synagogue ~: **6** bemata
Plath, Sylvia: **4** poet
spouse: Ted Hughes
work: Ariel
The Bell Jar
The Colossus
Lady Lazarus
platinum: **4** gray, grey **5** color, metal **6** blonde, bluish **7** blueish, element
alloy: **9** white gold
color kin: **3** ash **4** dove, drab **5** beige, dusty, merle, pearl, putty, slate, taupe **6** silver **7** grizzly **8** charcoal, gunmetal
platinum __: **5** blond **6** blonde
Platinum Blonde (1931 film)
cast: Jean Harlow
director: Frank Capra
platitude: **3** saw **5** maxim, motto, truth **6** cliché, phrase, saying, truism **7** bromide, proverb **8** buzzword, chestnut **10** shibboleth
platitudinous: **4** dull **5** corny, hokey, passé, stale, trite, vapid **6** common, jejune, old hat **7** clichéd, fatuous, humdrum, prosaic **8** bromidic, outdated, outmoded **9** hackneyed, prosaical **10** uninspired, unoriginal
Plato: **3** cat **4** Dana **5** Greek **11** philosopher
dialogue: **3** Ion
hangout: **4** stoa
parent: **7** Ariston **10** Perictione
subject of ~'s Symposium: **4** Eros
work: Apology
Critias
Ion
Laches
Letters
Lysis
Meno
The Republic
The Sophist
Platonic __: **4** love
platoon: **4** army, team, unit **5** group, squad, troop **6** outfit **7** company, phalanx **8** squadron **10** detachment
leader: **3** NCO **8** sergeant **10** lieutenant
member: **2** GI **7** recruit, soldier
subdivision: **5** squad
Platoon (1986 film)
cast: Tom Berenger, Willem Dafoe, Charlie Sheen, Forest Whitaker
director: Oliver Stone
extras: **6** troops
setting: **3** Nam **7** Vietnam
studio: **5** Orion
Platt: **6** Oliver
Platte: **5** river
locale: **8** Nebraska
tribe: **3** Oto **4** Otoe
tributary: **4** Loup
platter: **2** LP **4** disc, dish, disk, tray **5** plate **6** salver **7** charger
bottom: **5** B-side, side B
now: **2** CD
player: **4** hi-fi **6** stereo **10** phonograph
spinner: **2** DJ **6** deejay
top: **5** A-side, side A
__ Platter: **5** Pluto

Platters
members: Williams, Lynch, Robi, Reed, Taylor
song: Enchanted (1959)
The Great Pretender (1955)
Harbor Lights (1959)
He's Mine (1957)
I'm Sorry (1957)
It Isn't Right (1956)
My Prayer (1956)
One in a Million (1957)
Only You (1955)
On My Word of Honor (1957)
Smoke Gets in Your Eyes (1958)
To Each His Own (1960)
Twilight Time (1958)
With This Ring (1967)
You'll Never Never Know (1956)
(You've Got) The Magic Touch (1956)
Plattsburgh: **4** city, town
locale: **7** New York
platypus: **6** mammal
plaudits: **4** hand **5** éclat, honor, kudos **6** eulogy, homage, praise, salute **7** acclaim, big hand, ovation, tribute **8** accolade, applause, approval, encomium, flattery, good word **9** extolment, laudation, panegyric **10** exaltation
plausibility: **10** likelihood
plausible: **5** sound **6** doable, likely, viable **7** logical, tenable **8** apparent, credible, feasible, luculent, possible, probable, rational, specious, workable **9** deceptive, excusable, potential, practical **10** achievable, attainable, believable, convincing, defensible, imaginable, persuasive, reasonable
be ~: **4** wash **9** make sense
Plax: **9** mouthwash
competitor: **3** Act **5** Scope **6** Signal **7** Lavoris **9** Listerine **10** Fluorigard
play: **2** do **3** act, bet, fun, toy, vie **4** flop, game, give, jest, joke, lark, lick, pipe, ploy, risk, romp, room, show, skip, skit, trip, turn, work **5** caper, drama, farce, frisk, opera, prank, range, reach, revel, scope, serve, slack, smash, sound, space, sport, stage, stake, sweep, wager **6** cavort, comedy, fiddle, frolic, gamble, gambol, hazard, leeway, margin, one-act, render, tickle, tinker, trifle, turkey **7** carouse, compete, contend, disport, fribble, ham it up, musical, operate, pageant, pastime, portray, pretend, skylark, tragedy, writing **8** latitude, let loose, maneuver, movement, pleasure, recreate, simulate **9** amusement, diversion, elbowroom, enjoyment, free space, happiness, have a ball, make merry, melodrama, spectacle, stage show **10** fool around, manipulate, mess around, production, recreation, relaxation, roughhouse
again: **5** rerun
against: **3** pit **5** rival **6** oppose **7** compete
along: **5** agree, humor **6** comply **9** acquiesce, cooperate
a role: **3** act **5** emote, enact
around: **5** dally **6** trifle
a round: **4** golf
around (with): **6** dabble, fiddle, monkey, putter, tinker
at: **4** fake **5** feign **7** pretend **8** simulate
at full volume: **5** blast
at love: **3** toy **4** vamp **5** dally, flirt, tease **6** trifle **8** coquette
back: **6** repeat **7** recount **9** reiterate
backer: **5** angel
ball: **5** agree **6** comply **9** acquiesce, cooperate
beginning of a ~: **4** Act I **6** act one
bring into ~: **3** use **5** apply, exert **6** entail, resort
by ear: **5** ad-lib **6** invent, make up, whip up, wing it **7** offhand **9** extempore, impromptu, improvise **10** improvised, off the cuff
caller: **2** QB **3** ref, ump **5** coach **6** umpire **7** referee
cards: **3** bet, gin **4** ante, deal, meld, pass, ruff **5** stake, trump, wager **6** gamble **7** shuffle
chance to ~: **4** turn
child's ~: **4** easy, snap **5** cinch, cushy **6** facile, no prob, picnic, simple **7** no sweat **8** duck soup, painless, pushover **9** no problem, uncomplex **10** effortless, elementary
device: **5** aside
direction: **4** exit **5** enter **6** exeunt
down: **6** soften **8** belittle, derogate, minimize, moderate, shrug off **9** deprecate, disparage, gloss over, soft-pedal, underrate, whitewash **10** understate
ender: **3** boy, let, off, pen **4** back, bill, book, girl, goer, list, mate, room, suit, time, wear **5** going, house, maker, thing **6** ground, making, wright
fair ~: **6** equity **7** justice **8** equality
false: **4** sell **6** betray, renege **7** sell out **8** go back on
favorites: **4** side **8** side with
footsie: **5** dally, flirt **6** trifle
for a fool: **3** con, use **4** bilk, dupe, gull, hoax, rook, snow, take **5** cheat **6** delude, entrap, outwit, rip off, take in **7** deceive, defraud, ensnare, fake out, finagle, mislead, snooker, swindle **8** flimflam, hoodwink, outsmart, sucker in **9** bamboozle, victimize **10** manipulate
for time: **5** delay, stall
foul ~: **4** harm **5** wrong **6** dupery, murder **8** inequity, violence
free ~: **5** range, scope, space **9** elbow room
games: **3** toy, use **5** abuse **6** manage, misuse, trifle **7** exploit **8** maneuver **9** machinate **10** manipulate, stragegize
hooky: **3** cut **4** skip **6** go AWOL **7** abscond
host: **5** ask in, emcee, treat **6** invite
humorous ~: **4** skit **5** farce **6** comedy
in ~: **4** fair **5** alive
in the water: **4** swim, wade **5** float, slosh **6** paddle, splash
it by ear: **5** ad-lib **6** invent, make up, wing it
Japanese ~: **3** noh
keep in ~: **4** pass **5** shoot, throw **6** assist, joggle, juggle **7** dribble, shuffle
matchmaker: **5** set up
music: **3** bow **4** blow, pick, toot **5** pluck, segue, skirl, strum, thrum
nongamblers ~ for it: **5** kicks, sport **9** enjoyment
on words: **3** pun **9** equivoque
out of ~: **4** dead, foul
part: **3** act **4** Act I, Act V **5** Act II, Act IV, scene **6** Act III, Act One
past: **6** endure, ignore **7** persist **8** overlook **9** hang tough
politics: **6** pander **8** maneuver **9** machinate **10** manipulate, strategize
possum: **4** sham **6** freeze **7** pretend **9** dissemble
put in ~: **4** pass, toss **5** serve, throw **7** dribble, kick off
roster: **4** cast
serious ~: **5** drama **7** tragedy
short ~: **4** skit
something to ~: **3** uke **4** game, harp **5** bugle, drums, flute, organ, piano, sport **6** fiddle, guitar, violin **7** trumpet **9** accordion
stoolie: **3** rat **4** blab, sing **5** rat on, spill **8** inform on
successful ~: **3** hit **5** boffo, smash
the game: **5** yield **6** accept, comply **7** conform, go along **9** acquiesce, cooperate **10** keep in step
the market: **3** buy **4** sell **5** trade **6** invest **7** venture **9** speculate
the odds: **3** bet **5** wager **6** gamble
to the crowd: **3** ham **5** emote **7** ham it up, swagger, upstage
unsuccessful ~: **4** bomb, flop
up: **6** accent, stress **7** feature, magnify, promote **8** reassert **9** embroider, emphasize, highlight, publicize, punctuate, spotlight, underline **10** accentuate, underscore
up to: **4** fawn **5** cater **6** cajole, pander **7** flatter, wheedle **8** blandish, fawn over
with fire: **4** dare, risk **6** chance **7** venture **9** take a risk
play ___: **3** hob **4** ball, date, down, up to **5** along, games, havoc, hooky, money **6** possum
play ___ and loose: **4** fast
play ___ ear: **4** it by
play ___ fiddle: **6** second
play ___ in: **5** a role
play ___ one's hands: **4** into
play ___ time: **3** for
___ play: **4** draw, fair, foul, long, role **5** force, match, medal, out of, power **6** child's, double, one-act, triple
___-play: **4** role
Play-___: **3** Doh
Playa Azul
locale: **6** Ixtapa, Mexico
play-act: **4** play, pose **5** feign **6** fake it **7** perform, pretend **8** simulate
Play a Simple Melody
composer: Irving Berlin
Playback
author: Raymond Chandler
playback machine: **3** VCR
playbill: **7** program
listing: **3** bio **4** cast, role
playbook: **6** script
playboy: **4** rake, roué **7** swinger **8** sybarite **9** jet setter, libertine
Playboy (1962 song)
artist: Marvelettes
Playboy nickname: **3** Hef
Playboy of the Western World
author: John Synge
played
down: **6** low-key
out: **4** beat, worn **5** all in, banal, stale, tired, trite, weary **6** dished, done in, old hat **8** fatigued, overused **9** destitute, hackneyed **10** dissipated
___ Played On, The: **4** Band
player: **3** ham, pro **4** jock, lead, mime, star **5** actor, extra, mimic **6** artist, better, bettor, goalie, mummer, walk-on **7** actress, athlete, ingénue, soloist, stand-in, trouper **8** opponent, thespian, virtuoso **9** contender, performer, superjock **10** competitor, contestant, understudy
excellent ~: **3** ace, pro **4** whiz **5** crack **6** expert, master, talent **8** virtuoso **9** first-rate **10** A number one, specialist
intermediary: **3** rep **5** agent **9** go-between **10** negotiator
key ~: **3** CEO, VIP **4** boss, czar, exec, suit **5** brass, mogul, titan, wheel **6** honcho, leader, top dog, tycoon **7** big shot, magnate, witness **8** big wheel, director, governor, higher-up, kingfish, top brass **9** commander, executive **10** head honcho
minor ~: **3** cog **5** extra
music ~: **2** DJ **4** band, hi-fi, juke **5** combo, phono, radio **6** deejay, stereo **7** boombox, juke box **8** tape deck **9** orchestra **10** phonograph
nonvarsity ~: **5** scrub
paid ~: **3** pro **4** jock **5** actor **7** actress **8** thespian
player ___: **5** piano
___ player: **3** bit **4** disc, disk, tape, team **5** piano **6** record
Player, Gary: **6** golfer
players: **4** cast, team
first-string ~: **5** A-team **7** varsity
reserve ~: **5** bench
Player, The (1992 film)
cast: Peter Gallagher, Whoopi Goldberg, Tim Robbins, Greta Scacchi, Fred Ward
director: Robert Altman
play fast and ___: **5** loose
play for ___: **4** time **5** a fool, keeps
___ play for: **5** make a
playful: **3** fey **5** funny, happy, jolly, merry **6** frisky, impish, jocose, lively, unruly **7** coltish, jesting, naughty, puckish, teasing, waggish **8** humorous, mirthful, prankish, skittish, spirited, sporting, sportive **9** facetious, fun-loving, gamboling,

lightsome, sprightly, vivacious, whimsical **10** capricious, frolicsome, rollicking
animal: **3** dog, pet, pup **4** seal **5** otter, puppy **6** kitten
talk: **4** jive **6** banter **8** chit-chat
playfully: **5** in fun
playfulness: **3** fun **5** humor **7** jollity **8** jocosity, mischief
playgoer: **6** viewer **9** spectator
playgoers: **8** audience
playground: **4** park, yard **5** field
apparatus: **5** slide, swing **6** seesaw **10** monkey bars
cry: **4** whee
game: **3** tag
purpose: **3** fun **8** exercise
retort: **4** is so **5** am not, is too **6** are too
play hard __: **5** to get
playhouse: **5** odeon, odeum **7** theater, theatre **10** auditorium
playhouses, Greek: **4** odea
play in __: **6** Peoria
playing
hard ball: **8** ruthless **10** determined, relentless
hooky: **6** absent
it safe: **7** careful **8** cautious
marble: **3** mib, mig **4** migg **5** aggie, immie
with a full deck: **4** sane
with fire: **4** bold, rash **6** daring, unwise **8** reckless **10** indiscreet
playing card: **3** ace, six, ten, two **4** club, five, four, jack, king, nine, trey **5** deuce, eight, heart, joker, queen, seven, spade, three **7** diamond
Playing for Keeps
author: David Halberstam
Playing for Keeps (1957 song)
artist: Elvis Presley
__ Playing Our Song: **6** They're
__-playing record: **4** long
play into one's __: **5** hands
play it __: **4** cool, safe **5** by ear
Play It Again, Sam (1972 film)
cast: Woody Allen, Diane Keaton, Tony Roberts
Play It as It Lays
author: Joan Didion
play it close to the __: **4** vest
Play it, Sam! speaker: **4** Ilsa
Play It to the Bone (1999 film)
cast: Antonio Banderas, Lolita Davidovich, Woody Harrelson
Playland
author: Athol Fugard
Playmaker, The
author: Thomas Keneally
playmate: **4** chum **6** friend **7** partner **9** companion
nursery ~: **4** baby **6** infant **9** youngster
Play Me (1972 song)
artist: Neil Diamond
Play Misty for Me (1971 film)
cast: Clint Eastwood, Jessica Walter
director: Clint Eastwood
play on __: **5** words
play one's __ right: **5** cards
playpen
amusement: **3** toy
occupant: **3** tot **4** baby **6** infant

PL

plays
call the: **4** boss, lead **6** direct, manage
play second __: **6** fiddle
PlayStation
maker: **4** Sony
rival: **4** Xbox
Play That Funky Music (song)
artist: Vanilla Ice, Wild Cherry
play the __: **4** fool, game **5** field **6** horses, ponies
__ Play, The: **6** Insect
plaything: **3** top, toy **4** ball, doll, kite **6** blocks, teaset
playtime: **6** recess **10** recreation
Play Time (1967 film)
cast: Jacques Tati
director: Jacques Tati
play to the __: **4** hilt
play with __: **4** fire
playwright: **6** author, writer **9** dramatist, wordsmith **10** librettist
American ~: **4** Hart, Inge, Rabe, Rice **5** Akins, Albee, Hecht, Kanin, Mamet, Odets, O'Hara, Simon **6** Abbott, Crouse, Henley, Miller, O'Neill **7** Hellman, Kaufman, Lindsay, Shepard **8** Anderson, Connelly, Sherwood, Williams **9** Chayefsky, Fierstein, Hansberry, Van Druten
Australian ~: **6** Palmer, Porter **7** Seymour, Stewart
Austrian ~: **10** Schnitzler **11** Grillparzer
award: **4** Obie, Tony
British ~: **3** Fry, Gay, Kyd **4** Bolt, Gray **5** Arden, Brome, Eliot, Frayn, Nashe, Orton, Peele **6** Cibber, Coward, Dekker, Dryden, Jonson, Morgan, Pinero, Pinter, Rowley, Rudkin, Savage, Steele, Storey, Wesker **7** Barstow, Chapman, Delaney, Heywood, Marlowe, Nichols, Osborne, Shaffer, Shirley, Webster, Whiting **8** Congreve, Farquhar, Fielding, Rattigan, Sheridan, Stoppard **9** Ayckbourn, Middleton, Priestley, Wycherley **10** Galsworthy **11** Shakespeare
Czech ~: **5** Capek, Havel **7** Jirásek
existentialist ~: **5** Genet
French ~: **5** Camus, Genet, Hardy, Jarry, Sagan **6** Gréban, Grévin, Musset, Racine, Sardou, Scribe **7** Anouilh, Feydeau, Garnier, Ionesco, Molière, Régnard, Rolland, Romains, Rostand, Sedaine **8** Salacrou, Sarraute **9** Corneille
German ~: **4** Holz **5** Sachs **6** Brecht, Grabbe, Hebbel, Kaiser **7** Büchner, Freytag, Gutzkow, Horvath **8** Gryphius, Schiller **9** Hauptmann, Sudermann, Zuckmayer
Greek ~: **8** Menander **9** Aeschylus, Euripides **12** Aristophanes
Indian ~: **8** Kalidasa
Irish ~: **4** Shaw **5** Colum, Friel, Synge, Wilde, Yeats **6** O'Casey **8** Donleavy
Italian ~: **5** Betti, Gozzi **6** Oriani **7** Giacosa, Goldoni, Rovetta **10** Pirandello
Japanese ~: **7** Abe Kobo
New Zealand ~: **8** Sargeson
Nigerian ~: **7** Soyinka
Norwegian ~: **5** Ibsen
offering: **5** drama
Polish ~: **6** Fredro **8** Różewicz
Puerto Rican ~: **6** Arrivi
Roman ~: **6** Seneca **7** Plautus
Russian ~: **7** Chekhov
Scottish ~: **6** Barrie
Spanish ~: **4** Vega **6** Encina, Mihura, Sastre **7** Alberti **8** Calderón **9** Benavente **11** Pérez Galdós
Swedish ~: **9** Söderberg **10** Strindberg
Uruguayan ~: **7** Sánchez
plaza: **4** mall, park **5** court, green **6** common, square
Plaza: **3** car **4** auto **8** Plymouth
de la Revolución locale: **6** Havana
Plaza __: **5** Suite
plaza de __: **5** toros
Plaza Hotel
girl: **6** Eloise
Plaza Suite: **4** film, play
author: Neil Simon
cast: Lee Grant, Barbara Harris, Walter Matthau, Maureen Stapleton
plea: **3** out **4** call, suit **5** alibi, claim, story **6** appeal, demand, excuse, orison, prayer **7** apology, defense, pretext, request **8** argument, entreaty, petition
defendant's ~: **4** nolo
enter a ~: **3** sue
for help: **3** SOS **6** Mayday
plea-__: **7** bargain
__ plea: **4** cop a
plead: **3** ask, beg, sue **4** pray, urge **5** argue, crawl, press, speak **6** appeal, enjoin, reason **7** beseech, declare, entreat, implore, request, solicit **8** appeal to, petition **9** impetrate, importune **10** supplicate
for: **4** back **7** support **8** advocate, champion
pleader: **3** att. **4** atty. **6** lawyer **7** accused **8** advocate, attorney **9** apologist, counselor, defendant
Pleading Guilty
author: Scott Turow
plead the __: **5** Fifth
pleasant: **3** fun **4** cool, easy, fine, good, homy, mild, nice, okay, soft, warm **5** balmy, bland, civil, clear, great, homey, jolly, legit, moral, noble, suave, sunny, sweet **6** genial, gentle, jovial, kindly, lovely, polite, proper, smooth, social, urbane **7** affable, amiable, amusing, cordial, easeful, ethical, likable, welcome **8** all right, charming, cheerful, engaging, friendly, gladsome, gracious, heavenly, laudable, likeable, moderate, obliging, readable, splendid, superior **9** admirable, agreeable, congenial, convivial, enjoyable, excellent, favorable, palatable, reputable, temperate, unextreme, wonderful **10** acceptable, beneficial, creditable, delightful, diplomatic, enchanting, gratifying, personable, refreshing, satisfying, unagitated
combining form: **4** hedy-
odor: **5** aroma **7** incense, perfume **9** fragrance, redolence
surprise: **4** gift **5** treat **7** present
Pleasant Island, today: **5** Nauru
pleasantries, exchange: **4** chat, talk **5** greet **7** speak to **8** converse
pleasantry: **3** wit **4** jest, joke, quip **5** sally **6** bon mot **8** greeting, repartee **9** witticism **10** salutation
Pleasant Valley Sunday (1967 song)
artist: Monkees
Pleasantville (1998 film)
cast: Joan Allen, Jeff Daniels, William H. Macy, Tobey Maguire
please: **3** wow **4** grab, like, send, suit, want, will, wish **5** amuse, charm, cheer, elate, humor, score **6** appeal, divert, kindly, pamper, pander, regale, see fit, thrill, tickle, turn on **7** cater to, content, delight, enchant, gladden, gratify, hearten, indulge, overjoy, satisfy **8** interest **9** entertain, go over big, titillate **10** hit the spot, tickle pink
as you ~: **6** at will, freely
easy to ~: **3** lax **8** laid-back
hard to ~: **5** fussy, picky **6** choosy **7** choosey, finicky **8** exacting, finiking, finnicky **9** demanding, querulous
in Japan: **4** dozo
power to ~: **5** charm **8** charisma **9** magnetism
Please Come to Boston (1974 song)
artist: Dave Loggins
pleased: **4** glad **5** happy, merry, proud **6** blithe, cheery, elated, jovial, joyful, joyous, upbeat **7** content, gleeful, willing **8** blissful, cheerful, ecstatic, euphoric, exultant, jubilant, mirthful, relieved, thankful **9** rejoicing **10** complacent, flying high
be ~ by: **4** like, love **5** enjoy **9** delight in
look ~: **4** grin **5** smile
sounds: **3** ahs, ohs **4** aahs, oohs
with oneself: **4** smug, vain **5** proud **7** haughty **8** arrogant **9** conceited **10** complacent
pleased as __: **5** Punch
Please Don't Go (song)
artist: KC and the Sunshine Band, K.W.S., No Mercy
Please Don't Go Girl (1988 song)
artist: New Kids on the Block
Please do preceder: **4** May I **6** Shall I
Pleased to __ you: **4** meet
Please Love Me Forever (1967 song)
artist: Bobby Vinton
Please Mr. Please (1975 song)
artist: Olivia Newton-John
Please Mr. Postman (song)
artist: Carpenters, Marvelettes
Pleasence: **6** Donald
Please Please Me (1964 song)
artist: Beatles
__ pleaser: **5** crowd
Please Remember Me (1999 song)
artist: Tim McGraw
__ please the court: **4** If it

pleasing: **4** fine, good, nice, okay, rosy **5** ducky, great, legit, light, moral, nifty, noble, suave, sweet **6** comely, lovely, polite, pretty, proper, quaint, savory **7** amiable, easeful, ethical, likable, lilting, lovable, lyrical, musical, popular, welcome, winning, winsome **8** adorable, all right, alluring, charming, engaging, esthetic, fetching, gladsome, gorgeous, gracious, handsome, inviting, laudable, loveable, readable, splendid, stunning, suitable, superior, tasteful **9** admirable, agreeable, beautiful, congenial, enjoyable, excellent, palatable, reputable, rewarding, wonderful **10** acceptable, attractive, beneficial, creditable, delightful, enchanting, gratifying, personable, satisfying
to the ear: **5** on key **6** dulcet **7** lyrical, melodic, tuneful **9** melodious
to the palate: **5** tasty, yummy **9** delicious, flavorful **10** delectable

pleasurable: **4** nice **6** social **7** welcome **9** agreeable, enjoyable, luxurious **10** gratifying

pleasure: **3** fun, joy **4** buzz, ease, glee, kick, play, will, wish, zest **5** bliss, fancy, gusto, kicks, mirth, spice, sport, treat **6** choice, desire, gaiety, gayety, liking, relish, thrill, turn-on **7** command, delight, jollies, pursuit, rapture, revelry **8** felicity, gladness, radiance **9** amusement, diversion, enjoyment, festivity, happiness, jocundity, merriment **10** jubilation, preference, propensity, recreation, regalement, relaxation
at one's ~: **6** freely
boat: **5** yacht **7** cruiser **8** trimaran **9** catamaran
exclamation of ~: **3** aah, gee, hey, ooh, wow, yes **4** gosh, yeah **5** golly, zowie **6** whizzo, yippee **7** whoopee, whoopie **8** all right
get ~ from: **3** dig **4** like, love, want **5** enjoy, fancy, go for, savor **6** desire, dote on, relish **9** delight in, indulge in **10** appreciate, be mad about
give ~: **5** amuse **6** thrill **7** enchant, gladden, gratify, satisfy **8** enthrall **9** enrapture
obvious ~: **5** gusto **10** enthusiasm
show ~: **3** hum **4** glow, grin **5** laugh, smile **7** light up, whistle
sigh of ~: **3** aah
take ~: **4** live **5** enjoy, revel **6** relish, wallow **9** luxuriate
trip: **5** jaunt **6** cruise, junket, outing **9** excursion
with ~: **6** gladly **7** happily **9** willingly

Pleasure of His Company, The: **4** film, play
author: Cornelia Otis Skinner
cast: Fred Astaire, Lilli Palmer, Debbie Reynolds
director: George Seaton

Pleasures of Helen, The
author: Lawrence Sanders

pleat: **4** fold, tuck **5** crimp **6** crease, gusset, pucker, ruffle
alternative: **4** slit, vent **6** gather
__ pleat: **3** box **4** reet **5** knife

plebe: **4** tiro, tyro **5** cadet, newie **7** recruit
academy: **4** USMA, USNA
answer: **3** sir **5** no sir **6** yes sir

plebeian: **3** low **4** base, mean, rude **5** banal, lowly, small **6** coarse, common, humble, vulgar **7** ignoble, lowborn, peasant, popular **8** baseborn, commoner, ordinary **9** bourgeois, unrefined **10** lower-class, pedestrian, uncultured

plebeians: **4** herd **6** masses **8** riffraff **9** hoi polloi **10** lower class

plebiscite: **4** vote **6** ballot

plectrum: **4** pick
use a ~: **4** pick **5** plink, pluck, strum, thrum

pledge: **3** vow **4** avow, bail, bond, gage, hock, oath, pact, pawn, word **5** stake, swear, toast, token, troth, vouch, wager **6** assure, avowal, commit, devote, plight, surety **7** bargain, earnest, promise, warrant **8** contract, covenant, dedicate, guaranty, security, warranty **9** agreement, assurance, guarantee, liability, stipulate, subscribe, undertake **10** collateral, commitment, engagement
medieval ~: **4** gage
of fidelity: **5** troth
oneself: **3** vow **5** swear **7** promise
take the ~: **7** abstain, refrain
to wed: **5** troth **10** engagement

Pledge: **6** polish
alternative: **6** Behold, Endust **10** Liquid Gold, Old English

pledged: **5** bound, sworn **9** betrothed

Pledge of Allegiance last word: **3** all

Pledge, The
author: Howard Fast

Pledge, The (2001 film)
cast: Benicio Del Toro, Jack Nicholson, Vanessa Redgrave, Robin Wright
director: Sean Penn

Pleiades: **4** Maia **6** Merope **7** Alcyone, Celaeno, Electra, Halcyon, Sterope, Taygete **8** Halcyone
father: **5** Atlas
one of the ~: **4** star
pursuer: **5** Orion

Pleistocene: **5** Epoch **6** Ice Age

plenary: **4** full, open **5** total, uncut, whole **6** entire **7** general **8** absolute, complete, finished, sweeping, thorough **9** inclusive, unreduced **10** exhaustive, unabridged

plenipotentiary: **5** envoy **6** legate **8** diplomat, minister

plenish: **5** stock **6** fill up

plenitude: **3** lot **4** glut **6** argosy, bounty, wealth **9** abundance, amplitude, profusion, repletion **10** cornucopia, exuberance

plentiful: **4** full, lush, many, much, rich, rife **5** ample, large **6** bumper, enough, galore, lavish **7** copious, fertile, flowing, liberal, opulent, profuse, replete, teeming **8** abundant, complete, fruitful, generous, handsome, princely **9** abounding, bounteous, bountiful, capacious, chock-full, exuberant, lousy with, luxuriant, unsparing **10** sufficient
be ~: **4** teem **5** swarm **6** abound

plenty: **3** lot **4** a lot, a ton, ease, lots, many, much, peck, tons **5** ample, heaps, loads, piles **6** armful, enough, highly, lavish, masses, oodles, riches, stacks, wealth **7** but good, copious, liberal, profuse, volumes **8** abundant, generous, good deal, opulence, opulency **9** abounding, abundance, affluence, bounteous, bountiful, extremely, great deal, mountains, profusion **10** prosperity, sufficient
in ~ of time: **5** early
of nothing: **3** OOO **4** OOOO **5** OOOOO
old-style: **4** enow
Roman goddess of ~: **3** Ops
slangily: **4** enuf

__ Plenty o' Nuthin': **4** I Got

pleonasm: **8** verbiage

pleonastic: **5** wordy **7** gushing, verbose

Pleshette, Suzanne: **7** actress
spouse: Troy Donahue, Tom Poston
TV: The Bob Newhart Show

Plessy opponent: **8** Ferguson

plethora: **3** sea **4** glut, much **5** flood, ocean **6** deluge, excess **7** barrage, nimiety, overage, satiety, surfeit, surplus **8** overflow, overkill **9** abundance, profusion **10** exuberance, oversupply, redundancy

Plexiglas: **6** Lucite
component: **6** ketone

plexus: **4** rete **7** network
solar ~: **5** belly **7** stomach **10** midsection

__ plexus: **5** solar

pliable: **4** limp, soft **5** lithe, waxen **6** docile, gentle, limber, lissom, supple **7** elastic, lissome, plastic, rubbery, springy **8** amenable, bendable, flexible, formable, yielding **9** adaptable, lithesome, malleable, receptive, resilient, tractable **10** adjustable, responsive, submissive, unhardened

pliant: **4** limp, tame **5** lithe **6** broken, docile, limber, lissom, supple **7** lissome, plastic, subdued, trained **8** flexible, lamblike, obedient, resigned, yielding **9** formative, lightsome, lithesome, malleable, tractable **10** manageable, submissive

plié: **4** bend

pliers: **4** tool **7** forceps

plight: **3** fix, jam, lot, vow **4** case, hole, mess, pass, spot, word **5** pinch, state **6** corner, crisis, muddle, pickle, pledge, scrape, strait **7** dilemma, impasse, promise, straits, trouble **8** exigence, exigency, position, quagmire, quandary **9** betrothal, condition, deep water, emergency, extremity, situation **10** difficulty
light: **5** flare
one's troth: **3** wed **5** marry **10** tie the knot

Plimpton: **6** George, Martha **7** Shelley

plimsoll: **4** shoe **7** sneaker **8** footwear

plink: **5** pluck, strum, thrum

Plink, Plank, Plunk!
composer: Leroy Anderson

plinth: **4** base, foot, orlo, slab **5** block, socle

Pliny the Elder: **5** Roman **6** writer
work: Natural History

Pliny the Younger: **5** Roman **6** orator
where ~ served: **6** senate

plod: **3** lag **4** drag, grub, moil, plug, slog, toil, trek, wade, walk **5** clump, crawl, grind, labor, slave, stump, sweat, trail, tramp, tread, tromp **6** drudge, go slow, linger, lumber, trudge, waddle **7** galumph, schlepp, shuffle **8** keep at it, struggle **9** drag along, grind away, persevere

plodder: **4** hack **6** drudge

plodding: **4** poky, slow **6** draggy, stodgy **7** gradual, halting, humdrum, impeded, languid **8** dilatory, drawn-out, hesitant, slothful, sluggish, toddling **9** leisurely, lethargic, ponderous, prolonged, snaillike, unhurried **10** deliberate, monotonous, pedestrian, protracted

plop: **3** set, sit **4** drip, fall **5** plunk, thump **6** settle **7** deposit
down: **3** sit **4** flop

plot: **3** bed, fix, lot, way **4** brew, draw, land, mark, mold, plan, plat, ruse, scam, site, trap **5** chart, dodge, draft, frame, graph, hatch, patch, story, tract, trick **6** action, cook up, device, devise, gambit, garden, lay out, locate, map out, parcel, racket, scheme, sketch, survey, thread, wangle **7** acreage, collude, compute, concoct, connive, finagle, frame-up, outline, picture **8** conspire, contrive, engineer, home site, intrigue, maneuver, navigate, property, scenario, suspense **9** calculate, collusion, delineate, flower bed, machinate, narrative, story line, stratagem, visual aid **10** complicity, conspiracy
a course: **5** chart **8** navigate
again: **5** remap
device: **5** twist **10** red herring
element: **4** clue, love **5** humor, irony **6** climax, murder **7** mystery, revenge **8** suspense
garden ~: **3** bed
mathematically: **5** graph
measure: **4** acre
starter: **7** counter

plot __: **4** line

plottage: **4** area **5** acres

plotter: **9** intriguer
literary ~: **4** Iago

plotters: **5** cabal, junta
deed: **4** coup **9** coup d'état, overthrow

Plot That Thickened, The
author: P.G. Wodehouse

plotz: **5** faint, swoon **8** collapse

Plough and the Stars, The
author: Sean O'Casey

Plovdiv: **4** city, town
locale: **8** Bulgaria

plover: 4 bird 5 pewit, wader 6 peewit 7 dottrel, lapwing 8 dotterel, killdeer
pad: 4 nest
relative: 9 sandpiper
plow: 4 farm, till 6 furrow 8 reinvest, turn over 9 cultivate 10 cultivator
blade: 6 colter 7 coulter
ender: 3 boy, man, men 4 back 5 share
fit to ~: 4 rich 5 loamy 6 arable 7 fertile
follower: 6 harrow
into: 3 hit, ram 5 crash 7 collide
part: 4 sole 5 blade
puller: 2 ox 4 mule 5 horse
sole: 5 slade
starter: 4 snow
steel ~ inventor: 5 Deere
through: 4 plod, slog, wade
plow ___: 4 back, into 5 under
plowboy: 4 hick 5 yokel 6 rustic 7 bumpkin, hayseed 10 clodhopper, provincial
plowed land: 5 tilth
___ Plowman: 5 Piers
Plowright: 4 Joan
spouse: Laurence Olivier
ploy: 4 game, move, play, ruse, trap, wile 5 dodge, feint, shift, trick 6 device, gambit, scheme, tactic 7 gimmick, pretext, sleight, tactics 8 artifice, maneuver, strategy 9 chicanery, imposture, stratagem 10 red herring, subterfuge
advertising ~: 4 hype 5 promo 6 coupon, rebate
baseball ~: 4 bunt 5 steal 7 squeeze 8 pitchout
legal ~: 4 stay 5 alibi 6 appeal
pluck: 3 rob, tug 4 bilk, cull, draw, grab, grit, guts, jerk, pick, pull, rook, sand, take, tear, will, yank 5 cheat, heart, moxie, nerve, seize, spine, spunk, strum, thrum, twang, tweak, valor 6 chisel, clutch, daring, gather, mettle, rip out, snatch, spirit, starch, uproot 7 bravado, bravery, courage, defraud, extract, harvest, heroism, jerk out, prowess, swindle, take out, tear out, yank out 8 backbone, boldness, flimflam, gameness, gumption, temerity, tenacity, true grit, wrest out, yank away 9 derring-do, endurance, extirpate, fortitude, gallantry, gutsiness 10 confidence, enterprise, feistiness, moral fiber, resolution
up: 6 muster, summon
plucked in music: 4 pizz. 9 pizzicato
pluckiness: 4 grit 5 spunk 10 feistiness
plucky: 4 bold, game 5 brave, gutsy, nervy, stout 6 awless, daring, feisty, gritty, heroic, spunky, strong 7 aweless, dashing, defiant, doughty, gallant, impavid, staunch, valiant 8 fearless, heroical, intrepid, resolute, spirited, stalwart, unafraid, valorous 9 audacious, dauntless, dreadless, undaunted, unfearful, unfearing 10 courageous, mettlesome, undismayed, unflagging
plug: 2 ad 3 dam, nag, ram, wad 4 bung, clog, cork, fill, hype, lure, pack, plod, puff, push, seal, stop, toil, tout 5 block, boost, close, dam up, horse, lobby, promo, punch, study, wedge 6 equine, hype up, impede, stop up, talk up 7 advance, block up, closure, congest, hydrant, mention, occlude, promote, stopper, stopple 8 advocate, blockade, good word, obstruct 9 advertise, get behind, promotion, publicity, publicize, recommend, reference, sparkplug
along: 4 moil, slog 6 schlep, trudge
away: 4 work 5 labor 7 address, persist 8 keep at it, struggle 9 persevere
into: 3 tap 4 link 5 tie in, unite 6 hook up, link up, relate 7 connect 9 affiliate, interface
kind of electrical ~: 4 male 6 female
pull the ~ on: 3 end 4 halt, stop 5 cease, drain 9 terminate
starter: 3 ear 4 fire
up: 3 dam 4 clog, seal 5 block 7 seal off 8 obstruct
___ plug: 5 spark
Plug and ___: 4 Play
plugged: 5 tight
in: 3 hep, hip 4 wise 5 aware, savvy 6 posted, versed, wise to, with it 7 knowing, mindful 8 apprised, hooked up, informed 9 cognizant 10 conversant
plugged ___: 6 nickel
plugugly: 4 hood 5 rowdy, tough 7 hoodlum, ruffian
plum: 4 sloe, tree 5 bonus, color, cream, cushy, drupe, fruit, prize, prune 6 bluish, carrot, choice, damson, nugget, prized, purple, reward 7 blueish, premium, reddish 8 dividend, valuable, windfall 9 greengage, myrobalan
alternative: *see* purple color
cherry ~: 9 myrobalan
dried ~: 5 prune
family: 4 rose
Japanese ~: 6 loquat
like a ~ job: 5 cushy
product: 4 duff 6 brandy 7 pudding
relative: 6 almond 8 amethyst
starter: 5 sugar
sugar ~: 9 sweetmeat
wild ~: 4 sloe
plum ___: 4 duff 6 tomato 7 pudding
___ plum: 3 hog 6 cherry, damson
plumage: 4 down, tuft 6 plumes 8 feathers
grow ~: 6 fledge
soft ~: 4 down
plumb: 4 true 5 delve, erect, fully, gauge, probe, quite, smack, solve, sound 6 fathom, weight 7 dig into, exactly, examine, explore, measure, totally, unravel, upright 8 absolute, complete, directly, entirely, straight, vertical 9 delve into, downright, out-and-out, penetrate, precisely 10 absolutely, completely, thoroughly, to the limit
bob: 6 weight
crazy: 4 loco
make ~: 10 straighten
material: 4 lead
out of ~: 5 atilt 6 aslant 7 crooked, tilting 8 slanting 9 at an angle
plumb ___: 3 bob 4 line, loco
___ plumb: 3 off 5 out of
Plumb: 3 Eve
plumber
concern: 4 clog, drip, leak, main, pipe 5 drain, pipes 8 freeze-up
connection: 3 ell, tee 4 trap 5 elbow, joint
filler: 5 oakum
supply: 3 PVC 4 pipe
tool: 5 snake 7 plunger
plumbiferous: 4 lead 6 leaden
plumbing: 8 fixtures, hardware
inlet: 3 tap 4 cock, main 6 faucet
outlet: 5 drain
___ plumbing: 6 indoor
Plum Blossom
artist: Erté
plumbum: 4 lead
plume: 5 crest, penna, quill, remex 6 aigret, pinion 7 feather, panache, tectrix 8 aigrette
helmet ~: 5 crest 7 panache
nom de ~: 4 name 5 alias, title 6 anonym 7 pen name 8 cognomen 9 pseudonym
owner: 5 tante
source: 5 egret 7 ostrich
___ plume: 5 nom de
plumed cap: 5 shako
Plumed Serpent, The
author: D.H. Lawrence
Plum Island
author: Nelson DeMille
Plummer: 6 Amanda 11 Christopher
Plummer, Amanda: 7 actress
mother: Tammy Grimes
Plummer, Christopher: 5 actor
film: Aces High (1977)
Dragnet (1987)
Inside Daisy Clover (1965)
The Insider (1999)
The Man Who Would Be King (1975)
Somewhere in Time (1980)
The Sound of Music (1965)
Twelve Monkeys (1995)
spouse: Tammy Grimes
plummet: 3 dip 4 dive, drop, fall, sink, skid 5 crash, slide, slump, swoop 6 go down, plunge, tumble 7 decline, descend 8 collapse, decrease, downturn, nose-dive
plump: 4 full, ripe 5 beefy, bulky, burly, buxom, fubsy, large, obese, pudgy, pursy, round, stout, swell, tubby 6 chubby, chunky, fatten, fleshy, portly, pyknic, rotund, sprawl, stocky, zaftig, zoftig 7 adipose, paunchy 8 roly-poly 9 corpulent, filled-out 10 abdominous, overweight, well-padded
down: 4 drop, fall 5 plonk, plotz 8 collapse
not ~: 4 lean, slim, thin 6 skinny, svelte 7 slender
the pillows: 5 fluff
Plum, Professor game: 4 Clue
plum pudding ingredient: 4 suet
___-Plumr: 6 Liquid
plumule: 7 feather
plumy: 9 feathered
plunder: 3 gut, rob 4 haul, loot, raid, sack, swag, take 5 booty, harry, rifle, spoil, steal, strip, theft 6 fleece, forage, harrow, hijack, invade, maraud, prey on, rapine, ravage, snatch, spoils 7 despoil, jobbery, pillage, ransack 8 freeboot, highjack, lay waste, pickings, spoliate 9 depredate, devastate 10 run off with
old-style: 5 reave
plunderer: 5 thief 6 bandit, pirate, raider, robber, vandal, Viking 7 brigand, rustler 10 freebooter
plundering: 9 piratical, predatory, rapacious, vulturous
plunge: 3 dip 4 cast, dash, dive, drop, duck, dunk, fall, heel, jump, leap, push, rush, sink, stab, tear, toss, trip 5 forge, heave, lunge, lurch, pitch, slide, slump, stick, swoop, wager 6 career, charge, go down, header, hurtle, thrust, topple, tumble 7 descend, descent, dunking, immerse, mad rush, plummet, venture 8 downturn, flounder, nosedive, submerge 9 hit bottom 10 go the limit, go whole hog
ahead: 3 ram 4 race, rush, tear 6 hurtle, thrust
forward: 4 jump, leap 5 lunge, swoop 6 hurtle, pounce
into: 5 begin 6 attack, tackle 7 pitch in
take the ~: 3 wed 4 dare, risk 5 marry, start 6 chance, hazard 7 venture
take the ~ again: 5 rewed
plunk: 3 set 4 plop, thud 5 pluck, plump, twang
down: 3 pay, put 7 deposit
Plunkett, Jim: 2 QB 10 footballer
plural: 3 few 4 many, some 7 several
pronoun: 4 them, they 5 these, those
verb: 3 are 4 have
plurality: 4 bulk, mass, most 8 majority
plus: 3 and, too 4 also, boon, gain, perk 5 add-on, asset, bonus, extra 6 virtue 7 added to, benefit, besides, surplus 8 addition, positive 9 advantage, along with, including, lagniappe, what's more 10 additional, in addition
fours: 5 pants 8 breeches, knickers, trousers
in Spanish: 3 más
net ~ expenses: 3 sum 8 sum total
ne ~ ultra: 4 acme, A-one, apex, best, peak, tops 5 crest, crown, elite, prime 6 apogee, choice, far-out, finest, select, superb, unique, zenith 7 highest, maximum, optimal, optimum, paragon, perfect, stellar, sublime, supreme 8 choicest, exemplar, five-star, foremost, four-star, greatest, high spot, lodestar, nonesuch, paradigm, peerless, pinnacle, superior, topnotch, ultimate, very good 9 beau ideal, Endsville, excellent, exemplary, first-rate, high point, matchless, nonpareil, top-flight, unequaled, unrivaled 10 consummate, first-class, inimitable, out of sight, phenomenal, preeminent, touchstone

number next to a ~ sign: 6 addend
starter: 3 non
plus __: 4 sign 5 fours
plush: 4 lush, luxe, pile, posh, rich, soft 5 downy, furry, nappy, ritzy, silky, swank, swell, swish 6 costly, deluxe, fabric, fleecy, fluffy, lavish, ornate, snazzy, swanky 7 elegant, opulent, refined, squishy, velvety 8 cushiony, gorgeous, palatial, splendid 9 luxuriant, luxurious, sumptuous
item: 4 sofa 6 carpet 8 armchair
like a ~ toy: 4 soft 5 fuzzy 6 cuddly
Plutarch: 5 Greek 6 writer
subject: 4 Cato
work: Moralia
Parallel Lives
Pluto: 3 dog, god, orb 5 deity, Hades 6 planet
alias: 5 Orcus
brother: 7 Jupiter, Neptune
equivalent: 5 Hades
moon of ~: 6 Charon
owner: 6 Mickey
parent: 3 Ops 6 Saturn
sister: 4 Juno 5 Ceres, Vesta
wife: 10 Proserpina
plutocrat: 5 nabob 6 fat cat 7 Croesus, magnate 9 moneybags 10 capitalist, man of means
plutonium: 5 metal 7 element
Plutus
author: Aristophanes
pluvial: 5 rainy 6 hyetal
pluviometer input: 4 rain
pluvious: 5 rainy 6 hyetal
ply: 3 run, use 4 fold, sail, work 5 beset, exert, ferry, hound, layer, sheet, twist, wield 6 assail, attack, badger, employ, handle, harass, lamina, manage, pursue, regale, strand, work at 7 besiege, carry on, operate, utilize, wheedle 8 dispense, engage in, maneuver 9 persist in, thickness 10 manipulate
a needle: 3 sew 5 baste 6 stitch 9 embroider
one's trade: 4 work
the oars: 3 row 5 scull
Plymouth: 3 car 4 auto, city, port, town 10 automobile
landmark: 4 rock
locale: 4 Mass. 5 Devon 7 England 9 Minnesota
model: 3 GTX 4 Fury, Neon 5 Laser, Plaza, Savoy 6 Breeze, DeLuxe, Duster, Volare 7 Acclaim, Concord, Horizon, Prowler, Reliant, Valiant, Voyager 8 Gran Fury, Roadking, Suburban, Sundance 9 Barracuda, Belvedere, Cambridge, Cranbrook, Satellite, Sport Fury 10 Road Runner
Plymouth __: 4 Rock
Plymouth Rock: 3 hen 4 fowl 7 chicken
relative: *see* chicken
Plympton: 4 Bill
plywood: 5 panel
component: 5 layer
Plzen: 4 city, town
from ~: 5 Czech
Pm: 4 elem. 7 element 10 promethium
61 for ~: 4 at. no.
P.M.: 3 aft.
PMG employer: 4 USPS
__ P. Morgan: 4 Jaye
__ P. Morton: 4 Levi
pneuma: 4 soul 6 psyche
pneumatic __: 4 duct, pile, tire 5 drill
Pnin
author: Vladimir Nabokov
Po: 5 river 7 element 8 polonium
84 for ~: 4 at. no.
Basin city: 5 Milan
city on the ~: 5 Turin 6 Torino 7 Cremona
locale: 5 Italy
tributary: 4 Adda 7 Trebbia
PO
box item: 3 ltr. 4 card 6 letter, packet 8 postcard
branch ~: 3 sta. 7 station
busy mo. at the ~: 3 Dec. 8 December
competitor: 3 UPS 5 FedEx
concern: 3 pkg. 4 mail 6 letter 7 package
designation: 2 st. 3 RFD, rte., zip 4 addr., city 5 route, state 6 street 7 address, country, zip code
directive: 3 COD
stamp: 8 postmark
unit: 2 lb., oz. 5 ounce, pound
poach: 3 rob 4 boil, cook 5 filch, steal 6 coddle 7 intrude, ransack 8 encroach, trespass 10 run off with
something to ~: 3 egg
poached egg foundation: 5 toast
Pobble Who Has No Toes, The
author: Edward Lear
po boy: 3 sub 4 hero 5 hoagy 6 hoagie 9 submarine
Po' Boy Blues
author: Langston Hughes
pobre: 4 poor 7 Spanish
Pocahontas: 6 Indian
husband: 5 Rolfe
shelter: 4 tipi 5 tepee 6 teepee
transport: 5 canoe
Pocatello: 4 city, town
campus: 3 ISU
locale: 5 Idaho
pocket: 3 bag, net, wee 4 hide, hole, lift, lode, sack, take, tiny, vein 5 filch, pinch, pouch, small, steal, swipe, teeny 6 cavity, hollow, little, midget, minute, obtain, peewee, pilfer, streak, teensy 7 chamber, compact, conceal, opening, purloin, receive 8 portable, shoplift 9 miniature, undersize 10 diminutive, receptacle, vest-pocket
billiards: 4 pool
bread: 4 pita
container: 5 flask
contents: 4 keys, lint 5 hanky 6 change, hankie 8 billfold
edition: 9 miniature
ender: 4 book, size 5 knife
money: 4 cash, cent, dime 5 bills, coins, fiver, penny 6 change, nickel, single 7 coinage, quarter, ten-spot
protector: 4 flap, snap 6 button, zipper
starter: 4 pick
warm in the ~: 4 rich 5 flush 6 loaded 7 wealthy 8 well-to-do 9 well-fixed
watch ~: 3 fob
pocket __: 4 book, comb, veto 5 money
pocket-__: 4 size
__ pocket: 3 air 4 side 5 out of
__-pocket: 4 vest
pocketbook: 3 bag 4 tote 5 means, pouch, purse 6 clutch 7 handbag 8 reticule
__-pocket expenses: 5 out-of
pocketful of __, A: 3 rye
Pocketful of Miracles: 4 film, song
cast: Bette Davis, Glenn Ford, Hope Lange
composer: Sammy Cahn, Jimmy Van Heusen
director: Frank Capra
__ pockets: 4 deep
pocket-size: 4 tiny 5 small, teeny 6 teensy 9 miniature
Pocky
alternative: *see* cookie brand
poco: 4 a bit 6 little
Poco
song: Call It Love (1989)
Crazy Love (1979)
Heart of the Night (1979)
Poconos: 5 range
locale: 4 Penn.
__-pocus: 5 hocus
pod: 4 case, hull, husk 5 shell, shuck 6 jacket, school, sheath 7 capsule 8 seedcase 9 container 10 integument
contents: 3 pea 4 seed
cotton ~: 4 boll
edible ~: 4 okra 5 cacao, carob, chili 8 sugar pea
flax ~: 4 boll
member: 4 seal 5 whale
pungent ~: 5 chili
starter: 3 tri 4 deca, mega, octo, seed 5 tetra
Podhoretz, Norman: 6 writer 8 essayist
podia: 6 rostra
podiatrist concern: 3 toe 4 arch, foot
podium: 4 dais, foot 5 stage, stump 6 pulpit 7 lectern, rostrum, soapbox 8 platform
feature: 4 mike
speaker: 6 lector, orator 7 honoree 8 lecturer
take the ~: 4 talk 5 orate, speak
__ podrida: 4 olla
Podunk: 4 town 6 sticks
one from ~: 4 hick, rube 5 yokel
Poe, Edgar Allan: 4 poet 6 writer
cat: 8 Caterina
night visitor: 5 raven
work: Al Aaraaf
Alone
The Angel of the Odd
Annabel Lee
The Assignation
Astoria
The Balloon Hoax
The Bells
Berenice
The Black Cat
Bon-Bon
Bridal Ballad
The Business Man
The Cask of Amontillado
City in the Sea
The City in the Sea
The Coliseum
The Colloquy of Monos and Una
The Conqueror Worm
The Conversation of Eiros and Chamion
A Descent Into the Maelstrom
The Devil in the Belfry
Diddling
The Domain of Arnheim
A Dream
Dream-Land
Dreams
A Dream Within a Dream
The Duc de l'Omelette
Eldorado
Eleonora
An Enigma
Eulalie
Eureka
Evening Star
The Facts in the Case of M. Valdemar
Fairy-Land
The Fall of the House of Usher
For Annie
The Gold Bug
The Happiest Day
The Haunted Palace
Hop-Frog
How to Write a Blackwood Article
Imitatation
The Imp of the Perverse
In Youth I Have Known One
The Island of the Fay
Israfel
King Pest
Landor's Cottage
Lenore
Ligeia
Lionizing
The Literary Life of Tingum Bob, Esq.
Loss of Breath
Maelzel's Chess-Player
A Man of the Crowd
The Man That Was Used Up
The Masque of the Red Death
Mellonta Tauta
Mesmeric Revelation
Metzengerstein
Morella
MS. Found in a Bottle
The Murders in the Rue Morgue
The Mystery of Marie Roget
Mystification
Narrative of A. Gordon Pym
Never Bet the Devil Your Head
The Oblong Box
The Oval Portrait
The Philosophy of Composition
Philosophy of Furniture
The Pit and the Pendulum
The Power of Words
A Predicament
The Premature Burial
The Purloined Letter
The Quacks of Helicon
The Raven
Romance
Shadow-A Parable
Silence
Silence-A Fable
The Sleeper

Some Words With a Mummy
Song
Sonnet-To Science
The Spectacles
The Sphinx
Spirits of the Dead
A Tale of Jerusalem
A Tale of the Ragged Mounains
Tamerlane
The Tell-Tale Heart
Thou Art the Man
Three Sundays in a Week
To F.S.O.
To Helen
To Isadore
To M.L.S.
To My Mother
To One in Paradise
To Zante
Ulalume
A Valentine
The Valley of Unrest
Von Kempelen and His Discovery
William Wilson
X-ing a Paragrab

Poehler: 3 Amy

poem: 3 lai, ode 4 epic, epos, hymn, idyl, pean, rime, rune, song, waka 5 cento, ditty, elegy, epode, haiku, idyll, paean, rhyme, tanka, verse 6 ballad, monody, rondel, sonnet 7 ballade, canzone, rondeau, sestina, sextain, triolet, virelay, writing 8 canticle, cinquain, clerihew, limerick, palinode, quatrain, rondelet 9 free verse, telestich 10 blank verse, villanelle
- **17-syllable ~:** 5 haiku
- **3-line ~:** 5 haiku
- **Christmas ~ opener:** 4 'Twas
- **closing stanza:** 5 envoi
- **collection:** 5 divan
- **division:** 4 line 5 canto, envoi, stave, verse 6 stanza
- **epic ~:** 5 Iliad 6 Aeneid 7 Beowulf, Odyssey
- **heroic ~:** 4 epic, saga 5 epode 6 epopee 8 epopoeia
- **Japanese ~:** 4 waka 5 haiku, tanka
- **liturgical ~:** 5 psalm
- **long ~:** 4 epic, saga
- **lyric ~:** 3 ode 6 sonnet
- **medieval ~:** 3 lai, lay 6 aubade, ballad 7 ballade
- **morning ~:** 6 aubade
- **mournful ~:** 5 dirge, elegy
- **narrative ~:** 4 idyl 5 idyll
- **of lament:** 5 dirge, elegy 6 monody 8 threnody
- **pastoral ~:** 4 idyl 5 idyll 7 eclogue

poem lovely as a __: 4 tree

poesy: 4 poem, rime 5 rhyme, verse 6 poetry, rhymes

poet: 4 bard 5 odist, rimer 6 author, rhymer, writer 7 imagist 8 laureate, lyricist 9 balladist, rhymester, versifier
- **adverb for a ~:** 3 e'en, e'er, ere, o'er, oft, 'tis, yon 4 enow, ne'er, nigh, 'twas 5 afore, anear, 'neath
- **American ~:** 4 Dove, Hass, Tate 5 Benét, Plath, Pound, Wylie 6 Cullen, Dunbar, Kilmer, Kunitz, Lanier, Lowell, McKuen, Millay, Pinsky, Strand, Warren, Wilbur, Wilcox 7 Brodsky, Collins, Emerson, Jeffers, Kinnell, Lazarus, Markham, Nemerov, Rexroth, Roethke, Van Duyn, Whitman 8 Ginsberg, Levertov, MacLeish, Robinson, Rukeyser, Sandburg, Teasdale, Whittier 9 Dickinson 10 Longfellow
- **Argentine ~:** 6 Storni
- **Australian ~:** 4 Hope, Stow 6 Palmer, Porter, Wright 7 Brennan, Slessor, Stewart
- **Austrian ~:** 7 Bachman
- **beat for a ~:** 5 meter
- **Brazilian ~:** 7 Andrade 8 Bandeira
- **British ~:** 3 Gay, Pye 4 Gray, Gunn, Hood, Hunt, Owen, Pope, Read, Rowe, Tate 5 Blake, Byron, Carew, Clare, Davie, Donne, Eliot, Gower, Hardy, Keats, Monro, Peele, Powys, Raine, Rowse, Smart, Smith, Swift, Wyatt 6 Arnold, Austin, Brontë, Brooke, Bryher, Cibber, Cotton, Cowley, Cowper, Crabbe, Daniel, Dryden, Empson, Eusden, Fuller, Henley, Hughes, Jonson, Morris, Motion, Sidney, Symons, Waller, Warton 7 Bridges, Campion, Chapman, Chaucer, Collins, Crashaw, Drayton, Herrick, Heywood, Hopkins, Housman, Johnson, Marlowe, Marvell, Peacock, Quarles, Raleigh, Sassoon, Shelley, Sitwell, Skelton, Southey, Spender, Spenser 8 Betjeman, Browning, Day Lewis, de la Mare, Lovelace, Overbury, Richards, Rossetti, Shadwell, Suckling, Tennyson 9 Cleveland, Coleridge, Masefield, Sackville, Southwell, Swinburne, Whitehead 10 Chatterton, FitzGerald, Wordsworth 11 Shakespeare
- **Canadian ~:** 4 Page 5 Blais, Dudek, Klein, Pratt, Purdy, Scott, Smith 6 Avison, Carman, Hébert 7 Garneau, Newlove, Service, Souster 8 Sangster 9 Choquette, Fréchette, Grandbois, Gustafson
- **Chilean ~:** 5 Parra 6 Neruda 7 Mistral
- **Chinese ~:** 4 Li Po, Tufu 7 Wang Wei
- **Chuvash ~:** 4 Aigi
- **Colombian ~:** 5 Silva 6 Rivera
- **Cuban ~:** 5 Diego 7 Guillén
- **Czech ~:** 5 Havel, Holub 6 Neruda 7 Seifert
- **Danish ~:** 11 Stuckenberg
- **eye, to a ~:** 3 orb
- **Finnish ~:** 8 Runeberg
- **Flemish ~:** 7 Gezelle
- **foot for a ~:** 4 iamb 6 dactyl 7 spondee
- **French ~:** 4 Char 5 Bodel, Jacob, Jouve, Marot, Péguy, Perse, Scève 6 Breton, Desnos, Éluard, France, Grévin, Musset 7 Boileau, Chénier, Heredia, Michaux, Mistral, Prévert, Queneau, Régnier, Reverdy, Rimbaud, Ronsard 8 Chartier, Soupault 9 Corneille, Deschamps, Desportes, Froissart, Lamartine, Prudhomme 10 Baudelaire
- **German ~:** 4 Holz 5 Brant, Celan, Heine, Hesse, Rilke, Sachs, Storm 6 Brecht, Dehmel, George, Hebbel, Mörike 7 Fontane, Rückert 8 Brentano, Chamisso, Gryphius, Schiller, Schlegel 9 Nietzsche
- **Ghanaian ~:** 8 Anyidoho
- **Greek ~:** 4 Bion 5 Arion, Homer 6 Cavafy, Elytis, Hesiod, Ibycus, Pindar, Ritsos, Sappho 7 Agathon, Alcaeus, Palamas, Seferis 8 Anacreon 9 Aeschylus, Simonides
- **Hebrew ~:** 6 Bialik 8 Alterman 9 Greenberg
- **Hindu ~:** 5 Rishi
- **Hoosier ~:** 5 Riley
- **Hungarian ~:** 6 József
- **Indian ~:** 5 Iqbal 6 Moraes 7 Bharati 8 Kalidasa
- **inspiration for a ~:** 4 Muse 5 Erato
- **Ireland, to a ~:** 4 Erin
- **Irish ~:** 5 Colum, Moore, Wilde, Yeats 6 Boland, O'Grady 7 Parnell 8 MacNeice 9 Kavanaugh
- **Italian ~:** 5 Belli, Berni, Dante, Tasso 6 Marino, Oriani, Parini, Pavese 7 Ariosto, Boiardo, Colonna, Folengo, Foscolo, Montale, Morante, Pascoli, Pontano 8 Carducci, Pasolini, Petrarch 9 Boccaccio, D'Annunzio, Quasimodo, Sacchetti 10 Cavalcanti, Sannazzaro
- **Japanese ~:** 4 Issa 5 Basho, Buson, Ikkyu, Shiki 6 Hakuin, Ryokan 11 Akiko Yosano, Yosano Akiko
- **Lebanese ~:** 5 Accad, Adnan
- **Lycian ~:** 4 Olen
- **Martinican ~:** 7 Césaire
- **Mexican ~:** 3 Paz 4 Cruz 5 Nervo, Reyes
- **New Zealand ~:** 6 Adcock, Baxter, Curnow
- **Nicaraguan ~:** 5 Darío 8 Cardinal
- **Nigerian ~:** 5 Okara 7 Soyinka
- **Norman ~:** 4 Wace
- **of yore:** 4 bard, scop 5 scald, skald 8 minstrel
- **Old Norse ~:** 5 scald, skald
- **Persian ~:** 4 Omar, Sa'di 5 Hafez, Hafiz 7 Khayyám
- **Peruvian ~:** 4 Moro 6 Eguren
- **Polish ~:** 7 Herbert 8 Krasicki, Rózewicz 10 Mickiewicz
- **Portuguese ~:** 6 Camoes
- **pugilistic ~:** 3 Ali 11 Muhammad Ali
- **Roman ~:** 4 Ovid 6 Horace, Vergil 7 Juvenal, Persius 8 Catullus 9 Lucretius
- **Russian ~:** 3 Fet 4 Bely, Blok 5 Bedny, Bunin 6 Esenin 7 Nabokov, Sologub 8 Nekrasov, Sloukhin 9 Akhmatova, Pasternak, Zhukovsky 10 Mayakovsky, Zabolotsky
- **Scottish ~:** 4 Hogg, Muir 5 Burns, Scott, Spark 6 Dunbar 8 Campbell
- **Senegalese ~:** 7 Senghor
- **South African ~:** 6 Brutus, Plomer
- **Spanish ~:** 4 Mena, Ruiz, Vega 6 Berceo, Boscán, Encina 7 Alberti, Bousoño, Góngora, Guillén, Herrera, Jiménez, Salinas 8 Manrique
- **Swedish ~:** 6 Ekelöf 7 Bellman, Fröding 9 Karlfeldt 10 Gustafsson, Strindberg
- **Swiss ~:** 6 Keller 9 Spitteler
- **Turkish ~:** 6 Hikmet
- **Urdu ~:** 6 Ghalib
- **Venezuelan ~:** 5 Bello
- **Welsh ~:** 7 Herbert

poetic: 5 lyric 6 bardic, metric 7 idyllic, lilting, lyrical, musical 8 metrical, rhythmic, romantic, songlike 9 inspiring, melodious

poetic __: 7 justice, license

Poetica: 4 font 8 typeface

__ Poetica: 3 Ars

poetry: 3 art 4 rime 5 haiku, rhyme, verse 8 doggerel, limerick 10 literature

Poetry in Motion (1960 song)
- **artist:** Johnny Tillotson

Poetry Man (1975 song)
- **artist:** Phoebe Snow

__ Poets: 4 Lake

poets laureate (American):
- 2008- Kay Ryan
- 2007-2008 Charles Simic
- 2006-2007 Donald Hall
- 2004-2006 Ted Kooser
- 2003-2004 Louise Glück
- 2001-2003 Billy Collins
- 2000-2001 Stanley Kunitz
- 1997-2000 Robert Pinsky
- 1995-97 Robert Hass
- 1993-95 Rita Dove
- 1992-93 Mona Van Duyn
- 1991-92 Joseph Brodsky
- 1990-91 Mark Strand
- 1988-90 Howard Nemerov
- 1987-88 Richard Wilbur
- 1986-87 Robert Penn Warren

poets laureate (British):
- 2009- Carol Ann Duffy
- 1999-2009 Andrew Motion
- 1984-1998 Ted Hughes
- 1972-1984 John Betjeman
- 1968-1972 Cecil Day Lewis
- 1930-1967 John Masefield
- 1913-1930 Robert Bridges
- 1896-1913 Alfred Austin
- 1850-1892 Alfred Tennyson
- 1843-1850 William Wordsworth
- 1813-1843 Robert Southey
- 1790-1813 Henry Pye
- 1785-1790 Thomas Warton
- 1757-1785 William Whitehead
- 1730-1757 Colley Cibber
- 1718-1730 Lawrence Eusden
- 1715-1718 Nicholas Rowe
- 1692-1715 Nahum Tate
- 1689-1692 Thomas Shadwell
- 1668-1689 John Dryden

Poet's Notebook, A
- **author:** Edith Sitwell

__ Poets Society: 4 Dead

Pogo: 5 comic, strip
- **artist:** Walt Kelly
- **dog:** 10 Beauregard

pogonophobe
fear: **6** beards
pogo stick: **3** toy
pogs: **3** fad
pogy: **4** fish **8** menhaden **9** surfperch
Pohl, Frederik: **6** editor, writer
genre: **5** sci-fi
poi
base: **4** eddo, taro
party: **4** luau
poignancy: **6** pathos
poignant: **3** sad **4** keen **5** sharp, woful **6** biting, moving, tender, woeful **7** intense, piquant, piteous, pitiful, tearful **8** eloquent, pathetic, piercing, touching **9** affecting, emotional, exquisite, sorrowful, trenchant **10** expressive, pathetical
poilu: **6** French **7** soldier
ally: **5** Tommy
cap: **4** kepi
Poincaré, Raymond: **6** French **9** statesman
poinciana: **4** tree
family: **6** legume
relative: ***see*** legume tree
poinsettia: **5** plant **6** flower
point: **3** aim, dot, end, nib, nub, peg, set, tip, use **4** apex, barb, cape, crux, cusp, east, gist, goal, hint, idea, knub, lead, meat, pith, site, snag, spot, step, tend, text, time, tine, turn **5** drift, fleck, guide, heart, imply, issue, level, locus, moral, north, phase, pitch, prong, refer, score, sense, slant, south, speck, spike, spine, spire, stage, steer, sword, thing, thorn, train, where **6** burden, chakra, dagger, detail, direct, extent, finger, import, intent, kicker, marrow, moment, motive, nicety, object, period, reason, regard, signal, summit, thrust, tipoff, zero in **7** essence, feature, instant, meaning, message, minimum, pin down, purport, purpose, quality, quarter, respect, signify, sticker, suggest **8** argument, flyspeck, foreland, headland, indicate, interval, juncture, location, question, stiletto **9** designate, objective, punch line, situation, threshold **10** bottom line, particular, promontory, show the way
at any ~: **4** ever
at issue: **5** topic **8** argument
at that ~: **4** then **5** there
at the boiling ~: **3** hot **5** angry **6** fuming, raging **7** furious **8** bubbling, scalding, steaming
at this ~: **3** now **4** here **9** currently
a weapon: **3** aim
beside the ~: **4** moot **9** unrelated **10** extraneous, irrelevant
blue ~: **3** cat **7** Siamese
break ~: **5** ad out
breaking ~: **5** brink, limit **6** crisis **8** showdown
cardinal ~: **4** east, west **5** north, south
come to a ~: **5** taper
compass ~: **3** ENE, ESE, NNE, NNW, SSE, SSW, WNW, WSW **4** east, west **5** north, rhumb, south
crucial ~: **6** crisis, crunch **8** deadline
end ~: **3** cap **5** limit **7** ceiling
farthest ~: **3** end **5** brink **6** apogee, border, fringe **7** extreme **8** frontier **9** extremity, periphery
fine ~: **6** detail, nicety, nuance **9** condition, punctilio
focal ~: **3** hub **4** node, pith **5** focus, locus **6** center **8** cynosure **9** highlight
from this ~: **6** hereon
furthest ~: **4** edge **7** extreme **8** boundary **9** extremity
game ~: **3** run **4** goal **5** homer, score **6** basket **7** home run **9** field goal, touchdown
geometrical ~: **5** locus
get off the ~: **5** drift, stray **6** ramble, wander **7** deviate, digress, diverge **8** divagate
get the ~: **3** see **5** grasp **7** catch on **10** understand
halfway ~: **5** midst **6** center, median, middle
high ~: **3** tip, top **4** acme, apex, peak **5** crest, crown, limit **6** apogee, climax, summit, zenith **7** ceiling, maximum **8** pinnacle **10** prominence
in ~ of: **2** re **4** in re **5** as for **10** concerning
in ~ of fact: **6** indeed, really **8** actually
in question: **4** case **5** issue, theme, topic **6** affair, matter, thesis **7** problem, subject **8** business
joining ~: **4** link **5** ridge **8** juncture **9** stitching **10** connection
leading by a ~: **5** one up
low ~: **4** foot, pits, zero **5** abyss, chasm, floor, nadir **6** bottom, canyon, trough
main ~: **3** nub **4** core, crux, gist, knub, meat, pith **5** drift, heart **6** kernel, marrow, thrust, upshot **7** essence **9** substance **10** bottom line
make a ~ of: **6** repeat, stress **9** emphasize, stipulate, underline **10** underscore
of departure: **4** door, exit, gate, port **5** depot **8** terminal **9** threshold
of interest: **5** scene, vista **6** vision **7** display, exhibit **9** spectacle
of view: **4** mind, side, view **5** angle, light, slant **6** aspect, vision **7** feeling, opinion, outlook, posture
out: **4** cite, note, show, spot **5** input **6** adduce, advise, assert, denote, reason, record **7** comment, mention, specify, touch on **8** identify, indicate, register **9** touch upon
pen ~: **3** nib
rotating ~: **5** hinge **7** fulcrum
seal ~: **3** cat **7** Siamese
selling ~: **4** plus **5** asset, forte **6** virtue **7** benefit
size: **3** gem **4** pica, ruby **5** agate, elite **7** brevier, diamond, emerald, minikin **9** bourgeois, brilliant, excelsior, nonpareil
starter: **3** end, gun, pin **4** view **5** check, flash, knife, stand **6** needle **7** counter
starting ~: **4** base **5** basis, git-go **6** origin, source **8** base camp **9** beginning, threshold
sticking ~: **3** rub **4** beef **7** impasse
stopping ~: **3** end **5** limit **7** ceiling
strong ~: **5** asset, forte
the finger at: **5** blame **6** accuse, charge
the way: **4** lead **5** guide, spark, steer, teach, train, tutor, usher **6** orient **7** conduct **8** instruct **9** spearhead
to the ~: **3** apt **4** curt **5** ad rem, blunt, brief, crisp, frank, pithy, short, terse, tight **6** direct, gnomic **7** apropos, compact, concise, germane, laconic, summary, well-put **8** apposite, relevant, succinct **9** pertinent, trenchant **10** applicable
to this ~: **3** yet **5** so far **6** to date
turning ~: **3** hub **4** axis, axle, crux **5** hinge, pivot, rally **6** climax, crisis **8** juncture, landmark, zero hour **9** milestone
up: **3** toe **4** mark **6** accent, stress **9** highlight, italicize, punctuate, spotlight, underline **10** accentuate, illustrate, underscore
up to a ~: **6** partly **8** somewhat **9** partially
weak ~: **4** flaw, vice **5** fault **6** defect
point __: **5** guard **6** spread
point __ return: **4** of no
point-__: **5** blank **6** of-sale **8** and-shoot
__ point: **3** dew, pen, set **4** at no, game, sore **5** extra, flash, focal, grade, match, petit, price, to the **6** access **7** boiling, Brownie, decimal, melting, selling, talking, turning, vantage
Point __: **4** Ilio **5** Break, Reyes **6** Barrow
__ Point: **4** West
point-and-shoot result: **3** pic **4** snap **5** photo **7** picture **8** snapshot **10** photograph
__ point average: **5** grade
point-blank: **4** open **5** blunt, frank, smack **6** candid, direct, honest, openly **7** bluntly, frankly, sincere, up-front **8** candidly, directly, explicit, honestly, straight, truthful **9** outspoken, sincerely **10** explicitly, no-nonsense, truthfully, unmediated, unreticent
Point Break (1991 film)
cast: Gary Busey, Keanu Reeves, Patrick Swayze
point-by-point: **8** detailed **10** spelled out
Point Counter Point
author: Aldous Huxley
character: **4** Lucy **5** Hilda **6** Elinor, Webley **7** Bidlake
__ Pointe: **6** Grosse
pointed: **4** keen **5** pithy, sharp, short, smart, spiky, spiny, terse **6** acuate, barbed, spiked **7** cutting, prickly, pronged, pungent, right-on, telling **8** accurate, incisive, relevant, scathing **9** pertinent, sarcastic, trenchant **10** meaningful
arch: **5** ogive
as wit: **4** acid
comment: **4** barb **6** zinger
end: **4** cusp
not ~: **5** blunt **7** rounded
roof: **5** spire **7** steeple
tool: **3** awl **5** punch
weapon: **4** dart, shiv, snee **5** arrow, knife, lance, spear, sword **6** dagger **7** bayonet
pointer: **3** dog, rod, tip **4** clew, clue, dial, hint **5** arrow, canid, gauge, index **6** advice, canine, finger, hunter, needle, tipoff **7** warning **8** lodestar **9** indicator **10** suggestion
compass ~: **6** needle
CRT ~: **6** cursor
__ pointer: **5** laser
Pointer Sisters
hometown: Oakland
members: Ruth, Anita, June, Bonnie
song: American Music (1982)
Automatic (1984)
Dare Me (1985)
Fairytale (1974)
Fire (1978)
He's So Shy (1980)
How Long (1975)
I'm So Excited (1982)
Jump (For My Love) (1984)
Neutron Dance (1984)
Should I Do It (1982)
Slow Hand (1981)
Yes We Can Can (1973)
pointillism detail: **3** dot
pointillist: **6** Seurat
__-point landing: **5** three
pointless: **4** dull, flat, idle, vain **5** blunt, inane, no use, no-win, nutty, silly, vapid **6** absurd, futile, hollow, jejune, otiose **7** aimless, insipid, useless **8** bootless, ill-spent, needless **9** for naught, frivolous, fruitless, illogical, senseless, worthless **10** extraneous, irrelevant, ridiculous, unavailing
point of __: **4** view **5** honor, order
__ point of: **5** make a
point of no __: **6** return
__ point Siamese: **4** blue, seal
__ Point, The: **7** Turning
pointy shoes wearer: **3** elf
poise: **4** calm, cool, ease, tact, wait **5** asset, grace, hover **6** aplomb, polish, stasis, temper **7** balance, bearing, dignity, suspend **8** calmness, coolness, demeanor, elegance, patience, presence, serenity **9** assurance, composure, diplomacy, gallantry, sangfroid, stability, stabilize **10** confidence, equanimity, moderation, sedateness, self-esteem, steadiness
starter: **4** equi **7** counter
poised: **4** calm, cool **5** ready, suave **6** sedate, serene, stable, steady, urbane **7** assured, tactful **8** composed, graceful, mannered, polished, tranquil **9** collected, unruffled **10** phlegmatic, unagitated
remain ~: **5** hover
poison: **4** bane, evil, harm, kill, warp **5** ricin, taint, toxic, toxin, venom **6** infect **7** corrupt, henbane, pollute, subvert **8** impurity **9** herbi-

cide, infection, prejudice, undermine **10** adulterate
animal ~: **5** venom
another's ~: **4** meat
arrow ~: **4** inee, upas **5** urare **6** antiar, curara, curare
hemlock ~: **5** conin
ivy genus: **4** rhus
ivy symptom: **4** itch, rash
neutralizer: **8** antidote
poison __: **3** ivy, oak, pen **4** pill **5** sumac
Poison (1989 song)
artist: Alice Cooper
Poison Belt, The
author: Arthur Conan Doyle
Poisoned Stream, The
author: Hans Habe
Poison Ivy (1959 song)
artist: Coasters
poisonous: **5** nasty, toxic **6** septic **7** baleful, baneful, corrupt, harmful, hurtful, nocuous, noisome, noxious, vicious **8** venomous, viperous, virulent **9** injurious, malicious, unhealthy **10** contagious, malevolent, pernicious
combining form: **5** toxic- **6** toxico-
mulberry tree: **4** upas
plant: **5** sumac **6** sumach **7** henbane **8** mandrake **9** snakeroot **10** belladonna, jimsonweed, nightshade
snake: **3** asp **5** adder, cobra, krait, mamba, viper **7** rattler **10** copperhead
poison-pen __: **6** letter
Poitier, Sidney: **5** actor
film: All the Young Men (1960)
The Bedford Incident (1965)
Brother John (1970)
Cry, the Beloved Country (1951)
The Defiant Ones (1958)
Duel at Diablo (1966)
Edge of the City (1957)
Guess Who's Coming to Dinner (1967)
In the Heat of the Night (1967)
The Jackal (1997)
Let's Do It Again (1975)
Lilies of the Field (1963, AA)
The Organization (1971)
A Patch of Blue (1965)
A Piece of the Action (1977)
Porgy and Bess (1959)
Pressure Point (1962)
A Raisin in the Sun (1961)
Something of Value (1957)
Stir Crazy (1980)
To Sir, With Love (1967)
The Wilby Conspiracy (1975)
poivre: **6** pepper
partner: **3** sel
poke: **3** bag, dig, jab, jut, lag, pry **4** butt, idle, prod, push, root, slap, stab, stir **5** amble, annoy, dally, delay, elbow, goose, impel, jab at, lunge, mosey, nudge, pouch, probe, punch, purse, rouse, shlep, shove, snoop, stick, tarry **6** arouse, bonnet, dawdle, fiddle, fillip, jostle, justle, linger, loiter, meddle, propel, putter, schlep, shlepp, thrust **7** dawdler, intrude, laggard, project, shamble **8** hang back, knapsack, overhang, protrude, slugabed, stand out, stick out, straggle **9** drag along, gunnysack, interfere, lazybones, sunbonnet **10** dillydally, incitement
along: **5** crawl, dally, trail **6** dawdle, loiter **7** saunter, shuffle
around: **3** pry **5** snoop **7** rummage
full of holes: **6** riddle **8** disprove, puncture **9** discredit, perforate **10** prove false
fun at: **3** kid, rag, rib **4** jeer, mock, ride, twit **5** fleer, roast, scoff, taunt, tease **6** deride, needle **7** put down **8** ridicule
one's nose in: **3** pry **5** snoop **6** meddle **7** intrude **9** eavesdrop, interfere
out: **3** jut **5** bulge **7** project
starter: **3** cow **4** slow
poke __: **5** fun at
Pokémon: **4** game **5** anime **8** card game
poker: **4** game, tool **8** card game
action: **3** see **4** call, deal, fold **5** raise
bullet: **3** ace
call: **5** no bet
card: **3** ace, six, ten, two **4** five, four, jack, king, nine, trey **5** deuce, eight, joker, queen, seven, three **6** bullet
chip quantity: **5** stack
holding: **4** hand, pair **5** flush **6** aces up **10** royal flush
like some ~ hands: **3** pat
meet a ~ bet: **3** see
need: **4** deck, dice **5** chips, table
phrase: **4** I'm in **5** I call, I fold, I'm out **6** ante up, I raise
place: **5** stove **6** casino, hearth **8** fireside
ploy: **5** bluff
quit, in ~: **4** fold
raise, in ~: **4** bump
red-hot ~: **5** plant **6** flower
use a ~: **4** stir **5** stoke
variety: **4** brag, draw, hi-lo, stud **6** hold 'em **7** high-low, lowball **8** anaconda, baseball **9** freeze-out, penny ante
wager: **3** bet **4** ante, chip **5** kitty, money, stake
winnings: **3** pot **5** kitty
poker-faced: **5** blank, stoic, stony **6** glassy, stoney, wooden **7** neutral **9** impassive
Poker Flat
chronicler: **5** Harte
__-pokery: **7** jiggery
pokey: **3** can, jug, pen **4** jail, slow, stir **5** clink **6** cooler, lockup, prison **7** hoosgow, slammer **8** hoosegow, sluggish **9** calaboose
__-pokey: **5** hokey
Pokey: **5** Reese
poky: **4** jail, slow **5** tardy **6** cooler, draggy, lockup **7** gradual, halting, hoosgow, impeded, lagging, languid, slammer, tedious **8** crawling, creeping, dawdling, dilatory, dragging, drawn-out, hesitant, hoosegow, plodding, slothful, sluggish, toddling **9** leisurely, lethargic, prolonged, puttering, snaillike, unhurried **10** deliberate, protracted
pol: **10** ward heeler
concern: **4** vote **5** image
often: **6** orator **7** debater **9** sleazebag
Pola: **5** Negri
Poland: **6** nation **7** country
astronomer: **10** Copernicus
author: James A. Michener
capital: **6** Warsaw
chemist: **5** Curie
city: **4** Lódz **5** Posen, Radom **6** Gdansk, Kalisz, Kraków, Lublin, Poznan **7** Wroclaw
dance: **7** mazurka **8** mazourka **9** polonaise
export: **4** coal
gulf: **6** Danzig
harpsichordist: **9** Landowska
lancer: **4** ulan **5** uhlan
legislature: **4** Sejm
length measure: **4** mila
money: **5** grosz, zloty
mountain: **4** Rysy **5** Tatra
neighbor: **6** Russia **7** Belarus, Germany, Ukraine **8** Slovakia **9** Lithuania
Nobelist in Literature: **6** Milosz **7** Reymont **10** Szymborska **11** Sienkiewicz
Nobelist in Peace: **6** Walesa **7** Rotblat
Nobelist in Physics: **7** Charpak
org.: **4** NATO
pianist: **7** Hofmann **10** Paderewski, Rubinstein
playwright: **6** Fredro **8** Rózewicz
poet: **7** Herbert **8** Krasicki, Rózewicz **10** Mickiewicz
port: **6** Danzig, Gdansk, Gdynia **8** Szczecin
river: **4** Oder, Odra **5** Narew
saint: **7** Florian
soprano: **5** Raisa
stew: **5** bigos
writer: **6** Milosz, Mrozek **8** Borowski, Konwicki **10** Gombrowicz **11** Sienkiewicz
Poland China: **3** hog, pig **5** swine
Poland Spring: **5** water
competitor: **4** Naya **5** Evian **7** Perrier **8** Aquafina **9** Arrowhead
Polaner: **5** jelly
competitor: **5** Kraft **6** Knott's, Welch's **8** Smucker's
Polanski, Roman: **8** director
film: Chinatown (1974)
Cul-de-Sac (1966)
Death and the Maiden (1994)
Knife in the Water (1962)
Macbeth (1971)
The Pianist (2002, AA)
Repulsion (1965)
Rosemary's Baby (1968)
The Tenant (1976)
Tess (1979)
spouse: Sharon Tate
polar: **3** icy **4** cold **5** chill, nippy **6** arctic, biting, chilly, frigid, frosty, frozen, wintry **7** central, counter, extreme, glacial, guiding, ice-cold, numbing, opposed, pivotal, reverse, shivery, wintery **8** contrary, freezing, opposite **9** antipodal **10** antipodean
bear country: **6** Alaska, Arctic
departure point for ~ expeditions: **4** Etah
feature: **6** aurora, icecap
wear: **3** pac **5** parka **6** mukluk
polar __: **3** cap **4** bear **5** orbit
Polara: **3** car **4** auto **5** Dodge
Polar Express, The (2004 film)
cast: Tom Hanks
Polaris: **4** ICBM, star **8** lodestar
polarize: **6** divide
Polaroid: **4** film, lens **6** camera
competitor: ***see*** camera
inventor: **4** Land
Polaroid __ Camera: **4** Land
pole: **3** bar, rod, xat **4** axle, beam, bean, cane, mast, post, rail, spar, stud **5** perch, ridge, shaft, sprag, staff, stake, stave, stick, stilt **6** timber **7** railing **8** baluster, flagpole, terminus **9** extremity, flagstaff
along: **3** ski **4** raft, skee
antenna ~: **4** mast
bean ~: **5** stalk
boat to ~: **4** punt, raft **5** barge, ferry **7** gondola
clothes ~: **4** tree
dance with a ~: **5** limbo
ender: **3** axe, cat **4** star
Eskimo's ~: **3** xat **5** totem
fishing ~: **3** rod
make a totem ~: **5** carve
one with a striped ~: **6** barber
ship's ~: **4** boom, mast, spar **5** sprit
sport with a ~: **5** caber, kendo, vault
starter: **3** May, tad **4** bean, flag **5** catch, ridge
to pole: **10** everywhere
vaulter: **5** Bubka **7** Seagren **8** Richards
pole __: **4** bean, lamp **5** vault
__ pole: **3** ski **4** foul **5** totem **6** barber **7** fishing, utility
Pole: **4** Slav
__ Pole: **5** North, South
polecat: **5** fitch, skunk
relative: ***see*** weasel
polemic: **6** debate **7** dispute **8** argument
polemical: **8** juristic
polemics: **6** debate **8** argument **9** bickering, dialectic, wrangling
polenta: **5** grain
poles apart: **5** split **6** at odds, unlike **7** unalike, unequal **9** different, disparate, divergent **10** antithetic, dissimilar
poles connector: **4** axis
polestar: **3** hub **5** focus **7** Polaris **8** cynosure
police: **3** law **4** heat, tidy **5** guard, watch **6** patrol **7** control, protect
baton: **4** cosh **5** billy **9** billy club
blotter info: **2** MO **3** aka, DWI **5** alias **6** arrest
brass: **5** chief **7** marshal
bulletin: **3** APB **5** alert
car device: **5** siren
chase object: **5** felon **7** suspect
club, in India: **5** lathi **6** lathee
East German secret ~: **5** Stasi
ecol. ~: **3** EPA
headquarters: **7** station **8** precinct
insignia: **5** badge
line: **6** cordon
name on a ~ blotter: **3** Doe, Roe
officer: **3** cop, law **4** bear, fuzz, narc, nark **5** badge, bobby **6** copper, patrol **7** officer **8** blue-

PO

coat, gendarme **9** constable, detective
operation: **4** bust, raid, trap **5** sting **7** dragnet **10** undercover
order: **4** halt **6** freeze **7** hands up
org.: **3** FOP, PBA
patrol: **4** beat
procedure: **6** lineup
Russian secret ~: **3** KGB **4** NKVD, OGPU
school: **4** acad. **7** academy
slangily: **4** fuzz, heat **6** Smokey
squad: **4** vice
station: **4** jail, poky **6** lockup
target: **4** gang, perp **5** felon **7** suspect
team: **4** SWAT **5** squad
police __: **3** car, dog **5** force, power, state, wagon **6** action **7** officer, station
__ police: **5** state **6** secret **7** kitchen
Police
homeland: England
lead singer: Sting
song: De Do Do Do, De Da Da Da (1980)
Don's Stand So Close to Me (1981)
Every Breath You Take (1983)
Every Little Thing She Does Is Magic (1981)
King of Pain (1983)
Roxanne (1979)
Spirits in the Material World (1982)
Synchronicity II (1983)
Wrapped Around Your Finger (1984)
Police Story (1985 film)
cast: Jackie Chan
director: Jackie Chan
Police Woman (NBC drama)
cast: Angie Dickinson (Sgt. Pepper Anderson)
Earl Holliman (Lt. Bill Crowley)
employer: L.A.P.D.
policy: **3** way **4** code, line, rule, tact **5** stand, tenet **6** course, custom, system **7** posture, process, program, red tape, tactics **8** approach, behavior, channels, contract, doctrine, document, platform, practice, protocol, strategy **9** guideline, procedure **10** ground rule, management
hold a ~: **6** ensure, insure
noted ~ issuer: **6** Lloyd's
postscript: **5** rider
seller: **5** agent
policy __: **4** wonk
__ policy: **6** public **7** foreign
polio vaccine
developer: **4** Salk **5** Sabin
polis: **6** Athens, Sparta **9** city-state
polish: **3** rub, wax **4** buff, edit **5** class, clean, fix up, glaze, gloss, grace, poise, scour, scrub, sheen, shine, style, taste **6** better, enamel, enrich, finish, luster, redact, refine, reform, revise, smooth **7** brush up, burnish, correct, culture, develop, enhance, finesse, furbish, manners, perfect, retouch, shape up, sharpen, suavity, touch up, upgrade, varnish **8** breeding, brighten, cleanser, elegance, ornament, practice, spruce up, urbanity **9** gentility, meliorate, politesse, suaveness **10** ameliorate, brilliance, refinement, smoothness
apple ~: **4** fawn **5** toady **7** flatter **8** bootlick, butter up, suck up to
fingernail ~: **5** glaze, paint **6** enamel **7** lacquer, varnish
fingernail ~ brand: **5** Cutex
lacking ~: **5** crude **6** coarse, gauche **9** unrefined
off: **3** eat **4** down, wolf **5** eat up, scarf, use up, worst **6** devour, finish **7** consume, feast on, put away, scarf up **8** dispatch **9** dispose of, eliminate, liquidate, scarf down **10** consummate
prose: **4** edit **6** redact, revise
up: **4** cram **5** study **6** bone up, review
wood: **3** wax **4** sand **7** shellac
Polish: **8** language
see also Poland
Polish __: **3** ham **7** sausage
polished: **3** ace **4** nice, oily **5** level, light, shiny, sleek, slick, suave **6** bright, glassy, glossy, poised, polite, smooth, social, urbane, versed **7** courtly, elegant, genteel, refined, stylish, tactful **8** cultured, debonair, esthetic, highbred, ladylike, lettered, lustrous, mannerly, slippery, tasteful, well-bred **9** debonaire, processed **10** cultivated, debonnaire
Polish Wedding (1998 film)
cast: Gabriel Byrne, Claire Danes, Lena Olin
polite: **4** good, kind, mild, nice **5** bland, civil, suave **6** decent, formal, gentle, kindly, proper, smooth, social, subtle, urbane **7** affable, amiable, cordial, courtly, gallant, genteel, heedful, mindful, refined, tactful **8** amenable, amicable, cultured, discreet, friendly, gracious, highbred, ladylike, likeable, mannerly, obliging, pleasant, pleasing, polished, sociable, wellbred **9** attentive, civilized, concerned, courteous, judicious, sensitive, unselfish **10** chivalrous, diplomatic, neighborly, respectful, solicitous, thoughtful
address: **2** Ms. **3** Mrs., sir **4** ma'am, Miss **5** madam **6** Mister
fit for ~ society: **5** civil **7** genteel, refined
gesture: **3** bow **6** curtsy, salaam
language: **4** may I **6** if I may, pardon, please, thanks **8** excuse me, thank you
mot: **5** merci
not ~: **4** curt, rude **5** surly **7** brusque **9** impatient
remark: **10** pleasantry
politeness: **4** tact **7** amenity, manners **8** ceremony, civility, courtesy, niceties **9** deference, etiquette, gallantry, gentility, propriety **10** attentions
politesse: **6** polish **7** manners **8** niceties, protocol **9** etiquette, formality, propriety **10** refinement
politic: **4** cool, sane, wise **5** canny, sharp, smart, suave **6** adroit, artful, shrewd, smooth, subtle, urbane **7** prudent, tactful **8** cautious, delicate, discreet, sensible, suitable **9** advisable, courteous, expedient, judicious, provident, sagacious, sensitive, strategic **10** diplomatic, reasonable, thoughtful
body ~: **4** weal **5** state **6** nation, people **10** population
political
alliance: **4** bloc **5** junta
battlefield: **5** arena
benefactor: **6** fat cat
British ~ party: **4** Tory **6** Labour
campaign: **4** race
Canada ~ party: **7** Liberal **12** Conservative
cartoonist: **4** Nast
division: **4** ward **5** state
escapee: **6** émigré **7** refugee
event: **5** rally **6** caucus, debate **8** election **10** convention, referendum
faction: **5** cadre, lobby, party
football: **5** issue **7** problem
former ~ party: **4** Whig
gathering: **6** caucus **10** convention
housecleaning: **5** purge
illegal ~ money: **5** slush
influence: **4** pull
initials: **3** GOP
Israeli ~ party: **5** Likud, Mapam
Mexican ~ party: **3** PRI
organization: **7** machine
party offering: **5** slate
party VIP: **4** whip
patronage: **4** pork **10** pork barrel
payoff: **5** graft
platform part: **5** plank
ploy: **5** smear
position: **4** left **5** right, stand **8** platform
scandal suffix: **4** gate
symbol: **6** donkey **8** elephant
upset: **4** coup **5** purge **6** revolt, stroke **10** revolution
U.S. ~ party: **9** Socialist **10** Democratic, Republican **11** Independent, Libertarian
venue for ~ coverage: **5** CSPAN
political __: **5** party **6** asylum **7** science
Political Fictions
author: Joan Didion
politically __: **7** correct
Politically Incorrect (Comedy Central) host: Bill Maher
politician: **4** boss **6** heeler, leader **8** inflamer, lawmaker **9** demagogue, incumbent, statesman **10** campaigner, handshaker, legislator
concern: **4** poll **5** image **8** campaign
Georgia ~: **4** Nunn
picker: **5** voter
politick: **3** run **5** lobby, stump **8** campaign
politics: **6** civics **9** diplomacy **10** government, statecraft
play ~: **5** lobby, toady **6** pander **8** bootlick, maneuver **10** manipulate, strategize
__ politics: **4** play **5** party, power **6** office
Politics of Ecstasy
author: Timothy Leary
polka: **5** dance, music
polka __: **3** dot
Polk, James K.: **9** president
former occupation: **6** lawyer
middle name: **4** Knox
opponent: **4** Clay
veep: **6** Dallas
wife: **5** Sarah
__ Polk, LA: **4** Fort
poll: **4** list, vote **5** count, tally **6** ballot, census, number, sample, survey, voting **7** canvass, figures, returns **8** question, register, sampling **9** interview, straw vote **10** count noses
exit ~ participant: **5** voter
finding: **5** trend
starter: **3** red **5** catch
poll __: **3** tax **6** parrot **7** watcher
__ poll: **4** exit **5** straw **6** Gallup
pollack: **4** fish
cousin: **3** cod
Pollack, Sydney: **8** director
film: Absence of Malice (1981)
Changing Lanes (2002)
The Electric Horseman (1979)
The Firm (1993)
Havana (1990)
The Interpreter (2005)
Jeremiah Johnson (1972)
Out of Africa (1985, AA)
Sabrina (1995)
They Shoot Horses, Don't They? (1969)
Three Days of the Condor (1975)
Tootsie (1982)
The Way We Were (1973)
The Yakuza (1975)
Pollak: **5** Kevin
Pollan, Tracy
spouse: Michael J. Fox
pollen
bearer: **3** bee **4** wind **5** theca **6** anther, flower, stamen **7** blossom
grain: **5** spore
outer coat of a ~ grain: **5** exine
reaction to ~: **6** ah choo, sneeze **7** allergy
pollen __: **5** count
pollex: **5** thumb
Pollin: **3** Abe
pollinate: **9** fertilize
__-pollinate: **5** cross
pollinator: **3** bee **4** wind
polliwog: **7** tadpole
finally: **4** frog
pollock: **4** fish
kin: **3** cod
Pollock: **6** George **7** Jackson
Pollock (2000 film)
cast: Jennifer Connelly, Marcia Gay Harden, Ed Harris, Val Kilmer, Amy Madigan
director: Ed Harris
Pollock, Jackson: **6** artist **7** painter
spouse: Lee Krasner
__ polloi: **3** hoi
pollutant: **5** toxin **8** impurity
pollute: **4** foul, ruin, soil **5** alloy, dirty, spoil, stain, sully, taint **6** befoul, crud up, damage, debase, defile, infect, poison, smudge **7** begrime, blacken, corrupt, tarnish, vitiate **8** besmirch **9** desecrate, inebriate **10** adulterate, intoxicate

polluted: 4 foul 5 dirty, grimy, nasty, sooty 6 filthy, grubby, grungy, impure, rancid, rotten 7 corrupt, unclean 8 maculate, slovenly, vitiated 10 insanitary, unsanitary
not ~: 4 pure 5 clean 8 pristine
pollution: 4 ruin, smog 5 filth, smoke, taint 6 blight, damage, misuse 8 foulness, impurity 9 contagion, dirtiness 10 corruption, defilement, spoliation
air ~: 4 haze, smog 5 smaze
control org.: 3 EPA
ear ~: 4 roar, stir 5 blare, hoo-ha, noise 6 bedlam, clamor, hubbub, jangle, racket, scream, shriek, tumult, uproar 7 clangor, clatter, discord 8 brouhaha, disquiet 9 commotion, hue and cry 10 hullabaloo
ocean ~: 5 slick 8 oil slick 9 petroleum
___ pollution: 3 air 5 noise
Pollux: 4 star
parent: 4 Leda, Zeus
sister: 5 Helen
to Castor: 4 twin
Polly: 5 Adler 6 Bergen, Draper, parrot 8 Holliday
pad: 4 cage
to Tom: 4 aunt
Polly (play)
author: John Gay
Pollyanna: 5 novel 8 optimist
author: Cole Porter
polo: 4 game 5 shirt, sport 10 water sport
like the ~ set: 5 horsy 6 horsey
need: 4 pony, tack 5 boots, chaps, horse 6 bridle, helmet, mallet, saddle 9 kneeguard
period: 7 chukker
shirt brand: 4 Izod
team complement: 4 four
water ~ need: 3 net
___ polo: 5 water
Polo: 4 Teri 5 Marco
Polo Grounds: 7 stadium
star: 3 Ott
Polo, Marco: 7 Italian 8 explorer
locale: 4 Asia 5 China 6 Orient
polonaise: 5 dance, dress, music
polonium: 5 metal 7 element
Polonius
hiding place: 5 arras
son: 7 Laertes
Poltava: 4 city, town
locale: 7 Ukraine
poltergeist: 5 ghost 6 spirit 7 specter
Poltergeist (1982 film)
cast: Craig T. Nelson, Beatrice Straight, JoBeth Williams
director: Tobe Hooper
dog: 5 E. Buzz
poltroon: 4 wimp 5 sissy 6 coward, craven 7 chicken, dastard 8 recreant 9 fraidy-cat, jellyfish 10 scaredy-cat
poly: 6 fabric
ender: 4 math 5 ester
kin: 5 multi
see also polyester
poly ___: 3 sci
___-poly: 4 roly
___ Poly: 3 Cal
polyacrylonitrile: 5 Orlon
polychromatic: 6 motley 8 colorful 10 multi-color
polyester: 6 fabric 8 material 9 synthetic
fabric: 5 Kodel, nylon, rayon 6 Dacron
film: 5 Mylar
polyglot: 8 linguist
polygon corner: 5 angle
Polyhymnia: 4 Muse
domain: 4 song
parent: 4 Zeus 9 Mnemosyne
sister: 4 Clio 5 Erato 6 Thalia, Urania 7 Euterpe 8 Calliope 9 Melpomene 11 Terpsichore
polymath: 7 learned 10 generalist
___ polymerase: 3 DNA, RNA
polymerization
candidate: 5 ester
product: 5 latex
Polynesia: 4 isls. 5 isles 7 islands 9 South Seas
beer: 4 kava
carving: 4 tiki
celebration: 4 luau
chestnut: 4 rata
dance: 4 hula
fabric: 4 tapa
farewell: 5 aloha
flower: 5 lehua 6 orchid
food: 3 poi 4 taro 6 lau lau
garment: 5 pareo, pareu 6 sarong 8 lavalava 10 grass skirt
greeting: 5 aloha
plant: 2 ti
porch: 5 lanai
shrub: 4 kava
stone marker: 3 ahu
supernatural force: 4 mana
tongue: 5 Maori
tree: 4 palm 5 lehua
tuber: 4 taro
woman: 6 wahine
see also Hawaii
___ Polynesia: 6 French
polyp: 5 coral, hydra 10 sea anemone
Polyphemus: 5 giant 7 Cyclops
father: 8 Poseidon
polyphonic composition: 5 motet
polypody: 4 fern
polytech grad: 4 engr. 8 engineer
___ Polytechnique: 5 École
polytheist: 5 pagan
polyvinyl ___: 5 resin
pom: 6 canine, lap dog
pomace: 4 pulp
pomade: 8 ointment
apply ~: 5 slick
pome: 4 pear 5 apple, fruit 6 quince
pomegranate: 4 tree 5 fruit 6 purple
pomelo: 4 tree 5 fruit 6 citrus
relative: ***see*** citrus
Pomeranc: 3 Max
Pomeranian: 3 dog, pet, toy 5 canid, spitz 6 canine, lap dog
Pommard: 3 red 4 wine 7 red wine
origin: 6 France
pomme de ___: 5 terre
pommel: 3 zap 4 beat, belt, club, drub, hurt 5 flail, knock, pound, punch, smite, thump 6 batter, beat up, buffet, defeat, hammer, strike, thrash, thwack, wallop 7 trounce
pommel ___: 5 horse
pommes ___: 6 frites
pomology: 6 botany 7 science
study: 6 fruits
Pomona: 4 city, town
locale: 10 California
pomp: 4 ritz, show 5 éclat, state 7 display, fanfare, panoply 8 ceremony, grandeur, heraldry, splendor 9 formality, pageantry, solemnity, vainglory
pompadour: 4 coif 6 hairdo 7 upsweep 8 coiffure
Pompadour: 3 Mme. 6 Madame
Pomp and Circumstance
composer: Edward Elgar
pompano: 4 fish 8 palometa
Pompano Beach: 4 city, town
locale: 7 Florida
Pompeii: 4 city, town
art: 5 mural 6 fresco
city near ~: 6 Naples
court: 6 atrium
covering: 3 ash
heroine: 4 Ione
undoing: 7 volcano 8 eruption, Vesuvius
Pompeo: 5 Ellen
Pompey: 5 Roman
to Caesar: 3 foe 5 enemy
___ Pompilius: 4 Numa
pompom place: 3 cap, tam 4 shoe 7 curtain
pomposity: 4 airs, ritz 6 hubris, hybris 7 bombast, bravado, hauteur 9 arrogance, euphemism 10 floridness
pompous: 3 big 4 smug, vain 5 cocky, grand, proud, showy, stiff, tumid, windy 6 ritual, stuffy, turgid 7 courtly, flowery, fustian, haughty, hyped up, orotund, stately, stilted, stuck-up 8 affected, arrogant, boastful, decorous, inflated, pedantic, puffed up, snobbish, sonorous 9 big-headed, bombastic, conceited, dignified, egotistic, grandiose, high-flown, hubristic, imperious, overblown 10 big-talking, euphuistic, hoity-toity, pedantical, rhetorical
Ponca City: 4 town
locale: 8 Oklahoma
Ponce: 4 city, town
locale: 10 Puerto Rico
Ponce de León: 7 Spanish 8 explorer
Ponchielli, Amilcare: 7 Italian 8 composer
work: Dance of the Hours
poncho: 8 rain gear
relative: 6 sarape, serape
pond: 4 lake, mere, pool, tarn 5 basin, lough 6 lagoon 8 millpond 9 backwater, reservoir, water hole
big ~: 3 sea 5 ocean
blossom: 5 lotus 9 water lily
covering: 4 scum 5 algae
denizen: 3 eft, koi 4 alga, carp, fish, frog 7 tadpole
ender: 4 weed
floater: 3 pad
maker: 3 dam 6 beaver
salt ~: 9 backwater, tidewater
sound: 5 croak
starter: 4 fish, mill
___ Pond: 6 Walden
ponder: 3 see 4 mull, muse 5 brood, study, think, weigh 6 debate, digest, figure, ideate, puzzle, wonder 7 dwell on, examine, reflect, revolve 8 cogitate, consider, evaluate, look back, meditate, mull over, pore over, question, ruminate, turn over 9 brood over, dwell upon, reason out, speculate, sweat over 10 brainstorm, deliberate, introspect, meditate on, puzzle over, think about
Ponder Heart, The
author: Eudora Welty
ponderosa: 4 pine
Ponderosa: 5 ranch
brother: 3 Joe 4 Adam, Hoss 9 Little Joe
cook: 7 Hop Sing
patriarch: 3 Ben
ponderous: 3 big, dry 4 arid, dull, huge, slow 5 bulky, grave, heavy, hefty, large 6 boring, clumsy, dreary, leaden, prolix, stodgy, stuffy, taxing, wooden 7 awkward, hulking, humdrum, labored, lumpish, massive, onerous, stilted, tedious, verbose, weighty 8 cumbrous, lifeless, pedantic, plodding, sluggish, unwieldy 9 corpulent, graceless, important, laborious, lumbering, unwieldly 10 burdensome, cumbersome, enervating, galumphing, long-winded, monotonous, oppressive, pedantical, uninspired, well-padded
Pond in Winter, The
work: 6 Walden
Pond's
competitor: 5 Nivea 7 Jergens
pone: 9 corn bread 10 johnnycake
starter: 4 corn
___-Pong: 4 Ping
pongee: 4 silk 5 Honan 6 fabric
pongid: 3 ape
Pong producer: 5 Atari
poniard: 5 knife 6 dagger 7 sidearm 8 stiletto
ponies
play the: 3 bet 5 wager 6 gamble
Poni-Tails
song: Born Too Late (1958)
Ponselle, Rosa: 6 singer 7 soprano
role: 4 Aïda
specialty: 5 opera
Pons, Lily: 6 singer 7 soprano
specialty: 5 opera
spouse: André Kostelanetz
Pontchartrain: 4 lake
locale: 9 Louisiana
Ponte di ___: 6 Rialto
Ponte Vecchio river: 4 Arno
Pontiac: 3 car 4 auto, city, town 10 automobile
locale: 8 Michigan
model: 3 GTO 4 Vibe, Wave 5 Astre, Fiero 6 LeMans, Safari 7 Grand Am, Montana, Phoenix, Sunbird, Sunfire, Tempest, Torpedo, Torrent, Trans Am, Ventura 8 Catalina, Firebird, Solstice 9 Chieftain, Executive, Grand Prix, Star Chief 10 Bonneville, Grand Ville, Super Chief 11 Streamliner
Ponti, Carlo: 7 Italian 8 producer
spouse: Sophia Loren
pontiff: 4 pope 6 bishop, priest 7 prelate
vestment: 5 fanon, orale

pontifical: 5 papal 7 fustian 8 clerical, dogmatic
Pontifical ___: 4 Mass
pontificate: 5 orate, spout 6 preach 7 address, declaim, lecture 8 harangue, perorate 9 hold forth, sermonize
Pontius ___: 6 Pilate
Pont l'Évêque: 6 cheese, French
pontoon: 4 boat, game 6 bridge 8 card game
  alias: 9 blackjack, twenty-one, vingt-et-un
  plane: 5 hydro
pony: 3 pet 4 crib, ride, trot 5 dance, horse, money, mount 6 animal, equine 7 mustang 8 Shetland 9 racehorse
  cow ~: 5 paint, pinto 6 cayuse 7 mustang
  ender: 4 tail
  foot: 4 hoof
  frat ~: 4 crib
  Indian ~: 6 cayuse
  reply: 5 neigh, snort 7 whinney
  spotted ~: 5 paint, pinto
  up: 3 pay 4 ante, give 5 put up 6 chip in, donate, kick in, settle, supply 7 pitch in 9 do one's bit 10 contribute
  see also horse
___ pony: 3 cow 4 polo
Pony Express
  load: 4 mail 7 letters
  station: 4 Elko
ponytail: 2 do 4 coif 5 braid 6 hairdo 8 coiffure 9 hairstyle
  site: 4 nape
___ Pony, The: 3 Red
Pony Time (1961 song)
  artist: Chubby Checker
Ponzi scheme: 4 scam
___-poo: 5 cock-a 6 cutesy
pooch: 3 dog, mut 4 mutt 5 canid, doggy 6 beagle, bowwow, canine, doggie
  comment: 3 arf, yip 4 bark, woof, yelp
  lift a ~: 6 dognap
  name: 4 Fido, Fifi, Spot 5 Rover
  see also dog
___ poodle: 3 toy
poodle cut: 4 coif 6 hairdo 8 coiffure
poof, go: 6 vanish 9 disappear
pooh: 3 bah 5 pshaw 6 phooey 7 oh fudge
  see also baloney
Pooh: 4 bear
  creator: A.A. Milne
  pal: 3 Owl, Roo 6 Eeyore
Pooh ___: 3 Bah 6 Corner
pooh-bah: 6 fat cat
Pooh Goes Visiting
  author: A.A. Milne
pooh-pooh: 5 decry, scoff, scorn 6 deride, ignore, reject, slight 7 disdain, dismiss 8 minimize, ridicule 9 disregard, underplay
pool: 3 pot 4 bank, bath, fund, game, lake, mere, pond, ring, tank, tarn, well 5 basin, funds, group, immix, kitty, merge, share, sport, unite 6 lagoon, league, mingle, puddle, raffle, stakes 7 combine, jackpot, snooker 8 millpond, monopoly 9 billiards, reservoir 10 amalgamate, consortium, coordinate, join forces, natatorium
  accessory: 3 cue 4 rack 5 chalk 6 bridge
  amenity: 6 cabana, chaise 9 bath house
  clean the ~: 4 skim
  coral-reef ~: 6 lagoon
  dimension: 5 depth, width 6 length
  dirty ~: 5 guile 6 deceit, racket 7 knavery, swindle 9 duplicity
  distance: 3 lap
  division: 4 lane
  ender: 4 room, side
  enjoy the ~: 4 dive, swim, wade 5 float 6 paddle 9 dogpaddle
  fix a ~ cue: 5 retip
  hustler: 5 shark
  item in a ~: 4 gene
  money ~: 5 kitty
  mountain ~: 4 tarn
  open-air ~: 4 lido
  place: 3 bar, spa 4 hall, park, YMCA, YWCA 6 resort, saloon, tavern
  prepare for ~: 5 cue up
  problem: 5 algae
  resources: 5 unite 9 cooperate 10 join forces
  shot: 5 carom, massé 6 carrom
  starter: 4 cess 5 whirl
  table covering: 4 felt 5 baize
  wear: 6 bikini, trunks 7 maillot 8 swimsuit
  worker: 5 steno
pool ___: 3 cue 4 hall 5 shark, table
___ pool: 3 car, van 4 gene 5 dirty, motor 6 bumper, wading
Poole: 4 city, town
  locale: 6 Dorset 7 England
poolside
  area: 4 deck 5 patio
  recliner: 6 chaise
  turban: 5 towel
pools, like some: 6 heated
___ Pool, The: 4 Dead 6 Devil's
poop: 4 deck, info, news, tire 5 facts 6 gossip, notice 7 exhaust, fatigue, frazzle, lowdown 10 fuddy-duddy
  out: 4 fail, jade, tire 7 exhaust, fatigue, frazzle
poop ___: 3 out 4 deck
pooped: 4 beat, worn 5 all in, spent, tired, weary 6 bushed 7 drained, worn out 9 exhausted, prostrate 10 knocked out
___ pooped to pop: 3 too
poor: 3 low, off 4 bare, flat, junk, lame, mean, puny, slim, thin, weak 5 awful, broke, crude, lowly, needy, scant, seedy, small, sorry, spare 6 bad off, barren, faulty, feeble, flimsy, hard up, humble, in need, in want, meager, measly, modest, paltry, ragged, scanty, shabby, shoddy, skimpy, sleazy, slight, sloppy, sordid, sparse 7 lacking, limited, lowborn, pinched, pitiful, reduced, squalid 8 bankrupt, beggarly, below par, depleted, deprived, exiguous, God-awful, ill-fated, indigent, low-grade, luckless, mediocre, pathetic, strapped, trifling 9 deficient, destitute, flat broke, imperfect, insolvent, moneyless, penniless, penurious, third-rate, unfertile, worthless 10 down and out, fourth-rate, inadequate, low-quality, low-ranking, negligible, pathetical, second-rate, stone-broke, straitened, threadbare
  devil: 6 wretch
  in ~ health: 3 ill 4 sick 6 ailing, sickly, unwell 7 unsound
  in ~ shape: 4 torn, worn 5 ratty, unfit 6 beat-up, flabby, ragged, shabby 10 overweight, ramshackle
  in ~ taste: 4 loud 5 crude, tacky 6 coarse, flashy, vulgar 8 unseemly
  like a ~ excuse: 4 thin, weak 6 feeble 10 inadequate
  use ~ judgment: 4 flub, goof, muff 5 botch 6 bungle, foul up, mess up, slip up 7 blunder, go wrong, louse up, snarl up, stumble 9 mishandle, mismanage
  see also awful
poor ___ church mouse: 3 as a
___-poor: 4 dirt, land
poor-box contents: 4 alms
Poor Clare: 3 nun
poor dog
  what the ~ had: 4 none
___ poor example: 4 set a
Poor Folk
  author: Fyodor Dostoyevsky
Poor Little Fool (1958 song)
  artist: Ricky Nelson
poorly: 3 ill, low 4 sick 5 badly 6 adverb, ailing, sickly, unwell 7 failing 10 indisposed
  lit: 3 dim 4 dark 5 dusky, murky 6 gloomy, somber 7 shadowy 9 tenebrous
poor-mouth: 5 smear 8 minimize 9 deprecate
Poor Richard's Almanack feature: 3 saw 5 adage, maxim 6 saying
Poor Side of Town (1966 song)
  artist: Johnny Rivers
___! poor Yorick: 4 Alas
pop: 3 dad, hit, put, try 4 bang, Coke, leap, male, open, papa, shot, snap, sock, soda 5 burst, crack, daddy, drink, music, pappy, Pepsi, shoot, whack 6 appear, father, uncork 7 explode 8 beverage, Coca-Cola, Dr. Pepper, relative, shoot off 9 explosion, Pepsi-Cola, soft drink
  a ~: 3 per 4 each 6 apiece, for one
  artist: Andy Warhol, Robert Indiana
  a top: 5 uncap
  container: 3 can 6 bottle
  ender: 3 gun 4 corn, over
  fly: 5 bloop 6 looper
  in: 3 see 4 call, come 5 enter, visit 6 appear, arrive, drop by, show up, stop by 7 go to see, turn out
  off: 2 go 3 gab 5 leave 6 depart 7 chatter
  partner: 3 mom
  preppie's ~: 5 pater
  star: 4 idol
  starter: 3 may 5 lolli, lolly
  the cork: 4 open
  the question: 3 ask 7 propose
  to a toddler: 4 dada
  up: 4 come, show 5 arise, occur 6 appear, attend, blow in, emerge, happen, make it, roll in, sign in, spring 7 check in, clock in, hit town, punch in 8 breeze in 9 originate
pop ___: 3 art, fly, for, off, top 4 quiz, wine 5 psych 7 concert
Pop: 4 Iggy 6 Warner
Pop-___: 4 Tart
___ Pop: 3 Vox 5 Hop on, Jiffy
popcorn: 4 nosh 5 dance, snack
  holder: 3 tub
  how some ~ is popped: 5 in oil
  nuisance: 4 hull
  topper: 4 salt 6 butter
  unit: 6 kernel
popcorn ___: 6 shrimp
Popcorn: 5 Faith
Popcorn (1972 song)
  artist: Hot Butter
pope: 4 male, rank 6 bishop, cleric 7 pontiff, prelate 10 Holy Father
  calendar: 4 ordo
  cape: 5 orale
  council: 5 curia
  emissary: 6 legate
  headdress: 5 miter, tiara
  rite: 4 Mass
  teachings: 5 dogma
  who crowned Charlemagne: 3 Leo
  WWII ~: 4 Pius
Pope, Alexander: 4 poet 7 British 8 essayist, satirist
  work: The Dunciad
    Eloisa to Abelard
    Epistle to Dr. Arbuthnot
    An Essay on Criticism
    An Essay on Man
    Imitations of Horace
    Pastorals
    The Rape of the Lock
    Solitude
Popeil: 3 Ron
Pope John ___ II: 4 Paul
Pope of Greenwich Village, The (1984 film)
  cast: Daryl Hannah, Eric Roberts, Mickey Rourke
popes (with highest number):
  Adeodatus (II)
  Adrian (VI)
  Agapitus (II)
  Agatho
  Albert
  Alexander (VIII)
  Anacletus (II)
  Anastasius (IV)
  Anicetus
  Anterus
  Benedict (XVI)
  Boniface (IX)
  Caius
  Callistus (III)
  Celestine (V)
  Christopher
  Clement (XIV)
  Cletus
  Conon
  Constantine
  Cornelius
  Damasus (II)
  Dionysius
  Dioscorus
  Donus
  Eleutherius
  Eugene (IV)
  Eulabus

Eusebius
Eutychian
Evaristus
Fabian
Felix (V)
Formosus
Gelasius (II)
Gregory (XVI)
Hilary
Hippolytus
Honorius (IV)
Hormisdas
Hyginus
Innocent (XIII)
John Paul (II)
John (XXIII)
Julius (III)
Landus
Lawrence
Leo (XIII)
Liberius
Linus
Lucius (III)
Marcellinus
Marcellus (II)
Marcus
Marinus (II)
Martin (V)
Melchiades
Nicholas (V)
Novatian
Paschal (III)
Paul (VI)
Pelagius (II)
Peter
Philip
Pius (XII)
Pontian
Romanus
Sabinian
Sergius (IV)
Severinus
Silverius
Simplicius
Siricius
Sisinnius
Sixtus (V)
Soter
Stephen (X)
Sylvester (IV)
Symmachus
Telesphorus
Theodore (II)
Theodoric
Urban (VIII)
Ursinus
Valentine
Victor (IV)
Vigilius
Vitalian
Zachary
Zephyrinus
Zosimus

Popeye: **3** gob, tar **4** salt **6** sailor
affirmative: **3** aye
Bluto, to ~: **5** rival
cartoonist: **5** Segar
girlfriend: Olive Oyl
greeting: **4** ahoy
kid: **7** Swee' Pea
prop: **4** pipe
to Pipeye: **5** uncle
verb: **3** yam
Popeye (1980 film)
cast: Paul Dooley, Shelley Duvall, Ray Walston, Robin Williams
director: Robert Altman
popgun: **3** toy
Pop, Iggy
real name: James Jewel Osterberg
song: Candy (1991)
popinjay: **3** fop **4** dude **5** dandy **7** coxcomb **9** pretty boy **10** jack-a-dandy
popish: **5** papal
Popish Plot fabricator: **5** Oates
Popkin: **3** Leo
poplar: **4** tree **5** abele, alamo
family: **6** willow
relative: **5** aspen **10** cottonwood
Poplars
painter: Claude Monet
Pop Life (1985 song)
artist: Prince
poplin: **6** fabric **8** material
Popov: **5** vodka
competitor: **4** Skyy **5** Stoli **6** Rodnik, Starka **7** Absolut **8** Smirnoff **9** Grey Goose
popover: **6** pastry
Popp: **5** Lucia
poppa: **2** pa **3** dad **4** papa, pops **5** daddy **6** father, old man
partner: **5** momma
__ Poppa?: **6** Where's
Poppaea
husband: **4** Nero, Otho
Popper, Karl: **7** British **11** philosopher
popping: **4** busy
one's buttons: **5** proud
__-popping: **3** eye
Poppins: **4** Mary
Popp, Lucia: **6** singer **7** soprano
specialty: **5** opera
poppy: **3** red **4** seed **5** color, plant **6** flower **7** anodyne **8** orangish
color relative: ***see*** red color
ender: **4** cock
poppycock
see baloney
pops: **2** pa **3** dad **4** papa **5** daddy **6** father
Popsicle: **3** ice **4** nosh **5** snack
eat a: **4** lick
flavor: **5** grape **6** banana, cherry, orange
Popsicles and Icicles (1964 song)
artist: Murmaids
Pop Singer (1989 song)
artist: John Cougar Mellencamp
pop-top beverage: **4** beer, cola, soda **9** soft drink
populace: **3** mob **5** plebs **6** masses, people, public, voters **7** country **9** commoners, hoi polloi, multitude, residents
popular: **3** big, hot, mod, now **4** chic, okay, tony **5** known, liked, stock, toney, vogue **6** chi-chi, common, famous, modish, public, ruling, staple, trendy **7** à la mode, current, faddish, favored, general, in favor, in style, in vogue, leading, likable, selling, stylish, topical, voguish **8** accepted, approved, embraced, familiar, favorite, in demand, ordinary, pleasing, plebeian, run-after, societal, standard, up-to-date **9** customary, in fashion, preferred, prevalent, prominent, well-known, well-liked **10** all the rage, attractive, celebrated, fair-haired, mainstream, marketable, newfangled, prevailing, ubiquitous, widespread
place: **6** in spot
popular __: **4** song, vote **5** front **6** prices, singer
Popular __: **7** Science
__ Popular: **5** Banco
popularity: **4** fame **5** favor, kudos, vogue **6** demand, esteem, renown **7** acclaim **8** approval, currency **9** celebrity **10** admiration
popularize: **6** revive, spread **7** promote **8** simplify
popularly: **9** generally
populate: **5** dwell **6** live in, occupy, settle **7** dwell in, inhabit **8** reside in
populated
heavily ~: **5** dense, thick **7** crowded, teeming **8** crawling, swarming
thinly ~: **6** sparse
population: **4** folk, size **6** people, public **7** natives **8** citizens, denizens **9** residents
center: **3** urb **4** burb, city, town **5** exurb **6** suburb **10** metropolis
survey: **6** census
__ population growth: **4** zero
__ populi: **3** vox
populist: **9** socialist **10** democratic, self-ruling
populous: **5** dense, thick **6** jammed **7** crowded, peopled, teeming **8** crawling, swarming, thronged
populus tremula: **5** aspen
pop-up: **3** fly **5** bloop **6** looper
breakfast item: **4** Eggo
por __: **3** qué **5** favor
porcelain: **5** china **7** Limoges, pottery **8** ceramics, clayware, crockery **10** dinnerware
base: **4** clay, frit **6** kaolin **7** kaoline
British ~: **5** Spode
Chinese ~: **4** Ming
flower: **4** hoya
French ~: **6** Sèvres
Japanese ~: **5** Imari
porch: **4** stoa **5** lanai, lobby, stoop **6** piazza **7** balcony, ingress, veranda **8** verandah
classical ~: **4** stoa
furniture: **5** chair, swing **6** glider, rocker
Polynesian ~: **5** lanai
urban ~: **5** stoop
__ porch: **3** sun
porcine: **5** stout **7** hoggish, weighty
animal: **3** hog, pig **5** swine
home: **3** pen, sty
meal: **4** slop **5** swill
Muppet: **9** Miss Piggy
parent: **3** sow **4** boar
sound: **4** oink **5** grunt
youngster: **5** piggy, shoat, shote, shott **6** piggie, piglet
porcupine: **6** animal, mammal, rodent
female: **3** sow
like a ~: **5** spiny
male: **4** boar
part: **5** quill
relative: **6** agouti
young: **3** pup
see also rodent
pore: **4** read, scan **5** stoma, study **6** outlet, peruse **7** dig into, foramen, opening, orifice **8** aperture, look over, meditate **9** delve into **10** scrutinize
leaf ~: **5** stoma
over: **4** look, mull, read, sift **5** learn, study, think **6** peruse, ponder, regard **7** examine **8** consider **9** lucubrate **10** scrutinize
Porfirio: **4** Diaz
porgy: **4** fish, scup **5** bream, pargo **8** sea bream
Porgy
author: DuBose Heyward
Porgy and Bess: **5** opera
author: DuBose Heyward
composer: DuBose Heyward, George Gershwin, Ira Gershwin
Porgy and Bess (1959 film)
cast: Pearl Bailey, Dorothy Dandridge, Sammy Davis Jr., Sidney Poitier
director: Otto Preminger
Porizkova, Paulina: **5** model
spouse: Ric Ocasek
pork
barrel: **9** patronage
ender: **3** pie
fat: **4** lard
prepare ~ for wonton: **5** mince
rind: **4** nosh **5** snack
source: **3** hog, pig
pork __: **4** chop, loin **5** belly **6** barrel **7** sausage
__ pork: **4** salt **5** roast
porker: **3** hog, pig **5** swine
hangout: **3** pen, sty
nose: **5** snout
young ~: **5** shoat, shote, shott
porkpie: **3** hat
material: **4** felt
Porky
friend: **5** Darla **6** Spanky **7** Alfalfa, Petunia **9** Buckwheat
porous: **5** holey, leaky, light **6** leachy, spongy **8** pervious **9** absorbent, permeable, sievelike
rock: **4** tufa, tuff
porphyry: **4** rock **7** mineral
like ~: **7** igneous
porpoise: **6** animal, mammal **8** cetacean
relative: ***see*** cetacean
porridge: **4** mush, samp **5** gruel **6** burgoo, cereal **7** oatmeal
portion: **4** mess
__ Porridge Hot: **5** Pease
Porsche: **3** car **4** auto **6** German **9** Ferdinand **10** automobile
model: **5** Targa **7** Boxster, Carrera, Cayenne
Porsena: **4** Lars
port: **3** red **4** left, wine **5** docks, haven, wharf **6** harbor, refuge **9** anchorage
Germany ~: **6** Lübeck
holder: **5** glass **6** bottle, carafe
home ~: **4** base
in ~: **6** ashore, docked
kind of computer ~: **3** USB **4** game, SCSI **6** serial **8** parallel
leave ~: **4** sail **6** embark **7** set sail **8** go aboard
not in ~: **4** asea **5** at sea **7** en route **8** cruising
source: **5** grape **8** Portugal
starter: **3** air, car, jet, rap, sea **4** pass, tele **5** space, trans
when sailing north: **4** west
when sailing south: **4** east
__ port: **4** free, home
Port-__: **5** Salut

PO

Port.
see Portugal
portable: 5 handy, light **6** mobile, pocket **7** compact, folding, movable **8** haulable, moveable **10** convenient, conveyable, manageable
portage: 3 fee **5** track, trail **9** transport
item: 5 canoe
Portage: 4 city, town
locale: 7 Indiana **8** Michigan
portal: 4 adit, arch, door, gate **5** entry, way in **7** doorway, gateway, ingress, opening **8** entrance, entryway, hatchway **9** threshold
Shinto ~: 5 torii
Port Arthur: 4 city, port, town
locale: 5 Texas
Port-au-Prince: 4 city, town **7** capital
locale: 5 Haiti
port de __: 4 bras
Port du __: 5 Salut
porte-__: 7 cochere
portend: 4 bode, hint, loom, mean **5** augur, spell **6** herald, menace, warn of **7** bespeak, betoken, point to, predict, presage, promise, signify **8** forebode, foreshow, foretell, forewarn, indicate, prophesy, threaten **9** adumbrate, foretoken **10** foreshadow
portent: 4 omen, sign **5** hunch, vibes **6** augury, marvel, threat, wonder **7** caution, presage, warning **9** foretoken, harbinger, predictor **10** foreboding, forerunner, indication, prediction
portentous: 4 dire **5** grave, vatic, vital **6** solemn **7** bodeful, charged, crucial, fateful, ominous, pivotal, serious, weighty **8** critical, decisive, ill-fated, oracular, sinister **9** dangerous, important, momentous, prophetic **10** meaningful
porter: 3 ale **4** brew **5** drink **6** bearer, redcap, skycap **7** bellhop, carrier, janitor **8** beverage **10** doorkeeper, gatekeeper
ender: 5 house
Mideast ~: 5 hamal **6** hammal
relative: 4 beer **5** lager, stout
__-porter: 5 prêt-à
Porter: 3 Don, Hal **4** Cole **6** George, Quincy, Rodney, Sylvia **7** Eleanor, Wagoner
pen name: 6 O Henry
Porter, Cole: 8 composer
alma mater: 4 Yale
film score: Born to Dance
Broadway Melody of 1940
The Gay Divorcee
High Society
Les Girls
Night and Day
The Pirate
Rosalie
Something to Shout About
You'll Never Get Rich
hometown: 4 Peru
musical: Anything Goes
Can-Can
Du Barry Was a Lady
Fifty Million Frenchmen
Gay Divorce
Jubilee
Kiss Me, Kate
Leave It to Me!
Let's Face It
Mexican Hayride
The New Yorkers
Panama Hattie
Paris
Red, Hot and Blue!
Seven Lively Arts
Silk Stockings
Something for the Boys
Wake Up and Dream
song: Always True to You in My Fashion
Another Op'nin', Another Show
Anything Goes
At Long Last Love
Be a Clown
Begin the Beguine
Bingo Eli Yale
Blow, Gabriel, Blow
Brush Up Your Shakespeare
But in the Morning, No
Can-Can
C'est Magnifique
Don't Fence Me in
Easy to Love
Friendship
From This Moment on
Go Into Your Dance
I Concentrate on You
I Get a Kick out of You
I Hate Men
I Love Paris
It's De-Lovely
I've Got You Under My Skin
Just One of Those Things
Katie Went to Haiti
Let's Do It
Let's Misbehave
Love for Sale
Miss Otis Regrets
My Heart Belongs to Daddy
Night and Day
So in Love
Too Darn Hot
True Love
Well, Did You Evah!
What Is This Thing Called Love
Wunderbar
You'd Be So Nice to Come Home to
You Do Something to Me
You're the Top
Porter, Hal: 4 poet **6** writer **10** Australian, playwright
work: Criss-Cross
The Extra
The Paper Chase
porterhouse: 4 beef, meat **5** steak
alternative: 5 T-bone **6** rib-eye **7** sirloin
Porter, Katherine Anne: 6 writer
work: Flowering Judas
The Leaning Tower
Noon Wine
Old Mortality
Pale Horse, Pale Rider
Ship of Fools
Porter, Rodney: 7 British **8** Nobelist
__ Porter Stomp: 4 King
portfolio: 3 bag **4** case, file **5** album **6** folder **7** dossier **8** envelope **9** briefcase, container
item: 4 bond **5** asset, share, stock
option: 3 IRA **4** bond **5** stock
porthole: 4 vent **6** window
Porthos: 9 musketeer
partner: 5 Athos **6** Aramis **9** d'Artagnan
weapon: 5 sword
Port Huron: 4 city, town
locale: 8 Michigan
Portia: 4 moon
planet: 6 Uranus
Portia Faces Life: 9 radio show
portico: 4 stoa **5** porch **6** arcade **7** balcony, ingress
church ~: 6 parvis
seat: 6 exedra **7** exhedra
portiere: 5 arras **7** curtain, drapery
Portinari, Beatrice admirer: 5 Dante
__ port in a storm: 3 any
portion: 3 bit, cut, gob, leg, lot **4** deal, dole, doom, dose, fate, hunk, luck, lump, mete, part, slab, some, unit **5** allot, chunk, divvy, piece, quota, scrap, share, slice, split, taste **6** divide, dollop, factor, kismat, kismet, length, moiety, morsel, parcel, ration, sample **7** destiny, divvy up, dole out, element, excerpt, extract, fortune, helping, measure, mete out, prorate, quarter, section, segment, serving **8** allocate, dispense, dividend, division, fraction, fragment, interest, quantity, spoonful **9** allotment, apportion, partition **10** allocation, distribute, percentage
Portland: 4 city, port, town **5** Hoffa
bay: 5 Casco
county: 9 Multnomah
locale: 5 Maine **6** Oregon
newspaper: 9 Oregonian
river: 10 Willamette
time zone: 3 EDT, EST, PDT, PST
Portland __ Blazers: 5 Trail
Portland cement ingredient: 5 shale
Port Louis: 4 city, town **7** capital
locale: 9 Mauritius
portly
see obese
Portman: 4 Eric **6** Rachel **7** Natalie
Portman, Natalie: 7 actress
film: Anywhere but Here (1999)
Closer (2004)
Garden State (2004)
The Other Boleyn Girl (2008)
Star Wars Episode I: The Phantom Menace (1999)
V for Vendetta (2005)
portmanteau: 3 bag **5** trunk **6** valise
Port Moresby: 4 city, port, town **7** capital
locale: Papua New Guinea
Portnoy's Complaint
author: Philip Roth
Porto: 4 city, town
city near ~: 6 Lisboa, Lisbon
locale: 8 Portugal
Pórto Alegre: 4 city, town
locale: 6 Brazil
port of __: 4 call **5** entry
Portoferraio
island: 4 Elba
Port of Spain: 4 city, town **7** capital
locale: 8 Trinidad
Porto Novo: 4 city, town **7** capital
locale: 5 Benin
portrait: 3 art **5** image **6** canvas, figure, sketch **7** account, drawing, picture, profile **8** likeness, painting, snapshot, vignette **9** depiction, lineation, portrayal **10** photograph, silhouette
do a ~: 4 draw **5** paint **10** photograph
have a ~ done: 3 sit **4** pose
medium: 3 oil **4** film **7** pastels **8** charcoal **10** watercolor
__-portrait: 4 self
Portrait in Brownstone
author: Louis Auchincloss
Portrait in Sepia
author: Isabel Allende
Portrait of a Lady
author: T.S. Eliot
Portrait of a Lady, The: 5 novel
author: Henry James
character: 5 Merle, Pansy, Ralph **6** Archer, Caspar, Gemini, Isabel, Osmond, Rosier **8** Goodwood
dog: 7 Bunchie
Portrait of Bascom Hawke, A
author: Thomas Wolfe
Portrait of Berthe Morisot
artist: Édouard Manet
Portrait of the Artist as a Young Man, A: 5 novel
author: James Joyce
character: 5 Dante, Davin, Dolan, Nasty, Roche, Simon, Vance **6** Arnall, Cranly, Eileen **7** Dedalus, Stephen
portray: 2 do **3** act **4** copy, draw, limn, play, tell **5** enact, mimic, model, paint **6** depict, detail, parody, recite, render, sculpt, sketch **7** imitate, narrate, picture, recount **8** describe, simulate **9** adumbrate, delineate, interpret, represent **10** illustrate, photograph
portrayal: 4 role **6** acting, sketch **7** picture, recital, version **8** portrait **9** depiction, enactment, rendition
Port Said: 4 city, port, town
locale: 5 Egypt
Port Salut: 6 cheese
ports, between: 4 asea **5** at sea
portside: 4 left
portsider: 5 lefty **6** leftie **8** southpaw
Portsmouth: 4 city, port, town
locale: 4 Ohio **8** Virginia
town near ~: 5 Poole
Ports of Call
composer: Jacques Ibert
Port Stanley: 4 city, port, town
locale: 9 Falklands
Port St. Lucie: 4 city, town
locale: 7 Florida
Portugal: 6 nation **7** country
bay: 7 Setúbal
cape: 4 Roca
capital: 6 Lisboa, Lisbon
city: 4 Nisa **5** Braga, Évora, Olhao, Porto **6** Lisboa, Lisbon, Oporto **7** Amadora
explorer: 6 Cabral, da Gama **8** Magellan
folksong: 4 fado
former colony: 3 Goa **5** Macao, Macau, Timor
island: 6 Azores **7** Madeira

king: 4 Joao, Luis 5 Pedro 6 Afonso, Carlos, Manuel
leader: 7 Salazar
length measure: 4 vara
locale: 6 Europe, Iberia
money: 3 rei 5 conto 6 escudo 7 centavo, cruzado, milreis, moidore 8 johannes
neighbor: 5 Spain
Nobelist in Literature: 8 Saramago
Nobelist in Medicine: 5 Moniz
org.: 4 NATO
pilgrimage site: 6 Fatima
poet: 6 Camoes
port: 5 Porto 6 Lisbon, Oporto
river: 4 Miño 5 Minho, Tagus
wine: 4 port 7 Madeira, malmsey
Portuguese: 8 language
no, in ~: 3 nao
pronoun: 3 mim
title: 3 dom 4 dona
toast: 5 saude
wine, in ~: 5 vinho
Portuguese ___ dog: 5 water
Portuguese ___-of-war: 3 man
Portuguese West Africa today: 6 Angola
portulaca: 5 plant 6 flower 8 moss rose
posada: 3 inn
pose: 3 act, air, ask, sit 4 mask, mien, sham 5 feign, front, guise, mince, model, offer, put to, query, stand, strut 6 affect, facade, fake it, stance, submit, tender 7 advance, arrange, bearing, charade, playact, posture, present, pretend, profess, proffer, show off, suggest 8 attitude, carriage, pretense, propound, question, set forth, simulate 9 mannerism, put on airs, say cheese 10 false front, grandstand, masquerade, put forward
a question: 3 ask 6 baffle 7 inquire
for more pictures: 5 resit
for the camera: 3 mug 5 smile 9 say cheese
strike a ~: 5 model
Poseidon: 3 god 5 Greek
brother: 4 Zeus 5 Hades
Celtic ~: 3 Ler, Lir
child: 4 Idas 5 Orion 6 Aeolus, Triton 7 Pegasus, Proteus, Theseus 9 Charybdis 10 Polyphemus, Procrustes
domain: 3 sea 5 ocean
epithet: 5 Soter 7 Hippios 10 Phytalmios
equivalent: 7 Neptune
parent: 6 Cronos, Cronus
sculptor: 6 Milles
sister: 6 Hestia 7 Demeter
wife: 10 Amphitrite
Poseidon (2006 film)
cast: Jacinda Barrett, Richard Dreyfuss, Josh Lucas, Kurt Russell
Poseidon Adventure, The (1972 film)
cast: Jack Albertson, Ernest Borgnine, Red Buttons, Gene Hackman, Carol Lynley, Pamela Sue Martin, Roddy McDowall, Leslie Nielsen, Stella Stevens, Shelley Winters
director: Ronald Neame
poser: 4 koan 5 asker, dilly, model 6 enigma, puzzle, riddle, teaser, toughy 7 problem, stumper, toughie 9 conundrum, cover girl, pretender
give a ~ to: 5 throw 6 puzzle 7 buffalo, mystify, perplex 8 confound
poseur: 4 fake 5 phony 6 phoney 8 imposter, impostor 9 hypocrite, pretender
Posey: 5 Sandy 6 Parker
posh: 4 chic, lush, luxe, rich, tony 5 fancy, grand, plush, ritzy, smart, swank, swell, swish 6 classy, deluxe, la-de-da, la-di-da, lavish, lordly, luxury, modish, swanky, trendy 7 elegant, opulent, refined, upscale 8 lah-di-dah, palatial, splendid 9 exclusive, expensive, high-class, luxurious, sumptuous 10 upper-class
accommodations: 5 suite, villa 9 penthouse
posies: 8 bouquets
place for ~: 4 vase
posit: 3 put 5 place 6 affirm, assert, assume, thesis 7 premise, presume, proffer, situate, suggest 8 put forth, question 9 assertion, postulate, stipulate 10 assumption, contention, hypothesis, presuppose
position: 3 fix, job, lay, put 4 case, move, pose, post, rank, role, seat, side, site, slot, spot, view, work 5 angle, berth, caste, class, level, locus, mount, niche, phase, place, set at, situs, stand, state, stead, stick, terms, where 6 aspect, belief, billet, branch, cachet, career, instal, locale, locate, office, orient, plight, sphere, stance, status, theory, thesis 7 arrange, echelon, footing, install, opinion, outlook, posture, quality, quarter, setting, station, stature, straits, vacancy 8 attitude, bearings, doctrine, judgment, locality, location, prestige, standing 9 condition, sentiment, situation, viewpoint 10 employment, importance, nine-to-five, occupation, profession, reputation, standpoint
combining form: 5 stasi-
___ position: 4 pole 5 fetal, lotus
positioned: 3 set 5 fixed
as originally ~: 6 in situ
___ Positioning System: 6 Global
positive: 4 cold, firm, good, plus, real, sure 6 actual, aidful, benign, cheery, direct, upbeat, useful 7 assured, certain, decided, factual, genuine, helpful, settled 8 absolute, concrete, decisive, definite, explicit, forceful, in the bag, outright, remedial, resolved, salutary, sanguine, specific, verified 9 believing, confident, convinced, effectual, favorable, out-and-out, practical, satisfied 10 beneficial, conclusive, determined, guaranteed, inarguable, optimistic, photograph, productive, purposeful, undeniable, undisputed, worthwhile
be ~: 4 aver 5 swear 6 affirm, assert
make a ~ from a negative: 5 print
outlook: 4 hope 5 trust 6 morale 7 elation 8 buoyancy, calmness, easiness, idealism, optimism 9 assurance, certainty, good cheer, happiness, lightness 10 brightness, confidence, enthusiasm
sign: 4 plus
thinker: 5 Peale
vote: 3 aye, yea, yes
___ positive: 5 proof
___-positive: 4 Gram 5 false
positively: 6 and how, easily, gladly, wholly 7 exactly, flat out, go ahead 9 decidedly, expressly, favorably, no mistake, on the nose, precisely 10 inevitably, sure enough
see also of course
Positively ___!: 3 not
Positively 4th Street (1965 song)
artist: Bob Dylan
positron: 8 particle
posologist: 8 druggist 10 pharmacist
posse: 3 mob 4 crew, gang 7 pursuer
member: 6 deputy
movie: 5 oater 7 western
quest: 6 outlaw, robber 9 desperado
possess: 3 hog, own 4 bear, grab, have, hold, keep 5 boast, enjoy, seize, wield 6 lock up, madden, obtain, occupy, retain 7 acquire 8 hold on to, maintain 9 get hold of, latch onto 10 monopolize
old-style: 4 hath
possessed: 5 curst 6 cursed, raving 7 berserk, far gone, haunted, zealous 8 composed, consumed, fiendish, frenzied, obsessed 9 bedeviled, bewitched, collected, enchanted, fanatical 10 enthralled, hysterical, infatuated, spellbound
___-possessed: 4 self
Possessed, The
author: Fyodor Dostoyevsky
possession: 4 grip, hold 5 title 6 colony, effect, tenure 7 chattel, control, custody, tenancy 8 clutches, dominion, property 9 commodity, enjoyment, furniture, occupancy, ownership, territory
be in ~ of: 3 own 4 have
gain ~: 4 take
gain ~ again: 6 redeem
prized ~: 3 gem 5 jewel 8 heirloom, treasure, valuable
valuable ~: 5 asset
Possession
author: A.S. Byatt
possessions: 4 gear 5 goods, stuff 6 assets, estate, things, wealth 7 baggage, effects 8 chattels, property 10 belongings
possessive: 6 greedy 7 jealous, pronoun 9 tenacious
Dogpatch ~: 8 his'n her'n 9 our'n your'n
French ~: 3 mes, mon, tes, toi 4 a moi 5 notre, votre
German ~: 3 mie 4 mein 5 meine
Italian ~: 3 mia, mio, tua, tuo
Latin ~: 3 sua, suo
pronoun: 3 his, its, our 4 hers, mine, ours, your 5 their, whose
Quaker ~: 3 thy 5 thine
Spanish ~: 3 mia, mio 7 nuestra, nuestro
possessor: 5 owner 6 tenant 8 occupant 10 proprietor
posset: 5 drink 8 beverage
ingredient: 3 ale 4 milk, wine
possibilities: 7 promise 9 potential
possibility: 2 if 4 hope, odds, risk 5 break, fluke, maybe 6 chance, gamble, hazard, prayer, resort, toss-up 7 latency, opening, promise, surmise 8 fortuity, occasion, prospect 9 fair shake, liability 10 likelihood, lucky break
strong ~: 10 likelihood
within ~: 6 likely, viable 8 feasible
possible: 6 doable, latent, likely, viable 7 earthly, hopeful 8 apparent, credible, feasible, optional, probable, workable 9 available, plausible, potential, practical, promising, thinkable, uncertain 10 accessible, achievable, attainable, believable, contingent, imaginable, obtainable, realizable
least ~: 7 minimal, minimum
make ~: 5 set up 6 enable 7 approve, arrange
quite ~: 6 likely 8 feasible, probable
possibly: 5 maybe 7 perhaps 8 feasibly, probably 9 perchance
possum
comic-strip ~: 4 Pogo
honey ~: 4 tait
play ~: 4 fake, sham 5 feign 7 pretend 9 dissemble
___ possum: 4 play
post: 3 job, leg, set 4 base, beam, beat, fort, mail, mast, pale, pier, pile, pole, prop, race, rail, ride, seat, send, site, spot, stud, warn 5 after, brief, newel, perch, place, pylon, ready, remit, shaft, stake, stave, stilt 6 advise, assign, billet, column, fill in, inform, notify, office, pillar, record, update 7 forward, lookout, quarter, railing, situate, station, support, upright, vacancy 8 acquaint, baluster, banister, garrison, handrail, location, palisade, pedestal, position, province, quarters, register, transfer, vocation 9 make known, situation 10 assignment, employment, profession
ancient Roman racing ~: 4 meta
Army ~: 4 fort
banister ~: 5 newel
ender: 3 age, man 4 card, date, hole, mark, paid, pone 5 haste 6 master
go from pillar to ~: 3 gad 4 roam, rove 5 drift 6 ramble, wander 7 traipse
nautical ~: 4 bitt 7 bollard
starter: 3 bed, out 4 door, gate, lamp, mile, sign 5 guide
vertical ~: 4 beam 8 doorpost 9 doorframe
wooden ~: 3 rod 5 stake 6 picket, timber
post ___: 3 hoc 4 card, road, time 6 office
post-___: 3 ops 6 modern, season
___ post: 4 goal 6 parcel 7 command, trading

Post: **3** Ted **4** Mike **5** Emily, paper, Wiley **6** Markie, Wilbur **9** newspaper
cereal: **6** Oreo O's **9** Alpha Bits, Grape-Nuts, Honey Comb **10** Bran Flakes **11** Golden Crisp, Waffle Crisp
newspaper locale: **6** Denver **7** New York **10** Cincinnati
postage __: **3** due **5** meter, stamp
postal: **4** amok **6** raging **8** unhinged **9** murderous
abbr.: **3** APO, RFD, rte.
address word: **3** box
code: **3** zip
delivery: **2** ad **4** bill, card, mail **6** letter, parcel **7** air mail, package **8** circular, envelope, junk mail, magazine
equipment: **5** dater, scale
postaxial bone: **4** ulna
postcard: **4** mail **7** memento **8** souvenir
cost, once: **5** penny
message: **4** note
picture: **5** vista
__ postcard: **7** picture
Postcards From the Edge (1990 film)
cast: Richard Dreyfuss, Gene Hackman, Shirley MacLaine, Dennis Quaid, Meryl Streep
director: Mike Nichols
postdate: **6** follow **7** succeed
Post-Dispatch: **5** paper **9** newspaper
locale: **7** St. Louis
posted: **3** hep, hip **5** aware **6** au fait, versed **7** knowing, learned, located **8** familiar, informed **9** au courant, cognizant, conscious, on the beam, plugged in **10** conversant
it may be ~: **4** bail
keep ~: **4** tell **6** advise, inform
poster: **4** bill, sign **5** paper **6** banner **7** affiche, placard **9** billboard, broadside **10** broadsheet, photograph
GI ~: **5** pin-up
holder: **4** tack **7** push pin **9** thumbtack
info: **3** aka **5** alias **6** reward
Marine ~ words: **4** a few
surety ~: **6** bailor
Uncle Sam ~ words: I Want You
poster __: **5** child
__-poster bed: **4** four
posterity: **4** kids, seed **5** brood, heirs, issue, stock **6** family, future, scions **7** kinfolk, lineage, progeny **8** children, kinfolks, kinsfolk **9** offspring **10** descendant, successors
postern: **4** door, gate **7** gateway, ingress **8** back door, entrance, entryway
Postern of __: **4** Fate
postgame discussion: **5** recap **7** summary
Post-Gazette: **5** paper **9** newspaper
locale: **10** Pittsburgh
postgraduate
degree: **2** MA **3** MBA, MFA, PHD
requirement: **5** orals **6** thesis
posthaste: **3** PDQ **4** ASAP, fast, soon, stat **5** apace, quick, swift **6** at once, presto, pronto, speedy **7** fleetly, quickly, rapidly, swiftly **8** directly, in a flash, in a jiffy, in no time, pell-mell, promptly, speedily **9** forthwith, hurriedly, instantly, like a shot, on the spot
post hoc: **9** afterward
post hoc, __ propter hoc: **4** ergo
posting: **4** bill **6** notice
Post-it __: **4** note
postlarval: **5** pupal
Postlethwaite: **4** Pete
postman
assignment: **5** route
challenge: **3** dog, ice **4** rain, snow **5** sleet
Postman Always Rings Twice, The
author: James M. Cain
Postman, The
author: Roger Martin du Gard
Post, Markie: **7** actress
TV: The Fall Guy, Hearts Afire, Night Court
Postmaster General's org.: **4** USPS
Post, Mike: **8** composer
song: The Rockford Files (1975) The Theme from Hill Street Blues (1981)
postnasal __: **4** drip
post office: **4** game
buy: **5** stamp
creed word: **3** nor **4** rain, snow **5** sleet
do ~ work: **4** sort **5** weigh **7** collect, deliver
machine: **5** scale
poster datum: **3** aka **5** alias **6** reward
symbol: **5** eagle
unit: **5** ounce, pound
post-office __: **3** box
Poston, Tom: **5** actor
spouse: Suzanne Pleshette
TV: Mork & Mindy, Newhart
post-op destination: **3** ICU
postpone: **4** slow, stay **5** defer, delay, remit, sit on, stall, table, waive **6** hold up, put off, retard, shelve **7** adjourn, hold off, lay over, neglect, put back, suspend **8** hold over, prorogue **10** pigeonhole, reschedule
as a deadline: **6** extend
postponement: **4** stay **5** delay **7** respite **8** abeyance, reprieve
postprandial quaff: **4** port **6** brandy **7** liqueur
post-Reformation council: **5** Trent
postscript: **6** epilog **7** codicil **8** addendum, addition, appendix, epilogue **9** afterword **10** supplement
musical ~: **4** coda
write a ~: **3** add
post-season game: **4** bowl
post-shower sight: **6** fogbow **7** rainbow
post-tax profit: **3** net
postulant: **3** nun **9** applicant
postulate: **3** law **5** axiom, claim, given, posit **6** assert, assume, hazard, theory, thesis **7** believe, opinion, premise, solicit, suppose, theorem **8** theorize **9** predicate, speculate **10** assumption, conjecture, generalize, hypothesis, presuppose, put forward
postulation: **5** claim **6** belief **8** argument **9** assertion **10** allegation, assumption, contention
posture: **3** act, sit **4** mask, mien, pose **5** guise, mince, state **6** fake it, policy, stance **7** bearing, conduct, feeling, show off **8** attitude, carriage, position, presence **9** condition, sentiment, viewpoint **10** deportment, masquerade, standpoint
have poor ~: **3** sag **5** droop, slump, stoop
posturing: **8** pretense
Post, Wilbur pal: **4** Mr. Ed
posy: **5** bloom **6** flower **7** blossom, bouquet, nosegay
portion: **4** leaf, stem **5** petal
pot: **3** jar, jug, pan **4** bank, mint, olla, pool **5** basin, belly, crock, grass, kitty, plant, stake, wager **6** kettle, vessel **7** abdomen, amphora, caldron, stomach, tankard **8** cauldron, saucepan **9** container **10** jardiniere, receptacle
booster: **3** bet **4** ante **5** stake, wager
ender: **3** pie **4** herb, hole, hook, luck, shot **5** belly, bound, latch **6** boiler, holder, hunter **7** bellied
fragment: **5** shard, sherd
gambler's ~: **5** kitty, stake
go to ~: **4** rust **8** vegetate
hot ~: **4** stew **9** casserole
item: **3** IOU **4** cash, chip **5** money
lobster ~: **4** trap
monkey ~: **4** tree
pepper ~: **4** stew
protector: **6** enamel
starter: **3** tea **4** fuss, jack, toss **5** crack, flesh, sauce, stink, stock **6** coffee, flower
start the ~: **6** ante up
take the ~: **3** win
top: **3** lid **5** cover
pot __: **4** luck, shot **5** metal, roast **6** cheese, liquor **7** sticker
pot-__: **5** au-feu
__ pot: **3** hot, mud **4** bean, fire, go to, peat **5** paint **6** pepper, smudge **7** lobster, melting
__ Pot: **3** Pol **5** Crock
potable: **4** kava **5** drink, juice **6** liquor **8** beverage, libation, vermouth **9** aqua vitae, drinkable, inebriant
make ~: **6** desalt, filter, purify **10** desalinate, desalinize
nonpotent ~: **3** ade, pop, tea **4** soda **5** juice **6** coffee **7** herb tea, soda pop
potent ~: **3** ale, gin, rum, rye **4** beer, mead, port, sake, saki, wine **5** lager, stout, vodka **6** brandy, liquor, sherry, whisky **7** liqueur, whiskey
potage: **4** soup
potash: **3** lye **6** alkali
chemically: **3** KOH
potassium: **5** metal **7** element
hydroxide: **3** KOH, lye
nitrate: **5** niter
ore: **7** sylvite
potation: **5** draft, drink, quaff **8** beverage, libation **10** intoxicant
potato: **4** carb, spud **5** carbo, tuber **6** veggie **9** vegetable
alternative: **4** rice **5** pasta
baking ~: **5** Idaho
couch ~: **5** sloth **6** loafer **9** lazybones
dish: **4** soup **5** baked, fries, salad **8** au gratin **9** home fries, scalloped **10** hash browns
emulate a couch ~: **3** lie, veg **4** laze **6** veg out **7** recline
hot ~: **5** issue **7** problem
in Spanish: **4** papa
pancake: **5** latke
part: **3** eye **4** skin
preparer: **5** parer, ricer **6** peeler
salad ingredient: **3** egg **4** mayo **6** celery, pepper **10** mayonnaise
skin: **6** jacket **9** appetizer
sweet ~: **3** yam **7** ocarina
turnover: **5** knish
potato __: **4** chip, race, skin **5** knish, salad
__ potato: **3** hot **5** baked, couch, Idaho, sweet
...potato and __ potahto: **4** I say
potato chip: **4** nosh **5** snack **7** munchie
Brit's ~: **5** crisp
feature: **5** ridge
flavor: **5** chive **6** cheese
partner: **3** dip
Potato Eaters, The: **3** oil **8** painting
artist: Vincent Van Gogh
potatoes
brand: **6** Ore-Ida
partner: **4** meat
peeling ~ perhaps: **4** on KP
portion: **5** scoop
prepare ~: **4** bake, dice, mash, pare, peel, whip **5** grate
unit: **6** bushel
__ potatoes: **5** small **6** O'Brien
potatoes au __: **6** gratin
pot-au-feu: **4** meat, stew
Potawatomi: **6** Indian **7** Amerind
potbelly: **3** gut **6** paunch **7** stomach **9** spare tire
potbelly __: **5** stove
Potbelly: **3** pig **5** swine
potboiler: **4** yarn **5** novel, story **7** fiction **9** narrative
author: **4** hack
Potemkin (1925 film)
director: Sergei Eisenstein
Potemkin __: **7** village
Potemkin mutiny site: **5** Odesa **6** Odessa
potency: **3** vim, zip **4** dint, kick, sway, thew, zing **5** brawn, force, juice, might, power, punch, sinew, thews, vigor **6** energy, muscle **7** command, control, fitness, muscles, stamina **8** capacity, dominion, efficacy, strength, vitality **9** authority, beefiness, endurance, fortitude, hardiness, huskiness, influence, intensity, puissance, stoutness, toughness **10** brawniness, brute force, capability, horsepower, mightiness, robustness, sturdiness
lacking ~: **4** weak **6** feeble
potent: **4** hale, iron, male, wiry **5** beefy, burly, hardy, hefty, hunky, husky, lusty, solid, stiff, stout, tough **6** brawny, cogent, hearty, mighty, robust, rugged, sinewy, steely, stocky, strong, sturdy, virile **7** doughty, dynamic, telling, violent **8** athletic, forceful, indurate, muscular, powerful, puissant, stalwart,

vigorous 9 Atlantean, effective, Herculean, strapping, well-built 10 able-bodied, commanding, compelling, convincing, formidable, full-bodied, impressive, persuasive, red-blooded
starter: 4 omni

potentate: 3 aga 4 agha, amir, czar, emir, king, raja, shah, tsar, tzar 5 ameer, emeer, mogul, queen, rajah, ruler 6 gerent, sultan, tyrant 7 emperor, empress, monarch, pharaoh 8 maharaja 9 maharajah, sovereign
Mideast ~: 3 aga 4 agha, amir, emir 5 ameer, emeer 6 sultan
of yore: 4 czar, shah, tsar, tzar 7 pharaoh
Punjab ~: 4 raja 5 rajah 8 maharaja 9 maharajah

potential: 5 power 6 covert, doable, future, hidden, latent, likely, viable 7 ability, budding, dormant, earthly, lurking, makings, promise 8 aptitude, capacity, credible, feasible, implicit, inherent, possible, upcoming, workable 9 concealed, embryonic, plausible, practical, quiescent, thinkable 10 achievable, attainable, capability, imaginable, unrealized
client: 8 prospect
has the ~ to: 3 can, may

potentiality: 5 power 7 ability, latency 9 potential

pother: 3 ado, bug, vex 4 flap, fret, fuss, gall, rile, stir, to-do 5 annoy, chafe, harry, pique, upset, worry 6 bother, flurry, harass, hector, hubbub, nettle, pester, ruckus, rumpus, tumult, uproar 7 disturb, provoke, trouble, turmoil 8 irritate 9 commotion 10 hullabaloo

potherb: 4 mint 5 basil, orach, plant, thyme 6 catnip, orache, savory 7 oregano 8 rosemary 9 chamomile, spearmint 10 peppermint

pothole: 3 pit, rut
locale: 4 road 7 highway 8 pavement

pothook shape: 3 ess

potion: 4 balm, brew 5 drink, tonic 6 elixir, remedy 7 arcanum, mixture, philter 8 medicine 10 medication

__ potion: 4 love

potlatch: 5 feast

potluck: 4 meal 6 social 10 fund-raiser

potluck __: 6 dinner, supper

Pot Luck
author: Émile Zola

pot metal: 5 alloy
component: 4 lead 6 copper

pot of __: 4 gold

Potok, Chaim: 6 writer
work: The Book of Lights
The Chosen
In the Beginning
My Name Is Asher Lev
The Promise

Potomac: 4 city, town 5 river
city locale: 8 Maryland
city on the ~: 10 Washington
river locale: 8 Maryland, Virginia
river to the ~: 9 Anacostia 10 Shenandoah

potpie: 9 casserole 10 frozen food
veggie: 6 carrot, celery, potato

potpourri: 3 mix 4 hash, olio, stew 5 blend, combo 6 jumble, medley 7 farrago, goulash, mélange, mixture, variety 8 mishmash, mixed bag, pastiche 9 patchwork 10 assortment, collection, cumulation, hodgepodge, miscellany, salmagundi

Potsdam: 4 city, town
locale: 7 Germany
river: 5 Havel

potsherd: 8 artifact

potshot: 4 barb, slam
take a ~: 5 snipe

potsy: 4 game 9 hopscotch

pottage: 4 soup
buyer: 4 Esau

potter: 6 trifle 7 artisan 10 mess around
at times: 5 firer 6 hunter
clay: 5 argil 6 kaolin 7 kaoline 10 terra cotta
device: 4 kiln 5 wheel
mix: 4 slip 5 glaze, paste
name meaning ~: 7 Crocker
wheel kin: 5 lathe
work at a ~'s wheel: 5 throw

Potter: 2 H.C. 5 Carol 6 Dennis, Israel, Monica 7 Beatrix

Potter, Beatrix: 6 writer 7 British
work: Jemima Puddleduck
The Roly-Poly Pudding
The Tale of Benjamin Bunny
The Tale of Peter Rabbit
The Tale of Tom Kitten

Potter, Colonel: 7 Sherman
aide: 5 Radar 7 Klinger
program: 4 MASH

pottery: 3 art 4 clay, ware 6 jasper 8 ceramics, clayware, crockery 9 porcelain, stoneware 10 terra cotta
bake ~: 4 fire
blue ~ of Holland: 4 delf 5 delft
finish: 4 slip 5 glaze
flaw: 4 nick 5 crack
fragment: 5 shard, sherd 8 artifact
Iron Age ~ of Africa: 5 Urewe
Italian ~: 6 Faenza
material: 4 clay 5 argil 6 kaolin 7 kaoline 10 terra cotta

Potts: 5 Annie, Cliff

Pottstown: 4 city
locale: 4 Penn.

Potvin, Denis
milieu: 3 ice 4 rink 5 arena
org.: 3 NHL

pou __: 3 sto

pouch: 3 bag, sac 4 poke, sack 5 purse, swell 6 kitbag, packet, pocket 7 bladder, handbag, satchel, vesicle 8 carryall, knapsack, reticule, rucksack 9 container 10 pocketbook, receptacle
contents: 4 mail

pouched
animal: 3 roo 6 possum 7 hamster, opossum, pelican 8 chipmunk, kangaroo 9 marsupial

pouf: 4 coif 5 quilt 6 hairdo 7 hassock 8 coiffure

Poughkeepsie: 4 city, town
locale: 7 New York

Pouilly-__-Loire: 3 sur

pouilly-fuissé: 4 wine

poulard: 3 hen

poule
product: 4 oeuf

Poulenc, Francis: 6 French 8 composer
contemporary: 5 Satie

poult: 4 fowl 6 turkey 7 chicken 8 pheasant

poultice: 4 balm 6 remedy 8 dressing

poultry: 3 hen 4 duck, fowl, hens, meat 5 capon, ducks, fryer, geese, goose, quail 6 pullet, turkey 7 chicken, turkeys 8 chickens, pheasant, roosters 10 Cornish hen
housing: 4 coop
part: 4 wing 5 thigh 6 breast 8 dark meat 9 drumstick, white meat
plant worker: 5 sexer
product: 3 egg
seasoning: 4 sage

pounce: 4 dive, jump, leap 5 bound, fly at, lunge, seize, surge, swoop 6 ambush, attack, snatch, spring 8 drop down, fall upon
on: 3 nab 5 catch 6 ambush, snap up, waylay 10 buttonhole

pound: 3 hit, ram 4 bang, bash, beat, cake, club, drub, drum, lash, mall, mash, maul, mill, nail, pelt, pint, slam, thud, unit 5 baste, clout, crush, drive, grind, knock, money, paste, pulse, punch, smash, smite, stamp, stomp, throb, thump, tramp, whack, whang, whomp 6 batter, beetle, buffet, cudgel, defeat, hammer, kennel, larrup, pestle, pommel, powder, pummel, squash, strike, thrash, thwack, wallop 7 clobber, lambast, pulsate, thunder, trounce 8 give it to, lambaste, levigate 9 palpitate, pulverize, triturate
British ~: 4 quid
dweller: 3 cat, cur, dog 4 mutt 5 stray 6 canine
fraction: 5 ounce
fractions: 5 pence
into: 5 teach 7 ingrain 9 brainwash 10 evangelize
metric ~: 4 kilo
sound: 3 arf, grr, mew, yip 4 bark, meow, woof, yelp
the pavements: 5 tramp 7 job-hunt

pound __: 4 cake, sign

pound-__: 7 foolish

__-pound: 4 foot, half, inch

poundage: 6 weight
extra ~: 3 fat 4 flab 9 spare tire

pounder: 6 pestle 10 pile-driver

Pounder: 3 CCH

Pound, Ezra: 4 poet
birthplace: 5 Idaho
work: Cantos

pound-foolish: 8 wasteful

pounding: 4 ache 5 thump 6 athrob

pound of __: 5 flesh

pounds: 4 heft
1000 ~: 3 kip
about 2200 ~: 5 tonne
shillings, and pence: 3 LSD
take off ~: 4 diet, lose, slim
unwanted ~: 4 flab 9 spare tire

Poundstone: 5 Paula

__ Poupon: 4 Grey

pour: 3 jet, run, tip 4 emit, flow, gush, pump, rain, roll, rush, spew, spue, teem 5 crowd, drain, flood, issue, spill, spout, storm, surge, swarm 6 course, decant, deluge, drench, effuse, lavish, shower, splash, stream, throng 7 cascade, gush out, proceed, radiate, spew out, torrent 8 inundate 9 discharge
down the drain: 5 waste
forth: 4 emit, flow, gush, shed 5 erupt 6 effuse 9 discharge
oil on: 4 calm, ease 5 allay, salve 6 defuse, pacify, smooth, soften, soothe, stroke 7 appease, assuage, mollify, placate, relieve, sweeten 8 calm down 9 untrouble 10 conciliate, smooth over
out: 4 gush, spew, vent 5 empty, spill, spurt 6 decant, effuse, unload 7 confide
starter: 4 down

pour __: 4 it on

pour __ troubled waters: 5 oil on

pourboire: 3 tip 8 gratuity

pouring: 3 wet 5 rainy 6 stormy
aid: 6 funnel
sound: 4 glug

Pour Some Sugar on Me (1988 song)
artist: Def Leppard

pousse-__: 4 café

Poussin: 7 Nicolas

pout: 4 fume, mope, moue, sulk 5 brood, frown 6 glower
starter: 3 eel 4 horn

pouter: 4 bird 6 pigeon

pouting: 5 sulky 6 sullen

POV (PBS documentary)
creator: Marc Weiss

Po Valley city: 5 Parma

poverty: 4 debt, lack, need, want 6 dearth, famine, misery, penury 7 beggary, paucity, squalor 8 exiguity, hardship, scarcity, shortage, sparsity 9 indigence, necessity, privation 10 bankruptcy, deficiency, inadequacy, insolvency, meagerness, starvation

poverty __: 4 line 5 level

poverty-stricken: 4 poor 5 broke, needy, short 6 bad off, hard up, ill off, in need, in want, shabby 7 pinched, squalid, wanting 8 badly off, bankrupt, beggarly, dirt poor, indigent, stranded, strapped 9 destitute, insolvent, miserable, moneyless, penniless, penurious 10 down and out, pauperized, straitened

Povich, Maury: 2 MC 4 host 5 emcee
spouse: Connie Chung

pow: 3 bam, bop 4 sock, wham 5 noise, punch, whack 6 kaboom
response: 3 oof

POW: 2 GI 8 internee

powder: 4 dust, film, grit, meal, snow, talc 5 crush, flour, grate, grind, pound, smash 6 crunch, makeup, reduce 7 crumble, scatter 8 cosmetic, levigate, sprinkle 9 granulate, pulverize, triturate
baking ~: 6 leaven
bath ~: 4 talc 6 talcum

container: 4 horn
glass-polishing ~: 5 ceria
lover: 5 skier
needing ~: 5 shiny
photography ~: 6 amidol
reduce to ~: 5 grind 9 pulverize
room: 2 WC 3 lav 4 bath, john 8 lavatory
starter: 3 gun
take a ~: 2 go 3 lam, run 4 blow, bolt 5 lam it, leave 6 decamp, escape 7 vamoose 8 run for it, skip town 10 make tracks
powder __: 3 boy, keg 4 blue, horn, puff, room, snow
__ powder: 4 face, soap 5 black, chili, curry, onion, take a, tooth 6 baking, talcum 7 dusting
powdered __: 4 milk 5 donut, sugar
powder puff, use a: 3 dab
powdery: 3 dry 4 fine 5 dusty, loose, mealy 6 chalky, floury, grainy, gritty, ground, milled 7 friable 8 granular 9 crumbling 10 pulverized
residue: 3 ash 4 dust
Powell: 4 Adam, Boog, Dick, Jane, Paul 5 Cecil, Colin, Jesse 7 Anthony, Eleanor, Michael, William
successor: 4 Rice
Powell, Anthony: 6 writer 7 British
work: A Dance to the Music of Time
Powell, Colin: 7 general
Powell, Dick: 5 actor
spouse: June Allyson, Joan Blondell
Powell, Eleanor: 6 dancer 7 actress
film: Born to Dance (1936)
Broadway Melody of 1936 (1935)
Broadway Melody of 1940 (1940)
Rosalie (1937)
spouse: Glenn Ford
Powell, William: 5 actor
costar: 3 Loy
film: After the Thin Man (1936)
Another Thin Man (1939)
The Great Ziegfeld (1936)
The Kennel Murder Case (1933)
The Last Command (1928)
Life With Father (1947)
Manhattan Melodrama (1934)
Mister Roberts (1955)
My Man Godfrey (1936)
The Senator Was Indiscreet (1947)
Shadow of the Thin Man (1941)
The Thin Man (1934)
The Thin Man Goes Home (1944)
Ziegfeld Follies (1946)
spouse: Carole Lombard
power: 3 arm, law, vim 4 beef, cube, dint, gift, kick, pull, rule, sway, thew 5 brawn, clout, force, juice, means, might, punch, reach, right, say-so, sinew, skill, steam, thews, title, vigor 6 agency, energy, muscle, propel, square, talent, virtue, weight 7 ability, command, faculty, fitness, freedom, license, mastery, muscles, potence, potency, prowess, regency, stamina, strings, utility, voltage 8 capacity, dominion, dynamism, efficacy, energize, exponent, hegemony, imperium, kingship, leverage, momentum, prestige, strength, violence, vitality 9 authority, beefiness, endurance, fortitude, hardiness, huskiness, influence, intensity, magnetism, potential, privilege, puissance, stoutness, supremacy, toughness 10 ascendance, ascendancy, ascendence, ascendency, brawniness, brute force, capability, competence, government, horsepower, leadership, management, mightiness, robustness, ruggedness, sturdiness
colonial ~: 5 Spain 6 France 7 England
combining form: 4 dyna- 5 dynam-
decision-making ~: 4 veto 5 say-so
ender: 4 boat 5 house 6 broker
enforcement ~: 5 teeth 8 iron hand
exercise ~: 4 rule 5 wield 6 govern
friendly ~: 4 ally
give ~ to: 7 entitle, license 9 authorize
high ~: 3 nth
in Taoism: 3 teh
magic ~: 3 hex 4 mojo 5 spell
mental ~: 4 will 7 resolve
metaphorically: 5 reins
of choice: 7 freedom, liberty
org.: 3 REA, TVA
PA ~ plant: 3 TMI
paranormal ~: 3 ESP 10 sixth sense
personal ~: 8 clutches
plant: 5 hydro
problem: 5 surge 8 blackout, brown-out
put in ~ again: 7 reelect 9 reinstate
put out of ~: 4 oust, vote 5 exile, usurp 6 depose
Roman emblem of ~: 6 fasces
run without ~: 5 coast, glide
sea ~: 4 navy 5 fleet 6 armada
second ~: 6 square
source: 3 gas, oil, sun 4 atom, elec., fuel, wind 5 motor, steam 6 engine
starter: 3 man 4 fire, will 5 brain, horse, super, water 6 candle
staying ~: 5 might, vigor 7 stamina 8 patience, strength 9 endurance, tolerance
supernatural ~: 5 magic 6 voodoo
third ~: 4 cube
to please: 5 charm 8 charisma 9 magnetism
train: 6 engine
unit: 2 hp, kw 4 watt 8 kilowatt, megawatt
up: 5 start 6 turn on
voting ~: 5 agent, proxy 8 delegate 9 franchise
water ~: 5 hydro
power __: 3 saw, set 4 base, line, pack, play, tool, trip 5 brake, drill, elite, mower, plant, train 6 broker, supply
__ power: 3 air, man, nth, sea 4 gray, grey, land, veto, will, wind 5 green, solar, stock, water, world 6 atomic, buying, candle, flower, motive, police 7 nuclear, staying
Power: 6 Tyrone
Power, __ and Politics: 5 Pasta
Power and Glory
author: Karel Capek
Powerball: 5 lotto 7 lottery
PowerBook maker: 5 Apple
power-control mechanism: 5 servo
power-driven: 8 electric 10 electrical
__-powered: 4 high
powerful: 3 big, fit 4 able, hale, high, iron, loud, wiry 5 beefy, burly, hardy, hefty, hunky, husky, lusty, nervy, solid, stiff, stout, tough, vivid 6 brawny, cogent, hearty, mighty, potent, robust, rugged, ruling, sinewy, steely, stocky, strong, sturdy, virile 7 capable, doughty, dynamic, intense, orotund, supreme, telling, violent, weighty 8 athletic, dominant, dramatic, emphatic, forceful, indurate, muscular, puissant, stalwart, striking, vigorous 9 Atlantean, effective, effectual, energetic, extremely, heavy-duty, herculean, in control, paramount, sovereign, strapping, trenchant, well-built 10 able-bodied, commanding, compelling, convincing, formidable, impressive, omnipotent, overruling, persuasive, preeminent, prevailing, privileged, red-blooded
not ~: 4 puny, weak 6 anemic, feeble
one: 4 czar, lion, tsar 5 baron, mogul, mover, nabob, titan 6 shaker 7 magnate
__-powerful: 3 all
powerhouse: 5 titan 6 dynamo 8 live wire, stalwart, tough guy
powerless: 4 puny, weak 5 at bay, frail, wimpy 6 anemic, atonic, effete, feeble, flabby, flimsy, infirm, unable 7 anaemic, fragile, unarmed, wimpish 8 delicate, helpless, pithless 9 dependant, dependent, faltering, incapable, prostrate 10 handcuffed, impuissant, unequipped, vulnerable
render ~: 2 KO 4 kayo, slug 5 unarm 7 capture
Power Lunch
genre: 4 news 8 talk show
network: 4 CNBC
Powermaster: 3 car 4 auto 6 DeSoto
Power of Good-Bye, The (1998 song)
artist: Madonna
Power of Love (1972 song)
artist: Celine Dion, Huey Lewis and the News, Joe Simon, Luther Vandross
Power of Positive Thinking, The
author: Norman Vincent Peale
Power of Words, The
author: Edgar Allan Poe
Power Politics
author: Margaret Atwood
Powers: 4 Joey, Mala 5 Hiram 6 Boothe 8 Stefanie
Powers, Austin: 3 spy 5 agent
Powers, Stefanie
spouse: Gary Lockwood
powers that be: 3 ins
Powers That Be, The
author: David Halberstam
power-tool name: 4 Skil 5 Black 6 Decker
Power to the People (1971 song)
artist: John Lennon
power train part: 4 gear
Powhatan: 5 chief
daughter: 10 Pocahontas
son-in-law: 5 Rolfe
POW information: 4 name, rank 5 ser. no.
Pow, right in the __!: 6 kisser
Powter: 5 Susan
powwow: 4 chat, meet, talk 5 forum, rally 6 confab, confer, dialog, huddle, parley 7 consult, council, meeting, palaver 8 conclave, dialogue 9 gathering, touch base 10 conference, convention, discussion, round table
hold a ~: 6 huddle, parley 7 commune, palaver 8 converse 10 deliberate
Powys, J.C.: 4 poet 5 Welsh 6 writer
work: Wolf Solent
Powys, T.F.: 6 writer 7 British
work: The Left Leg
Mr Weston's Good Wine
The Two Thieves
Unclay
pox: 6 plague
starter: 3 cow 5 small, swine 7 chicken
ppd., not: 3 COD
Pr: 4 elem. 7 element 12 praseodymium
59 for ~: 4 at. no.
PR: 9 promotion, publicity
concern: 3 rep 5 image
gimmick: 2 ad 4 gift 5 promo 6 coupon, rebate 7 freebie, premium
job: 4 hype
person: 5 agent, flack 8 promoter 9 publicist 10 spin doctor
P.R.
see Puerto Rico
__ Prabang: 5 Luang
practicable: 3 fit 5 handy, utile 6 doable, likely, useful, viable 8 feasible, possible, workable
practical: 4 sane 5 handy, of use, sober, solid, sound, utile 6 doable, earthy, likely, usable, useful, viable 7 earthly, empiric, helpful, stopgap, useable, working, worldly 8 credible, feasible, positive, possible, rational, salutary, sensible, skillful, workable, workaday 9 effective, efficient, empirical, expedient, plausible, potential, pragmatic, realistic 10 achievable, attainable, economical, functional, hard-bitten, hard-boiled, hardheaded, imaginable, profitable, reasonable, unromantic
for all ~ purposes: 8 in effect 9 virtually
having ~ value: 5 handy, utile 6 usable, useful
joke: 4 dido, hoax 5 prank, trick 7 hotfoot
joker: 3 wag 4 zany 5 cutup, scamp
practical __: 4 joke 5 nurse

practicality: 7 utility 10 horse sense
practically: 4 most, near, nigh 5 about 6 all but, almost, nearly 7 close to, morally 8 as good as, as much as, in effect, not quite, well-nigh 9 basically, in essence, in the main, just about, virtually
Practical Magic (1998 film)
cast: Sandra Bullock, Stockard Channing, Nicole Kidman, Aidan Quinn
practice: 2 do 3 ism, job, ply, use, way 4 form, hone, mode, rite, rule, wont, work 5 apply, drill, habit, study, train, trick, usage 6 action, career, custom, dry run, follow, go over, lesson, manner, method, policy, polish, praxis, pursue, repeat, ritual, system, tune-up, warmup 7 carry on, clients, fashion, iterate, observe, perform, prepare, process, routine, sharpen, workout 8 business, engage in, exercise, function, habitude, live up to, localism, patients, rehearse, training, transact, vocation 9 clientele, operation, procedure, rehearsal, shakedown, specialty, tradition, treatment, undertake 10 convention, discipline, experience, observance, profession, repetition, run through, specialize
current ~: 5 vogue 7 fashion
customary ~: 4 rite 9 tradition
diligently: 3 ply 5 exert, sweat
expel from ~: 6 disbar
out of ~: 5 rusty
prohibited ~: 4 no-no, tabu 5 taboo
__ practice: 5 choir, group 6 family 7 general, private
practiced: 3 ace 4 able, deft, neat 5 adept, crack 6 expert, versed 7 capable, skilled, veteran 8 habitual, masterly, seasoned, skillful 9 efficient, masterful, qualified 10 consummate, conversant, proficient, well-versed
Practice, The (ABC drama)
PR
cast: Lara Flynn Boyle (Helen Gamble)
Steve Harris (Eugene Young)
Camryn Manheim (Ellenor Frutt)
Dylan McDermott (Bobby Donnell)
Kelli Williams (Lindsay Dole)
role: 6 lawyer
setting: Boston
Practice What You Preach (1994 song)
artist: Barry White
practitioner, general: 2 dr., MD 3 doc 5 medic 6 doctor, medico 8 sawbones 9 physician
__ Pradesh, India: 5 Uttar
Prado: 5 Perez 6 museum
artist: 4 Goya 5 Bosch 6 Rubens, Titian 7 El Greco, Murillo, Raphael 9 Velázquez
display: 3 art 9 paintings
locale: 5 Spain 6 Madrid
Prado, Perez
nickname: The King of the Mambo
song: Cherry Pink and Apple Blossom White (1955)
praetor
superior: 5 edile
Praetorian
employer: 6 caesar 7 emperor
Praetorian __: 5 guard
pragmatic: 4 sane 5 sober, sound 6 cogent, useful 7 empiric, logical, tenable 8 analytic, coherent, methodic, rational, sensible 9 empirical, expedient, officious, practical, realistic 10 analytical, consistent, hard-bitten, hard-boiled, hardheaded, unromantic
believer: 5 deist
Prague: 4 city, town 5 Praha 7 capital
city near ~: 5 Plzen, Tabor
resident: 5 Czech
river: 6 Moldau 7 Vlatava
Prague Symphony
composer: Wolfgang Amadeus Mozart
Praia: 4 city, town 7 capital
locale: 9 Cape Verde
prairie: 5 campo, llano, plain, plane, range 6 meadow, pampas 7 lowland, pasture, steppes 9 grassland
African ~: 4 veld 5 veldt
animal: 4 deer 6 coyote, ferret, rabbit 8 antelope 10 jackrabbit
predator: 6 coyote
schooner: 5 wagon
South American ~: 5 campo, pampa 6 pampas
prairie dog: 6 animal, rodent
female: 3 sow
male: 4 boar
predator: 6 ferret
relative: *see* rodent
young: 3 pup
Prairie State: 3 Ill. 8 Illinois
Prairie, The
author: James Fenimore Cooper
praisable: 6 worthy 7 fitting 8 laudable 9 admirable, deserving, estimable, righteous 10 creditable
praise: 4 cite, clap, hail, hymn, laud, puff, rave, sing, tout 5 adore, bless, boost, cheer, cry up, éclat, ensky, exalt, extol, glory, honor, kudos, thank 6 admire, cajole, credit, esteem, eulogy, extoll, homage, honors, puff up, regard, salute, stroke, thanks 7 acclaim, adulate, applaud, approve, big hand, bow down, build up, commend, dignify, elevate, endorse, ennoble, flatter, glorify, hosanna, indorse, laurels, lay it on, lionize, ovation, plaudit, smile on, tribute, worship 8 accolade, advocate, applause, approval, citation, encomium, eulogize, flattery, good word, gush over, hand it to, plaudits, proclaim, sanctify, sanction 9 adoration, adulation, celebrate, encourage, extolment, laudation, obeisance, panegyric, pay homage, recommend, reverence, warm fuzzy 10 admiration, aggrandize, appreciate, be gracious, compliment, exaltation, give thanks, make much of, panegyrize, pay tribute, sycophancy
ender: 6 worthy
from the audience: 5 brava, bravo 6 encore 9 standing O
high ~: 4 kudo 5 kudos 8 emcomium
hymn of ~: 3 ode 4 pean 5 paean, psalm
name meaning ~: 5 Judah 8 Thaddeus
offer faint ~: 4 damn
oneself: 4 brag, crow 5 boast
opposite: 5 knock 8 belittle
overblown ~: 4 hype, plug, puff, rave 5 promo 7 puffery 9 publicity
overly: 4 gush, hype, rave
shout of ~: 7 hosanna 10 hallelujah
word of ~: 4 good
Praise Singer, The
author: Mary Renault
Praise to the End
author: Theodore Roethke
praiseworthy: 4 fine, good, nice, okay 5 great, legit, moral, noble 6 proper 7 ethical, stellar 8 all right, laudable, pleasant, pleasing, splendid, superior, virtuous 9 admirable, agreeable, estimable, excellent, exemplary, honorable, reputable, righteous, wonderful 10 acceptable, beneficial, creditable
praline: 4 nosh 5 candy, snack, sweet
ingredient: 3 nut 5 pecan, sugar 6 almond 10 brown sugar
pram: 5 buggy 7 vehicle 8 carriage
pusher: 4 nana 5 nanny 6 nannie
Pran: 4 Dith
prance: 4 jump, leap, romp, skip, step, walk 5 bound, caper, dance, frisk, mince, strut, vault, waltz 6 cavort, frolic, gambol, parade, sashay, spring 7 flounce, show off, swagger 9 have a ball
Prancer: 8 reindeer
colleague: *see* reindeer
prank: 3 gag 4 dido, game, hoax, jape, jest, joke, lark, play, quiz, trap, trim 5 antic, caper, put-on, spoof, sport, trick 6 frolic 7 hotfoot 8 escapade, mischief 9 capriccio, high jinks, horseplay, vandalism 10 shenanigan, tomfoolery
prankster: 3 wag 4 brat, zany 5 clown, cutup, joker, scamp 6 jester, rascal 8 funnyman
praseodymium: 7 element 9 rare earth
prate: 3 gab, yak, yap 4 blab, carp, chat, gush, talk 5 bleat, run on 6 babble, patter, rattle, tattle, yammer 7 baloney, chatter 8 babbling, blabbing, chitchat, idle talk, nonsense, ramble on, slipslop, talk idly, tommyrot, trumpery 9 gossiping, jabbering, table talk 10 blathering, chattering, chew the rag, yackety-yak
see also baloney
pratfall, do a: 4 slip, trip 6 topple
prattle: 3 gab, jaw, yak, yap 4 blab, chat, gush, talk 6 babble, drivel, footle, gabble, gibber, gossip, jabber, patter, rattle, speech, tattle 7 blather, blether, chatter, twaddle 8 babbling, nonsense, ramble on, rattle on 9 gibberish 10 chew the rag, vocalizing
prattler: 6 gossip 10 chatterbox, motor mouth
Pravda: 9 newspaper
cofounder: Lenin
source: 4 Tass 8 ITAR-Tass
__ Prawer Jhabvala: 4 Ruth
prawn: 6 shrimp 7 seafood 10 crustacean
praxis: 3 use 4 wont 5 habit, usage 6 custom 8 practice 10 convention
pray: 3 ask, beg, sue 4 urge 5 plead 6 adjure, appeal, cry for, invoke 7 beseech, entreat, implore, request, solicit, worship 8 call upon, petition, say grace 9 importune 10 supplicate
in Latin: 3 ora
place to ~: 5 altar 6 chapel, church, shrine, temple 8 prie-dieu 9 cathedral
__ pray: 5 let us
Pray (1990 song)
artist: M.C. Hammer
prayer: 4 plea, suit 5 chant, grace 6 appeal, litany, mantra, novena, orison, rosary 7 request, service, worship 8 devotion, entreaty, petition, rogation 9 adoration, communion 10 invocation
beads: 4 mala 6 rosary
beginning: 5 O Lord
book: 6 missal, siddur 8 breviary
Catholic ~: 3 ave 6 novena, rosary
ending: 4 amen 5 svaha
Hopi ~ stick: 4 paho
hour: 4 sext 5 lauds, nones, prime 6 matins, tierce 7 complin, vespers 8 compline
house of ~: 4 shul 5 schul, zendo 6 chapel, church, shrine, temple 8 lamasery 9 cathedral, monastery, synagogue
Islamic ~: 4 raka 5 salah, salat
liturgical ~: 3 ave 5 kyrie 6 mantra 10 invocation
meal ~: 5 grace
not a ~: 8 high-risk, hopeless 10 impossible
start of a children's ~: 4 now I
synagogue ~: 5 shema 6 Hallel
vestment: 4 wrap 5 cloak
wear: 5 robes, shawl 8 vestment
prayer __: 3 rug 4 book, flag 5 beads, plant, shawl, wheel 7 meeting, service
__ prayer: 4 say a
Prayer for Owen Meany, A
author: John Irving
prayerful: 5 pious 9 religious
prayer wheel user: 4 lama 5 geshe, tulku 6 khenpo
praying
figure: 5 orans, orant 6 orante
mantis: 3 bug 6 insect
Praying for Rain
author: Jerome Weidman
Praying for Time (1990 song)
artist: George Michael
pre-__ show: 4 game
pre-__ student: 3 law, med
__ Pré: 5 Grand
preach: 4 talk 5 orate, scold 6 advise, exhort 7 address, lecture 8 admonish, harangue, homilize, moralize, perorate, prophesy 9 exprobate, preachify, sermonize 10 evangelize

preacher: **5** padre, vicar **6** cleric, curate, divine, father, orator, parson, pastor **7** apostle **8** chaplain, minister, reverend **10** evangelist, missionary
bird: **5** vireo
degree: **3** Th.D.
spot: **5** altar **6** church
word: **4** amen
Preacher: **3** Roe
__ Preacher Man: **6** Son-of-a
Preacher's Wife, The (1996 film)
cast: Gregory Hines, Whitney Houston, Courtney B. Vance, Denzel Washington
director: Penny Marshall
Preakness: **4** race **9** horse race
competitor: **4** pony **5** horse **9** racehorse
prize: **5** purse
preamble: **5** intro, proem **6** prolog **7** opening, preface, prelude **8** exordium, foreword, prologue **9** beginning
prearrange: **3** fix, rig **5** set up **7** bespeak, reserve **10** foreordain
prearranged: **3** set **5** meant **8** intended **10** purposeful, volitional
prebendary: **6** cleric
Precambrian: **3** Era
precarious: **4** iffy **5** dicey, hairy, risky, rocky, shaky, tight **6** chancy, jiggly, loaded, touchy, tricky, unfirm, unsafe, unsure, wabbly, wobbly **7** dubious, rickety **8** delicate, doubtful, dynamite, insecure, perilous, ticklish, unstable, unsteady **9** dangerous, hazardous, on thin ice, sensitive, uncertain **10** touch-and-go, unreliable
precariousness: **4** risk **6** danger **8** jeopardy
precaution: **4** care **7** defense **8** prudence, security, wariness **9** canniness, foresight, insurance, provision, safeguard **10** discretion, protection
as a ~: **6** in case **10** just in case
precede: **4** lead **5** usher **6** forego, lead to, ring in **7** forerun, go first, predate, preface, presage **8** announce, antedate, run ahead **9** come first, go ahead of, introduce **10** anticipate, come before
precedence: **4** lead, rank **8** priority **9** advantage, immediacy, seniority **10** importance, right of way
take ~: **8** outweigh
precedent: **4** rule **5** model **6** custom **7** example **8** exemplar, instance **9** authority, criterion, foregoing
__ precedent: **4** set a
preceding: **3** ere **4** late, past **5** older, prior, supra **6** before, former **7** ahead of, earlier, leading, one-time, prior to **8** anterior, long gone, previous, until now **9** aforesaid, erstwhile, foregoing, in advance **10** heretofore
precentor: **6** cleric
precept: **3** ism, law **4** rule **5** adage, axiom, bylaw, canon, dogma, edict, maxim, moral, motto, order, tenet, truth **6** behest, belief, byword, decree, dictum, lesson, ruling, saying **7** bidding, command, dictate, formula, mandate, statute **8** aphorism, doctrine **9** direction, guideline, ordinance, principle, teachings **10** convention, ground rule, injunction, regulation
cultural ~: **5** ethic, ethos **9** moral code
preceptor: **4** guru **5** tutor **6** expert, lector, master, sensei **7** teacher **9** abecedary, principal, professor **10** instructor
pre-Christmas period: **6** Advent
precinct: **4** area, ward, zone **5** field, limit **6** region, sector, sphere **7** quarter, section **8** district, division, vicinity **10** department
worker: **3** cop **9** policeman **11** policewoman
precious: **4** cute, dear, rare, rich **5** loved **6** adored, costly, cutesy, dainty, golden, prissy, prized, valued **7** finicky, lovable, mincing **8** adorable, idolized, loveable, overnice, uncommon, valuable **9** cherished, expensive, exquisite, priceless, recherché, treasured **10** fastidious, high-priced, invaluable, sweetheart
gem: **4** opal, ruby **5** jewel, pearl, stone, topaz **7** diamond, emerald **8** sapphire
metal: **4** gold **6** silver **8** platinum
resource: **4** time **5** water **6** health
see also sweetheart
Precious... (2009 film)
cast: Mo'Nique
Precious and Few (1972 song)
artist: Climax
precipice: **4** crag, edge **5** bluff, brink, cliff, scarp **6** height **8** mountain, palisade **10** escarpment, prominence
precipitance: **4** rush **5** haste, hurry, speed **8** rapidity **10** expedition
precipitate: **4** drop, hail, hurl, rain, rash, snow, spur **5** brash, cause, fling, hasty, hurry, sleet, spark, swift, throw **6** abrupt, hasten, launch, lead to, let fly, rushed, shower, sudden **7** advance, bring on, distill, drizzle, frantic, hurried, provoke, quicken, speed up, trigger **8** catapult, dizzying, engender, expedite, headlong, heedless, previous, reckless, sediment, sprinkle **9** breakneck, foolhardy, impatient, impetuous, impulsive **10** accelerate, uncautious
heavily: **4** pour, teem **5** flood
precipitateness: **4** rush **5** haste, hurry, speed **8** rapidity **10** expedition
precipitation: **4** hail, rain, snow **5** haste, sleet, storm **7** drizzle, wetness **8** moisture, rainfall, rapidity, rashness **9** hailstorm, rainstorm
that doesn't reach the ground: **5** virga
winter ~: **4** snow **5** sleet
precipitiously: **7** in a rush **8** pell-mell **9** headfirst
precipitous: **4** rash **5** hasty, rapid, sharp, sheer, steep, swift **6** abrupt, craggy, rushed, sudden **7** cragged, hurried **8** dizzying, headlong, heedless, plunging, reckless, straight **9** impetuous, impulsive
précis: **5** brief, recap **6** aperçu, digest, report, résumé, sketch, survey **7** outline, rundown, summary **8** abstract, syllabus, synopsis **10** abridgment, compendium, literature
Precis: **3** car **4** auto **10** Mitsubishi
precise: **4** fine, just, neat, nice, true **5** clean, clear, exact, fixed, fussy, level, picky, right, rigid, short, sound, valid **6** direct, minute, proper, spot-on, strict **7** bookish, careful, correct, express, factual, finicky, graphic, limited, literal, obvious, perfect, prudish, refined, regular, specify **8** absolute, accurate, clear-cut, concrete, decisive, definite, delicate, detailed, distinct, exacting, explicit, faithful, finiking, finnicky, flawless, incisive, methodic, on the dot, readable, rigorous, specific, truthful, unerring **9** definable, errorless, graphical, sensitive, stringent **10** definitive, fastidious, impeccable, inflexible, methodical, meticulous, on the money, particular, scientific, scrupulous, systematic, unmistaken, well-marked
don't be ~: **5** guess, round **8** estimate
precisely: **3** oui, pat **4** just, okay, to a T **5** good-o, plumb, quite, right, roger, sharp, smack, spang, uh-huh **6** agreed, dead-on, gladly, good-oh, indeed, just so, rather, really, righto, to a tee, yowzah **7** exactly, go ahead, indeedy, mais oui, quite so, right on, ten-four **8** all right, as you say, directly, smack-dab, squarely, thumbs up, verbatim, very well **9** be my guest, carefully, correctly, darn right, expressly, just right, literally, literatim, on the nose, sure thing, you said it **10** accurately, definitely, delicately, sure enough, that's right, unerringly
see also of course
precision: **4** care **5** rigor, truth **7** clarity **8** accuracy, fidelity, veracity **9** attention, clockwork, exactness **10** exactitude, factuality, perfection, refinement
preclude: **3** bar **4** curb, foil, omit, veto **5** avert, check, debar, deter **6** enjoin, forbid, hamper, hinder, impede, thwart **7** exclude, forfend, head off, inhibit, obviate, prevent, rule out, ward off **8** forefend, prohibit, stave off **9** foreclose, forestall, frustrate, interdict
precocious: **3** apt **5** early, quick, smart **6** bright, gifted, mature **7** forward **8** advanced, talented **9** brilliant **10** beforehand
precognition: **3** ESP **4** vibe **5** hunch, vibes **8** prophecy **9** intuition
pre-college: **4** el-hi
pre-Columbian: **3** old **7** ancient
civilization: **4** Inca, Maya **5** Aztec, Olmec **6** Mixtec **7** Zapotec
preconception: **4** bias, tilt **5** slant **6** notion **7** bigotry, leaning **8** delusion, illusion **9** prejudice **10** partiality
precondition: **2** if **4** must **9** condition, determine, necessity, requisite
precursor: **4** sign **6** herald, leader **7** symptom **8** ancestor, forebear, original, vanguard **9** harbinger, messenger, prototype **10** antecedent, forebearer, forefather, forerunner, progenitor
precursory: **10** antecedent
predacious: **6** fierce **8** ravaging **9** ferocious, on the hunt, vulturous **10** aggressive
predate: **7** precede **8** antecede
predating life, in geology: **5** azoic
predator: **3** cat, man, owl **4** hawk, lion, mako, orca, puma, wolf **5** dingo, eagle, harpy, human, shark, tiger **6** coyote, hunter **7** brigand, panther **9** carnivore, meat-eater, polar bear **10** highwayman
move like a ~: **5** prowl
nocturnal ~: **3** owl
quarry: **4** prey
Predator (1987 film)
cast: Arnold Schwarzenegger, Carl Weathers
Predators
home: **9** Nashville
org.: **3** NHL
rival: ***see*** hockey team
sport: **6** hockey
Predators, The
author: Harold Robbins
predatory: **6** greedy, lupine **7** wolfish **8** ravaging, ravening, ravenous, thieving, thievish **9** ferocious, marauding, on the hunt, pillaging, piratical, rapacious, raptorial, voracious, vulturine, vulturous **10** aggressive, plundering
predecessor: **6** father, mother **8** forebear **9** precursor
predestination: **3** lot **4** doom, fate **5** karma **6** kismet **7** fortune
predestine: **4** doom, fate **9** determine, preordain **10** foreordain
predestined: **5** fated **6** doomed **7** certain
predetermine: **3** rig
predetermined: **3** set **5** fated, fixed **7** decided, planned **8** destined **10** deliberate
predicament: **3** fix, jam, rub **4** bind, hole, knot, mess, node, pass, soup, spot, stew **5** event, pinch, state **6** clutch, corner, crisis, matter, muddle, pickle, plight, scrape, strait **7** dilemma, impasse, problem, rough go, trouble **8** exigence, exigency, hardship, headache, hot water, juncture, position, quagmire, quandary **9** deep water, imbroglio
Predicament, A
author: Edgar Allan Poe
predicate: **4** aver, base, rest **5** imply **6** affirm, assert **7** bespeak, connote, declare, express, profess, signify, suggest **8** indicate, intimate, maintain, proclaim, put forth, set forth **9** establish, postulate, represent
part: **4** verb
predict: **4** call, warn **5** augur, guess **6** divine, figure, gather, size up **7** betoken, foresee, portend, presage, project, surmise **8** envisage, envision, estimate, forebode,

forecast, foreshow, foretell, prophesy, soothsay, theorize 9 adumbrate, see coming 10 anticipate, conjecture, foreshadow, have a hunch, vaticinate

predictability: 8 sameness

predictable: 4 sure 5 usual 6 likely 7 certain 8 expected, foreseen, probable, reliable, sure-fire

prediction: 3 tip 4 omen, sign 5 guess, hunch 6 augury, oracle, tipoff 7 portent, warning 8 estimate, forecast, prophecy 9 horoscope, indicator, palmistry, prognosis 10 divination, expectancy, foreboding

weather ~: 3 dry 4 fair, gale, hail, rain, snow 5 clear, gusty, rainy, sleet, storm, sunny, windy 6 breezy, cloudy 7 tornado 8 overcast

predictor: 4 omen, seer, sign 5 augur, sibyl 6 shaman 7 diviner, portent, prophet 9 harbinger 10 forecaster, soothsayer

predilection: 4 bent; bias, dish 5 fancy, slant, taste 6 liking, relish 7 faculty, leaning 8 appetite, aptitude, attitude, cup of tea, druthers, fondness, penchant, tendency, weakness 9 proneness, sentiment 10 partiality, proclivity, propensity

predispose: 4 bend, bias, sway 5 prime 6 affect, govern, induce, prompt 7 dispose, impress, incline, inspire, prepare 8 activate, motivate 9 determine, encourage, influence, prejudice, stimulate

predisposed: 5 prone, ready 6 biased, liable, likely 7 partial, subject, tending, willing 8 amenable, inclined, prepared 9 agreeable

predisposition: 4 bent, bias 5 slant 6 liking 7 leaning 8 instinct, penchant, tendency, weakness 9 proneness

predominance: 4 sway 5 power 9 supremacy

predominant: 4 best, main, star 5 chief, first, major, prime 6 ruling, staple 7 central, leading, primary, rampant, supreme, weighty 8 forceful, powerful, reigning, superior 9 ascendant, governing, important, paramount, prevalent, principal, prominent, sovereign, uppermost

part: 4 bulk 8 majority 9 plurality 10 lion's share

predominantly: 6 mainly, mostly 7 largely, overall 9 primarily

predominate: 4 rule 5 reign 6 govern 7 command, prevail, surpass 8 hold sway, outweigh, overrule 9 sovereign

pre-election event: 4 poll 6 debate 8 campaign 10 convention

preemie: 4 baby 6 infant

preeminence: 4 fame 6 renown 8 dominion, prestige, priority 9 supremacy 10 precedence

preeminent: 3 top 4 A-one, arch, best, head, main, star, tops 5 chief, famed, first, grand, major, noble, noted 6 famous, ruling, utmost 7 honored, in front, leading, stellar, supreme 8 absolute, cardinal, dominant, foremost, greatest, peerless, powerful, renowned, superior, towering, ultimate 9 governing, important, matchless, number one, paramount, principal, prominent, topflight, unequaled, unrivaled, uppermost, virtuosic, worthiest 10 celebrated, consummate, unequalled, unrivalled

preeminently: 8 above all

preempt: 4 bump, take 5 co-opt, seize, usurp 6 assume, obtain 7 acquire 8 arrogate, take over 10 anticipate, commandeer, confiscate

preempted: 5 not on

preemptive __: 6 strike

preen: 5 gloat, groom, pride, primp, prink 6 doll up, dude up 7 dress up, gussy up, swank up 8 titivate 9 tittivate

preener: 3 fop 4 bird 5 dandy 7 peacock

pre-engage: 4 book 7 charter, reserve

preening, prone to: 4 smug, vain 5 proud 9 conceited 10 complacent

pre-entrée course: 4 soup 5 salad 9 appetizer

preestablished: 3 set 5 fixed

preexisting: 5 prior

preface: 5 begin, intro, proem, usher 6 launch, prolog 7 precede, prelude 8 commence, exordium, foreword, lead into, overture, preamble, prologue 9 beginning, introduce

prefer: 3 opt, put 4 cull, lean, like, love, pick, take, want 5 adopt, elect, fancy, favor, go for 6 choose, desire, opt for, select 7 elevate, fix upon 9 single out

charges: 3 sue 9 prosecute

preferable: 6 better 8 superior

preferably: 6 rather, sooner 7 instead 10 just as soon

preference: 4 bent, bias, pick, will 5 fancy, taste, voice 6 choice, desire, liking, option 7 leaning 8 cup of tea, decision, druthers, favorite, fondness, pleasure, priority, volition 9 advantage, proneness, selection, seniority 10 favoritism, propensity

preferment: 8 benefice 9 elevation

preferred: 3 pet 5 liked, named, taken 6 choice, chosen, culled, picked, select 7 elected, fancied, favored, popular 8 approved, endorsed, favorite, selected, set apart, superior 10 fair-haired, handpicked

group: 5 A-list, elite

item: 4 fave

prefigure: 8 foreshow 9 adumbrate, foretoken 10 foreshadow

pre-film feature: 5 short

prefixes (by meaning)

about: 4 peri-

above: 3 sur- 5 hyper-, super-, supra-

absence: 3 dis-, non-

accurate: 4 docu-

across: 3 dia- 5 trans-

adverse: 7 counter-

advocating: 3 pro-

after: 3 epi- 4 meta-, post- 5 infra-

again: 3 ana-

against: 3 cat- 4 anti-, cata-, cath- 6 contra-

all: 4 omni-

alone: 4 mono-

among: 5 inter-

around: 4 peri- 6 circum-

away: 3 apo-

backward: 3 ana- 5 retro-

bad: 3 dys-, mal-

before: 3 pre-, pro- 4 ante-, fore-

behind: 4 meta-, post- 5 retro-

below: 3 sub- 5 infra-, under- 6 contra-

beneath: 4 hypo- 5 under-

beside: 4 para-

besides: 3 epi-

between: 5 inter-

beyond: 3 out- 4 meta-, para- 5 extra-, hyper-, trans-, ultra- 6 preter-

billion: 4 giga-

both: 4 ambi- 5 amphi-

center: 3 mid-

Chinese: 4 Sino-

computer: 5 cyber-

contrary: 5 retro- 7 counter-

culture: 5 ethno-

double: 3 twi-

down: 3 cat- 4 cata-, cath-, hypo-

during: 3 dia- 5 intra-

earlier: 3 pre-, pro- 4 ante-, fore-

earth: 3 geo-

eight: 4 octa-, octo-

English: 5 Anglo-

environment: 3 eco-

equal: 3 iso-

Europe: 4 Euro-

excessive: 3 sur- 5 hyper-

excessively: 4 over- 5 ultra-

exclude: 3 dis-, for-

extra: 5 super-

fail: 3 for-

false: 6 pseudo-

farming: 4 agri-

Finnish: 5 Finno-

first: 5 archi-, proto-

fluorine: 6 fluoro-

foremost: 5 proto-

four: 5 tetra- 6 quadri-

French: 6 Franco-

front: 4 fore-

great: 4 maxi- 5 macro-

half: 4 demi-, hemi-, semi-

heat: 6 thermo-

higher: 5 super-, supra-

hundred: 5 centi-, hecto-

ill: 3 dys-, mal-, mis-

incorrect: 3 mis-

into: 5 intro-

inward: 5 intro-

itself: 4 self-

jointly: 3 col-, com-, con-

large: 4 maxi- 5 macro-

later: 4 meta-, post- 5 infra-

lesser: 5 under-

life: 3 bio-

light: 5 photo-

like: 3 sym-, syn-

long: 5 macro-

lower: 3 sub- 5 infra-

machine: 7 mechano-

many: 4 poly- 5 multi-

million: 4 mega-

modified: 3 neo-

more: 5 super-

much: 4 poly-

mutual: 5 inter-

nature: 3 eco-

near: 3 epi- 4 peri-, pros-

nearer: 3 cis-

nerve: 5 neuro-

new: 3 neo-

not: 3 dis-, non-

off: 3 apo-

oil: 5 petro-

omit: 3 for-

one: 3 uni- 4 mono-

one and a half: 6 sesqui-

on this side: 3 cis-

opposite: 3 dis- 4 anti- 7 counter-

outside: 5 extra-

outward: 5 extro-

over: 3 epi-, sur- 5 hyper-, super-

past: 4 para- 6 preter-

principal: 5 archi-

prior: 3 pre-, pro- 4 ante-

prohibit: 3 for-

quadrillionth: 5 femto-

quintillionth: 4 atto-

race: 5 ethno-

recent: 3 neo-

reciprocal: 5 inter-

related by remarriage: 4 step-

resembling: 5 quasi-

reverse: 3 dis-, non-

round: 4 peri- 6 circum-

same: 4 auto-, equi-

secondary: 3 sub-

self: 4 auto-

separate: 3 apo-

seven: 5 hepta-, septi-

since: 3 cis-

single: 4 mono-

six: 4 hexa-

small: 4 mini- 5 micro-

society: 5 socio-

solid: 6 stereo-

stars: 5 astro-

supporting: 3 pro-

surpass: 3 out-

surround: 6 circum-

ten: 4 deca-, deka-

tenth: 4 deci-

thoroughly: 3 per-

thousand: 4 kilo-

thousandth: 5 milli-

three: 3 tri-

through: 3 dia-, per- 5 trans-

together: 3 col-, com-, con-, sym-, syn-

too: 4 over-

toward: 4 pros-

transcending: 5 ultra-

true: 4 docu-

two: 3 twi- 5 amphi-

under: 3 sub- 4 hypo-

underneath: 5 intra-

unreal: 6 pseudo-

upon: 3 epi-

upward: 3 ana-

water: 4 aqua- 5 hydro-

with: 3 col-, com-, con-, sym-, syn-

within: 5 infra-, intra-, intro-

wrong: 3 mis-

wrongful: 3 mal-

see also combining forms

prefixes (by root)

agri-: 7 farming

ambi-: 4 both

amphi-: 3 two 4 both

ana-: 5 again 6 upward 8 backward

Anglo-: **7** English
ante-: **5** prior **6** before **7** earlier
anti-: **7** against **8** opposite
apo-: **3** off **4** away **8** separate
aqua-: **5** water
archi-: **5** first **9** principal
astro-: **5** stars
auto-: **4** same, self
bio-: **4** life
cat-: **4** down **7** against
cata-: **4** down **7** against
cath-: **4** down **7** against
centi-: **7** hundred
circum-: **5** round **6** around **8** surround
cis-: **5** since **6** nearer
col-: **4** with **7** jointly **8** together
com-: **4** with **7** jointly **8** together
con-: **4** with **7** jointly **8** together
contra-: **5** below **7** against
counter-: **7** adverse **8** contrary, opposite
cyber-: **8** computer
deca-: **3** ten
deci-: **5** tenth
deka-: **3** ten
demi-: **4** half
dia-: **6** across, during **7** through
dis-: **3** not **7** absence, exclude, reverse **8** opposite
docu-: **4** true **8** accurate
dys-: **3** bad, ill
eco-: **6** nature
epi-: **4** near, over, upon **5** after **7** besides
equi-: **4** same
ethno-: **4** race **7** culture
extra-: **6** beyond **7** outside
extro-: **7** outward
for-: **4** fail, omit **7** exclude **8** prohibit
fore-: **5** front **6** before **7** earlier
Franco-: **6** French
geo-: **5** earth
giga-: **7** billion
hecto-: **7** hundred
hemi-: **4** half
hepta-: **5** seven
hexa-: **3** six
hydro-: **5** water
hyper-: **4** over **5** above **6** beyond **9** excessive
hypo-: **4** down **5** under **7** beneath
infra-: **5** after, below, later, lower **6** within
inter-: **5** among **6** mutual **7** between **10** reciprocal
intra-: **6** during, within **10** underneath
intro-: **4** into **6** inward, within
iso-: **5** equal
kilo-: **8** thousand
macro-: **4** long **5** great, large
mal-: **3** bad, ill **8** wrongful
maxi-: **5** great, large
mechano-: **7** machine
mega-: **7** million
meta-: **5** after, later **6** behind, beyond
meth-: **6** methyl
micro-: **5** small
mid-: **6** center
milli-: **10** thousandth
mini-: **5** small
mis-: **3** ill **5** wrong **9** incorrect
mono-: **3** one **5** alone **6** single
multi-: **4** many
neo-: **3** new **6** recent **8** modified
neuro-: **5** nerve
non-: **3** not **7** absence, reverse
nucleo-: **7** nucleus
octa-: **5** eight
octo-: **5** eight
omni-: **3** all
out-: **6** beyond **7** surpass
over-: **3** too
para-: **4** past **6** beside, beyond
per-: **7** through **10** thoroughly
peri-: **4** near **5** about, round **6** around
petro-: **3** oil
photo-: **5** light
poly-: **4** many, much
post-: **5** after, later **6** behind
pre-: **5** prior **6** before **7** earlier
preter-: **4** past **6** beyond
pro-: **5** prior **6** before **7** earlier **10** advocating, supporting
pros-: **4** near **6** toward
proto-: **5** first **8** foremost
pseudo-: **5** false **6** unreal
quadri-: **4** four
quasi-: **10** resembling
retro-: **6** behind **8** backward, contrary
semi-: **4** half
septi-: **5** seven
Sino-: **7** Chinese
socio-: **7** society
stereo-: **5** solid
sub-: **5** below, lower, under **9** secondary
sulfo-: **6** sulfur
super-: **4** more, over **5** above, extra **6** higher
supra-: **5** above **6** higher
sur-: **4** over **5** above **9** excessive
sym-: **4** like, with **8** together
syn-: **4** like, with **8** together
tetra-: **4** four
thermo-: **4** heat
trans-: **6** across, beyond **7** through
tri-: **5** three
turbo-: **7** turbine
twi-: **3** two **6** double
ultra-: **6** beyond
under-: **5** below **6** lesser **7** beneath
uni-: **3** one
pre-game __: **4** show
pregnancy: **9** gestation, gravidity
pregnant: **6** gravid **7** pivotal **8** critical, decisive, enceinte, eventful **9** expectant, expecting, important, momentous, with child **10** meaningful
Prego: **10** pasta sauce
competitor: **4** Ragú **6** Prince **8** Classico **10** Newman's Own **11** Aunt Millie's
prehistoric: **7** ancient, antique **8** primeval **9** primaeval
axe head: **4** Celt
discovery: **4** fire
dwelling: **4** cave
Great Plains culture: **6** Folsom
invention: **5** wheel
shelter: **4** abri
stone tower: **6** chulpa **7** chullpa
tool: **3** axe **4** adze **5** burin **6** eolith
pre-holiday night: **3** eve
pre-Inca culture: **5** Chimu
preindication: **4** omen, sign **6** herald
pre-intermission period: **4** Act I **5** Act II
prejudge: **8** misjudge **9** prejudice
prejudice: **4** bias, harm, hurt, skew, sway **5** slant, spoil **6** ageism, damage, enmity, hinder, impair, injure, poison **7** bigotry, distort, incline, mindset **8** aversion, jaundice, prejudge **9** animosity, antipathy, detriment, influence, injustice **10** chauvinism, compromise, disservice, fanaticism, favoritism, inequality, narrowness, partiality, predispose, unfairness, unjustness
prejudiced: **6** biased, narrow, unfair, unjust **7** bigoted, insular, partial **8** one-sided, partisan **9** arbitrary, fanatical, jaundiced, parochial **10** interested, intolerant
Prejudices
author: H.L. Mencken
prejudicial: **6** biased, unjust **7** bigoted, harmful, hurtful **8** damaging **9** injurious
prelacy: **3** see **6** clergy **7** diocese **9** bishopric **10** episcopate
prelate: **4** pope **6** bishop, cleric **7** pontiff **8** cardinal, minister **10** archbishop
headdress: **5** miter
tribunal: **4** rota
pre-law exam: **4** LSAT
prelection: **4** talk **7** lecture **9** discourse
prelim: **5** event, intro, trial **6** lead-in
preliminary: **4** test **5** basic, first, pilot, prior, rough, trial **7** initial, opening, prelude, sketchy **9** beginning, elemental, preceding, prefatory, requisite
race: **4** heat **5** trial
text: **5** draft
Prell: **7** shampoo
competitor: **4** Flex, Pert **5** Suave, Wella **7** Finesse, Pantene
Prelog, Vladimir: **7** chemist **8** Nobelist **11** Yugoslavian
prelude: **5** intro, music, proem, start **6** prolog **7** preface **8** exordium, foreword, overture, preamble, prologue **9** beginning
Prelude: **3** car **4** auto **5** Honda
__ Préludes: **3** Les
Prelude to a Kiss (1992 film)
cast: Alec Baldwin, Kathy Bates, Ned Beatty, Meg Ryan
pre-marriage: **3** née
premature: **4** rash **5** early, hasty **6** unripe **7** forward, too soon **8** abortive, oversoon, previous, too early, untimely **9** overhasty, unfledged **10** half-cocked
Premature Burial, The
author: Edgar Allan Poe
prematurely: **5** early, short **7** betimes, too soon **8** too early **9** in advance **10** beforehand
premaxilla: **4** bone
locale: **3** jaw
Prem Chand: **6** Indian, writer
work: The Gift of a Cow
premed class: **4** anat., chem. **7** anatomy **9** chemistry
exam: **4** MCAT
premeditated: **5** fixed, meant, set-up **6** wilful **7** laid-out, planned, plotted, studied, willful **8** intended **9** contrived, voluntary **10** deliberate, purposeful, volitional
premier: **4** head, main **5** chief, first, prime **6** top dog **7** highest, initial, leading, opening, primary **8** champion, earliest, foremost, headmost, minister, official **9** beginning, inaugural, paramount, principal, topflight
Premier __: **3** Cru
premiere: **4** lead **5** debut **7** opening **9** beginning **10** first night
__ premiere: **5** world
Preminger, Otto: **8** director
brother: **4** Ingo
film: Advise & Consent (1962)
Anatomy of a Murder (1959)
Bonjour Tristesse (1958)
Carmen Jones (1954)
The Court-Martial of Billy Mitchell (1955)
Exodus (1960)
Forever Amber (1947)
Laura (1944)
The Man With the Golden Arm (1955)
The Pied Piper (1942)
Porgy and Bess (1959)
Stalag 17 (1953)
Such Good Friends (1971)
Where the Sidewalk Ends (1950)
Whirlpool (1949)
premise: **5** basis, given, posit, terms **6** ground, theory, thesis **7** grounds, thought **8** argument **9** assertion, postulate, reasoning **10** assumption, hypothesis
logical ~: **5** lemma
premises: **4** site **5** scene **6** bounds **7** grounds **8** property, vicinity
force off the ~: **4** boot, oust **5** evict
premium: **3** fee, gas **4** gift, perk, plum **5** bonus, extra, price, prize, value **6** bounty, carrot, costly, reward, select **7** freebee, freebie, payment, pension, subsidy **8** dividend, gasoline, giveaway, splendid, superior **9** excellent, unrivaled **10** perquisite, unrivalled
at a ~: **4** dear, high, rare **5** pricy, steep **6** costly, pricey, scarce **8** in demand, uncommon **9** expensive **10** exorbitant, high-priced, overpriced
currency ~: **4** agio
pay a ~ for: **6** ensure, insure
__ premium: **3** at a
premolar: **5** tooth
neighbor: **6** canine
premonition: **4** omen, sign **5** hunch, sense, vibes **7** feeling, inkling, portent, presage, warning **9** intuition, misgiving **10** foreboding
Prendergast school: **6** Ashcan
prenomen: **4** name
Prentiss, Paula: **7** actress
spouse: Richard Benjamin
prenup: **8** contract **9** agreement
preoccupation: **5** mania, thing **6** fetich, fetish, hang-up **8** fixation **9** immersion, obsession
preoccupied: **4** busy, lost, rapt **6** intent **7** bemused, engaged, faraway, pensive, unaware **8** absorbed, heedless, immersed, obsessed **9** engrossed, forgetful, oblivious, wrapped-up **10** distracted

preoccupy: 5 rivet 6 absorb, bemuse, divert, engage, fixate, obsess, occupy 7 consume, engross, enthral, immerse, inthral 8 distract, enthrall, inthrall

preordain: 3 fix, set 4 doom 5 impel, judge 6 choose, decide 7 destine, dictate, specify 8 identify 9 determine, establish 10 predestine

preordained: 5 fated 7 decided 8 destined

pre-owned: 4 used 6 resold 10 hand-me-down, secondhand
not ~: 3 new

prep: 5 groom, ready 6 get set, warm-up 8 get ready, rehearse 9 make ready, rehearsal
British ~ school: 4 Eton
school: 7 academy
school attire: 6 blazer

prepaid, not: 3 COD

preparation: 4 plan 5 basis, study 6 lotion 7 build-up, measure, mixture, prelude, workout 8 homework, lead time, medicine, practice, training 9 alertness, decoction, education, foresight, provision, readiness, rehearsal, safeguard

preparatory: 5 basic

prepare: 2 do 3 arm, fix, set 4 cook, gear, gird, make, plan, till, warm, warn 5 adapt, brace, coach, draft, endow, equip, frame, groom, hatch, learn, prime, ready, sauté, set up, shape, teach, train 6 adjust, devise, draw up, fill in, fit out, gear up, get set, ground, make up, outfit, school, season, supply, warm up 7 arrange, break in, build up, concoct, develop, dispose, fashion, fortify, furnish, look for, process, provide, psych up, qualify 8 assemble, contrive, get ready, mobilize, practice 9 condition, construct, fabricate, formulate 10 anticipate, predispose, square away, strengthen
in advance: 4 plan 7 arrange, charter, reserve

prepared: 3 fit, set 4 able, ripe, up on 5 fixed, handy, ready, set-up, wired 6 all set, primed, rigged 7 adapted, groomed, in order, on guard, planned, willing 8 adjusted, arranged, disposed, educated, inclined, skillful, watchful 9 available, psyched-up, qualified, rehearsed 10 accustomed

__-prepared: 3 ill 4 well

prepayment: 7 advance, deposit

preplanned: 5 meant 6 wilful 7 willful 9 voluntary 10 purposeful, volitional

Prepon: 5 Laura

preponderance: 4 bulk, glut, mass, most 6 excess 8 majority, plethora 9 plurality, supremacy 10 lion's share

preponderant: 6 ruling 8 dominant 9 paramount, prevalent, sovereign

preposition: 3 à la, bar, ere, for, fro, o'er, off, out, per, 'til, via 4 amid, as of, as to, atop, fore, in re, into, less, like, near, onto, over, pace, past, sans, save, than, till, unto, upon, word 5 about, above, after, aloft, along, among, après, midst, neath, since, under, until 6 across, amidst, mongst 7 amongst
poetic ~: 3 e'en, ere, o'er 5 neath

prepossessing: 4 nice 6 lovely, taking 7 likable, winsome 8 alluring, charming, engaging, fetching, handsome, magnetic, pleasant, pleasing, striking 9 appealing, beautiful, beguiling 10 attractive, bewitching, enchanting, impressive

preposterous: 3 mad 4 rich, tall, wild 5 balmy, goofy, inane, outré, sappy, silly, thick, wacky 6 absurd, far-out, whacky 7 asinine, bizarre, extreme, fatuous, foolish, too much 8 cockeyed, shocking 9 fantastic, laughable, ludicrous, monstrous, senseless, unheard-of 10 irrational, outrageous, ridiculous

preppie
parent: 5 mater, pater
wear: 5 tweed 6 blazer

prepupal phase: 5 larva

prerecord: 4 tape

pre-release software version: 4 beta

prerequisite: 4 must, need 5 state, vital 8 demanded, required 9 called for, de rigueur, essential, mandatory, necessary, necessity, provision, requisite 10 imperative, sine qua non

prerogative: 3 due 5 claim, droit, place, power, right, title 6 choice, option 7 freedom, liberty, warrant 8 immunity 9 advantage, authority, exemption, privilege
presidential ~: 4 veto

pres.
see president

presage: 4 bode, lead, mean, omen, sign, warn 5 augur, token 6 herald, threat 7 auspice, betoken, point to, portend, portent, precede, predict, promise, signify, warning 8 antecede, forebode, forecast, foreshow, foretell, forewarn, prophesy, threaten 9 adumbrate, foretoken, harbinger, introduce 10 come before, foreboding, foreshadow, indication, vaticinate

presbyter: 5 elder

preschooler: 3 kid, tot 9 youngster

prescience: 6 vision 9 foresight

prescient: 7 fatidic 8 oracular 9 farseeing, prophetic, vaticinal 10 farsighted

Prescott: 4 city, town
locale: 7 Arizona

prescribe: 3 set 4 bind, rule 5 enact, limit, order, treat 6 advise, assign, decree, direct, enjoin, impose, ordain 7 appoint, command, dictate, lay down, require, specify 8 instruct, proclaim 9 designate, establish, institute, legislate, recommend, stipulate

prescribed: 3 set 5 legal 6 formal 8 required 9 requisite 10 inevitable
amount: 4 dose
not ~: 3 OTC

prescript: 4 writ 9 ordinance 10 regulation

prescription: 3 law 4 dose, drug, rule 5 edict 6 decree, recipe, remedy 7 formula, mixture 8 medicine 9 direction, ordinance, treatment
abbr.: 2 cc. 3 alb., b.d.s., bib., cib., cuj., d.t.d., ead., gtt., liq., pil., p.r.n., q.i.d, Sig., t.d.s., t.i.d., ung., vin. 4 agit., coch., elix., ferv., filt., garg., quat., quor., trid., ungt. 5 calef., emuls., qq. hor., quinq., utend.
data: 4 dose 6 dosage 10 expiration
org.: 3 FDA

prescriptions
four times a day, in ~: 3 q.i.d.
honey, in ~: 3 mel
shake, in ~: 4 agit.
such, in ~: 3 tal.
the same, in ~: 3 ead.
three times a day, in ~: 3 t.i.d.

presence: 3 air, set 4 aura, ease, look, mien, wits 5 front, ghost, midst, poise, shade 6 entity, manner, shadow, spirit, troops, ubiety, wraith 7 bearing, charism, company, fantasm, posture, reality, specter 8 calmness, carriage, charisma, demeanor, nearness, phantasm, ubiquity, vitality 9 closeness, composure, existence, life force, occupancy, proximity, sangfroid 10 apparition, appearance, attendance, sedateness
in the ~ of: 6 before
of mind: 5 poise 6 aplomb 8 calmness 9 alertness, composure, sangfroid, stability

presence of __: 4 mind

present: 3 lay, now, put 4 gift, give, hand, here, lend, look, pose, show, time 5 award, favor, grant, in use, lay on, nonce, offer, pitch, put on, serve, stage, stake, state, there, today, voice 6 accord, at hand, at home, bestow, confer, donate, extant, extend, goodie, hand in, kick in, modern, nearby, on deck, on hand, relate, render, submit, tender, unfold, with us 7 current, declare, deliver, display, drop off, entrust, exhibit, expound, going on, handout, hold out, intrust, largess, on board, produce, proffer, propose, provide, recount, roll out, trot out 8 acquaint, donation, gratuity, hand over, largesse, nominate, nowadays, offering, put forth, up-to-date 9 attending, endowment, immediate, introduce, latter-day, on-the-spot, time being 10 contribute, promulgate, put forward
a case: 5 argue
arms: 6 salute
at ~: 3 now 5 today 7 already 8 promptly, right now, right off 9 forthwith, presently, right away 10 here and now, this minute
in its ~ state: 4 as is 6 as it is
itself: 5 occur 6 happen 7 develop
not ~: 4 away, gone 6 absent 9 elsewhere
prepare a ~: 4 wrap 8 decorate
starter: 4 omni
topper: 3 bow 6 ribbon
up to the ~: 5 as yet, so far 6 to date

present __: 4 arms 5 tense 7 perfect

present-__: 3 day

presentable: 2 OK 3 fit 4 okay, so-so 6 decent, not bad 8 adequate, all right, becoming, passable, suitable 9 tolerable 10 acceptable, good enough
make ~: 4 dust, tidy 5 clean, groom, sweep 6 neaten

presentation: 3 act 4 face, show 5 award, debut, offer, pitch 7 display, exhibit, present, program, recital, staging 8 bestowal, delivery, donation, offering, overture, proposal 9 coming out, conferral, launching, reception, rendition, statement
end a ~: 5 recap, sum up 9 summarize

present-day: 6 modern, recent 7 current

presentiment: 4 fear, sign 5 hunch, qualm, sense, vibes, worry 7 feeling, portent, presage 8 mistrust 9 intuition, misgiving 10 foreboding

Present Indicative
author: Noël Coward

presently: 3 now 4 anon, nigh, soon 5 today 6 at once 7 by and by, shortly 8 directly, hereupon, nowadays, promptly, right now, right off 9 following, forthwith, in a minute, in a moment, right away 10 at this time, before long, here and now, in good time, this minute, ultimately

preservation: 4 care 6 curing, saving, upkeep 7 canning, defense, tanning 8 freezing, pickling 9 salvation, upholding 10 conserving, protection

__-preservation: 4 self

preservative: 3 BHA, BHT 4 agar, EDTA, salt 5 brine, sugar 8 agar-agar

preserve: 3 can, dry, tin 4 corn, cure, jerk, keep, park, salt, save 5 guard, lay up, put up, smoke, souse, store 6 bottle, bronze, defend, encase, freeze, incase, keep up, kipper, pickle, record, refuge, rescue, retain, season, secure, shield, uphold 7 care for, mummify, process, protect, shelter, sustain 8 conserve, continue, maintain, mothball 9 dehydrate, safeguard, sanctuary, stabilize 10 perpetuate, protection
again: 5 recan
fodder: 6 ensile
nature ~: 4 park 9 sanctuary
veggies: 3 can, dry, ice 4 corn 5 frost 6 freeze, pickle 7 ice over

Preserve and Protect
author: Allen Drury

__ preserver: 4 life

Preserver, Hindu: 6 Vishnu

preserves: 3 jam 5 jelly 6 spread 7 compote 8 conserve 9 confiture, conserves, marmalade 10 confection
container: 3 jar

preside: 3 run, sit 4 lead, rule 5 chair 6 advise, direct, govern, handle, head up, manage 7 conduct, control, oversee 8 moderate 9 offi-

ciate, supervise **10** administer
over: **4** head, hold, lead **6** direct **7** conduct **9** supervise
president: **4** exec, head, suit **5** chief **6** leader, top dog **7** officer **9** executive
advisory group: **3** NSC
first one-term ~: **5** Adams
four years, for a ~: **4** term
honest ~: **3** Abe
initials: **3** CAA, DDE, FDR, GRF, GWB, HCH, HST, JAG, JEC, JFK, JKP, JQA, LBJ, MVB, RBH, RMN, RWR, USG, WGH, WHH, WHT, WJC **4** GHWB
maybe: **3** CEO **8** chairman
military title: **4** C in C
nickname: **3** Abe, Cal, Ike **4** Bill
pet: **3** Her, Him **4** Fala **5** Socks
prerogative: **4** veto
terse ~: **3** Cal
__ president: **4** vice
presidential __: **5** suite **7** primary
Presidential Papers, The
author: Norman Mailer
President of the U.S.: **4** Bush, Ford, Polk, Taft **5** Adams, Grant, Hayes, Nixon, Obama, Tyler **6** Arthur, Carter, Hoover, Monroe, Pierce, Reagan, Taylor, Truman, Wilson **7** Clinton, Harding, Jackson, Johnson, Kennedy, Lincoln, Madison **8** Buchanan, Coolidge, Fillmore, Garfield, Harrison, McKinley, Van Buren **9** Cleveland, Jefferson, John Adams, John Tyler, Roosevelt **10** Eisenhower, Gerald Ford, Washington
president pro __: **3** tem **7** tempore
Presidents' Day event: **4** sale
presiding officer: **4** head **5** chief **6** leader, top dog, warden **7** manager **8** director **9** executive **10** supervisor
presidio: **4** fort **8** fastness, fortress, garrison **10** stronghold
Presley: **4** Lisa **5** Elvis **9** Priscilla
Presley, Elvis: **5** actor **6** singer
contemporary: **5** Darin
film: Blue Hawaii (1961)
Change of Habit (1969)
Charro! (1969)
Clambake (1967)
Double Trouble (1967)
Easy Come, Easy Go (1967)
Flaming Star (1960)
Follow That Dream (1962)
Frankie and Johnny (1966)
Fun in Acapulco (1963)
G.I. Blues (1960)
Girl Happy (1965)
Girls! Girls! Girls! (1962)
Harum Scarum (1965)
It Happened at the World's Fair (1963)
Jailhouse Rock (1957)
Kid Galahad (1962)
King Creole (1958)
Kissin' Cousins (1964)
Live a Little, Love a Little (1968)
Love Me Tender (1956)
Loving You (1957)
Paradise, Hawaiian Style (1966)
Roustabout (1964)
Speedway (1968)
Spinout (1966)
Stay Away, Joe (1968)
Tickle Me (1965)
The Trouble With Girls (1969)
Viva Las Vegas (1964)
Wild in the Country (1961)
hometown: Tupelo, Mississippi
middle name: **4** Aron
nickname: The King
song: Ain't That Loving You Baby (1964)
All Shook Up (1957)
Any Way You Want Me (1956)
Are You Lonesome Tonight? (1960)
Ask Me (1964)
Big Boss Man (1967)
A Big Hunk O' Love (1959)
Blue Suede Shoes (1956)
Bossa Nova Baby (1963)
Burning Love (1972)
Can't Help Falling in Love (1961)
Crying in the Chapel (1965)
Devil in Disguise (1963)
Doncha' Think It's Time (1958)
Don't (1958)
Don't Be Cruel (1956)
Don't Cry Daddy (1969)
Do the Clam (1965)
Fame and Fortune (1960)
Flaming Star (1961)
Follow That Dream (1962)
A Fool Such As I (1959)
Frankie and Johnny (1966)
Good Luck Charm (1962)
Hard Headed Woman (1958)
Heartbreak Hotel (1956)
His Latest Flame (1961)
Hound Dog (1956)
I Beg of You (1958)
I Feel So Bad (1961)
If I Can Dream (1968)
If You Talk in Your Sleep (1974)
I Got Stung (1958)
I Gotta Know (1960)
I'm Yours (1965)
I Need Your Love Tonight (1959)
In the Ghetto (1969)
I Really Don't Want to Know (1971)
It's Now or Never (1960)
I Want You, I Need You, I Love You (1956)
I Was the One (1956)
Jailhouse Rock (1957)
Kentucky Rain (1970)
Kissin' Cousins (1964)
(Let Me Be Your) Teddy Bear (1957)
Little Sister (1961)
Love Letters (1966)
Love Me (1956)
Love Me Tender (1956)
Loving You (1957)
My Boy (1975)
My Wish Came True (1959)
One Broken Heart for Sale (1963)
One Night (1958)
Playing for Keeps (1957)
Promised Land (1974)
Puppet on a String (1965)
Return to Sender (1962)
Separate Ways (1972)
She's Not You (1962)
Steamroller Blues (1973)
Stuck on You (1960)
(Such an) Easy Question (1965)
Such a Night (1964)
Surrender (1961)
Suspicious Minds (1969)
Tell Me Why (1966)
Too Much (1957)
Treat Me Nice (1957)
U.S. Male (1968)
Viva Las Vegas (1964)
Way Down (1977)
Wear My Ring Around Your Neck (1958)
What'd I Say (1964)
The Wonder of You (1970)
You Don't Have to Say You Love Me (1970)
spouse: Priscilla Presley
Presley, Lisa Marie
spouse: Nicolas Cage, Michael Jackson
Presque Isle: **4** city, town
locale: **5** Maine
press: **3** beg, dun, get, hug, jam, jog, mob, nag, ram, sue, vex **4** cram, herd, hold, host, iron, lock, make, mash, mass, milk, mill, pack, pile, prod, push, rush, sell, spur, urge, vise **5** beset, bunch, clasp, cramp, crowd, crush, drove, egg on, flock, force, haste, horde, hurry, impel, level, lobby, media, offer, paper, plead, shove, sqush, steam, stuff, swarm, worry **6** assert, bustle, coerce, compel, demand, enfold, enjoin, estate, exhort, harass, harp on, hassle, hasten, infold, insist, lean on, mangle, plague, push on, reduce, smooth, squash, squish, squush, strain, stress, throng, thrust, work on **7** beseech, besiege, embrace, entreat, extrude, flatten, implore, newsmen, pin down, scrunch, squeeze, squoosh, torment, trouble, urgency **8** appeal to, bear down, blandish, bulldoze, compress, condense, insist on, petition, railroad, reporter, shoulder **9** columnist, confusion, emphasize, importune, magazines, multitude, news media, newspaper, promotion, publicist, publicity, publisher, unwrinkle, weigh down **10** buttonhole, journalism, journalist, newspapers, periodical, supplicate
agent: **5** flack **8** promoter **9** advertise
charges: **8** litigate
coverage: **3** ink
down: **4** tamp **7** depress
ender: **3** run, ure **4** gang, mark, room, work **5** board
for: **4** urge **6** demand, exhort **8** advocate, petition
for details: **4** pump
for money: **3** dun, sue **4** bill
for political action: **5** lobby
go to ~: **5** print **7** let roll
hot off the ~: **3** new **5** fresh **6** recent
into service: **3** use **5** avail **6** enlist **7** recruit
member: **6** editor, photog **8** reporter **10** journalist
on: **7** advance, proceed **8** continue **9** go forward, persevere
one's luck: **4** dare, push
one's suit: **3** sue, woo **5** court **7** propose
prepare a ~: **3** ink **5** reink
release: **4** news, word **5** aviso **6** notice, report **7** handout, message **8** bulletin, dispatch **9** statement **10** communiqué
secretary: **4** aide **9** assistant
starter: **4** wine **6** letter **7** clothes
the flesh: **5** lobby, stump **8** campaign, politick **10** shake hands
together: **5** purse
press __: **3** bed, box, fit, kit, run **4** gang, lord, stud, time **5** agent, baron, corps, party, proof **6** bureau **7** release
__ press: **3** web **4** body, drop, duck, free, go to, hand, wine **5** bench, cider, drill **6** cookie, rotary, vanity
Pressburger: **6** Emeric
press conference
format: **5** Q and A
gear: **4** mike **6** camera **10** microphone
pressed __: **4** duck
__-pressed: **4** hard
pressing: **4** dire, live, sore **5** acute, vital **6** crying, urgent **7** burning, crucial, exigent, hurry-up, instant, onerous, serious **8** critical, exigeant **9** demanding, immediate, important, insistent, necessary **10** compelling, imperative
situation: **4** crux, need **6** crisis **7** urgency **9** emergency
__ Press International: **6** United
press the __: **5** flesh
pressure: **4** heat, load, prod, pull, push, rush, sell, sway, urge **5** clout, drive, force, hurry, impel **6** burden, coerce, compel, crunch, demand, duress, hassle, insist, lean on, overdo, strain, stress, thrust, weight, work on **7** squeeze, straits, tension, tighten, trouble, urgency **8** coercion, deadline, exigence, exigency, politick, strength, threaten **9** adversity, constrain, heaviness, influence, necessity, strong-arm **10** compulsion, insistence, obligation, persuasion
apply ~: **4** push, urge **5** force **6** coerce, compel, lean on **7** squeeze **8** arm-twist **9** strong-arm
combining form: **3** bar- **4** baro-, tono- **5** piezo-
decrease ~: **4** ease
give in to ~: **4** obey **5** crack, yield **6** submit
grace under ~: **4** cool, tact **5** poise **6** aplomb **7** dignity **8** presence **9** assurance, composure, diplomacy, sang-froid **10** confidence, equanimity
measure: **3** atm., PSI
NASA ~ unit: **4** one G
put ~ on: **3** tax **5** crowd, lobby **6** strain
so to speak: **6** screws
starter: **3** acu
unit: **3** bar **4** torr **6** pascal **8** millibar **10** atmosphere
pressure __: **5** gauge, group, point, ridge **6** cooker
__ pressure: **3** air **4** peer **5** blood

__-pressure: 3 low 4 high

pressured: 5 tense 7 harried 10 overworked

pressurize: 3 bar 4 bind, curb, make 5 check, cramp, force, hem in, impel, stint 6 coerce, compel, hogtie, oblige, rein in, stifle 7 abstain, confine, control, harness, inhibit, require, squeeze, trammel 8 bottle up, hold back, moderate, pressure, prohibit, restrain 9 constrain, constrict 10 intimidate

Press Your Luck: 8 game show
  host: Peter Tomarken

pre-stereo system: 4 hi-fi 5 phono 10 phonograph

prestidigitation: 5 magic, trick 7 sorcery 8 wizardry 9 conjuring

prestidigitator: 4 mage 6 wizard 8 conjurer, conjuror, magician, sorcerer

prestige: 4 fame, rank, sway 5 clout, éclat, glory, honor, power, state 6 cachet, credit, esteem, regard, renown, repute, status, weight 7 control, dignity, laurels, stature 8 eminence, good name, position, standing 9 authority, celebrity, influence 10 importance, prominence, reputation

Prestige, The (2006 film)
  cast: Christian Bale, Michael Caine, Hugh Jackman, Scarlett Johansson

prestigious: 5 famed, great 6 famous 7 eminent, exalted, notable 8 esteemed, imposing, renowned 9 important, prominent, reputable, respected

presto: 3 PDQ 4 ASAP, fast, stat 5 apace, quick, tempo 6 at once 7 fleetly, hastily, quickly, rapidly, swiftly 8 in a flash, in a jiffy, in no time, pell-mell, right now, speedily 9 forthwith, hurriedly, instantly, like a shot, posthaste
  slower than ~: 7 allegro

presto __: 6 chango

Presto!: 4 poof, ta-da 5 ta-dah, there, voilà

Preston: 3 Sgt. 5 Billy, Kelly 6 Foster, Johnny, Robert 7 Sturges

Preston, Billy
  song: Nothing From Nothing (1964)
  Outa-Space (1972)
  Space Race (1973)
  Will It Go Round in Circles (1973)
  With You I'm Born Again (1980)

Preston, Johnny
  song: Cradle of Love (1960)
  Feel So Fine (1960)
  Running Bear (1959)

Preston, Kelly: 7 actress
  spouse: John Travolta

Preston, Robert: 5 actor
  film: Beau Geste (1939)
  How the West Was Won (1962)
  Junior Bonner (1972)
  The Music Man (1962)
  This Gun for Hire (1942)
  Union Pacific (1939)
  Victor/Victoria (1982)

Preston, Sergeant
  beat: 5 Yukon
  horse: 3 Rex
  org.: 4 RCMP

presumable: 6 likely 8 probable, specious 10 believable, convincing

presumably: 6 likely, surely 8 probably 9 assumably, doubtless, seemingly

presume: 4 dare, deem, feel, hold, take 5 guess, infer, posit, think, trust 6 assume, bank on, expect, figure, gather, impose, take it 7 believe, count on, imagine, intrude, suppose, surmise, suspect, venture 8 conclude, consider, infringe, misjudge, theorize 9 count upon, speculate, undertake 10 conjecture, jump the gun, presuppose, understand

presumed: 7 seeming 8 probable, putative, unproved 10 understood
  truth: 5 axiom, given

Presumed Innocent: 4 film 5 novel
  author: Scott Turow
  cast: Brian Dennehy, Harrison Ford, Raul Julia

presuming: 4 bold, sure 5 brave 6 secure, upbeat 7 assured, certain, hopeful, valiant 8 cocksure, fearless, intrepid, positive, sanguine, unafraid 9 assertive, collected, confident, convinced, dauntless, expectant, expecting, satisfied, undaunted 10 complacent, counting on, courageous, optimistic

presumption: 2 if 4 gall 5 basis, brass, cheek, guess, nerve, pride 6 belief, daring, theory, thesis 7 conceit, egotism, opinion, premise, surmise 8 audacity, boldness, chutzpah, rudeness, temerity 9 arrogance, brashness, contumely, impudence, insolence 10 assumption, conjecture, effrontery, likelihood

presumptive: 7 a priori 8 putative, specious

__ presumptive: 4 heir

presumptuous: 3 big 4 bold, pert, rude, smug 5 brash, cocky, fresh, lofty, nervy, proud, pushy, saucy 6 brassy, brazen, cheeky, lordly, uppity 7 forward, haughty, pompous, unasked 8 arrogant, assuming, cocksure, familiar, impudent, insolent, snobbish 9 audacious, conceited, egotistic, imperious, obtrusive, shameless 10 disdainful

presumptuousness: 5 brass, cheek, nerve 7 license 8 audacity

presuppose: 5 imply, infer, posit 6 assume 7 believe, presume 8 misjudge 9 postulate

presupposition: 5 given 6 belief, thesis 7 opinion, premise

prêt-à-__: 6 porter

pre-taped, not: 4 live

preteen: 3 kid 5 kiddy, minor 9 youngster 10 adolescent
  school: 4 elem. 10 elementary, junior high

pretend: 3 act 4 dupe, fake, fool, play, pose, sham 5 bluff, cheat, claim, cozen, feign, fudge, let on, mimic, put on 6 affect, allege, assume, delude, fake it, play at, pseudo, sucker 7 act as if, act like, beguile, deceive, fake out, imagine, imitate, mislead, playact, profess, purport, suppose 8 hoodwink, lay claim, malinger, simulate, spurious 9 disinform, dissemble, represent, whitewash 10 masquerade, play possum, put on an act
  to be: 8 disguise, double as

__ Pretend: 4 Let's

pretended: 4 fake, mock, sham 5 bogus, false, lying, phony, put-on, quack, quasi 6 phoney, pseudo, unreal 7 alleged, assumed, feigned, nominal 8 affected, so-called, spurious, strained, supposed 9 imaginary, insincere, professed, purported, vicarious 10 artificial, factitious, fictitious, ostensible

pretender: 4 fake 5 faker, fraud, knave, phony, poser, quack 6 phoney, poseur, rascal 7 upstart, wannabe 8 imposter, impostor 9 hypocrite

Pretenders
  song: Back on the Chain Gang (1983)
  Brass in Pocket (1980)
  Don't Get Me Wrong (1986)
  I'll Stand by You (1994)
  Middle of the Road (1984)
  vocalist: Chrissie Hynde

Pretenders, The
  author: Henrik Ibsen

__ Pretender, The: 5 Great

Pretend You Don't See Her
  author: Mary Higgins Clark

pretense: 3 act, gag 4 airs, cant, hoax, mask, pose, ritz, ruse, sham, show, veil, wile 5 bluff, claim, cloak, cover, decoy, feint, fraud, guise, put-on, shill, stall, stunt, title, trick 6 acting, deceit, dupery, excuse, facade, fakery, humbug, posing, veneer 7 charade, display, evasion, mockery, pretext, routine, schtick, snow job, swindle 8 artifice, disguise, feigning, trickery 9 deception, falsehood, hypocrisy, imposture, invention, posturing, semblance, shuffling 10 appearance, lip service, masquerade, pretension, simulation, subterfuge
  without ~: 4 open 5 naive 7 artless 8 innocent, trusting 9 ingenuous

__ pretenses: 5 false

pretension: 4 airs, ritz, show 5 claim, front, pride, title 6 hubris, hybris, vanity 7 big talk, bombast, bravado, conceit, display 8 ambition, pretense, snobbery 9 arrogance, hypocrisy, imposture, mannerism, vainglory 10 lip service, narcissism

pretentious: 3 big 4 arty, smug, vain 5 artsy, cocky, gaudy, lofty, proud, ritzy, showy, stagy, swank 6 flashy, garish, hollow, la-de-da, la-di-da, ornate, stagey, swanky, tawdry, too-too, turgid 7 fatuous, flowery, fustian, haughty, mincing, opulent, pompous, splashy, stilted, stuck-up 8 affected, arrogant, assuming, boastful, imposing, inflated, lah-di-dah, mannered, overdone, puffed up, snobbish, specious, superior 9 big-headed, bombastic, conceited, flaunting, grandiose, high-flown, high-toned, insincere, luxurious, overblown, tasteless, unnatural 10 hoity-toity, theatrical

preterit: 5 tense

preternatural: 3 odd 4 eery 5 eerie, weird 6 arcane, atypic, freaky, mystic, occult, quirky 7 bizarre, deviant, ghostly, offbeat, psychic, strange, uncanny, unusual 8 aberrant, abnormal, atypical, esoteric, freakish, mystical, peculiar, uncommon 9 anomalous, divergent, eccentric, fantastic, irregular, unearthly, unnatural 10 mysterious, unorthodox

pretext: 3 out 4 mask, plea, ploy, show, veil 5 alibi, basis, bluff, cloak, cover, feint, front, guise 6 cop-out, excuse 7 cover-up, evasion, grounds 8 pretense 9 deception, semblance 10 cover story, masquerade, subterfuge

Pretoria: 4 city, town 7 capital 8 asteroid
  coin: 4 rand
  locale: 3 RSA 11 South Africa

prettify: 4 deck 5 adorn, groom, preen, primp 6 bedeck 8 beautify, decorate, ornament 9 glamorize

pretty: 4 boss, cute, fair, fine, foxy, neat, nice 5 bonny, dishy, quite 6 bonnie, comely, dainty, dreamy, eyeful, fairly, kind of, lovely, rather, sort of 7 darling, winsome 8 adorable, alluring, becoming, charming, delicate, engaging, fetching, gorgeous, graceful, handsome, pleasing, skillful, somewhat, striking, stunning, tasteful 9 appealing, beauteous, beautiful, ravishing 10 attractive, delightful, moderately, reasonably
  boy: 3 fop 4 buck, dude 5 blade, dandy, spark, swell 7 coxcomb 8 popinjay 10 jack-a-dandy
  good: 4 fair, okay, tidy
  name meaning ~: 5 Linda, Lynda
  nice: 4 okay 6 not bad
  one: 5 cutey, cutie 8 cutie-pie
  penny: 4 dear, high 5 pricy, steep 6 bundle, costly, pricey 8 big bucks, precious 9 expensive, priceless 10 exorbitant, high-priced, overpriced
  sitting ~: 4 rich 6 loaded 7 wealthy, well-off 8 affluent, in clover, well-to-do 9 well-fixed 10 in the money, well-heeled

pretty __: 4 much 5 penny

pretty __ pretty does: 4 is as

__ pretty: 7 sitting

Pretty __: 4 Baby 5 Paper, Woman 6 Poison

__ Pretty: 5 I Feel 7 Sitting

pretty as a __: 7 picture

Pretty Baby (1978 film)
  cast: Keith Carradine, Susan Sarandon, Brooke Shields
  director: Louis Malle

Pretty Boy: 5 Floyd

Pretty Girl Is Like a Melody, A
composer: Irving Berlin
Pretty in Pink (1987 film)
cast: Jon Cryer, Andrew McCarthy, Molly Ringwald
Pretty Little Angel Eyes (1961 song)
artist: Curtis Lee
Pretty Paper (1963 song)
artist: Roy Orbison
pretty please, say: 3 beg **7** implore
— pretty sight: 4 not a
Pretty Woman (1990 film)
cast: Ralph Bellamy, Richard Gere, Julia Roberts
director: Garry Marshall
pretzel: 4 nosh **5** snack
topping: 4 salt **7** mustard
prevail: 3 win **4** lead, live, rule **5** carry, reign, stand **6** abound, endure, make it, obtain, pan out, remain, thrive **7** conquer, luck out, make out, prosper, succeed, triumph, work out **8** dominate, flourish, get ahead, go places, hold sway, make good, outweigh, overcome, overrule, prove out, surmount
against: 6 endure **7** survive, weather **9** withstand
on: 3 get **4** coax, make, move, sway **6** induce, prompt, reason, suck in **7** impress, win over **8** convince, motivate, persuade, talk into **9** argue into, get around, influence
over: 4 beat, whip **5** outdo **6** defeat **8** override, overrule
prevailing: 3 set **4** main **5** fixed, typic, usual **6** common, normal, ruling, wonted **7** current, general, in style, popular, rampant, regnant, regular, routine, supreme, typical **8** dominant, everyday, habitual, ordinary, orthodox, powerful, standard, superior **9** customary, operative, principal, universal, worldwide **10** accustomed
Préval: 4 Réne
prevalence: 9 frequency
prevalent: 4 rife **5** in use, typic, usual **6** common, normal, ruling, wonted **7** current, general, popular, rampant, regular, typical **8** dominant, familiar, frequent, habitual, infested, numerous **9** customary, extensive, paramount, pervasive, sovereign, universal **10** accustomed, prevailing, ubiquitous, widespread
prevaricate: 3 fib, lie **4** jive **5** dodge, evade, hedge **6** garble, invent, palter **7** deceive, distort, falsify, mislead, perjure, phony up, quibble **8** misquote, misspeak, tell a lie **9** dissemble, fabricate, misinform
prevarication: 3 fib, lie **4** tale **5** story **7** untruth **9** falsehood **10** taradiddle
prevaricator: 4 liar **6** fibber **8** deceiver, perjurer
prevent: 3 bar, dam **4** balk, cork, foil, halt, keep, stay, stem, stop **5** avert, avoid, baulk, block, check, debar, deter, limit, stimy, stymy **6** arrest, baffle, forbid, hamper, hinder, impede, muzzle, oppose, outlaw, retard, stifle, stymie, thwart **7** counter, exclude, forfend, head off, hold off, inhibit, obviate, occlude, repress, rule out, shut out, ward off **8** dissuade, forefend, handicap, hold back, obstruct, preclude, prohibit, restrain, restrict, sabotage, stave off **9** foreclose, forestall, frustrate, hamstring, intercept, interdict, interrupt, turn aside **10** anticipate, counteract, put an end to, put a stop to
from seeing: 4 hide, veil **6** screen **9** blindfold
in legalese: 5 estop
preventive: 4 drug **5** serum **9** defensive, deterrent **10** antiseptic
Prévert, Jacques: 4 poet **6** French
Previa: 3 van **6** Toyota
— preview: 5 sneak
previewer, movie: 5 rater **6** critic
Previn: 4 Dory **5** André
Previn, André: 9 conductor
spouse: Mia Farrow
previous: 3 old **4** last, late, past **5** prior **6** bygone, former **7** beloved, earlier, old-time, one-time, quondam **8** anterior, foregone, oversoon, sometime **9** erstwhile, foregoing, preceding, premature **10** antecedent
to: 3 ere **6** before
previously: 3 ere, née **4** once, then **5** ahead **6** before, erenow **7** already, earlier, long ago, time was **8** back when, formerly, hitherto, until now **9** at one time, a while ago, erstwhile, in advance, in the past **10** beforehand, beforetime, heretofore
Prévost, Abbé: 6 French, writer
work: Manon Lescaut
prewarn: 5 alert **6** inform, tip off **7** caution
pre-weekend cry: 4 TGIF
prexy: 4 boss, exec **6** leader **9** president **10** head honcho
often: 3 CEO **8** chairman
subordinate: 4 dean, veep
prey: 4 dupe, game, gull, kill, mark **5** patsy, ravin **6** hunted, martyr, pigeon, quarry, ravage, spoils, sucker, target, victim **7** cat's-paw, fall guy
bird of ~: 3 ern, owl **4** erne, hawk, kite **5** eagle **6** elanet, falcon, lanner **7** kestrel
grabber: 4 claw, fang **5** talon, tooth
move towards ~: 4 inch **5** bound, crawl, slink **6** pounce
on: 3 eat, mug, tax **4** hunt, raid **5** bleed, bully, haunt, seize, worry **6** attack, devour, fleece, ravage **7** consume, exploit, oppress, pillage, plunder, trouble **8** distress, freeboot **9** blackmail, depredate, strongarm, subjugate, terrorize, victimize **10** intimidate
on one's mind: 6 obsess, plague **9** preoccupy
search for ~: 5 prowl
— prey: 6 bird of
prez
see president
Priam: 4 king **6** Trojan
daughter: 6 Creusa **7** Laodice **8** Polyxena **9** Cassandra
home: 4 Troy
sister: 5 Cilla
son: 5 Axion, Paris **6** Hector **7** Troilus
wife: 6 Arisbe, Hecuba
Pribilofs: 4 isls. **5** isles **7** islands
locale: 6 Alaska **9** Bering Sea
price: 3 fee, fix, set, tab **4** bill, cost, dues, fare, hire, rate, toll, tune **5** quote, value, wages, worth **6** amount, bounty, charge, damage, demand, figure, mark up, outlay, ransom, reduce, retail, return, reward, tariff, ticket, upkeep **7** ceiling, damages, expense, payment, penalty, premium, sticker, tuition **8** appraise, discount, estimate, evaluate, mark down **9** appraisal, quotation, reckoning, sacrifice, valuation, wholesale **10** assessment
add-on: 3 tax **4** duty
again: 5 retag
beyond ~: 8 precious
ceiling: 3 cap
cut: 4 deal, sale **6** rebate, saving **7** bargain **8** discount **9** reduction
discuss ~: 4 deal **6** dicker **7** bargain
fixer: 6 cartel
give a ~: 5 quote
good ~: 4 deal **7** bargain
lower the ~: 3 cut **4** trim **5** slash **6** reduce
market ~: 5 quote, value **9** quotation
of admission: 3 fee **6** ticket
offer for a ~: 4 sell, vend **6** peddle **7** auction
pay the ~: 3 buy, get **8** purchase
raise the ~: 2 up **4** hike **5** bid up, run up
reducer: 6 coupon
remove ~ supports: 5 unpeg
set a ~: 3 ask
suggest a ~: 3 bid **5** offer
tag: 6 amount, outlay, ticket
ticket ~: 4 fare
word: 3 per **4** each **6** apiece
price —: 3 cut, tag, war **4** list **5** index, point, range **6** fixing **7** control, cutting, support
price — of the market: 3 out
— price: 3 at a, bid **4** base, list, spot, stop, unit **5** fixed, floor, upset **6** asking, beyond, market **7** sticker
Price: 3 Ray **4** Marc, Nick **5** Kelly, Lloyd **7** Anthony, Vincent **8** Leontyne, Reynolds
— Price: 5 T. Rowe
—-Price: 6 Fisher
Price Above Rubies (1998 film)
cast: Glenn Fitzgerald, Julianna Margulies, Renée Zellweger
priced
be ~ at: 4 cost **5** run to
reasonably ~: 6 budget
—-priced: 3 low **4** high
price-earnings —: 5 ratio
— Price Glory?: 4 What
— Price Hollywood?: 4 What
Price Is Right, The: 8 game show
announcer: 5 Olson, Pardo, Roddy
host: Bill Cullen, Bob Barker, Drew Carey
prop: 3 tag
shout: 5 lower **6** higher
Price, Leontyne: 6 singer **7** soprano
forte: 5 opera
role: 4 Aïda
priceless: 4 dear, rare, rich **5** droll **6** absurd, costly, prized, scream, valued **7** amusing, riotous **8** humorous, precious, valuable **9** cherished, excellent, expensive, hilarious, treasured **10** gut-busting, invaluable, out-of-sight, ridiculous
individual: 3 gem
Price, Lloyd
song: I'm Gonna Get Married (1959)
Personality (1959)
Stagger Lee (1959)
Price, Nick: 6 golfer **12** South African
price of —: 4 fame
price out of the —: 6 market
Prices may —: 4 vary
Price, Vincent: 5 actor
film: The Abominable Dr. Phibes (1971)
Champagne for Caesar (1950)
The Comedy of Terrors (1964)
The Conquerer Worm (1968)
Edward Scissorhands (1990)
The Fly (1958)
His Kind of Woman (1951)
The House of Seven Gables (1940)
House of Usher (1960)
House of Wax (1953)
House on Haunted Hill (1958)
The Invisible Man Returns (1940)
The Keys of the Kingdom (1944)
Laura (1944)
The Masque of the Red Death (1964)
Master of the World (1961)
Pit and the Pendulum (1961)
The Raven (1963)
Tales of Terror (1962)
The Ten Commandments (1956)
Theatre of Blood (1973)
Twice-Told Tales (1963)
The Whales of August (1987)
pricey: 4 dear, high **5** steep **6** costly **9** expensive **10** at a premium, exorbitant
prick: 3 jab, jag **4** bore, goad, hurt, prod, spur, stab **5** pique, punch, smart, spike, sting, thorn, wound **6** needle, pierce, twinge, whip up **7** pinhole, prickle, scratch **8** puncture **9** penetrate, perforate **10** incitement
starter: 3 pin
up one's ears: 6 listen
prickle: 4 barb **5** briar, brier, prick, smart, sting, thorn **6** nettle, tingle **7** bristle
prickly: 5 sharp, spiky, spiny **6** barbed, crabby, grumpy, knotty, thorny, touchy, tricky, trying **7** brambly, bristly, fretful, peevish, pointed, waspish **8** annoying, fretsome, grumpish, involved, petulant, snappish, ticklish **9** difficult, irritable **10** nettlesome, unamenable

plant: 5 brier 6 teasel 7 bramble, thistle 10 thorn apple
prickly __: 4 heat, pear
prickly pear: 5 fruit 6 cactus
locale: 6 desert
pricy
see pricey
pride: 3 ego 4 airs, brag, crow, face 5 boast, cream, preen, strut, vaunt 6 egoism, hubris, hybris, puff up, vanity 7 conceit, egotism, ego trip, emotion, hauteur, swagger, triumph 8 ornament, smugness, snobbery 9 arrogance, cockiness, gasconade, immodesty, insolence, loftiness, vainglory 10 narcissism, pretension, self-esteem
and joy: 8 treasure
burst with ~: 4 brag 5 boast, gloat, glory, kvell, strut 7 swagger
member: 3 cub 4 lion 7 lioness
successor: 4 fall
__ pride: 5 civic 6 ethnic
Pride: 7 Charley, Charlie, Hofstra
Pride __...: 5 goeth
pride and __: 3 joy
Pride and Joy (1963 song)
artist: Marvin Gaye
Pride and Prejudice: 5 novel
author: Jane Austen
character: 5 Darcy, Kitty, Lydia 6 Bennet
Pride and Prejudice (2005 film)
cast: Keira Knightley
Pride, Charley: 6 singer
song: Kiss an Angel Good Mornin' (1971)
Pride of the Yankees, The (1942 film)
cast: Walter Brennan, Gary Cooper, Teresa Wright
prie-__: 4 dieu 5 dieux
prie-dieu, use a: 4 pray 5 kneel
prier: 5 snoop 7 crowbar 9 buttinsky 10 Nosy Parker
priest: 4 abbé, imam, lama, monk, rank 5 druid, friar, geshe, padre, roshi, tulku, vicar 6 bishop, cleric, curate, divine, father, khenpo, parson, pastor, rector, sensei, shaman 7 adviser, advisor, holy man, pontiff 8 chaplain, minister, rinpoche 9 monsignor 10 archbishop
ancient Roman ~: 6 flamen
Asian ~: 4 lama 5 geshe, roshi, tulku 6 khenpo, sensei 8 rinpoche
calendar: 4 ordo
Celtic ~: 5 druid
cup: 7 chalice
ender: 3 ess
flock: 4 fold 5 laity 6 parish
French ~: 4 abbé
garment: 3 alb, zen 4 cope 5 amice, orale, robes 6 rakasu 8 vestment
headdress: 5 miter, mitre
in a Nash verse: 4 lama
item: 6 censer 7 incense
mantle: 4 cope
Muslim ~: 4 imam
name meaning ~: 5 Cohen
one-L ~: 4 lama
plate: 5 paten
school: 8 lamasery, seminary 9 monastery
stole: 5 amice
subordinate: 6 curate, deacon
__ priest: 4 high
Priest: 3 Pat
Priest (1994 film)
director: Antonia Bird
__ Priest: 5 Judas
__ priestess: 4 high
priesthood: 6 clergy
Priestley: 2 J.B. 5 Jason 6 Joseph
Priestley, Joseph: 7 British, chemist
priestly: 5 pious 8 clerical, hieratic 9 religious
combining form: 4 hier- 5 hiero-
not ~: 4 laic 6 laical
prig: 5 dandy, prude, snoot 6 carper, purist 7 caviler, fusspot, puritan 8 bluenose 9 formalist, nice Nelly, nitpicker, Victorian 10 fuddy-duddy, goody-goody
priggish: 4 prim, smug 5 staid, stiff 6 proper, stuffy 7 prudish 8 pedantic 10 goody-goody, pedantical
Prigogine, Ilya: 7 Belgian, chemist 8 Nobelist
prill: 3 ore
prim: 3 coy 4 nice, smug, tidy 5 fussy, rigid, stiff 6 choosy, demure, formal, prissy, proper, sedate, stuffy 7 choosey, correct, genteel, prudish, stilted, upright, uptight 8 decorous, priggish, reserved, starched 9 bluenosed, squeamish, Victorian 10 fastidious, fuddy-duddy, goody-goody, nitpicking, overmodest, particular, unassuming
ender: 4 rose
prima __ pares: 5 inter
prima ballerina: 6 dancer, étoile
Prima Ballerina
artist: Edgar Degas
primacy: 4 lead, rank 7 command 8 hegemony 9 supremacy 10 ascendance, ascendancy, ascendence, ascendency, leadership
prima donna: 4 diva 6 artist, singer 7 actress, artiste 8 vocalist
problem: 3 ego
prima facie: 6 likely 7 obvious
Primal Fear (1996 film)
cast: Richard Gere, Laura Linney, Edward Norton, Alfre Woodard
Prima, Louis: 6 singer 9 trumpeter
spouse: Keely Smith
Prima, Louis and Keely Smith
song: That Old Black Magic (1958)
Wonderland by Night (1960)
prim and __: 6 proper
primarily: 5 first 6 mainly, mostly 7 at first, chiefly, largely, overall 8 above all 9 basically, generally, in essence, initially 10 at the start, especially, on the whole, originally
primary: 3 key, top 4 arch, main 5 alpha, basal, basic, chief, first, major, vital 6 needed, simple, staple, urgent 7 central, crucial, highest, initial, leading, pivotal, premier, radical, special 8 cardinal, dominant, earliest, election, foremost, greatest, headmost, original, required, superior, ultimate 9 beginning, elemental, essential, governing, immediate, important, mandatory, necessary, number one, paramount, principal, uppermost 10 aboriginal, elementary, overriding, underlying
color: 3 red 4 blue, cyan 5 green 6 yellow 7 magenta
participant: 5 voter
school: 4 elem., el-hi 10 elementary
primary __: 4 care 5 color 6 school
Primary Colors: 4 book, film
author: Joe Klein
cast: Kathy Bates, Emma Thompson, John Travolta
director: Mike Nichols
primate: 3 ape, man 4 saki, titi 5 biped, chimp, drill, human, jocko, lemur, loris, magot, orang, potto, shrew 6 aye-aye, baboon, Bandar, bishop, galago, gelada, gibbon, grivet, guenon, howler, langur, macaco, mammal, monkey, rhesus, simian, uakari, vervet 7 colobus, gorilla, guereza, hoolock, macaque, sapajou, siamang, tamarin, tarsier 8 bush baby, capuchin, mandrill, mangabey, marmoset, talapoin 9 orangutan 10 Barbary ape, chimpanzee, orangutang
African ~: 5 chimp, drill, indri, lemur, potto 6 aye-aye, baboon, galago, gelada, grivet, guenon, vervet 7 colobus, gorilla, guereza 8 bush baby, mandrill, mangabey, talapoin 10 Barbary ape, chimpanzee
arboreal ~: 5 lemur, orang 6 gibbon 7 tarsier 9 orangutan
Asian ~: 5 orang 6 gibbon, langur 7 macaque, siamang, tarsier 9 orangutan 10 orangutang
Borneo ~: 5 orang 9 orangutan
Central American ~: 7 sapajou 8 capuchin, marmoset
genus: 4 homo
Gibraltar ~: 10 Barbary ape
hypothetical ~: 6 apeman
Indian ~: 5 loris 6 Bandar, rhesus 7 hoolock
nocturnal ~: 5 lemur, loris 6 aye-aye, galago 7 tarsier 8 bush baby
South American ~: 4 saki, titi 6 uakari 7 tamarin 8 capuchin, marmoset
tailless ~: 3 ape 5 loris
__ primavera: 5 pasta
prime: 3 fit 4 best, dawn, head, hour, main, morn, move, peak, pink, ripe, tops 5 bloom, brief, chief, coach, elite, first, grade, groom, heavy, prize, ready, start, sunup, train, vigor, youth 6 direct, excite, fill in, flower, get set, goodly, grade A, heyday, inform, master, notify, school, select, simple, spring, utmost, zenith 7 central, highest, initial, leading, morning, premier, prepare, provoke, sunrise, supreme, vintage 8 best days, cardinal, champion, daybreak, deciding, dominant, earliest, foremost, greatest, headmost, heavenly, majority, maturity, motivate, original, rehearse, ultimate, vitality, wondrous 9 essential, flowering, full-grown, galvanize, governing, make ready, matchless, nonpareil, number one, paramount, principal, top-drawer, unrivaled, uppermost, uttermost, wonderful 10 overriding, perfection, predispose, springtime, underlying, unrivalled, world-class
first ~: 3 two
for the picking: 4 ripe
in one's ~: 4 ripe 6 mature 8 vigorous
mover: 5 cause
not quite ~: 6 choice
of life: 8 fullness, maturity
past its ~: 3 old 5 moldy, passé, stale
the pump: 4 fund 9 subsidize
time: 3 ten 4 nine 5 eight, night, seven, ten p.m. 6 nine p.m. 7 eight p.m., evening, seven p.m.
see also wonderful
prime __: 3 rib 4 rate, ribs, time 5 mover
Prime (2005 film)
cast: Bryan Greenberg, Meryl Streep, Uma Thurman
Prime Cut (1972 film)
cast: Gene Hackman, Lee Marvin
primed: 3 set 5 ready 6 all set 7 groomed 8 prepared 9 rehearsed
Prime of Life, The
author: Simone de Beauvoir
Prime of Miss Jean Brodie, The: 4 film 5 novel
author: Muriel Spark
cast: Maggie Smith
director: Ronald Neame
primer: 4 book, coat, text 6 manual 8 handbook 10 schoolbook
topic: 4 ABCs 6 lesson
prime the __: 4 pump
primeval: 3 old 5 early, first 6 native, virgin 7 ancient 8 earliest, original, virginal 9 ancestral, unevolved 10 aboriginal
upheaval: 5 chaos
primitive: 3 old, raw 4 rude, wild 5 basic, crude, early, first, rough 6 animal, coarse, native, savage, simple 7 ancient, archaic, artless, austere, bestial, natural, radical, Spartan, untamed 8 barbaric, earliest, original, pristine 9 atavistic, barbarian, barbarous, childlike, inelegant, makeshift, unevolved, unrefined, vestigial 10 aboriginal, amateurish, elementary, indigenous, underlying, unpolished
primo: 4 A-one, best, fine, good, tops 5 first, great 6 unique 8 fabulous, topnotch, top-rated 9 excellent, first-rate, principal, topflight 10 first-class
Primo: 4 Levi 7 Carnera
__ primo cit.: 3 loc.
__ primo citato: 4 loco
primogenitary: 6 eldest
primordial: 3 old 5 basic, early, first 7 ancient 8 earliest, original 9 elemental, unevolved 10 aboriginal
primordial __: 4 soup
primp: 4 deck 5 fix up, groom, preen, prink 6 doll up, dude up 7 deck out, dress up, gussy up, smarten, spiff up, swank up 8 beautify, ornament,

pretty up, spruce up, titivate **9** smarten up, tittivate
primrose: 5 color, oxlip, plant **6** flower, yellow
color relative: ***see*** yellow color
primrose __: 4 path
primus __ pares: 5 inter
prince: 4 amir, emir, male, raja **5** ameer, emeer, Harry, Henry, mogul, noble, rajah, royal, ruler **6** Andrew, dynast, Edward, gerent **7** Charles, monarch, William **8** maharaja **9** maharajah, sovereign
Abyssinian ~: 3 ras
Bard's ~: 3 Hal
in disguise: 4 frog
Islamic ~: 4 amir, emir **5** ameer, emeer
of darkness: 5 devil, Satan **7** Lucifer
of India: 4 raja **5** rajah **8** maharaja **9** maharajah
operatic ~: 4 Igor
Trojan ~: 5 Paris
word for a TV ~: 5 fresh
prince __: 5 royal **6** regent **7** consort
__ prince: 5 crown
Prince: 10 pasta sauce
competitor: 4 Ragú **5** Prego **8** Classico **10** Newman's Own **11** Aunt Millie's
Prince (singer)
born: Prince Rogers Nelson
song: Alphabet St. (1988)
Batdance (1989)
Cream (1991)
Delirious (1983)
Diamonds and Pearls (1991)
Gett Off (1991)
I Hate U (1995)
I Wanna Be Your Lover (1979)
I Would Die 4 U (1984)
Kiss (1986)
Let's Go Crazy (1984)
Little Red Corvette (1983)
The Most Beautiful Girl in the World (1994)
Partyman (1989)
Pop Life (1985)
Purple Rain (1984)
Raspberry Beret (1985)
Sign 'O' the Times (1987)
Thieves in the Temple (1990)
U Got the Look (1987)
When Doves Cry (1984)
Prince __: 3 Ali, Hal **4** Igor **7** Valiant
Prince __ Island: 6 Edward
Prince __ Sound: 7 William
Prince Albert __: 4 coat
Prince and the Pauper, The: 5 novel
author: Mark Twain
character: 3 Tom **4** Hugo **5** Canty, Edith **6** Edward, Hendon
Prince Edward Island: 8 province
capital: Charlottetown
city: 6 Souris **8** Alberton, Cornwall
locale: 6 Canada
Prince Harry
school: 4 Eton
Prince Harry brother: 5 Wills
Prince Igor: 5 opera
composer: Aleksandr Borodin
princely: 5 noble, regal, ritzy, royal, swank **6** lavish, lordly, swanky **7** copious, liberal, profuse **8** abundant, generous, handsome, imperial, splendid **9** bountiful, luxurious, plentiful, sumptuous **10** altruistic, beneficent, benevolent, bighearted, unstinting
Prince of __: 5 Peace, Wales
__ Prince of Bel Air: 5 Fresh
Prince of Egypt, The (1998 film)
voice cast: Sandra Bullock, Ralph Fiennes, Val Kilmer, Michelle Pfeiffer
Prince of the City (1981 film)
cast: Jerry Orbach, Treat Williams
director: Sidney Lumet
Prince of Tides, The (1991 film)
cast: Blythe Danner, Nick Nolte, Barbra Streisand
director: Barbra Streisand
Prince of Wales: 4 heir **7** Charles
game: 4 polo
motto: 6 I serve **7** Ich Dien
princess: 4 rani **5** noble, royal, ruler, woman **6** gerent **7** monarch **9** sovereign
adornment: 5 tiara
British ~: 4 Anne
disturber: 3 pea
Golden Fleece ~: 5 Medea
of India: 4 rani **5** ranee **8** maharani
opera ~: 4 Aïda
Raj ~: 5 begum
princess __: 5 royal
__ princess: 5 crown
Princess __: 3 Ida **5** Daisy, Diana, phone **7** Caraboo, Cruises
Princess __, The: 5 Bride **7** Diaries
Princess and the Pea, The
author: Hans Christian Andersen
Princess Bride, The (1987 film)
cast: Billy Crystal, Cary Elwes, Peter Falk, Christopher Guest, Carol Kane, Mandy Patinkin, Chris Sarandon, Robin Wright
director: Rob Reiner
Princess Caraboo (1994 film)
cast: Jim Broadbent, Phoebe Cates, Wendy Hughes
Princess Casamassima, The
author: Henry James
Princess Daisy
author: Judith Krantz
Princess Diaries, The (2001 film)
cast: Julie Andrews, Hector Elizondo, Anne Hathaway
director: Garry Marshall
Princess Ida: 8 operetta
composer: W.S. Gilbert, Arthur Sullivan
Princess of Power: 5 She-Ra
__ Princess, The: 6 Little
__ Prince, The: 6 Little
Princeton: 4 city, town
athletes: 6 Tigers
league: 3 Ivy
locale: 9 New Jersey
Prince Valiant: 5 comic **10** comic strip
Aleta's kingdom, in ~: 10 Misty Isles
Arn's domain, in ~: 3 Orr
son: 3 Arn
trademark: 5 bangs
wife: 5 Aleta
Prince William
school: 4 Eton
Prince William __: 5 Sound
Princip: 7 Gavrilo
principal: 3 key, top **4** arch, dean, head, lead, main, star **5** basic, chief, first, grand, major, money, prime **6** assets, leader, master, rector, ruling, staple, top dog **7** capital, central, highest, leading, pivotal, premier, primary, stellar, supreme **8** cardinal, champion, crowning, deciding, director, dominant, foremost, greatest, headmost, superior **9** essential, governing, important, organizer, paramount, preceptor, sovereign, uppermost **10** headmaster, overriding, preeminent, prevailing
combining form: 4 arch-
dish: 6 entrée
in music: 5 primo
part: 4 bulk **8** majority **10** lion's share
Principal: 8 Victoria
principality: 6 nation **7** country
principally: 6 mainly, mostly **7** chiefly, largely, notably, overall **8** above all **9** basically, eminently, generally, in the main, primarily, supremely
Principal, The (1987 film)
cast: James Belushi, Rae Dawn Chong, Louis Gossett Jr.
Principia Mathematica
author: Bertrand Russell, Alfred North Whitehead
principle: 3 ism, law **4** code, fact, rule, sake, soul **5** axiom, basis, canon, credo, creed, dogma, ethic, ideal, maxim, tenet, truth **6** belief, dictum, ground, origin **7** dictate, formula, precept, probity, scruple, theorem **8** doctrine, morality, rudiment, standard, teaching **9** beginning, criterion, discovery, essential, integrity, knowledge, rationale **10** conviction, foundation, generality, honestness, hypothesis, principium, regulation
guiding ~: 3 saw **5** adage, axiom, credo, maxim, moral, motto, tenet **6** belief, byword, dictum, saying, slogan, war cry **7** epigram, precept, proverb **8** aphorism **9** battle cry, platitude, watchword
in ~: 7 ideally
palindromic ~: 5 tenet
universal ~: 3 law **5** axiom, given
__ Principle: 5 Peter
principled: 4 fair, just **5** moral, noble, right **6** trusty **7** ethical, upright **8** virtuous **10** scrupulous
principles: 4 code **5** creed, dogma, faith **6** ethics, morals, values **7** conduct, probity **8** ideology, morality, superego **9** character, integrity, rectitude **10** conscience
Principles and Practices of Medicine
author: William Osler
Prine: 4 John
Pringle: 6 Aileen
Pringle's
competitor: 4 Lay's, Wise **7** Doritos
prink: 4 trim **5** preen, primp **6** doll up, dude up **7** deck out, dress up, gussy up, spiff up **8** ornament, spruce up **9** smarten up
print: 4 book, copy, font, mark, step, type **5** issue, litho, photo, stamp, write **6** glossy, letter, medium, put out, run off **7** engrave, etching, impress, journal, let roll, letters, picture, publish, reissue, writing **8** halftone, magazine, put to bed, snapshot, typeface **9** engraving, go to press, lettering, newspaper, reproduce **10** characters, impression, lithograph, newsletter, periodical, photograph, typescript
check the fine ~: 4 pore **5** study **8** pore over
ender: 3 out
fine ~: 5 terms **7** details, strings **8** provisos **10** conditions, provisions
fit to ~: 5 newsy **7** topical
indelibly: 4 etch
photographic ~: 3 pos. **5** proof **8** positive
starter: 3 off **4** blue, foot, hand, news, wood **5** thumb, voice **6** finger
see also fingerprint
print __: 3 ads, run **4** shop **5** wheel
__ print: 4 fine **5** out of, small **7** contact
__-print: 5 large, out-of
printed __: 6 matter **7** circuit
printed material: 4 book, text, tome **6** manual, volume
printemps: 6 French, spring
Printemps
sculptor: Erté
printer
apprentice: 5 devil
goof: 4 typo **7** erratum
goofs: 6 errata
mark: 4 dele, fist, stet **5** caret, obeli **6** dagger, obelus
measure: 2 em, en **3** DPI **4** pica, quad **6** em dash, em quad, en dash, en quad
need: 3 ink **5** paper, press, toner **9** cartridge
option: 4 font **8** font size, typeface
part: 4 drum **6** feeder, roller **9** cartridge
speed: 3 cps, lpm
__ printer: 5 color, laser **6** ink-jet
printing: 3 run **4** type **5** issue **7** edition
compose for ~: 3 set **7** typeset
flourish: 5 swash **6** paraph
fluid: 3 ink
mold: 3 mat
process: 4 roto
printing __: 5 press
__ printing: 6 offset
Prinze Jr., Freddie: 5 actor
film: I Know What You Did Last Summer (1997)
I Still Know What You Did Last Summer (1998)
Scooby-Doo (2002)
She's All That (1999)
spouse: Sarah Michelle Gellar
prior: 4 abbé, monk, past, prev. **5** ahead, older **6** before, former **7** advance, brother, earlier, onetime **8** anterior, foregone, previous **9** foregoing, in advance, preceding **10** antecedent
combining form: 4 arch- **5** arche-, archi- **6** yester-
concern: 4 monk **7** brother

prefix: 3 pre-, pro- 4 ante-
superior: 5 abbot
to: 3 ere 5 afore, until 6 before, erenow 7 ahead of 9 in advance, preceding
prioress: 3 nun 6 sister
priority: 4 lead, rank 5 order 7 urgency 8 emphasis 9 immediacy, seniority, supremacy 10 ascendency, importance, precedence, preference, right of way
Priority ___: 4 Mail
priory: 5 abbey 8 cloister 9 monastery
Pripet: 5 river
city on the ~: 5 Pinsk
locale: 7 Belarus, Ukraine
___ pris: 5 parti
Priscilla: 4 Lane 6 Barnes 7 Presley
prism: 7 rainbow
prismatic: 10 iridescent
prison: 3 can, jug, pen 4 bars, brig, coop, gaol, jail, keep, poky, stir 5 clink, gulag, joint, pokey, tower 6 cooler, lockup 7 dungeon, slammer 8 bastille, big house, stockade 9 captivity 10 guardhouse
head: 6 warden
in Britain: 4 gaol
London ~: 7 Newgate
related: 5 penal
send to ~: 7 convict 8 sentence
unit: 4 cell
___ Prison Blues: 6 Folsom
prisoner: 3 con 5 felon, lifer 6 inmate 7 captive, convict, hostage 8 criminal, detainee, internee, jailbird, offender, yardbird 10 lawbreaker
take ~: 3 nab 4 bust 5 pinch, run in, seize 6 arrest, collar 7 capture 9 apprehend
wear: 5 irons 7 manacle, shackle, stripes
prisoner of ___: 3 war
Prisoner of Chillon, The
author: Lord Byron
Prisoner of Second Avenue, The: 4 play
author: Neil Simon
cast: Anne Bancroft, Jack Lemmon
character: 3 Mel 4 Edna 6 Edison
Prisoner of Zenda, The: 4 film
author: Anthony Hope
character: 4 Rose, Sapt 5 Josef 6 Flavia, Rudolf, Rupert
setting: 9 Ruritania
Prison of Ice
author: Dean Koontz
priss: 5 prude 8 bluenose 10 goody-goody
prissy: 4 prim 5 fussy, picky, sissy 6 demure, proper, stuffy 7 finicky, genteel, prudish 8 finiking, finnicky, overnice, precious 9 sissified, squeamish, Victorian 10 fastidious, goody-goody, particular, tight-laced
Pristina's province: 6 Kosovo
pristine: 3 new 4 pure 5 clean 6 unused, virgin, washed 7 aseptic 8 germ-free, hygienic, innocent, original, sanitary, spotless, unmarred, unsoiled, virginal 9 primitive, stainless, undamaged, undefiled, unspoiled, unsullied 10 antiseptic, immaculate, unpolluted
Pritchett, V.S.: 6 writer 7 British
work: Mr. Beluncle
___ prius: 4 nisi
privacy: 5 quiet 7 retreat, secrecy 8 solitude 9 aloneness, isolation, seclusion 10 retirement
allow some ~: 5 let be 10 leave alone
invade ~: 3 pry 4 nose, poke 5 mix in, snoop 6 horn in, impose, kibitz, meddle, worm in 7 barge in, break in, intrude, obtrude 9 eavesdrop, interfere, intervene
Privalova: 5 Irina
private: 2 GI 3 own 4 rank 5 inner, quiet 6 covert, hidden, inside, inward, lonely, masked, remote, secret, unseen, untold, veiled 7 cloaked, furtive, soldier, special 8 desolate, discreet, esoteric, hush-hush, interior, intimate, isolated, obscured, personal, reserved, secluded, separate, shrouded, solitary 9 concealed, disguised, exclusive, innermost, legionary, nonpublic, reclusive, secretive, withdrawn 10 classified, first-class, individual, restricted, tucked away, unattended, undercover, under wraps, unofficial
eye: 3 tec 4 dick, tail 6 shadow, shamus, sleuth 7 gumshoe 9 detective
having ~ knowledge: 4 in on
hoard: 5 stash 7 reserve 9 stockpile
make ~: 4 lock 5 fence 7 exclude, seclude 10 soundproof
not ~: 6 public
reply: 3 sir 5 no sir 6 yes sir
school: 4 acad. 7 academy
source: 5 cache, hoard, stash
teacher: 5 coach, tutor 7 trainer
private ___: 3 eye 5 brand, label 6 school, sector
private ___ class: 5 first
Private ___: 5 Lives 6 Dancer
Private Benjamin (1980 film)
cast: Armand Assante, Eileen Brennan, Goldie Hawn
Private Dancer (1985 song)
artist: Tina Turner
privateer: 4 ship 6 pirate 7 brigand, corsair 8 rapparee, sea rover 9 buccaneer 10 freebooter
Private Eyes (1981 song)
artist: Hall and Oates
___ Private Idaho: 5 My Own
Private Life of Henry VIII, The (1933 film)
cast: Robert Donat, Elsa Lanchester, Charles Laughton, Merle Oberon
director: Alexander Korda
Private Lives: 4 play
author: Noël Coward
character: 5 Chase, Elyot, Sibyl 6 Amanda, Prynne, Victor
privately: 5 alone, aside 6 inward 7 inwards, sub rosa 8 secretly 9 between us, entre nous, off-camera
privately-owned business: 5 indie
Private Pleasures
author: Lawrence Sanders
___ Private Ryan: 6 Saving
___ Privates: 4 Buck
Private Secretary (CBS/NBC sitcom)
cast: Don Porter (Peter Sands) Ann Sothern (Susie McNamara)
Private View, A
author: Václav Havel
privation: 4 lack, loss, need, want 6 misery, penury 7 absence, poverty 8 distress, hardship 9 indigence 10 bankruptcy, deficiency
privet: 5 hedge, shrub
privilege: 3 due 4 boon, rank 5 claim, favor, grant, honor, power, right, title 6 chance, option 7 benefit, charter, entitle, freedom, intitle, liberty, license 8 immunity, sanction 9 advantage, authority, exception, exemption, franchise, indemnity 10 birthright, concession, indulgence, perquisite
privileged: 4 free, rich 5 elite, flush 6 exempt, immune, loaded, monied, secret, select, vested 7 excused, favored, moneyed, special, wealthy, well-off 8 affluent, eligible, entitled, in clover, indulged, licensed, powerful, well-to-do 9 empowered, exclusive, qualified, well-fixed 10 fair-haired, in the dough, in the money, propertied, prosperous, well-heeled
group: 5 elite, haves 6 jet set
privy: 3 loo 6 covert, hidden, secret 7 latrine, private 8 hush-hush, outhouse, personal, secluded 9 concealed, innermost
to: 4 in on 5 aware 7 aware of, wised up 8 apprised, informed 9 cognizant, in the know 10 acquainted
privy ___: 4 coat, seal 5 purse
prix ___: 4 fixe
___ Prix: 5 Grand
prize: 3 cup, gem, pip, pry, top 4 haul, like, loot, love, pick, plum, swag 5 adore, award, catch, crown, dandy, honey, honor, jewel, kitty, medal, peach, pearl, prime, purse, stake, title, value 6 choice, esteem, honors, payoff, revere, reward, ribbon, spoils, trophy 7 care for, cherish, guerdon, jackpot, laurels, premium 8 accolade, citation, dividend, gold star, hold dear, pickings, topnotch, treasure, windfall, winnings 9 care about, first-rate, humdinger, medallion, recommend, rejoice in 10 appreciate, blue ribbon, decoration, first place, inducement, set store by
carnival ~: 6 kewpie 9 teddy bear
ender: 5 fight 6 winner 7 fighter
fighting: 4 ring 6 boxing
game-show ~: 3 car 4 cash, trip 6 cruise
take the ~: 3 win
prize ___: 4 ring 5 money
___ prize: 4 door 5 booby, first
___ Prize: 5 Nobel 8 Pulitzer
prized: 4 dear, plum 7 beloved, darling 8 precious, valuable 9 priceless
possession: 3 gem 5 asset 8 treasure, valuable
prizefighter: 3 pug 5 boxer 7 bruiser
org.: 3 WBA
wear: 4 robe 6 gloves, trunks
prizefighting: 5 sport 6 boxing
Prize, The (1963 film)
cast: Paul Newman, Edward G. Robinson, Elke Sommer
prizewinner: 5 champ 6 victor 8 champion, medalist
prizing: 7 valuing
Prizm: 3 car, Geo 4 auto 10 automobile
Prizzi's Honor (1985 film)
cast: Anjelica Huston, Robert Loggia, Jack Nicholson, Kathleen Turner
director: John Huston
pro: 3 ace, for 4 whiz 5 crack, maven, mavin 6 behind, expert, master, player, wizard 7 old hand, veteran 8 favoring, skillful 9 big-league, endorsing, in favor of 10 big leaguer, past master, specialist
bono: 4 free 6 gratis
opposite: 3 con 4 anti 6 contra
tem: 6 acting 7 interim
vote: 3 aye, yea, yes
pro ___: 3 tem 4 bono, rata 5 forma 6 patria
Pro ___: 4 Bowl
pro-am: 5 event 7 tourney 10 tournament
game: 4 golf
holder: 3 PGA
pro and ___: 3 con
probability: 4 odds 6 chance, toss-up 7 chances, outlook 8 prospect 10 likelihood
___ probability: 5 in all
probable: 3 apt 6 likely, odds-on 7 earthly, logical, regular, seeming 8 apparent, credible, expected, feasible, possible, presumed, rational 9 plausible, promising, thinkable 10 believable, contingent, in the cards, legitimate, ostensible, presumable, reasonable
not ~: 8 unlikely
probably: 5 maybe 6 adverb, likely 7 no doubt, perhaps 8 possibly 9 assumably, doubtless, like as not, perchance, seemingly 10 apparently, imaginably, most likely, presumably
___ probandi: 4 onus
probate concern: 4 will 6 estate
probationary: 5 trial 9 tentative
probe: 3 ask, dig 4 comb, hunt, poke, prod, pump, quiz, sift, test 5 delve, enter, grope, plumb, query, quest, study, touch 6 go into, search, verify 7 enquire, enquiry, examine, explore, fish for, inquire, inquiry, inspect, Pioneer, probing, pry into, ransack, rummage, Voyager 8 check out, follow up, look into, question, research, scrutiny, see about, sound out 9 catechize, criticize, delve into, feel about, penetrate, pick apart 10 inspection, poke around, scrutinize
___ probe: 3 DNA 5 space
Probe: 3 car 4 auto, Ford 10 automobile

probing, as a look: 6 shrewd 8 piercing 9 quizzical
probity: 4 good 5 honor 6 virtue 7 decency, honesty, loyalty 8 fairness, goodness, morality, veracity 9 character, good faith, innocence, integrity, principle, rectitude, sincerity 10 principles
problem: 3 ill, rub, woe 4 mess, snag 5 delay, doubt, hitch, issue, mix-up, poser, query, snarl, topic, vexer, worry 6 bother, crunch, enigma, glitch, hang-up, hassle, holdup, matter, misery, pickle, puzzle, riddle, scrape, teaser, unruly 7 bad news, bugaboo, dilemma, dispute, example, mystery, puzzler, squeeze, stumper, trouble 8 headache, hot water, obstacle, quandary, question 9 annoyance, conundrum, deep water, difficult, labyrinth, situation 10 can of worms, difficulty
no ~: 4 easy 6 simple 8 duck soup, kid stuff 10 child's play
problematic: 4 iffy, moot, open 5 shaky, vague 6 chancy, knotty, thorny, tricky, unsure 7 dubious, suspect, unknown 8 arguable, doubtful, puzzling 9 ambiguous, debatable, enigmatic, uncertain, unsettled, worrisome
Problems (1958 song)
artist: Everly Brothers
problem-solve: 5 think 8 consider, mull over 10 brainstorm
proboscis: 4 beak, nose 5 snoot, snout, trunk 6 beezer
Pro Bowl
contender: 3 AFC, NFC
site: 6 Hawaii
Probst: 4 Jeff
procedure: 3 way 4 mode, plan, step 5 setup, usage 6 action, agenda, course, custom, manner, method, policy, recipe, system 7 formula, measure, process, program, red tape, routine 8 approach, channels, practice, strategy 9 formality, mechanism, operation, technique 10 experiment, regulation, technology
according to ~: 4 duly
backup ~: 5 plan B
part: 4 step 5 phase, stage
question of ~: 3 how
usual ~: 4 wont 5 habit, usage 6 custom, policy, system 7 routine 8 practice 9 tradition 10 observance
proceed: 2 go 3 run 4 fare, move, pass, pour, rise, stem, wend 5 arise, ensue, get on, issue, march, start 6 derive, follow, happen, move on, pursue, push on, repair, result, resume, spring, take up, travel 7 advance, carry on, emanate, go ahead, journey, press on, push off 8 come from, continue, go on with, lengthen, progress 9 arise from, get to work, go forward, grow out of, originate, persevere 10 spring from, take action
briskly: 3 hie, jog, run 4 trot 5 hurry
(from): 4 flow 5 arise, issue 7 develop
laboriously: 4 plow, slog, wade 6 trudge
smoothly: 3 hum 4 flow, roll
proceedings: 4 acta 6 annals, doings, events 7 affairs, lawsuit, matters, minutes, records 8 archives, business, dealings, goings-on 9 documents 10 happenings
start legal ~: 3 sue 6 charge 8 litigate
proceeds: 3 pay 4 gain, gate, goes, take 5 funds, lucre, split, yield 6 income, profit, return, reward 7 returns, revenue 8 earnings, interest, receipts 9 royalties
process: 3 can, dry, way 4 fill, flow, flux, form, limb, mode, ship, step, wise, writ 5 candy, means, phase, smelt, smoke, stage, treat, trial 6 action, course, freeze, growth, handle, manner, method, policy, recipe, refine, screen, system 7 measure, prepare, program, routine, summons 8 channels, deal with, movement, practice, preserve, subpoena 9 dehydrate, evolution, freeze-dry, mechanism, operation, procedure, technique, transform, unfolding 10 litigation
due ~: 3 law 7 justice
due ~ championer: 4 ACLU
food: 3 can, fry 4 bake, boil, chew, cook, stew 5 broil, roast 6 digest, freeze 7 parboil 8 marinate, preserve 9 masticate
lumber: 3 cut, saw 4 mill
ore: 5 smelt 6 reduce, refine
part of a ~: 4 step 5 phase, stage
veggies: 4 chop, core, cube, dice, pare, peel 5 grate, slice
__ process: 3 due
__ processing: 4 data, word
procession: 3 run 4 file, line, rank 5 array, cycle, march, order, train 6 column, course, parade, review, series, string 7 caravan, cortege, pageant 8 movement, sequence 9 cavalcade, motorcade 10 succession
processor
food ~: 5 belly, corer, dicer, mixer, parer 6 enzyme, grater, peeler, slicer 7 blender, stomach
grain ~: 4 mill
wood ~: 3 saw 7 sawmill 8 chainsaw 10 lumberjack
word ~: 6 typist 8 software 9 secretary
__ processor: 4 data, food
Prochnow: 6 Jürgen
proclaim: 3 air 4 aver, avow, call, show, tell, vent 5 admit, break, spout, state, utter, voice 6 affirm, assert, blazon, clamor, evince, flaunt, herald, praise, spread 7 declare, deliver, divulge, enounce, expound, express, give out, profess, publish, purport, signify, trumpet 8 announce, antecede, disclose, manifest, shout out, sound off 9 advertise, broadcast, circulate, enunciate, make known, predicate, prescribe, pronounce, propagate 10 make public, promulgate
__-proclaimed: 4 self
proclaimer: 5 crier 6 hawker, herald, pedlar, pedler, vender, vendor 7 peddler 8 huckster 9 announcer
proclamation: 4 fiat 5 edict, order, ukase 6 decree, dictum, notice 7 release 9 broadcast, manifesto, statement
proclivity: 4 bent, bias, wont 5 taste 7 faculty, leaning 8 affinity, appetite, aptitude, attitude, druthers, instinct, penchant, tendency, weakness 9 direction, proneness 10 partiality, propensity
Procol Harum
song: A Whiter Shade of Pale (1967)
procrastinate: 3 lag 4 drag, idle, laze, loaf, poke, slow, stay, wait 5 amble, dally, defer, delay, mosey, stall, tarry 6 dawdle, linger, loiter, put off 7 adjourn, hold off, neglect, prolong, saunter, suspend 8 hang back, hesitate, let slide, lollygag, postpone, protract, slack off, straggle 9 goldbrick, temporize, waste time 10 dillydally
procrastinating: 4 lazy, poky, slow 6 draggy 7 gradual, halting, impeded, languid 8 dilatory, drawn-out, hesitant, slothful, sluggish, toddling 9 leisurely, lethargic, prolonged, snaillike, unhurried 10 deliberate, protracted
stop ~: 3 act 4 move 7 go ahead, proceed 9 get to work
procrastinator: 6 loafer 7 goof-off, slacker 9 goldbrick, lazybones
problem: 5 sloth 8 laziness
procreate: 5 beget, breed, spawn
Procrustean __: 3 bed
Procter & Gamble
detergent: 3 Era
shampoo: 5 Prell
soap: 4 Lava 5 Ivory
toothpaste: 5 Crest
proctor: 7 monitor 8 look over
cry: 4 time
Proctor-__: 5 Silex
procure: 3 buy, cop, get, win 4 book, earn, find, gain, grab, have, land, take 5 annex, score, seize 6 attain, come by, derive, effect, enlist, gather, induce, line up, obtain, pick up, secure, wangle 7 acquire, compass, provide, receive, recruit, solicit 8 hold on to, purchase 9 latch onto 10 accumulate, commandeer
Procyon: 4 star
prod: 3 cue, egg, jab, jog, nag 4 coax, goad, poke, push, spur, urge, wake 5 crowd, drive, egg on, elbow, goose, hound, impel, liven, nudge, press, prick, probe, punch, rouse, shove, spark, stick, waken 6 excite, exhort, fillip, incite, needle, poke at, prompt, propel, remind, stir up, thrust, urge on, whip up 7 provoke, refresh, wheedle 8 mnemonic, motivate, persuade, pressure 9 encourage, galvanize, stimulate 10 incitement
gently: 4 coax 5 nudge 6 cajole 8 persuade
__ prod: 6 cattle
prodigal: 4 free, lush 5 ample, flush 6 lavish, myriad, rakish, rascal, wanton 7 copious, liberal, profuse, spender, teeming, wastrel 8 abundant, generous, misspent, numerous, rakehell, reckless, swarming, vagabond, wasteful 9 abounding, bounteous, bountiful, countless, excessive, exuberant, libertine, luxuriant, luxurious, sumptuous, unthrifty 10 big spender, high roller, immoderate, munificent, numberless, profligate, squanderer
prodigal __: 3 son
prodigality: 5 waste 6 excess 7 license
prodigally: 9 in a big way
Prodigal Summer
author: Barbara Kingsolver
prodigious: 3 big 4 huge, vast 5 giant, great, jumbo, large 6 mighty 7 amazing, hulking, immense, mammoth, massive, sizable, titanic, uncanny, unusual 8 colossal, enormous, gigantic, king-size, oversize, singular, sizeable, striking, stunning, towering, uncommon, whapping, whopping 9 anomalous, elaborate, fantastic, herculean, humongous, marvelous, monstrous, overlarge, startling, voracious, wonderful 10 astounding, gargantuan, incredible, monumental, remarkable, stupendous, tremendous
prodigy: 3 ace 4 whiz 5 brain 6 expert, genius, marvel, phenom, rarity, talent, wizard, wonder 7 egghead, miracle, stunner, thinker, whiz kid 8 Einstein, highbrow, rare bird, virtuoso 9 sensation 10 mastermind, phenomenon, wunderkind
Prodigy
rival: 3 AOL
produce: 2 do 3 lay 4 bear, crop, form, give, make, reap, show 5 beget, breed, build, cause, crops, erect, fetch, forge, frame, fruit, goods, hatch, mount, offer, outgo, put on, put up, raise, shape, spawn, stage, stock, wares, write, yield 6 afford, author, create, design, devise, direct, effect, flower, fruits, greens, induce, invent, muster, parent, put out, render, return, secure, set off, supply, unfold, work up 7 advance, blossom, compose, deliver, develop, display, edibles, exhibit, fashion, furnish, harvest, perform, present, prosper, provide, provoke, pull off, realize, secrete, trigger, turn out 8 assemble, engender, generate, multiply, occasion, result in, set forth 9 construct, cultivate, establish, fabricate, foodstuff, originate, propagate, send forth, vegetable 10 accomplish, bring about, bring forth, contribute, effectuate, give rise to, put forward, regenerate, vegetables
a show: 5 stage
producer: 4 farm
seller: 6 grocer, market 7 grocery
unit: 4 peck, pint 5 bunch, pound, quart 6 bushel
produced
newly ~: 5 fresh 6 recent 7 just out

Producers, The (1968 film)
cast: Kenneth Mars, Zero Mostel, Gene Wilder
director: Mel Brooks
Producers, The (2005 film)
cast: Matthew Broderick, Will Ferrell, Nathan Lane, Uma Thurman
product: **4** line, opus, ware, work **5** brand, fruit, goods, issue **6** effect, legacy, output, result, upshot **7** outcome, results, spinoff **8** creation, offshoot **9** aftermath, commodity, handiwork, invention, outgrowth **10** derivative
Product 19: **6** cereal
competitor: ***see*** cereal
production: **4** film, opus, play, show, work **5** drama, movie, revue **6** growth, output, sitcom **7** musical, program, staging, turnout **8** creation, game show **9** formation, melodrama, spectacle, stage show **10** exposition, generation, handicraft
make a ~ out of: **4** carp **5** argue **6** play up **7** nitpick **10** exaggerate
stage ~: **4** play, skit **5** drama, revue **6** comedy, review **9** melodrama
target: **5** quota
productive: **4** rich **6** aidful, arable, benign, fecund, useful **7** dynamic, fertile, gainful, helpful **8** creative, fruitful, original, positive, prolific, remedial, salutary, valuable **9** effective, effectual, efficient, energetic, favorable, inventive, lucrative, luxuriant, rewarding **10** profitable, worthwhile
starter: **7** counter
productivity: **5** yield **6** output **8** capacity
proem: **5** intro **6** prolog **7** preface, prelude **8** foreword, preamble, prologue
prof: **3** don **5** tutor **7** teacher **10** instructor
see also professor
__ prof.: **4** asst. **5** assoc.
profanation: **6** misuse **9** violation
profane: **3** lay **4** cuss, foul, mock **5** abuse, crude, curse, dirty, nasty, swear, trash **6** befoul, coarse, debase, defile, filthy, impure, misuse, smutty, unholy, vulgar, wicked **7** abusive, godless, heathen, immoral, impious, mundane, obscene, raunchy, secular, ungodly, violate, worldly **8** indecent, temporal **9** atheistic, blaspheme, desecrate **10** irreverent
profanity: **4** no-no, oath **5** abuse, curse, filth, oaths **7** cursing, cussing, impiety **8** cussword, swearing **9** blasphemy, obscenity, sacrilege, swearword **10** execration
use ~: **4** cuss **5** curse, swear
profess: **4** aver, avow, pose, sing **5** admit, claim, feign, own up, teach, vouch **6** affirm, allege, assert, avouch, open up **7** declare, make out, pretend, promise, protest, purport **8** maintain, proclaim **9** dissemble, predicate
professed: **7** nominal **8** so-called **9** pretended **10** ostensible
profession: **3** art, biz, job, vow **4** game, line, post, slot, walk, work **5** craft, field, skill, trade **6** avowal, career, métier, office, sphere **7** calling, mission, pursuit, service **8** business, lifework, medicine, position, practice, vocation **9** admission, assertion, assurance, expertise, situation, specialty, statement, testimony **10** allegation, confession, contention, employment, livelihood, occupation, speciality, walk of life
professional: **3** ace **4** star, whiz **5** adept, brain, slick, yuppy **6** artist, doctor, expert, lawyer, wizard, yuppie **7** artiste, capable, hotshot, learned, old hand, skilled **8** licensed, polished, skillful, virtuoso **9** authority, competent, efficient, on the ball, practiced, qualified, superstar, technical, up to speed
pursuit: **3** job **6** career **9** specialty
Professional, The (1994 film)
cast: Jean Reno
director: Luc Besson
professor: **3** don **4** rank **5** brain, tutor **6** fellow, lector, pundit, savant **7** egghead, pedagog, scholar, teacher **8** academic, educator, emeritus, lecturer, longhair **9** abecedary, authority, pedagogue **10** instructor
aide: **2** TA **3** GTA
concoction: **4** exam, lect., quiz, test **7** lecture
degree: **3** Ph.D. **9** doctorate
title: **4** emer. **8** emeritus
professorial: **7** learned **9** pedagogic, scholarly
Professor Irwin __: **5** Corey
professors: **7** faculty
professorship: **5** chair
Professor, The
author: Charlotte Brontë
__ Professor, The: **5** Nutty
proffer: **3** bid **4** gift, give, hand, make, pose, show **5** posit, yield **6** extend, submit, tender **7** advance, commend, hold out, present, propose, provide, suggest **8** proposal **9** hold forth, volunteer **10** administer, contribute
proficiency: **5** craft, skill **6** talent **7** ability, know-how, mastery, sleight **8** artistry, facility, learning, literacy **9** expertise, technique
proficient: **3** ace, apt **4** able, deft, good, upon **5** adept, crack, handy, quick, ready, savvy, sharp, slick **6** adroit, at home, au fait, clever, expert, facile, gifted, good at, habile, nimble, up to it, versed, with it **7** capable, skilled, trained **8** aptitude, delicate, dextrous, graceful, masterly, seasoned, skillful, talented **9** competent, dexterous, effective, efficient, masterful, on the beam, practiced, qualified, up to speed **10** conversant
become ~: **5** excel **6** master
profile: **3** bio **4** face, form, vita **5** shape, study **6** figure, résumé, sketch, survey **7** contour, diagram, dossier, drawing, outline, skyline **8** analysis, likeness, portrait, side view, vignette **9** biography, lineament, lineation **10** silhouette
keep a low ~: **4** hide, lurk **6** hole up, lay low, lie low **7** conceal **8** lie doggo **9** take cover
__ profile: **3** low **4** high
Profiler (NBC drama)
cast: Ally Walker (Dr. Sam Waters)
Profiles in Courage: **4** book
author: John F. Kennedy
character: **4** Ross, Taft **5** Adams, Lamar **6** Benton, Norris **7** Houston, Webster
profit: **3** net, pay, use **4** earn, gain, gate, help, luck, reap, sake, skim, take **5** avail, clear, fruit, gravy, gross, lucre, score, serve, split, value, yield **6** income, output, return, reward, thrive **7** benefit, clean up, harvest, improve, prosper, realize, results, revenue, savings, surplus, takings, utility, welfare **8** earnings, interest, proceeds, receipts, winnings **9** advantage, increment, make money, well-being **10** bottom line, emoluments, percentage, prosperity
by: **3** use
ender: **3** eer
for no ~: **6** at cost **9** wholesale
from: **3** use **5** learn **7** utilize
make a ~: **3** net **4** turn **7** realize
opposite: **4** loss
profit __: **6** center, margin, motive, taking **7** sharing
__ profit: **3** net **5** gross, paper, turn a
profitable: **5** sweet **6** paying, useful **7** gainful, helpful **8** fruitful, salutary, valuable **9** covetable, desirable, efficient, expedient, fortunate, lucrative, practical, rewarding **10** beneficial, commercial, high-income, productive, well-paying, worthwhile
be ~: **3** pay
profitless: **4** vain **6** barren, futile **7** useless **8** bootless, misspent **9** fruitless, worthless
profligacy: **4** riot, vice **7** license **8** hedonism **9** depravity **10** corruption, indulgence
profligate: **4** fast, lewd, rake, roué, wild **5** loose **6** bad guy, lavish, rakish, rascal, wanton, wicked **7** corrupt, immoral, swinger, vicious, villain, wastrel **8** depraved, prodigal, rakehell, reckless, shameful, uncurbed, wasteful **9** abandoned, corrupted, dissolute, excessive, libertine, reprobate, shameless, unthrifty **10** dissipated, immoderate, licentious
profound: **4** deep, keen, sage, vast, wise **5** acute, great, heavy, meaty, sound, total, utter **6** occult, orphic, secret, shrewd, subtle **7** abysmal, erudite, extreme, intense, knowing, learned, radical, serious, sincere, weighty, yawning **8** absolute, abstruse, esoteric, hermetic, incisive, informed, mystical, thorough, unbroken **9** extensive, full-dress, heartfelt, innermost, intensive, out-and-out, pervasive, recondite, sagacious, scholarly **10** bottomless, consummate, deep-seated, discerning, exhaustive, fathomless, impressive, insightful, mysterious, pronounced, reflective, thoughtful, unknowable
profundity: **4** gulf **5** abysm, abyss, depth **6** wisdom **7** insight **8** deepness, sagacity **9** intellect
__ profundo: **5** basso
profuse: **4** full, lush, many, much, rank, rife **5** ample, thick **6** a lot of, divers, effuse, galore, gobs of, hearty, lavish, lots of, myriad, plenty, umteen, untold **7** a host of, aplenty, a slew of, copious, extreme, fulsome, heaps of, liberal, no end of, opulent, piles of, rampant, scads of, teeming, umpteen **8** a bunch of, abundant, an army of, effusive, frequent, fruitful, generous, infested, manifold, numerous, oodles of, princely, prodigal, prolific, scores of, swarming, umpsteen **9** abounding, alive with, a passel of, bounteous, bountiful, countless, excessive, exuberant, luxuriant, overblown, plentiful, profusive, quite a few, sumptuous, unsparing **10** dime a dozen, immoderate, inordinate, munificent, openhanded, unstinting, zillions of
profusely: **9** in a big way
profusion: **3** lot, sea, ton **4** glut, heap, host, load, mass, mess, pile, riot, slew **5** flood, ocean, stack **6** bounty, excess, galore, plenty, spread, wealth **7** barrage, legions, nimiety, surfeit, surplus **8** lushness, mountain, plethora, quantity **9** abundance, multitude, plenitude **10** congestion, cornucopia, exuberance, generosity, oversupply
profusive: **6** lavish **7** gushing, opulent, profuse **9** luxuriant
progenitor: **4** sire **6** mother, origin, parent **7** forbear **8** ancestor **9** archetype, precursor, prototype **10** antecedent, forebearer, forefather, forerunner
progenitors: **7** lineage **8** ancestry **10** family tree
progeny: **3** get, kin **4** cion, kids, race, seed, sons **5** heirs, issue, scion, spawn, stock, young **6** family, litter, scions **7** kindred, kinfolk, lineage **8** children, kinfolks, kinsfolk **9** inheritor, offspring, posterity **10** descendent
prognosis: **7** outlook, surmise **8** forecast **9** diagnosis **10** prediction, projection
prognostic: **4** omen, sign **7** fatidic, portent **9** vaticinal **10** indication, indicative
prognosticate: **5** augur **6** divine, herald **7** betoken, portend, predict, presage **8** forecast, foretell, prophesy, soothsay **9** adumbrate
prognostication: **4** omen, sign **6** oracle **7** portent **8** prophecy
prognosticator: **4** seer **5** augur **6** medium, oracle, shaman **7** diviner, prophet **9** predictor **10** forecaster, palm reader

program: **4** bill, book, card, plan, show **5** revue, set up, slate **6** agenda, budget, course, design, docket, lay out, line up, map out, method, policy, recipe, roster, series **7** catalog, details, listing, outline, process, project, work out **8** bulletin, calendar, pencil in, platform, playbill, proposal, schedule, sequence, strategy, syllabus **9** broadcast, catalogue, itinerary, procedure, timetable **10** curriculum, production, prospectus
business ~: **6** agenda **8** schedule
computer ~: **3** DOS **5** MS-DOS **7** Windows
interrupter: **2** ad **8** bulletin **9** news flash **10** commercial
regular ~: **4** soap **6** series, sitcom **7** regimen
programming
command: **4** go to
language: **3** Ada, APL, SQL **4** Alef, html, Icon, Java, LISP, Logo, Orca, Perl **5** Algol, Basic, Cecil, COBOL, Dylan, SISAL **6** Delphi, Eiffel, Erlang, Oberon, Pascal, Prolog, Sather, Scheme, Snobol **7** Fortran
web ~ language: **4** html, Java
Program, The (1993 film)
cast: Halle Berry, James Caan, Omar Epps
progress: **4** fare, gain, grow, hike, rate, work **5** forge, get on, go far, march, sweep **6** course, evolve, growth, inroad, look up, mature, motion, move on, thrive, travel **7** achieve, advance, blossom, build up, develop, headway, impetus, improve, journey, proceed, prosper, shape up, strides, success, upgrade **8** continue, get ahead, increase, momentum, movement **9** evolution, flowering, go forward, keep going, unfolding **10** accomplish, betterment, forge ahead, gain ground, shoot ahead, transition
in ~: **5** afoot, begun **6** at work **7** current, going on, ongoing **8** underway **9** happening, occurring
prevent ~: **5** stymy **6** hinder, impede **8** obstruct, sabotage
slight ~: **4** dent, step
progressing: **6** better **7** en route, ongoing **8** thriving **9** on the move **10** on the march
not ~: **5** stuck **8** moribund
progression: **3** run **4** flow, step **5** chain, order, scale, swing, train **6** course, growth, sequel, series **7** advance, current, headway **8** movement, progress, sequence **9** gradation **10** locomotion
progressive: **5** broad **6** modern **7** dynamic, gradual, growing, leftist, liberal, ongoing, radical **8** activist, advanced, positive, tolerant, unbroken, up-to-date **9** advancing, reformist
progressive __: **4** jazz, lens
__ Progress, The: **5** Rake's
prohibit: **3** ban, bar, nix **4** cork, deny, halt, kill, stay, stop, tabu, veto **5** block, debar, delay, estop, spike, stimy, stymy, taboo, tie up **6** abjure, censor, enjoin, forbid, freeze, hamper, hinder, hold up, impede, lock up, outlaw, reject, stymie **7** abolish, exclude, forfend, inhibit, obviate, prevent, put down, rule out, shut out **8** disallow, forefend, gridlock, obstruct, preclude, restrain, restrict **9** constrain, interdict, proscribe **10** keep in line
prohibited: **4** tabu **5** shady, taboo **6** banned, vetoed **7** illegal, illicit, wildcat **8** criminal, improper, outlawed, smuggled, unlawful, verboten, wrongful **9** felonious, forbidden, off-limits, out of line **10** contraband, not allowed
practice: **4** no-no, tabu **5** taboo
prohibition: **3** ban, bar **4** don't, no-no, tabu, veto **5** taboo **6** denial **7** embargo, refusal **8** negation **9** abatement, exclusion, interdict, restraint
word: **2** no **3** not **4** don't
Prohibition backer: **3** Dry **9** abstainer **10** teetotaler
prohibitive: **5** steep **7** sky-high **9** excessive, expensive **10** burdensome
project: **3** job, jut **4** baby, butt, cast, deal, hurl, plan, poke, task, toss, work **5** bulge, chore, draft, exude, fling, frame, gauge, heave, pitch, shoot, think, throw **6** affair, beetle, design, devise, launch, map out, matter, propel, reckon, scheme **7** ascribe, concern, overlap, predict, program, venture **8** activity, business, contrive, envision, estimate, forecast, overhang, proposal, protrude, see ahead, stand out, stick out, strategy, theorize, transmit **9** calculate, plan ahead, visualize **10** assignment, enterprise, stretch out
Project A (1983 film)
cast: Jackie Chan
projectile: **4** bolt, shot, slug **5** arrow **6** bullet **7** missile
game ~: **4** dart, puck **6** discus **7** Frisbee
long-range ~: **4** ICBM **7** missile
path: **3** arc **5** curve
projecting: **7** beetled, salient **9** obtrusive, prominent
projection: **3** jut, map, rim, tab **4** bump, eave, hump, knob, limb, lobe, sill, spur **5** bulge, guess, image, ledge, ridge, shelf, spine, tooth **8** estimate, forecast, overhang **9** appendage, extension, outthrust, prognosis **10** elongation
room unit: **4** reel
rounded ~: **4** dome, lobe
sharp ~: **3** jag **5** quill, spike, spine, thorn
projection __: **4** room **5** booth
__ projection: **4** rear **5** front
projectionist concern: **5** focus
projector
insert: **5** slide
part: **4** lens
screen: **4** wall **5** sheet
Prokhorov, Aleksandr: **7** Russian **8** Nobelist **9** physicist
Prokofiev, Sergei: **7** Russian **8** composer
work: Alexander Nevsky
The Love for Three Oranges
Peter and the Wolf
Russian Overture
Scythian Suite
War and Peace
__ prole: **4** sine
prolegomenon: **7** preface, prelude
proletarian: **4** pleb **5** lowly, prole **6** worker **7** popular **8** baseborn, commoner, plebeian
proletariat: **3** mob **4** herd **5** labor **6** masses, people, rabble **8** riffraff **9** hoi polloi, multitude **10** lower class
proliferate: **4** boom, rise, teem **5** breed, hatch, spawn, swarm **6** abound, expand, spread, step up **7** burgeon, enlarge, radiate, run riot, shoot up **8** bourgeon, escalate, increase, multiply, mushroom, snowball **9** propagate, reproduce, skyrocket, spread out **10** accelerate
proliferation: **6** growth, spread **8** increase
prolific: **4** lush, rank, rich **6** breedy, fecund, lavish **7** copious, fertile, profuse, teeming **8** abundant, creative, fruitful, swarming, thriving **9** abounding, bountiful, exuberant, luxuriant **10** generative, productive
be ~: **4** teem **5** swarm **7** run riot
prolix: **4** glib, long **5** gabby, windy, wordy **7** diffuse, lengthy, unterse, verbose, voluble **8** inflated, rambling **9** bombastic, garrulous, ponderous, redundant, talkative **10** bigmouthed, discursive, long-winded, loquacious, palaverous
not ~: **4** curt **5** brief, crisp, short, terse **10** to the point
prolixity: **8** verbiage **9** garrulity, wordiness
prolog
see prologue
prologue: **5** intro, proem **6** lead-in **7** preface, prelude **8** foreword, overture, preamble
prolong: **5** delay, renew, stall **6** expand, extend, retard, shelve **7** carry on, drag out, draw out, let ride, spin out, stretch, sustain **8** continue, hold back, hold over, increase, lengthen, maintain, protract, slow down **9** string out **10** perpetuate, stretch out
prolonged: **4** poky, slow, vast **6** draggy **7** gradual, halting, impeded, lagging, languid, lengthy **8** crawling, creeping, dawdling, dilatory, dragging, drawn-out, hesitant, plodding, slothful, sluggish, toddling **9** leisurely, lethargic, snaillike, unhurried **10** continuous, deliberate
account: **5** spiel **6** litany
prom: **4** ball, gala **5** dance, party **9** festivity
attendee: **4** teen **5** dater **6** junior, senior **8** chaperon **9** chaperone
attire: **3** tie, tux **4** gown, suit **6** formal, tuxedo **7** corsage
locale: **3** gym
partner: **4** date **6** escort
transport: **4** limo
unlikely ~ king: **4** nerd
promenade: **4** mall, stoa, turn, walk **5** amble, dance, march, paseo **6** flaunt, parade, ramble, stroll **7** display, exhibit, saunter, show off **8** ambulate **9** cavalcade
area: **4** deck
Prometheus: **4** moon **5** giant, Titan
author: André Maurois
brother: **5** Atlas **10** Epimetheus
parent: **7** Clymene, Iapetus
planet: **6** Saturn
punisher of ~: **4** Zeus **5** eagle
Prometheus __: **5** Bound **7** Unbound
Prometheus Bound: **4** play **9** sculpture
author: Aeschylus
sculptor: **3** Ney
Prometheus Deception, The
author: Robert Ludlum
Prometheus Unbound: **4** play **5** drama
author: Percy Bysshe Shelley
character: **4** Asia, Ione **5** Earth **7** Jupiter
promethium: **7** element **9** rare earth
emission: **7** beta ray
prominence: **3** tor **4** bump, crag, fame, hill, mesa, name, note, peak, rank, rise, spur **5** bluff, bulge, cliff, crest, knoll, kudos, mound **6** height, renown, status, summit, weight **7** hillock, stature **8** emphasis, headland, mountain, pinnacle, prestige, salience, standing, swelling **9** celebrity, elevation, greatness, high point, influence, precipice **10** high ground, importance, promontory, reputation
give ~: **6** play up **7** feature **9** publicize, spotlight
prominent: **3** big, top **4** high, main, star **5** chief, famed, great, large, noted **6** famous, marked, signal **7** big-name, bulging, evident, glaring, jutting, leading, notable, obvious, popular, salient **8** apparent, aquiline, beetling, foremost, renowned, stand-out, striking **9** arresting, big-league, brilliant, important, obtrusive, respected, topflight, well-known **10** celebrated, noticeable, preeminent, projecting, pronounced, protruding, protrusive, remarkable
feature: **3** jaw **4** nose
person: **3** VIP **4** lion, star **5** celeb, mover, nabob, titan **6** shaker, tycoon **7** magnate **9** celebrity
promise: **3** vow **4** avow, bind, bode, bond, hint, hope, oath, omen, pact, word **5** agree, augur, flair, say-so, spell, swear, token, troth, vouch **6** assure, avowal, engage, ensure, insure, parole, pledge, plight, talent **7** bargain, bespeak, betoken, betroth, compact, consent, declare, earnest, portend, presage, profess, warrant **8** affiance, aptitude, contract, covenant, forebode, foreshow, good omen, indicate, obligate, prospect, security, warranty **9** agreement, assurance, betrothal, foretoken, guarantee, insurance, potential, stipulate, subscribe, undertake **10** capability, commitment, engagement, foreshadow, likelihood, obligation, underwrite

break a ~: **6** betray, renege **7** violate
keep a ~: **4** meet **6** please **7** fulfill, gratify, perform **8** make good, reassure **9** discharge
partner: **4** lick
solemn ~: **3** vow **4** oath
to marry: **5** troth
to pay: **3** IOU **4** debt **9** debenture
word: **4** soon **5** later **8** tomorrow
written ~: **8** warranty **9** guarantee
Promise: **9** margarine
alternative: **6** Parkay, Shedd's **8** Imperial
Promise __ New Day, The: **3** of a
Promised Land: **4** Sion, Zion **6** Canaan
Promise her anything perfume: **6** Arpege
Promise of a New Day, The (1991 song)
artist: Paula Abdul
Promise of Joy, The
author: Allen Drury
Promises (1978 song)
artist: Eric Clapton
promises, like some: **4** kept **5** empty
Promises, Promises
author: Neil Simon
Promise, The
author: Chaim Potok
promising: **3** apt **4** able, rosy **5** happy, lucky **6** bright, gifted, golden, likely, rising, timely, upbeat **7** budding, hopeful, roseate **8** cheerful, cheering, possible, probable, talented **9** favorable, fortunate **10** auspicious, inspirited, optimistic, propitious, prosperous, reassuring
promissory note: **3** IOU **4** chit **5** T-bill, T-bond
receiver: **6** drawee **8** creditor
promo: **2** ad **4** hype, plug, puff **5** blurb **6** teaser **7** gimmick **9** publicity **10** commercial
promontory: **4** cape, head, hill, ness, spit **5** bluff, point **8** foreland, headland, landmark **10** prominence
promote: **3** aid **4** back, bump, flog, help, hype, lift, pass, plug, puff, push, sell, tout, urge **5** avail, boost, exalt, favor, lobby, pitch, raise, serve, speed, tempt **6** anoint, assist, better, foment, foster, hype up, incite, move up, second, talk up, uphold **7** advance, benefit, bolster, build up, develop, display, elevate, endorse, ennoble, espouse, feature, forward, further, improve, indorse, magnify, make for, nurture, push for, quicken, solicit, sponsor, support, trumpet, upgrade, work for **8** advocate, befriend, campaign, champion, graduate, increase, speak for **9** advertise, cooperate, cultivate, encourage, get behind, influence, patronize, publicize, recommend, stimulate, subsidize **10** aggrandize, contribute, facilitate, popularize, promulgate, rally round
aggressively: **4** flog, hype
another: **4** back **7** sponsor, support
in checkers: **5** crown
promoter: **5** agent, flack, PR man **7** handler, sponsor **8** advocate, exponent **9** expounder, publicist **10** missionary, press agent
promotion: **3** ads **4** hype, plug, rise **5** blurb, boost, pitch, press, raise, squib **6** brevet, hoopla **7** advance **8** advocacy, ballyhoo, espousal **9** elevation, patronage, publicity **10** betterment, exaltation, propaganda
basis: **5** merit
objective: **4** gate, take **5** sales **6** profit
promotive: **9** accessory, conducive, efficient **10** convenient
prompt: **3** cue, get, jog, tip **4** goad, hint, lead, move, prod, spry, spur, stir, urge, warn **5** alert, brisk, cause, eager, early, egg on, hasty, impel, nudge, quick, rapid, ready, swift **6** elicit, exhort, fillip, incite, induce, on time, propel, remind, speedy, timely, tipoff **7** bring up, counsel, inspire, instant, provoke, refresh, suggest, trigger, willing **8** activate, mnemonic, motivate, occasion, on the dot, persuade, punctual, reminder, vigilant, watchful **9** efficient, immediate, instigate, on the ball, on the nose, prevail on, stimulate, wide-awake **10** give rise to, in good time, predispose, responsive
more than ~: **5** early **7** too soon **8** too early **9** premature
not ~: **4** late **5** tardy **7** overdue
prompting: **6** behest **10** invitation
promptly: **3** now, PDQ **4** anon, fast, soon **5** right, sharp, today **6** at once, on time, pronto **7** flat out, hastily, quickly, rapidly, readily, swiftly **8** directly, on the dot, right now, right off, speedily **9** at present, forthwith, instantly, like a shot, posthaste, presently, right away, summarily **10** at this time, here and now, punctually, this minute
promptness: **5** haste, hurry **8** alacrity, celerity, dispatch, rapidity, velocity **9** eagerness, fleetness, readiness **10** expedition
promulgate: **3** sow **5** issue, strew, teach **6** decree, impose, spread **7** declare, display, expound, present, promote, publish, trumpet **8** announce, proclaim **9** advertise, broadcast, circulate, enunciate, make known, propagate
prone: **3** apt **4** flat **5** ready **6** liable, likely, supine **7** exposed, subject, tending, willing **8** disposed, face down, inclined **9** lying down, prostrate, reclining, recumbent **10** accustomed, horizontal
(to): **3** apt **7** of a mind, subject **8** disposed
proneness: **6** liking **7** leaning **8** penchant, tendency, weakness **9** liability **10** preference, proclivity, propensity
prong: **4** spur, tine **5** point **6** branch **7** stabber
pronghorn: **6** animal **8** antelope
relative: *see* antelope
__ pro nobis: **3** ora
pronoun: **3** all, any, few, her, him, his, its, one, our, she, thy, who, why, you **4** both, hers, mine, none, ours, some, that, thee, them, this, thou, what, whom **5** their, there, these, thine, those **6** itself **7** herself, himself **10** themselves
Brooklyn ~: **3** dem **4** dose **5** youse
demonstrative ~: **4** that, this **5** these, those
Dixie ~: **4** y'all **6** you all
feminine ~: **3** her, she **4** hers **7** herself
French ~: **3** lui, mes, qui, soi, tes, toi **4** nous, tien, vous **5** notre
German ~: **3** mie, sie **4** mein **5** einer, meine, unser
interrogative ~: **3** who, why **4** what, whom
Italian ~: **2** io, tu **3** mia, mio, noi **4** ella, esse, esso
Latin ~: **3** sua **4** quis
masculine ~: **3** him, his **7** himself
nonstandard ~: **3** yer **4** hern, his'n, ourn **5** yourn
Portuguese ~: **2** eu, tu **3** ela, ele, mim, nós, vós **4** elas, eles
possessive ~: **3** her, his, its, our **4** hers, ours, your **5** their, whose **10** themselves
Quaker ~: **3** thy **4** thee, thou **5** thine
reflexive ~: **6** itself **7** herself, himself **8** yourself **10** themselves
relative ~: **4** that **5** which
sharer's ~: **3** our **4** ours
Spanish ~: **2** tu, yo **3** esa, eso **4** ella **5** ellas, ellos, quien, usted **7** ustedes **8** nosotros
pronounce: **3** say **4** read, rule, talk **5** judge, speak, state, utter, voice **6** affirm, assert, decree, intone, ordain **7** declare, deliver, trumpet **8** proclaim, vocalize **9** emphasize, enunciate, verbalize **10** articulate
pronounced: **4** bold **5** acute, clear, vocal **6** marked, signal, strong **7** decided, evident, notable, obvious, salient, visible **8** clear-cut, definite, distinct, emphatic, profound, striking, vehement **9** prominent
pronouncement: **4** word **5** edict, ukase **6** decree, dictum, ruling **8** decision, judgment, sentence **9** manifesto, statement, utterance
__ pronounce you...: **4** I now
pronto: **3** now, PDQ **4** anon, ASAP, fast, soon, stat **5** quick, swift **6** at once **7** quickly **8** directly, promptly, right now, right off **9** posthaste, right away
pronunciation: **6** accent, speech **8** delivery
omit in ~: **4** slur **5** elide
symbol: **4** shwa **5** acute, grave, schwa, tilde **6** macron, umlaut **7** cedilla
proof: **4** data, lead, mark, sign, test **5** facts, goods, tight, title, token, trace, trial **6** galley, reason, skinny **7** grabber, grounds, picture, records, warrant, witness **8** acid test, argument, clincher, evidence, scrutiny, specimen **9** affidavit, documents, proofread, reasoning, testament, testimony **10** deposition, indication, paper trail, smoking gun, validation
cite as ~: **6** adduce, attest **7** certify
ender: **4** read **6** reader **7** reading
find: **4** typo **5** error, typos **6** errata **7** erratum
give ~: **4** aver **5** prove, swear **6** assure, depone, verify **7** bear out, certify, confirm, declare, stand by, testify, warrant, witness **8** vouch for
mark: **4** dele, stet **5** caret
math ~ abbr.: **3** QED
of employment: **5** badge **6** ID card
of ownership: **4** deed **5** paper, title **8** document
of purchase: **6** boxtop **7** receipt
printer's ~: **5** repro
starter: **4** bomb, fire, fool, goof, heat, leak, moth, oven, pick, rust **5** child, flame, light, shell, shock, sound, water **6** bullet, grease **7** burglar, scratch, shatter, weather
word: **4** ergo **9** therefore
Proof
author: Dick Francis
Proof of Life (2000 film)
cast: Russell Crowe, Pamela Reed, Meg Ryan
director: Taylor Hackford
proof of the __: **7** pudding
prop: **3** leg, set **4** beam, buoy, cane, hold, lean, post, rest, stay **5** brace, shore, staff, stand, strut **6** crutch, hold up, pillar, uphold **7** bolster, bracket, fortify, shore up, stiffen, support, sustain **8** buttress, mainstay **9** reinforce, stabilize, stanchion **10** strengthen
ender: **3** jet
propaganda: **4** hype, lies **7** handout, hogwash, release **8** doctrine, newspeak **9** diffusion, promotion, publicity
US ~ source: **3** VOA **4** USIA
propagandize: **3** lie **4** push **7** promote **8** persuade **9** brainwash, publicize
propagate: **3** sow **4** bear, grow, sire **5** beget, breed, raise **6** father, spread **7** diffuse, produce, publish, radiate **8** disperse, engender, generate, increase, multiply, proclaim, transmit **9** broadcast, circulate, cultivate, fertilize, make known, publicize, reproduce **10** distribute, promulgate
in a way: **5** clone
propane: **4** fuel
form of ~: **3** LPG **5** LP gas
propel: **3** oar, row, tow **4** goad, hurl, move, poke, pole, prod, push, send, spur, toss, urge **5** drive, eject, fling, force, heave, impel, power, scull, shoot, shove, slide, sling, spark, throw **6** launch, let fly, prompt, thrust **7** actuate, advance, project **8** activate, catapult, mobilize, motivate

propellant: **4** fuel **8** stimulus **9** explosive **10** rocket fuel
remove ~: **6** defuel
__-propelled: **3** jet **4** self
propeller: **3** fan, oar **5** screw
arm: **5** blade
site: **5** plane **6** beanie **8** aircraft, airplane
sound: **4** whir **5** whirr
__ propeller: **5** screw
__-propeller engine: **5** turbo
propeller-head: **4** nerd **5** dweeb
propensity: **4** bent, bias, turn **5** fancy, habit, knack, taste **6** liking **7** faculty, leaning **8** affinity, aptitude, capacity, penchant, pleasure, tendency, weakness **9** affection, appetence, proneness, sentiment **10** partiality, preference, proclivity
proper: **3** apt, due, fit, own **4** fair, fine, good, just, meet, nice, okay, prim, true, well **5** exact, great, legal, legit, licit, moral, noble, per se, pucka, pukka, right, sound, usual **6** au fait, august, comely, decent, demure, formal, honest, in line, kasher, kosher, lawful, modest, polite, prissy, seemly, stuffy, suited, timely **7** allowed, apropos, condign, correct, elegant, ethical, express, fitting, genteel, germane, in order, precise, prudish, refined, regular, special, stately **8** accepted, all right, apposite, assigned, becoming, decorous, highbrow, ladylike, laudable, mannerly, orthodox, personal, pleasant, pleasing, priggish, relevant, rightful, specific, splendid, straight, suitable, superior **9** admirable, agreeable, allowable, befitting, by the book, courteous, customary, de rigueur, equitable, excellent, opportune, permitted, pertinent, qualified, reputable, wonderful **10** acceptable, applicable, authorized, beneficial, creditable, defensible, individual, legitimate, particular, reasonable, respective, sanctioned, vindicable
be ~: **5** befit **6** beseem
in ~ style: **4** duly **6** aright
overly ~ one: **5** priss, prude **7** puritan **10** goody-goody
proper __: **4** name, noun
Proper Bostonians, The
author: Cleveland Amory
properly: **7** rightly **8** laudably, worthily **9** honorably
propertied: **4** rich **5** flush **6** loaded, monied **7** moneyed, wealthy, well-off **8** affluent, in clover, well-to-do **9** well-fixed **10** in the dough, in the money, privileged, prosperous, well-heeled
property: **3** lot **4** farm, home, land, plot **5** acres, claim, goods, house, means, money, place, stuff, thing, title, tract, trait, worth **6** assets, equity, estate, parcel, realty, riches, wealth **7** acreage, capital, chattel, effects, feature, grounds, quality **8** chattels, freehold, hallmark, holdings, premises **9** attribute, buildings, ownership, resources, substance **10** belongings, possession, real estate
attachment: **4** lien **8** mortgage
be the ~ of: **8** belong to
demarcation: **5** fence, stake
Federal ~ overseer: **3** GSA
hot ~: **5** asset **8** valuable
landed ~: **5** acres **6** estate
one with ~: **5** owner **6** squire **10** freeholder
ownable ~: **4** farm, home **5** acres, field, manor, ranch, tract **6** estate, parcel, realty **7** acreage, grounds, holding **9** farmstead **10** real estate
personal ~: **4** gear **5** goods, stuff **6** things **8** chattels
piece of ~: **3** lot **5** asset **6** spread **7** holding
stolen ~: **4** loot, swag **6** spoils **7** plunder
strip of ~: **6** devest
title: **4** deed **6** papers
property __: **3** tax
__ property: **4** real **7** private
prophecy: **6** augury, oracle, vision **8** forecast **10** divination, foreboding, prediction, revelation
prophesy: **4** warn **5** augur **6** divine, preach **7** betoken, foresee, portend, predict, presage **8** forebode, forecast, foreshow, foretell, forewarn, soothsay **9** adumbrate, see coming **10** foreshadow, vaticinate
combining form: **5** -mancy
prophet: **4** seer **5** augur, druid, magus, sibyl **6** auspex, herald, medium, oracle, reader, shaman, wizard **7** aruspex, diviner, palmist, seeress **8** haruspex, sorcerer **9** Cassandra, geomancer, messenger, predictor **10** astrologer, forecaster, prophesier, soothsayer
Biblical ~: **4** Amos, Ezra, Joel, Osee **5** Elias, Hosea, Jonah, Micah, Moses, Nahum **6** Daniel, Elijah, Elisha, Isaiah, Nathan, Samuel **7** Ezekiel, Malachi, Obadiah **8** Jeremiah **9** Zechariah, Zephaniah
female ~: **5** sibyl **9** Cassandra
of a ~: **5** vatic **7** vatical
of doom: **9** pessimist
prophetic: **5** vatic **6** mantic, occult **7** fatidic, ominous **8** Delphian, oracular, pythonic, sibyllic **9** prescient, sibylline, vaticinal, visionary **10** portentous, prognostic
Prophet, The
author: Sholem Asch, Kahlil Gibran
propinquity: **8** nearness, presence, relation, vicinity **9** closeness, proximity
propitiate: **4** calm **5** allay **6** pacify **7** assuage, mediate, mollify, placate, satisfy, sweeten **9** reconcile **10** recompense
propitiatory: **6** irenic **8** irenical **9** peaceable
propitious: **3** fit **4** rosy **5** happy, lucky, right **6** benign, golden, timely **7** hopeful **8** gracious, suitable **9** favorable, fortunate, opportune, promising, well-timed **10** auspicious, beneficial, felicitous, prosperous
propjet: **5** plane **6** engine **8** airplane
proponent: **5** urger **6** backer, friend, patron, votary **7** apostle, booster **8** advocate, champion, defender, endorser, espouser, exponent, partisan, upholder, votarist **9** apologist, protector, supporter **10** enthusiast, subscriber, vindicator
proportion: **3** cut, pct. **4** part, rate, size **5** allot, quota, ratio, scale, share **6** degree, ration **7** balance, harmony, measure, percent, segment **8** division, equation, fraction, symmetry **9** agreement, congruity, harmonize, integrate, magnitude **10** classicism, coordinate
blow out of ~: **6** play up **7** magnify **8** overplay **10** exaggerate
words: **4** is to
proportional: **4** even, just **7** uniform **8** balanced, relative **9** equitable
share: **3** cut **5** quota **9** allotment
proportionate: **4** even, just **5** equal, level **7** uniform **8** balanced, relative **9** equitable
proportions: **4** area, bulk, mass, size, span **5** range, scale, scope, width **6** extent, volume **7** breadth, expanse **9** amplitude, magnitude **10** dimensions
of epic ~: **3** big **4** huge, vast **5** giant, grand, great, gross, heavy, jumbo, large **6** cosmic **7** immense, mammoth, massive, monster, titanic **8** colossal, enormous, gigantic, oversize, spacious, terrific, towering, whopping **9** extensive, herculean, humongous, monstrous, walloping **10** gargantuan, monumental, overweight, prodigious, tremendous
proposal: **3** bid **4** bill, call, idea, plan, spec, suit **5** draft, offer, pitch, quote, terms, toast **6** appeal, feeler, layout, motion, scheme, tender, thesis **7** measure, outline, proffer, program, project **8** overture, question **10** brainchild, hypothesis, invitation, nomination, resolution, suggestion
starter: **7** counter
__ Proposal, A: **6** Modest
Proposals
author: Neil Simon
Proposal, The (2009 film)
cast: Sandra Bullock, Ryan Reynolds
propose: **3** aim, ask, bid, put, woo **4** hope, mean, move, name, plan, urge **5** offer, posit **6** advise, aspire, broach, design, expect, intend, submit, tender **7** advance, counsel, present, proffer, purpose, request, resolve, suggest **8** nominate, propound, put forth, set forth **9** determine, introduce, recommend, undertake **10** come up with, put forward
prepare to ~: **5** kneel
proposition: **3** ask, bid **4** deal, plan **5** offer, terms **6** motion, scheme, thesis **7** bargain, measure, proffer, propose, solicit, theorem, venture **8** contract, overture, question **9** agreement, principle, reasoning **10** resolution, suggestion
logical ~: **5** axiom, lemma **6** if-then
losing ~: **3** dog **4** bomb, diet, flop, no-go **6** bummer, fiasco **7** clinker, debacle, failure, washout
propound: **3** put **4** pose **5** state **6** assert, submit **7** declare, propose, suggest **8** advocate, set forth, theorize **10** put forward
__-propre: **5** amour
proprietary rights: **9** ownership
proprieties: **8** protocol
proprietor: **4** host **5** owner **6** holder **7** manager **8** landlady, landlord **9** possessor
proprietorship: **6** tenure **8** monopoly, property **9** ownership
__ proprietorship: **4** sole
propriety: **4** form **5** mense, mores, order, right **6** reason **7** concord, decency, decorum, dignity, fitness, modesty **8** breeding, ceremony, courtesy, delicacy, meetness, niceties, protocol **9** amenities, etiquette, formality, gentility, politesse, punctilio, rectitude, rightness **10** accordance, civilities, classicism, convention, politeness, refinement, seemliness
proprio __: **4** motu
propter __: **3** hoc
propulsion: **6** thrust **8** momentum
__ propulsion: **3** ion, jet **5** ionic
propylene __: **6** glycol
propylene derivative: **5** allyl
__ pro quo: **4** quid
prorate: **5** allot, scale, share **6** divide, ration **7** portion **9** apportion
pro re __: **4** nata
prorogue: **5** waive **6** put off, recess **8** postpone **9** terminate
prosaic: **3** dry **4** blah, drab, dull, flat, tame **5** banal, corny, ho-hum, hokey, lowly, passé, stale, trite, vapid **6** boring, common, jejune, old hat **7** clichéd, fatuous, humdrum, insipid, literal, mundane, routine, tedious **8** bromidic, everyday, lifeless, ordinary, outdated, outmoded, unlively, workaday **9** colorless, hackneyed **10** lackluster, monotonous, pedestrian, uneventful, uninspired, unoriginal
pros and __: **4** cons
ProScan: **2** TV **5** TV set **10** television
competitor: ***see*** electronics company
proscenium: **5** apron
proscenium __: **4** arch
prosciutto: **3** ham **4** meat
purveyor: **4** deli
proscribe: **3** ban, bar, nix **4** damn, tabu, veto **5** debar, exile, taboo **6** abjure, banish, enjoin, forbid, outlaw, reject **7** boycott, censure, condemn, enforce, exclude, rule out **8** denounce, disallow, prohibit, sentence **9** blacklist, interdict, repudiate **10** expatriate
proscribed: **4** tabu **5** taboo **7** illegal **8** smuggled **9** forbidden **10** contraband, not allowed
act: **4** no-no, tabu **5** taboo
proscription: **3** ban **4** no-no, tabu, veto **5** exile, taboo **7** embargo,

refusal 8 negation 9 expulsion 10 banishment

prose: 4 book, talk, text 5 essay, novel, story 6 letter, ramble, satire, speech, thesis 7 article, fiction, romance, writing 8 language, whodunit, workbook 10 bestseller, exposition, literature, nonfiction, short story
- **art of ~:** 4 rhet. 8 rhetoric
- **improve ~:** 4 edit 5 emend 6 revise 7 rewrite

__ prose: 6 purple

Prose __: 4 Edda

prosecute: 3 sue, try 4 wage 6 accuse, indict, pursue, summon 7 arraign, conduct, contest, wage war 8 litigate 9 go to court 10 put on trial

prosecution: 4 suit 5 trial 7 lawsuit 10 litigation

prosecutor: 2 DA 3 att. 5 trier 6 lawyer 8 attorney, litigant 9 detective
- **chief ~:** 2 AG
- **phrase:** 5 I rest

proselyte: 7 recruit 8 disciple, follower 9 layperson 10 catechumen

proselytize: 7 convert, recruit, win over 8 persuade

__ prosequi: 5 nolle

Proserpina
- **author:** John Ruskin
- **equivalent:** 10 Persephone
- **husband:** 5 Pluto
- **mother:** 5 Ceres

pro-shop purchase: 3 peg 4 club, iron, tees 5 visor, wedge 6 driver, putter 7 golf bag 8 golf club

prosit: 5 salud, skoal, toast 6 cheers, kampai, saluté 9 bene vobis

Prosky: 6 Robert

prosody, dictionary of: 6 gradus

prospect: 3 dig, pan 4 hope, seek, sift, view 5 drill, scene, sight, vista 6 chance, search, survey 7 chances, nominee, outlook, promise, scenery 8 look into, overlook, panorama 9 candidate, jobhunter, landscape 10 likelihood

prospective: 6 coming, future, likely 7 looming, pending, planned, would-be 8 destined, eventual, expected, hoped-for, imminent, intended, possible, proposed, soon-to-be 9 impending, in the wind, looked-for, potential, promising

prospector: 5 miner 9 sourdough 10 forty-niner
- **aid:** 3 map, pan 4 pick 6 shovel
- **find:** 3 ore 4 lode 6 nugget
- **property:** 4 mine 5 claim
- **test:** 5 assay

prospects: 7 outlook
- **good ~:** 4 hope 7 promise
- **like some ~:** 5 bleak

prospectus: 4 list, plan 7 catalog, program, summary 8 brochure, document, syllabus, synopsis 9 catalogue

prosper: 3 win 4 boom, gain, grow, live, rise 5 bloom, score, yield 6 arrive, do well, flower, hack it, make it, pan out, profit, thrive 7 advance, blossom, catch on, develop, luck out, make out, prevail, produce, succeed, triumph, work out 8 fare well, flourish, get ahead, go places, go to town, grow rich, hit it big, increase, make good, multiply, progress 9 bear fruit, luxuriate, make money 10 strengthen

Prosper: 7 Mérimée 9 Buranelli

prospering: 7 booming, roaring 8 thriving 9 doing well

prosperity: 4 boom, ease, gain, luck 6 bounty, growth, luxury, plenty, profit, riches, wealth 7 comfort, fortune, success, welfare 8 good life, good luck, increase, interest, opulence, opulency, thriving 9 abundance, affluence, expansion, good times, happiness, inflation, well-being 10 betterment
- **general ~:** 4 weal

Prospero: 8 magician, sorcerer
- **play:** The Tempest
- **servant:** 5 Ariel 7 Caliban

prosperous: 4 rich 5 flush, lucky, palmy 6 loaded, monied, timely 7 booming, moneyed, opulent, roaring, wealthy, well-off 8 affluent, blooming, in clover, thriving, well-to-do 9 doing well, favorable, fortunate, opportune, promising, well-fixed 10 auspicious, in the dough, in the money, privileged, propertied, propitious, successful, well-heeled
- **time:** 4 boom 6 uptick 7 upswing

Prost: 5 Alain

prostrate: 3 low, sap 4 deck, fell, flat, obey, tire, weak 5 drain, floor, kneel, kotow, level, prone, spent, tired, weary 6 abject, broody, fallen, grovel, kowtow, pooped, ravage, submit, supine 7 bow down, drained, exhaust, fatigue, flatten, frazzle, wearied, wear out, worn out 8 dejected, frazzled, helpless, obedient, overcome, overturn, paralyse, paralyze, tuckered 9 bring down, enervated, exhausted, knock down, lying down, overpower, overthrow, overwhelm, powerless, reclining, recumbent, tucker out 10 beseeching, debilitate, discourage, horizontal, knocked out, submissive
- **be ~:** 3 lie 7 recline
- **oneself:** 3 bow 5 kneel 9 pay homage

prostration: 3 bow 6 homage 9 reverence, weariness

prosy: 4 dull 5 vapid 6 common 7 humdrum, prosaic, tedious 8 lifeless, ordinary 9 prosaical 10 dullsville

Prot.: 4 Bapt., Epis., Luth., Meth. 5 Episc., Presb.
- ***see also*** Protestant

protactinium: 7 element

protagonist: 4 hero, lead, part, star 6 leader 7 heroine 8 champion, exponent 9 headliner, principal, title role

Protagoras: 5 Greek 6 orator 11 philosopher
- **specialty:** 7 Sophism

protean: 5 fluid 6 labile 7 erratic, mutable 8 shifting, unstable, variable, wavering 9 mercurial, uncertain, versatile 10 changeable

protect: 3 pad 4 hide, save, tend, veil, wrap 5 cover, guard, shade, watch 6 assure, convoy, cradle, defend, embank, encase, ensure, foster, harbor, incase, insure, patrol, pillow, police, rescue, screen, secure, shield 7 bulwark, care for, cover up, cushion, fortify, harbour, shelter, store up, support, ward off 8 champion, chaperon, conserve, insulate, maintain, preserve, scrimp on, shepherd 9 chaperone, guarantee, look after, safeguard, vaccinate, watch over 10 take care of

protected: 4 alee, safe 5 legal 6 immune, inside, lawful, secure 9 unanxious 10 guaranteed
- **place:** 5 haven 6 cocoon, refuge 8 preserve
- **species:** 4 nene 5 panda

protection: 3 lee, mac, net 4 care, coat, egis, ward 5 aegis, apron, armor, cover, guard, haven, parka 6 buffer, escrow, harbor, jacket, mantra, refuge, safety, shield 7 barrier, bulwark, custody, defense, harbour, keeping, lodging, mantram, padding, rampart, shelter, slicker, support, sweater 8 auspices, covering, immunity, overalls, preserve, raincoat, security, tutelage, umbrella 9 armaments, assurance, blackmail, extortion, insurance, macintosh, patronage, safeguard, sanctuary, tarpaulin 10 mackintosh, precaution 11 macfarelane
- **from harm:** 6 asylum, refuge, safety 7 shelter 9 sanctuary
- **money:** 3 ice
- **name meaning ~:** 6 Warren

__ protection factor: 3 sun

protective: 7 careful, heedful, jealous 8 fatherly, maternal, motherly, parental, paternal, vigilant, watchful 9 avuncular, custodial, defensive 10 solicitous
- **covering:** 4 tarp 5 armor, shell
- **garment:** 3 bib 5 apron, G-suit, smock 7 lab coat 8 overalls
- **glasses:** 6 shades 7 goggles
- **insert:** 5 liner 6 insole
- **layer:** 5 ozone, paint

protector: 5 guard 6 escort, keeper, knight, savior 7 saviour, shelter 8 champion, defender, guardian, watchdog, watchman 9 bodyguard, caretaker, companion, custodian, proponent 10 benefactor
- **chest ~:** 3 bib

__ protector: 5 chest, surge

__ Protector: 4 Lord

protectorate: 6 colony 7 outpost 8 province 9 territory 10 dependency, possession, settlement
- **former British ~:** 4 Aden 6 Gambia

protégé: 4 ward
- **helper:** 6 mentor

Protege: 3 car 4 auto 5 Mazda

protein
- **acid:** 5 amino
- **blood ~:** 6 globin
- **castor bean ~:** 5 ricin
- **coagulation ~:** 6 fibrin
- **corn ~:** 4 zein
- **digestive ~:** 6 enzyme
- **milk ~:** 6 casein
- **muscle ~:** 5 actin
- **shell:** 6 capsid
- **source:** 3 egg, soy 4 bean, beef, fish, food, meat, soya, tofu 6 legume, lentil 7 seafood
- **starter:** 4 meta
- **synthesis need:** 3 RNA
- **wheat ~:** 6 gluten

protest: 4 beef, buck, flak, kick, riot, yowl 5 argue, demur, fight, flack, gripe, knock, march, rally, rebel, say no, sit-in 6 affirm, assert, attest, avouch, clamor, differ, grouse, insist, love-in, object, oppose, outcry, picket, refuse, resist, revolt, squawk, squeal, strike, unrest 7 boycott, dissent, grumble, inveigh, quibble 8 backtalk, complain, disagree, maintain, question, sound off 9 bellyache, challenge, complaint, fulminate, grievance, make a fuss 10 asseverate, make a stand, make a stink
- **dummy:** 6 effigy
- **kid's ~:** 5 did so, not me 6 did not
- **non-violent ~:** 5 chant, march, sit-in, vigil 6 love-in
- **under ~:** 8 forcibly

protester: 5 rebel 6 picket 7 heretic 8 maverick, militant, renegade 9 dissident 10 iconoclast, malcontent

...__ protest too much: 4 doth

Proteus: 4 moon, seer
- **father:** 8 Poseidon
- **planet:** 7 Neptune

protoavis: 6 fossil

protocol: 4 form, pact 6 policy, ritual, treaty 7 compact, concord, customs, decorum, manners, red tape 8 behavior, ceremony, civility, courtesy, covenant, niceties 9 agreement, amenities, concordat, etiquette, formality, politesse, propriety, rigmarole 10 obligation, rigamarole

__ Protocol, The: 5 Sigma

proto ender: 3 zoa 4 zoan 5 plasm

proton site: 4 atom 7 nucleus

protoplasm: 5 cells 6 matter
- **component:** 5 lipid 6 lipide

protoprogenitor: 3 Eve 4 Adam

prototype: 4 norm 5 first, ideal, model 6 mock-up 7 example, paragon, pattern 8 ancestor, exemplar, original, paradigm, standard 9 criterion, precursor 10 antecedent, forerunner, progenitor

prototypical: 5 ideal, model 7 classic

protozoan: 5 ameba, monad 6 amoeba 10 paramecium
- **propeller:** 6 cilium 9 pseudopod

protract: 5 delay 6 drag on, expand, extend, ramble 7 draw out, prolong, spin out, stretch, suspend, sustain 8 continue, elongate, hold over, increase, lengthen 9 keep going, string out 10 stretch out

protracted: 4 long, poky, slow 6 draggy 7 gradual, halting, lagging, languid, lengthy 8 crawling, creeping, dawdling, dilatory,

dragging, drawn-out, hesitant, marathon, overlong, plodding, slothful, sluggish, toddling **9** extensive, leisurely, lethargic, snaillike, strung-out, unhurried **10** deliberate
not ~: **5** brief, short, terse **8** succinct **10** to the point
protractedness: **6** length
protractor
measure: **5** angle
unit: **6** degree
protrude: **3** jut **4** poke **5** bulge, swell **6** beetle, extend **7** butt out, overlap, project **8** overhang, stand out, stick out
protruding: **7** beetled, pendant, pendent, salient **8** aquiline **9** obtrusive, prominent
edge: **6** flange
protrusion: **3** nub **4** bump, hump, knob, knot, knub, lump, node **5** bulge, gnarl **6** nodule **8** swelling **10** projection
protrusive: **9** prominent
protuberance: **3** nub **4** bump, hump, knob, knot, knub, lump, node **5** bulge, gnarl **6** nodule **8** swelling
protuberant: **5** nodal **6** bunchy **7** bulging **9** obtrusive, prominent
proud: **3** big **4** smug, vain **5** cocky, fiery, grand, lofty, noble, regal **6** august, chesty, lordly, snooty, superb **7** haughty, honored, pleased, pompous, stately, stuck-up, sublime, upright **8** arrogant, boastful, cavalier, egoistic, gloating, glorious, imposing, majestic, puffed up, scornful, snobbish, spirited, splendid, superior **9** conceited, dignified, gratified, hubristic, imperious, red-letter **10** big-talking, disdainful, dismissive, egoistical, high-handed, hoity-toity, majestical, triumphant
do one ~: **3** win **7** achieve, succeed **10** accomplish
proud __ peacock: **3** as a
Proud __: **4** Mary
Proud __, The: **4** Ones **5** Rebel
proud as a peacock
network: **3** NBC
Proud Mary (song)
artist: Creedence Clearwater Revival, Ike and Tina Turner
Proust, Marcel: **6** French, writer
work: The Captive
Cities of the Plain
The Guermantes Way
The Past Recaptured
Remembrance of Things Past
Swann's Way
The Sweet Cheat Gone
Within a Budding Grove
prove: **3** fix, try **4** find, show, test **5** add up, assay, check, end up **6** affirm, attest, back up, evince, pan out, reason, result, settle, try out, uphold, verify **7** analyze, bear out, certify, confirm, examine, explain, justify, sustain, testify, turn out, warrant, witness **8** check out, document, evidence, indicate, manifest, validate **9** ascertain, determine, establish, make stick **10** experiment
out: **4** wash **7** prevail
something to ~: **6** theory, thesis **7** theorem
wrong: **5** belie, parry, rebut **6** debunk, negate, oppugn, refute **7** confute, explode **8** disprove, overturn **10** contradict, controvert, invalidate
Prove It All Night (1978 song)
artist: Bruce Springsteen
proven: **5** sound, tried, valid **7** genuine **8** reliable, verified **9** qualified **10** undeniable
provenance: **4** root **6** origin, source **9** etymology, inception **10** derivation
Provençal: **8** language
__ provençale: **3** à la
Provence
city in ~: **3** Aix **5** Arles
dance: **9** tambourin
department in ~: **3** Var
locale: **6** France
__-Provence: **5** Aix-en
provender: **4** chow, eats, feed, food, grub, meat **6** ration, viands **7** aliment, eatable, edibles, vittles **8** victuals **10** provisions, sustenance
preparer: **4** chef, cook
provide ~: **4** cook, feed **5** cater, serve **7** nourish
proverb: **3** saw **4** word **5** adage, axiom, gnome, maxim, moral, motto, truth **6** byword, dictum, phrase, saying, slogan, truism **7** epigram **8** aphorism, apothegm **9** platitude **10** apophthegm
proverbial: **5** known **6** famous **8** familiar **9** axiomatic, well-known
Proverbs: **4** book
follower: **4** Eccl.
preceder: **6** Psalms
Prove Your Love (1988 song)
artist: Taylor Dayne
provide: **3** fit **4** feed, give, keep, lend **5** allow, bring, cater, equip, fix up, grant, offer, put up, ready, serve, spare, stake, stock, treat, yield **6** afford, bestow, donate, fit out, impart, outfit, purvey, ration, render, supply **7** advance, appoint, deliver, furnish, prepare, present, procure, produce, proffer, require, satisfy, specify, support, sustain **8** accouter, accoutre, dispense, maintain, turn over **9** look after, replenish, stipulate **10** administer, contribute, take care of
for: **4** feed, keep **7** shelter, support, sustain **8** maintain **9** stipulate
more: **3** add **6** top off **9** replenish
temporarily: **4** lend, loan
provided: **8** granting **9** given that
that: **4** so as **6** in case **8** as long as
providence: **4** fate **5** karma **6** kismat, kismet **7** caution, fortune **9** foresight, frugality **10** discretion
Providence: **4** city, port, town **5** river
athletes: **5** Bears
conference: **7** Big East
locale: Rhode Island
school: **5** Brown
school south of ~: **3** URI
Providence (NBC drama)
cast: Mike Farrell (Dr. Jim Hansen)
Melina Kanakaredes (Dr. Sydney Hansen)
Concetta Tomei (Lynda Hansen)
provident: **4** wise **5** canny, chary, sober **6** frugal, saving, shrewd **7** careful, politic, prudent, sparing, thrifty **8** cautious, discreet, vigilant **9** judicious **10** deliberate, discerning, economical, farsighted, thoughtful
providential: **4** well **5** blest, happy, lucky **7** blessed, charmed, favored, on a roll **9** fortunate, on a streak **10** auspicious, felicitous, fortuitous, propitious
providing: **8** as long as, assuming, provided **9** given that, subject to, supposing **10** in the event
province: **3** job **4** area, duty, land, line, part, post, role, zone **5** arena, field, orbit, place, range, realm, shire, world **6** canton, charge, colony, county, domain, office, region, sphere **7** concern, demesne, purview, quarter, section **8** business, capacity, district, division, dominion, function **9** bailiwick, territory **10** department
Provincetown: **4** city, town
locale: **4** Mass. **7** Cape Cod
provincial: **4** hick, rude **5** local, rough, rural, yokel **6** common, little, narrow, rustic **7** bucolic, bumpkin, country, insular, limited, plowboy **8** homespun, outlying, pastoral, regional **9** backwoods, bucolical, hidebound, home-grown, parochial, sectarian, small-town **10** clodhopper
language: **6** patois **7** dialect
__ Provincial: **6** French
Provine: **7** Dorothy
proving __: **6** ground
provision: **3** rig **4** plan, term **5** catch, equip, joker, rider, stock, store, terms **6** clause, demand, fit out, kicker, outfit, ration, supply **7** article, furnish, strings, support **8** accouter, accoutre, catering **9** agreement, condition, endowment, fine print, foresight, insurance, requisite **10** limitation, precaution, small print
home contract ~: **6** escrow
make ~ for: **5** allow, set up **7** arrange, prepare
provisional: **4** test **5** trial **6** acting, pro tem **7** interim, limited, passing, stopgap, subject **9** dependant, dependent, ephemeral, makeshift, provisory, qualified, temporary, tentative, transient
government: **5** junta
worker: **4** temp
provisionary: **9** tentative
provisions: **3** kit **4** eats, fare, food, grub, meat **5** board, items **6** stores, viands **7** aliment, eatable, edibles, strings, victual, vittles **8** eatables, supplies, victuals **9** equipment, groceries, provender **10** sustenance
proviso: **4** term **5** catch, joker, rider, state **6** clause, demand, kicker **7** strings **9** agreement, condition, fine print, requisite **10** limitation, small print
provisory: **9** dependant, dependent, temporary, tentative
Provo: **4** city, town
athletes: **7** Cougars
locale: **4** Utah
neighbor: **4** Orem
school: **3** BYU
town near ~: **4** Lehi
__ provocateur: **5** agent
provocation: **4** spur **5** cause **6** injury, insult, reason, slight **7** affront, grounds, offense **8** occasion, vexation **9** annoyance, challenge, incentive, indignity
provocative: **4** racy **5** heady, juicy, pushy **6** erotic, lively, risqué, sultry, trying **7** defiant, irksome **8** alluring, annoying, exciting, inviting, tempting **9** insulting, offensive, provoking, ravishing, vexatious **10** irritating
provoke: **3** bug, egg, get, ire, irk, nag, vex **4** bait, defy, fire, fret, gall, goad, miff, move, prod, rile, roil, spur, stir **5** anger, annoy, cause, chafe, egg on, evoke, grate, hop up, hound, incur, peeve, pique, prime, raise, rouse, roust, spark, spite, start, taunt, tease, tempt, upset, waken **6** arouse, ask for, bother, elicit, enrage, excite, foment, incite, induce, insult, kindle, lead to, madden, needle, nettle, offend, pester, pother, prompt, put out, ruffle, stir up, whip up, work up **7** affront, aggress, bedevil, disturb, enflame, ferment, incense, inflame, inspire, perturb, produce, torment, trigger **8** engender, exercise, irritate, motivate, occasion **9** aggravate, call forth, challenge, displease, draw forth, galvanize, impassion, infuriate, instigate, stimulate, tantalize, titillate **10** exasperate
as a fight: **4** pick
provoked: **3** mad **5** huffy, irate, upset
easily ~: **5** fiery, short **7** grouchy **8** snappish **9** irascible
provoker: **5** tease **6** gadfly **9** aggressor
provolone: **6** cheese **7** Italian
prow: **3** bow **4** stem **5** front
away from the ~: **3** aft **6** astern
locale: **4** hull
opposite: **5** stern
part of the ~: **5** hawse **10** figurehead
prowess: **4** grit, guts **5** heart, might, nerve, pluck, power, skill, spunk, valor, vigor **6** daring, genius, mettle, starch, talent **7** ability, bravery, courage, heroism, mastery, stamina, stomach **8** boldness, facility, strength **9** derring-do, endurance, expertise, fortitude, gallantry, hardihood, readiness **10** efficiency, right stuff, virtuosity
prowl: **4** hunt, lurk, roam, rove, seek **5** creep, range, sculk, skulk, slink, sneak, stalk, steal **6** cruise, forage, search, wander, waylay **7** slither **8** scavenge **10** nose around
on the ~: **5** loose **7** escaped
prowl __: **3** car
prowler: **5** thief **6** robber **7** burglar **8** intruder
Prowler: **3** car **4** auto **8** Plymouth

Prowse: 6 Juliet
proximal: 4 near 9 immediate
opposite: 6 distal
proximate: 4 near, next, nigh 5 close, later 6 at hand, nearby 7 close by, closest, nearest 8 adjacent, imminent 9 bordering, following, immediate, impending, secondary 10 convenient, subsequent
proximity: 8 nearness, presence, vicinity 9 closeness, immediacy 10 contiguity
in close ~: 4 near 5 anear 6 hard by
place in ~: 6 appose
Proxmire: 7 William
proxy: 3 agt., rep, sub 5 agent, vicar 6 deputy 7 stand-in 8 delegate 9 alternate, appointee, go-between, surrogate 10 lieutenant, substitute
be ~ for: 7 stand in 9 represent 10 substitute
Proyas: 4 Alex
PRS, on the phone: 5 seven
prude: 4 prig 7 puritan 8 bluenose 9 nice Nelly, Victorian 10 goody-goody
prudence: 4 care, wits 5 sense 6 sanity, thrift, virtue, wisdom 7 caution, economy 8 judgment, sapience 10 discretion, expediency, horse sense, precaution
__ Prudence: 4 Dear
prudent: 4 safe, sage, sane, wary, wise 5 canny, chary, fussy, leery, sound 6 frugal, shrewd 7 careful, finicky, guarded, heedful, politic, sapient, sparing, tactful, thrifty 8 cautious, discreet, exacting, finiking, finnicky, keen-eyed, rational, rigorous, sensible, tactical, thorough, vigilant 9 advisable, assiduous, attentive, expedient, farseeing, judicious, observant, provident, realistic, sagacious 10 diplomatic, discerning, economical, farsighted, fastidious, longheaded, meticulous, particular, reasonable, scrupulous, thoughtful
be ~: 3 eke 5 skimp, stint 6 budget 7 refrain 9 economize
prudential
see prudent
Prudential
competitor: *see* insurance company
prudery: 7 modesty
Prudhoe Bay
craft: 5 kayak, oiler 6 tanker
dwelling: 4 iglu 5 igloo
locale: 6 Alaska
product: 3 oil 9 petroleum
Prudhomme: 4 Paul 5 Sully
Prudhomme, Paul: 4 chef
prudish: 4 prim, smug 5 fussy, rigid, stern, timid 6 demure, prissy, proper, strict, stuffy 7 finicky, genteel, mincing, precise, stilted, uptight 8 affected, finiking, finnicky, overnice, priggish, starched 9 puritanic, simpering, squeamish, Victorian 10 fastidious, goody-goody, overmodest
Pruett: 6 Jeanne
Prufrock creator: T.S. Eliot
prune: 3 cut, lop, mow, top 4 clip, crop, dock, pare, plum, snip, thin, trim 5 fruit, lower, shape, shave, shear 6 lop off, reduce, remove 7 abridge, curtail, cut back, scissor, shorten, snip off, thin out 8 condense, diminish, minimize, truncate 9 summarize 10 abbreviate
formerly: 4 plum
pastry filling: 6 lekvar
__ prune: 6 pitted
prunella: 6 fabric 8 material
pruning __: 4 hook 6 shears
pruning candidate: 4 tree 5 hedge, shrub
Prusiner, Stanley B.: 8 Nobelist
Prussia: 5 state
cavalryman: 4 ulan 5 uhlan
locale: 7 Germany
Prussian __: 4 blue
__-Prussian War: 6 Austro, Franco
pry: 3 spy 4 nose, peek, peep, peer, poke, root 5 force, heave, jimmy, lever, raise, snoop, stare, wrest, wring 6 butt in, elicit, extort, horn in, kibitz, meddle, search 7 crowbar, disjoin, enquire, extract, inquire, intrude, obtrude, ransack, wiretap 8 jerk away, listen in, question, quidnunc 9 disengage, eavesdrop, ferret out, force open, interfere, interpose 10 scrutinize
__ Pry: 4 Paul
Pryce: 8 Jonathan
prying: 4 busy, nosy 5 nosey 7 curious, ferrety 8 invasive 9 curiosity, intrusive, obtrusive 10 meddlesome, snoopiness
tool: 5 jimmy, lever 7 crowbar
Prynne, Hester daughter: 5 Pearl
Pryor, Richard: 5 actor 8 comedian
film: Blue Collar (1978)
Bustin' Loose (1981)
California Suite (1978)
Hit! (1973)
Lady Sings the Blues (1972)
Silver Streak (1976)
Stir Crazy (1980)
The Toy (1982)
psalm: 4 hymn, pean, song 5 chant, paean, verse 6 eulogy 7 chorale, introit 8 canticle
address: 5 O Lord
word: 3 yea 5 selah
Psalms: 4 book
follower: 8 Proverbs
preceder: 3 Job
singer: 6 cantor
psaltery: 6 string, zither
origin: 6 Europe
p's and q's: 7 manners 8 protocol 9 etiquette
mind one's ~: 6 behave 10 toe the line
PSAT: 4 exam, test
provider: 3 ETS
taker: 2 jr. 6 junior
pseudo: 4 fake, mock, sham 5 bogus, faked, false, phony, put-on, quack, quasi 6 ersatz, forged, phoney, unreal 7 assumed, feigned, plastic, pretend, suspect 8 spurious 9 imitation, imitative, pretended, simulated, synthetic, unnatural 10 artificial, fabricated, fictitious, fraudulent
pseudoaesthetic: 4 arty 5 artsy
pseudologist: 4 liar
pseudonym: 4 name 5 alias, title 6 anonym 7 pen name 8 cognomen 10 nom de plume
letters: 3 AKA
pseudopod possessor: 5 ameba 6 amoeba
pshaw: 3 bah, tut 4 drat, pooh 9 expletive
psi: 5 Greek 6 letter 9 telepathy
preceder: 3 chi
successor: 5 omega
P.S. I __ U: 3 Luv
P.S. I Love You (1964 song)
artist: Beatles
P.S. I Love You (2007 film)
cast: Gerard Butler, Hilary Swank
psoas site: 3 hip
psst!: 3 hey 6 hey you
cousin: 4 ahem
follower: 6 in here, listen
PSU
conference: 6 Big Ten
see also Penn State
psych: 4 stir 5 rouse, upset 6 arouse 7 agitate, enthuse 10 intimidate
out: 5 bluff, spook 6 rattle, unglue 7 disrupt, disturb, fluster, unnerve 8 unsettle 9 speculate 10 demoralize, discompose, disconcert, intimidate
up: 5 ready 6 incite 7 enthuse, hearten, inspire, prepare 8 embolden, enspirit, get ready, imbolden, inspirit, motivate 9 encourage
__ psych: 3 pop
psyche: 4 mind, self, soul 5 anima 6 pneuma, spirit 9 élan vital 10 inner child
component: 2 id 3 ego 8 superego
Psyche: 8 asteroid
daughter: 7 Volupta
lover: 4 Eros
__ Psyche: 5 Ode to
Psychedelic Shack (1970 song)
artist: Temptations
psyched up: 4 agog, high 5 eager, ready 6 on edge 8 prepared 10 inspirited
Psyche knot: 4 coif 6 hairdo 8 coiffure
psychiatrist: 7 analyst
Austrian ~: 5 Adler, Freud
org.: 3 APA
Swiss ~: 4 Jung
psychic: 4 seer 6 medium, mental, mystic, occult 8 mystical 9 sensitive, spiritual 10 palm reader, responsive, soothsayer, telepathic
power: 3 ESP 9 telepathy
sight: 4 aura
Psycho (1960 film)
cast: Martin Balsam, John Gavin, Janet Leigh, Vera Miles, Anthony Perkins
director: Alfred Hitchcock
locale: 5 motel
psycho ender: 6 babble
psychological: 6 mental 9 emotional
threshold: 5 limen
psychology: 7 science
appetite, in ~: 6 orexis
branch of ~: 7 haptics
starter: 4 meta, para
study: 4 mind
__ psychology: 3 ego, pop 4 mass
psychrophobe fear: 4 cold
pt.: 3 amt., qty. 4 meas.
compass ~: 3 dir., ENE, ESE, NNE, NNW, SSE, SSW, WNW, WSW
fraction: 2 oz.
high ~: 3 mtn. 4 elev.
multiple: 2 qt. 3 gal.
of speech: 2 vb 3 adj., adv. 4 conj.
see also point
Pt: 4 elem. 7 element 8 platinum
78 for ~: 4 at. no.
P.T.: 6 Barnum
PTA
member: 3 dad, mom 7 teacher
part of ~: 4 assn. 5 assoc. 6 parent 7 teacher
ptarmigan: 4 bird 6 grouse
PT boat: 7 warship
P-T connection: 3 QRS
PT Cruiser: 3 car 4 auto 8 Chrysler
pteriodsperm: 4 fern 5 plant
pterodactyl: 7 reptile
of film: 5 Rodan
Ptolemy: 8 Egyptian 10 astronomer
ptui: 3 fie 4 pooh 6 bunkum 8 nonsense
Pu: 4 elem. 7 element 9 plutonium
94 for ~: 4 at. no.
pub: 3 bar, inn 4 dive 5 joint 6 lounge, saloon, tavern 7 barroom, gin mill, taproom 8 alehouse, grogshop, taphouse 9 bierstube, roadhouse
expression: 5 on tap
fixture: 3 tap 9 dartboard, pool table
game: 4 pool 5 darts
order: 3 ale 4 beer, pint, suds 5 draft, lager, round, stein, stout 8 schooner
perch: 5 stool 8 barstool
projectile: 4 dart
pub-crawl: 6 barhop
puberty: 5 youth 8 minority 9 childhood 10 immaturity, pubescence
combining form: 4 hebe-
past ~: 5 adult 7 grown-up
pubescent: 5 young 8 immature 10 adolescent
public: 3 mob 4 city, folk, free, open 5 civic, civil, clear, known, overt, plain, state, urban 6 buyers, common, in view, masses, nation, patent, people, shared, social, voters, vulgar 7 country, exposed, federal, general, obvious, popular, society, visible 8 apparent, audience, citizens, clear-cut, communal, everyone, exoteric, explicit, manifest, national, ordinary, populace, societal, subjects, unhidden, unveiled 9 clientele, community, following, hoi polloi, multitude, municipal, published, statewide, universal, well-known 10 accessible, electorate, observable, population, recognized, supporters, unshrouded, widespread
announcer, formerly: 5 crier 9 town crier
area: 4 mall, park 5 plaza 6 square 7 commons
assembly: 4 diet 5 forum 7 meeting

figure: **3** VIP **4** lion, name, star **5** celeb **7** big name, notable **8** eminence, luminary, somebody **9** celebrity, dignitary, personage, superstar
general ~: **3** mob **4** folk, herd **5** world **6** masses, people, rabble **7** society **8** populace, riffraff **9** bourgeois, citizenry, hoi polloi, multitude, plebeians
good: **4** weal
house: **3** bar, inn, pub **5** lodge **6** saloon, tavern **7** barroom
in ~: **6** openly **7** overtly
land: **4** park **5** plaza **6** square **7** commons
make ~: **3** air **4** bare, leak, talk, vent **5** admit, break, speak, spill, voice **6** betray, expose, report, reveal, spread, unmask, unveil **7** come out, divulge, exhibit, lay bare, let slip, publish, uncover **8** announce, disclose, give away, proclaim **9** broadcast
notices: **2** ad
outcry: **5** stink **7** scandal
performance: **4** play **5** drama, opera, raree **6** ballet **7** concert
persona: **5** image
regard: **5** éclat **6** renown, repute **7** acclaim, stardom **8** eminence **9** celebrity, notoriety **10** popularity, prominence, reputation
sentiment: **5** pulse
servant: **3** rep **4** veep **5** mayor **7** officer, senator **8** alderman, governor **9** president, town clerk **10** politician
spat: **5** scene
speaker: **6** orator **10** campaigner, politician
transport: **2** el **3** bus, cab, jet **4** hack, taxi **5** ferry, metro, plane, train **6** subway **7** autobus, minibus **8** airplane
public __: **3** eye **4** debt, life, room **5** enemy, house, image, trust, works **6** domain, figure, health, option, policy, school, sector **7** affairs, library, opinion, servant, service
__ public: **6** notary
Public __ Administration: **5** Works
__ Public: **3** Joe **5** John Q.
__ publica: **3** res
publication: **4** book, text, tome **5** issue, novel, organ, print **6** annals, volume **7** booklet, edition, journal, leaflet, release, reprint, romance, writing **8** brochure, handbill, magazine, pamphlet, printing, whodunit **9** anthology, broadcast, newspaper, paperback, statement **10** bestseller, newsletter, periodical
book before ~: **2** ms. **10** manuscript
online ~: **5** e-book, e-zine
prepare for ~: **4** edit **6** censor, redact, revise **10** blue-pencil
slick ~: **3** mag **8** magazine
Public Citizen, Inc.
founder: Ralph Nader
public defender: **3** att. **4** atty. **6** lawyer **8** attorney **9** counselor
Public Enemies (2009 film)
cast: Christian Bale, Marion Cotillard, Johnny Depp
Public Enemy, The (1931 film)
cast: James Cagney, Mae Clarke, Jean Harlow
__ public eye: **5** in the
publicity: **2** ad **3** ink **4** hype, plug, puff **5** blurb, boost, flack, pitch, press, promo **6** hoopla, report, spread **7** billing, build-up, fanfare, handout, puffery, release, write-up **8** ballyhoo **9** attention, billboard, limelight, notoriety, promotion, spotlight **10** commercial, propaganda
generator: **4** sale **5** press, PR man, stunt **6** come-on **7** freebie **8** promoter
piece: **2** ad **5** promo **6** come-on, review **10** commercial
publicize: **3** air **4** bare, bill, flog, hype, plug, puff, push, sell, tout **5** boost, extol, pitch **6** extoll, herald, hype up, play up, spread, talk up **7** build up, promote, trumpet, write up **8** announce, headline, skywrite **9** advertise, billboard, broadcast, celebrate, circulate, make known, propagate, spotlight
publicized: **6** famous **8** renowned **9** notorious, well-known **10** celebrated
Public Men
author: Allen Drury
public-opinion __: **4** poll
publish: **3** air **4** bare, vend **5** issue, print, write **6** get out, put out, report, reveal, spread **7** lay bare **8** disclose, proclaim **9** circulate, propagate, ventilate **10** distribute, promulgate
publisher: **5** press **8** magazine **9** newspaper
ad: **5** blurb **6** review
crime: **5** libel
DC ~: **3** GPO
org.: **3** ABA
publishing: **5** media, press
employee: **6** editor **7** proofer **8** reporter **9** columnist **10** journalist
exec: **2** ed. **6** editor
problem: **6** errata **7** erratum
publishing __: **5** house
__ publishing: **7** desktop
Pucci, Emilio: **7** Italian **8** designer
Puccini, Giacomo: **7** Italian **8** composer
piece: **4** aria, opus, tema **5** opera
work: Edgar
Girl of the Golden West
La Boheme
La Rondine
Le Villi
Madame Butterfly
Manon Lescaut
Tosca
Turandot
puce: **5** color **6** purple **8** brownish, purplish
relative: ***see*** purple color
puck: **4** disc, disk
game: **6** hockey **9** ice hockey
stopper: **6** goalie
Puck: **3** imp **4** moon **6** sprite **8** Wolfgang
master: **6** Oberon
planet: **6** Uranus
pucka: **4** good **6** proper **7** genuine **8** reliable **9** authentic
pucker: **4** fold, knit, ruck, tuck **5** pinch, plait, pleat, purse **6** cockle, crease, furrow, gather, ruffle, rumple, shrink **7** crinkle, crumple, squeeze, wrinkle **8** compress, contract
up: **4** kiss **5** purse
puckered fabric: **6** plisse
Puckett: **4** Gary **5** Kirby
Puckett and the Union Gap, Gary
song: Lady Willpower (1968)
Over You (1968)
This Girl Is a Woman Now (1969)
Woman, Woman (1967)
Young Girl (1968)
Puckett, Kirby: **4** Twin **10** outfielder
puckish: **3** fey **5** elfin **6** impish **7** playful
creature: **3** elf **4** pixy **5** pixie **6** sprite **10** leprechaun
expression: **4** grin
puckster: **6** skater
org.: **3** NHL
sport: **6** hockey **9** ice hockey
P-U connection: **4** QRST
pudding: **4** flan **5** sweet **6** junket, mousse **7** custard, dessert, tapioca **8** flummery
ingredient: **3** egg **4** milk, plum, suet
plantain ~: **6** foofoo
thickened, as ~: **3** set
__ pudding: **4** plum, snow, suet **5** blood, bread, hasty
...pudding __ the eating: **4** is in
puddle: **4** pool
contents: **3** mud **4** rain **5** water
walk through a ~: **4** wade **5** slosh **6** splash
__ puddle: **3** mud
Puddleduck: **6** Jemima
puddle-jumper: **5** plane **8** airplane
take a ~: **3** fly
Pudd'nhead Wilson
author: Mark Twain
...puddy __!: **3** tat
pudgy
not ~: **4** lean, slim, thin, wiry **5** rangy **6** skinny, svelte **7** slender, willowy
see also obese
Pueblo: **4** city, town **5** tribe **6** Indian **7** Amerind
ancestor: **7** Anasazi
enemy: **3** Ute
locale: **8** Colorado
material: **5** adobe
New Mexico ~: **5** Acoma
people: **4** Hopi, Taos, Zuñi
site: **5** cliff
sunken chamber: **4** kiva
Puente, Tito: **7** drummer **10** bandleader
genre: **4** jazz **5** salsa
Puenzo: **4** Luis
puerile: **3** raw **4** weak **5** green, inane, silly, vapid, young **6** callow, infant, jejune, simple, stupid **7** babyish, fatuous, foolish, kiddish, trivial **8** childish, immature, juvenile, youthful **9** childlike, frivolous, infantile, senseless, unfledged **10** adolescent, nonserious, ridiculous, sophomoric
puerility: **5** youth **9** frivolity **10** callowness, immaturity
Puerto __: **4** Rico
Puerto Rico: **4** isle **6** island
capital: **7** San Juan
city: **4** Moca **5** Ponce **6** Caguas **7** Bayamón **8** Carolina
clock setting: **3** AST
instrument: **6** cuatro
writer: **5** Ferré **6** Arrivi
Puerto Vallarta: **4** city, town
locale: **6** Mexico **7** Jalisco
__-Puf: **3** Sta
puff: **3** air **4** blow, drag, gasp, gulp, gust, huff, hype, pant, plug, pull, waft, wind, wisp **5** blast, bloat, blurb, boost, draft, heave, pitch, promo, quilt, smoke, swell, whiff **6** breath, breeze, exhale, hairdo, inhale, overdo, pastry, praise, wheeze **7** breathe, distend, draught, enlarge, flatter, inflate, promote, upsweep **9** advertise, comforter, publicity, publicize **10** exaggerate, overpraise
along: **4** chug
ender: **4** ball
huff and ~: **4** blow, gasp, pant **6** wheeze
move on a ~ of air: **4** waft
of smoke: **4** wisp
out: **5** bulge **6** billow, blouse **7** balloon, inflate
piece: **5** blurb
up: **4** laud **5** bloat, elate, exalt, extol, pride, swell **6** billow, expand, extoll, praise **7** balloon, distend, enlarge, fill out, flatter, inflate, magnify **9** embroider, intumesce **10** exaggerate, overpraise
puff __: **5** adder, piece
__ puff: **5** cream **6** powder
Puff: **3** cat **6** dragon
puffball: **6** fungus **9** dandelion
Puff Daddy
real name: Sean Combs
song: All Night Long (1999)
Been Around the World (1998)
Can't Nobody Hold Me Down (1997)
Come With Me (1998)
I'll Be Missing You (1997)
It's All About the Benjamins (1997)
Lookin' at Me (1998)
Mo Money Mo Problems (1997)
No Time (1996)
Satisfy You (1999)
Someone (1997)
Victory (1998)
Puffed Rice: **6** cereal
competitor: ***see*** cereal
puffed-up: **4** smug, vain **5** proud, tumid **6** stuffy **7** fustian, pompous, swollen **8** gloating **9** conceited **10** big-talking
Puffed Wheat: **6** cereal
competitor: ***see*** cereal
puffer: **4** fish, fugu **9** globefish
puffery: **4** hype **6** hoopla **8** ballyhoo, flattery **9** publicity
puffin: **3** auk **4** bird
puffiness: **5** bloat, edema **6** oedema **8** swelling
puff-of-smoke sound: **4** poof

__ Puffs: 5 Cocoa
Puff (The Magic Dragon) (1963 song)
artist: Peter, Paul and Mary
puffy: 4 full 7 billowy, bloated, bulging, swollen 8 enlarged, inflamed, inflated 9 distended
__ Puffy Combs: 4 Sean
pug: 3 dog, toy 4 nose 5 boxer 6 canine 7 fighter 9 gladiator
ender: 4 mark
pug __: 4 mill, nose
Puget Sound: 5 inlet
locale: 6 Tacoma 7 Everett, Olympia, Pacific, Seattle 9 Bremerton 10 Washington
pugilism: 4 ring 6 boxing 10 fisticuffs
pugilist: 5 boxer 7 fighter, palooka 9 gladiator
asset: 5 reach
garb: 4 robe 6 gloves, trunks
milieu: 4 ring 5 arena
org.: 3 WBA, WBC
pay: 5 purse
punch: 2 KO 3 jab, TKO 6 one-two
seat: 5 stool
weapon: 4 fist
see also boxer
pugmark: 5 trace, trail
pugnacious: 4 mean, ugly 5 irate, nasty, salty, surly, tough 6 feisty, ornery 7 defiant, hateful, hawkish, hostile, martial, scrappy, warlike 8 contrary, fighting, inimical, menacing, militant, ructious, spiteful 9 bellicose, combative, malicious, truculent 10 aggressive, malevolent, unfriendly
pugnacity: 5 fight 6 temper 9 surliness 10 aggression
Pugni: 5 Cesar 6 Cesare
Pugsley: 6 Addams
puissance: 3 vim 4 dint, thew 5 brawn, force, might, power, thews, vigor 6 energy, muscle 7 fitness, muscles, potence, potency, stamina 8 vitality 9 beefiness, endurance, fortitude, hardiness, huskiness, stoutness, toughness 10 brawniness, brute force, mightiness, robustness, ruggedness, sturdiness
puissant: 4 hale, iron, wiry 5 beefy, burly, hardy, hefty, hunky, husky, lusty, stout, tough 6 brawny, hearty, mighty, potent, robust, rugged, sinewy, steely, stocky, sturdy, virile 7 doughty 8 almighty, athletic, forceful, indurate, muscular, powerful, stalwart, vigorous 9 Atlantean, herculean, strapping, well-built 10 able-bodied, red-blooded
Pujols, Albert
sport: 8 baseball
pukka: 4 good 6 proper 7 genuine 8 reliable 9 authentic
pukka __: 5 sahib
__ Pulaski: 4 Fort
pulchritude: 6 beauty
pulchritudinous: 4 cute, fair 5 bonny 6 bonnie, comely, lovely, pretty 7 winsome 8 alluring, gorgeous, handsome, striking, stunning 9 beautiful, ravishing 10 attractive
pule: 3 sob 4 bawl, mewl, wail, weep 5 whine 6 boohoo, snivel 7 blubber, grumble, whimper
puli: 3 dog 5 canid 6 canine
Pulitzer: 5 award, prize 6 Joseph
category: 5 drama, music 10 journalism, literature
rival: 4 Ochs 6 Hearst
pull: 3 lug, row, tow, tug 4 cull, drag, draw, haul, jerk, lure, pick, puff, tear, weed, yank 5 clout, heave, labor, pluck, power, trail, troll, truck, tug at, tweak, twist 6 allure, appeal, entice, entrée, evulse, gather, paddle, remove, snatch, sprain, strain, twitch, uproot, weight, wrench 7 attract, charism, extract, receive, stretch 8 charisma, intrigue, leverage, pressure, strength, traction 9 dislocate, influence, magnetism 10 attraction
a fast one: 3 con 4 fool 5 cheat, cozen, outdo, trick 6 delude, outwit 7 deceive, defraud, mislead, swindle 8 flimflam, hoodwink, outsmart 9 bamboozle
ahead of: 4 pass
a hoax: 5 bluff, cheat, feign, put on 7 mislead, pretend
an all-nighter: 4 cram
apart: 4 rend, tear 5 split 7 split up 9 find fault
a punch: 5 mince 6 soften
a switcheroo: 6 change 7 reverse 9 back-pedal
away: 4 lead 5 wrest 6 secede
back: 5 quail 6 recoil, retire 7 retract, retreat 8 hesitate, withdraw
down: 3 get, net 4 earn, fell, make, rase, raze 5 gross, level, lower, wreck 6 humble, ravage, reduce, remove 7 destroy, receive, subvert, unbuild 8 bulldoze, collapse, demolish, take home 9 dismantle, humiliate, knock over
for: 7 support 9 encourage 10 rally round
hard: 3 tug 4 jerk 5 pluck 6 wrench
in: 3 nab 4 bust, curb, draw, hook, lure, nail, park, rein, rope 5 check, pinch, snare, tempt 6 allure, arrest, arrive, bridle, collar, detain, entice, pick up 7 attract, tighten 8 appeal to, get there, restrain 9 apprehend
off: 2 do 3 win 4 skin 5 score 6 commit, detach, effect, manage, wangle 7 achieve, execute, perform, produce, succeed 8 conclude 10 accomplish, perpetrate, put through
one's leg: 3 guy, kid, rag, rib 4 fool, razz, twit 5 chaff, tease, trick 6 banter, take in 7 deceive, mislead
out: 2 go 4 exit, move, part, quit 5 leave, scram, split 6 beat it, be gone, decamp, defect, depart, go away, remove, renege, retire, secede 7 abandon, abscond, go south, retreat, ride off, take off 8 evacuate, hightail, separate, shove off, withdraw
out of: 8 give up on
over: 4 park
strings: 5 lobby, order, pluck 8 maneuver 10 manipulate
the lever: 3 opt 4 vote 5 elect 6 decide
the plug on: 3 end 4 stop 5 cease, drain 6 cancel 7 rescind
the strings: 4 rule 6 govern
the trigger: 4 fire 5 shoot
the wool over: 3 con, lie, rob, sap 4 bilk, butt, dupe, have, hoax, jerk, prey, scam, trap 5 cheat, fraud, shaft, trick 6 delude, fleece, lead on, outwit, rip off, rope in, suck in, take in 7 beguile, buffalo, chicane, deceive, defraud, mislead, swindle, two-time, wheedle 8 bulldoze, flimflam, hoodwink, inveigle, outsmart, sucker in 9 bamboozle, disinform, scapegoat
through: 4 heal, mend 5 rally 6 make it 7 get over, get well, rebound, recover, survive, triumph, weather 10 recuperate
together: 4 tidy 5 amass, unite 6 gather 7 collect
up: 4 halt, hike, stop 5 brake, raise 6 arrive 9 extirpate
up stakes: 4 move 5 leave 6 decamp
pull __: 3 for, off, out 4 away, back, down, rank 7 strings
pull __ one: 5 a fast
pull-__: 3 tab, top
__ pull: 4 bell 5 taffy 7 tractor
__-pull: 3 leg 4 push
pull a rabbit out of __: 4 a hat
...pulled out __: 5 a plum
pullet: 3 hen 4 bird, fowl 5 biddy, layer 7 chicken, poultry
pull in one's __: 5 horns
Pullman: 4 Bill, city, town
amenity: 5 berth
athletes: 7 Cougars
choice: 5 lower, upper
locale: 10 Washington
school: 3 WSU
Pullman __: 3 car 4 case
Pullman, Bill: 5 actor
film: Independence Day (1996)
The Last Seduction (1994)
Malice (1993)
Mr. Wrong (1996)
Sleepless in Seattle (1993)
Sommersby (1993)
Spaceballs (1987)
While You Were Sleeping (1995)
Zero Effect (1998)
pull one's __: 3 leg 6 weight 7 punches
pull-out: 7 retreat 10 withdrawal
pullover: 3 tee 6 anorak, blouse, jersey 7 sweater
pull the __ on: 4 plug
pull the __ out from under: 3 rug
pullulate: 3 bud 4 teem 7 burgeon 8 bourgeon, increase 9 germinate
pull up __: 6 stakes
pull-ups: 8 exercise
do ~: 4 chin
__ Pull Your Love: 4 Don't
pulmonary __: 4 vein 6 artery
pulmonary organ: 4 lung
pulp: 4 mash, mush, tree 5 crush, paste, purée 6 pomace, squash 7 tabloid 8 magazine 9 cellulose, dime novel, sarcocarp
ender: 4 wood
fruit ~: 5 flesh
like ~ fiction: 5 lurid
pulp __: 7 fiction
__ pulp: 4 wood
pulper: 6 logger 10 lumberjack
Pulp Fiction (1994 film)
cast: Samuel L. Jackson, Harvey Keitel, Uma Thurman, John Travolta
director: Quentin Tarantino
like ~: 6 R-rated
Uma in ~: 3 Mia
pulpit: 4 ambo 5 ambon, table 6 podium 7 lectern, rostrum 8 platform
address: 6 homily, sermon
pulpiteer: 5 padre, vicar 6 parson 8 minister, preacher
pulpy: 4 soft 5 mushy 6 liquid, spongy
fruit: 5 drupe, mango, peach 6 orange 7 apricot 10 grapefruit
pulque: 4 beer 5 drink, quaff 8 beverage 10 potato beer
drinker's place: 4 Peru 5 Andes
pulsar: 4 Mira, star
Pulsar: 3 car 4 auto 5 watch 6 Nissan 10 wristwatch
rival: ***see*** wristwatch
pulsate: 4 beat, drum, pump, roar, tick, wave 5 pound, quake, throb, thrum, thump 6 quaver, quiver, shiver 7 flutter, tremble, vibrate 9 oscillate, palpitate
pulsating: 6 athrob 7 vibrant
pulsation: 4 beat, tick 5 throb 9 frequency, vibration
pulse: 4 beat, drum, pump, thud, tick, wave 5 plant, pound, tempo, throb, thrum, thump 6 hammer, quiver, rhythm 7 cadence, cadency, shudder, tremble, vibrate 9 consensus, fluctuate, heartbeat, oscillate, palpitate, vibration, vital sign
pulverize: 4 mash, mill 5 crush, grate, grind, mince, pound, smash, wreck 6 crunch, defeat, ground, pestle, powder 7 atomize, break up, crumble, shatter 8 demolish, levigate 9 comminute, granulate, triturate
pulverized: 4 fine 7 powdery
pulverizer: 4 mano 6 metate, mortar, pestle
Pulver rank: 3 ens. 6 ensign
pulverulent: 5 dusty
puma: 3 cat 5 felid 6 animal, big cat, cougar, feline 7 panther
relative: ***see*** feline
Puma: 4 shoe 7 sneaker
competitor: 4 Nike 6 Adidas, Reebok
pumice: 4 rock 5 stone
feature: 4 pore
source: 4 lava
use ~: 6 abrade, smooth
pummel: 4 bang, beat, club, cuff, hurt, lash, mall, maul, pelt 5 baste, flail, knock, pound, punch, smite 6 beat on, beat up, beetle, buffet, hammer, strike, thrash, thwack, wallop 7 lambast 8 lambaste 9 fisticuff

pump: 3 ask 4 milk, pour, quiz, shoe 5 drain, eject, empty, grill, probe, pulse, shoot 6 siphon, syphon 7 draw out, inflate, pulsate 8 drive out, energize, footgear, footwear, force out, high heel, question
chamber: 4 sump
choice: 6 diesel 7 premium, regular
circulatory ~: 5 heart
fix a ~: 4 sole 6 resole
gas: 4 fill 6 fill up, fuel up, tank up
get a ~ flowing: 5 prime
iron: 4 lift 7 work out 8 exercise
ornament: 3 bow 4 clip
part: 6 insole, instep
prime the ~: 4 fund 5 stake 9 grubstake, subsidize
purchase: 3 gas 4 shoe 8 gasoline
unit: 3 gal. 5 liter, litre 6 gallon
up: 4 fill 5 bloat, liven, swell 6 expand, turn on, vivify 7 animate, balloon, distend, enlarge, enliven, inflate 8 activate, energize, vitalize 9 stimulate
pump __: 4 iron
__ pump: 3 air, gas 4 heat, sump
Pump __ Jam: 5 Up the
pumpernickel: 5 bread
relative: 3 rye 5 wheat, white 10 whole wheat
Pump House Gang, The
author: Tom Wolfe
Pumping Iron (1977 film)
cast: Lou Ferrigno, Arnold Schwarzenegger
pumpkin: 3 pie 4 pepo 5 color, fruit 6 orange, veggie 9 vegetable
color kin: 7 saffron 9 tangerine 10 terra cotta
ender: 4 seed
field: 5 patch
kin: 5 gourd
pie ingredient: 3 egg 4 milk 5 spice 6 ginger, nutmeg
smashing ~ sound: 5 splat
pumpkin __: 3 pie 4 head
pumpkin eater of rhyme: 5 Peter
Pumpkin Eater, The: 4 film 5 novel
author: Penelope Mortimer
cast: Anne Bancroft, Peter Finch, James Mason
pun: 3 mot 4 joke, quip 7 groaner 8 wordplay 9 equivoque, wisecrack, witticism
feedback: 2 ow 3 yow 4 ha-ha, ouch, yeow 5 groan, laugh, wince 7 chuckle
punch: 3 awl, bop, box, hit, jab, pep, rap, zip 4 bash, beat, belt, biff, bite, blow, brio, clip, cuff, hook, hurt, kick, left, plug, poke, prod, shot, slam, slap, slug, sock, tang, tool, whop, zest 5 clout, cross, drill, drink, drive, force, knock, nudge, pound, power, prick, right, smack, smash, smite, spark, spice, stamp, taste, thump, verve, vigor, whang, whomp 6 batter, buffet, energy, impact, lollop, one-two, pierce, pizazz, pommel, pummel, strike, thrash, thrust, thwack, wallop 7 cogency, lambast, potence, potency 8 beverage, haymaker, knock out, lambaste, puncture, uppercut, validity, vitality 9 fisticuff, haul off on, perforate 10 excitement, fruit drink, initiative, roundhouse
a clock: 4 work 8 report in
add ~ to: 5 pep up 7 enliven
boxer's ~: 3 jab 4 chop, hook, kayo 5 cross, right 6 one-two 8 haymaker, uppercut
competitively: 3 box
ender: 5 board
get the ~ line: 4 grin, howl, roar 5 groan, laugh 6 giggle, guffaw 7 chortle, chuckle, crack up, snicker, snigger
in: 4 come 5 enter, pop up 6 appear, arrive, attend, turn up
kin: 3 ade 5 juice
line: 5 point 6 climax, payoff
maker: 4 fist
out: 2 go 4 exit, quit 5 leave
pull a ~: 5 mince 6 soften
server: 4 bowl 5 ladle
sound: 3 pow 4 wham 5 kapow
spike the ~: 4 lace
starter: 3 key 4 gang 7 counter
without ~: 4 tame
punch __: 3 out 4 bowl, card, line
__ punch: 6 one-two, rabbit, sucker, Sunday
Punch: 5 clown 6 puppet
Judy, to ~: 4 wife
Punch-and-Judy __: 4 show
punchbowl: 5 jorum
partner: 5 ladle
puncheon: 3 tub
__ puncher: 5 clock 6 ticket
punches
pulling no ~: 5 frank 6 candid 8 straight
rolling with the ~: 5 stoic 7 stoical 8 flexible, resolute 9 resilient
roll with the ~: 4 cope 5 adapt 6 adjust, manage
punching __: 3 bag
punching tool: 3 awl
Punchline (1988 film)
cast: Sally Field, John Goodman, Tom Hanks
punchy: 5 dizzy, giddy, weary 6 addled 7 reeling 8 confused 10 bewildered, knocked out
punctilio: 6 detail, nicety, nuance 8 loose end, niceties 9 fine point, propriety 10 particular
punctilious: 5 exact, fussy, right, rigid 6 formal, minute, polite, proper, strict 7 careful, correct, finicky, precise, prudent, refined, upright 8 accurate, cautious, exacting, finiking, finnicky, orthodox, pedantic, rigorous, thorough 9 assiduous, attentive, judicious, observant 10 fastidious, meticulous, particular, pedantical, scrupulous
punctiliously: 4 to a T
punctual: 5 early, quick, ready 6 on time, prompt, steady, timely 7 regular 8 on the dot, reliable 10 dependable, on schedule, scrupulous
not ~: 4 late 5 tardy 7 delayed, overdue
punctually: 4 duly 5 sharp 6 on time 8 promptly
punctuate: 4 lace, mark 5 break 6 accent, divide, pepper, play up, stress 7 point up, scatter 8 separate, sprinkle 9 emphasize, highlight, interject, interrupt, spotlight, underline 10 accentuate, underscore
punctuation mark: 4 dash 5 colon, comma 6 em dash, en dash, hyphen, period 9 semicolon
puncture: 3 cut, jab, pit 4 bore, flat, hole, leak, nick, open, slit, stab 5 break, burst, drill, knife, prick, punch, stick 6 broach, debunk, empale, go flat, impale, pierce, riddle 7 deflate, flatten, opening, rupture 8 disprove, lacerate 9 penetrate, perforate
combining form: 5 -nyxis
result: 4 flat
sound: 4 hiss
pundit: 4 guru, sage 5 guide, solon, swami, swamy 6 critic, expert, master, mentor, savant, wizard 7 idea man, scholar, teacher, thinker 9 abecedary, authority, intellect, professor 10 specialist
like a ~: 7 learned 9 scholarly
pundits: 8 literati
pung: 4 sled 6 sledge, sleigh
relative: 4 luge 8 toboggan
pungency: 3 nip 4 bite, kick, odor, tang, zest 5 spice, sting 7 acidity 9 spiciness
pungent: 3 hot 4 acid, keen, racy, rank, rich, sour, tart 5 acrid, acute, salty, sharp, spicy, tangy, zesty 6 biting, bitter, red-hot, savory, spicey, strong 7 caustic, mordant, odorous, peppery, piquant, pointed, telling, zestful 8 aromatic, incisive, piercing, poignant, stinging, stinking, vinegary 9 flavorful, trenchant 10 astringent
Punic War city: 5 Utica 8 Carthage
punish: 3 fix, tar 4 beat, cane, damn, fine, flog, hurt, jail, lash, whip 5 abuse, debar, exile, expel, mulct, spank 6 amerce, avenge, ground, immure, misuse, paddle, strike, switch, thrash 7 chasten, correct, defrock, dismiss, execute, lambast, lecture, oppress, pay back, reprove, scourge, torment 8 admonish, chastise, imprison, lambaste, penalize, sentence 9 blacklist, castigate, dress down, exprobate 10 discipline, take to task
by fine: 6 amerce 8 penalize
punishing: 5 penal, tight 6 severe, uphill 7 arduous 8 grueling, punitive 10 relentless
stick: 6 ferula, ferule, switch
punishment: 3 rap, rod 4 fine 5 abuse, lumps 6 desert, lesson, rebuke, reward 7 beating, damages, deserts, forfeit, penalty, penance, redress 8 flogging, reprisal, sanction, sentence, spanking, whipping 9 execution, hell to pay, ostracism 10 correction, discipline, reparation
decide ~: 8 sentence
just ~: 6 desert
light ~: 4 slap
monetary ~: 4 fine
of ~: 5 penal
teen ~ perhaps: 4 no TV
punitive: 5 harsh, penal 8 vengeful 9 punishing 10 corrective, inflictive, vindictive
punitive __: 7 damages
Punjab
boss: 8 Warbucks
capital: 6 Lahore
friend: 3 Asp 5 Annie 6 Asp, The
native: 4 Sikh
river: 5 Indus
royalty: 4 raja, rani 5 rajah, ranee 8 maharaja 9 maharajah
wild sheep of ~: 5 urial
punk: 2 JD 4 blah, brat, coif, hood, runt 5 dinky, lousy, rowdy, thief, tough, twerp, twirp 6 crumby, crummy, hairdo, rotten, shabby, trashy 7 haircut, hoodlum, lowlife, ruffian, tinhorn 8 coiffure, hooligan, inferior 10 jackanapes
like ~ hairdos: 5 spiky
punk __: 4 rock
punkie: 4 gnat
punky: 6 rotten
Punky Brewster (NBC sitcom)
cast: Soleil Moon Frye (Punky Brewster)
dog: 7 Brandon
punster: 3 wag, wit 4 card 5 joker 8 funnyman
punt: 4 boat, kick
propeller: 5 poler
spender: 5 Irish
Punta __, FL: 5 Gorda
Punta Arenas: 4 city, port, town
locale: 5 Chile
Punta del __, Uruguay: 4 Este
punting game: 5 rugby 6 soccer 8 football
puny: 3 wee 4 baby, poor, thin, tiny, vain, weak 5 bitty, frail, light, petty, runty, small, teeny, wimpy 6 anemic, atomic, atonic, bantam, effete, feeble, flabby, flimsy, humble, infirm, little, meager, measly, minute, paltry, peewee, petite, sickly, skimpy, slight, teensy, two-bit 7 anaemic, fragile, shrimpy, stunted, trivial, wimpish 8 atomical, atomlike, delicate, helpless, niggling, pathetic, picayune, piddling, pithless, sawed-off, trifling, underfed 9 brawnless, emaciated, faltering, itsy-bitsy, itty-bitty, miniature, pint-sized, powerless, undersize, worthless 10 diminutive, inadequate, pathetical, teeny-weeny, undersized, vest-pocket, vulnerable
not ~: 6 strong
pup: 3 dog, pet 4 runt 5 canid, doggy, whelp, youth 6 canine, doggie, urchin 9 offspring, youngling, youngster 10 jackanapes
see also puppy
pup __: 4 tent
pupa: 3 bug 6 insect 9 chrysalis
eventually: 4 moth 9 butterfly
preceder: 5 imago, larva
protection: 6 cocoon
pupil: 4 tiro, tyro 5 tutee, youth 6 intern, junior, novice, senior 7 learner, scholar, student, trainee 8 academic, adherent, beginner, bookworm, disciple, follower,

freshman, neophyte **9** sophomore, youngster **10** apprentice, catechumen, tenderfoot
chore: **5** essay **6** lesson **8** homework
contraction: **6** miosis, myosis
covering: **4** uvea **6** cornea
gift: **5** apple
in French: **5** élève
locale: **3** eye **4** desk, iris **6** school **9** classroom
surrounder: **6** areola, areole
puppet: **3** toy **4** doll, dupe, pawn, tool **5** patsy **6** jackal, lackey, stooge, victim **7** cat's-paw, lacquey, manikin, nominal, servant **8** creature, mannikin, pushover **9** sycophant **10** figurehead, instrument, marionette, mouthpiece
rudimentary ~: **4** sock
puppet __: **4** show
__ puppet: **4** hand **6** finger
Puppet on a String (1965 song)
artist: Elvis Presley
puppy: **3** dog, pet **5** canid, whelp **6** canine
family: **6** litter
like a ~: **6** cuddly **10** cuddlesome
love: **5** ardor, crush **8** devotion, fondness **9** adoration, affection **10** admiration, attachment
pickup point: **4** nape
protest: **3** nip, yip **4** yelp **5** whine **7** whimper
smallest ~: **4** runt
starter: **3** mud **4** hush
without papers: **3** mut **4** mutt **5** stray
puppy __: **3** dog **4** love
__ puppy: **3** mud **4** hush, sand
Puppy Love (song)
artist: Paul Anka, Donny Osmond
__ pura: **4** aqua
Purcell: **5** Henry, Sarah **6** Edward
purchase: **3** buy, get **4** edge, gain, hold, sale, shop, take **5** order, steal **6** charge, come by, deal in, invest, obtain, pay for, pick up, redeem, secure **7** acquire, bargain, footing, procure, toehold **8** customer, foothold, invest in, leverage **9** advantage, influence, patronize **10** investment
alternative: **5** lease **6** rental
offer: **3** bid
__ Purchase: **6** Alaska **7** Gadsden **9** Louisiana
purchased, just: **3** new **5** fresh **8** brand-new
purchaser: **5** buyer, owner **6** patron **8** consumer, customer
boon: **4** sale **5** no tax **6** coupon, rebate **8** discount
purchasing __: **5** agent, power
purdah: **4** veil **6** screen **7** curtain **9** seclusion
Purdue: **6** school **10** university
athletes: Boilermakers
conference: **6** Big Ten
locale: **7** Indiana
Purdy: **2** Al **5** James
Purdy, Al: **4** poet **8** Canadian
Purdy, James: **6** writer
work: Color of Darkness
Dream Palace
Malcolm
Mourners Below
Narrow Rooms
The Nephew
On Glory's Course
pure: **4** good, mere, neat **5** clean, clear, fresh, lucid, moral, naked, plain, sheer, snowy, solid, stark, sweet, uncut, utter **6** chaste, devout, kasher, kosher, limpid, modest, sacred, simple, strong, unmixt, virgin **7** genuine, natural, perfect, refined, saintly, sterile, unmixed, upright **8** absolute, abstract, celibate, flawless, germfree, innocent, maidenly, outright, pellucid, pristine, sanitary, spotless, straight, thorough, unsoiled, virginal, virtuous **9** blameless, continent, downright, exemplary, faultless, guileless, guiltless, healthful, inviolate, lily white, out-and-out, pedigreed, righteous, spiritual, stainless, unalloyed, unclouded, uncorrupt, undefiled, undiluted, unsullied, untainted, untouched, wholesome **10** antiseptic, immaculate, impeccable, sterilized, unpolluted
ender: **4** bred **5** blood
name meaning ~: **7** Kathryn **9** Catherine, Katharine, Katherine
__-pure: **5** simon
Pure __ and Drug Act: **4** Food
pure as the __ snow: **6** driven
purebred: **8** pedigree
not a ~: **3** cur, mut **4** mutt **5** stray **8** alley cat
purée: **4** pulp, soup **6** bisque
purely: **3** all **4** just, only **5** quite **6** merely, simply, solely, wholly **7** totally, utterly **8** entirely **10** absolutely, altogether, completely, nothing but
Pure Reason exponent: **4** Kant
Purex: **6** bleach **9** detergent
competitor: *see* bleach **9** detergent
purfle: **5** adorn **6** finish **8** decorate, ornament **9** embellish
purgation: **8** emptying **9** catharsis, cleansing **10** evacuation
Purgatorio
author: Dante
Purgatory
author: William Butler Yeats
purge: **3** rid **4** coup, oust **5** atone, eject, empty, erase, expel **6** banish, delete, ouster, purify, remove, uproot **7** cleanse, cleanup, dismiss, expiate, expunge, forgive, root out, rout out, shake up, wipe out **8** clean out, clear out, empty out, evacuate, exorcise, exorcize, flush out, get rid of, sweep out, wash away **9** catharsis, cathartic, eliminate, eradicate, expulsion, expurgate, overthrow, witch hunt **10** do away with
purification: **5** grace **7** baptism, rebirth **8** ablution **9** atonement, catharsis, cleansing, expiation, salvation
purified: **5** clean **6** washed **7** refined **8** sanitary
purifier: **6** filter **7** alembic **10** antiseptic
purify: **4** free, sift, wash **5** atone, clean, clear, purge **6** aerate, censor, desalt, filter, rarify, redeem, refine, shrive, strain **7** absolve, clarify, cleanse, deterge, distill, expiate, freshen, improve **8** exorcise, exorcize, fumigate, sanctify, sanitize **9** deodorize, disinfect, oxygenate, sterilize, sublimate **10** desalinate, desalinize
Purim
month: **4** Adar
queen: **6** Esther
Purina: **7** cat food, dog food
alternative: *see* pet food brand
__ Purina: **7** Ralston
purist: **8** stickler **9** formalist **10** taskmaster
puritan: **4** prig **5** priss, prude **9** nice Nelly **10** goody-goody
Puritan: **10** cooking oil
alternative: **6** Crisco, Mazola, Wesson
Puritan __: **5** ethic
puritanical: **4** prim **5** sober **6** prissy, proper, severe, strict, stuffy **7** ascetic, austere, prudish **9** squeamish
Puritanism: **9** austerity
purity: **6** virtue **7** modesty **8** morality **9** innocence, integrity **10** perfection, simplicity
purl: **3** lap **4** knit, loop **6** gurgle, murmur, ripple, stitch **7** lapping
Purl: **5** Linda
purlieu: **4** area, land, site **5** haunt, limit **7** hangout
purlieus: **4** area **6** milieu **8** environs, vicinage, vicinity **9** outskirts
purloin: **3** rob **4** lift, take **5** filch, pinch, steal, swipe **6** pilfer, pocket, rip off, thieve **7** ransack **8** embezzle **10** run off with
Purloined Letter, The
author: Edgar Allan Poe
character: **5** Dupin
purloiner: **5** crook, felon, thief **6** bandit, robber **7** burglar, filcher **8** criminal, pilferer
puro: **5** cigar
purple: **5** livid **6** ornate **10** apoplectic, rhetorical
bluish ~: **4** plum **5** mauve **6** orchid **8** lavender
brownish ~: **4** puce
color: **4** plum, puce **5** grape, lilac, mauve **6** dahlia, orchid, violet **7** heather **8** amethyst, burgundy, eggplant, hyacinth, lavender, mulberry **9** raspberry **10** heliotrope
combining form: **7** purpuri-
flower: **3** mum **4** flag, iris **5** aster, lilac, tulip, vetch **6** betony, crocus, maypop, orchid, violet **7** figwort, fuchsia, heather, petunia, saffron, thistle **8** amaranth, boltonia, cyclamen, erigeron, foxglove, hepatica, hyacinth, lavender, wistaria, wisteria **9** candytuft, cockscomb, monkshood, wolfsbane **10** bluebottle, coneflower, cornflower, heliotrope, motherwort, pennyroyal
fruit: **4** plum, sloe **5** grape
grayish ~: **8** mulberry
in heraldry: **7** purpure
pinkish ~: **7** heather
reddish ~: **4** plum, ruby **5** lilac, murex **6** claret, orchid **7** carmine, crimson, fuchsia, magenta, petunia **8** cyclamen **9** cranberry, raspberry **10** heliotrope
purple __: **4** sage **5** prose **7** passion
__ purple: **5** royal
Purple __: **4** Dust, Haze, Rain **5** Heart
__ Purple: **4** Deep
Purple Decades, The
author: Tom Wolfe
Purple Dust
author: Sean O'Casey
Purple Heart: **5** award, medal
like a ~ recipient: **3** WIA
Purple People Eater, The (1958 song)
artist: Sheb Wooley
Purple Rain (1984 song)
artist: Prince
Purple Rose of Cairo, The (1985 film)
cast: Danny Aiello, Jeff Daniels, Mia Farrow, Dianne Wiest
director: Woody Allen
__ Purple, The: **5** Color
purport: **3** aim, nub **4** gist, idea, knub, mean, meat, pith **5** claim, drift, heart, imply, point, score, sense, tenor **6** allege, assert, burden, convey, denote, effect, hint at, import, intend, intent, matter, object, pose as, spirit, thrust, upshot **7** bearing, connote, contend, express, meaning, message, point to, pretend, profess, purpose, signify, suggest **8** allude to, indicate, intimate, maintain, proclaim **9** intention, objective, substance
purported: **7** nominal **8** so-called **9** pretended **10** ostensible
purpose: **3** aim, end, job, use **4** goal, hope, idea, plan, sake, will **5** angle, avail, cause, point, scope, sense **6** animus, design, desire, import, intend, intent, layout, method, motive, object, reason, spirit, target **7** meaning, mission, propose, purport, resolve, thought, utility **8** ambition, firmness, function, lifework, nominate, tenacity **9** direction, intention, objective, rationale **10** aspiration, motivation, resolution
answer the ~: **4** work **5** avail, serve
devious ~: **5** angle
lack of ~: **5** anomy **6** anomie
on ~: **9** expressly, willfully, wittingly **10** deliberate, designedly
serving a ~: **5** utile **6** useful
strength of ~: **4** will **7** resolve **8** tenacity **9** will power **10** resolution
to no ~: **4** vain **7** inutile **8** bootless
to the ~: **3** apt **8** relevant **9** pertinent
ultimate ~: **3** end **6** end-all, end use
without ~: **4** idly **7** blindly
__ purpose: **4** to no
__-purpose: **3** all **4** dual

purposeful: 4 firm 5 bound, can-do, fixed, meant, telic 6 intent, steady, wilful 7 dead set, decided, earnest, intense, planned, settled, staunch, studied, willful 8 intended, positive, resolute, stalwart 9 ambitious, committed, conscious, dedicated, iron-jawed, observant, steadfast, tenacious, voluntary 10 deliberate, determined, preplanned, volitional
purposeless: 4 idle, vain 5 empty, inane 6 adrift, random 7 aimless, inutile, useless 8 bootless, drifting, feckless, goalless, needless 9 desultory, haphazard, hit-or-miss, pointless, senseless, unhelpful, worthless
purposely: 8 by design 9 expressly, knowingly, willfully, wittingly 10 designedly, explicitly
purposes
at cross ~: 7 opposed
for all practical ~: 8 in effect 9 virtually
purr: 3 hum 6 murmur
it may ~: 3 cat 5 kitty 6 engine, feline, kitten
__ Purr-ee: 3 Gay
purse: 3 bag 4 knit, poke, sack, tote 5 award, bursa, funds, kitty, means, money, pinch, pouch, prize, stake 6 clutch, crease, pucker, reward 7 handbag, sporran, tighten, wrinkle 8 bankroll, billfold, carryall, finances, moneybag, pucker up, reticule, treasury, winnings 9 affluence, container, exchequer 10 pocketbook, receptacle
big ~: 4 tote 8 carryall
carrier: 5 strap 10 drawstring
contents: 2 ID 3 pen 4 cash, coin, comb, Mace 5 coins, hanky, money 6 hankie, powder 7 compact 8 billfold, lipstick 9 checkbook 10 credit card
ender: 7 strings
fastener: 4 snap 5 clasp 6 zipper 10 drawstring
geisha's ~: 4 inro
keeper of the ~ strings: 9 treasurer 10 controller
loosen the ~ strings: 3 buy 5 spend
snatcher: 5 thief
starter: 3 cut
purse __: 7 strings
purse-__: 5 proud
__ purse: 4 coin 5 privy 6 clutch
purser: 6 bursar 7 cashier 9 treasurer
purslane: 4 weed 5 plant
pursue: 3 bug, dog, ply, sue, tag, woo 4 call, date, hunt, rush, seek, shag, tail, wage 5 chase, chivy, court, harry, haunt, hound, quest, spark, stalk, trace, track, trail 6 aim for, aspire, badger, desire, follow, gun for, harass, hold to, keep on, plague, shadow, tackle, try for 7 attempt, bird-dog, carry on, conduct, fish for, go after, persist, proceed, run down 8 continue, engage in, follow up, hunt down, maintain, overtake, practice, quest for, run after, scout out 9 cultivate, persecute, persevere, prosecute, search out, shine up to, strive for, track down 10 prowl after, specialize, work toward
romantically: 3 woo 4 date 5 court 7 propose 9 send roses, sweet-talk
__, pursued by a bear: 4 Exit
pursuit: 3 biz, job 4 game, hunt, line, race, work 5 chase, hobby, quest, trail 6 career, racket, search, wooing 7 attempt, calling, enquiry, inquiry, mission, pastime, venture 8 activity, business, interest, lifework, pleasure, vocation 9 avocation, courtship, following, specialty 10 employment, enterprise, occupation, profession
in ~ of: 5 after 7 chasing 9 following
Pursuit of Happyness, The (2006 film)
cast: Thandie Newton, Jaden Smith, Will Smith
Pursuit of Love, The
author: Nancy Mitford
pursy
see obese
purvey: 5 cater, equip 6 outfit, supply 7 furnish, provide
purveyor: 6 grocer, source 8 supplier
Purviance: 4 Edna
purview: 3 ken 4 area 5 field, grasp, orbit, range, reach, realm, scope, sweep 6 length, radius, sphere 7 compass, horizon 8 confines, province 9 bailiwick, territory 10 boundaries, walk of life
Pusan: 4 city, port, town
locale: 10 South Korea
push: 2 go 3 jam, jog, pep, ram, tie 4 bump, goad, hawk, hype, jolt, move, plug, poke, prod, rush, sell, spur, sway, tout, urge, work, worm, zeal 5 boost, crowd, drive, egg on, elbow, exert, force, forge, goose, impel, labor, lobby, lunge, nudge, press, shove, spunk, stick, stuff, vigor, wedge 6 charge, coerce, effort, energy, fillip, harp on, hasten, hustle, hype up, incite, jostle, justle, lean on, muscle, oblige, peddle, plunge, propel, racket, sprout, squash, strain, strive, talk up, thrust, wiggle 7 advance, crusade, depress, further, inspire, promote, smuggle, speed up, squeeze, try hard 8 ambition, campaign, expedite, gumption, momentum, motivate, persuade, pressure, railroad, scramble, shoulder, stick out, stimulus, vitality 9 advertise, encourage, fast-track, get behind, go forward, influence, offensive, publicize, steamroll, strong-arm 10 enterprise, get up and go, go whole hog, incitement, initiative
ahead: 4 nose 7 advance
and shove: 5 crowd, elbow 8 shoulder
around: 5 bully 8 mistreat, threaten 10 intimidate
away: 5 shove 7 repulse
back: 5 repel 6 rebuff
back the boundaries: 5 widen 6 extend
button predecessor: 4 dial
down: 4 tamp 5 lower, press 6 squash 7 depress
ender: 3 pin 4 ball, cart, over 6 button
for: 4 urge 5 lobby 6 talk up 7 promote 8 advocate
forward: 4 goad, move, prod, push, spur, urge 5 boost, drive, press, shove, speed 6 attack, incite, induce, prompt, propel, stir up 7 actuate, inspire 8 motivate 9 influence, instigate, stimulate 10 accelerate
gentle ~: 3 jog 5 nudge
hard: 4 slam
in: 4 dent 5 barge, stave 7 intrude
off: 2 go 4 exit, part, quit 5 leave, start 6 beat it, begone, depart, repair, set out 7 get lost, head out, journey, proceed, set sail 8 hightail, light out, set forth 10 hit the road
on: 2 go 5 press 7 advance, proceed 8 continue 9 keep going
oneself: 4 toil 5 exert, slave 6 overdo 8 overwork
out of bed: 4 wake 5 awake, roust, waken 6 awaken, wake up
the buttons: 7 control
too far: 3 tax 4 task, tire, wear 6 exceed, impose, strain, weaken 7 oppress, wear out 8 overload, overtask, overwork 9 weigh down 10 overburden
to the limit: 3 tax 4 test
push __: 3 off 4 shot 5 broom, cycle, plate 6 around, button
pushcart
in Britain: 6 barrow
purchase: 3 ice 6 hot dog 7 flowers, pretzel 8 ice cream
__ push comes to shove: 4 when
pushed aside: 7 ignored, snubbed 9 unnoticed 10 overlooked
__-pusher: 5 paper 6 pencil
pusher nemesis: 4 narc, nark
__ pushers: 5 pedal
Pushing Tin (1999 film)
cast: Cate Blanchett, John Cusack, Angelina Jolie, Billy Bob Thornton
Push It (1987 song)
artist: Salt-n-Pepa
Pushkin, Aleksandr: 6 writer 7 Russian
hero: 5 Boris
work: The Bronze Horseman
The Captain's Daughter
Eugene Onegin
The Queen of Spades
push one's __: 4 luck
pushover: 4 dupe, easy, fool, lamb, snap, wimp 5 chump, cinch, cushy, patsy, softy 6 breeze, picnic, pigeon, puppet, simple, softie, stooge, sucker, victim 7 triumph 8 duck soup, easy mark, kid stuff, painless, weakling 9 jellyfish, no problem, receptive, soft touch 10 child's play, effortless
pushpin: 4 tack
push to the __: 4 wall
push-up: 8 exercise
muscle: 3 pec 4 pecs
pushy: 4 bold, loud, rude 5 bossy, brash, nervy 6 strong 7 forward, zealous 8 assuming, invasive, militant 9 ambitious, assertive, bumptious, insistent, obnoxious, obtrusive, offensive, officious 10 aggressive, meddlesome
be ~: 5 elbow 6 impose
pusillanimous: 5 timid 6 afraid, craven, yellow 7 chicken, fearful 8 cowardly, recreant, timorous 9 dastardly 10 frightened
puss: 3 cat, mug, yap 4 face 5 bazoo, felid, kitty, mouth, tabby 6 feline, kisser, kitten, mouser, tomcat, visage 8 features 9 grimalkin
starter: 4 sour
__ puss: 7 glamour
Puss-in-Boots: 3 cat
Pussy-Cat
boat: 8 pea-green
suitor: 3 owl
where the ~ went: 5 to sea
pussyfoot: 5 avoid, creep, dodge, evade, hedge, shirk, slink, sneak, steal, waver 6 tiptoe, weasel 7 shuffle, slither, whiffle 8 hesitate, sidestep 9 dissemble, hem and haw, vacillate 10 equivocate
pussy willow: 4 tree 5 ament, shrub 6 catkin
put: 3 lay, pop, set 4 give, levy, park, rest, word 5 couch, embed, imbed, place, plant, posit, rivet, stand, state, stick, utter, voice 6 assign, commit, employ, enjoin, impose, induce, insert, instal, invest, locate, phrase, prefer, reckon, render, settle, submit, tender 7 advance, consign, deposit, express, inflict, install, present, propose, require, set down, situate, station, suggest 8 position, propound 9 formulate, plunk down, translate, transpose 10 motionless
a crimp in: 5 block 6 hinder 8 obstruct
across: 6 convey, effect 7 explain 8 convince, spell out 9 make clear
a damper on: 5 quash 6 sadden 10 discourage, dishearten
a gloss on: 3 rub, wax 4 buff 5 shine 6 polish 7 burnish, varnish
a line through: 4 x out
a lock on: 6 ensure, secure 9 safeguard
a mark on: 3 tag 5 label
a match to: 3 lit 5 light, relit 6 ignite, kindle, set off 8 enkindle
an edge on: 4 hone 7 sharpen
an end to: 3 nix 4 stop 5 cease, sever 6 arrest, scotch, settle 7 abolish, prevent 8 abrogate, stamp out, suppress 9 close down, overthrow 10 do away with
another way: 5 resay 8 rephrase
a point on: 4 hone 7 sharpen
a question: 3 ask 4 pose 5 query 7 inquire
aside: 4 hold, keep, save 5 cache, defer, lay in, on ice, store, table, waive 6 shelve 7 deposit 8 hold on to, salt away, stow away 9 in reserve, stockpile

a spell on: 3 hex, zap 4 jinx 5 charm, curse 7 enchant 9 hypnotize

asunder: 5 sever, split 8 separate

at ease: 5 allay 6 assure 7 satisfy 8 reassure

at one's disposal: 5 offer 9 volunteer

at risk: 3 bet, lay 4 dare 5 stake, wager 6 chance, gamble, menace 7 imperil, venture 8 endanger, threaten 9 undermine 10 jeopardize

a value on: 3 tag 4 deem, rank, rate 5 gauge, grade, guess, judge, quote, scale, value, weigh 6 assess, charge, esteem, figure, regard, size up, survey 7 measure, valuate 8 appraise, classify, estimate, evaluate 9 determine

away: 3 box, eat, pen, tie 4 bind, cage, file, hold, jail, keep, pack, save, shut, stow 5 amass, bound, cache, chain, cramp, fence, hedge, hem in, hoard, lay by, lay in, lay up, limit, set by, stash, store, tie up 6 commit, coop up, detain, devour, fetter, garner, gobble, ground, hinder, hogtie, imbibe, immure, intern, lock up, murder, retain, save up, shut in, shut up 7 certify, confine, consume, deposit, enclose, feast on, impound, inclose, interne, isolate, reserve, scarf up, seclude, swallow, trounce 8 bottle up, hang onto, hold back, hold onto, imprison, maintain, salt away, sentence, set apart, set aside, straiten, surround, wolf down 9 constrain, grab a bite, overpower, polish off, scarf down, stockpile 10 accumulate

back: 6 return 7 replace, restore 8 postpone

back into service: 5 reuse

back on one's feet: 4 cure, heal, mend 5 treat

back to zero: 5 reset

between: 6 insert

by: 4 keep, save 5 cache, lay in, spare, stash, store 7 deposit, reserve, store up 8 hold on to, salt away, set aside, stow away 9 stockpile

down: 3 cut, dig, dis, hit, log, pan, pen 4 barb, gibe, gybe, jeer, jibe, land, mock, sink, slam, slap, slur, snub, stop, veto, zing 5 abase, abuse, crush, decry, enter, knock, libel, quash, quell, quiet, roast, scold, scorn, shame, sneer, spurn, still, taunt, tease, write 6 berate, debase, defame, defeat, demean, depone, deride, dump on, heckle, humble, ignore, impugn, insult, jibe at, malign, negate, offend, oppugn, quench, rebuff, rebuke, record, reject, slight, squash, subdue, vilify, zinger 7 affront, asperse, calumny, catcall, deflate, degrade, disdain, dismiss, mockery, obloquy, offense, rank out, repress, sarcasm, silence, slander, sneer at, specify, traduce 8 badmouth, belittle, contempt, denounce, derision, derogate, diminish, discount, minimize, prohibit, ridicule, stamp out, suppress, vanquish, vilipend 9 aspersion, blaspheme, cheap shot, contumely, denigrate, deprecate, discredit, disparage, find fault, humiliate, lash out at, poke fun at, subjugate 10 calumniate, defamation, disrespect, extinguish, opprobrium, transcribe

down, as money: 5 plunk 7 deposit

down for: 3 tag 4 slot 6 assign 7 earmark 8 allocate, delegate, set aside 9 apportion, designate

down for the count: 2 KO 4 deck, kayo 5 floor

down roots: 4 stay 6 linger, remain, settle 8 colonize

forth: 3 use 5 exert, offer, posit, voice 6 assert, submit 7 burgeon, present, propose 8 bourgeon, exercise 9 predicate

forward: 3 lay, say 4 move, pose 5 exert, issue, offer, raise 6 assert, submit, turn in 7 advance, declare, present, produce, propose, suggest, support 8 propound 9 introduce, postulate, recommend, volunteer

hard ~: 5 taxed 8 strained

in: 3 add, use 4 ante, dock, give, land 5 plant, spend, use up 6 devote, expend, instal, invest 7 consume, install, utilize 8 dedicate, exercise 9 interject, introduce 10 contribute

in a call: 4 dial, ring 5 phone

in a good word for: 4 laud, plug 8 champion 9 recommend

in an appearance: 4 come, show 6 attend, show up

in a nutshell: 4 trim 5 recap, sum up 6 digest 7 abridge, shorten 8 simplify 9 summarize

in a row: 4 even 5 align, aline, array, order 10 straighten

in a snit: 3 irk 4 miff, rile 5 anger, peeve, upset 7 agitate

in for: 5 apply 7 request 8 petition

in good shape: 5 fix up 6 neaten 10 straighten

in irons: 6 fetter 7 enchain, manacle, shackle, trammel 8 handcuff

in jeopardy: 3 bet 4 dare, risk 5 brave, stake, wager 6 chance, gamble, hazard

in mothballs: 5 store

in motion: 3 set 5 begin, start 8 commence

in office: 4 vote 5 elect

in order: 4 sort, tidy 6 assort 7 correct 8 organize, regulate, untangle

in place: 3 fix, set 6 instal 7 install

in play: 5 serve

in power: 5 elect 7 instate

in service: 3 use 5 avail 6 deploy 7 utilize

in something extra: 3 add, tip 7 augment

in the closet: 4 hang

in the hold: 4 lade, load, stow

into a funk: 6 bum out, deject 7 depress 8 dispirit, distress 10 discourage, dishearten

into circulation: 5 issue

into effect: 4 vote 5 enact, order 8 legalize 9 establish, institute, legislate

in touch: 5 refer 9 introduce

into words: 3 say 4 limn, talk 5 speak, state, utter, vocal, voice 6 phrase, relate, spoken 7 express 8 vocalize

in writing: 3 log 4 mark 5 enter 6 record 7 catalog, jot down, set down 8 mark down, take down 10 transcribe

money on: 3 bet 5 wager 6 gamble 7 venture

not ~ off: 9 undaunted

off: 3 lag 4 late, stay 5 dally, defer, delay, deter, evade, remit, repel, sit on, stall, table, tarry, waive 6 dawdle, dismay, linger, loiter, rattle, rebuff, retard, shelve 7 abeyant, adjourn, hold off, lighten, suspend 8 file away, hold over, lay aside, postpone, prorogue 10 dillydally, pigeonhole, reschedule

off-guard: 5 charm 6 disarm

on: 3 act, add, don, kid, lie 4 fake, fool, gain, hire, hoax, jest, levy, mock, ruse, sham, wear, worn 5 affix, apply, bluff, bogus, faked, farce, feign, fraud, front, light, phony, prank, spoof, stage, stake, tease, trick 6 affect, assume, ersatz, facade, forged, humbug, parody, phoney, pseudo, satire, unreal 7 assumed, confuse, deceive, feigned, lampoon, mislead, mockery, present, pretend, produce 8 activate, confound, mannered, pretense, simulate, spurious 9 activated, high-toned, imitation, imposture, pretended, simulated, synthetic, unnatural 10 artificial, caricature, fabricated, fictitious, fraudulent, masquerade

on account: 6 charge

on a happy face: 4 beam, glow, grin 5 smile

on airs: 4 pose 5 mince, strut 6 fake it 7 swagger

on an act: 4 fake 6 fake it 7 pretend 8 simulate 9 dissemble, misinform

on a pedestal: 5 adore, exalt, extol 6 esteem, extoll, praise 7 adulate, ennoble, glorify, idolize, worship 8 canonize, idealize, venerate

on a show: 3 act 5 amuse, stage

on board: 4 lade, load, ship, stow

on cloud nine: 5 cheer, elate, exult 6 buck up, perk up, uplift 7 delight, gladden, hearten 8 inspirit 9 make happy 10 exhilarate

on display: 4 show 5 array, shown

one over on: 3 con, get 4 fool, have 5 trick 6 delude, outwit 8 outsmart

one's cards on the table: 6 reveal 8 disclose

oneself out: 3 try 4 care 5 exert 6 bother 7 attempt

one's feet up: 4 laze, loaf, loll, rest 5 relax 6 repose, rest up, unwind 7 lay back, lie down, recline, sit back, take ten 8 take five 10 settle back, take a break, take it easy

one's finger on: 4 find 5 place 6 locate, recall 7 find out 8 discover, identify, remember 9 bring back

one's foot down: 4 step, walk 5 stamp, stomp, tread 6 demand, insist 7 protest 9 stand firm

one's hands on: 4 find 6 locate, turn up

ones' heads together: 6 confer

one's John Hancock on: 3 ink 7 endorse, initial 9 formalize

one's John Henry on: 3 ink 7 endorse, initial 9 formalize

one's mind to rest: 4 buoy 5 cheer 7 cheer up, comfort, console, hearten, satisfy 8 inspirit

one's two cents in: 3 add 5 opine 6 meddle 9 interfere

on guard: 4 warn 5 alarm, alert, awake, scare 6 arouse, clue in, inform, notify, tip off 7 apprise, caution, forearm, prepare 8 acquaint, forewarn

on hold: 5 defer, table 6 recess, shelve 7 suspend 8 postpone

on ice: 5 chill, delay, table 6 assure, shelve 7 confine, suspend 8 sentence

on notice: 4 warn 5 alert 6 inform, remind, signal, tip off 7 caution 8 admonish, forewarn, threaten

on one's feet: 5 boost 6 assist, buck up 7 bolster, support, sustain 10 facilitate

on one's thinking cap: 4 mull, muse 5 solve 7 analyze 8 consider, meditate 9 figure out

on paper: 3 pen 5 write 6 record

on tape: 6 record

on the back burner: 5 delay, table 6 shelve 7 suspend 8 postpone

on the dog: 6 flaunt 7 show off

on the feedbag: 3 eat

on the fire: 4 heat, warm 6 heat up, warm up

on the market: 4 sell, vend 5 offer 6 peddle 7 auction

on the payroll: 4 hire 5 staff 6 employ

on the radio: 3 air 8 transmit 9 broadcast

on the spot: 4 trap 5 abash 6 entrap 9 embarrass

on the tab: 4 bill 6 charge

on trial: 3 sue 9 prosecute

on view: 3 air 4 bare, show 6 expose, flaunt, lay out, parade, reveal 7 display, exhibit,

present, show off, trot out 8 showcase 10 illustrate
out: 3 bug, irk, vex 4 emit, gall, make, miff, rile, send 5 annoy, cross, douse, dowse, evict, exert, huffy, issue, peeve, pique, print, reach, snuff, spite, upset 6 badger, bother, harass, nettle, pester, piqued, quench, rattle, retire 7 disturb, go to sea, perturb, produce, provoke, publish, smother, torment, trouble 8 distress, irritate, squander 9 aggravate, disoblige, displease, eliminate, incommode 10 discommode, dispossess, exasperate, extinguish, impose upon, recompense
out a runner: 3 tag
out feelers: 3 ask 4 fish 5 probe, query 9 ask around
out of commission: 4 hurt 5 smash 6 injure 7 disable 8 sabotage
out of power: 4 oust 5 exile 6 depose
out with: 5 angry, irate, irked, vexed 9 indignant
over one's knee: 3 tan 4 lick, whip 5 smack, spank 6 punish, thrash, wallop 8 chastise 10 paddywhack
pen to paper: 5 write
pep into: 7 enliven, hearten 8 energize 10 exhilarate
pressure on: 3 tax 5 crowd, force, lobby
right: 3 fix 6 remedy 7 rectify, redress
starter: 3 out 7 through
stay ~: 3 fix 4 hold 5 stick
the arm on: 5 run in 9 shake down
the brakes on: 4 slow 6 slow up 8 slow down 10 decelerate
the chill on: 4 shun, snub 6 ignore, rebuff
the collar on: 3 nab 4 bust 5 run in 6 arrest 7 capture
the finger on: 4 name, tell 6 betray, inform, snitch, squeal, tattle
the kibosh on: 3 ban, end, nix, zap 4 curb, halt, stop, veto 5 check, quash, quell 6 forbid 7 abolish, contain, repress, squelch 8 cut short, suppress
the lid on: 3 gag 4 cork 5 cover, quash, quell 6 muffle, stifle 7 cover up
the pedal to the metal: 5 speed 6 barrel
the screws to: 5 force 6 coerce, compel 7 oppress 8 pressure
the top on: 3 cap 4 cork, seal 5 close, cover 7 stopper
the whammy on: 3 hex 4 damn, jinx 5 curse 7 bedevil, bewitch, condemn 9 imprecate
through: 3 end 6 effect, finish, wind up 7 achieve, execute, get done, pull off 8 bring off, complete, conclude, engineer 10 accomplish, bring about
through the wringer: 5 grill 7 torment 8 question 9 challenge
to bed: 5 close, print 6 finish 7 let roll 8 complete 10 consummate
to flight: 4 rout 5 panic, repel 7 overrun, repulse, scatter 8 chase out, stampede
together: 3 add, mix 4 form, join, make, mold 5 amass, build, frame, piece, rig up, set up 6 appose, create, derive, hook up, make up 7 combine, compile, prepare, work out 8 assemble
together again: 5 refit
to ~ it another way: 5 I mean
to rights: 4 tidy 5 clean, order 6 neaten, spruce 7 ordered, orderly 9 smarten up 10 straighten
to sea: 4 sail 6 launch 7 set sail, ship out 8 shove off 10 lift anchor
to shame: 4 beat, best 5 abase, outdo 6 exceed, humble, show up 7 eclipse, surpass 8 outclass, outshine, outstrip 9 humiliate 10 overshadow
to sleep: 4 bore, lull, rock, tire 9 hypnotize
to the proof: 3 try 4 test 5 assay
to the test: 3 try 5 prove
to use: 5 apply, avail, wield 7 utilize
to work: 3 use 4 hire 5 apply 6 employ, engage
two and two together: 3 add 5 solve 8 conclude
under a spell: 3 hex 5 charm 7 bewitch 9 hypnotize
under observation: 3 eye 4 tail 5 spy on 6 shadow 10 scrutinize
up: 3 bet, can, pay 4 ante, bunk, lift, make, post, rear, stay 5 board, build, built, erect, forge, house, lodge, pitch, raise, stake, wager 6 billet, canned, create, harbor, invest, lay out, lodged, supply, take in 7 auction, harbour, produce, provide, quarter, venture 8 assemble, domicile, nominate, preserve, ventured 9 construct, entertain, establish, fabricate, subscribe 10 contribute
up a fight: 6 oppose, resist 7 dissent 8 struggle
up a front: 3 lie 4 pose, sham 7 pretend
up a fuss: 4 balk, carp 5 baulk, demur 6 grouse, insist, refuse, resist 8 complain
up a smoke screen: 7 deceive 9 misinform
up for sale: 5 offer 7 auction
up money for: 4 back, fund 7 finance, sponsor 9 grubstake
upon: 7 oppress 8 bothered, keep down 9 disturbed, exploited
up to: 3 sic 4 abet, spur, urge 6 incite
up with: 3 let 4 bear, have, lump, okay, take 5 abide, admit, adopt, allow, brook, go for, stand, stick 6 accept, assent, comply, endure, permit, suffer, wink at 7 condone, include, let ride, stomach, sustain, swallow, undergo, welcome 8 accede to, assent to, overlook, sanction, stand for, submit to, tolerate 9 approve of, authorize, recognize, reconcile, sign off on 10 concur with, give the nod
well ~: 3 apt 6 cogent, timely 8 apposite, relevant, suitable 10 to the point
put __: 3 off, out 4 away, down, it to, over, upon 5 about, aside, forth, to bed, to use 6 across, option
put __ act: 4 on an
put __ and two together: 3 two
put __ block: 5 on the
put __ disadvantage: 3 at a
put __ dog: 5 on the
put __ face on: 5 a bold
put __ fight: 3 up a
put __ good word for: 3 in a
put __ in: 5 a dent, stock
put __ in it: 5 a sock
put __ in one's ear: 4 a bug
put __ in the water: 4 a toe
put __ on: 5 money
put __ on it: 4 a lid
put __ roots: 4 down
put __ sea: 5 out to
put __ show: 3 on a
put __ shut up: 4 up or
put __ to: 5 an end, a stop
put __ together: 5 heads, it all
put __ to pasture: 3 out
put __ writing: 4 it in
put-__: 4 down, upon
__-put: 4 hard, well
Put
father: 3 Ham
grandfather: 4 Noah
Put __ Hands Together: 4 Your
Put __ Happy Face: 3 on a
put a __ in: 5 crimp
put a __ in one's ear: 3 bug
Put a Little Love in Your Heart (song)
artist: Jackie DeShannon, Al Green, Annie Lennox
put an __ to: 3 end
put a tiger in your tank company: 4 Esso
putative: 7 alleged, assumed, imputed, reputed, seeming 8 presumed, reported, supposed
Put 'er __!: 5 there
put in __ word for: 5 a good
Put-in-Bay lake: 4 Erie
Putin, Vladimir: 7 Russian 9 statesman
Putnam: 6 George, Israel
put on __: 4 airs 5 an act, a show
put one's __ down: 4 foot
put one's __ in: 3 oar
put one's __ in order: 5 house
put one's __ on: 6 finger
put one's cards on the __: 5 table
put one's foot __: 4 down, in it
put on the __: 3 dog, map 4 ritz 5 block 7 feedbag
put out to __: 3 sea 7 pasture
putrefied: 6 rancid, rotten
putrefy: 3 rot 5 decay, go bad, spoil
putrescent: 6 rancid, rotten
putrid: 3 bad 5 awful, nasty 6 rancid, rotten, smelly 8 inedible, terrible
putsch: 4 coup 6 revolt 10 revolution
put something __ on: 4 over
putt: 4 shot 5 swing
easy ~: 5 gimme, tap-in
first to ~: 4 away
__ putt: 5 hole a
puttee: 6 gaiter 7 gambado, legging
putter: 4 club, fool, poke 6 dabble, diddle, doodle, fiddle, linger, piddle, tinker, trifle 7 fritter 8 golf club 10 goof around, mess around, play around
org.: 3 PGA
__-putter: 4 shot
putterer: 4 tiro, tyro 6 novice 7 amateur 8 beginner 9 greenhorn 10 dilettante
put the __ on: 3 arm 4 bite 5 skids 6 finger, kibosh 7 squeeze
put the __ to: 6 screws
put the __ to the metal: 5 pedal
__ Put the Bomp: 3 Who
putting __: 5 green
__-putting: 3 off
Puttin' on the Ritz: 4 song
composer: Irving Berlin
put to __: 3 bed, use 4 rest 5 shame 6 flight
put to the __: 4 test
putty: 4 gray, grey 6 cement 8 brownish 9 yellowish
kin: 3 ash
like: 8 yielding 9 malleable, tractable
relative: *see* gray color
user: 5 tiler
putty __: 5 knife
__ Putty: 5 Silly
put-up job: 4 ploy 5 frame 6 scheme 8 maneuver 9 strategem
put up or __ up: 4 shut
put up your __: 5 dukes
Put Your Hand in the Hand (1971 song)
artist: Ocean
Put Your Head on My Shoulder (1959 song)
artist: Paul Anka
Puyallup: 4 city, town 6 Indian 7 Amerind
locale: 10 Washington
Puzo, Mario: 6 writer
work: The Dark Arena
Fools Die
The Fortunate Pilgrim
The Fourth K
The Godfather
The Last Don
Omerta
The Sicilian
puzzle: 4 beat, faze, knot, maze, muse, snow 5 addle, floor, mix up, poser, rebus, stump, throw, vexer 6 baffle, bemuse, enigma, fuddle, jigsaw, marvel, ponder, riddle, secret, sudoku, teaser, wonder 7 becloud, buffalo, confuse, flummox, mystery, mystify, nonplus, paradox, perplex, problem, stagger, trouble 8 befuddle, bewilder, confound, entangle, mull over, quandary 9 bamboozle, brood over, conundrum, crossword, dumbfound, labyrinth, overwhelm 10 disconcert
direction: 4 down 6 across
do a ~: 4 work 5 solve
element: 4 clew, clue
fodder: 3 wds. 5 clues, words
help: 4 hint
need: 6 eraser, pencil
out: 5 crack, solve 6 decode

7 resolve, unravel 8 decipher, get right
over: 4 muse 6 ponder 8 meditate, question
part: 4 clue, grid, word 5 piece 7 picture
__ puzzle: 6 jigsaw, monkey 7 Chinese, picture
puzzled: 4 asea, lost 5 at sea, stuck 6 hung up, in a fog, thrown 7 at a loss, baffled, stumped 8 bollixed, clueless, confused, doubtful 9 buffaloed, flummoxed, mystified, perplexed 10 bewildered, nonplussed
exclamation: 3 duh, gee 4 gosh 5 golly 6 jiminy 7 jeepers 8 excuse me 9 beg pardon, come again
puzzlement: 4 koan 5 vexer 6 riddle, wonder 7 mystery 9 confusion, conundrum
puzzler: 4 snag 6 enigma, riddle 7 mystery, problem 9 conundrum
puzzling: 4 dark, hard 5 funny, mirky, murky, queer, tough, vague 6 arcane, knotty 7 cryptic, curious, elusive, elusory, obscure, unclear 8 abstruse, baffling, involved, nebulous, singular 9 ambiguous, confusing, cryptical, difficult, enigmatic, insoluble 10 indistinct, misleading, mysterious, mystifying, perplexing, surprising, unsettling
P-V connection: 5 QRSTU
PVC part: 4 poly 5 vinyl 8 chloride
pvt.: 2 GI
boss: 3 cpl., NCO, sgt.
like a ~: 3 enl.
see also private
P.W.: 5 Botha
pwr.: 4 elec.
source: 3 TVA 5 hydro
see also power
PX
part: 4 post 8 exchange
patron: 2 GI 3 NCO, PFC, sgt.
Pyewacket: 3 cat
Pygmalion: 4 play 5 drama 8 sculptor
author: George Bernard Shaw
love: 7 Galatea
sister: 4 Dido 6 Elissa
pygmy: 3 wee 5 small 9 miniature, undersize 10 diminutive, homunculus
pyknic
see obese
Pylades
wife: 7 Electra
Pyle: 5 Ernie, Gomer 6 Denver
pylon: 4 cone, pier, post 5 shaft, tower 6 column, marker, pillar 7 obelisk, support, upright 8 memorial, monolith, monument, pilaster
Pym: 4 John 7 Barbara
Pym, Barbara: 6 writer 7 British
work: Excellent Woman
A Few Green Leaves
Glass of Blessings
Quartet in Autumn
Some Tame Gazelle
A Very Private Eye
__ Pym Disposes: 4 Miss
Pynchon, Thomas: 6 writer
work: The Crying of Lot 49
Gravity's Rainbow
Low-Lands
Mason and Dixon
The Secret Integration
The Small Rain
V.
Vineland
Pyongyang: 4 city, town 7 capital
locale: 10 North Korea
Pyotr: 7 Kapitsa 9 Kropotkin
pyramid: 4 mass, pile, tomb 5 raise, stack 8 monument
builder: 5 Aztec, Mayan 6 Cheops 8 Egyptian
find: 4 gold 5 mummy 7 jewelry, Pharaoh 8 artifact
glass ~ architect: 3 Pei
glass ~ site: 5 Paris 6 France, Louvre
part: 4 apex, base 5 shaft, steps
site: 4 Giza, Nile 5 Egypt, Uxmal 6 Mexico, Thebes 7 Memphis 11 Chichén Itzá
Pyramus lover: 6 Thisbe
Pyrenees: 3 mts. 4 mtns. 5 range 9 mountains
bovine: 7 Alberes
chamois: 5 Izard
city: 3 Pau
locale: 5 Spain 6 Europe, France
native: 6 Basque
peak: 5 Aneto 6 Estats, Posets
region south of the ~: 6 Iberia
__-Pyrénées: 6 Basses, Hautes
pyretic: 3 hot 7 febrile 8 feverish
Pyrex: 5 glass 8 ovenware 9 glassware
pyrexia: 5 fever
pyrite: 3 ore 7 mineral
__ pyrite: 4 iron
pyro: 5 torch 7 firebug 8 arsonist 10 incendiary
pyromaniac: 5 torch 7 firebug 8 arsonist 10 incendiary
crime: 5 arson
pyrophobe fear: 4 fire
Pyrrha mother: 7 Pandora
pyrrhic: 4 foot
relative: 4 iamb 6 dactyl 7 anapest, spondee, trochee
Pyrrhic __: 7 victory
P.Y.T. (1983 song)
artist: Michael Jackson
Pythagoras: 5 Greek 11 philosopher 13 mathematician
Pythia: 5 sibyl 9 priestess
Pythian Games site: 6 Delphi
Pythias to Damon: 3 pal 6 friend
python: 5 snake 6 animal 7 reptile
relative: *see* snake
__ Python: 5 Monty
pythonic: 9 prophetic

Q: 6 letter
and A: 7 enquiry, inquiry
followers: 3 RST 4 RSTU 5 RSTUV
in phonetic alphabet: 6 Quebec
neighbor: 3 Tab
preceders: 3 NOP 4 MNOP 5 LMNOP
Q __: 4 and A
Q __ queen: 4 as in
Q-__: 3 Tip 4 Tips
'Q' __ Quarry: 5 Is for
__-Q: 4 Bar-B
Q & A (1990 film)
cast: Timothy Hutton, Nick Nolte
director: Sidney Lumet
Q&A
part of ~: 3 ans. 4 ques.
Qaddafi: 7 Muammar
Qantas
symbol: 5 koala
Qara __: 3 Qum
Qatar: 6 nation 7 country
capital: 4 Doha
group: 10 Arab League
leader: 4 amir, emir 5 ameer, emeer
locale: 4 Asia 6 Arabia
money: 4 rial 5 riyal 6 dirham
org.: 4 OPEC
Qatari: 4 Arab
neighbor: 5 Saudi
Qattara Depression: 6 desert
QB
armchair ~ channel: 4 ESPN
attacker: 2 LT, RT
bad ~ pass result: 3 int.
objective: 2 TD
org.: 3 NFL
protector: 2 LT, RT 3 end
see also football, quarterback
QB VII
author: Leon Uris
QE2: 4 ship 5 liner
letters: 3 HMS
line: 6 Cunard
QED part: 4 erat, quod
qintar: 4 coin 5 money
100 ~s: 3 lek
qirsh: 5 money
20 ~s: 5 riyal
'Q' Is for Quarry
author: Sue Grafton
Qom: 4 city, town 5 river
locale: 4 Iran
qoph: 6 Hebrew, letter
follower: 4 resh
preceder: 4 sadi 5 sadhe, tsade, tsadi
__ q's: 5 p's and
q's, p's and: 7 manners 9 etiquette, formality
mind one's ~: 6 behave 10 toe the line
qt.: 3 amt. 4 meas.
half: 2 pt.
multiple: 3 gal.
Q-tip: 4 swab, swob
target: 3 wax 6 earwax 7 cerumen
QT, on the: 5 close, slily, slyly 6 covert, hidden, secret 8 secretly 9 furtively, secretive, underhand 10 stealthily, undercover
qtr., first: 3 spr.
qty.: 3 amt., num. 4 meas.
food package ~: 3 doz. 4 nt. wt.
lab ~: 2 cc.
least ~: 3 min.
liquid ~: 2 oz., pt. 3 gal.
of the same ~: 5 equiv.
qua: 2 as 5 Latin
sine ~ non: 4 must, need 9 condition, essential, necessity, requisite
quack: 4 fake, sham 5 cheat, faker, fraud, knave, phony 6 humbug, phoney, pseudo 7 sharper, sharpie 8 imposter, impostor, swindler 9 charlatan, con artist, hypocrite, physician, pretended, pretender, simulator 10 medicaster, mountebank
ender: 6 salver
grass: 4 weed
quackery: 4 sham 5 fraud 8 pretense 9 deception, duplicity, hypocrisy, imposture, phoniness
Quacks of Helicon, The
author: Edgar Allan Poe
__ quack, there...: 5 Here a
quad: 4 four 5 court, space 6 campus 7 quarter 9 courtyard
building: 4 dorm
celeb: 4 BMOC
Quad __: 6 Cities
quadr-: 4 four
predecessor: 3 tri-
successor: 4 pent-
quadrangle: 4 yard 5 court 6 square 9 courtyard, enclosure
setting: 6 campus
quadratic: 6 square
quadriceps muscle: 6 vastus
quadrilateral: 5 rhomb 6 square 7 diamond, lozenge, rhombus 8 tetragon 9 trapezoid
type: 4 rect., rhom., trap. 7 rhombus 9 rectangle
quadrille: 4 game 5 dance 8 card game
quadrillion prefix: 4 peta-
quadrillionth prefix: 5 femto-
quadri- plus one: 5 penta-
quadrireme: 4 boat 5 craft 6 vessel 10 watercraft
quadruped: 3 ape, cat, cow, dog, elk, fox, gnu, pig, rat, sow, yak 4 bear, bull, deer, goat, hare, lion, lynx, mink, mole, puma, wolf 5 camel, hippo, horse, hyena, koala, lemur, llama, moose, mouse, panda, sheep, shrew, skunk, sloth, tapir, tiger, zebra 6 animal, badger, beaver, donkey, ermine, ferret, gerbil, gopher, jackal, jaguar, monkey, ocelot, rabbit, weasel, wombat 7 buffalo, echidna, gazelle, giraffe, hamster, leopard, muskrat, opossum, panther, raccoon 8 aardvark, anteater, antelope, chipmunk, dormouse, elephant, hedgehog, kangaroo, kinkajou, mongoose, platypus, reindeer, squirrel 9 bandicoot, groundhog, guinea pig, porcupine, woodchuck 10 rhinoceros
quads
kin: 3 abs 4 lats 5 traps
quaestor
subordinate: 5 edile 6 aedile
quaff: 3 ade, ale, nog, rum, sip, sup 4 beer, down, grog, gulp, mead, swig, toss 5 draft, drink, lager, stout, toddy 6 brandy, eggnog, guzzle, imbibe, liquor 7 iced tea, liqueut, partake, swallow 8 hot toddy, potation
quantity: 4 pint
see also beverage, drink
quag: 3 bog 5 swamp 9 marshland, quicksand
ender: 4 mire
quagga: 6 equine
relative: ***see*** equine
quagmire: 3 bog, fen, fix, jam 4 hole, mire, trap 5 marsh, pinch, swamp, waste 6 corner, morass, muddle, pickle, plight, scrape, slough 7 dilemma, impasse 8 headache, quandary 9 imbroglio, marshland, quicksand 10 difficulty, pretty pass
quahog: 4 clam 5 shell 7 bivalve, mollusc, mollusk 8 seashell 10 littleneck
Quaid, Dennis: 5 actor
film: The Alamo (2004)
Any Given Sunday (1999)
The Big Easy (1987)
Breaking Away (1979)
The Day After Tomorrow (2004)
D.O.A. (1988)
Dreamscape (1984)
Enemy Mine (1985)
Everybody's All-American (1988)
Far From Heaven (2002)
In Good Company (2004)
Innerspace (1987)
The Long Riders (1980)
The Parent Trap (1998)
Postcards From the Edge (1990)
The Right Stuff (1983)
The Rookie (2002)
The Savior (1998)
Suspect (1987)
Vantage Point (2008)
Wyatt Earp (1994)
spouse: Meg Ryan
Quai d'Orsay, view from the: 5 Seine
Quaid, Randy: 5 actor
film: Bye Bye, Love (1995)
Days of Thunder (1990)
Hard Rain (1998)
Independence Day (1996)
Kingpin (1996)
The Last Detail (1973)
The Last Picture Show (1971)
The Long Riders (1980)
Quick Change (1990)
quail: 4 bird, fear, fowl 5 colin, cower, droop, faint, quake, shake, start, wince 6 blanch, blench, cringe, falter, flinch, recoil, shrink 7 shudder, tremble 8 bobwhite, coturnix, draw back, game bird, pull back 9 lose heart 10 chicken out
group: 4 bevy 5 covey
hunter: 6 fowler
relative: ***see*** fowl
quaint: 3 odd, rum 4 cute 5 droll, funny, passé 6 freaky, Gothic 7 antique, baroque, bizarre, curious, erratic, oddball, offbeat, old-time, strange, unusual 8 adorable, charming, colonial, fanciful, old-timey, original, peculiar, pleasing, singular 9 eccentric, nostalgic, Victorian, whimsical 10 antiquated, enchanting, outlandish
in Britain: 4 twee
quake: 4 jerk, rock 5 cower, quail, seism, shake, shock 6 jitter, jounce, quiver, recoil, shiver, shrink, totter, tremor, wabble, wobble 7 pulsate, shudder, temblor, tremble, vibrate 8 upheaval 9 vibration 10 aftershock, convulsion
locale: 5 fault 9 fault line
make ~: 5 alarm, panic, scare 6 rattle 7 horrify, petrify, shake up, startle, terrify 8 frighten 10 intimidate
starter: 3 sea 4 moon 5 earth
Quaker __: 3 gun 4 Oats 7 meeting
Quaker cereal: 4 Life 5 Quisp 7 Oat Bran 9 Apple Zaps 10 Cap'n Crunch, Puffed Rice, Quaker Oats
Quaker Oats: 6 cereal
competitor: ***see*** cereal
Quakers: 4 sect 7 Friends
pronoun: 3 thy 4 thee, thou 5 thine
st.: 5 Penna.
verb: 3 art
Quaker State: Pennsylvania
quaking __: 5 aspen, grass
qualification: 4 need, term 5 goods, skill, stuff 6 caveat, string 7 ability, fitness, makings, proviso, stature 8 aptitude, capacity 9 attribute, condition, criterion, endowment, essential, exception, exemption, provision, requisite
form: 4 exam, test
without ~: 6 flatly
qualified: 3 apt, fit 4 able, good 5 adept, ready, tried 6 au fait, expert, fitted, proper, proven, tested, up to it, versed 7 bounded, capable, limited, partial, trained, veteran 8 adequate, eligible, equipped, licensed, modified, prepared, skillful, talented 9 certified, competent, cut out for, efficient, practiced, up to snuff, up to speed 10 contingent, instructed, privileged, proficient, restricted
become ~ for: 8 grow into
no longer ~: 5 rusty, stale 10 out of shape
qualifier: 2 if 3 but 6 adverb 9 adjective
qualify: 3 fit 4 lull, meet, name, pass, suit, vary 5 adapt, alter, cut it, endow, equip, get by, limit, ready, score, train 6 assign, change, enable, ground, hack it, impute, lessen, make it, modify, permit, reduce, season, soften, temper, weaken 7 ascribe, assuage, certify, empower, entitle, intitle, prepare, satisfy, suffice 8 check out, describe, diminish, mitigate,

moderate, modulate, regulate, restrain, restrict, sanction **9** attribute, authorize, condition, designate, measure up **10** capacitate, commission, make the cut, pass muster
for: **3** get, win **4** earn, gain, rate, reap **5** merit **6** attain, come by, derive, obtain, pick up, secure **7** deserve, procure, receive, warrant
qualities
making up good character: **5** arete
quality: **3** air **4** aura, kind, make, mark, rank, sort, tone **5** asset, class, fiber, grade, merit, point, state, thing, trait, value, worth **6** aspect, factor, flavor, goodly, nature, repute, status, virtue **7** caliber, earmark, essence, feature, footing, station, stature, texture, variety **8** position, property, standing, superior **9** attribute, character, condition, endowment, parameter **10** excellence, perfection, superbness
characteristic ~: **4** aura, odor **5** aroma, savor, smell
of poor ~: **3** bad **5** cheap, tacky, tatty **6** ragged, shabby, shoddy **8** mediocre
star ~: **5** charm **6** glamor **7** charism, glamour **8** charisma
suffix: **3** -ism **4** -ness, -ship
quality __: **4** time **5** point **6** circle **7** control
__-quality: **5** first **6** letter
Quality Inn: **5** motel
alternative: *see* motel
quality of __: **4** life
Quality of Mercy, The
author: Faye Kellerman
Quality Street
author: James M. Barrie
qualm: **3** rue **4** fear, pang **5** doubt, worry **6** regret, repent, twinge, unease **7** anxiety, scruple **8** disquiet, distrust, wariness **9** leeriness, misgiving, objection, suspicion **10** conscience, foreboding, hesitation, indecision, reluctance, skepticism, solicitude, uneasiness
have ~s: **5** doubt, worry **6** regret, repent
qualmish: **4** sick **6** queasy, queazy **9** squeamish
qualmless: **3** bad **5** wrong **6** amoral, wicked **10** licentious
__ quam videri: **4** esse
quandary: **3** fix, jam **4** bind, mess, spot **5** doubt **6** clutch, corner, muddle, pickle, plight, puzzle **7** dilemma, impasse, problem **8** exigence, exigency, juncture, quagmire **9** deep water **10** difficulty, perplexity
in a ~: **6** unsure **7** at a loss
Quang __: **3** Tri **4** Binh, Ngai
Quang Tri
locale: **3** Nam **7** Vietnam
__ qua non: **4** sine
Quant: **4** Mary
Quantico: **4** city, town
initials: **3** FBI **4** USMC
locale: **8** Virginia
quantify: **4** rate **5** gauge **7** measure
quantitative target: **5** quota
quantity: **3** lot, sum **4** bulk, deal, dose, hunk, load, mass, pile, size **5** batch, bunch, order, quota, store, total **6** amount, figure, length, number, supply, volume **7** measure, portion, variety **8** capacity **9** abundance, aggregate, allotment, multitude, profusion **10** collection, complement, cumulation
fixed ~: **4** unit
large ~: **3** gob, lot, sea, ton **4** acre, mass, much, peck, pile, raft, yard **5** ocean **6** boodle, galore, oodles **9** wholesale
liquid ~: **3** cup **4** pint **5** quart **6** gallon
miscellaneous ~: **6** job lot
small ~: **3** dab **4** dash, dram, drib, drop, iota, spot **5** ounce
__ quantity: **5** known
Quant, Mary: **7** British **8** designer
design: **3** mod **4** mini **9** miniskirt
Quanto è bella: **4** aria
Quanto rapita in estasi: **4** aria
quantum: **6** amount, ration
quantum __: **4** jump, leap
Quantum Leap (NBC sci-fi)
cast: Scott Bakula (Sam Beckett) Dean Stockwell (Al Calavicci)
computer: Ziggy
quantum mechanics: **7** science
Quantum of Solace (2008 film)
cast: Daniel Craig, Judi Dench, Olga Kurylenko
Quapaw: **6** Indian **7** Amerind **8** language
quarantine: **4** seal **6** cut off, enisle, shut in **7** isolate, seclude **8** solitude **9** detention, seclusion, segregate
in ~: **4** lone **5** alone, apart, aside **8** isolated, secluded, separate, solitary **9** by oneself
Quare Fellow, The
author: Brendan Behan
quark: **8** particle
+ antiquark: **5** meson
binder: **5** gluon
container: **4** atom
__ quark: **3** top **4** down **5** truth
quarrel: **3** row, war **4** beef, carp, feud, fray, fuss, rift, spar, spat, tiff, to-do **5** argue, brawl, broil, cavil, clash, fight, run-in, scrap, set-to, snarl **6** affray, barney, battle, bicker, breach, debate, differ, divide, dustup, fracas, haggle, hassle, jangle, ruckus, rumpus, strife, strive, take on, tangle, tumult **7** collide, contend, contest, discord, dispute, dissent, dustups, embroil, fall out, mix it up, quibble, rhubarb, wrangle **8** argument, catfight, complain, conflict, disagree, friction, object to, skirmish, squabble, struggle, vendetta **9** altercate, bickering, brannigan, break with, commotion, complaint, encounter, find fault, have it out, have words, imbroglio, lock horns, make a fuss, objection, take issue **10** bone to pick, contention, difference, difficulty, disapprove, dissension, dissidence, falling-out, fisticuffs
quarreling: **9** on the outs **10** discordant
quarrelsome: **4** ugly **5** cross, fiery, hasty, huffy, surly, testy **6** crabby, feisty, ornery, snappy, touchy, unruly **7** defiant, naughty, peevish, pettish, violent, warlike, wayward **8** brawling, choleric, churlish, contrary, fighting, militant, petulant, ructious, snappish, stubborn **9** bellicose, cat-and-dog, combative, excitable, fractious, hotheaded, irascible, irritable, litigious, querulous, splenetic, truculent, turbulent **10** out of sorts, pugnacious, rebellious
quarry: **3** pit **4** game, land, mine, prey, rock **6** source, target, victim **8** excavate **10** excavation
granite ~ locale: **5** Barre **7** Vermont
perhaps: **5** hider
yield: **3** gem, ore **4** rock **5** jewel, stone **6** gravel **7** crystal, mineral
quart: **4** unit
buy: **4** milk
eight ~s: **4** peck
ender: **3** ile
fraction: **2** pt. **3** cup **4** peck, pint
metric ~: **5** liter, litre
not quite a ~: **5** fifth
quarter: **4** area, bunk, coin, part, pity, post, quad, slum, spot, term, turf, ward, zone **5** board, cut up, grace, house, lodge, mercy, money, place, point, put up, tract **6** barrio, billet, canton, domain, fourth, ghetto, harbor, instal, lenity, locale, region, season, sector, take in **7** domicil, harbour, install, portion, section, shelter, station, two bits **8** clemency, district, domicile, lenience, leniency, locality, location, position, precinct, province, quadrant **9** direction, dismember, inner city, one-fourth, territory **10** compassion
bad ~: **4** slug
ender: **3** age, saw **4** ages, back, deck, tone **5** final, staff **6** master **8** finalist
give ~: **4** pity **5** spare **6** relent
half a ~: **3** bit **6** eighth
like a new ~: **5** shiny **6** agleam, bright **8** gleaming
note: **8** crotchet
of a quart: **3** cup
of eight: **3** two
starter: **4** fore, head, hind
third of a ~: **5** month
word on a ~: **3** God **4** unum **5** trust **6** dollar, States, United **7** America, liberty **8** pluribus
quarter __: **4** note, rest, tone **5** horse
__ quarter: **4** last **5** ask no, first
__-quarter: **5** three
__ Quarter: **5** Latin **6** French
quarterback: **4** lead **5** guide **6** direct **7** athlete, control, oversee **9** supervise
colleague: **6** center
great: **5** Baugh, Fouts, Kelly, Starr **6** Blanda, Dawson, Graham, Griese, Marino, Namath, Tittle, Unitas **7** Luckman, Montana **8** Bradshaw, Dan Fouts, Jim Kelly, Staubach, Y.A. Tittle **9** Bart Starr, Bob Griese, Dan Marino, Jurgensen, Len Dawson, Tarkenton **10** Joe Montana, Otto Graham, Sammy Baugh, Sid Luckman
move: **4** fade, pass **5** sneak
resource: **3** arm
signal: **3** hup **4** hike
tackle the ~: **4** sack
target: **3** end **8** receiver
the ~ takes it: **4** snap
quarterly: **8** magazine **10** periodical
Quartermaster __: **5** Corps
quarter-pint: **4** gill
Quarter Pounder: **6** burger **9** hamburger
part: **5** patty **6** pattie
quarters: **4** digs, dorm, flat, home, post, room, tent, yurt **5** abode, cabin, condo, house, lodge, money, place, ranch, roost, suite **6** billet, change **7** cottage, domicil, habitat, housing, lodging, shelter, station **8** barracks, chambers, domicile, dwelling, lodgment, sorority **9** apartment, residence **10** fraternity, habitation
at close ~: **4** near **6** nearby
cramped ~: **4** cell, coop **5** booth **6** alcove, recess **7** chamber, cubicle, dungeon **8** cloister
give ~ to: **4** rent **5** board, house, lodge, put up **6** billet, harbor, take in **7** shelter **9** entertain
in a sultan's palace: **5** haram, harem, harim **6** hareem
living ~: **4** home **5** abode, place
provide ~: **5** house
sailor's ~: **5** cabin **6** fo'c's'le
squalid ~: **3** sty **4** dump, slum **5** hovel **6** pigsty **8** cesspool, pesthole
starter: **4** head, hind
take up ~: **4** live, stay **5** abide, dwell, lodge, roost **6** occupy, reside, settle **7** inhabit, sojourn
temporary ~: **4** tent **7** bivouac
two ~: **4** half
winter ~: **3** den **4** lair
__ quarters: **5** close **6** call to
quartet: **4** four **5** combo, group **8** ensemble, foursome
alphabet ~: **4** ABCD, BCDE, CDEF, DEFG, EFGH, FGHI, GHIJ, HIJK, IJKL, JKLM, KLMN, LMNO, MNOP, NOPQ, OPQR, PQRS, QRST, RSTU, STUV, TUVW, UVWX, VWXY, WXYZ
deck ~: **4** aces, tens, twos **5** fives, fours, jacks, kings, nines, sixes **6** deuces, eights, queens, sevens, threes
double ~: **5** octet
half a ~: **3** duo, two **4** pair
member: **4** alto, bass **5** basso, tenor **7** soprano
minus one: **4** trio
plus five: **5** nonet
string ~ member: **5** cello, viola **6** violin
__ quartet: **5** piano **6** string
Quartet in Autumn
author: Barbara Pym
__ Quartet, The: **3** Raj
quarto, larger than: **5** folio
quartz: **4** rock **5** flint **7** mineral
deep-orange ~: **4** sard **5** agate, chert, topaz **6** jasper **7** sardine, sardius

fine-grained ~: 5 flint
grains: 4 sand
like ~: 4 hard 5 rocky, solid, stony
mineral in ~: 6 silica
pale yellow: 7 citrine
smoky ~: 3 gem
to Mohs: 5 seven
translucent ~: 10 chalcedony
violet: 8 amethyst
__ quartz: 4 rose
Quasar: 2 TV 5 TV set 10 television
alternative: *see* electronics company
quash: 3 end, nix 4 kill, stop, undo, veto, void 5 abate, annul, crush, estop, quell, rebut, sit on, trash 6 cancel, defeat, hush up, negate, quench, refute, repeal, revoke, scotch, squish, squush, subdue 7 abolish, blow out, destroy, nullify, put down, repress, rescind, reverse, scrunch, silence, smother, squeeze, squelch, squoosh, vitiate 8 abrogate, bottle up, dissolve, overcome, override, overrule, set aside, shut down, stamp out, suppress 9 extirpate, overthrow 10 annihilate, extinguish, invalidate
quasi: 4 as if, fake, mock, near, semi-, sham 6 almost, in part, kind of, partly, pseudo 7 nominal, seeming, virtual, would-be 8 apparent, so-called 9 pretended, synthetic 10 ostensible, resembling, supposedly
Quasimodo
creator: Victor Hugo
portrayer: Lon Chaney, Charles Laughton, Anthony Quinn
voice: Tom Hulce
Quatermain: 4 hero 5 Allan
Quaternary division: 6 ice age
__ Quatorze: 5 Louis
quatrain: 4 poem 5 verse
scheme: 4 ABAA, ABAB, ABBA
quatrainist, famous: 4 Omar
quatre: 4 four 6 French
follower: 4 cinq
preceder: 5 trois
__ quatre: 5 pas de
Quatre Evangiles
author: Émile Zola
quatri-
twice ~: 4 octa-, octo-
Quatro: 4 Suzi
quattordici: 7 Italian 8 fourteen
half of: 5 sette
quattro: 4 four 7 Italian
preceder: 3 tre
tre + ~: 5 sette
- tre: 3 una, uno
Quattro: 3 car 4 Audi, auto 10 automobile
quaver: 4 note 5 shake, trill 6 shiver, tremor, twitch, wabble, wobble 7 pulsate, tremble 10 eighth note
quavering: 5 reedy 6 shrill
quay: 4 dock, pier, port 5 berth, jetty, levee, wharf 7 landing 9 anchorage
ender: 3 age
Quayle: 2 VP 3 Dan 4 veep 7 Anthony
home: 3 Ind. 7 Indiana
predecessor: 4 Bush
successor: 4 Gore
__-que: 4 bar-b
Que __...: 4 sera
Que.: 4 prov.
neighbor: 2 NH 3 Ont. 4 Newf.
see also Québec
Qué __?: 4 pasa
Qué __ es?: 4 hora
queasiness: 5 upset 6 nausea 8 sickness
queasy: 3 ill 4 sick 5 queer, rocky, upset 6 uneasy, unwell 7 anxious, bilious, nervous 8 qualmish, troubled 9 squeamish, uncertain 10 indisposed
Québec: 4 city, prov., town 8 province
city: 4 Alma, Amos, Baie, Hull 5 Laval, Lévis, Rouyn, Sorel 6 Aylmer, Comeau, Granby, La Baie, Ste.-Foy, Val-d'Or, Verdun 7 Chambly, Lachine, La Salle, Mirabel, Noranda 8 Beauport, Brossard, Gatineau, Montréal, Rimouski, Sept-Iles, Ste.-Julie, St.-Hubert, St.-Jérôme 9 Côte-St.-Luc, Jonquière, Longueuil, Mascouche, Outremont, St.-Georges, St.-Lambert, St.-Laurent, St.-Léonard, Val-Belair, Westmount 10 Blainville, Boisbriand, Chicoutimi, Repentigny, Sherbrooke, St.-Constant, Ste.-Thérèse, St.-Eustache, St. Luc Anjou, Terrebonne
Indian: 6 Abnaki, Micmac 7 Abenaki, Naskapi 8 Wabanaki
locale: 6 Canada
neighbor: 5 Maine 7 New York
newspaper: 8 Le Soleil
peninsula: 5 Gaspé
school: 5 Laval 6 McGill 7 Bishop's 9 Concordia
see also French
Quechua: 4 Inca 5 Incan 6 Indian 7 Amerind 8 language
Queeg
ship: 5 Caine
queen: 3 ant, HRH, sov. 4 card 5 noble, piece, ruler, title, woman 6 dynast, victor 7 czarina, empress, monarch, sultana, tsarina, tzarina 8 face card 9 potentate, sovereign 10 chesspiece, Her Majesty
address: 4 ma'am
beater: 3 ace 4 king
ender: 4 side
fit for a ~: 5 regal, royal 9 luxurious
future ~ maybe: 4 pawn
home: 4 hive, nest 6 apiary, castle
in French: 5 reine
mate: 5 drone
name meaning ~: 6 Regina
Old Testament ~: 6 Esther
Spain ~: 5 reina
subject: 3 bee
topper: 5 crown, tiara
queen __: 3 bee 6 mother 7 consort, dowager, regnant
Queen: 4 Anne, band, Bess, Mary 6 Ellery 7 Beatrix, Latifah 8 Victoria 9 Elizabeth
Queen (rock group)
homeland: England
members: Mercury, May, Deacon, Taylor
song: Another One Bites the Dust (1980)
Body Language (1982)
Bohemian Rhapsody (1976)
Crazy Little Thing Called Love (1980)
Killer Queen (1975)
Somebody to Love (1976)
Under Pressure (1981)
We Are the Champions (1977)
You're My Best Friend (1976)
Queen __: 3 Mab, Mum 4 Anne, Bess, City, Mary 7 Latifah
Queen __ a Day: 3 for
Queen __ Hop: 5 of the
Queen __ lace: 5 Anne's
Queen __ Land: 4 Maud
Queen __ Nile: 5 of the
Queen __ War: 5 Anne's
__ Queen: 5 Dairy 6 Killer, Virgin 7 Dancing
Queen Anne's __: 3 War 4 lace
Queen-Anne's-Lace: 4 poem
author: William Carlos Williams
Queen City of the Rockies: 6 Helena
Queen Elizabeth: 4 boat, ship 5 liner
Queen, Ellery creator: Frederic Dannay, Manfred Lee
__ Queene, The: 6 Faerie
Queen for a Day (game show)
host: Jack Bailey
Queenie
author: Michael Korda
queenly: 5 noble, regal, royal 7 stately 8 imperial
Queen Mab
author: Percy Bysshe Shelley
Queen Mary: 4 boat, ship 5 liner
Queen Maud Range
locale: 9 Antartica
Queen of __: 5 Sheba 6 Heaven
Queen of Hearts (1981 song)
artist: Juice Newton
__, Queen of Scots: 4 Mary
Queen of Spades, The
author: Aleksandr Pushkin
Queen of the __: 4 Nile
Queen of the Damned, The
author: Anne Rice
Queen of the Hop (1958 song)
artist: Bobby Darin
Queen of the West, The: 4 Dale 5 Evans
Queen (rock group) (rock group)
song: Radio Ga-Ga (1984)
queen's __: 4 ware 5 scout 6 bounty 7 English, highway
queen's-__ openings: 4 pawn
Queens: 3 bor. 7 borough
locale: 3 NYC 7 New York
stadium: 4 Ashe, Shea
team: 4 Mets
Queensberry __: 5 rules
queens, game of: 5 chess
queenside castle, in chess: 3 OOO
queen-size __: 3 bed
Queensland: 5 state
capital: 8 Brisbane
city: 6 Cairns 8 Brisbane 10 Townsville
neighbor: 3 NSW
Queen, The (2006 film)
cast: James Cromwell, Helen Mirren
__ Queen, The: 3 May 4 Beet, Snow 6 Virgin 7 African
Queequeg captain: 4 Ahab
Queler: 3 Eve
quell: 4 calm, dull, ease, kill, lull, stop 5 abate, allay, check, crush, quash, queer, quiet, sit on, slake, still 6 becalm, defeat, hush up, pacify, quench, reduce, settle, soften, soothe, squash, stifle, subdue 7 appease, assuage, compose, conquer, control, head off, mollify, put down, repress, silence, smother 8 beat down, mitigate, moderate, overcome, shut down, stamp out, suppress, vanquish 9 alleviate, overpower, subjugate 10 extinguish
Quemoy: 4 isle 6 island
neighbor: 4 Mazu 5 Matsu
__ Que Nada: 3 Mas
quench: 3 end 4 cool, ruin, sate 5 allay, crush, douse, dowse, quash, quell, slake, wreck 6 dampen, put out, stifle 7 assuage, blow out, destroy, moisten, put down, relieve, satisfy, smother, squelch 8 decimate, demolish, mitigate, snuff out, suppress 9 alleviate 10 extinguish
quencher
thirst ~: 3 ade, ale, tea 4 beer 5 drink, juice, water
quenchless: 10 gluttonous, insatiable
Queneau, Raymond: 4 poet 6 French
work: The Bark Tree Zazie
Quentin: 5 Crisp 6 Massys 9 Tarantino
__ Quentin: 3 San
Quentin Durward
author: Walter Scott
Quentins
author: Maeve Binchy
Qué pasa? reply: 4 nada
quercus: 3 oak 4 tree
querulous: 4 edgy, sour 5 cross, fussy, huffy, testy, waspy, whiny 6 crabby, cranky, crusty, crying, grumpy, snappy, sullen, touchy, whiney 7 bearish, carping, finical, finicky, fretful, grouchy, nervous, peevish, scrappy, uptight, wailing, waspish, whining 8 captious, caviling, choleric, critical, finiking, finnicky, fretsome, grousing, grumpish, petulant, snappish 9 bemoaning, crotchety, demanding, deploring, fractious, grumbling, irascible, irritable, lamenting, plaintive, splenetic 10 censorious, out of sorts, whimpering
querulousness: 4 rage 5 spite, venom, wrath 6 enmity, malice, rancor, spleen 8 acrimony, ill humor 9 hostility, petulance, testiness 10 crabbiness, grumpiness, irritation, touchiness
query: 2 eh 3 ask, how, who, why 4 pose, quiz, seek, what, when 5 doubt, grill, issue, probe, where, which, whose 6 impugn, wonder 7 concern, dispute, enquire, enquiry, examine, inquire, inquiry, problem, request, solicit, suspect 8 distrust, mistrust, question, sound out 9 catechize, challenge, objection 10 disbelieve
mock-innocent ~: 5 who me

reporter's ~: 3 how, who, why 4 what, when 5 where
response: 5 reply 6 answer 8 comeback 9 rejoinder
ques.: 3 inq.
response: 3 ans.
Que Sera, Sera (1956 song)
artist: Doris Day
quest: 4 hunt, seek 5 chase, probe 6 pursue, search, voyage 7 crusade, enquiry, inquest, inquiry, journey, mission, pursuit 8 ambition, campaign, research 9 adventure, objective 10 enterprise, expedition, pilgrimage
object: 5 Grail 9 Holy Grail
__ quest: 6 vision
Quest: 3 van 6 Nissan
Quest __ Camelot: 3 for
__ Quest: 6 Galaxy
Questa notte: 4 aria
Quest for Camelot (1998 film)
voice cast: Cary Elwes, Eric Idle, Gary Oldman, Don Rickles, Jane Seymour
questing: 6 errant
question: 3 ask, how, pry, who, why 4 mull, poll, pose, pump, quiz, seek, what, when 5 demur, doubt, grill, hit up, issue, point, posit, probe, query, topic, where, which 6 debate, enigma, go over, impugn, matter, motion, needle, oppose, ponder, riddle, search, wonder 7 contest, dispute, enquire, enquiry, examine, impeach, inquire, inquiry, mystery, problem, protest, request, solicit, suspect 8 argument, ask about, distrust, hesitate, mistrust, petition, proposal, sound out 9 catechize, challenge, confusion, fight over, interview, misgiving, objection, speculate, suspicion 10 contention, controvert, difficulty, disbelieve, discussion, puzzle over
answer the ~: 5 field, reply 7 respond
anticipatory ~: 3 and
baffling ~: 5 poser 6 enigma, riddle 7 stumper, toughie
beyond ~: 4 sure, true 5 plain 6 surely
call into ~: 5 doubt 6 impugn, oppose 7 dispute 9 challenge
child's ~: 3 why
computer ~: 4 fail 5 abort, retry
French ~: 5 quand
gift recipient's ~: 5 for me
in ~: 4 open 7 at issue 10 suspicious
journalist's ~: 3 how, who, why 4 what, when 5 where
kind of ~: 5 essay, trick, yes/no
lamenter's ~: 5 why me
loaded ~: 4 bait, ruse, trap 6 ambush, come-on, device 8 maneuver 9 booby trap, deception 10 enticement, subterfuge
out of the ~: 2 no 3 nah, naw, nay, nix, non 4 nein, nope, nyet, uh-uh 5 I won't, ixnay, never, no how, no way 6 absurd, no deal, noways, nowise 7 I refuse 8 forget it, hopeless, I will not, negative, negatory 9 by no means, fat chance, forbidden, I think not 10 count me out, impossible, infeasible, not a chance, ridiculous, thumbs down
point in ~: 4 case 5 issue, theme, topic 6 affair, matter, thesis 7 problem, subject 8 business
pop the ~: 3 ask 7 propose
scientist's ~: 3 why
Spanish ~: 3 qué
tourist's ~: 5 where
question __: 4 mark
__ question: 5 essay, trick, yes-no 6 beyond, loaded 7 leading
__ Question, A: 6 Lover's
questionable: 4 iffy, moot, open, thin 5 fishy, queer, shady, shaky, vague 6 chancy, occult, unsure 7 cryptic, dubious, obscure, suspect, tenuous 8 arguable, doubtful, oracular, unlikely, unproven 9 ambiguous, cryptical, debatable, dubitable, enigmatic, equivocal, uncertain, undefined, unsettled 10 indefinite, unresolved, up for grabs, up in the air
questionables: 3 ifs 6 issues
questioner: 5 cynic 7 doubter, sceptic, scoffer, skeptic 8 examiner
conference ~: 5 media, press 8 reporter
motive ~: 5 cynic 7 doubter, skeptic
questioning: 7 curious, enquiry, inquiry 9 observant, quizzical, skeptical
sound: 2 eh 3 huh
questionnaire: 4 form, test
datum: 3 age, sex 4 name
Question of Mercy, A
author: David Rabe
__ questions: 4 four 6 twenty
__ questions?: 3 Any
quetzal: 4 bird 5 money
Quetzalcoatl: 3 god
worshiper: 5 Aztec 6 Toltec
queue: 3 row 4 coif, file, line, rank, tier 5 braid, chain, order, plait, train 6 column, hairdo, line up, series, string 7 pigtail 8 coiffure 10 succession
airport ~: 4 cabs 5 taxis
call to a ~: 4 next
queued up: 4 arow 6 in line, on line
Quezon City
island: 5 Luzon
quibble: 4 carp, spar, spat 5 argue, avoid, cavil, clash, dodge, evade, fudge, gripe, stall, whine 6 bicker, differ, hassle, niggle, pick at, waffle 7 dispute, evasion, nitpick, protest, quarrel, shuffle, sophism, wrangle 8 conflict, disagree, flip-flop, pettifog, squabble 9 altercate, argue over, chicanery, complaint, criticism, criticize, find fault, hem and haw, take issue 10 equivocate, split hairs
quibbler: 6 critic 10 fussbudget
quiche: 3 pie 6 pastry
alternative: 6 omelet 8 omelette
base: 5 crust
ingredient: 3 egg 5 bacon, Swiss 6 cheese 7 Gruyère
quick: 3 apt 4 able, anon, ASAP, curt, deft, fast, keen, rush, soon, spry 5 acute, adept, agile, alert, alive, brief, brisk, canny, fleet, hasty, nifty, rapid, ready, savvy, sharp, slick, smart, swift, tight 6 abrupt, active, adroit, astute, bright, clever, facile, flying, in a sec, liquid, lively, marrow, nimble, presto, prompt, pronto, racing, shrewd, snappy, speedy, sudden, winged 7 capable, cursory, express, hastily, hurried, instant, knowing 8 all there, dextrous, flitting, headlong, punctual, skillful, spirited 9 astucious, breakneck, competent, dexterous, effective, effectual, energetic, immediate, impatient, impetuous, mercurial, momentary, observant, on the ball, posthaste, rapid-fire, receptive, sprightly, whirlwind 10 discerning, double-time, hypersonic, insightful, perceptive, precocious, proficient, responsive, supersonic
be ~: 3 fly, hie, rip, run, zip 4 dart, dash, flit, move, race, rush, tear, whiz 5 hurry, scoot, smoke, speed, whisk 6 barrel, gallop, hasten, hustle, rocket, scurry 7 floor it, scamper 8 make time, step on it 9 make haste, shake a leg 10 accelerate, get a move on, lose no time, make tracks
ender: 3 set 4 lime, sand, step 6 silver
look: 4 peek, peep 6 aperçu
meal: 4 bite, nosh
on the uptake: 3 apt 4 glib 5 quick, sharp, smart, witty 6 adroit, astute, bright 9 astucious, receptive
too ~: 4 rash 5 hasty 10 headstrong
to the ~: 6 deeply, highly
to the helm: 3 yar 4 yare
turn: 3 zag, zig 4 jink
quick __: 3 fix 4 draw 5 bread, march, study
quick __ draw: 5 on the
quick __ wink: 3 as a
quick-__: 6 witted
__-quick: 6 double
Quick, __, the Flit!: 5 Henry
quick-and-dirty: 6 make-do 7 stopgap 8 slapdash 9 expedient, makeshift, temporary 10 improvised, pro tempore
Quick and the Dead, The (1995 film)
cast: Russell Crowe, Leonardo DiCaprio, Gene Hackman, Sharon Stone
director: Sam Raimi
quick as __: 5 a wink
Quick Change (1990 film)
cast: Geena Davis, Bill Murray, Randy Quaid, Jason Robards
Quick Draw: 3 dog 6 McGraw 7 sheriff
quicken: 3 fly, hie, rip, run, zip 4 dart, dash, flit, goad, grow, move, race, rush, spur, stir, tear, urge, wake, whet, zoom 5 hurry, impel, liven, pep up, pique, rouse, scoot, speed, touch, waken 6 arouse, awaken, barrel, excite, gallop, hasten, hustle, incite, kindle, move it, revive, rocket, scurry, step up, thrill, vivify 7 actuate, animate, enliven, floor it, hop to it, inspire, promote, refresh, scamper, speed up 8 activate, dispatch, energize, enspirit, expedite, increase, inspirit, motivate, step on it, vitalize 9 galvanize, hotfoot it, intensify, make haste, shake a leg, skedaddle, stimulate 10 accelerate, get a move on, hightail it, invigorate, revitalize, strengthen
Quicken
company: 6 Intuit
quickening: 7 revival 8 kindling
quicker-than-the-eye movement: 4 blur
Quick, Henry, the __!: 4 Flit
quicklime: 4 calx 5 oxide
quickly: 3 PDQ 4 ASAP, fast, soon, stat 5 apace, madly, right 6 adverb, presto, pronto 7 briefly, in brief, rapidly, readily, swiftly 8 directly, in a flash, in a jiffy, in no time, on the fly, on the run, pell-mell, promptly, right now, right off, speedily, suddenly, very soon 9 forthwith, hurriedly, instantly, like a shot, on the spot, posthaste, right away 10 here and now, swimmingly
quickness: 4 rush 5 haste, hurry, speed 8 alacrity, celerity, dispatch, legerity, rapidity, velocity 9 briskness, dexterity, diligence, eagerness, fleetness, readiness, smartness, swiftness 10 cleverness, expedition, nimbleness
quick on the __: 4 draw 6 uptake
Quick Pick: 6 tomato
relative: 4 Roma 6 Big Boy 9 beefsteak, Better Boy, Early Girl
quicksand: 4 mire, quag, trap 5 snare 7 pitfall 8 quagmire
Quicksand (1963 song)
artist: Martha & the Vandellas
quicksilver: 5 azoth, metal 6 fickle 7 mercury 9 mercurial
quick-tempered: 5 angry, cross, fiery, testy 6 cranky, snappy, touchy 7 grouchy, peppery, waspish 8 choleric, petulant, shrewish, snappish, wrathful 9 excitable, impatient, irascible, irritable, sensitive, splenetic
quick-witted: 3 apt 4 keen 5 acute, agile, alert, canny, ready, savvy, sharp, slick, smart, witty 6 astute, brainy, bright, clever, nimble, prompt, shrewd 7 jesting, knowing 8 humorous 9 astucious, brilliant, facetious, ingenious, inventive, on the ball, sprightly
quid: 4 chaw 5 money 9 sovereign
pro quo: 6 barter 8 exchange, reprisal 10 substitute
quiddity: 6 entity, nicety, nuance 7 essence 8 badinage, subtlety
quidnunc: 3 pry 5 snoop, yenta 6 gossip 7 meddler, Paul Pry, snooper 8 busybody 10 Nosy Parker
like a ~: 4 nosy 5 nosey
quid pro quo: 4 swap, swop 5 trade
Quién __?: 4 sabe
quiescence: 4 ease, lull, rest 6 repose, stasis 7 latency, silence 8 abeyance 10 inactivity

quiescent: **4** calm, cool **5** inert, quiet, still **6** at rest, latent, low-key, mellow, placid, sedate, serene **7** abeyant, amiable, at peace, dormant, equable, pacific, passive, relaxed, stoical, unmoved **8** amicable, composed, inactive, laid-back, peaceful, tranquil, unmoving **9** collected, easy-going, immovable, impassive, inanimate, potential, temperate, unexcited, unruffled **10** motionless, stationary, unagitated, untroubled

quiet: **3** gag, ice, lay, low, mum, shy **4** calm, cool, dumb, ease, easy, hush, lick, lull, meek, mild, mute, rest, soft, stop **5** allay, bated, can it, choke, close, faint, inert, light, muted, peace, piano, quell, relax, shush, slack, sober, still **6** becalm, clam up, cool it, deaden, docile, gentle, hushed, lonely, low-key, mellow, modest, muffle, muzzle, pacify, placid, repose, secret, sedate, serene, settle, shut up, silent, simple, smooth, soften, soothe, squash, stable, subdue **7** amiable, appease, assuage, at peace, console, cool out, dead air, easeful, equable, halcyon, harmony, leisure, mollify, muffled, orderly, pacific, privacy, private, put down, relaxed, relieve, restful, retired, satisfy, silence, squelch, stilled, stoical, subdued, unmoved **8** amicable, becalmed, calm down, calmness, composed, dampened, deadened, hushed up, inactive, isolated, laid-back, mitigate, moderate, murmured, palliate, peaceful, reserved, reticent, retiring, secluded, serenity, stagnant, stealthy, taciturn, tasteful, tone down, tranquil **9** cessation, clammed up, collected, contented, easy-going, impassive, inaudible, noiseless, peaceable, placidity, quiescent, reconcile, seclusion, secretive, soft-pedal, soundless, stillness, temperate, toned down, unexcited, unruffled, unuttered, voiceless, whispered **10** ameliorate, buttoned up, cool-headed, hold it down, low-pitched, motionless, nonviolent, relaxation, restrained, speechless, turned down, unagitated, unassuming, uneventful, unspeaking, untroubled
- **be ~:** **3** sit **4** hush **5** bag it, can it, shush **6** clam up, hush up, shut up **7** silence **8** pipe down
- **become ~:** **4** lull **5** abate, cease **6** recede **7** die down, subside **8** moderate
- **down:** **4** calm, hush, lull **5** abate **6** pacify, subdue, unwind **7** silence
- **exclamation of ~:** **3** shh **4** hush **5** shush **7** hushaby, silence
- **greeting:** **3** nod **4** wave
- **in music:** **5** tacet
- **make ~:** **6** muffle, shut up **7** silence
- **one:** **4** clam **5** mouse
- **on the ~:** **7** sub rosa **8** secretly
- **partner:** **5** peace
- **peace and ~:** **6** relief **8** solitude
- **period:** **4** calm, lull
- **suffix for ~:** **3** ude

quiet __: **3** sun **4** time

Quiet!: **3** shh **4** hush **5** bag it, can it, shush **6** hush up, shut up **7** silence **8** pipe down

quiet as a __: **4** lamb **5** mouse

Quiet City
- **composer:** Aaron Copland

Quiet Don, The
- **author:** Mikhail Sholokhov

Quiet Dust, The
- **author:** William Styron

quieten: **6** muffle **7** subside

quietly: **7** lightly **8** secretly
- **move ~:** **5** slink, steal **7** slither
- **very ~ in music:** **3** ppp

Quiet Man, The (1952 film)
- **cast:** Barry Fitzgerald, Victor McLaglen, Maureen O'Hara, John Wayne
- **director:** John Ford

quietness: **4** calm, ease **7** reserve, silence **8** calmness, serenity

Quiet on the __!: **3** set

__ Quiet on the Western Front: **3** All

quietude: **4** calm, hush, rest **5** peace, quiet **6** repose **8** serenity

quietus: **3** end **4** rest **7** silence

Quiet Village (1959 song)
- **artist:** Martin Denny

Quigley Down Under (1990 film)
- **cast:** Alan Rickman, Laura San Giacomo, Tom Selleck

quill: **3** pen **5** plume, spine **7** calamus, feather
- **ender:** **4** back, work, wort
- **partner:** **6** inkpot
- **tip:** **3** nib

Quiller-Couch, Anthony: **6** writer **7** British

Quiller Memorandum, The (1966 film)
- **cast:** Sir Alec Guinness, George Segal, Max von Sydow

Quills (2000 film)
- **cast:** Michael Caine, Joaquin Phoenix, Geoffrey Rush, Kate Winslet

quilt: **3** sew **4** pouf, puff **5** cover, duvet, piece **6** spread **7** bedding, blanket **8** bedcover, coverlet, coverlid **9** comforter, eiderdown, patchwork
- **crazy ~:** **4** olio **6** jumble, medley **7** mélange **8** mishmash, mixed bag, pastiche **9** pasticcio, patchwork, potpourri **10** assortment, hodgepodge, miscellany, salmagundi
- **material:** **4** batt, down **5** cloky, eider, patch **6** calico, cloque

quilting __: **3** bee

Quimby: **6** Ramona

quince: **4** pome, tree **5** fruit
- **family:** **4** rose
- **relative:** **4** pear, plum **5** apple, peach **6** almond, cherry, medlar **7** apricot **8** hawthorn, oiticica **10** blackthorn

Quincy: **4** city, town **5** Jones, Magoo **6** Josiah, Porter
- **locale:** **3** Ill. **4** Mass. **8** Illinois

__ Quincy Adams: **4** John

Quincy, M.E. (NBC drama)
- **cast:** Robert Ito (Sam Fujiyama) Jack Klugman (Dr. Quincy)

Quindlen: **4** Anna

Quine: **7** Richard

quinella: **3** bet **5** wager
- **kin:** **6** exacta **8** perfecta

quinine: **7** bitters
- **like ~:** **4** sour, tart **5** acerb **6** bitter **7** acerbic
- **water:** **5** tonic

Quinlan: **8** Kathleen

Quinn: **5** Aidan **6** Martin **7** Anthony **8** Cummings

__ Quinn: **6** Mighty

Quinn, Anthony: **5** actor
- **film:** Barabbas (1962)
  The Brave Bulls (1951)
  The Buccaneer (1958)
  A Dream of Kings (1969)
  The Guns of Navarone (1961)
  La Strada (1954)
  Lawrence of Arabia (1962)
  Lost Command (1966)
  Lust for Life (1956, AA)
  The Ox-Bow Incident (1943)
  Requiem for a Heavyweight (1962)
  Revenge (1990)
  Viva Zapata! (1952, AA)
  A Walk in the Clouds (1995)
  Warlock (1959)
  Zorba the Greek (1964)

Quintana __: **3** Roo

quintessence: **4** core, gist, meat, pith, root, soul, type **5** heart, model, stuff **6** kernel, marrow, spirit **7** epitome, essence, extract, paragon **8** quiddity **9** lifeblood, substance

quintessential: **5** ideal, model, typic **6** innate **7** classic, typical **9** necessary

quintet: **4** five **5** combo, group **6** pentad **8** ensemble, fivesome
- **alphabet ~:** **5** ABCDE, AEIOU, BCDEF, CDEFG, DEFGH, EFGHI, EIEIO, FGHIJ, GHIJK, HIJKL, IJKLM, JKLMN, KLMNO, LMNOP, MNOPQ, NOPQR, OPQRS, PQRST, QRSTU, RSTUV, STUVW, TUVWX, UVWXY, VWXYZ **6** vowels
- **string ~ member:** **4** bass **5** cello, viola **6** violin **10** double-bass

__ Quintet: **5** Trout

quintillion prefix: **3** exa-

quintillionth prefix: **4** atto-

Quinto: **7** Zachary

Quint's boat: **4** Orca

__ Quinze: **5** Louis

quip: **3** gag, mot, pun **4** barb, gibe, jape, jeer, jest, jibe, joke **5** ad-lib, crack, sally, spoof **6** banter, bon mot, insult, japery, retort, ripost, satire, zinger **7** epigram, mockery, offense, riposte **8** badinage, drollery, laconism, one-liner, repartee **9** wisecrack, witticism **10** pleasantry
- **ender:** **4** ster
- **quick with a ~:** **4** glib **5** witty

quipster: **3** wag, wit **4** card **5** clown, comic, joker **8** comedian, humorist **9** jokesmith **10** smart aleck

quipu maker: **4** Inca

quire
- **multiple:** **4** ream

quirk: **3** tic **4** kink, turn, whim **5** fancy, fluke, habit, thing, trait, trick, twist **6** fetich, fetish, foible, hang-up, oddity, vagary, whimsy **7** anomaly, caprice, conceit, whimsey **8** crotchet **9** aberrance, attribute, exception, mannerism **10** aberration

quirky: **3** odd **4** eery **5** eerie, funky, weird **6** atypic, freaky, tricky **7** bizarre, deviant, offbeat, strange, unusual **8** aberrant, atypical, freakish, peculiar, uncommon **9** anomalous, divergent, eccentric, fantastic, irregular **10** capricious, unorthodox

quirt: **4** lash, whip

Quisenberry: **3** Dan

quisling: **5** snake, viper **7** traitor **8** turncoat **10** subversive

Quisp: **6** cereal
- **competitor:** *see* cereal

quit: **2** go **3** end **4** drop, exit, fold, gone, halt, kick, part, stop **5** cease, close, forgo, leave, let up, yield **6** bow out, cop out, cut out, decamp, depart, desert, desist, expire, finish, forego, get out, give up, lay off, relent, resign, retire, secede, strike, vacate, wind up, wrap up **7** abandon, abscond, adjourn, bail out, break up, concede, conk out, drop out, forsake, pull out, push off, refrain, satisfy, scuttle, succumb, suspend, take off, walk out **8** abdicate, break off, check out, conclude, cut it out, give over, hang it up, kick over, knock off, leave off, light out, pack it in, renounce, run out on, say uncle, shove off, skip town, step down, swear off, withdraw **9** leave flat, liquidate, pull out of, stand down, surrender, take a hike, terminate, throw over, walk out on **10** call it a day, chicken out, give notice, go away from, knock it off, relinquish
- **ender:** **4** rent **5** claim

...__ quit!: **3** or I

quitch: **5** grass

quitclaim: **4** deed **8** abdicate

quite: **3** all, far **4** just, oh so, very, well **5** fully, plumb, sheer, stark **6** ever so, fairly, highly, hugely, in fact, in toto, pretty, purely, wholly **7** assuage, greatly, in truth, largely, totally, utterly **8** actually, entirely, for a fact, somewhat **9** decidedly, extremely, in reality, perfectly, seriously **10** altogether, completely, moderately, more or less, noticeably, reasonably, relatively, remarkably, thoroughly
- **a while:** **3** eon **4** aeon, days
- ***see also*** of course

quite __: **4** a few **6** enough

Quito: **4** city, town **7** capital
- **locale:** **7** Ecuador
- ***see also*** Spanish

quits, call it: **4** halt, stop **5** cease, yield

quittance: **7** receipt, redress

quitter: **4** wimp **5** mouse **6** coward **7** chicken **8** deserter, weakling **9** fraidy-cat, jellyfish **10** scaredy-cat

toss: 5 towel
word: 4 can't 5 uncle 6 cannot
quitting time for some: 3 six 4 five
quiver: 3 tic, wag 4 beat, jerk, lick, rock, stir 5 nidge, pulse, quake, shake, sheaf, spasm, throb 6 cringe, jitter, shiver, teeter, thrill, totter, tremor, twitch 7 pulsate, shimmer, shudder, sparkle, tremble, vibrate 8 convulse 9 oscillate, palpitate, vibration
carrier: 6 archer, bowman 9 Robin Hood 10 longbowman
item: 5 arrow
quivering: 5 jumpy, shaky 7 jittery 9 tremulous, vibration
motion: 3 tic 6 tremor
tree: 5 aspen
Quivers: 5 Robin
quivery: 7 fearful 8 trembling 9 tremulous
qui vive
on the ~: 4 wary 5 alert, aware, sharp 6 uneasy 7 heads-up, heedful, wakeful 8 keen-eyed, vigilant, watchful
Quixote, Don
see Don Quixote
quixotic: 6 dreamy 7 utopian 8 chimeric, delusive, fanciful, romantic 9 imaginary, visionary 10 chimerical, idealistic
quiz: 3 ask 4 exam, hoax, pump, test 5 check, grill, prank, probe, query 6 lesson 7 enquire, examine, inquire 8 blue book, querying, question 9 catechize, check up on, interview
answer: 4 true 5 false
quiz __: 3 kid 4 show
__ quiz: 3 pop
Quiz Kids, The: 9 radio show
Quiznos
rival: *see* restaurant chain
quiz show: 4 game
need: 5 booth 6 buzzer 10 contestant
radio ~: 4 Dr. IQ
VIP: 2 MC 4 host 5 emcee
Quiz Show (1994 film)
cast: Ralph Fiennes, Rob Morrow, Paul Scofield, John Turturro
character: 4 Herb 5 Barry 7 Enright, Goodwin, Stempel 8 Van Doren
director: Robert Redford
quizzical: 3 odd 4 arch 5 droll 6 show-me 7 amusing, comical, curious, mocking, off-beat, peering, probing, teasing 8 confused, derisive, peculiar, sardonic 9 bantering, eccentric, inquiring, laughable, searching, skeptical, whimsical 10 suspicious
quizzing: 7 enquiry, inquiry
Q-U link: 3 RST
Qum: 4 city, town 5 river
country: 4 Iran
__ Qum: 4 Qara 5 Qizil
Qumran inhabitant: 6 Essene
quo
quid pro ~: 6 barter 8 exchange, reprisal 10 substitute
status ~: 8 reaction 9 condition, situation
__ quo: 6 status
Quo __?: 5 Vadis
quod __ demonstrandum: 4 erat
quod __ faciendum: 4 erat
quodlibet, like a: 4 moot
quoin: 4 nook 5 wedge 8 keystone
quoits: 4 game 7 pastime
peg: 3 hob
play ~: 4 toss 5 throw
quondam: 3 old 4 erst, late, once, past 6 bygone, former 7 old-time, one-time 8 previous 9 erstwhile
Quonset hut: 8 barracks, quarters
quota: 3 cut, lot 4 goal, part, rate 5 chunk, floor, limit, piece, ratio, share, slice 6 ration 7 ceiling, measure, minimum, portion 8 quantity 9 allotment, allowance 10 allocation, assignment, complement, contingent, percentage, proportion
meeting the ~: 6 enough 8 adequate 10 acceptable, sufficient
off one's ~: 4 slow 6 behind 7 lagging 8 trailing 9 in arrears 10 delinquent
quotation: 3 bid 4 cost, rate, text 5 price 6 charge, citing, figure, saying, tender 7 cutting, excerpt, extract, passage 8 bid price, citation 9 reference, selection 10 recitation
attribution: 4 anon., Shak. 9 anonymous
quotation __: 4 mark
quotations: 8 analecta, analects
quote: 3 bid 4 cite, cost, rate 5 price, refer 6 adduce, attest, charge, figure, parrot, recite, repeat, retell, saying, tender 7 excerpt, extract, mention, passage, refer to 8 allude to, bid price, citation 9 recollect, reference, selection 10 paraphrase
source: 3 OTC 4 AMEX, NYSE 9 Bartlett's
Quoth the __...: 5 raven
quotidian: 5 daily, usual 6 common 7 diurnal, per diem, routine 8 everyday, ordinary 9 hackneyed
quotient: 5 ratio, share 6 result
Quo Vadis? (1951 film)
cast: Deborah Kerr, Robert Taylor, Peter Ustinov
character: 4 Nero 5 Actea, Aulus, Croto, Lygia, Peter, Ursus 6 Eunice, Seneca
director: Mervyn LeRoy
garb: 4 toga
q.v.
part of ~: 4 quod, vide
QVC: 7 channel
alternative: 3 HSN 7 ShopNBC
Q-V connection: 4 RSTU
Q-W connection: 5 RSTUV
QWERTY
alternative: 6 Dvorak
device: 7 keyboard

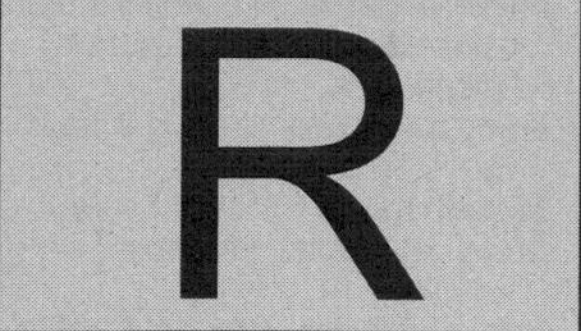

R: **6** letter, rating
and B: **4** soul **5** music
and R: **5** leave **7** time off **8** down time, furlough, vacation **10** recreation
followers: **3** STU **4** STUV **5** STUVW
give an ~: **4** rate
in phonetic alphabet: **5** Romeo
issuer: **4** MPAA
preceders: **3** OPQ **4** NOPQ **5** MNOPQ
R __: **4** and B, and D, and R
R __ rat: **4** as in
'R' __ Ricochet: **5** Is for
R2-D2: **5** robot
Ra: **3** god **4** boat, elem., ship **6** radium, sun god **7** element
88 for ~: **4** at. no.
enemy: **7** Apophis
symbol of ~: **4** Aten, Aton
__-Ra: **4** Amon
Rabat: **4** city, port, town **7** capital
locale: **7** Morocco
rabbet: **6** furrow, groove, joiner
rabbi: **3** Jew **6** cleric **8** chaplain, minister **10** theologian
detective: **5** Small
place: **4** shul **5** schul **9** synagogue
text: **5** Torah **6** Talmud
Rabbi Ben Ezra
author: Robert Browning
rabbinate: **6** clergy **8** ministry
rabbinical: **8** clerical
sch.: **3** sem.
rabbit: **3** fur, pet **4** cony **5** bunny, coney **6** animal, hopper, jumper, mammal **10** cottontail
breed: **6** angora
cousin: **4** hare
ears: **6** aerial, dipole **7** antenna
feature: **3** ear
female ~: **3** doe
fictional ~: **4** Br'er, Bugs **5** Mopsy, Peter, Roger **6** Flopsy **8** Crusader **9** Bugs Bunny **10** Cottontail
food: **5** salad **6** carrot, greens
foot: **3** paw
fur: **4** cony **5** coney, lapin
home: **5** hutch **6** burrow
like some ~ ears: **4** alop
male ~: **4** buck
starter: **4** jack
tail: **4** scut
Welsh ~ ingredient: **6** cheese
young: **5** bunny **6** kitten
rabbit __: **4** ball, ears, food, test **5** punch
__ rabbit: **5** Welsh
Rabbit: **2** VW **3** car **4** auto **10** automobile, Maranville, Volkswagen
Rabbit __: **5** Redux
__ Rabbit: **4** Br'er **5** Peter, White
Rabbit at Rest
author: John Updike
rabbit-eared bandicoot: **5** bilbi, bilby
Rabbit is Rich
author: John Updike
rabbitlike mammal: **4** mara, pika **6** agouti
__ rabbit out: **5** pull a
Rabbit Redux
author: John Updike
Rabbit, Run
author: John Updike
rabbit's foot: **5** charm **6** amulet **8** talisman
Rabbitt, Eddie
song: Drivin' My Life Away (1980)
I Love a Rainy Night (1980)
Step by Step (1981)
Suspicions (1979)
You and I (1982)
rabble: **3** mob **4** gang, herd, mass, pack, raff, ring, riot, scum **5** crowd, dregs, drove, flock, horde **6** masses, people, throng **7** beggary **8** riffraff **9** commoners, gathering, hoi polloi, multitude **10** lower class
in French: **8** canaille
Rabble in Arms
author: Kenneth Roberts
rabble-rouser: **7** inciter **8** agitator, inflamer **9** demagogue, firebrand **10** instigator
Rabe, David: **9** dramatist **10** playwright
spouse: Jill Clayburgh
work: The Basic Training of Pavlo Hummel
The Crossing Guard
Goose and Tomtom
Hurlyburly
I'm Dancing as Fast as I Can
In the Boom Boom Room
The Orphan
A Question of Mercy
Recital of the Dog
Sticks and Bones
Streamers
Those the River Keeps
Rabelais, François: **6** French, writer **8** humanist
work: Gargantua and Pantagruel
rabid: **3** mad **4** wild **5** feral, manic, ultra **6** crazed, ferine, raging, savage **7** beastly, berserk, bigoted, hog-wild, radical, untamed, violent, zealous **8** frenzied, in a furor, maniacal, obsessed, unbroken, vehement, white-hot, wild-eyed **9** delirious, fanatical, ferocious, unbridled, wrought-up **10** hysterical, infuriated
rabidity: **4** fury **5** wrath **6** frenzy **7** passion **8** ferocity **9** intensity, vehemence **10** fierceness
rabidly: **4** very **5** madly **7** acutely, greatly **9** devotedly, fervently, intensely, like crazy, zealously **10** thoroughly
rabies: **5** lyssa
like ~: **5** viral
Rabi, Isidor: **8** Nobelist **9** physicist, scientist
Rabindranath: **6** Tagore
Rabin, Yitzhak: **7** Israeli **8** Nobelist
predecessor: **4** Meir **6** Shamir
successor: **5** Begin, Peres
__-Ra-Boom-De-Ré: **4** Ta-Ra
raccoon: **3** fur **6** animal, mammal
cousin: **5** coati, panda **8** kinkajou
male ~: **4** boar
marking: **4** mask
to farmers: **6** bandit
Raccoon, city on the: **9** Des Moines
race: **3** fly, hie, rip, run, zip **4** bolt, clan, dart, dash, drag, flit, heat, meet, pelt, post, rill, rush, scud, sort, tear, tide, whiz, zoom **5** blood, breed, brook, chase, color, creek, derby, event, hurry, match, relay, rev up, rille, river, scoot, scram, shoot, spank, speed, tribe, whisk **6** barrel, careen, career, course, family, gallop, hasten, hurtle, hustle, Le Mans, move it, nation, people, rocket, runlet, runnel, scurry, slalom, sluice, sprint, stream **7** channel, compete, contest, culture, current, floor it, hop to it, lineage, progeny, pursuit, quicken, rivulet, scamper, scuttle, species, tear off **8** campaign, election, hightail, light out, make time, marathon, outstrip, scramble, step on it, undertow, waterway **9** go quickly, hotfoot it, shake a leg, skedaddle, streamlet, whip along **10** get a move on, go pell-mell, hightail it, lose no time, make tracks
an engine: **3** rev
auto ~: **4** Indy **5** rally **6** enduro, Le Mans **7** Daytona
combining form: **4** geno-, phyl- **5** ethno-, phylo-
competitor: **5** entry
course: **4** oval
downhill: **3** ski **4** skee
ender: **3** car, way **5** horse, track **6** course, runner
fabled ~ loser: **4** hare
human ~: **3** man **5** world **6** people **7** mankind
join the rat ~: **4** moil, slog, toil **5** labor, slave, sweat **6** drudge, hustle, strive **7** achieve, peg away **8** plug away **9** freelance, grind away, moonlight **10** buckle down
marker: **5** pylon
mythical ~: **7** Amazons
official: **5** timer **7** starter
out of the rat ~: **4** retd. **7** retired
place: **4** gate, tape
preliminary ~: **4** heat
prize: **5** medal, purse
rat ~: **3** rut **5** grind **7** society **8** drudgery **10** livelihood
starter: **3** gun **4** foot, head, mill, tail **5** horse
Triple Crown ~: **5** Derby **7** Belmont **9** Preakness
type of ~: **4** ten K **5** derby, relay **8** marathon
unit: **3** lap **4** mile, yard **5** meter
__ race: **3** rat **4** arms, drag, flat, foot, post, road, sack **5** horse, human, relay, stake
racecar: **3** GTO **6** hot rod
engine: **5** turbo
sound: **5** vroom **6** varoom
sponsor: **3** STP
racehorse: **3** nag **4** pony **5** pacer
certain ~: **4** mare **5** filly
racer: **5** miler, snake, yacht **6** animal, hot rod, jockey, runner **7** harrier, hurdler, reptile, speeder, trotter **8** dragster, sprinter **9** greyhound **10** speed demon
Aesop ~: **4** hare **8** tortoise
downhill ~: **3** ski **4** luge, skee, sled **5** skier
gauge: **4** tach
kid's ~: **4** kart **6** go-cart, go-kart
Olympics ~: **4** luge **5** rower, scull **10** marathoner
relative: ***see*** snake
track ~: **4** kart **5** horse **6** equine **8** sprinter
Racer's Edge, The: **3** STP
racetrack: **4** oval, turf **6** course
alternative: **3** OTB
Ancient Greek ~: **6** dromos
ancient Roman ~ marker: **4** meta
boundary: **4** rail
British ~: **5** Ascot, Epsom
California ~: **6** Del Mar **10** Santa Anita
circuit: **3** lap
combining form: **5** -drome
figure: **4** odds, tout **6** jockey
like ~ curves: **6** banked
margin: **4** neck, nose
NYC ~: **4** Big A **8** Aqueduct
painter of ~ scenes: Edgar Degas
prop: **4** gate
wager: **6** exacta **8** perfecta, quinella **9** quiniella
Rachael: **3** Ray
Rachael Leigh __: **4** Cook
Rachel: **4** Ward **5** Field, Weisz **6** Carson, Hunter **7** Jackson, McAdams, Roberts, Ticotin **9** de Queiròs
father: **5** Laban
husband: **5** Jacob
in Spanish: **6** Raquel
sister: **4** Leah
son: **6** Joseph **8** Benjamin
Rachel Papers, The
author: Martin Amis
Rachel, Rachel (1968 film)
cast: Joanne Woodward
director: Paul Newman
__ Rachel Wood: **4** Evan
Rachins: **4** Alan
rachis: **5** spine
Rachmaninoff: **5** Serge **6** Sergei, Sergey **7** pianist, Russian **8** composer
racial: **6** ethnic, lineal, tribal **7** genetic **8** national **9** ancestral, genetical **10** hereditary
Racine: **4** city, Jean, town
locale: **9** Wisconsin
see also French
Racine, Jean: **6** French **10** playwright
work: Andromaque
Britannicus
Esther
Iphigenie En Aulide
Phedre
racing: **4** fast **5** brisk, fleet, hasty, quick, rapid, sport, swift **6** speedy **7** express, hurried, instant **9** breakneck **10** double-time, supersonic
ancient Roman ~ post: **4** meta
car ~ org.: **4** NHRA **6** NASCAR
starter: **5** horse
vehicle: **4** bike, luge **5** scull, shell, yacht **6** hot rod **7** bicycle
world: **4** turf
see also race
racing __: **3** car **4** flag, form **5** skate
__ racing: **4** auto, drag, road, slot

5 horse 6 barrel 7 harness
Racing With the Moon (1984 film)
cast: Nicolas Cage, Elizabeth McGovern, Sean Penn
director: Richard Benjamin
racism: 4 bias 7 bigotry 9 apartheid, prejudice 10 unfairness
rack: 3 try 4 lamb, pain, tear 5 frame, shelf, stand, wring 6 clouds, harrow, holder, siphon, strain, stress, syphon, wrench 7 afflict, antlers, oppress, stretch, torment, torture, trestle 8 aggrieve, distress 10 excruciate
and ruin: 5 havoc 7 debacle 8 calamity, shambles 9 cataclysm
element: 6 antler
for fodder: 4 crib
one's brains: 4 mull 5 think 6 puzzle 8 ruminate
partner: 4 ruin
starter: 3 hat, hay 4 book, coat
up: 3 get, win 4 gain 5 incur, reach, score 6 attain, secure 7 achieve, acquire, realize 8 hold on to 10 accumulate
__ rack: 3 ski 5 on the, spice, towel
rack-and-__: 6 pinion
racket: 3 ado, bat, din, job, lay, row 4 fuss, game, plot, push, riot, roar, scam, stir, talk, to-do, work 5 babel, blare, brawl, cheat, clash, crash, crime, dodge, fight, fraud, graft, hoo-ha, noise, sound, storm, theft, trick 6 battle, career, clamor, fracas, hoopla, hubbub, jangle, outcry, paddle, rip-off, rumpus, scheme, squall, tumult, uproar 7 calling, clangor, clatter, con game, discord, jobbery, pursuit, ruction, shuffle, squeeze, swindle, turmoil, wrangle 8 artifice, cheating, intrigue, shouting, squabble, thievery, vocation 9 agitation, commotion, dirty pool, extortion, shakedown, specialty, swindling 10 clattering, conspiracy, corruption, dishonesty, free-for-all, hullabaloo, hurly-burly, illegality, livelihood, occupation, turbulence, underworld
ender: 3 eer
game: 6 squash, tennis 8 lacrosse, Ping Pong 9 badminton
make a ~: 5 shout
making a ~: 5 noisy
sports ~: 6 crosse, paddle
see also tennis
racketeer: 4 thug 5 crook, fraud 6 gunsel, outlaw 7 hoodlum, mobster 8 criminal, gangster 9 miscreant
racketeering statute: 4 RICO
rackety: 5 forte, noisy 7 blaring, booming, jarring, pealing, raucous, reboant, roaring 8 crashing, piercing, plangent, rumbling, sonorous, strident, turned up 9 big-voiced, clamorous, deafening 10 boisterous, resounding, stentorian, strepitous, thundering, uproarious, vociferous
racking: 5 acute 8 grueling 9 harrowing
__-racking: 5 nerve

RA

rack of __: 4 lamb
rack one's __: 5 brain
Rackstraw, Ralph: 3 gob, tar
raconteur: 7 reciter 10 anecdotist
racquet
see racket
racquetball: 4 game 5 sport
target: 4 wall
racy: 4 blue, lewd 5 bawdy, heady, lurid, salty, spicy, witty 6 erotic, lively, purple, ribald, risqué, smutty, snappy, spicey, vulgar 7 naughty, piquant, pungent, zestful 8 exciting, immodest, indecent, off-color, vigorous 9 energetic, sparkling, sprightly 10 indelicate, suggestive
hardly ~: 4 dull, flat, tame 5 bland 6 boring, jejune 7 humdrum, insipid, prosaic, routine, subdued, tedious 9 colorless 10 dullsville
rad
see wonderful
rad.
doubled: 3 dia. 4 diam.
Rada
locale: 7 Ukraine
Radames' love: 4 Aïda
radar
beacon: 5 racon
ender: 5 scope
flying ~ station: 5 AWACS
image: 3 pip 4 blip, echo, scan
laser ~: 5 lidar
measure: 3 mph
radar __: 4 trap
__ radar: 7 Doppler
Radar: 7 O'Reilly
home: 4 Iowa 7 Ottumwa
milieu: 4 MASH
Radarange maker: 5 Amana
Radbourne, Hoss: 6 hurler 7 pitcher
Radcliffe: 3 Ann 7 college
most ~ grads: 5 women
Radcliffe, Ann: 6 writer 7 English
work: The Mysteries of Udolpho
Radford: 5 Basil 7 Michael
Radha: 8 Mitchell
radial: 4 tire
British ~: 4 tyre
feature: 3 air 5 tread
opposite: 5 ulnar
perpendicular to ~: 5 axial
radial __: 3 saw 4 tire
radiance: 3 joy 4 glow 5 blaze, glare, gleam, light, sheen, shine 6 beauty, dazzle, gaiety, gayety, luster, warmth 7 aureola, aureole, delight, glitter, rapture, sparkle 8 gloriole, pleasure, splendor 9 happiness 10 brightness, brilliance, effulgence, loveliness, luminosity
surround with ~: 6 enhalo
radiant: 3 gay, lit 4 glad 5 aglow, happy, light, lucid, nitid, shiny, sunny 6 ablaze, agleam, bright, cheery, flashy, joyful, joyous, lucent 7 beaming, blazing, fulgent, glowing, lambent, shining 8 beatific, blissful, blooming, cheerful, dazzling, ecstatic, gleaming, glorious, luminous, lustrous, splendid 9 beautiful, brilliant, delighted, effulgent, gladdened, radiating, rapturous, refulgent, sparkling 10 flying high, glittering
be ~: 4 glow 5 gleam, shine 7 glisten, shimmer, sparkle 9 luminesce
radiate: 4 beam, cast, emit, glow, part, pour, send, shed, spew, spue 5 eject, expel, exude, flash, gleam, issue, shine, split, strew, yield 6 afford, branch, expand, ramble, ramify, spread 7 bestrew, cast out, deviate, diffuse, diverge, emanate, give off, give out, glitter, light up, scatter, send out 8 illumine, separate, shoot out, sprinkle, throw off, throw out, transmit 9 bifurcate, branch out, broadcast, circulate, irradiate, luminesce, propagate, send forth, spread out 10 distribute
radiation: 4 aura 5 light 6 spread 8 emission 9 emanation 10 divergence
cosmic ~ particle: 4 muon
emit ~: 5 decay
generator: 5 maser
give off focused ~: 4 lase
infrared ~: 4 heat
monitoring org.: 3 EPA
unit: 3 rem 5 curie 8 roentgen
radiator: 6 heater
output: 4 heat 5 steam
part: 4 coil, vane 5 grill 6 grille
sound: 3 sss 4 ssss
radical: 5 basal, basic, rabid, rebel, ultra, vital 6 bottom, entire, far-out, innate, native, primal, severe, way out 7 drastic, extreme, fanatic, lawless, leftist, liberal, natural, new-wave, organic, primary, restive, riotous, violent 8 advanced, cardinal, complete, inherent, maverick, militant, mutinous, nihilist, objector, original, pacifist, profound, recusant, reformer, renegade, sweeping, thorough, ultimate, ultraist 9 anarchist, essential, excessive, extremist, fanatical, firebrand, insurgent, intrinsic, primitive, seditious 10 avant-garde, deep-seated, immoderate, left-winger, nihilistic, rebellious, refractory, stupendous, underlying
change: 7 shake-up 8 upheaval 10 revolution
onetime ~ grp.: 3 SDS, SLA 4 SNCC
organic ~: 4 acyl, amyl, aryl 5 alkyl 6 acetyl
politically ~: 4 left
radical __: 4 chic
Radical Chic
author: Tom Wolfe
Radical, The
author: George Eliot
radicle: 4 root
radii: 4 rays 5 bones 6 spokes
radio: 2 AM, CB, FM 5 media 7 boombox, Walkman 8 receiver, transmit, wireless 9 shortwave
adjunct: 6 aerial 7 antenna
AMC series ~ station: 4 WENN
antenna: 6 dipole
band: 2 AM, CB, FM 3 VLF
broadcaster: 3 sta., stn. 7 station
button: 5 on/off
CB ~ knob: 3 vol. 6 volume 7 squelch
control: 4 knob 5 tuner 6 volume
detecting and ranging: 5 radar
discoverer of ~ waves: 5 Hertz
ender: 3 man, men 4 thon 5 meter, phone 9 broadcast, telegraph, telephone
enjoy a ~: 6 listen, tune in 8 listen in
first all-sports ~ station: 4 WFAN
first commercial ~ station: 4 KDKA
format: 4 news, rock, talk 6 call-in, oldies, sports
frequency band: 6 airway
freq. unit: 3 MHz
kind of ~: 4 AMFM
London ~: 3 BBC
message: 3 SOS
network: 3 ABC, CBS, MBS, NBC, NPR 6 Mutual
old ~ part: 4 tube
operator: 3 ham 4 Cber
overseer: 3 FCC
part: 4 dial 5 diode
put on the ~: 3 air 9 broadcast
receiver: 3 set
reply: 3 out 4 copy, over 5 roger, wilco
spots: 3 ads
stations: 5 media
studio need: 4 mike
studio sign: 5 on air
talk-show participant: 6 caller
transmitter: 5 tower
tube gas: 5 argon, xenon
type of ~ channel: 6 diplex
US ~ service: 3 VOA
worker: 2 DJ 6 deejay 8 engineer
radio __: 3 car 4 beam, star, taxi, tube, wave
__ radio: 4 AM FM, talk 5 clock, shock
Radio __: 4 Days, Ga-Ga 5 Flyer, Shack 7 Liberty
Radio __ Europe: 4 Free
__ Radio: 4 Talk 5 On the
radioactive: 3 hot
element: 5 radon 6 curium, radium 7 bohrium, dubnium, fermium, hassium, thorium, uranium 8 actinium, astatine, francium, nobelium, polonium 9 americium, berkelium, neptunium, plutonium 10 lawrencium, meitnerium, promethium, seaborgium, technetium 11 californium, copernicium, einsteinium, mendelevium, roentgenium 12 darmstadtium, protactinium 13 rutherfordium
gas: 5 radon
particle: 4 beta
radioactive __: 5 decay 6 dating
radiocarbon-dating developer: 5 Libby
Radio Days (1987 film)
cast: Jeff Daniels, Mia Farrow, Julie Kavner
director: Woody Allen
studio: 5 Orion
Radio Flyer: 5 wagon
Radio Flyer (1992 film)
cast: Lorraine Bracco, John Heard, Elijah Wood
dog: 5 Shane
Radio Free Europe
artist: R.E.M.
Radio Ga-Ga (1984 song)
artist: Queen
radiogram: 4 wire 5 cable, telex 7 message

radiograph: **4** x-ray
radioman's nickname: **6** Sparks
radio shows (old-time):
The Aldrich Family
Amos 'n' Andy
The Breakfast Club
Burns and Allen
Can You Top This?
Double or Nothing
Dr. I.Q.
Duffy's Tavern
Easy Aces
Fibber McGee and Molly
First Nighter
Front Page Farrell
The Great Gildersleeve
The Green Hornet
I Love a Mystery
Information, Please!
The Inner Sanctum Mysteries
It Pays to Be Ignorant
Jack Armstrong, the All-American Boy
John's Other Wife
Let's Pretend
Life Can Be Beautiful
Lights Out
Lora Lawton
Lorenzo Jones
Lum and Abner
Lux Radio Theatre
Ma Perkins
The March of Time
Mary Noble, Backstage Wife
Meet Corliss Archer
Melody Ranch
Mr. Keen, Tracer of Lost Persons
Myrt and Marge
One Man's Family
Our Gal Sunday
Pepper Young's Family
Portia Faces Life
The Quiz Kids
The Right to Happiness
The Road of Life
The Romance of Helen Trent
The Shadow
The Story of Mary Marlin
Suspense
Today's Children
Valiant Lady
Vic and Sade
Vox Pop
When a Girl Marries
Young Dr. Malone
Young Widder Brown
Your Hit Parade
__ Radio Theatre: **3** Lux
radish: **4** root **6** veggie **9** appetizer, vegetable
Japanese ~: **6** daikon
starter: **5** horse
Radisson: **5** hotel
alternative: ***see*** hotel
radium: **5** metal **7** element
radius: **4** bone, span **5** ambit, limit, orbit, range, reach, scope, space, spoke, sweep **6** extent, length **7** compass, expanse, purview **8** boundary, interval **9** extension
companion: **4** ulna
locale: **3** arm **7** forearm
radix: **4** root
RAdm employer: **3** USN
Radner, Gilda
spouse: Gene Wilder
Rado: **5** watch **10** wristwatch
alternative: ***see*** wristwatch
radon: **3** gas **7** element **8** noble gas
former name: **5** niton
like ~: **5** inert
Radziwill: **3** Lee
sister: **6** Jackie **10** Jacqueline
Rae: **3** Bob **4** John **9** Charlotte
__ Rae: **5** Norma
Rae Dawn __: **5** Chong
Rae, John: **8** explorer
Raf: **7** Vallone
RAF
auxiliary: **4** WAAF
award: **3** DFM
flyer: **4** Brit **6** airman
Rafael: **5** Nadal **7** Alberti, Kubelik **8** Palmeiro
__ Rafael, CA: **3** San
Rafelson: **3** Bob
Rafer: **7** Johnson
raff: **6** masses, rabble **9** commoners, hoi polloi, multitude
Rafferty: **5** Gerry
raffia: **4** palm
Raffin: **7** Deborah
raffish: **3** gay **4** fast, wild **5** cheap, crude **6** casual, coarse, jaunty, rakish, sporty, tawdry, trashy, vulgar **7** boorish, dashing, ill-bred, loutish, uncouth **8** bohemian, careless, unseemly **9** dissolute, tasteless, unrefined **10** picaresque
raffle: **4** game, lots, pool **5** flier, flyer **7** benefit, drawing, lottery **10** sweepstake
offering: **5** prize **6** chance
Rafsanjani: **5** Irani
raft: **3** lot, ton **4** boat, heap, host, pile, slew **5** bunch, craft, scads **6** oodles, passel **7** vehicle
noted papyrus ~: **3** Ra I **4** Ra II
propel a ~: **4** pole
user: **5** poler
wood: **5** balsa
__ raft: **4** life
Raft: **6** George
rafter: **4** beam **5** brace, joist **6** girder, timber **9** crossbeam
locale: **4** roof
thrill: **5** chute **6** rapids
Rafter, Patrick: **7** netster **9** tennis pro
milieu: **5** court
rafting: **5** sport
whitewater ~ site: **5** cañon **6** canyon
rafts: **4** a lot, much **5** no end, reams **6** highly **7** greatly
rag: **3** kid, rib **4** bait, gibe, jibe, mock, ride, twit **5** abuse, annoy, beset, blame, chide, cloth, harry, paper, roast, scoff, scold, scrap, shred, taunt, tease, tweak, wiper **6** badger, berate, bother, deride, duster, harass, heckle, noodge, pester, plague, rebuke, tatter **7** censure, chew out, lecture, reprove, tabloid, torment, toy with, upbraid **8** admonish, badinage, chastise, irritate, magazine, reproach, ridicule **9** castigate, dishcloth, dress down, dustcloth, make fun of, newspaper, persecute, poke fun at, reprimand **10** hand-me-down, make game of, periodical, take to task, tongue-lash, trifle with
chew the ~: **3** gab, jaw, rap, yak, yap **4** chat, talk **5** prate **6** gossip, jabber, parley, patter **7** blabber, blather, chatter, prattle **8** chitchat, schmooze **10** yakkety-yak
doll: **3** Ann **4** Andy
ender: **3** bag, man, men, tag, top **4** time, weed, wort
like a wet ~: **4** limp
man: **6** Joplin
starter: **4** dish, wash
use a ~: **4** wipe
rag __: **3** rug **4** doll **5** paper, trade
Rag __: **3** Mop **4** Doll
__ Rag: **5** Tiger
raga: **5** music
name: **4** Ravi **7** Shankar
ragamuffin: **3** bum **4** hobo, waif **5** gamin, tramp **6** beggar, gamine, orphan, sloven, urchin **7** vagrant **8** derelict, vagabond **9** foundling **10** panhandler
Rag Doll (1964 song)
artist: Four Seasons
rage: **3** bug, fad, ire **4** boil, fume, fury, gall, heat, huff, mode, rant, rave, tear, yell **5** anger, chafe, craze, erupt, freak, furor, go ape, mania, steam, storm, style, trend, vogue, wrath **6** blow up, choler, dander, frenzy, latest, lose it, rail at, scream, seethe, simmer, spleen, temper, uproar **7** bluster, bristle, carry on, dudgeon, emotion, explode, fashion, flare up, go crazy, in thing, madness, passion, rampage, run amok, run riot, run wild, tantrum, umbrage **8** boil over, ferocity, go postal, have a fit, outburst, paroxysm, run amuck, violence **9** blow a fuse, fireworks, fulminate, go bananas, go berserk, throw a fit, vehemence **10** bitterness, dernier cri, hit the roof, kick up a row, make a scene, resentment, turbulence
all the ~: **2** in **3** hip, hot, mod **4** tony **5** faddy, toney **6** chi-chi, modish, trendy **7** à la mode, current, in style, popular, stylish, voguish **8** up-to-date **9** in fashion
be all the ~: **4** rule
filled with ~: ***see*** angry
__ rage: **3** air **4** road
Rage
author: Stephen King
Rage of Angels
author: Sidney Sheldon
Rage to Live, A
author: John O'Hara
R-A-G-G-__...: **4** M-O-P-P
ragged: **4** fray, mean, poor, rent, torn, worn **5** badly, crude, dingy, erose, rough, seedy, tacky, tatty **6** broken, frayed, jagged, rugged, shabby, shaggy, shoddy, uneven **7** dressed, in holes, notched, patched, scraggy, scruffy, unkempt, worn-out **8** battered, frazzled, ill-kempt, in shreds, serrated, shredded, tattered **9** desultory, in tatters, irregular, lacerated, moth-eaten, ungroomed, unpressed **10** fragmented, threadbare, unfinished
become ~: **4** fray **5** shred
robin: **5** plant **6** flower
run ~: **4** tire **7** exhaust
ragged __: **4** edge
Ragged Dick
author: Horatio Alger
raggedy: **4** worn **5** erose
Raggedy __: **3** Ann, Man **4** Andy
Raggedy Ann or Andy: **4** doll
Raggedy Man (1981 film)
cast: Eric Roberts, Sissy Spacek
Raggedy Man, The: **4** poem
author: James Whitcomb Riley
Ragin' __: **6** Cajuns
raging: **3** hot, mad **4** ired, sore, wild **5** angry, cross, huffy, irate, livid, rabid, riled, rough, upset, wroth **6** ablaze, fierce, fuming, heated, ireful, peeved, raving, red-hot, savage, stormy **7** enraged, furious, on a tear, rampant, ranting, violent **8** blustery, choleric, frenzied, going ape, in a furor, incensed, inflamed, maddened, outraged, seething, volcanic, white-hot, wild-eyed, wrathful **9** indignant, irritated, resentful, seeing red, splenetic, turbulent **10** blustering, boiling mad, freaked out, hysterical, infuriated, tumultuous
Raging Bull (1980 film)
cast: Robert De Niro, Cathy Moriarty, Joe Pesci
director: Martin Scorsese
subject: **7** La Motta
raglan: **4** coat **6** jacket, sleeve **8** overcoat
Rag Mop (1950 song)
artist: Ames Brothers
Ragnar: **6** Frisch, Granit
ragout: **4** hash, meat, stew **5** salmi **6** salmis
ingredient: **5** onion
rags: **4** garb, gear, togs **5** array **6** attire, finery **7** clothes **8** castoffs, wardrobe **9** caparison
in ~: **4** poor **5** needy **8** tattered
like some ~: **5** linty
__ rags: **4** glad
Ragsdale: **7** William
rags-to-riches
author: Horatio Alger
Rags to Riches (1953 song)
artist: Tony Bennett
ragtag: **5** mangy **6** motley, shoddy **7** scruffy
ragtag and __: **7** bobtail
ragtime: **5** music
dance: **6** shimmy **10** turkey trot
master: **6** Joplin
Ragtime: **4** film **5** novel
author: E.L. Doctorow
cast: James Cagney, Elizabeth McGovern, Howard Rollins, Mary Steenburgen
director: Milos Forman
Ragú: **10** pasta sauce
alternative: **5** Prego **6** Prince **8** Classico **10** Newman's Own **11** Aunt Millie's
ragweed: **8** allergen
reaction: **5** achoo **6** ahchoo, hachoo **7** kerchoo
react to ~: **5** sniff **6** sneeze **7** sniffle
ragwort: **5** plant **6** flower
rah: **3** olé **4** yell **5** cheer, huzza **6** hooray, hurrah, hurray, huzzah
Rahal, Bobby: **5** racer **9** auto racer
milieu: **5** track
rah-rah: **4** keen **5** eager **6** ardent,

gung-ho 7 anxious, excited, fired up, keyed up, zealous 8 enthused, spirited 9 fanatical 10 passionate
Rahway: 4 city, town
locale: 9 New Jersey
raid: 3 rob 4 bust, loot, sack 5 blitz, foray, harry, rifle, sally, shell, storm, sweep, swoop 6 arrest, attack, forage, inroad, invade, maraud, pirate, prey on, ravage, sortie, strafe, strike 7 assault, break in, descent, despoil, overrun, pillage, plunder, ransack, round up, sacking, torpedo 8 fall upon, freeboot, invasion, lay waste, spoliate 9 air strike, depredate, descend on, devastate, incursion, intrude on, irruption, offensive, onslaught 10 plundering
site: 6 fridge
the fridge: 3 eat 4 nosh 5 munch, snack 6 nibble
___ raid: 3 air
Raid
competitor: 4 D Con
target: 3 ant 5 roach 6 insect
___ Raid: 7 Ulzana's
raider: 6 bandit, robber 7 brigand, corsair, invader 8 attacker 9 aggressor 10 freebooter
of old: 3 Hun
___ Raider: 4 Tomb
Raiders: 4 team 6 eleven 7 Colgate
home: 7 Oakland
org.: 3 AFC, NFL
rival: *see* NFL team
sport: 8 football
___ Raiders: 6 Nader's
Raiders of the Lost Ark (1981 film)
cast: Karen Allen, Harrison Ford
composer: John Williams
director: Steven Spielberg
snake: 3 asp
villain: 4 Nazi
Raiders, The
author: Harold Robbins
Raid on Entebbe
airline: 4 El Al
setting: 6 Uganda
weapon: 3 Uzi
___-raid shelter: 3 air
Ra II home: 4 Oslo
rail: 3 bar, jaw 4 bird, carp, pole, post, rant, rate, rave, rest, sora 5 blast, crake, fence, scold, train 6 berate, paling, revile, siding 7 barrier, censure, chew out, declaim, inveigh, lampoon, tell off, thunder, upbraid 8 banister, bloviate, complain, denounce, footrest 9 castigate, criticize, fulminate, go on about, make a fuss, marsh bird, transport 10 balustrade, tongue-lash, vituperate, wading bird
at: 3 hit, jaw 4 jeer, rage 5 abuse, blast, decry, scold 6 assail, attack, berate, hit out 7 condemn 8 denounce 9 criticize, fustigate 10 denunciate
ballet ~: 3 bar 5 barre
company: 6 Amtrak
connection: 3 tie
crossing sign: 4 STOP
ender: 3 car, way 4 bird, head, road
end of a ~: 5 newel
like a ~: 4 lank, lean, slim, thin 5 lanky, rangy, reedy 6 gangly, skinny, svelte, twiggy 7 scraggy, scrawny, slender, willowy 8 rawboned
lip: 6 flange
nautical ~: 6 gunnel 7 gunwale
relative: 4 coot 7 finfoot
rider: 4 hobo 5 tramp
starter: 4 hand, mono 5 guard
strike a ~: 5 carom 6 carrom
___ rail: 5 third
railing: 3 bar 4 pole, post, rest 5 abuse, fence 6 paling, siding 7 barrier 8 banister 10 balustrade
raillery: 3 wit 4 jest, joke, talk 5 chaff, humor, sport 6 banter, joking 7 jesting, joshing, ribbing 8 badinage, repartee, ridicule 9 funniness 10 jocoseness, persiflage
railroad: 4 line, push, tube 5 impel, metro, press 6 subway, tracks 7 lantern 9 train line
beam: 3 tie
branch ~: 6 feeder
car: 5 diner 6 engine 7 caboose 10 locomotive
cars: 5 train
device: 5 shunt
flare: 5 fusee, fuzee
mine ~: 4 tram
parking space: 4 yard
siding: 5 lie-by
station: 4 stop
stop: 3 sta., stn. 5 depot 7 station
switch: 3 wye
system: 6 Amtrak
terminal: 5 depot
unit: 3 car
rails: 5 track
distance between ~: 5 gauge
riding the ~: 6 aboard
Railsback: 5 Steve
railsplitter, famous: 3 Abe 7 Lincoln
railway: 5 track, train
overhead: 2 el
___ railway: 3 cog
raiment: 4 duds, garb, togs 5 dress 6 attire, livery, things 7 apparel, clothes, garment, threads 8 clothing, garments 9 trappings 10 Sunday best
in ~: 4 clad
Raimi: 3 Sam, Ted
Raimi, Sam: 8 director
film: Darkman (1990)
For Love of the Game (1999)
The Gift (2000)
The Quick and the Dead (1995)
A Simple Plan (1998)
Spider-Man (2002)
rain: 4 fall, hail, mist, pelt, pour, spit 5 flood, sleet, spate, storm, water 6 deluge, lament, lavish, patter, precip, shower, stream, volley 7 drizzle, monsoon, torrent 8 downpour, drencher, moisture, sprinkle 10 cloudburst
anti-acid ~ org.: 3 EPA
bit of ~: 4 drop
cats and dogs: 4 pelt, pour, teem 5 flood, spate
check: 4 stub 10 invitation
clearer: 5 wiper
collector: 4 eave, pond 9 reservoir
combining form: 4 hyet- 5 hyeto-, ombro-, pluvi- 6 pluvia-, pluvio-
dancer: 4 Hopi
delay coverup: 4 tarp 9 tarpaulin
drain: 4 sump
drain locale: 4 curb
ender: 3 bow, out 4 coat, drop, fall, wear 5 maker, spout, storm, water 6 making, squall
fine ~: 4 mist 7 drizzle
forest: 5 biome, selva 6 jungle
frozen ~: 4 hail 5 sleet
gear: 3 mac 7 slicker 9 macintosh 10 mackintosh
give a ~ check: 5 defer, delay 6 put off 7 suspend 8 postpone
in Japanese: 3 ame
like ~: 5 right
on: 4 soak 6 dampen, drench 7 moisten
or shine: 6 surely 10 definitely, for certain
out of the ~: 6 inside 7 indoors
right as ~: 5 sound
sign of ~: 5 cloud 6 nimbus
signs of ~: 5 nimbi
that doesn't reach the ground: 5 virga
without ~: 3 dry 4 arid, sere 7 parched
rain ___: 4 date, frog, tree 5 check, cloud, dance, delay, gauge 6 forest, shower
rain ___ and dogs: 4 cats
___ rain: 4 acid 7 driving, pouring
...rain, ___ sleet...: 3 nor
Rain: 7 Phoenix
author: W. Somerset Maugham
role: 5 Sadie 8 Thompson
setting: 5 Samoa 8 Pago Pago
Rain ___: 3 Man
___ Rain: 4 Hard 5 Black, Candy, In the 6 Purple, Summer
rainbow: 3 arc, bow 4 iris 5 curve, gamut, prism 6 motley 7 diverse 8 crescent, spectrum
fish: 5 smelt, trout
goddess: 4 Iris
like a ~: 5 arced 6 arcing
producer: 5 prism
segment: 3 hue, red 4 blue 5 color, green 6 indigo, orange, violet, yellow
rainbow ___: 5 trout
___ Rainbow: 4 Neon 5 Black, She's a 6 Broken 7 Finian's 8 Gravity's
Rainbow Falls site: 4 Hilo 6 Hawaii
Rainbow's End
author: James M. Cain
Rainbow, The
author: D.H. Lawrence
character: 4 Anna 5 Anton, Inger, Lydia, Tilly 6 Ursula
Rainbow Trail, The
author: Zane Grey
rain cats and ___: 4 dogs
raincheck: 6 ticket
take a ~: 4 wait
raincoat: 3 mac 6 jacket, poncho 7 cagoule, oilskin, slicker 9 macintosh, sou'wester 10 mackintosh, protection
feature: 6 lining
Raindrops (1961 song)
artist: Dee Clark
Raindrops Keep Fallin' on My Head (1969 song)
artist: B.J. Thomas
raindrop sound: 4 plop
Rainer: 4 Iris 5 Luise, Rilke
Rainer ___ Fassbinder: 6 Werner
Rainer ___ Rilke: 5 Maria
Rainer, Luise
Oscar: The Good Earth, The Great Ziegfeld
Oscar role: 4 O-lan
spouse: Clifford Odets
Raines: 3 Tim 4 Ella
Raines, Tim
sport: 8 baseball
Rainey: 2 Ma
rainfall measure: 4 inch
Rainier: 2 mt. 4 peak 5 mount 8 mountain
locale: 8 Cascades 10 Washington
rain in ___, The: 5 Spain
raining: 3 wet 7 showery
quit ~: 5 let up
Rain in Spain, The: 4 song 5 tango
composer: Alan Jay Lerner, Frederick Loewe
place: 5 plain 8 Hartford, Hereford 9 Hampshire
rainless: 3 dry 4 arid, sere 5 unwet 6 desert
expanse: 6 desert
Rainmaker, The (1956 film)
cast: Katharine Hepburn, Burt Lancaster
Rainmaker, The (1997 film)
cast: Matt Damon, Claire Danes, Danny DeVito, Jon Voight
director: Francis Ford Coppola
Rain Man (1988 film)
cast: Tom Cruise, Valeria Golino, Dustin Hoffman
director: Barry Levinson
Rainn: 6 Wilson
___ Rain on My Parade: 4 Don't
Rain on the Roof (1966 song)
artist: Lovin' Spoonful
rain or ___: 5 shine
___ Rain or Come Shine: 4 Come
Rain People, The (1969 film)
cast: James Caan, Robert Duvall, Shirley Knight
director: Francis Ford Coppola
Rains: 6 Claude
Rains ___, The: 4 Came
rainspout: 6 gutter
rainstorm: 8 downpour, drencher 10 cloudburst
Rain, The (song)
artist: Madonna, Oran Jones
Rain, the Park & Other Things, The (1967 song)
artist: Cowsills
Raintree County (1957 film)
cast: Montgomery Clift, Eva Marie Saint, Elizabeth Taylor
character: 4 Nell 6 Esther, Stiles
Rainwater: 3 Leo 6 Marvin
rainy: 3 wet 4 foul 5 moist, undry 6 hyetal, stormy 7 drizzly, pluvial, showery 8 pluvious 9 drizzling, inclement, showering
day fund: 7 nest egg, reserve, savings
days: 5 slump 9 recession 10 depression
not ~: 3 dry 4 arid, fair 5 clear, sunny
prepare for a ~ day: 4 plan, save 8 salt away
wind direction: 4 east
rainy ___: 3 day
Rainy Day People #12 & 35 (1975

song)
artist: Gordon Lightfoot
Rainy Days and Mondays (1971 song)
artist: Carpenters
Rainy Day Women (1966 song)
artist: Bob Dylan
Rainy Night in Georgia (1970 song)
artist: Brook Benton
Raisa: 4 Rosa 9 Gorbachev
see also Russian
Raisa, Rosa: 6 singer 7 soprano
specialty: 5 opera
raise: 2 up 3 pry, set, sow 4 bump, buoy, grow, heft, hike, incr., jack, levy, lift, rear, whet 5 add to, boost, breed, build, cause, dig up, erect, exalt, goose, heave, hoist, honor, lever, mount, pitch, plant, put up, rally, run up, set up, upend 6 better, broach, bump up, call up, drag up, draw up, emboss, foment, foster, gather, haul up, hike up, hold up, incite, jack up, jerk up, jump up, kindle, mark up, move up, muster, pick up, pull up, step up, stir up, uphold, uplift 7 advance, augment, boost up, bring up, care for, collect, dignify, elevate, enhance, enlarge, improve, inflate, magnify, nourish, nurture, produce, promote, provoke, pyramid, recruit, scale up, shoot up, support, upgrade, upheave 8 addition, dredge up, escalate, heighten, increase, mobilize, multiply, snowball, summon up 9 conjure up, construct, cultivate, elevation, increment, instigate, intensify, introduce, promotion, propagate 10 accelerate, invigorate, put forward, strengthen
a finger for: 3 aid 4 help 6 assist
a fuss: 5 act up
a red flag: 4 warn 5 alert 6 tip off 7 caution
Cain: 4 rage, rave, riot 5 brawl, clash 6 clamor, squawk 7 carouse
hackles: 3 irk 4 rile 5 anger, peeve, upset
hell: 5 party 9 make merry
high: 4 heft, hike 5 extol 6 hike up 7 build up, elevate, ennoble, glorify, idolize, lionize, worship
meet a ~: 3 see 4 call
one's hackles: 3 bug, get, try, vex 4 fret, gall, miff, rile 5 annoy, chafe, grate, harry, peeve, pique 6 abrade, bother, harass, hector, needle, nettle, pester, plague, rankle, ruffle 7 disturb, provoke 8 irritate 9 aggravate, displease
one's spirits: 4 buoy 5 cheer, elate 6 buck up, buoy up, solace 7 cheer up, comfort, console, enliven, gladden, hearten 8 brighten 9 encourage
one's voice: 3 cry 4 howl, roar, yell 5 shout, whoop 6 bellow, cry out, holler, scream, shriek, squeal 7 exclaim, screech
reason: 5 merit
starter: 4 fund
the roof: 5 gripe, revel, shout, storm 6 clamor, holler, squawk 7 grumble 8 complain 9 bellyache
raise __: 3 hob 4 Cain, hell
__ raise: 3 pay 5 merit
raise a __: 5 stink
raised: 5 lofty, steep, upped 7 upright
make a ~ design: 6 emboss
path: 4 berm, dike 5 berme, levee 8 causeway 10 embankment
Raise High the Roof-Beam, Carpenters
author: J.D. Salinger
__ raiser: 7 curtain
__-raiser: 4 fund, hair, hell
raise the __: 4 roof 5 devil 6 stakes
raisin: 4 blue 5 fruit 6 purply 8 purplish
center: 6 Fresno
originally: 5 grape
relative: *see* blue color, purple color
Raisin __: 4 Bran
raisin-and-rum cake: 5 babka
raisin bran: 6 cereal
Raisinets: 5 candy
alternative: 7 Goobers 8 Milk Duds
raising
goose bumps: 5 scary, weird 6 creepy, occult, spooky 7 ghostly, macabre, uncanny 9 unearthly 10 mysterious
hell: 4 wild 5 noisy 6 unruly 7 lawless, naughty, raucous 9 turbulent 10 boisterous, disorderly, tumultuous
the roof: 4 loud 7 blaring, booming, raucous, riotous, yelling 8 blasting, piercing, shouting 9 bellowing, clamorous, screaming 10 boisterous, uproarious, vociferous
__ raising: 4 barn
__-raising: 4 fund, hair 5 house
Raising Arizona (1987 film)
cast: Nicolas Cage, Holly Hunter, Trey Wilson
director: Joel Coen
Raising Helen (2004 film)
cast: Joan Cusack, Kate Hudson
director: Garry Marshall
raising the roof: 5 noisy
Raisin in the Sun, A: 4 film, play
author: Lorraine Hansberry
cast: Ruby Dee, Sidney Poitier
character: 4 Bobo, Karl, Lena, Ruth 5 Asagi 6 Joseph, Travis, Walter 7 Lindner, Younger 8 Beneatha
setting: 7 Chicago 8 Illinois
Raisin Nut Bran: 6 cereal
competitor: *see* cereal
raisins, soak: 5 plump
raison __: 5 d'état, d'être
raison d'être: 3 end 5 basis, cause 7 purpose 8 function 9 rationale
Raitt: 4 John 6 Bonnie
Raitt, Bonnie
song: I Can't Make You Love Me (1992)
Love Sneakin' Up on You (1994)
Something to Talk About (1991)
You Got It (1995)
Raj
headquarters: 5 Delhi
princess: 5 begum
servant: 4 amah
rajah: 5 Hindu, noble, ruler 6 gerent 7 monarch
land: 5 India
starter: 4 maha
wife: 4 rani 5 ranee
Rajiv: 6 Gandhi
mother: 6 Indira
see also India
Rajput
see India
Raj Quartet, The
locale: 5 India
title: 5 sahib
rake: 3 cad 4 comb, hunt, roué, scan, skim, tilt, tool, weed 5 clear, graze, ogler, scour, sweep 6 gather, harrow, rebuke, search, smooth, wanton 7 clean up, collect, ransack, rummage 8 lothario 9 libertine, scoundrel 10 garden tool, profligate
cousin: 3 hoe
in: 5 amass 6 gather, pile up 7 collect, round up
over the coals: 4 flay 5 roast, scold 6 berate 7 lambast, tell off 8 lambaste
part: 4 tine
starter: 4 muck
through: 5 rifle, scour 7 pillage, plunder, ransack
rake __: 3 off 4 it in
rakehell: 3 cad 5 knave, rogue, scamp, skunk 6 rascal 7 wastrel 8 prodigal, scalawag, sybarite 9 libertine, miscreant, reprobate, scoundrel 10 blackguard, jackanapes, ne'er-do-well, profligate, scapegrace
rake-off: 5 bribe 6 grease, payoff, payola 7 jobbery 8 kickback
rake over the __: 5 coals
raker starter: 4 muck
Rake's Progress, The: 5 opera
composer: 10 Stravinsky
raki: 5 drink 8 beverage
raking: 5 chore
starter: 4 muck
raking __: 4 bond 5 piece 6 course 7 cornice
rakish: 3 gay 4 airy, chic, fast, lewd, wild 5 dandy, loose, natty, saucy, sleek, smart, swank 6 breezy, dapper, flashy, jaunty, sinful, snazzy, spiffy, sporty, swanky, wanton 7 dashing, raffish 8 cavalier, charming, debonair, depraved, prodigal, uncurbed 9 abandoned, debauched, debonaire, dissolute, lecherous 10 debonnaire, dissipated, licentious, picaresque, profligate
Raleigh: 4 city, town 6 Walter
athletes: 8 Wolfpack
county: 4 Wake
locale: 4 N. Car.
neighbor: 6 Durham
school: 4 NCSU
Raleigh, Walter: 3 Sir 4 poet 7 English 8 courtier, explorer
rival: 5 Essex
work: Cynthia
rally: 4 call, fire, herd, meet, mock, spur, stir, urge, wake, whet 5 bandy, raise, renew, rouse, sit-in, steel, surge, unite, waken 6 arouse, awaken, bestir, charge, gather, kindle, muster, perk up, pick up, pow-wow, reform, revive, stir up, summon 7 brace up, collect, convene, enliven, fortify, get well, improve, marshal, meeting, protest, rebound, recover, refresh, regroup, renewal, restore, revival, round up, session, shape up 8 assemble, assembly, auto race, clambake, comeback, enspirit, inspirit, jamboree, mobilize, organize, recovery, redouble 9 challenge, come about, come along, encourage, gathering, get better, resurrect 10 assemblage, bounce back, call to arms, close ranks, come around, congregate, convention, invigorate, make a stand, reassemble, recuperate, rejuvenate, reorganize, resurgence, strengthen, turn around
pep ~ shout: 3 yay
road ~: 4 meet, race 7 contest
round: 4 back, help 5 boost, favor 6 assist, defend 7 bolster, endorse, promote, pull for, stand by, stick by, support 8 champion, side with 9 encourage, get behind 10 go to bat for, stand up for, stick up for
Wall Street ~: 5 runup
__ rally: 3 pep 4 road
rallying cry: 5 motto 6 slogan
Ralph: 4 Houk 5 Blane, James, Kiner, Nader, Smart, Waite 6 Bakshi, Branca, Bunche, Lauren, Meeker, Nelson, Thomas 7 Bellamy, Edwards, Ellison, Fiennes, Guldahl, Kramden, Macchio 8 Tresvant 9 Gustafson 10 Richardson
Ralph __ Abernathy: 5 David
Ralph __ Doister: 7 Roister
Ralph __ Emerson: 5 Waldo
Ralph __ Williams: 7 Vaughan
Ralph Roister Doister
author: Nicholas Udall
Ralston: 6 Dennis, Jobyna
Ralston __: 6 Purina
Ralston, Dennis: 7 netster 9 tennis pro
milieu: 5 court
ram: 3 hit, jam 4 beat, butt, cram, dash, male, plug, push, sink, slam, stab, tamp 5 Aries, crash, drive, force, pound, press, sheep, smash, stick, stuff, wedge 6 animal, batter, beetle, butter, hammer, hurtle, pack in, thrust 7 jam-pack, rear-end, run into, squeeze 8 bang into 9 barge into, broadside, crash into, smash into 10 barrel into, crunch into
battering ~: 6 engine
ender: 3 jet, rod 7 shackle
in: 4 cram 5 crowd, stuff 9 overcrowd
(in): 4 pack 5 shove
in Britain: 3 tup
mate: 3 ewe
remark: 3 baa, maa 5 bleat
sign of the ~: 5 Aries
young ~: 4 lamb
Ram: 4 Dass, sign 5 Aries, Singh
month: 3 Apr., Mar. 5 April, March
predecessor: 4 Fish
successor: 4 Bull
RAM
computer program: 3 TSR
counterpart: 3 ROM

part of ~: 6 access, memory, random
thing with ~: 2 PC 3 CPU, Mac 6 laptop 8 computer
Rama: 6 avatar
wife: 4 Sita
ramada: 5 arbor
Ramada Inn: 5 motel
alternative: *see* motel
offering: 2 rm. 4 room
Ramadan: 5 month
observance: 4 fast
Rama Lama Ding Dong (1961 song)
artist: Edsels
Raman, Chandrasekhara: 8 Nobelist 9 physicist, scientist
__ Rama Rau: 6 Santha
Ramayana: 4 epic, poem, saga
reader: 5 Hindu 6 Hindoo
setting: 5 India
ramble: 3 gad 4 fork, hike, roam, rove, tour, trip, turn, walk, wind 5 amble, climb, drift, jaunt, prose, range, run on, snake, spout, stray, trail, tramp, twist 6 babble, cruise, depart, drivel, extend, gossip, harp on, jabber, loiter, mumble, roving, sprawl, spread, stroll, trapes, travel, wander, zigzag 7 amplify, blather, blether, chatter, clamber, descant, digress, discant, diverge, dwell on, enlarge, excurse, journey, maunder, meander, radiate, roaming, saunter, traipse 8 ambulate, divagate, go astray, protract, rattle on, scramble, straddle, straggle 9 bat around, branch off, dwell upon, excursion, expatiate, gallivant, go on and on, percolate, promenade 10 knock about
on: 3 gab, jaw, yak, yap 4 blab 5 prate, speak, spout 6 gabble, gibber, jabber, yammer 7 blather, chatter, prattle
rambler: 4 rose 5 nomad, plant, rover 6 flower 7 pilgrim 8 gadabout, runagate, traveler, vagabond, wanderer 9 itinerant, journeyer
Rambler: 3 car 4 auto 6 Hudson 10 automobile
manufacturer: 3 AMC 4 Nash
Ramblers: 6 Loyola
rambling: 4 long 5 gabby, loose, windy, wordy 6 errant, gangly, prolix, random, strewn, zigzag 7 diffuse, erratic, lengthy, unterse, verbose, voluble 8 at length, confused, covering, episodic, gangling, rootless, trailing, vagabond 9 bombastic, desultory, excursive, garrulous, irregular, itinerant, scattered, sprawling, spreading, spread out, talkative, unplanned, vagarious, wayfaring 10 circuitous, digressive, discursive, disjointed, episodical, incoherent, long-winded, loquacious, palaverous, straggling
one: 5 nomad
Rambling __: 4 Rose 5 Wreck
Ramblin' Gamblin' Man (1969 song)
artist: Bob Seger
Rambling Rose (1991 film)
cast: Laura Dern, Robert Duvall, Diane Ladd
__ rambling wreck...: 3 I'm a
Ramblin Man (1973 song)
artist: Allman Brothers Band
Ramblin' Rose (1962 song)
artist: Nat King Cole
Rambo - First Blood Part II (1985 film)
cast: Richard Crenna, Sylvester Stallone
setting: 3 Nam 7 Vietnam
Rambouillet: 5 sheep
rambunctious: 4 loud 5 noisy, rough, rowdy 6 unruly 7 raucous 9 energetic, turbulent
become ~: 5 act up
ram down one's __: 6 throat
ramen: 4 soup
Ramey, Samuel: 4 bass 6 singer
specialty: 5 opera
rami: 8 branches
ramie: 5 shrub
family: 6 nettle
relative: 6 feijoa
ramification: 6 result, upshot 8 offshoot
ramiform: 8 arboreal
ramify: 6 branch 7 radiate
Ramirez, Manny
sport: 8 baseball
Ramis, Harold: 5 actor 8 director
film: Analyze This (1999)
Baby Boom (1987)
Bedazzled (2000)
Caddyshack (1980)
Ghostbusters (1984)
Groundhog Day (1993)
The Ice Harvest (2005)
National Lampoon's Vacation (1983)
Stripes (1981)
Year One (2009)
Ramiz: 4 Alia
ramjet: 5 plane 6 engine 8 airplane
__-ramjet: 5 turbo
ramkie: 6 guitar, string
Ramón: 7 Novarro
see also Spanish
Ramona
author: Helen Hunt Jackson
Ramone: 4 Joey 6 Dee Dee, Johnny
Ramos __ fizz: 3 gin
ramose: 8 arboreal 10 branchlike
Ramos, Joao de Deus: 4 poet
ramp: 4 adit 5 chute, grade, slant, slope 6 access, way off 7 gangway, incline, walkway 8 gradient 9 gangplank
alternative: 5 stair 8 elevator 9 escalator
ender: 3 age
highway ~: 4 exit 8 entrance
__ ramp: 4 exit
__-ramp: 3 off
rampage: 3 mad 4 fury, rage, riot, tear 5 binge, fling, spree, storm 6 blowup, frenzy, ruckus, tumult, uproar 7 ferment, go crazy, run riot, run wild, splurge, tantrum, tempest, turmoil 8 run amuck, violence, wingding 9 go berserk, go on a tear
on a ~: 4 amok 7 berserk, haywire
__ rampage: 3 on a
Rampal, Jean-Pierre: 6 French 7 flutist 8 flautist
rampant: 4 rank, rife, wild 6 raging, ruling, unruly, wanton 7 furious, growing, profuse, riotous, violent 8 dominant, epidemic, flagrant, infested, pandemic, vehement 9 clamorous, excessive, exuberant, fanatical, impetuous, impulsive, luxuriant, out of hand, prevalent, rampaging, spreading, tumultous, turbulent, unbridled, unchecked 10 aggressive, blustering, boisterous, epidemical, outrageous, prevailing, tumultuous, widespread
be ~: 4 rule
run ~: 4 rage, rant, rave 5 erupt, freak, storm 7 explode 8 freak out 9 go berserk 10 hit the roof
rampart: 4 fort, hill, wall 5 fence, guard, mound, redan, ridge 6 shield 7 barrier, bastion, bulwark, defense, parapet, support 8 fastness, security 9 barricade, earthwork, elevation, vallation 10 battlement, breastwork, embankment, protection, stronghold
ramparts
assail the ~: 5 arise, rebel 6 attack, charge
surrounder: 4 moat
Rampling: 9 Charlotte
ramrod: 4 ogre 6 tyrant 8 martinet, stickler 10 taskmaster
ram's __: 4 horn
Rams: 4 team 6 eleven 7 Fordham
div.: 3 NFC
home: 3 St. L. 7 St. Louis
org.: 3 NFC, NFL
rival: *see* NFL team
sport: 8 football
Ramsay: 4 Alec 7 William
Ramses I
son: 4 Seti
Ramses II
father: 4 Seti
Ramses river: 4 Nile
Ramsey: 4 Anne 5 Clark, Lewis, Logan 6 Norman
__ Ramsey: 3 Hec
ramshackle: 5 seedy, shaky 6 flimsy, shabby, unfirm, unsafe 7 rickety, run-down, squalid 8 decrepit, derelict, timeworn, unsteady, untended 9 crumbling, tottering 10 broken-down, jerry-built, tumbledown
ram's horn: 6 shofar 7 shophar
ramus: 6 branch
ran
at: 7 charged, set upon 8 attacked
ender: 4 sack
in: 6 busted, nabbed 7 pinched 8 arrested, collared 9 dropped by
on: 6 gabbed, prated 7 babbled, rambled 8 jabbered, prattled 9 blabbered, chattered, continued
to: 7 reached, totaled
up: 5 added 7 amassed 8 incurred 9 increased
__-ran: 4 also
Ran (1985 film)
director: Akira Kurosawa
rana: 4 frog
Rance: 6 Howard
ranch: 4 farm, King, land 5 finca 6 estate, spread 7 acreage 8 dressing, estancia, hacienda, quarters 9 farmstead, homestead, Ponderosa, Southfork
beast: 4 calf, dogy 5 dogey, dogie, horse, steer
beasts: 4 cows, herd 5 bulls, stock 6 calves, cattle, dogies 9 livestock, longhorns
do a ~ job: 5 brand 6 dehorn 7 round up
hand: 6 drover 8 buckaroo, wrangler
menace: 4 puma 6 bobcat, coyote 7 bay lynx
quarters: 4 bunk 9 bunkhouse
rope: 5 lasso, reata, riata
unit: 4 acre
vacationer: 4 dude
worker: 4 hand 6 cowboy, herder
ranch __: 4 mink 5 house
__ ranch: 4 dude
__ Ranch: 6 Melody
rancher: 6 cowboy, cowman 7 cowpoke 8 wrangler
need: 3 hay 5 lasso, water
perhaps: 5 Texan
tool: 4 prod 5 brand
__ Rancher: 5 Jolly
__ rancheros: 6 huevos
ranchero wrap: 6 sarape, serape
ranchland: 5 field
Rancho Cucamonga: 4 city, town
locale: 10 California
Rancho Deluxe (1975 film)
cast: Elizabeth Ashley, Jeff Bridges, Sam Waterston
Rancho Mirage: 4 city, town
locale: 10 California
__ Rancho, NM: 3 Rio
Ranch, The
author: Danielle Steel
rancid: 3 bad, off, old 4 foul, gamy, high, rank, sour 5 fetid, fusty, gamey, moldy, musty, nasty, reeky, sharp, stale 6 foetid, frowsy, frowzy, impure, putrid, rotten, smelly, soured, strong, turned 7 carious, curdled, gone bad, noisome, noxious, reeking, tainted, unclean 8 feculent, polluted, stinking, unsavory 9 loathsome, offensive, putrefied, repulsive, unhealthy 10 disgusting, malodorous, putrescent
become ~: 4 sour, turn
rancor: 4 bile, gall, hate 5 odium, pique, spite, venom, wrath 6 animus, enmity, grudge, hatred, malice, spleen 7 discord, dudgeon, ill will, sarcasm, umbrage 8 acerbity, acrimony, aversion, bad blood, variance 9 animosity, antipathy, harshness, hostility, malignity, mordacity, nastiness, vengeance, virulence 10 antagonism, bitterness, grumpiness, resentment, unkindness
rancorous: 4 evil 5 catty 6 bitter, malign 7 hateful, hostile 8 scathing, spiteful, vengeful, venomous, virulent 9 malicious, resentful, splenetic 10 implacable, malevolent, vindictive
rand: 5 money
starter: 6 Kruger
Rand: 3 Ayn 5 Sally
Rand __: 7 McNally
Randa: 6 Haines
Randal: 7 Kleiser
Randall: 4 Tony 7 Jarrell
Randall, Tony: 5 actor 8 comedian
film: 7 Faces of Dr. Lao (1964)
Let's Make Love (1960)

Lover Come Back (1961)
The Mating Game (1959)
Pillow Talk (1959)
Send Me No Flowers (1964)
Will Success Spoil Rock Hunter? (1957)
TV: The Odd Couple
Rand, Ayn: 6 writer
work: Atlas Shrugged
The Fountainhead
We the Living
Randi: 5 James, Oakes
Rand McNally
product: 3 map 5 atlas, globe
Randolph: 4 city, John, Ross, Stow, town 5 Boots, Joyce, Scott 8 Mantooth
locale: 4 Mass.
Randolph, Boots instrument: saxophone
__ Randolph Hearst: 7 William
random: 3 odd 4 spot 5 fluky, stray 6 casual, chance, flukey, patchy, spotty 7 aimless, erratic, oddball, unaimed 8 isolated, on-and-off, periodic, rambling, slapdash, sporadic 9 arbitrary, desultory, driftless, haphazard, hit or miss, irregular, spasmodic, unplanned 10 accidental, contingent, designless, disorderly, fortuitous, incidental, nonuniform, objectless, occasional, sporadical, unintended, willy-nilly
at ~: 7 blindly 8 by chance
notion: 4 whim 5 fancy, quirk 6 vagary 7 caprice, impulse 8 crotchet
random __: 4 line, walk 5 error 6 access, number
random-__ memory: 6 access
Random Harvest
author: James Hilton
Rand, Sally, gear: 3 fan
randy: 7 goatish, lustful 9 lubricous 10 lascivious
Randy: 4 Owen, Ross 5 Quaid 6 Newman, Shilts, Travis 7 Johnson, Meisner 9 Vanwarmer
skating partner: 3 Tai
Randy & the Rainbows
song: Denise (1963)
ranee's wrap: 5 saree
__ rang?: 3 You
range: 3 Erz, ken, Mts., row, run 4 Alai, Alps, area, band, Harz, Jura, oven, play, rank, roam, room, rove, site, size, span, sway, tier, trek, vary 5 align, aline, Altai, ambit, Andes, array, Atlas, Baird, Black, chain, class, drift, field, float, gamut, Ghats, Green, James, Lewis, orbit, order, prowl, reach, realm, ridge, Sayan, scale, scope, space, stove, stray, sweep, Tatra, tenor, tramp, Uinta, Urals, White, width 6 Anadir, assort, Balkan, bounds, Brooks, cruise, degree, differ, domain, Elburz, extend, extent, Kjölen, Kolyma, Kunlun, leeway, length, limits, line up, Ozarks, Pindus, Pontic, radius, ramble, region, series, sphere, spread, Taurus, Tetons, trapes, travel, wander, Zagros 7 Ala Dagh, Bighorn, bracket, breadth, Cariboo, compass, Darling, earshot, expanse, explore, freedom, habitat, horizon, Laramie, leisure, meander, migrate, Mitumba, Mustagh, Nan Ling, pasture, Poconos, prairie, Purcell, purview, Rhodope, Rockies, San Juan, Sawatch, Selkirk, soprano, St. Elias, stretch, Sudeten, Torngat, traipse, variety, Wasatch 8 ambulate, Cardamom, Cascades, Catoctin, Caucasus, Cevennes, classify, confines, distance, Flinders, latitude, Mogollon, mountain, Panamint, province, Pyrenees, spectrum, Stanovoi, straggle, Tian Shan, Tien Shan, traverse, vicinity, Wrangell 9 Admiralty, Aleutians, Apennines, Blue Ridge, dimension, diversity, Dolomites, Edsel Ford, encompass, fluctuate, gallivant, globe-trot, Himalayas, Hindu Kush, incidence, Karakoram, largeness, Mackenzie, magnitude, Queen Maud, repertory, Savoy Alps, selection, territory, Trans Alai 10 assortment, boundaries, Carnic Alps, Carpathian, categorize, dimensions, knock about, meadowland, parameters, Serra do Mar, St. Gotthard
Africa: 5 Atlas
animal: 4 calf, dogy 5 bison, dogey, dogie, steer 6 cayuse
Asia: 4 Alai, Ural 5 Altai, Urals 6 Kunlun 7 Kuenlun
ender: 4 land 6 finder
Europe: 4 Alps, Jura, Rhon, Ural 5 Alpes, Tatra, Urals 6 Cadore, Kjölen, Ortles, Pindus
feature: 5 timer
full ~: 4 A to Z 5 gamut, scope, sweep 6 extent 7 breadth, compass 8 spectrum
home on the ~: 5 tepee 6 wigwam
North America: 5 Lasal, Ozark, Teton, Uinta 7 Cascade, Rockies, Wasatch 10 Adirondack
of vision: 3 ken 4 view 5 sight 8 eyesight
out of ~: 3 far 4 away 6 remote 7 distant
out of ~ of: 6 beyond
over: 4 hike 5 cover, scout 6 search, survey, travel 7 explore 8 traverse
part: 3 mtn. 6 burner 8 mountain
South America: 5 Andes
starter: 4 down
within ~: 4 near 5 close 6 at hand, nearby 7 close-by 9 proximate
see also mountain
range __: 6 finder
__ range: 3 gas 5 price, rifle 6 firing 7 driving
__-range: 4 free, long 5 short
ranger: 6 warden
forest ~ at times: 5 guide
starter: 4 bush
__ ranger: 6 forest
Ranger: 3 car 4 auto 5 Edsel, NHLer 10 automobile, baseballer
rival: 10 hockey team
__ Ranger: 4 Lone 5 Night, Texas 6 Sloane
Rangers: 3 six, ten 4 team
home: 5 Texas 7 New York
milieu: 3 ice 4 rink
org.: 3 ALW, MLB, NHL
rival: ***see*** baseball team
sport: 6 hockey 8 baseball
__ Ranger, The: 4 Dude, Lone
ranginess: 4 size 5 sweep 6 length 7 breadth, compass, expanse
ranging: 6 mobile 7 migrant, nomadic 9 itinerant, migratory, transient
__-ranging: 4 wide
Rangoon: 4 city, port, town 6 Yangon 7 capital
locale: 5 Burma 7 Myanmar
royalty: 4 raja 5 rajah
rangy: 4 lank, lean, long, slim, tall, thin, wiry 5 lanky, leggy, reedy, weedy 6 gangly, skinny 7 slender, spindly 8 gangling 9 spindling 10 long-legged, long-limbed
__ Ranh Bay: 3 Cam
rani: 5 noble, ruler 6 gerent 8 princess
servant: 4 amah, ayah
spouse: 4 raja 5 rajah
wear: 4 sari 5 saree
ranid: 4 frog 9 amphibian
rank: 3 bad, fix, off, peg, row, tab 4 duke, earl, foul, gamy, high, line, lush, olid, rate, rich, seed, sort, sour, step, tier, type, wild 5 acrid, align, aline, array, baron, birth, caste, class, count, dense, fetid, funky, fusty, gamey, grade, gross, group, judge, level, major, moldy, musty, nasty, order, place, queue, range, sheer, stale, stand, stark, state, thick, total, utter 6 arrant, assign, assort, belong, column, estate, esteem, foetid, frowsy, frowzy, league, rancid, rating, rotten, series, size up, smelly, sphere, squire, status, stinky, string, strong, turned 7 arrange, blatant, colonel, dignity, duchess, echelon, extreme, footing, general, glaring, gone bad, measure, noisome, noxious, odorous, primacy, profuse, pungent, quality, rampant, reeking, station, stature, tainted, unclean 8 absolute, category, classify, complete, countess, estimate, evaluate, flagrant, graduate, immodest, leverage, mephitic, nobility, off-color, outright, position, prestige, priority, prolific, sergeant, standing, stinking, thorough, tropical, unsavory 9 authority, commander, downright, egregious, excessive, exuberant, gradation, hierarchy, low-minded, luxuriant, nefarious, out-and-out, overgrown, privilege, repellent, seniority, situation 10 categorize, consummate, disgusting, importance, indecorous, junglelike, malodorous, pigeonhole, precedence, procession, prominence, scurrilous
and file: 5 crowd, plebs 6 masses, people, public, rabble 8 plebeian
Army ~: 2 lt. 3 cpl., gen., maj., PFC, SFC, sgt 4 capt., corp. 5 lieut., lt. col., major 6 maj. gen. 7 captain, colonel, general, private 8 corporal, sergeant 10 lieutenant
Boy Scout ~: 4 Life, Star 5 Eagle
contestants: 4 seed
equal in ~: 5 level 10 comparable
front ~: 4 lead
grow ~: 3 rot
Navy ~: 3 cdr., CPO, ens., yeo. 4 capt., cmdr., RAdm. 5 lieut., lt. com. 6 ensign, seaman, yeoman 7 admiral, captain 10 lieutenant
of higher ~: 5 above, finer 6 better, senior 7 grander, greater 8 superior
out: 4 gibe, jeer, jibe, mock, slam, slur, snub 5 abuse, decry, libel, scorn, spurn, taunt 6 defame, deride, dump on, heckle, impugn, malign, offend, rebuff, slight, vilify 7 affront, asperse, degrade, disdain, put down, slander, traduce 8 belittle, denounce, ridicule, vilipend 9 denigrate, discredit, disparage, humiliate 10 calumniate, disrespect
partner: 4 file, name
raise in ~: 5 exalt 7 promote
reduce in ~: 4 bust 5 abase, break 6 demote 7 degrade 8 take down 9 downgrade
suffix: 4 -ship
with: 5 equal, match, rival 7 emulate 9 compare to
__ rank: 4 pull 5 break
rank and __: 4 file
Rankin: 3 Ian
ranking: 5 first 6 senior, status 7 echelon 9 hierarchy, seniority
Rankin, Judy: 6 golfer
rankle: 3 get, irk, vex 4 fret, gall, hurt, pain, rile 5 anger, annoy, chafe, grate, peeve, upset 6 bother, fester, harass, nettle, obsess, pester, plague 7 enflame, inflame, mortify, torment 8 embitter, imbitter, irritate 9 aggravate 10 exasperate
ranks
close ~: 4 ally 5 merge, rally, unite 8 assemble, coalesce, converge 9 integrate
in ~: 4 arow
ransack: 3 gut, pry, rob, see, spy 4 comb, hunt, lift, loot, peer, raid, rake, rape, rout, scan, seek 5 filch, harry, pinch, poach, probe, rifle, scour, seize, sound, spoil, steal, strip 6 ferret, forage, maraud, pilfer, ravage, ravish, rustle, search, thieve 7 despoil, explore, pillage, plunder, purloin, rummage 8 freeboot, lay waste, look into, overhaul, spoliate, take away 9 depredate, go through, shake down 10 scrutinize
ransom: 4 free, save 5 bribe, price 6 payoff, redeem, regain, rescue 7 deliver, payment, recover, release, set free 8 liberate 9 expiation 10 redemption
hold for ~: 6 abduct, hijack, kidnap, pirate
pay ~: 6 redeem
__ ransom: 5 king's
Ransom (1996 film)
cast: Mel Gibson, Delroy Lindo, Rene Russo, Gary Sinise
director: Ron Howard
Ransom __ Chief, The: 5 of Red
Ransom __ Olds: 3 Eli
Ransom of Red Chief, The
author: O. Henry

rant: 4 fume, rage, rail, rave, yell 5 go ape, orate, shout, spiel, spout, storm 6 bellow, blow up, gibber, holler, scream, tirade 7 bluster, bombast, carry on, declaim, fustian, go crazy, tantrum 8 bloviate, diatribe, go postal, harangue, have a fit, perorate, rhetoric 9 go bananas, go bonkers, go on about, make a fuss, throw a fit, utterance 10 hit the roof, make a scene

and rave: 6 ramble

rant and __: 4 rave

__ Ran the Circus: 3 If I

__ Ran the Zoo: 3 If I

ranting: 3 hot, mad 4 ired, sore 5 cross, huffy, irate, livid, riled, upset, wroth 6 ireful, peeved, raging, raving, red-hot, stormy, tirade 7 enraged, furious 8 choleric, harangue, incensed, inflamed, maddened, outraged, wrathful 9 bombastic, indignant, irritated, resentful, splenetic 10 freaked out, infuriated, vociferous

Rao, Raja: 6 Indian, writer

work: The Serpent and the Rope

Raoul: 4 Dufy 5 Walsh

__ Raoul: 6 Eating

rap: 3 gab, hit, pan, say, tap, yak 4 bark, beat, blow, cane, chat, chin, conk, drum, flak, peck, slur, talk, tick, yarn 5 blame, clout, crack, decry, flack, genre, idiom, knock, music, punch, smear, speak, swipe, thump, whack 6 gabble, hip-hop, jabber, malign, parley, rebuke, strike, vilify, yammer 7 censure, chatter, condemn, palaver, penalty, schmoos, slander 8 admonish, badmouth, chitchat, converse, denounce, schmoose, schmooze, sentence, vocalize 9 criticism, criticize, disparage, table talk, tête-à-tête, touch base 10 chew the fat, chew the rag, punishment, yackety-yak

beat the ~: 4 walk 6 get off, go free

bum ~: 5 frame 7 raw deal

ender: 8 scallion

give a ~: 4 care

music fan: 4 b boy, teen

on the knuckles: 5 scold 6 berate, punish, rebuke 7 censure, tell off, upbraid 8 admonish 9 reprimand

outlet: 3 MTV

sheet datum: 5 prior

star: 4 Ice-T, Jay-Z 5 Nelly, T-Pain 6 Coolio, Eminem, Ja Rule, Lil' Kim

starter: 3 rip

rap __: 4 full 5 group, music, sheet 7 session

__ rap: 3 bad, bum 7 gangsta

rapacious: 5 feral, venal 6 greedy, lupine, savage 7 furious, hoggish, lustful, preying 8 grasping, ravaging, ravening, ravenous, thieving, thievish 9 ferocious, marauding, murderous, predatory, raptorial, voracious, vulturous 10 aggressive, avaricious, gluttonous, insatiable, plundering

one: 3 hog 5 miser

rapacity: 5 greed 7 avarice 8 cupidity 9 esurience 10 grabbiness

Rapa Nui: 4 isle 6 Easter, island

Rapeé: 4 Ernö

Rape of the Lock, The

author: Alexander Pope

rapeseed __: 3 oil

Raph: 4 Alan

Raphael: 5 angel 6 artist, Sanzio 7 painter

homeland: 5 Italy

rapid: 4 fast, rush 5 brisk, fleet, hasty, quick, ready, swift 6 flying, prompt, racing, snappy, speedy, sudden, winged 7 cursory, express, hurried, instant 8 flitting, meteoric 9 breakneck, galloping, whirlwind 10 celeritous, double-time, harefooted, hypersonic, supersonic, ultrasonic

be ~: 3 hie 4 dash, race, tear 5 hurry, speed

growth environment: 3 den 4 nest 6 cradle

in music: 5 mosso

not ~: 4 poky, slow 6 draggy 7 gradual, halting, lagging 8 crawling, creeping, dawdling, dilatory, indolent, plodding, slothful, sluggish 9 leisurely, lethargic, ponderous, prolonged, snaillike, unhurried 10 protracted

pace: 4 clip

succession: 5 whirl 6 flurry

rapid __: 7 transit

rapid __ movement: 3 eye

rapid-__: 4 fire

Rapid __: 5 Shave

Rapidan: 5 river

locale: 8 Virginia

Rapid City: 4 town

locale: 4 S. Dak.

rapid-fire: 4 fast 5 hasty, quick, swift 6 speedy 7 hurried 9 breakneck 10 harefooted

rapidity: 3 bat, vel. 4 gait, pace, rush 5 haste, hurry, speed 8 alacrity, celerity, dispatch, velocity 9 briskness, fleetness, quickness, readiness, swiftness 10 expedition, promptness, speediness

rapidly: 3 PDQ 4 fast, soon 5 apace, madly 6 presto 7 briskly, flat out, fleetly, hastily, in a rush, in haste, quickly, swiftly 8 full tilt, in a flash, in a hurry, in a jiffy, in no time, pell-mell, promptly, speedily 9 forthwith, hurriedly, instantly, like a shot, posthaste 10 in high gear

rapids: 5 sault 6 chutes, dalles 10 white water

conveyance: 4 raft 5 kayak

__ Rapids, IA: 5 Cedar

rapier: 4 foil 5 blade, sword

cousin: 4 épée

rapierlike: 4 keen 5 honed, sharp 8 incisive

rapine: 7 looting, plunder, sacking, seizure

Rappahannock: 5 river

locale: 8 Virginia

Rappaport: 5 David

__ Rappaport: 5 I'm Not

rapparee: 6 pirate 7 brigand, corsair, sea wolf 8 marauder 9 buccaneer, privateer

rappel site: 5 cliff

rapper

bench ~: 5 gavel

friend: 3 bro

knock a ~: 3 dis

rave: 3 def, rad 4 phat

skill: 4 rime 5 rhyme

Rapper: 6 Irving

rapport: 4 bond, link, soul 5 unity 6 accord, cotton, groove 7 concord, empathy, harmony 8 affinity, goodwill, sympathy 9 agreement, belonging, communion, consensus, good vibes, simpatico, unanimity 10 friendship

rapprochement: 7 détente, harmony 9 agreement, softening

rapscallion: 3 cur, imp 4 heel, worm 5 churl, knave, rogue, scamp 6 rascal, wretch 7 lowlife, villain 8 picaroon, scalawag 9 miscreant, reprobate, scallawag, scallywag, scoundrel, vulgarian 10 blackguard, ne'er-do-well, scapegrace

rap sheet

datum: 5 theft 6 arrest

word: 3 AKA 5 alias

rapt: 4 awed, deep, lost 5 in awe, taken 6 dreamy, intent 7 all ears, bemused, charmed, focused, gripped 8 absorbed, beguiled, ecstatic, held fast, immersed, involved, ravished 9 awestruck, delighted, engrossed, entranced, gladdened, oblivious 10 blissed out, captivated, enraptured, enthralled, fascinated, hypnotized, mesmerized, moonstruck, spellbound, thoughtful, transfixed

ender: 3 ure

hold ~: 5 charm 6 absorb, allure, engage, occupy 7 enchant, engross, immerse 8 enthrall, entrance 9 fascinate, preoccupy

raptor: 3 owl 4 hawk 5 eagle 6 condor, eaglet, falcon

nest: 4 aery, eyry 5 aerie, eyrie

victim: 4 prey

raptorial: 5 feral 8 ravaging 9 on the hunt, predatory, rapacious

Raptors: 4 five, team

home: 7 Toronto

org.: 3 NBA

rival: see NBA team

sport: 10 basketball

rapture: 3 joy 4 cool, love 5 bliss, cheer, glory, spell 6 gaiety, gayety, heaven, trance 7 delight, ecstasy, elation, Elysium, nirvana, passion 8 buoyance, buoyancy, euphoria, felicity, gladness, lyricism, paradise, pleasure, radiance, radiancy, rhapsody 9 at-oneness, beatitude, cloud nine, communion, enjoyment, happiness, transport, well-being 10 ebullience, enthusiasm, exaltation, jubilation, ravishment

Rapture, The (1991 film)

cast: David Duchovny, Mimi Rogers

rapturous: 6 elated, joyful, joyous 7 excited, radiant 8 beatific, blissful, ecstatic, euphoric, heavenly, in heaven, jubilant, ravished, thrilled 9 delirious, overjoyed, rhapsodic 10 delightful

become ~: 5 faint, swoon

raptus: 5 bliss 7 delight, ecstasy 8 euphoria 10 excitement

Rapunzel pride: 4 hair 5 tress

Raquel: 5 Welch

rara avis: 3 gem 4 oner 6 oddity, wonder 7 oddball

rarae __: 4 aves

rare: 3 odd, red 4 thin 6 choice, exotic, lovely, scarce, seldom, select, single, sparse, superb, unique 7 extreme, oddball, several, special, strange, unusual, vintage 8 far apart, peerless, precious, singular, splendid, sporadic, uncommon, unlikely, unwonted 9 a cut above, exquisite, matchless, priceless, recherché, scattered, unheard of, unrivaled 10 at a premium, endangered, hard to find, improbable, infrequent, inimitable, invaluable, occasional, phenomenal, remarkable, sporadical, unexampled, unfrequent, unrivalled

earth: 5 metal 6 cerium, cesium, erbium 7 caesium, holmium, terbium, thulium, yttrium 8 europium, lutetium, samarium, scandium 9 neodymium, ytterbium 10 dysprosium, gadolinium, promethium 12 praseodymium

ender: 3 bit 4 ripe

like a ~ day in hell: 4 cool 6 chilly 8 freezing

not ~: 6 common 7 routine 8 familiar, frequent, ordinary 10 widespread

rarer than ~: 3 raw

rare __: 4 book 5 earth

rare as __ teeth: 4 hen's

__ rarebit: 5 Welsh

raree: 4 show 8 carnival, peep show

rarefaction: 6 vacuum

rarefied: 4 thin 5 lofty 6 select 7 exalted, refined, sublime, tenuous 8 eclectic, elevated, esoteric 9 selective, spiritual 10 unphysical

rarefy: 5 clean 6 purify, refine 7 cleanse, freshen

rarely: 6 little, seldom 7 notably 8 not often, scarcely 9 extremely, unusually 10 hardly ever, now and then, singularly, uncommonly

raring to go: 4 avid, keen 5 eager, itchy, ready 6 all set, on edge 9 hot to trot 10 inspirited

Raritan: 5 river 6 valley

locale: 9 New Jersey

rarity: 6 luxury, oddity, wonder 7 miracle, prodigy 9 curiosity 10 phenomenon

Rarotonga: 4 isle 6 island

island near ~: 4 Atiu

ras: 4 cape 8 headland

__ rasa: 6 tabula

rascal: 3 bum, cad, cur, imp 4 heel, liar, worm 5 bully, cheat, churl, demon, devil, felon, fraud, ganef, gonef, gonif, idler, knave, losel, rogue, rowdy, scamp, skunk, sneak, tough, tramp 6 bad guy, bad hat, beggar, daemon, daimon, goniff, loafer, monkey, robber, sinner, wretch 7 grafter, outcast, ruffian, varment, varmint, villain, wastrel 8 disgrace, hooligan, picaroon, prodigal, rakehell, recreant, scalawag, swindler 9 cardsharp, charlatan, hypocrite, miscreant, prankster, pretender, reprobate, scallawag, scallywag, scoundrel,

trickster, vulgarian **10** blackguard, black sheep, delinquent, holy terror, jackanapes, ne'er-do-well, profligate, scapegrace
rascality: 7 devilry, roguery **8** deviltry, mischief **10** dishonesty, impishness
rascally: 6 impish **7** knavish, naughty **9** miscreant **10** picaresque
Rascals
song: A Beautiful Morning (1968)
A Girl Like You (1967)
Good Lovin' (1966)
Groovin' (1967)
How Can I Be Sure (1967)
I've Been Lonely Too Long (1967)
People Got to Be Free (1968)
Rasche: 5 David
rash: 4 wave, wild **5** blind, brash, hasty, hives, spate **6** daring, litter, madcap, stupid, sudden, unwary, unwise, wanton **7** torrent **8** careless, eruption, headlong, heedless, immature, mindless, pell-mell, reckless **9** audacious, daredevil, desperate, foolhardy, hotheaded, impatient, impetuous, imprudent, impulsive, overhasty, premature, unadvised, unbridled, uncareful, unchecked, unguarded, unhearing, whirlwind **10** headstrong, ill-advised, incautious, indiscreet, regardless, succession, unthinking
act: 5 folly
not ~: 4 sane **5** lucid, sober, sound **6** steady **7** careful, logical, politic, prudent, tactful **8** cautious, discreet, moderate, rational, sensible, together **9** judicious, practical, pragmatic, provident, realistic, temperate **10** diplomatic, restrained, thoughtful
Rashad: 5 Ahmad **8** Phylicia
rasher: 5 bacon, piece, slice
rashly: 5 madly **7** in haste **8** pell-mell **9** headfirst
rashness: 5 folly, haste **7** courage **8** audacity **10** impatience, imprudence
goddess of ~: 3 Ate
Rashomon (1950 film)
cast: Toshiro Mifune
director: Akira Kurosawa
Raskolnikov's love: 5 Sonya
Rasmussen, Knud: 6 Danish **8** explorer
rasp: 3 rub **4** bray, file, tool **5** grate, grind **6** abrade, scrape, squeal, wheeze **7** grate on, scratch **9** grate upon
ender: 5 berry
raspberry: 3 boo **4** jeer, twit **5** color, fruit, shrub **6** purple **7** reddish **8** ice cream **10** Bronx cheer
alternative: ***see*** fruit, ice cream flavor
bit: 4 seed
cousin: 4 hoot
give the ~: 3 boo **4** hiss, hoot, mock **5** fleer, taunt **6** deride, heckle **7** catcall **9** make fun of
kin: 6 dahlia, kerria, orchid, spirea **7** bramble, heather, jetbead, petunia, spiraea **8** hardhack, lavender, mulberry, ninebark, photinia **9** firethorn
relative: ***see*** red color
sauce: 5 Melba
stem: 4 cane
__ raspberry: 5 black
Raspberry Beret (1985 song)
artist: Prince
rasping: 5 husky, roupy **7** grating, raucous **8** friction, gravelly, guttural, strident
sound: 5 skirr
raspy: 5 gruff, harsh, husky, rough, roupy, testy **6** coarse, froggy, hoarse **7** grating, throaty **8** gravelly, guttural **9** irritable **10** laryngitic
not ~: 6 smooth
rasse: 5 civet
Rasulala: 7 Thalmus
rat: 3 cur **4** degu, fink, nark, sing, tell, toad, turn **5** knave, namer, scamp **6** animal, bad guy, mammal, rodent, snitch, squeal, tattle **7** stoolie, tattler, traitor **8** apostate, fat mouth, informer, inform on, squeaker, turncoat **9** informant, miscreant, no-goodnik, scoundrel **10** taleteller, tattletale
catcher: 3 owl **4** trap **6** ferret
ender: 4 a-tat, fink, fish, line, tail, trap
female: 3 doe
join the ~ race: 4 moil, slog, toil **5** labor, slave, sweat **6** drudge, hustle, strive **7** achieve, peg away **8** plug away **9** freelance, grind away, moonlight **10** buckle down
male: 4 buck
milieu: 3 lab **4** maze **5** sewer, wharf
of film: 3 Ben **7** Willard
on: 4 sell **6** betray, give up, snitch, squeal, tattle, turn in **7** sell out **9** implicate
out of the ~ race: 4 retd. **7** retired
pack ~: 5 saver **6** animal, mammal, rodent, storer **7** amasser, hoarder **8** gatherer **9** collector
race: 3 rut **4** work **5** grind **7** society **8** drudgery **10** livelihood
race result: 6 stress
relative: ***see*** rodent
rug ~: 3 kid, tot **4** babe, baby **6** infant
smell a ~: 5 doubt **7** suspect **8** distrust, mistrust **10** disbelieve
starter: 4 musk
young: 3 pup **6** kitten
rat __: 4 pack, race
rat-__: 4 a-tat
rat-__ cactus: 4 tail
__ rat: 4 mole, pack **5** sewer, water, wharf, white **6** desert
__ Rat: 4 King
__ rata: 3 pro
rat!, A: 3 eek
ratafia: 5 drink **6** cookie **7** biscuit **8** beverage
ingredient: 4 wine **5** fruit, juice **6** almond, brandy **10** grape juice
ratal: 5 value, worth
rat-a-tat: 4 roll **5** spiel **6** babble, jabber, patter **7** chatter **9** yakety-yak
ratatouille: 4 stew
Ratatouille (2007 film)
director: Brad Bird
voice cast: Brad Garrett, Ian Holm, Patton Oswalt, Peter O'Toole
ratchet: 5 wheel **6** detent
partner: 4 pawl
ratchet __: 4 down
rate: 3 fee, jaw, pct., peg, set, tab, tag, tax **4** clip, cost, deem, dues, earn, gait, pace, rail, rank, time, toll **5** chide, count, grade, judge, merit, pitch, price, quota, quote, scale, score, set at, speed, tempo, terms, value, weigh **6** assess, assort, charge, degree, esteem, figure, reckon, regard, size up, survey, tariff, towage **7** adjudge, deserve, lecture, measure, percent, upbraid **8** appraise, classify, estimate, evaluate, progress, velocity **9** determine, incidence, quotation **10** have coming, percentage, pigeonhole, proportion
at any ~: 3 yet **10** all the same, in any event
ender: 5 payer **6** making
high: 3 dig **4** like, love **5** adore, enjoy, exalt, favor, go for **6** admire, prefer, relish, revere **7** cherish, idolize **8** hold dear, venerate **10** appreciate
of motion: 3 vel. **4** clip, pace **5** speed **8** velocity
poorly: 3 pan, rap **4** slam **5** knock **6** deride, oppugn **7** put down **8** lambaste **9** criticize, disparage
starter: 3 pro **5** birth
rate __: 4 base, card
__ rate: 3 cut, tax **4** bank, base, rack **5** at any, birth, heart, prime, pulse
__-rate: 3 cut, low
rated
highly ~: 3 AAA **4** A-one, best, one A, tops
X: 4 lewd, racy **5** spicy **6** erotic, risqué, sultry, torrid
ratel: 6 weasel
relative: ***see*** weasel
__-rate mortgage: 5 fixed
rater: 5 judge **6** critic **8** assessor **9** appraiser
film ~: 4 MPAA **6** critic
film ~ unit: 4 star
ratfink: 5 crumb **6** snitch **7** traitor **8** betrayer, informer, renegade, turncoat **10** tattletale
Rathbone, Basil: 5 actor
costar: Nigel Bruce
film: The Adventures of Robin Hood (1938)
The Adventures of Sherlock Holmes (1939)
The Dawn Patrol (1938)
Frenchman's Creek (1944)
The Hound of the Baskervilles (1939)
The House of Fear (1945)
If I Were King (1938)
The Mark of Zorro (1940)
Paris Calling (1941)
The Scarlet Claw (1944)
Sherlock Holmes and the Secret Weapon (1942)
Sherlock Holmes Faces Death (1943)
Son of Frankenstein (1939)
The Spider Woman (1944)
Tovarich (1937)
The Woman in Green (1945)
rather: 4 a bit, lief, some, so-so, very, well **5** first, kinda, sorta, uh-huh **6** enough, fairly, kind of, pretty, sooner, sort of **7** a little, instead **8** a good bit, by choice, passably, slightly, somewhat **9** averagely, something, to a degree, tolerably, willingly **10** just as soon, moderately, more or less, much sooner, noticeably, preferably, reasonably, relatively
suffix: 3 -ish
than: 4 over **8** in lieu of
would ~: 5 elect, favor **6** choose, opt for, prefer, select **10** like better
see also of course
Rather: 3 Dan
Rather, Dan: 6 anchor **10** journalist, newscaster
forte: 4 news
network: 3 CBS
rival: Peter Jennings, Tom Brokaw
Rather you __ me: 4 than
rathole: 3 hut **4** slum **5** hovel **6** pigpen
rathskeller: 3 bar, inn **6** eatery **10** restaurant
order: 3 ale **4** beer **5** lager, stein, wurst
...__ raths outgrabe: 4 mome
ratification: 6 assent **7** passage **8** adoption, sanction
ratify: 2 OK **4** bind, okay, pass, seal, sign **5** adopt, bless, go for **6** accept, affirm, attest, uphold **7** approve, bear out, certify, confirm, consent, endorse, indorse, license, sustain **8** accredit, sanction, validate **9** authorize, establish, make legal **10** commission
rating: 2 PG **3** TV-G, TV-M, TV-Y **4** mark, rank, tier, TV-PG **5** class, grade, level, order, score **6** degree, rebuke, status **8** category, judgment, standard **9** appraisal, valuation **10** assessment, evaluation
beef ~: 5 grade, prime **6** choice
bond ~: 3 AAA, Baa, BBB, CCC
dairy ~: 6 grade A
draft ~: 4 one A, two A **5** four F
film ~: 2 PG
film ~ org.: 4 MPAA
gasoline ~: 6 octane
high ~: 4 fine **5** prime **6** choice, superb **8** five-star, four-star, very good **9** excellent
perfect ~: 3 ten
sitcom ~: 4 TVPG
top ~: 4 A-one, one A **5** A plus
unit: 4 star
__ rating: 6 credit, octane **7** Nielsen
ratio: 4 sine **5** quota, scale **6** cosine **7** measure, tangent **8** equation, fraction, ten to one, two to one **10** comparison, percentage, proportion
indicator: 5 colon
math ~: 2 pi **3** cos, cot, sin, tan **4** sine **6** cosine **7** tangent **8** cosecant, fraction **9** cotangent
payout ~: 4 odds
phrase: 4 is to
__ ratio: 4 gear, loss **6** aspect
ratiocinate: 5 think **6** reason, reckon
ratiocination: 5 logic **6** reason **8** thinking **9** deduction, reasoning, reckoning
ratiocinator: 8 logician

ration: 3 bit, cut, lot 4 deal, dole, drag, food, give, meed, mete, part, save 5 allot, divvy, issue, limit, quota, share, store 6 assign, budget, divide, parcel, supply 7 control, deal out, dish out, divvy up, dole out, give out, hand out, helping, measure, mete out, pass out, portion, prorate, provide, quantum 8 allocate, conserve, disburse, dispense, division, restrict 9 allotment, allowance, apportion, parcel out, provender, provision 10 allocation, assignment, distribute, measure out, proportion, sustenance
  slip: 6 coupon
__-Ration: 4 Ken-L
rational: 4 calm, cook, cool, sane, wise 5 lucid, right, sober, sound 6 cogent, likely, mental, normal, stable 7 knowing, liberal, logical, prudent, regular, sapient, tenable 8 all there, analytic, balanced, cerebral, coherent, credible, luculent, methodic, probable, sensible, thinking, together 9 cognitive, collected, conscious, deductive, impartial, judicious, objective, observant, plausible, practical, pragmatic, realistic, reasoning, sagacious, synthetic, unslanted 10 analytical, believable, consistent, convincing, deliberate, discerning, farsighted, reasonable, reflective, thoughtful, unagitated
  ender: 3 ism
  mind: 3 ego
rationale: 5 logic, story 6 excuse, motive, reason, theory, whyfor 7 account, big idea, grounds, purpose, reasons, whatfor 9 incentive, principle, reasoning 10 definition, exposition, hypothesis, motivation, philosophy, sour grapes
rationalism: 5 sense 6 reason, sanity 8 judgment, sapience 9 intellect, mentality, soundness 10 moderation, philosophy
rationalist: 5 cynic 7 doubter, sceptic, skeptic 10 questioner
rationality: 4 wits 5 sense 6 reason, sanity 8 sapience
rationalization: 4 plea 6 reason 7 defense, pretext, thought 9 rationale
rationalize: 5 think 6 cop out, defend, reason, renege 7 explain, justify 9 extenuate, whitewash
rationing agcy., WWII: 3 OPA
rations: 4 chow, fare, food, grub 5 items 7 aliment 8 supplies, victuals
ratite: 3 emu, moa 4 emeu, kiwi, rhea 9 cassowary
  extinct ~: 3 moa
ratlike rodent: 4 vole
ratline: 4 rope
Ratner: 5 Brett
Ratoff: 7 Gregory
ratón chaser: 4 gato
__ Raton, FL: 4 Boca
Rat Pack member: 4 Dean, Dino, Joey 5 Frank, Peter, Sammy 6 Bishop, Martin 7 Lawford, Sinatra 10 Dean Martin, Joey Bishop
Rat Race
  author: Dick Francis
Rat Race (2001 film)
  cast: Rowan Atkinson, Whoopi Goldberg, Cuba Gooding Jr., Jon Lovitz
rat's __: 4 nest
Rats!: 3 fie 4 dang, darn, drat, heck, oath, oh no, pfui 5 pshaw 6 darn it, oh crud, phooey, shucks
ratskeller serving: 4 bier
Ratso: 5 Rizzo 6 Dustin
rats, to cats: 4 prey
rat-tail __: 6 cactus
rattan: 4 cane, palm
  artisan: 5 caner
ratter: 4 fink 5 snake 7 stoolie, tattler, traitor 8 betrayer, quisling, squealer, turncoat
Rat, The
  author: Günter Grass
Rattigan, Terrence: 7 British 9 dramatist 10 playwright
  work: French Without Tears
    Separate Tables
    While the Sun Shines
    The Winslow Boy
rattle: 3 cow, gab, jar, jaw, toy, yak 4 bang, chat, drum, faze, gush, jolt, list, rock, verb 5 abash, addle, adodo, clack, clank, get to, knock, prate, run on, scare, shake, sound, throw, upset 6 axatse, babble, baffle, bicker, bother, bounce, cackle, caxixi, dismay, flurry, gabble, harass, heckle, jabber, jangle, jiggle, jounce, judder, muddle, noodge, put off, put out, unglue 7 chatter, clatter, confuse, disrupt, disturb, flummox, fluster, nonplus, perplex, perturb, prattle, reel off, shake up, shatter, unnerve, vibrate 8 bewilder, confound, distract, frighten, irritate, psych out, unsettle, unstring 9 discomfit, embarrass, give a turn 10 demoralize, discompose, disconcert, percussion, run through
  chest ~: 4 rale
  ender: 3 box 4 trap 5 brain, snake
  off: 6 recite
  on: 3 gab, yak, yap 4 blab, talk 5 prate 6 babble, jabber, ramble 7 blather, chatter, prattle 8 divagate
__, Rattle and Roll: 5 Shake
rattlebrain
  see ninny
rattled: 5 shook, upset 6 addled 7 abashed, fuddled 9 unsettled
  it may get ~: 5 saber
rattleheaded
  see foolish
rattlepate
  see ninny
rattler: 5 snake 6 animal 7 reptile
  defense: 4 fang 5 venom
  position: 4 coil
  relative: *see* snake
rattles: 6 sistra 7 sistrum
rattlesnakes do it: 4 molt
rattletrap: 3 car 4 auto, heap 5 crate, lemon, wreck 6 jalopy, junker 7 clunker, flivver
rattling: 5 shaky 8 clashing 9 talkative
__-rattling: 5 saber
rattrap: 3 sty
Rattray: 7 Heather
ratty: 4 torn, worn 5 cheap, seedy, tacky 6 shabby 7 run-down, unkempt 8 dog-eared, tattered, wretched 9 moth-eaten 10 disheveled, gone to seed, in bad shape, threadbare
Ratzenberger: 4 John
raucous: 3 dry 4 loud 5 acute, brusk, forte, gruff, harsh, husky, noisy, rough, rowdy, sharp, thick 6 atonal, coarse, hoarse, shrill, unruly 7 blaring, blatant, booming, braying, brusque, grating, jarring, pealing, rackety, rasping, reboant, roaring 8 absonant, crashing, grinding, piercing, plangent, rumbling, sonorous, strident, turned up 9 big-voiced, clamorous, deafening, dissonant, squawking, tumultous, turbulent, unmelodic, unmusical 10 boisterous, discordant, disorderly, resounding, stentorian, stertorous, strepitous, thundering, tumultuous, uproarious, vociferant, vociferous
  sound: 4 blat 5 blare 6 clamor, racket
Raul: 5 Julia
  see also Spanish
Raunchy (1957 song)
  artist: Bill Justis, Billy Vaughan and His Orchestra, Ernie Freeman
RAV: 3 SUV 6 Toyota
ravage: 3 gut, rob 4 loot, prey, raid, rase, raze, ruin, sack, sink 5 cream, crush, erode, foray, harry, seize, smash, spoil, strip, total, trash, waste, wreck, wrest 6 damage, forage, harrow, impair, invade, maraud, pirate, prey on, waster 7 break up, capture, consume, corrupt, despoil, destroy, disrupt, overrun, pillage, plunder, ransack, shatter, trample 8 demolish, desolate, freeboot, lay waste, mutilate, pull down, spoliate, stamp out 9 depredate, desecrate, devastate, dismantle, overthrow, overwhelm, prostrate, sweep away 10 annihilate, extinguish, wreak havoc
ravager: 3 Hun 6 bandit, vandal
ravaging: 6 lupine 7 wolfish 8 ravenous 9 ferocious, predatory, rapacious, raptorial, voracious, vulturous 10 aggressive, predacious
rave: 4 boil, flip, fume, gush, rage, rail, rant 5 cry up, freak, go ape, go mad, kudos, shout, storm 6 babble, bubble, jabber, praise, review, scream, wander 7 acclaim, bluster, carry on, declaim, enthuse, explode, flare up, go crazy, thunder 8 bloviate, freak out, harangue, have a fit, splutter 9 blow a fuse, go bananas, go bonkers, raise Cain, throw a fit 10 effervesce, hit the roof, rhapsodize
  at: 4 slam 8 lace into 10 vituperate
  partner: 4 rant
ravel: 6 loosen, unwind 7 unravel, untwine, untwist, unweave 8 entangle, untangle 9 come apart
ravell'd __ of care..., The: 6 sleave
Ravel, Maurice: 6 French 8 composer
  work: Bolero
    Daphnis and Chloe
    Jeux d'eau
    La Valse
    Rhapsodie Espagnole
    Tzigane
Ravelstein
  author: Saul Bellow
raven: 3 jet 4 bird 5 black, sable 7 engorge
  call: 3 caw 5 croak
  cousin: 3 daw 4 crow
  haven: 4 nest
  relative: 3 jet 4 inky, onyx 5 ebony, sable, sooty
ravening: 6 lupine 7 lustful 9 predatory, rapacious, voracious
Ravenna: 4 city, town
  locale: 5 Italy
ravenous: 5 empty, feral, unfed 6 greedy, hungry, lupine 7 longing, peckish, piggish, starved, wolfish 8 covetous, desirous, edacious, esurient, famished, grasping, ravaging, starving 9 devouring, ferocious, insatiate, predatory, rapacious, voracious 10 avaricious, gluttonous, insatiable, omnivorous, very hungry
ravenousness: 6 hunger 7 craving, edacity, longing 8 appetite, cupidity, voracity 9 appetence, esurience
Ravens: 4 team 6 eleven
  home: 9 Baltimore
  org.: 3 AFC, NFL
  rival: *see* NFL team
  sport: 8 football
Raven's Wing
  author: Joyce Carol Oates
Raven, The: 4 poem
  author: Edgar Allan Poe
  emulate ~: 3 rap
  goddess: 6 Pallas
  opener: 4 once
  word: 4 upon 5 quoth 9 nevermore
raver: 6 ranter 7 windbag 8 blowhard 9 loudmouth
Ravi: 7 Shankar
ravin: 4 prey
ravine: 3 cut, gap 4 gulf, pass, rift, wadi, wady, wash 5 abyss, break, cañon, chasm, clove, ditch, flume, gorge, gulch, gully, notch 6 arroyo, canyon, coulee, defile, gullet, gulley, valley 7 crevice, fissure 8 crevasse
  South African ~: 5 kloof
raving: 3 hot, mad 4 ired, sore, wild 5 cross, huffy, irate, livid, manic, riled, upset, wroth 6 fierce, ireful, peeved, raging, red-hot, stormy 7 enraged, furious 8 choleric, harangue, incensed, inflamed, maddened, maniacal, outraged, white-hot, wrathful 9 fanatical, indignant, irritated, possessed, resentful, splenetic, wrought-up 10 freaked out, hysterical, infuriated
ravioli: 5 pasta 6 entrée
  alternative: *see* pasta
  kin: 6 dim sum, wonton 8 dumpling, kreplach
ravish: 4 ruin 5 charm, seize 6 abduct 7 bewitch, delight, enchant, enthral, inthral, overjoy, ransack, violate

8 enthrall, entrance, inthrall 9 captivate, enrapture, fascinate, spellbind, transport
ravished: 4 rapt 6 elated, joyful 7 gleeful, gripped 8 beguiled, ecstatic, euphoric, exultant, immersed, jubilant, thrilled 9 delighted, engrossed, entranced, overjoyed, rapturous, rhapsodic 10 captivated, enraptured, enthralled, fascinated, moonstruck, spellbound
ravishing: 4 cute 5 bonny 6 bonnie, comely, lovely, pretty 7 lovable, winsome 8 alluring, dazzling, gorgeous, handsome, loveable, striking, stunning 9 beautiful 10 attractive, delightful, enchanting
raw: 3 icy, new 4 cold, damp, dank, gory, nude, rude, sore 5 basic, bleak, chill, crass, crisp, crude, fresh, green, gross, harsh, naked, rough, seamy, stark, windy, young 6 biting, bitter, bloody, breezy, callow, chafed, chilly, coarse, earthy, frigid, frosty, frozen, grazed, ribald, risqué, smutty, tender, unclad, vulgar, wintry 7 abraded, bruised, cutting, exposed, fibrous, glacial, natural, numbing, obscene, painful, puerile, scraped, unbaked, uncouth, wintery 8 blustery, freezing, ignorant, immature, piercing, uncooked, untested, unversed 9 au naturel, blistered, inclement, irritated, primitive, roughhewn, scratched, sensitive, unclothed, uncovered, underdone, unrefined, unskilled, untrained, untutored 10 lascivious, uncultured, unfinished, unpolished, unschooled, unseasoned
ender: 4 hide 5 boned
in the ~: 4 bare, nude 5 naked 6 unclad 7 exposed 8 disrobed, stripped 9 unattired, unclothed, uncovered, undressed
nearly ~: 4 rare
raw __: 4 data, deal, silk 5 score, umber 6 fibers, sienna
rawboned: 4 lank, lean, thin 5 gaunt, lanky, spare 6 gangly, meager, skinny 8 gangling
animal: 5 scrag
rawhide: 4 whip 7 leather
Rawhide (CBS western)
cast: Paul Brinegar (Wishbone) Clint Eastwood (Rowdy Yates) Eric Fleming (Gil Favor) Sheb Wooley (Pete Nolan)
prop: 5 lasso, reata, riata 6 lariat
theme singer: Laine
Rawlings
competitor: 3 AMF 4 Voit 6 Wilson 8 Spalding 9 Brunswick
Rawlings, Marjorie Kinnan: 6 writer
work: The Yearling
Rawls: 3 Lou 5 Betsy
Rawls, Betsy: 6 golfer
Rawls, Lou
song: Lady Love (1978) Love Is a Hurtin' Thing (1966) A Natural Man (1971) You'll Never Find Another Love Like Mine (1976) Your Good Thing (1969)
Raw Material
author: Oliver La Farge
rawness: 4 cold 5 chill 10 immaturity, inclemency
ray: 4 beam, fish 5 flash, gleam, glint, light, manta, shaft, shred, skate, spark, spoke, trace 6 streak 7 flicker, glimmer, glitter, sunbeam 8 flatfish, moonbeam, particle 9 scintilla
combining form: 5 actin- 6 actino-
starter: 5 sting
ray __: 3 gun
__ ray: 4 beta 5 alpha, devil, gamma, manta 6 cosmic
Ray: 3 Amy, Man 4 Aldo, John, Kroc 5 Bloch, Evans, Floyd, Hamel, Meyer, Price 6 Bolger, Danton, Eberle, LaHood, Liotta, Parker, Romano, Schalk 7 Anthony, Charles, Conniff, Enright, Johnnie, Mancini, Milland, Rachael, Sharkey, Stevens, Walston 8 Bradbury, Goulding, Manzarek, Nicholas, Nitschke, Peterson, Satyajit, Winstone 9 Dandridge
Ray (2004 film)
cast: Jamie Foxx
Rayburn: 3 Sam 4 Gene
__ Ray Cyrus: 5 Billy
Raye: 6 Collin, Martha
ray gun, use a: 3 zap
__ Ray Hutton: 3 Ina
Ray, Johnnie
song: Cry (1951)
__ Ray Leonard: 5 Sugar
Raymond: 4 Alex, Burr, Gene 5 Davis, Flynn, Lully 6 Bailey, Carver, Massey 7 Queneau, Souster 8 Chandler, Poincaré 9 St. Jacques
ray of __: 4 hope
Ray of Light (1998 song)
artist: Madonna
rayon fabric: 3 rep 4 repp 5 moire, piqué, satin, surah, tulle, voile 6 chally, faille, jersey, pongee, poplin, velvet 7 challie, challis, charvet, chiffon, duvetyn, foulard, Mogador, organza, ottoman, silesia, taffeta 8 Celanese, chenille, marocain, Milanese, popeline, shantung 9 grenadine, sharkskin 10 seersucker
__ Ray Robinson: 5 Sugar
rays: 5 radii
catch some ~: 3 sun, tan 4 bask
Rays: 3 ten
home: 5 Tampa 8 Tampa Bay
org.: 3 ALE, MLB
see also baseball team
__-ray tube: 7 cathode
__ Ray Vaughan: 6 Stevie
Raz: 4 Kavi
raze: 4 bomb, ruin 5 level, smash, total, waste, wreck 6 efface, ravage, remove, topple 7 destroy, flatten, mow down, unbuild, wipe out 8 bulldoze, demolish, dynamite, pull down, take down, tear down 9 devastate, eradicate, extirpate, knock down 10 obliterate
razing: 8 leveling 10 bulldozing, demolition
remains: 5 ruins 6 debris, rubble
razor: 3 Bic 4 Atra 6 cutter, Schick, shaver 7 trimmer 8 Gillette
alternative: 4 Nair, Neet 10 depilatory
asset: 4 edge
cut: 2 do 8 coiffure 9 hairstyle
ender: 4 back, bill
filler: 5 blade
like a ~: 5 sharp
mishap: 3 cut 4 nick
ready a ~: 4 hone, whet 7 sharpen
sharpener: 5 strop
use a ~: 3 cut 5 shave
razor __: 4 clam, wire 5 blade
razor-__ auk: 6 billed
__ razor: 6 Occam's, safety 7 Ockham's
razorback: 3 hog, pig 4 boar 5 swine
Razorbacks: 3 Ark. 8 Arkansas
razor-billed bird: 3 auk 5 murre 6 auklet
razorlike: 4 keen 5 sharp
Razor's Edge, The
author: W. Somerset Maugham
razz: 3 kid, rib 4 hiss, jeer, twit 5 chaff, taunt, tease 6 banter, deride, heckle, needle 8 ridicule 9 make fun of 10 Bronx cheer
razzing: 8 derision 9 raspberry 10 Bronx cheer
razzle-dazzle: 5 éclat 8 trickery 10 virtuosity
Rb: 4 elem. 7 element 8 rubidium
37 for ~: 4 at. no.
RBI: 4 stat
R. Buckminster __: 6 Fuller
RC: 4 cola, soda 9 soft drink
competitor: 4 Coke 5 Pepsi
RCA: 2 TV 3 VCR 5 TV set 10 television
alternative: ***see*** electronics company
dog: 6 Nipper
RCA __: 4 Dome 6 Victor
RCMP: 8 Mounties
part of ~: 3 Mtd. 5 Royal 6 Police 7 Candian, Mounted
patrol zone: 3 NWT 5 Yukon
rank: 3 sgt.
rcpt.: 3 vou.
rct.: 2 GI
employer: 3 USN 4 USMC
rd.: 2 ln. 3 ave., hwy., rte., tpk. 4 pkwy., tnpk.
R.D.: 5 Laing
RDA formulator: 3 FDA
re: 4 as to, note 5 about, anent, as for 6 toward 7 towards 9 apropos of, as regards 10 concerning, in regard to
in ~: 4 as to 5 about, anent 10 concerning
Re: 4 elem. 7 element, rhenium
75 for ~: 4 at. no.
__ Ré: 5 Ile de
Rea: 5 Chris, Peggy 7 Gardner, Stephen
reach: 2 go, to 3 end, get, hit, ken, win 4 buck, come, drop, fall, gain, go on, go to, hand, join, land, lead, make, meet, move, pass, play, rise, room, show, sink, span, sway 5 ambit, climb, enter, equal, gamut, get at, get in, get to, grasp, lunge, orbit, power, range, realm, run to, scale, scope, score, seize, shoot, space, stand, sweep, swing, total, touch, width 6 affect, amount, arrive, attain, come at, come to, derive, extend, extent, gain on, land at, land on, length, make it, obtain, put out, rack up, radius, ring in, roll in, roll on, show up, sign in, spread, strain, strike, tamper, turn up 7 ability, achieve, breadth, carry to, check in, climb to, clock in, command, compass, contact, expanse, feel for, hit town, hold out, horizon, mastery, measure, purview, realize, stretch 8 amount to, approach, arrive at, capacity, come up to, distance, dominion, extend to, get there, go across, latitude, lengthen, maintain, overtake, wind up at 9 catch up to, dimension, encompass, extension, get hold of, get to know, go as far as, influence, largeness, magnitude, pass along, set foot in 10 accomplish, continue to, get a hold of, get as far as, get in touch, get through, shake hands
across: 4 span 6 bridge 8 traverse
a limit: 3 max 4 peak 6 max out
for: 6 grab at 9 stretch to
new heights: 4 grow, soar 5 bloom, climb 6 ascend, evolve, expand, rocket, sprout, thrive 7 burgeon, enlarge, prosper 8 increase, multiply, progress 9 skyrocket
out: 4 talk 6 extend 9 touch base
out blindly: 5 grope
out of ~: 3 far 7 distant 8 hopeless 10 infeasible
out of ~ of: 4 past 6 beyond
the top: 4 rise 5 climb 6 arrive, ascend 7 prosper, succeed, triumph 8 flourish, get ahead, surmount
within ~: 4 near, nigh, open 5 close, handy 6 at hand, doable, likely, nearby, viable 8 adjacent, credible, feasible, imminent, possible, workable 9 bordering, impending, plausible, potential, practical, proximate 10 achievable, attainable, convenient, imaginable
within ~ of: 4 near 6 nearby 7 close by, close to 10 adjacent to
__ reach: 5 close 6 within
reachable: 9 available 10 accessible, attainable
reached, not: 5 unmet
__ reaches: 5 outer, upper
__-reaching: 3 far
Reach Out I'll Be There (1966 song)
artist: Four Tops
reacquire: 6 recoup, regain 7 get back, reclaim, recover, win back 8 retrieve 9 recapture
react: 4 feel, take 5 reply, start 6 behave, recoil 7 counter, hit back, respond 8 backfire, talk back 9 boomerang, get back at 10 answer back, bounce back
to a bad joke: 4 moan 6 flinch 7 grimace 9 make a face
to funniness: 4 howl, roar 6 giggle, titter 7 chuckle, crack up
to onions: 3 cry 4 weep
to ragweed: 6 sneeze 7 sniffle
toward: 5 treat 6 handle, regard
unlikely to ~: 4 calm, cool 5 inert 6 serene

reactant: 8 catalyst
reaction: 3 hit, lip 4 echo, kick, sass, take 5 reply, right, vibes 6 answer, recoil, reflex, retort, return 7 feeling, opinion, outcome, rebound, relapse, retreat, Toryism 8 attitude, backfire, backlash, back talk, comeback, feedback, kickback, knee-jerk, response 9 boomerang, reception, rejoinder, revulsion, status quo, wisecrack 10 double-take, impression, reflection, regression, withdrawal
  atomic ~: 6 fusion 7 fission
  chemical ~: 5 redox 9 oxidation, reduction
  critical ~: 3 pan 4 rave
  get a ~ from: 6 arouse
  hostile ~: 4 flak 5 flack 6 outcry 7 dissent, protest 9 criticism
reaction ___: 4 time
___ reaction: 3 gut 5 chain
reactionaries: 5 right 9 right wing
reactionary: 4 tory 5 right 6 narrow 7 diehard, hard-hat 8 loyalist, orthodox, renegade, rightist, royalist 9 old-school
___ reactor: 6 atomic, fusion 7 breeder, nuclear
reactor, nuclear: 4 pile
  element: 5 boron
  part: 3 rod
  PA ~ site: 3 TMI
read: 4 look, pore, scan, skim, view 5 learn, sense, study 6 browse, decode, devour, go over, locate, peruse, rebuke, recite, record, regard, survey 7 deliver, dictate, dip into, make out, measure, observe 8 audition, bone up on, check out, construe, decipher, discover, look over, pore over, register 9 get to know, grind away, interpret, pronounce, translate 10 crack a book, understand
  ability to ~: 8 literacy
  able to ~: 8 literate
  back: 6 repeat
  between the lines: 3 bet 5 glean, guess, infer, judge, wager, weigh 6 assume, call it, deduce, figure, gather, intuit, reckon, size up, wonder 7 imagine, make out, presume, suppose, surmise, suspect 8 arrive at, conclude, construe, intimate 9 figure out, interpret, postulate, speculate 10 conjecture, have a hunch, understand
  easily ~: 5 clear, lucid, plain 7 legible 8 distinct
  ender: 3 out
  inability to ~: 6 alexia 10 illiteracy
  it may be ~: 4 lips, mind, palm 7 riot act
  make hard to ~: 6 encode
  one way to ~: 5 aloud
  out loud: 6 recite 7 narrate, perform
  starter: 5 proof
  the riot act to: 3 hit 4 flay, flog, slam 5 blast, chide, scold 6 berate, rebuke 7 bawl out, censure, chasten, chew out, condemn, lecture, reprove, upbraid 8 admonish, chastise, denounce, lambaste, reproach, sail into, tear into, threaten 9 castigate, criticize, dress down, excoriate, reprehend, reprimand 10 come down on, discipline, take to task, vituperate
  up on: 5 study 8 research 9 delve into
read ___: 3 out 4 up on 5 out of
read ___ weep: 5 'em and
read-___ memory: 4 only
___-read: 3 lip 4 must, well 5 sight, speed
readable: 4 easy, tidy 5 clean, clear, lucid, plain 6 clever, fluent, simple, smooth 7 amusing, flowing, graphic, legible, orderly, precise, regular 8 coherent, distinct, eloquent, engaging, exciting, explicit, gripping, inviting, pleasant, pleasing, relaxing 9 absorbing, appealing, brilliant, enjoyable, graphical, ingenious, rewarding 10 engrossing, gratifying, satisfying, worthwhile
  make ~: 5 crack 6 decode 7 decrypt 8 decipher 9 interpret, translate
Read all ___ it: 5 about
read between the ___: 5 lines
Reade, Charles: 6 writer 7 British
  work: The Cloister and the Hearth
Read 'Em and Weep (1983 song)
  artist: Barry Manilow
reader: 4 book, text 6 cleric, lector 7 prophet 8 lecturer 10 schoolbook
  avid ~: 8 bookworm
  manuscript ~: 6 editor
  need: 4 lamp 5 light
  omen ~: 4 seer 5 augur 6 auspex 7 prophet, psychic
  starter: 4 copy 5 proof
___ reader: 3 lay, lip 4 mind, palm
Reader's Digest lack, until 1955: 3 ads
Reader's Encyclopedia editor: 5 Benét
Reader, The (2008 film)
  cast: Ralph Fiennes, Kate Winslet
___ Reader, The: 4 Utne
readily: 4 lief 5 lieve 6 at once, easily, freely, gladly, openly 7 eagerly, quickly 8 in a jiffy, in no time, promptly, speedily 9 naturally, right away, summarily, willingly 10 cheerfully, swimmingly
readiness: 4 ease, zeal 5 skill, speed 7 address, aptness, fitness, fluency, prowess, sleight 8 alacrity, capacity, deftness, dispatch, facility, good will, keenness, maturity, rapidity, ripeness, tendency 9 dexterity, eagerness, eloquence, handiness, quickness 10 adroitness, efficiency, enterprise, expedience, expedition, generosity, promptness, volubility
  in ~: 5 on tap 6 all set, on call, on hand 8 geared up, prepared, warmed up
  state of ~: 5 alert 7 caution
reading: 5 grasp, study 6 lesson, review 7 account, perusal, recital, version 8 audition, learning, scrutiny 9 education, erudition, knowledge, narration, rehearsal, rendering, rendition, treatment 10 commentary, conception, impression, inspection, paraphrase, recitation
  compact ~: 5 brief 6 digest 7 summary 8 abstract, synopsis
  compass ~: 3 ENE, ESE, NNE, NNW, SSE, SSW, WNW, WSW 7 heading
  course ~: 4 text 8 textbook
  desk: 7 lectern
  gauge ~: 6 status 8 altitude 9 elevation
  give a ~: 6 recite, render 7 narrate 9 dramatize, interpret
  hold a ~: 5 drill 6 review, warm up 8 practice, rehearse 9 go through 10 run through
  light: 4 lamp
  light ~: 5 novel
  material: 3 mag 4 book, text, tome 5 novel, paper 8 magazine 9 newspaper
  required ~: 4 text 8 syllabus
  room: 3 den 5 study 7 library
  starter: 5 proof
reading ___: 4 desk, room 5 chair 6 notice 7 glasses
___ reading: 3 lip 4 mind 5 light
Reading: 2 RR 4 city, town 8 railroad
  locale: 4 Penn. 7 England 9 Berkshire
readjust: 4 suit 6 modify, revise, tailor 8 regulate
Read my ___!: 4 lips
read-only ___: 6 memory
readout: 3 LCD, LED
Read, Piers Paul book: 5 Alive
read the ___ act: 4 riot
ready: 3 apt, fit, fix, fox, get, set 4 deft, done, fain, game, gird, glad, keen, live, make, near, post, prep, ripe, spry 5 acute, adept, alert, brace, brief, can-do, eager, equip, fixed, groom, handy, happy, on tap, order, prime, prone, quick, rapid, sharp, smart, steel, tutor, wired 6 active, adroit, all set, ardent, astute, at hand, braced, bright, clever, cooked, expert, fill in, fit out, gear up, get set, in gear, in line, liquid, make up, mature, minded, nearby, on call, on hand, poised, primed, prompt, speedy, usable, warm up, wise up 7 arrange, covered, dynamic, equal to, fortify, heedful, incline, in order, in place, in shape, let in on, paratus, prepare, prepped, provide, psyched, psych up, put on to, qualify, skilled, useable, waiting, willing, zealous 8 adjusted, arranged, dextrous, disposed, equipped, geared up, get ready, inclined, masterly, mobilize, organize, prepared, punctual, rehearse, skillful, watchful 9 agreeable, astucious, available, brilliant, completed, dexterous, expectant, fitted out, on the ball, organized, psyched up, qualified, receptive, rehearsed 10 accessible, convenient, in position, keep posted, obtainable, on the brink, pave the way, perceptive, proficient, raring to go, square away, strengthen, time-saving
  be ~: 4 wait
  be ~ for: 5 await
  companion: 4 able 7 willing
  follower: 3 set
  (for): 4 game
  for action: 3 arm, fit 4 game 5 alert, eager
  for use: 9 available
  get ~: 3 fix, set 4 gird, pack, prep 5 brace, equip, groom, prime, ripen, train 6 gear up 7 arrange, prepare, psych up 8 mobilize 9 condition 10 square away
  (to): 4 open
  to fight: 7 hawkish, martial 8 militant 9 bellicose, combative 10 aggressive, pugnacious
  to fire: 5 armed
  to go: 7 in store 9 available 10 obtainable
ready ___: 4 room 5 money, or not, to eat
ready, ___, and able: 7 willing
ready-___: 3 mix 4 made
___ ready: 3 get 4 make 5 at the
___-ready: 4 make 5 cable 6 camera, combat
Ready, ___!: 5 set go
Ready, ___, fire!: 3 aim
___ Ready: 3 Get 4 We're 5 Yes I'm
Ready or not, here ___!: 5 I come
ready-to-___: 4 wear
Ready to Take a Chance Again (1978 song)
  artist: Barry Manilow
Ready to Wear (1994 film)
  director: Robert Altman
ready, willing, and ___: 4 able
reaffirm: 5 renew 6 stress
Reagan: 3 Ron 5 Nancy 6 Ronald 7 Maureen
Reagan, Ronald: 5 actor 9 president
  alma mater: 6 Eureka
  birthplace: 7 Tampico 8 Illinois
  cabinet member: 4 Bell, Dole, Haig, Lyng, Watt 5 Baker, Block, Bowen, Brady, Brock, Clark, Hodel, Lewis, Meese, Regan, Smith 6 Pierce, Verity 7 Bennett, Burnley, Cavazos, Donovan, Edwards, Heckler, Schultz 8 Carlucci 9 Baldridge
  child: 3 Ron 5 Patti 7 Maureen, Michael
  film: Bedtime for Bonzo (1951)
    Kings Row (1942)
    This Is the Army (1943)
  home: 10 California
  middle name: 6 Wilson
  opponent: 6 Carter 7 Mondale 8 Anderson
  parent: 4 Jack 5 Nelle
  previous occupation: 5 actor
  program: 3 SDI
  speechwriter: Peggy Noonan
  spouse: Jane Wyman, Nancy
  V.P.: 4 Bush
  was its pres.: 3 SAG
Reagle: 4 Merl
real: 4 coin, good, live, sure, true 5 basic, legit, money, right, solid, valid 6 actual, bodily, dinkum, honest, kasher, kosher, native 7 certain, de facto, evident, factual, genuine, natural, sincere 8 bona fide, concrete, definite, embodied, existing, explicit, material, original, physical, positive, rightful, tangible, verified 9 authentic, corporeal, decidedly, heartfelt, in earnest,

intrinsic, touchable, unfeigned, veracious, veritable **10** legitimate, sure-enough, true-to-life, undeniable, unimagined, verifiable
be ~: **4** live **5** exist **7** breathe
ender: **3** ism, ist
for ~: **2** so **4** true **6** honest, indeed, surely **7** genuine **9** seriously
get ~: **6** come on, wise up
McCoy: **5** legit
not ~: **3** bad **5** phony **6** ersatz, phoney, pseudo
world: **7** reality **9** actuality, existence
real __: **4** time **5** McCoy, wages, world **6** estate
real-__: **4** life
__ real: **3** for, get
Real __, The: **5** Glory **6** Blonde, McCoys
__ Real: **6** Camino
Real Blonde, The (1998 film)
cast: Daryl Hannah, Catherine Keener, Matthew Modine
real estate: **3** lot **4** bldg., home, land **5** asset, house **6** assets, ground, spread **7** acreage, grounds **8** building, property
abbr.: **2** BR, LR, rm. **3** blk., EIK, fpl., gar., MLS **4** bdrm., bsmt.
account: **6** escrow
chart: **4** plat
document: **4** deed **5** lease, title
investment: **4** REIT
seller: **5** agent **6** agency, broker
sign: **4** sold **5** to let **10** in contract
term: **4** relo
transaction: **6** resale
unit: **3** lot **4** acre, home **5** house **8** building, property
Real is rational man: **5** Hegel
realistic: **4** hard, sane, true **5** sober, sound **6** astute, earthy, shrewd **7** genuine, graphic, natural, prudent **8** faithful, lifelike, original, rational, sensible, truthful **9** astucious, authentic, graphical, practical, pragmatic **10** hard-bitten, hard-boiled, reasonable, true-to-life, unromantic
reality: **4** deed, esse, fact **5** being, facts, score, truth **6** entity, matter, object, verity **8** like it is, presence, realness, solidity, validity **9** actuality, certainty, existence, phenomena, substance, what's what **10** bottom line, brass tacks, phenomenon
in ~: **5** quite, truly **6** au fond, indeed, really **7** at heart, de facto **8** actually
old-style: **5** sooth
reality __: **5** check
__ reality: **7** virtual
Reality Bites (1994 film)
cast: Janeane Garofalo, Ethan Hawke, Winona Ryder, Ben Stiller
director: Ben Stiller
realizable: **6** liquid **8** feasible, knowable, possible **9** available **10** attainable
realization: **4** grip, life **5** grasp **7** success, thought **8** fruition
cry: **3** aha
__-realization: **4** self
realize: **2** do **3** get, net, see, win **4** earn, gain, know, make, reap **5** catch, clear, fancy, fetch, get it, go for, grasp, image, reach, reify, score, sense, think **6** attain, awaken, effect, finish, follow, fulfil, intuit, obtain, pick up, profit, rack up, take in, vision **7** achieve, acquire, bring in, catch on, compass, develop, discern, feature, fulfill, imagine, perfect, perform, produce, receive, sell for, succeed **8** bring off, carry out, complete, conceive, discover, envisage, envision, make good, perceive **9** actualize, apprehend, implement, learn from, liquidate, recognize, visualize **10** accomplish, appreciate, bring about, comprehend, consummate, effectuate, make good on, make happen, understand
realized: **4** done **8** finished
be ~: **5** occur **6** happen **8** come true
not ~: **5** unwon
realizing, without: **9** unwitting
Real Love (song)
artist: Doobie Brothers, Jody Watley, Mary J. Blige
really: **4** very, well **5** quite, truly **6** easily, honest, indeed, in fact, simply, verily **7** at heart, de facto, in truth **8** for a fact, honestly, in effect **9** assuredly, genuinely, literally, precisely, sincerely **10** absolutely, admittedly
see also of course
Really!: **5** no lie **6** do tell, so true
really big __: **4** show
__ Really Going Out With Him?: **5** Is She
__ Really Want to Do: **4** All I
realm: **3** job **4** land, turf, zone **5** arena, bourn, field, orbit, range, reach, scope, state, sweep, world **6** domain, empire, length, nation, region, sphere **7** compass, country, expanse, grounds, kingdom, purview **8** dominion, monarchy, province **9** dimension, territory **10** department, walk of life
suffix: **3** -dom
Real McCoys, The (ABC/CBS sitcom)
cast: Walter Brennan (Amos McCoy)
Richard Crenna (Luke McCoy)
Kathy Nolan (Kate McCoy)
Realms of Being
author: George Santayana
__ real nowhere man: **4** He's a
Real Peace
author: Richard Nixon
Realtor
see real estate
realty
see real estate
Real War, The
author: Richard Nixon
ream: **3** wad **4** bore, skim **5** scold, widen **7** defraud **9** penetrate
fraction: **5** quire, sheet
ream __: **3** out
reams: **5** piles, rafts, scads **6** masses, oceans, oodles, scores, stacks **7** bunches
reanimate: **6** revive **7** recruit, refresh **10** regenerate
reap: **3** cut, get, mow **4** earn, gain, take **5** clear, glean **6** derive, garner, gather, obtain, profit, secure, take in **7** bring in, collect, harvest, produce, receive **8** gather in
reaped row: **5** swath **6** swathe
reaper: **6** farmer **7** machine **9** harvester
follow the ~: **5** glean **6** garner, gather **7** collect, harvest
reaping: **4** crop **6** profit **7** farming, harvest
stalks left after ~: **4** halm **5** haulm
reappear: **6** return **8** come back
rear: **3** aft, end **4** back, form, heel, hind, lift, seat, side, tail **5** breed, build, erect, hoist, put up, raise, set up, stern, teach, tower, train **6** astern, behind, bottom, breech, dorsal, foster, parent, rise up, tag end **7** bring up, care for, educate, nourish, nurture, raise up, reverse, tail end, upheave **8** back seat, hindmost **9** construct, cultivate **10** hindermost
bringing up the ~: **4** last **6** behind, in back **7** lagging **8** trailing
bring up the ~: **3** lag **5** trail **6** follow
combining form: **7** opistho-
in the ~: **3** aft **4** last **5** aback, abaft **6** astern
up: **6** bridle, get mad, see red **7** bristle **8** get angry
rear __: **3** end **5** guard **7** admiral
rear-end: **3** ram **5** total **6** strike **7** wrack up **8** slam into **9** smash into
rear-ender: **5** crash, wreck **6** impact, pileup **7** smashup **8** accident **9** collision
rearmost: **3** end **4** hind, last **5** after **6** latter
rearrange: **5** alter, shift **6** change, reform, switch **7** reorder, shuffle **9** transpose **10** reposition
rearrangement: **5** shift **6** change
rearview mirror decoration: **4** dice
Rear Window (1954 film)
cast: Raymond Burr, Grace Kelly, Thelma Ritter, James Stewart
director: Alfred Hitchcock
remake star: **5** Reeve
reason: **3** aim, end, use, why, wit **4** call, case, goal, idea, mind, move, nous, root, sake, soul, talk, urge, wits **5** argue, basis, brain, cause, cover, infer, logic, point, proof, prove, sense, solve, study, think **6** acumen, adduce, bounds, brains, debate, decide, deduce, deduct, design, excuse, gather, ground, limits, motive, noesis, notion, object, sanity, senses, spring, target, whyfor, wisdom **7** account, apology, contend, defense, discuss, dispute, examine, grounds, impetus, justify, make out, marbles, purpose, reflect, resolve, suppose, warrant, whatfor, win over, work out **8** apologia, argument, cogitate, conclude, dissuade, draw from, judgment, lucidity, occasion, persuade, point out, saneness, sapience, talk into **9** causation, cerebrate, deduction, discourse, establish, figure out, incentive, induction, inference, intellect, intention, mentality, propriety, rationale, reasoning, soundness, speculate, syllogize, talk out of, thresh out, wherefore **10** antecedent, deliberate, dialectics, exposition, generalize, horse sense, inducement, moderation, motivation, philosophy
alleged ~: **5** alibi, bluff, cover, guise **6** excuse **7** cover-up, pretext **8** pretense **10** cover story
by ~ of: **5** due to **7** owing to
by ~ (of): **7** because
for any ~: **5** at all
for no ~: **4** idly
for this ~: **4** ergo, then, thus **5** hence **6** hereat **9** therefore
for what ~: **3** why
give a ~ for: **4** show **6** defend **7** clarify, clear up, explain, justify **8** spell out **9** expound on, make clear
having a ~: **6** causal
out: **5** educe, infer **6** deduce, derive, ponder
partner: **5** rhyme
rhyme or ~: **5** cause, logic, sense **6** motive
the ~ for: **6** behind **7** causing
(with): **5** plead
within ~: **4** fair **5** legit **7** logical **8** credible, rational, sensible **9** plausible, tolerable **10** legitimate
without ~: **4** idle **6** wanton **8** baseless, needless **9** causeless, illogical, senseless **10** gratuitous, groundless, unprovoked
without rhyme or ~: **4** idle **5** inane, nutty, silly, wacky **6** absurd **7** asinine, foolish, puerile **8** mindless **9** frivolous, half-baked, illogical, ludicrous, pointless **10** irrational, ridiculous
__ reason: **4** pure, with **6** within
Reason: **3** Rex **6** Rhodes
reasonable: **2** OK **3** fit, low **4** cool, fair, just, okay, sane, wise **5** cheap, legit, lucid, right, sober, sound, sweet, valid **6** decent, earned, honest, humane, likely, modest, on sale, proper, viable **7** average, bargain, cut-rate, knowing, liberal, logical, low-cost, natural, politic, prudent, sapient, tenable **8** arguable, cerebral, clear-cut, credible, deserved, discreet, feasible, luculent, moderate, probable, rational, sensible, suitable, together, tolerant, unbiased, uncostly **9** advisable, cognitive, conscious, equitable, excusable, half-price, impartial, judicious, low-priced, objective, plausible, practical, realistic, temperate, tolerable, unextreme **10** acceptable, admissible, analytical, believable, consequent, consistent, controlled, convincing, economical, legitimate, perceiving, percipient, reflective, restrained, thoughtful, thought-out, unagitated
seem ~: **5** add up **9** make sense
reasonableness: **6** sanity **10** likelihood
reasonably: **5** quite **6** enough, pretty, rather **10** apparently

reason-based
believer: 5 deist
faith: 5 deism
reasoned: 4 sane 8 coherent, dogmatic 10 dogmatical
reasoner: 7 casuist, sophist 8 logician
Reasoner: 5 Harry
reason for war in Latin: 10 casus belli
Reason in Art
author: George Santayana
reasoning: 5 logic, proof, sense 6 acumen, mental, noesis 7 premise, thought 8 analysis, argument, judgment, rational 9 conscious, deduction, dialectic, rationale, syllogism 10 dialectics, exposition, hypothesis, philosophy, thoughtful
valid ~: 5 sense 6 sanity 7 thought 9 coherence, deduction, good sense, induction, inference, rationale, syllogism
Reason in Science
author: George Santayana
Reason in Society
author: George Santayana
reasonless: 10 fallacious, gratuitous, irrational
__ Reason, The: 5 Age of
Reason to Believe (song)
artist: Carpenters, Rod Stewart
reassemble: 5 rally, reune
reassert: 6 accent, play up, stress 7 dwell on, iterate 9 emphasize, underline 10 accentuate, underscore
reassess: 6 review 10 reconsider, think twice
reassign: 5 shift 6 demote
reassignment: 5 shift
reassurance: 4 lift 5 boost 6 succor 7 comfort 10 comforting
reassure: 4 buoy, calm 5 brace, cheer 6 perk up, pick up, settle, uphold 7 bolster, cheer up, comfort, console, hearten, inspire, relieve, satisfy 8 convince, enspirit, inspirit 9 encourage, give a lift, guarantee
reassuring: 9 favorable, promising 10 comforting, supportive
words: 4 I'm OK 5 it's OK
Rea, Stephen: 5 actor
film: Angie (1994)
The Crying Game (1992)
Danny Boy (1982)
Interview With the Vampire... (1994)
Michael Collins (1996)
reata: 4 rope 5 lasso 6 lariat
kin: 4 bola
user: 5 roper 6 cowboy, gaucho
Reatta: 3 car 4 auto 5 Buick 10 automobile
Réaumur, René Ade: 6 French 9 physicist
reawaken: 5 renew 6 come to 8 rekindle 10 regenerate
Reb: 4 gray, grey
general: 3 Lee 5 Early 6 Stuart 7 Forrest, Jackson 10 Beauregard, Longstreet
letters: 3 CSA
state: 3 Ala., Fla., Tex. 4 Miss., N. Car., S. Car. 5 Texas 7 Alabama, Ark. Tenn., Florida, Georgia 8 Arkansas, Virginia 9 Louisiana, Tennessee 11 Mississippi 13 North Carolina, South Carolina
Yank, to a ~: 3 foe 5 enemy
__ Reb: 6 Johnny
Reba: 6 sitcom 8 McEntire
Reba (WB/CW sitcom)
cast: Joanna Garcia (Cheyenne Montgomery)
Steve Howey (Van Montgomery)
Reba McEntire (Reba Nell Hart)
Christopher Rich (Brock Hart)
rebate: 5 bonus, repay 6 deduct, reduce, refund, return 7 payback 8 decrease, diminish, discount, kickback 9 allowance, deduction, reduction
rebec: 6 string, violin
kin: 5 crwth
origin: 6 Europe
Rebecca: 4 film, West 5 novel 6 Romijn 8 DeMornay 9 Schaeffer
author: Daphne du Maurier
cast: Judith Anderson, Joan Fontaine, Laurence Olivier, George Sanders
director: Alfred Hitchcock
Rebekah
brother: 5 Laban
father: 7 Bethuel
husband: 5 Isaac
son: 4 Esau 5 Jacob
rebel: 4 defy, riot, rise 5 arise, fight, flout 6 defier, ignore, mutiny, oppose, opt out, resist, revolt, rise up, secede 7 boycott, disobey, dissent, drop out, heretic, protest, radical, traitor, violate 8 agitator, frondeur, maverick, mutineer, nihilist, overturn, renegade, resister, turncoat, ultraist 9 anarchist, break with, disregard, dissenter, dissident, fight back, insurgent, make waves, overthrow, protester, young Turk 10 go on strike, iconoclast, malcontent, schismatic, separatist, subversive
1850s ~: 5 Sepoy
1898 ~: 5 Boxer
African ~ org.: 5 SWAPO, UNITA
Nicaraguan: 6 Contra
rebel __: 4 yell
Rebel: 3 AMC, car 4 auto 7 Rambler 10 automobile
Rebel __ a Cause: 7 Without
__ Rebel: 4 He's a
rebellion: 6 heresy, revolt, rising, schism, unrest 7 dissent 8 apostasy, civil war, defiance, disorder, outbreak, uprising 9 commotion, defection, sundering 10 insurgence, insurgency, opposition, revolution
incite ~: 5 rouse 6 arouse, foment, stir up, whip up, work up 7 agitate 9 instigate
__ Rebellion: 5 Dorr's, Great, Sepoy, War of 6 Bacon's 7 Whiskey
rebellious: 4 wild 6 feisty, ornery, unruly 7 defiant, lawless, naughty, radical, wayward 8 contrary, disloyal, factious, indocile, mutinous, perverse, stubborn 9 alienated, bellicose, dissident, insurgent, obstinate, turbulent 10 disorderly, refractory, subversive, traitorous, unpeaceful
one: 6 defier
Rebel-Rouser (1958 song)
artist: Duane Eddy
Rebels
song: Wild Weekend (1963)
__ Rebels: 7 Running
Rebel, The
author: Albert Camus
Rebel, The (ABC/NBC western)
cast: Nick Adams (Johnny Yuma)
theme singer: Johnny Cash
Rebel Without a Cause (1955 film)
cast: Jim Backus, James Dean, Sal Mineo, Natalie Wood
director: Nicholas Ray
Rebel Yell (1984 song)
artist: Billy Idol
reboant: 5 forte, noisy 7 blaring, booming, jarring, pealing, rackety, raucous, roaring 8 crashing, piercing, plangent, rumbling, sonorous, strident, turned up 9 big-voiced, clamorous, deafening 10 boisterous, resounding, stentorian, strepitous, thundering, uproarious, vociferous
reboot, require a: 5 crash
rebound: 4 echo, heal, mend 5 carom, rally 6 bounce, carrom, glance, pick up, recoil, return, revive, spring 7 get well, recover, reflect 8 backfire, comeback, kick back, overcome, reaction, ricochet, snap back 9 boomerang, get better 10 bounce back, convalesce, recuperate, rejuvenate, spring back
shot after a ~: 5 tip-in
__ rebound: 5 on the
rebounding: 9 resilient
rebozo: 5 scarf
Rebozo: 4 Bebe
rebuff: 2 no 3 cut, dig, nix 4 barb, deny, gibe, go-by, jeer, jibe, mock, shun, slam, slap, slur, snub, veto 5 abuse, check, chide, decry, knock, libel, repel, scorn, spurn, taunt 6 bounce, defame, defeat, denial, deride, dump on, heckle, ignore, impugn, insult, malign, offend, oppose, pass on, pass up, put off, rebuke, refuse, reject, resist, slight, vilify 7 affront, asperse, beat off, calumny, catcall, censure, decline, degrade, disdain, dismiss, exclude, fend off, hold off, mockery, neglect, obloquy, offense, put-down, rank out, refusal, reprove, repulse, say no to, setback, slander, tell off, traduce 8 belittle, brush-off, contempt, denounce, derision, disallow, hard time, ignoring, push back, ridicule, send away, stave off, turn away, turn back, turndown, vilipend 9 aspersion, blackball, cast aside, cheap shot, contumely, denigrate, discredit, disparage, disregard, humiliate, lash out at, rejection, reprimand, repudiate 10 calumniate, defamation, discourage, disrespect, nonconsent, opposition, opprobrium, resistance, thumbs down
rebuild: 3 fix 6 reform 7 restore 8 overhaul
rebuilt: 5 fixed 9 good as new
rebuke: 3 fry, pay, rag, rap, rip, row, zap 4 flay, rake, read, slap, snub, twit 5 blame, chide, scold, sit on 6 berate, carp on, earful, jump on, lean on, lesson, monish, oppose, rating, rebuff 7 bawl out, censure, chew out, chiding, correct, go after, jawbone, lambast, lay into, lecture, put-down, refusal, reproof, reprove, repulse, rip into, tell off, tick off, upbraid 8 admonish, berating, denounce, hard time, lambaste, reproach, reproval, scolding, sound off 9 castigate, criticize, dress down, excoriate, exprobate, going-over, lash out at, ostracism, reprehend, reprimand, talking-to, tear apart 10 admonition, affliction, bawling-out, chewing-out, correction, punishment, take to task, telling-off, upbraiding
rebuker: 5 scold, shrew 6 chider 9 henpecker, termagant
rebus: 6 puzzle
rebut: 4 deny 5 belie, parry, quash 6 answer, negate, oppose, refute, retort 7 confute, counter, dispute, ward off 8 confound, disprove, overturn 9 discredit, shoot down 10 contradict, controvert, disconfirm, prove false, prove wrong
rebuttal: 6 answer, denial, retort, ripost 7 riposte 8 comeback, feedback, negation, response 9 rejoinder 10 refutation
rec __: 4 room
rec. __: 3 sec.
recalcitrance: 4 sass 7 bravado 8 back talk, defiance 10 opposition, resistance
recalcitrant: 4 wild 6 ornery, unruly, wilful 7 defiant, naughty, piggish, radical, wayward, willful 8 contrary, indocile, opposing, stubborn, untoward 9 fractious, obstinate, pigheaded, reluctant, resistant, resisting, unwilling 10 rebellious, refractory
be ~: 4 balk 5 demur 6 refuse, resist
recalibrate: 5 alter, right, shift 7 rectify, redress
recall: 4 cite, lift, mind, stir 5 annul, educe, evoke, flash, renew, rouse, think, unsay, waken 6 abjure, arouse, awaken, cancel, elicit, memory, recant, remind, repeal, retain, revive, revoke, summon 7 bethink, dismiss, extract, flash on, nullify, rescind, retract, reverse, suspend, think of 8 forswear, hark back, look back, nail down, override, overrule, palinode, recision, remember, take back, withdraw 9 anamnesis, annulment, discharge, dismantle, foreswear, hindsight, recognize, recollect, reinstate, reminisce, think back 10 bear in mind, disqualify, keep in mind, rescission, retraction, retrospect, revocation, withdrawal
cause: 6 defect
in Britain: 5 rub up
__ recall: 5 total
__ recall...: 3 As I
__ Recall: 5 Total 7 Perfect
recant: 4 deny, void 5 annul, unsay,

welsh 6 abjure, cancel, disown, recall, renege, repeal, revoke 7 back off, back out, disavow, nullify, rescind, retract 8 abnegate, abrogate, back down, call back, dial back, disclaim, forswear, renounce, take back, withdraw 9 back-pedal, backtrack, foreswear, repudiate, weasel out, worm out of 10 apostatize, contradict

recap: 4 tire 5 sum up 6 précis, review, wrap-up 7 recount, rundown, run over, summary 8 condense, synopsis 9 reiterate, summarize 10 highlights

recapitulate: 5 brief, sum up 6 detail, recite, rehash, repeat, replay, review, reword 7 iterate, outline, recount, restate, run over 8 hark back, rehearse, rephrase 9 epitomize, reiterate, summarize 10 paraphrase

recapitulation: 6 résumé 7 outline, recital, rundown, summary

recapture: 6 redeem, regain, rescue 7 get back, recover 8 retrieve, take back 9 reacquire

recast: 5 alter 6 modify, revise, reword 8 innovate 9 translate

recede: 3 die, dip, ebb 4 back, drop, fade, fall, sink, wane 5 abate, close, lapse, taper 6 depart, die off, go away, go back, lessen, narrow, reduce, retire, return, shrink 7 abridge, compact, curtail, decline, die down, dwindle, regress, relapse, retract, retreat, shorten, subside, tail off 8 compress, condense, contract, decrease, diminish, draw back, fall back, flow back, head away, level off, slack off, taper off, withdraw 9 disappear, drain away 10 abbreviate, retrograde, retrogress

receding: 9 on the wane

receipt: 3 vou. 4 chit, slip, stub 5 scrip 6 letter, notice, taking, ticket 7 arrival, getting, release, revenue, voucher 8 delivery, intaking 9 accession, acquiring, admission, admitting, discharge, quittance, sales slip 10 acceptance
word: 4 paid

— receipt: 5 sales 6 return

receipts: 3 get, net 4 gain, gate, take, wage 5 gross, lucre, money, wages 6 handle, income, profit, return, take-in, taking 7 revenue, royalty 8 cash flow, earnings, proceeds 9 royalties 10 bottom line

receivable: 3 due 4 owed 5 owing 6 coming

— receivable: 8 accounts

receivables: 6 income, inflow

receive: 3 cop, get, see, win 4 bear, draw, earn, gain, grab, have, hear, hold, host, make, meet, pull, reap, snag, take 5 admit, catch, clear, greet, learn, let in, seize 6 accept, assume, come by, corral, derive, endure, gather, incept, induct, instal, invite, listen, obtain, permit, pick up, pocket, redeem, secure, show in, suffer, take in 7 acquire, bring in, collect, inherit, install, partake, procure, realize, sustain, undergo, usher in, welcome 8 arrogate, come into, initiate, meet with, perceive, pull down 9 apprehend, encounter, entertain, get hold of, go through, introduce, latch onto 10 experience, fall heir to, let through, shake hands
as news: 5 catch, learn 6 pick up 7 find out 8 discover 9 get wind of
a visitor: 4 mark, view 5 greet, pop in 6 attend, behold 7 receive 9 recognize 10 anticipate
enthusiastically: 5 lap up
likely to ~: 5 in for

—-received: 4 well

receiver: 3 set 4 dish 5 donee, payee, phone, radio 9 inheritor
holder: 6 cradle
wide ~: 3 end 7 gridder 10 footballer

— receiver: 4 wide

receiving
area: 5 foyer, lobby 8 anteroom

receiving —: 3 end 4 line

recent: 3 new 4 late, past 5 fresh, novel, today, young 6 latter, modern 7 current, just out, newborn 8 contempo, neoteric, up-to-date 9 immediate, latter-day 10 newfangled, present-day
combining form: 2 ne- 3 neo- 4 ceno-
more ~: 5 later 6 latter 9 following
most ~: 4 last 6 latest, newest 8 up-to-date
not ~: 5 olden
past: 9 yesterday 10 not long ago

recently: 4 anew, just 5 newly 6 afresh, lately, of late 7 freshly, just now 8 latterly 9 currently, yesterday 10 not long ago

receptacle: 3 bin, box, can, cup, jug, pot, vat 4 bowl, case, pail, slot, tray, vase 5 pouch, purse, stein 6 ashcan, basket, bunker, hamper, holder, hopper, pocket, vessel 7 humidor 8 trash can 9 container, reservoir 10 repository
water ~: 5 basin

reception: 2 do 3 tea 4 ball 5 levee, party, salon 6 affair, at home, buffet, dinner, lounge, soiree, supper 7 banquet, matinee, meeting, receipt, welcome 8 function, greeting, reaction, response 9 accession, admission, encounter, enrolment, festivity, gathering, induction, treatment 10 absorption, acceptance, enrollment, salutation
aid: 4 dish 6 aerial 10 rabbit ears
area: 5 foyer, lobby, salon 6 lounge, parlor
in India: 6 durbar
interference: 4 snow 6 static
offering: 5 punch 6 canapé

reception —: 4 desk, room

receptionist's call: 4 next

receptive: 4 open 5 alert, quick, ready 6 bright 7 liberal, passive, pliable, sensory 8 amenable, catholic, friendly, pushover, swayable, tolerant 9 acceptant, favorable, observant, sensitive, sensorial, welcoming 10 accessible, hospitable, interested, open-minded, responsive

— receptor: 4 beta 5 alpha

recess: 3 bay, gap 4 apse, cell, cove, dent, drop, fork, halt, hole, lull, nook, rest, rise, slot, stop 5 angle, arbor, bower, break, crypt, heart, inlet, letup, mouth, niche, oriel, pause, shake, space 6 alcove, ambush, carrel, cavity, closet, corner, cranny, crutch, cutoff, depths, drop it, grotto, hiatus, hollow, indent, layoff, socket 7 adjourn, break up, carrell, closure, cubicle, holiday, interim, leisure, opening, reaches, respite, retreat, take ten, time-out 8 abeyance, break off, breather, call time, dissolve, downtime, free time, intermit, playtime, prorogue, sideline, take five, vacation 9 cessation, embrasure, happy hour, interlude, put on hold, terminate 10 depression, penetralia, pigeonhole, suspension, take a break

recession: 3 ebb 4 bust, slip 5 lapse, slide, slump 7 decline 8 bad times, collapse, downturn, reversal, shakeout 9 bottom-out, deflation, departure, hard times, inflation, rainy days 10 bankruptcy, depression, stagnation

Recessional
author: Rudyard Kipling

recessive —: 4 gene

recharging, in need of: 4 dead

recherché: 4 rare 6 arcane, exotic, unique 7 special, unusual 8 precious, singular, uncommon

recidivate: 5 lapse 6 revert 7 regress, relapse 8 fall back, slip back 10 retrogress

recidivism: 8 apostasy

Recife: 4 city, port, town
city near ~: 5 Natal
locale: 6 Brazil

recipe: 4 dish 6 design, method 7 formula, process, program 8 compound 9 direction, procedure, technique 10 directions
abbr.: 3 tbs., tsp. 4 tbsp.
amount: 3 cap 4 dash 5 pinch 6 cupful
direction: 3 add 4 bake, beat, boil, chop, dice, heat, stir 5 add in, sauté, scald
part: 4 step
phrase: 3 à la 8 au gratin

recipient: 5 donee, payee 6 sendee 7 legatee

reciprocal: 6 common, double, fellow, mutual, shared 7 related, similar 8 matching, relative, requited 9 alternate, bilateral, companion, dependant, dependent, duplicate, exchanged 10 changeable, coordinate, equivalent

reciprocally: 7 by turns, jointly 8 mutually, together 9 in concert
prefix: 5 inter-

reciprocate: 4 swap, swop 5 equal, match, repay, reply 6 return 7 requite, respond 8 exchange 9 alternate, retaliate

reciprocated: 6 mutual

reciprocity: 5 trade 8 exchange 9 tit for tat 10 quid pro quo

recision: 6 recall 7 voiding 9 canceling

recital: 3 gig 4 tale 5 fable, story 6 litany, report 7 account, concert, musical, reading, telling 8 delivery, musicale, relation 9 detailing, narration, narrative, portrayal, recountal, rehearsal, rendering, rendition, statement 10 recounting, repetition
give a ~: 4 play, sing 5 dance 7 perform
hall: 5 odeon, odeum 7 theater, theatre
instrument: 4 harp 5 organ, piano
offering: 4 duet, solo 5 piece 6 encore, sonata

Recital of the Dog
author: David Rabe

recitation: 3 say 4 talk 5 piece 6 appeal, lesson, litany, report, speech 7 address, lecture, monolog, oration, passage, telling 8 delivery, exercise, speaking 9 discourse, monologue, narrating, narration, quotation, rehearsal, rendering, selection, statement, utterance 10 confession, declaiming, discussion, recounting, vocalizing

recitative
kin: 4 aria 6 arioso

recite: 3 say 4 read, tell 5 chant, enact, quote, reply, speak, state, utter 6 answer, convey, detail, impart, incant, intone, parrot, relate, render, repeat, report, retell 7 address, declaim, deliver, enlarge, explain, itemize, lecture, mention, narrate, perform, picture, portray, recount, reel off 8 describe, rehearse, set forth 9 delineate, discourse, dramatize, enumerate, expatiate, hold forth, interpret, rattle off 10 account for
dramatically: 3 act 5 emote, orate 7 perform, playact
in a monotone: 5 thrum

reciter: 6 orator
verse ~: 4 poet 8 poetizer 9 sonneteer, versifier

reckless: 4 rash, wild 5 blind, brash, hasty, kooky 6 daring, kookie, madcap, unwary, unwise, wanton 7 lawless 8 carefree, careless, feckless, headlong, heedless, hopeless, mindless, off-guard, pell-mell, prodigal 9 audacious, breakneck, daredevil, desperate, foolhardy, haphazard, hotheaded, imprudent, negligent, unadvised, uncareful, unhearing, unheedful, venturous 10 ill-advised, incautious, indiscreet, profligate, regardless, sophomoric, unbothered, willy-nilly
activity: 5 stunt
one: 5 darer

Reckless Ecstasy
author: Carl Sandburg

recklessly: 5 madly 8 pell-mell 9 fervently, headfirst, like crazy

recklessness: 5 folly, haste 7 abandon 8 audacity

reckon: 3 add, put, sum, tot 4 call, cast, deem, foot, hold, make, rate, take, tell, tote, view 5 add up, count, fancy, gauge, guess, infer, judge, opine, place, tally, think, total, tot up 6 assess, assume, bank on, cipher, esteem, expect,

figure, gather, number, plan on, regard, rely on, size up, square, take it, tote up **7** account, believe, build on, compute, count on, imagine, measure, project, suppose, surmise, suspect, think of, tick off, trust in **8** appraise, conclude, consider, depend on, estimate, evaluate, keep tabs, look upon, theorize **9** build upon, calculate, count upon, enumerate, figure out, keep score **10** bargain for, conjecture, count heads, count noses, understand
with: **4** face **5** treat **6** handle **7** foresee **8** consider **10** bear in mind, take note of
(with): **4** cope, deal
__ reckoner: **5** ready
reckoning: **3** due, fee, IOU, sum, tab **4** bill, cost, debt **5** check, count, grunt, guess, price, score, tally **6** adding, charge, reward **7** account, bad news, invoice, working **8** addition, counting, estimate, figuring **9** appraisal, ciphering, dependant, dependent, statement, summation **10** arithmetic, assessment, estimation, settlement
final ~: **3** end **6** payoff, result, upshot **7** outcome **9** punch line **10** bottom line, conclusion, settlement
__ reckoning: **4** dead **5** day of
Reckoning, The
author: David Halberstam
reclaim: **6** redeem, reform, regain, rescue **7** get back, recover, salvage **8** retrieve, take back **9** reacquire **10** rejuvenate, repurchase
recline: **3** lay, lie, tip **4** cant, heel, lean, list, loll, rest, tilt **5** relax, slant, slope **6** lounge, repose, sprawl, unwind **7** lay down, lie down, stretch **10** stretch out
reclined: **4** lain
recliner: **4** lier, seat **5** chair **6** chaise, rocker **9** furniture
reclining: **5** prone **6** at rest **9** prostrate, recumbent
recluse: **3** nun **4** monk **5** friar, loner **6** hermit **7** ascetic, eremite, isolato **8** anchoret, cenobite, eremitic, hermetic, homebody, isolated, monastic, reserved, retiring, secluded, solitary **9** anchorite, religious, solitaire, withdrawn **10** antisocial, cloistered, hermitlike, monastical, troglodyte, unsociable
reclusive: **3** shy **5** aloof, loner **6** lonely, modest **7** ascetic, bashful, distant, private **8** eremitic, hermetic, isolated, monastic, reserved, reticent, retiring, secluded, shielded, solitary **9** diffident, nonpublic, withdrawn **10** antisocial, cloistered, hermitlike, monastical, unsociable
reclusiveness: **7** secrecy **8** solitude **9** hermitage, isolation, seclusion
recognition: **3** ken **4** fame, plum, puff, rave **5** award, honor, kudos, sense **6** avowal, credit, esteem, memory, notice, praise, recall, regard, renown, salute, thanks, tumble **7** acclaim, laurels, respect, strokes, tribute **8** approval, greeting, high sign, noticing **9** admission, allowance, attention, awareness, detection, discovery, gratitude, reception **10** acceptance, double take, perception
sound: **2** oh
words of ~: **4** I see **5** got it
__ recognition: **5** voice **6** speech **7** pattern
recognizable: **5** clear, plain, vivid **6** cogent **7** evident, express, obvious **8** apparent, distinct, explicit, knowable, manifest, palpable **9** graspable **10** spelled out
recognize: **3** nod, own, peg, see, tab, tag **4** avow, cite, espy, find, hail, know, make, nail, name, note, okay, spot, tell **5** admit, adopt, agree, allow, catch, go for, grant, greet, honor, place, sight, thank **6** accept, assent, comply, descry, detect, fess up, finger, notice, recall, remark, salute, verify **7** approve, bethink, concede, confess, discern, flash on, include, make out, mention, observe, realize, respect, welcome **8** accredit, diagnose, identify, perceive, pinpoint, remember, sanction, stand for **9** apprehend, entertain, put up with, recollect, sign off on **10** appreciate, bear in mind, comprehend, concur with, give the nod, keep in mind, understand
as an undercover cop: **4** name **6** finger
don't ~: **5** scorn **6** ignore
recognized: **5** known, noted, sound **6** public **8** official, orthodox, standard **9** canonical, customary, well-known
to be: **6** seen as
recoil: **4** balk, jerk, jump, kick, reel, turn **5** baulk, blink, carom, cower, demur, dodge, quail, quake, react, shake, shirk, start, stick, waver, wince **6** blanch, blench, bounce, carrom, cringe, falter, flinch, resile, return, shrink, spring, swerve, writhe **7** rebound, shudder, shy away, stickle, tremble **8** backfire, draw back, hesitate, pull back, reaction, step back, turn away, withdraw **10** shrink away, spring back
from: **4** duck, hate **5** abhor, avoid, dodge, skirt **6** detest, eschew, loathe **7** deplore, despise, disdain **8** execrate, sidestep **9** abominate
recollect: **4** cite, mind, stir **5** flash, place, quote, rouse, think, waken **6** arouse, awaken, recall, relive, remind, retain, revive, summon **7** bethink, flash on **8** hark back, remember **9** conjure up, recognize, reminisce **10** bear in mind, call to mind, keep in mind, look back on
recollection: **3** bio **6** memoir, memory **9** biography, life story
recolor: **3** dye
recombinant __: **3** DNA
recommence: **5** renew **6** pick up, reopen, resume, take up **7** restart **8** continue, go on with
recommend: **4** back, laud, move, plug, tout, urge **5** exalt, extol, favor, prize, refer, steer, value **6** advise, enjoin, esteem, exhort, extoll, hold up, praise, second, uphold **7** acclaim, advance, applaud, approve, confirm, counsel, endorse, glorify, indorse, justify, magnify, promote, propose, put on to, stand by, suggest **8** advocate, eulogize, front for, nominate, sanction, speak for, vouch for **9** celebrate, introduce, prescribe **10** come up with, compliment, felicitate, put forward
recommendation: **3** tip **4** plug **5** order **6** advice, motion, praise **7** counsel **8** advocacy, approval, blessing, good word, guidance, proposal, sanction **9** direction, reference
form of ~: **3** ltr. **6** letter
recompense: **3** due, fee, fix, pay **4** comp, wage **5** atone, repay, right, wages **6** amends, ante up, grease, make up, offset, pay for, put out, recoup, refund, return, reward, salary, square **7** balance, cough up, deserts, expiate, justice, pay back, payment, recover, redress, requite, satisfy **8** atone for, equalize, make good, retrieve, swing for **9** allowance, atonement, emolument, indemnify, make up for, reimburse, repayment, spring for **10** make amends, propitiate
old-style: **4** meed
recon: **3** spy **6** patrol **7** mission, overfly
goal: **5** intel
one on ~: **3** spy **5** scout **7** spotter
plane: **5** AWACS
reconcile: **3** fit, fix **4** cool, suit, tune **5** adapt, atone, fix up, quiet, yield **6** accept, accord, adjust, attune, make up, pacify, resign, settle, square, submit **7** appease, arrange, assuage, balance, compose, conform, correct, mediate, patch up, placate, rectify, resolve, reunite, win over **8** accustom, mitigate, regulate **9** acquiesce, arbitrate, get used to, harmonize, integrate, intercede, intervene, make peace, put up with **10** conciliate, coordinate, propitiate
reconciliation: **5** peace, truce **9** mediation
recondite: **4** dark, deep, hard **5** heavy **6** arcane, hidden, mystic, occult, orphic, secret **7** cryptic, learned, obscure **8** abstract, abstruse, academic, esoteric, hermetic, involved, mystical, pedantic, profound **9** concealed, cryptical, difficult, scholarly **10** far-fetched, mysterious, pedantical, unfamiliar, unknowable
recondition: **3** fix **4** mend **5** renew **6** change, revive **7** furbish, restore **8** overhaul **9** refurbish
reconnaissance: **4** look **6** survey **8** scouting
run ~: **3** spy **5** scout **6** patrol, survey **7** bird-dog
__ reconnaissance: **6** aerial
reconnoiter: **3** spy **5** range, scout, spy on, watch **6** survey **7** explore, inspect, observe **8** check out, scout out, stake out
reconnoiterer: **5** scout
reconsider: **6** rehash, review **7** revisit, reweigh, sleep on **8** mull over, reassess **9** reexamine, think over **10** think twice
reconstruct: **3** fix **4** copy, do up **5** alter, fix up, patch **6** deduce, doctor, recast, reform, remake, remold, repair, retool, revamp, rework **7** build up, correct, rebuild, remodel, replace, restore **8** make over, overhaul, recreate, renovate, reorient **9** modernize, replicate, reshuffle
Recontres
author: André Gide
record: **3** can, cut, dub, log, say, wax **4** book, copy, disk, file, film, list, mark, memo, note, post, read, show, tape **5** diary, enrol, enter, entry, paper, reign, score, story, table, tally, trace, video, write **6** annals, career, enroll, indite, insert, jacket, legend, memoir, notate, report, résumé, roster, script, scroll, ticket **7** almanac, archive, catalog, ceiling, chalk up, conduct, contain, dossier, explain, history, itemize, jot down, journal, lay down, maximum, minutes, monitor, point to, put down, set down, studies, witness, writing **8** archives, document, evidence, indicate, inscribe, mark down, memorial, monument, notation, point out, preserve, register, registry, tabulate, take down **9** audiotape, catalogue, chronicle, designate, directory, enumerate, inventory, keep count, keep score, put on file, statement, testimony, videotape, way of life, write down **10** background, experience, journalize, manuscript, memorandum, paper trail, photograph, put on paper, report card, tabulation, transcribe, transcript
academic ~: **6** grades
adjust the ~ book: **5** relog
as a complaint: **5** lodge
big ~ label: **3** MCA, RCA **6** Arista **7** Elektra **8** Atlantic, Columbia
break the ~ of: **3** top **4** beat, best, pass **5** outdo **6** better, exceed **7** eclipse, surpass **8** outshine, outstrip, surmount
British ~ label: **3** EMI
company: **5** label
cutter: **6** stylus
gold ~: **3** hit **5** smash **7** success, triumph **9** sensation
holder: **4** file **6** jacket, sleeve
jazz ~ label: **5** Verve
keeper: **5** clerk **6** scribe **9** archivist, historian **10** amanuensis
legal ~ book: **5** liber
like some ~ labels: **5** indie
mail-order ~ label: **4** K-Tel
make a ~: **3** cut **5** press
material: **5** vinyl
off the ~: **5** privy **6** secret **7** private, sub rosa **9** entre nous **10** unofficial

RE

old ~ label: **4** Atco, Okeh, Stax **5** Decca
org.: **4** RIAA
phonograph ~: **2** LP **4** disc, disk **5** album
player: **2** DJ **4** hi-fi, juke **5** phono **6** deejay, stereo **9** turntable **10** phonograph
producer's work: **3** mix
sample ~: **4** demo
speed: **3** rpm
surface: **4** side **5** A-side, B-side, side A, side B
track: **6** groove
without a ~: **5** clean
record __: **6** player
__ record: **4** gold, go on **5** on the, track
__-record: **4** tape **5** video
record book: **5** annal **6** annals
entry: **4** stat
suffix: **3** est
recorder: **4** wind **9** historian **10** bookkeeper, chronicler
cassette ~ letters: **3** mic
fodder: **4** tape
plug: **6** fipple
__ recorder: **4** tape **6** flight
recording: **2** CD, LP **4** tape **10** transcript
go back to the ~ studio: **5** remix
medium: **3** DAT **4** disc, disk, tape
studio apparatus: **5** mixer
tool: **4** mike
vinyl ~ type: **2** EP
__ recording: **4** tape **6** analog **7** digital
recordings: **4** trax
recording-tape
material: **5** Mylar
name: **3** TDK **6** Maxell **7** Memorex
records: **5** files, proof **6** annals **7** archive
book of public ~: **5** liber
check of ~: **5** audit
historical ~: **7** archive **9** chronicle
like old ~: **4** mono
place for ~: **5** shelf **7** cabinet
recount: **4** cite, echo, tell **5** cover, recap, state, track, voice **6** convey, depict, detail, recite, rehash, relate, repeat, report, set out, unload **7** itemize, iterate, mention, narrate, picture, portray, present, run down **8** describe, play back, rehearse **9** chronicle, delineate, enumerate, verbalize **10** run through
recountal: **4** saga, tale **5** diary, story **6** annals, memoir, report **7** history, journal, recital **9** chronicle, narration, narrative
recounted: **4** oral **5** vocal **6** spoken, verbal, voiced **7** uttered **9** vocalized
recounting: **7** recital **9** narration, narrative **10** recitation
recoup: **5** repay **6** redeem, refund, regain **7** get back, get well, recover, recruit, requite, satisfy, win back **8** make good, retrieve **9** make up for, reacquire, reimburse, repossess **10** compensate, recompense, remunerate
recourse: **3** aid, out **4** help **5** shift **6** appeal, option, refuge, remedy, resort, way out **8** resource **9** expedient
recover: **4** find, gain, grow, heal, mend, save **5** rally, renew **6** better, obtain, offset, perk up, pick up, ransom, recoup, redeem, regain, repair, rescue, resume, retake, revive **7** balance, catch up, get back, get over, get well, rebound, reclaim, recruit, refresh, replevy, restore, salvage, survive, win back **8** increase, make good, overcome, reoccupy, replevin, retrieve, snap back, take back **9** bring back, extricate, get better, reacquire, recapture, reimburse, repossess **10** bounce back, come around, compensate, convalesce, forge ahead, get in shape, recompense, recuperate, rediscover, rejuvenate
quick to ~: **9** resilient
recovered: **4** well **5** sound, whole **7** healthy
from: **4** over, past
recovering: **6** better **8** improved **9** healthier, improving, on the mend
recovery: **5** rally **7** revival **8** comeback
regimen: **5** rehab
recovery __: **4** room
recreancy: **9** defection, desertion **10** disloyalty
recreant: **5** false, knave, sissy, timid **6** afraid, bad hat, coward, craven, rascal, scared, untrue, yellow **7** chicken, crybaby, dastard, fearful, hellion, milksop, wimpish **8** apostate, betrayer, cowardly, defector, deserter, disloyal, poltroon, renegade, turncoat, two-faced **9** dastardly, faithless, fraidy-cat, jellyfish, spineless, two-timing **10** delinquent, frightened, perfidious, scaredy-cat, traitorous, unfaithful
recreate: **4** rest **5** enact, relax, revel **6** divert, unwind **7** refresh **9** replicate **10** regenerate
recreation: **3** fun **4** ball, ease, game, play, rest **5** games, hobby, mirth, R and R, sport **6** frolic, laughs, picnic, relief, repose, sports **7** disport, holiday, jollity, leisure, pastime, rollick **8** exercise, field day, free time, hilarity, interest, playtime, pleasure, vacation **9** amusement, athletics, avocation, diversion, enjoyment, festivity
place: **3** gym **4** park, YMCA, YMHA, YWCA, YWHA **9** gymnasium
recreation __: **4** room
recreational
activity: **4** game **5** sport **7** pastime **9** athletics
vehicle: **3** ATV **5** canoe
recreational __: **7** vehicle
recrimination: **5** blame
recriminatory: **8** vengeful
rec room: **3** den
item: **2** TV **3** VCR **5** TV set
recruit: **2** GI **4** gain, levy, pleb, tiro, tyro **5** draft, enrol, newie, plebe, raise, renew **6** airman, better, call up, engage, enlist, enroll, fill up, greeny, helper, induct, muster, novice, obtain, recoup, regain, repair, revive, rookie, sailor, select, sign on, sign up, supply, take in, take on **7** augment, build up, convert, deliver, draftee, impress, improve, jack tar, learner, new hand, procure, recover, refresh, restore, round up, soldier, store up, trainee, win over **8** beginner, initiate, mobilize, neophyte, newcomer, retrieve, selectee, shanghai **9** conscript, fledgling, greenhorn, layperson, legionary, novitiate, proselyte, reanimate, reinforce, replenish, repossess, volunteer **10** apprentice, call to arms, recuperate, strengthen, tenderfoot
fraternity ~: **6** rushee
like a new ~: **5** green
see also army, soldier
recruited, be: **6** enlist
recruiter: **5** hirer, scout
goal: **5** quota
regulating org.: **4** NCAA
recruiting poster word: **3** you **4** want
Recruit, The (2003 film)
cast: Colin Farrell, Al Pacino
recruit-to-be: **4** one A
rect-
kin: **4** orth-
__ recta: **4** cyma
rectangle: **6** isogon **7** polygon
shaped state: **3** Wyo. **4** Colo. **7** Wyoming **8** Colorado
rectangular: **2** ob. **6** oblong
dimension: **5** width **6** length
groove: **4** dado
rectification: **7** redress
rectifier, TV: **5** diode
rectify: **3** fix **4** cure, mend **5** amend, debug, emend, fix up, right, scrub **6** adjust, doctor, go over, pick up, reform, remedy, repair, revise, settle, square **7** clean up, correct, expiate, improve, launder, redress, shape up **8** dial back, make good, put right, regulate, set right **9** do justice, make right, make up for, reconcile **10** counteract, straighten
rectilinear: **6** in a row **8** straight **10** horizontal
rectitude: **4** good **5** honor **6** virtue **7** decency, honesty, justice, probity **8** goodness, morality, veracity **9** character, integrity, propriety **10** honestness, principles
recto: **4** page
opposite: **5** verso
rector: **5** padre **6** cleric, leader, parson, pastor, priest **8** minister **9** principal
assistant: **6** curate
representative: **5** vicar
Rector of Justin, The
author: Louis Auchincloss
rectory: **5** manse
rectus: **6** muscle
locale: **3** eye
recumbent: **4** flat **5** level, prone **6** supine **8** resupine **9** decumbent, lying down, prostrate, reclining, sprawling **10** horizontal, procumbent
be ~: **3** lie **4** laze, loll, rest **6** repose **7** lie down, recline
one: **4** lier
recuperate: **4** gain, heal, mend **5** rally **6** look up, perk up, pick up **7** get well, rebound, recover, recruit **9** come along, get better **10** ameliorate, bounce back, convalesce
recuperating: **9** on the mend
recur: **4** echo **5** cycle **6** repeat, return **7** persist **8** continue, intermit **9** come and go
recurrence: **6** return **7** atavism **9** duplicate, frequency
recurrent: **6** cyclic **7** regular **8** cyclical, frequent, habitual, haunting, iterated, periodic, unwaning **9** alternate, continual, continued, irregular, perennial, perpetual **10** monotonous, repetitive
recurrently: **4** much **5** again, often **8** ofttimes **10** oftentimes
recurring: **6** cyclic **8** periodic **9** perpetual
idea: **5** motif, theme **9** leitmotif
melody: **5** motif, thema
music with a ~ theme: **5** rondo
recusant: **7** lawless, radical **8** indurate
recyclable item: **3** can **5** empty, scrap **6** bottle **9** newspaper
recycle: **5** reuse
recycled: **4** used **10** hand-me-down, secondhand
recycling __: **3** bin
recycling station: **8** landfill
red: **3** hot **4** gory, Marx, port, rare, rose, rosy, ruby, rust, wine **5** aglow, brick, Gamay, Lenin, Médoc, Pinot, Rioja, ruddy **6** ablush, Barolo, bloody, blowsy, blowzy, cerise, cherry, claret, florid, garnet, Maoist, maroon, russet, Soviet, Stalin, titian **7** Amarone, Barbera, blowsed, blowzed, carmine, Chianti, Concord, crimson, flaming, flushed, fuchsia, glowing, magenta, Musigny, Pommard, scarlet, Trotsky **8** blushing, burgundy, Cabernet, cardinal, chestnut, Dolcetto, geranium, inflamed, Leninist, muscatel, port-wine, rubicund, sanguine **9** Bardolino, bloodshot, Bolshevik, Communist, irritated, lambrusco, rubescent, Stalinist, sunburned, table wine, vermilion, Zinfandel **10** Beaujolais, Chambertin
and yellow: **6** orange
be in the ~: **3** owe
bluish ~: **9** cranberry
brownish ~: **5** brick **6** maroon
color: **4** rose, ruby, rust, wine **5** brick, coral, grape, poppy, rusty, sandy **6** cerise, cherry, claret, garnet, maroon **7** carmine, crimson, fuchsia, magenta, pimento, scarlet, sultana, vermeil **8** amaranth, cardinal, dubonnet, geranium, rubicund **9** carnation, cranberry, vermilion **10** strawberry
combining form: **6** erythr- **7** erythro-
dark ~: **4** puce, winy **5** brick, winey
dog in football: **5** blitz
dwarf: **4** star
dye: **3** azo **5** eosin, henna **6** eosine, kermes
ender: **3** bud, bug, cap, eye, top **4** bait, bird, coat, fish, head, line, poll, root, wing, wood **5** brick, shank, shirt, start **6** breast, headed
entry in ~: **4** debt **5** debit

flag: 5 alarm 6 caveat 7 caution, warning
flower: 3 mum 4 lily 5 lehua, peony, poppy, tulip 6 cosmos, salvia 7 day lily, rambler 8 camellia, geranium, japonica, marigold, oleander, rockrose, tamarisk 9 amaryllis, candytuft, cockscomb, hollyhock, ohia lehua, Oswego tea, snow plant, woundwort 10 nasturtium, poinsettia
giant: 4 Mira, star 5 S star 7 Antares
herring: 4 ploy, ruse 5 decoy 9 diversion 10 camouflage
hot: 5 zesty 7 peppery, piquant, pungent 8 seasoned
in heraldry: 5 gules
ink: 4 debt, loss 7 arrears, deficit 8 mortgage 9 arrearage, debenture, liability 10 obligation
in the ~: 9 insolvent
in the face: 6 ablush
it turns ~: 6 litmus
letters: 4 USSR
light: 4 flag 6 signal 7 caution, warning
make see ~: 3 irk 4 rile 5 anger, peeve, upset 6 enrage, madden
man in ~: 5 Santa 10 Santa Claus
meat: 4 beef 5 steak
one in the ~: 4 ower
on the inside: 4 rare
orangish ~: 5 poppy
paint the town ~: 5 revel 6 barhop 7 carouse, roister 8 cut loose, let loose, live it up 9 celebrate, make merry, raise Cain, whoop it up
pinkish ~: 4 rose
preceder: 5 amber
purplish ~: 4 rose, ruby 5 grape, murex 6 claret 7 carmine, crimson, fuchsia, magenta, sultana 8 amaranth, dubonnet 9 cranberry
raise a ~ flag: 4 warn 5 alert 6 tip off 7 caution
roll out the ~ carpet: 5 greet, honor 7 lionize, receive, welcome
see ~: 4 boil, fume, rage 6 get mad, rear up, seethe 7 bristle, flame up 8 get angry 9 blow a fuse 10 hit the roof
seeing ~: 3 mad 5 angry, irate, livid, upset 6 raging 7 furious 9 indignant
tape: 4 maze 5 delay 6 policy, system 8 protocol 9 paperwork, procedure, rigmarole 10 impediment
turn ~: 5 blush, flush
turning litmus ~: 6 acidic
vegetable: 4 beet
wave a ~ flag: 6 enrage 7 caution 8 forewarn
what ~ means: 4 stop
wine: 4 port, rosé 5 gamay, Médoc, pinot, Rioja, tavel 6 barolo, claret 7 Chianti, Concord, Musigny, Pommard 8 burgundy, Cabernet, Dolcetto, muscatel 9 Bardolino, lambrusco, Zinfandel 10 Beaujolais, Chambertin
wrap in ~ tape: 5 sit on 8 withhold
yellowish ~: 4 rust 5 brick, coral, rusty, sandy

red __: 3 ant, bay, dog, fox, hat, ink, tag 4 card, cell, cent, clay, deer, flag, line, meat, rose, snow, star, tape, tide, wine 5 alert, algae, count, dwarf, giant, light, rover, state 6 carpet, pepper, salmon 7 herring, snapper
red __ beet: 3 as a
red __ cell: 5 blood
red-__: 3 dog, eye, hot 5 faced 6 handed, headed, letter, pencil 7 blooded
red-__ day: 6 letter
red-__ gravy: 3 eye
red-__ sale: 3 tag
__ red: 3 see 4 fire, Mars 5 blood, brick, in the 6 cherry
Red: 3 sea 4 NLer 5 Adair, Foley, Norvo, river, Smith 6 Barber, Grange, Sovine 7 Buttons, Holzman, Nichols, Ruffing, Skelton 8 Auerbach 10 baseballer
Hall-of-Famer: 5 Bench, Perez, Roush
jet: 3 MiG
leader: 3 Mao
River locale: 5 China, Texas 7 Vietnam 8 Oklahoma 9 Louisiana
role for ~: 4 Clem
Sea locale: 6 Africa, Arabia
see also Russia
Red __: 3 Sea, Sox 4 Army, Dust, Hats, Heat, Mass, Wing 5 Alert, Angus, Baron, China, Cloud, Cross, Guard, River, Ryder, Sonja 6 Jacket, Square 7 Lobster
Red __ at Morning: 3 Sky
Red __ Chili Peppers: 3 Hot
Red __ for a Blue Lady: 5 Roses
Red __ in the Sunset: 5 Sails
Red __ Morning: 5 Sky at
Red __ of Courage, The: 5 Badge
Red __, The: 4 Lily, Pony, Room 5 Baron, House, Shoes
Red, __ and Blue!: 3 Hot
Red-__ League, The: 6 Headed
Red-__ Woman: 6 Headed
__ Red: 3 Big 4 I Saw 5 Beach 6 Simply 7 Eric the, Erik the
redact: 4 edit 5 emend 6 polish, refine, revise 7 correct, tighten, touch up 8 fine-tune 10 blue-pencil
jointly: 6 coedit
redaction: 6 change 7 editing, rewrite 8 revision 10 emendation
redactor: 6 editor
word: 4 dele, stet
redan: 4 fort 7 rampart 9 fieldwork 10 battlement
Red and the Black, The
author: Stendhal
character: 4 Abbé 5 Sorel 6 Julien 7 de Rênal 8 de La Mole
Red and White Domes
artist: Paul Klee
red as __: 5 a beet
Red Badge of Courage, The: 5 novel
author: Stephen Crane
setting: 8 Civil War
Red Balloon
artist: Paul Klee

Red Bank Boogie
composer: Count Basie
red-blooded: 4 hale, iron, wiry 5 beefy, burly, hardy, hefty, hunky, husky, lusty, stout, tough 6 brawny, hearty, mighty, potent, robust, rugged, sinewy, steely, stocky, sturdy, virile 7 doughty 8 athletic, forceful, indurate, muscular, powerful, puissant, stalwart, vigorous 9 Atlantean, energetic, Herculean, strapping, well-built 10 able-bodied, courageous
Redbone: 4 Leon
redbreast: 4 bird 5 robin
redbud: 4 tree
family: 6 legume
relative: *see* legume tree
redcap: 6 porter
burden: 3 bag 7 luggage 8 suitcase
domain: 5 depot
red-carpet treader: 3 VIP 7 bigshot, notable 8 luminary 9 celebrity, dignitary
Red Cedar, city on the: 7 Lansing
Red Cloud: 6 Indian
residence: 4 tipi 5 tepee 6 teepee
Redcoat: 4 Tory
Continental, to a ~: 3 foe 5 enemy
general: 4 Howe
red-complexioned: 5 ruddy
Red Cross
concern: 6 famine
founder: Clara Barton
supply: 4 sera 5 blood, serum
volunteer: 5 donor
Redd: 4 Foxx
Red Delicious: 5 apple
relative: *see* apple
redden: 3 dye 4 chap, glow, pink, rose, ruby, rust, tint 5 blush, color, flush, paint, rouge, ruddy 6 bloody, mantle, pinken, raddle, rubify, rubric, ruddle 7 crimson, roughen, suffuse 8 irritate 9 encarmine, rubricate
crack and ~: 4 chap
reddened: 4 sore 5 angry, ruddy 6 florid, tender 7 bruised 8 inflamed, rubicund 9 indignant
Reddi __: 3 Wip
Redding: 4 city, Otis, town
locale: 10 California
Redding, Otis
song: (Sittin' On) The Dock of the Bay (1968)
reddish: 5 ruddy 6 rufous 8 sanguine
brown: 6 titian
color: 3 bay 4 bole, foxy, plum, rust, sand 5 brass, cocoa, coral, flame, henna, lilac, ocher, ochre, rusty, umber 6 auburn, copper, ginger, orchid, russet, sorrel, walnut 7 petunia 8 chestnut, cinnamon, hyacinth, mahogany, rubicund 9 raspberry, tangerine 10 heliotrope
red dog: 4 game 8 card game
Red Dragon (2002 film)
cast: Ralph Fiennes, Anthony Hopkins, Harvey Keitel, Edward Norton, Emily Watson
homeland: 9 Australia
Reddy, Helen
song: Ain't No Way to Treat a Lady (1975)
Angie Baby (1974)
Delta Dawn (1973)
I Am Woman (1972)
I Don't Know How to Love Him (1971)
Keep On Singing (1974)
Leave Me Alone (1973)
Peaceful (1973)
Somewhere in the Night (1975)
You and Me Against the World (1974)
You're My World (1977)
redecorate: 4 redo 6 do over 8 make over
redeem: 4 cash, free, meet, save 5 cover, loose, repay 6 acquit, buy off, call in, cash in, change, defray, fulfil, offset, pay off, purify, ransom, recoup, reform, refund, regain, rescue, set off, settle, take in, unbind 7 abide by, absolve, balance, buy back, deliver, fulfill, get back, manumit, perform, receive, reclaim, recover, redress, release, replevy, restore, salvage, satisfy, set free, trade in, unchain, win back 8 adhere to, atone for, carry out, exchange, liberate, make good, outweigh, purchase, replevin, retrieve, unfetter 9 discharge, extricate, make up for, recapture, reinstate, repossess 10 compensate, emancipate, make amends, repurchase
redeemer: 6 savior 7 messiah, saviour 9 liberator
redemption: 6 cash-in, ransom 7 freedom 9 atonement, salvation
slip: 6 coupon, ticket 7 voucher
Redemption
author: Leon Uris
Redenbacher: 7 Orville
redesigned: 3 new 7 updated
redeye: 5 gravy, hooch 6 flight, hootch, whisky 7 alcohol, whiskey
gravy source: 3 ham
Red Eye (2005 film)
cast: Rachel McAdams, Cillian Murphy
director: Wes Craven
red-faced: 4 rosy 5 ruddy 6 blowsy, blowzy 7 ashamed, blowsed, blowzed
Redford, Robert: 5 actor 8 director
film: All the President's Men (1976)
Barefoot in the Park (1967)
Brubaker (1980)
Butch Cassidy and the Sundance Kid (1969)
The Candidate (1972)
The Chase, (1966)
The Clearing (2004)
Downhill Racer (1969)
The Electric Horseman (1979)
The Great Gatsby (1974)
The Great Waldo Pepper (1975)
Havana (1990)
The Horse Whisperer (1998)
The Hot Rock (1972)
Indecent Proposal (1993)
Inside Daisy Clover (1965)
Jeremiah Johnson (1972)
Legal Eagles (1986)
The Legend of Bagger Vance (2000)
Lions for Lambs (2007)
The Milagro Beanfield War (1988)
The Natural (1984)

RE

Ordinary People (1980, AA)
Out of Africa (1985)
Quiz Show (1994)
A River Runs Through It (1992)
Sneakers (1992)
The Sting (1973)
Tell Them Willie Boy Is Here (1969)
Three Days of the Condor (1975)
An Unfinished Life (2005)
Up Close & Personal (1996)
The Way We Were (1973)
Redgrave: 4 Lynn 7 Michael, Vanessa
Redgrave, Lynn: 7 actress
film: Georgy Girl (1966)
Redgrave, Vanessa: 7 actress
film: Agatha (1979)
Blowup (1966)
Deep Impact (1998)
Déjà Vu (1998)
The Devils (1971)
Howards End (1992)
Isadora (1968)
Julia (1977, AA)
Mary, Queen of Scots (1971)
Morgan! (1966)
Murder on the Orient Express (1974)
The Pledge (2001)
A Rumor of Angels (2002)
The Seven-Per-Cent Solution (1976)
Yanks (1979)
red-handed: 6 guilty 8 blamable, culpable, in the act 9 blameable 10 censurable, delinquent
catch ~: 3 bag, get, nab, net 4 bust, grab, nail, trap 5 catch, pinch, run in, seize 6 arrest, collar, snatch 7 capture, startle 8 surprise 9 apprehend, burst in on
redhead: 4 Ball, duck, Eric, Erik, fowl, Lucy
become a ~: 3 dye
dye: 5 henna
relative: *see* duck
Red-Headed League, The
author: Arthur Conan Doyle
red-headed, name meaning: 5 Rufus
Red Heat (1988 film)
cast: James Belushi, Peter Boyle, Arnold Schwarzenegger
red-hot: 3 new 4 avid 5 afire, angry, candy, eager, faddy, fresh, surly, testy 6 aflame, ardent, baking, fervid, gung-ho, raving, snappy, sultry, torrid 7 angered, blazing, burning, fervent, flaming, grouchy, in a stew, intense, peevish, ranting, uptight, zealous 8 brand-new, broiling, in a pique, seething, sizzling, up-to-date 9 irritable, querulous, rancorous, scorching 10 blistering, freaked out, oppressive, passionate, sweltering
see also angry
Red, Hot and Blue!: 7 musical
composer: Cole Porter
Red Hot Chili Peppers
lead singer: Kiedis
song: Scar Tissue (1999)
Soul to Squeeze (1993)
Under the Bridge (1992)
Red House Mystery, The
author: A.A. Milne
redingote: 4 coat 5 dress 6 jacket
red-ink amount: 4 debt, loss 5 debit 7 deficit
redirect: 5 alter, deter 6 divert 7 reroute
Redlands: 4 city, town
locale: 10 California
red-letter: 5 proud 6 banner 7 special 8 historic 9 memorable
sign: 4 Exit
red-letter __: 3 day
Red Light Special (1995 song)
artist: TLC
Red Lily, The
author: Anatole France
redline: 4 drop, omit, snip, trim, X out 5 erase, scrub 6 cancel, delete, efface, excise, remove, rub off, rub out 7 blot out, exclude, expunge, scissor, scratch, wipe out 8 cross off, cross out 9 eliminate, expurgate, strike out 10 obliterate
__ Red Line, The: 4 Thin
redly: 6 ablush
Redmond: 4 city, town
locale: 10 Washington
redness: 5 flush
exemplar of ~: 4 beet
redo: 4 edit 5 fix up 6 change, modify, revise, update 7 remodel 8 make over, overhaul, renovate, work over 9 modernize, refurbish, replicate 10 redecorate
Red October: 3 sub 7 Russian 9 submarine
Red Oleanders
author: Rabindranath Tagore
redolence: 4 odor 5 aroma, scent, smell 6 stench 7 bouquet 9 balminess, fragrance
redolent: 5 spicy, sweet 6 spicey 7 odorous, scented 8 aromatic, fragrant 10 suggestive
Redondo Beach: 4 city, town
locale: 10 California
__ Red One, The: 3 Big
redouble: 5 rally 7 magnify 9 intensify
redoubt: 4 fort 7 citadel, defense 8 fastness, fortress 10 stronghold
Redoubt: 7 volcano
locale: 6 Alaska
redoubtable: 4 hale, iron, wiry 5 beefy, burly, hardy, hefty, hunky, husky, lusty, stout, tough 6 brawny, hearty, mighty, potent, robust, rugged, sinewy, steely, stocky, strong, sturdy, virile 7 awesome, doughty, valiant 8 athletic, fearsome, forceful, indurate, muscular, powerful, puissant, stalwart, vigorous 9 Atlantean, Herculean, strapping, well-built 10 able-bodied, red-blooded
red-pencil: 4 dele 5 bleep 6 censor, delete, excise, remove 8 cross off, cross out 9 expurgate, strike out 10 bowdlerize
Red Planet: 4 Mars
redpoll: 4 bird
Red Poll: 3 cow 4 bull 6 bovine, cattle
Red Pony, The
author: John Steinbeck
redraft: 6 revise 8 revision
Red Raiders: 9 Texas Tech
Red, Red Rose, A
author: Robert Burns
redress: 3 aid, pay 4 cure, ease, help, mend 5 amend, annul, atone, right 6 adjust, amends, avenge, cancel, change, make up, negate, offset, pay for, redeem, reform, refund, relief, remedy, repair, return, revise, reward, square 7 balance, correct, even out, expiate, justice, payment, rectify, relieve, renewal, restore 8 dial back, negative, put right, regulate, reprisal, requital, revision 9 amendment, atonement, balancing, do justice, expiation, frustrate, indemnity, make up for, quittance, remission, reworking, vengeance, vindicate 10 assistance, compensate, correction, counteract, make amends, neutralize, offsetting, punishment, recompense, remodeling, reparation, turn around
seek ~: 3 sue 8 litigate 9 prosecute
__ Red Riding Hood: 6 Little
Red River (1948 film): 5 oater 7 western
cast: Walter Brennan, Montgomery Clift, Joanne Dru, John Wayne
director: Howard Hawks
role: 4 Tess
Red River __: 3 War 6 Valley
Red River of the North
locale: 8 Manitoba 9 Minnesota
Red River Valley
locale: 4 N. Dak.
Red Roof Inn: 5 motel
alternative: *see* motel
Red Room, The
author: August Strindberg
Red Rose: 3 tea
alternative: 6 Lipton, Nestea, Salada, Tetley 7 Bigelow 8 Twinings
Red Roses for a Blue Lady (1965 song)
artist: Vic Dana
Reds: 4 nine, team
home: 10 Cincinnati
org.: 3 MLB, NLC
rival: *see* baseball team
sport: 8 baseball
Reds (1981 film)
cast: Warren Beatty, Diane Keaton, Jack Nicholson, Maureen Stapleton
director: Warren Beatty
role: 4 Emma, Reed 7 Goldman
Red Sea
access: 4 Suez 9 Suez Canal
ancient ~ kingdom: 5 Nubia
arm: 5 Akaba, Aqaba
boat: 3 dau, dow 4 dhow
country: 5 Egypt, Sudan, Yemen 7 Eritrea
gulf: 4 Suez
island: 5 Tiran
port: 5 Jedda, Jidda
region: 4 Asir 5 Hejaz, Hijaz, Negeb, Negev 6 Arabia, Hedjaz
strait: 5 Tiran
town: 4 Elat 5 Eilat, Elath
redshank: 4 bird
Red Shoes, The (1948 film)
cast: Moira Shearer
Redskins: 4 team 6 eleven
home: 10 Washington
org.: 3 NFC, NFL
rival: *see* NFL team
sport: 8 football
red snapper: 4 fish
Red Sox: 3 ten 4 team
Hall-of-Famer: 5 Doerr 6 Cronin 8 Williams 11 Yastrzemski
home: 6 Boston
nickname: 3 Yaz
org.: 3 ALE, MLB
rival: *see* baseball team
sport: 8 baseball
__ Red Spot: 5 Great
Red Square figure: 5 Lenin
redstart: 4 bird
residence: 4 nest
Red Storm: 10 Saint John's
red-tag __: 4 sale
redtop: 3 hay 5 grass
reduce: 3 cut, sag, sap 4 bant, bate, bump, bust, chop, clip, crop, curb, dice, diet, drop, ease, flag, mute, pare, ruin, slim, slow, thin, tire, trim, wane 5 abase, abate, allay, blunt, break, bring, crush, drain, drive, force, limit, lower, press, price, prune, quell, relax, shave, slash, smelt, taper 6 deaden, debase, deduct, defeat, demote, derate, digest, dilute, humble, impair, lessen, master, modify, narrow, powder, rebate, recede, shrink, soften, subdue, weaken 7 abridge, cheapen, compact, conquer, cripple, curtail, cut back, cut down, declass, deflate, degrade, demerit, deplete, depress, detract, disable, disrate, dwindle, exhaust, fall off, fatigue, lighten, mollify, qualify, scissor, shorten, thin out, whittle 8 bankrupt, bear down, beat down, bring low, close out, compress, condense, contract, decrease, diminish, discount, disgrade, downsize, enervate, enfeeble, mark down, minimize, mitigate, moderate, modulate, overcome, peter out, pull down, restrict, roll back, simplify, slim down, slow down, step down, take away, taper off, tone down, truncate, turn down, vanquish, wind down 9 attenuate, downgrade, go on a diet, humiliate, knock down, lose speed, overpower, pauperize, scale down, subjugate, telescope, undermine 10 abbreviate, debilitate, depreciate, devitalize, impoverish, lose weight
in rank: 4 bust 5 break 6 demote 7 degrade 8 take down 9 downgrade
speed: 4 slow 5 brake 8 slow down 10 decelerate
reduced: 3 cut, low 4 less, poor, slow 5 cheap, lower 6 on sale 7 limited, partial, sketchy 8 lessened, uncostly 9 condensed, half-price 10 compressed, synopsized, unfinished
in ~ circumstances: 5 needy
in value: 7 debased 8 degraded 9 worthless
reduce to __ of rubble: 5 a pile
reducing __: 5 agent
reduction: 3 cut 4 dent, drop, fall, lack, sale 5 let up 6 rebate, saving 7 bargain, cutback, decline, summary 8 decrease, discount,

rollback **9** abatement, allowance, decrement, deduction, lessening, remission, shrinkage **10** diminution
redundancy: 6 excess **8** overflow, plethora, verbiage
redundant: 5 extra, windy, wordy **6** de trop, excess, padded, prolix **7** surplus, verbose **8** needless, unneeded **9** bombastic, excessive **10** extraneous, inordinate, long-winded, loquacious
redux: 4 back **9** resurgent
___ Redux: 6 Rabbit **7** Phineas
Red Wheelbarrow, The
author: William Carlos Williams
redwing: 4 bird
Red Wings: 3 six **4** team
home: 7 Detroit
milieu: 3 ice **4** rink
org.: 3 NHL
rival: ***see*** hockey team
sport: 6 hockey
redwood: 4 tree
like a ~: 4 tall
relative: 7 sequoia
___ redwood: 5 giant
Redwood City: 4 town
locale: 10 California
Ree: 5 tribe **6** Indian **7** Amerind, Arikara
Reebok: 6 sneaks **8** sneakers
rival: 4 Avia, Keds, Nike **6** Adidas
reecho: 4 ring, roll
reed: 3 pen, sax **4** oboe, rush **5** grass, plant, stalk **6** bamboo **7** bassoon, bulrush, cattail, hautboy, papyrus **8** reed mace, woodwind **9** saxophone
ender: 3 man, men **4** bird, buck
giant ~: 3 nal
hollow ~: 6 bamboo
like a ~: 4 slim **6** skinny
weaver's ~: 4 slay, sley **6** sleigh
Reed: 3 Lou, Rex **4** Alan, John **5** Carol, Donna, Jerry, Jimmy **6** Alaina, Oliver, Pamela, Robert, Shanna, Walter, Willis **7** Ishmael
reedbuck: 8 antelope
relative: ***see*** antelope
Reed, Donna: 7 actress
film: From Here to Eternity (1953, AA)
It's a Wonderful Life (1946)
TV: Dallas, The Donna Reed Show
TV surname: 5 Stone
Reed-Hall: 6 Alaina
Reed, Ishmael: 4 poet **6** writer
Reed, Jerry
song: Amos Moses (1971)
When You're Hot, You're Hot (1971)
Reed, John: 6 writer **10** journalist
movie about ~: 4 Reds
work: Ten Days That Shook the World
Reed, Lou
song: Walk on the Wild Side (1973)
___ Reeds: 5 Lip My
Reed, Willis
milieu: 5 court
org.: 3 NBA
sport: 10 basketball
reedy: 4 slim, thin, weak **5** frail, rangy **6** piping, shrill, slight **7** slender **9** overgrown, quavering
reef: 3 bar, cay, key **4** bank, rock **5** atoll, ledge, ridge, shelf, shoal **7** barrier, sand bar
material: 5 coral
___ reef: 5 coral **7** barrier
reefer: 4 coat **6** jacket **9** outerwear
reek: 4 emit, fume **5** exude, fetor, smell, smoke, steam, stink **6** foetor, stench **7** malodor **9** effluvium, fetidness
reeked: 5 stank, stunk
___ Reekie: 4 Auld
reeking: 4 foul, rank **5** fetid, stale **6** foetid, rancid, rotten, smelly, stinky **7** noisome, noxious, odorous, squalid **8** mephitic, stinking **10** malodorous
reel: 4 keel, rock, roll, spin, sway, wind **5** dance, lurch, music, pitch, shake, spool, swing, swirl, twirl, waver, weave, wheel, whirl **6** careen, falter, recoil, rotate, teeter, totter, unwind, wabble, wobble **7** stagger, stumble **9** folk dance **10** spin around
contents: 4 film **5** movie
film ~ holder: 3 can
fishing ~ in Britain: 4 pirn
in: 4 land **6** entrap **7** retract
like a fly ~: 5 aspin
off: 4 tell **6** rattle, recite
out: 6 uncoil, unfold, unfurl, unwind
starter: 4 news
reel ___: 3 off
reelect: 6 return **9** reinstate
reelection runners: 3 ins
___-reeler: 3 one, two
reeling: 5 dazed, dizzy, shaky, tipsy, woozy **6** addled, punchy, wobbly **8** confused **9** befuddled **10** bewildered
Reeling in the Years (1973 song)
artist: Steely Dan
reel-to-reel ___: 4 tape
reenergize: 6 revive
reentry: 6 return
reequip: 9 refurbish
Rees: 5 Jerry, Roger
Reese: 5 Della, Mason, Pokey **6** Pee Wee **7** Lizette **11** Witherspoon
Reese, Della
real name: Delloreese Patricia Early
song: And That Reminds Me (1957)
Don't You Know (1959)
Not One Minute More (1959)
Reese, Pee Wee: 6 Dodger **9** shortstop
Reese, Pokey
sport: 8 baseball
Reese's: 5 candy **9** chocolate
alternative: ***see*** candy brand
Reese's ___: 6 Pieces
reestablish: 5 renew **6** recall **9** reinstate
reet ___: 5 pleat
reevaluate: 6 review **7** revisit
Reeve, Christopher: 5 actor
costar: 6 Kidder
film: Deathtrap (1982)
Noises Off (1992)
The Remains of the Day (1993)
Somewhere in Time (1980)
Speechless (1994)
Superman (1978)
Switching Channels (1988)
role: 4 Kent
work: Still Me
Reeves: 3 Del, Jim **5** Keanu **6** George, Martha
Reeves, George
role: 4 Kent **8** Superman
Reeves, Keanu: 5 actor
film: Bill & Ted's Excellent Adventure (1989)
Bram Stoker's Dracula (1992)
Dangerous Liaisons (1988)
The Day the Earth Stood Still (2008)
The Devil's Advocate (1997)
The Gift (2000)
Hardball (2001)
The Lake House (2006)
The Matrix (1999)
Much Ado About Nothing (1993)
My Own Private Idaho (1991)
Permanent Record (1988)
Point Break (1991)
River's Edge (1986)
Something's Gotta Give (2003)
Speed (1994)
Street Kings (2008)
Sweet November (2001)
A Walk in the Clouds (1995)
reexamine: 6 review **7** revisit **8** overhaul **10** reconsider
ref: 6 umpire **10** arbitrator
see also referee, reference
ref.: 2 bk.
book: 3 gaz. **4** dict., ency. **5** encyc. **6** encycl
multivolume ~ book: 3 OED
refashion: 5 alter **6** modify, reform
refection: 4 fare, meal **6** repast **7** aliment **8** victuals
refectory: 10 dining room
refer: 4 cite, send **5** apply, guide, point, quote **6** advert, allude, direct, look up, pass on, relate, resort, submit, turn to **7** concern, connect, consult, iterate, mention, pertain, speak of, suggest, touch on **8** accredit, relegate, turn over **9** appertain, recommend, touch upon
ender: 3 ent **4** ence
to: 4 cite, name, note **5** quote, touch **6** advert, regard, resort **7** bring up, mention, speak of, specify, touch on **9** touch upon
(to): 4 turn
referee: 3 try, ump **5** judge, zebra **6** umpire **7** adjudge, arbiter, mediate **8** moderate, official **9** arbitrate, go-between, interpose, negotiate, officiate **10** adjudicate, arbitrator, interceder
call: 3 TKO **4** foul, time **7** time out
count: 3 ten
employer: 3 NBA, NFL, NHL
order: 5 break
signal: 3 tee
reference: 4 cite, hint, note, plug, text **5** quote **6** look up, regard, remark, source **7** bring up, mention, stating, tribute, writing **8** allusion, archives, citation, evidence, good word, innuendo, relating, resource, workbook **9** attribute, character, quotation, thesaurus **10** connecting, cyclopedia, delegation, dictionary, indicating, mentioning, suggestion
book: 4 text, tome **6** manual
center: 7 library
field of ~: 3 run **4** area, play, span, sway, view **5** ambit, gamut, orbit, range, reach, realm, scale, scope, space, sweep, width **6** extent, margin, radius, sphere **7** breadth, compass, expanse, horizon, purview, subject **8** confines, latitude **9** amplitude, dimension
frame of ~: 4 idea, side, view **5** angle, light, slant, stand **6** aspect, stance, system **7** horizon, opinion, outlook, posture **8** attitude, position **9** viewpoint **10** estimation, philosophy, standpoint
have ~ to: 5 touch **6** bear on **7** concern, involve **8** deal with
indirect ~: 4 hint **8** allusion, innuendo **10** imputation, intimation, suggestion
in ~ to: 5 about, as for **9** apropos of, as regards
make ~: 5 refer **6** allude
mark: 6 obelus
marks: 5 obeli
quick ~: 5 index
use as a ~: 4 cite **6** quotee
reference ___: 4 book
___ reference: 5 cross
reference book: 5 atlas **7** almanac, lexicon **9** gazetteer **10** dictionary
direction: 3 see
name: 5 Roget **7** Webster
referendum: 4 vote **6** ballot, voting **8** election
choice: 2 no **3** yes
referring: 8 relative **10** delegation
to: 5 about **10** concerning
refill: 7 restock **9** replenish
in need of a ~: 3 dry **5** empty **7** drained **8** depleted **9** exhausted
refine: 4 edit, hone, thin **5** clean, round, sleek, slick, smelt **6** better, filter, finish, polish, purify, rarefy, rarify, redact, smooth, strain, temper **7** clarify, cleanse, develop, distill, elevate, explain, improve, perfect, process **8** civilize, polish up, round off, round out **9** cultivate, make clear
metal: 5 smelt
refined: 4 nice, posh, pure, thin **5** civil, clean, couth, exact, haute, noble, plush, ritzy, suave **6** classy, dainty, polite, proper, snazzy, spiffy, subtle, swanky, urbane, washed **7** aerated, courtly, drained, elegant, genteel, precise, sublime **8** cleansed, cultural, cultured, debonair, decorous, delicate, esthetic, filtered, graceful, gracious, highbred, highbrow, ladylike, lettered, mannerly, polished, purified, rarefied, strained, tasteful, well-bred **9** aesthetic, civilized, clarified, courteous, debonaire, dignified, distilled, processed, sensitive, spiritual, uplifting **10** boiled down, cultivated, debonnaire, discerning, expurgated, fastidious, high-minded, restrained
it's ~: 3 oil, ore
not ~: 3 raw **5** crass, rough **6** coarse, gauche
refinement: 4 chic, lore, tact **5** class,

grace, style, taste **6** beauty, change, finish, nicety, nuance, polish **7** amenity, culture, dignity, finesse, manners, suavity **8** breeding, civility, cleaning, courtesy, delicacy, draining, elegance, fineness, literacy, niceties, noblesse, subtlety, urbanity **9** education, erudition, gentility, knowledge, politesse, precision, propriety, suaveness **10** classicism
refinery: **7** factory
output: **5** metal
residue: **4** slag **5** dross
refinish furniture: **5** stain
refit: **5** renew **8** overhaul **9** refurbish
refitting: **10** adaptation, adjustment, alteration, conversion, remodeling
reflect: **4** cast, copy, echo, muse, show, stew **5** catch, flash, match, pause, reply, shine, sound, study, think, weigh **6** chew on, evince, follow, mirror, ponder, reason, repeat, return, reveal, revert, wonder **7** bear out, bespeak, display, emulate, exhibit, express, imitate, rebound, resound, reverse **8** cogitate, consider, give back, indicate, look back, manifest, meditate, mull over, register, resonate, ruminate **9** cerebrate, give forth, repercuss, reproduce, speculate, take after, throw back **10** deliberate, introspect, think about
light: **4** beam, glow **5** blaze, gleam, glint, shine **6** dazzle **7** flicker, glimmer, glisten, glitter, radiate, sparkle **8** illumine **9** coruscate, luminesce **10** incandesce
on: **4** mull **5** weigh **8** consider, mull over, turn over
time to ~: **4** lull, rest **5** break, pause **6** hiatus **7** respite **8** breather
reflection: **4** echo, idea, slam, slur, view **5** blame, image, light, study **6** glance, musing, remark, shadow **7** censure, obloquy, opinion, picture, thought **8** likeness, reaction, reproach, thinking **9** aspersion, brainwork, criticism, deduction, discredit, duplicate, imitation, stricture **10** appearance, cogitation, derogation
__ reflection: **4** upon
Reflections (1967 song)
artist: Supremes
Reflections __ Life: **4** of My
Reflections in a Golden Eye
author: Carson McCullers
Reflections on Ice-Breaking
poet: Ogden Nash
Reflections on the Death of a Porcupine
author: D.H. Lawrence
Reflections on Violence
author: Georges Sorel
reflective: **4** wise **5** shiny **6** glassy, solemn **7** pensive, wistful **8** profound, rational, studious, thinking **9** conscious, emulative, imitative, observant **10** reasonable, thoughtful
reflector: **5** glass **6** mirror
reflex: **6** hiccup **8** hiccough, knee-jerk, reaction **9** automatic
ending: **3** ive **5** ology
testing site: **4** knee
reflex __: **6** camera
__ reflex: **3** gag
Reflex
author: Dick Francis
reflexive pronoun: **6** itself, myself **7** herself, himself, oneself **9** ourselves **10** themselves
Reflex, The (1984 song)
artist: Duran Duran
refluence: **3** ebb
reflux: **3** ebb
reform: **4** cure, mend **5** alter, amend, emend, fix up, rally, renew **6** better, change, enrich, modify, polish, redeem, remake, remedy, repair, revise, rework, uplift **7** clean up, convert, correct, enhance, improve, rebuild, reclaim, rectify, redress, remodel, resolve, restore, shape up, sharpen, upgrade **8** make over, renovate, spruce up, swear off **9** amendment, meliorate, rearrange, refashion, transform **10** ameliorate, conversion, go straight, make amends, regenerate, reorganize
__ reform: **4** tort
reformation: **7** redress
starter: **7** counter
Reformation center: **6** Geneva
reformative: **8** remedial
reformatory: **3** pen **4** stir **5** joint, penal **6** lockup, prison **7** slammer **8** big house
reformer: **6** zealot **7** liberal, radical **8** advocate, champion, crusader, ultraist **10** campaigner
target: **4** slum
refractor, light: **5** prism **7** crystal, rainbow
refractory: **5** balky, tough **6** mulish, unruly, wilful **7** defiant, naughty, radical, wayward, willful **8** contrary, factious, indocile, perverse, stubborn **9** difficult, fractious, obstinate, pigheaded **10** bullheaded, disorderly, headstrong, rebellious, unamenable
refrain: **4** curb, halt, keep, pass, quit, song, stop, tune **5** avoid, cease, check, forgo, music, remit, verse **6** arrest, burden, chorus, desist, eschew, forego, give up, melody, pass up, resist, sit out, strain **7** abstain, back off, decline, forbear, inhibit **8** keep from, leave off, renounce, restrain, withhold **9** do without, interrupt, undersong
end of a childhood ~: **3** EIO **5** EIEIO
from: **4** duck, shun **5** avoid, defer, dodge, evade, forgo, shirk, spare, spurn **6** bypass, desist, eschew, forego **7** boycott, forbear **10** circumvent
mountaineer's ~: **5** yodel, yodle
part: **3** tra **4** fa la, la la **5** la-la's, tra la **6** fa la la **7** tra la la
please ~: **4** don't
refresh: **3** air, jog **4** cool, prod **5** brace, cheer, rally, renew, slake **6** perk up, prompt, regain, regale, repair, revive, update, vivify **7** brush up, disport, enliven, fortify, quicken, recover, recruit, restock, restore **8** enspirit, inspirit, recreate, renovate, revivify **9** deodorize, modernize, reanimate, refurbish, replenish, restitute, stimulate **10** exhilarate, invigorate, regenerate, rejuvenate, revitalize, strengthen
refresher course, take a: **6** bone up
refreshing: **3** new **4** cool **5** balmy, brisk, crisp, novel **6** lively, unique **7** bracing, cooling, welcome **8** original, pleasant **9** different, restoring **10** comforting, delightful, energizing, fortifying
refreshment: **3** ade **4** bite, eats, food, kick, meal, rest **5** drink, snack, treat **6** spread, tidbit, viands **8** pick-me-up, victuals
liquid ~: **5** drink, juice **8** beverage
stand: **5** kiosk
refried __: **5** beans
refrigerant: **6** dry ice, ethane **8** dimethyl
cryogenic ~: **4** neon
refrigerate: **3** ice **4** cool **5** chill **6** freeze **7** air-cool **8** preserve
refrigerated: **3** icy **4** cool, iced **5** algid, gelid **6** chilly, frosty, frozen **7** chilled **8** freezing
refrigeration: **4** cold **10** chilliness
refrigerator: **6** icebox
gas: **5** Freon
jar: **4** mayo **5** jelly
name: **5** Amana **6** Maytag **7** Kenmore **9** Whirlpool
refrigerator-__: **7** freezer
__ refrigerator: **6** walk-in
Refrigerator, The: **5** Perry
refuel: **3** eat **5** gas up
refueling area: **3** pit
refuge: **3** ark, den, lee **4** aery, exit, eyry, fort, hole, home, lair, nest, port **5** aerie, cover, eyrie, haven, oasis, shift **6** ambush, asylum, covert, escape, harbor, outlet, resort, safety, shield, way out **7** asylums, harbour, hideout, opening, retreat, shelter, stopgap **8** fastness, fortress, hideaway, immunity, preserve, recourse, resource, security **9** anchorage, expedient, harborage, hermitage, makeshift, safe haven, safe house, sanctuary **10** ivory tower, protection, stronghold
give ~: **4** hide, save **6** foster, harbor, rescue, shield **7** protect, shelter **8** insulate, keep safe **9** look after, safeguard
place of ~: **3** ark **4** fort, lair **5** haven, oasis **6** asylum **7** shelter **8** fortress **9** sanctuary
wayfarer ~: **5** hotel, lodge, motel **6** hostel **9** roadhouse
refugee: **2** DP **5** alien, exile **6** émigré **7** escapee, evacuee, outcast **8** defector, deserter, emigrant, outsider **9** foreigner **10** boat person, expatriate
request: **6** asylum
Refugee (1980 song)
artist: Tom Petty
Refugees, The
author: Arthur Conan Doyle
refulgence: **4** glow **5** light, shine **6** luster
refulgent: **5** aglow, light, lucid, nitid, shiny **6** ablaze, bright **7** beaming, glowing, radiant, shining **8** aglitter, dazzling, gleaming, luminous, lustrous, splendid **9** brilliant, sparkling **10** glistening, glittering
refund: **3** pay **5** remit, repay **6** adjust, give-up, rebate, recoup, redeem, return, reward, settle **7** balance, pay back, payment, redress, replace, restore **8** discount, give back, kickback, make good **9** allowance, discharge, indemnify, make up for, money back, reimburse, repayment **10** compensate, make amends, recompense, relinquish, remunerate, settlement
reason: **6** damage
refurbish: **4** do up, mend, redo **5** fix up, refit, rehab, renew **6** repair, revamp, spruce, update **7** clean up, gussy up, reequip, refresh, remodel, restore, retouch, retread, touch up, upgrade **8** overhaul, renovate, spruce up **9** modernize, restitute **10** rejuvenate
refusal: **2** no **3** ban, nix **4** pass, veto, writ **6** choice, denial, option, rebuff, rebuke **7** dissent, regrets, repulse **8** defiance, disfavor, negation, reversal, turndown **9** disavowal, exclusion, knockback, rejection, repulsion **10** abnegation, declension, disclaimer, enjoinment, forbidding, nonconsent, refutation, resistance, thumbs down
emphatic ~: **5** never, no how, no way
formal ~: **3** nay **4** veto
informal ~: **3** nah, naw **4** nope, uh-uh
in German: **4** nein
in Scottish: **3** nae
military ~: **5** no sir
words of ~: **4** not I **5** I won't, no how, no way **6** no deal **8** forget it **9** by no means, fat chance **10** count me out, not a chance
refuse: **3** nix **4** balk, deny, dump, dust, junk, muck, scum, shun, slag, slop **5** baulk, chaff, demur, dodge, dregs, dross, evade, filth, offal, repel, say no, scorn, spurn, swill, trash, waste **6** beg off, debris, desist, ignore, litter, loathe, pass up, rebuff, regret, reject, resist, scraps **7** abstain, decline, dissent, garbage, hogwash, hold off, hold out, protest, remains, repulse, residue, rubbish, send off, shut off, shut out **8** brush off, disallow, hold back, keep from, leavings, sediment, set aside, turn away, turn down, turn from, withdraw, withhold **9** disaccord, foreclose, frown upon, reprobate, repudiate, sweepings **10** disapprove
admission: **3** bar **5** block **6** forbid **7** exclude, keep out **9** freeze out
consent: **4** deny, veto **6** forbid, reject **7** decline **8** disallow, prohibit, turn down **9** interdict, proscribe **10** disapprove
hauler: **6** ashman **7** junkman
heap: **4** dump **8** junkyard, landfill
I ~: **2** no **3** nah, naw, nay, nix, non **4** nein, nope, nyet, uh-uh **5** ixnay, never, no how, noway **6** no deal, noways, nowise **8** forget it, negative, negatory

9 by no means, fat chance 10 count me out, not a chance, thumbs down

old-style: 4 nill

receptacle: 6 ashcan 8 trash can 10 garbage can

to deal with: 4 shun, snub 5 scorn, spurn 6 ignore, rebuff, reject 7 disavow, disdain, neglect, scoff at 8 turn down

to go: 5 demur 6 recoil 9 stop short

to obey: 4 balk 5 baulk, rebel 6 mutiny

refusenik word: 4 nyet

refuses: 4 won't

refutation: 2 no 6 answer, denial 7 refusal 8 rebuttal

refute: 3 top 4 burn, deny 5 belie, break, crush, evert, parry, quash, rebut 6 answer, cancel, debate, expose, impugn, naysay, negate, oppose, show up 7 confute, contend, convict, counter, dispute, explode, gainsay, reply to, silence, squelch 8 abnegate, burn down, demolish, disagree, disclaim, disprove, tear down 9 cancel out, disaffirm, discredit, dispose of, overthrow, repudiate, shoot down, vindicate 10 contradict, contravene, controvert, disconfirm, invalidate, prove false, prove wrong

reg.: 3 std.

Reg: 4 Owen 6 Grundy

Reg. __ Dept. Agr.: 5 Penna.

Reg. __ Off.: 5 U.S. Pat.

regain: 6 ransom, recoup, redeem 7 get back, reclaim, recover, recruit, refresh, salvage, win back 8 make back, retrieve, take back 9 reacquire, recapture, repossess

consciousness: 4 stir, wake 5 waken 6 awaken, come to, return, revive 7 recover 10 come around

one's health: 4 heal 5 rally 7 get well, rebound, recover 8 snap back 9 get better 10 convalesce, recuperate

regal: 5 grand, noble, proud, royal 6 august, kingly, lordly 7 courtly, haughty, queenly, stately 8 imperial, imposing, kinglike, majestic, palatial, princely, splendid 9 dignified, sovereign 10 majestical, statuesque

home: 6 castle, palace

letters: 3 HRH

Regal: 3 car 4 auto 5 Buick 10 automobile

__ Regal: 6 Chivas

Regalbuto: 3 Joe

regale: 3 ply 4 grab 5 amuse, feast, party, serve, treat 6 divert, please, spread 7 delight, gratify, have fun, nurture, refresh, satisfy 8 fracture 9 entertain, knock dead, laugh it up

regalement: 3 fun 5 cheer, mirth 7 delight 8 pleasure 9 amusement, diversion

regalia: 6 attire, finery, livery, symbol 7 clothes, uniform 9 trappings 10 Sunday best

item: 3 orb 5 tiara

Regan's father: 4 Lear

regard: 3 eye, see, spy 4 beam, care, deem, gaze, heed, hold, item, look, love, mark, mind, note, pipe, rate, read, sake, scan, take, view 5 assay, count, favor, flash, honor, judge, point, stare, store, think, treat, value, watch 6 admire, advert, aspect, assess, attend, behold, credit, detail, esteem, gaze at, homage, liking, look at, look on, matter, notice, praise, reckon, remark, repute, revere 7 account, apply to, bearing, believe, concern, dignity, eyeball, feature, observe, opinion, pertain, prizing, refer to, respect, stare at, suppose, surmise, thought, valuing, witness, worship 8 approval, bear upon, consider, devotion, estimate, fondness, good name, interest, listen to, look upon, once-over, overlook, perceive, pore over, prestige, relate to, relation, scrutiny, sympathy 9 advertise, affection, attention, curiosity, deference, pertain to, reference, relevance, reverence, think of as 10 admiration, attachment, cherishing, cognizance, connection, estimation, get a load of, observance, particular, reputation, scrutinize, self-esteem, solicitude, veneration

critical ~: 8 analysis, scrutiny 10 inspection

hastily: 4 peek, peep 6 glance, peek at, peep at 8 glance at

high ~: 4 love 6 esteem 10 attachment

highly: 5 adore, favor, prize 6 admire, revere 8 look up to

in high ~: 5 great 6 adored 7 beloved

public ~: 4 fame 5 éclat 6 renown, repute 7 acclaim, stardom 8 eminence 9 celebrity, notoriety 10 popularity, prominence, reputation

with interest: 4 gape, gawk 5 stare 10 rubberneck

with ~ to: 4 in re 5 about, anent, as for 6 toward 7 towards 9 apropos of

__-regarded: 4 well

regarded to be: 6 seen as

regardful: 5 aware 7 careful, duteous, dutiful, heedful, mindful 8 watchful 9 advertent, attentive, observant, observing 10 respectful, solicitous, thoughtful

regarding: 4 as to, look 5 about, anent, as for 6 toward 7 towards 9 apropos of

this: 6 hereto 8 hereunto

Regarding Henry (1991 film)

cast: Annette Bening, Harrison Ford

director: Mike Nichols

dog: 5 Buddy

Regarding Wave

author: Gary Snyder

regardless: 3 but, lax 4 deaf, rash, rude 5 altho, blind, crude, slack, still 6 anyhow, anyway, coarse, remiss 7 against 8 although, careless, derelict, heedless, listless, mindless, reckless 9 aside from, at any cost, in any case, negligent, unfeeling, unheeding, unmindful 10 for all that, in any event, incautious, neglectful

of: 7 despite

regards: 4 love 7 devoirs 8 greeting, respects 9 deference, greetings 10 best wishes, good wishes, salutation

as ~: 4 in re 5 about, anent 6 toward 7 towards 8 relative, relevant 10 concerning

__ regard to: 4 with

regatta: 4 race

entrant: 4 crew 5 racer, rower, scull, shell, yacht 6 boater

locale: 6 Henley

regency: 5 power 7 command 8 dominion 9 authority 10 leadership

__ Regency: 5 Hyatt

regenerate: 5 renew 6 change, reform, revive, uplift 7 produce, refresh, restore 8 enspirit, inspirit, reawaken, recreate, renovate, revivify 9 modernize, reanimate 10 rejuvenate

regent: 6 deputy 8 delegate, director 9 organizer

regent of the sun: 5 Uriel

Regents

song: Barbara-Ann (1961)

reggae: 5 music

musician, perhaps: 5 rasta

relative: 3 ska

Reggie: 7 Jackson

__ regia: 4 aqua

regime: 4 rule, sway 5 reign 6 system, tenure 7 dynasty 8 kingship 10 government, incumbency, leadership, management

__ régime: 6 ancien

regimen: 4 diet 6 course 9 treatment 10 discipline, weight plan

regiment: 4 army 5 corps, force, order, squad, troop 7 phalanx

regimentals: 7 uniform

regimentation: 8 severity 9 sternness 10 discipline, strictness

Regina: 4 city, town 7 capital

locale: 4 Sask. 6 Canada

Reginald: 4 Owen 5 Denny 8 Gardiner 10 VelJohnson

author: Saki

region: 3 ter. 4 area, belt, land, part, soil, terr., turf, walk, ward, zone 5 arena, block, field, place, range, realm, scene, scope, shire, tract, world 6 domain, ground, locale, sector, sphere, suburb 7 borough, country, demesne, expanse, quarter, section, stretch, terrain 8 clearing, confines, district, division, dominion, environs, locality, location, precinct, province, vicinity 9 bailiwick, territory

regional: 5 local 6 native 7 endemic, topical 8 sectoral 9 endemical, localized, parochial, sectional 10 indigenous

plants and animals: 5 biota

__ regions: 6 nether

__ Regions: 5 Polar

Regis: 6 Toomey 7 Philbin

Kelly to ~: 6 cohost

__ Regis: 5 Curia

register: 3 log, say 4 book, file, join, list, mark, note, poll, post, read, roll, rota, show, tell, till 5 diary, enrol, enter, entry, log in, scale, score, table, tally 6 annals, betray, dawn on, enlist, enroll, ledger, record, reveal, roster, scroll, sign on, sign up, sink in, strike 7 account, bespeak, catalog, check in, display, exhibit, express, impress, journal, point to, reflect, set down, weigh in, who's who 8 archives, disclose, indicate, inscribe, manifest, point out, roll call, schedule, take down 9 catalogue, chronicle, directory, inventory, keep count, keep score, sign up for, subscribe, write down 10 come home to, memorandum, tabulation, understand

as a complaint: 5 lodge

cash ~ calculation: 3 tax

cash ~ co.: 3 NCR

key: 6 no sale

ringer: 4 sale

signer: 5 guest 6 lodger, roomer 7 boarder, visitor

__ register: 4 cash 5 sales

Register: 5 paper 9 newspaper

locale: 6 Mobile 9 Des Moines

__ Register: 6 Lloyd's, Social 7 Federal

registered __: 4 mail 5 nurse

registration: 6 sign-up 10 enlistment, enrollment

registry: 6 patent, record

regnant: 6 ruling 7 supreme 8 dominant, in charge 9 sovereign 10 prevailing

regnat __: 7 populus

__ regni: 4 anno

regress: 3 ebb 4 sink, slip 5 lapse 6 go back, recede, revert 7 fall off, relapse, retreat, setback 8 fall away, fall back, return to, roll back, turn back 9 backslide, throw back 10 degenerate, lose ground, recidivate

ender: 3 ion, ive

regression: 3 ebb 5 lapse 7 setback 8 movement, reaction 9 decadence

regret: 3 rue, woe 4 care, dole, miss, moan, mope, pang, weep 5 demur, grief, mourn, qualm, worry 6 bemoan, bewail, grieve, lament, qualms, refuse, repent, repine, sorrow 7 anguish, apology, concern, cry over, deplore, remorse, scruple 8 weep over 9 annoyance, apologies, apologize, deprecate, heartache, misgiving, nostalgia, penitence 10 affliction, bitterness, conscience, contrition, disapprove, discomfort, heartbreak, misgivings, repentance, ruefulness, uneasiness

exclamation: 3 och 4 alas, rats 5 alack, sorry 6 shucks 7 Odzooks 8 Gadzooks, lackaday

express ~: 4 sigh

with ~: 5 sadly 8 grudging 9 reluctant

regretful: 3 sad 5 sorry 6 afraid, rueful 7 ashamed, humbled 8 contrite, mournful, penitent 9 repentant, sorrowful 10 apologetic, lamentable, remorseful

one: 4 ruer 6 atoner

regretfulness: 3 rue 6 qualms, regret 7 remorse 10 contrition, misgivings

regrets: 7 refusal 8 turndown

send ~: **5** say no **6** beg off, refuse **7** decline
with ~: **5** sadly
regrettable: **3** sad **4** dire **5** woful, wrong **6** woeful **7** pitiful, unhappy **8** dreadful, grievous, pitiable, shameful **10** afflictive, calamitous, deplorable, ill-advised, lamentable
regroup: **5** rally
regular: **3** gas, set **4** even, flat **5** daily, exact, fixed, level, paced, plain, plane, stock, typic, usual **6** client, common, cyclic, formal, lawful, no-lead, normal, proper, serial, smooth, stated, steady, wonted **7** classic, correct, general, in order, natural, ordered, orderly, precise, routine, sincere, typical, uniform **8** accepted, approved, arranged, balanced, bona fide, clean-cut, constant, everyday, expected, frequent, gasoline, habitual, measured, official, ordinary, orthodox, periodic, probable, punctual, rational, readable, rhythmic, standard, straight, unbroken, unwaning **9** accordant, automatic, congruous, consonant, continual, customary, efficient, momentary, organized, patterned, prevalent, recurrent, regulated, unvarying **10** accustomed, classified, consistent, dependable, frequenter, harmonious, invariable, legitimate, mechanical, methodical, prevailing, sanctioned, successive, systematic, true to type, unchanging, uneventful
fellow: **3** Joe
hangout: **5** haunt
regularity: **5** order **6** rhythm **8** symmetry **9** clockwork, constancy, exactness, fixedness, frequency **10** classicism
regularly: **3** oft **4** a lot, much **5** often **6** mostly, yearly **7** usually **9** eternally, generally, gradually, quite a bit, routinely **10** frequently, ordinarily, repeatedly
regulars: **5** trade **7** patrons **9** clientage, clientele, following, patronage
regulate: **3** fit, fix, run, set **4** rule, slow, time, true, tune **5** adapt, align, aline, guide, order, reset, shape **6** adjust, direct, govern, handle, manage, settle, square, temper, tune up **7** arrange, balance, conduct, control, correct, dispose, improve, measure, monitor, oversee, qualify, rectify, redress, shape up **8** allocate, classify, legalize, moderate, modulate, organize, readjust, restrict **9** determine, legislate, methodize, normalize, reconcile, supervise **10** coordinate, put in order, stereotype
Regulate (1994 song)
artist: Nate Dogg, Warren G
regulated: **5** paced **7** orderly, regular
be ~ by: **4** mind, obey **6** follow **7** observe, respect **8** adhere to **9** conform to
company: **4** util. **7** utility
item: **4** drug **8** narcotic
__ regulated militia...: **5** a well
regulation: **3** law **4** book, code, form, no-no, rule, tabu **5** bible, bylaw, canon, edict, order, taboo **6** decree, tuning **7** control, dictate, numbers, precept, statute **8** guidance, handling, managing, standard **9** customary, direction, directive, enactment, guideline, ordinance, prescript, principle, procedure **10** adjustment, discipline, government
regulations: **4** code **5** canon **6** policy **7** charter **9** etiquette
__ regulator: **7** voltage
regulator combining form: **4** -stat
Regulus: **4** star
constellation: **3** Leo
regurgitate: **4** spew, spue **5** eject, erupt, expel **8** disgorge **9** discharge
Reg. U.S. Pat. __: **3** Off.
rehab: **6** repair **7** restore **8** renovate **9** refurbish **10** rejuvenate
center: **6** clinic
rehabilitate: **4** cure, mend, save **5** clear, fix up, renew, right **6** adjust, better, change, enrich, polish, redeem, reform **7** convert, enhance, furbish, improve, rebuild, reclaim, recover, restore, salvage, shape up, sharpen, upgrade **8** make good, renovate, spruce up **9** meliorate, reeducate, refurbish, reinstate **10** ameliorate
rehabilitation: **7** redress, therapy
Rehan: **3** Ada
rehash: **5** weigh **6** repeat, review, rework **7** belabor, discuss, iterate, recount, rewrite, summary **9** reiterate, summarize **10** paraphrase, reconsider
rehashed: **9** imitative **10** derivative, unoriginal
rehearsal: **4** call, prep **5** drill **6** dry run, tryout **7** reading, recital, workout **8** practice, readying, relation **9** going-over, retelling, shakedown **10** experiment, recitation, repetition, run-through
__ rehearsal: **5** dress
Rehearsal of a Ballet
painter: Edgar Degas
rehearse: **3** act **4** hone, tell, test **5** drill, prime, ready, state, study, train **6** depict, do over, dry run, get set, go over, recite, relate, repeat, review, try out, tune up, warm up **7** iterate, narrate, recount, reenact, work out **8** describe, exercise, practice **9** go through, reiterate **10** experiment, prepare for, run through
rehearsed: **3** pat **4** glib **5** ready **6** primed **7** prepped **8** prepared
rehearsing, without: **5** ad-lib
reheat perhaps: **4** nuke
Rehm: **5** Diane
Rehnquist: **5** judge **7** Justice, William
Reichstein, Tadeus: **8** Nobelist
Reid: **3** Tim **4** Kate, Tara **5** Britt, Harry **6** Thomas
Reid, Thomas: **8** Scottish **11** philosopher
reign: **4** rule, sway **6** govern, record, regime, tenure **7** command, prevail **8** dominate, dominion, hold sway, kingship, monarchy **9** influence, supremacy **10** ascendance, ascendancy, ascendence, ascendency, incumbency, leadership
of terror: **5** purge **7** tyranny **9** despotism **10** oppression
over: **4** boss, head, helm, lead, rule **6** govern, head up, manage **7** command, control **8** dominate, domineer **9** supervise
reigning: **5** on top **8** dominant **9** sovereign
Reilly: **5** John C.
reimburse: **3** pay **5** repay **6** offset, recoup, refund, return, square **7** balance, pay back, recover, replace, requite, restore **8** make good, square up **9** indemnify, liquidate, make up for **10** compensate, recompense, remunerate
reimbursement: **6** rebate, refund **7** payment
reimpose: **7** put back, restore
Reims: **4** city, town
locale: **6** France
rein: **4** curb, slow, stop **5** check, leash, strap **6** bridle, halter, hamper, hinder, hold up, impede, muzzle, pull in, slow up, tether **7** contain, control, harness, smother, trammel **8** hold back, restrain, slow down **9** constrain, deterrent, restraint **10** constraint, keep a lid on
in: **10** keep in line
__ rein: **4** free
reina: **5** queen **7** Spanish
mate: **3** rey
reindeer: **4** deer **5** Comet, Cupid, octet, Vixen **6** Dancer, Dasher, Donder **7** Blitzen, Prancer, Rudolph
driver: **5** Santa **10** Santa Claus
herder: **4** Lapp **5** Yurak
part: **4** hoof **6** antler
relative: *see* deer
reined in: **6** curbed, pent-up **7** bridled, checked, stifled **8** held back **9** bottled-up, inhibited, repressed **10** restrained, restricted, suppressed
Reiner: **3** Rob **4** Carl **5** Fritz
Reiner, Carl: **5** actor **8** director
film: All of Me (1984)
Dead Men Don't Wear Plaid (1982)
The Gazebo (1959)
The Jerk (1979)
The Man With Two Brains (1983)
Ocean's Eleven (2001)
Oh, God! (1977)
son: **3** Rob
TV: Your Show of Shows
Reiner, Fritz: **7** maestro **9** conductor
Reiner, Rob: **5** actor **8** director
father: **4** Carl
film: Alex & Emma (2003)
The American President (1995)
The Bucket List (2007)
A Few Good Men (1992)
Ghosts of Mississippi (1996)
Misery (1990)
The Princess Bride (1987)
Rumor Has It... (2005)
Stand by Me (1986)
This Is Spinal Tap (1984)
When Harry Met Sally... (1989)
spouse: Penny Marshall
TV: All in the Family
reinforce: **4** gird, hype, line, prop, tone **5** add to, boost, brace, build, carry, cover, shore, steel **6** anneal, back up, beef up, harden, heat up, pick up, pillar, prop up, soup up, stress, stroke, temper, tone up **7** augment, bolster, brace up, build up, burgeon, develop, empower, enhance, enlarge, fortify, punch up, recruit, shore up, stiffen, support, sustain, toughen **8** bourgeon, buttress, energize, increase, indurate, multiply, vitalize **9** emphasize, encourage, intensify, undergird, underline **10** contribute, invigorate, strengthen, supplement
reinforced: **5** tough **6** rugged, strong, sturdy **7** durable **8** well-made **9** well-built
reinforcement: **3** aid **4** stay **5** brace **6** facing **7** buildup, support **8** buttress
steel ~ rod: **5** rebar
Reinhart in Love
author: Thomas Berger
Reinhold: **5** Judge **6** Glière **7** Niebuhr
Reinking: **3** Ann
reins: **4** helm
hold the ~: **4** rule **5** guide, reign, steer **6** direct, govern **7** command, control, oversee
reinstate: **6** recall, redeem, return **7** put back, reelect, restore **9** bring back
reintroduce: **6** recall **7** put back, restore **9** bring back
reinvent the __: **5** wheel
reinvest: **4** plow **8** plow back, roll over
reinvigorate: **6** revive **7** refresh **8** vitalize
Reis: **6** Irving
Reiser: **4** Paul, Pete
Reiser, Paul: **5** actor
costar: **4** Hunt
TV: Mad About You, My Two Dads
Reisz: **5** Karel
__ Reiter: **5** Blaue
reiterate: **3** rpt. **4** echo **5** ditto, recap, renew, resay, rub in **6** go over, harp on, parrot, rehash, repeat, retell **7** recheck, reprise, restate **8** play back, rehearse **9** come again, emphasize
reiterated: **4** many **7** regular **8** frequent, habitual, numerous, repeated **9** recurrent
reiteration: **4** echo
reiteratively: **4** anew **5** again **8** once more **10** repeatedly
Reitman, Ivan: **8** director
film: Dave (1993)
Ghostbusters (1984)
Junior (1994)
Kindergarten Cop (1990)
Legal Eagles (1986)
Meatballs (1979)
Six Days Seven Nights (1998)
Stripes (1981)
Twins (1988)
REIT part: **4** real **5** trust **6** estate **10** investment
Reivers, The: **4** film **5** novel
author: William Faulkner
cast: Will Geer, Steve McQueen
character: **3** Ned **4** Bobo, Boon, Otis, Reba **5** Maury, Sarah **6** Alison, Minnie
director: Mark Rydell
music: John Williams

reject: **3** ban, bar, nix **4** burn, deny, jilt, kill, shed, shun, veto **5** chuck, debar, ditch, repel, scoff, scorn, scout, scrap, spurn **6** abjure, bounce, disown, except, forbid, ignore, loathe, pass by, pass on, pass up, rebuff, refuse, second, slight, slough **7** abandon, cashier, cast off, cast out, decline, despise, disavow, discard, disdain, dismiss, exclude, forsake, kiss off, put down, repulse, rule out, say no to, toss out **8** abrogate, brush off, castaway, disallow, disclaim, discount, forswear, jettison, lay aside, pooh-pooh, prohibit, renounce, throw out, turn down **9** blackball, cast aside, discredit, eliminate, foreclose, foreswear, ostracize, proscribe, reprobate, repudiate, shoot down, throw away **10** contravene, disapprove, disbelieve
old-style: **4** nill
rejectamenta: **5** trash
rejected: **6** lonely **9** unpopular, unwelcome
rejecting: **6** except **8** negative **10** disdainful
rejection: **2** no **3** nix **4** no go, pass, veto **5** no way, spurn **6** bounce, denial, no dice, rebuff, slight **7** refusal, repulse **8** brush-off, hard time, negation, nihilism, turndown **9** defection, desertion, disbelief, dismissal, exception, exclusion, sundering **10** abdication, abnegation, nonconsent, thumbs down
exclamation: **3** nay, ugh **4** heck, pfui, phoo **6** phooey
rejection __: **4** slip
rejects: **4** junk **6** debris **8** castoffs, discards, leavings **9** sweepings
rejoice: **5** enjoy, exult, glory, revel **7** beatify, delight, satisfy, triumph **8** jubilate **9** celebrate, make merry **10** effervesce
in: **4** like **5** prize, savor **6** relish **8** hold dear **9** gloat over
rejoicing: **4** glad **5** happy, merry, mirth **6** blithe, cheery, elated, jovial, upbeat **7** gleeful, pleased, tickled, triumph **8** blissful, cheerful, ecstatic, euphoric, exultant, jubilant, laughter, mirthful, thrilled **9** delighted, happiness **10** exultation, risibility, triumphant
rejoin: **6** answer **7** respond
rejoinder: **3** ans. **5** reply **6** answer, retort, return, ripost **7** defense, riposte **8** comeback, reaction, rebuttal, repartee, response **9** wisecrack
rejuvenate: **4** do up **5** rally, rehab, renew **6** revive, spruce, update **7** enliven, rebound, reclaim, recover, refresh, restore, retread **8** renovate, revivify, spruce up, vitalize **9** modernize, refurbish, restitute **10** invigorate, regenerate
rejuvenation: **7** revival
rekindle: **6** revive **8** reawaken **10** revitalize
rel.: **3** bro., unc.
deg.: **3** Th.D.
school: **3** sem.
rel. __: **4** pron.
relapse: **4** fade, fail, sink **6** recede, return, revert, weaken, worsen **7** regress, setback **8** fall back, reaction, slip back, turn back **9** backslide, slide back **10** recidivate, retrogress
relate: **3** say **4** link, talk, tell **5** apply, cover, refer, spill, state, tie to, unite **6** clue in, cohere, convey, depict, detail, impart, orient, recite, report, reveal, set out **7** ascribe, concern, connect, divulge, express, itemize, narrate, pertain, present, recount **8** advise of, bear upon, belong to, describe, disclose, interact, rehearse **9** analogize, appertain, associate, chronicle, expound on, make sense, touch base, verbalize
to: **3** dig **4** grok **5** grasp **6** inform, regard **7** concern, involve **9** tie in with **10** comprehend, sympathize, understand
well: **2** go **4** jibe **5** fit in **6** cohere **7** conform
related: **3** kin **4** akin, like, oral **5** alike, joint **6** agnate, allied, enmesh, immesh, inmesh, linked, mutual, tied up **7** cognate, connate, germane, kindred, similar **8** incident, parallel, relevant **9** analogous, bracketed, connected, dependant, dependent, fraternal, pertinent **10** affiliated, associated, collateral, connatural, correlated, incidental, interwoven, reciprocal
item: **5** tie in
maternally: **5** enate
paternally: **6** agnate
relating to: **5** about
suffix: **3** -ile, -ine
relation: **3** dad, kin, mom, pop **4** aunt, bond, tale **5** niece, uncle **6** cousin, father, mother, nephew, regard, sister **7** bearing, brother, grandma, grandpa, kindred, kinship, kinsman, liaison, recital, sibling **8** affinity, alliance, grandson **9** great-aunt, rehearsal, statement **10** connection, great-uncle, kinsperson, similarity
in ~ to: **5** about **7** against, vis-à-vis **8** opposite
mathematical ~: **5** ratio **8** equation, fraction
with ~ to: **4** as to **5** anent, as for **9** regarding **10** concerning
__ relation: **5** blood
relations: **3** kin **5** terms **7** kinfolk **8** dealings, kinfolks, kinsfolk **9** coherence
break in ~: **4** rift **6** breach, schism **7** quarrel **10** falling-out
good ~: **5** amity, peace **6** comity **7** concord, harmony **8** goodwill **10** cordiality, fellowship, friendship
__ relations: **5** human, labor **6** public **7** foreign
relationship: **3** tie **4** bond, link **5** logic, ratio, tie in, tie-up **6** accord, affair, hookup, ration **7** analogy, contact, kinship, liaison, network, rapport, romance **8** affinity, alliance, exchange, likeness, marriage, nearness, parallel **9** relevance **10** connection
end a ~: **4** part **5** leave, split **7** break up, split up
relative: **3** bro, dad, kin, mom, pop, sib, sis, son **4** aunt, folk, near **5** about, blood, folks, in-law, niece, uncle **6** agnate, allied, cousin, father, in-laws, mother, nephew, parent, sister **7** apropos, brother, cognate, germane, grandma, grandpa, kinsman, reliant, sibling **8** apposite, parallel **9** analogous, as regards, connected, dependant, dependent, kinswoman, pertinent, referring **10** applicable, associated, concerning, connection, contingent, great-uncle, in regard to, kinsperson, pertaining, reciprocal, respective, stepfather, stepmother, stepparent, stepsister
through marriage: **5** in-law
__ relative: **5** blood
relatively: **5** quite **6** rather **8** somewhat
Relatively Speaking
author: Alan Ayckbourn
relatives: **3** fam., kin **5** folks **6** family **7** kindred, kinfolk **8** kinfolks, kinsfolk
relax: **3** ebb, lax, nap, sit, veg **4** bask, calm, ease, give, idle, laze, lift, loaf, loll, rest, slow **5** abate, coast, let go, let up, loose, lower, quiet, remit, slack, yield **6** cool it, ease up, go easy, lessen, loosen, lounge, modify, reduce, relent, repose, rest up, settle, soften, unbend, unwind, veg out, weaken **7** compose, cool off, ease off, goof off, lay back, let up on, lie down, lighten, recline, relieve, sit back, sit down, slacken, take ten **8** calm down, chill out, diminish, kick back, knock off, loosen up, mitigate, moderate, modulate, recreate, slack off, slow down, take five, tone down, wind down **9** hang loose, lie around, lighten up, mellow out, sit around, soft-pedal, untighten **10** liberalize, settle back, settle down, simmer down, take a break, take it easy
as rules: **4** bend
place to ~: **3** den
Relax!: **6** at ease
relaxation: **3** fun **4** ease, play, rest **5** peace, quiet **6** relief, repose **7** comfort, leisure, liberty, license, pastime, resting **8** free time, pleasure **9** amusement, diversion, enjoyment
relaxed: **4** calm, clam, cool, easy, homy, limp **5** homey, let up, loose, quiet, slack, staid, stoic, Type B **6** at ease, casual, low-key, mellow, placid, sedate, serene **7** amiable, at peace, easeful, equable, pacific, stoical, unmoved **8** amicable, carefree, composed, familiar, informal, laid-back, lounging, peaceful, tranquil **9** collected, easygoing, impassive, leisurely, quiescent, temperate, unexcited, unruffled **10** nonchalant, unagitated, untroubled
not ~: **4** edgy, taut **5** rigid, tense
relaxedness: **4** ease **5** peace, poise, quiet **6** aplomb **7** comfort, leisure, license **8** serenity **9** composure
relaxing: **4** cosy, cozy, easy **6** at ease, dreamy **7** easeful
relay: **4** race, send **5** carry **6** fork up, hand on, pass on, spread **7** deliver, hand off **8** hand down, hand over, transfer, transmit, turn over **9** broadcast, pass along, send forth
relay __: **4** race
__ relay: **6** medley
relay race
hand-off: **5** baton
length: **4** mile
portion: **3** leg
release: **3** axe, can, rid **4** boot, drop, emit, free, leak, news, open, oust, sack, undo, vent **5** clear, flash, issue, let go, let up, loose, slack, spare, spell, story, unbar, unmew, unpen, untie, yield **6** acquit, bounce, charge, excuse, exempt, lay off, let off, let out, loosen, notice, open up, pardon, ransom, redeem, relief, report, rescue, spring, unbind, unhand **7** absolve, bail out, cashier, commute, deliver, dismiss, drum out, floater, forgive, freedom, freeing, give off, give out, handout, let up on, liberty, manumit, receipt, set free, slacken, take out, turn out, unchain, unleash, unloose **8** clemency, delivery, dispense, furlough, get rid of, go easy on, liberate, lifeboat, offering, pink-slip, set loose, unfasten, unfetter **9** acquittal, cast loose, discharge, disengage, dismissal, exculpate, exemption, exonerate, extricate, lifesaver, publicity, salvation, surrender, terminate, turn loose, unshackle **10** abreaction, absolution, emancipate, liberation, propaganda, relinquish
press ~: **4** news, word **5** aviso **6** notice, report **7** handout, message **8** bulletin, dispatch **9** statement **10** communiqué
software ~: **3** ver. **7** version
upon: **5** let at
__ release: **4** news **5** cable, press
__-release: **4** slow, time, work **5** timed
released: **4** free **5** let go, loose **6** exempt, untied
be ~: **6** go free
just ~: **3** new
Release Me (song)
artist: Engelbert Humperdinck, Esther Phillips, Wilson Phillips
relegate: **3** lag **4** oust **5** eject, exile, expel, refer **6** assign, banish, charge, commit, credit, demote, deport, pass on, remove **7** commend, confide, consign, dismiss, entrust, expulse, intrust **8** accredit, displace, hand over, throw out, transfer, turn over **9** downgrade, ostracize, transport **10** expatriate
relegation: **9** dismissal, exclusion, expulsion
relent: **3** bow, ebb **4** drop, ease, fall, fold, give, melt, pity, quit, slow, wane **5** let go, let up, relax, spare, yield **6** cave in, comply, cool it, ease up, give in, give up, go soft, soften, weaken **7** back off, die away, die down, ease off, forbear, give way, lay back, slacken, subside **8** ease up on, go easy on,

have pity, loosen up, moderate, say uncle **9** acquiesce, lighten up, mellow out **10** capitulate, come around
don't ~: 5 press **6** demand, insist **7** persist **9** stand firm
relentless: 4 grim, hard, iron **5** bound, cruel, harsh, rigid, stern, stiff **6** dogged, fierce, hang in, savage, severe, strict **7** adamant, dead set, inhuman, nonstop **8** constant, obdurate, pitiless, rigorous, ruthless, sedulous, stubborn, unabated, unbroken, untiring, unwaning **9** continual, cutthroat, ferocious, hang-tough, incessant, merciless, obstinate, punishing, steadfast, stringent, sustained, tenacious, unbending, unpitying **10** implacable, inexorable, inflexible, iron-willed, undeterred, unflagging
relentlessly: 4 ever, hard **6** always **7** forever **8** evermore, for keeps **9** eternally **10** at all times, unendingly
relet: 8 sublease
relevance: 3 use **5** tie-in **6** regard **7** aptness, bearing, concern, fitness, utility **8** interest **10** connection, importance
have ~: 5 apply **6** relate **7** concern, pertain **8** bear upon **9** appertain, make sense
show ~: 5 tie in **7** connect **9** correlate
relevant: 3 apt, fit **5** ad rem **6** cogent, proper, tied in, timely **7** apropos, cognate, fitting, germane, logical, on point, pointed, related, well-put **8** apposite, material, suitable, valuable **9** as regards, bearing on, congruous, consonant, important, pertinent **10** applicable, concerning, felicitous, to the point
be ~: 5 apply, tie in **6** belong, relate **7** pertain **9** appertain
be ~ to: 6 bear on, regard **8** bear upon, belong to
not ~: 5 unapt **9** ill-suited **10** inapposite, malapropos, nongermane, out of order, out of place, unsuitable
not ~ to: 6 beside
reliability: 5 trust **7** loyalty **8** fidelity **9** sincerity
reliable: 4 firm, good, just, safe, sane, sure, true **5** loyal, pucka, pukka, solid, sound, tried **6** honest, proven, secure, stable, steady, trusty, worthy **7** careful, certain, devoted, durable, sincere, staunch, upright, willing **8** constant, credible, fail-safe, faithful, inerrant, punctual, straight, true-blue, truthful, unerring **9** foolproof, goofproof, honorable, incorrupt, reputable, rock solid, steadfast, unfailing, veracious **10** definitive, dependable, impeccable, infallible, inviolable, legitimate
not ~: 5 shaky **7** erratic
reliance: 5 faith, stock, trust **6** belief, credit **8** credence, security **9** assurance **10** confidence, conviction, dependance, dependence
__-reliance: 4 self
reliant: 8 relative **9** dependant, dependent
__-reliant: 4 self
Reliant: 3 car **4** auto **8** Plymouth **10** automobile
relic: 5 curio, scrap, token, trace, wreck **6** fossil, shadow **7** antique, memento, remnant, vestige **8** archaism, artefact, artifact, fragment, heirloom, keepsake, monument, souvenir, survival **9** antiquity **10** archaicism
relics: 5 ashes, ruins
relied upon, to be: 6 honest
relief: 3 aid **4** alms, balm, cure, dole, ease, hand, help, lift, rest **5** break, let up, model, spell **6** remedy, solace, succor **7** charity, comfort, redress, release, respite, support **8** breather, easement **9** abatement, diversion, softening **10** assistance, lightening, mitigation, palliative, recreation, relaxation, substitute, sustenance
cry of ~: 2 ah **3** aah **4** phew, sigh, whew, whoo **6** at last **7** finally **8** gracious
on ~: 5 needy
org.: 3 ARC **4** CARE, FEMA
source of ~: 4 balm **5** salve **6** lotion, remedy **7** anodyne, comfort, unguent **8** liniment, medicine, ointment **9** analgesic, emollient **10** medication, palliative
relief __: 3 map **7** pitcher
__ relief: 5 comic
__-relief: 3 bas
relieve: 3 aid, rid, rob **4** calm, cure, dull, ease, free, help, loot, vent **5** abate, allay, clear, quiet, relax, salve, slake, spare, spell **6** assist, exempt, let off, pacify, quench, rip off, rotate, soften, solace, soothe, succor, temper, unload **7** absolve, anodyne, appease, assuage, bail out, comfort, console, dismiss, let up on, lighten, mollify, redress, slacken, support, sustain **8** brighten, mitigate, moderate, palliate, reassure, unburden **9** alleviate, give a hand, untrouble **10** ameliorate, stand in for, substitute
from: 5 spare **6** excuse, exempt, pardon **7** bail out, forgive
of doubt: 6 assure **7** certify **8** convince **9** guarantee
of responsibility: 2 ax **4** fire, oust **5** let go **7** dismiss, suspend **8** furlough **9** discharge
relieved: 8 grateful, thankful **9** gratified
reliever: 6 hurler **7** pitcher
goal: 4 save
inning: 5 ninth **6** eighth **7** seventh
__-relievo: 4 alto, cavo **5** basso, mezzo
relig.: 4 Bapt., Cath., Prot. **5** theol.
religion: 3 Zen **4** Cath., cult, myth, Prot., sect **5** Baha'I, creed, deism, dogma, faith, Islam, piety, tenet **6** belief, church, Shinto **7** Jainism, Judaism, pietism, Rom. Cath. **8** Buddhism, doctrine, Hinduism, theology **9** Mormonism, mythology, orthodoxy **10** observance, persuasion
Religion and Science
author: Bertrand Russell
religion of Abraham, The: 5 Islam
religious: 3 dom, Fra, nun **4** holy, lama, monk, yogi **5** abbot, bonze, fakir, friar, godly, moral, pious, prior, rigid, sadhu, swami, tulku, yogin **6** abbess, cleric, devout, divine, father, hermit, mother, novice, sacred, sister, solemn, vestal, votary **7** ascetic, brother, caloyer, deistic, dervish, recluse, saintly, starets **8** Capuchin, cenobite, clerical, monastic, orthodox, priestly, prioress, reverent, theistic, Ursuline **9** anchorite, born-again, canonical, Carmelite, doctrinal, gyrovague, hesychast, pietistic, Poor Clare, postulant, prayerful, rasophore, righteous, sectarian, spiritual **10** Cistercian, cloistress, God-fearing, pontifical, sacerdotal, sacrosanct, scriptural, unswerving
art figure: 5 orans, orant **6** orante
building: 5 abbey **6** ashram, asrama, chapel, church, mosque, pagoda, priory, temple **7** convent **8** basilica, cloister, lamasery **9** cathedral, monastery, synagogue
ceremony: 4 Mass, rite **6** ritual **7** baptism, liturgy, service **9** communion, Eucharist, sacrament **10** observance
deg.: 3 SSD, STB, std., STM, Th.D.
dissent: 6 heresy **9** blasphemy, sacrilege
donation: 5 tithe
leader: 3 rev. **4** msgr., pope **5** rabbi **6** abbess, bishop, pastor, priest **8** cardinal, reverend **9** monsignor **10** archbishop
offshoot: 4 cult, sect
sayings: 5 logia
school: 3 sem. **7** yeshiva **8** seminary
scroll: 4 Tora **5** Torah
song: 4 hymn **5** psalm
symbol: 4 icon, ikon **5** eikon
very ~: 4 orth. **8** orthodox
virtue: 4 zeal **5** faith **8** devotion **9** reverence **10** devoutness, veneration
religiousness: 5 faith, piety **8** devotion, holiness **9** godliness, reverence **10** devoutness
Religulous (2008 film)
cast: Bill Maher
relinquish: 3 end **4** cede, drop, dump, give, lose, quit, sell, shed **5** chuck, demit, ditch, forgo, leave, let go, spare, waive, yield **6** forego, fork up, give up, opt out, refund, render, resign, vacate **7** abandon, discard, forfeit, forsake, kiss off, lay down, let go of, release **8** abdicate, abnegate, forswear, get rid of, hand over, jettison, lay aside, part with, renounce, sign away, throw out, turn over **9** cast aside, dispose of, foreswear, sacrifice, stand down, surrender, throw away
relinquishment: 6 waiver **7** cession **9** surrender **10** abdication
reliquary: 9 container **10** receptacle, repository
relish: 3 dig, zip **4** like, love, take, tang, zeal, zest **5** eat up, enjoy, fancy, go for, gusto, revel, savor, spice, taste **6** accept, catsup, desire, devour, flavor, liking, wallow **7** catchup, chutnee, chutney, ketchup, stomach **8** appetite, dressing, fondness, penchant, pleasure **9** condiment, delight in, enjoyment, flavoring, get high on, gloat over, luxuriate, rejoice in **10** appreciate, chili sauce, enthusiasm, love of life, partiality, piccalilli
excessively: 4 brag, crow **5** gloat **7** rub it in, swagger **9** whoop it up
fish ~: 4 alec
maker: 5 Heinz
with ~: 6 gladly **7** eagerly, happily
relish tray item: 5 olive **6** carrot, celery, pepper, pickle
relive: 8 remember, summon up **9** recollect, reminisce, think back
__ relleno: 5 chile
relocate: 4 move **5** carry, shift **7** migrate **8** displace, resettle, transfer **9** transpose **10** transplant
relocation: 4 move **5** shift **6** exodus **10** emigration, resettling
expert: 5 mover
reluctance: 5 qualm **8** aversion **9** timidness **10** diffidence, hesitation
reluctant: 3 coy, shy **4** loth, slow, wary **5** balky, chary, loath **6** afraid, averse, gun-shy **7** adverse, uneager **8** backward, grudging, hesitant **9** demurring, diffident, flinching, laggardly, tentative, uncertain, unwilling **10** indisposed, uneffusive, uninclined, unobliging
be ~: 4 balk **5** dally, demur, hedge, waver **6** recoil, waffle **7** hold off, shy away **8** hesitate, hold back, pull back **9** hem and haw, pussyfoot, vacillate **10** dillydally, equivocate, think twice
be more than ~: 5 dread
one: 6 balker
rely
on: 5 pivot, swear, trust **6** accept, assume, credit, expect, look to, reckon **7** believe, swear by **8** be sure of **9** believe in, calculate **10** set store by
(on): 4 bank, lean, rest **5** build, count, hinge **6** depend, gamble
too much: 7 presume
REM
engaged in ~: 6 asleep **8** sleeping
experience ~: 5 dream, sleep **7** slumber
part: 3 eye **5** rapid **8** movement
REM __: 5 sleep
R.E.M.
hometown: Athens, Georgia
lead singer: Michael Stipe
song: Bang and Blame (1995)
Drive (1992)
Everybody Hurts (1993)
Losing My Religion (1991)
Man on the Moon (1993)
The One I Love (1987)
Shiny Happy People (1991)
Stand (1989)
What's the Frequency, Kenneth? (1994)

remain: 3 lie, sit 4 bide, halt, hold, last, live, stay, wait 5 abide, cling, delay, dwell, exist, hover, lodge, perch, roost, squat, stand, stick, tarry, visit 6 endure, keep on, linger, occupy, reside 7 hang out, outlast, outlive, persist, prevail, sojourn, survive 8 continue, go unused, sit tight 9 persevere 10 hang around, sit through, stay a while, stick it out, wait around
undone: 4 hang 5 await, delay, stall
remainder: 3 end 4 rest, stub 5 dregs, scrap 6 excess 7 balance, oddment, remnant, residue, salvage, surplus 8 leavings, leftover, residuum 9 aftermath, carryover, liability 10 complement
leaving no ~: 6 evenly
remaining: 3 net, odd 4 left, over, sole 6 extant, with us 7 uneaten 8 leftover, residual 9 vestigial 10 unconsumed
combining form: 4 meno-
ones: 4 rest 6 others
remains: 4 rest 5 ashes, chaff, ruins, trace 6 refuse, shards 7 remnant, residue, vestige 8 leavings
remains __ seen: 4 to be
Remains of the Day, The (1993 film)
cast: Anthony Hopkins, Christopher Reeve, Emma Thompson
director: James Ivory
remake: 6 change, reform 9 modernize, replicate
remand: 4 jail 6 detain, immure, intern, lock up 7 confine 8 imprison
remark: 3 mot, say, see 4 barb, espy, mind, note, quip, word 5 ad lib, aside, crack, gloss, input, speak, state 6 advert, behold, bon mot, notice, phrase, regard 7 comment, declare, mention, observe 8 comeback, perceive, pick up on 9 assertion, recognize, reference, statement, utterance, wisecrack 10 observance, reflection
remarkable: 3 odd 4 rare 5 queer 6 famous, signal, unique 7 curious, notable, salient, uncanny, unusual 8 historic, singular, stunning, wondrous 9 arresting, important, memorable, prominent, unrivaled, wonderful 10 impressive, noteworthy, unrivalled
person: 4 oner 6 corker
thing: 4 lulu 5 dilly
see also wonderful
remarkably: 4 oh so, very 5 extra, quite, right 6 highly, vastly 7 greatly 8 markedly, terribly 9 eminently, extremely, unusually 10 especially, incredibly
remarks: 6 speech 8 analysis 9 voice-over 10 commentary
Remarque, Erich Maria: 6 German, writer
spouse: Paulette Goddard
work: All Quiet on the Western Front
A Time to Love and a Time to Die
remarriage: 6 digamy
Rembrandt: 5 Peale 6 artist, van Ryn 7 painter, van Rijn 10 toothpaste
alternative: ***see*** toothpaste
homeland: 7 Holland
work: 3 oil 8 portrait
remedial: 6 aidful, benign, iatric, useful 7 healing, helpful 8 curative, positive, salutary, sanative 9 effectual, favorable, medicinal 10 beneficial, corrective, productive, worthwhile
assistant: 5 coach, tutor 7 trainer
procedure: 7 therapy
workshop: 6 clinic
remedial __: 7 reading
remediless: 9 unfixable
remedy: 3 aid, fix 4 balm, cure, drug, ease, heal, help, pill 5 right, salve 6 doctor, elixir, physic, potion, reform, relief, repair, soothe 7 assuage, cure-all, expiate, panacea, rectify, redress, therapy 8 antidote, medicine, mitigate, palliate, put right, recourse, solution 9 alleviate, do justice, expiation, treatment 10 ameliorate, corrective, make good on, medication
old-fashioned ~: 5 tonic 6 elixir, potion 7 nostrum
secret ~: 7 arcanum
remember: 4 cite, mind 5 learn, place, think 6 call up, recall, relive, retain 7 bethink, observe 8 enshrine, hold dear, inshrine, look back, memorize, summon up, treasure 9 brood over, conjure up, dwell upon, give a darn, recognize, recollect, reminisce, think back 10 bear in mind, call to mind, keep in mind
a time to ~: 3 age, era 5 epoch
don't ~: 6 forget
thing to ~: 5 Alamo, Maine
words to ~: 3 saw 5 adage, axiom, maxim, motto 6 dictum, saying, slogan 7 epigram, precept, proverb 8 aphorism, apothegm
Remember (1964 song)
artist: Shangri-las
Remember __: 4 WENN
__ Remember: 3 I'll 5 This I, Try to
remembered, easily: 6 catchy
Remember Me
author: Mary Higgins Clark
Remember Me (1971 song)
artist: Diana Ross
Remember the __!: 5 Alamo, Maine
Remember the Titans (2000 film)
cast: Will Patton, Denzel Washington
Remember WENN
genre: 5 drama 6 comedy
network: 3 AMC
Remember You're Mine (1957 song)
artist: Pat Boone
remembrance: 4 gift 5 favor, relic, token 6 memory, recall, record 7 memento, present 8 keepsake, monument, reminder, souvenir 9 hindsight
Remembrance __: 3 Day
Remembrance of Things Past
author: Marcel Proust
remembrances: 7 regards 8 respects 9 greetings 10 best wishes
remex: 5 plume 7 feather
Remick, Lee: 7 actress
film: Anatomy of a Murder (1959)
Baby The Rain Must Fall (1965)
The Competition (1980)
Days of Wine and Roses (1962)
The Detective (1968)
The Europeans (1979)
Experiment in Terror (1962)
A Face in the Crowd (1957)
No Way to Treat a Lady (1968)
The Running Man (1963)
Telefon (1977)
remind: 4 hint, prod, warn 5 nudge 6 pester, prompt, recall 7 bethink, caution, suggest 9 recollect, reminisce
one of: 8 resemble
too often: 3 bug, nag 4 carp, harp 5 annoy, cavil, harry 6 badger, berate, harass, hector, needle, pester 7 henpeck, nitpick 8 browbeat, irritate 9 aggravate, importune
reminder: 3 cue 4 hint, memo, note, sign 5 nudge, token 6 notice, prompt 7 jotting, memento, trinket, warning 8 keepsake, mnemonic, souvenir 10 admonition, indication, memorandum, suggestion
remindful: 8 symbolic 9 evocative 10 suggestive
__ reminds me...: 4 That
Remington: 5 razor 6 shaver, Steele 8 Frederic
alternative: 5 Braun 6 Schick 7 Norelco
Remington-__: 4 Rand
Remington, Frederic: 6 artist 7 painter 8 sculptor
Remington Steele (NBC drama)
cast: Pierce Brosnan (Remington Steele)
Stephanie Zimbalist (Laura Holt)
cat: 4 Nero
producer: MTM
Remini: 4 Leah
reminisce: 5 think 6 recall, relive, remind 8 hark back, look back, remember 9 recollect, think back
reminiscence: 6 memory, recall
reminiscent: 8 mnemonic, redolent 9 evocative, nostalgic, remindful
remiss: 3 lax 4 lazy, loth, slow 5 hasty, loath, loose, slack 6 sloppy 7 belated 8 careless, derelict, dilatory, heedless, slapdash, slipshod, slothful 9 forgetful, imprudent, negligent, unmindful 10 delinquent, incautious, neglectful, nonchalant, regardless, unthinking, unthorough
be ~: 4 omit 5 shirk 6 ignore, pass by 7 neglect, slacken 8 overlook, pass over 9 disregard, gloss over
remission: 3 ebb 4 stay 5 letup 6 easing, ebbing, pardon, waning 7 amnesty, anodyne, decline, redress 8 abeyance, decrease 9 abatement, cessation, dwindling, lessening, reduction 10 diminution, subsidence, suspension
remissness: 6 laxity 7 laxness, neglect 8 laziness
remit: 3 pay 4 give, mail, post, send, ship 5 abate, defer, delay, relax, waive 6 cancel, excuse, modify, pardon, put off, refund, return, settle 7 absolve, deliver, forbear, forgive, forward, refrain, slacken, tail off 8 decrease, dispatch, fork over, mitigate, postpone, set right, transmit 9 exonerate
remittable: 9 allowable, excusable 10 condonable, defensible, forgivable, pardonable
remittance: 3 pmt. 7 payment 9 allowance, discharge
remitted in advance: 3 ppd. 7 prepaid
remitter: 5 payer
remnant: 3 bit, end 4 butt, dreg, heel, lees, orts, rest, snip, stub 5 crumb, dregs, dross, piece, relic, scrap, shard, sherd, shred, trace 6 excess, tag end 7 balance, frazzle, oddment, remains, residue, surplus, vestige 8 fragment, landmark, leavings, leftover, residuum 9 remainder
grill ~: 3 ash 6 cinder
remnants: 5 ruins 8 leavings 9 leftovers
Remo: 8 Williams
remodel: 4 redo 5 adapt, alter, renew, shape 6 change, do over, modify, reform 8 innovate, make over, renovate 9 modernize, refurbish, transform
remodeling: 6 change 7 redress 9 refitting 10 adaptation, alteration, correction
project: 3 ell 5 annex, attic 7 kitchen 8 basement
__ Remo, Italy: 3 San
remold: 5 alter
remonstrance: 5 blame 6 rebuke 7 censure 8 question
remonstrate: 4 warn 5 argue, chide, demur, scold 6 differ, object, reason 7 censure, contend, dispute, dissent, inveigh, protest 8 complain, reproach 9 take issue
remora: 4 fish, pega
ride: 5 shark
remorse: 3 rue 5 grief, guilt, shame 6 regret, sorrow 7 anguish, emotion 9 penitence 10 contrition, repentance, ruefulness
feel ~: 3 rue 6 regret, repent
sign of ~: 4 pang, tear
remorseful: 5 sorry 6 rueful 7 ashamed, humbled 8 contrite, penitent 9 chastened, regretful, repentant 10 apologetic
one: 4 ruer
remorseless: 4 grim, hard, mean 5 cruel, harsh 6 brutal, mortal, savage 7 callous, inhuman 8 hardened, indurate, inhumane, obdurate, pitiless, ruthless 9 merciless, murderous, shameless
remote: 3 far, icy, off, old 4 away, cold, cool, slim, wild 5 alien, alone, aloof, apart, outer 6 chilly, far-off, lonely, slight, uppity, yonder 7 distant, far away, foreign, glacial, obscure, outside, private, slender, strange, stuck-up, unknown 8 detached, far-flung, frontier, isolated, lonesome, outlying, reserved, secluded, snobbish, solitary, unlikely 9 bellicose, withdrawn 10 abstracted, antisocial, impersonal, improbable, insociable, negligible, out of range, unagitated, unamicable, unfamiliar
area: 6 Podunk 7 boonies 9 boondocks

button: 3 rec 4 mute, play 5 on-off, pause, reset 6 record, vol. off, volume. 7 channel
more ~: 7 farther, further
most ~: 4 last 7 extreme 8 farthest
target: 2 TV 3 VCR 5 TV set 8 CD player 9 DVD player
TV ~ control: 4 nemo
remote __: 7 control
remoteness: 6 length 8 distance 9 seclusion 10 alienation, detachment
removal: 8 excision, transfer 9 departure, dismissal, exclusion, expulsion, uprooting 10 deposition, extraction, transferal, unfrocking, withdrawal
combining form: 6 -ectomy
unlawful ~: 5 heist, theft 6 holdup, piracy 7 larceny, looting, robbery, robbing, swiping 8 burglary, poaching, stealing, thievery 9 pilferage, pilfering 10 plundering
remove: 3 rid 4 dele, doff, do in, drop, junk, kill, lift, oust, pull, rase, raze, shed, snip, take, undo, wean, wipe, x out 5 clear, drain, eject, erase, evict, expel, prune, purge, scoop, shear, strip, sweep 6 banish, bounce, censor, cut out, delete, depose, detach, dig out, divest, evulse, excise, exsect, lop off, rip out, unlade, unload, unseat, uproot 7 abscise, cart off, cashier, dismiss, drag off, exclude, excrete, expunge, exscind, extract, lighten, obviate, off with, pull out, root out, scratch, shake up, take off, take out, tear off, tear out, wipe out 8 cross off, cross out, dethrone, dislodge, displace, evacuate, exorcise, exorcize, get rid of, phase out, pull down, relegate, shake off, subtract, take away, throw out, transfer, white out, withdraw 9 carry away, clear away, discharge, dispose of, eliminate, eradicate, extirpate, liquidate, red-pencil, slip out of, transport 10 do away with, obliterate, transplant
a renter: 4 boot 6 bounce 7 boot out, kick out, toss out 8 force out 10 dispossess
feeling: 4 dull 6 deaden
gradually ~: 4 wean
oneself: 7 leave. go
(oneself): 6 absent
opposite: 5 put in 7 include, install
prefix: 3 dis-
rind: 4 pare, peel, skin
vital parts: 3 gut 4 sack 5 rifle 6 ravage 7 destroy, pillage, plunder, ransack 8 clean out, decimate
removed: 3 off 5 aloof 6 lonely 7 distant, missing 8 outlying, secluded, separate 9 withdrawn
__ remover: 5 paint 6 staple
remover, dirt: 8 cleanser 9 detergent
Remscheid region: 4 Ruhr
Remsen, Ira: 7 chemist
remuda: 6 horses, mounts 7 cayuses
remunerate: 3 pay 5 pay up, repay 6 ante up, recoup, refund, reward 7 guerdon, satisfy 8 shell out 9 indemnify, reimburse 10 compensate
remuneration: 3 fee, pay 4 wage 5 wages 6 profit, refund, reward, salary 7 payment 8 earnings 9 emolument
not taking ~: 6 unpaid 9 volunteer
remunerative: 7 gainful 9 lucrative, rewarding 10 good-paying, profitable, well-paying
Remus: 4 twin 5 Roman
parent: 4 Ares, Mars 10 Rhea Silvia
twin: 7 Romulus
Remus, Uncle
character: 3 Fox 4 Bear, Br'er 6 Rabbit 7 Br'er Fox 8 Br'er Bear 10 Br'er Rabbit
Remy: 4 wine
Ren: 3 dog 4 toon 5 Woods 9 Chihuahua
pal: 6 Stimpy
renaissance: 7 rebirth, revival
Renaissance: 5 style
composition: 5 motet
engraver: 5 Dürer
headdress: 6 cornet
instrument: 4 lute 5 rebec 6 rebeck
man: 10 generalist
painter: 5 Dürer 6 Titian 7 Raphael 9 Donatello 10 Botticelli 11 Fra Angelico
sword: 5 estoc
Renaissance __: 3 man 5 woman
__ Renaissance: 6 Harlem
Renaissance Man (1994 film)
cast: Danny DeVito, Gregory Hines, Cliff Robertson
director: Penny Marshall
renal: 7 hepatic, nephric
Renaldo: 6 Duncan
Renan, Ernest: 6 French, writer
renascence: 7 revival
Renascence and Other Poems
author: Edna St. Vincent Millay
Renata: 7 Tebaldi
Renault: 3 car 4 auto, Mary 5 Louis 10 automobile
model: 4 Clio 5 Le Car 6 Laguna, Megane 8 Dauphine
Renault, Louis: 8 Nobelist
Renault, Mary: 6 writer 7 English
work: The Charioteer
Fire from Heaven
The King Must Die
The Last of the Wine
The Persian Boy
The Praise Singer
Renay, Diane
song: Navy Blue (1964)
rend: 3 rip 4 rive, tear 5 break, rip up, sever, slash, split 6 cleave, divide, harrow, mangle, sunder 7 afflict, break up, disjoin, disturb, shatter, split up 8 distress, disunite, fracture, lacerate, rip apart, separate 9 pull apart, tear apart 10 break apart
old-style: 5 reave
Rendell: 4 Ruth
render: 2 do 3 bid, pay, put, say 4 cede, deal, give, melt, play 5 allot, grant, repay, yield 6 accord, afford, depict, donate, effect, fork up, hand in, impart, recite, return, sketch, supply, tender 7 furnish, pay back, perform, picture, portray, present, produce, provide, restore 8 dispense, fork over, hand down, hand over, melt down, shell out, turn over 9 interpret, translate 10 contribute, paraphrase, relinquish, transcribe
helpless: 4 bind 6 fetter, hamper, hobble 8 restrain 9 hamstring
speechless: 3 awe, wow 4 stun 5 amaze, floor 9 overwhelm
unconscious: 2 KO 4 drug, stun 5 floor, punch 7 flatten
rendered: 4 done 7 wrought
rendering: 7 reading, recital, version 9 depiction, execution 10 definition, recitation
Render therefore __ Caesar...: 4 unto
rendezvous: 4 date 5 haunt, tryst 6 gather, join up, liaise 7 hangout, meeting 9 encounter, forgather, get to know, heavy date, tête-à-tête 10 congregate, engagement
with: 3 see 4 meet
Rendezvous
artist: Erté
Rendezvous With Rama
author: Arthur C. Clarke
__-rending: 5 heart
rendition: 7 reading, recital, version 8 delivery 9 depiction, portrayal 10 definition, expression
Rendition (2007 film)
cast: Jake Gyllenhaal, Meryl Streep, Reese Witherspoon
Rene: 5 Russo 6 Goupil 7 Lacoste
René: 4 Char, Coty 5 Clair, Dubos 6 Cassin, Norman 7 Lacoste, Lalique 8 Favaloro, Levesque, Magritte 9 Descartes, Leibowitz
see also French
René __ Réaumur: 3 Ade
Renee: 6 Adoree, Taylor 7 Daalder, O'Connor 8 Richards
Renée: 7 Fleming 9 Zellweger
see also French
renegade: 5 exile, rebel, snake, stray 6 outlaw 7 escapee, hellion, heretic, radical, ratfink, runaway, traitor 8 apostate, betrayer, defector, derelict, deserter, disloyal, forsaker, frondeur, fugitive, maverick, mutineer, mutinous, recreant, resister, turncoat 9 dissenter, dissident, insurgent, protester 10 iconoclast, malcontent, schismatic
renege: 4 turn 6 cop out, recant 7 back out, pull out, retract, reverse, worm out 8 abrogate, go back on, withdraw 9 back-pedal, weasel out
renew: 4 mend 5 fix up, rally, refit, waken 6 extend, perk up, recall, reform, repair, resume, revive, take up, update 7 enliven, fortify, freshen, furbish, prolong, recover, recruit, refresh, remodel, restart, restore, retread, touch up 8 continue, overhaul, reaffirm, reawaken, renovate, spruce up 9 modernize, refurbish, reiterate, replenish, restitute, start over, transform 10 invigorate, recommence, regenerate, rejuvenate, revitalize, strengthen
renewable __: 6 energy
renewal: 5 rally 7 healing, redress 8 comeback, recovery
candidate: 4 slum
card: 6 insert
require ~: 5 lapse 6 expire, run out
__ renewal: 5 urban
renewed, not get: 5 lapse
Renfro: 3 Mel 4 Brad
Renfro, Mel
sport: 8 football
Reni: 5 Guido 7 Santoni
Reni, Guido: 6 artist 7 painter
homeland: 5 Italy
Rennes: 4 city, town
locale: 6 France
river: 4 Ille 7 Vilaine
Rennie: 7 Michael
Rennie, Michael: 5 actor
Renny: 6 Harlin
Reno: 4 city, Mike, town 5 Janet, Kelly
alternative: 5 Vegas 8 Las Vegas
city near ~: 4 Elko 6 Sparks
locale: 3 Nev. 6 Nevada
zone: 3 PDT, PST
see also casino
Renoir, Jean: 6 French 8 director
film: A Day in the Country (1946)
Grand Illusion (1937)
La Chienne (1931)
Nana (1926)
The River (1951)
Rules of the Game (1939)
The Southerner (1945)
film heroine: 5 Elena
Renoir, Pierre-Auguste: 6 artist, French 7 painter
associate: Claude Monet, Edgar Degas
subject: 4 nude
renounce: 4 deny, drop, dump, quit, turn 5 annul, demit, forgo, leave, spurn, waive 6 abjure, defect, desert, disown, eschew, forego, give up, opt out, recant, reject, resign 7 abandon, abstain, cast off, disavow, forbear, forsake, let go of, refrain, retract 8 abdicate, abnegate, disclaim, forswear, keep from, lay aside, part with, swear off, toss over 9 foreswear, repudiate, sacrifice, surrender 10 relinquish
renounced: 6 lonely 7 outcast 8 forsaken, isolated 9 by oneself
renouncement: 6 denial 7 refusal 8 apostasy 10 abdication
renovate: 4 mend, redo 5 alter, fix up, rehab, renew 6 change, reform, repair, revamp, update 7 furbish, refresh, remodel, restore, touch up 8 overhaul, spruce up 9 modernize, refurbish 10 regenerate, rejuvenate
renown: 4 fame, name 5 éclat, glory, honor 6 credit, luster, repute, status 7 acclaim, laurels, stardom 8 eminence, prestige, splendor 9 celebrity, notoriety 10 popularity, prominence, reputation
renowned: 4 star 5 famed, great, lofty, noted 6 famous, mighty, of note, signal 7 big-name, eminent, notable, storied 8 esteemed, extolled, glorious, historic, laureate, splendid 9 acclaimed, legendary, prominent, superstar, topflight, well-known 10 celebrated, preeminent
__-renowned: 5 world
rent: 3 let, rip 4 gash, hire, open, rift,

slit, take, tear, torn **5** break, cleft, crack, lease, lodge, slash, split **6** borrow, breach, engage, income, ragged, ripped, schism, sublet, tatter **7** charter, crevice, fissure, hire out, opening, rupture **8** fracture, overhead, sundered **9** lacerated **10** interspace
accommodation for ~: **2** rm. **3** inn **4** room **5** B and B, hotel, motel, suite **6** marina **7** lodging **10** motor lodge
apartment without ~: **5** condo
collector: **6** lessor **8** landlady, landlord
for ~: **5** to let, unlet **6** vacant
out again: **5** relet
payer: **6** lessee, tenant
rent __: **6** strike **7** control
rent-__: **4** a-car, free
rental: **4** flat **5** suite **7** vacancy
see also apartment
__-rent district: **3** low **4** high
rented: **5** in use **7** lived-in **8** occupied
renter: **5** guest, liver **6** lessee, lodger, tenant **8** occupant **10** inhabitant, vacationer
paper: **5** lease
remove a ~: **4** boot **5** evict **6** bounce **7** boot out, kick out, toss out **8** force out **10** dispossess
Renton: **4** city, town
locale: **10** Washington
rent-to-__: **3** own
renunciation: **6** denial **7** refusal **8** apostasy **10** abdication
Renuzit
alternative: **5** Glade **6** Wizard **7** Airwick, Stick-Up
__ reo: **7** absente
Reo: **3** car **4** auto **10** automobile
maker: **4** Olds
model: **5** Elite **6** Royale **11** Flying Cloud, Silver Cloud
part: **3** Eli **4** Olds **6** Ransom
rival: **5** Essex
reoccupy: **6** retake **7** recover
reoccur: **6** repeat **9** come again
reoccurring: **8** repeated, unending **9** continual, perpetual
reopen: **6** resume **7** restart **8** continue **10** recommence
reorder: **4** move **5** alter, shift **6** change, invert, switch **7** reverse **9** rearrange, transpose
reorganize: **5** rally **6** change, modify, reform **7** shake up **8** make over, overhaul
REO Speedwagon
lead singer: Cronin
song: Can't Fight This Feeling (1985)
Here With Me (1988)
In My Dreams (1987)
In Your Letter (1981)
Keep On Loving You (1980)
Keep the Fire Burnin' (1982)
One Lonely Night (1985)
Take It on the Run (1981)
That Ain't Love (1987)
rep: **3** agt., att. **4** atty., name **5** agent, proxy **6** cravat, deputy, fabric **8** attorney, good name **9** deal maker, middleman **10** mouthpiece, negotiator
see also representative
__ rep: **5** sales
Rep.: **3** pol.
counterpart: **3** Dem., Sen.
epithet: **3** GOP
not ~ or Dem.: **3** Ind.
see also Republican
__ Rep.: **3** Dom.
repair: **2** go **3** fix, hie, sew **4** cure, darn, mend, trim, vamp **5** amend, debug, emend, fixup, leave, patch, rehab, renew, resew, right **6** adjust, betake, doctor, modify, reform, remedy, revamp, stitch, tinker, travel **7** correct, journey, patch up, proceed, push off, recover, recruit, rectify, redress, refresh, replace, restore, retouch, retread, touch up **8** overhaul, renovate, retrieve **9** do justice, refurbish **10** adjustment
anew: **5** refix
beyond ~: **4** shot **5** kaput
bill part: **5** labor, parts
do a makeshift ~: **5** rig up
ender: **3** man, men **5** woman, women **6** people, person
needing ~: **6** broken, busted, faulty **7** cracked, damaged, haywire **9** defective, fractured, in the shop **10** inoperable, not working, on the blink, on the fritz, out of order
state of ~: **4** trim **5** shape **6** fettle **7** fitness **9** condition
to: **7** head for
repairer: **4** mech **5** fixer **8** mechanic
repairs: **6** upkeep
without ~: **4** as is
repair-shop substitute: **6** loaner
reparation: **3** pay **4** dues, fine **6** amends **7** apology, damages, payment, penance, redress **9** atonement, expiation, repayment **10** correction, punishment
make ~: **5** atone **7** redress, satisfy **9** reimburse
maker: **6** atoner
repartee: **3** wit **4** quip **5** sally **6** banter, bon mot, retort, ripost **7** riposte **8** badinage, chitchat, comeback, raillery, wordplay **9** rejoinder, table talk, witticism **10** persiflage, pleasantry
bit of ~: **3** mot **4** quip **5** crack **6** bon mot, retort, zinger **7** riposte **8** one-liner **9** wisecrack
repast: **4** meal **5** feast **6** dinner **7** aliment, banquet **8** victuals **9** collation, refection
enjoy a ~: **3** eat, sup **5** feast
quite a ~: **4** fete, gala **5** feast **6** spread **7** banquet **8** clambake
repay: **6** avenge, offset, rebate, recoup, redeem, refund, render, return, reward **7** get even, replace, requite, satisfy **8** give back, make good, settle up, square up **9** get back at, indemnify, liquidate, reimburse, retaliate **10** compensate, make amends, make good on, recompense, remunerate
must ~: **3** owe
repayment: **3** due **6** refund, reward **9** vengeance **10** recompense, reparation
repeal: **3** nix **4** kill, lift, void **5** annul, quash, scrub **6** cancel, negate, recall, recant, revoke **7** abolish, nullify, rescind, retract, reverse **8** abrogate, dissolve, override, overrule, overturn, set aside, withdraw **9** annulment, repudiate **10** invalidate
repeat: **3** say **4** copy, echo **5** clone, ditto, quote, recur, rerun, resay **6** do over, encore, harp on, parrot, recite, rehash, replay, retell, return, stress **7** imitate, iterate, narrate, recount, reflect, reoccur, reprise, restate, run over, stammer **8** drum into, multiply, play back, play over, practice, read back, reappear, rehearse **9** come again, duplicate, reiterate, replicate, reshowing
in music: **3** bis
performance: **6** déjà vu, encore
sign, in music: **5** segno
verbatim: **4** cite, copy, echo **5** mimic, quote **6** parrot, recite, repeat, retell **7** excerpt, extract
without ~: **4** once
repeated: **6** afresh **8** frequent, habitual, periodic, standing **9** perpetual **10** persistent, reiterated
exercises: **5** drill
repeatedly: **3** oft **4** much **5** again, often **8** ofttimes **9** many times, regularly **10** frequently
repeated pattern in heraldry: **4** semé
repeating, keep: **5** chant **6** intone
repel: **4** buck, defy **5** fight, parry, spurn **6** defeat, offend, put off, rebuff, refuse, reject, resist, revolt, sicken **7** disgust, fend off, hold off, repulse, turn off, ward off **8** beat back, drive off, fight off, frighten, gross out, push back, shake off, stave off, turn back, vanquish **9** chase away, displease, drive away, drive back, hold at bay, keep at bay, turn aside, withstand **10** antagonize
repellence: **4** hate **6** hatred, horror **7** disgust, dislike **8** aversion, distaste, loathing **9** antipathy, repulsion, revulsion **10** abhorrence, repugnance
repellent: **4** foul, icky, rank, ugly, vile **5** awful, gross, nasty, seamy **6** creepy, odious, sordid **7** beastly, ghastly, hateful, heinous, hideous, squalid **8** horrible, terrible, wretched **9** abhorrent, appalling, execrable, frightful, loathsome, monstrous, obnoxious, offensive, repugnant, revolting, unsightly **10** abominable, despicable, detestable, disgusting, forbidding, uninviting, unpleasant
__ repellent: **5** shark **6** insect
__-repellent: **5** water
repeller, evil: **5** charm, spell **7** periapt **8** talisman
repent: **5** atone **6** bewail, lament
of: **3** rue **6** regret **7** deplore **8** weep over
repentance: **5** guilt **6** regret, sorrow **7** penance, remorse **9** attrition, penitence **10** contrition
repentant: **5** sorry **7** subdued **8** contrite, penitent **9** regretful **10** apologetic, remorseful
one: **4** ruer **6** atoner
repercussion: **4** echo, flak **5** flack, waves **6** effect, impact, recoil, result, upshot **7** fallout, outcome **8** backlash, backwash, follow-up, reaction **9** aftermath
repertoire: **4** list **5** stock **6** dramas, operas, pieces **7** catalog **9** catalogue, inventory
repertory: **3** rep **5** range, shtik, stock, store **6** shtick, supply **10** collection, depository, repertoire
repertory __: **7** company, theater, theatre
repetition: **4** copy, echo, rote **5** chant, drill **6** chorus, encore, litany, rhythm **7** recital **8** practice, sameness **9** duplicate, frequency, iteration, rehearsal, tautology
mark of ~: **5** ditto
rapid ~ in music: **7** tremolo
request for ~: **4** what
rhetorical ~: **5** ploce
repetitious: **4** dull **5** stale, windy, wordy **6** boring, prolix **7** tedious, verbose **8** habitual **9** iterative, redundant, wearisome
repetitive: **7** verbose **8** unwaning **9** continual, recurrent
pattern: **5** cycle **6** series **7** routine
repetitiveness: **3** rut **5** ennui **6** tedium **7** boredom, routine **8** dullness, monotony, sameness **10** insipidity, uniformity
rephrase: **4** edit **5** amend **6** reword **9** translate **10** paraphrase
repine: **4** beef, fret, kick, moan, mope, wail **5** gripe, groan, whine **6** kvetch, lament, regret, squawk **7** grumble **8** complain, languish **9** bellyache, make a fuss
replace: **3** sub **4** oust **5** alter, repay, shift, spell **6** change, fill in, follow, refund, repair, return, switch **7** put back, restock, restore, succeed **8** displace, exchange, give back, supplant **9** antiquate, reimburse, replenish, supersede **10** compensate, substitute
ready to ~: **4** worn **6** broken, ruined
replacement: **3** sub **4** temp **6** change, fill-in **9** surrogate **10** substitute
vehicle: **6** loaner
Replacement Killers, The (1998 film)
cast: Jürgen Prochnow, Mira Sorvino, Chow Yun-Fat
replacing: **7** instead **8** in lieu of **9** instead of
replay: **6** do over, repeat
instant ~ technique: **5** slo-mo **10** slow motion, stop-action
__ replay: **7** instant
replenish: **4** fill **5** renew, stock **6** load up, make up, refill, reload, supply, top off **7** provide, recruit, refresh, replace, restock, restore
replenishments: **6** stores **7** rations **8** supplies **10** provisions
replete: **4** full, rife **5** alive, awash, laden, sated, thick **6** filled, full up, gorged, heaped, jammed, lavish, loaded, packed **7** charged, crammed, crowded, fraught, glutted, overfed, stuffed, teeming **8** abundant, brimming, infested, satiated, swarming **9** abounding,

chock-full, jam-packed, plenteous, plentiful
repletion: 4 glut 7 satiety, surfeit 8 plethora 9 plenitude
replevin: 4 writ 6 redeem 7 lawsuit, recover
replevy: 6 redeem 7 recover
replica: 4 copy, dupe 5 clone, ditto, image, match, model, repro, xerox 6 carbon, double, ectype 7 picture 8 knockoff, likeness 9 duplicate, facsimile, imitation, look-alike, miniature, photocopy 10 carbon copy, mimeograph
crude ~: 6 effigy
__ replicase: 3 RNA
replicate: 4 copy, redo 5 clone 6 do over, remake, repeat 7 imitate 8 recreate, simulate 9 reproduce
reply: 3 ans., lip, say 4 RSVP, sass 5 react 6 answer, letter, recite, retort, return, ripost 7 counter, defense, hit back, reflect, respond, riposte 8 antiphon, back talk, comeback, feedback, reaction, response 9 get back to, rejoinder, retaliate, utterance, wisecrack, write back
defiant ~: 5 never, no way
hedging ~: 5 maybe 7 perhaps 8 possibly 9 it could be, it might be
roll-call ~: 3 aye, nay, yea, yes 4 here 7 present
sarcastic ~: 4 I bet, sure
to: 5 field, rebut 6 answer, refute 7 counter, dispute 8 disclaim
wishy-washy ~: 7 perhaps 8 possibly 9 it could be, it might be, perchance
reply __: 4 card
Repo Man (1984 film)
cast: Emilio Estevez, Vonetta McGee, Harry Dean Stanton
répondez __ vous plaît: 3 s'il
report: 3 air, say 4 bang, boom, buzz, come, dirt, info, list, name, news, note, tale, talk, tell, wire, word 5 blast, brief, cable, crack, paper, rumor, scoop, sound, state, story, telex, theme 6 advise, cahier, canard, detail, digest, earful, exposé, gossip, impart, inform, letter, notice, notify, pass on, précis, recite, record, relate, repute, résumé, reveal, rumble, show up, tattle, tell on, turn up 7 account, article, check in, clock in, dossier, hearsay, history, itemize, mention, message, missive, narrate, outline, publish, recital, recount, release, rundown, scandal, summary, tidings, trumpet, version, weigh in, whisper, write-up 8 advise of, announce, describe, disclose, dispatch, document, telegram 9 broadcast, chronicle, circulate, discharge, explosion, expound on, grapevine, make known, narration, narrative, publicity, recountal, statement, telephone, term paper, touch base 10 communiqué, detonation, exposition, literature, make public, memorandum, recitation, reputation, whispering
ender: 3 age
false ~: 3 lie 5 libel, smear 7 calumny, slander, untruth 10 imputation
maker: 3 gun 7 firearm
on: 5 cover 6 relate, tell of 7 write up 9 talk about
unfounded ~: 3 lie 4 buzz, dirt, tale, talk, word 5 bruit, rumor 6 canard, earful, gossip, tattle 7 fiction, hearsay, whisper 9 falsehood, grapevine, invention 10 suggestion
weather ~ word: 3 dry, hot, wet 4 cold, cool, fair, hail, hazy, mild, rain, snow, warm 5 clear, foggy, humid, misty, sleet, storm, sunny 6 chilly, cloudy
report __: 4 card
__ report: 6 annual 7 weather
report card: 6 record
datum: 3 GPA 4 mark 5 grade
mark: 2 ef 3 bee, cee, dee 5 A plus, B plus, C plus, D plus 6 A minus, B minus, C minus, D minus
word: 5 tardy 6 absent
reported: 7 alleged, reputed 8 believed, putative, supposed
reporter: 3 cub 4 corr. 5 press 6 anchor, author, legman, writer 8 stringer 9 announcer, columnist, newshound, wordsmith 10 journalist, newscaster, newsperson, newswriter
angle: 5 focus, slant 9 viewpoint 10 standpoint
boss: 6 editor
coup: 5 scoop 9 exclusive
credit: 6 byline
news ~ of yore: 5 crier
often: 5 asker
question: 3 how, who, why 4 what, when 5 where
rookie ~: 3 cub
staple: 5 quote
__ reporter: 3 cub 5 court
reporting to: 5 under
__ Report, The: 4 Hite
repose: 3 lie 4 calm, ease, loaf, loll, rest 5 peace, quiet, relax, sleep 6 lounge, settle 7 leisure, lie down, recline, respite, slumber 8 calmness, free time, quietude 9 stillness 10 inactivity, quiescence, recreation, relaxation, stretch out, take it easy
in ~: 4 calm 5 quiet, still 6 at rest, placid, serene 7 dormant 9 quiescent
reposing: 6 at rest 8 lounging 9 incumbent
reposit: 5 lay up, store 7 put back
reposition: 4 move 5 alter, shift 6 change 7 shuffle 8 displace, maneuver, transfer 9 rearrange 10 move around
repository: 4 fund, safe, stge. 5 booth, depot, store, vault 6 closet, coffer, museum 7 arsenal, lockbox, storage 8 magazine, treasury 9 container, reservoir, warehouse 10 receptacle
repossess: 6 recoup, redeem, regain 7 get back, recover, recruit 8 retrieve, take back 9 reacquire
repp: 4 silk, wool 5 rayon 6 cotton, fabric 8 material
repp __: 3 tie
Repp: 8 Stafford
reprehend: 4 trim 5 chide, decry, knock, scold 6 berate, charge, rebuke 7 bawl out, censure, chew out, condemn, lecture, reprove, upbraid 8 chastise, denounce, reproach 9 castigate, criticize, dress down, fustigate 10 disapprove, take to task, tongue-lash
reprehensible: 4 vile 5 nasty, wrong 6 wicked 7 heinous, ignoble, lowdown, very bad 8 shameful, unseemly, unworthy, wrongful 9 miscreant, offensive 10 despicable, scandalous, villainous
most ~: 5 worst
reprehension: 5 blame 6 rebuke
represent: 4 limn, mean, show, tell 5 act as, enact, paint 6 act for, denote, depict, embody, imbody, mirror, pass as, sketch, typify 7 betoken, express, picture, portray, pretend, serve as, signify, suggest 8 appear as, describe, speak for, stand for 9 adumbrate, epitomize, exemplify, interpret, personify, predicate, symbolize 10 illustrate
representation: 3 map 4 icon, ikon, show, sign 5 eikon, image, totem 6 effigy, emblem, figure, sketch, statue, symbol 7 tableau 8 likeness, specimen 9 spectacle
representational: 7 graphic 9 graphical, realistic
representative: 3 agt., rep 5 agent, envoy, model, proxy, typal, typic 6 consul, deputy, jobber, legate, member, sample 7 example, officer, proctor, senator, typical 8 delegate, emissary, lawmaker, official, specimen, symbolic 9 appointee, councilor, depictive, messenger, realistic, surrogate 10 councillor, emblematic, mouthpiece
foreign ~: 3 amb. 5 envoy 6 consul, legate 8 delegate, diplomat, emissary, minister 10 ambassador
legal ~: 6 jurist, lawyer 7 adviser, advisor, counsel 8 advocate, attorney 9 barrister, solicitor 10 mouthpiece
Representative
locale: 5 House
representatives: 4 gild 5 guild, union 6 caucus, league 7 chamber, council, meeting 8 assembly, conclave, congress 9 committee, delegates, gathering 10 conference, convention, delegation
representing: 3 for 9 acting for 10 in behalf of, on behalf of
repress: 3 gag 4 bury, cork, curb, hold, stop, tame 5 check, crush, quash, quell 6 bottle, bridle, censor, deaden, fetter, hold in, keep in, muffle, muzzle, stifle, subdue 7 confine, contain, control, inhibit, prevent, put down, smother, squelch, swallow 8 blank out, restrain, stamp out, vanquish 9 interdict 10 discourage, keep a lid on, keep in line
repressed: 6 pent-up 7 subdued 9 forgotten, inhibited 10 unrecalled
repression: 9 abatement, restraint 10 constraint, domination
reprieve: 4 free, lull, stay 5 delay, grace, letup, pause, truce 6 pardon 7 forgive, respite 8 abeyance, breather 9 deferment, salvation 10 suspension
reprimand: 3 rag 4 slap 5 blame, chide, scold 6 berate, earful, jump on, lesson, rebuff, rebuke 7 censure, chew out, lambast, lecture, reprove, tell off, upbraid, what for 8 admonish, denounce, give it to, lambaste, reproach, reproval, scolding 9 castigate, criticize, dress down, exprobate, lash out at, light into, talking-to 10 bawling-out, come down on, take to task, upbraiding
reprint: 4 copy 5 print 6 ectype 7 edition 9 reproduce
reprisal: 7 redress, revenge 9 tit for tat, vengeance 10 punishment, quid pro quo
reprise: 6 encore, repeat 9 reiterate, reshowing
repro: 3 fax 4 copy, dupe, stat 6 ectype 7 replica 9 photocopy, Photostat
of yore: 5 mimeo 6 carbon 10 carbon copy, mimeograph
repro.
not a ~: 4 orig.
reproach: 3 rag, tax 4 slam, slur, twit 5 abuse, blame, chide, scold, shame, stain 6 berate, charge, rebuke, stigma 7 asperse, calumny, censure, condemn, reproof, reprove, scandal, tell off, upbraid 8 denounce 9 criticize, discredit, excoriate, frown upon, invective, reprehend, reprimand 10 impugnment, imputation, reflection, take to task
above ~: 5 clean 6 chaste 8 flawless, innocent, spotless, virtuous 9 blameless, faultless, guiltless
exclamation: 5 shame
exclamation of ~: 3 tch, tsk, tut 4 tush, well 6 tsk tsk, tut-tut
oneself: 5 atone 6 repent
__ reproach: 6 beyond
__-reproach: 4 self
reproachful: 7 injured, nagging 8 caviling, critical 9 querulous 10 derogatory, detractive
reprobate: 3 cur 4 heel, roué, worm 5 churl, knave, losel, rogue, rowdy, scamp, spurn 6 bad guy, bad hat, rascal, refuse, reject, varlet, wretch 7 lowlife, outcast, so-and-so, villain 8 picaroon, rakehell, scalawag, shameful 9 corrupted, criticize, debauched, dissolute, miscreant, scallawag, scallywag, scoundrel, shameless, vulgarian 10 blackguard, delinquent, disapprove, licentious, ne'er-do-well, profligate, scapegrace
reprobation: 5 blame 7 censure 9 criticism, reprimand
reproduce: 4 bear, copy, dupe, echo, sire 5 beget, breed, clone, hatch, mimeo, print, spawn, trace, xerox 6 carbon, father, pirate 7 produce, reflect, reprint 8 multiply, simulate

9 duplicate, photocopy, Photostat, propagate, replicate 10 mimeograph, photograph, transcribe
reproduction: 3 fax 4 copy, dupe, fake 5 clone, ditto, image, mimeo, model, xerox 6 carbon, double, ectype 7 replica 8 knockoff, likeness 9 duplicate, facsimile, imitation, look-alike, photocopy, Photostat 10 mimeograph
reproof: 3 rag, tax 4 slam, slur, twit 5 abuse, blame, chide, scold, shame, stain 6 berate, charge, lesson, rebuke, stigma 7 asperse, calumny, censure, condemn, lecture, scandal, tell off, upbraid 8 denounce, reproach, scolding 9 criticism, criticize, discredit, excoriate, frown upon, invective, reprehend, reprimand 10 imputation, reflection, take to task, upbraiding
reproval: 6 rebuke 7 censure, lecture 8 scolding 9 reprimand, talking-to 10 admonition, bawling-out, chewing-out, upbraiding
reprove: 3 rag, tax 4 warn 5 blame, chide, scold 6 berate, punish, rebuff, rebuke 7 censure, condemn, lecture, tell off, upbraid 8 admonish, denounce, reproach 9 criticize, excoriate, exprobate, lash out at, reprehend, reprimand 10 take to task
reptile: 3 asp, boa, uta 4 croc, T-Rex 5 aboma, adder, agama, anole, cobra, gator, gecko, krait, mamba, racer, skink, snake, teiid, viper 6 agamid, caiman, cooter, dhaman, dragon, elapid, gavial, goanna, iguana, lizard, moloch, python, ridley, taipan, turtle 7 markhor, rattler, serpent, snapper 8 anaconda, dinosaur, moccasin, ophidian, ringhals, stinkpot, tortoise 9 alligator, boomslang, chameleon, coachwhip, crocodile, hawksbill 10 bushmaster, copperhead, loggerhead, sidewinder
Africa: 5 mamba 8 ringhals 9 boomslang
Asia: 5 krait 6 dhaman, gavial
Australia: 6 goanna, moloch, taipan
combining form: 4 -saur 6 herpet-, -saurus 7 herpeto-
extinct ~: 4 T-Rex 8 dinosaur
like a ~: 5 scaly
Mexico: 3 uta 9 coachwhip
mythical ~: 6 dragon
New Guinea: 6 taipan
republic: 5 state 6 nation 9 democracy
see also country
__ republic: 6 banana
__ Republic: 5 Czech, Fifth, First, Khmer, Third 6 Fourth, Plato's, Second, Slovak, Weimar 7 People's
Republican: 3 GOP 5 party, river
forerunner: 4 Whig
Party birthplace: 3 Wis. 4 Wisc. 5 Ripon 9 Wisconsin
River locale: 6 Kansas 8 Colorado, Nebraska
Republican, Mr.: Robert Taft
__ Republic of Egypt: 4 Arab
Republic, The
author: Plato
repudiate: 4 deny, drop, dump, shun, veto, void 5 annul, flout, spurn 6 abjure, bounce, cancel, disown, loathe, pass on, rebuff, recant, refuse, refute, reject, repeal, revoke 7 abandon, abolish, cast off, disavow, disdain, dismiss, exclude, forsake, gainsay, let go of, nullify, rescind, retract, reverse 8 disallow, disclaim, forswear, go back on, renounce, take back, turn down 9 blackball, blacklist, break with, cast aside, foreswear, proscribe 10 contradict, contravene, disbelieve, disinherit
repudiated: 7 cast off, outcast 8 forsaken
repudiation: 5 blame, spurn 6 denial 7 refusal 8 apostasy, negation 10 abdication
exclamation of ~: 4 pfui, phoo 6 phooey
repugnance: 4 hate 5 odium 6 hatred, horror 7 disgust, dislike 8 aversion, distaste, loathing 9 antipathy, repulsion, revulsion 10 ill feeling, repellence
exclamation of ~: 3 ack, ick, ugh 4 yuck 5 yecch
feel ~: 4 hate 5 abhor 6 detest, loathe 7 despise 8 execrate 9 abominate
repugnant: 4 base, evil, foul, icky, ugly, vile 5 nasty, seamy, yucky 6 horrid, odious 7 hateful, hideous, noisome 8 gruesome, inimical, unsavory 9 abhorrent, invidious, loathsome, obnoxious, offensive, repellant, repellent, repulsive, revolting 10 abominable, detestable, disgusting, virtueless
repulse: 4 defy, rout, snub 5 parry, repel, spurn 6 defeat, offend, rebuff, rebuke, refuse, reject, revolt, sicken, thwart 7 disgust, fend off, hold off, refusal, turn off, ward off 8 alienate, drive off, fight off, hold back, nauseate, push away, stave off, turn away, turn back 9 drive back, force back, hold at bay, rejection
repulsion: 5 odium 6 hatred 7 disgust, refusal 8 aversion, distaste, loathing 9 antipathy, revulsion 10 abhorrence, repellence, repugnance
repulsive: 4 foul, icky, ugly, vile 5 nasty, slimy 6 creepy, grisly, horrid, odious, rancid 7 hateful, hideous, noisome, squalid 8 shocking, terrible 9 abhorrent, atrocious, execrable, loathsome, offensive, repellent, repugnant, revolting, unsightly 10 abominable, detestable, disgusting, forbidding, off-putting, unpleasant
measure of ~ force: 3 ESU
repurchase: 6 redeem 7 buy back, get back, reclaim 8 retrieve
reputability: 6 ethics, virtue 7 honesty, probity 9 integrity, rectitude 10 trustiness
reputable: 4 fine, good, nice, okay 5 great, legit, moral, noble, sound, tried 6 honest, proper, savory, worthy 7 ethical, upright 8 all right, esteemed, laudable, pleasant, pleasing, reliable, splendid, superior 9 admirable, agreeable, estimable, excellent, honorable, well-known, wonderful 10 acceptable, beneficial, creditable, dependable
reputation: 4 fame, name, odor 5 glory, state 6 credit, esteem, regard, renown, report 7 stature 8 eminence, good name, position, prestige, standing 9 celebrity, character, condition, influence, notoriety 10 importance, prominence
harm a ~: 5 smear
repute: 4 fame, name, odor 5 éclat, value 6 credit, esteem, regard, renown, report 7 quality 8 eminence, good name, prestige, standing 9 celebrity, character
high ~: 4 fame 5 glory 6 renown 7 acclaim 8 eminence, prestige 9 celebrity
ill ~: 5 odium, shame 6 infamy 7 obloquy 8 disfavor, disgrace, dishonor, ignominy 9 disesteem, disrepute, notoriety 10 opprobrium
of ill ~: 5 shady 7 crooked 8 infamous, shameful, unsavory 9 dishonest, notorious, unethical 10 inglorious, scandalous
reputed: 4 held, said 6 deemed 7 alleged, assumed, seeming, thought 8 believed, reckoned, regarded, reported, supposed 10 considered, ostensible
request: 3 ask, beg, bid, sue 4 call, plea, pray, seek, suit, urge 5 apply, hit up, lobby, offer, order, plead, query, touch 6 appeal, ask for, behest, demand, desire, hustle, invite, prayer, summon 7 beseech, bespeak, call for, enquire, enquiry, entreat, inquire, inquiry, propose, solicit 8 entreaty, petition, put in for, question 10 commercial, invitation, supplicate
again: 5 reask
polite ~: 4 may I 6 please
__ request: 4 upon
requiem: 4 Mass 5 dirge, elegy 6 lament
__ Requiem: 3 War 6 German
Requiem for a Heavyweight (1962 film)
cast: Jackie Gleason, Anthony Quinn, Mickey Rooney
Requiem for a Nun
author: William Faulkner
requiescence: 4 ease, rest 7 leisure
require: 3 ask, bid, put 4 bind, cost, lack, miss, need, take, tell, want, wish 5 crave, exact, force, order 6 adjure, compel, demand, desire, direct, enjoin, entail, expect, insist, oblige 7 command, involve, look for, provide, push for 8 call upon, instruct, obligate 9 constrain, prescribe, stipulate 10 depend upon, have use for, insist upon
required: 3 due, set 5 bound, major, vital 6 needed, urgent 7 binding, crucial, needful, pivotal, primary 8 impelled 9 called for, essential, important, mandatory, necessary 10 compulsory, imperative, obligatory, prescribed
beyond what's ~: 4 more 5 extra 8 optional 10 additional
is ~ to: 4 must 5 has to
reading: 4 text 8 syllabus, textbook
requirement: 4 must, need, want 5 state, terms 6 demand 7 dictate, proviso, urgency 8 exigence, exigency 9 condition, essential, extremity, necessity, provision 10 sine qua non
in Latin: 10 sine qua non
requirements: 5 terms 7 strings 10 conditions, provisions
meet ~: 2 do 4 pass, suit 5 serve 7 fulfill, qualify, satisfy, suffice
requisite: 3 due 4 must, need 5 terms, vital 6 demand 7 binding, needful, proviso 8 adequate, exigence, exigency, integral 9 condition, essential, extremity, mandatory, necessary, necessity, provision, right-hand 10 compulsory, imperative, obligatory, prescribed, sine qua non
requisition: 3 rob 5 claim, exact, order, seize 6 ask for, demand 7 request, require, solicit 8 apply for, put in for
requital: 6 amends 7 payment, redress, revenge 9 vengeance
requite: 3 pay 5 repay, right 6 avenge, recoup, reward 7 get even, revenge, satisfy 9 do justice, reimburse, retaliate 10 compensate, make amends, recompense
requited: 6 mutual, shared 8 conjoint, returned 9 bilateral 10 reciprocal
reroute: 6 detour, divert 8 redirect 9 sidetrack
rerun: 6 encore, repeat 9 reshowing
res __: 6 gestae 7 publica
res __ loquitur: 4 ipsa
__-res: 3 low 4 high
resale __: 5 value
__ Resartus: 6 Sartor
resay: 4 echo 6 parrot, repeat 7 iterate, restate 9 reiterate
__ Res. Bd.: 3 Fed.
reschedule: 5 defer, table 6 put off 8 postpone
rescind: 4 lift, void 5 annul, quash, scrub 6 cancel, negate, recall, recant, repeal, revoke 7 abolish, nullify, retract, reverse 8 abrogate, override, overrule, overturn, set aside 9 back-pedal, repudiate 10 invalidate
rescission: 6 recall 9 abolition, annulment
rescue: 3 aid 4 free, save 6 ransom, redeem, snatch, spring 7 bailout, deliver, freedom, heroics, heroism, protect, reclaim, recover, release, restore, salvage, set free, unloose 8 delivery, liberate, preserve, retrieve 9 extricate, recapture, safeguard, salvation
vehicle: 6 copter 8 aircraft 9 ambulance 10 helicopter
Rescue 911 (CBS) host: William Shatner
rescued: 6 untied 9 liberated
Rescue Me (song)
artist: Fontella Bass, Madonna
rescuer: 4 hero 6 savior 7 heroine, saviour 9 liberator

ocean ~: **4** USCG **10** Coast Guard
rescues, like some: 6 air-sea
research: 5 delve, dig up, probe, quest, study **6** look up, survey **7** enquiry, explore, inquiry, legwork, science **8** analysis, findings, learning, look into, read up on, scrutiny **10** groundwork, literature
aid: 5 index
do ~: 3 dig **4** seek **5** crack, delve, probe, study
funds: 5 grant **9** endowment **10** fellowship
govt. ~ sponsor: 3 NSF
paper: 6 thesis **8** treatise **9** monograph
place: 3 lab
project: 5 probe **6** thesis
subject: 6 lab rat
__ research: 6 market
resect: 6 cut out, excise
resection: 8 excision
reseda: 5 green **7** grayish
relative: *see* green color
resemblance: 7 analogy, kinship **8** affinity, likeness, parallel, sameness **9** closeness
resemble: 4 look, seem **5** match, mimic, rival **6** be like, mirror **7** pass for, smack of **8** look like, parallel, seem like, simulate **9** come close, take after **10** appear like, correspond
resembling: 3 à la **4** like **5** quasi **6** akin to **7** similar **8** parallel **9** analogous
combining form: 4 para- **5** quasi-
suffix: 3 -ine **4** -eous
resent: 4 mind **7** dislike **8** object to
resentful: 3 hot, mad **4** hurt, ired, sore **5** angry, cross, huffy, irate, irked, livid, riled, wroth **6** bitter, fuming, ireful, miffed, peeved, piqued, raging, raving, red-hot **7** angered, annoyed, enraged, envious, furious, hostile, jealous, ranting, teed off **8** choleric, incensed, inflamed, maddened, outraged, virulent, wrathful **9** indignant, irritable, irritated, jaundiced, malicious, rancorous, splenetic, ticked off **10** aggravated, freaked out, frustrated, infuriated, vindictive
resentment: 3 ire **4** fury, hate, huff, hurt, rage **5** anger, pique, spite, venom, wrath **6** animus, choler, grudge, malice, rancor, temper **7** dudgeon, ill will, offense, outrage, umbrage **8** acrimony, friction, vexation **9** animosity, annoyance, grievance, hostility, nastiness, surliness **10** sour grapes, unkindness
cause ~: 3 vex **4** miff, roil **5** anger, annoy, peeve, pique, upset **6** nettle, offend, put out **7** provoke **8** irritate **9** displease
show ~: 6 bridle **7** bristle
reservation: 5 doubt, order, place, qualm, query, terms **7** booking, enclave, proviso, scruple, strings **8** preserve **9** condition, hesitancy, misgiving, provision, territory **10** settlement
make a ~: 4 book
without ~: 5 fully **6** wholly **7** totally, utterly **8** entirely **10** absolutely, completely, thoroughly
reservations, with: 8 grudging
reserve: 3 own **4** book, fund, hold, mine, park, save, stow, take **5** cache, extra, hoard, lay up, order, put by, spare, stash, stock, store **6** assets, devote, engage, retain, secure, supply **7** bespeak, capital, caution, charter, earmark, lay away, modesty, nest egg, put away, rope off, savings, shyness, silence, store up **8** backbone, calmness, coldness, contract, distance, gold mine, hold back, keep back, maintain, schedule, set apart, set aside, stow away, withhold **9** aloofness, formality, insurance, inventory, quietness, reservoir, resources, restraint, reticence, sanctuary, secondary, stockpile, timidness **10** constraint, diffidence, prearrange, substitute
financial ~: 6 buffer **7** cushion
in ~: 4 held, kept **5** apart, aside, extra, on ice, on tap, saved, spare **6** stored **8** held back, kept back, put aside, set aside **9** held aside, kept aside
keep in ~: 5 put by, store **7** put away **8** put aside
without ~: 6 openly, wholly **7** frankly, plainly, readily, totally **8** candidly, directly, entirely, honestly, straight **9** all the way, to the hilt **10** completely, point-blank
__ reserve: 4 gold
__ Reserve Bank: 7 Federal
reserved: 3 coy, icy, shy **4** cold, cool, kept, mild, prim **5** aloof, close, quiet, sober, staid, taken **6** booked, demure, formal, humble, modest, placid, remote, sedate, serene, silent, steady **7** bashful, claimed, distant, engaged, indrawn, limited, private, recluse **8** cautious, composed, detached, laid away, moderate, retained, reticent, retiring, set apart, set aside, solitary, specific, taciturn **9** collected, diffident, reclusive, secretive, spoken for, unbending, withdrawn **10** antisocial, insociable, restricted, soft-spoken, unagitated, unamicable, unassuming, uneffusive, unsociable
in a ~ manner: 5 shyly
reserves: 5 means **6** assets **7** backlog, savings **9** resources
reservoir: 4 fund, lake, pond, pool, tank, tarn, well **5** basin, lough, stock, store **6** source, spring, supply **7** backlog, cistern **8** fountain **9** container, inventory, stockpile **10** receptacle, repository
filler: 4 rain **5** water
Reservoir Dogs (1992 film)
cast: Harvey Keitel, Michael Madsen, Tim Roth
director: Quentin Tarantino
reset: 5 adapt, align, fix up **6** adjust, modify **7** balance **8** fine-tune, modulate, regulate **9** calibrate
resettle: 4 move **8** emigrate, relocate **9** immigrate **10** transplant
resettling: 6 exodus **10** emigration, relocation
resew: 4 darn, mend **5** alter, patch **6** repair
res gestae: 4 acts **5** deeds **8** exploits
resh: 6 Hebrew, letter
predecessor: 4 koph, qoph
successor: 3 sin
reshape: 5 alter **6** change, modify **8** make over **9** customize, transform
reshaping: 6 change **8** revision **10** adjustment, alteration
reshowing: 5 rerun **6** repeat **7** reprise
reside: 3 lie **4** bide, live, nest, rest, stay **5** abide, dwell, exist, lodge, squat **6** belong, billet, inhere, locate, occupy, remain, settle, tenant **7** inhabit, sojourn
in: 6 occupy **7** inhabit **8** populate
residence: 4 co-op, digs, dorm, flat, hall, home, roof, seat **5** abode, condo, dacha, house, lease, manor, place, villa **6** datcha, estate, palace, tenure **7** address, domicil, embassy, habitat, housing, lodging, mansion, sojourn **8** domicile, dwelling, fireside, location, lodgment, quarters **9** apartment, dormitory, occupancy, townhouse **10** habitation, occupation, pied-à-terre, settlement
afterthought: 4 wing **5** add-on
change ~: 4 move **6** uproot **7** migrate **8** relocate
in one's ~: 4 home **6** at home
stately ~: 5 manor, villa **6** castle, estate, palace **7** chateau
tumbledown ~: 3 hut **5** shack **6** lean-to, shanty
see also home
Residence Inn: 5 motel
alternative: *see* motel
resident: 5 liver, local, voter **6** inmate, intern, lodger, native, tenant **7** citizen, denizen, dweller, interne **8** habitant, occupant, squatter, urbanite **9** indweller **10** inhabitant
a ~ of: 4 from
big house ~: 3 con **5** crook, lifer **7** convict **8** criminal, jailbird, prisoner, yardbird **10** lawbreaker
future ~: 6 intern **7** interne
kennel ~: 3 dog, pet **5** doggy, whelp **6** canine
nearby ~: 8 neighbor
suffix: 3 -ese, -ite, -ote
temporary ~: 6 lodger, renter, roomer, tenant **7** boarder
resident __: 5 alien
residential area: 5 exurb **6** suburb
residents: 4 folk **6** people **8** populace **9** citizenry, community **10** population
resider: 5 liver **6** native **7** citizen, denizen, dweller **8** habitant, occupant **10** inhabitant
residual: 3 net **4** left **5** extra **6** unused **7** balance, surplus **8** enduring, leftover **9** aftermath, lingering, remaining, vestigial **10** continuing, unconsumed
residue: 3 end **4** dreg, gunk, heel, orts, rest, rmdr., scum, silt, slag **5** dregs, dross, extra, trash **6** cinder, excess, refuse, scraps, sewage **7** balance, garbage, grounds, parings, remains, remnant, surplus **8** leavings, leftover, sediment, sewerage, shavings **9** leftovers, remainder, scourings, sweepings
grate ~: 3 ash **5** ember
greasy ~: 4 ooze **5** grime, slime
remove ~: 4 sift
volcano ~: 5 ember **6** cinder
residuum: 4 orts, slag **5** dregs, dross **6** scraps **7** remnant **8** leavings, leftover, sediment **9** leftovers, remainder, sweepings
resign: 4 quit **5** demit, leave, waive, yield **6** bow out, retire, secede, vacate **7** abandon, bail out, drop out, sign off, walk out **8** abdicate, hand over, hang it up, renounce, step down **9** reconcile, surrender, terminate **10** give notice, relinquish, stand aside
force to ~: 7 relieve
oneself: 3 bow **4** bend, fold **5** adapt, defer **6** accept, adjust, buckle, comply, give in, submit **7** truckle **9** acquiesce, get used to, make peace, reconcile, surrender **10** capitulate, come around
oneself to: 5 allow **6** permit, suffer **7** condone **8** stand for, tolerate
resignation: 6 notice **8** docility, meekness, patience, quitting, stoicism **9** departure, endurance, fortitude, passivity **10** abdication, equanimity, retirement, withdrawal
resigned: 4 calm, meek **5** stoic **6** docile, pliant **7** adapted, passive, patient, stoical, subdued **8** amenable, biddable, obedient, yielding **9** agreeable, compliant, peaceable, tractable **10** reconciled, submissive
resile: 6 recoil
resilience: 4 give, snap, tone **5** sinew **6** bounce, spring **7** stamina **9** tolerance
resilient: 5 hardy, tough **6** bouncy, limber, lissom, sinewy, spongy, strong, supple **7** buoyant, elastic, lissome, plastic, pliable, rubbery, springy **8** flexible, stretchy, yielding **9** adaptable, expansive **10** rebounding
be ~: 4 give **10** bounce back
resin: 3 gum, lac **4** glue **5** alkyd, amber, anime, copal, epoxy, myrrh, pitch **6** Dammar, guaiac, Lucite, mastic **7** shellac **8** shellack
component: 6 indene
fossil ~: 5 amber, copal
fragrant ~: 4 tolu **5** elemi **6** balsam
gum ~: 4 kino **5** myrrh **6** copalm
varnish ~: 5 anime, copal, damar **6** dammar
__ resin: 3 gum **5** amino, epoxy, vinyl
resist: 4 balk, buck, defy, stay, stem **5** baulk, demur, fight, flout, forgo, rebel, repel **6** assail, battle, bear up, combat, endure, forego, hinder, ignore, mutiny, oppose, rebuff, refuse, revolt, strike, suffer, thwart **7** abstain, contend, counter, dispute, forbear, hit back, hold out, protest, refrain, weather **8** confront, keep from, maintain, turn down **9** disregard, fight back, frustrate, persevere, stand up to, stonewall,

withstand **10** antagonize, contravene, go on strike, leave alone, strike back
resistance: 5 fight, stand **6** battle, combat, mutiny, rebuff **7** defense, dissent, refusal **8** defiance, fighting, friction, struggle, traction **9** endurance, tolerance **10** antagonism
air ~: 4 drag
of ~: 5 ohmic
symbol: 5 omega
unit: 3 ohm **5** abohm
__ resistance: 5 sales **7** natural
résistance, pièce de: 9 specialty
resistant: 5 stiff, tough **6** immune, stable **7** defiant **8** indocile **9** unwilling **10** impervious
combining form: 5 -proof
make ~: 8 immunize **9** stabilize
__-resistant: 4 fire **5** child, shock, water **6** crease, tamper **7** weather
resister: 5 rebel **8** frondeur, renegade **9** insurgent
__ resister: 7 passive
resistive: 5 balky **7** adverse, cynical **8** contrary, negative **9** defensive
Resnais: 5 Alain
resolute: 3 set **4** bent, bold, fast, firm, game, grim, hard, true **5** brave, fixed, gutsy, loyal, nervy, rigid, set on, stern, stout, tough **6** all-out, ardent, awless, daring, dogged, gritty, heroic, intent, plucky, severe, spunky, stable, steady, steely, strong, sturdy **7** adamant, aweless, dead-set, decided, defiant, doughty, earnest, gallant, hard-set, patient, serious, staunch, valiant **8** constant, decisive, diligent, emphatic, faithful, fearless, forceful, hellbent, heroical, intrepid, sedulous, spirited, stalwart, stubborn, tireless, unafraid, unshaken, untiring, valorous **9** audacious, dauntless, dreadless, hard-nosed, immovable, impliable, iron-jawed, masterful, steadfast, strenuous, tenacious, unbending, undaunted, unfearful, unfearing **10** conclusive, courageous, deliberate, determined, foursquare, hard-bitten, inexorable, inflexible, iron-willed, persistent, purposeful, undeterred, unflagging, unshakable, unswerving, unwavering, unwearying, unyielding
be ~: 4 last **6** endure, hold on, insist, linger **7** persist **8** plug away **9** hang tough, keep going, persevere, stand firm **10** tough it out
resolutely: 7 sternly **8** for keeps, intently **9** fervently, intensely, seriously, zealously **10** vigorously
resoluteness: 4 grit **8** decision **9** stability
resolution: 3 act, end **4** guts, will **5** close, heart, nerve, pluck, spunk, valor **6** ending, energy, finale, finish, intent, mettle, motion, ruling, spirit, upshot, windup, wrap-up **7** finding, loyalty, measure, outcome, purpose, verdict **8** backbone, decision, firmness, judgment, proposal, strength, tenacity, terminus, volition **9** breakdown, constancy, endurance, fixedness, fortitude, gallantry, hardiness, intention, willpower **10** conclusion, confidence, conversion, denouement, moral fiber
weaken the ~ of: 5 daunt **6** unglue **7** unnerve **8** dispirit **10** demoralize, discourage, dishearten, intimidate
__ resolution: 5 joint
__-resolution: 3 low **4** high
resolve: 2 do **3** end, fix **4** grit, rule, will **5** agree, steel, think **6** answer, decide, fathom, finish, intend, mettle, morale, pan out, reason, reform, settle, spirit, unfold **7** achieve, clear up, explain, impulse, iron out, mediate, propose, purpose, unravel, work out **8** conclude, decision, firmness, nail down, tenacity **9** determine, elucidate, intention, objective, puzzle out, reconcile, willpower **10** commitment, have in view
lacking ~: 4 weak **5** timid, wimpy **6** craven, scared, yellow **7** chicken, fearful, gutless **8** cowardly, recreant, timorous **9** dastardly, fraidy-cat, weak-kneed
resolved: 3 set **4** sure **5** clear **6** intent **7** assured, decided, serious **8** definite, hellbent, in the bag, positive **9** obstinate **10** conclusive, foursquare
be ~: 6 intend **9** persevere
resonance: 4 ring, tone, vibe **5** sound **9** vibration
resonant: 4 deep, full, loud, rich **6** in tune, mellow **7** booming, echoing, orotund, ringing, vibrant **9** melodious, throbbing **10** stentorian, thundering, thunderous
effect: 4 echo
not ~: 5 tinny
resonate: 4 peal, ring **5** sound, throb **7** reflect, vibrate
resort: 3 inn, spa, use **4** camp, hope, lido **5** apply, haven, hotel, lodge, motel, refer, shift **6** chance, course, employ, harbor, refuge **7** fat farm, hangout, harbour, lodging, measure, retreat, solicit, utilize **8** exercise, frequent, hideaway, recourse, resource **9** expedient, hot spring, make use of, sanctuary **10** expediency
accommodation: 5 cabin, condo, suite
activity: 4 golf **6** skiing, tennis **8** swimming
place: 4 isle
to: 6 invoke **7** utilize **10** fall back on
(to): 2 go **4** look, turn **5** refer, stoop
__ resort: 3 ski **4** last
resound: 4 boom, echo, gong, peal, ring, roar, roll, sing **5** clang **6** bellow, rumble **7** reflect, thunder, vibrate
resounding: 4 loud **5** boomy, forte, noisy **6** echoic **7** blaring, jarring, rackety, raucous, reboant **8** crashing, emphatic, piercing, plangent, sonorous, strident, turned up **9** big-voiced, clamorous, deafening **10** boisterous, stentorian, strepitous, uproarious, vociferant, vociferous
resource: 4 coal **5** asset, shift **6** refuge, resort **7** measure, mineral **8** recourse **9** expedient, ingenuity, petroleum, reference **10** capability, expediency, initiative, natural gas
natural ~: 3 oil, ore **4** coal **5** water **6** timber
precious ~: 4 time
shared ~: 4 pool
__ resource: 7 natural
resourceful: 4 able **5** ready, sharp, smart **6** active, adroit, artful, bright, clever, shifty, strong **7** capable **8** creative, dextrous, original, talented **9** dexterous, ingenious, inventive, versatile
resourcefulness: 7 ability **8** gumption **10** initiative
resources: 5 funds, kitty, lucre, means, money **6** assets, basics, budget, income, riches, wealth **7** backing, capital, nest egg, reserve, revenue, savings **8** bankroll, holdings, property, reserves **10** collateral, livelihood
financial ~: 5 means, purse **10** pocketbook
gather ~: 6 enlist, enroll, muster **7** procure, recruit, round up **8** mobilize
having the ~: 4 able
human ~: 5 staff **7** members, workers **9** employees, personnel, work force
pool ~: 5 unite **6** club up **9** cooperate **10** join forces
sans ~: 4 poor **5** broke, needy **8** beggarly, dirt poor, indigent **9** dead broke, destitute, penniless, penurious **10** down and out, down at heel, straitened
__ resources: 5 human
resp.: 3 ans.
respect: 3 awe **4** fear, heed, keep, mind, obey, sake **5** bow to, defer, facet, favor, honor, piety, point, spare, value **6** accept, admire, bend to, comply, detail, esteem, follow, fulfil, hallow, homage, regard, revere, uphold **7** abide by, agree to, dignity, fulfill, observe, pay heed, tribute, worship **8** adhere to, carry out, courtesy, listen to, look up to, venerate **9** conform to, consent to, deference, obeisance, recognize, reverence **10** admiration, appreciate, estimation, particular, self-esteem, set store by, toe the line, veneration
in any ~: 5 at all
in every ~: 4 to a T **6** to a tee, wholly **7** exactly
show ~: 3 bow **5** kneel **6** salute **7** lionize
term of ~: 3 sir **4** abba, ma'am, miss, sire **5** madam
with ~ to: 4 in re **5** about, as for **6** toward **7** towards **8** relative **9** apropos of, as regards, regarding **10** concerning
with ~ to this: 5 in hoc
__-respect: 4 self
Respect (1967 song)
artist: Aretha Franklin
respectability: 6 virtue **7** dignity **9** propriety
respectable: 4 done, fair, fine, good, nice, okay, so-so, tidy **5** clean, great, legit, moral, noble **6** decent, goodly, honest, modest, proper, savory, seemly, worthy **7** ethical, sizable, upright **8** all right, decorous, laudable, moderate, passable, pleasant, pleasing, sizeable, splendid, straight, suitable, superior, virtuous **9** admirable, agreeable, dignified, estimable, excellent, high-toned, honorable, reputable, tolerable, wholesome, wonderful **10** aboveboard, acceptable, beneficial, creditable
respected: 5 noted **9** dignified, estimable, prominent, venerable
one, maybe: 5 elder
Respect for Acting
author: Uta Hagen
respectful: 4 good **5** civil **6** filial, humble, polite **7** courtly, duteous, dutiful **8** admiring, gracious, highbred, mannerly, obedient **9** attentive, courteous, regardful
address: 3 sir **4** abba, ma'am **5** madam
not ~: 4 flip, pert, rude **5** brash, fresh, nervy, sassy, saucy **6** brassy, brazen, cheeky, snippy **7** defiant, forward **8** flippant, impudent, insolent **9** intrusive, out-of-line, sarcastic, shameless **10** irreverent
respecting: 4 as to **7** valuing
respective: 3 own **4** each **6** proper **7** several **8** personal, relative, separate, singular **9** bilateral **10** individual, particular
respects: 7 devoirs, regards **9** greetings
in all ~: 5 fully, quite **6** wholly
pay ~ to: 6 salute
Respect Yourself (1987 song)
artist: Bruce Willis
Respighi, Ottorino work: The Pines of Rome
respiration: 6 breath, eupnea **8** exhaling, inhaling **9** breathing **10** exhalation
combining form: 4 -pnea **5** -pnoea
respiratory: 9 breathing
organ: 4 gill, lung
passage: 6 airway
sound: 4 rale
woe: 6 asthma
respire: 4 sigh **6** exhale, inhale **7** breathe
respite: 3 gap, nap **4** lull, rest, stay **5** break, delay, letup, pause, R and R, truce **6** breath, easing, hiatus, recess, relief, repose **7** anodyne, leisure, time out **8** breather, downtime, furlough, reprieve, vacation **9** cessation, deferment, happy hour, interlude **10** moratorium, suspension
resplendence: 6 luster **8** radiance, radiancy **10** effulgence
resplendent: 4 rich **5** fancy, light, lucid, nitid, regal, royal, showy, vivid **6** bright, ornate, superb **7** beaming, blazing, flaming, glowing, lambent, radiant, shining, sublime **8** dazzling, gleaming, glorious, gorgeous, luminous, lustrous, splendid **9** brilliant, effulgent, refulgent, sparkling **10** glittering

respond: **3** act, nod, say **5** react, reply **6** answer, behave, retort **7** counter, get back **8** talk back **10** get in touch
ender: **3** ent
to: **5** act on **6** answer **7** confirm **9** write back
response: **3** lip **4** echo, sass **5** reply, vibes **6** action, answer, retort, ripost **7** defense, riposte **8** antiphon, back talk, comeback, feedback, kick-back, knee jerk, reaction, rebuttal **9** reception, rejoinder, sensation, utterance, wisecrack **10** double take
fence-sitting ~: **7** perhaps **8** possibly **9** it could be, it might be
military ~: **3** aye **5** no sir **6** aye aye, yes sir **9** aye aye sir
negative ~: **3** nah, nay **4** nope
noncommittal ~: **7** perhaps **8** possibly, probably **9** it could be, it might be
roll-call ~: **3** aye, nay, yea, yes
time: **3** lag
uncertain ~: **4** shot, stab **5** hunch **6** notion, theory **7** feeling, opinion, surmise, venture **9** suspicion **10** conjecture, hypothesis, prediction, projection
unequivocal ~: **2** no **3** nah, naw, nay, nix, non **4** nein, nope, nyet, uh-uh **5** ixnay, never, no how, no way **6** no deal, nowise **7** not ever **8** at no time, forget it, negative, not at all **9** by no means, fat chance **10** count me out, impossible, not a chance, thumbs down
unsure ~: **5** guess, maybe **6** I guess **7** maybe so, perhaps
response __: **4** time
__ response: **6** immune
responsibility: **3** job **4** beat, care, duty, load, onus, part, spot, task, work **5** blame, fault, guilt, place, power, trust **6** burden, charge, office, weight **7** concern, honesty, mission **8** contract, function, maturity, province **9** albatross, authority, liability **10** obligation
denial of ~: **7** refusal
duck ~: **5** evade **6** cop out, renege
relieve of ~: **2** ax **4** fire, oust **5** let go **6** lay off **7** dismiss, suspend **8** furlough **9** discharge
take ~: **5** own up **6** fess up **7** confess
responsible: **5** adult, loyal, right, sober, sound **6** bonded, guilty, honest, liable, mature, stable, steady, trusty **7** at fault, capable, obliged, pledged, to blame, willing **8** blamable, culpable, in charge, indebted, reliable, sensible **9** at the helm, blameable, competent, duty-bound, efficient, important, in control, incumbent, obligated, on the hook, qualified **10** chargeable
be ~ for: **3** own **4** lead **5** see to **7** sponsor **8** organize, shoulder
for: **6** behind
hold ~: **5** blame, thank **6** assign
not ~: **6** exempt **7** cleared **9** acquitted **10** exonerated, off the hook, vindicated
responsive: **3** yar **4** open, warm, yare **5** alive, awake, aware, quick, sharp **6** prompt, tender **7** pliable, psychic, vibrant **8** empathic, sentient **9** agreeable, conscious, emotional, observant, receptive, sensitive **10** empathetic, expressive, hospitable, interested, perceptive
rest: **3** gap, lay, lie, nap, nod, put, set, sit **4** calm, doze, ease, halt, idle, laze, lean, loaf, loll, lull, orts, prop, rail, rely, stay, stop, wait **5** break, hinge, letup, lie by, light, pause, peace, quiet, relax, roost, shelf, sleep, stand, truce **6** at ease, breath, cesura, depend, drowse, ease up, excess, lay off, lounge, others, recess, relief, repose, reside, settle, siesta, snooze, turn in, unwind **7** balance, caesura, holiday, leisure, liberty, lie down, overage, quietus, railing, recline, remains, remnant, residue, respite, sack out, silence, sit back, sit down, slumber, sojourn, support, surplus, take ten, time off **8** be seated, breather, calm down, calmness, downtime, interval, leavings, lie still, pedestal, pediment, quietude, recreate, reside in, stand for, take a nap, take five, vacation **9** cessation, do nothing, go to sleep, hang loose, hibernate, idle hours, interlude, leftovers, predicate, remainder, stillness **10** fall asleep, forty winks, inactivity, quiescence, recreation, relaxation, standstill, stretch out, take a break, take it easy
against: **6** lean on
area: **6** lounge
at ~: **4** idle **5** still **6** halted **7** napping **8** inactive, in repose, reposing, unmoving **9** not moving, quiescent, reclining **10** motionless, stationary
atop: **5** lie on
came to ~: **3** lit **4** alit
come to ~: **4** land **5** light, lodge **6** alight, settle
day of ~: **3** Sab. **7** Sabbath **8** vacation
give one's feet a ~: **5** relax
name meaning ~: **4** Noah
next to: **4** abut **5** touch **6** adjoin, border
(on): **4** base, hang, lean, rely **5** hinge **6** depend
put one's mind to ~: **4** buoy **5** allay, cheer **7** cheer up, comfort, console, hearten, satisfy **8** inspirit, reassure
room: **2** WC **3** lav **4** bath, john **6** lounge **7** latrine **8** lavatory
room sign: **5** in use
starter: **3** arm **4** back, foot, head
stop: **3** inn **5** hotel, lodge, motel **6** hostel **7** auberge, lodging **8** hostelry **9** roadhouse **10** motor court
the ~: **6** others
rest __: **4** area, room, stop
__ rest: **3** bed **4** chin **5** day of, lay to, put to **6** parade
restart: **5** renew **6** pick up, reopen, resume **8** continue, return to **10** recommence
restate: **5** resay **6** repeat **7** iterate **9** reiterate **10** paraphrase
restaurant: **3** bar, inn **4** café, dive **5** diner, grill, joint **6** bistro, eatery, in spot, saloon **7** canteen, drive-in **8** pizzeria, teahouse **9** brasserie, cafeteria, chophouse, hash house, lunchroom, nightclub **10** steakhouse
area: **9** food court
bill: **3** tab **5** check
chain: **3** KFC **4** IHOP **5** Arby's **6** Big Boy, Chili's, Denny's, Hardy's, Sbarro, Subway, Wendy's **7** Quiznos, Sizzler **8** Pizza Hut, Taco Bell **9** Applebee's, Bojangles', Captain D's, Chick-fil-A, Friendly's, McDonald's **10** Burger King, TGI Friday's **11** Famous Dave's, Ruby Tuesday **12** Golden Corral, Jack in the Box
choice: **5** order
employee: **4** chef, cook **5** valet **6** busboy, waiter **7** cashier, maître d' **10** dishwasher
forgo the ~: **5** eat in
freebie: **4** roll, salt **5** bread, sugar, water **6** catsup, pepper
furnishing: **5** table **10** tablecloth
go to a ~: **4** dine **6** eat out
group: **5** party
list: **4** menu **5** carte **10** bill of fare
offering: **5** lunch **6** brunch, buffet, dinner, supper **8** salad bar **9** breakfast
order: **4** to go
patron: **5** diner, eater, guest
requirement, maybe: **3** tie **5** shirt **6** jacket
work in a ~: **3** bus
__ Restaurant: **6** Alice's
rested: **5** fresh **7** revived
__-rested: **4** well
restful: **4** calm, cosy, cozy, snug **5** cozey, cozie, quiet **6** placid, serene **7** easeful, pacific **8** peaceful, tranquil **9** leisurely, peaceable
restfulness: **4** calm **6** repose **7** comfort **8** calmness
resting: **4** idle **5** in bed **6** asleep, at ease **7** abeyant **8** lounging **9** incumbent, unengaged **10** relaxation, unemployed
combining form: **5** stato-
on: **4** atop, over **5** above **8** touching
place: **3** bed, inn **4** lair, seat **5** perch **6** settee
restitute: **5** renew **7** refresh, restore **9** refurbish **10** rejuvenate
restitution: **6** amends, rebate, refund, return **7** redress **9** expiation, indemnity, repayment **10** paying back
exact ~: **6** avenge
make ~: **5** atone, repay **6** render **7** redress **8** square up
restive: **4** edgy **5** antsy, balky, itchy, jumpy, tense **6** ornery, uneasy, unruly **7** anxious, fidgety, fretful, froward, jittery, keyed up, nervous, radical, uptight **8** agitated, contrary, fluttery, fretsome, indocile, skittish, stubborn, troubled **9** concerned, excitable, ill at ease, impatient, obstinate, unsettled **10** high-strung
be ~: **4** fret **5** brood, worry
restiveness: **4** care **5** angst **6** dismay **7** anxiety, concern, fidgets **8** disquiet, distress
restless: **4** edgy **5** antsy, hyper, itchy, jumpy, nervy, tense **6** fitful, mobile, on edge, uneasy **7** anxious, fidgety, fretful, jittery, keyed up, nervous, on the go, uptight, wakeful, worried **8** agitated, feverish, fretsome, skittish, troubled **9** concerned, excitable, footloose, ill at ease, impatient, perturbed, strung out, turbulent, unsettled **10** highstrung
feeling: **3** yen **4** itch, urge **7** craving, longing **8** yearning **9** hankering
__ restless as a willow...: **4** I'm as
restlessness: **5** fever **6** nerves **7** anxiety, ferment, jitters, tension **8** disquiet, edginess, insomnia **9** agitation, antsiness, jumpiness **10** uneasiness
restock: **6** refill **7** refresh, replace **9** replenish
Reston: **4** city, town **5** James
locale: **8** Virginia
rest on one's __: **4** oars **7** laurels
restoration: **7** revival **8** comeback, recovery **9** salvation **10** renascence, resurgence
Restoration (1995 film)
cast: Robert Downey Jr., Sam Neill
restorative: **4** cure **5** tonic **6** potion, remedy **7** bracing, healthy **8** curative, pick-me-up, remedial **9** stimulant
restore: **3** fix **4** cure, heal, mend, undo **5** fix up, rally, rehab, renew, right **6** redeem, reform, refund, render, repair, rescue, return, revive, update **7** fortify, freshen, furbish, improve, patch up, put back, rebuild, recover, recruit, redress, refresh, replace, retouch, salvage, touch up, win back **8** give back, overhaul, reimpose, renovate, retrieve, revivify **9** bring back, modernize, refurbish, reimburse, reinstate, replenish, restitute **10** regenerate, rejuvenate, revitalize, strengthen
to health: **4** cure, heal **5** fix up, treat **6** doctor, remedy **7** patch up
restrain: **3** bar, dam, gag, pin, tie **4** bate, bind, curb, hold, jail, rein, rule, stem, stop, tame **5** chain, check, cramp, deter, hem in, leash, limit, sit on, tie up **6** arrest, bridle, dampen, detain, enjoin, fetter, forbid, govern, hamper, hinder, hogtie, impede, lock up, muzzle, pinion, pull in, rein in, slow up, stifle, subdue, temper, tether, thwart **7** confine, contain, control, curtail, harness, impound, inhibit, manacle, prevent, qualify, refrain, repress, smother, squelch, tie down, trammel **8** handcuff, handicap, hold back, imprison, moderate, obstruct, prohibit, restrict, slow down, straiten, suppress, tone down **9** constrain, crack down, hamstring, interdict **10** discourage, hold it down, keep a lid on, keep in line
restrained: **4** calm, cool, mild **5** muted, quiet, sober **6** low-key,

pent-up, silent 7 limited, refined, subdued, uptight 8 closed in, discreet, esthetic, hemmed in, moderate, on a leash, reined in, reticent, retiring, tasteful 9 classical, continent, temperate, unextreme, withdrawn 10 abstemious, reasonable, unagitated, unspeaking
restraining __: 5 order
restraint: 3 ban, bar 4 curb, rein, tabu, yoke 5 brake, check, irons, leash, limit, taboo, taste 6 arrest, bridle, chains, fetter, halter, tether 7 barrier, bondage, caution, control, economy, embargo, measure, reserve, squeeze, trammel 8 coercion, coolness, eschewal, patience 9 abatement, avoidance, captivity, detention, deterrent, endurance, hindrance 10 abstinence, classicism, compulsion, deterrence, discipline, government, impediment, imposition, inhibition, limitation, moderation, repression, self-denial, temperance
passive ~: 6 airbag
use ~: 6 go easy
without ~: 5 ad lib 6 at will, freely
__ restraint: 4 head 5 prior 7 passive
__-restraint: 4 self
restraint of __: 5 trade
restrict: 3 ban, tie 4 bind, curb, slow 5 bound, check, cramp, fence, hem in, limit, pen in, stint, tie up 6 arrest, define, fetter, forbid, ground, hamper, hang up, hobble, impede, intern, modify, narrow, ration, reduce, shut in, temper, tether 7 abridge, confine, contain, inhibit, pin down, prevent, qualify, trammel 8 handcuff, handicap, hold down, moderate, obstruct, prohibit, regulate, restrain, straiten 9 constrict, hamstring 10 abbreviate, come down on, keep a lid on, keep in line
restricted: 5 light, local, scant 6 closed, inside, narrow, pent-up, secret, single 7 insular, limited, private, special, topical 8 hemmed in, hush-hush, reined in, reserved, shielded, specific 9 confining, exclusive, nonpublic, qualified, technical 10 cloistered
not ~: 4 free, open 6 public 8 passable 9 unblocked 10 accessible, unreserved
restricted __: 4 area
restriction: 4 curb, no-no, rule, tabu 5 limit, taboo 6 bounds, lock-in 7 control, embargo, proviso, trammel 8 obstacle 9 condition, fine print, provision, restraint 10 regulation
restrictive: 5 tight 6 narrow 7 cramped, opposed 8 limiting, opposing 9 confining
restyle: 5 adapt, alter 6 adjust, change, modify 8 innovate 9 modernize, transform
result: 3 end 4 stem 5 arise, end up, ensue, fruit, occur, prove, score, total 6 accrue, answer, appear, come of, derive, effect, emerge, finish, follow, go well, happen, pan out, payoff, sequel, upshot 7 develop, fallout, outcome, proceed, product, succeed, turn out, work out 8 backwash, decision, flow from, fruition, offshoot, solution 9 aftermath, arise from, by-product, come about, culminate, eventuate, grow out of, outgrowth, terminate, transpire 10 completion, conclusion, denouement, impression, spring from
as a ~: 4 ergo 5 hence 6 hereby 7 through 9 therefore
as a ~ of: 5 due to 7 because, owing to
expected ~: 3 par 4 mean, norm 7 average 8 standard 9 benchmark, yardstick
from: 6 attend 9 originate
(from): 5 arise, issue
in: 5 beget, bring, cause 6 lead to, tend to 7 produce, redound
without ~: 4 vain 6 in vain 7 inutile, useless 8 bootless 9 for naught, pointless, to no avail, worthless 10 unavailing
resultant: 7 ensuing 9 derivable, secondary 10 consequent
resulting: 8 eventual 9 following 10 consequent, subsequent
resultingly: 4 ergo, thus 5 hence 9 therefore
results: 5 fruit 6 profit, return, reward 7 benefit, outcome, product
resume: 4 go on 5 renew 6 keep on, pick up, reopen, revert, take up 7 carry on, proceed, recover, restart 8 continue, go on with, return to 10 recommence
résumé: 3 bio 4 vita 6 digest, précis, record, report, review 7 outline, rundown, summary 8 abstract, synopsis
accent: 5 acute
detail: 4 jobs 7 address, hobbies 9 reference 10 experience
resupine: 9 recumbent
resurface: 3 tar 4 pave
resurgence: 5 rally 7 revival 8 comeback
resurgent: 5 redux
resurgently: 4 anew
resurrect: 5 rally 6 araise 9 bring back
resurrection __: 4 fern, gate 5 plant
Resurrection (1980 film)
cast: Ellen Burstyn, Sam Shepard
__ Resurrection: 5 Alien
Resurrection Mass time: 6 Easter
Resurrection Symphony
composer: Gustav Mahler
resuscitate: 4 wake 5 rally 6 revive 7 refresh
Reta: 4 Shaw
retail: 4 sell, vend 6 handle, market
big ~ season: 4 Xmas
business: 4 mart, shop 5 store 8 boutique
grouping: 4 line
ID: 3 SKU
retailer: 6 dealer, grocer, outlet, seller, trader 8 merchant 10 franchisee
concern: 4 sale 5 sales
retain: 3 own 4 have, hire, hold, keep, save 5 amass, cache, hoard, put by, store 6 absorb, clutch, employ, engage, garner, recall, save up, sign on, sign up, take on 7 cling to, husband, lay away, possess, put away, reserve 8 hang on to, hold on to, maintain, memorize, preserve, put aside, remember, withhold 9 recollect 10 accumulate
don't ~: 4 cede, fire 5 let go, loose, yield 6 lay off 7 abandon, dismiss, manumit, release, set free 8 cut loose 9 discharge, surrender
retainer: 3 fee 4 dike, wall 6 flunky 7 advance, deposit, flunkey, servant 8 follower 9 attendant
retainers: 5 staff, suite, train 6 escort 7 company, retinue 9 entourage, following, hangers-on 10 attendants
retaining __: 4 wall
retake: 7 get back, recover
retaliate: 3 pay 5 repay, reply, wreak 6 answer, return 7 counter, get even, hit back, pay back 9 get back at, pay in kind 10 strike back
for: 6 avenge 7 requite
retaliation: 6 rancor 7 revenge 8 reprisal 9 vengeance 10 punishment
bit of ~: 3 tit
retaliatory: 8 punitive, vengeful 10 vindictive
retard: 3 lag 4 balk, clog, slow 5 baulk, block, brake, check, delay, stall 6 arrest, baffle, dampen, detain, hamper, hang up, hinder, hold up, impede, put off, slow up 7 draw out, inhibit, prevent, prolong, set back, slacken, suspend 8 encumber, obstruct, postpone, slow down 10 decelerate
__-retardant: 4 fire 5 flame
rete: 4 mesh 6 plexus
retell: 5 quote 6 recite, repeat 7 iterate 9 reiterate
retention: 6 memory 9 detention, occupancy 10 absorption
retentive: 9 absorbent, tenacious
retentiveness: 6 memory, recall
retest, require a: 4 fail 5 flunk
reticence: 7 modesty, reserve, secrecy, silence 10 inhibition
reticent: 3 coy, shy 4 mute 5 aloof, close, quiet 6 modest, silent 7 bashful, distant 8 reserved, retiring, taciturn 9 diffident, reclusive, secretive, withdrawn 10 restrained, uneffusive
not ~: 4 bold 5 brash, gutsy, nervy 6 brassy, brazen, daring, heroic 7 defiant, doughty, forward, valiant 8 fearless, intrepid, resolute 9 audacious, dauntless, undaunted 10 courageous
reticulation: 3 web 7 lattice, network
reticule: 3 bag 5 pouch, purse 7 handbag 10 pocketbook
retina
cell: 3 rod 4 cone
neighbor: 4 lens
retinue: 4 crew 5 court, suite, train 6 escort 7 company, cortege, escorts 9 entourage, hangers-on, retainers 10 attendants
retire: 4 exit, quit 5 leave, sleep 6 decamp, depart, go away, put out, recede, resign, secede, turn in 7 give way, go to bed, pull out, retreat, sack out, saw logs, seclude, take off 8 abdicate, draw back, fall back, pull back, run along, withdraw 9 antiquate, go to sleep, hit the hay, rusticate 10 call it a day, give ground, hit the sack
signal to ~: 4 Taps 9 lights out
retired: 4 abed 5 in bed, quiet 6 lonely 9 withdrawn
retiree: 3 snr. 6 senior
benefits org.: 3 SSA
kitty: 3 IRA 7 nest egg, pension
residence: 5 condo
title: 7 emerita 8 emeritus
retirement: 4 exit 7 leisure, privacy 9 departure, seclusion 10 abdication
community caveat: 6 no kids
plan: 3 IRA 5 Keogh 7 pension, Roth IRA 8 Roth plan
retiring: 3 coy, shy 4 meek 5 aloof, lowly, quiet, timid 6 demure, humble, modest 7 bashful, distant, recluse 8 outgoing, reserved, reticent, sheepish, timorous 9 diffident, reclusive, shrinking, withdrawn 10 abdication, restrained, unassuming, uneffusive, unsociable
hardly ~: 4 bold 5 brash, nervy, pushy 7 forward 9 assertive, insistent, obtrusive 10 aggressive, meddlesome
retort: 3 ans., say 4 quip, snap 5 rebut, reply, sally 6 answer, ripost 7 alembic, counter, defense, respond, riposte 8 comeback, crucible, fire back, reaction, rebuttal, repartee, response 9 rejoinder, witticism
kid's ~: 4 is so 5 can so, did so, is too
retouch: 3 fix 4 edit, mend 5 emend, fix up, patch 6 doctor, modify, polish, repair, revise 7 brush up, enhance, improve, patch up, restore 9 refurbish
retrace steps: 6 return 8 turn back
retract: 4 turn 5 unsay 6 abjure, cancel, draw in, negate, recall, recant, recede, reel in, repeal, revoke, secede 7 call off, disavow, rescind, reverse, rule out, sheathe 8 abrogate, disclaim, forswear, go back on, pull back, renege on, renounce, take back, withdraw 9 back-pedal, foreswear, repudiate
as words: 5 unsay 6 recant 8 take back
retraction: 6 denial, recall 9 annulment 10 withdrawal
retread: 4 tire 5 patch, renew 6 lubber, repair 8 overhaul 9 refurbish 10 rejuvenate
retreading, in need of: 4 bald
retreat: 3 den, ebb 4 aery, exit, eyry, flee, lair, nest, nook, rout 5 aerie, cover, elude, eyrie, haunt, haven, leave, lodge, oasis, villa 6 asylum, beat it, corner, decamp, depart, escape, flight, go back, harbor, opt out, recede, recess, refuge, resort, retire, return, secede, shrink, vacate 7 back off, convent, harbour, privacy, pull out, regress, ride off, shelter 8 cloister, downturn, draw back, fall back, hideaway, log cabin, pull back, reaction, run for it, solitude, turn tail, withdraw 9 back-pedal, backtrack,

departure, disappear, disengage, hermitage, safe house, safe place, sanctuary, seclusion, sequester **10** evacuation, give ground, ivory tower, withdrawal
beat a hasty ~: **3** hie, rip, run **5** hurry, lam it **7** dash off
hasty ~: **3** lam **6** escape, flight **7** getaway
__ retreat: **5** beat a
retrench: **6** reduce **7** cut down **8** conserve **9** economize **10** cut corners
retribution: **6** payoff, refund, reward **7** justice, penalty, penance, redress, revenge **8** reprisal **9** reckoning, repayment, vengeance **10** punishment, recompense
bit of ~: **3** tit
divine ~: **5** wrath
exact ~: **5** repay **6** avenge **7** get even, hit back, pay back **9** retaliate **10** strike back
goddess of ~: **3** Ate
matter for ~: **3** tat
retributive: **5** penal **8** spiteful, vengeful **10** corrective, vindictive
retrieve: **3** get **5** fetch, field, go get **6** obtain, recoup, redeem, regain, repair, rescue **7** get back, reclaim, recover, recruit, restore, salvage, win back **9** reacquire, recapture, repossess **10** recompense
retriever: **3** dog, lab **5** canid **6** canine
__ retriever: **6** golden
retrocede: **3** die, ebb **4** ease, fade, fall, wane **5** let up **6** ease up, lessen, reflux **7** decline, die down, dwindle, ease off, slacken, subside, tail off **8** decrease, diminish, fade away, fall away, fall back, moderate, slack off, taper off, withdraw
retrograde: **4** sink **5** lapse **6** recede **7** decline **8** backward **10** degenerate
retrogress: **4** sink, slip **5** decay, slide **6** recede, revert, worsen **7** relapse **9** aggravate **10** degenerate, exacerbate, recidivate
retrogression: **5** lapse **7** relapse **8** apostasy, reaction **9** backslide **10** withdrawal
retrospect: **6** memory, recall **9** hindsight
retry: **6** hang in, hold on, keep on **7** persist, press on **8** continue, keep at it, plug away **9** hang tough, persevere
retsina: **4** wine
origin: **6** Cyprus, Greece
Rettig: **5** Tommy
Retton, Mary Lou: **7** gymnast
return: **3** net **4** earn, gain, wage **5** bring, fruit, lapse, price, recur, remit, repay, reply, wages, yield **6** bestow, come to, go back, income, profit, rebate, recede, recoil, refund, render, repeat, reseat, revert, reward **7** accrual, benefit, bring in, pay back, produce, put back, rebound, redress, reenter, reentry, reflect, relapse, replace, restore, results, retreat, revenue, revisit **8** comeback, dividend, earnings, give back, hand back, interest, move back, proceeds, reaction, reappear, receipts, roll back, send back, take back **9** carry back, come again, indemnify, reimburse, reinstate, rejoinder, retaliate, retrocede **10** bounce back, circle back, double back, homecoming, recompense, recurrence
get in ~: **4** earn, gain, reap **5** clear **6** derive, garner, profit, secure, take in **7** bring in, collect, harvest, receive **8** gather in
give in ~: **3** pay **6** avenge, reward **7** get even, requite **9** retaliate
investment ~: **5** yield **6** income, profit **7** revenue **8** earnings, proceeds
involuntary ~: **4** repo
never to ~: **4** gone **7** extinct **8** departed, vanished
the favor: **7** pay back, requite
to: **6** resume, revert **7** iterate, regress, restart **8** continue, go on with
to form: **4** heal, mend **5** rally **7** get well, rebound, recover **8** snap back **9** get better **10** bounce back, come around, convalesce, recuperate, rejuvenate, spring back
to office: **6** recall **7** reelect **9** bring back, reinstate
return __: **4** trip
__ return: **3** tax **5** joint **6** I shall
Return __ Jedi: **5** of the
Return __ Native, The: **5** of the
return-address word: **4** from
returned: **8** requited
Return of Buck Gavin, The
author: Thomas Wolfe
Return of the Jedi (1983 film)
beast: **4** Ewok
cast: Carrie Fisher, Harrison Ford, Mark Hamill, Billy Dee Williams
composer: John Williams
role: **3** Han **4** Leia, Luke, Oola, Solo, Yoda **5** Darth, Lando, Vader **7** Han Solo **9** Skywalker **10** Darth Vader
Return of the Native, The
author: Thomas Hardy
character: **3** Vye **4** Clym, Venn **5** Damon **6** Tamsin **7** Clement, Diggory, Wildeve **8** Eustacia, Thomasin **9** Yeobright
return on __: **6** assets, equity
returns: **4** poll, take **8** proceeds
calculation: **3** tax
expert: **3** CPA **4** acct. **7** auditor **10** accountant
org.: **3** IRS
__ Returns: **6** Batman
Return to Mars
author: Ben Bova
Return to Me (1958 song)
artist: Dean Martin
Return to Me (2000 film)
cast: Minnie Driver, David Duchovny, Robert Loggia, Carroll O'Connor
Return to Paradise (1998 film)
cast: Anne Heche, Joaquin Phoenix, Vince Vaughn
Return to Sender (1962 song)
artist: Elvis Presley
Reuben: **8** sandwich
brother: **3** Dan, Gad **4** Levi **5** Asher, Judah **6** Joseph, Simeon **7** Zebulun **8** Benjamin, Issachar, Naphtali
ingredient: **3** rye **5** kraut **6** cheese **8** rye bread **10** corned beef, sauerkraut
parent: **4** Leah **5** Jacob
sister: **5** Dinah
son: **5** Carmi **6** Hanoch, Hezron
Reuben, Reuben (1983 film)
cast: Tom Conti, Kelly McGillis
Reubens: **4** Paul
Reuel
father: **4** Esau
reunion: **7** meeting **8** assembly, conclave **9** gathering **10** convention
attendee: **3** rel., unc **4** alum, aunt, grad **5** niece, uncle **7** alumnus **8** relative
greeting: **3** hug
group: **3** fam., kin **4** clan **5** class **6** family
__ reunion: **5** class **6** family
Réunion: **4** isle **6** island
reunite: **6** gather **8** assemble **9** reconcile **10** conciliate
Reunited (1979 song)
artist: Peaches and Herb
reuse: **7** recycle
Reuters
rival: **3** UPI
Reuther
grp.: **3** UAW
rev: **3** gun **4** race **5** crank **7** crank up **10** accelerate
up: **6** excite **8** increase **9** intensify
rev.
address: **3** ser.
training: **5** theol.
Rev. __: **3** Ver.
revamp: **3** fix **4** mend **5** alter, fix up **6** repair, revise **7** improve, touch up **8** overhaul, renovate **9** modernize, refurbish, transform
Rêve
author: Émile Zola
reveal: **3** air, ope, say **4** bare, blab, leak, open, show, talk, tell **5** admit, break, let on, spill, unrip, utter **6** betray, decode, detail, evince, expose, fess up, impart, let out, relate, report, show up, turn up, unfold, unmask, unveil **7** add up to, bespeak, concede, confess, confide, declare, display, divulge, exhibit, express, give out, lay bare, let slip, mention, reflect, uncover, unearth **8** announce, decipher, disclose, evidence, give away, indicate, manifest, register, unburden, unclothe **9** make known, put on view **10** make public
oneself: **4** show **5** arise **6** appear, emerge **7** come out, peep out, surface
one's feelings: **4** avow, tell **5** admit, allow **6** fess up **7** concede, confess, divulge **8** disclose **9** make known
one's hunger: **8** salivate
revealed: **4** open **5** naked **7** visible **8** knowable, manifest
revealing: **6** low-cut **8** telltale **10** conclusive, expressive
reveille: **4** call **6** signal
opposite: **4** Taps
player: **5** bugle **6** bugler
respond to ~: **4** rise, wake **5** awake, get up **6** awaken
sound ~: **4** wake **5** awake, rouse, waken **6** arouse, awaken, wake up
__ Reveille: **3** 'Til
revel: **4** gala, lark, play **5** binge, enjoy, exult, gloat, glory, party, spree **6** bask in, cavort, frolic, gaiety, gambol, gayety, relish, wallow **7** blowout, carouse, delight, indulge, jollity, rejoice, roister, rollick, skylark, triumph **8** cut loose, hilarity, live it up, recreate **9** bacchanal, celebrate, festivity, have a ball, luxuriate, make merry, whoop it up **10** go on a spree, have a blast, have a fling, masquerade, saturnalia
cry: **4** evoe
in: **4** like, love **5** eat up, enjoy **6** devour **9** luxuriate
(in): **4** bask **7** delight
revelation: **3** tip **4** find, idea, info, jolt, leak, news, show, talk **5** augur, dream, scoop, shock, state, story **6** airing, answer, augury, avowal, baring, earful, espial, exposé, oracle, report, tipoff, vision, whammy **7** account, adviser, display, exhibit, finding, hearsay, insight, lowdown, message, miracle, outlook, release, scandal, shake-up, shocker, showing, stunner, tidings **8** betrayal, bulletin, exposure, forecast, prophecy, surprise **9** admission, assertion, bombshell, broadcast, detection, discovery, exclusive, eyeopener, foresight, intuition, news flash, statement, testimony, unmasking, unveiling, utterance **10** appearance, astuteness, communiqué, confession, deposition, disclosure, divination, divulgence, exhibition, exposition, expression, foreboding, prediction, prescience, profession, recitation, unbosoming, uncovering, unearthing, unexpected, wonderment
response: **3** aha
Revelation
name in ~: **3** Gog **5** Magog
preceder: **4** Jude
reveler: **9** wassailer
revelry: **3** fun, joy **5** mirth, party, spree **6** fiesta, gaiety, gayety **7** gayness, jollity, jubilee **8** carousal, festival, goings-on, hilarity, pleasure **9** festivity, high jinks, merriment, whoop-de-do **10** liveliness, risibility, saturnalia, sybaritism
revenant: **6** fantom **7** phantom, specter **10** apparition
revenge: **5** spite **6** avenge **7** get even, hit back, pay back, requite **8** reprisal, requital **9** get back at, stick it to, tit for tat, vengeance, vindicate
get ~: **9** retaliate
get ~ on: **3** fix, get **5** repay, set up **6** punish **7** pay back
Revenge (1990 film)
cast: Kevin Costner, Sally Kirkland, Anthony Quinn, Madeleine Stowe
revengefulness: **4** hate **6** animus, enmity, grudge, hatred, malice,

rancor 7 ill will 8 acrimony, bad blood 9 animosity, antipathy, hostility 10 antagonism
Revenge of the Nerds (1984 film)
cast: Timothy Busfield, Robert Carradine, Anthony Edwards
revenue: 3 net, pay **4** gain, gate, take **5** funds, gravy, lucre, means, money, split, wages, yield **6** income, payoff, profit, return, reward, salary, wealth **7** annuity, receipt **8** benefice, cash flow, earnings, interest, proceeds, receipts **9** dividends, emolument, resources **10** bottom line
deduction from ~: 5 debit
less outlays: 3 net **6** profit
of ~: 6 fiscal **8** economic, monetary **9** budgetary, financial, pecuniary
source: 4 sale **8** receipts
revenue __: 7 sharing
__ revenue: 5 gross
revenuer: 4 T-man
quest: 5 still
reverb __: 5 pedal
reverberant: 6 echoic **8** resonant
reverberate: 4 boom, echo, peal, ring, roar, roll **5** clang, sound **6** reecho **7** reflect, resound, thunder, vibrate
reverberation: 4 boom, echo, ring **5** clang, sound **6** report **8** reaction **9** vibration
revere: 4 laud, like, love **5** adore, ensky, exalt, go for, honor, prize, value **6** admire, esteem, hallow, regard **7** beatify, care for, cherish, defer to, glorify, idolize, magnify, observe, respect, worship **8** enshrine, hold dear, inshrine, look up to, treasure, venerate **9** care about
Revere: 4 Anne, city, Paul, town
co-rider: 5 Dawes
emulate ~: 4 ride **6** arouse
locale: 4 Mass.
Revere and the Raiders, Paul
song: Good Thing (1966)
Him or Me-What's It Gonna Be? (1967)
Hungry (1966)
Indian Reservation (1971)
Just Like Me (1965)
Kicks (1966)
vocalist: Mark Lindsay
Revere, Anne Oscar: National Velvet
revered: 5 hoary **6** sacred **7** beloved **9** venerable **10** celebrated
object: 4 icon, idol, ikon **5** eikon
reverence: 3 awe **4** fear **5** honor, piety, value **6** esteem, homage, praise, regard, wonder **7** respect, worship **8** devotion **9** adoration, deference, obeisance **10** admiration, devoutness, exaltation, veneration
show ~: 3 bow **5** kneel **9** genuflect
reverend: 5 padre **6** cleric, father, parson, pastor **8** minister, preacher
mother: 3 nun
residence: 5 manse
__ Reverend: 4 Most, Very **5** Right
Reverend Mr. Black (1963 song)
artist: Kingston Trio
reverent: 4 holy **5** pious **6** devout, loving **9** awestruck, religious, righteous
not ~: 6 unholy **7** godless, impious, ungodly **8** agnostic **9** atheistic
reverential: 5 lowly **6** loving **7** dutiful **9** awestruck
__ Revere's Ride: 4 Paul
reverie: 5 dream, study **6** musing, trance **7** fantasy, thought **8** daydream, head trip, phantasy **9** pipe dream **10** brown study, meditation
in ~: 5 moony **6** adream
indulge in ~: 4 muse **5** dream **7** reflect **8** daydream, meditate, ruminate **10** introspect
revers: 5 lapel
__ reversa: 4 cyma
reversal: 4 jolt **6** change, switch **7** licking, refusal, setback, tragedy, undoing **8** apostasy, flip-flop **9** about-face, inversion, one-eighty, recession, turnabout
auto ~: 3 uey **5** U-turn
Reversal of Fortune (1990 film)
cast: Glenn Close, Jeremy Irons, Ron Silver
role: 5 Claus, Sunny **8** von Bülow
reverse: 4 back, bath, blow, gear, lift, rear, turn, undo, void **5** annul, check, evert, polar, quash, shift, slump, upend, upset, verso, wrong **6** cancel, change, contra, invert, mishap, negate, oppose, recall, renege, repeal, revoke, switch **7** bad luck, counter, failure, inverse, nullify, overset, reflect, rescind, retract, setback **8** antipode, contrary, converse, exchange, flip-flop, flip side, negation, opposite, override, overrule, overturn, turn over **9** about-face, adversity, backpedal, mischance, other side, overthrow, repudiate, transpose, turnabout, underside, volte-face **10** antithesis, antithetic, double back, invalidate, misfortune, turn around
a decision: 8 override, overrule
go into ~: 4 back **5** shift **6** back up
in ~: 9 vice versa
oneself: 6 recant, renege **7** retract, retreat **8** flip-flop **9** back-pedal
prefix: 3 dis-, non-
reverse __: 5 video **7** English, osmosis
reversed: 8 opposite **9** inside out **10** upside-down
reversible: 9 revocable **10** changeable
Reversible Errors
author: Scott Turow
reversion: 7 atavism
revert: 4 turn **5** lapse **6** go back, resume, return **7** reflect, regress, relapse **9** backslide, throw back **10** change back, recidivate, retrogress
review: 3 pan **4** look, mull, rate, rave, slam **5** audit, blurb, check, drill, learn, organ, recap, study, sum up, trash, weigh **6** assess, bone up, column, go over, parade, rehash, résumé, survey **7** analyze, article, brush up, canvass, checkup, debrief, discuss, examine, hearing, inspect, journal, perusal, reading, revisit, rundown, run over, summary, touch on, write-up, writing **8** abstract, analysis, appraise, bone up on, critique, evaluate, hash over, look back, magazine, peculate, reassess, rehearse, scrutiny, synopsis **9** appraisal, comment on, criticism, criticize, newspaper, pick apart, reexamine, summarize, think over, touch upon **10** call to mind, commentary, discussion, inspection, look back on, periodical, procession, reconsider, reevaluate, run through, scrutinize, second look
bad ~: 3 pan **9** broadside
board: 5 panel **7** inquest **9** committee
good ~: 4 rave
legal ~: 6 appeal
__ review: 4 book, peer
reviewer: 5 rater **6** critic **8** examiner **9** evaluator, inspector
Review-Journal: 5 paper **9** newspaper
locale: 8 Las Vegas
revile: 3 jaw **4** hoot, rail **5** abuse, baste, libel, scoff, scorn, sully **6** assail, malign, vilify **7** despise, inveigh, run down, slander, tell off **8** backbite, denounce **9** blaspheme, denigrate, lash out at **10** blackguard, calumniate, villainize, vituperate
revilement: 5 abuse **6** tirade **7** calumny **9** invective **10** detraction, muckraking
reviler: 5 shrew **8** vilifier **9** detractor, henpecker
Revill: 5 Clive
revisal: 6 change **7** editing **9** amendment **10** adjustment, alteration, correction, emendation
revise: 3 cut, fix **4** edit, mend, redo, suit **5** adapt, alter, amend, debug, emend **6** change, doctor, modify, polish, recast, redact, reform, revamp, rework, update **7** clean up, correct, improve, perfect, rectify, redraft, redress, retouch, rewrite, scissor, touch up **8** emendate, overhaul **9** tighten up **10** blue-pencil
jointly: 6 coedit
Revised Standard __: 7 Version
reviser: 6 editor
revision: 6 change, update **7** editing, redraft, redress, rewrite **8** overhaul **9** amendment, redaction, reshaping **10** adjustment, alteration, correction, emendation
revisionist starter: 3 neo
revisit: 6 go back, return, review **8** come back **9** come again, reexamine **10** reconsider, reevaluate
revitalize: 5 renew **6** revive **7** freshen, inspire, quicken, refresh, restore **8** embolden, imbolden, rekindle **9** encourage **10** invigorate
revival: 5 rally **8** comeback, pick-me-up, recovery **9** awakening **10** quickening, renascence, resurgence
setting: 4 tent
shout: 4 amen
technique: 3 CPR
__ Revival: 5 Greek
revivalist: 3 neo
revive: 4 wake **5** awake, cheer, rally, renew, rouse, slake, waken **6** awaken, come to, perk up, recall **7** bring to, freshen, lighten, quicken, rebound, recover, recruit, refresh, restore **8** brighten, rekindle **9** bring back, modernize, reanimate, recollect **10** bounce back, come around, come to life, exhilarate, popularize, reenergize, regenerate, rejuvenate, revitalize
revived: 3 new **5** fresh **6** rested **7** like new
revivify: 7 hearten, refresh, restore **9** encourage **10** regenerate, rejuvenate
Revlon: 6 makeup
alternative: ***see*** cosmetic brand
revocable: 5 fluid **9** adaptable, temporary **10** changeable, reversible
revocation: 6 recall **9** abolition, annulment **10** withdrawal
revoke: 4 kill, lift, void **5** annul, erase, quash, scrub **6** cancel, negate, recall, recant, repeal **7** abolish, dismiss, expunge, nullify, rescind, retract, reverse **8** abrogate, disallow, disclaim, override, overrule, set aside, take back, withdraw **9** repudiate **10** invalidate
a legacy: 5 adeem
revolt: 4 coup, defy, riot, rise, turn **5** appal, flout, rebel, repel, shock **6** appall, ignore, loathe, mutiny, offend, oppose, putsch, resist, rise up, sicken **7** disgust, disobey, dissent, horrify, protest, repulse, treason, turn off, violate **8** civil war, defiance, gross out, overturn, sedition, uprising **9** break away, displease, disregard, make waves, overthrow, rebellion **10** insurgency, revolution
leader: 6 anarch **9** insurgent
revolting: 4 base, evil, foul, grim, icky, poor, ugly, vile **5** awful, gross, lousy, nasty, seamy, woful **6** crumby, crummy, dismal, horrid, odious, rotten, sickly, woeful **7** accurst, baleful, baneful, beastly, doleful, ghastly, hateful, heinous, hideous, noisome, obscene **8** accursed, dreadful, God-awful, grievous, horrible, inferior, shameful, shocking, stinking, terrible, wretched **9** abhorrent, appalling, atrocious, defective, execrable, frightful, insidious, insurgent, loathsome, low-minded, miserable, monstrous, offensive, repellant, repellent, repugnant, repulsive, unsightly **10** abominable, despicable, detestable, disastrous, disgusting, horrendous, uninviting, unpleasant, virtueless
find ~: 4 hate **5** abhor, scorn **6** detest, loathe **7** deplore, despise **8** execrate **9** abominate
revolution: 4 coup, spin, turn **5** cycle, golpe, orbit, round, storm, upset **6** change, circle, mutiny, putsch, revolt, strife **7** anarchy, circuit, shake-up **8** civil war, gyration, outbreak, rotation, upheaval, uprising, violence **9** bloodshed, coup d'état, overthrow, rebellion
line: 4 axis
starter: 7 counter
time for one ~: 4 year

Revolution (1968 song)
artist: Beatles
__ Revolution: 5 Texas **6** French **7** Chinese, English, October, Russian
revolutionary: 3 new **4** left **5** novel, rebel, ultra **6** anarch **7** lawless, radical **8** renegade **9** different, extremist, insurgent **10** avant-garde, innovative, subversive
Chinese ~: 3 Mao
core: 5 cadre
French ~: 5 Marat
Irish ~: 6 Fenian
path: 5 orbit
Russian ~: 5 Lenin
Revolutionary __: 3 War **5** Étude
Revolutionary Étude
composer: Frédéric Chopin
Revolutionary Road (2008 film)
cast: Leonardo DiCaprio, Kate Winslet
Revolutionary War
general: 4 Howe **5** Gates, Wayne **6** Arnold, de Kalb, Greene, Marion, Putnam **7** Clinton, Pulaski, Steuben **9** Lafayette **10** Cornwallis, von Steuben, Washington
hero: 5 Allen **10** Ethan Allen
spy: 4 Hale **10** Nathan Hale
revolutionize: 6 change, reform **8** innovate **9** transform
Revolutions of the Viaducts
artist: Paul Klee
revolve: 4 mull, muse, roll, spin, turn **5** orbit, pivot, swing, think, twirl, twist, wheel, whirl **6** circle, gyrate, ponder, rotate, swivel **8** go around, mull over, ruminate, turn over **9** pirouette **10** deliberate, think about
around: 5 orbit
revolver: 3 arm, gun **6** pistol **7** firearm
inventor: 4 Colt
revolving: 6 rotary
part: 5 rotor
revolving __: 4 door **6** charge, credit
revue: 4 show, skit **6** parody **7** program **10** production
line: 6 chorus
place: 6 casino
segment: 4 skit
revulsion: 4 hate **5** odium **6** hatred, horror **7** disgust, dislike **8** aversion, distaste, loathing, reaction **9** antipathy, repulsion **10** abhorrence, repellence, repugnance
revved up: 5 hyper
reward: 3 due, pay, tip **4** gift, meed, plum, wage **5** award, bonus, crown, favor, fruit, grant, gravy, honor, lucre, medal, merit, perks, price, prize, purse, repay, wages **6** bounty, carrot, desert, grease, payoff, profit, refund, return, tipoff, trophy **7** garland, goodies, guerdon, jackpot, laurels, payment, pension, premium, redress, requite, revenue, satisfy, strokes, subsidy **8** accolade, dividend, gratuity, kickback, proceeds **9** indemnify, lagniappe, reckoning, repayment, sweetener **10** compensate, inducement, punishment, recompense, remunerate, take care of
old-style: 4 meed
rewarding: 7 gainful **8** edifying, fruitful, pleasing, readable, valuable **9** well-spent **10** beneficial, fulfilling, gratifying, productive, profitable, satisfying, successful, worthwhile
reword: 5 alter **6** recast **7** clarify **9** translate **10** paraphrase
rework: 4 edit **6** modify, reform, rehash, revise
reworking: 6 rehash **7** redress **10** adaptation
rewrite: 4 copy, edit **6** rehash, revise **8** revision **9** redaction **10** emendation
rex: 4 king
Rex: 3 cat **4** Reed **5** Allen, felid, Smith, Stout **6** Barney, feline, Ingram, Morgan, Reason, Warner **7** Humbard **8** Harrison
colleague: 4 Erle **6** Agatha
__ Rex: 6 Arthur **7** Oedipus
Rexroth, Kenneth: 4 poet
rey: 6 Felipe **7** Alfonso **9** Ferdinand **10** Juan Carlos
mate: 5 reina
Rey: 6 Alvino **8** Fernando, Margaret **9** Alejandro
Reyes: 4 José
Reykjavik: 4 city, town **7** capital
locale: 4 Icel. **7** Iceland
Reynard, like: 3 sly **4** foxy
Reynard the Fox
author: John Masefield
Reynolds: 4 Burt, Jody, Lynn, Ryan **5** Allie, Price **6** Debbie, Freddy, Joshua **8** Marjorie
alternative: 4 Glad **5** Alcoa, Hefty **6** Ziploc **9** Saran Wrap
Reynolds, Burt: 5 actor
film: Boogie Nights (1997)
Breaking In (1989)
The Cannonball Run (1981)
City Heat (1984)
The Crew (2000)
Deliverance (1972)
The End (1978)
Hooper (1978)
The Longest Yard (1974)
The Man Who Loved Cat Dancing (1973)
Nickelodeon (1976)
Rent a Cop (1988)
Semi-Tough (1977)
Shamus (1973)
Smokey and the Bandit (1977)
Starting Over (1979)
Switching Channels (1988)
spouse: Loni Anderson, Judy Carne
TV: Evening Shade, Gunsmoke
Reynolds, Debbie: 7 actress
daughter: Carrie Fisher
film: How the West Was Won (1962)
The Mating Game (1959)
The Pleasure of His Company (1961)
The Rat Race (1960)
Singin' in the Rain (1952)
Tammy and the Bachelor (1957)
The Tender Trap (1955)
The Unsinkable Molly Brown (1964)
musical revival: 5 Irene
song: Tammy (1957)
spouse: Eddie Fisher
Reynolds, Joshua: 6 artist **7** British, painter
Reza: 7 Pahlavi
Reznor: 5 Trent
RF: 3 pos.
RFD part: 4 Free **5** Rural **8** Delivery
RFK, Mrs.: 5 Ethel
Rh: 4 elem. **7** element, rhodium
45 for ~: 4 at. no.
what the ~ factor is named for: 6 monkey, rhesus
Rh __: 6 factor
rhabdomantists do, what: 5 dowse
Rhaetian __: 4 Alps
Rhaiadr: 5 falls **9** waterfall
locale: 5 Wales
Rhames, Ving: 5 actor
film: Bringing Out the Dead (1999)
Con Air (1997)
Entrapment (1999)
Mission: Impossible II (2000)
Out of Sight (1998)
real first name: 6 Irving
rhapsodic: 6 elated **7** glowing, lilting, lyrical **8** blissful, ecstatic, in heaven, ravished, thrilled **9** bombastic, delighted, gladdened, overjoyed, rapturous
Rhapsodie Espagnole
composer: Maurice Ravel
rhapsodize: 4 rave, talk **5** orate **7** enthuse **9** go on about, hold forth
rhapsody: 5 music **7** rapture **8** lyricism **10** jubilation
__ Rhapsody: 4 Alto **6** Second
Rhapsody for Orchestra
composer: Antonín Dvorák
Rhapsody in Blue (1945 film)
cast: Robert Alda, Joan Leslie, Alexis Smith
subject: 8 Gershwin
rhea: 4 bird **6** ratite
cousin: 3 emu **4** emeu
Rhea: 4 moon **5** giant, Titan **7** Perlman **8** Caroline
brother: 6 Cronos, Cronus
daughter: 4 Hera **6** Hestia **7** Demeter
equivalent: 3 Ops
husband: 6 Cronos, Cronus
parent: 4 Gaea **6** Uranus
planet: 6 Saturn
son: 4 Zeus **5** Hades, Pluto **8** Poseidon
Rhea __: 6 Silvia
rhebok: 6 animal **8** antelope
relative: *see* antelope
Rhee: 7 Syngman
Rheem
alternative: 5 Trane **6** Lennox **7** Carrier, Fedders **9** Friedrich
Rheims: 4 city, town
locale: 6 France
__ Rheingold: 3 Das
Rhein port: 4 Köln
rhenium: 5 metal **7** element
rhesus: 6 animal, Bandar **7** macaque, primate
relative: *see* primate
rhesus __: 6 monkey
Rhesus __: 6 factor
rhetor: 6 orator
rhetoric: 4 bunk, rant **5** hooey **6** bunkum, hot air, speech **7** address, bombast, fustian, oration, oratory **8** buncombe **9** discourse, elocution, eloquence, gift of gab, hyperbole, verbosity, wordiness **10** balderdash, vocalizing
rhetorical: 4 glib **5** showy, tumid, windy, wordy **6** florid, mouthy, ornate, purple, turgid **7** flowery, pompous, stilted, unterse, verbose, voluble **8** eloquent, forensic, inflated, sonorous **9** bombastic, grandiose, high-flown, overblown **10** euphuistic, flamboyant
device: 5 ploce, trope **7** imagery
rhetorician: 6 orator
Rhett: 5 Akins **6** Butler
daughter: 6 Bonnie **10** Bonnie Blue
rival: 6 Ashley
rheum: 4 cold **7** catarrh
__-Rhin: 3 Bas **4** Haut
rhinal: 5 nasal
Rhine: 2 J.B. **4** wine **5** river
branch of the ~: 6 Ijssel
city on the ~: 4 Bonn, Köln **5** Basel, Basle, kleve, Mainz, Worms **6** Arnhem **7** Cologne **10** Düsseldorf, Strasbourg
ender: 4 land
feeder: 3 Aar **4** Aare, Main, Ruhr **5** Mosel **6** Neckar **7** Moselle
in Holland: 4 Rijn
locale: 7 Germany, Holland
region: 6 Alsace
wine: 4 hock
wine center: 5 Mainz
Rhine, J.B. field: 3 ESP
Rhinemann Exchange, The
author: Robert Ludlum
Rhinestone Cowboy (1975 song)
artist: Glen Campbell
rhinoceros: 5 beast **6** animal, mammal
beetle: 4 uang
cousin: 5 hippo, tapir
feature: 4 horn
female: 3 cow
home: 3 zoo **6** Africa
male: 4 bull
young: 4 calf
Rhinoceros
author: Eugène Ionesco
rhizome: 4 root
rho: 5 Greek **6** letter
predecessor: 2 pi
successor: 5 sigma
Rhoda (CBS sitcom)
cast: David Groh (Joe Gerard)
Valerie Harper (Rhoda Morgenstern)
Julie Kavner (Brenda Morgenstern)
Nancy Walker (Ida Morgenstern)
producer: MTM
Rhode: 5 nymph
brother: 6 Triton
father: 8 Poseidon
Rhode Island: 5 state
capital: 10 Providence
city: 7 Bristol, Newport, Warwick **8** Coventry, Cranston, Johnston, Westerly **9** Pawtucket **10** Cumberland, Providence, Woonsocket
Indian: 9 Wampanoag
motto: 4 Hope
nickname: 10 Ocean State
region: 4 N. Eng. **10** New England
school: 5 Brown
state flower: 6 violet
state mineral: 8 bowenite

state motto: 4 Hope
state shell: 6 quahog
state tree: 8 red maple
Rhode Island Red: 3 hen 4 fowl 7 chicken
relative: *see* chicken
Rhodes: 4 city, Hari, isle, port, town 5 Cecil 6 island
locale: 6 Greece
Rhodes __: 7 scholar
Rhodesian Ridgeback: 3 dog 5 canid 6 canine
rhodium: 5 metal 7 element
rhododendron: 5 plant 6 flower
relative: 6 azalea
rhodolite: 3 gem 6 garnet 8 gemstone
Rhody: 4 aunt
__ Rhody: 6 Little
rhombus: 5 shape
rhonchus: 5 snore
Rhonda: 7 Fleming
Rhone: 4 wine 5 river
city on the ~: 4 Lyon 5 Arles, Lyons 6 Geneva 7 Avignon
feeder: 5 Isère, Saône
locale: 6 France
tributary: 3 Ain
rhubarb: 3 pie 5 brawl, set-to 6 barney, fracas, hassle, rumpus 7 quarrel 8 argument 10 donnybrook
unit: 5 stalk
Rhue: 6 Madlyn
rhumba: 5 dance
Rhumba Is My Life
author: Xavier Cugat
rhum cake: 4 baba
rhyme: 3 ode 4 beat, poem, rune 5 ditty, meter, poesy, verse 6 poetry, rhythm, sonnet 7 cadence, cadency, couplet, measure, versify 8 doggerel, limerick, rondelet
maker: 4 bard, poet
or reason: 5 cause, logic, sense 6 motive
scheme: 4 AABA, AABB, ABAA, ABAB, ABBA, ABCA 6 ABACAB
without ~ or reason: 4 idle 5 inane, nutty, silly, wacky 6 absurd 7 asinine, foolish, puerile 8 mindless 9 frivolous, half-baked, illogical, ludicrous, pointless, senseless 10 irrational, ridiculous
rhyme __: 6 scheme
__ rhyme: 3 eye 7 nursery
Rhyme Pays
artist: Ice-T
rhymer: 4 bard, poet
rhymes: 5 poesy, verse 6 poetry
Rhymes: 5 Busta
__ Rhymes: 5 Busta
rhymester: 4 bard, poet 6 rhymer 9 sonneteer, versifier
Rhymes to Be Traded for Bread
author: Vachel Lindsay
rhyming __: 5 slang
rhyming game: 6 crambo
rhyolite: 4 lava 7 mineral
Rhys, Jean: 6 writer 7 British
work: Good Morning, Midnight
The Left Bank and Other Stories
Sleep It Off, Lady
Tigers are Better-Looking
Wide Sargasso Sea
rhythm: 4 beat, lilt, rime, time 5 meter, pulse, rhyme, swing, tempo, throb 6 accent, stress 7 cadence, cadency, measure, pattern 8 downbeat, symmetry 10 regularity, repetition
and blues: 5 music
body ~: 5 pulse
graceful ~: 4 lilt
instrument: 4 drum
__ rhythm: 4 beta, body 5 alpha
Rhythm __ Heart: 4 of My
__ Rhythm: 4 I Got
rhythm and __: 5 blues
Rhythm Heritage
song: Theme from S.W.A.T. (1976)
rhythmic: 4 even 5 paced 6 cadent, poetic, smooth, steady 7 lilting, lyrical, musical, regular 8 poetical 10 harmonious
movement: 5 dance
Rhythm Is Gonna Get You (1987 song)
artist: Gloria Estefan
Rhythm Nation (1989 song)
artist: Janet Jackson
Rhythm 'N' Blues (1955 song)
artist: McGuire Sisters
Rhythm of My Heart (1991 song)
artist: Rod Stewart
Rhythm of the Night (1985 song)
artist: DeBarge
RI
see Rhode Island
R.I.
neighbor: 4 Conn., Mass.
see also Rhode Island
ria: 5 creek, inlet 7 estuary, rivulet
RIAA, part of: 4 Amer., Assn. 5 Assoc 6 Record 7 America 8 Industry
rial: 5 money
locale: 4 Iran, Oman
rialto: 4 mart
Rialto Ripples
composer: George Gershwin
riant: 3 gay 7 gleeful, smiling 8 cheerful, laughing, mirthful
riata: 4 rope 5 lasso 6 lariat
end: 5 noose
rib: 3 kid, rag 4 bone, jape, joke, josh, mock, razz, twit, wale 5 chaff, costa, ridge, roast, taunt, tease 6 banter, deride, flange, needle, pick on, timber 8 ridicule 9 make fun of, poke fun at
combining form: 4 cost- 5 costo-, pleur- 6 pleuro-
ender: 4 wort 5 grass
leaf ~: 4 vein
order: 4 rack
relinquisher: 4 Adam
skyscraper ~: 6 girder
slangily: 4 slat
vault ~: 5 ogive 6 lierne
rib __: 4 cage 5 roast, steak, vault
rib-__ steak: 3 eye
__ rib: 5 prime
__ Rib: 5 Adam's
ribald: 3 raw 4 blue, lewd, racy 5 bawdy, crude, gross, juicy, nasty, salty, spicy 6 coarse, earthy, purple, risqué, smutty, spicey, unmeet, vulgar 7 naughty, obscene, raunchy 8 indecent, off-color, shameful 9 low-minded, salacious 10 indecorous, licentious, scurrilous
ribaldry: 8 lewdness 9 grossness, indecency, lubricity
riband: 4 cord, sash 5 badge 6 cordon
ribbed fabric: 3 rep 4 repp 5 pique, twill 6 faille, poplin, tricot 7 épinglé 8 corduroy 9 grosgrain
ribbing: 4 jest 5 roast 6 banter 8 badinage, raillery, ridicule 10 persiflage
ribbon: 4 band, belt, tape 5 medal, prize, shred, strip, title 6 cordon, edging, stripe, trophy 9 audiotape 10 decoration
blue ~: 5 prize 6 trophy 7 laurels
combining form: 4 taen-, -tene 5 taeni- 6 taenio-
earn a blue ~: 3 win 7 succeed, triumph
hair ~: 6 fillet
holder: 5 spool
trim: 9 picot. gimp
Ribbon: 5 falls 9 waterfall
locale: 8 Yosemite 10 California
__ ribbons: 5 cut to
ribbons, cut into: 5 shred
rib-eye: 3 cut 4 beef, meat 5 steak
Ribisi: 8 Giovanni
Ribisi, Giovanni: 5 actor
film: The Boiler Room (2000)
The Gift (2000)
The Mod Squad (1999)
The Other Sister (1999)
riboflavin: 3 vit. 7 vitamin 8 B vitamin, nutrient
ribonucleic __: 4 acid
ribosomal __: 3 RNA
ribs: 4 beef, meat
elbow in the ~: 3 jab 4 poke, prod 5 goose, nudge 6 tickle
source: 3 pig
spot: 5 grill 8 barbecue
__ ribs: 5 prime, short
rib-tickler: 4 hoot, jest, joke 6 gasser
rib-tickling: 4 rich 5 comic, funny 9 hilarious, priceless
Ric: 6 Ocasek
__ Rica: 5 Costa
__ Rican: 5 Costa 6 Puerto
rica, not: 5 pobre
Ricardo: 4 Lucy 5 David, Palma, Ricky 6 Cortez 9 Güiraldes, Montalban
costar: 5 Hervé
in English: 7 Richard
portrayer: 4 Ball, Desi, Lucy 5 Arnaz 7 Lucille
see also Spanish
Riccardo: 4 Muti 5 Drigo 8 Giacconi
in English: 7 Richard
Ricci: 4 Nina 6 Matteo 9 Christina
Ricci, Christina: 7 actress
film: The Addams Family (1991)
Addams Family Values (1993)
Anything Else (2003)
Black Snake Moan (2007)
Desert Blue (1999)
The Ice Storm (1997)
Monster (2003)
The Opposite of Sex (1998)
Sleepy Hollow (1999)
Speed Racer (2008)
rice: 4 carb 5 carbo, grain 6 cereal, Minute 7 Success 8 Carolina, side dish 9 Uncle Ben's
cake: 4 nosh 5 mochi, snack 6 nibble 7 munchie
cooker: 3 wok
dirty ~ cuisine: 5 Cajun
dish: 5 pilaf, pilau, pilaw 6 pilaff
field: 5 paddy
wine: 4 sake, saki
rice __: 4 cake, wine 5 paddy, paper
__ rice: 4 wild 5 brown, dirty
Rice: 3 Sam, Tim 4 Anne, univ. 5 Condi, Elmer, Jerry 8 Rosemary 9 Grantland 10 university
athletes: 4 Owls
conference: 3 WAC
locale: 5 Texas 7 Houston
Rice __: 4 Chex 8 Krispies
Rice-__: 5 a-Roni
__ Rice: 6 Minute
Rice, Anne: 6 writer
work: Beauty's Punishment
Beauty's Release
Belinda
Blackwood Farm
Blood and Gold
The Claiming of Sleeping Beauty
Cry to Heaven
Exit to Eden
Feast of All Saints
Interview With the Vampire
Lasher
Memnoch the Devil
Merrick
The Mummy
Pandora
The Queen of the Damned
Servant of the Bones
The Tale of the Body Thief
Taltos
The Vampire Armand
The Vampire Chronicles
The Vampire Lestat
Violin
Vittorio the Vampire
The Witching Hour
__ Rice Burroughs: 5 Edgar
Rice Chex: 6 cereal
competitor: *see* cereal
Rice, Elmer: 6 writer 10 playwright
work: The Adding Machine
Street Scene
We, the People
Rice Krispies: 6 cereal
competitor: *see* cereal
sound: 3 pop 4 snap 7 crackle
ricelike pasta: 4 orzo
Rice, Sam: 7 Senator 10 outfielder
Rice, Tim musical: 4 Aida 5 Chess, Evita
rich: 3 fat 4 deep, full, lush, luxe, oily, posh, rank, warm 5 droll, fancy, fatty, flush, funny, grand, haves, heavy, juicy, light, meaty, plush, ritzy, spicy, swank, sweet, tasty, vivid 6 absurd, bright, classy, costly, creamy, deluxe, fecund, gilded, landed, lavish, loaded, mellow, ornate, savory, spicey, strong, swanky, toothy, uptown 7 amusing, comical, copious, fertile, intense, liberal, moneyed, opulent, pungent, upscale, vibrant, wealthy, well-off 8 abundant, affluent, farcical, fruitful, gorgeous, humorous, in clover, luscious, old money, palatial, precious, prolific, resonant, sonorous, splendid, thriving, valuable, well-to-do 9 abounding, bounteous, bountiful,

deep-toned, delicious, diverting, doing well, elaborate, excessive, expensive, exuberant, flavorful, high-class, hilarious, laughable, ludicrous, luxuriant, luxurious, plentiful, priceless, succulent, sumptuous, very funny **10** exorbitant, expressive, full-bodied, gut-busting, high-priced, in the chips, in the dough, in the money, meaningful, nourishing, nutritious, overpriced, privileged, productive, propertied, prosperous, ridiculous, upper class, upper crust, well-heeled
as land: **7** fertile **8** farmable, tillable **10** cultivable
be ~ (in): **6** abound
be too ~: **4** cloy
grow ~: **4** gain **5** get on, score **6** arrive, batten, do well, profit, thrive **7** burgeon, make out, prosper, succeed **8** flourish, get ahead, go places, hit it big, make good **9** make money
not ~: **4** poor **8** indigent
one: **6** fat cat
one way to get ~: **5** lotto **7** inherit, lottery
striking it ~: **5** lucky **9** fortunate **10** fortuitous, prosperous, successful
supply: **4** lode, mine, vein
__ rich: **6** filthy
Rich: **4** Adam **5** Buddy, Eisen, Irene **6** Little **7** Charlie **8** Adrienne
Rich, Adrienne: **4** poet
Rich and Famous
author: John Guare
Rich and Famous (1981 film)
cast: Candice Bergen, Jacqueline Bisset
director: George Cukor
Rich and Famous host: **5** Leach
Richard: **3** Dix, Roe **4** Bach, Byrd, Eder, Egan, Ford, Gere, Kiel, Kind, Kuhn, Long, Marx, Moll, Todd **5** Adams, Arlen, Boone, Brome, Cliff, Conte, Daley, Ernst, Haydn, Kiley, Kline, Lewis, Masur, Nixon, Petty, Pryor, Quine, Simon, Stone, Synge **6** Armour, Avedon, Belzer, Beymer, Brooks, Burton, Condon, Crenna, Dawson, Deacon, Dehmel, Donner, Dysart, Greene, Grieco, Harris, Jordan, Leakey, Lester, Maltby, Pearce, Savage, Scarry, Steele, Taylor, Thomas, Thorpe, Tucker, Wagner, Wilbur, Wright **7** Branson, Carlson, Crashaw, Denning, Ellmann, Feynman, Gatling, Haldane, Jaeckel, Maurice, Roberts, Rodgers, Sanders, Simmons, Smalley, Strauss, Wallace, Widmark **8** Anderson, Basehart, Benjamin, Cromwell, Dreyfuss, Eberhart, Gephardt, Lovelace, Marquand, Matheson, Mulligan, Sarafian, Sheridan **9** Carpenter, Fleischer, Linklater, Llewellyn, Lockridge, Roundtree, Silvestri, Zsigmondy **10** Castellano, Clayderman, D'Oyly Carte, Farnsworth, Hofstadter
in Italian: **8** Riccardo
in Spanish: **7** Ricardo
Richard __: **3** III, Roe **4** Cory
Richard __ Anderson: **4** Dean
Richard __ Carte: **5** D'Oyly
Richard __ Dana: **5** Henry
Richard __ de Lion: **5** Coeur
__ Richard: **4** Poor **6** Little
Richard, Cliff
song: Devil Woman (1976)
Dreaming (1980)
A Little in Love (1981)
We Don't Talk Anymore (1979)
Richard Coeur de __: **4** Lion
Richard Cory
author: Edward Arlington Robinson
Richard Dean __: **8** Anderson
Richard Henry __: **4** Dana
Richard II
author: William Shakespeare
Richard III
author: William Shakespeare
Richard III (1955 film)
cast: Sir John Gielgud, Laurence Olivier, Ralph Richardson
director: Laurence Olivier
Richard III need: **5** horse
Richard, Maurice
milieu: **3** ice **4** rink **5** arena
org.: **3** NHL
Richards: **2** I.A. **3** Ann, Bob **4** Mary **5** Keith, Renee **6** Denise **7** Michael **8** Theodore **9** Dickinson
__ Richard's Almanack: **4** Poor
Richards, Bob: **7** athlete **8** Olympian **11** pole vaulter
Richards, Denise
spouse: Charlie Sheen
Richards, I.A.: **4** poet **7** British **8** linguist
Richards, Keith: **5** Stone
Richards, Mary player: **5** Moore
Richardson: **3** Ian **4** Owen, Tony **5** Bobby, Joely, Ralph **6** Robert, Samuel **7** Dorothy, Miranda, Natasha **8** Patricia
__ Richardson, AK: **4** Fort
Richardson, Dorothy: **6** writer **7** British
work: Fortunes of Richard Mahony
Richardson, Miranda: **7** actress
film: The Apostle (1997)
The Bachelor (1993)
The Crying Game (1992)
Dance With a Stranger (1985)
Empire of the Sun (1987)
Enchanted April (1991)
The Evening Star (1996)
Get Carter (2000)
Sleepy Hollow (1999)
Tom & Viv (1994)
film (voice): The King and I (1999)
Richardson, Natasha: **7** actress
film: Nell (1994)
The Parent Trap (1998)
mother: Vanessa Redgrave
spouse: Liam Neeson
Richardson, Owen: **8** Nobelist **9** physicist
Richardson, Samuel: **6** writer **7** British
work: Clarissa Harlowe
Pamela, or Virtue Rewarded
wrote: first modern English novel
Richard the __-Hearted: **4** Lion
Rich, Buddy: **7** drummer
genre: **4** jazz
Rich, Charlie
nickname: The Silver Fox
song: Behind Closed Doors (1973)
The Most Beautiful Girl (1973)
A Very Special Love Song (1974)
__ riche: **4** rime **7** nouveau
Richelieu: **8** Cardinal
riche, nouveau: **7** parvenu, upstart **9** arriviste
riches: **4** cash, gold, pelf, pile **5** lucre, means, money, worth **6** assets, clover, mammon, plenty, wealth **7** fortune **8** opulence, opulency, property, treasure **9** abundance, affluence, resources, substance **10** prosperity
hidden ~: **5** trove
Richet, Charles: **8** Nobelist **12** physiologist
Rich Girl (1977 song)
artist: Hall and Oates
Rich Harbor
artist: Paul Klee
Richie: **4** Rich **6** Havens, Lionel **7** Ashburn, Sambora
portrayer: **3** Ron
Richie, Lionel
lead singer of: The Commodores
song: All Night Long (1983)
Ballerina Girl (1987)
Dancing in the Ceiling (1986)
Endless Love (1981)
Hello (1984)
Love Will Conquer All (1986)
My Love (1983)
Penny Lover (1984)
Running with the Night (1983)
Say You, Say Me (1985)
Se La (1987)
Stuck on You (1984)
Truly (1982)
You Are (1983)
Richie Rich dog: **6** Dollar
Rich Kids (1979 film)
cast: Trini Alvarado, John Lithgow
Richler: **8** Mordecai
Rich Man, Poor Man: **5** novel **10** miniseries
author: Irwin Shaw
Rich Man, Poor Man (TV miniseries)
cast: Bill Bixby, Dorothy McGuire, Ed Asner, Nick Nolte, Peter Strauss, Susan Blakely
role: Asher Berg, Axel Jordache, Julie Prescott, Mary Jordache, Rudy Jordache, Smitty, Sue Prescott, Tom Jordache, Willie Abbott
Richmond: **4** city, town
county: **7** Henrico
locale: **6** Canada **7** Georgia, Indiana **8** Kentucky, Virginia **10** California
river: **5** James
was its cap.: **3** CSA
Richmond-__-Thames: **4** upon
richness: **4** luxe **6** luxury, wealth **8** grandeur, splendor, treasure **9** fecundity, fertility **10** exuberance, lavishness
Rich Project, Tony
song: Nobody Knows (1996)
Richter: **6** Burton, Conrad **7** Charles
concern: **5** quake, seism **6** tremor **10** earthquake
Richter __: **5** scale
Richter, Conrad: **6** writer
work: The Fields
The Light in the Forest
The Sea of Grass
The Town
The Trees
The Water of Kronos
Richter, Mordecai: **6** writer **8** Canadian
work: The Apprenticeship of Duddy Kravitz
Richthofen: **3** ace **5** Baron, flier, flyer, pilot **6** German **7** aviator, Manfred
ricin: **5** toxin **6** poison
rick: **4** pile **8** haystack
starter: **3** hay
Rick: **4** Dees **5** Barry, Jason, Mears **6** Astley **7** Moranis, Nielsen **8** Newcombe, Schroder
Rickenbacker: **3** ace **5** Eddie, flier, flyer, pilot **7** aviator
rickety: **4** sick, thin, weak **5** frail, rocky, shaky **6** flimsy, infirm, jiggly, shabby, unfirm, wabbly, wobbly **7** fragile, run-down, unsound **8** decrepit, delicate, insecure, unstable, unsteady, untended **9** breakable, dangerous, frangible, tottering **10** broken-down, jerry-built, precarious, ramshackle, tumbledown
not as ~: **5** safer
sound ~: **5** creak
rickey: **5** drink **8** beverage, cocktail
ingredient: **3** gin **4** lime
Rickey: **6** Branch **9** Henderson
Ricki: **4** Lake
Rickie __ Jones: **3** Lee
Rickles: **3** Don
Rickman: **4** Alan
Rickover: **5** Hyman **7** admiral
rickrack: **6** fringe
Rick's: **4** café
end of ~ toast: **3** kid
pianist: **3** Sam
rickshaw: **4** cart
Rickshaw Boy
author: Lao She
Ricky: **3** Jay **5** Zahnd **6** Martin, Nelson, Skaggs **7** Ricardo
landlord: **4** Fred **10** Ethel. Mertz
portrayer: **4** Desi **5** Arnaz
wife: **4** Lucy
rico: **4** rich **7** Spanish
not ~: **5** pobre
__ Rico: **6** Puerto
ricochet: **4** skip **5** carom **6** bounce, careen, carrom, glance **7** deflect, rebound **10** bounce back
Ricochet (1991 film)
cast: Denzil Washington, Ice-T, John Lithgow
Ricoh: **6** camera, copier
competitor: **5** Nikon, Xerox
ricotta: **6** cheese **7** Italian
rictus: **4** gape **5** mouth **6** gaping **7** opening
rid: **4** dump, fire, free, junk, lose, shed **5** clear, eject, expel, purge, scrap **6** dispel, divest, remove, unload, uproot **7** abolish, release, relieve, shake up, toss out **8** disabuse, liberate, shake off, stamp out, unburden **9** disburden, dispose of, eliminate, eradicate, extirpate, liberated, throw away **10** do away with, unhindered
get ~ of: **2** ax **3** axe, can, zap

4 boot, cede, drop, dump, junk, oust, sack, sell, shed 5 chuck, ditch, drain, eject, erase, expel, forgo, let go, purge, scrap, shake, yield 6 banish, bounce, depose, forego, give up, lay off, remove, unload 7 abandon, cashier, discard, dismiss, drum out, exclude, forfeit, forsake, release, wipe out 8 exorcise, exorcize, forswear, furlough, hand over, jettison, part with, pink-slip, shake off, stamp out, throw out, unburden 9 cast aside, discharge, eliminate, foreswear, liquidate, surrender, terminate, throw away 10 do away with, relinquish
of: 8 done with, free from
(of): 4 free 5 empty
__ riddance: 4 good
__ Riddance: 3 Bed
ridden starter: 3 bed
Riddick: 4 Bowe
riddle: 3 pit 4 maze, sift 5 poser, rebus, vexer 6 damage, enigma, impair, infest, pepper, pierce, puzzle, teaser 7 charade, mystery, paradox, pervade, problem, puzzler, stumper 8 permeate, puncture, question 9 conundrum, honeycomb, labyrinth, perforate 10 cryptogram, puzzlement
explanation: 3 key
starter: 4 what
Zen ~: 4 koan
Riddle: 6 Nelson
Riddle-me-__: 3 ree
Riddle, Nelson
song: Lisbon Antigua (1955)
Riddler foe: 6 Batman
ride: 3 bug, fly, nag, rag, run, vex 4 bait, fare, hack, lift, post, spin, taxi, trot, waft, whip 5 abuse, annoy, drift, drive, flume, get on, harry, hitch, hound, jaunt, motor, roast, taunt, tease, whirl 6 airing, badger, berate, bother, cruise, depend, Dodgem, gallop, go-cart, go-kart, harass, heckle, hector, jockey, junket, needle, outing, pester, plague, travel 7 bicycle, commute, henpeck, journey, joyride, mount up, oppress, torment, unnerve 8 carousel, log flume, ridicule, saddle up, travel on 9 excursion, hitchhike, move along, passenger, persecute, poke fun at, transport, tyrannize 10 Tilt-a-Whirl, tool around
ahead: 5 scout
allow to ~: 5 let on
free ~: 4 comp, lift, pass 7 license
go for a ~: 4 bike 5 motor 6 travel
herd on: 3 run 4 mind, tend 5 drive 6 direct 7 conduct, oversee 9 supervise, trample on, tyrannize 10 administer
let ~: 6 excuse, wink at 7 condone, forgive 8 overlook, shrug off, tolerate 9 put up with
off: 2 go 4 exit, flee 5 leave, split 6 beat it, be gone, decamp, depart 7 abscond, head out, move out, pull out, retreat, ship out, skip out 8 clear out, light out, run along, withdraw
(on): 4 rely 5 hinge 6 depend
out: 4 bear, take 5 brave 6 endure 7 subsist, survive, sustain, weather 8 navigate 9 withstand 10 see through
roughshod over: 5 bully 7 trample 9 trample on, tyrannize
seek a ~: 5 thumb
short ~: 3 hop 4 spin
shotgun: 5 watch 6 assist, defend, patrol, shield 7 protect 9 safeguard
starter: 3 hay
take for a ~: 3 gyp 4 bilk, dupe, gull, hoax, take 5 cheat, cozen, trick 6 fleece 7 deceive, defraud, mislead, swindle 8 flimflam, hoodwink 9 bamboozle
there for the ~: 5 along
thumb a ~: 5 hitch 9 hitchhike
to hounds: 4 hunt 5 chase, track 9 track down
via gravity: 5 coast
ride __: 3 out 4 down, high 7 shotgun
ride __ fall: 4 for a
ride __ on: 4 herd
__ ride: 4 free 5 let it
Ride! (1962 song)
artist: Dee Dee Sharp
Rideau Canal terminus: 6 Ottawa
Ride Captain Ride (1970 song)
artist: Blues Image
ride for __: 5 a fall
Ride Like the Wind (1980 song)
artist: Christopher Cross
rider: 4 fare 5 add-on, biker 6 cowboy, jockey 7 codicil, proviso 8 addendum, addition, commuter, horseman 9 amendment, bicyclist, passenger, provision 10 attachment, equestrian, hitchhiker, horsewoman, supplement
assistance: 5 leg up
attire: 5 habit 8 jodhpurs
command: 4 whoa 6 giddap 7 giddyap, giddyup
goad: 4 crop, spur 5 quirt
mishap: 4 buck 5 spill
payment: 4 fare
rail ~: 5 tramp
stance: 4 seat
strap: 4 rein
throw the ~: 4 buck
__ Rider: 4 Easy, Pale 6 Knight
__ Riders: 3 Sky 5 Rough
Riders of the Purple Sage
author: Zane Grey
Riders to the Sea
author: John Synge
__ Rides Again: 6 Destry
Ride, Sally: 9 astronaut
Ride With the Devil (1999 film)
cast: Jim Caviezel, Tobey Maguire, Skeet Ulrich
director: Ang Lee
ridge: 3 rib, rim 4 apex, dune, fold, hill, line, nurl, pole, reef, rise, ruck, seam, wale, weal, welt 5 arête, arris, bluff, chain, chine, crest, esker, knoll, knurl, ledge, mound, range, scarp, spine, stria 6 crease, cuesta, flange, furrow, sierra, upland 7 crinkle, hillock, hogback, moraine, parapet, rampart, wrinkle 8 backbone, mountain, pinnacle, swelling 9 elevation 10 high ground, projection
anatomical ~: 4 ruga 5 gyrus
botanical ~: 5 raphe 6 carina
button ~: 4 nurl 5 knurl
corduroy ~: 3 rib 4 wale
depression: 3 col
ender: 4 back, line, pole
fingerboard ~: 4 fret
fingerprint ~: 5 whorl
glacier ~: 4 kame 5 arête, esker, serac 7 moraine
ice ~: 7 hummock
rock ~: 4 crag
sand ~: 4 dune
seashell ~: 5 varix
__ Ridge Boys: 3 Oak
ridged: 5 rough 6 craggy, jagged, spiked 7 grooved, serrate, unlevel 8 crinkled, furrowed, serrated 10 corrugated
__ Ridge Mountains: 4 Blue
ridges: 5 rugae
glacial ~: 4 osar
__ Ridge, TN: 3 Oak
Ridgewood: 4 city, town
locale: 9 New Jersey
ridgy: 6 craggy, jagged, rugged, uneven 7 serrate 9 irregular
ridicule: 3 dig, kid, rag, rib 4 bait, barb, defy, gibe, haze, hiss, hoot, jape, jeer, jibe, jive, josh, lash, mock, razz, ride, slam, slap, slur, snub, twit 5 abuse, chaff, decry, farce, fleer, libel, mimic, roast, scoff, scorn, shame, sneer, spurn, taunt, tease 6 banter, debunk, defame, deride, dump on, expose, heckle, impugn, jeer at, jibe at, malign, needle, offend, parody, rebuff, satire, send-up, slight, vilify 7 affront, asperse, burlesk, calumny, catcall, deflate, degrade, disdain, lampoon, laugh at, mockery, mortify, obloquy, offense, putdown, rank out, ribbing, run down, sarcasm, slander, take off, traduce 8 belittle, contempt, denounce, derision, laugh off, pooh-pooh, raillery, satirize, sneeze at, vilipend 9 aspersion, burlesque, cheap shot, contumely, denigrate, discredit, disparage, humiliate, make fun of, poke fun at 10 calumniate, caricature, defamation, disrespect, make game of, opprobrium
Greek god of ~: 5 Momus
hold up to ~: 4 mock, twit 5 taunt 6 dump on, insult 7 disdain, lampoon, put down 8 belittle, satirize 9 burlesque 10 caricature
object of ~: 4 butt 5 sport 6 effigy
ridiculing: 7 jeering, satiric 8 derisive 9 satirical
ridiculous: 4 daft, rich 5 antic, crazy, daffy, droll, funny, goofy, goony, inane, nutty, sappy, silly, wacky 6 absurd, screwy, stupid, whacky 7 asinine, bizarre, comical, fatuous, foolish, puerile, suspect 8 cockeyed, farcical 9 facetious, fantastic, fatuitous, grotesque, hilarious, laughable, ludicrous, pointless, priceless, senseless, unearthly 10 hysterical, incredible, irrational, outlandish
idea: 5 folly 6 lunacy 7 fatuity, madness 8 nonsense 9 absurdity, silliness
riding: 5 sport 6 ahorse 9 annoyance
see also rider
riding __: 4 boot, crop 5 habit, mower
...riding on __: 5 a pony
ridley: 6 animal, turtle 7 reptile 9 amphibian, sea turtle
Ridley: 5 Scott
__ rid of: 3 get
Riefenstahl: 4 Leni
Rieger: 4 Alex
Riegert: 5 Peter
riel: 5 money
rien __ plus: 4 ne va
Rienzi
author: Edward Bulwer-Lytton
composer: Richard Wagner
Riesling: 4 wine 5 white
rife: 4 many 5 alive, awash, laden 6 common, filled, jammed, loaded, packed 7 copious, crammed, crowded, general, overrun, profuse, rampant, replete, stuffed, teeming 8 abundant, brimming, bursting, epidemic, infested, numerous, pandemic, swarming, thronged 9 abounding, chock-full, extensive, pervasive, plentiful, prevalent, universal 10 epidemical, ubiquitous, widespread
be ~: 4 rule 6 abound
(with): 5 alive, lousy
with vegetation: 4 rich, wild 5 dense, green 6 lavish 7 fertile, teeming, verdant 8 abundant, tropical 9 plentiful, succulent
riff: 6 melody
jazz ~: 4 vamp
Riff: 6 Berber
home: 6 Africa 7 Morocco
riffle (through): 4 leaf, scan, skim 5 thumb 6 browse
riffraff: 3 mob 4 scum 5 dregs 6 masses, people, rabble 7 beggary 9 commoners, hoi polloi, peasantry 10 lower class, underworld
associate with ~: 4 slum
Rifkin: 3 Ron
rifle: 3 arm, gun, gut, rob, Uzi 4 loot, M one, raid, sack 5 BB gun, steal, strip, yager 6 burgle, Garand, musket, rip off, search 7 despoil, firearm, pillage, plunder, ransack, rummage, shotgun 9 flintlock, go through 10 burglarize, Winchester
carrying a ~: 5 armed
ender: 3 man, men 4 bird 5 scope
mount: 5 bipod
part: 4 bead, butt 5 scope, sight, stock 6 barrel, breech
pellet: 2 BB 6 beebee
ready a ~: 3 aim
sight a ~ again: 5 reaim
rifle __: 5 range
__ rifle: 3 air 4 long
rifled __: 4 slug
Rifleman, The (ABC western)
cast: Chuck Connors (Lucas McCain)
Johnny Crawford (Mark McCain)
Paul Fix (Micah Torrance)
Rifle Regiment, The
composer: John Philip Sousa
rifles: 4 arms 8 weaponry 9 firepower
rift: 3 cut, gap 4 feud, gape, gash, gulf, rent, tear 5 abyss, break,

chasm, chink, cleft, crack, fault, gorge, gulch, gully, split **6** breach, cranny, gulley, hiatus, ravine, schism **7** crevice, fissure, opening, quarrel, rupture **8** aperture, cleavage, crevasse, division, fracture, squabble **10** alienation, falling-out, separation

rift ___: **3** saw **4** zone **6** valley
___ Rift Valley: **5** Great
rig: **3** arm, fit, fix, kit **4** fake, gear, semi, team **5** array, dress, equip, getup, lorry, set up, sulky, truck **6** attire, clothe, doctor, fit out, gear up, juggle, outfit, square, supply, tackle, tamper **7** appoint, bedrape, costume, falsify, furnish, trump up, turnout **8** accouter, accoutre, carriage, contrive, engineer, equipage, maneuver **9** apparatus, buckboard, caparison, equipment, improvise, machinery, provision **10** fiddle with, manipulate, prearrange, tamper with
as a sports event: **3** fix
big ~: **4** mack, semi **5** truck **9** transport
renter: **5** Ryder, U-Haul
starter: **7** thimble
up: **3** fix **4** garb **5** equip **6** attire, outfit **7** furnish **8** accouter, accoutre **9** caparison
___-rig: **4** jury
Rig-___: **4** Veda
Riga: **4** city, gulf, port, town **7** capital
locale: **6** Latvia
resident: **4** Lett
river: **5** Dvina
rigadoon: **5** dance
rigamarole: **9** goofiness
rigati: **5** pasta **7** noodles **8** macaroni
rigatoni: **5** pasta **7** noodles **8** macaroni
alternative: ***see*** pasta
sauce: **5** pesto **6** tomato **8** marinara
___ Rigby: **7** Eleanor
Rigby, Cathy: **7** gymnast
Rigel: **4** star
constellation: **5** Orion
Rigg, Diana: **4** Dame **7** actress
role: **4** Emma, Peel
TV: The Avengers
___-rigged: **4** jury
rigger starter: **3** out **4** down
rigging: **4** gear **6** outfit, tackle **9** caparison, trappings
make over the ~: **5** refit
overseer: **4** bo's'n **5** bosun
part of a ship's ~: **4** bibb
support: **4** mast, spar
Riggs, Bobby: **7** netster **9** tennis pro
milieu: **5** court
right: **3** apt, due, fit, fix **4** cure, fair, good, hale, just, meet, mend, nice, real, sane, true, very, well, wise **5** aptly, claim, emend, exact, fixed, hardy, ideal, legal, licit, lucid, moral, power, punch, smack, sound, spang, title, truth, utter, valid **6** actual, avenge, dead-on, decent, dexter, direct, equity, evenly, honest, justly, lawful, normal, proper, remedy, repair, seemly, spot on, square, virtue, wholly **7** condign, correct, ethical, factual, fitting, freedom, genuine, honesty, justice, legally, liberty, license, licitly, logical, merited, morally, perfect, precise, quickly, rectify, redress, requite, restore, sort out, totally, utterly **8** accuracy, accurate, all there, bona fide, deserved, directly, discreet, entirely, fairness, faithful, flawless, for suree, goodness, honestly, interest, lawfully, morality, on target, on the dot, orthodox, promptly, properly, rational, reaction, reliably, sensible, smack-dab, squarely, straight, suitable, suitably, truthful, unerring, validity, veracity, virtuous **9** actuality, authentic, authority, befitting, clockwise, correctly, equitable, errorless, ethically, exactness, exemption, faultless, favorable, favorably, fittingly, franchise, honorable, honorably, instantly, integrity, judicious, make up for, on the beam, on the mark, on the nose, opportune, out-and-out, perfectly, privilege, propriety, undoubted, veracious, veritable, vindicate **10** aboveboard, accurately, admissible, completely, exactitude, factuality, felicitous, infallible, lawfulness, legitimacy, legitimate, on the money, permission, perquisite, principled, propitious, reasonable, recompense, remarkably, scrupulous, unimagined, unmistaken, virtuously, watertight
angle: **2** el **3** ell
as rain: **5** sound
at ~ angles: **4** orth., perp. **5** plumb **10** orthogonal
at ~ angles to the keel: **5** abeam
at the ~ time: **3** apt **5** on cue **6** prompt **7** fitting **8** apposite, punctual **9** expedient **10** auspicious, convenient, felicitous
away: **3** now, PDQ **4** anon, ASAP, soon, stat **5** today **6** at once, pronto **7** quickly, readily, swiftly **8** directly, promptly **9** at present, forthwith, instantly, on the spot, presently **10** at this time, here and now, this minute
a wrong: **5** repay **6** avenge **7** get even, pay back, redress, requite **9** retaliate, retribute
be ~ for: **3** fit **4** suit **5** befit, match **6** become **7** apply to **9** agree with
by ~: **6** de jure
combining form: **4** orth-, rect- **5** dextr-, ortho-, recti- **6** dextro-
do all ~: **3** win **6** hack it, make it, manage, thrive **7** make out, prevail, prosper, succeed, triumph **8** flourish, go places, make good
ender: **3** ist **4** most, ness, ward
forgo a ~: **4** cede **5** forgo, waive **6** give up **8** sign away **10** relinquish
from the factory: **3** new **5** fresh **6** unused **8** brand-new **9** untouched
get ~: **5** solve **6** unlock **7** explain, unravel, work out **8** decipher **9** figure out, puzzle out
good ~ arm: **8** backbone, linchpin, mainstay
hand: **6** dexter
hang a ~: **4** turn
have a ~ to: **4** earn **5** merit **7** deserve
having the ~ stuff: **5** adept **6** suited, up to it **7** capable **8** skillful, talented **9** competent, efficient, qualified, up to snuff, up to speed **10** proficient
hitting the ~ notes: **5** on key
if all goes ~: **6** at best
ignorant of ~ and wrong: **6** amoral
in French: **9** n'est-ce pas?
in heraldry: **6** dexter
in one's ~ mind: **4** sane **5** lucid **8** sensible **10** reasonable
just ~: **4** to a T **5** ideal **6** to a tee **7** optimal, perfect, utopian **8** flawless **9** beautiful, correctly, exemplary, faultless, nonpareil, on the nose, perfectly, precisely **10** accurately, consummate
legal ~: **5** droit
look ~ through: **3** cut **4** shun, snub **5** scorn, spurn **6** ignore, insult, rebuff, slight **7** disdain, neglect, put down, tune out **8** brush off **9** blackball, disregard, humiliate, ostracize
make ~: **3** fix **5** atone, remit **6** adjust, remedy **7** correct, rectify, redress **8** disabuse
maker: **5** might
name meaning ~: **6** Dexter
not ~: **3** off **4** awry, left **5** amiss, wrong
now: **3** PDQ **4** anon, ASAP **5** as yet, today **6** at once, pronto **7** quickly, swiftly **8** promptly **9** at present, forthwith, instantly, on the spot, presently **10** at this time, the present, this minute
of access: **6** entrée **7** ingress, passage **10** admittance
off the bat: **6** at once, pronto **7** quickly, rapidly, swiftly **8** in a flash, in no time, on the fly **9** instantly, like a shot
of way: **8** priority **10** precedence
on: **3** yes **4** amen **5** exact **6** it is so **8** for a fact, specific **9** certainly, precisely **10** acceptable, positively
on the map: **4** east
party of the ~: **3** GOP
ship's ~ side: **4** stbd. **9** starboard
starter: **4** copy, down **5** birth, forth
stuff: **5** goods, knack, savvy, skill **6** talent **7** ability, faculty, know-how, prowess **8** aptitude, capacity, facility **9** dexterity, expertise **10** capability, competence, competency
to buy: **6** option
to the ~: **3** gee **4** away **5** aside
to vote: **9** franchise
see also of course
right ___: **3** off **4** away, face, hand, wing **5** angle, brain, field, guard, of way, stuff **6** tackle **7** fielder
right ___ and there: **4** then
right ___ money: **5** on the
right ___ the bat: **3** off
right ___ the horse's mouth: **4** from
right ___ up: **4** side
right-___: **4** wing **6** handed, hander, minded
right-___ man: **4** hand
___ right: **3** all **4** eyes **5** flush, hang a, stage
___, right!: **4** Yeah
___-right: **3** all **4** half
Right ___: **4** Bank **5** Guard
Right ___, The: **5** Stuff
right and wrong, uncaring of: **6** amoral
right-angled: **4** boxy **6** square
right as ___: **4** rain
Right Back ___: **4** at Ya
Right Back Where We Started From (1976 song)
artist: Maxine Nightingale
Right Bank
author: Elaine Neal
Right Bank attraction: **6** Louvre
right circular ___: **4** cone
righteous: **4** fair, good, holy, just, pure, smug **5** godly, moral, pious **6** devout, honest, trusty, worthy **7** angelic, dutiful, ethical, saintly, sincere, sinless, upright **8** elevated, innocent, reverent, virtuous **9** angelical, blameless, deserving, exemplary, guiltless, honorable, praisable, religious, veracious, wholesome **10** charitable, law-abiding, scrupulous
indignation: **4** fury **5** anger, pique **6** choler, dander **7** dudgeon, offense, outrage, umbrage **10** resentment
___-righteous: **4** self
Righteous Brothers
members: Medley, Hatfield
song: Ebb Tide (1965)
He (1967)
Just Once in My Life (1965)
Rock and Roll Heaven (1974)
Soul and Inspiration (1966)
Unchained Melody (1965)
You've Lost That Lovin' Feelin' (1964)
righteousness: **4** good **5** honor **6** virtue **7** justice, probity **8** goodness, moralism, morality
right from the ___ mouth: **6** horse's
rightful: **3** apt, due, fit **4** fair, just, real, true **5** jural, legal, legit, licit, valid **6** earned, kasher, kosher, lawful, proper, vested **7** allowed, condign, fitting, merited **8** bona fide, deserved, official, orthodox, suitable **9** befitting, by the book, canonical, permitted **10** authorized, legitimate, sanctioned **11** appropriate
rightfully: **8** lawfully
Right Guard: **9** deodorant
alternative: ***see*** deodorant
right-hand: **3** key **5** basic, vital **6** needed **7** crucial **9** important, necessary, requisite
person: **4** aide, asst. **6** helper **7** adviser, advisor **8** henchman, mainstay
___ Right In: **4** Walk
rightly: **4** ably, fine, well **6** nicely **7** adeptly, capably **8** expertly, properly, suitably **9** admirably, correctly, perfectly **10** accurately, adequately, splendidly
right-minded: **4** true **5** sound **6** worthy **7** ethical **8** virtuous
Right, Mr., not: **3** cad **4** heel

rightness: 8 justness, morality 9 propriety
righto
see of course
right of ___: 3 way
right off the ___: 3 bat
___ right of kings: 6 divine
Right on!: 4 amen, okay
right on the ___: 5 money
rights: 4 dibs 5 claim, title
by ~: 6 fairly, justly
have ~ to: 3 own 6 retain 7 control, possess
movement word: 3 lib
org.: 3 ADL 4 ACLU, EEOC, NLRB, SCLC 5 NAACP
put to ~: 5 clean, order 6 neaten, spruce 7 ordered, orderly 9 smarten up 10 straighten
set to ~: 6 remedy 7 restore 9 refurbish
strip of ~: 6 divest
to ~: 4 tidy, trim 7 orderly
___ rights: 3 air 5 civil, human 6 animal, states', women's
Rights ___, The: 5 of Man
___ Rights Amendment: 5 Equal
Rights of Man, The
author: Thomas Paine
Right Stuff, The: 4 book, film
author: Tom Wolfe
cast: Kathy Baker, Scott Glenn, Ed Harris, Barbara Hershey, Dennis Quaid, Sam Shepard, Fred Ward
org: 4 NASA
role: 3 LBJ 5 Glenn 6 Cooper, Yeager 7 Grissom, Schirra, Shepard, Slayton 9 Carpenter
right then and ___: 5 there
___ Right Thing: 5 Do the
right-thinking: 4 good 5 sound, valid 6 cogent, proper 7 correct, ethical, logical 8 accurate, credible, rational, sensible 9 competent, honorable 10 reasonable
Right Time of the Night (1977 song)
artist: Jennifer Warnes
right-to-___: 4 know
right-to-___ law: 4 work
Right Turn ___: 4 Only
___ right up!: 4 Step
___ right with the world: 4 All's
Right you ___!: 3 are
rigid: 3 set 4 firm, hard, iron, prim, snug, taut 5 balky, bossy, cruel, exact, fixed, harsh, picky, rocky, solid, stern, stiff, stony, tense, tight, tough 6 flinty, mulish, ornery, severe, static, steely, stoney, strict, stuffy, wooden 7 adamant, austere, dead set, diehard, hard-set, literal, precise, prudish, Spartan 8 absolute, concrete, contrary, despotic, exacting, hard-line, immobile, indurate, ironclad, locked in, obdurate, perverse, resolute, stubborn 9 demanding, difficult, draconian, hidebound, immovable, impliable, inelastic, obstinate, pigheaded, religious, sectarian, steadfast, stringent, unbending, unpliable, unsparing, unvarying 10 bullheaded, despotical, determined, hard-bitten, implacable, inexorable, inflexible, invariable, iron-fisted, iron-willed, no-nonsense, oppressive, relentless, tyrannical, unamenable, unchanging, unswerving, unyielding
not ~: 3 lax 5 slack 7 bending, relaxed
rigidify: 3 fix, set 7 tighten
rigidity: 6 starch 8 firmness, hardness
lose ~: 3 dip, sag 4 wilt 5 droop
rigmarole
see baloney
Rigney: 4 Bill
Rigoberta: 3 Tum
Rigoletto: 5 opera
character: 4 Duke 5 Borsa, Gilda 7 Ceprano, Marullo 8 Giovanna 9 Maddalena, Monterone
composer: Giuseppe Verdi
piece: 4 aria
sculptor: Erté
setting: 5 Italy 6 Mantua
rigor: 8 asperity, fidelity, hardness, hardship, iron hand, severity 9 austerity, diligence, exactness, harshness, precision, sternness 10 discipline, exactitude, inclemency, severeness, strictness, stringency
ending: 3 ous
rigorous: 4 firm, hard 5 bossy, cruel, exact, fussy, harsh, picky, stern, stiff, tough 6 bitter, Lenten, rugged, severe, strict, trying 7 austere, careful, correct, finicky, precise, prudent, Spartan 8 accurate, cautious, despotic, exacting, finiking, finnicky, hard-line, thorough 9 assiduous, attentive, demanding, draconian, inclement, judicious, observant, stringent, unbending, unsparing 10 despotical, fastidious, inflexible, iron-fisted, meticulous, no-nonsense, oppressive, particular, relentless, scrupulous, tyrannical
rigorously: 4 hard 6 keenly 8 severely 9 carefully
___ rigueur: 3 à la
rigueur, de: 6 proper 9 mandatory, necessary 10 compulsory
Rig-Veda god: 4 Agni
Riis, Jacob: 6 Danish, writer 8 reformer
work: How the Other Half Lives
The Making of an American
Rijeka: 4 city, port, town
locale: 7 Croatia
Rijksmuseum
artist: Frans Hals
Rikki Don't Lose That Number (1974 song)
artist: Steely Dan
Rikki-tikki-___: 4 Tavi
Riksdag
locale: 6 Sweden
rile: 3 bug, get, irk, vex 4 fret, gall, pain, stir 5 anger, annoy, get to, grate, peeve, pique, rouse, upset 6 arouse, bother, enrage, excite, fire up, hassle, madden, needle, nettle, offend, pother, put out, rankle, stir up, tee off, work up 7 agitate, disturb, enflame, grate on, incense, inflame, provoke, steam up, tick off 8 irritate 9 aggravate, displease, infuriate 10 exasperate, run afoul of
riled: 3 hot, mad 4 ired, sore, warm 5 angry, cross, het up, huffy, irate, livid, upset, wroth 6 fuming, galled, ireful, raging, raving, red-hot 7 enraged, furious, ranting 8 choleric, wrathful 9 indignant, irritated, resentful, splenetic 10 infuriated
riler: 7 inciter 8 agitator, fomenter 10 instigator
Riley: 3 Pat 7 Chester 8 Jeannine
life of ~: 4 ease
Riley, James Whitcomb
nickname: Hoosier Poet
work: Little Orphant Annie
The Old Swimmin' Hole
The Raggedy Man
When the Frost Is on the Punkin
Riley, Jeannie C.
song: Harper Valley P.T.A. (1968)
___ Riley, KS: 4 Fort
Riley, Mrs. Chester: 3 Peg
___-rilievo: 4 alto
Rilke, Rainer Maria: 4 poet 6 German
work: The Duino Elegies
The Sonnets to Orpheus
rill: 4 race 5 bourn, brook, creek, crick 6 runlet, runnel, stream 7 rivulet 9 streamlet
rille: 6 trench, valley
rim: 3 hem, lip, top 4 brim, brow, curb, edge, hoop, line, side 5 brink, frame, ledge, limit, mouth, ridge, skirt, verge 6 border, flange, margin 8 boundary, surround 9 extremity, outskirts, perimeter, periphery 10 projection
basketball ~: 4 hoop
circular ~: 5 felly 6 felloe
watch ~: 5 bezel
wheel ~: 6 flange
rim ___: 4 shot
___ Rim: 7 Pacific
___ rima: 5 terza 6 ottava
Rímac, city on the: 4 Lima
Rima's beloved: 4 Abel
Rimbaud, Arthur: 4 poet 6 French
rime: 4 hoar, poem 5 frost 9 hoarfrost, Jack Frost
Rime of the Ancient Mariner, The: 4 poem
author: Samuel Taylor Coleridge
rimer: 4 bard, poet 5 odist 9 versifier
Rimes, LeAnn
song: How Do I Live (1997)
Looking Through Your Eyes (1998)
Written in the Stars (1999)
Rimini: 4 city, town
locale: 5 Italy
___-rimmed glasses: 4 horn
rimose: 7 cracked
rimple: 6 furrow
rims, horn: 7 glasses 8 cheaters 10 spectacles
Rimsky-Korsakov, Nikolai: 7 Russian 8 composer
work: Capriccio Espagnol
Le Coq d'Or
Scheherazade
The Snow Maiden
The Tsar's Bride
rimy: 3 icy 5 gelid 6 frozen
rin
ten ~: 3 sen
Rinaldo: 5 opera
author: Torquato Tasso
composer: George Frideric Handel
rind: 4 bark, coat, hull, husk, peel, skin 5 cover, crust 6 albedo, casing, cortex 7 coating, peeling, surface 8 covering 10 integument
remove ~: 4 pare, peel, skin
remover: 5 parer 6 peeler
___ rinds: 4 pork
Rinehart, Mary Roberts: 6 writer
work: The Circular Staircase
The Door
The Man in Lower Ten
The Swimming Pool
Tish
The Yellow Room
ring: 3 mob 4 band, belt, bloc, bong, buzz, call, clan, dial, echo, gang, gird, gong, gyre, halo, hoop, link, loop, peal, pool, rink, toll, wind 5 arena, bunch, cabal, chime, clang, cycle, go off, hedge, hem in, junta, junto, knell, noise, party, phone, round, sound, torus, troop, wheel 6 call up, cartel, circle, clique, corona, engird, flange, gasket, girdle, jangle, jingle, league, outfit, rabble, reecho, summon, tinkle, troupe, wreath 7 annulet, annulus, bandlet, circuit, clangor, combine, compass, coterie, enclose, environ, faction, inclose, in-group, jewelry, resound, seal off, sing out, society, stadium, vibrate 8 alliance, bandelet, cincture, encircle, gloriole, ornament, resonate, surround 9 coalition, encompass, enwreathe, resonance, syndicate, telephone 10 federation, hippodrome
a bell: 6 recall 8 remember 9 recognize
anatomical ~: 6 areola, areole
bearer: 4 wife 5 bride, groom
boundary: 4 rope
combining form: 3 gyr- 4 cycl-, gyro- 5 cyclo-
competitor: 3 pug 5 boxer 7 fighter 8 pugilist
decision: 2 KO 3 TKO 4 draw, kayo
ender: 3 let 4 bolt, bone, dove, side, tail, toss, worm 6 leader, master
event: 4 bout 5 fight, match
face off in the ~: 3 box
foul: 4 butt, knee
in: 4 come, open 5 reach, start, usher 7 precede, welcome
(in): 5 usher
off: 6 hang up
official: 3 ref 7 referee
of light: 4 halo 7 aureola, aureole
org.: 3 WBA, WBC
out: 4 peal, toll 8 resonate
part: 3 gem 5 bezel, jewel
practice in the ~: 4 spar
Roman ~: 6 anello
rubber ~: 6 gasket
site: 3 ear 5 arena, pinky 6 big top, circus, finger
starter: 3 ear 4 bull
surface: 3 mat
tactic: 5 feint 6 clinch
thing on a ~: 3 key
three minutes in the ~: 3 rnd. 5 round
up: 4 call, dial 5 phone, total 9 tele-

phone, touch base
see also boxing
ring __: 3 off 4 toss, true 5 a bell 6 binder, finger
ring __ curtain: 5 up the
ring __ new year: 5 in the
ring __ the curtain: 4 down
ring-__: 6 porous, tailed
ring-__-the-rosey: 6 around
__ ring: 3 key 4 mood, nose, tree 5 brass 6 annual, boxing, growth, napkin, piston, signet 7 diamond, wedding
Ring: 7 Lardner
composer: 6 Wagner
goddess: 4 Erda
Ring __: 5 Cycle, Dings 6 Nebula
ring a __: 4 bell
ring-a-levio: 4 game
Ring and the Book, The: 4 poem
author: Robert Browning
character: 5 Guido
Ring and the Rose, The
author: William Makepeace Thackeray
ring around the __: 6 collar
ring-around-the-__: 5 rosey
Ring Around the Moon
author: Jean Anouilh
__-ring circus: 5 three
__ Ring des Nibelungen: 3 Der
ringdove: 4 bird
ringer: 4 bell 8 doorbell 9 accessory, imitation
bell ~: 6 caller 7 visitor
dead ~: 4 twin 5 image, match 6 double 7 picture 8 likeness 9 duplicate, facsimile, identical, look-alike 10 equivalent
register ~: 4 sale
__ ringer: 4 dead
ringing: 4 loud, peal 5 knell, sound 7 vibrant 8 resonant
sound: 4 bong, ding, peal, ting
ring in the __: 3 new
ringlet: 4 curl, lock 5 tress 10 lock of hair
ringlets: 4 coif 6 hairdo 8 coiffure
make ~: 4 coil, curl 5 swirl, twine, twirl, twist
ringlike: 5 curvy, round 6 curved 8 circular
Ringling: 4 John, Otto 5 Henry 6 Albert, Alfred, August 7 Charles
see also circus
Ringling __: 4 Bros.
ringmaster: 4 host 5 emcee
Ring My Bell (1979 song)
artist: Anita Ward
Ring Nebula constellation: 4 Lyra
Ringo: 3 Jim 5 Starr
colleague: 4 John, Paul 6 George
son: 3 Zak
Ringo (1964 song)
artist: Lorne Greene
Ring of Bright Water (1969 film)
cast: Virginia McKenna, Bill Travers
pet: 5 otter
Ring of Fire (1963 song)
artist: Johnny Cash
Ring of Thoth, The
author: Arthur Conan Doyle
rings: 4 tori 7 jewelry
mood ~: 3 fad 5 craze
run ~ around: 3 top 4 beat, best 5 outdo 7 surpass
tree ~: 6 annuli
__ rings: 5 onion, smoke
__ rings around: 3 run
ring-shaped: 5 toric 7 annular
Rings on __ fingers...: 3 her
ring-tailed animal: 4 coon 5 coati, genet 6 monkey
ringtoss: 4 game
game piece: 5 quoit
target: 3 peg
Ringwald, Molly: 7 actress
film: Betsy's Wedding (1990)
The Breakfast Club (1985)
Pretty in Pink (1987)
Sixteen Candles (1984)
ringworm: 5 tinea
rink: 5 arena
see also hockey
rink __: 3 rat
__ rink: 6 roller
rinky-dink: 5 cheap 6 flimsy, shabby, two-bit 8 outmoded, picayune 9 penny-ante, small-time 10 amateurish
Rinna: 4 Lisa
Rinna, Lisa
spouse: Harry Hamlin
rinpoche: 4 monk 6 cleric
rinse: 3 dip, wet 4 soak, tint, wash 5 bathe, clean, flush, henna 6 dampen, gargle 7 cleanse, dunking, immerse, launder, moisten, wash off 8 flush out 9 hair color
needing a ~: 5 foamy, soapy, sudsy 6 frothy 7 lathery
salon ~: 5 henna
Rinso
rival: 3 Duz, Fab 4 Tide
Rin Tin Tin: 3 dog 6 canine 8 shepherd
see also Adventures of Rin Tin Tin
Rinzai __: 3 Zen
río: 4 Ebro 5 river 7 Orinoco, Spanish
Rio: 3 car, Kia 4 auto, port 10 automobile
see also Rio de Janeiro
Rio __: 4 Lobo, Rita 5 Bravo, de Oro, Negro 6 Blanco, Cuarto, Grande 7 Piedras
Rio __ Plata: 4 de la
__ Rio: 3 Del 5 I Go to
Rio Bravo (1959 film): 5 oater
cast: Dean Martin, Ricky Nelson, John Wayne
composer: Dimitri Tiomkin
director: Howard Hawks
Rio de __: 3 Oro 7 Janeiro
Rio de Janeiro: 4 city, port, town
airline: 5 Varig
airport: 6 Galeao
dance: 5 samba
locale: 6 Brasil, Brazil
resident: 7 Carioca
Rio de la Plata: 5 river 7 estuary
locale: 3 Arg., Uru. 7 Uruguay 9 Argentina
Rio Grande: 5 river
capital of ~ do Norte: 5 Natal
city on the ~: 6 El Paso, Laredo 11 Albuquerque
locale: 5 Texas 8 Colorado 9 New Mexico
river to the ~: 5 Pecos 7 Conchos
Rio Grande (1950 film): 5 oater
cast: Ben Johnson, Maureen O'Hara, John Wayne
director: John Ford
Rioja: 3 red 4 wine 5 Pilar
like ~ wine: 4 seco
origin: 5 Spain
Rio Lobo (1970 film): 5 oater
cast: Jack Elam, Jennifer O'Neill, John Wayne
director: Howard Hawks
Riopan: 7 antacid
alternative: *see* antacid
Rio Rancho: 4 city, town
locale: 9 New Mexico
Rio Rita (1942 film)
cast: Bud Abbott, Lou Costello, Kathryn Grayson
__ Rios, Jamaica: 4 Ocho
riot: 3 mob, row 4 card, flap, fray, howl, rise, to-do 5 blast, brawl, chaos, mix-up, rebel, scene 6 bedlam, émeute, fracas, gasser, mutiny, rabble, racket, revolt, rise up, ruckus, rumble, rumpus, scream, strife, tumult, uproar 7 clutter, protest, rampage, ruction, run wild, triumph, turmoil 8 carousal, disorder, foofaraw, live it up, outbreak, run amuck, upheaval, uprising, violence 9 brannigan, commotion, confusion, go berserk, imbroglio, laughable, luxuriate, mobocracy, raise Cain, whoop it up 10 donnybrook, free-for-all, profligacy
cause a ~: 5 rouse 6 arouse, foment, incite, set off, whip up, work up 7 agitate, inflame 9 instigate
ending: 3 ous
read the ~ act to: 3 hit 4 flay, flog, slam 5 blast, chide, scold 6 berate, rebuke 7 bawl out, censure, chasten, chew out, condemn, lambast, lecture, reprove, upbraid 8 admonish, chastise, denounce, lambaste, reproach, sail into, tear into, threaten 9 castigate, criticize, dress down, excoriate, reprehend, reprimand 10 come down on, discipline, take to task, vituperate
run ~: 4 rage 6 abound, overdo 7 rampage 9 luxuriate
spray: 4 mace
stop a ~: 5 quash, quell 6 pacify 7 put down 8 beat down
riot __: 3 act, gun 5 squad
__ riot: 3 run 5 laugh
rioting: 5 brawl, chaos 6 fracas, mayhem, uproar 7 turmoil 8 disorder, violence 9 imbroglio
riotous: 4 lush, wild 5 funny, noisy 6 hectic, lavish 7 chaotic, lawless, opulent, radical, rampant, roaring 8 anarchic 9 insurgent, luxuriant, priceless, turbulent 10 anarchical, boisterous, disorderly, topsy-turvy, tumultuous
group: 3 mob 5 horde
__ Rio, TX: 3 Del
rip: 3 cut, fly, hie, jag, run, zip 4 claw, dart, dash, flit, hack, hole, race, rend, rent, rive, rush, slit, snag, tear, tide, zoom 5 burst, hurry, scoot, shred, slash, speed, split, spree 6 barrel, cleave, deride, gallop, hasten, hustle, move it, rebuke, rocket, scurry, wrench 7 blacken, disjoin, floor it, hop to it, quicken, scamper, yank off 8 badmouth, belittle, lacerate, mistreat, separate, step on it 9 castigate, criticize, denigrate, deprecate, hotfoot it, humiliate, shake a leg, skedaddle 10 come undone, get a move on, hightail it, laceration
ender: 3 rap, saw 4 cord
fix a ~: 5 resew
into: 5 abuse, roast 6 assail, attack, harass, impugn, malign, oppugn, rebuke, vilify 7 besiege, bombard, lambast 8 lambaste 9 lash out at 10 calumniate, vituperate
let ~: 5 begin, start 6 launch, set off, set out 7 kick off, lead off, take off, usher in 8 commence, get going, initiate, set about, set forth 10 inaugurate
off: 3 con, cop, gyp, nab, rob, use 4 dupe, flay, lift, loot, rook, soak, take 5 boost, cheat, filch, pinch, rifle, steal, swipe, trick 6 detach, fleece, pilfer, thieve 7 defraud, exploit, mislead, purloin, relieve, swindle 8 flimflam 10 overcharge, run a game on
on: 3 dis, rap 4 slam 5 knock 6 malign, vilify 7 asperse, put down, traduce 8 backbite, badmouth 9 criticize, denigrate, disparage
out: 5 pluck, unsew 6 remove, uproot 9 extirpate
up: 4 rend 5 shred, smear 6 vilify 7 destroy 9 tear apart
rip __: 3 off 4 cord, into, tide
rip-__: 3 off 7 roaring
Rip: 4 Torn 6 Sewell, Taylor 9 Van Winkle
Ripa: 5 Kelly
ripe: 3 due 4 aged 5 adult, plump, prime, ready 6 mature, mellow, stinky, timely 7 matured, overdue, ripened, skilled 8 blooming, prepared, seasoned, suitable 9 developed, favorable, filled out, full-grown, opportune, perfected 10 auspicious, well-versed
not ~: 5 green
starter: 4 rare
ripen: 3 age 4 grow 5 bloom 6 evolve, mature, mellow, season 7 blossom, develop 8 maturate 9 bear fruit
ripened: 5 adult 6 mature, mellow 9 full-grown
ripener: 4 ager
fruit ~: 6 ethene
ripeness: 8 fruition, maturity 9 readiness 10 perfection
ripening early: 4 rath 5 rathe
Riperton, Minnie
song: Lovin' You (1975)
Rip It Up (1956 song)
artist: Little Richard
Ripken: 3 Cal 6 Oriole
sport: 8 baseball
Ripley: 6 Robert 9 Alexandra
Ripley's Believe It or __: 3 Not
rip-off: 3 con 4 scam 5 cheat, fraud, heist, steal, theft, thief, trick 6 racket 7 robbery, swindle 8 swindler, thievery
artist: 5 cheat, shark 6 bilker, con

man **7** grifter, hustler, scammer **8** swindler **9** defrauder
riposte: 4 barb, quip **5** reply **6** answer, retort, zinger **8** comeback, rebuttal, repartee, response, wordplay **9** rejoinder, witticism
ripped: 4 rent, torn **7** asunder
ripping
good time: 3 gas **5** blast
see also wonderful
ripple: 3 lap **4** beat, lick, purl, wave **5** surge, swell **6** billow, gurgle, murmur, ruffle, rustle, tremor **7** flutter, vibrate, wavelet **8** undulate
design: 5 moiré
rippleless: 4 calm **6** serene, smooth **8** peaceful, tranquil
__ Ripples: 6 Rialto
rippling: 4 wavy **9** vibrating
riprap: 5 revet
rip-roaring: 5 noisy **6** hectic, stormy **8** exciting **9** thrilling
ripsnorter: 4 lulu **5** dilly, doozy **9** humdinger
Rip Van Winkle
author: Washington Irving
Rip Van Winkle dog: 4 Wolf
rise: 3 wax **4** dawn, go up, grow, hike, hill, incr., jump, leap, lift, loom, riot, soar, stem, upgo, wake **5** add to, awake, begin, bob up, boost, build, climb, crest, debut, get up, issue, knoll, mound, mount, onset, reach, rebel, ridge, scale, sit up, slope, stand, start, surge, swell, tower, waken, way up **6** appear, ascend, ascent, awaken, billow, crop up, derive, double, emerge, expand, gather, glacis, growth, height, jump up, move up, mutiny, origin, outset, pile up, recess, revolt, rocket, source, spiral, spring, step-up, upturn, wake up, well up **7** advance, augment, balloon, build up, burgeon, climb up, develop, elevate, emanate, flare up, hillock, hummock, improve, incline, infancy, mount up, proceed, prosper, roll out, speed up, stack up, stand up, start up, succeed, turn out, upclimb, upgrade, upslope, upsurge, upswing, uptrend **8** bourgeon, commence, eminence, escalate, flourish, go places, gradient, heighten, increase, levitate, mounting, multiply, surmount, upgrowth **9** acclivity, ascension, beginning, elevation, emergence, eventuate, inception, increment, inflation, intensify, originate, promotion, upwelling **10** appearance, appreciate, escalation, high ground, incipience, levitation, move upward, prominence, spring from, supplement
above: 5 outdo, tower **6** exceed **7** weather **8** overcome, surmount **9** cut across, transcend
and fall: 4 toss **6** billow, rhythm
and shine: 4 wake **5** get up, waken **6** awaken **7** turn out
cause to ~: 6 leaven
give ~ to: 5 beget, breed, cause, spawn **6** effect, induce, prompt **7** inspire, produce, trigger **8** engender, generate, occasion **10** bring about
in waves: 5 pitch, surge, swell **6** billow
on a wave: 5 scend
sharply: 4 zoom **5** surge **6** rocket **7** shoot up **9** skyrocket
starter: 3 sun **4** moon **5** earth
to the occasion: 4 cope **5** get by **6** manage
up: 4 rear, riot **5** rebel **6** mutiny, revolt
rise __ occasion: 5 to the
__-rise: 3 low, mid **4** high
Rise (1979 song)
artist: Herb Alpert
Risë: 7 Stevens
Rise and __!: 5 shine
Rise, Glory, Rise
composer: Thomas Arne
risen: 2 up **5** aloft, awake **6** high up **7** skyward **8** overhead, skywards **10** up in the air, up in the sky
not ~: 4 abed **5** in bed
Rise of Silas Lapham, The
author: William Dean Howells
character: 4 Anna, Lily **5** Corey, Irene, Nanny **6** Milton, Persis **7** Zerilla **8** Penelope
riser: 4 step
cousin: 5 tread
plus tread: 5 stair
__ riser: 5 early
rises
it ~ to the top: 5 cream
where hair ~: 4 nape
__ rise to: 4 give
Rise up so early in the __: 4 morn
'R' Is for Ricochet
author: Sue Grafton
rishi: 4 guru, poet, sage
risibility: 3 fun, joy **4** glee **5** cheer, mirth **6** gaiety, laughs, levity **7** revelry **8** gladness **9** amusement, happiness, merriment, rejoicing **10** jocularity
risible: 5 comic, droll, funny **6** har-har **7** comical **9** laughable, ludicrous
rising: 6 source, uphill **9** promising, rebellion
ground: 4 bank, hill **7** incline **8** gradient
in heraldry: 7 issuant
star: 5 comer
time: 4 dawn, morn **5** sunup
rising __: 4 star
__-rising flour: 4 self
Rising Sun: 4 film **5** novel
author: Michael Crichton
cast: Sean Connery, Harvey Keitel, Wesley Snipes
Rising Sun, Land of the: 5 Japan
risk: 3 bet, try **4** dare, face, play **5** brave, peril, stake, wager **6** chance, danger, gamble, hazard, menace, threat **7** imperil, pitfall, venture **8** endanger, exposure, jeopardy, long shot, openness, unsafety **9** adventure, liability, speculate **10** compromise, go for broke, insecurity, jeopardize, take a flyer
assessor: 5 rater
at ~: 6 liable **7** exposed, in peril **8** in danger **9** imperiled, on the line **10** endangered, in jeopardy
coverage: 3 ins. **9** insurance
not at ~: 4 safe **6** secure **9** protected
put at ~: 3 lay **5** stake, wager **6** chance, gamble **7** imperil, venture **8** endanger, threaten **9** undermine **10** jeopardize
take a ~: 3 bet **4** dare, defy **5** wager **6** gamble, hazard **7** presume, venture **9** challenge, speculate
taker: 4 doer **5** darer **6** better, bettor **7** gambler
underwrite a ~: 5 cover **6** ensure, insure, shield **7** protect, warrant **9** guarantee, indemnify
risk-__: 7 benefit
__ risk: 6 credit
__-risk: 4 high
Risk: 4 game **9** board game
author: Dick Francis
risked: 7 at stake, in peril **9** on the line **10** in jeopardy
risker: 7 gambler **9** daredevil **10** adventurer, speculator
riskless: 4 safe **6** secure **8** harmless
risky: 4 bold, iffy **5** dicey, hairy, rocky **6** chancy, daring, thorny, touchy, tricky, unsafe **7** fraught, parlous, unsound **8** insecure, perilous, ticklish, wide-open **9** dangerous, daredevil, desperate, difficult, foolhardy, hazardous, on thin ice, uncertain, unhealthy **10** jeopardous, out on a limb, precarious, touch-and-go, unreliable
business: 4 dare, spec **5** wager **6** hazard
Risky Business (1983 film)
cast: Tom Cruise, Rebecca De Mornay
risotto: 4 rice
risqué: 3 raw **4** blue, gamy, lewd, racy **5** bawdy, crude, gamey, lurid, salty, spicy **6** daring, purple, ribald, spicey, unmeet, vulgar, X-rated **7** naughty, obscene, off-base **8** immodest, improper, indecent, off-color **9** lubricous, offensive, out-of-line, salacious, unrefined **10** indecorous, indelicate, suggestive
rissole: 6 pastry **8** turnover
ristorante: 9 trattoria
offering: 4 vino, ziti **5** pasta, pollo, squid, zuppa **6** gelati, gelato **7** Chianti, lasagna, lasagne, spumoni, tortoni **8** linguine, linguini **9** antipasto
sauce: 5 pesto **6** tomato **8** marinara
Rit: 3 dye
Rita: 3 Gam **4** Dove **5** Cosby **6** Moreno, Rudner, Wilson **7** Johnson **8** Coolidge, Hayworth **10** Tushingham
Rita __ Brown: 3 Mae
__ Rita: 3 Rio
ritardando: 4 slow **6** slower
opposite: 5 accel.
undoer: 6 a tempo
Ritchard: 5 Cyril
Ritchie: 3 Guy **6** Petrie, Valens **7** Michael
Ritchie, Guy: 8 director
spouse: Madonna
rite: 4 form, Mass **7** baptism, liturgy, service **8** ceremony, exorcism, marriage, practice **9** communion, Eucharist, formality, sacrament, solemnity **10** bar mitzvah, ceremonial, observance
site: 5 altar
Rite __: 3 Aid
__ Rite: 5 Latin **6** Stride
Ritenour, Lee: 9 guitarist
rite of passage, teen: 4 prom
Rite of Spring
author: Andrew Greeley
Rite of Spring, The: 6 ballet
composer: 10 Stravinsky
Ritorna vincitor
singer: 4 Aïda
Ritsos, Yannis: 4 poet **5** Greek
Ritt: 6 Martin
Ritter: 3 Tex **4** John **6** Thelma
Ritter, John: 5 actor **8** comedian
father: 3 Tex
film: Noises Off (1992) They All Laughed (1981)
TV: 8 Simple Rules for Dating My Teenage Daughter, Hearts Afire, Three's Company
ritual: 4 form, Mass, rote **6** custom, formal, solemn **7** baptism, courtly, liturgy, pageant, pompous, service, stately **8** ceremony, decorous, exercise, exorcism, practice, protocol **9** dignified, formality, sacrament, solemnity, tradition **10** ceremonial, liturgical, observance
like some ~s: 5 pagan **9** religious
Ritual Bath, The
author: Faye Kellerman
ritualistic: 6 formal, proper, solemn **7** courtly, stately **8** decorous **9** dignified **10** ceremonial
ritualize: 4 keep **5** extol **7** glorify **8** adhere to **9** celebrate
ritz: 4 pomp **5** style **8** elegance, pretense **9** pageantry, pomposity **10** flashiness, peacockery, pretension
Ritz: 5 César, hotel **7** cracker
alternative: *see* cracker
home of The ~: 5 Paris
locale: 5 Paris
Ritz __: 7 Carlton **8** Brothers
ritzy: 4 chic, lush, posh, rich, tony **5** fancy, plush, sharp, showy, swank, swell, swish, toney **6** chichi, classy, deluxe, dressy, flashy, lavish, lordly, luxury, snazzy, swanky, urbane **7** elegant, opulent, refined, stylish **8** palatial, princely **9** elaborate, exclusive, expensive, high-class, high-toned, luxurious, sumptuous
group: 5 elite
not ~: 4 non-U **5** seedy
rival: 3 foe, tie, vie **4** meet, peer, side, vier **5** enemy, equal, match, touch **6** oppose **7** compete, contend, emulate, nemesis, opposer, vie with **8** approach, emulator, keep pace, opponent, opposing, rank with, resemble **9** adversary, challenge, contender, disputant, emulative, ill-wisher, measure up **10** antagonist, challenger, competitor, equivalent, keep up with, opposition
Rival: 7 dog food
alternative: *see* pet food brand
rivalry: 4 feud **5** fight, match **6** strife **7** contest **8** conflict, friction **10** con-

RI

tention, opposition

Rivals, The
author: Richard Sheridan
character: **5** Acres, Lydia **6** Lucius **8** Malaprop

rive: **3** rip **4** rend, tear **5** break, sever, smash, split **6** cleave, harrow, shiver, sunder **7** rupture, shatter **8** distress, fracture, separate **9** tear apart

riven: **4** torn **5** cleft, split **7** asunder **8** sundered

river: **3** Aar, Apa, Bug, Cam, Dal, Dee, Don, Fly, Han, Inn, Lek, Lot, Lys, Oka, Qom, Qum, Red, San, Tay, Ume, Usk, Wye **4** Aare, Adda, Aire, Amur, Arno, Aube, Avon, Bear, Beni, Bomu, Cher, Coco, Doon, Drin, East, Ebro, Eder, Eger, Elbe, flow, Geba, Gila, gush, Ille, Iowa, Isar, Juba, Kama, Kura, Lena, Liao, Maas, Main, Miño, Napo, Neva, Nile, Oder, Odra, Ohio, Ohre, Oise, Oulu, Ouse, Prut, race, Ruhr, Saar, Salt, Sava, Styr, Styx, Taff, Tana, Tees, Tyne, Uele, Ulúa, Ural, Vaal, Waal, Yalu, Yser, Yüen **5** Adige, Aisne, Apure, Argun, Atrak, Atrek, Benin, Benue, Boyne, Cauca, Chari, Clyde, Congo, Desna, Dnepr, Doubs, Douro, Drava, Drina, Dvina, Grand, Hondo, Indus, Isère, James, Japur, Jumna, Juruá, Kabul, Kafue, Karun, Kasai, Kuban, Lempa, Lethe, Liard, Loire, Marne, Mbomu, Memel, Meuse, Miami, Minho, Murat, Mures, Narew, Negro, Neman, Niger, Onega, Osage, Ouémé, Paran, Peace, Pearl, Pecos, Peene, Piave, Purús, Rhine, Rhone, Santa, Saöne, Seine, Shari, Siret, Slave, Snake, Somme, spate, Stone, Tagus, Tarim, Tiber, Tisza, Tobol, Trent, Tsana, Tumen, Tweed, Volga, Volta, Warta, Weser, White, Xingú, Yampa, Yaqui, Yazoo, Yukon, Zaire **6** Allier, Amazon, Angara, Atbara, attach, Bio-Bio, Brazos, Chenab, Clutha, Copper, Cuiabá, Cydnus, Danube, Dnestr, Donets, feeder, Fraser, Gambia, Ganges, Glomma, Harlem, Hudson, Humber, IJssel, Irtish, Irtysh, Isonzo, Javari, Javary, Jhelum, Jordan, Kagera, Kansas, Khabur, Kolyma, Lehigh, Liffey, Mamoré, Maumee, Mekong, Mersey, Mobile, Mohawk, Moldau, Molopo, Morava, Murray, Neckar, Neisse, Nelson, Niemen, Nueces, onrush, Orange, Orkhon, Ottawa, Pánuco, Patuca, Pee Dee, Platte, Pripet, Rovuma, Ruvuma, Sabine, Sambre, Santee, Scioto, Severn, Seyhan, Shashi, St. John, stream, Struma, Sutlej, Tanana, Thames, Thelon, Thjórs, Tigris, Ubangi, Ussuri, Vardar, Vltava, Wabash, Yakima, Yamuna, Yarmuk, Yarrow, Yellow **7** Alabama, Aruwimi, Ausuble, Berbice, Bermejo, Bighorn, Calabar, Catawba, Cauvery, Chagres, Charles, Conchos, Darling, Derwent, Detroit, Dnieper, Durwent, Garonne, Genesee, Guaporé, Helmand, Hooghly, Huang He, Iguassú, Karkheh, Klamath, Krishna, Limpopo, Livenza, Lualaba, Luapula, Madeira, Mangoky, Mantaro, Marañón, Maritsa, Moselle, Motagua, Narbada, Niagara, Orinoco, Orontes, Pechora, Potomac, Rapidan, Roanoke, Rubicon, Salween, Schelde, Scheldt, Selenga, Senegal, Shannon, Songhua, St. Clair, St. Croix, St. Johns, St. Marys, Tapajós, Trebbia, Truckee, Ucayali, Vistula, Wateree, Xi Jiang, Yenisei, Zambezi **8** Amu Darya, Araguaya, Arkansas, Berezina, Big Muddy, Blue Nile, Canadian, Cheyenne, Chindwin, Cimarron, Colorado, Columbia, Congaree, Delaware, Demerara, Dniester, Dordogne, Godavari, Granicus, Guadiana, Hamilton, Illinois, Kennebec, Kentucky, Klondike, Kootenay, Menderes, Nerbudda, Niobrara, Okavango, Ouachita, Paraguay, Parnaiba, Putumayo, Rio Bravo, Saguenay, Savannah, Shoshone, Suwannee, Syr Darya, Volturno, waterway **9** Allegheny, Anacostia, Aroostook, Churchill, Deschutes, Des Moines, Euphrates, Irrawaddy, Mackenzie, Macquarie, Magdalena, Merrimack, Minnesota, Penobscot, Richelieu, Rio Grande, Roosevelt, Tennessee, tributary, Wisconsin **10** Appomattox, Chao Phraya, Coppermine, Cumberland, Housatonic, inundation, outpouring, Pedernales, Republican, Schuylkill, Shenandoah, St. Lawrence, Tippecanoe, Willamette
Afghanistan: **5** Farah
Africa: **4** Nile, Tana, Uele, Vaal **5** Benue, Congo, Ebola, Niger, Tsana, Tsavo, Volta, Zaire **6** Atbara, Orange
Alaska: **5** Yukon
Albania: **4** Drin
Alps: **3** Aar **4** Aare **5** Isère, Rhone
area: **3** bed **4** fork **5** bayou, delta, mouth, oxbow, shore **6** rapids, source
Argentina: **5** Negro, Plata
Arizona: **4** Gila, Salt **8** Colorado
Asia: **4** Amur, Liao, Oxus, Yalu **6** Tigris
Australia: **5** Tamar
Austria: **3** Mur **4** Enns, Isar, Raab, Raba **5** Donau
barrier: **3** dam **4** dike **5** levee **10** embankment
Belgium: **3** Lys **4** Leie, Oise, Yser **5** Meuse, Senne
bend: **5** bight, elbow
Bolivia: **4** Beni
branch: **4** trib. **9** tributary
Brazil: **4** Acre **5** Negro, Purus, Xingu **6** Javari
Canada: **4** Nass **5** Liard, Trent, Yukon **6** Fraser, Ottawa **10** St. Lawrence
Caucasus: **4** Rion **5** Rioni
Chile: **6** Bíobío
China: **3** Han, Hsi, Ili **4** Liao, Yalu, Yuan, Yuen **5** Siang, Tarim
Colombia: **4** Meta
Colorado: **5** Yampa
combining form: **5** fluvi-, potam- **6** fluvio-, potamo-
Connecticut: **6** Thames
Croatia: **4** Sava
crosser: **5** ferry **6** bridge
crossing: **4** ford
curve: **4** bend
Czech: **4** Eger, Elbe, Hron, Iser, Oder, odra, Ohre
deity: **4** nais **5** nymph
depth measure: **3** fth. **10** fath.. fathom
Ecuador: **4** Napo
Egypt: **4** Nile
ender: **3** bed **4** bank, boat, head, side, ward, weed **5** front, wards
England: **3** Cam, Exe, Ure, Usk, Wye **4** Aire, Avon, Leam, Ouse, Tyne **5** Leame, Tamar, Trent **6** Thames
Europe: **4** Eder, Eger, Elbe, Oder, Odra, Oise, Saar **5** Meuse, Siret, Volga
feeder: **6** stream
fictional ~: **4** Kwai
France: **3** Lys **4** Aude, Eure, Ille, Leie, Oise, Orne, Saar, Yser **5** Aisne, Isère, Loire, Marne, Meuse, Rhone, Saône, Sarre, Seine, Selle, Somme, Yonne **6** Escaut
Georgia: **4** Rion **5** Coosa, Rioni
Germany: **3** Ems **4** Eder, Eger, Elbe, Isar, Naab, Oder, Odra, Ohre, Oste, Ruhr, Saar **5** Fulda, Rhine, Weser
Greece: **4** Arta
Guatamala: **5** Hondo
Hungary: **4** Eger, Raab, Raba **5** Tisza **6** Danube
Iberia: **4** Ebro, Miño **5** Douro, Minho, Tagus
Idaho: **5** Snake
India: **5** Indus, Jumna, Purna, Sarda **6** Ganges, Yamuna
in Spanish: **3** río
Iraq: **6** Tigris
Ireland: **4** Erne, Nore **5** Boyne
island: **3** ait **4** eyot
Italy: **2** Po **4** Arno, Nera **5** Adige, Oglio, Tiber
Japan: **3** Ota
Kansas: **5** Osage **6** Neosho
Kashmir: **5** Indus
Kazakhstan: **3** Ili **4** Ural **5** Tobol
Korea: **4** Yalu
Latvia: **5** Dvina
like a ~ bed: **5** silty, stony **6** stoney
Maine: **4** Saco
Malaysia: **5** Perak
mammal: **5** otter
Mexico: **5** Yaqui
Michigan: **5** Huron
Mississippi: **5** Yazoo
Nebraska: **4** Loup **6** Platte
Netherlands: **3** Lek **4** Maas, Rijn, Waal **5** Issel, Yssel **6** Ijssel
New York: **4** East **5** Tioga **6** Hudson
Norway: **4** Tana **5** Tsana
of forgetfulness: **5** Lethe
Oregon: **5** Rogue
overflow: **5** flood
Pakistan: **5** Indus
path: **4** flow **6** course **7** channel
Pennsylvania: **4** Ohio **6** Lehigh **8** Delaware **9** Allegheny
Peru: **5** Purus **6** Javari
Philippines: **5** Pasig
Poland: **4** Oder, Odra **5** Narew
Portugal: **4** Miño **5** Douro, Minho
rapids: **5** chute **6** dalles
Romania: **3** Olt **4** Prut **5** Siret
Russia: **3** Don, Oka, Oma **4** Lena, Neva, Seim, Seym, Yana **5** Aldan, Onega, Tobol **6** Angara, Kolima, Kolyma
Scotland: **3** Ayr, Dee, Esk, Tay **4** Doon, Lyon, Spey **5** Afton, Clyde, Devon, Lyons, Nairn, Tweed
sell down the ~: **5** rat on **6** betray, expose, fink on, give up, snitch, squeal, tattle, turn in **8** give away
Serbia: **4** Sava
Siberia: **4** Lena, Yana **5** Aldan
Slovenia: **4** Sava
source: **4** head
South America: **5** Negro, Plata **6** Amazon, Bíobío
Spain: **4** Ebro **5** Douro, Tinto
structure: **5** levee
Sweden: **3** Dal, Ume **4** Gota **5** Torne
Switzerland: **3** Aar **4** Aare **5** Reuss, Rhine, Rhone, Seuss
Tasmania: **5** Tamar
terminus: **5** mouth
Texas: **5** Pecos **6** Brazos, Nueces **9** Rio Grande **10** Pedernales
transport: **4** raft **5** barge, canoe, ferry **6** packet **7** steamer
Turkey: **4** Aras **5** Murat **6** Tigris
Turkmenistan: **4** Oxus
Ukraine: **4** Prut, Seim, Seym **5** Seret, Siret, Tisza
underworld: **4** Styx **5** Lethe
Uzbekistan: **4** Oxus
Venezuela: **3** Aro **5** Apure
vessel: **4** boat **5** craft, kayak **6** vessel **9** outrigger
Virginia: **5** James
Wales: **3** Dee, Usk, Wye
Wheeling's ~: **4** Ohio
world's longest ~: **4** Nile
Xanadu: **4** Alph
Yugoslavia: **4** Sava **5** Tisza

river __: **5** basin, otter

__ river: **5** up the

River __ Return: **4** of No

River __ Through It, A: **4** Runs

__ River: **4** Moon **5** Ol' Man

Rivera: **4** José **5** Chita, Diego **7** Geraldo, Mariano

__ Rivera, CA: **4** Pico

Rivera, Diego: **6** artist **7** painter **8** muralist
creation: **5** mural
homeland: **6** Mexico
spouse: Frida Kahlo

Rivera, José: **4** poet **6** writer **9** Colombian

__ River Anthology: **5** Spoon

riverbank: **5** shore
plant: **4** reed **5** sedge
steps, in India: **4** ghat **5** ghaut

riverbed: **6** canada
dry ~: **4** wadi, wady, wash
item: **5** stone

riverboat offering: **6** casino

Riverby
author: John Burroughs

River City
locale: 4 Iowa
Riverdale High student: 5 Betty, Moose 6 Archie 7 Jughead 8 Veronica
__ River, MA: 4 Fall
__ River, NJ: 4 Toms
River of Dreams, The (1993 song)
artist: Billy Joel
__ River of the North: 3 Red
River Runs Through It, A (1992 film)
cast: Emily Lloyd, Brad Pitt, Craig Sheffer, Tom Skerritt
director: Robert Redford
Rivers: 4 Joan 6 Johnny, Mickey 7 Melissa
__ River school: 6 Hudson
riverside: 4 bank 5 shore
Riverside: 4 city, town
locale: 4 Ohio 10 California
Rivers, Johnny
real last name: Ramistella
song: Baby I Need Your Lovin' (1967)
Maybelline (1964)
Memphis (1964)
Midnight Special (1965)
Mountain of Love (1964)
Muddy Water (1966)
Poor Side of Town (1966)
Rockin' Pneumonia (1972)
Secret Agent Man (1966)
Seventh Son (1965)
Slow Dancin' (1977)
Summer Rain (1967)
Swayin' to the Music (1977)
The Tracks of My Tears (1967)
Rivers to the Sea
author: Sara Teasdale
River, The (1951 film)
director: Jean Renoir
River Town, A
author: Thomas Keneally
River Wild, The (1994 film)
cast: Kevin Bacon, David Strathairn, Meryl Streep
rivet: 3 fix, put, tie 4 bolt, grip, stud 5 affix, infix, stare 6 absorb, anchor, arrest, attach, fasten, fixate, secure, thrill 7 enchain, engrain, engross, enthral, ingrain, inthral 8 bolt down, enthrall, fastener, interest, inthrall, intrigue, look hard, make fast, transfix 9 fascinate, preoccupy, spellbind
one's eyes: 5 focus 6 obsess, zero in 9 preoccupy
riveted: 4 firm 6 intent, rooted 7 focused 8 immobile
riveter: 5 drill
Riviera: 3 car 4 auto 5 Buick 6 resort 10 automobile
acquisition: 3 tan
locale: 6 France, Monaco
resort: 3 Eze 4 Biot, Nice 6 Cannes, Frejus, Gassin, Menton 7 Antibes, Cap d'Ail, Cogolin, Grimaud, Mougins, San Remo 8 Beaulieu, St. Tropez 9 Mandelieu, Ste. Maxime, St. Raphael 10 Beausoleil, Monte Carlo, Ramatuelle
wear: 6 bikini
__-Rivières, Que.: 5 Trois
__ Rivoli: 5 Rue de
rivulet: 3 ria 4 race, rill 5 bourn, brook, creek, rille 6 stream 9 streamlet
Rixey, Eppa: 6 hurler 7 pitcher
Riyadh: 4 city, town 7 capital
district: 4 Nejd
resident: 4 Arab 5 Saudi
riyal: 4 coin 5 money
fraction: 6 halala
spender: 6 Qatari
Rizzo: 5 Ratso 6 Enrico
of the Muppets: 3 rat
Rizzuto, Phil: 6 Yankee 7 Scooter 9 shortstop
rival: 5 Reese 6 Pee Wee
RKO: 6 studio
R.L.: 5 Stine
RLS part: 4 Robt. 5 Louis 6 Robert 9 Stevenson
rm. cooler: 2 AC
RMN: 4 pres.
opponent: 3 JFK
predecessor: 3 LBJ
successor: 3 GRF
VP: 3 NAR, STA
was his Vice President: 3 DDE
see also Richard M. Nixon
__ R. Murrow: 6 Edward
Rn: 4 elem. 5 radon 7 element
86 for ~: 4 at. no.
RN: 5 nurse
asset: 3 TLC
asst.: 3 LPN
colleague: 2 dr., GP, MD
employer: 3 HMO 4 hosp.
org.: 3 ANA
responsibility: 2 IV
station: 2 ER, OR 3 CCU, ICU
unit: 2 cc
RNA
ender: 3 ase
part of ~: 4 acid, ribo 7 nucleic
RNC org.: 3 GOP
rnd., not: 3 sqr.
roach: 4 pest 6 insect 7 sunfish
starter: 4 cock
Roach: 3 Hal, Jay, Max
Roach __: 5 Motel
Roach, Max: 7 drummer
genre: 4 jazz
road: 3 hwy., rte., way 4 belt, drag, lane, path, pike, walk 5 alley, byway, drive, means, route, track, trail 6 access, artery, avenue, bypath, course, street 7 freeway, highway, impetus, ingress, parkway, passage, thruway, viaduct 8 driveway, main drag, pavement, turnpike 9 boulevard, concourse 10 back street, expressway, Interstate, switchback, throughway
alternate ~: 6 detour
bend: 3 ess 4 turn 5 curve
burn up the ~: 4 race, rush, zoom 5 spank, speed
caution: 4 bump
charge: 4 toll
country ~ feature: 3 rut
covering: 3 tar 6 gravel 7 asphalt
crew member: 5 paver
do a ~ job: 3 tar 4 pave 5 retar, widen 6 repave
down the ~: 4 anon, soon, then 5 after, later 6 in a bit, in time 7 by and by, later on, someday 8 in a while, sometime 9 afterward, hereafter, presently 10 before long, eventually
ender: 3 bed, map, way 4 side, ster, work 5 block, house, stead 6 runner, worthy
get the show on the ~: 5 begin 6 launch 7 lead off 8 commence
go on the ~: 4 tour
guide: 3 map
hazard: 3 ice, rut 7 pothole
hit the ~: 2 go 4 blow, hike, rove, scat, walk, went 5 leave, scram, start 6 beat it, decamp, depart, set off, set out 7 push off, take off 8 hightail, set forth
inclination: 5 grade, slope
in Italian: 3 via
in Latin: 3 via 4 iter
junction: 4 fork, turn 6 branch
king of the ~: 4 hobo 5 tramp 7 drifter, vagrant 8 vagabond, wanderer
like some ~s: 3 icy 5 curvy, laned, rutty, stony 7 one-lane
noise: 4 honk, horn 5 siren
not on the ~: 4 home 6 at home
on the ~: 4 away 7 driving, en route, touring 9 traveling 10 journeying
rally: 4 meet 7 contest
service: 3 tow
service org.: 3 AAA
shoulder: 4 berm 5 berme
side ~: 4 lane 5 byway 6 by-path
sign: 3 dip, gas, slo 4 exit, slow, stop 5 merge, yield 6 danger, detour
signal: 5 flare
sign shape: 5 arrow 7 octagon 8 triangle
sign word: 4 thru, xing 5 ahead
situate back from the ~: 5 set in
split in the ~: 4 fork
starter: 4 rail 5 cross
take the wrong ~: 3 err 4 flub, goof, muff, slip 5 lapse, stray 6 boo-boo, bungle, foul up, fumble, mess up, slip up, wander 7 blunder, deviate, louse up, stumble 8 go astray 10 transgress
toll ~: 4 pike 7 highway 8 turnpike
treat an icy ~: 4 salt, sand
road __: 3 air, hog, map 4 gang, race, rage, show, test 5 atlas, rally 6 racing 7 company, warrior
__ road: 3 low 4 back, dirt, high, post, toll 5 on the, royal 6 access
Road __: 4 Trip 5 House, to Rio 6 Runner 7 Scholar
Road __ Taken, The: 3 Not
__ Road: 4 Silk, Tara 5 Abbey, Burma, Glory, On the 7 Freedom, Thunder, Tobacco
__ Road Again: 5 On the
roadblock: 3 bar 4 halt, snag, stop, wall 7 barrier 8 obstacle, obstruct 9 barricade 10 impediment
__ roadblock: 4 hit a
Road film
destination: 3 Rio 4 Bali 6 Utopia 7 Morocco 8 Hong Kong, Zanzibar 9 Singapore
name: 3 Bob 4 Bing, Hope 6 Crosby, Lamour 7 Dorothy
roadhouse: 3 inn, pub 5 hotel, lodge 6 tavern 8 rest stop, taphouse 9 nightclub
of yore: 4 inne
roadie equipment: 3 amp
Road Less Traveled, The
author: M. Scott Peck
road map
see map
Roadmaster: 3 car 4 auto 5 Buick 10 automobile
Road Not Taken, The: 4 poem
author: Robert Frost
road rally: 4 race
need: 3 map
Road Runner: 3 car 4 auto, bird, toon 8 Plymouth 10 automobile
cartoon backdrop: 4 mesa
foe: 5 Wile E. 6 coyote
sound: 4 beep
__ Roads: 7 Hampton
road-safety org.: 4 MADD, SADD
Road Scholar (1993 film)
director: Roger Weisberg
roadside
establishment: 3 inn 5 diner, motel, stand
offer: 5 hop in
problem: 6 litter
sign: 4 eats
warning: 5 flare
roadster: 3 car 4 auto 10 automobile
Roads to Freedom, The
author: Jean-Paul Sartre
road-test task: 5 U-turn 7 parking
Road, The
author: Cormac McCarthy
Road to Bali (1952 film)
cast: Bing Crosby, Bob Hope, Dorothy Lamour
Road to Gandolfo, The
author: Robert Ludlum
__ Road to Glory: 5 A Hard
Road to Hong Kong, The (1962 film)
cast: Joan Collins, Bing Crosby, Bob Hope, Dorothy Lamour
__ Road to Mandalay: 5 On the
Road to Mecca, The
author: Athol Fugard
Road to Morocco (1942 film)
cast: Bing Crosby, Bob Hope, Dorothy Lamour, Anthony Quinn
music: Jimmy Van Heusen, Johnny Burke
talker: 5 camel
Road to Omaha, The
author: Robert Ludlum
Road to Perdition (2002 film)
cast: Tom Hanks, Jennifer Jason Leigh, Paul Newman
Road to Rio (1947 film)
cast: Bing Crosby, Bob Hope, Dorothy Lamour
Road to Rome, The
author: Robert E. Sherwood
Road to Singapore (1940 film)
cast: Bing Crosby, Bob Hope, Dorothy Lamour
Road to Utopia (1945 film)
cast: Bing Crosby, Bob Hope, Dorothy Lamour
Road to Wellville, The (1994 film)
cast: Matthew Broderick, John Cusack, Bridget Fonda, Anthony Hopkins
Road to Xanadu, The
author: John Livingstone Lowes
Road to Yesterday, The (1925 film)
director: Cecil B. DeMille

RI

Road to Zanzibar (1941 film)
cast: Bing Crosby, Bob Hope, Dorothy Lamour
__-road vehicle: 3 off
roadway: 4 road **5** route **6** street **7** ingress
Roadwork
author: Stephen King
Roald: 4 Dahl **8** Amundsen, Hoffmann
roam: 3 gad **4** hike, rove, trek, walk **5** amble, drift, prowl, range, stray, tramp **6** ramble, trapes, travel, wander **7** digress, journey, maunder, meander, migrate, saunter, traipse **8** ambulate, gad about, nomadize, straggle, vagabond **9** bat around, bum around, gallivant, globetrot, run around **10** knock about
roamer: 5 nomad, rover **8** runagate, traveler, wanderer, wayfarer
roaming: 5 loose **6** astray, errant, ramble **7** nomadic **8** rootless, vagabond **9** itinerant, wayfaring
roan: 5 horse **6** equine, sorrel **8** chestnut
Roanoke: 4 city, isle, town **5** river **6** island
locale: 8 Virginia
Roanoke __, NC: 6 Rapids
roar: 3 bay, cry, din **4** bark, bawl, boom, call, drum, hoot, howl, peal, roll, yell **5** blast, crash, growl, laugh, noise, shout, sound, storm, voice **6** bellow, clamor, guffaw, holler, outcry, racket, rumble, scream, uproar **7** bluster, exclaim, explode, pulsate, resound, thunder, trumpet **8** laughter **9** explosion **10** belly laugh, clattering, detonation, hit the roof, horse laugh, vociferate
roaring: 4 loud **5** brisk, forte, noisy **6** active **7** booming, jarring, pealing, rackety, raucous, reboant, riotous **8** crashing, laughing, piercing, plangent, sonorous, strident, thriving, turned up **9** big-voiced, clamorous, deafening, turbulent **10** boisterous, prospering, prosperous, stentorian, strepitous, successful, uproarious, vociferous
__-roaring: 3 rip
Roaring Fork River, town on the: 5 Aspen
Roaring Girl, The
author: Thomas Middleton
Roaring Twenties: 3 era
roast: 3 kid, rag, rib **4** bake, burn, cook, flay, gala, gibe, haze, heat, jibe, meat, mock, ride, slur, twit **5** abuse, blast, broil, grill, knock, taunt, tease, toast **6** defame, deride, entrée, malign, parody, picnic, scorch, sizzle, vilify **7** lambast, lampoon, put down, ribbing, rip into, slander, swelter **8** badinage, badmouth, barbecue, belittle, denounce, lace into, lambaste, ridicule, tear into, travesty **9** criticize, denigrate, disparage, excoriate, festivity, light into, pick apart, poke fun at
device: 4 spit **6** baster
host: 2 MC **5** emcee, Friar
place: 4 oven **5** grill **8** barbecue
seasoning: 4 sage
table: 4 dais
wiener ~: 6 picnic **7** cookout
__ roast: 3 pot, rib **4** loin, rump **6** weenie
__-roasted: 3 dry
roaster: 3 pan **7** chicken **8** barbecue
roasting: 3 hot **6** steamy
Roast Pig essayist: 4 Elia
rob: 3 con, cop, mug, sap **4** lift, loot, raid, roll, sack, take **5** cheat, filch, harry, heist, pinch, pluck, poach, rifle, steal, strip, swipe **6** burgle, divest, fleece, hijack, hold up, hustle, pilfer, ravage, rip off, snitch, thieve **7** bereave, break in, defraud, deprive, despoil, do out of, pillage, plunder, promote, purloin, ransack, relieve, stick up, swindle **8** embezzle, highjack, liberate, spoliate **9** break into, depredate, knock over, strong-arm **10** burglarize, disinherit, dispossess
old-style: 5 reave
rob __: 5 blind
Rob: 4 Lowe **5** Cohen, Estes **6** Morrow, Petrie, Reiner **7** Epstein, Minkoff **9** Camiletti, Schneider
Rob __: 3 Roy
roband: 4 yarn
Robards, Jason: 5 actor
film: All the President's Men (1976, AA)
Any Wednesday (1966)
The Ballad of Cable Hogue (1970)
Black Rainbow (1991)
Divorce American Style (1967)
The Good Mother (1988)
Isadora (1968)
The Journey (1959)
Julia (1977, AA)
Long Day's Journey Into Night (1962)
Magnolia (1999)
Max Dugan Returns (1983)
Melvin and Howard (1980)
The Night They Raided Minsky's (1968)
Once Upon a Time in the West (1968)
The Paper (1994)
Parenthood (1989)
Philadelphia (1993)
A Thousand Clowns (1965)
spouse: Lauren Bacall
Robb: 3 Nen
robbed: 6 bereft
old-style: 4 reft
Robbe-Grillet, Alain: 6 French, writer
robber: 4 thug **5** cheat, crook, felon, fence, fraud, thief **6** bandit, looter, mugger, outlaw, pirate, raider, rascal **7** brigand, burglar, corsair, grafter, prowler, rustler, stealer **8** chiseler, hijacker, marauder, operator, pilferer, pillager, swindler **9** buccaneer, con artist, desperado, despoiler, plunderer, purloiner **10** cat burglar, pickpocket, shoplifter
accomplice: 5 fence
Asian ~: 6 dacoit, dakoit
chaser: 3 cop **6** lawman **7** officer
robber __: 5 baron
__ robber: 4 bank **5** train
Robber Bride, The
author: Margaret Atwood
Robbers' Roost
author: Zane Grey
Robbers, The
author: Friedrich von Schiller
robbery: 3 job **5** caper, heist, theft **6** felony, holdup, rip-off **7** break-in, larceny, mugging, stickup **8** burglary, thievery
__ robbery: 5 armed **7** highway
Robbie: 5 Nevil **6** Dupree
Robbins: 3 Tim, Tom **5** Marty **6** Harold, Jerome **9** Frederick
partner: 6 Baskin
Robbins, Harold: 6 writer
work: 79 Park Avenue
The Adventurers
The Betsy
The Carpetbaggers
Descent from Xanadu
The Dream Merchants
Dreams Die First
Goodbye, Janette
The Inheritors
The Lonely Lady
Memories of Another Day
Never Enough
Never Leave Me
Never Love a Stranger
Piranha
Pirate
The Predators
The Raiders
The Secret
Sin City
Spellbinder
The Stallion
Stiletto
A Stone for Danny Fisher
The Storyteller
Tycoon
Where Love Has Gone
Robbins, Jerome Oscar: West Side Story
Robbins, Marty
song: Don't Worry (1961)
El Paso (1959)
A White Sport Coat (1957)
Robbins, Tim: 5 actor **8** director
film: Antitrust (2001)
Bob Roberts (1992)
Bull Durham (1988)
Cadillac Man (1990)
Cradle Will Rock (1999)
Dead Man Walking (1995)
Five Corners (1988)
The Hudsucker Proxy (1994)
Human Nature (2001)
Miss Firecracker (1989)
Mystic River (2003, AA)
The Player (1992)
The Shawshank Redemption (1994)
Robby: 5 robot **6** Benson
robe: 3 aba **4** abba, gown, vest **5** cloak, dress, kanzu, simar, stola, talar **6** bertha, caftan, chimar, chimer, cyclas, dolman, kaftan, kimono, mantua, yukata **7** chimere, chrisom, garment, lounger, wrapper **8** bathrobe, covering, peignoir, vestment **9** djellabah, housecoat
African ~: 5 kanzu **9** djellabah
Arab ~: 3 aba **4** abba
church ~: 3 alb **6** chimar, chimer **7** chimere, chrisom
Japanese ~: 6 kimono, yukata
Roman ~: 5 stola, tunic **6** cyclas
starter: 4 bath, ward
Turkish ~: 6 dolman
woman's ~ of old: 5 simar
robe __: 5 de bal
__ robe: 3 lap
robed: 4 clad
Robert: 3 Bly, Ito **4** Adam, Alda, Bolt, Bork, Capa, Culp, Curl, Davi, Dole, Gray, Hass, Hays, Iler, John, Koch, Moog, Owen, Peel, Reed, Ryan, Shaw, Wise, Wuhl **5** Blake, Boyle, Burns, Clary, Clive, Crumb, Donat, Evans, Fiore, Fogel, Frost, Hamer, Henry, Hooke, Huber, Klein, Lucas, Mills, Moore, Morse, Musil, Novak, Noyce, Peary, Plant, Ruark, Scott, Solow, Stack, Towne, Urich, Vesco, Young **6** Altman, Bárány, Benton, Bochsa, Bunsen, Conrad, Coover, De Niro, Desnos, Downey, Duncan, Duvall, Florey, Fowler, Fuller, Fulton, Goulet, Graves, Greene, Hayden, Hegyes, Holley, Horton, Hutton, Jarvik, Loggia, Lowell, Ludlum, Mandan, Merton, Morley, Mugabe, Newton, Palmer, Parish, Pinsky, Prosky, Ripley, Rossen, Shayne, Taylor, Vaughn, Wagner, Walden, Walker, Webber, Wilder, Wilson **7** Aldrich, Beltran, Bridges, Creeley, Englund, Forster, Francis, Fulghum, Garnier, Goddard, Herrick, Horvitz, Indiana, Joffrey, Kennedy, Leonard, MacNeil, McNeill, Merrill, Mitchum, Mundell, Parrish, Patrick, Picardo, Preston, Redford, Service, Siodmak, Southey, Swanson, Walpole, Woolsey **8** Anderson, Benchley, Browning, Cummings, Flaherty, Foxworth, Heinlein, Laughlin, McNamara, Millikan, Mulligan, Mulliken, Robinson, Rockwell, Schuller, Schumann, Stephens, Sterling, Townsend, Woodward, Zemeckis **9** Armstrong, Carradine, Choquette, Furchgott, Guillaume, Rodriguez, Southwell, Stevenson **10** Hofstadter, La Follette, Merrifield, Montgomery, Richardson, Silverberg
Robert __: 4 E. Lee
Robert __ Leonard: 4 Sean
Robert __-Powell: 5 Baden
Robert __ Scott: 6 Falcon
Robert __ Stevenson: 5 Louis
Robert __ Waller: 5 James
Robert __ Warren: 4 Penn
Roberta: 5 Flack **6** Peters
Roberta (1935 film): 7 musical
cast: Fred Astaire, Irene Dunne, Ginger Rogers
composer: Jerome Kern, Otto Harbach
Robert Baden-__: 6 Powell
Robert De __: 4 Niro
Robert E. __: 3 Lee **8** Sherwood
Robert Edward __: 3 Lee
Robert F. __: 7 Kennedy
__ Robert Feller: 5 Rapid
Robert James __: 6 Waller
Robert Louis __: 9 Stevenson
Roberto: 5 Duran **6** Alomar **7** Benigni **8** Clemente **10** Rossellini
see also Spanish

Robert Penn __: 6 Warren
Roberts: 4 Emma, Eric, Nora, Oral, Tony 5 Cokie, Doris, Julia, Robin, Tanya 6 Austin, Rachel 7 Kenneth, Pernell, Richard
Robert's __ of Order: 5 Rules
__ Roberts: 3 Bob 6 Mister
Roberts, Eric: 5 actor
  sister: 5 Julia
Roberts, Julia: 7 actress
  brother: 4 Eric
  film: America's Sweethearts (2001)
    Charlie Wilson's War (2007)
    Closer (2004)
    Conspiracy Theory (1997)
    Duplicity (2009)
    Erin Brockovich (2000, AA)
    Everyone Says I Love You (1996)
    Flatliners (1990)
    Hook (1991)
    Michael Collins (1996)
    Mona Lisa Smile (2003)
    My Best Friend's Wedding (1997)
    Mystic Pizza (1988)
    Notting Hill (1999)
    Ocean's Eleven (2001)
    The Pelican Brief (1993)
    Pretty Woman (1990)
    Runaway Bride (1999)
    Sleeping With the Enemy (1991)
    Steel Magnolias (1989)
  spouse: Lyle Lovett
Roberts, Kenneth: 6 writer
  work: Arundel
    March to Quebec
    Northwest Passage
    Rabble in Arms
Robertson: 3 Don, Pat 4 Dale 5 Cliff, Oscar 6 Davies
Robertson, Cliff: 5 actor
  film: The Best Man (1964)
    Charly (1968, AA)
    The Girl Most Likely (1957)
    The Interns (1962)
    Three Days of the Condor (1975)
  spouse: Dina Merrill
Robertson, Oscar
  milieu: 5 court
  org.: 3 NBA
  sport: 10 basketball
Roberts, Oral city: 5 Tulsa
Roberts, Pernell: 5 actor
  TV: Bonanza, Trapper John, M.D.
__ Roberts Rinehart: 4 Mary
Roberts, Robin: 7 Phillie 13 pitcher. hurler
__ Roberts University: 4 Oral
Robert the Bruce: 4 Scot
  where ~ was crowned: 5 Scone
robes: 4 duds, garb, gear 5 getup 6 attire 7 apparel, clothes, costume, garment 8 clothing, garments 9 trappings
Robeson: 4 Paul
Robespierre: 10 Maximilien
  birthplace: 5 Arras
  foe: 6 Danton
Robic: 3 Ivo
robin: 4 bird 6 herald, nester 9 redbreast
  ragged ~: 5 plant 6 flower
  round ~: 4 plea 6 series 7 tourney 8 petition 10 conference, tournament
__ robin: 5 round
Robin: 4 Cook, Gibb, Luke 5 Adair, Leach, Moore, Yount 6 Givens, Trower, Wright, Zander 7 Cousins, Quivers, Roberts, Ventura 8 McNamara, Williams
  accessory: 3 bow 4 cape 5 arrow 6 quiver
  partner: 6 Batman
  portrayer in 1938: 5 Errol
Robin __: 4 Hood
Robin __ Penn: 6 Wright
__ Robin: 6 Rockin'
Robin and Marian (1976 film)
  cast: Sean Connery, Richard Harris, Audrey Hepburn, Robert Shaw
Robin and the Seven Hoods (1964 film)
  cast: Victor Buono, Bing Crosby, Sammy Davis Jr., Peter Falk, Dean Martin, Barbara Rush, Frank Sinatra
  character: 3 sot
Robin, Christopher creator: A.A. Milne
__ Robin Gray: 4 Auld
Robin Hood: 6 archer
  beneficiaries: 4 poor
  like ~'s men: 5 merry 6 merrie
  quarry: 4 rich
Robin Hood - Men in Tights (1993 film)
  cast: Cary Elwes, Richard Lewis, Roger Rees
  director: Mel Brooks
Robin Hood - Prince of Thieves (1991 film)
  cast: Kevin Costner, Morgan Freeman, Mary Elizabeth Mastrantonio, Alan Rickman, Christian Slater
...robins __ hair: 5 in her
Robins: 5 Laila
robin's-egg: 4 blue 5 color 8 greenish
Robinson: 4 Bill 5 Chris, David, Frank 6 Brooks, Crusoe, Jackie, Robert, Smokey 7 Jeffers
  Mrs. ~'s daughter: 6 Elaine
__ Robinson: 3 Mrs.
Robinson, Brooks: 6 Oriole 9 infielder
Robinson Crusoe
  author: Daniel Defoe
  character: 6 Friday
Robinson, Edward Arlington: 4 poet
  work: Luke Havergal
    The Man Against the Sky
    The Man Who Died Twice
    Miniver Cheevy
    Richard Corey
    Tristram
    Two Men
Robinson, Edward G.: 5 actor
  film: All My Sons (1948)
    Brother Orchid (1940)
    Bullets or Ballots (1936)
    The Cincinnati Kid (1965)
    Double Indemnity (1944)
    Dr. Ehrlich's Magic Bullet (1940)
    Five Star Final (1931)
    Flesh and Fantasy (1943)
    The Glass Web (1953)
    Good Neighbor Sam (1964)
    House of Strangers (1949)
    Key Largo (1948)
    Kid Galahad (1937)
    Larceny, Inc. (1942)
    Little Caesar (1930)
    The Little Giant (1933)
    Manpower (1941)
    The Prize (1963)
    The Red House (1947)
    Scarlet Street (1945)
    The Sea Wolf (1941)
    Seven Thieves (1960)
Robinson, Frank: 3 Red 6 Oriole 10 outfielder
Robinson, Jackie: 6 Dodger
Robinson, Robert: 7 chemist 8 Nobelist
Robinson, Smokey
  lead singer of: The Miracles
  song: Being With You (1981)
    Cruisin' (1979)
    Just to See Her (1987)
    One Heartbeat (1987)
Robinson, Sugar Ray: 5 boxer
  milieu: 4 ring
Robinson, Vicki Sue
  song: Turn the Beat Around (1976)
Robin Wright __: 4 Penn
Robitussin
  alternative: *see* cold remedy
  target: 5 cough
roble: 3 oak 4 tree
__ Robles, CA: 4 Paso
RoboCop (1987 film)
  cast: Nancy Allen, Dan O'Herlihy, Peter Weller
  character: 6 cyborg
  director: Paul Verhoeven
robot: 5 droid, golem 7 machine 9 automaton
  cousin: 6 cyborg
  folklore ~: 5 golem
  play: 3 R.U.R.
robotics cousin: 7 bionics
Robots (2005 film)
  voice cast: Halle Berry, Mel Brooks, Ewan McGregor, Robin Williams
rob roy: 5 drink 8 beverage, cocktail
  ingredient: 6 Scotch 7 bitters 8 vermouth
Rob Roy: 4 Scot
  author: Walter Scott
Rob Roy (1995 film)
  cast: John Hurt, Jessica Lange, Liam Neeson
Robson: 3 May 4 Mark, peak 5 Flora, mount 8 mountain
  locale: 6 Canada 7 Rockies
Robt. __: 4 E. Lee
Robur the Conqueror
  author: Jules Verne
robust: 3 fit 4 hale, iron, spry, well, wiry 5 beefy, burly, hardy, hefty, hunky, husky, large, lusty, sound, stout, tough 6 brawny, earthy, hearty, mighty, potent, rugged, sinewy, steely, stocky, strong, sturdy, virile 7 doughty, healthy 8 athletic, forceful, indurate, muscular, powerful, puissant, stalwart, thriving, vigorous 9 Atlantean, heavy-duty, Herculean, in the pink, strapping, well-built 10 able-bodied, boisterous, full-bodied, red-blooded
  not ~: 4 weak 5 frail 6 dainty, feeble, flimsy, infirm, slight 7 brittle, fragile, rickety, tenuous, unsound 8 delicate 9 breakable, frangible 10 vulnerable
robusta: 6 coffee
Robustelli, Andy
  sport: 8 football
robustness: 3 vim 4 dint, thew 5 brawn, force, might, power, sinew, thews, vigor 6 energy, health, muscle 7 fitness, muscles, potence, potency, stamina 8 strength, vitality 9 endurance, fortitude, hardiness, puissance 10 brute force
robustus, dinornis: 3 moa
Robyn: 5 Smith
roc: 4 bird
Roc (Fox sitcom)
  cast: Charles S. Dutton (Roc Emerson)
    Ella Joyce (Eleanor Emerson)
Roca: 4 cape
  locale: 6 Europe, Iberia 8 Portugal
Rocco: 4 Alex 7 Mediate
Roche: 6 Eugene
Rochelle: 6 Hudson
Rocher: 4 Yves
Rochester: 4 city, town
  clinic: 4 Mayo
  company: 5 Kodak
  county: 6 Monroe
  locale: 7 New York 9 Minnesota
  love: 4 Eyre
  to Benny: 5 valet
  ward: 5 Adele
Rochon: 4 Lela
rock: 3 gem, jar, ore, wag 4 crag, daze, jolt, lava, mica, reef, reel, roll, spar, stun, sway, talc, toss 5 agate, crust, dance, flint, genre, geode, jewel, lurch, magma, music, pitch, prase, quake, shake, shale, shelf, shock, solid, stone, swing 6 careen, gneiss, gravel, jasper, jiggle, jounce, mantle, marble, ophite, pebble, pillar, quarry, quartz, quiver, rattle, rubble, seesaw, teeter, totter, wabble, wobble 7 agitate, bastion, bedrock, boulder, bowlder, disturb, granite, igneous, librate, mineral, shake up, stagger, startle, stupefy, support, tremble, trinket, vibrate 8 feldspar, mainstay, surprise, unstring 9 oscillate 10 kryptonite
  and roll: 5 genre, music, pitch 6 boogie
  between a ~ and a hard place: 6 in a fix, in a jam
  bottom: 4 zero 5 nadir, worst
  cavity: 3 vug 4 vugg, vugh
  climber's gear: 5 piton
  coating: 6 lichen
  collapse: 6 cave-in
  combining form: 4 petr-, saxi- 5 petri-, petro-
  concert need: 3 amp
  crystals: 5 druse
  detritus: 4 sand 5 scree
  don't ~ the boat: 3 bow 4 mind 5 agree, yield 6 accede, accept, assent, comply, give in, relent, submit 7 go along, respect 8 play ball 9 acquiesce, cooperate 10 come around
  ender: 4 fish, rose, weed, work 5 bound, shaft, slide 8 hounding
  flowing ~: 4 lava
  fracture: 5 fault

genre: 3 emo, rap 4 acid, hard, punk 5 metal 6 grunge
igneous ~: 4 sima 6 basalt, dunite, gabbro, norite, pumice 7 diorite, felsite, picrite, syenite 8 aphanite, dolerite, obsidian
igneous ~ source: 4 lava
inscribed ~: 5 stela, stele
isolated ~: 4 scar
jagged ~: 3 tor 5 arête 8 pinnacle 10 escarpment
layer: 4 vein 5 shelf 6 mantle
like a ~: 4 hard 5 solid 6 firmly 7 lithoid 9 lithoidal
name meaning ~: 5 Craig, Peter
partner: 4 roll
porous ~: 4 tufa, tuff
ridge: 4 crag 5 arête
rugged ~: 3 tor 4 crag
salt: 4 NaCl 6 halite
scratch: 5 stria
sheet: 5 nappe
shelf: 5 ledge
shelter: 4 abri
solid: 5 loyal 6 honest, trusty 7 certain, ethical, staunch 8 faithful, reliable, surefire 9 honorable, steadfast, unfailing 10 consistent, dependable, infallible
starter: 3 bed 4 sham
steep ~: 3 tor 4 crag 5 arête, bluff, cliff, scarp 8 overhang, pinnacle 9 precipice 10 escarpment, prominence
suffix: 3 -ite
the boat: 5 rebel, upset 6 revolt
thin layers of ~: 5 folia
valueless ~: 6 gangue
volcanic ~: 4 lava, tuff 5 magma
rock __: 4 salt 5 candy, hound, 'n' roll 6 bottom, garden, steady
rock-__: 4 a-bye
__ rock: 3 art 4 acid, folk, glam, hard, punk, soft
__-rock: 4 jazz 5 blues
Rock: 5 Chris 6 Hudson 7 Blossom
Rock __ game hen: 7 Cornish
Rock-__: 3 ola
Rock-__ baby...: 4 a-bye
__ Rock: 3 Cop, Pet 4 I Am a 5 Ayers, Like a, Limbo
Rock-a-Bye Your Baby With a Dixie Melody (song)
artist: Al Jolson, Jerry Lewis
rock and __: 3 rye 4 roll
rock and roll classic: 4 oldy 5 oldie
Rock and Roll Dreams Come Through (1994 song)
artist: Meat Loaf
Rock and Roll Heaven (1974 song)
artist: Righteous Brothers
Rock and Roll Is __ to Stay: 4 Here
Rock and Roll Music (1976 song)
artist: Beach Boys
__ Rock and Roll Music: 4 I Dig
Rock and Roll Part 2 (1972 song)
artist: Gary Glitter
Rock and Roll Waltz (1956 song)
artist: Kay Starr
rock and rye: 5 drink 8 beverage, cocktail
ingredient: 7 whiskey 9 rock candy
Rock Around the Clock (1955 song)
artist: Bill Haley and His Comets
__ Rock, Australia: 5 Ayers
__ Rock Cafe: 4 Hard
Rockcliffe: 8 Fellowes
rock climbing: 5 sport
Rock Cornish __ hen: 4 game
Rock Creek: 4 Park
Rockefeller: 4 John 5 David 6 Nelson 8 Winthrop
handout: 4 dime
__ Rockefeller: 7 oysters
rocker: 4 seat 5 chair 6 cradle 8 recliner 9 furniture
part: 3 arm 4 back, seat, slat
place: 5 porch
rocket: 3 fly, hie, rip, run, zip 4 bomb, dart, dash, flit, leap, race, rise, rush, soar, tear, Thor, zoom 5 climb, hurry, scoot, speed 6 Ariane, barrel, gallop, hasten, hustle, move it, scurry 7 floor it, hop to it, missile, quicken, scamper, shoot up 8 step on it 9 hotfoot it, shake a leg, skedaddle 10 get a move on, hightail it
booster ~: 5 Agena, Atlas
deviation: 3 yaw
ender: 3 eer
French ~: 6 Ariane
fuel ingredient: 3 LOX 5 nitro
gasket: 5 O-ring
housing: 4 silo
interceptor: 3 ABM
launch: 4 shot 7 liftoff, takeoff 8 blastoff
no ~ scientist: *see* ninny
org.: 4 NASA
path: 3 arc
scaffold: 6 gantry
scientist: 5 brain 6 genius 7 egghead, scholar
section: 5 stage
starter: 3 sky 5 retro
top: 4 nose 5 ogive 8 nose cone
rocket __: 4 ship 7 science
__ rocket: 3 ion
rocketeer: 7 Goddard 9 astronaut, cosmonaut
Rocketeer, The (1991 film)
cast: Alan Arkin, Jennifer Connelly, Timothy Dalton
Rocket Gibraltar (1988 film)
cast: Suzy Amis, Patricia Clarkson, Burt Lancaster
Rocket Man (1972 song)
artist: Elton John
Rockets: 4 five, team
home: 7 Houston
org.: 3 NBA
rival: *see* NBA team
sport: 10 basketball
Rockette: 6 dancer
Rocket, The: Maurice Richard, Rod Laver
rockfish
California ~: 4 rena
Rockford: 4 city, town
city near ~: 6 De Kalb
locale: 8 Illinois
Rockford Files, The (NBC drama)
cast: Noah Beery Jr. (Joseph Rockford) James Garner (Jim Rockford)
theme song: Mike Post
rockhound science: 4 geol. 7 geology
Rockies: 3 mts. 4 mtns., nine, team 5 range
beast: 3 elk 4 dall, pika, puma 6 cougar 7 bighorn, panther 8 cimarron
brew: 5 Coors
city: 6 Denver, Helena
explorer: 4 Pike
highest of the ~: 6 Elbert
hrs.: 3 MDT, MST
locale: 3 Ida., Mex., Nev., Wyo. 4 Alta., Ariz., Colo., Mont., Utah 5 Idaho, Yukon 6 Alaska, Canada, Mexico, Nevada 7 Alberta, Arizona, Montana, Wyoming 8 Colorado 9 New Mexico
mountain: 4 Yale 5 Bross, Eolus, Evans 6 Antero, Elbert, Oxford, Robson, Wilson 7 Belford, Cameron, Harvard, Lincoln, Shavano, Sherman 8 Columbia, Democrat, Sneffels 9 Bierstadt, Pikes Peak, Princeton
org.: 3 MLB, NLW
park: 5 Banff
range: 5 Teton, Uinta
rival: *see* baseball team
ski resort: 4 Vail 5 Aspen
sport: 8 baseball
team home: 8 Colorado
tribe: 3 Ute
wind: 7 chinook
zone: 3 MDT, MST
Rockin' Around the Christmas Tree (1960 song)
artist: Brenda Lee
rocking: 4 spry 5 brisk, merry, peppy, perky, vital, zesty 6 active, bouncy, jaunty 7 vibrant, zestful 8 animated, spirited, vigorous 9 energetic, exuberant, vivacious
rocking __: 5 chair, horse
Rockin' Good Way, A (song)
artist: Brook Benton, Dinah Washington
Rocking the Boat
author: Gore Vidal
Rockin' Pneumonia (1972 song)
artist: Johnny Rivers
Rockin' Robin (song)
artist: Bobby Day, Michael Jackson
word: 5 tweet
R.O.C.K. in the U.S.A. (1986 song)
artist: John Cougar Mellencamp
Rock Island: 4 city, town
locale: 8 Illinois
Rock Island Line (1956 song)
artist: Lonnie Donegan
rocklike: 4 firm, hard 5 solid 6 rugged, strong
Rock Me (1969 song)
artist: Steppenwolf
Rock Me Gently (1974 song)
artist: Andy Kim
rock-'n'-__: 4 roll
Rockne: 5 Knute
Rock'n Me (1976 song)
artist: Steve Miller Band
Rock 'n' Roll Is King artist: ELO
Rock of Ages: 4 hymn
Rock On (song)
artist: David Essex, Michael Damian
Rock & Roll Music (1957 song)
artist: Chuck Berry
rocks: 3 ice 5 cubes
growth on ~: 4 moss
hot ~: 4 lava 5 magma 6 basalt, pumice, scoria 8 obsidian
like some ~: 5 mossy
not on the ~: 4 neat 8 straight
on the ~: 4 iced 8 deprived, stranded 9 destitute, insolvent
science of ~: 9 petrology
__ rocks: 5 on the
rock salt: 6 halite 7 mineral
rockslide: 9 earthfall
Rock Star (2001 film)
cast: Jennifer Aniston, Mark Wahlberg
Rock Steady (song)
artist: Aretha Franklin, Whispers
rock-strewn: 5 stony 6 stoney
rock the __: 4 boat
Rock, The (1996 film)
cast: Nicolas Cage, Sean Connery, Ed Harris
__ Rock, The: 3 Hot
Rock the Boat (1974 song)
artist: Hues Corporation
Rock the Casbah (1982 song)
artist: Clash
Rockville: 4 city, town
locale: 8 Maryland
Rockville Centre: 4 city, town
locale: 7 New York
Rockwell: 4 font, Kent 6 Norman, Robert 8 typeface
Rockwell, Norman: 6 artist 7 painter 11 illustrator
Rock Wit'cha (1989 song)
artist: Bobby Brown
Rock With You (1979 song)
artist: Michael Jackson
rocky: 3 ill 4 firm, hard, iffy, sick 5 dizzy, rigid, risky, rough, shaky, solid, stony 6 chancy, craggy, flinty, jagged, jouncy, lithic, pebbly, queasy, queazy, rugged, steady, steely, stoney, tricky, wabbly, wobbly 7 arduous, cragged, dubious, rickety, unlevel 8 concrete, doubtful, gravelly, indurate, perilous, ticklish, unsteady 9 difficult, hazardous, petrified, uncertain 10 precarious, unyielding
debris: 5 scree, talus
height: 3 tor 4 crag 5 cliff
ledge: 3 tor 5 arête, cliff 8 pinnacle 9 precipice 10 escarpment, prominence
not ~: 6 smooth
Rocky: 3 SUV 8 Burnette, Daihatsu, Graziano, Marciano, squirrel
enemy: 5 Boris 7 Natasha
to Bullwinkle: 3 pal
Rocky (1976 film)
cast: Burgess Meredith, Talia Shire, Sylvester Stallone, Carl Weathers, Burt Young
character: 5 Creed 6 Adrian, Apollo, Balboa, Mickey, Paulie
composer: Bill Conti
dog: 6 Butkus
Rocky __ Friends: 6 and His
Rocky __ Picture Show, The: 6 Horror
Rocky and His Friends dog: 9 Mr. Peabody
Rocky Balboa (2006 film)
cast: Sylvester Stallone, Milo Ventimiglia, Burt Young
director: Sylvester Stallone
Rocky Horror Picture Show, The (1975 film)
cast: Barry Bostwick, Tim Curry, Susan Sarandon
hero: 4 Brad

Rocky II (1979 film): **6** sequel
cast: Burgess Meredith, Talia Shire, Sylvester Stallone, Carl Weathers, Burt Young
director: Sylvester Stallone
Rocky III (1982 film)
cast: Burgess Meredith, Mr. T, Talia Shire, Sylvester Stallone, Carl Weathers, Burt Young,
director: Sylvester Stallone
villain: **4** Lang
Rocky IV (1985 film)
cast: Dolph Lundgren, Mr. T, Brigitte Nielsen, Talia Shire, Sylvester Stallone, Burt Young,
director: Sylvester Stallone
setting: **6** Russia
villain: **4** Ivan **5** Drago
Rocky Mount: **4** city, town
locale: **4** N. Car.
Rocky Mountain: **4** park
see also Rockies
Rocky Mountain ___: **4** goat, High
Rocky Mountain High (1973 song)
artist: John Denver
Rocky Mountain News: **5** paper **9** newspaper
locale: **6** Denver
rocky road: **6** flavor **8** ice cream
alternative: ***see*** ice cream flavor
rococo: **5** style **6** florid, ornate **7** flowery **10** flamboyant
too ~: **4** arty **5** artsy
rod: **3** bar, gat, gun, pin **4** axle, bolt, cane, pole, rung, spit, wand, whip **5** baton, birch, dowel, piece, poker, shaft, spike, staff, stake, stave, stick, swish **6** cudgel, heater, pistol, roscoe, switch **7** pointer, scepter **8** baluster, cylinder **9** truncheon **10** discipline, punishment
combining form: **6** -bacter, rhabdo-
construction ~: **5** rebar
divining ~: **4** twig **6** dowser
hot ~: **4** auto **5** racer **6** go fast **7** fast car **8** dragster **9** drive fast, racing car **10** speed demon
item on a ~: **5** towel
nautical ~: **7** bobstay
of authority: **4** mace
punishing ~: **6** ferula, ferule
starter: **3** ram **4** push **6** golden, silver
wheel ~: **4** axle **5** spoke
___ rod: **3** fly, hot, tie **4** fuel **6** Aaron's, piston **7** curtain, dowsing, fishing
Rod: **5** Carew, Laver **6** McKuen, Taylor **7** Gilbert, Langway, Serling, Steiger, Stewart
Rodan (1956 film)
like ~: **6** dubbed
setting: **5** Japan, Tokio, Tokyo
rod and ___: **4** reel
Rodd: **6** Marcia
Roddenberry: **4** Gene
___ rodder: **3** hot
Roddick: **4** Andy
Roddy: **3** Rod **8** McDowall
rodent: **3** rat **4** cavy, degu, hare, jird, mara, paca, vole **5** coypu, gundi, mouse, shrew, xerus **6** agouti, animal, beaver, gerbil, gopher, jerboa, mammal, marmot, murine, suslik **7** hamster, lemming, mole rat, muskrat, pack rat, rice rat, sand rat, souslik, visacha, wood rat **8** capibara, capybara, chipmunk, cricetid, dormouse, spiny rat, squirrel, trade rat, tuco-tuco, water rat, wharf rat **9** chickaree, groundhog, guinea pig, porcupine, woodchuck **10** chinchilla, prairie dog
Africa: **4** jird **5** gundi, xerus **6** gerbil, jerboa **7** mole rat
aquatic ~: **5** coypu **6** beaver **7** muskrat
Asia: **4** jird **6** gerbil, jerboa, suslik **7** hamster, souslik
burrowing ~: **4** degu, jird, mole **6** gerbil, gopher **7** hamster, mole rat, visacha **8** tuco-tuco **9** groundhog, woodchuck **10** prairie dog
Central America: **4** paca **6** agouti **8** spiny rat
desert ~: **5** gundi
Europe: **6** suslik **7** hamster, lemming, mole rat, souslik
Mexico: **7** rice rat
mouselike ~: **4** vole **6** jerboa **7** lemming
rabbitlike ~: **4** mara **6** agouti
reaction to a ~: **3** eek
South America: **4** cavy, mara, paca **5** coypu **6** agouti **7** rice rat, visacha **8** capibara, capybara, spiny rat, tuco-tuco **9** guinea pig **10** chinchilla
rodents, old-style: **5** meece
rodeo: **5** sport
compete in a ~: **4** ride, rope
mount: **4** bull **5** bronc, steer **6** Brahma, bronco **7** broncho
need: **5** chute, lasso, noose, reata, riata **6** barrel, lariat
performer: **5** rider, roper
yell: **5** wahoo, whoop
Rodeo: **3** SUV **5** Isuzu **6** ballet
author: Larry McMurtry
composer: Aaron Copland
Rodeo ___: **5** Drive
Roderick Hudson
author: Henry James
Roderick Random
author: Tobias Smollett
Roderick, the Last of the ___: **5** Goths
Rodgers: **4** Bill **6** Jimmie **7** Richard
Rodgers, Jimmie
song: Are You Really Mine (1958)
Honeycomb (1957)
Kisses Sweeter Than Wine (1957)
Oh-Oh, I'm Falling in Love Again (1958)
Secretly (1958)
Rodgers, Richard: **8** composer
collaborator: Lorenz Hart, Oscar Hammerstein, Stephen Sondheim
musical: Allegro
Babes in Arms
The Boys From Syracuse
By Jupiter
Carousel
A Connecticut Yankee
Dearest Enemy
Do I Hear a Waltz?
Flower Drum Song
The Garrick Gaieties
The Girl Friend
Heads Up!
Higher and Higher
I'd Rather Be Right
I Married an Angel
Jumbo
The King and I
Me and Juliet
No Strings
Oklahoma!
On Your Toes
Pal Joey
Peggy-Ann
Pipe Dream
Present Arms
Simple Simon
The Sound of Music
South Pacific
Spring Is Here
Too Many Girls
Two by Two
song: Bali Ha'i
Bewitched, Bothered and Bewildered
Blue Moon
Climb Ev'ry Mountain
A Cockeyed Optimist
Do-Re-Mi
Edelweiss
The Gentleman Is a Dope
Getting to Know You
Happy Talk
Hello, Young Lovers
I Cain't Say No
I Could Write a Book
I Enjoy Being a Girl
If I Loved You
Isn't It Romantic
It Might as Well Be Spring
It's a Grand Night for Singing
I Whistle a Happy Tune
I Wish I Were in Love Again
Johnny One Note
June Is Bustin' Out All Over
The Lady Is a Tramp
Little Girl Blue
Manhattan
Many a New Day
Mimi
The Most Beautiful Girl in the World
Mountain Greenery
My Favorite Things
My Funny Valentine
My Heart Stood Still
Oh, What a Beautiful Mornin'
Oklahoma
People Will Say We're in Love
Shall We Dance?
Some Enchanted Evening
The Sound of Music
The Surrey With the Fringe on Top
The Sweetest Sounds
Ten Cents a Dance
There Is Nothin' Like a Dame
There's a Small Hotel
This Can't Be Love
Thou Swell
Where or When
With a Song in My Heart
A Wonderful Guy
You'll Never Walk Alone
Younger Than Springtime
___ Rodham Clinton: **7** Hillary
Rodin, Auguste: **6** artist **8** sculptor
homeland: **6** France
work: **4** Adam, nude **6** St. John **7** Kiss, The, Ugolino **9** Bather, The, Le Penseur **10** Thinker, The
Rodman, Dennis
milieu: **5** court
org.: **3** NBA
sport: **10** basketball
spouse: Carmen Electra
Rodney: **6** Caesar, Porter
Rodnik: **5** vodka
competitor: **4** Skyy **5** Popov, Stoli **6** Starka **7** Absolut **8** Smirnoff **9** Grey Goose
Rodnina: **5** Irina
Rodolfo's beloved: **4** Mimi
rodomontade: **6** hot air **7** bluster, bombast **8** boasting, bragging, claptrap **9** gasconade, vainglory
Rodrigo in English: **8** Roderick
Rodrigues: **5** Percy
Rodriguez: **6** Robert
Rodzinski, Artur: **9** conductor
roe: **3** egg, ova **4** buck, deer, eggs, hind, stag **6** animal, caviar **7** caviare, seafood
ender: **4** buck
lobster ~: **5** coral
relative: ***see*** deer
source: **4** shad **8** sturgeon
___ roe: **4** crab
Roe: **4** Jane **5** Tommy **7** Allison, Richard **8** Preacher
Roebling: **4** John
roebuck: **4** deer, male
Roebuck partner: **5** Sears
Roeg, Nicolas: **8** director
film: Insignificance (1985)
The Man Who Fell to Earth (1976)
spouse: Theresa Russell
roentgenogram: **4** x-ray
Roentgen, Wilhelm: **6** German **9** physicist
discovery: **4** X-ray
Roeper: **7** Richard
colleague: **5** Ebert
Roethke, Theodore: **4** poet
work: The Far Field
Open House
Praise to the End
The Waking
Words for the Wind
Roe, Tommy
hometown: Atlanta
song: Dizzy (1969)
Everybody (1963)
Hooray for Hazel (1966)
Jam Up Jelly Tight (1969)
Sheila (1962)
Sweet Pea (1966)
Roe vs. ___: **4** Wade
___ rogas: **3** uti
rogation: **6** prayer
Rogen: **4** Seth
roger
see of course
roger ___: **5** wilco
Roger: **4** Mudd, Rees **5** Bacon, Ebert, Maris, Moore, Smith, Taney, Vadim **6** Allers, Corman, du Gard, Miller, Mosley, Rabbit, Sperry **7** Clemens, Daltrey, Livesey, Maltbie, McGuinn, Zelazny **8** Staubach, Weisberg, Williams **9** Bannister, Bresnahan, Christian, Donaldson, Guillemin, Whittaker
in German: **6** Rutger
Roger ___: **5** and Me
___ Roger: **5** Jolly
Roger and Me (1989 film)
director: Michael Moore

Roger B. __: **5** Taney
Roger E. __: **6** Mosley
Rogers: **3** Roy **4** Buck, Fred, Mimi, Will **5** Buddy, Kenny, mount, Wayne **6** Ginger **7** Hornsby **8** mountain
partner: **5** Evans **7** Astaire
Rogers, Buddy
spouse: Mary Pickford
Rogers, Ginger: **7** actress
film: The Barkleys of Broadway (1949)
Carefree (1938)
Flying Down to Rio (1933)
Follow the Fleet (1936)
The Gay Divorcee (1934)
Kitty Foyle (1940, AA)
The Major and the Minor (1942)
Roberta (1935)
Shall We Dance (1937)
Stage Door (1937)
The Story of Vernon & Irene Castle (1939)
Swing Time (1936)
Top Hat (1935)
Vivacious Lady (1938)
spouse: Lew Ayres
__ Rogers in the 25th Century: **4** Buck
Rogers, Kenny
member of: New Christy Minstrels
song: But You Know I Love You (1969)
Coward of the County (1979)
Don't Fall in Love With a Dreamer (1980)
The Gambler (1978)
I Don't Need You (1981)
Islands in the Stream (1983)
Just Dropped In (1968)
Lady (1980)
Love Will Turn You Around (1982)
Lucille (1977)
Ruby, Don't Take Your Love to Town (1969)
She Believes in Me (1979)
Something's Burning (1970)
We've Got Tonight (1983)
You Decorated My Life (1979)
Rogers, Mimi: **7** actress
spouse: Tom Cruise
Rogers, Roy: **6** cowboy
dog: **6** Bullet
horse: **7** Trigger
real name: **4** Slye
spouse: Dale Evans
__ Rogers St. Johns: **5** Adela
Rogers, Wayne: **5** actor
TV: MASH
Rogers, Will: **5** actor **6** writer **8** humorist
film: A Connecticut Yankee (1931)
Doubting Thomas (1935)
Dr. Bull (1933)
Judge Priest (1934)
Life Begins at Forty (1935)
State Fair (1933)
horse: **8** Soapsuds
prop: **4** rope **5** lasso
work: The Cowboy Philosopher on Prohibition
The Illiterate Digest
Sanity is Where You Find It
Roget: **5** Peter
entry: **3** syn. **7** synonym
rogue: **3** cad, cur **4** heel, toad, worm **5** cheat, churl, crook, demon, devil, fraud, knave, losel, scamp, stray **6** bad egg, bad guy, con man, daemon, daimon, goonda, outlaw, picaro, rascal, rotter **7** bad news, bounder, brigand, dastard, lowlife, outcast, stinker, varment, varmint, villain, wastrel **8** blighter, criminal, deceiver, hooligan, picaroon, rakehell, scalawag, spalpeen, swindler **9** charlatan, con artist, defrauder, miscreant, reprobate, scallawag, scallywag, scoundrel, trickster, vulgarian **10** blackguard, black sheep, mountebank, ne'er-do-well, scapegrace
Rogue River Feud
author: Zane Grey
roguery: **7** devilry, knavery **8** deviltry, mischief **9** rascality
rogues' __: **7** gallery
roguish: **3** sly **4** arch, base **5** rowdy **6** shifty **7** jesting, jocular, knavish **8** sporting, sportive **9** deceitful, deceptive **10** frolicsome, picaresque
Roh __ Woo: **3** Tae
Rohmer: **3** Sax **4** Eric
roi: **4** king **5** Louis **6** French **7** Louis IV **8** Louis XIV, Louis XVI, monarque
spouse: **5** reine
__ Roi: **3** Ubu
roil: **3** irk, vex **4** bait, gall, miff, stir **5** anger, annoy, chafe, churn, muddy, peeve, pique, swirl **6** badger, harass, hector, plague, ruffle, stir up, tee off **7** agitate, becloud, bedevil, churn up, cloud up, disturb, enflame, incense, inflame, provoke, tick off **8** disquiet, irritate **9** aggravate, displease **10** exasperate
roiled: **5** mirky, muddy, murky, rough **6** turbid **9** turbulent
roister: **4** romp **5** revel **6** gambol **7** carouse **9** have a ball
Rojas, Manuel: **6** writer **7** Chilean
Roker: **2** Al **5** Roxie
Rolaids: **7** antacid
alternative: ***see*** antacid
Roland: **4** hero **5** Joffe, Young **7** Gilbert **8** Emmerich
love: **4** Aude
role: **3** bit, job **4** duty, hero, lead, part, star, task **5** cameo, extra, guise, place, stint, super, title **6** aspect, office, status, walk-on **7** ingénue **8** business, capacity, function, position, province **9** character, portrayal, situation **10** appearance
assign a ~: **4** cast
brief ~: **5** cameo
role __: **5** model
__ role: **5** cameo, title
roleo
entrant: **6** logger
roleo, compete in a: **4** birl
role-playing __: **4** game
Rolex: **5** watch **10** wristwatch
alternative: ***see*** wristwatch
rolfing: **7** massage
roll: **3** bun, hum, rob, wad, yaw **4** bolt, boom, bowl, coil, echo, flow, furl, hank, keel, list, loop, peal, pour, reel, roar, rock, spin, sway, toss, turn, verb, wind, wrap **5** bagel, bialy, bread, drive, glide, growl, heave, level, lurch, money, pitch, spool, surge, swirl, table, trill, twirl, twist, wheel, whirl, whirr **6** billow, census, gyrate, kaiser, lumber, muster, reecho, roster, rotate, rumble, scroll, stream, swivel, totter, tumble, waddle, wallow **7** catalog, operate, rat-a-tat, resound, revolve, thunder, trundle **8** cylinder, drumbeat, get going, gyration, overturn, register, schedule, turn over, undulate **9** cannonade, catalogue, directory, get moving, luxuriate **10** somersault, tabulation
back: **5** lower, skimp **6** deduct, lessen, reduce, return **7** regress, tail off **8** decrease, downsize **10** underspend
bakery ~: **3** bun **5** bagel, bialy
by: **6** elapse
call: **6** muster **8** register
ender: **3** mop, out, way **4** away, back, over
expert: **5** baker
in: **4** come **5** enter, pop up, reach **6** appear, arrive, show up, wallow **7** turn out **8** get there **9** luxuriate
in the aisles: **4** howl, roar **5** laugh **6** guffaw **7** break up, crack up **8** convulse
jelly ~: **7** dessert **10** confection
let ~: **5** print **6** run off **8** put to bed **9** go to press
on: **2** go **3** fly **4** flow, go by, pass **6** pass by **7** glide by **8** tick away **9** transpire
on a ~: **3** hot **5** blest, lucky **7** blessed, charmed, favored **9** fortunate **10** auspicious, felicitous, fortuitous
out: **4** rise, wake **5** arise, get up, waken **6** awaken, smooth, spread, unfurl **7** exhibit, flatten, present, turn out **9** introduce
out of bed: **4** rise, wake **5** awake, get up, rouse, waken **6** awaken, bestir
out the red carpet: **5** greet, honor **7** lionize, receive
over: **8** reinvest **9** overpower, surrender
(over): **4** mull **5** think
starter: **3** bed, log, pay **4** bank **5** jelly, steam
the eyes: **4** leer, look, ogle **5** stare **6** goggle
topping: **5** onion **6** sesame **10** sesame seed
up: **4** furl, wrap **5** amass, lay up **6** arrive, garner
with the punches: **4** cope **5** adapt **6** adjust, manage **8** overlook
roll __: **3** bag, bar, out, top **4** back, book, call, film, over
roll __ the punches: **4** with
roll __ the red carpet: **3** out
roll-__ desk: **3** top
__ roll: **3** egg, on a **5** honor, jelly, music, onion, piano, sweet **6** barrel, French, kaiser, spring **7** chicken, lobster
__-roll: **5** rock-'n'
Roll __ Beethoven: **4** Over
Roll __ bones!: **3** dem
rollaway feature: **6** caster
rollback: **6** saving **8** discount **9** reduction **10** concession
__-roll bar: **4** anti
roll call
response: **3** aye, nay, yea, yes **4** here
Rolle: **6** Esther
rolled __: **4** gold, oats **5** roast
Rollei: **6** camera
alternative: ***see*** camera
roller: **4** bird, wave **5** surge, wheel **6** caster
ender: **5** skate
high ~: **7** spender **8** prodigal **10** big spender
starter: **5** steam, stone
roller __: **4** rink **5** derby, skate **6** hockey **7** coaster
__ roller: **4** high
Rollerball (1975 film)
cast: Maud Adams, James Caan, John Houseman
rollerblader's wear: **5** skate **6** helmet
roller coaster: **4** ride **5** dance
cry: **4** whee
feature: **3** dip
like a ~: **4** fast **5** loopy
operator: **5** carny **6** carney
roller derby: **5** sport
track: **4** oval
rollers: **4** dice
use ~: **3** set
__ Rollers: **4** High
roller skating: **5** sport
accessory: **3** key
place: **4** rink
rollick: **4** lark, romp **5** caper, frisk, revel **6** cavort, frolic, gambol **9** have a ball, luxuriate **10** recreation
rollicking: **3** gay **4** glad **5** happy, jolly, merry **6** frisky, hearty, jaunty, jovial, joyful, joyous, lively **7** jesting, playful, romping **8** carefree, cheerful, spirited, sporting, sportive **9** exuberant, fun-loving, hilarious, sprightly **10** boisterous, frolicsome
Rollie: **7** Fingers
Rollin: **4** Hand **5** Betty
rolling: **4** open **5** hilly **6** active **8** gyration, thriving
get things ~: **4** open **5** begin, cause, start **6** launch, tackle **8** commence **10** lead the way
in dough: **4** rich **5** flush **6** loaded, monied **7** moneyed, wealthy, well-off **8** affluent, well-to-do **9** well-fixed **10** privileged, propertied, prosperous, well-heeled
really ~: **4** fast **5** brisk, fleet, quick, rapid, swift **6** flying, speedy
starter: **3** log **5** steam
stone: **5** rover **7** drifter, vagrant **8** wanderer
stone lack: **4** moss
with the punches: **5** stoic **7** stoical **9** resilient
rolling __: **3** pin **4** in it, mill, stop **5** stock
__-rolling: **4** high
Rolling __: **5** Stone **6** Stones
rolling in the __: **6** aisles
Rolling Rock
rival: ***see*** beer
rolling stock repository: **4** yard
Rolling Stone: **3** mag **8** magazine
founder: Jann Wenner
__ Rolling Stone: **5** Like a

Rolling Stones
members: Jagger, Richards, Jones, Wyman, Watts, Wood
song: 19th Nervous Breakdown (1966)
Ain't Too Proud to Beg (1974)
Angie (1973)
As Tears Go By (1966)
Beast of Burden (1978)
Brown Sugar (1971)
Dandelion (1967)
Emotional Rescue (1980)
Fool to Cry (1976)
Get Off My Cloud (1965)
Happy (1972)
Harlem Shuffle (1986)
Have You Seen Your Mother, Baby? (1966)
Heart of Stone (1965)
Honky Tonk Women (1969)
(I Can't Get No) Satisfaction (1965)
It's All Over Now (1964)
It's Only Rock 'n Roll (1974)
Jumpin' Jack Flash (1968)
Lady Jane (1966)
The Last Time (1965)
Miss You (1978)
Mixed Emotions (1989)
Mothers Little Helper (1966)
Paint It, Black (1966)
Ruby Tuesday (1967)
She's a Rainbow (1968)
Start Me Up (1981)
Time Is on My Side (1964)
Tumbling Dice (1972)
Undercover of the Night (1983)
Waiting on a Friend (1981)
Wild Horses (1971)
Rollins: 4 Easy **5** Sonny **6** Howard
Rollins, Sonny: 11 saxophonist
genre: 4 jazz
___ Roll Morton: 5 Jelly
roll-on: 9 deodorant
alternative: 5 spray **7** aerosol
rollout: 6 launch
roll out the ___ carpet: 3 red
Roll Out the ___: 6 Barrel
Roll Over Beethoven (1956 song)
artist: Chuck Berry
rollover subj.: 3 IRA
rolls
like ~: 5 crisp **6** crusty
remove from the ~: 6 delist
shop: 6 bakery **10** patisserie
Rolls-Royce: 3 car **4** auto **7** British **10** automobile
model: 7 Phantom **8** Camargue, Corniche, Park Ward **10** Silver Dawn, Silver Spur **11** Silver Cloud, Silver Ghost
part: 4 boot, tyre **6** bonnet
___ Roll Symphony: 4 Drum
rolltop: 4 desk **9** furniture, secretary **10** escritoire
Roll With It (1988 song)
artist: Steve Winwood
roll with the ___: 7 punches
Rolonda: 5 Watts
Rölvaag, Ole: 6 writer
work: Giants in the Earth
roly-poly
see obese
Roly-Poly Pudding, The
author: Beatrix Potter
ROM
medium: 2 CD **4** disc, disk
part: 3 mem. **4** only, read **6** memory
Roma: 4 city, town **6** Downey, tomato
composer: Georges Bizet
hill count in ~: 5 sette
locale: 5 Italy **6** Italia
relative: 6 Big Boy **9** beefsteak, Better Boy, Early Girl, Quick Pick
___-Romagna, Italy: 6 Emilia
Romain: 4 Gary **7** Rolland
romaine: 3 cos **7** lettuce
roman: 4 type **8** typeface
alternative: 6 italic **7** italics
roman ___: 5 à clef
roman-___: 6 fleuve
Roman: 4 Ruth **8** aquiline, Polanski **9** classical
see also Latin, Rome
Roman ___: 4 arch, nose **5** Curia **6** candle, collar, Empire **7** holiday, numeral
___-Roman: 5 Greco **6** Graeco
___ romana: 4 alla
___ Romana: 3 Pax **5** Curia
roman à clef: 4 book **5** novel **7** fiction
___ Romana Rota: 5 Sacra
romance: 3 woo **4** book, idyl, love, tale **5** amour, fling, genre, idyll, novel, prose, story **6** affair, glamor, legend, wooing **7** fantasy, fiction, glamour, liaison, mystery, passion **8** intrigue **9** adventure, courtship, fairy tale, love story, melodrama, narrative, sentiment **10** attachment, flirtation, tear-jerker
in French: 5 amour
language: 6 French, Ladino **7** Italian, Spanish **8** Romanian, Rumanian **9** Provençal, Sardinian **10** Portuguese
of yore: 4 gest **5** geste
Romance
author: Edgar Allan Poe
___ Romance: 4 True **5** A Fine **7** Crimson, Murphy's
___ Romance, A: 4 Fine **6** Little
Romance of Helen Trent, The: 9 radio show
Romancero gitano
poet: Frederico García Lorca
romances
name: Barbara Cartland, Danielle Steel
Romancing the Stone (1984 film)
cast: Danny DeVito, Michael Douglas, Kathleen Turner
cat: 5 Romeo
Roman Curia office: 6 datary
Roman de Brut
author: Wace
___ Roman Empire: 4 Holy
Roman/Greek god equivalents:
Amor - Eros
Apollo - Apollo
Aurora - Eos
Bacchus - Dionysus
Cupid - Eros
Demeter - Ceres
Diana - Artemis
Jove - Zeus
Juno - Hera
Jupiter - Zeus
Mars - Ares
Mercury - Hermes
Minerva - Athena
Neptune - Poseidon
Ops - Rhea
Pax - Irene
Pluto - Hades
Proserpina - Persephone
Saturn - Cronos
Sol - Helios
Venus - Aphrodite
Vesta - Hestia
Vulcan - Hephaestus
Roman Holiday (1953 film)
cast: Eddie Albert, Audrey Hepburn, Gregory Peck
Romania: 6 nation **7** country
ancient: 5 Dacia
capital: 9 Bucharest
city: 4 Arad, Iasi **5** Bacau, Sibiu **6** Braila, Brasov, Galati, Oradea **9** Bucharest, Constanta
conductor: 6 Perlea **10** Comissiona
dance: 4 hora **5** horah
gymnast: 8 Comaneci
locale: 3 Eur. **6** Europe **7** Balkans
money: 3 ban, leu, ley
neighbor: 7 Hungary, Moldova, Ukraine **8** Bulgaria **10** Yugoslavia
Nobelist in Medicine: 6 Palade
Nobelist in Peace: 6 Wiesel
port: 6 Braila **9** Constanta
region: 5 Banat
river: 3 Olt **4** Prut **5** Siret
tennis pro: 7 Nastase
violinist: 6 Enesco
Romanian: 8 language
Roman numeral: *see* page 1007
Romano: 3 Ray **6** cheese
source: 3 ewe **5** sheep
___ Romanorum: 5 Gesta
Romanov: 7 Mikhail
title: 4 tsar
see also Russian
Romans, book before: 4 Acts
Romansh language: 5 Ladin
Roman Spring of Mrs. Stone, The
author: Tennessee Williams
romantic: 4 fond, wild **5** corny, mushy, soppy **6** ardent, dreamy, erotic, exotic, loving, poetic, sirupy, sloppy, syrupy, tender **7** amatory, amorous, hugging, idyllic, kissing, maudlin, utopian **8** charming, colorful, enamored, exciting, idealist, poetical, quixotic **9** amatorial, fairytale, fantastic, glamorous, legendary, nostalgic, visionary **10** chivalrous, enchanting, idealistic, lovey-dovey, mysterious, passionate, quixotical, starry-eyed
beginning: 3 neo
ender: 3 ist
inspiration: 4 moon
offering: 4 rose
one: 5 lover, Romeo **6** suitor **8** lothario
outing: 4 date
work: 4 poem **5** novel **6** ballad
___-Roman wrestling: 5 Greco **6** Graeco
Rombauer: 4 Irma
Romberg: 7 Sigmund
Rom. Cath. off: 3 mgr. **4** msgr.
Rome: 4 city, town **5** apple **6** Harold **7** capital
Bishop of ~: 4 pope **7** pontiff
city near ~: 5 Terni **6** Naples
fountain: 5 Trevi
lake near ~: 6 Albano
like ~: 5 hilly **7** eternal
locale: 5 Italy **7** Georgia, New York
relative: *see* apple
river: 5 Tiber
see also Italy, Latin
Rome (ancient)
amphitheaters: 6 arenae
army: 6 legion
augur: 6 auspex
bathtub: 6 labrum
biographer: 9 Suetonius
boxing glove: 6 cestus
bronze: 3 aes
bust: 4 herm
calendar date: 4 ides **5** nones **7** calends, kalends
carriage: 5 rheda
censor: 4 Cato
commoner: 4 pleb
council: 6 Senate
emblem of power: 6 fasces
emperor: 4 Nero, Otho **5** Galba, Nerva, Titus **6** Caesar, Julius, Trajan **7** Hadrian **8** Augustus, Caligula, Claudius, Tiberius **9** Vitellius
festivals: 4 ludi
foe: 4 Goth, Pict
games: 4 ludi
garment: 4 toga **5** stola, tunic **6** abolla, birrus, byrrus, cyclas **7** paenula
god: 3 Dis **4** Jove, Mars **5** Cupid, Janus, Pluto **6** Saturn, Vulcan **7** Bacchus, Jupiter, Mercury, Neptune **8** Silvanus
goddess: 3 Nox, Ops **4** Juno, Spes **5** Ceres, Diana, Flora, Parca, Salus, Venus, Vesta **6** Aurora **7** Fortuna, Minerva
historian: 4 Cato, Livy **7** Sallust, Tacitus **9** Suetonius
household god: 3 lar
household gods: 5 lares
initials: 4 SPQR
language: 5 Latin
marketplace: 5 forum
money: 2 as **3** aes **5** libra, semis, uncia **6** aureus, talent, triens **7** denarii, sextans **8** denarius, sesterce **9** dupondius, sestertia, sestertii **10** sestertium, tripondius
official: 5 edile **6** aedile, lictor
orator: 4 Cato
philosopher: 6 Seneca
pitcher: 4 olpe
playwright: 6 Seneca **7** Plautus, Terence
poet: 4 Ovid **6** Horace, Vergil **7** Juvenal, Persius **8** Catullus **9** Lucretius
port: 5 Ostia
priest: 6 flamen
province: 4 Gaul **5** Dacia, Lycia
racetrack marker: 4 meta
racing post: 4 meta
resort: 5 Gaeta
road: 4 iter
rooms: 5 atria
saint: 5 Agnes **6** Agatha **7** Cecilia, Clement, Crispin **8** Paulinus **9** Dionysius, Valentine **11** Christopher
satirist: 6 Horace **7** Juvenal
shield: 6 ancile
spear: 4 pila **5** pilum
spectacles: 4 ludi

Roman Numerals

1 - I
2 - II
3 - III
4 - IV
5 - V
6 - VI
7 - VII
8 - VIII
9 - IX
10 - X
11 - XI
12 - XII
13 - XIII
14 - XIV
15 - XV
16 - XVI
17 - XVII
18 - XVIII
19 - XIX
20 - XX
21 - XXI
22 - XXII
23 - XXIII
24 - XXIV
25 - XXV
26 - XXVI
27 - XXVII
29 - XXIX
30 - XXX
31 - XXXI
32 - XXXII
34 - XXXIV
35 - XXXV
36 - XXXVI
39 - XXXIX
40 - XL
41 - XLI
42 - XLII
43 - XLIII
44 - XLIV
45 - XLV
46 - XLVI
47 - XLVII
49 - XLIX
50 - L
51 - LI
52 - LII
53 - LIII
54 - LIV
55 - LV
56 - LVI
57 - LVII
58 - LVIII
59 - LIX
60 - LX
61 - LXI
62 - LXII
63 - LXIII
64 - LXIV
65 - LXV
66 - LXVI
67 - LXVII
69 - LXIX
70 - LXX
71 - LXXI
72 - LXXII
74 - LXXIV
75 - LXXV
76 - LXXVI
79 - LXXIX
80 - LXXX
81 - LXXXI
85 - LXXXV
90 - XC
91 - XCI
92 - XCII
93 - XCIII
94 - XCIV
95 - XCV
96 - XCVI
97 - XCVII
99 - XCIX
100 - C
101 - CI
102 - CII
103 - CIII
104 - CIV
105 - CV
106 - CVI
107 - CVII
108 - CVIII
109 - CIX
110 - CX
111 - CXI
112 - CXII
113 - CXIII
114 - CXIV
115 - CXV
116 - CXVI
117 - CXVII
119 - CXIX
120 - CXX
121 - CXXI
122 - CXXII
124 - CXXIV
125 - CXXV
126 - CXXVI
129 - CXXIX
130 - CXXX
131 - CXXXI
135 - CXXXV
140 - CXL
141 - CXLI
142 - CXLII
144 - CXLIV
145 - CXLV
146 - CXLVI
149 - CXLIX
150 - CL
151 - CLI
152 - CLII
153 - CLIII
154 - CLIV
155 - CLV
156 - CLVI
157 - CLVII
159 - CLIX
160 - CLX
161 - CLXI
162 - CLXII
164 - CLXIV
165 - CLXV
166 - CLXVI
169 - CLXIX
170 - CLXX
171 - CLXXI
175 - CLXXV
180 - CLXXX
190 - CXC
191 - CXCI
192 - CXCII
194 - CXCIV
195 - CXCV
196 - CXCVI
199 - CXCIX
200 - CC
201 - CCI
202 - CCII
203 - CCIII
204 - CCIV
205 - CCV
206 - CCVI
207 - CCVII
209 - CCIX
210 - CCX
211 - CCXI
212 - CCXII
214 - CCXIV
215 - CCXV
216 - CCXVI
219 - CCXIX
220 - CCXX
221 - CCXXI
225 - CCXXV
230 - CCXXX
240 - CCXL
241 - CCXLI
245 - CCXLV
250 - CCL
251 - CCLI
252 - CCLII
254 - CCLIV
255 - CCLV
256 - CCLVI
259 - CCLIX
260 - CCLX
261 - CCLXI
265 - CCLXV
270 - CCLXX
290 - CCXC
291 - CCXCI
295 - CCXCV
300 - CCC
301 - CCCI
302 - CCCII
304 - CCCIV
305 - CCCV
306 - CCCVI
309 - CCCIX
310 - CCCX
311 - CCCXI
315 - CCCXV
320 - CCCXX
340 - CCCXL
350 - CCCL
351 - CCCLI
355 - CCCLV
360 - CCCLX
390 - CCCXC
400 - CD
401 - CDI
402 - CDII
403 - CDIII
404 - CDIV
405 - CDV
406 - CDVI
407 - CDVII
409 - CDIX
410 - CDX
411 - CDXI
412 - CDXII
414 - CDXIV
415 - CDXV
416 - CDXVI
419 - CDXIX
420 - CDXX
421 - CDXXI
425 - CDXXV
430 - CDXXX
440 - CDXL
441 - CDXLI
445 - CDXLV
450 - CDL
451 - CDLI
452 - CDLII
454 - CDLIV
455 - CDLV
456 - CDLVI
459 - CDLIX
460 - CDLX
461 - CDLXI
465 - CDLXV
470 - CDLXX
490 - CDXC
491 - CDXCI
495 - CDXCV
500 - D
501 - DI
502 - DII
503 - DIII
504 - DIV
505 - DV
506 - DVI
507 - DVII
508 - DVIII
509 - DIX
510 - DX
511 - DXI
512 - DXII
513 - DXIII
514 - DXIV
515 - DXV
516 - DXVI
517 - DXVII
519 - DXIX
520 - DXX
521 - DXXI
522 - DXXII
524 - DXXIV
525 - DXXV
526 - DXXVI
529 - DXXIX
530 - DXXX
531 - DXXXI
535 - DXXXV
540 - DXL
541 - DXLI
542 - DXLII
544 - DXLIV
545 - DXLV
546 - DXLVI
549 - DXLIX
550 - DL
551 - DLI
552 - DLII
553 - DLIII
554 - DLIV
555 - DLV
556 - DLVI
557 - DLVII
559 - DLIX
560 - DLX
561 - DLXI
562 - DLXII
564 - DLXIV
565 - DLXV
566 - DLXVI
569 - DLXIX
570 - DLXX
571 - DLXXI
575 - DLXXV
580 - DLXXX
590 - DXC
591 - DXCI
592 - DXCII
594 - DXCIV
595 - DXCV
596 - DXCVI
599 - DXCIX
600 - DC
601 - DCI
602 - DCII
603 - DCIII
604 - DCIV
605 - DCV
606 - DCVI
607 - DCVII
609 - DCIX
610 - DCX
611 - DCXI
612 - DCXII
614 - DCXIV
615 - DCXV
616 - DCXVI
619 - DCXIX
620 - DCXX
621 - DCXXI
625 - DCXXV
630 - DCXXX
640 - DCXL
641 - DCXLI
645 - DCXLV
650 - DCL
651 - DCLI
652 - DCLII
654 - DCLIV
655 - DCLV
656 - DCLVI
659 - DCLIX
660 - DCLX
661 - DCLXI
665 - DCLXV
670 - DCLXX
690 - DCXC
691 - DCXCI
695 - DCXCV
700 - DCC
701 - DCCI
702 - DCCII
704 - DCCIV
705 - DCCV
706 - DCCVI
709 - DCCIX
710 - DCCX
711 - DCCXI
715 - DCCXV
720 - DCCXX
740 - DCCXL
750 - DCCL
751 - DCCLI
755 - DCCLV
760 - DCCLX
790 - DCCXC
800 - DCCC
801 - DCCCI
805 - DCCCV
810 - DCCCX
850 - DCCCL
900 - CM
901 - CMI
902 - CMII
903 - CMIII
904 - CMIV
905 - CMV
906 - CMVI
907 - CMVII
909 - CMIX
910 - CMX
911 - CMXI
912 - CMXII
914 - CMXIV
915 - CMXV
916 - CMXVI
919 - CMXIX
920 - CMXX
921 - CMXXI
925 - CMXXV
930 - CMXXX
940 - CMXL
941 - CMXLI
945 - CMXLV
950 - CML
951 - CMLI
952 - CMLII
954 - CMLIV
955 - CMLV
956 - CMLVI
959 - CMLIX
960 - CMLX
961 - CMLXI
965 - CMLXV
970 - CMLXX
990 - CMXC
991 - CMXCI
995 - CMXCV
1000 - M
1001 - MI
1002 - MII
1003 - MIII
1004 - MIV
1005 - MV
1006 - MVI
1007 - MVII
1008 - MVIII
1009 - MIX
1010 - MX
1011 - MXI
1012 - MXII
1013 - MXIII
1014 - MXIV
1015 - MXV
1016 - MXVI
1017 - MXVII
1019 - MXIX
1020 - MXX
1021 - MXXI
1022 - MXXII
1024 - MXXIV
1025 - MXXV
1026 - MXXVI
1029 - MXXIX
1030 - MXXX
1031 - MXXXI
1035 - MXXXV
1040 - MXL
1041 - MXLI
1042 - MXLII
1044 - MXLIV
1045 - MXLV
1046 - MXLVI
1049 - MXLIX
1050 - ML
1051 - MLI
1052 - MLII
1053 - MLIII
1054 - MLIV
1055 - MLV
1056 - MLVI
1057 - MLVII
1059 - MLIX
1060 - MLX
1061 - MLXI
1062 - MLXII
1064 - MLXIV
1065 - MLXV
1066 - MLXVI
1069 - MLXIX
1070 - MLXX
1071 - MLXXI
1075 - MLXXV
1080 - MLXXX
1090 - MXC
1091 - MXCI
1092 - MXCII
1094 - MXCIV
1095 - MXCV
1096 - MXCVI
1099 - MXCIX
1100 - MC
1101 - MCI
1102 - MCII
1103 - MCIII
1104 - MCIV
1105 - MCV
1106 - MCVI
1107 - MCVII
1109 - MCIX
1110 - MCX
1111 - MCXI
1112 - MCXII
1114 - MCXIV
1115 - MCXV
1116 - MCXVI
1119 - MCXIX
1120 - MCXX
1121 - MCXXI
1125 - MCXXV
1130 - MCXXX
1140 - MCXL
1141 - MCXLI
1145 - MCXLV
1150 - MCL
1151 - MCLI
1152 - MCLII
1154 - MCLIV
1155 - MCLV
1156 - MCLVI
1159 - MCLIX
1160 - MCLX
1161 - MCLXI
1165 - MCLXV
1170 - MCLXX
1190 - MCXC
1191 - MCXCI
1195 - MCXCV
1200 - MCC
1201 - MCCI
1202 - MCCII
1204 - MCCIV
1205 - MCCV
1206 - MCCVI
1209 - MCCIX
1210 - MCCX
1211 - MCCXI
1215 - MCCXV
1220 - MCCXX
1240 - MCCXL
1250 - MCCL
1251 - MCCLI
1255 - MCCLV
1260 - MCCLX
1290 - MCCXC
1300 - MCCC
1301 - MCCCI
1305 - MCCCV
1310 - MCCCX
1350 - MCCCL
1400 - MCD
1401 - MCDI
1402 - MCDII
1404 - MCDIV
1405 - MCDV
1406 - MCDVI
1409 - MCDIX
1410 - MCDX
1411 - MCDXI
1415 - MCDXV
1420 - MCDXX
1440 - MCDXL
1450 - MCDL
1451 - MCDLI
1455 - MCDLV
1460 - MCDLX
1490 - MCDXC
1500 - MD
1501 - MDI
1502 - MDII
1503 - MDIII
1504 - MDIV
1505 - MDV
1506 - MDVI
1507 - MDVII
1509 - MDIX
1510 - MDX
1511 - MDXI
1512 - MDXII
1514 - MDXIV
1515 - MDXV
1516 - MDXVI
1519 - MDXIX
1520 - MDXX
1521 - MDXXI
1525 - MDXXV
1530 - MDXXX
1540 - MDXL
1541 - MDXLI
1545 - MDXLV
1550 - MDL
1551 - MDLI
1552 - MDLII
1554 - MDLIV
1555 - MDLV
1556 - MDLVI
1559 - MDLIX
1560 - MDLX
1561 - MDLXI
1565 - MDLXV
1570 - MDLXX
1590 - MDXC
1591 - MDXCI
1595 - MDXCV
1600 - MDC
1601 - MDCI
1602 - MDCII
1604 - MDCIV
1605 - MDCV
1606 - MDCVI
1609 - MDCIX
1610 - MDCX
1611 - MDCXI
1615 - MDCXV
1620 - MDCXX
1640 - MDCXL
1650 - MDCL
1651 - MDCLI
1655 - MDCLV
1660 - MDCLX
1690 - MDCXC
1700 - MDCC
1701 - MDCCI
1705 - MDCCV
1710 - MDCCX
1750 - MDCCL
1800 - MDCCC
1900 - MCM
1901 - MCMI
1902 - MCMII
1904 - MCMIV
1905 - MCMV
1906 - MCMVI
1909 - MCMIX
1910 - MCMX
1911 - MCMXI
1915 - MCMXV
1920 - MCMXX
1940 - MCMXL
1950 - MCML
1951 - MCMLI
1955 - MCMLV
1960 - MCMLX
1990 - MCMXC
2000 - MM
2001 - MMI
2002 - MMII
2003 - MMIII
2004 - MMIV
2005 - MMV
2006 - MMVI
2007 - MMVII
2009 - MMIX
2010 - MMX
2011 - MMXI
2012 - MMXII
2014 - MMXIV
2015 - MMXV
2016 - MMXVI
2019 - MMXIX
2020 - MMXX
2021 - MMXXI
2025 - MMXXV
2030 - MMXXX
2040 - MMXL
2041 - MMXLI
2045 - MMXLV
2050 - MML
2051 - MMLI
2052 - MMLII
2054 - MMLIV
2055 - MMLV
2056 - MMLVI
2059 - MMLIX
2060 - MMLX
2061 - MMLXI
2065 - MMLXV
2070 - MMLXX
2090 - MMXC
2091 - MMXCI
2095 - MMXCV
2100 - MMC
2101 - MMCI
2102 - MMCII
2104 - MMCIV
2105 - MMCV
2106 - MMCVI
2109 - MMCIX
2110 - MMCX
2111 - MMCXI
2115 - MMCXV
2120 - MMCXX
2140 - MMCXL
2150 - MMCL
2151 - MMCLI
2155 - MMCLV
2160 - MMCLX
2190 - MMCXC
2200 - MMCC
2201 - MMCCI
2205 - MMCCV
2210 - MMCCX
2250 - MMCCL
2300 - MMCCC
2400 - MMCD
2401 - MMCDI
2405 - MMCDV
2410 - MMCDX
2450 - MMCDL
2500 - MMD
2501 - MMDI
2502 - MMDII
2504 - MMDIV
2505 - MMDV
2506 - MMDVI
2509 - MMDIX
2510 - MMDX
2511 - MMDXI
2515 - MMDXV
2520 - MMDXX
2540 - MMDXL
2550 - MMDL
2551 - MMDLI
2555 - MMDLV
2560 - MMDLX
2590 - MMDXC
2600 - MMDC
2601 - MMDCI
2605 - MMDCV
2610 - MMDCX
2650 - MMDCL
2700 - MMDCC
2900 - MMCM
2901 - MMCMI
2905 - MMCMV
2910 - MMCMX
2950 - MMCML
3000 - MMM
3001 - MMMI
3002 - MMMII
3004 - MMMIV
3005 - MMMV
3006 - MMMVI
3009 - MMMIX
3010 - MMMX
3011 - MMMXI
3015 - MMMXV
3020 - MMMXX
3040 - MMMXL
3050 - MMML
3051 - MMMLI
3055 - MMMLV
3060 - MMMLX
3090 - MMMXC
3100 - MMMC
3101 - MMMCI
3105 - MMMCV
3110 - MMMCX
3150 - MMMCL
3200 - MMMCC
3400 - MMMCD
3500 - MMMD
3501 - MMMDI
3505 - MMMDV
3510 - MMMDX
3550 - MMMDL
3600 - MMMDC
3900 - MMMCM

statuary: 4 herm
theaters: 4 odea
trumpets: 5 tubae
underworld: 5 Orcus
vase stone: 5 murra 6 murrha
vessel: 6 bireme, galley 7 trireme 10 quadrireme
victory site: 4 Zama
wars: 5 Punic
writer: 4 Livy 5 Pliny 7 Martial, Sallust, Tacitus 9 Suetonius
see also Latin
Rome __ apple: 6 Beauty
Rome __ built...: 5 wasn't
__ Rome: 4 Tony
Rome Beauty: 5 apple
relative: ***see*** apple
Romeo: 4 roué 5 lover, swain 6 suitor 7 Don Juan 8 Casanova, lothario, lover boy 9 inamorato
rival: 5 Paris
__ Romeo: 4 Alfa
Romeo and Juliet: 4 play 7 tragedy
author: William Shakespeare
character: 4 John 5 Friar, Paris, Peter 6 Samson, Tybalt 7 Capulet, Escalus, Gregory 8 Benvolio, Lawrence, Mercutio, Montague 9 Balthasar, Friar John
emulate ~: 5 elope
event: 5 tryst
scene: 4 tomb
setting: 5 Italy 6 Verona
Romeo and Juliet (1968 film)
cast: Olivia Hussey, Leonard Whiting
director: Franco Zeffirelli
Rome of Hungary, The: 4 Eger
Romeo Is Bleeding (1994 film)
cast: Lena Olin
Romeo & Juliet (1996 film)
cast: Claire Danes, Brian Dennehy, Leonardo DiCaprio, John Leguizamo
Romeo Must Die (2000 film)
cast: Aaliyah, Jet Li, Delroy Lindo, Henry O
Romero: 5 Cesar 6 George
Romero, George A.: 8 director
film: Dawn of the Dead (1978) Knightriders (1981) Martin (1978) Night of the Living Dead (1968)
Rome wasn't built __: 6 in a day
Romijn, Rebecca
spouse: John Stamos
Rommel: 5 Erwin 9 Desert Fox
battle: 9 El Alamein
Romney: 4 Mitt 5 sheep 6 George
Romola
author: George Eliot
character: 4 Tito 5 Nello, Piero, Tessa
romp: 3 fun 4 lark, play, rout, skip 5 antic, caper, cut up, frisk, spree 6 cavort, frolic, gambol, prance 7 carouse, disport, roister, rollick, scamper 8 cakewalk, good time, recreate 9 have a ball, make merry, whoop it up
romper: 6 jumper
romper __: 4 room
romping: 3 gay 5 happy, merry, peppy, zesty 6 bouncy, feisty, frisky, jaunty, jovial, joyful, joyous, lively 7 coltish 8 carefree, cheerful, spirited 9 exuberant, fun-loving 10 frolicsome
Romulan: 5 alien
Romulo: 6 Carlos 8 Gallegos
Romulus: 4 twin 5 Roman 6 eponym
daughter: 5 Prima
parent: 4 Ares, Mars, Rhea
son: 7 Aollius
twin: 5 Remus
Romy: 9 Schneider
Ron: 3 Cey, Ely, Mix 4 Gant, Mann, Wood 5 Brown, Glass, Kovic, Moody, Santo 6 Guidry, Holden, Howard, Nessen, Reagan, Rifkin, Silver 7 Leflore, Leibman, Palillo, Perlman, Shelton, Swoboda, Weasley, Winston 8 Clements, Turcotte 9 Greschner, Underwood
Rona: 5 Jaffe 7 Barrett
Ronald: 4 Ross 5 Coase, Isley, Neame 6 Colman, Reagan, Searle 7 Firbank, Norrish
rond de __: 5 jambe
rondelet: 4 poem 5 rhyme, verse
Rondo: 3 Don
Ronee: 7 Blakley
Ronettes
song: Be My Baby (1963)
Roni (1988 song)
artist: Bobby Brown
__-Roni: 5 Rice-a
Ronnie: 4 Lott 5 Dyson 6 Milsap 7 Van Zant 8 McDowell, Montrose
Ronnie (1964 song)
artist: Four Seasons
Ronny: 3 Cox 6 Howard
Ronny & the Daytonas
song: G.T.O. (1964)
__ Ron Ron: 5 Da Doo
Ronsard, Pierre de: 4 poet 6 French
Ronson
competitor: 3 Bic 5 Zippo
Ronstadt, Linda
song: All My Life (1990) Blue Bayou (1977) Different Drum (1967) Don't Know Much (1989) Heat Wave (1975) How Do I Make You (1980) Hurt So Bad (1980) It's So Easy (1977) Ooh Baby Baby (1978) Somewhere Out There (1987) That'll Be the Day (1976) When Will I Be Loved (1975) You're No Good (1975)
Röntgen, Wilhelm: 8 Nobelist 9 physicist
Ronzoni __ buoni: 4 sono
roo: 4 joey 6 jumper
Roo
creator: A.A. Milne
friend: 3 Owl 4 Pooh 6 Eeyore, Piglet, Winnie
parent: 5 Kanga
rood: 5 cross 7 measure 8 crucifix
four ~s: 4 acre
__ Rood: 4 Holy
roof: 3 top 4 dome, peak 6 shield, summit, zenith 7 ceiling, gambrel, lodging, mansard, shelter 8 covering, housetop, overhead, top level 9 residence
attachment: 4 dish 6 aerial, gutter, leader
beam: 6 header
curved ~: 4 dome 6 cupola
ender: 3 top 4 line, tree
fix a ~: 5 retar
go through the ~: 4 grow, rise, soar 5 mount, surge 6 ascend 7 burgeon, mount up 8 escalate, increase 9 intensify, skyrocket 10 appreciate
hanging: 6 icicle
hit the ~: 4 flip, rage, rant, rave, roar, snap 5 storm 6 blow up, bridle, get mad, see red 7 explode 8 have a fit 9 blow a fuse, throw a fit
nester: 5 stork
problem: 4 drip, leak
projection: 4 eave
raise the ~: 5 gripe, revel, shout, storm 6 clamor, holler, squawk 7 grumble 8 complain 9 bellyache
raising the ~: 4 loud 5 noisy 7 blaring, booming, raucous, riotous, yelling 8 blasting, piercing, shouting 9 bellowing, clamorous, screaming 10 boisterous, uproarious, vociferous
runoff: 4 rain
send through the ~: 5 anger 6 enrage, fire up, madden 7 incense, inflame, provoke 9 infuriate 10 exasperate
starter: 3 sun
support: 5 truss
topper: 3 epi 4 vane 6 aerial
to the ~: 6 loaded, packed 7 crowded, replete, stuffed 9 chock-full, jam-packed
type of ~: 5 gable 6 A-frame, thatch
under the ~: 6 indoor, inside 7 indoors
worker: 5 tiler
__ roof: 3 hip 5 gable 7 gambrel, mansard
roofer
material: 3 tar 4 tile 5 nails, slate
need: 3 adz, zax 4 adze 6 ladder
Roof of the World, The: 5 Tibet
rooftop
tell from the ~: 5 shout
Rooftop Singers
song: Walk Right In (1963)
rook: 3 con 4 bilk, bird, burn, crow, dupe, gull, have, hoax, nick 5 cheat, cozen, gouge, pluck, sting, trick 6 castle, chisel, fleece, rip off 7 beguile, defraud, mislead, swindle 8 flimflam, swindler 9 blackbird 10 chess piece, run a game on
place: 6 corner
sound: 3 caw
Rook: 5 Susan
Rooker: 7 Michael
__ Rookh: 5 Lalla
rookie: 4 tiro, tyro 5 newie 6 novice 7 recruit 8 freshman, neophyte, newcomer 9 fledgling 10 apprentice, first-timer, tenderfoot
like a ~: 5 green
military ~: 4 pleb 5 plebe 10 rct. Recruit
promising ~: 5 comer
Rookie of the Year: 5 award
Rookie, The (2002 film)
cast: Rachel Griffiths, Dennis Quaid
room: 3 den, way 4 cave, cell, dorm, flat, hall, play 5 attic, cabin, lodge, niche, place, range, reach, salon, scope, slack, space, study, vault 6 alcove, cellar, chance, garret, leeway, lounge, margin, office, parlor, volume 7 boudoir, chamber, compass, cubicle, expanse, library, license, lodging, nursery, opening, vacancy 8 basement, capacity, latitude, lodgment, occasion, quarters, vastness 9 allowance, apartment, clearance, cubbyhole, free space, largeness 10 auditorium
and board: 4 keep 7 lodging, pension
asset: 4 view
at the top: 4 loft 5 attic 6 garret
book ~: 3 den 5 study 7 library
British ~: 6 bed-sit
college ~: 4 dorm, hall 7 commons
connector: 4 hall 5 foyer 8 corridor
cooler: 3 fan 9 window fan 10 ceiling fan
decorate a ~: 5 panel, paper
dining ~: 4 mess 8 chow hall, mess hall 9 cafeteria, refectory 10 triclinium
divider: 4 wall 9 partition
ender: 4 ette, mate
extension: 3 ell 5 add-on
furnace ~: 6 cellar
furnishings: 5 decor
home ~: 3 den, lav 4 bath, loft 5 attic, study 6 cellar, parlor 7 boudoir, kitchen 8 basement
in French: 5 salle
in Latin: 6 camera
in Spanish: 4 sala
lecture ~: 10 auditorium
make ~ for: 3 add 5 admit 6 append, edge in, insert 7 include 9 interject
measure: 4 area, sq. ft. 5 width 6 length
out of ~: 4 full
partner: 5 board
place to rent a ~: 3 inn 5 hotel, motel
powder ~: 4 john
rest ~: 4 john
starter: 3 bar, bed, gun, leg, sun, tap, tea 4 ante, back, ball, bath, bunk, club, coat, dark, head, home, mail, mush, news, play, pool, rest, sick, ward, ware, wash, work 5 board, check, class, cloak, court, elbow, green, grill, guard, house, lunch, press, sales, state, stock, store 6 school
storage ~: 5 attic 6 cellar 8 basement
strong ~: 5 vault
take a ~: 4 stay 5 lodge 7 sojourn 8 stop over
temple ~: 6 adytum
to move: 4 give 5 space, width 6 leeway 8 latitude
underground ~: 8 basement
unfinished ~: 4 loft 6 garret
visitor ~: 6 parlor 7 gallery 10 living room
wiggle ~: 4 play 5 space 7 freedom 8 latitude
with ~ to spare: 4 vast, wide 5 ample, broad 7 sizable 8 spacious 9 capacious, expansive

10 voluminous
work the ~: 3 mix 6 hobnob, mingle 9 circulate 10 fraternize
room __: 5 clerk 7 divider, service
__ room: 3 box, day, gun, mud, rec, sea, war 4 back, chat, city, game, jury, mail, men's, pump, shed, tack, twin 5 board, chart, clean, elbow, front, guest, ready, squad, steam 6 boiler, common, dining, double, family, living, locker, powder, public, romper, rumpus, throne, trophy, wiggle 7 banquet, control, cutting, drawing, fitting, Florida, reading, running, sitting, utility, waiting
Room __: 5 to Let 7 Service
Room __ One More: 3 for
Room __ Top: 5 at the
Room __ View, A: 5 With a
__ Room: 4 East, In My 5 Panic, White 6 Jacob's
Room 222 (ABC sitcom)
cast: Michael Constantine (Seymour Kaufman)
Lloyd Haynes (Pete Dixon)
Denise Nicholas (Liz McIntyre)
Karen Valentine (Alice Johnson)
room and __: 5 board
Room at the Top (1959 film)
cast: Laurence Harvey, Simone Signoret
Room at the Top (1990 song)
artist: Adam Ant
__-room comedy: 7 drawing
roomer: 5 guest, liver 6 lessee, lodger, tenant 10 inhabitant, vacationer
roominess: 5 space, width 7 breadth 9 amplitude
rooming house: 3 inn 5 hotel 7 lodging
British ~: 3 kip
roommate: 3 pal 4 mate 5 buddy, crony 6 cohort, escort, fellow, friend 7 compeer, consort 8 intimate, sidekick 9 associate, companion, confidant
Room of One's Own, A
author: Virginia Woolf
rooms: 5 lodge, suite 6 billet 7 housing, lodging 8 quarters
Room Service (1938 film)
cast: Lucille Ball, Chico Marx, Groucho Marx, Harpo Marx, Ann Miller
studio: 3 RKO
room-service prop: 4 cart, tray
Rooms on Fire (1989 song)
artist: Stevie Nicks
Room, The
author: Harold Pinter
__ Room, The: 3 Red, War 5 Black, Small 6 Boiler, Yellow 7 L-Shaped
room to swing __: 4 a cat
Room With a View, A: 4 film 5 novel
author: E.M. Forster
cast: Helena Bonham Carter, Denholm Elliott, Maggie Smith
character: 4 Lucy, Vyse 5 Cecil
director: James Ivory
setting: 5 Italy 8 Florence
view: 4 Arno
roomy: 3 big 4 wide 5 ample, broad, large, loose 7 sizable 8 far-flung, generous, sizeable, spacious, sweeping 9 capacious, cavernous, expansive, extensive, spread out, uncrowded 10 commodious, voluminous, widespread
Roone: 7 Arledge
Rooney: 3 Art 4 Andy 5 Annie 6 Mickey
Rooney, Mickey: 5 actor
film: The Black Stallion (1979)
The Bold and the Brave (1956)
Boys Town (1938)
Girl Crazy (1943)
Huckleberry Finn (1939)
The Human Comedy (1943)
It's a Mad Mad Mad Mad World (1963)
Killer McCoy (1947)
Life Begins for Andy Hardy (1941)
Love Finds Andy Hardy (1938)
National Velvet (1944)
Night at the Museum (2006)
Requiem for a Heavyweight (1962)
Young Tom Edison (1940)
spouse: Ava Gardner
Roosevelt: 5 Grier 7 Eleanor 8 Theodore
Roosevelt, Eleanor
work: My Days
On My Own
This I Remember
This Is My Story
Roosevelt, Franklin Delano: 9 president
alma mater: 6 Groton 7 Harvard
biographer: 5 Alsop
cabinet member: 4 Hull, Knox 5 Ickes, Roper 6 Edison, Farley 7 Hopkins, Perkins, Stimson, Wallace
child: 4 Anna, John 5 James 7 Elliott
film portrayer: 7 Bellamy 8 Herrmann
home: 7 New York 8 Hyde Park
mother: 4 Sara
opponent: 5 Dewey 6 Hoover, Landon 7 Willkie
predecessor: 6 Hoover
successor: 6 Truman
V.P.: 6 Garner, Truman 7 Wallace
wife: 7 Eleanor
__ Roosevelt Longworth: 5 Alice
Roosevelt, Theodore: 8 Nobelist 9 president
alma mater: 7 Harvard
child: 5 Alice, Ethel 6 Archie, Kermit 7 Quentin
home: 7 New York
opponent: 4 Debs 6 Parker
predecessor: 8 McKinley
successor: 4 Taft
V.P.: 9 Fairbanks
wife: 5 Alice, Edith
roost: 3 sit 4 home, live, nest, rest, seat, stay 5 dwell, house, light, lodge, perch, squat 6 alight, remain, settle 7 domicil, habitat, housing, shelter, sojourn 8 domicile, henhouse, quarters 9 birdhouse
rule the ~: 4 boss, head, lead 5 order 6 direct, manage 7 command, control 8 dominate
sitter: 3 hen
rooster: 4 cock, fowl, male 6 bantam 7 chicken, poultry
mate: 3 hen
name meaning ~: 4 Hahn
pride: 4 comb 5 crest
replacement: 5 alarm 10 alarm clock
sound: 4 crow
time: 4 dawn 5 sunup
walk like a ~: 5 strut
Rooster Cogburn (1975 film)
cast: Katharine Hepburn, John Wayne
root: 3 dig, fix, nub, pry 4 base, beer, beet, core, font, germ, grub, hunt, knub, nose, poke, seek, soul, stem, stub, well 5 amole, basis, cause, delve, embed, imbed, lodge, orris, radix, tuber 6 bottom, burrow, carrot, center, ferret, forage, ground, insert, jicama, marrow, motive, origin, radish, reason, search, source, spring, turnip 7 essence, grounds, implant, keynote, parsnip, radicle, rhizome, rummage, unearth 9 beginning, causation, etymology, substance, vegetable 10 derivation, foundation, mainspring, provenance, underlying
chopper: 3 adz 4 adze
combining form: 4 rhiz- 5 -rhiza, rhizo- 6 -rrhiza
edible ~: 3 oca, oka, yam 4 beet, eddo, taro 5 tuber 6 carrot, jicama
ender: 3 age 4 hold, worm 5 stalk, stock
for: 5 cheer, favor 7 applaud 8 advocate 9 encourage
hair: 6 fibril
malady: 3 rot
out: 5 purge 6 remove, uproot 7 abolish, unearth 9 eradicate, extirpate 10 do away with
starter: 3 red, tap 4 alum, beet, musk, pink, poke, rose 5 arrow, birth, blood, bread, briar, colic, coral, orris, putty, snake 6 balsam, bitter, canker, dragon, ginger, orange 7 crinkle
take ~: 6 settle, sprout 7 develop 8 spring up 9 germinate
word: 6 etymon
root __: 3 rot 4 beer, crop, hair, knot, test 5 field, graft 6 cellar, doctor, system 7 climber
__ root: 4 cube, take 6 bitter, square
Root: 5 Elihu
root beer: 4 soda 5 drink 8 beverage 9 soft drink
alternative: 4 cola
brand: 4 Dad's 5 Barqs
plus ice cream: 5 float
rooted: 3 set 4 firm 5 fixed, solid 6 frozen, inborn, inbred, stable, static 7 riveted, settled 8 constant, definite, embedded, immobile, ironclad 9 immovable, ingrained, permanent 10 deep-seated, inveterate, motionless, stationary, unchanging
__-rooted: 4 deep
Root, Elihu: 8 diplomat, Nobelist
rooter: 3 fan, pig 4 buff 7 admirer, booster, devotee, fancier 8 follower, partisan 9 supporter 10 aficionado, enthusiast
cry: 3 rah, yay
__-Rooter: 4 Roto
rooters: 6 claque
rootless: 5 shaky 6 roving 7 nomadic, roaming 8 drifting, rambling, vagabond 9 itinerant, wandering, wayfaring 10 journeying
plant: 4 alga
rootlessness: 5 anomy 6 anomie
roots: 6 origin 7 descent, genesis, lineage 8 ancestry, heritage, homeland, pedigree 9 ancestors, bloodline, forebears, genealogy 10 extraction, family tree, fatherland, motherland, native land, native soil
put down ~: 4 stay 6 linger, remain, settle 8 colonize
__ roots: 5 grass
Roots
author: Alex Haley
Roots (ABC miniseries): 4 saga
cast: John Amos (Kunta Kinte)
LeVar Burton (Kunta Kinte)
Leslie Uggams (Kizzy)
Ben Vereen (Chicken George)
Emmy winner: 5 Asner
historian: 5 griot
rope: 3 tie 4 bind, bond, cord, lace, line, vang 5 cable, lasso, leash, twine 6 hawser, lariat, pull in, ratlin, secure, strand, string, tether 7 cordage, lanyard, ratline 8 ligature
at the end of one's ~: 7 frantic, panicky 8 frenzied, strained, wretched 9 desperate, miserable
climber: 5 faker, fakir, faqir 6 faquir
cowboy ~: 5 lasso, reata, riata 6 lariat
ender: 4 walk
fasten a ~: 3 tie 4 bind, knot 5 belay
feature: 4 knot 5 bight, noose
horse guiding ~: 5 longe
in: 4 coax, dupe, fool, gull, hoax, hook, lure, trap 5 cheat, decoy, lasso, shill 6 delude, entice, entrap, fleece 7 attract, beguile, ensnare, mislead 8 inveigle 9 captivate, disinform, victimize
injury: 4 burn
jump ~: 3 toy 4 game, skip
knot: 4 loop 5 noose, snare
nautical ~: 3 tye 4 vang 6 cablet, earing, gilguy, hawser 7 bobstay, bowline, outhaul, ratline 8 buntline, gantline, girtline
off: 5 fence 6 divide 7 reserve 8 set apart 9 partition
open a ~: 5 unrig, untie 6 loosen
separate strands of ~: 5 feaze, feeze, unlay
source: 4 bast, coir, hemp, jute, riem 5 abaca, istle, ixtle, oakum, sisal 6 baobab
starter: 3 man 4 bolt, foot 5 tight
target: 4 calf, dogy 5 dogey, steer 6 doggie
twist: 4 kink
rope __: 3 off, tow 4 yarn 6 bridge
rope-__: 5 a-dope
__ rope: 4 jump, skip
Rope (1948 film)
cast: John Dall, Farley Granger, James Stewart
director: Alfred Hitchcock
Rope-a-dope boxer: 3 Ali

Roper: 4 Elmo
report: 4 poll
ropes
learn the ~: 5 adapt, study, train **6** adjust, bone up, master **9** acclimate
on the ~: 5 at bay, spent, tired **6** in a fix, in a jam **7** in a mess, rundown, trapped, up a tree, worn out **9** enervated, exhausted **10** in hot water
show the ~: 5 coach, teach, train, tutor **6** school **7** educate **8** instruct
__ ropes: 5 on the
ropy: 4 oozy **5** thick, tough **6** viscid **7** fibrous, stringy, viscose, viscous **8** cordlike **9** glutinous
roque: 4 game
need: 6 mallet
Roquefort: 6 cheese
hue: 4 bleu, blue
Rorem: 3 Ned
rorqual: 3 sei **5** whale **6** animal, mammal **8** cetacean
relative: ***see*** cetacean
Rorschach: 4 test
image: 4 blot **7** ink blot
Rory: 7 Calhoun
Rosa: 4 Mota **5** Parks, Raisa **6** Chacel **7** Bonheur **8** Ponselle
see also Spanish
__ Rosa: 5 Monte, Santa
Rosalie (1937 film)
cast: Nelson Eddy, Eleanor Powell
Rosalie (musical)
composer: Cole Porter
Rosalind: 4 Chao, moon **7** Russell
planet: 6 Uranus
role for ~: 4 Mame
Rosalyn: 5 Yalow
Rosalynn: 6 Carter
child: 3 Amy **4** Chip
to Jimmy: 4 wife
__ Rosalynn Carter: 7 Eleanor
Rosamond
composer: Thomas Arne
Rosanna: 8 Arquette
Rosanna (1982 song)
artist: Toto
Rosanne: 4 Cash
Rosa Parks Day month: 3 Dec. **8** December
Rosario: 6 Dawson
rosary: 3 ave **5** beads **6** prayer
part: 3 ave **4** bead, gaud
Rosary, The
composer: Ethelbert Nevin
rosa, sub: 7 furtive, illegal **8** hush-hush, on the sly, secretly **9** entre nous, furtively, privately
roscoe: 3 gat, gun, rod **5** piece **6** heater, pistol **7** firearm
Roscoe: 4 Ates **5** Karns **8** Arbuckle, Conkling
Roscoe Lee __: 6 Browne
rose: 3 red **4** pink **5** color, got up, plant, sat up, shrub **6** damask, flower, redden, went up **7** climbed, crimson, rambler, stood up **9** table wine, vermilion **10** floribunda, multiflora, sweetbrier
chafer: 3 bug **6** insect
combining form: 4 rhod- **5** rhodo-
ender: 3 bay, bud, hip **4** bush, fish, root, wood
enjoy a ~: 5 smell
extract: 4 atar, otto **5** athar, attar, ottar
family plant: 4 sloe **5** avens **6** kerria, spirea **7** bramble, jetbead, spiraea **8** hardhack, ninebark, photinia **9** firethorn, raspberry
family tree: 4 pear, plum **5** apple, peach **6** almond, cherry, medlar, quince **7** apricot **8** hawthorn, oiticica, photinia **10** blackthorn
fruit: 3 hip
holder: 4 stem
locale: 3 bed
of Sharon: 6 althea
oil: 5 nerol **6** neroli
pest: 5 aphid, aphis
protection: 5 thorn
relative: ***see*** red color
starter: 4 prim, rock
rose __: 3 oil **4** hips **5** water
rose-__ glasses: 7 colored
__ rose: 3 dog, old, red, tea **4** moss, musk, wild
rosé: 4 pink, wine **5** tavel
alternative: 6 claret
Rose: 3 Axl **4** Pete **5** Billy, Byrne, David, Marie, Tokyo **7** Bernard, Charlie, Kennedy **8** Macaulay
like Abie's ~: 5 Irish
Rose __: 4 Bowl **5** Marie, Royce **6** Garden, Madder, of Lima
Rose __ rose...: 3 is a
__ Rose: 4 Lida **5** Only a, Tokyo **7** Ramblin'
Roseanne: 4 Barr
like ~'s speech: 5 nasal
spouse: Tom Arnold
Roseanne (ABC sitcom)
cast: Sara Gilbert (Darlene Conner)
John Goodman (Dan Conner)
Laurie Metcalf (Jackie Harris)
Roseanne (Roseanne Conner)
roseate: 4 pink **6** bright **9** promising **10** optimistic
Roseau: 4 city, town **7** capital
locale: 8 Dominica
Rose, Billy
spouse: Fanny Brice
Rose Bowl
kickoff: 6 parade
org.: 4 NCAA
Rosebud: 4 sled
owner: 4 Kane
...rosebuds while __: 5 ye may
rose-colored: 7 hopeful **8** sanguine **10** optimistic
glasses: 4 hope **8** idealism, optimism **10** positivism
Rose, David: 8 composer **9** conductor
song: The Stripper (1962)
spouse: Judy Garland, Martha Raye
Rose Garden (1970 song)
artist: Lynn Anderson
Rose is a rose...
author: Gertrude Stein
__ Rose Lee: 5 Gypsy
Rose Madder
author: Stephen King
Rose Marie (1936 film)
cast: Nelson Eddy, Jeanette MacDonald
org.: 4 RCMP
rosemary: 4 herb **5** shrub, spice
family: 4 mint
relative: 4 sage **8** lavender
Rosemary: 4 Lane, Rice **6** Casals, De Camp **7** Clooney
portrayer: Mia Farrow
Rosemary's Baby: 4 film **5** novel
author: Ira Levin
cast: John Cassavetes, Mia Farrow, Ruth Gordon
director: Roman Polanski
Rosenberg: 4 Alan **6** Stuart
Rosenbloom: 5 Maxie
Rosencrantz
friend: 6 Hamlet
Rosencrantz and Guildenstern Are Dead
author: Tom Stoppard
__ Rosenkavalier: 3 Der
Rosenthal: 5 china **8** Emmanuel
competitor: 5 Lenox **6** Mikasa
Rosenthal, Emmanuel: 9 conductor
rose of __: 5 China **6** Heaven, Sharon
Rose of __: 4 Lima **6** Tralee
__ Rose of Cairo, The: 6 Purple
Rose of Lima: 5 saint
__ Rose of Texas, The: 6 Yellow
Rose, Pete
forte: 4 hits **7** singles
sport: 8 baseball
roses
bed of ~: 4 ease **6** luxury **7** comfort **8** good life, opulence
coming up ~: 5 lucky
gather ~: 3 cut **4** clip, snip
run for the ~: 5 Derby
__ roses: 5 bed of
Roses __ red...: 3 are
__ Roses: 5 Bed of, Guns N', Paper
Roses Are Red (1962 song)
artist: Bobby Vinton
__ Roses for a Blue Lady: 3 Red
__ Rose's Jumbo: 5 Billy
Rose Tattoo, The: 4 film, play
author: Tennessee Williams
cast: Burt Lancaster, Anna Magnani
Rose, The (1979 film)
cast: Alan Bates, Frederic Forrest, Bette Midler
Rose, The (1980 song)
artist: Bette Midler
Rosetta
locale: 4 Nile **5** Egypt
Rosetta Stone
language: 5 Greek
material: 6 basalt
Rosewall, Ken: 7 netster **9** tennis pro
milieu: 5 court
Rosey: 5 Grier
Rosh __: 6 Hodesh **7** Chodesh, Hashana, Hashono
Rosie: 5 Daley, Perez **6** Casals **8** O'Donnell
fastener: 5 rivet
former rival: 5 Oprah
__ Rosie O' Grady: 5 Sweet
rosin: 9 colophony
ender: 4 weed
source: 4 pine
Rosinante: 5 horse **6** equine
rosiness: 5 blush, flush
Rosmersholm
author: Henrik Ibsen
Ross: 3 sea, Ted **4** city, John, town **5** Betsy, Diana, James, Lanny, Perot **6** Hunter, Marion, Martin, Nellie, Ronald **7** Herbert, McElwee **9** Katharine, Macdonald, McWhirter
locale: 10 Antarctica, New Zealand
Ross __ Shelf: 3 Ice
Rossano: 6 Brazzi
Ross, Betsy: 10 seamstress
emulate ~: 3 sew
need: 6 needle, thread
product: 4 flag
Ross, Diana
born: Diane Earle
lead singer of: The Supremes
song: Ain't No Mountain High Enough (1970)
All of You (1984)
Endless Love (1981)
I'm Coming Out (1980)
It's My Turn (1980)
Love Hangover (1976)
Mirror, Mirror (1982)
Missing You (1985)
Muscles (1982)
Remember Me (1971)
Swept Away (1984)
Theme from Mahogany (1975)
Touch Me in the Morning (1973)
Upside Down (1980)
Why Do Fools Fall in Love (1981)
You're a Special Part of Me (1973)
Rossellini: 7 Roberto **8** Isabella
Rossellini, Isabella: 7 actress
film: Blue Velvet (1986)
Cousins (1989)
Death Becomes Her (1992)
Fearless (1993)
Immortal Beloved (1994)
mother: Ingrid Bergman
Rossellini, Roberto
spouse: Ingrid Bergman
Rossen: 6 Robert
Rossetti: 5 Dante **9** Christina
Rossetti, Christina: 4 poet **7** British
Rossetti, Dante Gabriel: 4 poet **7** British
work: The Blessed Damozel
The House of Life
Rosshalde
author: Hermann Hesse
Rossi: 4 Aldo
Rossini, Gioacchino: 7 Italian **8** composer
genre: 5 opera
work: The Barber of Seville
Comte Ory
Mosè
Tancredi
William Tell
Ross Island volcano: 6 Erebus
Rossiya
see Russian
Ross, James: 7 British **8** explorer
Ross, John: 8 explorer, Scottish
Ross, Katharine: 7 actress
film: The Betsy (1978)
Butch Cassidy and the Sundance Kid (1969)
The Final Countdown (1980)
The Graduate (1967)
The Stepford Wives (1975)
Tell Them Willie Boy Is Here (1969)
spouse: Sam Elliott
Rossner: 6 Judith
Ross Sea bay: 6 Whales

__ Ross Trophy: 3 Art
Rossum: 4 Emmy
Rostand, Edmond: 6 French 10 playwright
character: 6 Roxane
work: Cyrano de Bergerac
Rosten, Leo: 6 writer 8 humorist
specialty: 7 Yiddish
roster: 4 bill, list, roll, rota 5 index 6 agenda, lineup, muster, record 7 catalog, listing, program 8 register, schedule 9 catalogue, directory, inventory
listing: 4 name 6 member 7 surname
on the ~: 6 active
Rostov-__: 5 on-Don
Rostropovich, Mstislav: 7 cellist, Russian
rostrum: 4 dais 5 stage 6 podium, pulpit 7 lectern 8 platform
Roswell: 4 city, town
locale: 7 Georgia 9 New Mexico
rosy: 3 red 4 pink 5 coral, fresh, palmy, ruddy 6 bright, upbeat 7 flushed, glowing, hopeful 8 blooming, blushing, cheerful, pleasing, red-faced, rubicund, sanguine 9 favorable, hunky-dory, looking up, promising 10 auspicious, optimistic
feature: 5 cheek
hardly ~: 3 wan 4 ashy, pale 5 ashen
make ~: 5 flush 6 redden
not ~: 4 dire, dour, glum, grim 5 black, bleak, harsh, woful 6 gloomy, morose, somber, woeful 7 ominous 8 hopeless 9 cheerless, depressed, frightful
opposite: 4 gray, grim, pale 5 ashen, bleak 6 dismal, gloomy, pallid 8 hopeless 12 inauspicious
rosy-cheeked: 3 fit 4 hale, well 5 hardy, ruddy, sound 6 robust 7 healthy 8 vigorous 9 in the pink
rosy-fingered goddess: 6 Aurora
rot: 3 eat 4 mold, rust, sink, turn 5 decay, go bad, spoil, taint 6 blight, canker, fester, molder, perish, wither 7 baloney, compost, corrode, corrupt, crumble, decline, degrade, go stale 8 go to seed, languish, stagnate 9 break down, corrosion, decompose, fall apart, lie fallow, overripen 10 degenerate, go to pieces
ender: 3 gut
starter: 5 tommy
see also baloney
rota: 6 roster 8 register
Rota, Nino: 7 Italian 8 composer
rotary: 7 turning 8 spinning, whirling 9 revolving
motion: 5 twirl, twist
tool: 5 auger, drill
rotary __: 3 hoe 4 dial, plow, pump, wing 5 press, valve 6 engine, tiller
Rotary __: 4 Club
rotate: 4 eddy, jink, reel, roll, spin, turn 5 pivot, spell, swing, twirl, twist, wheel, whirl 6 circle, follow, gyrate, switch, swivel 7 relieve, revolve, succeed 8 exchange, go around, turn over 9 alternate, change off, pirouette, take turns
to an astronaut: 3 yaw
rotating: 6 awhirl
piece: 3 cam
point: 5 hinge, pivot 7 fulcrum
rotation: 4 spin, turn 5 orbit 8 gyration 10 revolution
line: 4 axis
__ rotation: 4 crop
rotational: 5 axial
device: 4 pawl
speed: 3 rps
rotator __: 4 cuff
ROTC
relative: 3 OCS, OTC, OTS
rote: 5 habit 6 groove, ritual 7 routine 10 repetition
by ~: 10 from memory
Rote, Kyle: 2 QB
sport: 8 football
rotelle: 5 pasta 7 noodles
rotgut: 5 booze 6 whisky 7 alcohol, whiskey 10 intoxicant
Roth: 3 Eli, Tim 4 Mark 6 Philip 7 Lillian, William
Roth __: 3 IRA
Roth, David Lee
lead singer of: Van Halen
song: California Girls (1985) Just Like Paradise (1988)
Rothko, Mark: 6 artist 7 painter
Roth, Mark: 6 bowler
milieu: 5 alley
org.: 3 PBA
Roth, Philip: 6 writer
spouse: Claire Bloom
work: The Anatomy Lesson
Everyman
Exit Ghost
The Ghost Writer
Goodbye, Columbus
The Humbling
Indignation
Letting Go
My Life as a Man
Portnoy's Complaint
When She Was Good
Zuckerman Bound
Zuckerman Unbound
Rothstein: 6 Arnold
rotini: 5 pasta 8 macaroni
rotisserie: 4 oven 5 grill 8 barbecue
Rotisserie __: 8 Baseball
roto-__: 6 tiller
Roto-__: 6 Rooter
rotor
ender: 5 craft
noise: 4 whir 5 whirr
Roto-Rooter
alternative: 5 Drano
rotten: 3 bad, bum, off 4 foul, grim, mean, poor, punk, rank, sick, sour, vile 5 amiss, awful, dirty, fetid, gross, lousy, moldy, nasty, punky, reeky, sorry, woful, wrong 6 crumby, crummy, dismal, filthy, foetid, horrid, odious, putrid, rancid, scurvy, shabby, smelly, spoilt, strong, wicked, woeful 7 accurst, baleful, baneful, beastly, bruised, corrupt, crooked, decayed, doleful, ghastly, gone bad, noisome, noxious, odorous, spoiled, tainted, unclean, vicious 8 accursed, depraved, dreadful, God-awful, grievous, horrible, inedible, infamous, inferior, overripe, polluted, shameful, stinking, terrible, two-faced, wretched 9 abhorrent, appalling, atrocious, crumbling, dastardly, deceitful, defective, dishonest, execrable, faithless, frightful, insidious, loathsome, mercenary, miserable, moldering, nefarious, offensive, putrefied, revolting, unhealthy, worm-eaten 10 abominable, deplorable, despicable, detestable, disastrous, disgusting, horrendous, lamentable, malodorous, scurrilous, unpleasant, villainous
be ~: 4 reek 5 smell, stink
bunch: 6 bad lot
combining form: 4 sapr- 5 sapro-
feeling ~: 3 ill
kid: 3 imp 4 brat, punk 5 demon, rowdy, scamp, tough 6 rascal 7 hellion, hoodlum, ruffian 8 hooligan
luck: 6 mishap 7 setback 8 bad break, calamity 9 adversity, mischance
spoil ~: 4 baby 6 pamper
rotten __ core: 5 to the
Rotten: 6 Johnny
__ Rotten Scoundrels: 5 Dirty
rotter: 3 cad 4 heel, roué 5 rogue 6 bad egg, bad guy 8 picaroon 9 scoundrel 10 blackguard
Rotterdam: 3 spt. 4 city, port, town 7 seaport
locale: 7 Holland, New York
river: 4 Maas 5 Meuse
see also Netherlands
Rottweiler: 3 dog 5 canid 6 canine
rotund: 5 beefy, fubsy, obese, plump, pudgy, pursy, round, stout 6 chubby, chunky, fleshy, portly, pyknic, stocky, zaftig, zoftig 7 adipose, paunchy 8 globular, roly-poly 9 corpulent, filled-out 10 abdominous, overweight, well-padded
Rouben: 9 Mamoulian
roué: 3 cad 4 rake, wolf 5 Romeo 6 masher, rotter 7 bounder, Don Juan, playboy, swinger 8 Casanova, lothario, lover boy, sybarite 9 ladies' man, libertine 10 profligate, sensualist, voluptuary
Rouen: 4 city, town
locale: 6 France
river: 5 Seine
town near ~: 6 Dieppe
Rouen Cathedral
artist: Claude Monet
rouge: 3 bet, red 5 blush, paint 6 French, makeup, redden 7 blusher 8 cosmetic 9 beauty aid
apply ~: 6 redden
__ rouge: 3 vin
__ Rouge: 5 Baton, Khmer 6 Moulin
rouge et noir: 4 game 8 card game
rough: 3 raw 4 curt, hard, mean, rude, ugly, wild 5 brash, brusk, bumpy, crass, crude, cruel, gruff, hairy, harsh, heavy, husky, jaggy, nasty, nubby, raspy, rocky, rowdy, rutty, scaly, seamy, short, stern, stony, surly, tight, tough, uncut, vague, wooly 6 abrupt, biting, bitter, broken, brutal, choppy, coarse, craggy, crusty, fierce, gauche, hackly, hoarse, hubbly, jagged, jouncy, knobby, knotty, ragged, raging, ridged, roiled, rugged, rustic, rutted, savage, severe, shaggy, smutty, sticky, stoney, stormy, thorny, trying, tufted, uneven, unmeet, uphill, vulgar, woolly 7 arduous, austere, bearish, bristly, brusque, brutish, chapped, cragged, crinkly, crudely, drastic, extreme, gnarled, grating, grouchy, hard-won, harshly, inexact, jarring, loutish, naughty, onerous, raucous, ruffled, scraggy, scruffy, sketchy, Spartan, stubbly, uncivil, uncouth, unlevel, vicious, violent 8 abrasive, churlish, grueling, homemade, impolite, impudent, leathery, no picnic, scabrous, scratchy, strident, tactless, toilsome, ungentle, ungently, unshaven 9 demanding, difficult, draconian, estimated, ferocious, graceless, imperfect, imprecise, inclement, inelegant, irregular, laborious, makeshift, primitive, strenuous, stringent, tasteless, turbulent, uncourtly, unfeeling, ungroomed, unrefined, untrained, untutored, unwrought, violently 10 amateurish, corrugated, disordered, disorderly, formidable, indecorous, indelicate, laryngitic, nonuniform, oppressive, provincial, tumultuous, unbecoming, uncultured, unfinished, ungracious, unmannerly, unpleasant, unpolished, unprepared
draft: 6 sketch 7 outline
ender: 3 age, dry 4 back, cast, neck, shod 5 dried, house, rider 6 caster 7 casting
handling: 4 harm 5 abuse 6 misuse
it: 4 camp 7 camp out 10 pitch a tent
not ~: 4 calm, easy, kind, mild, pure 5 balmy, civil, exact, suave 6 benign, classy, docile, genial, gentle, kindly, mellow, placid, serene, smooth, tender, urbane 7 amiable, clement, courtly, genteel, lenient, pacific, precise, refined, subdued 8 cultured, gracious, laid back, mannerly, merciful, moderate, pleasant, polished, purified 9 civilized, courteous, dignified, easygoing, leisurely, processed, temperate 10 cultivated
out: 4 plan 5 draft 6 sketch 7 outline, suggest 8 block out 9 adumbrate
partner: 5 ready 6 tumble
sketch: 4 plan 5 draft 7 croquis, outline
time: 5 slump 6 downer 8 dry spell, tailspin
up: 3 hit 4 bash, hurt, mall, maul 5 abuse 6 batter, beat up 8 maltreat, mistreat 9 manhandle 10 slap around
rough __: 3 cut 5 stuff
rough-__: 4 hewn
Rough __: 6 Riders
roughage: 4 bran 5 fiber
rough-and-__: 5 ready 6 tumble
Rough Boy
artist: ZZ Top
rough-cut: 4 hewn
roughen: 4 chap 5 crack 6 abrade,

redden 7 callous, coarsen, wrinkle 9 corrugate

rough-hew: 5 shape

rough-hewn: 3 raw 4 rude 5 wooly 6 rugged, woolly 7 lowbred 10 unfinished

roughhouse: 4 play 5 abuse, brawl 8 mistreat 9 misbehave

Roughing It
author: Mark Twain

Roughing It in the Bush
author: Susanna Moodie

roughly: 4 hard, or so 5 about, circa 6 approx., around, nearly 8 severely 9 generally

rough-mannered: 4 curt, rude 5 blunt, gruff, harsh, surly 6 coarse, crabby, crusty, grumpy 7 bearish, boorish, brusque, grating, grouchy, loutish, uncivil 8 churlish, impolite, inurbane, tactless 10 unfriendly, ungracious, unmannerly

roughneck: 4 bozo, goon, thug 5 rowdy, tough 7 ruffian

roughness: 4 chop, woof 7 texture 8 violence 10 coarseness

roughrider: 5 tamer

roughshod, ride: 5 bully 6 defeat 7 trample 9 overpower, trample on, tyrannize

rough-sounding: 6 hoarse

roulade: 4 meat 6 entrée

roulette: 4 game
bet: 3 odd, red 4 even, noir
need: 5 wheel
opponent: 5 house
play ~: 3 bet

round: 3 cut, lap, run 4 bout, full, oval, ring, turn 5 bowed, curvy, cycle, orbed, orbit, pivot, plump, pudgy, route, salvo, semis, stage, steak, tubby, wheel, whirl, whole 6 arched, around, chubby, coiled, course, curled, curved, curvey, entire, finals, looped, nearly, refine, rotund, series, sphere 7 bulbous, circuit, concave, globule, gunshot, orotund 8 circular, disklike, division, globular, outburst, ringlike, roly-poly, schedule, sequence 9 discharge, egg-shaped, filled-out, globelike, spherical 10 abdominous, ball-shaped, curvaceous, disk-shaped, elliptical, pear-shaped, revolution, succession
ender: 4 bell, worm 5 about, house
not perfectly ~: 4 oval 5 ovoid 8 elliptic 10 elliptical
off: 3 cap, end, top 6 beef up, finish 7 augment, touch up 8 conclude, estimate, finalize 9 culminate
out: 3 cap, end 5 close, swell 6 fatten, fill in, finish, refine, top off 7 perfect 8 complete, conclude, finalize 9 culminate, terminate 10 complement, supplement
prefix: 4 peri- 6 circum-
rally ~: 4 back, help 5 boost, favor 6 assist, defend 7 bolster, endorse, promote, pull for, stand by, stick by 8 champion, side with 9 encourage, get behind 10 go to bat for, stand up for, stick up for
robin: 4 plea 6 series 7 tourney
8 petition 10 conference, tournament
starter: 4 bell
table: 5 forum 6 parley, powwow 9 symposium 10 conference
thing: 3 orb 4 ball 5 globe 6 circle, sphere
trip: 4 tour 5 jaunt 6 junket, travel 7 circuit, journey 9 excursion
up: 4 bead, cull, herd, raid 5 amass, drive, group, rally, snare 6 arrest, corral, gather, muster, rake in 7 capture, cluster, collect, convene, convoke, marshal, recruit, wrangle 8 assemble 10 accumulate, congregate

round ___: 3 lot, off, out 4 file, hand, trip, turn 5 robin, steak, table

___ round: 3 top 4 come 5 bring 6 bottom

___-round: 3 all 4 year 5 out-of

roundabout: 5 wordy 6 outing 7 devious, evasive, oblique, winding 8 indirect, tortuous 10 circuitous, collateral
not ~: 5 blunt, clear, frank, plain 6 candid, direct, head-on 7 express, precise 8 explicit, straight 10 forthright, point-blank, to the point
way: 6 detour

Roundabout (1972 song)
artist: Yes

Round and Round (song)
artist: Perry Como, Ratt

___-Round-a-Rosie...: 5 Ring-a

roundball
see basketball

round-bellied: 5 obese, plump, pudgy, tubby 6 chubby, portly, rotund 7 paunchy 9 corpulent 10 abdominous

rounded: 4 full, oval 5 blunt, lobar, lobed, orbed 6 convex, obtuse 7 bulbous, shapely 8 globular 9 spherical
protuberance: 4 knop

___-rounded: 4 well

rounders: 5 sport

Rounders (1998 film)
cast: Matt Damon, Gretchen Mol, Edward Norton, John Turturro

round hill, name meaning: 6 Gordon

roundhouse: 5 punch 8 uppercut

roundish: 4 oval 5 ovate, ovoid 8 elliptic 9 egg-shaped 10 elliptical

round of ___: 4 beef, golf

rounds: 4 ammo, beat, tour 5 route 6 patrol 10 ammunition
go a few ~: 3 box 4 spar 5 fight
make the ~: 3 mix 4 walk 5 watch 6 hobnob, mingle, patrol, police 7 inspect 9 socialize

Rounds for Squares
composer: PDQ Bach

Round Table
adventure: 5 quest
member: 3 Kay, Tor 4 Bors, Eric 5 Driam, Ector, Floll, Lucan, Yvain, Ywain 6 Ewaine, Gareth, Gawain, Hector, knight 7 Galahad, Mordred, Pelleas, Tristan 8 Lancelot, Percival, Tristram
quest: 5 Grail 9 Holy Grail
title: 3 sir

...Round the ___ Oak Tree: 3 Ole

round-the-clock: 6 steady 7 nonstop 8 constant, unending 9 ceaseless, incessant 10 continuous, relentless

___ Round the Mountain: 5 Comin'

Roundtree, Richard: 5 actor
film: Shaft (1971)
Shaft in Africa (1973)
Shaft's Big Score! (1972)

roundup: 4 herd 5 drive 6 muster 7 summary 9 gathering
group: 4 herd 6 beeves, cattle, strays
need: 4 prod 5 brand, lasso 6 herder
site: 5 range

Roundup: 3 car 4 auto 5 Edsel 10 automobile

Round up the ___ suspects: 5 usual

roundworm: 4 nema

roup: 9 huskiness 10 hoarseness

roupy: 5 husky, raspy 6 hoarse 7 grating, rasping 8 gravelly, scratchy

Rourke, Mickey: 5 actor
film: Animal Factory (2000)
Barfly (1987)
Diner (1982)
The Pope of Greenwich Village (1984)
Rumble Fish (1983)
White Sands (1992)
The Wrestler (2008)

rouse: 4 call, fire, goad, move, poke, prod, rile, spur, stir, wake, whet 5 awake, drive, get up, hop up, liven, pique, rally, start, tempt, waken 6 awaken, bestir, buck up, excite, fire up, foment, incite, kindle, recall, revive, stir up, thrill, vivify, wake up, work up 7 actuate, agitate, animate, disturb, enflame, enliven, ferment, fortify, freshen, hearten, inflame, inspire, provoke, quicken, startle, trigger 8 activate, embolden, engender, enkindle, enspirit, get going, heighten, imbolden, inspirit, interest, motivate, psyche up, summon up 9 electrify, encourage, enhearten, galvanize, impassion, influence, instigate, recollect, stimulate 10 exhilarate, intoxicate, invigorate

roused: 5 astir, awake 8 up in arms 9 wrought up

___-rouser: 6 rabble

Roush, Edd: 3 Red 10 outfielder

rousing: 5 brisk 6 lively 7 bracing, dashing 8 animated, spirited, vigorous 9 energetic, thrilling 10 fortifying, impressive

Rousseau and Revolution
author: Will Durant

Rousseau, Jean Jacques: 6 French, writer 11 philosopher
work: Confessions
Émile
The Social Contract

roust: 4 stir 5 waken 6 awaken, stir up 7 disturb, drag out, kick out, provoke, shake up, yank out 8 drive out
ender: 5 about
(from): 5 drive, heave

roustabout: 4 hand 7 laborer

rout: 3 zap 4 beat, best, bury, do in, drub, lick, stir, whip 5 cream, crush, eject, expel, score, skunk, swamp, total, trash, upset, whomp, worst 6 defeat, dispel, finish, legion, thrash, wallop 7 beating, clobber, conquer, debacle, failure, overrun, pasting, ransack, repulse, retreat, rummage, scatter, shutout, torpedo, trounce, washout, wipeout 8 conquest, disaster, drive off, drive out, drubbing, gouge out, stampede, vanquish, walkover 9 chase away, landslide, overpower, overthrow, overwhelm, slaughter, thrashing, trouncing 10 demoralize
out: 4 find 5 dig up, purge 7 uncover, unearth 8 discover

route: 3 run, way 4 beat, lane, line, path, pike, road, send, ship 5 byway, guide, means, round, steer, steps, track, trail 6 access, artery, avenue, byroad, course, detour, direct, rounds, street 7 address, beeline, channel, circuit, consign, forward, freeway, heading, highway, ingress, parkway, passage, roadway 8 dispatch, shepherd, short cut, transmit, turnpike 9 boulevard, direction, itinerary 10 Interstate, throughway
alternate ~: 6 bypass, detour
direct ~: 7 beeline
en ~: 6 aboard, coming, midway 7 driving 8 embarked, motoring, on the way 9 advancing, in transit, on the road, traveling
en ~ in a way: 4 asea 5 at sea
go the ~: 6 finish 9 culminate
in Latin: 3 via
in Spanish: 3 vía
jet ~: 3 arc 4 lane 6 airway, flyway, skyway 7 airlane
narrow ~: 6 strait
ocean ~: 4 lane 6 seaway 7 passage, sea lane
recommender: 3 AAA 8 Auto Club
secondary ~: 4 lane 6 byroad

___ route: 3 air 4 star 5 rural, trade

Route 66 (CBS adventure)
cast: George Maharis (Buz Murdock)
Martin Milner (Tod Stiles)

router: 4 tool

Routh: 7 Brandon

routine: 3 act, job, rut, way 4 dull, rote, rule, tack, tame, wont 5 cycle, daily, drill, grind, habit, ho-hum, order, spiel, stock, trite, typic, usage, usual 6 boring, common, custom, groove, method, normal, system, tedium, wonted 7 formula, general, generic, humdrum, mundane, process, prosaic, regular, schtick, tedious, typical, workout 8 everyday, familiar, frequent, habitual, habitude, monotony, ordinary, orthodox, periodic, practice, pretense, standard, workaday 9 customary, generical, procedure, prosaical, quotidian, technique, treadmill, unvarying 10 accustomed, daily grind, dullsville, mechanical, prevailing, uneventful, widespread
dull ~: 3 rut 4 rote 5 chore, grind
fixed ~: 7 rat race 8 monotony 9 treadmill

routine-bound: 6 in a rut

routinely: 5 often 7 as a rule, usually 8 commonly, normally 9 generally, in general, in the main, regularly 10 by and large, frequently, habitually, ordinarily
rove: 3 gad 4 roam, trek, walk 5 amble, drift, prowl, range, stray, tramp 6 ramble, travel, wander 7 explore, journey, maunder, meander, migrate, saunter 8 ambulate, gad about, nomadize, straggle, traverse 9 bum around, gallivant, itinerate, run around 10 hit the road, knock about
Rove: 4 Karl
rover: 5 gypsy, nomad 6 roamer 7 drifter, pilgrim, rambler, voyager 8 fugitive, gadabout, runagate, traveler, vagabond, wanderer, wayfarer 9 itinerant, journeyer, meanderer, sojourner, transient 10 adventurer
sea ~: 6 pirate 7 corsair 8 freeboot 9 buccaneer 10 freebooter
__ rover: 3 red, sea 5 lunar
Rover: 3 dog 5 pooch 6 canine
doc: 3 DVM, vet
friend: 4 Fido, Spot
remark: 3 arf 4 bark, woof 6 bowwow
Rover __: 3 Boy
__ Rovers: 4 Wild 5 Irish
roving: 6 errant, ramble 7 erratic, migrant, nomadic 8 rootless, vagabond 9 itinerant, migratory, wayfaring
row: 4 feud, file, fray, fuss, line, pull, rank, riot, spat, stir, tier, tiff, to-do 5 aisle, brawl, chain, clash, fight, furor, melee, mix-up, noise, queue, range, run-in, scene, scrap, scull, set-to, storm, train, words 6 affray, barney, blowup, clamor, column, dustup, fracas, frenzy, furrow, hassle, kickup, lineup, racket, rebuke, ruckus, rumpus, scrape, series, string, tumult, uproar 7 contest, dispute, ferment, quarrel, scuffle, trouble, wrangle 8 argument, ballyhoo, brouhaha, catfight, conflict, sequence, skirmish, squabble, struggle 9 altercate, commotion, hue and cry, imbroglio 10 difference, donnybrook, falling-out, free-for-all, hullabaloo, succession
ender: 4 boat, lock
in a ~: 6 alined, linear, unbent 7 aligned, lined up, unbowed 8 straight 10 single-file, unswerving
kick up a ~: 5 anger 6 burn up, fire up, madden, offend 7 incense 9 infuriate, instigate
long ~ to hoe: 4 task, toil 5 chore, grind, labor 6 burden 8 headache
put in a ~: 4 even 5 align, aline, array, order 10 straighten
starter: 4 corn, shed, wind 5 fence, hedge
row __: 5 house
__ row: 3 in a 4 home, skid, tone
__ Row: 4 Park, Skid 5 Kings 6 Savile 7 Cannery
rowan: 3 ash 4 tree
fruit: 4 sorb
Rowan: 3 Dan 4 Carl 8 Atkinson
Rowan and Martin's Laugh-In (NBC comedy)
cast: Ruth Buzzi
Judy Carne
Henry Gibson
Goldie Hawn
Arte Johnson
Dick Martin
Gary Owens
Dan Rowan
Alan Sues
Jo Anne Worley
rowboat: 3 gig 4 dory 5 scull, skiff 6 bateau, caique, dinghy, galley, vessel, wherry 7 batteau 8 inrigger
need: 3 oar
pin: 5 thole
problem: 4 leak
rowdy: 4 goon, loud, lout, punk, thug, wild 5 brute, bully, fiend, noisy, rough, tough, wooly, yahoo 6 heller, hoiden, hoyden, mugger, rascal, unruly, vandal, woolly 7 brawler, brutish, hellion, hoodlum, lawless, naughty, raucous, roguish, ruffian 8 hooligan 9 miscreant, out of hand, reprobate, roughneck, scoundrel, turbulent 10 boisterous, disorderly, hopping mad, tumultuous, unpeaceful, vociferant
be ~: 5 act up
rowdydow: 3 ado 4 flap, to-do 5 melee 6 hubbub 10 hullabaloo
rowed combining form: 8 -stichous
Rowe, Nicholas: 4 poet 7 British
rower: 3 oar 5 racer 7 oarsman, sculler
craft: 5 canoe, kayak, skiff
foremost ~: 6 bow oar
rowing: 5 sport
muscles used in ~: 5 delts
team: 4 crew 5 eight, octad
team member: 3 oar
Rowland: 3 Roy 4 Hill 5 Evans 8 Sherwood
Rowlands, Gena: 7 actress
son: Nick Cassavetes
spouse: John Cassavetes
Rowley, William: 7 British 10 playwright
work: The Changeling
Rowlf of the Muppets: 3 dog
Rowling, J.K.: 6 writer 7 British
honour: 3 OBE
Row, Row, Row Your Boat: 5 round
end: 6 a dream
rows
combining form: 5 -stich
series of ~: 4 bank, tier 5 level 7 section, stratum
Rowse, A.L.: 4 poet 7 British
__ row to hoe: 4 hard, long
Roxana: 3 Zal
Roxane
lover: 6 Cyrano
Roxann __-Dawson: 5 Biggs
Roxanne: 4 Hart
Roxanne (1979 song)
artist: Police
Roxanne (1987 film)
cast: Shelley Duvall, Daryl Hannah, Steve Martin
Roxette
members: Fredriksson, Gessle
song: Dangerous (1990)
Dressed for Success (1989)
Fading Like a Flower (1991)
It Must Have Been Love (1990)
Joyride (1991)
Listen to Your Heart (1989)
The Look (1989)
Roxie: 4 Hart 5 Roker
Roxy Music co-founder: 3 Eno
Roy: 4 Bean, Cohn, Head 5 Acuff, Clark, Innis 6 Disney, Fuller, London, Rogers 7 Del Ruth, Emerson, Huggins, Orbison, Rowland, Thinnes, Wilkins 8 Boulting, Eldridge, Hamilton, Scheider 9 Firestone, Gabrielle 10 Campanella
royal: 4 blue, fern, king, palm, sail 5 grand, lofty, noble, regal, ruler 6 august, gerent, kingly, lordly, superb 7 courtly, exalted, queenly, stately, supreme, viceroy 8 dynastic, high-born, highbred, imperial, imposing, kinglike, majestic, princely, splendid 9 patrician, sovereign 10 autocratic, majestical
address: 4 sire
battle ~: 4 to-do 5 brawl, clash, fight, run-in, set-to 6 affray, dustup, fracas, ruckus, rumpus, tangle 7 quarrel, rhubarb, ruction, wrangle 8 brouhaha 9 imbroglio
command: 4 fiat 5 edict 6 decree
ender: 3 ist 4 mast
fur: 6 ermine
headgear: 5 crown, tiara 7 coronet
home: 6 castle, palace
letters: 3 HIH, HRH, HSH
part of a ~ flush: 3 ace, ten 4 jack, king 5 queen
starter: 5 penny
symbol: 3 orb
royal __: 4 blue, fern, fizz, lily, mast, palm, road 5 flush, jelly 6 family, purple
__ royal: 6 battle, prince
Royal: 3 car 4 auto, Dano 5 Dodge 8 Chrysler 10 automobile
Hall-of-Famer: 5 Brett
Royal __: 3 Oak 4 Anne 5 Flash, Teens 7 Academy, Society, Wedding
Royal __ Hall: 6 Albert
Royal __, MI: 3 Oak
Royal Ascot time: 4 June
Royal, Billy Joe
song: Down in the Boondocks (1965)
Royal Crown: 3 pop 4 cola, soda 9 soft drink
alternative: ***see*** soft drink
__ royale: 4 café
Royale: 3 car, Reo 4 auto, Olds 10 automobile, Oldsmobile
__ Royale: 6 Casino
__ Royale, MI: 4 Isle
__ Royale National Park: 4 Isle
Royal Family, The
author: Edna Ferber
Royal Firewater Musick
composer: PDQ Bach
Royal Guardsmen
song: Snoopy vs. the Red Baron (1966)
__ Royal Highness: 3 Her, His
Royal Hunt of the Sun, The
author: Peter Shaffer
royal jelly producer: 3 bee
Royals: 3 ten 4 team
home: 10 Kansas City
org.: 3 ALC, MLB
rival: ***see*** baseball team
sport: 8 baseball
Royal Teens
song: Short Shorts (1958)
Royal Tenenbaums, The (2001 film)
cast: Gene Hackman, Anjelica Huston, Gwyneth Paltrow, Ben Stiller
royalties: 6 income 8 earnings, proceeds, receipts
org.: 3 BMI 5 ASCAP
royalty: 5 crown, lords, noble 6 income 8 kingship, nobility, receipts
receiver: 6 author, singer 8 composer
Royal Wedding (1951 film)
cast: Fred Astaire, Peter Lawford, Jane Powell
director: Stanley Donen
Royce, Josiah: 6 writer 8 essayist 11 philosopher
Roy G. __: 3 Biv
Roy, Gabrielle: 6 writer 8 Canadian
work: The Tin Flute
Roy G. Biv part: 3 hue, red 4 blue 5 color 6 indigo, orange, violet, yellow
__ Roy Hill: 6 George
Royko: 4 Mike
Roz: 4 Ryan 5 Chast
Rozanov, Vasily: 6 writer 7 Russian
Rozelle: 4 Pete
Różewicz, Tadeusz: 4 poet 6 Polish 10 playwright
RPI: 6 school
locale: 4 Troy 7 New York
part of ~: 4 Inst., Poly
rival: 3 MIT
RPM
indicator: 4 tach
part of ~: 3 min., per, rev. 6 minute
step up the ~s: 3 gun, rev 4 race
RPS part: 3 Per, Rev., Sec. 6 Second
RR
driver: 4 engr.
info: 3 ETA, ETD
mail place: 3 RPO
sign abbreviation: 4 xing
stop: 3 dep., sta., stn.
see also railroad, train
R&R: 5 leave 7 time off 8 furlough, vacation
locale: 3 USO
part of ~: 4 rest 10 recreation
R-rated
like some ~ movies: 4 gory
or higher: 5 adult
R's
have trouble saying ~: 4 lall
three ~ org.: 3 AFT, NEA, UFT
RSVP: 3 ans. 5 reply 6 answer
insert: 4 card, encl. 7 SASE. SAE
part: 3 s'il 4 vous 5 plaît 8 répondez
RSV, part of: 3 Rev., Ver. 7 Revised, Version 8 Standard
RSX: 3 car 4 auto 5 Acura 10 automobile
Rt. __: 3 Hon., Rev.
rte.: 2 av., st. 3 ave., hwy., tpk. 4 hgwy., tnpk. 9 itinerary
where ~ s meet: 3 jct.
see also route

rt.-hand man: **2** lt. **3** ADC **4** asst.
RT quarry: **2** QB
rt. to left: **3** ccw
Ru: **4** elem. **7** element **9** ruthenium
44 for ~: **4** at. no.
Ruanda-__: **6** Urundi
Ruark: **6** Robert
rub: **3** mop, pat **4** bark, buff, fray, lick, rasp, snag, wear, wipe **5** apply, brush, catch, chafe, erase, gloss, grate, graze, grind, hitch, knead, scour, scrub, shine, smear, touch **6** abrade, caress, hangup, hurdle, polish, scrape, smooth, spread, stroke **7** burnish, dilemma, massage, problem, scratch **8** drawback, friction, irritate, levigate, obstacle **9** annoyance, hindrance, tight spot **10** difficulty, impediment
clean: **4** wipe **5** erase **6** delete, efface **7** expunge, wipe off **10** obliterate
down: **4** file, wear **5** erode **6** abrade **7** massage
elbows: **3** mix **6** hobnob, mingle **9** socialize **10** fraternize
ender: **3** off, out **4** down
in: **6** harp on, repeat, stress **7** belabor, iterate **9** emphasize, reiterate
it in: **4** crow **5** gloat **7** swagger
off: **5** erase **6** delete **7** blot out, expunge, wipe out **9** eradicate **10** obliterate
on: **3** dab **4** coat **5** apply, cover, smear **6** spread
the wrong way: **3** get, ire, irk, vex **4** fret, gall, miff, rack, rile, roil **5** annoy, chafe, grate, harry, hound, peeve **6** abrade, harass, nettle, offend, pester, pick on, plague, rankle **7** afflict, agonize, anguish, bedevil, oppress, torment, torture **8** aggrieve, distress, irritate **9** persecute
rub __: **3** out **4** down, it in
rub __ with: **6** elbows
rub-a-dub-dub craft: **3** tub
Rubáiyát, The: **4** poem
author: Omar Khayyám
word: **4** enow
rubbed
be ~ wrong way: **4** mind **8** object to
rubber: **3** ule **4** shoe, tree **6** balata, caucho, eraser, galosh, golosh, lissom **7** galoshe, lissome **8** footwear, overshoe
burn ~: **3** hie, zip **4** bolt, dash, rush, zoom **5** hurry, speed **6** barrel, career, hasten, hustle, scurry **8** step on it **9** hotfoot it, make haste, shake a leg **10** accelerate
city: **5** Akron
ender: **4** neck
product: **4** ball, tire **6** eraser, gasket
synthetic ~: **4** buna **5** latex **8** neoprene
tire ~: **5** tread
tree: **3** ule **7** seringa
tree mover of song: **3** ant
rubber __: **4** ball, band, game, tree **5** check, match, plant, stamp **6** cement
rubber-__: **5** faced
rubber-__ circuit: **7** chicken
__ rubber: **4** burn, foam **5** India
Rubber Ball (1960 song)
artist: Bobby Vee
Rubberband Man, The (1976 song)
artist: Spinners
Rubber Duckie
singer: **5** Ernie
rubber-duck owner: **6** bather
rubberized canvas: **4** tarp
rubberneck: **3** eye **4** gawk, gaze, look, ogle, peer, view **5** ogler, stare, watch **6** gawker **7** witness **8** busybody **9** spectator
rubber stamp: **2** OK **4** okay, sign **6** accept, affirm, ratify **7** certify **8** validate
partner: **6** inkpad
word: **4** paid, void **8** received
rubber tree
mover of song: **3** ant
rubbery: **5** mushy **6** bouncy, limber, spongy, supple **7** elastic, pliable **8** flexible **9** resilient
Rubbia, Carlo: **8** Nobelist **9** physicist
rubbing: **7** massage **8** abrasion, friction
liquid: **3** alc. **7** alcohol
out: **7** erasure
the wrong way: **5** nasty **7** caustic, galling **8** abrasive, annoying **10** irritating, unpleasant
rubbing __: **7** alcohol
rubbish: **4** junk **5** chaff, dregs, dross, offal, scrap, swill, waste **6** debris, grunge, litter, refuse, rubble, shards **7** baloney, garbage **8** leavings **9** sweepings
pile: **4** dump, heap **7** ash heap **8** junkyard, landfill
see also baloney
rubble: **4** rock **5** ruins, trash, waste **6** debris **7** garbage, rubbish
reduced to ~: **7** in ruins
reduce to ~: **8** demolish
Rubble: **5** Betty **6** Barney
rubdown, require a: **4** ache
rube: **3** oaf **4** clod, hick **5** looby, yahoo, yokel **6** gaffer, rustic **7** bumpkin, hayseed **9** hillbilly
__ rube: **3** hey
Rube: **6** Foster **7** Waddell **8** Goldberg, Marquard
rubellite: **3** gem **8** gemstone
Ruben: **5** Dario **6** Blades, Joseph, Sierra
Rubenesque: **5** buxom
Rubens, Peter Paul: **6** artist **7** painter
homeland: **8** Flanders
subject: **4** nude
rubescent: **3** red
Rubicon: **5** river
crosser: **6** Caesar
land across the ~: **4** Gaul
locale: **5** Italy
rubicund: **3** red **4** rosy **5** ruddy **6** blowsy, blowzy, florid **7** blowsed, blowzed, flushed, reddish **8** reddened **9** rufescent
relative: ***see*** red color
rubidium: **5** metal **7** element
rubify: **6** redden
Rubik: **4** Erno
Rubik's Cube: **4** game **5** craze **6** puzzle
Rubinstein: **3** Ida **5** Anton, Artur **6** Arthur, Helena
rival: **4** Avon **5** Almay **6** Lauder **7** Mary Kay
Rubinstein, Anton: **7** pianist, Russian
Rubinstein, Artur: **6** Polish **7** pianist
birthplace: **4** Lodz
ruble: **5** money
fraction: **5** kopek **6** copeck, kopeck
locale: **6** Russia
rub one's __ in: **4** nose
rub one's __ of: **5** hands
rubric: **5** title **6** legend, redden
rubricate: **6** redden
rub the __ way: **5** wrong
ruby: **3** gem, red **5** color, jewel **6** redden **7** carmine, crimson, mineral **8** corundum, gemstone **9** vermilion
alternative: ***see*** point size
month: **4** July
relative: ***see*** red color
synthetic ~: **5** boule
Ruby: **3** Dee **5** Harry **6** Keeler
spouse: **5** Ossie
Ruby __: **4** Baby **7** Tuesday
Ruby and the Romantics
song: Our Day Will Come (1963)
Ruby Baby (1962 song)
artist: Dion
Ruby, Don't Take Your Love to Town (1969 song)
artist: Kenny Rogers
Ruby, Harry: **8** composer
collaborator: **6** Kalmar
song: Ev'ryone Says I Love You
Hooray for Captain Spaulding
I Wanna Be Loved by You
Nevertheless
Three Little Words
Who's Sorry Now
Ruby Tuesday
rival: ***see*** restaurant chain
Ruby Tuesday (1967 song)
artist: Rolling Stones
ruche: **4** fold, lace, trim **6** ruffle
ruck: **4** fold, mass **5** ridge **6** crease, pucker **7** wrinkle **9** hoi polloi
ender: **4** sack
up: **4** muss **6** rumple **7** crumple **8** dishevel
Ruck: **4** Alan
__ Rucker, AL: **4** Fort
rucksack: **3** bag **4** pack **5** pouch **6** kitbag **8** backpack
ruckus: **3** ado, din, row **4** flap, fray, fuss, riot, stir, to-do **5** brawl, furor, hoo-ha, melee **6** clamor, frenzy, hoo-hah, hoopla, hubbub, pother, uproar **7** quarrel, rampage, scuffle, wrangle **8** argument, brouhaha, conflict, disorder, friction **9** commotion **10** hullabaloo
ruction: **4** riot, to-do **5** melee **6** fracas, frenzy, hubbub, racket, tumult, uproar **7** wrangle **8** skirmish **10** free-for-all, hullabaloo
ructious: **7** hawkish, hostile, martial, warlike **8** militant **9** bellicose, combative **10** aggressive, pugnacious
Rudd: **4** Paul **6** Hughes
rudder: **4** helm **5** blade **7** control
ender: **4** fish, post **5** stock
locale: **3** aft **5** stern **6** astern
support: **4** skeg
toward the ~: **3** aft **5** abaft **6** astern **8** rearward
use the ~: **5** pilot, steer **6** direct **8** maneuver, navigate
rudderless: **8** unguided
Ruddigore
composer: Arthur Sullivan, W.S. Gilbert
ruddiness: **5** blush, flush
ruddle: **3** ore **6** redden
ruddy: **3** red **4** duck, pink, rosy **5** fresh **6** blowsy, blowzy, florid, redden **7** blowsed, blowzed, bronzed, crimson, flushed, glowing, reddish, scarlet **8** blooming, blushing, reddened, red-faced, rubicund, sanguine **9** rufescent
not ~: **3** wan **4** ashy, pale **5** ashen
rude: **3** raw **4** bold, curt, flip, loud, mean, pert, wild **5** bawdy, blunt, brash, brusk, crass, crude, fresh, gross, gruff, harsh, nervy, pushy, rough, sassy, saucy, sharp, short, surly **6** abrupt, awless, brassy, brazen, cheeky, coarse, hoiden, hoyden, incult, rustic, savage, simple, snippy, vulgar **7** abusive, aweless, boorish, brusque, crabbed, forward, ill-bred, loutish, lowbred, offhand, selfish, uncivil, uncouth **8** assuming, churlish, flippant, heedless, impolite, impudent, indecent, insolent, inurbane, liverish, plebeian, snippety, tactless, unseemly, unsubtle **9** audacious, backwater, difficult, graceless, insulting, makeshift, obnoxious, offensive, officious, out of line, primitive, roughhewn, shameless, tasteless, truculent, ungallant, unrefined **10** indecorous, indelicate, peremptory, provincial, regardless, uncultured, ungracious, unmannerly, unthinking
be ~ to: **3** dis **6** insult
comment: **3** dig **4** barb, slam, slap, slur **5** crack, taunt **6** insult **7** affront, offense
look: **4** leer **5** sneer, stare
not ~: **4** kind, nice **6** genial, kindly, polite, proper **7** affable, amiable, cordial, likable, refined **8** charming, cultured, decorous, friendly, gracious, pleasant, pleasing, polished **9** civilized, courteous, exemplary, simpatico **10** fastidious, personable, scrupulous
one: **3** cad **4** boor, bozo, lout **5** churl
Rudel, Julius: **9** conductor
rudeness: **3** lip **4** sass **5** brass, cheek, mouth, nerve **6** insult **8** acerbity, acrimony, audacity, temerity **9** impudence, indecorum **10** disrespect, effrontery, indelicacy, inurbanity, misconduct, unkindness
reaction to ~: **4** slap
Rudge: **7** Barnaby
Rudi: **3** Joe **9** Gernreich
rudiment: **4** germ, seed **5** basis **6** embryo **9** principle
rudimentary: **5** basic, crude, early, prime, rough **6** coarse, larval, latent, simple **7** initial, primary **8** immature, original **9** beginning, elemental, embryonic, inelegant, makeshift, primitive, unrefined, vestigial **10** amateurish, unpolished
life: **4** germ, seed **5** virus **6** embryo

7 microbe 8 pathogen 9 bacterium
prefix: 3 pro-
rudiments: 4 ABCs 6 basics
Rudner, Rita: 5 comic 8 comedian
Rudolf: 3 Max 4 Abel, Bing, Hess, lake 5 Friml 6 Diesel, Eucken 7 Nureyev, Steiner 9 Mössbauer
locale: 5 Kenya
Rudolf, Max: 9 conductor
Rudolph: 4 Alan, Mate 5 Dirks, Isley, Wilma 6 Marcus 8 Giuliani 9 Valentino
costar: 4 Lila
in Italian: 7 Rodolfo
in Spanish: 7 Rodolfo
master: 5 Santa
Rudolph the __-Nosed Reindeer: 3 Red
Rudolph, Wilma: 6 runner 8 sprinter
Rudy: 4 Maté 5 Wiebe 6 Gatlin, Solari, Vallee 8 Giuliani, Huxtable
Rudy (1993 film)
cast: Sean Astin, Ned Beatty
Rudyard: 7 Kipling
rue: 4 herb 5 grief, mourn 6 bemoan, bewail, grieve, lament, qualms, regret, repent 7 deplore, remorse 8 repent of 10 contrition
family shrub: 7 skimmia 9 jaborandi
Rue: 10 McClanahan
costar: 3 Bea 5 Betty 7 Estelle
Rue de __: 6 la Paix, Rivoli
rueful: 3 sad, wry 7 doleful 8 penitent 9 miserable, regretful 10 apologetic, lamentable, lugubrious, remorseful
sigh: 4 ah me
ruefulness: 4 pity 6 regret 7 remorse 9 penitence
Ruehl, Mercedes: 7 actress
film: The Fisher King (1991, AA)
Lost in Yonkers (1993)
Married to the Mob (1988)
Rue Morgue
creator: Edgar Allan Poe
culprit: 3 ape
__ Rue My Heart Is Laden: 4 With
ruer: 6 atoner
like a ~: 5 sorry 8 contrite, penitent 9 regretful, repentant 10 apologetic, remorseful
word: 4 alas
rue the __: 3 day
rufescent: 5 ruddy 8 rubicund
ruff: 4 bird, fish, mane 5 scarf 6 collar 9 sandpiper
female ~: 3 ree 5 reeve
in bridge: 5 trump
material: 4 lace
starter: 4 wood 5 cross
Ruffalo: 4 Mark
Ruff and Reddy: 5 toons 7 cartoon
cat: 4 Ruff
dog: 5 Reddy
ruffian: 4 goon, hood, punk, thug 5 brute, bully, knave, rowdy, scamp, tough, yahoo 6 apache, bad guy, goonda, heller, mauler, rascal 7 brigand, hoodlum 8 gangster, hooligan, plugugly, tough guy 9 miscreant, roughneck, scoundrel
Ruffin: 5 David, Jimmy
Ruffing, Red: 6 hurler, Yankee 7 pitcher
ruffle: 3 irk, vex 4 faze, fret, gall, miff, muss, roil, tuck, wave 5 abash, anger, annoy, chafe, frill, jabot, peeve, pique, plait, pleat, ruche, shake, tease, upset 6 bother, crease, excite, flurry, harass, mess up, muss up, needle, nettle, noodge, pucker, ripple, rumple, tangle, tousle, touzle 7 agitate, crinkle, disturb, flounce, fluster, flutter, perturb, provoke, shake up, wrinkle 8 dishevel, froufrou, furbelow, irritate, unsettle 9 corrugate, discomfit 10 disarrange, discompose, disconcert, intimidate
feathers: 3 irk, vex 5 annoy, peeve 6 bother, nettle 8 irritate
ruffled: 5 irate, rough, upset 6 shaggy 7 nervous, tousled 9 turbulent
Ruffles feature: 5 ridge
rufous: 7 reddish
Rufus: 6 Sewell, Thomas
Rufus T. __: 7 Firefly
rug: 3 rya, wig 4 shag 5 kilim, Saruk 6 Berber, carpet, kaross, Kirman, runner, Sarouk, Saxony, toupee 8 bearskin 9 broadloom, carpeting, hairpiece
cleaner: 3 vac 6 beater, vacuum
color variation: 6 abrash
coverage: 4 area
cut a ~: 5 dance
exporter: 4 Iran
fabric: 5 frise, nylon
feature: 3 nap 4 pile
fiber: 5 sisal
knot: 5 sehna
like a bug in a ~: 4 snug
like some ~s: 4 oval
make a ~: 5 weave
Persian ~: 5 kilim 6 Kirman
rat: 3 kid, tot 4 babe, baby 6 infant
Scandinavian ~: 3 rya
wear a hole in the ~: 4 pace
__ rug: 3 rag 4 area, cut a 5 grass, throw 6 hooked, prayer, Wilton 7 Bokhara, Bukhara, Kashmir, Persian, scatter, Turkish 8 Cashmere
ruga: 5 ridge 7 wrinkle
rugby: 5 shirt, sport
formation: 5 scrum 9 scrummage
kick: 4 punt
position: 4 back, wing 6 centre, hooker 7 flanker, forward
score: 3 try
Rugby: 4 city, town
locale: 7 England
Rugby __: 5 shirt 6 jersey
rugged: 3 big, fit 4 hale, hard, iron, wild, wiry, worn 5 beefy, bumpy, burly, hardy, harsh, hefty, hilly, hunky, husky, lusty, ridgy, rocky, rough, solid, sound, stony, stout, tough, wooly 6 brawny, craggy, hearty, jagged, mighty, potent, ragged, robust, savage, severe, shaggy, sinewy, steely, sticky, stocky, stoney, strong, sturdy, taxing, trying, uneven, virile, woolly 7 arduous, cragged, doughty, unlevel 8 athletic, forceful, furrowed, heavyset, indurate, leathery, muscular, no picnic, powerful, puissant, rigorous, rocklike, stalwart, vigorous, well-made, wrinkled 9 Atlantean, demanding, difficult, energetic, heavy-duty, Herculean, inclement, irregular, roughhewn, strapping, strenuous, weathered, well-built 10 able-bodied, formidable, red-blooded, reinforced
rock: 3 tor
ruggedness: 5 brawn, force, might, power, vigor 6 muscle 7 stamina 8 strength 9 fortitude, puissance
Ruggles: 6 Wesley 7 Charles, Charlie
Rugrats kid: 3 Dil
Ruhr: 5 river 6 valley
city: 4 Hamm 5 Essen, Herne
locale: 7 Germany
ruin: 3 end, mar, sap, zap 4 bane, bust, dash, do in, doom, fall, harm, loss, maim, rase, raze, sack, sink, undo 5 blast, botch, break, crush, decay, havoc, level, queer, smash, spoil, taint, total, waste, wrack, wreck 6 beggar, blight, blow up, damage, debase, deface, defeat, finish, fleece, foul up, go sour, injure, mangle, mess up, penury, quench, ravage, ravish, reduce, topple 7 break up, butcher, consume, corrupt, debacle, debauch, degrade, despoil, destroy, disable, disrupt, failure, flatten, louse up, nemesis, pillage, pollute, scourge, screw up, scuttle, shamble, shatter, subvert, undoing, wipe out 8 bankrupt, bring low, bulldoze, calamity, clean out, cut short, decimate, demolish, desolate, disaster, dissolve, downfall, lay waste, spoilage, spoliate, straiten, take down, tear down, Waterloo, wreckage 9 bring down, cataclysm, desecrate, devastate, dismantle, knock down, overthrow, perdition, pollution, shoot down, take apart, undermine 10 annihilate, bankruptcy, corruption, desolation, disruption, extinction, impoverish, insolvency, invalidate, lead astray, obliterate, subversion
cause of ~: 4 bane 6 plague 7 scourge 8 anathema, calamity, downfall
in the kitchen: 4 char, sear 5 singe 6 scorch 9 carbonize
partner: 4 rack
rack and ~: 7 debacle 8 calamity, shambles 9 cataclysm
ruination: 3 end 4 bane, doom 5 havoc, waste 6 blight, plague 7 debacle, undoing 8 calamity, collapse, disaster, downfall 9 detriment, disrepair, nightmare, perdition 10 bankruptcy
ruined: 4 lost, shot, sunk, worn 5 broke, kaput 6 doomed, fallen, shabby, undone 7 injured, worn-out 8 bankrupt, ill-fated, in pieces 9 insolvent, penniless 10 irremedial
be ~: 4 bust, fail 7 founder 8 collapse
ruinous: 3 bad, ill 4 dire 5 fatal, sorry, toxic 6 costly, deadly, malign, shabby, tragic 7 adverse, baleful, baneful, fateful, harmful 8 damaging, luckless, negative, tragical, wasteful 9 dangerous, ill-omened, injurious, murderous, pestilent 10 calamitous, disastrous, immoderate, pernicious, shattering
ruins: 5 ashes, shell 6 debris, relics, rubble 7 remains 8 landmark, remnants, wreckage
fall into ~: 5 decay 7 crumble 8 collapse
in ~: 5 kaput 6 undone 9 destroyed 10 devastated
__ Ruins National Monument: 5 Aztec
Ruiz: 4 Juan
Rukeyser: 5 Louis 6 Muriel
rule: 3 law, reg., run 4 code, find, head, lead, line, mode, no-no, norm, sway, wont 5 axiom, bylaw, canon, edict, gnome, judge, maxim, model, moral, order, power, reign, stick, tenet, usage 6 assize, custom, decide, decree, dictum, direct, empire, govern, manage, ordain, policy, regime, ruling, settle, system, truism 7 command, conduct, control, dictate, dynasty, formula, measure, oppress, precept, preside, prevail, resolve, routine, statute, theorem 8 aphorism, conclude, dominate, domineer, dominion, hegemony, hold sway, kingship, lord over, normalcy, override, practice, regulate, restrain, sentence, standard, take over 9 authority, be rampant, criterion, determine, directive, dominance, establish, guideline, influence, normality, ordinance, precedent, prescribe, principle, pronounce, reign over, supremacy, underline 10 adjudicate, administer, ascendance, ascendancy, ascendence, ascendency, domination, generality, government, leadership, observance, principium, regulation, run the show, suzerainty, take charge
against: 3 nix 4 veto 5 annul 6 revoke 8 disallow, override, overturn, set aside, turn down 10 invalidate
as a ~: 6 mostly 7 largely, usually 8 commonly, normally 9 generally, in general, in the main, most times, routinely 10 by and large, frequently, on the whole, ordinarily
combining form: 5 -archy, -cracy
ground ~: 6 policy 7 precept
mob ~: 7 anarchy 8 disorder, nihilism
out: 3 ban, bar, nix 4 tabu, veto 5 avert 6 bypass, except, forbid, ignore, reject 7 dismiss, exclude, forfend, obviate, prevent, retract, ward off 8 forefend, overlook, preclude, prohibit, stave off 9 disregard, eliminate, forestall, proscribe
the roost: 4 boss, head, lead 6 direct, manage 7 command, control
unwritten ~: 4 wont 5 usage 6 custom, policy 7 folkway 8 practice 9 etiquette, precedent 10 convention, observance
rule __: 3 out
rule __ road: 5 of the
__ rule: 3 as a, gag, mob 4 foot, home, unit 5 board, chain, house,

phase, plumb, slide **6** closed, golden, ground, Oxford, zigzag **7** caliper, Cramer's, folding, general, hearsay, sliding, special
__-rule: **4** self
Rule: **3** Ann **6** Janice
Golden ~ word: **4** unto **6** others
Rule, Britannia
composer: Thomas Arne
ruled: **4** liny **5** liney **8** governed
__ Ruled the World: **3** If I
Rule, Janice: **7** actress
spouse: Ben Gazzara
rule of __: **5** thumb
rule of the __: **4** road
ruler: **3** bey, dey, emp., oba, sov. **4** amir, boss, czar, doge, emir, khan, king, lord, raja, rani, shah, tsar, tzar **5** ameer, calif, chief, crown, emeer, kalif, mogul, nawab, pacha, pasha, queen, rajah, royal, scale, stick **6** archon, caesar, caliph, despot, dynast, exarch, gerent, kaiser, kaliph, khalif, leader, master, mikado, prince, satrap, shogun, sultan, top dog, tyrant **7** czarina, emperor, empress, headman, monarch, pharaoh, sultana, tsarina, T-square, tzarina, viceroy **8** dictator, governor, heptarch, kingfish, maharani, oligarch, overlord, princess, superior, suzerain **9** chieftain, commander, maharajah, potentate, sovereign, yardstick
absolute ~: **4** tsar **6** despot, tyrant
Arabian Nights ~: **5** calif, kalif **6** caliph, kaliph, khalif
Aztec ~: **9** Montezuma
combining form: **4** -arch, -crat **5** -ocrat
hereditary ~: **4** king
length: **4** foot
Muslim ~: **3** aga **4** agha, amir, emir **5** ameer, calif, emeer, kalif, mogul **6** caliph, kaliph, khalif
part: **4** inch
Persia ~: **6** satrap
...ruler of the Queen's __: **5** navee
rulers, interim: **5** junta
rules
break the ~: **4** defy **5** cheat, flout **7** disobey **9** disregard
government ~ to some: **6** jungle, morass **9** labyrinth
in the ~: **4** good **5** legal, legit, licit, valid **6** kosher **9** allowable, warranted **10** acceptable, admissible, legitimate
__ rules: **4** work **6** ground
Rules __ rules: **3** are
rules of __: **5** order
Rules of Engagement (2000 film)
cast: Samuel L. Jackson, Tommy Lee Jones, Ben Kingsley
__ Rules of Games: **6** Hoyle's
Rules of the Game (1939 film)
director: Jean Renoir
__ rules the gods...: **4** Love
rule the __: **5** roost
ruling: **3** law **4** main **5** chief, edict, order, ukase **6** decree, dictum **7** central, current, finding, leading, pivotal, popular, precept, rampant, regnant, supreme, verdict **8** cardinal, decision, dominant, judgment, powerful, sentence **9** directive, executive, ordinance, prevalent, principal, sovereign **10** overriding, preeminent, prevailing, resolution, widespread
body: **4** govt. **10** government
class: **5** elite, lords **7** royalty **8** nobility
ruly: **4** tame **10** manageable
rum: **5** drink, quaff, tafia **6** liquor, taffia **7** Bacardi **8** beverage **10** intoxicant
bay ~: **10** aftershave
brand: **7** Bacardi
cake: **4** baba
drink: **4** grog
ender: **6** runner
mixer: **4** Coke, cola **8** Coca-Cola
run ~: **7** bootleg, smuggle
source: **4** Cuba **7** Jamaica
__ rum: **3** bay **5** demon **7** Jamaica
Rum __ Tugger: **3** Tum
rumaki: **8** Hawaiian **9** appetizer
wrapper: **5** bacon
rumal: **5** scarf
Ruman: **3** Sig
Rum and Coca-Cola (1945 song)
artist: Andrews Sisters
Rumania
see Romania
rumba: **4** step **5** dance, music
relative: **5** mambo
Rumba King: **5** Cugat
rumble: **4** boom, fray, peal, riot, roar, roll, talk, word **5** brawl, fight, growl, melee, sound **6** frenzy, mumble, murmur, mutter, report **7** contest, ferment, grumble, resound, thunder, wrangle **8** violence **10** donnybrook
weapon: **4** shiv
rumble __: **4** seat
Rumble Fish (1983 film)
cast: Matt Dillon, Dennis Hopper, Diane Lane, Mickey Rourke
director: Francis Ford Coppola
Rumble in the Jungle: **4** bout **5** fight, match
boxer: **3** Ali **7** Foreman
site: **5** Zaire
rumbling: **5** forte, noisy **7** jarring, rackety, raucous, reboant, roaring **8** piercing, plangent, sonorous, strident, turned up **9** big-voiced, clamorous, deafening **10** boisterous, stentorian, strepitous, uproarious, vociferous
Rumer: **6** Godden
ruminant: **3** cow, elk, gnu, kob, roe **4** axis, deer, guib, kudu, oryx, pudu, puku, shou, sika, topi **5** addax, bison, bongo, bovid, camel, chiru, eland, goral, korin, llama, moose, nyala, okapi, oribi, saiga, serow, steer **6** alpaca, animal, bovine, chammy, chital, dik-dik, duiker, guemal, hangul, huemul, impala, koodoo, lechwe, nilgai, rhebok, sambar, sambur, shammy, shamoy, thamin, vicuña, wapiti **7** blaubok, blesbok, brocket, buffalo, caribou, chamois, defassa, gazelle, gemsbok, gerenuk, giraffe, grysbok, muntjac, muntjak, nylghai, nylghau, sambhar, sambhur, sassaby **8** antelope, blesbuck, bontebok, bushbuck, gemsbuck, reedbuck, reindeer, steenbok, steinbok **9** barasingh, blackbuck, pronghorn, sitatunga, springbok, waterbuck **10** hartebeest, wildebeest
chew: **3** cud
stomach: **5** rumen **6** omasum
stomachs: **5** omasa
ruminate: **4** mull, muse **5** brood, study, think, weigh **6** chew on, digest, figure, look at, ponder **7** examine, reflect, revolve, sleep on **8** chew over, cogitate, consider, look back, meditate, mull over, see about, turn over **9** reflect on, speculate, sweat over, think over **10** deliberate, introspect, toss around
over: **4** call, deem, feel, heed, mull, muse, view **5** count, judge, study, think, weigh **6** credit, debate, digest, look at, ponder, reckon, regard, take up **7** balance, believe, examine, inspect, presume, reflect, sleep on, suppose, surmise, suspect **8** allow for, cogitate, consider, deal with, envisage, look upon, meditate, see about **9** enter into, reflect on, speculate **10** reckon with, toss around, understand
ruminater: **5** muser
rumination: **5** study **7** thought **9** deduction **10** cogitation
rummage: **4** comb, fish, grub, hunt, muss, rake, root, rout, seek **5** delve, probe, rifle, scour, upset, waste **6** dig out, forage, jumble, litter, search **7** explore, ransack **8** leavings **10** poke around
sale: **5** bazar **6** bazaar
rummage __: **4** sale
Rummies
author: Peter Benchley
rummy: **3** gin **4** game **5** toper **8** card game
group: **4** meld
variety: **3** gin **4** tonk **7** canasta, cooncan **8** conquian **10** panguingue
__ rummy: **3** gin **5** knock
rumor: **3** lie, say **4** buzz, dirt, news, tale, talk, wind, word **5** bruit, on dit, story **6** canard, earful, gossip, report, tattle **7** fiction, hearsay, lowdown, scandal, whisper **9** circulate, falsehood, grapevine, invention, undertone **10** suggestion
ender: **6** monger
result, maybe: **5** panic, scare
starter: **5** I hear
rumor __: **4** mill
Rumor __...: **5** has it
Rumor __ it...: **3** has
Rumor Has It (2005 film)
cast: Jennifer Aniston, Kevin Costner, Shirley MacLaine, Mark Ruffalo
director: Rob Reiner
rumormonger: **5** yenta **7** tattler **8** quidnunc
Rumor of Angels, A (2002 film)
cast: Ray Liotta, Catherine McCormack, Vanessa Redgrave
rumors: **4** talk **5** noise **6** gossip
spread ~: **3** pan **4** blab, slam, slur, talk **5** libel, smear, sully, taint **6** defame, gossip, malign, tattle, vilify **7** asperse, slander, tarnish, traduce **8** backbite, badmouth, besmirch **9** denigrate, discredit, disparage **10** calumniate, scandalize, stigmatize, throw mud at, vituperate
Rumors
author: Neil Simon
Rumpelstiltskin: **5** troll
rumple: **4** fold, muss **5** crimp, crush **6** crease, muss up, pucker, ruck up, ruffle, tangle, tousle, touzle **7** crinkle, scrunch, wrinkle **8** dishevel, disorder **9** bedraggle
rumpled: **5** messy, mussy **6** matted, unneat, untidy **7** tousled, unkempt **10** disheveled
Rumpleteazer: **3** cat
creator: T.S. Eliot
rumpus: **3** ado, din, row **4** fray, riot, spat, tiff, to-do **5** brawl, clash, hoo-ha, melee, mix-up, scrap **6** affray, clamor, dustup, fracas, frenzy, hoo-hah, hoopla, hubbub, pother, racket, shindy, tumult, uproar **7** clatter, dispute, quarrel, rhubarb, scuffle, wrangle **8** argument, brouhaha, disorder, friction, squabble **9** commotion, encounter **10** hullabaloo
raising a ~: **5** noisy
room: **3** den
rumpus __: **4** room
rum raisin: **8** ice cream
alternative: *see* ice cream flavor
rum-running: **9** smuggling **10** contraband
run: **3** air, fly, hie, jog, own, ply, rip, use, zip **4** bolt, boss, dart, dash, flee, flit, flow, flux, gait, gush, hare, head, keep, last, leak, lift, lope, melt, move, oper., pace, pelt, pour, race, ride, rule, rush, sail, scud, shag, skim, skip, spin, step, sway, tear, ten K, thaw, tick, tide, tour, trip, trot, vary, verb, whiz, work, zoom **5** bleed, bound, carry, creek, cycle, dog it, drift, drive, elope, glide, hurry, issue, jaunt, lam it, leg it, range, round, route, scoot, scope, score, shoot, smoke, speed, spell, spill, spirt, spout, spurt, steer, stick, stump, trend **6** barrel, beat it, bustle, canter, career, course, cut out, decamp, depart, direct, escape, extend, flight, gallop, govern, handle, hasten, head up, hustle, ladder, manage, move it, ordain, outing, period, rocket, scurry, season, series, spread, sprint, streak, stream, string, whoosh **7** abscond, command, compete, conduct, contend, control, dash off, floor it, hop to it, journey, joy ride, keep fit, leak out, liquefy, liquify, make off, operate, oversee, passage, perform, preside, proceed, quicken, scamper, scuttle, skip out, skitter, stretch, take off, tear off **8** cheese it, clear out, continue, duration, function, hightail, latitude, light out, organize, politick, printing, regulate, scramble, sequence, skip town, ski slope, stampede, step on it, televise, turn tail, unfreeze **9** broadcast, excursion, flow along, get moving, go quickly, go swiftly,

hotfoot it, look after, make haste, officiate, shake a leg, skedaddle, streamlet, supervise, transport **10** administer, coordinate, get a move on, get hopping, hightail it, kiss babies, lose no time, make a break, make tracks, procession, ride herd on, shake hands, succession, take flight
across: **4** find, meet **5** hit on **7** hit upon **8** bump into, chance on, come upon **9** encounter, stumble on **10** chance upon
afoul of: **3** irk **4** rile **5** peeve
after: **3** dog, woo **4** hunt, seek, tail **5** chase, hound **6** follow, pursue, shadow **8** hunt down
a game on: **2** do **3** con **4** bilk, burn, clip, dupe, fool, gull, hoax, rook, scam, snow **5** cheat, gouge, hocus, set up, shaft, sting, trick **6** fleece, hustle, rip off, rope in, take in **7** deceive, defraud, fake out, swindle **8** flimflam, hoodwink **9** bamboozle, four-flush, shake down, victimize
aground: **4** fail **5** wreck **8** stranded
ahead: **4** lead **5** scout **7** precede **8** antecede, go before **10** show the way, trail-blaze
along: **2** go **4** move **5** leave **6** be gone, depart, go away, retire **7** head out, ride off **8** shove off **9** get moving
amok: **4** rage, riot **5** storm **7** rampage **8** have a fit
around: **3** gad **4** roam, rove **9** gallivant **10** equivocate, knock about
at: **6** attack, charge
(at): **5** lunge
away: **2** go **3** fly **4** bail, bolt, flee, skip **5** break, elope **6** cop out, decamp, defect, escape, get out, go AWOL **7** abscond, make off, take off **8** fugitate, hightail, light out, turn tail **10** hightail it
away from: **4** jilt, skip **5** ditch, split **6** desert, escape, maroon, strand **7** abandon, forsake **9** leave flat
batted in: **3** RBI **5** ribby
circles around: **3** top **4** beat, best **5** outdo **6** outwit **8** outsmart **9** overwhelm
counter to: **4** vary **5** belie **6** differ, oppose **7** deviate, diverge **8** conflict, contrast, disagree
cut and ~: **7** go south **8** fugitate
down: **4** find, quit, slam, slur, stop **5** abase, abuse, cease, chase, decry, knock, seedy, trace, track **6** defame, impugn, malign, pursue, revile, search, vilify **7** asperse, degrade, detract, recount **8** backbite, badmouth, belittle, derogate, diminish, minimize, overtake, peter out, research, ridicule, throw mud **9** blaspheme, criticize, denigrate, deprecate, discredit, disparage, enumerate, frown upon, humiliate, make fun of, pick apart, search out, summarize **10** blackguard, calumniate, speak ill of, vituperate
dry ~: **4** test **5** trial **8** practice **9** rehearsal
end ~: **9** deviation, diversion, variation **10** aberration, deflection, red herring
ender: **3** off, out, way **4** away, back, down **5** about **6** around
(for): **7** compete **8** campaign
for it: **3** fly **4** blow, bolt, flee, skip **5** leave, scoot, scram, split **6** bug out, cut out, decamp, escape, skidoo **7** abscond, bail out, get away, make off, retreat, scamper, skip out, vamoose **8** clear out, fugitate, skip town, turn tail **9** skedaddle **10** fly the coop
help ~: **6** cohost **8** co-manage
hot and cold: **4** yo-yo **5** hedge **6** dither, seesaw, waffle, wobble **8** straddle **9** hem and haw, pussyfoot
in: **3** nab **4** bust, call, jail **5** pinch **6** arrest, collar, detain, pick up **7** capture **8** handcuff **9** apprehend
in neutral: **4** idle
interference for: **3** aid **4** help **6** assist, defend **7** support **8** advocate
in the long ~: **7** finally, overall **8** after all **10** eventually, ultimately
into: **3** ram, see **4** butt, find, meet, snag **5** total **6** accost, fall on, strike **8** come upon, fall upon, happen on, meet with **9** encounter, stumble on
(into): **5** empty
into the ground: **6** overdo **7** belabor, overuse **8** overplay
its course: **3** ebb **4** ease, fade, flag, stop, wane **5** abate, let up, relax **6** ease up, lessen, recede **7** die down, dwindle, ease off, slacken, subside, tail off **8** blow over, diminish, fade away, moderate, peter out, taper off **10** slacken off
last: **4** lose
leisurely ~: **3** jog **4** lope, trot
make a ~ at: **6** tackle **7** attempt **9** undertake
off: **2** go **3** fly, hie **4** bolt, flee, gone, skip **5** drain, elope, leave, print, split **6** escape **7** abscond **8** chase out, clear out, slip away **9** enumerate **10** break loose, mimeograph
off at the mouth: **3** gab, yak **4** blab **6** babble, jabber **7** blather, blether
off the page: **5** bleed
off with: **4** lift, take **5** heist, pinch, poach, steal, swipe **6** abduct, hijack, kidnap, pilfer, snatch, thieve **7** plunder, purloin **10** spirit away
on: **3** gab, yak, yap **4** talk **5** prate **6** rattle **7** chatter, maunder **8** continue
on the ~: **7** fleeing, hastily, in a rush, in haste, quickly, swiftly **8** escaping, in flight, speedily **9** hurriedly
out: **3** end **4** skip, stop **5** cease, dry up, end up, lapse, spill, use up **6** defect, elapse, escape, expire, finish, lapsed, wind up **7** deplete, exhaust, expired **8** conclude, finish up, jump bail **9** dissipate, terminate
(out): **4** give **5** peter
out of: **4** lack **5** use up **7** exhaust
out of gas: **3** sag **4** drop, flag, fold, tire, yawn **5** stall, weary **6** fizzle **7** dwindle, poop out **8** collapse, overwork
out of town: **4** oust **5** eject **6** depose, remove, unseat **7** cashier, drum out, kick out **9** overthrow
out on: **4** jilt, quit **6** desert **7** abandon, forsake **8** forswear **9** foreswear **10** go away from
over: **4** brim, echo, gush, lick, pass **5** recap, spill **6** exceed, repeat, review **7** do again, iterate, surpass, trample **8** go beyond **9** summarize
ragged: **7** exhaust
rampant: **4** rage, rant, rave **5** erupt, freak, storm **7** explode **8** freak out **9** go berserk **10** hit the roof
reconnaissance: **3** spy **6** patrol, survey **7** bird-dog
rings around: **4** best **5** outdo **7** surpass
riot: **4** rage **6** abound, overdo **7** rampage **9** luxuriate
rum: **7** bootleg
scared: **5** panic **10** chicken out
smoothly: **3** hum **4** purr **7** prosper
the show: **4** rule **6** direct, manage **7** oversee **8** dominate **9** supervise **10** administer
things: **4** lead **5** reign, steer
through: **3** reh., use **4** blow, leaf, lose, scan, skim, stab **5** spear, spend, use up, waste **6** empale, expend, finish, impale, infest, lavish, misuse, pierce, rattle, review **7** consume, exhaust, recount **8** look over, practice, rehearse, squander, transfix **9** dissipate, throw away **10** gamble away
to: **4** cost **5** reach, total
together: **3** mix **4** meld **5** blend, merge, unite **6** mingle **7** combine **8** intermix **9** integrate
trial ~: **4** test **5** trial, whirl **10** experiment
up: **3** sew **5** amass, incur, raise **6** stitch **7** magnify **8** increase **10** accumulate
up the flagpole: **5** raise
wild: **4** rage, riot **7** rampage **8** cut loose **9** go berserk
(with): **3** mix **6** hobnob, mingle **7** consort **9** associate, socialize **10** fraternize
words together: **6** garble, mumble
run __: **3** off, out **4** amok, away, down, into, over, riot, wild **5** after, along, amuck, out of, out on, short **6** across, scared **7** against, through
run __ around: **5** rings
run __ gas: **5** out of
run __ ground: **5** to the
run __ in: **6** batted
run __ of: **3** out **5** afoul, short
run __ on: **3** out
run __ the clock: **3** out
run __ the ground: **4** into
run __ with: **3** off **4** away
run-__-mill: **5** of-the
__ run: **3** dry, end, ice, ski **4** back, bomb, dead, home, long, milk **5** on the, press, print, split, trial **6** earned
__-run: **4** long **5** after, short
Run __, Run Deep: **6** Silent
Run __ Your Life: **3** for
Run, __, run!: **4** Spot
Run-__: **3** D.M.C. **6** Around
__ Run: **4** Bull **5** Trial **6** Logan's
__, Run: **6** Rabbit
run a __ ship: **5** tight
runabout: **4** auto, boat **5** craft
runagate: **5** nomad, rover **6** roamer **7** drifter, rambler **8** gadabout, vagabond, wanderer, wayfarer **9** itinerant, sojourner, transient
runaround: **5** delay, dodge, hedge **6** bypass **7** evasion **8** sidestep **9** avoidance
Runaround Sue (1961 song)
artist: Dion
__ run average: **6** earned
runaway: **4** romp, wild **6** bolter, truant **7** at large, escapee **8** deserter, forsaker, fugitive, offender, renegade **9** absconder **10** delinquent, lawbreaker, on the loose
of rhyme: **4** dish **5** spoon
Runaway (song)
artist: Del Shannon, Janet Jackson
Runaway Bride (1999 film)
cast: Joan Cusack, Hector Elizondo, Richard Gere, Julia Roberts
cat: **7** Italics
director: Garry Marshall
dog: **7** Skipper
Run Away Child, Running Wild (1969 song)
artist: Temptations
Runaway Jury (2003 film)
cast: John Cusack, Gene Hackman, Dustin Hoffman, Rachel Weisz
Runaway Train (1985 film)
cast: Rebecca De Mornay, Eric Roberts, Jon Voight
Runaway Train (1993 song)
artist: Soul Asylum
__ Run Baker: **4** Home
runcible spoon: **7** utensil
feature: **4** tine **5** prong
Runciman, Steven: **6** writer **7** British **9** historian
Rundgren, Todd: **6** singer
song: Hello It's Me (1973) I Saw the Light (1972)
rundle: **4** rung, step
Run-D.M.C.
album: King of Rock (1985)
genre: **3** rap
members: Darryl McDaniels, Jason Mizell, Joseph Simmons
song: Down with the King (1993) Walk This Way (1986)
rundown: **5** brief, recap **6** précis, report, résumé, review, sketch **7** account, outline, summary **8** briefing, scenario, synopsis **9** statement
dwelling: **4** dive, slum **5** hovel
give the ~: **6** fill in, inform, report, update **7** apprise
run-down: **3** old **4** drab, mean, sick, weak, worn **5** dingy, dumpy,

mangy, ratty, seamy, seedy, tacky, tired, weary **6** ailing, beat-up, crumby, crummy, grungy, mangey, peaked, shabby, shoddy, sickly, sleazy, used up **7** drained, rickety, scruffy, squalid, worn-out **8** below par, decrepit, derelict, desolate, fatigued, forsaken, tattered, time-worn, untended **9** abandoned, crumbling, enervated, exhausted, neglected **10** in bad shape, on the ropes, ramshackle, threadbare, uncared-for
area: **4** slum **5** slurb **7** skid row
dwelling: **4** dump **5** hovel
rune: **4** poem, rime **5** rhyme, verse **6** letter
letter: **3** edh
Runeberg, Johan: **4** poet **7** Finnish
Run for Your Life (NBC drama)
cast: Ben Gazzara (Paul Bryan)
rung: **3** bar, rod **4** step **5** level, spoke, stage, stave, tread **6** degree, rundle **10** crosspiece
runic: **7** magical, obscure **8** mystical
run-in: **3** row **4** tiff, to-do **5** brush, clash, fight, set-to **6** dustup, fracas, hassle, tussle **7** contest, dispute, quarrel **8** argument, conflict, skirmish **9** encounter, imbroglio **10** falling-out
run into the __: **6** ground
runlet: **5** brook **6** stream
run like __: **5** a deer
__-run movie: **5** first
runnel: **4** race, rill **5** creek, rille **6** stream **9** streamlet
runner: **3** Coe, rug, ski **4** skee, Tyus **5** Flo-Jo, Hayes, Keino, Lewis, loper, miler, Nurmi, Ovett, Owens, racer, scout **6** bearer, Benoit, Bikila, carpet, Devers **7** Ashford, athlete, carrier, courier, entrant, harrier, hurdler, nominee, Rudolph, Shorter, Zátopek **8** Bob Hayes, Kip Keino, sprinter **9** candidate, Carl Lewis, messenger **10** Gail Devers, Jesse Owens, Joan Benoit, Paavo Nurmi, Steve Ovett, Wyomia Tyus
British ~: **3** Coe **5** Ovett **10** Steve Ovett
concern: **4** pace
Czech ~: **7** Zátopek
distance ~: **5** miler **10** marathoner
downhill ~: **3** ski **4** skee **5** skier
Ethiopian ~: **6** Bikila
Finnish ~: **5** Nurmi **10** Paavo Nurmi
goal: **4** tape
Kenyan ~: **5** Keino **8** Kip Keino
put out a ~: **3** tag
starter: **3** gun, rum **4** fore, race, road **5** front
unit: **3** lap **4** mile, yard **5** meter **9** kilometer
__ runner: **4** base **5** front, pinch
__ Runner: **4** Road **5** Blade **6** Indian
runners: **5** field, slate
carry it: **4** sled
of song: **4** mice
__ Runner, The: **6** Indian
runner-up: **5** loser **6** second
__ Runneth Over: **5** My Cup
Runnin' Down a Dream (1989 song)
artist: Tom Petty
running: **4** live, on TV **5** alive, fluid, going, sport **6** active, flight, liquid, usable **7** cursive, flowing, useable, working **8** handling, straight, unbroken **9** continual, direction, incessant, operation, operative **10** continuous, management
a fever: **3** ill **4** sick **6** ailing, unwell **9** bedridden **10** indisposed
combining form: **4** drom- **5** -drome, dromo- **7** -dromous
hot and cold: **4** torn **7** not sure **8** hesitant, waffling, wavering **9** equivocal, uncertain, undecided, unsettled **10** ambivalent, indecisive, irresolute, of two minds, on the fence
in ballet: **5** couru
in the ~: **8** eligible **9** qualified
late: **5** tardy **6** behind, held up, hung up **7** delayed, overdue **8** detained **10** unpunctual
mate: **2** VP **4** veep **6** veepee
over: **4** full **5** awash, flush, laden **6** jammed **7** brimful, copious, crammed, crowded, profuse, replete, stuffed, teeming **8** brimming, bursting **9** bounteous, chock-full, plenteous, plentiful **10** voluminous
partner: **3** off
place: **4** oval **5** track
smoothly: **6** in sync
still in the ~: **5** alive
stop ~: **4** fail **6** unplug **7** conk out, go kaput, turn off **8** shut down **9** break down
together: **6** branch, feeder **7** joining, meeting **8** blending, mingling **9** confluent, tributary **10** concurrent
wild: **7** haywire
running __: **3** gag **4** back, gear, head, joke, mate, room, shoe, time **5** board, light, start
running __ jump: **5** broad
Running __: **3** Dog **4** Bear, Wild **6** Rebels, Scared
__ Running: **4** Come **6** Silent
Running Bear (1959 song)
artist: Johnny Preston
Running Dog
author: Don DeLillo
running man: **5** dance
Running Man, The: **4** film **5** novel
author: Richard Bachman (Stephen King)
cast: Maria Conchita Alonso, Richard Dawson, Yaphet Kotto, Arnold Schwarzenegger
Running on Empty (1988 film)
cast: Judd Hirsch, Christine Lahti, River Phoenix
director: Sidney Lumet
Running Rebels, The: **4** UNLV
__ Runnings: **4** Cool
Running Scared (1961 song)
artist: Roy Orbison
Running with the Night (1983 song)
artist: Lionel Richie
Runnin' Rebels: **4** UNLV
runny: **4** thin, weak **5** fluid, soupy, unset **6** liquid, watery
not ~: **3** set **5** solid
Runnymede: **6** meadow
document: **10** Magna Carta
locale: **6** Surrey **7** England
run-of-__: **7** the-mill
runoff site: **4** eave, roof
run-of-the-mill: **4** dull, so-so **5** banal, plain, stock, trite, usual, vapid **6** common, medium, normal **7** average, general, generic, regular, routine, same old **8** everyday, familiar, frequent, mediocre, middling, ordinary, standard **9** generical, tolerable **10** dullsville, widespread
run out of __: **3** gas
run out the __: **5** clock
Run River
author: Joan Didion
Run Silent, Run Deep (1958 film)
cast: Clark Gable, Burt Lancaster
__ Runs Through It, A: **5** River
runt: **3** lad, pup **4** punk **5** dwarf, puppy, scrub **6** midget, peewee, shrimp **8** half-pint **9** pipsqueak
run the __: **4** risk, show
run-through: **4** test **5** drill **9** rehearsal
run to __: **4** seed **5** earth
Run to Him (1961 song)
artist: Bobby Vee
run to the __: **6** ground
Run to You (1984 song)
artist: Bryan Adams
runty: **4** puny **5** small **7** stunted **8** pint-size, sawed-off
run up __: **4** a tab
runway: **5** strip **6** tarmac **7** landing
hit the ~: **3** lit **4** alit, land **6** alight
move on the ~: **4** taxi
work on the ~: **4** pave **6** repave
Run with the __ and hunt...: **4** Hare
Runyon, Damon: **6** writer
work: Blue Plate Special Guys and Dolls
rupee: **4** coin **5** money
100 ~s: **4** lakh
fraction: **4** pice **5** paisa
ten million ~s: **5** crore
Rupert: **6** Brooke, Holmes **7** Everett, Murdoch
Rupp, Adolph: **5** coach
milieu: **5** court
sport: **10** basketball
rupture: **4** feud, open, rend, rent, rift, rive, tear **5** break, burst, clash, crack, erupt, sever, split **6** breach, divide, schism, sunder **7** disrupt, divorce, fissure, opening, shatter, split-up **8** disunion, division, fracture, puncture, separate **10** come undone, falling-out, separation
R.U.R.
author: Karel Capek
character: **4** Gall **5** Domin **6** Helena, Primus **7** Alquist
language: **5** Czech
machine: **5** robot
rural: **4** calm, farm, hick **6** rustic, silvan, sylvan **7** bucolic, country, georgic **8** agrarian, Arcadian, farmlike, outlying, pastoral **9** agronomic, backwoods, bucolical **10** provincial
addr.: **3** RFD
agcy.: **3** FCA, TVA
area: **7** boonies, country **9** backwoods
club: **3** FFA **5** Four-H
crossing: **5** stile
not ~: **5** civic, urban **9** municipal
road: **2** ln. **4** lane
sight: **3** inn **4** farm, well **5** field
structure: **3** pen, sty **4** barn, shed, silo **5** fence **9** farmhouse
rural __: **5** route
rural __ delivery: **4** free
__ R Us: **4** Toys
Rusalka: **5** opera
composer: Antonín Dvorák
ruse: **3** con, jig **4** flam, game, hoax, juke, plot, ploy, sham, trap, wile **5** angle, blind, bluff, craft, dodge, feint, fraud, guile, put-on, shift, stunt, trick, twist **6** deceit, device, dupery, gambit, humbug, scheme, switch **7** chicane, evasion, gimmick, sleight, snow job, swindle **8** artifice, game plan, intrigue, maneuver, pretense, scenario **9** booby trap, chicanery, curveball, deception, imposture, stratagem **10** red herring, subterfuge
Rusedski: **4** Greg
rush: **3** fly, hie, rip, run, woo, zip **4** bolt, dart, dash, flit, flow, flux, gush, gust, leap, pelt, pile, pour, push, race, reed, scud, tear, tide, whiz, zoom **5** blitz, flood, haste, hasty, hurry, lunge, panic, plant, press, quick, rapid, scoot, sedge, shoot, sough, spate, speed, spirt, spurt, storm, surge, swash, swoop, whirl, whisk **6** action, attack, barrel, bustle, careen, career, charge, course, deluge, flurry, gallop, hasten, hurtle, hustle, influx, move it, plunge, pursue, rocket, scurry, sprint, streak, stream, thrash, thrill, urgent, whoosh **7** assault, besiege, dash off, floor it, hop to it, hotfoot, hurried, hurry-up, quicken, scamper, speed up, torrent, urgency **8** celerity, expedite, gang up on, hightail, outbreak, overcome, pressure, rapidity, scramble, step on it **9** avalanche, hastiness, horsetail, hotfoot it, make haste, onslaught, quickness, shake a leg, skedaddle **10** accelerate, burn rubber, get a move on, get hopping, go pell-mell, go whole hog, hightail it, lose no time, make tracks
give the bum's ~ to: **4** boot, oust **6** bounce **7** boot out, cast out, kick out, turn out **8** throw out **9** chase away
in: **5** enter **6** arrive
in a ~: **7** fleeing, hastily, quickly, rapidly, swiftly **8** escaping, on the run, speedily **9** hurriedly
mad ~: **4** dash **5** furor, hurry, panic **6** bustle, frenzy, plunge, scurry **7** ferment, scamper, turmoil **8** outburst, stampede
milieu: **3** bog, fen **5** marsh, swamp **7** wetland
together: **5** bunch, swarm **6** stream, throng **7** cluster **10** congregate
rush __: **4** hour
__ rush: **3** in a **4** bum's, gold
Rush: **7** Barbara **8** Geoffrey, Limbaugh, Merrilee
Rush!: **4** ASAP, stat **6** pronto
Rush and the Turnabouts, Merrilee
song: Angel of the Morning (1968)
Rushdie, Salman: **6** critic, Indian, writer
work: Midnight's Children Satanic Verses

rushed: **5** hasty **6** hectic **7** hurried **8** headlong
rusher, NFL: **2** FB **8** fullback
rushes, covered with: **5** sedgy
Rush, Geoffrey: **5** actor
  film: Frida (2002)
    Lantana (2001)
    Les Misérables (1998)
    Quills (2000)
    Shakespeare in Love (1998)
    Shine (1996, AA)
    The Tailor of Panama (2001)
rush hour
  component: **3** car **4** auto
  problem: **3** jam **5** tie up **7** traffic
  speed: **5** crawl
  train: **3** exp. **7** express
Rush Hour (1998 film)
  cast: Jackie Chan, Chris Tucker
rush-hour speed: **5** creep
__ Rush In: **5** Fools
rushing: **5** sough **6** abrupt **7** hurried **8** headlong **9** impetuous
  sound: **5** whish **6** whoosh
Rushing: **5** Jimmy
Rushmore: **5** Mount
  face: **7** Lincoln **9** Jefferson, Roosevelt **10** Washington
  locale: **4** S. Dak.
Rush, Rush (1991 song)
  artist: Paula Abdul
__ Rush, The: **4** Gold
Rusie, Amos: **5** Giant **6** hurler **7** pitcher
rusk: **5** bread, toast **8** zwieback
Rusk: **4** Dean
Ruskin, John: **6** critic, writer **7** British
  work: Deucalion
    Modern Painters
    Proserpina
    Sesame and Lilies
    The Seven Lamps of Architecture
    The Stones of Venice
Russ: **3** Tim **5** Meyer **6** Morgan **7** Columbo, Tamblyn **8** Hamilton
Russ.: **4** lang.
  neighbor of ~: **3** Est., Fin., Ukr
  see also Russia
__ Russe: **6** Ballet
Russel: **6** Crouse
Russell: **3** Ken **4** Andy, Bill, Gail, Jane, John, Keri, Kurt, Leon, Mark, peak **5** Baker, Bobby, Crowe, Hulse, mount, Myers, rouse **6** Brenda, Harold, Nipsey **7** Johnson, Markert, Theresa **8** Bertrand, mountain, Rosalind
  2000: **5** index **10** stock index
  locale: **10** California
Russell __ College: **4** Sage
Russell, Bertrand: **6** writer **7** British **8** Nobelist, reformer **11** philosopher
  work: The ABC of Relativity
    Common Sense and Nuclear Warfare
    Has Man a Future?
    A History of Western Philosophy
    Religion and Science
    Unarmed Victory
Russell, Bill
  milieu: **5** court
  org.: **3** NBA
  sport: **10** basketball
Russell, Harold Oscar: The Best Years of Our Lives
Russell, Jane: **7** actress
  film: Gentlemen Prefer Blondes (1953)
    The Outlaw (1943)
    The Paleface (1948)
    Son of Paleface (1952)
  in The Outlaw: **3** Rio
Russell, Kurt: **5** actor
  film: Backdraft (1991)
    The Best of Times (1986)
    Dreamer (2005)
    Escape From New York (1981)
    Executive Decision (1996)
    Overboard (1987)
    Poseidon (2006)
    Silkwood (1983)
    Stargate (1994)
    Tequila Sunrise (1988)
    Tombstone (1993)
    Unlawful Entry (1992)
    Used Cars (1980)
    Vanilla Sky (2001)
  role: **4** Earp **9** Wyatt Earp
__ Russell Lowell: **5** James
Russell, Mark: **8** humorist, satirist
  instrument: **5** piano
Russell, Rosalind: **7** actress
  film: Auntie Mame (1958)
    Gypsy (1962)
    His Girl Friday (1940)
    Picnic (1955)
    Rosie! (1967)
    Sister Kenny (1946)
    The Women (1939)
  role: **4** Mame
__ Russell terrier: **4** Jack
Russell, Theresa: **7** actress
  film: The Believer (2002)
    Black Widow (1987)
    Impulse (1990)
    Insignificance (1985)
    Straight Time (1978)
    Wild Things (1998)
  spouse: Nicolas Roeg
Russell, William Howard: **6** writer **7** British **10** journalist
Russert: **3** Tim
russet: **3** red **4** rust **5** apple, brown, color **6** veggie **7** reddish **9** vegetable, yellowish
  relative: *see* apple, brown color
Russia: **6** nation **7** country
  aircraft: **3** MiG
  antelope: **5** saiga
  auto: **3** Zil **4** Lada
  ballet: **5** Kirov **7** Bolshoi
  ballet dancer: **5** Lifar **7** Massine, Nureyev, Pavlova, Ulanova **8** Danilova, Nijinsky **11** Baryshnikov, Youskevitch
  bass: **9** Chaliapin
  bay: **5** Dvina, Onega
  beer: **5** kvass, quass
  bovine: **7** Istoben
  capital: **6** Moscow
  cellist: **12** Rostropovich
  chemist: **9** Mendeleev
  city: **3** Ufa **4** Omsk, Orel, Orsk, Perm, Tula **5** Kazan, Penza, Serov, Sochi, Tomsk **6** Kaluga, Moscow, Rostov, Samara **7** Irkutsk, Ulan-Ude
  collective: **5** artel
  commune: **3** mir
  composer: **3** Cui **6** Glière, Glinka **7** Arensky, Borodin **8** César Cui **9** Prokofiev **10** Stravinsky **11** Moussorgsky **12** Shostakovich **19** Scriabin. Tchaikovsky
  conductor: **8** Smallens **9** Goldovsky, Markevich **11** Kostelanetz **12** Koussevitzky
  cooperative: **5** artel
  council: **4** Duma
  country home: **5** dacha **6** datcha
  czar: **4** Ivan, Paul **5** Ivan V, Paul I, Peter **6** Feodor, Ivan IV, Ivan VI, Peter I **7** Feodor I, Ivan III, Peter II, Romanov **8** Nicholas, Peter III **9** Alexander **10** Alexander I
  distance unit: **5** verst **6** verste, werste
  dog: **6** borzoi
  drink: **5** vodka
  dry measure: **3** lof
  emperor: **4** czar, tsar, tzar
  epic hero: **4** Igor
  figure skater: **5** Kulik **9** Ilia Kulik
  fur: **5** sable
  girl's nickname: **5** Tasha
  gulf: **8** Taganrog
  gymnast: **6** Korbut **10** Olga Korbut
  hemp: **4** rine
  high jumper: **6** Brumel
  John, in ~: **4** Ivan
  journalist: **8** Sloukhin
  lake: **5** Onega **6** Ladoga, Peipus
  legislature: **4** Duma
  log house: **4** isba, izba
  money: **5** kopec, kopek, ruble **6** copeck, kopeck, rouble
  mountain: **4** Alai **5** Altai, Sayan, Urals **6** Anadir, Elbrus, Elbruz, Kolyma **8** Caucasus
  native: **5** Osset **6** Ossete
  neighbor: **5** China **6** Latvia, Norway, Poland **7** Belarus, Estonia, Finland, Georgia, Ukraine **8** Mongolia **9** Lithuania **10** Azerbaijan, Kazakhstan, North Korea
  newspaper: **6** Pravda **8** Izvestia
  Nobelist in Chemistry: **7** Semenov
  Nobelist in Economics: **11** Kantorovich
  Nobelist in Literature: **5** Bunin **7** Brodsky **9** Pasternak, Sholokhov **12** Solzhenitsyn
  Nobelist in Medicine: **6** Pavlov
  Nobelist in Peace: **8** Sakharov **9** Gorbachev
  Nobelist in Physics: **4** Tamm **5** Basov, Frank **6** Landau **7** Alferov, Kapitsa **9** Cherenkov, Prokhorov
  noble: **5** boyar **6** boyard
  once: **4** USSR
  painter: **7** Chagall **9** Kandinsky
  pancake: **5** blini, bliny
  peasant: **5** mujik
  people: **4** Mari
  pianist: **6** Gilels **9** Ashkenazy
  place-name suffix: **4** grad
  poet: **3** Fet **4** Bely, Blok **5** Bedny, Bunin **6** Esenin **7** Nabokov, Sologub **8** Nekrasov, Sloukhin **9** Akhmatova, Pasternak, Zhukovsky **10** Mayakovsky, Zabolotsky **11** Akhmadulina, Yevtushenko
  pole vaulter: **5** Bubka
  port: **4** Omsk **7** Yakutsk **8** Murmansk **9** Archangel, Leningrad
  revolutionary: **3** Red **5** Lenin **9** Bolshevik, Menshevik
  river: **3** Don, Oka, Oma **4** Lena, Neva, Seim, Seym, Yana **5** Onega, Tobol **6** Angara, Kolima, Kolyma
  rodent: **6** gerbil
  saint: **4** Olga **6** Nevski **8** Nicholas, Vladimir
  scientist: **9** Mendeleev
  sea: **4** Aral, Azov **5** White **6** Sivash **7** Okhotsk
  secret police: **4** OGPU
  spacecraft: **3** Mir **5** Lunik, Soyuz **6** Vostok **7** Sputnik, Voskhod
  spy org.: **3** KGB
  symbol: **4** bear
  tennis pro: **10** Kournikova
  tent: **4** yurt
  village: **3** mir
  violinist: **5** Elman **8** Milstein, Oistrakh **9** Zimbalist
  volcano: **5** Alaid **6** Tiatia **8** Karymsky **9** Tolbachik
  weight: **4** pood
  writer: **4** Grin **5** Babel, Gogol, Gorky **6** Daniel, Ivanov, Krylov, Kuprin, Olesha, Panova, Yashin **7** Aksakov, Amalrik, Bryusov, Chekhov, Fadayev, Gladkov, Katayev, Nabokov, Pushkin, Rozanov, Sologub, Tolstoy **8** Aksyonov, Andreyev, Bulgakov, Karamzin, Nekrasov, Saltykov, Sloukhin, Turgenev, Zamyatin **9** Goncharov, Sholokhov, Sinyavsky **10** Zoshchenko **11** Aleshkovsky, Dostoyevsky **12** Solzhenitsyn
__ Russia $1200: **4** I Owe
Russia House, The (1990 film)
  cast: Sean Connery, Michelle Pfeiffer, Roy Scheider
Russian: **8** dressing, language
  neighbor: **4** Esth, Finn, Pole **6** Korean **7** Chinese, Latvian **8** Estonian, Georgian **9** Mongolian, Norwegian, Ukrainian **10** Lithuanian
  no, in ~: **4** nyet
  peace, in ~: **3** mir
  space station: **6** Salyut
  typical ~: **4** Ivan
  yes, in ~: **2** da
Russian __: **8** dressing
__ Russian: **5** Black
Russian America
  capital: **5** Sitka
Russian Bear
  ingredient: **5** vodka
Russian Blue: **3** cat **5** felid **6** feline
Russian Girl, The
  author: Kingsley Amis
Russian Overture
  composer: Sergei Prokofiev
Russians __ Coming..., The: **3** Are
__ Russia Today: **6** Inside
__ Russia With Love: **4** From
Ruslan and Ludmilla
  composer: Mikhail Glinka
Russo-Japanese __: **3** War
Russo, Rene: **7** actress
  film: The Adventures of Rocky and Bullwinkle (2000)
    Big Trouble (2002)
    Get Shorty (1995)
    In the Line of Fire (1993)
    Lethal Weapon 3 (1992)

Lethal Weapon 4 (1998)
Outbreak (1995)
Ransom (1996)
Showtime (2002)
The Thomas Crown Affair (1999)
Tin Cup (1996)

__-Russo War: 5 Finno

rust: 3 eat, red, rot **4** film, mold **5** brown, color, decay, eat at, erode, oxide **6** auburn, blight, fungus, patina, patine, redden, russet, wither, yellow **7** coating, corrode, crumble, eat away, go stale, go to pot, oxidize, reddish, tarnish **8** go to seed, stagnate **9** corrosion, iron oxide, lie fallow, oxidation, yellowish **10** brown shade, degenerate
ender: 5 proof
relative: *see* orange color, red color

rust __: 4 belt

rustic: 4 boor, hick, hind, homy, rube, rude **5** crude, homey, plain, rough, rural, yokel **6** coarse, farmer, folksy, gaffer, gauche, silvan, simple, sylvan **7** austere, boorish, bucolic, bumpkin, country, hayseed, loutish, outdoor, peasant, plowboy, redneck, uncouth **8** agrarian, Arcadian, churlish, farmlike, homemade, homespun, pastoral **9** backwoods, bucolical, hillbilly **10** clodhopper, provincial, unpolished
fellow: 5 swain
lodging: 3 inn **4** camp **5** B and B
poem: 4 idyl **5** idyll
structure: 4 barn **5** cabin, lodge
way: 4 lane

rustle: 4 sigh, stir **5** filch, sough, speed, steal, swipe, swish **6** gather, murmur, patter, ripple, thieve **7** crackle, crinkle, flutter, ransack, whisper **9** crepitate
up: 3 get **4** find **5** scout **6** gather

rustler: 5 crook, thief **6** bandit, outlaw, robber **7** stealer **8** criminal, marauder **9** larcenist, plunderer **10** bushranger
target: 4 herd **6** cattle

rustling: 5 sough, swish, theft **6** rustle **8** thievery
sound: 5 swish

Ruston: 4 city, town
athletes: 8 Bulldogs
locale: 9 Louisiana
school: 3 LTU

RU

rustproof coating: 4 zinc

rusty: 3 old, red **4** soft, weak **5** stale, stiff **6** yellow **7** decayed, reddish **8** corroded, impaired, oxidized, sluggish **9** deficient, neglected, unpliable, yellowish **10** out of shape

Rusty: 5 Hamer, Staub **6** Draper **8** Cundieff

rut: 3 job **5** ditch, gouge, grind, habit, slump, track, trail **6** custom, furrow, groove, hollow, trench **7** channel, pattern, pothole, rat race, routine **8** flatness, monotony **9** treadmill **10** daily grind
in a ~: 5 bored, stuck **8** stagnant **10** bogged down, stultified, uncreative

__ rut: 3 in a

rutabaga: 5 tuber **6** turnip, veggie **9** vegetable

Rutger: 5 Hauer
in English: 5 Roger

Rutgers
conference: 7 Big East
locale: 9 New Jersey

ruth: 4 pity **5** heart, mercy **6** lenity, pardon **7** ache for, console, empathy, feel for **8** bleed for, clemency, go easy on, kindness, lenience, sympathy **9** tolerance **10** compassion, humaneness, tenderness

Ruth: 2 Dr. **4** Babe **5** Buzzi, Orkin, Roman **6** Etting, Gordon, Hussey **7** McKenny, Rendell, slugger, St. Denis, Warrick **8** Ginsburg **10** Chatterton, Westheimer
follower: 6 Samuel
homeland: 4 Moab
husband: 4 Boaz
mother-in-law: 5 Naomi
preceder: 6 Judges
sister-in-law: 5 Orpah
son: 4 Obed

Ruth __ Ginsburg: 5 Bader

Ruth __ Jhabvala: 6 Prawer

__ Ruth: 4 Baby

Ruth, Babe: 6 George, Yankee **7** Bambino, slugger **10** outfielder
rival: 4 Cobb **6** Gehrig, Ty Cobb **9** Lou Gehrig
stat: 3 HRs, RBI **6** homers
sultanate: 4 swat
topper: 5 Aaron
uniform number: 5 three

Ruth, Dr. subject: 3 sex

ruthenium: 5 metal **7** element

Rutherford: 3 Ann **5** Hayes, Kelly **6** Ernest **8** Margaret
concern: 4 atom

Rutherford, Ernest: 7 chemist **8** Nobelist **9** physicist, scientist

ruthful: 3 lax **4** easy, kind, mild, soft **5** loose **6** gentle, kindly **7** clement, sparing **8** flexible, laid-back, merciful, placable, tolerant **9** assuasive, compliant, easygoing, forgiving, indulgent, miserable **10** forbearing, permissive, unexacting

ruthless: 4 cold, grim, hard, mean **5** cruel, harsh, nasty, stern, stony, tough **6** animal, bitter, brutal, fierce, mortal, savage, stoney, unkind, wanton **7** beastly, callous, hurtful, inhuman, vicious **8** barbaric, fiendish, inhumane, pitiless, sadistic, vengeful **9** barbarian, barbarous, cutthroat, dog-eat-dog, ferocious, heartless, inclement, merciless, monstrous, murderous, truculent, unfeeling, unpitying **10** implacable, ironfisted, relentless, unmerciful, unyielding, vindictive

ruthlessly: 4 hard **5** felly **9** viciously

ruthlessness: 5 venom **6** malice, rancor **7** cruelty, tyranny **8** coldness, ferocity, savagery, severity, violence **9** barbarism, brutality, depravity, despotism, harshness **10** inhumanity, oppression

Ruthless People (1986 film)
cast: Danny DeVito, Bette Midler, Judge Reinhold, Helen Slater

Ruth Prawer __: 8 Jhabvala

Ruthville: 9 bleachers

rutile: 3 ore **7** mineral
synthetic ~: 7 titania

rutin: 8 vitamin P

Rutland: 4 city, town **6** county
locale: 7 England, Vermont

Rutledge: 3 Ann

Ruttan: 5 Susan

rutted: 5 bumpy, rough **8** potholed

Ruy __ chess opening: 5 Lopez

Ruy Blas Overture
composer: Felix Mendelssohn

Ruy Díaz de Bivar: 3 Cid **5** El Cid

RV: 6 camper **9** motor home, Winnebago
fuel: 3 LNG
haven: 3 KOA
park convenience: 6 hookup
park the ~: 6 encamp
part of ~: 3 rec., veh. **7** vehicle

RV (2006 film)
cast: Jeff Daniels, Cheryl Hines, Robin Williams

R-V connectors: 3 STU

Rwanda: 6 nation **7** country
capital: 6 Kigali
lake: 4 Kivu
money: 5 franc
neighbor: 5 Congo **6** Uganda **7** Burundi **8** Tanzania
people: 4 Hutu, Tusi **5** Tussi, Tutsi **6** Watusi **7** Watutsi

Rx
abbr.: 2 cc. **3** alb., b.d.s., bib., cib., cuj., d.t.d., ead., gtt., liq., pil., p.r.n., q.i.d, sig., t.d.s., t.i.d., ung., vin. **4** agit., coch., elix., ferv., filt., garg., quat., quor., trid., ungt. **5** calef., emuls., qq. hor., quinq., utend.
amount: 4 dose **6** dosage
not needing an ~: 3 OTC
writer: 2 dr., GP, MD **3** doc **5** doser **6** doctor
writers org.: 3 AMA

Ry: 6 Cooder

rya: 3 rug **4** shag **6** carpet

Ryan: 3 Meg, Roz **4** Jeri **5** Irene, Nolan, O'Neal, Peggy **6** Robert, Sheila, Stiles **7** Gosling **8** Reynolds, Seacrest **9** Cornelius, Phillippe

Ryan, Meg: 7 actress
film: City of Angels (1998)
Courage Under Fire (1996)
DOA (1988)
The Doors (1991)
Hanging Up (2000)
Innerspace (1987)
Joe Versus the Volcano (1990)
Kate and Leopold (2001)
Prelude to a Kiss (1992)
Proof of Life (2000)
Sleepless in Seattle (1993)
When a Man Loves a Woman (1994)
When Harry Met Sally... (1989)
You've Got Mail (1998)
spouse: Dennis Quaid

Ryan, Nolan: 6 hurler **7** pitcher
once: 3 Met **5** Angel, Astro **6** Ranger

Ryan's __: 4 Hope

Ryan's daughter: 5 Tatum

Ryan's Daughter (1970 film)
cast: Trevor Howard, Leo McKern, Sarah Miles, John Mills, Robert Mitchum
director: David Lean

__ Ryan's Express: 3 Von

Ryan's Hope (ABC): 4 soap **9** soap opera

Rybinsk Reservoir site: 5 Volga

Rydell: 4 Mark **5** Bobby

Rydell, Bobby
born: Robert Ridarelli
song: The Cha-Cha-Cha (1962)
Forget Him (1963)
Kissin' Time (1959)
Swingin' School (1960)
Volare (1960)
We Got Love (1959)
Wild One (1960)

Ryder: 5 Mitch **6** Alfred, Winona
offering: 3 rig, van **5** truck
rival: 5 U-Haul

Ryder Cup: 6 trophy
sport: 4 golf

__ Ryder Open: 5 Doral

Ryder, Winona: 7 actress
film: The Age of Innocence (1993)
Bram Stoker's Dracula (1992)
Edward Scissorhands (1990)
Girl, Interrupted (1999)
Heathers (1989)
How to Make an American Quilt (1995)
Little Women (1994)
Mermaids (1990)
Night on Earth (1991)
Reality Bites (1994)

rye: 3 liq. **5** bread, drink, grain **6** cereal, liquor, whisky **7** whiskey **8** beverage
ender: 5 grass
grass: 6 darnel
mold: 5 ergot
partner: 3 ham

rye __: 5 bread, grass **6** whisky **7** whiskey

__ rye: 4 wild **5** ham on **6** Jewish

Ryeland: 5 sheep

Ryerson: 3 RPU **6** school
locale: 6 Canada **7** Ontario, Toronto

Ryman Auditorium show: 4 Opry

Ryne: 5 Duren **8** Sandberg

Ryukyus: 4 isls. **5** isles **7** islands
locale: 5 Japan
part: 4 Kume **5** Amami, Iheya **6** Kerama, Miyako, O-shima **7** Iishima, Okinawa
port: 4 Naha

Ryun, Jim: 5 miler **6** runner

6
on a phone: 3 MNO
7 (1992 song)
artist: Prince
7-__: 6 Eleven
7 Faces of Dr. Lao (1964 film)
cast: Barbara Eden, Tony Randall
director: George Pal
7th Heaven (WB drama)
cast: Jessica Biel (Mary Camden)
Stephen Collins (Eric Camden)
Catherine Hicks (Annie Camden)
Barry Watson (Matt Camden)
7
on a phone: 3 PRS
7 UP: 3 pop 4 soda 6 uncola 9 soft drink
alternative: *see* soft drink
16 Blocks (2006 film)
cast: Mos Def, Bruce Willis
16 Candles (1958 song)
artist: Crests
__ 17: 6 Stalag
60 Minutes (CBS news)
feature: 6 exposé
reporter: Bob Simon
Ed Bradley
Steve Kroft
Dan Rather
Harry Reasoner
Andy Rooney
Morley Safer
Diane Sawyer
Scott Pelley
Lesley Stahl
Meredith Vieira
Mike Wallace
61* subject: 5 Maris
__ 66: 5 Route
__ 67: 4 Expo
__ '70s Show: 4 That
76ers: 4 five
home: 12 Philadelphia
org.: 3 NBA
rival: *see* NBA team
77 Dream Songs
author: John Berryman
77 Sunset Strip (ABC drama)
cast: Edd Byrnes (Kookie)
Roger Smith (Jeff Spencer)
Efrem Zimbalist Jr. (Stu Bailey)
restaurant: 5 Dino's
79 Park Avenue
author: Harold Robbins
622 event: 5 Hijra 6 Hegira, Hijrah
704 Hauser (CBS sitcom)
cast: John Amos
707: 3 jet 5 plane
714
Badge ~ holder: 6 Friday
747: 3 jet 5 plane
alternative: 6 Airbus
767: 3 jet 5 plane
777: 3 jet 5 plane
1776
character: 5 Adams
1776 (1972 film)
cast: William Daniels, Howard da Silva, Ken Howard
$64,000 Question, The (game show)
host: Hal March
S: 3 dir. 4 elem., size 6 letter, sulfur 7 element
16 for ~: 4 at. no.
follower: 3 TUV 4 TUVW 5 TUVWX
in phonetic alphabet: 6 Sierra
mispronounce ~: 4 lisp
preceders: 3 PQR 4 OPQR 5 NOPQR
S __: 4 and L
S __ 500: 4 and P
S __ Green Stamps: 4 and H
S __ Sam: 4 as in
S. __: 3 Afr., Sgt. 4 Amer.
'S' __ Silence: 5 Is for
__ 6: 5 Motel
S.A.: 4 cont.
country: 3 Arg., Bol., Col., Par., Uru. 4 Braz., Ecua. 5 Venez.
see also South America
Saab: 3 car 4 auto, Elie 7 Swedish 10 automobile
competitor: 5 Volvo
model: 4 Aero
Saale
city on the ~: 5 Halle
Saar: 5 basin, river
locale: 6 France 7 Germany
Saarinen: 4 Eero 5 Eliel
Saatchi product: 3 ads
Sabara: 5 Daryl
Sabatini, Gabriela: 7 netster 9 tennis pro
Sabbath activity: 4 rest
sabbatical: 5 leave 6 hiatus 7 leisure 8 free time, vacation
Sabbatical
author: John Barth
__ Sabe: 4 Kemo
saber: 3 arm, saw 4 stab 5 blade, knife, sword
alternative: 4 épée, foil 6 rapier
deflect a ~: 5 parry
handle: 4 hilt
set-to: 4 duel
saber-__ tiger: 7 toothed
Saberhagen, Bret: 6 hurler 7 pitcher
Saberjet
erstwhile foe: 3 MiG
sabers: 8 weaponry
sabertooth: 3 cat 5 felid, tiger 6 feline
Sabin __: 7 vaccine
Sabin, Albert: 9 physician
contemporary: 4 Salk
sable: 3 fur 4 dark 5 black, color 6 animal, weasel 9 pitch-dark 10 pitch-black
relative: *see* black color, weasel
Sable: 3 car 4 auto, cape, Merc 7 Mercury 10 automobile
sabot: 4 clog, shoe 8 footwear 10 wooden shoe
ender: 3 age
sound: 4 clop
sabotage: 4 do in, harm 5 block, wreck 6 damage, hamper, hinder 7 destroy, disable, disrupt, subvert, take out, torpedo 8 mischief, obstruct, undercut 9 frustrate, treachery, undermine, vandalism, vandalize 10 demolition, disruption, subversion
saboteur: 5 enemy 9 ill-wisher 10 subversive
Saboteur (1942 film)
cast: Robert Cummings, Priscilla Lane
director: Alfred Hitchcock
sabre
see saber
Sabre and Spurs
composer: John Philip Sousa
Sabres: 3 six 4 team
home: 7 Buffalo
milieu: 3 ice 4 rink
org.: 3 NHL
rival: *see* hockey team
sport: 6 hockey
Sabrina (1954 film)
cast: Humphrey Bogart, Audrey Hepburn, William Holden
director: Billy Wilder
Sabrina (1995 film)
cast: Harrison Ford, Greg Kinnear, Julia Ormond
director: Sydney Pollack
Sabrina the Teenage Witch (ABC sitcom)
cast: Beth Broderick (Zelda Spellman)
Melissa Joan Hart (Sabrina Spellman)
Caroline Rhea (Hilda Spellman)
cat: Salem
Sabu: 5 actor 6 Indian
film: Black Narcissus (1947)
Cobra Woman (1944)
Drums (1938)
Elephant Boy (1937)
Jungle Book (1942)
The Thief of Bagdad (1940)
sac: 3 wen 4 cyst 5 bursa, pouch, theca 7 bladder, blister, capsule, vesicle 8 follicle 9 container, marsupium
air ~: 8 alveolus
anatomical ~: 5 bursa
combining form: 3 asc- 4 asco-
fungus spore ~: 5 ascus 6 aecium
gland ~: 6 acinus
pollen ~: 5 theca
starter: 3 ovi
__-sac: 5 cul-de
SAC
counterpart: 5 NORAD
headquarters: 5 Omaha
part: 3 Air 7 Command 9 Strategic
saccharin
discoverer: Ira Remsen
saccharine: 5 mushy, sappy, sweet 6 honied, sirupy, sugary, syrupy 7 candied, cloying, honeyed, mawkish 9 disarming, oversweet
sacellum: 6 chapel, shrine, temple 7 oratory
sacerdotal: 8 hieratic 9 religious
Sacha: 6 Guitry
sachem: 5 chief
Sacher torte: 4 cake 7 dessert
sachet: 5 aroma 7 perfume
item: 5 petal
Sachs: 4 Hans 5 Nelly
__ Sachs: 7 Goldman
Sachs, Nelly: 4 poet 6 German, writer 8 Nobelist 10 playwright
work: Eli
Journey Into a Dustless Room
O the Chimneys
sack: 2 ax 3 axe, bag, bed, can, gut, rob 4 base, boot, drop, fire, loot, oust, raid, ruin, wine 5 dress, harry, let go, pouch, purse, rifle, spoil, steal, strip, waste 6 bounce, harrow, lay off, maraud, pocket, ravage, tackle 7 cashier, despoil, destroy, dismiss, drum out, garment, pillage, plunder, ransack, release 8 demolish, desolate, displace, freeboot, furlough, get rid of, lay waste, pink-slip, spoliate 9 container, depredate, desecrate, devastate, discharge, terminate
a student: 5 expel
designer: 4 Dior
ender: 5 cloth
in the ~: 4 abed
leave the ~: 4 rise, wake 5 arise, awake, waken 6 awaken
material: 5 gunny 6 burlap
out: 4 rest 5 crash, sleep 6 retire, turn in 7 go to bed, saw logs 8 take a nap 9 go to sleep, hit the hay
remove from a ~: 5 unbag
sad ~: 5 schmo 6 schmoe, wretch
starter: 3 hop, ran 4 grip, knap, pack, ruck, wool 5 gunny
time: 5 sleep 7 slumber
sack __: 3 out 4 race, time 5 dress
__ sack: 3 sad
__ Sack: 5 Hacky
sackbut: 4 wind 8 trombone 10 instrument
sackcloth
and ashes: 7 penance
wearer: 6 atoner
sacked out: 4 abed 5 in bed 6 asleep, dozing 7 dormant, napping 8 dreaming, snoozing 9 somnolent 10 sawing logs, slumbering
sacker: 7 brigand
Rome ~: 4 Goth
Sackett: 5 Jubal
__ sack had seven cats...: 4 Each
Sacks: 6 Oliver
__ Sack, The: 3 Sad
Sackville-West, Victoria: 4 poet 7 British
sacque: 5 dress
sacra: 9 vertebrae
Sacra __ Rota: 6 Romana
sacrament: 4 rite 6 ritual 7 baptism, liturgy, penance 8 marriage 9 communion, Eucharist, matrimony 10 holy orders
sacramental __: 4 wine
sacramental oil: 6 chrism 7 chrisom
Sacramento: 3 mts. 4 city, mtns., town 5 range 6 valley 7 capital 9 mountains
arena: 4 Arco
locale: 3 Cal. 10 California
newspaper: 3 Bee
team: 5 Kings
Valley tribe: 5 Maidu
Sacra Romana __: 4 Rota
Sacre __!: 4 bleu
sacred: 4 holy, pure 5 blest, godly, pious 6 divine, iconic, solemn 7 blessed, revered, saintly 8 hallowed, iconical, numinous 9 cherished, dedicated, enshrined, inviolate, religious, spiritual, venerable 10 inviolable, sanctified
combining form: 4 hier- 5 hiero-

hold ~: **5** exalt **6** hallow **8** enshrine, inshrine, sanctify **10** consecrate
image: **4** icon, idol, ikon **5** eikon
make ~: **6** anoint
spot: **5** altar **6** shrine
writings: **4** Veda **5** Bible, Koran
sacred __: **3** cow
Sacred and Profane
author: Faye Kellerman
Sacred Fount, The
author: Henry James
Sacred Wood, The
author: T.S. Eliot
sacrifice: **4** cede, cost, lose, loss **5** forgo, let go, offer, price **6** forego, give up, victim **7** forbear, forfeit, offer up **8** libation, offering, part with, renounce **9** surrender **10** abnegation, contribute, relinquish
diamond ~: **3** fly **4** bunt
Hebrew ~: **6** corban, korban
site: **5** altar
sacrifice __: **3** fly, hit **4** bunt
sacrificial __: **4** lamb
sacrilege: **3** sin **5** crime **6** heresy **7** impiety, mockery **9** blasphemy, profanity, violation **10** disrespect
sacrilegious: **7** impious, profane
sacrosanct: **4** holy **6** sacred **9** immutable, inviolate, religious
sacrum: **4** bone
locale: **6** pelvis
sad: **4** mopy **5** funky, mopey, teary, woful **6** gloomy, rueful, shabby, tragic, triste, woeful **7** crushed, elegiac, grieved, hurting, painful, pensive, piteous, pitiful, subdued, tearful, wistful **8** bereaved, crushing, dolorous, grievous, mournful, pathetic, pitiable, poignant, touching, tragical **9** long-faced, plaintive, regretful, upsetting **10** deplorable, despairing, lachrymose, lamentable, pathetical
be ~: **5** mourn **6** grieve, sorrow
expression: **4** ah me, pout
in ~ shape: **6** bad off
occurrence: **7** tragedy
one: **5** moper, schmo **6** schmoe, wretch
sound: **3** sob **4** sigh
to say: **4** alas
see also gloomy
sad __: **4** sack
Sada: **8** Thompson
Sadaharu: **2** Oh
Sadat: **4** Arab **5** Anwar, Jihan
Sadat, Anwar
predecessor: **6** Nasser
sadden: **4** hurt, pain **6** bum out, darken, deject, dismay, grieve **7** depress, oppress, trouble, turn off **8** dispirit, distress, drag down, keep down **9** bring down, weigh down **10** disappoint, discourage, dishearten
saddened: **5** sorry **7** unhappy **10** melancholy
saddening: **5** bleak **6** dismal, dreary, gloomy, somber **7** joyless **8** hopeless, mournful **9** cheerless, dejecting, upsetting **10** depressing, lugubrious, melancholy, oppressive
saddle: **3** lay, tan, tax **4** load, meat **5** blame **6** burden, lumber **7** oppress **8** encumber, keep down **9** weigh down
be in the ~: **3** run **7** operate **9** supervise
elephant ~: **6** houdah, howdah
ender: **3** bag, bow **4** back, tree **5** cloth
horse: **4** hack, pony **5** mount, steed **7** hackney, palfrey **9** Appaloosa
irritant: **3** bur
loop: **3** lug
material: **7** leather
part: **4** girt, horn **5** girth **6** cantle
starter: **4** pack, side
strap: **6** latigo
tighten a ~: **5** cinch
up: **4** ride
saddle __: **4** shoe, soap, sore **5** horse **6** stitch
__ saddle: **7** English, Western
saddlebag: **8** knapsack
saddlemaker tool: **3** awl
__ Saddles: **7** Blazing
Sade
born: Helen Folasade Adu
homeland: Nigeria
song: Paradise (1988)
Smooth Operator (1985)
The Sweetest Taboo (1985)
__/Sade: **5** Marat
Sade, Marquis de: **6** French, writer
work: Justine
sadhe: **6** Hebrew, letter
predecessor: **2** pe **3** peh
successor: **4** koph, qoph
sadhu: **4** monk **5** friar
sadi: **6** Hebrew, letter
predecessor: **2** pe **3** peh
successor: **4** koph, qoph
Sadie: **5** Frost **7** Hawkins **8** Thompson
Sadie Hawkins Day creator: Al Capp
__ Sadie Thompson: **4** Miss
sadist: **6** abuser
sadistic: **4** mean, sick **5** cruel, harsh, nasty **6** animal, brutal, fierce, savage, unkind, wanton **7** beastly, callous, hurtful, vicious **8** barbaric, fiendish, inhumane, perverse, pitiless, ruthless, vengeful **9** barbarous, cutthroat, ferocious, merciless, monstrous, truculent **10** vindictive
Sadler: **7** Elliott
Sadler, Barry: **4** SSgt.
song: The Ballad of the Green Berets (1966)
sadly: **4** alas **9** unhappily
sadness: **3** woe **4** funk, pain **5** blahs, blues, dolor, gloom, grief, mopes **6** bummer, downer, misery, pathos, sorrow **7** anguish, dismals, emotion, letdown **8** blue funk, distress, glumness, mourning **9** bleakness, dejection, heartache, pessimism, poignancy **10** depression, desolation, gloominess, heartbreak, heavy heart, infelicity, loneliness, melancholy, woefulness
show ~: **3** cry, sob **4** weep
Sad Sack girlfriend: **5** Sadie
__ Sad, Serbia: **4** Novi
Sad Songs (1984 song)
artist: Elton John
SAE: **3** enc. **4** encl. **9** enclosure
__ sae weary...: **4** and I
safari: **4** tour, trek **5** jaunt **7** caravan, journey **9** excursion **10** expedition
camp: **4** base
concern: **5** spoor, trail
helmet material: **4** pith
leader: **5** bwana **6** hunter
park: **3** zoo
servant: **6** bearer
sight: **3** gnu **5** hippo, okapi, rhino
souvenir: **5** photo
safari __: **4** park, suit **5** shirt **6** jacket
Safari: **3** car, GMC, van **4** auto **7** Pontiac **10** automobile
__ Safari: **6** Surfin'
__ Safari, A: **7** Swingin'
safe: **2** OK **4** cosy, cozy, okay, snug, sure, till, wary **5** clear, cozey, cozie, sound, vault **6** secure, steady, tended, unhurt **7** careful, certain, checked, guarded, healthy, lockbox, prudent **8** cautious, discreet, harmless, home-free, nontoxic, reliable, risk-free, riskless, treasury, tucked in, unharmed, unmarked **9** foolproof, goofproof, innocuous, innoxious, preserved, protected, strongbox, unanxious, undamaged, uninjured, unscathed, untouched, wholesome **10** depository, impervious, in the clear, inviolable, repository, unhindered, unpolluted
ender: **5** guard, light **7** cracker, keeping
environmentally ~: **5** green
from the elements: **6** inside **7** indoors
house: **6** asylum **7** hideout, retreat **9** sanctuary
keep ~: **4** hide **5** guard **6** assure, back up, defend, foster, harbor, patrol, police, screen, secure, shield **7** fortify, protect, shelter, ward off **8** chaperon, fight for, preserve, shepherd **9** look after, safeguard, watch over **10** take care of
make ~: **6** declaw, ensure, secure
not ~: **3** out
partner: **5** sound
place: **4** bank **6** refuge **7** retreat
playing ~: **7** careful, prudent **8** cautious
starter: **5** vouch
to be ~: **6** in case **10** just in case
safe __: **5** haven, house **6** harbor
safe-__ box: **7** deposit
safe-__ pass: **7** conduct
__-safe: **4** fail
Safe!: **4** call
safe and __: **5** sound
Safeco
competitor: *see* insurance company
safe-conduct: **4** pass **6** permit **7** passage **8** passport
Safe Conduct
author: Boris Pasternak
safecracker: **4** yegg **5** thief **6** robber **7** burglar
need: **4** soup **5** nitro
safe-deposit box: **5** vault
safeguard: **4** egis, fend, keep, tend **5** aegis, armor, cover, watch **6** buffer, convoy, defend, ensure, escort, harbor, insure, patrol, rescue, screen, secure, shield, surety **7** bulwark, defense, harbour, protect, shelter, store up **8** chaperon, conserve, preserve, scrimp on, security **9** chaperone, companion, cut back on, insurance, look after, watch over **10** precaution, protection
Safeguard: **4** soap
alternative: *see* soap
safekeeping: **4** care **5** trust **6** charge **7** custody **8** wardship **9** salvation **10** protection
Safer, Morley: **8** reporter **10** journalist
colleague: Ed Bradley, Steve Kroft, Scott Pelley, Bob Simon, Lesley Stahl, Mike Wallace
network: **3** CBS
__ safe than sorry: **6** better
safety: **5** cover **6** asylum, refuge **7** freedom, shelter **8** immunity, security **9** assurance, sanctuary **10** protection
device: **3** net **6** airbag **8** seat belt
hwy. ~ org.: **4** MADD, SADD
measure: **10** precaution
place of ~: **6** asylum
provide ~: **7** shelter
specifications: **4** code
valve: **4** duct, vent **5** spout **6** nozzle, outlet **7** channel
safety __: **3** net, pin **4** belt **5** glass, match, razor, valve
Safety __: **4** Last **5** First
safety-deposit __: **3** box
Safety Last (1923 film)
cast: Harold Lloyd
safflower: **3** oil **5** plant **6** flower
saffron: **5** color, plant, spice **6** flower, orange, yellow **8** orangish **9** condiment
dish: **4** rice **6** paella
family: **4** iris
relative: *see* see orange color, yellow color
source: **6** crocus
Safid __: **3** Rud
Safin: **5** Marat
Safire, William: **6** writer
concern: **5** usage
S. Africa
see South Africa
sag: **3** bag, bow, dip, sap **4** bend, cant, drop, fail, fall, flag, flex, flop, give, lean, list, loll, sink, slip, tire, wane, wilt **5** blunt, bulge, curve, droop, lower, slump, stoop, yield **6** cave in, dangle, falter, go limp, impair, reduce, shrink, slouch, soften, tumble, weaken **7** decline, deplete, drop off, exhaust, fatigue, give way **8** collapse, diminish, downturn, enervate, enfeeble, hang down, languish, sink down **9** attenuate, downslide, hang loose, undermine, worsening **10** debilitate, depression, devitalize
SAG: **5** union
former ~ president: **4** Duke **5** Asner **6** Cagney, Heston, Reagan
member: **5** actor
part: **5** Guild **6** Actors, Screen
saga: **4** epic, tale, yarn **5** novel, story **6** legend **9** adventure, chronicle, narrative, recountal
Icelandic ~: **4** edda

like a ~: **6** epical
poetic ~: **4** epos
__ Saga: 5 Olaf's
sagacious: 3 apt **4** cagy, foxy, keen, wise **5** acute, cagey, canny, savvy, sharp, smart **6** astute, shrewd, strong **7** knowing, politic, prudent, sapient **8** profound, rational, sensible **9** astucious, judicious **10** discerning, farsighted, insightful, perceptive
sagacity: 3 wit **4** wits **5** depth, sense **6** acumen, sanity, wisdom **7** insight **8** judgment, sapience **9** intellect **10** profundity
Sagal: 5 Katey
Sagan: 4 Carl **9** Françoise
Sagan, Françoise: 6 French, writer **10** playwright
work: Bonjour Tristesse A Certain Smile
__ Saga, The: 7 Forsyte
sage: 4 guru, herb, wise **5** brain, green, magus, shrub, smart, Solon **6** expert, master, mentor, Nestor, oracle, pundit, savant **7** erudite, grayish, knowing, learned, mahatma, prudent, sapient, scholar, Solomon, thinker **8** harmless, highbrow, profound, sensible **9** authority, graybeard, intellect, judicious, pansophic, seasoning, Solomonic, venerable **10** discerning, specialist
ender: 5 brush
family: 4 mint
Hindu ~: 5 rishi
like a ~: 7 learned
relative: *see* green color
Roman ~: 4 Cato
scarlet ~: 5 plant **6** flower
Sägebrecht: 8 Marianne
Sagebrush State: 3 Nev. **6** Nevada
__ Sage College: 7 Russell
Sage of Concord: Ralph Waldo Emerson
Sager, Carole Bayer
spouse: Burt Bacharach
sages: 8 literati
Muslim ~: 5 ulema
New Testament ~: 4 Magi
Saget: 3 Bob
sagging: 4 limp **5** baggy, loppy, seedy, slack **6** adroop, broody, droopy, floppy **7** concave, flaccid **8** dangling, dejected **9** pendulous **10** ill-fitting
__-saghyz: 3 kok
Saginaw: 3 bay **4** city, port, town
Bay lake: 5 Huron
locale: 8 Michigan
Sagittarius: 4 sign **6** archer
month: 3 Dec., Nov. **8** December, November
predecessor: 7 Scorpio
projectile: 5 arrow
successor: 9 Capricorn
sago: 4 palm
saguaro: 5 fruit, plant **6** cactus, flower
locale: 6 desert
part: 5 spine
Saguaro: 4 park
locale: 7 Arizona
Sagwa, the Chinese Siamese Cat
author: Amy Tan
Sahara: 3 SUV **4** Jeep **6** desert
beast: 5 camel
like the ~: 3 dry **4** arid, sere, vast **5** sandy
massif: 5 Adrar
mountains: 5 Atlas
nation: 4 Chad, Mali **5** Egypt, Libya, Niger
nomad: 6 Berber, Tuareg
region: 5 Sahel
robe: 3 aba **4** abba
scarcity: 4 rain **5** water
sight: 4 dune
stop-off: 5 oasis
wind: 6 simoom
Sahara (2005 film)
cast: Penélope Cruz, Matthew McConaughey, Steve Zahn
__ Sahara: 7 Spanish, Western
Sahel: 6 desert
locale: 5 Sahara
sahib
address: 3 sri
cousin: 5 bwana
land: 5 India
prefix: 3 mem
__ sahib: 5 pukka
Sahl, Mort: 5 comic **8** comedian, humorist, satirist
said: 4 oral **5** vocal **6** spoken, verbal **7** reputed **9** vocalized
all ~ and done: 5 ended
old-style: 5 spake
you ~ it: *see* of course
__ said: 4 'Nuff
__ said...: 3 as I, so I
__ Said: 4 I Am...I, Mama, Port
__ Said a Mouthful: 3 You
__ Said and Done: 3 All
__ Said, 'HA!': 3 God
Said I Loved You...But I Lied (1994 song)
artist: Michael Bolton
__ said it!: 3 You
Said, Sultan Qabus bin: 5 Omani
__ said than done: 6 easier
__ said there'd be days like this: 4 Mama
Saigon: 4 city, port, town
locale: 3 Nam **7** Vietnam
sail: 3 fly, ply, run **4** flit, skim, soar **5** drift, float, glide, leave, pilot, speed, sweep **6** cruise, embark, jigger, junket, travel, voyage **7** cast off, go to sea, head out, ship out **8** navigate, put to sea, shove off
adjust a ~: 4 trim **5** rerig
before the wind: 4 scud
corner: 4 clew
edge: 4 luff
ender: 4 boat, fish **5** board, cloth, plane **6** planer **7** boarder
fit a ~ to: 3 rig
for home: 6 head in
holder: 4 mast **5** sprit
into: 4 lace **5** abuse, scold
into the wind: 4 luff
lash down a ~: 4 frap
over: 4 leap
raise a ~: 5 hoist
reduce ~: 4 reef
securer: 6 batten
set ~: 6 embark **7** push off, ship out **8** put to sea, shove off
small ~: 5 royal
starter: 3 lug, sky, top, try **4** head, main, stay **5** sprit **7** foretop **8** forestay, studding
support: 4 gaff, spar
through: 3 ace **6** breeze
triangular ~: 3 jib **5** raffe **6** lateen, raffee, raffie
type of ~: 3 jib **4** mule **5** mizen **6** gunter, jigger, lateen, mizzen, raffee **7** spanker, spencer **9** spinnaker
under ~: 4 asea **5** at sea
__ sail: 3 set
Sail
constellation: 4 Vela
Sail __ Ship of State!: 3 on O
sailboat: 3 cat **4** dory, yawl **5** ketch, skiff, sloop, yacht **6** galley **7** galleon, pinnace **8** schooner, tall ship, trimaran **9** catamaran **10** knockabout, windjammer
stabilizer: 4 keel
sailcloth: 6 canvas, fabric
...sailed the __ blue...: 5 ocean
Sailfish: 4 boat **5** skiff
sailing: 4 asea **5** at sea, sport **6** cruise **10** navigation
maneuver: 4 tack
of ~: 8 nautical
smooth ~: 4 snap **6** picnic
starter: 4 wind **5** board
vessel: 4 bark, boat, ship, yawl **5** craft, ketch, skiff, sloop **6** barque
Sailing (1980 song)
artist: Christopher Cross
Sailing to Byzantium
author: William Butler Yeats
Sail on (1979 song)
artist: Commodores
sailor: 3 gob, hat, tar **4** bo's'n, hand, salt, swab, swob **5** bosun, middy **6** ensign, pirate, sea dog, seaman **7** boatman, captain, crewman, jack tar, mariner, matelot, matelow, old salt, recruit, skipper, yachter, yachtie **8** coxswain, deckhand, helmsman, salty dog, seafarer, traveler, water dog **9** boatswain, first mate, yachtsman **10** midshipman **11** yachtswoman
accommodation: 5 berth
depth measure: 6 fathom
direction: 4 alee, port **5** aport **6** astern **9** starboard
drink: 3 rum **4** grog
East Indian ~: 6 lascar **7** lashkar
exclamation ~: 3 aye **4** ahoy **5** avast **6** aye aye **7** heave ho
guide: 4 buoy **6** beacon, Pharos **10** lighthouse
like a ~ on leave: 6 ashore
line: 5 brail
on standby: 3 RNR **4** USAR
pal: 5 matey
patron: 4 Elmo
pride: 4 knot
quarters: 6 fo'c's'le
shift: 5 watch
sighting: 4 land
song: 6 chanty
spy grp.: 3 ONI
unskilled ~: 6 lubber **10** landlubber
where a ~ goes: 5 to sea
wooden-shoe ~: 3 Nod **6** Wynken **7** Blynken
sailorly: 5 naval **8** nautical
Sailor on Horseback
author: Irving Stone
sailors: 4 crew **5** hands
Sailor's Song start: 5 to sea
Sailor Who Fell from Grace with the Sea, The
author: Yukio Mishima
sails: 6 canvas
__ Sails in the Sunset: 3 Red
sail the __ seas: 5 seven
...sail the __ blue: 5 ocean
saint: 5 angel, model
Alexandrian ~: 10 Athanasius
American ~: 5 Seton
Avila ~: 6 Teresa
Bohemian ~: 10 Wenceslaus
British ~: 4 Bede, More **5** Alban, Baeda **6** Anselm **7** Dunstan **8** Boniface, Cuthbert **10** Thomas More
combining form: 4 hagi- **5** hagio-
ender: 3 dom
French ~: 5 Denis, Denys, Giles **6** Ansgar, Fiacre **7** Bernard, Louis IX, Vianney **8** Lawrence **9** Genevieve, Joan of Arc **10** Bernadette
Greek ~: 5 Cyril
Hungarian ~: 7 Stephen
Irish ~: 5 Aidan, Kevin **7** Patrick
Italian ~: 5 Paolo, Pius X **7** Ambrose, Gregory **8** Benedict **10** Philip Neri **11** Bonaventure
Muslim ~: 3 pir
North African ~: 7 Cyprian **9** Augustine
Peruvian ~: 10 Rose of Lima
Polish ~: 7 Casimir, Florian
Roman ~: 5 Agnes **6** Agatha **7** Cecilia, Clement, Crispin **8** Paulinus **9** Dionysius, Valentine **11** Christopher
Russian ~: 4 Olga, Gleb **5** Boris **6** Nevski **8** Nicholas, Vladimir **10** Theodosius
Serbian ~: 4 Sava
Spanish ~: 7 Dominic **8** Ignatius
Welsh ~: 5 David
Saint: 8 Eva Marie **10** footballer
Saint __: 4 Joan, Pete **6** Helena, Moritz
Saint __ and Miquelon: 6 Pierre
Saint __ and Nevis: 5 Kitts
Saint __ College: 4 Olaf
Saint __ Cross: 7 Andrew's, George's
Saint __ Day: 7 George's
Saint __ de Paul: 7 Vincent
Saint __ Eve: 5 Agnes'
Saint __ fire: 5 Elmo's
Saint __ Merici: 6 Angela
Saint __ Mountains: 5 Elias
Saint-__: 5 Saens **6** Tropez
Saint-__, France: 4 Malo
Saint Agnes' __: 3 Eve
Saint Andrews: 5 links **6** course **10** golf course
locale: 8 Scotland
Saint Andrew's __: 5 Cross
Saint Anthony's __: 4 fire **5** Cross
Saint Augustine: 4 city, town
locale: 3 Fla. **7** Florida
Saint Bernard: 3 dog **5** canid **6** canine
beat: 4 Alps
fictional ~: 4 Neil
Sainte-Beuve, Charles: 6 French, writer **9** historian
sainted: 4 holy **9** canonized

Saint Elias: 4 peak **5** mount **8** mountain
Saint Elmo's ___: 4 fire
Sainte-Marie, Buffy: 6 singer
Saint-Exupéry, Antoine de: 6 French, writer **7** aviator
work: The Little Prince
Night Flight
Southern Mail
Wind, Sand, and Stars
Saint-Gaudens: 8 Augustus
Saint George's ___: 3 Day **5** Cross
Saint Helens: 4 peak **5** mount **8** mountain
locale: 10 Washington
sainthood, fit for: 4 holy
Saint James, Susan: 7 actress
TV: Kate & Allie, McMillan and Wife, The Name of the Game
Saint Joan
author: George Bernard Shaw
Saint-John: 5 Perse
Saint John Passion
composer: J.S. Bach
Saint John's: 10 university
athletes: 8 Johnnies, Red Storm
locale: 7 Jamaica, New York **9** Minnesota
longtime ~ coach: 9 Gagliardi
Saint Kitts and Nevis org.: 3 OAS
Saint Laurent: 4 Yves
birthplace: 4 Oran
Saint Lawrence ___: 6 Seaway
saintliness: 5 piety **8** morality
Saint Louis: 4 city, port, town
bridge: 4 Eads
landmark: 4 arch
pro team: 4 Rams **5** Blues **9** Cardinals
Saint Lucia: 4 isle **6** island, nation **7** country
money: 4 cent **6** dollar
org.: 3 OAS
saintly: 4 good, holy, pure **5** blest, godly, moral, pious **6** devout, divine, sacred **7** angelic, blessed, sincere **8** beatific, seraphic, virtuous **9** angelical, religious, righteous **10** benevolent, seraphical
Saint Mark, symbol of: 4 lion
Saint Maybe
author: Anne Tyler
___-Saint-Michel: 4 Mont
Saint Nick
see Santa Claus
Saint Patrick's Day event: 6 parade
Saint Paul: 6 writer **9** cathedral **10** evangelist
architect of ~: 4 Wren
feature: 4 dome
locale: 6 London **7** England
longtime dean of ~: 4 Inge
once: 4 Saul
story of ~: 4 Acts
Saint Peter's
feature: 4 dome
locale: 4 Rome **7** Vatican
service: 4 Mass
Saint Petersburg: 4 city, port, town
Ballet once: 5 Kirov
locale: 6 Russia **7** Florida
neighbor: 5 Tampa
river: 4 Neva
setting: 3 EDT, EST
saints
roll of ~: 5 canon
saint's ___: 3 day
Saints: 4 team **6** eleven
home: 10 New Orleans
org.: 3 NFC, NFL
rival: *see* NFL team
sport: 8 football
Saints (patron):
Adelard (gardeners)
Agatha (bellringers)
Agnes (young girls)
Albertus Magnus (scientists)
Aloysius (teenagers)
Amand (innkeepers)
Ambrose (beekeepers)
Andrew (fishermen)
Andronicus (silversmiths)
Anne (mothers, housewives)
Anthony of Padua (lost articles, travelers)
Anthony the Abbot (basket makers, butchers)
Antony (domestic animals)
Apollonia (dentists)
Augustine (brewers)
Barbara (architects, thunderstorms)
Bartholomew (plasterers)
Benedict (students)
Bernadette (shepherds)
Bernard (skiers)
Blaise (throat ailments, wild animals)
Casimir of Poland (bachelors)
Catherine of Alexandria (philosophers)
Catherine of Siena (Italy)
Cecilia (music)
Christopher (travelers)
Clare (embroiderers, television)
Claude (sculptors)
Clement (marble workers)
Cosmas (barbers, pharmacists, physicians)
Crispin (shoemakers)
Cyril (resolving of schisms)
Damian (barbers, pharmacists, physicians)
David (doves, poets, Wales)
Denis (France)
Denys (France)
Dismas (prisoners)
Dominic (astronomers)
Dunstan (goldsmiths, blacksmiths)
Eligius (jewelers, metalworkers)
Elmo (sailors)
Eustachius (hunters)
Florian (firefighters, Poland)
Francis de Sales (writers)
Francis of Assisi (animals, ecologists)
Francis Xavier (foreign missions)
Gabriel the Archangel (postal workers, radio)
Genesius (actors, theater)
Genevieve (disasters, Paris)
George (England)
Gertrude (fear of rats and mice)
Giles (the poor)
Gregory (music)
Herbert (drought relief)
Hilary (snake bite victims)
Hubert (dogs, hunters)
Ignatius (soldiers)
Isidore of Seville (computer users)
Isidore the Farmer (farmers)
James the Greater (Chile)
Januarius (blood banks, Naples, volcanoes)
Jerome (librarians)
Joan of Arc (soldiers)
John Bosco (boys)
John of God (booksellers, hospitals)
John of the Cross (contemplatives)
John the Apostle (writers)
John the Baptist (lambs)
John Vianney (priests)
Jude (lost causes)
Kevin (blackbirds)
Lawrence (cooks, fire prevention)
Lidwina (skaters)
Louis IX (barbers)
Luke (physicians, painters, glassworkers)
Margaret (pregnant women)
Mark (lawyers, lions)
Martha (cooks, housewives, servants)
Martin de Porres (barbers, hairdressers)
Martin of Tours (horsemen, soldiers)
Mary Magdalene (sinners)
Matthew (accountants, bankers, tax collectors)
Maurice (swordsmiths, weavers)
Medard (bad weather)
Methodius (resolving of schisms)
Michael (flyers, paratroopers)
Monica (married women)
Nicholas of Myra (bakers, brides, pawnbrokers)
Our Lady of Guadalupe (Mexico)
Patrick (fear of snakes, Ireland)
Paul (snake bite victims)
Perpetua (cows)
Peter (fishermen, longevity)
Polycarp (earaches)
Rene Goupil (anesthetists)
Roch (dogs, dog lovers)
Rose of Lima (florists, the Americas, Philippines)
Sava (Serbia)
Scholastica (bad weather)
Sebastian (archers)
Stephen (bricklayers, stonemasons)
Teresa of Avila (headaches)
Thomas Aquinas (schools, learning)
Thomas (architects)
Thomas More (English, civil servants)
Valentine (lovers)
Vincent de Paul (charities, volunteers)
Vitus (comedians, dancers)
Zita (lost keys, maids)
Saint-Saëns, Camille: 6 French **8** composer
___ Saints' Day: 3 All
Saint-Simon, Comte de: 6 French **11** philosopher
specialty: rationalism
___ Saints in Three Acts: 4 Four
Saint, The (1997 film)
cast: Val Kilmer, Elisabeth Shue
Saint, The (NBC adventure)
cast: Roger Moore (Simon Templar)
Saint Vincent and the Grenadines: 4 isls. **5** isles **6** nation **7** country, islands
locale: 10 West Indies
money: 4 cent **6** dollar
org.: 3 OAS
Saint Vincent de ___: 4 Paul
Saipan: 4 isle **6** island
island near ~: 4 Guam
saison: 3 été
___ sais quoi: 4 je ne
Sajak, Pat: 2 MC **4** host **5** emcee
boss: Merv Griffin
colleague: Vanna White
purchase from ~ perhaps: 3 an a, an e, an i, an o
Sakakawea: 4 lake **9** reservoir
dam: 8 Garrison
locale: 4 N. Dak.
river: 8 Missouri
Sakall: 2 S.Z.
Sakamoto, Kyu
song: Sukiyaki (1963)
Sakata: 6 Harold
sake: 3 aim **4** gain, good, wine **5** cause, drink, score **6** behalf, motive, profit, reason, regard **7** benefit, concern, purpose, respect, welfare **8** beverage, interest **9** advantage, objective, principle, well-being
for the ~ of: 7 because
starter: 4 keep, name
see also saki
saker: 4 bird **6** falcon
___ sakes alive!: 4 Land
Sakharov, Andrei: 8 Nobelist **9** physicist
saki: 4 wine **5** drink **8** beverage
base: 4 rice
Saki: 5 alias **6** writer
pen name of: H.H. Munro
work: Beasts and Super Beasts
The Chronicles of Clovis
Esme
Reginald
The Square Egg
The Unbearable Bassington
Sakmann, Bert: 6 German **8** Nobelist
Saks: 4 Gene
sal ___: 4 soda
Sal: 3 gal **4** mule **5** Bando, Mineo **6** Maglie **7** Viscuso
canal: 4 Erie
___ Sal: 5 My Gal
sala: 4 room **7** Spanish
site: 4 casa
salaam: 3 bow **5** greet **8** greeting
___ Salaam: 5 Dar es
Salacia
husband: 7 Neptune
salacious: 4 lewd **6** ribald, risqué, smutty **8** uncurbed **10** lubricious, scurrilous, unbecoming
salad: 4 slaw **5** mache **6** course **7** Waldorf **8** coleslaw, side dish **9** macédoine, tabbouleh **10** salmagundi
bowl wood: 4 teak
cheese: 4 bleu, blue
complete a ~: 5 dress
days: 5 youth
deli ~: 4 slaw
follower: 6 entrée
green: 5 cress **6** borage **7** spinach
help with the ~: 4 toss
ingredient: 3 udo **4** cuke, mayo **5** onion **6** carrot, celery, endive
like some ~ dressings: 5 zesty **6** creamy
order: 5 no oil
salad ___: 3 bar, oil **4** bowl, days, fork **5** green, plate **6** greens

— salad: 3 egg 4 tuna 5 chef's, fruit, Greek, pasta 6 Caesar, garden, potato, tossed 7 spinach, Waldorf
Salada: 3 tea
alternative: 6 Lipton, Nestea, Tetley 7 Bigelow, Red Rose 8 Twinings
— Salad Annie: 4 Polk
salad-bar habitué: 5 vegan
salad dressing: 4 Roka 5 aioli, house, ranch 6 French 7 Italian, Russian 8 Wish-Bone 9 Seven Seas 10 bleu cheese, honey Dijon, mayonnaise 11 Good Seasons
bottle: 5 cruet
ingredient: 3 oil 7 vinegar
Saladin citadel site: 5 Cairo
Salam, Abdus: 8 Nobelist 9 Pakistani, physicist
salamander: 3 eft, olm 4 newt 6 mud eel 7 axolotl 8 mudpuppy 9 amphibian
salami: 4 meat 5 Genoa 7 cold cut, sausage
salary: 3 fee, pay 4 take, wage 5 bacon, money, wages 6 income 7 revenue, stipend 8 earnings 9 emolument 10 recompense
get a ~: 4 earn, work
increase: 5 raise
less deductions: 3 net
limit: 3 cap
list: 7 payroll
— salary: 4 base
Salazar: 3 Ken
Salchow: 4 jump
sport: 10 ice skating
Saldana: 3 Zoe 7 Theresa
sale: 4 deal 7 auction, bargain, special 8 discount, disposal, markdown, purchase 9 clearance, reduction, vendition
bake ~: 7 benefit 10 fund-raiser
disclaimer: 4 as is
for ~: 9 available
incentive: 6 rebate
item for ~: 4 good, ware
item marking: 3 irr. 5 irreg. 9 imperfect, irregular
offer for ~: 5 put up 6 market
on ~: 3 low 5 cheap 7 cut-rate, good buy, low-cost, reduced, slashed, thrifty 8 uncostly 9 half-price 10 economical, marked down, reasonable
put up for ~: 5 offer
rummage ~: 5 bazar 6 bazaar 7 benefit 10 fund-raiser
starter: 5 whole
word: 3 off 4 only, save 5 limit
— sale: 3 tag, tax 4 bake, fire, wash, yard 5 short, white 6 forced, garage, jumble, public, red-tag 7 rummage
Salem: 3 cat 4 city, town
city near ~: 6 Eugene
county: 6 Marion
locale: 4 Mass. 6 Oregon 8 Virginia
river: 10 Willamette
—-Salem: 7 Winston
Salem's Lot
author: Stephen King
Sale of the Century: 8 game show
Salerno: 4 city, port, town 8 province
commune: 5 Eboli
Gulf of ~ resort: 6 Amalfi
locale: 5 Italy
sales: 5 trade
attraction: 6 come-on, rebate 8 discount 9 clearance
bonus: 5 spiff
ender: 3 man, men 4 girl, lady, room 5 clerk, woman, women 6 ladies, people, person
goal: 5 quota
group: 5 force
pitch: 2 ad 4 line 5 spiel
rep's client: 3 acc. 7 account
sample: 4 demo
slip: 4 rcpt. 7 receipt
slip entry: 3 tax 5 price
talk: 4 puff 5 pitch
venue: 4 mall, mart, shop 5 store 6 market 8 boutique
sales —: 3 rep, tax 4 slip, talk 5 check 7 receipt
salesperson: 3 rep 5 agent, clerk 6 closer, hawker, vender, vendor 7 employe 8 employee, merchant
lines: 4 puff, sell 5 offer, spiel 6 patter 9 promotion
Sales, Soupy: 4 host 5 comic 8 comedian
dog: 9 White Fang 10 Black Tooth
missile: 3 pie
salicylate: 5 ester
salicylic —: 4 acid
salient: 5 sharp 6 famous, marked, signal 7 central, jutting, notable, obvious, weighty 8 striking 9 arresting, important, intrusive, obtrusive, pertinent, prominent, trenchant 10 impressive, noticeable, projecting, pronounced, protruding, remarkable
Salieri, Antonio: 7 Italian 8 composer
rival: Wolfgang Amadeus Mozart
Saliers: 5 Emily
Salinas: 4 city, town 5 Pedro
locale: 10 California
saline: 5 salty 8 brackish
solution: 5 brine
symbol: 4 NaCl
Salinger, J.D.: 6 writer
work: The Catcher in the Rye
For Esme-with Love and Squalor
Franny and Zooey
A Perfect Day for Bananafish
Raise High the Roof-Beam, Carpenters
Salisbury: 4 city, town
locale: 8 Maryland, Rhodesia
today: 6 Harare
Salisbury —: 5 Plain, steak
Salisbury Plain river: 4 Avon
saliva: 4 spit 5 drool
antibody in ~: 3 IGA
eject ~: 4 spit
salivary —: 5 gland
salivate: 5 drool 7 slobber
Salk, Jonas: 9 physician
contemporary: 5 Sabin
product: 5 serum 7 vaccine
salle: 4 room 6 French 7 chambre
salle à —: 6 manger
Sallie —: 3 Mae
sallow: 3 wan 4 dull, pale, waxy 5 ashen, mealy, pasty 6 anemic, chalky, pallid, peaked, sickly 7 anaemic, bilious 8 liverish 9 albescent, bloodless, jaundiced, unhealthy, yellowish 10 exsanguine
sally: 3 wit 4 joke, quip, raid 5 burst, foray, jaunt, leave 6 assail, attack, junket, onrush, outing, retort, sortie 7 assault, go forth, outflow, outrush 8 burst out, outburst, repartee 9 excursion, irruption, offensive, onslaught, stream out 10 expedition, outpouring, pleasantry
forth: 2 go 5 start 6 set off, set out
lunn: 4 cake
sally —: 4 lunn 5 forth
Sally: 4 Rand, Ride, song 5 Field 6 Bowles, Eilers 7 Hemings, musical 8 Kirkland 9 Kellerman, Struthers
composer: Jerome Kern
Sally — Alley: 5 in Our
Sally — Raphael: 5 Jessy
— Sally: 4 Aunt, Axis 7 Mustang
Sally Ann —: 5 Howes
Sally Bowles
author: Christopher Isherwood
Sally G (1974 song)
artist: Paul McCartney
Salma: 5 Hayek
salmagundi: 3 mix 4 hash, olio, stew 5 salad 6 jumble, medley 7 farrago, mélange, mixture 8 mishmash, mixed bag, pastiche 9 pasticcio, patchwork, potpourri 10 hodgepodge, miscellany
Salman: 7 Rushdie
salmi: 4 game 6 ragout
like ~: 5 spicy 6 spicey
salmon: 3 lox 4 chum, coho, fish, masu, pink, tyee 5 cohoe, color 6 kipper, orange 7 sockeye 9 yellowish
Chinook ~: 4 tyee
cured ~: 7 gravlax
emulate ~: 5 spawn
ender: 5 berry
mature ~: 4 kelt
Pacific ~: 4 chum, coho 5 cohoe
relative: 4 nude 5 melon 6 damask 7 apricot 8 flamingo 9 carnation
serving: 5 steak
smoked ~: 3 lox 4 nova
three-year-old ~: 4 mort
young: 4 jack, parr 5 smolt 6 grilse, samlet
— salmon: 3 red 4 coho, lake, pink 7 chinook, Pacific, sockeye
Salmon
son: 4 Boaz
salmonlike fish of Japan: 3 ayu
Salmon P. —: 5 Chase
Salome: 4 Jens 5 opera
composer: Richard Strauss
role: 5 Herod 8 Herodias, Jokanaan 9 Narraboth
setting: 7 Galilee
to Herod: 5 niece
Salomé
author: Oscar Wilde
salon: 4 shop 6 parlor, soiree 7 gallery 8 assembly, boutique, tea party 9 reception 10 art gallery, living room
color: 5 henna
concern: 4 hair 5 nails
creation: 4 coif 6 hairdo
item: 6 curler
job: 3 dye, set 4 perm, tint 5 rinse 6 facial
product: 3 dye, gel 4 curl, wave 5 spray
sound: 4 snip
worker: 6 barber
— salon: 3 art 6 beauty
Salonen, Esa-Pekka: 7 Finnish 9 conductor
Salonga: 3 Lea
saloon: 3 bar, inn, pub 4 dive 6 lounge, tavern 7 barroom, taproom 8 alehouse, taphouse 9 speakeasy 10 restaurant
chit: 3 tab 6 bar tab
entertainer: 5 B-girl
habitué: 6 barfly
light: 4 neon
order: 3 ale 4 beer 5 booze
seat: 5 stool
smashers assn.: 4 WCTU
salsa: 3 dip 4 salt 5 dance, music, sauce, spice 6 relish 8 dressing 9 condiment, flavoring, seasoning
club dance: 5 rumba 6 rhumba
holder: 4 chip 5 nacho
like ~: 3 hot 4 mild 5 tangy, zesty
salt: 3 gob, tar 4 cure, NaCl, swab, swob, zest 6 borate, deicer, flavor, iodate, kipper, living, pickle, sailor, sea dog, seaman, season 7 acetate, bromate, citrate, crewman, jack tar, mariner, matelot, matelow, nitrate, nitrite, sulfate, sulfite, swabbie 8 benzoate, deckhand, dry humor, fluoride, preserve, seafarer, stearate, tartrate 9 carbonate, condiment, cyclamate, phosphate, seasoning, shellback 10 bluejacket
acid ~: 5 ester
add ~: 6 flavor, season
away: 4 bank, hide, keep, save 5 amass, cache, hoard, lay by, lay up, put by, spare, stash, store 6 invest, pile up 7 deposit, store up 8 hold on to, lay aside, put aside, set aside 9 stockpile 10 accumulate
bit: 5 grain, pinch
combining form: 3 hal- 4 hali-, halo-, sali-
deposit: 4 lick
ender: 3 box 4 bush, wort 5 peter, water, works 6 cellar, shaker
his wife turned to ~: 3 Lot
in French: 3 sel
mines: 4 work 6 office
preserve with ~: 4 corn
rock ~: 4 NaCl 6 halite
rub ~ in the wound: 3 vex 4 fret, rack 5 harry, hound 6 harass, pester, pick on, plague, rankle 7 afflict, agonize, anguish, bedevil, oppress, torment, torture 8 aggrieve, distress, irritate 9 persecute
spread ~: 5 deice
treat ~: 6 iodize
tree: 4 atle
water: 3 sea 5 brine, ocean
see also sailor
salt —: 4 away, cake, dome, flat, lake, lick, mine, pork 5 marsh, water 6 shaker
salt — earth: 5 of the
salt — taffy: 5 water
salt-—: 3 box
— salt: 3 bay, sea 4 rock 5 attic, Epsom, table 6 celery, garlic

Salt: 5 river 8 Jennifer
  city on the ~: 4 Mesa 5 Tempe 7 Phoenix
  locale: 7 Arizona
Salt ___ City: 4 Lake
SALT: 4 pact 6 treaty
  concern: 3 ABM 4 ICBM, nuke 5 H-bomb
  part: 4 Arms 5 Talks 9 Strategic 10 Limitation
  participant: 3 USA 4 USSR
salt and ___: 6 pepper
saltate: 4 jump, leap
saltbox topper: 4 roof
saltbush: 5 orach, shrub 6 orache
___ Salt Desert: 5 Great
salted peanuts: 5 snack
Salten, Felix: 6 writer 9 Hungarian
  work: Bambi
saltine: 5 bread 7 cracker 9 appetizer
  brand: 5 Zesta 7 Premium
___ Salt Lake: 5 Great
Salt Lake City
  athlete: 3 Ute
  city near ~: 4 Orem
  grp.: 3 LDS
  locale: 4 Utah
  newspaper: 7 Tribune
  river: 6 Jordan
saltlike: 6 haloid
salt-marsh shrub genus: 3 iva
Salt-n-Pepa: 4 trio
  genre: 3 rap
  members: James, Denton, Roper
  song: Do You Want Me (1991)
    Push It (1987)
    Shoop (1993)
    Whatta Man (1994)
Salton Sea: 4 lake
saltpeter: 5 niter
  source: 5 Chile
___ salts: 4 bath 5 Epsom
saltwater: 5 brine 6 marine 8 maritime
Salt-Water Ballads
  author: John Masefield
saltwater taffy: 5 candy
salty: 3 dry 4 blue, racy, tart 5 bawdy, briny, tangy, taste, witty 6 coarse, earthy, lively, ribald, risqué, saline 7 piquant, pungent 8 alkaline, brackish, off-color 10 indelicate, pugnacious
salty dog: 5 drink 6 sailor 7 jack tar 8 beverage, cocktail
  ingredient: 3 gin 5 vodka 10 grapefruit
salubrious: 4 good 7 healthy 8 hygienic, sanitary 9 healthful, wholesome 10 beneficial
salubrity: 8 wellness
Salud!: 5 skoal, toast 6 cheers, kampai
Saludos ___!: 6 amigos
Saluki: 3 dog 5 canid 6 canine
___-Salut: 4 Port
salutary: 4 good 6 aidful, benign, useful 7 gainful, healthy, helpful 8 curative, positive, remedial, sanative, valuable 9 effectual, favorable, healthful, practical, wholesome 10 beneficial, productive, profitable, worthwhile
salutation: 3 bow 4 hail, kiss 5 hallo, hello, title 6 speech 7 address, regards, welcome 8 greeting 9 reception 10 apostrophe, good wishes, pleasantry
  word: 3 sir 4 dear, sirs 6 madame
salutations: 7 regards 8 respects
salute: 3 bow, nod 4 hail, laud, wave 5 exalt, extol, greet, honor, kudos, toast 6 extoll, homage, kampai, praise 7 acclaim, address, applaud, commend, flatter, gesture, glorify, plaudit, tribute, welcome 8 accolade, encomium, flattery, good word, greeting 9 laudation, panegyric, pay homage, recognize 10 exaltation, panegyrize
Salvador: 4 city, Dali, town 5 Luria 7 Allende
  author: Joan Didion
  formerly: 5 Bahia
  locale: 6 Brasil, Brazil
___ Salvador: 3 San
salvage: 4 junk, loot, save, take 5 glean 6 obtain, redeem, regain, rescue 7 get back, reclaim, recover, restore 8 retrieve 9 remainder
salvation: 6 escape, pardon, rescue 7 freedom, release 8 delivery, lifeline, reprieve 10 liberation, redemption
Salvation Army: 7 charity
  temp: 5 Santa 10 bell-ringer
  trainee: 5 cadet
Salvatore: 9 Quasimodo
salve: 4 balm, ease 5 cream 6 lotion, remedy, soothe 7 anodyne, assuage, comfort, mollify, relieve, unction, unguent 8 dressing, lenitive, liniment, medicine, ointment, palliate 9 alleviate, emollient, lubricant, mollifier, untrouble 10 medication, palliative
  apply ~: 5 rub in
  ingredient: 4 aloe
salver: 4 tray 7 platter
salvia: 5 plant 6 flower
  cousin: 4 sage
salvo: 4 bang, fire, hail 5 blast, burst, shout 6 volley 7 barrage, ovation, tribute 8 outburst 9 broadside, cannonade, discharge, explosion, fusillade
Salwen: 3 Hal
Salzburg: 4 city, town
  environs: 4 Alps
  locale: 3 Aus. 4 Aust. 7 Austria
  river: 3 Mur
Sam: 4 Bass, Colt, Hill, Huff, Nunn, Rice, Wood 5 Adams, Cooke, Ervin, Jaffe, Neill, Raimi, Sills, Snead, Spade, uncle, Wyche 6 Levene, Malone, Mendes, Taylor, Walton 7 Bottoms, Clemens, Elliott, Houston, Kinison, McCloud, Rayburn, Shepard, Spiegel 8 Bischoff, Crawford, Levenson, Phillips 9 Donaldson, Peckinpah, Wanamaker, Waterston
Sam ___: 4 Hill 7 the Sham
Sam ___ belt: 6 Browne
Sam-___: 3 I-Am
___ Sam: 3 I Am 5 Uncle
Sam Adams product: 3 ale
Sam and Dave
  members: Moore, Prater
  song: Hold On! I'm a Comin' (1966)
    I Thank You (1968)
    Soul Man (1967)
Samantha: 3 Fox 4 Sang 5 Eggar 6 Mathis
  aunt: 5 Clara
  mother: 6 Endora
Samar: 4 isle 6 island
  island near: 5 Leyte
  locale: Philippines
Samaria, south of: 5 Judea 6 Judaea
Samaritan
  be a ~: 3 aid 4 help
___ Samaritan: 4 Good
samarium: 5 metal 7 element
Samarra: 4 city, town
  locale: 4 Irak, Iraq
  river: 6 Tigris
samba: 4 step 5 dance, music
  variation: 7 carioca
Sambora, Richie
  spouse: Heather Locklear
same: 4 dupe, ibid., idem, like, twin 5 alike, clone, ditto, equal, exact, level, xerox 6 coeval, double, on a par 7 pronoun, similar, uniform 8 constant, likewise, matching, unvaried 9 aforesaid, analogous, congruous, duplicate, identical, perpetual, similarly, unaltered, unchanged, unfailing, unvarying 10 carbon copy, coincident, comparable, compatible, consistent, equivalent, invariable, synonymous, tantamount, true to type, two of a kind, unchanging
  at the ~ time: 5 along 8 meantime 9 meanwhile
  at the ~ time as: 5 while 6 during, whilst
  be the ~: 4 gybe, jibe 5 agree, match, tally 6 concur, square 8 coincide, dovetail 10 correspond
  combining form: 3 aut-, hom-, iso-, syn- 4 auto-, equi-, homo-, taut- 5 homeo-, tauto-
  consider the ~: 6 equate
  in prescriptions: 3 ead.
  in the ~ way: 3 too 4 also 6 as well 8 likewise 9 similarly
  In the ~ way: 9 similarly, uniformly 10 comparably
  just the ~: 3 yet 5 still 6 anyhow, anyway, at that, even so, though 7 however 9 at any rate
  make the ~: 8 equalize
  of the ~ height: 4 even 6 square 8 parallel
  of the ~ opinion: 3 one 5 joint 6 agreed 8 in accord 9 concerted, unanimous, undivided 10 like-minded
  starter: 4 self
Same ___ Me: 3 Ole
___ same boat: 5 in the
___ same breath: 5 in the
samech: 6 Hebrew, letter
  predecessor: 3 nun
  successor: 4 ayin
Same here!: 5 ditto, me too, so do I
samekh: 6 Hebrew, letter
  predecessor: 3 nun
  successor: 4 ayin
sameness: 3 par 5 unity 6 parity, tedium, unison 7 analogy, oneness 8 equality, likeness, monotony 9 alikeness 10 repetition, similarity, uniformity
same old ___: 5 grind, story
Same Old Lang Syne (1980 song)
  artist: Dan Fogelberg
same-old-same-old: 3 rut 4 dull 7 rat race, routine 9 treadmill
___ same time: 5 at the
Same Time, Next Year: 4 film, play
  author: Bernard Slade
  cast: Alan Alda, Ellen Burstyn
___ same token: 5 by the
___ same wavelength: 5 on the
Sami: 4 Lapp 9 Laplander
samisen: 4 lute 6 string 10 instrument
  origin: 5 Japan
Sammee: 4 Tong
Sammi: 5 Davis, Smith
Samms: 4 Emma
Sammy: 4 Cahn, Fain, Kaye, Sosa 5 Baugh, Davis, Hagar, Johns 6 Turner
Sammy ___ Jr.: 5 Davis
Samoa: 4 isls. 5 isles 7 islands
  capital: 4 Apia
  island: 5 Upolu 6 Hivaoa, Savaii
  neighbor: 5 Tonga
  port: 8 Pago Pago
  studier of ~: 4 Mead
Samos: 4 isle 6 island
  locale: 6 Aegean, Greece
  site of ancient ~: 5 Ionia
  storyteller of ~: 4 Esop 5 Aesop
samovar: 3 urn
  serving: 3 tea
Samoyed: 3 dog, pet 5 canid, spitz 6 canine
  burden: 4 sled
sampan: 4 boat 5 skiff
sample: 3 bit, eat, sip, try 4 bite, case, clip, demo, lick, part, poll, test, unit 5 model, piece, savor, taste, token 6 morsel, survey, swatch 7 display, examine, example, handout, inspect, partake, pattern, portion, section, segment 8 fragment, instance, specimen, spoonful, standard 10 experience, experiment
  sign by a free ~: 5 try me
___ sample: 5 floor
sampler statement: 5 motto
sampling: 4 case, poll 8 instance, specimen
___ sampling: 6 random
Sampras, Pete: 7 netster 9 tennis pro
  milieu: 5 court
  rival: 6 Agassi
Sampson: 4 Will
Sam's Club
  rival: 3 BJ's 6 Costco
Samson: 5 he-man, opera
  composer: George Frideric Handel
  father: 6 Manoah
  tempter: 7 Delilah
Samson Agonistes
  author: John Milton
Samson and Delilah (1949 film)
  cast: Hedy Lamarr, Victor Mature
  director: Cecil B. DeMille
  setting: 4 Gaza
Samsung country: 5 Korea
Sam the Sham and the Pharaohs
  song: Lil' Red Riding Hood (1966)
    Wooly Bully (1965)
Samuel: 4 Colt, Ting 5 Adams, Alito, Baker, Morse, Pepys, Ramey

6 Barber, Butler, Daniel, Fuller, Selvon 7 Beckett, Goldwyn, Gompers, Jackson, Johnson 9 Coleridge, Hahnemann 10 Duesenberg, Richardson
parent: 6 Hannah 7 Elkanah
preceder: 4 Ruth
son: 4 Joel 6 Abijah
teacher: 3 Eli
Samuel __ Coleridge: 6 Taylor
Samuel __ Morison: 5 Eliot
Samuel de __: 9 Champlain
Samuel F.B. __: 5 Morse
Samuel L. __: 7 Jackson
Samuelson, Paul: 8 Nobelist 9 economist
Samurai: 3 SUV 6 Suzuki
__ Samurai, The: 5 Seven
__ s'amuse: 5 Le roi
San __: 4 Blas, José, Juan, Remo 5 Bruno, Diego, Dimas, Mateo, Pablo, Pedro 6 Angelo, Antone, Felipe, Isidro, Marcos, Marino, Martín, Rafael, Simeon, Ysidro 7 Antonio, Gabriel, Gennaro, Quentin
San __ Bay: 5 Pablo
San __ Capistrano: 4 Juan
San __ Chargers: 5 Diego
San __ Chicken: 5 Diego
San __ Day: 7 Jacinto
San __ fault: 7 Andreas
San __ Hill: 4 Juan
San __ Mountains: 4 Juan 7 Gabriel
San __ Obispo: 4 Luis
San __ Potosí: 4 Luis
San __ scale: 4 Jose
San __ Spurs: 7 Antonio
San __ Valley: 7 Joaquin
Sana: 4 city, town 7 capital
locale: 5 Yemen
San Angelo: 4 city, town
locale: 5 Texas
San Antonio: 4 city, town
county: 5 Bexar
landmark: 5 Alamo
locale: 5 Texas
pro team: 5 Spurs
San Antonio Rose (1961 song)
artist: Floyd Cramer
sanative: 5 tonic 6 iatric 7 healing 8 curative, remedial, salutary 9 healthful, medicinal 10 corrective
sanatorium: 8 hospital
sanatory: 7 healthy
San Bernardino: 3 mts. 4 city, mtns., town 5 range 6 valley 9 mountains
locale: 10 California
San Bruno: 4 city, town
locale: 10 California
Sanchez: 5 Sonia
Sanchez, Oscar Arias: 8 Nobelist 10 Costa Rican
Sancho __: 5 Panza
San Clemente: 4 isle 6 island
locale: 10 California
sanctified: 4 holy 5 blest 6 divine, sacred, solemn
sanctify: 4 keep 5 adore, bless, deify, exalt, extol 6 anoint, devote, extoll, hallow, praise, purify 7 absolve, cleanse, glorify, worship 8 canonize, dedicate, enshrine, inshrine, set apart 10 consecrate, panegyrize
sanctimonious: 4 smug 5 false, pious 7 bigoted, prudish 8 unctuous 9 deceiving, insincere
sanction: 2 OK 3 ban, let, nod 4 abet, back, okay, pass, tabu, writ 5 allow, bless, brook, leave, taboo 6 accept, assent, decree, invest, permit, praise, ratify, suffer 7 approve, backing, boycott, certify, command, confirm, consent, embargo, empower, endorse, go-ahead, indorse, liberty, license, mandate, penalty, qualify, support, warrant 8 accede to, accredit, approval, assent to, blessing, legalize, sentence, stand for, tolerate, validate, vouch for 9 approve of, authorize, clearance, encourage, get behind, give leave, privilege, put up with, recognize, recommend, subscribe 10 commission, give the nod, green light, injunction, legitimize, permission, punishment, sufferance, underwrite
sanctioned: 5 jural, legal, legit, licit, sound, valid 6 kasher, kosher, lawful, proper 7 regular 8 official, orthodox, rightful, verified 9 by the book, canonical 10 legitimate
__ Sanction, The: 3 Loo 5 Eiger
sanctity: 5 piety 8 holiness
sign of ~: 4 halo
sanctuary: 3 den 4 aery, bema, eyry, hole, lair, park, port 5 aerie, altar, cover, eyrie, haven, oasis, zendo 6 asylum, bethel, chapel, church, covert, harbor, hole-up, refuge, resort, safety, shrine, temple 7 chancel, convent, defense, harbour, hideout, reserve, retreat, shelter 8 cloister, hideaway, preserve 9 anchorage, cathedral, harborage, hermitage, safe house, seclusion 10 ivory tower, protection, tabernacle
African ~: 6 casbah
give ~: 7 protect
Greek ~: 5 secos, sekos
Sanctuary
author: William Faulkner, Faye Kellerman
sanctum: 3 den 4 lair 5 haven, oasis 6 shrine
inner ~: 6 adytum
__ Sanctum Mysteries, The: 5 Inner
sand: 3 tan 4 dune, grit 5 pluck, scour, shore, valor 6 abrade, smooth, yellow 7 reddish 8 abrasive, brownish
bar: 4 reef 5 shoal
creation: 6 castle
dab: 4 fish
dune: 4 seif
ender: 3 bag, bar, box, bur, hog, lot, man, men, pit 4 bank, fish, spur, worm, wort 5 blast, paper, piper, stone, storm 6 bagger, castle 7 blaster
fine ~: 4 silt
hill: 4 dune
kind of ~: 4 slag
lance: 4 fish
product: 5 glass
relative: *see* yellow color
starter: 5 green, quick
trap: 6 bunker, hazard
unit: 5 grain
sand __: 3 bar, dab, eel 4 crab, dune, trap 5 shark 6 castle, dollar
Sand: 4 Paul 6 George
Sandahl: 7 Bergman
sandal: 4 clog, geta, shoe, zori 5 jelly, thong 7 go-ahead 8 flip-flop, footgear, footwear, huarache
ender: 4 wood
Japan ~: 4 zori
part: 5 strap
sandals: 5 flats
sandarac: 4 tree
family: 7 cypress
relative: 7 juniper 10 arborvitae
wood: 5 thuja, thuya
sandbag: 5 cheat, force 7 inhibit, swindle 8 obstruct, undercut 9 undermine
sandbank: 5 shelf, shoal
Sandberg, Ryne
sport: 8 baseball
sandbox
need: 4 pail
patron: 3 kid, tot 4 tike, tyke
__ Sandbox: 5 Up the
Sandbox, The
author: Edward Albee
Sandburg, Carl: 4 poet 6 writer
work: Abraham Lincoln - The Prairie Years
Abraham Lincoln - The War Years
A.E.F.
The American Songbag
Chicago
Chicago Poems
Cornhuskers
Fog
Good Morning, America
Grass
Harvest Poems
Honey and Salt
The People, Yes
Reckless Ecstasy
Rootabaga Stories
Smoke and Steel
sand-castle
destroyer: 4 wave
locale: 5 beach
Sandcastle, The
author: Iris Murdoch
Sande, Earl: 6 jockey
milieu: 5 track
Sandel, Cora: 6 writer 9 Norwegian
__ sander: 4 belt, disk 7 orbital
Sander: 7 Vanocur
Sanders: 5 Deion 6 George 7 Harland, Richard 8 Lawrence
Sanders, Deion: 10 baseballer, footballer
nickname: 4 Neon
Sanders, George: 5 actor
persona: 3 cad
spouse: Zsa Zsa Gabor
Sanders, Harland: 3 Col. 7 Colonel
company: 3 KFC
Sanders, Lawrence: 6 writer
work: The Anderson Tapes
Caper
Capital Crimes
The Case of Lucy Bending
The Dream Lover
The Eighth Commandment
The First Deadly Sin
The Fourth Deadly Sin
Guilty Pleasures
The Loves of Harry Dancer
Love Songs
The Marlow Chronicles
McNally's Alibi
McNally's Caper
McNally's Chance
McNally's Dilemma
McNally's Folly
McNally's Gamble
McNally's Luck
McNally's Puzzle
McNally's Risk
McNally's Secret
McNally's Trial
The Passion of Molly T
The Pleasures of Helen
Privat Pleasures
The Second Deadly Sin
The Seduction of Peter S
The Seventh Commandment
The Sixth Commandment
Stolen Blessings
Sullivan's Sting
Tales of the Wolf
The Tangent Factor
The Tangent Objective
The Tenth Commandment
The Third Deadly Sin
The Timothy Files
Timothy's Game
The Tomorrow File
Sand, George: 5 alias 6 French, writer
friend: 6 Chopin
work: Agendas
The Bagpipers
The Black City
Consuelo
Country Waif
The Devil's Pool
Elle et lui
François le Champi
The Gallant Lords of Bois-Dori
Histoire de Ma Vie
Horace
Indiana
La Mare au diable
La Petite Fadette
La Ville Noire
Lavinia
Lélia
Le Marquis de Villemer
Le menunier d'Angibault
Les Maîtres Mosaïstes
Les Maîtres Sonneurs
Lucrezia Floriani
Mademoiselle Merquem
Marianne
The Master Mosaic Workers
The Master Pipers
Mauprat
The Miller of Angibault
Nanon
Narcisse
Nohant
She & He
Simon
Valentine
A Winter on Majorca
sandhill: 5 crane
Sandhurst school: 3 RMA
San Diego: 4 city, port, town
athletes: 6 Aztecs
attraction: 3 zoo
city near ~: 6 Del Mar, La Mesa
locale: 10 California
newspaper: 7 Tribune
pro team: 6 Padres 8 Chargers
school: 4 SDSU

San Diego __: **7** Chicken
San-Diego-to-Santa-Ana dir.: **3** NNW
Sandinista foe: **6** Contra
Sandler, Adam: **5** actor
film: Anger Management (2003)
Big Daddy (1999)
Click (2006)
The Longest Yard (2005)
Reign Over Me (2007)
Spanglish (2004)
The Waterboy (1998)
The Wedding Singer (1998)
song: The Chanukah Song (1995)
__ Sandman: **5** Enter **6** Mister
Sandoz: **4** Mari
sandpaper: **4** buff **6** abrade
covering: **4** grit
like ~: **4** fine **5** rough **6** coarse, gritty
Sand Pebbles, The (1966 film)
cast: Richard Attenborough, Candice Bergen, Richard Crenna, Steve McQueen
director: Robert Wise
sandpiper: **4** bird, knot, ruff **5** snipe, stint **6** dunlin, willet **8** grayback, peetweet, redshank **10** sanderling
female ~: **3** ree **5** reeve
relative: **6** curlew
Sandpipers
song: Guantanamera (1966)
Sandpiper, The (1965 film)
cast: Charles Bronson, Richard Burton, Eva Marie Saint, Elizabeth Taylor
director: Vincente Minnelli
Sandra: **3** Dee **6** Haynie **7** Bullock **8** Bernhard
Sandra __ O'Connor: **3** Day
Sandrich: **3** Jay **4** Mark
Sand Rivers
author: Peter Matthiessen
Sandro: **10** Botticelli
sands: **5** shore **8** littoral
Sands: **5** Diana, Tommy
__ Sands Missile Range: **5** White
sands of __: **4** time
Sands of Iwo Jima (1949 film)
cast: John Agar, Adele Mara, John Wayne
director: Allan Dwan
Sands of Time, The
author: Sidney Sheldon
Sands, Tommy
song: Teen-Age Crush (1957)
spouse: Nancy Sinatra
sandstone: **5** wacke **7** mineral **9** graywacke
sand-trap club: **5** wedge
Sandusky: **4** city, town
lake: **4** Erie
locale: **4** Ohio
sandwich: **3** sub **4** gyro, hero **5** bread, po boy **6** hoagie, reuben **7** Dagwood **9** hamburger, interpose
bread: **3** rye **4** pita **5** white **9** sourdough **10** whole wheat
deli ~: **3** sub **4** hero **5** hoagy **6** hoagie
filler: **3** ham **4** tuna **5** jelly **6** cheese, salami, turkey **7** bologna, chicken **8** tuna fish **9** roast beef **10** corned beef
garnish: **5** caper
grilled ~: **4** melt
knuckle ~: **4** fist
need: **5** bread **7** filling
remnant: **5** crumb
shop: **4** deli
spread: **4** mayo **6** catsup **7** ketchup, mustard **10** mayonnaise
tiny ~: **6** canapé
wrapper: **4** foil **5** Saran **6** Baggie **7** tin foil
sandwich __: **3** bag **5** board
__ sandwich: **4** club, hero, open **5** Cuban **6** Reuben **7** Dagwood, knuckle, western
sandwich-board: **2** ad
words: **5** eat at
Sandwich Islands: **6** Hawaii
sandy: **3** red **5** blond, flaxy, light **6** blonde, flaxen, gritty **7** arenose, arenous **8** gravelly **9** arenulous, tow-headed, yellowish
area: **5** beach
islet: **5** atoll
Sandy: **3** dog **4** Gary, Lyle **5** Posey **6** Dennis, Duncan, Koufax, Nelson
owner: **5** Annie
__ Sandy Desert: **5** Great
sandy-haired: **5** blond **6** blonde
sane: **3** fit **4** well, wise **5** lucid, right, sober, sound **6** normal, steady **7** healthy, logical, politic, prudent **8** all there, balanced, credible, feasible, moderate, oriented, rational, reliable, sensible, together **9** competent, judicious, practical, pragmatic, realistic **10** discerning, fair-minded, reasonable, thoughtful
San Fernando: **6** valley
neighbor: **6** Encino
Sanford: **5** Clark **6** Isabel
Sanford and Son (NBC sitcom)
cast: Redd Foxx (Fred Sanford)
Whitman Mayo (Grady Wilson)
LaWanda Page (Esther Anderson)
Demond Wilson (Lamont Sanford)
producer: Lear
__ Sanford Brown: **5** Georg
San Franciscan Nights (1967 song)
artist: Animals
San Francisco: **3** bay **4** city, port, town
1906 ~ event: **5** quake
Bay tribe: **5** Miwok
county north of ~: **5** Marin
district: **6** Castro
like ~: **5** hilly
locale: **10** California
newspaper: **8** Examiner **9** Chronicle
pro team: **6** Giants, Niners
setting: **3** PDT, PST
street: **6** Haight **7** Ashbury
tower: **4** Coit
transit system: **4** BART
San Francisco (1936 film)
cast: Clark Gable, Jeanette MacDonald, Spencer Tracy
San Francisco (1967 song)
artist: Scott McKenzie
sang-__: **5** froid
Sang: **8** Samantha
San Gabriel: **3** mts. **4** city, mtns., town **5** range **9** mountains
locale: **10** California
Sanger: **8** Margaret **9** Frederick
sang-froid: **5** poise **6** aplomb **8** calmness, coolness, presence **9** composure **10** equanimity, sedateness
San Giacomo, Laura: **7** actress
film: Quigley Down Under (1990)
sex, lies, and videotape (1989)
TV: Just Shoot Me
sanglier: **6** fabric **8** material
Sangre de Cristo: **3** mts. **4** mtns. **5** range **9** mountains
locale: **8** Colorado **9** New Mexico
sangría: **5** drink **8** beverage
container: **6** carafe
ingredient: **4** wine **10** fruit juice
sanguinary: **9** ferocious
sanguine: **3** red **4** rosy, sure **5** happy, ruddy **6** blowsy, blowzy, bright, elated, florid, upbeat **7** assured, blowsed, blowzed, buoyant, certain, crimson, flushed, glowing, hopeful, reddish, scarlet **8** cheerful, positive **9** believing, confident, convinced, presuming, satisfied **10** flying high, inspirited, optimistic
Sanibel: **4** isle **6** island
locale: **7** Florida
sanitary: **4** pure **5** clean **6** washed **7** aseptic, healthy, sterile **8** germfree, hygienic, pristine, purified, spotless, unsoiled **9** healthful, unsullied, untouched, wholesome **10** antiseptic, immaculate, salubrious, uninfected, unpolluted
sanitation: **7** hygiene
sanitize: **6** censor, degerm, purify **7** absolve, cleanse **9** deodorize, disinfect, expurgate, sterilize
sanitized: **5** clean
sanity: **3** wit **4** wits **5** logic, sense **6** acumen, reason, senses, wisdom **7** balance **8** lucidity, prudence, sagacity **9** lucidness, soundness, stability
Sanity is Where You Find It
author: Will Rogers
San Jacinto: **6** battle
San Jacinto __: **3** Day
San Joaquin Valley city: **6** Fresno
San Jose: **4** city, town
athletes: **8** Spartans
conference: **3** WAC
county: **10** Santa Clara
locale: **10** California
pro team: **6** Sharks
river: **6** Coyote **9** Guadalupe
San José: **4** city, town **7** capital
locale: **9** Costa Rica
see also Spanish
San Juan: **4** city, port, town
locale: **10** Puerto Rico
suburb: **6** Cataño
see also Spanish
San Juan Hill: **6** battle
locale: **4** Cuba
San Juan Mountains peak: **5** Eolus
Sanka: **4** java **5** decaf **6** coffee
alternative: **5** Yuban **7** Folgers, Melitta, Nescafé, Savarin **9** Hills Bros.
San Leandro: **4** city, town
locale: **10** California
__ San Lucas: **4** Cabo
San Luis Obispo: **4** city, town
locale: **10** California
San Marcos: **4** city, town
locale: **5** Texas **10** California
San Marino
currency: **4** euro
former currency: **4** lira, lire
neighbor: **5** Italy **6** Italia
San Martín: **4** José
San Mateo: **4** city, town
locale: **10** California
San Pablo: **3** bay **4** city, town
locale: **10** California
neighbor: **4** Napa
San Rafael: **4** city, town
county: **5** Marin
locale: **10** California
San Ramon: **4** city, town
locale: **10** California
San Remo: **4** city, port, town
locale: **5** Italy **7** Riviera
sans: **5** minus **6** French **7** lacking, needing, without
sans __: **4** égal **5** serif, souci
sans-__: **7** culotte
San Salvador: **4** city, town **7** capital
locale: **10** El Salvador
see also Spanish
sansei: **8** Japanese
grandparent: **5** issei
parent: **5** nisei
San Simeon
builder: **6** Hearst
Sanskrit: **5** Indic **8** language
canon: **5** agama
classic: **4** Gita
cousin: **4** Pali
language: **5** Vedic
syllable: **2** om **3** aum
Sansom: **3** Art **7** William
sans souci: **8** carefree
Santa
see Santa Claus
Santa __: **3** Ana **4** Anna, Cruz, Rosa, Ynez **5** Anita, Clara, Claus, Lucia, Maria **6** Monica **7** Barbara
Santa __ and Pooh Box: **3** Roo
Santa __ Canyon: **5** Elena
Santa __ Islands: **4** Cruz **7** Barbara
Santa __ Valley: **4** Ynez
Santa __ winds: **3** Ana
Santa Ana: **4** city, town, wind
base near ~: **6** El Toro
city near ~: **6** Irvine
county: **6** Orange
locale: **10** California
Santa Anita: **5** track **9** racetrack
locale: **10** California
transaction: **3** bet **5** wager
Santa Anna: **7** general, Mexican
battleground: **5** Alamo
Santa Baby
artist: Eartha Kitt
Santa Barbara: **4** city, soap, town **7** islands
city near ~: **4** Ojai
locale: **10** California
Santa Catalina: **4** isle **6** island
locale: **10** California
Santa Clara: **4** city, town
locale: **10** California
Santa Claus: **10** benefactor
artist: Thomas Nast
bane: **4** soot
busy time: **3** Dec. **4** Xmas, yule **8** December **9** Christmas
delivery: **3** toy **4** gift **7** present
helper: **3** elf **8** reindeer
jingle: **5** reins
letter to ~: **4** list
prop: **4** pipe
reindeer, before Rudolph: **5** octet
vehicle: **4** sled
Santa Clause, The (1994 film)
cast: Tim Allen, Wendy Crewson, Judge Reinhold

SA

Santa Claus Is Coming to Town
composer: J. Fred Coots, Haven Gillespie
Santa Cruz: 4 city, town **7** islands
city on the ~: 6 Tucson
locale: 7 Bolivia **10** California
Santa Fe: 3 SUV **4** city, town **5** trail **7** Hyundai
brick: 5 adobe
locale: 9 New Mexico
town near ~: 4 Taos
Santa Fe Trail, The
author: Vachel Lindsay
Santa Maria: 4 boat, city, ship, town
companion: 4 Niña **5** Pinta
locale: 10 California
Santa Monica: 4 city, town
locale: 10 California
Santana, Carlos
homeland: Mexico
song: Black Magic Woman (1970)
Evil Ways (1970)
Oye Como Va (1971)
Smooth (1999)
Santa Roo and Pooh Box
author: A.A. Milne
Santa Rosa: 4 city, town
locale: 10 California
Santa's Twin
author: Dean Koontz
Santayana, George: 6 writer **7** Spanish **11** philosopher
work: The Last Puritan
Persons and Places
Realms of Being
Reason in Art
Reason in Science
Reason in Society
The Sense of Beauty
Skepticism and Animal Faith
santé, à votre: 5 salud, skoal, toast **6** cheers, French
Santha __ Rau: 4 Rama
Santiago: 4 city, port, town **7** capital, Saundra
locale: 4 Cuba **5** Chile **6** Mexico **9** Nuevo León
river: 7 Mapocho
see also Spanish
Santo: 3 Ron
Santo Domingo: 4 city, town **7** capital
locale: 6 Dom. Rep. **10** Hispaniola
see also Spanish
Santoni: 4 Reni
Santorini: 4 isle **6** island **7** volcano
formerly: 5 Thera, Thira
locale: 6 Greece
Santos: 4 city, port, town
locale: 6 Brazil
product: 6 coffee
Sanyo
alternative: *see* electronics company
Sanzio: 7 Raphael
Sao __: 4 Luis **5** Jorge, Paulo **6** Miguel **7** Vicente
Sao __ and Principe: 4 Tomé
Saône: 5 river
city on the ~: 4 Lyon **5** Lyons, Mâcon
locale: 6 France
river to the ~: 5 Doubs
__-Saône: 5 Haute
Sao Paulo: 4 city, town
city near ~: 3 Itu
locale: 6 Brazil
river: 5 Tietê
Saorstát __: 7 Éireann
Sao Tomé: 4 city, isle, town **6** island **7** capital
Sao Tomé and Principe: 6 nation **7** country
sap: 3 rob, sag, tax **4** butt, cosh, dupe, flag, gull, nerd, ruin, tire, wane **5** bleed, blunt, drain, erode, fluid, ninny, schmo, trash, waste, weary, wreck **6** burn up, cudgel, impair, liquid, nectar, pigeon, reduce, schmoe, shrink, soften, weaken **7** deplete, destroy, exhaust, fall guy, fatigue, schnook, subvert, unnerve, vitiate **8** bludgeon, easy mark, enervate, enfeeble, fool away, lunkhead, softhead, squander, weakling, wear down **9** attenuate, dissipate, prostrate, schlemiel, thickhead, undermine **10** debilitate, devitalize, noodlehead
as energy: 4 tire **5** leach **6** expend, lessen **7** deplete, exhaust, fatigue, suck dry, tire out **8** diminish, wear down **10** debilitate, devitalize, impoverish
collect ~: 3 tap
derivative: 5 sirup, syrup
ender: 4 head, ling, wood **6** headed, sucker
fermented palm ~: 4 arak **6** arrack
petrified ~: 5 amber
source: 5 maple
spout: 5 spile
starter: 4 pine, wine
sucker: 5 aphid, aphis
see also ninny
Saperstein: 3 Abe
saphead
see ninny
sapid: 5 tasty, yummy **6** savory, toothy **8** luscious **9** delicious, flavorful, nectarous, palatable, toothsome **10** appetizing, delectable
sapience: 3 wit **4** wits **5** sense **6** reason, wisdom **7** insight **8** judgment, prudence, sagacity **9** knowledge
sapiens, homo: 3 man **4** race **5** biped, human **6** person
sapient: 4 sage, wise **5** smart **6** brainy **7** erudite, knowing, learned, prudent **8** rational, sensible **9** judicious, sagacious **10** reasonable
sapless: 3 dry **4** arid
sapling: 3 boy, kid **4** girl, tree **5** child, youth **8** juvenile **9** youngster
sapodilla: 4 plum, tree **5** fruit **6** sapota **9** evergreen
sap: 6 chicle
tree: 4 shea **6** balata **7** almique **8** alamiqui
saponaceous: 5 soapy
sapor: 4 tang **5** taste **6** flavor
sapota: 4 tree **5** fruit **9** sapodilla
Sapp: 6 Warren
sapped: 5 drawn **9** exhausted
Sapphic __: 3 ode
sapphire: 3 gem **4** blue **5** color, jewel **7** mineral **8** corundum, gemstone
month: 4 Sept. **9** September
relative: *see* blue color
synthetic ~: 5 boule
__ sapphire: 4 star
Sappho: 4 poet **5** Greek
Sapporo: 4 city, town
city near ~: 5 Otaru
locale: 5 Japan
sappy: 4 zany **5** corny, goony, goosy, inane, mushy, silly **6** absurd, drippy, liquid, slushy, sticky, stupid **7** fatuous, foolish, maudlin, mawkish **8** overdone **9** illogical **10** ridiculous, saccharine, weak-minded
stuff: 5 sirup, syrup
sapsago: 6 cheese
Saps at Sea (1940 film)
cast: Oliver Hardy, Stan Laurel
sapsucker: 4 bird
Sara: 3 Lee, Mia **7** Allgood, Gilbert **8** Paretsky, Teasdale
Sara (song)
artist: Fleetwood Mac, Starship
saraband: 4 step **5** dance
Sarabandes
composer: Erik Satie
Saracen: 4 Arab
to a Crusader: 3 foe **5** enemy
Saragossa: 4 city, town
locale: 5 Spain
river: 4 Ebro
Sarah: 5 Miles **6** Fergie, Hughes **7** Purcell, Siddons, Vaughan **8** Caldwell, Ferguson **9** Bernhardt, Churchill, McLachlan
husband: 7 Abraham
maid of ~: 5 Hagar
son: 5 Isaac
Sarah __ Gellar: 8 Michelle
Sarah __ Hale: 7 Josepha
Sarah __ Jewett: 4 Orne
Sarah __ Parker: 7 Jessica
Sarah __ Siddons: 6 Kemble
Sarah Bishop
author: Scott O'Dell
Sarah Lawrence: 7 college
grad: 5 woman **6** alumna
Sarajevo: 4 city, town **7** capital
locale: 6 Bosnia **7** Balkans
Sara Lee employee: 5 baker
Sara, Mia
spouse: Jason Connery
Saranac __: 5 Lakes
Sarandon: 5 Chris, Susan
Sarandon, Susan: 7 actress
film: Alfie (2004)
Atlantic City (1981)
The Banger Sisters (2002)
Bull Durham (1988)
The Client (1994)
Compromising Positions (1985)
Dead Man Walking (1995, AA)
The Great Waldo Pepper (1975)
Light Sleeper (1992)
Little Women (1994)
Lorenzo's Oil (1992)
Pretty Baby (1978)
The Rocky Horror Picture Show (1975)
Shall We Dance? (2004)
Sweet Hearts Dance (1988)
Thelma & Louise (1991)
Twilight (1998)
White Palace (1990)
The Witches of Eastwick (1987)
role: 3 nun
Saran Wrap
alternative: 4 foil, Glad **5** Hefty **6** Ziploc **8** Reynolds, wax paper
sarape: 5 scarf, shawl
__ sarà sarà: 3 che
Sara Smile (1976 song)
artist: Hall and Oates
Sarasota: 4 city, town
locale: 7 Florida
Saratoga: 3 car **4** auto, city, town **6** battle **8** Chrysler **10** automobile
event: 4 race
general: 5 Gates **8** Burgoyne
locale: 7 New York **10** California
Saratoga Springs: 3 spa **4** city, town
locale: 7 New York
Saratoga Trunk
author: Edna Ferber
Sarawak
locale: 6 Borneo **8** Malaysia
people: 4 Iban
sultanate: 6 Brunei
tribe: 5 Dayak
Sarazen, Gene: 6 golfer
sarcasm: 3 cut, dig **4** acid, gibe, jeer, jibe **5** irony, scorn, taunt **6** banter, rancor, satire **7** mockery, put-down **8** acerbity, acrimony, contempt, cynicism, derision, ridicule, scoffing **9** aspersion, criticism, wisecrack **10** bitterness, enantiosis, lampooning, unkindness
sarcastic: 3 dry, wry **4** acid, mean **5** acerb, edged, nasty, saucy, sharp, snide **6** biting, bitter, ironic, ornery **7** abusive, acerbic, caustic, cutting, cynical, jeering, mocking, mordant, pointed, satiric **8** arrogant, captious, critical, derisive, incisive, sardonic, scornful, sneering, stinging, taunting **9** acidulous, corrosive, facetious, irascible, offensive, satirical, scorching **10** backhanded, derogatory, scurrilous
sarcocarp: 4 pulp
sardine: 4 fish, sild **5** sprat
holder: 3 tin
sardines
packed like ~: 5 in oil, solid **6** jammed
Sardinia: 4 isle **6** island
city: 8 Cagliari
locale: 5 Italy, Medit.
sheep: 7 mouflon **8** moufflon
sardonic: 3 dry, wry **5** sharp **6** bitter, ironic **7** caustic, cutting, cynical, mocking, mordant, satiric **8** derisive, incisive, scathing, scornful, sneering **9** quizzical, sarcastic, satirical, trenchant **10** disdainful
humor: 7 sarcasm
sardonyx: 3 gem **8** gemstone
Sardou, Victorien: 6 French **10** playwright
saree: 4 garb, gown, wrap
kin: 6 chadar, chador **7** chaddar, chuddar
wearer: 4 rani **5** ranee
Sarek: 5 alien **6** Vulcan
son: 5 Spock
Sargasso: 3 sea
locale: 10 West Indies
__ Sargasso Sea: 4 Wide
sarge: 3 NCO **6** noncom
superior: 5 looey, looie, louie
Sargent: 4 Dick **6** Joseph **7** Malcolm
Sargent, John Singer: 6 artist **7** painter
Sargent, Malcolm: 7 British **9** conductor

...as
...pe
...ani **5** ranee
...Cutty
...to, Domingo: 6 writer
...ateman **9** Argentine
...ork: Facundo
...arnoff, David org.: 3 RCA
sarong: 5 skirt **7** garment
  Malaysian ~: 4 kain
  relative: 4 sari **5** saree
Saros: 4 gulf
  locale: 6 Aegean
Saroyan: 4 Aram **7** William
Saroyan, William: 6 writer
  work: The Bicycle Rider in Beverly Hills
    The Daring Young Man on the Flying Trapeze
    The Human Comedy
    The Laughing Matter
    My Heart's in the Highlands
    My Name Is Aram
    The Time of Your Life
Sarrazin: 7 Michael
sarsaparilla: 5 drink **8** beverage
Sarsgaard: 5 Peter
Sarton, May: 4 poet
  work: The Small Room
Sartoris
  author: William Faulkner
Sartre, Jean-Paul: 6 critic, French, writer **8** Nobelist **11** philosopher
  contemporary: 5 Camus
  work: Being and Nothingness
    Dirty Hands
    The Flies
    Intimacy
    Nausea
    No Exit
    The Roads to Freedom
SAS: 7 airline
  competitor: 3 KLM
Sasdy: 5 Peter
SASE: 3 enc. **4** encl. **9** enclosure
  part: 4 self **7** stamped **8** envelope **9** addressed
  use an ~: 5 reply
sash: 3 obi **4** belt, faja **5** scarf **6** cordon, girdle, riband **9** framework, waistband **10** cummerbund
  filler: 4 pane
  place: 5 waist
  stopper: 4 sill
Sasha: 5 Cohen **8** Mitchell
sashay: 5 amble, glide, mince, mosey, strut **6** prance **7** saunter
sashayed: 4 went
sashimi: 4 fish
  alternative: 5 sushi
Sask.: 4 prov.
Saskatchewan: 8 province
  capital: 6 Regina
  city: 5 Craik, Unity **6** Regina **7** Avonlea, Eastend, Melfort, Nipawin, Tisdale, Weyburn, Wynyard, Yorkton **8** Moose Jaw **9** Saskatoon
  Indian: 4 Cree **9** Saulteaux
  lake: 9 Athabasca
  locale: 6 Canada
  neighbor: 3 Alb., Man. **4** Alta., Mont., N. Dak. **7** Alberta, Montana **8** Manitoba
Sasquatch: 5 giant **7** Bigfoot
  kin: 4 yeti
sass: 3 lip **4** guff **5** cheek, mouth, reply, sauce **8** audacity, back talk, boldness, contempt, defiance, get fresh, get smart, mouth off, reaction, response, rudeness, talk back **9** brashness, flippancy, freshness, fresh talk, impudence, insolence, sauciness **10** answer back, brazenness, disrespect, effrontery, impishness, incivility, talk back to
Sass: 6 Sylvia
sassafras: 4 tree
  family: 6 laurel
  relative: 7 avocado, camphor **8** cinnamon
sassafras ___: 3 oil, tea
Sassanid: 3 Era
sassiness
  see sass
Sassoon: 5 Vidal **9** Siegfried
Sassoon, Siegfried: 4 poet **6** writer **7** British
  work: Counter-Attack and Other Poems
    Memoirs of a Fox-Hunting Man
sassy: 4 bold, flip, pert, rude **5** brash, fresh, lippy, nervy, saucy, smart **6** awless, brazen, cheeky, jaunty, lively, snippy **7** aweless, defiant, forward, uncivil **8** derisive, flippant, impolite, impudent, insolent, snippety **9** out of line **10** irreverent, ungracious
  girl: 5 missy
  one: 4 snip
...sat ___ tuffet...: 3 on a
Sat.: 3 day
  follower: 3 Sun.
  preceder: 3 Fri.
SAT: 4 exam, test
  college counterpart: 3 GRE
  fill-in: 6 answer
  part: 4 Test **8** Aptitude **10** Scholastic
  preparer: 3 ETS
  section: 4 math **7** English
  taker: 2 sr. **4** teen **6** senior
Satan: 5 devil **6** diablo **7** Evil One, Lucifer, Old Nick **8** evildoer, Old Harry **9** Beelzebub **10** Old Scratch
  ally: 5 Magog
satanic: 4 dark, evil, vile **6** horrid, wicked **7** demonic, hateful, heinous, hellish, malefic **8** daemonic, devilish, diabolic, fiendish, horrible, infernal, sinister **9** abhorrent, demonical, execrable, loathsome, monstrous, nefarious **10** abominable, despicable, detestable, diabolical, iniquitous, malevolent, villainous
satchel: 3 bag **4** grip **5** pouch
  binder: 5 strap
Satchel: 5 Paige
  mom: 3 Mia
Satchmo
  see Louis Armstrong
...sat down beside ___...: 3 her
sate: 4 cloy, fill, glut **5** gorge, stuff **7** appease, engorge, satisfy, surfeit **8** overfeed, overfill **10** gormandize, oversupply
sated: 4 full **5** blasé **7** replete **8** cramfull **10** world-weary
sateen: 6 fabric **8** material
  like ~: 6 glossy
satellite: 4 moon **8** partisan **9** ancillary **10** collateral
  broadcast: 4 feed
  community: 5 exurb
  early ~: 3 OGO **4** Echo, ESSA **5** Tiros **6** Comsat
  Earth ~: 4 moon
  job: 3 spy **4** scan **5** recon **7** surveil
  launcher: 4 NASA **6** Ariane
  NASA ~ launcher: 5 Agena
  path: 5 orbit
  reconnaissance ~: 5 Samos
  Soviet: 5 Lunik **7** Sputnik
  tracker: 5 NORAD
  see also moon
satellite ___: 3 DNA **4** dish
___ satellite: 7 weather
Satellite: 3 car **4** auto **8** Plymouth
satiate: 4 cloy, fill, glut, jade, pall, sate **5** gorge, slake, stuff **7** gratify, indulge, satisfy, surfeit **8** overfill **10** gormandize
satiated: 3 fed **4** full, sick **5** blasé **7** replete **10** world-weary
Satie, Erik: 6 French **8** composer
  work: Gymnopédies
    Mercure
    Ogives
    Parade
    Sarabandes
    Socrate
satiety: 4 glut **7** surfeit **8** fullness, plethora **9** repletion
satin: 5 cloth, sleek **6** fabric **8** material
  like ~: 4 soft **5** silky **6** smooth
Satin ___: 4 Doll
satins: 6 finery
satiny: 4 soft **5** silky, sleek **6** flossy, glossy, smooth **8** lustrous, slippery
satire: 3 wit **4** quip, skit **5** farce, genre, irony, prose, put-on, spoof **6** comedy, parody, send-up **7** burlesk, lampoon, mockery, sarcasm, takeoff **8** ridicule, travesty **9** burlesque **10** caricature, enantiosis
  magazine: 3 Mad
Satires
  author: Horace
satirical: 6 biting, bitter, ironic **7** burlesk, caustic, cutting, cynical, mocking, mordant **8** farcical, incisive, sardonic, spoofing, stinging, taunting **9** burlesque, facetious, parodying, sarcastic **10** lampooning, ridiculing
  comedy: 5 sotie **6** sottie
  production: 5 revue **6** review
satirist: 8 humorist
  British ~: 4 Pope **5** Nashe, Swift **9** Thackeray
  Roman ~: 6 Horace **7** Juvenal
satirize: 4 lash, mock, twit **5** sneer, spoof **6** parody **7** burlesk, lampoon **8** ridicule **9** burlesque **10** caricature
satisfaction: 3 joy **4** ease, zest **5** bliss, pride **6** luxury, refund, regard, relief, reward **7** comfort, content, damages, delight, emotion, justice, rapture, redress, revenge, satiety **8** fruition, gladness, pleasure, serenity **9** amusement, atonement, enjoyment, happiness, well-being
  exact ~: 6 avenge
  exclamation: 3 aah, ooh, yum **5** uh-huh, voilà **6** yum-yum
  express smug ~: 5 gloat
  get ~ from: 3 dig **4** like **5** boast, eat up, enjoy, go for, savor **6** dote on, wallow **7** revel in **8** flip over, thrill to **9** delight in **10** appreciate
  seek ~ in court: 3 sue
Satisfaction (1965 song)
  artist: Rolling Stones
  starter: 5 I can't
satisfactory: 2 OK **3** A-OK **4** fair, fine, good, jake, nice, okay, okeh, okey, so-so, tidy, well **5** ample, great, legit, moral, noble, right, solid, sound, valid **6** decent, enough, proper **7** average, ethical, up to par **8** adequate, all right, laudable, passable, pleasant, pleasing, splendid, suitable **9** admirable, agreeable, competent, excellent, palatable, reputable, sufficing, tolerable, up to grade, up to snuff, wonderful **10** acceptable, beneficial, creditable
satisfied: 4 full, sure **5** clear, happy **7** certain, content **8** positive, relieved, sanguine, thankful **9** believing, confident, contented, fulfilled **10** complacent, optimistic
  not ~: 5 unmet
  not easily ~: 5 picky
___-satisfied: 4 self
Satisfied (1989 song)
  artist: Richard Marx
satisfy: 2 do **3** pay **4** cloy, fill, glut, jade, meet, quit, sate, suit **5** amuse, atone, avail, elate, equip, get by, gorge, pay up, quiet, repay, score, serve, slake **6** answer, assure, fulfil, pacify, pander, pay off, please, quench, recoup, redeem, regale, reward, sell on, settle, square, supply **7** appease, assuage, cheer up, clear up, comfort, content, delight, enthral, fulfill, furnish, gladden, gratify, indulge, inthral, mollify, observe, perform, placate, provide, qualify, rejoice, requite, satiate, suffice, surfeit, win over, work out **8** come up to, complete, convince, enthrall, inthrall, make good, persuade, reassure, square up, tide over **9** conform to, discharge, indemnify, liquidate, put at ease **10** accomplish, compensate, comply with, conciliate, do the trick, exhilarate, hit the spot, pass muster, propitiate, recompense, remunerate
satisfying: 4 good, nice **5** solid, sound **6** cogent, worthy **7** welcome **8** pleasant, pleasing, readable **9** agreeable, enjoyable, rewarding **10** believable, convincing, delectable, delightful, gratifying
Satisfy You (1999 song)
  artist: Puff Daddy, R. Kelly
S. Atlantic
  see South Atlantic
Sato, Eisaku: 8 Japanese, Nobelist
Satori in Paris
  author: Jack Kerouac
satrap: 5 ruler **6** despot, gerent
saturate: 3 sop, wet **4** dunk, glut, soak **5** bathe, douse, dowse, imbue, souse, steep, tinge, water

SA

6 dampen, drench, embrue, imbrue, infuse 7 immerse, moisten, pervade, suffuse, surfeit 8 humidify, overfill, permeate, waterlog 9 penetrate 10 impregnate

saturated: 3 wet 4 damp 5 juicy, soggy, soppy, undry 6 sodden 7 wettish

saturated __: 3 fat

saturation: 4 glut 9 immersion 10 absorption

Saturday
morning TV fare: 4 toon 7 cartoon
night ritual: 4 bath
night special: 3 gun
to some: 7 Sabbath

Saturday in the Park (1972 song)
artist: Chicago

Saturday Night (1975 song)
artist: Bay City Rollers

Saturday Night __: 4 Live 5 Fever

__ Saturday Night: 7 Another

Saturday Night and Sunday Morning
author: Alan Sillitoe

Saturday Night Fever (1977 film)
cast: Karen Lynn Gorney, Donna Pescow, John Travolta
director: John Badham
setting: 5 disco 7 New York 8 Brooklyn

Saturday Night Live (NBC comedy)
bit: 4 skit
cat: 7 Toonces

Saturday Night Special (1975 song)
artist: Lynyrd Skynyrd

Saturn: 3 car, god, orb 4 auto 10 automobile
daughter: 4 Juno 5 Ceres, Vesta
ender: 4 alia
equivalent: 6 Cronos
model: 3 Ion, Vue
moon: 3 Pan 4 Rhea 5 Atlas, Dione, Janus, Mimas, Titan 6 Helene, Phoebe, Tethys 7 Calypso, Iapetus, Pandora, Telesto 8 Hyperion 9 Enceladus 10 Epimetheus, Prometheus
neighbor: 6 Uranus
ring phenomenon: 4 ansa
sister: 3 Ops
son: 5 Pluto 7 Jupiter
wife: 3 Ops

saturnalia: 5 blast, revel 7 revelry

saturniid: 3 bug 6 insect

saturnine: 3 sad 4 blue, dour, glum, ugly 5 moody, sulky, surly 6 broody, crabby, crusty, dismal, gloomy, morbid, morose, somber, sullen 7 unhappy 8 dejected, downcast, liverish 9 depressed, sorrowful 10 dispirited, lugubrious, melancholy

Satya __: 4 Yuga

Satyajit: 3 Ray

satyr: 3 Pan 4 faun 6 lecher 7 Silenus 9 libertine
in part: 4 goat
trait: 4 lust

sauce: 3 lip 4 gall, guff, sass 5 booze, brass, cheek, gravy, hooch, mouth, nerve, pesto 6 catsup, hootch, liquor, Mornay, whisky 7 alcohol, Alfredo, catchup, chutnee, chutney, ketchup, soubise, Tabasco, topping, velouté, whiskey 8 audacity, back talk, béchamel, boldness, dressing, marinara, pertness 9 aqua vitae, béarnaise, brashness, condiment, flavoring, freshness, hard stuff, impudence, inebriant, insolence, sassiness 10 bordelaise, brassiness, brazenness, cheekiness, intoxicant
basil ~: 5 pesto
ender: 3 box, pan, pot 4 boat
fish ~: 4 alec
flavoring: 4 miso
hit the ~: 4 tope 5 booze, drink
holder: 3 can
Mexican ~: 4 mole
pasta ~: 5 pesto 7 Alfredo 8 marinara
raspberry ~: 5 Melba
source: 4 soya
starter: 5 apple
sundae ~: 5 fudge
tend the ~: 4 stir
Tex-Mex ~: 5 salsa
thickener: 4 roux

__ sauce: 3 hot, soy 4 clam 5 brown, chili, cream, white 6 butter, Mornay, tartar, tomato 7 Tabasco

saucepan: 3 pan, pot 6 boiler

saucer: 4 bowl, dish, disk 5 plate
emulate a flying ~: 5 hover
flying ~: 3 UFO

saucer __: 4 dome

__ saucer: 6 cup and, flying

sauciness: 3 lip 4 gall, sass 5 mouth 7 license 9 flippancy 10 impishness

saucy: 4 bold, flip, pert, rude, smug 5 brash, fresh, nervy, sassy, smart 6 awless, bantam, brassy, brazen, cheeky, rakish, snippy 7 aweless, forward, uncivil 8 flippant, impolite, impudent, insolent, snippety, volatile 9 audacious, combative, intrusive, out-of-line, sarcastic, shameless, sprightly 10 irreverent, ungracious
miss: 4 minx

__ Saud: 3 Ibn

Saudi Arabia: 6 nation 7 country
capital: 6 Riyadh
city: 4 Taif 5 Jedda, Jidda, Mecca 6 Jiddah, Medina
desert: 5 Dahna, Nefud 6 Syrian
group: 4 OPEC 10 Arab League
gulf: 4 Aden 5 Akaba, Aqaba
money: 4 rial 5 girsh, gursh, qirsh, qursh, riyal 6 ghirsh, halala, qurush
neighbor: 3 UAE 4 Irak, Iraq, Oman 5 Katar, Qatar, Yemen 6 Jordan, Kuwait
port: 5 Jedda, Jidda 6 Jiddah
region: 4 Asir, Nejd
VIP: 5 sheik 6 shaikh, sheikh

sauerbraten: 4 meat 6 German 8 pot roast

Sauk: 5 tribe 6 Indian 7 Amerind 8 language

Sauk Centre: 4 city, town
locale: 9 Minnesota

Saul: 4 king, poem 6 Bellow 7 Chaplin 8 oratorio
author: Robert Browning
composer: George Frideric Handel
cousin: 5 Abner
daughter: 6 Michal
father: 4 Kish
grandfather: 3 Ner
son: 5 Ishvi 6 Armoni 8 Jonathan 10 Malchishua
wife: 7 Ahinoam

Saul of __: 6 Tarsus

sault: 6 rapids 9 waterfall

Sault Ste. Marie: 4 city, town
locale: 6 Canada 7 Ontario 8 Michigan

sauna: 6 hot tub 7 thermae 9 caldarium, steam bath 10 sudatorium
need: 5 towel
output: 5 steam
site: 3 spa

Saunders: 4 Merl 8 Jennifer

Saundra: 8 Santiago

saunter: 3 gad, lag 4 idle, laze, loaf, roam, rove, walk 5 amble, dally, drift, mosey, stall, tarry 6 airing, canter, dawdle, linger, loiter, lounge, ramble, sashay, stroll, toddle, trapes, wander 7 meander, traipse 8 ambulate, lollygag, straggle 9 poke along, promenade, waste time 10 dillydally

saurian: 6 lizard

-saurus starter: 5 stego 6 bronto

sausage: 4 meat 5 wurst 6 banger, boudin, kishke, kiskha, salami 7 bologna 8 kielbasa 9 bratwurst, pepperoni 10 knockwurst, liverwurst
combining form: 6 allant- 7 allanto-
meat: 4 pork
seasoning: 4 sage 6 fennel
segment: 4 link
skin: 6 casing

__ sausage: 5 blood 6 Polish, summer, Vienna

Sausalito: 4 city, town
alternative: *see* cookie brand
county: 5 Marin
locale: 10 California

saut de basque: 4 leap

sauté: 3 fry 4 cook, leap 5 brown 6 braise, panfry 7 prepare

Sauterne: 3 vin 4 wine 5 white 9 white wine
see also French

Sauvignon: 5 grape
relative: *see* wine

Sauvignon Blanc: 4 wine

Sava: 5 river
city on the ~: 6 Zagreb 8 Belgrade
locale: 6 Bosnia 7 Croatia 8 Slovenia
river to the ~: 5 Drina

savage: 4 grim, mall, maul, mean, rude, wild 5 beast, brute, cruel, feral, fiend, harsh, nasty, rabid, rough, swine, tough 6 animal, bitter, brutal, crazed, ferine, fierce, lupine, raging, rugged, unkind, wanton 7 beastly, bestial, callous, furious, hellish, hurtful, inhuman, lawless, monster, untamed, vicious, violent, wolfish 8 barbaric, demoniac, fiendish, infernal, inhumane, pitiless, ruthless, sadistic, vengeful 9 atrocious, barbarian, barbarous, cutthroat, ferocious, heartless, hellhound, inclement, merciless, monstrous, primitive, rapacious, truculent, unpitying 10 infuriated, relentless, vindictive

Savage: 3 Ben, Doc 4 Fred 7 Richard

Savage Island today: 4 Niue

Savage Paris
author: Émile Zola

savagery: 4 fury 6 ferity 7 crue 8 ferocity, violence 10 inhuma

Savalas, Telly: 5 actor
film: The Dirty Dozen (1967) Kelly's Heroes (1970)
like ~: 4 bald
TV: Kojak

Savana: 3 GMC, van

savanna: 3 lea, ley 4 moor 5 plain, veldt 9 grassland
dweller: 3 gnu
kin: 5 campo, veldt
tree: 6 baobab

Savannah: 4 city, port, town 5 river
locale: 7 Georgia

savant: 4 sage 6 expert, master, pundit 7 scholar, thinker 8 highbrow 9 authority, literatus, professor 10 specialist

Savant: 4 Doug

savarin: 4 cake
ingredient: 3 rum

Savarin: 6 coffee
alternative: 5 Sanka, Yuban 7 Folgers, Melitta, Nescafé 9 Hills Bros.

save: 3 bar, but 4 balm, bank, free, hold, keep 5 amass, cache, guard, hoard, lay by, lay up, put by, set by, skimp, spare, stash, stint, stock, store 6 defend, except, garner, gather, obtain, pile up, ransom, ration, redeem, rescue, retain, scrimp, secure, shield, spring, unless 7 bail out, collect, deliver, deposit, husband, lay away, protect, put away, recover, reserve, salvage, sustain, unchain 8 conserve, file away, gather up, hang onto, hide away, hold back, hold onto, lay aside, liberate, maintain, omitting, preserve, put aside, retrench, salt away, set apart, set aside, sock away, stow away, treasure, withhold 9 economize, except for, excepting, extricate, outside of, safeguard, stash away, stockpile, unshackle 10 accumulate, cut corners, emancipate, underspend
alternative: 5 spend
as coupons: 4 clip
computer files: 6 back up
for: 3 but 6 except
one's neck: 4 free, save 6 let off, pardon, rescue 7 bail out, manumit, release, set free, unchain 9 extricate, unshackle

save __: 4 face

saved __ bell: 5 by the

Save It for Me (1964 song)
artist: Four Seasons

save one's __: 6 breath

saver: 7 pack rat 9 depositor
like a ~: 6 frugal 7 thrifty
of fable: 3 ant
starter: 4 life, time

__ saver: 6 screen

saves, what a certain stitch: 4 nine

Save the Best for Last (1992 song)
artist: Vanessa Williams

Save the Last Dance for Me (1960 song)
artist: Drifters

Save the Tiger (1973 film)
cast: Jack Gilford, Jack Lemmon

... 5 How to

...on

... film of 1950: 3 Kim

...ingy, thrift 7 economy, ...g, sparing 8 discount, price ... rollback 9 deduction, provi-...ent, reduction

starter: 4 life, time

saving __: 5 grace

__-saving: 4 face 5 labor, space

Saving All My Love for You (1985 song)

artist: Whitney Houston

Saving Private Ryan (1998 film)

cast: Edward Burns, Matt Damon, Vin Diesel, Tom Hanks, Tom Sizemore

composer: John Williams

craft: 3 LST

director: Steven Spielberg

setting: 4 D-day 6 France 8 Normandy

savings: 4 cash 5 cache, funds, kitty, means, stake, store 6 assets, profit 7 capital, deposit, nest egg, reserve 8 reserves 9 resources

account: 2 CD 3 IRA

account addition: 3 int. 8 interest

protector: 4 FDIC 5 FSLIC

savings __: 4 bank, bond 7 account

savings and __: 4 loan

Savion: 6 Glover

savior: 4 hero 5 freer 7 messiah, rescuer 8 defender, redeemer 9 deliverer, liberator, preserver, protector

Savior, The (1998 film)

cast: Nastassja Kinski, Dennis Quaid

saviour

see savior

Savoca: 5 Nancy

Savoie

see Savoy

__-Savoie: 5 Haute

savoir-__: 5 faire, vivre

savoir faire: 4 tact 5 grace, poise, skill, style 6 aplomb, polish 7 culture, finesse, know-how, suavity 8 breeding, urbanity 9 gentility, suaveness 10 refinement

Savonarola: 5 chair 8 Girolamo

savor: 3 sip 4 bask, feel, like, live, mark, odor, tang, zest 5 enjoy, gloat, gusto, scent, smack, smell, spice, taste, tinge, verve 6 appeal, bask in, degust, flavor, relish, sample 7 cherish, dwell on, feast on, partake 9 degustate, delight in, dwell upon, get high on, gloat over, rejoice in 10 appreciate, attraction, enticement, experience

savory: 4 good, herb, nice, rich 5 sapid, spicy, tangy, tasty, yummy 6 spicey, toothy 7 piquant, pungent 8 fragrant, luscious, noshable, pleasing, tempting 9 ambrosial, delicious, flavorful, nectarous, palatable, reputable, toothsome 10 appetizing, delectable

Savoy: 3 car 4 auto, font 5 duchy, hotel 8 Plymouth, typeface 10 automobile

dance: 5 stomp

locale: 6 France

savvy: 3 apt, hep, hip 4 able, wise 5 adept, aware, get it, knack, quick, sense, sharp, skill 6 adroit, astute, clever, expert, shrewd, up to it, versed, wisdom, wise to, with it 7 ability, erudite, finesse, know-how, knowing, mindful, tuned in 8 apprised, informed, instinct, judgment, skillful 9 astucious, cognizant, competent, erudition, expertise, intellect, in the know, plugged in, sagacious 10 appreciate, competence, comprehend, horse sense, insightful, proficient, right stuff, shrewdness, streetwise, understand

about: 4 onto, up on

saw: 3 cut 4 lore, tool, word 5 adage, axiom, gnome, maxim, moral, motto 6 bisect, byword, cliché, cutter, dictum, saying, truism 7 bromide, epigram, proverb 8 aphorism, apothegm, Atticism, dissever, laconism 9 platitude 10 apophthegm, folk wisdom, shibboleth, woodcutter

cut: 4 kerf

down: 4 fell

ender: 3 fly, yer 4 buck, dust, fish, mill 5 bones, dusty, horse

I ~: 4 vidi

logs: 3 nap 5 crash, sleep, snore, snort 6 nod off, retire, snooze, turn in 7 drop off, sack out, slumber, snuffle, zonk out 8 take a nap 9 hit the hay 10 hit the sack

part: 5 tooth

starter: 3 jig, pit, rip, see 4 back, buck, hack, hand, whip 5 sight 7 quarter

saw __: 3 log 4 wood

saw-__: 7 toothed

__ saw: 3 bow, pad, pit 4 band, buzz, fret, gang, grub, hole, rift 5 chain, crown, miter, muley, panel, power, saber, table 6 coping, planer, radial, scroll 7 bracket, compass, keyhole, musical

__ saw a purple cow...: 6 I never

Sawatch: 3 mts. 4 mtns. 5 range 9 mountains

locale: 8 Colorado

mountain: 4 Yale 6 Antero 7 Harvard, Shavano 9 Princeton

sawbones: 2 dr., MD 3 doc 6 doctor 7 surgeon 9 physician

sawbuck: 3 ten 4 bill 5 money 6 tenner 7 ten-spot 8 banknote, currency

fraction: 3 fin, one 5 fiver

sawbucks

hundred ~: 4 one G 5 G-note

ten ~: 3 cee 5 C-note

Sawchuk, Terry: 8 puckster

milieu: 3 ice 4 rink 5 arena

org.: 3 NHL

sawed-off: 4 puny 5 runty, short

..... saw Elba: 4 ere I

sawlike: 8 serrated

__-Saw, Margery Daw: 3 See

sawmill

machine: 5 edger

output: 5 board 6 lumber

sawn: 3 cut

sawtooth: 8 serrated

Sawyer: 3 Tom 5 Diane 7 Forrest

Sawyer, Diane

spouse: Mike Nichols

Sawyer, Tom

craft: 4 raft

friend: 4 Finn, Huck

half brother: 3 Sid

sax: 4 reed, wind 8 woodwind 10 instrument

ender: 4 horn, tuba

__ sax: 4 alto, bass 5 tenor 7 soprano

Sax: 5 Steve 6 Rohmer 7 Adolphe

Sax by the Fire

artist: John Tesh

Saxe-Coburg-__: 5 Gotha

saxhorn: 4 tuba, wind 10 instrument

saxifrage: 4 itea 6 willow 7 syringa

Saxon: 4 John

contemporary: 4 Jute

__-Saxon: 5 Anglo

saxony: 4 yarn 6 fabric 8 material

Saxony: 5 state

city: 5 Riesa

locale: 7 Germany

once: 5 duchy

river: 5 Weser

saxophonist: 4 Getz, Sims 5 Young 6 Barnet, Bechet, Beneke, Carter, Dorsey, Gordon, Herman, Kenny G, Parker 7 Coleman, Desmond, Hawkins, Rollins 8 Adderley, Coltrane, Marsalis, Mulligan, Stan Getz, Zoot Sims 9 Tex Beneke

saxtuba: 4 wind 8 woodwind 10 instrument

say: 3 add, bid, gab, jaw, rap, yak 4 aver, avow, talk, tell 5 about, claim, guess, imply, judge, let on, opine, orate, reply, rumor, speak, spiel, state, utter, voice 6 affirm, allege, answer, assert, attest, convey, decide, inform, intone, pipe up, recite, record, relate, remark, render, repeat, report, retort, reveal 7 breathe, bring up, control, declare, dictate, divulge, express, mention, observe, opinion, respond, suggest 8 announce, bring out, disclose, intimate, maintain, register, rephrase, set forth, throw out, vocalize 9 enunciate, give forth, insinuate, make known, pronounce, verbalize 10 articulate, asseverate, conjecture, for example, put forward, recitation

again: 4 echo 6 repeat 7 recount, run over 9 reiterate

cheese: 4 grin, pose 5 smile

dare ~: 7 venture

goodbye: 4 part 5 leave 6 go home

grace: 4 pray 6 invoke

have one's ~: 4 vote 5 speak 7 speak up 8 speak out

hello: 5 greet 7 welcome

I do: 3 wed 5 marry 10 tie the knot

imperfectly: 4 lisp, slur 6 mumble

inadvertently: 4 blab 5 blurt 7 let slip

indirectly: 5 couch

in fun: 3 kid 4 fool, gibe, jape, jest, joke, josh 5 clown, crack 9 kid around

it isn't so: 4 deny

it's so: 6 attest

loud and clear: 7 speak up 8 speak out

more: 3 add

needless to ~: ***see*** of course 9 obviously

no: 3 nix 4 deny, shun, veto 5 spurn 6 bounce, forbid, pass on, rebuff, refuse, reject, resist 7 decline, disdain, dismiss, exclude, protest 8 disallow, turn down 9 blackball

one with nothing to ~: 4 mime 5 mimer

over and over: 5 chant

pretty please: 3 beg

sad to ~: 4 alas

silently: 5 mouth

softly: 7 whisper

starter: 3 nay 4 dare, gain, hear 5 sooth

that is to ~: 3 viz. 5 to wit 6 namely

the word: 9 authorize, give leave

the wrong thing: 3 err

unable to ~ no: 5 timid 6 docile 7 lenient, servile, slavish 8 lamblike, yielding 9 spineless 10 obsequious, submissive

uncle: 4 quit 5 yield 6 fess up, give up, relent, submit 7 concede 9 acquiesce

under oath: 5 swear 6 attest, depone, depose 7 testify, witness

what they ~: 4 buzz, talk 5 rumor 6 gossip 7 hearsay 9 grapevine

what you think: 5 opine

wrongly: 3 lie

yea or nay: 4 vote

yes: 2 OK 3 nod 4 okay 5 agree, allow, yield 6 accede, accept, assent, permit 7 approve, consent, go along

say __: 3 aah 4 no to, what, when 5 uncle

__ say!: 3 I'll

__ say...: 5 Sad to

Say

it isn't so: 4 Oh, no!

Say __: 3 ahh 4 Si Si

Say __ only a paper moon: 3 it's

Say __ Will: 3 You

Say again?: 3 huh 4 what

Say Anything... (1989 film)

cast: John Cusack, Ione Skye, Lili Taylor

director: Cameron Crowe

__ Say a Word: 4 Don't

Say cheese!: 5 smile

__ Say Die: 5 Never

sayer: 7 speaker 8 declarer 9 announcer

Sayer, Leo

song: Long Tall Glasses (I Can Dance) (1975)
More Than I Can Say (1980)
When I Need You (1977)
You Make Me Feel Like Dancing (1976)

Sayers: 4 Gale 7 Dorothy

Sayers, Dorothy: 6 writer 7 British

sleuth: Lord Peter Wimsey

work: Busman's Honeymoon
The Nine Tailors
Strong Poison
Whose Body?

Sayers, Gale

sport: 8 football

SA

Say goodnight, __: 6 Gracie
...say goodnight till it be __: 6 morrow
Say, Has Anybody Seen My Sweet Gypsy Rose (1973 song)
artist: Tony Orlando & Dawn
Say Hey Kid, The: Willie Mays
saying: 3 saw 4 word 5 adage, axiom, maxim, moral, motto, quote, squib 6 byword, cliché, dictum, homily, logion, phrase, slogan, truism 7 epigram, precept, proverb 8 aphorism, laconism 9 platitude, quotation, utterance
nothing: 3 mum 4 mute 5 quiet 6 silent 7 aphonic 8 nonvocal, taciturn, wordless 9 secretive, soundless, voiceless 10 pantomimic, speechless, tongue-tied
sayings: 4 lore 8 analecta, analects
collected ~: 3 ana
religious ~: 5 logia
Say It Isn't So (1983 song)
artist: Hall and Oates
Say It Loud - I'm Black and I'm Proud (1968 song)
artist: James Brown
__ Say It's Wonderful: 4 They
Say It With Music
composer: Irving Berlin
Sayles: 4 John
__ say more?: 5 Need I
Say My Name (2000 song)
artist: Destiny's Child
__ say, not...: 5 Do as I
...say, not __: 5 as I do
__ Say Nothin' Bad: 4 Don't
Sayonara (1957 film)
cast: Marlon Brando, Red Buttons, James Garner, Ricardo Montalban, Martha Scott, Miyoshi Umeki
director: Joshua Logan
Sayonara!: 3 bye 4 ta-ta 5 adieu, later 7 goodbye 8 farewell
in French: 5 adieu
in Hawaiian: 5 aloha
in Italian: 4 ciao
in Latin: 3 ave 4 vale
in Spanish: 5 adios
__ says: 5 Simon
Say Say Say (1983 song)
artist: Michael Jackson, Paul McCartney
say-so: 2 OK 4 okay, word 5 order, power, voice 6 dictum 7 opinion, promise 9 assertion, authority, clearance
says old-style: 5 saith
__ Say the Darndest Things: 4 Kids
Say what?: 3 huh
Say You'll Be There (1997 song)
artist: Spice Girls
Say You, Say Me (1985 song)
artist: Lionel Richie
Sb: 4 elem. 7 element 8 antimony
51 for ~: 4 at. no.
SBA: 6 lender
part of ~: 5 Admin., Small 8 Business
Sbarro
rival: *see* restaurant chain
SbE: 3 hdg.
SBLI part: 3 Ins. 4 Bank, Life 7 Savings 9 Insurance
__ S. Buck: 5 Pearl
__ S. Burroughs: 7 William
Sc: 4 elem. 7 element 8 scandium
21 for ~: 4 at. no.
S.C.
see South Carolina
scabbard: 6 sheath 7 sheathe
insert: 5 sword
Scacchi: 5 Greta
scad: 3 lot, ton 4 load
scads: 4 a lot, a ton, lots, many, much, raft, wads 5 acres 6 flocks, hoards, oodles, scores 7 bushels, legions 8 zillions
of: 6 divers, myriad, umteen, untold 7 copious, profuse, umpteen 8 abundant, manifold, numerous, umpsteen 9 bountiful, countless, quite a few
scaffold: 5 frame 8 platform, skeleton
rocket ~: 6 gantry
Scaggs, Boz
song: JoJo (1980)
Lido Shuffle (1977)
Lowdown (1976)
Scala: 3 Gia
scalawag: 5 knave, rogue, scamp 6 bad hat, rascal 7 bounder 8 blighter, picaroon, rakehell, spalpeen 9 miscreant, reprobate, scoundrel 10 blackguard, ne'er-do-well, scapegrace
scald: 4 burn, cook, heat 6 scorch 7 parboil 9 cauterize
starter: 3 sun 4 leaf
scalding: 3 hot 6 torrid
scale: 3 pan, top 4 film, go up, norm, rate, rise, size, skin 5 climb, flake, gamut, gauge, layer, mount, plate, range, ratio, reach, ruler, scope, shell, strip 6 adjust, ascend, degree, extent, ladder, lamina, series, shinny, spread 7 balance, breadth, clamber, coating, measure, prorate, shinney 8 register, spectrum, surmount 9 barometer, calibrate, continuum, dimension, gradation, hierarchy, sliderule, yardstick 10 proportion
allowance: 4 tare
bottom of a ~: 3 one
bump on the ~: 3 pip 4 blip
down: 4 pare, trim 5 lower 6 lessen, reduce 7 cut back 8 downsize
drawing: 4 plan 9 blueprint
earthquake ~: 7 Richter
entire ~: 4 A to Z 5 field, gamut, range, reach, scope, sweep 6 extent 7 breadth 8 panorama, spectrum
hardness ~: 4 Mohs
hydrometer ~: 5 Baume
interval: 5 fifth, sixth, third 6 octave
kind of ~: 5 major, minor
note: 2 do, fa, la, mi, re, ti, ut 3 sol
off: 9 exfoliate
on a small ~: 8 slightly
part: 3 pan
segment: 4 note, tone
starter: 4 down
temperature ~: 3 Fah. 4 Fahr 6 Kelvin 7 Celsius 10 Fahrenheit
thin ~: 6 lamina
top of a ~: 3 ten
uncomfortability ~: 3 THI
unit: 2 lb., oz. 4 gram 5 ounce, pound
up: 5 boost, raise 7 augment, greaten 8 escalate, increase 9 intensify
scale __: 5 model
__ scale: 4 gray, Mohs, wage 7 Richter, sliding
__-scale: 4 full 5 grand, large, small
scaled-down: 9 miniature
scaleless fish: 3 eel
__ scale of one to ten: 3 on a
scales
heavenly ~: 5 Libra
tip the ~: 5 weigh 8 outweigh
Scales: 4 sign 5 Libra
month: 3 Oct., Sep. 4 Sept. 7 October 9 September
predecessor: 6 Virgin
successor: 8 Scorpion
Scalia: 7 Antonin
scallion: 6 veggie 9 vegetable
cousin: 4 leek 5 onion
starter: 3 rap
scallop: 4 curl, loop, pink 5 curve, shell 8 seashell
__ scallop: 3 bay, sea
scaloppine ingredient: 4 veal
scalp: 4 skin
scalpel: 5 knife 6 lancet
like a ~: 5 sharp
scaly: 5 rough 7 scutate 8 lamellar, squamose, squamous
scam: 3 con, gyp 4 bilk, do in, dupe, fool, hoax, plot 5 bunco, cheat, cozen, dodge, fraud, sting 6 con job, dupery, humbug, hustle, racket, rip-off 7 beguile, con game, deceive, defraud, mislead, swindle 8 artifice, flimflam, hoodwink, maneuver, trickery 9 deception 10 run a game on
artist: 3 con 5 cheat 6 conman 7 hustler
scamp: 3 bum, cad, cur, imp, rat 4 brat, heel, toad, worm 5 churl, knave, louse, rogue 6 bad boy, bad hat, monkey, rascal, urchin 7 bounder, dastard, lowlife, ruffian, stinker 8 blighter, picaroon, rakehell, scalawag, spalpeen 9 miscreant, no-goodnik, prankster, reprobate, scallawag, scallywag, scoundrel, vulgarian 10 blackguard, holy terror, jackanapes, malefactor, ne'er-do-well, scapegrace
scamper: 3 fly, hie, rip, run, zip 4 bolt, dart, dash, flee, flit, race, romp, rush, skip, tear, trot, whip, zoom 5 hurry, scoot, shoot, speed 6 barrel, bustle, gallop, hasten, hustle, move it, rocket, scurry, sprint 7 floor it, hop to it, mad rush, make off, quicken, scuttle 8 fugitate, run for it, step on it 9 hotfoot it, shake a leg, skedaddle, speed away 10 get a move on, hightail it
scampi
ingredient: 5 prawn 6 garlic, shrimp
scan: 3 eye, pan 4 leaf, look, peer, pore, rake, read, skim, view 5 check, scour, study, sweep, watch 6 browse, look up, peruse, regard, riffle, screen, search, size up, survey 7 dip into, examine, inspect, monitor, ransack 8 digitize, look over, read over 9 speed-read 10 glance over, inspection, run through, scrutinize
__ scan: 3 CAT, MRI, NMR, PET 5 brain
Scand.
see Scandinavia
scandal: 3 mud 4 dirt, flap, news, tale, talk 5 crime, juice, libel, rumor, shame, stink 6 exposé, gossip, infamy, report 7 hearsay, outrage, slander 8 disgrace, dishonor, reproach 9 discredit, disrepute, improbity, sensation 10 dirty linen, wrongdoing
combining form: 4 -gate
ender: 3 ous 6 monger
sheet: 3 rag 9 newspaper
Scandal (1989 film)
cast: Bridget Fonda, John Hurt, Joanne Whalley
Scandal in Bohemia, A
author: Arthur Conan Doyle
scandalize: 4 slur 5 appal, shock 6 appall, defame 7 horrify, outrage, slander 9 denigrate
scandalmonger: 7 tattler 8 busybody
scandalous: 4 foul, lewd, ugly 5 juicy, lurid, seamy, shady, spicy 6 spicey, wicked 7 heinous 8 flagrant, horrible, improper, libelous, shameful, shocking 9 atrocious, desperate, egregious, gossiping, invidious, monstrous, offensive 10 defamatory, deplorable, disgusting, outrageous, scurrilous
city: 5 Sodom 8 Gomorrah
Scandinavia
bard: 5 scald, skald
city: 4 Oslo, Oulu 8 Helsinki 9 Stockholm 10 Copenhagen
country: 6 Norway, Sweden 7 Denmark, Finland
epic: 4 edda
flier: 3 SAS
folklore creature: 5 nisse, troll
god: 4 Frey, Odin, Thor 5 Othin
goddess: 4 Norn
gods: 5 Vanir
gulf: 7 Bothnia
land, to natives: 5 Norge, Suomi 7 Sverige
language, to natives: 5 Norsk
one of a trio in ~ myth: 4 Norn
plateau: 5 fjeld
range: 6 Kjölen
rodent: 7 lemming
royal name: 4 Erik, Olaf, Olav
rug: 3 rya
sea: 6 Baltic 7 Barents
sight: 5 fiord, fjord
toast: 5 skoal
Scandinavian: 4 Dane, Finn, Lapp 5 Norse, Swede 9 Norwegian
scandium: 5 metal 7 element
scanner: 3 CAT, MRI, NMR, OCR, PET 7 monitor
checkout ~ ID: 3 UPC
scant: 3 low, shy 4 bare, mere, poor, slim, thin 5 short, skimp, spare, tight 6 little, meager, narrow, paltry, scarce, skimpy, sparse, spotty 7 cramped, limited, minimal, scrimpy, slender, sparing, wanting 8 one or two 9 confining, deficient, hardly any, scattered 10 a handful of, compressed, contracted, inadequate, restricted
scantiness: 4 lack, want 6 dearth 7 paucity 8 exiguity, scarcity, shortage, sparsity 10 deficiency, inadequacy

scantling: 4 stud
scantly: 6 hardly
scanty: 3 shy 4 bare, lean, poor, slim, thin 5 light, short, small, spare, tight 6 exotic, little, meager, measly, scarce, skimpy, slight, sparse, spotty 7 limited, minimal, scrimpy, slender, sparing, trivial, wanting 8 exiguous, uncommon 9 deficient, miserable, scattered 10 inadequate
scape
ender: 4 goat 5 grace
starter: 3 ice, sea 4 city, land, mind, moon, town 5 beach, cloud, dream, lunar, night, water 6 street
scapegoat: 4 butt, dupe, gull, mark 5 patsy 6 azazel, sucker, target, victim 7 fall guy 10 blame-taker
burden: 5 blame
scapegrace: 3 cur 5 knave, rogue, scamp 6 bad guy, bad hat, rascal 7 bounder 8 blighter, rakehell, scalawag, spalpeen 9 reprobate, scallawag, scallywag, scoundrel 10 blackguard, ne'er-do-well
scapula: 4 bone 5 blade
locale: 8 shoulder
neighbor: 7 humerus
scar: 3 mar 4 flaw, hurt, line, mark, nick, scab, welt 5 brand, slash, wound 6 crater, damage, deface, defect, fright, injure, stigma 7 blemish, scratch 8 cicatrix 9 cicatrice 10 traumatize
seed ~: 5 hilum
scarab: 3 bug 6 amulet, beetle, insect 7 periapt 8 talisman
scarabaeid: 6 chafer
Scaramouche (1952 film)
cast: Stewart Granger, Janet Leigh
Scarborough __: 4 Fair, lily
Scarborough Fair (1968 song)
artist: Sérgio Mendes & Brasil '66, Simon and Garfunkel
herb: 4 sage 5 thyme 7 parsley 8 rosemary
scarce: 3 few, shy 4 bare, rare, slim, thin 5 scant, short 6 exotic, scanty, sparse 7 limited, slender, unusual 8 far apart, sporadic, uncommon, valuable 9 deficient 10 at a premium, inadequate, infrequent, occasional, sporadical
make oneself ~: 2 go 4 hide 5 scram 6 lie low 7 abscond, push off 8 withdraw
scarce as __ teeth: 4 hen's
scarcely: 4 just 6 barely, hardly, little, rarely, seldom 8 narrowly, slightly 10 hardly ever
ever: 6 rarely, seldom
scarcity: 4 lack, want 6 dearth 7 paucity, poverty 8 exiguity, shortage, sparsity 10 deficiency, inadequacy, meagerness, scantiness
scare: 3 cow 4 funk, turn 5 alarm, alert, daunt, deter, panic, shock, spook, start, upset 6 dismay, fright, menace, rattle 7 horrify, petrify, shake up, startle, terrify 8 frighten, paralyse, paralyze, threaten 9 close call, give a turn, terrorize 10 close shave, discourage, intimidate
ender: 4 crow 6 monger
off: 4 shoo 5 deter 8 frighten
up: 3 get 4 find 5 amass, group 6 gather, obtain, secure 7 acquire, collect, convene 8 assemble, scrounge 10 accumulate
word: 3 boo
scarecrow
innards: 5 straw
wish: 5 brain
Scarecrow (1973 film)
cast: Gene Hackman, Al Pacino
Scarecrow and Mrs. King (CBS drama)
cast: Bruce Boxleitner (Lee Stetson)
Kate Jackson (Amanda King)
scared: 5 funky, jumpy, timid 6 afeard, afraid, aghast, craven, divine, gun-shy, shaken, trepid 7 afeared, anxious, chicken, fearful, nervous, panicky, spooked, wimpish 8 cowardly, fearsome, hesitant, recreant, startled, timorous 9 nerveless, petrified, terrified, tremulous 10 frightened
be ~ of: 4 fear 5 dread
looking ~: 4 ashy, pale 5 ashen
run ~: 5 panic 10 chicken out
scared __: 5 stiff
__ Scared: 7 Running
__ Scared Stupid: 6 Ernest
scaredy-cat: 4 wimp 6 coward, craven, yellow 7 chicken, quitter, wimpish 8 poltroon, recreant
scarf: 3 boa, eat 4 gulp, ruff, sash, wolf, wrap 5 ascot, barbe, curch, do-rag, fichu, lungi, nubia, rumal, shawl, stole, throw 6 cravat, devour, fraise, gobble, guzzle, madras, pugree, rebosa, reboso, rebozo, riboso, ribozo, sarape, serape, tippet, wimple 7 bandana, consume, muffler, paisley, pugaree, sautoir 8 babushka, bandanna, covering, kaffiyeh, kerchief, mantilla, puggaree, wolf down 9 comforter, headcloth, headdress, neckpiece, polish off 10 fascinator
British ~: 5 ascot
crocheted ~: 5 nubia
down: 3 eat 4 bolt, gulp, wolf 5 eat up 6 devour, gobble, inhale 7 feast on 9 grab a bite, polish off
embroidered ~: 6 fraise
ender: 4 skin
feathery ~: 3 boa
liturgical ~: 5 amice, stole
make a ~: 4 knit
neck ~: 5 dicky 6 dickey, dickie
of India: 5 rumal
Scottish ~: 5 curch
starter: 4 head
support: 4 nape
scarf __: 4 down
Scarface (1983 film)
cast: Steven Bauer, Mary Elizabeth Mastrantonio, Al Pacino, Michelle Pfeiffer
director: Brian De Palma
Scaria: 4 Emil
scaring-away shout: 4 scat, shoo 5 scram 6 begone 7 amscray
Scarlatti: 8 Domenico
Scarlatti Inheritance, The
author: Robert Ludlum
scarlet: 3 red 5 color, ruddy 8 sanguine
relative: *see* red color
runner: 4 bean
sage: 5 plant 6 flower
the ~ letter: 4 red A
turn ~: 5 blush 6 redden
scarlet __: 7 tanager
Scarlet __, The: 6 Letter
Scarlet Feather
author: Maeve Binchy
Scarlet Knights: 7 Rutgers
Scarlet Letter, The: 5 novel
author: Nathaniel Hawthorne
character: 5 Pearl, Roger 6 Arthur, Hester, Prynne 10 Bellingham, Dimmesdale
Scarlet Pimpernel, The
author: Baroness Emmuska Orczy
scarlet runner: 6 legume, veggie 9 vegetable
Scarlett: 5 belle, O'Hara 6 Sylvia 9 Johansson
daughter: 4 Ella 10 Bonnie Blue
home: 4 Tara 7 Atlanta, Georgia
love: 5 Rhett 6 Ashley
mother: 5 Ellen
scarp: 5 bluff, cliff, ridge 9 declivity, precipice
like a ~: 5 steep
__-scarred: 6 battle
Scarry, Richard: 5 Swiss 6 writer
Scar Tissue (1999 song)
artist: Red Hot Chili Peppers
__-scarum: 5 harum
Scarwid: 5 Diana
scary: 4 eery 5 eerie, hairy 6 creepy, spooky 7 macaber, macabre, uncanny 8 alarming, chilling, daunting, fearsome, menacing, shocking 9 frightful, unearthly, unnerving 10 disturbing, horrendous, horrifying, terrifying
feeling: 4 fear 5 alarm, angst, dread, panic 6 fright, horror, terror 7 anxiety
Scary Movie (2000 film)
cast: Jon Abrahams, Carmen Electra, Shannon Elizabeth
director: Keenen Ivory Wayans
scat: 4 flee, shoo 5 music, scram 6 beat it, begone 7 amscray, buzz off, get lost, vamoose 8 clear out 9 skedaddle, take a hike 10 hightail it, hit the road
do ~: 4 sing
queen: 4 Ella
scathe: 4 slam 7 lambast 8 lambaste 9 castigate, criticize, excoriate
scathing: 5 cruel, harsh, sharp 6 biting, bitter, severe 7 caustic, cutting, pointed, searing 8 critical, incisive, sardonic, stinging, virulent 9 rancorous, scorching, trenchant, truculent, vitriolic
Scatman: 8 Crothers
scatter: 3 sow 4 cast, flee, part, rout, shed, spew, spue 5 fling, spill, spray, strew, throw 6 dispel, divide, fan out, lavish, litter, powder, shower, spread 7 bestrew, diffuse, disband, diverge, migrate, radiate, spatter, split up 8 disorder, disperse, disunite, separate, sprinkle, squander 9 broadcast, dissipate, punctuate 10 besprinkle, distribute
ender: 3 gun 4 good, shot 5 brain 7 brained
scatter __: 3 pin, rug 4 shot
scatterbrained: 4 daft 5 ditsy, ditzy, dizzy, giddy, silly 6 goosey, madcap 7 flighty 8 skittish 9 forgetful, illogical
scattered: 4 rare, sown, thin 5 scant 6 effuse, scanty, skimpy, sparse, spotty 7 diffuse 8 far apart, rambling, separate, sporadic 9 somewhere 10 disorderly, dissipated, infrequent, sporadical, unfrequent
scattering: 3 few 6 litter 7 handful 8 stampede 9 diffusion 10 dispersion
scaup: 4 bird, duck, fowl 8 bluebill
emulate a ~: 4 dive
scavenge: 5 prowl 6 forage
scavenger
beach ~: 3 ern 4 erne, gull
canine ~: 5 hyena 6 hyaena, jackal
scavenger __: 4 hunt
Sc.D.: 3 deg.
Scedrin: 6 Rodion
scena: 4 solo
scenario: 4 idea, plan, plot, ruse 5 setup 6 design, scheme, script, sketch 7 outline, rundown, summary 8 game plan, strategy, time line 9 story line 10 screenplay
scend: 5 heave
scene: 3 ado, row, set 4 fuss, riot, site, spot, to-do, view 5 arena, event, furor, hoo-ha, place, scape, sight, stage, venue, vista 6 hoo-hah, locale, milieu, region 7 episode, lookout, outlook, picture, setting, tableau, tantrum, theater, theatre, wrangle 8 backdrop, brouhaha, incident, locality, location, outburst, panorama, premises, prospect, squabble, standing, strategy 9 commotion, happening, landscape, situation, spectacle 10 background, exhibition, hullabaloo, occurrence
bad ~: 4 mess, riot 6 downer, uproar 10 unpleasant
do a ~: 3 act 7 perform
how to enter a ~: 5 on cue
locale: 3 set
make a ~: 3 act 4 rage, rant 5 act up, upset 7 trouble
make the ~: 4 come, show 5 visit 6 appear, arrive, attend, emerge, stop by 7 turn out
of action: 5 arena, venue 6 sphere
quit the ~: 2 go 4 part 5 leave
shift, in a movie: 4 wipe
stealer: 3 ham 6 emoter
scene __ crime: 5 of the
__ scene: 3 mob 4 drop 5 on the 6 street
scène, mise en: 5 stage
scenery: 3 set 4 view 5 scape, stage, vista 6 nature 7 terrain 8 backdrop, panorama, prospect, stage set 9 landscape, spectacle
bit of ~: 4 drop
chewer: 3 ham 6 emoter
suffix: 5 -scape
Scenes From a Mall (1991 film)
cast: Woody Allen, Bill Irwin, Bette Midler
Scenes From a Marriage (1973 film)
cast: Bibi Andersson, Liv Ullmann
director: Ingmar Bergman

SC

Scenes From Childhood
composer: Robert Schumann
__ Scenes of Winter: 6 Chilly
scenic: 5 grand **8** dramatic, striking **9** beautiful, panoramic **10** impressive
scent: 4 aura, hint, nose, odor, tang **5** aroma, odour, savor, sense, smell, sniff, spoor, track, trail, whiff **6** detect **7** bouquet, cologne, essence, incense, perfume **9** fragrance, get wind of, redolence
air-freshener ~: 4 pine **5** lilac
animal ~: 5 spoor, trail
brand: 5 Opium **6** Chanel **9** Obsession
maker: 4 atar, otto **5** athar, attar, ottar
on the ~ of: 5 after **9** following
throw off the ~: 7 mislead
scented: 5 balmy, olent, sweet **7** odorous **8** aromatic, redolent **9** ambrosial
Scent of a Woman (1992 film)
cast: Gabrielle Anwar, Chris O'Donnell, Al Pacino
director: Martin Brest
scepter: 3 rod **4** wand **5** staff
hold the ~: 4 rule **6** govern **7** command
mock ~: 6 bauble
partner: 3 orb
wielder: 5 ruler **8** governor
sch.
see school
Schacht: 2 Al
Schaech, Johnathon
spouse: Christina Applegate
Schaeffer: 7 Rebecca
Schafer: 7 Natalie
Schaffner: 8 Franklin
Schalk: 3 Ray
Schatzberg: 5 Jerry
schav: 4 soup
ingredient: 6 sorrel
Schayes, Dolph: 5 cager
milieu: 5 court
org.: 3 NBA
sport: 10 basketball
schedule: 4 bill, book, card, list, plan, roll **5** chart, round, set up, slate, table **6** agenda, docket, lineup, roster **7** appoint, arrange, program, reserve **8** calendar, organize, pencil in, register, time line **9** itinerary, timetable **10** tabulation
abbr.: 3 arr., dep., ETA, ETD, TBA
ahead of ~: 5 early
behind ~: 4 late **5** tardy **7** overdue
busy ~: 5 whirl
on ~: 6 timely **8** punctual
position: 4 slot
tough ~: 5 grind
scheduled: 3 due, set **5** on tap
schedules, like some: 5 light, tight
Scheherazade: 6 ballet
composer: Nikolai Rimsky-Korsakov
hero: 3 Ali
specialty: 4 tale
subject: 3 roc
Scheib: 4 Earl
Scheider, Roy: 5 actor
film: 2010 (1984)
All That Jazz (1979)
The French Connection (1971)
Jaws (1975)
Last Embrace (1979)
Marathon Man (1976)
The Russia House (1990)
Schelde: 5 river
see also Scheldt
Scheldt
city on the ~: 5 Ghent **7** Antwerp
feeder: 3 Lys **4** Leie
locale: 6 France **7** Belgium
Schell: 5 Maria **10** Maximilian
Schelomo
composer: Ernest Bloch
schema: 6 method
schematic detail, briefly: 4 spec
scheme: 3 aim, job, way **4** brew, form, hoax, idea, plan, plot, ploy, ruse **5** angle, cabal, cadre, craft, dodge, hatch, pitch, plan A, plan B, setup, shift, trick, twist **6** course, design, device, format, hookup, hustle, layout, method, racket, system **7** collude, connive, diagram, drawing, finagle, frame-up, gimmick, network, outline, pattern, picture, project, sleight, tactics, trump up, wrangle **8** conspire, game plan, intrigue, maneuver, proposal, put-up job, scenario, strategy **9** blueprint, cast about, framework, machinate, speculate, stratagem **10** brainchild, conspiracy, subterfuge, suggestion
color ~: 5 décor
crooked ~: 3 con **4** scam **5** setup **6** racket
in Britain: 4 rede
__ scheme: 5 color, Ponzi, rhyme **7** pyramid
schemer: 5 snake **6** con man
schemers: 5 cabal
scheming: 3 sly **4** foxy, wily **5** slick **6** artful, crafty, shifty, shrewd, subtle, tricky **7** cunning, devious, furtive, knavish **8** slippery **9** conniving, deceitful, deceptive, designing, underhand
Schenectady: 4 city, town
locale: 7 New York
Schenkel: 5 Chris
Schepisi: 4 Fred
Scherzo __ Flat Minor: 3 in E
Schiaparelli: 4 Elsa **8** Giovanni
Schick: 4 Bela **5** razor
alternative: 3 Bic **4** Atra **8** Gillette
Schick __: 4 test
Schickele: 5 Peter
alias: 7 PDQ Bach
Schiele, Egon: 7 painter **8** Austrian
Schiffer: 7 Claudia
Schifrin: 4 Lalo
Schildkraut: 6 Joseph
Schiller, Friedrich von: 4 poet **6** German **9** historian **10** playwright
collaborator: 6 Goethe
work: Don Carlos
The Maid of Orleans
The Robbers
Wilhelm Tell
Schilling, Curt
sport: 8 baseball
Schindler: 5 Oskar **6** Emelie, Emilie
Schindler's List: 4 book, film
author: Thomas Keneally
cast: Ralph Fiennes, Ben Kingsley, Liam Neeson
composer: John Williams
director: Steven Spielberg
villain: 4 Nazi
schipperke: 3 dog **5** canid **6** canine
Schippers, Thomas: 9 conductor
Schirra, Wally: 9 astronaut
schism: 4 rent, rift **5** break, chasm, space, split **6** breach **7** dissent, faction, parting, rupture **8** cleavage, disunion, division, fracture **9** rebellion **10** disruption, divergence, separation
__ Schism: 5 Great
schismatic: 5 rebel **8** forsaker, renegade **9** dissident, heretical, sectarian
schist: 7 mineral
Schlafly: 7 Phyllis
Schlatter: 7 Charlie
schlemiel: 3 oaf, sap **4** clod, fool, gull, jerk **5** looby, patsy
question: 5 why me
schlep: 3 lug **4** cart, drag, haul, plod, poke, tote, walk **5** carry, fetch **6** convey, trudge
Schleptet
composer: PDQ Bach
Schlesinger: 4 John **6** Arthur
Schlessinger: 5 Laura
Schliemann, Heinrich: 6 German, writer **13** archaeologist
discovery: Troy, Mycenae
Schlitz: 4 beer
alternative: *see* beer
schlocky: 5 cheap, junky, tacky **6** cheesy, shoddy, tawdry **7** chintzy
schmaltz: 3 goo **4** corn **5** slush **6** bathos
schmaltzy: 5 corny, mushy **7** maudlin, mawkish **8** affected
Schmeling, Max: 5 boxer
milieu: 4 ring
Schmidt: 3 Joe **4** Mike **6** Helmut
Schmidt, Mike: 7 Phillie
sport: 8 baseball
schmo: 3 oaf, sap **4** dolt, fool, jerk, nerd **5** dufus, klutz, yahoo **6** doofus **7** sad sack **9** blockhead **10** dunderhead, nincompoop, noodlehead
like a ~: 5 dense, inept **7** hapless
schmooze: 3 gab, rap, yak **4** chat **6** gossip, hobnob, parley **8** causerie, converse **9** tête-à-tête **10** chew the rag
Schnabel, Artur: 7 pianist **8** Austrian
schnapps: 3 gin **5** drink **8** beverage
schnauzer: 3 dog, pet **5** canid **6** canine
feature: 5 beard
like a ~ coat: 4 wiry
Schneider: 3 Rob **4** John, Paul, Romy
Schneitzhoeffer: 4 Jean
__ schnitzel: 6 Wiener
Schnitzler, Arthur: 8 Austrian **10** playwright
work: La Ronde
Leutnant Gustl
Light o' Love
Professor Bernhardi
schnook: 3 sap **6** pigeon, sucker
schnoz: 4 beak, nose **5** snoot, snout **6** beezer, honker
ender: 3 ola
Schoedsack: 6 Ernest
__ schoen: 5 danke
Schoenberg, Arnold: 8 composer
style: 6 atonal
Schoendienst, Red: 8 Cardinal
sport: 8 baseball
scholar: 4 coed, sage **5** brain, pupil **6** critic, pundit, savant **7** egghead, learner, student, teacher, thinker **8** academic, bookworm, highbrow, longhair, mandarin **9** abecedary, authority, intellect, literatus, professor, undergrad **10** specialist
assistant: 7 famulus
classical ~: 8 humanist
wish: 5 grant
__ scholar: 6 Rhodes
Scholar-Gipsy, The
author: Matthew Arnold
scholarly: 4 wise **7** bookish, erudite, learned **8** academic, cerebral, cultured, educated, highbrow, lettered, literary, literate, longhair, profound, studious, well-read **9** pedagogic, recondite, technical
scholarship: 4 lore **5** award, grant, prize **7** letters, reading, subsidy **8** learning, literacy **9** erudition
criterion: 4 need
endower: 6 Rhodes
recipient: 7 grantee
scholastic: 7 bookish **8** academic, pedantic **9** classical **10** pedantical
Scholastic Aptitude __: 4 Test
Scholes, Myron: 8 Canadian, Nobelist **9** economist
school: 3 ism, pod **4** acad., coll., form, sect, univ. **5** class, coach, drill, edify, genre, group, guide, lycée, prime, swarm, teach, train, tutor, verse **6** belief, ground, inform, litter, lyceum **7** academy, break in, college, educate, nurture, outlook, prepare **8** devotees, instruct, seminary **9** adherents, alma mater, cultivate, disciples, enlighten, followers, following **10** discipline, halls of ivy, persuasion, university
absence from ~: 5 hooky **6** hookey
administrator: 4 dean, supt. **9** principal
aim: 9 education
boarding ~: 4 acad., prep **7** academy
clanger: 4 bell
closet: 6 locker
community ~: 2 JC
country ~ teacher: 4 marm
dance: 4 prom
division: 5 grade
do well in ~: 5 learn
ender: 3 bag, boy, man, men **4** book, girl, marm, mate, room, work, yard **5** child, house **6** fellow, master **7** teacher **8** children, mistress
essay: 6 thesis
founded in 1440: 4 Eton
French ~: 5 école, lycée
furniture: 4 desk
grade ~ subject: 3 Eng. **4** geog. **5** arith. **7** English **9** geography **10** arithmetic
grounds: 4 quad **6** campus
group: 3 PTA **4** fish **5** class, grade
issue: 6 busing
kid: 5 pupil **7** student
middle ~: 2 JH
not in ~: 6 absent
nursery ~: 4 pre-K

officers' ~: 3 OTC, OTS
of fish: 5 shoal
of the old ~: 5 passé 7 veteran
of thought: 3 ism
onetime ~ subject: 4 rhet. 8 rhetoric
ordeal: 4 exam, test
org.: 3 NEA, PTA
paper: 5 essay, theme
period: 4 term 7 quarter, session 8 semester
plebe ~: 4 USMA, USNA
police ~: 7 academy
prep ~: 7 academy
primary ~: 4 elem. 10 elementary
publication: 5 paper 8 yearbook 9 newspaper
spinner: 5 globe
sports org.: 4 NCAA
staffer: 2 TA 7 teacher 9 professor 10 instructor
subject: 3 alg., bio., Eng., ESL, mus., RRR, sci. 4 econ., geog., hist., math 5 arith., music 7 algebra, biology, English, history, science, three Rs 9 economics, geography 10 arithmetic
supply: 4 glue 5 paper, paste, ruler 7 binders, pencils, tablets
tabloid program for ~: 3 NIE
tech ~: 4 inst. 9 institute
tool: 2 PC 5 ruler
vehicle: 3 bus
work: 6 lesson
worker: 4 aide 5 nurse 7 teacher
school ___: 3 age, bus, day, tie 4 year 5 board, night
___ school: 3 day, med, old 4 free, high, prep 5 Bible, charm, grade, night, trade 6 Ashcan, dental, magnet, middle, normal, public, reform, riding, summer, Sunday 7 evening, grammar, medical, nursery, primary, private
School ___: 3 Day 4 Days, Daze, Ties 5 Is Out, of Law
schoolbook: 4 text 6 primer, reader 7 speller 8 workbook
schoolchild: 3 boy, lad 4 girl, miss 5 minor, pupil, youth 9 stripling, youngster
___ School Confidential: 4 High
Schoolcraft, Henry Rowe: 6 writer 8 explorer
School Day (1957 song)
artist: Chuck Berry
schooldays: 9 childhood 10 juvenility
School Daze (1988 film)
cast: Tisha Campbell, Giancarlo Esposito, Laurence Fishburne
director: Spike Lee
schooled: 6 expert 8 literate 10 well-versed
be ~ in: 4 know
School for Scandal, The
author: Richard Sheridan
School for Wives, The
author: Molière
schooling: 6 lesson 7 tuition 8 learning, training, tutelage 9 education, knowledge 10 upbringing
School Is Out (1961 song)
artist: Gary U.S. Bonds
schoolmarm
reply to a: 4 yes'm
rod: 6 ferule
schoolmarmish: 4 prim
school of ___: 7 thought
school of ___ knocks: 4 hard
School of ___: 3 Law 4 Mind
___ School of Design: 7 Parsons
School of Rock (2003 film)
cast: Jack Black, Joan Cusack
schoolroom: 4 hall
schools, like most: 4 coed
School's Out (1972 song)
artist: Alice Cooper
___ school tie: 3 old
School Ties (1992 film)
cast: Matt Damon, Brendan Fraser, Chris O'Donnell
schoolwork
do ~: 9 grind away
holder: 6 binder
School Zone: 4 sign
warning: 4 slow
schooner: 3 mug 4 boat 6 argosy 8 sailboat
contents: 3 ale 4 beer
feature: 4 mast
prairie ~: 5 wagon
team: 4 oxen
___ schooner: 7 prairie
Schopenhauer: 6 Arthur
Schorr: 6 Daniel
schottische: 4 step 5 dance
Schrader: 4 Paul
Schreiber: 4 Liev 5 Avery
Schreiber, Liev: 5 actor
film: The Hurricane (1999)
Kate and Leopold (2001)
Phantoms (1998)
Spring Forward (2000)
The Sum of All Fears (2002)
Taking Woodstock (2009)
A Walk on the Moon (1999)
Schreiner, Olive: 6 writer 12 South African
work: The Story of an African Farm
Schroder: 4 Rick 5 Ricky
Schrödinger, Erwin: 8 Nobelist 9 physicist
Schroeder: 3 Pat 6 Barbet 8 Patricia
schtick: 7 routine 8 pretense
Schubert, Franz: 8 Austrian, composer
composition: 4 lied
string work: 5 octet 7 octette
work: Tragic Symphony
Trout Quintet
Unfinished Symphony
Schuck: 4 John
schul: 6 temple 7 synagog 9 synagogue
Schulberg, Budd: 6 writer
work: The Disenchanted
The Harder They Fall
What Makes Sammy Run?
Schuller, Robert: 10 evangelist
Schultz: 4 Carl 8 Theodore
Schultz, Dutch: 5 alias 8 gangster
Schultz, Theodore: 8 Nobelist 9 economist
Schulz: 4 Axel 7 Charles
Schumacher: 4 Joel
Schumann, Robert: 6 German 8 composer
wife: 5 Clara
work: Manfred Overture
Scenes From Childhood
schuss: 3 ski 4 skee
ender: 6 boomer
Schuster, Max: 9 publisher
partner: 5 Simon
Schütz, Heinrich: 6 German 8 composer
Schuyler: 5 James 6 Colfax, Philip
Schuylkill: 5 river
locale: 4 Penn. 5 Phila.
schwa: 5 sound 6 symbol
Schwab: 7 Charles
Schwartz: 6 Melvin 7 Delmore 8 Berthold
Schwartz, Delmore: 4 poet 6 writer
work: Genesis
Shenandoah
Summer Knowledge
The World Is a Wedding
___ Schwarz: 3 FAO
Schwarzenegger, Arnold: 5 actor
film: Batman & Robin (1997)
Commando (1985)
Conan the Barbarian (1982)
Eraser (1996)
Junior (1994)
Kindergarten Cop (1990)
Last Action Hero (1993)
Predator (1987)
Pumping Iron (1977)
Red Heat (1988)
The Running Man (1987)
Stay Hungry (1976)
The Terminator (1984)
Total Recall (1990)
True Lies (1994)
Twins (1988)
middle name: 5 Alois
spouse: Maria Shriver
Schwarzkopf: 6 Norman 9 Elisabeth
biography collaborator: 5 Petre
like ~: 3 ret. 7 retired
rank: 3 gen. 7 general
Schweitzer, Albert: 6 German 8 Nobelist 9 physician
Schwimmer: 5 David
sci.
see science
___ sci: 4 poli, poly
sciatic: 5 nerve
science: 3 bio., bot. 4 anat., biol., chem., geol., phys. 5 logic, ology, theol. 6 astron., botany, method, optics, osmics 7 anatomy, biology, ecology, geodesy, haptics, myology, orology, physics, zoology, zymurgy 8 agrology, avionics, bryology, forestry, gemology, genetics, horology, learning, medicine, mycology, pharmacy, pomology, research, taxonomy, theology, zymology 9 acoustics, astronomy, chemistry, cosmology, dentistry, economics, ethnology, geography, geoponics, hydrology, ichnology, knowledge, mechanics, ophiology, petrology, sociology, technique, telemetry, zoography 10 archeology, biophysics, demography, discipline, embryology, entomology, ergonomics, exobiology, geophysics, hydraulics, metallurgy, mineralogy, morphology, psychology, seismology, topography 11 aeronautics, agriculture, aquaculture, biodynamics, criminology, electronics, herpetology, ichthyology, lichenology, meteorology, myrmecology, ornithology, thermionics, volcanology 12 horticulture
behavioral ~: 5 psych. 10 psychology
builder's ~: 4 arch. 6 archit.
center: 3 lab
combining form: 4 -logy 5 -sophy
course cost: 6 lab fee
cyborg ~: 7 bionics
divine ~: 5 theol. 8 theology
earth ~: 4 geol. 7 geology
environmental ~: 4 ecol. 7 ecology 8 oecology
farming ~: 3 agr. 11 agriculture
gardener's ~: 4 hort. 12 horticulture
insect ~: 5 entom. 10 entomology
life ~: 3 bot. 4 biol., zool. 6 botany 7 biology, zoology
like ~: 6 amoral
magazine: 4 Omni
mapping ~: 5 topog. 10 topography
medieval ~: 7 alchemy
of reasoning: 5 logic
of selling: 4 mktg. 9 marketing
of smell: 6 osmics
of touch: 7 haptics
physical ~: 6 astron. 7 geology, physics 9 astronomy, mechanics
poison ~: 3 tox. 10 toxicology
program: 4 Nova
social ~: 3 eco. 4 econ. 9 economics
starter: 3 bio, con, pre 4 omni
the sweet ~: 6 boxing
science ___: 7 fiction
___ science: 3 big 4 food, hard, life, soft, soil 5 earth, exact, space 6 rocket, social 7 library, natural
___ Science: 5 Weird 7 Popular
Science and the Modern World
author: Alfred North Whitehead
science fiction: 5 genre
award: 4 Hugo
character: 2 ET 5 alien, droid, robot 6 cyborg
father: 5 Verne
film: 4 Tron 5 Alien 6 Aliens
magazine: 6 Analog
setting: 6 future
understand, in ~: 4 grok
vehicle: 3 UFO
weapon: 5 laser 6 phaser
Science Guy, The: 3 Nye
sciences partner: 4 arts
scientia ___ potentia: 3 est
scientific: 7 learned, logical, precise 9 deductive, objective, technical
combining form: 5 -logic
scientific ___: 6 method
Scientific American Frontiers
host: 4 Alda
scientist: 3 Ohm, Ray 4 Baer, Berg, Bohr, Born, Cohn, Davy, Gray, Hahn, Hess, Koch, Kuhn, Mead, Rabi, Ryle, Todd, Urey 5 Banks, Black, Boyle, Bragg, Brahe, Crick, Curie, Dewar, Dirac, Esaki, Euler, Evans, Fabre, Fermi, Fitch, Gamow, Gauss, Hedin, Henry, Hertz, Hooke, Joule, Libby, Lyell, Nobel, Pauli, Raman, Ruska, Sagan, Soddy, Stern, Tesla, Volta, Vries, Young 6 Adrian, Ampère, Binnig, Buffon, Bunsen, Carrel, Carter, Carver, Cuvier, Dalton, Darwin, Draper, Finsen, Franck, Frazer, Galton, Gesner, Halley, Hubble, Huxley, Kelvin, Kepler,

Leakey, Mendel, Müller, Napier, Nernst, Newton, Pascal, Peirce, Perkin, Perrin, Piazzi, Planck, Ramsay, Remsen, Rohrer, Sanger, Sitter, Solvay, Stokes, Strabo, Susumu, Torrey, Watson, Yukawa **7** Agassiz, Borlaug, Celsius, Compton, Coulomb, Crookes, Doppler, Faraday, Fleming, Fourier, Fresnel, Galilei, Galvani, Goddard, Hodgkin, Hopkins, Huggins, Huygens, Lamarck, Laplace, Marconi, Maxwell, Meitner, Oersted, Pasteur, Pauling, Piccard, Ptolemy, Réaumur, Scheele, Thomson, Tyndall, Wallace, Wegener, Woolley **8** Ångström, Avogadro, Blackett, Breasted, Chadwick, Einstein, Foucault, Friedman, Herschel, Lagrange, Linnaeus, Mercator, Millikan, Rayleigh, Roentgen, Sakharov, Sorensen, Tombaugh, Van Allen, Weismann **9** Arrhenius, Berthelot, Berzelius, Cavendish, Eddington, Gay-Lussac, Kirchhoff, Lavoisier, Mendeleev, Michelson, Pausanias, Priestley **10** Archimedes, Copernicus, Fahrenheit, Fraunhofer, Heisenberg, Hipparchus, Malinowski, Rutherford, Schliemann, Torricelli **11** al-Khwarizmi, Aristarchus, Joliot-Curie, Omar Khayyám, Oppenheimer, Sherrington, van der Waals
Arabic ~: 11 al-Khwarizmi
association: 3 ACS
Austrian ~: 5 Pauli **6** Mendel **7** Doppler, Meitner
Belgian ~: 6 Solvay
British ~: 3 Ray **4** Davy, Ryle, Snow **5** Banks, Black, Boyle, Bragg, Crick, Dirac, Evans, Hooke, Joule, Lyell, Soddy, Young **6** Adrian, Dalton, Darwin, Galton, Halley, Huxley, Kelvin, Leakey, Newton, Perkin, Ramsay, Sanger, Stokes **7** Crookes, Faraday, Hodgkin, Hopkins, Huggins, Thomson, Tyndall, Wallace, Woolley **8** Blackett, Chadwick, Herschel, Rayleigh **9** Cavendish, Eddington, Priestley **10** Malinowski, Rutherford **11** Sherrington
Danish ~: 4 Bohr **5** Brahe **6** Finsen **7** Oersted **8** Sorensen
Dutch ~: 5 Vries **6** Sitter **7** Huygens **11** van der Waals
Egyptian ~: 7 Ptolemy
Flemish ~: 8 Mercator
French ~: 5 Curie, Fabre **6** Ampère, Buffon, Carrel, Cuvier, Franck, Pascal, Perrin **7** Coulomb, Fourier, Fresnel, Lamarck, Laplace, Pasteur, Réaumur **8** Foucault, Lagrange **9** Berthelot, Gay-Lussac, Lavoisier **11** Joliot-Curie
German ~: 3 Ohm **4** Baer, Born, Cohn, Hahn, Koch, Kuhn **5** Gauss, Hertz, Ruska, Stern **6** Binnig, Bunsen, Kepler, Müller, Nernst, Planck **7** Wegener **8** Einstein, Roentgen, Weismann **9** Kirchhoff **10** Fahrenheit, Fraunhofer, Heisenberg, Schliemann
Greek ~: 6 Strabo **9** Pausanias **10** Archimedes, Hipparchus **11** Aristarchus
Indian ~: 5 Raman
Italian ~: 5 Fermi, Volta **6** Piazzi **7** Galilei, Galvani, Marconi **8** Avogadro **10** Torricelli
Japanese ~: 5 Esaki **6** Susumu, Yukawa
Kenyan ~: 6 Leakey
no rocket ~: 3 dim, oaf **4** ditz, fool, jerk, slow **5** dense, dopey, dummy, dunce, thick **6** lubber, nitwit, oafish, obtuse **7** boorish, doltish, dullard, jackass, loutish **8** dumbbell **9** blockhead, simpleton **10** nincompoop
Persian ~: 4 Omar **7** Khayyám
Polish ~: 5 Curie **10** Copernicus
question: 3 how, why
rocket ~: 5 brain **6** genius **7** scholar
Russian ~: 9 Mendeleev
Scottish ~: 4 Todd **5** Dewar **6** Frazer, Napier **7** Fleming, Maxwell
Soviet ~: 8 Sakharov
Swedish ~: 5 Hedin, Nobel **7** Celsius, Scheele **8** Ångström, Linnaeus **9** Arrhenius, Berzelius
Swiss ~: 5 Euler **6** Gesner, Rohrer **7** Piccard
workplace: 3 lab
__ scientist: 3 mad **6** rocket
sci-fi
see science fiction
scilicet: 6 namely
scimitar: 5 blade, sword
cousin: 5 saber
scintilla: 3 bit, jot, ray **4** atom, hint, iota, mite, mote, whit **5** gleam, glint, grain, shred, spark, speck, touch, trace **7** glimmer, minimum, modicum
scintillate: 5 blink, flare, flash, gleam, shine **6** dazzle **7** glimmer, glisten, glitter, shimmer, sparkle, twinkle **9** coruscate
scintillating: 5 brisk, smart, witty **6** bright, lively, lucent **7** beaming, buoyant, dynamic, piquant, radiant, shining **8** dazzling, exciting, flashing, gleaming, glinting, luminous, lustrous, shimmery, spirited **9** brilliant, ebullient, sparkling, sprightly, twinkling, vivacious
scintillation: 5 gleam, light, spark **7** shimmer, sparkle
scion: 3 kid, son **4** heir, seed, slip **5** child, graft, issue, sprig **6** branch, sprout **7** heiress, progeny **8** daughter, grandson, offshoot **9** inheritor, offspring, posterity, successor **10** descendant
Sciorra: 9 Annabella
Scioto: 5 river
city on the ~: 8 Columbus
locale: 4 Ohio
Scipio: 5 Roman
rival: 4 Cato
Scirocco: 2 VW **3** car **4** auto **10** automobile, Volkswagen
scissor: 2 ax **3** axe, cut, lop **4** chop, clip, crop, edit, hack, omit, pink, snip, trim **5** erase, prune, sever, shear, shred, slash **6** censor, cleave, delete, digest, excise, reduce, revise, shears **7** abridge, expunge **8** leave out **9** capsulize, expurgate
ender: 4 tail
__ Scissorhands: 6 Edward
scissors __: 4 hold, jack, kick
__ scissors: 4 nail
sclaff outcome: 5 divot
__ S. Cobb: 5 Irvin
scoff: 3 boo, pan, rag **4** gibe, gybe, jeer, jibe, mock **5** fleer, flout, knock, laugh, scorn, sneer, spurn **6** deride, jibe at, reject, revile, slight **7** disdain, laugh at, poke fun **8** belittle, discount, pooh-pooh, ridicule **9** discredit, poke fun at
at: 5 flout, scorn, taunt **6** deride **8** belittle, discount **9** discredit, frown upon, make fun of **10** disbelieve, make game of
ender: 3 law
scoffer: 5 cynic **7** doubter, killjoy, sceptic, skeptic **9** pessimist **10** questioner
scoffing: 4 gibe, jibe **5** snide **7** jeering, mockery, sarcasm **8** derision, derisive **9** skeptical
scofflaw: 8 criminal
Scofield: 4 Paul
Scoggins: 5 Tracy
Scolari: 5 Peter
scold: 3 jaw, nag, rag **4** flay, lash, rail, ream, snub **5** abuse, baste, blame, chide, shrew **6** berate, chider, critic, hector, jump on, preach, rebuke, virago **7** bawl out, censure, chasten, chew out, henpeck, lambast, lecture, needler, put down, rebuker, reprove, tell off, upbraid **8** admonish, chastise, denounce, fishwife, harridan, lace into, lambaste, reproach, sail into, tear into **9** castigate, criticize, disparage, dress down, excoriate, exprobate, find fault, fustigate, henpecker, light into, objurgate, reprehend, reprimand, termagant, Xanthippe **10** castigator, denunciate, take to task, tongue-lash, vituperate
scolding: 5 abuse **6** earful, lesson, rebuke **7** censure, lecture, reproof **8** critical, reproval **9** reprimand **10** impugnment, upbraiding
words: 4 no-no
__'s Coming: 3 Eli
sconce: 4 head **5** skull **6** noggin, noodle **7** cranium **9** braincase
spot: 4 wall
scone: 6 pastry **7** biscuit, teacake
like ~: 4 oaty **5** oaten
partner: 3 tea
__ S. Connell Jr.: 4 Evan
Scooby-Doo: 3 dog **4** film **7** cartoon
cast: Sarah Michelle Gellar, Matthew Lillard, Freddie Prinze Jr.
scooch: 5 slide
scoop: 3 dip **4** bail, beat, dirt, info, lift, news, skim **5** empty, gouge, ladle, spade, spoon, story, truth **6** bailer, bucket, burrow, deepen, dig out, dipper, dredge, gather, hollow, pick up, remove, report, shovel, take up, trowel **7** lowdown, sweep up, utensil **8** excavate **9** clear away, exclusive **10** depression, revelation
get the ~: 5 learn
long-handled ~: 4 bail **5** ladle **6** dipper
receptacle: 4 cone
Scoop
author: Evelyn Waugh
scooped out: 5 round **6** curved, dented, dished, hollow, sunken **7** concave, sagging **8** indented **9** depressed, excavated
scoot: 3 fly, hie, rip, run, zip **4** bolt, dart, dash, flee, flit, race, rush, skip, tear, zoom **5** hurry, scram, shoot, spank, speed **6** barrel, gallop, hasten, hustle, move it, rocket, scurry, sprint, streak **7** floor it, hop to it, make off, quicken, rush off, scamper **8** fugitate, run for it, scramble, step on it **9** hotfoot it, make haste, shake a leg, skedaddle **10** get a move on, get hopping, hightail it, make tracks
scoot __: 4 over
scooter
Italian ~: 5 Vespa
kin: 5 moped **6** go-cart, go-kart
__ scooter: 5 motor
scop: 4 bard, poet **8** minstrel
scope: 3 run **4** area, play, room, size, span, sway, view **5** ambit, depth, field, gamut, orbit, range, reach, realm, scale, space, sweep, width **6** degree, extent, leeway, margin, radius, region, sphere, spread, survey, vision **7** breadth, compass, expanse, freedom, horizon, leisure, liberty, look out, measure, purpose, purview, stretch **8** capacity, confines, distance, latitude, wideness **9** amplitude, dimension, elbowroom, extension, full range, incidence, largeness **10** boundaries
camera lens ~: 5 field
of great ~: 3 big **4** vast **5** broad
out: 3 see **4** case **5** check, watch
starter: 3 oto **4** endo, peri, tele **5** fiber, micro, radar, rifle **6** stetho
use a ~: 3 aim
Scope: 9 mouthwash
alternative: 3 Act **4** Plax **6** Signal **7** Lavoris **9** Listerine **10** Fluorigard
use ~: 6 gargle
Scopes Trial
lawyer: 5 Bryan **6** Darrow
locale: 9 Tennessee
org.: 4 ACLU
scorch: 4 bake, burn, char, cook, heat, melt, sear, slur **5** broil, parch, roast, scald, singe, smear **6** vilify, wither **7** blacken, blister, frizzle, lambast, shrivel, slander, swelter **8** lambaste **9** carbonize
scorched: 3 dry **6** torrid **7** parched
scorched-__ policy: 5 earth
scorching: 3 hot **4** fire, warm **5** fiery **6** red-hot, sultry, torrid **7** burning **8** scathing, tropical **9** sarcastic **10** sweltering
score: 3 bag, cut, get, mar, run, sum, tab, win **4** bill, debt, earn, gain, gash, goal, mark, nick, rate, rout, sake, slit **5** chalk, count, facts, gouge, grade, notch, point, reach, slash, tally, theft, total, truth

6 basket, charge, deface, furrow, groove, grudge, incise, pick up, pile up, please, profit, rack up, rating, record, result, scrape, thrill, twenty **7** account, achieve, chalk up, luck out, outcome, procure, prosper, pull off, purport, qualify, reality, realize, satisfy, scratch, serrate, succeed, triumph **8** come home, conquest, lacerate, register, thievery **9** go over big, grievance, reckoning **10** crosshatch, hit pay dirt, obligation
baseball ~: **3** run
below D: **5** flunk
bowling ~: **3** pin **5** spare **6** strike
ender: **4** card **5** board **6** keeper **7** keeping
even the ~: **3** tie **5** repay **6** avenge **7** revenge **9** retaliate
exam ~: **4** mark, rank **6** rating
final ~: **5** total
football ~: **2** TD **3** PAT **6** safety **9** fieldgoal, touchdown
golf ~: **3** ace **5** bogey, bogie, eagle, one up **6** birdie
half a ~: **3** ten **6** decade
hockey ~: **4** goal
horseshoes ~: **6** leaner, ringer
in French: **5** vingt
keep ~: **3** add, sum **5** count, sum up, tally, total, tot up **6** figure, record **7** compute **8** register **9** enumerate
notation: **5** G clef, tacet **6** a tempo, da capo
settle the ~: **3** get **5** repay **6** avenge
starter: **4** four **5** three
tennis ~: **3** ace **4** ad in **5** ad out
unit: **5** point
__ score: **3** box, hog, raw **4** back, foot, line **5** Apgar, piano **7** partial
scoreboard
division: **6** inning
heading: **3** RHE
statistic: **3** hit, out, run **5** error
scorecard
abbr.: **3** yds.
word: **3** out, par
scoreless, hold: **5** skunk **7** shut out
scores: **3** lot **4** army, lots, many, tons, wads **5** hosts, loads, reams, scads **6** clouds, crowds, divers, droves, flocks, hoards, legion, masses, myriad, oodles, swarms, umteen, untold **7** copious, legions, myriads, numbers, profuse, throngs, umpteen **8** abundant, billions, manifold, millions, numerous, umpsteen, very many **9** bountiful, countless, multitude, quite a few, trillions **10** multitudes
Score, The (2001 film)
cast: Angela Bassett, Marlon Brando, Robert De Niro, Edward Norton
director: Frank Oz
scoria: **4** lava, slag **7** mineral
scorn: **3** boo, dig, dis **4** barb, defy, gibe, hate, hoot, jeer, jibe, mock, shun, slam, slap, slur, snub, twit **5** abhor, abuse, decry, flout, libel, scoff, sneer, spurn, taunt, trash **6** defame, demean, deride, disown, dump on, hatred, heckle, hoot at, ignore, impugn, insult, jeer at, jibe at, malign, offend, rebuff, refuse, reject, revile, slight, vilify **7** affront, asperse, calumny, catcall, contemn, degrade, despise, disavow, disdain, high-hat, laugh at, mockery, neglect, obloquy, offense, put down, rank out, sarcasm, scoff at, slander, sneer at, sniff at, traduce **8** belittle, contempt, denounce, derision, pooh-pooh, ridicule, sneeze at, spit upon, turn down, vilipend **9** arrogance, aspersion, contumely, denigrate, deprecate, discredit, disparage, disregard, humiliate, invective, ostracize **10** calumniate, defamation, disbelieve, disrespect, look down on, opprobrium
scorned: **9** unpopular
scornful: **5** proud, snide **7** cynical, haughty, jeering, mordant **8** cavalier, derisive, sardonic **9** sarcastic, vitriolic **10** derogatory, minimizing, pejorative
Scorpio: **4** sign
month: **3** Nov., Oct. **7** October **8** November
predecessor: **5** Libra **6** Scales **7** Balance
star in ~: **7** Antares
successor: **6** Archer **11** Sagittarius
Scorpio Illusion, The
author: Robert Ludlum
scorpion: **3** bug **8** arachnid
product: **5** venom
water ~ genus: **4** nepa
Scorpius neighbor: **3** Ara
Scorsese, Martin: **8** director
film: The Age of Innocence (1993)
Alice Doesn't Live Here Anymore (1974)
The Aviator (2004)
Bringing Out the Dead (1999)
Cape Fear (1991)
Casino (1995)
The Color of Money (1986)
The Departed (2006, AA)
Gangs of New York (2002)
GoodFellas (1990)
The King of Comedy (1983)
The Last Temptation of Christ (1988)
The Last Waltz (1978)
Mean Streets (1973)
New York, New York (1977)
Raging Bull (1980)
Taxi Driver (1976)
Who's That Knocking at My Door? (1968)
scot
starter: **4** wain
scot-__: **4** free
Scot: **4** Celt, Gael **6** Newman **9** Dalrymple **10** Glaswegian, Highlander
ancient ~ ally: **4** Pict
see also Scotland
scotch: **4** foil, kill **5** crush, quash **6** thwart **7** nullify, scuttle **8** stamp out **9** frustrate **10** neutralize, put an end to
starter: **3** hop **6** butter
Scotch: **5** drink **6** liquor, whisky **7** whiskey **8** beverage
like ~: **4** aged
partner: **4** soda
product: **4** tape
relative: **3** rye
Scotch __: **3** egg **4** mist, pine, rose, tape **6** Gaelic, whisky **7** terrier
scotch and __: **4** soda
scoter: **4** bird, coot, duck, fowl
relative: ***see*** duck
scot-free: **10** in the clear, on the loose
__ Scotia: **4** Nova
Scotland
accent: **4** burr
anthropologist: **6** Frazer
bacteriologist: **7** Fleming
ballet dancer: **7** Shearer
bovine: **5** Angus, Luing **8** Ayrshire, Galloway
boy: **3** lad **6** laddie
capital: **9** Edinburgh
cheese: **7** crowdie
chemist: **4** Todd **5** Dewar
city: **3** Ayr **4** Oban **5** Perth, Troon **6** Dundee, Irvine, Wishaw **7** Airdrie, Falkirk, Glasgow, Paisley, Renfrew **8** Aberdeen, Bearsden, Dumfries, Greenock, Stirling **9** Edinburgh
dance: **4** reel **5** fling **9** écossaise **10** strathspey
economist: **5** Smith
explorer: **4** Park, Ross **11** Livingstone
former county: **5** Nairn **6** Argyll
game pole: **5** caber
hat: **3** tam
historian: **7** Carlyle
household: **4** clan
inventor: **4** Watt
island: **4** Iona, Mull, Skye, Uist **5** Arran, Tiree, Tyree **8** Hebrides
lake: **4** Ness **5** Maree **6** Lomond
landowner: **5** laird
land tenure system: **4** udal
language: **4** Erse **6** Celtic, Gaelic
mathematician: **6** Napier
miss: **4** lass **6** lassie
money: **4** merk, rial, ryal **5** plack **6** bawbee **7** unicorn
mountain: **8** Ben Nevis
musician: **5** piper
name prefix: **3** Mac
neighbor: **3** Eng. **7** England
Nobelist: **7** Macleod
noble: **5** thane, thegn
pattern: **5** plaid
philosopher: **5** Smith
physicist: **5** Dewar **7** Maxwell
playwright: **6** Barrie
poet: **4** Hogg, Muir **5** Burns, Scott, Spark **6** Dunbar **8** Campbell
port: **3** Ayr **7** Glasgow **8** Greenock **9** Edinburgh, Scapa Flow
pudding: **6** haggis
river: **3** Awe, Ayr, Dee, Esk, Tay **4** Doon, Lyon, Spey **5** Afton, Clyde, Devon, Lyons, Nairn, Tweed
scientist: **4** Todd **5** Dewar **6** Frazer, Napier **7** Fleming, Maxwell
skirt: **4** kilt **7** filibeg **8** philibeg
sound: **5** Sleat
tartan: **4** kilt
terrier: **5** cairn
tongue: **4** Erse
writer: **3** Tey **5** Scott, Smith, Spark **6** Buchan, Cronin **7** Boswell, Carlyle **8** Mitchell **9** Stevenson
Scotland, Pa. (2002 film)
cast: James LeGros, Maura Tierney, Christopher Walken
Scotland Yard: **3** CID
Scots __: **6** Gaelic
Scott: **2** Oz, S.R. **4** Baio, Caan, Dred, Eric, Hoch, Jack, Tony, Wolf **5** Brady, Glenn, Linda, Pippa, Turow **6** Bakula, Gordon, Joplin, Martha, Ridley, Robert, Walter, Wilson **7** Cynthia, McGehee, Willard, Zachary **8** Campbell, Debralee, Hamilton, Lizabeth, McKenzie, Randolph, Winfield **9** Carpenter **10** paper towel
alternative: **4** Viva **6** Bounty, Brawny, Marcal **7** Charmin **8** Northern, Soft Weve **10** Cottonelle, White Cloud
__ Scott: **5** Great
Scott, Dred: **5** slave
chief justice: **5** Taney
__ Scott Forester: **5** Cecil
Scott, George C.: **5** actor
film: Bank Shot (1974)
The Changeling (1979)
Dr. Strangelove (1964)
Firestarter (1984)
The Flim Flam Man (1967)
The Hospital (1971)
The Hustler (1961)
The List of Adrian Messenger (1963)
Movie Movie (1978)
The New Centurions (1972)
Not With My Wife You Don't! (1966)
Oklahoma Crude (1973)
Patton (1970, AA)
Petulia (1968)
They Might Be Giants (1971)
spouse: Colleen Dewhurst, Trish Van Devere
Scott-Heron: **3** Gil
Scotti: **4** Vito
Scotti, Antonio: **6** singer **7** Italian
Scottie, FDR's: **4** Fala
Scottie, Pippen
sport: **10** basketball
Scottish __: **4** rite, star **6** Gaelic **7** terrier
Scottish Fold: **3** cat, pet **5** felid **6** feline
Scottish Symphony
composer: Felix Mendelssohn
Scottish words
adverb: **3** nae **4** syne
ago: **4** syne
alder: **3** arn
askew: **4** agee
church: **4** kirk
estuary: **5** firth, frith
exclamation: **3** och
fish: **3** ged
fishing boat: **6** baldie
goblet: **4** tass
have: **3** hae
hill: **4** brae
John: **3** Ian
knife: **5** skean, skene
lake: **4** loch
no: **3** nae
number: **3** ane, twa
pants: **5** trews
scarf: **5** curch
shoe: **5** gilly **6** gillie
since: **4** syne

to: **3** tae
turnip: **4** neep
waterfall: **3** lin **4** linn
yes: **2** ay **3** aye
__ Scott Key: **7** Francis
__ Scott King: **7** Coretta
__ Scott Lee: **5** Jason
Scotto, Renata: **4** diva **6** singer **7** Italian, soprano
Scott, Ridley: **8** director
film: Alien (1979)
American Gangster (2007)
Black Hawk Down (2001)
Black Rain (1989)
Blade Runner (1982)
Body of Lies (2008)
The Duellists (1977)
G.I. Jane (1997)
Gladiator (2000)
Hannibal (2001)
Kingdom of Heaven (2005)
Matchstick Men (2003)
Someone to Watch Over Me (1987)
Thelma & Louise (1991)
White Squall (1996)
Scott, Robert Falcon: **7** British **8** explorer
Scottsdale: **4** city, town
locale: **7** Arizona
Scott, Steve: **5** miler **6** runner
__ Scott Thomas: **7** Kristin
Scott, Tony: **8** director
film: Crimson Tide (1995)
Days of Thunder (1990)
Enemy of the State (1998)
The Fan (1996)
The Last Boy Scout (1991)
Revenge (1990)
Top Gun (1986)
True Romance (1993)
Scott, Walter: **3** Sir **4** poet **6** writer **8** Scottish
work: The Antiquary
The Bride of Lammermoor
Guy Mannering
The Heart of Midlothian
Ivanhoe
Kenilworth
The Lady of the Lake
The Lay of the Last Minstrel
Marmion
Quentin Durward
Rob Roy
The Talisman
Waverley
Scotty: **7** Beckett
__ Scotus: **4** Duns
scoundrel: **3** cad, cur, rat **4** heel, rake, toad, worm **5** cheat, churl, creep, crook, devil, ganef, gonef, gonif, knave, losel, rogue, rowdy, scamp, sneak, swine, thief, viper **6** bad egg, bad guy, bad hat, goniff, maggot, rascal, rotter, varlet, weasel, wretch **7** bad news, bounder, lowlife, ruffian, so-and-so, varment, varmint, villain **8** picaroon, rakehell, scalawag, swindler **9** miscreant, reprobate, scallawag, scallywag, vulgarian **10** blackguard, black sheep, mountebank, ne'er-do-well, scapegrace
Scoupe: **3** car **4** auto **7** Hyundai **10** automobile
scour: **3** rub **4** buff, comb, find, grub, hunt, rake, sand, scan, seek, wash **5** brush, clean, flush, scrub **6** abrade, forage, polish, pumice, search **7** burnish, cleanse, enquire, inquire, ransack, rummage **9** ferret out, track down
Scourby: **9** Alexander
scourge: **3** tan **4** bane, beat, belt, cane, flog, lash, pest, ruin, slam, whip **5** blast, curse, flail, knout, whale **6** blight, plague, punish, terror, thrash **7** afflict, lambast, torment **8** calamity, lambaste **9** castigate, excoriate, horsewhip, terrorize **10** affliction, flagellate, infliction
of mortals: **4** Ares
Scourge of God: **6** Attila
scouring
need: **3** S.O.S. **6** Brillo **7** soap pad
starter: **3** off
scouring __: **3** pad
scourings: **4** dirt **5** trash **7** residue
scouse: **4** stew
scout: **3** spy **4** case, look **5** guide, recce, recon, snoop, watch **6** escort, patrol, picket, reject, runner, search, survey **7** bird-dog, explore, lookout, observe, outpost, servant, soldier, spotter **8** check out, explorer, front man, outrider, rustle up, vanguard **9** ferret out, range over, recruiter **10** advance man, look down on
act: **4** deed **8** good deed
destination: **4** camp
ender: **6** master
handiwork: **4** knot
out: **4** find, hunt, seek **6** pursue, search **7** hunt for, look for **8** hunt down **9** search for, track down
pledge word: **4** duty
recitation: **4** oath
sew-on: **5** badge **10** merit badge
shelter: **4** tent
unit: **3** den **5** troop
__ scout: **6** talent
Scout: **3** Cub **4** Life, Star **5** Eagle, horse, pinto, steed **6** equine **7** Brownie, Cadette **8** Explorer **10** Tenderfoot
rider: **5** Tonto
__ Scout: **3** Boy, Cub, Sea **4** Girl **5** Eagle
scow: **4** boat, ship **5** barge **8** flatboat
Scowcroft: **5** Brent
scowl: **4** lour, sulk **5** frown, glare, lower **6** glower **7** grimace **8** threaten **9** dirty look, make a face
scrabble: **6** shinny **7** clamber, shinney
starter: **4** hard
Scrabble: **4** game **9** board game
inventor: **5** Butts
maker: **6** Hasbro
need: **4** rack, tile, word **5** board
unit: **6** letter
versatile ~ tile: **5** blank
scrag: **4** nape, neck **6** scruff **8** beanpole **10** string bean
scraggy: **4** lank, lean, slim, thin, wiry **5** gaunt, lanky, rough, spare **6** dainty, gangly, meager, ragged, skinny, slight, slinky, svelte, twiggy, uneven **7** gracile, scrawny, slender, spidery, willowy **8** gangling **9** sylphlike
scram: **2** go **3** hie **4** exit, flee, move, race, scat **5** leave, scoot, split **6** beat it, begone, bug out, decamp, depart, get out, go away **7** abscond, buzz off, get lost, make off, pull out, take off, vamoose **8** cheese it, clear out, fugitate, hightail, run for it, shove off **9** disappear, skedaddle, take a hike **10** go fly a kite, hightail it, hit the road, make tracks, take flight
Scram!: **3** git **4** away, blow, scat, shoo **5** leave **6** beat it, begone, get out
scramble: **3** run, vie **4** hash, push, race, rush **5** addle, climb, melee, mix up, scoot **6** bustle, encode, garble, hasten, jockey, jostle, jumble, justle, litter, muddle, muss up, ramble, scurry, shinny, strive, tussle **7** clamber, clutter, compete, scuffle, scuttle, shinney, shuffle, snarl up **8** mishmash, straggle, struggle **9** commotion, confusion, make haste, scrimmage **10** disarrange, free-for-all
a message: **6** encode
something to ~: **4** yolk
scrambled: **8** pell-mell **10** disorderly
scrambled __: **4** eggs
Scranton: **4** city, town
city near ~: **6** Elmira
locale: **4** Penn.
scrap: **3** bit, ort, rag, rid, row **4** atom, bite, bout, chip, dump, fray, hunk, iota, junk, lump, mite, part, shed, spat, tiff, whit **5** abort, argue, brawl, brush, chuck, chunk, clash, crumb, ditch, fight, grain, melee, patch, piece, relic, set-to, shard, sherd, shred, slice, spark, speck, trace, trash, waste **6** barney, bicker, fracas, hassle, morsel, reject, rumpus, sliver, tussle **7** abandon, contest, discard, dispute, fall out, garbage, modicum, oddment, portion, quarrel, remnant, rubbish, scuffle, snippet, toss out, uneaten, useless, vestige, wrangle **8** argument, conflict, demolish, fragment, get rid of, have at it, jettison, junkyard, leftover, mouthful, particle, pittance, skirmish, squabble, struggle, throw out **9** eighty-six, encounter, fistfight, have words, remainder, square off, throw away **10** difference, free-for-all, smithereen
ender: **4** book, heap
scrapbook: **5** album
need: **4** glue **5** paste, photo **7** memento
scrape: **3** eke, fix, jam, rub **4** bark, claw, file, gall, mess, pare, peel, rasp, skin, snag, spot, wear **5** chafe, clean, grate, graze, grind, pinch, score, shave, skimp, spare, stint, wound **6** abrade, boo-boo, bruise, corner, injury, lesion, pickle, plight, scrimp **7** dilemma, problem, scratch, shuffle, trouble **8** abrasion, exigence, exigency, irritate, quagmire, squeak by **9** economize, excoriate, tight spot **10** difficulty, underspend
as a knee: **4** bark **5** graze **6** abrade, scrape
away at: **5** erode **6** abrade
bow and ~: **4** fawn **5** court, kneel, kotow, toady **6** grovel, kowtow **8** bootlick, fawn upon, suck up to **10** curry favor, pay court to
by: **3** eke **5** exist **6** eke out, make do, manage **7** make out, subsist, survive
treatment: **6** iodine **7** Band-Aid
up: **5** amass, glean **6** garner, gather, obtain **7** acquire, collect **8** assemble
scraped: **3** raw **4** hurt
scraper: **4** tool
starter: **3** sky
use a ~: **5** deice
scraping: **5** trash, waste **6** refuse **7** garbage, grating, residue **8** friction, leftover
scrappy: **6** feisty **7** hostile **8** militant **9** querulous, truculent **10** pugnacious, unflagging
scraps: **5** trash, waste **6** refuse **7** residue **8** leftover, residuum
scratch: **3** cut, eke, mar, rub **4** claw, drop, etch, flaw, gash, hurt, mark, nick, rasp, scar, snub, tear, work, zero **5** abort, annul, bills, erase, funds, grate, graze, prick, score, wound **6** boo-boo, cancel, damage, deface, defect, delete, incise, injury, lesion, moolah, remove, scrape, scrawl **7** blemish, engrave, redline **8** abrasion, lacerate, scribble, withdraw **9** eliminate, terminate **10** laceration
ender: **5** board, proof
from ~: **4** anew, over **6** afresh
not up to ~: **3** bad **4** poor, weak **5** rusty **6** faulty, flawed **7** lacking, wanting **8** impaired, inferior **9** defective, deficient, imperfect **10** inadequate, incomplete
out: **5** erase **6** cancel, efface, excise
out a living: **6** scrape
pad: **6** tablet **8** foolscap
rock ~: **5** stria
without a ~: **4** safe **5** whole **8** unharmed **9** untouched
see also moolah
scratch __: **3** awl, hit, pad, wig **4** coat, line, test **5** paper, sheet
__ scratch: **4** from, up to
__ Scratch: **3** Old
scratch and __: **5** sniff
scratched out: **3** x'ed
__ scratcher: **4** back
__ scratches: **3** hen
scratching-post covering: **6** carpet
scratchy: **5** husky, itchy, rough, roupy **6** coarse, gritty **8** abrasive
scrawl: **5** write **6** doodle **7** scratch, writing **8** longhand, scribble, squiggle
scrawly: **6** sloppy **9** illegible **10** unreadable
scrawny: **4** bony, lank, lean, slim, thin, wiry **5** boney, gaunt, lanky, spare, weedy **6** dainty, gangly, ill-fed, meager, skinny, slight, slinky, svelte, twiggy **7** angular, gracile, runtish, scraggy, slender, spidery, willowy **8** angulose, angulous, gangling **9** sylphlike
scream: **3** cry, jar **4** bawl, card, hoot, howl, rage, rant, rave, riot, roar, wail, yell, yowl **5** blare, cheer,

comic, joker, laugh, panic, shout, whoop **6** bellow, cry out, holler, outcry, shriek, squeal **7** screech, sing out **8** comedian, funnyman **9** caterwaul, character, laughable, priceless, sensation **10** comedienne, vociferate

cartoon ~: **3** eek

Scream (1995 song)

artist: Janet Jackson, Michael Jackson

Scream (1996 film)

cast: David Arquette, Drew Barrymore, Neve Campbell, Courteney Cox, Jamie Kennedy, Matthew Lillard, Rose McGowan, Skeet Ulrich

director: Wes Craven

screamer: **4** bird **7** pennant **8** headline

Screamin' ___ Hawkins: **3** Jay

screaming: **5** noisy, showy **7** blatant **9** deafening

screaming-___: **7** meemies

scree: **5** talus **6** debris **8** detritus

screech: **3** cry **4** bawl, yell, yelp, yowl **5** groan, shout **6** holler, scream, shriek, squawk, squeak, squeal **9** caterwaul **10** vociferate

screech ___: **3** owl

screeching: **5** noisy **6** shrill **8** jangling, strident

screed: **4** talk **6** tirade **8** diatribe, harangue **9** philippic

screen: **3** net, VDT **4** cull, hide, mask, mesh, scan, sift, sort, veil, wall **5** blind, cloak, cover, gauge, grade, grill, guard, hedge, shade, shoji, sieve, unmix **6** awning, canopy, defend, enveil, filter, grille, mantle, select, shadow, shield, strain, winnow **7** conceal, curtain, divider, examine, lattice, obscure, pick out, process, protect, seclude, secrete, shelter, shut off, shut out, wall off **8** block out, evaluate, security, separate, terminal **9** eliminate, partition, safeguard **10** camouflage

again: **5** rerun

blinker: **6** cursor

computer ~: **3** CRT, VDT **7** monitor **8** terminal

ender: **4** land, play **5** saver **6** writer

from view: **4** hide **6** enisle **7** conceal, confine, isolate **8** cloister, separate **9** keep apart, segregate, sequester **10** quarantine

image unit: **5** pixel

Japanese ~: **5** shoji

local ~: **4** nabe

partner: **5** stage

perforated ~: **5** grill **6** grille

silver ~: **5** films **6** cinema, flicks, movies **7** filmdom **8** pictures

starter: **3** off, sun **4** silk, wind **5** smoke

screen ___: **4** grid, pass, test **5** saver

___ screen: **4** fire **5** small, smoke, split, video **6** silver

___-screen: **3** off **4** wide

Screen ___: **4** Gems

Screen ___ Guild: **6** Actors

screened: **5** shady **6** hidden, select **9** unexposed

screening device: **5** sieve, V-chip

screenplay: **5** movie **6** script **8** scenario

Screens, The

author: Jean Genet

screenwriter: **6** writer **9** dramatist, scenarist

screw: **4** turn, wind **5** helix, twist, wring **6** fasten, spiral, wrench **7** contort **8** fastener, flathead **9** propeller

backing: **6** cap nut

ender: **4** ball, worm **6** driver

starter: **3** air, set **4** cork, jack **5** thumb

thread: **5** helix

up: **4** blow, flub, goof, muff, ruin, undo **5** botch, louse, spoil **6** blow it, bobble, boggle, bungle **7** confuse **9** mishandle, mismanage

screw ___: **3** cap

screw-___: **3** top

___ screw: **4** wood **5** Allen **8** Phillips

screwball: **4** kook, zany **5** flake, nutty, pitch

screw-cutting tool: **3** die

screwdriver: **4** tool **5** drink **8** beverage, cocktail

impromptu ~: **4** dime

ingredient: **5** vodka

screw-shaped: **6** spiral **7** helical

Screwtape Letters, The

author: C.S. Lewis

screwup: **4** flub, mess, slip **5** lapse, snafu, upset **6** muddle **7** blunder, mistake

screwy: **4** zany **5** flaky, goofy, inane, silly, wacky **6** absurd, flakey, whacky **7** fatuous, unsound **8** cockeyed, specious **9** illogical, senseless, untenable **10** groundless, ridiculous

Scriabin, Alexsandr: **7** Russian **8** composer

scribble: **3** jot **5** write **6** doodle, scrawl **7** scratch, writing **8** longhand

scribbles: **8** graffiti

scribe: **5** clerk, write **6** author, copier, penner, writer **7** copyist **8** annalist, essayist **9** columnist, scrivener, secretary, wordsmith **10** amanuensis, chronicler, journalist

Biblical ~: **4** Ezra

Dead Sea Scrolls ~: **6** Essene

Scribner: **7** Charles

scrim: **6** fabric **7** drapery **8** backdrop, material

scrimmage: **4** tilt **5** clash, fight, melee, mix-up **6** battle, fracas **8** scramble, skirmish

starter: **4** snap

scrimp: **4** save **5** hoard, spare, stint **6** meager, scrape **7** cut back **8** conserve **9** economize **10** cut corners, underspend

scrimping: **6** stingy **7** economy **9** frugality **10** economical

scrimpy: **5** scant **6** meager, scanty, skimpy, sparse

scrimshaw material: **5** ivory **6** baleen

Scripps: **5** Ellen

script: **4** book, copy, text **5** lines, story **6** dialog, record **7** letters, writing **8** dialogue, document, libretto, longhand, playbook, scenario **10** manuscript, penmanship, screenplay

alter a ~: **4** edit

as directed by the ~: **5** on cue

direction: **4** exit, fade **5** enter **6** fade in

ender: **3** ure **6** writer

ignore the ~: **5** ad-lib

lines: **6** dialog

starter: **4** Act I, manu, type

writer: **6** author **9** dramatist, scenarist **10** playwright

script ___: **4** girl **6** doctor, reader

___ scripta: **3** lex

scriptural doctrine: **6** cabala, kabala **7** cabbala, kabbala

scripture: **5** Bible **7** the Word

excerpt: **5** verse

Hindu ~: **4** Veda

Muslim: **5** Koran

___ Scripture: **4** Holy

scrivener: **6** scribe **7** copyist **10** amanuensis, journalist

scrod: **4** fish **7** codfish, haddock, seafood

scroll: **4** coil, roll **6** record **8** register

ancient ~ writer: **6** Essene

holder: **3** ark

synagogue ~: **4** Tora **5** Torah

scrolled: **6** spiral

Scrooge: **5** miser, saver **8** tightwad **9** skinflint

comment: **3** bah

nephew: **6** Donald

play ~: **5** stint

portrayer: George C. Scott, Alistair Sim

Scrooge (1970 film)

cast: Albert Finney, Alec Guinness

director: Ronald Neame

Scrooged (1988 film)

cast: Karen Allen, John Forsythe, Bill Murray

scrounge: **3** beg, bum **4** grub, hunt **5** cadge, filch, leech, mooch **6** forage, pilfer, sponge **7** finagle, scare up, wheedle **8** freeload **9** panhandle

scrounger: **5** leech **6** beggar **8** parasite

scrub: **3** mop, mut, rub **4** buff, drop, mutt, runt, stop, wash **5** abort, bathe, brush, clean, erase, scour **6** abrade, cancel, delete, lather, polish, repeal, revoke, shelve **7** abandon, abolish, call off, cleanse, correct, deterge, launder, mongrel, rectify, rescind, stunted, thicket **8** abrogate, brighten, inferior **9** disinfect, pipsqueak, terminate **10** do away with

ender: **4** land

up: **4** lave, wash

scrub ___: **3** jay, oak **4** fowl, pine, suit **5** brush, nurse

___ Scrub: **4** Soft

scrubber, back: **5** loofa, luffa **6** loofah

scrubbing: **4** bath

need: **3** S.O.S. **5** brush **6** Brillo **7** soap pad

scrubby: **5** small **6** humble **8** slipshod

scrubland: **5** heath

scrubs: **5** B team

Scrubs (NBC comedy/drama)

cast: Zach Braff (J.D. Dorian) Sarah Chalke (Elliot Reid) Donald Faison (Christopher Turk) Ken Jenkins (Bob Kelso) John C. McGinley (Perry Cox) Judy Reyes (Carla Espinosa)

scruff: **4** nape, neck **5** nucha, scrag

hair: **7** hackles

scruffy: **4** mean **5** mangy, messy, rough, seedy, sorry, tacky **6** mangey, ragged, ragtag, shabby, shoddy, unneat, untidy **7** run-down, unkempt **8** slipshod, slovenly, tattered, untended **9** ungroomed **10** bedraggled, threadbare

Scruggs, Earl: **8** banjoist

partner: **5** Flatt

scrum game: **5** rugby

scrumptious: **4** nice **5** sapid, tasty, yummy **6** lovely, savory **8** heavenly, luscious **9** ambrosial, delicious, exquisite, flavorful, palatable, succulent, toothsome **10** appetizing, delectable

scrunch: **4** mash **5** munch, press, quash, smash **6** rumple, squash, squint **7** squeeze, wrinkle

scruple: **4** balk **5** baulk, demur, doubt, grain, pause, qualm **6** falter, regret, twinge **7** anxiety, measure **8** hesitate **9** misgiving, principle **10** conscience, hesitation, solicitude, think twice, uneasiness

scruples: **6** morals **8** superego **10** conscience, inner voice

three ~: **4** dram

without ~: **6** amoral

Scruples

author: Judith Krantz

scrupulous: **4** fair, just, nice, true **5** chary, exact, frank, fussy, legit, moral, right **6** honest, minute, square, strict **7** careful, correct, dutiful, earnest, ethical, factual, finicky, precise, prudent, sincere, upright **8** accurate, cautious, credible, exacting, finiking, finnicky, methodic, punctual, rigorous, sedulous, straight, thorough, truthful **9** assiduous, attentive, honorable, judicious, observant, righteous, squeamish, veracious **10** deliberate, fastidious, forthright, meticulous, on the level, particular, principled, upstanding

scrupulousness: **4** care **5** honor **7** honesty, loyalty

scrutinize: **3** eye, see, spy **4** case, comb, look, ogle, peer, pore, scan, sift, view **5** assay, audit, check, probe, study, watch, weigh **6** look at, peruse, regard, review, search, survey **7** compare, dissect, examine, explore, inspect, observe, pry into, ransack **8** look into, look over, peer into, pore over **9** criticize, enter into, pick apart, take stock

scrutiny: **4** look, test **5** audit, check, probe, proof, study, watch **6** regard, review, survey **7** enquiry, inquiry, perusal, reading, thought **8** analysis, eagle eye, research **9** attention, probation **10** inspection, weather eye

bear ~: **4** wash

SCTV (TV comedy)

bit: **4** skit

cast: Catherine O'Hara, Eugene

Levy, Harold Ramis, John Candy, Rick Moranis, Robin Duke
scuba
diving: 5 sport
gear: 4 tank
tank supply: 3 air
user: 5 diver
weapon: 5 spear
Scuba Duba
author: Bruce Jay Friedman
scud: 3 run 4 race, rush 5 glide, sweep
Scud downer: 3 ABM
Scudéry, Madeleine de: 6 French, writer
work: Clélie
scudo: 4 coin 5 money
scuff: 3 mar 4 gall, mule, walk, wear 6 abrade 7 shuffle 8 abrasion
scuffle: 3 row 4 bout, cuff, fray, fuss, tilt 5 brawl, clash, fight, melee, scrap 6 affray, barney, fracas, jostle, justle, ruckus, rumpus, tussle 7 grapple, mix it up, shuffle, wrangle, wrestle 8 brouhaha, scramble, skirmish, struggle 9 commotion 10 donnybrook, free-for-all
memento: 5 mouse 6 fat lip, shiner 8 black eye
scull: 3 row 4 boat 7 rowboat
ancient ~: 6 bireme 7 trireme
implement: 3 oar
squad: 4 crew
scullcap, ancient: 6 pileus
scullery: 7 kitchen
sculling: 5 sport
Scully: 3 Vin 4 Dana 5 agent
partner: 6 Mulder
sculpt: 4 mold 5 carve, model, shape 6 chisel, incise 7 portray, whittle 9 give shape
sculpted-heads
island: 6 Easter
sculptor: 3 Arp 5 Moore, Rodin 6 artist, Calder, French, Giotto 7 Borglum, Cellini, Noguchi, Picasso, Pisarro 8 Dubuffet 9 Donatello, Remington 12 Michelangelo
American ~: 6 Calder, French 7 Borglum, Noguchi 9 Remington
British ~: 5 Moore
Dada ~: 3 Arp
deg.: 3 MFA
French ~: 3 Arp 5 Rodin 8 Dubuffet
funding source: 3 NEA
Greek ~: 5 Myron 6 Scopas
Italian ~: 6 Giotto 7 Cellini 9 Donatello 12 Michelangelo
material: 3 ice 4 clay, jade 5 stone
mobile ~: 6 Calder
need: 6 chisel
Renaissance ~: 9 Donatello
Spanish ~: 7 Picasso, Pisarro
subject: 4 head 5 torso
Western ~: 9 Remington
work: 4 bust
sculpture: 3 art, cut, hew 4 bust, cast, mold, work 5 carve, model, shape 6 incise, medium, mobile, statue 7 contour, fashion, whittle
1498 ~: 5 Pietà
kind of ~: 4 bust, head 5 torso
mineral: 9 alabaster

Parthenon ~: 6 Athena, Athene
scum: 3 mob 4 dirt, film 5 algae, crust, dregs, dross, froth, slime, trash, waste 6 rabble, refuse, vermin 7 lowlife, residue 8 riffraff 9 miscreant 10 lower class
scummy: 5 slimy, sorry 6 shabby
scup: 5 porgy
scuppernong
relative: *see* grape
scurf: 8 dandruff
scurrility: 6 insult 9 blasphemy, invective 10 detraction, muckraking
scurrilous: 3 low 4 lewd, mean, rank 5 dirty, gross, nasty 6 coarse, filthy, ribald, rotten, smutty, vulgar 7 abusive, obscene, raunchy 8 indecent, libelous 9 insulting, offensive, salacious, sarcastic, shameless 10 scandalous
scurry: 3 fly, hie, rip, run, zip 4 dart, dash, flee, flit, race, rush, skim, tear, zoom 5 haste, hurry, scoot, spank, speed, whisk 6 barrel, bustle, gallop, hasten, hustle, move it, rocket, sprint 7 floor it, hop to it, mad rush, quicken, scamper 8 scramble, step on it 9 hotfoot it, shake a leg, skedaddle, tear along 10 burn rubber, get a move on, get hopping, hightail it
__-scurry: 5 hurry
scurvy: 3 low 6 rotten, sordid, stingy 7 pitiful 9 miserable
scut: 4 tail
ender: 4 work
scutate: 5 scaly
scuttle: 3 run 4 pail, quit, race, ruin, sink 5 ditch, wreck 6 defeat, scotch 7 abandon, destroy, forsake, scamper 8 give up on, scramble 9 back out of, container, pull out of
coal ~: 3 hod
load: 4 coal
scuttlebutt: 4 buzz, dirt, poop, talk, word 5 rumor 6 gossip, report 7 hearsay
scuttled: 6 sunken 9 submerged
scuzzy: 5 gross
scythe: 3 mow 5 knife
handle: 5 snath 6 snathe
path: 5 swath 6 swathe
use a ~: 3 cut 4 reap
Scythian lamb: 4 fern
Scythian Suite
composer: Sergei Prokofiev
S. Dak.
see South Dakota
SDI
concern: 3 ABM 4 ICBM
part: 3 Def. 7 Defense 9 Strategic 10 Initiative
SDS protest target: 3 SSS
__ se: 3 per 5 inter
Se: 4 elem. 7 element 8 selenium
34 for ~: 4 at. no.
Se __: 5 Ri Pak
Se __ español: 5 habla
SE: 3 dir., hdg.
Se7en (1995 film)
cast: Morgan Freeman, Gwyneth Paltrow, Brad Pitt, Kevin Spacey
sea: 3 Red 4 Aral, Azov, Dead, deep, Java, Kara, main, Ross, Sulu 5 Banda, Black, briny, China, Coral, Egean, Irish, Japan, North, ocean, spate, swell, Timor, waves, White 6 Aegean, Baltic, Bering, Inland, Ionian, Laptev, Sagami, Salton, Sivash, Tasman, Yellow 7 Andaman, Arabian, Arafura, Barents, Caspian, Celebes, Galilee, legions, Marmara, Okhotsk, Sibuyan, Weddell 8 Adriatic, Amundsen, Beaufort, Bismarck, Labrador, Ligurian, plethora, Sargasso 9 abundance, Caribbean, East China, Greenland, Hudson Bay, multitude, Norwegian, profusion 10 Philippine, South China, Tyrrhenian
Africa ~: 3 Red
Alaska ~: 6 Bering 8 Beaufort
anemone: 5 polyp 6 animal
Antarctica ~: 4 Ross 7 Weddell 8 Amundsen
Arabia ~: 3 Red
Arctic ~: 4 Kara 7 Barents
arm of the ~: 5 fiord, fjord, inlet
Asia ~: 4 Aral, Kara, Savu, Sawu, Sulu 5 Banda, China, Coral, Timor 6 Flores, Inland, Laptev, Sagami, Yellow 7 Andaman, Arafura, Marmara 8 Bismarck 9 East China 10 South China
at ~: 4 lost 6 addled, adrift, afloat, in a fog, unsure 7 at a loss, baffled, bemused, in a daze, muddled, out of it, puzzled, sailing, stumped 8 clueless, confused, cruising, drifting, floating, offshore, steaming, voyaging, yachting 9 befuddled, flummoxed, mystified, perplexed, sailoring, uncertain, under sail 10 bewildered, nonplussed
Australia ~: 5 Coral, Timor 6 Tasman 7 Arafura
away from the ~: 6 inland
barrier: 4 dike
bass: 4 fish 7 grouper 9 blackfish
be stationary at ~: 5 lie to
bottom: 3 bed 7 benthos
bream: 4 fish
Canada ~: 8 Labrador 9 Hudson Bay
change course, at ~: 4 tack
chicken of the ~: 4 tuna
color: 4 blue
cow: 6 dugong
creature: 4 salp 5 salpa, squid, whale, whelk
dog: 3 gob, tar 4 salt 6 sailor 7 jack tar, mariner
dog quaff: 3 rum 4 grog
dogs: 4 crew
ender: 3 bed, man, men, way 4 bird, cock, food, fowl, girt, gull, jack, lift, mark, port, sick, side, wall, ward, ware, weed 5 board, borne, coast, farer, floor, going, mount, plane, quake, scape, shell, shore, train, wards, water 6 faring, jacker, strand, worthy
Eurasia ~: 5 Black 7 Caspian
Europe ~: 4 Azov 5 Egean, Irish, North 6 Aegean, Baltic, Ionian 7 Barents 8 Adriatic, Ligurian 10 Tyrrhenian
extension: 3 arm 4 gulf
foam: 5 spume
grape: 5 fruit
Greek personification of the ~: 6 Pontos, Pontus

greenery: 4 alga
Greenland ~: 8 Labrador
holly: 6 eryngo
horse: 4 fish
in French: 3 mer
inland ~: 4 Aral, lake
in Latin: 4 mare
lettuce: 4 ulva
like the ~: 5 briny, salty
lion: 6 animal, mammal
lunar ~: 4 mare
mean ~ level: 5 geoid
mew: 4 bird
Mideast ~: 4 Dead 7 Galilee
motion: 4 tide
mythical ~ nymph: 4 Ione
New Zealand ~: 4 Ross 6 Tasman
Norwegian ~ monster: 7 krakens
not at ~: 6 ashore
nymph: 5 siren 6 nereid
of the ~: 6 marine 8 maritime, nautical
Pacific ~: 5 Coral
Philippines ~: 4 Sulu 7 Celebes, Sibuyan
pollution: 5 slick
power: 6 armada
put to ~: 4 sail 6 launch 7 set sail, ship out 8 shove off
raven: 4 fish
resort: 4 Lido
robber: 6 pirate 7 brigand, corsair 8 freeboot 9 buccaneer 10 freebooter
Russia ~: 4 Aral, Azov 5 White 6 Sivash 7 Okhotsk
shocker: 3 eel
swell: 4 surf, wave
swirl: 4 eddy 9 maelstrom
treat ~ water: 6 desalt 10 desalinate, desalinize
urchin: 7 echinus
voyage: 4 sail, trip 6 cruise, junket, travel 7 journey 8 crossing
wall: 4 dike, mole 5 levee 10 breakwater
West Indies ~: 8 Sargasso 9 Caribbean
wolf: 8 rapparee
sea __: 3 bag, cow, dog, fan, fox, hog, mew, pen 4 bass, calf, duck, duty, fire, foam, gate, gull, lane, legs, lily, lion, mile, mist, moss, salt, slug, star, wall, wolf 5 chest, devil, eagle, floor, grape, green, holly, horse, level, otter, poppy, power, purse, raven, robin, rover, snail, snake, trout 6 breeze, change, nettle, robber, turtle, urchin 7 anemone, biscuit, cabbage, captain, feather, lamprey, scallop, serpent, swallow
__ sea: 4 open 5 all at
__-sea: 4 deep
Sea __: 4 Calm, Hunt 5 Scout 6 Cruise 7 Islands
Sea __, The: 4 Hawk, Wolf 6 Wolves 7 Gypsies
Sea-__ Airport: 3 Tac
__ Sea: 3 Red 4 Aral, Dead, Java, Kara, Ross, Sulu 5 Banda, Black, China, Coral, Irish, North, Timor, White 6 Aegean, Baltic, Bering, Euxine, Flores, Inland, Ionian, Laptev, Salton, Tasman, Yellow 7 Andaman, Arabian, Arafura,

Barents, Caspian, Celebes, Chukchi, Icarian, Weddell
Sea and Sardinia
author: D.H. Lawrence
Sea Around Us, The
author: Rachel Carson
Seabee: 4 doer 7 builder
motto: 5 Can Do
organization: 3 USN 4 Navy
seabird: 3 auk, ern, mew 4 coot, erne, gull, skua, tern 5 booby, jager, solan, yager 6 auklet, bonxie, gannet, jaeger, petrel, puffin 7 dovekey, dovekie, pelican 9 albatross, cormorant, guillemot, mallemuck, mollymawk, mollymoke 10 sheathbill
Seabiscuit: 5 horse 9 racehorse
Seabiscuit (2003 film)
cast: Jeff Bridges, Chris Cooper, Tobey Maguire
seaboard: 5 coast
Seaborg, Glenn: 7 chemist 8 Nobelist
Sea Breeze
ingredient: 5 vodka 9 cranberry 10 grapefruit
Sea Calm
author: Langston Hughes
seacoast: 5 beach, shore 6 strand 9 shoreline
seacock: 5 valve
Seacrest: 4 Ryan
seadog: 6 fogbow
seafarer: 3 gob, tar 4 salt 6 sailor 7 jack tar, mariner 8 helmsman, traveler
seafaring: 5 naval 6 marine, travel 8 maritime, nautical 10 navigation
seafood: 3 cod, eel, roe 4 clam, crab, sole 5 gaper, perch, prawn, scrod 6 schrod, shrimp
course: 4 bisk 6 bisque
garnish: 5 lemon
how to pack ~: 5 in ice
Seagal, Steven: 5 actor
spouse: Kelly LeBrock
seagirt land: 4 isle
seagoing: 5 naval 8 maritime, nautical
initials: 3 HMS, ONI, USS
see also nautical
Seagren, Bob: 11 pole vaulter
seagull: 3 mew 4 bird
cousin: 4 tern
hangout: 4 pier
Seagulls
artist: Erté
Seagull, The
author: Anton Chekhov
character: 4 Dorn, Ilia, Nina 5 Boris, Irina, Masha, Simon, Sorin
Seahawks: 4 team 6 eleven
div.: 3 NFC
home: 7 Seattle
org.: 3 NFL
rival: *see* NFL team
sport: 8 football
Sea Hunt (TV drama)
apparatus: 5 scuba
cast: Lloyd Bridges (Mike Nelson)
___ Sea Islands: 5 South
seal: 3 bar, cap, dam, gum 4 bolt, clog, cork, lock, mark, plug, sear, shut, stop, tape 5 block, brown, close, dam up, latch, sigil, stamp 6 animal, assure, attest, barker, cachet, cement, clinch, clog up, emblem, encase, ensure, fasten, gasket, lock up, mammal, plug up, ratify, secure, settle, signet, stop up, tape up 7 close up, closure, confirm, occlude, shutter, sticker, stopper, wall off 8 blockade, button up, finalize, hallmark, obstruct, validate 9 assurance, guarantee, medallion 10 coat of arms, escutcheon, imprimatur, quarantine, underwrite, waterproof
affix a ~: 5 stamp 8 validate
a tub: 4 calk 5 caulk, grout
baby ~: 3 pup 4 calf 5 whelp
break the ~: 6 launch
eared ~: 5 otary
ender: 4 skin
female: 3 cow
fur ~: 5 matka
group: 3 pod
home: 3 sea, zoo 5 ocean
in the juices: 4 sear
kin: 6 walrus
male: 4 bull
movie ~: 5 André
of approval: 2 OK 4 okay 6 cachet 8 sanction
papal ~: 5 bulla
point: 3 cat 5 felid 6 feline
prepare to ~: 4 lick
relative: *see* brown color
seal ___: 3 dog, off 4 ring 5 brown
seal ___ Siamese: 5 point
___ seal: 3 fur, pin 4 hair, harp, monk 5 eared, great, privy 6 Arctic, harbor, hooded 7 bearded
___-seal: 4 heat
Seal
org.: 3 USN
song: Crazy (1991)
Fly Like an Eagle (1996)
Kiss From a Rose (1995)
sealant: 6 cement
roofing ~: 3 tar
sealed: 5 tight 6 closed 7 assured 8 airtight, destined 9 leakproof, nonporous
with cement: 5 luted
sealed ___: 3 bid
Sealed With ___: 5 a Kiss
Sealed With a Kiss (1962 song)
artist: Brian Hyland
sea-level: 4 flat 10 unelevated
sealing ___: 3 wax
Seal in the Bedroom, The
author: James Thurber
Seals: 3 Dan, Jim
___ Seals: 6 Easter 9 Christmas
Seals and Crofts
members: Jim Seals, Dash Crofts
song: Diamond Girl (1973)
Get Closer (1976)
Summer Breeze (1972)
sealskin
canoe: 5 kayak
mukluk: 5 kamik
wearer: 6 Eskimo
Sealy
competitor: 5 Serta 7 Simmons
seam: 3 hem, sew 4 line, link, lode, tuck, vein 5 joint, layer, ridge 6 furrow, suture 7 closure, coal bed, deposit, stratum 8 junction, juncture, vinculum 9 stitching 10 connection
coal ~: 4 vein
filler: 5 grout
make a ~: 3 sew
open a ~: 5 unrip 6 let out
style: 4 welt
tapered ~: 4 dart
___ seam: 4 coal
seaman: 3 gob, tar 4 rank, salt 6 sailor 7 jack tar, mariner, swabbie 8 deckhand 10 bluejacket
saint: 4 Elmo
see also sailor
___ seaman: 4 able
Seaman's Friend, The
author: Richard Henry Dana
seamount
flat-topped: 5 guyot
seams
bursting at the ~: 4 full 7 crammed
join at the ~: 4 tack 5 baste 6 repair, stitch
seamstress: 6 tailor 10 dressmaker
inset: 6 gusset
strip: 4 welt
work: 6 edging
Seamus: 6 Heaney
seamy: 3 low, raw 4 base 5 rough 6 coarse, shabby, sordid 7 ignoble, run-down, squalid, unkempt 8 degraded, depraved, shameful, unsavory, wrinkled 9 execrable, offensive, repellent, repugnant, revolting 10 abominable, despicable, detestable, scandalous, unpleasant
Sean: 4 Bean, Penn 5 Astin, Combs, Young 6 Lennon, O'Casey 7 Connery 8 MacBride, O'Faolain
in English: 4 John
Sean ___ Combs: 5 Puffy
Sean ___ Flanery: 7 Patrick
Sean ___ Lennon: 3 Ono
Seanad ___: 7 Eireann
séance: 7 meeting, session, sitting
figure: 5 ghost
like a ~: 4 eery 5 eerie
sound: 3 rap
___ Sean Connery: 3 Sir
___ Sean Leonard: 6 Robert
Sea of ___: 4 Azov, Love 5 Crete, Japan 7 Galilee, Marmara, Marmora, Okhotsk
Sea of Azov
feeder: 3 Don
gulf: 8 Taganrog
Sea of Death
author: Jorge Amado
Sea of Grass, The
author: Conrad Richter
Sea of Japan feeder: 5 Tumen
Sea of Love (1989 film)
cast: Ellen Barkin, John Goodman, Al Pacino
Sea of Love (song)
artist: Honeydrippers, Phil Phillips With the Twilights
Sea of Okhotsk feeder: 4 Amur
Sea of Tranquillity site: 4 Moon
seaplane: 8 aircraft
attachment: 5 float
seaport: 6 harbor 7 harbour
SeaQuest ___: 3 DSV
sear: 3 dry, fry 4 burn, char, cook, heat, seal 5 brand, brown, dry up, grill, parch, singe 6 braise, scorch, sizzle, wither 7 blacken, frizzle, shrivel 8 barbecue 9 carbonize, cauterize, dehydrate, desiccate
search: 3 dig, pry, spy 4 comb, fish, grub, hunt, look, rake, root, scan, seek, sift 5 check, delve, frisk, grope, probe, prowl, quest, rifle, scour, scout, snoop, study, sweep 6 ferret, forage, lookup, survey 7 dragnet, examine, explore, inspect, legwork, look for, pursuit, ransack, rummage, run down 8 poke into, prospect, question, scout out 9 cast about, feel about, ferret out, go through, range over, shakedown, track down, witch hunt 10 inspection, scrutinize
blindly: 5 grope
diligently: 4 comb 5 delve, scour
ender: 5 light
engine find: 3 URL
for: 4 seek 5 trace 6 look up 7 scout up 8 scout out
for prey: 5 prowl
go in ~ of: 5 quest 6 aspire, gun for, pursue 7 hunt for, long for, look for 8 yearn for 9 track down
high heaven: 4 comb 6 forage 7 ransack
in ~ of: 5 after 9 following
in ~ of adventure: 6 errant
Internet ~ engine: 5 Yahoo! 6 Google
out: 5 dig up 6 locate, pursue 9 challenge
party: 5 posse
thorough ~: 5 sweep
search ___: 5 party 6 engine 7 warrant
Search ___ Tomorrow: 3 for
___ Search: 4 Star
Searchers
homeland: England
song: Love Potion Number Nine (1964)
Needles and Pins (1964)
___ Search for Meaning: 4 Man's
Search for Signs of Intelligent Life in the Universe, The (1991 film)
cast: Lily Tomlin
Search for Tomorrow (CBS/NBC): 4 soap 9 soap opera
Searchin' (1957 song)
artist: Coasters
searching: 7 in-depth 8 complete, piercing, thorough 9 full-dress, inquiring, observant, quizzical 10 exhaustive
___-searching: 4 soul
Searching for Bobby Fischer (1993 film)
cast: Joan Allen, Joe Mantegna
Searching for Caleb
author: Anne Tyler
Searchin' So Long (1974 song)
artist: Chicago
searchlight: 7 lantern
Search me!: 6 I dunno
Search, The
author: C.P. Snow
Searcy: 4 Nick
searing: 3 hot 8 scathing
Searle: 6 Ronald
Sears: 5 store 8 retailer
competitor: 5 K-Mart 6 Target 7 Penney's, Walmart
partner: 7 Roebuck
Sears ___: 5 tower
seas: 5 seven 6 heptad

__ seas: 4 high
seascape: 4 view 6 nature 7 picture 8 painting
artist: Winslow Homer
Seascape
author: Edward Albee
__ Sea Scrolls: 4 Dead
Sea Serpent constellation: 5 Hydra
seashell: 5 capiz, conch, cowry, murex, snail, whelk 6 chiton, cockle, cowrie, limpet, mussel, oyster, quahog, triton, volute, winkle 7 abalone, bivalve, crinoid, scallop 8 ammonite, argonaut, baculite, escallop, frustule, nautilus, ram's-horn, univalve 9 belemnite, giant clam, pink conch 10 blue mussel, crown conch, eyed cowrie, periwinkle, quahog clam
sharp point on a ~: 5 mucro
seashore: 5 beach, coast 6 strand
recess: 5 inlet
seasickness in French: 8 mal de mer
seaside: 5 coast, shore 7 coastal 8 littoral
resort: 4 lido
sidler: 4 crab
town: 4 port
season: 3 age, dry, run 4 fall, lace, salt, term, time 5 admix, drill, enure, inure, pep up, ripen, space, spell, spice, train 6 autumn, flavor, harden, length, mature, mellow, pepper, period, spring, summer, temper, winter 7 prepare, qualify, quarter, spice up, toughen, weather 8 accustom, indurate, interval, preserve 9 acclimate, condition
ticketholder: 6 abonne
__ season: 4 open 5 out of, silly 6 closed 7 monsoon
__-season: 3 off 4 post
Season: 6 Hubley
seasonable: 6 timely 8 apposite, suitable 9 expedient, favorable, judicious, opportune 10 convenient, felicitous
seasonal: 3 odd 8 periodic 9 migratory
drink: 6 eggnog
song: 4 noel 5 carol
visitor: 5 Santa 6 St. Nick
worker: 7 migrant
seasoned: 3 old 4 deft, ripe 5 hardy, slick, spicy, tough 6 adroit, au fait, expert, mature, mellow, nimble, red-hot, spicey 7 capable, skilled, trained, veteran 8 dextrous, graceful, masterly, skillful 9 competent, dexterous, efficient, masterful, practiced 10 acclimated, proficient
become ~: 8 practice
highly ~: 5 spicy 6 spicey, strong 7 peppery, piquant
seasoning: 4 file, herb, mint, sage, salt, zest 5 curry, spice, thyme 6 fennel, flavor, garlic, ginger, pepper 8 dressing, jalapeño 9 condiment, flavoring 10 background, experience
German ~: 4 salz
Seasonings, The
composer: PDQ Bach
seasons
four ~: 4 year 5 cycle
__ Seasons: 4 Four 5 Sweet, Three
season's growth: 5 yield 7 harvest
Seasons in the Sun (1974 song)
artist: Terry Jacks
Seasons of the Soul
poet: Allen Tate
Seasons, The
painter: Erté
__ Seasons, The: 4 Four
__-seas over: 4 half
Seastrom: 6 Victor
seat: 3 hub, pew, sit, ush 4 base, hold, post, sofa, spot, town 5 abode, bench, booth, cause, chair, couch, divan, heart, perch, place, plant, roost, see in, stool, usher 6 center, daybed, escort, estate, exedra, instal, locate, nestle, pillow, rocker, settee, settle 7 capital, cushion, install, instate, mansion, ottoman, situate, station 8 bleacher, enthrone, inthrone, location, position, recliner 9 davenport, easy chair, establish, footstool, lawn chair, residence, situation, wing chair 10 foundation
back ~: 4 rear
backless ~: 5 stool
be in the driver's ~: 3 run 5 steer 6 direct 7 operate, oversee 9 supervise
belt: 5 strap
bird ~: 5 perch
bishop's ~: 9 cathedral
booster ~ user: 5 child
bridge ~: 4 East, West 5 North, South
catbird ~: 7 lookout
cathedral ~: 7 diocese
church ~: 3 pew
court ~: 4 banc 5 bench
cover: 6 dosser
cushionlike ~: 4 pouf
elephant ~: 6 houdah, howdah
ender: 4 back, mate, work
for several: 4 sofa 6 settee 9 davenport
leave one's ~: 4 rise 5 arise, get up, stand 6 jump up
material: 4 cane
of government: 7 capital
piano ~: 5 stool
porch ~: 5 swing
portico ~: 6 exedra 7 exhedra
show to one's ~: 5 usher 6 lead in
starter: 4 love
sunbather's ~: 6 chaise
take a back ~ (to): 5 defer
theater ~: 3 box, row 4 loge 5 aisle
tot: 3 lap 4 knee
weave a chair ~: 4 cane
seat __: 4 back, belt
seat-__-pants: 5 of-the
__ seat: 3 box, car, hot 4 back, jump, love 5 aisle, have a, house, take a 6 banana, bucket, county, rumble, window 7 bicycle, booster, catbird, driver's, ejector
seat-belt feature: 5 strap 6 buckle 7 release
__-seat driver: 4 back
seated: 9 sedentary
be ~: 4 rest
__-seated: 4 deep
__-seater: 3 two
__ Sea, The: 3 Big 5 Cruel
Sea, the Sea, The
author: Iris Murdoch
SEATO: 4 pact
counterpart: 4 NATO
kin: 5 ASEAN
part: 3 Org. 4 Asia, East 5 South 6 Treaty
seat-of-the-__: 5 pants
Seaton: 6 George
seats
near the stage: 4 row A, row B, row C
section of ~: 4 tier
series of ~: 6 gradin 7 gradine
Seats of the Mighty, The
author: Gilbert Parker
Seattle: 4 city, port, town
arena: 3 Key
athletes: 7 Huskies
county: 4 King
locale: 10 Washington
neighbor: 6 Tacoma
pro team: 8 Mariners, Seahawks
sound: 5 Puget
suburb: 8 Lynnwood
time zone: 3 PDT, PST
Seattle Slew: 5 horse 9 racehorse
to Swale: 4 sire
Seaver, Tom: 3 Met 6 hurler 7 pitcher
seawater mineral: 4 NaCl, salt
seaway: 5 canal, ocean
seaweed: 4 alga, kelp 5 algae, arame, dulse, fucus, laver, plant, sloke 6 hijiki, wakame 9 carrageen, Irish moss, sargassum
brown ~: 5 fucus 6 wakame
edible ~: 5 arame, dulse, laver
food wrapped in ~: 5 sushi
product: 4 agar, nori 5 kombu 8 agar-agar
red ~: 5 dulse, laver
Sea Wolf, The
author: Jack London
SeaWorld attraction: 4 seal 5 Shamu
sebaceous __: 5 gland
Sebastian: 3 Coe 4 crab, John 5 Brant, Cabot, saint
__ Sebastián: 3 San
__ Sebastian Bach: 6 Johann
Sebastian, John
song: Welcome Back (1976)
Seberg: 4 Jean
Sebring: 3 car 4 auto, race 8 auto race, Chrysler 10 automobile
sec: 3 dry 4 jiff 5 jiffy, trice 6 minute, moment 7 instant
drier than ~: 4 brut
in a ~: 3 PDQ 4 soon 5 quick 7 shortly 8 very soon
__ sec: 3 arc, in a 6 triple
__ sec.: 3 fin., rec.
__-sec: 4 demi
SEC: 8 agcy. conf.
part: 4 Comm., Exch. 5 South 7 Eastern 8 Exchange 10 Commission, Securities
school: 3 LSU 6 Auburn 7 Alabama, Florida, Georgia 8 Arkansas, Kentucky 9 Tennessee 10 Vanderbilt 11 Mississippi
Secada, Jon
song: Do You Believe in Us (1992)
If You Go (1994)
Just Another Day (1992)
__ secco: 6 fresco
secede: 4 quit 5 leave, rebel, split 6 defect, depart, desert, resign, retire 7 drop out, pull out, retract, retreat 8 pull away, separate, withdraw 9 break away, break with
__ Secession: 5 War of
sechs: 3 six 6 German
sechzehn: 6 German 7 sixteen
Seckel: 4 pear 5 fruit
relative: 4 Bosc 5 Anjou 6 Comice 8 Bartlett
seclude: 4 hide 6 enisle, immure, retire, screen 7 conceal, confine, enclose, inclose, isolate, secrete, shut off, shut out 8 cloister, separate, withdraw 9 ostracize, segregate, sequester 10 quarantine
secluded: 4 lone 5 alone, privy, quiet 6 covert, cut off, hidden, lonely, remote, secret, single, unseen 7 cloaked, furtive, insular, private, recluse, removed, shut off 8 deserted, hermetic, hush-hush, isolated, lonesome, shielded, solitary 9 out of view, reclusive, sheltered, unexposed, withdrawn 10 cloistered, tucked away, undercover, under wraps
place: 3 den 4 cell, glen, lair, nest, nook, vale 5 abbey 6 alcove, ashram, asrama, friary, priory 7 convent, nunnery, retreat 8 cloister, lamasery 9 courtyard, hermitage, monastery, sanctuary
seclusion: 5 quiet 6 hiding 7 privacy, retreat, secrecy, shelter 8 hideaway, solitude 9 aloneness, hermitage, isolation, sanctuary 10 quarantine, remoteness, retirement, withdrawal
second: 4 aide, back, base, echo, help, jiff, next, tick, time, twin, wink 5 extra, flash, jiffy, least, looie, lower, shake, trice 6 assist, back up, helper, latter, lesser, minute, moment, reject, uphold 7 another, approve, endorse, forward, further, indorse, instant, promote, support 8 inferior, runner-up 9 assistant, encourage, get behind, recommend, subscribe, twinkling 10 additional, bat of an eye, lieutenant, subsequent, substitute, succeeding
combining form: 4 deut- 5 deuto-
draft: 4 redo
finish ~: 4 fail, lose 5 place 9 fall short
go into ~: 5 shift
in a ~: 4 anon, soon 8 directly
in command: 2 VP 4 veep 6 veepee
man: 4 Cain
of two: 6 latter
person: 3 Eve, you
section: 5 part B
showing: 5 rerun
sight: 3 ESP 8 prophecy
sound of a ~: 4 tick
split ~: 4 jiff, wink 5 flash, jiffy, trice 6 minute, moment
starter: 4 nano 5 micro
this ~: 6 at once 8 right now
time: 4 anew 5 again
to none: 4 A-one, best, tops 5 first, prime 8 peerless 9 unequaled 10 preeminent
to the ~: 5 exact

second __: 4 base, best, gear, hand, home, mate, self, unit, wind 5 class, floor, sight, story 6 banana, cousin, estate, fiddle, growth, nature, string 7 baseman, officer, reading, thought
second __ motion: 5 law of
second-__: 4 foot, rate 5 class, guess
second-__ man: 5 story
__ second: 3 arc 4 leap 5 split
Second __ Around, The: 4 Time
Second __ Rose: 4 Hand
Second __ War: 5 World
Second Amendment
supporter: 3 NRA
word: 4 arms
secondary: 4 less, side 5 lower, minor, petty, small 6 backup, junior, lesser 7 reserve, subject, trivial 8 inferior, ulterior 9 alternate, ancillary, auxiliary, dependant, dependent, proximate, resultant, small-time, tributary, vicarious 10 collateral, consequent, contingent, derivative, incidental, low-ranking, peripheral, subsequent, subsidiary
prefix: 3 sub-
to: 5 under
secondary __: 4 road 6 market, school
second baseman
Hall of Fame ~: 3 Fox 5 Carew, Doerr, Evers 6 Frisch, Gordon, Lajoie, Morgan 7 Collins, Hornsby, Lazzeri 8 Robinson, Rod Carew, Sandberg 9 Joe Gordon, Joe Morgan, Mazeroski, Nap Lajoie, Nellie Fox 10 Bobby Doerr 12 Schoendienst
Second Best (1994 film)
cast: John Hurt, William Hurt
second-class: 4 hack, junk, poor 5 cheap, lower, tacky 6 common, shoddy, tawdry 8 inferior, low-grade, mediocre
Second Coming, The
author: William Butler Yeats
Second Deadly Sin, The
author: Lawrence Sanders
second-fiddle: 5 lower, minor 6 lesser
__ second fiddle: 4 play
Second Generation, The
author: Howard Fast
secondhand: 4 used, worn 8 indirect, preowned, recycled 9 emulative, imitative, vicarious 10 derivative, indirectly
it may be ~: 5 smoke
second-hand
item: 5 timer
movement: 5 sweep
Secondhand Lions (2003 film)
cast: Michael Caine, Robert Duvall
second-in-command: 4 aide 5 agent 6 acting, deputy, helper 9 assistant 10 lieutenant
naval ~: 4 exec
second-nature: 6 inbred, rooted 9 ingrained
Second of May, The
painter: Francisco de Goya
second-place finisher: 5 loser
second-quality: 3 irr. 5 irreg. 9 irregular
second-rate: 4 hack, junk, poor 5 cheap, dinky, lousy, minor, tacky 6 cheesy, common, crumby, crummy, lesser, shoddy, tawdry 8 déclassé, inferior, low-grade, mediocre, ordinary
material: 5 tripe
Second Rhapsody
composer: George Gershwin
seconds: 10 irregulars
sixty ~: 6 minute
store: 6 outlet
second-sequel letters: 3 III
Second Sex, The
author: Simone de Beauvoir
__ Seconds Over Tokyo: 6 Thirty
Second Stage, The
author: Betty Friedan
second-story
job: 5 caper, crime, heist, theft 6 felony 7 break-in, larceny, robbery
man: 5 thief 6 robber 7 burglar
__-Second Street: 5 Forty
second-string: 5 lower, minor 6 lesser
second-stringer: 2 JV 3 sub 5 scrub 6 jayvee
Second Time Around, The
composer: Sammy Cahn, Jimmy Van Heusen
second to __: 4 none
Second Wind
author: Dick Francis
secours: 4 lift
secrecy: 4 hush 6 hiding 7 mystery, privacy, silence 8 darkness, muteness, solitude 9 isolation, reticence, seclusion 10 confidence, covertness
breach of ~: 4 leak
secret: 3 sly 4 dark, deep 5 close, inner, privy, quiet, trick 6 arcane, cabala, closet, covert, enigma, hidden, inmost, inside, inward, kabala, latent, lonely, masked, mystic, occult, puzzle, unseen, untold, veiled 7 arcanum, cabbala, cloaked, cryptic, encoded, furtive, kabbala, mystery, obscure, on the QT, private, uncanny, unknown 8 abstruse, backdoor, esoteric, hush-hush, intimate, mystical, obscured, oracular, password, personal, profound, secluded, shrouded, stealthy, ulterior 9 concealed, cryptical, disguised, incognito, innermost, in the dark, nonpublic, recondite, underhand, unnoticed 10 classified, enshrouded, mysterious, privileged, restricted, tucked away, undercover, under wraps, undetected, undivulged, unrevealed
agent: 3 spy 5 spook
combining form: 5 crypt-, krypt- 6 crypto-, krypto-
divulge a ~: 4 blab, tell 5 spill 7 whisper
ender: 3 ive
govt. group: 3 CIA, NSA, ONI
in ~: 8 on the sly 9 entre nous
information: 3 tip 6 tipoff
keep ~: 4 hide, mask, veil 5 cache, cloak, couch, cover, sit on 6 hush up 7 conceal, cover up, obscure 8 disguise, suppress 10 camouflage
like an open ~: 5 known
make ~: 6 encode 7 encrypt
motive: 5 angle
not keep a ~: 3 gab 4 blab, leak, tell 5 blurt, let on, spill 6 squeal, tattle, tip off 7 divulge, let slip 8 blurt out, give away
observer: 3 spy 5 spier
one who can't keep a ~: 5 sieve
place: 6 recess
plan: 4 plot
self: 4 soul
society: 4 tong 5 cabal
writing: 4 code 10 cryptogram
secret __: 5 agent 6 ballot, police
__ secret: 4 deep, open 5 in on a, state, trade
__-secret: 3 top
Secret: 9 deodorant
alternative: *see* deodorant
Secret (1994 song)
artist: Madonna
Secret __: 4 Love 5 Agent 7 Service
Secret __, The: 5 Storm 6 Garden
__ Secret: 3 Pop
Secret Agent Man (1966 song)
artist: Johnny Rivers
secretary: 4 aide, asst., desk 5 clerk 6 helper, scribe, typist 7 copyist, rolltop 8 minister, official 9 assistant, attendant, gal Friday, man Friday 10 amanuensis, escritoire, girl Friday
at times: 5 filer, steno
slip: 4 typo
stat.: 3 wpm
work: 4 memo 6 letter
secretary-__: 7 general
__ secretary: 5 press 6 pocket, social 7 foreign, private
__ Secretary: 4 Home
secretary of __: 5 labor, state 6 energy 7 defense
secrete: 4 bury, emit, hide, mask, palm, stow, veil 5 cache, cloak, couch, cover, exude, stash, sweat 6 effuse, harbor, screen, shroud 7 conceal, cover up, curtain, give off, harbour, obscure, produce, seclude, wall off 8 disguise, perspire, stow away 9 discharge, sequester, stash away 10 camouflage
Secret Garden (1997 song)
artist: Bruce Springsteen
Secret Integration, The
author: Thomas Pynchon
secretion: 6 liquid
odorous ~: 4 musk
skin ~: 5 sebum
toxic ~: 5 venom
secretive: 3 coy, mum 4 cagy 5 cagey, close, quiet 6 covert, hushed, silent, sneaky, zipped 7 cryptic, furtive, on the QT, private 8 reserved, reticent, stealthy, taciturn, thieving, thievish 9 clammed up, cryptical, enigmatic, in the dark, nonpublic, underhand, withdrawn 10 backstairs, buttoned up, in chambers, mysterious, undercover, unsociable, unspeaking
sort: 3 spy 5 hider
Secret Life of Bees, The (2008 film)
cast: Dakota Fanning, Jennifer Hudson, Queen Latifah
Secret Life of Walter Mitty, The: 4 film 5 novel
author: James Thurber
cast: Boris Karloff, Danny Kaye, Virginia Mayo
Secret Love (1953 song)
artist: Doris Day
secretly: 7 on the QT, quietly, sub rosa 8 covertly, hush-hush, inwardly, on the sly 9 between us, entre nous, furtively, obscurely, privately 10 intimately, on the quiet, personally, stealthily, under cover, unobserved
Secretly (1958 song)
artist: Jimmie Rodgers
Secret of __, The: 4 Nimh
Secret of My Success, The (1987 film)
cast: Michael J. Fox, Helen Slater
director: Herbert Ross
secrets: 6 arcana
__ Secret Senses, The: 7 Hundred
Secret Service agent: 4 G-man, T-man
Secret Sharer, The
author: Joseph Conrad
Secret Storm, The (CBS): 4 soap 9 soap opera
Secret, The
author: Harold Robbins
sect: 3 set 4 bloc, camp, cult, side, wing 5 faith, group, order 6 church, school 7 faction, Quakers, Shakers 8 division, religion 10 Mennonites, persuasion
Buddhist ~: 3 Zen
Hindu ~ member: 4 Jain, yogi 5 Jaina, yogin
Indian ~ members: 4 Sikh
Islam ~: 5 Sunni 6 Shi'ite
Jamaican ~ member: 5 rasta
Jewish ~ member: 5 Hasid
Mennonite ~: 5 Amish
Muslim ~: 4 Sufi 5 Sunni 6 Shi'ite
sectarian: 5 bigot, rigid 6 narrow, zealot 7 bigoted, fanatic, insular, limited 8 adherent, clannish, cliquish, dogmatic, partisan 9 dissident, dogmatist, exclusive, extremist, factional, heretical, parochial, religious 10 dogmatical, provincial, schismatic, separatist
suffix: 3 -ist, -ite
section: 3 cut, leg 4 area, belt, bite, hunk, link, lump, part, site, slot, spot, tier, unit, wing, zone 5 block, chunk, field, piece, place, share, slice, split, strip, tract 6 branch, clause, length, moiety, parcel, region, sample, sphere 7 bracket, chapter, element, passage, portion, quarter, segment 8 category, district, division, fraction, fragment, locality, location, precinct, province, vicinity 9 component, partition, territory 10 department
combining form: 4 tomo-
cross ~: 6 sample 8 specimen
first ~: 5 part A, part I 7 part one
prefix for ~: 3 mid
second ~: 5 part B 7 part two
__ section: 5 conic, cross 6 golden, rhythm
sectional: 4 sofa 5 local, zonal 6 zonary 7 divided, limited 8 regional 9 factional 10 fractional

sections, divided into: **5** paned
sector: **4** area, part, side, spot, zone **5** arena, tract **6** locale, region **7** quarter, segment, stratum **8** category, district, division, locality, precinct **9** territory
___ sector: **6** public **7** private
secular: **3** lay **4** laic **5** civil **6** laical **7** earthly, profane, worldly **8** temporal **9** layperson
___ secund.: **4** dieb.
securable: **9** available **10** attainable, obtainable
secure: **3** bag, bar, buy, dam, fix, get, ice, pin, tie, win **4** bind, bolt, clog, cork, cosy, cozy, earn, fast, firm, gain, gird, have, hook, know, land, lash, lock, moor, nail, plug, reap, rope, safe, save, seal, shut, sure, tack, take, tape, yoke **5** annex, block, bound, catch, chain, cinch, clamp, close, cover, cozey, cozie, dam up, fixed, grasp, guard, hitch, latch, leash, on ice, order, rivet, seize, solid, sound, tie up, tight, truss **6** accept, anchor, assure, at ease, attach, attain, batten, buy out, cement, clinch, clog up, collar, come by, defend, effect, embank, engage, enlist, ensure, fasten, harbor, insure, line up, locked, lock up, obtain, pick up, plug up, rack up, seal up, shield, stable, steady, stop up, strong, sturdy, tether **7** achieve, acquire, bespeak, bulwark, capture, certain, chalk up, collect, harbour, padlock, procure, produce, protect, receive, reserve, scare up, seal off, settled, shutter, staunch, succeed, tie down, tighten **8** anchored, blockade, button up, carefree, definite, entrench, fastened, harmless, home-free, in the bag, locked on, obstruct, preserve, purchase, reliable, riskless, shielded, tucked in, unharmed **9** confident, fortified, guarantee, immovable, indemnify, protected, safeguard, sheltered, stabilize, thumbtack, unanxious, undamaged, untouched **10** batten down, button down, dependable, nailed down, perpetuate, underwrite
  a boat: **4** moor **6** anchor
  a contract: **4** land
  a package: **3** tie
  a tent: **3** peg
  by tying down: **5** belay
  place: **4** nest
  position: **8** foothold
  together: **3** sew
secured: **4** firm **6** in hand
securely: **4** fast **9** immovably
securities: **5** means **8** holdings
  dealer: **3** arb **6** broker, trader
  like some ~: **3** OTC
  offering: **3** IPO **4** bond **5** issue, stock
security: **4** bail, bond, ease, egis, gage **5** aegis, cover, guard, token **6** pledge, refuge, safety, screen, shield, surety, tenure, wealth **7** defense, earnest, freedom, hostage, promise, rampart, shelter, warrant **8** immunity, reliance, strength **9** assurance, certainty, guarantee, insurance, safeguard, stability **10** collateral, confidence, precaution, protection
  equipment: **6** camera
  give as ~: **4** hock, pawn **8** mortgage
  government ~: **5** E bond, T-bill, T-bond, T-note
  holder: **6** bailee
  org.: **3** CIA, NSA, ONI, OSS
  problem: **4** leak **6** breach
security ___: **4** risk **5** guard **6** police, thread **7** analyst, blanket
___ security: **6** social
___-security: **7** maximum
Security Council
  denial: **4** veto
  former ~ member: **4** USSR
secy.
  see secretary
Sedaka, Neil
  hometown: Brooklyn
  song: Bad Blood (1975)
    Breaking Up Is Hard to Do (1962)
    Calendar Girl (1960)
    The Diary (1958)
    Happy Birthday, Sweet Sixteen (1961)
    Laughter in the Rain (1974)
    Little Devil (1961)
    Next Door to an Angel (1962)
    Oh! Carol (1959)
    Stairway to Heaven (1960)
Sedalia: **4** city, town
  locale: **8** Missouri
sedan: **3** car **4** auto **7** carrier, hardtop **10** automobile, touring car
  large ~: **4** limo **9** limousine
  take in a ~: **4** bear
Sedan: **4** city, town **6** battle
  locale: **6** France
  river: **4** Maas **5** Meuse
Sedan de Ville: **3** car **4** auto **8** Cadillac
Sedaris: **3** Amy
sedate: **4** calm, cool, drug, prim **5** quiet, sober, staid, stoic **6** at ease, demure, gentle, low-key, mellow, placid, poised, serene, settle, somber, steady **7** amiable, at peace, equable, pacific, relaxed, serious, stoical, unmoved **8** amicable, carefree, composed, decorous, laid-back, peaceful, reserved, tranquil **9** collected, dignified, easygoing, impassive, quiescent, temperate, unexcited, unruffled **10** deliberate, nonchalant, unagitated, untroubled
sedateness: **4** calm, cool **5** poise **6** aplomb **7** balance, dignity **8** presence, serenity **9** assurance, composure, placidity, sang-froid, stability **10** dispassion, equanimity
sedative: **4** drug **6** opiate **7** anodyne **8** hypnotic, medicine **9** analgesic, calmative, soporific **10** anesthetic, medication, painkiller
sedentary: **3** lax **4** idle, lazy **5** inert, unfit **6** asleep, draggy, seated, torpid **7** dormant, passive, settled, sitting **8** inactive, indolent, slothful, sluggish **9** desk-bound, lethargic **10** disengaged, motionless, stationary
Seder: **5** feast
  celebrant: **3** Jew
  fare: **4** lamb **5** matzo **6** matzah, matzoh
sedge: **5** brush **7** bulrush, papyrus
Sedgwick: **4** Edie, Kyra **6** Edward
Sedgwick, Kyra: **7** actress
  spouse: Kevin Bacon
sedgy area: **3** fen **5** marsh, swamp
sediment: **4** dreg, gunk, lees, silt, slag **5** dregs, trash, waste **6** debris, refuse, solids **7** deposit, grounds, residue **8** residuum **9** settlings
sedimentary: **4** rock
sedition: **6** revolt, unrest **7** treason **8** civil war
seditious: **7** lawless, radical **8** disloyal **9** insurgent **10** incendiary, subversive
Sedona: **3** Kia, van **4** city, town
  locale: **7** Arizona
Seduction of Joe Tynan, The (1979 film)
  cast: Alan Alda, Barbara Harris, Meryl Streep, Rip Torn
Seduction of Peter S, The
  author: Lawrence Sanders
___ Seduction, The: **4** Last
sedulous: **5** stout **7** earnest **8** diligent, resolute, studious, tireless, untiring **9** assiduous, laborious, motivated **10** determined, persistent, relentless, scrupulous, unflagging
sedulously: **4** hard
see: **3** eye, get, peg, spy **4** be at, date, espy, feel, gape, gawk, gaze, know, look, mark, meet, note, peek, peep, peer, show, spot, tell, view, wake **5** get it, grasp, greet, learn, pop in, sight, stare, think, usher, visit, waken, watch, weigh **6** advert, attend, behold, detect, drop by, escort, fathom, follow, gaze at, go with, intuit, look at, notice, peek at, peer at, ponder, regard, remark, stop in, survey, take in **7** catch on, cognize, consult, diocese, discern, examine, find out, glimpse, imagine, inspect, make out, observe, picture, prelacy, ransack, realize, receive, run into, so there, take out, unearth, witness **8** appraise, discover, drop in on, envision, foretell, identify, look upon, meet with, perceive, pick up on, scope out **9** accompany, ascertain, bishopric, encounter, figure out, go out with, interview, penetrate, recognize, visualize **10** anticipate, appreciate, comprehend, confer with, episcopacy, experience, eyewitness, get a load of, get the idea, I told you so, scrutinize, understand
  about: **5** probe **6** tend to **8** attend to, consider, look into **10** take care of
  after: **4** tend **5** watch **8** shepherd
  ahead: **7** portend, predict, project **8** prophesy **10** anticipate
  cause to ~ red: **3** irk **4** rile **5** anger, peeve, upset **6** enrage, madden
  come to ~: **5** visit
  daylight: **5** get it **7** realize **9** recognize
  ender: **3** saw
  eye to eye: **4** gybe, jibe **5** agree **6** accede, accord, assent, comply, concur **7** approve, consent, go along **8** coincide **9** acquiesce, harmonize
  face to face: **5** greet **7** run into **8** bump into, confront **9** run across
  fit: **5** deign **6** please **10** condescend
  go to ~: **5** pop in, visit **6** attend, call on, drop by, look up, stop in, travel **7** sojourn, swing by **8** pay a call, stay with
  hard to ~: **3** dim **4** hazy **5** faint, fuzzy, murky, muzzy, vague **6** bleary, blurry, far-off, opaque **7** blurred, clouded, muddled, obscure, shadowy, unclear **8** nebulous **10** indistinct
  how others ~ us: **5** image **9** depiction **10** appearance, conception, impression, perception, projection
  in: **4** seat **5** admit, greet, usher **6** escort **7** welcome
  in court: **3** sue **8** litigate
  old friends: **5** reune
  partner: **4** wait
  plain to ~: **5** clear, overt **7** obvious
  red: **4** boil, fume, rage **6** get mad, rear up, seethe **7** bristle, flame up **8** get angry **9** blow a fuse **10** hit the roof
  socially: **4** date
  something to ~: **5** sight **6** eyeful
  starter: **5** sight
  the error of one's ways: **5** atone **6** repent
  the light: **7** realize
  through: **4** help, last, stay **5** stick **6** keep at, remain **7** achieve, persist, ride out, survive **8** tide over **9** penetrate, persevere
  to: **2** do **3** fix **4** tend **6** advert, attend, handle **7** address, care for, monitor, sit with **9** look after **10** take care of
  what you ~: **4** view **5** image, vista
  you later: **3** bye **4** ciao, ta-ta **5** adieu, adios, aloha, later **6** bye-bye, shalom, so long **7** cheerio, goodbye **8** au revoir, farewell, sayonara, toodle-oo
see ___: **3** out, red **4** to it **5** about, after, stars **6** double, things **7** through
see-___: **4** thru **7** through
___ see...: **5** Let me
___-see: **4** look, must
See ___ care!: **3** if I
See ___ Later, Alligator: **3** You
See ___, pick it up...: **4** a pin
See ___ run: **4** Spot
___ See: **4** Holy
seeable: **6** visual
___ See About Me: **4** Come
___ See Clearly Now: **4** I Can
seed: **3** egg, nut, pip, pit, sow **4** cion, core, germ, idea, kids, ovum **5** acorn, anise, benne, benny, cumin, grain, heirs, issue, ovule, plant, poppy, scion, spark, spawn, spore, start **6** embryo, fennel, gamete, kernel, origin, pippin, scions, sesame, source **7** caraway, concept, inkling, kinfolk, mustard, nucleus, progeny **8** germ cell, kinfolks, kinsfolk, particle, rudiment

SE

9 beginning, broadcast, coriander, inheritor, offspring, posterity 10 successors
aromatic ~: 5 anise, cumin 6 fennel
bacteria ~: 5 spore
combining form: 4 cocc- 5 cocci-, cocco-
company: 6 Burpee
covering: 3 pod 4 aril, boll, hull, husk 5 testa
destination: 4 soil
dill ~: 4 anet
edible ~: 3 nut 4 chia 5 piñon
ender: 3 bed, pod 4 time 5 eater
fern ~: 5 spore
fit to ~: 6 arable
fruit ~: 3 pip
gone to ~: 4 soft 5 passé, ratty 9 enervated 10 dissipated
go to ~: 3 rot 4 rust 5 decay 8 stagnate, vegetate
grain: 6 kernel
hard-roll ~: 5 poppy 6 sesame
immature ~: 5 ovule
maple ~: 6 samara
perk: 3 bye
plant ~: 5 spore
plant with two ~ leaves: 5 dicot 7 dicotyl
remover: 3 gin
ridge: 5 raphe
scar: 5 hilum
scatter ~: 3 sow
starter: 3 all, hay 4 bird, flax, moon, tick, worm 5 stick 6 cotton 7 pumpkin
winged ~: 5 maple
seed __: 4 corn 5 money, pearl
__ seed: 4 go to 5 anise, poppy, run to 6 canary, fennel, sesame 7 caraway
__ Seed: 5 Demon 6 Dragon
seedbed: 4 soil
seedcase: 3 pod
seed-catalog offering: 6 hybrid
__ seeding: 5 cloud
seedless orange: 5 navel
seedling: 4 tree 5 plant
container: 4 flat, tray
plant a ~: 5 unpot
seed-money
govt. ~ agency: 3 SBA
seedpod, clingy: 3 bur
seeds
plant ~: 3 sow 6 garden
sow the ~ of: 6 arouse
__ Seed, The: 3 Bad 4 Wild
seedtime: 6 spring
seedy: 4 mean, poor, torn, worn 5 dingy, faded, grody, mangy, ratty, tacky, tired 6 beat-up, crumby, crummy, grotty, grubby, mangey, ragged, shabby, shoddy, sickly, sleazy, sordid 7 run down, sagging, scruffy, squalid, unkempt 8 decaying, decrepit, flagging, slovenly, tattered, untended 9 neglected, overgrown, ungroomed 10 bedraggled, disheveled, threadbare
establishment: 4 dive 5 joint 9 flophouse, speakeasy
__ See for Miles: 4 I Can
Seeger: 4 Alan, Pete
Seeger, Alan: 4 poet
work: I Have a Rendezvous with Death
Seeger, Pete: 6 folkie 8 banjoist
__ see here!: 3 Now
See if __!: 5 I care
seeing: 5 sense, sight 6 vision
prevent from ~: 9 blindfold
red: 3 mad 4 sore 5 angry, irate, livid 6 raging 7 furious 9 indignant
starter: 3 far 5 sight
that: 5 since 7 because, whereas
Seeing __ dog: 3 Eye
__ seeing things?: 3 Am I
__ Seeing You: 5 I'll Be
__ See It: 3 As I 4 I Can
See It Now (CBS) host: Edward R. Murrow
seek: 3 aim, ask, beg, dig, try 4 comb, hunt, look, nose, root, want 5 chase, covet, crave, delve, essay, prowl, query, quest, scour, trace 6 aspire, beg for, bid for, desire, dig for, forage, gun for, invite, look up, pursue, search, strive 7 attempt, bird-dog, dragnet, enquire, entreat, explore, find out, fish for, go after, hunt for, inquire, long for, look for, ransack, request, rummage, scout up, solicit 8 endeavor, petition, plead for, probe for, prospect, quest for, question, run after, scout out, sniff out, yearn for 9 cast about, ferret out, hanker for, search for, track down
a handout: 3 beg 5 hit up
another opinion: 3 ask 4 talk 5 refer 6 call in, confer, huddle, look to, parlay, powwow, turn to 7 consult 9 negotiate, touch base 10 brainstorm
a ride: 5 thumb
charity: 3 beg
employment: 5 apply 8 petition
favor: 4 fawn 10 ingratiate
office: 3 run 5 stump 7 contend 8 politick
redress: 3 sue 8 litigate 9 prosecute
shelter: 9 take cover
(to): 6 aspire
to win: 5 chase, court, spark 6 pursue 10 bill and coo
Seek __ shall find: 5 and ye
seeker: 6 hunter 9 applicant, candidate, job-hunter
asylum ~: 5 alien 6 émigré
evade the ~: 4 hide, lurk 5 ditch 6 hole up, lie low 8 disguise, tuck away 9 hibernate, sequester, take cover 10 camouflage
information ~: 5 asker
office ~: 3 pol 9 candidate 10 politician
query: 3 how, who, why 4 what, when 5 where 7 how many, how much
target: 5 hider
thrill ~: 8 hedonist
__ seeker: 3 job 6 office, status
Seekers
homeland: Australia
song: Georgy Girl (1966)
I'll Never Find Another You (1965)
__ Seekers: 3 New
seeking: 5 after
combining form: 5 -petal
seem: 4 hint 5 feign, imply, sound 6 appear, assume, strike 7 suggest 8 feel as if, intimate, look as if, look like, resemble 9 insinuate, sound like
like: 7 smack of 8 resemble
See Me, Feel Me (1970 song)
artist: Who, The
seeming: 4 look, show 5 quasi 6 likely 7 evident, nominal, outside, reputed 8 apparent, presumed, probable, putative, specious, supposed 9 semblance 10 ostensible
seemingly: 4 as if 6 likely 8 just like, probably 9 doubtless, evidently, outwardly 10 apparently, ostensibly, presumably
seemliness: 8 niceties 9 etiquette, propriety
seemly: 3 apt, fit 4 good, nice 5 moral, right 6 decent, modest, proper 7 correct, fitting 8 apposite, becoming, decorous, suitable 9 advisable, befitting
__ seems: 4 so it
Seems Like Old Times (1980 film)
cast: Chevy Chase, Charles Grodin, Goldie Hawn
seen: 6 visual 7 visible
as ~ fit: 4 duly
easily ~: 4 open 5 overt, plain 9 prominent
never before ~: 6 all-new 8 brand-new
seldom ~: 4 rare 6 exotic, scanty, scarce 8 uncommon
...seen and not __: 5 heard
See No __: 4 Evil
see one's __ clear: 3 way
seep: 4 drip, flow, leak, ooze, soak 5 drain, exude, leach, sweat 6 filter, osmose 7 dribble, trickle 8 filter in, filtrate, permeate, transude 9 penetrate, percolate
ender: 3 age
(into): 3 get
seepage: 9 discharge
collector: 3 pit 5 bilge
seer: 4 Demo, guru, Olen 5 augur, Crius, Iamus, Iapis, Idmon, Maeon, Manto, Sabbe, sibyl, swami, swamy, Vanus 6 Andros, Apollo, Asilas, Carnus, Daphne, medium, Merops, Mopsus, mystic, oracle, Pholus, Scirus, viewer, wizard 7 Aesacus, Ampycus, aruspex, Asbolus, Calchas, diviner, Ennomus, Glaucus, Helenus, Laocoon, Laokoon, Lavinia, palmist, Phineus, prophet, Proteus, psychic, Rhamnes, Telemus, Thestor, witness 8 Alcander, haruspex, Melampus, Munichus, observer, onlooker, Phrasius, Polyidus, presager, Tiresias 9 Amphiarus, Aristaeus, Cassandra, Herophile, predictor, spectator, theurgist, Thiodamas, Tolumnius, visionary, Xenocleia 10 eyewitness, forecaster, foreteller, mind reader, palm reader, Polyphides, soothsayer
asset: 3 ESP
card: 5 tarot
ender: 3 ess 6 sucker
need: 4 omen
pertaining to a ~: 5 vatic 7 vatical
site: 6 Delphi
starter: 5 sight
Seeress of __, The: 4 Kell
seersucker: 6 fabric 8 material
seesaw: 4 rock, tilt, toss 5 lurch, pitch, waver 6 teeter, totter 7 librate, whiffle 8 exchange, hesitate 9 alternate, fluctuate, oscillate, vacillate
quorum: 3 two
site: 4 park
See-saw, Margery __: 3 Daw
See See Rider (1966 song)
artist: Animals
See Spot run textbook: 6 reader
seethe: 4 boil, burn, foam, fume, rage, soak, stew 5 churn, froth, souse, storm, surge 6 bubble, see red, simmer 7 bristle, ferment, flame up, smolder 8 smoulder
with activity: 3 hum
see the __: 5 light
seething: 5 aboil, irate, wroth 6 raging, red-hot, tumult
see-through: 4 thin 5 clear, gauzy, sheer 6 limpid 10 diaphanous
material: 5 glass
See You in September (1966 song)
artist: Happenings
See You Later, Alligator (1956 song)
artist: Bill Haley and His Comets
__ See You Smile: 5 When I
__ See You, The: 5 More I
Seferis: 6 George 7 Giorgos
Sega
rival: 3 NES 5 Atari
Segal: 4 Alex 5 Erich 6 George
Segal, George: 5 actor
TV: Just Shoot Me
Segar, E.C.: 10 cartoonist
character: 3 Oyl 5 Bluto, Olive, Wimpy 6 Popeye 7 Swee'Pea 8 Olive Oyl
Seger, Bob
song: Against the Wind (1980)
American Storm (1986)
Even Now (1983)
Fire Lake (1980)
Hollywood Nights (1978)
Like a Rock (1986)
Night Moves (1977)
Old Time Rock & Roll (1989)
Ramblin' Gamblin' Man (1969)
Shakedown (1987)
Shame on the Moon (1982)
Still the Same (1978)
Tryin' to Live My Life Without You (1981)
Understanding (1984)
We've Got Tonite (1978)
You'll Accomp'ny Me (1980)
segment: 3 bit, cut, leg 4 part, unit, zone 5 block, piece, share, slice, strip, wedge 6 length, member, moiety, parcel, sample, sector 7 portion, section 8 division, fraction 9 component 10 proportion
__ segment: 4 line
__ segno: 3 dal
sego lily state: 4 Utah
Segovia, Andrés: 7 Spanish 9 guitarist
segregate: 5 sever, split 6 cut off, divide, island 7 isolate, seclude, split up 8 close off, insulate, separate, set apart 9 sequester, single out 10 disconnect, dissociate, quarantine
segregated: 5 apart 9 exclusive
segue: 4 link 6 lead-in 10 connection, transition

SE

Segura, Pancho: **7** netster **9** Ecuadoran, tennis pro
milieu: **5** court
Se habla __: **6** inglés
__ se habla Español: **4** Aquí
Sehorn, Jason
spouse: Angie Harmon
sei: **5** whale **8** cetacean
relative: ***see*** cetacean
Seidelman: **5** Susan
Seiji: **5** Ozawa
Seiko: **5** watch
alternative: ***see*** wristwatch
Seiler: **5** Lewis
seine: **3** net **4** fish **7** fish net
like a ~: **5** meshy, netty
Seine: **5** river
city on the ~: **5** Melun, Paris, Rouen **6** Troyes
landscapist: **5** Monet
locale: **6** France
tributary: **4** Aube, Eure, Oise **5** Marne
seiner: **6** angler **9** fisherman
Seinfeld (NBC sitcom)
cast: Jason Alexander (George Costanza)
Estelle Harris (Estelle Costanza)
Wayne Knight (Newman)
Julia Louis-Dreyfus (Elaine Benes)
Michael Richards (Cosmo Kramer)
Jerry Seinfeld (Jerry Seinfeld)
Jerry Stiller (Frank Costanza)
seis: **3** six **7** Spanish
seism: **5** quake **6** tremor **10** earthquake
seismic __: **3** gap
seismograph
part: **6** stylus
part of a ~ reading: **5** L wave
reading: **5** quake **6** tremor **10** earthquake
seismologist
concern: **5** fault, quake
field: **7** geology
seize: **3** bag, get, nab **4** bust, fist, gain, glom, grab, grip, hold, jail, lift, nail, snag, snap, take, tear, trap **5** annex, catch, clasp, exact, force, grasp, pinch, pluck, reach, snare, usurp, wrest **6** abduct, ambush, arrest, assume, clench, clinch, clutch, collar, detain, hijack, intern, kidnap, obtain, occupy, pick up, pounce, prey on, ravage, ravish, secure, snap up, snatch, tackle, wrench **7** capture, embrace, grapple, impound, interne, overrun, possess, preempt, procure, ransack, receive **8** arrogate, carry off, highjack, hold fast, overcome, take over, throttle **9** apprehend, extradite, intercept, latch onto, overpower, overwhelm, pitch into **10** commandeer, comprehend, confiscate, spirit away, take hold of
eagerly: **6** jump at
old-style: **5** reave
power: **5** usurp
__ Seize: **5** Louis
seized
item: **4** repo
old-style: **4** reft
seize the day: **4** live
in Latin: **9** carpe diem
Seize the Day: **4** film **5** novel
author: Saul Bellow
cast: Jerry Stiller, Robin Williams
Seize the Night
author: Dean Koontz
seizure: **4** bust, grab, loot, turn **6** collar, rapine, snatch **7** capture **9** abduction **10** annexation, assumption, kidnapping, occupation, usurpation
Seizure
author: Robin Cook
Sejm: **10** parliament
locale: **6** Poland
Sekely: **5** Steve
Sekt: **4** wine **6** German
Sela: **4** Ward
Se La (1987 song)
artist: Lionel Richie
Selassie: **5** Haile
country: **8** Ethiopia
title: **3** Ras
worshiper: **5** Rasta
Selby: **5** David
Selby Jr., Hubert
work: Last Exit to Brooklyn
seldom: **6** hardly, little, rarely **8** far apart, scarcely, sporadic **9** sometimes **10** hardly ever, infrequent, occasional, sporadical, uncommonly, unfrequent
seen: **4** rare **6** exotic, scanty, scarce **8** uncommon
used: **5** dusty, rusty
select: **3** opt, peg, tab, tag, tap, top **4** A-one, best, cull, fine, mark, name, pick, rare, sort, take, tops **5** elect, elite, first, glean, key on, prime **6** assign, choice, choose, chosen, deluxe, gather, go into, goodly, opt for, picked, prefer, screen, weeded, winner **7** appoint, excerpt, extract, fix upon, limited, pick out, pin down, premium, recruit, sort out, special, vintage **8** bookmark, draw lots, handpick, identify, nominate, rarefied, screened, superior, topnotch **9** excellent, exclusive, exquisite, first-rate, number one, preferred, single out, unrivaled **10** first-class, handpicked, preferable, privileged, settle upon, unrivalled, world-class
at random: **4** draw
from a menu: **5** order
group: **5** A-list, elite
on a computer: **5** click
selectee: **7** recruit, soldier **9** appointee
selection: **3** cut **4** pick **5** quote, range, stock **6** choice, option **7** culling, excerpt, extract, picking **8** adoption, decision, election **9** anthology, quotation **10** assignment, assortment, collection, nomination, preference, recitation
__ selection: **7** natural
selective: **5** picky **6** choosy **7** careful, choosey **8** rarefied **9** judicious **10** discerning, particular
Selective __ System: **7** Service
Selena
song: I Could Fall in Love (1995)
Selena (1997 film)
cast: Jennifer Lopez, Edward James Olmos, Jon Seda
Selene: **7** goddess
brother: **6** Helios
daughter: **6** Pandia
equivalent: **4** Luna
lover: **8** Endymion
mother: **4** Thia
realm: **4** moon
sister: **3** Eos
son: **9** Narcissus
selenic: **5** lunar
selenium: **7** element
selenology: **9** astronomy
Seles, Monica: **7** netster **9** tennis pro
milieu: **5** court
self: **3** ego, you **4** atma, soul **5** anima, atman, being **6** nature, person, psyche **8** identity **9** character **10** individual
combining form: **3** aut- **4** auto-
ender: **3** dom **4** same
Hindu ~: **4** atma **5** atman
pride: **3** ego
starter: **3** her, him, one, our, thy **4** your
self-__: **4** help, made, pity, rule, will **5** doubt, image, study, worth **6** denial, esteem, styled, taught **7** assured, control, defense, evident, imposed, reliant, respect, service, serving, starter
self-__ flour: **6** rising
self-__ man: **4** made
self-__ millionaire: **4** made
self-__ turkey: **7** basting
self-__ watch: **7** winding
__ self: **6** second
self-absorption: **6** egoism **7** conceit, egotism
self-admiration: **5** pride **6** egoism **7** conceit, egotism
self-admiring: **4** vain **9** conceited
self-aggrandizing: **8** boastful
self-assertive: **5** brash, pushy **6** strong **9** bumptious
self-assurance: **5** brass, poise **6** aplomb, morale **8** presence
self-assured: **6** poised, secure **8** composed
self-basting: **5** moist
self-centered: **4** smug, vain **5** cocky **6** little, stuffy **7** fustian, haughty, pompous, selfish, stuck-up, worldly **8** arrogant, boastful, egoistic, snobbish **9** big-headed, egotistic **10** egoistical
one: **6** egoist **7** egotist
self-cleaning __: **4** oven
self-command: **5** poise
self-concern: **6** egoism **7** egotism
self-condemnation: **6** regret
self-condemnatory: **5** sorry
self-confidence: **5** poise **6** aplomb, morale
destroy ~: **5** abash
self-confident: **4** sure **6** poised, secure **7** assured, certain, hotshot **8** fearless
self-conscious: **3** shy **5** stiff **6** uneasy, unsure **7** anxious, awkward, bashful, nervous, stilted **8** mannered, sheepish, strained **9** ill-at-ease, uncertain
make ~: **5** abash
self-contained: **5** whole **6** closed **8** reserved, reticent
self-contented: **4** smug **8** arrogant
self-contradiction: **7** paradox
self-control: **4** will **5** poise **6** aplomb, temper **7** balance, reserve **8** patience, sobriety **9** restraint, reticence, sang-froid, stability, willpower **10** temperance
lose one's ~: **4** flip, slap, snap **5** crack, go ape, smack, smash, whack **6** injure, insult, lose it **7** thunder **9** go bonkers
Self Control (1984 song)
artist: Laura Branigan
self-controlled: **4** cool **5** sober, stoic **7** stoical **9** temperate
self-defense
art: **4** judo **6** aikido, karate, kung fu
expert: **6** judoka
school: **4** dojo
spray: **4** mace
self-denial: **9** austerity, restraint **10** abnegation, abstinence
self-denying: **7** ascetic, austere
self-determination: **7** liberty, license
self-discipline: **4** will **9** restraint, willpower
self-disgust: **5** shame **6** regret
self-effacing: **3** coy, shy **5** mousy **6** demure, humble, modest, mousey **8** reserved, retiring **9** diffident **10** unassuming
self-employed: **5** indie
self-esteem: **3** ego **5** poise, pride **6** egoism, regard **7** dignity, egotism, hauteur, respect
self-evident: **5** clear, plain **6** patent **7** obvious, visible **8** apparent, manifest **9** axiomatic
self-explanatory: **5** clear, plain **6** simple **7** obvious, visible **8** apparent, manifest
self-government: **7** freedom, liberty
self-help category: **5** how-to
self-image: **3** ego
self-importance: **3** ego **5** pride **6** hubris, hybris **7** conceit, hauteur **10** pretension
self-important: **4** smug, vain **5** proud **6** snooty, stuffy **7** fustian, haughty, pompous, stuck-up **8** arrogant, snobbish **9** bigheaded, conceited, officious **10** hoity-toity
one: **3** ass
self-indulgence: **7** license **8** pleasure
self-indulgent: **6** effete **9** luxurious
self-interest: **6** egoism
selfish: **3** big **4** mean, rude **5** brash, nervy, small, tight **6** grabby, greedy, little, sordid, stingy **7** boorish, hoggish, miserly, worldly **8** egoistic, grasping, heedless, impolite, tactless, ulterior, ungiving **9** egotistic, mercenary, penurious **10** avaricious, egocentric, egoistical, skinflinty, ungenerous, ungracious, ungrateful, unthinking
one: **3** hog, pig **5** taker **6** egoist **7** egotist
selfishness: **5** greed **7** avarice
selfless: **3** big **10** altruistic, bighearted
self-love: **6** egoism, vanity **7** conceit, egotism **10** narcissism
self-loving: **10** egocentric, egoistical
self-named: **8** so-called
self-possessed: **4** calm, cool, sure **6** placid, poised, sedate, serene, steady **7** assured, patient, relaxed **8** balanced, composed, peaceful,

tranquil **9** collected, easygoing, nerveless **10** untroubled
self-possession: 5 poise **6** aplomb **7** balance **8** calmness, presence **9** restraint
Self-Reliance: 5 essay
author: Ralph Waldo Emerson
self-reliant: 4 sure **6** secure **7** assured, valiant **9** autonomic, confident **10** autonomous
self-reproach: 5 shame **6** regret **7** remorse **9** penitence **10** repentance
self-reproachful: 5 sorry
self-respect: 3 ego **5** pride **7** conceit, dignity
self-restraint: 4 will **7** control, reserve **9** sang-froid **10** discipline, temperance
self-righteous: 4 smug **5** pious **7** canting, preachy **8** superior
person: 4 prig
self-ruling: 4 free **8** populist **10** autonomous, democratic
self-sacrificing: 5 chary **7** prudent, thrifty **9** provident **10** economical
selfsame: 4 like, twin, very **9** identical
self-satisfied: 4 smug, vain **5** proud **7** pleased **8** puffed up **9** conceited, egotistic
act ~: 5 gloat
self-seeker: 6 egoist **7** egotist **10** narcissist
self-service
ending: 4 -omat **5** -teria
self-serving: 8 ulterior
one: 5 taker
self-styled: 7 nominal, wannabe, would-be **8** so-called **9** soi-disant
self-sufficient: 4 unit **5** proud **6** closed **9** competent, confident, on one's own
self-sustaining: 6 closed **7** insular **8** solitary
self-willed: 4 wild **7** wayward **8** indocile, perverse, stubborn **9** obstinate, pigheaded **10** headstrong
self-worship: 5 pride **6** egoism, vanity **7** egotism
Selick: 5 Henry
Selig: 3 Bud
Selkirk: 9 Alexander
Selkirk Rex: 3 cat **5** felid **6** feline
sell: 4 dump, fail, hawk, push, sham, shed, show, snow, vend **5** close, cross, lobby, pitch, press, rat on, spiel, spoof, trade **6** barter, betray, deal in, delude, give up, handle, hustle, market, peddle, retail, take in, unload **7** auction, beguile, deceive, dispose, mislead, promote, traffic, triumph, win over **8** contract, convince, exchange, get rid of, give away, hand over, part with, persuade, pressure, transact, transfer **9** deliver up, disinform, dispose of, influence, liquidate, move goods, play false, publicize, surrender, sweet talk, wholesale **10** auction off, relinquish
a bill of goods: 2 do **3** con, rob **4** bilk, burn, clip, dupe, fool, gull, have, hoax, nick, rook, scam, take, trim **5** cheat, cozen, fraud, gouge, mulct, pluck, set up, shaft, stiff, sting, trick **6** diddle, extort, fleece, hustle, outwit, rip off, sucker **7** deceive, defraud, finagle, sandbag, swindle **8** flimflam, hoodwink, outsmart **9** bamboozle, four-flush, shake down, victimize **10** run a game on
abroad: 6 export
aggressively: 4 flog, hype
buy and ~: 4 deal **5** trade **7** traffic **8** exchange
cheap: 4 dump
door to door: 6 peddle
down the river: 5 rat on **6** betray, expose, fink on, give up, snitch, squeal, tattle, turn in **7** sell out **8** give away
ender: 3 off, out **4** back
for: 4 cost **5** bring, fetch, yield **6** charge **7** realize
hard ~: 5 spiel **6** patter **8** cajolery **10** persuasion
off: 6 divest **9** liquidate
on: 5 lobby **7** satisfy
out: 5 cross, rat on **6** betray, give up **7** deceive, mislead, violate **8** give away **9** deliver up, play false, surrender
try to ~: 7 solicit
sell __: 3 off, out **4** date **5** short
sell __ hotcakes: 4 like
sell __ of goods: 5 a bill
sell __ the river: 4 down
__ sell: 4 hard, soft
Sellecca, Connie: 7 actress
spouse: Gil Gerard, John Tesh
Selleck, Tom: 5 actor
film: 3 Men and a Baby (1987)
Her Alibi (1989)
In & Out (1997)
Quigley Down Under (1990)
TV: Magnum, p.i.
seller: 5 agent **6** broker, dealer, grocer, hawker, pedlar, pedler, trader, vender, vendor **7** peddler **8** marketer, merchant, retailer **10** auctioneer, franchisee, shopkeeper
caveat: 4 as is
short ~: 4 bear
spots: 3 ads
starter: 4 book
tip ~: 4 tout
__ seller: 4 best **5** short
Sellers, Peter: 5 actor
film: The Battle of the Sexes (1960)
Being There (1979)
Casino Royale (1967)
Dr. Strangelove (1964)
I Love You, Alice B. Toklas (1968)
Lolita (1962)
The Mouse That Roared (1959)
Murder by Death (1976)
The Optimists (1973)
The Party (1968)
The Pink Panther (1964)
A Shot in the Dark (1964)
There's a Girl in My Soup (1970)
tom thumb (1958)
Waltz of the Toreadors (1962)
Woman Times Seven (1967)
The World of Henry Orient (1964)
The Wrong Arm of the Law (1962)
spouse: Britt Ekland
selling __: 5 point
__-selling: 4 best
sell-off: 7 auction
sellout: 3 hit **6** throng **9** treachery
notice: 3 SRO
__ sells seashells...: 3 She
Selma: 4 city, town **5** Blair **7** Diamond **8** Lagerlöf
locale: 7 Alabama
Selman: 7 Waksman
seltzer: 4 fizz, soda **5** mixer **8** beverage
make ~: 6 aerate
seltzer __: 5 water
__ Seltzer: 5 Bromo
__-Seltzer: 4 Alka
selva: 10 rain forest
selvage: 3 end **5** verge **6** margin
Selvon, Samuel: 6 writer **11** Trinidadian
Selznick, David O.
spouse: Jennifer Jones
semana: 4 week **7** Spanish
semantic: 10 linguistic
semaphore: 4 code
sender: 5 waver
__ Sematary: 3 Pet
Sembello, Michael
song: Maniac (1983)
semblance: 3 air **4** aura, cast, face, feel, form, look, mask, mood, show, veil **5** front, guise, image, shape **6** aspect, facade, simile, veneer **7** analogy, bearing, feeling, pretext, seeming, showing **8** likeness, likening, pretense **9** imitation **10** appearance, atmosphere, comparison, complexion, similarity, similitude
Semele: 8 oratorio
composer: George Frideric Handel
father: 6 Cadmus
lover: 4 Zeus
sister: 3 Ino
son: 7 Bacchus **8** Dionysus
semester: 4 term
ender: 4 exam, test **5** final
semesters, two: 4 year
semi: 3 rig **5** lorry, truck **6** big rig, hauler **9** transport
British ~: 5 lorry
compartment: 3 cab
drive a ~: 4 haul
fuel: 6 diesel
semi-: 4 half **5** quasi
semibreve: 4 note
semicircle: 3 arc, bow
semicircular: 5 round
semicircular __: 5 canal
semicolon: 4 dots, mark
semiconductor: 5 diode
concentration: 3 LSI
giant: 5 Intel
impurity: 6 dopant
metal: 6 indium **7** silicon **9** germanium
semidiameter: 6 radius
semiliquid: 3 gel **5** mushy
seminal: 7 primary **8** original **9** formative **10** innovative
seminar: 4 talk **5** class **6** course **8** elective **10** conference
follower: 5 Q and A
seminary: 6 school **7** academy
degree: 3 STB, STM, Th.D.
subject: 3 rel. **8** religion
text: 5 Bible
Seminole: 5 tribe **6** Indian **7** Amerind, athlete
chief: 7 Osceola
Seminole __: 4 Wars
Seminoles' school: 3 FSU
semiprecious __: 5 stone
semiquaver: 4 note
semirural region: 5 exurb
semisolid: 3 gel **5** mushy
Semite: 3 Jew **4** Arab
ancient ~: 6 Essene
Semitic: 6 Jewish **8** language
deity: 4 Baal
kingdom: 4 Moab
language: 6 Arabic, Hebrew **7** Amharic, Aramaic **8** Akkadian
Semi-Tough (1977 film)
cast: Jill Clayburgh, Kris Kristofferson, Burt Reynolds
semolina: 5 grain, wheat
product: 5 pasta **9** spaghetti
semper __: 7 fidelis, paratus
Semper Fidelis: 5 march, motto
composer: John Philip Sousa
org.: 4 USMC
vower: 6 Marine
__ semper tyrannis: 3 sic
__ Semple McPherson: 5 Aimee
sempre: 6 always
__ sempre: 4 ora e
Senate: 10 upper house
airer: 5 CSPAN
ancient Roman ~ house: 5 curia
assistant: 4 aide, page
counterpart: 5 House
garb: 4 toga
influencer: 8 lobbyist
locale: 4 Rome **5** Italy **6** Canada, France, Mexico
member: 8 lawmaker **10** legislator
official: 4 whip
output: 3 law **4** bill
six years, for the ~: 4 term
vote: 3 aye, nay, yea
senator: 8 lawgiver
Senator: 6 iceman
Hall-of-Famer: 4 Rice **7** Johnson, Sam Rice
Senators: 3 six **4** team
home: 6 Ottawa
milieu: 3 ice **4** rink
org.: 3 NHL
rival: see hockey team
sport: 6 hockey
send: 3 fax **4** cast, drop, emit, fire, hurl, mail, move, post, ship, stir, wire **5** charm, drive, elate, fling, grant, issue, refer, relay, remit, route, shoot, sling, telex **6** assign, commit, convey, detail, direct, excite, impart, let fly, please, propel, put out, thrill, turn on **7** advance, consign, delight, deliver, dismiss, enchant, enthral, enthuse, forward, freight, give off, inthral, radiate **8** delegate, dispatch, enthrall, hurry off, inthrall, televise, transfer, transmit **9** broadcast, bundle off, circulate, electrify, enrapture, pass along, stimulate, titillate, transport **10** exhilarate, intoxicate
a letter: 4 mail **5** write **10** correspond, epistolize
a message to: 4 wire
a package: 4 ship
away: 6 banish, deport, rebuff **7** dismiss **8** chase out

away for: 5 order
back: 6 remand, return
ender: 3 off
for: 4 page 6 muster, summon
forth: 4 bear, emit, gush, shed, spew, spue 5 eject, expel, exude, issue, relay, yield 6 launch 7 cast out, diffuse, emanate, give off, produce, radiate 8 generate, throw off 9 discharge
forward: 7 advance
hit ~: 5 e-mail
money: 5 remit
off: 4 beam 6 export, launch, refuse 7 dismiss 8 disperse
out: 4 emit 5 exude, issue 7 radiate
overnight: 4 rush 6 hasten 7 speed up 8 expedite 10 accelerate
packing: 2 ax 3 axe, can, rid 4 boot, drop, fire, oust, sack 5 eject, evict, exile, expel, let go 6 banish, bounce, depose, lay off 7 cashier, dismiss, drum out, release, turn out 8 chase out, furlough, get rid of, pink-slip 9 discharge, terminate
regrets: 5 say no 6 beg off, refuse 7 decline
skyward: 4 loft
starter: 3 god
through the roof: 5 anger 6 enrage, fire up, madden 7 incense, inflame, provoke 9 infuriate 10 exasperate
to another: 5 refer
to Coventry: 4 shun, tabu 5 taboo
to the bottom: 4 sink
up: 4 loft, mock 6 launch 7 imitate, lampoon 8 ridicule
word to: 6 inform, notify

send __: 3 for, off, out 5 forth 6 flying 7 packing
send-__: 2 up
Sendak, Maurice: 6 writer
Sending __ Love: 5 All My
Send in the Clowns starter: 4 Isn't
__ Send Me: 3 You
Send Me No Flowers (1964 film)
cast: Doris Day, Rock Hudson, Tony Randall
sendoff: 5 start 8 farewell 9 launching
Send One Your Love (1979 song)
artist: Stevie Wonder
send-up: 5 spoof 6 comedy, parody, satire 7 lampoon, mockery, takeoff 8 travesty 10 caricature, impression
Seneca: 3 car 4 auto, lake 5 Dodge, Roman, tribe 6 Indian 7 Amerind 8 language 10 playwright 11 philosopher
ally: 6 Cayuga, Mohawk, Oneida 8 Onondaga 9 Tuscarora
enemy: 4 Erie
locale: 7 New York
specialty: 8 Stoicism
student: 4 Nero
Seneca __ Conference: 5 Falls
Senegal: 5 river 6 nation 7 country
capital: 5 Dakar
city: 5 Dakar, Thiès
language: 5 Wolof 7 Malinke
locale: 6 Africa
money: 5 franc
neighbor: 4 Mali 6 Gambia, Guinea 10 Mauritania
people: 4 Fula 5 Wolof 6 Fulani
poet: 7 Senghor
port: 5 Dakar
River locale: 4 Mali
senescent: 4 aged 5 aging 6 ageing 7 ancient, elderly, wizened 8 grizzled 9 geriatric, getting on, up in years
__ Seng Index: 4 Hang
senhor: 3 man 5 title 6 mister 10 Portuguese
senhora: 4 dona, lady 5 title 10 Portuguese
daughter: 5 filha
senhorita: 4 miss 5 title 10 Portuguese
senior: 3 old 4 head, year 5 elder, major, older, pupil 6 higher 7 leading 8 old-timer, superior 9 collegian, first-born, matriarch, patriarch 10 golden-ager
citizen group: 4 AARP
exam: 4 GMAT, LSAT
former ~: 4 alum, grad 6 alumna 7 alumnus
goal: 6 degree 7 diploma
member: 4 dean 5 doyen
year highlight: 4 prom
senior __: 4 debt, prom 7 citizen
Senior Bowl team: 5 North, South
seniority: 4 rank 7 ranking 8 priority, standing 9 advantage 10 precedence, preference
greater in ~: 5 older 9 first-born
having more ~: 5 older
senna: 5 shrub
source: 6 cassia
Senne: 5 river
city on the ~: 8 Brussels
locale: 7 Belgium
Sennett: 4 Mack
señor: 3 man 5 title 6 Latino 7 Spanish
shawl: 6 sarape, serape
squiggle: 5 tilde
wife: 6 esposa, marida
señora: 4 lady, wife 5 title 6 Latina 7 Spanish
husband: 6 esposo, marido
shawl: 6 rebozo
squiggle: 5 tilde
señorita: 5 title 6 Latina 8 fraülein
squiggle: 5 tilde
sensation: 3 hit, wow 4 feel, kick, stir, vibe 5 flash, furor, smash, vibes 6 marvel, scream, splash, thrill, tingle, wonder 7 emotion, feeling, miracle, passion, prodigy, scandal, stunner, triumph 8 response, surprise 9 agitation, awareness, bombshell, commotion 10 excitement, gold record, impression, perception, phenomenon
causer: 5 nerve
without ~: 4 numb 9 unfeeling
sensational: 5 juicy, livid, lurid, rough, showy, spicy 6 coarse, moving, sultry, vulgar 7 pointed, salient 8 dramatic, eloquent, exciting, shocking, stirring, stunning, wondrous 9 agitating, arresting, emotional, prominent, revealing, thrilling, wonderful 10 scandalous
see also wonderful
sensationalism: 4 hype 6 hoopla
sensationless: 4 numb 9 unfeeling
Sens Cathedral
artist: Camille Corot
sense: 3 get, use, wit 4 aura, core, feel, gist, hear, hold, know, meat, mind, read, soul, tact, wits 5 drift, grasp, logic, point, savvy, scent, sight, smell, stuff, taste, tenor, think, touch, value, worth 6 absorb, acuity, brains, detect, divine, import, intuit, matter, notice, nuance, pick up, reason, sanity, seeing, smarts, spirit, take in, thrust, upshot, wisdom 7 ability, believe, catch on, discern, faculty, feeling, hearing, insight, meaning, message, observe, purport, purpose, realize, summary 8 aptitude, capacity, function, instinct, judgment, keenness, overtone, perceive, prudence, sagacity, sapience 9 apprehend, awareness, intellect, intuition, knowledge, reasoning, sharpness, smartness, substance 10 anticipate, appreciate, atmosphere, cleverness, cognizance, definition, denotation, impression, perception, understand
a ~: 5 smell, taste, touch 6 seeing, vision 7 hearing
common ~: 3 wit 4 tact, wits 5 logic 6 sanity, wisdom 8 gumption, judgment 9 practical, pragmatic 10 discretion
general ~: 4 gist, tone, vein 5 drift, tenor, theme, trend 6 burden, intent 7 essence, meaning, purport 9 substance
horse ~: 5 savvy 6 acumen, brains, reason, wisdom 7 insight 8 judgment, prudence, sagacity 9 ingenuity, reasoning, sharpness 10 astuteness, perception, shrewdness
make ~: 4 jell 5 add up, fit in 6 cohere, figure, relate, square 7 conform, connect 8 dovetail 9 hold water 10 correspond
make ~ of: 6 decode 9 figure out
making ~: 10 reasonable
moral ~: 8 superego 10 conscience, small voice
not making ~: 9 illogical
of a ~: 4 otic 5 aural
of humor: 3 wit 9 wittiness 10 cleverness
organ: 3 ear, eye 4 nose, skin 6 tongue
sixth ~: 3 ESP 8 instinct 9 intuition, telepathy
__ sense: 3 in a 4 talk 5 horse, moral, sixth 6 common
__ Sense: 6 Common
Sense and Sensibility: 4 film 5 novel
author: Jane Austen
cast: Hugh Grant, Alan Rickman, Emma Thompson, Kate Winslet
character: 4 Anne, Lucy 5 Fanny 6 Elinor 8 Marianne
director: Ang Lee
sensei: 6 master 7 teacher
art: 3 Zen 4 judo 6 karate
locale: 5 Japan
milieu: 4 dojo
senseless: 3 mad 4 idle, null, numb, vain 5 blind, flaky, goony, inane, no-win 6 flakey, insane, wanton 7 trivial 8 headless 9 half-baked, unfeeling, unmeaning 10 irrational, unthinking
knock ~: 4 kayo 5 floor 6 lay out 9 overpower
see also inane
senselessness: 5 folly 6 idiocy 8 nonsense
sense of __: 4 self 5 humor, smell
Sense of Beauty, The
author: George Santayana
Sense of Wonder, The
author: Rachel Carson
senses: 6 reason, sanity
bring to one's ~: 5 alert 6 wake up
Senses Working Overtime
artist: XTC
sensibility: 5 taste 7 feeling, finesse, insight, reality 8 attitude, judgment, keenness 9 awareness, intuition, rationale
sensible: 4 sage, sane, wise 5 aware, lucid, right, smart, sober, solid, sound 6 astute, cogent, shrewd, steady, trusty 7 knowing, logical, mindful, politic, prudent, sapient, tenable 8 all there, analytic, coherent, discreet, informed, methodic, physical, rational, together 9 advisable, astucious, attentive, cognizant, conscious, judicious, observant, practical, pragmatic, realistic, sagacious, temperate, unextreme 10 analytical, consistent, discerning, farsighted, legitimate, observable, reasonable, unromantic
be ~ of: 3 see 4 know 5 grasp 6 fathom 7 cognize, discern 8 perceive 9 apprehend 10 understand
of: 6 wise to
sensing device: 5 radar, sonar
sensitive: 3 raw 4 fine, keen, kind, soft, sore 5 sharp 6 gentle, kindly, liable, polite, subtle, tender, touchy, tricky, wise to 7 feeling, gallant, heedful, knowing, mindful, nervous, painful, politic, precise, psychic, refined, tactful, tuned in 8 delicate, discreet, gracious, obliging, reactive, skittish, ticklish, unstable 9 cognizant, conscious, courteous, emotional, excitable, formative, irritable, judicious, observant, receptive, unselfish 10 diplomatic, discerning, high-strung, perceiving, perceptive, precarious, responsive, thoughtful, unhardened, vulnerable
one: 6 empath
people get them: 5 vibes
sensitivity: 3 ear 4 tact 5 heart 7 allergy, feeling, finesse 8 delicacy, keenness, subtlety, sympathy 9 awareness, tolerance
sensitivity __: 5 group
Sensodyne: 10 toothpaste
alternative: *see* toothpaste
sensor: 6 feeler
sensory: 5 aural, optic 6 neural, ocular, phonic, visual 7 audible, lingual, tactile 8 acoustic, afferent, auditory, hearable 9 olfactive, olfactory, receptive 10 acoustical, ophthalmic

sensualist: 4 roué 8 hedonist 9 epicurean
__-sent: 6 heaven
Senta: 6 Berger
sentence: 3 rap 4 jail, rule, term, text, time 5 blame, edict, hitch, judge, order 6 dictum, punish, ruling, settle 7 adjudge, censure, condemn, confine, convict, impound, mete out, passage, penalty, put away, verdict 8 decision, imprison, judgment, penalize, sanction 9 proscribe, utterance 10 punishment
  analyze a ~: 5 parse
  break: 3 dot 4 dash 5 colon, comma 6 period 8 ellipsis
  one whose ~ is complete: 5 ex-con
  part: 4 verb, word 6 adverb, clause, object, phrase 7 subject 9 adjective, predicate
  pass ~: 5 judge 7 convict
  reduce a ~: 6 pardon 7 commute
  serve a ~: 6 do time
  server: 3 con 5 lifer 6 inmate 7 convict 8 jailbird, prisoner, yardbird
  structure: 7 grammar
sentences, like some: 5 run-on
sententious: 7 laconic 8 pedantic 9 axiomatic 10 pedantical
sentience: 4 life 9 awareness
sentient: 5 aware 7 knowing 9 conscious, observant 10 responsive
sentiment: 4 bias, love, view 5 slant, toast 6 belief, pathos 7 emotion, feeling, leaning, opinion, passion, posture, romance, thought 8 attitude, judgment, penchant, position 9 affection, inclining 10 compliment, conviction, partiality, persuasion, propensity
sentimental: 4 soft 5 corny, hokey, mushy, sappy, silly, soppy, sweet, vapid, weepy 6 dreamy, drippy, loving, sirupy, sugary, syrupy, tender 7 maudlin, mawkish, tearful 8 affected, dewy-eyed, effusive, poignant, romantic, schmalzy, shmaltzy, touching 9 emotional, nostalgic, schmaltzy
  one: 5 softy 6 softie
  overly ~: 4 icky 5 gushy, mushy, sappy, soupy, weepy
sentimentality: 3 goo 4 corn, glop, mush 5 slush 6 bathos
Sentimental Journey, A
  author: Laurence Sterne
sentinel: 5 guard, watch 6 patrol, picket, sentry 7 lookout 8 guardian, watchman 10 doorkeeper, gatekeeper
Sentinel: 5 paper 9 newspaper
  locale: 7 Orlando
Sentinel, The (2006 film)
  cast: Michael Douglas, Eva Longoria, Kiefer Sutherland
Sentra: 3 car 4 auto 6 Nissan
  cousin: 6 Altima
sentry: 5 guard, watch 6 picket 7 lookout 8 sentinel 10 doorkeeper, gatekeeper
  duty: 5 vigil, watch
  like a good ~: 5 alert, awake
  order: 4 halt
__ Sen Yung: 6 Victor
Seoul: 4 city, town 7 capital
  GI: 3 ROK
  locale: 5 Korea
  river: 3 Han
SEP: 3 IRA
sepals
  flower ~: 5 calyx
separable: 10 dissoluble
separate: 3 one, rip 4 fork, free, lone, only, part, rend, rive, sift, skim, snap, sole, sort, tear, undo, vary, wean 5 alone, apart, break, fence, group, leave, loose, other, sever, split, unfix, unmix, unpeg 6 assign, assort, bisect, blouse, branch, cleave, cut off, depart, detach, divide, filter, go away, loosen, parted, screen, secede, single, spread, strain, sunder, unique, unlike, unlink, unwind, varied, winnow 7 asunder, break up, deviate, disjoin, dissect, distant, diverge, diverse, divided, divorce, insular, isolate, private, pull out, radiate, removed, rope off, rupture, scatter, seclude, several, severed, split up, tear off, unalike, unravel, variant, various 8 alienate, break off, classify, close off, come away, contrast, cut apart, cut in two, detached, discrete, disjoint, distinct, disunite, estrange, insulate, isolated, laminate, peculiar, set apart, singular, solitary, sundered, uncouple 9 bifurcate, come apart, different, disengage, divergent, draw apart, interrupt, intervene, partition, punctuate, scattered, segregate, sequester, single out, take leave, unrelated 10 autonomous, come undone, disconnect, disjointed, distribute, far between, individual, particular, respective, unattached
  go ~ ways: 4 fork, part 5 leave, split 7 break up, disband, diverge, pull out, scatter, split up
  in a ~ place: 5 aside
  prefix: 3 apo-
Separate __: 4 Ways 5 Lives 6 Tables
Separate __, A: 5 Peace
separated: 4 lone 5 alone, apart, cleft, in two 6 single 7 asunder 8 sundered 10 disjointed
Separate Lives (1985 song)
  artist: Phil Collins, Marilyn Martin
separately: 5 alone, apart, aside, per se 6 apiece, singly, solely 8 one by one
Separate Ways (song)
  artist: Journey, Elvis Presley
separating: 7 between
separation: 3 gap 4 gape, rift 5 break, space, split 6 schism 7 breakup, divorce, parting, rupture, split-up, veering 8 cleavage, contrast, distance, disunion, division, farewell 9 defection, departure, exclusion, partition, severance, sundering 10 alienation, comparison, detachment, difference, disruption, divergence, extraction
separation of __: 6 powers
separatist: 5 rebel 9 dissident, sectarian
Sephardic language: 6 Ladino
Sephia: 3 car, Kia 4 auto
sepia: 3 ink 5 brown, color 7 grayish
  relative: *see* brown color
Sepoy Mutiny center: 5 Delhi
Sept-__: 4 Iles
septa-
  predecessor: 4 hexa-
  successor: 4 octa-, octo-
September: 5 month
  birthstone: 8 sapphire
  predecessor: 3 Aug. 6 August
  sign: 5 Libra, Virgo 6 Scales, Virgin 7 Balance
  successor: 3 Oct. 7 October
September 13: 4 ides
September 5: 5 nones
September Morn (1980 song)
  artist: Neil Diamond
septembre: 4 mois 5 month 6 French 9 September
  follower: 7 octobre
  preceder: 4 août
septic: 5 germy, toxic 8 virulent 9 poisonous 10 insanitary
septic __: 4 tank
septillion combining form: 5 yotta-
septillionth combining form: 5 yocto-
septum: 4 wall 8 membrane
sepulchral: 6 somber 9 cavernous, unearthly
sequel: 5 chain, issue, story 6 ending, epilog, payoff, result, series 7 closing, outcome, spin-off 8 epilogue, follow-up 9 aftermath, finishing 10 conclusion
  title starter: 3 son 5 son of
sequence: 3 row, run 4 flow 5 array, chain, cycle, order, round, suite, train 6 course, series, streak, string 7 program 8 grouping, ordering 9 gradation, placement 10 catenation, continuity, graduation, perpetuity, procession, succession
sequential: 4 next 5 later 6 serial 9 following
sequentially: 6 in turn
sequester: 4 hide 6 cut off, set off 7 isolate, retreat, seclude, secrete 8 cloister, close off, draw back, ensconce, hide away, insulate, separate, set apart, withdraw 9 segregate 10 commandeer, confiscate
sequestered: 5 quiet 6 hidden, lonely 7 insular, private, recluse 8 secluded, solitary 9 reclusive 10 cloistered
sequin: 5 money 7 spangle 10 decoration
sequins, apply: 5 sew on
__ sequitur: 3 non
sequoia: 4 tree
  locale: 10 California
  relative: 7 redwood
__ sequoia: 5 giant
Sequoia: 3 SUV 4 park 6 Toyota
  locale: 10 California
ser.
  see sermon
sera: 4 whey 8 vaccines 10 antitoxins, antivenins, inoculants
__ sera: 5 buona
Serafita
  composer: Ruggiero Leoncavallo
seraglio: 5 haram, harem, harim 6 hareem
  chamber: 3 oda 4 odah
serai: 3 inn 6 imaret
  site: 5 oasis
serape: 5 scarf, shawl
seraph: 5 angel
seraphic: 4 holy 5 pious 7 angelic, saintly 8 heavenly 9 angelical, celestial
__ será, será: 3 qué
Serb: 4 Slav 6 Balkan
Serbia: 6 nation 7 country
  bovine: 4 Busa
  capital: 8 Belgrade
  city: 3 Nis 5 Vrsac 7 Novi Sad 8 Belgrade, Podorica, Subotica 10 Kragujevac
  dance: 4 kolo
  former capital: 3 Nis
  neighbor: 6 Bosnia 7 Albania, Croatia, Hungary, Romania 8 Bulgaria
  saint: 4 Sava
sere: 3 dry 4 arid 5 unwet 7 bone-dry, dried up, parched, wizened 8 dried out, droughty, rainless, withered 9 infertile, juiceless, shriveled, unfertile, waterless 10 dehydrated, desertlike, desiccated
Serena: 8 Williams
  sister: 5 Venus
serenade: 4 sing 5 music 6 ballad
  dawn ~: 4 alba
  instrument: 4 lute
  the moon: 3 bay 4 howl
Serenade
  author: James M. Cain
  painter: Jan Steen
__ Serenade, The: 6 Donkey
serendipitous: 5 blest, lucky 6 casual 7 blessed, charmed, favored, helpful, on a roll 9 fortunate, on a streak 10 auspicious, felicitous, fortuitous
serendipity: 4 luck 6 chance 8 fortuity, good luck
Serendipity (2001 film)
  cast: Kate Beckinsale, John Cusack, Jeremy Piven
serene: 4 calm, cool, easy, even, fair, meek, mild 5 clear, quiet, sober, staid, still, stoic 6 at ease, gentle, low-key, mellow, placid, poised, sedate, smooth, steady 7 amiable, at peace, content, equable, halcyon, idyllic, pacific, patient, relaxed, restful, stoical, unfazed, unmoved 8 amicable, carefree, composed, in repose, laid-back, pastoral, peaceful, reserved, tranquil 9 collected, easygoing, impassive, peaceable, quiescent, temperate, unexcited, unruffled, unworried 10 Apollonian, nonchalant, rippleless, unagitated, untroubled
__ Serene Highness: 3 Her
Serengeti: 5 plain
  animal: 4 lion 5 eland, hyena, zebra 6 hyaena, impala
  dweller: 5 Masai 6 Maasai
  group: 5 pride
  locale: 6 Africa 8 Tanzania
Serenissima
  author: Erica Jong
__ Serenitatis: 4 Mare
serenity: 4 calm, ease 5 peace, poise, quiet 7 concord, harmony 8 calmness, quietude 9 composure, placidity, quietness, stillness 10 equanimity, sedateness

serf: **4** esne, hand, peon **5** helot, slave **6** thrall, vassal, worker **7** bondman, chattel, colonus, peasant, servant, subject, villain, villein
ender: **3** dom
of a ~: **6** feudal
serfdom: **4** yoke **7** slavery **9** servitude
serge: **5** cloth, twill **6** fabric **8** material
bane: **4** lint
Serge: **5** Lifar **8** Reggiani **9** Diaghilev
sergeant: **3** NCO **4** rank, York **6** Friday, noncom, Pepper **7** officer, Preston, Snorkel
address: **3** APO
call: **3** hep, hup
command: **4** halt **5** march **6** at ease
denial: **5** no sir
like a ~: **8** enlisted
major: **3** NCO
mess ~: **4** cook
subordinate: **3** PFC, pvt. **7** private **8** corporal
superior: **2** lt. **5** lieut. **10** lieutenant
voice: **4** bark, roar, snap, yell **5** growl, shout, snarl
sergeant __: **5** major
__ sergeant: **3** top **5** drill, first, lance, staff **6** master
Sergeant Preston of the Yukon (CBS drama)
cast: Richard Simmons (Sgt. Preston)
dog: **4** King
horse: **3** Rex
Sergeant York (1941 film)
cast: Walter Brennan, Gary Cooper, Joan Leslie
composer: Max Steiner
director: Howard Hawks
Sergei: **6** Esenin **7** Aksakov **9** Prokofiev **10** Eisenstein
see also Russian
Sergey: **4** Brin **5** Bubka **8** Korolyov **9** Diaghilev, Prokofiev
see also Russian
Sergio: **5** Leone **6** García **7** Franchi
Sérgio: **6** Mendes
Sergiu: **10** Comissiona
Se Ri __: **3** Pak
__ seria: **5** opera
serial: **5** story **7** ensuing, going on, regular, sequent **9** continual, continued, following **10** continuing, sequential, succeeding, successive
link: **5** nexus
serial __: **5** comma **6** number, rights
Serial Mom (1994 film)
cast: Ricki Lake, Kathleen Turner, Sam Waterston
director: John Waters
series: **3** row, run, set **4** file, flow, line, list, rank, suit, tier **5** array, chain, cycle, group, order, queue, range, round, scale, suite, train **6** catena, column, course, parade, sequel, sitcom, streak, string **7** battery, program **8** category, sequence **9** gradation, soap opera **10** continuity, procession, round robin, succession
connected ~: **5** nexus
ender: **3** etc.
last of a ~: **3** end
repeating ~: **5** cycle
separator: **5** comma
starter: **4** mini
__ Series: **5** World
__ serif: **4** sans
serious: **3** bad, big **4** deep, dire, grim, hard, ugly **5** acute, grave, heavy, major, sober, solid, staid, stern, tough **6** devout, fervid, honest, no joke, sedate, severe, solemn, somber, urgent **7** arduous, crucial, deadpan, earnest, fervent, genuine, pensive, sincere, subdued, weighty **8** grievous, menacing, pressing, profound, resolute, resolved, sobering, studious, terrible **9** big-league, dangerous, difficult, humorless, important, laborious, momentous, strenuous, unamusing, unsmiling **10** deliberate, determined, formidable, inexpiable, meaningful, no-nonsense, portentous, thoughtful
offense: **4** tort **5** arson, crime, heist, theft **6** felony, holdup **7** assault, robbery, treason **8** burglary, delictum **10** kidnapping
Serious: **5** Yahoo
seriously: **4** hard, very **5** badly, quite **6** cool it, sorely **7** for real, gravely, soberly, sternly, to heart **8** actively, for keeps, intently, sedately, severely, solemnly, terribly, urgently **9** fervently, harmfully, intensely, sincerely, zealously **10** critically, deplorably, grievously, menacingly, perilously, resolutely, vigorously
not ~: **5** in fun
seriousness: **5** depth **6** fervor, import, moment, weight **7** earnest, gravity, urgency **8** enormity, sobriety **9** heaviness, sincerity, solemnity, staidness, sternness
Serkin, Peter: **7** pianist
Serling, Rod: **2** MC **5** emcee
TV: Night Gallery, The Twilight Zone
sermon: **4** talk **6** advice, homily, lesson, speech, tirade **7** address, lecture, monolog, oration, service **8** harangue **9** discourse, monologue, preaching **10** vocalizing
Buddha ~: **5** sutra
deliver a ~: **6** preach
ender: **4** amen, ette
passage: **4** text
spot: **5** mount
Sermon __ Mount: **5** on the
sermonist: **5** padre **6** orator **8** preacher
sermonize: **5** orate, speak, spout, teach **6** preach **7** address, lecture **8** perorate **9** discourse, exprobate, pound into
serous: **5** fluid **6** liquid **7** aqueous
Serpens: **13** constellation
neighbor: **5** Libra
star in ~: **4** Alya
serpent: **3** asp **5** adder, krait, snake, viper **6** animal, hisser **7** reptile, traitor **8** ophidian
combining form: **4** ophi- **5** ophio-
ender: **3** ine
home: **4** Eden
like a ~: **5** scaly
Pharaoh's ~: **6** uraeus
sound: **4** hiss
__ serpent: **3** sea
Serpent and the Rainbow, The
setting: **5** Haiti
Serpent and the Rope, The
author: Raja Rao
serpentine: **3** sly **4** arch, wavy, wily **5** slick, snaky **6** artful, crafty, curved, shifty, shrewd, tricky **7** crooked, cunning, mineral, sinuous, winding **8** tortuous, twisting, writhing **9** dangerous, deceptive **10** meandering
form: **3** ess
line: **9** arabesque
mottled ~: **4** verd **5** verde
serpent's mouth
name meaning ~: **7** Phineas
Serpent's Tooth
author: Faye Kellerman
Serpico: **4** book, film
author: Peter Maas
cast: Al Pacino
director: Sidney Lumet
dog: **5** Alfie
Serra, Junípero: **5** padre **10** missionary
serrate: **5** ridgy, score **6** jagged, ridged, uneven **7** unlevel **8** lacerate
serrated: **5** sharp **6** jagged, ragged, ridged, scored, zigzag **7** notched, sawlike, toothed **8** indented, sawtooth **10** saw-toothed
Serta
competitor: **5** Sealy **7** Simmons
Sert, José: **6** artist **7** painter, Spanish
serum: **4** whey **7** vaccine **8** medicine **9** antitoxin **10** medication
give ~: **6** inject
milk ~: **4** whey
__ serum: **5** blood, truth **6** immune
serv.
see service
Servadac: **6** Hector
servant: **4** amah, cook, hand, help, maid, mozo, page, serf **5** slave, valet **6** butler, drudge, flunky, helper, lackey, live-in, menial, minion, puppet, server, thrall **7** flunkey, lacquey, villein **8** domestic, factotum, follower, hireling, retainer **9** attendant, launderer
civil ~: **7** officer **8** official **10** politician
garb: **6** livery
of India: **4** amah, ayah, maty **5** matee
starter: **3** man **4** bond, maid
__ servant: **5** civil **6** public
Servant of the Bones
author: Anne Rice
servants: **4** help **5** staff
Servants of Twilight, The
author: Dean Koontz
serve: **2** do **3** act, aid, fit, hit **4** feed, give, help, pass, play, suit, tend, toil, work **5** avail, do for, labor, nurse **6** accept, act for, answer, assist, attend, dish up, fulfil, handle, oblige, profit, regale, set out, squire, supply, wait on **7** benefit, care for, carry on, deliver, dish out, fulfill, perform, present, promote, provide, satisfy, suffice, work for **8** attend to, function, minister, wait upon **9** discharge, look after, officiate, put in play **10** administer, distribute, do one's duty, minister to
a meal: **4** feed, wait **6** wait on
as: **9** represent
a sentence: **6** do time
drinks: **4** pour
out-of-bounds ~: **5** fault
voided ~: **3** let
well: **3** ace
wine: **6** decant
serve one __: **5** right
server: **4** tray **6** carhop, waiter **7** servant **8** waitress **9** attendant, lazy Susan
handout: **4** menu
__ server: **7** process
service: **3** aid, job, use **4** duty, help, mass, mend, rite, sext, turn, wear, work **5** asset, avail, favor, labor, nones, prime, terce, value **6** action, combat, matins, prayer, ritual, sermon, supply, wait on **7** benefit, liturgy, offices, station, utility, vespers, worship **8** business, ceremony, compline, courtesy, function, kindness, military, overhaul, wait upon **10** active duty, assistance, employment, observance, profession, usefulness
agency: **5** VISTA
area: **5** plaza
award: **3** tip
bad ~ result: **5** no tip
be of ~: **5** avail, stead
branch: **3** USA, USN **4** Army, Navy, USAF, USMC **7** Marines **8** Air Force
charge: **3** fee
church ~: **4** Mass **7** worship
club: **3** VFW **4** Elks, YMCA, YMHA, YWCA, YWHA **5** Lions **6** Amvets, Rotary **7** Kiwanis
compel into ~: **9** conscript
end ~: **6** resign
error: **3** let **5** fault
game: **6** tennis
lip ~: **4** cant **7** mockery **8** pretense **9** hypocrisy, phoniness **10** pharisaism, pretension, sanctimony
morning ~: **5** terce **6** matins
of ~: **5** utile **6** aidful, useful
out of ~: **6** closed
paid ~: **6** employ
part of a ~: **3** cup **4** dish, fork **5** knife, plate, spoon
people: **8** military
perfect ~: **3** ace
press into ~: **3** use **6** enlist
put back into ~: **5** reuse
religious: **4** mass, sext **5** nones, prime, terce **6** matins **7** liturgy, vespers **8** compline
stay in the ~: **4** reup
tree fruit: **4** sorb
see also air force, army, military, navy
service __: **4** road **6** center, charge, module **7** station
service __ smile: **5** with a
__ service: **3** air, lip, tea **4** curb, debt, food, maid, news, room, wire **5** civil **6** active, postal, prayer, public, silent, social **7** foreign, yeoman's
__-service: **4** full, self
__ Service: **4** Room **6** Forest, Secret
serviceable: **4** good **5** handy, of use, utile **6** aiding, usable, useful

7 durable, helpful, useable 8 salutary, valuable 9 assistive, operative, practical
service-academy freshman: 4 pleb 5 plebe
serviceperson: 7 recruit, soldier, warrior
career ~: 5 lifer
Service, Robert: 4 poet 8 Canadian
work: The Shooting of Dan McGrew
__ services: 5 armed, human
services of, obtain the: 3 use 4 book, hire 5 enrol 6 employ, engage, enlist, enroll, line up, secure, sign up, take on 7 appoint, charter, recruit, reserve 8 contract 10 commission
service station: 6 garage
job: 3 LOF 4 lube 6 tune-up
purchase: 3 gas 8 gasoline
servicewoman: 3 WAC, WAF
serviette in America: 6 napkin
servile: 3 low 4 base, mean, meek, oily, ugly 5 lowly 6 abject, craven, humble, menial 7 fawning, ignoble, passive, slavish, subject, wimpish 8 beggarly, obedient, obeisant, unctuous 9 adulatory, groveling 10 despicable, submissive
be ~: 3 bow 4 fawn 5 kotow, slave 6 grovel, kowtow 8 fawn over
one: 5 toady 6 lackey 7 lacquey
servility: 8 humility 10 submission
serving: 5 piece, plate, share 6 active, entrée 7 portion
a purpose: 5 of use, utile
piece: 4 bowl, tray 5 plate
utensil: 5 ladle, spoon
__-serving: 4 self
servitor: 5 toady 6 fawner, flunky 7 flunkey 8 courtier, follower 9 attendant, flatterer, sycophant 10 bootlicker
servitude: 3 job 4 work, yoke 5 bonds 6 chains, thrall 7 bondage, peonage, serfdom, slavery 9 captivity, obedience, vassalage
symbol: 4 yoke
sesame: 3 til 4 teel
confection: 5 halva 6 halvah 7 halavah
open ~: 6 ticket 8 password 10 hocus-pocus
plant: 3 til 5 benne, benny
product: 4 seed
seeds: 5 benne, benny
sesame __: 3 oil 4 seed 5 paste
__ sesame: 4 open
Sesame and Lilies
author: John Ruskin
Sesame Street
character: 3 Sam, Zoe 4 Bert, Elmo 5 Ernie, Oscar 6 Kermit, Muppet, Rosita 7 Big Bird
lesson: 4 ABCs
network: 3 PBS
__ Sese Seko: 6 Mobutu
sess.: 3 mtg.
session: 4 meet, term 5 forum, rally 6 caucus, huddle, period 7 hearing, meeting, sitting, workout 8 assembly 9 concourse, gathering 10 conference, discussion
be in ~: 3 sit 4 meet 7 convene
bull ~: 3 gab, jaw, rap, yak 4 chat, talk 7 palaver 10 conference, discussion
court ~: 5 trial 6 assize
full-group ~: 6 plenum
returned to ~: 5 remet, resat
schedule: 6 agenda
training ~: 6 lesson
__ session: 3 jam, rap 4 bull 5 joint, skull
Sessue: 8 Hayakawa
sestina: 4 poem 5 verse
set: 2 TV 3 aim, dip, fit, fix, gel, kit, lay, mob, pat, put 4 band, bent, body, camp, cast, clan, clot, crew, curl, drop, fast, firm, gang, jell, levy, make, mien, name, pack, park, plop, post, prop, rate, rest, sect, sink, sort, sure, team, tune, wave 5 affix, align, aline, allot, apply, array, batch, bunch, class, clump, covey, crowd, embed, fixed, given, group, imbed, inlay, limit, lodge, mount, order, party, place, plant, plunk, point, price, raise, ready, rigid, scene, sited, solid, stage, staid, stake, stand, stick, stiff, suite, telly, tight, trite, usual 6 adjust, agreed, anchor, assess, assign, braced, bundle, circle, clique, clutch, decide, decree, direct, fasten, firm up, gaggle, gelate, go down, harden, impose, incite, inlaid, insert, instal, intent, jelled, little, locate, narrow, ordain, orient, outfit, placed, primed, rooted, series, stable, stated, strict, whip up, zero in 7 arrange, assured, battery, certain, cluster, congeal, coterie, decided, deposit, descend, dictate, dispose, doublet, encrust, faction, implant, incrust, in-group, install, in stone, lay down, limited, located, petrify, prepare, regular, scenery, situate, special, specify, stiffen, subside, thicken 8 allocate, arranged, assembly, cemented, concrete, constant, decide on, decisive, definite, demeanor, embedded, ensconce, estimate, hardened, indurate, initiate, instruct, ironclad, locked in, pinpoint, prepared, presence, receiver, regulate, required, resolute, resolved, situated, solidify, specific, standard, stubborn 9 agree upon, appointed, coagulate, concluded, confirmed, customary, delineate, designate, determine, disappear, establish, immovable, in granite, instigate, introduce, iron-jawed, make ready, obstinate, preordain, prescribe, ready to go, scheduled, specified, stabilize, steadfast, stipulate, stringent, tenacious, unbending 10 assemblage, assortment, collection, compendium, decide upon, deportment, determined, entrenched, fraternity, gelatinize, inflexible, in position, positioned, prescribed, prevailing, sound stage, stipulated, television, undoubtful, unwavering, unyielding
about: 5 begin, enter, start 6 assume, launch, let rip, tackle, take up 8 approach, get going 9 undertake
against: 3 pit 6 down on, oppose 8 alienate
all ~: 5 ready 6 primed 7 groomed 8 prepared 10 raring to go
apart: 4 part, save 5 lay by, lay up, sever, split, store 6 cut off, detach, devote, divide, enisle, unlink 7 disjoin, earmark, isolate, lay away, put away, reserve, rope off, split up, store up 8 break off, dedicate, disunite, reserved, sanctify, separate, uncouple 9 preferred, segregate, sequester 10 disconnect, pigeonhole
aside: 4 hold, save 5 allot, allow, amass, annul, lay by, lay up, put by, quash, store, table, waive 6 cancel, devote, refuse, repeal, revoke 7 abeyant, abolish, earmark, lay away, put away, rescind, reserve, rope off, store up 8 allocate, laid away, override, overrule, overturn, reserved, salt away 9 designate, in reserve, supersede 10 pigeonhole
at: 4 rate 6 assail, attack 7 go after, lay into 8 appraise, assailed, attacked, position 9 appraised, establish, went after 10 positioned
at odds: 6 divide 7 break up, disrupt, quarrel 8 alienate, disunite, estrange 9 disaffect
back: 4 mire, slow 5 delay 6 detain, hang up, hinder, hold up, impede, retard, slow up 7 bog down, reverse 8 slow down 9 depressed
by: 7 lay away, put away
cry: 6 places
dead ~: 5 rigid 8 resolute, stalwart 9 immovable, obstinate 10 inexorable, purposeful, relentless, unwavering, unyielding
down: 3 lay, lit, put 4 alit, copy, land, note 5 enter, light, lower, place, write 6 record 8 register 9 chronicle, formulate
ender: 3 off, out 4 back, line 5 screw
eyes on: 3 see, spy 6 look at, regard
firmly: 5 embed, posit, rivet 6 anchor
foot in: 5 enter, get to, reach 6 come to 8 arrive at
forth: 2 go 3 say 4 give, pose, show, tell 5 begin, couch, leave, speak, start, state, voice, write 6 depart, detail, embark, let rip, recite, travel 7 declare, expound, express, go ahead, head out, itemize, move out, narrate, produce, propose, push off 8 commence, describe, get going, propound, start out, vocalize 9 enunciate, expound on, introduce, predicate, verbalize 10 articulate, hit the road
free: 5 clear, let go, loose, unpen, untie 6 loosen, ransom, redeem, rescue, unbind, unhand 7 absolve, manumit, release, unloose 8 liberate 9 discharge, liberated 10 unhindered
get ~: 3 fix 4 prep 5 equip, prime, ready 6 fit out, gear up, warm up 7 arrange, prepare 8 mobilize, organize, rehearse 10 pave the way, square away
in: 5 began, begin, start 6 arrive, harden 7 arrived, implant, started 8 commence, hardened, take hold 9 commenced 10 take effect
in motion: 3 act 4 open, spur 5 begin, impel, shake, spark, start 6 launch 7 trigger 8 activate, mobilize, touch off 9 originate 10 lead the way
in one's ways: 4 firm, iron 5 balky, fixed, rigid, stern, stiff, stony 6 dogged, mulish, ornery 7 adamant, piggish, willful 8 contrary, indurate, obdurate, perverse, resolute, stubborn 9 fractious, hard-nosed, immovable, obstinate, pigheaded, tenacious, unbending 10 bullheaded, hard-bitten, hardheaded, headstrong, inflexible, refractory, unshakable, unyielding
in stone: 5 solid 6 steady 7 adamant 9 immovable, permanent, unbending 10 inexorable
jet ~: 5 elite, haves 7 in-crowd, society 8 well-to-do 9 beau monde 10 glitterati, haute monde, socialites, upper crust
leaders ~ it: 4 pace
matched ~: 4 pair
movie ~: 3 lot 10 sound stage
off: 2 go 4 fire 5 begin, grace, leave, shoot, start 6 depart, embark, ignite, incite, let rip, redeem 7 explode, garnish, go ahead, move out, produce, trigger 8 commence, contrast, detonate, get going, outweigh, start out 9 discharge, sequester 10 hit the road, sally forth
on: 6 affect, assail, attack 7 assault, lay into 8 resolute
(on): 8 hellbent
one back: 4 cost
on end: 5 tip up
one's cap for: 3 woo 4 date 5 court 6 pursue 7 take out 9 cultivate
one's hand to: 3 ink 4 sign
one's heart on: 4 pine, want, wish 5 yearn 6 desire
one's sights on: 3 see 6 aim for, behold, look at
on its way: 6 convey, propel 8 dispatch
out: 2 go 3 lay 4 show, tell 5 begin, leave, plant, serve, start 6 define, depart, detail, embark, let rip, relate, travel 7 display, explain, go ahead, itemize, push off, recount, specify, take off 8 commence, describe, get going 9 elucidate, undertake 10 hit the road, sally forth
out on: 5 enter
right: 3 fix 6 adjust 7 correct, rectify 8 disabuse 10 make good on
sail: 6 embark 7 push off, ship out 8 go aboard, put to sea, shove off 9 leave port
side by side: 5 check, liken, weigh

SE

6 equate, oppose, size up **7** analyze, balance, compare, examine, inspect, stack up **8** contrast, parallel **9** correlate **10** correspond, scrutinize
start a ~: **5** serve
starter: **3** off, sun **4** back, bone, hand, head, lock, moon, type **5** heavy, quick, thick **6** tumble
store by: **5** prize, value **6** accept, bank on, esteem, rely on **7** count on, respect, trust in **8** depend on, hold with **9** count upon
straight: **3** fix **5** right **6** orient **7** correct **8** disabuse **9** reconcile
the pace: **4** lead
to: **7** pitch in, quarrel
to rights: **6** remedy **7** restore **9** refurbish
up: **3** fix, rig **4** back, book, form, hoax, rear **5** begin, build, erect, found, frame, mount, pitch, raise, start, trick **6** create, entrap, instal, launch, lay for **7** arrange, compose, elevate, install, prepare, program, swindle, usher in **8** assemble, engineer, generate, initiate, organize, schedule **9** construct, establish, institute, introduce, originate, subsidize, victimize **10** constitute, inaugurate, prearrange
(up): **4** line
upon: **3** mob **5** lunge, ran at **6** assail, attack, have at, waylay **7** assault, lay into
VIP: **4** star
set ___: **3** off, out **4** back, down, free, sail, shot, upon **5** about, a date, apart, aside, a trap, forth, piece, point
set ___ by: **5** store
set ___ example: **4** a bad **5** a good, a poor
set ___ for: **5** a date, a trap
set ___ in: **4** foot
set ___ standard: **5** a high
set ___ to: **4** fire
___ set: **3** all, box, get, jet, tea **4** data, dead, desk, nail, null **5** chess, horsy, smart, stage **6** socket **7** dinette
___-set: **4** deep, hard, mind
Set
brother: **4** Isis **6** Osiris
victim: **6** Osiris
___ Set: **4** Desk **7** Erector
seta: **7** bristle
setback: **4** blow, jolt, loss, snag **5** delay, hitch **6** defeat, glitch, hiccup, holdup, mishap, outlay, rebuff **7** bad luck, letdown, licking, regress, relapse, reverse, tragedy, trouble **8** accident, hard luck, hiccough, obstacle, reversal, slowdown **9** about-face, hindrance **10** difficulty, impediment, misfortune, regression
Seth: **5** Rogen **6** Kantor, Thomas **9** Pecksniff
brother: **4** Abel, Cain
parent: **3** Eve **4** Adam
son: **4** Enos **5** Enosh
set in ___: **6** motion
set in one's ___: **4** ways
set on ___: **4** fire
Seton: **4** Anya **6** Ernest **9** Elizabeth
Seton ___ University: **4** Hall
Seton, Anya: **6** writer
work: Dragonwyck
Foxfire
My Theodosia
set one ___: **4** back, wise
Seton, Elizabeth Ann: **5** saint
set one's ___ for: **3** cap
set one's ___ in order: **5** house
set one's ___ on: **4** eyes **5** heart **6** sights
Seton Hall: **10** university
athletes: **7** Pirates
conference: **7** Big East
locale: **9** New Jersey
sètte: **5** seven **7** Italian
follower: **4** otto
preceder: **3** sei
settee: **4** seat, sofa **5** bench, couch, divan **7** seating **8** loveseat **9** furniture
setter: **3** dog **5** canid **6** canine
starter: **3** pin **4** pace, type **5** photo, trend
___ setter: **3** jet, job **5** Irish **6** Gordon **7** English
set the ___: **4** pace
set the ___ for: **5** stage
set the ___ on fire: **5** world
Set the Night to Music (1991 song)
artist: Roberta Flack, Maxi Priest
Set This House on Fire
author: William Styron
setting: **4** site **5** scene, stage, venue **6** locale, medium, milieu **7** context, horizon **8** ambience, backdrop, distance, location, mounting, position **9** framework, situation **10** adjustment, background
starter: **3** off **4** film, pace, type **5** trend
switch ~: **2** on **3** off **4** stop
___ setting: **5** place, stage
settle: **3** end, fix, lay, pay, put, sit **4** calm, land, live, lull, park, plop, rest, rule, seal, seat, sink, stay **5** abide, agree, allay, clear, droop, dwell, judge, light, lodge, order, pay up, perch, pitch, place, prove, quell, quiet, relax, remit, roost, solve, spend, squat, stand, still **6** adjust, alight, assure, belong, choose, clinch, decide, define, encamp, figure, finish, harden, instal, locate, make up, pay off, pony up, redeem, refund, repose, reside, sedate, soothe, square, verify **7** achieve, appoint, arrange, bed down, clean up, clear up, confirm, descend, dispose, inhabit, install, iron out, mediate, rectify, resolve, satisfy, specify, squelch, subside, work out **8** colonize, complete, conclude, dispatch, ensconce, finalize, make good, nail down, reassure, regulate, sentence, square up, take root, transact **9** arbitrate, determine, discharge, dispose of, establish, homestead, liquidate, make peace, negotiate, reconcile, stabilize, touch down **10** adjudicate, come to rest, compromise, put an end to
a deal: **3** ice
a debt: **3** pay **5** pay up, remit, repay **9** discharge
a score: **3** get **5** repay **6** avenge
back: **4** laze **5** relax
down: **5** light, marry, relax **6** gentle, mature, mellow, nestle **7** cool off **8** blow over
in: **4** nest **5** lodge **6** encamp, nestle **7** inhabit
on: **3** tap **4** cull, name, pick, take, vote **5** adopt, draft, elect, favor **6** assign, choose, decide, desire, opt for, prefer, select **7** appoint, pick out **8** delegate, draw lots, nominate **9** designate, determine, single out
upon: **4** name
settle ___: **4** down, into
settled: **3** lit **4** alit, firm, over, sure **5** given, staid **6** intent, mature, secure, stable, static, steady **7** assured, certain, decided **8** constant, decisive, definite, in the bag, ironclad, occupied, positive **9** permanent, sedentary **10** conclusive, inevitable, inveterate, purposeful, unchanging, undoubtful
in: **10** accustomed
thickly ~: **5** dense, urban **8** populous
settlement: **4** base, deal, mise, pact, town **6** accord, colony, diktat, hamlet, payoff, refund, treaty **7** compact, outpost, payment **8** contract, covenant, decision, defrayal **9** agreement, community, discharge, occupancy, reckoning, residence **10** adjustment, compromise, conclusion, foundation
settlement ___: **5** house
settle one's ___: **4** hash
settler: **7** pioneer **8** colonist, newcomer **9** colonizer **10** inhabitant
dispute ~: **6** umpire **7** arbiter
migration: **4** trek
settlings: **5** dregs **7** deposit, grounds
set-to: **3** row **4** bout, fray, spat, tiff, tilt **5** brawl, brush, clash, fight, melee, run-in, scrap, words **6** fracas, tussle **7** contest, quarrel, rhubarb, wrangle **8** argument, brouhaha, catfight, conflict, skirmish, squabble, struggle **9** encounter **10** contention, donnybrook
setup: **4** form, plan, trap **5** order **6** design, entrap, format, layout, scheme, system **7** machine, pitfall **8** easy mark, scenario, strategy **9** framework, procedure, structure
set up ___: **4** shop
Setzer: **5** Brian
___ seul: **3** pas
Seurat, Georges: **6** artist, French **7** painter
Seurat's Lunch
artist: Ben Shahn
Seuss, Dr.
real name: Theodor Seuss Geisel
work: The 500 Hats of Bartholomew Cubbins
And to Think That I Saw It on Mulberry Street
The Butter Battle Book
The Cat in the Hat
The Foot Book
Fox in Socks
Green Eggs and Ham
Hop on Pop
Horton Hatches the Egg
Horton Hears a Who
How the Grinch Stole Christmas
Hunches in Bunches
I Can Read With My Eyes Shut
If I Ran the Circus
If I Ran the Zoo
I Had Trouble Getting to Solla Sollew
King's Stilts
The Lorax
McElligot's Pool
Norval the Great
Oh Say Can You Say
Oh, the Places You'll Go!
Oh, the Thinks You Can Think!
On Beyond Zebra
There's a Wocket in My Pocket!
Thidwick: The Big-Hearted Moose
What Was I Scared Of?
Yertle the Turtle
You're Only Old Once!
___ Seuss Geisel: **7** Theodor
Sevareid: **4** Eric
Sevastopol: **4** city, port, town
locale: **6** Crimea, Russia
seven: **3** VII **6** heptad, number
best of ~: **6** series
biggest of ~: **4** Asia **7** Pacific
combining form: **4** hept-, sept- **5** hepta-, septi-
days: **4** week
ender: **4** teen
in French: **4** sept
in German: **6** sieben
in Italian: **5** sette
in Japanese: **4** nana
in Portuguese: **4** sete
in Spanish: **5** siete
man has ~ of them: **4** ages
one of ~: **3** sea **9** continent
times a week: **7** diurnal
seven ___ sins: **6** deadly
seven-___ boots: **6** league
seven-___ cake: **5** layer
seven-___ stud: **4** card
Seven ___: **4** Seas **5** Sages
Seven ___ Arts: **6** Lively
Seven ___ Itch, The: **4** Year
Seven ___ of Architecture, The: **5** Lamps
Seven ___ of Rome: **5** Hills
Seven ___ of the World: **7** Wonders
Seven ___ of Wisdom: **7** Pillars
Seven ___ to Baldpate: **4** Keys
Seven ___ to Noon: **4** Days
Seven ___ War: **5** Weeks', Years'
Seven Against Thebes
author: Aeschylus
Seven Brides for Seven Brothers (1954 film)
cast: Howard Keel, Jane Powell, Russ Tamblyn
director: Stanley Donen
Seven Cities of ___: **6** Cibola
Seven Days in May: **4** film **5** novel
author: Fletcher Knebel
cast: Kirk Douglas, Ava Gardner, Burt Lancaster, Fredric March
Seven Descents of Myrtle, The
author: Tennessee Williams
Seven Dwarfs
any of the ~: **4** toon **5** miner
one of the ~: **3** Doc **5** Dopey, Happy **6** Grumpy, Sleepy, Sneezy **7** Bashful
workplace: **4** mine
Seven Gothic Tales
author: Isak Dinesen

Seven Hills of __: 4 Rome
Seven Keys to Baldpate
author: Earl Derr Biggers
Seven Lamps of Architecture, The
author: John Ruskin
seven-league __: 5 boots
Seven Lively Arts: 7 musical
composer: Cole Porter
Seven-Per-Cent Solution, The (1976 film)
cast: Alan Arkin, Robert Duvall, Vanessa Redgrave, Nicol Williamson
director: Herbert Ross
Seven Pillars of Wisdom
author: T.E. Lawrence
Seven Pounds (2008 film)
cast: Rosario Dawson, Woody Harrelson, Will Smith
sevens: 4 game 6 fan-tan
Seven Samurai, The (1954 film)
cast: Toshiro Mifune
director: Akira Kurosawa
Seven Seas: 8 dressing
alternative: 8 Wish-Bone 11 Good Seasons
Seven Storey Mountain, The
author: Thomas Merton
seventeen-__ locust: 4 year
Seventeen (1955 song)
artist: Boyd Bennett and his Rockets, Fontane Sisters
Seventeen (novel)
author: Booth Tarkington
dog: 6 Flopit 8 Clematis
seventh
day activity: 4 rest
heaven: 6 utopia 7 rapture 8 empyrean, paradise
in ~ heaven: 4 glad 5 happy, merry 6 blithe, cheery, elated, jovial, joyful, joyous, upbeat 7 gleeful, pleased, tickled 8 blissful, cheerful, ecstatic, euphoric, exultant, jubilant, mirthful, thrilled 9 delighted, overjoyed, rejoicing
seventh __: 6 heaven
seventh-__ stretch: 6 inning
Seventh __, The: 4 Seal, Veil
Seventh-__ Adventist: 3 Day
Seventh Commandment, The
author: Lawrence Sanders
Seventh Seal, The (1957 film)
cast: Bibi Andersson, Max von Sydow
director: Ingmar Bergman
Seventh Son (1965 song)
artist: Johnny Rivers
Seventy-Six Trombones instrument: 6 cornet
seven-up: 4 game 5 pitch 8 card game 9 old sledge
Seven Wise Men home: 6 Greece
Seven Wonders __ World: 5 of the
Seven Wonders site: 6 Rhodes
Seven Year Itch, The (1955 film)
cast: Tom Ewell, Marilyn Monroe
director: Billy Wilder
Seven Years in Tibet
setting: 4 Lasa 5 Lhasa
Seven Years' War loser: 6 Russia
sever: 3 cut, hew, lop 4 part, rend, rive, slit, tear 5 carve, slash, slice, split 6 bisect, cleave, cut off, detach, divide, lop off, sunder, unlink 7 abandon, abscind, chop off, disband, disjoin, dissect, divorce, hack off, rupture, scissor, split up, tear off 8 break off, cut apart, cut in two, disjoint, dissolve, disunite, separate, set apart, shear off, slice off, uncouple 9 interrupt, partition, segregate, terminate 10 disconnect, dissociate, put an end to, put asunder
severable: 10 dissoluble
several: 4 a few, many, rare, some 6 divers, legion, plural 7 diverse, handful, special, various 8 assorted, distinct, numerous, separate, specific 9 different 10 infrequent, particular, respective, sprinkling
ender: 4 fold
more than ~: 4 a lot, lots, many
severance: 7 fission 9 defection, sundering 10 separation
severance __: 3 pay
Severance: 4 Joan
severe: 3 bad 4 dour, firm, grim, hard, sore 5 acute, bleak, bossy, cruel, exact, grave, harsh, heavy, hefty, nasty, picky, plain, rigid, rough, sharp, sober, stark, stern, stiff, tough 6 barren, biting, bitter, brutal, fierce, mortal, rugged, strict, strong, taxing, trying, wicked 7 arduous, ascetic, austere, caustic, cutting, drastic, extreme, intense, mordant, onerous, radical, serious, Spartan, violent, weighty 8 critical, despotic, exacting, grievous, grueling, hard-line, incisive, obdurate, pitiless, resolute, rigorous, scathing, terrible, terrific, toilsome 9 bare-bones, dangerous, demanding, difficult, draconian, hard-nosed, inclement, intensive, merciless, punishing, strenuous, stringent, unadorned, unbending, unfeeling, unsmiling, unsparing 10 astringent, despotical, forbidding, implacable, inexorable, inflexible, iron-fisted, ironhanded, iron-willed, no-nonsense, oppressive, relentless, tyrannical, unpleasant
more ~: 5 worse
severed: 4 torn 8 separate
severely: 4 hard 5 badly 6 firmly 7 acutely, gravely, harshly, roughly, sharply, sternly 8 forcibly, markedly, strictly, urgently 9 extremely, intensely, painfully, seriously, viciously 10 critically, powerfully, rigorously
Severinsen: 3 Doc 4 Carl
severity: 5 rigor 6 degree 7 cruelty, gravity, tyranny 8 iron hand, violence 9 intensity 10 inclemency, oppression
Severn: 4 city, town 5 river 6 Darden
city on the ~: 9 Annapolis
feeder: 3 Usk
locale: 8 Maryland
River locale: 5 Wales 7 England
tributary: 3 Wye 4 Avon
Severo: 5 Ochoa
Severus: 5 Roman 6 Caesar
Sevigny: 5 Chloë
Sevilla: 4 city, town
locale: 5 Spain
Seville: 3 car 4 auto, city, port, town 5 David 6 citrus, orange 8 Cadillac
locale: 5 Spain
orange: 6 bitter
relative: *see* citrus
worker: 6 barber, Figaro
Seville and the Chipmunks, David
Chipmunks: Alvin, Simon, Theodore
song: Alvin's Harmonica (1959) The Chipmunk Song (1958) Witch Doctor (1958)
Sèvres: 4 city, town 5 china
locale: 6 France
Se vuol ballare: 4 aria
sew: 3 hem 4 bind, darn, mend, seam, tack 5 baste, patch, piece, quilt, run up 6 fasten, repair, stitch, suture 9 embroider
loosely: 4 tack 5 baste
on: 5 affix
up: 3 end, ice 5 close 6 assure, clinch, finish, stitch 8 complete, conclude, finalize, nail down, transact 10 accomplish, consummate, make sure of, monopolize
sewan: 4 peag 5 beads 6 wampum
Seward: 4 city, town 7 William
locale: 6 Alaska
purchase: 6 Alaska
Seward Peninsula
cape: 4 Nome
city: 4 Nome
locale: 6 Alaska
Seward's Folly: 6 Alaska
Sewell: 3 Joe, Rip 4 Anna 5 Rufus
sewer: 3 sty 4 pipe 5 drain 7 conduit, culvert 10 storm drain
entrance: 7 manhole
org.: 5 ILGWU
__ sewer: 5 storm
sewing: 9 housework
kit item: 3 awl 5 spool 6 button, needle
machine attachment: 6 hemmer
machine part: 6 bobbin
sewing kit: 4 etui 5 etwee
stitch: 4 purl
trim: 5 inkle
sewing __: 3 awl, kit 5 table 6 circle, needle 7 machine
sex: 6 gender
appeal: 5 oomph
__ sex: 4 fair
Sex and the City (HBO sitcom)
cast: Kim Cattrall (Samantha Jones)
Kristin Davis (Charlotte York)
Cynthia Nixon (Miranda Hobbes)
Chris Noth (Mr. Big)
Sarah Jessica Parker (Carrie Bradshaw)
Sex and the Single Girl (1964 film)
cast: Lauren Bacall, Tony Curtis, Henry Fonda, Natalie Wood
sexes, for both: 4 coed
sex, lies, and videotape (1989 film)
cast: Peter Gallagher, Andie MacDowell, Laura San Giacomo, James Spader
director: Steven Soderbergh
sextant successor: 5 loran
sextet: 4 band 8 ensemble
sextillion combining form: 5 zetta-
sextillionth combining form: 5 zepto-
sexton: 6 beadle
Sexton, Anne: 4 poet
work: Live or Die
Sexy Eyes (1980 song)
artist: Dr. Hook
Seychelles: 4 isls. 5 isles 6 nation 7 country, islands
capital: 8 Victoria
island: 4 Mahé 7 La Digue, Praslin
money: 4 cent 5 rupee
Seyfried: 6 Amanda
Seymour: 4 Alan, Anne, Cray, Jane 6 Cassel
__ Seymour Hoffman: 6 Philip
Seymour, Jane: 7 actress
film: Live and Let Die (1973) Somewhere in Time (1980)
TV: Dr. Quinn Medicine Woman
Sez who?: 6 oh yeah
S.F.
see San Francisco
Sfax: 4 city, town
locale: 7 Tunisia
SFC: 3 NCO
SFO: 7 airport
SFX, part of: 7 effects, special
__ S. Gilbert: 7 William
__ S. Grant: 7 Ulysses
sgt.
see sergeant
__ sgt.: 4 tech.
Sgt. Bilko (1996 film)
cast: Dan Aykroyd, Phil Hartman, Steve Martin
Sha __: 4 La La, Na Na
__ Shabbat: 4 Oneg
shabby: 3 sad 4 bare, drab, junk, mean, poor, punk, torn, worn 5 cheap, dingy, dinky, dowdy, faded, mangy, petty, ratty, seamy, seedy, shady, sorry, tacky, tatty, tired 6 crumby, crummy, frayed, frowsy, frowzy, frumpy, humble, mangey, meager, paltry, ragged, rotten, ruined, scummy, shoddy, sleazy, sordid, stingy, unjust, unkind, unneat 7 chintzy, decayed, ignoble, low-down, miserly, pitiful, rickety, ruinous, run-down, scruffy, squalid, unkempt, worn-out 8 beggarly, decaying, decrepit, desolate, shameful, slipshod, tattered, time-worn, untended, unworthy, wretched 9 miserable, moth-eaten, neglected, ungroomed 10 bedraggled, broken-down, despicable, ramshackle, threadbare, undeserved
dresser: 5 frump
shabby-__: 7 genteel
shack: 3 hut 4 shed 5 abode, bower, cabin, house, hovel, hutch, lodge 6 lean-to, shanty 7 cottage, shelter
like a ~: 5 crude
__ Shack: 4 Love 5 Radio, Sugar
Shackelford: 3 Ted
shackle: 3 tie 4 band, bind, bond, cuff, gyve, iron, yoke 5 chain, cramp, tie up 6 fetter, hamper, hogtie, pinion 7 enchain, leg iron, manacle 8 enfetter, handcuff 9 hamstring 10 impediment
site: 5 ankle
starter: 3 ram
shackles: 8 trammels 9 bracelets
Shackleton, Ernest: 3 Sir 7 British 8 explorer
shad: 4 fish 7 herring
ender: 3 fly 4 blow, bush 5 berry
product: 3 roe

shade: **3** dim, hue **4** cast, dash, hide, hint, mask, tint, tone, veil **5** bedim, blind, bogey, color, cover, ghost, gloom, haunt, stain, tinct, tinge, touch, trace, umbra **6** amount, awning, breath, canopy, darken, deepen, degree, fantom, nuance, screen, shield, spirit, trifle, wraith **7** becloud, blacken, conceal, cover up, curtain, dimness, fantasm, obscure, phantom, protect, shelter, shutter, specter, umbrage **8** coolness, covering, darkness, disguise, penumbra, phantasm, presence, tone down **9** adumbrate, gradation, obscurity, suspicion, variation **10** apparition, camouflage, gloominess, suggestion
starter: **3** eye, sun **4** lamp **5** night
see also color
shade __: **4** tree
__ shade: **6** window
__ Shade: **7** Evening
shaded: **5** leafy
Shade of Difference, A
author: Allen Drury
__ Shade of Pale, A: **6** Whiter
__ Shade of Winter: **5** A Hazy
shader: **4** tree
shades: **7** glasses **10** sunglasses
reason for ~: **5** glare
shadiness: **8** venality **10** corruption, illegality
shading: **4** tint **6** nuance
mark with ~: **5** hatch
shadow: **3** dim, dog, spy, tag **4** dark, dusk, gray, grey, haze, hint, kohl, pall, soul, tail, veil **5** bedim, cloud, cover, gloom, relic, shred, spare, spy on, stalk, tinge, touch, trace, trail, umbra, watch **6** darken, fantom, makeup, pursue, screen, shield, spirit **7** becloud, dimness, eclipse, epigone, minimum, obscure, phantom, shelter, specter, umbrage, vestige, whisper **8** darkness, imitator, overcast, penumbra, presence, run after **9** accompany, adumbrate, obscurity, suspicion, track down **10** intimation, reflection, silhouette, suggestion
astronomical ~: **5** umbra
beyond the ~ of a doubt: **6** surely
cast a ~: **8** overhang
combining form: **4** scia-, scio-, skia-
eliminator: **5** razor
ender: **3** box **5** graph
eye ~: **4** kohl **5** liner **6** makeup
five o'clock ~: **5** beard **7** stubble
locale: **3** lid **6** eyelid
shadow __ frame: **3** box
__ shadow: **3** eye
Shadow: **3** car **4** auto **5** Dodge
Shadow __, The: **5** knows
Shadow and Act
author: Ralph Ellison
Shadow-A Parable
author: Edgar Allan Poe
shadowbox: **4** spar
Shadowboxer (1996 song)
artist: Fiona Apple
Shadow Dancing (1978 song)
artist: Andy Gibb
Shadowfires
author: Dean Koontz
Shadow Flies, The
author: Rose Macaulay
shadowing: **7** eclipse
Shadowland (1988 album)
artist: k.d. lang
Shadowlands (1993 film)
cast: Anthony Hopkins, Debra Winger
Shadow of a Doubt (1943 film)
cast: Macdonald Carey, Joseph Cotten, Teresa Wright
director: Alfred Hitchcock
Shadow of a Sun, The
author: A.S. Byatt
Shadow of the Vampire (2000 film)
cast: Willem Dafoe, Cary Elwes, John Malkovich
shadow of Virtue, The: **4** fame
Shadow on the Trail
author: Zane Grey
__ Shadows: **4** Dark
Shadows and Fog (1992 film)
cast: Woody Allen, Kathy Bates, John Cusack, Mia Farrow
director: Woody Allen
Shadows on the Rock
author: Willa Cather
shadows, remain in the: **4** lurk
Shadow, The: **9** radio show
garment: **4** cape
nemesis: **4** evil
Shadow, The (1994 film)
cast: Alec Baldwin, Peter Boyle, Penelope Ann Miller
shadowy: **3** dim **4** dark, hazy **5** black, dusky, faded, fuzzy, mirky, murky, muted, vague **6** bleary, blurry, gloomy, hidden, ill-lit, somber **8** nebulous **9** hard to see, lightless, tenebrous, unlighted **10** indistinct
Shadrach (1998 film)
cast: Harvey Keitel, Andie MacDowell
shady: **3** dim **4** dark, foul **5** dusky, leafy, queer, vague, wrong **6** cloudy, louche, shabby, shifty, shoddy, somber, tricky **7** corrupt, covered, crooked, devious, dubious, illegal, suspect **8** arboreal, darkened, infamous, off-color, screened, shameful, slippery, unsavory **9** dishonest, notorious, sheltered, tree-lined, underhand, unethical **10** fly-by-night, inglorious, prohibited, scandalous, suspicious, umbrageous
deal: **5** cheat **6** con job **10** corruption
place: **5** arbor, bower, grove **6** gazebo
walk: **4** mall
Shadyac: **3** Tom
Shady Business, A
author: Honoré de Balzac
SHAEF
commander: **3** DDE
sector: **3** ETO
Shaffer: **4** Paul **5** Peter **7** Anthony
Shaffer, Anthony
spouse: Diane Cilento
Shaffer, Peter: **7** British **10** playwright
work: Amadeus
Black Comedy
Equus
Five Finger Exercise
The Royal Hunt of the Sun
shaft: **3** bar, pit, ray, rod **4** axis, axle, beam, duct, dupe, mine, pole, post, well **5** cheat, pylon, stalk **6** column, fleece, pillar, tongue, tunnel **7** defraud, javelin, mislead, passage, swindle, two-time, upright **8** flimflam **10** passageway, run a game on
air ~: **6** intake
auto: **3** cam **4** axle
column ~: **5** scape
combining form: **5** scapi-
end of a ~: **4** adit
feathered ~: **5** arrow
groove: **6** keyway
light ~: **3** ray **4** beam **7** sunbeam **8** moonbeam
mine ~: **3** pit **5** winze
starter: **3** cam **4** jack, mine, rock **5** crank, drive **7** counter
worker: **5** miner
__ shaft: **3** air **4** wind **5** drive
Shaft (1971 film)
cast: Moses Gunn, Richard Roundtree
director: Gordon Parks
Shaft (2000 film)
cast: Christian Bale, Samuel L. Jackson, Vanessa Williams
Shaft Theme (1971 song)
artist: Isaac Hayes
shag: **3** nap, rug, run, rya **4** bird, pile **5** chase, dance **6** carpet, hairdo
cousin: **3** bob
ender: **4** bark
shaggy: **5** bushy, furry, hairy, nappy, rough **6** pilose, pilous, ragged, rugged, unneat **7** hirsute, ruffled, unkempt, unshorn **8** uncombed **10** long-haired
animal: **3** yak **4** bear **5** bison, bruin
blossom: **6** dahlia
coat: **4** hair
combining form: **4** dasy-
__ Shaggybreeches: **6** Ragnar
shaggy cap: **8** mushroom
Shaggy D. A., The (1976 film)
cast: Tim Conway, Dean Jones, Suzanne Pleshette
shaggy-dog
story: **4** joke
unlike a ~ story: **5** short
Shaggy Dog, The (1959 film)
cast: Annette Funicello, Jean Hagen, Tommy Kirk, Fred MacMurray
dog: **7** Chiffon
Shaggy Dog, The (2006 film)
cast: Tim Allen, Kristin Davis, Danny Glover
shaggymane: **8** mushroom
Shah: **5** exile, Jahan, Jehan, ruler, title **6** gerent **7** Krishna, monarch
land: **4** Iran **6** Persia
language: **5** Farsi
name: **4** Reza
Shah Jahan
building site: **4** Agra
wife: **5** Mahal
Shahn, Ben: **6** artist **7** painter
Shaka __: **4** Zulu
shake: **3** jar, jog, wag **4** bump, flap, flit, foil, jerk, jolt, lose, move, reel, rock, sway, tick, toss, wake, wave, whip, wink **5** alarm, avoid, churn, cower, dance, daunt, dodge, drink, elude, greet, quail, quake, swing, upset, waken, worry **6** bother, dismay, dither, dodder, frappe, jiggle, joggle, jostle, jounce, justle, minute, quaver, quiver, rattle, recess, recoil, ruffle, second, shimmy, shiver, stir up, totter, tremor, unglue, wabble, waggle, weaken, wobble **7** agitate, chatter, disturb, flicker, flitter, fluster, flutter, horrify, perturb, shimmer, shudder, stagger, startle, tremble, unnerve, vibrate **8** brandish, convulse, disquiet, distress, frighten, get out of, sprinkle, throw off, unsettle, unstring **9** discomfit, fluctuate, make waves, oscillate, palpitate, take aback **10** demoralize, discompose, disconcert, earthquake, intimidate
a fist at: **8** threaten
a leg: **3** fly, hie, rip, run, zip **4** dart, dash, flit, move, race, rush, stir, tear, zoom **5** hurry, scoot, speed **6** barrel, boogie, gallop, hasten, hustle, move it, rocket, scurry **7** floor it, hop to it, quicken, scamper, speed up **8** step on it **9** hotfoot it, skedaddle **10** burn rubber, get a move on, get hopping, hightail it
down: **4** bilk, test **5** bleed, bully, frisk **6** coerce, extort, lean on **7** ransack, squeeze **9** blackmail **10** experiment, run a game on
ender: **3** out **4** down
fair ~: **6** chance
hands: **6** make up
hands on: **4** seal **5** agree, close **6** clinch, settle **7** confirm **8** finalize
hands with: **4** meet **5** greet
ingredient: **4** milk
in prescriptions: **4** agit.
off: **3** rid **4** drop, foil, lose, shun **5** avoid, clear, dodge, elude, evade, outdo, repel **6** remove **7** discard **8** dislodge, get rid of, unburden **10** escape from, knock loose
starter: **4** hand, head
up: **3** jar, mix, rid **4** faze, jolt, stun **5** addle, alarm, churn, purge, roust, scare, shock, upset **6** rattle, remove, ruffle **7** agitate, disturb, perturb, startle, stupefy, trouble, unnerve **8** bewilder, clean out, clear out, convulse, disquiet, distress, mistreat, overturn, surprise, unsettle **10** disconcert, reorganize
violently: **5** upset **6** quiver **7** agitate, disturb **8** unsettle **10** discompose
shake __: **3** off **4** a leg, down **5** hands
__ shake: **4** fair, milk **6** square
Shake (1965 song)
artist: Sam Cooke
Shake __: **4** It Up **5** 'N Bake
shake a __: **3** leg
shake a __ at: **5** stick
shakedown: **6** racket, search **7** jobbery, swindle **8** practice **9** blackmail, extortion, rehearsal **10** experiment
shakedown __: **6** cruise, flight
Shakedown (1987 song)
artist: Bob Seger

Shake It Up (1981 song)
artist: Cars
shake like ___: 5 a leaf
shaken: 5 fazed 6 addled, scared, uneasy 8 unstrung 9 unsettled
it may be ~: 3 leg 4 fist
shake one's ___: 4 head
shakeout: 8 upheaval 9 recession
shaker: 3 VIP 6 afuché, cabasa, dynamo 8 chocalho
contents: 4 NaCl, salt
mover and ~: 4 doer 5 mogul 6 leader
___ shaker: 4 bone, salt 6 pepper
Shaker ___: 3 Hts.
Shake, Rattle and Roll (1954 song)
artist: Bill Haley and His Comets
Shaker Heights: 4 city, town
locale: 4 Ohio
Shakers: 4 sect
founder: Ann Lee
Shaker, Why Don't You Sing
author: Maya Angelou
shakes: 7 jitters, tension, willies
have the ~: 6 shiver
in two ~ of a lamb's tail: 3 now 4 anon, soon 6 at once, in a sec, pronto 7 hastily, quickly, rapidly, shortly 8 directly, promptly, right now, speedily 9 forthwith, in a minute, in a second, right away 10 this moment
no great ~: 4 so-so 8 mediocre, ordinary
two ~ of a lamb's tail: 3 sec 4 jiff 5 jiffy, trice
Shakespearean ___: 6 sonnet
Shakespeare in Love (1998 film)
cast: Judi Dench, Joseph Fiennes, Gwyneth Paltrow, Geoffrey Rush
Shakespeare, William: 4 bard, poet 7 British 10 playwright
adverb: 4 anon
contemporary: 5 Bacon
cry: 3 fie
device: 5 aside
edition: 5 Folio
forest: 5 Arden
forte: 5 drama
king: 4 Lear
muse: 5 Erato
plaint: 4 alas
prince: 3 Hal
product: 4 play
river: 4 Avon
segment: 3 act 5 scene
shrew: 4 Kate
sprite: 5 Ariel
suffix: 3 ana, est, eth
teen: 5 Romeo 6 Juliet
theatre: 5 Globe
verb: 4 hast, hath 5 seest
very foolish fond old man: 4 Lear
villain: 4 Iago
wife: 4 Anne
work: All's Well That Ends Well
Antony and Cleopatra
As You Like It
The Comedy of Errors
Coriolanus
Cymbeline
Hamlet
Henry IV
Henry V
Henry VI
Julius Caesar
King John
King Lear
Love's Labour's Lost
Macbeth
Measure for Measure
The Merchant of Venice
The Merry Wives of Windsor
A Midsummer Night's Dream
Much Ado About Nothing
Othello
Pericles
Richard II
Richard III
Romeo and Juliet
The Taming of the Shrew
The Tempest
Timon of Athens
Titus Andronicus
Troilus and Cressida
Twelfth Night
Two Gentlemen of Verona
The Winter's Tale
shake-up: 5 purge, upset 10 revolution
Shake Your Body (1979 song)
artist: Jackson 5
Shake Your Booty (1976 song)
artist: KC and the Sunshine Band
Shake Your Groove Thing (1979 song)
artist: Peaches and Herb
Shake Your Love (1987 song)
artist: Debbie Gibson
shaking: 9 tremulous, vibration
hands: 6 custom, ritual 9 formality 10 convention
starter: 5 earth
shako: 3 hat 8 headgear
feature: 5 plume
Shakur: 5 Tupac
shaky: 4 weak 5 dizzy, jumpy, rocky, tense, timid 6 aquake, flimsy, infirm, jiggly, uneasy, unfirm, unsafe, unsure, wabbly, wobbly 7 aquiver, dubious, jittery, nervous, quaking, reeling, rickety, suspect, tenuous, unclear, unsound 8 doubtful, insecure, perilous, rattling, rootless, unstable, unsteady, wavering, yielding 9 dangerous, faltering, jellylike, quivering, spasmodic, squeamish, teetering, tentative, tottering, trembling, tremorous, tremulous, uncertain, unsettled 10 frightened, indecisive, precarious, ramshackle, suspicious, unbalanced, unreliable, up in the air
Shalala: 5 Donna
Sha La La (song)
artist: Al Green, Manfred Mann
shale: 7 mineral
product: 3 oil
rock formed from ~: 5 slate
Shaler: 4 city, town
locale: 4 Penn.
Shalhoub, Tony: 5 actor
TV: Monk
Shalimar Gardens
locale: 5 India 6 Lahore
Shalit, Gene: 6 critic
shall: 4 will 6 plan to 8 intend to
ender: 4 owed 5 owing
...___ shall die: 3 or I
___ Shall Have Music: 4 They
Shall I compare thee to a summer's day?: 4 poem 6 sonnet
author: William Shakespeare
...shall not ___ from the earth: 6 perish
shallot: 5 onion 6 allium, veggie 9 vegetable
kin: 4 leek 6 garlic
shallow: 3 low 4 dull, flat, vain, weak 5 inane, petty, shelf, shoal 6 flimsy, narrow, paltry, simple, slight 7 cursory, sketchy, surface, trivial, unsound, vacuous 8 ignorant, piddling, skin-deep, trifling 9 frivolous, half-baked 10 nonserious, uncritical, unprofound, unthinking
Shall we? answer: 4 Let's
Shall We Dance (1937 film): 7 musical
cast: Fred Astaire, Ginger Rogers
music: George and Ira Gershwin
Shall We Dance (2004 film)
cast: Richard Gere, Jennifer Lopez, Susan Sarandon
Shall We Dance?
composer: Oscar Hammerstein, Richard Rodgers
___-shally: 6 shilly
shalom: 5 hello, peace 6 Hebrew 7 goodbye 8 greeting
Shalom: 6 Harlow 8 Aleichem
sham: 3 act, ape, lie 4 cant, copy, fake, hoax, jive, mock, pose, ruse, sell, show 5 bluff, bogus, cheat, dummy, false, farce, feign, feint, fraud, lying, phony, put on, quack, quasi, shuck, spoof, trick 6 deceit, dupery, ersatz, facade, fake it, fakery, forged, humbug, phoney, pseudo, sucker, unreal, untrue 7 assumed, cover-up, falsity, feigned, forgery, imitate, mislead, mockery, pretend, snow job, swindle 8 artifice, flimflam, imposter, impostor, pretense, simulate, so-called, spurious, travesty 9 charlatan, contrived, deception, falsehood, hypocrisy, imitation, imposture, insincere, invention, mare's nest, phoniness, pretended, simulated, synthetic, ungenuine 10 artificial, caricature, fabricated, factitious, false front, fictitious, fraudulent, misleading, mountebank, play possum, substitute, subterfuge
___ sham: 6 pillow
___ Sham: 6 Sam the
Shamah
grandfather: 4 Esau
shaman: 5 druid 6 cleric, healer, priest, wizard 7 prophet
find: 4 omen
specialty: 5 spell
wisdom: 4 lore
Shambala (1973 song)
artist: Three Dog Night
shamble: 4 poke, ruin, walk 6 loiter, lumber 7 shuffle
shambles: 4 mess 5 babel, botch, chaos, havoc, mix-up, wreck 6 bedlam, mess-up, muddle 7 anarchy, clutter 8 disarray, disorder, madhouse 9 confusion, maelstrom 10 hodgepodge
shame: 3 fie 4 blot, pang, pity, soil 5 abase, abash, guilt, odium, smear, stain 6 debase, defile, humble, infamy, show up, stigma 7 chagrin, decency, degrade, emotion, modesty, mortify, put down, remorse, scandal 8 calamity, contempt, derision, disfavor, disgrace, dishonor, ignominy, reproach, ridicule, take down 9 abashment, discredit, disrepute, embarrass, frown upon, humiliate, penitence, shoot down 10 contrition, disconcert, disgruntle, opprobrium, stigmatize
ender: 5 faced
feel ~ over: 3 rue
put to ~: 4 beat, best 5 abase, outdo 6 exceed, humble, show up 7 eclipse, mortify, surpass 8 outclass, outshine, outstrip 9 humiliate 10 overshadow, tower above
Shame ___!: 5 on you
Shame!: 3 fie, tsk, tut 6 tsk tsk, tut-tut
___ Shame: 4 It's a
shamed: 5 sorry 6 fallen 7 abashed 8 penitent
be ~: 8 lose face
shamefaced: 3 shy 5 sorry 8 sheepish
shameful: 4 base, lewd, vile 5 awful, seamy, shady, sorry, wrong 6 impure, odious, ribald, shabby, shoddy, sordid, vulgar 7 corrupt, ignoble, immoral, obscene, unclean 8 degraded, God-awful, immodest, indecent, infamous, inferior, unworthy 9 dastardly, degrading, nefarious, notorious, reprobate 10 diabolical, inglorious, mortifying, outrageous, profligate, scandalous, unbecoming, villainous
see also awful
shameless: 4 bold, lewd, mean, open, rude 5 brash, saucy, tacky 6 arrant, brassy, brazen, cheeky, wanton, wicked 7 blatant, corrupt, forward, immoral 8 depraved, flagrant, immodest, improper, impudent, indecent, insolent, unchaste 9 abandoned, audacious, barefaced, dissolute, graceless, reprobate, unabashed 10 disgusting, outrageous, profligate, scurrilous, unblushing
be ~: 6 flaunt
Shame on the Moon (1982 song)
artist: Bob Seger
Shamir, Yitzhak: 2 P.M. 7 Israeli
predecessor: 5 Begin, Peres
successor: 5 Peres, Rabin
shampoo: 4 Flex, lave, Pert, wash 5 Breck, clean, Prell, Suave, Wella 6 Tegrin 7 Finesse, Pantene
additive: 4 aloe 6 balsam
bottle word: 5 rinse 6 repeat
feature: 6 lather
measure: 2 pH
oil: 6 jojoba
Shampoo (1975 film)
cast: Warren Beatty, Julie Christie, Carrie Fisher, Lee Grant, Goldie Hawn
director: Hal Ashby
screenwriter: 5 Towne
shampoos, like some: 5 low pH
___ Shamra, Syria: 3 Ras
shamrock: 6 clover
isle: 4 Eire, Erin 7 Ireland
Shamsky: 3 Art
shams, pillow: 5 linen
Shamu: 4 orca
shamus: 2 PI 3 cop, tec 4 narc, nark 5 agent, snoop 6 sleuth

7 gumshoe, officer 9 constable, detective, operative 10 bloodhound, private eye
Shana: 9 Alexander
Sha Na Na
number: 4 oldy 5 oldie
Shandling: 5 Garry
shandy: 5 drink 8 beverage
ingredient: 4 beer 8 lemonade
shandygaff: 5 drink 8 beverage
ingredient: 4 beer 10 ginger beer
Shane: 5 Gould 7 Maxwell 8 MacGowan
Shane (1953 film): 5 oater 7 western
cast: Jean Arthur, Brandon de Wilde, Van Heflin, Alan Ladd, Jack Palance
shanghai: 4 levy 5 draft, force 6 abduct, enlist, induct, kidnap 7 impress, recruit, soldier, warrior 8 inductee 9 conscript 10 commandeer
Shanghai: 4 city, fowl, port, town 7 chicken
locale: 5 China
relative: *see* chicken
river: 7 Huangpu
Shanghai Knights (2003 film)
cast: Jackie Chan, Owen Wilson
Shanghai Noon (2000 film)
cast: Jackie Chan, Lucy Liu, Owen Wilson
director: Tom Dey
Shangri-la: 4 Eden 6 heaven, utopia 7 Elysium 8 paradise
cleric: 4 lama
creator: James Hilton
locale: 4 Asia 5 Tibet
Shangri-las
hometown: Queens
song: Leader of the Pack (1964)
Remember (Walkin' in the Sand) (1964)
Shani: 6 Wallis
Shania: 5 Twain
shank: 3 gam, leg 4 crus, meat, shin, stab
of the ~: 6 crural
__ shank: 4 lamb
Shankar, Ravi: 6 Indian 8 sitarist
daughter: Norah Jones
genre: 4 raga
instrument: 5 sitar
shanks'
by ~ mare: 5 afoot
go by ~ mare: 4 slog, walk 5 leg it, march 6 foot it, hoof it, trudge
Shanna: 4 Reed
Shannen: 7 Doherty
Shannon: 3 Del 4 city, font, town 5 river, Tweed 6 Miller 8 typeface 9 Elizabeth
locale: 4 Eire, Erin 7 Ireland
Shannon (1976 song)
artist: Henry Gross
Shannon, Del
song: Hats Off to Larry (1961)
Keep Searchin' (We'll Follow the Sun) (1964)
Runaway (1961)
Shannon's __: 3 Way
__ Shan Range: 3 Nan
__-shanter: 4 tam-o'
shanty: 3 hut 4 dump, shed, song 5 cabin, house, hovel, lodge, shack 6 lean-to 7 cottage
shape: 3 fit, hew, pat 4 bend, body, case, cast, form, grow, look, make, mint, mold, oval, pear, plan, trim, turn, work 5 adapt, build, carve, forge, frame, guide, guise, knead, model, prune, rhomb, stamp, state, thing 6 beetle, chisel, circle, create, define, devise, embody, fantom, fettle, figure, format, health, imbody, modify, sculpt, sketch, square, tailor, work up 7 chassis, contour, develop, fashion, fitness, octagon, outline, pattern, phantom, prepare, produce, profile, remodel, rhombus, whittle 8 assemble, block out, jaundice, octangle, pentagon, physique, regulate, roughhew, symmetry, take form, triangle 9 condition, construct, curvature, fabricate, lineament, lineation, sculpture, semblance, structure, trapezoid 10 appearance, embodiment, manipulate, silhouette, streamline
beat into ~: 5 forge
bend out of ~: 4 warp
bent out of ~: 5 irate, upset 6 raging 7 furious
get in ~: 3 jog 4 hone, sort, tidy, tone 5 train 7 arrange, rebound, recover, work out 8 exercise, organize
give ~: 4 cast, form, mold 5 forge, model 6 design, sculpt 7 fashion, whittle
in bad ~: 4 soft 5 ratty, unfit 6 bad off, shabby, shoddy 7 pitiful, rundown 8 untended
in good ~: 3 fit 4 able, buff, hale, lean, neat, tidy, trim 5 hardy, ready, sound 6 robust, strong 7 healthy, orderly
lick into ~: 5 coach, groom 8 organize
out of ~: 4 bent, soft 5 rusty, stiff, unfit 6 flabby, sickly 7 untoned 8 lopsided 9 enervated, unhealthy
put in good ~: 5 fix up 6 neaten 10 straighten
starter: 4 ship
take ~: 3 gel 4 form, jell, loom
up: 3 fix 4 form, tidy 5 groom, rally 6 better, enrich, evolve, polish, reform 7 correct, develop, enhance, improve, rectify, sharpen, upgrade 8 progress, regulate 9 come along, condition, go forward, meliorate 10 ameliorate, go straight
__ shape: 4 take
shapeable: 7 plastic 8 formable
__-shaped curve: 4 bell
__-Shaped Room: 4 The L
__-shaped tone: 4 pear
shapeless: 3 lax 5 baggy, vague 8 abnormal, amorphic, deformed, formless, nebulous, unformed 9 amorphous, anomalous, irregular, malformed 10 indefinite, indistinct
mass: 4 blob, glob
Shape Of My Heart (2000 song)
artist: Backstreet Boys
SHAPE
org. that includes: 4 NATO
shaper: 4 adze, file, mold 5 swage
Shapes of Things (1966 song)
artist: Yardbirds
Shape up or __ out!: 4 ship
Shaphat
son: 6 Elisha
shaping: 10 adjustment
tool: 3 die 4 adze 5 gouge, lathe 6 chisel
Shapiro: 4 Karl 5 Artie
Shaq: 5 O'Neal
Shar-__: 3 Pei
shard: 3 bit 4 chip 5 piece, scrap 7 remnant 8 fragment, potsherd
starter: 3 pot
shards: 5 chaff, trash 6 debris 7 remains, rubbish
share: 3 cut, due, lot 4 bite, deal, dose, lend, mete, part, pool, take, wage 5 allot, chunk, claim, cut in, divvy, piece, quota, slice, split, stake, taste, wages, yield 6 assign, bestow, divide, parcel, ration 7 divvy up, dole out, give out, go Dutch, helping, measure, mete out, partake, percent, portion, prorate, section, segment, serving, split up 8 dispense, dividend, division, fraction, fragment, go in with, interest, kickback, pittance, quotient 9 allotment, allowance, apportion, parcel out, partake of, partition 10 allocation, commission, distribute, experience, percentage, proportion, take part in
a side with: 4 abut
a view: 5 agree, match 6 accord, concur 7 conform 9 harmonize 10 go together
biggest ~: 4 bulk
billing: 6 costar
don't ~: 3 hog 10 monopolize
earning: 8 dividend
ender: 4 crop 5 owner 6 holder
fair ~: 4 half
fifty-fifty: 5 halve
ideas: 10 brainstorm
lion's ~: 3 all 4 bulk, mass, most 8 majority
one unlikely to ~: 3 pig
proportional ~: 5 quota
starter: 4 plow, ride
the load: 4 ease, help 6 assist, join in 7 pitch in, relieve 9 cooperate, lend a hand 10 see through
__ share: 5 lion's 6 market
__-share: 4 cost, time
sharecrop: 4 farm
sharecropper: 6 tenant
beast: 4 mule
shared: 5 joint 6 common, mutual, public 8 communal, requited 9 corporate, unanimous 10 collective, reciprocal
feeling: 5 unity 7 empathy, rapport 8 affinity, sympathy
resource: 4 pool
shareholder: 5 owner 8 investor
sharer word: 3 our 4 ours
shares: 5 slice, stock
how some ~ sell: 5 at par
Share the Land (1970 song)
artist: Guess Who
Sharett, Moshe: 2 P.M. 7 Israeli
predecessor: 9 Ben-Gurion
successor: 9 Ben-Gurion
Shari: 5 Lewis 9 Belafonte
Sharif, Omar: 5 actor
film: Doctor Zhivago (1965)
Funny Girl (1968)
Lawrence of Arabia (1962)
The Tamarind Seed (1974)
__ sharing: 3 tax 6 profit 7 revenue
__-sharing: 3 job 4 code, time
Sharing the Night Together (1978 song)
artist: Dr. Hook
shark: 4 fish, mako, tope 5 cheat, crook, fraud, knave, nurse 6 con man, usurer, wizard 7 cheater, dogfish, grifter, hustler, sharper, sharpie 8 chiseler, predator, swindler, thresher 10 hammerhead
ender: 4 skin
environment: 3 sea 5 ocean
feature: 3 fin
flick: 4 Jaws
Hawaiian ~: 4 mano
loan ~: 5 leech 6 lender, usurer 7 Shylock
nurse ~: 4 gata
__ shark: 4 blue, bull, card, loan, mako, pool, sand 5 nurse, tiger
Sharkey: 3 Ray
__ Sharkey: 3 C.P.O.
Sharks: 3 six 4 gang, team
home: 7 San Jose
milieu: 3 ice 4 rink
org.: 3 NHL
rival: *see* hockey team
sport: 6 hockey
shark's fin: 4 soup
Shark Tale (2004 film)
voice cast: Jack Black, Robert De Niro, Angelina Jolie, Will Smith, Renée Zellweger
Shark Trouble
author: Peter Benchley
Sharm al-__: 6 Sheikh
Sharman, Bill: 5 cager
Sharon: 4 Leal, Tate 5 Ariel, Gless, Stone 7 Farrell 8 Lawrence
rose of ~: 6 althea
Sharon, Ariel: 2 P.M. 7 Israeli
predecessor: 5 Barak
sharp: 3 apt, hot, sly 4 able, acid, chic, cold, curt, fast, fine, foxy, keen, rude, sore, sour, tart, wily, wise 5 acerb, acrid, acute, adept, alert, angry, brisk, class, clean, clear, crisp, edged, fresh, harsh, honed, natty, nifty, quick, ready, ritzy, savvy, short, slick, smart, snaky, spiky, spiny, steep, stiff, swank, tined, vivid, windy 6 abrupt, acidic, acuate, adroit, apical, artful, astute, barbed, biting, bitter, brainy, briery, bright, classy, clever, crafty, dapper, dressy, expert, fierce, jagged, keenly, lively, marked, nimble, on time, ornery, peaked, pointy, rancid, severe, shrewd, shrill, snappy, spiked, square, strong, sudden, swanky, thorny, trendy, tricky 7 acerbic, acutely, austere, caustic, cunning, cutting, dashing, exactly, extreme, hurtful, in focus, in style, intense, knowing, learned, legible, odorous, peppery, piquant, pointed, politic, prickly, pungent, raucous, salient, stylish, tapered, violent, voguish, whetted 8 abrasive, abruptly, clear-cut, critical, definite, distinct, explicit, handsome, incisive, keen-eyed, lynx-eyed, on the dot, piercing,

poignant, promptly, sardonic, scathing, serrated, shooting, skillful, slippery, spirited, squarely, stabbing, stinging, suddenly, swindler, tactless, vigilant, vigorous, vinegary, virulent 9 acidulous, acuminate, acuminous, agonizing, astucious, brilliant, excellent, ingenious, inventive, keen-edged, knifelike, observant, on the ball, on the nose, precisely, sagacious, sarcastic, sensitive, splintery, trenchant, underhand, unethical, vitriolic 10 accurately, astringent, discerning, first-class, insightful, knife-edged, needlelike, perceptive, proficient, punctually, rapierlike, responsive, ungracious, well-marked
  combining form: 3 oxy-
  corner: 5 angle
  dresser: 5 dandy
  end: 5 point, spike
  ender: 7 shooter
  flavor: 3 nip, zip 4 bite, kick, tang, zest 6 relish 8 piquancy, pungency 9 spiciness, zestiness
  make ~: 4 hone, whet
  make a ~ turn: 4 veer
  part: 3 jag 4 edge 5 thorn
  practice: 7 swindle 8 trickery
  starter: 4 card
  turn: 3 jog, zag, zig 6 dogleg, zigzag
sharp __ tack: 3 as a
sharp-__: 3 cut, set 4 eyed 5 eared, edged, nosed 6 witted 7 tongued
__ sharp: 4 look
Sharp: 3 Don 6 Dee Dee 7 Phillip
  competitor: 4 Sony
sharp as __: 5 a tack
sharp-cornered: 7 angular, pointed 8 angulose, angulous
Sharp, Dee Dee
  song: Do the Bird (1963)
    Mashed Potato Time (1962)
    Ride! (1962)
    Slow Twistin' (1962)
Sharpe: 7 William
Shar-Pei: 3 dog 5 canid 6 canine 7 Chinese
sharpen: 4 file, hone, whet 5 fix up, grind, strop, taper 6 adjust, better, enrich, polish, reform 7 enhance, improve, shape up, upgrade 8 practice, spruce up 9 acuminate, condition, intensify, meliorate 10 ameliorate
sharpened: 4 keen 5 honed 6 acuate
sharpener: 4 hone 5 strop
sharper: 5 cheat, fraud, knave, quack, shark 6 con man 7 cheater 8 chiseler, swindler
  Sharper __, The: 5 Image
sharp-eyed: 4 wary 5 alert 9 observant
sharp-flavored: 5 tangy
sharpie: 5 knave 6 bad guy
Sharpie: 3 pen 6 marker
sharp-looking: 5 natty 6 spiffy
sharply: 4 hard 8 intently, severely
sharpness: 3 nip 4 bite, edge, tang 5 depth, sense, spice 6 acuity, acumen 8 judgment, keenness 9 intensity, smartness 10 bitterness, cleverness, horse sense

sharps
  key with four ~: 6 E major
  key with three ~: 6 A major
sharpshooter: 5 yager 6 archer 8 marksman
  need: 5 rifle, scope
  org.: 3 NRA
sharp-smelling: 5 acrid
Sharpsteen: 3 Ben
sharp-tasting: 5 tangy 6 bitter 7 pungent
Sharpton: 2 Al
sharp-tongued: 4 acid 5 salty, sassy
  one: 5 shrew
sharp-witted: 6 astute 9 astucious
__ S. Hart: 7 William
Shasta: 3 mtn. 4 lake, peak 5 mount, tribe 8 mountain
  daisy: 5 plant 6 flower
  locale: 8 Cascades 10 California
Shatner, William: 5 actor
  film: Free Enterprise (1999)
    Judgment at Nuremberg (1961)
    Miss Congeniality (2000)
    Star Trek Generations (1994)
    Star Trek III: The Search for Spock (1984)
    Star Trek II: The Wrath of Khan (1982)
    Star Trek IV: The Voyage Home (1986)
    Star Trek-The Motion Picture (1979)
    Star Trek VI: The Undiscovered Country (1991)
  TV: Boston Legal, Rescue 911, Star Trek, T.J. Hooker
Shatt-al-Arab: 5 river
  island in the ~: 6 Abadan
  locale: 4 Irak, Iraq
  port on the ~: 5 Basra, Busra 6 Busrah
shatter: 4 dash, rend, rive, ruin, snap, undo 5 blast, break, burst, crack, crash, crush, smash, split, total, upset, wreck 6 crunch, impair, madden, rattle, ravage, shiver 7 destroy, disable, explode, implode, rupture, smatter, stagger, torpedo, wrack up 8 demolish, dissolve, dynamite, fracture, fragment, splinter 9 devastate, dumbfound, overwhelm, pulverize
  ender: 5 proof
shatterable: 7 fragile
shattered: 5 spent 6 broken, undone 8 in pieces
Shattered
  author: Dick Francis, Dean Koontz
__-shattering: 5 earth
Shaud: 5 Grant
Shaughnessy: 7 Maxwell
Shaun: 7 Cassidy
shave: 3 cut, mow 4 clip, crop, kiss, pare, peel, skim, skin, snip, thin, trim 5 brush, graze, lower, plane, prune, shear, shred, slash, slice, strip, touch 6 barber, cut off, reduce, scrape, sliver 7 cut away, cut back, cut down, shingle, snip off, tonsure, whittle
  prepare to ~: 5 strop
__ shave: 5 close
__-shave: 5 after
Shave __ haircut...: 4 and a
__ Shave: 5 Burma, Rapid 7 Lectric

Shavelson: 8 Melville
shaven: 6 smooth 8 glabrous, hairless
__-shaven: 5 clean 6 smooth
shaver: 3 boy, kid, lad, tad, tot 4 tike, tyke 5 child, razor, youth 6 barber
  aid: 4 foam 6 lather
  electric ~: 5 Braun 7 Norelco 9 Remington
  insert: 5 blade
  lotion: 6 bay rum
  wood ~: 5 plane
Shaver: 5 Helen
shavetail: 2 lt. 5 lieut. 10 lieutenant
  academy: 3 OCS, OTS
shaving: 3 bit 4 chip 5 flake 6 sliver 8 splinter
  mishap: 4 nick
  site: 4 sink
shaving __: 4 soap 5 brush, cream
__ shaving: 5 point
shaving cream: 3 gel 4 foam
  additive: 4 aloe
shavings: 5 trash 7 residue 8 kindling
Shaw: 4 Reta, Stan 5 Artie, Irwin 6 George, Robert 7 Bernard
Shaw, Artie: 11 clarinetist
  genre: 4 jazz
  spouse: Ava Gardner, Evelyn Keyes
Shaw, George Bernard: 5 Irish 6 critic, writer 8 Nobelist 10 playwright
  contemporary: 5 Yeats
  work: Androcles and the Lion
    Arms and the Man
    Back to Methuselah
    Buoyant Billions
    Caesar and Cleopatra
    Candida
    Captain Brassbound's Conversion
    The Devil's Disciple
    Fanny's First Play
    Heartbreak House
    John Bull's Other Island
    Major Barbara
    Man and Superman
    The Man of Destiny
    Mrs. Warren's Profession
    The Philanderer
    Pygmalion
    Saint Joan
    Widowers' Houses
    You Never Can Tell
Shaw, Irwin: 6 writer
  work: Bury the Dead
    Love on a Dark Street
    Mixed Company
    Rich Man, Poor Man
    The Young Lions
shawl: 4 wrap 5 cloak, manta, scarf, stole, throw 6 afghan, sarape, serape 8 covering, mantilla
  Indian ~: 5 pattu
  triangular ~: 5 fichu
shawm: 4 wind 10 instrument
  descendant: 4 oboe
Shawn: 3 Ted 4 Dick 5 Estes 6 Colvin 7 Mullins, Wallace
Shawnee: 4 city, town 5 tribe 6 Indian 7 Amerind 8 language
  locale: 6 Kansas 8 Oklahoma
Shaw, Robert: 5 actor
  film: Black Sunday (1977)
    The Deep (1977)
    From Russia With Love (1963)
    Jaws (1975)
    A Man for All Seasons (1966)
    Robin and Marian (1976)
    The Sting (1973)
    The Taking of Pelham One Two Three (1974)
Shawshank Redemption, The (1994 film)
  cast: Morgan Freeman, Bob Gunton, Tim Robbins
  extra: 5 lifer 6 inmate
  highlight: 6 escape
  setting: 5 Maine 6 prison
shay: 6 chaise 7 vehicle
  one-hoss ~ owner: 6 deacon
Shayne: 6 Robert 7 Michael
Shayne, Michael
  portrayer: 5 Nolan
shazam: 6 presto
she: 3 gal, her 4 lady 5 woman 6 female, madame 7 pronoun 8 daughter
  he and ~: 4 they
  in French: 4 elle
  in Spanish: 4 ella
she-__: 4 wolf 5 devil
she-__ soup: 4 crab
She
  author: H. Rider Haggard
Shea: 4 John 7 stadium 8 ballpark
  player: 3 Met 5 NY Met
sheaf: 5 batch, bunch, stack 6 bundle, quiver 10 collection
She Ain't Worth It (1990 song)
  artist: Bobby Brown, Glenn Medeiros
shear: 3 cut, mow 4 chop, clip, crop, trim 5 prune, sever, shave 6 cut off, dehair, fleece, lop off, remove 7 cut back, scissor, snip off 8 truncate
  ender: 5 water
__ shear: 4 wind
Shearer: 5 Harry, Moira, Norma
Shearer, Moira: 6 dancer 7 actress 8 danseuse 9 ballerina
  film: The Red Shoes (1948)
Shearer, Norma: 7 actress
  spouse: Irving Thalberg
shearing
  candidate: 3 ewe, ram 5 sheep
  output: 4 wool
Shearing, George: 7 pianist
shears: 7 cutters 8 clippers, scissors
  use dressmaker's ~: 4 pink
__ shears: 5 grass 7 pinking, pruning
Shearson partner: 6 Lehman
shearwater: 4 bird
Shea Stadium: 8 ballpark
  see also Shea
sheath: 3 pod 4 skin 5 dress, skirt 6 casing, jacket 7 outside 8 membrane 10 integument
  plant ~: 5 ocrea 6 ochrea
sheathe: 4 case, wrap 6 encase, incase 7 retract
  with metal: 4 clad
sheathing: 4 case, skin
sheaves, grain: 5 shock
Sheb: 6 Wooley
Sheba
  creator: William Inge
  locale: 5 Yemen 6 Arabia
shebang, the whole: 3 all 5 works 10 everything
Shebat: 5 month 6 Hebrew
  follower: 4 Adar
She Believes in Me (1979 song)
  artist: Kenny Rogers

__ she blows!: 4 Thar
She Bop (1984 song)
artist: Cyndi Lauper
Sheboygan: 4 city, town
locale: 9 Wisconsin
She Came to Stay
author: Simone de Beauvoir
Shecky: 6 Greene
__ She Coo?: 4 Who'd
she-crab __: 4 soup
She Cried (1962 song)
artist: Jay and the Americans
shed: 3 hut, rid 4 beam, cast, cede, doff, drop, dump, emit, lose, molt, sell, skin, slip 5 chuck, ditch, exude, forgo, scrap, shack, spill, strip, yield 6 forego, give up, hangar, lean-to, reject, remove, shanty, shower, slough 7 abandon, cast off, diffuse, discard, drop off, forfeit, forsake, let fall, let go of, radiate, scatter, shelter, take off, undress 8 exuviate, forswear, get out of, get rid of, hand over, jettison, part with, sprinkle, throw off, throw out 9 cast aside, disburden, dispose of, exfoliate, foreswear, give forth, pour forth, send forth, slough off, surrender, throw away, toolhouse 10 relinquish
feathers: 4 molt 5 moult
light: 5 shine
light on: 7 clarify, explain 8 illumine, simplify
pounds: 4 diet, slim
Shetland Islands ~: 4 skeo
something to ~: 4 tear
starter: 3 cow 4 wood 5 blood, water
tears: 3 cry, sob 4 bawl, mewl, pule, wail, weep 6 boohoo, snivel 7 blubber, whimper
shed __: 5 a tear
shed __ on: 5 light
__-shedding: 4 load
Shedd's: 6 spread 9 margarine
alternative: 6 Parkay 7 Promise 8 Imperial
She-Devil (1989 film)
cast: Roseanne Barr, Ed Begley Jr., Linda Hunt, Meryl Streep
She Done Him Wrong (1933 film)
cast: Cary Grant, Gilbert Roland, Mae West
She'd Rather Be With Me (1967 song)
artist: Turtles
shee: 5 fairy
Sheed, Wilfrid: 6 writer
Sheedy: 4 Ally
Sheehan: 4 Neil 5 Patty
Sheehan, Patty: 6 golfer
Sheehy: 4 Gail
sheen: 3 wax 4 glow 5 glaze, gleam, glint, gloss, light 6 finish, luster, patina, patine, polish 7 burnish, glitter, shimmer 8 radiance, radiancy 9 shininess 10 brightness, luminosity
give a ~: 5 shine
Sheen: 6 Fulton, Martin 7 Charlie, Michael
Sheena: 6 Easton
Sheena, Queen of the Jungle
chimp: 4 Neal
Sheen, Charlie: 5 actor
brother: Emilio Estevez
father: Martin
film: The Arrival (1996)
Eight Men Out (1988)
Hot Shots! (1991)
Lucas (1986)
Major League (1989)
Platoon (1986)
Terminal Velocity (1994)
The Three Musketeers (1993)
Wall Street (1987)
Young Guns (1988)
spouse: Denise Richards
TV: Two and a Half Men
Sheen, Martin: 5 actor
film: The American President (1995)
Apocalypse Now (1979)
Catch-22 (1970)
The Final Countdown (1980)
Firestarter (1984)
Gettysburg (1993)
Man, Woman and Child (1983)
Wall Street (1987)
son: Charlie, Emilio Estevez
TV: The West Wing
sheep: 3 ram 4 lamb, meat 5 argal, bovid, shapu, stock, toady, urial 6 animal, aoudad, argali, bharal, merino, yes man 7 Babbitt, bighorn, burrhel, Cheviot, mouflon 8 assenter, cimarron, Cotswold, emulator, follower, moufflon 9 followers, livestock 10 conformist
African ~: 6 aoudad, dorper
Asian ~: 3 sha 5 argal, shapu, urial 6 argali, bharal 7 burrhel, Karakul
bear a ~: 4 yean
black ~: 5 rogue 6 bad guy, rascal 9 miscreant, scoundrel 10 delinquent
breed: 5 Devon 6 dorper, Oxford, Romney 7 Cheviot, Karakul, Lincoln, Ryeland, Suffolk 8 Columbia, Cotswold, Dartmoor 9 Hampshire, Leicester, Montadale, Southdown, Wiltshire 10 Corriedale, Dorset Horn, Shropshire
cloned ~: 5 Dolly
coat: 6 fleece
Corsican ~: 7 mouflon 8 moufflon
ender: 3 dog 4 cote, fold, skin 5 berry, shank 6 herder
female ~: 3 ewe
foot: 4 hoof
grease: 5 suint
group: 4 fold 5 drove, flock
like a ~: 4 meek 6 docile, fleecy, lanose
like some ~: 5 shorn
male ~: 3 ram
New Zealand ~: 10 Corriedale
pen: 4 cote, fold
product: 4 wool
Rockies ~: 4 Dall 7 bighorn 8 cimarron
seeds for pottery ~: 4 chia
shave ~: 5 shear
sound: 3 baa, maa 4 blat 5 bleat
Spanish ~: 6 merino
young ~: 3 teg 4 lamb, tegg 8 yeanling
sheep-__: 3 dip
sheepdog: 6 collie, herder
Hungarian ~: 4 puli 6 kuvasz
__ sheepdog: 7 Belgian, English
sheepfold: 4 cote
sheepish: 3 shy 4 tame 5 ovine, silly, sorry, timid 6 docile 7 abashed, ashamed, bashful, fearful 8 retiring 9 chagrined, diffident, flinching, mortified 10 shamefaced, uneffusive
sheepshank: 4 knot
sheepskin: 3 fur 6 degree 7 diploma
alternative: 3 GED
cap: 6 calpac 7 calpack
holder: 4 alum, grad
leather: 4 roan
sheeptick: 3 ked
sheer: 4 airy, fine, lacy, main, mere, pure, rank, soft, thin, turn 5 erect, filmy, gauzy, gross, light, lucid, naked, quite, stark, steep, total, utter 6 arrant, fabric, flimsy, limpid, simple, slight, smooth, swerve, unmixt 7 chiffon, extreme, fragile, perfect, totally, unmixed, upright 8 absolute, complete, delicate, entirely, finespun, gossamer, outright, pellucid, straight, thorough, vertical 9 downright, out-and-out, unalloyed, undiluted 10 altogether, completely, confounded, diaphanous, see-through, to the limit
drop: 5 cliff 9 precipice
fabric: 4 lawn, leno 5 gauze, ninon, toile, voile 6 barege, dimity 7 batiste, chiffon 9 georgette
off: 4 veer 6 swerve
sheet: 3 ply 4 area, coat, film, leaf, page, pane, slab, slip 5 layer, panel, paper, plate, verso 6 lamina, veneer 7 bedding, blanket, coating, expanse, overlay, stratum, stretch, surface 8 bedcover, bed linen, covering, membrane 9 lightning, newspaper, tarpaulin
cheat ~: 4 crib, trot
four-page ~: 5 folio
glass ~: 4 pane
metal ~: 4 foil 5 plate 6 latten
paper ~: 4 leaf
scandal ~: 9 newspaper
starter: 3 fly 4 clip, main, spec, work 5 baker, broad 6 spread
thin ~: 6 lamina
sheet __: 5 metal, music
__ sheet: 3 cue, end, fly, ice, rap, tip 4 bath, crib, dope, lead, spec, tear, time 5 style 6 baking, cookie 7 balance, scandal, scratch
__-sheet: 5 short
sheet-music feature: 5 lyric, notes 6 chords, lyrics
sheets: 5 linen 6 linens, tablet 10 scratch pad
24 ~: 5 quire
come down in ~: 4 pour, rain
Sheffer: 5 Craig
Sheffield: 4 city, town 6 Johnny
artisan: 6 cutler
city near ~: 5 Leeds
locale: 7 England 9 Yorkshire
She & He
author: George Sand
sheik: 4 Arab, male 5 Saudi
ender: 3 dom
peer: 4 amir, emir 5 ameer, emeer
robe: 3 aba 4 abba
wives: 5 haram, harem, harim 6 hareem
sheikdom
group: 3 UAE
Mideast ~: 5 Dibai, Dubai
musical ~: 5 Araby
Sheik of __, The: 5 Araby
Sheik, The (1921 film)
cast: Rudolph Valentino
sheila: 4 girl 5 woman 6 Aussie
Sheila: 4 Ryan 5 James 6 Kelley, MacRae
Sheila (1962 song)
artist: Tommy Roe
Sheila E.
last name: Escovedo
song: The Glamorous Life (1984)
Sheilah: 6 Graham
shekel: 4 coin 5 money
fraction: 5 agora
locale: 6 Israel
shekels
see moolah
Shelagh: 7 Delaney
Shelby: 5 Foote, Lynne 6 Steele
Sheldon: 6 Sidney 7 Glashow, Harnick, Leonard
Sheldon, Sidney: 6 writer
work: The Best Laid Plans
Bloodline
The Doomsday Conspiracy
If Tomorrow Comes
Master of the Game
Memories of Midnight
Morning Noon and Night
The Naked Face
Nothing Lasts Forever
The Other Side of Midnight
Rage of Angels
The Sands of Time
The Sky is Falling
The Stars Shine Down
Stranger in the Mirror
Tell Me Your Dreams
Toby
Windmills of the Gods
shelf: 4 bank, berm, rack, reef, rest, rock 5 berme, layer, ledge, shoal 6 mantel, mantle 7 console, counter, shallow 8 cupboard, sandbank 10 projection
chimney ~: 3 hob
on a ~: 4 atop
on the ~: 4 idle 6 unused 7 dormant 8 inactive
starter: 4 book 6 mantel
take off the ~: 3 use
underwater ~: 4 reef
shelf __: 4 life 6 talker
__ shelf: 3 ice 5 on the
shell: 3 pod 4 bark, boat, bomb, case, coat, face, fire, hull, husk, peel, raid, skin 5 conch, cowry, crust, frame, murex, ruins, scale, shuck, snail, whelk 6 chiton, cockle, cowrie, facade, limpet, mussel, oyster, quahog, triton, veneer, volute, winkle 7 abalone, bivalve, bombard, chassis, coating, crinoid, grenade, outside, scallop, surface 8 ammonite, argonaut, baculite, carapace, covering, escallop, fire upon, frustule, magazine, nautilus, pericarp, piecrust, ram's-horn, skeleton, univalve 9 belemnite, cannonade, container, explosive, framework, giant clam, pink conch, structure 10 blue

mussel, crown conch, eyed cowrie, integument, periwinkle, quahog clam, watercraft
abalone ~: 5 ormer
abandoned ~: 4 hulk
ender: 4 back, bark, fire, fish 5 proof 6 flower 7 fishery, shocked
game: 5 cheat 7 swindle 8 trickery 9 collusion
lining: 5 nacre
necklace ~: 4 puka
out: 3 pay 4 ante, fork, give 5 spend 6 ante up, divide, expend, fork up, pay for, render 8 disburse, dispense, fork over, hand over 10 remunerate
peanut ~: 4 husk
pie ~: 5 crust
propel a ~: 3 oar, row 5 scull
protein ~: 6 capsid
put into a ~: 6 enhusk
ridge: 5 varix
ship ~: 4 hull
spiral ~: 5 conch
starter: 3 egg, nut, sea 4 band, bomb, clam, lamp 6 cockle 8 tortoise
shell __: 3 out 4 game 5 steak
__ shell: 4 band, clam, half, taco
__-shell: 4 hard, soft
Shell: 3 Art, gas 8 gasoline
former ~ rival: 4 Esso
rival: 5 Amoco, Exxon, Getty, Mobil 6 Conoco, Texaco 7 Chevron
shellac: 4 drub, lick, whip 5 cream, resin, tromp, worst 6 defeat, wallop 7 clobber, lambast, varnish 8 lambaste 9 overpower
shellacking: 4 bath, rout 6 defeat 7 beating, debacle, licking
Shell and Head sculptor: 3 Arp
Shell, Art
sport: 8 football
shellback: 4 salt 7 veteran
__-shell clam: 4 hard, soft
__-shell crab: 4 hard, soft
Shelley: 4 Hack, Long, Mary, poet 6 Berman, Duvall 7 Fabares, Winters
Shelley, Mary: 6 writer 7 British
work: Frankenstein
Shelley, Percy Bysshe: 4 poet 7 British
alma mater: 4 Eton
biography by Maurois: 5 Ariel
contemporary: 5 Byron, Keats
work: Adonais
Alastor
The Cenci
The Cloud
Hymn to Intellectual Beauty
Ode to Liberty
Ode to the West Wind
Ozymandias
Prometheus Unbound
Promethus Unbound
Queen Mab
To a Skylark
shellfish: 4 clam, crab 6 limpet
eater: 5 otter
shelling: 4 fire 5 blitz 6 volley 7 barrage 9 cannonade
shells: 4 ammo 5 chaff, pasta 7 noodles 10 ammunition
alternative: *see* pasta
__ She Lovely?: 4 Isn't
she loves
in Latin: 4 amat
She loves me... unit: 5 petal
She Loves You (1964 song)
artist: Beatles
word: 4 yeah
shelter: 3 den, hut, lee, pad, pen 4 cave, co-op, cove, hide, home, keep, need, nest, port, roof, shed, tent, yurt 5 admit, condo, cover, guard, haven, house, joint, lodge, roost, shack, shade, tower 6 asylum, awning, billet, covert, defend, foster, hangar, harbor, hostel, kennel, lean-to, refuge, safety, screen, shadow, shield, take in, wigwam 7 chamber, conceal, cover up, defense, enclose, habitat, harbour, hideout, housing, inclose, lodging, protect, quarter, retreat 8 dwelling, ensconce, hideaway, hold on to, preserve, quarters, security, surround, umbrella 9 anchorage, apartment, harborage, hermitage, protector, safeguard, sanctuary, seclusion, watch over 10 protection, take care of
adoptee: 3 cat, dog 4 mutt 5 stray
animal ~: 4 barn, cote, fold, shed
as in a cove: 5 embay
crude ~: 3 hut 6 dugout, lean-to
farm ~: 4 barn, shed
give ~ to: 4 hide 5 house 6 billet, harbor, shield 7 conceal, protect
leafy ~: 5 arbor, bower 6 recess 7 pergola
marine ~: 4 cove
military ~: 4 tent 8 barracks
org.: 5 ASPCA
rustic ~: 5 cabin
seek ~: 9 take cover
__ shelter: 3 tax 4 bomb 6 animal 7 air-raid
__ Shelter: 5 Gimme
sheltered: 4 cosy, cozy, snug 5 cozey, cozie, shady 6 covert, inside, secure 7 indoors 8 secluded, shielded, tucked in 10 cloistered
nautically: 4 alee
spot: 4 cove, dale
Shelters of Stone, The
author: Jean Auel
character: 4 Ayla
sheltie: 3 dog 5 canid 6 canine
charge: 5 sheep
Shelton: 3 Ron
shelve: 4 drop, hold, stay 5 delay, scrub, table, waive 6 freeze, hang up, hold up, put off, slow up 7 adjourn, dismiss, hold off, prolong, suspend 8 file away, hold over, lay aside, mothball, postpone, put aside, sideline 10 inactivate, pigeonhole
shelved: 7 abeyant
shelves, fill the: 5 stock
Shem
brother: 3 Ham 7 Japheth
father: 3 Noe 4 Noah
son: 3 Lud 4 Aram, Elam 6 Asshur 10 Arpachshad
Shemp: 6 Howard
brother: 3 Moe 5 Curly
partner: 5 Larry
Shenandoah: 4 park 5 river 6 valley
author: Delmore Schwartz
locale: 8 Virginia
shenanigan: 3 gag 4 jape, lark 5 antic, caper, prank, stunt, trick 6 frolic 8 escapade
shenanigans: 7 foolery 8 jocosity, mischief 10 tomfoolery
Shensi: 8 province
capital: 4 Sian
city: 5 Yanan, Yenan
locale: 5 China
Shep: 6 Fields
Shepard: 3 Sam 4 Alan, Jean 5 Vonda
Shepard, Alan org.: 4 NASA
Shepard, Sam: 5 actor 10 playwright
film: Baby Boom (1987)
Country (1984)
Crimes of the Heart (1986)
Days of Heaven (1978)
Frances (1982)
The Pelican Brief (1993)
Resurrection (1980)
The Right Stuff (1983)
Steel Magnolias (1989)
Thunderheart (1992)
shepherd: 3 dog, pet 4 herd, lead, show, tend 5 canid, guard, guide, route, steer 6 canine, collie, direct, leader, pastor 7 conduct, oversee, protect 8 chaperon, guardian, minister, see after 9 chaperone, look after, watch over
Biblical ~: 4 Abel
charge: 5 flock
god: 3 Pan
locale: 3 lea 6 meadow
staff: 5 crook
__ shepherd: 6 German
Shepherd: 4 Jean 6 Cybill
Shepherd, Cybill: 7 actress
film: Chances Are (1989)
The Heartbreak Kid (1972)
The Last Picture Show (1971)
Taxi Driver (1976)
Texasville (1990)
TV: Moonlighting
Shepherd Moons (1991 song)
artist: Enya
shepherd's __: 3 pie 5 check, plaid
shepherd's purse: 4 weed
__ sher!: 3 Fer
Sher: 6 Antony
Shera: 4 Mark
Sheraton: 5 hotel
alternative: *see* hotel
sherbet: 3 ice 7 dessert
flavor: 4 lime 5 fruit, lemon 6 orange
Shere: 4 Hite
Sheree: 5 North
Sheree J. __: 6 Wilson
Shere Khan: 5 tiger
Sheridan: 3 Ann 7 Richard 10 Nicollette
Sheridan, Nicollette
spouse: Harry Hamlin
Sheridan, Richard: 7 British 9 statesman 10 playwright
work: The Duenna
The Rivals
The School for Scandal
sheriff: 6 lawman 7 officer
aide: 6 deputy 7 bailiff
band: 5 posse
cry: 6 drop it
symbol: 4 star 5 badge
TV ~: 4 Lobo
__ sheriff: 6 deputy
Sherilyn: 4 Fenn
Sherlock: 6 Holmes 9 detective
brother: 7 Mycroft
Sherman: 4 tank 5 Allan, Allie, Bobby, mount 6 Lowell 7 Hemsley, Vincent 8 mountain
Sherman, Allan
song: Hello Mudduh, Hello Fadduh! (1963)
Sherman Antitrust __: 3 Act
Sherman, Bobby
song: Easy Come, Easy Go (1970)
Julie, Do Ya Love Me (1970)
La La La (1969)
Little Woman (1969)
Sherman Oaks: 4 city, town
locale: 10 California
town near ~: 6 Encino
Sherpa: 5 guide
home: 5 Nepal
sighting: 4 yeti
Sherr: 4 Lynn
Sherrill: 6 Milnes
sherry: 4 wine
city: 4 Xera 5 Jerez, Xeres
dry ~: 4 fino
Sherry: 7 Jackson, Lansing
Sherry (1962 song)
artist: Four Seasons
Sherwood: 6 forest 7 Rowland 8 Anderson
Sherwood, Robert E.: 10 playwright
work: Abe Lincoln in Illinois
Idiot's Delight
The Road to Rome
There Shall Be No Night
Sheryl: 3 Lee 4 Crow
Sheryl __ Ralph: 3 Lee
She's __: 4 Gone, Mine 5 a Fool, a Lady
She's a Fool (1963 song)
artist: Lesley Gore
She's a Heartbreaker (1968 song)
artist: Gene Pitney
__, She Said: 6 Murder
She's a Lady (1971 song)
artist: Tom Jones
composer: Paul Anka
She's All I Ever Had (1999 song)
artist: Ricky Martin
She's All That (1999 film)
cast: Rachael Leigh Cook, Matthew Lillard, Freddie Prinze Jr.
She's Always a Woman (1978 song)
artist: Billy Joel
She's a Rainbow (1968 song)
artist: Rolling Stones
She's a Woman (1964 song)
artist: Beatles
She's Gone (1976 song)
artist: Hall and Oates
She's Got a Way (1981 song)
artist: Billy Joel
She's Gotta Have It (1986 film)
cast: Tommy Redmond Hicks, Tracy Camilla Johns, Spike Lee, John Canada Terrell
character: 4 Nola
director: Spike Lee
She's Having a Baby (1988 film)
cast: Kevin Bacon, Alec Baldwin, Elizabeth McGovern
director: John Hughes
She's Like the Wind (1988 song)
artist: Patrick Swayze

She's Lookin' Good (1968 song)
artist: Wilson Pickett
She's Not There (1964 song)
artist: Zombies
She's Not You (1962 song)
artist: Elvis Presley
She's Out of My Life (1980 song)
artist: Michael Jackson
She stood in tears amid the ___ corn: 5 alien
She Stoops to Conquer
author: Oliver Goldsmith
character: 4 Kate, Tony 6 Marlow
___ She Sweet?: 4 Ain't
Shetland: 4 isls., pony 5 horse, isles 7 islands
Shetland Islands
fishing grounds: 4 Haaf
hut: 4 skeo
neighbor: 5 Faroe 6 Faeroe
Shevardnadze: 6 Eduard
Shevat: 5 month 6 Hebrew
predecessor: 5 Tevet
successor: 4 Adar
She Walks in Beauty
author: Lord Byron
She Was a Phantom of Delight: 4 poem
author: William Wordsworth
___ She Was Good: 4 When
She Wore a Yellow Ribbon (1949 film): 5 oater 7 western
cast: John Agar, Joanne Dru, John Wayne
director: John Ford
She Works Hard for the Money (1983 song)
artist: Donna Summer
___, She Wrote: 6 Murder
shh: 5 quiet 8 pipe down
Shia: 7 LaBeouf
Shiba Inu: 3 dog 5 canid 6 canine
shibboleth: 3 saw 5 motto 6 phrase 9 catchword, platitude
shield: 4 egis, fend, hide, keep, mail, roof, save, tend, veil 5 aegis, armor, badge, cover, guard, haven, house, shade 6 buffer, bumper, defend, embank, ensure, fender, harbor, insure, refuge, screen, secure, shadow 7 bulwark, conceal, cover up, defense, harbour, protect, rampart, shelter, ward off 8 absorber, armament, preserve, security 9 safeguard, stonewall 10 escutcheon, protection
archer's ~: 5 pavis 6 pavise
Athena's ~: 4 egis 5 aegis
border: 4 orle
camera-lens ~: 4 gobo
combining form: 4 scut- 5 aspid-, scuti- 6 aspido-
division in heraldry: 4 ente
in heraldry: 10 escutcheon
knob: 4 umbo
old ~: 3 écu 5 targe 6 ancile
starter: 4 wind
sun ~: 5 visor, vizor
shield ___: 3 law
___ shield: 4 heat
Shield: 4 soap
alternative: *see* soap
___ Shield: 6 Desert
shielded: 6 hidden, secure 8 secluded 9 insulated, reclusive, sheltered, withdrawn 10 cloistered, restricted
Shields: 3 Ren 6 Brooke
Shields, Brooke: 7 actress
film: The Blue Lagoon (1980)
Brenda Starr (1989)
Pretty Baby (1978)
spouse: Andre Agassi
TV: Suddenly Susan
shift: 3 job, tip 4 bout, move, ploy, ruse, slip, stir, tack, tilt, time, tour, turn, vary, veer, wile 5 alter, budge, dodge, dress, drift, fault, slide, spell, stint, swing, trick, waver 6 change, divert, gambit, manage, modify, period, refuge, resort, scheme, squirm, swerve, switch, waffle 7 chemise, deviate, disturb, evasion, lighten, replace, reverse, shuffle, stopgap, veering 8 artifice, camisole, displace, exchange, flip-flop, lingerie, maneuver, movement, move over, reassign, recourse, relocate, resource, transfer 9 about-face, deviation, dislocate, expedient, fluctuate, hem and haw, rearrange, transpose, vacillate, variation 10 alteration, changeover, conversion, deflection, expediency, move around, relocation, reposition, substitute, subterfuge, switch over, transition, turn around
starter: 4 down, gear, make
work ~: 4 days 6 nights
shift ___: 3 key 4 lock 5 gears
___ shift: 3 day 5 night, stick, swing
shifting: 5 fluid 7 erratic, mutable, protean 8 floating, unstable, variable 9 irregular, mercurial, momentary, uncertain, unsettled 10 changeable, nonuniform
___ shifting: 4 time
shiftless: 4 idle, lazy 5 slack 6 otiose 8 dallying, fainéant, feckless, indolent, slothful 9 apathetic, do-nothing, negligent 10 neglectful, unreliable
one: 5 idler 10 ne'er-do-well
shiftlessness: 5 sloth
Shift neighbor: 3 Alt, Tab 5 Enter
shifty: 3 sly 4 cagy, foxy, wily 5 cagey, lying, shady, slick, slimy 6 crafty, louche, shrewd, sneaky, tricky 7 crooked, cunning, devious, dodging, elusive, elusory, evasive, furtive, roguish 8 guileful, scheming, slippery, stealthy 9 conniving, deceitful, deceptive, dishonest, ingenious, insidious, insincere, inventive, shuffling, underhand 10 contriving, fly-by-night, fraudulent, mendacious, serpentine, unfaithful, unreliable, untruthful
one: 6 dodger
Shigeta: 5 James
Shih Tzu: 3 dog, pet, toy 5 canid 6 canine, lap dog
shiitake: 8 mushroom
Shi'ite: 4 Arab 5 Irani
caliph: 3 Ali
faith: 5 Islam
God: 5 Allah
holy city: 5 Najaf
holy man: 4 imam 5 imaum
Shikoku: 6 island
city: 5 Kochi
locale: 5 Japan
shill: 4 bait, lure, tout 5 decoy, plant, tempt, trick 6 allure, come-on, entice, lead on, rope in, suck in 7 insider 8 inveigle, pretense 9 accessory, deception
shillelagh: 4 club 5 staff 6 cudgel 9 truncheon
land: 4 Eire, Erin 7 Ireland
shilling: 3 bob 4 coin 5 money
21 ~s: 6 guinea
fraction: 5 penny
Shilling for Candles, A
author: Josephine Tey
Shillong region: 5 Assam
shilly-shally: 4 drag, poke, vary, yo-yo 5 hedge, waver 6 seesaw 7 dubiety 8 hesitate 9 dubiosity, hem and haw, oscillate, vacillate
Shiloh: 5 novel 6 battle
author: Shelby Foote
locale: 9 Tennessee
Shilts: 5 Randy
shim: 5 strip, wedge
___ Shimbun: 5 Asahi
shimmer: 4 glow 5 blink, flare, flash, gleam, glint, gloss, shake, sheen, shine, spark 6 glance, luster, quiver 7 flicker, glimmer, glisten, glitter, spangle, sparkle, twinkle 8 blinking 9 irradiate, luminesce 10 incandesce, luminosity
shimmering: 5 aglow 6 bright 7 vibrant 8 lustrous 10 iridescent
shimmier
of song: 4 Kate
shimmy: 4 step 5 dance, shake 6 jiggle, judder, totter, wabble, wiggle, wobble 7 shudder, vibrate 8 lingerie
Shimmy, Shimmy, Ko-Ko-Bop (1960 song)
artist: Little Anthony and the Imperials
Shimon: 5 Peres
Shimura: 7 Takashi
shin: 4 calf, go up 5 climb, shank, tibia 6 Hebrew, letter 7 clamber, foreleg, leg bone
armor: 6 greave
ender: 3 dig 4 bone, leaf 7 plaster
neighbor: 5 ankle
predecessor: 3 sin
successor: 3 tau, tav, taw
topper: 4 knee
shin ___: 5 guard 6 splint
shinbone: 5 tibia
shindig: 4 ball, bash, fest, fete, gala, luau 5 party 6 affair 7 blowout, jubilee 8 clambake, jamboree 9 festivity
shine: 3 rub, wax 4 beam, buff, glow, show 5 blaze, brush, excel, flame, flare, flash, glare, glaze, gleam, glint, glitz, gloss, light, sleek 6 buff up, dazzle, finish, luster, mirror, patina, patine, polish 7 burnish, deflect, flicker, furbish, glimmer, glisten, glister, glitter, lighten, radiate, reflect, shimmer, sparkle, twinkle 8 bedazzle, brighten, illumine, radiance, radiancy, stand out 9 coruscate, freshness, irradiate, luminesce 10 brightness, brilliance, effulgence, illuminate, incandesce, luminosity, refulgence
alternative: 4 rain
in ad-speak: 3 glo
intermittently: 5 blink
lose ~: 4 dull 7 tarnish
partner: 4 rise
rain or ~: 6 surely 10 definitely, for certain
rise and ~: 4 wake 5 awake, waken 6 awaken 7 turn out
spoil a ~: 4 dull 5 scuff
starter: 3 sun 4 moon, shoe 5 earth 6 monkey
take a ~ to: 4 like
up to: 3 woo 5 court 6 pursue 7 flatter 8 butter up 9 cultivate, patronize 10 curry favor
___-shine: 4 spit
Shine (1996 film)
cast: Armin Mueller-Stahl, Geoffrey Rush
Shine a Little Love (1979 song)
artist: ELO
___, shine, for thy light is come...: 5 Arise
shiner: 4 fish, star 5 mouse 6 bruise 8 black eye
___ Shines Bright, The: 3 Sun
___ shine to: 5 take a
shingle: 3 lap 5 shave 7 overlap
abbr.: 2 MD 3 DDS, esq.
hang up one's ~: 4 open
site: 4 roof
words: 5 at law
shining: 3 lit 5 aglow, clean, clear, light, lucid, nitid, sunny, vivid 6 ablaze, aglare, agleam, bright, flashy, golden, lucent, washed 7 fulgent, lambent, radiant 8 glorious, luminous, lustrous, spotless 9 brilliant, refulgent
Shining Star (song)
artist: Earth, Wind & Fire, Manhattans
Shining, The: 4 film 5 novel
author: Stephen King
cast: Scatman Crothers, Shelley Duvall, Jack Nicholson
director: Stanley Kubrick
mirrored word in ~: 6 redrum
Shining Through (1992 film)
cast: Michael Douglas, Melanie Griffith, Liam Neeson, Joely Richardson
shinny: 5 climb, mount, scale, sport 6 ascend 7 clamber 8 scrabble, scramble
Shinto: 8 Japanese, religion
gateway: 5 torii
god: 4 Kami
shiny: 3 lit 5 aglow, clear, light, nitid, sleek, slick, sunny 6 ablaze, agleam, bright, flashy, glassy, glossy, smooth 7 beaming, blazing, fulgent, glowing, lambent, radiant 8 aglimmer, dazzling, gleaming, luminous, lustrous, polished 9 brilliant, burnished, refulgent, sparkling 10 glimmering, glistening, glittering, reflective, unpowdered
coating: 5 glaze 6 enamel
Shiny Happy People (1991 song)
artist: R.E.M.
ship: 3 dau, dow, tug 4 boat, brig, dhow, haul, move, scow, send, yawl 5 barge, craft, liner, oiler, razee, remit, route, xebec, zebec 6 caique, direct, drakar, embark, export, galley, lugger, tanker, tender, vessel, zebeck 7 chebeck,

clipper, coaster, consign, deliver, felucca, forward, freight, frigate, process, vehicle **8** dispatch, ironclad, transfer, transmit **9** bundle off, destroyer, freighter, hydrofoil, submarine, transport **10** icebreaker, ocean liner, spacecraft, watercraft
abroad: **6** export
anchor a ~: **5** lay to
any ~: **3** her, she
auxiliary ~: **4** dory **6** tender **8** lifeboat
beam: **4** keel
bed: **4** bunk
bottom: **4** hull
canvas: **4** sail
capacity measure: **3** ton
cargo: **4** bulk
cargo ~: **5** oiler **6** argosy, coaler, tanker
clumsy ~: **3** ark, tub
colors: **6** ensign
crane: **5** davit
cruise ~: **5** liner **6** vessel
cruise ~ accommodation: **5** cabin
cruise ~ stop: **3** POC **10** port of call
Cunard ~: **4** QE II
curved plank: **3** sny
deck: **4** poop **5** orlop **6** fo'c's'le
drainage area: **5** bilge
ender: **3** lap, man, men, way **4** load, mate, side, worm, yard **5** board, borne, shape, wreck **6** master, wright
engine part: **4** pump
en route on a ~: **4** asea **5** at sea
fictional ~: **5** Caine
floor: **4** deck
give up the ~: **6** resign
go by ~: **4** sail
guidance system: **5** loran, radar
holder: **6** anchor
in the ~ hold: **4** alow
journal: **3** log
leave the ~: **6** debark **9** disembark
line: **6** inhaul
loading area: **4** quay
Mediterranean ~: **5** xebec, zebec **6** caique, zebeck **7** chebeck
memorable ~: **5** Maine
merchant ~: **6** argosy
multimasted ~: **8** schooner
officer: **4** mate **5** bosun
off the ~: **6** ashore
of the desert: **5** camel
of the Middle Ages: **3** nao
on a ~: **6** aboard
origin: **4** port
out: **4** part, sail **5** leave **6** embark, export **7** abandon, ride off, set sail **8** go aboard, put to sea, shove off
personnel: **4** crew
pirate ~: **5** rover, xebec, zebec **6** zebeck **7** chebeck
plank: **4** wale
pole: **4** boom, mast, spar
post: **4** bitt **7** bollard
prison: **4** brig
prow: **4** nose
Roman ~: **6** bireme, galley **7** trireme
rope: **3** tye
rusted-out ~: **4** hulk
sailing ~: **4** bark **5** ketch, skiff
side: **4** port **9** starboard
slot: **4** slip **5** berth
stall a ~: **6** becalm
starter: **3** air, kin **4** amid, flag, head, king, lady, star **5** court, light, space, steam, troop **6** amidst, battle, fellow, friend, master
storage area: **4** hold
strip a ~: **5** unrig **6** demast
tall ~: **8** sailboat
three-masted ~: **5** xebec, zebec **6** zebeck **7** chebeck
timber: **4** mast
to a poet: **4** keel
turn a ~: **4** tack
wake of a ~: **5** track
wheel: **4** helm **6** tiller
wood: **4** teak
see also boat
ship __: **3** out
__ ship: **5** cargo **6** cruise, mother, rocket **7** clipper, Liberty, sailing
__-ship: **3** air **4** drop
Ship __!: **4** ahoy
shipboard
buddy: **4** mate
romance: **4** idyl **5** fling, idyll
Shipley: **3** Tom
__ & Shipley: **6** Brewer
shipload: **5** cargo
shipmate: **6** sailor **7** mariner
shipmates: **4** crew
shipment: **4** load **5** batch, cargo, order **6** export, lading **7** arrival, freight **8** delivery **9** wagonload
ship of __: **3** war **5** state
Ship of Fools: **4** film **5** novel
author: Katherine Anne Porter
cast: José Ferrer, Vivien Leigh, Simone Signoret, Oskar Werner
character: **3** Rac, Ric **4** Elsa, Graf, Lola, Lutz, Pepe, Tito **5** Greta, Käthe, Lizzi **6** Theile
director: Stanley Kramer
ship of the desert: **5** camel
shipper: **8** merchant
shipping: **9** transport **10** navigation
abbr.: **3** COD, FOB, ppd. **4** recd.
hazard: **4** floe, reef
like some ~ rates: **5** zonal **6** zonary
paper: **7** invoice
route: **4** lane **5** canal
unit: **3** ton
shipping __: **3** out **4** lane **5** clerk
Shipping News, The (2001 film)
cast: Cate Blanchett, Judi Dench, Julianne Moore, Kevin Spacey
ships
group of ~: **5** fleet **6** armada
of ~: **5** naval **8** nautical
starter: **4** amid
ship's __: **6** papers, stores
Ships (1979 song)
artist: Barry Manilow
shipshape: **4** good, neat, taut, tidy, trim **5** kempt **6** spruce **7** orderly **8** well-kept **10** fastidious
make ~ again: **5** refit
ship-shaped clock: **3** nef
ship-to-shore
vehicle: **6** amtrac **7** amtrack
shipworm: **5** borer **6** teredo
shipwreck: **4** hulk, sink **5** wreck **6** maroon, strand
cause: **4** reef
visitor: **5** diver
Shipwreck: **5** Kelly
shipwrecked: **7** aground
Shiraz: **4** city, town
locale: **4** Iran
shire: **5** Derby, Devon, Essex **6** county, region, Surrey **8** province
starter: **3** Ayr **4** York **9** Worcester
Shirelles
hometown: Passaic
song: Baby It's You (1962)
Dedicated to the One I Love (1961)
Foolish Little Girl (1963)
Mama Said (1961)
Soldier Boy (1962)
Will You Love Me Tomorrow (1960)
Shirer, William L.: **6** writer **9** historian
Shire, Talia: **7** actress
brother: Francis Ford Coppola
film: The Godfather (1972)
Rocky (1976)
Rocky II (1979)
nephew: Nicolas Cage
shirk: **4** duck, loaf, lurk, shun, slip **5** avoid, cheat, dodge, dog it, elude, evade, parry, sculk, skulk, slack, slink, snake, sneak **6** bypass, cop out, eschew, recoil **7** abstain, default, goof off, neglect, shy from, slacken **8** flee from, get out of, malinger, sidestep **9** get around, goldbrick, pussyfoot, slough off **10** circumvent, malingerer, shuffle off
shirker: **3** bum **5** idler **6** truant **8** fainéant, layabout, parasite **9** goldbrick **10** malingerer, ne'er-do-well
like a ~: **4** lazy
Shirley: **4** Anne, Grau **5** Booth, Eaton, Ellis, James, Jones **6** Bassey, Knight, Manson, Temple **7** Jackson **8** Chisholm, MacLaine **9** Muldowney
author: Charlotte Brontë
__ & Shirley: **7** Laverne
Shirley Temple: **5** drink **8** beverage
Shirley Temple __: **5** Black
Shirley Valentine (1989 film)
cast: Pauline Collins, Tom Conti
shirr: **4** bake, cook
shirred item: **3** egg
shirt: **3** tee, top **4** polo **5** kurta, middy, rugby, tunic, V-neck **6** banian, banyan, blouse, camise, halter, Henley, jersey, khurta **7** blouson, bustier, chemise, cover-up, dashiki, hauberk, maillot, singlet, tank top **8** daishiki, guernsey **9** garibaldi **10** button-down
accessory: **3** tie
armor ~: **7** hauberk
athletic ~: **6** jersey
ender: **4** tail **5** dress, waist **6** sleeve
feature: **5** V-neck
hair ~: **7** penance **9** penitence **10** contrition
keep one's ~ on: **4** bide, wait **5** abide **6** cool it, hold on **7** stand by, sweat it **8** sit tight
like a stuffed ~: **5** stiff
loose ~: **6** camise
lose one's ~: **4** fold **6** go bust
measurement: **4** neck **6** sleeve
neaten a ~: **4** tuck
of India: **5** kurta **6** banian, banyan, khurta
part: **3** arm **6** button, collar, sleeve
preceder: **5** sport
ruffle: **5** jabot
size: **3** lge., med. **5** large, small **6** medium, x-large
sleep ~: **9** nightgown
starter: **3** red **5** brown, night, sweat, under
stuffed ~: **4** snob **5** snoot **7** elitist
__ shirt: **3** tee **4** body, hair, polo **5** aloha, dress, Rugby, sport **6** muscle, safari **7** stuffed
shirtwaist: **5** dress
shish: **6** skewer
shish __: **5** kebab, kebob
shish kebab
necessity: **4** spit **6** skewer
shiv: **4** dirk **5** blade, knife **6** weapon
user: **4** hood, thug
Shiva: **9** Destroyer
believer: **5** Hindu **6** Hindoo
coequal: **6** Brahma, Vishnu
wife: **4** Kali
shiver: **4** jerk, rive **5** burst, crack, quake, shake, smash **6** dither, freeze, quaver, quiver, tingle, tremor, twitch **7** flutter, pulsate, shatter, shudder, smatter, tremble, vibrate **8** fragment, splinter **9** palpitate
shiverer's utterance: **3** brr
shivering, fit of: **4** ague
shiver me __: **7** timbers
shiver-producing: **4** eery **5** eerie
shivers: **7** jitters, willies
shivery: **3** icy **4** cold, cool **5** chill, nippy, polar **6** arctic, biting, chilly, frigid, frosty, frozen, wintry **7** numbing, wintery **8** freezing **10** frightened
shlemiel: **3** oaf **5** klutz
shlep: **3** lug **4** drag, haul **5** carry, fetch
shmo: **3** oaf **4** jerk
Shmoo creator: Al Capp
Shmuel: **5** Agnon
SHO: **7** channel
alternative: *see* movie channel
shoal: **4** reef, spit **5** shelf **6** lagoon **7** sand bar, shallow **8** sandbank
__ Shoals: **6** Muscle
shoat: **3** hog, pig **5** swine
home: **3** pen, sty **6** pigpen, pigsty
shock: **3** awe, jar, mop, wow **4** blow, bump, daze, hair, jolt, mass, numb, pile, rock, stun, tuft, wisp **5** abash, amaze, anger, appal, clash, crash, flood, floor, mound, quake, scare, start, upset, wreck **6** appall, dismay, fright, impact, injury, insult, offend, revolt, sicken, stroke, stupor, terror, trauma, tremor, wallop, whammy **7** agitate, astound, disgust, disturb, horrify, jarring, outrage, shake up, stagger, startle, stupefy, terrify, tragedy **8** astonish, bowl over, collapse, disquiet, distress, frighten, hysteria, overcome, paralyse, paralyze, surprise, unsettle **9** bombshell, breakdown, buffeting, collision, displease, electrify, encounter, eye-opener, galvanize, overwhelm, terrorize, trepidity **10** antagonize,

concussion, earthquake, excitement, scandalize, scare stiff, traumatize
absorber: 3 pad 6 buffer, bumper
exclamation: 2 oy 4 gasp, yipe 5 yikes, yipes 7 omigosh
in ~: 4 agog
partner: 3 awe
starter: 5 after, shell
shock __: 4 wave 5 radio 6 troops
__ shock: 6 future 7 culture, sticker
Shock
author: Robin Cook
shocked: 5 agasp, upset 6 aghast, jolted 8 overcome 10 dumbstruck, speechless
act ~: 5 start
in a ~ state: 5 agape
more than ~: 4 numb
shocker: 10 revelation
shocking: 4 ugly, vile 5 awful, gross, lurid, outré, scary, utter 6 grisly, odious, tragic, unholy 7 fearful, ghastly, glaring, hateful, heinous, hideous, ungodly 8 dreadful, flagrant, grievous, gruesome, horrible, horrific, infamous, shameful, terrible, terrific, tragical 9 appalling, atrocious, desperate, loathsome, monstrous, offensive, repulsive, revolting, unheard-of 10 abominable, detestable, disgusting, formidable, horrifying, outrageous, petrifying, scandalous, stupefying, surprising
shade: 4 pink
Shocking __: 4 Blue
Shockley, William: 8 Nobelist 9 physicist
shod: 6 booted
it may be ~: 4 hoof
starter: 4 slip 5 rough
shoddy: 3 low 4 base, junk, poor 5 cheap, dingy, gaudy, junky, lousy, mangy, seedy, shady, sorry, tacky, tinny 6 cheapo, cheesy, common, grungy, mangey, paltry, ragged, ragtag, shabby, sleazy, tawdry, trashy 7 run-down, scruffy, squalid 8 el cheapo, inferior, schlocky, shameful, untended 9 makeshift, ungroomed 10 broken-down, inglorious, jerry-built, second-rate
shoe: 3 moc, pac 4 boot, cack, clog, flat, geta, mule, pump 5 gilly, heels, sabot, sling, sneak, spike, stogy, thong, wader 6 bootee, bootie, brogan, brogue, buskin, chopin, chukka, galosh, gillie, golosh, kiltie, loafer, oxford, patten, rubber, sandal, stogie, wedgie 7 chopine, galoshe, ghillie, gumboot, high-low, jodhpur, ski boot, slipper, sneaker, wingtip 8 balmoral, brake pad, elevator, flip-flop, footgear, footwear, high-heel, Mary Jane, moccasin, platform, plimsoll, sneakers, Top-Sider 9 ankle boot, high heels, sling-back, spike heel 10 clodhopper, wellington, white bucks
ankle-length ~: 3 bal 6 chukka 7 high-low, jodhpur
baby ~: 6 bootee, bootie
backless ~: 4 mule 5 thong 8 flip-flop
beach ~: 5 thong
blemish: 5 scuff
brand: 4 Avia, Nike 5 Bally 6 Adidas, Reebok 8 Converse 9 Florsheim 10 New Balance
calf-length ~: 7 gumboot
canted ~: 6 wedgie
canvas ~: 7 sneaker 8 plimsoll, Top-Sider
clerk query: 4 size
cowpuncher's ~: 4 boot
deerskin ~: 3 moc 8 moccasin
divided-toe ~: 5 thong 8 flip-flop
dressy ~: 5 heels, spike 6 oxford 7 wingtip 9 high heels, spike heel
ender: 3 box, pac 4 bill, horn, lace, pack, tree 5 maker, shine 6 string
fix a ~: 4 sole 6 cobble, resole
form: 4 last
gym ~: 5 sneak 7 sneaker
heavy ~: 5 stogy 6 stogie 10 clodhopper
insert: 4 foot, lift, tree
Japanese ~: 4 geta
knee-length ~: 10 wellington
light ~: 3 moc 7 slipper 8 moccasin
like a ~: 5 soled
liner: 3 pac
low-cut ~: 4 flat, pump 6 brogue, gillie, oxford, sandal 7 ghillie, slipper 9 ankle boot, Mary Janes
mark up a ~: 5 scuff
material: 5 suede 6 canvas 7 leather
part: 3 toe 4 arch, heel, sole, vamp, welt 5 shank, upper 6 eyelet, insole, instep 7 outsole
plastic ~: 7 ski boot
polish brand: 4 Kiwi
preserver: 4 tree
rubber ~: 7 gumboot, sneaker 8 plimsoll, Top-Sider
running ~: 6 jogger
salesperson, at times: 5 lacer
size: 4 six A, six B, six C, six D, six E, ten A, ten B, ten C, ten D, ten E 5 five A, five B, five C, five D, five E, four A, four B, four C, four D, four E, nine A, nine B, nine C, nine D, nine E 6 eight A, eight B, eight C, eight D, eight E, seven A, seven B, seven C, seven D, seven E 7 eleven A, eleven B, eleven C, eleven D, eleven E, twelve A, twelve B, twelve C, twelve D, twelve E
slip-on ~: 6 loafer
spike: 5 cleat
starter: 3 gum 4 over, snow 5 horse
stat: 4 size 5 width
strapless ~: 4 pump
string: 4 lace
suede ~: 6 chukka
thick-soled ~: 4 clog 5 sabot 6 buskin, chopin, patten 7 chopine
tighten a ~: 5 retie
tongueless ~: 6 gillie 7 ghillie
walking ~: 4 flat 8 balmoral
waterproof ~: 4 boot 5 wader 6 galosh, rubber
width: 2 AA, EE 3 AAA, EEE 4 AAAA, EEEE
woman's ~: 4 flat, heel, pump 5 sling 8 balmoral
wooden ~: 4 clog, geta 5 sabot
work ~: 4 boot 6 brogan
__ shoe: 3 gym 5 brake, track 6 Oxford, saddle, tennis, wooden 7 jogging, running
__-shoe: 4 soft
shoebox
datum: 4 size 5 width
letters: 3 AAA, EEE
__ shoe fits...: 5 If the
shoehorn: 4 cram 6 insert
shoelace
alternative: 6 Velcro
feature: 4 knot
fix a ~: 5 retie
hole: 6 eyelet
tip: 5 aglet 6 aiglet
shoeless: 6 unshod 8 barefoot
Shoeless Joe
author: W.P. Kinsella
shoemaker
at times: 5 soler
bottle: 3 dye
helper: 3 elf
mold: 4 last
tool: 3 awl
Shoemaker, Bill: 6 jockey
milieu: 5 track
Shoemaker-Levy: 5 comet
Shoemaker, Willie: 6 jockey
milieu: 5 track
shoer: 7 farrier 10 blacksmith
concern: 4 hoof
Shoeshine (1946 film)
director: Vittorio De Sica
Shoes of the Fisherman, The
author: Morris West
__ Shoes, The: 3 Red
shoestring: 5 light 6 little
shoestring __: 5 catch 6 tackle
__ shoestring: 3 on a
shoestrings: 6 lacing
shofar: 4 wind 8 ram's horn
origin: 6 Hebrew
shogi: 4 game 8 Japanese
master: 3 dan
shogun: 5 ruler 6 gerent 8 Japanese
capital: 3 Edo 4 Yedo 5 Yeddo
extra: 6 geisha
sash: 3 obi
vassal: 6 daimio, daimyo
warrior: 5 ninja
Shogun
author: James Clavell
Sholem: 4 Asch
Sholokhov, Mikhail: 6 writer 7 Russian 8 Nobelist
work: The Quiet Don
Shondell: 4 Troy
sho' nuff: 3 yep, yup
shoo: 3 git 4 away, scat 5 scram 6 beat it, begone 7 dismiss 8 wave away 9 chase away, drive away, scare away
shoo-__ pie: 3 fly
Shoo-Be-Doo-Be-Doo-Da-Day (1968 song)
artist: Stevie Wonder
shooby-doo
go ~: 4 scat
shoo-fly pie: 6 pastry
shook: 4 agog 5 upset 6 aghast 7 gyrated, rattled, stunned 8 confused, got rid of, quivered, shimmied, trembled, vibrated 9 perturbed, unsettled 10 high-strung
__ Shook Up: 3 All
Shoop (1993 song)
artist: Salt-n-Pepa
Shoop Shoop Song, The (1964 song)
artist: Betty Everett
refrain: 6 na na na
shoot: 3 bag, bud, gun, hie, hit, pop, run, zap 4 bolt, dart, dash, emit, film, fire, hurl, lick, pass, pump, race, rush, send, slip, snap, soar, stem, tear, twig, zoom 5 blast, chase, expel, flash, fling, graft, photo, plant, reach, scoot, sling, speed, spire, spirt, sprig, spurt, start, throw, whisk 6 charge, darn it, hasten, hurtle, ignite, launch, let fly, member, open up, propel, set off, spring, sprout, stolon, strafe, streak 7 barrage, bombard, cutting, explode, pick off, project, scamper, torpedo 8 catapult, dispatch, fire upon, open fire, spring up 9 bring down, discharge, germinate, new growth 10 photograph
again: 6 remake
ahead: 4 pass 5 outdo 8 progress 9 go forward
(at): 3 aim
at, as tin cans: 5 plink
director's ~: 4 take 5 scene
down: 3 nix 4 fell, flay, ruin, slam, veto 5 rebut, shame 6 debase, debunk, refute, reject 7 deflate, degrade, explode 8 belittle 9 disparage, eradicate, find fault, humiliate
ender: 3 out 4 down
for: 3 try 5 aim at 6 aspire, strive 8 aspire to
forth: 3 jet 4 spew, spue 5 erupt
for the green: 4 chip 5 slice
from ambush: 5 snipe
get ready to ~: 3 aim 5 focus, point
in and out: 6 dartle
off: 3 pop 4 fire 5 erupt 7 explode 8 detonate 9 discharge, fulminate
off one's mouth: 4 brag 5 spout 7 bluster
oneself in the foot: 3 err 4 flub, goof 5 gum up 6 blow it, bungle, foul up, fumble, goof up, mess up 7 blunder, louse up 9 mishandle, mismanage
out: 4 emit 5 eject, flash, spirt, spurt 7 burgeon, radiate 8 bourgeon
plant ~: 4 twig 5 spire
slender ~: 4 wand
starter: 3 off 4 crap, snap 7 trouble
the breeze: 3 gab, jaw, rap 4 blab, chat 5 prate, speak 6 gossip, jabber 7 blather, blether, chatter 8 chitchat, talk idly 10 chew the fat, chew the rag
the curl: 4 surf
the moon: 6 gamble
up: 4 soar, zoom 5 raise 6 mature, rocket, spring, sprout, thrive 7 burgeon 8 bourgeon, mushroom
shoot __: 3 for 4 down 5 hoops
shoot __ one's mouth: 3 off
shoot __ the hip: 4 from
__ shoot: 5 photo 6 bamboo, turkey

Shoot!: 3 ask 4 darn, drat 5 ask me
shoot-'em-up: 5 oater 7 western 10 horse opera
shooter: 3 gun 6 gunman
ammo: 2 BB 3 pea
circus ~: 6 cannon
marble: 3 mib, taw 5 agate, aggie
need: 6 camera
pellet ~: 5 BB gun 6 airgun
request: 5 smile 9 say cheese
spot: 6 rapids
starter: 3 pea 4 trap 5 sharp 7 trouble
__ shooter: 3 pea 6 square
__-shooter: 3 six
shoot from the __: 3 hip
shooting: 5 sharp 6 murder
area: 5 range
clay-pigeon ~: 5 skeet
end of ~: 4 wrap
game: 5 skeet
position: 5 prone
range shout: 3 aim 4 fire 5 ready
star: 5 plant 6 flower, meteor
star path: 3 arc
shooting __: 4 iron, star 5 match 6 script 7 gallery
__ shooting: 4 trap 5 skeet
Shooting an Elephant
author: George Orwell
Shooting of Dan McGrew, The
author: Robert Service
__ shootin' match, the: 5 whole
Shootist, The (1976 film): 5 oater 7 western
cast: Lauren Bacall, Richard Boone, Ron Howard, Hugh O'Brian, James Stewart, John Wayne
__ Shoot Me: 4 Just
shootout: 4 duel
__ shoots: 6 bamboo
shoot the __: 5 works 6 breeze, chutes, rapids
Shoot the Moon (1982 film)
cast: Karen Allen, Albert Finney, Diane Keaton
shop: 3 buy 4 deli, mart, mill 5 plant, salon, stand, store, trade 6 bakery, garage, market, office, outlet 7 factory, hunt for, look for, splurge 8 boutique, business, emporium, purchase, showroom
at: 9 patronize
chic ~: 5 salon
close up ~: 10 call it a day
ender: 4 lift, talk, worn 6 keeper
for: 3 buy
in the ~: 6 broken
machine: 5 lathe 6 jigsaw
set up ~: 4 open
specialty ~: 8 boutique
starter: 4 bake, book, hock, pawn, work 5 sweat, sweet 6 barber
talk: 4 cant 5 argot, lingo 6 jargon
tool: 3 awl 4 vise 6 hammer, pliers
without buying: 6 browse
shop __: 6 around 7 steward
__ shop: 3 job, pro, tea 4 body, chop, malt, open, swap, talk 5 cycle, fix-it, print, set up, union 6 beauty, closed, coffee, thrift 7 butcher, machine
__-shop: 5 sweet 6 window
shopaholic hangout: 4 mall
Shop Around (song)
artist: Captain & Tennille, Miracles
Shop Around the Corner, The (1940 film)
cast: Frank Morgan, James Stewart, Margaret Sullavan
director: Ernst Lubitsch
__ Shop Boys: 3 Pet
shopkeeper: 6 grocer, seller, trader 8 merchant
shoplift: 5 boost, steal, swipe 6 pocket, thieve
shoplifter: 5 thief 6 klepto
ShopNBC: 7 channel
alternative: 3 HSN, QVC
__ Shop of Horrors: 6 Little
shoppe descriptor: 4 olde
shopper: 6 patron 8 consumer, customer
aid: 3 bag 4 cart, list
channel: 3 HSN, QVC
clipping: 6 coupon
concern: 5 price
find: 3 buy 7 bargain
lure: 4 free, sale 5 no tax 6 rebate
often: 5 toter
stop: 4 mall, mart 5 salon, store 8 boutique
window ~: 4 eyer 7 browser
shopping: 9 patronage
center: 4 mall, mart 5 bazar, plaza, store 6 arcade, bazaar, market
extravaganza: 5 spree
go ~: 3 buy 5 spend
shopping __: 3 bag 4 cart, list, mall 5 plaza, spree 6 center
__ shopping: 6 window 7 one-stop
Shop 'Til You Drop: 8 game show
host: Pat Finn
shopworn: 5 corny, hokey, stale, trite 10 threadbare
Shor: 5 Toots
shore: 4 bank, brim, hold, land, prop, sand 5 beach, brace, brink, coast, sands 6 anneal, bear up, border, margin, uphold 7 bolster, bulwark, seaside, support, sustain 8 buttress, lakeside, littoral, seacoast, underpin 9 coastland, coastline, reinforce, riverbank, riverside, waterside 10 embankment, strengthen, waterfront
away from the ~: 6 inland
ender: 4 bird, line, ward 5 front, wards
feature: 3 bay 4 cove 5 bight, inlet
find: 5 conch, shell
leave: 8 furlough
leave ~: 4 sail 7 set sail 8 shove off
make ~: 4 land
starter: 3 off, sea 4 back, lake, long 5 along
up: 4 gird, hold, prop, tone 5 brace, build, shore, steel 6 anneal, harden, temper, uphold 7 bolster, burgeon, develop, empower, enhance, fortify, stiffen, support, sustain, toughen 8 bourgeon, buttress, energize, indurate, underpin, vitalize 9 intensify, reinforce, undergird 10 invigorate, strengthen
shore __: 4 bird 5 leave 6 dinner, patrol
__ shore: 3 lee
Shore: 5 Dinah, Eddie, Ernie, Pauly
shorebird: 3 ern 4 erne, gull, tern 5 heron, oxeye, stilt, wader 6 avocet, curlew, dunlin, godwit, plover, willet 7 tattler 9 dowitcher, sandpiper, turnstone 10 greenshank, yellowlegs
shoreline indentation: 3 bay 4 cove, gulf 5 basin, bayou, bight, fiord, firth, fjord, inlet 6 lagoon 7 estuary
shorn: 3 cut 4 bare 7 clipped, fleeced 8 glabrous, hairless, tonsured
short: 3 low, shy, wee 4 curt, flat, rude, slim 5 blunt, brief, brusk, coast, crisp, gruff, huffy, needy, pithy, rough, scant, sharp, small, spare, squat, terse, testy, tight 6 abrupt, curtly, direct, gnomic, in need, little, meager, petite, scanty, scarce, skimpy, snappy, snippy, sparse, stocky, stubby, sudden 7 briefly, brusque, cartoon, compact, concise, cursory, failing, friable, hastily, hurried, lacking, laconic, limited, missing, needing, passing, pointed, precise, squatty, stunted, summary, tersely, uncivil, wanting 8 abridged, fleeting, flitting, impolite, knee-high, lessened, off-guard, sawed-off, sea-level, snippety, strapped, succinct, suddenly, travelog, unawares 9 brusquely, condensed, curtailed, decreased, deficient, ephemeral, hurriedly, irascible, minimovie, momentary, pint-sized, temporary, transient, truncated, two-reeler, undersize 10 boiled down, by surprise, compressed, diminished, diminutive, evanescent, inadequate, succinctly, summarized, to the point, travelogue, undersized, unelevated, unenduring, ungracious
and stocky: 5 squat
and sweet: 5 brief, pithy, terse 7 laconic
a ~ time ago: 6 lately, of late 8 recently 9 yesterday
at ~ notice: 9 summarily
be ~: 4 snap
be ~ of: 4 lack, need
come up ~: 3 owe 4 fail, lack, lose
cut ~: 3 bob, end, nip 4 crop, ruin, stop 5 elide, shave 7 curtail, silence, suspend 8 compress, condense 9 interrupt, synopsize, telescope, terminate 10 unfinished
cut ~ as a tail: 4 dock
distance: 3 hop 4 inch
end: 4 stub 5 least
ender: 3 age, cut 4 cake, fall, hair, hand, horn, list, stop, wave 5 bread 6 change, coming, haired 7 sighted
fall ~: 4 fail, lack, lose, miss 7 let down, lose out
haul: 3 hop, run 6 outing 7 day trip
in ~: 7 briefly 9 concisely
in a ~ time: 4 anon, fast, soon
in ~ supply: 6 exotic, scanty, scarce, sparse 8 uncommon
in the ~ term: 6 for now
of: 5 low on 6 except 10 leaving out
of cash: 4 poor 5 needy
period: 3 bit 5 spell, trice
seller: 4 bear
stop ~: 4 balk 5 baulk 10 abbreviate
supply: 6 dearth
time: 4 msec., nsec. 7 instant
trip: 5 jaunt, whirl 6 dayhop, errand, outing
version: 6 digest
short __: 3 run, ton 4 fuse, game, haul, iron, line, list, ribs, sale, time 5 order, story 6 seller, shrift 7 circuit, subject
short __ of the stick, the: 3 end
short-__: 3 cut, day, run 4 laid, term 5 lived, range, sheet 6 handed, spoken, winded
short-__ cook: 5 order
short-__ memory: 4 term
__ short: 3 cut, for, run 4 fall, sell
Short: 5 Bobby 6 Martin
shortage: 4 lack, need, want 5 lapse 6 dearth, famine 7 deficit, failure, paucity, poverty 8 leanness, scarcity, sparsity, weakness 9 tightness 10 deficiency, inadequacy, scantiness
Short, Bobby: 7 pianist
shortbread: 6 cookie
shortcake: 7 dessert
Short Circuit (1986 film)
cast: Steve Guttenberg, Ally Sheedy
short-circuit
sight: 5 spark
shortcoming: 3 sin 4 flaw, lack, need, vice, want 5 catch, debit, fault, lapse, minus 6 defect, foible, hurdle 7 barrier, demerit, failing, frailty 8 drawback, handicap, obstacle, weakness 9 detriment, hindrance, infirmity, liability, weak point 10 impediment
Short Cuts (1993 film)
cast: Jack Lemmon, Andie MacDowell, Julianne Moore
director: Robert Altman
shorten: 3 bob, lop 4 chop, clip, crop, dock, edit, pare, snip, trim 5 prune, slash 6 digest, lessen, narrow, recede, reduce, shrink 7 abridge, commute, compact, curtail, cut back, cut down 8 abstract, boil down, compress, condense, contract, decrease, diminish, minimize, simplify, truncate 9 capsulize, summarize, synopsize, telescope 10 abbreviate, blue-pencil
a garment: 3 hem 5 alter
grass: 3 mow
sideburns: 5 razor, shave
shortened: 3 cut 4 less 7 capsule, partial, sketchy 10 unfinished
shortening: 4 lard
brand: 6 Crisco
Shorter, Frank: 6 runner
shortfall: 4 lack, need 7 arrears, deficit 8 exiguity, underage 10 inadequacy
short-fused: 9 excitable, irritable 10 intolerant
shorthair: 3 cat 5 felid 6 feline
shorthand
expert: 5 steno
stat: 3 wpm
short-haul: 5 brief 7 passing 8 fleeting, flitting 9 momentary, temporary, transient 10 transitory
Short History of the World, A
author: H.G. Wells
short-lived: 5 brief, swift 6 little 7 passing 8 fleeting, flitting, temporal, volatile 9 ephemeral, momentary, temporary, transient 10 fly-by-night, pro tempore, transitory

shortly: 4 anon, soon 6 awhile, in a bit, in a sec 7 briefly 8 directly, hereupon 9 in a moment, presently 10 in good time
Short, Martin: 5 actor 8 comedian
film: Father of the Bride (1991)
Innerspace (1987)
Three Amigos! (1986)
TV: Saturday Night Live
shortness: 4 lack 10 impatience
__ short of: 3 run
short-order place: 5 diner
employee: 4 cook
Short People (1977 song)
artist: Randy Newman
__ short run: 5 in the
shorts: 4 BVDs 5 pants 6 boxers, briefs, trunks, undies 7 cutoffs, drawers, jockeys 8 bermudas, bloomers, breeches, hot pants, knickers, skivvies 9 underwear 10 lederhosen
class: 3 gym
stat: 5 waist
__ shorts: 3 gym 4 walk 5 boxer 6 Jockey 7 Bermuda, walking
short-sheeting: 5 prank
Short Shorts (1958 song)
artist: Royal Teens
shortsighted: 4 rash 6 myopic, unwary, unwise 7 foolish 8 careless 9 imprudent
one: 5 myope
short-spoken: 4 curt 5 brief, terse
shortstop: 7 athlete 9 intercept, interrupt 10 baseballer
gear: 5 glove
Hall of Fame ~: 5 Banks, Reese, Smith, Yount 6 Cronin, Ripken, Wagner 7 Appling, Rizzuto, Vaughan 8 Aparicio, Boudreau 9 Cal Ripken, Joe Cronin 10 Ernie Banks, Ozzie Smith, Robin Yount
locale: 7 infield
stat: 6 assist, putout
Short Symphony
composer: Aaron Copland
short-tempered: 5 huffy, irate, moody, surly, testy 6 crabby, cranky, crusty, feisty, grumpy, ireful, ornery, snarly, touchy 7 bearish, bilious, crabbed, fretful, grouchy, peevish, waspish 8 choleric, fretsome, grumpish, petulant, snappish 9 fractious, irascible, irritable, querulous, splenetic
Short-Tempered Clavier, The
composer: PDQ Bach
short-term: 5 brief 9 transient 10 transitory
short-term __: 6 memory
shortwave: 4 band 5 radio
broadcaster: 3 ham
US ~ service: 3 VOA
short-winded: 5 brief, pursy, terse
__ Shorty: 3 Get
Shoshone: 3 Ute 5 river, tribe 8 Comanche 9 waterfall
language family: 5 Numic
river locale: 7 Wyoming
structure: 4 tipi 5 tepee 6 teepee
Shoshone Falls
locale: 5 Idaho
Shostakovich, Dmitri: 7 Russian 8 composer
work: The Age of Gold
Festival Overture
Leningrad Symphony
October Symphony
shot: 3 BBs, lob, nip, pop, try 4 ammo, ball, bang, dart, dram, gone, hypo, slap, slug, stab, time, turn, worn 5 blast, break, burst, crack, drink, fling, guess, kaput, noise, photo, punch, smash, spent, tense, throw, whack, whirl 6 beebee, bullet, chance, effort, gamble, pellet, ruined, used up 7 attempt, damaged, far-gone, liftoff, missile, vaccine, venture, worn-out 8 endeavor, marksman, occasion, slam dunk, washed-up 9 discharge, fisticuff, injection, in tatters, wild guess 10 ammunition, conjecture, photograph, projectile
a ~: 4 each 6 apiece
bar ~: 5 snort
basketball ~: 4 dunk 5 lay up, tip-in 8 slam dunk
big ~: 3 VIP 4 king, lion, name 5 mogul, nabob, nawab, wheel 6 fat cat, kahuna, tycoon 7 notable 8 higher-up, official 9 authority, celebrity, dignitary, personage
billiards ~: 5 carom, massé 6 carrom
camera ~: 4 zoom 6 fade-in
cheap ~: 3 dig 4 barb, gibe, jibe, slam, slap, slur, snub 5 abuse, libel, scorn, taunt 6 insult, rebuff, slight 7 affront, calumny, catcall, disdain, low blow, mockery, obloquy, offense, put-down, slander 8 contempt, derision, ridicule 9 aspersion, contumely 10 defamation, disrespect, opprobrium
down: 8 dejected
ender: 3 gun
follower: 6 chaser
get a ~: 4 snap 10 photograph
give a ~: 8 immunize 9 vaccinate
glass: 6 jigger
golf ~: 4 chip, putt 5 drive, gimme, pitch, shank, tap-in
go like a ~: 3 hie, run 4 race, rush 5 speed 6 streak
hot ~: 6 dynamo, wizard 9 personage
in the arm: 4 lift 5 boost, tonic 8 pick-me-up, stimulus
in the dark: 3 bet 4 risk, stab 5 guess 6 gamble 9 guesswork
like a ~: 3 PDQ 4 fast 5 apace 6 presto 7 fleetly, hastily, quickly, rapidly, swiftly 8 in a flash, in a jiffy, in no time, pell-mell, promptly, speedily 9 forthwith, hurriedly, instantly, posthaste
prepare to be ~: 4 pose
put: 5 event, sport
short ~: 4 putt 5 lay-up
small ~: 4 dram
soccer ~: 4 kick 6 header
starter: 3 big, bow, ear, eye, gun, hot, out, pot 4 bird, buck, head, over, snap 5 blood, grape, sling, under 7 scatter, trouble
sure ~: 3 ace
take a ~: 3 try 5 guess 8 theorize 10 conjecture
tennis ~: 3 lob 4 dink 5 smash 6 volley 8 backhand, forehand
volleyball ~: 4 dink 5 spike
wide ~: 4 miss
shot __: 3 put 4 hole 5 clock, glass, metal, noise, tower 6 effect
shot-__: 6 putter
__ shot: 3 big, hot, mug, pot, rim, set 4 bank, bird, boom, chip, draw, drop, dunk, foul, hook, jump, long, moon, push, slap, trap 5 cheap, like a, massé, matte, tight 7 booster, parting
__-shot: 3 one 5 guest
__ Shot: 3 Big 4 Bank, Slap 7 Warning
__ shot at: 5 have a, take a
__-shot deal: 3 one
shotgun: 3 arm 5 rifle 6 coerce 7 firearm
diameter: 5 gauge
ride ~: 5 watch 6 assist, defend, patrol, shield 7 protect 8 advocate 9 safeguard
__ shotgun: 4 ride
Shotgun __: 5 Slade
shotguns: 8 weaponry
shot in the __: 3 arm 4 dark
Shot in the Dark, A (1964 film)
cast: George Sanders, Peter Sellers, Elke Sommer
director: Blake Edwards
shot putter: Al Oerter
shots: 4 ammo 10 ammunition
call the ~: 4 boss, lead, rule 5 order 6 direct, govern, manage, settle 7 dictate, oversee 8 dominate 9 supervise
series of ~: 5 salvo
__ Shots!: 3 Hot
should: 4 must 5 ought 6 in case 7 had best 9 had better
Shoulda listened!: 6 told ya
shoulder: 4 bear, meat, pack, push, take 5 carry, elbow, nudge, press, shove 6 accept, assume, flange, hustle, take on 7 go about, support 9 push aside, undertake
bag: 5 purse 9 haversack
cold ~: 3 cut 4 snub 5 spurn 6 rebuff, slight 7 refusal, repulse 9 rejection
combining form: 3 omo-
enhancer: 3 pad
gesture: 5 shrug
muscle: 4 delt
part: 5 blade
road ~: 4 berm 5 berme
something to ~: 5 blame
to shoulder: 7 abreast
with a chip on one's ~: 6 bitter 9 resentful
wrap: 5 shawl
shoulder __: 3 bag 4 arms, belt 5 blade, strap 7 harness, holster
__ shoulder: 4 cold, soft
__-shouldered: 5 round 6 square
__ shoulders with: 3 rub
shoulder to __: 5 cry on
Should I Do It (1982 song)
artist: Pointer Sisters
shout: 3 bay, cry, yap 4 bark, bawl, call, hoot, howl, rant, rave, roar, yell 5 cheer, hallo, huzza, salvo, sound, speak, utter, voice, whoop 6 bellow, clamor, cry out, halloa, halloo, holler, huzzah, outcry, scream, shriek, squawk, squeal, tumult, yammer 7 belt out, call out, exclaim, screech, sing out, thunder 8 laughter, let loose, outburst, vocalize 10 vociferate
shout __: 4 down
Shout (song)
artist: Joey Dee and the Starliters, Tears for Fears
shouting: 5 aroar, noise, noisy 6 racket 10 vociferous
match: 3 row 8 argument
within ~ distance: 4 near 6 nearby
shove: 3 jab, jam 4 cram, grub, move, poke, prod, push, tuck 5 boost, crowd, elbow, forge, impel, nudge, press, slide, stuff 6 hustle, insert, jostle, justle, propel, thrust 8 bulldoze, shoulder 9 strong-arm
it may come to ~: 4 push
off: 2 go 4 exit, part, quit, sail 5 leave, scram, split 6 beat it, be gone, decamp, depart, go away 7 head out, pull out, set sail, ship out, vamoose 8 clear out, hightail, put to sea, run along, start out
upward ~: 4 lift, push 5 heave, hoist 6 assist, thrust
shove __: 3 off
shove __ one's throat: 4 down
shovel: 4 tool 5 gouge, scoop, spade
ender: 4 head, nose
in: 3 eat
use a ~: 3 dig
__ shovel: 5 power, steam
show: 3 act, air, gig, see 4 bare, come, expo, face, fair, film, give, look, play, pomp, sell, sham, time, view 5 array, drama, flick, front, guide, guise, mount, movie, occur, offer, pop up, prove, reach, revue, shine, sight, sport, stage, steer, teach 6 adduce, appear, arrive, assert, attend, blow in, cinema, circus, comedy, confer, denote, depict, detail, direct, effect, emerge, escort, evince, expose, flaunt, lay out, mirror, parade, record, reveal, review, set out, splash, spread, turn up, unfold, unfurl, unveil, vanity 7 act with, bespeak, betoken, burlesk, clarify, concert, display, divulge, exhibit, explain, express, glitter, pageant, picture, present, pretext, produce, proffer, program, reflect, seeming, signify, sparkle, testify, trot out, turn out, uncover 8 brandish, bring out, carnival, disclose, discover, document, evidence, flourish, indicate, instruct, manifest, point out, pretense, proclaim, register, set forth, shepherd, spell out, splendor, stick out 9 accompany, burlesque, determine, elucidate, establish, fireworks, make clear, make known, make plain, pageantry, put on view, represent, semblance, spectacle, symbolize, testify to 10 appearance, evincement, exhibition, exposition, false front, grandstand, illustrate, impression, occurrence, pretension, production, vaudeville
affection: 4 kiss 5 spoon 6 caress
again: 5 reair, rerun

approval: 3 nod 4 buoy, clap, yell 5 cheer, shout, whoop 6 buck up, perk up, praise, scream, uplift 7 acclaim, applaud, elevate, enliven, gladden, hearten, root for, support 8 enspirit, inspirit, reassure 9 encourage 10 brighten up, exhilarate, strengthen
around: 5 usher 9 accompany
clearly: 6 detail 7 specify
contempt: 4 jeer, mock 5 scoff
curiosity: 3 ask 8 question
delight: 4 beam, glow, grin 5 smile
disapproval: 3 boo 4 hiss 5 frown
disdain: 4 jeer 5 shrug, sniff
displeasure: 4 pout 5 frown
disrespect: 4 snub 6 slight
do a ~: 3 act 4 sing 6 appear 7 perform
do better than ~: 5 place
elation: 4 beam 5 smile 7 light up
embarrassment: 5 blush 6 redden
ender: 3 biz, man, men, off 4 boat, case, down, girl, time 5 piece, place 6 finale 7 stopper
excitement: 4 rave 6 bubble 7 delight, enthuse, rejoice, sparkle 10 effervesce
failure: 4 bomb 6 turkey
false ~: 3 act 4 sham 8 pretense
fatigue: 3 nod 4 yawn
fear: 3 run 5 cower, quake, wince 6 cringe
feelings: 5 emote, react
for ~: 5 fancy 6 dressy, ornate 9 beautiful, elaborate, exquisite 10 decorative, ornamental, ostensibly
get the ~ on the road: 5 begin 6 launch 7 lead off 8 commence
give the ~ away: 4 blab, leak, talk 5 spill 6 tattle
glee: 4 grin 5 smile 7 sparkle
hesitation: 5 waver 6 falter, wobble 9 hem and haw, vacillate
improvement: 4 gain, mend 6 look up, pick up 7 advance, shape up 8 progress 9 come along, get better 10 recuperate
in: 5 usher 7 receive, welcome
industrial ~: 4 expo
irritation: 4 boil, fume, rage, rant, rave 5 chafe 6 blow up, seethe
need: 6 ticket
no ~: 4 AWOL 7 absence 8 absentee
off: 4 brag, pose, tout, wear 5 boast, flash, model, sport, strut 6 expose, fake it, flaunt, parade, prance 7 bluster, display, exhibit, posture, swagger, trot out 8 brandish, overplay 9 advertise, promenade 10 grandstand, wave around
one's face: 5 pop in, visit 6 appear, arrive, attend, blow in, drop in, emerge, roll in, turn up 7 check in, clock in, punch in, turn out 8 breeze in
one's heels: 3 hie, run
otherwise: 4 deny 5 belie, quash, rebut 6 negate, refute 7 confute, dispute 8 confound, disprove, overturn 9 discredit, shoot down 10 contradict, disconfirm
partner: 4 tell 6 cohost
patience: 5 abide, await
position: 5 third
put on a ~: 3 act 5 amuse, stage
relevance: 5 tie in 7 connect 9 correlate
respect: 3 bow 5 honor, kneel 7 lionize
run the ~: 4 rule 6 direct, manage 7 oversee 8 dominate 9 supervise 10 administer
sadness: 3 cry, sob 4 bawl, wail, weep 6 bewail
short ~: 3 act 4 skit
SRO ~: 3 hit 5 smash
stage ~: 4 play 5 drama, revue 6 review 10 production
starter: 4 Act I, side, song 5 floor
the ropes: 5 coach, teach, train, tutor 6 school 7 educate 8 instruct
the way: 4 lead 5 guide, point 6 direct, lead in, lead on 7 pioneer
to advantage: 7 flatter
to a seat: 5 usher 6 escort 7 usher in
traveling ~: 6 circus 8 carnival
up: 4 come 5 enter, get in, outdo, pop in, reach, shame, visit 6 appear, arrive, attend, blow in, defeat, drop in, expose, refute, report, reveal, roll in, unmask 7 eclipse, lay bare, turn out, uncloak, weigh in 8 belittle, breeze in, get there, outshine, unshroud 9 discredit, embarrass 10 invalidate, overshadow, put to shame
use: 4 fade, fray, wear 5 decay, erode, scuff 6 abrade, weaken 7 corrode, crumble, wear out, weather 8 wear down
venue: 5 stage 8 Broadway
Western ~: 5 oater, rodeo
show __: 3 biz, off
show __ order: 5 cause
show-__: 7 stopper, through
__ show: 3 dog, ice 4 chat, game, late, quiz, road, talk 5 floor, horse, light, raree, trade 6 best in, one-man, puppet, talent 7 picture, pregame, variety
Show: 5 Grant
__ Show: 4 Quiz
show and __: 4 tell
showboat: 4 brag 10 grandstand
Show Boat: 5 novel 7 musical
author: Edna Ferber
character: 3 Kim 4 Andy 5 Ellie, Julie 7 Cap'n Andy, Gaylord, Ravenal
composer: Oscar Hammerstein, Jerome Kern
prop: 4 bale
tune: 4 Bill
showcase: 4 expo 5 array 7 display, exhibit, feature 8 headline
showdown: 4 duel 5 clash 6 climax, crisis 7 meeting 8 skirmish 9 unfolding
Showdown
author: Jorge Amado
shower: 4 hail, lave, mist, pelt, pour, rain, shed, wash 5 spray, throw 6 lavish, splash 7 barrage, moisten, scatter, smother, spatter 8 ablution, sprinkle
affection: 4 dote 5 adore
alternative: 3 tub 4 bath
baby ~ gift: 7 bootees, booties
ender: 4 head
feature: 5 drain
kudos on: 4 laud 5 extol 6 extoll, praise, puff up 7 acclaim, applaud, commend 10 compliment
meteor ~: 5 Lyrid 6 Cygnid, Leonid
sealer: 5 grout
sponge: 5 loofa
starter: 7 thunder
take a ~: 4 lave, wash 5 bathe
shower __: 5 stall
__ shower: 4 rain 6 bridal, meteor
__ Showers: 5 April
showery: 3 wet 5 rainy 6 hyetal 7 pluvial, raining
month: 3 Apr. 5 April
Show Girl tune: 4 Liza
showgoer: 6 viewer 9 spectator
showgoers: 8 audience
showiness: 5 glitz 7 glitter
showing: 7 display 9 semblance 10 exhibition
advance ~: 6 prevue 7 preview
cinema ~: 4 film 5 movie, short
first ~: 5 debut 8 premiere
second ~: 5 rerun
with more ~: 5 nuder
show-me: 9 quizzical, skeptical
Show Me State: 8 Missouri
Show Me the Meaning of Being Lonely (2000 song)
artist: Backstreet Boys
Show Me the Way (song)
artist: Peter Frampton, Styx
Show Must Go On, The (1974 song)
artist: Three Dog Night
shown: 6 taught 8 manifest 9 on display
show of __: 5 hands
__ show of: 5 make a
showoff: 3 ham 4 zany 6 gascon, hotdog 7 boaster, egotist 8 braggart 9 daredevil, swaggerer
__ Show of Shows: 4 Your
show one's __: 4 face, hand 5 heels, teeth
show one the __: 4 door
showpiece: 3 art 8 nicknack 10 knickknack
showroom: 4 mart, shop 5 store 6 outlet 7 gallery
car: 4 demo
caveat: 4 as is
operator: 6 dealer
__ Show, The: 4 Gong, Late, Lucy, T.A.M.I. 5 Cosby 6 Muppet, Truman
__ showtime!: 3 It's
Showtime: 7 channel
alternative: *see* movie channel
offering: 5 movie
Showtime (2002 film)
cast: Robert De Niro, Eddie Murphy, Rene Russo
director: Tom Dey
show to __: 5 a seat
showy: 4 arty, bold, gala, loud 5 artsy, fancy, gaudy, jazzy, ritzy, swank, vivid 6 chichi, flashy, florid, frilly, garish, glitzy, lavish, ornate, snazzy, swanky, tawdry, tinsel 7 dashing, flowery, glaring, opulent, pompous, splashy 8 gorgeous, imposing, overdone, peacocky, striking 9 decorated, elaborate, grandiose, high-flown, luxurious, screaming, sumptuous, tasteless 10 expressive, flamboyant, ornamental, ornamented, rhetorical, theatrical
ornament: 4 gaud 6 bauble, geegaw, gewgaw
something ~: 9 spectacle
shoyu ingredient: 3 soy
Shrapnel: 5 Henry
__ shrdlu: 6 etaoin
shred: 3 bit, cut, jot, rag, ray, rip 4 atom, fray, iota, part, snip, tear, whit, wisp 5 crumb, grain, grate, mince, ounce, piece, scrap, shave, slice, speck, strip, trace 6 ribbon, shadow, sliver, stitch, tatter, tear up 7 frazzle, modicum, remnant, scissor, smidgen, smidgin, snippet, vestige 8 fragment, particle, smidgeon 9 scintilla
shredded wheat: 6 cereal
shreds
cut to ~: 6 impugn
in ~: 4 torn 6 ragged
Shrek (2001 film)
character: 4 ogre
voice cast: Cameron Diaz, John Lithgow, Eddie Murphy, Mike Myers
Shreveport: 4 city, town
county: 5 Caddo
locale: 9 Louisiana
school: 3 LSU
shrew: 3 nag 5 harpy, momus, scold, vixen 6 animal, beldam, blamer, chider, grouch, kvetch, mammal, nagger, noodge, ogress, virago, whiner 7 beldame, caviler, needler, primate, rebuker, reviler 8 fishwife, grumbler, harridan, spitfire 9 henpecker, termagant, Xanthippe 10 castigator, complainer
kin: 4 mole
__ shrew: 4 tree 5 otter
shrewd: 3 sly 4 cagy, cute, deep, foxy, keen, neat, wily, wise 5 acute, cagey, canny, quick, savvy, shark, sharp, slick, smart 6 artful, astute, brainy, clever, crafty, shifty, smooth, tricky 7 cunning, cutting, knowing, politic, probing, prudent 8 guileful, piercing, profound, scheming, sensible, slippery 9 astucious, designing, farseeing, ingenious, in the know, judicious, provident, realistic, sagacious, underhand 10 discerning, far-sighted, insightful, keen-witted, longheaded, perceptive, serpentine, streetwise
shrewdness: 3 wit 4 wits 5 craft, wiles 6 acumen, wisdom 8 gumption, judgment 9 smartness 10 cleverness, discretion, horse sense
shriek: 2 ow 3 cry, eek, yow 4 bawl, howl, ouch, wail, yell, yeow 5 blare, laugh, shout, sound, whoop 6 bellow, holler, scream, shrill, squawk, squeal 7 screech 8 laughter 9 caterwaul 10 vociferate
__ shrift: 5 short
shrill: 4 high, yell 5 acute, reedy, sharp, sound 6 brassy, piping,

SH

shriek, squeak, squeal, treble **7** blaring, blatant, clarion, grating, raucous **8** clanging, jangling, metallic, piercing, strident **9** deafening, unmusical **10** clangorous, discordant, screeching, vociferous
noise: **6** scream, shriek **7** whistle
shrimp: **4** runt
prepare ~: **6** devein
relative: **5** prawn
sense organ: **4** palp **6** palpus
tiny ~: **5** krill
shrimp ___: **5** salad **6** creole, scampi
___ shrimp: **5** brine, jumbo **7** popcorn
shrimp cocktail: **9** appetizer
shrimper gear: **3** net
Shrimpton: **4** Jean
shrimpy: **4** puny, tiny **5** small **6** little
shrine: **5** altar, zendo **6** adytum, chapel, church, temple **7** sanctum **8** monument, sacellum **9** sanctuary **10** tabernacle
Buddhist ~: **5** stupa **6** Ajanta
French ~: **7** Lourdes
innermost ~: **6** adytum
Muslim ~: **4** Kaba **5** Kaaba, Kabah **6** Kaabah
Texas ~: **5** Alamo
Shriner: **3** Wil **4** Herb
gathering: **5** lodge
hat: **3** fez
shrink: **3** ebb, sag, sap **4** curb, drop, fail, flag, tire, wane **5** blunt, cower, demur, lower, quail, quake, start, waste, wince, wizen **6** blanch, cringe, crouch, draw up, flinch, huddle, impair, lessen, narrow, pucker, recede, recoil, reduce, soften, wither **7** abridge, analyst, compact, curtail, cut down, decline, deflate, deplete, drop off, dwindle, exhaust, fall off, fatigue, retreat, shorten, shrivel, shudder, shy away, wrinkle **8** compress, condense, contract, decrease, diminish, downsize, draw back, enervate, enfeeble, hang back, hesitate, minimize, peter out, withdraw **9** attenuate, constrict, undermine **10** abbreviate, debilitate, devitalize
back: **5** wince **6** flinch
ender: **3** age **4** able
from: **4** shun **5** avoid, dread **6** blench, detest **7** retreat
shrink-___: **4** pack, wrap
shrinkage: **4** lack, loss **5** theft **8** decrease **9** reduction
shrinking: **3** coy, shy **4** lack **5** timid **6** averse, demure, modest **7** bashful, fearful, nervous **8** blushing, reserved, retiring **9** diffident, flinching, unwilling, withdrawn
shrinking ___: **6** violet
shrive: **6** purify
shrivel: **3** dry **4** sear, wilt **5** decay, dry up, parch, stale, wizen **6** go limp, scorch, shrink, welter, wither **7** dwindle, mummify, wrinkle **8** contract, decrease, emaciate **9** dehydrate, desiccate
shriveled: **3** dry **4** sere, thin **5** unwet **6** little **9** juiceless
from heat: **7** parched **10** desiccated
Shriver: **3** Pam **5** Maria **6** Eunice **7** Sargent
Shriver, Maria
spouse: Arnold Schwarzenegger
Shropshire: **5** sheep **6** county
city: **7** Telford
locale: **7** England
Shropshire Lad, A: **4** poem
author: A.E. Housman
shroud: **4** hide, pall, veil, wrap **5** cloak, cover **6** enveil, enwrap, inwrap **7** conceal, secrete, shut off, shut out, smother **8** disguise **9** dissemble **10** camouflage
city: **5** Turin
shrouded: **5** misty **6** covert, hidden, masked, secret, unseen **7** furtive, private **8** hush-hush, ulterior **9** out of view, unexposed **10** undercover, under wraps, undetected
Shroud of ___: **5** Turin
Shrove ___: **6** Monday, Sunday **7** Tuesday
Shrovetide Revelers
artist: Frans Hals
Shrove Tuesday follower: **4** Lent
Shroyer, Sonny
role: **4** Enos
shrub: **3** bay, box, fig, kat, qat **4** aloe, anil, bush, coca, gumi, hebe, ilex, itea, karo, kava, khat, ocra, okra, okro, pich, rose, sage, sloe, sola, sunn, titi, tree **5** aalii, akala, alder, birch, briar, brier, buchu, caper, cubeb, elder, erica, ficus, gorse, guava, hakea, hazel, heath, henna, holly, ixora, lilac, maqui, mulga, peony, plant, ramee, ramie, retem, salal, senna, sumac, toyon, urena, yapon **6** abelia, acacia, annona, aucuba, azalea, cassia, cercis, cleome, coffee, cornel, dahoon, daphne, fatsia, feijoa, jojoba, kalmia, kerria, mimosa, myrtle, nardin, nettle, papaya, pawpaw, pituri, privet, spirea, storax, sumach, tobira, willow, yaupon **7** agarita, arbutus, banksia, boxwood, bramble, buckeye, cumquat, currant, deutzia, dogwood, figwort, filbert, fuchsia, geebung, goldcup, guarana, guayule, hoptree, jasmine, jetbead, juniper, karanda, kumquat, logania, mahonia, mahuang, mesquit, nandina, quassia, rhatany, rhodora, skimmia, spiraea, syringa **8** abutilon, albizzia, algerita, barbasco, barberry, bauhinia, bayberry, beverage, bignonia, bluewood, buddleia, camellia, caragana, cassiope, cat's-claw, cinchona, columnea, corkwood, cowberry, divi-divi, euonymus, evonymus, firebush, gardenia, guaiacum, hardhack, hornbeam, huisache, inkberry, justicia, lancepod, lavender, leadwort, magnolia, mangrove, mesquite, mezereon, mezereum, milkwort, myoporum, ninebark, ocotillo, oleander, oleaster, photinia, rosemary, saltbush, snowball, snowbush, sweetsop, tamarisk, wistaria, wisteria **9** blueberry, bouvardia, deerberry, firethorn, forsythia, hackberry, hydrangea, jaborandi, jessamine, kalanchoe, mistletoe, monacillo, raspberry, sagebrush, sugarbush **10** blackthorn, frangipani, gooseberry, ornamental
Arabian ~: **5** retem
Asian ~: **4** gumi **5** ramee, ramie
bog ~ fruit: **9** cranberry
desert ~: **5** retem **6** jojoba
evergreen ~: **5** erica, gorse, salal **6** dahoon
flowering ~: **5** lilac **6** abelia, acacia, azalea
fruit: **6** annona **8** barberry **9** bearberry, blueberry
Hawaiian ~: **5** olona
Indian hemp ~: **4** pooa **5** pooah
medicinal ~: **5** senna, sumac **6** sumach
miniature ~: **6** bonsai
New Zealand ~: **4** karo
of India: **4** sola, sunn
poisonous ~: **5** sumac **6** sumach
prickly ~: **5** briar, gorse **7** bramble **8** hawthorn
row: **5** hedge
South African ~: **6** narras
southern ~: **4** titi
spiny ~: **5** furze, gorse
see also plant
shrubbery: **5** brush, hedge **6** bushes, hedges **10** vegetation
maintain ~: **4** clip **5** prune
shrug: **7** gesture
indication: **6** apathy
off: **6** ignore, slight, wink at **7** let ride, neglect **8** minimize, overlook, play down, sneeze at **9** disregard, gloss over, underplay
___ Shrugged: **5** Atlas
shrunken: **3** dry **5** tight **6** narrow
shtick: **3** act **6** comedy **9** repertory
shuck: **3** pod **4** hull, husk, peel, sham, skin **5** shell, strip **7** uncover **9** throw away **10** integument
shuck and ___: **4** jive
Shucks!: **4** darn, drat, durn, heck, rats **6** darn it
shudder: **4** fear, wave **5** pulse, quail, quake, shake **6** dither, gyrate, jitter, quiver, recoil, shimmy, shiver, shrink, tremor, twitch **7** tremble, twitter **8** convulse
shuddering: **9** tremulous
shuddersome: **6** creepy **7** fearful, hateful **8** dreadful
Shue: **6** Andrew **9** Elisabeth
Shue, Elisabeth: **7** actress
brother: **6** Andrew
film: Back to the Future Part II (1989)
Back to the Future Part III (1990)
Cocktail (1988)
Cousin Bette (1998)
The Karate Kid (1984)
Leaving Las Vegas (1995)
The Marrying Man (1991)
The Saint (1997)
Soapdish (1991)
shuffle: **3** lag, pad **4** drag, limp, plod, walk **5** bandy, dance, hedge, mix up, scuff, shift, trail **6** change, juggle, jumble, linger, litter, loiter, lumber, muddle, racket, scrape, waddle **7** confuse, disrupt, disturb, quibble, scuffle, shamble, stumble **8** disarray, disorder, exchange, intermix, scramble, straggle **9** dislocate, poke along, pussyfoot, rearrange **10** disarrange, discompose, reposition
along: **5** amble, mosey **7** saunter
ender: **5** board
fast ~: **5** fraud **7** swindle **8** trickery
follower: **3** cut **4** deal
off: **2** go **4** exit, move **5** leave, shirk **6** depart, go away
___ Shuffle: **4** Lido **6** Harlem
shuffleboard: **4** game **5** sport
locale: **4** deck
Shuffle Off to Buffalo
composer: Al Dubin, Harry Warren
___-shuffler: **5** paper
shuffling: **6** shifty **8** pretense
___ shui: **4** feng
shul: **6** temple **7** synagog **9** synagogue
scroll: **4** Tora **5** Torah
teacher: **5** rabbi, rebbe
Shula, Don: **5** coach
sport: **8** football
Shulman: **3** Max
Shumway, Gordon alias: **3** Alf
shun: **4** bilk, duck, omit, snub, veto **5** avoid, ditch, dodge, elude, evade, forgo, parry, scorn, shirk, spurn **6** beware, bounce, bypass, escape, eschew, forego, ignore, pass on, pass up, rebuff, refuse, reject **7** abstain, despise, disdain, dislike, dismiss, exclude, forbear, neglect, palm off, shy from **8** disallow, flee from, keep from, shake off, sidestep, turn away, turn down **9** blackball, cast aside, freeze out, get around, ostracize, repudiate **10** circumvent, shrink from
shunned: **9** abandoned, unpopular
shunt: **4** turn **5** avert **6** bypass, divert, switch **8** file away, lay aside **9** push aside, sidetrack, turn aside
___ shu pork: **3** moo
Shusaku: **4** Endo
shush: **5** quiet **6** shut up **7** be quiet, silence, squelch **8** pipe down, suppress **9** keep still
Shuster: **3** Joe
shut: **3** bar, dam **4** bolt, cage, clog, cork, draw, lock, plug, seal, slam **5** block, close, dam up, latch, tight **6** bolted, clog up, closed, fasten, fold up, lock up, plug up, seal up, secure, stop up **7** board up, close up, confine, enclose, exclude, inclose, occlude, seal off, wall off **8** airtight, blockade, button up, closed up, close off, folded up, imprison, obstruct **9** close down **10** batten down
almost ~: **4** ajar
down: **3** end **4** fold, halt, stop **5** cease, close, quash, quell, stall **6** arrest, closed, finish, squash **7** conquer, suspend, turn off
ender: **3** eye, off, out **4** down
in: **3** pen **4** pent **6** begird, encase, immure, pent-up **7** confine, enclose, impound, isolate **8** confined, imprison, restrict **9** barricade **10** quarantine
off: **3** bar **4** hide, kill, mask, stem, veil **5** block, close, cover, debar, evict **6** refuse, screen, shroud **7** conceal, exclude, keep out, lock out, seclude, tune out **8** blockade, block out, obstruct,

secluded **9** beleaguer, ostracize, overpower
one's eyes to: 6 ignore, wink at **9** disregard
out: 3 ban, bar, top, win **4** mask, rout, tabu, veil **5** blank, close, cover, debar, evict, skunk **6** forget, refuse, screen, shroud **7** boycott, conceal, exclude, occlude, prevent, seclude **8** blockade, disallow, fence off, obstruct, prohibit **9** beleaguer, foreclose, ostracize, unwelcome
up: 3 gag **4** cage **5** box in, choke, quiet, shush, still **6** immure, muzzle, stifle, stow it **7** confine, impound, silence **8** imprison
wouldn't ~ up: 5 ran on
shut __: 3 off, out **4** down
shut __ on: 4 down
shutdown: 8 stoppage
computer ~: 5 crash
Shute, Nevil: 6 writer **7** British
work: No Highway
On the Beach
Pied Piper
A Town Like Alice
shuteye: 3 nap **4** doze **5** sleep **6** catnap, snooze **7** slumber
getting some ~: 6 asleep, dozing **7** dormant, napping **8** dreaming, snoozing **9** sacked out, somnolent **10** slumbering
shut-in: 7 patient
shutoff: 5 valve
shut one's __ to: 4 eyes
shutout: 4 rout, zero
like a ~: 5 no-run
score, in Britain: 3 nil
shutter: 3 dam **4** bolt, clog, cork, lock, plug, seal **5** block, close, dam up, latch, shade **6** clog up, lock up, plug up, seal up, secure, stop up **7** seal off **8** blockade, button up, obstruct
ender: 3 bug
part: 6 louver, louvre
sound: 5 click
shutterbug
see photographer
shut the __ on: 4 door
shuttle: 3 bus **5** ferry **6** flight, jitney **8** exchange
ender: 4 cock **5** craft
org.: 4 NASA
take a ~: 3 fly **4** ride
use a ~: 3 tat **5** weave
__ shuttle: 5 space
shuttlecock: 4 bird
Shut up!: 4 hush **5** can it, Quiet, Zip it **7** be quiet **8** pipe down **9** keep still
shy: 3 coy **4** meek, slim, wary **5** aloof, chary, leery, loner, mousy, quiet, scant, short, start, throw, timid, wince **6** averse, demure, humble, modest, mousey, scanty, scarce, silent, skimpy **7** bashful, distant, failing, fearful, lacking, needing, nervous, uneager **8** backward, cautious, cowardly, hesitant, reserved, reticent, retiring, sheepish, skittish, unsocial **9** deficient, diffident, flinching, recessive, reclusive, reluctant, shrinking, unassured, unwilling, withdrawn **10** inadequate, indisposed, shamefaced, unassuming, uneffusive, unsociable
away: 4 turn **6** blench, flinch, recoil, shrink **8** hesitate
be ~: 3 owe **4** lack **7** wanting
ender: 4 lock, ness, ster
from: 4 duck, shun **5** avoid, dodge, evade, shirk **6** bypass, eschew **7** abstain **8** flee from **10** circumvent
make ~: 5 abash
__-shy: 3 gun **6** camera
__ Shy: 5 He's So, Twice
Shyer: 7 Charles
shylock: 6 lender, usurer **8** creditor **9** loan shark
Shylock's Daughter
author: Erica Jong
shyness: 7 modesty, reserve **9** abashment, timidness **10** constraint, diffidence, insecurity
shyster: 5 knave **6** bad guy
sí
see of course, yes
Si: 3 cat **4** elem. **7** element, silicon
14 for ~: 4 at. no.
S.I.: 3 mag **8** Hayakawa, Newhouse
Siamese: 3 cat, Tai **4** Thai **5** felid **6** feline **8** language
coin: 4 baht
old ~ coin: 5 tical
remark: 3 mew **4** meow **5** miaou, miaow, miaul
twin: 3 Eng
weight: 3 pai
Siamese __: 3 cat **4** twin
Siamese fighting __: 4 fish
sib: 3 bro, kin, rel., sis **6** sister **7** brother **8** relative
see also sibling
Sibelius, Jean: 7 Finnish **8** composer
work: Finlandia
Siberia: 5 limbo
antelope: 5 saiga
city: 4 Omsk **5** Tomsk
feature: 5 taiga **6** tundra
lake: 6 Baikal
language: 5 Yakut
locale: 4 Asia **6** Russia
mountain: 6 Anadir, Kolyma
people: 5 Tatar, Yakut, Yupik, Yurak **6** Evenki
river: 4 Lena, Yana **5** Aldan
sea: 4 Kara **6** Laptev
Siberian: 3 cat **4** cold **5** felid **6** feline, frigid, frosty, frozen **7** ice-cold **8** freezing
Siberian __: 5 Husky
__-Siberian Railroad: 5 Trans
sibilance: 4 hiss, lisp
sibilant: 3 ess **4** hiss, soft
sound: 3 sss **5** swish
sibilate: 4 hiss, lisp **5** swish **7** whisper
sibling: 3 bro, kin, sis **8** relation, relative
child: 5 niece **6** nephew
colt's ~: 5 filly
having no ~: 4 only
often: 6 coheir
starter: 4 step
victim of ~ rivalry: 4 Abel
__ Si Bon: 4 C'est
sibyl: 4 seer **5** augur **6** medium, oracle, Pythia **7** diviner, palmist, prophet, seeress **8** Amalthea **9** Cassandra, predictor **10** forecaster, prophetess, soothsayer
sibyllic: 7 fatidic **9** vaticinal
Sibyl, The
author: Pär Lagerkvist
sic: 4 thus **6** attack **8** verbatim **9** literally
sic __: 6 passim
sic __ gloria mundi: 7 transit
sic __ tyrannis: 6 semper
Sichuan city: 6 Luchou, Luchow, Luzhou
Sicilian __: 5 pizza
Sicilian, The
author: Mario Puzo
Sicily: 4 isle **6** island
city: 4 Enna **6** Ragusa **7** Catania, Messina, Palermo **8** Siracusa
commune: 5 Riesi
islands off ~: 5 Egadi **6** Lipari
locale: 5 Italy
money: 4 tari **5** scudi, scudo
neighbor: 5 Malta
peak: 4 Etna **5** Aetna
port: 7 Trapani
sea off ~: 5 Medit. **6** Ionian
volcano: 4 Etna **5** Aetna
wine: 5 corvo **7** Marsala
sick: 3 bad, ill, low **4** down, weak **5** fed up, frail, green, gross, jaded, lousy, rocky, tired, upset, weary **6** ailing, feeble, infirm, laid up, morbid, morose, peaked, poorly, queasy, queazy, rotten, unwell, wabbly, wobbly **7** macaber, macabre, rickety, run-down, unsound **8** confined, delicate, feverish, ghoulish, impaired, infected, qualmish, sadistic **9** afflicted, bedridden, declining, defective, disgusted, imperfect, in a bad way, miserable, squeamish, suffering, tottering, unhealthy **10** broken-down, displeased, indisposed, out of sorts
and tired: 5 fed up, weary
at heart: 3 sad **4** blue, glum **5** moody, mopey, morose, woful **6** gloomy, morose, woeful **7** doleful **8** dejected, dolorous, downcast, grieving, mournful, troubled **9** cheerless, depressed, miserable, saturnine, sorrowful, woebegone **10** despondent, dispirited, melancholy
bay: 8 hospital **9** infirmary
become ~ with: 3 get
be ~ of: 4 hate **5** abhor **6** detest, loathe
ender: 3 bed, out **4** room
feel ~: 3 ail
(of): 5 bored, tired
partner: 5 tired
starter: 3 air, car, sea **4** home, love **5** green, heart, space
sick __: 3 bay, day, pay **4** call, list **5** leave
sick __ dog: 3 as a
sicken: 3 ail **4** tire **5** repel, shock, upset, weary **6** affect, offend, revolt **7** afflict, derange, disgust, fend off, hold off, repulse, turn off, unhinge **8** alienate, disorder, drive off, gross out, languish, unsettle **9** indispose
sickle: 4 tool **5** knife
ender: 4 bill
hammer and ~: 6 emblem
swing a ~: 4 reap
sickle-shaped: 5 arced, bowed **7** falcate **8** crescent, falcated, meniscus
sickly: 3 low, wan **4** down, pale, puny, weak **5** faint, pasty, seedy **6** ailing, feeble, infirm, laid up, morbid, morose, pallid, peaked, pining, poorly, sallow, unwell **7** cloying, languid, mawkish, noxious, run-down, unsound **8** below par, delicate, dragging, liverish, off-color **9** afflicted, bedridden, miserable, revolting, squeamish, unhealthy **10** indisposed, lackluster, out of shape
sickness: 3 bug, ill **6** malady **7** ailment, disease, illness, malaise **8** disorder, syndrome **9** complaint, condition, ill health, infirmity **10** affliction, queasiness, unwellness
__ sickness: 6 motion
Sick Rose, The: 4 poem
author: William Blake
Sic semper tyrannis shouter: 5 Booth
sic transit __ mundi: 6 gloria
Sicut __ in principio: 4 erat
Sid: 5 Bream, Levin, Stone **6** Caesar, Melton **7** Catlett, Gillman, Grauman, Luckman, Vicious
Sidamo home: 6 Africa **8** Ethiopia
Siddhartha
author: Hermann Hesse
Siddig: 9 Alexander
Siddons: 5 Sarah
side: 3 foe, lee, rim **4** camp, edge, face, hand, jamb, join, loin, part, rear, sect, team, view, wall **5** angle, cause, facet, flank, front, jambe, limit, minor, party, phase, rival, slant, stand, verge **6** aspect, behalf, belief, border, bottom, haunch, lesser, margin, sector, stance **7** faction, lateral, opinion, surface, version **8** attitude, boundary, coleslaw, division, flanking, indirect, interest, marginal, position, skirting **9** ancillary, auxiliary, combatant, direction, elevation, off-center, perimeter, periphery, secondary, viewpoint **10** appearance, collateral, contestant, hypotenuse, incidental, standpoint, subsidiary, tangential
at one ~ of (prefix): 4 para-
by side: 4 near **7** abreast, lateral **8** parallel, together
by the ~ of: 4 with **5** along
combining form: 5 later-, pleur- **6** lateri-, latero-, pleuro-
dark ~: 4 evil **9** pessimism
dish: 4 rice, slaw **5** salad **6** potato **8** coleslaw **9** vegetable
ender: 3 arm, bar, car, man, way **4** band, kick, line, long, rite, show, slip, spin, step, walk, wall, ward, ways, wise **5** board, burns, light, piece, swipe, track, wards **6** saddle, stroke, winder **9** splitting
flip ~: 6 option **7** reverse **9** inversion **10** antithesis
from ~ to side: 7 athwart
head for the other ~: 5 cross
larger on one ~: 4 awry **5** askew **6** canted, uneven **7** crooked,

unequal 8 cockeyed, lopsided, top-heavy 9 irregular 10 off-balance, unbalanced
lean to one ~: 4 list
left ~: 4 port
move side to ~: 3 wag 6 zigzag
on one's ~: 5 loyal
on the ~: 5 extra 10 additional
on the far ~ of: 6 across 7 athwart
on the ~ of: 3 for, pro 6 behind 10 supporting
on the opposite ~: 6 across
other ~: 3 foe 5 enemy 7 reverse 8 opposite 9 ill-wisher, inversion 10 antithesis, opposition
port ~: 4 left
put to one ~: 7 isolate 8 separate
right ~: 9 starboard
set side by ~: 5 check, liken, weigh 6 appose, equate, oppose, size up 7 analyze, balance, compare, examine, inspect, stack up 8 contrast, parallel 9 correlate 10 correspond, scrutinize
starboard ~: 5 right
starter: 3 air, bay, bed, day, off, out, sea, sub, top, way 4 back, curb, dock, down, fire, hill, king, lake, land, pool, port, ring, road, ship, surf 5 along, beach, blind, broad, court, green, plane, queen, river, state, table, track, trail, under, water 6 ground, hearth, silver, stream 7 country, slicken 8 mountain
thorn in the ~: 4 bane, pain, pest 7 bugbear 8 nuisance 9 annoyance
to one ~: 2 by 3 off 5 apart, askew
to side: 6 across
view: 7 contour, profile 10 silhouette
with: 4 ally, back, join 5 agree, align, aline, favor 6 uphold 7 support 8 champion 9 cooperate, encourage 10 rally round, sympathize
side ___: 3 arm, bet 4 band, dish, step, trip, with 5 chair, horse, money, table 6 effect, pocket, street
___ side: 4 flip 5 blind, on the, sunny 6 strong 7 distaff
___-side: 6 demand, supply
___ Side: 4 East, West 5 North, South
sidearm: 4 Colt, dirk 5 blade, knife, Luger 6 dagger 7 cutlass, poniard 8 stiletto
sideboard: 5 table 8 credenza 9 furniture
sideburn: 4 hair
shortener: 5 razor
sidecar: 5 drink 8 beverage, cocktail
ingredient: 6 brandy 10 lemon juice
occupant: 5 rider
___-sided: 3 one, two 4 many, open 5 sober 6 double
sided starter: 3 lop
sidekick: 3 pal 4 aide, ally, chum, mate 5 amigo, buddy, crony 6 cohort, friend 7 compeer, comrade, partner 8 alter ego, follower, henchman, roommate 9 associate, colleague, companion, confidant 10 compatriot, well-wisher
cowboy's ~: 4 pard
Sidekick: 3 SUV 6 Suzuki
sideline: 5 hobby 6 recess, shelve 9 avocation, indispose
shout: 3 rah
sidelined: 4 lame 6 unable 7 dormant 8 stranded 9 abandoned
sidelines
on the ~: 7 neutral 8 inactive
put on the ~: 5 bench
sidelong: 7 asquint, athwart, lateral 9 laterally
sideman instrument: 3 axe
side of ___: 4 beef
___ Side of Midnight, The: 5 Other
___ Side of Paradise: 4 This
___ side of the coin, the: 5 other
sidepiece: 4 jamb 5 jambe
___-Sider: 3 Top
sidereal: 6 astral
siderite: 3 ore 7 mineral
constituent: 4 iron
sides
change ~: 4 turn 6 defect
slopping over the ~: 5 awash
starter: 3 off 5 sober
take ~: 6 choose
___ sides: 4 take
sideshow
attraction: 4 geek 5 freak
worker: 5 carny 6 barker
sideslip: 4 skid, veer 6 swerve
___ Sides Now: 4 Both
sidesplitter: 4 hoot, joke, riot 6 scream
sidesplitting: 4 rich 5 funny 7 comical 8 humorous 9 priceless 10 uproarious
sidestep: 3 zig 4 duck, shun 5 avert, avoid, dodge, elude, evade, fence, hedge, parry, shirk, skirt 6 bypass, detour, swerve 8 get out of 9 pussyfoot, runaround 10 circumvent, work around
___ Side Story: 4 West
Side Street (1950 film)
director: Anthony Mann
sidestroke: 4 swim
sideswipe: 3 hit 5 crash 9 collision, criticism
___ Side, The: 3 Far
sidetrack: 4 turn 5 avert, shunt 6 divert 7 deflect, reroute 8 lead away
sidetracked, get: 5 stray 6 ramble, wander 7 digress, meander
___ side up: 5 right, sunny
sidewalk: 6 street 8 pavement
activity: 4 sale
amusement: 5 raree
artist need: 5 chalk
edge: 4 curb
game: 5 jacks, potsy 9 hopscotch
hazard: 5 grate
joint: 5 chink, crack 7 crevice
London ~: 4 kerb
material: 6 cement
stand: 5 kiosk
superintendent: 7 meddler 8 busybody
sidewalk ___: 4 café, sale 5 Santa 6 artist
___ sidewalk: 6 moving
Sidewalks of New York (2001 film)
cast: Edward Burns, Rosario Dawson, Heather Graham, Stanley Tucci
sidewall protection: 4 eave
sideward: 7 lateral
sideways: 6 aslant, aslope 7 asquint, athwart, lateral, sloping 8 slanting 9 laterally, obliquely, slantwise, to the edge 10 indirectly, slantingly
Sideways (2004 film)
cast: Thomas Haden Church, Paul Giamatti, Virginia Madsen
sidewinder: 5 snake 6 animal 7 reptile
relative: *see* snake
sidewise: 8 flanking
Sidi ___: 4 Ifni
siding: 4 rail, spur 7 railing
material: 4 wood 5 steel, vinyl 8 aluminum, tarpaper
producer: 5 Alcoa
railroad ~: 5 lie by
sidle: 4 edge, inch 5 slink, sneak 7 slither
Sidney: 4 Hook 5 Furie, Lumet, Toler 6 Altman, Bechet, George, Hayers, Howard, Lanier, Philip, Sylvia 7 Gilliat, Poitier, Sheldon 8 Franklin, Kingsley, Lanfield
Sidney J. ___: 5 Furie
Sidney, Philip: 3 Sir 4 poet 6 writer 7 British
work: Arcadia
Astrophel and Stella
Sidney, Sylvia: 7 actress
spouse: Bennett Cerf
Sido
author: Colette
Sidra: 4 gulf
locale: 5 Libya
sieben: 5 seven 6 German
Siebert: 6 Muriel 7 Charles
siècle ___: 3 d'or
___-siècle: 5 fin-de
siege: 5 box in, storm 6 attack, battle 8 blockade, encircle, surround 9 cordon off
lay ~ to: 4 gird 5 beset, box in, hem in 6 begird, circle 7 fence in 8 blockade, encircle 9 beleaguer, close in on, encompass
___ Siege: 5 Under
Siegel: 3 Don 5 Bugsy, Jerry
Siege, The (1998 film)
cast: Annette Bening, Tony Shalhoub, Denzel Washington, Bruce Willis
director: Edward Zwick
___ siege to: 3 lay
Siegfried: 4 hero 5 opera 7 Sassoon
composer: 6 Wagner
role: 4 Erda, Mime 5 Wotan 6 Fafner 9 Sieglinde
setting: 5 Rhine 7 Germany
Siegfried ___: 4 Line
Siegfried and ___: 3 Roy
Siegmeister: 4 Elie
Siena: 4 city, town
locale: 5 Italy 7 Tuscany
Sienkiewicz: 6 Henrik, Henryk
sienna: 5 brown, color 9 yellowish
relative: *see* brown color, yellow color
___ sienna: 3 raw 5 burnt
Sienna: 3 van 6 Toyota
Siepi, Cesare: 4 bass
sierra: 5 ridge 8 mountain
Sierra: 3 car 4 auto 5 Dodge, Ruben 7 Gregory
Sierra ___: 4 lily 5 Leone, Madre 6 Madres, Nevada
___ Sierra: 4 High
Sierra Club pioneer: 4 Muir
Sierra Leone: 6 nation 7 country
bovine: 5 n'dama
capital: 8 Freetown
city: 5 Koidu 6 Makeni 8 Freetown
lingua franca: 4 Krio
money: 4 cent 5 leone
neighbor: 6 Guinea 7 Liberia
people: 5 Mende, Temne
Sierra Madre: 3 mts. 4 mtns. 5 range 9 mountains
locale: 6 Mexico 7 Wyoming 8 Colorado 9 Guatemala
Sierra Maestra country: 4 Cuba
Sierra Nevada: 3 mts. 4 mtns. 5 range 9 mountains
locale: 10 California
mountain: 4 Muir, Sill 5 Lyell 7 Granite, Langley, Russell, Tyndall, Whitney 9 El Capitan 10 Williamson
resort: 5 Tahoe
siesta: 3 nap 4 doze, rest 5 sleep 6 catnap, snooze
end a ~: 4 wake 5 awake, get up, waken 6 awaken
unit: 4 wink
siete: 5 seven 7 Spanish
sieve: 4 sift 6 filter, screen, strain 8 colander, strainer
like a ~: 5 leaky 6 porous
Sif
husband: 4 Thor
like ~'s hair: 6 golden
sift: 3 pan 4 comb, part, size, sort 5 drain, glean, grade, probe, sieve, unmix 6 assort, filter, go into, purify, riddle, screen, search, strain, winnow 7 analyze, dig into, enquire, examine, explore, inquire 8 colander, evaluate, look into, pore over, prospect, separate 9 delve into, go through 10 scrutinize
in Britain: 3 lue
through: 4 cull 7 examine
___ sifter: 5 flour, sugar
sifting, needing: 5 lumpy
Sig: 4 Arno 5 Ruman
sigh: 2 ah 3 aah, sob 4 ache, ah me, blow, gasp, howl, lust, moan, pant, pine 5 crave, dream, groan, mourn, sough, sound, whine, yearn 6 exhale, hanker, hunger, lament, murmur, rustle, sorrow, thirst, wheeze 7 long for, respire, suspire, whisper 8 aspirate, complain, languish 10 exhalation
for: 4 long, pine, want, wish 5 crave, yearn
sighing: 5 sough
sight: 3 aim, eye, ken, see 4 espy, eyes, find, look, mess, show, slob, spot, view 5 scene, sense, vista 6 aperçu, behold, descry, eyeful, fright, glance, parade, seeing, vision 7 discern, display, exhibit, eyeshot, eyesore, glimpse, make out, observe, outlook, pageant, viewing 8 perceive, prospect 9 great deal, recognize, spectacle 10 appearance, exhibition, inspection, perception, visibility
combining form: 4 -opia, opto- 5 -opsia

ender: 3 saw, see 4 line, seer 6 seeing
related: 5 optic
starter: 3 eye 4 bomb, hind
sight __: 3 gag 6 unseen
sight __ sore eyes: 3 for
sight-__: 4 read
__ sight: 5 out of 6 second
__-sighted: 3 far 4 long 5 clear, sharp
sighted starter: 3 far 4 near 5 short
Sighted sub, sank __: 4 same
sighting: 6 espial
__ sight of: 5 catch
sights
get in one's ~: 5 aim at
set one's ~ on: 6 aim for, behold
take in the ~: 4 look, tour
sightsee: 4 tour
sightseer: 7 tourist, visitor 8 onlooker, traveler 10 vacationer
need: 3 map 6 camera
sigil: 4 seal, sign 6 signet
sigma: 3 ess, sum 5 Greek 6 letter
predecessor: 3 rho
successor: 3 tau
Sigma: 3 car 4 auto 10 Mitsubishi
Sigma __: 3 Chi
Sigma Protocol, The
author: Robert Ludlum
sigmatism: 4 lisp
sigmoid: 6 curved
curve: 3 ess
Sigmund: 5 Freud 7 Romberg
daughter: 4 Anna
sign: 2 OK 3 cue, ink, nod 4 bell, clew, clue, flag, hint, lead, logo, mark, name, note, okay, omen, type, wave, wink 5 augur, badge, board, crest, index, light, proof, title, token, trace, track, write 6 augury, beacon, cipher, emblem, herald, letter, motion, notice, poster, ratify, symbol 7 auspice, caution, confirm, endorse, express, gesture, indorse, initial, inkling, insigne, placard, portent, presage, symptom, vestige, warning, whistle, witness 8 evidence, forecast, giveaway, hallmark, indicate, inscribe, insignia, landmark, lodestar, mnemonic, reminder 9 assurance, authorize, autograph, billboard, foretoken, formalize, guidepost, handwrite, harbinger, indicator, precursor, predictor, subscribe 10 denotation, divination, foreboding, indication, intimation, prediction, prognostic, suggestion, underwrite
a contract: 3 ink
advertising ~: 4 neon
arithmetic ~: 4 plus 5 minus, times 6 divide
away: 4 cede 5 forgo, waive 6 forego, give up 9 surrender 10 relinquish
bad ~: 4 omen
be a ~ of: 6 denote 7 suggest
combining form: 7 symbolo-
direction ~: 5 arrow
ender: 3 age 4 post 5 board
first ~: 5 onset
for: 6 accept
give the high ~: 3 tip 5 alert 6 advise, signal, tip off 7 caution 8 forewarn
high ~: 4 wink 5 alarm, alert 6 motion
in: 4 come 5 pop up, reach 6 arrive 8 get there
language: 3 ASL
large ~: 6 banner
off: 3 end 4 stop 6 resign
off on: 2 OK 4 okay 5 admit, adopt, allow, go for 6 accept, assent, comply, permit 7 approve, confirm, include, welcome 8 stand for, validate 9 put up with, recognize 10 concur with, give the nod
of the future: 4 omen 6 augury, herald 7 portent, presage 9 foretoken, harbinger
on: 4 hire, join 5 draft, enrol, enter, log in 6 employ, engage, enlist, enroll, join up, retain 7 recruit 8 register
on the dotted line: 5 agree
over: 4 cede 5 trust 8 transfer
starter: 7 counter
telltale ~: 4 odor
up: 4 hire, join 5 draft, enrol, enter 6 employ, engage, enlist, enroll, join up, muster, retain 7 recruit 8 register 9 volunteer
zodiac ~: 3 Leo, Ram 4 Bull, Crab, Fish, Goat, Lion 5 Aries, Libra, Twins, Virgo 6 Archer, Cancer, Gemini, Pisces, Taurus 7 Balance, Scorpio 8 Aquarius, Scorpion 9 Capricorn 11 Sagittarius
sign __: 3 off, out 8 language
__ sign: 3 air, hex, sun 4 call, cent, fire, high, plus, stop 5 earth, equal, minus, peace, pound, times, water 6 dollar, equals 7 percent, radical
signal: 2 OK 3 cue, nod, SOS 4 beck, beep, bell, blip, call, feed, flag, hail, okay, omen, warn, wave, wink, word 5 alarm, alert, bleep, flare, flash, great, point, token 6 beacon, beckon, denote, famous, herald, marked, Mayday, motion, tocsin, wigwag 7 blinker, gesture, go-ahead, notable, salient, warning, whistle 8 indicate, language, lodestar, mnemonic, movement, password, red light, renowned, striking, wave down 9 harbinger, indicator, memorable, momentous, prominent 10 green light, indication, individual, lighthouse, noteworthy, noticeable, pronounced, remarkable
at the ~: 5 on cue
booster: 3 amp
caller: 2 QB
danger ~: 3 red 5 alert
device: 5 pager 6 beeper
distress ~: 3 SOS 5 flare 7 warning
electronic ~: 4 blip 5 bleep
eye ~: 4 wink
fire ~: 4 bell
hand ~: 4 clap, wave
nautical ~: 4 bell
phone ~: 4 busy
receiver: 5 tuner
sonar ~: 4 echo
traffic ~: 4 honk, horn 5 green, light
transmit a ~: 4 beam
turn ~: 5 arrow
visual ~: 3 bat 5 blink, flick 6 squint 7 flutter, twinkle 8 high sign
signal __: 3 box 5 board, corps
__ signal: 3 fog 4 busy, hand, time, turn 5 storm 7 traffic
Signal: 9 mouthwash
alternative: 3 Act 4 Plax 5 Scope 7 Lavoris 9 Listerine 10 Fluorigard
signalize: 9 celebrate
signally: 8 markedly 10 especially
signals
call the ~: 4 lead 6 direct 7 control, oversee 11 quarterback
signatory: 5 inker 7 witness
signature: 4 name 5 stamp 7 imprint, writing 8 longhand 9 autograph, John Henry
attestor: 2 NP
follower: 2 PS
imitate a ~: 5 forge
song: 5 theme
signature __: 4 loan, song, tune
__ signature: 3 key 4 time
Signe: 5 Hasso
Signed, Sealed, Delivered I'm Yours (1970 song)
artist: Stevie Wonder
signer: 5 inker 7 witness
need: 3 pen
signet: 4 seal 5 sigil
signet __: 4 ring
significance: 4 heft, meat, note, pith 5 drift, force, heart, merit, point, sense, stuff, value, worth 6 accent, credit, effect, impact, import, kicker, moment, stress, virtue, weight 7 bearing, gravity, meaning, message, purport 8 emphasis, interest, prestige 9 authority, influence, magnitude, punch line, relevance, substance 10 prominence
have ~ for: 6 bear on 7 concern
statistical ~ measure: 5 t-test
significant: 3 big 4 high, rich 5 great, major, meaty, sound, valid, vital 6 cogent 7 central, fateful, helpful, knowing, notable, salient, serious, special, telling, weighty 8 critical, denoting, eloquent, forceful, historic, material, powerful, pregnant, relevant, symbolic, ultimate 9 important, memorable, momentous, operative
other: 4 love, mate, wife 5 hubby 7 beloved 9 boyfriend 10 girlfriend
significant __: 5 other
significantly: 3 far 5 quite 6 rather 8 somewhat
signification: 7 purport 9 magnitude
signifier: 10 indication
signify: 4 bear, bode, mark, mean, show, tell, wink 5 carry, imply, point, spell, weigh 6 convey, denote, evince, import, intend 7 add up to, bespeak, betoken, connote, exhibit, express, portend, presage, purport, suggest 8 announce, disclose, evidence, foreshow, indicate, intimate, manifest, proclaim, stand for 9 insinuate, predicate, represent, symbolize
signoff: 3 end 8 last word
word: 4 love, over 5 later, see ya
Sign of Four, The
author: Arthur Conan Doyle
sign of the __: 5 cross, times 6 zodiac
signor: 2 Mr. 3 sir 5 title 6 mister 7 Italian 9 gentleman
signora: 3 Mrs. 4 lady 5 title 7 Italian
Signoret, Simone: 6 French 7 actress
film: The Crucible (1957) Diabolique (1955) Room at the Top (1959, AA) Ship of Fools (1965)
spouse: Yves Montand
signorina: 2 Ms. 4 Miss 5 title 7 Italian
Sign o' the Times: 4 film, song
artist: Prince
cast: Sheena Easton, Prince, Sheila E.
director: Prince
__ signo vinces: 5 in hoc
signs
indicate by ~: 4 bode
read the ~: 7 predict
show ~ of: 7 promise
__ signs: 4 life 5 vital
Signs (song)
artist: Five Man Electrical Band, Tesla
__ signum: 4 ecce
sign-up: 10 enlistment
Sigourney: 6 Weaver
uncle: 7 Doodles
Sigrid: 6 Undset
Sigurd
dragon slain by ~: 6 Fafnir
horse: 5 Grani
successor: 4 Atli
Sigurd the Volsung: 4 epic, poem
author: William Morris
Sikes: 3 Dan 7 Cynthia
Sikh: 5 Hindu 6 Indian
dagger: 6 kirpan
founder: Nanak
Sikkim: 5 state
bovine: 4 Siri
locale: 5 India
people: 6 Lepcha
Sikorsky: 4 Igor
s'il __ plaît: 4 vous
silage: 3 hay 4 feed, oats 6 fodder
Silas: 4 Paul 5 Deane 10 evangelist
companion: 4 Paul
Silas Marner: 5 novel
author: George Eliot
character: 4 Cass, Dane 5 Aaron, Dolly, Eppie, Molly, Nancy
silence: 3 gag, nix 4 calm, dull, hush, lull, mute, stop, sulk 5 dry up, peace, quash, quell, quiet, shush, sit on, still 6 clam up, cool it, cut off, dampen, deaden, muffle, muzzle, refute, shut up, stifle, subdue 7 be quiet, close up, dead air, put down, quietus, reserve, secrecy, squelch 8 choke off, cut short, hush-hush, muteness, pipe down, suppress, throttle 9 keep still, quiet down, quietness, reticence, stillness, tongue-tie 10 censorship, extinguish, keep it down, quiescence, sullenness
break ~: 3 say 4 talk 5 speak
exclamation for ~: 4 hush 5 shush 7 hushaby
in music: 4 rest
__ silence: 5 eerie, stony

Silence
author: Harold Pinter
Silence-A Fable
author: Edgar Allan Poe
silenced: **4** mute **5** quiet
Silence is Golden (1967 song)
artist: Tremeloes
Silence of Colonel Bramble, The
author: André Maurois
Silence of the Lambs, The (1991 film)
cast: Jodie Foster, Scott Glenn, Anthony Hopkins
character: **6** Lecter **7** Clarice **8** Hannibal, Starling
director: Jonathan Demme
studio: **5** Orion
silencer: **3** gag
court ~: **5** gavel
in America: **7** muffler
Silencers, The (1966 film)
cast: Victor Buono, Dahlia Lavi, Dean Martin, Stella Stevens
hero: **4** Helm
Silences
author: Tillie Olsen
silent: **3** mum, shy **4** hush, mute **5** faint, movie, muted, quiet, still, tacit **6** curbed, hushed, sullen, unsaid **7** aphonic, bashful, checked, implied, laconic, unheard **8** hushed up, implicit, nonvocal, reserved, reticent, stealthy, taciturn, unspoken, unvoiced, wordless **9** clammed up, inhibited, noiseless, secretive, soundless, voiceless, withdrawn **10** buttoned up, incoherent, indistinct, restrained, speechless, tongue-tied, unsociable, unspeaking
approval: **3** nod
be ~: **6** shut up **9** keep still
be ~ in music: **5** tacet
communication: **3** ESP
entertainer: **4** mime **5** Harpo, mimer
fall ~: **5** quiet **8** pipe down **9** keep still
film accompaniment: **5** organ
language: **3** ASL
make ~: **5** quiet
one: **4** clam
strike ~: **3** awe, wow **4** stun **5** amaze
silent __: **4** vote **5** alarm **6** butler **7** auction, partner, service
Silent __: **3** Cal **5** Movie, Night **6** Spring **7** Running
Silent Clowns, The
author: Walter Kerr
Silent Honor
author: Danielle Steel
Silent Movie (1976 film)
cast: Mel Brooks, Dom DeLuise, Marty Feldman, Bernadette Peters
director: Mel Brooks
Silent Night: **4** noel **5** carol, novel
author: Mary Higgins Clark
word: **5** sleep
Silent Partner
author: Jonathan Kellerman
Silent Running (1986 song)
artist: Mike + the Mechanics
Silent Spring
author: Rachel Carson
topic: **3** DDT
__ silent type, the: **6** strong
Silent, upon a peak in __: **6** Darien
Silent World, The (1956 film)
director: Jacques-Yves Cousteau, Louis Malle
Silesian: **5** Czech
river: **4** Oder, Odra
__-Silex: **7** Proctor
silhouette: **4** form, line **5** shape **6** shadow **7** contour, outline, profile **8** likeness, portrait, side view **9** adumbrate, lineament, lineation
Silhouette: **3** van **4** Olds **10** Oldsmobile
Silhouettes
song: Get a Job (1958)
Silhouettes (song)
artist: Herman's Hermits, Rays
silica: **5** flint **6** quartz **7** mineral
form of ~: **4** opal
trap, as ~ gel: **6** adsorb
silica __: **3** gel
silicate: **4** mica, talc **6** garnet, zircon **9** rhodolite **10** tourmaline
silicon: **7** element
alloy: **7** Everdur **9** barberite
slice: **5** wafer
Silicon __: **5** Alley **6** Valley
silicone: **9** lubricant
Silicon Valley name: **5** Intel
silk: **5** cloth **6** damask, fabric **8** material
ancient ~ fabric: **6** byssus
corn ~: **5** floss
cotton: **5** ceiba
dye: **5** eosin **6** eosine
ender: **4** weed, worm **6** screen
fabric: **3** rep **4** repp **5** crape, crepe, gazar, Honan, moire, pekin, piqué, plush, satin, surah, tulle, voile **6** armure, byssus, camaca, camaka, camoca, damask, faille, gloria, jersey, pongee, poplin, samite, tricot, tussah, tusseh, tusser, tussor, tussur, velvet **7** charvet, chiffon, duvetyn, foulard, grogram, Mogador, organza, ottoman, sarsnet, tabaret, tabinet, taffeta, tussore **8** chambray, chenille, marocain, Milanese, paduasoy, popeline, sarcenet, sarsenet, tabbinet **9** charmeuse, grenadine **10** peau de soie
French ~ center: **4** Lyon **5** Lyons
in French: **4** soie
replacement: **5** nylon
source: **4** worm **6** cocoon
thread: **4** poil
watered ~: **5** moiré
silk __: **3** hat
silk-__: **6** tassel
__ silk: **3** net, raw **4** corn, spun, wild
Silk __: **4** Road
silk-cotton tree: **5** ceiba
silken: **4** soft **5** plush, sleek **6** flossy, glossy, satiny, smooth, tender **7** velvety **8** delicate, lustrous, slippery **9** luxurious, satinlike
silklike fabric: **5** ramee, ramie
silk-making region: **5** Assam
silks: **6** finery
Silk Stalkings (CBS/USA drama)
cast: Rob Estes (Sgt. Chris Lorenzo)
Mitzi Kapture (Sgt. Rita Lance)
silk-stocking: **4** dude **5** elite, noble **6** gentry **8** nobleman, well-born **9** patrician **10** upper-class
Silk Stockings (1957 film): **7** musical
cast: Fred Astaire, Cyd Charisse
Silkwood: **5** Karen
Silkwood (1983 film)
cast: Cher, Kurt Russell, Meryl Streep
director: Mike Nichols
silkworm: **3** bug **5** larva **6** insect
Assam ~: **3** eri **4** eria
silky: **4** soft **5** plush, sleek **6** flossy, glossy, satiny, smooth, tender **7** velvety **8** delicate, lustrous, slippery **9** luxurious, satinlike
sound: **5** swish
sill: **5** ledge **9** threshold **10** projection
opposite: **6** lintel
sitter: **5** plant
starter: **3** mud **4** door **6** ground, window
__ sill: **6** window
__ Sill: **4** Fort
Silla: **5** Felix
Sillanpää, Frans Eemil: **6** writer **7** Finnish **8** Nobelist
Sillas: **5** Karen
silliness: **3** rot **4** bosh **5** folly **6** footle, humbug, levity, lunacy **7** fatuity, foolery, inanity **8** jocosity, nonsense **9** absurdity, frivolity, goofiness
Sillitoe, Alan: **6** writer **7** British
work: The Loneliness of the Long Distance Runner
Saturday Night and Sunday Morning
Sills: **3** Sam **7** Beverly
Sills, Beverly: **4** diva **6** singer **7** soprano
former company: **3** Met
specialty: **5** opera
silly: **4** daft, dopy, soft, zany **5** apish, daffy, dazed, dippy, dizzy, dopey, droll, empty, funny, giddy, goofy, goony, goose, goosy, inane, loony, nutty, sappy, trite, wacky **6** absurd, cuckoo, giggly, gooney, jejune, jocose, looney, screwy, simple, unwise, whacky **7** amusing, asinine, comical, doltish, fatuous, flighty, foolish, jocular, puerile, unsound, vacuous, waggish, witless **8** anserine, anserous, bonehead, childish, cockeyed, farcical, humorous, ignorant, immature, mindless, sheepish, specious, trifling **9** brainless, dim-witted, facetious, fatuitous, foolhardy, frivolous, half-baked, illogical, ill-suited, imprudent, laughable, lightsome, ludicrous, nitwitted, pointless, senseless, untenable, whimsical **10** addlepated, boneheaded, cockamamie, groundless, half-witted, ill-advised, irrational, nonserious, ridiculous, unprofound, weak-minded
one: *see* ninny
silly __: **5** billy **6** season
silly __ goose: **3** as a
silly-__: **5** sider
Silly Love Songs (1976 song)
artist: Paul McCartney
Silly me!: **3** Duh
Silly Putty
handful: **4** glob
holder: **3** egg
__ silly question,...: **4** Ask a
Silly Symphony: **7** cartoon
silo
contents: **4** ICBM **5** grain **6** fodder, forage
neighbor: **4** barn
Silone, Ignazio: **6** writer **7** Italian
work: Bread and Wine
silt: **3** mud **4** ooze **7** deposit, residue **8** alluvium, sediment
deposit: **5** delta
depositor: **5** flood
remove ~: **6** dredge
windblown ~: **5** loess
silva: **5** trees **8** woodland
Silva: **4** José **5** Henry
Silvana: **7** Mangano
Silvano
composer: Pietro Mascagni
silver: **4** coin, gray, grey, pale **5** color, metal, plate, white **6** argent, bright, change, moolah, pearly, plated, whiten **7** element, whitish **8** flatware, lustrous, sterling **9** valuables
alloy: **7** amalgam **8** electrum
bar: **5** ingot
braid: **5** orris
dollar: **6** cactus
ender: **3** eye, rod, tip **4** back, fish, side, ware, weed, work **5** berry, point, smith
fabric: **4** lamé
German ~: **6** albata
in heraldry: **6** argent
measure: **8** sterling
Navaho ~: **6** concha
ore: **9** argentite, sylvanite **10** polybasite
piece of ~: **4** fork **5** knife, spoon
relative: *see* gray color **10** white color
source: **3** ore **4** mine, vein
starter: **5** quick
take the ~: **5** place
uncoined ~: **5** sycee
see also moolah
silver __: **3** age, fox **4** bell **5** medal, plate, spoon **6** bullet, dollar, iodide, lining, screen **7** jubilee, nitrate, wedding
silver-__: **6** plated **7** tongued
Silver: **3** Ron **5** horse, steed **6** equine
companion: **5** Scout
State: **6** Nevada
Silver __: **4** Star **5** Bells **6** Streak
Silverado (1985 film)
cast: Rosanna Arquette, Kevin Costner, Scott Glenn, Danny Glover, Kevin Kline
director: Lawrence Kasdan
role: **3** Mal **4** Jake
__ Silver, away!: **4** Hi-yo
Silverberg: **6** Robert
Silver Chalice, The
author: Thomas Costain
Silver Cloud: **3** car, Reo **4** auto **10** automobile, Rolls-Royce
Silver Comet: **5** train
Silver Dawn: **3** car **4** auto **10** automobile, Rolls-Royce
silver fizz: **5** drink **8** beverage, cocktail
ingredient: **3** gin **4** soda **5** vodka **8** egg white **10** lemon juice

Silver Ghost: 3 car 4 auto 10 automobile, Rolls-Royce
silver-gray: 3 ash
Silverheels: 3 Jay
  partner: 5 Moore
  role: 5 Tonto
silver-lining
  locale: 5 cloud
Silverman: 5 Belle 8 Jonathan
___ silver platter: 3 on a
Silvers: 4 Phil
___ Silver Sands: 5 White
Silver Seraph: 3 car 4 auto 10 automobile, Rolls-Royce
Silver Shadow: 3 car 4 auto 10 automobile, Rolls-Royce
silverside: 4 fish
Silvers, Phil
  role: 5 Bilko
Silver Spirit: 3 car 4 auto 10 automobile, Rolls-Royce
Silver Spring: 4 city, town
  locale: 8 Maryland
Silver Springs, city near: 5 Ocala
Silver Spur: 3 car 4 auto 10 automobile, Rolls-Royce
Silver Star: 5 medal
Silverstein: 4 Shel
Silverstone: 6 Alicia, estate
  owner: 6 Tipton
Silverstone, Alicia: 7 actress
  film: Batman & Robin (1997)
    Blast From the Past (1999)
    Clueless (1995)
Silver Streak (1976 film)
  cast: Jill Clayburgh, Richard Pryor, Gene Wilder
silver-tongued: 4 glib 5 suave, sweet 8 eloquent 10 articulate, rhetorical, well-spoken
silverware: 4 fork 5 knife, spoon 7 utensil
Silver Wedding
  author: Maeve Binchy
Silver Wraith: 3 car 4 auto 10 automobilr, Rolls-Royce
silvery: 4 gray, grey 5 smoky, white 6 argent 7 melodic, musical 9 melodious
___ Silvia: 3 Rea 4 Rhea
silviculture: 8 forestry
s'il vous plait: 6 French, kindly, please
Sim: 8 Alastair
Simba: 3 cat 4 lion
  uncle: 4 Scar
___ Simbel: 3 Abu
Simchas ___: 5 Torah
Si, me ne vo, Contessa: 4 aria
Simenon, Georges: 6 French, writer
  sleuth: Inspector Maigret
Simeon: 5 saint
  brother: 3 Dan, Gad 4 Levi 5 Asher, Judah 6 Joseph, Reuben 7 Zebulun 8 Benjamin, Issachar, Naphtali
  parent: 4 Leah 5 Jacob
  sister: 5 Dinah
___ Simeon: 3 San
___ Simeone Chorale: 5 Harry
Simhat ___: 5 Torah
simian: 3 ape 5 jocko, orang 6 baboon, monkey 7 primate
Simian Line, The (2001 film)
  cast: Harry Connick Jr., Cindy Crawford, Lynn Redgrave

similar: 3 kin 4 akin, like, same, such, twin 5 alike 6 akin to, allied, on a par 7 cognate, kindred, related, uniform 8 matching, parallel 9 analogous, congruent, congruous, consonant, identical 10 coincident, coinciding, comparable, equivalent, like-minded, reciprocal, resembling
  be ~: 8 resemble
  combining form: 5 homeo-
  prefix: 3 syn- 4 para-
  think ~: 5 liken 6 equate
similarity: 6 parity 7 analogy, kinship 8 affinity, likeness, parallel, relation, sameness 9 agreement, alikeness, closeness, community, congruity, look-alike, semblance 10 comparison, conformity
  suffix: 3 -oid
similarly: 4 also, same 5 alike 6 in kind 8 likewise
  to: 4 like
simile: 5 image 8 likeness, likening 9 semblance 10 comparison
  center: 3 as a 4 as an
  start: 5 like a
___ simile: 4 epic
similitude: 8 likeness, metaphor 9 semblance
Simi Valley: 4 city, town
  locale: 10 California
simmer: 4 boil, burn, cook, foam, fume, heat, rage, stew, warm 5 churn, froth, smart 6 braise, bubble, seethe 7 ferment, parboil, smolder 8 smoulder 10 effervesce
  down: 4 calm 5 relax 7 compose, cool off
simmer ___: 4 down
simmering: 5 aboil, on low
Simmons: 2 Al 4 Gene, Jean 7 Richard 8 mattress
  competitor: 5 Sealy, Serta
Simms: 4 Phil 7 William
Simms, Phil: 2 QB
  sport: 8 football
Simms, William: 4 poet 6 writer
  work: Beauchampe
    Charlemont
    Woodcraft
simoleon: 4 bill, buck, clam 6 dollar 7 smacker 8 banknote, frogskin 9 greenback
simoleons
  see moolah
simon-___: 4 pure
Simon: 3 Joe 4 Gray, Neil, Paul, Ward 5 Carly, Estes, Le Bon, Wells 6 Claude, Cowell, Legree, Simone, Stevin, Wincer 7 Kuznets, Oakland, Richard 8 7 Herbert, chipmunk 10 Wiesenthal
  author: George Sand
  brother: 5 Jesus
Simon ___: 4 says 5 Peter
___ Simon: 6 Simple
Simón: 7 Bolívar
Simon and Garfunkel: 3 duo
  members: Paul Simon, Art Garfunkel
  song: At the Zoo (1967)
    The Boxer (1969)
    Bridge Over Troubled Water (1970)
    Cecilia (1970)
    The Dangling Conversation (1966)
    El Condor Pasa (1970)
    Fakin' It (1967)
    A Hazy Shade of Winter (1966)
    Homeward Bound (1966)
    I Am a Rock (1966)
    Mrs. Robinson (1968)
    My Little Town (1975)
    Scarborough Fair (1968)
    The Sounds of Silence (1965)
    Wonderful World (1978)
Simon Birch (1998 film)
  cast: Ashley Judd, Oliver Platt
Simon Boccanegra: 5 opera
  composer: Giuseppe Verdi
  setting: 5 Genoa, Italy
Simon, Carly
  song: Anticipation (1972)
    Haven't Got Time for the Pain (1974)
    Jesse (1980)
    Mockingbird (1974)
    Nobody Does It Better (1977)
    You Belong to Me (1978)
    You're So Vain (1972)
  spouse: James Taylor
Simon, Claude: 6 French, writer 8 Nobelist
Simone: 4 Nina, Weil 5 Simon 8 Signoret 10 de Beauvoir
Simone (2002 film)
  cast: Catherine Keener, Al Pacino, Winona Ryder
Simone, Nina: 7 pianist
  genre: 4 jazz
Simon Fraser University
  location: 6 Canada 7 Burnaby
Simon, Herbert: 8 Nobelist 9 economist
Simoniz: 3 wax 6 car wax
Simon, Neil: 10 playwright
  character: 5 Felix, Oscar
  nickname: 3 Doc
  spouse: Marsha Mason
  work: Barefoot in the Park
    Biloxi Blues
    Brighton Beach Memoirs
    Broadway Bound
    California Suite
    Chapter Two
    Come Blow Your Horn
    Fools
    The Gingerbread Lady
    The Good Doctor
    I Ought to Be in Pictures
    Jake's Women
    Last of the Red Hot Lovers
    Laughter on the 23rd Floor
    London Suite
    Lost in Yonkers
    The Odd Couple
    Plaza Suite
    Prisoner of Second Avenue
    Promises, Promises
    Proposals
    Rumors
    The Star-Spangled Girl
    The Sunshine Boys
    Sweet Charity
    They're Playing Our Song
Simon of the Desert (1965 film)
  director: Luis Buñuel
Simon, Paul
  song: 50 Ways to Leave Your Lover (1976)
    Kodachrome (1973)
    Late in the Evening (1980)
    Loves Me Like a Rock (1973)
    Me and Julio Down by the Schoolyard (1972)
    Mother and Child Reunion (1972)
    Slip Slidin' Away (1977)
  spouse: Edie Brickell, Carrie Fisher
Simon Says player: 4 aper
___-Simon scale: 5 Binet
Simon & Simon (CBS drama)
  cast: Gerald McRaney (Rick Simon)
    Jameson Parker (A.J. Simon)
  dog: 7 Marlowe
simp
  see ninny
simpatico: 4 nice 7 rapport 8 likeable 10 compatible, harmonious
simper: 4 grin 5 smile, smirk
simple: 4 bare, dull, easy, homy, mere, mild, naif, pure, rude, slow, snap, soft 5 basic, cinch, clean, clear, crude, cushy, dense, frank, goosy, green, homey, inane, light, lowly, lucid, naive, naked, plain, prime, quiet, sheer, silly, stark, thick 6 breeze, common, direct, earthy, facile, feeble, folksy, honest, humble, modest, picnic, rustic, single, unmixt 7 amateur, artless, asinine, austere, classic, foolish, literal, lowborn, natural, no sweat, primary, puerile, shallow, Spartan, unfussy, unmixed, witless 8 absolute, backward, childish, discreet, duck soup, gullable, gullible, homemade, homespun, ignorant, inexpert, informal, innocent, mindless, ordinary, painless, pastoral, pushover, readable, trusting, unartful, untaxing, walkover, workable 9 backwater, brainless, childlike, credulous, dimwitted, easy as pie, guileless, ingenuous, nitwitted, no problem, primitive, senseless, unadorned, unalloyed, unblended, uncomplex, unlabored, unstudied, untrimmed 10 child's play, effortless, elementary, half-witted, illiterate, manageable, soft-headed, unaffected, unassuming, uncombined, undeniable, uneducated, unexacting, uninvolved, unschooled
  ender: 6 minded 7 hearted
  something ~: 4 snap 6 breeze
___ simple: 3 fee
Simple ___: 5 Simon
simple as ___: 3 ABC
___ Simple Melody: 5 Play a
simpleminded: 4 dopy, dull 5 dense, dopey, silly 6 obtuse 7 doltish, foolish, witless 9 dim-witted
  one: 4 naif
Simple Plan, A (1998 film)
  cast: Bridget Fonda, Bill Paxton, Billy Bob Thornton
  director: Sam Raimi
Simple Simon: 7 musical
  composer: Lorenz Hart, Richard Rodgers
  treat: 3 pie
Simple Simon met a ___: 6 pieman
Simple Symphony
  composer: Benjamin Britten
simpleton
  see ninny

Simple Twist of Faith, A (1994 film)
cast: Stephen Baldwin, Gabriel Byrne, Steve Martin, Catherine O'Hara
simplicity: **4** ease **6** candor, purity **7** clarity, modesty, naivety **8** chastity, easiness **9** austerity, clearness, ignorance, innocence, integrity, plainness **10** classicism
simplified: **10** elementary
simplify: **4** ease **5** clear **6** lay out, reduce **7** abridge, clarify, clear up, cut down, explain, shorten **8** boil down, make easy, spell out **9** break down, elucidate, interpret, make clear, make plain, translate **10** facilitate, popularize, streamline, unscramble
simply: **4** just, mere, only **6** barely, easily, in fact, merely, openly, purely, really, solely, wholly **7** clearly, frankly, lightly, plainly, totally, utterly **8** candidly, commonly, directly, honestly, modestly **9** literally, naturally, sincerely **10** absolutely, completely, nothing but, ordinarily
Simpson: **2** O.J. **3** Abe **4** Alan, Bart, Lisa, Mona **5** Adele, Homer, Louis, Marge **6** Ashlee, desert, Maggie **7** Jessica, Valerie
Simpson, Jessica
song: I Wanna Love You Forever (1999)
Simpson, Louis: **4** poet
Simpson, O.J.
sport: **8** football
Simpsons, The (Fox sitcom)
bar: **4** Moe's
bartender: **3** Moe
beer: **4** Duff
bus driver: **4** Otto
cat: **8** Scratchy, Snowball
clerk: **3** Apu
disco lover: **3** Stu
grandfather: **3** Abe
mouse: **5** Itchy
neighbor: **3** Ned
shout: **3** doh
teacher: **4** Edna
voice cast: Nancy Cartwright (Bart Simpson)
Dan Castellaneta (Homer Simpson)
Julie Kavner (Marge Simpson)
Yeardley Smith (Lisa Simpson)
Simpson, Valerie
spouse: Nickolas Ashford
Sims: **3** Kym **4** Zoot
Sims, Zoot: **11** saxophonist
genre: **4** jazz
simulacrum: **4** copy, icon, ikon **5** eikon, image **9** imitation
simulate: **3** act, ape, lie **4** copy, fake, lift, mock, play, pose, sham **5** bluff, cheat, feign, fence, forge, mimic, phony, put on, steal **6** affect, assume, borrow, fake it, invent, mirror, phoney, pirate, play at **7** act like, concoct, deceive, imitate, playact, portray, pretend **8** disguise, knock off, resemble **9** fabricate, replicate, reproduce **10** equivocate, put on an act
simulated: **4** fake, mock, sham **5** bogus, false, phony, put-on, quack **6** ersatz, phoney, pseudo, unreal **7** assumed **8** spurious **9** emulative, imitation, imitative, synthetic **10** artificial, factitious, fictitious, fraudulent
simulation: **3** act **8** pretense **9** imitation
__ simulator: **6** flight
simultaneous: **10** concurrent
simultaneously: **5** along **6** at once, in sync **8** meantime, together **9** at one time, meanwhile
sin: **3** err **4** evil, lust, vice **5** anger, cheat, crime, error, fault, guilt, lapse, lying, stray, wrong **6** Hebrew, letter, offend, wander **7** avarice, demerit, deviate, do wrong, impiety, misdeed, offense **8** go astray, iniquity, peccancy, trespass **9** backslide, blasphemy, evildoing, misbehave, sacrilege, veniality, violation **10** immorality, infraction, misconduct, peccadillo, transgress, wickedness, wrongdoing
deadly ~: **4** envy, lust **5** pride, sloth, wrath **7** avarice **8** gluttony
lead into ~: **6** entice, entrap
predecessor: **4** resh
successor: **4** shin
sin __: **3** tax
__ sin: **3** arc **6** deadly, mortal
Sinai: **4** peak **5** mount **8** mountain
city near ~: **4** Gaza
desert near ~: **5** Negeb, Negev
locale: **4** Asia **7** Mideast
Sinatra: **4** Tina **5** Frank, Nancy
Sinatra, Frank: **5** actor **6** singer
film: Anchors Aweigh (1945)
Can-Can (1960)
Come Blow Your Horn (1963)
The Detective (1968)
Dirty Dingus Magee (1970)
The First Deadly Sin (1980)
From Here to Eternity (1953, AA)
Guys and Dolls (1955)
High Society (1956)
The Joker Is Wild (1957)
The Manchurian Candidate (1962)
The Man With the Golden Arm (1955)
Not as a Stranger (1955)
Ocean's Eleven (1960)
On the Town (1949)
Pal Joey (1957)
Robin and the Seven Hoods (1964)
Some Came Running (1959)
Take Me Out to the Ball Game (1949)
The Tender Trap (1955)
Tony Rome (1967)
Von Ryan's Express (1965)
Young at Heart (1954)
hometown: Hoboken
song: All the Way (1957)
Can I Steal a Little Love (1957)
Hey! Jealous Lover (1956)
High Hopes (1959)
How Little We Know (1956)
It Was a Very Good Year (1966)
Learnin' the Blues (1955)
Love and Marriage (1955)
My Way (1969)
Same Old Saturday Night (1955)
Somethin' Stupid (1967)
Strangers in the Night (1966)
The Tender Trap (1955)
That's Life (1966)
Witchcraft (1958)
spouse: Mia Farrow, Ava Gardner
Sinatra, Nancy
song: How Does That Grab You, Darlin'? (1966)
Somethin' Stupid (1967)
Sugar Town (1966)
These Boots Are Made for Walkin' (1966)
spouse: Tommy Sands
Sinbad: **4** hero
emulate ~: **4** rove
number of voyages of ~: **5** seven
transport: **3** roc
since: **3** ago, for **4** as of **7** because, whereas **8** as long as, from then, until now **9** therefore **10** inasmuch as
in French: **3** des
in Scottish: **4** syne
prefix: **3** cis-
Since __ for You: **5** I Fell
Since __ Have You: **5** I Don't
Since __ You, Baby: **4** I Met
since Hector was __: **4** a pup
sincere: **4** dear, just, naif, open, real, true, warm **5** frank, meant, naive, plain **6** actual, candid, devout, direct, fervid, hearty, honest, infelt, square **7** artless, cordial, earnest, fervent, genuine, natural, regular, saintly, serious, up-front **8** bona fide, credible, faithful, innocent, like it is, out-front, profound, reliable, true-blue, truthful **9** dead-level, guileless, heartfelt, honorable, ingenuous, on the line, outspoken, righteous, unfeigned, unguarded **10** aboveboard, forthright, no-nonsense, on the level, point-blank, scrupulous, sure enough, unaffected, unimagined
sincerely: **4** true **5** truly **6** deeply, really, simply **7** frankly **8** candidly, for keeps, heartily, honestly **9** earnestly, genuinely, seriously **10** aboveboard, point-blank, profoundly, truthfully
in Latin: **7** ex animo
Sincerely (1955 song)
artist: McGuire Sisters, Moonglows
sincerity: **4** zeal **5** heart, honor, truth **6** candor, fervor, warmth **7** honesty, loyalty, probity **8** devotion, goodwill, openness, veracity **9** frankness, good faith, innocence, integrity **10** cordiality
Since you __...: **5** asked
Since You __ Me: **5** Asked
Since You've Been Gone (1968 song)
artist: Aretha Franklin
Sin City
author: Harold Robbins
Sin City (2005 film)
cast: Jessica Alba, Benicio Del Toro, Clive Owen, Mickey Rourke, Bruce Willis
Sinclair: **5** Lewis, Madge, Upton
rival: **4** Esso **7** Flying A
Sinclair, Upton: **6** writer
work: Boston
The Jungle
King Coal
Oil!
World's End
sine: **5** ratio
reciprocal: **5** cosec
sine __: **3** die **4** wave **5** curve
__ sine: **3** arc
Sinéad: **7** O'Connor
__ sine numine: **3** nil
sine qua non: **4** gist, must, need **7** essence **9** condition, essential, necessity, requisite
sinew: **4** beef, thew **5** brawn, force, power, thews, vigor **6** muscle, tendon **7** potence, potency **8** strength **9** toughness **10** resilience, robustness
sinewy: **4** hale, iron, lean, wiry **5** beefy, burly, hardy, hefty, hunky, husky, lusty, nervy, stout, tough **6** brawny, hearty, mighty, potent, robust, rugged, steely, stocky, strong, sturdy, virile **7** doughty, stringy **8** athletic, forceful, indurate, muscular, powerful, puissant, stalwart, vigorous **9** Atlantean, Herculean, resilient, strapping, well-built **10** able-bodied, red-blooded
sinful: **3** bad **4** dark, evil **5** cruel **6** guilty, rakish **7** harmful, immoral **8** depraved **10** inexpiable, iniquitous, villainous
sing: **3** hum, pur, rat **4** belt, blab, fink, laud, pipe, purr, talk, tune **5** carol, chant, chirp, croon, honor, sound, trill, troll, tweet, whine, yodel, yodle **6** betray, depone, inform, intone, lament, praise, snitch, tattle, turn in, warble **7** belt out, confess, descant, discant, glorify, perform, profess, resound, tell all, testify **8** melodize, serenade, vocalize **9** celebrate, harmonize **10** cantillate
ender: **4** song **5** spiel
falsetto: **5** yodel, yodle
how to ~: **5** on key
one's own praises: **4** brag, crow **5** boast
out: **3** cry **4** call, ring, yell **5** shout **6** bellow, holler, scream
softly: **5** croon
the blues: **4** mope, wail **5** be sad **6** bemoan, lament, sorrow **7** despair
the praises of: **4** laud **5** exalt, extol **6** extoll **7** glorify
without words: **3** hum
sing-__: **4** song **5** along
Sing (1973 song)
artist: Carpenters
Sing __ of sixpence...: **5** a song
Sing __ songs for me...: **5** no sad
Sing __ With Mitch: **5** Along
__ Sing: **3** Hop
Sing Along With Mitch (NBC music)
cast: Mitch Miller, Leslie Uggams
__ Sing and I'm Happy: **5** Let Me
Singapore: **4** city, isle, town **6** island, nation **7** capital, country
capital: **9** Singapore
language: **5** Malay
locale: **4** Asia
money: **4** cent **6** dollar
Singapore sling: **5** drink **8** beverage, cocktail
ingredient: **3** gin

Sing a Song (1975 song)
artist: Earth, Wind & Fire
Sing Down the Moon
author: Scott O'Dell
singe: **3** fry **4** burn, char, heat, sear **6** scorch **7** blacken, torrefy, torrify **8** overheat **9** carbonize
singer: **4** alto, bass, diva **5** basso, tenor **6** artist, canary **7** artiste, chanter, crooner, intoner, soloist, warbler, yodeler **8** melodist, minstrel, musician, songbird, songster, vocalist **9** chanteuse, choralist, chorister, serenader **10** troubadour
gig: **6** lounge
starter: **4** folk **6** master
work: **5** vocal
__ singer: **3** pop **4** folk, jazz **5** torch **6** gospel **7** country, popular
Singer: **4** Lori, Marc **5** Bryan, Isaac
Singer, Bryan: **8** director
film: The Usual Suspects (1995) X-Men (2000)
Singer, Isaac Bashevis: **6** writer **7** Yiddish **8** Nobelist
work: Enemies, a Love Story
The Estate
The Family Moskat
The Magician of Lublin
The Manor
The Penitent
Satan in Goray
Shosha
The Slave
singers: **5** choir **6** chorus **8** ensemble
__ Singer, The: **4** Jazz **7** Wedding
Singh: **3** Ram **5** Vijay
Singh, Vijay: **6** Fijian, golfer
singing: **5** music
group: **5** choir **6** chorus
style: **6** arioso, doo-wop
suitable for ~: **5** melic
syllables: **4** la la **5** tra la
the blues: **3** low **4** down **6** morose **8** downcast **9** sorrowful
voice: **4** alto, bass **5** basso, mezzo, pipes, tenor **7** soprano **8** baritone
singing __: **8** telegram
__ singing: **4** folk, part, scat
Singing Cowboy, The: **5** Autry
Singing Nun
song: Dominique (1963)
Singin' in the Rain (1952 film): **7** musical
cast: Cyd Charisse, Jean Hagen, Gene Kelly, Donald O'Connor, Debbie Reynolds
director: Stanley Donen, Gene Kelly
studio: **3** MGM
__ Sing in the Sunshine: **4** We'll
single: **3** hit, odd, one **4** lone, only, rare, sole, solo, unal **5** alone, loner, unwed **6** dollar, lonely, simple, unique, unmixt **7** unitary, unmixed **8** bachelor, distinct, divorced, eligible, especial, isolated, original, peerless, secluded, separate, solitary, specific, uncommon, unshared, wifeless **9** exclusive, on one's own, separated, unalloyed, unblended, undivided, unmarried, unrivaled **10** individual, particular, restricted, spouseless, unattached, unfettered, unrivalled
combining form: **3** mon- **4** hapl-, mono- **5** haplo-
entity: **4** item, unit **5** monad
having a ~ element: **5** unary
in ~ file: **4** arow
new ~: **2** ex
no more: **3** wed
out: **3** opt **4** cite, name, pick, take **5** elect, key on **6** choose, opt for, prefer, select **7** fix upon **8** decide on, handpick, identify, separate **9** designate, segregate **10** settle upon
softly-hit ~: **5** bloop
time: **4** once
single __: **4** file
single-__: **4** foot, knit, shot **5** space **6** family, handed, minded, suiter
single-__ bookkeeping: **5** entry
single-__ reflex camera: **4** lens
__ single: **3** RBI **4** bunt
single-file: **6** in a row
single-minded: **5** rigid **6** intent, steady **8** stubborn **9** steadfast, unbending
single-mindedness: **4** will **7** loyalty, purpose **9** willpower
single-name
singer: **4** Cher **5** Björk **6** Fergie, Prince **7** Beyoncé, Madonna, Tiffany
supermodel: **4** Iman **6** Twiggy
singleness: **5** unity **7** loyalty
single-purpose: **5** ad hoc
singles __: **3** bar
singles party: **5** mixer
singlet: **5** shirt
in America: **10** undershirt
singleton: **5** loner **10** individual
Singleton: **4** John **5** Penny
__ Singleton Copley: **4** John
Single White Female (1992 film)
cast: Bridget Fonda, Jennifer Jason Leigh, Steven Weber
singly: **3** but **4** each **5** alone, apart **6** apiece, solely **8** one by one **10** one at a time, separately
sing one's __: **7** praises
Sing Sing: **6** prison
locale: **7** New York
resident: **3** con **5** felon **6** inmate **8** prisoner
singsong: **6** intone **10** monotonous
__ Sings the Blues: **4** Lady
sing the __: **5** blues
singular: **3** odd, one **4** lone, only, rare, sole, solo, unal **5** alone, loner, queer **6** atypic, quaint, unique **7** certain, curious, eminent, oddball, special, strange, uncanny, unusual **8** atypical, definite, especial, original, peculiar, puzzling, separate, solitary, striking, uncommon, unwonted **9** eccentric, exclusive, marvelous, recherché, unheard-of **10** individual, noteworthy, outlandish, particular, phenomenal, prodigious, remarkable, respective, unexampled, unordinary
singularity: **5** quirk **6** oddity **8** identity **9** mannerism
Sinise: **4** Gary
Sinise, Gary
TV: CSI: NY
sinister: **3** bad, ill **4** base, dark, evil, grim, left, ugly, vile **5** lurid, nasty **6** creepy, malign **7** baleful, baneful, corrupt, doomful, harmful, hurtful, malefic, ominous, satanic, unlucky **8** lowering, menacing, perverse **9** dishonest, ill-boding, injurious, malignant, obnoxious, satanical **10** disastrous, forbidding, foreboding, malevolent, pernicious, portentous, villainous, virtueless
look: **4** leer
opposite: **6** dexter
sinistral: **4** left
sink: **3** bog, dip, ebb, fen, lay, ram, rot, sag, set **4** dive, drop, fail, fall, flag, hole, mire, ruin, slip, stab, tire, verb, wane, wilt **5** abate, basin, decay, drill, drive, droop, drown, embed, imbed, lapse, lower, marsh, reach, slide, slope, slump, spoil, stick, stoop, swamp, swoop, waste, wreck **6** cave in, debase, defeat, demean, engulf, fall in, go down, hollow, ingulf, lessen, plunge, ravage, recede, settle, thrust, weaken, worsen **7** capsize, decline, degrade, depress, descend, destroy, drop off, dwindle, fatigue, founder, go broke, go under, immerse, let down, plummet, put down, regress, relapse, scuttle, subside, succumb, tail off, triumph, venture **8** bankrupt, cast down, collapse, decrease, demolish, diminish, excavate, flounder, submerge, submerse, vanquish, washbowl **9** aggravate, backslide, bring down, devastate, disappear, force down, humiliate, overwhelm, shipwreck **10** degenerate, depreciate, depression, exacerbate, go bankrupt, go downhill, impoverish, retrograde, retrogress
alternative: **4** swim
ender: **3** age **4** hole
feature: **4** trap **5** drain
in: **8** register **9** penetrate
like the kitchen ~: **5** soapy, sudsy
one's teeth into: **3** nip **4** bite
starter: **7** counter
to the bottom: **6** settle
trap shape: **3** ess
__ sink: **3** dry **4** heat, slop **7** kitchen
sinker: **5** donut, pitch **6** weight **8** doughnut
ender: **4** ball
material: **4** lead
sub ~: **6** ashcan
sinkhole: **6** hollow **10** depression
Sin Killer
author: Larry McMurtry
sinking: **3** low **4** down **7** descent
sinking __: **4** fund
sinking ship deserter: **3** rat
sink one's __ into: **5** teeth
sink or __: **4** swim
Sink the Bismarck (1960 song)
artist: Johnny Horton
Sink the Bismarck!
author: C.S. Forester
sinless: **5** clean **6** chaste **8** innocent **9** faultless, guiltless, righteous **10** immaculate, impeccable
sinner: **6** rascal **8** criminal, evildoer
former ~: **6** atoner
Sinn Fein
land: **4** Eire **7** Ireland
org.: **3** IRA
Sino-: **7** Chinese
Sin of Father Mouret
author: Émile Zola
Sino-Japanese __: **3** War
Sinope: **4** moon
planet: **7** Jupiter
Sint __: **7** Maarten
__ Sin to Tell a Lie: **4** It's a
sinuate: **4** coil, curl, kink, loop, wind **5** crimp, curve, snake, swirl, twine, twirl, twist, whorl **6** spiral, tangle **7** entwine, intwine, meander, wreathe **9** convolute, corkscrew **10** intertwine
sinuosity: **3** arc, bow **4** arch, bend, coil, curl, loop, ogee, turn **5** crook, curve, orbit, twist, whorl **6** camber, circle, spiral **7** contour, ellipse, flexure, rainbow **8** parabola **9** arabesque, concavity, hyperbola **10** trajectory
sinuous: **4** bent, viny, wavy **5** curvy, lithe, snaky **6** curved, curvey, supple, zigzag **7** coiling, crooked, devious, turning, vagrant, winding **8** flexuous, indirect, tortuous, twisting, writhing **9** lithesome, meandrous **10** circuitous, convoluted, meandering, serpentine, undulating
shape: **3** ess
sinus: **6** cavity **10** depression
cavity: **6** antrum
Sinutab
alternative: *see* cold remedy
Sinyavsky, Andrey: **6** writer **7** Russian
Siobhan: **7** McKenna
Siouan: **8** language
Indian: **3** Oto **4** Crow, Otoe **5** Omaha **6** Mandan **8** Missouri **10** Assiniboin
language: **4** Iowa **5** Kansa, Osage, Ponca **6** Dakota, Quapaw **7** Catawba, Hidatsa
Sioux: **5** tribe **6** Dakota, Indian, Lakota **7** Amerind, Lakhota
Sioux __: **3** War **4** City **5** Falls
Sioux __ Sue: **4** City
Sioux City: **4** city, town
locale: **4** Iowa
Sioux Falls: **4** town
locale: **4** S. Dak.
sip: **3** lap, nip, try **4** test, toss **5** drink, enjoy, quaff, savor, taste, touch **6** imbibe, sample **7** drink in, partake, swallow **8** spoonful **10** thimbleful
loudly: **5** slurp
more than a ~: **4** swig
siphon: **3** tap **4** draw, hose, pipe, pump, rack **5** drain **7** channel, extract **8** transmit
sipper: **5** straw
sir: **2** he **3** guy, him **4** chap, male, tuan **5** bloke, title **6** feller, fellow, knight, mister **7** effendi **9** gentleman
counterpart: **4** ma'am **5** madam
Hindu ~: **4** babu **5** baboo
Indian: **5** saheb, sahib
in Spanish: **5** señor
__, sir!: **3** Yes
Sir __: **4** Duke **5** Nigel **7** Mix-a-Lot
Sir __ Belch: **4** Toby
Sir __ John: **5** Elton
Sir Duke (1977 song)
artist: Stevie Wonder

sire: 3 dad 4 male, papa 5 beget, breed, spawn 6 father 7 creator 8 ancestor, stallion 9 propagate, reproduce 10 progenitor
mate: 3 dam
siren: 4 Bara, vamp 5 alarm, alert, houri, lurer, nymph, vixen 6 mud eel 7 Aglaope, enticer, Lorelei, manatee, Pisinoe, tempter, warning, whistle 8 alluring, Leucosia, sea nymph, tempting 9 beguiling, enchanter, temptress 10 bewitching, enchanting, Parthenope, Thelxiepia
sound: 4 wail
siren ___: 4 song
Sirens
sculptor: Erté
___ Sirenum: 4 Mare
Sir Francis ___: 5 Drake
Sir Galahad: 4 poem
author: Alfred Tennyson
Sirius: 4 star 6 Sothis 7 Dog Star
owner: 5 Orion
sirloin: 4 beef, meat 5 steak
Sir Mix-___: 4 a-Lot
Sir Nigel
author: Arthur Conan Doyle
sirocco: 4 wind
___, Sir, That's My Baby: 3 Yes
Sirtis: 6 Marina
sis
see sister
sisal: 5 agave, fiber
sisal ___: 4 hemp
'S' Is for Silence
author: Sue Grafton
Siskel: 4 Gene
Sisler, George: 8 Cardinal 10 baseballer
sissified: 6 effete, prissy
sissy: 4 nerd, wimp, wuss 5 nerdy, weeny 6 craven, moaner, prissy 7 chicken, crybaby, dastard, mincing 8 mama's boy, poltroon, recreant, weakling 9 fraidy cat, jellyfish 10 namby-pamby, pantywaist
lack: 5 spine
like a ~: 5 timid
sissy ___: 3 bar
Sissy: 6 Spacek
sister: 3 kin, nun, rel., sib 6 female 7 kinsman, sibling 8 relation, relative 9 kinswoman 10 kinsperson
child: 5 niece 6 nephew
ender: 4 hood
group: 3 sor. 8 sorority
parent's ~: 4 aunt 5 aunty
sib: 3 bro
starter: 4 step
superior: 6 abbess
sister-___: 5 in-law
___ sister: 3 big, lay, sob 4 half, soul 6 foster
Sister ___: 3 Act 5 Kenny, Sarah 6 Carrie, Sledge 7 Souljah
___ Sister: 6 Little
Sister Act (1992 film)
cast: Whoopi Goldberg, Harvey Keitel, Maggie Smith
role: 3 nun
setting: 4 Reno
Sister Carrie
author: Theodore Dreiser
character: 3 Bod 4 Ames, Sven 6 Drouet, Hanson, Meeber, Minnie
Sister Golden Hair (1975 song)
artist: America
sisterhood: 5 order
Sisterhood of the Traveling Pants, The (2005 film)
cast: Alexis Bledel, America Ferrera, Blake Lively
sisterly: 4 kind 5 thick
Sister of ___: 5 Mercy 7 Charity, Loretto
___ sisters: 5 weird
Sisters
artist: Erté
Sisters (1973 film)
cast: Charles Durning, Margot Kidder
director: Brian De Palma
Sisters (NBC drama)
cast: Ashley Judd (Reed Halsey)
Patricia Kalember (Georgie Whitsig)
Swoosie Kurtz (Alex Barker)
Julianne Phillips (Frankie Reed)
Sela Ward (Teddy Reed)
___ Sisters: 7 Andrews, McGuire, Pointer
Sister Sledge
song: He's the Greatest Dancer (1979)
We Are Family (1979)
Sisters of Charity
founder: Elizabeth Seton
Sistine ___: 6 Chapel 7 Madonna
Sistine Chapel
locale: 4 Rome 7 Vatican
work: 5 mural 6 fresco
Sisyphean: 7 endless, eternal
Sisyphus: 4 king
parent: 6 Aeolus 7 Enarete
wife: 6 Merope
sit: 3 lie 4 meet, park, plop, pose, rest, seat, wait 5 brood, cover, light, model, perch, relax, roost, squat, usher 6 bear on, groove, hunker, instal, lounge, occupy, remain, settle, sprawl 7 convene, install, posture, preside 8 assemble, bear upon, ensconce, plop down 9 officiate, watch over 10 deliberate, take a chair, take it easy
around: 4 laze, loaf, rest 5 relax 6 linger, unwind
down: 4 land, plop, rest 5 light, relax 6 strike
in: 6 attend, strike
in on: 5 audit, visit 7 observe
not ~ well: 3 irk, vex 4 gall, rile 5 anger, annoy, chafe, grate 6 bother, nettle, pester, rankle 8 irritate 10 exasperate
on: 5 hatch, quash, quell 6 put off, rebuke, squash, stifle 7 secrete, silence, squelch 8 hold back, incubate, postpone, restrain, suppress, withhold 10 keep in line, monopolize
on one's hands: 7 abstain
on the fence: 5 waver 7 abstain, quibble 8 hesitate 9 pussyfoot
out: 5 forgo 6 forego 7 abstain, refrain
place to ~: 3 lap 4 sofa 5 bench, chair, perch
spread out: 6 sprawl
starter: 5 house
still for: 3 let 5 abide, allow 6 accept 8 tolerate
through: 6 endure, remain
tight: 4 stay, wait 6 remain 7 stay put
unable to ~ still: 5 antsy 7 fidgety
up for: 5 await
sit ___: 3 out 4 down, in on, upon 5 tight 6 around
sit ___ by: 4 idly
sit-___ strike: 4 down
___-sit: 3 bed 4 baby
Sita
husband: 4 Rama
sitar: 6 string 10 instrument
motif: 4 raga
origin: 5 India
sitarist: 7 Shankar
sitcom: 6 series 10 production
award: 4 Emmy
demo: 5 pilot
material: 5 humor
sit-down: 6 strike 8 stoppage
affair: 6 dinner
site: 3 fix, lay 4 area, base, home, plot, post, slot, spot 5 haunt, locus, place, point, range, scene, venue, where 6 ground, layout, locale, locate 7 habitat, hangout, purlieu, section, setting, station, theater, theatre 8 locality, location, position, premises, wherever
starter: 4 camp, dump
___ site: 3 Web
sited: 3 set
sit-in: 5 rally 7 protest 10 substitute
Sitka: 4 city, Emil, town
locale: 6 Alaska
Sitka ___: 6 spruce
sit on one's ___: 5 hands
sitophobe fear: 4 food
sitter: 5 model 8 caretake, guardian, watchdog 9 attendant, caretaker, custodian
bane: 4 brat
___ sitter: 3 pet 4 baby 5 aisle, house
___-sitter: 3 bed 4 farm 5 fence
sitting: 4 idle 7 session 9 sedentary
duck: 4 butt, dupe, goat, prey 6 pigeon, sucker, target, victim
on: 4 atop
place: 5 roost, stoop
pretty: 4 rich, safe 6 loaded 7 wealthy, well-off 8 affluent, in clover, thriving, well-to-do 9 well-fixed 10 well-heeled
room: 5 salon 6 lounge, parlor 7 boudoir
starter: 5 house
sitting ___: 4 duck, room 6 pretty
Sitting ___: 4 Bull
Sitting Bull: 5 chief, Sioux
foe: 6 Custer
(Sittin' On) The Dock of the Bay (1968 song)
artist: Otis Redding
Sittin' Up in My Room (1996 song)
artist: Brandy
situate: 3 put, set 4 post, seat 5 place, posit 6 locate, orient 8 ensconce
situated, get: 3 set 5 dwell, lodge, perch, roost, set up 6 locate, orient, settle
situation: 3 job 4 case, hire, mode, pass, post, rank, role, seat, site, spot, trim 5 event, locus, place, point, scene, stage, state, thing, trade 6 billet, locale, matter, office, plight, sphere, status 7 footing, picture, problem, setting, station, vacancy 8 ball game, bearings, instance, latitude, like it is, locality, location, position, size of it, standing 9 adversity, condition, placement, status quo 10 employment, engagement, occurrence, profession, standpoint, walk of life
accept the ~: 4 cope 5 adapt 6 face it, manage
bad ~: 3 fix 4 bind, drag, mess, spot 5 pinch 6 scrape 8 quagmire
no-win ~: 4 bind 7 dilemma 8 dead heat, deadlock, quandary, standoff 9 stalemate
situation ___: 4 room 6 comedy
___ situation: 5 no-win
___ sit under the apple tree...: 4 Don't
situs: 6 locale 8 position
Sitwell: 5 Edith 6 Osbert
Sitwell, Edith: 4 Dame, poet 7 British
work: A Poet's Notebook
Still Falls the Rain
sitz ___: 4 bath
Sivan: 5 month 6 Hebrew
predecessor: 4 Iyar
successor: 6 Tammuz
Siva worshiper: 5 Hindu 6 Hindoo
six: 5 hexad 6 hexade, number
combining form: 3 hex-, sex- 4 hexa-, sexi- 5 sexti-
ender: 4 teen 5 pence
feet: 6 fathom
games in tennis: 3 set
in dice: 4 sise
in German: 5 sechs
in Italian: 3 sei
in Japanese: 4 roku
in Portuguese: 4 seis
in Spanish: 4 seis
outs: 6 inning
to Mohs: 10 orthoclase
years, for senators: 4 term
six ___ and half...: 5 of one
six-___: 3 gun 4 pack, spot 6 footer 7 shooter
___-six: 4 deep 6 eighty
Six ___: 6 Crises
Six ___ a-laying...: 5 geese
Six ___ Riv Vu: 3 Rms
Six Characters in Search of an Author
author: Luigi Pirandello
Six Crises
author: Richard Nixon
Six Days Seven Nights (1998 film)
cast: Harrison Ford, Anne Heche
director: Ivan Reitman
Six-Day War
hero: 5 Dayan
Six-Day War site: 5 Sinai
Six Degrees of Separation: 4 film, play
author: John Guare
cast: Stockard Channing, Mary Beth Hurt, Ian McKellen, Will Smith, Donald Sutherland
Sixers: 4 five, team 6 cagers
org.: 3 NBA

sixes
at ~ and sevens: 4 hazy 5 aback, dizzy, messy, muddy, upset, wooly 6 cloudy, hectic, punchy, woolly 7 abashed, chaotic, haywire, out of it, puzzled, shook up 8 anarchic, confused, mistaken, nebulous, pell-mell, rambling 9 misguided, quizzical, slaphappy, spaced out, unsettled 10 anarchical, disjointed, disorderly, indefinite, in disarray, indistinct, out to lunch, topsy-turvy, upside-down
double ~: 7 boxcars
pair of ~: 5 dozen
Six Feet Under
genre: 5 drama
network: 3 HBO
Six Flags attraction: 4 ride
Six Flags New England
locale: 6 Agawam
six-mile
about a ~ run: 4 ten K
Six Million Dollar Man, The (ABC adventure)
cast: Richard Anderson (Oscar Goldman)
Martin E. Brooks (Dr. Rudy Wells)
Lee Majors (Col. Steve Austin)
employer: OSI
hometown: Ojai
six-pack: 5 hexad
unit: 3 can
six-pack __: 3 abs
__ Six-pack: 3 Joe
six-packs, four: 4 case
sixpenny __: 4 nail
six-pointer: 2 TD 9 touchdown
six-shooter: 3 arm, gun 6 pistol
six-sided
crystal: 4 snow
solid: 4 cube
sixteen
one of ~ in a game: 4 pawn
one of ~ teeth: 5 upper
oz.: 5 one lb.
tablespoons: 3 cup
__ sixteen: 5 sweet
Sixteen __: 4 Tons 7 Candles, Reasons
__ Sixteen: 4 Only 5 You're
Sixteen Candles (1984 film)
cast: Paul Dooley, Anthony Michael Hall, Molly Ringwald
director: John Hughes
Sixteen Reasons (1960 song)
artist: Connie Stevens
sixteenth __: 4 note, rest
Sixteen Tons (1955 song)
artist: Tennessee Ernie Ford
sixth __: 5 sense
Sixth Commandment, The
author: Lawrence Sanders
sixth-grader: 5 'tween
sixth sense: 3 ESP 8 instinct 9 intuition, telepathy
Sixth Sense, The (1999 film)
cast: Toni Collette, Haley Joel Osment, Bruce Willis
director: M. Night Shyamalan
__-Six Trombones: 7 Seventy
Sixtus: 4 pope 7 pontiff
sixty: 10 threescore
grains: 4 dram
minutes: 4 hour
seconds: 6 minute
sixty-__-dollar question: 4 four
Six Weeks (1982 film)
cast: Dudley Moore, Mary Tyler Moore
sizable: 3 big 4 good, huge, much, tall, tidy, vast 5 ample, burly, giant, great, gross, hefty, husky, jumbo, large, major, roomy 6 decent, goodly 7 hulking, immense, mammoth, massive, titanic 8 colossal, enormous, gigantic, handsome, spacious, towering, whapping, whopping 9 capacious, extensive, Herculean, humongous, overlarge, strapping 10 gargantuan, large-scale, monumental, prodigious, stupendous, tremendous, voluminous
size: 4 area, bulk, girt, mass, sift, tall 5 girth, jumbo, large, range, scale, scope, small, width 6 amount, extent, height, junior, length, medium, petite, spread, volume 7 bigness, breadth, caliber, content, stature, stretch, tonnage, tunnage 8 capacity, classify, enormity, hugeness, quantity, vastness 9 amplitude, dimension, extension, greatness, immensity, intensity, largeness, magnitude, ranginess, substance 10 dimensions, extra large, population, proportion
adjust the ~ of: 6 zoom in 7 zoom out
cut down to ~: 5 shame 6 demean, humble 7 deflate 8 belittle, minimize 9 humiliate
geometric ~: 4 area 6 volume
large ~: 9 greatness
starter: 3 mid 4 down
test for ~: 5 try on
the ~ of it: 7 outlook 8 position 9 situation
up: 3 eye 4 case, rank, rate, scan, sort 5 assay, gauge, judge 6 assess, reckon, survey, verify 7 compare, look out, measure, predict 8 appraise, check out, estimate, evaluate 9 determine, speculate
__-size: 3 lap, mid 4 bite, desk, full, king, life, pint, twin 5 legal, queen 6 letter, pocket 7 economy, Olympic
__-size car: 3 mid
__-sized: 3 man 4 bite, full, good, king, pint
__ size fits all: 3 one
Sizemore: 3 Tom
sizzle: 3 fry 4 cook, hiss, sear, spit, whiz 5 broil, grill, roast, swish 6 wheeze 7 crackle, frizzle, sputter, whisper
Sizzler
rival: *see* restaurant chain
sizzling: 3 hot 4 warm 6 red-hot, sultry, toasty, torrid 7 burning, summery 8 ovenlike, tropical, white-hot 10 sweltering
S.J.: 8 Perelman
SJD: 6 degree
SJU
see Saint John's
ska: 5 music
kin: 7 calypso
Skagerrak
port: 4 Oslo
river to the ~: 6 Glomma
Skaggs: 5 Ricky
Skagway: 4 city, town
locale: 6 Alaska
Skala: 5 Lilia
Skara __: 4 Brae
skat: 4 game 8 card game
low card: 5 seven
skate: 3 ray 4 fish, skim, slip 5 dance, glide, slide
bottom: 5 blade
ender: 5 board
kin: 5 manta
kind of ~: 6 in-line
on thin ice: 4 risk
starter: 5 cheap
__ skate: 3 ice 5 speed 6 hockey, racing, roller
skate-boarding: 5 sport
skate on __ ice: 4 thin
skater: 6 carhop
fictional ~: 4 Hans 7 Brinker
figure: 5 eight
game: 6 hockey
jump: 4 axel, flip, loop, lutz 7 Salchow, toe loop
manuever: 4 jump, lift, spin, step 6 spiral
milieu: 3 ice 4 rink 5 arena
need: 3 ice 4 rink
org.: 3 ISU, NHL
spin: 3 sit 5 camel 7 layback
__ skater: 3 ice 6 figure
skating: 5 sport
figure ~ event: 3 men 5 pairs 6 ladies
__ skating: 4 pair 5 pairs, speed 6 figure, in-line
__ S. Kaufman: 6 George
sked
see schedule
skedaddle: 3 fly, git, hie, lam, rip, run, zip 4 bolt, dart, dash, flee, flit, race, rush, scat, shoo, skip, tear, zoom 5 leave, scoot, scram, spank, speed 6 barrel, cut out, decamp, gallop, get out, hasten, hustle, move it, rocket, scurry 7 abscond, floor it, go south, hop to it, make off, quicken, scamper 8 fugitate, run for it, step on it, turn tail 9 hotfoot it, shake a leg 10 get a move on, hightail it
Skee-Ball site: 6 arcade
skeet: 4 game 5 sport
Skeet: 6 Ulrich
Skeeter: 5 Davis
skein: 4 hank, knot 6 tangle 9 labyrinth
call: 4 honk
grounded ~: 6 gaggle
material: 4 silk, wool
unit: 5 goose
skeleton: 4 bone, cage, slim 5 bones, draft, frame, shell 6 design, sketch, slight 7 outline, slender, summary, support 9 framework, structure
in the closet: 5 shame 6 secret 7 scandal
starter: 3 exo 4 endo
skeleton __: 3 key 4 crew
__-skelter: 6 helter
Skelton: 3 Red 4 John
Skelton, Red: 5 actor 8 comedian
character: 4 Clem
persona: 4 hobo
wife: 4 Edna
skep: 6 basket
skeptic: 5 cynic 7 atheist, doubter, infidel, killjoy, scoffer 8 apostate, nihilist 9 dissenter, pessimist, worrywart 10 questioner, unbeliever
skeptical: 4 wary 5 chary, leery 6 show-me, unsure 7 cynical, dubious, guarded 8 cautious, doubtful, doubting, hesitant, scoffing 9 faithless, heretical, jaundiced, quizzical, uncertain 10 dissenting, hesitating, suspicious
comment: 3 bah 4 as if, I bet 5 how so
skepticism: 5 doubt, qualm, query 6 wonder 7 dubiety 8 distrust, mistrust, nihilism, wariness 9 disbelief, dubiosity, leeriness, misgiving, suspicion 10 hesitation
Skepticism and Animal Faith
author: George Santayana
Skerritt, Tom: 5 actor
film: Alien (1979)
The Big Town (1987)
Contact (1997)
MASH (1970)
A River Runs Through It (1992)
Steel Magnolias (1989)
TV: Picket Fences
sketch: 3 art, map 4 copy, draw, form, limn, plan, plot, skit 5 brief, cameo, chart, draft, piece, shape, trace 6 depict, design, detail, doodle, figure, lay out, map out, précis, render, survey 7 account, cartoon, croquis, develop, diagram, drawing, outline, picture, portray, profile, rundown, summary, version 8 block out, describe, likeness, portrait, rough out, scenario, skeleton, syllabus, synopsis, vignette 9 adumbrate, blueprint, delineate, depiction, floor plan, landscape, lineation, portrayal, represent, synopsize 10 compendium, figuration, illustrate
ender: 3 pad 4 book
literary ~: 5 cameo
thumbnail ~: 3 bio 7 outline, profile
__ Sketch: 5 Etch a
sketcher need: 6 eraser, pencil
Sketches by __: 3 Boz
sketchy: 3 cut 4 thin 5 crude, rough, vague 6 coarse, faulty, patchy, skimpy, slight 7 cursory, outline, partial, reduced, shallow, tenuous 8 abridged, half-done 9 condensed, curtailed, defective, depthless, imperfect, shortened 10 diminished, expurgated, inadequate, incomplete, unfinished
skew: 4 bias, skid, tilt, veer 5 slant, slope, twist 6 squint, squirm, swerve 7 deflect, distort, diverge, oblique 8 angle off, misquote, misstate 9 misrender, misreport, prejudice, turn aside 10 deflection, divergence
skewed: 3 wry 4 awry, bent 5 askew 6 angled, biased, warped 7 angular, beveled, crooked, oblique, on a bias, slanted, twisted 8 angulose, angulous, cockeyed, diagonal, lopsided, slanting, tortu-

SI

ous **9** contorted, crossways, crosswise, distorted, malformed **10** asymmetric, transverse
skewer: 3 pin **4** spit, stab **5** spear, spike **6** empale, impale **8** transfix
meat ~: 5 shish
tidbit: 5 cabob, kabab, kabob, kebab, kebob
ski: 5 glide **6** runner, schuss
area: 3 run **5** piste, slope, trail
dwelling: 5 lodge **6** chalet
ender: 3 bob **4** wear **6** bobber, mobile
gear: 3 bib **4** mask, pole **7** goggles
instructor: 3 pro
jacket: 6 anorak
lift: 4 J-bar, T-bar
maneuver: 4 stem
need: 4 snow
part: 4 prow
position: 4 tuck
resort: 4 Alta, Vail **5** Aspen, Banff, Tahoe **6** Gstaad
slope bump: 5 mogul
slope machine: 3 tow **4** lift
wood: 3 ash
ski __: 3 bum, pro, run, tow **4** boot, jump, lift, mask, pole, rack, suit **5** pants
__ ski: 5 water
__-ski: 5 après, hydro
Ski-__: 3 Doo
__ Ski: 3 Jet
skiagraph: 4 x-ray
skid: 4 skew, slew, slip, slue, veer **5** drift, glide, slide **6** sledge, slough, swerve **7** plummet **8** fishtail, sideslip
starter: 3 non **4** anti, tail
skid __: 3 row
skidoo: 3 fly **4** flee **5** scram, split **8** fugitate, run for it
skid-prone: 3 icy
skids, hit the: 4 fail, sink **5** slump **7** decline
skier: 3 Moe **5** Killy, Mahre, Tomba **6** Street **7** Klammer
Austrian ~: 7 Klammer
French ~: 5 Killy
Italian ~: 5 Tomba
Olympian ~: 3 Moe
showoff ~: 6 hotdog
see also ski
skies: 9 firmament
__ skies: 5 to the
__ Skies: 4 Blue
skies they were __ and sober, The: 5 ashen
skiff: 4 boat, dory **5** barca, canoe, kayak **6** dinghy, dugout, sampan **7** catboat, pirogue, rowboat, Sunfish **8** sailboat, Sailfish **9** catamaran
body: 4 hull
propel a ~: 3 row
tool: 3 oar
Ski Hall of Fame site: 4 Vail
skiing: 5 sport
see also ski
__ skiing: 5 grass **6** alpine
skill: 3 art, job **4** ease, gift, head, line, tact, work **5** clout, craft, goods, knack, moxie, power, savvy, stuff, touch, trade, trick **6** smarts, talent **7** ability, command, cunning, faculty, finesse, know-how, masonry, mastery, prowess, sleight **8** aptitude, artistry, capacity, deftness, facility, hang of it, juggling **9** adeptness, carpentry, dexterity, diplomacy, expertise, handiness, ingenuity, readiness, smartness, technique **10** capability, cleverness, competence, competency, efficiency, experience, green thumb, leadership, nimbleness, profession, right stuff, toolmaking, virtuosity
having ~: 4 able
in Chinese: 6 kung fu
in Italian: 4 arte
to a sore loser: 4 luck
skilled: 3 ace, apt **4** able, deft, good, ripe **5** adept, crack, handy, ready, slick **6** adroit, au fait, expert, gifted, habile, nimble, up to it, versed **7** capable, learned, tactful, trained **8** delicate, dextrous, graceful, masterly, seasoned **9** competent, dexterous, efficient, masterful, practiced, versatile **10** conversant, proficient
in: 6 good at
occupation: 5 craft
one: 3 wiz **4** tech, whiz **6** master, techie
skilled __: 5 labor
skillet: 3 pan **6** frypan **9** frying pan
use a ~: 3 fry **5** sauté
skillful: 3 ace, apt, old, pro, vet **4** able, cool, deft, fine, good, neat, whiz **5** adept, canny, crack, great, handy, quick, ready, savvy, sharp, slick, smart **6** adroit, artful, au fait, brainy, clever, expert, facile, fluent, habile, nimble, pretty, primed, up to it, versed **7** capable, cunning, knowing, learned, tactful, trained, tuned in, versant, veteran **8** dextrous, graceful, masterly, prepared, seasoned, talented **9** competent, dexterous, efficient, excellent, ingenious, judicious, masterful, practical, practiced, qualified **10** proficient, well-versed
facetiously: 3 ept
skillfully: 4 neat, well **8** laudably, very well, worthily **10** delicately, swimmingly
skillfulness: 4 ease **5** knack **8** facility **9** dexterity
skills, basic: 4 ABCs
skim: 3 dip, fly, run, top **4** dart, film, kiss, leaf, milk, read, ream, sail, scan, skip, soar **5** coast, cream, defat, float, glide, graze, ladle, scoop, shave, skate, skirr, slide, sweep **6** browse, low-fat, peruse, profit, riffle, scurry **7** fat-free, lightly, skitter **8** glance at, separate **9** brush over **10** glance over, go smoothly, hydroplane, run through
along: 4 flit, skip
milk lack: 3 fat
the cream: 5 defat
skimmer: 3 hat **4** bird **5** A-line, dress
skimp: 3 eke **4** save **5** scant, screw, spare **6** scrape, slight **7** cut back, stretch **8** conserve, roll back, withhold **9** economize **10** cut corners, underspend
on: 5 stint **7** cut down
skimpiness: 4 want **10** inadequacy
skimpy: 3 shy **4** poor, puny, thin, weak **5** brief, lousy, scant, short, spare, tight **6** faulty, feeble, frugal, little, meager, measly, scanty, scrimp, sparse, spotty, stingy **7** chintzy, failing, lacking, miserly, scrimpy, sketchy, wanting **8** exiguous, piddling **9** deficient, illiberal, penurious, scattered **10** inadequate, skinflinty, ungenerous
skin: 3 fur **4** bare, bark, coat, film, flay, hide, hull, husk, pare, peel, pelt, rind, shed, trim **5** cover, crust, derma, flesh, graze, layer, organ, scale, scalp, shave, shell, shuck, strip **6** abrade, casing, corium, cut off, defeat, dermis, jacket, scrape, sheath, slough **7** coating, leather, outside, pull off, surface, swindle **8** carapace, membrane **9** container, epidermis, excoriate, parchment, sheathing **10** integument
alive: 4 flay **6** vilify **9** criticize
and bones: 4 lank, thin **5** spare
animal ~: 3 rug **4** hide, pelt
bare ~: 4 buff
blemish: 3 wen, zit **4** wart
by the ~ of one's teeth: 6 barely **8** narrowly
combining form: 4 derm-, scyt- **5** -derma, dermo-, scyto- **6** dermat-, -dermis **7** dermato-
cream: 5 toner
damager: 3 sun **5** UV ray
diving: 5 sport
ender: 5 flint, tight
feature: 4 pore
fold: 6 dewlap
get under one's ~: 3 irk, vex **4** rile **5** annoy, peeve, pique, upset
hardened ~: 6 callus
irritation: 5 uredo
layer: 5 derma
lotion ingredient: 4 aloe
of the ~: 6 dermal, dermic
opening: 5 stoma
secretion: 5 sebum
sensation: 5 touch
shed ~: 4 molt
shrinker: 4 alum
soother: 5 salve
starter: 3 doe, kid, oil, pig **4** bear, buck, calf, cape, coon, deer, goat, lamb, mole, seal, swan, wine, wool **5** onion, scarf, shark, sheep, snake
tone: 4 look **5** flesh **6** aspect **8** coloring **10** appearance, complexion
skin __: 4 care, game **5** diver **6** diving
skin-__: 4 deep, dive
Skin __: 6 Bracer
skin-and-bones
see skinny
skin-deep: 7 shallow, trivial **8** external **10** unprofound
skin-dive: 4 swim
skinflint: 5 miser, piker **7** miserly, Scrooge **8** tightwad **10** cheapskate, pinchpenny
skinflinty: 4 near **5** cheap, small, tight **6** greedy, skimpy, stingy **7** miserly, selfish **8** ungiving **9** penurious **10** avaricious
skink: 6 animal, lizard **7** reptile
Skinnay: 5 Ennis
__-skinned: 4 thin **5** thick
__ skinner: 4 mule
Skinner: 2 B.F. **4** Otis
Skinner __: 3 box
__ Skinner Blues: 4 Mule
Skinner, Cornelia Otis: 6 writer
work: The Ape in Me
Our Hearts Were Young and Gay
The Pleasure of His Company
skinny: 4 bony, dirt, info, lank, lean, slim, thin, wiry **5** boney, gaunt, lanky, proof, rangy, spare **6** dainty, gangly, latest, meager, skinny, slight, slinky, svelte, twiggy **7** gracile, lowdown, scraggy, scrawny, slender, spidery, starved, willowy **8** gangling, rawboned, starving **9** emaciated, sylphlike
one: 4 wisp
skinny-dip: 4 swim
Skinny Legs and All (1967 song)
artist: Joe Tex
__ skin of one's teeth: 5 by the
Skin of Our Teeth, The
author: Thornton Wilder
'Skins
see Redskins
skintight: 4 snug **5** close
skip: 3 bob, cut, fly, hop, run **4** bolt, flee, flit, jump, leap, lope, miss, omit, pass, play, romp, skim, slur, snub, trip, verb **5** avoid, bound, caper, dance, forgo, frisk, graze, scoot, skirr, skirt **6** bounce, bypass, canter, cavort, desert, escape, eschew, forego, forget, gambol, glance, go past, hasten, ignore, pass up, prance, run off, run out, slight, spring, tiptoe **7** exclude, make off, neglect, run away, scamper, skitter **8** fugitate, jump over, leapfrog, leave out, omission, overlook, pass over, ricochet, run for it, skim over **9** disregard, exclusion, miss out on, oversight, play hooky, skedaddle **10** bounce over, fly the coop, hippety-hop
ender: 4 jack
meals: 4 fast
out: 2 go **3** fly, run **4** flee, move, quit **5** elope, leave **6** escape **7** abscond, go south, make off, ride off **8** jump bail, run for it
out on: 4 jilt **5** dodge **6** desert **7** abandon
past commercials: 3 zap
stones: 3 dap
sweets: 4 diet
syllables: 5 elide
skip __: 4 bail, rope, town **5** a beat **6** tracer
Skip: 7 Homeier
Skip __ Lou: 4 to My
__ Skip: 5 My Dog
__, skip and a jump: 3 hop
skipjack: 4 tuna
skipper: 4 boss **5** steer **6** leader, master, sailor **7** captain, headman, jack tar, oversee **8** director, helmsman, kingfish **9** commander
be a ~: 8 navigate
nickname: 4 cap'n
place: 4 helm **6** bridge
starter: 3 mud
Skipper
friend: 6 Barbie
Skippy
alternative: 3 Jif **8** Peter Pan

Skipworth: **6** Alison
skirmish: **3** row **4** fray, spat, tiff, tilt **5** brush, clash, fight, melee, mix-up, run-in, scrap, set-to **6** action, attack, battle, combat, dustup, fracas, tussle **7** contest, dispute, quarrel, ruction, scuffle **8** argument, conflict, showdown, squabble, struggle **9** encounter, scrimmage, square off **10** donnybrook, engagement
set for a ~: **5** armed
skirr: **3** fly **4** flee, skim, skip
skirt: **3** hem, rim **4** brim, duck, edge, hoop, kilt, maxi, midi, mini, skip, tutu **5** A-line, avoid, brink, dodge, dress, elude, evade, flank, hedge, pagne, pareu, verge **6** border, bypass, detour, dirndl, escape, fringe, hobble, ignore, margin, peplum, sarong, sheath **7** filibeg, pollera **8** culottes, go around, lavalava, lie along, philibeg, sidestep, surround **9** crinoline, get around, perimeter, periphery **10** circumvent, equivocate, fustanella, work around
accessory: **4** belt
African ~: **5** pagne
alter a ~: **3** sew **5** rehem
alternative: **5** pants **6** slacks **8** culottes
Balkan ~: **10** fustanella
edge: **3** hem
feature: **4** dart, gore, slit, vent **5** plait, pleat, waist
length: **4** maxi, midi, mini
movement: **5** swish
panel: **6** insert
partner: **6** bodice
Polynesian ~: **5** pareu **6** sarong **8** lavalava
Scottish ~: **4** kilt **7** filibeg **8** philibeg
short ~: **4** mini **6** peplum
South American ~: **7** pollera
strapped ~: **6** jumper
wearer: **4** lady **5** woman **6** female
skirt ___: **5** steak
___ skirt: **4** hoop, hula **6** hobble, poodle
skit: **4** play **5** revue, spoof **6** parody, satire **7** lampoon **8** blackout
collection: **5** revue **6** review
Skitch: **9** Henderson
skitter: **3** run **4** skid, skim, skip **5** slink **6** spring **7** slither
skittish: **3** coy, shy **4** edgy **5** antsy, dizzy, giddy, itchy, jumpy, leery, nervy, peppy, tense, timid **6** demure, fickle, lively, uneasy **7** anxious, excited, fearful, fidgety, flighty, jittery, keyed up, nervous, playful, restive, uptight **8** agitated, restless, troubled, volatile **9** alarmable, concerned, excitable, frivolous, ill at ease, sensitive, tremulous, whimsical **10** capricious, high-strung, unreliable
Skittle Players
artist: Jan Steen
skivvies: **6** briefs, shorts, undies **8** lingerie **9** underwear
skiwear: **5** parka
skoal: **5** prost, toast **6** cheers, kampai, prosit
Skokie: **4** city, town
locale: **8** Illinois
Skopje: **4** city, town **7** capital
locale: **9** Macedonia
skosh: **3** bit, tad **4** iota **7** smidgen, smidgin **8** smidgeon
Skou, Jens: **6** Danish **7** chemist **8** Nobelist
skulk: **4** lurk **5** creep, prowl, shirk, slink, sneak **6** lay for **7** slither **9** lie in wait **10** nose around
skull: **4** bone, head **6** noodle, sconce **7** cranium **9** braincase
cavity: **5** sinus
combining form: **5** crani- **6** cranio-
ender: **3** cap
protuberance: **5** inion
seam: **5** raphe
starter: **4** numb
skull ___: **7** session
Skull and Bones
member: **3** Eli **5** Yalie
skullcap: **6** beanie, pileus **8** yarmulke
skunk: **3** cur **4** rout, toad **5** grape, sneak **6** animal, bad hat, defeat, rascal, weasel **7** polecat, shut out, stinker **8** rakehell
African ~: **5** zoril **7** zorilla, zorille
Bambi ~: **6** Flower
cabbage family: **4** arum
defense: **4** odor **5** scent
ender: **4** weed
relative: ***see*** weasel
young: **3** kit
skunk ___: **5** works **7** cabbage
Skunk: **5** river
city on the ~: **4** Ames
locale: **4** Iowa
skunky: **7** odorous
sky: **5** azure, ether **6** aether, canopy, heaven **7** heavens **8** empyrean **9** firmament **10** atmosphere, outer space
battle: **6** air war
blow ~ high: **5** rebut **8** disprove **9** discredit, shoot down **10** invalidate
clear ~: **5** ether **6** aether
color: **4** blue **5** azure
Egyptian ~ goddess: **3** Nut
ender: **3** box, cap, way **4** dive, hook, jack, lark, line, sail, walk, ward **5** diver, light, wards, write **6** diving, rocket, writer **7** scraper
fall from the ~: **4** hail, rain, snow
hit the ~: **3** fly **4** soar **6** aviate
in the ~: **4** over **6** aerial **8** overhead
light: **3** sun **4** moon, star **6** albedo, aurora
maybe: **5** limit
path: **6** airway
pie in the ~: **5** dream
pilot: **5** padre **6** cleric, priest
science: **9** astronomy
tilt toward the ~: **5** tip up
traveler: **5** comet **6** meteor
up in the ~: **5** above, aloft, risen **6** aerial
sky ___: **4** blue **5** diver, pilot, train **6** diving **7** marshal
sky-___: **3** cam **4** high, hook
___ sky: **5** to the
___-sky: **4** blue
Sky: **9** Masterson
___ Sky: **4** Blue **6** Liquid, Yellow **7** October, Vanilla
___ Sky at Morning: **3** Red
___ sky at night...: **3** Red
sky-blue: **5** azure, lapis
skycap: **5** toter **6** porter
concern: **3** bag **7** luggage
Sky Captain and the World of Tomorrow (2004 film)
cast: Jude Law, Gwyneth Paltrow, Giovanni Ribisi
skydive: **4** jump
skydiving: **5** sport
need: **5** chute **9** parachute
Sky Dragon hero: **4** Chan
Skye: **4** Ione, isle **6** island
Skye, Ione: **7** actress
father: Donovan
Skyhawk: **3** car **4** auto **5** Buick **10** automobile
sky-high: **4** tall **5** aloft, lofty **9** excessive, expensive
Sky is Falling, The
author: Sidney Sheldon
Skylab
org.: **4** NASA
sighting: **5** comet
skylark: **4** bird, play **5** revel, sport
Skylark: **3** car **4** auto **5** Buick **10** automobile
___ Skylark: **3** To a
___-sky law: **4** blue
skylight site: **4** roof **7** ceiling
skyline: **7** profile
feature: **5** spire, tower
obscurer: **3** fog **4** haze, smog
skylit area: **6** atrium
___ Skynyrd: **6** Lynyrd
skyrocket: **4** leap, soar, zoom **5** mount, surge
skyscraper: **5** tower **7** edifice **9** structure
support: **5** I-beam **6** girder
skyscraping: **4** high, tall **5** lofty **7** soaring **8** elevated, towering, uplifted
___ Sky, The: **3** Big
Skywalker, Luke: **4** hero, Jedi
father: **6** Anakin **10** Darth Vader
foe: **5** Vader
member of ~'s army: **4** Ewok
skyward: **5** above, aloft, lofty **6** uphill **8** overhead
skywrite: **9** advertise, publicize
Skyy: **5** vodka
competitor: **5** Popov, Stoli **6** Rodnik, Starka **7** Absolut **8** Smirnoff **9** Grey Goose
S&L
device: **3** ATM
offering: **2** CD **3** IRA **4** mtge.
payment: **3** int.
protector: **4** FDIC
unit: **3** acc. **4** acct.
see also bank
slab: **3** bar, bit, cut **4** cake, hunk, lump **5** block, board, chunk, ingot, layer, piece, plate, sheet, slice, stave, stela, stick, stone, strip, table, wedge **6** billet **7** boulder, bowlder, cutting, portion **9** flagstone
slack: **3** lax **4** dull, ease, idle, lazy, limp, play, room, slow, soft, wane, weak **5** abate, baggy, dodge, inert, let up, loose, quiet, relax, shirk, taper, tardy **6** droopy, excess, feeble, flabby, flimsy, floppy, infirm, leeway, lessen, loosen, remiss, sloppy, slow-up, supine **7** drop off, dwindle, ease off, flaccid, goof off, hanging, laggard, lay back, neglect, passive, relaxed, release, sagging, unready, untoned **8** careless, dangling, decrease, derelict, dilatory, diminish, flexible, heedless, inactive, indolent, listless, malinger, slothful, slovenly, slowdown, sluggish, stagnant, unsteady, unstrict **9** do-nothing, easygoing, forgetful, imprudent, leisurely, lethargic, loitering, negligent, shiftless, slow-paced, unheedful **10** delinquent, neglectful, permissive, regardless, slow-moving, sluggardly
cut some ~: **6** relent
off: **3** ebb **4** fade, idle, loaf, wane **5** abate, dally, let up, relax **6** cop out, dawdle, ease up, recede, soften **7** dwindle, lighten, subside **8** fade away, malinger, peter out, tone down, wind down **9** goldbrick, retrocede
slack-___: **5** jawed
slacken: **3** die, ebb, lag, lax **4** ease, idle, lull, slow, tire, wane **5** abate, delay, dodge, let up, loose, relax, remit, shirk, taper **6** dampen, lessen, loiter, loosen, modify, relent, retard, unwind **7** drop off, dwindle, ease off, goof off, lay back, neglect, release, relieve, subside, tail off **8** decrease, diminish, head away, level off, moderate, slow down **9** lighten up, retrocede **10** liberalize
slackened: **5** loose **9** leisurely
slackening: **3** ebb **5** letup **8** slowdown
slacker: **5** idler **6** loafer, truant **7** goof-off, shirker **8** layabout, parasite **9** do-nothing, goldbrick **10** malingerer
bane: **3** job **4** work
slack-jawed: **4** agog **5** agape **6** gaping
slackness: **6** laxity **7** laxness, license, neglect **8** laziness
slacks: **5** jeans, pants **6** chinos, khakis **8** breeches, flannels, trousers **10** hiphuggers
measure: **5** waist **6** inseam
slag: **5** dregs, dross **6** cinder, scoria **7** residue **8** residuum, sediment
slake: **4** cool **5** allay, quell **6** obtund, pacify, quench, revive **7** appease, assuage, mollify, refresh, relieve, satiate, satisfy **8** palliate
slalom: **4** race **5** event
curve: **3** ess
marker: **4** gate
need: **3** ski
site: **5** slope
___ slalom: **5** giant
slam: **3** bat, dig, hit, jab, pan, ram **4** bang, barb, bash, beat, belt, blow, boom, clap, damn, dash, ding, flay, gibe, hurl, jeer, jibe, mock, shut, slap, slug, slur, snub, swat, wham **5** abuse, blast, burst, close, crack, crash, decry, fling, knock, libel, pound, punch, scorn, smack, smash, smear, sneer, sound, spurn, swipe, taunt, thump, whack **6** attack, batter, cudgel, defame, deride, dump on, hammer, heckle, impugn, insult, jibe at, malign, offend, rebuff, review, scathe, slight, strike, thwack, vilify, wallop **7** affront, asperse, banging, calumny, catcall, clobber, degrade, disdain, lambast, mockery,

obloquy, offense, potshot, putdown, rank out, reproof, run down, scourge, slander, traduce **8** badmouth, belittle, contempt, denounce, derision, lace into, lambaste, lash into, reproach, ridicule, throw mud, uppercut, vilipend **9** aspersion, castigate, cheap shot, contumely, criticism, criticize, denigrate, discredit, disparage, humiliate, light into, shoot down **10** calumniate, defamation, disrespect, opprobrium, reflection, villainize
component: **5** trick
dance: **4** mosh
grand ~: **5** homer **7** home run, success, triumph, victory **9** landslide
into: **3** ram **7** rear-end
slam __: **4** dunk **5** dance **7** dancing
__ slam: **4** body **5** belly, grand
slam-bang
see wonderful
slam dunk: **4** shot **5** stuff
alternative: **5** lay-up
target: **4** hoop
slammer: **3** can, jug, pen **4** coop, jail, poky, stir **5** joint, pokey **6** cooler, lockup, prison **8** hoosegow
Slammin' Sammy: **4** Sosa **5** Snead
rival: **6** Big Mac
Slam the Door Softly
author: Clare Boothe Luce
slander: **3** dig, lie, mud, pan, rap, tar **4** barb, blot, dirt, gibe, hurt, jeer, jibe, mock, slam, slap, slur, snub, tale **5** abuse, belie, curse, decry, libel, roast, scorn, slime, smear, sneer, spurn, sully, taunt, wrong **6** accuse, assail, attack, damage, defame, defile, deride, dump on, heckle, impugn, injure, insult, malign, offend, rebuff, revile, scorch, slight, smirch, vilify **7** affront, asperse, blacken, calumny, catcall, degrade, detract, disdain, mockery, obloquy, offense, put-down, rank out, scandal, tarnish, traduce **8** backbite, badmouth, belittle, besmirch, black eye, contempt, denounce, derision, derogate, dishonor, ridicule, sling mud, tear down, throw mud, vilipend **9** aspersion, blaspheme, cheap shot, contumely, denigrate, discredit, disparage, humiliate **10** backbiting, calumniate, defamation, depreciate, detraction, disrespect, impugnment, imputation, muckraking, opprobrium, scandalize, villainize
ammo: **3** mud
slanderous: **7** vicious **9** injurious, invidious **10** defamatory, derogatory
slang: **4** cant, talk **5** argot, lingo **6** jargon, patois, pidgin **7** dialect, neology **8** jive talk, language, localism **9** Briticism, neologism **10** street talk, vernacular
slangy suffix: **3** -ese, -ola **4** -aroo, -eroo
slant: **3** tip **4** beam, bend, bent, bias, cant, heel, lean, list, look, ramp, side, skew, tilt, veer, view, warp **5** angle, bevel, color, focus, fudge, grade, level, light, phase, pitch, point, slope, splay, stand, twist **6** aspect, camber, direct, garble, stance, swerve, weight **7** decline, descend, deviate, distort, diverge, incline, leaning, opinion, outlook, recline **8** angle off, approach, attitude, diagonal, emphasis, gradient, judgment, misquote, skewness, strategy **9** direction, influence, prejudice, sentiment, viewpoint **10** conviction, deflection, diagonally, distortion, divagation, divergence, partiality, standpoint
ender: **4** ways, wise
slant-__ desk: **3** top
slanted: **5** askew, bevel, leant **6** aslope, leaned, skewed **7** crooked **8** diagonal, partisan
type: **6** italic **7** italics
slanting: **5** atilt **6** skewed **7** oblique, sideway **8** diagonal, sideways, sidewise
surface: **4** ramp
slantwise: **7** sideway **8** sideways **9** at an angle, obliquely, on the bias **10** diagonally
slap: **3** box, dig, hit, lap **4** bang, barb, bash, beat, blow, bust, chop, clap, cuff, gibe, hurt, jibe, lick, poke, shot, slam, slur, snub, sock, spat, swat, wham **5** abuse, crack, knock, libel, punch, scorn, smack, spank, swipe, taunt, thump, whack **6** insult, rebuff, rebuke, slight, strike, thwack, wallop **7** affront, calumny, catcall, disdain, lambast, mockery, obloquy, offense, putdown, slander **8** contempt, derision, lambaste, ridicule **9** aspersion, cheap shot, contumely, reprimand **10** defamation, disrespect, opprobrium
around: **7** rough up
ender: **4** dash, jack **5** happy, stick
in the face: **4** slam, slur **5** smear **6** rebuke, slight **7** affront, obloquy, offense, repulse **9** aspersion, cheap shot, rejection **10** backbiting, defamation, detraction, opprobrium
on: **3** add **4** link **5** affix **6** attach
on the wrist: **5** chide, scold **6** rebuke **7** lecture, reprove, upbraid **8** admonish, reproach **9** reprehend, reprimand
starter: **4** back
the cuffs on: **3** nab **5** run in **6** arrest
together: **4** make **5** rig up **7** throw up
with: **8** penalize
slap __: **4** down, shot
slap __ wrist: **5** on the
slapdash: **5** hasty, messy **6** random, remiss, untidy **7** cursory, hurried, offhand **8** careless, pell-mell, slipshod, slovenly **9** haphazard, makeshift, negligent, temporary, unheedful **10** last-minute, unthinking, unthorough, willy-nilly
slaphappy: **5** dizzy, giddy **6** addled, spacey **7** out of it **8** confused **9** befuddled
slapjack: **4** game **8** card game
__-slapper: **4** knee **5** thigh
Slap Shot (1977 film)
cast: Lindsay Crouse, Paul Newman, Michael Ontkean
slap-shot projectile: **4** puck
Slapsie __ Rosenbloom: **5** Maxie
slapstick: **4** zany **5** farce, funny, genre **6** comedy
noise: **5** splat
prop: **3** pie
slash: **3** axe, cut, rip **4** chop, clip, crop, drop, gash, hack, mark, pare, rend, rent, slit, tear **5** carve, lower, score, sever, shave, slant, slash, slice, split, wound **6** cleave, incise, injure, mangle, open up, pierce, reduce, streak, stroke **7** abridge, curtail, cut back, cut down, lambast, scissor, shorten, solidus, virgule, whittle **8** close out, decrease, diagonal, discount, incision, lacerate, lambaste, mark down **10** abbreviate, laceration, separatrix
slash-and-__: **4** burn
slashed: **3** low **4** torn **5** cheap **6** on sale **7** incised **9** lacerated
it may be ~: **5** price
slasher movie, like a: **4** gory
slat: **4** lath **5** board **6** batten, louver, louvre
slate: **4** blue, gray, grey, list, sked **5** color **6** agenda, bluish, lineup, tablet **7** blueish, grayish, mineral, program, runners **8** blue-gray, nominate, schedule **10** blackboard
need: **5** chalk **6** eraser
once: **5** shale
relative: *see* gray color
tool: **3** zax
wipe the ~ clean: **5** erase **6** pardon **7** absolve, forgive, release **8** overlook
Slate: **4** e-mag **5** e-zine
Slater: **5** Helen **9** Christian
slather: **6** spread
Slatkin, Leonard: **9** conductor
Slaughter: **4** Enos **5** Frank
Slaughterhouse-Five
author: Kurt Vonnegut Jr.
Slav: **4** Pole, Serb **5** Croat, Czech **6** Balkan, Slovak **7** Russian **8** Moravian **9** Bulgarian, Ukrainian
slave: **4** esne, grub, hand, help, moil, peon, plod, serf, slog, toil, work **5** grind, labor **6** drudge, jackal, menial, thrall, toiler, vassal, victim, worker **7** bondman, captive, chattel, laborer, servant, villein **8** liniment, struggle, work hard **9** Nat Turner, Spartacus, sycophant, workhorse
ancient ~: **4** esne
driver: **6** despot, master, tyrant **8** dictator, martinet **10** taskmaster
operatic ~: **4** Aïda
wages: **7** peanuts **8** pittance
slave __: **6** driver
__ slave: **4** wage **6** galley
__ Slave: **6** Marche
__ Slave Lake: **5** Great
slaver: **5** drool **6** drivel **7** lay it on, slobber
slavery: **4** toil, work, yoke **5** grind **6** chains, drudge, thrall **7** bondage, peonage, serfdom **8** drudgery, serfhood, thraldom **9** captivity, feudalism, indenture, servitude, thralldom, vassalage **10** constraint
Slave, The
sculptor: Erté
Slavic
cake: **5** babka
cold soup: **5** schav
dance: **4** kolo **8** kazatsky
sovereign: **4** czar, tsar
__-Slavic: **5** Balto
slavish: **4** meek **6** menial **7** fawning, servile **9** adulatory, groveling **10** submissive
Slavonic Dances
composer: Antonín Dvorák
slaw: **5** salad **8** side dish
starter: **4** cole **7** cabbage
Slawomir: **6** Mrozek
slay: **3** zap **4** do in **5** smite **8** dispatch
__ Slayer, The: **4** Deer
Slay Ride
author: Dick Francis
Slayton: **4** Deke
sleazebag: **3** rat **4** crud, dirt **5** skunk, slime, trash
sleazy: **3** low **4** base, limp, mean, poor, vile **5** cheap, dirty, grody, mangy, seedy, tacky **6** common, flimsy, mangey, paltry, shabby, shoddy, sordid, tawdry, trashy **7** run-down, squalid **8** slovenly **9** loathsome **10** broken-down, disgusting
sled: **3** toy **4** luge, pung **6** sledge, sleigh, troika **7** coaster, go-devil, Rosebud, vehicle **8** toboggan
racing ~: **4** luge **8** skeleton
runner: **5** blade
starter: **3** bob
sled __: **3** dog
__ sled: **3** dog
sledding
go ~: **5** coast, glide, slide
need: **4** hill, snow **5** slope
__ sledding: **5** rough, tough
sled dog: **5** husky
command: **4** mush
heroic ~: **5** Balto
sledge: **4** dray, skid **6** hammer
ender: **6** hammer
__ Sledge: **6** Sister
sledgehammer: **4** mall, maul
Sledgehammer (1986 song)
artist: Peter Gabriel
Sledge, Percy: **6** singer
song: When a Man Loves a Woman (1966)
sleek: **4** neat, oily, tidy, trim **5** natty, satin, shine, shiny, silky, slick, swank **6** dapper, glassy, glossy, jaunty, rakish, refine, satiny, silken, smooth, snazzy, spiffy, sporty, swanky **7** groomed **8** lustrous, polished, slippery, spruce up **9** lubricous **10** glistening
sleep: **3** nap, nod, zzz **4** doze, rest, yawn **5** crash, snore **6** catnap, drowse, nod off, repose, retire, siesta, snooze, torpor, trance, turn in **7** bed down, bedtime, conk off, drop off, fall out, latency, pass out, sack out, saw logs, saw wood, shuteye, slumber, zonk out **8** dormancy, dullness, languish, lethargy, take a nap **9** dreamland, hibernate, hit the hay, torpidity **10** catch a wink, estivation, forty winks, hit the sack

aid: 5 Nytol 6 Compoz, Unisom 7 Sominex
combining form: 4 hypn- 5 hypno-, somni-
cycle: 3 REM
deep ~: 4 coma 5 sopor
disorder: 5 apnea 6 apnoea
disturber: 5 light, noise
emerge from ~: 4 wake 5 awake, get up, waken 6 awaken
ender: 4 over, walk, wear
go to ~: 3 nap 4 rest 6 retire, turn in 7 lie down, sack out 8 abdicate 9 hit the hay 10 hit the sack
lightly: 4 doze 6 snooze
lose ~ (over): 4 fret 5 sweat
on: 8 consider, mull over 10 reconsider
place to ~: 3 bed, inn 8 quarters
put to ~: 4 bore, lull, tire 9 hypnotize
restlessly: 4 toss
scene: 5 dream
sound: 3 zzz 5 snore
spoiler: 5 alarm
unit: 4 wink
wear: 3 PJs 5 teddy 7 jammies, pajamas 9 nightgown 10 nightshirt

sleep __: 4 on it, over, sofa
sleep-__ camp: 4 away
__ sleep: 3 REM 4 go to 6 beauty
sleeper: 3 car, spy 4 sofa
compartment: 5 berth
legendary ~: 3 Rip
upside-down ~: 5 sloth
sleeper __: 3 car 4 seat
Sleeper (1973 film)
cast: Woody Allen, John Beck, Diane Keaton
director: Woody Allen
dog: 4 Rags
role: 4 Erno
Sleepers (1996 film)
cast: Kevin Bacon, Robert De Niro, Dustin Hoffman, Jason Patric
director: Barry Levinson
Sleeper, The
author: Edgar Allan Poe
sleep-inducing: 8 hypnotic 9 soporific
sleepiness: 8 laziness, lethargy 9 lassitude
sleeping: 4 abed 5 in bed, not up, under 6 latent 7 dormant 8 dormient 9 unmindful 10 unrealized
bag stuffing: 5 kapok
Chinese ~ platform: 4 kang
place: 3 bed, cot 4 bunk
stop ~: 4 wake 5 awake, get up, waken 6 awaken
sleeping __: 3 bag, car
Sleeping __: 6 Beauty
Sleeping Bag (1985 song)
artist: ZZ Top
Sleeping Beauty
author: Ross Macdonald
__ Sleeping Beauty: 3 To a
Sleeping Beauty, The: 6 ballet
composer: Peter Tchaikovsky
__ sleeping dogs lie: 3 let
Sleeping Prophet, The: 5 Cayce
sleeping sickness carrier: 6 tsetse, tzetze 8 glossina
__ Sleep in the Subway: 4 Don't
Sleep It Off, Lady
author: Jean Rhys
Sleepless in Seattle (1993 film)
cast: Tom Hanks, Bill Pullman, Meg Ryan
director: Nora Ephron
role: 5 Annie
sleeplessness: 6 nerves 8 insomnia
sleep like __: 4 a log, a top
sleeplike state: 8 hypnosis
__ Sleeps Tonight, The: 4 Lion
__ Sleep, The: 3 Big
sleepy: 4 dopy, dozy, dull, lazy, logy, slow 5 dopey, heavy, tired, weary 6 draggy, drowsy, groggy, snoozy, torpid 7 nodding, out of it, yawning 8 fatigued, hypnotic, inactive, listless, sluggish 9 heavy-eyed, lethargic, somnolent, soporific 10 knocked out, slumberous
be ~: 3 nod 6 drowse
ender: 4 head
get ~: 4 doze 5 droop 6 drowse
make ~: 9 hypnotize
sign: 4 yawn
Sleepy: 5 dwarf
colleague: *see* dwarf
sleepyhead
advice to a ~: 5 get up
sleepyheaded: 7 languid 8 sluggish 9 lethargic
Sleepy Hollow
schoolmaster: 5 Crane
Sleepy Hollow (1999 film)
cast: Johnny Depp, Christina Ricci, Miranda Richardson
director: Tim Burton
Sleepy John: 5 Estes
__ Sleepy People: 3 Two
Sleepy Time Gal lyricist: 4 Egan
sleet: 3 ice 4 rain 5 storm
sleeve
band: 6 armlet
end: 4 cuff
filler: 3 arm
it may be up one's ~: 3 ace
part: 5 wrist
type of ~: 6 dolman
__ sleeve: 3 air, cap 4 wind 5 set-in 6 dolman, raglan
__-sleeve: 5 shirt
sleeveless
blouse: 5 shell
cloak: 3 aba 4 abba
dress: 6 jumper
top: 4 vest
sleigh: 4 pung, sled
driver: 5 Santa
puller: 5 horse 8 reindeer
sleigh __: 3 bed 5 bells
Sleigh Ride
composer: Leroy Anderson
sleight: 4 ploy, ruse 5 knack, magic, skill, trick 6 gambit, scheme 7 gimmick 8 artifice, deftness, facility, maneuver 9 adeptness, dexterity, expedient, readiness, stratagem 10 adroitness, subterfuge
sleight-of-hand: 5 magic, trick
Sleipnir: 5 horse, steed 6 equine
owner: 4 Odin 5 Othin
slender: 3 off 4 bare, fine, lank, lean, slim, thin, trim, weak, wiry 5 faint, lanky, light, lithe, rangy, reedy, scant, small, spare, stick, wispy 6 dainty, feeble, gangly, little, meager, minute, narrow, remote, scanty, scarce, skinny, slight, slinky, stalky, svelte, twiggy 7 fragile, gracile, outside, scraggy, scrawny, spidery, tenuous, wanting, willowy, wispish 8 beanpole, exiguous, gangling 9 beanstalk, deficient, lithesome, sylphlike, waferlike 10 inadequate, negligible, threadlike
one: 4 wisp 5 sylph
slenderize: 4 slim
sleuth: 2 PI 3 spy, tec 5 snoop 6 shamus 7 gumshoe 9 detective
cry: 3 aha 4 ah so
ender: 5 hound
find: 4 clew, clue
game: 4 Clue
job: 4 case 5 caper
Sleuth (1972 film)
cast: Michael Caine, Laurence Olivier
character: 4 Milo, Wyke 6 Tindle
slew: 3 wad 4 gobs, host, lots, raft, skid 5 bunch, ocean, pivot 6 myriad, passel 7 legions, numbers, zillion 9 multitude, profusion, turn about
a ~ of: 4 many 6 legion, myriad, umteen, untold 7 copious, profuse, umpteen 8 abundant, manifold, numerous, umpsteen 9 bountiful, countless, quite a few
__ Slew: 7 Seattle
Slezak: 5 Erika 6 Walter
slice: 3 cut, lot 4 bite, chip, chop, gash, hack, hunk, part, slab, slit, stab 5 carve, knife, piece, quota, scrap, sever, share, shave, shred, slash, split, strip, wedge, wound 6 cleave, divide, incise, morsel, parcel, pierce, rasher, shares, sliver, sunder 7 dissect, helping, percent, portion, section, segment 8 division, fraction, fragment, triangle 9 allotment, allowance, ownership, subdivide 10 commission, laceration, percentage
destination, often: 5 rough
in four: 7 quarter
in two: 5 halve
off: 3 lop 4 trim 5 sever
pizza ~: 6 eighth
thick ~: 4 slab
thin: 5 shave 7 shaving
up: 5 split 6 divide 10 distribute
Slice: 4 soda 9 soft drink
maker: 5 Pepsi
slice of __: 4 life
slicer place: 4 deli
slick: 3 icy, oil, pat, sly 4 cagy, deft, foxy, glib, oily, slip, trim, waxy, wily, wise 5 adept, cagey, canny, quick, sharp, shiny, sleek, slimy, smart, soapy, spill 6 adroit, artful, au fait, clever, crafty, expert, flossy, glassy, glazed, glossy, greasy, nimble, refine, shifty, shrewd, smooth, tricky, urbane 7 capable, cunning, elegant, groomed, knowing, skilled, slither, stylish, trained 8 dextrous, graceful, guileful, masterly, polished, scheming, seasoned, skillful, slippery, slithery, spruce up, unctuous, wondrous 9 competent, deceitful, deceptive, dexterous, efficient, ingenious, insidious, insincere, inventive, lubricate, lubricous, masterful, talkative, top-drawer, unethical, wonderful 10 lubricated, periodical, persuasive, proficient, serpentine, streetwise, well-spoken
contents: 3 oil
get ~: 5 ice up
make ~: 9 lubricate
on top: 4 bald
opposite: 4 pulp
see also wonderful
Slick: 5 Grace
slicker: 3 mac 4 coat 6 jacket 7 oilskin 8 raincoat 10 protection
__ slicker: 4 city
__ Slickers: 4 City
slide: 3 dip 4 dive, drop, fall, flow, lurk, sink, skid, skim, slip, tilt, trip, veer 5 coast, decay, drift, glide, lapse, lurch, shift, shove, skate, slink, slump, sneak, spill, steal, swoop 6 go down, plunge, propel, scooch, stream, thrust, tumble 7 decline, descend, descent, drop off, fall off, plummet, slither 8 downturn, move down, move over, toboggan 9 aggravate, move along, recession, worsening 10 degenerate, exacerbate, go smoothly, hit the dirt, lose ground, photograph, retrogress, take it easy
back: 7 relapse
by: 6 elapse
dye: 5 eosin 6 eosine
let ~: 4 omit 6 wink at 7 neglect 8 overlook
on snow: 3 ski 4 skee
over: 5 elide
prepare a ~: 5 stain
site: 4 park
starter: 3 mud 4 back, down, land, rock
water ~: 5 chute, flume
slide __: 4 rule
__ slide: 3 mud
slider: 5 curve, pitch
objective: 4 base
__ Slidin' Away: 4 Slip
sliding
door: 6 fusuma
door groove: 5 regle
part: 4 bolt
sliding __: 5 scale
Sliding Doors (1998 film)
cast: John Hannah, Gwyneth Paltrow, Jeanne Tripplehorn
slight: 3 cut, dig, off 4 barb, defy, fail, gibe, jeer, jibe, lank, lean, mere, mock, omit, poor, puny, skip, slam, slap, slim, slur, snub, thin, tiny, weak, wiry 5 abuse, chill, decry, faint, frail, lanky, libel, light, lithe, minor, petty, reedy, scant, scoff, scorn, sheer, skimp, small, sneer, spare, spurn, stick, taunt, teeny, wispy, wrong 6 dainty, defame, deride, dump on, feeble, flimsy, forget, gangly, heckle, ignore, impugn, insult, little, malign, meager, minute, modest, offend, paltry, rebuff, reject, remote, scanty, skinny, slinky, sparse, subtle, svelte, teensy, twiggy, vilify 7 affront, asperse, calumny,

catcall, contemn, degrade, despise, disdain, fragile, gracile, mockery, neglect, obloquy, offense, outside, passing, put-down, rank out, scraggy, scrawny, shallow, sketchy, slender, slender, spidery, tenuous, traduce, trivial, willowy, wispish 8 belittle, brush-off, call-down, contempt, delicate, denounce, derision, discount, exiguous, feathery, gangling, marginal, overlook, piddling, pooh-pooh, ridicule, shrug off, trifling, unlikely, vilipend 9 aspersion, attenuate, cheap shot, contumely, denigrate, discredit, disparage, disregard, humiliate, lithesome, rejection, sylphlike, undersize 10 calumniate, defamation, diminutive, disrespect, negligible, opprobrium, weightless
amount: 4 hint, tint, wisp 5 tinge, touch, whiff
difference: 5 shade
lead: 9 advantage, head start
odor: 4 hint 5 sniff, trace 6 breath 9 suspicion
progress: 4 dent
Slight Ache, A
author: Harold Pinter
slighter: 4 less 6 lesser
slightest: 5 least 7 minimal, minimum 8 littlest 9 narrowest
in the ~: 5 at all
not in the ~: 5 no how
slightly: 4 a bit, a tad 5 a mite 6 hardly, kind of, partly, rather 7 a little, faintly, lightly 8 somewhat 9 to a degree 10 marginally, moderately
Slightly Scarlet (1956 film)
cast: Arlene Dahl
Sligo: 3 Bay 4 city, town
locale: 4 Eire, Erin 7 Ireland
slim: 3 off, shy 4 lank, lean, poor, thin, trim, weak, wiry 5 faint, lanky, lithe, rangy, reedy, scant, short, small, spare, stick 6 dainty, feeble, flimsy, gangly, meager, narrow, reduce, remote, scanty, scarce, skinny, slight, slinky, stalky, svelte, twiggy 7 fragile, gracile, outside, scraggy, scrawny, slender, spidery, tenuous, wanting, willowy 8 beanpole, gangling 9 attenuate, beanstalk, deficient, lithesome, sylphlike 10 improbable, inadequate, lose weight, negligible, slenderize, threadlike
down: 4 diet, lose 6 reduce
Slim: 7 Pickens, Whitman
Slim __: 3 Jim
slime: 3 goo, mud 4 crud, glop, guck, gunk, mire, muck, ooze, scum 5 sloke 6 fungus, sludge 7 lowlife, slander 10 sleazeball
slime mold: 6 fungus
slimming device: 6 corset, girdle
slim to __: 4 none
slimy: 3 wet 4 icky, miry, oozy, vile 5 dirty, gooey, mucky, muddy, slick, yucky, yukky 6 greasy, scummy, shifty 7 viscose, viscous 8 slippery 9 glutinous, loathsome 10 despicable
one: 4 slug 5 snail
sling: 3 lob 4 cast, fire, hurl, send, shoe, toss 5 chuck, drink, fling, heave, hoist, pitch, shoot, swing, throw 6 dangle, launch, let fly, propel 7 suspend 8 beverage, catapult, cocktail, footwear, hang over 9 throw over
ender: 4 shot
ingredient: 3 gin 9 lime juice 10 lemon juice
missile: 2 BB 4 rock
mud: 4 slur 5 smear 7 slander
part: 4 band 5 strap
shape: 3 wye
sling-back: 4 shoe 8 footwear
slinger
hash ~: 4 cook
ink ~: 6 writer 8 reporter 9 columnist 10 journalist, newswriter
starter: 3 gun, mud
...slings and ___...: 6 arrows
slingshot
alternative: 3 bow 5 BB gun
slink: 4 lurk, slip 5 coast, cower, crawl, creep, glide, prowl, sculk, shirk, sidle, skulk, slide, snake, sneak, steal 7 creep by, meander, skitter 8 glissade, undulate 9 pussyfoot 10 nose around
slinking: 5 snaky 7 furtive 8 stealthy
slinky: 4 lank, lean, slim, thin, wiry 5 lanky, spare 6 dainty, gangly, skinny, slight, svelte, twiggy 7 furtive, gracile, scraggy, scrawny, slender, spidery, willowy 8 gangling 9 sylphlike
Slinky: 3 toy 4 coil 6 spring
shape: 5 helix
slip: 3 err, sag, tag 4 bomb, bust, cion, dock, drop, fall, flop, flub, gaff, goof, knot, lose, lurk, miss, move, muff, pier, shed, sink, skid, trip 5 berth, decay, error, fault, fluff, flunk, gaffe, glide, jetty, lapse, lurch, plant, scion, sheet, shift, shirk, shoot, skate, slick, slide, slink, slump, sneak, steal, strip, wharf 6 blow it, boo-boo, bungle, falter, flit by, foozle, foul-up, howler, lapsus, sliver, ticket, totter, tumble 7 abscond, blooper, blunder, chemise, decline, drop off, erratum, failure, fall off, faux pas, founder, go under, go wrong, landing, misdeed, misstep, mistake, receipt, regress, screw-up, slither, stumble, wash out 8 fall flat, flounder, giveaway, glissade, lay an egg, lingerie, misjudge, omission 9 aggravate, backslide, indecorum, oversight, petticoat, recession, strike out, underwear 10 degenerate, diminution, exacerbate, imprudence, inaccuracy, infraction, lose ground, peccadillo, pillowcase, retrogress
away: 2 go 3 fly 4 exit, flee, lose 5 elope, fly by, leave 6 be gone, depart, elapse, escape, run off 7 head out 8 sneak out
back: 7 relapse 10 recidivate
by: 4 edge 5 drift 6 elapse
ender: 3 way 4 case, knot, over, page, shod, slop, ware 5 cased, cover 6 stitch, stream
exclamation: 4 oh-oh, oops, uh-oh
ferry ~: 4 pier 5 berth
give the ~: 4 foil, lose 5 avoid, dodge, elude, evade, leave, shake 8 shake off, throw off
give the pink ~: 2 ax 3 axe 4 fire, oust, sack 7 dismiss 9 discharge
in: 5 enter 6 arrive
into: 3 don 4 wear 5 put on
keyboard ~: 4 typo 7 erratum, mistake 8 misprint 10 inaccuracy
let ~: 4 blab, leak, miss, tell 5 blurt, spill 6 betray, expose, forget, reveal, unmask, unveil 7 divulge, exhibit, lay bare, uncover 8 disclose 9 make known 10 make public
off: 6 escape 7 undress 8 get out of
of the tongue: 5 gaffe 7 blunder, faux pas, mistake
one over on: 4 fool
one's mind: 6 forget
out: 2 go 5 leave
past: 4 edge 5 elude
redemption ~: 6 coupon, ticket 7 voucher
sales ~: 7 receipt
ship ~: 4 dock 5 wharf
starter: 3 cow 4 land, side
through one's fingers: 4 flee, skip 6 escape, pass by, run off, run out 7 abscond, bail out, duck out, get away, make off, run away 9 break away, steal away 10 fly the coop
up: 3 err 4 goof, trip 5 lapse 7 mistake 8 overlook
slip __: 4 a cog, away
slip __ the cracks: 7 between
slip-__ pliers: 5 joint
__ slip: 3 let 4 buck, call, pink 5 cover, sales 6 credit 7 deposit
slip a __: 3 cog
slipknot: 5 noose
slip-on: 3 moc 6 loafer 8 moccasin
slipover: 7 sweater
slipper: 8 footwear
backless ~: 4 mule 5 scuff
material: 5 glass 7 leather
onyx ~: 5 shell 8 seashell
slipper __: 4 sock
__ slipper: 5 house 6 ballet, carpet 7 bedroom
__-slipper: 5 lady's
slippers like Dorothy's: 4 ruby
slippery: 3 icy, wet 4 cagy, eely, foxy, glib, oily, waxy, wily 5 cagey, glacé, shady, sharp, silky, sleek, slick, slimy, soapy 6 crafty, glassy, glazed, greasy, louche, satiny, shifty, shrewd, smooth, sneaky, tricky, unsafe, wiggly 7 cunning, devious, elusive, elusory, evasive 8 guileful, insecure, perilous, polished, scheming, slithery, unctuous, unstable, unsteady, variable 9 deceptive, dishonest, lubricous, uncertain, underhand, unethical 10 changeable, glistening, lubricated, lubricious, unreliable
get ~: 5 ice up 6 freeze
make ~: 3 oil 9 lubricate
one: 3 eel 6 dodger
on ~ ground: 4 iffy 5 dicey, hairy, risky 6 chancy, daring, touchy, tricky, unsafe 7 fraught 8 ticklish 9 dangerous, desperate, foolhardy, hazardous 10 precarious, touch-and-go
slippery __: 3 elm 5 slope
slippery __ eel: 4 as an
Slippery When __: 3 Wet
Slippin' and Slidin' (1956 song)
artist: Little Richard
Slipping-Down Life, A
author: Anne Tyler
slipshod: 3 bad, lax 5 hasty, junky, loose, messy, tacky 6 faulty, remiss, shabby, sloppy, untidy 7 botched, ill-done, scrubby, scruffy, unkempt 8 careless, fouled-up, slapdash, slovenly, tattered 9 haphazard, hit-or-miss, imperfect, imprudent, neglected, negligent, screwed-up, unheedful, unmindful 10 bedraggled, disheveled, inaccurate, incautious, jerry-built, last-minute, nonchalant, uncritical, unthinking, unthorough, willy-nilly
Slip Slidin' Away (1977 song)
artist: Paul Simon
slipslop
see baloney
slip-up: 4 boot, flub, goof, muff 5 boner, botch, error, fault, fluff, gaffe, lapse 6 boo-boo, bungle, fumble, miscue 7 blunder, faux pas, misdeed, misstep, mistake 9 indecorum, oversight
slit: 3 cut, rip 4 gash, hole, nick, open, rent, slot, tear, torn, vent 5 cleft, crack, knife, lance, score, sever, slash, slice, split 6 crenel, incise, louver, pierce 7 crevice, cut open, fissure, incised, keyhole, opening 8 aperture, cleavage, crenelle, incision, peephole, puncture, sundered 9 lacerated, split open 10 buttonhole, interspace, interstice, laceration
garment ~: 4 vent
organ-pipe ~: 4 flue
slither: 4 lurk, slip, wind 5 coast, cower, creep, glide, prowl, sculk, sidle, skulk, slick, slide, snake, sneak, steal 7 creep by, meander, skitter 8 glissade, undulate 9 pussyfoot 10 nose around
Slither (1973 film)
cast: Peter Boyle, James Caan, Sally Kellerman
slitherer: 4 worm 5 snake
slithery: 4 eely 5 slick 8 slippery 9 lubricous
slithy
creatures: 5 toves
what the ~ toves did: 4 gyre
sliver: 3 bit 4 chip, slip, snip 5 crumb, flake, piece, scrap, shave, shred, slice, thorn 6 paring 7 flinder, shaving, snippet 8 fragment, splinter
Sliver: 4 film 5 novel
author: Ira Levin
cast: William Baldwin, Tom Berenger, Sharon Stone
slivovitz: 5 drink 6 brandy 8 beverage
flavor: 4 plum
maker: 4 Serb
Sloan: 4 John 6 Alfred, Wilson
Sloane: 7 Everett
slob: 5 sight 6 lubber 9 litterbug
slobber: 4 drip, spit 5 drool, froth 6 drivel, slaver 7 dribble, slabber 8 salivate

__ Slobbovia: **5** Lower
sloe: **4** plum, tree **5** fruit, shrub **10** blackthorn
  family: **4** rose
  relative: *see* rose family plant
sloe __ fizz: **3** gin
sloe-__: **4** eyed
slog: **4** grub, path, plod, toil, trek, wade, walk, work **5** slave, trail, tramp, tread **6** lumber, trudge, wallop
slogan: **4** word **5** idiom, motto **6** byword, jingle, phrase, saying, war cry **7** proverb **9** battle cry, catchword, trademark, watchword **10** expression
  ending: **3** eer
  like a ~: **6** catchy
  maker: **5** adman
  repeated ~: **5** chant
sloop: **4** boat **5** craft, yacht **8** sailboat **10** knockabout, watercraft
Sloop John B (1966 song)
  artist: Beach Boys
slop: **4** drip **5** dance, slosh, slush, smear, spill, spray, swill, waste **6** liquid, refuse, smudge, splash, wallow **7** spatter **8** overflow, splatter **9** litterbug
slop __: **4** bowl, pail, sink
slope: **3** dip, tip **4** bank, bend, bias, cant, drop, fall, hill, lean, list, ramp, rise, sink, skew, sway, tilt **5** angle, bevel, chute, grade, pitch, slant, splay, way up **6** ascend, ascent, cuesta **7** descend, descent, incline, leaning, recline **8** diagonal, drop away, gradient, hillside **9** declivity, deviation, downgrade, obliquity, steepness **10** declension, deflection
  downward: **4** drop **7** descend
  downward ~: **4** drop **7** descent **9** declivity
  fortification ~: **5** talus
  gentle ~: **6** glacis **9** acclivity
  Hawaiian steep ~: **4** pali
  Highlands ~: **4** brae
  hollow: **6** corrie
  rugged ~: **4** scar **6** escarp
  steep ~: **5** chute, cliff, scarp
  upward: **4** rise **5** climb **6** ascend
  upward ~: **4** bank, hill, rise **5** grade **6** ascent, glacis **7** hillock, incline **8** gradient, hillside **9** acclivity, elevation
__ Slope: **5** North
slopes, hit the: **3** ski **4** skee, sled
sloping: **5** bevel **6** aslant, uphill **7** sideway **8** sideways, sidewise
  sharply ~: **5** steep
slopping
  over the sides: **5** awash
  the hogs: **5** chore
sloppy: **3** lax **4** poor **5** dirty, hasty, loose, messy, muddy, mushy, mussy, slack, tacky **6** blowsy, blowzy, clumsy, frowsy, frowzy, grungy, remiss, sludgy, slushy, unneat, untidy **7** awkward, blowsed, blowzed, botched, mawkish, splashy, squalid, unclean, unkempt **8** careless, romantic, slipshod, slovenly **9** imprudent, negligent, unmindful **10** bedraggled, disheveled, incautious, nonchalant, unthinking, unthorough
  stuff: **3** goo
Sloppy Joe: **4** beef **7** sweater **8** sandwich
slosh: **3** lap **4** slop, wade, wash **5** plash, spill **6** splash **8** overflow **9** spill over
  around: **6** wallow
slot: **3** cut, job **4** file, hole, site, slit, spot, time, work **5** niche, notch, place, space **6** groove, recess, socket **7** channel, earmark, keyhole, opening, section, specify, station, vacancy **8** aperture, position, standing **9** designate **10** department, depository, interspace, job opening, letter drop, livelihood, occupation, pigeonhole, profession
  filler: **3** tab **5** hirer
  spot: **6** casino
slot __: **3** car **5** racer **7** machine
sloth: **2** ai **3** sin **4** bear, unau **5** idler **6** acedia, animal, laxity, mammal, torpor **7** dawdler, inertia, languor, laxness **8** hebetude, idleness, laziness, lethargy, loginess, otiosity **9** fainéance, indolence, inertness, torpidity **10** inactivity, stagnation
  act the ~: **4** laze
  group: **8** edentata
  home: **4** tree
slothful: **3** lax **4** idle, lazy, logy, poky, slow **5** inert, slack, tardy **6** asleep, draggy, otiose, remiss, torpid **7** dormant, gradual, halting, impeded, lagging, languid, passive **8** crawling, creeping, dallying, dawdling, dilatory, dragging, drawn-out, fainéant, hesitant, inactive, indolent, lifeless, plodding, sluggish, toddling **9** apathetic, do-nothing, leisurely, lethargic, loitering, negligent, prolonged, sedentary, shiftless, snaillike, unhurried **10** deliberate, disengaged, neglectful, protracted, sluggardly
slot machine
  city: **4** Reno **5** Tahoe, Vegas
  feature: **3** arm
  input: **4** coin
  play the ~: **3** bet **5** wager **6** gamble
  symbol: **3** bar **4** plum **5** lemon **6** cherry, orange **10** watermelon
slotted __: **5** spoon
slouch: **3** bow, lag, sag **4** bend, flex, lean, loaf, loll, tilt, wilt **5** droop, slump, stoop **6** crouch, linger, loafer, lounge, sprawl **8** loiterer **9** lazybones, slump over
Slouching Towards Bethlehem
  author: Joan Didion
slough: **3** bog, fen **4** molt, shed, skin **5** marsh, swamp **6** loiter, reject **8** quagmire
  off: **4** molt, shed **5** shirk
Slovakia: **6** nation **7** country
  capital: **10** Bratislava
  city: **6** Kosice **10** Bratislava
  Danube, in ~: **5** Dunaj
  mountain range: **5** Tatra
  neighbor: **6** Poland **7** Austria, Hungary, Ukraine
  tennis pro: **6** Hingis
sloven: **3** pig **9** litterbug **10** ragamuffin
Slovenia: **6** nation **7** country
  capital: **9** Ljubljana
  city: **7** Maribor **9** Ljubljana
  neighbor: **5** Italy **7** Austria, Croatia, Hungary
  river: **4** Sava
slovenly: **4** icky **5** dingy, dirty, dowdy, grimy, grody, loose, lousy, messy, mussy, piggy, seedy, slack, sooty, tacky **6** blowsy, blowzy, filthy, fouled, frowsy, frowzy, frumpy, grubby, grungy, piggie, pigpen, sleazy, sloppy, soiled, sordid, unneat, untidy **7** blowsed, blowzed, botched, raunchy, scruffy, smudged, squalid, stained, tainted, unclean, unkempt, unswept **8** befouled, begrimed, careless, heedless, maculate, messed up, polluted, slapdash, slipshod **9** blackened, negligent, tarnished, ungroomed **10** bedraggled, besmirched, disheveled, disordered, disorderly, topsy-turvy, unsanitary
slow: **3** dim, lag, off **4** beam, curb, damp, dull, late, lazy, poky, stem, tame **5** abate, brake, check, choke, delay, dense, dunce, inert, pokey, relax, slack, stall, stunt, tardy, thick, unapt **6** adagio, arrest, behind, dampen, detain, draggy, dreamy, drowsy, ease up, hamper, hang up, hinder, hold up, impede, leaden, lessen, loiter, reduce, rein in, relent, remiss, retard, simple, sleepy, stolid, torpid **7** belated, bog down, curtail, cut back, cut down, delayed, ease off, fall off, glacial, gradual, halting, impeded, inhibit, laggard, lagging, languid, limited, lumpish, reduced, set back, slacken, tedious **8** backward, cautious, crawling, creeping, dawdling, decrease, delaying, detained, dilatory, diminish, hindered, hold back, inactive, indolent, lifeless, listless, moderate, peter out, plodding, postpone, regulate, restrict, road sign, slothful, sluggish, wind down **9** backwater, dimwitted, leisurely, lethargic, lighten up, lingering, loitering, negligent, ponderous, prolonged, reluctant, snaillike, unhurried **10** decelerate, deliberate, dull-witted, phlegmatic, postponing, protracted, uneventful, unpunctual, unreactive
  burn: **5** pique **6** temper **9** surliness **10** irritation
  do a ~ burn: **4** fume, stew **5** react **6** seethe
  down: **4** damp, loaf, rein, tire **5** brake, check, delay, deter, let up, relax, stall, tie up **6** arrest, dampen, detain, hamper, hang up, hinder, impede, lessen, reduce, rein in, retard, unwind, weaken **7** fall off, inhibit, prolong, set back, slacken, tail off **8** decrease, encumber, hold back, make late, obstruct, peter out, restrain **10** decelerate
  ender: **4** down, poke
  go ~: **4** plod **5** crawl
  in music: **5** largo, lento, tardo **6** adagio
  in retail: **4** dead
  interval: **4** lull
  one: **2** ox **4** poke, worm **5** sloth, snail
  on the uptake: **3** dim **5** dense **6** obtuse
  signal: **5** amber **6** yellow
  take it ~: **4** laze **6** go easy
  up: **3** lag **4** rein **5** abate, check, delay **6** impede, rein in, retard, shelve **7** set back **8** hold back, restrain **10** decelerate
slow __: **4** burn **6** cooker, motion
slow-__: **6** footed, moving, witted
__ slow: **6** take it
Slow __: **6** Dancin' **7** Twistin'
__ Slow Boat to China: **3** On a
slowdown: **3** jam **4** lull **5** delay, letup, slack, slump, tie-up **6** arrest, strike **7** decline, drop-off, falloff, setback **8** downturn, tarrying **9** downtrend, worsening **10** slackening
slower
  in music: **3** rit. **4** rall. **8** ritenuto **10** ritardando
  traffic ~: **4** bump **9** speed bump
Slow Hand (1981 song)
  artist: Pointer Sisters
slowly: **5** largo **6** adagio **7** loathly **8** bit by bit **9** languidly, leisurely, piecemeal
slow-moving: **4** lazy, logy **5** slack **6** torpid **8** sluggish **9** lethargic
slow on the __: **6** uptake
slowpoke: **5** snail **6** lagger **7** dawdler, laggard **8** lingerer, loiterer **9** latecomer
Slow Twistin' (1962 song)
  artist: Chubby Checker, Dee Dee Sharp
slow-witted: **4** dull **5** dense, thick
SLR: **6** camera
slub: **4** burl
sludge: **4** gook, guck, ooze, slop **5** slime
slue: **4** skid, veer **5** pivot **6** swerve **9** turn about
sluff
  see slough
slug: **3** bat, hit, nip **4** bash, beat, belt, blow, deck, hurt, pest, shot, slam, sock, swat, swig, wham **5** clout, drink, drone, flail, paste, punch, smash, smite, thump, whack **6** bullet, strike, wallop **7** clobber, laggard, mollusk **8** uppercut **9** gastropod, haul off on
  cousin: **5** snail
  ender: **4** fest
  it out: **3** box **5** fight **6** battle
  like a ~: **4** fake **5** bogus, slimy
__ slug: **3** sea
slugabed: **4** poke **5** idler **7** dawdler **9** do-nothing, lazybones
slugfest: **4** fray **6** boxing **10** donnybrook
sluggard: **5** drone, idler, sloth, snail **6** loafer, truant **7** dawdler, slacker **8** layabout, loiterer **9** do-nothing, lazybones **10** ne'er-do-well
  bane: **3** job **4** work
slugged, old-style: **4** smit **5** smote
Slugger, Louisville: **3** bat
slugging __: **5** it out
sluggish: **3** lax, off **4** blah, dopy, down, dull, idle, lazy, logy, poky, slow, weak **5** dopey, heavy, inert, leady, pokey, rusty, slack **6** asleep,

bovine, draggy, drippy, drowsy, leaden, sleepy, stupid, sullen, torpid **7** dormant, gradual, halting, impeded, lagging, languid, lumpish, passive **8** crawling, creeping, dawdling, dilatory, dragging, drawn-out, hesitant, inactive, indolent, laid-back, lifeless, listless, plodding, slothful, stagnant, toddling **9** apathetic, leisurely, lethargic, lymphatic, ponderous, prolonged, sedentary, snaillike, unhurried **10** deliberate, disengaged, languorous, phlegmatic, protracted, slow-moving, slumberous, unreactive
one: **5** sloth
sluggishness: **5** sloth **7** inertia, languor, latency **8** laziness, lethargy **9** lassitude
sluice: **4** race, tide **5** flume, surge **6** gutter, stream
ender: **3** box, way
slum: **3** sty **4** dump **6** ghetto, pigsty, sordid **7** piggery, quarter, rathole, skid row **9** inner city
ender: **4** lord
outer city ~: **5** slurb
Sluman, Jeff: **6** golfer
slumber: **3** nap **4** doze, rest **5** sleep **6** drowse, repose, snooze, stupor, torpor **7** languor, latency, saw logs, shut-eye **8** dormancy, lethargy, sack time **10** forty winks, inactivity
see also sleep
slumbering: **4** abed **6** asleep **7** dormant **9** sacked out, somnolent
slumberland: **5** sleep
slumberous: **6** drowsy, sleepy **8** sluggish **9** lethargic, somnolent
slumber-party attire: **3** PJs **7** pajamas
Slumdog Millionaire (2008 film)
cast: Dev Patel, Freida Pinto
slumgullion: **4** hash, stew
slump: **3** dip, low, nod, rut, sag **4** bend, drop, fall, flag, flex, flop, funk, loll, sink, slip, wilt **5** crash, decay, droop, dumps, hunch, panic, pitch, slide, stoop **6** cave in, downer, go down, plunge, slouch, sprawl, topple, trough, tumble **7** decline, descend, descent, dessert, drop off, failure, falloff, plummet, reverse, tail off **8** bad times, blue funk, collapse, decrease, downturn, dry spell, keel over, nosedive, slowdown, tailspin **9** downslide, downswing, downtrend, hard times, recession, worsening **10** degenerate, depression, falling-off, go downhill, stagnation
slumping, stop: **5** sit up
Slums of Beverly Hills (1998 film)
cast: Alan Arkin, Marisa Tomei
slung: **6** hurled, tossed **9** suspended
slur: **3** cap, dig, rap **4** barb, blot, chop, gibe, jeer, jibe, mock, onus, skip, slam, slap, snub, zing **5** abuse, brand, cut up, decry, elide, knock, libel, odium, roast, scorn, smear, spurn, stain, taunt **6** defame, deride, dump on, expose, garble, heckle, impugn, insult, malign, mumble, offend, rebuff, scorch, slight, smirch, stigma, vilify, zinger **7** affront, asperse, blacken, blemish, blister, calumny, catcall, degrade, detract, disdain, mockery, obloquy, offense, putdown, rank out, run down, slander, spatter, stutter, traduce **8** backbite, belittle, besmirch, black eye, contempt, denounce, derision, disgrace, innuendo, reproach, ridicule, tear down, throw mud, vilipend **9** aspersion, black mark, cheap shot, contumely, denigrate, discredit, disparage, humiliate, insinuate, stricture **10** accusation, calumniate, defamation, disrespect, imputation, opprobrium, reflection, scandalize, villainize, vituperate
in music: **5** glide
slurp: **3** lap, sip **5** drink, lap up **6** guzzle **7** swallow
slush: **3** mud **4** mire, mush, slop **7** schmalz, shmaltz **8** schmaltz **9** mushiness, soppiness
slush __: **4** fund, pile
slushy: **3** wet **5** muddy, mushy, sappy **6** sloppy **7** maudlin
beverage: **6** frappé
Slutskaya: **5** Irina
SLX: **3** SUV **5** Acura
sly: **3** coy **4** arch, cagy, foxy, wily **5** cagey, canny, sharp, slick, smart, snaky, sneak **6** artful, astute, clever, covert, crafty, feline, impish, secret, shifty, shrewd, smooth, sneaky, subtle, tricky **7** crooked, cunning, devious, elusive, elusory, evasive, furtive, knavish, roguish, vulpine **8** bluffing, delusive, guileful, plotting, scheming, sneaking, stealthy **9** astucious, conniving, deceitful, deceptive, designing, dishonest, ingenious, insidious, underhand **10** intriguing, serpentine
one: **3** fox **9** intriguer
on the ~: **7** sub rosa **8** covertly, in secret, secretly, sneakily **9** furtively **10** stealthily, undercover
sly __ fox: **3** as a
__ sly: **5** on the
Sly: **5** Stone **8** Stallone
Sly and the Family Stone
song: Dance to the Music (1968)
Everyday People (1969)
Family Affair (1971)
Hot Fun in the Summertime (1969)
Stand! (1969)
Thank You (Falettinme Be Mice Elf Agin) (1970)
slyly: **7** asquint **10** guilefully
slyness: **3** art **4** wile **5** craft, guile **6** deceit
Sm: **4** elem. **7** element **8** samarium
62 for ~: **4** at. no.
sma: **3** wee
one: **5** bairn
smack: **3** box, hit **4** bang, beat, belt, blow, boat, buss, chop, clap, clip, cuff, kiss, lash, lick, slam, slap, sock, spat, swat, tang, thud **5** clout, crack, flail, knock, plumb, punch, right, savor, spank, swipe, taste, thump, tinge, touch, whack, whang **6** buffet, strike, trifle, wallop **7** clearly, clobber, exactly, lay into **8** directly, squarely, uppercut **9** fisticuff, precisely **10** accurately, osculation, point-blank, suggestion
dab: **8** directly
ender: **4** eroo
of: **5** smell **7** suggest **8** look like, resemble, seem like
one's lips: **5** eat up, enjoy, gloat, savor **6** devour, relish **7** feast on
smack-dab: **5** right **9** precisely
smacker: **4** bill, buck, clam **6** dollar **8** banknote, frogskin **9** greenback
smackers
see moolah
Smacks: **6** cereal
competitor: ***see*** cereal
small: **3** off, toy, wee **4** baby, base, mere, mini, poor, puny, size, slim, tiny **5** bitty, dinky, light, minor, petty, runty, short, sorry, teeny, weeny, young **6** atomic, bantam, elfish, elvish, humble, lesser, little, meager, midget, minute, modest, narrow, paltry, petite, pocket, scanty, shrimp, slight, teensy **7** cramped, ignoble, limited, nominal, outside, pitiful, scrubby, selfish, slender, stunted, trivial **8** atomical, atomlike, exiguous, immature, inferior, marginal, picayune, piddling, plebeian, trifling **9** lowercase, miniature, minuscule, pint-sized, secondary, undersize **10** bush-league, diminutive, humiliated, inadequate, low-ranking, negligible, skinflinty, undersized, ungenerous
combining form: **4** micr-, mini- **5** micro -
ender: **3** pox **4** time **5** timer
suffix: **3** -let, -ule **4** -ette
small __: **3** fry **4** talk **5** hours, print, stuff, world **6** change, screen
small __ advisory: **5** craft
small-__: **4** bore, time, town **5** scale **6** minded
small-__ court: **6** claims
Small Craft Warnings
author: Tennessee Williams
Smallens, Alexander: **7** Russian **9** conductor
smaller: **4** less **5** lower, minor
get ~: **3** ebb **4** wane **6** lessen, narrow, reduce, shrink **7** decline, deflate, drop off, dwindle, shrivel **8** contract, decrease, diminish **9** waste away
make ~: **6** lessen, shrink **7** dwindle **8** minimize
to a ~ extent: **5** fewer, lower, minor **7** limited, reduced, without **8** inferior **9** excepting, secondary, shortened **10** diminished
smallest: **5** least **7** minimal, minimum **8** littlest **9** narrowest
part: **8** molecule
small-fry: **5** minor **6** lesser
__ Small Hours: **3** Wee
small-minded: **5** petty **6** little, narrow, sordid **7** bigoted **9** parochial
smallmouth __: **4** bass
Small Rain, The
author: Thomas Pynchon
Small Room, The
author: May Sarton
small screen
see television
Small Soldiers (1998 film)
cast: Kirsten Dunst, Phil Hartman, Jay Mohr
small-time: **5** dinky, local, minor, petty **6** lesser, two-bit **9** parochial, secondary **10** provincial
Small Time Crooks (2000 film)
cast: Woody Allen, Hugh Grant, Elaine May, Tracey Ullman
director: Woody Allen
Small Town
author: Sloan Wilson
Small Town (1985 song)
artist: John Cougar Mellencamp
Smallville (WB/CW sci-fi)
cast: Sam Jones III (Pete Ross)
Kristin Kreuk (Lana Lang)
Allison Mack (Chloe Sullivan)
Annette O'Toole (Martha Kent)
Michael Rosenbaum (Lex Luthor)
John Schneider (Jonathan Kent)
Tom Welling (Clark Kent)
Small Wonder
author: Barbara Kingsolver
Small world, __ it?: **4** isn't
Small World
composer: Stephen Sondheim, Jule Styne
__ Small World: **4** It's a
smarmy: **4** oily
smart: **3** apt, hip, sly **4** able, ache, bold, burn, chic, fine, good, hurt, keen, neat, pain, pert, posh, sage, trim, whiz, wise **5** acute, adept, agile, alert, brisk, canny, crisp, faddy, fresh, natty, nervy, nifty, prick, quick, ready, sassy, saucy, sharp, slick, sting, swank, swell, swish, throb **6** astute, brainy, brazen, bright, clever, crafty, dapper, dressy, genius, gifted, lively, modish, nimble, rakish, shrewd, simmer, snappy, spruce, suffer, swanky, trendy, twinge, with it **7** cunning, dashing, elegant, erudite, groomed, knowing, learned, pointed, politic, prickle, sapient, stylish, voguish **8** cerebral, cracking, flippant, impudent, insolent, masterly, sensible, skillful, spirited, vigorous, well-read **9** astucious, brilliant, effective, eggheaded, energetic, exclusive, in fashion, ingenious, inventive, judicious, on the ball, sagacious, sprightly **10** discerning, insightful, keen-witted, precocious
aleck: **7** wise guy **8** quipster, wiseacre
get ~: **4** sass **8** mouth off, talk back
group: **5** Mensa
one: **5** brain **6** genius **8** Einstein, wiseacre
talk: **4** sass
smart __: **3** off, set **4** bomb, card **5** aleck, money
smart __ whip: **3** as a
__-smart: **6** street
Smart: **3** Amy **5** Ralph **7** Maxwell
__ Smart: **3** Get
smart-alecky: **4** bold, flip, pert, wise **5** fresh, lippy, nervy, sassy, saucy **6** brazen **7** forward **8** cocksure, derisive, flippant, impudent **9** sarcastic

smarten: 5 primp 7 educate 8 ornament, spruce up
  up: 4 tidy, trim 5 groom, primp, prink, spiff 6 neaten 7 get wise 8 beautify 9 glamorize
smarting: 4 achy, sore 9 irritated
Smart, Maxwell: 3 spy 5 agent
  portrayer: Don Adams, Steve Carell
smartmouth: 5 sassy, saucy 8 back talk, impudent
smartness: 4 wits 5 craft, guile, sense, skill 6 acumen, brains 7 finesse 8 aptitude, keenness 9 canniness, ingenuity, quickness, sharpness 10 adroitness, astuteness, brightness, cleverness, shrewdness
smarts: 5 sense, skill 6 acumen 8 aptitude, keenness 9 intellect, mentality
___ smarts: 6 street
Smart Start: 6 cereal
  competitor: *see* cereal
Smart Women
  author: Judy Blume
smarty: 8 wiseacre 9 know-it-all 10 jackanapes
smarty-___: 5 pants
smash: 3 hit, jar, ram, wow 4 bang, bash, belt, boom, clap, play, rase, raze, rive, ruin, shot, slam, slug, sock, swat, undo, welt, wham 5 blast, break, burst, crack, crash, crush, pound, punch, smite, sound, spoil, sqush, stave, trash, whack, wreck 6 bash in, batter, big hit, defeat, impact, pile-up, powder, ravage, shiver, squash, squish, squush, topple, tumble, wallop, winner 7 break up, clobber, collide, crackup, debacle, destroy, disrupt, failure, flatten, implode, scrunch, shatter, squoosh, success, triumph 8 accident, breaking, collapse, decimate, demolish, destruct, disaster, downfall, fracture, fragment, knockout, overturn, splinter, stampede, tear down, uppercut, vanquish 9 breakdown, collision, devastate, haul off on, knock down, overpower, overthrow, pulverize, sensation 10 annihilate, gold record, shattering
  and grab: 4 loot 5 rifle 7 plunder
  ender: 4 eroo
  into: 3 hit, ram 4 bump 6 strike 7 rear-end
  letters: 3 SRO
smash ___: 3 hit
smashed: 3 lit 5 tight 6 broken, undone 8 in pieces
___ smasher: 4 atom
___ Smasher: 3 Spy
smashing
  atom ~: 7 fission
  find ~: 4 love 5 adore
  see also wonderful
Smashing ___: 8 Pumpkins
smashup: 5 crash, wreck 6 impact 7 rear-end 8 accident
smatter: 6 shiver 7 shatter
smattering: 3 few 5 tinge, touch 6 snatch 7 handful
smaze: 3 fog
  cousin: 4 smog
Smeal: 7 Eleanor
smear: 3 dab, mud, pan, rap, rub, tar 4 blob, blot, blur, coat, daub, foul, lick, slam, slop, slur, soil 5 abuse, apply, bribe, cover, dirty, libel, rip up, rub on, shame, spray, stain, sully, taint 6 bedaub, befoul, crud up, defame, defile, impugn, malign, mess up, scorch, smudge, spread, streak, vilify 7 asperse, blacken, blister, lambast, overlay, plaster, slander, spatter, tarnish, traduce 8 backbite, badmouth, belittle, besmirch, denounce, discolor, innuendo, lambaste, sling mud, throw mud 9 aspersion, denigrate, discredit, disparage, lubricate, poor-mouth 10 calumniate, defamation, imputation, spread over, stigmatize, villainize
  on: 5 apply
smeared: 5 grimy, sooty 7 unclean
Smee: 4 mate 6 pirate
smell: 4 funk, odor, reek, tang 5 aroma, fetor, odour, savor, scent, sense, sniff, snuff, stink, trace, trail, whiff 6 breath, detect, foetor, inhale, stench 7 bouquet, essence, incense, perfume, suspect 8 identify, perceive 9 emanation, fetidness, fragrance, get wind of, redolence, suspicion
  a rat: 5 doubt 7 suspect 8 distrust, mistrust 10 disbelieve
  detector: 4 nose
  mask the ~ of: 6 purify 7 freshen, sweeten 8 sanitize 9 deodorize
  (of): 5 smack
  out: 3 spy 4 espy, find 5 catch, hit on, trace 6 detect, expose, locate, unmask 7 discern, uncover 8 discover, identify, pinpoint 9 ascertain, track down
  science of ~: 6 osmics
  sense of ~: 4 nose
smell ___: 4 a rat
Smell!
  author: William Carlos Williams
smeller: 4 nose 5 snoot 6 beezer, honker, schnoz
smelling ___: 5 salts
___ Smell of Success: 5 Sweet
smelly: 4 foul, olid, rank 5 fetid, funky, musty, reeky, stale 6 foetid, frowsy, frowzy, putrid, rancid, rotten, stinky, strong 7 noisome, noxious, odorous, reeking 8 mephitic, stinking 10 malodorous
smelt: 4 fish 6 inanga, reduce 7 process 8 sparling
smeltery
  input: 3 ore
  leftover: 4 slag 5 dross
  oxide: 4 calx
Smetana, Bedrich: 5 Czech 8 composer
  work: The Bartered Bride
    M Vlast
smidge: 4 iota
smidgen: 3 bit, dab, jot, tad 4 atom, dash, drop, iota, mite, snip, spot, whit, wisp 5 crumb, grain, pinch, shred, skosh, speck, trace 7 minimum, modicum 8 particle
Smight: 4 Jack
smile: 4 beam, grin, luck 5 laugh, smirk 6 simper 9 say cheese 10 expression
  bring a ~ to: 5 amuse
  derisive ~: 5 sneer
  feature: 6 dimple
  sly ~: 4 leer 5 smirk
  upon: 4 help 5 bless, favor, grace, shine 9 encourage
  upside-down ~: 5 frown, scowl
Smile (song)
  artist: Tupac, Vitamin C
___ Smile: 4 Sara
___ Smile, A: 7 Certain
___ Smile Be Your Umbrella: 4 Let a
___ Smile Without You: 4 Can't
smiley ___: 4 face
Smiley: 3 spy 5 agent
Smiley, Jane novel: 3 Moo
Smiley's People
  author: John le Carré
smiling: 5 riant, sunny 8 laughing 9 lightsome
  keep ~: 5 cheer 6 divert, please, tickle 7 delight 9 entertain
Smiling Faces Sometimes (1971 song)
  artist: Undisputed Truth
smilodon: 5 tiger
smirch: 4 blot, slur, soil, spot 5 smear, stain, sully, taint 6 bedaub 7 begrime, besmear, calumny, slander, tarnish 8 backbite, discolor 10 calumniate, imputation
smirk: 4 grin, leer 5 fleer, smile, sneer 6 jibe at, simper 7 grimace, snicker, snigger 9 make a face 10 expression
  cousin: 4 leer
Smirnoff: 5 vodka, Yakov
  competitor: 4 Skyy 5 Popov, Stoli 6 Rodnik, Starka 7 Absolut 9 Grey Goose
smite: 3 zap 4 bash, conk, flog, slay, slug, sock 5 flail, pound, punch, smash, visit, whack, whomp 6 batter, buffet, cudgel, hammer, pommel, pummel, strike, thrash, thwack, wallop 7 lambast, torment 8 bludgeon, lambaste 10 lay waste to, strike down
smith: 5 shoer 7 farrier 10 horseshoer
  starter: 3 gun, tin 4 gold, iron, lock, song, tune, word 5 black, white 6 copper, silver
Smith: 2 E.E., O.C. 3 A.J.M., Bob, Hal, Ian, Lee, Liz, Red, Rex 4 Adam, John, Kate, Kent, Kerr, Lane, Seba, Stan, Will 5 Betty, Bubba, Dodie, Jacob, Jaden, Keely, Kevin, Ozzie, Patti, Robyn, Roger, Sammi 6 Alexis, Bessie, Brooke, Cotter, Emmitt, H. Allen, Horton, Jaclyn, Joseph, Maggie, Stevie, Sydney, Thorne, Vernon 7 college, Lillian, Michael, Pinetop 8 Hamilton, Margaret, Yeardley
  grad: 5 woman 6 alumna
  partner: 6 Corona, Wesson
___ Smith: 6 Granny, Nevada
Smith, Adam: 6 writer 8 Scottish 9 economist
  work: The Wealth of Nations
Smith, Alexis: 7 actress
  spouse: Craig Stevens
___ Smith and Jones: 5 Alias
Smith Brothers: 9 cough drop
  competitor: 6 Luden's
  feature: 5 beard
Smith, Emmitt
  sport: 8 football
smithereens: 5 atoms 6 pieces, scraps 8 flinders 9 particles
Smithers: 3 Jan
Smithfield ___: 3 ham
Smith, Hannibal group: 5 A-Team
Smith, Horton: 6 golfer
Smith, John perhaps: 5 alias
Smith, Kate
  film: The Big Broadcast (1932)
Smith, Keely
  spouse: Louis Prima
Smith, Lee: 6 hurler 7 pitcher
Smith, Lillian
  work: Strange Fruit
Smith, Maggie: 4 Dame 7 actress
  film: California Suite (1978, AA)
    The First Wives Club (1996)
    Murder by Death (1976)
    Othello (1965)
    The Prime of Miss Jean Brodie (1969, AA)
    A Room With a View (1986)
    Sister Act (1992)
Smith, O.C.
  song: Little Green Apples (1968)
Smith, Ozzie: 8 Cardinal 9 shortstop
Smith, Rex
  song: You Take My Breath Away (1979)
Smith, Robyn
  spouse: Fred Astaire
Smith, Roger
  spouse: Ann-Margret
Smith, Sammi
  song: Help Me Make It Through the Night (1971)
Smith, Snuffy: 4 toon 5 comic 7 cartoon 10 comic strip
  baby: 5 Tater
  dog: 8 Ol' Bullet
Smithsonian: 6 museum
  diamond: 4 Hope
  locale: 10 Washington
Smith, Stan: 7 netster 9 tennis pro
  milieu: 5 court
Smith, Thorne: 6 writer 8 humorist
  creation: 6 Topper
Smith & Wesson: 3 gun
Smith, Will: 5 actor
  film: Ali (2001)
    Enemy of the State (1998)
    Hancock (2008)
    Hitch (2005)
    I Am Legend (2007)
    Independence Day (1996)
    I, Robot (2004)
    The Legend of Bagger Vance (2000)
    Men in Black (1997)
    The Pursuit of Happyness (2006)
    Six Degrees of Separation (1993)
    Wild Wild West (1999)
  song: Gettin' Jiggy Wit It (1998)
    Men in Black (1997)
    Wild Wild West (1999)
  spouse: Jada Pinkett
  TV: Fresh Prince of Bel Air
smithy: 5 forge 9 ironworks
  item: 4 shoe 9 horseshoe
  tool: 5 anvil, tongs 6 hammer
Smitrovich: 4 Bill
Smits, Jimmy: 5 actor
  film: My Family/Mi Familia (1995)
    Old Gringo (1989)

Price of Glory (2000)
TV: L.A. Law, N.Y.P.D. Blue, The West Wing
smitten: **4** gaga **5** crazy, taken **6** in love **7** far gone **8** enamored **10** infatuated
smock: **4** coat **5** apron, frock **6** camise, duster **7** coverup, garment
smog: **3** fog **4** haze, mist **5** vapor **8** haziness **9** pollution
cousin: **5** smaze
smoke: **3** cig, run **4** cure, fume, puff, reek, tree **5** cigar, color, hurry, vapor **6** inhale, kipper, stogie **7** cheroot, incense, light up, process, smolder **8** fastball, preserve, smoulder **9** pollution
and mirrors: **6** deceit
bit of ~: **4** puff, wisp
detector: **5** alarm
emitter: **4** flue
ender: **5** house, stack **6** jumper, screen
go up in ~: **4** burn, fail **6** ignite
out: **4** find **5** learn **6** expose, locate
put up a ~ screen: **9** misinform
rid of ~: **6** air out
signal: **5** plume
tree: **6** fustet
smoke __: **3** out **4** bomb **5** alarm **6** screen
smoke-__ room: **6** filled
__ smoke: **3** sea **4** up in **5** frost **7** prairie
Smoke (1995 film)
cast: Stockard Channing, William Hurt, Harvey Keitel
smoke and __: **7** mirrors
Smoke and Steel
author: Carl Sandburg
smoked fish: **3** eel, lox **6** salmon **7** herring
Smoke Gets in Your Eyes (1958 song)
artist: Platters
composer: Otto Harbach, Jerome Kern
smokehouse worker: **5** curer
smokejumper's need: **5** chute
Smoke on the Water (1973 song)
artist: Deep Purple
Smokeout sponsor: **3** ACS
smokescreen: **10** camouflage
Smokescreen
author: Dick Francis
Smoke Signals (1998 film)
director: Chris Eyre
smokestack: **4** flue **6** funnel
like a ~: **5** sooty
Smokey: **4** bear **6** Stover **8** Robinson
Smokey and the Bandit (1977 film)
cast: Sally Field, Jackie Gleason, Burt Reynolds
director: Hal Needham
dog: **4** Fred
__ Smokies: **5** Great
Smokin' Aces (2007 film)
cast: Ben Affleck, Andy García, Alicia Keys
smoking: **3** hot **7** on a roll
smoking __: **3** gun **6** jacket
__-smoking: **3** non
Smoking or __?: **3** non
Smokin' in the Boys Room (song)
artist: Brownsville Station, Mötley Crüe
smoky: **4** fumy, gray, grey, hazy **5** black, dingy, grimy, mirky, murky, sooty, thick **6** fuming **7** burning, silvery **8** begrimed, vaporous **10** smoldering
__ Smoky Mountains: **5** Great
smolder: **4** boil, burn, fume, stir **5** smoke, steam **6** bubble, fester, seethe, simmer **7** consume, explode, ferment **9** fulminate
smoldering: **5** smoky **6** latent **10** unrealized
Smollett, Tobias: **6** writer **7** British
work: Peregrine Pickle Roderick Random
smooch: **3** pet **4** buss, kiss, neck **5** spoon **8** osculate **10** osculation
__-Smoot: **6** Hawley
smooth: **3** pat, rub, sly **4** calm, ease, easy, even, file, flat, glib, iron, mild, nice, oily, rake, sand, soft, wily **5** adept, allay, bland, clear, fluid, flush, glaze, gloss, grind, level, light, plain, plane, press, quiet, sheer, shiny, silky, sleek, slick, suave, sweet, touch **6** artful, crafty, creamy, facile, finish, flossy, fluent, genial, gentle, glassy, glazed, glossy, legato, liquid, mellow, polish, polite, refine, satiny, serene, shaven, shrewd, soften, stable, steady, stroke, tricky, urbane **7** appease, assuage, burnish, comfort, flatten, flowing, iron out, mollify, perfect, planate, politic, regular, roll out, uniform, varnish, velvety **8** dextrous, graceful, hairless, lustrous, mitigate, palliate, peaceful, pleasant, polished, readable, rhythmic, slippery, soothing, tranquil, unbroken, unctuous, untaxing **9** agreeable, alleviate, dexterous, lubricate, make peace, talkative, unruffled, unvarying **10** continuous, effortless, facilitate, horizontal, integrated, invariable, lubricated, mirrorlike, monotonous, nonchalant, pave the way, persuasive, rippleless, uneventful, untroubled, unwrinkled
along: **4** slip **5** slide
in music: **6** legato
in phonetics: **4** lene
make ~: **4** sand **5** shave **9** lubricate
on: **6** spread
out: **4** even, iron
over: **6** defuse, defuze, disarm, lessen, pacify, soften, soothe **7** mollify **8** moderate **9** untrouble
sailing: **4** snap **6** picnic
the way: **5** set up **6** loosen **7** further, lighten **8** expedite, mitigate, moderate, simplify
very ~: **5** silky
smooth-__: **4** talk **5** faced **6** shaven, spoken **7** tongued
Smooth (1999 song)
artist: Santana
smooth as __: **4** silk **5** satin
Smooth Criminal (1988 song)
artist: Michael Jackson
smoothly: **4** even, well **6** legato **7** lightly **10** swimmingly
in music: **6** legato
smoothness: **4** ease, tact, woof **6** polish **7** fluency, texture **8** facility, fluidity **9** clockwork, dexterity
Smooth Operator (1985 song)
artist: Sade
smooth-pated: **4** bald
smooth-shaven: **9** beardless
smooth-spoken: **4** glib, oily **5** slick, suave, vocal **6** fluent
smorgasbord: **4** meal **5** feast **6** buffet
enjoy a ~: **3** eat
item: **3** ham **5** pasta, roast, salad
smother: **4** heap, lick, rein, trim **5** cover, douse, dowse, quash, quell, snuff **6** hush up, muffle, put out, quench, shower, shroud, stifle **7** blow out, control, envelop, lambast, oppress, repress, squelch **8** inundate, keep down, lambaste, restrain, stamp out, suppress, surround **9** keep quiet, overwhelm **10** extinguish
smothered: **6** pent-up
Smothers: **3** Tom **4** Dick **5** Tommy
Smothers Brothers: **3** duo **4** pair
Smothers, Tom hobby: **4** yo-yo
SMU
athlete: **7** Mustang
conference: **3** WAC
locale: **5** Texas **6** Dallas
Smucker's: **3** jam **5** jelly
alternative: **5** Kraft **6** Knott's, Welch's **7** Polaner
smudge: **3** dab **4** blob, blot, blur, daub, foul, mark, slop, soil, spot **5** blear, dirty, grime, smear, stain, sully, taint **6** bedaub, befoul, blotch, crud up, defile **7** begrime, besmear, blacken, blemish, plaster, pollute, spatter, tarnish **8** besmirch
garage ~: **3** oil
smudged: **5** dirty, grimy, sooty **6** filthy, grubby, grungy **7** unclean **8** maculate, slovenly, unwashed **10** unsanitary
smug: **4** prim, vain **5** cocky, proud, saucy **6** stuffy **7** content, fustian, haughty, hotshot, pompous, prudish, stuck-up **8** arrogant, boastful, cocksure, egoistic, gloating, priggish, puffed-up, snobbish, superior **9** big-headed, conceited, hubristic, overproud, righteous **10** big-talking, complacent, egoistical
be ~: **5** gloat
look: **4** grin, leer **5** smirk, sneer **6** simper
one: **4** prig
smuggle: **4** deal, hide, push **5** sneak **6** export, pirate **7** bootleg, snake in
smuggled: **7** illegal **9** forbidden **10** prohibited, proscribed
smuggler unit: **4** kilo
smuggling: **10** contraband, rum-running
smugness: **5** pride **6** vanity **7** conceit
smurf: **5** dance
Smurf: **4** toon **7** cartoon
cat: **6** Azrael
color: **4** blue
smush: **8** compress
smut: **5** filth, grime **6** fungus **8** lewdness **9** lubricity
Smuts, Jan: **4** Boer
smuttiness: **8** lewdness **9** bawdiness, crassness, indecency, vulgarity **10** coarseness, earthiness, indelicacy
smutty: **3** raw **4** foul, lewd, racy **5** bawdy, crude, dirty, nasty, rough **6** coarse, filthy, ribald, risqué, vulgar, X-rated **7** immoral, obscene, profane, raunchy **8** improper, indecent, off-color, unwashed **9** low-minded, salacious **10** indelicate, scurrilous
Smyrna: **4** city, port, town
locale: **5** Ionia **6** Aeolia **7** Georgia **9** Tennessee
Smyrna __: **3** fig
Smyslov, Vasily
forte: **5** chess
Smyth: **5** Patty
Sn: **3** tin **4** elem. **7** element
50 for ~: **4** at. no.
S.N.: **7** Behrman
snack: **3** eat, tea **4** bite, eats, gorp, grub, Ho Ho, meal, nosh, nuts, Oreo, taco **5** break, candy, chips, goody, knish, munch, nacho, piece, s'more, sweet **6** canapé, Fritos, goodie, morsel, nibble, pepita, tidbit **7** Cheetos, Doritos, falafel, goodies, munchie, peanuts, popcorn, pretzel **8** candy bar, carnitas, fast food, junk food, munchies, pick-me-up, pretzels, rice cake **9** collation, corn chips, pork rinds
like ~ dispensers: **6** coin-op
snack __: **3** bar **5** table
snacks, like some: **5** salty, sweet
snafu: **3** err **4** goof, muff **5** boner, botch, chaos, error, hitch, mix up **6** bollix, foul-up, glitch, mishap, muddle **7** mistake, screwup **8** disorder, rat's nest **9** mare's nest
snag: **3** bar, bug, get, jag, nab, rip, rub, run **4** clog, curb, grab, knot, nail, stub, tear, trap **5** block, brake, catch, crimp, hitch, point, seize, stick **6** arrest, crunch, glitch, hamper, hang-up, holdup, hurdle, kicker, obtain, pickle, scrape, snatch, tangle **7** acquire, barrier, ensnare, insnare, pitfall, problem, puzzler, receive, setback **8** blockade, drawback, entangle, grab away, obstacle, tangle up **9** hindrance, roadblock, tight spot **10** bottleneck, difficulty, impediment, limitation
__ snag: **4** hit a
snail: **4** apod **5** conch, whelk **7** abalone, dawdler, mollusc, mollusk **8** escargot, seashell, slowpoke **10** periwinkle
home: **5** shell
kin: **4** slug
snail __: **4** mail **6** darter
snaillike: **4** poky, slow **5** slimy, tardy **6** apodal, draggy **7** apodous, gradual, halting, impeded, lagging, languid **8** crawling, creeping, dawdling, dilatory, dragging, drawn-out, hesitant, plodding, slothful, sluggish, toddling **9** leisurely, lethargic, prolonged, unhurried **10** deliberate, protracted
snail-mail
alternative: **3** fax
__ snail's pace: **3** at a
snake: **3** asp, boa, cur **4** apod, coil, curl, fink, lurk, toad, turn, wind

5 adder, cobra, creep, curve, dance, knave, krait, mamba, racer, shirk, slink, snake, sneak, steal, swirl, twist, viper, weave 6 animal, bad guy, elapid, hisser, python, ramble, ratter, taipan 7 meander, rattler, reptile, schemer, serpent, sinuate, slither, wriggle 8 betrayer, cerastes, moccasin, ophidian, quisling, renegade, ringhals, rinkhals, turncoat 9 coachwhip, intriguer, slitherer 10 bushmaster, copperhead, fer-de-lance, sidewinder
African ~: 3 asp 5 cobra, mamba 8 ringhals 9 boomslang
Asian ~: 5 krait 6 dhaman, taipan
charmer's partner: 5 cobra
combining form: 4 ophi- 5 ophio-
covering: 5 scale
dancer: 4 Hopi
emulate a ~: 4 molt 5 crawl, slink 7 slither
ender: 4 bird, bite, fish, head, root, skin, weed 5 mouth, stone
in the grass: 5 knave, rogue, sneak 7 traitor 8 turncoat 9 scoundrel
like a ~: 5 scaly 6 apodal 7 apodous
mesmerize a ~: 5 charm
Mexican ~: 9 coachwhip
oil: 6 humbug
oil, supposedly: 4 cure
on Pharaoh's headdress: 3 asp
place for a ~: 5 drain
poison: 5 venom
poisonous ~: 3 asp 5 adder, cobra, krait, mamba, viper
science: 9 ophiology
shape: 3 ess
sound: 3 sss 4 hiss, siss, ssss
starter: 6 rattle
tooth: 4 fang
snake __: 3 oil, pit 4 eyes, foot 5 dance 6 doctor 7 charmer
__ snake: 3 fox, mud, rat, sea 5 coral, water 6 garter 7 hognose
Snake: 5 river
locale: 5 Idaho 7 Wyoming 10 Washington
snakebite plant: 5 guaco
Snake Eater (1989 film)
cast: Lorenzo Lamas
snake eyes: 3 two
roll ~: 4 lose
snakelike fish: 3 eel 5 moray 7 lamprey
snaky: 3 sly 4 wavy 5 sharp 6 aspish, coiled, crafty, curved, sneaky, subtle, vipery, zigzag 7 crooked, devious, lurking, sinuous, twisted, winding 8 entwined, flexuous, guileful, indirect, slinking, tortuous, twisting, two-faced, venomous, writhing 9 deceitful, insidious, meandrous 10 convoluted, meandering, serpentine, traitorous, treasonous
character: 3 ess
shape: 4 coil
snap: 2 go 3 nip, pep, pic, pop 4 bark, bean, bite, dash, ease, easy, élan, flip, game, grab, grip, jerk, kick, vent, yank, yell, zest 5 break, catch, cinch, clack, click, crack, cushy, flare, flash, flick, go ape, grasp, growl, grunt, lurch, photo, seize, shoot, snarl, snick, split, verve, vigor 6 bite at, breeze, clutch, cookie, fasten, fillip, lose it, picnic, retort, simple, snatch 7 crackle, give way, go crazy, grumble, lash out, no sweat, panache, shatter 8 break off, card game, duck soup, fastener, fracture, go postal, kid stuff, painless, pushover, separate, vitality, vivacity, walkover, workable 9 animation, briskness, come apart, easy as pie, go bananas, go berserk, go bonkers, no problem 10 child's play, effortless, get up and go, hit the roof, photograph, resilience, unexacting
alternative: 6 button, Velcro, zipper
back: 6 bounce 7 rebound, recover
call: 3 hut 6 hut one, hut two
cold ~: 5 frost
out of it: 5 rally 6 revive 9 take heart
starter: 6 ginger
to attention: 6 salute
to it: 6 hasten
up: 3 get, nab 4 grab, take 5 seize 8 pounce on
snap __: 3 pea 4 back, bean
snap __ it: 5 out of
__ snap: 4 cold 6 ginger
Snap! __! Pop!: 7 Crackle
snap-brim: 3 hat 6 fedora
snap one's __ off: 4 head
snapper: 4 croc, fish, jocu, sesi 5 gator 6 animal 7 reptile 9 alligator, crocodile
photo ~: 6 camera
starter: 7 whipper
trapper: 3 net 5 seine
__ snapper: 3 red
snappiness: 5 spice 10 impatience
snapping __: 6 turtle
snappish: 4 curt, edgy, sour, tart 5 huffy, moody, surly, testy, upset 6 crabby, cranky, crusty, feisty, fretty, grumpy, ireful, morose, ornery, snarly, touchy 7 bearish, bilious, crabbed, fretful, grouchy, huffish, nervous, peevish, peppery, prickly, waspish 8 choleric, fretsome, growling, grumpish, petulant 9 crotchety, fractious, irascible, irritable, querulous, splenetic
snappy: 4 chic, edgy, fast, pert, racy, sour, tart 5 brisk, crisp, cross, fleet, gruff, hasty, huffy, nasty, quick, rapid, sharp, short, smart, spicy, swank, swift, terse, testy 6 abrupt, classy, crabby, dapper, fretty, gnomic, lively, modish, ornery, speedy, spicey, sudden, swanky, touchy, trendy 7 dashing, grouchy, huffish, instant, peevish, peppery, stylish, voguish 8 petulant, spirited 9 breakneck, energetic, fractious, immediate, irascible, irritable, on-the-spot, querulous, sprightly 10 harefooted
make it ~: 3 hie 4 rush
snapshot: 3 pic 5 photo, print 6 candid 7 picture 8 portrait 10 photograph
collection: 5 album
snapshots: 3 pix
snap the __: 4 whip
snare: 3 bag, gin, nab, net, web 4 bait, drum, hook, land, lure, mire, trap 5 catch, decoy, noose, seize, tempt, trick 6 arrest, cobweb, come-on, corral, dupery, enmesh, entice, entrap, immesh, inmesh, pilfer, pull in 7 capture, involve, pitfall, round up 8 entangle, interest 9 booby trap, deception, quicksand 10 allurement, enticement, entrapment, temptation
snare __: 4 drum
snarl: 3 jam, web 4 bark, gnar, knot, maze, mesh, mess, muck, snap 5 bully, chaos, gnarl, growl, gum up, jam-up, swarm, tie-up, twist 6 enmesh, immesh, inmesh, jumble, jungle, knot up, mess up, morass, muddle, mutter, tangle 7 clutter, confuse, embroil, ensnare, entwine, grumble, insnare, intwine, mistake, perplex, problem, quarrel, thunder 8 disarray, disorder, entangle, mishmash, obstacle, threaten 9 confusion, labyrinth 10 complexity, complicate, congestion, difficulty, traffic jam
up: 3 err 6 jumble, muddle, tousle, touzle 7 confuse 8 dishevel, disorder, scramble 10 complicate
snarleyyow: 3 dog 6 canine
snarly: 5 surly 6 crusty, ornery 7 bearish 8 snappish 9 irritable, splenetic 10 out of sorts
snatch: 3 bit, nab, win 4 gain, grab, grip, jerk, jump, loot, nail, pull, snag, snap, take, tear, yank 5 catch, clasp, grasp, piece, pinch, pluck, seize, spell, steal, theft, wrest 6 abduct, assume, clutch, collar, jump at, kidnap, pilfer, pounce, rescue, wrench 7 capture, grapple, oddment, plunder, seizure, snippet 8 fragment, grab away, jerk away, thievery 10 commandeer, run off with, smattering, spirit away
Snatch (2000 film)
cast: Benicio Del Toro, Dennis Farina, Brad Pitt
director: Guy Ritchie
snazziness: 5 style
snazzy: 5 dandy, jazzy, natty, plush, ritzy, showy, sleek, swank 6 classy, dapper, flashy, jaunty, rakish, spiffy, sporty, swanky 7 refined, stylish 10 flamboyant
Snead, Sam: 6 golfer
sneak: 3 cur, pad, sly 4 case, heel, hide, lurk, shoe, slip, toad, worm 5 cower, crawl, creep, evade, glide, louse, mooch, prowl, sculk, shirk, sidle, skulk, skunk, slide, slink, snake, steal, swipe 6 ambush, delude, rascal, weasel, wretch 7 cheater, deceive, gumshoe, slither, smuggle, traitor 8 informer, stealthy 9 con artist, miscreant, pussyfoot, scoundrel 10 ambushment, nose around
along: 5 sidle
a look: 3 pry, see, spy 4 peek, peep, peer 5 snoop 6 glance 7 glimpse
alternative: 3 moc
around: 5 steal
attack: 6 ambush 10 ambushment
away: 7 abscond
by: 4 pass 6 elapse
in: 5 crash, enter 10 infiltrate
off: 5 elope 6 desert 8 slip away
peek: 6 prevue 7 preview
up on: 8 surprise
sneak __: 5 a peek, thief 6 attack 7 preview
sneaker: 4 shoe 7 gym shoe, high top 8 footwear
brand: 4 Avia, Keds, Nike, Puma 6 Adidas, Reebok
in Britain: 8 plimsoll
part: 3 toe 4 lace, sole 6 eyelet
Sneakers (1992 film)
cast: Dan Aykroyd, Ben Kingsley, Mary McDonnell, Robert Redford
sneakily: 8 on the sly
sneaky: 3 low, sly 4 base, mean, wily 5 nasty, snaky, snide 6 covert, feline, shifty, tricky 7 devious, furtive, knavish 8 guileful, indirect, slippery, stealthy, thieving, thievish 9 deceitful, deceptive, dishonest, insidious, malicious, secretive, underhand, unethical 10 unfaithful, unreliable
maneuver: 4 ploy
sneaky __: 4 pete
snee: 4 dirk 5 knife 6 dagger
sneer: 4 dump, gibe, grin, jeer, jest, jibe, leer, mock, slam, twit 5 crack, decry, fleer, flout, scoff, scorn, smirk, spurn, swipe, taunt 6 deride, insult, jibe at, slight 7 affront, burlesk, condemn, contemn, detract, disdain, grimace, lampoon, put down, slander, snicker, sniff at, snigger 8 belittle, ridicule, satirize, sneeze at 9 burlesque, dirty look, disparage 10 caricature, expression, look down on
sneering: 5 snide 7 cynical 8 derision, sardonic 9 sarcastic
sneeze
at: 4 mock 5 scorn, sneer, spurn 6 ignore 7 dismiss 8 brush off, laugh off, ridicule, shrug off 9 disregard
ender: 4 weed, wort
response: 8 bless you
sound: 5 achoo 6 ahchoo, hachoo 7 kerchoo
Sneezy: 5 dwarf
colleague: ***see*** dwarf
Snellen __: 4 test 5 chart
Snerd partner: 6 Bergen 7 Klinker
Sneva, Tom: 5 racer 9 auto racer
milieu: 5 track
__ S. Ngor: 5 Haing
snick: 3 cut 4 snap 5 click
snick-__: 5 a-snee
snick and __: 4 snee
snicker: 5 laugh, smirk, sneer, te-hee 6 giggle, guffaw, hee-haw, heehee, teehee, titter 7 chortle, chuckle 8 laughter
derisive ~: 3 heh
ender: 4 snee
snickering: 8 giggling, laughing
Snickers: 3 bar 5 candy 8 candy bar 9 chocolate
alternative: ***see*** candy brand
snide: 4 base, mean 5 catty, nasty 6 sneaky, unkind 7 caustic, hateful,

hurtful 8 derisive, scoffing, scornful, sneering, spiteful 9 insulting, malicious, sarcastic 10 derogatory, evil-minded
remark: 4 barb 5 crack 6 zinger
Snider: 3 Dee 4 Duke
Snider, Duke: 6 Dodger 10 outfielder
teammate: 3 Roe 5 Reese 6 Hodges 7 Erskine, Furillo 8 Newcombe, Robinson
sniff: 4 odor 5 aroma, scent, smell, whiff 6 detect, inhale 7 inspire, snuffle 9 breathe in 10 inhalation
around: 3 pry 4 nose
at: 5 scorn, sneer 7 contemn, disdain 10 look down on
out: 4 seek 6 detect, locate 9 track down
sniffle: 10 inhalation
sniffles: 4 cold
have the ~: 3 ail
sniffy: 7 haughty
snifter: 5 glass 6 goblet
contents: 6 brandy, cognac
snig: 3 eel
sniggler: 5 eeler
snare: 6 eelpot
spot: 6 eelery
snip: 3 bit, cut, nip 4 brat, clip, crop, minx, mite, nick, trim 5 crumb, fleck, prune, shave, shred, speck, touch 6 cut off, delete, hoiden, hoyden, morsel, remove, sliver, trifle 7 abridge, cut back, cut into, cutting, remnant, scissor, shorten, smidgen, smidgin 8 clipping, fragment, smidgeon 10 thimbleful
and tuck: 5 alter
off: 5 prune, shave, shear
snipe: 4 bird, fowl, jeer 5 wader 9 criticize, sandpiper
(at): 4 fire
relative: *see* fowl
Snipes, Wesley: 5 actor
film: The Art of War (2000)
Blade (1998)
Demolition Man (1993)
Down in the Delta (1998)
The Fan (1996)
Jungle Fever (1991)
Mo' Better Blues (1990)
Murder at 1600 (1997)
Passenger 57 (1992)
Rising Sun (1993)
U.S. Marshals (1998)
The Waterdance (1992)
White Men Can't Jump (1992)
snippet: 3 bit 4 wisp 5 scrap, shred, trace 6 little, sliver, snatch 7 oddment 8 clipping 9 sound bite
snippy: 4 curt, flip, pert, rude, tart 5 brusk, fresh, gruff, nervy, sassy, saucy, short 6 abrupt, awless, brazen, cheeky 7 aweless, brusque, uncivil 8 churlish, flippant, impolite, impudent, insolent 9 irascible, irritable, out of line
snit: 4 huff, stew 5 pique, tizzy 6 lather, temper 7 tantrum 8 hissy fit 9 huffiness, surliness
in a ~: 3 mad 4 sore 5 cross, huffy, irate, upset, vexed
put in a ~: 3 irk 4 miff, rile 5 anger, peeve, upset 7 agitate
snitch: 3 rat, rob 4 blab, fink, lift, loot, nark, sing, take, tell 5 filch, rat on, steal, swipe 6 squeal, tattle 7 ratfink, tattler, traitor 8 fat mouth 10 taleteller, tattletale
in British ~: 4 nark
on: 4 name 6 turn in
snivel: 3 cry, sob 4 bawl, mewl, pule, wail, weep 5 whine 6 boohoo 7 blubber, grumble, whimper 8 languish
sniveling: 5 weepy 7 tearful, wet-eyed
SNL: Saturday Night Live
Sno-__: 3 Cat 4 Caps, Cone
snob: 5 snoot 6 egoist 7 Brahmin, elitist, high-hat, upstart 8 braggart, highbrow 9 swellhead 10 downlooker, narcissist
put-on: 4 airs
snob __: 6 appeal
snobbery: 4 airs 5 pride 10 narcissism, pretension
snobbish: 4 smug, vain 5 aloof, cocky, proud 6 la-de-da, la-di-da, lordly, remote, snooty, stuffy, uppity 7 fustian, haughty, high-hat, pompous, stuck-up 8 arrogant, boastful, lah-di-dah, superior 9 bigheaded, conceited, egotistic, exclusive, hubristic 10 hoity-toity
set: 6 clique
snobbishness: 7 hauteur
Snobol: 8 language
alternative: *see* computer language
Sno-Caps: 4 nosh 5 candy, snack
Snodgress: 6 Carrie
snood: 3 net 7 hairnet 8 headband
snooker: 3 con 4 game, pool 5 trick
need: 3 cue 5 table
snookums
see sweetheart
Snooky: 6 Lanson
snoop: 3 pry, spy 4 lurk, peek, peep, peer, poke 5 noser, prier, pryer, scout, spy on, yenta 6 butt in, ferret, gossip, meddle, search, shamus, sleuth 7 gumshoe, intrude, meddler 8 busybody, quidnunc 9 detective, eavesdrop, interfere 10 nose around, poke around, sneak a look
prone to ~: 4 nosy 5 nosey
Snoop __: 4 Dogg
Snoop Doggy Dogg: 6 rapper
born: Calvin Broadus
rival: 5 Dr. Dre
song: Come and Get With Me (1998)
Dre Day (1993)
Gin & Juice (1994)
Nuthin' But a 'G' Thang (1993)
What's My Name? (1993)
snoopiness: 6 prying 8 interest, meddling, nosiness 9 curiosity
snoopy: 4 busy, nosy 5 nosey 7 curious, ferrety, peering 8 invasive 10 meddlesome
one: 5 prier, pryer
Snoopy: 3 dog 6 beatle
brother: 4 Olaf 5 Spike
enemy: 8 Red Baron
sister: 5 Belle
Snoopy, Come Home (1972 film)
director: Bill Melendez
Snoopy vs. the Red Baron (1966 song)
artist: Royal Guardsmen
snoot: 4 beak, nose, snob 6 beezer, schnoz 7 grimace, high-hat, schnozz 8 highbrow 9 proboscis, schnozzle 10 high-hatter, schnozzola
snootiness: 4 airs
snooty: 5 aloof, lofty, proud 6 la-de-da, la-di-da, uppity 7 haughty 8 arrogant, boastful, cavalier, lah-di-dah, snobbish 9 hubristic 10 disdainful
one: 4 snob
snooze: 3 nap 4 doze, rest, yawn 5 sleep 6 catnap, drowse, nod off, siesta 7 drop off, saw logs, slumber 10 fall asleep, forty winks
end one's ~: 4 wake
sound: 3 zzz
snoozing: 4 abed 6 asleep 7 dormant 9 sacked out, somnolent, unmindful 10 sawing logs
snoozy: 4 lazy 6 drowsy, sleepy 7 languid 9 lethargic, soporific
Snopes: 4 Flem
snore: 5 sleep 6 wheeze 7 saw logs, saw wood, snuffle 8 rhonchus
sound: 3 zzz
snorkel: 4 tube
alternative: 5 scuba
snorkeler
site: 6 lagoon
view: 5 coral
Snorkel, Sergeant bulldog: 4 Otto
Snorri Sturluson
work: Edda
Olaf's Saga
snort: 3 nip 4 belt, huff, pant, swig 5 drink, laugh, whiff 6 inhale 8 laughter 9 jiggerful 10 inhalation
of disgust: 3 hah, ugh 5 humph
snorting starter: 3 rip
snout: 4 beak, nose 5 trunk 6 muzzle, schnoz 7 schnozz 9 proboscis, schnozzle 10 schnozzola
snow: 3 lie 4 bilk, dupe, fool, hoax, sell 5 bluff, cheat, outdo, storm, trick, white 6 delude, powder, puzzle, take in 7 beguile, deceive, mislead, two-time, wheedle 8 bewilder, blizzard, fast-talk, flurries, hoodwink, inundate, inveigle, pettifog 9 bamboozle, disinform, four-flush, influence, overwhelm, victimize 10 run a game on
bump in ~: 5 mogul
creation: 4 fort
crystal: 5 flake
ender: 3 cap, man 4 ball, bell, bird, bush, drop, fall, melt, plow, shoe, suit 5 berry, blink, board, bound, brush, drift, flake, storm 6 capped, mobile
glider: 4 luge, sled 8 toboggan
goose: 4 fowl
granular ~: 4 firn, névé
job: 3 lie 4 hoax, ruse, sham 5 cheat, feint, fraud 6 deceit, dupery, humbug 7 swindle 8 artifice, trickery 9 deception, imposture 10 persuasion, subterfuge
light ~: 6 flurry
like ~: 4 cold, pure 5 white
lover: 5 skier
melter: 4 NaCl, salt 6 halite
melting ~: 5 slush
move ~: 4 blow, plow 5 sweep 6 shovel
navigate on ~: 3 ski 4 skee
pertaining to ~: 5 nival
relative: *see* white color
sign of ~: 6 nimbus
skier's ~: 4 corn
under: 5 swamp 6 deluge, engulf, ingulf 8 inundate 9 overwhelm
snow __: 3 day, job, pea 4 cone, crab, crop, lily, line, tire 5 board, goose, guard, under 6 blower, flurry 7 leopard, thrower
snow-__: 4 clad 5 white 6 capped
...snow, __ rain...: 3 nor
Snow: 2 C.P. 4 Hank 6 Phoebe
Snow __: 4 Belt
snowball: 4 grow 5 plant, raise, shrub 6 flower 7 burgeon, dessert, enlarge 8 bourgeon, ice cream, increase
alternative: 6 gelati, gelato, sundae 7 parfait, spumone, spumoni, tortoni
impact sound: 5 splat
relative: 5 elder 6 abelia
sometimes: 4 ammo
snowbank: 5 drift
snowbird: 5 junco
Snowbird (1970 song)
artist: Anne Murray
snowboarding: 5 sport
Snow-Bound: 4 poem
author: John Greenleaf Whittier
snowcapped: 8 towering
Snow, C.P.: 6 writer 7 British
work: Corridors of Power
The New Men
The Search
Strangers and Brothers
Snowe: 7 Olympia
snowfield: 4 firn
snowflake-like: 4 lacy
Snow Leopard, The
author: Peter Matthiessen
Snow Maiden, The: 5 opera
composer: Nikolai Rimsky-Korsakov
snowman
abominable ~: 4 yeti
nose: 6 carrot
wear: 3 hat 4 pipe 5 scarf
Snowmass: 6 resort 9 ski resort
locale: 8 Colorado
snowmobiler: 5 rider
Snow, Phoebe
song: Poetry Man (1975)
snowplow target: 5 drift
Snow Queen, The
author: Hans Christian Andersen
snowshoe
alternative: 3 ski 4 skee
snowshoe __: 4 hare 6 rabbit
snowslide: 9 avalanche
Snows of Kilimanjaro, The
author: Ernest Hemingway
Snows of Kilimanjaro, The (1952 film)
cast: Ava Gardner, Susan Hayward, Gregory Peck
snowstorm: 8 blizzard
Snow-Storm, The: 4 poem
author: Ralph Waldo Emerson
Snow Walker, The
author: Farley Mowat
Snow White
and her friends: 5 octad, octet
friend: *see* dwarf 5 dwarf
snowy: 3 wet 4 cold, pure 5 clean, white 6 washed, wintry 7 niveous,

wintery **8** spotless, unsoiled **9** laundered **10** immaculate
month: **3** Dec., Feb., Jan. **7** January **8** December, February
snowy __: **3** owl **5** egret
Snowy: **6** bleach
alternative: **5** Purex, Vivid **6** Clorox **8** Borateem
snub: **3** cut, dig **4** barb, duck, gibe, go by, jeer, jibe, mock, shun, slam, slap, slur **5** abuse, decry, libel, scold, scorn, spurn, taunt **6** defame, deride, dump on, heckle, humble, ignore, impugn, insult, little, malign, offend, pass up, rebuff, rebuke, reject, slight, vilify **7** affront, asperse, boycott, calumny, catcall, censure, contemn, degrade, disdain, high-hat, mockery, neglect, obloquy, offense, putdown, rank out, repulse, scratch, slander, traduce, upstage **8** belittle, brushoff, contempt, denounce, derision, pass over, ridicule, skip over, vilipend **9** aspersion, blackball, contumely, denigrate, discredit, disparage, disregard, humiliate, indignity, ostracize **10** calumniate, defamation, disrespect, opprobrium
snub-__: **5** nosed
snuck: **5** crept **7** prowled, skulked
snuff: **5** douse, dowse, smell **10** extinguish
bring up to ~: **5** rehab **6** repair
ender: **3** box
out: **5** douse, dowse **6** quench **7** blow out **8** suppress **10** extinguish
up to ~: **3** fit **4** able, good **5** sound **7** capable **9** competent, qualified **10** acceptable
__ snuff: **4** up to
snug: **4** cosy, cozy, firm, homy, safe, soft, taut, tidy, trim, warm **5** close, comfy, cozey, cozie, cushy, homey, rigid, stiff, tight **6** nestle **7** compact, livable, restful, tighten **8** homelike, intimate, liveable, tucked in **9** cuddled up, sheltered **10** convenient
bug locale: **3** rug
make ~: **4** tuck **6** nestle
spot: **3** den **4** nest **6** hearth
snug __ bug...: **3** as a
snuggery: **3** den
snuggle: **3** hug **4** neck **5** spoon **6** bundle, burrow, caress, cozy up, cuddle, curl up, huddle, nestle, nuzzle **8** ensconce, huddle up
Snuggle
alternative: **5** Downy **6** Bounce **9** Cling Free **10** Final Touch
snuggly: **4** soft **6** cuddly **7** lovable **8** huggable, loveable **10** cuddlesome
snugness: **4** ease **7** comfort **8** coziness
Snyder: **3** Tom **4** Gary, Liza
Snyder, Gary: **4** poet
work: The Back Country
Regarding Wave
Turtle Island
so: **4** a lot, ergo, lots, then, thus, true, very **5** hence, quite **6** actual, indeed **7** correct, factual, for real, that way **8** accurate, likewise, truthful **9** certainly, in this way, therefore **10** definitely, positively, unimagined, unmistaken
in Latin: **3** sic **4** ergo
much as: **4** even
so __: **3** far **4** as to, long, much, that, what **5** far as
so __ and yet...: **4** near
so __ as: **3** far **4** long, much
so __ I know: **5** far as
so __ me: **4** help
so __ so good: **3** far
so-__: **5** and-so **6** called
__ so: **3** how **4** ever
__ so!: **5** T'aint
__ so?: **3** How
__-so: **3** say
...so __ as a day in June?: **4** rare
So __: **3** Bad, Big, Sad **4** be it, Fine, Rare
So __!: **4** long **5** I lied, sue me, there
So __ in Love: **4** Much
So __ Is Paris: **4** This
So __ to you, Fuzzy-Wuzzy: **4** 'eres
So!: **3** aha
soak: **3** dip, sog, wet **4** dunk, seep, wash **5** bathe, clean, douse, dowse, flood, imbue, rinse, souse, steep, toper, water **6** absorb, dampen, drench, embrue, imbrue, infuse, pour on, rain on, rip off, seethe, soften, splash, take in **7** exploit, immerge, immerse, moisten **8** infusion, irrigate, marinate, permeate, pour into, saturate, submerge, waterlog **9** four-flush, penetrate, percolate **10** impregnate, infiltrate, overcharge
again: **5** rewet
fibers: **3** ret
in: **6** absorb **9** penetrate
up: **3** mop, sop **5** drink, learn **6** absorb, draw in, gather, ingest, osmose, take in **7** drink in, swallow **10** assimilate
up some sun: **3** tan **4** bask
soaked: **3** wet **5** adrip, soggy, soppy **6** sodden, sweaty **8** drenched **10** bedraggled
soaking: **3** dip, wet **4** bath **5** soggy **7** dunking **8** bibulous
site: **6** hot tub
so-and-so: **4** jerk **5** rogue, scamp **7** stinker **8** somebody **9** reprobate, scoundrel
soap: **3** Lux **4** Dial, Dove, Lava, suds, Tone, wash, Zest **5** Camay, clean, Coast, Ivory **6** Boraxo, Caress, lather, Shield **7** bubbles **8** cleanser, Lifebuoy **9** detergent, Palmolive, Safeguard **11** Irish Spring
acid: **5** oleic
bubbles: **4** foam **6** lather
ender: **3** box **4** bark, suds, wort **5** berry, stone
ingredient: **3** lye **4** aloe **6** alkali, potash
like a ~: **7** maudlin
opera: **5** drama, story **6** serial, series **9** imbroglio
plant: **5** amole
remove ~: **5** rinse
soft ~: **7** coaxing, palaver **8** cajolery, nonsense **9** wheedling **10** persuasion
target: **4** dirt **5** grime
unit: **3** bar **4** cake
work with ~: **5** carve
soap __: **3** pad **4** dish **5** chips, opera **6** bubble, flakes, powder
__ soap: **4** soft **6** saddle **7** shaving
Soap (ABC sitcom)
cast: Jimmy Baio (Billy Tate)
Diana Canova (Corrine Tate)
Billy Crystal (Jodie Dallas)
Cathryn Damon (Mary Campbell)
Robert Guillaume (Benson)
Katherine Helmond (Jessica Tate)
Robert Mandan (Chester Tate)
Richard Mulligan (Burt Campbell)
Jennifer Salt (Eunice Tate)
Robert Urich (Peter Campbell)
Sal Viscuso (Father Timothy Flotsky)
Ted Wass (Danny Dallas)
spin-off: **6** Benson
soapberry: **4** akee, tree **5** genip **6** lichee, litchi, longan, lungan **7** genipap, leechee
soapbox: **5** stump **6** podium **7** lecture, oration **8** platform
get on a ~: **5** orate **6** preach **7** address, declaim, lecture **8** harangue, proclaim
Soap Box Derby site: **5** Akron
Soapdish (1991 film)
cast: Robert Downey Jr., Sally Field, Carrie Fisher, Whoopi Goldberg, Kevin Kline, Cathy Moriarty, Elisabeth Shue
SoapNet: **7** channel
alternative: *see* cable channel
soapstone: **4** talc **8** steatite
soapy: **5** foamy, slick, sudsy **6** frothy **7** foaming, lathery **8** lathered, slippery, unrinsed **9** lubricous
soar: **3** fly **4** go up, leap, lift, rise, sail, skim **5** arise, climb, glide, shoot, tower, vault **6** ascend, aspire, move up, rocket **7** fly high, shoot up, take off **8** escalate, take wing **9** hang glide, skyrocket
above: **8** overlook
soaring: **4** high, tall **5** aloft, lofty, surge **6** flight, flying **8** elevated, towering, uplifted **9** on the wing
soave: **4** wine **5** white **7** Italian
like ~: **3** sec
sob: **3** cry **4** bawl, howl, mewl, moan, pule, sigh, wail, weep **5** mourn, whine **6** boohoo, lament, snivel **7** blubber, whimper **9** break down, cry a river, shed tears **10** take it hard
sob __: **5** story **6** sister
__ so bad: **3** not
So Bad (1984 song)
artist: Paul McCartney
__ So Bad: **4** Hurt **5** I Feel
sobbing: **5** tears, weepy **6** lament **7** in tears, tearful **9** sniveling **10** lachrymose, waterworks
So be it: **4** amen
sober: **4** calm, cool, dark, dull, sane, soft **5** grave, lucid, plain, quiet, solid, sound, staid, stoic **6** demure, dreary, low-key, sedate, serene, severe, solemn, somber, steady **7** ascetic, austere, careful, deadpan, pensive, serious, stoical, subdued **8** coherent, composed, forgoing, moderate, rational, reserved, sensible **9** abstinent, clear-eyed, collected, continent, eschewing, humorless, impartial, judicious, practical, pragmatic, provident, realistic, temperate, toned down, unamusing, unexcited, unextreme, unruffled, unslanted **10** abnegating, abstaining, abstemious, controlled, coolheaded, hard-bitten, no-nonsense, on the wagon, reasonable, restrained, thoughtful, unagitated, unhumorous
ender: **5** sides
sober __ judge: **3** as a
sober-__: **5** sided **6** headed, minded
Sobieski: **4** John **6** Leelee
So Big
author: Edna Ferber
sobriety: **8** eschewal **10** abstinence, moderation, temperance
sobriquet: **3** tag **4** name **5** title **6** handle **7** agnomen, epithet, moniker **8** cognomen, monicker, nickname
soca: **5** dance, music
kin: **7** calypso
so-called: **4** mock, sham **5** quasi **7** alleged, nominal **8** supposed **9** allegedly, pretended, professed, purported, self-named **10** ostensible, self-styled
in French: **9** soi-disant
soccer: **5** sport
former ~ org.: **4** NASL
game fraction: **4** half
goal: **3** net
in Britain: **8** football
kick: **4** punt
position: **3** LFB, RFB **4** wing **6** goalie
score: **4** goal
shoe feature: **5** cleat
shot: **4** kick **6** header
star: **4** Pelé
stat: **6** assist
team: **6** eleven
soccer __: **3** mom **4** ball
sociable: **4** easy, kind, warm **5** close, suave **6** chummy, clubby, genial, jovial, kindly, polite **7** affable, amiable, cordial **8** amicable, familiar, fireside, friendly, gracious, intimate, likeable, outgoing **9** congenial, convivial, expansive **10** accessible, benevolent, buddy-buddy, gregarious, hospitable, neighborly, personable, solicitous
be ~: **3** mix **6** hobnob, mingle
social: **3** bee **4** nice **5** civil, mixer, party **6** common, polite, public **7** cordial **8** communal, familiar, fireside, friendly, luncheon, mannerly, pleasant, polished **9** community, congenial, convivial, organized **10** collective, gregarious, hospitable, neighborly
activity: **3** bee, tea **5** dance, doing, party **6** affair, soiree **8** function
asset: **4** tact **7** manners **9** propriety
blunder: **5** gaffe
call: **5** visit
climber: **4** snob **7** elitist, upstart
dud: **4** geek, nerd **5** dweeb
elite: **5** A-list **6** jet set

ender: 3 ism, ist, ite
engagement: 4 date
graces: group: 3 set 4 clan, club
insect: 3 ant, bee
lack of ~ grace: 9 gaucherie
lack of ~ standards: 5 anomy 6 anomie
science: 7 history 9 economics
starter: 4 anti
stratum: 5 caste, class, elite 6 sphere
social __: 3 bee 4 work 6 worker 7 climber, compact, dancing, science, service, studies, welfare
__ social: 3 box
Social Contract, The
author: Jean Jacques Rousseau
socialist: 4 left 7 leftist 8 populist
Socialist: 5 party
five-time ~ candidate: 4 Debs
Socialist __ party: 5 Labor
socialite: 9 jet setter
teen: 3 deb
socialize: 3 mix 4 join 5 go out 6 hobnob, mingle 7 consort, hang out 8 chum with 9 associate, entertain, get around, pal around 10 fraternize
social-page word: 3 née
Social Register: 4 list
folk: 5 A-list, cream, elite
word: 3 née
societal: 6 public 7 popular 8 national
attitudes: 5 mores
breakdown: 5 anomy 6 anomie
unit: 4 clan
society: 4 clan, club, gang, gild, ring 5 elite, group, guild, order, tie-in, union, world 6 circle, clique, gentry, jet set, jungle, league, nation, outfit, people, public 7 company, culture, network, rat race, who's who 8 alliance, folkways, humanity, sodality 9 beau monde, community, humankind, institute, syndicate, top drawer 10 fellowship, friendship, haute monde, membership, upper class, upper crust
column word: 3 née
dictates of ~: 5 mores 8 protocol
dregs of ~: 6 rabble 8 riffraff 9 hoi polloi
event: 5 debut 9 cotillion
girl: 3 deb
high ~: 5 elite 6 bon ton, jet set 8 nobility 9 beau monde
honor ~ letter: 3 phi 4 beta 5 kappa
secret ~: 4 tong 5 cabal
__ society: 4 café, high 5 honor 6 Dorcas, humane, secret
__ Society: 4 High 5 Amana, Bible, Great, Royal 6 Fabian 7 Audubon
Society Island: 6 Mooréa, Tahiti 8 Bora Bora
Society of __: 7 Friends
Society's Child (1967 song)
artist: Janis Ian
sociology: 7 science
sock: 3 bop, hit, pop, pow 4 bang, beat, belt, blow, chop, clip, cuff, ding, nail, slap, slug, swat, wham 5 clout, flail, paste, punch, smack, smash, smite, swipe, whack, whang 6 anklet, argyle, buffet, strike, wallop 7 hosiery 8 haymaker, knee-high, uppercut
away: 4 hide, save 5 hoard, store 7 deposit 8 conserve
dealer: 6 hosier
ender: 4 eroo
fix a ~: 4 darn, mend
holder: 6 drawer
hop: 5 dance
Japanese ~: 4 tabi
kin: 6 bootee, bootie
like an old ~: 5 holey
part: 3 toe 4 foot, heel
starter: 4 wind
support: 6 garter
unit: 4 pair
sock __: 3 hop 4 away
__ sock: 3 air 4 crew, knee, tube 7 slipper
Sock __ me!: 4 it to
sockdolager: 4 lulu, oner
socked in: 5 foggy, misty
socket: 4 slot 6 cavity, recess
eye ~: 5 orbit
nautical ~: 7 gudgeon
socket __: 3 set 6 wrench
__ socket: 3 eye 4 wall
sockeye: 4 fish 6 salmon
Sock it to me! sayer: 5 Carne
socko: 5 boffo 7 boffola 8 terrific 10 impressive, successful
socks: 4 hose 7 hosiery
knock one's ~ off: 3 awe, wow 4 stun 5 amaze 6 thrill
sort ~: 5 match
__ socks: 4 knee 5 bobby, sweat
Socks: 3 cat
__ Socks: 5 Fox in
Socony today: 5 Mobil
Socrate
composer: Erik Satie
Socrates: 5 Greek 11 philosopher
friend: 5 Crito
pupil: 5 Plato
wife: 5 shrew 9 Xanthippe
Socratic __: 5 irony 6 method
sod: 4 land, lawn, turf 5 divot, earth, field, grass, sward 6 ground, meadow, swarth 7 pasture 9 grassland 10 greensward, native land
ender: 6 buster
grass: 5 Bahia
home: 5 hogan
like ~: 5 rooty
__ Sod: 3 Old 4 Auld
soda: 3 pop 4 cola, fizz 5 cream, drink, mixer, tonic 6 bubbly, cherry, leaven, orange 7 seltzer 8 beverage 9 soft drink
accessory: 5 straw
bottle unit: 3 can 4 case 5 liter, ounce
club ~: 4 fizz 5 mixer
high-caffeine ~: 4 Jolt
make ~ water: 6 aerate
open a ~ bottle: 5 uncap
partner: 6 Scotch
without club ~: 4 neat
soda __: 3 ash, pop 4 jerk 5 bread, water 7 cracker
__ soda: 3 sal 4 club, diet 5 cream 6 baking, celery 7 caustic, washing
soda fountain
in New England: 3 spa
order: 4 cola, malt 5 float, shake
seat: 5 stool
worker: 4 jerk
sodality: 5 order, union 6 league 7 society 10 fellowship, friendship, trade union
sodden: 3 wet 4 damp 5 muddy, soggy, soppy, steep, undry 6 drench, soaked, torpid, watery 7 wettish 8 dripping 9 saturated 10 bedraggled
Soddy, Frederick: 7 chemist 8 Nobelist
Söderberg, Hjalmar: 6 writer 7 Swedish 10 playwright
Soderbergh, Steven: 8 director
film: Che (2008)
Erin Brockovich (2000)
Full Frontal (2002)
Ocean's Eleven (2001)
Out of Sight (1998)
sex, lies, and videotape (1989)
Solaris (2002)
Traffic (2000, AA)
sodium: 5 metal 7 element
chloride: 4 NaCl, salt
combining form: 4 natr- 5 natro-
compound: 5 niter 6 alkali
form of ~ carbonate: 5 trona
hydroxide: 3 lye 4 NaOH
sodium-__ lamp: 5 vapor
Sodom: 4 city, town
escapee: 3 Lot
neighbor: 8 Gomorrah
__ So Easy: 3 It's
So Emotional (1987 song)
artist: Whitney Houston
soeur: 6 French, sister
soever starter: 3 how, who 4 what, when, whom 5 where, which 6 whence 7 whither
sofa: 4 seat 5 couch, divan 6 canapé, daybed, lounge, settee 7 seating, vis-à-vis 8 love seat 9 davenport, furniture, sectional, tête-à-tête
bed: 5 futon
part: 3 arm, leg 4 back 7 cushion
sofa __: 3 bed
__ sofa: 5 sleep
So far __ can tell...: 3 as I
So Far Away (1971 song)
artist: Carole King
so far so __: 4 good
__ so fast!: 3 Not
Sofer: 4 Rena
__ So Few: 5 Never
so few, to Churchill: 3 RAF
__ Soffel: 3 Mrs.
soffit location: 4 eave
Sofia: 4 city, town 7 capital, Coppola
locale: 8 Bulgaria
__ Sofia Museum: 5 Reina
So Fine (1981 film)
cast: Ryan O'Neal, Jack Warden
__ So Fine: 3 He's 4 Feel
soft: 3 dim, fat, lax, low 4 cosy, cozy, daft, dull, easy, fine, hazy, kind, limp, meek, mild, pale, snug, weak 5 bland, comfy, cozey, cozie, cushy, downy, dusky, faint, fluid, furry, light, loose, mealy, mushy, muted, nappy, pappy, piano, pithy, plush, pulpy, quiet, rusty, sheer, silky, silly, slack, sober, soggy, sweet, timid 6 benign, creamy, cuddly, docile, doughy, dulcet, flabby, fleecy, fleshy, flimsy, fluffy, gentle, kindly, liquid, low-key, mellow, padded, pallid, pastel, satiny, silken, simple, smooth, spongy, supple, tender 7 amiable, clement, diffuse, ductile, elastic, fatuous, flaccid, flowing, foolish, lenient, plastic, pliable, ruthful, snuggly, sparing, squashy, squishy, subdued, untoned, velvety, witless 8 bendable, cushiony, delicate, feathery, flexible, formless, laid-back, lenitive, merciful, moderate, moldable, murmured, overripe, pampered, placable, pleasant, sibilant, silklike, soothing, tolerant, twilight, unstrict, yielding 9 assuasive, caressing, compliant, courteous, cushioned, easygoing, forgiving, indulgent, malleable, melodious, sensitive, spineless, temperate, toned down, untrained, whispered 10 cuddlesome, effortless, forbearing, gelatinous, gone to seed, manageable, namby-pamby, out of shape, permissive, pianissimo, squeezable, starchless, unexacting, unhardened
ender: 4 ball, head, ware, wood 5 bound, cover 6 headed 7 hearted
go ~: 4 melt, thaw 6 loosen, relent, warm up 7 defrost 8 languish, unfreeze 10 deliquesce
in French: 3 bas
in music: 5 piano
palate: 5 velum
soap: 7 coaxing, palaver 8 cajolery, nonsense 9 wheedling 10 persuasion
sound: 3 coo 5 whish
spot: 4 love 6 liking 8 fondness, velleity, weakness
touch: 6 pigeon, sucker, victim 8 pushover
soft __: 4 coal, lens, line, news, rock, sell, soap, spot 5 drink, focus, goods, money, pedal, touch, water 6 palate 7 landing
soft-__: 3 top 4 shoe 5 cover, pedal, shell 6 headed 7 hearted
soft-__ clam: 5 shell
soft-__ crab: 5 shell
soft-__ egg: 6 boiled
Soft __: 4 Cell 5 Scrub
Soft and Dri: 9 deodorant
alternative: *see* deodorant
softball path: 3 arc
softcover: 4 book
soft drink: 2 A&W 3 7 Up, Tab 4 Coke, Dad's, Jolt, Nehi 5 Barq's, Fanta, Hires, Pepsi, Slice 6 Fresca, Nestea, Sprite 7 Snapple 8 beverage, Coca-Cola, Diet Rite, Dr. Brown's, Dr. Pepper, Gatorade 9 Canada Dry, Pepsi-Cola, Schweppes 10 Mello Yello, Royal Crown 11 Mountain Dew
unit: 4 case 6 carton
soften: 3 sag, sap 4 bend, calm, ease, flag, mash, melt, mute, soak, tame, thaw, tire, wane 5 abate, allay, blunt, break, knead, lower, mince, quell, quiet, relax, still, yield 6 deaden, defuse, defuze, impair, lessen, mellow, modify, muffle, obtund, reduce, relent, shrink, smooth, soothe, subdue, temper, weaken 7 appease, assuage, commute, deplete, exhaust, fatigue, lighten, moisten, mollify, qualify, relieve 8 diminish, dissolve,

enervate, enfeeble, humanize, mitigate, moderate, modulate, palliate, play down, slack off, tone down, turn down, unfreeze **9** alleviate, attenuate, lighten up, tenderize, undermine, water down **10** come around, debilitate, devitalize, liberalize, smooth over
__ softener: **5** water **6** fabric
softening: **6** relief **7** anodyne **9** abatement **10** comforting
agent: **4** aloe
softer in music: **3** dim. **7** decresc. **10** diminuendo
softhearted: **3** lax **4** easy, kind, mild, soft, warm **5** loose **6** gentle, kindly, tender **7** clement, lenient, ruthful, sparing **8** flexible, laid-back, merciful, placable, tolerant **9** assuasive, compliant, easygoing, forgiving, indulgent **10** forbearing, permissive, unexacting
become ~: **4** melt, thaw
softheartedness: **5** mercy **8** clemency
softie: **4** dupe, wimp **6** sucker **8** weakling
like a ~: **7** lenient
softly in music: **3** ppp. **9** sotto voce
__ Softly to Me: **4** Come
Soft 'N __: **3** Dri
softness: **4** woof **5** sound **6** lenity **7** texture **8** lenience
soft-pedal: **4** calm, lull, mute **5** quiet, relax **6** lessen, pacify, temper **8** minimize, moderate, play down, tone down **9** alleviate, whitewash **10** understate
Soft Scrub: **8** cleanser
alternative: **4** Ajax, Bab-O **5** Comet **6** Bon Ami
soft-sell: **4** coax **5** lobby **6** low-key
soft-shell: **4** clam, crab **7** lenient
soft-shoe: **5** dance
__ soft shoe, the: **3** old
softsoap: **3** lie **4** coax **5** lobby **6** cajole **7** flatter, lay it on, wheedle **8** blandish
soft-spoken: **5** suave **6** humble **8** reserved **9** courteous
software
bundled ~: **5** suite
company: **5** Lotus, Roxio **6** Intuit **9** Microsoft
convenience: **5** macro
fix ~: **5** debug
former statistical ~: **5** Dbase
Internet ~: **6** applet
medium: **5** CD-ROM
Microsoft ~: **4** Word **5** Excel **6** Access **10** PowerPoint
option list: **4** menu
problem: **3** bug
purchaser: **4** user
release: **7** version
runner: **2** PC **3** Mac
test: **4** beta
tycoon: **5** Gates
user: **6** hacker
Web ~: **7** browser
write ~: **4** code **7** program
Soft Weve: **6** tissue
alternative: **5** Scott **6** Marcal **7** Charmin **8** Northern **10** Cottonelle, White Cloud
softy
see softie

sog: **4** soak **6** drench **7** moisten
sogginess: **3** dew **5** vapor **7** wetness **8** dampness, humidity, moisture
soggy: **3** wet **4** damp, dank, soft **5** humid, moist, mucky, muddy, muggy, mushy, soppy, undry **6** clammy, soaked, sodden, spongy, steamy, sticky, stuffy, sultry, watery **7** soaking, sopping, wettish **8** drenched, dripping **9** saturated **10** bedraggled, sopping wet
ground: **3** bog, mud
mixture: **4** glop
Soglow: **4** Otto
__ so good: **5** so far
__ So Good: **4** Feel **5** Feels, Hurts
So good...it's gone food: **4** Spam
So help me!: **6** honest, really
Soho
locale: **3** NYC **6** London **7** England, New York **9** Manhattan
So I __!: **4** lied
Soichiro: **5** Honda
soi-disant: **7** wannabe **8** so-called **10** self-styled
soil: **3** mar, tar **4** blot, clay, dirt, dust, foul, home, land, loam, mess, muck, soot, spot, turf **5** crumb, dirty, earth, grime, humus, loess, muddy, shame, smear, spoil, stain, sully, taint **6** bedaub, befoul, bemire, crud up, debase, defile, embrue, ground, imbrue, malign, mess up, muck up, muss up, region, smudge, spread **7** begrime, besmear, blacken, corrupt, country, degrade, dry land, pollute, seedbed, spatter, tarnish, topsoil **8** besmirch, discolor, disgrace, farmland, homeland **9** bedraggle, homestead **10** terra firma
additive: **4** lime, peat **5** mulch
aerator: **4** root, worm
combining form: **4** agro -
component: **4** clay **5** humus **6** alkali
cultivated ~: **5** tilth
embankment: **4** berm **5** berme
farm ~: **4** dirt, land **5** earth
kind of ~: **4** clay, loam **5** humus
layer: **5** solum
like some ~: **5** loamy **6** acidic, clayey
science of ~: **8** agrology
soggy ~: **3** mud
starter: **3** top
turn the ~: **6** aerate
windborne ~: **5** loess
__ soil: **7** potting
soil agriculture science: **9** geoponics
soiled: **5** dirty, grimy, muddy, sooty **6** filthy, grubby, grungy **7** squalid, unclean **8** befouled, begrimed, maculate, slovenly, unwashed, vitiated **9** blackened **10** bedraggled, besmirched, germ-ridden, unsanitary
__-Soiler: **4** Free
So in Love
composer: Cole Porter
soir: **6** French **7** evening
soiree: **4** fete, gala **5** party, salon **6** affair **9** festivity, reception
snack: **6** canapé

Soirées de Médan
author: Émile Zola
__ soit qui...: **4** Honi
sojourn: **4** bide, nest, rest, stay, stop **5** abide, dwell, lodge, perch, roost, squat, tarry, visit **6** linger, remain, reside **7** inhabit, layover **8** stay over, stopover, vacation **9** residence, tarriance **10** pilgrimage, stay a while
sojourner: **5** guest, rover **8** runagate **9** journeyer **10** vacationer
Sojourner: **5** Truth
Sokolov: **4** Ivan
sol: **4** note
preceder: **2** fa
successor: **2** la
Sol: **3** sun **4** star **5** Hurok **7** Phoebus
equivalent: **6** Helios
sister: **3** Eos **6** Aurora
__-Sol: **4** Pine
solace: **4** balm **5** allay, cheer, peace **6** relief, soothe, succor **7** assuage, cheer up, comfort, compose, condole, console, hearten, relieve **8** mitigate, sympathy **9** alleviate, disburden, encourage, untrouble **10** condolence
sought ~ from: **5** ran to
solan: **4** bird **5** diver, goose **6** gannet
solar
cycle: **4** year
gap between ~ and lunar year: **5** epact
output: **4** heat **5** light
ring: **6** corona
wind particle: **3** ion
wind phenomenon: **6** aurora
solar __: **3** day **4** cell, heat, wind, year **5** cycle, flare, panel, power **6** energy, plexus, system **7** battery, eclipse, heating
Solara: **3** car **4** auto **6** Toyota
Solar Barque
author: Anaïs Nin
Solari: **4** Rudy
Solaris
author: Stanislaw Lem
Solaris (2002 film)
cast: George Clooney, Natascha McElhone
sold
on, as a cause: **5** wed to
out: **4** bare, gone **5** empty **7** crowded **8** depleted
Soldati: **5** Mario
solder: **4** fuse, join, weld **5** alloy, braze, metal, stick **6** cement, fasten
flux: **5** borax
material: **3** tin
tool: **4** iron
soldered: **4** firm
soldering __: **4** iron
soldier: **2** GI **5** cadet, guard, scout **6** gunner, gyrene, knight, marine **7** draftee, fighter, officer, private, recruit, trooper, veteran, warrior **8** commando, guerilla, infantry, selectee **9** combatant, conscript, guerrilla, legionary, mercenary, musketeer, volunteer, warmonger **10** Green Beret
absent ~: **4** AWOL
address: **3** APO, FPO
assignment: **4** duty, post
break: **5** leave, R and R **8** furlough
burden: **6** kitbag

camp: **5** étape
career ~: **5** lifer
cavalry ~: **6** hussar
Civil War ~: **3** reb **4** gray, grey
distaff ~: **4** WAAC
down under: **5** Anzac
fare: **4** Spam
French ~: **5** poilu
group: **3** USO, VFW **5** Amvet
horse ~: **6** lancer
I.D.: **6** dogtag
Korean ~: **3** ROK
lodging: **4** base **6** billet, casern **7** caserne **8** barracks
mounted ~: **7** dragoon
Muslim ~: **5** ghazi
Nepalese ~: **6** Gurkha
of fortune: **4** merc **9** mercenary **10** adventurer
onetime ~ of India: **5** Sepoy
rank: **2** BG, lt. **3** col., cpl., gen., maj., NCO, PFC, sgt. **4** capt. **5** lieut., lt. col., lt. gen., major **6** maj. gen. **7** captain, colonel, general, private **8** corporal, sergeant **10** lieutenant
retired ~: **3** vet **7** veteran
Tatar ~: **4** ulan **5** uhlan
tin ~: **3** toy
toy ~: **5** GI Joe
tune: **5** march
Turkish ~: **5** Nizam
uniform: **3** ODs **4** camo, drab **5** khaki, olive
U.S. ~: **4** Yank **5** GI Joe **8** doughboy
WWI ~: **5** Anzac, poilu
WWII ~: **3** WAC **5** GI Joe
see also army, military
__ soldier: **3** tin **4** foot
__ Soldier: **7** Unknown
Soldier Boy (1962 song)
artist: Shirelles
Soldier Field: **5** arena **7** stadium
locale: **7** Chicago **8** Illinois
soldierly: **7** martial, warlike **8** military
soldier of __: **7** fortune
Soldier of Love (1989 song)
artist: Donny Osmond
soldiers: **4** army **5** force, troop **6** grunts **7** cavalry **8** infantry
ten Roman ~: **6** decade
Soldier's Daughter Never Cries (1998 film)
cast: Barbara Hershey, Kris Kristofferson, Leelee Sobieski
soldiers of fortune group: **5** A-Team
Soldier's Pay
author: William Faulkner
sole: **3** ace, odd, one **4** fish, lone, only **5** alone **6** cobble, entrée, single, unique **7** halibut, seafood **8** flatfish, flounder, isolated, separate, singular, unshared **9** exclusive, matchless, nonpareil, remaining, unequaled, unmarried **10** individual, one and only, particular
attachment: **5** cleat
combining form: **4** pedi- **5** pedio-
ender: **5** plate, print
of the ~: **5** volar
part: **5** tread
plow ~: **5** slade
protector: **3** tap
starter: **4** turn **5** inner
__ sole: **5** Dover, lemon

—-sole: **4** half
solecism: **5** error, gaffe **6** misuse **7** mistake
popular ~: **4** ain't
solecistic: **10** illiterate
Soledad: **6** O'Brien
Soleil — Frye: **4** Moon
— Soleil: **5** Le Roi
solely: **3** all, but **4** only **5** alone, per se **6** merely, purely, simply, singly, wholly **7** totally **8** entirely **10** completely, nothing but, separately, singularly
solemn: **4** glum, holy **5** grand, grave, heavy, sober, staid **6** august, divine, formal, ritual, sacred, somber **7** austere, deadpan, intense, learned, serious, stately, subdued, weighty **8** brooding, downbeat, hallowed, imposing, majestic **9** awestruck, dignified, humorless, momentous, religious, unamusing, venerable **10** ceremonial, devotional, impressive, liturgical, majestical, no-nonsense, portentous, reflective, sanctified, unhumorous
word: **3** vow **4** oath
— Solemnis: **5** Missa
solemnity: **4** pomp, rite **6** ritual **7** dignity **8** splendor **9** austerity, formality
solemnize: **4** keep **7** observe **9** celebrate
solemnness: **9** formality
— Solennelle: **5** Messe
— Solent: **4** Wolf
Sole Survivor
author: Dean Koontz
soleus: **6** muscle
locale: **4** calf
solfeggio syllable: **2** do, fa, la, mi, re, ti, ut **3** sol
solicit: **3** ask, beg, bum, sue, woo **4** call, hawk, pray, seek, tout, urge **5** crave, exact, hit on, hit up, lobby, mooch, plead, query, steer **6** appeal, ask for, demand, desire, drum up, hustle, invoke, peddle, resort, sponge, sue for **7** beseech, canvass, enquire, entreat, implore, inquire, procure, promote, request **8** approach, campaign, come on to, petition, plead for, question **9** impetrate, importune, panhandle, postulate **10** pass the hat, supplicate, whistle for
solicitant: **9** candidate
solicitation: **4** call, care, plea **6** appeal **7** request
solicitor: **5** asker **6** lawyer, legist **7** counsel **9** barrister, counselor
solicitor —: **7** general
solicitous: **4** avid, keen, kind **5** close, eager **6** ardent, caring, chummy, clubby, genial, kindly, loving, polite, tender, uneasy **7** affable, amiable, anxious, careful, cordial, devoted, earnest, fearful, heedful, mindful, nervous, thirsty, worried, zealous **8** amicable, friendly, intimate, outgoing, sociable, troubled **9** attentive, brotherly, concerned, convivial, impatient, regardful **10** benevolent, buddy-buddy, neighborly, protective
be ~: **4** mind **5** hover
one: **5** carer
phrase: **5** I care, try me
solicitude: **3** TLC **4** care, heed **5** qualm, worry **6** regard, unease **7** anxiety, concern, scruple, thought **8** disquiet, kindness **9** affection, attention, eagerness **10** discretion
solid: **3** set **4** cube, firm, good, hard, hunk, lump, pure, real, rock, sure **5** beefy, block, cubic, dense, fixed, hardy, heavy, hefty, husky, rigid, rocky, sober, sound, stiff, stony, stout, thick, tight, valid **6** cogent, decent, intact, massed, potent, rooted, rugged, secure, stable, steady, steely, stocky, stoney, strong, sturdy, trusty, united, unmixt, worthy **7** compact, durable, genuine, learned, logical, serious, solvent, telling, unmixed, upright **8** accurate, complete, concrete, constant, material, palpable, physical, powerful, reliable, rocklike, sensible, stalwart, tangible, unbroken, well-made **9** compacted, condensed, continued, estimable, excellent, like a rock, nonporous, practical, steadfast, touchable, unalloyed, unanimous, undivided, unfailing, well-built **10** compressed, continuous, convincing, dependable, hard-packed, impervious, law-abiding, satisfying, set in stone, unshakable, unwavering, unyielding, upstanding
combining form: **5** stere-
geometric ~: **4** cube **5** prism, torus **6** sphere **7** pyramid
geometry calculation: **6** volume
gold: **7** optimum **8** peerless, splendid **9** marvelous
in physics: **5** state
on ~ ground: **6** ashore
rock: **5** loyal **6** honest, stable, steely, trusty **7** certain, ethical, staunch **8** faithful, reliable, surefire **9** honorable, steadfast, unfailing **10** consistent, dependable, infallible
semirigid ~: **3** gel
solid — rock: **3** as a
solid-—: **5** state
Solid (1985 song)
artist: Ashford and Simpson
Solid —: **5** South
solidarity: **5** unity **6** accord **7** concord, oneness **9** coherence, unanimity **10** friendship
Solidarity: **5** union
city: **6** Gdansk
Solid Gold host: **4** Dees **5** McCoo
solidified: **4** hard **5** stiff, thick **7** jellied
solidify: **3** fix, gel, set **4** cake, clot, jell **5** unite **6** cake up, firm up, freeze, gelate, harden **7** congeal, encrust, stiffen, thicken **8** condense **9** coagulate **10** gelatinize
solidifying agent: **4** agar **8** agar-agar
solidity: **4** pith **7** reality **8** firmness **9** stability
lose ~: **4** melt, thaw
symbol of ~: **4** rock
solidly built: **5** beefy, stout **6** strong
solids: **8** sediment
solidus: **4** coin **5** money
soliloquist, like a: **5** alone
soliloquize: **5** orate **6** recite
soliloquy: **4** talk **7** monolog **9** monologue
phrase: **4** to be **5** or not
sung ~: **4** aria
woeful ~: **6** lament
solipsist: **6** egoist **7** egotist
preoccupation: **4** self
Solis: **5** Hilda
solitaire: **4** game **5** jewel **7** jewelry, recluse **8** card game
how ~ is played: **5** alone
variety: **8** canfield, patience
Solitaire (song)
artist: Laura Branigan, Carpenters
solitarian: **6** hermit
solitarily: **5** alone, per se
solitary: **3** odd, one **4** lone, monk, only, stag **5** alone, aloof, stark, unwed **6** hermit, lonely, remote, single, unique **7** distant, eremite, oddball, private, recluse **8** anchoret, deserted, desolate, eremitic, forsaken, hermitic, isolated, lonesome, reserved, secluded, separate, singular, unsocial **9** anchorite, reclusive, withdrawn **10** antisocial, cloistered, friendless, hermitical, individual, unattended, unsociable
combining form: **4** erem-, soli- **5** eremo-
one: **5** loner **6** hermit
Solitary Man (1970 song)
artist: Neil Diamond
Solitary Reaper, The
author: William Wordsworth
— solita storia: **3** E La
solitude: **7** privacy, retreat, secrecy **9** aloneness, emptiness, isolation, seclusion **10** desolation, detachment, loneliness, quarantine, withdrawal
seeker: **5** loner **6** hermit
Solitude
author: Alexander Pope
— Solitude: **5** Ode on
solo: **4** aria, lone **5** alone **6** single, unique **7** unaided **8** singular **9** by oneself **10** one-man band, unassisted, unescorted
passage in music: **7** cadenza
performer: **4** diva
vocal ~: **4** aria **5** scena **6** arioso
Solo: **3** Han **8** Napoleon
Solo, Han: **4** hero
ally: **4** Leia, Luke **6** Obi-Wan
foe: **5** Darth, Vader
portrayer: Harrison Ford
soloist: **6** player, singer **8** musician
Soloist, The (2009 film)
cast: Robert Downey, Jr., Jamie Foxx, Catherine Keener
Solomon: **4** king, sage
composer: George Frideric Handel
daughter: **7** Taphath
like ~: **4** wise
parent: **5** David **9** Bathsheba
queen: **5** Sheba
son: **8** Rehoboam
Solomon and Sheba (1959 film)
cast: Yul Brynner, Gina Lollobrigida
Solomonic: **4** sage, wise
Solomon Islands: **6** nation **7** country
capital: **7** Honiara
money: **4** cent **6** dollar
one of the ~: **4** Buka, Savo **7** Malaita **8** Choiseul
— Solomon's Mines: **4** King
solon: **4** sage **6** pundit **8** lawmaker
Solo, Napoleon: **3** spy **5** agent
employer: **5** UNCLE
Solondz: **4** Todd
So long!: **3** bye **4** ciao, ta-ta **5** adieu, adios, aloha, I'm off, later **6** bye-bye, shalom **7** goodbye **8** sayonara
in French: **5** adieu
in Hawaiian: **5** aloha
in Italian: **4** ciao
in Latin: **3** ave **4** vale
in Spanish: **5** adios
Solothurn river: **3** Aar **4** Aare
solstice: **6** height
— solstice: **6** summer, winter
Solstice
author: Joyce Carol Oates
Solstices
author: Louis MacNeice
Solti, Georg: **9** conductor
soluble: **10** explicable
soluble —: **3** RNA
—-soluble: **3** fat **5** water
solus: **5** alone
solution: **3** key, mix **5** blend, fluid, juice **6** answer, elixir, liquid, remedy, result, ticket **7** extract, mixture, pay dirt, solvent **8** compound, emulsion, quick fix
alcohol ~: **8** tincture
caustic ~: **6** alkali
corrosive ~: **4** acid **5** oleum
darkroom ~: **5** fixer, toner
high-pH ~: **6** alkali
hydroxide ~: **3** lye
inelegant ~: **5** kluge **6** kludge
low-pH ~: **4** acid
salt ~: **5** brine
— solution: **6** saline
Solvay, Ernest: **7** chemist
solve: **2** do **3** fix, get, hit **4** have, lick, work **5** crack, plumb **6** answer, decide, decode, fathom, pan out, reason, settle, unlock **7** achieve, clarify, clear up, explain, expound, find out, hit upon, iron out, make out, unravel, work out **8** construe, deal with, decipher, get right, think out, untangle **9** determine, elucidate, enlighten, figure out, interpret, puzzle out **10** account for, illuminate
hard to ~: **5** nasty, tough **6** knotty
solvent: **5** solid, sound **6** acetal, afloat, eluant, hexane, hexone, liquid, liquor **7** acetone **8** cleanser, solution **10** in the black, turpentine
alcohol ~: **6** acetal
financially ~: **6** afloat
glycerol-based ~: **6** acetin
perfumery ~: **5** aldol **9** acetaldol
use a ~: **5** elute
solver: **7** puzzler
need: **6** eraser
quest: **6** answer
shout: **3** aha
Solway Firth: **5** inlet
locale: **7** England **8** Irish Sea, Scotland
tributary: **3** Esk **4** Eden
Solzhenitsyn, Aleksandr: **6** writer **7** Russian **8** Nobelist

formerly: 5 exile
work: Cancer Ward
The First Circle
The Gulag Archipelago
Som.
see Somalia
soma: 4 body
Somali: 3 cat 5 felid 6 feline 7 Current 8 language
home: 5 Kenya 6 Africa, Jibuti 7 Somalia 8 Djibouti, Ethiopia
Somalia: 6 nation 7 country
capital: 9 Mogadishu
group: 10 Arab League
gulf: 4 Aden
locale: 6 Africa
money: 4 cent 8 shilling
neighbor: 5 Kenya 8 Djibouti, Ethiopia
__ so many words: 5 not in
somatic: 6 bodily 8 corporal, physical
somber: 3 dim, sad 4 blue, dark, dire, down, drab, dull, glum, gray, grey, grim 5 black, bleak, dingy, dusky, grave, mirky, murky, shady, sober, staid, woful 6 cloudy, dismal, dreary, gloomy, morbid, morose, sedate, solemn, sullen, woeful 7 deadpan, doleful, elegiac, hurting, joyless, obscure, serious, shadowy, unhappy, weighty 8 darkened, dejected, desolate, downcast, funereal, mournful, overcast, sourpuss, troubled 9 bummed out, cheerless, heartsick, humorless, miserable, saddening, saturnine, sorrowful, tenebrous, unamusing, woebegone 10 chapfallen, depressing, depressive, dispirited, lackluster, lugubrious, melancholy, no-nonsense, oppressive, sepulchral, tenebrific, unhumorous
in a ~ way: 5 sadly
music: 5 dirge
sombrero: 3 hat 7 Mexican
some: 3 any 4 a bit, a few, part 6 rather 7 a little, handful, portion, pronoun, several 8 a good bit 9 a number of 10 moderately
ender: 3 day, how, one, way 4 body, time, ways, what 5 place, thing, times, where
in French: 3 des
starter: 3 awe, irk, two, win 4 fear, four, game, glad, glee, hand, lone, long, tire, toil 5 light, three, tooth, whole 6 bother, frolic, meddle
Some __ meat and canna eat: 3 hae
somebody: 3 one, VIP 4 name, star 5 nabob 6 anyone, person 7 notable, so-and-so, whoever 8 luminary 9 celebrity, dignitary, personage, superstar
Somebody __ de bay: 5 bet on
Somebody __ Me: 5 Loves
Somebody __ Moon: 5 Else's
Somebody __ My Gal: 5 Stole
Somebody in Boots
author: Nelson Algren
Somebody Loves Me
composer: George Gershwin
Somebody's Baby (1982 song)
artist: Jackson Browne
Somebody's Darling
author: Larry McMurtry
Somebody to Love (song)
artist: Jefferson Airplane, Queen
Somebody Up There Likes Me (1956 film)
cast: Pier Angeli, Paul Newman
Some Came Running: 4 film 5 novel
author: James Jones
cast: Shirley MacLaine, Dean Martin, Frank Sinatra
director: Vincente Minnelli
Some Can Whistle
author: Larry McMurtry
someday: 3 yet 4 anon, soon, then 5 after 6 in a bit, in time 7 anytime, by and by, later on 8 in a while 9 afterward, hereafter 10 before long, eventually, ultimately
Someday (song)
artist: Mariah Carey, Glass Tiger, Sugar Ray
Some Day My __ Will Come: 6 Prince
Someday We'll Be Together (1969 song)
artist: Supremes
Some Enchanted Evening
composer: Oscar Hammerstein, Richard Rodgers
singer: 5 Emile
Some Guys Have All the Luck (1984 song)
artist: Rod Stewart
somehow: 6 anyway, in a way
somehow or __: 5 other
Some Kind of Wonderful (1974 song)
artist: Grand Funk
Some Kind of Wonderful (1987 film)
cast: Mary Stuart Masterson, Craig Sheffer, Eric Stoltz, Lea Thompson
Some Like It Hot (1959 film)
cast: Joe E. Brown, Tony Curtis, Jack Lemmon, Marilyn Monroe, George Raft
director: Billy Wilder
role: 4 Kane 5 Sugar
__ Some Lovin': 5 Gimme
Some of __ Days: 5 These
someone: 6 entity, person
someone __ problem: 5 else's
Someone (1997 song)
artist: Puff Daddy, SWV
__ Someone Happy: 4 Make
Someone to Watch Over Me: 4 song
composer: George Gershwin, Ira Gershwin
Someone to Watch Over Me (1987 film)
cast: Tom Berenger, Lorraine Bracco, Mimi Rogers
__ some rays: 4 grab 5 catch
Somers: 5 Brett 6 Joanie 7 Suzanne
somersault: 4 flip, roll 6 tumble
somersaulter: 7 gymnast
Somers, Brett
spouse: Jack Klugman
Somersetshire river: 3 Exe
Somerville: 4 city, town
locale: 4 Mass.
Some Tame Gazelle
author: Barbara Pym
something: 3 tip 5 being 6 entity, object, rather, tipoff 7 article 9 commodity, substance 10 individual
something __: 3 new, old 4 blue, else 8 borrowed
__ something: 4 up to 5 start
Something (1969 song)
artist: Beatles
Something for the Boys: 7 musical
composer: Cole Porter
Something Happened
author: Joseph Heller
Something Happened on the Way to Heaven (1990 song)
artist: Phil Collins
__ something I said?: 4 Is it 5 Was it
Something of Value
author: Robert Ruark
__ something over on: 3 put 4 slip
Something's Burning (1970 song)
artist: Kenny Rogers
Something's Gotta Give (1955 song)
artist: Sammy Davis Jr., McGuire Sisters
Something's Gotta Give (2003 film)
cast: Diane Keaton, Jack Nicholson, Amanda Peet, Keanu Reeves
__ Something to Me: 5 You Do
Something to Talk About (1991 song)
artist: Bonnie Raitt
Something Unspoken
author: Tennessee Williams
Something Wicked This Way Comes
author: Ray Bradbury
Somethin' Stupid (1967 song)
artist: Frank Sinatra, Nancy Sinatra
sometime: 3 old, yet 4 anon, ever, late, once, soon, then 5 after 6 any day, in a bit, in time, one day 7 by and by, later on 8 in a while, previous 9 afterward, hereafter 10 before long, eventually, on occasion, ultimately
sometimes: 6 seldom 7 usually 8 off and on 10 frequently, now and then, on occasion
Sometimes __ We Touch: 4 When
Sometimes a Great Notion
author: Ken Kesey
Sometimes Love Just Isn't Enough (1992 song)
artist: Don Henley
Sometimes you feel like __...: 4 a nut
somewhat: 4 a bit 5 a mite, quite, sorta 6 fairly, in part, kind of, little, partly, pretty, rather, sort of 7 a little, not much 8 bearably, slightly 9 partially, to a degree, tolerably 10 moderately, more or less, relatively
prefix: 4 semi-
suffix: 3 -ish
somewhere: 5 about 6 around 9 scattered 10 ultimately
else: 3 out 4 away 6 absent
get ~: 6 arrive
Somewhere in the Night (song)
artist: Barry Manilow, Helen Reddy
Somewhere in Time (1980 film)
cast: Christopher Plummer, Christopher Reeve, Jane Seymour, Teresa Wright
Somewhere, My Love (1966 song)
artist: Ray Conniff
dedicatee: 4 Lara
Somewhere Out There (1987 song)
artist: James Ingram, Linda Ronstadt
Some Words With a Mummy
author: Edgar Allan Poe
__ some Z's: 5 catch
Sominex: 8 sleep aid
alternative: 5 Nytol 6 Compoz, Unisom
Somme: 5 river 6 battle
city on the ~: 6 Amiens
locale: 6 France
sommelier: 6 server, waiter 7 steward
concern: 4 wine 6 cellar
cooler: 3 ice
Sommer: 4 Elke 5 Jaime, Josef
Sommersby (1993 film)
cast: Jodie Foster, Richard Gere, James Earl Jones, Bill Pullman
director: Jon Amiel
Sommers, Jamie bionic implant: 3 ear
somniferous: 6 sleepy 8 hypnotic 9 soporific
somnolent: 4 dozy, lazy 5 yawny 6 asleep, dozing, drowsy, groggy, sleepy, torpid 7 dormant, napping 8 dreaming, inactive, snoozing 9 heavy-eyed, lethargic, sacked out, soporific 10 half-asleep, slumbering, slumberous
Somnus
father: 3 Nyx
...so much __ by so many to so few: 4 owed
so much in music: 5 tanto
son: 2 he 3 boy, kid, lad 4 cion, male 5 child, scion 6 junior, laddie 7 dauphin, kinsman 8 relative, young man 10 descendant
in Gaelic: 3 Mac
Jr.'s ~ perhaps: 3 III
starter: 3 god 4 step 5 grand
son __ gun: 3 of a
son-__: 5 in-law
__ son: 6 foster, native
__ Son: 6 Native 7 Seventh
sonant: 6 spoken
sonar
kin: 5 radar
pulse: 4 ping
signal: 4 echo
use ~: 6 locate
sonata: 4 opus, solo 5 music, piece
ender: 4 coda
movement: 4 trio 5 rondo
Sonata: 3 car 4 auto 7 Hyundai
__ Sonata: 6 Autumn, Spring
Sondergaard: Gale: 7 actress
Sondheim, Stephen: 8 composer
collaborator: Leonard Bernstein, Richard Rodgers, Jule Styne
musical: Company
Do I Hear a Waltz?
Follies
A Funny Thing Happened on the Way to the Forum
Gypsy
Into the Woods
A Little Night Music
Pacific Overtures
Passion
Sunday in the Park With George
Sweeney Todd
West Side Story
Sondra: 5 Locke

song: 3 air 4 aria, glee, hymn, lied, noel, oldy, pean, poem, tune 5 carol, chant, ditty, lyric, music, oldie, opera, paean, piece, psalm, verse, vocal 6 anthem, ballad, chanty, chorus, melody, number, shanty, strain 7 ballade, chanson, chantey, chorale, lullaby, refrain, shantey 8 birdcall, canticle 9 barcarole 10 plainchant
classic ~: 4 oldy 5 oldie
combining form: 4 melo-
eighteenth-century ~: 4 glee
ender: 4 bird, fest 5 smith 6 writer
German art ~: 4 lied
in music: 5 canto
name meaning ~: 6 Carmen
starter: 4 even, folk, sing 5 plain 6 cradle
syncopated ~: 3 rag
song __: 5 cycle
__ song: 3 art 4 folk, for a, part, swan, work 5 siren, theme, torch 7 popular
__-song: 4 part, sing
Song: 4 Aree
author: Edgar Allan Poe
Song __, The: 5 Is You
__ Song: 4 Goat, Last, Love, Lute, No-no, Your 5 Sing a 6 Annie's, Cradle, Danny's
__ Song, A: 6 Summer
song-and-dance
show: 5 revue 6 review
__ Song Before I Go: 5 Just a
songbird: 3 jay, tit 4 chat, lark, wren 5 finch, junco, mavis, pipit, robin, serin, vireo 6 bulbul, canary, linnet, oriole, parula, phoebe, singer, thrush, tityra, tomtit 7 babbler, bunting, cotinga, creeper, skylark, sparrow, swallow, tanager, wagtail, waxwing 8 bellbird, blackcap, bobolink, cardinal, nuthatch, redstart, thrasher, titmouse, whinchat, white-eye, woodlark 9 bullfinch, chaffinch, chickadee, crossbill, currawong, frogmouth, goldfinch, pardalote 10 chiffchaff, flycatcher, honeyeater
Songbird (1987 song)
artist: Kenny G
songbook, church: 6 hymnal
Song Flung up to Heaven, A
author: Maya Angelou
Song for Mama, A (1997 song)
artist: Boyz II Men
songful: 5 lyric 6 in tune 7 lilting, lyrical, musical
__ Song Go...: 5 I Let a
__ Song in My Heart: 5 With a
Song Is __, The: 3 You 5 Ended
Song Is Ended, The
composer: Irving Berlin
Song Is You, The
composer: Jerome Kern
songlike: 5 lyric 6 arioso, poetic 7 lyrical 8 poetical
Song of __: 7 Solomon
Song of Bernadette, The: 4 film 5 novel
author: Franz Werfel
cast: Jennifer Jones
Song of Hiawatha, The: 4 poem
author: Henry Wadsworth Longfellow
tribe: 6 Ojibwa 7 Ojibway 8 Chippewa
Song of India (1949 film)
cast: Sabu
Song of Los, The
author: William Blake
Song of Myself: 4 poem
author: Walt Whitman
Song of Old Hawaii, A accompaniment: 3 uke 7 ukulele
Song of Roland, The: 4 epic, poem 6 French
character: 4 Aude, Emir, Ives, Ivor 5 Ogier, Othon 6 Anseis, Oliver
Song of Rosemary
author: Ira Levin
__ song of sixpence...: 5 Sing a
Song of Solomon follower: 6 Isaiah
Song of the Chattahoochee, The
author: Sidney Lanier
Song of the Golden Calf: 4 aria
Song of the Lark, The
author: Willa Cather
Song of the Open Road: 4 poem
author: Walt Whitman
Song of the South (1946 film)
cast: James Baskett, Bobby Driscoll, Ruth Warrick
role: 5 Remus
song: Zip-a-Dee-Doo-Dah
title: 4 Br'er
__ Songs: 3 Sad 4 Love
Songs and Sonnets
author: John Donne
Songs for a Summer Day
author: Archibald MacLeish
__ Songs for Me: 5 No Sad
songsmith: 8 composer, lyricist
Songs of the Sierras
author: Joaquin Miller
__ Songs, The: 3 Old 5 Dream
Song Sung Blue (1972 song)
artist: Neil Diamond
Songs Without Words
composer: Felix Mendelssohn
__ Song Trilogy: 5 Torch
songwriter: 8 composer, lyricist
org.: 3 BMI 5 ASCAP
Sonia: 5 Braga 9 Sotomayor
sonic
rebound: 4 echo
starter: 5 ultra
sonic __: 4 boom
sonic boom source: 3 SST
Sonics: 4 five, team
home: 7 Seattle
org.: 3 NBA
Sonic the Hedgehog maker: 4 Sega
Sonja: 5 Henie
Sonnenfeld, Barry: 8 director
film: The Addams Family (1991)
Addams Family Values (1993)
Big Trouble (2002)
Get Shorty (1995)
Men in Black (1997)
Wild Wild West (1999)
sonnet: 4 poem, rime 5 rhyme, verse
cousin: 3 ode
like a ~: 5 lyric
measure: 4 iamb
stanza: 5 octet 6 sestet 7 octette
__ sonnet: 7 English, Italian
sonneteer: 4 bard, poet 9 rhymester
Sonnets From the Portuguese
author: Elizabeth Barrett Browning
Sonnets to __: 5 Delia
Sonnets to Orpheus, The
author: Rainer Maria Rilke
Sonnet-To Science
author: Edgar Allan Poe
sonny: 3 boy, kid 4 male
Sonny: 4 Bono 5 James, Tufts 6 Liston 7 Rollins 8 Corleone 9 Jurgensen
Sonny __: 3 Boy
Sonny and Cher: 3 duo 4 team
song: All I Ever Need Is You (1971)
Baby Don't Go (1965)
The Beat Goes On (1967)
A Cowboys Work Is Never Done (1972)
I Got You Babe (1965)
Laugh at Me (1965)
Sonny Boy (1928 song)
artist: Al Jolson
son of __: 4 a gun
Son of __ Baba: 3 Ali
Sonofagun!: 4 darn, rats 6 darn it, phooey
Son-of-a Preacher Man (1968 song)
artist: Dusty Springfield
Son of Flubber (1963 film)
cast: Tommy Kirk, Fred MacMurray, Keenan Wynn
Son of Frankenstein (1939 film)
cast: Boris Karloff, Bela Lugosi, Basil Rathbone
role: 4 Ygor
son of in Arabic: 3 ibn
Son of Paleface (1952 film)
cast: Bob Hope, Roy Rogers, Jane Russell
Son of Rosemary
author: Ira Levin
Son of the Circus, A
author: John Irving
Son of the Sheik (1926 film)
cast: Vilma Banky, Rudolph Valentino
Son of the Sun: 4 Inca
Sonoma: 4 city, town
firm: 5 Gallo
locale: 10 California
neighbor: 4 Napa
Sonora: 4 city, town 5 state
city: 7 Nogales
Indian: 4 Seri
locale: 6 Mexico 10 California
Sonoran: 6 desert
sonority: 4 tone
sonorous: 4 deep, full, loud, rich 5 forte, noisy, sweet 6 dulcet, in tune 7 blaring, booming, jarring, lyrical, melodic, orotund, pealing, pompous, rackety, raucous, reboant, roaring, stilted, tuneful, vibrant 8 crashing, piercing, plangent, resonant, rumbling, strident, turned up 9 big-voiced, clamorous, deafening, deep-toned, melodious 10 boisterous, euphonious, harmonious, resounding, rhetorical, stentorian, strepitous, thundering, thunderous, uproarious, vociferous
sons: 5 issue 7 kinfolk, progeny 8 kinfolks, kinsfolk
Sons
author: Pearl S. Buck
Sons __ Pioneers: 5 of the
__ Sons: 5 All My
Sons and Lovers: 5 novel
author: D.H. Lawrence
role: 5 Clara, Dawes, Edgar, Morel 6 Agatha
Sons of __: 7 Liberty
Sons of Katie Elder, The (1965 film): 5 oater 7 western
cast: Martha Hyer, Dean Martin, John Wayne
Sons of the Desert (1933 film)
cast: Oliver Hardy, Stan Laurel
Sontag, Susan: 6 writer 8 essayist
work: The Benefactor
Death Kit
I, Etcetera
Illness as Metaphor
Sony: 2 TV 3 VCR 5 TV set 10 television
acquisition: 5 Loew's
alternative: *see* electronics company
founder: Masuru Ibuka, Akio Morita
Soo: 4 Jack
Soo __: 5 Locks 6 Canals
sooey: 7 hog call
__ so often: 5 every
soon: 4 anon, nigh, then 5 after 6 any day, in a bit, in a sec, in time, pronto 7 betimes, by and by, erelong, fleetly, hastily, in a wink, later on, quickly, rapidly, shortly, someday 8 directly, hereupon, in a jiffy, in a while, promptly, sometime, speedily 9 afterward, any day now, any minute, any second, forthwith, hereafter, in a minute, in a moment, in a second, in due time, instantly, posthaste, presently, right away 10 any time now, before long, eventually, in good time
as ~ as: 4 once
just as ~: 6 gladly, rather 7 instead 10 preferably
sooner than ~: 6 at once
(to): 5 about
too ~: 5 early 9 premature
Soon
composer: George Gershwin, Ira Gershwin
sooner: 6 prefer, rather 7 earlier 10 beforehand, preferably
or later: 3 yet 4 anon 5 after 6 at last, in a bit, in time 7 by and by, finally, later on, someday 8 in a while, in the end, sometime 9 afterward, hereafter 10 before long, eventually, inevitably
than expected: 5 early 9 in advance, premature
Sooner: 9 Oklahoman
sooner or __: 5 later
soot: 4 dirt, soil 5 grime 9 lampblack
collector: 4 flue
particle: 4 smut
soothe: 3 pat 4 balm, calm, ease, help, hush, lick, love, lull 5 allay, cheer, quell, quiet, salve, still 6 becalm, defuse, defuze, gentle, make up, pacify, remedy, settle, soften, solace, stroke, subdue, temper 7 appease, assuage, compose, console, cool off, mollify, placate, relieve, sweeten 8 butter up, calm down, mitigate, palliate, play up to, unburden 9 alleviate, pour oil on, untrouble 10 conciliate, make nice to, smooth over
sooth ender: 3 say 5 sayer
soother: 4 balm 6 balsam, lotion 7 anodyne 9 analgesic

baby ~: **4** talc
muscle ~: **6** hot tub
skin ~: **4** aloe **5** salve
sprain ~: **6** ice bag **7** ice pack
stomach ~: **5** Bromo **6** bicarb
throat ~: **6** hot tea
soothing: **4** calm, mild, soft **5** balmy, bland, sweet **6** dreamy, dulcet, smooth **7** anodyne **8** lenitive, tranquil **9** demulcent, emollient, soporific
plant: **4** aloe
word: **5** there
soothsay: **7** predict **8** foretell, prophesy
soothsayer: **4** seer **5** augur, sibyl **6** oracle, wizard **7** aruspex, diviner, prophet, psychic **8** haruspex **9** predictor **10** forecaster
observance: **4** omen
of a ~: **5** vatic **7** vatical
sooty: **4** dark **5** black, dirty, grimy, smoky **6** filthy, fouled, grubby, grungy, soiled **7** dirtied, smeared, smudged, stained, tainted, unclean **8** befouled, begrimed, maculate, polluted, slovenly, smirched **9** besmeared, blackened, tarnished **10** besmirched, fuliginous, unsanitary
relative: **3** jet **4** inky, onyx **5** ebony, raven, sable
sooty ___: **4** tern
sooty mold: **6** fungus
sop: **3** wet **4** blot, dunk **5** bribe, souse, steep **6** absorb, drench, grease, payola, soak up, splash **7** moisten **8** pacifier, saturate **10** concession
starter: **4** milk, sour **5** sweet
up: **6** absorb, draw in, gather, ingest, osmose, retain, take in **7** drink in, swallow **10** assimilate
soph
see sophomore
sopher: **6** scribe **7** copyist, scholar, teacher
Sophia: **5** Loren
in Russian: **5** Sonia
sophic: **4** wise
Sophie: **6** Tucker **7** Germain, Marceau
___-Sophie Mutter: **4** Anne
Sophie's Choice: **4** film **5** novel
author: William Styron
cast: Kevin Kline, Meryl Streep
sophism: **6** dupery **7** fallacy, quibble **9** deception **10** invalidity
sophist: **8** logician, reasoner
sophistic: **6** faulty, flawed **7** invalid, unsound **8** specious **9** illogical **10** fallacious, irrational
sophisticated: **3** hep, hip **4** chic, cool, into, nice, wise **5** blasé, couth, sharp, slick, smart, suave **6** jet-set, mature, modern, smooth, subtle, uptown, urbane, with it **7** complex, elegant, genteel, knowing, refined, studied, wised up, worldly **8** advanced, citified, cultured, delicate, involved, polished, schooled, seasoned, tolerant, well-bred **9** elaborate, high-toned, in the know, intricate, practiced, skeptical **10** cultivated
gathering: **5** salon
miss: **3** deb
quality: **5** class, style
Sophisticated ___: **4** Lady
sophistication: **4** tact **5** class, poise, style **6** wisdom **7** culture, finesse, manners **8** elegance, judgment, maturity **9** composure
lacking ~: **4** naif **5** naive
showy ~: **5** glitz
sophistry: **7** fallacy **9** casuistry, chicanery
Sophocles: **5** Greek **10** playwright
forte: **5** drama
work: Ajax
Antigone
Electra
Oedipus at Colonus
Oedipus Rex
sophomore: **4** year **5** pupil **7** student **9** collegian, undergrad
future ~: **5** frosh
past ~: **6** junior
team: **6** jayvee
sophomoric: **4** naif **5** brash, naive, young **6** callow **7** asinine, foolish, puerile **8** immature, reckless, youthful **9** half-baked
sopor: **8** lethargy
soporific: **4** dopy, dozy, dull **5** balmy, dopey **6** drowsy, opiate, sleepy, snoozy **7** calming, nodding, numbing, tedious **8** hypnotic, sedative, soothing **9** deadening, somnolent **10** anesthetic, dullsville, enervating, monotonous
soppiness: **5** slush
sopping: **3** wet **4** damp **5** soggy, undry **7** wettish
soppy: **3** wet **5** mushy, soggy **6** soaked, sodden **7** maudlin, mawkish **8** drenched, romantic **9** saturated **10** bedraggled
soprano: **4** Alda, Bori, high, Lind, Pons, Popp **5** Calvé, Eames, Freni, Horne, Melba, Mills, Moffo, Moore, Patti, Price, Raisa, range, Sills, voice **6** Battle, Berger, Callas, Farrar, Garden, Kanawa, Norman, Peters, singer, Steber, Upshaw **7** Crespin, Farrell, Fleming, Lehmann, Nilsson, Tebaldi, Traubel **8** Albanese, Flagstad, Ponselle, vocalist **10** Galli-Curci, Sutherland, Tetrazzini
Australian ~: **5** Melba **10** Sutherland
Austrian ~: **4** Popp
between ~ and tenor: **4** alto
British ~: **6** Garden
Catfish Row ~: **4** Bess
certain ~: **5** mezzo
French ~: **4** Pons **5** Calvé **7** Crespin
German ~: **6** Berger **7** Lehmann
Italian ~: **5** Freni, Patti **7** Tebaldi **8** Albanese **10** Galli-Curci, Tetrazzini
New Zealand ~: **4** Alda
Norwegian ~: **8** Flagstad
note: **5** high C
Polish ~: **5** Raisa
Spanish ~: **4** Bori
specialty: **5** trill
Swedish ~: **4** Lind **7** Nilsson
soprano ___: **3** sax **4** clef
___-soprano: **5** mezzo
Sopranos, The (HBO drama)
cast: Lorraine Bracco (Dr. Jennifer Melfi)
Edie Falco (Carmela Soprano)
James Gandolfini (Tony Soprano)
Nancy Marchand (Livia Soprano)
chef: **5** Artie
matriarch: **5** Livia
___ sop to Cerberus: **5** give a
Sopwith ___: **5** Camel
Sor ___ Cruz: **5** Juana
sora: **4** bird, rail
milieu: **5** marsh
So Rare (1957 song)
artist: Jimmy Dorsey
sorbet: **3** ice **7** dessert
sorbic ___: **4** acid
Sorbo: **5** Kevin
Sorbonne site: **5** Paris **6** France
sorcerer: **4** mage **5** magus, witch **6** wizard **7** charmer, diviner, prophet, warlock **8** conjurer, conjuror, magician **9** enchanter
African ~ of fiction: **3** She
assistant: **7** famulus
of Greek myth: **5** Medea
Sorcerer's Apprentice, The
composer: Paul Dukas
Sorcerer, The
composer: W.S. Gilbert, Arthur Sullivan
sorcery: **3** hex, obi **4** jinx **5** magic, obeah, spell, vodun **6** voodoo **7** alchemy, devilry, evil eye **8** black art, deviltry, witchery, witching, wizardry **10** black magic, divination, hocus-pocus, mumbo-jumbo, necromancy, witchcraft
Sordello
author: Robert Browning
sordid: **3** bad, low **4** base, foul, mean, poor, slum, ugly, vile **5** cheap, dirty, dowdy, grimy, mangy, nasty, seamy, seedy, sorry, venal **6** abject, filthy, grubby, impure, mangey, scurvy, shabby, sleazy, vulgar **7** bestial, corrupt, ignoble, low-down, selfish, squalid, unclean, vicious **8** covetous, degraded, shameful, slovenly, wretched **9** corrupted, low-minded, mercenary, miserable, repellant, repellent **10** avaricious, degenerate, despicable, ungenerous
sordidness: **6** misery **7** squalor
sordino: **4** mute
___ sordino: **3** con
sore: **3** hot, mad, raw **4** achy, hurt, ired, lame **5** acute, angry, blain, cross, huffy, irate, irked, livid, riled, sharp, stung, upset, vexed, wroth **6** aching, bitter, chafed, fuming, in a pet, injury, ireful, lesion, miffed, pained, peeved, piqued, raging, raving, red-hot, severe, tender **7** annoyed, blister, bruised, burning, enraged, furious, grieved, hurting, in a snit, irksome, painful, ranting, steamed, teed off **8** abrasion, annoying, burned up, choleric, grieving, incensed, inflamed, maddened, offended, outraged, pressing, reddened, smarting, swelling, troubled, wrathful **9** afflicted, affronted, aggrieved, indignant, irritated, resentful, seeing red, sensitive, splenetic, ticked off **10** freaked out, hopping mad, infuriated, unpleasant
be a ~ loser: **4** mope, sulk
ender: **4** head
feel ~: **4** ache, hurt **6** resent
make ~: **3** ire, irk **4** rile **5** anger, peeve, upset **6** injure
point: **5** nerve **8** weakness
spot: **4** ache **8** irritant
starter: **3** eye **4** foot
sore ___: **5** loser, point **6** throat
___ sore: **6** saddle
sorehead: **5** grump **6** grouch
Sorel: **7** Georges
sorely: **5** badly **9** seriously
soreness: **4** ache, hurt, kink, pain **10** discomfort
Sorenstam, Annika: **6** golfer **7** Swedish
Sorento: **3** Kia, SUV
sorghum: **5** grain **6** fodder
grain ~: **4** milo **5** doura, durra, kafir **6** dourah, hegari
product: **5** sirup, syrup
structure: **4** silo
Sorkin: **5** Aaron **6** Arleen
sorority: **4** club **5** order **7** coterie, society
gathering: **5** mixer
letter: **2** mu, nu, pi, xi **3** chi, eta, phi, psi, rho, tau **4** beta, iota, zeta **5** alpha, delta, gamma, kappa, omega, sigma, theta **6** lambda **7** epsilon, omicron, upsilon
member: **4** coed **6** sister
opposite: **4** frat **10** fraternity
seek a ~: **4** rush
sorority ___: **5** house
sorrel: **4** roan, tree **5** brown, color, horse **6** equine **7** reddish
family: **5** heath
relative: *see* brown color
soup: **5** schav
wood ~: **3** oca, oka **6** oxalis
Sorrell: **5** Booke
sorrow: **3** woe **4** ache, moan, pain, pity, sigh **5** agony, blues, dolor, gloom, grief, groan, mourn, tears, trial, worry **6** bemoan, bewail, grieve, lament, misery, regret **7** agonize, anguish, bad news, carry on, deplore, despair, emotion, grieved, remorse, sadness, trouble, weeping **8** distress, grieving, hardship, languish, mourning, the blues **9** dejection, heartache, lamenting, penitence, suffering **10** affliction, depression, desolation, heartbreak, heavy heart, infelicity, melancholy, misfortune, repentance, woefulness
exclamation: **4** alas **5** alack **8** lackaday, welladay, wellaway
express ~: **3** sob **4** weep **5** mourn **6** grieve
express ~ for: **4** pity **6** bemoan, bewail
in music: **6** dolore
sign of ~: **4** tear
with ~: **5** sadly
sorrowful: **6** gloomy, in pain, tragic **7** elegiac, hurting, painful, piteous, tearful **8** dolorous, grieving, grievous, mournful, poignant, tragical **9** affecting, afflicted, plaintive, regretful, sniveling **10** lamentable
in a ~ way: **5** sadly
one: **4** ruer

sound: 4 moan, sigh 5 groan
words: 4 ah me
see also gloomy
sorrowfully
in music: 8 doloroso
sorry: 3 bad, sad 4 base, dire, grim, oops, poor, ugly, vile 5 bleak, needy, small, woful 6 abject, dismal, gloomy, paltry, rotten, scummy, shabby, shamed, shoddy, sordid, tragic, woeful 7 apology, ashamed, grieved, hapless, ill-done, joyless, pitiful, ruinous, scruffy, unhappy, unlucky 8 beggarly, contrite, dejected, downcast, excuse me, grievous, indigent, inferior, luckless, mea culpa, mournful, pathetic, penitent, saddened, shameful, sheepish, touching, tragical, trifling, unusable, wretched 9 chastened, depressed, destitute, miserable, plaintive, regretful, repentant, worthless 10 apologetic, deplorable, depressing, despicable, despisable, despondent, detestable, distressed, inadequate, melancholy, pathetical, remorseful, shamefaced
be ~: 3 rue 6 regret, repent
Sorry!: 4 oops 8 excuse me
__ Sorry Now: 4 Who's
Sorry Seems to Be the Hardest Word (1976 song)
artist: Elton John
sort: 3 ilk, lot, peg, set, tab 4 body, comb, cull, file, form, kind, make, mold, pick, race, rank, sift, type 5 array, batch, brand, breed, class, genre, genus, grade, group, index, order, stamp, style, suite 6 assort, choose, clutch, divide, family, kidney, manner, nature, number, parcel, person, screen, select, size up, stripe, winnow 7 arrange, bracket, catalog, collate, fashion, quality, species, variety 8 category, classify, graduate, organize, separate, specimen, typecast 9 catalogue, character, deficient 10 categorize, distribute, pigeonhole
sort __: 3 out
__ sort: 3 of a
sorta: 4 a bit 5 kinda 6 in a way, kind of, rather 8 somewhat, yes and no 10 more or less, not exactly
sortie: 4 raid 5 foray, sally 6 attack, battle, charge 7 assault, mission 9 irruption, offensive, onslaught
sort of
suffix: 3 -ish
sorts
be out of ~: 3 ail 4 pout, sulk
out of: *see* gloomy 3 ill 4 curt, mean, mopy, sick, sour 5 angry, balky, cross, fed up, fussy, gruff, huffy, mopey, nasty, riled, sharp, short, testy, tired, upset, vexed, whiny 6 ailing, bitter, bummed, cranky, crusty, droopy, feisty, fretty, gloomy, grumpy, ornery, peaked, peeved, piqued, poorly, put out, snarly, snippy, stewed, touchy, unwell 7 annoyed, bearish, bilious, carping, crabbed, fretful, griping, grouchy, huffish, let down, nettled, not well, peevish, pensive, pouting, prickly, subdued, uncivil, waspish, whining, worried 8 below par, brooding, cast down, caviling, choleric, churlish, contrary, critical, fretsome, growling, grumpish, incensed, offended, perverse, petulant, provoked, snappish, snarling 9 aggrieved, crotchety, disgusted, dyspeptic, fractious, grumbling, impatient, in the pits, irascible, irritable, long-faced, querulous, resentful, splenetic, truculent 10 censorious, displeased, ill-humored, ill-natured, indisposed, in the dumps, ungracious, unpleasant
Sorvino: 4 Mira, Paul
SOS: 4 help 6 signal 7 soap pad, warning
motorist's ~: 5 flare
receiver: 4 USCG
response: 3 aid
rival: 6 Brillo
SOS (1975 song)
artist: ABBA
So Sad (1960 song)
artist: Everly Brothers
Sosa, Sammy
sport: 8 baseball
__ So Shy: 3 He's
so-so: 2 OK 3 avg. 4 blah, fair, okay 5 ho-hum 6 medium, modest, not bad, rather 7 average 8 adequate, lukewarm, mediocre, middling, moderate, not great, ordinary, passable, passably 9 not too bad, tolerable, tolerably, unnotable 10 acceptable, adequately, fairly good, mezza-mezza, moderately, pedestrian, pretty good
sostenuto: 5 pedal
__ So Stories: 4 Just
So's your old man: 6 retort
sot: 4 lush, wino 5 souse, toper 6 barfly, bibber 7 guzzler, tippler, tosspot 9 inebriate
Sot-__ Factor, The: 4 Weed
So that's it!: 3 aha, oho 4 I see
Sotheby's: 10 auctioneer
patron: 6 bidder
signal at ~: 3 nod
So there!: 3 hah, see
Sothern, Ann: 7 actress
TV: My Mother the Car, Private Secretary
Sothis: 6 Sirius 7 Dog Star
so to __: 5 speak
Soto __: 3 Zen
__ so to bed: 3 and
Sotomayor: 5 Sonia
Soto, Talisa: 7 actress
spouse: Benjamin Bratt
sotto voce: 6 softly 7 quietly 9 whispered
remark: 5 aside
Sot-Weed Factor, The
author: John Barth
sou: 4 coin 5 money 8 pittance
without a ~: 4 poor 5 needy
soubise: 5 sauce
ingredient: 5 onion
soubrette: 4 maid
souchong: 3 tea 8 beverage
__ souci: 4 sans
Soudan to Fuzzy-Wuzzy: 3 'ome
Souez: 3 Ina
soufflé, like a: 4 airy, eggy 5 light
sought-after: 3 hot 7 popular
souk: 4 mart 5 bazar 6 bazaar, market
shopper: 4 Arab
soul: 3 ego 4 body, life, mind, root, self 5 anima, ardor, being, bosom, cause, force, ghost, heart, human, music, sense, stuff, umbra 6 bottom, energy, fantom, fervor, genius, marrow, mortal, person, pneuma, psyche, reason, shadow, spirit 7 courage, essence, feeling, phantom, rapport, thought 8 creature, interior, nobility, vitality, vivacity 9 animation, character, élan vital, intellect, life force, personage, principle, substance 10 conscience, human being, individual
heart and ~: 4 pith 6 wholly 8 entirely 10 completely, thoroughly
in French: 3 âme
in Hinduism: 4 atma 5 atman
in Spanish: 4 alma
living ~: 5 being, human 6 mortal, person 10 human being, individual
mate: 3 bud, pal 4 body 5 buddy 6 friend 8 alter ego
not a ~: 4 none 5 no one 6 nobody
soul __: 4 cake, food, mate 5 music 6 sister 7 brother
__ soul: 5 nary a
Soul: 5 David, Jimmy
Soul __: 3 Man 5 on Ice, Train
Soul and Inspiration (1966 song)
artist: Righteous Brothers
Soule: 4 Olan
soulful: 5 funky 6 moving 7 intense, lyrical 9 emotional 10 expressive
__ soul man: 3 I'm a
Soul Man (1967 song)
artist: Sam and Dave
__ Soul Music: 5 Sweet
__ Soul Picnic: 6 Stoned
__ Souls' Day: 3 All
Souls on Fire
author: Elie Wiesel
sound: 3 din, fit, hum, jar 4 bang, bark, blow, boom, buzz, clap, cool, deep, echo, emit, fair, firm, good, gulf, hale, just, look, moan, note, ping, play, ring, roar, safe, sane, seem, sing, slam, spry, thud, tone, toot, true, well, wise, word 5 audio, blare, burst, clack, clang, clank, clink, crash, creak, drone, exact, hardy, legal, legit, licit, loyal, lucid, music, noise, pitch, plumb, right, shout, smash, sober, solid, speak, tenor, thump, tight, total, valid, vital, voice, whine, whole 6 babble, cackle, cogent, entire, hearty, intact, jabber, jangle, kasher, kosher, melody, murmur, patter, proper, proven, racket, rattle, report, robust, rugged, rumble, secure, shriek, shrill, squawk, squeak, stable, static, strong, sturdy, tinkle, unhurt, up to it 7 channel, chatter, clatter, correct, durable, ethical, explode, harmony, healthy, learned, logical, measure, perfect, precise, prudent, ransack, reflect, ringing, solvent, telling, tenable, thunder, trumpet, upright, vibrant, vibrate, whisper 8 accepted, accurate, all there, analytic, coherent, complete, credible, detonate, faithful, flawless, language, laughter, luculent, methodic, orthodox, profound, rational, received, reliable, resonate, sensible, softness, thorough, together, tonality, unbroken, unflawed, unharmed, unmarked, vigorous, virtuous, well-made 9 advisable, canonical, competent, effective, effectual, faultless, holding up, honorable, in the pink, judicious, plausible, practical, pragmatic, realistic, recovered, reputable, resonance, undamaged, undecayed, uninjured, unscathed, untouched, up to snuff, vibration, well-built, wholesome 10 analytical, clattering, consequent, consistent, convincing, defensible, dependable, impeccable, intonation, legitimate, modulation, reasonable, recognized, sanctioned, satisfying, standing up, undeniable, unimpaired, unmistaken
bite: 4 clip
booster: 3 amp
combining form: 4 phon-, soni-, sono-
ender: 3 man, men 5 board, proof, stage, track
quality in music: 6 timbre
science of ~: 9 acoustics
stage: 3 set
unit: 3 bel 7 decibel
sound __: 3 off, out 4 bite, wave 5 stage, truck 6 effect 7 barrier
sound __ bell: 3 as a
sound __ dollar: 3 as a
__ sound: 5 white 6 Motown
__ Sound: 4 Hobe 5 Puget 6 Kalmar, Norton 7 McMurdo, Pamlico
Sound and the Fury, The
author: William Faulkner
sounded: 4 oral 9 vocalized
__ sounder: 5 depth
Sounder (1972 film)
cast: Kevin Hooks, Cicely Tyson, Paul Winfield
director: Martin Ritt
sounding __: 4 lead, line 5 board 6 rocket 7 balloon, machine
take a ~: 5 plumb
soundless: 3 mum 4 calm 5 quiet, still 6 hushed, silent 8 nonvocal 9 inaudible, noiseless
communication: 3 ASL
soundlessness: 5 quiet
soundly: 4 well
soundness: 4 wits 5 vigor 6 health, reason, sanity 8 strength, validity 9 integrity, stability 10 legitimacy
Sound of Music, The (1965 film)
cast: Julie Andrews, Christopher Plummer
character: 3 Max 4 Elsa, Kurt, Rolf 5 Georg, Gretl, Liesl, Maria, Marta, Trapp 6 Abbess, Berthe, Gruber, Louisa, Mother, Rainer, Sister, Sophia, Ursula 7 Schmidt 8 Brigitta, von Trapp 9 Detweiler, Friedrich, Schraeder 10 Margaretta
director: Robert Wise
extra: 3 nun
setting: 4 Alps 7 Austria
song: 5 Maria 6 Do-Re-Mi

Sound of Music, The (musical)
composer: Oscar Hammerstein, Richard Rodgers
Sound of Waves, The
author: Yukio Mishima
soundproof: 6 deaden
soundproofing unit: 5 sabin
sounds
harmonious ~: 5 music
making ~: 5 vocal
Sounds of Silence, The (1965 song)
artist: Simon and Garfunkel
sound system
component: 5 phono **6** stereo **9** turntable
soundtrack
component: 5 vocal
prepare a ~: 3 dub, mix
soup: 3 fog, mix **4** bisk, miso, mist **5** broth, dashi, fumet, gumbo, nitro, purée, ramen, schav **6** bisque, borsch, course, menudo, oxtail, potage, tomato, turtle, won ton **7** borscht, borshch, cholent, chowder, egg drop, mixture, pottage, she-crab **8** alphabet, bouillon, callaloo, consommé, gazpacho, julienne, mulligan, split pea **9** beef broth, bird's nest, madrilène, mazto ball, pepper pot, shark's fin, vegetable **10** avgolemono, hot and sour, minestrone, mock turtle
alphabet ~ letter: 6 noodle
base: 5 stock
beet ~: 6 borsch **7** borscht
chilled ~: 5 schav **8** gazpacho **9** madrilène
Chinese ~: 6 won ton **7** egg drop **9** bird's-nest **10** hot and sour
crabmeat ~: 8 callaloo
duck ~: 4 snap **5** cinch, cushy **6** picnic, simple **7** no sweat **8** easy task, painless, pushover, workable **9** uncomplex **10** child's play, effortless, elementary, unexacting
eat ~ loudly: 5 slurp
ender: 5 spoon
flavoring: 4 miso
follower: 6 entrée
herb: 4 dill
holder: 3 can, cup **4** bowl **6** tureen
Indian: 3 dal
ingredient: 3 pea **4** bean, beet, corn, leek, lima, ocra, okra, okro **5** onion **6** barley, lentil
in the ~: 9 desperate **10** despairing
Italian ~: 10 minestrone
Japanese ~: 4 miso **5** dashi, ramen **6** larmen
okra ~: 5 gumbo
pea ~: 3 fog
safecracker ~: 5 nitro
sorrel ~: 5 schav
Spanish ~: 6 menudo
staple: 4 bone
sushi-bar ~: 4 miso
thick ~: 5 purée **6** bisque
thin ~: 5 broth
to nuts: 4 A to Z **6** all-out **7** in-depth **8** complete, from A to Z, sweeping, thorough **9** extensive **10** exhaustive, meticulous
up: 9 reinforce
utensil: 5 ladle, spoon
warmer: 6 hot pot
soup __: 4 bowl **5** plate, spoon **6** du jour **7** kitchen
__ soup: 3 pea **4** duck **5** in the
__ Soup: 4 Duck
soup-and-fish: 5 tails
soupçon: 3 dab, nip **4** dash, hint **5** pinch, taste, tinge, touch, trace, whiff **6** breath, little, morsel, nibble, tidbit, trifle **7** minimum, whisper **8** spoonful
soup du __: 4 jour
souped-up
auto: 5 racer **6** hot rod
sound: 5 vroom **6** varoom
__-souper: 3 pea
__ soup fog: 3 pea
soup-to-__: 4 nuts
soupy: 4 thin **5** misty, runny **6** watery
Soupy: 5 Sales
__ soup yet?: 4 Is it
sour: 3 bad, off **4** acid, dour, keen, mean, rank, tart, turn **5** acerb, acrid, musty, sharp, spoil, tarty, taste, testy **6** acetic, acidic, biting, bitter, crabby, curdle, lemony, morose, off-key, on edge, rancid, rotten, snappy, sullen, turned, unripe **7** acerbic, acetose, acetous, acidify, caustic, curdled, cutting, cynical, envenom, gone bad, grouchy, off-tune, peevish, peppery, piquant, pungent, unhappy, waspish **8** alienate, churlish, embitter, grudging, imbitter, inedible, liverish, snappish, stinging, unsavory, vinegary **9** acidulate, acidulous, clabbered, fermented, irascible, irritable, jaundiced, querulous **10** astringent, bad-tasting, disenchant, embittered, exacerbate, ill-natured, unfriendly, ungenerous, unpleasant
compound: 4 acid
ender: 3 sop **4** ball, puss, wood **5** dough
expression: 5 scowl, sneer
go ~: 4 ruin, turn **5** addle, spoil, taint **6** curdle, mildew **7** acidify
grapes: 6 excuse, reason **9** rationale
hit a ~ note: 5 clash **6** jangle, rattle
make ~: 8 acerbate
note: 5 clash **6** jangle, off-key **7** discord **9** cacophony **10** disharmony
sour __: 3 gum **4** mash, note **5** cream **6** cherry, grapes
__ sour: 6 whisky **7** whiskey
sourball: 4 crab **5** candy, crank, grump **6** grouch **8** grumbler **10** curmudgeon
source: 4 font, fund, germ, head, mine, rise, root, seed, text, well **5** basis, birth, cause, onset, start **6** author, expert, father, matrix, mother, origin, parent, quarry, rising, spring, supply **7** dawning, opening **8** begetter, fountain, gold mine **9** authority, beginning, etymology, inception, informant, paternity, reference, reservoir **10** antecedent, authorship, birthplace, connection, derivation, originator, provenance, specialist, wellspring
idea ~: 4 seed **5** spark **6** kernel
source __: 4 book, code
__-source: 4 sole
Sources of Strength
author: Jimmy Carter
Source, The
author: James A. Michener
sour cream: 3 dip **5** dairy
companion: 5 blini, bliny
partner: 5 chive
serving: 6 dollop
sourdine: 4 mute
sourdough: 5 bread, miner
be a ~: 8 prospect
gear: 3 pan
mix: 5 dough
quest: 3 ore **4** gold **5** claim
soured: 6 rancid
sour grapes coiner: 4 Esop **5** Aesop
sourness: 6 flavor **7** acidity **8** acerbity
sourpuss: 4 crab, mope **5** crank, grump **6** grouch, kvetch, somber **7** killjoy **9** gloomy Gus, pessimist, worrywart
like a ~: 4 dour **5** surly
look: 5 scowl, sneer
sour-tasting: 4 tart **5** acerb
sous-__: 4 chef
Sousa, John Philip: 8 composer **10** bandleader
work: The Beau Ideal
The Bride Elect
El Capitan
The Fairest of the Fair
The Free Lance
The Gallant Seventh
The Gladiator
Globe and Eagle
The Glory of the Yankee Navy
Golden Jubilee
Hands Across the Sea
The High School Cadets
The Invincible Eagle
Jack Tar
King Cotton
The Liberty Bell
Manhattan Beach
Marching Along
The Rifle Regiment
Sabre and Spurs
Semper Fidelis
The Stars and Stripes Forever
The Thunderer
The Washington Post
sousaphone: 4 horn, tuba, wind **5** brass
__ Sousatzka: 6 Madame
souse: 3 dip, sop, sot, wet **4** dunk, lush, soak, wino **5** brine, douse, dowse, drown, steep, toper, water **6** deluge, drench, embrue, imbrue, pickle, seethe **7** dunking, guzzler, immerse, tippler **8** marinate, preserve, saturate, submerge, submerse, waterlog **9** inebriate **10** impregnate, intoxicate
south: 5 point **9** direction
combining form: 5 austr- **6** austro-
ender: 3 ern, paw **4** east, land, ward **5** bound, wards **6** lander, wester **7** eastern, western **8** eastward, westerly, westward
go ~: 4 bolt, flee, quit **5** split **6** beat it, decamp, defect, escape **7** abscond, make off, pull out, skip out, vamoose **9** cut and run, disappear, skedaddle, steal away **10** fly the coop, hightail it, make a break
in Spanish: 3 sur
of: 5 below
South: 3 Joe **5** Dixie
South __: 4 Bend, Park, Pole, Seas, Side **5** Korea, Yemen **7** America, Pacific, Vietnam
South __ Islands: 3 Sea **6** Orkney
South __ Ocean: 7 Pacific
South __ Sea: 5 China
South __ Zone: 6 Frigid
South-__ Africa: 4 West
__ South: 3 Old **4** Deep, Goin' **5** Solid
South Africa: 6 nation **7** country
bishop: 4 Tutu
bovine: 4 Tuli **8** Bonsmara
capital: 8 Cape Town, Pretoria
city: 6 Benoni, Durban, Soweto **8** Cape Town, Pretoria
encampment: 5 lager **6** laager
golfer: 3 Els **5** Price **6** Player **8** Ernie Els **9** Nick Price **10** Gary Player
grazing area: 4 veld **5** veldt
hill: 3 kop **5** kopje **6** koppie
iris: 4 ixia
language: 4 Taal, Xosa, Zulu **5** Sotho, Swazi, Xhosa **7** Ndebele **9** Afrikaans
lowland: 4 vlei
money: 4 cent, rand
national park: 6 Kruger
neighbor: 7 Lesotho, Namibia **8** Botswana, Zimbabwe **9** Swaziland **10** Mozambique
Nobelist in Chemistry: 4 Klug
Nobelist in Literature: 8 Gordimer
Nobelist in Peace: 4 Tutu **5** Klerk **6** Lutuli **7** Mandela
people: 4 Xosa **5** Sotho, Swazi, Xhosa **6** Basuto, Tswana **7** Ndebele **8** Khoekhoe, Khoikhoi, Matabele
plateau: 6 Karroo
poet: 6 Brutus, Plomer
port: 6 Durban **8** Cape Town
province: 5 Natal
ravine: 5 kloof
region: 5 Natal **6** Ciskei
river: 4 Vaal **6** Orange
sheep: 6 dorper
shrub: 6 narras
territory: 5 Venda
village: 4 stad **5** craal, kraal
waterfall: 6 Tugela
weasel: 8 muishond
wind: 4 berg
writer: 4 Head **5** Paton **6** Cloete, Fugard, Plomer **7** Coetzee **8** Abrahams, Gordimer, Jacobson **9** Schreiner **10** Van der Post
South African Dutch: 4 Taal
South America: 9 continent
airline: 5 Varig
bird: 4 guan, rhea **5** potoo **6** condor, quezal **7** finfoot, hoatzin, quetzal, tinamou **8** caracara, curassow, guacharo, hoactzin, ovenbird, screamer, troupial
bovine: 4 nata
brandy: 5 pisco
camel: 5 llama **6** alpaca, vicuña **7** guanaco
cape: 4 Horn

capital: 4 Lima 5 La Paz, Quito, Sucre 6 Bogotá 7 Caracas, Cayenne 8 Asunción, Brasilia, Santiago 10 Montevideo, Paramaribo 11 Buenos Aires
cowboy: 6 charro, gaucho 7 llanero, vaquero
current: 6 El Niño
dance: 5 tango
deer: 4 pudu 6 guemal, huemul 7 brocket
desert: 7 Atacama, Sechura 10 Patagonian
explorer: 5 Cabot 8 Vespucci
farm: 5 finca
feline: 4 puma 6 cougar, margay, ocelot 7 panther
fish: 6 aimara 7 piranha, scalare 8 bloodfin, characin
gulf: 9 Guayaquil
Indian: 4 Inca, Moxo, Tama 5 Carib 6 Arawak, Aymara, Galibi, Jivaro, Kechua, Lengua, Yahgan 7 Chibcha, Guarani, Kechuan, Quechua, Quichua 8 Caingang, Quechuan 9 Tehuelche 10 Araucanian
island: 6 Chiloe
language: 4 Tupi 7 Spanish
mat: 4 yapa
monkey: 3 sai 4 titi 6 howler
mountain: 4 Solo, Toro 5 Cachi, Chani, Cusco, Cuzco, Galan, Laudo, Negro, Pular, Quela 6 Ampato, Bonete, Juncal, Pissis, Sajama 7 Huandoy, Illampu, Palermo, San Juan 8 Ancohuma, Coropuna, El Condor, El Muerto, Famatina, Illimani, Polleras, Solimana, Tortolas, Yerupaja 9 Aconcagua, Antofalla, Condoriri, Huascarán, Incahuasi, Marmolejo, Pumasillo, Salcantay, Tupungato 10 Chimborazo, Mercedario, Nacimiento, Parinacota, Tres Cruces
mountains: 5 Andes
nation: 4 Peru 5 Chile 6 Brazil, Guyana 7 Bolivia, Ecuador, Uruguay 8 Colombia, Paraguay, Suriname 9 Argentina, Venezuela
opossum: 5 yapok
parrot: 5 macaw 6 Amazon
plain: 5 pampa
port: 3 Rio
prairie: 5 pampa
primate: 4 saki, titi 6 uakari 7 tamarin 8 capuchin, marmoset
region: 6 Guiana
reptile: 5 aboma
river: 3 Apa 4 Arno, Beni, Napo 5 Apure, Cauca, Japur, Juruá, Negro, Paran, Purús, Santa, Xingú 6 Amazon, Bio-Bio, Cuiabá, Javari, Javary, Mamoré 7 Berbice, Bermejo, Guaporé, Iguassú, Madeira, Mantaro, Marañón, Orinoco, Tapajós, Ucayali 8 Araguaya, Demerara, Paraguay, Parnaiba, Putumayo 9 Magdalena, Roosevelt
rodent: 4 cavy, mara, paca 5 coypu 6 agouti 7 rice rat, visacha 8 capibara, capybara, spiny rat, tuco-tuco 9 guinea pig 10 chinchilla
shrub: 6 feijoa 7 guarana, rhatany 9 jaborandi
skirt: 7 pollera
strongman: 4 jefe
tanager: 4 yeni 5 lindo
tree: 4 ombu 6 carapa, rubber 7 wallaba 8 andiroba, crabwood, piassava
unit of length: 4 vara
volcano: 4 Ruiz 6 Láscar, Puracé, Sangay 7 El Misti, Galeras 8 Cotopaxi
weasel: 5 tayra
wind: 5 zonda

___ South America: 6 Inside
South American: 6 Andean, Latina, Latino
South Atlantic: 5 ocean 7 current
island: 8 St. Helena 9 Ascension
South Australia capital: 8 Adelaide
___ South Bay: 5 Great
South Bend: 4 city, town
locale: 7 Indiana
sch.: 3 NDU
south by ___: 4 east, west
South Carolina: 5 state
capital: 8 Columbia
city: 5 Aiken 6 Easley, Sumter 7 Taylors 8 Anderson, Columbia, Florence, Rock Hill 9 Greenwood, St. Andrews 10 Charleston, Goose Creek, Greenville
conference: 3 SEC
island: 6 Parris
neighbor: 7 Georgia
port: 10 Charleston
school: 7 Citadel, Clemson
state amphibian: 10 salamander
state beverage: 4 milk
state bird: 4 wren
state dance: 4 shag
state flower: 9 jessamine
state fruit: 5 peach
state game bird: 10 wild turkey
state gemstone: 8 amethyst
state hospitality beverage: 3 tea
state insect: 6 mantid
state stone: 7 granite
state tree: 8 palmetto
word in ~ motto: 5 spero
South China Sea
bay: 6 Brunei
city on the ~: 6 Danang
gulf: 4 Siam 6 Tonkin 8 Thailand
inlet: 5 Subic
island: 6 Hainan, Taiwan 7 Formosa 8 Hong Kong 9 Singapore
locale: 5 China 6 Taiwan 7 Vietnam
old ~ kingdom: 4 Anam 5 Annam
river to the ~: 6 Mekong 7 Xi Jiang
South Dakota: 5 state
capital: 6 Pierre
city: 4 Lead 5 Huron, Onida 6 Custer, Pierre 8 Aberdeen, Deadwood 9 Rapid City, Watertown 10 Sioux Falls
county: 5 Lyman
Indian: 10 Miniconjou
mountain: 6 Harney
national park: 8 Badlands, Wind Cave
neighbor: 3 Neb., Wyo. 4 Iowa, Minn., Mont., Nebr. 7 Montana, Wyoming 8 Nebraska 9 Minnesota

Southeast Asian: 3 Lao, Tai 4 Thai
Buddhism: 9 Theravada
fruit: 6 durian 8 rambutan 9 carambola
gulf: 4 Siam 6 Tonkin 8 Thailand
language: 3 Tai, Yao 4 Miao 5 Malay
nation: 4 Laos 5 Burma 7 Myanmar, Vietnam 8 Malaysia, Thailand
people: 5 Hmong
wild ox: 4 gaur
southeaster: 4 wind
Southeastern Conference
school: 3 LSU 4 Miss. 6 Auburn 7 Alabama, Florida, Georgia 8 Arkansas, Kentucky 9 Tennessee 10 Vanderbilt
southerly: 4 wind
southern ___: 6 lights
Southern: 5 Terry
Southern ___: 3 Cal 4 Alps 5 belle, Cross
Southern Alps: 3 mts. 4 mtns. 5 range 9 mountains
locale: 10 New Zealand
Southern California
see USC
Southern Comfort: 5 drink 8 beverage
Southern Mail
author: Antoine de Saint-Exupéry
Southern Methodist University
see SMU
Southern Nights (1977 song)
artist: Glen Campbell
Southey, Robert: 4 poet 7 British
group: Lake Poets
work: The Battle of Blenheim
Southfield: 4 city, town
locale: 8 Michigan
South Florida
athletes: 5 Bulls
locale: 5 Tampa
Southfork: 5 ranch
matriarch: 5 Ellie
South Frigid ___: 4 Zone
South, Joe
song: Games People Play (1969) Walk a Mile in My Shoes (1970)
South Jordan: 4 city, town
locale: 4 Utah
South Korea: 6 nation 7 country
capital: 5 Seoul
city: 4 Tegu 5 Ansan, Cheju, Seoul, Ulsan 6 Chonju, Inchon 7 Kwangju
legislature: 6 Kukhoe
money: 3 won 4 chon, jeon
Nobelist in Peace: 10 Kim Dae Jung
port: 5 Pusan
sea: 9 East China
south-of-the-border
see Mexico
South Orange: 4 city, town
athletes: 7 Pirates
locale: 9 New Jersey
school: 9 Seton Hall
South Pacific
cairn: 3 ahu
capital: 4 Apia, Suva 5 Agana 6 Majuro, Manila, Nouméa, Tarawa 7 Honiara, Papeete 8 Funafuti, Pago Pago, Port-Vila 9 Nuku'alofa
cloth: 4 tapa
explorer: 4 Cook 5 Davys 6 Tasman 7 Dampier, Johnson 9 Heyerdahl, Vancouver
feature: 4 isle 5 atoll
garment: 5 pareo, pareu
island: 3 Aru 4 Aroe, Arru, Bali, Cook, Fiji, Niue, Reao, Savo 5 atoll, Samar, Samoa, Tonga, Upolu 6 Easter 7 Oceania, Society, Vanuatu 9 Australia, Marquesas, New Guinea
islander: 6 kanaka
nation: 4 Fiji 5 Tonga
port: 4 Apia
shrub: 8 snowbush
spot: 6 lagoon
staple: 4 taro
South Pacific (1958 film): 7 musical
cast: Rossano Brazzi, Mitzi Gaynor, Ray Walston
character: 4 Liat 5 Abner, Cable, Emile, Ngana 6 Billis, Jerome, Joseph, Luther, Nellie 7 Forbush, Stewpot 8 de Becque 10 Bloody Mary
director: Joshua Logan
South Pacific (musical)
composer: Oscar Hammerstein, Richard Rodgers
South Pacific ___: 5 Ocean 7 Current
South Park
cat: 5 Kitty
character: 4 chef
dog: 6 Sparky
puppet: 5 Mr. Hat
southpaw: 5 lefty 6 leftie 7 pitcher 9 portsider
South Platte: 5 river
city on the: 6 Denver
locale: 8 Colorado, Nebraska
South Pole
bird: 6 Adélie 7 penguin
explorer: 5 Scott 8 Amundsen
South Street (1963 song)
artist: Orlons
South Temperate ___: 4 Zone
South Vietnam
former ~ rebel org.: 3 NLF
___ South Wales: 3 New
Southwest: 7 airline
alternative: *see* airline, U.S.
Southwest Conference team: 3 SMU
southwester: 4 wind
Southwestern
barbecue: 5 asado
copse: 4 mott 5 motte
dwelling: 5 adobe
lizard: 3 uta
painter: 7 O'Keeffe
plant: 5 yucca
predator: 4 puma
school: 4 UTEP
sight: 4 mesa 6 cactus, desert
state: 5 Texas 6 Nevada 7 Arizona 9 New Mexico
tree: 5 alamo, piñon
souvenir: 4 gift 5 curio, relic, token 7 memento, vestige 8 keepsake, landmark, reminder
souvenir ___: 5 sheet
souvlaki ingredient: 4 lamb
sou'wester: 3 hat 4 coat, wind 6 jacket 8 raincoat
___ So Vain: 5 You're

sovereign: **4** best, coin, czar, king, quid, tops, tsar, tzar **5** chief, crown, lofty, money, queen, regal, royal, ruler **6** gerent, leader, master, prince, ruling, top dog, utmost **7** emperor, empress, guiding, highest, majesty, monarch, regnant, supreme, viceroy **8** absolute, autocrat, dominant, imperial, majestic, powerful, princess, reigning **9** ascendant, directing, effective, excellent, monarchal, paramount, potentate, prevalent, principal, unlimited **10** autonomous, commanding, majestical
sovereignty: **4** rule, sway **5** power, reign, state **6** empire, nation **7** command, liberty, primacy **8** dominion, kingship **9** ascendant, dominance, supremacy
emblem of ~: **3** orb
Soviet: **3** Red
cosmonaut: **7** Gagarin
farm: **5** artel
first lady: **5** Raisa
first ~ premier: **5** Lenin
plane: **3** MiG
political division: **3** SSR
press arm: **4** Tass
secret org.: **3** KGB **4** OGPU
spacecraft: **3** Mir **4** Luna **5** Lunik, Soyuz **7** Sputnik
workers' group: **5** artel
see also Russia, USSR
Soviet __: **5** Union **6** Russia
__ Soviet: **7** Supreme
__-Soviet: **4** Sino
sow: **3** hog, pig, she **4** grow, seed, till, toss **5** fling, plant, raise, strew, swine **6** animal, female, spread **7** bestrew, implant, scatter **9** broadcast, propagate **10** promulgate
chow: **4** slop **5** swill
dissension: **6** divide
ender: **5** belly, bread
fit to ~: **6** arable
home: **3** pen, sty **6** pigpen, pigsty
mate: **4** boar
offspring: **4** gilt **6** farrow
opposite: **4** reap
syllable: **4** oink
the seeds of: **6** arouse
time to ~: **6** spring
wild oats: **3** err, sin **5** act up, cut up, stray **7** carry on, go wrong **8** go astray **9** misbehave **10** fool around
__ so weiter: **3** und
sower: **6** farmer, seeder **7** planter, strewer
So what __ is new?: **4** else
sown: **4** semé **6** seeded **9** broadcast, dispersed, implanted, scattered, spread out **10** propagated
sow one's __ oats: **4** wild
so written: **3** sic
...sow's __: **3** ear
__ sow, so shall...: **4** As ye
Sox
see Red Sox, White Sox
__ Soxx: **4** Bob B.
soy: **6** legume, veggie **9** vegetable
ender: **4** bean, milk
sauce fungus: **4** koji
soy __: **3** oil **4** milk **5** flour, sauce
soybean: **6** legume, veggie **9** vegetable
product: **3** oil **4** miso, tofu
Soyinka, Wole: **4** poet **6** writer **8** essayist, Nigerian, Nobelist **10** playwright
Soylent __: **5** Green
Soyuz launcher: **4** USSR
Sp.
see Spanish
SP: Shore Patrol
employer: **3** USN
quarry: **4** AWOL
spa: **3** Ems, gym **4** bath, Enna, well **5** Baden, Epsom, Evian, Ischl, Troon, Vichy **6** Bad Ems, hot tub, resort, spring **7** Jacuzzi **9** hot spring, Marienbad, whirlpool, Wiesbaden **10** Baden-Baden, health club, Hot Springs, Lake Placid
British ~: **4** Bath
feature: **5** sauna
French ~: **5** Evian
German ~: **3** Ems **5** Baden **6** Bad Ems
Hungarian ~: **4** Eger
Sicilian: **4** Enna
__ spa: **3** day **6** health
space: **3** bit, gap, way **4** area, hole, play, room, slot, span, spot, term, time, turf, void, zone **5** arena, blank, field, lapse, range, reach, scope, spell, tract, while **6** extent, hiatus, lacuna, leeway, length, margin, period, radius, recess, schism, season, sphere, spread, vacuum, volume **7** breadth, expanse, headway, opening, stretch, vacancy, vacuity **8** aperture, capacity, distance, duration, headroom, infinity, interval, latitude, location, omission **9** elbowroom, expansion, interlude, largeness, territory **10** interstice, separation
breathing ~: **4** lull, pore **5** pause **8** vacation
chimp: **4** Enos
empty ~: **6** vacuum **7** vacancy
ender: **4** port, ship, sick, ward **5** borne, craft, farer **6** bridge
first American woman in ~: **4** Ride
free ~: **4** play, room **6** leeway **8** headroom **9** clearance, elbowroom
join up in ~: **4** dock, link
like outer ~: **4** vast
open ~: **5** glade **8** clearing, headroom **9** clearance, elbowroom
org.: **4** NASA
out: **6** forget **8** daydream **10** woolgather
outer ~: **3** sky **6** vacuum
program: **6** Apollo, Gemini **7** Mercury
starter: **3** air, sun **4** aero, back, head, work **5** crawl
telescope: **6** Hubble
to a poet: **5** ether **6** aether
two-dimensional ~: **4** area
visitor from ~: **2** ET **5** alien, comet
space __: **3** bar **5** cadet, opera, probe **6** flight, heater, travel **7** capsule, science, shuttle, station
space-__: **6** saving
space-__ continuum: **4** time
__ space: **3** air **4** deep, free, open **5** crawl, outer, white **7** parking
Space
author: James A. Michener
Space __: **3** Age **4** Camp, Race **7** Cowboys
__-Space: **4** Outa
Spaceballs (1987 film)
cast: Mel Brooks, John Candy, Rick Moranis, Bill Pullman
character: **5** Vespa
director: Mel Brooks
Space Cowboys (2000 film)
cast: Clint Eastwood, James Garner, Tommy Lee Jones, Donald Sutherland
director: Clint Eastwood
spacecraft: **4** ship **5** probe
alien ~: **3** UFO
compartment: **3** pod
frame: **6** gantry
spaced-out: **6** in a fog, sparse **8** confused, mindless **10** disjointed
spaceflight
combining form: **4** astr- **5** astro-
Space Flight Center
locale: **7** Alabama, Florida
Space Invaders producer: **5** Atari
Spacek, Sissy: **7** actress
film: Affliction (1998)
Blast From the Past (1999)
Carrie (1976)
Coal Miner's Daughter (1980, AA)
Crimes of the Heart (1986)
The Grass Harp (1996)
In the Bedroom (2001)
JFK (1991)
The Long Walk Home (1990)
Marie (1985)
Missing (1982)
Raggedy Man (1981)
The Straight Story (1999)
role: **4** Lynn **7** Loretta
Space Merchants, The
author: Frederik Pohl
Space Race (1973 song)
artist: Billy Preston
space shuttle
assent: **3** A-OK
org.: **4** NASA
space station: **6** Skylab
org.: **4** NASA
Russian ~: **3** Mir **6** Salyut
supply: **3** air
__ Space Telescope: **6** Hubble
Space, the __ frontier: **5** final
spacewalk: **3** EVA
spacey: **3** odd **5** dazed **7** unaware **8** confused **9** slaphappy
Spacey, Kevin: **5** actor
film: American Beauty (1999, AA)
Beyond the Sea (2004)
The Big Kahuna (2000)
Glengarry Glen Ross (1992)
L.A. Confidential (1997)
Midnight in the Garden of Good and Evil (1997)
The Negotiator (1998)
Outbreak (1995)
Pay It Forward (2000)
Se7en (1995)
The Shipping News (2001)
Superman Returns (2006)
A Time to Kill (1996)
The Usual Suspects (1995, AA)
film (voice): a bug's life (1998)
S. Pacific
see South Pacific
spacious: **3** big **4** airy, huge, open, vast, wide **5** ample, broad, great, large, roomy **7** immense, sizable **8** enormous, far-flung, generous, infinite, sizeable, sweeping **9** boundless, capacious, cavernous, expansive, extensive, limitless, uncrowded **10** commodious, voluminous, widespread
spaciousness: **4** room **6** extent, length **9** amplitude
spackle: **7** plaster
Spad: **5** plane **7** biplane **8** airplane
foe: **6** Fokker
spade: **4** tool **5** scoop
calling a ~ a spade: **6** candor **9** outspoken
ender: **4** fish, work
use a ~: **3** dig
Spade: **3** Sam **5** David
spadefoot: **4** toad
spadelike tool: **4** spud
Spader, James: **5** actor
film: sex, lies, and videotape (1989)
Stargate (1994)
White Palace (1990)
Wolf (1994)
TV: Boston Legal
spades: **4** suit
at times: **5** trump
in ~: **9** decidedly
Spade, Sam: **2** PI **3** tec **6** shamus, sleuth **7** gumshoe **9** detective
partner: **6** Archer
work: **4** case **5** caper
spadework: **4** prep **8** planning **11** preparation
spaghetti: **5** pasta **7** noodles
alternative: ***see*** pasta
drainer: **5** sieve
sauce: **4** Ragú **5** Prego **6** Prince **8** Classico **10** Newman's Own **11** Aunt Millie's
topping: **5** pesto, sauce **8** marinara
western director: **5** Leone
spaghetti __: **5** sauce, strap **6** squash **7** Western
Spahn, Warren: **5** Brave **6** hurler **7** pitcher
Spain: **6** España, nation **7** country
appetizers: **5** tapas
art gallery: **5** Prado
bay: **4** Vigo **6** Biscay
bovine: **7** Alberes, Cachena, Retinta
capital: **6** Madrid
castles in ~: **6** revery **7** reverie
cellist: **6** Casals
city: **4** Leon, Lugo, Reus, Vigo **5** Avila, Elche, Gijón, Palma, Palos **6** Bilbao, Madrid, Málaga, Murcia, Toledo **7** Alacant, Córdoba, Granada, Sevilla, Seville **8** Valencia, Zaragoza **9** Barcelona, Las Palmas
conductor: **6** Iturbi
dance: **4** jota **6** bolero **7** alegras, bourrée **8** chaconne, fandango **9** malaguena, paso doble, zapateado **10** seguidilla
explorer: **6** Balboa, Cortés **7** Pizarro **8** Coronado **11** Ponce de León
golfer: **6** García **11** Ballesteros

guitarist: **5** Charo **7** Segovia
gulf: **5** Cádiz
gypsy: **6** gitano
hero: **5** El Cid
invader of ~: **4** Moor
island: **6** Canary
jacket: **7** zamarra
kettledrum: **6** atabal
king: **3** rey **9** Ferdinand **10** Juan Carlos
language: **6** Basque **9** Castilian
legislature: **6** Cortes
linear measure: **4** vara
locale: **6** Europe, Iberia
maize grinding stone: **4** mano
money: **3** bit **4** duro, real **5** dobla **6** doblon, escudo, peseta **7** centimo, pistole **8** doubloon **9** pistareen
mountain: **5** Aneto, Teide **6** Estats, Posets **8** Pyrenees
neighbor: **6** France **7** Andorra, Morocco **8** Portugal **9** Gibraltar
Nobelist in Literature: **4** Cela **7** Jiménez **9** Benavente, Echegaray **10** Aleixandre
Nobelist in Medicine: **11** Ramón y Cajal
org.: **4** NATO
painter: **4** Dali, Goya, Gris, Miró, Sert **7** El Greco, Picasso, Pisarro **9** Velázquez
philosopher: **6** Marías **7** Unamuno
pianist: **6** Iturbi **8** Larrocha
playwright: **4** Vega **6** Encina, Mihura, Sastre **7** Alberti **8** Calderón **9** Benavente
poet: **4** Mena, Ruiz, Vega **6** Berceo, Boscán, Encina **7** Alberti, Bousoño, Góngora, Guillén, Herrera, Jiménez, Salinas **8** Manrique **11** Altoaquirre
port: **4** Adra, Vigo **5** Cadiz **6** Bilbao **8** Alicante, La Coruña **9** Algeciras, Barcelona, Cartagena
princess: **5** Elena
queen: **3** Ena **5** reina, Sofia **8** Isabella
railway: **5** Renfe
region: **4** Jaén, León, Lugo **5** Alava, Avila, Cádiz, Ceuta, Soria **6** Aragon, Burgos, Cuenca, Gerona, Huelva, Huesca, Lérida, Málaga, Murcia, Orense, Teruel, Toledo, Zamora **7** Almería, Badajoz, Cáceres, Córdoba, Galicia, Granada, La Rioja, Melilla, Navarre, Segovia, Sevilla, Vizcaya **8** Albacete, Alicante, Asturias, Baleares, Castilla, La Mancha, Palencia, Valencia, Zaragoza **9** Andalusia, Barcelona, Cantabria, Castellón, Catalonia, Las Palmas, Salamanca, Tarragona **10** Pontevedra
river: **4** Ebro **5** Douro, Tinto
saint: **6** Teresa **7** Dominic, Isidore, Vincent **8** Ignatius
sculptor: **7** Picasso, Pisarro
sheep: **6** merino
stately ~ dance: **8** saraband **9** sarabande
stewpot: **4** olla
surrealist: **4** Dali, Miró
tenor: **7** Domingo **8** Carreras
weight unit: **6** arroba
wine: **4** Cava **5** rioja, tinto **6** Malaga **8** Albariño, Montilla
with, in ~: **3** con
writer: **3** Aub **4** Cela **5** Benet **6** Alemán, Chacel, Marías, Matute **7** Alarcón, Arrabal **8** Marquina **9** Cervantes, Gironella **11** Pérez Galdós **12** Blasco Ibañez, Martínez Ruiz **13** Ortega y Gasset **14** Martínez Sierra
see also Spanish
__ Spake Zarathustra: **4** Thus
Spalding: **2** Al **4** Gray **6** Albert
competitor: **3** AMF **4** Voit **6** Wilson **8** Rawlings **9** Brunswick
spalpeen: **5** rogue, scamp **6** bad guy **8** scalawag **9** scallawag, scallywag **10** scapegrace
spam: **5** e-mail
like ~: **8** unwanted
Spam: **4** meat
eater: **2** GI
ingredient: **3** ham
maker: **6** Hormel
span: **3** age **4** arch, ford, hand, life, link, pair, team, term, time **5** cover, cross, range, reach, scope, space, spell, sweep, vault, width **6** amount, bridge, extent, length, period, radius, spread **7** breadth, connect, measure, stretch, twosome, viaduct **8** bestride, comprise, distance, duration, go across, interval, latitude, pass over, straddle, traverse **9** cross over, encompass, extension, longevity **10** generation, transverse, wingspread
life ~: **4** time **8** lifetime
of existence: **4** days, life **5** years **6** course, period
spic and ~: **5** clean
starter: **4** wing
__ span: **4** life
Span.
see Spanish
spanakopita: **5** Greek **6** pastry
cheese: **4** feta
ingredient: **7** spinach
Spandau __: **6** Ballet
Spandau, last prisoner at: **4** Hess
spandex: **6** fabric **8** material
brand: **5** Lycra
spang: **5** right **7** exactly **8** directly, squarely **9** precisely
spangle: **4** trim **5** fleck **6** bauble, sequin **7** glitter, shimmer **10** decoration
__-Spangled Banner, The: **4** Star
__-Spangled Girl, The: **4** Star
__ Spangled Rhythm: **4** Star
spaniel: **3** dog **5** canid **6** canine, yes man
__ spaniel: **5** field, water **6** cocker
Spanish: **8** language
start of many ~ place names: **3** San **5** Santa, Santo
see also Spain
Spanish __: **4** Eyes, heel, iris, Main, moss, rice **5** onion, Steps **6** Armada, guitar, Harlem, omelet, Sahara **8** omelette
Spanish __ War: **5** Civil
Spanish Eyes (1965 song)
artist: Al Martino
Spanish Flea (1966 song)
artist: Herb Alpert and the Tijuana Brass
Spanish Guitar Player
artist: Édouard Manet
Spanish Harlem (song)
artist: Aretha Franklin, Ben E. King
Spanish Main: **9** Caribbean
cargo: **3** oro
chest: **4** arca
coin: **4** real
Spanish Prisoner, The (1998 film)
cast: Ben Gazzara, Steve Martin, Campbell Scott
director: David Mamet
Spanish Smile, The
author: Scott O'Dell
Spanish Steps
locale: **4** Rome
Spanish Tragedy, The
author: Thomas Kyd
__ Spanish Trail: **3** Old
Spanish words
adverb: **3** mas, que **4** nada
all: **4** todo
among: **5** entre
another: **4** otra, otro
are: **3** son **4** esta **5** están
article: **3** las, los, una, uno
aunt: **3** tía
be: **3** ser
bear: **3** oso
beast: **5** tigre
between: **5** entre
boss: **3** amo
bull: **4** toro
but: **3** mas
chamber: **4** sala
cheer: **3** olé **4** viva
child: **4** niña, niño
conjunction: **3** mas **4** pero
day: **5** lunes **6** jueves, martes, sábado **7** domingo, viernes **9** miércoles
definitely: **4** sí sí
diminutive suffix: **3** -ita, -ito
direction: **3** sur **4** este **5** norte, oeste
east: **4** este
eight: **4** ocho
everything: **4** toda, todo
exclamation: **5** salud **6** arriba
face: **4** cara
farewell: **5** adios
father: **5** padre
female: **4** ella
fingernail: **3** una
friend: **5** amiga, amigo
fruit: **4** pina
gentleman: **3** don **5** señór **6** Latino
gold: **3** oro
hall: **4** sala
Helen: **5** Elena
home: **4** casa
honorific: **4** dona
hour: **4** hora
I love you: **5** te amo
interrogative: **3** qué **4** cómo
is: **4** esta
January: **5** enero
kid: **4** niña, niño
king: **3** rey
kiss: **4** beso
lady: **3** sra. **4** dama, dona **6** Latina, señora **8** señorita
letter: **3** uve
love: **4** amor
marking: **5** tilde
meat: **5** carne
miss: **4** srta. **8** señorita
mister: **5** señor
month: **3** mes **4** mayo **5** abril, enero, julio, junio, marzo **6** agosto **7** febrero, octubre **9** diciembre, noviembre **10** septiembre
more: **3** más
Mr.: **5** señor
Mrs.: **3** sra. **6** señora
Ms.: **4** srta. **8** señorita
nickname: **4** mote
nil: **4** nada
number: **3** dos, uno **4** diez, octo, seis, tres **5** cinco, nueve, siete **6** quarto
one: **3** una, uno
other: **4** otra, otro
ourselves: **3** nos
parent: **5** madre, padre
plus: **3** más
potato: **4** papa
preposition: **3** por **5** entre
priest: **5** padre
pronoun: **4** ella, esta, este, todo **5** quien
queen: **5** reina
question: **3** qué
river: **3** río
room: **4** sala
route: **3** vía
saint: **5** santo
she: **4** ella
soul: **4** alma
south: **3** sur
sun: **3** sol
this: **4** esta, este
three: **4** tres
toast: **5** salud
to be: **3** ser
tot: **4** niña, niño
two: **3** dos
uncle: **3** tío
us: **3** nos
walk: **4** anda
water: **4** agua
wave: **3** ola
way: **3** vía
will be: **4** será
with: **3** con
year: **3** año
yes: **2** sí
spank: **3** box, hie, tan, zip **4** beat, belt, cane, cuff, dart, dash, flog, hide, hurt, lash, lick, race, slap, trim, welt, whip, whup, zoom **5** clout, scoot, smack, whack **6** buffet, hustle, larrup, paddle, punish, scurry, sprint, thrash, thwack, wallop **7** clobber **8** chastise **9** skedaddle **10** get a move on, make tracks, paddywhack
spanker: **4** mast, sail
relative: **3** jib
spanking: **3** new **4** fast, fine **5** swift **7** licking **10** punishment
spanking __: **3** new
Spanky: **9** McFarland
dog: **4** Pete **5** Petey
friend: **5** Darla, Porky **7** Alfalfa **9** Buckwheat
Spanky and Our Gang
song: Like to Get to Know You (1968)
Sunday Will Never Be the Same (1967)

spanner: **6** wrench
spanning: **6** across
Spano: **7** Vincent
spar: **3** box **4** beam, boom, gaff, mast, pole, tilt **5** fight, joust **6** bicker **7** dispute, mineral, quarrel, quibble, wrangle **8** bowsprit **9** shadowbox
heavy ~: **6** barite **7** barytes
long ~: **4** yard
nautical ~: **4** boom, gaff **5** sprit **8** bowsprit
SPAR counterpart: **3** WAC
spare: **3** odd **4** bare, bony, free, give, lank, lean, more, pity, poor, save, slim, thin, tire, wiry **5** allow, avoid, boney, extra, forgo, gaunt, grant, lanky, leave, let be, let go, mince, other, pinch, put by, scant, short, skimp, stick, stilt, stint **6** afford, backup, bestow, dainty, excuse, exempt, forego, frugal, gangly, give up, let off, meager, modest, option, pardon, relent, scanty, scrape, scrimp, shadow, skimpy, skinny, slight, slinky, sparse, stingy, supply, svelte, twiggy, unused **7** absolve, bail out, forbear, forgive, forsake, gracile, haggard, in store, provide, release, relieve, reserve, respect, scraggy, scrawny, slender, spidery, surplus, willowy **8** dispense, exiguous, gangling, go easy on, in excess, leftover, part with, rawboned, salt away, save from, unwanted **9** do without, emergency, in reserve, sylphlike **10** additional, economical, fifth wheel, relinquish, substitute, unoccupied
difficult ~: **5** split
from: **6** exempt
get a ~: **4** bowl
the expense of: **5** grant, offer **6** afford, bestow, impart, render **7** furnish, provide
tire: **4** flab **5** belly **6** paunch **7** stomach
tire locale: **5** trunk, waist
to ~: **5** ample **6** galore
unit: **3** pin
with room to ~: **4** vast, wide **5** broad **7** sizable **8** spacious **9** capacious, expansive **10** voluminous
with time to ~: **5** early
spare __: **3** rib **4** part, ribs, time, tire
Spare the ___: **3** rod
sparing: **3** lax **4** easy, kind, mild, soft, wary **5** chary, close, loose, scant, tight **6** decent, frugal, gentle, humane, kindly, saving, scanty, stingy, tender **7** careful, clement, lenient, prudent, ruthful, thrifty **8** flexible, gracious, laid-back, merciful, placable, taciturn, tolerant, ungiving **9** assuasive, compliant, easygoing, indulgent, provident **10** abstemious, altruistic, avaricious, benevolent, economical, forbearing, permissive, unexacting, unwasteful
be ~: **5** skimp, stint **9** economize
spark: **3** arc, jot, ray, vim, woo **4** beam, fire, germ, glow, hint, idea, kick, lead, life, love, prod, seed, spur, stir, zest, zing **5** court, flare, flash, gleam, glint, grain, light, liven, pique, punch, scrap, start, trace, verve, vigor **6** arouse, excite, foster, ignite, incite, kindle, propel, pursue, spirit, stir up **7** animate, enliven, flicker, glitter, inspire, minimum, nucleus, provoke, shimmer, trigger, vestige **8** activate, engender, enkindle, motivate, touch off, vitality, vivacity **9** animation, galvanize, impassion, inamorato, life force, originate, pretty boy, scintilla, stimulate **10** bring about, enthusiasm, exuberance, friskiness, jack-a-dandy, liveliness
plug: **6** dynamo **8** catalyst
producer: **5** flint
vital ~: **3** vim, zip **4** brio, dash, élan, fire, soul, zest, zing **5** being, gusto, heart, nerve, oomph, pluck, verve, vigor **6** animus, bounce, energy, esprit, psyche, spirit **7** essence, passion **8** vitality **9** animation, life force **10** enthusiasm, excitement, exuberance, get-up-and-go, liveliness
spark __: **4** plug
sparkle: **3** pep, vim, wit, zap, zip **4** beam, dash, fizz, glow, kick, life, show, wink **5** blink, dance, flash, gleam, glint, glitz, light, shine **6** bubble, dazzle, esprit, fizzle, gaiety, gayety, glance, luster, quiver, spirit **7** flicker, glimmer, glisten, glitter, panache, shimmer, twinkle **8** radiance, radiancy, vitality, vivacity **9** animation, coruscate, élan vital, freshness, irradiate **10** brilliance, effervesce, effulgence, incandesce, liveliness
sparkler: **3** gem, ice **4** ring **5** jewel, tiara **7** jewelry, trinket **8** firework
sparkling: **3** lit **4** racy **5** aglow, clean, fresh, peppy, shiny, witty **6** ablaze, agleam, bright, flashy, glinty, lively, washed **7** beaming, fulgent, lambent, piquant, radiant, vibrant **8** dazzling, luminous, lustrous, spirited, unsoiled **9** brilliant, exuberant, refulgent, vivacious
make ~: **6** aerate
sparkling __: **4** wine **5** water
Spark, Muriel: **4** poet **6** writer **8** Scottish
work: Memento Mori The Prime of Miss Jean Brodie
Sparks: **3** Ned **4** city, town **5** Jared **8** radioman
agreement: **5** roger
city west of ~: **4** Reno
locale: **6** Nevada
post: **5** radio
Sparky: **4** Lyle **8** Anderson
sparrow: **4** bird **5** finch
ender: **5** grass
sparse: **3** low **4** lean, poor, rare, thin **5** light, scant, short, spare **6** little, meager, scanty, scarce, skimpy, slight **7** scrimpy, sporadic **8** exiguous, far apart, sporadic **9** dispersed, scattered, uncrowded **10** inadequate, infrequent, occasional, sporadical
sparsity: **4** lack, need, want **6** dearth **7** absence, paucity, poverty **8** exiguity, scarcity, shortage **9** scantness **10** deficiency, inadequacy, meagerness
Sparta: **4** city, town **5** polis
ally: **4** Elis
locale: **6** Greece
magistrate: **5** ephor
rival: **5** Argos **6** Athens
river: **3** Iri
Spartacus: **4** film **5** novel, slave
author: Howard Fast
cast: Tony Curtis, Kirk Douglas, Nina Foch, John Gavin, Charles Laughton, Laurence Olivier, Jean Simmons, Peter Ustinov
director: Stanley Kubrick
setting: **4** Rome **5** arena
Spartan: **4** firm, font, hard **5** apple, bossy, cruel, Greek, harsh, picky, plain, rigid, rough, stark, stern, tough **6** barren, severe, simple, strict **7** ascetic, austere **8** despotic, exacting, hard-line, rigorous, typeface **9** bare-bones, demanding, draconian, primitive, stringent, unadorned, unbending, unsparing **10** despotical, inflexible, iron-fisted, no-nonsense, oppressive, tyrannical
relative: ***see*** apple
theater: **5** odeon
worker: **5** helot
Sparv: **7** Camilla
spasibo: **5** danke, merci **6** thanks **7** gracias **8** thank you
spasm: **3** fit, tic **4** ache, jerk, kink, pain, pang **5** burst, cramp, crick, spell, start, throe **6** frenzy, hiccup, quiver, twinge, twitch **8** hiccough, outburst, paroxysm **10** convulsion
spasmodic: **5** jerky, shaky **6** choppy, fitful, random, spotty, uneven **7** erratic, snatchy **8** far apart, on-and-off, periodic, sporadic, variable **9** irregular, momentary, twitching **10** changeable, convulsive, disjointed, hysterical, infrequent, sporadical, unfrequent
Spassky, Boris
forte: **5** chess
spat: **3** ado, row **4** flap, fuss, slap, tiff, to-do **5** argue, clash, scrap, set-to, smack **6** barney, dustup, gaiter, rumpus, strife **7** dispute, gambado, legging, mix it up, quarrel, quibble, wrangle **8** argument, brouhaha, catfight, disagree, skirmish, squabble **9** altercate, bickering, have words, imbroglio **10** difference, falling-out
public ~: **5** scene
spot: **5** ankle
suffix: **3** ula
spate: **3** fit, sea **4** flow, gush, rain, rash, rush, tide **5** burst, flood, river, spirt, spurt **6** deluge, stream **7** freshet, torrent **8** downpour, overflow **10** flash flood, inundation
of activity: **5** spasm
spatter: **3** dot, wet **4** daub, slop, slur, soil, spit, spot **5** dirty, douse, dowse, plash, smear, spray, stain, strew **6** mottle, shower, smudge, splash, squirt **7** asperse, dribble, scatter, speckle, stipple **8** disperse, sprinkle **9** broadcast, discharge **10** calumniate
spatterdash: **6** gaiter
__ S. Patton: **6** George
spatula, use a: **4** flip
spawn: **3** roe **4** make, seed, sire **5** beget, breed, brood, hatch, issue **6** create, father, parent **7** produce, progeny **8** engender, generate, multiply **9** offspring, originate, reproduce **10** bring forth, give rise to
spawner
salt-water ~: **3** eel
upstream ~: **4** shad **6** salmon
spay: **3** fix **5** alter **6** neuter
SPCA: Society for the Prevention of Cruelty to Animals
speak: **3** air, gab, gas, jaw, lip, rap, say, yak **4** bark, blab, chat, pipe, talk, tell **5** mouth, orate, pitch, plead, shout, sound, spiel, spout, state, stump, utter, voice **6** assert, confer, convey, intone, mumble, murmur, mutter, parley, pipe up, recite, remark, yammer **7** address, chatter, declaim, declare, deliver, dictate, express, lecture, testify, whisper **8** converse, modulate, ramble on, set forth, vocalize **9** discourse, enunciate, expatiate, get across, hold forth, make known, pronounce, sermonize, touch base, verbalize **10** articulate, chew the fat, make public, yakkety-yak
against: **6** oppose **7** gainsay
at length: **3** jaw, yak **4** rant **5** run on, spout **6** expand, preach, rattle **7** address, amplify, declaim, descant, enlarge, lecture, maunder **8** harangue, perorate, sound off **9** discourse, elaborate, expatiate, explicate, hold forth, sermonize, speechify **10** dissertate
doth ~: **5** saith
ender: **4** easy
excitedly: **6** burble, gibber
for: **4** laud **6** back up, defend, esteem, foster, praise, uphold **7** bespeak, commend, endorse, espouse, indorse, promote, support, sustain **8** advocate, champion **9** recommend, represent, vindicate **10** compliment
haltingly: **3** haw, hem **5** drawl **6** mumble **7** sputter, stumble
highly of: **4** hail, laud, tout **5** exalt, extol, honor **6** extoll, praise **7** acclaim, applaud, approve, commend, endorse, indorse **8** hand it to **9** recommend **10** compliment
highly of oneself: **4** brag, crow **5** boast
ill of: **3** pan **4** slur **5** abase, knock, smear **6** defame, deride, impugn, malign, smirch, vilify **7** asperse, put down, rip into, run down, slander **8** backbite, badmouth, belittle, besmirch, tear down, throw mud **9** criticize, denigrate, deprecate, disparage, fling dirt **10** calumniate, depreciate, villainize
imperfectly: **4** lisp, slur **7** stutter
in a monotone: **5** drone

irritably: **4** bark, snap
lovingly: **3** coo
of: **4** name **5** refer, touch **7** discuss, mention, refer to, touch on **9** touch upon
out: **4** avow, yell **6** assert, insist **7** declare **8** sound off **9** make plain **10** stand up for
publicly: **5** orate
right to ~: **5** floor
roughly: **4** rasp **5** croak
rudely: **4** sass
so to ~: **4** as if **8** as it were, in effect **10** implicitly
starter: **3** new **6** double
suddenly: **5** blurt
to: **7** contact **8** approach **10** get a hold of
up: **6** assert, insist **7** declare **8** sound off **9** make plain
wildly: **4** rage, rant, rave, roar, yell **5** storm
with forked tongue: **3** fib **4** dupe **5** bluff, fudge, guile **6** delude **7** deceive, falsify, mislead **8** misspeak **9** dissemble, misinform
with one's hands: **4** sign
without notes: **5** ad-lib
speak __: **3** for, out
speak __ to: **4** down
__ speak: **4** so to
speakeasy: **5** joint **6** saloon, tavern **7** barroom **9** nightclub
offering: **5** booze **10** bathtub gin
speaker: **5** sayer **6** lector, orator **8** lecturer
asset: **3** wit
ender: **4** ship **5** phone
like a cheap ~: **5** tinny
need: **4** mike **5** intro **10** microphone
part: **3** amp **6** woofer **7** tweeter
pause: **2** er, uh, um
request: **5** floor
spot: **4** dais **6** podium
starter: **4** loud
system: **4** hi-fi **6** stereo
__ speaker: **7** keynote
Speaker, Tris: **6** Indian **10** outfielder
speaking: **9** utterance **10** recitation
ability: **5** oracy
generally ~: **7** overall
manner of ~: **4** tone **5** idiom, usage
not ~ to: **5** mad at
plain ~: **5** prose
speaking __: **4** part, role
__ speaking: **6** public
__ Speaks: **4** Seth **5** Harpo
spear: **4** spit, stab **5** kebab, lance, spike, stick **6** empale, impale, pierce, skewer, weapon **7** assagai, assegai, harpoon, javelin, missile, trident **9** lancinate
carrier: **4** supe **5** extra
ender: **3** man, men **4** fish, head, mint, wort
fish ~: **3** gig **7** leister
god, name meaning: **5** Oscar
handle: **5** shaft
name meaning ~: **5** Barry
Roman ~: **5** pilum
rule, name meaning: **6** Gerald
strength, name meaning: **8** Gertrude
thrower: **6** atlatl
tip: **4** pike
spear __: **3** gun **7** carrier
spear-__: **7** carrier, thrower
spearhead: **4** lead, spur **7** go first, pioneer
spearmint: **4** herb
Spears: **7** Britney
spec: **6** detail **8** standard
special: **3** pet, set **4** best, gala, main, meal, rare, sale **5** chief, major **6** choice, festal, marked, proper, select, unique **7** certain, defined, express, festive, limited, primary, private, several, unalike, unusual **8** definite, isolated, peculiar, personal, singular, smashing, uncommon **9** different, earmarked, exclusive, important, memorable, momentous, recherché, red-letter **10** designated, individual, occasional, particular, privileged, restricted
ender: **3** ist
interest group: **3** org., soc. **4** assn., bloc **5** assoc., lobby **6** caucus
issue: **5** extra **6** annual
nothing ~: **5** plain, usual **7** average, routine, typical **8** ordinary, standard
Saturday night ~: **3** gun
something ~: **4** oner
treat as ~: **5** favor
special __: **5** agent **6** orders **7** effects, session
special __ of relativity: **6** theory
Special __: **3** Ops **6** Forces
Special Delivery
author: Danielle Steel
Special Forces
cap: **5** beret
unit: **5** A-Team
weapon: **3** Uzi
specialist: **3** ace, pro **4** guru, sage **5** adept, maven, mavin **6** doctor, expert, old pro, pundit, savant, source **7** devotee, old hand, scholar, veteran **8** virtuoso **9** authority, physician
suffix: **5** -arian, -ician
__ specialist: **7** mission, payload
Specialist, The (1994 film)
cast: Sylvester Stallone, Rod Steiger, Sharon Stone, James Woods
cat: **5** Timer
director: Luis Llosa
spécialité __ maison: **4** de la
specialized: **9** technical
special K: **5** dance
Special K: **6** cereal
competitor: *see* cereal
special laurel __ go, A: **4** ere I
__ Special Love Song: **5** A Very
specially: **8** uniquely **9** expressly
specialty: **3** bag, job **4** area, game, work **5** field, forte, hobby, major, niche, thing **6** career, domain, métier, number, racket **7** feature, pursuit **8** cup of tea, practice, vocation, weakness **9** commodity **10** department, discipline, magnum opus, occupation, profession
specie
see moolah
species: **3** lot **4** kind, race, sort, type **5** breed, class, group, likes, order, taxon **6** nature, number, strain **7** variety **8** category, division **10** collection
category above ~: **5** genus
division: **3** sex
Species (1995 film)
cast: Natasha Henstridge, Ben Kingsley, Michael Madsen, Forest Whitaker
specific: **3** set **4** item, such **5** exact, fixed **6** dead-on, detail, finite, proper, single, unique **7** certain, express, flat-out, limited, precise, right on, several **8** bull's-eye, clear-cut, concrete, definite, detailed, distinct, explicit, on target, outright, peculiar, positive, reserved **9** definable, different, downright, drawn fine **10** definitive, individual, occasional, particular, restricted
be ~: **4** name **6** define
__-specific: **4** site **6** gender
specifically: **5** to wit **6** as such, namely **7** clearly, exactly **8** in detail, minutely **9** expressly, pointedly, precisely, specially
specification: **4** code, term **6** clause, detail **7** proviso **8** standard **9** blueprint, condition, provision, requisite
specified: **3** set **5** given **9** necessary
those not ~: **6** others
specify: **3** fix, peg, set, tab, tag **4** cite, list, name, slot **5** label, limit, state **6** assign, define, detail, finger, lay out, set out, settle **7** itemize, mention, pin down, precise, provide, put down, refer to **8** describe, indicate, nominate, point out, spell out **9** blueprint, condition, designate, determine, elaborate, enumerate, establish, preordain, prescribe, stipulate **10** button down
specimen: **3** bit **4** case, copy, part, sort, type, unit **5** model, piece, proof **6** person, sample, swatch **7** example, exhibit, pattern, variety **8** exemplar, instance, landmark, sampling **10** embodiment, individual
specious: **4** vain **5** false, inane, silly, wacky, wrong **6** absurd, faulty, made-up, screwy, untrue, whacky **7** fatuous, in error, inexact, seeming, unsound **8** captious, cockeyed, delusive, spurious **9** beguiling, deceptive, erroneous, illogical, incorrect, plausible, senseless, sophistic, untenable **10** artificial, fallacious, flattering, groundless, inaccurate, misleading, ostensible, presumable, ungrounded
speck: **3** bit, dab, dot, jot, tad **4** atom, blot, drop, flaw, iota, lick, mark, mite, mote, snip, spot, whit **5** crumb, fault, fleck, grain, pinch, point, scrap, shred, stain, touch, trace **6** defect, little, tittle, trifle **7** blemish, freckle, glimmer, granule, lentigo, minimum, modicum, smidgen, smidgin, splotch **8** molecule, particle, pinpoint, smidgeon **9** scintilla
starter: **3** fly
speckle: **4** spot **5** fleck **7** spatter **8** sprinkle
specklebelly: **5** goose
speckled: **6** dotted, flaked, mosaic, motley, patchy, spotty **7** dappled, flecked, mottled, spotted, studded **8** brindled, freckled, peppered, stippled **9** sprinkled **10** variegated
specs: **6** frames **7** details, glasses **8** cheaters **10** directions, eyeglasses
see also spectacles
spectacle: **4** play, show, view **5** drama, event, movie, scene, sight **6** circus, comedy, marvel, parade, wonder **7** display, pageant, picture, scenery, tableau **8** splendor **9** cavalcade, curiosity **10** exhibition, exposition, phenomenon, production
combining form: **4** -cade **5** -orama
make a ~ of: **7** show off
spectacles: **6** frames **7** glasses, lorgnon **8** cheaters, horn-rims, wire-rims **9** lorgnette **10** eyeglasses
big name in ~: **4** Lomb **6** Bausch, Pearle
piece: **4** lens
support: **3** ear **4** nose
Spectacles, The
author: Edgar Allan Poe
spectacular: **4** epic **6** daring, marked, scenic **8** dramatic, meteoric, scenical, stunning, wondrous **9** thrilling, wonderful
see also wonderful
spectator: **3** fan **4** eyer, seer **5** gazer **6** looker, viewer **7** watcher, witness **8** beholder, looker-on, observer, onlooker, playgoer, showgoer **9** bystander, moviegoer, perceiver, stander-by **10** eyewitness
spectator __: **5** sport
spectators: **5** crowd **7** gallery **8** audience **9** listeners **10** attendance
Spectator, The
writer: Richard Steele
specter: **5** ghost, shade, spook **6** fantom, shadow, spirit, wraith **7** bugbear, phantom **8** presence, revenant **10** apparition
Specter: **5** Arlen
Spector: **4** Phil **6** Ronnie
Spectra: **3** car, Kia **4** auto **10** automobile
spectral: **4** eery **5** eerie **7** ghostly **9** ghostlike, imaginary, unearthly **10** immaterial
type: **5** N star, O star, S star
spectre
see specter
__ spectrograph: **4** mass
__ spectrometer: **4** mass
spectrophobe
fear: **6** ghosts
spectrum: **5** gamut, range, scale
band: **3** red **4** blue **5** green **6** indigo, orange, violet, yellow
displayer: **5** prism **7** rainbow
__-spectrum: **5** broad
Spectrum: **5** arena
locale: Philadelphia
speculate: **3** bet **4** dare, muse, risk **5** guess, infer, opine, think, wager, weigh **6** assume, call it, figure, gamble, hazard, ponder, reason, review, scheme, size up, wonder **7** presume, reflect, suppose,

surmise, suspect, venture, wildcat **8** chew over, cogitate, consider, give odds, make book, question, ruminate, theorize **9** figure out, pipe-dream, postulate **10** brainstorm, conjecture, deliberate, excogitate, experiment, generalize, have a hunch, kick around, take a fling
speculation: 3 bet **4** game, look, risk, shot, stab **5** guess, hunch, wager **6** belief, chance, gamble, hazard, plunge, reason, review, theory **7** backing, opinion, surmise, thought, venture **8** card game, gambling, studying, thinking **9** brainwork, guesswork
speculative: 4 iffy **5** risky **6** chancy **8** academic **9** tentative, uncertain, visionary
venture: 5 flier, flyer
speculator: 3 arb **6** risker **7** gambler **9** financier **10** adventurer
__ Spee: 4 Graf
speech: 4 talk, word **5** idiom, lingo, pitch, prose, spiel, stump, voice **6** accent, appeal, debate, dialog, eulogy, homily, jargon, medium, parley, sermon, tirade, tongue **7** address, bombast, dialect, diction, keynote, lecture, monolog, oration, oratory, pep talk, prattle, remarks, voicing **8** dialogue, diatribe, harangue, language, parlance, rhetoric **9** chalk talk, discourse, elocution, monologue, utterance **10** allocution, apostrophe, commentary, discussion, expressing, expression, filibuster, invocation, recitation, salutation, vernacular, vocalizing
colloquial ~: 5 slang **10** vernacular
combining form: 4 lalo-, -laly **5** -lalia **6** glosso-, glotto-
ender: 5 maker **6** writer
figure of ~: 5 image, trope **7** imagery, similar **8** metaphor
free ~: 7 liberty
hesitation: 2 er, uh, um
instructive ~: 6 sermon
like some ~: 5 nasal
long ~: 8 rhetoric
loss of ~: 6 alogia
of ~: 4 oral
of a ~ sound: 6 apical
part of ~: 4 noun, verb **6** adverb **7** pronoun **9** adjective **11** conjunction, preposition **12** interjection
pattern: 6 accent
raucous ~: 4 yaup, yawp
regional ~: 6 patois
slow ~: 5 drawl
sound: 4 lene
source: 6 larynx
specialized ~: 5 lingo
violent ~: 4 rant
__ speech: 4 free **5** stump **7** keynote
speechify: 5 orate **8** perorate
speechless: 3 mum **4** awed, cool, mute **5** blank, dazed, quiet **6** aghast, amazed, silent **7** aphonic, shocked **8** nonvocal, overcome, taciturn, wordless **9** astounded, clammed up, noiseless, voiceless **10** bewildered, tongue-tied, unspeaking
one: 4 mime **5** mimer
render ~: 3 awe, wow **4** stun **5** amaze, floor **7** astound, nonplus, stupefy **8** astonish **9** overwhelm
Speechless (1994 film)
cast: Bonnie Bedelia, Geena Davis, Michael Keaton, Christopher Reeve
speed: 3 aid, fly, hie, rip, run, zip **4** belt, bomb, clip, dart, dash, flit, gait, hare, help, lick, pace, pelt, race, rate, rush, sail, tear, whiz, zoom **5** boost, flash, haste, hurry, impel, scoot, shoot, steam, tempo, whisk **6** barrel, breeze, career, course, gallop, gear up, hasten, hurtle, hustle, move it, rocket, rustle, scurry, spring, step up, streak **7** advance, agility, floor it, forward, further, headway, hop to it, press on, promote, quicken, scamper, take off, tear off, urgency **8** alacrity, celerity, cut along, dispatch, expedite, fastness, go all out, hightail, make time, momentum, rapidity, step on it, velocity **9** briskness, eagerness, fast-track, fleetness, get moving, hotfoot it, make haste, quickness, rapidness, readiness, shake a leg, skedaddle, swiftness **10** burn rubber, double-time, expedition, facilitate, get a move on, hightail it, liveliness
at a fast ~: 5 apace **7** rapidly **9** sprinting
combining form: 4 drom- **5** dromo-, tacho-
contest: 4 race
demon: 5 racer **6** hot rod
ender: 3 way **4** boat, ster, well **6** writer
inhibitor: 4 bump
lose ~: 3 lag **4** slow **5** brake, check, choke, delay, let up, relax, stall, unlax **6** ease up, go easy, loiter, reduce, unwind, weaken **7** bog down, lay back, sit back **8** moderate, slack off, slow down, wind down **9** soft-pedal **10** decelerate, settle back, simmer down
LP ~: 3 rpm
measure ~: 4 time **5** clock
no ~ demon: 5 sloth, snail **8** slowpoke
rate of ~: 4 clip, pace **8** velocity
resume ~ in music: 6 a tempo
spurt: 5 burst
starter: 3 God **6** ground
unit: 3 kph, mph
up: 4 push, rise, rush **6** hasten **7** quicken **8** expedite, get going **9** get moving, shake a leg **10** accelerate, facilitate, get a move on
up to ~: 7 capable **9** competent, qualified **10** proficient
speed __: 4 bump, trap **5** brake, chess, demon, limit, skate **7** skating
speed-__: 4 read
__ speed: 3 air **4** film, full, good, up to, warp **5** flank **7** shutter
__-speed: 3 ten **4** high
Speed (1994 film)
cast: Sandra Bullock, Jeff Daniels, Dennis Hopper, Keanu Reeves
director: Jan De Bont
vehicle: 3 bus
Speed __: 5 Racer
__ speed ahead: 4 full
__-speed bike: 3 ten **5** three
speeder: 5 racer
nemesis: 3 cop **5** radar
speedily: 3 PDQ **4** fast, soon **5** apace, madly **6** presto **7** fleetly, hastily, in a rush, in haste, quickly, rapidly, readily, swiftly **8** in a flash, in a hurry, in a jiffy, in no time, on the fly, on the run, pell-mell, promptly **9** forthwith, hurriedly, instantly, like a shot, posthaste, summarily **10** in high gear
speediness: 5 hurry **8** celerity, rapidity **9** fleetness
Speedo material: 5 latex
speedometer: 4 dial **5** gauge
part: 6 needle
reading: 3 kph, mph **8** velocity
__-speed pitch: 3 off
Speed Racer (2008 film)
cast: John Goodman, Emile Hirsch, Christina Ricci, Susan Sarandon
speed-read: 4 scan
speed skater: 4 Enke **5** Blair **6** Heiden
speed skating: 5 sport
Speed Stick: 9 deodorant
alternative: deodorant
Speed-the-__: 4 Plow
__-speed transmission: 4 five, four
__ Speedwagon: 3 REO
speedway: 9 race track
area: 3 pit
letters: 4 IROC, NHRA **6** NASCAR
speedy: 4 fast **5** agile, brisk, fleet, hasty, quick, rapid, ready, swift **6** active, flying, lively, nimble, prompt, racing, snappy, winged **7** express, hurried, instant **8** headlong, meteoric **9** breakneck, galloping, immediate, lightning, posthaste, quick-fire, rapid-fire, whirlwind **10** double-time, harefooted, hypersonic, supersonic, ultrasonic
Speedy Gonzales: 4 toon **5** mouse
Speedy Gonzales (1962 song)
artist: Pat Boone
Speke, John: 8 explorer
river explored by: 4 Nile
speleology topic: 4 cave
spell: 3 bit, fit, hex, jag, run **4** bout, free, jinx, mean, span, term, time, tour, turn **5** allow, charm, hitch, imply, lie by, magic, patch, shift, space, spasm, stint, throe, trick, vodun, while **6** allure, amulet, attack, course, denote, glamor, herald, hexing, import, intend, lay off, period, relief, rotate, season, snatch, streak, trance, voodoo, whammy **7** add up to, cantrip, connote, express, glamour, illness, point to, portend, promise, rapture, release, relieve, replace, signify, sorcery, stretch, suggest **8** amount to, exorcism, foretell, indicate, interval, take over, talisman, witchery **9** hypnotism, interlude, mesmerism **10** bewitching, enchanting, hocus-pocus, mumbo-jumbo, tour of duty, witchcraft
breathing ~: 4 lull, rest **5** pause **6** recess **7** respite **8** reprieve
cold ~: 4 snap
dry ~: 5 slump **6** drouth **7** drought
ender: 4 bind, down **6** binder **7** binding
for a ~: 6 awhile
out: 4 cite, mean, show **6** define, detail **7** clarify, explain, expound, itemize, specify **8** construe, simplify **9** elucidate, enumerate, interpret, put across, stipulate, translate
put a ~ on: 3 hex, zap **4** jinx, mojo **5** charm, curse **7** bewitch, conjure, enchant
under a ~: 5 hexed **9** possessed
spell __: 3 out **7** checker
spell-__: 5 check
__ spell: 3 dry **4** cold
spellbind: 4 grip **5** charm, rivet **6** ravish **7** bewitch, enchant, enthral, inthral **8** enthrall, entrance, inthrall, transfix **9** captivate, enrapture, fascinate, hypnotize, mesmerize, transport
spellbinder: 6 orator **8** magician
Spellbinder
author: Harold Robbins
spellbinding: 5 magic, siren **7** magical **8** hypnotic
spellbound: 4 held, lost, rapt **5** agape, in awe **6** amazed, enrapt, hooked **7** bemused, charmed, far gone, gripped **8** caught up, held fast, immersed, ravished **9** bewitched, enchanted, petrified, possessed **10** fascinated, infatuated
hold ~: 5 charm **7** enchant **8** enthrall, entrance, transfix **9** captivate, fascinate, hypnotize
Spellbound (1945 film)
cast: Ingrid Bergman, Leo G. Carroll, Gregory Peck
director: Alfred Hitchcock
spelldown: 3 bee
spelled out: 5 clear, plain, vivid **6** cogent **7** evident, express, obvious **8** apparent, distinct, explicit, manifest, palpable **9** graspable
speller: 4 book, text **8** textbook
spelling
alternative ~: 7 variant
contest: 3 bee
error: 4 typo **7** erratum
game: 5 ghost
spelling __: 3 bee
Spelling: 4 Tori **5** Aaron
Spelling, Aaron
spouse: Carolyn Jones
Spelling, Tori father: 5 Aaron
__ spell on: 5 cast a
spelt: 5 wheat
spelunker: 5 caver
hat attachment: 4 lamp
Spencer: 4 John **5** Diana, Tracy **6** Tracie **7** Herbert
Spencerville
author: Nelson DeMille
spend: 3 buy, pay, use **4** blow, drop, fill, give, idle, kill, laze, pass **5** apply, drain, drift, empty, exert, pay up, put in, use up, waste **6** ante up, bestow, confer, defray, devote,

SP

donate, employ, expend, finish, invest, lavish, lay out, misuse, occupy, outlay, pay out, settle **7** consume, cough up, deplete, exhaust, fork out, fritter, hand out, let pass, pay down, play out **8** allocate, cast away, disburse, dispense, shell out, squander **9** dissipate, go through, liquidate, spring for, throw away, while away **10** come across, contribute, run through
as time: **5** put in
ender: **6** thrift
freely: **4** blow **6** lavish **7** splurge **8** squander
place to ~ the night: **3** inn **5** B and B, hotel, motel **8** motor inn **10** campground, motor lodge
prepare to ~ the night: **6** encamp
reluctant to ~: **5** cheap, tight **6** frugal **10** skinflinty
spender: **5** sport **7** wastrel **8** prodigal **10** high roller
phrase: **4** on me
Spender, Stephen: **3** Sir **4** poet **7** British
spending: **5** outgo **6** outlay **8** dazzling
expedition: **5** spree
govt. ~ watchdog: **3** GAO, OMB
limit: **3** cap
plan: **6** budget
some Congressional ~: **4** pork
spending __: **4** orgy **5** money
__ spending: **7** deficit
__-spending: **4** free
spendthrift: **6** waster **7** wastrel **8** prodigal, wasteful **9** imprudent **10** squanderer
spendthrift __: **5** trust
Spengler: **6** Oswald
Spenser, Edmund: **4** poet **7** British
heroine: **3** Una
work: Astrophel
The Faerie Queene
Spenser: For Hire (ABC drama)
cast: Avery Brooks (Hawk)
Robert Urich (Spenser)
Spenserian __: **6** sonnet, stanza
spent: **4** dead, done, gone, limp, lost, shot, used, weak, worn **5** blown, had it, tired, weary, wiped **6** bleary, bushed, dished, done in, effete, pooped, used up, wasted **7** all gone, drained, far-gone, wearied, worn out **8** burnt-out, consumed, depleted, dog-tired, expended, fatigued, finished, lifeless, tired out, washed-up, weakened **9** disbursed, enervated, exhausted, played-out, prostrate, shattered **10** dissipated, knocked out, on the ropes, thrown away
__-spent: **3** ill
__ Spent My Summer Vacation: **4** How I
Sperry: **5** Elmer, Roger
partner: **4** Rand
successor: **6** Unisys
spew: **3** jet **4** emit, gush, pour, spit **5** belch, egest, eject, erupt, expel, exude, flood, heave, issue, spirt, spume, spurt **6** spit up, spread, spritz, squirt **7** bring up, cascade, cast out, diffuse, emanate, give off, pour out, radiate, scatter, spit out **8** disgorge, throw off **9** cast forth, discharge, flow forth, send forth **10** break forth, shoot forth
sphagnum: **4** moss, peat
Spheeris: **8** Penelope
sphenoid: **4** bone
locale: **5** skull **7** cranium **9** braincase
sphere: **3** job, orb, sun **4** area, ball, rank, turf, zone **5** ambit, apple, arena, bourn, class, Earth, field, globe, orbit, plane, range, realm, round, scope, space, world **6** circle, domain, ground, jungle, locale, marble, milieu, planet, region **7** compass, element, globule, grounds, purview, section, station, stratum, terrain **8** baseball, capacity, dominion, function, locality, position, precinct, province **9** bailiwick, situation, territory **10** basketball, department, discipline, employment, profession, walk of life
curve: **5** rhumb
of conflict: **5** arena
of influence: **4** area **5** orbit **6** domain
shaped like a ~: **5** orbed
starter: **3** bio, eco **4** hemi, meso **5** tropo
tiny ~: **4** bead
Sphere: **4** film **5** novel
author: Michael Crichton
cast: Peter Coyote, Dustin Hoffman, Samuel L. Jackson, Sharon Stone
director: Barry Levinson
spherical: **5** orbed, orbic, round **6** global **7** globate, globoid, globose, rounded **8** globated, globular
spheroid: **3** pea **7** globule
spheroidal: **6** oblate
spherule: **4** bead, blob **7** globule
sphinx: **6** enigma
Sphinx
answer to ~'s riddle: **3** man
author: Robin Cook
in part: **4** lion
locale: **4** Giza **5** Egypt
parent: **6** Orthus **7** Echidna
Sphinx, The
author: Edgar Allan Poe
Sphynx: **3** cat **5** felid **6** feline
Spica: **4** star
constellation: **5** Virgo
spic and span: **4** mint, neat, tidy, trim **5** clean **7** orderly **8** spotless
spice: **3** pep, zip **4** bite, guts, kick, mace, tang, zest **5** anise, aroma, basil, clove, color, cumin, curry, gusto, liven, punch, savor **6** cassia, cloves, fennel, flavor, garlic, ginger, nutmeg, pepper, relish, season, spirit, stacte **7** cayenne, enliven, mustard, paprika, pimento, saffron **8** allspice, cardamom, cardamon, cinnamon, jalapeño, pimiento, piquancy, pleasure, pungency, rosemary, turmeric **9** condiment, coriander, fenugreek, flavoring, fragrance, hot pepper, poppy seed, red pepper, seasoning, sharpness **10** black cumin, excitement, liveliness, snappiness
early source of ~: **6** Orient
ender: **4** bush **5** berry
holder: **4** rack
starter: **3** all
up: **5** add to **6** pepper, season **7** enhance, enliven, improve **8** heighten **9** interlard
without ~: **5** bland **9** tasteless
Spice __: **5** Girls **7** Islands
__ Spice: **3** Old
Spice Girls
members: Victoria Adams (Posh), Melanie Brown (Scary), Emma Bunton (Baby), Melanie Chisholm (Sporty), Geri Haliwell (Ginger)
song: 2 Become 1 (1997)
Goodbye (1998)
Say You'll Be There (1997)
Stop (1998)
Too Much (1998)
Wannabe (1997)
Spice Islands: **8** Moluccas
spiciness: **4** tang **6** flavor **8** pungency
Spic & Span: **7** cleaner
alternative: **5** Brite, Lysol **6** Top Job **7** Lestoil, Mr. Clean, Pine Sol **9** Fantastik, Step Saver
spicy: **3** hot **4** blue, keen, racy, rich **5** fiery, juicy, tasty, zesty, zippy **6** erotic, red hot, ribald, risqué, savory, snappy, strong, vulgar, wicked, X-rated **7** gingery, peppery, piquant, pungent, zestful **8** aromatic, fragrant, off-color, perfumed, poignant, redolent, seasoned, spirited, unseemly **9** flavorful **10** appetizing, flavorsome, indelicate, scandalous
spider: **6** frypan **8** arachnid
combining form: **6** arachn- **7** arachno-
creation: **3** web **6** cobweb
defense: **5** venom
emulate a ~: **4** spin **5** weave
like a ~ web: **4** lacy
nest: **5** nidus
web: **3** net
web victim: **3** fly
spider __: **3** web **6** monkey
Spider: **3** car **4** auto **9** Alfa Romeo
Spider-Man
villain: **5** Venom **6** Doc Ock **7** Electro
Spider-Man (2002 film)
cast: Willem Dafoe, Kirsten Dunst, Tobey Maguire
director: Sam Raimi
Spider-Man 2 (2004 film)
cast: Kirsten Dunst, Tobey Maguire, Alfred Molina
director: Sam Raimi
Spiders & Snakes (1973 song)
artist: Jim Stafford
spidery: **4** lank, lean, slim, thin, wiry **5** lanky, spare **6** dainty, gangly, skinny, slight, slinky, svelte, twiggy **7** gracile, scraggy, scrawny, slender, willowy **8** gangling **9** sylphlike
Spiegel: **3** Sam
__ Spiegel: **3** Der
spiel: **3** say **4** line, rant, sell, tale, talk **5** pitch, speak, spout, state, story **6** patter, speech **7** address, lecture, oration, routine **8** harangue, hard sell **9** utterance **10** sales pitch, vocalizing
ad ~: **4** hype
give a carnival ~: **4** bark
starter: **4** sing
Spielberg, Steven: **8** director
film: AI: Artificial Intelligence (2001)
Always (1989)
Amistad (1997)
Catch Me If You Can (2002)
Close Encounters of the Third Kind (1977)
The Color Purple (1985)
Empire of the Sun (1987)
E.T. The Extra-Terrestrial (1982)
Hook (1991)
Indiana Jones and the Kingdom of the Crystal Skull (2008)
Indiana Jones and the Last Crusade (1989)
Indiana Jones and the Temple of Doom (1984)
Jaws (1975)
Jurassic Park (1993)
The Lost World: Jurassic Park (1997)
Minority Report (2002)
Munich (2005)
Raiders of the Lost Ark (1981)
Saving Private Ryan (1998, AA)
Schindler's List (1993, AA)
The Sugarland Express (1974)
The Terminal (2004)
War of the Worlds (2005)
spouse: Kate Capshaw, Amy Irving
spier: **7** spotter, watcher
Spies
author: Michael Frayn
Spies Like Us (1985 film)
cast: Dan Aykroyd, Chevy Chase
director: John Landis
Spies Like Us (1985 song)
artist: Paul McCartney
spiff: **5** bonus
up: **5** groom, primp, prink **6** spruce **7** garnish, smarten **8** brighten **9** embellish
spiffy: **5** dandy, fancy, natty, sleek, swank **6** classy, dapper, jaunty, rakish, snazzy, sporty, spruce, swanky **7** refined **9** gussied up
spigot: **3** tap **5** valve **6** faucet
tree ~: **5** spile
spike: **3** ear, pin, rod, tap **4** barb, lace, nail, shoe, spit **5** cleat, lance, piton, point, prick, spear, stake, stalk, stick, thorn **6** empale, impale, pierce, skewer, tamper **8** footwear, high heel, prohibit, transfix **9** intensify **10** adulterate
birch ~: **5** ament **6** catkin
game: **10** volleyball
grain ~: **3** awn, ear
volleyball ~: **4** kill
spike __: **4** heel
Spike: **3** Lee **4** Owen **5** Jones, Jonze **8** Milligan
formerly: **3** TNN
spiked: **5** sharp, spiny **6** jagged **7** pointed
spikelet part: **6** arista
spiky: **4** acid **5** sharp **6** peaked, thorny **7** acerbic, peevish, pointed, prickly **8** abrasive
hair style: **4** punk
spile: **5** spout **6** spigot
fluid: **3** sap

spill: **3** run, tip **4** blab, blow, drip, drop, emit, fall, leak, lose, pour, shed, slop, tell **5** empty, let on, slide, slosh, spirt, spout, spray, spurt, upset **6** betray, header, inform, relate, reveal, run out, splash, squeal, squirt, stream, tattle, tumble **7** divulge, dribble, dump out, let slip, overrun, pour out, run over, scatter, tip over **8** disclose, disgorge, flow over, give away, overfill, overflow, overpour, overturn, slop over, splatter, sprinkle, throw off, well over **9** discharge, knock over
clean a ~: **5** mop up, sop up **6** wipe up
consequence: **5** stain
ender: **3** age, way **4** back, over
oil ~: **5** slick
over: **4** brim, gush **5** slosh
take a ~: **4** fall, slip, trip
the beans: **3** rat **4** blab, blat, leak, sing, talk, tell **5** blurt, let on **6** tattle **7** confess
__ spill: **3** oil
Spillane, Mickey: **6** writer
sleuth: Mike Hammer
work: The Delta Factor
The Girl Hunters
I, the Jury
Kiss Me, Deadly
Survival: Zero
Tomorrow I Die
The Twisted Thing
spill one's __: **4** guts
spill the __: **5** beans
spillway: **5** flume
spin: **3** run **4** jink, reel, ride, roll, turn **5** crank, drive, pivot, swirl, twirl, twist, weave, wheel, whirl **6** gyrate, outing, rotate, spiral, swivel **7** joyride, revolve **8** go around, gyration, rotation **9** oscillate, pirouette **10** revolution
a yarn: **4** tell **6** relate **7** narrate
doctor: **5** PR man
doctor concern: **5** image
ender: **3** off, out **5** drift
go for a ~: **4** ride **5** drive
imparter: **5** wrist
in ballet: **7** fouetté
out: **7** prolong, stretch **8** lengthen, protract
skater ~: **5** camel
starter: **3** top **4** back, down, side, tail
the bottle: **4** game
spin __: **3** off, out **6** doctor **7** control
spin __ top: **5** like a
spin-__: **3** dry, off
Spin __: **4** City
spinach: **6** veggie **9** vegetable
like ~: **5** leafy
spinach __: **3** pie
spinachlike plant: **5** orach **6** orache
spinal __: **4** cord **6** column
spinal column part: **6** sacrum
spinal cord
combining form: **4** myel- **5** myelo-
lining: **6** endyma
terminus: **5** brain
Spin City (ABC sitcom)
cast: Barry Bostwick (Randall Winston)
Connie Britton (Nikki Faber)
Michael J. Fox (Michael Flaherty)
Richard Kind (Paul Lassiter)
Alan Ruck (Stuart Bondek)
dog: **4** Rags
spindle: **4** axis, axle **6** empale, impale **8** baluster
spindly: **4** lank, thin, weak **5** lanky, leggy, rangy, weedy **6** gangly **7** stringy **14** gangling. skinny
spindrift: **4** surf **5** spray, spume
spine: **4** back, grit, guts **5** briar, chine, moxie, pluck, point, quill, ridge, thorn **6** mettle, rachis **7** bramble, courage, hogback, rhachis **8** backbone, decision, gumption **9** fortitude, stiffness, vertebrae, willpower **10** moral fiber, projection
item: **5** title **6** author
part: **6** coccyx
where the ~ starts: **4** nape
spinel: **3** gem **4** ruby **5** balas **7** mineral **8** gemstone
spineless: **4** meek, soft, weak **5** timid **6** feeble, yellow **7** fawning, fearful, gutless **8** cowardly, pithless, recreant **9** forceless, nerveless, squeamish, weak-kneed **10** amoebalike, frightened, inadequate, irresolute, namby-pamby, spiritless, submissive, weak-willed
one: **4** wimp, worm **5** sissy
Spiner, Brent: **5** actor
role: **4** Data
TV: Star Trek: The Next Generation
spinet: **5** organ, piano **8** keyboard
spine-tingling: **4** eery **5** eerie, scary **6** spooky **8** exciting
Spingarn: **4** Joel
Spingarn Medal awarder: **5** NAACP
Spinks: **4** Leon **7** Michael
Spinks, Leon: **5** boxer
defeater: **3** Ali
milieu: **4** ring
Spinks, Michael: **5** boxer
milieu: **4** ring
spin like __: **4** a top
spinnaker: **4** sail
support: **4** mast
spinner: **2** DJ **3** top **4** gyro, lure, reel **6** deejay
Spinners
song: Could It Be I'm Falling in Love (1973)
Cupid (1980)
I'll Be Around (1972)
I'm Coming Home (1974)
One of a Kind (1973)
The Rubberband Man (1976)
Then Came You (1974)
'They Just Can't Stop It' the (Games People Play) (1975)
Working My Way Back to You (1980)
spinning: **5** areel **6** awhirl, rotary **8** gyration
one's wheels: **6** in a rut
sound: **4** whir **5** whirr
spinning __: **5** jenny, wheel
Spinning Wheel (1969 song)
artist: Blood, Sweat & Tears
spinoff: **6** sequel **7** product, variant **9** by-product, outgrowth **10** derivative
spin one's __: **6** wheels
Spinoza, Baruch: **5** Dutch **6** writer **11** philosopher
spins, part that: **5** rotor
spin the __: **6** bottle
spinule: **5** thorn
spiny: **5** sharp **6** barbed, briery, hispid, spiked, thorny **7** bristly, pointed, prickly, pronged, thistly **9** acanthoid, spiculate
spiral: **4** coil, curl, loop, rise, spin, turn, wind **5** curve, helix, screw, twist, whorl **6** coiled, curled, volute **7** curling, entwine, helical, intwine, sinuate, whorled, winding **8** circling, circular, cochlear, curlicue, curlycue, flourish, gyration, scrolled **9** arabesque, corkscrew, sinuosity **10** tendrillar
combining form: **3** gyr- **4** gyro- **5** helic- **6** helico-
molecule: **3** DNA
motion: **8** gyration
spiral __: **6** galaxy, nebula **7** binding
spiral-__: **5** bound
spirals: **5** pasta **7** noodles
alternative: ***see*** pasta
spire: **3** tip, top **4** acme, apex, peak **5** crest, crown, point, shoot, stalk, tower **6** apogee, belfry, flèche, sprout, summit, turret, vertex **7** steeple **8** pinnacle
ornament: **6** finial
spirea: **5** plant, shrub **6** flower
family: **4** rose
relative: **4** sloe **6** kerria **7** bramble, jetbead **8** hardhack, ninebark, photinia **9** firethorn, raspberry
spiring: **5** lofty
spirit: **3** air, pep, vim, zip **4** dash, élan, fire, gist, grit, guts, jazz, life, mood, soul, tone, vein, will, zeal, zest **5** ardor, force, genie, ghost, gusto, heart, humor, moxie, nerve, oomph, pluck, sense, shade, spark, spice, spook, spunk, style, umbra, valor, verve, vigor **6** action, animus, brandy, energy, esprit, fantom, flavor, genius, intent, kelpie, liquor, mettle, morale, psyche, shadow, sprite, temper, vision, warmth, wraith **7** bravery, courage, essence, fantasm, feeling, incubus, meaning, outlook, passion, phantom, purport, purpose, resolve, sparkle, specter **8** attitude, backbone, boldness, fervency, phantasm, presence, strength, vitality **9** animation, character, élan vital, fortitude, intention, life force, substance, willpower **10** apparition, atmosphere, enterprise, enthusiasm, exuberance, liveliness, moral fiber, motivation, resolution
African ~: **4** ngai
antithesis: **5** flesh
away: **5** seize, sneak, steal **6** abduct, kidnap, snatch **10** run off with
Chinese ~: **5** hsien
evil ~: **5** demon, ghoul **6** daemon, daimon
free ~: **8** bohemian
guardian ~: **5** angel **6** daemon, genius
household ~: **3** Lar
imbue with ~: **6** ensoul, insoul
in French: **3** âme
in music: **4** brio
Irish ~: **5** Pooka
Islamic ~: **3** jin **4** djin, jinn **5** djinn, genie, jinni **6** djinni
lose ~: **6** weaken
of a culture: **5** ethos
show team ~: **3** rah **4** root
water ~: **5** kelpy **6** kelpie
spirit __: **3** gum
__ spirit: **4** evil, free
Spirit: **3** AMC, car **4** auto **5** Dodge
Spirit __: **4** Cave, Lake
__ Spirit: **4** Holy **5** Great **6** Blithe
Spirit and the Flesh, The
author: Pearl S. Buck
spirited: **3** hot **4** avid, bold, game, keen, pert, spry **5** alert, alive, brave, crisp, eager, fiery, gutsy, jazzy, lit up, lusty, nervy, peppy, perky, proud, quick, sharp, smart, spicy, vital, zesty, zingy, zippy **6** active, ardent, bouncy, bright, feisty, frisky, gritty, gung-ho, lively, plucky, snappy, spicey, spunky **7** animate, burning, coltish, dashing, gingery, peppery, piquant, playful, rocking, romping, rousing, vibrant, zealous, zinging **8** animated, fearless, intrepid, resolute, vigorous **9** audacious, dauntless, energetic, exuberant, sparkling, sprightly, strenuous, unfearing, vivacious **10** courageous, expressive, hot-blooded, mettlesome, passionate, rollicking
__-spirited: **3** low **4** high, mean, poor **6** public
spiritedness: **4** zest **8** buoyance, buoyancy
Spirit in the Sky (1970 song)
artist: Norman Greenbaum
spiritless: **3** low **4** arid, blah, blue, down, dull, flat, limp, meek, tame **5** leady, tepid, timid, vapid **6** broken, draggy, drippy, droopy, jejune, leaden, torpid **7** languid, subdued, unmoved **8** cast down, dejected, downcast, lifeless, listless **9** apathetic, bloodless, depressed, enervated, exanimate, impassive, inanimate, lethargic, spineless
__ spirito: **3** con
Spirit of '76, The instrument: **4** drum, fife
Spirit of Goodyear: **5** blimp **8** zeppelin
Spirit of St. Louis builder: **4** Ryan
Spirit of St. Louis, The: **4** book, film
author: Charles Lindbergh
cast: James Stewart
director: Billy Wilder
Spirit of the Border, The
author: Zane Grey
spirits: **4** grog **5** booze, drink, hooch **6** fettle, hootch, liquor, whisky **7** alcohol, liqueur, whiskey **9** aqua vitae, firewater, hard stuff, moonshine **10** intoxicant
be in high ~: **4** crow **5** exult **6** bubble **7** enthuse, rejoice **9** make merry **10** effervesce, jump for joy
dampen the ~ of: **6** sadden **10** discourage
good ~: **3** joy, pep **4** élan, glee, life, mood **5** cheer, mirth **6** gaiety, gayety, levity **7** elation,

jollity, rapture **8** buoyance, buoyancy, euphoria, felicity, gladness, hilarity **9** happiness, joviality, merriment, well-being **10** enthusiasm, exuberance, joyfulness
guardian ~: **5** Lares
in high ~: **3** gay **5** happy, jolly, riant **6** cheery, elated **7** chipper **8** cheerful, exultant, sanguine
in low ~: **3** sad **4** blue, down, glum **6** gloomy
lift the ~ of: **5** elate **7** hearten
low ~: **3** woe **4** mood **5** blues **7** sadness **8** glumness **10** depression, woefulness
raise one's ~: **4** buoy **5** cheer, elate **6** buck up, buoy up, solace **7** cheer up, comfort, console, enliven, gladden **8** brighten **9** encourage
with low ~: **5** sadly
see also liqueur, liquor

___ spirits: **4** high
Spirits of the Dead
author: Edgar Allan Poe
Spirits that ___ on mortal thoughts: **4** tend
spiritual: **4** airy, holy, hymn, pure, song **5** inner **6** divine, mystic, sacred **7** ghostly, psychic, refined **8** bodiless, ethereal, mystical, platonic, rarefied **9** celestial, ineffable, religious, unearthly, unworldly **10** devotional, immaterial, intangible, mysterious, unphysical
being: **4** soul
discipline: **4** yoga
formula: **5** credo
teacher: **4** guru, lama, yogi **5** rabbi, rebbe
word in a ~: **4** amen
spiritualist: **4** seer **7** psychic
board: **5** Ouija
spirituality: **8** religion
Spiro: **5** Agnew
spirogyra: **4** alga **5** algae
___ spiro, spero: **3** dum
spiry: **6** coiled **7** helical
spit: **3** rod **4** hiss, rain, spew, spue **5** drool, spear, spike, water **6** saliva, sizzle, squirt **7** dribble, slobber, spatter, sputter **8** splutter, sprinkle, transfix **9** brochette, discharge **10** promontory
ender: **4** ball, fire
out: **4** spew, spue, tell **5** eject
partner: **6** polish
put on a ~: **6** empale, impale
starter: **4** turn
upon: **5** scorn
spit ___: **4** curl
spit ___ ocean: **5** in the
spit-___: **5** shine
spit and ___: **6** polish
spitchcock: **3** eel
spite: **3** vex **4** crab, gall, harm, hate, hurt **5** annoy, beset, peeve, venom, wrong **6** enmity, grudge, hang up, harass, hatred, injure, malice, needle, nettle, offend, put out, rancor, spleen **7** cruelty, get even, ill will, louse up, provoke, revenge, umbrage **8** acrimony, bad blood, begrudge, contempt, defiance, meanness **9** animosity, antipathy, discomfit, hostility, nastiness, persecute, vengeance **10** grumpiness, resentment, unkindness
in ~ of: **3** tho, yet **5** altho **6** though **8** although, ignoring **10** even though
in ~ of that: **6** even so
spiteful: **4** evil, mean, ugly **5** angry, catty, cruel, dirty, nasty, snide, surly **6** barbed, malign, ornery, unkind, wicked **7** hateful, hostile, hurtful, vicious **8** inimical, vengeful, venomous, virulent **9** bellicose, malicious, malignant, rancorous, splenetic **10** derogatory, ill-natured, malevolent, minimizing, pugnacious, unfriendly, vindictive
one: **5** hater, meany, viper **6** meanie
spitefulness: **5** venom **6** malice, rancor
spitfire: **5** hussy, shrew, vixen **6** chider, virago **9** henpecker, termagant
Spitfire: **5** plane **7** fighter **8** airplane
org.: **3** RAF
Spitsbergen: **4** isle **6** island
locale: **6** Arctic
spitting
exclamation: **4** ptui **6** ptooey
image: **4** copy, twin **5** clone, match **6** double **7** picture **8** likeness **9** duplicate, look-alike **10** dead ringer
spitting ___: **5** image
spitz: **3** dog **5** canid **6** canine **7** Samoyed **8** chow chow **10** Pomeranian
Spitz, Mark: **7** swimmer
splash: **3** lap, sop, wet **4** blob, dash, pour, show, slop, soak, spot, stir, wade **5** bathe, burst, douse, dowse, drown, flair, lobby, slosh, spill, spray, strew **6** dabble, drench, effect, gurgle, paddle, shower, spread, squirt, wallow **7** display, moisten, spatter, splurge, triumph **8** splatter, sprinkle **9** broadcast, sensation **10** spattering
ender: **4** down **5** board, guard
splash ___: **4** down **5** guard
Splash (1984 film)
cast: John Candy, Tom Hanks, Daryl Hannah
director: Ron Howard
___ Splash: **6** Splish
splashboard: **6** fender
splashdown: **7** landing
splashy: **5** gaudy, showy, swank **6** ornate, sloppy, swanky **8** splendid **9** grandiose, well-known **10** flamboyant
splat: **5** strip
Splat! cousin: **4** plop
splatter: **4** slop **5** spill, throw **6** splash **7** moisten
safeguard: **3** bib **5** apron **6** napkin
splay: **5** flare, slant, slope, squat **6** expand, spread
spleen: **3** ire **4** hate, rage **5** anger, gland, organ, spite, venom, wrath **6** enmity, hatred, malice, rancor **8** acrimony **9** hostility, petulance, testiness **10** crabbiness, grumpiness, irritation, touchiness, unkindness
vent one's ~: **4** boil, fume, rant, rave, yell **5** erupt, steam, wrath **6** blow up, rail at, scream, seethe **7** explode, rampage, run riot, run wild **8** boil over, have a fit, outburst, paroxysm, run amuck, violence **9** blow a fuse, fulminate, go berserk **10** hit the roof, kick up a row
spleenwort: **4** fern
splendid: **3** fat **4** luxe, posh, rare, rich **5** plush, proud, regal, royal **6** bright, costly, deluxe, lavish, lordly, ornate, swanky **7** beaming, capital, elegant, eminent, gallant, glowing, premium, radiant, splashy, supreme **8** gorgeous, imperial, lustrous, majestic, palatial, peerless, princely, renowned, wondrous **9** expensive, grandiose, luxurious, magnifico, matchless, refulgent, solid gold, sumptuous, unrivaled, wonderful, wunderbar **10** celebrated, flamboyant, glittering, impressive, majestical, unrivalled
see also wonderful
splendidly: **7** rightly **8** laudably, worthily
Splendid Splinter, The: **8** Williams
splendiferous: **5** showy
splendor: **4** luxe, pomp, show **5** éclat, glory, light **6** dazzle, luster, luxury, renown **7** display, glitter, majesty, pageant **8** ceremony, elegance, grandeur, heraldry, radiance, radiancy, richness **9** solemnity, spectacle **10** brightness, brilliance, effulgence, kingliness, luminosity
Splendor in the Grass: **4** film, play
author: William Inge
cast: Warren Beatty, Natalie Wood
director: Elia Kazan
splenetic: **4** acid **5** angry, surly, testy **6** crabby, cranky, crusty, feisty, grumpy, morose, ornery, raving, snarly, touchy **7** bearish, bilious, crabbed, fretful, grouchy, peevish, ranting, waspish **8** fretsome, grumpish, petulant, snappish, vengeful, venomous, virulent **9** crotchety, fractious, irritable, malicious, querulous, rancorous **10** freaked out, ill-humored, out of sorts, vindictive
see also angry
splice: **3** tie, wed **4** join, knit, link, mate, mesh, yoke **5** braid, graft, hitch, joint, marry, plait, unite, weave **7** entwine, intwine **8** junction, juncture **9** interlace, interlink **10** interweave
film: **4** edit
thing to ~: **4** gene
___ splicing: **4** gene
___ splint: **4** shin
splinter: **3** jag **4** chip, part **5** burst, crack, flake, piece, smash, split, stave **6** needle, paring, shiver, sliver **7** flinder, shatter, shaving **8** fracture, fragment
group: **4** bloc, cult, sect **7** faction
ore ~: **5** spall
splintery: **5** sharp **9** breakable
Splish Splash (1958 song)
activity: **4** bath
artist: Bobby Darin
split: **2** go **3** gap, lam, rip **4** blow, bolt, exit, flee, fork, gape, gone, gulf, hack, left, open, part, rend, rent, rift, rive, slit, snap, tear, torn, went **5** allot, apart, be off, break, burst, chasm, chink, cleft, crack, divvy, forky, halve, in two, leave, riven, scram, sever, share, slash, slice **6** beat it, begone, bisect, branch, breach, broken, cleave, cloven, cut off, cut out, damage, decamp, depart, desert, detach, divide, forked, get out, go away, profit, run off, schism, secede, spread, sunder, unlink **7** abscond, asunder, break up, carve up, cracked, crack-up, crevice, deviate, disband, discord, disjoin, diverge, divided, divorce, divvy up, faction, fissure, get lost, give way, go forth, go south, head out, incised, isolate, make off, mete out, opening, portion, pull out, radiate, revenue, ride off, rupture, section, shatter, slice up, take off, walk out **8** allocate, bisected, break off, check out, cleavage, detached, dissever, disunion, disunite, division, divorced, fracture, fragment, fugitate, hightail, laminate, proceeds, run for it, separate, set apart, shove off, splinter, sundered, uncouple **9** apportion, bifurcate, bundle off, come apart, dichotomy, disengage, disunited, lacerated, parcel out, partition, pull apart, segregate, subdivide, take leave **10** alienation, come undone, difference, disconnect, disruption, dissension, distribute, divergence, go fly a kite, interspace, percentage, poles apart, put asunder, separation
combining form: **5** schiz-
component: **3** pin
hairs: **5** cavil **6** niggle **7** nitpick, quibble **8** pettifog
it may be ~: **4** atom
off: **5** spall
old-style: **5** reave
one's sides: **4** roar **5** laugh **6** guffaw
second: **4** jiff, wink **5** flash, jiffy, trice **6** minute, moment **7** instant
they may be ~: **4** ends
up: **4** part, rend **5** apart, break, halve, sever, share **6** bisect, divide, parcel, sunder **7** disjoin, scatter **8** fragment, separate **9** apportion, partition, pull apart, segregate
split ___: **3** end, off **4** ends **5** hairs **6** screen, second, ticket
split-___: **5** level
split-___ soup: **3** pea
___ split: **4** baby, dodo **6** banana
___-split: **7** lickety
Split: **4** city, town
locale: **7** Croatia
split-level: **5** house
___-splitter: **4** rail
splitter's
log ~ aid: **3** ram **4** froe, frow **5** chock, wedge
splitting: **7** fission
starter: **3** ear **4** side
splitting ___: **3** adz **4** adze **5** hairs
split-up: **7** parting, rupture **10** detachment, separation

splotch: 4 blob, mark, spot **5** speck, stain
splotchy: 4 pied **7** mottled
splurge: 4 shop **5** binge, fling, spree, waste **6** splash **7** rampage **9** celebrate
splutter: 4 rave, spit **7** spatter, stutter
Spock, Benjamin: 2 MD **6** doctor
  specialty: 10 pediatrics
Spock, Mr.: 5 alien **6** Vulcan
  colleague: 4 Kirk, Sulu **5** McCoy, Scott, Uhura **7** Chekhov
  father: 5 Sarek
  mother: 6 Amanda
  successor: 4 Data
Spode: 5 china **6** Josiah
  competitor: 5 Lenox **6** Mikasa **9** Rosenthal
spoil: 3 mar, pet, rot **4** baby, blot, harm, hurt, ruin, sack, sink, soil, sour, turn, undo **5** addle, botch, decay, favor, go bad, go off, gum up, humor, queer, smash, sully, taint, trash, upset, waste, wreck **6** befoul, coddle, crud up, curdle, damage, dampen, dandle, debase, deface, defile, dote on, go sour, impair, infect, injure, mangle, mess up, mildew, molder, muck up, oblige, pamper, ravage, squash **7** acidify, blemish, cater to, corrupt, crumble, destroy, go to pot, indulge, pillage, plunder, pollute, ransack, screw up, tarnish, turn bad, vitiate **8** demolish, desolate, disgrace, dote upon, freeboot, give in to **9** break down, decompose, depredate, desecrate, devastate, disfigure, prejudice, spoon-feed, take apart **10** overpamper
  ender: 3 age **5** sport
  for: 4 want, wish
spoilage: 4 ruin **5** decay
spoiled: 3 bad, off **4** gamy **5** gamey, moldy, musty, stale **6** bratty, rotten **8** inedible
  child: 4 brat
spoiled __: 4 brat
spoiler: 5 doter, louse
spoils: 3 cut **4** gain, loot, make, pelf, prey, swag, take **5** booty, goods, graft, prize **6** trophy **7** pillage, plunder, squeeze **8** pickings
spoils __: 6 system
Spoils of Poynton, The
  author: Henry James
Spokane: 4 city, town
  athlete: 3 Zag
  event of 1974: 4 Expo **10** World's Fair
  locale: 10 Washington
  school: 7 Gonzaga
spoke: 3 bar, ray, rod **4** rung **6** radius **8** baluster
  intersection: 3 hub
  place: 5 wheel
  umbrella ~: 3 rib
spoken: 4 oral, said, told **5** aloud, vocal **6** phonic, sonant, verbal, voiced **7** lingual, uttered **8** narrated, phonetic **9** announced, expressed, mentioned, recounted, unwritten, vocalized **10** articulate
  for: 5 in use, taken **6** chosen **7** engaged **8** reserved
  in French: 3 dit
  not ~ of: 4 tabu **5** taboo
  statement: 5 parol
__-spoken: 4 fair, free, well **5** plain, rough, short **6** smooth
spokesperson: 5 agent, mouth, sayer **6** deputy, talker **7** prophet, speaker, stand-in **8** advocate, champion, delegate, mediator **9** proponent **10** mouthpiece
spoliate: 3 rob **4** raid, ruin, sack **5** waste, wreck **6** maraud, ravage **7** despoil, destroy, pillage, plunder, ransack **8** demolish, desolate **9** desecrate, devastate
spoliation: 5 decay **9** pollution
spondee: 4 foot
  relative: 4 iamb **6** dactyl **7** anapest, pyrrhic, trochee
spondulicks
  see moolah
sponge: 3 dry, mop **4** bath, cake, wash, wipe **5** cadge, clean, dab at, leech, loofa, luffa, mooch **6** cadger, loofah, wipe up **7** moocher, solicit **8** deadbeat, freeload, hanger-on, parasite, scrounge **10** freeloader
  gourd: 5 loofa, luffa **6** loofah
  like a ~: 6 porous **9** permeable
  on: 3 beg **5** cadge, mooch **8** freeload
  out: 5 erase **6** efface **7** expunge **10** obliterate
  target: 5 spill
  up: 6 absorb
  use a ~: 3 sop **4** wipe **5** sop up
sponge __: 4 bath
__ sponge: 4 bath
SpongeBob SquarePants (Nick sitcom)
  voice cast: Clancy Brown (Eugene Krabs)
    Rodger Bumpass (Squidward Tentacles)
    Bill Fagerbakke (Patrick Star)
    Tom Kenny (SpongeBob)
    Carolyn Lawrence (Sandy Cheeks)
    Doug Lawrence (Sheldon Plankton)
sponger: 3 bum **5** drone, leech, mooch **6** cadger, loafer **7** moocher **8** hanger-on, parasite **10** freeloader
sponge-toy brand: 4 Nerf
spongy: 4 soft **5** light, mushy, pulpy, soggy **6** leachy, porous **7** elastic, rubbery, springy, squishy **8** bibulous, cushiony, flexible, yielding **9** absorbent, resilient
  rubber: 4 foam
  wet and ~: 5 muddy **6** swampy
  wet ~ area: 3 bog, fen **5** marsh, swamp
sponsor: 4 back, fund, help **5** angel, endow, stake **6** backer, foster, patron, surety **7** finance, promote, support **8** adherent, advocate, bankroll, financer, guardian, mainstay, promoter, vouch for **9** answer for, financier, godparent, grubstake, guarantee, guarantor, patronize, subsidize, supporter, sustainer **10** benefactor, connection, grubstaker, underwrite
  message: 2 ad **5** a word
sponsored child: 6 godson **11** goddaughter
sponsorship: 4 egis **5** aegis, start **7** backing **8** auspices **9** patronage
spontaneity: 4 élan **7** abandon
spontaneous: 4 free, naif **5** ad-lib, naive, unbid **6** casual, simple **7** natural, offhand, up-front, willing **8** informal, unartful, unbidden, unforced **9** automatic, impetuous, impromptu, impulsive, unguarded, unplanned, unstudied, voluntary
spontaneously: 5 ad lib **9** extempore, naturally
spontoon: 7 javelin
spoof: 4 fake, fool, game, hoax, jest, joke, mock, quip, sell, sham, skit **5** bluff, cheat, phony, prank, put on, trick **6** deceit, parody, phoney, satire, send-up **7** burlesk, deceive, imitate, lampoon, mockery, take off **8** parodize, travesty, trickery **9** burlesque, deception, imposture, wisecrack **10** caricature
spoofing: 7 jesting, satiric **9** satirical
spook: 3 spy **4** stir **5** alarm, ghost, haunt, scare, upset **6** fantom, goblin, spirit, wraith **7** fantasm, fluster, petrify, phantom, specter, startle, terrify, trouble, unnerve **8** distress, frighten, phantasm, psych out, threaten, unsettle **9** give a turn, terrorize **10** intimidate, scare stiff
spooked: 5 jumpy, timid **6** afraid, scared, trepid **7** anxious, chicken, fearful, jittery, nervous, panicky **8** cowardly, fearsome, hesitant, timorous
spooky: 4 eery **5** eerie, scary, weird **6** creepy **7** eidolic, ghostly, macaber, macabre, ominous, uncanny **8** haunting **9** frightful, unearthly **10** mysterious
  sound: 4 moan **5** creak
spool: 4 reel, roll, wind **6** bobbin, unwind
  in Britain: 4 pirn
  toy: 4 yo-yo
spoon: 3 woo **4** club, iron, lure, wood **5** court, ladle, scoop **6** cuddle, smooch **7** snuggle, stirrer, utensil **8** golf club, pitch woo **9** three wood **10** bill and coo
  companion, in rhyme: 4 dish
  ender: 4 bill **5** drift
  greasy ~: 4 café **5** diner **6** eatery **10** restaurant
  out: 5 ladle
  starter: 3 tea **4** soup **5** table **7** dessert
spoon-__: 3 fed **4** feed
__ spoon: 4 soup **5** sugar **6** coffee, greasy, silver **7** slotted **8** runcible
spoonbill: 4 bird
  relative: 4 ibis **5** stork
spoon-feed: 4 baby **5** spoil **6** pamper **7** cater to, indulge
spoonful: 3 sip **4** bite **5** taste **6** dollop
  starter: 3 tea **5** table
__ Spoonful: 5 Lovin'
spoon-playing
  locale: 4 knee
Spoon River Anthology
  author: Edgar Lee Masters
spoony, make: 6 enamor
spoor: 5 piste, scent, trace, track, trail **9** footprint **10** impression
sporadic: 3 odd **4** rare **6** broken, random, scarce, seldom, sparse, spotty **7** erratic **8** far apart, isolated, on and off, periodic, uncommon **9** hit-or-miss, irregular, scattered, spasmodic **10** flickering, infrequent, nonuniform, occasional, unfrequent
sporadically: 6 hardly, seldom **8** fitfully
spore: 4 cell, seed
  case: 5 theca
  case cluster: 6 telium
  combining form: 4 coni- **5** conio-
  fern ~ cluster: 5 sorus
  fungus ~: 6 oidium
  fungus ~ sac: 5 ascus **6** aecium
  mark: 5 hilum
  mold ~ sac: 5 ascus
  producer: 4 fern
  starter: 4 endo
__ spore: 4 mold
spork: 7 utensil
sporran: 5 purse
  it's worn with a ~: 4 kilt
  sporter: 4 Scot
sport: 3 don, fun, toy **4** butt, chap, crew, épée, game, golf, jest, judo, luge, mock, play, polo, pool, show, sumo, wear **5** darts, fight, games, kendo, mirth, model, prank, rodeo, rugby **6** action, aikido, antics, boxing, diving, frolic, gaiety, gambol, gayety, have on, hiking, hockey, joking, karate, kung fu, pelota, racing, riding, rowing, shinny, skiing, soccer, squash, tennis, tubing **7** archery, birling, bowling, buffoon, camping, contest, cricket, croquet, curling, cycling, display, disport, exhibit, fencing, fishing, gambler, hunting, hurling, jai alai, jesting, jollity, jujitsu, kidding, mockery, pastime, rafting, running, sailing, show off, skating, skylark, surfing, teasing, tenpins **8** aerobics, baseball, canoeing, derision, dressage, duelling, escapade, exercise, falconry, football, handball, high-jump, interest, jousting, lacrosse, laughter, long-jump, ninepins, Ping Pong, pleasure, pole-jump, raillery, rounders, sculling, softball, swimming, trifling, tumbling, yachting **9** amusement, athletics, badminton, bicycling, billiards, broad-jump, decathlon, diversion, dog racing, enjoyment, horseplay, ice hockey, merriment, plaything, pole vault, skydiving, sprinting, water polo, wrestling **10** acrobatics, auto-racing, ballooning, basketball, big spender, deck tennis, fly-casting, fly fishing, gymnastics, horse-shoes, iceboating, ice dancing, ice fishing, ice-skating, kickboxing, lawn tennis, liveliness, pentathlon, recreation, ski jumping, skin diving, tomfoolery, volleyball **11** backpacking, bobsledding, hang-gliding, horse racing, parachuting, racquetball, scuba diving, shot-putting, table tennis, tobogganing, water skiing, windsurfing
  be a ~: 3 pay **5** treat
  make ~ of: 3 kid **4** jape
  starter: 5 spoil
sport __: 3 car, ute **4** fish **5** shirt
sport-__: 3 ute

— **sport:** **3** be a **5** blood **7** contact
Sportage: **3** Kia, SUV
sporting: **3** gay **4** fair, game, wild **5** antic, merry **6** frisky, impish, jaunty, joyous, lively **7** larkish, playful, roguish **8** athletic, generous **9** full of fun, sprightly **10** frolicsome, rollicking
event: **4** game, meet, race **5** match
sporting —: **3** dog **6** chance
sporting-goods
company: **3** AMF **4** Voit **6** Wilson **8** Rawlings, Spalding **9** Brunswick
Sporting Life
friend: **4** Bess
sportive: **3** gay **4** game, wild **5** antic, jolly, merry **6** frisky, impish, jaunty, joyous, lively **7** coltish, jocular, larkish, playful, roguish **8** generous **9** full of fun, gamboling, sprightly, vivacious **10** frolicsome, rollicking
sportiveness: **8** jocosity, mischief
sports: **9** athletics **10** recreation
award: **3** MVP
center: **3** gym **5** arena **7** stadium **9** gymnasium
championship: **5** title
college ~ org.: **3** AAU **4** NCAA
commentator's patter: **5** color
deal: **5** trade
ender: **3** man, men **4** cast, wear **5** woman, women **6** caster, writer
enthusiast: **3** fan
event: **4** bowl, game, meet, race
extra period in ~: **2** OT **8** overtime
fan: **9** spectator
group: **4** team **6** league **10** conference
legend: **5** great
network: **4** ESPN
official: **3** ref, ump **5** judge, timer **6** umpire **7** referee
page item: **4** stat **5** recap, score
position: **5** coach **7** manager, trainer
rig, as a ~ event: **3** fix
schedule word: **4** away, home
shoe attachment: **5** cleat
show feature: **5** slo-mo **6** replay
surprise: **5** upset
tally: **5** point
team: **5** squad
unguarded, in ~: **4** open
violation: **4** foul
sports —: **3** bar, car **6** jacket
Sports —: **6** Afield
Sports Arena team: **3** USC
sports car: **3** GTI, GTO, Jag **4** auto **5** Miata, 'Vette **6** Camaro, Jaguar **7** Mustang **8** Corvette **10** automobile
noseguard: **3** bra
org.: **4** IMSA
sportscaster
hockey ~ cry: **5** score
need: **4** mike
shout: **3** yes
SportsCenter network: **4** ESPN
Sports Challenge: **8** game show
host: Dick Enberg
sportsman: **6** hunter
sportsmanly: **4** fair **5** clean
sportsmanship: **7** honesty **8** courtesy, fairness, fair play, goodwill **9** integrity
Sportsman's Sketches, A
author: Ivan Turgenev
sports medicine: **7** science
sportswear: **7** clothes
label: **4** Izod
sporty: **5** natty, sleek, swank **6** dapper, jaunty, rakish, snazzy, spiffy, swanky **7** dashing, raffish
spot: **2** ad **3** dab, dot, fix, jam, job, jot, nip, pad, see, spy **4** blob, blot, blur, daub, drop, espy, find, flaw, hole, iota, look, lump, mark, mess, post, seat, site, slot, soil, view **5** berth, catch, dirty, drink, fleck, joint, light, lobby, locus, odium, patch, pinch, place, point, scene, sight, space, speck, stain, sully, taint, trace, track, where **6** billet, blotch, cavern, crud up, dapple, descry, detect, dollop, little, locale, locate, lounge, notice, pepper, pickle, plight, random, scrape, sector, smudge, splash, stigma, streak, stripe, turn up **7** blemish, dilemma, discern, freckle, glimpse, hangout, lentigo, look out, make out, observe, pick out, quarter, section, smidgen, smidgin, spatter, speckle, splotch, station, stipple, tarnish, trouble **8** besmirch, diagnose, discover, flyspeck, identify, locality, location, meet with, molecule, particle, perceive, pinpoint, point out, position, quandary, smidgeon, sprinkle **9** bespatter, encounter, ferret out, lay eyes on, light upon, little bit, nightclub, recognize, situation **10** connection, difficulty, imputation
combining form: **5** macul- **6** maculi-, maculo-
ender: **3** lit **5** light
starter: **3** eye, hot, sun **5** night
spot —: **4** news **5** check, of tea, price
spot-—: **4** weld **5** check
— **spot:** **3** hot, in a **4** soft, warm **5** black, blind, on the, sweet, tight **6** beauty **7** trouble
Spot: **3** dog
owner: **4** Dick, Jane
spotless: **4** neat, pure **5** blank, clean, snowy **6** chaste, decent, modest, virgin, washed **7** shining **8** flawless, gleaming, hygienic, innocent, pristine, sanitary, unsoiled, virginal, virtuous **9** blameless, faultless, guiltless, laundered, lily-white, stainless, undefiled, unspoiled, unstained, unsullied, untouched **10** immaculate, inculcable, unpolluted
spotlight: **4** fame **5** stage **6** accent, play up, stress **7** feature, point up **8** interest, showcase **9** attention, emphasize, notoriety, public eye, publicity, publicize, punctuate, underline **10** accentuate, illuminate, illustrate, underscore
filter: **3** gel
in the ~: **5** famed, noted **6** famous **7** eminent
— **Spot run:** **3** See
spots
fix some bare ~: **5** resod
hit the high ~: **4** skim **5** recap **8** simplify **9** summarize
hit the low ~: **4** slum
mark with ~: **6** dapple
spotted: **4** pied **5** dirty **6** calico, flecky **7** flecked, mottled, unclean **8** brindled, maculate, speckled
animal: **4** fawn, paca **5** civet, genet, ounce **6** jaguar, ocelot
horse: **5** paint, pinto
spotted —: **3** owl
spotter: **3** spy **5** scout, spier **7** lookout
Spottiswoode: **5** Roger
spotty: **4** thin **5** scant **6** patchy, pimply, random, scanty, skimpy, uneven **7** blotchy, erratic, unequal **8** on-and-off, periodic, speckled, sporadic **9** desultory, irregular, piecemeal, scattered, spasmodic, vagarious **10** flickering, sporadical, unfrequent
spousal: **6** bridal, wedded **7** marital, nuptial
spouse: **3** man **4** male, mate, wife **5** bride, groom, hubby, woman **6** missis, missus, mister **7** consort, husband, partner **8** helpmate **9** companion **10** better half, bridegroom
family member: **5** in-law
former ~: **2** ex
spouseless: **5** unwed **6** single **9** unmarried **10** unattached
spouse-to-be: **6** fiancé **7** fiancée
spout: **3** jet, lip, run, tap, yak **4** brag, emit, go on, gush, pipe, pour, rant, talk, vent, yell **5** boast, eject, erupt, expel, exude, orate, speak, spiel, spile, spill, spirt, spray, spurt, surge **6** effuse, nozzle, outlet, patter, ramble, squirt, stream **7** cascade, chatter, conduit, declaim, lecture, opening **8** bloviate, fountain, harangue, overflow, proclaim, ramble on, water jet **9** discharge, expatiate, go on and on, hold forth, sermonize, waterfall
as a whale: **4** blow
geothermal ~: **6** geyser
starter: **4** down, rain **5** water
spout —: **3** off
— **spout:** **4** eave **5** eaves
spouted vessel: **3** jug **7** pitcher
spouting: **5** agush **8** harangue
spr.
see spring
— **Sprach Zarathustra:** **4** Also
Spradlin: **2** G.D.
sprain: **4** pull, turn **5** twist **6** injury, strain, wrench
site: **5** ankle, wrist
soother: **3** ice **6** arnica, ice bag **7** ice pack
sprat: **4** fish **7** herring, sardine **8** brisling
Sprat, Jack
diet: **4** lean
no-no: **3** fat
Sprat, Mrs.
diet: **3** fat
no-no: **4** lean
sprawl: **3** lie, sit **4** flop, loll, trip **5** drape, plump, slump **6** extend, lounge, ramble, slouch, spread, tumble **7** recline, stretch **8** straddle, straggle **9** spread out
— **sprawl:** **5** urban
sprawling: **9** recumbent
spray: **3** fog, wet **4** dust, foam, limb, mist, slop **5** froth, smear, spill, spout, sprig, spume, throw, water **6** dampen, shower, splash, spread, spritz, squirt **7** aerosol, atomize, bouquet, corsage, diffuse, drizzle, moisten, scatter, spatter **8** atomizer, dispense, droplets, hose down, irrigate, sprinkle **9** spindrift, sprinkler, vaporizer **10** sprinkling
banned ~: **3** DDT **4** Alar
defensive ~: **4** mace
fine ~: **4** mist
garden ~: **6** fogger
ocean ~: **4** foam, surf, wave **5** froth, spume **8** breakers **9** spindrift
plane ~: **6** deicer
small ~: **5** sprig
starter: **4** hair
spray —: **3** can, gun **5** paint
— **spray:** **4** hair **5** nasal
Spray —: **5** 'N Wash
— **Spray:** **5** Ocean
spread: **3** jam, lay, lie, rub, run, sow, wax **4** cast, coat, daub, farm, flow, grow, luau, meal, oleo, open, part, show, size, soil, span, spew, spue **5** array, bloat, cover, feast, flare, jelly, level, lunch, quilt, ranch, range, reach, relay, rub on, scale, scope, smear, space, splay, split, spray, strew, sweep, table, tract, widen, width **6** branch, butter, dilate, estate, expand, extend, extent, fan out, layout, lekvar, period, ramble, regale, splash, sprawl, uncoil, unfold, unfurl, unroll, unwind **7** arrange, banquet, bestrew, blanket, blowout, breadth, broaden, burgeon, compass, develop, deviate, diffuse, display, diverge, enlarge, even out, expanse, flatten, open out, overlay, pervade, publish, radiate, roll out, scatter, slather, stretch, suffuse, untwist **8** bedcover, bourgeon, covering, dilation, disperse, distance, escalate, heighten, increase, latitude, lengthen, multiply, mushroom, overgrow, proclaim, separate, smooth on, straggle, transmit, widening **9** advertise, bifurcate, branch off, broadcast, circulate, collation, comforter, diffusion, dispersal, expansion, extension, largeness, make known, margarine, marmalade, preserves, profusion, propagate, publicity, publicize, radiation, suffusion **10** dispersion, distribute, escalation, make public, outstretch, plantation, popularize, promulgate, tablecloth
around: **5** share, strew
bread ~: **3** jam **4** mayo, oleo **5** jelly **6** butter **7** ketchup, mustard
cracker ~: **4** Brie, pâté
ender: **5** sheet
fancy ~: **3** roe **6** caviar **7** caviare
for drying: **3** ted
lie ~ out: **4** flop, loll **5** slump **6** lounge, slouch, sprawl **7** stretch
like wildfire: **7** overrun

nondairy ~: **4** oleo
on: **5** apply
out: **3** fan **4** open, sown **5** add to, flare, roomy, widen **6** effuse, expand, extend, open up, sprawl, uncoil, uncurl, unfold, unfurl **7** augment, broaden, diffuse, enlarge, flatten, radiate, stretch **8** extended, rambling **9** diversify
over: **5** cover, smear **7** blanket, overrun, swaddle
quickly: **8** mushroom
rumors: **3** pan **4** blab, slam, slur, talk **5** libel, smear, sully, taint **6** defame, gossip, malign, tattle, vilify **7** asperse, slander, tarnish, traduce **8** backbite, badmouth, besmirch **9** denigrate, discredit, disparage **10** calumniate, scandalize, stigmatize, throw mud at, vituperate
starter: **3** bed **4** wide, wing
thickly: **7** plaster, slather
thin: **6** sparse
through: **7** pervade **8** permeate
spread __: **5** eagle
__ spread: **5** photo, point
__ Spread: **6** Shedd's
spread-eagle: **8** boastful, rambling **9** bombastic
lie ~: **6** sprawl
spreader: **5** knife
__ spreader: **4** salt **6** butter
spreading: **5** viral **7** rampant **8** rambling **9** epizootic **10** contagious, infectious
tree: **6** banian, banyan **8** chestnut
spread oneself __: **4** thin
spread-out: **4** vast, wide
spreadsheet
abbr.: **3** YTD
material: **4** data **6** number
pro: **3** CPA
shortcut: **5** macro
software: **5** Excel, Lotus
unit: **3** row **4** cell **6** column
Sprechen __ deutsch?: **3** sie
spree: **3** jag, rip **4** ball, bash, bust, lark, romp, tear, toot **5** binge, caper, fling, party, revel **6** bender, frolic, gambol, junket **7** blowout, rampage, revelry, splurge **8** field day, jamboree, wild time, wingding **9** carousing, high jinks
go on a ~: **5** revel, spend **7** carouse
Spree
city on the ~: **6** Berlin
sprig: **3** boy, kid, lad **4** cion, heir, limb, twig, wand **5** scion, shoot, spray, youth **6** branch **7** cutting **8** half-pint, juvenile **9** youngster
sprightliness: **4** dash, élan, jazz **6** energy, esprit, spirit **8** vitality, vivacity **9** animation, briskness **10** get up and go
sprightly: **3** fun, gay **4** airy, busy, good, keen, pert, racy, spry **5** agile, alert, alive, astir, brisk, elfin, fresh, hyper, jolly, light, peppy, perky, quick, saucy, smart, zappy, zingy, zippy **6** active, blithe, bouncy, breezy, bright, cheery, chirpy, clever, dapper, jaunty, joyous, lively, nimble, snappy **7** animate, chipper, dashing, dynamic, playful, working, zinging **8** animated, bustling, cheerful, grooving, spirited, sporting, sportive **9** assiduous, energetic, exuberant, facetious, fairylike, vivacious **10** frolicsome, keen-witted, rollicking
spring: **3** fly, hop, jog, lop, spa **4** bolt, buck, coil, come, flow, free, grow, gush, jump, leap, limb, rise, root, save, skip, stem, tide, trip, well **5** arise, begin, birth, bound, cause, fount, hatch, issue, let go, lunge, pop up, prime, shoot, speed, start, vault **6** appear, arrive, bounce, derive, emerge, gambol, geyser, hurdle, motive, origin, pardon, pounce, prance, reason, recoil, rescue, season, source, sprout, whence **7** absolve, budding, budtime, burgeon, come out, descend, develop, emanate, genesis, impetus, proceed, rebound, release, shoot up, skitter **8** bourgeon, buoyance, buoyancy, commence, flow from, fountain, mushroom, seedtime **9** beginning, flowering, originate, reservoir **10** bounciness, elasticity, hippety hop, resilience
acrobatic ~: **5** nip-up
back: **6** bounce, recoil **7** rebound
chicken: **5** youth **9** youngster
combining form: **4** cren- **5** creno-
ender: **4** buck, halt, hare, head, tail, tide, time, wood **5** board, house
for: **5** spend, treat **8** squander **9** entertain **10** recompense
(for): **3** pay
(from): **4** come, rise **5** arise **6** result **7** proceed
from a ~: **6** fontal
harbinger: **5** robin
having ~ fever: **6** draggy **7** languid **8** sluggish **9** lethargic
hot ~: **3** spa **6** geyser, resort
like ~ flowers: **6** abloom
month: **3** May **4** June **5** April, March
nymph: **5** naiad
observance: **4** Lent **5** Pasch, seder **6** Easter **8** Passover
of ~: **6** vernal
opposite: **4** fall, neap **6** autumn
ready to ~: **6** coiled
sign: **3** bud **4** thaw **5** Aries **6** Gemini, Taurus
something on: **7** startle **8** surprise
sound: **5** boing
starter: **3** bed, off **4** hair, hand, head, main, well **5** inner
to mind: **5** occur
up: **5** arise, shoot **6** appear, emerge **8** mushroom, take root
spring __: **3** for **4** lamb, roll, tide **5** a leak, break, fever **7** chicken, equinox
__ spring: **3** air, box, hot **7** mineral, thermal
Spring: **8** Byington
Spring __; fall back: **5** ahead **7** forward
__ Spring: **6** Silent
spring-ahead setting: **3** DST
springboard, use a: **4** dive **5** vault
springbok: **6** animal **8** antelope
relative: *see* antelope
spring-break time: **6** Easter
Spring Collection
author: Judith Krantz
springe: **4** trap
springer: **3** dog **5** canid **6** canine **7** spaniel
Springer: **5** Jerry
Springfield: **4** city, Rick, town **5** Dusty, rifle
county: **8** Sangamon
locale: **4** Ohio **6** Oregon **8** Illinois, Missouri, Virginia
river: **8** Sangamon
__ Springfield: **7** Buffalo
Springfield, Dusty
song: I Only Want to Be With You (1964)
Son-of-a Preacher Man (1968)
Wishin' and Hopin' (1964)
You Don't Have to Say You Love Me (1966)
Springfield, Rick
song: Affair of the Heart (1983)
Don't Talk to Strangers (1982)
I've Done Everything for You (1981)
Jessie's Girl (1981)
Love Somebody (1984)
springiness, show: **4** flex, give
Spring is like a perhaps hand: **4** poem
author: e.e. cummings
springlike: **4** mild **5** leafy **6** vernal
name meaning ~: **6** Vernon
springs
warm ~: **7** thermae
__ Springs: **4** Palm **5** Alice, Coral **6** Tarpon
__ springs eternal: **4** Hope
__ Springs National Park: **3** Hot
Spring Sonata
composer: Ludwig van Beethoven
Springsteen, Bruce
nickname: The Boss
song: Better Days (1992)
Born in the U.S.A. (1984)
Born to Run (1975)
Brilliant Disguise (1987)
Cover Me (1984)
Dancing in the Dark (1984)
Fade Away (1981)
Glory Days (1985)
Human Touch (1992)
Hungry Heart (1980)
I'm Goin' Down (1985)
I'm on Fire (1985)
My Hometown (1985)
One Step Up (1988)
Prove It All Night (1978)
Secret Garden (1997)
Streets of Philadelphia (1994)
Tunnel of Love (1987)
War (1986)
spouse: Julianne Phillips
Spring Symphony
composer: Benjamin Britten
spring training
locale: **7** Arizona, Florida
springy: **5** agile **6** bouncy, limber, lissom, spongy, supple **7** buoyant, elastic, lissome, pliable **8** flexible, stretchy, yielding **9** resilient
sprinkle: **3** dot, wet **4** dash, drip, dust, mist, rain, shed, spit, spot, stud **5** bedew, shake, spill, spray, strew, throw, water **6** dampen, dragée, dredge, pepper, powder, shower, splash, spritz, squirt **7** asperse, baptize, bestrew, drizzle, moisten, radiate, scatter, spatter, speckle **8** christen, humidify, irrigate **9** punctuate
with: **5** admix
sprinkled: **8** speckled
in heraldry: **4** semé
sprinkler: **5** spray
sprinkling: **3** bit, few **4** dash, dust, hint **5** spray, taste, tinge, touch, trace **6** strain **7** dusting, handful, mixture, several **8** spoonful **9** admixture, powdering
sprint: **3** run **4** dart, dash, race, rush, tear, whiz **5** scoot, spank **6** gallop, hasten, scurry, streak **7** scamper
__ sprint: **4** wind
Sprint: **3** car, Geo **4** auto **10** automobile
competitor: **3** MCI
sprinter: **4** Tyus **5** Flo-Jo, Hayes, Lewis, loper, Owens, racer **6** Devers, runner **7** Ashford, Rudolph **8** Bob Hayes **9** Carl Lewis **10** Gail Devers, Jesse Owens, Wyomia Tyus
event: **4** dash
goal: **4** tape
need: **5** speed
path: **4** lane
problem: **3** mud
prop: **5** block
sprit: **4** pole, spar
ender: **4** sail
starter: **3** bow
sprite: **3** elf, fay, imp, Mab, nix **4** nixy, peri, pixy, Puck **5** Ariel, faery, fairy, gnome, nisse, nixie, nymph, pixie, pooka, sylph **6** faerie, goblin, kelpie, kobold, Oberon, spirit **7** brownie, gremlin, Titania **9** hobgoblin **10** leprechaun, Tinker Bell
Sprite: **9** soft drink
alternative: *see* soft drink
spritelike: **5** elfin
spritely: **6** elfish, elvish
spritz: **4** spew, spue **5** spirt, spray, spurt **6** squirt **8** sprinkle, water jet
spritzer: **5** drink **8** beverage
ingredient: **4** soda, wine
sprocket: **4** gear **5** tooth
sprout: **3** boy, bud **4** cion, grow, push **5** bloom, plant, scion, shoot, spear, spire **6** emerge, spring **7** burgeon, develop, shoot up **8** bourgeon, mushroom, offshoot, take root, vegetate **9** germinate **10** effloresce
sprouting: **5** green **6** growth
__ sprouts: **4** bean
spruce: **4** neat, tidy, tree, trim **5** clean, color, crisp, dandy, kempt, natty, nifty, smart **6** classy, dapper, neaten, spiffy **7** elegant, groomed, orderly, stylish **8** well-kept **9** evergreen, refurbish, shipshape **10** fastidious, neat as a pin, rejuvenate
family: **4** pine
genus: **5** picea
in Britain: **4** trig
relative: **3** fir **7** hemlock **8** tamarack
up: **3** fix **4** tidy, trim, wash **5** adorn, brush, clean, groom, primp, prink, renew, sleek, slick, spiff **6** better, enrich, neaten, polish, reform **7** arrange, deck out,

enhance, freshen, furbish, garnish, sharpen, smarten **8** decorate, emblazon, ornament, renovate **9** embellish, meliorate, refurbish **10** ameliorate, rejuvenate
__ spruce: **5** Sitka
spruced up: **4** neat
Spruce Goose: **5** plane **8** airplane
builder: Howard Hughes
sprung: **5** let go **6** arisen
spry: **4** busy, pert, wiry **5** agile, alert, alive, astir, brisk, fleet, fresh, lithe, peppy, perky, quick, ready, sound, zippy **6** active, adroit, dapper, frisky, limber, lively, nimble, prompt, robust, supple **7** chipper, dynamic, healthy, on the go, rocking, working **8** animated, bustling, spirited, vigorous **9** assiduous, energetic, lightsome, lithesome, sprightly, vivacious **10** frolicsome, full of life
spud: **4** pipe **5** Idaho, tater, tuber **6** potato
bud: **3** eye
covering: **4** skin
state: **5** Idaho
spumante: **4** wine **7** Italian
__ spumante: **4** Asti
spume: **4** foam, spew, spue, surf **5** froth, spray **6** lather **7** sea foam **9** spindrift **10** effervesce
spumoni: **7** dessert **8** ice cream
alternative: **6** gelati, gelato, sundae **7** parfait, tortoni **8** snowball
spumy: **5** barmy
spun
out: **4** long
starter: **4** home
wool: **4** yarn
spun __: **4** silk, yarn **5** glass, rayon, sugar
__-spun: **4** fine, hard
spunk: **4** élan, grit, guts, push **5** drive, heart, moxie, nerve, pluck, valor **6** daring, hutzpa, mettle, spirit **7** bravado, bravery, chutzpa, courage, hutzpah, panache, prowess **8** audacity, backbone, chutzpah, gameness, gumption, tenacity, true grit, vitality **9** derring-do, endurance, fortitude, gutsiness, toughness **10** confidence, doggedness, feistiness, initiative, moral fiber, pluckiness, resolution
spunky: **4** bold, game **5** gutsy, nervy **6** awless, daring, feisty, gritty, heroic, plucky **7** aweless, defiant, doughty, gallant, staunch, valiant **8** fearless, heroical, intrepid, resolute, spirited, stalwart, unafraid, valorous **9** audacious, dauntless, dreadless, undaunted, unfearful **10** courageous, mettlesome, undismayed, unflagging
spur: **4** abet, barb, goad, limb, prod, push, stir, urge **5** drive, egg on, favor, goose, hop up, impel, key up, liven, pique, press, prick, prong, rally, rouse, spark **6** arouse, awaken, exhort, fillip, fire up, foment, incite, induce, motive, needle, prompt, propel, siding, stir up, turn on, urge on, whip up, work up **7** actuate, animate, impetus, impulse, inspire, provoke, put up to, quicken, trigger **8** catalyst, embolden, excitant, imbolden, motivate, offshoot, stimulus **9** actuation, encourage, galvanize, impassion, incentive, instigate, spearhead, stimulate **10** activation, incitement, inducement, motivation, projection, prominence
attachment: **5** rowel
on the ~ of the moment: **5** ad-lib **6** rashly **7** brashly, hastily, offhand **8** abruptly, headlong, pellmell, suddenly **9** headfirst, offhanded, unplanned
rocky ~: **5** arête
sporter: **4** boot
starter: **4** lark, long, sand
spur-__-moment: **5** of-the
spurious: **3** bum **4** bent, fake, mock, sham **5** bogus, dummy, faked, false, phony, put-on **6** ersatz, forged, framed, phoney, pirate, pseudo, unreal, untrue **7** assumed, feigned, pretend **8** affected, delusive, specious **9** contrived, deceitful, deceptive, erroneous, imitation, pretended, simulated, synthetic, unfounded, ungenuine **10** apocryphal, artificial, fabricated, fallacious, fictitious, fraudulent, mendacious, misleading, substitute, unverified
spurn: **3** cut, nix **4** defy, drop, dump, gibe, jeer, jibe, jilt, mock, shun, slam, slur, snub, veto **5** abuse, decry, flout, flush, libel, repel, scoff, scorn, sneer, taunt **6** bounce, defame, deride, dump on, heckle, ignore, impugn, loathe, malign, offend, pass by, pass on, pass up, rebuff, refuse, reject, slight, vilify **7** abstain, affront, asperse, blow off, boycott, contemn, decline, degrade, despise, disdain, dismiss, exclude, forsake, let go of, neglect, put down, rank out, repulse, slander, sneer at, traduce **8** belittle, brush off, denounce, disallow, forswear, keep from, renounce, ridicule, sneeze at, turn away, turn back, turn down, vilipend **9** blackball, cast aside, denigrate, discredit, disparage, disregard, foreswear, humiliate, rejection, reprobate, repudiate **10** calumniate, contravene, disapprove, disrespect, look down on, steer clear
Spurs: **4** five, team
former org.: **3** ABA
home: **10** San Antonio
org.: **3** NBA
rival: *see* NBA team
sport: **10** basketball
spurt: **3** fit, jet, run **4** boom, flow, gush, jump, ooze, rush, spew, spue, wash **5** erupt, issue, shoot, spasm, spate, spill, spout, surge **6** access, effuse, emerge, flurry, geyser, spritz, squirt, stream **7** flow out, outpour, pour out **8** effusion, eruption, fountain, outburst, overflow, shoot out **9** commotion, discharge, explosion **10** accelerate, outpouring
speed ~: **5** burst
__ Spur, The: **5** Naked
Sputnik (1958 film)
cast: Mischa Auer
sputter: **4** spit **6** fizzle, mutter, sizzle **7** stammer, stutter
Spuyten __ Creek: **6** Duyvil
spy: **3** pry, see **4** Berg, Bond, Hale, Helm, look, mole, peek, peep, peer, Solo, spot, tail, view **5** agent, plant, recon, scout, snoop, trail, watch **6** detect, meddle, notice, patrol, peeper, Philby, regard, search, shadow, sleuth, Smiley, take in **7** examine, eyeball, fish out, glimpse, Harriet, look for, lookout, Moe Berg, observe, ransack, sleeper, spotter, watcher **8** CIA agent, come upon, discover, emissary, informer, Mata Hari, Matt Helm, observer, smell out, stake out, take note **9** detective, eavesdrop, James Bond, lay eyes on, operative, set eyes on **10** get a load of, Nick Carter, scrutinize, sneak a look
Biblical ~: **5** Caleb
device: **3** bug
disguise: **5** cover
ender: **5** glass **6** master
fictional ~: **4** Bond, Helm, Solo **6** Smiley **8** Matt Helm **9** James Bond
first name in ~ stories: **3** Ian
in the sky: **5** AWACS
Japanese ~: **5** ninja
kind of ~: **4** mole **5** ninja, plant
name: **4** Hari, Mata
on: **3** bug **4** case, tail **5** snoop, trail, watch **6** follow, shadow **7** observe, surveil **8** check out, stake out
org.: **3** CIA, KGB, NSA, ONI
Revolutionary War ~: **4** Hale **5** André
starter: **7** counter
upon: **5** watch
work: **5** recon
writing: **4** code **10** cryptogram
Spy __: **4** Hard, Kids
__ Spy, A: **7** Perfect
Spybey: **4** Dina
Spyder: **3** car **4** auto **6** Toyota
spyglass part: **4** lens
Spy Hard (1996 film)
cast: Charles Durning, Marcia Gay Harden, Leslie Nielsen, Nicollette Sheridan
spying: **9** espionage **10** undercover
Spy in the House of Love, A
author: Anaïs Nin
Spy Kids (2001 film)
cast: Antonio Banderas, Carla Gugino, Daryl Sabara, Alexa Vega
Spyri, Johanna: **5** Swiss **6** writer
work: Heidi
Spyro __: **4** Gyra
Spy, The
author: James Fenimore Cooper
Spy vs. Spy mag: **3** Mad
Spy Who Came in From the Cold, The: **4** film **5** novel
author: John le Carré
cast: Claire Bloom, Richard Burton, Oskar Werner
director: Martin Ritt
Spy Who Loved Me, The: **4** film **5** novel
author: Ian Fleming
cast: Barbara Bach, Richard Kiel, Roger Moore
role: **4** Anya
squab: **4** bird **6** pigeon **7** hassock
squabble: **3** ado, row **4** feud, flap, fuss, rift, spat, tiff **5** argue, brawl, clash, fight, scene, scrap, set-to, words **6** barney, bicker, dustup, fracas, hassle, niggle, racket, rumpus, strife **7** dispute, fall out, quarrel, quibble, wrangle **8** argument, disagree, skirmish **9** bickering, encounter, have words, imbroglio **10** contention, difference
squad: **4** army, band, crew, gang, team, unit **5** corps, force, group, hands, party, troop **6** detail, outfit, troupe **7** brigade, company, platoon **8** division, regiment **9** battalion **10** detachment
squad __: **3** car
__ squad: **4** bomb, goon, riot, taxi
squad car device: **5** siren
squadron: **4** unit **5** corps, force **6** patrol **7** platoon
__ Squad, The: **3** Mod
squalid: **3** low **4** base, foul, mean, poor, ugly **5** dingy, dirty, fetid, grimy, mangy, nasty, seamy, seedy **6** filthy, foetid, horrid, impure, mangey, shabby, shoddy, sleazy, sloppy, soiled, sordid **7** decayed, ignoble, odorous, reeking, rundown, unclean, unkempt **8** gruesome, horrible, slovenly, untended, wretched **9** miserable, offensive, repellent, repulsive **10** abominable, broken-down, despicable, disgusting, disheveled, ramshackle
area: **3** sty **4** dump, slum **5** hovel **6** pigsty **8** cesspool, pesthole
squall: **4** gale, gust, wail, weep, wind, yowl **5** blast, furor, noser, storm **6** racket, tumult **7** tempest, turmoil **9** commotion, windstorm **10** hurly-burly, turbulence
starter: **4** rain
squalor: **6** misery **7** poverty **10** sordidness
squamous: **5** scaly
squander: **3** eat, sap **4** blow, burn, lose **5** drain, spend, trash, use up, waste **6** burn up, expend, frivol, lavish, misuse, put out, trifle **7** cash out, consume, deplete, exhaust, play out, scatter **8** fool away, misspend **9** dissipate, go through, spring for, throw away, while away **10** frivol away, gamble away, run through
squandered: **4** gone **7** all gone
squanderer: **7** wastrel **8** prodigal
square: **3** fit, fix, rig **4** area, boxy, even, fair, gybe, jibe, just, knot, nerd, park, true, unit **5** adapt, agree, align, aline, block, clear, court, dated, equal, frank, legit, level, match, moral, nerdy, pay up, plaza, power, right, shape, sharp, tally, unhip **6** accord, adjust, buy off, cohere, common, decent, even up, honest, isogon, pay off, reckon, settle, stuffy, trusty **7** balance, boxlike, clear up, comport, conform, ethical, factual, rectify, redress, satisfy, sincere, upright

8 balanced, check out, clear off, coincide, credible, equalize, multiply, orthodox, outdated, out-front, quadrate, regulate, straight, truthful, unbiased 9 do justice, equitable, four-sided, harmonize, impartial, ingenuous, liquidate, make sense, objective, out-of-date, outspoken, quadratic, reconcile, reimburse, uncolored, unfeigned, unslanted, veracious 10 aboveboard, button-down, correspond, equal-sided, evenhanded, forthright, fuddy-duddy, on-the-level, quadrangle, recompense, scrupulous
accounts: 5 repay 6 avenge
away: 5 ready 6 get set, settle 7 prepare 8 get ready
ceramic ~: 4 tile
coin: 6 klippe
column: 4 anta
footage: 4 area
from ~ one: 4 anew, over 5 again 6 afresh
game-board ~: 5 start
off: 3 war 4 feud, tilt 5 clash, fight, scrap, set-to 6 action, battle, combat, tussle 7 contend, contest, dispute 8 conflict, disagree, struggle 9 lock horns 10 engagement
off against: 4 face
one: 4 nerd 5 getgo, start 6 origin 9 beginning
setting: 4 town
starter: 4 four
town ~: 5 plaza 7 commons
up: 3 pay 5 repay 6 pay off, settle 7 pay back, satisfy 8 equalize, make good 9 reimburse
(with): 5 agree 7 conform
square __: 3 off, one 4 away, deal, foot, inch, knot, meal, mile, root, sail, yard 5 dance 7 dancing, shooter
square __ a round hole: 5 peg in
__ square: 3 cut, try 4 word 5 on the, out of
__ Square: 3 Red 4 Soho 5 Times
squared __: 6 circle
__-squared: 3 pi r
square dance: 7 hoedown
attire: 6 dirndl
call: 3 gee 6 do-si-do, sashay 7 dos-à-dos
dancer tie: 4 bolo
for 4 couples: 9 quadrille
group: 5 octad, octet 7 octette
instrument: 6 fiddle
official: 4 cuer 6 caller
partner: 3 gal, guy
site: 4 barn
Square Egg, The
author: Saki
squarely: 4 just 5 flush, right, sharp, smack, spang 9 precisely
Square Root of Wonderful, The
author: Carson McCullers
squares
one of three ~: 4 meal
set of ~: 4 grid
square-shooting: 6 candid, honest
squaretail: 4 fish
squaring the __: 6 circle
squarish: 4 boxy
squash: 3 jam 4 cram, game, kill, mash, pepo, pulp, push 5 crowd, crush, lie on, pound, press, quell, quiet, sit on, smash, spoil, sport, tread 6 bruise, cushaw, humble, stifle, veggie 7 deflate, depress, distort, flatten, put down, scrunch, squeeze, squelch, stamp on, trample, wedge in 8 compress, macerate, shut down, suppress 9 humiliate, vegetable 10 annihilate, extinguish
coat: 4 rind
court feature: 4 wall
kin: 5 gourd
shot: 5 carom 6 carrom
__ squash: 5 acorn, lemon
squashy: 4 soft 5 mushy
squat: 3 low, nil, sit, zip 4 boxy, nada, wide 5 broad, dumpy, heavy, hunch, lodge, perch, pudgy, roost, short, splay, stoop, thick, tubby, zilch 6 chunky, crouch, hunker, lie low, locate, naught, nought, remain, reside, settle, stocky, stubby 7 nothing, sojourn 8 entrench, heavyset, thickset 9 crouching 10 hunker down
__-squat: 6 diddly, doodly
squatness: 5 width
squatter: 7 pioneer 8 resident
squatty: 3 low 5 short
squawbush: 5 sumac 6 sumach
squawk: 3 caw, cry, yap 4 beef, crow, hoot, yaup, yell, yelp 5 croak, gripe, groan, noise, shout, sound, whine, whoop 6 cackle, grouse, holler, plaint, repine, shriek, squeal, yammer 7 grumble, protest, screech 8 complain 9 bellyache, complaint, grievance, make a fuss, raise Cain
squawk __: 3 box
squawking: 7 raucous 8 strident
Squaw Man, The (1931 film)
director: Cecil B. DeMille
squeak: 3 cry 4 pipe, talk, time, yelp 5 cheep, creak, sound, whine 6 shrill, squeal 7 screech
by: 6 scrape 7 nose out
fix a ~: 3 oil 6 grease 9 lubricate
past, in sports: 4 edge
squeaker: 3 rat 5 hinge, mouse
squeaky clean: 4 pure 6 chaste, honest 9 righteous
squeal: 3 rat, yip 4 blab, howl, rasp, talk, tell, wail, yell, yelp, yowl 5 bleat, cheep, creak, rat on, shout, spill 6 betray, holler, scream, shriek, shrill, snitch, squawk, squeak, tattle 7 protest, screech 8 complain, inform on 9 make a fuss 10 tattletale
comic-book ~: 3 eek
on: 6 turn in 7 sell out
squealer: 3 pig, rat 4 fink, nark 6 ratter 7 tattler 8 fat mouth, turncoat 10 taleteller, tattletale
squeamish: 4 prim, sick 5 dizzy, fussy, shaky, upset 6 prissy, queasy, queazy, sickly 7 finicky, mincing, prudish 8 delicate, finiking, finnicky, qualmish 9 disgusted, spineless, unsettled 10 fastidious, particular, scrupulous
squeegee: 3 mop 5 wiper
use a ~: 4 wipe
squeezable: 4 soft
squeeze: 3 hug, jam, nip, ram 4 clip, cram, grip, hold, mash, milk, pack, push, vise 5 bleed, choke, clasp, crowd, crush, force, pinch, press, quash, sqush, stuff, wedge, wring 6 clinch, clutch, crunch, eke out, enfold, extort, infold, insert, jostle, justle, lean on, pucker, racket, spoils, squash, squish, squush, strait, thrust, wrench 7 embrace, extract, oppress, problem, scrunch, squoosh, tighten, wedge in 8 compress, contract, pressure, throttle 9 constrict, extortion, handclasp, hold tight, influence, overcrowd, restraint, shake down 10 congestion, pressurize
by: 3 eke 4 edge
dry: 5 wring
ender: 3 box
in: 3 jam 4 tuck 7 bunch up 9 interject, overcrowd
out liquid: 6 squirt
put the ~ on: 5 force 6 coerce 7 oppress 8 pressure
together: 7 bunch up
squeeze __: 3 off, out 4 play 6 bottle 7 through
__ squeeze: 5 tight
squeezebox: 8 keyboard 9 accordion
Squeeze Box (1976 song)
artist: Who, The
squeezed: 6 juiced 7 crammed, crowded 9 compacted, condensed, jam-packed 10 compressed
__ squeeze play: 7 suicide
squeezer: 3 boa 6 python
squeezings: 5 juice
squelch: 3 gag, nix 4 halt, kill, stop 5 crush, quash, quiet, shush, sit on 6 censor, hush up, muffle, quench, refute, settle, squash, stifle, subdue, thwart 7 abolish, censure, oppress, repress, silence, smother 8 black out, restrain, stamp out, strangle, suppress 9 keep quiet 10 extinguish, keep in line
squib: 7 lampoon, lighter 9 promotion
news ~: 4 item
squid: 7 calamar, mollusc, mollusk 8 calamari
cousin: 7 octopus
weapon: 3 ink
Squier: 5 Billy
squiffed: 5 tipsy 6 blotto
squiggle: 4 curl, mark 6 scrawl, squirm
in a series: 5 comma
señor's ~: 5 tilde
squiggly: 4 wavy
squinch: 4 wink
squint: 4 leer, look, peek, peep, peer, skew, view, wink 6 glance 7 glimpse 8 lopsided
squint-__: 4 eyed
squire: 4 beau, date, gent, lead, rank 5 owner, serve 6 assist, attend, escort 7 step out 8 chaperon, courtier, landlord 9 accompany, chaperone, companion, landowner
squires: 6 gentry
squirm: 4 skew, toss, wind, worm 5 shift, twist 6 fidget, thrash, twitch, wiggle, writhe 7 agonize, wriggle 8 flounder, squiggle
squirrel: 5 xerus 6 animal, mammal, rodent, suslik 7 souslik 9 chickaree
abode: 4 tree
African ~: 5 xerus
away: 4 hide, save 5 amass, cache, hoard, put by, stash, store 6 pile up 7 deposit, harvest, reserve 8 conserve, put aside, set apart, set aside
ender: 4 fish
female: 3 doe
food: 3 nut 5 acorn
fur: 4 vair
ground ~: 6 gopher
male: 4 buck
noise: 7 chitter
relative: *see* rodent
young: 3 pup 6 kitten
squirrely: 4 daft
squirt: 3 boy, imp, jet 4 emit, flow, spew, spit, spue 5 child, eject, kiddy, spill, spirt, spout, spray, spurt, twerp, twirp 6 nobody, splash, spritz, stream 7 moisten, spatter 8 sprinkle, water jet 9 nonentity
gun: 3 toy
squirt __: 3 can, gun
squish: 3 jam 4 mash 5 crowd, crush, press, quash, smash 7 squeeze, wedge in
squishy: 3 wet 4 oozy, soft 5 downy, furry, mushy, nappy, plush 6 fleecy, fluffy, spongy 7 velvety 8 cushiony, yielding
toy: 4 Nerf
Sr: 4 elem. 7 element 9 strontium
38 for ~: 4 at. no.
Sri Lanka: 4 isle 6 Ceylon, island, nation 7 country
capital: 7 Colombo
deer: 4 axis 6 chital, sambar, sambur 7 sambhar, sambhur
export: 3 tea 5 pekoe
fish: 5 danio
language: 5 Tamil 10 Singhalese
money: 4 cent 5 rupee
neighbor: 5 India
people: 5 Tamil, Vedda 6 Veddah
port: 5 Galle 7 Colombo
primate: 5 lemur, loris
temple city: 5 Kandy
wood: 5 ebony
SRO: 7 crowded 9 chock-full
show: 3 hit 5 smash
SS: 3 pos.
he plays behind the ~: 2 LF
see also shortstop
S.S.: 7 McClure, Van Dine
SSA part: 3 Sec., Soc. 5 Admin. 6 Social 8 Security
SSE: 3 dir., hdg.
opposite: 3 NNW
SSgt.: 3 NCO 7 officer
employer: 4 USAF
s-shaped: 5 curvy, snaky 6 curved, curvey
curve: 4 ogee
SSN: 2 ID
part: 3 Soc. 6 Number, Social 8 Security
SSR
former ~: 6 Latvia 7 Estonia, Ukraine 9 Lithuania
part of ~: 6 Soviet 8 Republic 9 Socialist
SSS
classification: 4 one A
concern: 5 draft

part: 3 Sys. 4 Syst. 6 System 7 Service 9 Selective
SST: 3 jet 7 Tupolev 8 aircraft, Concorde
crossing: 3 Atl. 8 Atlantic
go by ~: 3 fly 6 aviate
part of ~: 5 sonic, super 9 transport
term: 4 Mach
SSW: 3 dir., hdg.
opposite: 3 NNE
st.
see street
St.
see Saint
St. __: 4 Ives, Paul 5 Croix
St. __ and Miquelon: 6 Pierre
St. __ Blues: 5 Louis
St. __-bread: 5 John's
St. __ College: 4 Olaf
St. __ cross: 7 Andrew's
St. __ Day: 5 John's
St. __ Eve: 5 John's
St. __ fire: 5 Elmo's
St. __ Island: 6 Simons
St. __-l'École: 3 Cyr
St. __ Mountains: 5 Elias
St. __-Nevis: 5 Kitts
St. __ Palace: 6 James's
St. __ Square: 6 Peter's
St.-__: 4 Malo
sta.
see station
Sta-__: 3 Flo, Puf
stab: 3 cut, jab, ram, try 4 ache, blow, chop, clip, gash, gore, hurt, pang, plow, poke, shot, sink 5 brand, carve, crack, drive, fling, guess, knife, lance, lunge, prick, saber, shank, slice, spear, stick, whack, whirl, wound 6 chance, cleave, effort, empale, gamble, impale, injure, open up, pierce, plunge, skewer, thrust, twinge 7 attempt, bayonet, venture 8 endeavor, incision, lacerate, piercing, puncture 9 penetrate, perforate, wild guess 10 laceration
in the back: 4 sell 5 cross 6 betray 7 sell out 9 duplicity, treachery
starter: 4 back
take a ~ at: 3 try 5 essay, guess 7 attempt, venture 8 theorize 10 conjecture
Stabat __: 5 Mater
stabber: 5 prong
stabbing: 5 sharp 8 piercing
stabile: 5 fixed 6 steady 10 unchanging
coiner: 3 Arp
Stabile: 2 Ed
stability: 5 poise 6 aplomb, fixity, sanity, wisdom 7 balance, support 8 backbone, cohesion, firmness, maturity, security, solidity, strength 9 adherence, assurance, composure, constancy, endurance, equipoise, fixedness, integrity, solidness, soundness, toughness 10 continuity, durability, permanence, perpetuity, sedateness, steadiness
period of ~: 3 pax
stabilize: 3 fix, set 4 bolt, even, firm, prop, trim 5 brace, poise 6 anchor, fasten, firm up, fixate, freeze, ossify, secure, settle, steady, uphold 7 balance, stiffen, support, sustain 8 buttress, equalize, maintain, preserve 9 establish
stabilizer: 4 gyro
combining form: 4 -stat
food ~: 4 agar 8 agar-agar
nautical ~: 7 ballast
plane ~: 3 fin
sailboat ~: 4 keel
surfboard ~: 4 skeg
stabilizer __: 3 bar
stable: 3 set 4 calm, even, fast, firm, good, sure 5 fixed, level, quiet, solid, sound, stout, tight 6 manger, nailed, poised, rooted, secure, smooth, static, steady, strong, sturdy 7 abiding, durable, equable, lasting, settled, staunch, uniform 8 anchored, balanced, constant, definite, enduring, ironclad, long-term, rational, reliable, resolute, stalwart, together 9 immutable, permanent, resistant, steadfast, temperate, unvarying, well-built 10 deep-rooted, dependable, invariable, motionless, stationary, staying put, unchanging, unwavering
area: 4 mews
baby: 4 colt, foal 5 filly
bed: 5 straw
hand: 5 groom, shoer
noise: 4 clop 5 neigh, snort
parent: 3 dam 4 mare, sire
sustenance: 4 feed, oats
unit: 5 stall
worker of India: 4 sice, syce 5 saice
see also horse
__ stable: 6 livery
stableboy: 5 groom 6 lackey 7 lacquey
play about a ~: 5 Equus
Stabler, Ken: 2 QB 5 Snake
__ stables: 6 Augean
staccato: 8 detached
mark: 3 dot
not ~: 6 legato
Stacey: 4 Dash
stack: 3 lot 4 bank, heap, hill, keep, load, mass, pack, pile 5 amass, bunch, drift, hoard, mound, sheaf 6 bank up, bundle, heap up, pileup 7 chimney, pyramid 8 hold on to, mountain 9 great deal, multitude, profusion, stockpile 10 accumulate, collection, cumulation
blow one's ~: 4 rant 6 seethe 7 flare up, flip out
material: 3 hay
starter: 3 hay 5 smoke
the deck: 5 cheat 9 victimize
up: 4 rise, test 5 total 6 gather 7 compare 10 accumulate
up against: 5 equal, weigh
Stack, Robert: 5 actor
role: 4 Ness
TV: The Name of the Game, The Untouchables
stacks: 3 lot 4 lots 5 reams 6 myriad, plenty
frequent the ~: 4 read
stack-up: 8 accident
Stacy: 5 Keach 6 Hollis 8 Lattisaw
Stacy, Hollis: 6 golfer
Stade, Frederica von: 5 mezzo 6 singer 7 soprano
specialty: 5 opera
stadium: 4 bowl, park, ring 5 arena, field, venue 7 diamond 8 coliseum, gridiron 9 colosseum, gymnasium
cry: 3 rah, yay 6 charge
display: 4 wave
employee: 5 usher
feature: 4 dome, gate, loge, ramp, tier 5 level
football ~: 4 bowl
gofer: 6 bat boy
habitué: 3 fan
hoverer: 5 blimp
instrument: 5 organ
sound: 3 boo, rah 4 hiss, roar 5 chant, cheer 6 hoorah, hooray, hurrah, hurray
Stadler, Craig: 6 golfer, Walrus
stadt: 7 München 8 Nürnberg
Staël, Madame de: 6 French, writer
work: Corinne
Delphine
staff: 3 man, rod 4 cane, cast, club, crew, help, hire, mace, pole, prop, team, wand 5 aides, baton, cadre, court, crook, force, hands, stave, stick 6 agents, fasces 7 crosier, crozier, employe, faculty, scepter, support, workers 8 caduceus, deputies, employee, flagpole, legation, officers, servants, teachers 9 employees, entourage, personnel, retainers, truncheon, work force 10 alpenstock, assistants, operatives, shillelagh
ceremonial ~: 4 mace
cut: 3 RIF 6 layoff
figure: 4 clef, note 5 C clef, F clef, G clef
notation: 4 flat 5 sharp
officer: 4 aide 8 adjutant
of life: 5 bread 7 aliment
opening: 3 job 4 slot
shepherd ~: 5 crook
starter: 3 tip 4 flag, pike, wait 7 quarter
__ staff: 7 general
staffer: 4 aide 8 employee
nonpermanent ~: 4 temp
staff of __: 4 life
Stafford: 2 Jo 3 Jim 4 Jean, Repp 5 Terry 7 William
Stafford, Jean: 6 writer
work: The Catherine Wheel
A Winter's Tale
Stafford, Jim: 6 singer
song: Spiders & Snakes (1973)
Wildwood Weed (1974)
Staffordshire: 6 county
city: 7 Cannock
locale: 7 England
stag: 3 roe 4 buck, deer, hart, lone 5 alone, party 6 animal 8 dateless, solitary 10 unescorted
attendee: 2 he 3 man 4 male
ender: 5 hound
feature: 6 antler
mate: 3 doe 4 hind
stag __: 4 line
Stag at __, The: 3 Eve
stage: 3 lap, leg, set 4 give, node, pass, play, rung, show, step, stop, tier, time 5 arena, coach, drama, enact, frame, grade, level, mount, notch, phase, point, put on, round, scene, stand, venue 6 boards, degree, length, locale, moment, period, podium, status 7 arrange, execute, footing, landing, perform, plateau, present, process, produce, rostrum, scenery, setting, show biz, theater, theatre 8 bring out, Broadway, division, engineer, juncture, landmark, locality, organize, platform 9 gradation, limelight, situation, spotlight 10 footlights
alone on ~: 4 sola 5 solus
area: 3 pit 5 apron, riser, wings
award: 4 Obie, Tony
beginning: 4 Act I
center ~: 9 spotlight
curtain: 5 arras, scrim
direction: 4 exit 5 enter 6 exeunt
door symbol: 4 star
ender: 4 hand 5 coach, craft
extra: 4 supe
fill time on ~: 4 vamp
gear: 3 mic, set 4 mike, prop 5 decor
get ~ fright: 6 freeze
get off the ~: 4 exit
go on ~: 3 act 5 enter 7 perform
name: 5 alias
org.: 4 ANTA
represent on ~: 5 enact
seats near the ~: 4 row A, row B, row C
set the ~: 5 dress
setting: 5 scene
show: 4 play 5 drama, revue 6 review 10 production
signal: 3 cue
starter: 3 off 4 back, down 5 sound
success: 3 hit 5 smash
whisper: 5 aside 6 murmur
stage __: 3 set 4 door 6 fright 7 manager, setting, whisper
stage-__: 6 manage
stage-__ Johnny: 4 door
__ stage: 5 sound
Stagecoach (1939 film): 5 oater
cast: John Carradine, Andy Devine, Thomas Mitchell, Claire Trevor, John Wayne
director: John Ford
stagecoach puller: 4 team 5 horse
stagecraft: 6 acting
staged: 9 unnatural
Stage Door: 4 film, play
author: Edna Ferber, George S. Kaufman
cast: Katharine Hepburn, Adolphe Menjou, Ginger Rogers
stagehand: 4 crew, grip 6 flyman
concern: 3 set 4 prop
stage light: 4 spot 5 klieg
covering: 3 gel
stages, in: 9 gradually 10 step by step
Stage to Mesa City: 5 oater
Stagg: 4 Amos
stagger: 3 wow 4 jolt, reel, rock, stun, sway 5 amaze, floor, lurch, pitch, shake, shock, stump, waver 6 boggle, careen, dither, falter, linger, puzzle, teeter, topple, totter, wabble, wobble, zigzag 7 astound, founder, nonplus, overlap, perplex, shatter, stammer, startle, stumble, stupefy 8 astonish, bewilder, bowl over, confound, hesitate, surprise, unstring 9 alternate, devastate, dumbfound, overpower, overwhelm, take aback, vacillate

staggering: **3** big **4** vast **5** dizzy **6** untold **8** striking **9** marvelous, wonderful **10** formidable
Stagger Lee (1959 song)
artist: Lloyd Price
staghorn __: **4** fern
staging: **5** stand **10** production
staging __: **4** area, post
stagnant: **4** dull, foul, idle **5** dirty, inert, quiet, slack, stale, still **6** filthy, halted, in a rut, static, stuffy **7** odorous, passive **8** brackish, immobile, inactive, lifeless, listless, moribund, sluggish, unmoving **10** motionless, stationary
stagnate: **3** rot **4** drag, idle, rust **5** decay, stall **6** fester, stifle **7** decline, go stale **8** go to seed, languish, vegetate **9** hibernate, lie fallow **10** stand still
stagnation: **5** sloth, slump **6** acedia, torpor **7** inertia, languor **8** doldrums, idleness, laziness, otiosity **9** faineance, indolence, recession, torpidity **10** depression
sign of ~: **5** algae
__ St. Agnes, The: **5** Eve of
stagy: **5** hammy **8** affected, overdone **9** overacted, unnatural **10** histrionic, theatrical
Stahl: **4** John, Nick **6** Lesley
staid: **3** set **4** calm, cool **5** fixed, grave, sober, stoic **6** at ease, demure, formal, low-key, mellow, placid, sedate, serene, solemn, somber, steady, stodgy, stuffy **7** at peace, deadpan, earnest, relaxed, serious, settled, stoical, weighty **8** carefree, composed, decorous, laid-back, priggish, reserved, tranquil **9** collected, dignified, humorless, impassive, temperate, unamusing, unexcited, unruffled **10** nonchalant, no-nonsense, unagitated, unhumorous, untroubled
stain: **3** dye, mar, tar **4** blot, blur, daub, foul, mark, slur, soil, spot, tint, woad **5** brand, color, dirty, odium, paint, shade, shame, smear, speck, sully, taint, tinct, tinge **6** bedaub, befoul, blotch, crud up, damage, debase, defect, defile, embrue, finish, imbrue, malign, mottle, smirch, smudge, stigma **7** begrime, besmear, blacken, blemish, corrupt, debauch, deprave, pigment, pollute, spatter, splotch, tarnish, varnish **8** besmirch, black eye, coloring, discolor, disgrace, dishonor, impurity, infusion, maculate, reproach, tincture **10** demoralize, imputation, stigmatize
common ~: **3** ink **4** food **5** grass
driveway ~: **3** oil
escutcheon ~: **4** blot
lab ~: **5** eosin **6** eosine
starter: **4** tear **5** blood **7** counter
stained: **5** dirty, grimy, sooty **6** filthy, grubby, grungy **7** unclean **8** maculate, slovenly, vitiated **10** unsanitary
stained __: **5** glass
stainless: **4** pure **5** clean **6** chaste, washed **8** innocent, pristine, rustless, spotless, unsoiled **9** blameless, faultless, undefiled, unspoiled, unsullied **10** immaculate, impeccable, unpolluted
stainless steel: **5** alloy
component: **4** iron **8** chromium
stair: **4** step
alternative: **4** ramp **8** elevator **9** escalator
ender: **3** way **4** case, well
part: **4** rail, step **5** riser, tread
post: **5** newel
starter: **4** back
__ staircase: **6** moving, spiral
stairs
like some ~: **6** creaky
starter: **4** back, down
take the ~: **4** walk **5** climb
__ Stairsteps: **4** Five
__ Stair, The: **7** Winding
stairway: **6** flight
entrance ~: **5** stoop
moving ~: **9** escalator
section: **7** landing
Stairway to Heaven (song)
artist: Led Zeppelin, Neil Sedaka
Stairway to the __: **5** Stars
stake: **3** bet, peg, pot, rod, set **4** ante, back, fund, game, lend, loan, pale, play, pole, post, risk **5** award, claim, kitty, means, peril, prize, purse, put on, put up, share, spike, stave, stick, wager **6** chance, gamble, furnish, hazard, invest, marker, paling, picket, pledge, supply, timber **7** concern, delimit, finance, funding, imperil, present, provide, savings, sponsor, support, venture **8** bankroll, interest, make book **9** speculate, subsidize **10** capitalize, investment, jeopardize, underwrite
at ~: **6** risked **7** gambled, in peril **8** invested, involved **9** concerned, on the line **10** endangered, in jeopardy
ender: **3** out **6** holder
like a ~: **5** palar
out: **3** spy **4** mark **5** claim, spy on, watch **6** survey **7** surveil
put on a ~: **6** empale, impale
something to ~: **5** claim
starter: **4** grub
stake __: **3** out **4** race
stakeout: **5** vigil, watch
Stakeout (1987 film)
cast: Richard Dreyfuss, Emilio Estevez, Aidan Quinn, Madeleine Stowe
stakes: **4** pool **7** jackpot
pull up ~: **6** decamp
starter: **5** sweep
stakes __: **4** race
__ Stakes: **7** Belmont
staking starter: **4** pain
stalactite
form a ~: **4** drip
shape: **6** icicle
site: **4** cave **6** cavern
stalag
resident: **3** POW
Stalag 17 (1953 film)
cast: William Holden, Otto Preminger
director: Billy Wilder
role: **3** POW **6** Animal
stalagmite
form a ~: **4** drip
site: **4** cave **6** cavern
stale: **3** dry, old **4** arid, drab, dull, flat, hard, rank, weak, worn **5** banal, corny, dated, dried, faded, fetid, fuggy, fusty, hokey, musty, passé, rusty, tired, trite, vapid **6** cliché, common, foetid, frowsy, frowzy, jejune, old hat, rancid, smelly, spoilt, stuffy, watery **7** clichéd, decayed, fatuous, fogyish, humdrum, insipid, parched, prosaic, reeking, shrivel, spoiled, worn-out **8** bromidic, dried out, obsolete, outdated, outmoded, overused, shopworn, stagnant, stinking, timeworn, well-used, well-worn, zestless **9** hackneyed, out-of-date, played out, prosaical, tasteless **10** antiquated, dullsville, malodorous, threadbare, uninspired, unoriginal, yesterday's
ender: **4** mate
go ~: **3** rot **4** mold, rust, tire **5** decay **7** crumble **8** stagnate
stalemate: **3** tie **4** draw, game **5** delay, pause **6** arrest **7** impasse **8** cul-de-sac, deadlock, gridlock, standoff, tarrying **10** standstill
Stalin: **3** Red **6** Joseph **7** Russian
predecessor: **5** Lenin
realm: **4** USSR
stalk: **3** dog **4** axis, halm, hunt, pace, reed, stem, tail, walk **5** chase, haulm, haunt, hound, march, prowl, shaft, spike, spire, stick, straw, trace, track, trail, trunk **6** ambush, follow, pester, pursue, shadow, stride **7** bird-dog, pedicel, pedicle, support **8** approach, flush out **9** creep up on, track down
crunchy ~: **6** celery
food: **4** corn
grass ~: **4** reed
of bananas: **4** hand, stem
plant ~: **5** scape, stipe
remove a ~: **6** destem
starter: **3** eye **4** bean, corn, foot, leaf, root
__ stalk: **4** corn **6** celery
stalker: **6** hunter
starter: **4** deer
Stalker
author: Faye Kellerman
stalking-__: **5** horse
__ Stalkings: **4** Silk
stalks: **6** fodder
left after reaping: **4** halm **5** haulm
stalky: **4** slim **7** slender
stall: **3** die, lag **4** crib, halt, idle, laze, loaf, mart, slow, stay, stop, wait **5** amble, block, booth, brake, check, dally, delay, hedge, kiosk, mosey, stand, still, stimy, stymy, tarry **6** arrest, becalm, corral, dawdle, hamper, hinder, linger, loiter, market, put off, retard, stymie **7** buy time, cubicle, hold off, prolong, quibble, saunter, suspend **8** footdrag, kill time, lollygag, obstruct, postpone, pretense, shut down, slow down, stagnate, stand off, straggle **9** accessory, hem and haw, interrupt, stonewall, waste time **10** accomplice, dillydally, equivocate, filibuster, stand still
starter: **4** book, foot, head, whip
__ stall: **6** shower
stalled: **3** out **6** static **10** gridlocked, motionless
stalling, stop: **3** act **6** decide
stallion: **4** male, roan, sire **5** horse, mount **6** equine
future ~: **4** colt
mate: **4** mare
sound: **5** snort
stopper: **4** whoa
Stallion, The
author: Harold Robbins
__ Stallion, The: **5** Black
Stallone: **5** Frank **9** Sylvester
Stallone, Sylvester: **5** actor
film: Assassins (1995)
Cliffhanger (1993)
Cop Land (1997)
Demolition Man (1993)
First Blood (1982)
F.I.S.T. (1978)
Get Carter (2000)
The Lords of Flatbush (1974)
Nighthawks (1981)
Rambo (2008)
Rambo: First Blood Part II (1985)
Rambo III (1988)
Rocky (1976)
Rocky Balboa (2006)
Rocky II (1979)
The Specialist (1994)
film (voice): Antz (1998)
nickname: **3** Sly
spouse: Brigitte Nielsen
Stallworth, John
sport: **8** football
stalwart: **3** big, fit **4** bold, game, hale, iron, wiry **5** beefy, bound, brave, burly, gutsy, hardy, hefty, hunky, husky, lusty, nervy, solid, stout, tough **6** awless, brawny, daring, gritty, hearty, heroic, mighty, plucky, potent, robust, rugged, sinewy, spunky, stable, steely, stocky, strong, sturdy, virile **7** aweless, dead set, defiant, doughty, gallant, staunch, valiant **8** athletic, fearless, forceful, heroical, indurate, intrepid, muscular, powerful, puissant, resolute, unafraid, valorous, vigorous **9** Atlantean, audacious, dauntless, dreadless, Herculean, strapping, tenacious, undaunted, unfearful, unfearing, well-built **10** able-bodied, courageous, dependable, powerhouse, purposeful, red-blooded, undismayed
stalwartness: **4** grit, guts **5** valor **7** bravery
stamen: **5** organ
part: **6** anther
site: **6** flower
Stamford: **4** city, town
locale: **4** Conn.
stamin: **6** fabric **8** material
stamina: **3** vim, zip **4** dint, grit, guts, legs, thew **5** brawn, force, heart, might, moxie, power, thews, vigor **6** energy, mettle, muscle, starch **7** fitness, muscles, potence, potency, prowess **8** backbone, strength, vitality **9** beefiness, endurance, fortitude, gutsiness, hardiness, huskiness, lustiness, puissance, stoutness, tolerance, toughness **10** brawniness, brute

ST

force, continuity, durability, mightiness, resilience, robustness, ruggedness, sturdiness
stammer: 2 er, uh, um **4** halt, stop **5** lurch **6** falter, jabber, mumble, repeat, wabble, wobble **7** sputter, stagger, stumble, stutter **8** hesitate **9** hem and haw
stammering: 10 hesitation, incoherent
Stamos, John: 5 actor
spouse: Rebecca Romijn
stamp: 3 cut, fix, ilk, lot **4** beat, cast, etch, form, mark, mint, mold, seal, sort, type **5** brand, clomp, crush, drive, label, pound, print, punch, shape, tramp **6** emblem, enseal, hammer, incuse, makeup, offset, step on, symbol **7** approve, earmark, engrave, fashion, impress, imprint, sticker, trample **8** hallmark **9** signature **10** impression
agcy.: 4 USPS
album sticker: 5 hinge
apparatus: 5 inker
backing: 3 gum **4** glue
bank ~: 3 NSF
coin ~: 3 die
dampen a ~: 4 lick
down: 5 tromp
give a ~ of approval: 2 OK **4** okay, pass **5** bless **6** ratify **7** approve, certify, confirm, consent, endorse, license **8** sanction, validate **9** authorize, sign off on
holder: 5 album
library ~: 5 dater
of approval: 2 OK **4** okay **8** blessing, sanction
office: 3 rcd. **4** recd. **8** received
office ~: 4 paid, recd
on: 5 tread **6** squash
ornamental ~: 4 seal
out: 3 end, rid **5** crush, erase, quash, quell **6** ravage, scotch **7** abolish, destroy, put down, repress, smother, squelch **8** get rid of, suppress **9** close down, eliminate, eradicate **10** extinguish, obliterate, put an end to
passport ~: 4 visa
place in a ~ album: 5 mount
P.O. ~: 8 postmark
purchase: 4 coil, pane **5** sheet **7** booklet
rubber ~: 6 ratify
stamp __: 3 pad, tax **5** album
__ stamp: 3 tax **4** date, food, time **5** green **6** rubber **7** postage, trading
Stamp: 7 Terence
Stamp __: 3 Act
stampede: 3 run **4** dash, rout, tear **5** chase, crash, hurry, panic, smash **6** charge, flight, onrush **7** mad rush **10** scattering
group: 4 herd
__ Stampede: 7 Calgary
stamping: 10 impression
ground: 4 turf
machine: 3 die
need: 3 pad
Stan: 3 Lee **4** Getz, Shaw **5** Drake, Smith **6** Kenton, Lathan, Laurel, Mikita, Musial **7** Barstow, Dragoti, Freberg **9** Coveleski **10** Berenstain
and Ollie foul-up: 4 mess
cohort: 5 Ollie
stance: 4 pose, side **5** slant, stand **7** bearing, conduct, posture **8** attitude, carriage, position **9** viewpoint **10** deportment, standpoint
belligerent ~: 6 akimbo
political ~: 8 platform
starter: 6 happen
stanch: 4 stem, stop **6** arrest
stanchion: 4 beam, pile, prop, stay **5** brace **6** picket, pillar **7** support **8** buttress
stand: 2 go **3** put, set **4** base, bear, cope, hold, lump, pose, prop, rack, rank, rest, rise, shop, side, stay, take, view **5** abide, allow, angle, arise, booth, brook, easel, erect, frame, get up, grove, kiosk, mount, pause, place, reach, slant, stage, stall, state, stick, table, treat **6** accept, belief, endure, handle, hang on, jump up, linger, locate, notion, obtain, occupy, remain, settle, stance, submit, suffer, take up **7** bracket, counter, dispose, lectern, opinion, prevail, staging, station, stomach, support, sustain, undergo, weather **8** attitude, bear with, carriage, continue, live with, platform, position, tolerate **9** encounter, put up with, viewpoint **10** contention, engagement, experience, resistance
against: 6 oppose
apart: 6 differ
around: 4 idle, loaf
art ~: 5 easel
aside: 4 quit **6** resign **8** withdraw
before: 4 face
behind: 4 avow, back **7** endorse, espouse, indorse, support, warrant **8** attest to, champion
by: 3 aid **4** help, wait **5** await, tarry **6** attest, cleave, hold on, uphold **7** support, sustain **8** attest to, lose time, maintain **9** recommend **10** rally round
(by): 4 hang
can't ~: 4 hate **5** abhor **6** detest, loathe **7** dislike
down: 4 quit **5** leave **8** withdraw **9** step aside **10** relinquish
ender: 3 off, out **4** down, pipe **5** point, still **6** offish, patter
firm: 6 insist **7** persist **9** persevere
flip-chart ~: 5 easel
for: 3 let **4** back, cope, hold, mean, okay, rest, stay, take, wear **5** abide, admit, adopt, allow, brook, favor, imply **6** accept, assent, comply, denote, embody, endure, handle, hang on, imbody, permit, submit, suffer, take up, typify **7** betoken, condone, include, signify, stomach, suggest, support, sustain, swallow, undergo, weather, welcome **8** advocate, champion, hold dear, indicate, live with, overlook, sanction, tolerate **9** approve of, epitomize, exemplify, personify, put up with, recognize, represent, sign off on, symbolize, withstand **10** concur with, experience, give the nod, illustrate
in: 3 sub **8** pinch-hit **10** substitute
in for: 5 cover, spell **7** relieve
in line: 4 wait **5** await
in the way: 3 bar **4** clog **6** hinder, impede **9** foreclose
let it ~: 4 stet
make a ~: 4 dare, defy **5** claim, fight, query, rally **6** accost, object, take on, threat **7** contest, dispute, protest, vie with **8** confront, denounce, face down, question **9** challenge, discredit, stimulate, vindicate **10** contradict, controvert, insist upon
open-mouthed: 4 gape, gawk, ogle **5** stare **6** goggle
out: 3 jut **4** bulk, loom, poke **5** bulge, excel, shine **6** beetle, emerge **7** project **8** overhang, protrude **9** prominent
over: 8 bestride
pat: 4 stay
place to ~: 8 foothold
starter: 3 cab, ink **4** band, book, hand, hard, head, kick, news, wash, with **5** grand, night
still: 5 stall **6** freeze **8** stagnate
take a ~: 3 opt **4** vote **5** judge **6** choose, decide, oppose **9** determine
the gaff: 4 cope, last **5** brook **6** endure, hang on, keep on, stay on **7** carry on, hold out, outlast, survive, weather **9** put up with **10** get through, stick it out
the test of time: 4 last **6** endure **7** survive
three-legged ~: 5 easel
together: 5 unite **6** club up
two-legged ~: 5 bipod
up: 4 jilt, rise, wear **5** arise **6** verify **7** survive **9** volunteer
up for: 6 defend **7** endorse, espouse, indorse, support, testify **9** guarantee **10** rally round
up to: 4 defy, face, meet **5** brave **6** oppose, resist **7** sustain **8** confront **9** challenge, withstand
vehicle: 3 cab **4** taxi **7** taxicab
way to ~: 3 pat **4** tall **5** in awe, on end **6** akimbo
stand __: 3 for, off, out, pat **4** down, over, tall, up to **5** guard, up for
stand __ by: 4 idly
stand __ of: 5 in awe
stand-__: 5 alone
__ stand: 3 cab **4** home, taxi **5** music, take a **7** witness
Stand (1989 song)
artist: R.E.M.
Stand __: 4 by Me
Stand! (1969 song)
artist: Sly and the Family Stone
stand a __: 6 chance
stand-alone: 4 unit
Stand and Deliver (1987 film)
cast: Edward James Olmos, Lou Diamond Phillips
standard: 3 law, par, set **4** code, flag, mean, norm, rule, test **5** axiom, basic, canon, ethic, gauge, grade, ideal, level, model, stock, typic, usual, value **6** banner, belief, common, emblem, ensign, ethics, figure, ideals, median, medium, morals, normal, rating, sample, staple, symbol, wonted **7** average, classic, correct, example, measure, paragon, pattern, pennant, popular, regular, routine, typical, vanilla **8** accepted, approved, everyday, exemplar, habitual, mediocre, official, ordinary, orthodox, paradigm, streamer **9** archetype, banderole, barometer, benchmark, canonical, criterion, customary, guideline, principle, prototype, yardstick **10** acceptable, definitive, prevailing, recognized, regulation, stereotype, touchstone, uneventful
below ~: 4 poor
deviation symbol: 5 sigma
ender: 4 bred
not ~: 7 variant
standard-__: 4 bred **6** bearer
__ standard: 4 gold **6** double, living
Standard and __: 5 Poor's
standardization: 8 sameness
standardize: 4 type **5** order **6** reform **9** normalize
standardized: 7 regular
standard of __: 6 living
Standard Oil
of California: 7 Chevron
of Indiana: 5 Amoco
of New Jersey: 4 Esso **5** Exxon
of New York: 5 Mobil
standards: 5 ethos, mores **6** morals, values **8** morality
lacking ~: 6 amoral
lack of social ~: 5 anomy **6** anomie
org.: 4 ANSI
Standards and Practices
employee: 6 censor
__ Standard Time: 5 Yukon **6** Alaska, Bering, Hawaii **7** Central, Eastern, Pacific
__ Standard Version: 7 Revised
Stand Back (1983 song)
artist: Stevie Nicks
Stand by Me (1986 film)
cast: Corey Feldman, River Phoenix, Wil Wheaton
director: Rob Reiner
Stand by Me (song)
artist: Ben E. King, John Lennon
stand by one's __: 4 guns
standby troops: 4 USAR, USNR **5** USAFR
Stand By Your Man (1968 song)
artist: Tammy Wynette
standee lack: 3 lap **4** seat
Stander: 6 Lionel
stander-by: 9 spectator
stand in __ of: 3 awe
stand-in: 3 sub **4** temp **5** agent, proxy **6** backup, double, player **8** delegate **9** alternate, look-alike, surrogate **10** substitute, understudy
standing: 4 mark, rank, slot, term **5** caste, class, clout, erect, fixed, level, light, on end, place, scene, state, terms **6** cachet, credit, repute, status **7** dignity, footing, quality, station, stature, stratum, upright **8** capacity, eminence, existing, good name, position, prestige, repeated **9** character, condition, permanent, perpetual, seniority, situation **10** continuing, estimation, prominence, reputation, stationary
around: 4 idle

financial ~: 5 worth 8 net worth
have ~: 4 rank, rate
high ~: 4 note 5 glory, honor 6 esteem, renown 7 acclaim, dignity 8 eminence, prestige 9 celebrity, greatness, magnitude, reverence 10 importance, prominence
of long ~: 3 old 5 early, hoary 6 age-old, senior 7 ancient, lasting, vintage 8 enduring 9 perennial, venerable 10 immemorial
of longer ~: 5 older 6 senior
one's ground: 9 unbending
out: 7 obvious
pat: 6 static 9 unbending
room only: 3 SRO 4 full 5 close, tight 6 filled, jammed, packed 7 crammed, cramped, crowded, sold out, stuffed 8 brimming, thronged 9 chock-full, congested, jam-packed 10 wall-to-wall
social ~: 5 caste 6 estate
starter: 4 free, with
tall: 4 bold, game 5 brave, gutsy, nervy, tough 6 gritty, heroic, plucky, strong 7 assured, doughty, valiant 8 fearless, heroical, resolute, unafraid, valorous 9 confident, dauntless, undaunted 10 courageous, mettlesome, red-blooded
the one left ~: 5 champ
standing __: 4 army 5 order, water
standing __ foot: 5 on one
standing __ jump: 5 broad
standing __ only: 4 room
standing __ roast: 3 rib
Standing in the Shadows of Love (1966 song)
artist: Four Tops
Standing on the Corner (1956 song)
artist: Four Lads
stand in good __: 5 stead
Standing Room Only
author: Alan Ayckbourn
standings column: 3 won 4 lost, ties, wins 6 losses
Standish: 5 Miles, Myles
stand-in: 5 Alden
Stand like Druids of __...: 3 eld
standoff: 3 tie 4 draw 7 impasse 8 deadlock 9 stalemate
like a ~: 5 tense
__ standoff: 7 Mexican
standoffish: 3 icy, shy 4 cold, cool 5 aloof, stiff 6 chilly, frigid, modest, remote 7 bashful, distant, glacial, haughty, hostile, recluse 8 eremitic, inimical, reserved, reticent, retiring, solitary 9 diffident, reclusive, withdrawn
one: 4 snob 5 snoot
stand one's __: 6 ground
standout
see wonderful
standpoint: 4 side, view 5 angle, slant 6 stance, vision 7 mind-set, opinion, outlook, posture 8 attitude, position 9 direction, situation
St. Andrews: 4 city, port, town 10 golf course
locale: 8 Scotland
stands: 9 bleachers
__ stands: 4 as it
__ stands now...: 4 As it
standstill: 4 halt, hole, rest, stay, stop, wait 5 check, delay, pause 6 corner 7 dead end, impasse 8 deadlock, dead stop, gridlock, inaction, stoppage 9 cessation, checkmate, stalemate
at a ~: 4 calm 6 hung up, static
bring to a ~: 4 stem, stop 5 cease 6 arrest, becalm
__ standstill: 3 at a
Stand, The
author: Stephen King
dog: 5 Kojak
stand to __: 6 reason
stand up __: 3 for
stand-up: 5 comic 8 comedian
bit: 3 gag 4 joke 7 monolog 8 one-liner 9 monologue
need: 4 mike 5 stool, water 10 microphone
Stanford: 5 Moore, White 6 Leland, school
athletes: 8 Cardinal
conference: 6 Pac-Ten
locale: 10 California
rival: 4 UCLA
Stanford-__ test: 5 Binet
Stanislavsky: 10 Konstantin
Stanislavsky __: 6 Method, System
Stanislaw: 3 Lem
Stanky: 5 Eddie
Stanley: 3 Kim 5 Adams, Baker, Cohen, Donen, Elkin, Jaffe, Tucci 6 Jordan, Kramer, Kunitz 7 Baldwin, Kubrick, Wendell 8 Holloway, Kowalski, Prusiner 10 Livingston
__ Stanley: 6 Morgan
Stanley and the Women
author: Kingsley Amis
Stanley Cup: 5 award, prize 6 trophy
org.: 3 NHL
__ Stanley Gardner: 4 Erle
Stanley, Henry Morton: 3 Sir 7 British 8 explorer
concern: 6 Africa
Stanley & Iris (1990 film)
cast: Robert De Niro, Jane Fonda
director: Martin Ritt
__ Stanley Range: 4 Owen
Stanley Steamer: 3 car 4 auto
contemporary: 3 Reo
stannum: 3 tin
Stansfield: 4 Lisa
Stan the Man teammate: 4 Enos
St. Anthony's __: 5 cross
Stanton, Elizabeth Cady: 8 feminist
colleague: Lucretia Mott
Stanwyck, Barbara: 7 actress
spouse: Robert Taylor
TV: The Big Valley
stanza: 4 text 5 verse
concluding ~: 5 envoi
Greek ~: 5 epode
sonnet ~: 5 octet 6 sestet 7 octette
Stanza: 3 car 4 auto 6 Nissan
stapes: 4 bone
locale: 3 ear
staph: 3 bug 8 pathogen
staple: 3 key 4 main, tack 5 affix, basic, chief 6 attach, fasten 7 bracket, popular, primary 8 standard 9 essential, important, necessary, principal
staple __: 3 gun 7 remover
Stapledon, Olaf: 6 writer 7 British 8 essayist 11 philosopher
work: Odd John
Staples Center player: 5 Laker
Staple Singers
one of the ~: 4 Cleo
song: If You're Ready (1973)
I'll Take You There (1972)
Let's Do It Again (1975)
Stapleton: 4 Jean 7 Maureen
star: 3 ace, sun 4 draw, hero, idol, lead, main, name, role 5 actor, chief, great, light, major 6 bigwig, famous, player, top dog 7 actress, capital, feature, heroine, leading, top draw 8 dominant, favorite, headline, luminary, pentacle, red dwarf, red giant, renowned, somebody, topliner, twinkler, virtuoso 9 brilliant, celebrity, dignitary, headliner, paramount, principal, prominent, supernova, top banana, well-known 10 celebrated, leading man, preeminent, white dwarf 11 leading lady
attribute: 4 fame
binary ~: 6 Sirius
blazing ~: 5 plant 6 flower
combining form: 4 astr- 5 -aster, astro-, sider- 6 -astero, sidero-
constellation's brightest ~: 5 alpha 6 lucida
Dog ~: 6 Sirius
Earth's ~: 3 Sol, sun
ender: 3 dom, lit 4 doms, dust, fish, gaze, ship, wort 5 board, burst, gazer, light 6 flower, gazing, struck
evening ~: 5 Venus 6 Hesper, planet, Vesper 8 Hesperus
followers: 4 fans, Magi 6 fandom
giver: 5 rater 6 critic
gold ~: 5 award, prize 6 trophy 7 laurels
hitch it to a ~: 5 wagon
in Andromeda: 6 Almach, Mirach
in Aquila: 6 Altair 7 Alshain, Tarazed
in Aries: 5 Hamal 8 Sheratan
in Auriga: 5 Al Kab 6 Almaaz 7 Capella
in Bootes: 4 Izar 6 Nekkar 7 Muphrid, Seginus 8 Arcturus
in Cancer: 6 Al Tarf 7 Acubens
in Canes Venatici: 5 Chara
in Canis Major: 5 Wezen 6 Adhara, Aludra, Mirzam, Sirius 7 Gomeisa
in Canis Minor: 7 Procyon
in Capricorn: 5 Dabih 6 Algedi 7 Nashira
in Carina: 5 Avior 7 Canopus
in Cassiopeia: 5 Segin 6 Achird, Shedar 7 Ruchbah
in Centaurus: 5 Hadar 7 Menkent
in Cepheus: 6 Alfirk
in Cetus: 4 Mira 6 Menkar
in Columba: 5 Phact
in Coma Berenices: 6 Diadem
in Corona Borealis: 5 Gemma 7 Nusakan 8 Alphecca
in Corvus: 7 Alchiba, Algorab
in Crater: 5 Alkes
in Crux: 6 Mimosa
in Cygnus: 4 Sadr 5 Deneb 7 Albireo
in Delphinus: 7 Rotanev 8 Sualocin
in Draco: 4 Adib 6 Thuban 7 Eltanin, Giausar 8 Rastaban
in Eridanus: 4 Beid, Keid 5 Cursa 6 Acamar
in Gemini: 5 Tejat, Wasat 6 Alhena, Castor, Pollux, Propus 7 Mekbuda
in Grus: 6 Al Nair
in Hydra: 7 Alphard
in Leo: 5 Zosma 7 Algieba, Rasalas, Regulus 8 Algenubi, Denebola
in Lepus: 5 Arneb, Nihal
in Lupus: 6 Kakkab
in Lyra: 4 Vega 7 Sheliak, Sulafat
in Ophiuchus: 5 Sabik 8 Cebalrai
in Orion: 5 Rigel, Saiph 7 Alnilam, Alnitak, Mintaka 9 Bellatrix 10 Betelgeuse
in Pegasus: 4 Enif 6 Markab, Scheat 7 Algenib
in Perseus: 5 Algol 6 Menkib, Mirfak
in Phoenix: 5 Ankaa
in Pisces: 8 Alrescha
in Puppis: 4 Naos 6 Tureis
in Sagitta: 4 Sham
in Sagittarius: 5 Nunki 6 Alnasl, Rukbat
in Scorpio: 6 Girtab, Lesath, Shaula 7 Al Niyat, Antares 8 Dschubba, Graffias
in Serpens: 4 Alya
in Taurus: 3 Ain 4 Maia 5 Atlas 6 Elnath, Merope 7 Alcyone, Pleione 9 Aldebaran
in Ursa Major: 5 Alcor, Dubhe, Merak, Mizar 6 Alioth, Alkaid, Phecda 7 Muscida, Talitha
in Ursa Minor: 6 Kochab, Yildun 7 Pherkad, Polaris
in Vela: 5 Regor 6 Suhail
in Virgo: 4 Awwa 5 Spica 6 Zaniah 7 Porrima
in Vulpecula: 5 Anser
K ~: 8 Arcturus 9 Aldebaran
look like a ~: 5 shine
M ~: 7 Antares 10 Betelgeuse
male ~: 4 hero, hunk
N ~: 3 sun
name meaning ~: 6 Stella 7 Estella, Estelle
place: 3 sky 5 space
quality: 5 charm 6 glamor 7 charism, glamour 8 charisma
rising ~: 5 comer
starter: 3 all, day 4 load, lode, pole 5 earth, super
system: 6 galaxy
type of ~: 5 dwarf
utilize a falling ~: 4 wish
variable ~: 4 Mira, nova
star __: 3 cut, map 4 turn 5 chart 6 system 7 chamber, cluster
star-__: 6 struck 7 crossed, studded
__ star: 3 red, sea, sun 4 gold 5 dwarf, guest, radio 6 binary 7 blazing, evening, falling, morning, neutron
__-star: 3 all, one, two 4 five, four 5 three
Star: 5 paper, Scout 6 skater 8 puckster 9 newspaper
locale: 7 Toronto 10 Kansas City
Star __: 4 Trek, Wars 6 Search 7 Chamber, Witness

Star! (1968 film)
cast: Julie Andrews
Star-__ tuna: 4 Kist
__ Star: 3 All, Dog, Tin **4** Rock **5** Demon, Lucky, North, Polar **6** Bronze, Little, Silver **7** Evening, Flaming, Shining
starboard: 5 right
opposite: 4 port
Starbuck: 4 mate
captain: 4 Ahab
Starbucks: 6 coffee
employee: 7 barista
order: 4 chai **5** latte, mocha **6** au lait
Star-Bulletin: 5 paper **9** newspaper
locale: 8 Honolulu
starch: 3 pep **4** grit, guts **5** nerve, pluck, valor, vigor **6** energy, farina, mettle **7** bravery, courage, prowess, stamina, stiffen **8** boldness, ceremony, gumption, patience, rigidity, tenacity, vitality **9** formality, fortitude, stiffness **10** get up and go
combining form: 4 amyl- **5** amylo-
medium: 5 spray
source: 4 corn, taro
starchy: 4 prim **5** rigid, stiff **6** formal **7** prudish **9** impliable **10** inflexible
compound: 4 amyl
food: 4 carb
foodstuff: 4 sago **5** salep
root: 4 taro
vegetable: 3 yam **4** spud **5** tater, tuber **6** potato
Starcraft: 3 GMC, van
star-crossed: 5 curst **6** cursed, doomed, jinxed **7** accurst, hapless, unblest, unlucky **8** accursed, ill-fated, luckless **9** unblessed, unfavored **10** ill-starred
stardom: 4 fame **6** renown **9** celebrity
achieve ~: 6 arrive
Stardust (2007 film)
cast: Claire Danes, Robert De Niro, Michelle Pfeiffer
Stardust Memories (1980 film)
cast: Woody Allen, Jessica Harper, Charlotte Rampling
director: Woody Allen
stare: 3 eye, fix, pry, see **4** beam, bore, gape, gaup, gawk, gawp, gaze, leer, look, ogle, peer, view **5** focus, glare, rivet, watch **6** glower, goggle, marvel, regard, take in, wonder **7** eyeball **8** eagle eye **10** give the eye, rubberneck
stare __: 4 down
__ stare: 5 blank
stares, like some: 3 icy **5** stony
__ Starfighter, The: 4 Last
Starfire: 3 car **4** auto, Olds **10** Oldsmobile
starfish part: 3 arm, ray
__-Star Game: 3 All
Stargate (1994 film)
cast: Jaye Davidson, Kurt Russell, James Spader
stargazer: 9 visionary
science: 9 astronomy
sight: 4 nova
time: 5 night
stargazers, Biblical: 4 Magi
Stargell, Willie: 6 Pirate **10** outfielder
__-star general: 3 one, two **4** five, four **5** three
staring: 5 agape, agaze **6** aglare

Starion: 3 car **4** auto **10** Mitsubishi
Star Is Born, A (1937 film)
cast: Janet Gaynor, Fredric March
Star Is Born, A (1954 film)
cast: Judy Garland, James Mason
Star Is Born, A (1976 film)
cast: Kris Kristofferson, Barbra Streisand
stark: 3 raw **4** bald, bare, cold, grim, pure, rank **5** bleak, blunt, clear, gross, harsh, naked, plain, quite, sheer, stiff, utter **6** barren, chaste, dreary, patent, severe, simple, strong, unclad **7** austere, blasted, Spartan, utterly **8** absolute, desolate, forsaken, glabrous, infernal, outright, palpable, solitary, stripped, undraped **9** bare-bones, cheerless, downright, glaringly, out-and-out, unadorned, unalloyed, unclothed, uncovered **10** absolutely, altogether, completely, consummate, depressing, thoroughly
stark-__: 5 naked
Stark: 6 Willie **8** Johannes
Starka: 5 vodka
competitor: 4 Skyy **5** Popov, Stoli **6** Rodnik **7** Absolut **8** Smirnoff **9** Grey Goose
Starker, Janos: 7 cellist **9** Hungarian
starkers: 4 bare, nude **5** naked **9** unattired
Star-Kist: 4 tuna
alternative: 9 Bumble Bee
starkness: 9 austerity
Starkville: 4 city, town
athletes: 8 Bulldogs
locale: 4 Miss.
school: 3 MSU
Starland Vocal Band
song: Afternoon Delight (1976)
Star-Ledger: 5 paper **9** newspaper
locale: 6 Newark
starless: 4 dark **5** black
starlet: 7 actress
quest: 4 fame, role
Starlight Express: 7 musical
composer: Andrew Lloyd Webber
footwear: 5 skate
starlike: 6 astral
flower: 5 aster
starling: 4 bird **8** oxpecker
relative: 4 mina, myna **5** minah, mynah
Starling: 7 Clarice
Starman (1984 film)
cast: Jeff Bridges
Star of __: 5 David **9** Bethlehem
__-Star Pictures: 3 Tri
__ Star Program: 6 Energy
Starr: 3 Kay, Ken **4** Bart **5** Belle, Edwin, Ringo **6** Brenda **7** Kenneth
Starr, Bart: 2 QB
sport: 8 football
__-starred: 3 ill
__-star review: 4 four
starring __: 4 role
starring, also: 4 with
Starr, Kay
song: My Heart Reminds Me (1957)
Rock and Roll Waltz (1956)
Starr, Ringo: 7 drummer
born: Richard Starkey
group: The Beatles
song: Back Off Boogaloo (1972)
It Don't Come Easy (1971)
No No Song (1975)
Oh My My (1974)
Only You (1974)
Photograph (1973)
You're Sixteen (1973)
spouse: Barbara Bach
starry: 6 astral
Starry __, The: 5 Night
starry-eyed: 4 owly **6** enrapt **8** romantic, youthful **9** idealized, visionary
Starry Night: 3 oil **8** painting
artist: Vincent Van Gogh
stars
check out the ~: 4 gaze
give ~ to: 3 peg **4** rate **5** scale, set at, weigh **6** size up **8** classify, evaluate
in the ~: 5 fated
science: 9 astronomy
worth no ~: 5 awful
stars (with constellations)
Acamar: Eridanus
Achird: Cassiopeia
Acubens: Cancer
Adhara: Canis Major
Adib: Draco
Ain: Taurus
Albireo: Cygnus
Alchiba: Corvus
Alcor: Ursa Major
Alcyone: Taurus
Aldebaran: Taurus
Alfirk: Cepheus
Algedi: Capricorn
Algenib: Pegasus
Algenubi: Leo
Algieba: Leo
Algol: Perseus
Algorab: Corvus
Alhena: Gemini
Alioth: Ursa Major
Al Kab: Auriga
Alkaid: Ursa Major
Alkes: Crater
Almaaz: Auriga
Almach: Andromeda
Al Nair: Grus
Alnasl: Sagittarius
Alnilam: Orion
Alnitak: Orion
Al Niyat: Scorpio
Alphard: Hydra
Alphecca: Corona Borealis
Alrescha: Pisces
Alshain: Aquila
Altair: Aquila
Al Tarf: Cancer
Aludra: Canis Major
Alya: Serpens
Ankaa: Phoenix
Anser: Vulpecula
Antares: Scorpio
Arcturus: Bootes
Arneb: Lepus
Atlas: Taurus
Avior: Carina
Awwa: Virgo
Beid: Eridanus
Bellatrix: Orion
Betelgeuse: Orion
Canopus: Carina
Capella: Auriga
Caph: Cassiopeia
Castor: Gemini
Cebalrai: Ophiuchus
Chara: Canes Venatici
Cursa: Eridanus
Dabih: Capricorn
Deneb: Cygnus
Denebola: Leo
Diadem: Coma Berenices
Dschubba: Scorpio
Dubhe: Ursa Major
Elnath: Taurus
Eltanin: Draco
Enif: Pegasus
Gemma: Corona Borealis
Giausar: Draco
Girtab: Scorpio
Gomeisa: Canis Minor
Graffias: Scorpio
Hadar: Centaurus
Hamal: Aries
Izar: Bootes
Kakkab: Lupus
Keid: Eridanus
Kochab: Ursa Minor
Lesath: Scorpio
Maia: Taurus
Markab: Pegasus
Mebsuta: Gemini
Megrez: Ursa Major
Meissa: Orion
Mekbuda: Gemini
Menkar: Cetus
Menkent: Centaurus
Menkib: Perseus
Merak: Ursa Major
Merope: Taurus
Mimosa: Crux
Mintaka: Orion
Mira: Cetus
Mirach: Andromeda
Mirfak: Perseus
Mirzam: Canis Major
Mizar: Ursa Major
Muphrid: Bootes
Muscida: Ursa Major
Naos: Puppis
Nashira: Capricorn
Nekkar: Bootes
Nihal: Lepus
Nunki: Sagittarius
Nusakan: Corona Borealis
Phact: Columba
Phecda: Ursa Major
Pherkad: Ursa Minor
Pleione: Taurus
Polaris: Ursa Minor
Pollux: Gemini
Porrima: Virgo
Procyon: Canis Minor
Propus: Gemini
Rasalas: Leo
Rastaban: Draco
Regor: Vela
Regulus: Leo
Rigel: Orion
Rotanev: Delphinus
Ruchbah: Cassiopeia
Rukbat: Sagittarius
Sabik: Ophiuchus
Sadr: Cygnus
Saiph: Orion
Scheat: Pegasus
Segin: Cassiopeia
Seginus: Bootes
Sham: Sagitta
Shaula: Scorpio
Shedar: Cassiopeia
Sheliak: Lyra

Sheratan: Aries
Sirius: Canis Major
Spica: Virgo
Sualocin: Delphinus
Suhail: Vela
Sulafat: Lyra
Talitha: Ursa Major
Tarazed: Aquila
Tejat: Gemini
Thuban: Draco
Tureis: Puppis
Vega: Lyra
Wasat: Gemini
Wezen: Canis Major
Yildun: Ursa Minor
Zaniah: Virgo
Zosma: Leo
__ stars: 3 see
Stars: 3 six 4 team
home: 6 Dallas
milieu: 3 ice 4 rink
org.: 3 NHL
rival: *see* hockey team
sport: 6 hockey
Stars above!: 6 Dear me
Stars and __: 4 Bars 7 Stripes
Stars and Bars: 4 flag
inits.: 3 CSA
Stars and Stripes: 4 flag 8 Old Glory
Stars and Stripes Forever, The: 5 march
composer: John Philip Sousa
Starship
aka: Jefferson Airplane, Jefferson Starship
song: It's Not Over (1987)
Nothing's Gonna Stop Us Now (1987)
Sara (1986)
We Built This City (1985)
starship letters: 3 NCC
Starsky and Hutch (ABC drama)
cast: David Soul (Hutch)
Paul Michael Glaser (Starsky)
Starsky & Hutch (2004 film)
cast: Ben Stiller, Owen Wilson
Stars Like Dust, The
author: Isaac Asimov
Star-Spangled Banner: 4 flag 8 Old Glory
Star-Spangled Banner, The: 6 anthem
contraction: 3 o'er
opener: 4 O say
writer: 3 Key
Star-Spangled Girl, The
author: Neil Simon
Stars Shine Down, The
author: Sidney Sheldon
__ Star State: 4 Lone
start: 3 jar, shy 4 bolt, buck, dart, dawn, draw, edge, jerk, jump, lead, leap, open, rise, seed, step, wade 5 arise, begin, birth, bound, break, bulge, crank, enrol, found, get-go, git-go, issue, leave, light, onset, prime, quail, react, rouse, scare, set in, set up, shock, shoot, spark, spasm, wince 6 advent, arouse, blanch, blench, bounce, create, day one, depart, dive in, embark, enroll, fire up, flinch, go to it, ignite, jump in, launch, let rip, origin, outset, recoil, ring in, set off, set out, shrink, source, spring, take up, tee off, turn on, twitch, whip up 7 aggress, dawning, develop, genesis, go ahead, infancy, jump off, kickoff, leadoff, opening, pioneer, power up, prelude, proceed, provoke, push off, sendoff, takeoff, trigger, usher in, vantage 8 activate, approach, blastoff, commence, draw back, entrance, exordium, get going, initiate, set about, set forth, strike up, surprise, touch off 9 advantage, allowance, beginning, countdown, enter upon, establish, first step, get moving, get to work, inception, instigate, institute, introduce, originate, square one, strike out 10 conception, convulsion, envisaging, foundation, hit the road, inaugurate, incipience, initiation, jump the gun, sally forth
start __ under: 5 a fire
__ start: 4 head 5 false 6 flying 7 housing, running
__-start: 4 jump, kick 5 boost
started
get ~: 4 move 5 begin, crank, found 7 proceed, take off 8 turn over, initiate
Star-Telegram: 5 paper 9 newspaper
locale: 7 Ft. Worth
__ starter: 4 kick
__-starter: 4 self
__ starters: 3 for
starting: 4 from 8 original 10 initiatory
from: 4 as of
point: 4 base 5 basis, gitgo 6 origin, source 9 beginning, threshold
up: 3 new 8 brand-new
starting __: 4 gate, line, over 5 block
Starting Over (1979 film)
cast: Candice Bergen, Jill Clayburgh, Burt Reynolds
startle: 3 awe, jar 4 bolt, jolt, jump, rock, stun 5 alarm, amaze, floor, rouse, scare, shake, shock, spook 6 fright 7 agitate, astound, shake up, stagger, terrify 8 affright, astonish, frighten, surprise 9 galvanize, give a turn, take aback, terrorize 10 scare stiff
startled: 5 agasp 6 afraid, scared 10 dumbstruck
cry: 4 yipe 5 yikes, yipes 7 omigosh
startling: 8 dramatic, striking, uncommon 9 different, wonderful 10 prodigious, unexpected, unforeseen
Start Me Up (1981 song)
artist: Rolling Stones
Start playing!: 5 hit it
Star Trek (2009 film)
cast: Eric Bana, Chris Pine, Zachary Quinto, Zoe Saldana
Star Trek (NBC sci-fi)
cast: Majel Barrett (Nurse Christine Chapel)
James Doohan (Lt. Cmdr. Scott)
DeForest Kelley (Dr. Leonard McCoy)
Walter Koenig (Ens. Pavel Chekov)
Nichelle Nichols (Lt. Uhura)
Leonard Nimoy (Cmdr. Spock)
William Shatner (Capt. James Kirk)
George Takei (Lt. Sulu)
extra: 5 alien
setting: 5 space
ship: 10 Enterprise
speed: 4 warp
studio: 6 Desilu
weapon: 6 phaser
weapon setting: 4 stun
Star Trek - Deep Space Nine (TV sci-fi)
cast: René Auberjonois (Odo)
Avery Brooks (Cmdr. Benjamin Sisko)
Terry Farrell (Jadzia Dax)
Colm Meaney (Miles O'Brien)
Alexander Siddig (Dr. Julian Bashir)
Nana Visitor (Major Kira Nerys)
Star Trek Generations (1994 film)
cast: Malcolm McDowell, William Shatner, Patrick Stewart
Star Trek III: The Search for Spock (1984 film)
cast: James Doohan, DeForest Kelley, William Shatner
director: Leonard Nimoy
Star Trek II: The Wrath of Khan (1982 film)
cast: DeForest Kelley, Ricardo Montalban, Leonard Nimoy, William Shatner
Star Trek: Insurrection (1998 film)
cast: LeVar Burton, Michael Dorn, Jonathan Frakes, Gates McFadden, Marina Sirtis, Brent Spiner, Patrick Stewart
Star Trek IV: The Voyage Home (1986 film)
cast: Catherine Hicks, DeForest Kelley, Leonard Nimoy, William Shatner
director: Leonard Nimoy
Star Trek Nemesis (2002 film)
cast: LeVar Burton, Jonathan Frakes, Brent Spiner, Patrick Stewart
Star Trek-The Motion Picture (1979 film)
cast: Stephen Collins, DeForest Kelley, Leonard Nimoy, William Shatner
director: Robert Wise
Star Trek: The Next Generation (TV sci-fi)
cast: LeVar Burton (Lt. Geordi La Forge)
Denise Crosby (Lt. Tasha Yar)
Michael Dorn (Lt. Worf)
Jonathan Frakes (Cmdr. Will Riker)
Whoopi Goldberg (Guinan)
Gates McFadden (Dr. Beverly Crusher)
Colm Meaney (Miles O'Brien)
Marina Sirtis (Deanna Troi)
Brent Spiner (Lt. Cmdr. Data)
Patrick Stewart (Capt. Jean-Luc Picard)
Wil Wheaton (Wesley Crusher)
cat: 4 Spot
foe: 4 Borg
Star Trek VI: The Undiscovered Country (1991 film)
cast: DeForest Kelley, Leonard Nimoy, William Shatner
Star Trek: Voyager (UPN sci-fi)
cast: Robert Beltran (Chakotay)
Roxann Biggs-Dawson (B'Elanna Torres)
Jennifer Lien (Kes)
Robert McNeill (Lt. Tom Paris)
Kate Mulgrew (Capt. Kathryn Janeway)
Ethan Phillips (Neelix)
Robert Picardo (The Doctor)
Tim Russ (Tuvok)
Jeri Ryan (Seven of Nine)
Garrett Wang (Ens. Harry Kim)
Star Tribune: 5 paper 9 newspaper
locale: 6 St. Paul 10 Twin Cities 11 Minneapolis
Start the Revolution Without Me (1970 film)
cast: Donald Sutherland, Gene Wilder
starved: 4 thin 5 drawn, empty, faint, unfed 6 hungry, peaked, skinny 7 craving, haggard, peckish, pinched 8 edacious, esurient, famished, ravenous, underfed, weakened 9 emaciated, hungering, insatiate, voracious 10 gluttonous
starving: 4 thin 5 drawn, empty, faint, unfed 6 hungry, skinny 7 craving, haggard, pinched 8 famished, ravenous, underfed, weakened 9 emaciated, hungering, insatiate, voracious
Star Wars
aka: 3 SDI
Star Wars (1977 film)
cast: Peter Cushing, Carrie Fisher, Harrison Ford, Alec Guinness, Mark Hamill
director: George Lucas
foe: 6 Empire
knight: 4 Jedi
music: John Williams
planet: 5 Endor
role: 3 Han 4 Leia, Luke, Solo 5 Darth, Vader 6 Kenobi, Obi-Wan 9 Skywalker 10 Artoo Detoo
weapon: 5 laser
Star Wars Episode 1: The Phantom Menace (1999 film)
cast: Jake Lloyd, Ewan McGregor, Liam Neeson, Natalie Portman
director: George Lucas
music: John Williams
role: 3 Ani
starwort: 5 aster
Starz: 7 channel
alternative: *see* movie channel
stash: 4 bury, hide, save, stow 5 cache, hoard, put by, store, trove 6 pileup 7 conceal, deposit, harvest, lay away, put away, reserve, secrete 8 conserve, ensconce, hide away, salt away, stow away
stasis: 5 poise 7 balance 8 stoppage 9 equipoise 10 inactivity, quiescence
stat: 3 avg., CPI, ERA, GNP, GPA, now, PDQ, RBI, TDs, THI 4 ASAP 5 datum, hurry, net wt., repro 6 at bats, at once, pronto 7 assists, quickly 8 chop-chop 9 duplicate, facsimile, photocopy, posthaste, right away 10 this minute
starter: 4 aero, rheo 5 photo
state: 3 air, put, say 4 avow, case, form, land, mode, mood, pass, pomp, rank, tell, time, trim, vent

5 event, glory, phase, pitch, realm, shape, speak, spiel, stand, style, union, utter, voice **6** affirm, allege, assert, cachet, depone, dither, fettle, lather, nation, nature, pickle, plight, public, recite, relate, remark, report, temper **7** chances, chime in, country, declare, dignity, display, element, enounce, explain, expound, express, footing, majesty, mention, narrate, observe, outlook, posture, present, proviso, quality, recount, specify, testify, welfare **8** announce, attitude, bring out, capacity, category, ceremony, describe, dominion, grandeur, juncture, maintain, occasion, position, prestige, proclaim, propound, rehearse, republic, set forth, standing, throw out **9** character, community, condition, elucidate, enumerate, enunciate, expound on, interpret, make clear, pronounce, situation, stipulate, territory, verbalize **10** articulate, ceremonial, federation, government, imperative, limitation, occurrence, reputation
combining form: **6** -phoria
ender: **4** room, side, wide **5** craft, house
in French: **4** état
solemnly ~: **5** swear
starter: **4** down **5** inter
suffix: **3** -age, -dom, -ism **4** -ence, -ness, -ship
U.S. ~: **3** Ala., Ark., Cal., Del., Fla., Haw., Ida., Ill., Ind., Kan., Ken., Neb., Nev., Ore., Tex., Wis., W. Va., Wyo. **4** Alas., Ariz., Colo., Conn., Iowa, Mass., Mich., Minn., Miss., Mont., N. Car., N. Dak., Nebr., N. Mex., Ohio, Okla., Penn., S. Car., S. Dak., Tenn., Utah, Wash., Wisc. **5** Calif., Idaho, Maine, Penna., Texas **6** Alaska, Hawaii, Kansas, Nevada, Oregon **7** Alabama, Arizona, Florida, Georgia, Indiana, Montana, New York, Vermont, Wyoming **8** Arkansas, Colorado, Delaware, Illinois, Kentucky, Maryland, Michigan, Missouri, Nebraska, Oklahoma, Virginia **9** Louisiana, Minnesota, New Jersey, New Mexico, Tennessee, Wisconsin **10** California, Washington **11** Connecticut, Mississippi, North Dakota, Rhode Island, South Dakota **12** New Hampshire, Pennsylvania, West Virginia **13** Massachusetts, North Carolina, South Carolina
state __: **3** aid **4** bank, bird, tree **5** of war, visit **6** flower, police, prison, secret **7** trooper
state __ art: **5** of the
__ state: **3** in a **6** buffer, police **7** altered, welfare
__-state: **4** city **5** out-of, solid **6** nation
State __: **4** Fair
State __ Union address: **5** of the
__ State: **3** Bay, Gem **4** Ball, Kent, Penn **5** Aloha **7** Buckeye
__-State: **3** all
State and Main (2000 film)
cast: Alec Baldwin, Philip Seymour Hoffman, William H. Macy, Sarah Jessica Parker
director: David Mamet
State College: **4** city, town
locale: **4** Penn.
statecraft: **8** politics **9** diplomacy **10** government
stated: **3** set **5** given **6** verbal **7** nominal, regular
State Farm
competitor: *see* insurance company
stateliness: **8** grandeur, nobility, splendor
stately: **4** high **5** grand, large, lofty, noble, proud, regal, royal, stiff **6** august, formal, kingly, lordly, portly, proper, ritual, solemn, superb **7** courtly, elegant, gallant, haughty, massive, opulent, pompous, queenly, sublime **8** decorous, elevated, gracious, highbrow, imperial, imposing, majestic, measured, palatial, towering **9** dignified, grandiose, luxurious, sumptuous, venerable **10** ceremonial, high-minded, impressive, majestical, monumental, statuesque
home: **5** manor
Stately Wayne __: **5** Manor
statement: **3** tab **4** bill, news, word **5** input, voice **6** avowal, budget, charge, dictum, record, remark, report **7** account, comment, invoice, mention, picture, recital, theorem **8** relation **9** admission, affidavit, assertion, assurance, manifesto, narrative, reckoning, testimony, utterance **10** allegation, communiqué, confession, exposition, expression, indictment, profession, recitation
brief ~: **4** note **9** sound bite
confidential ~: **5** aside
detailed ~: **6** report
entry: **5** asset, debit **6** credit **8** net worth **9** liability
false ~: **3** lie **4** tale
formal ~: **5** edict **6** dictum
itemized ~: **4** bill **7** invoice
make a ~: **3** say **4** aver, talk **5** speak
__ statement: **4** bank **5** make a, proxy, sworn **6** income **7** fashion
Staten Island: **3** bor. **7** borough
locale: **3** NYC
transport: **5** ferry
state of __: **3** war **5** grace **7** affairs
__ state of affairs: **4** a sad
State of Grace (1990 film)
cast: Ed Harris, Gary Oldman, Sean Penn, Robin Wright
State of Play (2009 film)
cast: Ben Affleck, Russell Crowe, Rachel McAdams, Helen Mirren
State of Shock (1984 song)
artist: Jackson 5
State of Siege
author: Albert Camus
State of the __ address: **5** Union
state-of-the-art: **3** new **6** modern, superb **7** current **8** advanced, up-to-date
State of the Union (1948 film)
cast: Katharine Hepburn, Spencer Tracy
director: Frank Capra
State of the World (1991 song)
artist: Janet Jackson
stateroom: **5** cabin **8** quarters
state-run game: **5** lotto
states' __: **6** rights
__ States: **4** Gulf **5** Assam, Malay, Papal **6** Balkan, Baltic, Border, Punjab **7** Altered, Barbary, Trucial
state's evidence
turn ~: **4** sing **7** testify
__ statesman: **5** elder
statesmanship: **4** tact **5** poise **7** finesse **8** delicacy, politics **9** diplomacy
__ States of America: **6** United
__ States of Brazil: **6** United
__ States of Indonesia: **6** United
statesperson: **8** lawmaker **10** politician
States, The: **3** USA **5** US of A **7** America
__ State Warriors: **6** Golden
Statham: **5** Jason
static: **4** firm **5** fixed, inert, rigid, sound, still, stuck **6** halted, rooted, stable, sticky, strife **7** passive, settled, stalled, stopped, uniform **8** constant, definite, immobile, inactive, ironclad, lifeless, stagnant, unmoving **9** immovable, permanent, unvarying **10** changeless, contention, deadlocked, gridlocked, invariable, motionless, stationary, unchanging
not ~: **6** moving **7** kinetic **8** in motion
problem: **5** cling
static __: **5** cling
station: **3** CRT, job, put, VDT **4** base, duty, park, post, rank, seat, site, spot, stop **5** allot, caste, class, depot, grade, house, level, locus, lodge, order, pitch, place, plant, stand **6** assign, deploy, estate, instal, locate, office, sphere **7** appoint, footing, install, lookout, quality, quarter, service, stratum **8** entrench, garrison, location, position, quarters, standing, terminal **9** character, crow's nest, establish, situation **10** commission, department, employment, occupation, walk of life
abbr.: **3** arr., dep., ETA, ETD
bus ~: **4** stop **5** depot
ender: **5** house **6** master
live beneath one's ~: **4** slum
posting: **4** sked **8** schedule
pull into the ~: **6** arrive
starter: **4** work
wagon: **3** car **4** auto
work ~: **3** CRT, VDT **4** desk **6** office **7** cubicle
station __: **5** agent, break, house, wagon
__ station: **3** aid, air, bus, gas, ice, key, pay, way **4** base, fire, flag, hill, work **5** earth, pilot, power, radio, space, train **6** battle, ground, police **7** coaling, comfort, docking, filling, service, weather
__ Station: **4** Penn **5** Power, Union **7** Savage's **8** Victoria
stationary: **3** pat **4** firm, idle **5** fixed, inert **6** at rest, moored, parked, rooted, stable, static **8** anchored, immobile, stagnant, standing, unmoving **9** immovable, permanent, quiescent, sedentary **10** stock-still
be ~ at sea: **5** lie to
stationary __: **5** front **7** bicycle
stationer: **8** merchant, retailer
supply: **3** pen **5** paper **6** eraser, pencil
stationery: **5** paper **8** envelope
amount: **4** ream **5** quire
brand: **5** Eaton
station-house ritual: **6** lineup
__ Station Zebra: **3** Ice
statistic: **3** avg. **4** mean, mode **5** datum, index **6** median, number **7** average, per cent
statistical
significance measure: **5** t-test
statistician no-no: **4** bias
statistics: **3** nos. **4** data **5** table **7** numbers **10** tabulation
vital ~: **5** story **6** résumé **7** profile
__ statistics: **5** vital
Statler Brothers
song: Flowers on the Wall (1965)
stator partner: **5** rotor
statue: **4** bust, icon, ikon **5** eikon, model, piece **6** bronze, effigy, figure, marble, trophy **8** likeness, memorial, monument **9** sculpture
armless ~: **5** Venus
base: **5** socle
headless ~: **5** torso
leaf: **3** fig
of a god: **4** idol
place: **4** apse **5** niche
play ~: **6** freeze
support: **4** base
Statue of Liberty
feature: **5** crown, torch **6** tablet
inscription starter: **4** give
poet: **7** Lazarus
ship that brought the ~: **5** Isère
skin: **6** copper
statues, island of large: **6** Easter
statuesque: **4** tall, trim **5** grand, regal **7** stately **8** graceful, imposing, majestic **9** beautiful **10** curvaceous, majestical
statuette: **4** Emmy, Tony **5** model, Oscar **8** figurine
stature: **4** rank, size **5** merit, value, worth **6** cachet, growth, height, virtue **7** ability, caliber, dignity, quality **8** capacity, eminence, position, prestige, standing **9** elevation **10** competence, importance, prominence, reputation
gain ~: **4** grow
status: **3** job **4** mode, rank, role **5** caste, class, grade, level, merit, place, stage **6** cachet, credit, degree, estate, league, rating, renown **7** caliber, dignity, footing, quality, ranking **8** capacity, eminence, position, prestige, standing **9** character, condition, situation **10** importance, prominence
have ~: **4** rank, rate
raise in ~: **5** exalt
suffix: **4** -ship
status __: **3** quo **6** symbol
statute: **3** act, law **4** bill, rule **5** bylaw, canon, edict **6** decree **7** measure, precept **9** enactment, ordinance **10** regulation

statute __: 4 mile
statutory: 5 jural, legal, licit 6 lawful, vested 7 enacted 9 canonical 10 legitimate
Staubach, Roger: 2 QB
sport: 8 football
Staub, Rusty
sport: 8 baseball
St. Augustine
author: Rebecca West
staunch: 4 bold, fast, firm, game, stem, stop, sure, true 5 gutsy, hardy, liege, loyal, nervy, stiff, stout, tough 6 ardent, awless, daring, gritty, heroic, plucky, secure, spunky, stable, steady, strong, sturdy, trusty 7 aweless, defiant, devoted, doughty, dutiful, gallant, valiant 8 constant, faithful, fearless, heroical, intrepid, reliable, resolute, stalwart, true-blue, unafraid, untiring, valorous 9 allegiant, audacious, dauntless, dedicated, dreadless, rock solid, steadfast, tenacious, undaunted, unfailing, unfearful 10 courageous, dependable, inflexible, iron-willed, purposeful, undeterred, unflagging, unwavering, unyielding
staunchness: 4 grit 5 nerve, valor 7 loyalty 8 fidelity, tenacity
Staunton: 4 city, town
locale: 8 Virginia
Stautner: 5 Ernie
stave: 3 rod 4 cane, pale, pole, post, rung, slab 5 crush, smash, staff, stake, stick, verse 6 paling, picket 7 fend off, support 8 splinter
in: 4 cave, push 5 pound, press
off: 5 avert, deter, parry, repel 6 defend, rebuff 7 obviate, prevent, repulse, rule out 8 forefend, hold back, preclude, turn back 9 hold at bay
stave __: 3 off
Stavros
rival: 3 Ari
stay: 3 lag 4 bide, bunk, curb, halt, hang, hold, last, live, nest, prop, rest, stem, stop, wait 5 abide, brace, break, check, dally, defer, delay, dwell, exist, lodge, pause, perch, put up, roost, stall, stand, stick, tarry, truce, visit, waive 6 arrest, column, detain, endure, hang in, hinder, inhere, insert, intern, linger, loiter, occupy, put off, remain, reside, resist, settle, shelve 7 adjourn, hang out, holiday, layover, prevent, respite, sojourn, support, suspend, ward off 8 buttress, continue, hold back, intermit, lateness, obstruct, postpone, prohibit, reprieve, sit tight, stand for, stand pat, stopover, stopping, vacation 9 cessation, deferment, hang about, remission, stanchion, take a room 10 brave it out, hang around, standstill, stick it out, suspension, wait around
away from: 4 duck, miss, shun 5 avoid, dodge, evade, shirk 6 bypass, eschew 7 abstain 10 circumvent
a while: 5 abide, dwell 6 hold on, linger, remain 7 sojourn 8 continue
didn't ~: 4 left, went
ender: 4 sail
for: 5 await
invite to ~: 5 ask in
on: 4 last 5 stick 6 endure
over: 4 bunk 5 lodge 7 sojourn
place to ~: 3 inn 5 B and B, hotel, lodge, motel 8 motor inn 10 motor lodge
put: 3 fix 4 hold 5 stick
starter: 3 bob 4 back, jack, main
the course: 5 stand 7 persist 9 persevere
with: 4 keep
stay __: 3 out, put 5 loose
stay-__: 5 press
__ stay: 6 collar
Stay (song)
artist: Four Seasons, Maurice Williams and the Zodiacs
stay-at-home: 5 loner 6 hermit
Stayin' Alive (1977 song)
artist: Bee Gees
staying
power: 5 might, vigor 7 stamina 8 patience 9 endurance, tolerance
put: 6 stable
staying __: 5 power
Stay of Execution
author: Stewart Alsop
stay the __: 6 course
__ Stay Together: 4 Let's
St. Bartholomew: 4 isle 6 island
St. Catharines: 4 city, town
locale: 6 Canada 7 Ontario
school: 5 Brock
St. Cloud: 4 city, town
locale: 7 Florida 9 Minnesota
St. Croix: 4 isle 5 river 6 island
locale: 9 Minnesota, Wisconsin 10 West Indies
native: 6 Cruzan
St. Cyr: 4 Lily
St. Cyr-__: 6 l'École
std.
see standard
Ste-__-Eglise: 4 Mère
Ste.-__-des-Plaines: 4 Anne
Ste.-__, Quebec: 3 Foy
stead: 4 lieu 5 place 8 bed frame, location, position
ender: 4 fast
starter: 3 bed 4 farm, home, road
Stead, Christina: 6 writer 10 Australian
work: The Man Who Loved Children
steadfast: 3 set 4 firm, sure, true 5 fixed, liege, loyal, rigid, solid 6 ardent, gritty, intent, stable, steady, strong, sturdy, trusty 7 abiding, adamant, devoted, dutiful, hard-set, intense, staunch 8 constant, enduring, faithful, hellbent, immobile, implicit, reliable, resolute, stubborn, tireless, true-blue 9 allegiant, dedicated, immovable, immutable, obstinate, permanent, rock solid, tenacious, unbending, undaunted, unfailing, unmovable 10 changeless, dependable, determined, foursquare, hard-bitten, inflexible, iron-willed, persistent, purposeful, relentless, unflagging, unswerving, unwavering, unyielding
steadfastness: 4 grit 5 nerve, valor 7 loyalty, purpose, resolve 8 backbone, fidelity, tenacity 9 stability, tolerance 10 resolution
symbol of ~: 4 rock
steadily: 7 fixedly 8 intently
steadiness: 5 poise 6 aplomb 8 calmness, strength 9 certainty, constancy, fixedness, stability, tolerance 10 equanimity
Steadman: 6 Alison
steady: 4 calm, cool, even, fast, firm, safe, sane, sure, true 5 brace, fixed, level, liege, loyal, paced, rocky, sober, solid, staid, tight, wooer 6 ardent, poised, secure, sedate, serene, smooth, stable, strong 7 abiding, balance, certain, durable, endless, equable, eternal, gradual, intense, nonstop, patient, regular, settled, stabile, staunch, stiffen, uniform 8 constant, enduring, faithful, habitual, punctual, reliable, reserved, resolute, rhythmic, sensible, unbroken, unending, unshaken, untiring, unwaning 9 allegiant, ceaseless, continual, immovable, incessant, patterned, perennial, perpetual, stabilize, steadfast, temperate, undivided, unextreme, unvarying, valentine 10 changeless, consistent, continuous, dependable, persistent, phlegmatic, purposeful, set in stone, sweetheart, true to type, unaffected, unagitated, unchanging, undeterred, unflagging, unswerving, untroubled, unwavering
go ~: 3 pin, see, woo 4 date
keep ~: 3 fix, set 4 prop 6 freeze, secure, steady 7 balance, support 8 maintain, preserve 9 stabilize
succession: 6 stream
see also sweetheart
steady-__: 5 going 6 handed
__ steady: 4 rock
Steady __ goes!: 5 as she
Steady as __ goes!: 3 she
Steady Eddie: 5 Lopat
steady-going: 5 loyal
steak: 4 loin, meat, rump 5 chuck, filet, flank, round, T-bone 6 entrée, rib-eye 7 red meat, sirloin
ender: 5 house
grade: 5 prime 6 choice
like overcooked ~: 5 tough
like prime ~: 4 aged
on the hoof: 5 steer
order: 4 rare, well 6 medium 8 well-done
prepare ~: 4 sear 5 broil 8 barbecue
so to speak: 4 turf
starter: 4 beef
tenderize ~: 4 cube 5 pound
steak __: 3 set 5 Diane, knife 7 tartare
__ steak: 3 rib 4 club, cube, tuna 5 cubed, round, shell, skirt, strip, Swiss, T-bone 6 cheese, minute, pepper, rib-eye, tartar 7 Chicago, chopped, Hamburg
steak au __: 6 poivre
steakhouse: 6 eatery 10 restaurant
steak tartare, like: 3 raw
steal: 3 buy, rob 4 copy, flit, glom, lift, loot, lurk, sack, slip, take 5 cheat, creep, filch, glide, heist, pinch, poach, prowl, rifle, slide, slink, snake, sneak, strip, swipe, theft 6 abduct, burgle, divert, hijack, hold up, kidnap, pilfer, pirate, pocket, rip off, snatch, snitch, thieve, tiptoe 7 bargain, break in, defraud, despoil, larceny, pillage, plunder, purloin, ransack, slither, stick up, swindle 8 carry off, embezzle, good deal, highjack, liberate, peculate, purchase, shoplift, simulate, thievery, withdraw 9 great deal, pussyfoot 10 burglarize, plagiarize, run off with, spirit away
a march on: 5 one-up
a scene: 5 emote 7 overact
away: 2 go 3 fly 5 elope 6 escape 7 abscond, go south
(away): 4 slip
cattle: 6 rustle
from: 3 mug, rob 9 knock over
old-style: 3 nim
steal a __ on: 5 march
Steal Away (1980 song)
artist: Robbie Dupree
stealer: 5 thief 6 robber 7 burglar, rustler
scene ~: 3 ham
stealing: 5 theft 7 larceny 8 burglary, thievery 10 plagiarism
combining form: 5 klept- 6 klepto-
Stealing Beauty (1996 film)
cast: Sinead Cusack, Joseph Fiennes, Jeremy Irons, Liv Tyler
director: Bernardo Bertolucci
Stealing Home (1988 film)
cast: Jodie Foster, Mark Harmon
steal one's __: 5 heart 7 thunder
Stealth: 3 car 4 auto 5 Dodge
steal the __: 4 show
stealthily: 8 on the sly, secretly
stealth warrior: 5 ninja
stealthy: 3 sly 4 wily 5 catty, quiet, sneak 6 covert, crafty, feline, secret, shifty, silent, sneaky 7 catlike, cunning, furtive 8 hush-hush, skulking, slinking, sneaking, thieving, thievish 9 deceitful, enigmatic, insidious, noiseless, secretive, underhand 10 undercover, under wraps
steam: 3 gas, irk, vim 4 boil, cook, fume, mist, rage, reek 5 anger, might, peeve, power, press, speed, sweat, upset, vapor, vigor 6 blanch, energy, enrage, muscle, tee off 7 moisten, smolder, tick off 8 have a fit, smoulder, strength, vitality 10 exhalation
bath: 5 sauna
blow off ~: 4 rant, rave, vent, yell 6 holler, scream
conveyor: 4 pipe
cook with ~: 5 scald
ender: 4 boat, roll, ship 6 fitter, roller
give off ~: 4 reek
head of ~: 5 force
like ~: 7 gaseous
lose ~: 4 slow
sound: 4 hiss
source: 6 boiler, geyser 7 furnace
turn on the ~: 5 hurry 7 speed up
up: 3 fog 4 mist, rile 5 anger, befog, cloud 6 enrage, madden 7 enflame, inflame 9 instigate, stimulate
steam __: 3 box, fog 4 bath, beer, coal, heat, iron, room 5 chest,

organ, point, table **6** boiler, engine, fitter, hammer, jacket, shovel **7** heating, turbine
Steam __: **4** Heat
Steamboat __: **6** Willie **7** Springs
steamed: **4** sore **5** angry, het up, irate, upset, wroth **6** fuming, galled **7** furious **8** incensed, volcanic
get ~ up: **4** boil, burn, fume, stew **5** froth **6** see red, seethe, simmer **7** bristle, smolder
steam engine developer: **4** Watt
steamer: **3** wok **4** boat, clam **5** liner **6** vessel
steamer __: **3** rug **4** clam **5** chair, trunk **6** basket
__ steamer: **5** tramp **6** paddle
steaminess: **8** humidity
steaming: **3** hot **5** aboil, angry, at sea, irate, riled, upset **10** equatorial
steamroll: **4** push **5** forge **6** defeat
steamroller: **4** whip **6** hector **8** stalwart **9** overwhelm
Steamroller Blues (1973 song)
artist: Elvis Presley
steamroom site: **3** spa
steamship: **4** boat **5** liner
steamy: **3** hot, wet **4** damp, dank, hazy **5** humid, misty, moist, muggy, soggy, undry **6** clammy, erotic, fogged, sticky, stuffy, sultry, sweaty, torrid **7** boiling, wettish **8** roasting, tropical **10** oppressive, passionate, sweltering
get ~: **5** fog up
Ste.-Anne-__-Plaines: **3** des
stearate: **4** salt **5** ester
stearic __: **4** acid
stearin: **5** ester
__ Stearns: **4** Bear
Stearns, Turkey: **10** outfielder
steatite: **4** talc
Steber, Eleanor: **6** singer **7** soprano
role: **4** Elsa
specialty: **5** opera
Stedman: **6** Edmund, Graham
steed: **4** Arab, mare **5** bronc, horse, mount, pacer **6** bronco, equine **7** Arabian, broncho, charger, courser **8** war-horse **10** Bucephalus
Cockney ~: **4** 'orse
stopper: **4** whoa
see also horse
Steed, John: **7** Avenger
partner: **4** Emma, Gale, King, Peel, Tara
steel: **4** gird, tone **5** alloy, brace, build, metal, nerve, rally, ready, shore **6** anneal, beef up, buck up, harden, prop up, temper, tone up **7** bolster, brace up, build up, burgeon, develop, empower, enhance, fortify, hearten, resolve, shore up, stiffen, toughen **8** bourgeon, buttress, embolden, energize, imbolden, indurate, vitalize **9** encourage, intensify, reinforce **10** invigorate, strengthen
additive: **5** boron **6** cobalt **8** chromium
base: **4** iron **6** carbon
beam: **4** I-bar, L bar **5** H-beam, I-beam **6** girder
by-product: **4** slag
city: **3** Pgh. **4** Gary **10** Pittsburgh
ender: **4** head, work, yard **5** works **6** worker
factory: **4** mill
fine ~: **6** Toledo
German ~ center: **4** Ruhr **5** Essen
like ~ wool: **4** wove **5** woven
man of ~: **5** robot
oneself: **7** prepare
plow inventor: **5** Deere
reinforcement rod: **5** rebar
structural column: **5** lally
use ~ wool: **5** scour, scrub
what stainless ~ doesn't do: **4** rust
steel __: **4** band, blue, drum, gray, grey, mill, trap, wool **6** guitar
__ steel: **4** cold **6** carbon, chrome
Steel: **4** Dawn **8** Danielle
Steel __: **4** Pier
__ Steel: **5** Man of
steel-belted buy: **4** tire
Steel, Danielle: **6** writer
work: Accident
Amazing Grace
Answered Prayers
Bittersweet
Coming Out
The Cottage
Daddy
Echoes
Five Days in Paris
The Ghost
The Gift
A Good Woman
Granny Dan
Heartbeat
Honor Thyself
The House on Hope Street
The House
H.R.H.
Impossible
Irresistible Forces
Jewels
Journey
The Kiss
The Klone and I
Leap of Faith
Lightning
Lone Eagle
The Long Road Home
Malice
Matters of the Heart
Message from Nam
Miracle
Mirror Image
Mixed Blessings
No Greater Love
Once in a Lifetime
One Day at a Time
The Ranch
Ransom
Rogue
Safe Harbour
Second Chance
Silent Honor
Sisters
Southern Lights
Special Delivery
Sunset in Saint Tropez
Toxic Bachelors
Vanished
The Wedding
Wings
Steele: **5** Tommy **7** Richard
Steele, Richard: **3** Sir **6** writer **7** British **8** essayist **10** playwright
partner: Joseph Addison
publication: **6** Tatler **7** Tattler **9** Spectator
Steelers: **4** team **6** eleven
coach: **4** Noll
home: **10** Pittsburgh
org.: **3** AFC, NFL
rival: ***see*** NFL team
sport: **8** football
steelhead: **4** fish **5** trout
steelie
alternative: **5** agate
Steel Magnolias (1989 film)
cast: Olympia Dukakis, Sally Field, Daryl Hannah, Shirley MacLaine, Dolly Parton, Julia Roberts, Sam Shepard, Tom Skerritt
director: Herbert Ross
dog: **5** Rhett
steelworkers
former ~ union chief: **4** Abel
steely: **3** icy **4** firm, hale, hard, iron, wiry **5** beefy, burly, hardy, hefty, hunky, husky, lusty, rigid, rocky, solid, stern, stiff, stony, stout, tough **6** brawny, flinty, hearty, mighty, potent, robust, rugged, sinewy, stocky, stoney, strong, sturdy, virile **7** adamant, doughty, ferrous, hard-set **8** athletic, blue-gray, concrete, forceful, hardened, indurate, intrepid, muscular, powerful, puissant, resolute, stalwart, vigorous **9** Atlantean, Herculean, impliable, strapping, unbending, undaunted, well-built **10** able-bodied, adamantine, determined, inflexible, iron-willed, red-blooded, unyielding
Steely Dan
album: **3** Aja
song: Do It Again (1972)
Hey Nineteen (1980)
Reeling in the Years (1973)
Rikki Don't Lose That Number (1974)
Steen: **3** Jan
steenbok: **6** animal **8** antelope
relative: ***see*** antelope
Steenburgen, Mary: **7** actress
film: Back to the Future Part III (1990)
Cross Creek (1983)
Dead of Winter (1987)
Goin' South (1978)
Melvin and Howard (1980, AA)
A Midsummer Night's Sex Comedy (1982)
Miss Firecracker (1989)
Nixon (1995)
One Magic Christmas (1985)
Parenthood (1989)
Philadelphia (1993)
Ragtime (1981)
Time After Time (1979)
role in Back to the Future III: **5** Clara
spouse: Ted Danson, Malcolm McDowell
TV: Ink
Steen, Jan: **5** Dutch **6** artist **7** painter
steep: **3** sop **4** boil, brew, cook, damp, dear, fill, high, soak, tall **5** bathe, erect, imbue, lofty, pricy, sharp, sheer, souse, stiff **6** costly, drench, infuse, invest, pickle, pricey, raised, sodden **7** arduous, engrain, extreme, immerse, ingrain, moisten, pervade, suffuse **8** dizzying, marinade, marinate, permeate, saturate, submerge, towering, vertical, waterlog **9** breakneck, excessive, expensive **10** exorbitant, high-priced, immoderate, impregnate, inordinate, outrageous, overpriced, straight-up
descent: **6** escarp
in brine: **5** souse
place: **5** cliff
rock: **3** tor **4** crag **5** arête, bluff, cliff, scarp **8** overhang, pinnacle **9** precipice **10** escarpment, prominence
slope: **5** chute, scarp
steeper, get: **4** rise
steeple: **3** tip **5** spire, tower **6** belfry, flèche, turret **8** pinnacle **9** bell tower, campanile
adornment: **3** epi
ender: **4** bush, jack **5** chase
feature: **4** bell
Gothic ~: **6** flèche
part: **6** belfry
steeplechase: **4** race **5** sport **9** horse race
obstacle: **5** fence **6** hurdle
steeply pitched: **6** gabled
steepness: **5** pitch, slope
Steep Trails
author: John Muir
steer: **3** run, tip **4** helm, herd, land, lead, male, show **5** Angus, drive, guide, pilot, point, route, usher **6** advice, bovine, Brahma, cattle, direct, escort, govern, handle, jockey, manage, tipoff **7** captain, conduct, control, counsel, operate, skipper, solicit, suggest **8** longhorn, maneuver, navigate, shepherd, take over **9** influence, recommend **10** manipulate, take charge
as a ship: **4** conn
clear of: **4** duck, omit, shun **5** avoid, dodge, elude, evade, shirk, skirt, spurn **6** beware, bypass, eschew, lay off **7** abstain, shy from **8** flee from, sidestep **10** circumvent
easy to ~: **3** yar **4** yare
enclosure: **6** corral
(for): **3** aim, try
handler: **5** roper **6** cowboy
mark on a ~: **5** brand
throw a ~: **4** rope
towards: **7** head for
wrong: **8** misguide **9** misinform
steer __ of: **5** clear
__ steer: **3** bum
steering: **10** navigation
adjustment: **5** toe-in
apparatus: **4** helm
steering __: **4** gear **5** wheel **6** column
__ steering: **5** power
steersman: **3** cox
Stefan: **5** Zweig **6** Edberg, George
Stefani: **4** Gwen
Stefanie: **6** Powers
Steffens: **7** Lincoln
Steffi: **4** Graf
Ste.-Foy: **4** city, town
locale: **6** Canada, Québec
Stegner, Wallace: **6** writer
stegodon: **8** elephant
Steichen: **6** Edward
Steiger, Rod: **5** actor
film: Al Capone (1959)
The Chosen (1981)

Cry Terror (1958)
Doctor Zhivago (1965)
F.I.S.T. (1978)
Hands Over the City (1963)
Happy Birthday, Wanda June (1971)
The Harder They Fall (1956)
In the Heat of the Night (1967, AA)
Jubal (1956)
No Way to Treat a Lady (1968)
Oklahoma! (1955)
On the Waterfront (1954)
The Pawnbroker (1965)
The Specialist (1994)
W.C. Fields and Me (1976)
spouse: Claire Bloom
stein: 3 mug **4** dish **6** beaker, holder, vessel **7** tankard **9** container **10** receptacle
contents: 3 ale **4** beer **5** lager
Stein: 3 Ben **7** William **8** Gertrude
part of a ~ quote: 3 is a **4** rose **5** a rose
Steinbeck, John: 6 writer **8** Nobelist
birthplace: 7 Salinas
work: Cannery Row
East of Eden
The Grapes of Wrath
In Dubious Battle
Of Mice and Men
The Pearl
The Red Pony
Sweet Thursday
Tortilla Flat
Travels with Charley
The Wayward Bus
The Winter of Our Discontent
Steinberg, William: 9 conductor
steinbok: 8 antelope
relative: ***see*** antelope
Steinbrenner: 6 George **7** The Boss
Steinem: 6 Gloria
Steiner: 3 Max **4** Fred **6** Rudolf
Steiner, Max: 8 composer
film score: The Big Sleep
The Caine Mutiny
Casablanca
Dark Victory
Gone With the Wind
Intermezzo
Key Largo
King Kong
Marjorie Morningstar
Mildred Pierce
Now, Voyager
Sergeant York
A Summer Place
The Treasure of the Sierra Madre
White Heat
steinful: 3 ale
Stein, Gertrude: 6 writer
work: The Autobiography of Alice B. Toklas
Three Lives
Steinitz, William
forte: 5 chess
Stein, Jean
work: 4 Edie
Steinmetz: 3 Sol **7** Charles
Stein Song
state: 5 Maine
town: 5 Orono
Steinway: 5 grand, piano
stela
see stele
stele: 4 slab **6** column, marker **8** memorial, monument
St. Elias: 2 mt. **3** mtn. **4** peak **5** mount, range **8** mountain
locale: 6 Canada
Stella: 5 Adler **7** Stevens **8** Kowalski
Stella __: 4 d'Oro **5** Maris **6** Dallas **7** Polaris
stellar: 6 astral **8** sidereal
prefix: 5 astro-
see also wonderful
stellar __: 4 wind
St. Elmo's __: 4 fire
St. Elmo's Fire (1985 film)
cast: Emilio Estevez, Rob Lowe, Andrew McCarthy, Demi Moore, Judd Nelson, Ally Sheedy
St. Elmo's Fire (1985 song)
artist: John Parr
St. Elsewhere (NBC drama)
area: 2 ER **3** ICU
cast: Bonnie Bartlett (Ellen Craig)
Ed Begley Jr. (Dr. Victor Ehrlich)
William Daniels (Dr. Mark Craig)
Ed Flanders (Dr. Donald Westphall)
Stephen Furst (Dr. Elliot Axelrod)
Mark Harmon (Dr. Robert Caldwell)
Howie Mandel (Dr. Wayne Fiscus)
Kavi Raz (Dr. V.J. Kochar)
Denzel Washington (Dr. Phillip Chandler)
producer: MTM
setting: 6 Boston
stem: 3 bow, dam **4** axis, curb, flow, head, limb, prow, rise, root, stay, stop, twig **5** arise, block, check, issue, jam up, shoot, stick, stock, straw, trunk **6** arrest, branch, cut off, derive, hinder, oppose, resist, result, spring, stanch, stop up **7** control, curtail, develop, emanate, pedicel, pedicle, prevent, proceed, shut off, staunch **8** come from, hold back, peduncle, restrain **9** originate, withstand **10** keep in line
angle: 4 axil
berry ~: 4 cane
bulb-like ~: 4 corm
center: 4 pith
ender: 4 ware
(from): 4 come **5** arise **6** derive
hops ~: 4 bine
joint: 4 node **8** juncture, swelling
main ~: 5 trunk
mushroom ~: 5 stipe
opposite: 5 stern
pipe ~: 5 shank
plant ~: 5 stalk
stem __: 4 cell
stem-__: 6 winder
__ stem: 4 main **5** brain
__ Ste. Marie: 5 Sault
__-stemmed rose: 4 long
stem the __: 4 tide
__ stem to stern: 4 from
stem-to-stern timber: 4 keel
stemware: 5 glass **6** goblet **7** glasses
Sten: 3 gun **4** Anna
role: 4 Nana
stench: 4 funk, odor, reek **5** odour, smell, stink **7** malodor **9** effluvium, fetidness, redolence
stencil: 7 pattern
copy from a ~: 5 mimeo
cutter: 6 stylus
Stendhal: 6 French, writer
real name: 5 Beyle
work: The Charterhouse of Parma
The Red and the Black
Stenerud, Jan
sport: 8 football
Stengel, Casey: 7 manager
Mrs. ~: 4 Edna
sport: 8 baseball
stenographer: 5 clerk **6** writer **10** amanuensis
item: 3 pad
slip: 4 typo
stat.: 3 wpm
work: 6 letter
Stenson: 6 Henrik
stentorian: 4 loud **5** forte, noisy, vocal **7** blaring, booming, jarring, pealing, rackety, raucous, reboant, roaring **8** crashing, piercing, plangent, resonant, rumbling, sonorous, strident, turned up **9** big-voiced, clamorous, deafening **10** boisterous, resounding, strepitous, thundering, thunderous, uproarious, vociferant, vociferous
step: 3 act, run **4** gait, hoof, move, pace, rank, rung, trip, trot, walk **5** dance, grade, level, means, notch, phase, point, print, riser, rumba, samba, stage, stair, start, stoop, trace, track, trail, tread, troop **6** action, canter, degree, gallop, motion, prance, rhumba, rundle, shimmy, stride, tiptoe, trapes, trudge **7** advance, descend, measure, process, traipse **8** ambulate, footfall, maneuver, saraband **9** footprint, gradation, increment, procedure, sarabande **10** proceeding
all over: 9 trample on, tyrannize
aside: 4 move **9** stand down
back: 6 recoil
ballet ~: 3 pas **5** coupé, pique, tombé **7** déboîté, emboîté, pas alle **8** glissade **9** pas marché
by step: 8 bit by bit, in stages **9** gradually, piecemeal
dance ~: 5 rumba, samba, waltz **6** cha cha, chassé, do-si-do, rhumba **7** dos-à-dos, fox trot
down: 4 quit **5** leave, light **6** reduce, resign **8** abdicate, decrease
ender: 3 son **4** wise **5** child **6** family, father, ladder, mother, parent, sister **7** brother, sibling **8** children, daughter
false ~: 4 trip **7** mistake
forward: 7 advance **8** progress **9** volunteer
front ~: 5 stoop
heavily: 5 stomp, tromp
in: 5 enter **7** mediate **9** intercede, interfere, interpose, intervene, lend a hand, negotiate, take a hand **10** take action
in ~: 8 together **9** consonant **10** conforming, going along, harmonious
in French: 3 pas
keep a ~ ahead of: 5 one-up, outdo
keep in ~: 4 obey **6** comply, follow **7** abide by, agree to, conform **10** toe the line
long ~: 6 stride
measured ~: 4 pace
miss a ~: 6 falter
off: 6 alight
on: 5 stamp, tread **7** trample
on it: 2 go **3** fly, hie, rev, rip, run, zip **4** bolt, dart, dash, flit, race, rush, tear, zoom **5** hurry, scoot, speed **6** barrel, gallop, hasten, hustle, rocket, scurry **7** quicken, scamper, speed up **9** shake a leg, skedaddle **10** accelerate, burn rubber, get hopping
out with: 3 see, woo **4** date **5** court **6** escort, squire
over: 8 bestride
part: 5 riser
quick ~: 4 trot
request to take a giant ~: 4 may I
starter: 4 door, foot, lock, over, side **5** quick
take the first ~: 5 start
up: 4 bump, grow, lift **5** add to, boost, build, hurry, raise, speed, stair **6** hasten **7** augment, fortify, improve, magnify, quicken **8** escalate, expedite, increase **9** increment, intensify **10** accelerate, strengthen, supplement
up or down: 4 rung
walk in ~: 5 march
watching one's ~: 4 wary **5** canny, chary, leery **7** careful, guarded, heedful, prudent **8** cautious, vigilant, watchful **9** judicious **10** deliberate, scrupulous
watch one's ~: 6 behave, beware **7** look out **10** toe the line
step __: 3 off, out **4** down, on it, turn **5** aside
step __ gas: 5 on the
step __ rear: 5 to the
step __ the bar: 4 up to
__ step: 4 baby, side **5** dance, false, goose, out of
__-step: 3 one, two **4** high
Step __: 5 Saver **6** Lively
Step __!: 4 on it
Step __ crack...: 3 on a
__ step at a time: 3 one
Step Brothers (2008 film)
cast: Will Ferrell, John C. Reilly
Step by Step (song)
artist: New Kids on the Block, Eddie Rabbitt
Stepfanie: 6 Kramer
Stepford Wives, The: 4 film **5** novel
author: Ira Levin
cast: Peter Masterson, Paula Prentiss, Katharine Ross
Stephane: 8 Mallarmé
Stephanie: 5 Mills **6** Faracy, Miller **7** Beacham **9** Zimbalist
Stephen: 3 Fry, Rea **4** Boyd, King, pope **5** Crane, Dorff, Furst, Herek, saint **6** Austin, Bishop, Breyer, Dobyns, Foster, Frears, Harper, Leslie, Stills **7** Baldwin, Collins, Decatur, Douglas, Hawking, Langton, Leacock, McNally, pontiff, Spender **8** Sondheim **10** Gyllenhaal
Stephen __ Benet: 7 Vincent
Stephen __ Gould: 3 Jay
Stephen J. __: 7 Cannell

Stephen Jay __: 5 Gould
Stephen, King mother: 5 Adela
Stephen of __: 5 Blois
Stephens: 6 Darrin, Robert 8 Samantha 9 Alexander
Stephenson: 6 George
Stephen Vincent __: 5 Benet
Stepin: 7 Fetchit
Step on it!: 5 hurry 6 faster
step on one's __: 4 toes
step on the __: 3 gas
steppe: 4 moor 5 plain, plane 6 meadow 7 lowland
antelope: 5 saiga
cousin: 5 llano
horse: 6 tarpan
Steppenwolf
author: Hermann Hesse
song: Born to Be Wild (1968)
Magic Carpet Ride (1968)
Rock Me (1969)
Steppin' __: 3 Out 5 Stone
Steppin' __ With My Baby: 3 Out
stepping
ender: 5 stone
place: 4 rung
stepping-__ place: 3 off
Steppin' Out (song)
artist: Joe Jackson, Tony Orlando & Dawn
Steppin' Out With My Baby
composer: Irving Berlin
Steppin' Stone (1966 song)
artist: Monkees
Step right in!: 5 enter
steps: 3 way 4 path 5 route 6 course 8 movement
over a fence: 5 stile
retrace one's ~: 6 return 8 turn back
riverbank ~ in India: 4 ghat 5 ghaut
series of ~: 5 stair 6 gradin 7 gradine
take ~: 3 act 4 pace, walk 7 get busy
__ steps: 5 giant 7 library
Steps
author: Jerzy Kosinski
__ Steps: 7 Spanish
Step Saver: 7 cleaner
alternative: 5 Brite, Lysol 6 Top Job 7 Lestoil, Mr. Clean, Pine Sol 9 Fantastik
step to the __: 4 rear
step-up: 4 rise 5 raise 8 increase
-ster cousin: 3 -ist, -ite
stereo: 4 hi-fi 5 phono 7 boombox, Walkman 8 binaural, two-track, Victrola 10 phonograph
ancestor: 4 hi-fi, mono
component: 5 tuner 7 speaker 9 turntable
control: 4 bass 5 fader 6 treble, volume
erstwhile relative: 4 quad
input: 4 tape 8 cassette
run the ~: 4 play
stereotype: 3 dub 4 type 5 label 6 cliché, custom, define 7 average, catalog, example, fashion, formula, pattern 8 regulate, standard 9 catalogue, formality, normalize
stereotyped: 5 stale, stock, trite 7 clichéd 8 ordinary, overused 9 hackneyed, played out
stereotypes
use: 4 type 5 label 8 typecast
sterile: 7 aseptic
sterilize: 5 clean 6 degerm, purify 7 cleanse 8 fumigate, sanitize 9 autoclave, disinfect 10 pasteurize
sterilized: 4 pure 5 clean 10 antiseptic
sterilizer: 10 antiseptic
sterlet: 4 fish 8 sturgeon
sterling: 6 silver 9 honorable
fractions: 5 pence
starter: 5 pound
see also wonderful
sterling __: 6 silver
__ sterling: 5 pound
Sterling: 3 Jan 5 Brown, Tisha 6 Hayden, Robert 8 Holloway
stern: 3 aft 4 back, firm, grim, hard, rear 5 bossy, cruel, harsh, picky, rigid, rough, tough 6 bitter, crusty, flinty, severe, steely, strict 7 ascetic, austere, hard-set, prudish, serious, Spartan 8 coercive, despotic, exacting, frowning, hard-core, hard-line, resolute, rigorous, ruthless, stubborn 9 by the book, demanding, draconian, hang-tough, hard-nosed, hard-shell, imperious, impliable, mortified, stringent, unbending, unpitying, unsparing 10 adamantine, astringent, autocratic, bullheaded, despotical, forbidding, hard-bitten, hard-boiled, hard-headed, implacable, inexorable, inflexible, iron-fisted, ironhanded, iron-willed, no-nonsense, oppressive, relentless, tyrannical, unmerciful, unyielding
ender: 3 way 4 most, post, ward 5 wards 8 foremost
not ~: 3 lax 4 easy 7 lenient
opposite: 4 stem
toward the ~: 3 aft 5 abaft
Stern: 4 Emil, Otto 5 Isaac 6 Daniel, Howard
author: Bruce Jay Friedman
__ Stern: 3 Der
Sterne, Laurence: 6 writer 7 British
work: A Sentimental Journey
Tristram Shandy
Sternhagen: 7 Frances
Stern, Isaac: 9 violinist
need: 3 bow 5 resin
sternness: 5 rigor 8 iron hand 9 austerity
sternum: 4 bone 10 breastbone
sternward: 3 aft 5 abaft
steroid: 5 lipid 6 lipide
stertorous: 7 raucous 8 strident 10 breathless
stet: 7 leave in
opposite: 4 dele
stethoscope sound: 5 thump
St.-Étienne: 4 city, town
city near ~: 4 Lyon 5 Lyons
locale: 5 Loire 6 France
Stetson: 3 hat 10 university
athletes: 7 Hatters
locale: 6 DeLand 7 Florida
wearer: 5 Texan
Stettin river: 4 Oder, Odra
Steuben __: 5 glass
Steubenville: 4 city, town
locale: 4 Ohio
Steve: 3 Sax 4 Biko, Owen, Zahn 5 Allen, Earle, James, Kroft, Miner, Ovett, Perry 6 Barron, Binder, Brodie, Canyon, Carell, Carver, Forbes, Garvey, Gatlin, Harris, Kanaly, Martin, Miller, Sekely 7 Buscemi, Carlton, Cauthen, Cochran, Forrest, Largent, Mandell, Marriot, McQueen, Winwood, Wozniak, Yzerman 8 Lawrence, Lukather 9 Bedrosian, Railsback 10 Guttenberg
Steve Allen Show regular: 3 Nye
stevedore: 5 lader 6 loader
concern: 5 cargo
org.: 3 ILA
__-steven: 4 even
Steven: 3 Chu 4 Culp, Hill, Jobs 5 Bauer, Weber 6 Bochco, Seagal 8 Runciman, Weinberg 9 Spielberg 10 Soderbergh
in French: 7 Etienne
in Spanish: 7 Estéban
Stevens: 3 Art, Cat, Ray 4 Mark, Risë 5 April, Craig, Inger 6 Andrew, Connie, George, Stella 7 Wallace
Stevens, Andrew
spouse: Kate Jackson
Stevens, Cat
song: Another Saturday Night (1974)
Moon Shadow (1971)
Morning Has Broken (1972)
Oh Very Young (1974)
Peace Train (1971)
Wild World (1971)
Stevens, Connie
song: Kookie, Kookie (Lend Me Your Comb) (1959)
Sixteen Reasons (1960)
spouse: Eddie Fisher
Stevens, Craig
spouse: Alexis Smith
Stevens, George: 8 director
film: Alice Adams (1935)
A Damsel in Distress (1937)
The Diary of Anne Frank (1959)
Giant (1956, AA)
Gunga Din (1939)
I Remember Mama (1948)
The More the Merrier (1943)
A Place in the Sun (1951, AA)
Shane (1953)
Swing Time (1936)
Vivacious Lady (1938)
Woman of the Year (1942)
Stevens, Inger: 7 actress
TV: The Farmer's Daughter
Stevenson: 2 B.W. 3 Jan 5 Adlai 6 McLean, Parker, Robert
Stevenson, Jan: 6 golfer
Stevenson, Parker
spouse: Kirstie Alley
Stevenson, Robert Louis: 4 poet 6 writer 8 Scottish
home: 5 Samoa
work: The Body Snatcher
A Child's Garden of Verses
Kidnapped
The Master of Ballantrae
The Strange Case of Dr. Jekyll and Mr. Hyde
Treasure Island
Stevens Point: 4 city, town
locale: 9 Wisconsin
Stevens, Ray
song: Ahab, the Arab (1962)
Everything Is Beautiful (1970)
Gitarzan (1969)
The Streak (1974)
Stevens, Risë: 5 mezzo 6 singer 7 soprano
specialty: 5 opera
Stevens, Wallace: 4 poet
work: The Emperor of Ice Cream
The Man with the Blue Guitar
Owl's Clover
Peter Quince at the Clavier
Sunday Morning
Steverino: 5 Allen
__, Steverino!: 4 Hi-ho
__ Steve, The: 5 Tao of
Stevie: 5 Nicks, Smith 6 Wonder
Stevie __ Vaughan: 3 Ray
stew: 3 mix 4 boil, brew, cook, dahl, flap, fret, fume, fuss, hash, huff, olla, snit, sulk 5 adobo, bigos, blaff, brood, chafe, daube, gumbo, sweat, think, tizzy, worry 6 braise, burgoo, crisis, dither, fuming, hot pot, jumble, lather, medley, ragout, scouse, seethe, simmer, tumult 7 agonize, ferment, goulash, haricot, mélange, mixture, reflect, swelter, tsimmes, turmoil, tzimmes 8 cioppino, couscous, étouffée, fretting, matelote, mishmash, mixed bag, mulligan, pot-au-feu 9 Brunswick, casserole, cassoulet, commotion, confusion, inebriate, lobscouse, pepper pot, potpourri, succotash 10 blanquette, carbonnade, intoxicate, miscellany, salmagundi, turbulence
beef ~: 5 daube 10 carbonnade
Belgian ~: 10 carbonnade
British ~: 6 hot pot
Cajun ~: 8 étouffée
cooker: 5 crock
corn ~: 9 succotash
crayfish ~: 8 étouffée
East Indian ~: 4 dahl
fish ~: 8 cioppino, matelote
in a ~: 6 pacing, peeved 9 concerned 10 distressed
ingredient: 4 leek
lamb ~: 7 haricot 10 blanquette
lentil ~: 4 dahl
mutton ~: 7 haricot
North African ~: 8 couscous
okra ~: 5 gumbo
(over): 5 brood 7 agonize
Philippine ~: 5 adobo
pod: 4 ocra, okra, okro
Polish ~: 5 bigos
sailor's ~: 6 scouse 9 lobscouse
spicy ~: 4 olla 5 salmi 6 salmis
veal ~: 10 blanquette
vegetable: 5 onion 6 carrot
vegetable ~: 7 tsimmes, tzimmes
West Indian ~: 5 blaff 9 pepper pot
white-bean ~: 9 cassoulet
__ stew: 3 in a 5 Irish 9 Brunswick
steward: 5 agent 6 factor, keeper, lackey 7 curator, lacquey 8 watchdog 9 caretaker, custodian 10 manservant
ender: 3 ess
__ steward: 4 shop, wine
Steward, Rod
spouse: Alana Hamilton
Stewart: 2 Al 3 J.I.M., Jon, Rod 4 Amii, Dave, John, Mary 5 Alsop, James, Payne 6 Dugald, Elaine, French, Jackie, Martha 7 Douglas, Granger, Patrick 8 Copeland

Stewart, Al
song: Time Passages (1978)
Year of the Cat (1977)
Stewart, Jackie: **5** racer **8** Scottish **9** auto racer
Stewart, James: **5** actor
film: Bandolero! (1968)
Bell, Book and Candle (1958)
Born to Dance (1936)
Broken Arrow (1950)
Call Northside 777 (1948)
The Cheyenne Social Club (1970)
Destry Rides Again (1939)
The Far Country (1955)
The FBI Story (1959)
filmAnatomy of a Murder (1959)
Flight of the Phoenix (1966)
The Glenn Miller Story (1954)
The Greatest Show on Earth (1952)
Harvey (1950)
How the West Was Won (1962)
It's a Wonderful Life (1946)
It's a Wonderful World (1939)
The Man From Laramie (1955)
The Man Who Knew Too Much (1956)
The Man Who Shot Liberty Valance (1962)
Mr. Smith Goes to Washington (1939)
The Philadelphia Story (1940, AA)
Rear Window (1954)
Rope (1948)
Shenandoah (1965)
The Shootist (1976)
The Shop Around the Corner (1940)
The Spirit of St. Louis (1957)
The Stratton Story (1949)
Thunder Bay (1953)
Vertigo (1958)
Vivacious Lady (1938)
Winchester '73 (1950)
You Can't Take It With You (1938)
Ziegfeld Girl (1941)
Stewart, Mary: **6** writer **7** British
work: Airs Above the Ground
The Crystal Cave
The Gabriel Hounds
The Hollow Hills
The Ivy Tree
The Last Enchantment
Madam, Will You Talk?
Touch Not the Cat
The Wicked Day
Stewart, Patrick: **3** Sir **5** actor
film: Conspiracy Theory (1997)
Star Trek Generations (1994)
Star Trek: Insurrection (1998)
X-Men (2000)
TV: Star Trek: The Next Generation
Stewart, Payne: **6** golfer
Stewart, Rod
homeland: England
song: All for Love (1993)
Baby Jane (1983)
Crazy About Her (1989)
Da Ya Think I'm Sexy? (1978)
Downtown Train (1989)
Forever Young (1988)
Have I Told You Lately (1993)
Hot Legs (1978)
I'm Losing You (1971)
Infatuation (1984)
Lost in You (1988)
Love Touch (1986)
Maggie May (1971)
The Motown Song (1991)
My Heart Can't Tell You No (1989)
Passion (1980)
Reason to Believe (1993)
Rhythm of My Heart (1991)
Some Guys Have All the Luck (1984)
This Old Heart of Mine (1990)
Tonight's the Night (1976)
Young Turks (1981)
You're in My Heart (1977)
You Wear It Well (1972)
spouse: Alana Hamilton, Rachel Hunter, Penny Lancaster
stewed: **5** huffy, tight, tipsy **6** blotto **9** irrigated
fruit: **5** sauce
fruit dessert: **5** grunt
stew in one's ___ juice: **3** own
stewpot, Spanish: **4** olla
St. George's: **4** city, isle, town **6** island **7** capital
locale: **7** Bermuda, Grenada
St. Helens
locale: **8** Cascades **10** Washington
Stheno sister: **6** Medusa
Stich: **7** Michael
stick: **3** bar, bat, dig, jab, jam, lay, pin, put, ram, rod, run, set **4** bear, bind, bond, cane, clog, club, fuse, glue, gore, join, last, mast, poke, pole, prod, push, rule, sink, slab, slim, snag, stab, stay, stem, twig, wand, weld **5** abide, affix, baton, catch, clasp, cling, drive, jam up, lodge, paste, place, plant, plunk, ruler, spare, spear, spike, staff, stake, stalk, stand, stave, strip, stuff, swish, unite, wedge **6** adhere, attach, baffle, billet, branch, cement, cleave, cohere, cudgel, empale, endure, fasten, hold on, impale, insert, instal, linger, pierce, plunge, recoil, remain, slight, solder, stay on, suffer, switch, take it, thrust, timber **7** install, persist, slender, stay put, support, weather **8** beanpole, bludgeon, freeze to, hold fast, position, puncture, tolerate, transfix **9** billy club, penetrate, put up with, slap ender, truncheon, withstand **10** see through
alternative: **6** carrot
around: **4** bide, last, stay, wait **5** abide, tarry **6** linger, remain
billiards ~: **3** cue
bobby's ~: **4** cosh
by: **3** aid **6** uphold **7** support **10** go to bat for
conductor's ~: **5** baton
cotton on a ~: **4** Q-tip
ender: **3** pin, ups **4** ball, seed, tail, weed **5** tight **6** handle **7** handler
game: **6** hockey **8** lacrosse
in one's craw: **4** rile
into: **6** pierce
it out: **4** last, stay, take **6** endure, hang on, remain **7** subsist, weather **9** challenge
it to: **5** blame **6** impugn **7** revenge
lick and ~: **4** seal
make ~: **5** prove **6** attach
meat on a ~: **5** cabob, kabab, kabob, kebab, kebob
night ~: **5** baton **9** billy club
on: **3** add **5** affix **6** attach, empale, fixate, impale
one's neck out: **5** crane **6** gamble **7** venture **9** speculate
one's nose in: **6** meddle
on the ~: **5** alert, awake, aware **7** heads-up
out: **3** jut **4** poke, pout, push, show **5** bulge, pouch **6** extend **7** extrude, obtrude, project **8** overhang, protrude
out a hand to: **3** aid **4** abet, help **6** assist
pointed ~: **4** goad
riding ~: **4** crop
starter: **3** big, dip, joy, lip, non **4** chop, crab, drum, flag, mall, maul, slap, yard **5** broom, match, night **6** candle, single
to: **4** obey **5** cling **6** keep at **7** abide by **8** continue **9** accompany
together: **4** bond, glue, join, tape **5** clump, unite **6** cement, cleave, cohere
to one's guns: **6** insist **7** persist **9** persevere
up: **3** mug, rob **4** loot **5** steal
up for: **3** aid **4** back, help **6** defend, uphold **7** support, sustain **10** rally round, speak up for
walking ~: **3** bug **4** cane **5** staff **6** insect
stick ___: **3** out **4** it to **5** shift, up for **6** around, figure
stick ___ in the water: **4** a toe
stick-___-ive: **4** to-it
stick-___-mud: **5** in-the
___ stick: **3** big, cue **4** fish, pogo, salt **5** night **6** hockey **7** swagger, swizzle, walking
___ Stick: **4** Chap
stickball
locale: **6** street
marker: **5** sewer
stick by one's ___: **4** guns
Stick 'em up!: **5** reach
sticker: **3** bur, pin, tab, tag **4** barb, seal **5** decal, label, point, price, stamp, thorn **6** ticket
sticker ___: **5** price, shock
___ sticker: **3** pot **4** frog **6** bumper
sticker-shock site: **6** car lot
stickiness: **8** humidity
sticking: **8** cohesion **9** adherence
out: **9** obtrusive
point: **3** rub **4** beef **5** thorn
to one's guns: **3** set **4** firm **5** dug in **6** dogged, steely, strong **7** adamant, decided, do-or-die **8** hard-line, locked in, resolute **9** iron-jawed, steadfast, tenacious, unbending **10** unswayable, unyielding
sticking ___: **5** place, point
stick-in-the-mud: **4** fogy **5** fogey **6** fossil, square **7** diehard, old fogy
stickler: **6** purist, ramrod **7** fusspot **8** martinet **9** nitpicker **10** fussbudget
stick-on: **5** decal, label
stick one's ___: **5** oar in
stick one's ___ out: **4** neck
sticks: **5** wilds **6** claves, Podunk **7** boonies **8** frontier **9** backwoods, boondocks, outskirts **10** wilderness
it comes in ~: **3** gum
one from the ~: **4** rube **5** yokel **7** hayseed
starter: **6** fiddle
Sticks and Bones
author: David Rabe
stickshift selection: **3** low **4** gear, park **5** first, third **6** second **7** reverse
stick-to-itiveness: **4** grit, zeal **8** tenacity
stick to one's ___: **4** guns, ribs
stickum: **4** bond, glue **5** paste **6** cement **8** adhesive, fixative, mucilage
stickup: **3** job **5** heist, theft **6** holdup **7** robbery **8** thievery
Stick-Ups
alternative: **5** Glade **6** Wizard **7** Airwick, Renuzit
sticky: **4** damp, dank, icky **5** close, gluey, gooey, gummy, gunky, hairy, humid, mucky, muggy, nasty, rough, sappy, soggy, tacky, tight **6** clammy, clayey, knotty, rugged, sirupy, static, steamy, stuffy, sultry, sweaty, syrupy, thorny, tricky **7** awkward, clayish, painful, viscose, viscous **8** adhesive, clinging, delicate, tropical **9** difficult, glutinous, laborious, strenuous, tenacious **10** formidable, oppressive, sweltering, unpleasant
place: **4** mire
situation: **4** bind
stuff: **3** goo, gum **4** glue, goop, gunk **5** sirup, syrup
sweet: **3** bun **5** honey
sticky ___: **3** bun **6** wicket **7** fingers
Sticky ___: **4** Note
sticky-fingered: **8** thieving, thievish
Stieglitz, Alfred
need: **4** lens **6** camera
spouse: Georgia O'Keeffe
stiff: **3** set **4** cold, dear, firm, hard, high, lame, prim, snug, taut, wiry **5** aloof, brisk, cruel, exact, fixed, great, harsh, heavy, rigid, rusty, sharp, solid, stark, steep, stony, tense, thick, tight, tough, undue **6** creaky, forced, formal, frigid, frozen, jelled, numbed, potent, severe, steely, stoney, strict, strong, trying, wooden, worker **7** arduous, austere, bookish, brittle, chilled, default, distant, drastic, extreme, hard-set, jellied, labored, pompous, starchy, stately, staunch, stilted, swindle, uptight **8** annealed, cemented, exacting, grueling, hardened, immobile, mannered, ossified, pitiless, powerful, priggish, rigorous, starched, strained, stubborn, towering, ungainly, unlimber, vigorous **9** congealed, difficult, excessive, expensive, fatiguing, graceless, hidebound, impliable, laborious, obstinate, petrified, resistant, strenuous, stringent, thickened, unbending, unnatural, unpliable, victimize **10** artificial, contracted, exorbitant, formidable, hardheaded, headstrong, high-priced, inexorable, inflexible, insociable, mechanical,

oppressive, out of shape, relentless, solidified, unamenable, unbendable, ungraceful, unyielding
bindle ~: **3** bum **4** hobo **5** tramp
having a ~ upper lip: **5** stoic
in the joints: **4** achy
keep a ~ lower lip: **4** fume, mope, sulk **5** brood, frown **6** glower
keep a ~ upper lip: **4** cope **6** bear up, endure, hang in
working ~: **6** worker **7** laborer
stiff __ board: **3** as a
stiff __ lip: **5** upper
stiff-__: **3** arm **6** necked
__ stiff: **5** bored **7** working
stiffen: **3** fix, gel, set **4** clot, firm, gird, jell, prop, tone **5** brace, build, chill, shore, steel, tense **6** anneal, beef up, cement, curdle, freeze, gelate, harden, ossify, prop up, starch, steady, temper, tone up **7** bolster, brace up, build up, burgeon, congeal, develop, empower, enhance, fortify, inflate, petrify, shore up, support, thicken, tighten, toughen **8** bourgeon, buttress, condense, energize, indurate, solidify, vitalize **9** coagulate, intensify, reinforce, stabilize **10** gelatinize, inspissate, invigorate, strengthen
stiff-necked: **3** set **4** prim **5** stern **6** wilful **7** willful **8** stubborn **9** pigheaded
stiffness: **4** kink **5** cramp, spine **6** starch **7** tension, texture **8** distance, hardness **9** austerity
lose ~: **3** sag **4** wilt **5** droop
__ stiff upper lip: **5** keep a
stifle: **3** gag **4** cork, curb, hush, stop **5** check, choke, quell, sit on **6** clam up, dampen, deaden, hush up, keep in, muffle, muzzle, quench, shut up, squash **7** contain, cover up, prevent, repress, silence, smother, squelch, torpedo **8** black out, restrain, stagnate, strangle, suppress, throttle **9** choke back, clamp down, constrain, crack down, keep quiet, keep still **10** extinguish, hold it down, keep a lid on, keep in line
stifled: **4** weak **6** pent-up **8** reined in
stifling: **5** close **6** stuffy, sultry, torrid **8** tropical **10** equatorial, oppressive, sweltering
stigma: **4** blot, mark, scar, slur, spot **5** blame, brand, odium, shame, stain, taint **6** blotch **7** blemish **8** disgrace, dishonor, reproach **9** black mark, disrepute **10** imputation
stigmatize: **5** brand, shame, smear, stain, sully, taint **6** defame **7** asperse **8** denounce, disgrace, throw mud **9** discredit, implicate **10** calumniate
stile: **7** ingress
starter: **4** turn
Stiles: **4** Ryan **5** Julia
stiletto: **5** knife, point **6** bodkin, dagger **7** poniard, sidearm
use a ~: **4** stab
stiletto __: **4** heel
Stiletto
author: Harold Robbins
still: **3** lay, tho, yet **4** calm, ease, even, hush, idle, lull, stop **5** as yet, inert, photo, quell, quiet, stall **6** and yet, at rest, but yet, even so, halted, muffle, muzzle, placid, serene, settle, shut up, silent, soften, soothe, static, though **7** alembic, assuage, dormant, even now, however, put down, silence **8** calmness, even then, immobile, inactive, in repose, overcome, peaceful, stagnant, unmoving, until now **9** in any case, noiseless, peaceable, quiescent, soundless, to this day, voiceless **10** all the same, at this time, in any event, motionless, regardless, untroubled
and all: **3** yet **6** though
be ~: **5** relax **8** calm down
in the game: **4** live **5** alive
keep ~: **3** gag **4** hush **5** choke, quiet, shush **6** muzzle, shut up, stifle **7** silence **8** pipe down
life: **6** canvas **8** painting
not ~: **5** antsy, hyper, jumpy, noisy **6** moving, on edge **7** fidgety, jittery **8** restless
product: **5** hooch **6** hootch **9** moonshine
sit ~ for: **3** let **5** abide, allow **6** accept **8** tolerate
stand ~: **5** stall **6** freeze **8** stagnate
standing ~: **6** static
still __: **4** life **5** water
__-still: **5** stock
Still (song)
artist: Bill Anderson, Commodores
Still __: **4** Life **5** I Rise
still and __: **3** all
Still Breathing (1998 film)
cast: Brendan Fraser, Celeste Holm, Ann Magnuson
Still Crazy (1998 film)
cast: Stephen Rea
Stille __: **5** Nacht
stilled: **5** quiet **6** silent **8** hushed up
Stiller, Ben: **5** actor **8** director
film: The Cable Guy (1996)
The Heartbreak Kid (2007)
Keeping the Faith (2000)
Meet the Fockers (2004)
Meet the Parents (2000)
Night at the Museum (2006)
Permanent Midnight (1998)
Reality Bites (1994)
The Royal Tenenbaums (2001)
Starsky & Hutch (2004)
There's Something About Mary (1998)
Tropic Thunder (2008)
Zero Effect (1998)
Zoolander (2001)
parent: Anne Meara, Jerry Stiller
Stiller, Jerry: **5** actor **8** comedian
spouse: Anne Meara
TV: Seinfeld
Still Falls the Rain
author: Edith Sitwell
__ Still Felt: **5** In Joy
Still I Rise
author: Maya Angelou
Still Life
author: A.S. Byatt
still life subject: **4** ewer, pear **5** fruit **6** banana
Still Life with Coffee
artist: Joan Miró
Still Me
author: Christopher Reeve
stillness: **4** calm, hush, lull, rest **5** peace, quiet **6** repose **7** silence **8** calmness, serenity
Stillness at Appomattox, A
author: Bruce Catton
__ Still of the Night: **5** In the
Stillson __: **6** wrench
Stills, Stephen
member: Crosby, Stills & Nash
song: Love the One You're With (1970)
Still the One (1976 song)
artist: Orleans
__ Still the One: **5** You're
Still the Same (1978 song)
artist: Bob Seger
Stillwatch
author: Mary Higgins Clark
Stillwater: **4** city, town
athletes: **7** Cowboys
locale: **8** Oklahoma
school: **3** OSU
stilt: **4** bird, pole, post **5** lanky, spare **7** support **9** elongator, shorebird
cousin: **5** egret, stork **6** avocet
stilted: **4** prim **5** stiff **6** forced, formal, stuffy, turgid, wooden **7** bookish, flowery, genteel, labored, pompous, prudish **8** affected, decorous, inflated, mannered, pedantic, sonorous **9** bombastic, high-flown, overblown, ponderous, unnatural **10** artificial, pedantical, rhetorical, theatrical
Stilton: **6** cheese
Stimpy: **3** cat **4** toon
pal: **3** Ren
stimulant: **4** whet **5** tonic **6** bracer, coffee **8** pick-me-up **9** analeptic, energizer, incentive
stimulate: **3** jog **4** abet, goad, grab, help, hook, prod, send, spur, stir, urge, wake, whet **5** drive, evoke, hop up, impel, juice, key up, liven, pep up, pique, rouse, spark, waken **6** arouse, bestir, excite, fillip, fire up, foment, incite, kindle, perk up, prompt, pump up, stir up, thrill, tickle, turn on, vivify, wake up, work up **7** actuate, animate, enflame, enliven, inflame, inspire, juice up, liven up, massage, nurture, promote, provoke, quicken, refresh, sharpen, steam up, trigger **8** activate, energize, engender, enspirit, inspirit, interest, motivate, vitalize **9** challenge, electrify, entertain, fascinate, galvanize, impassion, instigate, titillate **10** accelerate, exhilarate, invigorate, predispose
stimulating: **5** brisk, crisp, fresh **6** lively, strong **7** bracing, healthy, piquant **8** readable **9** evocative
hardly ~: **4** blah **5** vapid **6** boring **8** tiresome
stimulation: **4** kick **5** spice
stimulus: **4** fuel, goad, kick, push, spur, urge **5** force, tonic **6** bracer **7** impetus, impulse **8** catalyst, pick-me-up **9** incentive **10** incitement, inducement, propellant
respond to a ~: **5** react
Stine: **2** R.L.
sting: **3** con **4** bilk, bite, burn, gull, hoax, hurt, pain, pang, rook, scam, trap **5** fraud, pique, prick, setup, smart, snare, wound **6** con job, dupery, entrap, humbug, injury, needle, offend, tingle **7** con game, prickle, swindle **8** irritate, pungency, trickery **9** deception, victimize **10** overcharge, run a game on
artist: **6** conman
ender: **3** ray
FBI ~: **6** Abscam
get in a ~: **6** entrap
react to a ~: **5** wince
take the ~ out: **4** lull **5** allay **6** lessen, smooth, soothe, temper **7** mollify
target: **4** mark **5** patsy **6** pigeon, victim
Sting
born: Gordon Sumner
song: All for Love (1993)
All This Time (1991)
Fortress Around Your Heart (1985)
If You Love Somebody Set Them Free (1985)
We'll Be Together (1987)
stinger: **3** bee **4** barb, wasp **5** drink **6** hornet **8** beverage, cocktail
flying ~: **3** bee **4** wasp **6** hornet
ingredient: **6** brandy
jellyfish ~: **5** cnida
part of an insect's ~: **5** oopod
stinginess: **6** thrift **9** frugality, parsimony
stinging: **4** acid, cold, sour **5** itchy, sharp **6** biting, bitter **7** caustic, cutting, intense, painful, peppery, piquant, pungent, satiric **8** scathing **9** sarcastic, satirical, vitriolic
comment: **4** barb
insect: **3** bee **4** wasp **6** hornet
Sting like a bee boxer: **3** Ali
stingo: **4** beer
stingray: **4** fish
Sting Ray: **3** car **4** auto **5** Chevy **8** Corvette **9** Chevrolet, sports car **10** automobile
Sting, The (1973 film)
cast: Paul Newman, Robert Redford, Robert Shaw
director: George Roy Hill
game: **5** poker
stingy: **4** mean **5** chary, cheap, close, petty, spare, tight **6** frugal, greedy, meager, measly, paltry, saving, scurvy, shabby, skimpy **7** chintzy, miserly, selfish, sparing, thrifty **8** churlish, grasping, grudging, skimping, ungiving **9** illiberal, mercenary, pennywise, penurious, scrimping **10** avaricious, economical, inadequate, pinchpenny, skinflinty, ungenerous
be ~: **5** skimp, stint
one: **5** miser, piker **10** cheapskate
stink: **4** fuss, odor, reek, to-do **5** fetor, furor, odour, smell **6** foetor, stench, uproar **7** malodor, scandal **8** brouhaha, fetidity, foulness **9** commotion, complaint, fetidness, grievance, hue and cry
ender: **3** bug, pot **4** aroo, ball, eroo, horn, weed, wood **5** stone
make a ~: **7** protest
social ~: **4** flap
stink __: **3** bug **4** bomb
__ stink: **5** make a
stinker: **3** cur **4** toad **5** knave, louse, rogue, scamp, skunk **6** bad egg, bad guy **10** holy terror

stinking: **3** bad **4** base, foul, grim, olid, poor, rank, vile **5** awful, fetid, funky, lousy, nasty, reeky, stale, woful **6** crumby, crummy, dismal, foetid, frowsy, frowzy, horrid, odious, rancid, rotten, smelly, strong, sweaty, woeful **7** accurst, baleful, baneful, beastly, doleful, ghastly, noisome, noxious, odorous, pungent, reeking, unclean **8** accursed, dreadful, God-awful, grievous, horrible, inferior, mephitic, shameful, terrible, unsavory, wretched **9** abhorrent, appalling, atrocious, defective, execrable, frightful, insidious, loathsome, miserable, offensive, revolting **10** abominable, deplorable, despicable, detestable, disastrous, disgusting, horrendous, lamentable, malodorous
__ Stinks: **4** Love
stinky
see stinking
stint: **3** bit, job **4** bird, curb, duty, lack, role, save, task, term, time, tour, turn, work **5** chore, hitch, limit, shift, spare, spell **6** grudge, scrape, scrimp **7** inhibit, skimp on, stretch **8** begrudge, hold back, restrict, withhold **9** constrain, economize, sandpiper **10** assignment, constraint, cut corners, engagement, penny-pinch, tour of duty
stinted: **6** meager **10** inadequate
Stipe: **7** Michael
stipend: **3** fee, pay **4** take, wage **5** grant, wages **6** salary **7** pension **8** benefice, gratuity, largesse **9** allowance, emolument
stipple: **3** dot **4** spot **5** fleck, paint **7** spatter, speckle
stipulate: **3** set **4** name **5** agree, posit, state **6** detail, impose, pledge **7** bargain, lay down, promise, provide, require, specify **8** contract, spell out **9** condition, designate, guarantee, prescribe **10** insist upon, provide for
stipulated: **3** set **9** customary
stipulation: **2** if **4** term **5** order **6** clause, string **7** promise, proviso **8** contract, covenant **9** agreement, condition, fine print, provision, requisite
stir: **3** ado, din, get, jog, mix, pen, row **4** beat, fire, flap, fuss, jail, move, poke, poky, rile, rout, send, spur, to-do, toss, wake, whet, whip **5** awake, blend, budge, clink, furor, get up, hoo-ha, hop up, jails, joint, pique, pokey, psych, rally, rouse, roust, shift, spark, spook, waken, whisk **6** action, affect, arouse, awaken, buck up, bustle, come to, cooler, excite, fidget, flurry, hoopla, hubbub, incite, kindle, lockup, muddle, pother, prison, prompt, quiver, racket, recall, ruckus, rustle, splash, thrill, tumult, uproar, wake up, whip up, work up **7** agitate, enflame, ferment, flutter, hearten, hoosgow, inflame, inspire, provoke, quicken, slammer, smolder, swizzle, tremble, trigger, turmoil **8** activate, big house, brouhaha, disorder, disquiet, embolden, energize, enspirit, hoosegow, imbolden, inspirit, interest, motivate, psyche up, smoulder **9** calaboose, commotion, electrify, encourage, enhearten, galvanize, get moving, impassion, make waves, move about, recollect, sensation, shake a leg, stimulate, transport **10** excitement, get a move on, invigorate
add, then ~: **5** mix in
cause a ~: **5** act up
in: **3** add
the air: **3** fan
up: **3** get **4** brew, fire, goad, prod, rile, roil, spur, urge, wake **5** anger, churn, egg on, impel, liven, raise, rally, rouse, roust, shake, spark, stoke, waken **6** arouse, awaken, excite, foment, incite, jostle, justle **7** ferment, fluster, provoke, trouble **8** motivate **9** impassion, instigate, stimulate
stir-__: **3** fry **5** crazy, fried
Stir __: **4** It Up **5** Crazy
Stir Crazy (1980 film)
cast: Richard Pryor, Gene Wilder
director: Sidney Poitier
stir-fry pan: **3** wok
Stir It Up (1973 song)
artist: Johnny Nash
stirred: **7** touched
up: **4** agog **9** turbulent **10** disordered
stirrer: **5** spoon
__ stirreth up strifes: **6** Hatred
stirring: **5** about, afoot, alive, astir, awake **6** lively, motion, moving **7** graphic **8** electric, eloquent, imposing, in motion, movement, touching **9** emotional, evocative, graphical, thrilling **10** expressive, impressive, intoxicant, passionate
stirrup: **4** bone
and hammer partner: **5** anvil
bone: **6** stapes
locale: **3** ear
stitch: **3** sew **4** knit, mend, pain, pang, purl, tack **5** baste, cable, patch, run up, sew up, shred **6** misery, repair, suture, twinge **7** crochet **8** particle **9** embroider
hidden ~: **6** inseam
loosely: **5** baste
sewing ~: **4** purl
starter: **3** hem, top **4** back, slip, whip **7** feather
without a ~: **4** bare, nude **5** naked
__ stitch: **4** knot, lock, loop, purl, rope, slip, tent **5** cable, catch, chain, close, flame, picot, satin **6** garter, kettle, ladder, saddle **7** blanket, running
__-stitch: **5** cross
Stitch
friend: **4** Lilo
__ & Stitch: **4** Lilo
stitches
be in ~: **5** laugh
line of ~: **4** seam
...St. Ives, __ a man...: **4** I met
St. Jacques: **7** Raymond
St. James's __: **6** Palace
St. John: **4** Jill **5** Betta
St.-John: **5** Perse
St. John, Jill
spouse: Jack Jones, Robert Wagner
St. John's: **4** city, town **7** capital **10** university
conference: **7** Big East
locale: **6** Canada **7** Antigua
school: **8** Memorial
school locale: **6** Queens **7** Jamaica, New York
St. John's Night
author: Henrik Ibsen
St. Joseph: **4** city, town **7** aspirin **9** analgesic **10** painkiller
alternative: *see* pain reliever brand
locale: **8** Missouri
stk.
see stock
St. Kitts and Nevis: **4** isls. **5** isles **6** nation **7** country, islands
capital: **10** Basseterre
locale: **10** West Indies
St. Laurent: **4** Yves
birthplace: **4** Oran
St. Lawrence: **4** gulf **5** river **6** seaway
city on the ~: **8** Montreal
explorer: **7** Cartier
river to the ~: **6** Ottawa **8** Saguenay **9** Richelieu
St.-Lô: **4** city, town
locale: **6** France, Manche
St. Louis: **4** city, port, town
locale: **8** Missouri
pro team: **4** Rams **5** Blues **9** Cardinals
river: **11** Mississippi
St. Louis Blues
composer: W.C. Handy
St. Lucia: **4** isle **6** island, nation **7** country
capital: **8** Castries
St. Malo: **4** city, gulf, port, town
locale: **6** France
river: **5** Rance
__ St. Mark, The: **5** Eve of
stoa: **5** Greek **6** arcade **7** portico
stoat: **6** ermine, weasel
relative: *see* weasel
stock: **3** kin **4** clan, cows, fill, folk, fund, have, herd, hogs, keep, line, mdse., mine, pigs, save, stem **5** amass, array, asset, banal, basic, breed, broth, cache, carry, count, equip, faith, flock, goods, hoard, lay in, paper, plant, sheep, store, swine, tribe, trite, trust, typic, uplay, usual, wares **6** assets, beasts, cattle, common, cravat, deal in, family, flower, gather, handle, horses, liquor, load up, normal, origin, outfit, shares, strain, supply **7** animals, backlog, capital, descent, furnish, kindred, lineage, popular, produce, progeny, provide, regular, reserve, routine, typical, variety, worn-out **8** ancestry, bouillon, everyday, gold mine, judgment, material, ordinary, overused, pedigree, reliance, standard, stow away, supplies **9** blue chips, customary, forebears, hackneyed, inebriant, inventory, parentage, posterity, provision, repertory, replenish, reservoir, selection **10** background, collection, confidence, dependance, dependence, estimation, evaluation, extraction, investment, threadbare, uninspired
acquisition pgm.: **4** ESOP
buy ~: **6** invest
counterpart: **4** bond
diet: **3** hay
ender: **3** ade, age, man, men, pot **4** fish, pile, room, yard **5** owner **6** broker, holder, jobber, piling, taking **7** breeder, holding **8** breeding **9** brokerage
have in ~: **4** keep, sell **5** carry **6** handle
holder: **6** corral
in ~: **4** here **9** available **10** obtainable
in trade: **5** asset
lock, ~ and barrel: **5** whole **6** in toto, wholly
of goods: **4** line
product: **4** soup
starter: **3** bit, die, gun, pen **4** feed, head, live, root, tail **5** drill **6** rudder **8** laughing
take ~: **10** scrutinize
take ~ in: **6** accept **7** believe
take ~ of: **4** note **5** audit **6** assess, survey
ticker inventor: **6** Edison
ticker output: **4** tape
see also stock market
stock __: **3** boy, car **4** book, shot **5** clerk, horse **6** broker, ledger, market, option, ticker **7** buyback, company, footage
stock-__: **5** route, still
stock-__ race: **3** car
__ stock: **4** open, take **5** no-par, out of, penny **6** common, equity, summer **7** capital, glamour, rolling
__ Stock: **6** Summer
stockade: **4** brig, jail, wall **5** fence **6** corral, prison **8** imprison **9** enclosure
stockaded village: **5** craal, kraal
__, stock and barrel: **4** lock
Stockard: **8** Channing
Stockhausen: **9** Karlheinz
stockholder: **8** investor
distribution: **8** dividend
vote: **5** proxy
Stockholm: **4** city, port, town **7** capital
airline to ~: **3** SAS
lake: **5** Malar
locale: **6** Sweden
prize: **5** Nobel
stock in __: **5** trade
__ stock in: **3** put **4** take
stocking: **7** hosiery
cap: **5** toque, tuque
filler: **3** leg
in French: **3** bas
material: **4** mesh, silk **5** lisle
no longer ~: **5** out of
part: **3** toe **4** foot
run in Britain: **6** ladder
shade: **4** ecru
snag: **3** run
starter: **4** blue
stuffer: **3** toy **4** coal, gift
stocking __: **3** cap **4** mask **6** stitch **7** stuffer
__ stocking: **4** body
__-stocking: **4** silk
stockings: **4** hose **6** nylons **7** hosiery, legwear
make ~: **4** knit

ST

stockings __ hung..., The: **4** were
__ Stockings: **4** Silk
__-Stocking Tales: **7** Leather
stockman: **6** cowboy **7** cowpoke **8** wrangler
stock market: **3** OTC **4** AMEX, mart, NYSE **6** bourse, NASDAQ **10** Wall Street
figure: **3** low **4** high **6** volume
gamble: **5** flier, flyer
holding: **3** lot
listing: **5** quote
membership: **4** seat
new ~ entry: **3** IPO
option: **3** put **4** call
phrase: **5** at par
remove from the ~: **6** delist
statistic: **5** yield
unit: **5** share
volatility measurement: **4** beta
stockpile: **4** heap, mass, pile, save **5** amass, cache, hoard, put by, store, trove **6** garner, gather, load up, supply **7** arsenal, backlog, buildup, collect, lay away, put away, reserve **8** gather up, hold on to, put aside, salt away **9** gathering, inventory, reservoir, warehouse **10** accumulate, collection, cumulation
stockroom: **9** warehouse
need: **6** ladder
stocks and __: **5** bonds
stock-still: **5** inert **6** frozen **8** immobile, unmoving **10** motionless, stationary
Stockton: **4** city, John, town
locale: **10** California
Stockton-on-__: **4** Tees
Stockwell, Dean: **5** actor
TV: Quantum Leap
stocky: **4** hale, iron, wiry **5** burly, hardy, hefty, hunky, husky, lusty, obese, short, solid, squat, tough **6** brawny, chunky, hearty, mighty, potent, robust, rugged, sinewy, steely, stubby, sturdy, virile **7** doughty **8** athletic, forceful, heavyset, indurate, muscular, powerful, puissant, stalwart, vigorous **9** Atlantean, filled-out, Herculean, strapping, well-built **10** able-bodied, red-blooded
see also obese
stockyard group: **4** herd
stodgy: **4** dull **5** dowdy, heavy, staid, unfun **6** boring, formal, stuffy **7** labored, tedious **8** pedantic, plodding **9** ponderous **10** enervating, monotonous, pedantical, pedestrian, unexciting
one: **4** fogy **5** fogey **7** old fogy **8** old fogey
stogie: **4** boot, shoe **5** cigar, smoke **8** footwear
cousin: **5** claro
stoic: **4** calm, cool **5** aloof, sober, staid **6** at ease, low-key, mellow, placid, sedate, serene, stolid **7** at peace, austere, patient, relaxed, unmoved **8** carefree, composed, detached, enduring, laid-back, resigned, tranquil **9** apathetic, collected, impassive, temperate, unexcited, unruffled **10** nonchalant, phlegmatic, poker-faced, unagitated, untroubled
one: **6** iceman
philosopher: **4** Zeno
stoical
see stoic
stoicism: **8** patience **9** austerity
founder: **4** Zeno
practice ~: **5** enure, inure
Stoic, The
author: Theodore Dreiser
Stojko: **5** Elvis
stoke: **4** feed, fuel **6** stir up
ender: **4** hold, hole
Stokely: **10** Carmichael
Stoker, Bram: **6** writer
work: Dracula
Stokowski, Leopold: **9** conductor
stola: **4** gown, robe **5** tunic
stole: **3** boa, fur **4** wrap **5** amice, scarf, shawl **7** garment, orarion, orarium **8** fur piece
material: **4** mink **5** sable **10** chinchilla
stolen: **3** hot
goods: **4** loot, swag **5** booty
goods outlet: **5** fence
Stolen Blessings
author: Lawrence Sanders
Stolen Kisses (1968 film)
director: François Truffaut
Stolen Summer (2002 film)
cast: Bonnie Hunt, Kevin Pollak, Aidan Quinn
Stoli: **5** vodka
rival: **4** Skyy **5** Popov **6** Rodnik, Starka **7** Absolut **8** Smirnoff **9** Grey Goose
stolid: **4** cool, dull, dumb, slow **5** dense, heavy, inert, stoic **6** bovine, obtuse, wooden **7** lumpish, passive, stoical **8** lubberly **9** apathetic, impassive, lethargic, unruffled **10** phlegmatic, unagitated, unreactive
stolidity: **7** laxness **8** laziness
Stolle, Fred: **7** netster **9** tennis pro
milieu: **5** court
Stoller: **4** Mike **5** Ilona
Stoloff: **3** Ben **6** Morris
stolon: **5** shoot
Stoltz: **4** Eric
Stolze: **4** Lena
stoma: **4** pore
stomach: **3** gut, maw, pot, tum **4** bear, craw, lump, take **5** abide, belly, brook, stand, stick, taste, tummy, valor **6** accept, endure, liking, omasum, paunch, relish, suffer **7** abdomen, gizzard, prowess, sustain, swallow **8** appetite, bear with, overlook, potbelly, stand for, tolerate **9** put up with, spare tire
animal ~: **3** maw **4** craw
butterflies in the ~: **6** nerves
combining form: **4** celi- **5** celio-, coeli-, gastr-, ventr- **6** coelio-, gastro-, ventri-, ventro-
complaint: **5** growl **6** rumble
cow ~: **5** rumen **6** omasum
ender: **4** ache
have no ~ for: **4** hate **5** abhor **6** detest, loathe **7** dislike
muscles: **3** abs
of the ~: **7** gastric
on one's ~: **5** prone
part of the ~: **6** cardia
problem: **3** gas **4** acid **5** agita
soother: **5** Bromo **6** bicarb
tightener: **5** sit up
turn one's ~: **6** revolt, sicken
stomach __: **4** acid
stomp: **4** step **5** clump, crush, dance, pound, storm, tramp **6** stride **7** clobber, trample, trounce
around: **4** rage
__ Stomp: **7** Bristol
Stompin' __ Savoy: **5** at the
stomping ground: **4** turf **5** haunt **6** domain, locale, region, sphere **7** hangout, quarter **8** locality **9** territory
stone: **3** gem, ore, pit **4** crag, pelt, rock, slab **5** flint, grain, jewel, throw **6** gravel, jasper, pebble **7** boulder, bowlder, crystal, jewelry, mineral, trinket **8** landmark, monument **9** inebriate **10** intoxicate
altar ~: **5** mensa
ancient ~ implement: **6** amgarn
artifact: **6** eolith
basin: **6** lavabo
cherry ~: **3** pit
chip: **5** galet, spall **6** gallet, garret
combining form: **4** -lith, petr-
ender: **3** cat, fly **4** chat, crop, fish, wall, ware, wash, work, wort **5** mason **6** cutter, roller, worker
face with ~: **5** revet
grinding ~: **4** mano
hollow ~: **5** geode
launcher: **5** sling **9** slingshot
leave no ~ unturned: **4** seek **5** scour **6** search, strive **7** persist, ransack, rummage **9** persevere
lily: **6** fossil
marker: **4** carn **5** cairn
masonry ~: **6** ashlar, ashler
monument: **5** stela, stele
paving ~: **4** sett **5** favus **6** cobble
piece: **4** slab
precious ~: **3** gem **4** ruby **5** jewel **7** emerald
prehistoric ~ tower: **6** chulpa **7** chullpa
rolling ~: **5** rover **7** drifter, vagrant **8** wanderer
Roman vase ~: **5** murra **6** murrha
set in ~: **5** solid **6** steady **7** adamant **9** immovable, unbending **10** inexorable
starter: **3** cap, gem, key, mud, oil, pot, sun, tin **4** blue, brim, burr, cope, curb, drip, fire, flag, flow, foot, free, gall, gold, hail, holy, iron, jack, lime, load, lode, marl, mile, mill, moon, pipe, sand, silt, soap, toad, turn, vein, whet **5** birth, blood, brown, chalk, cling, field, green, grind, pitch, rhine, snake, stink, touch **6** cherry, cobble, corner, hearth **8** stepping
turn to ~: **6** freeze **7** petrify
stone __: **4** bass, crab, lily, mint, pine **5** china, fruit, plant **6** curlew, fungus, marten **7** lantern, parsley
stone-__: **5** broke, faced
stone-__ wheat: **6** ground
__ stone: **5** set in **7** Blarney, Rosetta
__-stone: **4** rune
Stone: **3** Sid, Sly **4** Ezra, Lucy, Matt **5** Lewis, river **6** Irving, Jagger, Norman, Oliver, Sharon **7** Milburn, Richard **8** Phillips
locale: **9** Tennessee
Stone __: **3** Age **4** Kiss, Love
Stone __, GA: **8** Mountain
Stone __ Pilots: **6** Temple
__ Stone: **7** Moabite, Rolling, Steppin'
Stone Age
relic: **6** eolith
Stone Boy, The (1984 film)
cast: Glenn Close, Robert Duvall
stone-broke: **4** poor **8** strapped **9** destitute
stonecrop: **5** orpin, sedum
stonecutter tool: **6** chisel
Stoned Love (1970 song)
artist: Supremes
Stoned Soul Picnic (1968 song)
artist: Fifth Dimension
composer: Laura Nyro
Stone for Danny Fisher, A
author: Harold Robbins
...stone gathers no __: **4** moss
stone-ground __: **5** wheat
Stonehenge: **8** monument
builder: **4** Celt **5** druid
river near ~: **4** Avon
Stone, Irving: **6** writer
work: Adversary in the House
The Agony and the Ecstasy
Depths of Glory
Love Is Eternal
Lust for Life
The Origin
Sailor on Horseback
Stone Kiss
author: Faye Kellerman
stonelike: **4** hard **7** lithoid **9** lithoidal
Stone Love (1987 song)
artist: Kool and the Gang
Stone of __: **5** Scone
Stone, Oliver: **8** director
film: Alexander (2004)
Any Given Sunday (1999)
Born on the Fourth of July (1989, AA)
The Doors (1991)
JFK (1991)
Nixon (1995)
Platoon (1986, AA)
Talk Radio (1988)
U Turn (1997)
Wall Street (1987)
World Trade Center (2006)
stones
companions: **6** sticks
skip ~: **3** dap
throw ~ at: **3** pan, rap **4** pelt, slam **5** blame, decry, knock, sneer **6** malign, vilify **7** censure, condemn, put down, run down, slander, traduce **8** backbite, badmouth, belittle, denounce, derogate **9** criticize, denigrate, disparage, reprehend **10** calumniate
__ Stones: **7** Rolling
Stone, Sharon: **7** actress
film: Above the Law (1988)
Basic Instinct (1992)
Casino (1995)
Catwoman (2004)
He Said, She Said (1991)
The Mighty (1998)
The Muse (1999)
The Quick and the Dead (1995)
Sliver (1993)
The Specialist (1994)

Sphere (1998)
Total Recall (1990)
film (voice): Antz (1998)
Stones of Venice, The
author: John Ruskin
stone's throw away, a: 4 near **5** close **6** nearby
stonewall: 5 block, evade, hedge, stall, stimy, stymy **6** hold up, impede, resist, shield, stymie **7** cover up **8** obstruct **9** dissemble **10** equivocate
Stonewall: 7 Jackson
stoneware: 6 jasper **7** pottery **8** ceramics
stone-wash: 6 abrade
stonewashed
fabric: 5 denim
garment: 5 jeans
stoneworker: 5 mason
stonewort: 4 alga
Stoney End (1970 song)
artist: Barbra Streisand
composer: Laura Nyro
stony: 3 icy **4** cold, firm, hard **5** blank, chill, cruel, rigid, rocky, rough, solid, stiff **6** chilly, flinty, jouncy, lithic, rugged, steely **7** adamant, callous, deadpan, hostile, ice-cold **8** concrete, gravelly, hardened, indurate, obdurate, pitiless, ruthless, stubborn, uncaring **9** heartless, impassive, impliable, merciless, unbending, unfeeling, unpitying, unsmiling **10** hard-bitten, inexorable, inflexible, poker-faced, unwavering
stony-__: 5 faced **7** hearted
stooge: 4 dupe, fool, pawn, tool **5** patsy, toady **6** jackal, lackey, puppet, victim **7** cat's-paw, lacquey **8** henchman, kowtower, pushover **9** underling
Stooge: 3 Moe **5** Curly, Larry, Shemp **8** Curly Joe
count: 5 three
Stookey, Paul: 6 singer
member of: Peter, Paul & Mary
song: Wedding Song (There Is Love) (1971)
stool: 4 seat **5** perch **7** ottoman **8** footrest **9** furniture
part: 3 leg
starter: 3 bar **4** camp, foot, step, toad
user: 5 comic **8** comedian
__ stool: 7 ducking, milking
stoolie
see stool pigeon
stool pigeon: 3 rat **4** fink, nark, tool **5** namer **6** canary, ratter **7** tattler, traitor **8** informer, turncoat **9** informant **10** tattletale
stoop: 3 sag **4** bend, duck, flex, lean, orch, sink, step **5** deign, droop, hunch, kneel, kotow, lower, porch, slump, squat, swoop **6** crouch, hunker, kowtow, oblige, slouch **7** bow down **8** bend down, lose face, resort to **9** patronize **10** condescend, double over
ender: 4 ball
stooped: 4 bent **6** droopy
__ Stoops to Conquer: 3 She
stop: 3 bar, end, fix, gag, nip, tab, tie **4** clog, cork, drop, foil, halt, hush, kill, lift, lull, park, plug, quit, rest, seal, stay, stem, veto **5** avast, belay, block, brake, break, cease, check, close, delay, depot, leave, letup, light, lodge, pause, quash, quell, quiet, scrub, stage, stall, still, stump, stunt, tarry, tie up, visit **6** arrest, becalm, cool it, cutoff, cut out, desist, draw up, ending, expire, finish, forbid, freeze, give up, hamper, hinder, hold it, impede, lay off, linger, muzzle, outlaw, period, pull up, recess, rein in, run out, stifle, tackle, thwart, wait up, wind up, wrap up **7** adjourn, back off, closure, congest, disrupt, embargo, fetch up, f-number, inhibit, layover, occlude, prevent, put down, refrain, repress, sign off, silence, sojourn, squelch, stammer, station, staunch, suspend, turn off, ward off **8** blockade, blockage, break off, choke off, conclude, cut short, guard cry, hang it up, hold back, knock off, leave off, obstruct, peter out, prohibit, restrain, shut down, suppress, surcease, terminus **9** barricade, cessation, close down, forestall, frustrate, hesitancy, intercept, interdict, interrupt, roadblock, terminate **10** call it a day, cold-turkey, conclusion, disruption, do away with, knock it off, put an end to, standstill
as a ship: 5 lay to
brief ~: 5 pause **6** recess
by: 4 call **5** pop in, visit **6** drop in
don't ~: 4 go on **5** run on **6** keep at **8** continue
ender: 3 gap **4** cock, over **5** light, watch
for: 6 pick up
legally: 5 embar
rest ~: 5 B and B, hotel, lodge, motel **6** hostel **7** auberge, lodging **8** hostelry **9** roadhouse **10** motor court, motor lodge
starter: 3 non **4** back, door **5** short
try to ~: 5 deter **10** discourage
up: 3 dam **4** bolt, clog, cork, lock, plug, seal, shut, stem **5** block, close, latch, stuff **6** impede, secure **7** occlude, seal off, shutter **8** blockade, obstruct
with: 5 end at
worrying: 5 relax **6** unwind **7** cool off, lay back **8** calm down, loosen up **9** hang loose **10** settle down, simmer down
stop __: 3 off, out **4** over, sign **5** order **6** clause, motion **7** payment
stop __ dime: 3 on a
stop-__: 5 and-go
stop-__ order: 4 loss **5** limit
stop-__ photography: 6 action
__ stop: 3 pit **4** flue, full, reed, rest **5** truck **6** double **7** glottal, rolling, whistle
__-stop: 7 whistle
Stop (1998 song)
artist: Spice Girls
Stop __!: 5 thief
Stop!: 4 halt, whoa **5** avast **6** enough, hold it, quit it
__ Stop: 3 Bus **4** Can't, Don't
Stop and Smell the Roses (1974 song)
artist: Mac Davis
stop at __: 7 nothing
stopcock: 3 tap **6** faucet
Stop Draggin' My Heart Around (1981 song)
artist: Stevie Nicks, Tom Petty
stopgap: 5 ad hoc, shift **6** ersatz, fill-in, refuge **7** Band-Aid, interim, measure **9** contrived, emergency, expedient, impromptu, makeshift, practical, temporary **10** improvised, jury-rigged, pro tempore, substitute
Stop! In the Name of Love (1965 song)
artist: Supremes
stoplight
color: 3 red **5** amber, green **6** yellow
heed a ~: 5 brake
stop-listen link: 4 look
__ Stop Loving You: 5 I Can't
Stop Making Sense (1984 film)
director: Jonathan Demme
stopover: 3 inn **4** camp, stay **5** B and B, hotel, lodge, motel, oasis, visit **6** hostel **7** auberge, lodging, sojourn **8** hostelry **9** roadhouse **10** motor court, motor lodge
stoppage: 3 jam **4** halt **5** block, check, delay, tie-up **6** arrest, cutoff, holdup, layoff, stasis **7** closure, lockout, sit-down, walkout **8** abeyance, blockade, blockage, downtime, gridlock, shutdown, tarrying **9** abatement, cessation, interlude, occlusion **10** standstill, suspension
__ stoppage: 4 work
Stoppard, Tom: 3 Sir **7** British **10** playwright
work: Enter a Free Man
Every Good Boy Deserves Favour
Jumpers
The Real Inspector Hound
The Real Thing
Rosencrantz and Guildenstern Are Dead
stopped: 5 let up **6** frozen, static **10** gridlocked
up: 5 tight
stopper: 3 top **4** cork, plug, seal **5** block **7** closure, occlude
__-stopper: 3 gob **4** show
stopping
device: 5 brake
point: 5 limit
Stopping by Woods on a Snowy Evening: 4 poem
author: Robert Frost
stopple
see stopper
Stop pouring!: 4 When
__ stops here, The: 4 buck
__-stop shopping: 3 one
stop-sign sides: 5 eight
Stop Stop Stop (1966 song)
artist: Hollies
Stop talking!: 3 shh **4** hush **5** bag it, can it **6** shut up
__ Stop the Rain: 5 Who'll
Stop the World I Want To Get Off
character: 4 Evie
stopwatch: 5 timer
button: 5 reset
storage
area: 3 bin **4** crib, hold, loft, shed, silo **5** attic, chest, depot, hutch, shelf, trunk, vault **6** armory, cellar, closet, garage, locker, recess **7** cabinet **8** basement, cupboard, landfill, magazine, wardrobe **9** warehouse **10** depository, repository
food ~ area: 5 hutch, shelf **6** closet, pantry **7** cabinet **8** cupboard
storage __: 4 cell **7** battery
__ storage: 4 cold, dead, main, real **5** cache **7** virtual, working
storax: 4 tree **5** shrub
Storch: 5 Larry
store: 3 can, lot **4** bank, deli, fund, hide, hold, keep, load, lode, mart, mine, pile, save, shop, stow, well **5** amass, cache, depot, fount, hoard, lay in, lay up, place, put by, stash, stock, super, uplay, vault, wares **6** bakery, freeze, garner, larder, load up, market, outlet, pantry, pile up, ration, regard, retain, save up, supply, wealth **7** arsenal, backlog, deposit, harvest, husband, lay away, nest egg, put away, reserve, savings, Staples **8** boutique, business, cumulate, emporium, fountain, gold mine, hang onto, hide away, hold onto, lock away, lodgment, magazine, maintain, mothball, pack away, pharmacy, preserve, put aside, quantity, salt away, set apart, set aside, showroom, sock away, treasury **9** abundance, inventory, provision, repertory, reservoir, stockpile, superette, warehouse **10** accumulate, collection, cumulation, five-and-ten, keep on hand, repository
be in ~: 4 loom
be in ~ for: 4 look, wait **5** await **10** anticipate
ender: 4 room, wide **5** front, house, owner **6** keeper
enjoy a ~: 4 shop **6** browse
event: 4 sale
factory ~: 6 outlet
group: 5 chain
in ~: 5 on tap, spare **6** at hand, coming **8** destined, imminent **9** impending, ready to go
information: 4 file **5** enter **6** record **7** archive, catalog **8** document, preserve, tabulate
makeshift ~: 5 stand
offering: 5 goods
owner: 10 proprietor
set ~ by: 5 prize, value **6** accept, bank on, esteem, rely on **7** count on, respect, swear by, trust in **8** depend on, hold with **9** count upon
sign: 4 open **6** closed
starter: 4 book, drug
up: 5 amass, lay by, lay in, put by **6** garner **7** recruit, reserve **8** conserve, hold on to, salt away, set apart, set aside **10** accumulate
worker: 5 clerk **7** cashier
store __: 5 brand
store-__: 6 bought
__ store: 3 box **4** cold, dime, men's **5** chain, combo, ship's **6** anchor

7 company, country, general, grocery, package, ten-cent, variety
__ store by: 3 set 5 set no
storefront
feature: 4 neon 6 awning, canopy, display
storehouse: 4 fund 5 cache, depot, trove 6 museum 7 arsenal 8 magazine, treasury 10 depository
storekeeper: 6 grocer, seller, trader 8 merchant
storer: 7 pack rat
storeroom: 5 attic
stores: 8 supplies 10 provisions
__ stores: 3 sea 5 naval, ship's, small
__ Store, The: 3 Big
storied: 5 famed 6 fabled, famous 7 eminent, honored 8 mythical, renowned 9 legendary, well-known 10 celebrated
stories
body of legendary ~: 6 mythos
handed-down ~: 4 lore
__ Stories, The: 6 Berlin
stork: 4 bird 5 wader 6 argala, jabiru 7 marabou 8 marabout 9 flinthead
cousin: 4 ibis 5 crane, egret, heron
like a ~: 5 leggy
visit: 5 birth
storm: 3 row 4 blow, boil, door, fray, fury, fuss, gale, gust, hail, howl, pour, rage, raid, rain, rant, rave, roar, rush, snow, tear, to-do, wind 5 beset, blast, blitz, burst, foray, furor, melee, onset, siege, sleet, stomp 6 assail, attack, charge, invade, lather, outcry, precip, racket, seethe, squall, temper, tumult, volley 7 assault, barrage, besiege, bluster, bombard, cyclone, ferment, monsoon, outrage, passion, rampage, run amok, tantrum, tempest, thunder, tornado, turmoil, twister 8 blizzard, downpour, have a fit, hysteria, invasion, outbreak, outburst, upheaval, violence 9 blow a fuse, broadside, cannonade, commotion, discharge, fusillade, hurricane, hysterics, intrude on, onslaught, whirlwind 10 cloudburst, convulsion, free-for-all, hit the roof, revolution
center: 3 eye
dust ~: 4 wind
electromagnetic ~: 6 aurora
ender: 5 bound
eye of the ~: 4 calm, lull
look like a ~: 5 lower
out of: 7 abandon
pellets: 4 hail 5 sleet
posting: 5 alert
preceder: 4 calm
refuge: 6 cellar
sci-fi ~ material: 3 ion
sewer: 5 drain
starter: 4 barn, fire, hail, rain, sand, snow, wind 5 brain 7 thunder
take by ~: 4 rush 6 attack
up a ~: 10 vigorously
storm __: 3 out, pit 4 boat, coat, door, sash 5 drain, house, sewer, surge, track, watch 6 cellar, center, signal, window 7 warning
storm __ teacup: 3 in a
__ storm: 3 ice 4 dust
Storm: 3 car, Geo 4 auto, Gale 7 Theodor
__ Storm: 6 Desert, Summer
Storm and __: 6 Stress
Storm Fear
author: Robert Frost
storminess: 8 violence 10 turbulence
storming: 8 wrathful 10 infuriated
stormless: 4 calm 5 still 8 peaceful, tranquil
Storm Operation
author: Maxwell Anderson
__ Storm, The: 3 Ice 6 Mortal, Secret 7 Perfect
stormy: 3 hot, wet 4 cold, foul, wild 5 angry, gusty, irate, rainy, rough, windy, wroth 6 fierce, heated, raging, raving 7 furious, howling, pouring, ranting, violent 8 blustery, menacing, vehement, wrathful 9 inclement, turbulent 10 coming down, passionate, riproaring, tumultuous
stormy __: 6 petrel
Stormy Monday (1988 film)
cast: Melanie Griffith, Tommy Lee Jones, Sting
Stormy Weather: 4 song
artist: Lena Horne, Ethel Waters
composer: Harold Arlen, Ted Koehler
Stormy Weather (1943 film): 7 musical
cast: Cab Calloway, Lena Horne, Bill Robinson
Storrs: 4 city, town
athletes: 7 Huskies
school: 5 U. Conn.
Storting: 10 parliament
locale: 4 Oslo 6 Norway
story: 3 bio, fib, lie 4 book, epic, myth, news, plea, plot, saga, tale, tier, yarn 5 alibi, drama, fable, floor, level, novel, prose, rumor, scoop, spiel 6 canard, comedy, excuse, exposé, gossip, legend, memoir, record, report, script, sequel, serial 7 account, article, baloney, boloney, episode, feature, fiction, history, mystery, parable, recital, release, romance, tragedy, untruth, version, writing 8 allegory, anecdote, folktale, libretto, news item, strategy, tall tale, teleplay, thriller, white lie, whodunit 9 adventure, biography, chronicle, dime novel, fairy tale, falsehood, narration, narrative, potboiler, rationale, recountal, soap opera 10 allegation, confession, literature
animal ~: 5 fable
cover ~: 7 pretext
credit: 6 byline
ender: 4 book 5 board 6 teller, writer
end of ~: 6 period
fairy ~: 4 lore, myth, tale 5 fable 6 legend 7 fantasy, fiction 8 allegory, delusion, folktale 9 falsehood, invention
false ~: 3 lie 6 canard
fish ~: 3 fib, lie 4 tale, yarn 7 fiction
folk ~: 4 myth, tale 5 fable 6 legend 9 tradition
funny ~: 4 joke
heroic ~: 4 epic, gest 5 geste
in Britain: 4 rede
inconsistency: 4 hole
inside ~: 4 dope 5 scoop, truth 7 lowdown
life ~: 3 bio 4 biog. 6 memoir 7 memoirs 9 biography
line: 3 arc 4 plot 8 scenario
long ~: 4 epic, saga 5 novel
made-up ~: 5 novel 7 fiction
old ~: 4 myth 6 legend
sensational ~: 6 exposé
suppress a ~: 4 kill
suspect's ~: 5 alibi
tall ~: 3 lie 4 tale, yarn 9 invention
tell a ~: 7 narrate, recount
upper ~: 4 loft 5 attic
with a lesson: 4 myth 5 fable 7 parable 8 allegory, apologue
story __: 4 line
__ story: 3 sob, war 4 dope, fish, folk, half, lead, life, news, tall 5 cover, fairy, ghost, photo, short 6 horror, inside, second 7 bedtime, feature, running, success
__-story: 4 back
__ Story: 3 Toy 4 Love 5 Tokyo 6 Orrie's, Police 7 Bedtime
storybook: 6 unreal
__-story man: 6 second
Story of __ H, The: 5 Adele
Story of Alexander Graham Bell, The (1939 film)
cast: Don Ameche
Story of an African Farm, The
author: Olive Schreiner
Story of a Novel, The
author: Thomas Wolfe
Story of Civilization, The
author: Will Durant
Story of Louis Pasteur, The (1936 film)
cast: Paul Muni
Story of Mary Marlin, The: 9 radio show
Story of Philosophy, The
author: Will Durant
Story of Vernon & Irene Castle, The (1939 film): 7 musical
cast: Fred Astaire, Ginger Rogers
storyteller: 4 liar 6 fibber 8 fabulist, narrator, novelist 9 raconteur
ancient ~: 4 Esop 5 Aesop
Storyteller, The
author: Harold Robbins
storytelling: 9 narration
dance: 4 hula
__ Story, The: 3 FBI, Zoo 4 Nun's 6 Jolson
stotinki
100: 3 lev
stout: 3 big 4 bold, brew, hale, iron, wiry 5 ample, brave, bulky, burly, drink, hardy, hefty, hunky, husky, loyal, lusty, nervy, obese, solid, tough 6 brawny, chunky, hearty, heroic, mighty, plucky, potent, robust, rugged, sinewy, stable, steely, strong, stubby, sturdy, virile 7 doughty, hulking, impavid, porcine, staunch, valiant 8 athletic, beverage, fearless, forceful, heroical, indurate, intrepid, muscular, powerful, puissant, resolute, sedulous, stalwart, valorous, vigorous 9 Atlantean, corpulent, dauntless, filled-out, Herculean, strapping, tenacious, undaunted, unfearing, well-built 10 able-bodied, courageous, determined, invincible, red-blooded, undismayed
cousin: 3 ale 4 beer
ingredient: 4 malt
make ~: 6 fatten
vessel: 3 mug 4 toby 5 stein
see also obese
stout-hearted: 4 bold, game 5 brave, gutsy, nervy 6 awless, daring, gritty, heroic, plucky, spunky, sturdy 7 aweless, defiant, doughty, gallant, staunch, valiant 8 fearless, heroical, intrepid, resolute, stalwart, unafraid, valorous 9 audacious, dauntless, dreadless, undaunted, unfearful 10 courageous
one: 4 hero
Stouthearted __: 3 Men
stoutness: 3 vim 4 dint, thew 5 brawn, force, might, power, thews, vigor 6 energy, muscle 7 fitness, muscles, potence, potency, stamina 8 strength, vitality 9 endurance, fortitude, puissance 10 brute force, fleshiness
Stout, Rex: 6 writer
sleuth: Nero Wolfe
work: The Doorbell Rang
Fer-de-Lance
stove: 4 kiln, oven 5 forge, range 6 heater 7 furnace 9 fireplace
accessory: 5 timer
ender: 3 top 4 pipe
part: 4 oven 6 burner, gas jet
right off the ~: 3 hot
Stove __ Stuffing: 3 Top
__-stove league: 3 hot
stovepipe: 3 hat, lid
connection: 4 flue
like a ~: 5 sooty
stovetop item: 3 pan, pot 6 boiler 7 skillet
stow: 4 bury, hide, load, pack, save 5 amass, cache, hoard, lay in, place, put by, stash, stock, store, stuff 6 bundle, closet, garner, pile up 7 conceal, deposit, harvest, put away, reserve, secrete 8 ensconce, pack away, put aside 9 store away, warehouse
on board: 4 lade
Stow: 8 Randolph
stowaway: 5 hider
Stowe: 4 city, town 9 ski resort
activity: 6 skiing
equipment: 3 ski 4 skee
locale: 7 Vermont
sight: 3 tow 4 snow, T-bar 5 slope
Stowe, Harriet Beecher: 6 writer
character: 3 Eva, Tom 5 Simon, Topsy 6 Legree
work: Dred
The Minister's Wooing
Oldtown Folks
Uncle Tom's Cabin
Stowe, Madeleine: 7 actress
film: The General's Daughter (1999)
The Last of the Mohicans (1992)
Revenge (1990)
Stakeout (1987)
Twelve Monkeys (1995)
The Two Jakes (1990)
Unlawful Entry (1992)
We Were Soldiers (2002)
spouse: Brian Benben

STP
competitor: 4 Fram
St. Paul: 4 city, town
composer: Felix Mendelssohn
county: 6 Ramsey
locale: 9 Minnesota
river: 11 Mississippi
St. Peter's: 6 square 8 basilica
St. Petersburg: 4 city, port, town
county: 8 Pinellas
locale: 6 Russia 7 Florida
newspaper: 5 Times
Strad: 6 violin
relative: 5 Amati
substance for a ~: 5 rosin
straddle: 4 span 5 mount 6 ramble, sprawl 8 bestride, fence-sit 9 vacillate
straddle the ___: 5 fence
straddling: 4 atop 6 across
the fence: 6 middle
Stradivari: 7 Antonio
teacher: 5 Amati
strafe: 4 raid 6 fire at
straggle: 3 lag 4 drag, idle, laze, loaf, poke, roam, rove, tail 5 amble, dally, drift, mosey, range, stall, stray, tarry, trail 6 dawdle, linger, loiter, ramble, sprawl, spread, wander 7 meander, saunter, shuffle 8 lollygag, scramble 9 limp along, string out, waste time 10 dillydally
straggler: 7 laggard 8 lingerer, wanderer
straight: 3 due 4 even, fair, hand, just, neat, pure, tidy, true 5 blunt, erect, exact, frank, legal, legit, level, moral, plain, plumb, right, sheer 6 candid, decent, direct, honest, in a row, ih line, linear, openly, proper, square, strong, trusty, unbent, unmixt 7 aligned, correct, ethical, exactly, factual, frankly, in order, nonstop, orderly, regular, running, summary, unbowed, unmixed, upright 8 accurate, candidly, credible, directly, orthodox, out-front, outright, reliable, truthful, unbiased, unbroken, uncurled, vertical, virtuous 9 authentic, downright, equitable, honorable, out-and-out, undiluted, unfailing, veracious 10 aboveboard, continuous, evenhanded, forthright, from the hip, horizontal, inflexible, invariable, law-abiding, on the level, point-blank, scrupulous, successive, unmediated, unrelieved, unswerving
be ~: 5 level
combining form: 4 orth-, rect- 5 ortho-, recti-
don't keep ~: 4 bend, warp 5 curve, slant 6 buckle, deform 7 contort, distort
ender: 3 way 4 away, edge 5 arrow, edged 6 jacket 7 forward
go ~: 6 reform 7 shape up
in a ~ line: 8 directly
like a ~ line: 4 one-D
line: 3 row
make ~ lines: 4 rule
man: 4 foil 6 feeder, stooge
not ~: 3 wry 4 wavy 5 askew, atilt, curly 6 angled, aslant, aslope 7 crooked
off the ~ and narrow: 4 awry, lost 5 amiss 6 adrift, afield 7 missing, roaming 9 wandering
set ~: 3 fix 5 right 7 correct 8 disabuse 9 reconcile
topper: 5 flush
up: 4 neat, over
up and down: 5 plumb
with a ~ face: 9 seriously, sincerely
straight ___: 3 man, off, pin 4 away, face, time 5 angle, arrow, flush, poker, razor 6 ticket, whisky 7 shooter, whiskey
straight ___ arrow: 4 as an
straight ___ the heart: 4 from
straight-___: 3 arm, out 4 edge, line 5 ahead, chain, faced, laced
straight-___-the-shoulder: 4 from
___ straight: 3 set 5 shoot 6 inside
Straight: 8 Beatrice
author: Dick Francis
straight-A ___: 7 student
straight and ___: 6 narrow
straight-arrow: 6 honest 8 orthodox 9 veracious
straightaway: 3 now, PDQ 4 anon, ASAP, soon 5 apace, today 6 at once, presto, pronto 7 fleetly, hastily, quickly, rapidly, readily, swiftly 8 directly, in a flash, in a jiffy, in no time, pell-mell, promptly, right now, right off, speedily 9 at present, forthwith, hurriedly, instantly, like a shot, posthaste, presently, right away 10 at this time, here and now, this minute
Straight, Beatrice
Oscar: Network
Straight Dope, The
columnist: 5 Adams
straightedge: 5 ruler
straighten: 3 fix 4 even, tidy, true 5 align, aline, level 6 adjust, line up, neaten, unbend, uncoil, uncurl, unfold 7 compose, correct, rectify, untwist
out: 3 aid 5 right 6 settle 7 correct, improve, rectify 8 organize, untangle 9 seriously
up: 4 rise, tidy 5 clean 7 rectify
___ straight face: 5 keep a
straightforward: 4 easy, just, open 5 blunt, brusk, clear, frank, legit, level, plain, right, vivid 6 abrupt, candid, cogent, direct, honest, patent, simple, square 7 brusque, evident, express, factual, genuine, obvious, right-on, routine, sincere, up-front, upright 8 apparent, clear-cut, credible, definite, distinct, explicit, impolite, like it is, manifest, palpable, readable, tactless, truthful 9 barefaced, graspable, guileless, honorable, outspoken, unfeigned, unguarded, veracious 10 forthright, free-spoken, indelicate, on the level, scrupulous, spelled out
be ~: 5 level
not ~: 3 sly 4 foxy, wily 5 false, shady 6 artful, crafty, shifty, sneaky, subtle, tricky 7 crooked, cunning, devious, evasive, oblique 8 guileful, indirect, scheming, slippery 9 deceitful, designing, dishonest, insidious, insincere, underhand 10 circuitous, misleading, roundabout
straightforwardly: 4 true 6 simply
straightforwardness: 6 candor 7 honesty 9 sincerity
straight-laced
see strait-laced
straightness: 6 candor 7 honesty 9 sincerity
symbol of ~: 5 arrow
straight-out: 6 direct, flatly 8 specific, thorough
straight-shooting: 6 candid, honest 7 sincere
Straight Story, The (1999 film)
cast: Sissy Spacek, Harry Dean Stanton
director: David Lynch
Straight Time (1978 film)
cast: Dustin Hoffman, Theresa Russell
straight-up: 5 steep 8 vertical
Straight Up (1988 song)
artist: Paula Abdul
strain: 3 air, tax, try, tug 4 ache, care, moil, ooze, pain, pull, push, rack, sift, song, tear, tire, toil, toll, tone, tune, turn, vein, work 5 blood, breed, brunt, drive, exert, labor, leach, music, press, reach, sieve, stock, sweat, tinge, touch, trace, twist, unmix 6 burden, effort, family, filter, injure, injury, melody, nerves, purify, refine, screen, sprain, streak, stress, strive, temper, trauma, warble, weaken, weight, wrench 7 anxiety, descant, descent, discant, distort, fatigue, lineage, measure, overtax, peg away, refrain, species, stretch, tension, tighten, trouble, variety 8 ancestry, bear down, distress, endeavor, exertion, go all out, overload, overwork, pedigree, pressure, separate, struggle, tautness 9 leitmotif, lixiviate, overexert, percolate, suspicion, tightness, weigh down 10 bear down on, difficulty, extraction, go for broke, sprinkling, suggestion
starter: 3 eye
under a ~: 5 tense
strain ___ gnat: 3 at a
strained: 4 taut 5 false, stiff, tense, tight, wired 6 forced, uneasy 7 awkward, hard-put, intense, labored, refined, uptight 9 contrived, difficult, laborious, miserable, pretended, strung out, unnatural, unrelaxed 10 far-fetched
strainer: 5 sieve 6 sifter 8 colander
strait: 4 bind, mess, neck, pass 5 pinch 6 crisis, plight 7 channel, dilemma, narrows, passage, squeeze 8 distress, hardship 9 deep water, emergency, extremity 10 difficulty, passageway, perplexity
ender: 6 jacket
opposite: 7 isthmus
turbulent ~: 7 euripus
strait-___: 5 laced
Strait: 6 George
Australia: 6 Torres
Gulf of Aqaba ~: 5 Tiran
Persian Gulf ~: 5 Ormuz 6 Hormuz
Red Sea ~: 5 Tiran
___ Strait: 3 Rae 4 Bass, Cook, Rion 5 Cabot, Davis, Korea, Menai, Sunda, Tiran 6 Bering, Hainan, Taiwan, Torres 7 Formosa 8 Macassar, Makassar
straiten: 4 curb, ruin 5 break, limit 6 hamper, hinder, impede 7 confine 8 bankrupt, restrain, restrict 9 pauperize 10 impoverish, keep in line
straitened: 4 poor 5 broke, needy 6 bad off, hard up, ill off, in debt, in need, in want 7 pinched 8 badly off, bankrupt, beggarly, deprived, indigent, strapped, wiped out 9 destitute, insolvent, moneyless, penniless, penurious 10 down and out, pauperized
Strait Is the Gate
author: André Gide
straitjacket: 8 restrain 9 restraint
strait-laced: 4 firm, hard, prim 5 bossy, cruel, picky, rigid, staid, stern, stiff, tough 6 narrow, prissy, proper, severe, square, strict 7 austere, prudish, puritan, Spartan 8 despotic, exacting, hard-line, priggish, rigorous 9 demanding, draconian, squeamish, stringent, unbending, unsparing 10 despotical, inflexible, iron-fisted, no-nonsense, oppressive, tyrannical
one: 5 priss, prude
Strait of ___: 5 Canso, Dover, Ormuz 6 Hormuz, Melaka 7 Malacca, Otranto 8 Magellan 9 Belle Isle 10 Juan de Fuca
Strait of Malacca
island: 6 Penang
straits: 6 plight 8 position, pressure 9 emergency, indigence 10 insolvency
dire ~: 6 crisis, penury 7 trouble
in dire ~: 5 needy 6 hard-up
___ straits: 4 dire
Stram: 4 Hank
strand: 3 ply 4 hair, lock, rope, wisp, yarn 5 beach, cable, coast, fiber, tress, twine 6 desert, enisle, length, maroon, string, thread 7 abandon, cowlick, forsake, isolate, let down 8 cast away, filament, littoral, seacoast, seashore
at an airport: 5 ice in
___ strand: 3 DNA
stranded: 6 ashore 7 aground, beached, wrecked 8 castaway, deserted, grounded, helpless, homeless, marooned, passed up 9 abandoned, foundered, penniless, sidelined 10 high and dry, on the rocks, run aground
Stranded
sculptor: Erté
strange: 3 fey, new, odd, off 4 eery, lost, rare 5 alien, apart, crazy, eerie, funny, novel, queer, weird 6 atypic, exotic, far-out, freaky, quaint, quirky, remote, unique, way-out 7 awkward, bizarre, curious, deviant, erratic, faraway, foreign, oddball, offbeat, unalike, uncanny, uncouth, unknown, untried, unusual 8 aberrant, abnormal, atypical, freakish, isolated,

peculiar, singular, uncommon **9** anomalous, different, divergent, eccentric, fantastic, grotesque, irregular, marvelous, unearthly, unheard of, unnatural, unrelated, wonderful **10** astounding, irrelevant, miraculous, mysterious, mystifying, newfangled, outlandish, out of place, perplexing, remarkable, unexplored, unfamiliar, unorthodox, unseasoned
combining form: **3** xen- **4** xeno-
in a ~ way: **5** oddly
strange __ may seem: **4** as it
Strange Case of Dr. Jekyll and Mr. Hyde, The
author: Robert Louis Stevenson
Strange, Curtis: **6** golfer
Strange Fruit: **4** song **5** novel
artist: Billie Holiday
author: Lillian Smith
Strange Interlude: **4** film, play
author: Eugene O'Neill
cast: Clark Gable, Norma Shearer
character: **3** Ned **4** Nina **5** Leeds
Strangelove: **2** Dr.
Strange Magic
artist: ELO
strangeness: **6** oddity
stranger: **5** alien **7** drifter, incomer, migrant, tourist, unknown, visitor **8** intruder, newcomer, outsider, squatter, wanderer **9** foreigner, immigrant, itinerant, outlander, transient **10** interloper
Stranger __ Paradise: **4** Than
Stranger __ Shore: **5** on the
__ Stranger: **5** Hello **7** Welcome
Stranger From the Tonto
author: Zane Grey
__ Stranger Here Myself: **3** I'm a
Stranger in the Mirror
author: Sidney Sheldon
Stranger Is Watching, A
author: Mary Higgins Clark
Strangers
author: Dean Koontz
__ Strangers: **7** Perfect
Strangers and Brothers
author: C.P. Snow
Strangers in Good Company (1991 film)
director: Cynthia Scott
Strangers in the Night (1966 song)
artist: Frank Sinatra
__ Strangers Marry: **4** When
Strangers on a Train: **4** film **5** novel
author: Patricia Highsmith
cast: Farley Granger, Ruth Roman, Robert Walker
composer: Dimitri Tiomkin
director: Alfred Hitchcock
Stranger, The
author: Albert Camus
Stranger, The (1946 film)
cast: Edward G. Robinson, Orson Welles, Loretta Young
director: Orson Welles
Strange Victory
author: Sara Teasdale
strap: **3** tie **4** band, belt, lace, lash, rein, whip, yoke **5** hitch, leash, thong **6** handle, latigo **7** binding, harness **8** seat belt **9** watchband
closure: **5** dring
decorative ~: **5** patte
ender: **4** hang **6** hanger
starter: **4** boot **5** black
__ strap: **4** chin
straphanger: **5** rider **8** commuter
purchase: **5** token
strapless: **5** dress
top: **4** tube
strapped: **4** poor **5** broke, needy, short **6** bad off, hard up, ill off, in a fix, in a jam, in deep, in need, in want **7** pinched **8** badly off, bankrupt, beggarly, deprived, dirt poor, indigent **9** destitute, insolvent, moneyless, penniless, penurious **10** down and out, pauperized, stone-broke, straitened
for time: **4** late **5** tardy
strapping: **3** big, fit **4** hale, iron, wiry **5** beefy, burly, hardy, hefty, hunky, husky, lusty, stout, tough **6** brawny, hearty, mighty, potent, robust, rugged, sinewy, steely, stocky, strong, sturdy, virile **7** doughty, hulking, sizable **8** athletic, forceful, indurate, muscular, powerful, puissant, sizeable, stalwart, vigorous **9** Atlantean, Herculean, well-built **10** able-bodied, red-blooded
Strasberg: **3** Lee **5** Susan
subject: **6** acting
Strasbourg: **4** city, town
locale: **6** Alsace, France
river: **3** Ill
Strassman, Marcia: **7** actress
TV: MASH, Welcome Back Kotter
stratagem: **4** move, plot, ploy, ruse, trap, wile **5** craft, dodge, trick **6** deceit, device, dupery, gambit, scheme, tactic **7** finesse, gimmick, knavery, measure, sleight, tactics **8** artifice, intrigue, maneuver **9** chicanery, deception, expedient, imposture **10** subterfuge
Stratas: **6** Teresa
strategic: **3** key **5** vital **6** clever, tricky **7** crucial, cunning, planned, politic **8** cardinal, critical, decisive **9** dishonest, important, necessary **10** calculated, deliberate, diplomatic, imperative
Strategic __ Command: **3** Air
Strategic __ Initiative: **7** Defense
strategist: **9** tactician
strategize: **4** plan
strategy: **4** game, plan, ploy **5** angle, craft, dodge, scene, setup, slant, story **6** design, gambit, method, policy, scheme, system **7** cunning, gimmick, program, project, tactics **8** approach, artifice, game plan, scenario, time line **9** blueprint, expedient, procedure, treatment **10** expediency
fallback ~: **5** plan B
game: **4** Risk
original ~: **5** plan A
session: **6** huddle
Strategy of Peace, The
author: John F. Kennedy
Stratemeyer, Edward L.: **6** writer
book series: Hardy Boys, Nancy Drew, Rover Boys, Tom Swift
Stratford-__-Avon: **4** upon
Stratford's river: **4** Avon
Strathairn: **5** David
stratify: **8** laminate
Stratocaster: **6** guitar
maker: **6** Fender
stratocumulus: **5** cloud
stratosphere, in the: **4** high **6** high up
stratum: **3** bed **4** seam, tier, vein **5** caste, class, grade, layer, level, plane, sheet **6** lamina, sector, sphere, streak **7** station **8** standing
social ~: **5** caste, class, elite **6** sphere **7** station **8** standing
stratus: **5** cloud
Stratus: **3** car **4** auto **5** Dodge **10** automobile
Straub: **5** Peter
Strauss: **4** Levi **5** Peter **6** Johann **7** Richard
Strauss, Johann: **8** Austrian, composer
work: Blue Danube Waltz
Die Fledermaus
Emperor Waltz
Tales from the Vienna Woods
Strauss, Richard: **6** German **8** composer
genre: **5** opera
work: Also Sprach Zarathustra
Der Rosenkavalier
Don Quixote
Salome
Till Eulenspiegel
Stravinsky, Igor: **7** Russian **8** composer
work: Agon
The Firebird
Petrushka
Rite of Spring
Symphony of Psalms
straw: **3** hay, jot **4** feed, iota, stem, tube **5** blade, chaff, color, stalk **6** fodder, silage, sipper, trifle, yellow **7** padding **8** least bit
bit of ~: **4** wisp
boss: **6** gerent **7** manager **8** overseer **10** figurehead, supervisor
covering: **5** mulch
ender: **4** worm **5** berry, board **6** flower
in the wind: **4** omen, sign **5** token **6** augury, herald, signal **7** portent, presage, warning **9** foretoken, harbinger, indicator **10** indication
last ~: **5** limit
like a ~: **5** tubal
man: **6** effigy
pile: **4** rick
product: **3** hat, mat
relative: *see* yellow color
starter: **3** bed **4** jack
unit: **4** bale **5** sheaf
use a ~: **3** sip **4** suck
vote: **4** poll
straw __: **3** hat, man **4** boss, mite, poll, vote, wine **5** color **6** yellow
straw __ wind: **5** in the
__ straw: **4** last **5** man of
__ Strawberries: **4** Wild
strawberry: **3** pie, red **5** fruit **6** flavor **8** ice cream
alternative: *see* ice cream flavor
relative: *see* red color
tree: **7** arbutus
strawberry __: **5** blond **6** blonde, tomato
__-strawberry: **4** cran
Strawberry: **6** Darryl
once: **3** Met
Strawberry Alarm Clock
song: Incense and Peppermints (1967)
Strawberry Fields Forever (1967 song)
artist: Beatles
straw-colored: **5** flaxy **6** flaxen
Straw Dogs (1971 film)
cast: Susan George, Dustin Hoffman
director: Sam Peckinpah
straw in the __: **4** wind
straws
catch at ~: **5** argue, cavil **7** quibble
draw ~: **6** choose
stray: **3** cur, err, sin **4** dogy, lost, roam, rove, waif **5** dogey, dogie, drift, range **6** animal, depart, errant, orphan, ramble, random, wander **7** deviate, digress, diverge, do wrong, go wrong, maunder, meander, mongrel, vagrant **8** alley cat, divagate, homeless, isolated, maverick, renegade, straggle, wanderer **9** abandoned, foundling, gallivant **10** incidental, occasional, unattached
animal: **4** dogy, waif **5** dogey, rogue **6** doggie
dog: **3** mut **4** mutt
home for a ~: **5** pound
Strayhorn, Billy: **7** pianist **8** composer
genre: **4** jazz
straying: **6** afield, errant **7** veering **9** departure **10** digression, discursion
streak: **3** bar, ray, run **4** band, beam, dash, daub, hint, line, mark, rush, spot, tear, vein, welt, zoom **5** layer, scoot, shoot, slash, smear, spell, stria, strip, tinge, touch, trace **6** marble, period, pocket, series, sprint, strain, stripe **7** element, stratum **8** sequence **9** suspicion **10** suggestion
like a blue ~: **4** fast **5** quick, rapid
losing ~: **3** dip, sag **5** panic, slide, slump **6** plunge **7** decline, falloff, reverse **8** bad times, downturn, dry spell, slowdown **9** downslide, downswing, downtrend, hard times, recession
on a ~: **3** hot **5** blest, lucky **7** blessed, charmed, favored **9** fortunate **10** auspicious, felicitous, fortuitous
talk a blue ~: **3** yak **5** run on **6** yammer
winning ~: **3** run **4** roll
__ streak: **3** on a **4** blue
__ Streak: **6** Silver
streaked: **4** liny, rowy **5** liney **7** mottled **8** brindled
streaking: **3** fad
streaks, full of: **4** liny **5** liney
Streak, The (1974 song)
artist: Ray Stevens
Streaky: **3** cat
stream: **3** jet, run **4** emit, flow, gush, kill, pour, race, rain, rill, roll, rush, tide **5** bourn, brook, creek, drift, flood, glide, issue, rille, river, slide, spate, spill, spirt, spout, spurt, surge, swarm **6** bourne, branch, course, emerge, influx, motion, onrush, parade, runlet, runnel, sluice, squirt **7** cascade, current, freshet, rivulet, torrent, trickle

8 continue, fountain 9 tributary 10 air current, inundation, outpouring
combining form: 4 rheo- 5 fluvi- 6 fluvio-
cross a ~: 4 ford
ender: 3 bed 4 line, side
fast-flowing ~: 3 jet 4 kill
flow like a ~: 4 purl
gentle ~ of poetry: 5 Afton
movement: 6 inflow 7 outflow
starter: 3 mid 4 down, main, mill, slip 5 blood
__ stream: 3 air, jet
__ Stream: 4 Gulf
streamer: 4 flag 5 title 6 banner, ensign 7 pennant 8 standard
Streamers: 4 film, play
author: David Rabe
cast: Matthew Modine
director: Robert Altman
streaming: 6 active
streamlet: 3 run 4 race, rill 5 bourn, brook, creek, rille 6 runlet, runnel 7 rivulet 9 tributary
streamline: 5 shape 7 improve 8 simplify 9 modernize 10 centralize
streamlined: 4 trim 5 sleek
Streep, Meryl: 7 actress
film: Adaptation (2002)
Before and After (1996)
The Bridges of Madison County (1995)
A Cry in the Dark (1988)
Death Becomes Her (1992)
The Deer Hunter (1978)
Defending Your Life (1991)
The Devil Wears Prada (2006)
Doubt (2008)
Falling in Love (1984)
The French Lieutenant's Woman (1981)
Heartburn (1986)
The Hours (2002)
Ironweed (1987)
Julie & Julia (2009)
Kramer vs. Kramer (1979, AA)
Lions for Lambs (2007)
Mamma Mia! (2008)
The Manchurian Candidate (2004)
Manhattan (1979)
Music of the Heart (1999)
One True Thing (1998)
Out of Africa (1985)
Postcards From the Edge (1990)
Prime (2005)
The River Wild (1994)
The Seduction of Joe Tynan (1979)
She-Devil (1989)
Silkwood (1983)
Sophie's Choice (1982, AA)
street: 3 way 4 drag, lane, road 5 byway, court, drive, place, route 6 artery, avenue 7 ingress, parkway, passage, roadway, terrace 8 pavement 9 back alley, boulevard, concourse, territory
across the ~: 4 near 5 close 6 nearby
art: 5 mural
band: 4 gang
border: 4 curb
common ~ name: 3 Elm 4 Main 5 Maple
crosser: 6 avenue 10 pedestrian
ender: 3 car 4 wise 5 light, scape
eyesore: 6 litter
French ~ name starter: 5 rue de
in French: 3 rue
in Italian: 3 via
in Spanish: 5 calle
kid: 4 waif 5 gamin, stray 6 gamine, orphan, urchin 9 foundling 10 ragamuffin
language: 5 slang
maneuver: 5 U-turn
man in the ~: 6 people
noise: 5 siren
on easy ~: 4 rich 7 wealthy, well-off 8 well-to-do 10 in the chips, prosperous
on the other side of the ~: 8 opposite
performer: 4 mime 5 mimer 6 busker
person: 7 vagrant
posting: 4 sign
prohibiting cars: 4 mall
short ~: 4 lane 5 alley, court, place
show: 5 raree
sign: 4 slow, stop 5 arrow, yield
talk: 5 slang
street __: 4 name 6 hockey, smarts 7 cleaner, fighter
street-__: 5 smart
__ street: 4 back, easy, side, stop 5 cross, on the 6 one-way, two-way 7 through
Street: 5 Della 6 Picabo
Street __: 5 Angel, Scene 6 Dreams
__ Street: 4 Back, Easy, Grub, Lime, Main, Side, Wall 5 Baker, Fleet, South 6 Harley, Hester, Lonely, Sesame 7 Downing, Lombard, Quality, Scarlet
__ Street Blues: 4 Hill 5 Basin, Beale
streetcar: 4 tram
building: 4 barn
charge: 4 fare
Streetcar Named Desire, A: 4 film, play
author: Tennessee Williams
cast: Marlon Brando, Kim Hunter, Vivien Leigh, Karl Malden
character: 4 Stan 5 Mitch, Pablo 6 DuBois, Eunice, Stella 7 Blanche, Stanley 8 Kowalski
director: Elia Kazan
setting: 9 Louisiana 10 New Orleans
street-corner call: 4 taxi
street-corner sign: 4 walk 8 don't walk
Street, Della
boss: 5 Mason
portrayer: 4 Hale
Street Dreams (1996 song)
artist: Nas
Street Kings (2008 film)
cast: Hugh Laurie, Keanu Reeves, Forest Whitaker
Street of Dreams (1991 song)
artist: Nia Peeples
Street, Picabo: 5 skier
streets
like some ~: 4 thru 6 gaslit
where ~ meet: 6 corner
__ Streets: 4 City, Mean
Street Scene: 4 play
author: Elmer Rice
character: 3 Abe, Sam 4 Anna, Rose 6 Kaplan
street-smart
see streetwise
Streets of Fire (1984 film)
cast: Diane Lane, Rick Moranis
Streets of Laredo
author: Larry McMurtry
Streets of Philadelphia (1994 song)
artist: Bruce Springsteen
Streets of San Francisco, The (ABC drama)
cast: Michael Douglas (Insp. Steve Keller)
Karl Malden (Det. Lt. Mike Stone)
__ Street, USA: 4 Main
__ Street Where You Live: 5 On the
streetwise: 4 onto 5 canny, savvy, slick 6 crafty, shrewd
Streisand, Barbra: 6 singer 7 actress
film: All Night Long (1981)
For Pete's Sake (1974)
Funny Girl (1968, AA)
Hello, Dolly! (1969)
Meet the Fockers (2004)
The Mirror Has Two Faces (1996)
Nuts (1987)
On a Clear Day You Can See Forever (1970)
The Owl and the Pussycat (1970)
The Prince of Tides (1991)
A Star Is Born (1976)
Up the Sandbox (1972)
The Way We Were (1973)
What's Up, Doc? (1972)
Yentl (1983)
role: 5 Brice
song: Evergreen (1977)
Guilty (1980)
I Finally Found Someone (1996)
My Heart Belongs to Me (1977)
No More Tears (1979)
People (1964)
Stoney End (1970)
The Way We Were (1973)
What Kind of Fool (1981)
Woman in Love (1980)
You Don't Bring Me Flowers (1978)
spouse: James Brolin, Elliott Gould
strength: 3 vim, zip 4 beef, dint, guts, kick, pull 5 asset, brawn, clout, depth, fiber, force, forte, juice, might, nerve, power, sinew, steam, thews, vigor 6 degree, energy, fervor, health, muscle, spirit, virtue, volume, weight 7 ability, bravery, cogency, courage, fitness, potence, potency, prowess, stamina 8 efficacy, firmness, mainstay, momentum, pressure, security, tenacity, validity, vitality 9 fortitude, hardiness, intensity, magnitude, soundness, stability, stoutness, substance, tolerance, toughness, vehemence, willpower 10 brawniness, brute force, durability, resolution, robustness, ruggedness, steadiness, sturdiness
lose ~: 3 lag 4 fade, fail, wilt
name meaning ~: 5 Ethan
of mind: 4 will 5 spine 7 resolve 8 backbone, decision, firmness, tenacity 9 fortitude, will power 10 resolution
regain ~: 5 rally 7 recover
sap the ~ of: 4 tire 5 drain 6 weaken 7 exhaust, wear out 8 enervate, enfeeble, paralyse, paralyze 9 attenuate, prostrate, undermine 10 debilitate, demoralize, devitalize
source of ~: 5 unity
test for ~: 6 stress
tower of ~: 6 pillar 7 bastion 9 supporter
__ strength: 3 wet 5 brute 7 tensile
strengthen: 3 wax 4 back, feed, gird, prop 5 add to, brace, build, cheer, mount, raise, rally, ready, renew, shore, sinew, steel 6 anneal, beef up, deepen, extend, firm up, harden, step up, temper, thrive, tone up, uphold 7 animate, augment, bear out, bolster, build up, burgeon, confirm, develop, empower, enhance, enlarge, enliven, fortify, hearten, justify, nourish, nurture, prepare, prosper, quicken, recruit, refresh, restore, shore up, stiffen, support, sustain, toughen 8 bourgeon, buttress, embolden, enspirit, flourish, heighten, imbolden, increase, indurate, inspirit, multiply 9 encourage, establish, intensify, reinforce, undergird, vulcanize 10 accentuate, contribute, invigorate
__ strength of: 5 on the
strenuous: 4 hard 5 eager, heavy, lusty, rough, stiff, tough 6 active, ardent, rugged, severe, sticky, strong, taxing, thorny, trying, uphill 7 arduous, dynamic, earnest, labored, onerous, operose, serious, zealous 8 grueling, resolute, spirited, tireless, tiresome, toilsome, vigorous 9 ambitious, combative, demanding, difficult, effortful, energetic, herculean, laborious, murderous 10 aggressive, determined, exhausting, formidable, oppressive
strenuously: 4 hard 8 mightily
strep __: 6 throat
strepitous: 5 forte, noisy 7 blaring, booming, jarring, pealing, rackety, raucous, reboant, roaring 8 crashing, piercing, plangent, rumbling, sonorous, strident, turned up 9 big-voiced, clamorous, deafening 10 boisterous, resounding, stentorian, thundering, uproarious, vociferous
stress: 3 tax 4 beat, care, fear, heat, rack 5 dread, force, labor, press, rub in, worry 6 accent, burden, crunch, harp on, hassle, import, nerves, overdo, play up, repeat, rhythm, strain, trauma, weight 7 anxiety, belabor, dwell on, feature, iterate, measure, point up, stretch, tension, trouble, urgency 8 emphasis, headline, pressure, reaffirm, reassert 9 dwell upon, emphasize, go on about, highlight, intensify, italicize, punctuate, reinforce, spotlight, tightness, underline 10 accentuate, importance, insistence, make much of, oppression, overextend, traumatize, underscore

feeling no ~: 6 at ease 7 content, relaxed 8 carefree, composed, tranquil
lack of ~: 6 atonia
result: 5 agita, ulcer
stress __: 4 test
__-stress analyzer: 5 voice
stressed: 4 taut 5 drawn, tense 8 emphatic 10 high-strung
stress-free: 4 calm 6 sedate, serene
stressful: 5 tense 6 jangly, taxing, trying 10 enervating
event: 6 crisis
stressless sound: 4 shwa 5 schwa
stretch: 3 eke, leg, run, way 4 area, grow, land, pull, rack, size, span, term, time, tour 5 cover, crane, patch, range, reach, scope, sheet, skimp, space, spell, stint, sweep, swell, tract, while, widen 6 blow up, bridge, dilate, expand, extend, extent, length, overdo, period, region, sprawl, spread, strain, stress, tauten, unfold, unroll 7 broaden, drag out, draw out, enlarge, expanse, inflate, overlap, prolong, recline, spin out, tighten 8 distance, duration, elongate, lengthen, misquote, overplay, protract 9 overstate, spread out, string out 10 exaggerate
fabric: 5 Lycra 7 spandex
out: 3 lie 4 rest 6 extend, repose, unfold 7 project, prolong, recline 8 protract
over: 4 span
starter: 4 back, home
the truth: 3 fib 10 exaggerate
stretch __: 3 out
stretch a __: 5 point
stretchable: 7 elastic, springy
stretched: 4 taut, thin 5 tight
in ballet: 5 tendu 7 allongé
stretcher: 6 gurney, litter
stretching: 9 expansive, extension
combining form: 4 tono-
stretch one's __: 4 legs
stretchy: 6 lissom, supple 7 elastic, lissome, springy 9 lethargic, resilient
cord: 6 bungee
strew: 3 sow 4 cast 5 throw 6 litter, splash, spread 7 diffuse, radiate, scatter, spatter 8 disperse, sprinkle 9 broadcast, cast about, circulate, toss about 10 distribute, promulgate
strewn: 7 diffuse 8 rambling
in heraldry: 4 semé
stria: 4 vein 5 ridge 6 streak 7 channel, fluting
striation: 4 vein 6 stripe
__-stricken: 3 awe 5 grief, panic 6 terror, wonder 7 poverty
strict: 3 set 4 firm, grim, hard 5 close, exact, harsh, rigid, stern, stiff, total, tough, utter 6 formal, severe, stuffy 7 austere, hard-set, literal, perfect, precise, prudish, Spartan, uptight 8 absolute, complete, despotic, exacting, rigorous 9 demanding, draconian, stringent, unbending 10 despotical, forbidding, inflexible, ironfisted, meticulous, no-nonsense, oppressive, particular, relentless, scrupulous
strictly: 5 truly 8 severely 9 literally
strictness: 5 rigor 8 hardness, iron hand 9 austerity, exactness 10 discipline
stricture: 4 slur, tabu 5 taboo 9 criticism 10 impediment, limitation, reflection
stride: 4 gait, pace, step, walk 5 march, stalk, stomp, tramp, tread, tromp 6 length, trapes 7 traipse 8 footstep
break ~: 6 falter
easy ~: 4 lope
Stride __: 4 Rite
stridency: 5 noise 9 cacophony
strident: 4 loud 5 forte, harsh, noisy, rough, vocal 6 brassy, off-key, shrill 7 blaring, blatant, booming, clarion, grating, jarring, pealing, rackety, rasping, raucous, reboant, roaring, squawky 8 clashing, crashing, jangling, piercing, plangent, rumbling, sonorous, turned up 9 big-voiced, clamorous, deafening, dissonant, outspoken, unmusical 10 boisterous, discordant, resounding, screeching, stentorian, stertorous, strepitous, thundering, uproarious, vociferant, vociferous
sound: 3 din 5 blare, noise
Stride Rite: 4 shoe
brand: 4 Keds
strides
make: 4 move 7 improve 8 progress
Stride Toward Freedom
author: Martin Luther King
stridulate: 4 rasp
stridulent: 7 grating
stridulous: 5 noisy
strife: 3 war 4 feud, fuss, riot, spat 5 brawl, clash, fight, words 6 affray, battle, blowup, combat, hassle, static, tumult, unrest, uproar 7 contest, discord, dispute, dissent, faction, quarrel, rivalry, trouble, warfare 8 argument, conflict, disunity, fighting, friction, squabble, struggle, tug of war, variance 9 animosity, bickering, wrangling 10 contention, difference, difficulty, disharmony, dissension, dissidence, dissonance, revolution
personification of ~: 4 Eris
starter: 5 loose
strigine youngster: 5 owlet
strike: 3 box, hit, rap, tap, wap 4 bang, bash, beat, blow, boff, bonk, cane, club, conk, cuff, find, flog, lash, lick, peck, pelt, quit, raid, seem, slam, slap, slug, sock, swat, sway, whap, whop, x out 5 blitz, clash, clout, crash, drive, erase, flail, knock, lunge, occur, pound, punch, reach, sit in, smack, smite, swipe, thump, touch, whack, whang 6 assail, attack, batter, buffet, delete, fillip, hammer, harrow, impact, invade, locate, picket, pommel, pummel, punish, resist, thwack, wallop 7 assault, bombard, boycott, clobber, collide, impress, inspire, lambast, occur to, protest, rear-end, run into, sit down, uncover, unearth, walkout 8 bludgeon, bump into, chastise, discover, fall upon, fire upon, interest, lambaste, register, slowdown 9 arbitrate, deal a blow, discovery, haul off on, intrude on, smash into 10 chance upon, come across, come to mind, happen upon
back: 6 resist 9 retaliate
caller: 3 ump 5 union 6 umpire
down: 4 fell 5 smite
end a ~: 6 settle
ender: 3 out 4 over 5 bound 7 breaker
go on ~: 5 rebel 6 picket, resist, revolt 7 protest, walk out
ignorer: 4 scab
issue: 5 wages 6 demand, salary 8 benefits
monitoring agcy.: 4 NLRB
on ~: 3 out
out: 3 fan, nix 4 bomb, bust, dele, fail, flop, lose, slip, trip 5 begin, elide, erase, flunk, start, whiff 6 blow it, cancel, censor, delete, falter 7 blunder, expunge, founder, go under, go wrong, misstep, stumble 8 fall flat, flounder, lay an egg 9 leave home, red-pencil
ready to ~: 6 coiled
try for a ~: 4 bowl
strike __: 3 oil, out, pay 4 camp, down, home, zone 5 a pose, force
strike __ for liberty: 5 a blow
strike __ the iron is hot: 5 while
__ strike: 3 air 4 rent 5 first 6 called 7 general, sit-down, wildcat
__-strike: 3 ten
strike a __: 4 pose
strikebreaker: 4 scab
strike it __: 4 rich
strike or spare in bowling: 4 mark
strikeout: 5 whiff
all-time ~ king: 4 Ryan
striker: 6 picket
strikes
three ~: 3 out
unable to throw ~: 4 wild
__ Strikes Back, The: 6 Empire
__-strikes law: 5 three
__ Strikes Out: 4 Fear
Strike up the band!: 5 hit it
Strike Up the Band: 7 musical
composer: 8 Gershwin
song: 4 Soon
striking: 4 cute 5 bonny, jazzy, lofty, showy, vivid 6 bonnie, cogent, comely, lovely, marked, pretty, scenic, signal 7 awesome, bizarre, graphic, salient, telling, unusual, visible, winsome 8 alluring, charming, dazzling, dramatic, dynamite, emphatic, fabulous, flagrant, forceful, forcible, gorgeous, handsome, imposing, powerful, scenical, singular, stunning, wondrous 9 arresting, beautiful, graphical, marvelous, memorable, prominent, ravishing, startling, wonderful 10 attractive, commanding, compelling, expressive, impressive, noteworthy, noticeable, prodigious, pronounced, remarkable, staggering, surprising
be ~: 8 stand out
strikingly: 7 greatly 8 markedly 9 eminently, extremely 10 especially, incredibly
Strindberg, August: 6 writer 7 Swedish 10 playwright
work: The Dance of Death Miss Julie The Red Room
string: 3 kit, oud, row, run, saz, tie, uke, uti 4 bass, bean, biwa, ch'in, cord, file, harp, kora, koto, lace, line, lira, lute, lyre, mvet, pipa, rank, rope, ruan, team, tier, vina, viol, yarn 5 banjo, bolon, cello, chain, chang, cobza, crwth, Dobro, fidla, kerar, ko-kiu, nguru, qanun, quena, queue, rebab, rebec, sitar, suite, train, twine, veena, viola 6 bagana, buzuki, chakay, fiddle, guitar, kissar, lacing, lirica, ramkie, rebeck, santir, series, strand, valiha, violin, zither 7 bandore, baryton, cithara, cittern, gittern, kantele, kithara, machete, mandola, obukano, pandora, quinton, samisen, tambura, theorbo, ukelele, ukulele 8 archlute, autoharp, bass viol, bousouki, bouzouki, clarsach, cymbalom, dulcimer, filament, harp lute, mandolin, psaltery, sequence, surbahar, yang chin 9 balalaika, long fiber 10 instrument, procession, succession
along: 3 lie, toy 4 dupe, fool 5 dally 6 follow, lead on, trifle 7 deceive, promise 8 play with 9 misinform
clean with ~: 5 floss
fastening: 4 knot
holder: 5 kiter
in music: 5 corda
out: 6 extend, line up 7 prolong, stretch 8 elongate, lengthen, protract, straggle
piece on a ~: 4 bead
player: 3 cat 6 kitten, lyrist 7 bassist, cellist, violist 9 violinist
quartet member: 5 cello, viola 6 violin
starter: 3 bow, ham 4 draw, shoe 5 heart, latch
strong ~: 6 catgut
together: 4 link 6 extend 7 stretch
string __: 4 bass, bean 5 along 6 player 7 quartet
__ string: 3 on a 5 apron 6 second
string bean: 5 scrag 6 legume, veggie 9 vegetable
like a: 4 lank, thin 5 lanky 6 skinny, svelte
stringency: 5 rigor 9 austerity
stringent: 3 set 4 firm, hard 5 bossy, cruel, harsh, picky, rigid, rough, stern, stiff, tight, tough 6 forced, severe, strict 7 austere, binding, precise, Spartan 8 despotic, exacting, forceful, hard-line, rigorous 9 by the book, demanding, draconian, unbending, unsparing 10 compelling, despotical, inflexible, ironfisted, no-nonsense, oppressive, relentless, tyrannical
stringer: 8 reporter 10 journalist
__-string guitar: 6 twelve
strings: 5 power, terms 7 proviso 9 fine print, provision 10 conditions, provisions
in music: 5 corde
no ~: 9 boundless, limitless, unlimited
pull ~: 5 lobby, order, pluck 8 maneuver 10 manipulate
pull the ~: 6 govern

__ strings: 4 pull 5 purse
stringy: 4 lank, lean, long, ropy, thin, wiry 5 lanky, ropey, tough 6 gangly, sinewy 7 fibrous, gristly, spindly 8 gangling
strip: 3 bar, gut, rob 4 band, bare, belt, flay, hull, husk, lath, peel, sack, shed, skin, slab, slip, tape 5 board, empty, harry, layer, patch, rifle, scale, shave, shred, shuck, slice, steal, stick, thong 6 denude, divest, expose, fillet, ravage, remove, ribbon, runway, streak, tongue 7 bereave, deprive, despoil, disrobe, lay bare, peel off, pillage, plunder, ransack, section, segment, take off, uncover, undress 8 displace, freeboot, get out of, unclothe 9 depredate, dismantle, excoriate, slip out of
leather ~: 4 rein 5 thong
off: 4 flay 6 flench, flense 9 excoriate
of wood: 4 lath, slat
panel ~: 5 splat
raised ~: 5 ridge
reinforcing ~: 6 batten
starter: 3 air 4 film 5 field
suffix: 4 ling
thin ~: 4 shim
wooden ~: 4 lath
strip __: 4 mall 5 steak 6 mining
__ strip: 4 drag 5 comic, panel 6 Möbius 7 landing, parking, weather
__ Strip: 4 Gaza
Strip city: 5 Vegas 8 Las Vegas
stripe: 3 bar, ilk 4 band, line, sort, spot, vein, welt 5 class, layer, order 6 border, makeup, nature, ribbon, streak 7 variety 9 striation 10 decoration
of the same ~: 5 alike
raised ~: 4 welt
starter: 3 pin
zoologist's ~: 5 vitta
__ stripe: 5 candy, chalk 6 pencil
striped: 4 liny 5 liney, tabby
animal: 4 kudu 5 bongo, skunk, tiger, zebra 6 koodoo
fabric: 7 gingham 8 bayadere
name meaning ~: 5 Rajiv
striped __: 4 bass
__ striper: 5 candy
stripes: 7 uniform
person in ~: 3 ref 5 zebra 7 referee
remove ~ from: 6 demote
Stripes (1981 film)
cast: John Candy, Bill Murray, Warren Oates, Harold Ramis, Sean Young
director: Ivan Reitman
stripling: 3 boy, kid, lad, tad 4 baby, teen 5 child, minor, youth 6 teener 7 preteen 8 half-pint, juvenile, teenager, young man 9 schoolboy, young lady, youngster 10 adolescent, schoolgirl
stripped: 4 bare 5 naked, plain, stark 8 in the raw 9 in the buff, in the nude
be ~ of: 7 forfeit
stripped-__: 4 down
Stripper, The (1962 song)
artist: David Rose
__ stripping: 7 weather
strips: 7 funnies
cut into ~: 6 flitch
make ~: 4 tear
Stritch: 6 Elaine
strive: 3 aim, try, vie 4 moil, push, seek, toil, work 5 aim to, essay, exert, fight, labor, sweat 6 aspire, jockey, strain, tackle, take on 7 attempt, compete, contend, go after, quarrel, wrestle 8 bear down, endeavor, go all out, scramble, shoot for, struggle 10 go for broke, go the limit
for: 5 aim at 6 pursue
striving: 6 effort 8 endeavor, exertion
towards a goal: 5 nisus
strobe-light gas: 5 xenon
strobilus: 4 cone 8 pine cone
stroganoff: 6 entrée 9 casserole
__ stroganoff: 4 beef
Stroheim,: 8 Erich von
Stroh's: 4 beer
rival: *see* beer
stroke: 3 hit, pat, pet, rub 4 blow, coup, feat, laud, lick, love, luck, lull, tick 5 brush, shock, spell, touch 6 caress, pacify, praise, smooth, soothe, tickle 7 comfort, flatter 8 fawn over, flourish, inveigle, kowtow to, movement 9 reinforce, untrouble
along: 4 swim
green ~: 4 putt
light ~: 3 dab, pat
of genius: 4 coup, feat 7 exploit, triumph
of luck: 5 break, fluke 7 godsend 8 blessing, windfall
starter: 3 key 4 back, side 6 breast, ground, master
__ stroke: 5 cross 6 ground, master 7 penalty
stroking: 7 coaxing 8 cajolery, flattery 9 wheedling
stroll: 4 hike, turn, walk 5 amble, dance, jaunt, mosey, paseo, tramp 6 airing, foot it, junket, linger, loiter, ramble, trapes, wander 7 meander, saunter, traipse 8 ambulate 9 promenade
stroller: 4 pram 8 wanderer 10 pedestrian
occupant: 3 tot
Stroll in the Air, A
author: Eugène Ionesco
Strom: 8 Thurmond
Stromboli: 4 isle 6 island 7 volcano
locale: 5 Italy 6 Europe
strong: 3 big, fit, hot 4 able, bold, deep, fast, firm, hale, hard, high, keen, loud, pure, rank, rich, sure, well, wiry 5 acute, beefy, brave, brute, burly, eager, fetid, fixed, great, gutsy, hardy, heady, hefty, husky, lusty, macho, nervy, pushy, sharp, solid, sound, spicy, stark, stiff, stout, tight, tough, vivid 6 active, biting, brawny, bright, cogent, fervid, fierce, foetid, hearty, living, marked, mighty, plucky, potent, rancid, robust, rotten, rugged, secure, severe, sinewy, smelly, spicey, stable, steady, steely, sturdy, unmixt, virile 7 capable, drastic, durable, extreme, fervent, glaring, handful, healthy, intense, noisome, odorous, orotund, piquant, pungent, staunch, telling, unmixed, violent, weighty 8 athletic, clear-cut, dazzling, distinct, emphatic, enduring, forceful, forcible, indurate, leathery, muscular, powerful, resolute, rocklike, stalwart, stinking, straight, untiring, vehement, vigorous, well-made 9 brilliant, dedicated, effective, energetic, hard-nosed, heavy-duty, herculean, resilient, sagacious, steadfast, strapping, strenuous, tenacious, trenchant, unbending, undiluted, well-built 10 able-bodied, aggressive, compelling, convincing, courageous, determined, formidable, full-bodied, iron-willed, malodorous, passionate, persuasive, pronounced, reinforced, unyielding
coming on ~: 4 bold 7 zealous 9 undaunted
ender: 3 box, man 4 hold
going ~: 5 palmy 7 booming, healthy, roaring, rolling 8 thriving 9 advancing 10 prospering, prosperous, successful
grow ~: 5 train 7 work out 8 exercise, pump iron
inclination: 3 yen 4 itch, urge 7 craving, impulse, passion 8 appetite, yearning 9 hankering
interest: 4 zeal, zest 5 ardor, mania 6 fervor, thirst 7 craving 8 devotion 9 intensity, obsession 10 dedication, enthusiasm
name meaning ~: 7 Valerie
not ~: 4 puny, weak 5 frail, tinny 6 feeble, flimsy
point: 5 asset, forte
starter: 4 head
strong __: 4 suit 5 point
strong __ ox: 4 as an
strong __ type: 6 silent
strong-__: 3 arm 6 minded, willed
strong-arm: 3 cow, mug, rob 4 push 5 bleed, bully, force, forge, shove 6 coerce, compel, hector, menace, prey on 8 pressure, prey upon 9 force upon, terrorize 10 intimidate
tactics: 6 duress 7 tyranny 8 coercion, violence 9 extortion 10 oppression
strongbox: 4 safe 5 chest, vault 6 coffer 7 lockbox 8 treasury
ancient ~: 4 arca
Strong Enough (1995 song)
artist: Sheryl Crow
stronger: 6 better
grow ~: 5 rally 6 arouse, perk up, pick up, revive 7 get well, improve, rebound, recover, shape up 8 come back 9 get better 10 bounce back, come around, recuperate, rejuvenate, turn around
make ~: 6 beef up
stronger than dirt cleaner: 4 Ajax
strongest: 4 best
stronghold: 4 fort, keep 5 tower 6 castle, refuge 7 bastion, bulwark, citadel, defense, rampart, redoubt 8 fastness, fortress, garrison, presidio
castle ~: 4 keep
mountain ~: 4 aery, eyry 5 aerie, eyrie
Old Irish ~: 4 rath
strongly: 4 hard, well 6 keenly 8 forcibly, mightily, urgently
strongman: 4 jefe 8 dictator
mythical ~: 5 Atlas 8 Heracles, Hercules
rule: 5 junta
Strong Man, The (1926 film)
director: Frank Capra
strong-minded: 4 firm 6 all-out 7 decided 8 decisive, emphatic, forceful, resolute 9 obstinate 10 conclusive, unswerving, unwavering
Strong Poison
author: Dorothy Sayers
strong-smelling: 4 olid, rank 5 sharp 6 rancid
strong-willed: 8 hellbent, resolute 9 masterful, tenacious 10 purposeful
strontium: 5 metal 7 element
ore: 9 celestite
strop: 4 edge, hone, whet 7 sharpen
stropped item: 5 razor
Strother: 6 Martin
Stroud: 6 Robert
Strouse, Charles
musical: Annie
Applause
Bye Bye Birdie
Golden Boy
struck: 4 hurt
down, old-style: 4 smit
out: 3 x'ed
starter: 3 awe 4 dumb, moon, star 7 thunder
__-struck: 4 star
structural: 5 modal 7 organic
frame: 5 truss
member: 4 I-bar 5 H-beam, I-beam
steel ~ column: 5 lally
suffix: 4 -plex
structural __: 5 steel
structure: 4 cage, form, make 5 build, frame, house, order, setup, shape, shell 6 design, fabric, figure, format, makeup, nature, system 7 anatomy, complex, edifice, grammar, lattice, network 8 building, organism, skeleton 9 apparatus, fabricate, formation, framework, machinery 10 morphology, skyscraper
crude ~: 5 shack 6 lean-to
science: 7 anatomy 10 morphology
sentence ~: 7 grammar
__ structure: 5 power 6 social
structured: 8 methodic
strudel: 4 cake 6 pastry 7 dessert
__ strudel: 5 apple
struggle: 3 row, try, vie, war 4 agon, bout, buck, cope, plod, tilt, toil, work 5 agony, brawl, brush, clash, essay, fight, grind, labor, pains, scrap, set-to, slave, sweat, trial 6 battle, combat, effort, hassle, hustle, strain, strife, strive, tackle, take on, tussle, writhe 7 attempt, compete, contend, contest, grapple, quarrel, scuffle, trouble, vie with, warfare, wrangle, wrestle 8 conflict, endeavor, exertion,

flounder, long haul, plug away, scramble, skirmish, violence **9** bump heads, encounter, lock horns, square off **10** contention, difficulty, free-for-all, resistance
against: **6** resist **9** withstand
Greek hero's ~: **4** agon
long ~: **5** siege
__ struggle: **5** class, power
Strug, Kerri: **7** gymnast
strum: **5** plink, pluck, thrum
__ S Truman: **5** Harry
__-strung: **4** high
strung-out: **4** long, taut **5** tense **6** jangly **8** fluttery, restless, strained **10** distressed, protracted
strut: **4** beam, pose, prop, step, walk **5** dance, march, mince, pride, swank, sweep **6** flaunt, parade, prance, sashay **7** flounce, peacock, show off, support, swagger **8** auto part **9** put on airs **10** grandstand
__ strut: **4** oleo
Strut (1984 song)
artist: Sheena Easton
__ Strut: **7** Soulful
Struthers: **5** Sally
strut one's __: **5** stuff
St. Swithin's __: **3** Day
Stu: **5** Erwin **7** Gilliam, Jackson **9** Sutcliffe, Symington
Stuart: **3** J.E.B., Mel **4** Chad, city, Mary, town **5** Erwin **6** Cloete, Gloria, Gordon **7** Gilbert, Heisler, Whitman **8** Horowitz, Margolin **9** Rosenberg
last ~ monarch: **4** Anne
locale: **7** Florida
Stuart __ Flexner: **4** Berg
Stuart, J.E.B.: **3** reb **7** general
Stuart Little: **4** book, film
author: E.B. White
cast: Geena Davis, Michael J. Fox, Jeffrey Jones, Nathan Lane, Hugh Laurie, Jonathan Lipnicki, Chazz Palminteri, Jennifer Tilly
__ Stuart Masterson: **4** Mary
__ Stuart Mill: **4** John
stub: **3** end, tag, tip **4** butt, root, snag, tail **5** stump **6** tag end, ticket, tipoff **7** receipt, remnant, tail end **8** short end **9** rain check, remainder
one's toe: **3** err
stub __: **4** a toe
__ stub: **5** check
stubble: **5** beard **7** bristle
clear ~: **5** shave
remover: **5** razor
site: **4** chin
stubbly: **5** nubby, rough **7** bristly
stubborn: **3** set **4** firm, hard, iron **5** balky, fixed, rigid, stern, stiff, stony, tough **6** cussed, dogged, feisty, mulish, ornery, stoney, unruly, wilful **7** adamant, defiant, hard-set, naughty, piggish, restive, wayward, willful **8** contrary, factious, hellbent, indocile, indurate, obdurate, perverse, resolute, untoward **9** fractious, hard-nosed, immovable, impliable, obstinate, pigheaded, steadfast, tenacious, unbending **10** bullheaded, determined, hard-bitten, hardheaded, headstrong, inexorable, inflexible, iron-willed, persistent, rebellious, refractory, relentless, self-willed, unshakable, unyielding
be ~: **6** resist **7** persist **9** persevere
one: **3** ass **4** cuss, mule **6** balker **7** baulker, holdout
stubborn __ mule: **3** as a
Stubborn Hope
poet: Dennis Brutus
stubbornness: **4** will **8** tenacity
Stubbs: **4** Levi **6** George
stubby: **5** short, squat, stout, thick **6** little, stocky, stumpy **8** heavyset, thickset
Stubby: **4** Kaye
stucco: **7** encrust, incrust, plaster
backing: **4** lath
site: **4** wall
stuck: **5** mired **6** caught, in a fix, in a jam, in a rut, lodged, static **7** adhered, at a loss, baffled, in a bind, puzzled, trapped **8** confused **9** buffaloed, immovable **10** gridlocked
be ~ on: **4** like, love **5** adore
get ~: **4** mire **5** lodge **6** wallow
in place: **3** set
it may be ~ out: **4** neck
on: **6** fond of
on oneself: **4** smug, vain
stuck __ rut: **3** in a
Stuck on You (song)
artist: Elvis Presley, Lionel Richie
stuck-up: **4** smug, vain **5** aloof, cocky, proud **6** remote, snooty, stuffy **7** fustian, haughty, pompous **8** arrogant, boastful, snobbish, superior **9** big-headed, conceited, hubristic **10** big-talking
person: **4** snob **5** snoot
Stuck With You (1986 song)
artist: Huey Lewis and the News
stud: **4** beam, bolt, boss, game, hunk, male, pole, post **5** he-man, poker **7** earring, tie tack **8** card game, cufflink, fastener, lothario, sprinkle **9** scantling
challenge: **5** I call
ender: **4** book, fish, work **5** horse
progeny: **4** colt, foal **5** filly
site: **3** ear **4** lobe
stud __: **5** poker
studded: **5** beset **6** inlaid **8** speckled
studded __: **4** tire
__-studded: **4** star
Studebaker: **3** car **4** auto **10** automobile
model: **4** Hawk, Lark **5** Regal **6** Avanti, Pelham **7** Daytona, Sky Hawk, St. Regis **8** Champion, Dictator, Scotsman **9** Broadmoor, Commander, President **10** Challenger
student: **4** coed, grad **5** pupil, tutee, youth **6** intern, junior, novice **7** interne, learner, scholar **8** academic, disciple, freshman, graduate, observer **9** sophomore, undergrad, youngster **10** apprentice
award: **5** grant
become a ~: **5** enrol **6** enroll **8** register
book: **4** text
center: **4** quad **6** campus
eager ~ plea: **4** me me
first-year ~: **5** frosh **8** freshman
former ~: **4** alum, grad **6** alumna **7** alumnus **8** graduate
in French: **5** élève
last-year: **2** sr. **3** snr. **6** senior
ordeal: **4** exam, test **5** essay, final **7** midterm
place: **4** desk, dorm **6** school **7** college **9** dormitory **10** university
sack a ~: **5** expel
second-year ~: **4** soph **9** sophomore
stat: **3** GPA
third-year: **2** jr. **6** junior
unpopular ~: **4** geek, nerd
vehicle: **3** bus
student __: **4** body **5** nurse, union **7** council, teacher
__ student: **6** pre-law, pre-med
studied: **6** wilful **7** labored, learned, planned, plotted, willful **8** affected, designed, gone into **9** conscious, unnatural **10** calculated, deliberate, purposeful
__ studies: **5** black **6** social, women's
studio: **4** loft **7** atelier
feature: **3** set **5** easel **6** camera
film ~: **3** lot
former ~: **3** RKO **6** Desilu
movie ~: **3** Fox, MGM **6** Disney **7** Miramax, New Line **8** Columbia **9** Paramount, Universal **10** Dreamworks, Warner Bros.
studious: **4** busy **5** eager **6** intent **7** bookish, careful, earnest, learned, serious **8** academic, diligent, highbrow, sedulous, well-read **9** assiduous, attentive, motivated, scholarly **10** meditative, reflective, thoughtful
studiously: **4** hard **10** designedly
studly: **5** macho, manly **6** virile
Studs: **6** Terkel
Studs Lonigan
author: James T. Farrell
study: **3** con, den, dig, eye **4** case, cram, heed, look, mull, muse, plug, pore, read, room, scan **5** assay, grind, learn, paper, probe, think, train, weigh **6** bone up, debate, digest, go over, lesson, master, peruse, ponder, reason, revery, review, search, survey, take up **7** analyze, canvass, dissect, enquiry, examine, inquiry, inspect, library, observe, perusal, profile, reading, reflect, reverie, thought **8** analysis, check out, consider, learning, likeness, look into, meditate, mull over, polish up, pore over, practice, read up on, rehearse, research, scrutiny **9** attention, brood over, criticize, education, enter into, get to know, grind away, lucubrate, pick apart, sweat over, think over **10** crack a book, deliberate, experiment, reflection, rumination, scrutinize
brown ~: **4** muse **6** revery, trance **7** reverie **10** detachment
course of ~: **5** major **9** specialty
group: **7** seminar
hard: **4** cram, pore
session: **6** lesson
study __: **4** hall **5** group
__ study: **4** area, case, home, time **5** brown, quick **6** motion, nature
__-study: **4** self
Study in Scarlet, A
author: Arthur Conan Doyle
Study of History, A
author: Arnold Toynbee
__-study program: **4** work
stuff: **3** jam, kit, pad, ram, wad **4** cram, fill, gear, glut, guff, junk, load, pack, push, sate, soul, stow **5** cloth, crowd, goods, gorge, items, press, ram in, sense, shove, skill, stick, trash, wedge **6** fabric, fatten, matter, stop up, tackle, things **7** baloney, compact, congest, effects, engorge, luggage, objects, overeat, satiate, shove in, squeeze **8** compress, material, movables, property, slam-dunk **9** equipment, overcrowd, substance, trappings **10** belongings, gormandize
starter: **3** dye **4** feed, food **5** bread
see also baloney
__ stuff: **3** hot, kid **4** hard **5** green, right, rough, small
__ Stuff: **3** Hot **5** Mr. Big
stuffed: **4** full, rife **5** close, laden, thick **6** loaded, packed **7** compact, fraught, replete, teeming **8** brimming **9** chock-full, condensed, congested, jam-packed, stoppered **10** compressed, gridlocked, obstructed, overfilled
delicacy: **5** derma **6** kishke, kiskha
in cookery: **5** farci
shirt: **4** prig, snob **5** snoot **7** elitist
stuffed __: **5** derma, shirt **7** cabbage, peppers
Stuffed Shirts
author: Clare Boothe Luce
stuffiness: **3** ego **6** egoism **7** conceit, egotism **8** humidity
stuffing: **3** pad **6** filler **7** filling, padding **8** dressing
flavoring: **4** sage
stuff one's __: **4** face
__ Stuff, The: **5** Right
stuffy: **4** blah, damp, dank, dull, prim, smug **5** bland, close, heavy, ho-hum, humid, muggy, musty, rigid, soggy, staid, stale, thick, unfun **6** boring, clammy, formal, prissy, proper, square, steamy, sticky, stodgy, strict, sultry **7** airless, blocked, bookish, clogged, haughty, high-hat, pompous, prudish, stilted, stuck-up, tedious **8** priggish, puffed up, snobbish, stagnant, stifling, tiresome **9** conceited, humorless, ponderous, Victorian **10** big-talking, egocentric, oppressive, sweltering
Stuka: **5** plane **6** bomber **8** airplane
stultify: **6** thwart **7** nullify, vitiate **9** frustrate, hamstring
stumble: **3** dud, err **4** bomb, bust, fall, flop, halt, lose, loss, muff, reel, slip, trip **5** error, fluff, flunk, lurch, waver **6** blow it, bumble, defeat, falter, fiasco, header, mishap, teeter, topple, totter, trudge, turkey, wabble, wobble **7** blunder, debacle, founder, go under, go wrong, misstep, shuffle, stagger, stammer, stutter, washout **8** downfall, fall flat, flounder, hesitate, lay an egg **9** indecorum, strike out **10** chance upon, come across, happen upon
across: **5** hit on **6** strike

ender: **3** bum
on: **4** find **5** learn **6** detect, locate **7** run into, uncover, unearth **8** bump into, chance on, discover **9** run across **10** chance upon
verbal ~: **2** er, uh, um
stumblebum: **2** ox **3** oaf **4** lout **5** klutz, looby **6** galoot, lubber
stumbling: **5** gawky **6** clumsy, klutzy, oafish **7** awkward, gawkish, halting, unadept **8** bungling, ungainly **9** all thumbs, graceless, maladroit, unskilled **10** hesitation, unskillful
block: **3** bar, rub **4** snag **5** catch, hitch **6** hurdle, kicker **7** barrier, pitfall, problem, setback **8** drawback, handicap, obstacle **9** hindrance **10** impediment
Stumblin' In (1979 song)
artist: Suzi Quatro
stump: **3** end, leg, nub, run, vex **4** butt, foil, fool, knub, plod, stop, stub, talk, tour, walk **5** clomp, clump, floor, speak, stamp, stimy, stomp, stymy, tramp **6** baffle, lumber, nubbin, outwit, podium, puzzle, speech, stymie, trudge **7** buffalo, confuse, galumph, mystify, nonplus, perplex, stagger, tail end **8** bewilder, campaign, confound, hustings, platform **9** dumbfound, frustrate
for: **4** help **6** assist **7** endorse, indorse, support **8** advocate
source: **4** tree
take the ~: **5** orate, speak **7** address
__ stump: **3** off, up a
stumped: **4** asea **5** at sea **7** at a loss, puzzled, up a tree **8** confused
stumper: **4** koan **5** poser **6** enigma, riddle **7** problem, toughie
__ Stumper: **8** Saturday
stumpy: **5** thick **6** stubby
stun: **2** KO **3** awe, jar, wow **4** daze, faze, jolt, kayo, numb, rock **5** amaze, appal, floor, shock **6** appall, baffle, bedaze, bemuse, benumb, deaden, lay out **7** astound, confuse, flummox, nonplus, petrify, shake up, stagger, startle, stupefy, terrify **8** astonish, bedazzle, bewilder, blow away, bowl over, confound, knock out, overcome, paralyse, paralyze, surprise, transfix **9** dumbfound, overpower, overwhelm, take aback **10** discompose, scare stiff
gun: **5** taser
with sound: **6** deafen
stung: **4** sore **5** burnt **6** burned **7** injured
be ~ by conscience: **3** rue **5** atone **6** regret
__ Stung: **4** I Got
stunned: **4** agog **5** agasp, in awe, shook **6** aghast, jolted **7** in a daze **8** overcome **9** awestruck **10** dumbstruck
appear ~: **4** gape
stunner: **6** beauty, eyeful, looker, marvel, vision **7** miracle, prodigy **8** knockout **9** sensation
stunning: **4** cute **5** bonny **6** bonnie, comely, lovely, pretty, superb **7** amazing, awesome, winsome **8** adorable, alluring, dazzling, fetching, gorgeous, handsome, heavenly, pleasing, smashing, striking **9** arresting, beautiful, brilliant, marvelous, number one, ravishing **10** attractive, impressive, prodigious, remarkable, stupendous
stunt: **3** act **4** deed, feat, ruse, slow, stop **5** caper, dwarf, thing, trick **6** hinder, impede **7** exploit, gimmick **8** activity, pretense **10** shenanigan
performer: **5** clown **7** acrobat **9** daredevil
stunted: **3** low **4** puny, tiny **5** runty, scrub, short, small **6** bantam, little, peewee **7** dwarfed **9** pint-sized, undersize **10** diminutive, undersized
animal: **4** runt
tree: **5** scrub
Stunt Man, The (1980 film)
cast: Barbara Hershey, Peter O'Toole
stupe
see ninny
stupefaction: **3** awe **4** daze **5** shock **8** hypnosis
stupefied: **4** logy **5** agape **9** lethargic **10** bewildered
stupefy: **4** daze, drug, numb, rock, stun, zonk **5** addle, amaze, besot, floor, shock **6** bemuse, benumb, boggle, dazzle, muddle **7** astound, confuse, petrify, shake up, stagger, terrify **8** astonish, bewilder, blow away, bowl over, confound, knock out, paralyse, paralyze, surprise **9** dumbfound, inebriate, overwhelm **10** intoxicate, scare stiff
stupendous: **3** big **4** huge, vast **5** jumbo, large **6** cosmic, mighty, peachy **7** hulking, immense, mammoth, massive, radical, sizable, titanic, too much **8** colossal, cosmical, enormous, gigantic, king-size, oversize, sizeable, stunning, towering, whapping, whopping, wondrous **9** Herculean, humongous, monstrous, overlarge, unrivaled, wonderful **10** gargantuan, monumental, out of sight, unrivalled
see also wonderful
Stupid __ Tricks: **3** Pet
Stupid Cupid (1958 song)
artist: Connie Francis
stupor: **4** daze **5** shock, swoon **6** apathy, torpor, trance **7** inertia, languor, slumber **8** dullness, hypnosis, lethargy, loginess, numbness **9** indolence, lassitude **10** somnolence
sturdiness: **3** vim **4** dint, thew **5** brawn, force, might, power, thews, vigor **6** energy, muscle **7** fitness, muscles, potence, potency, stamina **8** strength, vitality **9** endurance, fortitude, puissance **10** brute force
sturdy: **4** firm, hale, iron, wiry **5** beefy, burly, hardy, hefty, hunky, husky, lusty, solid, sound, stout, tight, tough **6** brawny, hearty, mighty, potent, robust, rugged, secure, sinewy, stable, steely, stocky, strong, virile **7** doughty, durable, healthy, hulking, staunch **8** athletic, forceful, indurate, muscular, powerful, puissant, resolute, stalwart, vigorous, well-made **9** Atlantean, fortified, Herculean, steadfast, strapping, tenacious, well-built **10** able-bodied, determined, red-blooded, reinforced
sturgeon: **4** fish **6** beluga **7** sterlet
product: **3** roe **6** caviar **7** caviare
Sturgeon, Theodore: **6** writer
genre: **5** sci-fi
Sturges: **4** John **7** Preston
Sturges, Preston: **8** director
film: Christmas in July (1940)
The Great McGinty (1940)
Hail the Conquering Hero (1944)
The Lady Eve (1941)
The Miracle of Morgan's Creek (1944)
The Palm Beach Story (1942)
Sullivan's Travels (1941)
Unfaithfully Yours (1948)
Sturm und Drang: **5** drama **6** tumult **7** turmoil **8** upheaval
stutter: **4** slur **6** falter, mumble **7** sputter, stammer, stumble **8** hesitate, splutter
Stuttgart: **4** city, town
locale: **7** Germany
river: **6** Neckar
Stutz Bearcat: **3** car **4** auto **10** automobile
contemporary: **3** Reo **5** Essex
Stuyvesant: **5** Peter
St. Vincent and the Grenadines: **6** nation **7** country
capital: **9** Kingstown
locale: **10** West Indies
__ St. Vincent Millay: **4** Edna
sty: **3** pen **4** dump, slum **5** hovel, sewer **6** pigpen **7** piggery, rathole **8** cesspool, pesthole **9** enclosure, hordeolum
baby: **4** gilt **5** shoat, shote, shott **6** piglet
comment: **4** oink **5** grunt
dweller: **3** hog, pig, sow **5** swine
fare: **4** slop **5** swill
free from the ~: **5** unpen
starter: **3** pig
Stygian: **3** dim **4** dark, evil **6** nether **9** lightless
style: **3** air, cut, dub, fad, tag, way **4** call, coif, dash, ease, élan, form, kind, mode, name, rage, sort, term, tone, type, vein **5** class, craze, decor, flair, genre, genus, grace, label, model, state, taste, tenor, thing, title, trend, vogue **6** aplomb, beauty, bon ton, custom, design, flavor, format, glamor, Gothic, luxury, manner, method, nature, pizazz, polish, rococo, spirit, tailor, temper **7** baroque, bearing, comfort, costume, diction, fashion, glamour, Moorish, panache, pattern, suavity, wording **8** approach, artistry, delicacy, elegance, grandeur, language, phrasing, Sheraton, urbanity **9** character, classical, designate, nattiness, ritziness, smartness, suaveness, technique, treatment **10** art nouveau, complexion, dapperness, denominate, flashiness, modishness, refinement, Romanesque, snazziness, swankiness
cramp one's ~: **5** spite **8** obstruct
in ~: **3** hip, mod **4** tony **5** natty, sharp, swank, toney **6** chi-chi, classy, dapper, dressy, modish, trendy **7** à la mode, current, dashing, elegant, popular, voguish **10** all the rage, prevailing
in the ~ of: **3** à la
no longer in ~: **3** old, out **4** past **5** dated, dowdy, dusty, fusty, passé **6** bygone, old hat, quaint **7** ancient, archaic, fogyish **8** decrepit, long gone, medieval, obsolete, timeworn **10** antiquated, superseded
starter: **4** free, life
style __: **5** sheet
__ style: **3** old **4** hair, high, type **5** out of **6** family
Style: **7** channel
alternative: ***see*** cable channel
__-styled: **4** self
stylet: **5** probe
styling goo: **3** gel **5** gelee
stylish: **3** hip, mod, now **4** chic, neat, tony **5** class, dashy, faddy, funky, haute, jazzy, natty, nifty, ritzy, sharp, slick, smart, swank, swell, swish, toney **6** chichi, classy, dapper, dressy, flossy, knobby, modern, modish, snappy, snazzy, spruce, swanky, trendy, uptown **7** à la mode, current, dashing, elegant, genteel, in vogue, popular, voguish **8** artistic, handsome, polished, up-to-date **9** exclusive, high-class, in fashion **10** all the rage, artistical
too ~: **4** arty **5** artsy
stylishness: **3** ton **4** chic **5** vogue
stylist: **6** barber
activity: **3** cut, dye **8** makeover
challenge: **3** mop
creation: **4** coif **6** hairdo
supply: **3** gel **4** comb **5** spray **9** hairspray
Stylistics
hometown: Philadelphia
song: Betcha By Golly, Wow (1972)
Break Up to Make Up (1973)
I'm Stone in Love With You (1972)
You Are Everything (1971)
You Make Me Feel Brand New (1974)
stylograph: **3** pen
stylus: **3** pen
holder: **3** arm **7** tonearm
target: **6** groove
Stylus: **3** car **4** auto **5** Isuzu **10** automobile
stymie: **4** balk, foil, tree, undo **5** baulk, block, cramp, crimp, stall, stump **6** baffle, corner, defeat, hamper, hang up, hinder, hogtie, impede, thwart **7** dead-end, inhibit, nonplus, prevent, ward off **8** confound, obstruct, prohibit **9** frustrate, stonewall
stymied: **5** stuck **6** in a fix, in a jam
Styne, Jule: **8** composer
collaborator: Sammy Cahn, Bob Merrill, Stephen Sondheim
musical: Bells Are Ringing
Do Re Mi

Funny Girl
Gentlemen Prefer Blondes
Gypsy
Hallelujah, Baby!
High Button Shoes
Lorelei
Sugar
song: Diamonds Are a Girl's Best Friend
Don't Rain on My Parade
Everything's Coming Up Roses
Five Minutes More
I Don't Want to Walk Without You, Baby
It's Been a Long, Long Time
It's Magic
I've Heard That Song Before
Just in Time
Let Me Entertain You
Make Someone Happy
The Party's Over
People
Saturday Night Is the Loneliest Night of the Week
Small World
Three Coins in the Fountain
styptic: **4** alum **7** binding **10** astringent
pencil coverup: **4** nick
Styrofoam: **7** padding, plastic
Styron, William: **6** writer
work: The Confessions of Nat Turner
In the Clap Shack
Lie Down in Darkness
The Long March
The Quiet Dust
Set This House on Fire
Sophie's Choice
Styx: **5** river
daughter: **4** Nike
locale: **5** Hades
tributary: **5** Lethe **6** Aornis **7** Acheron, Cocytus
Styx (rock group)
hometown: Chicago
song: Babe (1979)
The Best of Times (1981)
Come Sail Away (1977)
Don't Let It End (1983)
Lady (1975)
Lorelei (1976)
Mr. Roboto (1983)
Show Me the Way (1981)
Too Much Time on My Hands (1981)
suave: **4** cool, glib, oily **5** bland, civil **6** genial, poised, polite, smooth, urbane **7** affable, cordial, courtly, gallant, politic, refined, tactful, worldly **8** charming, cultured, debonair, finished, gracious, obliging, pleasant, pleasing, polished, sociable, unctuous, well-bred **9** agreeable, civilized, courteous, debonaire, high-toned **10** cultivated, debonnaire, diplomatic, soft-spoken
Suave: **7** shampoo
competitor: **4** Flex, Pert **5** Prell, Wella **7** Finesse, Pantene
suaveness: **4** tact **5** couth, style **6** polish **8** courtesy **11** savoir faire
sub: **4** hero, temp **5** hoagy, proxy, sit in, U-boat, under **6** backup, deputy, fill in, hoagie **7** replace, stand-in **8** pinch-hit, sandwich **9** alternate, fill in for, surrogate **10** understudy
concern: **5** depth
detector: **5** asdic, sonar
device: **5** scope **7** torpedo **9** periscope
door: **5** hatch
hazard: **4** mine **6** ashcan
locale: **3** sea **4** deep **5** ocean
on sonar: **3** pip **4** blip
outlet: **4** deli
sub __: **4** rosa, voce **5** verbo **6** judice
sub-__: **4** zero **5** level **7** Saharan
Subaru: **3** car **4** auto **6** import **10** automobile
competitor: **5** Honda, Isuzu **6** Toyota
model: **3** SVX, WRX **5** Justy, Leone **6** Legacy, Loyale **7** Impreza, Outback **8** Forester
subatomic particle: **2** xi **4** kaon, muon, pion **5** axion, boson, gluon, meson, quark, tauon **6** baryon, hadron, K meson, lepton, photon, proton **7** fermion, hyperon, neutron, nucleon, pi meson, tachyon **8** deuteron, electron, graviton, neutrino, positron
subcompact: **3** car **4** auto **10** automobile
subconscious: **4** mind **5** inner **6** hidden, inmost, latent, psyche **9** intuitive **10** archetypal
subdivide: **5** halve, slice, split **9** partition
minutely: **4** cube, dice **5** mince
subdivision: **3** arm **4** part **5** class, group, split, tract **6** branch, sector **7** element, section, segment **9** community
subdue: **3** cow **4** beat, curb, lull, mute, tame **5** abate, break, crush, quash, quell, quiet, worst **6** bridle, deaden, defeat, gentle, govern, humble, mellow, muffle, pacify, reduce, soften, soothe, temper **7** appease, conquer, control, oppress, put down, repress, silence, squelch, trample, triumph **8** keep down, mitigate, moderate, overcome, restrain, strangle, suppress, surmount, tone down, vanquish **9** humiliate, overpower, quiet down, subjugate **10** keep in line
subdued: **3** dim, low, sad **4** meek, mild, soft, tame **5** bated, faint, grave, muted, piano, quiet, sober, yoked **6** broken, broody, docile, gentle, hushed, low-key, mellow, pliant, solemn, subtle **7** neutral, serious, trained **8** dejected, delicate, downcast, lamblike, murmured, obedient, resigned, tasteful **9** chastened, compliant, repentant, repressed, toned down, tractable, whispered **10** manageable, restrained, spiritless, submissive
color: **3** ash, tan **4** gray, grey, navy **5** beige, brown, mauve, ocher, ochre, umber
Subic __: **3** Bay
subjacent: **5** lower **6** lesser
subject: **3** apt **4** item, noun, serf, text **5** class, issue, liege, model, motif, prone, ruled, theme, thing, topic, under **6** client, course, liable, likely, vassal **7** captive, exposed, inflict, patient, servile, villein **8** enslaved, governed, inferior, obedient **9** dependant, dependent, guinea pig, leitmotif, secondary, tentative **10** answerable, contingent, controlled, discipline, vulnerable
subject __: **6** matter
subjection: **7** loyalty **9** captivity, liability **10** domination
subjective: **6** biased, mental **8** illusive, illusory, personal **9** arbitrary, emotional, intuitive
subjectivity: **4** bias **9** prejudice **10** favoritism, preference
Subject Was Roses, The (1968 film)
cast: Jack Albertson, Patricia Neal, Martin Sheen
subjoin: **3** add **5** affix
subjugate: **4** tame **5** crush, quell **6** defeat, prey on, reduce, subdue **7** conquer, enslave, enthral, inthral, oppress, put down, triumph **8** bring low, dominate, enthrall, inthrall, keep down, overcome, prey upon, suppress, vanquish **9** overpower
subjugation: **6** defeat **7** slavery, victory **9** servitude
subjugator: **4** hero **6** master, victor, winner **8** champion **9** conqueror **10** vanquisher
sublet: **4** rent **5** lease
sublimate: **6** purify **7** ennoble
sublime: **4** high **5** lofty, proud **7** refined, stately **8** elevated, empyreal, empyrean, ethereal, gorgeous, imposing, majestic, rarefied, towering, ultimate, wondrous **9** celestial, unrivaled, wonderful **10** majestical, unrivalled
see also wonderful
subliminal: **6** mental **9** intuitive
sublimity: **5** glory **8** grandeur, nobility **9** elevation, greatness **10** perfection
submachine gun: **3** Uzi
submarine
see sub
__ Submarine: **6** Yellow
submerge: **3** dip **4** duck, dunk, sink, soak **5** douse, dowse, drown, flood, lower, souse, steep, swamp **6** deluge, drench, engulf, ingulf, plunge **7** descend, founder, go under, immerse **8** inundate, overflow **9** hit bottom, overwhelm
submerged: **4** sunk **6** sunken **8** immersed, scuttled **9** engrossed **10** underwater
submerse: **3** dip **4** sink **5** bathe, souse, swamp
submission: **3** bid **6** assent **7** loyalty **8** docility, humility, meekness, yielding **9** deference, endurance, obedience, orthodoxy, passivity, servility, surrender **10** compliance, conformity
contest ~: **5** entry
editorial: **5** draft **10** manuscript
submissive: **4** easy, meek, mild, tame **5** lowly, timid **6** abject, broken, docile, humble, pliant **7** dutiful, orderly, passive, pliable, servile, slavish, subdued, trained, willing **8** amenable, gracious, lamblike, obedient, resigned, yielding **9** agreeable, compliant, groveling, malleable, prostrate, spineless, tractable **10** governable, manageable
submit: **3** bid, bow, put **4** bend, cave, fold, obey, pose **5** defer, kotow, offer, refer, stand, yield **6** assert, buckle, comply, endure, give in, hand in, kowtow, suffer, tender, turn in **7** advance, contend, present, proffer, propose, succumb, suggest, truckle **8** nominate, propound, put forth, say uncle, stand for **9** acquiesce, prostrate, reconcile, surrender **10** capitulate, come around, put forward, toe the line
subnormal: **7** lacking **9** defective, deficient
subordinate: **4** aide, asst., less, side **5** gofer, lower, lowly, minor, slave, under **6** deputy, flunky, gopher, helper, junior, lesser, second, stooge **7** flunkey, servant **8** adjuvant, henchman, inferior **9** accessory, ancillary, assistant, attendant, auxiliary, dependant, dependent, gal Friday, man Friday, overwhelm, satellite, secondary, subaltern, tributary, underling **10** girl Friday
subordinate __: **6** clause
subordinates: **5** staff
subordination: **4** sway **5** might **7** control, mastery **9** supremacy, upper hand **10** domination, occupation, oppression
suborn: **5** bribe **7** corrupt, falsify
suborned: **5** false **7** corrupt **9** on the take
Subotica: **4** city, town
locale: **6** Serbia
subpar hole: **3** ace **5** eagle **6** birdie
subpoena: **4** call, cite, writ **5** paper **6** summon **7** process, summons, warrant
sub rosa: **6** secret **7** furtive, illegal **8** hush-hush, on the sly, secretly **9** entre nous, furtively, privately, underhand **10** undercover
subscribe: **3** buy **4** back, give, sign **5** agree, bless, boost, enrol, favor, grant, put up **6** ante up, chip in, donate, enroll, pledge, second, sign up **7** approve, endorse, indorse, pitch in, promise, support **8** advocate, register, sanction **9** acquiesce, autograph, get behind **10** contribute, underwrite
subscriber: **6** patron, reader **9** proponent, supporter **10** benefactor
subscribing, keep: **5** renew **6** extend, update **7** prolong **8** continue
subscription
card: **6** insert
unit: **5** issue
subsequent: **4** next **5** after, later **6** coming, future, second **7** ensuing **8** eventual, upcoming **9** following, posterior, proximate, resulting, secondary **10** consequent, succeeding
subsequently: **4** anon, next, then **5** after, hence, later, since **6** behind **7** ensuing, finally, someday **8** in back of, in the end **9** afterward, following **10** succeeding
subservience: **4** fear **8** docility, humility, meekness **9** cowardice, servility

subservient: **4** meek, mild **5** slave, under **6** abject, docile, menial, useful **7** fawning, ignoble, servile, slavish **8** cowering, cringing, resigned **9** prostrate
be ~: **4** fawn **5** cower **6** cringe, grovel, kowtow **8** bootlick
subside: **3** die, ebb, set **4** ease, fall, lull, sink, wane **5** abate, lapse, let up, lower **6** go down, lessen, recede, relent, settle **7** decline, die down, dwindle, quieten, slacken, tail off **8** blow over, collapse, contract, decrease, diminish, head away, level off, moderate, peter out, slack off, taper off **9** lighten up, retrocede **10** de-escalate
subsidence: **5** lysis **9** abatement, remission
subsidiary: **4** side **5** minor, under **6** backup, branch, lesser **9** ancillary, auxiliary, secondary **10** collateral, incidental
subsidize: **3** aid **4** abet, back, fund, help **5** endow, juice, set up, stake **7** finance, promote, sponsor, support **8** bankroll **9** encourage, grubstake **10** capitalize, contribute, supplement, underwrite
subsidy: **3** aid **4** gift **5** bonus, grant **6** bounty, reward **7** alimony, backing, bequest, payment, pension, premium, support **8** donation, largesse **9** allowance, endowment, patronage **10** assistance, fellowship, honorarium
subsist: **3** are **4** last, live **5** exist **6** endure, hang on, manage **7** breathe, ride out, survive **8** continue, get along, scrape by **9** keep going, stay alive **10** stick it out
subsistence: **4** life **5** means, wages **6** income, living, salary, upkeep **7** aliment, capital, support **8** earnings **9** provision, resources **10** livelihood
subsoil: **3** bed **4** dirt **5** earth
substance: **3** nub **4** body, core, gist, guts, heft, knub, meat, pith, root, size, soul **5** drift, fiber, focus, force, heart, means, sense, stuff, tenor, theme, thing, value, worth **6** burden, import, kernel, marrow, matter, moment, riches, spirit, thrust, upshot, wealth **7** content, essence, keynote, meaning, purport, reality **8** contents, material, property, strength, sum total, validity **9** actuality, affluence, essential, lifeblood, something **10** importance
full of ~: **4** rich **5** meaty, pithy **7** weighty **8** profound
in ~: **6** nearly **9** virtually
lacking ~: **4** thin **5** inane **8** ethereal
sum and ~: **3** nub **4** core, gist **5** heart, theme **6** kernel
Substance of Fire, The
author: Jon Robin Baitz
substandard: **3** bad, low, off **4** poor, weak **7** wanting **8** inferior
substantial: **3** big, key **4** firm, good, much, real, rich, tidy, true, vast **5** ample, beefy, bulky, hardy, heavy, hefty, large, meaty, solid, sound, stout, thick, valid **6** actual, goodly, hearty, rugged, stable, steady, strong, sturdy **7** durable, for real, gainful, massive, serious, sizable, visible, wealthy, weighty, well-off **8** abundant, concrete, definite, explicit, generous, material, physical, positive, sizeable, stalwart, tangible, valuable, well-made, well-to-do **9** corporeal, important, momentous, objective, well-built
substantiality: **4** size **7** reality **9** stability
substantially: **4** well **6** mainly **7** heavily, largely **9** in essence, in the main
substantiate: **4** test **5** prove, vouch **6** affirm, attest, ratify, verify **7** bear out, certify, confirm, justify, support **8** attest to, check out, evidence, flesh out, validate **9** establish, vindicate
substantiation: **5** proof **8** acid test, evidence **9** testimony
substantive: **4** noun, real **5** meaty **6** actual **7** pronoun
substitute: **4** mock, sham, swap, swop, temp **5** agent, cover, false, ghost, other, proxy, shift, sit-in, spare, vicar **6** act for, backup, change, deputy, ersatz, fill in, relief, second, switch **7** another, plastic, relieve, replace, reserve, stand-in, stopgap **8** cover for, displace, exchange, pinch-hit, spurious **9** alternate, assistant, auxiliary, expedient, fill in for, makeshift, surrogate, temporary **10** artificial, equivalent, pro tempore, quid pro quo, understudy
name meaning ~: **4** Seth
substitution: **6** change **8** exchange
substratum: **3** bed **4** base **5** layer **7** support **10** foundation, groundwork
substructure: **5** basis **7** support
subsume: **4** have **7** contain, include
subsumed: **5** under
subterfuge: **3** lie **4** hoax, ploy, ruse, sham, trap, wile **5** blind, bluff, craft, dodge, feint, fraud, shift, trick **6** deceit, device, dupery, humbug, scheme **7** evasion, knavery, pretext, sleight, snow job, swindle **8** artifice, maneuver, pretense **9** chicanery, deception, expedient, fourberie, imposture, stratagem **10** hanky-panky
subterranean: **4** deep **5** below **6** buried, hidden **7** abysmal **9** cavernous
area: **4** mine **5** crypt **6** cavern, cellar, grotto **8** basement
creature: **3** bat **4** mole **5** gnome, troll
lockup: **6** donjon **7** dungeon
passageway: **6** dromos
subtle: **3** sly **4** deep, fine, keen, nice **5** faint, snaky **6** artful, astute, clever, low-key, polite, slight, tricky **7** devious, implied, logical, politic, refined, subdued, tactful, tenuous **8** abstruse, delicate, discreet, finespun, guileful, illusive, indirect, inferred, profound, scheming **9** astucious, courteous, designing, exquisite, ingenious, insidious, judicious, sensitive **10** diplomatic, intriguing, perceptive, suggestive, thoughtful
indication: **4** clue, hint **5** trace **10** suggestion
not ~: **5** broad **7** obvious
signal: **3** nod **4** wink **7** gesture
subtlety: **4** tact **5** craft **6** nicety, nuance **7** finesse, mystery **8** delicacy, quiddity **9** diplomacy **10** refinement
subtract: **4** take **6** deduct, remove **7** compute, detract **8** decrease, diminish, discount, knock off, take away, withhold **9** calculate
subtraction: **9** lessening, reduction
result: **10** difference
word: **4** less **5** minus
suburb: **4** town **6** hamlet **7** village
suburban: **8** outlying
resident: **8** commuter
status symbol: **4** pool **6** hot tub
tool: **5** mower
Suburban: **3** car, GMC, SUV **4** auto **5** Chevy, Dodge **8** Plymouth **9** Chevrolet **10** automobile
subversion: **4** ruin **7** undoing **8** betrayal, sabotage
subversive: **5** rebel **7** harmful, traitor **8** disloyal, frondeur, quisling, saboteur **9** insurgent, seditious **10** incendiary, rebellious
subvert: **4** oust, ruin, undo **5** upset, wreck **6** debase, depose, poison, topple, tumble, unseat **7** abolish, conquer, corrupt, deprave, destroy, vitiate **8** demolish, overturn, pull down, sabotage, undercut, vanquish **9** discredit, overthrow, undermine
subway: **4** tube **5** metro **6** tunnel **8** railroad
access: **5** stair, stile **9** escalator
alternative: **2** el **3** bus, car **4** auto, taxi **7** car pool
artwork: **5** mural **8** graffiti
fare: **5** token
NYC ~: **3** BMT, IRT, MTA
of song: **6** A Train
power source: **4** rail
station: **4** stop
take the ~: **7** commute
Subway
rival: *see* restaurant chain
succeed: **2** go **3** win **4** boom, pass, rise, take, work **5** avail, bloom, click, ensue, go far, score, trail, worst **6** accede, arrive, assume, follow, fulfil, go next, go well, hack it, make it, manage, pan out, pay off, result, rotate, secure, thrive **7** achieve, acquire, blossom, come off, conquer, fulfill, go after, inherit, make out, prevail, prosper, pull off, realize, replace, triumph, turn out, work out **8** carry off, come into, displace, flourish, go places, hit it big, make a hit, make good, overcome, postdate, supplant, surmount, take over **9** come after, supersede **10** accomplish, do the trick
don't ~: **4** fail, flop **6** fizzle **9** strike out
one likely to ~: **5** comer
__ Succeed in Business...: **5** How to
succeeding: **4** next **5** after, later **6** behind, second, serial **7** ensuing **8** in back of **9** following, posterior **10** attainment, subsequent
succès __: **3** fou **7** d'estime
success: **3** hit, win **4** fame, luck, palm **5** éclat, smash **6** big hit, growth **7** fortune, triumph, victory, welfare **8** eminence, fruition, progress, walkover **9** grand slam, happiness, well-being **10** ascendance, ascendancy, ascendence, ascendency, attainment, gold record, gravy train, prosperity
achieve ~: **6** arrive
assure ~: **3** ice
exclamation: **4** ta-da **5** voilà **6** I did it
path to ~: **5** rungs **6** ladder
sign of ~: **3** SRO
success __: **5** story
Success: **4** rice
alternative: **6** Minute **8** Carolina **9** Uncle Ben's
author: Martin Amis
successful: **4** huge **5** boffo, going, happy, lucky, on top, palmy, socko **6** banner, paying **7** booming, notable, ongoing, on track, roaring, wealthy, well-off, winning **8** at the top, blooming, fruitful, thriving, unbeaten **9** effectual, favorable, fortunate, lucrative, rewarding **10** flying high, prosperous, victorious
be ~: **3** win **6** thrive **7** prevail **8** flourish, get ahead, make good
successfully: **4** well **10** swimmingly
succession: **3** row, run **4** line, rash, turn **5** chain, cycle, order, queue, round, suite, train **6** course, series, string **7** lineage **8** kingship, sequence **9** accession, gradation **10** continuity, procession
in ~: **6** lineal **7** running
rapid ~: **6** flurry
steady ~: **6** stream
successive: **4** next **6** in a row, in turn, serial **7** ensuing, regular **8** straight, unbroken **9** following **10** consequent
successively: **5** on end **6** in a row
successor: **4** cion, heir **5** scion **7** heiress **8** follower **10** descendant
succinct: **4** curt **5** blunt, brief, brusk, crisp, pithy, short, terse, tight **7** brusque, compact, concise, laconic, summary **9** condensed **10** boiled down, synopsized, to the point
succor: **3** aid **4** help, lift **6** assist, relief, solace, uphold **7** comfort, help out, relieve, support **8** kindness, minister **9** encourage **10** assistance
succotash: **4** stew
ingredient: **4** corn, lima **8** lima bean
Succoth celebrator: **3** Jew
succulent: **4** aloe, good, lush, nice, rich **5** agave, juicy, moist, sedum, tasty, undry, yummy **6** cactus, divine, liquid, mellow, savory, toothy **8** heavenly, luscious **9** delicious, kalanchoe, nectarous **10** appetizing
succumb: **3** bow **4** cave, fall, fold, lose, quit, sink, wilt **5** yield **6** buckle, give in, submit **7** founder, give way, go under **8** collapse **9** break down, surrender **10** capitulate

SU

such: **4** akin, like, very **5** alike **6** on a par **7** similar **8** parallel, specific **9** analogous, uniformly **10** comparable, equivalent, especially
as: **4** like **5** to wit **6** namely **10** for example
as ~: **5** per se **8** in itself
at ~ time as: **4** when
in ~ a way: **4** as if, so as, thus
in prescriptions: **3** tal.
starter: **4** none
__ Such As I: **5** A Fool
Such Good Friends (1971 film)
cast: Dyan Cannon, James Coco, Jennifer O'Neill
director: Otto Preminger
suck: **6** draw in, inhale
dry: **3** sap **5** drain **7** exhaust **8** enervate
in: **4** dupe, fool, lure, nick, sway, trap **5** decoy, shill, trick **6** absorb, entrap, inhale **7** deceive, defraud, ensnare, mislead **8** hoodwink **9** bamboozle, prevail on
up: **6** absorb, draw in, gather, gobble, ingest, inhale, osmose, take in **7** drink in, swallow **10** assimilate
up to: **4** fawn **5** toady **6** cajole, pander **7** flatter **8** bootlick
sucker: **3** ass, oaf, sap **4** boob, butt, clod, dolt, dupe, fish, fool, gull, lamb, pawn, prey, sham, tool **5** candy, cheat, chump, clown, cluck, dummy, dunce, joker, ninny, patsy, softy **6** delude, dimwit, lummox, nitwit, pigeon, remora, softie, turkey, victim **7** buffoon, dingbat, dullard, fall guy, fathead, half-wit, jackass, pinhead, pretend, saphead, schnook, swindle, two-time **8** bonehead, dumbbell, easy mark, meathead, numskull, pushover **9** birdbrain, blockhead, disinform, lamebrain, numbskull, scapegoat, simpleton, soft touch, victimize **10** dunderhead
eat a ~: **3** lap **4** lick
in: **4** dupe, fool, lure, nick, sway, trap **5** decoy, shill, trick **6** absorb, entrap **7** deceive, defraud, ensnare, mislead **8** hoodwink **9** bamboozle
on a stick: **5** lolly **8** lollipop
play for a ~: **3** use **7** exploit
starter: **4** goat, seer **5** blood
sucker __: **5** punch
__ sucker: **6** all-day
Suckling, John: **4** poet **7** British
Sucre: **4** city, town **7** capital
locale: **7** Bolivia
sucrose: **5** sugar
suction: **6** intake **8** leverage
fish with a ~ disk: **4** goby
prefix: **4** lipo
suction __: **3** cup **4** pump
Sudafed
alternative: *see* cold remedy
Sudan: **6** nation **7** country
capital: **8** Khartoum
desert: **6** Libyan, Nubian **7** Arabian
language: **7** Shilluk
money: **7** piaster, piastre **8** millieme
most of ~: **6** Sahara
neighbor: **4** Chad **5** Congo, Egypt, Kenya, Libya **6** Uganda **7** Eritrea **8** Ethiopia
old name for ~: **4** Kush
people: **4** Beja, Nuer **5** Dinka, Zande **6** Azande, Nubian **7** Shilluk, Turkana
region: **6** Darfur, Gezira
river: **4** Nile
sudatorium: **5** sauna **9** steam bath
Sudbury: **4** city, town
locale: **6** Canada **7** Ontario
sudden: **4** fast, rash **5** acute, fleet, hasty, quick, rapid, sharp, short, swift **6** abrupt, snappy **7** hurried **8** headlong, meteoric **9** immediate, impetuous, impromptu, impulsive **10** unexpected, unforeseen
all of a ~: **3** bam **8** abruptly
attack: **4** raid **5** blitz, foray **6** ambush
happening: **5** burst **7** flare-up **8** outbreak **9** explosion
impact: **3** jar **4** jolt **5** shock **9** collision
rise: **5** spike, surge **6** upturn **7** upsurge
sudden-__ overtime: **5** death
Sudden Impact (1983 film)
cast: Bradford Dillman, Clint Eastwood, Pat Hingle, Sondra Locke
director: Clint Eastwood
dog: **8** Meathead
suddenly: **4** bang, then **5** bingo, sharp, short **6** astart **7** briefly, quickly, swiftly, unaware **8** abruptly, unawares **9** all at once, thereupon
in music: **6** subito
Suddenly (song)
artist: Olivia Newton-John, Billy Ocean
Suddenly Last Summer (1983 song)
artist: Motels
Suddenly, Last Summer (1959 film)
author: Tennessee Williams
cast: Montgomery Clift, Katharine Hepburn, Elizabeth Taylor
Suddenly Susan (NBC sitcom)
cast: Judd Nelson (Jack Richmond)
Brooke Shields (Susan Keane)
sudoku: **6** puzzle
suds: **3** ale **4** beer, brew, foam, head, soap **5** froth **6** lather **7** brewski, bubbles **8** cleanser **10** malt liquor
get rid of the ~: **5** rinse
place: **3** bar, mug, pub **5** stein **6** tavern, washer **8** alehouse, schooner **10** Laundromat
starter: **4** soap
sudsy: **7** foaming **8** unrinsed
sue: **3** beg, bid **4** pray, urge **5** plead, press **6** accuse, appeal, demand, indict, pursue **7** apply to, beseech, contest, entreat, implore, request, solicit **8** appeal to, litigate, petition, plead for **9** fight over, importune, prosecute **10** supplicate
Sue: **4** Lyon **6** Eugène **7** Grafton **8** Thompson
Sue __ Ewing: **5** Ellen
Sue __ honey: **3** Bee
Sue __ Langdon: **3** Ane
__ Sue: **5** Peggy
__ Sue Anderson: **7** Melissa
suede: **3** kid **7** leather **8** goatskin
feature: **3** nap
__ Suede Shoes: **4** Blue
Sue, Eugène: **6** French, writer
work: The Mysteries of Paris
__ Sue Got Married: **5** Peggy
__ Sue, Just You: **5** Sweet
__ Sue Martin: **6** Pamela
suer: **8** litigant **9** plaintiff **10** petitioner
__ Sue Robinson: **5** Vicki
Sues: **4** Alan
suet: **6** tallow **7** pudding
cousin: **4** lard
__ suey: **4** chop
Suez: **4** city, gulf, port, town **5** canal **7** isthmus
locale: **5** Egypt
Suez Canal
fueling station: **4** Aden
opera for the opening of the ~: **4** Aïda
suffer: **2** go **3** ail, bow, let **4** ache, bear, cope, have, hurt, lump, take **5** abide, allow, bleed, brave, droop, leave, smart, stand, stick, yield **6** accept, endure, grieve, permit, resist, submit, take it, writhe **7** agonize, license, receive, stomach, support, survive, sustain, swallow, undergo, wait out **8** bear with, languish, live with, meet with, sanction, stand for, tolerate **9** acquiesce, go through, put up with, withstand **10** experience
defeat: **4** fail, fall, lose **5** yield **6** go down
from: **5** catch
the consequences: **3** pay
sufferer: **6** victim **7** patient **8** casualty
suffering: **3** woe **4** ache, hell, hurt, pain, sick **5** agony, dolor, grief, trial **6** misery, ordeal, sorrow, trauma **7** anguish, passion, pitiful, torment, torture, travail, trouble **8** distress, hard luck, hardship **9** adversity, endurance, heartache, miserable **10** affliction, difficulty, discomfort, heartbreak, misfortune, oppression
__-suffering: **4** long
__ suffer the slings...: **4** or to
suffice: **2** do **4** pass, suit **5** avail, get by, serve **6** answer, fulfil **7** content, fulfill, qualify, satisfy **10** hit the spot
Suffice __ say...: **4** it to
sufficient: **3** due **4** full **5** ample **6** decent, enough, plenty, up to it **8** adequate, all right **9** competent, plentiful, tolerable, up to grade **10** acceptable
nonstandardly: **4** enuf, 'nuff
to a poet: **4** enow
__-sufficient: **4** self
suffixes (by meaning)
advocate: **5** -arian
aggregate: **3** -age
art: **3** -ery
attendee: **4** -goer
believer: **5** -arian
capable: **4** -able, -ible
capacity: **7** -ability, -ibility
collection: **3** -age, -ana, -ery **4** -iana
condition: **3** -dom
deserving: **6** -worthy
direction: **3** -ern
doer: **4** -ator
drink: **3** -ade
enzyme: **3** -ase
expert: **7** -meister
fit for: **6** -worthy
fitness: **7** -ability, -ibility
garden: **4** -etum
imitation: **3** -een **4** -ette
jurisdiction: **3** -dom
lacking: **4** -free
language: **3** -ese
like: **4** -eous **5** -esque
long-running: **5** -athon
nationality: **3** -ese, -ish
occupation: **3** -eer, -eur **4** -euse, -ster
office: **3** -dom
place: **3** -ery **5** -arium
practice: **3** -ery
process: **3** -age
procession: **4** -cade
producer: **5** -arian
product: **3** -ade
realm: **3** -dom
resembling: **4** -eous
resident: **3** -ese
resistant: **5** -proof
scenery: **5** -scape
skill: **7** -manship
somewhat: **3** -ish
specialist: **5** -ician
spectacle: **4** -cade
state: **3** -age, -dom
study: **5** -ology
times: **4** -fold
trade: **3** -ery
typical: **3** -ish
vehicle: **6** -mobile
view: **5** -scape
worthy: **4** -able, -ible
see also combining forms
suffixes (by root)
-ability: **7** fitness **8** capacity
-able: **6** worthy **7** capable
-ade: **5** drink **7** product
-age: **5** state **7** process **9** aggregate **10** collection
-ana: **10** collection
-arian: **8** advocate, believer, producer
-arium: **5** place
-ase: **6** enzyme
-athon: **4** long
-ator: **4** doer
-cade: **9** spectacle **10** procession
-dom: **5** realm, state **6** office **9** condition
-een: **9** imitation
-eer: **10** occupation
-eous: **4** like **10** resembling
-ern: **9** direction
-ery: **3** art **5** place, trade **8** practice **10** collection
-ese: **8** language, resident
-esque: **4** like
-ette: **9** imitation
-etum: **6** garden
-eur: **10** occupation
-euse: **10** occupation
-fold: **5** times
-free: **7** lacking
-goer: **8** attendee
-iana: **10** collection
-ibility: **7** fitness **8** capacity
-ible: **6** worthy **7** capable
-ician: **10** specialist
-ish: **7** typical **8** somewhat
-manship: **5** skill
-meister: **6** expert
-mobile: **7** vehicle
-ology: **5** study

SU

-proof: 9 resistant
-scape: 4 view 7 scenery
-ster: 10 occupation
-worthy: 6 fit for 9 deserving
suffocating: 5 close 6 stuffy, sultry 10 sweltering
Suffolk: 3 pig 4 city, town 5 swine 6 county 10 sheep breed
city: 7 Ipswich
locale: 7 England 8 Virginia
suffrage: 4 vote 5 voice 7 liberty 9 franchise
letters: 3 SBA
suffuse: 3 mix 5 bathe, cover, flood, imbue, steep, tinge 6 embrue, imbrue, redden, spread 7 pervade 8 permeate, saturate 9 penetrate 10 overspread
sugar: 5 cubes, lumps, sweet 6 hexose 7 glucose, lactose, maltose, sucrose, sweeten 8 dextrose, fructose, levulose 9 muscovado, sweetener
add ~: 7 sweeten
combining form: 4 gluc-, glyc-, sucr- 5 gluco-, glyco-, sucro- 7 sacchar- 8 sacchari-, saccharo-
ender: 4 coat, plum
in woody tissue: 5 xylan
metabolism chemical: 3 ATP
portion: 3 cup 4 cube, loaf, lump 6 cupful 8 spoonful, teaspoon 10 tablespoon
source: 4 beet, cane, carb 5 maple
suffix: 3 -ose
syrup: 5 glaze
see also sweetheart
sugar __: 3 pea, pie 4 beet, bowl, cane, cone, corn, palm, pine, tree 5 apple, basin, candy, grove, maple, spoon, tongs 6 sifter
__ sugar: 4 beet, cane, corn, malt, milk, palm, spun 5 brown, fruit, grape, maple, table 6 invert, simple
Sugar: 7 musical
composer: Jule Styne
Sugar __: 3 Act, Ray 4 Moon, Town 5 Blues, Daddy, Shack
Sugar __ Leonard: 3 Ray
Sugar __ Mountain: 4 Loaf
Sugar __ Robinson: 3 Ray
sugarbush: 5 grove, shrub 7 orchard 9 evergreen
family: 6 cashew
product: 3 sap 5 sugar, syrup
relative: 5 sumac 6 sumach
tap a ~: 5 spile
unit: 4 tree 5 maple
sugarcane
cutter: 4 bolo
eater: 6 agouti
exporter: 4 Maui 7 Jamaica 10 West Indies
product: 3 rum 5 sugar 8 molasses
sugarcoat: 4 ease 5 glaze 7 sweeten 9 whitewash
sugar-coated: 5 glacé, sweet, tasty 6 glazed 7 candied 9 palatable
Sugarfoot (ABC western)
cast: Will Hutchins (Tom Brewster)
sugar-free: 4 lite 5 no-cal
Sugarland Express, The (1974 film)
cast: William Atherton, Goldie Hawn, Ben Johnson
director: Steven Spielberg
Sugar Lips
artist: Al Hirt
Sugar Loaf Mountain
locale: 3 Rio
sugarplum: 5 candy, sweet
Sugar Ray: 5 boxer 7 Leonard 8 Robinson
Sugar Shack (1963 song)
artist: Fireballs
Sugar, Sugar (1969 song)
artist: Archies
Sugartime (1958 song)
artist: McGuire Sisters
Sugar Town (1966 song)
artist: Nancy Sinatra
sugary: 5 mushy, sweet 6 honied 7 candied, honeyed 9 sweetened 10 saccharine
suggest: 3 put, say, tip 4 hint, mean, move, pose, seem, warn 5 argue, evoke, get at, imply, infer, let on, offer, opine, point, posit, refer, spell, steer 6 advert, advise, allude, broach, denote, hint at, prompt, remind, submit, tip off, typify 7 advance, commend, connote, counsel, make out, mention, point to, proffer, propose, purport, signify, smack of 8 advocate, allude to, indicate, intimate, lead up to, motivate, nominate, propound, rough out, stand for, theorize, throw out 9 adumbrate, insinuate, introduce, predicate, recommend, represent, symbolize, volunteer 10 conjecture, put forward
itself: 5 occur
strongly: 4 urge 8 armtwist, pressure
suggested: 5 tacit 7 implied 9 advisable
suggestible: 5 naive 8 gullible 9 receptive
suggestion: 3 tip 4 aura, clew, clue, hint, idea, lead, lick, plan, sign, tint, wind 5 pitch, rumor, shade, smack, taste, tinge, touch, trace 6 advice, breath, feeler, motion, notion, scheme, shadow, strain, streak, tipoff, trifle 7 glimmer, inkling, pointer, warning, whisper 8 allusion, innuendo, overtone, proposal, reminder 9 amendment, reference, suspicion, undertone 10 hypothesis, indication, intimation, invitation
formal ~: 6 motion
starter: 4 auto
suggestions: 5 input
open to ~: 8 amenable 9 receptive
suggestive: 6 subtle 8 symbolic 9 evocative, remindful 10 expressive, indicative, meaningful
Suggs, Louise: 6 golfer
sui __: 5 juris 7 generis
Sui: 4 Anna
Suicide Blonde (1990 song)
artist: INXS
sui generis: 4 rare 6 unique 10 unexampled
Suisse range: 5 Alpes
suit: 2 do 3 fit 4 case, exec, gear, plea 5 adapt, befit, cause, clubs, getup, match, serve, trial, yuppy 6 action, adjust, answer, appeal, attire, become, belong, beseem, gerent, hearts, livery, modify, outfit, please, prayer, revise, series, spades, tailor, tuxedo, wooing, yuppie 7 conform, costume, flatter, garment, lawsuit, manager, qualify, request, satisfy, suffice, threads, uniform 8 clothing, diamonds, ensemble, entreaty, petition, proposal, readjust 9 agree with, courtship, executive, reconcile 10 litigation, pass muster, proceeding
accessory: 3 tie 6 cravat
award: 7 damages
change to ~: 5 adapt, alter, slant 6 tailor
ender: 4 case
fabric: 4 wool 5 serge, tweed, twill
feature: 4 vent 5 lapel 6 crease
file ~: 3 sue 8 litigate
follow ~: 3 ape 4 copy, echo 6 parrot 7 imitate
grounds for a ~: 4 tort 5 abuse, crime, libel, smear, wrong 6 attack 7 calumny, slander 10 defamation
legal ~: 4 case
maker: 6 tailor
measurement: 5 chest, waist 6 inseam, sleeve
monkey ~: 3 tux 5 tails 6 tuxedo
neaten a ~: 5 brush, press, steam
one of a ~: 3 ace, six, ten, two 4 club, five, four, jack, king, nine 5 deuce, eight, heart, queen, seven, spade, three 7 diamond
piece: 4 vest 5 pants 6 jacket 8 trousers
pocket item: 4 keys 5 hanky 6 change, hankie, wallet
power ~: 5 trump
press one's ~: 3 woo 5 court, spark 7 propose
starter: 3 law 4 jump, pant, play, snow, swim 7 counter
strong ~: 5 armor, forte
two-piece ~: 6 bikini
up: 4 garb, wear 5 array, dress 6 attire
suit __ tee: 3 to a
__ suit: 3 cat, dry, gym, Mao, ski, wet 4 body, flak, long, tank, zoot 5 anti-G, civil, dress, pants, sweat, track, union 6 diving, flight, follow, monkey, safari, strong 7 bathing, jogging, leisure
suitable: 2 OK 3 apt, due, fit, pat 4 fine, good, just, meet, okay, ripe 5 happy, right 6 decent, fitted, proper, seemly, timely, up to it, useful 7 apropos, condign, correct, fitting, germane, helpful, perfect, politic 8 adequate, apposite, becoming, decorous, deserved, feasible, pleasing, relevant, rightful 9 advisable, allowable, befitting, competent, expedient, favorable, in keeping, opportune, pertinent, up to grade 10 acceptable, applicable, compatible, convenient, propitious, reasonable, seasonable
absolutely ~: 5 ideal 7 perfect
make ~: 5 adapt 6 change, modify, tailor
position: 5 niche
suitableness: 6 accord, parity 7 concord, fitness, harmony 9 agreement, coherence, congruity, propriety 10 accordance, conformity, consonance, proportion, similarity
suitably: 7 rightly 8 laudably, worthily
suitcase: 3 bag 4 grip 5 trunk 6 valise 7 baggage, luggage
fill a ~: 4 pack
suite: 4 flat 5 condo, group, rooms, train 6 office, rental, series, string 7 battery, cortege, retinue 8 sequence 9 apartment, entourage, hangers-on, retainers 10 attendants, succession
musical ~ ender: 5 gigue
__ suite: 6 bridal
__ Suite: 5 Czech, Plaza 6 London, Petite 7 Holberg
__-suited: 3 ill 4 well
Suite: Judy Blue Eyes (1969 song)
artist: Crosby, Stills & Nash
__-suiter: 3 one, two 5 three 6 single
suitor: 3 man 4 beau, date, love 5 Romeo, swain, woman, wooer 6 fellow 7 admirer 8 cavalier, courtier, litigant, lover boy, paramour 9 boyfriend, inamorato 10 girlfriend, supplicant, sweetheart
what a ~ pitches: 3 woo
Suits me!: 3 yes 4 fine, okay 5 swell 8 very well
suit to a __: 3 tee
suk: 5 bazar 6 bazaar
Sukiyaki (song)
artist: A Taste of Honey, Kyu Sakamoto
Sula
author: Toni Morrison
Sulawesi: 4 isle 6 island 7 Celebes
locale: 9 Indonesia
neighbor: 6 Borneo
sulfa drug: 10 antibiotic
sulfur: 7 element 8 nonmetal
combining form: 4 thia-, thio- 5 thion-
sulk: 4 fume, moon, mope, pout, tiff 5 brood, frown, gripe, grump, lower, scowl 6 glower, grouse 7 bad mood, silence
in Britain: 4 mump
sulky: 3 rig 4 cart, dour, glum, grim, mopy 5 huffy, moody, mopey, surly 6 crabby, gloomy, grouty, grumpy, in a pet, morose, sullen 7 grouchy, peevish, pouting 8 grumpish, liverish, petulant 9 saturnine 10 ill-natured
Sulla: 5 Roman 7 general 8 dictator
opponent: 6 Marius
Sullavan: 8 Margaret
spouse: Henry Fonda, Leland Hayward
sullen: 4 dark, dour, dull, glum, grim, mopy, sour, ugly 5 cross, gruff, heavy, huffy, moody, mopey, pouty, surly, testy, upset 6 bitter, cloudy, crabby, dismal, gloomy, grumpy, morose, ornery, silent, somber 7 hostile, peevish, pouting, sulking, uptight, vicious 8 brooding, churlish, darkened, frowning, grumpish, liverish, lowering, perverse, petulant, sluggish 9 cheerless, glowering, irritable, obstinate, querulous, saturnine, truculent 10 ill-humored, ill-natured, out of sorts, unsociable
look: 5 frown, scowl 7 grimace
look ~: 4 lour, mope, pout, sulk 5 brood

sullied: **4** foul **5** dirty **6** impure **7** unclean **8** maculate, vitiated **10** bedraggled
Sullivan: **2** Ed **3** Pat **4** Anne **5** Barry, Frank, Louis, Susan **6** Arthur **8** Kathleen
Sullivan, Arthur: **3** Sir **7** British **8** composer
collaborator: W.S. Gilbert
work: The Gondoliers
The Grand Duke
HMS Pinafore
Iolanthe
The Mikado
Patience
The Pirates of Penzance
Princess Ida
Ruddigore
The Sorcerer
Trial by Jury
Utopia, Ltd.
The Yeoman of the Guard
Sullivan, Ed: **2** MC **4** host **5** emcee
network: **3** CBS
Sullivan, Pat cat: **5** Felix
Sullivan's Travels (1941 film)
cast: Veronica Lake, Joel McCrea
director: Preston Sturges
Sullivan Trophy org.: **3** AAU
sully: **3** mar **4** blot, blur, foul, soil, spot **5** dirty, smear, spoil, stain, taint **6** befoul, crud up, deface, defame, defile, embrue, imbrue, malign, revile, smudge, vilify **7** asperse, begrime, besmear, blacken, blemish, pollute, slander, tarnish **8** backbite, besmirch, discolor, disgrace, dishonor, maculate, throw mud **9** denigrate **10** adulterate, calumniate, stigmatize, villainize
Sully: **9** Prudhomme
sulphur: **7** element
sultan: **5** ruler **6** gerent **7** emperor
cousin: **4** amir, emir **5** ameer, emeer
decree: **5** irade
Ottoman ~: **5** Selim
pride: **5** haram, harem, harim, wives **6** hareem
sultana: **3** red **5** queen, ruler **6** raisin **8** purplish
sultanate
Gulf ~: **4** Oman
Malay ~: **6** Brunei
old Arabian ~: **4** Nejd
Sultan of Sulu, The
author: George Ade
Sultan of Swat: Babe Ruth
sultriness: **4** heat **6** allure **8** humidity
sultry: **3** hot **4** damp, dank **5** close, heavy, humid, lurid, muggy, soggy **6** baking, clammy, erotic, red-hot, steamy, sticky, stuffy, toasty, torrid **7** boiling, summery **8** broiling, ovenlike, sizzling, stifling, tropical **9** scorching **10** equatorial, oppressive, passionate, sweltering
weather: **7** dog days
Sulu: **3** sea
locale: **6** Borneo
Sulu Archipelago
island: **4** Jolo **6** Sibutu **7** Basilan
sum: **3** add, all, tot **4** body, bulk **5** add up, count, gross, score, tally, total, tot up, value, whole, works **6** amount, number, reckon **7** compute, epitome, essence, payment, tally up **8** entirety, integral, quantity, totality **9** aggregate, calculate, keep score, reckoning **10** bottom line
and substance: **3** nub **4** core, gist **5** heart, tenor, theme
component: **6** addend, augend
double-check a ~: **5** readd
in Latin: **3** I am
of the parts: **5** whole
to ~ up: **4** last **6** lastly **7** finally
trifling ~: **3** sou **5** groat
up: **3** add **5** close, count, recap, tally, total **6** digest, figure, review, typify **7** examine, outline **8** conclude, condense, estimate **9** calculate, enumerate, epitomize, keep score, synopsize
up to: **5** equal, total
sum __: **5** total
__ sum: **3** dim **4** lump, tidy
sumac: **4** tree **5** shrub **9** squawbush
family: **6** cashew
genus: **4** rhus
relative: **5** mango **6** cashew, fustet, mastic **9** pistachio, sugarbush
Sumac: **3** Yma
Sumatra: **4** isle **6** island
animal: **5** rhino
city: **5** Medan **6** Padang **9** Palembang
island off ~: **4** Nias **5** Banka **6** Bangka
locale: **4** Asia **9** Indonesia
people: **5** Batak
port: **6** Padang
primate: **5** orang **7** siamang **9** orangutan **10** orangutang
volcano: **7** Kerinci
Sumerian city: **4** Kish, Uruk **5** Eridu **6** Lagash
sum, es, __: **3** est
__-sum game: **4** zero
Sumida: **5** river
city on the ~: **5** Tokio, Tokyo
summa cum __: **5** laude
summarily: **7** readily, swiftly **8** promptly, speedily **9** forthwith, on the spot
summarize: **4** trim **5** brief, prune, recap **6** digest, rehash, review, survey **7** abridge, compile, cut down, outline, run down, run over, shorten **8** abstract, boil down, compress, condense **9** capsulize, inventory, synopsize, telescope **10** abbreviate
summary: **4** core, curt, gist **5** brief, pithy, recap, sense, short, table, terse **6** aperçu, digest, gnomic, précis, rehash, report, résumé, review, sketch, survey, wrap-up **7** epitome, essence, extract, outline, pandect, roundup, rundown, version **8** abstract, analysis, recapped, scenario, skeleton, straight, succinct, syllabus, synopsis **9** inventory, momentary, reduction, temporary **10** abridgment, compendium, highlights, literature, prospectus, tabulation, to the point
career ~: **4** vita **6** résumé
news ~: **5** recap **6** review **8** synopsis
summation: **6** ending, wrap-up **8** addition **9** reckoning
summer: **5** adder **6** season **7** dog days
appliance: **2** AC **3** fan
attire: **3** tee **6** Capris, halter, shades, shorts **7** cut-offs **8** swimsuit **10** sunglasses
clock setting: **3** CDT, CST, DST, EDT, EST, MDT, MST, PDT, PST
cooler: **3** ade, fan, ice, pop **4** pool, soda **6** breeze, ice tea **7** iced tea, limeade **8** lemonade
dessert: **4** cone **6** malted, sundae **7** Sno-cone **8** ice cream **9** milkshake
ender: **4** time **5** house
escape: **4** camp, lake, pool **5** cabin **8** vacation
fabric: **4** poly **5** linen, nylon, voile **6** cotton **7** acrylic, chiffon **9** polyester
feature: **4** heat **8** humidity
follower: **4** fall
forecast: **3** hot **4** rain, warm **5** humid, muggy, sunny
in French: **3** été
month: **3** Aug., Jul., Jun., Sep. **4** July, June, Sept. **6** August **9** September
pest: **3** ant, fly **4** gnat **5** midge **8** horse fly, mosquito
preceder: **6** spring
retreat: **5** shade
shade: **3** tan
shoe: **5** thong **6** sandal **8** flip-flop
sign: **3** Leo **5** Virgo **6** Cancer
TV fare: **5** rerun
summer __: **4** camp **5** stock **6** school, squash
__ summer: **6** Indian
Summer: **5** Donna **7** Phoenix
Summer __: **4** Rain, Wind **5** Brave, Games, Girls, Stock, Storm **6** Breeze, Nights
Summerall: **3** Pat
Summer and Smoke: **4** film, play
author: Tennessee Williams
cast: Laurence Harvey, Una Merkel, Geraldine Page
director: Peter Glenville
heroine: **4** Alma
Summer Brave
author: William Inge
Summer Breeze (1972 song)
artist: Seals and Crofts
summer camp
do a ~ activity: **3** row **4** hike, swim
Summer, Donna: **6** singer
nickname: Queen of Disco
song: Bad Girls (1979)
Dim All the Lights (1979)
Heaven Knows (1979)
Hot Stuff (1979)
I Feel Love (1977)
Last Dance (1978)
Love Is in Control (1982)
Love to Love You Baby (1975)
MacArthur Park (1978)
No More Tears (1979)
On the Radio (1980)
She Works Hard for the Money (1983)
The Wanderer (1980)
Summer Games
see Olympics
Summer Girls (1999 song)
artist: LFO
summerhouse: **6** gazebo **8** pavilion
Summer House, The (1993 film)
cast: Jeanne Moreau, Joan Plowright
Summer in the City (1966 song)
artist: Lovin' Spoonful
Summer Knowledge
author: Delmore Schwartz
__ Summer Long: **3** All
__ Summer Night: **3** One
Summer Nights (1978 song)
artist: Olivia Newton-John, John Travolta
Summer of __, The: **5** Katya
Summer of '42 (1971 film)
cast: Gary Grimes, Jerry Houser, Jennifer O'Neill
Summer of '42 Theme (1971 song)
artist: Peter Nero
Summer of '49
author: David Halberstam
Summer Place, A: **4** film **5** novel
author: Sloan Wilson
cast: Sandra Dee, Troy Donahue, Richard Egan, Dorothy McGuire
director: Delmer Daves
music: Max Steiner
Summers: **4** Marc
Summer Sisters
author: Judy Blume
Summer Song, A (1964 song)
artist: Chad & Jeremy
Summer Stock (1950 film)
cast: Eddie Bracken, Judy Garland, Gene Kelly
__ Summer, The: **7** Endless
Summertime: **4** aria, song
composer: George Gershwin, DuBose Heyward
Summertime (1955 film)
cast: Rossano Brazzi, Katharine Hepburn
director: David Lean
__ Summertime: **5** In the
Summertime and the __ is easy: **5** livin'
Summertime Blues (1958 song)
artist: Eddie Cochran
Summer Wishes, Winter Dreams (1973 film)
cast: Martin Balsam, Sylvia Sidney, Joanne Woodward
summery: **3** hot **4** warm **5** balmy, humid, muggy, sunny **6** sultry, toasty **7** boiling, estival **8** broiling, ovenlike, sizzling, tropical **10** sweltering
summit: **3** tip, top **4** acme, apex, head, peak, roof **5** crest, crown, point, spire **6** apogee, climax, height, tipoff, vertex, zenith **7** maximum **8** capstone, meridian, pinnacle **9** crescendo, high point **10** prominence
approach the ~: **5** climb, mount **6** ascend
attendee: **2** P.M. **6** leader **8** diplomat **9** president
combining form: **5** apico-
summit __: **7** meeting
summon: **3** bid **4** beep, call, cite, hail, levy, page, ring, tell **5** draft, evoke, order, rally **6** ask for, beckon, call to, gather, invite, invoke, muster, recall **7** command, convene, convoke, pluck up, request, send for **8** assemble, mobilize, muster

up, subpoena 9 call forth, prosecute, recollect
up: 6 recall, relive
summoner: 5 pager 6 beeper
summons: 4 psst, writ 5 paper 7 process, warrant 8 citation, subpoena
sumo: 5 sport 9 wrestling
home: 5 Japan
like ~ wrestlers: 5 obese
Sum of All Fears, The (2002 film)
cast: Ben Affleck, James Cromwell, Morgan Freeman, Liev Schreiber
sump: 4 well 5 drain 7 cistern 8 cesspool 10 catch basin
sump __: 4 pump
__-sum payment: 4 lump
sumptuous: 4 dear, lush, luxe, posh, rich 5 fancy, grand, plush, ritzy, showy, swank, swish, ultra 6 costly, deluxe, flashy, frilly, glitzy, lavish, lordly, ornate, swanky 7 elegant, opulent, profuse, stately 8 gorgeous, imposing, luscious, palatial, princely, prodigal, splendid 9 decorated, elaborate, expensive, luxuriant, luxurious 10 impressive
meal: 4 feed 5 feast 6 spread 7 banquet
sumptuousness: 4 luxe 6 luxury, wealth 7 glamour 8 elegance, grandeur, splendor
sums, do: 3 add 4 tote 5 total 6 figure
__ Sumter: 4 Fort
sun: 3 orb, Sol, tan 4 ager, bask, star 5 light 6 figure, sphere 7 daystar 8 daylight, fireball, luminary
Babylonian ~ god: 3 Utu
block: 5 cloud, shade, smaze 6 lotion, shades 10 sunglasses
combining form: 4 heli-, soli- 5 helio-
cool ~: 5 K star
dancer: 3 Ute 6 Dakota
disk: 4 Aten, Aton
dry in the ~: 4 bake
Egyptian ~ god: 4 Aten, Aton
emulate the ~: 5 shine
ender: 3 dog, lit, set, tan 4 bath, beam, bird, burn, dial, down, fish, less, rise, roof, room, spot, ward 5 baked, bathe, burnt, burst, dress, light, scald, shade, shine, shiny, space, stone, wards 6 bather, bonnet, downer, flower, screen, tanned 7 bathing, glasses
Greek ~ god: 6 Apollo, Helios
hang in the ~: 3 air, dry
hat: 4 topi 5 topee
in French: 6 soleil
in Latin: 3 sol
in Spanish: 3 sol
lie in the ~: 3 tan 4 bask, laze, loll 5 relax 6 lounge 9 luxuriate
of the ~: 5 solar
once around the ~: 4 year
orbiter: 5 comet 6 planet 8 asteroid
red ~: 5 N star
Roman ~ god: 3 Sol
screen: 5 visor, vizor 6 lotion
spot: 6 facula
toward the rising ~: 4 east
toward the setting ~: 4 west
sun __: 3 god 4 bear, deck, disk, lamp, sign 5 block, dance, porch, visor 6 parlor 7 glasses
sun-__: 5 cured, dried
Sun: 5 paper 9 newspaper
ender: 3 day
locale: 6 Ottawa 7 Calgary, Toronto 8 Edmonton, Las Vegas 9 Baltimore, Vancouver
Sun __: 4 Belt, City, King 6 Devils, Valley
Sun __ Moon: 5 Myung
Sun __-sen: 3 Yat
__ Sun: 6 Rising
Sun Also Rises, The: 4 film 5 novel
author: Ernest Hemingway
cast: Mel Ferrer, Ava Gardner, Tyrone Power
character: 4 Bill, Cohn, Jake 5 Brett, Pedro 6 Ashley, Barnes, Gorton, Robert, Romero 7 Michael, Montoya 8 Campbell 10 Bill Gorton, Jake Barnes, Robert Cohn
director: Henry King
sunbathe: 3 tan 4 bask
to excess: 4 burn 7 blister
sunbather: 6 basker, tanner
need: 5 towel 6 lotion 7 glasses
seat: 6 chaise
sunbeam: 3 ray 5 light
Sunbird: 3 car 4 auto 7 Pontiac
sunblock: 6 lotion
apply ~: 3 dab, pat, rub 5 rub on 6 smooth
ingredient: 4 aloe, PABA
it's blocked by ~: 2 UV
letters: 3 SPF
sunbonnet: 3 hat 4 poke
Sun Bowl site: 6 El Paso
sunburned: 3 red 4 pink 7 flaking, peeling
sunburn remedy: 4 aloe 5 cream 6 lotion 7 Noxzema
Sun City: 4 town
locale: 7 Arizona
sundae: 5 treat 7 dessert
alternative: 4 cone 7 parfait 8 snowball
ingredient: 7 berries 8 ice cream
sauce: 5 fudge
topping: 4 nuts 6 cherry 8 hot fudge
Sundance: 3 car 4 auto 8 Plymouth
Sundance Film Festival
entry: 5 indie
locale: 4 Utah
Sundance Kid: 5 alias 6 outlaw
girlfriend: 4 Etta 5 Place
sidekick: 5 Butch 7 Cassidy
Sunday: 5 Billy
best: 4 duds, garb, gear, rags, togs, wear 5 array, dress, frock, getup, mufti 6 attire, civies, finery, livery, outfit, things 7 apparel, civvies, clothes, costume, raiment, regalia, threads 8 ensemble, frippery, garments, wardrobe 9 trappings 10 habiliment
book: 6 hymnal
closing: 4 amen
excursion: 5 drive
section: 6 comics 7 funnies 8 magazine
service: 4 Mass
Sunday __: 4 best 5 punch 6 driver, school 7 clothes
Sunday-__-meeting: 4 go-to
__ Sunday: 3 Low 4 Palm 5 Black, Great, Super 6 Advent, Easter, Shrove 7 Mid-Lent, Passion, Trinity
__ Sunday Afternoon: 3 On a, One
Sunday, Bloody Sunday (1971 film)
cast: Peter Finch, Glenda Jackson
Sunday in the Park With George: 7 musical
composer: Stephen Sondheim
Sunday Morning: 4 poem
author: Wallace Stevens
Sunday Will Never Be the Same (1967 song)
artist: Spanky and Our Gang
sunder: 4 part, rend, rive, tear 5 break, crack, sever, slice, split 6 breach, cleave, divide 7 disjoin, divorce, rupture, split up 8 fracture, separate
sundered: 3 cut 4 rent, slit, torn 5 apart, cleft, riven, split 6 broken, parted 7 cracked 8 separate 9 separated
Sun Devils
home: 5 Tempe
school: 3 ASU
sundial: 9 timepiece 10 timekeeper
numeral: 3 III, VII, XII 4 IIII, VIII
part: 6 gnomon
Sun Dial, The
author: Don Marquis
sundown: 4 dusk 5 night 7 evening 8 twilight 9 nightfall
Sundown (1974 song)
artist: Gordon Lightfoot
sundowner: 4 hobo 5 drink, tramp 8 libation
Sundowners, The (1960 film)
cast: Deborah Kerr, Robert Mitchum, Peter Ustinov
sundries case: 4 etui 5 etwee
sundry: 3 odd 4 many 6 divers, legion, varied 7 diverse, oddball, unalike, various 8 assorted, manifold, multiple 9 different
Sunfire: 3 car 4 auto 7 Pontiac
sunfish: 5 bream, roach 7 crappie 8 bluegill
ocean ~: 4 mola
sunflower: 5 plant
center: 4 disc, disk
family member: 5 aster
product: 3 oil 4 seed
support: 4 stem 5 stalk
Sunflowers: 3 oil 8 painting
artist: Vincent Van Gogh
setting: 5 Arles
Sunflower State: 3 Kan. 6 Kansas
sung: 5 vocal 6 choral
correctly ~: 5 on key
sunglare, respond to: 5 blink 6 squint 7 squinch
sunk: 5 kaput 6 doomed, ruined 7 done for 8 washed-up 9 submerged 10 humiliated
sunken: 3 low 6 hollow 7 concave 8 immersed, scuttled 9 depressed, submerged, submersed 10 underwater
fence: 4 ha-ha
ship explorer: 5 diver
Sun King's number: 3 XIV
sunless: 4 dark, gray, grey, hazy 5 foggy 6 cloudy 8 darkened, overcast 9 tenebrous, unlighted
Sun Life
competitor: *see* insurance company
Sunlight: 9 detergent
competitor: 3 Joy 4 Ajax, Dawn 7 Cascade 9 Palmolive 10 Electrasol
sunlit: 6 bright
Sun Myung __: 4 Moon
Sunne Rising, The: 4 poem
author: John Donne
Sunni: 4 sect 6 Muslim
faith: 5 Islam
sunny: 3 gay 4 fair, fine, mild, warm 5 clear, happy, jolly, light, merry, perky, shiny 6 blithe, bright, cheery, chirpy, daylit, genial, jovial, joyful, joyous 7 beaming, buoyant, clement, glowing, radiant, shining, smiling, summery, well-lit 8 carefree, cheerful, jubilant, laughing, mirthful, pleasant 9 brilliant, cloudless, ebullient, unclouded 10 bright-eyed, flying high, optimistic
color: 6 canary, golden, orange, yellow 8 daffodil
side: 5 south
Sunny: 7 musical
composer: Jerome Kern
Sunny (1966 song)
artist: Bobby Hebb
sunny-side up: 5 light
item: 3 egg
Sunny von __: 5 Bülow
Sunoco: 3 gas 8 gasoline
rival: 4 Arco, Hess 5 Exxon, Getty, Mobil, Shell 7 Chevron
sunrise: 4 dawn, morn 5 light, prime 6 aurora 7 morning 8 cockcrow, daybreak, daylight
color: 4 pink
goddess: 3 Eos 6 Aurora
locale: 4 east
time before ~: 5 night
to sunset: 3 day
__ Sunrise: 7 Tequila
Sunrise at Campobello (1960 film)
cast: Ralph Bellamy, Hume Cronyn, Greer Garson
Sunrise Serenade
composer: Frankie Carle
Sunrise Sunset: 4 song 5 waltz
composer: Jerry Bock, Sheldon Harnick
sunroom: 8 solarium
Suns: 4 five, team
home: 7 Phoenix
org.: 3 NBA
rival: *see* NBA team
sport: 10 basketball
sunscreen: 6 lotion
abbr.: 3 SPF
ingredient: 4 aloe, PABA
sunset: 3 eve 4 dusk 5 night 7 evening 8 eventide, twilight 9 nightfall
direction: 4 west
hue: 3 red
sunrise to ~: 3 day
time after ~: 5 night
Sunset: 4 city, town
locale: 7 Florida
Sunset (1988 film)
cast: James Garner, Mariel Hemingway, Malcolm McDowell, Bruce Willis
director: Blake Edwards

Sunset Blvd. (1950 film)
cast: William Holden, Erich von Stroheim, Gloria Swanson
director: Billy Wilder
Sunset Boulevard: 7 musical
composer: Andrew Lloyd Webber
Sunset in Saint Tropez
author: Danielle Steel
Sunset Limited: 5 train
Sunset Pass
author: Zane Grey
___ Sunset, The: 4 Last
sunshade: 3 cap, hat **5** visor, vizor **6** awning, canopy **7** parasol **8** umbrella
sunshine: 5 light **8** daylight
line: 6 isohel
sunshine ___: 3 law
Sunshine: 6 cookie
competitor: ***see*** cookie manufacturer
Sunshine and Snow
artist: Claude Monet
Sunshine Boys, The: 4 film, play
author: Neil Simon
cast: George Burns, Walter Matthau
director: Herbert Ross
Sunshine of Your Love (1968 song)
artist: Cream
Sunshine on My Shoulders (1974 song)
artist: John Denver
Sunshine State: 7 Florida
Sunshine Superman (1966 song)
artist: Donovan
sunshiny: 4 fair **9** cloudless, unclouded
sunspot center: 5 umbra
___ sunt: 3 ubi
suntan ___: 3 oil **6** lotion
suntan lotion ingredient: 4 aloe, PABA
letters: 3 SPF
Sun-Times: 5 paper **9** newspaper
locale: 7 Chicago
sunup: 4 dawn, morn **5** early, prime **7** morning **8** daybreak, daylight **10** first light
direction: 4 east
Sun Valley: 4 city, town
enjoy ~: 3 ski **4** skee
locale: 3 Ida. **5** Idaho
Sun Valley Serenade (1941 film)
cast: Sonja Henie
Sun Yat-___: 3 sen
suo ___: 4 jure, loco
sup: 3 eat **4** dine **8** chow down **9** have a bite **10** break bread
super: 3 big **4** role, tops **5** crack, large **7** immense **8** director, watchdog, wondrous **9** caretaker, custodian, extremely, fantastic, organizer, top-drawer, unrivaled, wonderful, wunderbar **10** unrivalled, world-class
see also wonderful
Super ___: 3 Mex **4** Bowl, Glue **6** Sleuth, Sunday **7** Tuesday
Super ___ Bros.: 5 Mario
Super 8: 5 motel
alternative: ***see*** motel
superabundance: 4 glut, much **5** ocean **6** excess **8** overflow **9** amplitude
superabundant: 4 rich **6** plenty **8** prodigal **9** luxuriant, plentiful
superannuated: 3 old **4** aged **5** aging **6** ageing **7** ancient, elderly, wizened **8** grizzled, obsolete, outmoded **9** geriatric, getting on, senescent, up in years
Superannuated Man, The
author: Charles Lamb
superannuation: 7 pension
superb: 4 best, rare **5** first, lofty, proud, royal **7** elegant, exalted, optimal, stately, supreme **8** elevated, majestic, peerless, stunning **9** matchless, unrivaled, virtuosic, wonderful, wunderbar **10** consummate, impressive, majestical, unrivalled
see also wonderful
Super Bowl: 5 event
org.: 3 NFL
sight: 5 blimp **7** airship **9** dirigible
Superboy
girlfriend: 4 Lana, Lang
supercharger: 5 turbo
Super Chief: 3 car **4** auto **5** train **7** Pontiac **10** automobile
supercilious: 4 smug, vain **5** cocky, lofty, proud **6** snobby, uppity **7** fustian, haughty, pompous, stuck-up **8** arrogant, boastful, cavalier, egoistic, scornful, snobbish, superior **9** big-headed, egotistic, imperious, quizzical
super-duper
see super
superego: 6 ethics **8** scruples **10** conscience
supererogatory: 7 unasked **9** excessive
superficial: 4 glib, side, weak **5** empty, hasty, light, outer, rough, slick, vague **6** casual, flimsy, hollow, slight **7** cursory, hurried, outward, partial, passing, seeming, shallow, sketchy, summary, surface, trivial, vacuous **8** affected, apparent, cosmetic, exterior, external, skin-deep **9** depthless, desultory, frivolous **10** uncritical
superfluity: 4 glut **6** excess, frills **7** surplus **8** overflow, plethora
superfluous: 4 over **5** extra, spare **6** de trop, excess, lavish **7** profuse, surplus, useless **8** left over, needless, overmuch, residual, unneeded, unwanted **9** abounding, excessive, overblown, redundant, remaining
Superfly (1972 film)
cast: Ron O'Neal
Superfly (1972 song)
artist: Curtis Mayfield
Superfortress: 5 plane **6** bomber **8** airplane, warplane
Superfudge
author: Judy Blume
super G: 6 slalom **7** ski race
supergiant: 4 star **5** Rigel **7** Antares **10** Betelgeuse
super giant ___: 6 slalom
Supergirl
cat: 7 Streaky
home: 4 Argo
superintend: 3 run **4** boss, mind **5** watch **6** direct, govern, manage **7** command, oversee **8** regulate **9** officiate
superintendent: 4 boss, head **5** chief, super **6** keeper, leader, master, warden **7** curator, manager **8** director, governor, guardian, overseer **9** caretaker, conductor, custodian, inspector, principal, straw boss, zookeeper **10** headmaster
superior: 3 CEO, VIP **4** exec, head, jefe, smug, tops **5** above, bossy, brass, chief, cocky, crack, elder, finer, hirer, lofty, moral, noble, on top, proud, ruler, upper **6** better, deluxe, expert, goodly, higher, honcho, leader, proper, select, senior, top dog, uppity **7** elegant, eminent, exalted, foreman, grander, greater, haughty, high-hat, leading, manager, premium, primary, stuck-up, vintage **8** arrogant, brass hat, cavalier, champion, director, dominant, enviable, higher-up, in charge, insolent, laudable, peerless, snobbish, towering, wondrous **9** a cut above, agreeable, bodacious, chieftain, exceeding, executive, matchless, overlying, paramount, preferred, principal, reputable, unrivaled, wonderful **10** beneficial, commanding, creditable, disdainful, noteworthy, preeminent, preferable, prevailing, surpassing, unrivalled, world-class
see also wonderful
___ superior: 6 mother
Superior: 4 lake
locale: 7 Ontario **8** Michigan **9** Minnesota, Wisconsin
superiority: 4 edge, lead, pull, rank **5** power, value **7** vantage **8** eminence, goodness, position, prestige, priority, whip hand **9** advantage, authority, dominance, influence, landslide, seniority, supremacy, upper hand
superiority ___: 7 complex
superlative: 4 A-one, best, rare, tops **5** crack, great, prime **6** divine, superb **7** all-time, capital, highest, optimum, perfect, stellar, supreme **8** gilt-edge, greatest, peerless, splendid, sterling, ultimate **9** excellent, masterful, matchless, unequaled, unrivaled **10** unrivalled
superliner: 5 train
Superman: 4 hero
alias: Clark Kent
attire: 4 cape
birth name: 5 Kal-El
cover: 8 reporter
dog: 6 Krypto
foe: Lex Luthor
girlfriend: Lois Lane
home: 10 Metropolis
newspaper: 6 Planet
parent: 4 Lara **5** Jor-El
portrayer: 4 Alyn, Cain **5** Reeve, Routh **6** Reeves
symbol: 3 ess
Superman (1978 film)
cast: Ned Beatty, Marlon Brando, Jackie Cooper, Gene Hackman, Margot Kidder, Valerie Perrine, Christopher Reeve, Susannah York
director: Richard Donner
role: 4 Otis
Superman (1979 song)
artist: Herbie Mann
Superman II (1980 film)
cast: Ned Beatty, Gene Hackman, Margot Kidder, Christopher Reeve
villain: 3 Zod **4** Ursa
Superman Returns (2006 film)
cast: Kate Bosworth, Brandon Routh, Kevin Spacey
supermarket: 5 store **7** grocery **8** emporium
employee: 5 clerk **6** bagger **7** cashier, stocker
feature: 4 cart, line
freebie: 3 bag **4** sack
saver: 6 coupon
section: 5 aisle, dairy
tabloid: 5 Globe
work at the ~: 3 bag
see also grocery
supermodel: 3 Alt **4** Iman, Klum, Moss **5** Banks, Tiegs **6** Alexis, Twiggy **7** Benitez **8** Brinkley, Bundchen, Campbell, Carol Alt, Crawford, Kate Moss, Schiffer **9** Heidi Klum, Kim Alexis, Porizkova, Tyra Banks **10** Macpherson, Turlington
plus-size ~: 4 Emme
single-name ~: 4 Iman **6** Twiggy
supernal: 6 divine **7** angelic **8** ethereal, heavenly **9** ambrosial, angelical, celestial
supernatural: 4 dark, eery **5** eerie, weird **6** fantom, hidden, mystic, occult, secret, spooky **7** ghostly, phantom, psychic, uncanny, unknown **8** heavenly, mystical, numinous, spectral **9** invisible, marvelous, unearthly, unnatural
being: 3 imp **5** ghost, haunt, spook **6** spirit **7** phantom, specter
occurrence: 6 séance **7** miracle
power: 5 magic **6** occult, voodoo **8** wizardry **10** witchcraft
Supernatural Thing (1975 song)
artist: Ben E. King
supernova: 4 star
supernumerary: 5 extra **9** excessive
Super Password
host: Bert Convy
superpower, former: 4 USSR
supersede: 6 follow **7** abolish, discard, outmode, replace, succeed **8** displace, override, overrule, set aside, supplant **9** antiquate, discharge
superseded: 5 passé **8** obsolete, outmoded, unusable
supersensory: 7 psychic
Supersition (1972 song)
artist: Stevie Wonder
supersonic: 4 fast **5** brisk, fleet, hasty, quick, rapid, swift **6** flying, racing, speedy **7** express, hurried, instant **9** breakneck **10** double-time
speed unit: 4 Mach
transport: 3 jet, SST **5** plane **7** Tupolev **8** Concorde
SuperSonics: 4 five, team
home: 7 Seattle
org.: 3 NBA
rival: ***see*** NBA team
sport: 10 basketball
superstar: 4 hero, idol, name **5** celeb, great **8** luminary,

renowned, somebody, virtuoso **9** celebrity, headliner, personage, well-known
Superstar (1971 song)
artist: Carpenters
superstition: **4** fear, lore, tabu **5** magic, taboo **6** notion
supervene: **5** ensue **6** follow
supervise: **3** run **4** boss, head, lead, mind, tend **5** chair, guard, watch **6** direct, govern, handle, manage **7** command, conduct, control, inspect, monitor, oversee, preside **8** chaperon, overlook, regulate **9** chaperone, check up on, look after **10** administer, ride herd on, run the show
supervision: **4** care, rule **5** trust **6** charge **7** command, conduct, control, custody, running **8** auspices, guidance, handling, tutelage **9** direction, oversight
supervisor: **4** boss, head **5** chief, hirer **6** gerent, keeper, master, top dog **7** curator, foreman, headman, manager, monitor **8** brass hat, director, employer, governor, guardian, higher-up, overseer, watchdog **9** caretaker, conductor, custodian, executive, inspector, organizer, straw boss, zookeeper
supine: **4** flat, lazy **5** slack **6** face-up **7** languid **8** listless **9** lethargic, prostrate, recumbent
opposite: **5** prone
supper: **4** feed, meal **6** buffet, dinner, spread **7** banquet, potluck **9** reception
club: **6** bistro **7** cabaret **10** restaurant
ender: **4** time
fix ~: **5** eat in
have ~: **3** eat **4** dine
__ Supper: **4** Last
Supper Club
radio host: **4** Como
supplant: **4** oust **5** usurp **6** change, follow, unseat **7** cast out, replace, succeed **8** displace, force out **9** supersede
supple: **4** limp, soft, spry, wiry **5** agile, lithe **6** limber, lissom, pliant, svelte **7** ductile, elastic, lissome, plastic, pliable, rubbery, sinuous, springy, willowy **8** flexible, graceful, stretchy, yielding **9** adaptable, lightsome, lithesome, malleable, resilient
supplement: **3** add, eke, pad **4** grow, rise **5** add-on, add to, annex, build, extra, rider **6** append, beef up, eke out, enrich, extend, insert, jazz up, option, step up **7** adjunct, augment, broaden, build up, codicil, enhance, enlarge, fill out, fortify **8** addendum, addition, additive, appendix, buttress, complete, escalate, increase, round off, round out **9** accessory, accompany, amendment, appendage, extension, increment, reinforce, subsidize **10** attachment, complement, contribute, elongation, postscript
dietary ~: **4** iron **7** mineral, vitamin
__ supplement: **6** Sunday
supplementary: **3** new **4** more **5** added, extra, fresh, other, spare **7** adjunct, further **9** ancillary, auxiliary, secondary **10** additional, subsidiary
Suppliant Women, The
author: Aeschylus
supplicant: **5** lover **6** beggar, pauper, suitor
supplicate: **3** beg, sue **4** pray **5** plead, press **6** adjure, appeal, demand **7** beseech, entreat, implore, request, solicit **8** petition **9** importune
supplication: **4** plea, suit **6** appeal, demand, litany, prayer **7** request **8** entreaty, petition
supplier: **6** jobber, seller, vendor **8** retailer **10** wholesaler
supplies: **3** kit **4** food **5** items, stock **6** outfit, stores **7** rations **9** equipment, inventory, materials **10** provisions
supply: **3** arm, rig **4** drop, feed, fill, find, fund, give, lend, mine **5** bring, cache, cater, endow, equip, fix up, grant, hoard, put up, serve, spare, stake, stock, store, yield **6** afford, amount, fulfil, kick in, load up, outfit, pony up, purvey, ration, render, source, vittle **7** appoint, backlog, deliver, fulfill, furnish, prepare, produce, provide, recruit, reserve, satisfy, service, surplus, sustain, victual **8** accouter, accoutre, dispense, hand over, material, minister, quantity, turn over **9** inventory, provision, repertory, replenish, reservoir, stockpile **10** administer, come up with, contribute
anew: **5** refit **10** replentish
depot: **5** étape **6** armory **9** warehouse
full ~: **7** satiety, surfeit **8** plethora **9** plenitude **10** saturation
hidden ~: **5** cache, hoard, stash
in short ~: **4** rare **5** scant **6** exotic, scanty, scarce, sparse **8** uncommon
rich ~: **4** mine, vein
supply-__ economics: **4** side
__ Supply: **3** Air
supply and __: **6** demand
support: **3** aid, fan, job, leg **4** abet, back, base, bear, earn, egis, feed, food, fund, gird, hand, help, hold, keep, lift, pier, post, prop, rest, rock, stay **5** aegis, allow, boost, brace, carry, cheer, endow, favor, found, guard, guide, means, money, nurse, pylon, raise, shore, staff, stake, stalk, stand, stave, stick, stilt, strut **6** assist, back up, bottom, buoy up, column, cradle, crutch, defend, foster, ground, handle, hold up, living, pay for, pillar, prop up, relief, second, succor, suffer, timber, uphold, upkeep, verify **7** advance, alimony, approve, backing, bolster, bracket, care for, comfort, endorse, espouse, finance, footing, fortify, forward, further, help out, indorse, justify, lectern, loyalty, nourish, nurture, payment, pension, promote, protect, provide, pull for, rampart, relieve, shore up, sponsor, stand by, stick by, stiffen, subsidy, sustain **8** abutment, advocacy, advocate, approval, auspices, banister, bankroll, blessing, buttress, champion, chaperon, espousal, exponent, foothold, mainstay, maintain, platform, plead for, plump for, sanction, shoulder, side with, skeleton, speak for, stand for **9** agree with, allowance, chaperone, encourage, establish, flotation, get behind, insurance, patronage, patronize, provision, reinforce, stability, stabilize, stanchion, subscribe, subsidize, testimony, undergird, underside, vindicate **10** assistance, foundation, friendship, go to bat for, groundwork, livelihood, perpetuate, protection, provide for, put forward, rally round, speak up for, stand up for, stick up for, strengthen, substratum, sustenance, underwrite
obtain, as ~: **5** draft **6** muster **7** recruit **8** mobilize
support __: **4** hose **5** group
__ support: **4** arch, tech **5** child, moral, price
supporter: **3** aye, fan **4** ally **5** angel, giver, urger **6** backer, cohort, friend, helper, patron, rooter, votary **7** admirer, apostle, devotee, grantor, sponsor **8** adherent, advocate, believer, champion, defender, disciple, endorser, espouser, exponent, financer, follower, henchman, mainstay, partisan, upholder **9** apologist, assistant, auxiliary, comforter, expounder, proponent **10** benefactor, enthusiast, subscriber, well-wisher
combining form: **4** -crat **5** -ocrat
supporting: **3** for, pro **6** all for, behind **9** in favor of
__-supporting: **4** self
supporting factor: **4** crux, root **5** cause **6** motive, reason **7** footing, grounds, premise, pretext **8** evidence **9** criterion, principle **10** assumption, foundation
supportive: **3** for **7** helpful **8** fatherly, motherly, parental **9** favorable **10** reassuring
Support Your Local Gunfighter (1971 film)
cast: Jack Elam, James Garner, Suzanne Pleshette
Support Your Local Sheriff (1969 film)
cast: Walter Brennan, James Garner
supposable: **6** likely **10** believable, imaginable
suppose: **4** deem, feel, take **5** fancy, grant, guess, infer, opine, think, trust **6** assume, expect, figure, gather, reason, reckon, regard, what if **7** believe, daresay, imagine, presume, pretend, surmise, suspect **8** conceive, conclude, consider, estimate, theorize **9** postulate, speculate **10** conjecture, understand
old-style: **4** trow, ween
supposed: **7** nominal, reputed, seeming **8** apparent, putative, reported, so-called, unproved **9** imaginary, pretended **10** ostensible
supposedly: **4** as if **5** quasi **9** doubtless **10** apparently
supposing: **9** given that, providing
even ~: **6** though
that: **8** as long as
supposition: **4** idea **5** doubt, given, guess, hunch, rumor **6** belief, notion, theory, thesis **7** concept, opinion, premise, surmise, thought **9** condition, guesswork, suspicion
suppress: **3** gag, nix **4** bury, curb, hide, hush, kill, stop, tame **5** check, crush, elide, leash, quash, quell, shush, sit on **6** arrest, bottle, bridle, censor, cut off, deaden, defeat, hold in, hush up, muffle, muzzle, quench, squash, stifle, subdue **7** abolish, conceal, conquer, contain, cover up, inhibit, oppress, put down, repress, silence, smother, squelch **8** beat down, hold back, hold down, keep down, overcome, restrain, snuff out, stamp out, throttle **9** keep quiet, overpower, overthrow, put a lid on, subjugate **10** annihilate, extinguish, keep a lid on, keep in line, keep secret, put an end to
suppressed: **6** latent, pent-up, untold **9** forgotten **10** unrecalled
supra: **9** preceding
opposite: **5** infra
__ supra: **3** ubi **4** vide
Supra: **3** car **4** auto **6** Toyota
__ supra citato: **4** loco
supranormal: **7** psychic, uncanny **10** paranormal
supremacy: **4** lead, rule, sway **5** power, reign **6** empire **7** command, control, primacy, victory **8** dominion, hegemony, kingship, priority **9** advantage, authority, dominance, influence **10** ascendance, ascendancy, ascendence, ascendency, domination, excellence, government, leadership, perfection
__ Supremacy, The: **6** Bourne
supreme: **3** top **4** best, head, last, main **5** chief, final, first, grand, ideal, noble, prime, royal **6** all-out, divine, master, ruling, utmost **7** dessert, highest, in front, leading, maximum, perfect, regnant, topmost **8** absolute, almighty, cardinal, crowning, dominant, foremost, greatest, headmost, peerless, powerful, splendid, towering, ultimate **9** excellent, first-rate, high-class, marvelous, matchless, nonpareil, paramount, principal, sovereign, topflight, unequaled, unmatched, unrivaled, uppermost, virtuosic, worthiest **10** consummate, first-class, inimitable, overriding, preeminent, prevailing, surpassing, unrivalled
Supreme __: **5** Being, Court **6** Soviet
Supreme Court: **6** ennead
complement: **4** nine
position: **4** seat
work: **6** appeal, ruling **7** hearing

supremely: 4 very 7 greatly 8 above all 9 perfectly 10 especially
Supremes
 hometown: Detroit
 members: Ross, Wilson, Ballard, Birdsong
 song: Baby Love (1964)
  Back in My Arms Again (1965)
  Come See About Me (1964)
  Floy Joy (1972)
  The Happening (1967)
  I Hear a Symphony (1965)
  I'm Gonna Make You Love Me (1968)
  I'm Livin' in Shame (1969)
  In and Out of Love (1967)
  Love Child (1968)
  Love Is Here and Now You're Gone (1967)
  Love Is Like an Itching in My Heart (1966)
  My World Is Empty Without You (1966)
  Nothing But Heartaches (1965)
  Reflections (1967)
  Someday We'll Be Together (1969)
  Stoned Love (1970)
  Stop! In the Name of Love (1965)
  Up the Ladder to the Roof (1970)
  Where Did Our Love Go (1964)
  You Can't Hurry Love (1966)
  You Keep Me Hangin' On (1966)
__ Sur: 3 Big
sura: 7 chapter
 compilation: 5 Koran, Quran
surcease: 3 end 4 halt, stop 5 close, delay 6 desist, ending, finish, wind up 8 break off, complete, conclude, leave off, wind down 9 finish off, terminate 10 conclusion
surcharge: 3 fee, tax 5 add-on 6 excise
sure: 3 set 4 fast, firm, real, safe, true 5 bound, clear, fixed, solid, valid 6 secure, stable, steady, strong 7 assured, certain, cinched, decided, genuine, settled, staunch 8 absolute, clinched, composed, constant, definite, enduring, fail-safe, for a fact, inerrant, in the bag, positive, reliable, resolved, sanguine, unerring, unshaken 9 assertive, certified, confident, convinced, doubtless, downright, foolproof, goofproof, persuaded, satisfied, steadfast, unfailing, unvarying 10 conclusive, dependable, determined, documented, guaranteed, inevitable, infallible, legitimate, optimistic, unarguable, unchanging, undeniable, undisputed, undoubtful, unshakable, unwavering
 as hell: 5 truly 9 certainly, doubtless 10 absolutely, definitely, positively, undeniably
 ender: 6 footed
 feel ~ of: 4 rely 5 bet on, trust 6 bank on 7 believe
 for ~: 3 yes 5 natch, quite, truly 6 indeed, rather, you bet 7 certain, exactly, quite so 8 definite, manifest, of course 9 certainly, darn right, naturally, you betcha 10 absolutely, by all means, conclusive, definitely, guaranteed, positively, that's right, unarguable, undeniable
 make ~: 5 check 6 affirm, verify 7 confirm 9 ascertain, guarantee
 make ~ of: 3 ice 5 sew up
 victory: 5 cinch 9 certainty
 yeah, ~: 4 as if, I bet
 see also of course
Sure: 9 deodorant
 competitor: ***see*** deodorant
sure as __: 7 shootin'
surefire: 9 foolproof, rock solid 10 guaranteed
surefooted: 5 agile 6 nimble
surely: 2 OK 4 okay, okeh, okey 6 and how, easily, indeed, really 7 clearly, for real, plainly 8 for a fact 9 decidedly, no mistake 10 definitely, far and away, for certain, inevitably, inexorably, infallibly, invariably, manifestly, presumably
 see also of course
Surely you __!: 4 jest
sureness: 5 trust 8 accuracy, optimism 10 confidence, conviction
...sure plays __ pinball: 5 a mean
surety: 4 bail, egis, gage 6 pledge 7 hostage, sponsor 8 security, warranty 9 certainty, guarantee, safeguard 10 collateral, conviction
 agreement: 4 bond
 poster: 6 bailor
surf: 4 foam, wave 5 froth, spume, surge, swell, waves 7 hang ten 8 breakers, hang five, sea spray 9 spindrift 10 catch a wave
 and turf: 3 duo 6 entree
 droplets: 4 mist 5 spray, spume 6 mizzle 7 drizzle
 ender: 5 board
 get ready to ~: 5 log in, log on
 like the ~: 5 aroar, foamy 6 frothy 7 foaming, roaring 8 frothing 10 thundering
 motion: 4 tide, wave 5 swell 6 roller
 murmur: 4 rote
 place to ~: 3 Net, Web 8 Internet
 starter: 4 body, wind
surf-__: 5 'n 'turf
__-surf: 7 channel
Surf: 9 detergent
 competitor: ***see*** detergent
Surf __: 4 City
surface: 3 nap, top 4 area, face, pave, peel, rind, side, skin, wall 5 arise, cover, level, outer, plane, sheet, shell 6 appear, come up, crop up, emerge, facade, finish, loom up, move up, veneer 7 expanse, flare up, outside, outward, shallow, texture 8 apparent, cosmetic, covering, exterior, external 9 periphery 10 peripheral
 beneath the ~: 5 inner 6 latent
 flat ~: 5 plane
 measurement: 4 area
 on the ~: 7 outward 9 outwardly
surface-to-__: 3 air
surf and __: 4 turf
Surfaris
 song: Wipe Out (1963)
surfboard
 application: 3 wax
 stabilizer: 4 skeg
 use a ~: 4 ride 7 hang ten 8 hang five
Surf City (1963 song)
 artist: Jan & Dean
surfeit: 4 cloy, cram, fill, glut, jade, load, orgy, pall, sate 5 gorge 6 excess 7 nimiety, satiate, satiety, satisfy 8 bellyful, overfeed, overfill, overflow, overkill, plethora, saturate 9 profusion, repletion 10 gormandize, oversupply
surfeited: 5 blasé, jaded 10 world-weary
surfer
 challenge: 5 crest, swell 6 comber
 hangout: 3 net, Web 5 beach 8 Internet
 Internet ~: 4 user
 need: 4 wave 5 board, modem 8 computer
 shopping place: 3 Net, Web 4 eBay 8 Internet
 wannabe: 5 ho-dad
 worry: 5 shark
Surfer Girl (1963 song)
 artist: Beach Boys
Surfin' __: 3 USA 4 Bird 6 Safari
Surfin' Safari (1962 song)
 artist: Beach Boys
Surfin' U.S.A. (1963 song)
 artist: Beach Boys
Surf's Up (2007 film)
 voice cast: Jeff Bridges, Zooey Deschanel, Jon Heder, Shia LaBeouf
surge: 3 jet 4 eddy, flow, gush, jump, leap, pour, rise, roll, rush, surf, wash, wave, zoom 5 arise, climb, drive, flood, heave, lunge, mount, rally, spirt, spout, spurt, swash, swell, swirl 6 billow, deluge, growth, influx, onrush, pounce, ripple, roller, seethe, sluice, stream, upturn, well up 7 barrage, breaker, overrun, soaring, upswing 8 effusion, increase, outbreak, outburst, overflow, swelling, undulate, upgrowth 9 crescendo, upwelling, well forth 10 move upward, outpouring
 estuary ~: 5 eager, eagre
 ocean ~: 4 tide, wave 5 swell 6 comber
__ surge: 5 storm
surgeon: 2 dr., MD 6 doctor 9 physician
 attire: 4 gown 6 scrubs
 dressing: 5 gauze
 glove: 5 latex
 prefix: 5 neuro
 procedure: 9 operation
 surname: 4 Mayo
 tool: 5 clamp, laser, probe 6 lancet, stylet 7 curette, forceps, scalpel
 word: 4 stat
surgeon __: 7 general
__ surgeon: 4 oral, tree
surgery: 9 operation, treatment
 before ~: 5 pre-op
 locale: 2 OR 8 hospital
 perform ~: 7 operate
 prepare for ~: 5 scrub
 starter: 5 micro
__ surgery: 5 laser 7 plastic
Suriname: 6 nation 7 country
 capital: 10 Paramaribo
 language: 6 Arawak
 money: 6 dollar, gilder, gulden 7 guilder
 neighbor: 6 Brazil, Guyana
 org.: 3 OAS
Sur la plage
 artist: Edgar Degas
surliness: 9 short fuse
surly: 4 cold, cool, dark, dour, glum, mean, rude, ugly 5 brusk, cross, gruff, huffy, irate, nasty, rough, sulky, testy 6 chilly, crabby, cranky, crusty, dismal, feisty, fretty, gloomy, grouty, grumpy, ireful, morose, ornery, sullen 7 bearish, bilious, brusque, glacial, grouchy, hateful, hostile, peevish, uncivil, vicious 8 choleric, churlish, contrary, frowning, growling, grumpish, inimical, inurbane, liverish, lowering, perverse, snappish, snarling, spiteful 9 bellicose, cheerless, crotchety, fractious, irascible, irritable, malicious, saturnine, splenetic, ungallant 10 ill-humored, ill-natured, malevolent, out of sorts, pugnacious, unfriendly, ungracious
__-sur-Marne: 7 Châlons
surmise: 4 deem, feel, idea 5 fancy, guess, hunch, infer, opine, think, trust 6 assume, deduce, expect, gather, notion, reckon, regard, take it, theory, thesis 7 imagine, opinion, predict, presume, suppose, suspect, thought, venture 8 conclude, consider, estimate, theorize 9 deduction, guesswork, inference, prognosis, speculate, suspicion 10 assumption, conclusion, conjecture, hypothesis, understand
surmount: 3 cap, top 4 best, lick, pass, rise 5 clear, scale, tower, vault 6 better, defeat, exceed, hurdle, subdue 7 conquer, prevail, succeed, weather 8 overcome, vanquish 9 negotiate, rise above, transcend
surname: 4 name 6 handle 8 cognomen 10 patronymic
 common ~: 5 Jones, Smith
 follower: 3 née
surpass: 3 cap, top 4 beat, best, lead, lick, pass 5 break, excel, outdo, tower, trump 6 better, exceed, outrun 7 eclipse, outpace, outrank, outstep, overrun, run over 8 go beyond, outclass, outmatch, outshine, outstrip, outweigh, overstep 9 transcend 10 outperform, overshadow, put to shame, tower above
surpassing: 5 above 6 beyond 7 ahead of, supreme 8 superior, towering, ultimate 9 unequaled, unrivaled 10 unrivalled
surplice: 5 cotta
surplus: 3 odd 4 glut, over, rest 5 extra, flood, spare 6 de trop, excess, margin, profit, supply, unused 7 balance, nimiety, overage, overrun, remnant, residue 8 leftover, overflow, plethora, residual 9 overstock, profusion, redundant, remainder 10 inordinate, lavishness, oversupply, unconsumed
__ surplus: 3 war 7 capital

surprise: **3** awe, jar, nab **4** daze, jolt, rock, stun, trap, turn **5** alarm, amaze, catch, floor, shock, start, treat, upset **6** ambush, dazzle, dismay, lay for, marvel, waylay, whammy, wonder **7** astound, capture, confuse, godsend, miracle, nonplus, perplex, shake up, stagger, startle, stupefy **8** astonish, blow away, bowl over, confound, discover, drop in on, unsettle **9** amazement, bombshell, burst in on, bushwhack, curveball, dumbfound, electrify, eyeopener, lie in wait, overwhelm, sensation, sneak up on, take aback **10** come down on, disconcert, revelation, unexpected, unforeseen, wonderment
  attack: **4** raid **5** foray **6** ambush **10** ambushment
  by ~: **5** aback, short **8** unawares
  ending: **5** twist
  nice ~: **5** bonus, treat
  win: **5** upset
surprise __: **5** party **6** ending
surprised: **4** numb **5** agape **7** in shock, stunned **10** taken aback
Surprise Symphony
  composer: Joseph Haydn
surreal: **5** weird **6** far-out **7** bizarre **8** freakish **9** fantastic, grotesque **10** incredible
Surrealist: **6** artist **7** painter
  French ~: **6** Tanguy
  German ~: **5** Ernst
  predecessor: **4** Dada
  Spanish ~: **4** Dali, Miró, Varo
  Swiss ~: **4** Klee
surrender: **3** bow **4** cave, cede, drop, dump, fall, fold, give, lose, quit, sell, shed **5** chuck, ditch, forgo, leave, let go, waive, yield **6** fess up, forego, fork up, give in, give up, go down, resign, submit, toss in, unhand **7** abandon, concede, consign, entrust, forfeit, forsake, intrust, lay down, release, sell out, succumb **8** abdicate, forswear, get rid of, hand over, jettison, part with, renounce, roll over, say uncle, sign away, throw out, turn over **9** cast aside, deliver up, dispose of, extradite, foreswear, sacrifice, throw away, white flag **10** abdication, abnegation, capitulate, concession, relinquish, submission
  cry of ~: **5** I quit, uncle
  flag color: **5** white
Surrender (1961 song)
  artist: Elvis Presley
Surrender (1987 film)
  cast: Peter Boyle, Michael Caine, Sally Field, Steve Guttenberg
__ Surrender: **5** Never, Sweet
surreptitious: **3** sly **6** covert, hidden, masked, secret, sneaky, unseen, veiled **7** cloaked, devious, furtive, on the QT, private **8** hush-hush, obscured, on the sly, secluded, shrouded, sneaking, stealthy **9** concealed, disguised, underhand **10** undercover, under wraps
surreptitiously: **7** sub rosa **8** on the sly, secretly **9** furtively, in private, underhand **10** undercover

surrey: **5** buggy
  puller: **5** horse **6** equine
  trim: **6** fringe
Surrey: **4** city, town **5** shire **6** county
  city: **5** Egham, Epsom **7** Staines, Sunbury
Surrey With the Fringe on Top, The
  composer: Oscar Hammerstein, Richard Rodgers
surrogate: **3** sub **5** agent, proxy, vicar **6** acting, backup, deputy, fill-in **7** stand-in **8** delegate **9** alternate, appointee, vicarious **10** substitute
surround: **3** mob, rim **4** edge, gird, hoop, ring, wrap **5** bathe, beset, bound, bower, boxin, embay, fence, hedge, hem in, skirt, verge **6** begird, border, circle, cordon, encase, enfold, engird, engulf, enlace, enwrap, fringe, girdle, incase, infold, ingulf, inlace, inwrap **7** besiege, compass, confine, embrace, enclave, enclose, envelop, environ, fence in, inclose, shelter, smother **8** blockade, cincture, encircle, neighbor **9** beleaguer, close in on, encompass **10** circumvent, lay siege to
  prefix: **6** circum-
surrounded: **3** mid **4** amid **5** among **6** amidst, mongst **7** amongst, between
surroundings: **4** area **6** medium, milieu **7** climate, habitat, scenery, setting **8** ambiance, ambience, environs, location, position, purlieus, vicinity
__-sur-Saône: **7** Châlons
__-sur-Seine: **4** Ivry **7** Neuilly
surveillance: **3** bug **4** look, tail **5** recon, vigil, watch **6** spying **7** lookout, wiretap **8** eagle eye, scrutiny, security, stake-out **9** vigilance
  device: **3** bug **4** mike **5** radar, sonar **6** camera **7** wiretap **9** satellite **10** microphone
  engage in ~: **3** spy
  keep under ~: **4** tail **5** guard, trace, watch **6** follow, patrol, police, shadow **7** baby-sit, observe, protect **9** chaperone, safeguard
  outfit: **3** CIA, FBI, NSA
survey: **3** eye, map, see **4** case, look, plot, poll, rate, read, scan, view **5** assay, audit, cover, scope, scout, study **6** assess, census, digest, look at, précis, review, sample, search, size up, sketch, voting **7** canvass, enquiry, examine, explore, inquiry, inspect, legwork, measure, monitor, observe, outline, oversee, perusal, profile, summary, valuate **8** analysis, appraise, critique, estimate, evaluate, look over, look upon, overlook, overview, prospect, research, scrutiny, stake out **9** check over, range over, summarize **10** compendium, inspection, scrutinize
  instrument: **6** alidad **7** compass, transit
survival __: **3** kit
survival of the __: **7** fittest
Survival: Zero
  author: Mickey Spillane

survive: **4** bear, last, live **5** cut it, exist, get by **6** endure, handle, linger, live on, make do, manage, remain, revive, suffer **7** carry on, hold out, make out, outlast, outlive, outwear, persist, recover, ride out, stand up, subsist, sustain, wait out, weather **8** continue, live down, overcome **9** persevere, withstand **10** get through, keep afloat, make the cut, see through, tough it out
__ Survive: **5** I Will
surviving: **5** alive **6** extant, with us **9** remaining
__ survivor: **4** sole
Survivor (2001 song)
  artist: Destiny's Child
Survivor (CBS)
  host: Jeff Probst
  immunity token: **4** idol
  shelter: **3** hut
  team: **5** tribe
Survivor (rock group)
  hometown: Chicago
  song: Burning Heart (1985)
    Eye of the Tiger (1982)
    High on You (1985)
    Is This Love (1986)
    The Search Is Over (1985)
__ Survivors: **4** Soul
Susan: **3** Dey **4** Rook **5** Anton, Clark, Lucci, Olsen **6** Faludi, George, Oliver, Powter, Ruttan, Sontag **7** Anspach, Blakely, Hayward, Tyrrell **8** Glaspell, Sarandon, Sullivan **9** Hampshire, Seidelman, Strasberg
  black-eyed ~: **5** plant **6** flower **9** perennial **10** wildflower
  lazy ~: **4** tray **6** server
Susan __ James: **5** Saint
__ Susan: **4** lazy
Susanin: **4** Ivan
Susann: **10** Jacqueline
Susanna: **5** Hoffs **6** Moodie
  composer: George Frideric Handel
Susannah: **4** York
Susanne: **6** Langer
Susan Saint __: **5** James
susceptible: **4** easy, naif, open, soft **5** naive, prone **6** liable, swayed **7** exposed, given to, pliable, psychic, subject, taken in, tending, touched **8** affected, gullable, gullible, inclined, wide open **9** receptive, sensitive
  not ~: **6** immune
sushi: **4** fish **5** snack **9** appetizer
  bar soup: **4** miso
  ingredient: **3** eel, egg **4** fish, nori, rice, tofu, tuna **5** algae, unagi **6** sea eel, wasabi **7** octopus, seaweed
  like ~: **3** raw
  source: **5** Japan
  wrap: **4** kelp
suspect: **4** fear, feel, hold, moot, open, take **5** doubt, fishy, guess, query, shady, shaky, smell, think **6** assume, expect, gather, louche, pseudo, reckon, unsure, wonder **7** believe, dubious, imagine, presume, suppose, surmise, unclear **8** conclude, consider, distrust, doubtful, mistrust, question, theorize, unlikely **9** smell a rat, speculate, uncertain **10** conjecture, disbelieve, have a hunch, incredible, ridiculous, understand
  check a ~: **5** frisk **7** pat down
  need: **5** alibi
__ suspect: **5** prime
Suspect (1987 film)
  cast: Cher, Liam Neeson, Dennis Quaid
__ Suspects, The: **5** Usual
suspend: **3** bar **4** file, halt, hang, pend, quit, stay, stop **5** break, cease, check, debar, defer, delay, poise, sling, stall, swing, table, waive **6** arrest, dangle, depend, freeze, hold up, lay off, put off, recall, recess, retard, shelve **7** adjourn, break up, hold off, neglect **8** cut short, intermit, lay aside, postpone, protract, put on ice, shut down **9** interrupt **10** inactivate, pigeonhole
suspended: **5** slung **6** frozen, on hold **7** abeyant, dormant, hanging **10** up in the air
  hang ~: **5** float, hover
suspenders: **6** braces
  alternative: **4** belt
suspense: **4** plot **5** doubt **7** anxiety, tension **10** expectancy
suspenseful: **8** dramatic
suspension: **4** halt, stay **5** break, delay, letup, pause, truce **6** arrest, cutoff, freeze, recess **7** latency, respite, time-out **8** abeyance, breather, dormancy, downtime, lateness, reprieve, solution, stoppage **9** armistice, cessation, deferment, dismissal, exclusion, expulsion, remission **10** leaving off, putting off
suspension __: **6** bridge
suspicion: **4** clew, clue, hint, idea **5** doubt, guess, hunch, qualm, shade, smell, tinge, touch, trace, whiff **6** belief, notion, shadow, strain, streak, trifle **7** feeling, glimmer, inkling, opinion, surmise, vestige, whisper **8** bad vibes, cynicism, distrust, jealousy, mistrust, question, wariness **9** chariness, guesswork, leeriness, misgiving, nonbelief **10** assumption, conjecture, gut feeling, impression, intimation, skepticism, suggestion
  above ~: **5** clean **8** innocent **9** blameless, guiltless **10** inculpable, in the clear
Suspicion (1941 film)
  cast: Joan Fontaine, Cary Grant
  director: Alfred Hitchcock
__ Suspicion: **5** Above
Suspicions (1979 song)
  artist: Eddie Rabbitt
suspicious: **4** cagy, wary **5** cagey, chary, fishy, funny, leery, phony, queer, shady, shaky **6** louche, phoney, unsure **7** careful, cynical, dubious, guarded, jealous, unusual, uptight **8** cautious, doubtful, doubting, hesitant, peculiar, watchful **9** diffident, equivocal, green-eyed, ill at ease, irregular, jaundiced, out of line, quizzical, skeptical, uncertain, wondering **10** far-fetched
Suspicious Minds (1969 song)
  artist: Elvis Presley
suspire: **4** sigh **6** exhale

Susquehanna: 5 river, tribe
city on the ~: 5 Owego **10** Harrisburg
locale: 4 Penn. **7** New York **8** Maryland
suss (out): 6 figure
Sussex: 3 cow **4** bull, fowl **6** bovine, cattle, county **7** chicken
city: 7 Bexhill, Crawley **8** Brighton, Hastings **10** Eastbourne
locale: 7 England
relative: *see* chicken
Susskind, David: 2 MC **4** host **5** emcee
Sussudio (1985 song)
artist: Phil Collins
sustain: 3 aid **4** back, bear, buoy, feed, help, hold, keep, prop, save **5** abide, brace, brook, carry, nurse, prove, shore, stand **6** afford, assist, convey, defend, endure, foster, hang in, ratify, suffer, supply, uphold, verify **7** approve, bolster, comfort, confirm, endorse, fortify, indorse, justify, nourish, nurture, prolong, provide, receive, relieve, ride out, shore up, stand by, stomach, support, survive, undergo **8** bankroll, bear with, befriend, buttress, continue, preserve, protract, stand for, tolerate, validate **9** keep alive, keep going, lend a hand, put up with, reinforce, stabilize, stand up to, withstand **10** experience, perpetuate, provide for, speak up for, stick up for, strengthen
sustained: 7 chronic **8** constant **9** chronical, perennial, unabating **10** relentless
in ballet: 7 soutenu
in music: 6 tenuto
sustaining: 7 ongoing **10** alimentary, comforting, continuing, nutritious
sustenance: 3 aid, job **4** diet, fare, food, fuel, grub, keep, meat **5** bacon, bread **6** living, ration, relief, upkeep, viands **7** aliment, edibles, support, victual **8** eatables, victuals **9** nutrition, provender **10** assistance, livelihood, provisions
spiritual ~: 5 manna **6** prayer
take ~: 3 eat, sup **4** dine
susurrus: 6 murmur **7** whisper
Sutcliffe: 3 Stu
Sutherland: 4 Earl, Joan **6** Donald, Kiefer
Sutherland, Donald: 5 actor
film: The Act of the Heart (1970)
Backdraft (1991)
Bethune (1977)
Buffy the Vampire Slayer (1992)
The Day of the Locust (1975)
The Dirty Dozen (1967)
Disclosure (1994)
Don't Look Now (1973)
The Eagle Has Landed (1977)
Eye of the Needle (1981)
The Great Train Robbery (1979)
Heaven Help Us (1985)
Instinct (1999)
Invasion of the Body Snatchers (1978)
JFK (1991)
Kelly's Heroes (1970)
Klute (1971)
MASH (1970)
Max Dugan Returns (1983)
National Lampoon's Animal House (1978)
Ordinary People (1980)
Panic (2000)
Six Degrees of Separation (1993)
Space Cowboys (2000)
Start the Revolution Without Me (1970)
Steelyard Blues (1973)
Without Limits (1998)
son: 6 Kiefer
Sutherland, Joan: 4 Dame, diva **6** singer **7** soprano **10** prima donna
milieu: 5 opera
solo: 4 aria
Sutherland, Kiefer: 5 actor
father: 6 Donald
film: Bright Lights, Big City (1988)
Crazy Moon (1986)
Dark City (1998)
A Few Good Men (1992)
Flatliners (1990)
Freeway (1996)
Mirrors (2008)
Phone Booth (2003)
The Sentinel (2006)
The Three Musketeers (1993)
Young Guns (1988)
__ Sutra: 4 Kama
Sutter: 4 John
Sutter's __: 4 Mill
Sutton: 3 Don, Hal **4** John **5** Frank **6** Willie
Sutton, Don: 6 Dodger, hurler **7** pitcher
Sutton, Hal: 6 golfer
Sutton, Willie
emulate ~: 3 rob **5** steal
suture: 3 sew **4** seam **6** stitch
combining form: 6 -rhaphy **7** -rrhaphy
material: 4 silk **6** catgut
Suu Kyi, Aung San: 8 Nobelist
SUV: 3 ute **7** vehicle
Suva: 4 city, town **7** capital
locale: 4 Fiji
Suvari: 4 Mena
Suwannee: 5 river
locale: 7 Florida, Georgia
Suzanne: 4 Vega **6** Somers **7** Farrell **9** Pleshette
composer: Leonard Cohen
suzerain: 4 lord **5** ruler **6** gerent
suzerainty: 4 rule
__ suzette: 5 crêpe
Suzi: 6 Quatro
Suzuki: 3 car **4** auto **6** Ichiro, import **10** automobile
model: 5 Aerio, Swift **6** Esteem, Vitara **7** Samurai **8** Sidekick
Suzuki, Ichiro
sport: 8 baseball
Suzy: 4 Amis **6** Parker **7** Chaffee
svelte: 4 lank, lean, slim, thin, trim, wiry **5** lanky, lithe, spare **6** dainty, gangly, lissom, skinny, slight, slinky, supple, twiggy **7** gracile, scraggy, scrawny, slender, spidery, willowy **8** gangling, graceful **9** lithesome, sylphlike
Sven: 5 Hedin
Svenson: 2 Bo
Sverdrup __: 7 Islands
svgs. __: 4 acct.
SVX: 3 car **4** auto **6** Subaru **10** automobile
swab: 3 gob, mop, tar **4** Q-tip, salt, wash, wipe **5** clean, mop up **6** sailor **7** cleanse, jack tar, mariner **10** applicator
salutation: 4 ahoy **5** avast
target: 3 wax **6** earwax
swabbie: 3 gob, tar **4** salt **6** seaman **7** jack tar
swaddle: 3 lap **4** tuck, wrap **5** cover **6** enwrap, inwrap
swaddling __: 5 bands **7** clothes
swag: 4 loot, tilt **5** booty, prize **6** boodle, spoils **7** festoon, garland, jobbery, plunder **9** valuables
Aussie's ~: 5 bluey
Swaggart: 5 Jimmy
swagger: 4 brag, crow **5** boast, bully, gloat, pride, strut, swank, swash **6** hector, parade, prance **7** bluster, conceit, peacock, rub it in, show off, triumph **8** brandish, domineer, flourish **9** arrogance, put on airs **10** grandstand, lord it over
stick: 4 cane
swagger __: 5 stick
swaggerer: 5 bully **6** gascon **7** showoff **8** blowhard, braggart
swaggering: 4 vain **6** jaunty **8** arrogant, blustery, boastful, cocksure **10** blusterous
swagman: 6 Aussie
Swahili: 5 Bantu **8** language
freedom, in ~: 5 uhuru
honorific: 5 bwana
swain: 3 lad **4** beau, love, male **5** adore, flame, lover, Romeo, wooer **6** adorer, suitor **7** admirer, gallant **8** lover boy **9** boyfriend, inamorato **10** sweetheart
offering: 4 rose **5** candy **10** chocolates
starter: 3 cox **4** boat
Swain: 9 Dominique
SWAK
part of ~: 4 kiss, with **6** sealed
site: 6 letter **8** envelope **10** billet-doux, love letter
swale: 5 swamp **6** valley **7** lowland
swallow: 3 buy, eat, nip, sip **4** belt, bird, bolt, down, drop, gulp, lump, swig, take, toss, wolf **5** abide, drink, quaff, slurp, sop up, swill, taste **6** absorb, accept, devour, digest, draw in, endure, engulf, gather, gobble, guzzle, herald, imbibe, ingest, ingulf, inhale, martin, osmose, soak up, suck up, suffer, take in **7** believe, consume, dispose, drink in, fall for, put away, repress, stomach **8** chug-a-lug, dispatch, spoonful, stand for, tolerate, wash down **9** put up with **10** assimilate
don't ~: 5 doubt **6** reject **7** laugh at **8** pooh-pooh **10** disbelieve
ender: 4 tail
home: 4 nest
lookalike: 4 gull **5** swift
nervous ~: 4 gulp
prepare to ~: 4 chew **9** masticate
sea ~: 4 bird, tern
__ swallow: 3 sea **4** barn, tree **5** cliff **7** chimney
swallowtail: 4 coat **9** butterfly
swami: 4 guru, seer **5** Hindu **6** Hindoo, master, pundit
swamp: 3 bog, fen, mud **4** load, mire, moor, quag, rout, sink, wash **5** bayou, beset, crowd, drown, flood, marsh, swale, waste **6** defeat, deluge, drench, engulf, ingulf, morass, muskeg, slough **7** besiege, bottoms, lowland, overrun, peat bog, trounce **8** inundate, overflow, overload, quagmire, submerge, submerse, waterlog, wetlands **9** backwater, marshland, overcrowd, overpower, overwhelm, snow under **10** everglades, overburden
Australian ~ monster: 6 bunyip
denizen: 4 croc, frog **5** crane, egret, gator, heron, snake **6** caiman, cayman **9** alligator, crocodile
grass: 5 sedge
hazard: 4 croc **5** gator, snake **6** caiman, cayman **7** reptile **9** alligator, crocodile, quicksand
pink: 5 plant **6** flower
sound: 5 croak
tree: 6 tupelo **7** live oak
swamp __: 3 gas
__ Swamp: 6 Dismal
swamped: 4 busy **5** awash **7** deluged **10** overworked
swampy: 3 low, wet **4** miry **5** boggy, fenny, muddy **6** marshy, quaggy **7** paludal **8** low-lying
__ Swampy: 4 Camp
swan: 4 bird
female ~: 3 pen
genus: 4 olor
male ~: 3 cob
song: 3 end **4** last **6** ending
young ~: 6 cygnet
swan __: 4 dive, song
__ swan: 4 mute **6** tundra **7** Bewick's, whooper **9** trumpeter
Swan: 5 Billy
city on the ~: 5 Perth
constellation: 6 Cygnus
Swan, Billy
song: I Can Help (1974)
Swanee (1920 song)
artist: Al Jolson
composer: Irving Caesar, George Gershwin
swank: 4 chic, posh, rich, tony **5** dandy, fancy, grand, haute, natty, plush, ritzy, sharp, showy, sleek, smart, strut, style, swank, swish, toney **6** chichi, classy, dapper, deluxe, dressy, flashy, jaunty, lavish, lordly, modish, rakish, snappy, snazzy, spiffy, sporty, trendy, with-it **7** dashing, elegant, opulent, refined, splashy, stylish, swagger, upscale, voguish **8** palatial, peacocky, princely, splendid **9** exclusive, expensive, glamorous, luxurious, nattiness, sumptuous **10** flamboyant
up: 5 preen, primp
Swank, Hilary: 7 actress
film: Amelia (2009)
Boys Don't Cry (1999, AA)
Insomnia (2002)
Million Dollar Baby (2004, AA)
The Next Karate Kid (1994)
spouse: Chad Lowe
swanky
see swank

Swan Lake: **6** ballet
composer: Peter Tchaikovsky
role: **5** Benno, Odile **6** Odette **8** Princess, Wolfgang **9** Siegfried
Swann, Lynn
sport: **8** football
__ swans a-swimming...: **5** seven
Swansea: **4** city, port, town
locale: **5** Wales
Swanson: **6** Gloria, Kristy, Robert
Swanson, Gloria: **7** actress
role: **5** Norma, Sadie
spouse: Wallace Beery
swap: **4** deal **5** bandy, trade, truck **6** barter, change, switch **7** bargain **8** exchange **9** negotiate, transpose **10** horse-trade, quid pro quo, substitute
swap __: **4** meet, shop
sward: **3** lea, ley, sod **4** lawn, turf **5** field, grass **6** meadow **9** grassland
starter: **5** green
swarm: **3** jam, mob **4** army, bevy, herd, host, mass, pack, pour, teem **5** bunch, covey, crawl, crowd, crush, drove, flock, flood, horde, press, snarl, troop **6** abound, legion, myriad, school, stream, throng **7** cluster, numbers, overrun **9** gathering, multitude **10** congregate
home: **4** hive **7** beehive, bee tree
swarming: **4** busy, rife **5** alive, dense, thick **6** active, packed **7** crowded, teeming **8** infested, thronged
swarms: **4** lots **6** flocks **7** legions
Swarm, The menace: **4** bees
swarth
see sward
swarthy: **3** tan **4** dark **5** black, dusky, swart, tawny
far from ~: **4** fair, pale **5** light
swash: **4** rush **5** boast, surge **6** onrush, parade **7** bluster, bravado, swagger
ender: **7** buckler **8** buckling
swashbuckle: **5** boast **7** bluster, swagger
swashbuckler: **5** Athos **6** Aramis **7** Porthos **9** D'Artagnan
weapon: **5** sword
swashbuckling: **4** bold **5** brave **6** daring, rakish **7** dashing, gallant, raffish **8** colorful, fearless, spirited **9** impetuous **10** flamboyant
actor: Errol Flynn
swat: **3** box, hit, zap **4** beat, belt, biff, blow, cuff, ding, slam, slap, slug, sock **5** clout, knock, smack, smash, swipe, whack, whang **6** buffet, larrup, strike, wallop **7** clobber **9** haul off on
SWAT __: **4** team
swatch: **4** snip **6** sample
Swatch: **5** watch
competitor: *see* wristwatch
swath: **3** row **4** belt, path
swathe: **3** lap **4** tape, wrap **5** dress **6** enfold, infold **7** bandage **8** muffle up
__ swatter: **3** fly
S.W.A.T. Theme (1976 song)
artist: Rhythm Heritage
sway: **3** get, run, wag, win **4** bend, bias, keel, lean, move, push, reel, rock, roll, rule, tilt, toss, turn, wave, yo-yo **5** budge, carry, clout, dance, lobby, lurch, might, power, range, reach, reign, scope, shake, slope, sweep, swing, waver, weave **6** affect, careen, dangle, empire, govern, induce, regime, strike, suck in, teeter, totter, wabble, waddle, waffle, wobble **7** control, convert, deviate, impress, incline, inspire, potence, potency, stagger, vibrate, win over **8** dominate, dominion, hegemony, impact on, kingship, motivate, persuade, pressure, prestige, undulate **9** authority, brainwash, fluctuate, hem and haw, influence, oscillate, prejudice, prevail on, supremacy **10** domination, leadership, predispose
hold ~: **4** head, rule **5** reign **6** direct, govern, manage **7** command, control, prevail **8** dominate, overrule **9** influence
swayed: **9** influence
easily ~: **4** meek, soft, weak **5** naive, timid **7** pliable **10** indecisive, irresolute
Swayin' to the Music (1977 song)
artist: Johnny Rivers
Swayze, Patrick: **5** actor
film: Dirty Dancing (1987)
Ghost (1990)
Grandview, U.S.A. (1984)
Point Break (1991)
Swaziland: **6** nation **7** country
bovine: **5** Nguni
capital: **7** Mbabane
city: **7** Manzini, Mbabane
locale: **6** Africa
money: **9** lilangeni
neighbor: **10** Mozambique
Swe.
see Sweden
swear: **3** vow **4** aver, avow, cuss **5** curse, vouch **6** affirm, assert, assure, attest, pledge **7** certify, declare, profane, promise, testify, warrant **8** maintain **9** blaspheme, guarantee **10** asseverate
by: **4** rely **5** trust **6** bank on, rely on **7** believe, count on **8** depend on **9** believe in, count upon
ender: **4** word
falsely: **3** lie **7** perjure
in: **6** adjure, induct **7** instate
off: **4** quit **5** forgo **6** abjure, eschew, forego, reform **7** forsake **8** renounce
word: **4** oath **5** curse **9** expletive
swearing: **4** vice **7** cursing, cussing **9** blasphemy, profanity
Swearin' to God (1975 song)
artist: Frankie Valli
swearword: **4** oath **5** curse **9** expletive, profanity
sweat: **3** job **4** care, drip, fret, glow, moil, ooze, plod, seep, stew, toil, wilt, work **5** chafe, exert, exude, grind, labor, steam, worry **6** effort, egesta, lather, strain, strive **7** agonize, excrete, secrete, swelter, work out **8** drudgery, exertion, moisture, perspire, struggle **9** give a darn, percolate
bit of ~: **4** bead, drop
combining form: **4** hidr- **5** hidro-
ender: **3** box **4** band, shop **5** house, pants, shirt
it out: **4** wait **5** worry **6** endure
no ~: **4** easy, snap **5** cinch **6** simple **8** duck soup **9** easy as pie **10** child's play, effortless
out: **5** await **6** endure
over: **4** mull **5** study, think, weigh **6** debate, ponder **7** revolve **8** cogitate, ruminate **9** cerebrate **10** deliberate, kick around
source: **4** pore **5** gland
sweat __: **3** out **4** suit **5** blood, gland, it out, socks **6** equity **7** bullets
__ sweat: **4** cold
Sweat: **5** Keith
sweatband site: **5** wrist
sweater: **4** wrap **5** V-neck, wooly **6** jersey, woolly **7** kashmir **8** cardigan, cashmere, cowlneck, crew neck, pullover, slipover **10** protection, turtleneck
fabric: **4** poly, wool **5** Orlon **6** angora, cotton, mohair
letter: **2** mu, nu, pi, xi **3** chi, eta, phi, psi, rho, tau **4** beta, iota, zeta **5** alpha, delta, gamma, kappa, omega, sigma, theta **6** lambda **7** epsilon, omicron, upsilon
make a ~: **4** knit
needing a ~: **4** cold, cool **5** nippy, windy **6** chilly, drafty
part: **3** arm **4** neck
size: **2** sm., XL **3** lge., med. **5** large, small **6** medium
sweat of one's __: **4** brow
sweatshirt part, maybe: **4** hood **5** pouch
__, Sweat & Tears: **5** Blood
sweaty: **3** hot, wet **4** damp, warm **5** moist, undry **6** clammy, soaked, steamy, sticky, stinky **7** glowing, wettish **8** drenched, dripping **10** perspiring, sweltering
Sweden: **6** nation **7** country
astronomer: **7** Celsius **8** Ångström
bath: **5** sauna
botanist: **8** Linnaeus
bovine: **5** Fjall
canal: **4** gota
capital: **9** Stockholm
car: **4** Saab **5** Volvo
chemist: **5** Nobel **7** Scheele **8** Svedberg, Tiselius **9** Arrhenius, Berzelius
city: **4** Lund, Umea **5** Gavle, Luleå, Malmö, Ystad **6** Kalmar, Upsala **7** Uppsala **8** Göteborg, Halmstad **9** Stockholm
district: **3** lan
economist: **5** Ohlin **6** Myrdal
explorer: **5** Hedin **12** Nordenskjold
furniture chain: **4** IKEA
geographer: **5** Hedin
golfer: **9** Sorenstam
island: **5** Oland **7** Gotland
lake: **5** Malar
legislature: **7** Riksdag
money: **3** ore **5** krona
mountain: **6** Kjölen
native: **4** Lapp
neighbor: **6** Norway **7** Denmark, Finland
Nobelist in Chemistry: **8** Svedberg, Tiselius **9** Arrhenius **15** von Euler-Chelpin
Nobelist in economics: **5** Ohlin **6** Myrdal
Nobelist in Literature: **5** Sachs **7** Johnson **8** Lagerlöf **9** Karlfeldt, Martinson **10** Lagerkvist **13** von Heidenstam
Nobelist in Medicine: **6** Granit **8** Carlsson, Theorell, von Euler **9** Bergström **10** Gullstrand, Samuelsson
Nobelist in Peace: **6** Myrdal **8** Branting **9** Arnoldson, Söderblom **12** Hammarskjöld
Nobelist in Physics: **5** Dalén **6** Alfvén **8** Siegbahn
philosopher: **10** Swedenborg
physicist: **5** Dalén **6** Alfvén **8** Ångström **9** Arrhenius
playwright: **9** Söderberg **10** Strindberg
poet: **6** Ekelöf **7** Bellman, Fröding **9** Karlfeldt **10** Gustafsson, Strindberg
port: **5** Gavle, Luleå, Malmö, Ystad **6** Kalmar **8** Göteborg, Halmstad **9** Stockholm
river: **3** Dal, Ume **4** Gota **5** Torne
rock group: **4** ABBA
rug: **3** rya
sea: **6** Baltic
soprano: **4** Lind **7** Nilsson
tennis pro: **4** Borg
toast: **5** skoal
waterfall: **6** Handol, Skykje
writer: **5** Weiss **6** Bremer, Moberg, Myrdal, Wägner, Wahlöö **7** Bergman, Johnson, Sjöwall **8** Almqvist, Lagerlöf, Matinson **9** Söderberg **10** Lagerkvist
Swede neighbor: **4** Dane, Finn **9** Norwegian
Swedish: **8** language
Swedish __: **3** ivy **6** turnip **7** massage
Swedish Nightingale, The: **4** Lind
Swee' __: **3** Pea
Sweeney: **2** D.B. **5** Julia
Sweeney Todd: **4** film **7** musical
composer: Stephen Sondheim
prop: **5** razor
Sweeney Todd (2007 film)
cast: Helena Bonham Carter, Johnny Depp, Alan Rickman
director: Tim Burton
sweep: **3** arc, fly, mop, pan **4** area, bend, comb, flit, lick, play, raid, rake, sail, scan, scud, skim, span, sway, wing, zoom **5** ambit, broom, brush, clean, clear, curve, gamut, glide, orbit, range, reach, realm, scope, strut, swing, vista, whisk **6** career, course, extent, glance, length, radius, remove, spread, tidy up, vacuum **7** breadth, clean up, clear up, compass, expanse, flounce, purview, stretch, triumph **8** clear out, confines, flourish, latitude, panorama, progress **9** extension, full range, landslide, ranginess **10** boundaries, clean house
away: **4** toss **6** ravage, ravish **7** destroy, discard, enchant **9** overwhelm
clean ~: **7** triumph, victory **9** landslide
ender: **4** back **6** stakes
off one's feet: **5** besot, charm,

tempt **6** allure, entice, rope in **7** attract, beguile, bewitch, enchant **8** entrance **9** captivate, fascinate, infatuate
upward: 4 rise, soar **5** climb **6** ascend
__ sweep: 5 clean **7** chimney
sweeper: 4 fish, maid **5** broom **7** janitor
starter: 4 mine
__ sweeper: 6 carpet, vacuum
sweeping: 3 big **4** epic, vast, wide **5** broad, chore, large, roomy, total **6** all-out, global **7** blanket, general, overall, plenary, radical **8** extended, far-flung, spacious, thorough, whole-hog **9** all-around, capacious, expansive, extensive, full-dress, housework, inclusive, universal, wholesale **10** exhaustive, large-scale, soup-to-nuts, unspecific, widespread
sweepings: 4 dust, junk **5** trash, waste **6** litter, refuse **7** garbage, rejects, residue, rubbish **8** residuum
sweep one off one's __: 4 feet
sweep-second __: 4 hand
sweepstakes: 6 raffle **7** contest, lottery
__ Sweepstakes: 5 Irish
sweet: 3 jam, new, pet **4** cake, dear, kind, mild, pure, rich, soft **5** balmy, candy, clean, fresh, lolly, mushy, snack, taste, treat **6** bonbon, dainty, dulcet, gentle, goodie, honied, in tune, kindly, lovely, loving, mellow, pastry, sirupy, smooth, sugary, syrupy, taking, tender, washed **7** amiable, angelic, beloved, candied, cloying, darling, dearest, dessert, honeyed, likable, lovable, melodic, musical, pudding, scented, sugared, treacly, tuneful, winning, winsome **8** amicable, aromatic, charming, engaging, euphonic, fragrant, friendly, generous, gumdrops, heavenly, junk food, ladylove, loveable, luscious, nectared, perfumed, pleasant, pleasing, precious, redolent, sonorous, soothing **9** agreeable, ambrosial, angelical, appealing, beautiful, cherished, chocolate, courteous, delicious, enjoyable, lucrative, melodious, nectarous, preserves, sugarplum, toothsome, treasured, unselfish, wholesome **10** attractive, confection, delectable, delightful, euphonical, euphonious, gratifying, harmonious, profitable, reasonable, saccharine, thoughtful, unhardened
be ~ on: 4 like, love **5** adore **6** admire **7** care for
ender: 3 sop **4** meat, shop **5** bread, briar, brier, heart
food: 3 bar, jam, pie **4** cake, tart **5** candy, honey, jelly **6** bonbon, cookie, mousse, pastry **7** brownie **8** ice cream **9** marmalade, preserves **10** confection
girl of song: 3 Sue
on: 6 fond of, keen on **8** mad about
science: 6 boxing
shop: 6 bakery **10** patisserie
starter: 4 semi **6** bitter, meadow
suffix: 3 -ose
talk: 4 sell **7** blarney, coaxing, palaver **8** cajolery, flattery **9** wheedling **10** endearment, inducement, persuasion
too ~: 4 icky **6** cutesy **7** cutesie, gushing, mawkish
sweet __: 3 bay, gum, pea **4** corn, roll, spot, talk **5** cider, tooth **6** clover, potato **7** william
Sweet: 5 Dolph **7** Blanche
Sweet __: 3 Pea **4** Lady, Love, Mary **5** Afton, Thing **6** Dreams **7** Adeline, Charity, Liberty, Seasons
Sweet __ Brown: 7 Georgia
Sweet __, Just You: 3 Sue
Sweet __ O'Grady: 5 Rosie
Sweet Afton
author: Robert Burns
sweet-and-__: 4 sour
...sweet and __ you: 5 so are
Sweet and Innocent (1971 song)
artist: Donny Osmond
Sweet and Lowdown (1999 film)
cast: Samantha Morton, Sean Penn, Uma Thurman
director: Woody Allen
Sweet and Low-Down
composer: George Gershwin, Ira Gershwin
Sweet are the __ of adversity: 4 uses
Sweet as apple cider girl: 3 Ida
Sweet Bird of Youth: 4 film, play
author: Tennessee Williams
cast: Shirley Knight, Paul Newman, Geraldine Page
sweetbrier: 4 rose
Sweet Caroline (1969 song)
artist: Neil Diamond
Sweet Charity: 4 film, play **7** musical
author: Neil Simon
cast: Shirley MacLaine, Ricardo Montalban
director: Bob Fosse
Sweet Cherry Wine (1969 song)
artist: Tommy James and the Shondells
Sweet Child o' Mine (1988 song)
artist: Guns N' Roses
__ Sweet Day: 3 One
Sweet Dreams
author: Michael Frayn
Sweet Dreams (1985 film)
cast: Ed Harris, Jessica Lange
subject: Patsy Cline
Sweet Dreams (song)
artist: Air Supply, Eurythmics
sweeten: 3 pay **4** mull **5** sugar **6** enrich, pacify, soothe **7** appease, assuage, mollify, placate **8** soften up **9** alleviate, candy-coat, deodorize, sugar-coat **10** conciliate, propitiate
sweetened: 5 tasty **6** sugary **10** appetizing
sweetener: 3 tip **4** lure **5** Equal, honey, sirup, sugar, syrup **6** reward **8** gratuity, largesse, molasses **9** saccharin **10** enticement
natural ~: 5 honey **8** cinnamon
sweeten the __: 3 pot
__ Sweeter Than Wine: 6 Kisses
Sweeter Than You (1959 song)
artist: Ricky Nelson
Sweetest __, The: 5 Taboo, Thing **6** Sounds
Sweetest Sounds, The
composer: Richard Rodgers
Sweetest Taboo, The (1985 song)
artist: Sade
Sweetest Thing, The (1981 song)
artist: Juice Newton
Sweetest Thing, The (2002 film)
cast: Christina Applegate, Selma Blair, Cameron Diaz
sweetheart: 2 jo **3** hon, luv, pet **4** baby, beau, dear, doll, jill, love, wife **5** amour, angel, chéri, cooky, cutey, cutie, deary, ducky, flame, honey, leman, lover, lovey, novia, novio, sugar, swain **6** bon ami, chérie, cookie, dautie, dearie, steady, suitor **7** admirer, beloved, darling, dearest, dear one, pigsney, schatzi, squeeze, tootsie **8** chou-chou, cutie pie, dowsabel, dulcinea, ladylove, lovebird, macushla, paramour, precious, snookums, sugar pie, treasure, truelove **9** bonne amie, boyfriend, companion, dreamboat, inamorata, inamorato, petit chou, valentine **10** girlfriend, heartthrob, honeybunch, mavourneen, turtledove
of yore: 5 leman
sweetheart __: 4 deal
Sweetheart of Sigma __, The: 3 Chi
Sweet Hearts Dance (1988 film)
cast: Jeff Daniels, Don Johnson, Elizabeth Perkins, Susan Sarandon
Sweet Hitch-Hiker (1971 song)
artist: Creedence Clearwater Revival
Sweet Home Alabama (1974 song)
artist: Lynyrd Skynyrd
Sweet Home Alabama (2002 film)
cast: Candice Bergen, Patrick Dempsey, Josh Lucas, Mary Kay Place, Reese Witherspoon
sweetie
see sweetheart
__ sweet it is!: 3 How
Sweet Liberty (1986 film)
cast: Alan Alda, Michael Caine, Bob Hoskins, Michelle Pfeiffer
director: Alan Alda
Sweet Little Sixteen (1958 song)
artist: Chuck Berry
Sweet Lorraine (1987 film)
cast: Trini Alvarado, Maureen Stapleton
Sweet Love (song)
artist: Anita Baker, Commodores
sweetly
in music: 5 dolce
sweetmeat: 5 candy, fudge, lolly, taffy, toffy **6** bonbon, dainty, nougat, toffee **7** caramel **8** lollipop **9** chocolate, sugar plum **10** confection, peppermint
sweet-natured: 4 kind, nice **6** genial, polite **7** helpful, likable **8** friendly **10** thoughtful
sweetness and __: 5 light
Sweet 'N Low
rival: 5 Equal
sweet nothings
whisper ~: 3 coo, woo
Sweet Nothin's (1960 song)
artist: Brenda Lee
Sweet November (2001 film)
cast: Greg Germann, Keanu Reeves, Charlize Theron
Sweet Old Fashioned Girl, A (1956 song)
artist: Teresa Brewer
Sweet Pea (1966 song)
artist: Tommy Roe
sweet potato: 3 yam **6** veggie **7** ocarina **9** vegetable
sweet potato __: 3 pie
Sweet Seasons (1972 song)
artist: Carole King
Sweet Sixteen org.: 4 NCAA
sweet-smelling: 5 balmy **7** scented **8** aromatic, fragrant, perfumed, redolent **9** ambrosial
Sweet Smell of Success: 4 film, play
author: Clifford Odets
cast: Tony Curtis, Burt Lancaster
sweet-sounding: 4 soft **6** dulcet **7** lyrical, melodic, musical **9** melodious
Sweet Swan of __: 4 Avon
sweet-talk: 3 con **4** coax **5** lobby, tempt **6** cajole, enamor, entice, induce **7** flatter, wheedle **8** blandish, inveigle, persuade
Sweet Talkin' Guy (1966 song)
artist: Chiffons
Sweet Thing (1976 song)
artist: Chaka Khan
Sweet Thursday
author: John Steinbeck
swell: 3 fop, sea, wax **4** flow, grow, gush, posh, pout, puff, rise, surf, wash, wave **5** add to, belly, bloat, bulge, heave, mount, plump, plush, pouch, ritzy, slick, smart, surge, swish, widen **6** abound, beef up, billow, blow up, deluxe, dilate, expand, extend, fatten, gather, growth, modish, puff up, pump up, ripple, uprise, well up **7** amplify, augment, balloon, broaden, burgeon, coxcomb, distend, elegant, enlarge, fill out, inflate, magnify, stretch, stylish, thicken, voguish **8** bloating, bourgeon, escalate, fancy Dan, gay blade, heighten, increase, lengthen, mushroom, protrude, round out, undulate, wondrous **9** crescendo, desirable, intensify, intumesce, luxurious, pretty boy, upwelling, wonderful **10** accumulate, undulation
as the sea: 5 heave
at sea: 4 surf, tide, wave **6** roller
British ~: 4 toff
ender: 4 fish, head
in space: 3 A-OK
person: 4 dear **5** peach **7** sweetie **10** sweetheart
starter: 6 ground
time: 3 gas **5** blast
see also wonderful
__ Swell: 4 Thou
swelled head: 3 ego **5** pride, quirk **6** egoism, vanity **7** conceit, egotism, hauteur, swagger **8** self-love, smugness **9** arrogance, immodesty, vainglory **10** pretension, stuffiness
swelling: 4 bump, corn, knob, lump, node, nurl, sore, wale, welt **5** blain, bulge, edema, gnarl, knurl, ridge, surge **6** bruise, bunion, injury, nodule, oedema **7** blister **8** dilation, increase **9** contusion, expansion,

inflation, puffiness **10** distention, prominence
reducer: **3** ice **6** ice bag **7** ice pack
swell with __: **5** pride
swelter: **4** bake, boil, cook, heat, wilt **5** broil, roast, sweat **6** scorch **8** humidity, perspire
sweltering: **3** hot **4** warm **5** close, fiery, humid **6** baking, red-hot, steamy, sticky, stuffy, sultry, sweaty, toasty, torrid **7** airless, burning, stewing, summery **8** broiling, ovenlike, sizzling, stifling, tropical **9** scorching **10** equatorial
Swenson: **3** May **4** Inga
swept: **4** neat, tidy **5** clean **7** in order
starter: **4** back, wind
Swept Away (1984 song)
artist: Diana Ross
swerve: **3** dip, yaw, zag, zig **4** bend, duck, skew, skid, slew, slue, tack, turn, vary, veer, wind **5** lurch, sheer, shift, slant, swing, waver, wince **6** careen, divert, recoil, slough **7** deflect, deviate, diverge **8** sheer off, sideslip, sidestep **9** turn aside
swift: **4** bird, fast **5** apace, brief, brisk, fleet, hasty, quick, rapid **6** abrupt, clever, flying, nimble, prompt, pronto, racing, snappy, speedy, sudden, winged **7** cursory, express, flat-out, hurried, instant **8** cracking, full tilt, headlong, meteoric, spanking **9** breakneck, galloping, lightning, posthaste, rapid-fire, whirlwind **10** double-time, hypersonic, short-lived, supersonic, ultrasonic, unexpected
combining form: **5** tachy-
ender: **4** ness
__ swift: **7** chimney
Swift: **3** car, Kay, Tom **4** auto **5** David **6** Suzuki **8** Jonathan **10** automobile
Swift, Jonathan: **6** writer **7** British **8** satirist
colleague: Alexander Pope, Richard Steele
creature: **5** Yahoo
work: Drapier's Letters
Gulliver's Travels
A Modest Proposal
The Tale of a Tub
swiftly: **3** PDQ **4** ASAP, fast, stat **5** apace **6** presto, pronto **7** briefly, flat out, fleetly, hastily, in a rush, in haste, quickly, rapidly **8** full tilt, in a flash, in a hurry, in a jiffy, in no time, on the fly, on the run, pell-mell, promptly, right now, right off, speedily, suddenly **9** forthwith, hurriedly, instantly, like a shot, posthaste, right away, summarily **10** in high gear
swiftness: **4** pace **5** haste, hurry, speed **8** alacrity, celerity, dispatch, rapidity, velocity **9** fleetness, quickness **10** expedition
Swifty: **5** Lazar
swig: **4** belt, chug, gulp, slug **5** draft, drink, quaff, snort **6** guzzle, imbibe **7** swallow **8** mouthful, toss down
quick ~: **4** belt **5** snort
small ~: **3** sip, tot **4** dram
swill: **4** chug, gulp, slop, swig **5** dregs, offal, quaff, waste **6** guzzle, liquid, refuse **7** garbage, hogwash, rubbish, swallow
eater: **3** hog, pig, sow **4** boar
swim: **3** dip **4** dive **5** bathe, crawl, float **6** paddle **8** skin-dive, take a dip **9** dog paddle, freestyle, scuba-dive **10** backstroke, keep afloat, sidestroke
alternative: **4** sink
brief ~: **3** dip
competition: **4** meet
ender: **4** suit, wear
make one's head ~: **5** amaze **6** dazzle **7** impress
place to ~: **3** gym, sea **4** lake, pond, pool, the Y, YMCA, YWCA **5** beach, ocean, river **6** lagoon, stream **8** seashore
with the tide: **4** cope **5** adapt **6** adjust
swim __: **3** fin **4** mask
__ swim: **5** in the
swim against the __: **4** tide
swimmer: **4** Otto **5** Dyken, Ender, Evans, Gould, Spitz **6** Biondi, Crabbe, Fraser, Phelps
Australian ~: **5** Gould **6** Fraser
German ~: **4** Otto **5** Ender
playful ~: **4** seal **5** otter
see also fish
swimming: **5** sport **6** afloat, natant
combining form: **4** nect- **5** necto-
convenience: **6** cabana
gear: **3** fin **4** mask **5** wings **7** goggles **10** water wings
go ~: **5** bathe
hazard: **5** cramp, shark **9** jellyfish
in it: **4** rich **5** flush **7** wealthy **8** affluent **9** well-fixed **10** well-heeled
motion: **5** crawl **10** backstroke
spot: **4** hole, lake, pond, pool **5** beach, river **6** stream **8** seashore
unit: **3** lap
swimming __: **4** hole, pool
swimmingly: **4** fine, well **5** great **6** easily **7** handily, happily, quickly, readily **8** adroitly, laudably, smoothly, very well **9** as planned, favorably, hands down **10** skillfully
swimming pool
problem: **5** algae
site: **3** gym, spa **4** the Y, YMCA, YWCA **6** resort
sound: **5** plash **6** splash
Swimming Pool, The
author: Mary Roberts Rinehart
swim wear: **6** bikini, trunks **7** maillot **8** one-piece, two-piece
brand: **6** Speedo
part: **3** bra
Swinburne, Algernon: **4** poet **7** British
work: Astrophel
Atalanta in Calydon
Dolores
Hymn to Proserpine
swindle: **2** do **3** con, gyp, job, rob **4** bilk, burn, clip, dupe, flam, flay, fool, gull, have, hoax, hose, nick, rook, ruse, scam, sham, skin, take, trim, work **5** bunco, cheat, cozen, feint, fraud, gouge, mulct, pluck, set up, shaft, steal, stiff, sting, theft, trick **6** chisel, chouse, con job, deceit, diddle, dupery, euchre, extort, fleece, humbug, hustle, outwit, racket, rip off, sucker, take in **7** con game, deceive, defraud, fast one, finagle, sandbag, snow job **8** artifice, flimflam, hoodwink, outsmart, thievery **9** bamboozle, deception, dirty pool, extortion, four-flush, imposture, shakedown, shell game, victimize **10** illegality, run a game on, subterfuge
swindler: **4** rook **5** cheat, crook, fraud, ganef, gonef, gonif, knave, quack, rogue, shark, sharp, thief **6** bad guy, conman, dodger, forger, goniff, gouger, rascal, rip-off, robber **7** grifter, hustler, sharper, sharpie **8** chiseler, imposter, impostor, operator **9** absconder, charlatan, con artist, defrauder, inveigler, scoundrel, trickster **10** mountebank
take: **5** grift
swine: **3** cad, cur, hog, pig, sow **4** boar, boor, Kele, lout, toad **5** Bazna, beast, brute, Duroc, Hezuo, louse, piggy, shoat, shote, shott, stock, Welsh **6** animal, barrow, Jinhua, Minzhu, Mukota, oinker, piggie, piglet, porker, savage, tusker **7** bounder, grunter, Iberian, Lacombe, lowlife, Meishan, Mong Cai, peccary, Suffolk **8** babirusa, blighter, Hereford, Landrace, Pietrain, Potbelly, Tamworth **9** Berkshire, Hampshire, razorback, scoundrel, Yorkshire
combining form: **3** hyo-
ender: **3** pox **4** herd
food: **4** slop **5** swill
little ~: **3** pig **4** gilt **5** shoat, shote, shott **6** piggie, piglet
place: **3** pen, sty **4** farm **6** pigpen, pigsty
swine __: **3** flu
swing: **3** wag **4** beat, flap, hang, jazz, keel, lilt, reel, rock, sway, toss, tour, trip, turn, vary, veer, wave **5** curve, dance, flail, guide, lunge, lurch, meter, music, pivot, reach, shake, shift, sling, sweep, tempo, twirl, wheel, whirl **6** change, dangle, direct, leeway, manage, rhythm, rotate, swerve, swivel, travel, wabble, waggle, wangle, wobble **7** cadence, cadency, librate, measure, revolve, suspend, vibrate, work out **8** flourish, free hand, latitude, undulate **9** fluctuate, influence, negotiate, oscillate, vacillate **10** ebb and flow, equivocate
around: **4** slew, slue, spin, turn **5** avert, pivot, whirl **6** slough, swivel
by: **4** call **5** visit **6** stop in
ersatz ~: **4** tire
half a ~: **3** fro
loose: **4** flap, hang **6** dangle
music: **4** jive
partner: **4** sway
place for a ~: **4** lawn, limb, park, tree, yard **5** bough, porch **10** playground
ready to ~: **5** at bat
swing __: **3** leg **4** door, loan **5** music, shift
Swing __: **4** Time
Swing __, Sweet Chariot: **3** Low
Swing and sway bandleader: **4** Kaye
swinger: **4** roué **5** flirt, Romeo **6** golfer, hepcat **7** Don Juan **8** Lothario **9** jet-setter, libertine **10** profligate
Swinger: **3** car **4** auto **5** Dodge
swinging: **5** loose **6** lively **9** pendulous
swinging __: **4** door
Swinging on a Star
beast: **3** pig **4** fish, mule **6** monkey
composer: Johnny Burke, Jimmy Van Heusen
Swing Time (1936 film): **7** musical
cast: Fred Astaire, Ginger Rogers
music: Dorothy Fields, Jerome Kern
studio: **3** RKO
swinish: **6** greedy **7** hoggish, loutish
remark: **4** oink
Swinton, Tilda: **7** actress
film: Michael Clayton (2007, AA)
Orlando (1992)
swipe: **3** cop, hit, nab, rap, rob **4** bash, blow, clip, cuff, gibe, glom, hook, jibe, lick, lift, loot, nick, slam, slap, sock, swat, take, wipe **5** clout, filch, heist, knock, lunge, pinch, smack, sneak, sneer, steal, taunt **6** assume, pilfer, pocket, rip off, snitch, strike, thieve, wallop **7** lash out, purloin **8** liberate, shoplift, uppercut **10** run off with
starter: **4** side
take a ~ at: **3** dis **4** swat **5** decry **6** impugn, insult, malign **7** lash out, put down
swirl: **4** boil, coil, curl, eddy, reel, roil, roll, turn, wash, wave **5** churn, crimp, snake, surge, twirl, whirl, whorl **6** bustle, swoosh, tumult, unrest **7** agitate, sinuate, tempest, turmoil **8** disorder, gyration **9** circulate, confusion, maelstrom, whirlpool **10** spin around
swirling: **6** roiled **9** turbulent
swish: **3** lap, rod **4** posh, tony, wash, whiz **5** grand, plush, ritzy, smart, sound, stick, swank, swell, toney, whisk, woosh **6** classy, deluxe, rustle, sizzle, trendy, whoosh, with-it **7** elegant, stylish **8** flourish, rustling, sibilate **9** exclusive, sumptuous, whooshing **10** sibilation
Swiss: **4** font **5** steak **6** alpine, cheese **8** typeface
like ~ cheese: **5** holey
partner: **3** ham, rye
see also Switzerland
Swiss __: **4** Alps **5** chard, Guard, steak **6** cheese, muslin
Swiss army __: **5** knife
Swiss Family Robinson: **4** book
author: Johann David Wyss
character: **5** Emily, Fritz **6** Ernest
dog: **4** Duke, Turk
Swit: **7** Loretta
costar: **4** Alda, Farr
role: **5** nurse **7** Hot Lips **8** Houlihan
sitcom: **4** MASH
switch: **3** rod, wag **4** limb, ruse, swap, swop, tack, turn, veer, whip **5** shift, shunt, stick, trade **6** button, change, cudgel, divert, ferule, punish, rotate, toggle **7** convert, replace, reverse **8** exchange, modulate, reversal, variance **9** about-

face, alternate, change off, inversion, oscillate, rearrange, take turns, transpose, turnabout **10** alteration, flagellate, substitute
activator: **4** clap
asleep at the ~: **3** lax **5** slack **6** remiss **9** negligent
bait and ~: **4** scam **7** con game
electric ~: **5** relay **6** dimmer
ender: **4** back, eroo **5** blade, board
hit the ~: **4** kill, stop **5** douse, light **6** kindle, turn on **7** turn off **8** activate
position: **2** on **3** off
sides: **6** defect
switch __: **3** box, off **5** gears **6** hitter
__ switch: **6** dimmer, toggle
Switch (CBS drama)
cast: Eddie Albert (Frank McBride) Charlie Callas (Malcolm Argos) Sharon Gless (Maggie) Robert Wagner (Pete Ryan)
switchback: **4** road **5** curve
switchblade: **4** shiv **5** knife
switchboard
employee: **8** operator
letters: **3** ext.
switcheroo: **6** change **8** reversal
pull a ~: **9** back-pedal
Switching Channels (1988 film)
cast: Ned Beatty, Christopher Reeve, Burt Reynolds, Kathleen Turner
Swithin: **5** saint
Switzerland: **6** nation **7** country
Alp: **4** Jura, Zupo **5** Eiger **6** Castor **7** Bernina **8** Jungfrau **9** Mont Blanc, Monte Rosa **10** Matterhorn, St. Gotthard
archeological site: **4** Biel
artist: **4** Klee
bovine: **6** Herens **9** Simmental
cabin: **6** chalet
canton: **3** Uri, Zug **4** Bern, Jura, Vaud **5** Berne **6** Aargau, Geneva, Glarus, Schwyz, Ticino, Valais, Zurich **7** Lucerne, Thurgau **8** Fribourg, Obwalden **9** Neuchâtel, Nidwalden, Saint Gall, Solothurn
capital: **4** Bern **5** Berne
cheese: **7** Gruyère, sapsago **8** Emmental **9** Emmenthal, Jarlsberg **10** Emmentaler
chocolatier: **5** Lindt
city: **3** Zug **4** Sion **5** Basel, Basle, Vevey **6** Geneva, Genève, Zurich **8** Lausanne
conductor: **8** Ansermet
educator: **6** Piaget
export: **5** clock, watch **6** cheese **9** chocolate
lake: **3** Zug **4** Biel, Thun **6** Bienne, Brienz, Geneva, Lugano, Zurich **7** Lucerne **8** Maggiore **9** Neuchâtel
language: **6** French, German **7** Italian
legendary hero: **4** Tell
mathematician: **5** Euler
money: **5** franc, rappe **7** centime
mountain: **3** alp
natural historian: **6** Gesner
neighbor: **5** Italy **6** France **7** Austria, Germany
Nobelist in Chemistry: **5** Ernst **6** Karrer, Werner **7** Ruzicka **8** Wüthrich
Nobelist in Literature: **9** Spitteler
Nobelist in Medicine: **4** Hess **5** Arber **6** Kocher, Müller **10** Reichstein **11** Zinkernagel
Nobelist in Peace: **5** Gobat **6** Dunant **8** Ducommun
Nobelist in Physics: **6** Müller, Rohrer
physicist: **6** Müller, Rohrer **7** Piccard
pianist: **6** Cortot **7** Fischer
poet: **6** Keller **9** Spitteler
province: **6** canton
psychologist: **3** Neo **6** Piaget
river: **3** Aar **4** Aare **5** Reuss, Rhine, Rhone
ski resort: **5** Davos **6** Gstaad
state: **6** canton
strain: **5** yodel, yodle
waterfall: **6** Simmen
writer: **5** Meyer, Ramuz, Spyri **6** Frisch, Piaget
swivel: **3** pan **4** jink, look, roll, spin, turn, veer **5** hinge, joint, pivot, swing, twist, wheel, whirl **6** rotate **7** librate, revolve **9** oscillate, pirouette
swivel __: **5** chair
swizzle: **4** stir
ingredient: **3** rum
swizzle __: **5** stick
Swoboda: **3** Ron
swollen: **5** puffy, tumid **6** turgid **7** bloated, bulging **8** enlarged, inflamed, inflated **9** distended, tumescent
'S Wonderful
composer: George Gershwin, Ira Gershwin
swoon: **5** faint, plotz **6** go limp **7** crumple, pass out, syncope **8** black out, fall over, keel over
swoop: **3** dip, fly **4** dive, drop, fall, raid, rush, sink **5** slide, stoop **6** go down, plunge, pounce **7** descend, descent, plummet **8** downrush, nosedive
down on: **4** dive **6** ambush, pounce, snap up, waylay
up: **4** grab **5** scoop, seize **6** snatch
swoosh: **5** swirl
Nike ~: **4** logo
Swoosie: **5** Kurtz
swop
see swap
__ Swope: **6** Putney
sword: **4** épée, fern, foil **5** blade, knife, point, saber, sabre **6** anlace, cutlas, rapier, Toledo **7** anelace, bayonet, cutlass **8** claymore, scimitar, scimiter **9** cold steel, Excalibur
combining form: **4** xiph- **5** xiphi-, xipho-
ender: **4** bill, fish, play, tail
fencing ~: **4** épée, foil **5** saber **6** rapier
fight: **4** duel, epée **7** fencing
handle: **4** haft, hilt
medieval ~: **5** estoc
name meaning ~: **6** Brenda
short ~: **6** dagger
Turkish ~: **5** kilij
wield a ~: **5** lunge, parry, slash **6** pierce
Sword Blades and Poppy Seed
author: Amy Lowell
swordfish: **6** entrée
constellation: **6** Dorado
Swordfish (2001 film)
cast: Halle Berry, Don Cheadle, Hugh Jackman, John Travolta
director: Dominic Sena
Sword in the Stone, The
author: T.H. White
bird: **3** owl
dog: **5** Tiger **6** Talbot
swords
cross ~: **4** buck, defy, duel, spar, tilt **5** argue, clash, fight **6** attack, battle, bicker, combat, debate, engage, oppose, resist, tussle **7** contend, contest, dispute, quarrel, wrangle **8** conflict, confront, disagree, do battle, struggle **9** duke it out, have it out, lock horns, slug it out
sword-shaped: **6** ensate
swordsman: **5** blade **6** fencer
swordsmanship: **4** épée **5** kendo **7** fencing
sworn: **6** avowed **7** pledged
statement: **3** vow **4** oath
sworn __: **5** enemy
sybarite: **4** roué **7** playboy **8** hedonist, rakehell **9** bon vivant, libertine **10** voluptuary
delight: **4** ease **8** pleasure
sybaritic: **9** dissolute, epicurean, luxurious
sybaritism: **6** excess **7** license, revelry **8** hedonism **9** decadence, depravity **10** indulgence
Sybil: **4** Leek **7** Danning **9** Thorndike
sycamore: **4** tree
Sychaeus
wife: **4** Dido
sycophancy: **6** praise **8** flattery **9** adulation, servility
sycophant: **3** fan **5** leech, slave, toady **6** fawner, flunky, lackey, minion, puppet, yes man **7** doormat, flunkey, groupie, lacquey **8** adulator, courtier, groveler, hanger-on, kowtower, parasite, servitor **9** flatterer **10** bootlicker, handshaker, politician
answer: **3** yes
sycophantic: **6** menial **7** fawning, slavish **8** toadying, unctuous **9** groveling
sycophants: **6** claque **7** fan club **9** entourage, following
Sycorax: **4** moon
planet: **6** Uranus
Syd: **4** Hoff **7** Barrett, Chaplin
Sydney: **4** city, port, town **5** Penny, Smith **7** Brenner, Chaplin, Pollack
locale: **3** NSW **9** Australia
__ Sydow: **6** Max von
Sykes: **5** Peter, Wanda
Sylk-E. __: **4** Fyne
syllable
last ~: **6** ultima
next-to-last ~: **6** penult
third-to-last ~: **10** antepenult
syllabub: **7** dessert
ingredient: **4** wine **5** cider, cream
syllabus: **4** list, plan, text **6** précis, sketch **7** program, summary **10** prospectus
syllogism: **5** logic **9** reasoning
word: **4** ergo
words: **4** is to
syllogistics: **5** logic
syllogize: **6** reason
sylph: **5** nymph **6** sprite
__ Sylphides: **3** Les
sylphlike: **4** slim **5** light **6** slight **7** gracile, slender, willowy **8** graceful
sylva: **8** woodland
Sylva: **7** Koscina
sylvan: **5** bosky, rural, woody **6** rustic, wooded, woodsy **8** arboreal, forested, pastoral **9** arboreous
area: **5** glade, grove, trees, woods **6** forest
deity: **3** Pan **4** faun **5** satyr
Sylvan historian, to Keats: **3** urn
Sylvania: **2** TV **5** TV set **10** television
alternative: ***see*** electronics company
sylvanite: **3** ore **7** mineral
Sylvester: **3** cat **4** pope **7** pontiff **8** Stallone
to Tweety: **3** tat **8** puddy tat
Sylvester and the Magic Pebble
author: William Steig
Sylvia: **4** Syms **5** Miles, Plath **6** ballet, Porter, Sidney, Warner **7** Delibes
Sylvia's Mother (1972 song)
artist: Dr. Hook
Sylvie and Bruno
author: Lewis Carroll
__ Sylvius: **6** Aeneas
Symaethis
son: **4** Acis
symbiosis: **5** union **7** benefit **10** dependence
symbol: **4** icon, ikon, logo, mark, note, sign **5** badge, crest, eikon, image, index, model, motif, stamp, token, totem **6** design, device, emblem, figure, letter **7** imprint, insigne, numeral, pattern, regalia **8** colophon, hallmark, heraldry, ideogram, insignia, metaphor, standard **9** attribute, character, indicator, trademark **10** denotation, embodiment, indication
__ symbol: **3** UPC **5** peace **6** status
symbolic: **5** token **7** nominal **10** denotative, emblematic, figurative, indicatory, suggestive
symbolize: **4** mean, show **6** denote, embody, imbody, mirror **7** betoken, connote, express, signify, suggest **8** indicate, stand for **9** adumbrate, epitomize, exemplify, personify, represent **10** illustrate
Symington: **3** Stu **6** Stuart
symmetrical: **4** trim **5** equal **7** regular, shapely, uniform **8** balanced
not ~: **4** alop, awry **7** crooked **9** irregular, out of line **10** unbalanced
symmetry: **4** form **5** order, shape **6** rhythm **7** balance, harmony **8** equality, evenness, neatness **9** agreement, equipoise **10** conformity, proportion, regularity
sympathetic: **4** easy, kind, open, soft, warm **5** close, noble, sweet **6** benign, caring, chummy, clubby, decent, genial, gentle, humane, kindly, loving, polite, tender **7** affable, amiable, clement,

cordial, helpful, lenient, likable, sparing, tactful, tuned in **8** all heart, amenable, amicable, friendly, gracious, intimate, merciful, outgoing, pleasant, sociable, tolerant **9** agreeable, concerned, congenial, convivial, fraternal, receptive, sensitive, simpatico, vicarious **10** altruistic, benevolent, buddy-buddy, neighborly, responsive, solicitous, supportive
be ~: **4** care **6** listen **9** empathize
not ~: **4** cold **5** stony **6** stoney **8** uncaring **9** impatient
sympathize: **4** pity **5** agree **7** ache for, comfort, console, feel for **8** bleed for, relate to, side with **9** empathize **10** understand
sympathizer: **6** backer, patron **8** partisan **9** supporter **10** benefactor
sympathy: **3** aid **4** pity **5** heart, mercy, unity **6** accord, lenity, liking, pathos, regard, solace, warmth **7** comfort, emotion, rapport, thought **8** affinity, feelings, kindness, lenience **9** agreement, tolerance **10** compassion, connection
words of ~: **5** I care
sympathy __: **6** strike
symphonic: **7** lyrical **10** harmonious, orchestral
movement: **5** largo, rondo **7** prelude
symphonic __: **4** band, poem
Symphonic Ode
composer: Aaron Copland
Symphonie Espagnole
composer: Édouard Lalo
Symphonie Fantastique
composer: Hector Berlioz
symphony: **4** opus, work **5** music, piece **9** orchestra
__ Symphony: **3** Toy **4** Linz **5** Clock, Dante, Faust, Paris, Short **6** Choral, Eroica, Prague, Simple, Spring, Tragic **7** Haffner, Italian, Jupiter, Kaddish, Manfred, October, Unbegun
Symphony in Black
artist: Erté
Symphony of a Thousand
composer: Gustav Mahler
Symphony of Psalms
composer: Igor Stravinsky
Symphony, The
author: Sidney Lanier
symposium: **4** talk **5** forum **7** meeting **8** assembly **10** conference, discussion, round table
Symposium
subject of Plato's ~: **4** Eros
symptom: **4** hint, mark, sign **5** token **7** warning **8** evidence **9** precursor **10** indication
ender: **4** atic
symptomatic: **10** indicative, suggestive
Syms: **6** Sylvia
synagogue: **4** shul **5** schul **6** temple
attender: **3** Jew
container: **3** ark
language: **6** Hebrew
official: **5** rabbi, rebbe **6** cantor, chazan
platform: **4** bema
platforms: **6** bemata
prayer: **5** shema
scroll: **4** Tora **5** Torah
vestment: **5** ephod
sync: **6** kilter **7** harmony **9** agreement
be in ~: **4** jibe **5** agree **6** accord **8** coincide
get in ~: **5** adapt **6** adjust, attune **10** coordinate
in ~: **4** same **7** fitting, matched **8** suitable, together **9** accordant, agreeable, congruent, consonant, simpatico **10** coinciding, compatible, concurrent, consistent, harmonious, like-minded
out of ~: **3** off
__-sync: **3** lip **5** out-of
synch: **6** accord **7** harmony **9** harmonize **10** coordinate
__-synch: **3** lip **5** out-of
synchronal: **9** concerted, confluent **10** coexistent, coexisting, coincident, coinciding, collateral, compatible, concurrent, consistent, convergent, converging, harmonious, incidental, like-minded
Synchronicity II (1983 song)
artist: Police
synchronous __: **5** orbit
Syncopated Clock, The
composer: Leroy Anderson
syncopation: **6** rhythm
syncope: **5** faint, swoon
syndicate: **3** mob **4** bloc, gang, ring **5** board, chain, group, merge, trust, union **6** cartel **7** combine, company, council, society **8** megacorp, monopoly **9** gangsters **10** federation, monopolize, underworld
crime ~ head: **3** don **4** capo **9** godfather
syndicated prose: **6** column
syndication
air in ~: **5** rerun
syndrome: **6** malady **7** ailment, complex **8** disorder, sickness **9** complaint, condition, infirmity
__ Syndrome, The: **5** China
syne: **3** ago **5** since
synecdoche: **5** trope
synergize: **8** interact **9** cooperate
Synge, John: **5** Irish **10** playwright
work: Playboy of the Western World
Riders to the Sea
Syngman: **4** Rhee
synod: **7** council **8** assembly, conclave, ecclesia
synonym
opposite: **3** ant. **7** antonym
synonymist: **5** Roget
synonymous: **4** like, same **5** alike, equal **9** identical **10** equivalent, two of a kind
synopsis: **5** brief, recap, table **6** digest, précis, résumé, review, sketch **7** capsule, epitome, outline, pandect, rundown, summary **8** abstract **10** abridgment, compendium, highlights, prospectus, tabulation
synopsize: **5** recap, sum up **6** digest, sketch **7** outline **8** abstract, boil down, condense **9** capsulize, summarize, telescope
synopsized: **3** cut **4** firm **5** dense, short, solid, terse, thick **6** cut off, gnomic, packed **7** capsule, compact, concise, crammed, cutback, cut down, reduced, stuffed **8** abridged, cut short, digested, squeezed, succinct **9** compacted, condensed, curtailed, shortened **10** abstracted, compressed, summarized
syntax: **7** grammar
unit: **4** word **5** morph **6** phrase **8** sentence **9** paragraph
synthesis: **5** blend, union, unity **6** fusion **7** amalgam **8** compound, pastiche **9** composite, formation, immixture
antithesis and ~: **5** logic
synthesize: **4** fuse, join, make **5** blend, merge, unify, unite **7** combine **8** coalesce **9** integrate **10** amalgamate
__ synthesizer: **4** Moog
__ synthetase: **3** RNA
synthetic: **4** fake, mock, sham **5** bogus, false, phony, quasi **6** ersatz, phoney, pseudo **7** plastic **8** rational, spurious **9** imitation, simulated, unnatural **10** artificial, fabricated
fabric: **4** poly **5** Arnel, Dynel, Kodel, Lycra, nylon, Orlon, rayon **6** Ban-Lon, Dacron, Kevlar **7** Gore-Tex, spandex **9** polyester
synthetic __: **5** fiber **6** rubber
Syr.
see Syria
Syracuse: **4** city, town
athletes: **9** Orangemen
city near ~: **5** Utica **6** Oneida
conference: **7** Big East
lake near ~: **6** Oneida
locale: **7** New York
team color: **6** orange
to Buffalo dir.: **3** WSW
Syria: **6** nation **7** country
ancient ~: **4** Aram
ancient city in ~: **4** Ebla
ancient kingdom in ~: **4** Moab
bovine: **6** Baladi, Jaulan
capital: **8** Damascus
city: **4** Hama, Homs **6** Aleppo **8** Damascus
leader: **5** Assad
money: **7** piaster, piastre
mountain: **6** Hermon
neighbor: **4** Irak, Iraq **5** Egypt **6** Israel, Jordan, Turkey **7** Lebanon
resident: **4** Arab **5** Druse, Druze
shrub: **5** retem
Syrian __ Republic: **4** Arab
Syriana (2005 film)
cast: George Clooney, Matt Damon
syringe: **4** hypo
syrinx: **4** wind **7** panpipe
syrup: **7** topping
alternative: **5** honey
brand: **4** Eggo, Karo **8** Log Cabin
flavoring: **5** maple
source: **3** sap **4** corn **5** maple, sorgo **6** sorgho
sugar ~: **5** glaze
__ syrup: **4** corn **5** cough, maple
syrupy: **5** mushy, sweet, thick **6** sticky **7** honeyed, maudlin, mawkish, viscose, viscous **8** romantic **9** oversweet **10** saccharine
system: **3** ism, way **4** form, mode, plan, rule, unit **5** means, order, setup **6** custom, hookup, manner, method, policy, regime, scheme, theory **7** complex, machine, network, pattern, process, red tape, routine **8** ideology, practice, strategy, totality **9** machinery, mechanism, operation, procedure, structure, technique **10** philosophy
starter: **3** eco
__ system: **4** farm, star **5** buddy, honor, merit, point, quota, solar **6** expert, immune, metric, spoils **7** decimal, exhaust, nervous, support, turnkey
systematic: **4** neat, tidy **6** formal **7** logical, orderly, precise, regular **8** accurate, coherent, habitual, methodic **9** efficient, organized
systematize: **4** plan, sort **5** array, group, order **6** codify **7** arrange, dispose **8** classify, organize, regulate, tabulate **9** establish, institute, methodize
systems __: **7** analyst
systems go, all: **3** A-OK **5** ready **8** prepared
S.Z.: **6** Sakall
Szechuan pan: **3** wok
Szell, George: **9** conductor
Szigeti, Joseph: **9** Hungarian, violinist
Szilard: **3** Leo
Szwarc: **7** Jeannot

T

2
mult. by ~: 3 dbl.
wks. off: 3 vac.
x 4: 5 board
2%: 4 milk
2 Become 1 (1997 song)
artist: Spice Girls
2 Legit 2 Quit (1991 song)
artist: M.C. Hammer
2-pointer, easy: 4 dunk
#2: 4 veep 6 veepee
$2 window action: 5 wager
3 A.M. Eternal (1991 song)
artist: KLF
3Com Park player: 5 Niner
3-D
exam: 3 MRI
graph line: 5 z-axis
quality: 5 depth
___-3 fatty acid: 5 omega
3-in-___ Oil: 3 One
3 Men and a Baby (1987 film)
cast: Ted Danson, Steve Guttenberg, Tom Selleck, Nancy Travis
director: Leonard Nimoy
3 Musketeers: 3 bar 5 candy 8 candy bar 9 chocolate
alternative: *see* candy brand
3 P.M. in a monastery: 5 nones
3rd Rock from the Sun (NBC sitcom)
cast: Jane Curtin (Dr. Mary Albright)
Kristen Johnston (Sally Solomon)
John Lithgow (Dick Solomon)
French Stewart (Harry Solomon)
3 Women (1977 film)
cast: Shelley Duvall, Sissy Spacek
director: Robert Altman
3:10 to Yuma (2007 film)
cast: Christian Bale, Russell Crowe, Peter Fonda
10: 7 sawbuck
10 (1979 film)
cast: Julie Andrews, Bo Derek, Dudley Moore
director: Blake Edwards
theme: 6 Bolero
10 ___ or less: 5 items
___-10: 3 Pac
10cc
homeland: England
song: I'm Not in Love (1975)
The Things We Do for Love (1977)
10-cent
former ~ coin: 5 disme
10K: 4 race
10 Lb. Penalty
author: Dick Francis
10 Things I Hate About You (1999 film)
cast: Heath Ledger, Julia Stiles
10-year-old: 5 'tween
12: 7 boxcars
dozen: 3 gro. 5 gross
every ~ months: 4 yrly. 6 yearly
___ 12: 4 Adam
___-12: 6 carbon
12 Angry Men (1957 film)
cast: Martin Balsam, Ed Begley, Lee J. Cobb, Henry Fonda, Jack Klugman, E.G. Marshall, Jack Warden
director: Sidney Lumet
12-pack: 6 carton
12-year-old: 5 'tween
13 ___ Madeleine: 3 Rue
___ 13: 6 Apollo
___-13: 6 carbon
13 Days to Glory subject: 5 Alamo
13 Going on 30 (2004 film)
cast: Jennifer Garner, Mark Ruffalo
13th Warrior, The (1999 film)
cast: Antonio Banderas, Diane Venora
20%: 5 fifth
20-mule team load: 5 borax
21
exceed: 4 bust
over ~: 5 of age
21 (2008 film)
cast: Kate Bosworth, Laurence Fishburne, Kevin Spacey
___ 21: 7 Century
23 ___: 6 Skidoo
24
every ~ hours: 4 a day 5 daily
horas: 3 día
sheets: 5 quire
24/7 (1999 song)
artist: Kevon Edmonds
24 (Fox drama)
cast: Anil Kapoor (Omar Jassan)
Mary Lynn Rajskub (Chloe O'Brian)
Kiefer Sutherland (Jack Bauer)
Annie Wersching (Renee Walker)
24-hour ___: 3 flu
24-karat: 4 pure 7 optimum
24-pack: 6 carton
25 or 6 to 4 (1970 song)
artist: Chicago
26 Miles (1958 song)
artist: Four Preps
27 Dresses (2008 film)
cast: Katherine Heigl, James Marsden
28 Days (2000 film)
cast: Sandra Bullock, Diane Ladd, Viggo Mortensen
30 Manhattan East
author: Hillary Waugh
30 Rock (NBC sitcom)
cast: Alec Baldwin (Jack Donaghy)
Tina Fey (Liz Lemon)
Jane Krakowski (Jenna Maroney)
Jack McBrayer (Kenneth Parcell)
Tracy Morgan (Tracy Jordan)
creator: Tina Fey
35mm: 6 camera
setting: 5 f-stop
35 Up (1991 film)
director: Michael Apted
38th-parallel land: 5 Korea
38 Special
lead singer: Donnie Van Zant
song: Caught Up in You (1982)
Second Chance (1989)
39 Steps, The (1935 film)
cast: Madeleine Carroll, Robert Donat
director: Alfred Hitchcock
___ 200: 5 Dutch
227 (NBC sitcom)
cast: Marla Gibbs (Mary Jenkins)
Jackée Harry (Sandra Clark)
Alaina Reed-Hall (Rose Lee Holloway)
Hal Williams (Lester Jenkins)
___ 235: 7 uranium
237 milliliters: 3 cup
___ 238: 7 uranium
___ 239: 7 uranium
1040: 4 form 7 IRS form, tax form
completer: 5 filer
data: 6 income
figure: 3 net
form ~ deduction: 4 dues
form ~ ID: 3 SSN
imprinter: 3 GPO
submitter: 5 filer
1055 conqueror: 6 Norman
1300: 5 one p.m.
2001: A Space Odyssey (1968 film)
beast: 3 ape
cast: Keir Dullea, Gary Lockwood
computer: 3 Hal
director: Stanley Kubrick
studio: 3 MGM
2010 (1984 film)
cast: John Lithgow, Helen Mirren, Roy Scheider
director: Peter Hyams
20/20 (ABC news)
host: Hugh Downs
2200
about ~ pounds: 5 tonne
3000 Miles to Graceland (2001 film)
cast: Kevin Costner, Courteney Cox, Kurt Russell, Christian Slater
3280.8 ft.: 3 kil.
10,000 Maniacs
song: Because the Night (1993)
More Than This (1997)
vocalists: Natalie Merchant, Mary Ramsey
10,000 meters: 4 ten K
$10,000/25,000 Pyramid, The
genre: game show
host: Dick Clark, Bill Cullen, Donny Osmond
20,000 Leagues Under the Sea (1954 film)
captain: 4 Nemo
cast: Kirk Douglas, Paul Lukas, James Mason
seal: 4 Esme
T: 5 shirt 6 letter
followers: 3 UVW 4 UVWX 5 UVWXY
in phonetic alphabet: 5 Tango
model ~: 4 Ford
preceders: 3 QRS 4 PQRS 5 OPQRS
to a ~: 4 well 6 just so 7 exactly 8 laudably, very well, worthily 9 correctly, just right, on the nose, perfectly, precisely 10 accurately, flawlessly
to Morse: 3 dah 4 dash
use a ~ square: 5 aline
T ___: 4 and E, cell
T ___ Tom: 4 as in
T-___: 3 bar, Man 4 bill, bone
T-___ lift: 3 bar
T-___ steak: 4 bone
T. ___ Pickens: 5 Boone
T. ___ Price: 4 Rowe
___ T: 3 to a
'T' ___ Trespass: 5 Is for
'T' ___ Undertow: 5 Is for
___-T: 3 Ice
Ta: 4 elem. 7 element 8 tantalum
73 for ~: 4 at. no.
Ta-___-Boom-De-Ré: 4 Ra-Ra
TA: 4 aide, asst.
superior: 4 prof 9 professor
tab: 3 IOU, tag 4 bill, chit, cost, flag, flap, list, name, rank, rate, sort, stop 5 check, label, price, score, title 6 amount, charge, choose, credit, marker, outlay, select, tariff, ticket 7 account, bar bill, earmark, invoice, specify, sticker 8 bookmark, identify, indicate, nominate 9 appendage, liability, reckoning, recognize, statement 10 projection
pick up the ~: 4 foot 5 treat 6 defray 9 subsidize
put on one's ~: 3 owe 6 charge 8 purchase
settle the ~: 3 pay 5 pay up
use the ~ key: 6 indent
___-tab: 4 pull
Tab: 3 key, pop 4 cola, soda 6 Hunter 9 soft drink
alternative: *see* soft drink
neighbor: 5 Shift
tabard: 4 cape, coat 6 jacket
Tabard Inn serving: 3 ale
tabaret: 6 fabric 8 material
Tabasco: 5 sauce
quality: 4 zest 5 spice
see also Spanish
tabbouleh: 5 salad
tabby: 3 cat, pet 4 puss 5 felid 6 feline 7 striped 8 brindled 9 grimalkin
sound: 3 mew, pur 4 meow, purr 5 miaou, miaow, miaul
tabernacle: 5 abbey 6 chapel, church, shrine, temple 8 basilica 9 cathedral, sanctuary
singer: 4 alto, bass 5 choir, tenor 7 soprano
Tabitha
brother: 4 Adam
grandma: 6 Endora
table: 3 bar 4 dais, desk, food, list, meal, menu, mesa, roll, slab 5 bench, board, defer, delay, graph, index, stand, waive 6 agenda, buffet, legend, pulpit, put off, record, shelve, spread, upland, vanity 7 console, cuisine, desk top, diagram, dresser, lectern, plateau, summary, suspend 8 appendix, file away, flatland, lay aside, postpone, put aside, put on ice, register, schedule, set aside, synopsis, victuals 9 furniture, inventory, sideboard, tableland, visual aid 10 bill of fare, compendium, gastronomy, pigeonhole, reschedule, statistics
accessory: 4 lamp
at the ~: 6 eating, gaming
cover: 5 cloth, scarf
decoration: 5 doily 6 doyley
d'hôte: 4 fare, food, meal 6 dinner
ender: 3 top 4 land, mate, side, ware 5 cloth, spoon 8 spoonful
follower: 5 spoon

insert: 4 leaf
makeshift ~: 5 spool
material: 3 oak 4 data 8 mahogany
part: 3 leg 4 leaf
place at the ~: 4 seat
prepare the ~: 3 lay, set
put one's cards on the ~: 6 reveal
remove dishes from the ~: 3 bus
round ~: 6 parley, powwow 9 symposium 10 conference
scrap: 3 ort
staple: 4 salt 5 sugar 6 pepper
starter: 4 time, turn, work 5 round
talk: 3 gab, rap 5 prate 6 banter, gabble, gibber, gossip 7 chatter, palaver 8 chin-chin, chitchat, repartee
tea ~: 4 cart
tennis: 4 game 5 sport
TV dinner ~: 4 tray
with folding leaves: 5 tip up
writing ~: 7 rolltop 9 secretary
table __: 3 saw 4 lamp, salt, talk, wine 5 d'hôte, linen, stake, sugar 6 tennis 7 manners
table-__: 3 hop
__ table: 3 bag, bed, end, tax, tea 4 card, head, pool, side, sofa, tray 5 night, on the, poker, snack, stack, tip-up, water 6 bridge, coffee, dining, dinner, gaming, picnic, sewing 7 drawing, folding, gateleg, nesting, Parsons, tilt-top
tableau: 4 view 5 scene 7 picture 8 panorama 9 depiction, spectacle
__-table book: 6 coffee
tablecloth: 6 spread
material: 5 linen 6 damask
tabled: 6 put off 7 abeyant, shelved 8 deferred, set aside 9 postponed, suspended
table-hop: 3 mix 6 hobnob, mingle 7 consort, hang out 9 socialize 10 fraternize
tableland: 4 mesa 5 table 7 plateau
African ~: 5 karoo
tables
attend ~: 5 serve
turn the ~: 5 shift 6 oppose 7 revenge, reverse 9 retaliate
__ tables: 4 wait
tablespoons, sixteen: 3 cup
tablet: 3 pad 4 dose, pill 5 slate 6 sheets, troche 7 capsule, lozenge, memo pad, notepad 8 medicine, memorial, monument, notebook 10 medication, scratch pad
alternative: 6 gelcap
table tennis: 4 game 5 sport
see also Ping Pong
tablets, two: 4 dose 6 dosage
tableware: 4 dish, fork 5 china, forks, glass, knife, spoon 6 dishes, knives, spoons 7 glasses, utensil 8 utensils
tabloid: 3 rag 4 pulp 5 paper 7 journal 9 newspaper
boss: 6 editor
like some ~ headlines: 4 racy 5 lurid 6 risqué 7 graphic 8 shocking 9 low-minded
pages: 3 ads
topic: 3 UFO 5 alien, celeb 6 exposé, gossip

taboo: 3 ban, bar, law 4 don't, no-no, veto 5 magic 6 banned, forbid, outlaw, vetoed 7 exclude, illegal, illicit, keep out, rule out, shut out 8 anathema, criminal, disallow, improper, leave out, outlawed, prohibit, sanction, unlawful, verboten, wrongful 9 blackball, exclusion, felonious, forbidden, frowned on, interdict, off-limits, ostracize, proscribe, restraint, stricture, unallowed 10 limitation, not allowed, prohibited, proscribed, regulation
tabor: 4 drum
Tabor: 4 city, peak, town 8 mountain
ancient site near Mt. ~: 5 Endor
from ~: 5 Czech
peak locale: 6 Israel
taboret: 7 hassock
Tabriz: 4 city, town
locale: 4 Iran
town near ~: 4 Ahar
tabs
keep ~: 5 gauge, judge 6 assess, figure, notice 7 account, compute, measure 8 appraise, evaluate, watch out 9 calculate
keep ~ on: 4 tend 5 check, track, watch
tabu
see taboo
tabula __: 4 rasa
tabulate: 3 add 4 list 5 chart, index, order 6 assort, codify, figure, record 7 arrange, catalog 8 classify 9 catalogue, enumerate, formulate, keep count 10 categorize
tabulation: 4 list 5 index, tally 6 record, roster 7 catalog, summary 8 counting, register
__ tac: 3 tie
__ Tac Dough: 3 Tic
tach reading: 3 rpm 4 revs
tacit: 4 mute 5 quiet 6 silent, unsaid 7 assumed, implied, virtual 8 hinted at, implicit, indirect, inferred, unspoken, unstated, unvoiced, wordless 9 alluded to, intimated, suggested, unwritten 10 undeclared, understood
taciturn: 3 mum 4 cold, curt, dour, mute 5 aloof, close, quiet 6 morose, silent 7 distant, laconic, sparing 8 brooding, reserved, reticent 9 impassive, secretive, withdrawn 10 antisocial, speechless
one: 4 clam
taciturnity: 7 silence
Tacitus: 5 Roman 6 writer 9 historian
work: Annales
Germania
Historiae
tack: 3 add, fix, hem, sew, tag, yaw 4 bend, brad, glue, line, nail, path, turn, veer, yoke 5 affix, annex, baste, paste, shift 6 append, attach, course, fasten, method, secure, staple, stitch, swerve, switch, zigzag 7 heading, routine, tangent 8 approach 9 direction
kin: 3 pin 7 pushpin
like a ~: 5 sharp
material: 5 brass
on: 3 add 4 link 5 affix, annex 6 append, attach
starter: 4 hard, tick 5 thumb

up a hem: 3 sew 5 baste 6 stitch
__ tack: 3 tie
tackle: 3 kit, rig, tie, try 4 gear, grab, halt, hook, line, nail, sack, stop, wade 5 begin, block, goods, hoist, seize, stuff, throw, tools, upset 6 accept, attack, have at, launch, lifter, outfit, pursue, strive, take on, work on 7 athlete, attempt, get busy, go about, go for it, grapple, pitch in, rigging 8 confront, deal with, engage in, material, materiel, set about, struggle 9 apparatus, bring down, equipment, intercept, machinery, pitch into, trappings, undertake 10 embark upon, implements, make a run at
block and ~: 4 lift 5 hoist 6 lifter, pulley 10 dumbwaiter
teammate: 3 end 4 back 5 guard 6 center, tackle 8 fullback, halfback 11 quarterback
the quarterback: 4 sack
see also football
__-tackle: 5 touch
tackle box item: 4 hook, line, lure, reel 5 float, snell
tacks
brass ~: 5 facts 7 reality 9 actuality, essential 10 foundation
down to brass ~: 5 pithy
get down to brass ~: 6 detail 7 account, itemize, specify 9 make clear, stipulate
__-tack-toe: 4 tick
tacky: 5 cheap, crass, crude, dingy, dowdy, faded, gaudy, gluey, gooey, messy, ratty, seedy 6 coarse, flashy, frumpy, garish, grubby, ragged, shabby, shoddy, sleazy, sloppy, sticky, tawdry, vulgar 7 chintzy, kitschy, rundown, scruffy, uncouth 8 adhesive, outmoded, schlocky, slipshod, slovenly 9 inelegant, out-of-date, shameless, tasteless, unstylish 10 broken-down, second-rate, threadbare, unbecoming, unsuitable
not ~: 5 smart 6 classy, modish, urbane 7 elegant, refined, stylish, voguish 8 esthetic, polished, tasteful 9 dignified, exquisite, glamorous
stuff: 4 glue, goop
__-tacky: 5 ticky
Tacloban's
island: 5 Leyte
taco: 7 Mexican
chip brand: 7 Doritos
ingredient: 4 beef 5 salsa 6 cheese
__ Taco: 3 Del
Taco Bell
dog: 5 Dinky
rival: *see* restaurant chain
Tacoma: 4 city, port, town
locale: 4 Wash. 10 Washington
tact: 5 asset, poise, sense, skill 6 comity, policy 7 aptness, control, finesse, suavity 8 civility, courtesy, delicacy, judgment, subtlety, urbanity 9 diplomacy, gallantry, good taste, suaveness 10 discretion, perception, politeness, refinement, smoothness
ender: 3 ics, ile
lack of ~: 5 gaffe 7 faux pas

9 gaucherie
tactful: 4 kind, wise 5 aware, civil, suave 6 gentle, kindly, poised, polite, subtle, urbane 7 gallant, heedful, mindful, politic, prudent, skilled 8 delicate, discreet, gracious, obliging, polished 9 courteous, judicious, observant, sensitive, unselfish 10 diplomatic, perceptive, thoughtful
tactfully: 7 lightly 9 carefully 10 cautiously, delicately, gracefully, skillfully
tactic: 4 ploy, ruse 5 means 8 artifice, maneuver 9 expedient, stratagem 10 expediency
tactician: 7 planner 10 mastermind, strategist
tactics: 4 plan, ploy 5 means, trick 6 course, method, policy, scheme 7 defense 8 approach, campaign, channels, strategy 9 stratagem, technique
strong-arm ~: 6 duress 7 tyranny 8 coercion, violence 9 extortion 10 oppression
__ tactics: 5 scare
tactile: 7 sensory, sensual 9 sensorial
tactless: 4 rude 5 blunt, brash, brusk, crude, frank, gruff, harsh, hasty, inept, nervy, rough, sharp 6 abrupt, candid, clumsy, gauche, stupid, unkind, vulgar 7 awkward, boorish, brusque, selfish, unadept, uncivil 8 bungling, heedless, impolite, inurbane, unsubtle 9 impolitic, imprudent, maladroit, outspoken, tasteless, unfeeling, ungallant, untactful 10 blundering, indelicate, indiscreet, ungracious, unpolished, unthinking
__-tac-toe: 3 tic
tad: 3 bit, boy, jot 4 iota, mite, tike, tyke 5 child, skosh, speck 7 smidgen, smidgin 8 small fry, smidgeon 9 little bit, little boy, youngster
ender: 4 pole
__ tad: 5 just a
Tad: 5 Mosel 7 Lincoln
father: 3 Abe
ta-da: 5 there, voilà 6 I did it
Tadeusz: 8 Borowski, Konwicki, Rózewicz
tadpole: 4 frog, toad 5 larva 9 amphibian
cousin: 3 eft
Tadzhikistan
see Tajikistan
tae kwon do
relative: 4 judo 6 karate
TAE part: 4 Alva, Thos. 6 Edison, Thomas
__ Tae Woo: 3 Roh
__ Tafari: 3 Ras
Taff: 5 river
city on the ~: 7 Cardiff
locale: 5 Wales
taffeta: 5 weave 6 fabric, faille
sound: 5 swish
taffrail, toward the: 3 aft
taffy: 5 candy, treat 9 sweetmeat
like ~: 5 chewy, gooey 6 sticky
taffy __: 4 pull 5 apple
__ taffy: 7 Turkish
tafia: 3 rum
source: 5 Haiti

Taft
preceder: 9 Roosevelt
successor: 6 Wilson
__ Taft Benson: 4 Ezra
Taft-Hartley __: 3 Act
Taft, William Howard: 9 president
alma mater: 4 Yale
former occupation: 6 lawyer
home: 4 Ohio
opponent: 4 Debs 5 Bryan
state: 4 Ohio
V.P.: 7 Sherman
wife: 5 Helen
tag: 2 ID 3 add, dog, dub, pin, tab, tap 4 call, card, flap, game, heel, logo, mark, name, note, pick, rate, slip, stub, tack, tail, term 5 affix, badge, chase, label, style, title, touch, trail 6 append, attend, button, emblem, fasten, follow, marker, pursue, select, shadow, ticket 7 earmark, specify, sticker, voucher 8 christen, identify, indicate, nickname, subtitle 9 accompany, designate, recognize, sobriquet, track down, trademark
along: 4 come, link 5 trail
attach, as a name ~: 5 pin on
cry: 5 not it
end: 4 rear, tail
ender: 4 line 5 along
ID ~: 5 badge, label
on: 3 add 4 link 5 affix 6 append 8 vinculum
price ~: 3 tab 4 cost 5 total, value 6 amount, charge, outlay
red ~ event: 4 sale
starter: 3 rag 4 hang, name
up: 9 touch base
words: 4 as is
tag __: 3 end 4 line, sale, team 5 along
tag __ with: 5 along
__ tag: 3 dog, ear, red 5 phone, price
__ tag!: 5 Guten
Tag, __ it!: 5 you're
__ Tag: 5 Lazer
tagalong's cry: 5 ditto, me too
__-taggle: 6 raggle
Tag Heuer: 5 watch 10 wristwatch
alternative: *see* wristwatch
Tagliabue, Paul org.: 3 NFL
tagliarini: 5 pasta 7 noodles
tag-on abbr.: 3 etc.
Tagore, Rabindranath: 3 Sir 4 poet 6 Indian, writer 8 Nobelist
work: Chitra
The Crescent Moon
Fireflies
The Golden Boat
One Hundred Poems of Kabir
Red Oleanders
tagrag and __: 7 bobtail
tag-renewal org.: 3 DMV
__-tag sale: 3 red
Tagus: 5 river
city on the ~: 6 Lisbon, Toledo
locale: 5 Spain 6 Iberia 8 Portugal
tahini base: 6 sesame
Tahiti: 3 île 4 isle 6 island
dish: 4 taro
garment: 5 pareo, pareu
Island near ~: 7 Raiatea 8 Pitcairn
novel set in ~: 4 Omoo
port: 7 Papeete
see also French
Tahnee: 5 Welch
mother: 6 Raquel
Tahoe: 3 SUV 4 lake 5 Chevy 6 resort 9 Chevrolet
alternative: *see* cookie brand
locale: 6 Nevada 10 California
visitor: 5 skier
Tahoma: 4 font 8 typeface
tahr: 4 goat
relative: 4 ibex 6 Angora 7 markhor 8 markhoor
tai __: 3 chi
tai __ ch'uan: 3 chi
__ tai: 3 mai
__-tai: 3 mao
Tai: 7 Siamese 9 Babilonia
language: 3 Lao 4 Shan
tail: 3 dog, end, eye, lag, spy, tag 4 rear, rump, scut, stub 5 hound, spy on, stalk, track, trail, train 6 behind, follow, pursue, shadow, tag end, wagger 8 follower, run after, straggle 9 appendage, extremity, posterior, track down 10 conclusion
combining form: 3 uro- 4 caud-, cerc- 5 caudi-, caudo-, cerco-
end: 4 back, rear, stub 5 stump
ender: 3 fin 4 back, bone, coat, gate, pipe, race, skid, spin, wind 5 board, gater, light, piece, stock 6 gating
in two shakes of a lamb's ~: 3 now 4 soon 6 at once, in a sec, pronto 7 hastily, quickly, rapidly, shortly 8 directly, promptly, right now, speedily 9 forthwith, in a minute, in a second, right away 10 this moment
lacking a ~: 5 anury 7 acaudal
of a ~: 6 caudal
off: 3 ebb 4 drop, ease, fade, fall, pale, sink, wane 5 abate, let up, lower, remit, slump 6 lessen, recede, weaken 7 decline, die down, dwindle, lighten, slacken, subside, thin out 8 decrease, diminish, head away, moderate, peter out, roll back, slow down 9 retrocede
shake a ~: 4 lose
starter: 3 bob, cat, cur, fan, fox, pig, pin, rat, wag 4 bang, coat, dove, duck, fish, high, horn, pony, ring, whip 5 broad, horse, shirt, sprig, stick, sword, white 6 cotton, spring, square, triple, yellow 7 bristle, flicker, scissor, swallow
turn ~: 3 run 4 bolt, flee 6 escape 7 retreat, run away, take off 8 fugitate, run for it 9 cut and run, skedaddle
two shakes of a lamb's ~: 4 jiff 5 jiffy, trice 6 moment, second
tail __: 3 end, fin, off 4 wind
__ tail: 4 turn
tailbone: 6 coccyx
__-tail cactus: 3 rat
__-tailed: 3 fan, pin 4 ring 5 bushy
__-tailed deer: 5 black, white
tailless
cat: 4 Manx
primate: 3 ape 5 chimp, loris, orang 7 gorilla 9 orangutan 10 chimpanzee
tailor: 3 fit 4 gear, suit 5 adapt, alter, shape, style 6 adjust, attune, fitter, hemmer, modify 7 alterer, arrange, fashion, measure 8 clothier, readjust 9 couturier, outfitter 10 custom-make, dressmaker
anew: 5 refit
don at the ~: 5 try on
do ~ work: 3 fit, hem 5 alter, plait, pleat, rehem, resew
measure: 6 inseam
need: 3 pin 4 iron, tape 5 chalk, cloth 6 needle, shears 8 scissors
of song: 3 Sam
work: 3 hem 4 seam 5 plait, pleat
tailor-__: 4 made
__-tailor: 4 hand 6 custom
tailored
not custom-~: 3 RTW
tailor-made: 6 fitted
Tailor of Panama, The (2001 film)
cast: Pierce Brosnan, Jamie Lee Curtis, Geoffrey Rush
__, Tailor, Soldier, Spy: 6 Tinker
tails: 4 coat 6 jacket 10 monkey suit
accompaniment: 3 tie
make heads or ~ of: 3 see 6 fathom, follow, pick up 9 figure out 10 comprehend, understand
tailspin: 5 slump 7 descent 8 nosedive 9 rough time
tailward: 3 aft 6 astern
taint: 3 mar, rot, tar 4 blot, blur, foul, ruin, soil, spot, tint, turn 5 abuse, brand, decay, dirty, muddy, smear, spoil, stain, sully 6 befoul, blight, crud up, debase, defame, defect, defile, doctor, embrue, go sour, imbrue, infect, malign, poison, smudge, stigma 7 asperse, begrime, blacken, blemish, corrupt, pollute, tarnish, vitiate 8 besmirch, discolor, disgrace, dishonor, impurity, throw mud 9 discredit, disrepute, pollution 10 adulterate, defilement, imputation, stigmatize, villainize
tainted: 3 off 4 foul, gamy, rank 5 gamey, grimy, sooty 6 filthy, grubby, grungy, impure, rancid, rotten 7 corrupt, unclean 8 inedible, maculate, slovenly, vitiated 10 germ-ridden, malodorous, unsanitary
taintless: 4 pure 5 clean 6 chaste 7 ethical, sterile 8 germfree, hygienic, innocent, pristine, sanitary, spotless, unsoiled, virtuous 9 exemplary, honorable, incorrupt, stainless, undefiled, unspoiled, unspotted, unsullied, untouched, wholesome 10 immaculate, impeccable, inculpable, sterilized
'tain't opposite: 3 'tis
Tai-Pan
author: James Clavell
Taipei: 4 city, town 7 capital
locale: 6 Taiwan 7 Formosa
Taiwan: 4 isle 6 island, nation, strait 7 country
capital: 6 Taipei
city: 6 Taibei, Tainan, Taipei
computer company: 4 Acer
ender: 3 ese
island: 4 Mazu 5 Matsu 7 Formosa
island near ~: 3 Lan
money: 4 cent 6 dollar
port: 6 Tainan 7 Chilung, Keelung 9 Kaohsiung
sea: 9 East China 10 South China
Taiwanese: 5 Asian
Taiwan Strait
island: 4 Amoy 6 Jinmen, Kinmen, Quemoy 7 Chinmen 10 Pescadores
taj: 3 cap 9 headdress
wearer: 6 Muslim
Tajikistan: 6 nation 7 country
capital: 8 Dushanbe
mountain: 9 Lenin Peak, Trans Alai
neighbor: 5 China 10 Kyrgyzstan, Uzbekistan
once: 3 SSR
region: 5 Pamir 6 Pamirs
Taj Mahal: 4 tomb
feature: 4 dome
locale: 4 Agra 5 India
Tajo: 5 Italo
take: 2 go 3 bag, buy, con, cut, eat, get, lug, nab, opt, rob, use, win 4 bear, beat, bilk, book, cart, cull, deem, down, dupe, earn, gate, grab, grip, gull, hack, haul, have, hire, hold, lead, lift, loot, lump, nail, need, pack, pick, reap, rent, tote, trap, verb 5 abide, admit, adopt, booty, bring, brook, carry, catch, charm, cheat, clasp, drink, drive, elect, ferry, fetch, filch, grasp, guide, lease, lucre, marry, pilot, pinch, pluck, react, see as, seize, share, stand, steal, swipe, trick, truck, usher, yield 6 abduct, accept, arrest, assume, borrow, choose, clutch, collar, convey, deduct, demand, derive, devour, endure, entrap, escort, fleece, go with, handle, hang in, haul in, hijack, imbibe, ingest, inhale, obtain, opt for, output, pay for, pick up, pilfer, pocket, prefer, profit, reckon, regard, relish, remove, rip off, salary, secure, select, snap up, snatch, snitch, spoils, suffer 7 acquire, bewitch, call for, capture, charter, collect, conduct, contain, deceive, defraud, deliver, enchant, ensnare, extract, imagine, impound, include, insnare, lighten, opinion, plunder, preempt, presume, procure, profits, purloin, receive, require, reserve, returns, revenue, ride out, salvage, stipend, stomach, succeed, suppose, suspect, swallow, swindle, two-time, utilize, weather, welcome 8 arrogate, bear with, carry off, carve out, decide on, flimflam, gather up, handpick, highjack, hoodwink, liberate, live with, look upon, proceeds, purchase, reaction, receipts, shoulder, stand for, submit to, subtract, tolerate, transmit 9 accompany, apprehend, bamboozle, captivate, fascinate, four-flush, hang tough, intercept, lay hold of, piggyback, put up with, single out, transport, withstand 10 commandeer, confiscate, settle upon, stick it out
aback: 4 faze, stun 5 shake 7 astound, nonplus, stagger,

startle **8** astonish, bowl over, surprise **9** discomfit, dumbfound, give a turn **10** disconcert
a break: 4 rest **5** pause, relax **6** lay off, recess, rest up, unwind **8** intermit, loosen up
account of: 6 reckon **7** measure
a chance: 4 bite, dare, risk **5** wager **6** gamble, hazard **7** venture **9** speculate
a crack at: 3 try **7** venture
action: 4 move **6** step in **7** proceed
action against: 3 sue
a dim view of: 5 knock, scorn **7** censure, deplore, put down, run down **8** belittle, derogate, disfavor **9** deprecate, disesteem, disparage, poor-mouth **10** disapprove
advantage of: 3 use **4** gull, have, milk **5** abuse, cozen, wrong **6** impose, play on, prey on **7** deceive, exploit, utilize **8** hoodwink, play upon **9** victimize
advantage (of): 5 avail
advice: 4 heed, obey **5** adopt **6** accept, attend, follow, harken, listen, regard **7** abide by, hear out, observe **8** adhere to, consider, pick up on **9** entertain **10** bear in mind
a fling: 4 risk **6** gamble, hazard **7** venture
a flyer: 6 gamble **7** venture
after: 6 follow **7** emulate, reflect **8** resemble
a gander: 3 eye **4** look, peer, scan, view
a hand: 6 butt in, step in **7** barge in, mediate **9** intercede
a header: 4 fall, risk, trip **6** topple, tumble
a hike: 2 go **4** blow, exit, part, quit, scat **5** leave, scram **6** begone, get out **8** light out, withdraw **10** go fly a kite
a holiday: 4 loaf, rest, slow **5** break, pause, relax **6** unwind **8** recreate, slack off, slow down, vacation
a load off: 3 sit **5** relax **6** unload **7** lighten
along: 4 lead, tote **5** bring, guide, usher **6** convey, escort **7** conduct **9** transport
a look at: 3 eye, see **4** case **5** assay, gauge, probe, scout, try on **6** assess, size up, verify **7** confirm, examine, inspect, qualify **8** appraise, check out, evaluate, follow up
a loss: 7 devalue **8** give up on
amiss: 6 resent
a nap: 7 saw logs
another look: 5 audit, check, weigh **6** assess, go over, rehash, survey **7** analyze, examine, inspect, revisit **8** appraise, critique, evaluate, reassess **9** reexamine, think over **10** reconsider, reevaluate, run through, scrutinize
apart: 4 ruin, undo **5** level, spoil, unrig, unrip, wreck **6** detach, tinker **7** destroy, dissect **8** demolish, tear down **9** devastate, dismantle, knock down **10** demoralize, disconnect
a powder: 2 go **3** lam **4** blow, bolt, exit, flee, scat **5** lam it, leave, scram **6** escape **7** abandon, vamoose
a quick look: 4 leaf, skim **5** check **6** browse, riffle, size up, survey **7** monitor **8** look over **10** glance over, run through
a risk: 4 dare, defy **6** gamble, hazard **7** presume, venture **9** challenge, speculate
a room: 4 stay **7** sojourn **8** stop over
as fact: 6 accept **7** believe, suppose, surmise **9** postulate
as gospel: 3 buy **6** accept, credit, rely on **7** swallow, swear by
as one's own: 5 adopt, co-opt **6** accept **7** espouse
a stand: 3 opt **4** vote **5** judge **6** choose, decide, oppose **9** determine
at face value: 4 rely **5** bet on **6** accept, assume, bank on, commit, credit, expect, lean on, look to, rely on **7** believe, consign, count on, entrust, presume, suppose, swear by **8** depend on, rely upon
away: 4 less, wipe **5** minus **6** abduct, deduct, reduce, remove **7** ransack **8** decrease, diminish, discount, subtract, withdraw
a wrong turn: 3 err **5** stray **6** slip up **8** go astray, trespass **10** transgress
back: 5 rewin, unsay **6** recall, recant, regain, return, revoke **7** disavow, forgive, reclaim, recover, retract **8** disclaim, exchange, withdraw **9** recapture, repossess, repudiate
bets: 8 give odds
by the hand: 5 guide, steer, usher **6** assist, direct, escort **7** bolster, conduct **9** encourage
can't ~: 4 hate **5** abhor **6** detest, loathe **7** despise **8** execrate **9** abominate
care of: 3 pay **4** feed, mall, maul, tend **5** act on, nurse, see to, watch **6** advert, attend, foster, handle, reward **7** address, babysit, execute, nurture, protect, provide, shelter, sit with **8** attend to, cope with, deal with, maintain, minister, see about, transact **9** cultivate, do justice, look after, overpower, watch over **10** accomplish, compensate, consummate
care of a tot: 4 mind **5** watch **7** oversee **9** look after
charge: 4 lead, rule **5** steer **6** head up **7** command
cover: 3 den **4** hide, wait **6** hole up, lie low **7** shelter
don't ~ no for an answer: 7 persist, protest **8** speak out **9** stand firm
down: 3 jot **4** land, note, rase, raze, ruin, undo **5** abase, level, lower, shame, wreck, write **6** debase, demean, humble, record, topple **7** deflate, degrade, destroy, devalue, mortify **8** belittle, bulldoze, demolish, disgrace, inscribe, register **9** deprecate, devaluate, devastate, discredit, dismantle, disparage, humiliate **10** journalize, transcribe
down a peg: 5 abase, lower, shame **6** demean, demote, humble, reduce **7** degrade, mortify **8** belittle **9** downgrade
effect: 4 tell, work **5** enure, inure, set in **6** happen
ender: 3 off, out **4** away, down, over
everything: 7 possess **10** monopolize
exception: 5 demur **6** differ **7** protest, quarrel
exception to: 4 mind **5** cavil, demur **6** object, oppose, resent **7** dissent **8** question **9** challenge, deprecate
five: 4 rest **5** break, pause, relax **6** recess, rest up **8** intermit
flight: 2 go **3** lam, run **4** bolt, flee, wing **5** scram, split **6** depart, escape **8** fugitate **9** disappear
for a ride: 3 con, gyp **4** bilk, dupe, gull, hoax, scam **5** cheat, cozen, trick **6** fleece **7** deceive, defraud, mislead, swindle **8** flimflam, hoodwink **9** bamboozle
for a time: 6 borrow
forcibly: 5 seize, wrest
forever: 4 drag **5** dally, stall, tarry **10** dillydally
for granted: 5 posit **6** assume **7** believe, presume, suppose **9** postulate
form: 3 gel **4** jell **5** shape **8** incubate
for oneself: 3 hog **7** possess **10** monopolize
give and ~: 4 swap, swop **5** bandy, share, trade **8** exchange
hard to ~: 5 nasty, rough **7** galling **8** abrasive, annoying, grinding **10** irritating, unpleasant
heed: 4 mind **5** watch **6** beware, listen **7** hearken
heed of: 4 mind **6** notice **7** observe **8** listen to
heist ~: 4 loot **5** booty **7** plunder
hold: 3 fix
hold of: 3 bag, nab **4** bust, grab, grip, nail, snag **5** catch, grasp, pinch, snare **6** abduct, arrest, collar, detain, hijack, obtain, secure, snap up, snatch, tackle **7** capture, impound, overrun, procure, receive **8** carry off **9** apprehend, overwhelm **10** commandeer, confiscate
home: 3 net **4** earn **5** clear **8** pull down
how much to ~: 4 dose **6** dosage
in: 3 con, eat, eye, lie, see, spy **4** bilk, dupe, earn, fool, gull, have, hear, hoax, make, nick, note, reap, sell, snow, soak, view **5** admit, adopt, bluff, board, catch, cheat, cover, grasp, gross, hocus, house, learn, lodge, put up, sense, sop up, stare, trick, visit **6** absorb, attend, betray, billet, delude, devour, digest, follow, gather, incept, ingest, notice, osmose, outwit, pick up, redeem, soak up, suck up **7** beguile, contain, deceive, defraud, embrace, glimpse, include, mislead, observe, quarter, realize, receive, recruit, shelter, swallow, swindle, two-time **8** comprise, contract, flimflam, hoodwink, outsmart, perceive **9** apprehend, bamboozle, disinform, encompass, four-flush **10** assimilate, comprehend, understand
in a guest: 5 greet **6** invite **7** welcome
in law: 5 seise
into account: 4 heed, note **5** cover **6** regard **7** respect **8** consider
into custody: 3 nab **4** book, nail **5** pinch, run in, seize **6** arrest **9** apprehend
issue: 5 argue, clash **6** differ, oppose **7** quarrel, quibble **8** conflict, disagree
it: 5 abide, infer, stick **6** deduce, gather, reckon, suffer **7** imagine, presume, surmise **9** withstand **10** understand
it easy: 3 sit **4** idle, laze, loaf, lull, rest **5** coast, relax, slide, unlax **6** lounge, repose, rest up, unwind **8** loosen up **9** luxuriate
it hard: 3 cry, sob **4** bawl, howl, keen, moan, mope, wail, weep **5** brood, mourn **6** bemoan, bewail, grieve, lament
it on the lam: 3 fly, run **4** flee **6** escape
lodgings: 3 let **4** rent **5** lease **8** sublease
no note of: 6 ignore **7** neglect **8** brush off, skip over **9** disregard
notice: 4 heed **5** sit up, watch **6** listen
nourishment: 3 sup **4** dine, nosh **5** feast, graze **6** ingest **7** consume, partake **9** have a bite, have a meal **10** gormandize
off: 2 go **3** fly, hie, run **4** blow, bolt, dash, doff, exit, flee, move, part, quit, shed, soar **5** begin, climb, elope, leave, mimic, scram, speed, split, strip **6** ascend, aviate, beat it, decamp, deduct, depart, desert, divest, embark, get out, let rip, remove, retire, set out **7** abscond, disrobe, head out, lampoon, pull out, undress, vamoose **8** clear out, get out of, hightail, light out, turn tail, withdraw **9** disappear, slip out of **10** go fly a kite, hit the road
off after: 4 hunt, tail **5** chase, stalk **6** follow, pursue, shadow **7** hunt for
off weight: 4 diet, slim, thin **6** shrink **7** lighten **8** slim down
on: 2 do **3** add, pit, vie **4** face, hire **5** adopt, annex, fight, match,

worry 6 accept, affect, assume, attach, employ, engage, enlist, join in, oppose, retain, strive, tackle 7 acquire, attempt, compete, contend, embrace, espouse, grapple, quarrel, recruit, venture, vie with 8 deal with, endeavor, shoulder, struggle 9 agree to do, challenge, have a go at, pitch into
one's breath away: 3 awe, wow 5 amaze 6 boggle, excite, thrill 7 astound, stagger 8 astonish
one's leave: 2 go 4 exit 5 split 6 beat it, depart, go away, move on, retire 7 make off, pull out, push off 8 blast off, hightail, light out, set forth, shove off, slip away, withdraw
one's time: 5 dally, delay, mosey, relax, stall, tarry 6 dawdle, linger, loiter 7 goof off 8 lollygag 10 dillydally
on faith: 5 trust 6 accept, assume 7 believe
on the ~: 5 venal 7 corrupt 8 suborned 9 dissolute
out: 3 see 4 date, dele 5 court, erase, pluck, treat 6 deduct, delete, murder, remove, wallop 7 expunge, release 8 diminish, sabotage 9 eliminate, overpower
over: 4 grab, rule 5 adopt, co-opt, seize, spell, steer, usurp 6 assume, manage, occupy 7 inherit, preempt, succeed 10 commandeer, fall heir to, monopolize
over for: 5 cover 6 fill in, follow 7 relieve, replace, succeed 8 supplant
part: 4 join 5 opt in 6 accept, assist, engage, join in 8 deal with 9 cooperate
part in: 4 join 5 enter, share
partner: 4 give
place: 4 fall 5 occur 6 befall, betide, happen 9 come about, eventuate, transpire 10 come to pass
pleasure: 4 live 5 revel 6 wallow
pleasure in: 5 eat up, enjoy
prepare to ~ off: 4 taxi
responsibility: 6 fess up 7 confess
root: 6 settle, sprout 7 develop 8 spring up 9 germinate
shape: 3 gel 4 form, jell, loom
sides: 6 choose, prefer
steps: 7 get busy
stock of: 4 note 5 audit 6 assess, survey
ten: 4 rest 5 break, pause, relax 6 recess, rest up 8 intermit
the ~: 4 gate 8 proceeds, receipts
the bit in one's teeth: 4 defy 5 rebel 6 revolt 7 disobey 9 break away
the edge off: 5 blunt 6 lessen, pacify, smooth, soothe, temper 8 mitigate, tone down
the elevator: 4 rise 5 climb 6 ascend
the floor: 4 talk 5 orate, speak, spout 6 recite 7 lecture 9 hold forth, sermonize, speechify
the heat off: 5 allay, let up, relax 6 lessen, relent 7 lighten, slacken 8 mitigate, moderate 9 alleviate, disburden
the lead: 4 head, rule 5 exact, order, reign 6 direct, enjoin, govern, handle, manage 7 command, control, dictate, mandate, oversee 8 dominate, instruct 9 officiate, supervise
the liberty: 4 dare 6 impose 8 be so bold 9 go so far as
the plunge: 3 wed 4 dare 5 marry, start 7 venture
the sting out: 4 lull 5 allay 6 lessen, smooth, soothe, temper
the wheel: 4 helm 5 drive, pilot 8 navigate
the wind out of: 6 defeat, hamper, hinder, hogtie, hold up, impede, stymie 8 obstruct 9 frustrate, hamstring, undermine
the wraps off: 4 bare 6 expose, reveal 7 lay bare, uncover
the wrong road: 4 flub, goof, muff, slip 5 lapse, stray 6 boo-boo, bungle, foul up, fumble, mess up, slip up, wander 7 blunder, deviate, louse up, stumble 8 go astray 10 transgress
thief ~: 4 cash, jack 5 bills, booty, dough, graft, lucre, money 6 dinero, moolah, snatch 7 plunder, scratch 8 bankroll
to: 4 like 7 care for 10 fall back on
to heart: 4 obey 6 follow 7 abide by, observe, respect
to mean: 4 draw, make 5 glean, guess, infer, think 6 assume, decode, deduce, derive, gather 7 imagine, surmise 8 conclude, construe 10 understand
to task: 3 rag 5 blame, decry, scold 6 berate, punish, rebuke 7 censure, contemn, lecture, reprove, tell off 8 denounce, reproach 9 inculpate, reprehend, reprimand 10 denunciate
to the cleaners: 3 gyp 4 bilk 6 fleece 7 deceive, defraud, swindle 8 hoodwink
turns: 4 vary 5 spell 6 rotate, switch 8 exchange, trade off 9 alternate, change off
umbrage: 6 object, resent
up: 4 lift 5 adopt, alter, renew, scoop, stand, start, study 6 assume, attack, choose, occupy, resume 7 address, embrace, espouse, proceed 8 commence, consider, continue, engage in, initiate, set about, stand for 10 monopolize, recommence
up quarters: 4 live, stay 5 abide, lodge, roost 6 occupy, reside, settle 7 inhabit, sojourn
up with: 4 join 8 befriend 9 associate
up (with): 7 consort
take __: 3 for, off, out, ten 4 a dip, a hit, a nap, a vow, back, care, down, five, hold, part, root, wing 5 a bath, a dive, after, a hike, apart, a peek, a rest, a risk, a seat, a stab, a trip, a walk, cover, heart, issue, pains, place, shape, sides, steps, stock, turns 6 charge, effect, flight
take __ account: 4 into
take __ after: 3 off, out
take __ an answer: 5 no for
take __ a peg: 4 down
take __ at: 5 a shot, a stab
take __ breath: 5 a deep
take __ check: 5 a rain
take __ cleaners: 5 to the
take __ down: 5 lying
take __ faith: 4 it on
take __ for the worse: 5 a turn
take __ from: 4 a cue, away
take __ grain of salt: 5 with a
take __ granted: 3 for 5 it for
take __ in: 5 stock
take __ in the dark: 5 a shot
take __ leave it: 4 it or
take __ of: 4 care 6 notice 7 account
take __ off: 5 a load
take __ on: 4 pity 5 a toll, it out
take __ peg: 5 down a
take __ ride: 4 for a
take __ slack: 5 up the
take __ stride: 4 it in
take __ the chin: 4 it on
take __ the garden path: 4 down
take __ the lam: 4 it on
take __ the waist: 4 in at
take __ to: 6 kindly
take __ toll: 3 its
take __ view: 4 a dim
take-__: 5 along 6 charge
take-__ pay: 4 home
__ take: 5 on the 6 double
Take __!: 4 care, that 5 a seat
Take __ a compliment!: 4 it as
Take __ from me!: 4 a tip
Take __ leave it!: 4 it or
Take __ on the Reading: 5 a Ride
Take __ out of crime!: 5 a bite
Take __, She's Mine: 3 Her
Take __ song and make it better: 4 a sad
Take __ the Limit: 4 It to
Take __ to the Ball Game: 5 Me Out
Take __ Train: 4 The A
Take __ your leader: 4 me to
take a __: 4 bath, dive, hike, seat, walk 5 stand 6 powder
take a __ at: 4 shot, stab 5 whack
take a __ on: 4 toll
take a __ to: 5 shine
take a __ view: 3 dim
Take a Bow (1994 song)
 artist: Madonna
Take a Chance on Me (1978 song)
 artist: ABBA
take a crack __: 4 at it
take a dim __: 4 view
Take a Girl Like You
 author: Kingsley Amis
Take a hike!: 4 scat 5 scram 6 beat it 7 amscray, buzz off, get lost 8 scramola
__ take all: 6 winner
__ Take an Old-Fashioned Walk: 4 Let's
...__ take arms...: 4 or to
take by __: 5 storm 8 surprise
take-charge: 8 forceful
takedown: 7 lampoon
take down __: 4 a peg
take down the __ path: 6 garden
Take Five (1961 song)
 artist: Dave Brubeck
take for __: 5 a ride 7 granted
Take Good Care of My Baby (1961 song)
 artist: Bobby Vee
Take Her, __ Mine: 4 She's
take-home: 3 net, pay 4 wage 5 wages
Takei, George
 role: 4 Sulu
take in __: 6 stride
take into __: 7 account
take it __: 5 out on
take it __ chin: 5 on the
take it __ lam: 5 on the
take it __ man: 5 like a
take it __ oneself: 4 upon
Take It Away (1982 song)
 artist: Paul McCartney
Take it easy!: 3 bye 4 ta-ta 5 adios, aloha, later, see ya 6 bye-bye, shalom, so long 7 goodbye 8 au revoir, sayonara
take it in __: 6 stride
take it like __: 4 a man
take it on the __: 3 lam 4 chin
Take It on the Run (1981 song)
 artist: REO Speedwagon
take it or leave it: 4 as is
take its __: 4 toll
Take It to the Limit (1976 song)
 artist: Eagles
take lying __: 4 down
__ Take Manhattan: 3 I'll
Take Me __: 5 Along
Take Me __ Am: 3 as I
Take Me Home (song)
 artist: Cher, Phil Collins
Take Me Home, Country Roads (1971 song)
 artist: John Denver
Take Me Home Tonight (1986 song)
 artist: Eddie Money
Take Me Out to the Ball Game: 5 waltz
Take Me Out to the Ball Game (1949 film)
 cast: Gene Kelly, Frank Sinatra, Esther Williams
Take Me There (1998 song)
 artist: Mase, Mya
Take me to your __: 6 leader
Take my __, please!: 4 wife
taken: 3 occ. 4 rapt 5 burnt, in use 6 burned 8 occupied, reserved 9 preferred, spoken for
aback: 5 agape, fazed 6 shamed 7 abashed, ashamed, at a loss, fuddled, puzzled 9 astounded, befuddled, chagrined, flustered, in a dither, mortified, mystified, perplexed, staggered, stupefied, surprised 10 astonished, bewildered, bowled over, confounded, dumbstruck, speechless
advantage of: 4 used 7 put upon 9 exploited
alone: 5 per se
care of: 4 done 8 finished
down: 3 low, sad 4 blue, glum, mopy 5 moody, mopey 6 gloomy, morose 7 forlorn, unhappy 8 dejected, desolate, liverish, wretched 9 aggrieved, bummed-out, cheerless, depressed, in the pits, miser-

able, sorrowful, woebegone **10** despairing, despondent, dispirited, in the dumps, lugubrious, melancholy, out of sorts, spiritless
easily ~ in: **4** naif **5** naive **6** unwary **8** gullible, ignorant, lamblike, trustful, trusting, wide-eyed
for granted: **5** given, tacit **6** unsaid **7** assumed **8** implicit, unspoken, unstated, unvoiced **9** axiomatic **10** understood
not ~ care of: **5** unmet
not ~ in by: **4** onto
old-style: **4** taen
with: **4** into **8** obsessed, turned on **9** wild about
taken __: **4** with **5** aback
Taken (2009 film)
cast: Maggie Grace, Famke Janssen, Liam Neeson
taken-back item: **4** repo
take notice in Latin: **8** nota bene
takeoff: **5** spoof, start **6** ascent, comedy, parody, satire, send-up **7** burlesk, lampoon, mockery **8** ridicule, travesty **9** beginning, burlesque, departure, imitation **10** caricature, impression
artist: **4** aper **5** mimic
do a ~: **3** ape **4** mime **5** mimic **8** simulate **9** duplicate
hr.: **3** ETD
vertical ~: **4** jato
take off __: **5** after
Take one!: **5** try it
take one's __: **4** part, time **5** leave
take one's __ away: **6** breath
take one's __ off to: **3** hat
Take on Me (1985 song)
artist: A-HA
takeout: **4** food
call for ~: **5** eat in, order **7** order in
counter call: **4** next
for ~: **4** to go
shop: **4** deli **8** pizzeria
take out __: **4** an ad **5** after, a loan
takeover: **3** LBO **4** coup **6** buyout, merger **7** triumph **9** coup d'état **10** assumption, occupation, usurpation
taker: **5** buyer, donee **6** better, bettor **8** acceptor, customer **9** con artist **10** pickpocket, plagiarist
odds ~: **6** player **7** gambler, wagerer **8** gamester
starter: **4** care, poll
__ taker: **6** census
__ Take Romance: **3** I'll
__ takers?: **3** Any
takes
what it ~: **5** drive, knack, savvy, skill **6** talent **7** ability, faculty, know-how, prowess **8** aptitude, capacity, facility, gumption **9** expertise, potential **10** capability, initiative, right stuff
__ Takes a Chance: **5** A Lady
__ Takes a Wife, The: **6** Doctor, Farmer
__ Takes Command: **5** Grant
__ Takes Time: **4** Love
take the __: **3** hit, rap **4** cake, fall, heat, road **5** bench, count, field, Fifth, floor, stand **6** plunge
take the __ by the horns: **4** bull
take the day __: **3** off
Take the Money and Run (1969 film)
cast: Woody Allen
director: Woody Allen
Take the Money and Run (1976 song)
artist: Steve Miller Band
Take These Chains From My Heart (1963 song)
artist: Ray Charles
Take this!: **4** here
take to __: **4** task **5** heart
take to one's __: **5** heels
take to the __: **6** bricks
take-up __: **4** reel
take up the __: **5** slack
take with a __ of salt: **5** grain
Take your time!: **6** no rush
taking: **5** sweet **7** receipt, winning, winsome **8** receipts **10** assumption
after: **3** à la
it easy: **5** still **8** inactive, unmoving **10** motionless
one's time: **3** lax **4** easy, lazy, slow **5** slack **6** calmly, casual, gentle, lazily, slowly **7** relaxed **8** casually, laid-back **9** gradually, languidly, unhurried **10** composedly, deliberate, indolently
out the garbage: **3** job **4** duty, task **5** chore **9** housework
__ taking: **6** profit
__-taking: **5** leave
Taking __ of Business: **4** Care
Taking of Pelham 123, The (2009 film)
cast: John Travolta, John Turturro, Denzel Washington
Taking of Pelham One Two Three, The (1974 film)
cast: Martin Balsam, Walter Matthau, Robert Shaw
takings: **5** booty, yield **6** profit
Tal: **7** Mikhail
talaria: **5** wings **7** sandals
like ~: **4** alar **5** alary
Talbot: **4** Lyle, Nita
Talbot Odyssey, The
author: Nelson DeMille
talc: **6** powder **7** mineral **8** steatite **9** soapstone **10** bath powder
to Mohs: **3** one
talcum __: **6** powder
Talcum is walcum
poet: Ogden Nash
tale: **3** fib, lie **4** epic, myth, saga, yarn **5** fable, novel, rumor, spiel, story **6** canard, excuse, legend, report **7** account, evasion, fiction, megilla, parable, recital, romance, scandal, slander, untruth, version, western, whapper, whopper **8** anecdote, chestnut, relation, sob story, whodunit **9** chronicle, deception, dime novel, falsehood, fish story, folk story, invention, mendacity, moonshine, narration, narrative, recountal, rigmarole, tall story **10** concoction, fairy story, inaccuracy, short story, taradiddle
ancient ~: **4** myth **5** fable
contrived a ~: **4** wove
ender: **6** bearer, teller **7** bearing
epigrammatic ~: **4** myth, tale, yarn **5** story **6** legend **7** parable **8** allegory
fairy ~: **4** yarn **5** story **7** romance
fairy ~ villain: **5** giant **7** monster
heroic ~: **4** edda, epic, gest, saga **5** conte, geste
in Britain: **4** rede
malicious ~: **5** rumor **6** canard **7** untruth **9** falsehood
starter: **4** folk, tell **6** tattle
tall ~: **4** yarn **5** story **9** invention
tell a ~: **4** spin **7** narrate
teller: **4** liar **7** tattler
tale __: **5** of woe
__ tale: **4** folk, tall **5** fairy
Tale __ Cities, A: **5** of Two
Tale __ Tub: **3** of a
__ Tale, A: **5** Bronx **7** Winter's
__-Tale Heart, The: **4** Tell
talent: **3** ace **4** bent, gift, head, nose, turn, whiz **5** craft, flair, forte, knack, money, power, skill, touch **6** artist, genius **7** ability, faculty, know-how, prodigy, promise, prowess **8** aptitude, artistry, capacity, facility **9** endowment, ingenuity **10** capability, green thumb, right stuff
have no ~: **5** stink
having ~: **4** able
scout: **3** rep **5** agent **8** promoter **9** middleman
seeker: **5** scout
show device: **4** gong
talent __: **4** show **5** scout
talented: **3** ace **4** deft, good **5** adept, crack **6** adroit, clever, gifted **7** capable **8** artistic, masterly, skillful **9** ingenious, masterful, promising, qualified, versatile **10** artistical, precocious, proficient
be ~: **3** top **4** lead **5** excel, outdo, shine **7** surpass **8** outclass, outshine, outstrip **10** overshadow
Talented Mr. Ripley, The: **4** film **5** novel
author: Patricia Highsmith
cast: Cate Blanchett, Matt Damon, Jude Law, Gwyneth Paltrow
tale of __: **3** woe
Tale of __ Saltan, The: **4** Tsar
Tale of a Tub, The
author: Jonathan Swift
Tale of Benjamin Bunny, The
author: Beatrix Potter
Tale of Genji, The
author: Murasaki Shikibu
Tale of Jerusalem, A
author: Edgar Allan Poe
Tale of Peter Rabbit, The
author: Beatrix Potter
Tale of the Body Thief, The
author: Anne Rice
Tale of the Ragged Mounains, A
author: Edgar Allan Poe
Tale of the Tape measure: **5** reach **6** height, weight
Tale of Tom Kitten, The
author: Beatrix Potter
Tale of Two Cities, A: **5** novel
author: Charles Dickens
character: **3** Cly **5** Lorry, Lucie, Pross, Roger **6** Carton, Darnay, Ernest, Jarvis, Sydney **7** Charles, Defarge, Gaspard, Manette, Stryver, Thérèse **8** Roger Cly **9** Alexander
director: Jack Conway
setting: **5** Paris **6** France, London **7** England
tales: **4** lore **7** legends
tell ~: **3** gab, yak **4** blab, dish **6** gossip, tattle **8** schmooze
Tales __ Jazz Age: **5** of the
Tales __ South Pacific: **5** of the
Tales __ the Hood: **4** From
Tales __ Wayside Inn: **3** of a
__ tale's best for winter: **4** A sad
Talese: **3** Gay, Nan
Talese, Gay: **6** writer
work: Fame and Obscurity
Honor Thy Father
The Kingdom and the Power
Thy Neighbor's Wife
Unto the Sons
Tales from Shakespeare
author: Elia, Charles Lamb
Tales From the Crypt
like ~: **4** eery **5** eerie
Tales from the Vienna Woods
composer: Johann Strauss
Tales of Adventure
author: Jack London
Tales of a Wayside Inn: **4** poem
author: Henry Wadsworth Longfellow
town: **4** Atri
Tales of Hoffman: **5** opera
character: **6** Andrès, Luther, Stella **7** Antonia, Hermann, Lindorf, Olympia **9** Coppélius, Giulietta, Nathaniel **10** Nicklausse
composer: Jacques Offenbach
setting: **5** Italy **6** Munich, Venice **7** Germany **9** Nuremberg
Tales of the Jazz Age
author: F. Scott Fitzgerald
Tales of the South Pacific
author: James A. Michener
Tales of the Wolf
author: Lawrence Sanders
Tales of Wells Fargo (NBC western)
cast: Dale Robertson (Jim Hardie)
__ Tale, The: **6** Reeve's **7** Winter's
tale told by an __, A: **5** idiot
tali: **10** ankle bones
Talia: **5** Shire
__ talionis: **3** lex
Talisa: **4** Soto
talisman: **4** mojo **5** charm, spell **6** amulet, scarab **7** periapt
Talisman, The
author: Stephen King, Walter Scott
talk: **3** gab, jaw, lip, rap, rot, say, yak **4** bunk, buzz, cant, chat, hint, jive, sing, vent, word, yack, yarn **5** argot, argue, drawl, drone, forum, lingo, noise, orate, pitch, prate, prose, rumor, run on, slang, speak, spiel, spout, stump, utter, visit, voice, words **6** accost, babble, banter, broach, confab, confer, dialog, earful, gabble, gossip, homily, hot air, huddle, inform, intone, jabber, jargon, mumble, parley, patois, patter, powwow, preach, racket, reason, relate, report, reveal, rumble, rumors, screed, sermon, speech, squeak, squeal, tattle **7** address, blather, blether, bombast, buzzing,

TA

canvass, chatter, chime in, commune, confess, confide, consult, contact, declaim, descant, dialect, dictate, discant, discuss, divulge, express, hearsay, lecture, meeting, monolog, network, oration, palaver, prattle, rubbish, scandal, seminar, tell all **8** badinage, causerie, chitchat, colloquy, converse, dialogue, exchange, harangue, innuendo, interact, language, locution, nonsense, parlance, persuade, raillery, rattle on, reach out, verbiage, vocalize **9** comment on, discourse, grapevine, hold forth, interface, interview, monologue, negotiate, pronounce, soliloquy, symposium, tête-à-tête, thrash out, touch base, utterance, verbalize **10** articulate, chew the fat, chew the rag, discussion, groupthink, peroration, persiflage, prelection, recitation, rhapsodize, vocalizing
about: **5** state **7** clarify, comment, discuss, mention **8** report on, set forth, spell out **9** interpret
amorously: **3** coo
baby ~: **3** goo, mom **4** lisp, mama, papa **5** mamma **6** goo-goo
back: **4** sass **5** react **6** answer **7** respond **8** get fresh, mouth off
back ~: **3** jaw, lip **4** echo, guff, sass **5** cheek, mouth, reply, sauce **8** defiance, reaction, response **9** impudence, insolence, wisemouth **10** smartmouth
big: **4** brag, crow **5** boast, vaunt **6** overdo **7** bluster, lay it on **9** gasconade
big ~: **9** hyperbole **10** pretension
chalk ~: **6** lesson, speech **7** address, lecture, oration **8** training
chick ~: **5** cheep
don't ~: **6** clam up
down: **3** pan **5** knock **8** belittle, derogate, minimize **9** criticize, disparage, underplay **10** depreciate
down to: **5** agree, deign, lower, stoop, yield **9** acquiesce, patronize, vouchsafe **10** condescend
effusively: **4** gush, rave **9** pour forth
empty ~: **3** gas, pap **4** wind **5** prate **6** humbug
ender: **4** back, fest
fast ~: **4** bull, bunk **5** prate **6** banter, hot air, humbug, patter **7** baloney, blarney, blather **8** malarkey **9** banana oil **10** applesauce, balderdash
foolish ~: ***see*** baloney
formal ~: **6** speech **7** oration
fresh ~: **3** lip **4** guff, sass **5** cheek, sauce **9** impudence, insolence, sauciness
full of back ~: **5** lippy
give a ~: **5** orate, speak **6** preach **7** address, declaim, deliver, expound, lecture **9** discourse, hold forth
give a pep ~: **4** urge **6** charge **8** admonish **9** encourage
have a ~ with: **3** see
hoarsely: **4** rasp
idle ~: **3** gab, gas, yap **4** wind **5** mouth, prate **6** babble, cackle, gossip **8** babbling, chitchat **9** loquacity
idly: **5** prate **6** babble, gibber **7** blather, blether
insider ~: **5** argot, idiom, lingo **6** jargon, patois
insincere ~: **4** cant, jive **6** bunkum **8** buncombe
into: **3** con **4** coax, goad **6** reason **7** win over **8** convince, persuade **9** prevail on
jive ~: **5** argot, lingo, slang **6** patois **8** parlance **10** vernacular
like: **3** ape **4** echo, mock **5** mimic **6** follow, mirror, parrot **7** copycat, imitate, portray **8** resemble, ridicule **9** make fun of
like a child: **4** lisp
local ~: **5** lingo **6** patois
loose ~: **6** gossip **7** hearsay
low: **7** whisper
monotonously: **5** drone, whine
nonsense: **4** jive **5** prate **6** footle, gabble, ramble, wander **7** blather, blether
out of: **5** deter **6** reason **8** dissuade **10** discourage
over: **6** air out **7** discuss, hash out **9** bat around **10** deliberate, kick around
over again: **6** rehash
pep ~: **6** speech **7** address, lecture, oration
playful ~: **5** humor **6** banter, joking **7** jesting, joshing, kidding, ribbing, teasing **8** badinage, chitchat, raillery, repartee **10** persiflage
rhythmically: **3** rap
session: **5** forum **8** assembly, colloquy **9** symposium **10** conference
slowly: **5** drawl
small ~: **4** chat **6** banter, gossip **7** palaver **8** babbling, chitchat
starter: **4** shop **5** cross
straight: **5** level
street ~: **5** slang
sweet ~: **4** sell **7** blarney, coaxing, palaver **8** cajolery **9** wheedling **10** endearment, inducement, persuasion
table ~: **3** gab, rap **5** prate **6** banter, gabble, gibber, gossip **7** chatter, palaver **8** chin-chin, chitchat, repartee
tech ~: **5** lingo **6** jargon
the talk: **4** brag **5** boast **6** flaunt, parade **7** show off, swagger **10** grandstand
to: **7** contact **8** approach **9** interview **10** get a hold of
too much: **3** gab, gas, jaw, yak, yap **5** drone, run on **6** ramble, rattle **7** drone on
unclearly: **4** slur **6** babble
up: **4** hype, plug, push, tout **7** promote, push for **8** ballyhoo **9** get behind, publicize
wildly: **4** rant, rave
worthless ~: ***see*** baloney
talk __: **3** big, out **4** back, down, into, over, shop, show **5** radio, sense **6** around, turkey
__ talk: **3** big, pep **4** baby, back, girl, town **5** chalk, cross, sales, small, sweet, table **6** pillow
__ talk?: **5** Can we
__-talk: **4** fast **6** double, smooth
Talk __ Town, The: **5** of the
__ Talk: **4** Baby **5** Happy **6** Pillow
talkathon: **7** gabfest **10** filibuster
talkative: **4** glib, long **5** gabby, slick, vocal, windy, wordy **6** chatty, fluent, mouthy, prolix, smooth **7** diffuse, gossipy, lengthy, unterse, verbose, voluble **8** effusive, eloquent, rambling, rattling **9** bombastic, expansive, garrulous **10** articulate, bigmouthed, chattering, discursive, long-winded, loquacious, palaverous
less ~: **5** muter
one: **6** gasbag, gossip, magpie, yakker **8** prattler **10** chatterbox
talkativeness: **9** garrulity, loquacity, prolixity, verbosity, wordiness
talked: **5** spoke
at length: **5** ran on
impolitely: **5** swore
old-style: **5** spake
talker: **6** orator **7** speaker **8** lecturer
excessive ~: **6** gossip, magpie, yakker **8** prattler
proverbial ~: **5** money
__ talker: **5** shelf
talkie: **4** film, show **5** flick, movie **7** picture
attraction: **5** sound
__-talkie: **6** walkie
__ Talkin': **4** Jive
talking
not ~: **3** mum **4** mute **5** quiet **6** silent **8** nonvocal, taciturn **9** voiceless **10** speechless
stop ~: **6** shut up **8** pipe down
talking __: **4** book, down, head **5** chief, point **7** machine, picture
__-talking: **5** trash
Talking __: **5** Heads
Talking Peace
author: Jimmy Carter
talking-to: **6** earful, rebuke **7** lecture **8** reproval, scolding **9** reprimand **10** upbraiding
Talking Trees, The
author: Sean O'Faolain
__ Talkin' Guy: **5** Sweet
Talk is __: **5** cheap
talk it __: **4** over
Talk of Angels (1998 film)
cast: Frances McDormand, Franco Nero
Talk Radio (1988 film)
cast: Alec Baldwin, Eric Bogosian, Ellen Greene
director: Oliver Stone
__ Talks: **5** Garbo
talk show
host: **4** Leno, Paar **5** Allen, Dinah, Oprah, Rosie, Shore **6** Carson, O'Brien **7** Winfrey **8** O'Donnell **9** Letterman
partner: **6** cohost
radio ~ participant: **6** caller
talk through one's __: **3** hat
Talk to Me (1985 song)
artist: Stevie Nicks
__ Talk to Strangers: **4** Don't
talky: **5** wordy **6** chatty **7** verbose, voluble **9** garrulous **10** bigmouthed, long-winded, loquacious
tall: **3** big **4** high, lank, long, size **5** giant, great, lanky, lathy, leggy, lofty, rangy, steep **6** absurd, alpine, gangly **7** sizable, sky-high, soaring, willowy **8** elevated, gangling, sizeable, towering, uplifted **9** overblown **10** exorbitant, farfetched, improbable, long-legged, statuesque
in Spanish: **4** alto
stand ~: **5** tower
standing ~: **4** bold, game **5** brave, gutsy, nervy, tough **6** gritty, heroic, plucky, strong **7** assured, doughty, valiant **8** fearless, heroical, resolute, unafraid, valorous **9** confident, dauntless, undaunted **10** courageous, mettlesome, red-blooded
tale: **3** lie **4** yarn **5** story **9** invention
tall __: **3** oil, one **4** tale **5** drink, order, story
tall, __, and handsome: **4** dark
__ tall: **5** stand **7** walking
Tallahassee: **4** city, town **7** capital
athletes: **9** Seminoles
county: **4** Leon
locale: **3** Fla. **7** Florida
school: **3** FSU
tallboy: **5** glass **6** goblet
Tallchief, Maria: **6** dancer **8** danseuse **9** ballerina
taller, get: **4** grow
Talley's Folly
author: Lanford Wilson
Tallinn: **4** city, port, town **7** capital
locale: **7** Estonia
native: **4** Esth
tallith feature: **6** fringe
tallness: **5** reach **6** height, length **7** stature **8** altitude **9** elevation
tallow: **4** lard, suet **6** grease **9** lubricate
acid in ~: **5** oleic
combining form: **5** steat- **6** steato-
product: **4** soap **6** candle
Tall Paul (1959 song)
artist: Annette Funicello
__ Tall Sally: **4** Long
Tallulah: **8** Bankhead
tally: **3** add, sum **4** gybe, jibe, list, poll, tell **5** add up, agree, chalk, count, gauge, score, sum up, total, tot up **6** census, figure, notate, number, reckon, record, square, voting **7** account, catalog, chalk up, compute, conform, itemize **8** check out, coincide, mark down, numerate, register **9** calculate, catalogue, enumerate, head count, inventory, keep count, keep score, reckoning **10** bottom line, correspond, count heads
mark: **5** notch
Talmadge: **5** Norma
Talmadge Girls, The
author: Anita Loos
Talman: **7** William
Tal, Mikhail
forte: **5** chess
Talmud
follower: **3** Jew
language: **6** Hebrew

scholar: 4 gaon 5 rabbi, rebbe
section: 6 Gemara
Talmud __: 5 Torah
talon: 4 claw 6 ungual, unguis
Taltos
author: Anne Rice
talus: 4 bone 5 ankle, scree
decoration: 6 anklet
tam: 3 cap, hat, lid 8 balmoral
cousin: 5 beret
wearer: 4 Scot
Tama: 8 Janowitz
__ tamale: 3 hot
Tamar
brother: 7 Absalom
father: 5 David
Tamara: 7 Jenkins 9 Karsavina
tamarack: 4 tree 5 larch
relative: 3 fir 4 pine 6 spruce 7 hemlock
tamarind: 4 tree 5 fruit 6 veggie 9 vegetable
family: 6 legume
relative: *see* legume tree
Tamarind Seed, The (1974 film)
cast: Julie Andrews, Omar Sharif, Sylvia Syms
tamarisk: 4 atle, tree 5 plant, shrub 6 flower
Tamblyn: 4 Russ 5 Amber
Tambor: 7 Jeffrey
tambourine: 3 riq 4 drum 6 chimta 8 pandéiro
__ Tambourine: 5 Green
Tamburlaine the Great
author: Christopher Marlowe
tame: 4 bust, curb, dull, flat, meek, mild, slow, weak 5 bland, break, check, train, unfun, vapid, yoked 6 boring, bridle, broken, busted, docile, feeble, gentle, govern, jejune, pacify, placid, pliant, soften, subdue, temper 7 conquer, diluted, enslave, harness, humdrum, insipid, muzzled, prosaic, repress, routine, subdued, tedious, trained 8 amenable, biddable, domestic, harmless, lamblike, obedient, restrain, sheepish, suppress, tone down, unafraid, unlively 9 civilized, colorless, compliant, dry-as-dust, harnessed, prosaical, subjugate, tractable, wearisome 10 cultivated, dullsville, manageable, monotonous, spiritless, submissive, unexciting, white-bread
tamed: 6 broken 7 crushed, subdued 10 spiritless
tamer: 6 catman 9 Petruchio 10 roughrider
need: 4 hoop, whip
place: 6 circus
Tamerlane: 5 Timur
author: Edgar Allan Poe
Tam Glen
author: Robert Burns
Tamiami __: 5 Trail
__ Tamid: 3 Ner
Tamil Nadu
capital: 6 Madras
Taming of the Shrew, The: 4 play
author: William Shakespeare
character: 3 Sly 6 Bianca, Curtis, Gremio, Grumio, Tranio 8 Baptista, Lucentio 9 Biondello, Hortensio, Katharina, Petruchio, Vincentio 11 Christopher
setting: 5 Italy, Padua
Tamiroff: 4 Akim
Tammany Hall
boss: 5 Tweed
foe: 4 Nast
Tammi: 7 Terrell
Tamm, Igor: 8 Nobelist 9 physicist
Tammuz: 5 month 6 Hebrew
predecessor: 5 Sivan
successor: 2 Av
Tammy: 6 Grimes 7 Wynette
Tammy (1957 song)
artist: Ames Brothers, Debbie Reynolds
Tammy __ Bakker: 4 Faye
tam-o'-shanter: 3 cap, hat
Tam O'Shanter
author: Robert Burns
tamp: 3 jam, ram 4 cram, pack 7 pat down 8 pack down, push down 9 pound down
Tampa: 3 bay 4 city, port, town
athletes: 5 Bulls
city near ~: 5 Largo 6 St. Pete
clock setting: 3 EDT, EST
locale: 3 Fla. 7 Florida
newspaper: 4 Trib 7 Tribune
pro team: 4 Rays 9 Lightning 10 Buccaneers
school: 3 USF
tamper: 3 cut, fix, rig 4 cook 5 alter, bribe, get to, plant, reach, spike 6 butt in, change, doctor, fiddle, horn in, meddle, tinker 7 corrupt, intrude, phony up 8 mess with 9 interfere, interlope, muck about 10 fiddle with, manipulate
don't ~ with: 5 let be 7 leave be 8 let alone 10 deregulate
with: 3 fix, rig 5 fudge 6 change, damage, doctor, juggle, monkey
(with): 6 fiddle, monkey
tam-tam: 4 bell, gong 5 chime
TAMU
conference: 9 Big Twelve
see also Texas A&M
tan: 3 sun 4 buff, drab, drub, flog, lick, sand, whip 5 brown, color, cream, flail, olive, spank, taupe 6 almond, bronze, darken, defeat, larrup, saddle, swarth, thrash, thwack, wallop 7 bronzed, natural, neutral, scourge, swarthy 8 brownish, sunbathe 9 yellowish 10 light brown, olive-brown
a hide: 6 punish
get a ~: 3 sun 4 bask 8 sunbathe
leather: 4 cure
relative: *see* brown color
starter: 3 sun
__-tan: 3 fan
tanager: 4 bird, yeni 5 lindo
Tan, Amy: 6 writer
work: The Bonesetter's Daughter
The Hundred Secret Senses
The Joy Luck Club
The Kitchen God's Wife
Moon Lady
The Opposite of Fate
Sagwa, the Chinese Siamese Cat
Saving Fish from Drowning
Tanana: 5 Frank, river 6 Indian 7 Amerind
locale: 6 Alaska
Tanana, Frank
sport: 8 baseball
Tanaro
city on the ~: 4 Asti
Tancredi
composer: Gioacchino Rossini
tandem __: 4 bike 7 bicycle, trailer
tandoor: 4 oven
tandoori-baked bread: 3 nan
__ T. and the MGs: 6 Booker
Tandy, Jessica: 7 actress
film: The Birds (1963)
Butley (1974)
Cocoon (1985)
Driving Miss Daisy (1989, AA)
Fried Green Tomatoes (1991)
Nobody's Fool (1994)
spouse: Hume Cronyn, Jack Hawkins
Tandy product: 2 PC 8 computer
tang: 3 nip, zip 4 bite, hint, kick, odor, zest 5 aroma, drink, punch, sapor, savor, scent, smack, smell, spice, taste 6 flavor, relish 8 piquancy, pungency 9 sharpness, spiciness 10 aftertaste
lacking ~: 5 bland, vapid
T'ang: 7 Chinese, dynasty
capital: 4 Sian
follower ~: 4 Liao
tangelo: 4 tree, ugli 5 fruit 6 citrus
relative: *see* citrus
tangent: 4 tack 5 ratio
cousin: 4 sine 6 cosine, secant
go off on a ~: 5 stray 6 ramble, wander 7 digress
Tangent Factor, The
author: Lawrence Sanders
tangential: 4 side 6 beside 7 close by 8 touching 9 alongside, bordering, excursive, proximate 10 digressive, side-by-side
remark: 5 aside 10 digression
to: 4 near
Tangent Objective, The
author: Lawrence Sanders
tangerine: 4 tree 5 color, fruit 6 citrus, orange 7 reddish, satsuma
relative: *see* citrus, orange color
tangerine-shaped: 6 oblate
tangibility: 7 reality
tangible: 4 real 5 solid 6 actual 7 evident, obvious, visible 8 concrete, definite, embodied, explicit, manifest, material, palpable, physical 9 corporeal, objective, touchable 10 detectable, observable, unimagined, verifiable
Tangier: 4 city, port, town
locale: 7 Morocco
tanginess: 4 zest, zing 6 flavor
tangle: 3 mat, mix, mop, web 4 coil, foul, kink, knot, maze, mesh, mess, muss, snag, trap 5 melee, mix up, skein, snarl, twist 6 enlace, enmesh, entrap, immesh, inmesh, jumble, jungle, morass, muddle, ruffle, rumple, tousle, touzle 7 clutter, embroil, ensnare, insnare, mistake, quarrel, sinuate 8 dishevel, entangle 9 confusion, implicate, labyrinth, patchwork 10 disarrange, intertwine, interweave
with: 3 box, vie 4 feud, spar 5 argue, brawl, clash, fight 6 attack, bicker, combat, defend, go at it, hassle, oppose, resist, rumble, take on 7 contend, dispute, grapple, lay into, mix it up, protest, quarrel, scuffle, wage war, wrangle 8 do battle, squabble 9 altercate, challenge, scrimmage, square off 10 put up a fuss
tangled: 5 afoul, kinky 6 knotty, matted, thorny 7 chaotic, complex, jumbled, knotted, mixed up, tousled 8 involved, pell-mell 9 difficult, intricate 10 disorderly, topsy-turvy
get ~: 3 mat 4 knot 5 snarl, twist
Tanglewood Festival
locale: 4 Mass. 5 Lenox
tango: 5 dance, music
feature: 3 dip
requirement: 3 duo, two 4 pair 6 couple 7 twosome
Tango
author: Slawomir Mrozek
__ Tango: 4 Blue
Tango and __: 4 Cash
__ Tango in Bayreuth: 4 Last
__ Tango in Paris: 4 Last
Tanguay: 3 Eva
Tanguy: 4 Yves
tangy: 4 tart 5 minty, salty, zesty, zippy 6 acetic, biting, lemony, savory 7 piquant, pungent 9 flavorful
tania: 4 taro
tank: 3 vat 4 pool 6 panzer 7 cistern, Sherman, vehicle 8 aquarium 9 container, reservoir
closer: 6 gas cap
filler: 3 gas 4 fuel 8 gasoline
fill the ~: 4 fuel 5 gas up
level: 4 full 5 empty
starter: 4 anti
think ~ output: 6 notion, theory 7 concept 8 proposal 10 brainstorm
top: 5 shirt
when ~ warfare began: 3 WWI
tank __: 3 car, top 4 farm, suit, town
__ tank: 3 gas 5 glass, scuba, spray, think 6 septic 7 holding, Sherman
tanka: 4 poem 8 Japanese
kin: 5 haiku
tankard: 3 mug, pot 5 stein
contents: 3 ale 4 beer 5 stout 6 porter
tanker: 4 boat, ship 5 oiler 6 vessel
cargo: 3 oil 5 crude 8 crude oil
insignia, once: 4 Esso
leak: 5 spill
__ tanker: 3 oil, ore
tankful: 3 gas
Tank Girl (1995 film)
cast: Ice-T, Lori Petty
tanned: 5 brown 6 bronze, bronzy
not ~: 4 pale
starter: 3 sun
tannenbaum: 3 fir
Tanners
houseguest: 3 Alf
Tannhäuser: 5 opera
composer: 6 Wagner
role: 5 Venus 7 Hermann, Wolfram 9 Elisabeth
setting: 7 Germany 9 Thuringia
song: 4 aria
tannic __: 4 acid
tanning: 7 licking 8 flailing, flogging, whipping

bark for ~: **5** sumac **6** sumach
need: **3** sun **4** hide
solution: **4** bate
tanning __: **3** bed **6** parlor
tanning-lotion letters: **3** SPF **4** PABA
tannin source: **5** sumac **6** sumach
tan one's __: **4** hide
tantalize: **4** bait **5** charm, taunt, tease, worry **6** entice, lead on **7** provoke, torment **8** interest **9** fascinate, frustrate, titillate
tantalizing: **5** juicy, siren **8** tempting
tantalum: **5** metal **7** element
Tantalus
daughter: **5** Niobe
father: **4** Zeus
son: **6** Pelops **7** Broteas
wife: **12** Clytemnestra
tantamount: **4** like, same **5** equal **6** as good, on a par **9** duplicate, identical **10** comparable, coordinate, equivalent
tantara: **5** blare **7** fanfare **8** flourish
tante: **4** aunt **6** French
possession: **5** plume
spouse: **5** oncle
tanto: **6** so much **7** too much
tantrum: **3** fit **4** rage, snit, tiff **5** scene, storm **6** blowup, temper **7** flare-up, rampage **8** outburst, paroxysm **9** explosion, hysterics **10** conniption
throw a ~: **4** rant
thrower: **3** imp **4** brat **5** child **9** youngster
__ tantrum: **6** temper
Tanya: **6** Tucker **7** Roberts
Tanzania: **6** nation **7** country
capital: **6** Dodoma
city: **5** Mbeya, Moshi, Tanga, Ujiji **6** Dodoma, Iringa, Kigoma, Mtwara, Musoma, Mwanza, Songea, Tabora **8** Morogoro, Zanzibar
island: **5** Pemba **8** Zanzibar
lake: **5** Nyasa **6** Malawi **8** Victoria **10** Tanganyika
language: **5** Masai **6** Maasai
locale: **3** Afr. **6** Africa
money: **4** cent **5** senti **8** shilling
mountain: **4** Meru
neighbor: **5** Kenya **6** Malawi, Rwanda, Uganda, Zambia **7** Burundi **10** Mozambique
people: **3** Yao **5** Chaga, Makua, Masai, Ngoni, Nguni **6** Chagga, Dorobo, Maasai, Sukuma **7** Makonde **8** Nyamwezi **9** Wandorobo
region: **5** Tanga
tanzanite: **3** gem **8** gemstone
Tao
homophone: **3** Dow
literally: **3** way
Taoism: **3** rel. **8** religion
power in ~: **3** teh
Tao of Pooh, The
author: Benjamin Hoff
Taormina mount: **4** Etna **5** Aetna
Taos: **4** city, town **6** Indian **7** Amerind
locale: **4** N. Mex. **9** New Mexico
Tao Te Ching
author: Lao-tzu
tap: **3** bug, dab, pat, rap, tag, use **4** draw, drum, milk, name, open, peck, tick **5** draft, drain, flick, knock, spike, spile, spout, thrum, thump, touch, valve **6** assign, broach, choose, draw on, faucet, fillip, lounge, nozzle, patter, select, siphon, spigot, strike, syphon, unplug **7** appoint, bibcock, exploit, hydrant, petcock, utilize **8** draw upon, keep time, nominate, stopcock **9** designate, eavesdrop, siphon off, unstopper **10** settle upon
choice: **3** ale **4** beer **5** draft, stout **6** porter
ender: **4** room, root
on ~: **4** open **5** ready **7** in store **9** available, in reserve, ready to go, scheduled **10** at the ready, convenient, obtainable, time-saving
problem: **4** drip, leak **5** crack **7** dribble, trickle
starter: **4** heel, wire
word: **3** hot **4** cold
tap __: **3** off **4** bell, bolt, into **5** dance, pants, water **6** dancer
Tap (1989 film)
cast: Sammy Davis Jr., Gregory Hines
tapas: **9** appetizer **10** finger food
tap-dance: **6** hoof it
tape: **4** band, bind, bond, line, mend, seal, wrap **5** strip, truss, video **6** edging, fasten, record, ribbon, secure, swathe, wrap up **7** bandage **8** cassette **9** prerecord **10** finish line, transcribe, transcript
beginning: **6** leader
clear a ~: **5** erase **6** delete
ender: **4** line, worm
format: **3** VHS **4** Beta
half: **5** side A, side B
linen ~: **5** inkle
machine: **3** VCR
measure: **5** ruler
player: **7** boombox
put on ~: **6** record
recorder measure: **3** ips
red ~: **4** maze **5** delay **6** policy, system **8** protocol **9** paperwork, procedure, rigmarole **10** impediment
reel: **5** spool
sample ~: **4** demo
starter: **5** audio, video
wrap in red ~: **5** delay, sit on
tape __: **4** deck **5** drive, grass **6** player **7** measure
tape-__: **6** record
__ tape: **3** red **4** duct **6** Scotch, ticker **7** masking, tracing
Tape (2001 film)
cast: Ethan Hawke, Robert Sean Leonard, Uma Thurman
__-tape parade: **6** ticker
taper: **5** abate, light, slack **6** candle, lessen, narrow, recede, reduce **7** sharpen, slacken **8** diminish
off: **4** fade, flag, wane **5** abate, close, drain **6** lessen, narrow, recede, reduce **7** die away, dwindle, subside, thin out **8** decrease, diminish, peter out, wind down **9** retrocede
part: **4** wick
taper __: **3** off
tape recorder
attachment: **3** mic **10** microphone
button: **3** fwd, rec, rew **4** play **5** pause **6** record, rewind **7** forward
tapered: **5** sharp **6** fusate, narrow, pointy, terete **7** pointed
tapestry: **5** arras **6** carpet **7** drapery
fiber: **5** ramee, ramie
make a ~: **5** weave
motif: **6** bocage
Norman Conquest ~: **6** Bayeux
spot ~: **4** wall
thread: **4** weft
taphouse: **3** bar, pub **6** saloon, tavern
tap-in: **5** gimme
tapioca: **6** junket
source: **6** casava
tapir: **6** animal, mammal
cousin: **5** rhino
feature: **5** snout
Tappan
alternative: ***see*** appliance brand
Tappan __ Bridge: **3** Zee
tapped: **7** abroach
item: **3** keg **5** maple **9** maple tree
out: **5** broke **8** bankrupt, depleted, strapped **9** insolvent, penniless
tapper: **5** gavel
starter: **4** wire
vein ~: **5** miner
taproom: **3** bar, pub **4** dive **6** lounge, saloon, tavern
taps
like some ~: **5** leaky **6** drippy
Taps: **4** tune **9** bugle call
instrument: **5** bugle
time, at times: **3** ten **5** ten p.m.
tar: **3** gob **4** drum, goop, pave, salt, soil, swab, swob **5** pitch, smear, stain, taint **6** crud up, impugn, larrup, sailor, sea dog, seaman, thrash **7** asphalt, bitumen, crewman, encrust, incrust, mariner, matelot, matelow, old salt, swabbie, tarnish **8** deckhand, seafarer **10** bluejacket
coal ~ extract: **6** cresol
ender: **3** mac **4** weed **5** paper
in Spanish: **4** brea **6** la brea
juniper ~: **4** cade
pits locale: **6** La Brea **10** Los Angeles
source: **4** coal, pine
whale the ~ out of: **3** tan **4** rout **6** defeat, ravage **9** overpower
see also sailor
tar __: **4** baby, ball
__ tar: **4** coal, pine, wood
Tar __: **4** Baby, Heel
__ Tar: **4** Jack
Tara: **4** Kemp, Reid **6** estate **8** Lipinski **10** Fitzgerald
family name: **5** O'Hara
land of ~: **4** Eire, Erin **7** Ireland
locale: **7** Atlanta, Georgia
taradiddle: **3** fib
see also baloney
taradiddler: **4** liar
tar and __: **7** feather
tarantella: **5** dance
Tarantino: **7** Quentin
tarantula: **3** bug **6** insect
leg count: **5** eight
like a ~: **5** fuzzy, hairy
toxin: **5** venom
Ta-Ra-Ra-Boom-__: **4** De-Ré
Tara Road
author: Maeve Binchy
Taras Bulba
author: Nikolai Gogol
Tarawa: **4** city, town **7** capital
locale: **8** Kiribati
Tar Baby
author: Toni Morrison
Tar-Baby, The
author: Joel Chandler Harris
Tarbell, Ida: **6** writer **9** muckraker
work: History of the Standard Oil Company
tarboosh cousin: **3** fez
tarde: **7** Spanish **9** afternoon
activity: **6** siesta
tardy: **4** late, lazy, poky, slow **5** slack **6** behind, held up, hung up **7** belated, delayed, languid, overdue, past due, unready **8** dawdling, detained, dilatory, slothful **9** laggardly, leisurely, lethargic, snaillike **10** behindhand, behind time, delinquent, unpunctual
be ~: **3** lag **4** idle **5** dally, delay, mosey, tarry, trail **6** dawdle, linger, loiter **10** dillydally
make ~: **5** laten
somewhat ~: **6** latish
tare: **4** weed **5** vetch
Targa: **3** car **4** auto **7** Porsche **9** sports car **10** automobile
target: **3** aim, end **4** butt, goal, goat, gull, mark, prey **5** aim at, focus, patsy **6** intent, object, pigeon, quarry, reason, victim **7** purpose **8** ambition, bull's-eye **9** intention, objective, scapegoat **10** ground zero
face the ~: **3** aim
on ~: **3** apt **7** apropos
target __: **4** date
__ target: **6** moving
target practice game: **5** skeet
Tar Heel State: **4** N. Car.
school: **3** UNC **4** Elon
tariff: **3** fee, tab, tax **4** cost, duty, fare, levy, rate, toll **5** price **6** charge, excise, impost, towage **7** expense **8** exaction **10** assessment
pact: **4** GATT **5** NAFTA
Tarkanian: **5** Jerry
Tarkenton, Fran: **2** QB
sport: **8** football
Tarkington, Booth: **6** writer
work: Alice Adams
The Gentleman From Indiana
The Magnificent Ambersons
Monsieur Beaucaire
Penrod
Seventeen
tarmac
area: **5** apron
lay down ~: **4** pave
reached the ~: **4** alit
roll on the ~: **4** taxi
tarn: **4** lake, pond, pool **5** lough **9** reservoir
tarnish: **3** dim, mar, tar **4** blot, dull, foul, rust, soil, spot **5** dirty, oxide, smear, spoil, stain, sully, taint **6** befoul, damage, darken, deface,

defame, defile, malign, smudge 7 begrime, blacken, blemish, corrode, oxidize, pollute, slander 8 besmirch, discolor, disgrace, throw mud 10 imputation

tarnished: 5 dirty, grimy, sooty 6 filthy, grubby, grungy 7 unclean 8 maculate, slovenly, vitiated 10 unsanitary

taro: 5 aroid, tania, tuber 6 veggie 9 rootstock, vegetable
- **product:** 3 poi
- **root:** 4 eddo
- **tuber:** 4 corm

tarot card: 3 Sun 4 Fool, King, Moon, Page, Star 5 Death, Devil, Queen, Tower, World 6 Hermit, Knight, Lovers 7 Chariot, Emperor, Empress, Justice 8 Magician, Strength 9 Hanged Man, Judgement 10 Hierophant, Temperance
- **group:** 6 arcana
- **reader:** 4 seer 7 prophet, psychic
- **reading:** 10 prediction
- **suit:** 4 cups 5 wands 6 swords 9 pentacles

tarp
- *see* tarpaulin

tarpaulin: 5 sheet 6 canvas 8 covering 10 protection

tarragon: 4 herb

tarry: 3 lag 4 bide, drag, idle, laze, loaf, poke, stay, stop, wait 5 abide, amble, dally, delay, mosey, pause, stall, trail, visit 6 dawdle, linger, loiter, remain 7 saunter, sojourn, stand by 8 footdrag, hold back, lollygag, stop over, straggle 9 temporize, waste time 10 dillydally, filibuster, goof around, hang around, wait around

tarsal
- *see* tarsus

tarsus: 4 bone
- **adornment:** 6 anklet
- **locale:** 4 foot 5 ankle
- **starter:** 4 meta

tart: 3 pie 4 acid, cake, sour 5 acerb, acrid, salty, sharp, tangy, testy, zingy 6 acidic, biting, bitter, crabby, lemony, pastry, snappy, snippy 7 acerbic, caustic, cutting, dessert, piquant, popover, pungent, zinging 8 snappish, snippety, vinegary 9 acidulous, trenchant 10 astringent
- **fruit:** 4 sloe 5 berry, lemon 9 crab apple
- **ingredient:** 5 dough, flour, fruit, sugar
- **substance:** 4 acid
- **thief of fiction:** 5 knave

tartan: 4 kilt, sett 5 plaid 6 fabric
- **trousers:** 5 trews
- **wearer:** 4 clan, Scot

tartar: 5 sauce
- **grape ~:** 5 argal, argol
- **sauce ingredient:** 5 caper

tartar ___: 5 sauce, steak

___ tartare: 5 steak

Tartarian ___: 5 aster

tartaric ___: 4 acid

tartness: 6 flavor 7 acidity 8 acerbity, acrimony 10 bitterness
- **with ~:** 6 acidly

tartrate: 4 salt 5 ester

___-Tarts: 3 Pop

tart-tongued: 4 mean 5 catty, nasty 7 hateful, vicious 8 spiteful, venomous 9 rancorous 10 backbiting, ill-natured

Tartu: 4 city, town
- **locale:** 7 Estonia
- **resident:** 4 Esth

Tartuffe: 4 play 6 comedy
- **author:** Molière
- **character:** 5 Damis, Orgon 6 Dorine, Elmire, Valère 7 Cléante, Mariane

tarty: 4 sour

Tarzan: 4 hero 5 he-man 6 ape man
- **companion:** 3 ape 5 chimp
- **home:** 6 jungle
- **lion:** 4 Numa 5 simba
- **love:** 4 Jane
- **mother:** 5 Alice
- **portrayer:** 3 Ely 4 Brix 5 Henry, Scott 6 Barker, Crabbe, O'Keefe, Ron Ely 7 Lambert, Lincoln 9 Lex Barker, Mike Henry 10 Herman Brix 11 Gordon Scott, Miles O'Keefe, Weissmuller
- **son:** 3 Boy
- **title:** 4 earl
- **transport:** 4 vine 5 liana, liane

Tarzan (1999 film)
- **voice cast:** Glenn Close, Minnie Driver, Tony Goldwyn, Rosie O'Donnell

Tarzan (NBC/CBS adventure)
- **cast:** Ron Ely (Tarzan) Manuel Padilla Jr. (Jai)

Tarzan, the Ape Man (1932 film)
- **cast:** Maureen O'Sullivan, Johnny Weissmuller

Taschhorn: 3 Alp

taser: 3 gun 7 stun gun

Tashi ___: 4 Lama

Tashkent: 4 city, town 7 capital
- **city near ~:** 3 Osh
- **language:** 5 Usbeg, Usbek, Uzbeg, Uzbek
- **locale:** 4 Asia 10 Uzbekistan

Tashlin: 5 Frank

task: 3 job 4 duty, onus, part, role, toil, work 5 chore, grind, labor, stint, thing 6 burden, charge, errand, lesson 7 mission, project 8 activity, business, function, headache, homework, overload 9 millstone 10 assignment, enterprise, obligation
- **simple ~:** 4 snap 6 breeze
- **unpleasant ~:** 4 onus

task ___: 5 force

taskmaster: 5 taxer 6 ramrod 8 martinet, stickler

Tasman: 3 sea 4 Abel
- **locale:** 9 Australia 10 New Zealand

Tasman, Abel Janszoon: 5 Dutch 8 explorer

Tasmania: 4 isle 6 island
- **capital:** 6 Hobart
- **fish:** 6 inanga
- **mountain:** 4 Ossa
- **pine:** 4 huon
- **river:** 5 Tamar

Tasmanian ___: 4 wolf 5 devil, tiger

Tasmanian devil: 9 marsupial
- **relative:** *see* marsupial

___-Tass: 4 Itar

tasse: 3 cup 6 French
- **contents:** 3 thé 4 café
- **starter:** 4 demi

tassel: 4 tuft
- **corn ~:** 4 silk

tasseled
- **cap:** 3 fez, tam
- **hem:** 6 fringe

Tasso, Torquato: 4 poet 7 Italian
- **patron:** 4 Este
- **work:** Aminta Jerusalem Delivered Rinaldo

taste: 3 bit, eat, nip, sip, try, zip 4 bite, chew, dash, drop, hint, kick, know, lick, sour, tang, test, zest, zing 5 enjoy, fancy, flair, gusto, punch, salty, sapor, savor, sense, share, smack, style, sweet, tinge, touch 6 bitter, canapé, flavor, ginger, liking, little, morsel, nibble, palate, polish, relish, sample, tidbit, trifle 7 culture, decorum, leaning, portion, soupçon, stomach, swallow 8 appetite, delicacy, elegance, fondness, judgment, mouthful, penchant, piquancy, sapidity, spoonful, weakness 9 encounter, partake of, restraint 10 excellence, experience, partiality, preference, proclivity, propensity, refinement, savoriness, sprinkling, suggestion
- **again:** 5 retry
- **bad ~:** 9 crassness, indecorum, vulgarity 10 coarseness, indelicacy
- **ender:** 5 maker
- **get a ~ of:** 3 try 6 sample
- **good ~:** 4 tact 5 taste 7 culture
- **have no ~ for:** 4 hate 5 abhor 6 detest 7 despise, dislike 9 abominate
- **having a ~ for:** 6 fond of 9 partial to
- **like:** 7 smack of
- **like a ~ bud:** 5 ovoid
- **small ~:** 3 nip, sip 4 bite, lick 6 sample
- **starter:** 5 after
- **stimulus:** 5 aroma
- **tease the ~ buds:** 4 whet

taste ___: 3 bud 4 test

tasteful: 4 fine, nice 5 quiet 6 classy, pretty, seemly 7 elegant, refined, subdued 8 artistic, charming, cultured, esthetic, graceful, handsome, pleasing, polished 9 ambrosial, beautiful, exquisite 10 artistical, cultivated, gratifying, harmonious, restrained

tastefulness: 5 charm, class, grace, style, taste 6 beauty, luxury, polish 7 dignity 8 elegance 9 gentility 10 refinement

tasteless: 4 blah, dull, flat, loud, mild, rude, thin, weak 5 bland, cheap, crass, crude, gaudy, gross, plain, rough, showy, stale, tacky, vapid 6 boring, coarse, flashy, garish, ornate, tawdry, vulgar, watery 7 insipid, raffish, raunchy, uncouth, vanilla 8 improper, off-color, tactless, unlovely, unsalted, unsavory, unseemly, unsubtle 9 graceless, inelegant, savorless, unrefined 10 flavorless, indecorous, indelicate, outlandish, unbecoming, unpolished, unseasoned

Taste of Honey, A (1965 song)
- **artist:** Herb Alpert and the Tijuana Brass

taster
- **need:** 4 fork 5 spoon

Taster's Choice: 6 coffee
- **alternative:** 5 Sanka, Yuban 7 Folgers, Melitta, Nescafé, Savarin 9 Hills Bros.

tasty: 4 good, nice, rich 5 sapid, spicy, yummy, zesty 6 dainty, delish, divine, mellow, savory, spicey, toothy 7 piquant, zestful 8 heavenly, luscious, noshable 9 ambrosial, delicious, flavorful, nectarous, palatable, succulent, sweetened, toothsome, with a kick 10 appetizing, delectable, flavorsome

tat
- **give tit for ~:** 5 spite 6 avenge 7 get even, pay back, revenge 9 retaliate
- **tit for ~:** 7 revenge 8 exchange, reprisal 9 interplay, vengeance

___-tat: 4 rat-a

ta-ta: 3 bye 5 later, see ya 6 goodby, so long 7 goodbye 8 farewell
- **in French:** 5 adieu 8 au revoir
- **in Hawaiian:** 5 aloha
- **in Italian:** 4 ciao
- **in Latin:** 3 ave 4 vale
- **in Spanish:** 5 adios

tatami: 3 mat 8 Japanese
- **material:** 5 straw

Tatar: 7 Crimean
- **chief:** 4 khan
- **soldier:** 4 ulan 5 uhlan

Tatar Strait, river into the: 4 Amur

Tate: 5 Allen, Laura, Nahum 6 Sharon

Tate, Allen: 4 poet 6 writer
- **work:** Ode to the Confederate Dead

Tate Gallery display: 3 art

tater: 4 spud 5 tuber 9 vegetable
- *see also* potato

Tater ___: 4 Tots

Tate, Sharon: 7 actress
- **spouse:** Roman Polanski

Tati: 7 Jacques

Tatiana: 5 Murin 8 Troyanos

Tatis, Fernando
- **sport:** 8 baseball

Tatler, The essayist: 6 Steele 7 Addison

___-tat-tat: 4 rat-a

tatter: 3 rag 4 rent, tear 5 shred

tatterdemalion: 4 waif 6 urchin 10 ragamuffin

tattered: 4 worn 5 mangy, ratty, seedy 6 in rags, mangey, ragged, shabby 7 in holes, run-down, scruffy, worn-out 8 slipshod, untended 9 ungroomed 10 threadbare

Tattered Tom
- **author:** Horatio Alger

tatters, in: 4 shot, torn 6 ragged

tatting: 4 lace

tattle: 3 rat 4 blab, chat, fink, leak, sing, talk 5 prate, rat on, rumor,

spill 6 babble, gossip, jabber, report, snitch, squeal, tell on 7 chatter, hearsay, prattle 8 informer, telltale 9 informant
ender: 4 tale
on: 6 give up, turn in 8 give away
__-tattle: 6 tittle
tattler: 3 rat 4 bird, fink, nark 5 namer 6 canary, gossip, ratter, snitch, squeal 7 ratfink, traitor 8 bigmouth, busybody, fat mouth, informer, squealer, telltale, turncoat 9 informant 10 talebearer, taleteller
tattletale
see tattler
tattletale __: 4 gray, grey
Tattletales: 8 game show
host: Bert Convy
tattoo: 4 call 6 design, signal 9 bugle call
place: 3 arm
popular ~: 3 Mom
__ Tattoo, The: 4 Rose
tatty: 4 worn 5 cheap 6 frayed, ragged, shabby 8 decrepit, ill-kempt 9 moth-eaten
Tatum: 3 Art 5 Goose, O'Neal 6 Edward
dad: 4 Ryan
Tatum, Art: 7 pianist
genre: 4 jazz
Tatyana: 3 Ali
tau: 5 Greek 6 letter
predecessor: 5 sigma
successor: 7 upsilon
tau __: 5 cross
taught: 4 wise 5 shown 8 educated, well-bred
be ~: 5 learn, study 6 absorb, master, soak up 7 major in, minor in 9 brush up on 10 get down pat
information ~: 6 lesson
__-taught: 4 self
taunt: 3 cut, dig, egg, guy, jab, rag, rib, vex 4 barb, gibe, goad, haze, jape, jeer, jest, jibe, mock, razz, ride, slam, slap, slur, snub, twit 5 abuse, chaff, crack, decry, get on, libel, roast, scorn, sneer, spurn, swipe, tease 6 banter, bother, defame, deride, dump on, harass, heckle, impugn, insult, jeer at, jibe at, malign, needle, noodge, offend, rebuff, slight, vilify 7 affront, asperse, calumny, catcall, degrade, disdain, laugh at, mockery, obloquy, offense, provoke, put down, rank out, sarcasm, scoff at, slander, snigger, torment, traduce 8 belittle, contempt, denounce, derision, ridicule, vilipend 9 aspersion, cheap shot, contumely, denigrate, discredit, disparage, humiliate, make fun of, poke fun at, tantalize 10 calumniate, defamation, disrespect, make game of, opprobrium
taunting: 7 jeering, satiric 8 derisive 9 annoyance, sarcastic, satirical
exclamation: 3 oho
one: 5 darer
taupe: 4 gray, grey 5 color 8 brownish
relative: *see* gray color
Taupin: 6 Bernie
Taurog: 6 Norman
Taurus: 3 car 4 auto, Ford, sign 5 range 9 mountains 10 automobile
locale: 4 Asia 6 Turkey
month: 3 Apr., May 5 April
nebula in ~: 4 crab
neighbor: 5 Orion
predecessor: 5 Aries
ruler of ~ in astrology: 5 Venus
successor: 6 Gemini
taut: 4 firm, snug, trim 5 drawn, rigid, stiff, tense, tight 7 nervous, wound up 8 fluttery, strained, stressed 9 shipshape, stretched, unrelaxed 10 highstrung, inflexible, unyielding
not ~: 5 loose, slack
tauten: 4 tidy 7 stretch, tighten 9 constrict
tautness: 6 strain 7 tension 9 tightness
lose ~: 3 sag
tautological: 7 verbose 9 redundant
tautology: 8 verbiage 10 repetition
tautomeric compound: 4 enol
Tautou: 6 Audrey
tav: 6 Hebrew, letter
predecessor: 4 shin
tavern: 3 bar, inn, pub 4 dive 5 hotel, joint, lodge 6 bistro, lounge, saloon 7 barroom, gin mill, taproom 8 alehouse, grog shop, hostelry, lodgment, taphouse 9 honky-tonk, nightspot, roadhouse, speakeasy
old-style: 4 inne
supply: 3 ale 4 beer, grog 5 lager, stout 6 liquor
visit ~s: 6 barhop
see also bar
__ Tavern: 6 Duffy's
Tavist
alternative: *see* cold remedy
taw: 5 aggie 6 Hebrew, letter
predecessor: 4 shin
...taw a __ tat!: 5 puddy
tawdry: 4 loud, mean 5 cheap, crude, gaudy, jazzy, junky, showy, tacky 6 brazen, common, flashy, garish, glitzy, ornate, shoddy, sleazy, tinsel, vulgar 7 blatant, chintzy, raffish 8 gimcrack, schlocky 9 tasteless 10 glittering, second-rate
things: 6 kitsch
tawn: 5 flaxy 6 flaxen
tawny: 3 tan 5 blond, brown, color 6 blonde, golden, swarth, yellow 7 old gold, saffron, swarthy 8 brindled 9 yellowish
animal: 3 owl 4 lion
combining form: 5 fusco-, pyrrh-, pyrro- 6 pyrhho-
relative: *see* brown color
tawny __: 4 port
Tawny: 6 Kitaen
tax: 3 sap, try 4 bite, dues, duty, fine, lade, levy, load, rate, tire, toll, wear 5 blame, enact, exact, tithe, weary 6 accuse, assess, burden, charge, cumber, custom, demand, excise, impose, impost, impugn, impute, indict, lumber, prey on, saddle, strain, stress, tariff, towage, weaken 7 arraign, censure, exhaust, expense, extract, impeach, oppress, reprove, tribute, wear out 8 encumber, exaction, overload, overtask, overwork, reproach 9 inculpate, surcharge, weigh down 10 assessment, imposition, overburden
basis: 5 ratal
determine a ~: 4 rate 5 gauge, value 6 assess 8 appraise, evaluate
do a ~ calculation: 6 deduct
ender: 3 man, men 5 payer 6 paying
expert: 3 acc., CPA 4 acct. 10 accountant
form: 4 W two
form part: 5 line A
import ~: 4 duty, levy 6 charge, excise, impost, tariff 10 assessment
month: 3 Apr. 5 April
of old: 4 geld, sess
org.: 3 IRS
shelter: 3 IRA 5 Keogh 7 Roth IRA 8 Roth plan
tax __: 4 code, deed, lien, rate, sale 5 exile, haven, stamp, table, title 6 return 7 evasion, sharing, shelter
tax-__: 4 free 6 exempt
__ tax: 3 gas, sin, use 4 gift, poll 5 nanny, sales, stamp 6 estate, excise, hidden, income, luxury 7 payroll
__-tax: 5 after
taxable __: 6 income
Taxation without representation
coiner: 4 Otis
tax-bracket __: 5 creep
Taxco: 4 city, town
locale: 6 Mexico
see also Spanish
tax-deferred __: 7 annuity
taxed: 5 laden, weary 7 fraught 10 encumbered
taxes
before ~: 5 gross
earn after ~: 3 net 4 make 5 clear
evade ~: 4 duck 5 cheat, dodge 6 scheme
__ taxes: 5 No new
taxi: 3 cab, car 4 auto, hack, ride 5 sedan 7 vehicle 8 transfer 9 transport 10 automobile
Asian ~: 5 cyclo
device: 5 meter
driver: 4 hack 5 cabby 6 cabbie, hackie
drop-off point: 4 curb
ender: 3 cab, way 5 meter
fee: 4 fare
forerunner: 6 hansom
go by ~: 4 ride
passenger: 4 fare
summon a ~: 4 flag, hail 8 flag down
water ~: 4 boat 5 ferry 6 launch 7 gondola
taxi __: 5 squad, stand 6 dancer, driver
__ taxi: 3 air 5 radio, water
Taxi (1972 song)
artist: Harry Chapin
Taxi (ABC/NBC sitcom)
cast: Tony Danza (Tony Banta) Danny DeVito (Louie De Palma) Marilu Henner (Elaine Nardo) Judd Hirsch (Alex Rieger) Carol Kane (Simka Gravas) Andy Kaufman (Latka Gravas)
dog: 5 Buddy
__ Taxi: 7 Tijuana
Taxi Driver (1976 film)
cast: Peter Boyle, Robert De Niro, Jodie Foster, Harvey Keitel, Cybill Shepherd
director: Martin Scorsese
taxing: 5 heavy, hefty, tough 6 leaden, rugged, severe, tiring, trying, uphill 7 arduous, onerous, operose, tedious, wearing, weighty 8 exacting, grievous, grueling 9 demanding, ponderous, strenuous, stressful, wearisome 10 burdensome, enervating, oppressive
taxol source: 3 yew
taxon: 5 class, genus, order 6 phylum 7 species 8 category
taxonomic
division: 5 class, genus, order 6 family, phylum 7 kingdom, species
divisions: 5 phyla
suffix: 3 -ota, -ote 4 -ella
taxpayer: 5 filer, voter 6 earner 7 citizen
fear: 5 audit 8 scrutiny 10 inspection
ID: 3 SSN
Tay: 5 river 7 Garnett
city on the ~: 5 Perth
Firth of ~ port: 6 Dundee
locale: 8 Scotland
Tayback: 3 Vic
Taye: 5 Diggs
__ Tayloe Ross: 6 Nellie
Taylor: 3 Don, Dub, Jim, Rip, Rod, Sam 4 Lili, Otis 5 Dayne, Deems, James, Renee 6 Joseph, Robert 7 Johnnie, Richard, Zachary 8 Caldwell, Hackford, Lawrence 9 Elizabeth
Taylor, Andy: 8 Griffith
aunt: 3 Bee
son: 4 Opie
__ Taylor Bradford: 7 Barbara
__ Taylor Coleridge: 6 Samuel
Taylor, Elizabeth: 4 Dame 7 actress
film: Butterfield 8 (1960, AA)
Cat on a Hot Tin Roof (1958)
Cleopatra (1963)
Father of the Bride (1950)
Father's Little Dividend (1951)
Giant (1956)
Ivanhoe (1952)
The Last Time I Saw Paris (1954)
Life With Father (1947)
The Mirror Crack'd (1980)
National Velvet (1944)
A Place in the Sun (1951)
Raintree County (1957)
The Sandpiper (1965)
Suddenly, Last Summer (1959)
The Taming of the Shrew (1967)
The V.I.P.s (1963)
Who's Afraid of Virginia Woolf? (1966, AA)
spouse: Richard Burton, Eddie Fisher, Larry Fortensky, Nicky Hilton, Mike Todd, John Warner, Michael Wilding
Taylor, James
song: Fire and Rain (1970)
Handy Man (1977)
Her Town Too (1981)
How Sweet It Is (1975)

Mockingbird (1974)
You've Got a Friend (1971)
spouse: Carly Simon
Taylor, Johnnie
song: Disco Lady (1976)
I Believe in You (1973)
Who's Making Love (1968)
Taylor, Lawrence
sport: 8 football
Taylor, Renee: 7 actress
spouse: Joseph Bologna
TV: The Nanny
Taylor, Robert: 5 actor
spouse: Barbara Stanwyck
__ Taylor Thomas: 8 Jonathan
Taylor-Young: 5 Leigh
Taylor, Zachary: 9 president
former occupation: 7 soldier
opponent: 4 Cass
V.P.: 8 Fillmore
wife: 8 Margaret
Tb: 4 elem. **7** element, terbium
65 for ~: 4 at. no.
T-bar: 4 bolt, lift **6** ski tow **7** ski lift
terrain: 5 slope
user: 5 skier
Tbilisi: 4 city, town **7** capital
locale: 7 Georgia
T-Bird: 3 car **4** auto, Ford **10** automobile
rival: 5 'Vette
T-bone: 4 meat **5** steak
source: 4 loin
T-Bone: 6 Walker
T. Boone __: 7 Pickens
TBS
alternative: *see* cable channel
tbsp.: 3 amt. **4** meas.
fraction: 3 tsp. **4** fl. oz.
Tc: 4 elem. **7** element **10** technetium
43 for ~: 4 at. no.
Tchaikovsky, Peter: 7 Russian **8** composer
work: 1812 Overture
Eugene Onegin
Manfred Symphony
Marche Slave
The Nutcracker
Pathétique Symphony
Romeo and Juliet
Sleeping Beauty
Swan Lake
tchr.: 4 prof. **5** instr.
deg.: 3 Ed.B., Ed.D., MSE **7** Ed.M. MSEd.
org.: 3 AFT, NEA, UFT
place: 3 sch.
see also teacher
TCU
rival: 3 SMU
TD: 4 stat
passer: 2 QB
scorer: 2 FB, HB
six, for a ~: 3 pts.
te __: 3 amo
te-__: 3 hee
Te: 4 elem. **7** element **9** tellurium
52 for ~: 4 at. no.
Te __: 4 Deum
T.E.: 8 Lawrence
tea: 4 brew, chai, meal **5** bohea, congo, cuppa, drink, fluid, hyson, party, pekoe, snack **6** congou, Lipton, Nestea, oolong, Salada, Tetley, tisane **7** Bigelow, cambric, lapsang, Red Rose **8** beverage, camomile, Earl Grey, souchong, Twinings **9** chamomile, elevenses, gunpowder, reception, yerba maté **10** Darjeeling
additive: 4 herb, milk, mint **5** honey, sugar
Arabian ~: 3 qat
black ~: 5 bohea, congo, oopak **6** congou, oopack
brewer: 3 urn **7** samovar
ceremony need: 4 raku
Chinese ~: 3 cha **5** bohea, congo **6** congou
cup of ~: 3 bag **5** field **7** leaning **9** specialty **10** preference
ender: 3 cup, pot **4** cake, cart, room, shop, time **5** berry, house, spoon **6** cupful, kettle **8** spoonful
genus: 4 thea
have ~: 5 drink
high ~: 4 meal
holder: 3 bag, cup **4** cozy **5** caddy
Indian ~ source: 5 Assam
in French: 3 thé
leaf reader: 7 psychic
leaves: 4 lees **5** dregs **8** sediment
make ~: 4 brew **5** steep
medicinal ~: 5 tansy
party: 5 salon
quantity: 3 cup **4** spot
serve ~: 4 pour
time: 3 aft. **4** four **6** four p.m. **9** afternoon
tea __: 3 bag, set **4** ball, cozy, gown, rose, shop, tray, tree **5** break, caddy, dance, maker, money, party, table, towel, wagon **6** garden **7** biscuit, service
__ tea: 3 hot **4** beef, herb, high, iced, mint, pink **5** black, cup of, green, Texas **6** herbal, spot of **7** jasmine
Tea __ Two: 3 for
Téa: 5 Leoni
Tea and Sympathy
author: Robert Anderson
TEAC
rival: 4 Bose
teacake: 5 scone
teacart: 5 wagon
teach: 4 form, rear, show **5** brief, coach, drill, edify, guide, imbue, train, tutor **6** advise, direct, ground, impart, inform, instil, school **7** break in, educate, engrain, explain, expound, implant, ingrain, instill, lecture, nurture, prepare, profess **8** exercise, initiate, instruct, polish up **9** brainwash, catechize, cultivate, enlighten, inculcate, interpret, irradiate, pound into, sermonize **10** discipline, evangelize, illustrate, promulgate
a lesson to: 6 punish
easy to ~: 3 apt **5** quick
teacher: 4 guru, prof **5** coach, guide, instr., tutor **6** lector, master, mentor, pundit **7** adviser, advisor, pedagog, scholar, trainer **8** educator, lecturer **9** abecedary, assistant, counselor, pedagogue, preceptor, professor **10** instructor, missionary
charge: 5 class
college ~: 4 prof **6** docent, lector **8** lecturer **9** professor **10** instructor
country ~: 4 marm **10** schoolmarm
degree: 3 Ed.B., Ed.D., Ed.M., M.Ed., MSE **4** MSEd
figuratively: 4 lamp
Hindu ~: 4 guru **5** swami, swamy
Islamic ~: 5 mulla **6** mullah
name meaning ~: 5 Enoch **6** Lehrer
need: 3 map, pen **4** desk **5** chalk, paper, ruler **6** eraser
note from the ~: 5 see me
org.: 3 AFT, NEA, UFT
place: 3 sch. **4** acad., coll., univ. **6** school **7** academy, college **10** high school, university
private ~: 5 tutor
religious ~: 3 nun **5** rabbi, rebbe
roster: 4 roll
starter: 6 school
student ~: 6 intern, novice **7** interne, trainee **10** apprentice
__ teacher: 7 student
__-Teacher Association: 6 Parent
teachers: 5 staff **7** faculty **9** lecturers
teacher's __: 3 pet
Teachers (1984 film)
cast: Judd Hirsch, Ralph Macchio, Nick Nolte, JoBeth Williams
Teacher's Pet (1958 film)
cast: Doris Day, Clark Gable, Gig Young
teaching: 4 lore **5** drill, tenet **6** homily, lesson **7** tuition **8** doctrine, pedagogy, training **9** education, paedagogy, principle **10** profession
teaching __: 3 aid
teachings: 5 creed, dogma, tenet **6** belief **7** precept **8** doctrine
Teach Your Children (1970 song)
artist: Crosby, Stills & Nash
teacup
like a ~: 5 eared
part: 3 ear, lip **4** brim **6** handle
Tea for Two: 4 duet, song
composer: Irving Caesar, Vincent Youmans
Teagarden, Jack: 10 trombonist
genre: 4 jazz
Teague: 5 Lewis
teahouse: 10 restaurant
hostess: 6 geisha
Teahouse of the August Moon, The (1956 film)
cast: Marlon Brando, Glenn Ford
teak: 4 tree, wood **5** color **8** hardwood
family: 7 verbena
teakettle
part: 5 spout
sound: 3 sss **4** hiss, ssss
teal: 4 bird, blue, duck, fowl **5** color **8** greenish
faux ~: 5 decoy
relative: *see* blue color, duck
team: 3 duo, rig, set **4** band, body, club, crew, gang, pair, side, span, trio, unit, yoke **5** bunch, cadre, corps, group, hands, party, squad, staff, troop **6** lineup, outfit, string, tandem, troupe **7** company, coterie, faction, platoon, varsity, workers **8** athletic, ball club, foursome, partners **10** contingent
B ~: 6 scrubs
be on a ~: 4 play
drop from the ~: 3 cut
ender: 4 mate, ster, work
goal: 3 win
leader: 3 mgr. **5** coach **7** manager
member: 5 horse **6** player **10** contestant
show ~ spirit: 4 root **5** cheer **7** cheer on
the other ~: 3 foe **4** them **5** enemy
up: 3 wed **4** bond, join, link, pair **5** marry, merge, unite **6** couple, hook up **7** combine, conjoin, connect, pair off **8** side with, tag along **9** affiliate, interface, tie in with **10** amalgamate, assist with, go partners
team __: 6 player
__ team: 3 tag **4** farm, SWAT **5** dream, drill
__, team!: 3 Yay, Yea
__-team: 6 double
__-Team: 4 The A
teammate: 7 partner **8** co-worker **9** colleague
Te Amo: 5 cigar
team player, not a: 5 loner, rebel
Teamster: 6 hauler **7** trucker
unit: 4 semi **5** local
Teamsters: 5 union
team-supporting word: 3 rah
teamwork obstacles: 4 egos
tea party
attendee: 5 Alice
host a ~: 4 pour
__ Tea Party: 6 Boston
teapot: 6 kettle
cover: 4 cozy
feature: 5 spout
tempest in a ~: 3 ado **4** fuss
Teapot Dome victim: 4 Fall
tear: 3 cut, fly, hie, rip, run, zip **4** bolt, bust, claw, dart, dash, flit, fray, gash, grab, hole, hurt, part, pull, race, rack, rage, rend, rent, rift, rive, rush, slit, snag, weep, yank, zoom **5** binge, break, crack, hurry, pluck, scoot, seize, sever, shoot, shred, slash, speed, split, spree, storm, whisk, wrest **6** barrel, bender, breach, careen, career, cleave, crying, damage, divide, gallop, hasten, hurtle, hustle, impair, injure, mangle, move it, plunge, rocket, scurry, snatch, sprint, strain, streak, sunder, tatter, wrench **7** divulse, droplet, fissure, floor it, frazzle, globule, hop to it, opening, quicken, rampage, rip open, rupture, scamper, scratch **8** carousal, jerk away, lacerate, moisture, mutilate, separate, stampede, step on it, teardrop, zip along **9** come apart, fulgurate, hotfoot it, pull apart, shake a leg, skedaddle **10** come undone, get a move on, get hopping, hightail it, laceration, make tracks
apart: 3 cut, hew, rip **4** chop, part, rend, rive **5** rip up, sever, slash, split **6** avulse, cleave, divide, rebuke **7** disjoin **8** dissever, disunite, separate
channel: 4 duct
down: 4 rase, raze, ruin, slur **5** level, libel, smash, wreck **6** malign, refute, topple, vilify **7** degrade, destroy, slander, unbuild **8** badmouth, belittle, bulldoze, demolish, diminish,

disprove **9** denigrate, devastate, discredit, dismantle, take apart **10** calumniate
dryer: 5 hanky **6** hankie
ender: 4 down, drop **5** stain **6** jerker
go on a ~: 4 rage **5** storm
holder: 3 sac
into: 4 lash **5** roast, scold **6** assail, attack, have at, oppugn, vilify **9** excoriate **10** vituperate
(into): 4 lace
mend a ~: 5 resew
off: 3 hie, lop, run **4** race **5** sever, speed **6** detach, loosen, remove **7** disjoin **8** separate, unfasten **10** disconnect
old-style: 5 reave
on a ~: 4 wild **5** rowdy **6** unruly **7** lawless, raucous **9** fractious **10** boisterous, disorderly, disruptive, rebellious
open: 5 unrip
out: 5 pluck **6** remove, uproot **9** extirpate
out a seam: 5 unrip
partner: 4 wear
small ~: 4 slit
try to ~: 5 rip at
up the road: 4 zoom **5** spank
wear and ~: 3 use **6** damage **8** breakage **9** shrinkage **10** impairment
tear __: 3 gas, off, out **4** away, down, into **5** sheet
tear-__: 6 jerker
__ tear: 3 hot, on a
__ Teardrops: 6 Lonely
tearful: 3 sad **5** moist, upset, weepy, woful **6** crying, woeful **7** bawling, maudlin, sobbing, weeping, wet-eyed **8** blubbery, dolorous, mournful, pathetic, poignant **9** lamenting, sniveling, sorrowful **10** blubbering, distressed, lachrymose, lamentable, pathetical, whimpering
tearjerker: 4 play **5** drama, flick, movie, story **7** romance
kitchen ~: 5 onion
quality: 6 pathos
tear-jerking: 3 sad **5** mushy **7** maudlin, mawkish **8** romantic, touching **9** sorrowful
tear one's __ out: 4 hair
tearoom cousin: 4 café **6** bistro **10** restaurant
tears: 5 drops **6** crying, egesta, lament, sorrow **7** sobbing, wailing, weeping **8** distress, grieving, moisture **10** blubbering, waterworks, whimpering
antibody in ~: 3 IGA
combining form: 7 lacrimo-
dim with ~: 4 blur **5** blear, cloud
in ~: 5 weepy **7** bawling, sobbing, weeping **8** broken up **9** sniveling
like ~: 5 salty
move to ~: 3 get **5** upset **6** affect
near ~: 5 misty
shed ~: 3 cry, sob **4** bawl, mewl, pule, wail, weep **6** boohoo, snivel **7** blubber, whimper
__ tears: 5 baby's, Pele's **9** crocodile
Tears for Fears
song: Everybody Wants to Rule the World (1985)
Head Over Heels (1985)
Shout (1985)
Sowing the Seeds of Love (1989)
Tears, Idle Tears
author: Alfred Tennyson
Tears in Heaven (1992 song)
artist: Eric Clapton
Tears of a Clown, The (1970 song)
artist: Miracles
Tears on My Pillow (1958 song)
artist: Little Anthony and the Imperials
teary: 3 sad, wet **5** blear, moist, weepy **6** crying **7** bawling, maudlin, mawkish, sobbing, unhappy **8** broken up, choked up **9** emotional, misty-eyed, sniveling **10** blubbering, lachrymose
Teasdale: 4 Sara **6** Verree
Teasdale, Sara: 4 poet
work: Dark of the Moon
Flame and Shadow
Love Songs
Rivers to the Sea
Strange Victory
tease: 3 dog, kid, rag, rib, toy, vex **4** bait, be at, comb, gibe, gnaw, goad, guye, jest, jibe, jive, joke, josh, mock, pest, razz, ride, twit **5** annoy, chaff, devil, flirt, harry, nudge, put on, rag on, roast, taunt, tweak, worry **6** badger, banter, bother, harass, heckle, hector, kidder, lead on, needle, pester, pick on, plague **7** bedevil, disturb, fluff up, provoke, put down, torment, toy with **8** backcomb, bullyrag, coquette, ridicule **9** aggravate, beleaguer, importune, make fun of, persecute, poke fun at, tantalize, titillate **10** make eyes at
teasel: 5 plant **6** flower
teaser: 4 bait, pest **5** poser, promo, vexer **6** enigma **7** problem, stumper **9** conundrum, promotion
starter: 5 brain
teasing: 5 sport **6** banter **7** naughty, playful **8** badinage **9** annoyance, quizzical, vexatious **10** allurement
teasingly: 5 in fun
teaspoon, use a: 4 stir
Teatro __ Scala: 4 alla
Tebaldi, Renata: 4 diva **6** singer **7** soprano
role: 5 Tosca
specialty: 5 opera
tec: 2 PI **6** Holmes, shamus, sleuth **7** Columbo, gumshoe **8** hawkshaw, Sherlock **10** Mike Hammer, private eye
tech: 4 geek, guru, nerd
starter: 3 bio
talk: 5 argot, lingo **6** jargon
tech. __: 3 sgt.
__-tech: 3 low, sci **4** high
__ Tech: 5 Texas **7** Georgia
techie: 4 geek, guru, nerd
__ Te Ching: 3 Tao
technetium: 7 element
technical: 8 abstruse, detailed **9** scholarly **10** industrial, mechanical, restricted, scientific, vocational
word: 4 term
technical __: 4 foul **6** school
technicality: 5 point **6** detail, nicety **7** minutia **8** loophole **9** fine point, punctilio
technician: 4 guru **6** expert **8** mechanic, repairer **9** authority **10** specialist
__ technician: 4 x-ray **6** dental
technique: 3 art, way **4** mode **5** craft, knack, means, skill, style, trick **6** manner, method, recipe, system **7** know-how, process, routine, science, tactics **8** approach, artistry, facility, hang of it **9** execution, procedure
combining form: 4 -urgy
technology: 3 sci. **7** science **9** procedure
__ technology: 3 low **4** high
Tech TV
alternative: *see* cable channel
__ tectonics: 5 plate
tectonics event: 5 quake, seism **6** tremor
tectrix: 5 plume
__ Tecumseh Sherman: 7 William
Ted: 3 Key **4** Mack, Post, Ross, Wass **5** Demme, Lange, Lewis, Raimi, Shawn, Weems, Wilde **6** Baxter, Berman, Danson, Hughes, Husing, Knight, Koppel, Nugent, Turner **7** Bessell, Cassidy, Kennedy, Lindsay **8** Kotcheff, McGinley, Nicolaou, Sorensen, Tetzlaff, Williams **10** Kluszewski
Caroline, to ~: 5 niece
Maria, to ~: 5 niece
TED defeater: 3 FDR, HST
teddy __: 4 bear
Teddy: 7 Kennedy **9** Roosevelt
1904 opponent: 5 Alton
Eleanor, to ~: 5 niece
mom: 4 Rose
Teddy Bears
song: To Know Him, Is to Love Him (1958)
Teddy Grahams
alternative: *see* cookie brand
tedious: 3 dry **4** arid, drab, dull, flat, poky, slow, tame **5** banal, bland, dusty, heavy, ho-hum, prosy, unfun, vapid, wordy, yawny **6** boring, dreary, jejune, stodgy, stuffy, taxing, tiring **7** endless, humdrum, insipid, irksome, lengthy, operose, painful, prosaic, routine, verbose **8** annoying, dragging, drudging, lifeless, tiresome **9** fatiguing, laborious, ponderous, prosaical, soporific, wearisome **10** dullsville, enervating, exhausting, monotonous, uneventful, unexciting
account: 6 litany **10** recitation
be ~: 4 bore, pall
one: 4 bore, drag, drip, pain, pest, pill **5** creep **8** nuisance **10** wet blanket
routine: 3 rut **5** grind **8** drudgery
tediousness: 6 tedium **8** monotony **9** heaviness
tedium: 5 ennui, grind **7** boredom, routine **8** banality, doldrums, drabness, dullness, flatness, monotony, sameness **9** weariness **10** dreariness, melancholy
sign of ~: 4 yawn
__ & Ted's Excellent Adventure: 4 Bill
tee: 3 peg **5** joint, shirt **8** pullover **10** undershirt
ender: 5 total
off: 3 irk **4** miff, rile, roil **5** anger, annoy, drive, peeve, start, steam, upset **6** enrage **7** pitch in **9** infuriate **10** exasperate
(off): 4 tick
partner: 5 jeans
preceder: 3 ess
to a ~: 8 very well **9** on the nose, precisely **10** positively
up: 5 start
user: 6 golfer
tee __: 3 off **4** time **5** shirt
tee-__: 3 hee
__ tee: 3 to a **4** golf
teed off: 3 mad **4** sore **5** angry, irate, upset **7** steamed **9** disgusted, resentful
tee-hee: 6 giggle, titter **7** snicker, snigger
teem: 4 brim, pour, swim **5** crawl, crowd, swarm **6** abound, bustle, deluge, wallow **7** bristle, overrun **8** overflow **9** pullulate
teeming: 3 wet **4** full, lush, many, rife **5** alive, dense, laden, thick **6** aswarm, fecund, filled, imbued, jammed, loaded, packed **7** brimful, crammed, crowded, fertile, profuse, replete, stuffed **8** abundant, brimfull, bursting, fruitful, infested, numerous, populous, prodigal, prolific, swarming, thronged **9** bristling, chock-full, exuberant, luxuriant, plentiful
teen: 3 kid **4** girl **5** child, minor, youth **6** Archie **8** juvenile **9** childhood, stripling, youngster **10** adolescent, bobbysoxer
activist org.: 4 SADD
big day: 4 prom **10** graduation
channel: 3 MTV **5** Spike
concern: 6 curfew
culture: 6 hip-hop
desire: 3 car **4** auto **6** wheels **10** automobile
ender: 3 age **4** aged, ager
exclamation: 3 rad
former ~: 5 adult **7** grownup
hangout: 4 mall **6** arcade
mustache: 4 wisp
outcast: 4 geek, nerd
punishment, perhaps: 4 no TV
room, often: 4 mess **5** chaos, wreck **7** clutter, eyesore **8** disarray, shambles
sentence ender: 6 and all
socialite: 3 deb
starter: 3 six, ump **4** four, nine **5** seven
woe: 3 zit **4** acne

teen __: 4 idol
__-teen: 3 mid
Teen: 6 Harold
Teen __: 4 Beat, Wolf **5** Angel
Teena: 5 Marie
teenage: 5 young **8** juvenile **10** adolescent
Teen-Age Crush (1957 song)
artist: Tommy Sands
Teen Age Idol (1962 song)
artist: Ricky Nelson
Teenage Mutant __ Turtles: 5 Ninja

Teen Age Prayer (1955 song)
artist: Gale Storm
teenager: **3** kid **4** girl **5** child, minor, youth **8** juvenile **9** stripling, youngster **10** adolescent
see also teen
Teenager in Love, A (1959 song)
artist: Dion and the Belmonts
Teenager's Romance, A (1957 song)
artist: Ricky Nelson
__ Teen-age Werewolf: **5** I Was a
Teena Marie
real name: Mary Christine Brokert
song: Lovergirl (1985)
Teen Angel (1960 song)
artist: Mark Dinning
teenie-__: **6** weenie
teensy-__: **6** weensy
Teen Wolf (1985 film)
cast: Michael J. Fox
teeny-__: **5** weeny **6** bopper
teenybopper: **4** girl, miss **10** adolescent, schoolgirl
teeny-weeny: **3** wee **4** baby, itsy, puny, tiny **5** bitsy, bitty, teeny, weeny **6** atomic, bantam, little, minute, peewee, petite, teensy **8** atomical, atomlike **9** itsy-bitsy, itty-bitty, miniature, pint-sized, undersize **10** diminutive, vest-pocket
teeter: **4** reel, rock, sway **5** lurch, pivot, waver, weave **6** falter, jiggle, quiver, seesaw, topple, totter, wabble, wobble **7** balance, flutter, stagger, stumble, tremble, whiffle **9** fluctuate, oscillate, vacillate
ender: **5** board **6** totter
teetering: **5** shaky **6** jiggly, unfirm, wabbly, wobbly **8** unstable, unsteady
teeter-totter: **6** seesaw **9** oscillate
teeth: **5** vigor
bare one's ~: **4** dare **5** snarl
by the skin of one's ~: **4** just **6** barely **8** narrowly, scarcely
device with ~: **3** saw **4** comb, gear, rake
enough to sink one's ~ into: **5** meaty
grit one's ~: **5** gnarl, gnash, steel **6** clench
kick in the ~: **4** slur **6** rebuff, rebuke **7** repulse **9** rejection
like some ~: **6** capped
of ~: **6** dental
science of ~: **9** dentistry
straighteners: **6** braces
take the bit in one's ~: **4** defy **5** rebel **6** revolt **7** disobey **9** break away
to the ~: **5** fully **8** entirely **10** completely
use one's ~: **3** nip **4** bite, chew, gnaw
see also tooth
__ teeth: **4** baby **5** false, to the
teething __: **4** ring
teetotaler: **3** dry **9** abstainer **10** nondrinker
grp.: **4** WCTU
Teflon company: **6** DuPont
Tegucigalpa: **4** city, town **7** capital
locale: **8** Honduras
see also Spanish
Tegus
city on the ~: **6** Toledo
te-hee: **6** giggle, titter **7** snicker, snigger
Teheran: **4** city, town **7** capital
city near ~: **3** Qom, Qum
language: **5** Farsi
locale: **4** Iran
VIP: **4** imam **5** imaum
Teicher, Louis: **7** pianist
partner: **8** Ferrante
Teilhard de Chardin, Pierre: **6** French, writer **10** theologian **11** philosopher
specialty: **9** mysticism
work: The Divine Milieu
The Phenomenon of Man
Tejo
city on the ~: **6** Toledo
Te Kanawa, Kiri: **4** Dame, diva **5** Maori **6** singer **7** soprano
solo: **4** aria
specialty: **5** opera
Tel __: **4** Aviv **6** Amarna
Telamon: **8** Argonaut
father: **6** Aeacus
son: **4** Aias, Ajax
Tel Aviv: **4** city, town
airport: **3** Lod
locale: **3** Isr. **6** Israel
port near ~: **4** Gaza **5** Haifa
telecast: **4** news, on TV, show **7** program
like some ~s: **4** live
signal: **5** audio, video
telecom letters: **3** GTE, ITT, MCI
telecommuter workplace: **4** home **6** at home
telecopy: **3** fax
tele ender: **4** gram, path, play, port, thon, type, vise **5** graph, metry, pathy, phone, photo, scope **7** commute
Telefon (1977 film)
cast: Charles Bronson, Tyne Daly, Lee Remick
Telefone (1983 song)
artist: Sheena Easton
telegram: **4** news, wire **5** cable, flash, telex **6** report **7** message **8** teletype **9** cablegram, radiogram
sender: **5** wirer
word: **4** stop
telegraph: **4** wire
datum: **3** dah, dit, dot **4** dash
inventor: **5** Morse
operator: **5** coder
part: **3** key **5** relay
receiver: **5** inker
sound: **5** clack
starter: **5** radio
telekinetic: **7** psychic
Telemachus parent: **8** Odysseus, Penelope
Telemann, Georg: **6** German **8** composer
telemarketer: **6** caller
device: **6** dialer
telemetry: **7** science
telepathic: **6** mental **7** psychic
telepathist: **4** seer
telepathy: **3** ESP, psi **10** sixth sense
__ telepathy: **6** mental
telephone: **4** buzz, call, dial, horn, ring **5** phone **6** blower, notify, report, ring up **7** contact **9** broadcast, touch base **10** get a hold of
button: **3** ABC, DEF, GHI, JKL, MNO, PRS, TUV, WXY **4** OPER, PQRS, star, WXYZ **9** pound sign
charge: **4** toll
company: **4** util. **7** utility
device: **4** jack **5** modem **6** dialer **7** headset
exclamation: **8** greeting **10** salutation
greeting: **5** hello
inventor: **4** Bell
line: **4** cord **5** trunk
number part: **3** ext. **8** area code, exchange **9** extension
part: **4** cord, wire **6** cradle **8** receiver
starter: **5** radio
user: **5** party **6** caller
wait on the ~: **4** hold
see also phone
telephone __: **3** tag **4** bank, book, pole **5** booth
Telephone Line (1977 song)
artist: ELO
telephoto __: **4** lens
teleplay: **5** story **6** script
TelePromp__: **3** Ter
telescope: **3** cut **6** Hubble, reduce **7** abridge, shorten **8** abstract, boil down, compress, condense, cut short, truncate **9** capsulize, summarize, synopsize **10** abbreviate
adjust a ~: **5** focus
part: **4** lens **5** optic **8** eyepiece **9** magnifier
view: **4** moon **6** cosmos, galaxy, planet **8** Milky Way
Telescopium neighbor: **3** Ara
telesthesia: **3** ESP **9** intuition, telepathy
Telesto: **4** moon
planet: **6** Saturn
telethon: **6** appeal **7** benefit **10** fundraiser
Teletubby: **2** Po **5** Dipsy **6** Laa-Laa **10** Tinky Winky
fan: **3** kid, tot
televise: **3** air **4** send **8** transmit **9** broadcast
television: **3** box, JVC, NEC, RCA, set **4** Sony, tube **5** media, telly **6** Quasar, Zenith **7** Emerson, Hitachi, monitor, ProScan, Samsung, Toshiba **8** boob tube, idiot box, Magnavox, Sylvania **9** goggle box, Panasonic
fare: **4** news, show, talk **5** drama **6** series, sitcom **8** game show, talk show
former ~ brand: **6** Dumont
letters on a ~: **3** UHF, VHF
like early ~: **4** live
signal component: **5** audio, video
tube gas: **4** neon
tuner: **4** dial
see also TV
__ television: **6** public
Television, Mr.: **5** Berle
tell: **3** air, bid, rat, say, see **4** blab, know, leak, warn **5** learn, let on, level, order, speak, spill, state, tally, utter, voice, weigh **6** advise, clinch, clue in, convey, deduce, depict, detail, direct, divine, enjoin, fill in, impart, inform, notify, number, open up, recite, reckon, relate, report, reveal, set out, snitch, squeal, summon, tip off, unveil **7** apprise, apprize, breathe, bring up, command, compute, confess, declare, discern, divulge, explain, express, find out, give out, lay bare, lay open, let in on, let know, let slip, make out, mention, narrate, portray, recount, reel off, require, signify, spit out, uncover, whisper **8** acquaint, announce, call upon, describe, disclose, discover, identify, instruct, let it out, militate, numerate, perceive, proclaim, register, rehearse, set forth, throw out **9** ascertain, authorize, calculate, chronicle, determine, enumerate, expound on, leave word, make known, put before, recognize, represent **10** comprehend, keep posted, take effect, understand
again: **5** resay
all: **3** air **4** bare, blab, sing, talk **6** fess up **8** unburden **9** name names
ender: **4** tale
hear ~: **5** learn **6** listen
of: **5** cover **7** bespeak, narrate, recount **9** adumbrate
off: **4** lash, rail **5** chide, scold **6** berate, rebuff, rebuke, revile **7** censure, lecture, reprove, upbraid **8** admonish, reproach **9** lash out at, reprimand **10** take to task
on: **3** rat **6** give up, report, tattle, turn in
partner: **4** kiss, show
tales: **3** gab, yak **4** blab, dish **6** gossip, tattle **8** schmooze
the judge: **3** sue **5** argue **6** appeal **7** declare **8** petition
tell __: **3** off **4** a fib, a lie
tell __ glance: **3** at a
tell-__ book: **3** all
__ tell!: **4** Pray
Tell: **7** Wilhelm, William
Tell __: **5** Her No, Me Why
Tell __ About It: **3** Her
Tell __ I Love Her: **5** Laura
Tell __ My Heart: **4** It to
Tell __ story: **3** me a
Tell __ Sweeney!: **4** it to
Tell __ the judge!: **4** it to
Tell __ the Marines!: **4** it to
Tell-__ Heart, The: **4** Tale
tell-all: **4** book **6** exposé
teller: **5** clerk **7** cashier **9** paymaster
cry: **4** next
fish story ~: **6** fibber **8** deceiver
place: **4** bank, cage **5** booth, S and L
starter: **4** tale **5** story **7** fortune
whopper ~: **4** liar **6** fibber **7** deluder **8** deceiver
Teller: **6** Edward
partner: **4** Penn **8** Jillette
Tell Her About It (1983 song)
artist: Billy Joel
Tell Her No (1965 song)
artist: Zombies
telling: **5** solid, sound, valid **6** cogent, marked, potent, strong **7** graphic, logical, pointed, pungent, recital **8** decisive, forceful, forcible, material, powerful, striking **9** effective, effectual, graphical, trenchant **10** conclusive, convincing, expres-

sive, impressive, persuasive, recitation, unarguable
it like it is: 5 blunt, frank **6** candid, candor, direct, honest **7** honesty, up-front **8** straight, veracity **9** outspoken **10** aboveboard, forthright, free-spoken, from the hip, point-blank, unreserved
off: 6 rebuke, tirade **7** reproof **8** harangue, scolding **9** reprimand, talking-to
___ telling me!: 5 You're
telling-off: 6 earful, rebuke
Tell it ___ Marines!: 5 to the
tell it like ___: 4 it is
Tell It Like It Is (song)
artist: Heart, Aaron Neville
Tell It to My Heart (1987 song)
artist: Taylor Dayne
Tell It to the Rain (1966 song)
artist: Four Seasons
Tell Laura I Love Her (1960 song)
artist: Ray Peterson
___ tell me!: 4 Don't
Tell Me How Long the Train's Been Gone
author: James Baldwin
Tell me more!: 4 Go on
Tell Me Something Good (1974 song)
artist: Chaka Khan
Tell Me Why (song)
artist: Exposé, Elvis Presley
Tell Me Your Dreams
author: Sidney Sheldon
___ Tells Me So, The: 5 Bible
telltale: 6 tattle **7** tattler **9** revealing **10** meaningful
sign: 4 odor
Tell-Tale Heart, The
author: Edgar Allan Poe
Tell Them Willie Boy Is Here (1969 film)
cast: Robert Redford, Katharine Ross
Telluride: 4 city, town
enjoy ~: 3 ski **4** skee
locale: 8 Colorado
tellurium: 5 metal **7** element
Tell, William: 6 archer, bowman
home: 3 Uri **11** Switzerland
target: 5 apple
weapon: 3 bow **5** arrow
telly: 2 TV **3** set **4** tube **5** TV set **10** television
network: 3 BBC
Telly: 7 Savalas
Telma: 7 Hopkins
Telstar (1962 song)
artist: Tornadoes
tema: 5 motif
temblor: 5 quake, seism **6** tremor **8** upheaval **10** earthquake
temerarious: 8 reckless
temerity: 4 gall **5** brass, cheek, nerve, pluck **6** daring **7** courage, license **8** audacity, boldness, chutzpah, defiance, rudeness **9** impudence **10** effrontery
temp: 3 sub **6** fill-in, helper **7** stand-in **9** assistant, fill in for, makeshift **10** substitute
employer: 4 firm **6** agency, office **7** company
temp.
scale: 3 Fah. **4** Fahr
unit: 3 deg.
Tempe: 4 city, town
athletes: 9 Sun Devils
locale: 4 Ariz. **7** Arizona
river: 4 Salt
school: 3 ASU
temper: 3 ire **4** bile, calm, cool, curb, ease, fury, gird, heat, lull, mood, rage, snit, tame, tiff, tone, vein **5** allay, anger, build, humor, Irish, poise, shore, state, steel, storm, style, trend, wrath **6** animus, anneal, beef up, choler, dampen, dander, esprit, harden, lessen, makeup, modify, nature, pacify, prop up, refine, season, soften, soothe, spirit, strain, subdue, tone up, weaken **7** assuage, bad mood, bolster, brace up, build up, burgeon, develop, empower, enhance, fortify, leaning, mollify, passion, qualify, relieve, shore up, stiffen, tantrum, toughen **8** bourgeon, buttress, calmness, energize, humanize, ill humor, indurate, mitigate, moderate, modulate, outburst, palliate, regulate, restrain, restrict, slow burn, tone down, vitalize **9** character, composure, huffiness, intensify, petulance, pugnacity, reinforce, short fuse, soft-pedal, surliness **10** equanimity, grumpiness, impatience, invigorate, keep in line, resentment, strengthen, sullenness, touchiness
even ~: 8 patience **9** composure **10** sedateness
fit of ~: 3 pet **4** rage, snit **5** blast, blaze, flash, scene, storm, surge **6** access, attack, flurry, frenzy, outcry, tirade **7** flare-up, tantrum, torrent **8** eruption, outbreak, outburst, paroxysm, upheaval **9** discharge, explosion, hysterics **10** conniption, outpouring
ill ~: 4 bile, fury, rage **5** anger, wrath **6** enmity, rancor **7** sarcasm, umbrage **8** acerbity, acrimony, rudeness, sourness, tartness **9** surliness **10** bitterness
lose one's ~: 4 rage, rant, roar, yell **6** blow up
temper ___: 7 tantrum
___ temper: 3 ill
tempera: 5 paint
temperament: 4 bent, cast, mood, soul, vein **5** humor, stamp **6** makeup, mettle, nature, spirit **7** outlook **8** attitude **9** character, mentality **10** complexion
temperamental: 3 hot **5** fiery, hyper, moody **6** cussed, fickle, ornery, touchy, wilful **7** erratic, froward, waspish, willful **8** petulant, ticklish, unstable, variable, volatile **9** emotional, excitable, explosive, hotheaded, impatient, irritable, mercurial, sensitive, uncertain
temperance: 6 virtue **8** eschewal, sobriety **9** austerity, restraint **10** abnegation, abstinence, moderation
advocate: 3 dry **4** WCTU
temperate: 4 calm, cool, easy, even, fair, kind, mild, soft, warm, zone **5** balmy, quiet, sober, staid, stoic, tepid **6** at ease, benign, gentle, low-key, medium, mellow, modest, placid, sedate, serene, stable, steady **7** amiable, at peace, clement, equable, pacific, relaxed, stoical, unmoved, warmish **8** amicable, carefree, composed, discreet, laid-back, moderate, peaceful, pleasant, sensible, tranquil **9** abstinent, agreeable, collected, continent, easy-going, impassive, quiescent, unexcited, unextreme, unruffled **10** abstemious, nonchalant, phlegmatic, reasonable, restrained, unagitated, untroubled
Temperate ___: 4 Zone
temperature: 4 heat **5** fever **6** warmth **7** climate, degrees, pyrexia **8** body heat
extreme: 3 low **4** high
freezing ~: 5 teens
high ~: 4 heat **5** fever
measure: 6 degree, Kelvin **7** Celsius **10** Centigrade, Fahrenheit
___ temperature: 4 ran a, room, run a
___-tempered: 3 bad, hot, ill **4** even, good **5** quick, short, sweet
___-Tempered Clavier, The: 4 Well **5** Short
tempering: 9 abatement, reduction **10** diminution, mitigation, moderation, palliation, subsidence
tempest: 4 blow, gale, wind **5** blast, furor, storm, swirl **6** squall, tumult, uproar **7** bluster, cyclone, rampage, tornado, typhoon **8** blizzard, upheaval **9** hurricane, windstorm **10** convulsion
in a teapot: 3 ado **4** fuss
tempest-___: 4 tost **6** tossed
Tempest: 3 car **4** auto **5** Marie **7** Pontiac **10** automobile
tempest in a ___: 6 teacup, teapot
Tempestt: 7 Bledsoe
Tempest, The: 4 play **6** comedy
author: William Shakespeare
role: 5 Ariel **6** Alonso **7** Antonio, Caliban, Gonzalo, Miranda **8** Prospero, Stephano, Trinculo **9** Ferdinand, Sebastian
tempestuous: 4 wild **5** fiery, rough **6** fierce, heated, raging, stormy **7** excited, furious, intense, lawless, violent **8** agitated, feverish **9** emotional, turbulent, unbridled **10** tumultuous
tempestuousness: 4 fire, fury **7** passion **8** savagery **9** intensity **10** turbulence
___ Templar: 7 Knights
Templar, Simon: The Saint
portrayer: Val Kilmer, Roger Moore
template: 7 pattern
temple: 4 fane, shul **5** abbey, schul, zendo **6** chapel, church, mosque, pagoda, shrine, temple **7** synagog **8** pantheon, sacellum **9** cathedral, sanctuary, synagogue **10** tabernacle
ancient Greek ~: 4 naos **6** hieron
Buddhist ~: 3 wat
chamber: 4 naos **5** cella **6** adytum
combining form: 7 temporo-
of India: 4 rath **5** ratha
table: 5 altar
teacher: 5 rabbi, rebbe
tongue: 6 Hebrew
worshiper: 3 Jew
temple ___: 6 orange
Temple: 4 city, town **7** Shirley
athletes: 4 Owls
locale: 4 Penn. **5** Phila., Texas
___ Temple Black: 7 Shirley
Temple of ___: 4 Ares **7** Artemis
Temple of the Golden Pavilion, The
author: Yukio Mishima
___ Temple Pilots: 5 Stone
temples: 4 naoi
Temple, Shirley: 7 actress
costar: 5 Ebsen **8** Robinson
film: The Bachelor and the Bobby-Soxer (1947)
Fort Apache (1948)
Heidi (1937)
The Little Colonel (1935)
Little Miss Marker (1934)
The Little Princess (1939)
The Littlest Rebel (1935)
Poor Little Rich Girl (1936)
Wee Willie Winkie (1937)
spouse: John Agar
Temple, The
author: Jerome Weidman
Templeton: 4 Alec
tempo: 4 beat, pace, rate, time **5** grave, largo, lento, meter, pulse, speed, swing **6** adagio, presto, rhythm, vivace **7** allegro, andante, cadence, cadency, measure **8** downbeat, moderato, momentum, velocity
a ~: 6 in time
modified ~: 6 rubato
Tempo: 3 car **4** auto, Ford, Nino **10** automobile
temporal: 3 lay **4** laic **5** civil **6** laical, mortal **7** earthly, mundane, passing, profane, secular, worldly **8** banausic, fleeting, fugitive, material, physical **9** ephemeral, momentary, transient **10** evanescent, short-lived, transitory, unhallowed
temporal ___: 4 lobe
temporarily: 6 for now **7** briefly **8** meantime **9** meanwhile
temporary: 5 ad hoc, brief, short **6** acting, make-do, pro tem **7** interim, migrant, passing, stopgap, summary **8** fleeting, flitting, fugitive, slapdash **9** alternate, ephemeral, makeshift, migratory, momentary, overnight, provisory, revocable, transient **10** changeable, evanescent, jury-rigged, perishable, short-lived, substitute, transitory, unenduring
resident: 6 lodger, roomer **7** boarder
___ tempore: 3 pro
temporize: 4 duck **5** dally, delay, dodge, evade, hedge, skirt, stall, tarry, waver **6** put off, waffle **8** hesitate, postpone, sidestep **9** hem and haw, pussyfoot **10** equivocate
___-temps: 5 entre
tempt: 3 oil, woo **4** bait, coax, dare, draw, hook, lure, urge, whet **5** charm, decoy, rouse, shill, snare **6** allure, appeal, beckon, cajole, entice, entrap, incite, induce,

invite, lead on, pull in **7** attract, beguile, bewitch, mislead, promote, provoke **8** appeal to, butter up, interest, inveigle, motivate, persuade, play up to **9** captivate, fascinate, influence, mousetrap, sweet-talk
fate: **4** dare
temptation: **4** bait, lure, trap, urge **5** decoy, snare **6** allure, carrot, come-on **9** incentive **10** attraction, enticement, inducement, invitation
lead into ~: **4** hook, lure, trap **5** snare, trick **6** entice, entrap, lead on, reel in, rope in, suck in **7** deceive
Temptations
song: Ain't Too Proud to Beg (1966)
All I Need (1967)
Ball of Confusion (1970)
Beauty Is Only Skin Deep (1966)
Cloud Nine (1968)
I Can't Get Next to You (1969)
I'm Gonna Make You Love Me (1968)
I'm Losing You (1966)
I Wish It Would Rain (1968)
Just My Imagination (1971)
Masterpiece (1973)
The Motown Song (1991)
My Girl (1965)
Papa Was a Rollin' Stone (1972)
Psychedelic Shack (1970)
Run Away Child, Running Wild (1969)
The Way You Do the Things You Do (1964)
You're My Everything (1967)
Temp, The (1993 film)
cast: Lara Flynn Boyle, Faye Dunaway, Timothy Hutton
tempting: **5** siren, yummy **6** savory **8** alluring, charming, enticing, fetching, inviting **9** palatable **10** appetizing, intriguing
one: **5** lurer **7** enticer
temptress: **4** vamp **5** lurer, siren
tempura mix: **6** batter
tempus fugit: **9** time flies
ten: **5** decad **6** decade, number **7** perfect, respite, sawbuck **9** honor card
combining form: **3** dec-, dek- **4** deca-, deka- **5** decem-
in French: **3** dix
in German: **4** zehn
in Italian: **5** dieci
in Portuguese: **3** dez
in Spanish: **4** diez
take ~: **4** rest **5** break, pause, relax **6** recess, rest up **8** intermit
to Mohs: **7** diamond
to one: **4** odds
ten __: **5** to one
ten-__: **4** four, spot **5** speed **6** strike
ten-__ bike: **5** speed
ten-__ hat: **6** gallon
ten-__ shotgun: **5** gauge
ten-__ store: **4** cent
__ ten: **3** top **4** hang, take **5** one to
Ten __ a Dance: **5** Cents
Ten __ a-leaping: **5** lords
Ten __ Frederick: **5** North
Ten __ scholar: **6** o'clock
Ten __ That Shook the World: **4** Days
Ten __ War: **5** Years'
tenable: **5** sound **6** cogent, viable **7** logical **8** analytic, arguable, coherent, credible, methodic, rational, sensible **9** excusable, plausible, pragmatic **10** analytical, believable, condonable, consistent, defensible, reasonable, vindicable
tenacious: **3** set **5** fixed, hardy, nervy, stout, tight, tough **6** clingy, dogged, gritty, mulish, sticky, strong, sturdy **7** adamant, durable, staunch **8** clinging, hellbent, obdurate, resolute, stalwart, stubborn, untiring **9** obstinate, retentive, steadfast, unbending **10** courageous, determined, hard-bitten, iron-willed, persistent, possessive, purposeful, relentless, undeterred, unflagging, unshakable, unswerving, unyielding
tenacity: **4** grit, guts **5** moxie, nerve, pluck, spunk **6** starch **7** courage, purpose, resolve **8** backbone, chutzpah, firmness, strength **9** assiduity, diligence, endurance, gutsiness, hardiness, obstinacy **10** confidence, doggedness, moral fiber, resolution
tenancy: **9** occupancy, ownership **10** occupation, possession
tenant: **5** guest, liver **6** holder, leaser, lessee, lodger, occupy, renter, reside, roomer **7** boarder, dweller, inhabit **8** occupant, resident **9** addressee, possessor **10** inhabitant
awaiting a ~: **5** unlet
find a ~: **4** rent
find a new ~: **5** relet
organization: **4** co-op
pact: **5** lease
tenant __: **6** farmer
tenantless: **5** to let **6** vacant
Tenant of Wildfell Hall, The
author: Anne Brontë
Tenants, The
author: Bernard Malamud
Tenant, The (1976 film)
cast: Isabelle Adjani, Roman Polanski
director: Roman Polanski
ten-armed animal: **5** squid
ten-cent __: **5** store
Ten Cents a Dance
composer: Lorenz Hart, Richard Rodgers
Ten Commandments
recipient: **5** Moses
repository: **3** ark
word: **3** not, thy **5** shalt
Ten Commandments, The (1956 film): **4** epic
cast: Judith Anderson, Anne Baxter, Yul Brynner, John Carradine, Yvonne De Carlo, John Derek, Nina Foch, Cedric Hardwicke, Charlton Heston, Debra Paget, Vincent Price, Edward G. Robinson, Martha Scott
director: Cecil B. DeMille
role: **4** Seti **5** Aaron, Moses **6** Dathan **7** Pharaoh, Rameses
__ Ten Conference: **3** Big, Pac
tend: **4** bear, feed, head, keep, lead, lean, look, mind, till **5** do for, drift, groom, guard, labor, nurse, point, see to, serve, trend, verge, watch **6** foster, handle, manage, shield, wait on **7** baby-sit, care for, cater to, conduce, dispose, incline, nurture, oversee, protect, redound, sit with, verge on **8** maintain, minister, result in, see after, shepherd, wait upon **9** cultivate, gravitate, look after, safeguard, supervise, watch over **10** administer, keep tabs on, minister to, move toward, ride herd on, take care of
a fire: **5** stoke
a horse: **5** brush
an orchard: **3** lop, mow, top **4** clip, crop, snip, trim **5** shear
to: **4** mind **5** nurse, serve **6** wait on **8** see about, wait upon **9** look after
towards: **5** favor
(towards): **4** lean
Ten Days That Shook the World
author: John Reed
tendency: **3** way **4** bent, bias, tide, wont **5** drift, habit, trend **6** course, liking **7** bearing, current, heading, impulse, leaning, mindset **8** penchant, velleity, weakness **9** appetence, direction, liability, proneness, readiness **10** likelihood, partiality, proclivity, propensity
combining form: **6** -phoria
suffix: **3** -ive
tendentious: **6** biased **7** partial
tender: **3** bid, put, raw **4** boat, fond, give, hand, hurt, kind, lush, mild, pose, ship, soft, sore, warm, weak **5** frail, green, mushy, offer, quote, silky, sweet, yield, young **6** accord, aching, callow, caring, decent, feeble, gentle, hand in, humane, kindly, loving, moving, render, submit, turn in, vernal **7** amatory, amorous, bruised, clement, commend, cordial, fragile, hugging, kissing, lenient, lighter, painful, present, proffer, propose, sparing **8** all heart, delicate, gracious, immature, inflamed, maternal, merciful, nominate, overture, parental, poignant, proposal, reddened, romantic, tolerant, touching, yielding, youthful **9** amatorial, childlike, emotional, forgiving, irritated, quotation, sensitive, volunteer **10** administer, altruistic, benevolent, contribute, lovey-dovey, responsive, solicitous, unhardened, vulnerable
age: **5** teens, youth **6** cradle **7** infancy, puberty **8** minority **9** childhood, juniority **10** immaturity, juvenility, schooldays
an offer: **3** ask, bid **5** quote **6** invite, submit **7** proffer, propose **10** make a pitch
become ~: **6** soften
ender: **4** foot, loin **7** hearted
feeling: **4** pity **5** heart, mercy **6** lenity **7** charity, empathy, quarter **8** clemency, kindness, lenience, sympathy **9** sentiment, tolerance **10** compassion, condolence, humaneness
legal ~: *see* moolah
loving care: **7** concern
starter: **3** bar **4** goal
tender __: **5** offer
__ tender: **5** legal
Tender __: **4** Love **7** Mercies, Vittles
tenderfoot: **4** dude, tiro, tyro **5** newie, pupil, young **6** greeny, intern, novice, rookie **7** entrant, interne, learner, new hand, recruit, trainee **8** beginner, initiate, neophyte, newcomer **9** fledgling, greenhorn **10** apprentice, dilettante, first-timer, uninitiate
Tenderfoot: **5** Scout **8** Boy Scout
org.: **3** BSA
tender-hearted: **4** kind, soft **6** caring, kindly **8** merciful **9** concerned
one: **5** softy **6** softie
tender-heartedness: **5** mercy **6** lenity **8** clemency, humanity, kindness, mildness, patience, softness, sympathy **10** compassion, generosity, gentleness, indulgence, moderation, toleration
Tender Is the Night
author: F. Scott Fitzgerald
character: **3** Abe **4** Beth, Clay, Hoyt **5** Diver, Elsie **6** Barban, Collis, Kaethe, Nicole, Speers
tenderize: **6** soften
tenderloin: **4** meat **5** filet
tenderly: **6** gently, softly **7** lightly
in music: **7** pietoso
treat ~: **4** baby, love **6** coddle, cosset, dote on, pamper **7** cater to, indulge
Tender Mercies (1983 film)
cast: Robert Duvall, Tess Harper
tenderness: **4** love, pain, pity **5** heart, mercy **8** lenience **9** affection **10** attachment, compassion
Tender Trap, The: **4** song
artist: Frank Sinatra
composer: Sammy Cahn, Jimmy Van Heusen
tending: **3** apt **5** prone **6** liable, likely **8** inclined
(to): **8** disposed
to (suffix): **3** -ish
tendon: **5** chord, sinew **6** muscle
tendon-bone connector: **5** bursa
tendril: **4** hair **5** fiber **6** strand **8** filament
tenebrific: **4** dark, drab, dull **5** black, bleak, mirky, murky **6** dismal, dreary, gloomy, somber **7** austere **9** cheerless **10** depressing, oppressive
tenebrous: **3** dim **4** dark **5** dusky, mirky, murky, unlit, vague **6** dismal, gloomy, opaque, somber **7** obscure, shadowy, sunless **8** lowering **9** ambiguous, equivocal, unlighted
tenement
locale: **4** slum
__ Tenenbaums, The: **5** Royal
__ tenens: **5** locum
Tenerife: **4** isle **6** island
locale: **8** Canaries
tenet: **3** ism **4** rule, view **5** bylaw, canon, credo, creed, dogma, ethos, faith **6** belief, policy, thesis **7** precept **8** doctrine, ideology, platform, teaching **9** principle, teachings **10** conviction

tenfold: **6** denary
ten-four
  buddy: **4** CBer
ten-gallon __: **3** hat
Ten-hut! opposite: **6** at ease
Tenley: **8** Albright
__ Ten List: **3** Top
Tennant: **4** Andy, Emma **8** Victoria
Tennant, Victoria
  spouse: Steve Martin
tenner: **4** bill **8** banknote
  half a ~: **3** fin
Tennessee: **5** river, state **8** Williams
  athlete: **3** Vol
  capital: **9** Nashville
  city: **5** Alcoa **6** Smyrna **7** Bristol, Jackson, Lebanon, Memphis **8** Bartlett, Columbia, Franklin, Gallatin, Oak Ridge **9** Brentwood, Cleveland, East Ridge, Kingsport, Knoxville, Maryville, Nashville **10** Cookeville, Germantown, Morristown
  conference: **3** SEC
  neighbor: **7** Alabama, Georgia **8** Arkansas, Kentucky, Missouri, Virginia
  pro team: **6** Titans
  River locale: **7** Alabama **8** Kentucky
  River tributary: **3** Elk
  school: **10** Vanderbilt
  state flower: **4** iris
  state gem: **5** pearl
  state reptile: **9** box turtle
  state wild animal: **7** raccoon
Tennessee __: **7** warbler
Tennessee __ Authority: **6** Valley
Tennessee __ Ford: **5** Ernie
Tennessee __ horse: **7** walking
Tennesseean: **5** paper **9** newspaper
  locale: **9** Nashville
Tennessee Waltz beginning: **4** I was
Tenney: **3** Jon
Tennille: **4** Toni
  partner: **6** Dragon **7** Captain
tennis: **4** game **5** sport
  area: **5** court **8** baseline
  Argentine ~ pro: **5** Vilas
  Australian ~ pro: **4** Hoad **5** Court, Laver **6** Fraser, Rafter, Stolle **7** Emerson, Lew Hoad **8** Newcombe, Rod Laver, Rosewall **9** Goolagong **10** Fred Stolle, Roy Emerson
  Brazilian ~ pro: **5** Bueno **10** Maria Bueno
  call: **3** let **4** long **5** fault
  cup: **5** Davis
  Czech ~ pro: **5** Kodes, Lendl **8** Jan Kodes **9** Ivan Lendl **10** Mandlikova **11** Navratilova
  Ecuadorean ~ pro: **6** Segura
  edge: **4** ad in **5** ad out
  exchange: **5** rally **6** volley
  French ~ pro: **7** Lacoste
  need: **3** net **4** ball **5** court **6** racket
  official: **3** ref, ump **6** umpire **7** referee
  org.: **4** USTA **5** USLTA
  pro: **4** Ashe, Borg, Hoad, King, Wade **5** Budge, Bueno, Court, Evert, Kodes, Laver, Lendl, Moody, Riggs, Seles, Smith, Vilas **6** Agassi, Austin, Casals, Fraser, Gibson, Hingis, Kramer, Marble, Rafter, Segura, Stolle, Tilden **7** Connors, Emerson, Lacoste, Lew Hoad, McEnroe, Nastase, Ralston, Sampras, Trabert **8** Capriati, Connolly, Don Budge, Gonzales, Jan Kodes, Newcombe, Rod Laver, Rosewall, Williams **9** Bjorn Borg, Davenport, Goolagong, Ivan Lendl, Stan Smith **10** Arthur Ashe, Bill Tilden, Bobby Riggs, Chris Evert, Jack Kramer, Kournikova, Mandlikova **11** Navratilova
  Romanian ~ pro: **7** Nastase
  Russian ~ pro: **10** Kournikova
  score: **3** ace **4** love **5** forty **6** thirty **7** fifteen
  shot: **3** lob **4** chop, dink **5** slice, smash **6** volley **8** backhand, forehand
  six games in ~: **3** set
  Slovakian ~ pro: **6** Hingis
  stadium: **4** Ashe
  start a ~ game: **5** serve
  status: **3** bye **4** seed
  surface: **4** clay, lawn **5** grass
  Swedish ~ pro: **4** Borg **9** Bjorn Borg
  teacher: **3** pro
  term: **3** ace, all, bye, let, lob, net, ref, set, ump **4** ad in, game, love, seed **5** ad out, court, deuce, fault, match, point, serve, smash **6** do-over, racket, rubber, umpire, volley **7** doubles, referee, service, singles, topspin **8** backhand, baseline, forehand, overspin
  tie: **5** deuce
  tourney: **6** U.S. Open **9** Wimbledon **10** French Open
  unit: **3** set **4** game **5** match
  wear: **6** anklet, shorts, sneaks **8** headband, sneakers **9** wristband
  Yugoslavian ~ pro: **5** Seles
tennis __: **4** ball, shoe **5** elbow
__ tennis: **4** deck, lawn **5** table **6** paddle
Tennis, __?: **6** anyone
tennis elbow site: **4** ulna
Tenn. neighbor: **3** Ala., Ark., Ken. **4** Miss, N. Car., Virg.
  see also Tennessee
Ten North Frederick
  author: John O'Hara
Tennyson, Alfred: **4** Lord, poet **7** British
  character: **3** Ida **4** Enid **6** Elaine
  work: Charge of the Light Brigade
    Crossing the Bar
    Enoch Arden
    Idylls of the King
    In Memoriam
    The Lady of Shalott
    Locksley Hall
    The Lotus-Eaters
    Mariana
    Maud
    Oenone
    Tears, Idle Tears
Tenochtitlán
  resident: **5** Aztec
tenon: **6** insert **8** dovetail
tenor: **4** clef, gist, male, mood, pith, tone, vein **5** drift, Lanza, Pears, range, sense, sound, style, theme, trend, voice **6** burden, Caruso, intent, Peerce, singer, Tucker **7** caroler, Corelli, current, Domingo, essence, meaning, purport, Vickers **8** Carreras, Melchior, vocalist **9** chorister, direction, Jan Peerce, Pavarotti, substance **10** Mario Lanza, Peter Pears
  British ~: **5** Pears **10** Peter Pears
  colleague: **4** alto, bass **5** mezzo **7** soprano **8** baritone **9** contralto
  Danish ~: **8** Melchior
  Italian ~: **6** Caruso **7** Corelli **9** Pavarotti
  Spanish ~: **7** Domingo **8** Carreras
  starter: **7** counter
tenor __: **3** cor, sax **4** clef, horn
ten-pack: **6** carton
tenpenny __: **4** nail
ten-percenter: **3** agt., rep **5** agent
tenpins: **4** game **5** sport **7** bowling
  participant: **6** kegler **7** kegeler
ten-point type: **5** elite
tense: **4** edgy, shot, taut **5** antsy, drawn, hyper, itchy, jumpy, key up, rigid, shaky, stiff, tight, wired **6** jangly, on edge, uneasy **7** anxious, excited, fidgety, fretful, harried, in knots, jittery, keyed up, nervous, restive, stiffen, tighten, uptight, worried, wound up **8** agitated, distress, fluttery, fretsome, in a tizzy, preterit, restless, skittish, strained, troubled, unnerved, worked up **9** concerned, excitable, ill at ease, knotted up, pressured, stressful, strung out, unbending, unsettled, up the wall **10** distressed, highstrung, overstrung
  be ~: **5** worry **6** simmer
  vb. ~: **3** fut. **4** impf., pres., pret. **6** imperf.
__ tense: **4** past **6** future **7** present
tenseness: **6** nerves, strain, stress **7** anxiety
__, tens, hundreds: **5** units
tension: **5** drama, worry **6** nerves, shakes, strain, stress, unease, unrest **7** anxiety, jitters **8** disquiet, edginess, pressure, suspense, tautness **9** hostility, intensity, stiffness, tightness **10** uneasiness
  lose ~: **3** sag
  treatment: **3** rub **7** massage
__-tension: **3** low **4** high
ten-speed: **4** bike **5** cycle, racer **7** bicycle
  part: **4** gear
  rider: **5** biker
ten-spot, half a: **5** fiver
tent: **4** camp, tipi, yurt **5** dress, tepee **6** big top, teepee, wigwam **7** camp out, shelter **8** barracks, covering, pavilion, quarters
  Asian ~: **4** yurt
  dismantle a ~: **5** unpeg
  dweller: **5** nomad
  fabric: **4** duck **6** canvas
  flap: **3** fly
  holder: **3** peg **5** stake
  pitch a ~: **7** rough it
  set up a ~: **4** camp, stay **5** abide, pitch **6** encamp
  set up a ~ again: **5** repeg
  show: **4** fair **6** big top, circus **8** carnival
__ tent: **3** pup **6** circus
tentacle: **3** arm **5** organ **6** feeler
tentative: **4** iffy **5** shaky, trial **6** acting, unfirm, unsure, wabbly, wobbly **7** halting, interim, subject **8** cautious, doubtful, hesitant, unproved **9** dependant, dependent, faltering, provisory, reluctant, uncertain, undecided, unsettled **10** contingent, indecisive, indefinite, irresolute, unfinished
tenterhook: **4** nail
tenterhooks
  be on ~: **5** sweat, worry
  on ~: **4** edgy **5** antsy, itchy, jumpy, tense **6** on edge, queasy, queazy, uneasy **7** alarmed, anxious, jittery, keyed up, nervous, restive, uptight, worried **8** agitated, qualmish, restless, skittish, troubled **9** concerned, excitable, ill at ease **10** high-strung
tenth: **5** tithe **6** decile
  combining form: **4** deci-
Tenth Commandment, The
  author: Lawrence Sanders
Tenth Man, The
  author: Paddy Chayefsky
ten thousand combining form: **5** myria-
Tentmaker: **4** Omar **7** Kháyyam
tenuous: **4** slim, thin, weak **5** faint, frail, light, shaky **6** flimsy, slight, subtle, unfirm **7** dubious, sketchy, slender **8** doubtful, ethereal, exiguous, gossamer, nebulous, rarefied
  fragment: **4** wisp
tenure: **3** job **4** hold, term **5** reign **6** regime **7** holding **8** duration, security **9** longevity, occupancy, ownership, residence **10** incumbency, occupation, possession
Ten Years' __: **3** War
Tenzing: **6** Norgay
  colleague: **6** Edmund
Teo: **4** Fabi
tepee: **4** tent **5** abode **6** wikiup **7** wickiup, wickyup
  like a ~: **5** conic **7** conical
tepid: **4** cool, mild, warm **7** languid, warmish **8** lifeless, lukewarm, milkwarm, moderate, not so hot **9** apathetic, temperate, unextreme **10** spiritless, unagitated
tequila: **5** drink **8** beverage
  source: **5** agave
Tequila (1958 song)
  artist: Champs
Tequila Sunrise (1988 film)
  cast: Mel Gibson, Raul Julia, Michelle Pfeiffer, Kurt Russell
  director: Robert Towne
teratoid: **8** aberrant, freakish **9** monstrous
terbium: **5** metal **7** element
Ter Borch, Gerard: **6** artist **7** painter
  homeland: **7** Holland **11** Netherlands
tercel: **4** bird, hawk, male **6** falcon
Tercel: **3** car **4** auto **6** Toyota **10** automobile
tercet: **7** triplet
Terence: **5** Roman, Stamp, Young **6** Fisher **10** playwright
Terence __ D'Arby: **5** Trent

Teresa: 5 saint 6 Brewer, Mother, Wright 7 Stratas
Teresa of __: 5 Avila
tergiversate: 5 fence, hedge, waver 6 seesaw, waffle 8 flip-flop, hesitate 9 vacillate 10 equivocate
tergiversator: 9 chameleon
Terhune: 6 Albert
  canine: 3 Lad
Teri: 4 Garr, Polo 6 Austin, Copley 7 DeSario, Hatcher
teriyaki: 4 meat
  ingredient: 4 soya 6 ginger
Terkel, Studs: 6 writer
  work: The Good War
    Working
term: 3 dub, tag 4 call, name, span, time, tour, word 5 hitch, label, limit, phase, space, spell, stint, style, title 6 course, length, period, phrase, season, tenure 7 baptize, caption, quarter, session, stretch 8 christen, confines, describe, duration, interval, nominate, semester, sentence, standing, subtitle 9 condition, designate, occupancy, provision 10 denominate, expression
term __: 5 paper 6 limits
term.
  marking: 3 neg., pos.
__-term: 4 full, long, near 5 short
termagant: 4 crab 5 harpy, scold, shrew, vixen 6 chider, virago 7 needler, rebuker, violent 8 brawling, grumbler, harridan, shrewish, spitfire 9 henpecker, turbulent, Xanthippe 10 disorderly
terminable: 7 bounded, limited 10 dissoluble, measurable
terminal: 3 CRT, end, sta., stn., VDT 4 base, last 5 anode, depot, final 6 distal, screen 7 cathode, display, extreme, monitor, station 8 eventual, ultimate 10 concluding
  approach the ~: 4 taxi
  battery ~: 3 neg., pos. 5 anode 7 cathode 8 negative, positive
  info: 3 arr., ETA, ETD
  of a ~: 6 anodal
__ terminal: 5 video 6 dial-up
Terminal
  author: Robin Cook
Terminal Man, The: 4 film 5 novel
  author: Michael Crichton
  cast: Joan Hackett, George Segal
Terminal, The (2004 film)
  cast: Tom Hanks, Stanley Tucci, Catherine Zeta-Jones
  director: Steven Spielberg
Terminal Velocity (1994 film)
  cast: James Gandolfini, Nastassja Kinski, Charlie Sheen
terminate: 2 ax 3 axe, can, end 4 boot, drop, fire, halt, lift, oust, quit, sack, stop 5 abort, annul, cease, close, lapse, let go, limit, scrub, sever 6 bounce, cancel, cut off, expire, finish, lay off, recess, resign, result, run out, wind up, wrap up 7 abolish, adjourn, break up, cashier, dismiss, drum out, release, scratch 8 complete, conclude, cut short, dissolve, furlough, get rid of, intermit, obstruct, pack it in, pink-slip, prorogue, round off, round out, surcease, wind down 9 culminate, discharge, eliminate, eventuate, liquidate 10 call it a day, consummate, extinguish
terminated: 3 out 4 done, over 6 lapsed 7 all over, through 8 done with
termination: 3 end 4 halt 5 close, limit 6 cut-off, demise, ending, expiry, finale, finish, period, result, windup, wrap-up 7 closure, outcome, passing 8 curtains, surcease 9 abatement, cessation 10 conclusion
Terminator 2 - Judgment Day (1991 film)
  cast: Edward Furlong, Linda Hamilton, Arnold Schwarzenegger
  director: James Cameron
  dog: 3 Max
Terminator, The (1984 film)
  cast: Michael Biehn, Linda Hamilton, Arnold Schwarzenegger
  director: James Cameron
  role: 5 Sarah
terminer's partner: 4 oyer
terminology: 5 argot, lingo 6 jargon 7 lexicon, wording 8 language, locution, phrasing
terminus: 3 end 4 pole, stop 5 close 6 ending, finale, finish, windup, wrap-up 10 conclusion, denouement, resolution
terminus __: 4 a quo
terminus ad __: 4 quem
termitarium: 4 nest
termite: 3 bug 5 borer 6 insect
  group: 5 swarm
  home: 4 nest
  kin: 3 ant
  meal: 4 wood
__-term memory: 4 long 5 short
term paper
  abbr.: 4 et al., ibid. 5 op. cit. 6 loc. cit.
terms: 4 rate 5 truce 6 points, treaty 7 details, footing, payment, premise, proviso, strings 8 position, proposal, standing 9 agreement, fine print, provision, relations, requisite 10 conditions, small print
  be on good ~ with: 4 know
  bring to ~: 7 mediate 9 negotiate, reconcile
  come to ~: 5 agree, level, yield 6 make up, settle 7 bargain, work out 10 capitulate
  on good ~: 4 kind 5 close, thick 6 chummy, clubby, genial, kindly 7 affable, amiable, cordial 8 amicable, friendly, intimate, outgoing, peaceful, sociable 9 convivial 10 benevolent, buddy-buddy, neighborly, solicitous
Terms of Endearment: 4 film 5 novel
  author: Larry McMurtry
  cast: Jeff Daniels, Danny DeVito, John Lithgow, Shirley MacLaine, Jack Nicholson, Debra Winger
  director: James L. Brooks
tern: 4 bird 5 noddy 7 seabird 9 shorebird 10 sea swallow
  in England: 5 starn
  relative: 4 gull
terne metal: 5 alloy
  component: 3 tin 4 lead
ternion: 4 trio 6 triple
Terpsichore: 4 Muse
  colleague: *see* Muse
  parent: 4 Zeus 9 Mnemosyne
terpsichorean: 6 dancer, hoofer 8 coryphée, Rockette 9 ballerina, chorus boy 10 chorus girl
  work: 5 dance 6 ballet
terra __: 4 alba 5 cotta, firma
Terra
  in Greek myth: 4 Gaia
terrace: 4 yard 6 street 7 balcony 8 platform
Terrace at Le Havre
  painter: Claude Monet
terra cotta: 4 clay 6 orange 7 pottery 8 brownish, clayware, crockery
  relative: *see* orange color
terra firma: 4 land, soil 5 earth, shore 6 ground
  on ~: 6 ashore
terrain: 4 area, land, turf 5 field 6 domain, ground, region, sphere 7 contour, country, grounds, habitat, scenery 8 confines, dominion 9 landscape, territory 10 topography
terra incognita: 6 enigma 7 mystery
__-terrain vehicle: 3 all
__-terre: 5 pied-à
Terre
  author: Émile Zola
__-Terre: 5 Basse
Terre Haute: 4 city, town
  locale: 3 Ind. 7 Indiana
  sch.: 3 ISU
Terrell, Tammi: 6 singer
  song: Ain't No Mountain High Enough (1967)
    Ain't Nothing Like the Real Thing (1968)
    If I Could Build My Whole World Around You (1967)
    You're All I Need to Get By (1968)
    Your Precious Love (1967)
Terrence: 6 Howard, Malick 7 McNally 8 Rattigan
terrene: 7 earthly, worldly 8 material
terrestrial: 6 global 7 earthly, terrene 8 telluric 9 earthlike
Terri: 5 Clark, Gibbs, Treas
terrible: 4 base, hard, vile 5 awful 6 mortal, severe 7 awesome, dreaded, extreme, hellish, painful, serious, violent 8 God-awful, grievous 9 dangerous, desperate, harrowing, ill-omened, obnoxious, repulsive, unnerving 10 disturbing, horrifying
  be ~: 5 stink
  combining form: 3 din- 4 dein-, dino- 5 deino-
  enfant ~: 4 brat 5 devil, scamp
  feeling ~: 3 ill, low 4 hurt, sick 6 ailing, infirm, queasy, unwell 7 laid low 8 below par 9 in a bad way, miserable 10 out of sorts
  see also awful
terrible __: 4 twos
__ terrible: 6 enfant
Terrible Swift Sword
  author: Bruce Catton
...__ terrible thing to waste: 3 is a
terribly: 4 much, very 5 badly 6 highly 7 awfully, gravely, greatly 8 horribly, markedly 9 decidedly, extremely, fearfully, in a big way, intensely, seriously, unhappily, unusually 10 dreadfully, remarkably, thoroughly
terrier: 3 dog, pet 5 canid, pooch 6 canine 8 wirehair
  fictional ~: 4 Asta
  like a ~ coat: 4 wiry
__ terrier: 3 fox, rat 4 bull, Skye 5 Cairn, Irish, silky, Welsh 6 Border, Boston, Scotch 7 Norfolk, Norwich, Tibetan, wheaten 8 Airedale
terrific: 4 huge 5 awful, harsh 6 fierce, severe 7 extreme, fearful, immense, intense 8 dreadful, enormous, gigantic, horrible, horrific, laudable, shocking 9 appalling, deafening, excessive, frightful, monstrous 10 thunderous
  time: 4 ball, gala 5 blast, party, spree
  see also wonderful
Terrific!: 3 wow 4 fine 5 great, super 9 marvelous, wonderful
terrified: 5 ashen, funky, timid 6 afraid, aghast, scared, trepid 7 anxious, chicken, fearful, nervous, panicky 8 cowardly, fearsome, hesitant, timorous 10 frightened
terrify: 3 awe 4 stun 5 alarm, appal, chill, daunt, haunt, scare, shock, spook 6 adread, appall, dismay, freeze, menace 7 horrify, petrify, startle, stupefy 8 frighten, paralyse, paralyze 9 terrorize 10 intimidate, scare stiff
terrifying: 5 dread, scary 6 creepy, grisly 7 dreaded, ghastly, hideous 8 gruesome, horrible 9 appalling, harrowing 10 formidable
territorial: 8 colonial, regional
territorial __: 6 waters
territory: 4 area, belt, land, turf, walk, ward, zone 5 arena, block, field, range, realm, space, state, tract 6 colony, domain, empire, extent, locale, nation, parish, region, sector, sphere, street 7 country, enclave, expanse, grounds, habitat, mandate, purview, quarter, section, terrain 8 boundary, confines, district, dominion, locality, province, vicinity 9 community 10 boundaries, possession
__ Territory: 5 Yukon 6 Dakota, Indian
terror: 3 awe 4 fear, funk 5 alarm, dread, panic, shock 6 dismay, fright, horror, phobia 7 anxiety, scourge 9 trepidity
  cry of ~: 4 oh no 5 oh God
  holy ~: 3 cad, cur, imp, rat 4 brat, toad 5 churl, demon, knave, louse, rogue, scamp 6 bad boy, rascal, urchin 7 bounder, dastard, hellion, lowlife, ruffian, stinker 8 blighter, picaroon, scalawag, spalpeen 9 miscreant, prankster, reprobate, scoundrel 10 blackguard, malefactor, ne'er-do-well, scapegrace

reign of ~: **5** purge **7** tyranny **9** despotism **10** oppression
terrorist: **4** thug **5** enemy **9** anarchist, ill-wisher
'70s ~ org.: **3** SLA
terrorize: **3** awe, cow **5** alarm, appal, bully, haunt, panic, scare, shock, spook **6** appall, coerce, dismay, fright, hector, menace, prey on **7** dragoon, horrify, oppress, petrify, scourge, startle, terrify **8** bludgeon, browbeat, bulldoze, frighten, prey upon, threaten **9** strong-arm **10** intimidate, scare stiff
Terror, The
author: Edgar Wallace
terry: **5** cloth **6** fabric **8** material
product: **4** robe **5** towel **9** washcloth
Terry: **3** Eli **4** Bill **5** Ellen, Jacks, Moore **6** Carter **7** Farrell, Gilliam, Sawchuk **8** Bradshaw, McMillan, Southern, Stafford **9** Pendleton
Terry, Bill: **5** Giant
terse: **4** curt, lean **5** blunt, brief, brusk, close, crisp, pithy, short, tight **6** abrupt, gnomic, snappy **7** brusque, clipped, compact, concise, cryptic, laconic, pointed, summary **8** clear-cut, incisive, succinct **9** axiomatic, condensed, cryptical, trenchant **10** aphoristic, boiled down, elliptical, synopsized, to the point
terseness: **7** brevity **8** laconism
Tertiary Period epoch: **6** Eocene
terza __: **4** rima
Teseo
composer: George Frideric Handel
Teshigara: **7** Hiroshi
Tesh, John: **7** pianist
former colleague: Mary Hart
genre: **6** New Age
spouse: Connie Sellecca
Tesla __: **4** coil
Tesla, Nikola: **9** physicist, scientist
rival: **6** Edison
Tess: **6** Harper **9** Trueheart
Tess (1979 film)
cast: Peter Firth, Nastassja Kinski
director: Roman Polanski
Tess __ d'Urbervilles: **5** of the
tessellate: **5** inlay
tessellated: **6** inlaid
Tessie: **5** O'Shea
Tess of the d'Urbervilles
author: Thomas Hardy
character: **3** Izz **4** Alec, Hope, Jack, Joan **5** Angel, Chant, Clare, Crick, Farmy, Felix, Groby, Huett, James, Mercy, Nancy, Retty **6** Liza-Lu, Marian, Sorrow **7** Abraham, Dark Car, Modesty, Richard **8** Car Darch, Cuthbert, Izz Huett, Tringham **10** Angel Clare, Christiana, Farmy Groby, Mercy Chant
test: **2** go **3** sip, try **4** comp, exam, oral, quiz **5** assay, check, essay, final, gauge, grill, probe, proof, prove, taste, trial, try on **6** assess, dry run, enduro, handle, lesson, ordeal, sample, tryout, verify **7** analyze, confirm, examine, match up, midterm, midyear, pop quiz, stack up **8** analysis, audition, blue book, check out, crucible, gauntlet, rehearse, scrutiny, standard, trial run, validate **9** catechism, challenge, countdown, criterion, give it a go, probation, shake down, true-false, yardstick **10** evaluation, experiment, inspection, run-through, touchstone, ultrasound
acid ~: **5** proof, trial
British ~: **6** A level
coll. student: **3** GRE **4** GMAT, LSAT, MCAT
command to ~ takers: **4** open **5** begin, start
comparison ~ item: **6** Brand X
HS proficiency ~: **3** GED
kind of ~ question: **5** essay **9** true-false
medical ~: **3** ECG, EEG, EKG, MRI **4** X-ray
one's endurance again: **5** retax
response: **3** ans. **4** true **5** false **6** answer
stand the ~ of time: **4** last **6** endure
the waters: **4** poll **5** query **6** survey
venue: **3** lab **5** class **9** classroom
version: **4** beta
test __: **3** ban **4** case, tube **5** drive, match, paper, pilot **7** pattern
test-__ treaty: **3** ban
__ test: **3** DNA **4** acid, beta, Dick, oral, road **5** Binet, blood, essay, taste **6** breath, litmus, Schick, screen, stress **7** Snellen **9** true-false
__-test: **4** high **5** field, shock **6** flight
testa: **8** seed coat
cousin: **4** aril
testament: **4** will **5** proof **8** covenant **9** guarantee **10** instrument
__ Testament: **3** New, Old
Testament, The
author: Elie Wiesel
Testarossa: **3** car **4** auto **7** Ferrari **10** automobile
testator's bequest: **6** estate
testatrix: **5** woman
Testaverde, Vinny: **2** QB
sport: **8** football
test-ban __: **6** treaty
__ Test Dummies: **5** Crash
tested: **5** tried, valid **9** qualified
they may be ~: **5** wills
__-tested: **4** time
tester: **4** coin, vial **5** money **6** bottle **8** examiner **9** inspector
output: **5** scent **7** perfume
testify: **4** show, sing **5** argue, prove, speak, state, swear, vouch **6** affirm, allege, assert, avouch, depone, depose **7** bespeak, certify, declare, swear to, warrant, witness **8** vouch for **10** stand up for
prepare to ~: **5** swear
testimonial: **5** honor, medal, salvo **6** homage, salute **7** ovation, tribute, warrant, witness **8** citation, memorial, monument **9** reference
testimony: **5** proof **6** avowal, record **7** grounds, support, witness **8** evidence **9** admission, affidavit, statement **10** deposition, indication, profession
disparage ~: **5** rebut
give ~: **5** swear, vouch **6** assert, depone, depose **7** certify, declare, warrant, witness
give false ~: **7** perjure
hearer: **4** jury **5** judge, juror
preceder: **4** oath
testiness: **6** spleen, temper **10** irritation
test of __: **4** time **5** wills **8** strength
test tube: **4** vial **5** phial
glass: **5** Pyrex
testy: **4** edgy, mean, sour, tart **5** cross, huffy, moody, raspy, short, surly **6** crabby, cranky, crusty, fretty, grouty, grumpy, in a pet, ireful, morose, on edge, ornery, snappy, sullen, touchy **7** annoyed, bearish, crabbed, fretful, grouchy, huffish, peevish, peppery, uptight, waspish **8** captious, choleric, fretsome, growling, grumpish, liverish, petulant, snappish **9** crotchety, excitable, fractious, impatient, irascible, irritable, querulous, splenetic **10** out of sorts
mood: **4** snit
tet: **6** Hebrew, letter
predecessor: **4** heth **5** cheth
successor: **3** yod **4** yodh
Tet
locale: **3** Nam **7** Vietnam
tetched: **3** mad **7** bananas, lunatic
tetchy: **7** peevish
__ tête: **5** mal de
tête-à-tête: **3** rap **4** chat, sofa, talk, word **5** couch, tryst **6** confab, dialog **7** schmoos **8** causerie, dialogue, schmoose, schmooze **9** interview **10** discussion, rendezvous
teth: **6** Hebrew, letter
predecessor: **4** heth **5** cheth
successor: **3** yod **4** yodh
tether: **3** tie **4** bind, cord, know, lead, moor, rein, rope **5** chain, hitch, leash, tie up **6** fasten, halter, hobble, hopple, lariat, picket, secure **7** harness **8** restrain, restrict **9** restraint **10** keep in line
tetherball: **4** game
Tethys: **4** moon **5** giant, Titan
daughter: **5** Argia, Metis
husband: **7** Oceanus
parent: **4** Gaea **6** Uranus
planet: **6** Saturn
Tetley: **3** tea
alternative: **6** Lipton, Nestea, Salada **7** Bigelow, Red Rose **8** Twinings
Teton: **5** range, tribe **6** Indian, Lakota **7** Amerind, Lakhota
range locale: **5** Idaho **7** Wyoming
__ Teton National Park: **5** Grand
tetra: **4** fish
tetra-: **4** four
plus one: **5** penta-
predecessor: **3** tri-
twice ~: **4** octa-, octo-
__ tetra: **4** neon
tetrad: **8** foursome
half a ~: **4** dyad
tetrarch: **4** king
__ tetrazzini: **7** chicken
Tetrazzini, Luisa: **6** singer **7** soprano
specialty: **5** opera
Tetris: **4** game **9** video game
tetr- successor: **4** pent-
Tetzlaff: **3** Ted
Teut.: **3** Ger.
Teuton
early: **4** Goth
Teutonic
combining form: **7** Germano-
god: **3** Tiu
goddess: **4** Erda, Norn
see also German
Tevere
city on the ~: **4** Roma
Tevet: **5** month **6** Hebrew
predecessor: **6** Kislev
successor: **6** Shevat
Tevin: **8** Campbell
Tevye: **7** Russian
portrayer: Zero Mostel, Topol
wife: **5** Golde
Tewes: **6** Lauren
Tewksbury: **5** Peter
Tex: **3** Joe **5** Avery **6** Beneke, Ritter **7** McCrary
Tex (1982 film)
cast: Matt Dillon, Meg Tilly
Tex-__: **3** Mex
Tex.
neighbor: **3** Ark., Mex. **4** N. Mex., Okla.
see also Texas
__-Tex: **4** Gore
Texaco: **8** gasoline
former ~ rival: **4** Esso **7** Flying A **8** Sinclair
rival: **4** Gulf, Hess **5** Amoco, Exxon, Getty, Mobil **7** Chevron
Texaco Star Theater
star: Milton Berle
Texans
home: **7** Houston
org.: **3** AFC, NFL
rival: ***see*** NFL team
sport: **8** football
Texas: **5** novel, state **6** Guinan
author: James A. Michener
bay: **9** Galveston
capital: **6** Austin
city: **4** Eola, Waco **5** Alice, Allen, Alvin, Bryan, Cisco, Ennis, Hurst, Olney, Pampa, Paris, Pharr, Plano, Tioga, Tyler **6** Austin, Conroe, Dallas, Del Rio, Denton, DeSoto, El Paso, Euless, Frisco, Irving, Keller, Laredo, Lufkin, Odessa, Orange, Seguin, Spring, Temple, Uvalde **7** Abilene, Baytown, Bedford, Coppell, Denison, Garland, Houston, Killeen, La Porte, Lubbock, Midland, Mission, Rowlett, San Juan, Sherman, Socorro, Watauga, Weslaco **8** Amarillo, Beaumont, Benbrook, Burleson, Cleburne, Deer Park, Edinburg, Fort Hood, Longview, MacAllen, Marshall, Mesquite, Pasadena, Pearland, Victoria **9** Arlington, Big Spring, Cedar Hill, Cedar Park, Corsicana, Eagle Pass, Fort Worth, Galveston, Grapevine, Harlingen, Kerrville, Lancaster, MacKinney, Mansfield, Plainview, Rosenberg, Round Rock, San Angelo, San Benito, San Marcos, Southlake, Sugar Land, Texarkana, The Colony **10** Atascocita, Carrollton, Cloverleaf, Georgetown,

Greenville, Haltom City, Huntsville, Kingsville, League City, Lewisville, Port Arthur, Richardson, San Antonio, Waxahachie
collegian: 5 Aggie, Miner
conference: 9 Big Twelve
county: 4 Cass, Coke, Frio, Hays, Kerr, Rusk, Webb 5 Bexar, Comal, Crane, Duval, Ector, Erath, Foard, Garza, Gregg, Irion, Llano, Milam, Nolan, Pecos, Starr, Titus 6 Brazos, Castro, Concho, DeWitt, Dimmit, Donley, Karnes, Kenedy, Kimble, Lavaca, Loving, Medina, Menard, Motley, Nueces, Oldham, Panola, Scurry, Shelby, Upshur, Uvalde, Yoakum, Zapata, Zavala 7 Aransas, Briscoe, Coryell, Hidalgo, Jim Hogg, Kleberg, Live Oak, Navarro, Refugio, San Saba, Swisher, Tarrant, Willacy 8 Atascosa, Comanche, Crockett, Hansford, Jim Wells, Maverick, Presidio, Tom Green, Val Verde, Van Zandt 9 Deaf Smith, Jeff Davis, Matagorda, Palo Pinto
desert: 10 Chihuahuan
dish: 5 chile, chili 6 chilli
Indian: 9 Karankawa
leaguer: 3 fly
national park: 7 Big Bend
neighbor: 4 Gulf 6 Mexico 8 Arkansas, Oklahoma 9 Louisiana, New Mexico
port: 7 Houston 9 Galveston
pro team: 4 Mavs 5 Spurs, Stars 6 Astros 7 Cowboys, Rangers 9 Mavericks
river: 5 Pecos 6 Brazos, Nueces 9 Rio Grande 10 Pedernales
school: 3 SMU, TCU 4 Rice, UTEP 5 Lamar 6 Baylor
state dish: 5 chili
state fiber: 6 cotton
state fish: 4 bass
state flower: 10 bluebonnet
state gem: 5 topaz
state large mammal: 8 longhorn
state musical instrument: 6 guitar
state pepper: 8 jalapeno
state shell: 5 whelk
state small mammal: 9 armadillo
state sport: 5 rodeo
state tree: 5 pecan
state vegetable: 10 sweet onion
tourist site: 5 Alamo
University of ~ locale: 6 Austin
Texas __: 3 tea 4 Tech 5 A and M 6 Ranger 7 leaguer
Texas __ M: 4 A and
Texas A&M
athletes: 6 Aggies
conference: 9 Big Twelve
rival: 3 SMU
Texas Chain Saw Massacre, The (1974 film)
director: Tobe Hooper
Texas Christian
locale: 9 Fort Worth
Texas-El Paso conference: 3 WAC
Texas Longhorn: 3 cow 4 bull 6 bovine, cattle
__, Texas Ranger: 6 Walker
Texas tea: 3 oil
Texas Tech
athletes: 10 Red Raiders
conference: 9 Big Twelve
locale: 7 Lubbock
Texas Troubadour, The: Ernest Tubb
Texas two-step: 5 dance
Texasville: 4 film 5 novel
author: Larry McMurtry
cast: Timothy Bottoms, Jeff Bridges, Annie Potts, Cybill Shepherd
director: Peter Bogdanovich
Tex, Joe
song: Hold What You've Got (1965)
I Gotcha (1972)
Skinny Legs and All (1967)
Tex-Mex
item: 4 taco 5 chile, chili, nacho, salsa 6 chilli, fajita 7 burrito
prepare ~ beans: 5 refry
text: 4 book, copy, idea, line 5 issue, point, prose, theme, topic, verse, words 6 manual, matter, primer, reader, script, source, stanza, thesis 7 content, extract, passage, speller, subject, wording 8 argument, contents, document, handbook, libretto, main body, material, sentence, syllabus, workbook 9 paragraph, quotation, reference 10 assignment, schoolbook, transcript
addendum: 5 index
authoritative ~: 4 book 5 Bible 6 manual 8 handbook 9 guidebook, scripture, vade mecum
change ~: 3 fix 4 edit 5 alter, emend 6 doctor, polish, refine, revise 7 correct, improve, rewrite, touch up 8 rephrase 10 blue-pencil
ender: 4 book
mistakes: 6 errata
preliminary ~: 4 plot 5 draft 7 outline
reviewer: 6 editor 8 compiler, redactor
starter: 5 plain
work on ~ together: 6 coedit
textbook: 4 tome 5 guide 6 manual, primer, reader, volume 10 compendium
category: 4 elhi
division: 4 quiz, test, unit 5 drill 6 lesson 7 reading 8 exercise
textile: 5 cloth 6 fabric 8 material
component: 4 noil, yarn 5 fiber 6 strand, thread
dye: 5 eosin 6 eosine
lubricant: 5 olein 6 oleine
machine: 4 loom
texture: 4 wale, woof
unit: 6 dye lot
worker: 4 dyer
see also fabric
textiles: 5 cloth
texture: 3 nap 4 feel, warp, woof 5 grain, touch, weave 6 makeup 7 essence, feeling, quality, surface 8 fineness, softness 9 character, roughness, stiffness 10 coarseness, smoothness
Tey, Josephine: 6 writer 8 Scottish
work: The Daughter of Time
The Franchise Affair
Miss Pym Disposes
__ T. Firefly: 5 Rufus
T.G.I. __: 7 Friday's
TGIF
part of ~: 3 Fri., God, It's 5 Thank 6 Friday
sayer: 6 worker
TGI Friday's
rival: ***see*** restaurant chain
Th: 4 elem. 7 element, thorium
90 for ~: 4 at. no.
T.H.: 5 White
Thackeray, William Makepeace: 6 writer 7 English
work: The Book of Snobs
Henry Esmond
Pendennis
The Ring and the Rose
Vanity Fair
The Virginians
Thai: 5 Asian 7 Siamese 8 language
Thailand: 4 gulf 6 nation 7 country
capital: 7 Bangkok
cat: 5 korat
dance: 4 khon
export: 4 teak
language: 3 Lao 5 Hmong
money: 3 att 4 baht 5 tical
native: 3 Lao 4 Miao
neighbor: 4 Laos 7 Myanmar 8 Cambodia, Malaysia
old name for ~: 4 Siam
org. for ~: 5 ASEAN
royal name: 4 Rama
temple: 3 wat
Thaïs: 5 opera
author: Anatole France
composer: Jules Massenet
role: 6 Albine, Nicias 7 Crobyle, Myrtale, Palemon 8 Athanaël
setting: 5 Egypt 10 Alexandria
Thal: 4 Eric
Thalassa: 4 moon
planet: 7 Neptune
thalassic: 5 naval 6 marine 7 aquatic 8 maritime, nautical
thalassophobe fear: 3 sea
Thalberg, Irving
spouse: Norma Shearer
thaler: 5 money
Thalia: 4 Muse 5 Grace
colleague: ***see*** Grace, Muse
parent: 4 Zeus
__ T. Hall: 3 Tom
thallium: 5 metal 7 element
Thalmus: 8 Rasulala
Thames: 5 river
city on the ~: 6 London
county on the ~: 5 Essex
craft: 4 punt
locale: 7 England
school on the ~: 4 Eton
tributary: 3 Wey
__ than: 4 less 5 other
__ than a breadbox: 6 bigger
__ Than a Feeling: 4 More
__-than-air: 7 heavier, lighter
Thanatopsis
author: William Cullen Bryant
Thanatos Syndrome, The
author: Walker Percy
Thandie: 6 Newton
thane: 4 lord 5 title 8 nobleman
group: 4 clan
__ than ever: 4 more
thank: 5 blame, bless 6 credit, praise 9 bow down to, recognize 10 appreciate
thank __: 3 you 6 heaven 7 heavens 8 goodness
thank-__ card: 3 you
Thank __ for Little Girls: 6 Heaven
thankful: 7 content, pleased 8 beholden, grateful, indebted, relieved 9 gratified, satisfied
Thank God I Found You (2000 song)
artist: Mariah Carey
Thank God I'm a Country Boy (1975 song)
artist: John Denver
Thank Heaven for Little Girls
composer: Alan Jay Lerner, Frederick Loewe
show: 4 Gigi
thankless: 4 vain 6 futile 7 useless 8 wretched 9 fruitless, miserable, unwelcome 10 ungracious, ungrateful, unpleasant, unreturned
thanks: 5 danke, merci 6 credit, grazie, praise 7 gracias, spasibo 8 blessing 9 gratitude
give ~: 6 praise 10 appreciate
give ~ to: 4 laud 5 bless, exalt, extol, honor 7 glorify
Londoner's ~: 3 tas
to: 7 because, through 10 by virtue of
__ thanks: 4 many
Thanks __ the Memory: 3 for
Thanks a __!: 3 lot 4 heap 7 million
Thanksgiving
day: 4 Thur. 5 Thurs.
month: 3 Nov. 8 November
offering: 3 yam 4 bird, corn 5 feast, maize 6 turkey
parade producer: 5 Macy's
parade sight: 5 float, Santa 10 Santa Claus
VIP: 6 carver
where ~ is in October: 6 Canada
Thanks, I __ that!: 6 needed
thanks to God in Latin: 10 Deo gratias
Thank U (1998 song)
artist: Alanis Morissette
thank-you __: 4 card, note
Thank You... (1970 song)
artist: Sly and the Family Stone
thank-you card
subject: 4 gift 5 award, favor 7 present 8 donation
__-than-life: 6 bigger, larger
__ than meets the eye: 4 more
__ Than Springtime: 7 Younger
__-than-thou: 6 holier
Thant, U
birthplace: 5 Burma
__ Than You Know: 4 More
thar: 6 yonder
Thar __ blows!: 3 she
Tharp: 5 Twyla
that: 4 as if 7 pronoun
after ~: 4 next, then 5 since 10 thereafter
at ~: 7 besides 10 all the same, as it stands, in addition
at ~ place: 3 yon 5 there 6 yonder
at ~ time: 4 then 9 thereupon
be ~ as it may: 6 anyhow, anyway, even so 7 however
being ~: 3 for 5 since 7 because, whereas

being the case: 4 ergo, if so, then, thus 5 hence 9 therefore
by ~ time: 7 already
failing ~: 4 else
following ~: 4 next 5 later 9 thereupon 10 afterwards
for all ~: 6 though 7 however 10 regardless
given ~: 3 tho 6 though 8 although, assuming, provided 9 providing, subject to, supposing 10 in the event
in spite of ~: 6 even so
is: 5 id est
is to say: 3 viz. 5 to wit 6 namely
it follows ~: 4 ergo, then, thus 9 therefore
kind of: 7 similar
not ~: 4 this
on ~ occasion: 4 when 9 thereupon
provided ~: 4 so as 6 in case 8 as long as
this and ~: 4 both 10 miscellany
this or ~: 6 either
that __ say: 4 is to
that __ you do!: 5 thing
__ that!: 5 Fancy 7 Imagine
...that __ men's souls: 3 try
That __: 4 Girl 5 is all
That __ Black Magic: 3 Old
That __ Cat!: 4 Darn
That __ Feeling: 7 Certain
That __ Gang of Mine: 3 Old
That __ hay!: 4 ain't
That __ is, so was he made: 4 as he
That __ it!: 4 does 5 tears
That __ it all!: 4 says
That __ lady...: 5 was no
That __ Then, This Is Now: 3 Was
That '70s Show (Fox sitcom)
cast: Topher Grace (Eric Forman) Mila Kunis (Jackie Burkhart) Ashton Kutcher (Michael Kelso) Danny Masterson (Steven Hyde) Laura Prepon (Donna Pinciotti)
__ that a dainty dish...: 5 Wasn't
__ that again?: 4 How's
That ain't __!: 3 hay
That Ain't Love (1987 song)
artist: REO Speedwagon
__ That a Shame: 4 Ain't
__ that be: 6 powers
That Certain Feeling
composer: George Gershwin, Ira Gershwin
thatch: 3 mop 5 cogon, reeds, straw 6 leaves, rushes
palm ~: 4 atap, nipa
Thatcher: 5 Torin 8 Margaret
Thatcher, Margaret: 2 P.M. 4 Tory 7 British
predecessor: 9 Callaghan
successor: 5 Major
__ That Could Happen: 5 Worst
That Darn Cat! (1965 film)
cast: Dean Jones, Hayley Mills
That Don't Impress Me Much (1999 song)
artist: Shania Twain
__ That Dream: 4 Darn 6 Follow
__ That Failed, The: 5 Light
That feels good!: 3 aah
__ That Ghost: 4 Hold
That Girl (ABC sitcom)
cast: Ted Bessell (Don Hollinger) Marlo Thomas (Ann Marie)
That Girl (song)
artist: Maxi Priest, Stevie Wonder
__ That Girl: 4 Who's
__ that glitters...: 3 All
__ that got away, the: 3 one
__ That Got Away, The: 3 Man
__ that has gits: 4 Them
__ That Heaven Allows: 3 All
That hurts!: 2 ow 3 oof, yow 4 ouch, yeow
__ That I Marry, The: 4 Girl
that is __: 5 to say
That is...: 5 I mean
that is in Latin: 5 id est
__ That Jack Built, The: 5 House
__ That Jazz: 3 All
That Lady (1973 song)
artist: Isley Brothers
That'll Be the Day (1974 film)
cast: David Essex, Ringo Starr
That'll Be the Day (song)
artist: Buddy Holly and the Crickets, Linda Ronstadt
That makes sense!: 3 aha 6 I get it
...that married dear old __: 3 Dad
__ that matter: 3 for
__ that men do..., The: 4 evil
That old black magic ___...: 5 has me
That Old Black Magic
composer: Harold Arlen, Johnny Mercer
That Old Black Magic (1958 song)
artist: Louis Prima and Keely Smith
That rings __!: 5 a bell
__ That Roared, The: 5 Mouse
That's __: 4 Life 5 Amore
That's __!: 3 all 4 a gas, a lie 5 a wrap
That's __, folks!: 3 all
That's __ for you to say: 4 easy
That's __ how-do-you-do!: 5 a fine
That's __ off my mind!: 5 a load
That's __ she wrote: 3 all
That's a __!: 4 no-no, wrap
That's a joke, __!: 3 son
That's a laugh!: 3 hah 4 ha-ha
That's a lie!: 5 not so
That's all __ wrote: 3 she
That's All! (1983 song)
artist: Genesis
That's all, folks! voice: Mel Blanc
That's All I Want from You (1954 song)
artist: Jaye P. Morgan
That's all there __ it!: 4 is to
That's All You Gotta Do (1960 song)
artist: Brenda Lee
That's amazing!: 3 gee, wow 5 golly
That's Amore
composer: Jack Brook, Harry Warren
That's a pity: 3 tsk 4 alas 5 alack 6 tsk tsk
That's a relief!: 4 phew
That's a riot!: 4 ha-ha
That's a surprise!: 5 hello
That's cheating!: 6 no fair
That's enough for me: 6 I'm good
That's Entertainment! (1974 film)
director: Jack Haley Jr.
hosts: Fred Astaire, Bing Crosby, Gene Kelly, Peter Lawford, Liza Minnelli, Donald O'Connor, Debbie Reynolds, Mickey Rooney, Frank Sinatra, James Stewart, Elizabeth Taylor
studio: 3 MGM
That's hilarious!: 4 ha-ha 6 hee-hee
That's it!: 3 aha 5 bingo
That's Life (1966 song)
artist: Frank Sinatra
That's Life! (1986 film)
cast: Julie Andrews, Jack Lemmon
that's life in French: 9 c'est la vie
That's My Desire (song)
artist: Frankie Laine
That's no lie!: 6 really
That's not __ idea!: 4 a bad
That's not the __ of it: 4 half
That's obvious!: 3 duh
That's okay: 6 no prob
That's one small step for ___...: 4 a man
That sounds like __: 5 a plan
__ that special?: 4 Isn't
that's right: 4 amen
see also of course
That's Rock 'N' Roll (1977 song)
artist: Shaun Cassidy
That's the __!: 6 ticket
That's the last __!: 5 straw
That's the truth!: 6 honest
That's the Way (1975 song)
artist: KC and the Sunshine Band
That's the Way It Is (1999 song)
artist: Celine Dion
That's the Way I've Always Heard It Should Be (1971 song)
artist: Carly Simon
That's the Way Love Goes (1993 song)
artist: Janet Jackson
That's the Way Love Is (1969 song)
artist: Marvin Gaye
That's What Friends Are For (1985 song)
artist: Elton John, Gladys Knight, Dionne Warwick, Stevie Wonder
That's What Love Is for (1991 song)
artist: Amy Grant
That's what you think!: 3 hah
that thing you do! (1996 film)
cast: Tom Hanks, Johnathon Schaech, Tom Everett Scott, Liv Tyler
director: Tom Hanks
setting: 4 Erie, Penn.
__ That Time Forgot, The: 4 Land
That Touch of __: 4 Mink
__ That Tune: 4 Name
That Uncertain Feeling
author: Kingsley Amis
That was close!: 4 phew, whew
That was no ___...: 4 lady
That Was Then, This Is Now (1986 song)
artist: Monkees
That will do!: 6 enough
__ that you can be: 5 Be all
thaumaturge: 6 wizard 8 magician, sorcerer
thaumaturgic: 5 magic 7 magical, uncanny 8 mystical, wizardly 10 bewitching, enchanting, miraculous
thaumaturgy: 5 magic 7 sorcery
thaw: 3 run 4 flow, flux, fuse, melt, warm 6 ice out, loosen, open up, soften, unbend, warm up 7 defrost, détente, liquefy, liquify, melting 8 dissolve, fluidize, melt away, unfreeze 10 deliquesce
out: 5 deice 7 defrost 8 unfreeze
Thayer: 6 Ernest
Th.D.: 3 deg.
curriculum: 3 rel. 5 relig.
the: 7 article
in French: 3 les
in German: 3 das, der, die
in Spanish: 3 las, los
thé: 3 tea 6 French
holder: 5 tasse
thé __: 7 dansant
The __ Circus: 6 Family
The __, OR: 6 Dalles
__ the 13th: 6 Friday
Thea
daughter: 4 Arne
father: 6 Chiron 7 Cheiron
__ the above: 5 all of 6 none of
__ the act: 4 in on
__ the air: 4 up in 5 clear
__-the-air: 4 over
__ the Americas: 5 Ave. of
__ the ancient yuletide carol: 5 Troll
__ the Angels Sing: 3 And
__, the Ape Man: 6 Tarzan
__ the Apostle: 4 John
__ the Arab: 4 Ahab
__ the arm on: 3 put
theater: 3 art 4 barn, hall, site 5 arena, drama, movie, odeon, odeum, scene, stage 6 boards, cinema, kabuki, locale, lyceum 7 drive-in 8 coliseum, locality 9 colosseum, playhouse 10 auditorium, footlights, hippodrome, movie house, opera house
abbr.: 3 SRO
area: 4 loge, tier 5 foyer, lobby 6 lounge 7 balcony 9 box office, orchestra 13 orch. Mezzanine
attendees: 5 house 8 audience
award: 4 Obie, Tony
buy: 3 tix, tkt. 5 ducat 6 ticket
chain: 5 Loews
cheer: 5 brava, bravo 6 hurrah, huzzah
company: 3 rep 4 cast 6 troupe 9 repertory
drop: 5 scrim 7 curtain
ender: 4 goer 5 going
funder: 3 NEA
Greek ~: 5 odeon, odeum
in French: 4 cine
Japanese ~: 3 noh 6 kabuki
light: 4 neon
local ~: 4 nabe
location: 4 row A
name: 4 Roxy 5 Bijou 6 Lyceum
offering: 4 film, play, show 5 drama, farce, movie, revue 6 comedy, review 7 musical 10 production
org.: 4 ANTA
passage: 5 aisle
platform: 5 stage
seating: 3 box, row
sign: 4 Exit
sound system: 5 Dolby
souvenir: 4 stub 7 program 8 Playbill
success: 3 hit 4 boff 5 boffo, smash 7 boffola

summer ~ often: 4 barn
walk-on, for short: 4 supe
warning: 3 shh 4 hush 5 quiet
work in a ~: 3 ush 5 usher
see also Broadway
theater __: 4 arts 5 of war
theater-__-round: 5 in-the
__ theater: 3 art 4 IMAX 5 arena, movie 6 dinner, little, shadow, street, summer
Theater
First Lady of the ~: Helen Hayes
__ Theater: 5 Ford's
theatergoer: 9 spectator
__ the 'A' Train: 4 Take
theatre
see theater
__ Theatre: 5 Abbey, Globe
Theatre of the absurd
writer: Jean Genet
theatrical: 4 camp 5 campy, hammy, showy, stagy 6 flashy, stagey 7 stilted 8 affected, dramatic, mannered, operatic 9 grandiose, unnatural 10 artificial, flamboyant, histrionic
bit: 3 act 4 skit
overly ~: 4 arty 5 artsy
see also theater
__ the back: 5 pat on
__, the Bad, and the Ugly, The: 4 Good
__ the bag: 4 hold
__ the bag!: 5 It's in
__ the ball: 5 carry
__ the Ball Is Over: 5 After
__ the ball rolling: 4 keep
__ the Band Played On: 3 And
__ the Baptist: 4 John
__ the Barbarian: 5 Conan
__ the bat: 3 off
Thebe: 4 moon
planet: 7 Jupiter
__ the beans: 5 spill
__ the Bear: 4 Jack
__ the Beasts and Children: 5 Bless
__ the Beat Around: 4 Turn
__ the Beat Goes On: 3 And
__ the beef?: 6 Where's
__ the Beguine: 5 Begin
__, the Beloved Country: 3 Cry
__ the belt: 5 below
__ the bench: 4 take, warm
__ the bend: 6 around
Thebes: 4 city 5 ruins
ancient city near ~: 6 Abydos
land: 5 Egypt
river: 4 Nile
site of ancient ~: 5 Luxor
__ the best: 3 for
__ the best for last: 4 save
__ the best of: 3 get 4 have
__ the bill: 4 fill, foot
__ the birdie: 5 watch
__ the birds: 3 for
__ the Bismarck!: 4 Sink
__ the bite on: 3 put
__ the Blame on Mame: 3 Put
__ the block: 5 put on
__ the blue: 5 out of
__ the Blue Horizon: 6 Beyond
__ the blues: 4 sing
__ the board: 4 go by
__-the-board: 6 across
__ the boards: 5 tread
__ the Boardwalk: 5 Under
__ the boat: 4 miss, rock
__ the Body Electric!: 5 I Sing
__ the book at: 5 throw
__ the books: 3 hit 4 cook
__-the-books: 3 off
__ the boom: 5 lower
__ the Boss?: 4 Who's
__ the bottle: 4 spin
__ the bough breaks...: 4 When
__ the Boys: 3 For 6 Follow
__ the Boys Are: 5 Where
__ the breeze: 5 shoot
__ the bridge: 5 under
__ the buck: 4 pass
__ the bud: 5 nip in
__ the bull by the horns: 4 grab, take
__ the bullet: 4 bite
__ the bushes: 4 beat
theca: 3 sac
contents: 5 spore 6 pollen
__ the cake: 3 cut 4 take
__ the calmly gathered thought: 4 unto
__ the candle at both ends: 4 burn
__ the cat: 4 bell
__ the cat out of the bag: 3 let
__ the ceiling: 3 hit
__ the Champions: 5 We Are
__ the chase: 5 cut to
__ the Children: 4 Save
__ the chutes: 5 shoot
__ the circumstances: 5 under
__ the Circus, A: 5 Son of
__ the city: 5 key to
__ the clear blue sky: 5 out of
__-the-clock: 5 round 6 around
__ the Clock: 4 Beat
__ the cloth: 5 man of
__ the Clouds Roll By: 4 Till
__ the cold: 5 out in
__ the compass: 3 box
__ the Confessor: 6 Edward
__ the Conquering Hero: 4 Hail
__ the Conqueror: 5 Pelle, Robur 7 William
__ the coop: 3 fly 4 blow
__ the corner: 4 turn
__-the-counter: 4 over 5 under
__ the course: 4 stay
__ the Covenant: 5 Ark of
__ the Cow: 5 Elsie
__ the cows come home: 4 till
__ the crack of dawn: 4 up at
__ the Craziest Dream: 4 I Had
__ the cud: 4 chew
__-the-cuff: 3 off
The CW
rival: 3 ABC, CBS, Fox, NBC, PBS
Theda: 4 Bara
colleague: 4 Pola
__ the Dark, A: 5 Cry in
__ the day: 3 rue, win 5 carry, seize
__ the Deal, The: 5 Art of
__ the deck: 3 hit 5 clear, stack
__ the deep end: 3 off 5 go off
__ the Defiant!: 4 Damn
__ the devil: 5 raise
__ the Devil: 4 Beat 7 Memnoch
__ the devil his due: 4 give
__ the dice: 4 load
__ the difference: 5 split
__ the dirt: 4 dish
__, the doctor!: 5 My son
__ the dog: 5 put on
__ the Dog: 3 Wag 7 Walking
__ the dogs: 4 go to
__ the door: 4 show
__ the door on: 4 shut 5 close
__ the door open: 5 leave
__-the-dots: 7 connect
__ the Dragon: 5 Enter
__ the drain: 4 down
__ the drop on: 3 get 4 have
__ the drum: 4 beat
__ the Drum Slowly: 4 Bang
__ the dust: 4 bite
thee: 7 pronoun
belonging to ~: 5 thine
__ the Earth Move: 5 I Feel
__ the Earth Stood Still, The: 3 Day
__ the east, and Juliet...: 4 It is
__ the edge: 4 over
__ the eight ball: 6 behind
__ the elbows: 4 up to 5 out at
__ the Elder: 5 Pliny
__ the end of my rope!: 4 I'm at
__ the end of Rico?: 6 Is this
__ the End of Time: 4 Till
__ the Entertainer: 6 Cedric
__ the envelope: 4 push
__-thee-well: 4 fare
__ the Explorer: 4 Dora
__ the eye: 4 give
__ the eye can see: 5 far as
__ the face of: 5 fly in
__ the Fair: 6 Philip
__ the faith: 4 keep
__ the fall: 4 take
__ the Fall: 5 After
__ the Family: 5 All in
__ the Fanatic: 3 Eli
__ the Farmer: 7 Isidore
__ the fat: 4 chew
__ the feedbag: 5 put on
__ the field: 4 play, take
__ the fields we go...: 3 O'er
__ the Fifth: 4 take
__, the final frontier: 5 Space
__ the finish: 4 in at
__ the fire?: 6 Where's
__ the first stone: 4 cast
__ the Fleet: 6 Follow
__ the flesh: 5 press
__ the floor: 4 take
__ the floor with: 3 mop 4 wipe
__ the fool: 3 act 4 play
__ the Force be with you!: 3 May
__ the fort: 4 hold
__ the Fox: 7 Reynard
__ the Frog: 6 Kermit
theft: 3 job 5 caper, crime, fraud, heist, pinch, score, steal 6 felony, holdup, piracy, racket, ripoff, snatch 7 break-in, larceny, lifting, looting, mugging, plunder, robbery, robbing, stickup, swindle, swiping 8 banditry, burglary, filching, fleecing, poaching, rustling, stealing, thievery 9 extortion, pilferage, pilfering, swindling 10 illegality, peculation, plagiarism, plundering, purloining
combining form: 5 klept- 6 klepto-
__ theft: 5 grand, petty
Theft, A
author: Saul Bellow
__ Theft Auto: 5 Grand
__ the Fugue, The: 5 Art of
__ the fur fly: 4 make
__ the game: 4 play
__ the games begin: 3 Let
__ the gate: 3 get
__ the Giant: 5 André
__ the Giant Killer: 4 Jack
__ the gold: 5 go for
__ the good: 5 all to
__ the good life: 4 live
__ the Good Times: 3 For
__ the Good Times Roll: 3 Let
__ the grade: 4 make
__ the Gray Flannel Suit, The: 5 Man in
__ the Great: 4 Ivan, Nate 5 Elmer, Herod, James, Peter 6 Alfred, Darius, Norval, Pompey 7 Charles 9 Alexander, Catherine, Frederick 10 Theodosius
__ the greatest!: 5 You're
__ the Great Pumpkin, Charlie Brown: 3 It's
__ the Greek: 4 Nick 5 Jimmy, Zorba
__ the green: 5 rub of
__ the Grinch Stole Christmas: 3 How
__ the Grouch: 5 Oscar
__ the ground: 3 off 5 ear to, run to
__ the ground running: 3 hit
__ the ground up: 4 from
__ the gun: 4 jump 5 under
__ the habit: 4 kick
__ the half of it: 3 not
__ the hat: 4 pass
__ the hatch: 4 down
__ the hatchet: 4 bury
__ the Hat, The: 5 Cat in
__ the hay: 3 hit
__ the head of the class: 4 go to
__ the heart: 4 from
__ the heat: 4 take
__ the heck: 4 what
__ the heels: 5 out at
__! The Herald Angels Sing: 4 Hark
__ the high spots: 3 hit
__-the-hill: 4 over
__ the hills: 5 old as
__ the hilt: 4 up to
__ the hit: 4 take
__ the Hittite: 5 Uriah
__ the hole: 5 ace in
__ the Hood: 5 Boyz N
__ the hook: 3 get, off
__ the Hoople: 4 Mott
__ the Horrible: 5 Hägar
__ the horses: 4 play
__ the hour: 5 man of
__ the house: 5 man of
__ the hump: 4 over
__ the Hutt: 5 Jabba
__ the ice: 5 break
__ the iceberg: 5 tip of
their: 4 pron. 7 pronoun
like ~: 4 poss. 10 possessive
not ~: 3 our 4 your
Their __ Hour: 6 Finest
Their Eyes Were Watching God
author: Zora Neale Hurston
Their Finest Hour
author: Winston Churchill
__ the Iron Mask, The: 5 Man in
theirs: 4 pron. 6 others 7 pronoun
like ~: 4 poss. 10 possessive
not ~: 4 ours 5 yours
Theirs __ to reason why...: 3 not
theistic: 6 divine 9 religious
__ the Jackal, The: 5 Day of
__ the jackpot: 3 hit
__ the jump on: 3 get 4 have
__ the jungle: 5 law of
__ the Kid: 5 Billy
__, The Killer Whale: 4 Namu

__ the King's Men: 3 All
__ the kitty: 4 feed
__ the Knife: 4 Mack
__ the knot: 3 tie
__ the knuckles: 5 rap on
__ the land: 5 law of, lay of
__ the land of the free: 3 o'er
__ the land, the: 5 fat of
__ the Last Dance for Me: 4 Save
__ the Last Rose of Summer: 3 'Tis
__ the law: 5 above
__ the leader: 6 follow
__ the lead out: 3 get
__ the least: 5 not in, to say
__ the Liar: 5 Jakob
__ the lid off: 4 blow
__ the lie to: 4 give
__ the Life, A: 5 Day in
__ the lifeboats!: 3 Man
__ the light: 3 see
__ the light fantastic: 4 trip
__ the lily: 4 gild
__ the limit!, The: 4 sky's
__ the line: 3 toe 4 down, draw, hold 5 above, below, end of
__-the-line: 5 top-of
__ the Line: 5 I Walk
__ the lines: 7 between
__ the lion: 5 beard
__ the Lion-Hearted: 7 Richard
__ the Little Girl Dance: 3 Let
Thelma: 4 Todd 6 Ritter 7 Houston
Thelma & Louise (1991 film)
  cast: Geena Davis, Harvey Keitel, Michael Madsen, Susan Sarandon
  director: Ridley Scott
__ the Locust, The: 5 Day of
__ the loneliest number: 5 One is
__ the Lonely: 4 Only
Thelonious: 4 Monk
__ the Look: 4 U Got
__ the Looking-Glass: 7 Through
__ the Lovin': 5 After
them: 4 side 5 enemy, those 6 others 7 pronoun
  author: Joyce Carol Oates
  belonging to ~: 5 their
  ender: 6 selves
  to us: 3 foe 5 enemy
...them __ hills!: 4 thar
Them __ Eyes: 5 There
Them! (1954 film)
  creature: 3 ant
thema: 6 thesis
__ the Magic Dragon: 4 Puff
__ the Magnificent: 8 Suleiman
__ the Man: 4 Stan
__ the manger: 5 dog in
__ the map: 5 put on
__ the mark: 3 toe 5 shy of
__ the market: 4 play
__ the mat: 4 go to
__ the matter?: 5 What's
__ the mayo!: 4 Hold
theme: 4 gist, idea, text 5 essay, motif, paper, tenor, topic 6 melody, report, thesis 7 keynote, message, subject, writing 8 argument, exercise 9 discourse, leitmotif, substance, term paper 10 exposition, literature
  park feature: 4 maze, ride
theme __: 4 park, song
__ Theme: 5 Lara's, Love's, Tara's 6 Nadia's
__ the Menace: 6 Dennis
__ the Merciless: 4 Ming
__ the merrier!, The: 4 more
__ the message: 3 get
__ the midnight oil: 4 burn
__ the mill: 7 through
__-the-mill: 5 run-of
__-the-minute: 4 up-to
Themis: 5 giant, Titan
  daughter: 5 Irene 6 Clotho 7 Atropos 8 Lachesis
  parent: 4 Gaea 6 Uranus
__ the Money and Run: 4 Take
__ the Moocher: 6 Minnie
__ the Mood for Love: 4 I'm in
__ the moon: 5 man in
__ the Moon: 4 I See 5 Lasso, Man on, Shoot
__ the morning!: 4 Top o'
__ the Morning, No: 5 But in
__ the most of: 4 make
__ the most part: 3 for
__ the music: 4 face
__ the music!: 4 Stop
__ the mustard: 3 cut
then: 4 anon, ergo, if so, next, soon, thus, when 5 after, again, hence, later 6 in a bit, in time, just as, not now 7 by and by, further, later on, someday 8 formerly, in a while, sometime, suddenly, years ago 9 after that, afterward, all at once, following, hereafter, in the past, therefore, thereupon 10 afterwards, at that time, back in time, before long, eventually, in that case, previously
  as of ~: 5 until
  back ~: 4 once, past
  between ~ and now: 5 since
  by ~: 7 already
  even ~: 5 still
  now and ~: 6 rarely, seldom 7 at times 9 sometimes 10 on occasion
  or ~: 9 otherwise
Then __ will guide the planets...: 5 peace
Then __ You: 4 Came
Then Again, Maybe I Won't
  author: Judy Blume
__ the nail on the head: 3 hit
then and __: 5 there
__ then and there: 5 right
thenar: 4 palm
__ the Nation: 4 Face
__ the Navigator: 5 Henry
Then Came You (1974 song)
  artist: Spinners, Dionne Warwick
thence: 9 from there, therefrom
  ender: 5 forth 7 forward
__ the Needle: 5 Eye of
__ the nerve!: 5 Of all
__ the news today...: 5 I read
Then He Kissed Me (1963 song)
  artist: Crystals
__ the Night: 4 Into 5 Seize 7 Because
__ the Night Away: 7 Twistin'
__ the night before Christmas...: 4 'Twas
__ the Nightlife: 5 I Love
__ then I wrote...: 3 And
Then punctual as __...: 5 a star
__ Then There Were None: 3 And
Then You Can Tell Me Goodbye (1967 song)
  artist: Casinos
Theo: 5 Kojak 7 van Gogh 8 Huxtable
__ & Theo: 7 Vincent
__ the Obscure: 4 Jude
theocratical: 5 papal 8 churchly, clerical, pastoral, priestly 9 apostolic, religious 10 pontifical, rabbinical
theodolite: 7 transit
Theodor: 5 Herzl, Storm 6 Geisel 7 Fontane, Mommsen, Schwann 8 Svedberg
Theodor __ Geisel: 5 Seuss
Theodora
  composer: George Frideric Handel
Theodore: 4 pope 5 Bikel 7 Dreiser, pontiff, Roethke, Schultz 8 chipmunk, Richards, Rousseau, Sturgeon 9 Roosevelt
  brother: 5 Alvin, Simon
  Eleanor, to ~: 5 niece
  in Russian: 6 Feodor, Fyodor
Theodore H. __: 5 White
Theodore Roosevelt Award giver: 4 NCAA
Theodoric: 4 pope 7 pontiff
__ the ointment: 5 fly in
__ Theologica: 5 Summa
theological: 6 divine 7 deistic 8 churchly, theistic 9 canonical, doctrinal, religious
  doctrine: 7 kenosis
theology: 3 rel. 5 faith, relig. 8 religion
__ the One: 4 I Was, She's 5 Still, You're
Theophilus North
  author: Thornton Wilder
theorbo: 4 lute 6 string
  origin: 6 Europe
Theorell, Axel: 8 Nobelist
theorem: 3 law 4 rule 5 axiom, truth 6 dictum, thesis 7 formula, opinion 9 deduction, postulate, principle, statement 10 assumption, principium
  auxiliary ~: 5 lemma
  initials: 3 QED
theoretical: 4 moot, pure 5 ideal 6 unreal 7 assumed, logical, nominal, on-paper 8 abstract, academic, notional, pedantic, presumed, supposed, unproved 9 tentative 10 pedantical
theoretically: 7 ideally, on paper
theorist: 5 muser 7 idea man, thinker 9 visionary
theorize: 4 feel 5 guess, infer, think 6 assume, expect, ideate, reckon, wonder 7 believe, imagine, predict, presume, project, suggest, suppose, surmise, suspect 8 estimate, propound 9 formulate, postulate, speculate, take a shot, take a stab 10 anticipate, conjecture
theory: 3 ism 4 idea, view 5 basis, guess, hunch 6 belief, system, thesis 7 concept, feeling, opinion, premise, surmise, thought 8 argument, doctrine, position 9 inference, postulate, rationale, suspicion 10 assumption, conception, conjecture, hypothesis, philosophy, principium
  combining form: 4 -logy
  in ~: 7 ideally
__ theory: 4 game 6 domino
Theory of Semiotics, A
  author: Umberto Eco
theos: 3 god
__ the other: 5 one or
__ the other cheek: 4 turn
__ the Other Half Lives: 3 How
__ the other shoe: 4 drop
__ the pace: 3 set
__ the pale: 6 beyond
__ the pants: 4 wear
__ the Parents: 4 Meet
__ the pavement: 5 pound
__ the peace: 4 keep
__ the Perverse, The: 5 Imp of
__ the phone: 4 hold
__ the picture!: 4 I get
__ the Pinhead: 5 Zippy
__ the piper: 3 pay
__ the pity!: 5 More's
__ the plank: 4 walk
__ the plug on: 4 pull
__ the plunge: 4 take
__ the point: 3 get 6 beside
__ the ponies: 4 play
__ the Pooh: 6 Winnie
__ the pot: 7 sweeten
__ the present: 3 for
__ the President's Men: 3 All
__ the Press: 4 Meet
__ the pump: 5 prime
__ the punch: 6 beat to
__ the question: 3 beg, pop 4 begs 5 out of
__ the quick: 5 cut to
Thera: 4 isle 6 island 9 Santorini
  locale: 6 Greece 8 Cyclades
__ the races!: 5 Off to
__ the Races, A: 5 Day at
__-the-rack: 3 off
TheraFlu
  alternative: *see* cold remedy
__ the rag: 4 chew
__ the rage: 3 all
__ the Rainbow: 4 Over
__ The Rain Must Fall: 4 Baby
__ the ramparts...: 3 O'er
__ the rap: 4 beat, take
therapeutic: 7 healing, medical 8 curative, remedial, salutary 9 analeptic 10 beneficial
  datum: 4 dose 6 dosage
__ the rapids: 5 shoot
therapist: 6 doctor, healer, shrink 7 analyst
  degree: 3 MSW
  org.: 3 APA
therapy: 4 cure 5 rehab 6 remedy 7 healing 8 analysis, medicine 9 treatment
  starter: 4 sero 5 aroma
__ the raven...: 5 Quoth
there: 3 yon 4 here, yond 5 voilà 6 on hand, yonder 7 present, pronoun, thither 10 over yonder
  all ~: 4 sane 5 lucid, quick, right, sound 6 intact 8 rational, sensible 10 reasonable
  almost ~: 4 near 5 close
  always ~: 6 trusty 9 unfailing
  ender: 3 for 4 fore, from, unto, upon, with 5 about, after, under 6 abouts, withal 7 against
  for the ride: 5 along
  from ~ on: 4 then 6 thence
  get ~: 4 be at, come, go to, land 5 enter, light, pop in, pop up,

reach 6 alight, appear, arrive, attend, blow in, make it, pull in, roll in, show up, sign in, turn up 7 check in, clock in, fetch up, hit town 8 breeze in 9 disembark, touch down 10 drop anchor
get ~ fast: 3 run 4 dash, rush, tear, whiz, zoom 5 hurry, speed, whisk 6 hasten, scurry 7 scamper
go here and ~: 3 gad 4 roam, rove, trek 5 drift, range 6 ramble, travel, wander 7 explore, journey, meander, traipse 9 bat around, bum around, gallivant, run around 10 knock about
hang in ~: 3 try 6 endure 9 withstand
here and ~: 5 about 6 around 7 in spots 8 rambling 9 irregular, sometimes, somewhere
it's neither here nor ~: 7 nowhere
means of getting ~: 4 belt, lane, path, pike, road, ship 5 guide, route, trail 6 access, artery, avenue, detour, street 7 channel, freeway, highway, parkway, passage, roadway, thruway, viaduct 8 short cut, turnpike 9 boulevard, itinerary 10 expressway, throughway
not ~: 3 off, out 4 away, AWOL, gone, here 6 absent 7 missing 9 elsewhere
over ~: 3 yon 4 afar, yond 6 yonder
partner: 4 here, then
the one ~: 4 that
the ones ~: 5 those
way out ~: 5 eerie, weird 7 strange
___ there: 3 all, get
___ there?: 4 Who's
There ___ atheists...: 5 are no
There ___ bad boys: 5 are no
There ___ be a law!: 6 oughta
There ___ crooked man...: 4 was a
There ___ Frigate...: 4 is no
There ___ My Baby: 4 Goes
There ___ tavern...: 3 is a
There ___ tide...: 3 is a
There!: 5 voilà
There! ___ Said It Again: 3 I've
___ There: 3 Hey 4 Over 5 Being, I'll Be
thereabouts: 4 or so
thereafter: 4 next 5 later 9 after that, following
there and ___: 4 then
There are ___ that make us happy: 6 smiles
Thereby hangs ___: 5 a tale
___-the-record: 3 off
___ the Red: 4 Eric, Erik
___ there, done that: 4 been
___ There Eyes: 4 Them
therefore: 2 so 4 ergo, then, thus 5 and so, hence, since 6 whence 9 as a result, to that end 10 inasmuch as
___ There for You: 5 I'll Be
therefrom: 6 thence
There Goes My Baby (1959 song)
artist: Drifters
There Goes My Baby (1994 film)
cast: Dermot Mulroney, Rick Schroder, Kelli Williams
There is ___!: 4 a God
There is ___ in the affairs...: 5 a tide
There is no ___ team: 3 I in
There is no Frigate like ___: 5 a book
There Is Nothin' Like a Dame
composer: Oscar Hammerstein, Richard Rodgers
There! I've Said It Again (1963 song)
artist: Bobby Vinton
There'll be ___ time...: 4 a hot
There'll Be Sad Songs (1986 song)
artist: Billy Ocean
___ There Lonely Girl: 3 Hey
theremin: 10 instrument
There oughta be ___!: 4 a law
There's ___ every crowd!: 5 one in
There's ___ here but...: 5 no one
There's ___ in my soup!: 4 a fly
There's ___ in My Soup: 5 a Girl
There's ___ in team: 3 no I
There's ___ of Hush: 5 a Kind
There's ___ Out Tonight: 5 a Moon
Theresa: 5 Maria 7 Russell, Saldana
of Avila: 3 nun 5 saint
___ Theresa: 5 Maria
There's a fly ___ soup!: 4 in my
There's a Girl in My Soup (1970 film)
cast: Goldie Hawn, Peter Sellers
There's a Kind of Hush (song)
artist: Carpenters, Herman's Hermits
There's a Moon Out Tonight (1961 song)
artist: Capris
There's a place ___: 5 for us
There's a Rainbow Round My Shoulder (1928 song)
artist: Al Jolson
There's a Small Hotel
composer: Lorenz Hart, Richard Rodgers
There's a Wocket in My Pocket!
author: Dr. Seuss
Thérèse: 3 Ste. 6 sainte
see also French
___ Thérèse, Que.: 3 Ste.
Thérèse Raquin
author: Émile Zola
There Shall Be No Night
author: Robert E. Sherwood
___ there's life ...: 5 Where
There's many ___ 'twixt...: 5 a slip
There's never ___ around...: 4 a cop
There's no ___ like home: 5 place
There's no ___ team: 3 I in
There's No Business Like Show Business
composer: Irving Berlin
There's no future ___: 4 in it
(There's) No Gettin' Over Me (1981 song)
artist: Ronnie Milsap
There's Only One of You (1958 song)
artist: Four Lads
There's Something About Mary (1998 film)
cast: Cameron Diaz, Matt Dillon, Ben Stiller
director: Bobby Farrelly, Peter Farrelly
dog: 5 Puffy
The results ___: 5 are in
There, there!: 5 it's OK
thereupon: 4 then
___ the Revolution Without Me: 5 Start
There was ___ woman...: 5 an old
___ There Was You: 4 Till
___ there yet?: 5 Are we
There you ___!: 3 are
___ the Right Moves: 3 All
___ the Ring: 7 Closing
___ the riot act: 4 read
___ the ritz: 5 put on
___ the Riveter: 5 Rosie
thermae: 4 spas 5 baths, sauna 10 hot springs
thermal: 3 hot 4 warm 6 heated
starter: 3 geo
___ thermal unit: 7 British
___ thermidor: 7 lobster
thermochemistry: 7 science
study: 4 heat
thermodynamics: 7 science
study: 4 heat 6 energy
___ thermodynamics: 5 law of
thermometer: 5 gauge 10 instrument
marking: 5 notch 6 degree 9 gradation
part: 4 bulb, merc. 5 glass 7 mercury
scale: 6 Kelvin 7 Celsius 10 Centigrade, Fahrenheit
___ thermometer: 3 gas 4 oral 7 drybulb, wet-bulb
thermonuclear: 6 atomic 8 atomical
reaction: 6 fusion 7 fission
Thermopylae: 6 battle
locale: 6 Greece
victor: 6 Xerxes
warrior: 7 Persian, Spartan
thermos: 5 flask 6 bottle 7 canteen 9 container
___ the road: 3 hit 4 down 5 end of
___-the-road: 4 over
___ the Road Jack: 3 Hit
Theron, Charlize: 7 actress
film: Aeon Flux (2005)
Cider House Rules (1999)
The Curse of the Jade Scorpion (2001)
The Devil's Advocate (1997)
Hancock (2008)
The Italian Job (2002)
The Legend of Bagger Vance (2000)
Men of Honor (2000)
Mighty Joe Young (1998)
Monster (2003, AA)
North Country (2005)
Sweet November (2001)
Trial and Error (1997)
___ the roof: 3 hit 5 raise
___ the Roof: 4 Up on
___ the roost: 4 rule
___ the ropes: 4 know
theropod: 5 biped 8 dinosaur
___ the Rose: 5 So Red
___ the Roses, The: 5 War of
___ the rounds: 4 make
Theroux, Paul: 6 writer
work: The Family Arsenal
The Great Railway Bazaar
The Mosquito Coast
The Old Patagonian Express
O-Zone
___ the rug out: 4 pull
___ the running: 5 out of
___ the sack: 3 hit
___ the Sailor: 6 Popeye, Sinbad
___ the same: 3 all 4 just
___ the Same Old Song: 3 It's
thesaurus: 4 book, list 5 lexis 7 lexicon 9 reference 10 vocabulary
compiler: 5 Roget
detail: 3 syn. 7 synonym
___ the scale: 3 tip
___ the scene: 4 make
___-the-scenes: 6 behind
___ the score: 4 even, know
these: 7 pronoun
not ~: 5 those 6 others
These ___ Things: 7 Foolish
___ the Sea: 5 Under 6 Beyond
These are the ___...: 5 times
___ the season...: 3 'Tis
___ the seas run dry...: 3 'til
These Boots Are Made for Walkin' (1966 song)
artist: Nancy Sinatra
___ these days...: 5 One of
These Eyes (1969 song)
artist: Guess Who
Theseus
parent: 6 Aegeus, Aethra 8 Poseidon
stepmother: 5 Medea
victim of ~: 8 Minotaur
___ the seven seas: 4 sail
___ the Sham: 3 Sam
___ the Sheik, The: 5 Son of
___-the-shelf: 3 off
___ the Sheriff: 5 I Shot
___ the Short: 5 Pepin
___ the shots: 4 call
___ the show: 3 run 5 steal
___ the show on the road: 3 get
___ the side of caution: 5 err on
thesis: 4 idea, text, view 5 essay, logic, paper, posit, prose, tenet, thema, theme, topic 6 belief, theory 7 opinion, premise, surmise, theorem, writing 8 argument, downbeat, position, proposal, treatise 9 discourse, monograph, postulate, term paper 10 contention, exposition
starter: 3 syn 4 meta
___ the Sixth Happiness: 5 Inn of
___ the skids on: 3 put
___ the sky: 5 pie in
___ the slip: 4 give
___ the Snowman: 6 Frosty
___ the socks off: 5 knock
thespian: 5 actor, mimic 6 player 7 actress, trouper 9 performer 10 histrionic
org.: 3 AEA, SAG 5 AFTRA
quest: 4 part, role
signal: 3 cue 6 prompt
work: 6 acting
workplace: 5 stage
___ the spot: 3 hit
___ the squeeze on: 3 put
Thessalonians: 4 book
follower: 7 Timothy
preceder: 10 Colossians
Thessaloníki: 4 city, port, town
locale: 6 Greece
Thessaly, mountain in: 4 Ossa
___ the stage for: 3 set
___ the stakes: 5 raise
___ the stand: 4 take
___ the Stars Get in My Eyes: 4 I Let
___ the stick: 5 get on
___ the Stoic: 4 Zeno
___ the storm: 7 weather

— the street: 5 man in, man on
— the Strong Survive: 4 Only
— the sun: 5 under
— the Sun in the Morning: 4 I Got
theta: 5 Greek 6 letter
predecessor: 3 eta
successor: 4 iota
—-the-table: 5 under
— the tables: 4 turn
— the tail on the donkey: 3 pin
—, the Tattooed Lady: 5 Lydia
— the Teenage Witch: 7 Sabrina
— the teeth of: 5 fly in
— the Terrible: 4 Ivan
— the test: 5 put to
— the Things You Are: 3 All
— the thought: 6 perish
— the ticket!: 5 That's
— the tide: 4 stem, turn
— the Tiger: 4 Save 5 Eye of
— the time: 4 pass 5 all of
— the time being: 3 for
— the time for all...: 5 Now is
— the time of day: 4 pass
— the times: 6 behind
— the Times: 5 Sign o'
— the Time To Fall In Love: 4 Now's
— the Toiler: 6 Tillie
— the top: 4 over
— the Top: 5 You're
— the top of one's head: 3 off
— the torch: 4 pass
— the torpedoes...: 4 Damn
— the town red: 5 paint
— the track: 3 off
— the trail: 5 hot on
— the transom: 4 over
— the trick: 4 turn
— the Triffids, The: 5 Day of
— the tubes: 4 down
— the tune: 4 call
— the Turtle: 6 Yertle
— the twain shall meet: 4 ne'er 5 never
— the Two of Us: 4 Just
theurgist: 4 seer
— the use!: 5 What's
— the valley of death...: 4 Into
— the Vampire Slayer: 5 Buffy
— & the Vandellas: 6 Martha
thew: 3 vim 4 dint 5 brawn, force, might, power, sinew, vigor 6 energy, muscle 7 fitness, muscles, potence, potency, stamina 8 vitality 9 beefiness, endurance, fortitude, hardiness, huskiness, puissance, stoutness, toughness 10 brawniness, brute force, mightiness, robustness, sturdiness
— the wagons: 6 circle
— the wall: 3 hit, off 4 go to
—-the-wall: 3 off
— the walls: 5 climb
— the Walrus: 3 I am
— the way: 3 all 4 lead, pave 5 out of
— the way it is: 5 That's
— the wayside: 4 go by
— the Way You Are: 4 Just
— the weather: 5 under
— the West Was Won: 3 How
— the West Wind: 5 Ode to
— the wheel: 6 behind
— the whip: 4 snap 5 crack
— the whistle: 4 blow
...— the whole thing!: 4 I ate
— the Wild Wind: 4 Reap
— the Wind: 6 Saddle 7 Against, Inherit
— the window: 5 go out
— the wire: 5 under
—-the-wisp: 5 will-o'
Thewlis: 5 David
— the wolf from the door: 4 keep
— the woods: 5 out of
— the Woods: 4 Into
— the woodwork: 5 out of
— the word!: 4 Mum's
— the works: 5 gum up, shoot
— the world: 5 man of, way of
— the World: 5 End of, Joy to, Top of, We Are
— the World Go Away: 4 Make
— the World in Eighty Days: 6 Around
— the World Needs Now: 4 What
— the world of: 5 think
— the world on fire: 3 set
— the Worlds, The: 5 War of
— the worst of it: 3 get 4 have
— the wrong horse: 4 back
— the wrong way: 3 rub
thews: 5 brawn, might, power, sinew, vigor 6 muscle 8 strength
thewy: 5 beefy, hefty, tough 6 brawny, robust, sinewy, strong, virile 7 hulking 8 athletic, muscular, pumped up 9 herculean, well-built 10 able-bodied
they: 4 pron. 5 those 6 others, people 7 pronoun
in Italian: 4 esse, esso
what ~ say: 4 buzz, talk 6 gossip 7 hearsay 9 grapevine
They — Be Giants: 5 Might
They — Expendable: 4 Were
They — Have Music: 5 Shall
They — Horses, Don't They?: 5 Shoot
They — It's Wonderful: 3 Say
They — Laughed: 3 All
They — serve...: 4 also
They — the Wind Maria: 4 Call
They All Laughed
composer: George Gershwin, Ira Gershwin
They All Laughed (1981 film)
cast: Ben Gazzara, Audrey Hepburn, John Ritter
director: Peter Bogdanovich
— They Are A-Changin', The: 5 Times
They called her frivolous —: 3 Sal
They Call the Wind Maria
composer: Alan Jay Lerner, Frederick Loewe
They Can't Take That Away From Me
composer: George Gershwin, Ira Gershwin
They Didn't Believe Me
composer: Jerome Kern
They Don't Know (song)
artist: Jon B, Tracey Ullman
— the year: 5 man of
— They Fall, The: 6 Harder
They laughed when —...: 4 I sat
They'll — Every Time: 4 Do It
They Might Be Giants (1971 film)
cast: Jack Gilford, George C. Scott, Joanne Woodward
— the Younger: 5 Pliny
They're —!: 3 off
They're — Our Song: 7 Playing
They're Biting
painter: Paul Klee
They're Coming to Take Me Away, Ha-Haaa! (1966 song)
artist: Napoleon XIV
They're Playing Our Song
author: Neil Simon
...— they say: 4 or so
They Say It's Wonderful
composer: Irving Berlin
...they shall — the whirlwind: 4 reap
They Shoot Horses, Don't They? (1969 film)
cast: Jane Fonda, Michael Sarrazin, Susannah York, Gig Young
director: Sydney Pollack
— the Yum Yum Tree: 5 Under
They worshipped from —: 4 afar
THI: 4 stat.
part: 4 temp. 5 index 8 humidity
Thia: 5 giant, Titan
brother: 8 Hyperion
daughter: 3 Eos 6 Selene
parent: 4 Gaea 6 Uranus
son: 6 Helios
thiamine: 3 vit. 7 vitamin 8 B vitamin
deficiency: 8 beriberi
thick: 3 dim, fat 4 deep, dopy, dull, full, hard, logy, rank, ropy, slow, wide 5 broad, bulky, burly, bushy, caked, close, dense, dopey, foggy, gooey, gummy, gunky, heavy, husky, midst, mirky, muddy, murky, obese, pudgy, ropey, smoky, solid, squat, stiff, tight 6 chummy, chunky, clotty, clubby, gloppy, heaped, jammed, jelled, middle, obtuse, opaque, packed, simple, sirupy, stocky, stubby, stuffy, stumpy, stupid, syrupy, turbid, viscid 7 bulbous, clotted, compact, crammed, crowded, curdled, devoted, jellied, massive, obscure, profuse, raucous, replete, stuffed, teeming, viscose, viscous 8 abundant, familiar, friendly, ignorant, intimate, lubberly, numerous, populous, sisterly, swarming, thickset, thronged 9 abounding, bristling, brotherly, clabbered, condensed, congealed, dim-witted, jam-packed, jellylike, populated, thickened 10 boneheaded, buddy-buddy, coagulated, compressed, dull-witted, gelatinous, half-witted, hard-packed, impervious, palsy-walsy, slow-witted, solidified
be ~ with: 4 know, teem 5 swarm 6 abound, infest
combining form: 4 pycn- 5 pachy-, pycno-
in the ~ of: 3 mid 4 amid 5 among 6 amidst, mongst 7 amongst
lay it on ~: 8 overplay
piece: 4 hunk, slab 5 block, chunk, wedge
thick-—: 4 knee 5 soled 6 witted 7 skinned, skulled
thick and —: 4 thin
thick as a —: 5 brick, plank
thick-bodied: 5 squat, stout
Thicke: 4 Alan
thicken: 3 add, gel, set 4 cake, clot, curd, jell 5 swell, widen 6 curdle, deepen, expand, fatten, freeze, gelate, harden 7 acidify, clabber, clobber, congeal, enlarge, stiffen 8 buttress, condense, solidify 9 coagulate 10 gelatinize, inspissate
thickened: 5 stiff, thick 7 jellied
thickening agent: 4 agar, guar 5 algin 7 guar gum 8 agar-agar
— thickens, The: 4 plot
Thicker Than Water (1977 song)
artist: Andy Gibb
thicket: 4 bosk, bush, wood 5 brake, brush, clump, copse, hedge, scrub, woods 6 jungle 7 coppice
thickhead: 2 ox 3 oaf, sap 4 boor, clod, dolt, fool, lout 5 chump, clown, dunce 6 dimwit, lummox 7 bungler, jackass 9 blockhead, simpleton
thickheaded: 4 daft, dopy, slow 5 dense, dopey 6 obtuse 7 doltish, foolish, lumpish, witless 8 mindless 9 dim-witted
thickness: 3 ply 5 depth, layer, width
thickset: 4 boxy 5 beefy, burly, dense, husky, obese, pudgy, squat, stout, thick 6 brawny, chunky, stocky, stubby
thick-skinned: 4 hard, numb 5 tough 7 callous 8 hardened, obdurate 9 unfeeling 10 hard-boiled
thick-witted: 3 dim 4 dopy, dull, dumb, slow 5 crass, dense, dopey 6 bovine, oafish, obtuse, simple, stolid, stupid 7 boorish, doltish, fatuous, loutish, lumpish 9 pig-headed
Thidwick: The Big-Hearted Moose
author: Dr. Seuss
thief: 4 punk, yegg 5 cheat, crook, felon, ganef, gonef, gonif 6 bandit, goniff, klepto, lifter, mugger, outlaw, pirate, rip-off, robber, vandal 7 brigand, burglar, filcher, footpad, heister, prowler, rustler, stealer 8 criminal, cutpurse, hijacker, marauder, picklock, pilferer, swindler 9 embezzler, hold-up man, larcenist, peculator, plunderer, privateer, purloiner, scoundrel, scrounger 10 bushranger, cat burglar, highwayman, pickpocket, plagiarist, shoplifter
be a ~: 3 rob 4 loot, sack 5 steal, strip
customer: 5 fence
jewel ~: 6 iceman
job: 5 heist 7 robbery
take: 4 cash, jack, loot, swag 5 bills, booty, dough, graft, lucre, money 6 dinero, moolah, snatch 7 plunder, scratch 8 bankroll
— thief: 5 horse, sneak
Thief of Bad Gags, The: 5 Berle
Thief of Bagdad, The (1940 film)
cast: Sabu
— Thief, The: 5 King's 7 Bicycle
—-Thierry: 7 Château
thieve: 3 nip, rob 4 lift, loot 5 boost, filch, heist, pinch, steal, swipe 6 burgle, pilfer, rip off 7 purloin, ransack 8 embezzle, shoplift 10 burglarize, run off with
thievery: 3 job 5 heist 7 larceny, robbery 8 burglary, stealing 9 pilfering 10 illegality, purloining

___ thieves: 5 den of
Thieves' Carnival
author: Jean Anouilh
Thieves in the Temple (1990 song)
artist: Prince
thievish: 6 sneaky 7 crooked, cunning, piratic 8 stealthy 9 dishonest, larcenous, pilfering, predatory, rapacious, secretive 10 fraudulent
thigh: 6 haunch
ender: 4 bone
it's above the ~: 3 hip
muscle: 4 quad 6 biceps, rectus, vastus
muscles: 5 recti, vasti
site: 3 leg
terminus: 5 groin
thigh-___: 7 slapper
thighbone: 5 femur
thighbones: 6 femora
thigh-highs: 4 hose 7 hosiery
thigh-rotation
muscle: 5 psoas
muscles: 5 psoae, psoai
thimble ender: 3 rig 4 weed 5 berry
thimbleful: 3 sip 4 snip
Thimble Theatre
name: 3 Oyl 5 Bluto, Olive, Wimpy 6 Popeye 7 Swee' Pea 8 Olive Oyl
Thimphu: 4 city, town 7 capital
locale: 6 Bhutan
thin: 3 wan 4 bony, edit, fade, fine, lacy, lame, lank, lean, poor, puny, rare, slim, trim, weak, wiry 5 boney, filmy, gaunt, gauzy, gawky, lanky, lathy, light, lousy, prune, rangy, reedy, runny, scant, shave, sheer, soupy, spare, tinny, water, weedy, wispy 6 dainty, dilute, faulty, feeble, flimsy, gangly, lessen, limpid, liquid, meager, narrow, peaked, reduce, refine, scanty, scarce, skimpy, skinny, slight, slinky, sparse, spotty, svelte, twiggy, wasted, watery, weaken 7 cut back, diffuse, diluted, fragile, gawkish, gracile, haggard, lacking, lighten, pinched, refined, rickety, scraggy, scrawny, sketchy, slender, spidery, spindly, starved, stringy, tenuous, vitiate, weed out, willowy, wispish, wizened 8 decrease, delicate, disperse, exiguous, gangling, gossamer, raillike, rarefied, rawboned, skeletal, starving, twiglike, wisplike 9 attenuate, cut back on, dispersed, emaciated, permeable, scattered, shriveled, stretched, sylphlike, tasteless, uncrowded, untenable, waferlike, water down 10 adulterate, attenuated, diaphanous, improbable, inadequate, indistinct, see-through, threadlike
combining form: 4 lept- 5 lepto-
covering: 7 coating
limb: 4 wand 5 sprig, stick
not ~: 5 broad, bulky, heavy, husky, obese, plump, pudgy, squat, thick 6 brawny, chubby, chunky, stocky 8 thickset
one: 5 scrag 8 beanpole 10 string bean
on ~ ice: 5 risky 6 unsafe 8 perilous 9 uncertain 10 precarious
out: 4 bald 5 prune 7 tail off 8 taper off
piece: 5 slice 8 splinter
thin-___: 7 skinned
___ thin: 4 wear
___-thin: 5 paper, wafer
thin as ___: 5 a rail, a reed
thine: 5 yours
not ~: 4 mine
Thine ___ kingdom...: 5 is the
Thine alabaster ___ gleam: 6 cities
...thine own self be ___: 4 true
thing: 3 bag, fad, job 4 duty, fact, feat, form, gear, idea, item, noun, task, tool, work 5 craze, dodad, event, facet, forte, gizmo, mania, means, point, quirk, shape, stunt, style, trait, trend 6 affair, aspect, detail, device, dingus, doodad, entity, factor, fetich, fetish, figure, gadget, hang-up, matter, notion, object, phobia, widget 7 article, concept, episode, feature, machine, quality, subject, thought 8 attitude, business, creature, fixation, idée fixe, incident, material, occasion, property, vocation 9 apparatus, commodity, doohickey, equipment, happening, implement, mechanism, obsession, situation, specialty, substance 10 individual, instrument, livelihood, occurrence, particular, phenomenon, proceeding
harmful ~: 5 curse 6 blight, plague, poison 7 scourge 8 calamity 9 detriment
improper ~: 5 taboo 9 dirty pool
in ~: 3 fad 4 mode, rage 5 craze, trend, vogue 7 fashion 8 last word
indispensable ~: 4 need 9 essential, necessity, requisite 10 imperative, obligation, sine qua non
in Latin: 3 res
living ~: 5 beast, being 6 animal, person 8 creature, organism
not a ~: 3 nil, zip 4 nada, none, zero 5 aught, zilch 6 naught, nought 7 nothing
one's ~: 5 skill 9 specialty
starter: 3 any 4 play, some 5 every
too much of a good ~: 4 glut 5 flood 7 surfeit, surplus 8 overload 10 indulgence, oversupply
wicked ~: 4 evil, vice 5 crime 7 misdeed, offense 8 atrocity, iniquity, trespass 9 sacrilege 10 misconduct
___ thing: 3 new 4 sure 5 first, young
Thing
Addams Family's ~: 4 hand
___ Thing: 4 Good, Wild
thingamajig: 5 dodad, gismo, gizmo 6 device, dingus, doodad, gadget, whosis, widget
___ thing at a time: 3 one
___ Thing Called Love: 4 This
thing of beauty..., A
author: John Keats
thing of beauty is ___ forever, A: 4 a joy
___ Thing on My Mind, The: 4 Last
things: 4 duds 5 goods, stuff 6 attire 7 apparel, baggage, clothes, effects, garment, luggage, raiment 8 chattels, clothing 9 trappings 10 belongings
all living ~: 5 world 6 nature 8 universe
how ~ are: 6 status 7 reality 9 situation
in philosophy: 5 entia
one of those ~: 4 that
work ~ out: 6 manage
___ things: 3 see 6 seeing
Things (1962 song)
artist: Bobby Darin
Things ___ for Love, The: 4 We Do
___ Things: 4 Last, Wild 7 Needful
Things could be ___!: 5 worse
___ Things Mean a Lot: 6 Little
Things of This World
author: Richard Wilbur
___ things up: 5 patch
Things We Lost in the Fire (2007 film)
cast: Halle Berry, David Duchovny, Benicio del Toro
Things You Can Tell Just by Looking at Her (2001 film)
cast: Kathy Baker, Glenn Close, Cameron Diaz, Calista Flockhart
thingy: 5 dodad, gismo, gizmo 6 device, dingus, doodad, gadget, whosis, widget 7 whatsis
___ thing you do!: 4 that
think: 3 see 4 deem, feel, hold, muse, stew 5 brood, fancy, guess, infer, judge, sense, study, weigh 6 assume, deduce, esteem, expect, gather, ideate, ponder, reason, recall, reckon, regard, wonder 7 analyze, believe, daresay, examine, feature, foresee, imagine, presume, project, realize, reflect, resolve, revolve, sort out, suppose, surmise, suspect 8 appraise, cogitate, conceive, conclude, consider, envisage, envision, estimate, evaluate, look upon, meditate, mull over, perceive, remember, ruminate, theorize, turn over 9 cerebrate, determine, figure out, recollect, reminisce, speculate, sweat over, visualize 10 call to mind, comprehend, conjecture, deliberate, have in mind, understand
about: 4 view 5 study 6 ponder 7 reflect, revolve 8 consider, mull over, turn over
alike: 4 jibe, mesh 5 agree 6 accord, concur 9 harmonize
back: 6 recall, relive 8 remember 9 reminisce
better of: 3 rue 6 regret
hard: 5 focus 6 fixate
highly of: 4 love 5 adore, favor, value 6 admire, esteem, revere 7 idolize, respect 8 look up to, venerate 9 reverence
I ~ not: 3 nah, naw, nay, nix, non 4 nein, nope, nyet, uh-uh 5 ixnay, never, no how, no way 6 no deal, noways, nowise 8 forget it, negative, negatory 9 by no means, fat chance 10 count me out, thumbs down
little of: 4 skip, snub 5 let go, scorn, spurn 6 forget, ignore, rebuff, slight 7 disdain, dismiss, let pass, tune out 8 discount, laugh off, let slide, pass over, shrug off 9 disregard, gloss over, pay no mind 10 brush aside
no more of: 6 forget, ignore 8 discount, overlook, pass over 9 disregard
of: 5 hit on 6 recall, reckon 7 imagine
of as: 6 look on
old-style: 4 trow
out: 4 plan 5 solve 6 reason 7 analyze
over: 4 mull, muse 5 study, weigh 6 digest, review 8 consider, meditate, ruminate 9 entertain 10 reconsider
(over): 4 chew, pore
piece: 4 Op-Ed 5 essay, paper, theme, tract 7 article 8 critique, treatise 10 exposition
similar: 6 equate
starter: 5 group 6 double
the worst of: 4 hate 5 abhor 6 detest, loathe 7 despise, dislike 8 execrate 9 abominate
too much of: 8 overrate
twice: 5 pause 7 scruple 8 reassess 10 reconsider
up: 5 fancy, hatch 6 create, design, devise, invent 7 concoct, devises, imagine 8 conceive, contrive 9 formulate, improvise, originate 10 mastermind
(up): 4 make 5 dream
think ___: 4 tank 5 aloud, piece, twice
think ___ about: 5 twice
think ___ of: 4 much 6 better, little 7 nothing
Think
company: 3 IBM, NCR
Think (1968 song)
artist: Aretha Franklin
thinkable: 6 likely 8 feasible, possible, probable 9 potential 10 believable, imaginable
thinker: 3 ace 4 sage, whiz 5 brain 6 pundit, savant 7 egghead, idea man, prodigy, scholar 8 Einstein, highbrow, theorist, virtuoso 9 intellect 10 mastermind
pause: 2 er, uh, um
Thinker, The: 6 statue
artist: Auguste Rodin
Think I'm in Love (1982 song)
artist: Eddie Money
thinking: 6 mental, motive 7 logical, pensive, thought 8 analytic, cerebral, rational 10 analytical, philosophy, reflection, reflective, thoughtful
clear ~: 5 logic, sense 6 reason, sanity, thesis, wisdom 9 coherence, deduction, dialectic, good sense, induction, inference, rationale, reasoning, syllogism 10 philosophy
not ~ straight: 5 woozy 8 confused
twice: 7 prudent
way of ~: 4 mind, view 9 mentality, sentiment, viewpoint
thinking ___: 3 cap
___ thinking: 7 wishful

__-thinking: 5 right 7 forward
Thinking Eye, The
artist: Paul Klee
Thinking Reed, The
author: Rebecca West
Think nothing __!: 4 of it
Think of Laura (1983 song)
artist: Christopher Cross
ThinkPad
producer: 3 IBM
think tank
name: 4 Rand
output: 4 idea 6 notion, theory 7 concept 8 proposal 10 brainstorm
think the __ of: 5 world
Thin Man, The: 4 film 5 novel
author: Dashiell Hammett,
cast: Myrna Loy, William Powell
character: 4 Mimi, Nick, Nora, Shep 5 Clyde 6 Wynant 7 Charles
director: W.S. Van Dyke
dog: 4 Asta
Thinnes: 3 Roy
thinness symbol: 4 dime, rail, reed 5 razor, wafer
Thin red line of __: 5 'eroes
Thin Red Line, The: 4 film 5 novel
author: James Jones
cast: Adrien Brody, Jim Caviezel, Sean Penn
__ Thins: 5 Wheat
thin-skinned: 5 testy 6 feisty, tender, touchy 8 choleric, liverish, petulant 9 fractious, humorless, irritable, querulous, sensitive
thin-voiced: 5 reedy
third: 8 fraction
combining form: 4 trit- 5 trito-
degree: 3 Ph.D. 5 probe 7 torture 8 question
finish ~: 4 lose, show
give the ~ degree: 4 pump, quiz 5 grill 8 question
section: 5 part C
to the ~ power: 5 cubed, cubic
third __: 3 ear, eye, man 4 base, gear, mate, rail 5 class, party 6 degree, estate, person 7 baseman
third-__: 4 rate 5 class
Third __: 5 Order, World 7 Worlder
Third __ Blind: 3 Eye
third baseman
Hall of Fame ~: 5 Boggs, Brett 7 Johnson, Mathews, Schmidt, Traynor 8 Robinson 9 Dandridge, Ed Mathews, Wade Boggs 10 Pie Traynor
Third Deadly Sin, The
author: Lawrence Sanders
Third Man, The: 4 film 5 novel
author: Graham Greene
cast: Joseph Cotten, Alida Valli, Orson Welles
director: Carol Reed
role: 4 Lime 5 Harry
Third Miracle, The (1999 film)
cast: Ed Harris, Anne Heche
Third Night, The
author: Thomas Wolfe
third-place award: 6 bronze
third-rate: 3 bad 4 poor 5 cheap, lousy 6 cheesy, crumby, crummy 7 ill-done 8 inferior, pathetic 9 miserable 10 pathetical
third-stringer: 5 scrub
Third World area: 6 Africa
thirst: 3 yen 4 long, lust, need, pant, pine, sigh, want, wish 5 yearn 6 desire, drouth, hunger 7 craving, drought, dryness, longing, passion 8 appetite, keenness, yearning 9 appetence, eagerness, esurience, hankering
for: 4 want 5 covet, crave 6 desire
(for): 4 long, lust, pant, pine
quencher: 3 ade, ale, tea 4 beer, cola, soda 5 drink, juice, water
satisfy ~: 5 slake 6 quench
thirst-quenching sound: 4 glug
thirsty: 3 dry 4 arid, avid, keen 5 eager, unwet 6 greedy, hungry 7 bone-dry, craving, parched, wishful 8 desirous, droughty, yearning 9 absorbent, waterless 10 dehydrated, solicitous
(for): 4 wild
make ~: 5 parch
Thirteen Clocks, The
author: James Thurber
Thirteen Conversations About One Thing (2001 film)
cast: Alan Arkin, Matthew McConaughey, John Turturro
thirteenth-century traveler: 4 Polo
Thirty days __ September...: 4 hath
thirty-eight: 3 gun 6 pistol, weapon 7 firearm 8 revolver
thirtysomething (ABC drama)
cast: Timothy Busfield (Elliot Weston)
Polly Draper (Ellyn)
Mel Harris (Hope Steadman)
Peter Horton (Gary Shepherd)
Melanie Mayron (Melissa Steadman)
Ken Olin (Michael Steadman)
Patricia Wettig (Nancy Weston)
dog: 7 Grendel
Thirty Years' __: 3 War
this: 5 hence 7 pronoun
after ~: 5 hence, later 9 from now on, hereafter 10 henceforth
and that: 4 both 10 miscellany
at ~ juncture: 3 now 4 here 5 as yet, today 8 promptly, right now, right off 9 forthwith, presently, right away 10 here and now
at ~ time: 3 now 8 until now 9 presently
before ~: 5 prior 8 hitherto, until now
can't be: 4 oh no
concerning ~: 6 hereof
for ~ reason: 4 ergo, then, thus 6 hereat
found at ~ place: 6 herein
from ~ point: 6 hereon 8 evermore
from ~ time forward: 6 always 9 endlessly, eternally 10 henceforth
in ~ fashion: 4 thus 6 like so, thusly 7 that way
in Latin: 3 hic
in ~ place: 4 here 6 herein
in Spanish: 4 esta, esto
instant: 3 now, PDQ 4 anon, ASAP, soon 5 today 6 at once 7 quickly 8 in no time, promptly, right now, right off 9 at present, forthwith, instantly, posthaste, presently, right away 10 here and now
in ~ way: 4 thus 6 hereby
like ~ in prescriptions: 3 tal.
not ~: 4 that
or that: 6 either
regarding ~: 6 hereto 8 hereunto
to ~ day: 5 still 8 until now
to ~ point: 3 yet 4 here 5 so far 6 hither
up to ~ time: 3 yet 6 ere now, of late 7 thus far 8 until now 10 heretofore, previously
way: 4 thus 6 like so
with ~ action: 6 hereby
this __ and age: 3 day
this __ of: 4 side
this __ of tears: 4 vale
This __: 4 Is It, Kiss, Time 5 House
This __ Army: 5 Is the
This __ Army, Mr. Jones: 5 Is the
This __ be!: 4 can't
This __ Be: 4 Will
This __ Be Love: 4 Can't
This __ Country: 4 Is My
This __ Earth: 6 Island
This __ Feeling: 5 Happy
This __ fine how-do-you-do!: 3 is a
This __ for Hire: 3 Gun
This __ Heart of Mine: 3 Old
This __ House: 3 Old
This __ I Ask: 5 Is All
This __ in Love with You: 4 Guy's
This __ joke!: 4 is no
This __ Kisses: 5 Year's
This __ man, he played...: 3 old
This __ Moment: 5 Magic
This __ of Paradise: 4 Side
This __ on me!: 4 one's
This __ outrage!: 4 is an
This __ recording: 3 is a
This __ Song: 4 Is My
This __ stickup!: 3 is a
This __ sudden!: 4 is so
This __ test: 3 is a
This __ the Dream's on Me: 4 Time
This __ Up: 3 End 4 Side
__ This a Lovely Day: 4 Isn't
this and __: 4 that
__ This and Heaven Too: 3 All
Thisbe's love: 7 Pyramus
This Boy's Life (1993 film)
cast: Ellen Barkin, Robert De Niro, Leonardo DiCaprio
This Brunette Prefers Work
author: Anita Loos
This can't be!: 4 oh no
This Can't Be Love
composer: Lorenz Hart, Richard Rodgers
__ this corner...: 5 And in
This Diamond Ring (1965 song)
artist: Gary Lewis and the Playboys
This early?: 6 so soon
__ This Earth: 5 Not of
This Girl Is a Woman Now (1969 song)
artist: Gary Puckett and the Union Gap
This Girl's in Love With You (1969 song)
artist: Dionne Warwick
This Gun for Hire: 4 film 5 novel
author: Graham Greene
cast: Alan Ladd, Veronica Lake, Robert Preston
This Guy's in Love With You (1968 song)
artist: Herb Alpert
This I Remember
author: Eleanor Roosevelt
This is __: 5 a test
This is __-brainer!: 3 a no
This Is __ Ask: 4 All I
This Is __ Life: 4 Your
This Is __ Tap: 6 Spinal
This Is for the Lover in You (1996 song)
artist: Babyface, LL Cool J, Jody Watley
This Is It (1979 song)
artist: Kenny Loggins
This Is Just to Say
author: William Carlos Williams
This Island __: 5 Earth
__ This Is My Beloved: 3 And
This Is My Song (1967 song)
artist: Petula Clark
This Is My Story
author: Eleanor Roosevelt
This is not __ time: 5 a good
This is only __: 5 a test
This Is Spinal Tap (1984 film)
cast: Christopher Guest, Michael McKean, Rob Reiner
director: Rob Reiner
This Is the Army (1943 film): 7 musical
cast: Joan Leslie, George Murphy, Ronald Reagan
composer: Irving Berlin
This is the thanks __?: 4 I get
This Is Your __: 4 Life
This Kiss (1998 song)
artist: Faith Hill
This little __ went to market...: 6 piggie
This Magic Moment (1969 song)
artist: Jay and the Americans
This Masquerade (song)
artist: George Benson, Carpenters
This means __!: 3 war
This minute!: 3 now, PDQ 4 ASAP 6 pronto 9 right away
__ This Moment On: 4 From
This must weigh __!: 4 a ton
This Old Heart of Mine (1990 song)
artist: Rod Stewart
This Old House (PBS how-to)
host: Bob Vila
This Ole House (1954 song)
artist: Rosemary Clooney
This one __ me!: 4 is on
this one in Spanish: 4 esta, esto
This one's __!: 4 on me
This One's for the Children (1989 song)
artist: New Kids on the Block
This One's for You (1976 song)
artist: Barry Manilow
This Perfect Day
author: Ira Levin
__ this ring...: 4 With
...this sceptred __: 4 isle
This Side of Paradise
author: F. Scott Fitzgerald
This Time I Know It's for Real (1989 song)
artist: Donna Summer

This Time the Dream's on Me
composer: Harold Arlen, Johnny Mercer
thistle: 4 burr, weed 5 plant 6 flower 7 bramble
down: 5 pappi 6 pappus
relative: 6 arnica
thistly: 5 spiny 6 thorny
This Used to Be My Playground (1992 song)
artist: Madonna
this vale of ___: 5 tears
This was their ___ hour: 6 finest
___ this way...: 4 Come, Walk
This weighs ___!: 4 a ton
This Will Be (1975 song)
artist: Natalie Cole
This won't hurt ___!: 4 a bit
___ this world: 5 out of
This Year's Kisses
composer: Irving Berlin
thither: 4 yond 5 there 6 yonder
move hither and ~: 3 gad 4 roam, rove 5 range 6 ramble, wander 7 meander, traipse 8 ambulate, nomadize 9 bum around, gallivant, globe-trot
thither and ___: 3 yon
thith, thpeak like: 4 lisp 8 sibilate
Tho: 5 Le Duc
thole: 3 pin 7 oarlock
insert: 3 oar
Thom: 4 Gunn, Mc An
Thomas: 2 B.J. 3 Cal, Ira, Kid, Kyd 4 Arne, Cech, Cole, Dave, Debi, Gray, Hood, Ince, Irma, Mann, More, Nast, Reid, Seth 5 Betty, Carew, Chong, Danny, Dewey, Dolby, Dylan, Foley, Frank, Hardy, Helen, Henry, Isiah, Marlo, Moore, Nashe, Paine, Ralph, Rufus, saint, Timmy, Tryon, Wolfe, Wyatt, Young 6 Berger, Browne, Dekker, Eakins, Edison, Gibson, Hobbes, Huxley, Malory, Merton, Morgan, Starzl, Warton, Weller, Wolsey 7 à Becket, à Kempis, Aquinas, Beecham, Calabro, Campion, Carlyle, Costain, Cranmer, Donnall, Erastus, Heather, Heywood, Malthus, Noguchi, Parnell, Peacock, Pynchon, Richard 8 Bernhard, Bulfinch, Campbell, Clarence, Keneally, Kinsella, Lawrence, Macaulay, Mitchell, Overbury, Shadwell 9 De Quincey, Gallaudet, Jefferson, Middleton, Sackville, Schippers 10 Chatterton, Haliburton
doubting ~: 7 sceptic, skeptic
Thomas ___ Benton: 4 Hart
Thomas ___ Church: 5 Haden
___-Thomas: 5 Terry
Thomas, B.J.
song: Hooked on a Feeling (1968)
I Just Can't Help Believing (1970)
I'm So Lonesome I Could Cry (1966)
Raindrops Keep Fallin' on My Head (1969)
Thomas Crown Affair, The (1968 film)
cast: Faye Dunaway, Steve McQueen
Thomas Crown Affair, The (1999 film)
cast: Pierce Brosnan, Rene Russo
Thomas, Debi: 6 skater
rival: 4 Witt
Thomas, Dylan: 4 poet 5 Welsh
work: Do not go gentle into that good night...
Under Milk Wood
Thomas E. ___: 5 Dewey
Thomas, Frank
sport: 8 baseball
Thomas Hart ___: 6 Benton
Thomasina: 3 cat
Thomas, Isiah: 8 hoopster
milieu: 5 court
org.: 3 NBA
sport: 10 basketball
Thomas, Kristin Scott: 7 actress
film: Angels & Insects (1995)
Four Weddings and a Funeral (1994)
Gosford Park (2001)
The Horse Whisperer (1998)
Life as a House (2001)
Thomas, Lowell milieu: 5 radio
Thomas, Marlo
spouse: Phil Donahue
Thomas, Michael Tilson: 9 conductor
Thomas, Richard: 5 actor
TV: The Waltons
Thomas Stearns ___: 5 Eliot
Thomasville: 4 city, town
locale: 4 N. Car.
Thompson: 3 Kay, Lea, Sue 4 Emma, Gina, Jack, J. Lee, Sada 5 David, Sadie 6 Ernest 7 Francis
Thompson, Emma: 7 actress
film: Carrington (1995)
Howards End (1992, AA)
In the Name of the Father (1993)
Judas Kiss (1999)
Junior (1994)
Last Chance Harvey (2008)
Love Actually (2003)
Much Ado About Nothing (1993)
Nanny McPhee (2005)
Peter's Friends (1992)
Primary Colors (1998)
The Remains of the Day (1993)
Sense and Sensibility (1995)
spouse: Kenneth Branagh
Thompson, Kay
kid: 6 Eloise
Thompson, Lea: 7 actress
film: All the Right Moves (1983)
Back to the Future (1985)
Some Kind of Wonderful (1987)
TV: Caroline in the City
Thompson seedless: 5 grape
Thompson submachine ___: 3 gun
Thompson Twins: 4 trio
song: Doctor! Doctor! (1984)
Hold Me Now (1984)
King for a Day (1986)
Lay Your Hands on Me (1985)
Thomson: 5 Bobby 6 George, Joseph, Virgil 7 William
Thomson, Virgil: 8 composer
work: Four Saints in Three Acts
The Mother of Us All
thong: 4 lace, shoe, whip 5 strap, strip 6 lacing 7 leather 8 flip-flop, footwear
oxhide ~: 4 riem
thon starter: 4 tele 5 radio, walka
't Hooft: 8 Gerardus
Thor: 3 god 5 Norse 9 Heyerdahl
brother: 3 Tiu
father: 4 Odin 5 Othin
son: 3 Ull
wife: 3 Sif
Thora: 5 Birch
thoracic ___: 4 duct 6 artery
thorax: 5 chest, trunk
Thoreau, Henry David: 6 writer
work: Civil Disobedience
Walden
thorium: 5 metal 7 element
isotope: 6 ionium
thorn: 3 bur 4 barb, burr 5 briar, brier, point, prick, spike, spine, trial 6 sliver 7 barbule, bramble, bristle, prickle, spicule, spinule, sticker 8 apiculus, irritant 9 annoyance 10 impediment
be a ~: 3 irk 4 rile 5 annoy 6 pester
in the side: 4 bane, pain, pest 6 bother, gadfly, hassle 7 bugbear 8 irritant, nuisance 9 annoyance
like a ~: 5 spiny
mishap: 5 prick
starter: 3 box, haw 4 buck 5 black
Thorn Birds, The: 5 novel 10 miniseries
author: Colleen McCullough
setting: 9 Australia
Thorn Birds, The (ABC saga)
cast: Barbara Stanwyck (Mary Elizabeth Cleary Carson)
Jean Simmons (Fee Armstrong Cleary)
Rachel Ward (Meggie Cleary)
Richard Chamberlain (Father Ralph)
Thornburgh predecessor: 5 Meese
Thorndike, Sybil: 4 Dame 7 actress
Thorne: 5 Smith
Thorne-Smith: 8 Courtney
Thornfield
governess: 4 Eyre
thorn in one's ___: 4 side
Thornton: 6 Wilder
Thornton, Billy Bob: 5 actor
film: All the Pretty Horses (2000)
The Apostle (1997)
Armageddon (1998)
Bandits (2001)
Homegrown (1998)
The Man Who Wasn't There (2001)
Monster's Ball (2001)
One False Move (1992)
Pushing Tin (1999)
A Simple Plan (1998)
spouse: Angelina Jolie
thorny: 4 hard 5 risky, rough, sharp, spiky, spiny, tough 6 barbed, knotty, sticky, tricky, trying, uphill 7 arduous, awkward, brambly, bristly, complex, hard-won, irksome, onerous, prickly, tangled, thistly 8 baffling, grueling, ticklish, toilsome, worrying 9 dangerous, demanding, difficult, laborious, strenuous, vexatious 10 bothersome, formidable, irritating, nettlesome, oppressive, perplexing
plant: 4 rose 5 briar, brier 7 bramble
thorough: 4 full, pure, rank 5 clean, exact, fussy, sheer, sound, total, uncut, utter, whole 6 all-out, arrant, entire, minute 7 careful, finicky, in-depth, orderly, overall, perfect, plenary, prudent, radical 8 absolute, cautious, complete, detailed, exacting, finiking, finished, finnicky, from A to Z, itemized, outright, profound, rigorous, sweeping, whole-hog 9 assiduous, attentive, downright, efficient, elaborate, expansive, extensive, full-dress, intensive, judicious, observant, out-and-out, searching, undivided, unreduced 10 blow-by-blow, consummate, exhaustive, fastidious, meticulous, particular, scrupulous, soup-to-nuts, unabridged
thoroughbred: 4 pure 5 horse 6 equine, unmixt 7 unmixed 8 pedigree 9 blueblood, pedigreed, racehorse 10 aristocrat
mother: 3 dam 4 mare 5 filly 6 equine
no ~: 3 nag
thoroughfare: 2 av., rd., st. 3 ave., way 4 blvd., drag, lane, pike, road 5 paseo, route 6 artery, avenue, street 7 freeway, highway, parkway, passage, roadway 8 causeway, toll road, turnpike 9 boulevard, concourse 10 expressway, interstate
thoroughgoing: 4 full, pure, rank 5 exact, sheer, total, utter, whole 6 all-out, arrant, entire, minute, plenty 7 allover, careful, in-depth, perfect, radical 8 absolute, complete, detailed, from A to Z, itemized, outright, profound, straight, sweeping, whole-hog 9 assiduous, downright, efficient, intensive, out-and-out
thoroughly: 4 hard, very, well 5 fully, plumb, quite, stark 6 au fond, highly, hugely, wholly 7 but good, flat out, in depth, notably, totally, utterly 8 entirely, from A to Z, in detail, laudably, terribly, very well, whole hog, worthily 9 carefully, downright, earnestly, every inch, extremely, inside out, intensely, like a book, perfectly, to the full, up-and-down 10 absolutely, altogether, completely, to the limit
prefix: 3 per-
Thoroughly Modern Millie (1967 film)
cast: Julie Andrews, Carol Channing, Mary Tyler Moore
composer: Sammy Cahn, Jimmy Van Heusen
thoroughness: 5 rigor
thorp: 4 town 6 hamlet 7 village 9 community 10 settlement
Thorpe: 3 Jim 4 Otis 7 Richard
Thorpe, Jim: 10 decathlete
sport: 8 football
Thorson: 5 Linda
those: 4 them, they 7 pronoun
not ~: 5 these
not these or ~: 6 others
one of ~ things: 4 that
Those ___ But Goodies: 6 Oldies
Those ___ the Days: 4 Were

Those Lazy-Hazy-Crazy Days of Summer (1963 song)
artist: Nat King Cole
Those Lips, Those Eyes (1980 film)
cast: Tom Hulce, Frank Langella, Glynnis O'Connor
Those Oldies But Goodies (1961 song)
artist: Little Caesar and the Romans
Those the River Keeps
author: David Rabe
Those Were the Days (1968 song)
artist: Mary Hopkin
__ Those Years Ago: 3 All
thou: 3 gee, you 4 one G 5 G-note, grand 7 pronoun
objectively: 4 thee
Thou __: 5 Swell
Thou __ not be false...: 5 canst
Thou Art the Man
author: Edgar Allan Poe
though: 3 but, yet 5 altho, still, while 6 albeit, even if, much as, whilst 7 despite, granted, however, whereas 8 after all, allowing 10 all the same, for all that
though __ and thin: 5 thick
__, though I walk...: 3 Yea
thought: 3 aim 4 care, heed, hope, idea, plan, soul, view 5 drift, fancy, guess, image, logic, study, thing 6 albeit, belief, caring, design, musing, notion, regard, revery, theory 7 concept, concern, feeling, knowing, opinion, premise, purpose, reputed, reverie, surmise 8 judgment, kindness, scrutiny, sympathy, thinking 9 attention, brainwork, deduction, inference, intention, intuition, knowledge, reasoning, sentiment 10 aspiration, assumption, brainchild, brainstorm, cogitation, conception, conclusion, conjecture, conviction, discerning, estimation, hypothesis, impression, meditation, perception, philosophy, reflection, rumination, solicitude
be lost in ~: 4 muse 5 dream 8 daydream 9 fantasize
capricious ~: 4 whim
combining form: 4 ideo-, -noia
course of ~: 5 logic, tenor, train
have a ~: 6 ideate
lose one's train of ~: 6 wander
lost in ~: 4 rapt 5 taken 6 intent 7 bemused, gripped 8 absorbed, immersed, involved 9 engrossed, oblivious 10 fascinated
on second ~: 6 rather 7 instead
provoker: 4 Muse
second ~: 5 qualm 7 scruple 10 retrospect
sound of deep ~: 3 hmm
starter: 5 afore, after, merry
train of ~: 5 logic 9 reasoning
venture a ~: 3 say 5 guess 7 comment, suppose, surmise
well ~ out: 4 sane 7 logical 8 sensible
without ~: 4 idly
thoughtful: 4 deep, keen, kind, rapt, sane, wise 5 aware, canny, civil, sober, sweet 6 astute, brainy, caring, decent, intent, kindly, loving, musing, polite, subtle 7 careful, gallant, heedful, helpful, logical, mindful, pensive, politic, prudent, serious, tactful, wistful 8 absorbed, discreet, generous, gracious, obliging, profound, rational, studious, thinking, well-bred 9 astucious, attentive, concerned, courteous, engrossed, judicious, observant, pondering, provident, reasoning, regardful, sensitive, unselfish 10 charitable, deliberate, diplomatic, expressive, forbearing, reasonable, reflective
one: 5 carer, muser
thoughtfulness: 4 care, tact 6 effort, regard 7 concern 8 interest, prudence 9 alertness, assiduity, attention, diligence 10 discretion, precaution
though thick and __: 4 thin
thoughtless: 4 rash, rude 5 blind, brash, crass, hasty, inane, nervy, short, silly 6 madcap, remiss, shabby, stupid, unkind, unwary, unwise 7 boorish, flighty, foolish, selfish, vacuous, witless 8 careless, headlong, heedless, impolite, listless, mindless, reckless, slapdash, tactless, uncaring 9 hotheaded, imprudent, negligent, senseless, unadvised, unguarded, unheeding, unmindful 10 ungracious, unthinking
thoughtlessly: 7 lightly 8 absently, pell-mell
thoughtlessness: 5 folly 7 abandon, neglect 8 omission 9 disregard, frivolity, looseness, oversight, stupidity 10 negligence, wantonness
__-thought-of: 4 well
__ Thought of You, The: 4 Very
thought-out: 10 considered, deliberate, reasonable, well-chosen
__-thought-out: 4 well
thought-provoking: 4 deep 5 heavy, meaty, pithy 7 complex, intense, serious, weighty 8 profound 10 mysterious
thoughts
have second ~: 4 balk 5 baulk 6 falter, regret 8 question
offer for one's ~: 5 penny
offer one's ~: 3 say 5 opine 7 comment, observe, suppose, surmise
one with second ~: 4 ruer
__ Thou Now O Soul: 6 Darest
thousand
and one: 4 a lot, gobs, lots, many, tons 5 heaps, piles, scads 6 myriad, oodles, scores, untold 7 copious, profuse, teeming, umpteen 8 manifold, numerous 9 abundance, countless, multitude
combining form: 4 kilo- 5 chilo-, milli-
dollar bill: 3 gee 5 G-note 6 big one
grams: 4 kilo
G's: 3 mil 7 million
Thousand __: 4 Oaks 7 Islands
Thousand __, A: 5 Acres, Stars 6 Clowns
thousand and one __, A: 4 uses
Thousand-and-Second Tale of Scheherazade, The
author: Edgar Allan Poe
Thousand Clowns, A (1965 film)
cast: Martin Balsam, Barbara Harris, Jason Robards
director: Fred Coe
Thousand Days queen: 4 Anne
Thousand Island: 7 Russian 8 dressing
alternative: 5 ranch 6 French 7 Italian 10 bleu cheese
Thousand Oaks: 4 city, town
locale: 10 California
thousandth combining form: 5 milli-
...__ thousand times...: 3 no a
__ thou slain the Jabberwock?: 4 Hast
Thou Swell
composer: Lorenz Hart, Richard Rodgers
...thou vain world, __: 5 adieu
thpeak like thith: 4 lisp 8 sibilate
thrall: 4 esne, peon, serf 5 slave 7 chattel, slavery 9 servitude
thralldom: 7 bondage, slavery 9 captivity, servitude, vassalage 10 internment
thrash: 3 hit, tan, tar, zap 4 beat, belt, bury, cane, drub, flap, flog, jerk, lash, lick, mall, maul, pelt, rout, rush, toss, trim, whip 5 baste, birch, crush, flail, knock, paste, pitch, pound, punch, smite, spank, thump, trash, whack, worst 6 batter, beat up, buffet, defeat, hammer, larrup, paddle, pommel, pummel, punish, squirm, thrash, thresh, wallop, writhe 7 chasten, clobber, lambast, overrun, scourge, trounce, wriggle 8 chastise, lambaste, work over 9 castigate, overwhelm, slaughter
out: 4 talk 5 argue 6 debate 7 discuss
thrash __: 3 out
Thrashers
home: 7 Atlanta, Georgia
org.: 3 NHL
rival: *see* hockey team
sport: 6 hockey
thrashing: 4 rout 6 defeat, hiding 7 licking 8 flogging
thread: 4 lace, line, plot, poil, vein, wisp, yarn 5 fiber, filum, lisle, twine 6 enlace, inlace, strand 8 filament
ball: 4 clew
bits: 4 fuzz, lint
combining form: 3 mit-, nem- 4 fili-, mito-, nema-, nemo- 5 nemat- 6 nemato-
cotton ~: 5 lisle
embroidery ~: 5 floss
ender: 3 fin 4 bare, worm
hanging by a ~: 5 risky 6 unsafe 9 uncertain
holder: 5 spool
knot: 4 burl, node
weight unit: 6 denier
threadbare: 3 old 4 dull, poor, worn 5 banal, dingy, musty, ratty, seedy, stale, stock, tacky, tired, trite 6 beat-up, frayed, ragged, shabby, used-up 7 clichéd, in holes, rundown, scruffy, worn-out 8 bathetic, decrepit, dog-eared, overused, shopworn, tattered, timeworn, well-used, well-worn 9 hackneyed, imitative, moth-eaten, ungroomed 10 bedraggled
become ~: 4 fray, tear, wear 5 shred
threadlike: 4 ropy, slim, thin 5 filar, ropey 6 narrow 7 slender
threads: 4 fila, garb, gear, suit, togs 5 array, dress 6 attire, livery 7 apparel, clothes, raiment 8 garments, wardrobe 10 Sunday best
fabric ~: 4 weft, woof
provide with ~: 5 cover 6 attire, clothe, outfit, tog out 7 costume, furnish 8 accouter
threadwork: 4 lace
threat: 4 omen, risk 5 bluff, peril 6 danger, hazard, menace 7 portent, presage, warning 9 blackmail, challenge 10 foreboding
ender: 4 else 6 or else
urban ~: 3 mob 4 pack, ring
__ threat: 4 idle 5 empty 6 triple, veiled
threaten: 3 cow 4 loom, warn 5 augur, bully, scare, scowl, snarl, spook 6 coerce, impend, loom up, menace 7 advance, imperil, portend, presage 8 admonish, approach, browbeat, endanger, forebode, forewarn, frighten, hang over, overhang, pressure 9 blackmail, terrorize, undermine 10 foreshadow, intimidate, jeopardize, push around
threatening: 4 dire, grim, ugly 5 black, close, loury, scary 6 at hand, lowery, stormy, unsafe 7 baleful, baneful, fateful, looming, ominous, serious, warning 8 alarming, bullying, imminent, lowering, menacing, minatory, overcast, perilous, scowling, sinister 9 dangerous, ill-boding, impending 10 pugnacious
three: 4 trey, trio 5 triad 6 number, triple
ender: 4 some 5 pence, penny, score
in French: 5 trois
in German: 4 drei
in Italian: 3 tre
in Japanese: 3 san
in Portuguese: 4 tres
in Spanish: 4 tres
it had ~ parts: 4 Gaul
or four: 3 few 4 a few 7 several
prefix: 3 ter-, tri-
proverbially: 5 crowd
R's org.: 3 AFT, NEA, UFT
squared: 4 nine
to Mohs: 7 calcite
three __ kind: 3 of a
three __ match: 3 on a
three-__: 3 ply 4 peat 6 bagger, decker, handed, master, square, suiter 7 pointer, quarter, wheeler
three-__ bike: 5 speed
three-__ bulb: 3 way
three-__ circus: 4 ring
three-__ fire: 5 alarm
three-__ general: 4 star
three-__ hit: 4 base
three-__ landing: 5 point
three-__ length: 7 quarter
three-__ limit: 4 mile

three-__ monte: 4 card
three-__ race: 6 legged
three-__ sloth: 4 toed
three-__ suit: 5 piece
three-__ time: 7 quarter
Three __: 4 Ages 5 Fires, Hours, Kings, Lives 7 Degrees, Seasons, Secrets, Sisters
Three __!: 6 Amigos
Three __ a Horse: 5 Men on
Three __ a Lady: 5 Times
Three __ Fishies: 6 Little
Three __ Girls: 5 Smart
Three __ in the Fountain: 5 Coins
Three __ Island: 4 Mile
Three __ Night: 3 Dog
Three __ of Eve, The: 5 Faces
Three __ of the Condor: 4 Days
Three __ on a Horse: 3 Men
Three __ Words: 6 Little
Three Amigos! (1986 film)
  cast: Chevy Chase, Steve Martin, Martin Short
Three Bears
  one of the ~: 4 Baby, Mama, Papa
Three Blind __: 4 Mice
three-card monte: 3 con 4 game, scam 8 card game
Three Coins in the Fountain (1954 film)
  cast: Dorothy McGuire, Jean Peters, Clifton Webb
  composer: Sammy Cahn, Jule Styne
  locale: 4 Rome 5 Italy, Trevi
  title song: Frank Sinatra
Three-Cornered Hat, The: 6 ballet
  composer: Manuel de Falla
Three Days of the Condor (1975 film)
  cast: Faye Dunaway, Robert Redford, Cliff Robertson, Max von Sydow
  director: Sydney Pollack
Three Degrees
  song: TSOP (1974)
    When Will I See You Again (1974)
three-dimensional: 5 cubic, solid
  figure: 3 sph. 4 cube 5 globe, prism 6 sphere 7 pyramid
three-dog
  night: 4 cold 6 chilly, frigid 8 freezing
Three Dog Night
  members: Hutton, Wells, Negron
  song: Black & White (1972)
    Celebrate (1970)
    Easy to Be Hard (1969)
    Eli's Coming (1969)
    Joy to the World (1971)
    Liar (1971)
    Mama Told Me (1970)
    Never Been to Spain (1972)
    An Old Fashioned Love Song (1971)
    One (1969)
    Pieces of April (1972)
    Shambala (1973)
    The Show Must Go On (1974)
    Try a Little Tenderness (1969)
three-dollar bill
  like a ~: 4 fake 5 phony
Three Faces of Eve, The (1957 film)
  cast: Lee J. Cobb, David Wayne, Joanne Woodward

threefold: 5 trine 6 triple 7 ternary
Three Kings (1999 film)
  cast: George Clooney, Ice Cube, Spike Jonze, Mark Wahlberg
three-legged __: 4 race
Three Little Words: 4 song
  composer: Burt Kalmar, Harry Ruby
  one of the: 3 you 4 love
Three Lives
  author: Gertrude Stein
__ Three Lives: 4 I Led
three men __ tub: 3 in a
three-mile __: 5 limit
Three Mile __: 6 Island
three-minute __: 3 egg
Three Musketeers, The
  author: Alexandre Dumas (père)
  character: 5 Athos 6 Aramis, Milady 7 Porthos 9 D'Artagnan
Three Musketeers, The (1993 film)
  cast: Chris O'Donnell, Charlie Sheen, Kiefer Sutherland
  director: Stephen Herek
three of __: 5 a kind, clubs 6 hearts, spades 8 diamonds
Three of a Kind
  author: James M. Cain
three-peat coiner: Pat Riley
threepence: 4 coin 5 money
Threepenny Opera, The: 7 musical
  author: Bertolt Brecht
  composer: Kurt Weill
three-piece __: 4 suit
three-point __: 4 line, play 7 landing
three-quarter __: 4 time 5 armor 6 length, nelson 7 binding
three-ring __: 6 binder, circus
Three's Company (ABC sitcom)
  cast: Priscilla Barnes (Terri Alden)
    Joyce DeWitt (Janet Wood)
    Norman Fell (Stanley Roper)
    Richard Kline (Larry Dallas)
    Don Knotts (Ralph Furley)
    Audra Lindley (Helen Roper)
    John Ritter (Jack Tripper)
    Suzanne Somers (Chrissy Snow)
threescore: 5 sixty
three-seater: 4 sofa
Three Sisters: 4 play
  author: Anton Chekhov
  role: 4 Ivan, Olga 5 Irina, Masha 6 Andrey, Fyodor 7 Natasha
Three Soldiers
  author: John Dos Passos
threesome: 4 trin, trio 5 trine 6 triple
three-speed __: 4 bike
three-spot: 4 trey
three-star __: 7 general
three-star off.: 3 gen. 5 lt. gen.
three-step: 6 cha-cha
Three Stooges
  laugh: 4 nyuk
  one of the ~: 3 Joe, Moe 4 Fine 5 Curly, Larry, Shemp 6 Besser, De Rita, Howard 8 Curly Joe
three-striper: 3 NCO, sgt. 8 sergeant
Three Sundays in a Week
  author: Edgar Allan Poe
Three Tall Women
  author: Edward Albee
Three Teeny Preludes
  composer: PDQ Bach
__ Three Times: 5 Knock

Three Times a Lady (1978 song)
  artist: Commodores
three-toed __: 5 sloth
three-way __: 4 bulb
three-way circuit: 3 wye
Three Weeks
  author: Elinor Glyn
three-wheeled taxi: 5 cyclo
three-wheeler: 5 trike 8 tricycle
three-year-old: 3 kid, tot 4 tike, tyke
threnody: 5 dirge, elegy 6 lament 7 keening
thresher __: 5 shark
threshing: 7 farming, reaping 10 harvesting
  aid: 5 flail 6 scythe
  refuse: 4 husk 5 chaff, waste 7 remains
threshold: 3 eve 4 dawn, door, edge, gate, line, sill 5 brink, entry, point, verge 6 border, origin, outset, portal 7 doorway, ingress, opening 8 doorstep, entrance 9 beginning, inception
  cross the ~: 4 go in 5 enter, pop in 6 blow in, come in, step in 8 breeze in
  opposite: 6 lintel
  psychological ~: 5 limen
thrice
  combining form: 3 ter-
  in prescriptions: 3 ter
thrift: 5 plant 6 flower, saving 7 economy 8 prudence 9 austerity, frugality, parsimony 10 stinginess
  starter: 5 spend
thriftless: 6 lavish 8 wasteful
thrift shop: 5 store
  transaction: 6 resale
thrifty: 4 mean 5 canny, chary, cheap, close, tight 6 frugal, on sale, stingy 7 careful, prudent, sparing 8 ungiving 9 provident 10 economical, unwasteful
  be ~: 4 save
  one: 5 saver
Thrifty: 9 car rental 10 auto rental
  alternative: *see* car rental
thrill: 3 fun, wow 4 bang, glow, kick, move, rush, send, stir 5 blast, cheer, elate, flash, juice, key up, kicks, rouse, score, throb 6 arouse, charge, excite, fire up, please, quiver, tickle, tingle, turn on 7 animate, delight, emotion, enchant, enthuse, flutter, gladden, gratify, happify, hearten, impress, inspire, quicken, tremble, vibrate 8 blow away, entrance, pleasure 9 adventure, electrify, enjoyment, enrapture, fascinate, fireworks, galvanize, go over big, inebriate, sensation, stimulate, titillate, transport 10 exhilarate, intoxicate
  seeker: 8 hedonist, sybarite 9 bon vivant, libertine 10 sensualist
  to: 4 love 5 adore, eat up, enjoy, go for 6 dote on 7 revel in 8 flip over 9 delight in, get high on 10 appreciate, experience
Thrilla in Manila: 4 bout 5 fight, match
  boxer: 3 Ali 7 Frazier
thrilled: 4 agog, glad 5 happy, merry 6 blithe, cheery, jovial, joyful, joyous, upbeat 7 gleeful 8 blissful, cheerful, ecstatic, euphoric, exultant, jubilant, mirthful, ravished 9 delirious, overjoyed, rapturous, rejoicing, rhapsodic 10 flying high
thriller: 4 book 5 novel, story 7 mystery 9 narrative
__-thriller: 6 techno
Thriller (1984 song)
  artist: Michael Jackson
Thriller sequel: 3 Bad
thrilling: 3 fab 4 boss, wild 5 heady, kicky 7 rousing 8 dramatic, electric, exciting, fabulous, gripping, riveting, stirring, wondrous 9 emotional, exquisite, trembling 10 delightful, enchanting, impressive, intoxicant, miraculous, passionate, rip-roaring
  not ~: 4 blah, drab, dull, flat 5 banal, bland, ho-hum, vapid 6 boring 7 humdrum 8 lifeless 9 wearisome 10 dullsville, lackluster, monotonous, pedestrian, spiritless
Thrill of It All, The (1963 film)
  cast: Doris Day, James Garner
thrive: 2 go 3 wax, win 4 boom, grow, live 5 bloom, get on 6 abound, arrive, batten, do well, hack it, make it, pan out, profit 7 advance, blossom, burgeon, develop, luck out, make out, prevail, prosper, shoot up, succeed, triumph, work out 8 bourgeon, flourish, get ahead, go places, grow rich, increase, make good, mushroom, progress 9 bear fruit, luxuriate 10 strengthen
thriving: 4 rich, well 5 palmy 6 robust 7 booming, cooking, growing, healthy, roaring, rolling, wealthy, well-off 8 affluent, blooming, home free, prolific, well-to-do 9 advancing, doing well, luxuriant 10 burgeoning, developing, prospering, prosperity, prosperous, successful, well-heeled
throat: 3 maw 4 neck 6 gullet
  armor: 6 gorget
  bird's ~: 6 gorget
  bug: 5 staph, strep
  clearer: 4 ahem
  combining form: 3 der- 4 dero- 6 bronch- 7 broncho-, pharyng-
  feature: 6 dewlap
  frog in one's ~: 4 rasp 7 scratch 10 hoarseness
  infection: 5 strep
  jump down one's ~: 5 blame, chide, scold 6 berate, lean on, rebuke 7 bawl out, chew out, go after, lay into, lecture, reprove, rip into, tell off, upbraid 8 admonish, lambaste 9 dress down, reprimand, tear apart 10 take to task
  of the ~: 5 gular
  problem: 4 frog, lump
  projection: 5 uvula
  rinse one's ~: 6 gargle
  soother: 6 hot tea
  starter: 3 cut
  upper ~: 4 gula
__ throat: 4 sore 5 strep
throaty: 5 gruff, husky, raspy, velar 6 froggy, hoarse 8 gravelly, guttural 10 laryngitic
throb: 4 ache, beat, hurt, pain, pang, thud, tick 5 pound, pulse, smart, thump 6 quiver, rhythm, thrill, tingle, twinge 7 flutter, pitapat,

pulsate, tremble, vibrate **8** resonate **9** heartbeat, palpitate, pulsation, vibration
starter: **5** heart
throbbing: **4** ache, achy, beat **7** painful, vibrant **8** resonant **9** vibration
throe: **3** fit **4** ache, pain, pang **5** spasm, spell **6** misery, twinge **7** seizure **8** paroxysm, upheaval
thrombus: **4** clot
throne: **4** seat **5** chair
cover: **6** canopy, dosser
locale: **4** dais **6** castle, palace
name meaning ~: **5** Cyrus
put on the ~: **6** enseat
seize the ~: **5** usurp
sit on the ~: **4** rule **5** reign **6** govern
sitter: **4** czar, king **5** queen, ruler **7** monarch, pharaoh
take the ~: **6** accede, ascend
Throne: **7** Malachi
Throneberry: **4** Marv
Throne of Saturn, The
author: Allen Drury
throng: **3** jam, mob **4** army, bevy, herd, host, many, mass, pack, pour **5** bunch, crowd, crush, drove, flock, group, horde, press, swarm, troop **6** gather, huddle, legion, muster, rabble **7** company, numbers, sellout, turnout **8** assembly **9** concourse, gathering, multitude **10** assemblage, concursion
throngs: **4** lots **6** flocks, hoards, scores **7** legions
__ Thro' the Rye: **5** Comin'
throttle: **3** gag **5** seize, wring **6** muzzle, stifle **7** inhibit, occlude, silence, squeeze **8** obstruct, suppress
open up the ~: **4** race **5** speed
through: **3** for, per, via **4** done, fini, free, over, past, with **5** clear, ended, finis, using **6** during, within **7** all done, between, by way of, nonstop, wound up **8** complete, finished, in and out, washed-up **9** as a result, because of, by means of, concluded, wrapped up **10** by virtue of, terminated
ender: **3** out, put, way
prefix: **3** dia-, per- **5** trans-
starter: **4** feed **5** break, where **6** follow
through __-colored glasses: **4** rose
__ through: **3** get, put, run, see **4** come, fall, look, walk, work **5** break, carry, think **6** follow, muddle, squeak **7** squeeze
__-through: **3** see **4** pass, read, rust, show **5** drive
Through a Glass, Darkly (1962 film)
cast: Harriet Andersson, Max von Sydow
director: Ingmar Bergman
__ through hoops: **4** jump
__ through one's fingers: **4** slip
__ through one's hat: **4** talk
__ through one's teeth: **3** lie
throughout: **4** over **6** during **7** all over, overall **8** every bit, to the end **9** up-and-down **10** everywhere
through the __: **4** mill
__ through the cracks: **4** fall
Through the Looking-Glass
author: Lewis Carroll
__ through the nose: **3** pay
throughway: **4** road **5** route
throw: **3** boa, fit, lob, peg, shy **4** buck, cast, dash, dump, flip, hurl, lick, pass, pelt, roll, shot, toss **5** addle, bandy, chuck, flick, fling, floor, heave, impel, let go, mix up, pitch, scarf, shawl, shoot, sling, spray, stone, strew, upset **6** afghan, baffle, launch, let fly, pepper, propel, puzzle, rattle, shower, tackle, unseat **7** area rug, blanket, bombard, confuse, deliver, disturb, fluster, muffler, mystify, nonplus, project, scatter, unhorse, unnerve **8** astonish, befuddle, bewilder, catapult, confound, coverlet, coverlid, mantilla, splatter, sprinkle, unsettle **9** dumbfound, give a turn **10** disconcert
a ~: **4** each
a curve to: **4** stun **6** delude **7** stupefy **8** misquote, surprise
a fit: **4** rage, rant, rave, yell **5** go ape **10** hit the roof
a monkey wrench into: **5** block **6** hamper, hinder **7** disrupt **8** obstruct **9** frustrate, undermine
around: **5** spray, strew **7** scatter
a stone's ~ away: **4** near **5** close **6** nearby
away: **3** rid **4** blow, drop, dump, junk, lose, shed **5** chuck, ditch, scrap, shuck, spend, waste **6** reject **7** abandon, cast off, discard, fritter, let go of **8** get rid of, jettison, squander, throw out **9** dispose of, dissipate **10** run through
back: **6** revert **7** reflect, regress
cold water on: **5** deter **6** sadden **8** dispirit
dice ~: **3** six, ten, two **4** five, four, nine **5** eight, seven, three **6** eleven, twelve **7** boxcars **9** snake eyes
down the gauntlet: **4** defy **9** challenge **10** make a stand
ender: **4** away, back
for a loop: **4** faze, stun **5** addle, upset **6** baffle **7** fluster, stagger **9** take aback
in: **3** add **6** donate **9** interject, introduce
in one's hand: **4** fold, quit **5** yield **6** submit **7** concede **9** surrender
in the towel: **4** give, quit **5** yield **6** resign **7** concede, succumb **9** surrender
into a panic: **5** scare, spook **8** frighten
in together: **3** mix, wed **4** band, join, link, pool, yoke **5** admix, blend, group, marry, merge, unite **6** league, mingle, team up **7** bunch up, combine **9** affiliate, aggregate, commingle, integrate, syndicate **10** amalgamate
in with: **4** join, link **5** unite **7** support
in (with): **9** affiliate
light on: **4** show **5** solve **6** answer, unfold **7** clarify, explain, expound **8** illumine, simplify, spell out **9** bring home, elaborate, elucidate, interpret, make plain, translate **10** illuminate, illustrate
like a bad ~: **4** wide, wild **6** errant
mud at: **4** slam, slur **5** knock, libel, smear, sully, taint, wrong **6** defame, malign, vilify **7** asperse, blacken, run down, slander, tarnish, traduce **8** backbite, badmouth, besmirch, dishonor **9** denigrate, discredit, disparage **10** calumniate, stigmatize, vituperate
off: **4** beam, emit, lose, shed, spew, spue, trip **5** eject, elude, evade, expel, exude, issue, shake, spill, trick **6** delude, escape, outrun **7** cast out, confuse, deceive, diffuse, emanate, excrete, mislead, radiate, unnerve **8** confound, unburden, unsettle **9** disinform, exfoliate, misdirect, send forth, take aback
off guard: **4** stun **5** shake **7** astound, nonplus, stagger **8** astonish, bowl over, surprise **9** discomfit, dumbfound **10** disconcert
oneself into: **6** attack, have at, take up **7** address, focus on **8** engage in **9** have a go at, undertake **10** plug away at, take care of
one's lot in with: **3** wed **4** join **5** marry **6** go with, hook up
one's weight around: **5** bully **6** hector **7** oppress **8** browbeat, domineer **9** tyrannize **10** intimidate
on the pile: **3** add
open: **6** turn on **8** activate
out: **2** ax **3** axe, ban, say **4** boot, cast, drop, dump, emit, junk, nail, oust, shed, spew, spue, tell, veto, void **5** chuck, ditch, eject, evict, expel, forgo, scrap, state, utter, waste **6** depose, forego, give up, reject, remove **7** abandon, bring up, chime in, comment, exclude, forsake, lighten, mention, radiate, suggest **8** forswear, get rid of, jettison, part with, relegate, turn down **9** cast aside, dispose of, eliminate, foreswear, ostracize **10** relinquish
out of whack: **4** skew **7** distort
over: **4** drop, dump, jilt, quit **5** leave, sling, upset **6** desert **7** abandon, forsake **9** eighty-six, walk out on **10** finish with, go away from
overboard: **4** dump, hurl, junk **5** chuck, ditch, eject, heave, scrap **6** unload **7** abandon, cast off, deep-six, discard, lighten **8** jettison
stones at: **3** pan, rap **4** pelt, slam **5** blame, decry, knock, sneer **6** malign, vilify **7** censure, condemn, put down, run down, slander, traduce **8** backbite, badmouth, belittle, denounce, derogate **9** criticize, denigrate, disparage, reprehend **10** calumniate
the book at: **6** punish **7** condemn, convict **8** sentence
together: **4** make **5** build, hatch **6** devise
underhand ~: **4** toss **5** pitch
water on: **6** drench, splash **8** saturate **10** extinguish
throw __: **3** off, out, rug **4** a fit, away, back, over **6** pillow
throw __ kiss: **3** me a
throw __ loop: **4** for a
throw __ on: **5** light
throw __ the gauntlet: **4** down
__ throw: **4** free **6** hammer, stone's **7** javelin
throw a __: **3** fit
throwaway: **6** dodger **7** handout, offhand **8** handbill, pamphlet **10** disposable
throwaways: **5** lagan, ligan **6** jetsam, jetsom
throwback: **6** legacy **7** atavism, atavist **8** archaism **10** archaicism
of a ~: **6** atavic
throw down the __: **8** gauntlet
thrower
tantrum ~: **3** imp **5** child **9** youngster
__ thrower: **4** snow
throw for __: **5** a loop, a loss
Throwing It All Away (1986 song)
artist: Genesis
throw in the __: **5** towel
__-throw line: **4** free
Throw Momma From the Train (1987 film)
cast: Billy Crystal, Danny DeVito, Anne Ramsey
director: Danny DeVito
role: **4** Owen
throw one's __ around: **6** weight
throw one's __ in the ring: **3** hat
throw the __ at: **4** book
throw up one's __: **5** hands
thru: **3** o'er, via
ender: **3** way
__-thru: **3** see **5** drive
thrum: **3** tap **5** drone, pluck, pulse, strum **7** pulsate
thrush: **4** bird, chat **5** mavis, shama, veery **7** redwing **8** redstart, wheatear, whinchat **9** blackbird, fieldfare, stonechat
Hawaiian ~: **4** omao
home: **4** nest
relative: **5** ousel, ouzel, robin **6** dipper
thrust: **3** jab, jam, ram **4** butt, core, crux, gist, jerk, meat, pith, poke, prod, push, sink, stab, tilt **5** blitz, boost, drive, elbow, embed, force, forge, heave, imbed, impel, lunge, nudge, point, press, punch, sense, shove, slide, stick **6** effect, empale, impale, import, jostle, justle, pierce, plunge, propel, upshot **7** impetus, meaning, purport, squeeze **8** momentum, pressure, transfix **9** impulsion, interject, onslaught, penetrate, substance **10** incitement, propulsion
forward: **5** sally
in: **5** embed, imbed
out: **6** exsert
thwart a ~: **5** parry
upon: **3** tax **4** heap, pour **5** exact, foist, force, order **6** bestow, compel, decree, deluge,

demand, enjoin, impose, lavish, shower **7** dictate, inflict **9** institute, stipulate
thrusting
weapon: 4 épée **5** estoc, spear
thruway: 4 road **5** route **8** turnpike
entrance: 4 ramp
warning: 3 SLO
Thu.: 3 day
thud: 3 bam, jar **4** bang, fall **5** clonk, clump, clunk, knock, noise, pound, pulse, smack, sound, throb, thump, thunk, whomp
thug: 4 goon, hood **5** brute, rowdy, tough **6** bandit, gunsel, menace, mugger, outlaw, robber **7** brigand, gorilla, hoodlum, ruffian, torpedo **8** criminal, gangster, hard case, hired gun, hooligan, plugugly, tough guy **9** desperado, racketeer, roughneck, terrorist **10** highwayman, triggerman
group: 3 mob **4** gang **5** cabal **9** syndicate **10** Cosa Nostra, underworld
knife: 4 shiv
thulium: 5 metal **7** element **9** rare earth
thumb: 4 leaf **5** digit **6** finger, pollex
a ride: 5 hitch **9** hitchhike
bird's ~: 5 alula
ender: 3 nut **4** hole, nail, tack **5** print, screw
fleshy part of a ~: 4 soft
green ~: 3 art **4** gift **5** flair, knack, touch **6** genius, talent **7** faculty, know-how **8** aptitude, facility, instinct **9** expertise
one's nose at: 4 defy, mock **5** flout, rebel, scoff, spurn **6** deride
rule of ~: 4 norm **8** standard
site: 4 fist, hand, mitt
through: 4 scan **6** browse
(through): 3 run **4** leaf, page, read, scan, skim
under one's ~: 4 weak **7** subject **8** helpless **9** dependant, dependent, powerless **10** vulnerable
thumb __: 5 a ride, index
__ thumb: 5 green
__ Thumb: 3 Tom
thumbnail: 3 bio **5** brief, short, small **7** concise, outline, profile
thumb one's __ at: 4 nose
thumbprint feature: 5 whorl
thumbs
all ~: 5 gawky, inept, unapt **6** cloddy, clumsy, klutzy, oafish **7** awkward, gawkish, unadept **8** bumbling, bungling, fumbling, ungainly **9** graceless, lumbering, maladroit, stumbling, unskilled **10** unskillful
be all ~: 4 flub, slip **5** botch **6** bungle, fumble, goof up, mess up **7** blunder, louse up, screw up
birds' ~: 6 alulae
twiddle one's ~: 4 idle, laze **5** shirk **6** lounge **7** goof off, sit back **8** malinger, mark time, slack off **9** do nothing
__ thumbs: 3 all
thumbs down: 2 no **3** nah, naw, nay, nix, non **4** nein, nope, nyet, uh-uh, veto **5** I won't, ixnay, never, no how, no way **6** no deal, noways, nowise, rebuff **7** I refuse, refusal **8** forget it, I will not, negative, negatory **9** blacklist, by no means, fat chance, I think not, rejection **10** count me out, not a chance
give a ~ to: 3 nix, pan **4** deny, rate, veto **6** refuse, refute, reject
vocal ~: 3 boo **4** hiss, jeer **7** catcall **8** ridicule **9** sibilance **10** sibilation
voter: 4 anti
worth two ~: 3 bad **5** awful, gross, lousy **7** beastly, ghastly, ungodly **8** dreadful, horrible, horrific, terrible **9** appalling, atrocious, frightful, revolting **10** abominable, deplorable, disgusting, horrendous
thumbs up
critic: 5 Ebert **10** Roger Ebert
give a ~ to: 2 OK **4** okay, rate **6** accept, assent, permit **7** approve **9** recommend
see also of course
Thummim's Biblical partner: 4 Urim
thump: 3 hit, jar, rap, tap, wap **4** bang, bash, beat, blow, cuff, drum, fall, plop, slam, slap, slug, thud, tick, whap, whop **5** clonk, clout, clump, clunk, knock, lobby, pound, pulse, punch, smack, sound, throb, thunk, whack **6** batter, beat up, buffet, impact, pommel, pummel, strike, thwack, wallop **7** pulsate **8** pounding **9** fisticuff, haul off on
for: 4 back **6** foster **7** endorse, espouse, further, indorse, promote, support **8** advocate, champion
thumping: 3 big **5** hefty, large
Thun: 4 lake, town
river: 3 Aar **4** Aare
thunder: 3 din **4** boom, clap, drum, echo, peal, rail, rave, roar, roll, yell **5** blast, crack, crash, growl, pound, shout, snarl, sound, storm **6** bellow, deafen, go boom, rumble **7** declaim, explode, resound **8** bloviate, detonate **9** cannonade, discharge, fulminate
ender: 4 bird, bolt, clap, head **5** cloud, stone, storm **6** shower, struck
god: 4 Thor
sound: 4 boom, clap, peal, roar **5** blast, crash **9** cannonade, explosion
unit: 4 bolt, peal
Thunder Alley (ABC sitcom)
cast: Ed Asner (Gil Jones)
Thunderball: 4 film **5** novel
author: Ian Fleming
cast: Claudine Auger, Sean Connery
role: 5 Fiona, Largo **6** Emilio
theme singer: Tom Jones
Thunder Bay: 4 city, port, town
locale: 3 Ont. **6** Canada **7** Ontario
Thunderbird: 3 car **4** auto, Ford **10** automobile
thunderbolt: 4 jolt, roar **6** boomer **7** thunder **8** surprise
thunderclap: 4 roar **6** boomer
Thunderer, The: 5 march
composer: John Philip Sousa
thunderhead: 5 cloud **7** cumulus
Thunderhead's mother: 6 Flicka
Thunderheart (1992 film)
cast: Graham Greene, Val Kilmer, Sam Shepard
thundering: 3 big **4** loud **5** aroar, forte, noisy **7** blaring, booming, jarring, pealing, rackety, raucous, reboant, roaring **8** crashing, piercing, plangent, resonant, rumbling, sonorous, strident, turned up **9** big-voiced, clamorous, deafening **10** boisterous, resounding, stentorian, strepitous, uproarious, vociferous
Thundering Herd, The
author: Zane Grey
Thunder in Paradise (TV action)
cast: Carol Alt (Kelly LaRue)
thunderous: 8 resonant, sonorous, terrific **9** deafening **10** stentorian
Thunder Out of China
author: Theodore H. White
thundershower: 4 rain
thunderstorm product: 4 rain **5** ozone
thunderstruck: 4 awed **5** agape, dazed, in awe **6** aghast, amazed **7** floored, shocked, stunned **9** astounded **10** astonished, bowled over, speechless, taken aback
reaction: 3 awe **5** shock **6** dazzle, terror, wonder **8** surprise **9** amazement, reverence
Thurber, James: 6 writer
work: Alarms and Diversions
Fables for Our Time
The Male Animal
The Middle-Aged Man on the Flying Trapeze
The Seal in the Bedroom
The Secret Life of Walter Mitty
The Thirteen Clocks
Thurgood, Marshall: 5 judge **7** justice
thurible: 6 censer
use a ~: 5 cense
Thüringen: 5 state **6** German
city: 5 Gotha **6** Weimar
thurm: 3 cut **5** carve, shape **6** chisel, incise, sculpt **7** engrave
Thurman: 3 Uma **6** Munson
Thurman, Uma: 7 actress
film: The Avengers (1998)
Batman & Robin (1997)
Be Cool (2005)
Dangerous Liaisons (1988)
Final Analysis (1992)
Gattaca (1997)
The Golden Bowl (2001)
Henry & June (1990)
Kill Bill (2003)
Les Misérables (1998)
Mad Dog and Glory (1993)
My Super Ex-Girlfriend (2006)
Prime (2005)
The Producers (2005)
Pulp Fiction (1994)
Sweet and Lowdown (1999)
Tape (2001)
The Truth About Cats and Dogs (1996)
spouse: Ethan Hawke, Gary Oldman
Thurmond: 4 Nate **5** Strom
Thurmond, Nate
milieu: 5 court
org.: 3 NBA
sport: 10 basketball
Thurmond, Strom: 3 sen. **7** senator
Thurs.: 3 day
follower: 3 Fri.
preceder: 3 Wed.
__ Thursday: 4 Holy **5** Sweet **6** Maundy
Thursday eponym: 4 Thor
Thurston: 6 Harris, Howell
thus: 3 sic **4** ergo, then **5** hence **6** hereby, in kind, like so **9** as follows, therefore **10** for example, in such a way
far: 3 yet **5** as yet **8** until now
in Latin: 3 sic
thus __: 3 far
Thus Spake Zarathustra
author: Friedrich Nietzsche
thwack: 3 bop, hit, jab, tan **4** bash, beat, belt, blow, cane, conk, slam, slap, swat **5** crown, flail, knock, paste, pound, punch, smite, spank, thump, whang, whomp **6** batter, buffet, pommel, pummel, strike, wallop **7** lambast, lay into **8** lace into, lambaste, uppercut
thwart: 3 nip **4** balk, beat, curb, dash, defy, foil, halt, mock, stop **5** avert, baulk, block, cheat, check, cramp, crimp, cross, elude, queer, stimy, stymy, upset **6** baffle, defeat, hamper, hinder, hogtie, hold up, impede, oppose, outwit, resist, scotch, stymie **7** buffalo, counter, nonplus, prevent, repulse, squelch, trammel, ward off **8** handcuff, obstruct, outflank, override, overrule, preclude, restrain, turn back **9** discomfit, forestall, frustrate, hamstring, undermine **10** circumvent, contravene, counteract, disappoint
THX 1138 (1978 film)
cast: Robert Duvall,, Donald Pleasance
director: George Lucas
thy: 4 your
Thy kingdom __...: 4 come
thyme: 4 herb
thymus: 5 gland
Thy Neighbor's Wife
author: Gay Talese
thyroid: 5 gland
Thyrsis
author: Matthew Arnold
Thy word is __ unto...: 5 a lamp
ti: 4 note
follower: 2 do
preceder: 2 la **4** so la
Ti: 4 elem. **7** element **8** titanium
22 for ~: 4 at. no.
Tia: 5 Mowry **7** Carrere
Tia __: 5 Juana, Mária
Tia Maria: 5 drink **8** beverage
Tiananmen __: 6 Square
Tiant, Luis: 6 hurler **7** pitcher
tiara: 5 crown **6** diadem **7** coronet, jewelry
inset: 3 gem **5** bijou, jewel, stone **8** gemstone
Tibbets, Col. mom: 5 Enola
Tibbett, Lawrence: 6 singer **8** baritone, barytone
specialty: 5 opera

Tibbs: 6 Virgil
Tiber: 5 river
feeder: 4 Nera
locale: 4 Rome 5 Italy
Tiberius: 5 Roman 6 Caesar
mother: 5 Livia
see also Latin
Tibet
beast: 5 panda
bovine: 3 yak
Buddhism: 6 Tantra 9 Vajrayana
capital: 4 Lasa 5 Lassa, Lhasa
creature: 4 yeti
deer: 4 shou
equine: 5 kiang
explorer: 5 Hedin 6 Norgay 9 David-Neel
gazelle: 3 goa
icon: 5 tanka
language: 4 Naga
locale: 4 Asia
monastery: 5 gompa
monk: 4 lama
mountain: 5 Kamet 6 Cho Oyu, Kangto, Lhotse, Makalu 7 Everest 8 Changtzu, Pauhunri 9 Himalayas 10 Chomo Lhari
mysticism: 8 dzogchen
neighbor: 5 India, Nepal
Nobelist in Peace: 9 Dalai Lama
people: 4 Nosu
river rising in ~: 5 Indus
sheep: 6 bharal 7 burrhel
Tibetan: 5 Asian 8 language
ocean, in ~: 5 Dalai
__-Tibetan: 4 Sino
tibia: 4 bone, shin 8 shinbone
connectors: 5 tarsi
locale: 3 leg
neighbor: 5 ankle, talus 6 fibula, tarsus
Tiburon: 3 car 4 auto 7 Hyundai 10 automobile
tic: 3 fit 4 jerk 5 spasm 6 oddity, quiver, twinge, twitch 9 mannerism
tic-__-toe: 3 tac
Tic __ Dough: 3 Tac
Tic-__: 3 Tac
tick: 3 bug, rap, run, tap 4 beat, blow, dash, line, mark, pest, wink 5 check, clack, click, cross, flash, flick, pulse, shake, throb, thump 6 acarid, insect, minute, moment, second, stroke 7 instant, operate, pulsate, tapping 8 clicking 9 checkmark, pulsation, twinkling 10 indication
away: 2 go 4 pass 6 elapse, roll on
ender: 4 bird, seed, tack
maker: 5 clock, watch 10 wristwatch
off: 3 ire, irk, vex 4 list, miff, rile, roil 5 anger, annoy, count, peeve, steam, upset 6 enrage, number, rebuke, reckon 8 distress 9 enumerate
(off): 3 tee
tick __: 3 off
tick-__-toe: 4 tack
__ tick: 3 dog 4 hard, plus, seed, soft, wood 5 minus 6 cattle 7 harvest
__-tick: 5 ricky
Tick __: 4 Tock
tickbird: 3 ani
animal followed by a ~: 5 rhino
ticked off: 3 mad 4 sore 5 angry, irate, upset 6 galled 9 resentful
ticker: 5 clock, heart, watch
ticker __: 4 tape
__ ticker: 5 stock
ticker-tape __: 6 parade
ticket: 3 key, tab, tag 4 card, chit, cite, list, mark, note, pass, slip, stub 5 badge, board, check, ducat, label, paper, price, slate, token 6 coupon, docket, entrée, invite, marker, notice, permit, record 7 license, passage, receipt, sticker, voucher 8 citation, document, passport, password, solution 9 admission, raincheck 10 credential, open sesame
abbr.: 4 orch.
again: 5 retag
choose a ~: 4 vote
endorser: 5 voter
free ~: 4 comp, pass
leftover: 4 stub
office sign: 3 SRO
punishment: 4 fine
risk a ~: 5 speed
word on a ~: 3 row 4 seat 5 admit
word on a track ~: 3 win 4 show 5 place
writer: 5 citer 7 officer, trooper 9 meter maid, policeman
__ ticket: 4 lift, meal 5 split 6 season
__-ticket: 3 big 4 high
ticketholder, season: 6 abonne
__-ticket item: 3 big
tickets, overcharge for: 5 scalp
Ticket to Ride (1965 song)
artist: Beatles
Ticket to the Moon
artist: ELO
ticking: 5 alive 6 fabric, living
tickle: 3 pat, pet 4 itch, play 5 amuse, brush, charm, cheer, elate, goose, touch 6 caress, divert, excite, please, stroke, thrill, tingle, turn on 7 beguile, delight, enchant, gratify 8 convulse, interest 9 entertain, make laugh, stimulate, titillate, vellicate
response: 5 te-hee 6 giggle
tickle __: 4 pink
tickled: 4 glad 5 happy, merry 6 blithe, cheery, jovial, joyful, joyous, upbeat 7 content, gleeful, pleased 8 blissful, cheerful, ecstatic, euphoric, exultant, jubilant, mirthful 9 delighted, overjoyed, rejoicing 10 flying high
feeling: 4 glee
it may be ~: 3 rib 5 fancy
Tickle Me __: 4 Elmo
tickler: 4 list, memo, note 7 jotting 8 reminder 10 memorandum
rib ~: 3 pun 4 jest, joke 5 antic, farce, laugh 6 banter 8 drollery
tickler __: 4 file
tickle the __: 7 ivories
__-tickling: 3 rib
ticklish: 4 nice 5 dicey, goosy, itchy, risky, rocky, tight 6 chancy, fickle, goosey, thorny, touchy, tricky, trying, unsafe 7 awkward, prickly 8 critical, delicate, perilous, unstable, unsteady, variable, volatile 9 dangerous, difficult, mercurial, sensitive, uncertain 10 capricious, changeable, inconstant, precarious, touch-and-go
situation: 5 pinch 6 plight
tick-tack-toe: 4 game
Tick Tock
author: Dean Koontz
ticky-__: 5 tacky
Tico: 10 Costa Rican
Ticonderoga: 4 Fort
Ticotin: 6 Rachel
tic-tac-__: 3 toe
Tic Tac
alternative: 5 Certs 6 Binaca, Mentos 7 Altoids, Clorets, Dentyne
Tic Tac Dough: game show
host: Gene Barry, Wink Martindale
tic-tac-toe: 4 game
nonwinner: 3 OOX, OXO, OXX, XOO, XOX, XXO
result: 3 tie 4 draw 8 standoff 9 stalemate
side: 3 Xes
win: 3 OOO, XXX
tidal
bore: 5 eager, eagre
motion: 3 ebb 4 flow 6 waning 7 outflow
wave: 4 bore 6 tumult 7 tempest, tsunami, turmoil 8 disaster, upheaval 9 cataclysm
tidal __: 4 bore, wave 5 basin
tidbit: 4 bite 5 crumb, goody, snack, taste, treat 6 goodie, morsel, nibble 7 soupçon 8 delicacy, mouthful, spoonful 9 collation
juicy ~: 4 buzz, dirt, talk, word 5 rumor 6 report 7 hearsay, scandal
tide: 3 ebb, rip, run 4 drag, eddy, flow, flux, neap, race, rush, time, wave 5 drift, flood, ocean, spate, trend 6 assist, billow, course, sluice, spring, stream, vortex 7 current, torrent 8 movement, tendency, undertow 9 direction, whirlpool 10 inundation
cause: 4 moon
double ~ phenomenon: 5 agger
ender: 3 rip, way 4 land, mark 5 water 6 waiter
lapped by the ~: 5 awash
low ~: 3 ebb
over: 3 aid 4 help 6 assist 7 satisfy 9 help along 10 see through
ride the ~: 4 surf 7 hang ten
starter: 3 rip 4 even, noon, Yule 5 flood 6 Easter, spring 7 Passion 9 Christmas
swim with the ~: 4 cope 5 adapt 6 adjust
__ tide: 3 ebb, lee, low, red, rip 4 high, neap 5 flood
Tide: 9 detergent
alternative: ***see*** detergent
__ Tide: 3 Ebb 7 Crimson
Tide Is High, The (1980 song)
artist: Blondie
Tide, The: 4 Bama
Tidewater Tales, The
author: John Barth
tidiness: 5 order
tidings: 4 dirt, info, news, word 6 advice, report 7 message 8 bulletin 9 greetings
tidy: 4 fair, good, neat, nice, prim, snug, trig, trim, vast 5 ample, clean, crisp, fix up, frame, groom, kempt, large, order, sleek 6 decent, goodly, neaten, police, spruce, tauten 7 chipper, cleanly, groomed, healthy, in order, largish, ordered, orderly, shape up, sizable 8 adequate, generous, handsome, methodic, passable, readable, sizeable, spruce up, straight, to rights, well-kept 9 good-sized, organized, shipshape, smarten up, tolerable 10 acceptable, fastidious, methodical, neat as a pin, pretty good, straighten, systematic
not ~: 5 messy 7 in a mess, jumbled 8 messed up, slovenly 9 cluttered, jumbled up 10 disheveled, disorderly, in disarray, out of order, topsy-turvy
up: 4 dust 5 clean, groom, sweep 6 neaten 7 arrange 8 organize
tie: 3 fix, gag, wed 4 band, bind, bond, clog, cord, curb, do up, draw, duty, gird, hold, join, knot, know, lace, lash, link, meet, moor, push, rope, stop, yoke 5 ascot, brace, cinch, delay, deuce, equal, hitch, joint, leash, level, limit, marry, match, nexus, rival, rivet, strap, touch, truss, unite 6 anchor, attach, batten, begird, bundle, clinch, couple, cravat, enlace, even up, fasten, fetter, hamper, hinder, hook on, hookup, inlace, lace up, lacing, ligate, lock up, outfit, secure, splice, string, tackle, tether, zipper 7 balance, bandage, bracket, confine, conjoin, connect, foulard, kinship, liaison, loyalty, network, shackle, tighten, trammel 8 alliance, dead heat, deadlock, fastener, ligament, ligation, ligature, make fast, neckwear, obstruct, parallel, restrain, restrict, standoff, vinculum 9 break even, entrammel, fastening, indenture, interlace, measure up, stalemate 10 allegiance, attachment, commitment, connection, four-in-hand, keep up with, obligation
a horse: 6 tether
black ~: 6 tuxedo 10 monkey suit
department: 4 men's
down: 4 lash 6 fasten, pinion, secure 8 restrain
fabric: 3 rep 4 repp, silk 7 charvet, Mogador
feature: 4 knot
holder: 3 pin, tac 4 stud 5 clasp
in: 4 link 5 merge 6 belong, mingle, relate 7 connect 8 catenate 9 correlate 10 connection, coordinate
in a ~: 4 even 5 drawn
like some ~s: 4 loud 5 gaudy 6 clip-on, flashy
off: 6 ligate
on: 5 affix 6 attach 7 connect
place: 4 neck
starter: 3 hog 4 neck 5 cross
tack: 4 stud 7 jewelry
the knot: 3 wed 4 mate 5 marry 10 get hitched
tightly: 5 truss
together: 4 join, loop, yoke 7 conjoin
up: 4 bind, clog, curb, dock, even, halt, hold, join, knot, moor, stop, wrap 5 delay, leash, limit,

match, truss 6 engage, fasten, fetter, hamper, hinder, impede, ligate, occupy, pinion, secure, tether 7 confine, shackle, trammel 8 deadlock, encumber, finalize, handicap, keep busy, obstruct, prohibit, restrain, restrict, slow down 9 entrammel 10 traffic jam
up loose ends: 6 finish 8 complete, finalize
up the phone: 3 gab, rap, yak 4 chat, talk
Western ~: 4 bola, bolo
tie __: 3 bar, rod, tac 4 clip, down, line, tack 5 clasp, one on
tie __ on: 3 one
tie-__: 3 dye
__ tie: 3 bow 4 bola, bolo 5 black, power, twist, white 6 clip-on, string
__-tie: 3 hog 6 tongue
Tie a Yellow Ribbon... (1973 song)
artist: Tony Orlando & Dawn
tree: 3 oak
tiebreaker: 2 OT 8 overtime
tied: 4 even 5 equal, tight 6 even up, liable 7 at deuce
fit to be ~: 3 mad 4 wild 5 angry, irate, livid, riled, vexed 6 fuming, heated, piqued, raging, red-hot 7 boiling, enraged, furious, intense, steamed, violent 8 incensed, up in arms, wrathful 9 bummed-out, indignant 10 hysterical, infuriated
in: 6 united 8 in league, relevant
not ~ down: 4 free 5 loose 7 unbound 8 cut loose, detached 9 footloose, unchained, unengaged, unimpeded 10 autonomous, disengaged, unattached, unconfined, unhampered, unhindered, unshackled
up: 4 busy 5 tight 7 engaged, in knots, related 8 immersed, obsessed, occupied
with hands ~: 5 at bay 8 helpless
__-tied: 6 tongue
tie-dyed fabric: 4 ikat 5 batik 6 battik
Tiegs: 5 model 6 Cheryl
tie-in: 7 society 8 junction, juncture 9 relevance 10 connection
tieless: 6 casual
Tie Me Kangaroo Down, Sport (1963 song)
artist: Rolf Harris
Tien Shan: 5 range
locale: 4 Asia 5 China 10 Kyrgyzstan
Tiepolo: 8 Giovanni
tier: 3 row 4 bank, deck, file, line, rank 5 class, grade, group, lacer, layer, level, order, queue, range, story 6 course, league, rating, series, string 7 echelon, gallery, section, stratum 8 category, grouping 9 mezzanine 10 pigeonhole
fly ~: 9 fisherman
__-tier: 3 two
Tierney: 4 Gene 5 Maura
Tierney, Gene: 7 actress
film: A Bell for Adano (1945)
The Ghost and Mrs. Muir (1947)
Laura (1944)
spouse: Oleg Cassini
Tierra del Fuego: 4 isle 6 island
co-owner: 3 Arg. 5 Chile 9 Argentina
native: 3 Ona 6 Yahgan
range: 5 Andes
tiers __: 4 état
__ Ties: 6 Family, School
Tietê
city on the ~: 8 Sao Paulo
tie the __: 4 knot
tie-up: 3 jam 4 link 5 delay, snarl 6 logjam 8 blockage, slowdown, stoppage 10 bottleneck, congestion, traffic jam
tiff: 3 ado, fit, pet, row 4 huff, miff, spat, sulk 5 argue, clash, fight, pique, run-in, scrap, set-to, words 6 barney, bicker, dustup, rumpus, temper 7 bad mood, dispute, quarrel, tantrum, wrangle 8 argument, skirmish, squabble 9 altercate, bickering 10 difference, falling-out, irritation
tiffany: 6 fabric 8 material
Tiffany: 4 Chin, font 5 Louis 7 Bolling 8 typeface
Tiffany (singer)
last name: Darwish
song: All This Time (1988)
Could've Been (1987)
I Saw Him Standing There (1988)
I Think We're Alone Now (1987)
Tiffany __: 4 lamp 5 glass
Tiffin: 6 Pamela
tiffin, take: 3 eat, sup 4 dine
Tige: 3 dog 7 Andrews
tiger: 3 cat 4 Tony 5 beast, felid 6 animal, big cat, feline, mammal 8 go-getter 9 Shere Khan 10 sabertooth
by the tail: 9 obsession
home: 3 zoo
like a ~: 4 wild 7 striped
prehistoric ~: 8 smilodon
relative: *see* feline
swallowtail: 3 bug 6 insect
tooth: 4 fang
young: 3 cub
tiger __: 3 cat 4 lily, moth 5 shark, snake
__ tiger: 5 paper 6 Bengal
Tiger: 5 Woods 10 baseballer
Hall-of-Famer: 4 Cobb 6 Kaline, Ty Cobb 8 Al Kaline 9 Greenberg, Newhouser
org.: 3 PGA
Tiger (1959 song)
artist: Fabian
Tiger __: 3 Bay, Rag 4 Beat, Eyes 5 Shark 6 Lilies
Tiger Beat reader: 4 teen
Tiger Eyes
author: Judy Blume
Tiger in your tank company: 4 Esso
tigerish: 4 wild 5 feral 6 fierce, savage 7 furious, intense, vicious 8 menacing 9 barbarous, ferocious, merciless, predatory, rapacious, voracious 10 passionate
Tiger Lilies
author: Sidney Lanier
Tigers: 3 ten 4 team 6 Auburn 7 Clemson 9 Grambling, Princeton
home: 7 Detroit
org.: 3 ALC, MLB
rival: *see* baseball team
sport: 8 baseball
__ Tigers: 6 Flying
Tigers are Better-Looking
author: Jean Rhys
tiger's-eye: 3 gem 6 quartz 8 gemstone
Tiger Walks, A (1964 film)
cast: Sabu
Tigger
creator: A.A. Milne
pal: 3 Owl, Roo 4 Pooh 6 Eeyore
Tigger Comes to the Forest
author: A.A. Milne
Tighe: 5 Kevin
tight: 3 set 4 fast, firm, high, mean, near, shut, snug, taut, tied 5 blind, boozy, bound, cheap, close, dense, drawn, fixed, proof, quick, rigid, rough, scant, short, solid, sound, stiff, tense, terse, thick, tipsy, tough 6 bolted, buzzed, firmly, frugal, gnomic, greedy, loaded, locked, nailed, narrow, scanty, sealed, secure, skimpy, stable, steady, stewed, sticky, stingy, stoned, strong, sturdy, tied up, tricky, trying 7 arduous, blocked, choking, clasped, clumped, compact, concise, cramped, crowded, cutting, laconic, miserly, pickled, plugged, selfish, slammed, smashed, snapped, sparing, thrifty 8 clear-cut, cramping, critical, crushing, enduring, exacting, fastened, grasping, hermetic, intimate, ironclad, perilous, pinching, shrunken, strained, succinct, ticklish, ungiving 9 compacted, dangerous, difficult, hazardous, hidebound, leakproof, nonporous, padlocked, penurious, plastered, punishing, stopped up, stretched, stringent, tenacious, unbending, upsetting, worrisome 10 avaricious, compressed, contracted, disturbing, hard-packed, impervious, inebriated, inflexible, nip and tuck, obstructed, precarious, skinflinty, smothering, to the point, unyielding, waterproof, watertight
ender: 3 wad 4 rope
grip: 4 lock 6 clinch, clutch 7 squeeze
hold ~: 5 clasp, cling 6 clench 7 squeeze
not ~: 3 lax 4 free 5 baggy, loose, slack 6 limber, sloppy, undone 7 relaxed 8 loosened, rambling, slipshod, unhooked 10 disjointed, unbuttoned, unfastened
not ~ in Britain: 5 lowse
pack ~: 3 jam, ram 4 cram, fill, load, tamp, tuck 5 crowd, crush, press, stuff 6 squash 7 squeeze 8 compress, overfill 9 overcrowd
sit ~: 4 stay, wait 7 stay put
spot: 3 fix, jam, rub 4 bind, snag 5 pinch 6 corner, crunch, hassle, pickle, plight, scrape
starter: 3 air, gas 4 skin 5 stick, water
tight __: 3 end 4 shot, spot
tight __ drum: 3 as a
tight-__: 4 knit 6 fisted, lipped 7 mouthed
__ tight: 3 sit 4 hand
__ tight budget: 3 on a
tighten: 3 fix, tie 4 bind, edit, grip, snug 5 cinch, close, cramp, crush, pinch, purse, screw, tense 6 batten, clench, fasten, harden, hold in, lace up, narrow, pull in, redact, secure, strain, tauten 7 congeal, squeeze, stiffen, stretch, toughen 8 compress, condense, contract, pressure, rigidify, strangle 9 constrict
a lid: 5 twist
one's belt: 5 skimp 9 economize
up: 4 edit 6 redact
tightened: 4 firm
tightening, belt: 6 layoff 7 cutback 8 decrease 9 lessening, reduction 10 diminution
tight-fisted: 4 mean 5 cheap 6 greedy, skimpy, stingy 7 chintzy, miserly, sparing 8 grasping, stinting 9 penurious 10 skinflinty
one: 5 miser, piker
tight-fitting: 4 snug
tight-laced: 6 prissy
tight-lipped: 3 mum 4 mute 5 quiet, tacit 6 silent 8 reticent, taciturn 9 secretive, voiceless 10 speechless
tightly: 9 immovably
tightness: 7 tension 8 shortage
tightrope
walk a ~: 4 dare
Tight Rope (1972 song)
artist: Leon Russell
tights: 4 hose 7 leotard 8 leggings
wearer: 6 dancer 9 ballerina
__ tight ship: 4 ran a, run a
tightwad: 5 miser, piker 7 Scrooge 9 skinflint 10 cheapskate, pinchpenny
tigon: 3 cat 5 felid 6 feline, hybrid
Tigra: 3 car 4 auto, Opel 10 automobile
Tigran: 9 Petrosian
Tigris: 4 boat, ship 5 river
ancient city near the ~: 6 Arbela
city on the ~: 5 Amara, Mosul 7 Baghdad
locale: 4 Irak, Iraq 6 Turkey
river to the ~: 7 Karkheh
Tijuana: 4 city, town
locale: 4 Baja 6 Mexico
see also Spanish
Tijuana Taxi (1966 song)
artist: Herb Alpert and the Tijuana Brass
__ Tikes: 6 Little
tiki: 4 idol 8 figurine
Tiki: 6 Barber
__-Tiki: 3 Kon
Tikkanen: 3 Esa
__-tikki-tavi: 5 Rikki
til: 6 sesame
Tilda: 7 Swinton
tilde: 4 mark
topper: 3 ESC
Tilden, Bill: 7 netster 9 tennis pro
milieu: 5 court
tile: 4 pave 5 inlay 6 domino 7 encrust, incrust, tessera
convex ~: 6 imbrex
dotted ~: 6 domino
install ~: 3 lay, set
__ tile: 6 carpet 7 ceiling, ceramic, parquet
tiled: 6 inlaid

tiler
job: 4 roof 5 floor 7 kitchen
need: 5 grout, putty
till: 3 box, dig, hoe, sow, yet 4 farm, grow, plow, safe, tend, tray, turn, work 5 dress, kitty, labor, mulch, plant, vault 6 before, drawer, garden, harrow 7 cash box, prepare 8 money box, register, treasury, turn over 9 cultivate, meanwhile
co.: 3 NCR
ender: 3 age
fit to ~: 6 arable 7 fertile 8 farmable, plowable 10 cultivable
now: 5 as yet, so far, still
slot: 4 ones, tens 5 fives 8 twenties
Till: 4 Eric
Till __ Was You: 5 There
tillage: 4 land 5 field 7 farming
Tillamook __: 3 Bay
tiller: 4 helm 5 reins, wheel 6 farmer, handle 7 control
locale: 3 aft 4 rear 6 astern
tool: 3 hoe
__-tiller: 4 roto
Till Eulenspiegel
composer: Richard Strauss
Tilley: 7 Eustace
Tillie: 5 Olsen
Tillie and Gus (1933 film)
cast: W.C. Fields, Baby LeRoy
Tillie the __: 6 Toiler
Tillis: 3 Mel, Pam
Tillotson: 6 Johnny
Tillstrom: 4 Burr
till the __ come home: 4 cows
Till the Clouds Roll By
composer: Jerome Kern
Till the Day I Die
author: Clifford Odets
Till the End of Time (1945 song)
artist: Perry Como
Till We Meet Again
author: Judith Krantz
composer: Raymond Egan
Tilly: 3 Meg 8 Jennifer
Tilsit: 6 cheese
__ Tilson Thomas: 7 Michael
tilt: 3 dip, tip, yaw 4 bend, bias, bout, cant, cock, drop, duel, fall, heel, lean, list, meet, rake, skew, spar, swag, sway, turn 5 angle, bevel, break, clash, fight, grade, joust, lurch, pitch, set-to, shift, slant, slide, slope, upset 6 attack, careen, charge, combat, fracas, seesaw, slouch, thrust, tussle 7 contend, contest, incline, leaning, recline, scuffle, tourney 8 conflict, gradient, skirmish, struggle 9 collision, encounter, overthrow, scrimmage 10 declension, tournament
at full ~: 5 amain 8 pell-mell
competitor: 6 knight 7 warrior 8 horseman
full ~: 4 fast 5 swift 7 rapidly, swiftly
toward: 5 favor 6 prefer
tilt-__ table: 3 top
__ tilt: 4 full
Tilt-a-Whirl: 4 ride
tilted: 4 alop 5 alist, bevel, leant 6 aslant, aslope 9 at an angle
tilth: 4 farm, land, soil 5 acres, earth, field, tract 6 ground 7 acreage, tillage
__ 'Til the Sun Shines, Nellie: 4 Wait
tilting: 5 alist 8 lopsided
Tilton: 8 Charlene
'Til Tuesday
lead singer: Aimee Mann
song: Voices Carry (1985)
__ 'Til You Drop: 4 Shop
Tim: 4 Holt, Hunt, Mara, Reid, Rice, Roth, Russ, Tiny 5 Allen, Curry, Keefe 6 Burton, Conway, Hunter, McGraw, Raines, Whelan 7 Meadows, Robbins, Russert 8 Cratchit, Matheson, McCarver, McIntire 9 Considine 10 Kazurinsky
__ Tim: 4 Tiny
timber: 3 log, rib 4 balk, beam, boom, club, mast, pole, tree, wood 5 board, frame, grove, joist, plank, stake, stick, trees, woods 6 forest, girder, lumber, rafter 7 support 8 hardwood, woodland
ender: 4 head, land, line, work
foundation ~: 4 sill
made of ~: 6 wooden
mine ~: 5 brace, sprag, stull
problem: 4 knot 5 gnarl 6 dryrot
ship: 3 sny 4 bibb, keel, mast 6 inwale, poppet 7 cathead, futtock, stemson 8 stempost
tool: 3 axe, saw 4 adze
use ~ for support: 5 shore
wolf: 4 lobo
timber __: 4 wolf
timberland: 4 wood 5 woods 6 forest 8 wildwood 9 backwoods
__ Timberlane: 4 Cass
timberline
above the ~: 6 alpine
__ Timbers: 6 Fallen
Timberwolves: 4 five, team
home: 9 Minnesota
org.: 3 NBA
rival: *see* NBA team
sport: 10 basketball
timbre: 4 tone 5 pitch 6 accent 10 inflection
Timbuktu: 4 town
locale: 4 Mali
river near ~: 5 Niger
time: 3 age, bit, day, era 4 ager, bout, date, hour, life, pace, past, peak, rate, shot, show, slot, span, term, tide, tour, turn, week, year 5 break, clock, epoch, month, point, shift, space, spell, stage, state, stint, tempo, while 6 chance, extent, future, heyday, heydey, length, look-in, moment, period, rhythm, season, second, squeak 7 instant, leisure, measure, opening, present, stretch 8 duration, eternity, infinity, instance, interval, juncture, lifespan, occasion, regulate, sentence 9 allotment 10 chronology, generation
ahead of ~: 5 early 9 in advance 10 beforehand
ahead of its ~: 3 new 8 advanced 10 innovative
allowance: 5 grace
ancient ~: 4 yore 9 antiquity
and again: 3 oft 4 a lot, much 5 often 9 quite a bit, regularly, routinely 10 frequently, habitually
another ~: 4 anew, anon, over, soon, then 5 after, again 6 in a bit 7 by and by, later on, someday 8 in a while, sometime 9 afterward, hereafter 10 before long, eventually
appointed ~: 4 date, hour 5 H-Hour 8 zero hour
a second ~: 4 anew, over 5 again
a short ~ ago: 5 newly 6 lately 7 just now 8 latterly, recently
a single ~: 4 once
at a future ~: 3 yet 5 later 10 eventually, ultimately
at a later ~: 9 following 10 afterwards, before long, subsequent
at any ~: 3 e'er 4 ever 8 even once
at no ~: 4 ne'er 5 never 7 not ever
at one ~: 8 back when, formerly, hitherto, together 9 a while ago, in the past 10 heretofore, previously
at such ~ as: 4 when
at that ~: 4 then 9 thereupon
at the present ~: 3 now 5 today
at the right ~: 3 apt 5 on cue 6 prompt 7 fitting 8 apposite, punctual 9 expedient 10 auspicious, convenient, felicitous
at the same ~: 5 along 6 in sync 8 together 9 meanwhile
at the same ~ as: 5 while 6 during, whilst
at the same ~ (prefix): 3 syn-
at this ~: 3 now 4 here 5 still, today 8 promptly, right now, right off, until now 9 forthwith, presently, right away 10 here and now
at what ~: 4 when
back in ~: 3 ago
behind ~: 4 late 5 tardy 7 overdue 8 detained
being: 5 nonce 7 present
bide one's ~: 4 wait 5 delay, tarry 6 lie low 7 stand by
by that ~: 7 already
call ~: 5 pause 6 recess
can do it: 4 heal, mend
combining form: 5 chron- 6 chrono-
correct the ~: 5 reset
current ~: 3 now 7 present
delay: 3 lag
display: 3 LCD, LED
earlier in ~: 5 prior 10 previously
ender: 4 card, less, work, worn 5 piece, saver, table 6 keeper, saving, server, worker 7 keeping
extra ~: 5 slack, space 6 leeway, margin 8 latitude
fool away ~: 4 idle, laze, loll 5 dally, dream, shirk, stall 6 dawdle, loiter, lounge 7 hang out 8 malinger, slack off 9 goldbrick 10 dillydally, fool around, knock about
for a ~: 6 awhile
for all ~: 3 e'er 4 ever 7 finally
for the ~ being: 3 now 9 meanwhile, temporary
free ~: 4 ease 6 recess, repose 7 holiday, leisure, liberty 8 vacation 10 recreation, relaxation, sabbatical
from that ~: 4 then
from this ~ forward: 5 for ay 6 always, for aye 7 forever 8 evermore 9 endlessly, eternally 10 henceforth
from time to ~: 10 now and then
further in ~: 4 anon 5 after 8 eventual 9 afterward 10 thereafter
galactic ~ period: 3 age
gap: 4 stay 5 delay, hitch, pause, stall 6 holdup 7 respite, setback 8 interval, reprieve, slowdown, stoppage 9 deferment, extension, interlude 10 standstill, suspension
get on, as ~: 5 laten
give a hard ~: 3 irk, nag, vex 5 annoy, tease, upset 6 harass, hassle 7 torment
gone by: 4 past
good ~: 3 fun, gas 4 ball, lark, romp 5 blast 6 laughs
hard ~: 4 bind 5 trial 6 crisis, crunch, hassle, ordeal, rebuff, rebuke 7 squeeze, trouble 8 distress 9 adversity, emergency, rejection 10 misfortune, upbraiding
have a bad ~: 6 suffer
have a good ~: 5 enjoy, party 6 cavort 7 carouse, skylark 8 cut loose, live it up 9 celebrate, make merry, whoop it up
have a good ~ with: 5 enjoy
high ~: 4 noon 5 spree
high old ~: 5 caper, fling, revel, spree 6 frolic, gambol, picnic 7 rollick
hit the big ~: 6 arrive, make it, thrive 7 prosper, succeed 8 make good
important ~: 3 age, era 5 epoch
in ~: 4 anon, soon, then 5 after, later 6 a tempo, not now 7 by and by, later on, someday 8 bit by bit 9 afterward, hereafter 10 before long, eventually, ultimately
infinite ~: 7 forever 8 eternity
in good ~: 4 anon, soon 6 prompt 7 by and by, erelong, shortly 8 punctual 9 presently 10 beforehand, before long
in ~ in music: 6 a tempo
in no ~: 3 PDQ 4 fast 5 apace 6 presto 7 fleetly, hastily, quickly, rapidly, readily, swiftly 8 pell-mell, speedily 9 forthwith, hurriedly, instantly, like a shot, posthaste
in the ~ left: 4 till 5 still
in the nick of ~: 9 opportune 10 felicitous
it's about ~: 5 enfin 6 at last 7 finally
keep ~ manually: 4 clap
kill ~: 5 stall 8 lallygag
length of ~: 4 span 5 sweep
limit: 6 curfew
limited ~: 4 span, term, tour 5 hitch, phase 6 period, tenure 7 stretch 8 duration, interval, semester, sentence
line: 4 plan 6 agenda 7 outline 8 game plan, scenario, schedule, strategy 9 blueprint, framework 10 big picture

long ~: 3 age, eon 4 aeon, ages 5 years 7 century, decades, forever
lose no ~: 3 fly, hie, run 4 dash, race, rush, tear 5 hurry, scoot, speed 6 hasten 10 get hopping
make ~ with: 3 woo 4 date 5 court 6 pursue 7 take out
mark ~: 4 drag, idle, laze, loaf, tick, wait 5 abide, stall 6 loiter, lounge 8 vegetate
most of the ~: 6 mainly 7 as a rule, overall, usually 8 as a whole 9 generally, in general 10 by and large, on the whole
not give the ~ of day: 3 cut 4 shun, snub 5 spurn 6 ignore, rebuff, slight 8 brush off
occupy ~ and space: 4 last, live 7 breathe 8 continue
of ~: 8 temporal
of a ~: 4 eral
of day: 4 dawn, dusk, hour, morn, noon 5 sunup 6 sunset 7 evening, morning, sunrise 9 afternoon
off: 4 rest 5 leave, R and R 6 recess 7 holiday, leisure 8 furlough, vacation
of one's life: 4 ball 5 blast
of ~ past: 5 olden
on ~: 5 sharp 6 prompt 8 promptly, punctual 10 punctually
once upon a ~: 6 before, erenow 9 in the past
one at a ~: 6 singly 9 piecemeal
opportune ~: 4 shot 6 chance 8 occasion
out: 5 break, pause 7 respite
palindromic ~: 3 eve 4 noon
partner: 4 tide
pass, as ~: 5 spend, while
play for ~: 5 dally, delay, stall 6 put off 8 postpone 9 temporize
pleasant ~: 4 idyl 5 idyll
point in ~: 4 date, hour 5 point, stage 6 moment
rough ~: 6 downer 8 dry spell, tailspin
science of ~: 8 horology
short ~: 3 bit, sec 4 jiff, msec. 5 jiffy, trice 6 minute, moment 10 nanosecond
some ~ ago: 4 once 6 before 7 earlier 8 formerly 9 in the past 10 heretofore, originally, previously
spare ~: 4 ease, rest 7 freedom, holiday, leisure, liberty, respite 8 vacation 10 recreation, sabbatical
spend, as ~: 5 put in
stand the test of ~: 4 last 6 endure, hold up
starter: 3 air, any, bed, big, day, nap, rag, tea, war 4 down, flex, half, life, long, meal, mean, noon, over, seed, show, some, zone 5 afore, after, lunch, night, peace, small 6 before, dinner, spring, summer, supper, winter
take ~ off: 4 rest 5 pause, relax
take one's ~: 5 dally, delay, mosey, relax, stall, tarry 6 dawdle, linger, loiter 7 goof off 8 lollygag 10 dillydally
taking one's ~: 3 lax 4 easy, lazy, slow 5 slack 6 calmly, casual, gentle, lazily, slowly 7 relaxed 8 casually, laid-back 9 gradually, languidly, leisurely, unhurried 10 composedly, deliberate, indolently
teller: 4 dial 5 clock, watch 10 wristwatch
terrific ~: 4 gala 5 blast, party, spree
to reflect: 4 lull, rest 5 break 6 hiatus 7 respite 8 breather
to the end of ~: 3 e'er 4 ever 7 forever 8 evermore
unit: 2 hr., mo. 3 day, eon, era, min., sec. 4 aeon, half, hour, span, term, week, year 5 epoch, month, space, spell 6 decade, minute, moment, period, second 7 century, quarter 10 millennium
up to this ~: 3 yet 5 as yet 6 ere now, of late 7 thus far 8 hitherto, until now 10 heretofore, previously
vacation ~: 3 Aug., Jul. 4 July 6 August, summer 7 dog days
very long ~: 3 age 4 ages 7 century 9 centuries, millennia 10 millennium
was: 4 once 10 previously
waste ~: 3 lag 4 futz, idle, kill, laze, loaf, moon, mope 5 amble, dally, mosey, stall, tarry 6 dawdle, diddle, linger, loiter, lounge, trifle 7 saunter 8 lollygag, straggle 10 dillydally, fool around
wild ~: 5 spree
working ~: 5 stint
zone abbr.: 3 CDT, CST, EDT, EST, MDT, MST, PDT, PST
time __: 3 lag, was 4 bomb, line, loan, lock, warp, zone 5 clock, frame, limit, of day, sheet, stamp 6 killer, signal 7 capsule, deposit, machine
time __ half: 4 and a
time __ mind: 5 out of
time __ time: 5 after
time-__: 3 lag, out 5 lapse, share 6 tested 7 binding, honored, release, sharing
time-__ photography: 5 lapse
__ time: 3 air, big, buy, cut, tee 4 at no, comp, dead, face, fast, full, gain, good, hang, hard, high, in no, keep, kill, lead, lose, make, mark, peak, post, real, sack, slow, true, word, zone 5 at one, buy on, drive, equal, in due, local, many a, press, prime, quick, quiet, short, spare, waltz 6 access, at this, bottom, crunch, double, family, travel, triple 7 braking, Central, connect, curtain, Eastern, elapsed, Pacific, quality, release, running
__-time: 3 all, old, one 4 lead, long, part 5 first, small
Time: 3 mag 8 magazine
contents: 4 news
founder: Briton Hadden, Henry Luce
onetime ~ film critic: 4 Agee
staffer: 6 editor 8 reporter
Time (1983 song)
artist: Culture Club
Time __: 3 Inc.
Time __, A: 5 To Die
Time __ Bottle: 3 in a
Time __ Let Me: 4 Won't
Time __ Life: 4 of My
Time __ My Side: 4 Is on
Time __ Season: 5 of the
Time __ the essence: 4 is of
__ Time: 3 Bad, Big, Our 4 Play, Pony, This 5 Magic, One Mo', Swing 6 Crying, Father, Kissin'
Time After Time (1979 film)
cast: Malcolm McDowell, Mary Steenburgen, David Warner
Time After Time (song)
artist: Inoj, Cyndi Lauper
time and __: 4 tide 5 again, a half
Time and Time Again
author: Alan Ayckbourn
__ Time Around, The: 6 Second
__ Time at All: 3 Any
Time Bandits (1981 film)
cast: John Cleese, Sean Connery, Shelley Duvall
Time Bomb
author: Jonathan Kellerman
time-capsule event: 6 burial
__-time Charlie: 4 good
Timecode (2000 film)
cast: Salma Hayek, Jeanne Tripplehorn
time-consuming: 4 long, slow 7 lengthy, spun-out 8 drawn-out, unending 10 long-winded, protracted
__-time continuum: 5 space
Timecop (1994 film)
cast: Mia Sara, Jean-Claude Van Damme
timed-__: 7 release
__-timed: 3 ill 4 well
timed, perfectly: 5 on cue
__ Time Gal: 6 Sleepy
time-honored: 3 old 4 trad. 6 age-old 7 classic, regular
__ Time I Get to Phoenix: 5 By the
Time in a Bottle (1973 song)
artist: Jim Croce
__ Time I Saw Paris, The: 4 Last
Time is money: 3 saw 5 adage, maxim
Time Is on My Side (1964 song)
artist: Rolling Stones
Time Is Ripe, The
author: Clifford Odets
Time Is Tight (1969 song)
artist: Booker T. and the MGs
timekeeper: 5 alarm, clock, watch 6 ticker 7 sundial 9 hourglass 10 alarm clock, wristwatch
timeless: 6 eterne 7 abiding, eternal, undying 8 enduring, immortal, unending 9 deathless, perennial, perpetual, unceasing
Timeline
author: Michael Crichton
Time, Love and Tenderness (1991 song)
artist: Michael Bolton
timely: 3 apt, fit, now, pat 4 meet, ripe 5 happy, lucky 6 likely, modern, prompt, proper, with it 7 apropos, fitting, germane, helpful, hopeful 8 apposite, punctual, relevant, suitable, towardly, up-to-date 9 expedient, favorable, judicious, opportune, pertinent, promising 10 auspicious, convenient, felicitous, propitious, prosperous, seasonable
in a ~ fashion: 5 on cue
time-machine destination: 4 past 6 future
Time Machine, The
author: H.G. Wells
Time Machine, The (1960 film)
cast: Yvette Mimieux, Rod Taylor, Alan Young
character: 4 Eloi 5 Weena 7 Morlock
director: George Pal
Time Machine, The (2002 film)
cast: Orlando Jones, Samantha Mumba, Guy Pearce
director: Simon Wells
__ Time, Next Year: 4 Same
__ time no see!: 4 long
time of __: 3 day
Time of My Life
author: Alan Ayckbourn
Time of My Life, The (1987 song)
artist: Bill Medley, Jennifer Warnes
time of one's __: 4 life
Time of the Season (1969 song)
artist: Zombies
Time of Your Life, The
author: William Saroyan
time on one's __: 5 hands
time-out: 3 nap 4 lull 5 pause 6 recess, siesta 7 interim 8 interval 9 cessation 10 suspension
time out of __: 4 mind
Time out of Mind (1997 album)
artist: Bob Dylan
timepiece: 5 clock, watch 7 sundial 9 hourglass
sound: 4 tick, tock
timer: 5 clock, watch 6 gadget 9 hourglass, stopwatch
place: 7 kitchen
__ timer: 3 egg
__-timer: 3 big, old 4 full, part
times
abreast of the ~: 7 current 8 up-to-date
a number of ~: 9 regularly 10 frequently, repeatedly
at ~: 3 occ. 9 not always 10 now and then, on occasion
at all ~: 4 ever 6 always 10 unendingly
at various ~: 6 cyclic 8 cyclical, frequent, repeated, seasonal, sporadic 9 recurrent, recurring, spasmodic 10 occasional
bad ~: 5 slump 9 recession 10 depression
behind the ~: 3 out 5 dated, fusty 6 square 8 outdated, outmoded 9 out-of-date
good ~: 3 fun 6 laughs 10 prosperity
hard ~: 3 woe 5 slump 9 adversity, recession 10 depression, woefulness
in ~ past: 4 once 7 earlier 8 formerly, hitherto, until now 10 heretofore, previously
in these ~: 3 now 5 today 9 at present
keep up with the ~: 5 adapt, alter 6 adjust, change, modify, revise 7 conform, convert, remodel 8 accustom 9 acclimate 10 assimilate, come around

many ~: 3 oft 5 often 6 mostly 10 frequently, repeatedly
most ~: 7 as a rule, largely, usually 9 generally, in general 10 by and large, frequently, on the whole
olden ~: 4 past, yore 5 antiq. 9 antiquity, yesterday
seven ~ a week: 7 diurnal
starter: 3 oft 4 some 5 often 7 between
suffix: 4 -fold
these ~: 8 today. now
Times: 4 font 5 paper 9 newspaper
locale: 7 New York 10 Los Angeles
Times __: 5 Roman 6 Square
__ Times: 3 Old 4 Good, Hard 6 Modern
__ Times a Lady: 5 Three
Time's Arrow
author: Martin Amis
__ Times at Ridgemont High: 4 Fast
timesaver: 4 tool 6 gadget
time-saving: 5 handy, on tap, ready 6 nearby 7 close by, helpful, in reach 9 expedient, immediate, opportune 10 convenient, economical
Times-Dispatch: 5 paper 9 newspaper
locale: 8 Richmond
time-share: 5 lease 6 sublet 7 rent out 8 sublease
time-shifting device: 3 VCR
time-slot abbr.: 3 TBA
Times of Your Life (1975 song)
artist: Paul Anka
Times-Picayune: 5 paper 9 newspaper
locale: 10 New Orleans
Times Roman: 4 font 8 typeface
Times Square
light: 4 neon
locale: 3 NYC 7 New York 9 Manhattan
timetable: 4 card, list, sked 5 sched. 6 agenda, docket 7 program 8 schedule
abbr.: 3 arr., ETA, ETD
time-tested: 3 old 5 tried
Time to Kill, A (1996 film)
cast: Sandra Bullock, Samuel L. Jackson, Matthew McConaughey, Kevin Spacey
Time to leave!: 4 c'mon 6 let's go
__ time to time: 4 from
time-wasting: 3 lax 4 lazy, slow, vain 5 slack, tardy 6 remiss 8 dallying, delaying, dilatory, tarrying 9 snail-like, unhurried
Time Won't Let Me (1966 song)
artist: Outsiders
timeworn: 3 old 5 dated, dusty, hoary, passé, stale, trite 6 eroded, old-hat, shabby 7 archaic, rundown 8 decrepit, obsolete, out of use 9 crumbling, hackneyed, out-of-date, weathered 10 antiquated, broken-down, ramshackle, threadbare
time-worn: 8 well-used
Time wounds all __: 5 heels
Timex: 5 watch 10 wristwatch
alternative: *see* wristwatch
timid: 3 coy, shy 4 meek, soft, weak 5 cowed, mousy, pavid, shaky 6 afraid, craven, demure, feeble, gentle, gun-shy, humble, modest, mousey, scared, trepid, yellow 7 abashed, alarmed, anxious, bashful, bullied, chicken, daunted, fearful, nervous, panicky, prudish, spooked, wimpish 8 badgered, blushing, cowardly, cowering, fearsome, hesitant, recreant, retiring, sheepish, skittish, unnerved, wavering 9 dastardly, diffident, flinching, nerveless, petrified, shrinking, spineless, terrified, trembling, tremulous, unassured, withdrawn 10 ambivalent, browbeaten, capricious, frightened, indecisive, irresolute, namby-pamby, spiritless, submissive, uneffusive, unsociable
not ~: 4 bold, pert 5 brash, brave, fresh, gutsy, nervy, pushy, saucy 6 brassy, brazen, cheeky, daring, flashy, heroic, plucky, spunky 7 dashing, defiant, forward, gallant, valiant 8 fearless, forceful, immodest, impudent, intrepid, resolute, spirited, unafraid, valorous 9 audacious, confident, dauntless, shameless, undaunted, unfearing 10 courageous, incautious, unreserved
one: 4 wimp 5 sissy 6 coward 7 chicken
timidity: 4 fear 7 modesty 8 cold feet, humility 9 cowardice, weak knees 10 constraint, diffidence, faint heart, insecurity
timidly: 5 shyly 7 charily, lightly
timidness: 7 modesty, reserve, shyness 8 meekness 9 hesitancy, mousiness 10 constraint, diffidence, insecurity, reluctance
timing __: 4 belt 5 chain
__-timing: 3 two
Timon of Athens
author: William Shakespeare
Timor: 3 sea 4 isle 6 island
island group near ~: 4 Leti 5 Letti
locale: 5 Malay
Nobelist in Peace: 4 Belo 10 Ramos-Horta
sea near ~: 4 Savu, Sawu
__ Timor: 4 East
timorous: 4 weak 5 faint, jumpy, mousy 6 afraid, craven, mousey, scared, trepid 7 abashed, alarmed, anxious, bashful, chicken, daunted, fearful, nervous, panicky, spooked, wimpish 8 cowardly, fearsome, hesitant, retiring 9 petrified, terrified 10 frightened
timothy: 3 hay 5 grass
Timothy: 4 Daly 5 Aluko, Leary, saint 6 Dalton, Dwight, Hutton 7 Bottoms, Findley 8 Busfield, Olyphant
follower: 5 Titus
mother: 6 Eunice
Timothy Files, The
author: Lawrence Sanders
Timothy Mouse
friend: 5 Dumbo
Timothy's Game
author: Lawrence Sanders
tin: 3 can 5 metal 6 canful 7 element, package, stannum 8 preserve 9 baking pan, container
alloy: 6 bronze, oreide, oroide, pewter 8 calamine, gunmetal
anniversary: 5 tenth
can eater: 4 goat
combining form: 5 stann- 6 stanno-
containing ~: 7 stannic
ear: 6 asonia
ender: 4 horn, type, work 5 smith, stone
lizzie: 3 car 4 auto 10 automobile
ore: 8 stannite
organ: 3 ear
plate: 4 tain
remove from a ~: 5 uncan
tin __: 3 can, ear, god, hat 4 foil 5 plate 6 lizzie 7 soldier
tin-__: 3 pan, pot
__ tin: 3 pie 6 baking
Tin __: 3 Cup, Man, Men
Tin __ Alley: 3 Pan
Tin __, The: 4 Drum, Star 5 Flute
Tina: 3 Fey 4 Cole 5 Brown 6 Louise, Turner 7 Sinatra, Yothers 8 Majorino, Weymouth
Tinbergen: 3 Jan 8 Nikolaas
Tin Can Tree
author: Anne Tyler
tinct: 3 dye, hue 4 tone 5 color, shade, stain, tinge 7 colored, pigment 8 coloring, flavored
tincture: 3 dye, hue 4 odor, tint 5 color, stain, tinge, trace 7 pigment 8 infusion, medicine 10 medication
Tin Cup (1996 film)
cast: Kevin Costner, Don Johnson, Cheech Marin, Rene Russo
tinder: 5 twigs 6 amadou 8 kindling
ender: 3 box
Tinderbox, The
author: Hans Christian Andersen
Tin Drum, The
author: Günter Grass
tine: 3 bug 5 point, prong 6 insect
tool with ~s: 4 fork 5 spork 7 trident 9 pitchfork
tinea: 6 insect 8 ringworm
tined: 5 forky, sharp 6 forked
tineid: 4 moth
Tin Flute, The
author: Gabrielle Roy
ting-__: 5 a-ling
tinge: 3 bit, dye, hue, nib 4 cast, dash, drop, hint, lick, tint, tone, wash 5 color, imbue, pinch, savor, shade, smack, stain, taste, tinct, touch, trace 6 nuance, shadow, strain, streak 7 modicum, pigment, soupçon, suffuse, whisper 8 colorant, coloring, dyestuff, infusion, jaundice, saturate, tincture 9 suspicion, undertone 10 coloration, complexion, impregnate, infiltrate, intimation, smattering, sprinkling, suggestion
with: 5 admix
tingle: 4 itch 5 creep, itchy, sting, throb 6 shiver, thrill, tickle, tinkle 7 prickle, twitter 9 sensation
tingling: 4 itch, numb 5 itchy
__-tingling: 5 spine
tingly: 4 numb 5 itchy
tinhorn: 4 punk 5 cheap, minor 7 gambler 9 small-time
tiniest: 5 least 7 minimum
tinker: 3 fix, toy 4 mess, play 6 dabble, doodle, fiddle, monkey, puddle, putter, repair, tamper 8 fool with, mess with 9 muck about, take apart 10 fiddle with, mess around, play around, trifle with
with: 6 adjust
Tinker Bell: 5 fairy, pixie 6 sprite
Tinker, Grant
spouse: Mary Tyler Moore
tinker's __: 3 dam 4 damn
Tinker, Tailor, Soldier, Spy
author: John le Carré
Tinker to __ to Chance: 5 Evers
Tinkertoy
alternative: 4 Lego
tinkle: 4 ding, ring, ting 5 chime, chink, clink, plink, sound 6 jangle, jingle, murmur, tingle
Tinky Winky: 9 Teletubby
Tin Man
need: 3 oil 5 heart
portrayer: Jack Haley
tool: 3 axe
Tin Man (1974 song)
artist: America
Tin Men (1987 film)
cast: Danny DeVito, Richard Dreyfuss, Barbara Hershey
director: Barry Levinson
tinny: 4 thin 5 cheap 6 flimsy, shoddy
not ~: 6 strong 7 durable
sound: 4 ping
Tin Pan Alley
org.: 3 BMI 5 ASCAP
product: 4 song, tune
Tin Pan Alley (1940 film)
cast: Alice Faye, Betty Grable, Jack Oakie
director: Walter Lang
tinsel: 5 gaudy, showy 6 bauble, flashy, garish, tawdry 7 glitter 10 decoration
strand: 6 icicle
time: 4 Noel, yule 8 December, yuletide 9 Christmas
use ~: 6 bedeck
Tinseltown
see Hollywood, Los Angeles
tint: 3 dye, hue 4 cast, dash, glow, hint, tone, wash 5 color, flush, paint, rinse, shade, stain, taint, tinge, touch, trace 6 affect, chroma, redden 7 pigment, shading 8 coloring, jaundice, tincture 9 influence 10 coloration, complexion, luminosity, suggestion
starter: 4 aqua
see also color, dye
Tintagel
composer: Arnold Bax
Tintern Abbey
author: William Wordsworth
river: 3 Wye
__ Tin Tin: 3 Rin
tintinnabulate: 4 peal, ring 5 chime 6 tinkle
tintinnabulation: 4 ding, peal, ring 5 knell 8 ding-dong
Tintoretto: 6 Jacopo
tintype: 5 photo 7 picture 10 photograph
color: 5 sepia

tinware: 4 tole
Tin Woodman
see Tin Man
tiny: 3 wee 4 baby, itsy, mini, puny 5 bitsy, bitty, dinky, dwarf, eensy, light, micro, small, teeny, weeny 6 atomic, bantam, little, midget, minute, pee-wee, petite, pocket, slight, teensy 7 cramped, minikin, minimum 8 atomical, atomlike, trifling 9 fairylike, itsy-bitsy, itty-bitty, miniature, minuscule, pint-sized, undersize 10 diminutive, minuscular, negligible, pocket-size, teeny-weeny, vest-pocket
amount: 3 bit, dab, jot, ppm, sip 4 atom, drib, iota, mote, whit 5 crumb, grain, ounce, pinch, shred, speck, touch 6 morsel, sliver, tidbit
bug: 3 ant 4 gnat, mite 5 midge
mark: 3 dot 5 fleck 6 tittle
Tiny __: 3 Tim 5 Alice
Tiny Alice
author: Edward Albee
Tiny Bubbles (song)
artist: Don Ho
Tiny Tim
born: Herbert Khaury
instrument: 3 uke 7 ukulele
song: Tip-Toe Thru' the Tulips With Me (1968)
Tiomkin, Dimitri: 7 Russian 8 composer
film score: The Alamo
Dial M for Murder
Friendly Persuasion
Giant
The Guns of Navarone
The High and the Mighty
High Noon
It's a Wonderful Life
Meet John Doe
Mr. Smith Goes to Washington
The Old Man and the Sea
Rio Bravo
Strangers on a Train
Town Without Pity
tip: 3 bug, cap, cue, end, fee, nib, nip, top 4 apex, bang, bend, butt, buzz, cant, cash, clew, clue, cusp, doff, dope, dump, edge, gift, give, head, heel, hint, info, lead, lean, list, news, peak, perk, pour, stub, tilt, warn, word 5 bonus, crown, empty, money, point, shift, slant, slope, spill, spire, steer, upend, upset 6 advice, advise, careen, dollar, height, one-way, prompt, reward, summit, topple, unload, upturn, vertex 7 capsize, caution, handout, hot lead, incline, inkling, lookout, overset, pointer, recline, steeple, suggest, warning, whisper 8 forecast, forewarn, gratuity, heel over, mnemonic, overturn, turn over 9 extremity, knock over, knowledge, lagniappe, pourboire, something, sweetener 10 honorarium, perquisite, prediction, recompense, suggestion, topple over
ender: 3 toe, top 4 cart, ster 5 staff
give a ~ to: 4 tell, warn 5 alert, brief, edify, teach 6 advise, clue in, fill in, impart, inform, notify, reward 7 apprise, caution, counsel, educate, let in on, let know 8 acquaint, forewarn
leave no ~ to: 5 stiff
off: 4 tell, tout, warn 5 alert 6 advise, clue in, inform, notify 7 apprise, apprize, caution, let in on, let know, prewarn, suggest 8 forewarn, intimate
of the ~: 6 apical
one's hand: 4 show, tell 6 expose, reveal 7 divulge, lay bare, lay open, uncover 8 disclose 9 make known
one's hat to: 4 hail 5 cheer, greet, honor 6 praise, salute 7 applaud, commend 10 compliment
one's topper: 4 doff 5 unhat
over: 4 cant, fall 5 spill, upend, upset 6 topple 7 capsize 8 overturn
(over): 4 keel 6 topple
seller: 4 tout
starter: 4 wing 6 finger, silver
to one side: 3 sag 4 lean, list, rock, sway, tilt 5 lurch, slant, slope 6 careen, totter, wobble 7 incline, stagger
tip __: 5 sheet
__ tip: 4 foul, wing
Tip: 6 O'Neill
Tip-__: 4 Toes
tip-off: 3 cue 4 dope, hint, news, word 6 notice 7 inkling, warning, whisper 8 forecast 9 knowledge 10 prediction, suggestion
__ tip of one's tongue: 5 on the
tip of the __: 7 iceberg
tip one's __: 3 cap, hat 4 hand
Tippecanoe: 5 river
locale: 7 Indiana
__-tip pen: 4 felt
Tipper: 4 Gore
spouse: 6 Al Gore
Tipperary
locale: 4 Eire, Erin 7 Ireland
tippet: 4 cape, wrap 5 scarf
Tippi: 6 Hedren
daughter: 7 Melanie
tipple: 5 drink 6 guzzle, imbibe
tippler: 3 sot 4 lush, wino 5 souse, toper 6 barfly, bibber 7 guzzler, tosspot
debt: 6 bar tab
tippy: 6 wabbly, wobbly 8 unstable, unsteady
tippy-__: 3 toe
tips: 6 income 9 emolument
tip-sheet buyer: 6 bettor 7 wagerer
tipster: 4 fink, tout 8 informer 9 informant
tipsy: 3 lit 4 high 5 dazed, dizzy, drunk, happy, merry, oiled, tight, woozy 6 addled, loaded, mellow, stewed 7 fuddled, reeling 8 besotted, unsteady 9 irrigated 10 inebriated, in one's cups
tip the __: 5 scale 6 scales
tiptoe: 4 skip, step 5 steal 9 pussyfoot 10 walk on eggs
move on ~: 5 creep, slink
Tip-Toes: 7 musical
composer: George Gershwin, Ira Gershwin
Tip-Toe Thru' the Tulips With Me (1968 song)
artist: Tiny Tim
tiptop: 4 acme, apex, best, peak 6 apogee, height, zenith 8 champion
see also wonderful
tirade: 4 rant 5 abuse, anger 6 screed, sermon, speech 7 censure, dispute, lecture, ranting 8 berating, diatribe, harangue, jeremiad, outburst 9 invective, philippic 10 revilement, upbraiding, vocalizing
deliver a ~: 4 rage, rant, rave, yell 5 storm
tiramisu: 4 cake 7 dessert, Italian
Tirana: 4 city, town 7 capital
locale: 7 Albania
Tirane: 4 city, town 7 capital
locale: 7 Albania
tire: 3 irk, sag, sap, tax, try, vex 4 bore, bush, drop, fade, fail, flag, fold, jade, pain, pall, poop, sink, wane, wear, wilt, yawn 5 annoy, blunt, crawl, drain, droop, faint, recap, spare, weary, wheel, worry 6 deject, harass, impair, radial, soften, strain, weaken 7 bias-ply, burn out, deplete, depress, disgust, exhaust, fatigue, give out, go stale, overtax, poop out, retread, slacken, vitiate, wear out 8 collapse, dispirit, distress, enervate, enfeeble, irritate, overwork, peter out, slow down, wear down 9 attenuate, displease, prostrate, undermine, whitewall 10 debilitate, devitalize, dishearten, exasperate, overburden, overstrain, put to sleep
attachment: 3 lug, rim 5 valve 6 hubcap, lug nut
bicycle ~ feature: 5 spoke
brand: 5 Kelly 6 Cooper, Dunlop 7 General, Pirelli 8 Goodrich, Goodyear, Michelin, Uniroyal 9 Firestone 11 Bridgestone
contents: 3 air
do a ~ job: 5 align, aline
ender: 4 some
extra ~: 5 spare
fixed-up ~: 5 recap
leaky ~ sound: 3 sss 4 ssss
like an old ~: 4 bald
out: 5 drain, weary 7 exhaust, fatigue, frazzle 8 enervate, enfeeble
(out): 4 poop 5 peter 6 tucker
part: 4 belt, tube 5 tread
place for a ~ swing: 4 limb
pressure meas.: 3 psi
spare ~: 4 flab 5 belly 6 paunch 7 stomach 9 bay window
tool: 4 jack, pump
town: 5 Akron
track: 3 rut
trouble: 4 flat 8 puncture
tire __: 4 iron 5 chain
__ tire: 4 flat, snow 5 spare 6 belted, radial 7 bias-ply, studded
tired: 3 old 4 beat, dull, lazy, limp, sick, worn 5 all in, bored, corny, empty, faint, fed up, irked, jaded, musty, seedy, spent, stale, trite, weary, wiped 6 asleep, bleary, bushed, dished, done in, droopy, drowsy, pooped, shabby, sleepy, wasted 7 annoyed, done for, drained, haggard, insipid, rundown, worn out 8 careworn, consumed, drooping, fatigued, finished, flagging, outdated, outmoded, wiped out 9 burned out, enervated, exhausted, hackneyed, irritated, out-of-date, overtaxed, played out, prostrate 10 broken-down, collapsing, distressed, dullsville, half-asleep, knocked out, on the ropes, overworked, petered out, prostrated, threadbare, warmed-over
appear ~: 4 yawn
get ~: 4 fade, flag, jade 5 droop, weary 8 languish, peter out, slow down
(of): 4 sick
partner: 4 sick
__-tired: 3 dog
__ Tired: 4 I'm So
tiredness: 6 anemia 7 anaemia, fatigue, languor 9 lassitude 10 exhaustion
Tired of Waiting for You (1965 song)
artist: Kinks
tireless: 5 eager, grind, hyper, perky 6 active 7 jumping, on the go 8 diligent, resolute, sedulous, vigorous 9 energetic, incessant, laborious, steadfast, strenuous, unwearied 10 determined, persistent, undeterred, unflagging, unwearying
Tiresias: 4 seer 5 Greek
tiresome: 4 drag, dull, flat, hard, yawn 5 heavy, hefty, ho-hum, tough, unfun, vapid, yawny 6 boring, dreary, jading, jejune, stuffy, trying, uncool 7 arduous, humdrum, irksome, lengthy, nowhere, onerous, operose, tedious, too much, wearing 8 a bit much, annoying, boresome, dragging, drudging, exacting, wearying 9 demanding, difficult, fatiguing, laborious, strenuous, vexatious, wearisome 10 burdensome, dullsville, enervating, enervative, exhausting, irritating, monotonous, oppressive, unrelieved
become ~: 4 bore, pall, wear
one: 4 bore, drag, pest, pill
tiresomeness: 3 rut 5 ennui 6 tedium 7 boredom 8 monotony 10 dreariness, insipidity, uniformity
Tiriac: 3 Ion
tiring: 4 hard 6 taxing 7 onerous, tedious 10 enervating, exhausting
tiro
see tyro
Tirtoff, Romain de: 4 Erté 6 artist 7 Russian
'tis
answer: 5 'taint
in the past: 4 'twas
'Tis
author: Frank McCourt
Tisa: 6 Farrow
sister: 3 Mia
tisane: 3 tea 7 herb tea 8 beverage 9 herbal tea
'Tis a pity!: 4 alas 5 alack 6 too bad
Tiselius: 4 Arne
'T' Is for Trespass
author: Sue Grafton
'Tis good to keep __ egg: 5 a nest
Tish
author: Mary Roberts Rinehart
Tisha: 8 Campbell, Sterling

Tishah __: 3 b'Av
Tishri: 5 month 6 Hebrew
predecessor: 4 Elul
successor: 7 Heshvan
Tisiphone: 4 Fury
sister: 6 Alecto 7 Megaera
...'tis of __: 4 thee
tissue: 3 web 4 tela 5 paper, telae 6 muscle 8 gift wrap, membrane
additive: 4 aloe
body ~: 4 tela 5 flesh, telae
build new ~: 4 heal
combining form: 4 hist- 5 histi-, histo-, -plasm 6 histio-
connective ~: 6 fascia
connector: 6 areola, areole
fluid: 5 lymph
of ~: 5 telar
plant ~: 5 xylem 6 cambia
separators: 5 septa
soft ~: 4 flab
target: 4 tear 5 tears
tissue __: 5 paper
__ tissue: 6 facial
tissuelike: 4 soft, thin 5 filmy, gauzy, light, sheer 8 delicate, finespun, gossamer
tit: 4 bird
ender: 3 bit 4 lark, mice 5 mouse
for tat: 7 revenge 8 exchange, reprisal 9 interplay, vengeance
give ~ for tat: 5 spite 6 avenge 7 get even, pay back, revenge 9 retaliate
tit __ tat: 3 for
titan: 5 giant, whale 8 colossus 9 leviathan
Titan: 4 ICBM, moon, Rhea, Thia 5 Atlas, Coeus, Crius, Dione 6 Cronus, Phoebe, Tethys, Themis 7 Eurybia, Iapetus, missile, Oceanus 8 Hyperion 9 Menoetius, Mnemosyne 10 Epimetheus, footballer, Prometheus
locale: 4 silo
parent: 4 Gaea 6 Uranus
planet: 6 Saturn
rocket stage: 5 Agena
Titania: 4 moon 6 sprite
planet: 6 Uranus
spouse: 6 Oberon
titanic: 3 big 4 huge, vast 5 giant, great, jumbo, large 6 mighty 7 hulking, immense, mammoth, massive, sizable 8 colossal, enormous, gigantic, king-size, oversize, sizeable, towering, whapping, whopping 9 herculean, humongous, monstrous, overlarge 10 gargantuan, monumental, prodigious, stupendous, tremendous
Titanic: 4 boat, ship 5 liner
undoing: 4 berg 7 iceberg
Titanic (1997 film)
cast: Kathy Bates, Leonardo DiCaprio, Frances Fisher, Bill Paxton, David Warner, Kate Winslet, Billy Zane
director: James Cameron
titanium: 5 metal 7 element
alloy: 7 nitinol
ore: 8 ilmenite
titanothere: 10 rhinoceros
Titans
home: 9 Tennessee
org.: 3 AFC, NFL
rival: *see* NFL team
sport: 8 football
Titans, The
author: André Maurois
Titan, The
author: Theodore Dreiser
tit-for-tat: 6 in kind
tithe: 3 tax 4 levy 5 tenth 6 donate 8 offering
titian: 3 red 5 color 6 orange
Titian: 6 artist 7 Italian, painter
work: 3 art
Titicaca: 4 lago, lake
locale: 4 Peru 7 Bolivia
titillate: 4 grab, hook, send 5 amuse, tease 6 arouse, excite, please, thrill, tickle, turn on 7 grapple, palpate, provoke 8 interest, intrigue, switch on 9 entertain, fascinate, stimulate, tantalize 10 tickle pink
titillation: 8 pleasure
titivate: 5 preen, primp
title: 3 dub, due, tab, tag 4 call, dame, deed, dibs, duke, earl, head, miss, name, role, sign, term 5 baron, brand, claim, close, count, crest, crown, label, medal, merit, nomen, power, prize, proof, right, style 6 banner, degree, desert, handle, header, laurel, legend, ribbon, rights, rubric 7 address, baptize, caption, dauphin, duchess, epithet, heading, holding, license, moniker 8 baroness, christen, cognomen, countess, document, headline, monicker, pretense, property, streamer, subtitle 9 authority, designate, honorific, occupancy, ownership, privilege, pseudonym, sobriquet 10 commission, decoration, denominate, nom de plume, possession, pretension, salutation
ender: 6 holder
proof of ~: 4 deed
title __: 4 bout, deed, page, role
__ title: 4 half 7 working
titled: 5 elite, lofty, noble 8 elevated, imperial, well-born 9 honorable, patrician 10 upper-class
man: 4 duke, earl, lord, peer 5 baron 7 marquis 8 marquess, viscount
woman: 4 dame 7 duchess 8 baroness, countess
titleholder: 5 champ, owner 6 victor, winner 8 champion
titleless one: 4 pleb 7 peasant 8 commoner, plebeian
titmouse: 4 bird
home: 4 nest
relative: 9 chickadee
__ titmouse: 6 tufted
Tito: 4 Broz 6 Puente 7 Jackson
titter: 4 ha-ha 5 laugh, te-hee 6 cackle, giggle, guffaw, hee-hee 7 break up, chortle, chuckle, crack up, snicker, snigger 8 laughter
tittle: 3 dot, jot 4 atom, iota, mite 5 grain, speck
tittle-__: 6 tattle
Tittle, Y.A.: 2 QB 5 Giant
sport: 8 football
titular: 7 nominal 8 honorary 10 in name only
Titus: 4 book 5 Roman, saint 6 Caesar
follower: 8 Philemon
preceder: 7 Timothy
Titus (1999 film)
cast: Anthony Hopkins, Jessica Lange
Titus Andronicus: 4 play
author: William Shakespeare
role: 5 Aaron 6 Chiron, Lucius, Mutius, Tamora 7 Alarbus, Lavinia, Martius, Publius, Quintus 8 Aemilius 9 Bassianus, Demetrius
Titusville: 4 city, town
locale: 7 Florida
Tiu worshiper: 4 Celt 6 Celtic
Tiverton's river: 3 Exe
tix: 6 ducats, passes
tizzy: 4 flap, huff, snit, stew 5 hoo-ha, upset 6 dither, frenzy, lather 9 agitation
in a ~: 4 agog 5 het up, manic, tense, upset 6 jangly 7 abashed, anxious, excited, frantic 8 fluttery, frenetic, frenzied 9 perturbed 10 distressed, infuriated
__ tizzy: 3 in a
T.J. Hooker (ABC/CBS drama)
cast: James Darren (Off. Jim Corrigan)
Heather Locklear (Off. Stacy Sheridan)
William Shatner (Sgt. T.J. Hooker)
Adrian Zmed (Off. Vince Romano)
TKO caller: 3 ref 7 referee
Tl: 4 elem. 7 element 8 thallium
81 for ~: 4 at. no.
TLC: 7 channel, concern 9 attention 10 solicitude
alternative: *see* cable channel
dispenser: 2 RN 3 LPN 5 carer, doter, nurse
part: 4 care 6 loving, tender
TLC (rock group)
members: Watkins, Lopes, Thomas
song: Ain't 2 Proud 2 Beg (1992)
Baby-Baby-Baby (1992)
Creep (1994)
Diggin' on You (1995)
No Scrubs (1999)
Red Light Special (1995)
Unpretty (1999)
Waterfalls (1995)
What About Your Friends (1992)
Tm: 4 elem. 7 element, thulium
69 for ~: 4 at. no.
T-man: 3 agt., Fed 5 agent 8 revenuer
TMC: 7 channel
alternative: *see* movie channel
TM, where to register a: 3 PTO
TN
see Tennessee
__ T. Nelson: 5 Craig
T-note
relative: 2 CD
tnpk.: 2 rd. 3 hwy., rte.
TNT: 7 channel 9 explosive
alternative: *see* cable channel
ingredient: 5 niter
mixture: 6 amatol
part: 3 tri 5 nitro 7 toluene
use ~: 5 blast, wreck 7 explode 8 demolish, dynamite
to: 5 until
in Scottish: 3 tae
to __: 3 wit 4 a man, a tee, boot, date 5 a turn, blame, spare
to __ and to hold: 4 have
to __ intents and purposes: 3 all
to __ nothing of: 3 say
to __ of: 5 speak
to __ phrase: 5 coin a
to __ the band: 4 beat
to __ the least: 3 say
to __ with: 5 start
__ to: 3 due, get, has, hop, lay, lie, put, see, set 4 come, fall, look, next, so as, take, turn 5 add up, alive, bring, cater, ought, owing, prior, privy, put it, refer, stand 6 amount, lead up, thanks
__-to: 3 set 4 lean 7 talking
...to __ few: 5 name a
To __ a Mockingbird: 4 Kill
To __ and a bone...: 4 a rag
To __ and Back: 4 Hell
To __ and Have Not: 4 Have
To __ a Thief: 5 Catch
To __ breeze unfurled: 6 April's
To __ For: 3 Die
To __, From Prison: 6 Althea
To __ go where no man...: 6 boldly
To __ His Own: 4 Each
To __ is human: 3 err
To __ it may concern: 4 whom
To __ Mockingbird: 5 Kill a
To __ not to...: 4 be or
To __ own self...: 5 thine
To __ their golden eyes: 3 ope
To __ the Truth: 4 Tell
To __, With Love: 3 Sir
to a __: 3 man, tee 4 turn 5 fault, woman 6 degree
to a __-thee-well: 4 fare
__ to Abelard: 6 Eloisa
__ to account: 4 call
__ to a crisp: 5 burnt 6 burned
__ to a customer: 3 one
toad: 3 cad, cur, rat 4 heel, worm 5 knave, rogue, scamp, skunk, snake, sneak, swine 6 anuran, bad guy, hopper, wretch 7 lowlife, paddock, stinker, tadpole 9 amphibian, scoundrel, spadefoot 10 blackguard, natterjack
ender: 4 fish, flax 5 eater, stone, stool
feature: 4 wart
group: 4 knot
home: 4 pond
like a ~: 5 warty
relative: 4 frog
tree ~: 4 hyla
__ toad: 4 tree 6 horned
toadeater: 5 sheep 6 fawner, flunky, jackal, lackey, minion, stooge, yes man 7 Babbitt, doormat, flunkey, lacquey 8 adulator, assenter, bootlick, courtier, emulator, groveler, kowtower, parasite, servitor, truckler, yeasayer 9 applauder, flatterer, sycophant 10 bootlicker, conformist, handshaker
toadflax: 4 weed
toadies: 6 claque
toadstool: 5 plant 6 fungus
unlike a ~: 6 edible
toady: 3 bow 4 fawn 5 cower, crawl, kneel, kotow, sheep 6 fawner, flunky, grovel, jackal, kowtow, lackey, minion, stooge, submit, yes

man 7 Babbitt, doormat, flatter, flunkey, lacquey 8 adulator, assenter, bootlick, courtier, emulator, fawn over, groveler, kowtower, kowtow to, parasite, servitor, truckler, yeasayer 9 applauder, flatterer, sycophant 10 bootlicker, conformist, handshaker
act the ~: 5 kotow 6 kowtow
like a ~: 7 servile
to a fare-__-well: 4 thee
__ to a halt: 5 bring, grind
__ to a head: 4 come
__-to-air: 6 ground 7 surface
__ to a Kill: 5 A View
__ to a Kiss: 7 Prelude
__ to Alaska: 5 North
to all __ and purposes: 7 intents
To All the Girls I've Loved Before (1984 song)
artist: Julio Iglesias, Willie Nelson
To a Louse
author: Robert Burns
To Althea from Prison
author: Richard Lovelace
__ to America: 6 Coming
To a Mountain Daisy: 3 ode 4 poem
author: Robert Burns
To a Mouse: 3 ode 4 poem
author: Robert Burns
To an Athlete Dying Young
author: A.E. Housman
to and __: 3 fro
__ to a Nightingale: 3 Ode
To a Poor Old Woman: 4 poem
author: William Carlos Williams
__ to arms: 4 call
To a Skylark: 3 ode 4 poem
author: Percy Bysshe Shelley
__ to a Small Planet: 5 Visit
To Asra
author: Samuel Taylor Coleridge
toast: 3 dry 4 burn, cook, heat, rusk, warm 5 bread, brown, crisp, drink, grill, honor, parch, prost, roast, salud, salut, skoal 6 cheers, pledge, prosit, salute 7 drink to, l'chayim, lehayim, tribute 8 ceremony, here's how, lechayim, libation, proposal 9 happy days, sentiment 10 compliment, here's to you
Cockney ~ start: 4 'eres
edge: 5 crust
ender: 6 master 8 mistress
finish the ~: 5 drink
French ~ word: 5 santé, votre
in French: 5 salut
in German: 6 prosit
In German: 5 prost
in Hebrew: 6 l'chaim
in Portuguese: 5 saude
in Scandinavia: 5 skoal
in Spanish: 5 salud
like ~: 5 brown, crisp 6 crusty 7 crumbly, crunchy
necessity: 5 drink, glass 6 goblet
of the town: 3 VIP 4 hero 5 celeb 6 big gun 7 big name 8 luminary 9 celebrity
Scandinavian ~: 5 skoal
sound of a ~: 5 clink
topper: 3 jam 4 oleo 5 jelly 6 butter
where ~ s are proposed: 4 dais
word: 3 mud 6 health
__ toast: 4 milk 5 Melba 6 French
To a Steam Roller
poet: Marianne Moore
Toasted Oatmeal: 6 cereal
competitor: *see* cereal
toaster __: 4 oven 6 pastry
toastmaster: 2 MC 4 host 5 emcee 7 hostess 10 introducer
Toast of New York, The (1937 film)
director: Rowland V. Lee
toasty: 3 hot 4 cosy, cozy, warm 6 sultry 7 boiling, summery 8 broiling, ovenlike, sizzling, tropical 10 sweltering
__ to a T: 3 fit 4 suit
__ to a turn: 4 done
__ to Autumn: 3 Ode
To Autumn: 3 ode 4 poem
author: John Keats
To a Waterfowl: 3 ode 4 poem
author: William Cullen Bryant
tobacco: 4 shag 6 burley
dryer: 4 oast
Tobacco Road
author: Erskine Caldwell
character: 3 Ada, Lov 4 Dude 6 Bensey, Bessie, Jeeter, Lester
Toback: 5 James
Tobago: 4 isle 6 island
neighbor: 4 Trin. 8 Trinidad
__ to Bali: 4 Road
__-to-basics: 4 back
to be
in French: 4 être
in Italian: 3 ser
in Latin: 4 esse
in Spanish: 3 ser 5 estar
like ~: 3 irr. 5 irreg. 9 irregular
part of ~: 3 are, was 4 been, were
to be __: 4 fair, sure
Tobe: 6 Hooper
To be __...: 5 or not
To Be a Lover (1986 song)
artist: Billy Idol
__ to bear: 5 bring
to beat the __: 4 band
__ to Beauty: 3 Ode
__ to be born...: 5 A time
__ to bed: 3 put 5 And so
__ to Be Happy: 5 I Want
__ to Be Hard: 4 Easy
__ to Be in Love: 5 I Need
To Be or Not to Be (1983 film): 6 remake
cast: Anne Bancroft, Mel Brooks, Jose Ferrer
director: Mel Brooks
dog: 5 Mutki
__ to Berlin: 7 Goodbye
Tobermory
author: Saki
__ to be seen: 7 remains
__ to Be There: 3 Got
__ to be tied: 3 fit
__ to Be Wild: 4 Born
__ to Be With You: 4 Born, Nice
To Be with You (1992 song)
artist: Mr. Big
Tobey: 7 Maguire
__ to Be You: 5 It Had
To Be Young, Gifted and Black
author: Lorraine Hansberry
Tobias: 5 Asser 6 Andrew, George 8 Smollett
__ to Billie Joe: 3 Ode
__ to black: 4 fade
Toblerone: 5 candy, Swiss 9 chocolate
__ to blows: 4 come
toboggan: 4 sled 5 slide 6 bobcat
area: 5 chute 6 ice run
cousin: 4 luge
go by ~: 5 slide
tobogganing: 5 sport
__-to book: 3 how
__ to Bountiful, The: 4 Trip
Tobruk: 4 city, town
locale: 5 Libya
...to buy __ hog: 4 a fat
...to buy __ pig: 4 a fat
toby: 3 jug, mug 5 stein
contents: 3 ale 4 beer, brew 5 stout 6 porter
Toby: 5 Belch, Keith, Tyler 6 Harrah
author: Sidney Sheldon
__ to Byzantium: 7 Sailing
To Catch a Thief (1955 film)
cast: Cary Grant, Grace Kelly
director: Alfred Hitchcock
Toccata Festiva
composer: Samuel Barber
To Celia
author: Ben Jonson
__ to Come: 6 Things
__ to Cook Book, The: 5 I Hate
__-tocopherol: 5 alpha
__ to Creation: 3 Ode
tocsin: 4 bell 5 alarm, alert 6 signal 7 warning
tod: 3 ivy 4 mass 5 clump 6 weight 7 measure
Tod: 8 Browning
__ Tod: 4 Ase's
__ to Dance: 4 Born
today: 3 now 6 at once, modern, recent 7 present 8 promptly, right now, right off, up-to-date 9 at present, currently, forthwith, in this era, presently, right away 10 at this time, aujourd'hui, here and now, the present, this minute
__ today: 4 as of
Today __ a man!: 3 I am
__ Today: 3 USA
__ today, gone...: 4 Here
__ today, hot tamale: 5 Chili
Today's Children: 9 radio show
Today Show, The
chimp: 5 Beebe, Muggs
host: 5 Lauer 6 Gumbel, Pauley 8 Garroway
rival: 3 GMA
weatherman: 5 Roker
Todd: 3 Ann 4 Mike, Tony 6 Duncan, Haynes, Thelma 7 Bridges, Richard, Solondz, Sweeney 8 Rundgren 9 Alexander
toddle: 4 walk 6 waddle 7 saunter
toddler: 3 tot 4 baby, tike, tyke 5 child 6 infant, moppet, rug rat 8 juvenile
glassful: 4 wawa
mishap: 5 spill
perch: 3 lap 4 knee
question: 3 why
ritual: 3 nap
school: 4 pre-K
vehicle: 5 trike
watch a ~: 3 sit
wear: 6 diaper
words to a ~: 3 nos 4 noes
see also tot
toddlers: 8 small fry
__ Todd Lincoln: 4 Mary
toddling: 4 poky 6 draggy 7 gradual, halting, impeded, lagging, languid 8 dilatory, drawn-out, hesitant, plodding, slothful, sluggish 9 leisurely, lethargic, prolonged, snaillike, unhurried 10 deliberate, protracted
Todd, Mary
spouse: 3 Abe 7 Abraham, Lincoln
Todd, Mike
spouse: Joan Blondell, Elizabeth Taylor
Todd, Sweeney street: 5 Fleet
toddy: 4 palm 5 drink 8 beverage
hot ~ spice: 5 clove
__ toddy: 3 hot
To Die For (1995 film)
cast: Matt Dillon, Illeana Douglas, Nicole Kidman, Joaquin Phoenix
director: Gus Van Sant
dog: 6 Walter
__ to differ!: 4 I beg
to-do: 3 row 4 flap, fuss, riot, spat, stir 5 fight, furor, hoo-ha, mania, melee, run-in, scene, stink, storm, whirl 6 bother, bustle, clamor, flurry, fracas, frenzy, hassle, hoopla, hubbub, matter, pother, racket, ruckus, rumpus, tumult, unrest, uproar 7 ferment, quarrel, ruction, trouble, turmoil 8 activity, brouhaha, busyness, disorder, disquiet, foofaraw, rowdydow 9 agitation, commotion 10 difficulty, donnybrook, excitement, hullabaloo, hurly-burly
list: 6 agenda
list entry: 3 job 4 item, task 5 chore 6 errand 7 project
to-do __: 4 list
__-to-do: 4 well
__ to Duty: 3 Ode
toe: 5 digit 6 dactyl, hallux, member 7 minimus 9 appendage, extremity
combining form: 6 dactyl- 7 dactylo-
ender: 3 cap 4 hold, nail
hurt one's ~: 4 stub
in the water: 4 test
starter: 3 tip
stubber's cry: 2 ow 3 yow 4 ouch, yeow
the line: 4 heed, mind, obey 5 agree, bow to, defer, yield 6 accept, adhere, behave, bend to, comply, follow, fulfil, listen, submit 7 conform, consent, fulfill, observe, respect 8 carry out 10 keep in step
topper: 4 nail 6 enamel, polish
tot's ~: 5 piggy 6 piggie
woe: 4 corn, gout 6 agnail, bunion
toe __: 4 clip, loop, pick 5 dance
__ toe: 3 big
__-toe: 5 tippy
To Each His Own (1960 song)
artist: Platters
__ to earth: 3 run
__-to-earth: 4 down
To Earthward: 4 poem
author: Robert Frost
__-toed: 3 web 6 pigeon
__-toed sloth: 3 two 5 three
toehold: 5 ledge, niche, way in 6 access
toe-in: 6 camber
toeing the line: 5 loyal 8 obedient

toe loop: **4** jump
where to do a ~: **3** ice **4** rink
toenail: **6** unguis
To err is __: **5** human
toes
on one's ~: **4** atip, wary **5** alert, awake, ready **7** heads-up, heedful, mindful **8** cautious, vigilant, watchful **9** attentive, observant, wide-awake
tread on one's ~: **3** bug, get, irk, try, vex **4** gall, miff, rile **5** annoy, grate, peeve, pique **6** bother, enrage, nettle, offend, ruffle **7** affront, agitate, disturb, incense, inflame, outrage, provoke **8** distress, irritate **9** infuriate **10** antagonize, exasperate
To E.T.
author: Robert Frost
toe the __: **4** line, mark
Toe, The: Lou Groza
toe-to-toe, go: **5** fight **6** battle
__ to Exhale: **7** Waiting
__ to Extremes: **3** I Go
...to fetch __ of water: **5** a pail
toff: **4** dude **5** dandy **9** pretty boy **10** jack-a-dandy
toffee: **5** candy **8** ice cream **9** sweetmeat
alternative: *see* ice cream flavor
like ~: **5** chewy **7** crunchy
Toffler: **5** Alvin
__-to-five: **4** nine
__-to-fiver: **4** nine
To form __ perfect Union...: **5** a More
To F.S.O.
author: Edgar Allan Poe
tofu: **6** legume **8** bean curd
base: **3** soy **4** soya
tog: **4** coat **5** dress **6** clothe, outfit **7** garment
out: **4** deck, garb **5** array, dress **6** attire, clothe **7** bedrape
toga: **7** garment
alternative: **5** tunic
venue: **4** frat, Rome **5** Forum **10** fraternity
__ to get: **4** hard
together: **3** one **4** calm, cool, sane **5** as one, at one, lucid, sound, whole **6** at once, en bloc, in step, in sync, intact, stable **7** en masse, en suite, jointly, unapart **8** as a group, combined, commonly, composed, in unison, mutually, rational, sensible, unitedly **9** all at once, at one time, collected, in concert **10** conjointly, hand in hand, phlegmatic, reasonable, side by side, unagitated
in music: **4** a due
prefix: **3** col-, com-, con-, sym-, syn-
__ together: **3** get, put **4** hang, pull **6** cobble
__-together: **3** get
__ Together: **3** Get **4** Come **5** Get It, Happy
Together Again (1997 song)
artist: Janet Jackson
Together Forever (1988 song)
artist: Rick Astley
togetherness: **5** synch, unity **7** rapport **9** proximity
__ to get ready...: **5** three
toggery: **4** garb **6** attire **7** clothes
toggle __: **4** bolt **6** switch
To Gillian on Her 37th Birthday (1996 film)
cast: Claire Danes, Peter Gallagher, Michelle Pfeiffer
__ to Give It Up: **3** Got
Tognazzi: **3** Ugo
__ to go: **5** rarin' **6** raring
__ to go!: **3** Way
Togo: **6** nation **7** country
capital: **4** Lomé
language: **3** Ewe, Gbe
locale: **3** Afr. **6** Africa
money: **5** franc
neighbor: **5** Benin, Ghana
people: **3** Ewe **6** Yoruba
__-to-God: **6** honest
to go. like: **3** irr. **5** irreg. **9** irregular
__-to-goodness: **6** honest
to-go order: **3** BLT **5** pizza **6** burger, hot dog **8** sandwich **9** hamburger
__-to-ground: **3** air
__ to grow on: **3** one
togs: **4** duds, gear **5** dress, getup, jeans **6** attire, outfit **7** apparel, clothes, jerseys, raiment, threads **8** clothing, ensemble, garments, glad rags, wardrobe **9** jumpsuits **10** Sunday best
to have __ hold: **5** and to
To Have and Have Not: **4** film **5** novel
author: Ernest Hemingway
cast: Lauren Bacall, Humphrey Bogart
director: Howard Hawks
__ to heart: **4** take
To Helen
author: Edgar Allan Poe
To Hell and Back (1955 film)
cast: Audie Murphy
To His Coy Mistress: **4** poem
author: Andrew Marvell
__ to Hold Your Hand: **5** I Want
__ to home: **5** close
To Homer: **3** ode **4** poem
author: John Keats
to-ho shouter: **6** hunter
toil: **3** job **4** grub, moil, plod, plug, slog, task, wade, work **5** grind, labor, pains, serve, slave, sweat **6** drudge, effort, strain, strive **7** peg away, slavery, travail **8** drudgery, endeavor, exercise, exertion, hardship, industry, struggle **9** grind away, grunt work, hard labor, lucubrate, slave away **10** nine-to-five
ender: **4** some
toil and __: **7** trouble
toile: **6** fabric **8** material
toiler: **5** labor, slave **6** drudge, worker
toilet: **2** WC **3** lav, loo **4** john **7** latrine **8** bathroom, lavatory, rest room
water: **5** scent **7** cologne, perfume **9** fragrance
toilet __: **3** set **4** soap **5** water
toiletries case: **4** etui **5** etwee **6** kitbag
__ toilette: **5** eau de
toilet water: **5** scent
toiling away: **4** at it, busy
toils: **3** web **4** mesh
toilsome: **4** hard **5** heavy, rough, tough **6** severe, thorny, trying, uphill **7** arduous, hard-won, labored, onerous, operose **8** grueling **9** demanding, difficult, herculean, laborious, strenuous **10** formidable, oppressive
To Isadore
author: Edgar Allan Poe
__ to it: **3** get, hop, see
__-to-it-ive: **5** stick
__-toity: **5** hoity
To Jerusalem and Back
author: Saul Bellow
__ to Joy: **3** Ode
Tokar: **6** Norman
tokay: **5** gecko **6** lizard
Tokay: **4** wine **5** grape, white
origin: **7** Hungary
relative: *see* wine
toke: **3** tip
token: **4** coin, gage, gift, hint, mark, note, omen, pawn, sign **5** badge, favor, index, proof, relic, trace **6** emblem, herald, pledge, sample, signal, symbol, ticket **7** earnest, memento, minimal, nominal, presage, promise, symptom, vestige, warning **8** evidence, gratuity, indicium, keepsake, reminder, security, souvenir **10** expression, indication
by the same ~: **3** and, yet **4** also **6** as well **7** besides, further **8** moreover
taker: **4** slot
user: **4** fare **5** rider **9** passenger
Tokens
song: The Lion Sleeps Tonight (1961)
__ to Kill: **4** Born, Hard **5** A Time **7** Dressed, Licence
To Kill a Mockingbird: **4** film **5** novel
author: Harper Lee
cast: Robert Duvall, Gregory Peck, Brock Peters
character: **3** Boo, Jem **4** Dill **5** Ewell, Finch, Scout **6** Radley **7** Atticus **9** Boo Radley
screenwriter: **5** Foote
Toklas: **5** Alice **6** Alice B.
friend: **5** Stein
__-to-know: **5** right
__-to-know basis: **4** need
To Know Him, Is to Love Him (1958 song)
artist: Teddy Bears
To know me __...: **4** is to
__ to Know You: **7** Getting
Toko-Ri structure: **6** bridge
Tokyo: **4** city, port, town **7** capital
airport: **6** Narita
area: **5** Ginza
destroyer: **5** Rodan
former name: **3** Edo **4** Yedo **5** Yeddo
locale: **5** Hondo, Japan **6** Honshu
river: **6** Sumida
town near ~: **5** Nagai, Urawa
Tokyo __: **3** Bay **4** Rose
Tokyo Woes
author: Bruce Jay Friedman
told: **4** oral **6** spoken, verbal
be ~: **4** hear **5** catch, learn **6** pick up **7** find out, receive **8** discover **9** ascertain, get wind of **10** understand
do as ~: **4** mind, obey **6** behave, comply, listen **7** abide by, respect **8** take heed **10** toe the line
I ~ you so: **3** see
__ told: **3** all
__-told: **5** twice
...__ told by an idiot: **5** a tale
Told by an Idiot
author: Rose Macaulay
__ Told Ev'ry Little Star: **3** I've
__ Told Me: **4** Mama **6** Nobody
__-Told Tales: **5** Twice
tole: **9** metalware **10** enamelware
material: **3** tin
__ to leap tall buildings...: **4** Able
Toledo: **4** city, town
athletes: **7** Rockets
conference: **3** MAC
county: **5** Lucas
lake: **4** Erie
locale: **4** Ohio **5** Spain **6** España
newspaper: **5** Blade
product: **5** steel
river: **4** Tejo **5** Tegus
see also Spanish
Toler: **6** Sidney
role: **4** Chan
tolerable: **2** OK **4** fair, okay, so-so, tidy **6** decent, medium, not bad, venial **7** average, livable **8** adequate, all right, bearable, liveable, mediocre, middling, moderate, ordinary, passable **9** endurable, unnotable **10** acceptable, admissible, forgivable, good enough, reasonable, sufficient
tolerably: **4** so-so **6** rather **8** somewhat **10** adequately, moderately
tolerance: **5** grace, mercy **6** leeway **7** charity, freedom, license, stamina **8** altruism, clemency, goodwill, humanity, kindness, lenience, leniency, patience, strength, sympathy **9** endurance, fortitude, hardiness **10** compassion, indulgence, resilience, resistance, steadiness
tolerant: **3** big, lax **4** easy, fair, just, kind, meek, mild, soft, wide **5** broad, loose, noble **6** gentle, humane, kindly, tender **7** clement, lenient, liberal, patient, ruthful, sparing **8** catholic, flexible, laid-back, merciful, moderate, placable, unstrict **9** assuasive, compliant, condoning, easygoing, forgiving, indulgent, receptive **10** benevolent, charitable, forbearing, open-minded, permissive, reasonable, unexacting, unhardened
tolerate: **3** let **4** bear, bide, have, lump, take **5** abide, allow, brook, humor, stand, stick **6** accept, endure, excuse, permit, suffer, wink at **7** blink at, condone, indulge, let ride, stomach, sustain, swallow, undergo **8** accede to, assent to, bear with, live with, sanction, stand for, tough out **9** approve of, authorize, consent to, put up with, withstand **10** understand
can't ~: **4** hate **5** abhor **6** detest, loathe **7** despise
toleration: **6** lenity **9** allowance, endurance **10** indulgence
__ to Liberty: **3** Ode

__ to life: 4 come, true 5 bring
__ to light: 4 come 5 bring
__ to Live: 5 A Rage
__ to Live!: 5 I Want
To Live and Die __: 4 in L.A.
Tolkien, J.R.R.: 6 writer 7 British
creature: 3 Ent, orc 6 hobbit
work: The Fellowship of the Ring
The Hobbit
The Lord of the Rings
The Return of the King
The Silmarillion
The Two Towers
toll: 3 fee, tax 4 bong, cost, duty, fare, gong, levy, peal, rate, ring 5 chime, clang, knell, price 6 charge, damage, impost, losses, strain, tariff, towage 7 penalty, ring out, tribute 8 exaction 10 assessment
ender: 4 gate 5 booth, house
road: 3 tpk. 4 pike, tnpk. 5 route 7 highway 8 turnpike
stop: 5 stile
take a ~ on: 3 tax 6 strain
toll __: 3 bar 4 call, line, road 6 bridge
Toll __ cookies: 5 House
tollbooth site: 5 plaza
toll collector, name meaning: 7 Travers
toll-free __: 4 call
tollhouse: 6 cookie
__ toll on: 5 take a
Tolomeo
composer: George Frideric Handel
__ to Look At: 6 Lovely
__ to Love: 4 Easy 7 Goodbye, Someone
Tolstoy, Leo: 6 writer 7 Russian
title: 5 Count
work: Anna Karenina
The Cossacks
The Death of Ivan Ilyich
War and Peace
Toltec: 5 Nahua 6 Indian 7 Amerind
city: 4 Tula
To Lucasta, Going to the Wars
author: Richard Lovelace
__ to lunch: 3 out
tom: 3 cat 4 male 6 turkey 7 gobbler
ender: 3 boy, cat, cod, tit 4 fool 7 foolery
mate: 3 hen
Tom: 3 cat, Mix 4 Bell, Gola, Joad, kite 5 Brown, Conti, Dewey, Drake, Ewell, Foley, Gries, Hanks, Hulce, Jones, Kalin, Mboya, Petty, Ridge, Sneva, Swift, Tryon, uncle, Waits, Wolfe, Wopat 6 Arnold, Bosley, Brokaw, Clancy, Conway, Cruise, Harkin, Harmon, Hayden, Landry, Lehrer, Lester, Noonan, Parker, Poston, Sawyer, Seaver, Snyder, Watson 7 Bradley, DiCillo, Glavine, Holland, Johnson, Kennedy, Robbins, Selleck, Shadyac, Shipley, Welling 8 Berenger, Cochrane, Heinsohn, Laughlin, Sizemore, Skerritt, Smothers, Stoppard 9 Courtenay
Tom & __: 3 Viv
Tom __: 5 Thumb 6 Dooley 7 Collins
Tom, __ and Harry: 4 Dick
tomahawk: 2 ax 3 axe 7 hatchet
Tom and Jerry: 5 drink 8 beverage, cocktail
bulldog: 5 Spike
cat: 3 Tom
dog: 5 Jerry
ingredient: 3 egg, rum 4 eggs, milk
__ to Marry a Millionaire: 3 How
Tomás: 10 Torquemada
tomato: 4 Roma, soup 5 fruit, sauce 6 Big Boy, cherry, veggie 9 beefsteak, Better Boy, Early Girl, love apple, Quick Pick, vegetable
container: 3 can
impact sound: 5 splat
pest: 5 aphid, aphis
plant support: 5 stake
product: 5 aspic, paste, purée, sauce
sauce ingredient: 5 basil, purée
__ tomato: 4 plum 6 cherry
__ to maturity: 5 yield
Tomba, Alberto: 5 skier 7 Italian
Tombaugh, Clyde: 10 astronomer
discovery: 5 Pluto
tomboy: 6 hoiden, hoyden
Tomb Raider heroine: 4 Lara 5 Croft
Tombstone: 4 town 5 pizza
alternative: 5 Jeno's, Tony's 6 Ellio's 7 Celeste, Totino's 8 DiGiorno 10 Freschetta
locale: 4 Ariz. 7 Arizona
marshal: 4 Earp
newspaper: 7 Epitaph
Tombstone (1993 film)
cast: Powers Boothe, Val Kilmer, Kurt Russell
tomcat: 3 gib 4 male, puss 6 feline
Tom Collins ingredient: 3 gin 4 lime, soda 5 lemon
Tom Corbett, Space Cadet
role: 5 Astro
Tom, Dick and Harry: 4 trio 5 males
Tom, Dick, or Harry: 4 male
Tom Dooley (1958 song)
artist: Kingston Trio
tome: 2 bk. 3 vol 4 book, opus 6 volume 7 classic, writing 9 great work 10 magnum opus
home: 5 shelf 9 bookshelf
__ Tomé and Principe: 3 Sao
__-to-measure: 4 made
Tomei: 6 Marisa 8 Concetta
Tomei, Marisa: 7 actress
film: In the Bedroom (2001)
My Cousin Vinny (1992, AA)
Only You (1994)
The Paper (1994)
Slums of Beverly Hills (1998)
What Women Want (2000)
__ to mention: 3 not
__ to Me Only With Thine Eyes: 5 Drink
__ to Methuselah: 4 Back
tomfool: 3 lug, mad, oaf 4 boor, clod, daft, dolt, dope, goof, jerk, lout, mutt, rube, yo-yo 5 batty, chump, daffy, dunce, flaky, goofy, inane, nutty, silly, wacky 6 absurd, dimwit, freaky, galoot, lummox, nitwit, screwy 7 asinine, bumbler, bumpkin, dingbat, fathead, fumbler, half-wit, jackass, jughead, palooka, pinhead 8 bonehead, dumbbell, dummkopf, goofball, lunkhead, meathead, numskull 9 birdbrain, blockhead, ding-a-ling, harebrain, ignoramus, illogical, lamebrain, laughable, ludicrous, senseless, simpleton 10 dunderhead, muttonhead, off-the-wall, ridiculous, stumblebum
tomfoolery: 3 fun 4 jape, jest 5 antic, caper, humor, prank, sport, trick 6 antics, capers, pranks 7 inanity 8 mischief 9 escapades, funniness, goofiness 10 friskiness, hanky-panky, impishness, jocoseness
__ to middling: 4 fair
__ to mind: 4 come 5 bring
Tom Jones: 4 film 5 novel
author: Henry Fielding
cast: Albert Finney, Hugh Griffith, Susannah York
character: 6 Blifil, Sophia
director: Tony Richardson
Tomlin, Lily: 7 actress 10 comedienne
film: All of Me (1984)
The Beverly Hillbillies (1993)
Big Business (1988)
The Late Show (1977)
Nashville (1975)
Nine to Five (1980)
TV: Rowan & Martin's Laugh-In
To M.L.S.
author: Edgar Allan Poe
Tommie: 4 Agee 5 Aaron
Tommies
of WWI: 3 BEF
Tommy: 3 Lee, Moe, Roe 4 Bolt, John, Kirk, Page, Tune 5 Aaron, Boyce, Chong, James, opera, Sands 6 Armour, Dorsey, Norden, Rettig, Steele 7 Edwards, Henrich, Lasorda, soldier 8 Hilfiger, Smothers
ally: 5 poilu
band: Who, The
Tommy (1975 film)
cast: Ann-Margret, Roger Daltrey
Tommy __: 3 gun 6 Atkins
Tommy __ Jones: 3 Lee
tommy ender: 3 rot
Tommy gun: 4 Sten
Tommyknockers, The
author: Stephen King
tommyrot
see baloney
__ to Morocco: 4 Road
tomorrow: 6 future, mañana
preceder: 5 today
Tomorrow: 4 song
composer: Martin Charnin, Charles Strouse
musical: 5 Annie
Tomorrow File, The
author: Lawrence Sanders
Tomorrow I Die
author: Mickey Spillane
Tomorrow Never Dies (1997 film)
cast: Pierce Brosnan, Judi Dench, Teri Hatcher, Jonathan Pryce, Michelle Yeoh
__-to-mouth: 4 hand
Tom Sawyer: 5 novel
author: Mark Twain
character: 3 Joe, Sid 4 Finn, Mary, Muff 5 Becky, Polly 8 Injun Joe, Thatcher 9 Aunt Polly, Joe Harper 10 Muff Potter 11 Huckleberry
__ Tom's Cabin: 5 Uncle
Toms, David: 6 golfer
Tom's Diner (1990 song)
artist: Suzanne Vega
Tom's of Maine: 10 toothpaste
alternative: ***see*** toothpaste
Tom T. __: 4 Hall
Tom Terrific dog: 7 Manfred
tom thumb (1958 film)
cast: Peter Sellers, Russ Tamblyn
director: George Pal
Tom Thumb
author: Henry Fielding
tom-tom: 4 drum
Tom, Tom, the Piper's __: 3 Son
Tom & Viv (1994 film)
cast: Willem Dafoe, Miranda Richardson
__ to My Lou: 4 Skip
To My Mother
author: Edgar Allan Poe
Tomy product: 3 toy
ton: 4 chic, lots, raft 5 bunch, ocean, scads, style, vogue 6 oodles, passel 8 mountain 9 profusion
bon ~: 4 chic, dash 5 class, style, vogue
fraction: 2 lb. 3 cwt. 5 pound
hit like a ~ of bricks: 3 jar 4 jolt, kayo, stun 5 shock 6 bedaze 7 astound, flummox, horrify, nonplus, outrage, stagger, stupefy, terrify 8 astonish, bewilder, blow away, bowl over, confound, knock out, paralyze, surprise, unsettle 9 dumbfound, overpower, overwhelm, take aback 10 discompose
starter: 4 mega 6 double
__ ton: 3 bon, net 4 long 5 short 6 metric
tonal: 5 on key 7 melodic, musical 8 harmonic
combination: 5 chord, triad
tonality: 5 sound 6 accent 10 inflection
tone: 3 air, hue 4 aura, beep, cast, feel, gird, mood, note, tint, vein 5 blend, build, chime, color, drift, humor, pitch, shade, shore, sound, steel, style, tenor, tinct, tinge, trend, voice 6 accent, anneal, beef up, firm up, flavor, harden, manner, prop up, spirit, strain, temper, timbre 7 bolster, brace up, build up, burgeon, cadence, cadency, develop, empower, enhance, fortify, quality, shore up, stiffen, toughen 8 ambiance, ambience, attitude, bourgeon, buttress, coloring, emphasis, energize, indurate, sonority, vitalize 9 character, condition, intensify, reinforce, resonance 10 elasticity, inflection, intonation, invigorate, modulation, resiliency
down: 3 dim 4 fade, mute, tame 5 lower, mince, quiet, relax, shade 6 dampen, darken, deaden, lessen, modify, muffle, obtund, reduce, soften, subdue, temper 7 let up on 8 mitigate, moderate, modulate, restrain, slack off 9 soft-pedal 10 keep in line
earth ~: 5 beige, brown, ocher, ochre, umber
emotional ~: 3 air 4 aura, mood

5 humor, state, tenor 6 nature, spirit, temper 7 climate, feeling 8 attitude 9 character
hushed ~: 6 murmur
prefix for ~: 4 mono
skin ~: 4 look 5 flesh 6 aspect 8 coloring 10 appearance, complexion
up: 4 firm 7 work out 8 exercise 9 condition 10 strengthen
tone __: 3 arm, row 4 down, poem
tone-__: 4 deaf
__ tone: 4 dial, half 5 earth
__-tone: 3 two 5 touch
Tone: 4 soap 8 Franchot
alternative: *see* soap
toned: 3 fit 4 hale, trim 5 agile, burly, hardy, tough 6 brawny, robust, strong 7 healthy 8 athletic, muscular 9 strapping 10 able-bodied
down: 3 dim, low 4 soft 5 faint, piano, quiet, sober 6 low-key 7 subdued
__-toned: 4 high 6 copper
Tone, Franchot: 5 actor
spouse: Joan Crawford
toneless: 4 weak 5 unfit 6 flabby 7 droning, flaccid, uniform 8 singsong 9 unvarying 10 monotonous, out of shape
Tone Loc: 6 rapper
born: Anthony Smith
song: Funky Cold Medina (1989) Wild Thing (1988)
tone of __: 5 voice
__-tone phone: 5 touch
toner: 6 dry ink, imager 9 skin cream
tonette: 4 wind 5 flute 10 instrument
Tong: 6 Sammee
Tonga: 4 isle 6 island, nation 7 country
capital: 9 Nuku'alofa
neighbor: 4 Fiji, Niue 5 Samoa
tongs: 7 forceps
__ tongs: 3 ice
tongue: 5 argot, idiom, lingo, organ, shaft, strip, voice 6 glossa, lingua, patois, speech 7 clapper, dialect 8 language, parlance 10 vernacular
bone: 5 hyoid
clicking sound: 3 tsk 6 tsk tsk
combining form: 4 -glot
covering: 4 coat
hinged ~: 4 pawl
hold one's ~: 6 clam up, shut up 7 silence
in cheek: 7 as a joke 8 jokingly 9 jestingly, kiddingly
mollusk's ~: 6 radula
neighbor: 5 uvula
one with a forked ~: 4 liar
part: 6 frenum 7 fraenum
partner: 6 groove
part of a dog's ~: 5 lytta
sharp of ~: 4 tart 5 acerb 6 bitter 7 caustic 9 sarcastic
slip of the ~: 5 gaffe 7 blunder, faux pas, mistake
speak with forked ~: 3 fib, lie 4 dupe 5 bluff, fudge, guile 6 delude 7 deceive, falsify, mislead 8 misspeak 9 dissemble, misinform
see also language
tongue __: 7 twister
tongue-__: 3 tie 4 lash, tied 7 lashing
tongue-burning: 6 bitter
__-tongued: 4 acid, long 5 loose, sharp 6 silver, smooth
tongue-in-cheek: 7 jesting, playful
tongue-lash: 3 jaw, nag, rag 4 carp, harp, lash, rail, whip 5 scold 6 berate 7 upbraid 9 castigate, dress down, reprehend
tongue-lashing: 5 abuse 6 rebuke, tirade 9 reprimand
give a ~: 3 rag 5 blame, decry, scold 6 berate, punish, rebuke 7 censure, contemn, reprove, tell off 8 denounce, reproach 9 inculpate, reprehend, reprimand 10 denunciate
tonguelike part: 6 ligula
tongues do it: 3 wag 4 lash
tongue-tie: 3 gag 7 silence
tongue-tied: 3 mum 4 mute 6 silent 7 at a loss 8 choked up, nonvocal, wordless 9 voiceless 10 dumbstruck, incoherent, speechless, unspeaking
tongue-wagging: 6 drivel, patter 7 chatter, palaver, prattle 8 chitchat
Toni: 5 Basil 6 Fisher 7 Bambara, Braxton 8 Collette, Morrison, Tennille
tonic: 4 drug, soda 5 drink 6 bracer, elixir, fillip, pickup, potion 7 cordial, healthy 8 curative, medicine, pick-me-up, sanative, stimulus 9 stimulant 10 invigorant, medication
amount: 4 dose 6 dosage
companion: 3 gin
ingredient: 7 bitters
starter: 3 iso
water: 4 fizz, soda 5 mixer 7 seltzer 8 club soda
tonic __: 5 water
Tonight (song)
artist: Ferrante & Teicher, New Kids on the Block
Tonight, I Celebrate My Love (1983 song)
artist: Peabo Bryson, Roberta Flack
Tonight She Comes (1985 song)
artist: Cars
Tonight Show
bandleader: 5 Melis 10 Severinsen
host: 4 Leno, Paar 5 Allen 6 Carson, O'Brien
regular: 3 Nye 7 McMahon
theme composer: Paul Anka
Tonight's the Night (1976 song)
artist: Rod Stewart
Tonight, Tonight, Tonight (1987 song)
artist: Genesis
Tonight You Belong to Me (1956 song)
artist: Patience & Prudence
toning target: 4 flab 6 muscle
Tonio Kroger
author: Thomas Mann
__-tonk: 5 honky
Tonka product: 3 toy 5 Gobot, truck
Tonkin: 4 gulf
locale: 3 Nam 5 Hanoi 7 Vietnam
tonnage: 4 size 5 cargo 6 weight
to no __: 5 avail
Tono-__: 6 Bungay
__ to none: 4 slim
tons: 4 a lot, lots, many, much, scad 5 loads, ocean 6 hoards, oodles, plenty, scores 7 legions 10 inundation
__ Tons: 7 Sixteen
tonsil neighbor: 5 uvula
tonsorial
artist: 6 barber, shaver
challenge: 3 mop
item: 4 comb 5 razor, strop
procedure: 3 cut 4 clip, trim 5 shave
__ ton soup: 3 won
tonsure: 5 shave
tonsured: 5 shorn
tontine: 4 pact 6 pledge
Tonto: 3 cat 4 hero 6 Indian
friend: 8 Kemo Sabe 10 Long Ranger
horse: 5 Scout
__-to-nuts: 4 soup
tony: 3 mod 5 ritzy, swank, swish 6 chichi, classy, modish, swanky, trendy 7 à la mode, current, in style, popular, stylish, upscale, voguish 9 high-toned, in fashion 10 all the rage
Tony: 3 Dow 4 Bill, Lema, Peña, Rome, Sarg, Todd, Zale 5 award, Blair, Danza, Gwynn, horse, Kubek, Oliva, Perez, Scott, tiger 6 Curtis, equine, Martin 7 Bennett, Dorsett, Goldwyn, Kushner, La Russa, Lazzeri, Musante, Orlando, Perkins, Randall, Roberts, Soprano, Trabert 8 Lo Bianco, Luraschi, Shalhoub 9 Franciosa 10 Richardson
daughter: 8 Jamie Lee
of cereal fame: 5 tiger
relative: 4 Obie 5 Oscar
rider: Tom Mix
Tonya: 7 Harding
Tony's: 5 pizza
alternative: 5 Jeno's 6 Ellio's 7 Celeste, Totino's 8 DiGiorno 9 Tombstone 10 Freschetta
Tony the Tiger favorite word: 5 great
too: 3 yet 4 also, ever, more, most, over, plus, very 5 along 6 adverb, as well, beyond, either, overly, to boot, unduly 7 awfully, besides, further 8 likewise, moreover, overmuch 9 extremely 10 improperly, in addition
familiar: 4 dull, flat 5 banal, corny, hokey, stale, tired, vapid 6 common, jejune, old hat 7 clichéd, insipid, prosaic, routine 8 bromidic, ordinary, shopworn, timeworn 9 hackneyed 10 pedestrian, uninspired, unoriginal, warmed-over
fast: 4 rash 5 brash 6 abrupt, madcap 8 careless, headlong, heedless, pell-mell, reckless, slapdash 9 foolhardy, impetuous, impulsive
feed ~ well: 4 cloy, glut 5 gorge, stuff 7 surfeit 8 overfill 10 gormandize
frank: 9 impolitic 10 indiscreet
frugal: 4 mean, near 5 cheap 6 greedy, stingy 7 miserly 9 penurious
get ~ excited over: 4 gush 7 enthuse
get ~ personal: 3 spy 5 snoop, stare 6 butt in, horn in, meddle 7 intrude, obtrude, wiretap 8 question 9 interfere
give ~ much: 4 cloy, glut 5 gorge 7 surfeit
go ~ far: 4 hype 6 pile on 7 belabor, lay it on, stretch 8 overplay 9 overstate 10 exaggerate
go ~ fast: 4 tear, whiz, zoom 6 barrel
little too late: 9 deficient, half-baked, shortfall 10 inadequate
me ~: 5 ditto
much: 5 ultra, undue 6 de trop, excess, overly 8 tiresome, to a fault 9 excessive, overblown 10 inordinate, outrageous, stupendous, unbearable, untempered
much (French): 6 de trop
much of a good thing: 4 glut 5 flood 7 surfeit, surplus 8 overload 10 indulgence, oversupply
only ~: 4 very 6 highly, overly 7 greatly 9 extremely, intensely, unusually 10 strikingly, uncommonly
prefix: 4 over-
too __ by half: 6 clever
too __ for comfort: 5 close
too __ for one's britches: 3 big
too __ to be true: 4 good
too __ to handle: 3 hot
too __ to pop: 6 pooped
Too __ cooks...: 4 many
Too __ Hot: 4 Darn
Too __ the Phalarope: 4 Late
Too __, Too Little, Too Late: 4 Much
__ too bad: 3 not
Too bad!: 3 tsk 4 alas, pity 5 alack 6 tsk tsk
Too Busy Thinking About My Baby (1969 song)
artist: Marvin Gaye
too clever by __: 4 half
Too Close for Comfort (ABC sitcom)
cast: Lydia Cornell (Sara Rush) Nancy Dussault (Muriel Rush) Ted Knight (Henry Rush) Deborah Van Valkenburgh (Jackie Rush)
Too Darn Hot
composer: Cole Porter
Toodle-oo!: 3 bye 4 ciao, ta-ta 5 adieu, adios, I'm off, later 6 bye-bye, so long 7 goodbye 8 farewell
Toody, Gunther: 3 cop
portrayer: 4 Ross
uncle: 4 Igor
Too Far to Go
author: John Updike
Too Funky (1992 song)
artist: George Michael
too good __ true: 4 to be
Too Hot (1980 song)
artist: Kool and the Gang
tool: 3 awl, axe, bit, hoe, lag, saw, zax 4 adze, dupe, file, froe, frow, jack, mark, pawn, pick, rake, rasp, vise 5 agent, anvil, auger, burin, chump, clamp, drill, edger, gizmo, gouge, knife, lathe, lever, means,

organ, patsy, plane, poker, punch, snake, spade, thing **6** chisel, device, dibble, engine, flunky, gadget, gimlet, hammer, harrow, jackal, lackey, linger, mallet, medium, minion, pliers, puppet, router, shovel, sickle, stooge, sucker, trowel, victim, wrench **7** cat's-paw, flunkey, hacksaw, hatchet, hayfork, ice pick, lacquey, machine, mattock, nail set, scalpel, utensil, vehicle **8** clippers, easy mark, forceps, hireling **9** accessory, apparatus, appliance, greenhorn, implement, machinery, mechanism, timesaver **10** accomplice, figurehead, instrument, jackhammer

along: 3 zip **4** ride **5** drive, motor, steer **7** advance, journey

boring ~: 10 jackhammer

building: 4 shed

carpentry ~: 3 adz, saw **4** adze, vise **5** bevel, clamp, drill, level, plane **6** chisel, hammer, jigsaw, pliers

chef's ~: 4 mill **5** corer, dicer, parer, ricer, whisk **6** beater, slicer

cutting ~: 3 axe, saw **4** adze **5** blade, knife **6** bowsaw, stylus **7** scalpel

ender: 3 box **5** maker

forester's ~: 7 hatchet

garden ~: 3 hoe **4** hose, rake **5** edger, spade **6** dibble

handle: 4 haft **5** helve

orthopedist's ~: 4 x-ray **10** radiograph

partner: 3 die

point: 3 nib

prehistoric ~: 3 axe **4** adze **6** eolith

rotary ~: 5 auger

yard ~: 4 rake **5** edger, mower

tool ___: 3 kit

___ tool: 4 hand **5** power

tool and ___: 3 die

___ Too Late: 3 It's **4** Born

Too Late for Goodbyes (1985 song)

artist: Julian Lennon

Too Late the Phalarope

author: Alan Paton

Too Late to Say Goodbye (1990 song)

artist: Richard Marx

toolbox item: 3 nut **4** bolt, nail, T-nut **5** screw

toolhouse: 4 shed

tools: 3 kit **4** gear **6** tackle **8** hardware **9** equipment

good with ~: 4 able, deft **5** adept, handy **6** adroit **7** skilled **8** skillful **9** dexterous

Too Many ___ in the Sea: 4 Fish

Too many cooks...: 3 saw **5** adage, maxim

Toomey: 4 Bill **5** Regis

Toomey, Bill: 10 decathlete

Too Much (song)

artist: Elvis Presley1, Spice Girls

Too Much Heaven (1978 song)

artist: Bee Gees

too much in music: 5 tanto **6** troppo

Too Much Time on My Hands (1981 song)

artist: Styx

Too Much, Too Little, Too Late (1978 song)

artist: Johnny Mathis, Deniece Williams

toon: 4 tree **9** character

art: 3 cel **4** cell

Toonces: 3 cat

___ to One, A: 7 Million

To One in Paradise

author: Edgar Allan Poe

Toonerville ___: 7 Trolley

to one's ___: 4 face, name **5** taste

to one's ___ content: 6 heart's

___ to oneself: 4 keep

___ to one's guns: 5 stick

___ to one's heart: 5 close

___ to one's heels: 4 take

___ to one's knees: 5 bring

___ to one's knitting: 5 stick

___ to one's ribs: 5 stick

___ to one's word: 4 true

too pooped ___: 5 to pop

___ Too Proud to Beg: 4 Ain't

Too-Ra-___...: 5 Loo-ra

___ to order: 4 call

___-to-order: 4 made

___ too shabby!: 3 Not

toot: 4 beep, blow, honk, pipe **5** binge, blast, fling, sound, spree **6** bender **10** inhalation

one's own horn: 4 brag, crow **5** boast, vaunt **7** talk big

___ toot: 3 on a

tooter: 5 piper

tooth: 3 cog **4** fang, tusk **5** molar **6** canine, cuspid, liking **7** grinder, incisor **8** sprocket **10** projection

and nail: 5 madly **6** wildly **8** fiercely, savagely **9** violently

cleaner: 5 brush, floss **7** dentist

combining form: 4 dent- **5** denti-, dento-, odont- **6** odonto-

doctor's degree: 3 DDS, DMD

doctor's org.: 3 ADA

ender: 4 ache, pick, some, wort **5** brush, paste **6** powder

extract a ~: 4 yank

filling: 5 crown, inlay **7** amalgam

fix a ~: 4 fill

for a tooth: 7 revenge

gear ~: 3 cog

holder: 3 jaw **4** gums **5** mouth

long in the ~: 4 aged **5** aging, hoary **6** ageing **7** ancient, elderly, wizened **8** grizzled **9** geriatric, getting on, senescent, up in years

of a ~: 6 dental

part: 4 cusp, pulp, root **5** crown **6** dentin, enamel **7** dentine

partner: 4 nail

starter: 3 dog, eye **4** buck

sweet ~: 4 urge **6** desire, hunger **9** addiction

taker: 5 fairy

topper: 3 cap **5** crown

trouble: 4 ache **5** decay **6** caries, cavity

tooth ___: 5 decay, fairy

___ tooth: 3 dog, egg **4** baby, milk **5** sweet **6** wisdom

tooth and ___: 4 nail

toothbrush brand: 3 Tek **5** Oral B, Reach **7** Colgate

___-tooth check: 6 hound's

___-tooth comb: 4 fine

toothed: 8 serrated

bar: 5 ratch

device: 3 saw **4** comb, gear, rake

toothpaste: 3 Aim **5** Crest, Gleem, Topol **7** Close-Up, Colgate, Viadent **9** Aquafresh, Mentadent, Pepsodent, Rembrandt, Sensodyne **10** Pearl Drops, Ultra Brite **11** Tom's of Maine

1950s ~: 5 Ipana

approving org.: 3 ADA

kind of ~: 3 gel

open, as ~: 5 uncap

unit: 4 tube

toothpicks, like some: 5 minty

toothpick, treat on a: 6 canapé

toothsome: 5 sapid, sweet, tasty, yummy **6** edible, savory **8** luscious **9** ambrosial, delicious, flavorful, nectarous, palatable **10** appetizing, delectable

make ~: 7 sweeten

___-tooth tiger: 5 saber

tootle: 4 beep, blow, honk **5** blare

toot one's own ___: 4 horn

too-too: 5 artsy, ultra **6** la-de-da, la-di-da, overly **7** mincing **8** lah-di-dah

Toots: 4 Shor

tootsie

see sweetheart

Tootsie (1982 film)

cast: Dabney Coleman, Geena Davis, Charles Durning, Teri Garr, Dustin Hoffman, Jessica Lange, Bill Murray

director: Sydney Pollack

Tootsie Roll: 5 candy, snack, sweet

tootsy: 4 foot

tootsy-___: 6 wootsy

Toot Toot Tootsie (1922 song)

artist: Al Jolson

Too Young (1972 song)

artist: Donny Osmond

top: 3 ace, cap, end, fox, ice, lid, rim, tip **4** acme, A-one, apex, beat, best, boss, cork, cusp, dock, fine, head, lead, lick, peak, roof, skim, trim, whip **5** break, chief, climb, cover, cream, crest, crown, elite, excel, limit, major, one up, outdo, prize, prune, scale, shirt, spire, tower, upper **6** apogee, better, blouse, bodice, choice, cut off, defeat, exceed, finest, finial, height, lop off, outfox, outwit, refute, select, summit, utmost, vertex, zenith **7** ceiling, dreidel, eclipse, garnish, highest, leading, maximum, overrun, primary, shut out, spinner, stopper, supreme, surface, surpass **8** covering, dominant, five-star, foremost, go beyond, greatest, lingerie, loftiest, outclass, outshine, outsmart, outstrip, outweigh, pinnacle, round off, surmount, truncate **9** beginning, excellent, first-rate, high point, number one, paramount, plaything, principal, prominent, uppermost **10** first-class, preeminent, tower above, upper limit

again: 5 reice

at ~ speed: 4 fast **5** apace **7** hastily, quickly, rapidly, swiftly **8** in no time, speedily **9** hurriedly, posthaste

at the ~: 5 aloft **6** apical **8** unbeaten **10** successful

banana: 4 boss **5** brass, ruler **6** honcho, kahuna, leader **7** kingpin, skipper **8** kingfish **9** big cheese, big kahuna, commander **10** head honcho

be on ~: 4 rule

big ~: 4 show, tent **6** circus **9** spectacle

blow one's ~: 4 rage, rant, rave **5** erupt, freak **7** flare up, flip out

brass: 5 chief, mogul **8** kingfish, official **9** commander **10** management

come out on ~: 3 ace, win **7** prevail, triumph **8** overcome

dog: 4 boss, head, jefe, king, star **5** champ, chief, first, Mr. Big, ruler **6** bigwig, gerent, honcho, leader, master, winner **7** captain, headman, manager, premier **8** big wheel, brass hat, cardinal, champion, director, foremost, governor, higher-up, kingfish, official, overseer, superior **9** authority, big cheese, commander, executive, number one, personage, president, principal, sovereign **10** supervisor

draw: 4 star

ender: 4 coat, knot, mast, most, sail, side, soil, spin **5** lofty, notch **6** minnow, stitch **7** gallant

floor: 4 loft **6** garret

from the ~: 4 anew, over **6** afresh, de novo

from ~ to bottom: 5 thoro **8** complete, thorough

get ~ billing: 4 star

go at ~ speed: 3 run **4** dash, race, rush, tear, whiz **5** scoot **6** gallop, scurry, sprint, streak **7** scamper

group: 4 best **5** A-list, elite **6** choice, gentry, jet set, select **7** in crowd, society **8** literati, nobility, old money **9** exclusive, high-class **10** blue bloods, glitterati, privileged, upper class, upper crust

jar ~: 3 cap **5** cover

level: 4 acme, apex, head, peak, roof **5** crest, crown **6** apogee, heyday, summit, zenith **7** maximum **8** mountain, pinnacle

off: 3 cap, end **4** fill **5** crown **8** round out **9** culminate, replenish **10** complement

off the ~ of one's head: 5 ad-lib **7** offhand **9** extempore, impromptu, unplanned **10** improvised, off-the-cuff, unprepared

on ~: 5 above, ahead **7** winning **8** dominant, reigning, superior, unbeaten **9** in command, in the lead **10** successful, triumphant, victorious

on ~ of: 3 o'er **4** over, upon **5** above **6** shrewd **7** besides

on ~ of the world: 4 glad **5** happy, merry **6** blithe, cheery, elated, jovial, joyful, joyous, upbeat **7** gleeful, pleased, tickled **8** bliss-

ful, cheerful, ecstatic, euphoric, exultant, jubilant, mirthful, thrilled 9 delighted, overjoyed, rejoicing
out: 4 peak
over the ~: 7 bonkers
put the ~ on: 3 cap 4 cork, seal 5 close, cover 7 stopper
rating: 3 ten 4 A-one 5 A plus
reach the ~: 4 rise 5 climb 6 arrive, ascend 7 prosper, succeed, triumph 8 flourish, get ahead, surmount
room at the ~: 4 loft 5 attic 6 garret
spot: 4 lead 5 first 9 front rank, title role 10 first place
starter: 3 car, lap, rag, red, tip 4 desk, flat, hard, hill, main, roof, tree 5 black, house, stove, table 6 bubble 7 counter 8 mountain
take it from the ~: 4 redo
take off the ~: 4 skim
to bottom: 7 totally 10 thoroughly
top ___: 3 dog, gun, hat, off, ten 4 kick, tier 5 brass, round 6 banana, dollar
top-___: 4 down, hole 5 heavy, level 6 drawer, flight, secret
top-___-line: 5 of-the
___ top: 3 big, box, peg, pop 4 tank, tube 6 halter
___-top: 3 pop 4 pull, soft 5 screw 6 carrot
Top ___: 3 Cat, Gun, Hat
Top ___ mornin'!: 4 o the
Top ___ World: 5 of the
Top-___: 5 Sider
___ to pay: 4 hell
___ to pay, the: 5 devil
topaz: 3 gem 5 color, jewel 7 citrine, mineral 8 gemstone
month: 3 Nov. 8 November
to Mohs: 5 eight
Topaz: 3 car 4 auto 5 novel 7 Mercury 10 automobile
author: Leon Uris
top-billed one: 4 star
topcoat: 3 mac 6 jacket, raglan, ulster 9 macintosh 10 mackintosh
___-top desk: 4 roll 5 slant
top-drawer: 3 AAA, ace, top 4 A-one, best, fine, one A 5 adept, elite, great, prime, slick, super 6 choice, finest, goodly, worthy 7 exalted 8 champion, fabulous 9 important, memorable
tope: 4 fish 5 stupa 6 bibble, guzzle, imbibe 9 hoist a few
Topeka: 4 city, town
county: 7 Shawnee
locale: 3 Kan. 6 Kansas
river: 6 Kansas
toper: 3 sot 4 lush, soak, wino 5 rummy, souse 6 barfly, bibber 7 guzzler, tippler, tosspot 10 bar crawler
bill: 6 bar tab
___ to Perdition: 4 Road
topflight: 3 AAA, ace 4 A-one, best, fine, one A 5 adept, crack, dandy, elite, great, prime, primo, super 6 expert, famous, finest, grade A, superb 7 eminent, optimal, premier, stellar, supreme 8 choicest, five-star, foremost, four-star, greatest, peerless, renowned, selected, splendid, sterling, superior, ultimate 9 excellent, exemplary, first-rate, high-class, matchless, nonpareil, paramount, prominent, unequaled, unrivaled, wonderful 10 celebrated, first-class, preeminent, unrivalled, world-class
Top Gun (1986 film)
cast: Tom Cruise, Val Kilmer, Kelly McGillis
director: Tony Scott
Top Hat (1935 film): 7 musical
cast: Fred Astaire, Ginger Rogers
composer: Irving Berlin
studio: 3 RKO
top-heavy: 7 leaning, tilting 8 lopsided, one-sided, unsteady 10 off-balance, unbalanced
Topher: 5 Grace
topic: 4 case, subj., text 5 field, issue, motif, thema, theme 6 affair, matter, thesis 7 problem, subject 8 argument, business, question
hot ~: 5 issue 7 problem 8 argument 10 contention
list: 6 agenda
topical: 3 apt, new 4 live 5 local, newsy 6 modern, timely 7 current, insular, limited, popular 8 regional, thematic 9 parochial 10 newsworthy, particular, restricted
___ to pick: 4 bone
___ to Pieces: 3 I Go 5 I Fall
Top Job: 7 cleaner
alternative: 5 Brite, Lysol 7 Lestoil, Mr. Clean, Pine Sol 9 Fantastik, Step Saver
Topkapi (1964 film)
cast: Melina Mercouri, Robert Morley, Maximilian Schell, Peter Ustinov
topknot: 4 coif, tuft 5 crest 6 hairdo 8 coiffure
___ to play: 4 come
___ to please!: 5 We aim
topless towers of ___, The: 5 Ilium
topliner: 4 star
topminnow: 4 fish 5 guppy
topmost: 3 top 4 head 5 upper 6 apical 7 highest, maximal, maximum, supreme 8 greatest 9 paramount
topnotch
see wonderful
Topo ___: 5 Gigio
top-of-the-line: 4 aces, A-one, best, fine, posh 5 elite, first, great, plush, prime, primo, ritzy, super, swank, swish 6 choice, costly, deluxe, finest, select, superb, swanky 7 highest, leading, optimum, opulent, premier, ranking 8 choicest, five-star, foremost, superior, very good 9 excellent, expensive, first-rate, high-class, high-grade, luxurious, matchless, nonpareil, number one, numero uno, sumptuous, unequaled, unrivaled 10 consummate, first-class, out of sight, perfection, super-duper, unrivalled
Top of the World (1973 song)
artist: Carpenters
topog.: 3 sci.
topographic
feature: 2 mt. 3 mtn. 4 cape, gulf, lake, spit 6 valley 8 mountain
map info: 4 elev. 9 elevation
topography: 6 layout 7 science, terrain
Topol: 10 toothpaste
alternative: *see* toothpaste
Topol (actor)
film: Fiddler on the Roof (1971)
topper: 3 cap, hat, lid 6 capper 8 headgear, headwear
kitchen ~: 3 cap 5 cover
tooth ~: 5 crown
see also hat
Topper (1937 film)
cast: Constance Bennett, Cary Grant, Roland Young
Topper (TV sitcom)
cast: Leo G. Carroll (Cosmo Topper)
Anne Jeffreys (Marion Kerby)
Robert Sterling (George Kerby)
dog: Neil
topping: 5 above, icing 8 frosting
toppings, minus: 5 plain
topple: 3 tip 4 fall, flop, oust, rase, raze, ruin, trip 5 crash, level, pitch, slump, smash, upend, upset, wreck 6 depose, falter, go down, plunge, teeter, totter, tumble, unseat 7 capsize, destroy, founder, stagger, stumble, subvert, tip over, unhorse 8 bulldoze, collapse, demolish, keel over, overturn, take down, tear down, turn over 9 bring down, devastate, dismantle, knock down, knock over, overthrow, take apart 10 hit the dirt
top-priority: 6 urgent
Topps
rival: 5 Fleer
top-rated: 3 AAA 4 A-one, best, fine, one A 5 first, great, primo
top round: 4 beef, meat
tops: 4 best 5 crack, first, great, limit, prime, primo, super 6 choice, select, wizard 7 capital, highest, in front, perfect 8 fabulous, foremost, four-star, greatest, peerless, superior 9 excellent, first-rate, high-grade, number one, paramount, sovereign, unequaled 10 first-class, preeminent, super-duper, unexcelled
high ~: 6 sneaks 8 sneakers
what ~ do: 4 spin
top-secret org.: 3 NSA
top-shelf: 4 posh 5 fancy, grand, plush, ritzy 6 choice, deluxe, select, swanky 7 opulent 8 palatial, splendid, superior 9 exclusive, high-class 10 first-class
Top-Sider: 4 shoe 8 footwear
___-top sneakers: 4 high
topsoil: 4 dirt, loam, soil 5 earth 6 ground
layer: 5 solum
___ Top Stuffing: 5 Stove
Topsy
friend: 3 Eva
___ to Psyche: 3 Ode
Topsy II (1958 song)
artist: Cozy Cole
topsy-turvy: 5 askew, messy, mussy, on end 6 unneat, untidy 7 chaotic, jumbled, mixed-up, muddled, riotous, tangled, upended 8 confused, inverted, littered, pell-mell, slovenly 9 cluttered, inside-out 10 disorderly
turn ~: 5 upend, upset 6 invert, jumble, muss up 7 derange 8 disarray, unsettle
Top Ten, Letterman's: 4 list
toque: 3 hat
feature: 5 plume
material: 6 velvet
wearer: 5 woman
tor: 4 crag, hill, peak 8 mountain, pinnacle 10 prominence, rocky ledge
Torah: 10 Pentateuch
authority: 5 rabbi, rebbe
medieval ~ commentary: 5 zohar
place: 3 ark 4 shul 5 schul 9 synagogue
place marker: 3 yad
Tora! Tora! Tora! (1970 film)
cast: Martin Balsam, Toshio Masuda
character: 4 Tojo
torch: 4 burn 5 flare, light 6 ignite 7 firebug, lantern 8 arsonist, burn down, flambeau 10 incinerate, pyromaniac
carry a ~: 4 pine 5 adore 6 suffer
crime: 5 arson 9 pyromania
in America: 10 flashlight
starter: 4 blow
use an acetylene ~: 4 weld
torch ___: 4 song 6 singer
___ torch: 4 tiki
Torch ___ Trilogy: 4 Song
Torch-Bearers, The
author: Alfred Noyes
torched: 3 lit
toreador: 7 matador
toreador ___: 5 pants
Toreador Song: 4 aria
composer: Georges Bizet
opera: 6 Carmen
___ to reason: 5 stand
___ to Remember: 3 Try
___ to Remember, A: 4 Walk 5 Night
___ to Remember, An: 6 Affair
Toren: 5 Marta
torero: 7 matador
cape color: 4 rojo
Torero Saluting
painter: Édouard Manet
___ to rest: 3 lay, put
tori: 5 rings
Tori: 4 Amos 8 Spelling
father: 5 Aaron
role: 5 Donna
___ to ribbons: 3 cut
___ to riches: 4 rags
___ to Ride: 6 Ticket
___ to rights: 4 dead
torii: 4 gate 7 gateway
Torin: 8 Thatcher
Torino: 3 car 4 auto, city, Ford, town 5 Turin 10 automobile
locale: 5 Italy 6 Italia
river: 5 the Po
___ Torino: 4 Gran
___ to Rio: 3 I Go 4 Road
Tork, Peter: 6 Monkee
colleague: 5 Jones 6 Dolenz 7 Nesmith
Tormé, Mel: 6 singer
technique: 4 scat
torment: 3 nag, rag, try, vex 4 bait, fret, gall, haze, hell, hurt, pain, rack, ride 5 abuse, agony, angst, annoy, bully, curse, devil, grind, harry, haunt, hound, press, smite, taunt, tease, worry, wound

6 badger, bother, harass, harrow, heckle, menace, misery, noodge, ordeal, pester, pick on, plague, punish, put out, rankle 7 afflict, agonize, anguish, bedevil, depress, henpeck, oppress, provoke, scourge, torture, travail, trouble 8 aggrieve, distress, irritate, lacerate, mistreat 9 heartache, martyrdom, persecute, suffering, tantalize 10 affliction, excruciate, heartbreak, infliction, oppression
tormented: 7 worried 8 obsessed 9 miserable 10 distraught, distressed
tormenting: 5 abuse 9 agonizing, harrowing
tormentor: 4 pest 5 bully 6 tyrant 10 browbeater, persecutor
torn: 4 rent, slit 5 burst, cleft, ratty, riven, seedy, split 6 broken, gashed, ragged, ripped, shabby, sliced, unsure 7 asunder, cracked, cut open, damaged, divided, mangled, severed, slashed, snapped 8 impaired, in shreds, ruptured, sundered, wavering, wrenched 9 fractured, in tatters, lacerated, uncertain, undecided 10 irresolute, of two minds
all ~ up: 3 low, sad 4 glum 5 tense, upset 6 gloomy, morose 7 anxious, doleful, forlorn, frantic, in a funk, unhappy, worried 8 dejected, downcast, grieving, wretched 9 bummed-out, cheerless, depressed, exercised, in despair, miserable, sorrowful, strung out, tormented, woebegone 10 despairing, despondent, dispirited, distraught, distressed, melancholy
apart, old-style: 4 reft
tornado: 4 wind 5 storm 7 cyclone, tempest, twister 9 hurricane, whirlwind, windstorm
part: 6 funnel
refuge: 6 cellar 7 shelter 8 basement
Tornadoes
song: Telstar (1962)
Tornami a dir che m'ami: 4 duet
Torn Between Two Lovers (1967 song)
artist: Mary MacGregor
Torn Curtain (1966 film)
cast: Julie Andrews, Paul Newman
director: Alfred Hitchcock
Torn, Rip: 5 actor
spouse: Geraldine Page
toro: 4 bull 7 Spanish
at times: 5 gorer
opponent: 7 matador, picador
target: 4 capa
Toronado: 3 car 4 auto, Olds 10 automobile, Oldsmobile
Toronto: 4 city, port, town
former name: 4 York
locale: 3 Ont. 6 Canada 7 Ontario
newspaper: 3 Sun 4 Star
pro team: 7 Raptors 8 Blue Jays 10 Maple Leafs
school: 4 York 7 Ryerson
Toronto Argonauts' org.: 3 CFL
torpedo: 4 bomb, fish, hero, raid, rout, thug 5 blast, shoot, wreck 6 cancel, stifle 7 destroy, shatter 8 abrogate, demolish, sabotage, undercut 9 overpower, undermine
WWII ~ vessel: 5 E-boat
torpedoes: 4 ammo 9 munitions 10 ammunition
torpid: 3 lax 4 dopy, dull, idle, lazy, logy, numb, slow 5 dopey, heavy, inert 6 asleep, draggy, drowsy, latent, leaden, sleepy, sodden 7 dormant, languid, passive 8 benumbed, comatose, fainéant, inactive, indolent, lifeless, listless, slothful, sluggish 9 apathetic, lethargic, paralyzed, sedentary, somnolent, unhurried 10 disengaged, languorous, motionless, slow-moving, spiritless, unreactive
torpidity: 5 sleep, sloth 6 acedia 7 inertia, languor 8 hebetude, idleness, laziness, lethargy 9 faineance, indolence, inertness 10 stagnation
torpor: 4 coma 5 sleep, sloth 6 acedia, apathy 7 inertia, languor, latency, slumber, vacuity 8 doldrums, dormancy, hebetude, idleness, laziness, lethargy, loginess, otiosity 9 faineance, inanition, indolence, inertness, lassitude 10 inactivity, stagnation
Torquato: 5 Tasso
Torquemada: 5 Tomás
Torrance: 4 city, town
locale: 10 California
Torre: 3 Joe 5 Frank
torrefy: 4 heat 5 parch, singe
Torre, Joe
sport: 8 baseball
Torrence: 4 Dean 6 Ernest
Torrens: 4 lake
city on the ~: 8 Adelaide
locale: 9 Australia
torrent: 4 flux, gush, hail, pour, rain, rash, rush, tide 5 blaze, burst, flood, spate 6 deluge, onrush, stream 7 cascade, niagara 8 cataract, downpour, effusion, outburst, overflow 9 avalanche, cataclysm, waterfall 10 cloudburst, inundation, outpouring
Torrey __: 4 pine
Torricelli, Evangelista: 7 Italian 9 physicist
torrid: 3 dry, hot 4 arid 5 fiery 6 ardent, erotic, heated, red-hot, steamy, sultry 7 blazing, boiling, burning, fervent, flaming, intense, parched 8 broiling, parching, scalding, scorched, sizzling, stifling, tropical, white-hot 9 scorching 10 blistering, equatorial, hot-blooded, oppressive, passionate, sweltering
torridity: 4 heat 8 warmness
Torrijos: 4 Omar
torsion: 5 twist
torsion __: 3 bar
torso: 3 bod 4 body, form 5 trunk 6 figure 8 physique
tort: 5 crime, libel, wrong 8 trespass
ender: 3 oni
torte: 4 cake 6 pastry 7 dessert 10 confection
like a ~: 4 rich
part: 4 nuts 5 layer
shop: 6 bakery
__ torte: 6 Linzer, Sacher
tortellini: 5 pasta 7 noodles
alternative: ***see*** pasta
topping: 5 pesto, sauce 8 marinara
tortilla: 7 Mexican
chip: 4 nosh 5 nacho, snack
dish: 4 taco 6 fajita, flauta
flour: 4 masa 8 cornmeal
like a ~: 4 flat
topper: 5 salsa
Tortilla Flat: 5 novel
author: John Steinbeck
role: 4 Tito 5 Pablo, Pilon 6 Sweets 7 Dolores
tortoise: 6 animal 7 reptile
feature: 5 shell
like a ~: 4 poky, slow 6 draggy 7 halting, lagging, languid 8 crawling, creeping, dawdling, dilatory, dragging, drawn-out, plodding, slothful, sluggish, toddling 9 leisurely, lethargic, snail-like, unhurried 10 deliberate, protracted
opponent: 4 hare
Tortoise and the Hare, The: 5 fable
source: 4 Esop 5 Aesop
tortoni: 7 dessert 8 ice cream
alternative: 6 gelati, gelato, sundae 7 parfait, spumone, spumoni 8 snowball
__ Tortugas: 3 Dry
tortuous: 4 bent, mazy, wavy 5 snaky 6 skewed, zigzag 7 bending, complex, crooked, curving, devious, sinuous, snaking, twisted, verbose, winding 8 indirect, involved, twisting 9 ambiguous, entangled, intricate 10 circuitous, convoluted, meandering, roundabout, serpentine
tortured: 5 woful 6 woeful 9 miserable
torturous: 4 hard 5 harsh 6 brutal, severe, taxing, trying 7 onerous 8 crushing, grueling 9 demanding, difficult, harrowing, herculean, punishing, strenuous 10 enervating, exhausting
__ to ruin, the: 4 road
__ to Run: 4 Born 7 Nowhere
torus: 4 ring 5 donut 8 doughnut 9 inner tube
Torvill: 5 Jayne
partner: 4 Dean
Tory: 5 Major 8 loyalist
opponent: 4 Whig
to say __ of: 7 nothing
__ to say...: 5 I mean
to say the __: 5 least
Tosca: 5 opera
composer: Giacomo Puccini
piece: 4 aria
role: 5 Mario 6 Cesare 7 Scarpia 8 Spoletta
setting: 4 Rome 5 Italy
trio: 4 acts
Toscanini, Arturo: 7 Italian 9 conductor
__ to seed: 3 run
to see, like: 3 irr. 5 irreg. 9 irregular
__ to sell: 6 priced
__ to Sender: 6 Return
tosh
see baloney
__ to shame: 3 put
Toshiba: 2 TV 5 TV set 10 television
alternative: ***see*** electronics company
Toshiro: 6 Mifune
__-to-shore: 4 ship
__ to Silence: 3 Ode
__ to Singapore: 4 Road
To Sir, With Love (1967 film)
cast: Judy Geeson, Sidney Poitier
director: James Clavell
theme singer: Lulu
...to skin __: 4 a cat
To Sleep
author: John Keats
__ to Smoochy: 5 Death
__ to sow...: 5 A time
__ to spare: 4 room
toss: 3 bob, lob, sip, sow 4 cast, flip, hurl, jolt, keel, rock, roll, stir, sway 5 bandy, chuck, fling, heave, lurch, pitch, quaff, shake, sling, strew, swing, throw 6 buffet, jiggle, joggle, launch, let fly, plunge, propel, seesaw, squirm, thrash 7 agitate, deep-six, discard, flounce, flutter, project, swallow 8 flounder, get rid of 9 dispose of, eighty-six
about: 5 bandy, strew 7 flutter
and turn: 4 fret 5 brood, worry 7 agonize
around: 6 debate 7 discuss 8 consider
back: 4 down, gulp, swig, tope 5 drink, quaff 6 guzzle, imbibe 7 put away
dice ~: 3 six, ten, two 4 five, four, nine, roll 5 eight, seven, three 6 eleven, twelve 7 boxcars 9 snake eyes
down: 3 eat, use 4 bolt, gulp, ruin, wolf 5 drain, drink, eat up, empty, erode, gorge, put in, scarf, spend, use up 6 absorb, devour, digest, engulf, expend, feed on, finish, guzzle, imbibe, ingest, ingulf, inhale, nosh on, obsess, prey on, ravage 7 consume, corrode, deplete, destroy, engross, exhaust, partake, play out, put away, scarf up, smolder, snack on, swallow, utilize, wear out 8 gobble up, nibble on, smoulder, squander 9 devastate, dissipate, go through, polish off, preoccupy 10 lay waste to, monopolize, run through
ender: 3 pot
it in: 4 quit 6 give up 9 surrender
out: 3 rid 4 drop, junk 5 eject, evict, scrap 6 depose, reject 7 let go of
toss __: 3 off 6 around
toss and __: 4 turn
tossed __: 5 salad
__-tossed: 7 tempest
tossed-off: 5 ad-lib 6 casual 9 extempore, impromptu, whipped-up 10 improvised, unscripted
Tossin' and Turnin' (1961 song)
artist: Bobby Lewis
tossing and turning: 5 awake 8 restless
tosspot: 3 sot 4 lush, wino 5 toper 7 tippler

__-tost: 7 tempest
tostada cousin: 4 taco
__ to stern: 4 stem
__ to suggestions: 4 open
tot: 3 add, cub, kid 4 babe, baby, dram, tike, tyke 5 child, kiddy, wee un 6 infant, jigger, kiddie, moppet, nipper, reckon, rug rat 7 crawler, creeper, toddler 8 juvenile, small fry 9 youngster
cry: 5 Mommy
first word: 4 dada, mama
in Spanish: 4 niña, niño
place: 3 lap 4 crib 7 nursery, playpen 8 bassinet 9 high chair
query: 3 why
refresher: 4 wawa
take care of a ~: 4 mind 5 watch 7 baby-sit, oversee 9 look after
time-out: 3 nap
toe: 5 piggy 6 piggie
tool: 6 crayon
toy: 4 doll 5 Legos
up: 3 add, sum 5 count, tally 6 figure, number, reckon 9 keep score
vehicle: 4 sled 5 trike, wagon 6 go-cart, go-kart 8 tricycle
watcher: 4 nana 5 nanny 6 nannie, sitter 10 babysitter
wear: 3 bib 6 diaper
see also baby
total: 3 add, all, sum 4 body, bulk, full, mass, rank, rase, raze, rout, ruin, tote 5 add up, clean, count, crash, crush, equal, gross, reach, run to, score, sheer, sound, sum up, tally, uncut, utter, whole, wreck, yield 6 all-out, amount, budget, come to, entire, figure, global, number, pile up, ravage, reckon, result, ring up, strict, volume 7 balance, compute, destroy, flat-out, full-out, general, in-depth, jackpot, mount up, overall, perfect, plenary, rear-end, run into, shatter, stack up, trounce 8 absolute, amount to, complete, comprise, demolish, entirety, finished, implicit, integral, livelong, outright, profound, quantity, sweeping, the works, thorough 9 aggregate, calculate, devastate, downright, enumerate, full-dress, inclusive, keep score, out-and-out, overpower, overwhelm, undivided, universal, unlimited, unreduced, wholesale 10 bottom line, consummate, count heads, exhaustive, final score, unabridged
again: 5 readd
as a ~: 5 in all
component: 6 addend
starter: 3 tee
total __: 4 loss 5 bases 6 recall 7 eclipse
__ total: 3 sum
Total: 6 cereal
competitor: *see* cereal
Total Eclipse of the Heart (song)
artist: Nicki French, Bonnie Tyler
totaled: 4 beat 5 kaput, ran to 7 done for, wrecked 8 finished, wiped out 10 demolished
totalitarian: 8 absolute, despotic, dictator, one-party 9 fascistic 10 despotical
totalitarianism: 7 tyranny
totality: 3 sum 5 gross, unity, whole 6 system 8 ensemble, entirety 9 aggregate, integrity
totalizer numbers: 4 odds
totally: 3 all 4 only 5 fully, plumb, quite, right, sheer 6 bodily, in full, purely, simply, solely, wholly 7 flat out, utterly 8 all in all, entirely, whole hog 9 every inch, full blast, inside out, perfectly, to the hilt 10 absolutely, altogether, completely, thoroughly, to the limit
Total Recall (1990 film)
cast: Arnold Schwarzenegger, Sharon Stone, Rachel Ticotin
director: Paul Verhoeven
setting: 4 Mars
__ to task: 4 call, take 5 bring
tote: 3 lug 4 bear, cart, haul, pack, take 5 add up, bring, carry, ferry, fetch, purse, shlep, total 6 convey, reckon, schlep, shlepp 7 handbag, portage 8 carryall, transfer 9 transport 10 bring along, count heads, pocketbook
board numbers: 4 odds
easy to ~: 5 light
up: 3 add, sum 5 count, tally, total 6 figure, reckon 7 compute 9 calculate, enumerate 10 count heads
tote __: 3 bag 5 board
__ to tears: 4 bore
To Tell the Truth: 8 game show
contestant: 4 liar
host: Bud Collyer, Garry Moore, Bill Cullen
regular: 4 Bean, Cass 9 Orson Bean, Peggy Cass
totem: 3 xat 6 column, emblem, symbol
make a ~: 5 carve
material: 4 tree, wood 5 trunk
totem __: 4 pole
Totem __ Tabu: 3 und
Totem and Taboo
author: Sigmund Freud
Totenberg: 4 Nina
Totentanz
composer: Franz Liszt
toter: 6 bearer, hauler, porter, skycap 7 carrier 9 schlepper 10 backpacker
__ to terms: 4 come 5 bring
__ to that!: 4 Amen
to the __: 3 max, sky 4 fore, good, hilt 5 gills, nines, point, skies, teeth 6 letter 7 fullest
to the __ born: 6 manner
to the __ degree: 3 nth
to the __ of: 4 tune
to the __ of the earth: 4 ends
__ to the Beach: 4 Back
__ to the chase: 3 cut
__ to the Chief: 4 Hail
__ to the Church on Time: 5 Get Me
__ to the cleaners: 4 take
__ to the core: 6 rotten
__ to the draw: 4 beat
__ to the Future: 4 Back 5 North
__ to the Galatians: 7 Epistle
__ to the good: 3 all
__ to the ground: 3 run
To the Hilt
author: Dick Francis
__ to the last drop: 4 Good
To the Last Man
author: Zane Grey
To the Lighthouse
author: Virginia Woolf
to the manner __: 4 born
__ to the Marines!: 6 Tell it
__ to the Mob: 7 Married
__ to the Moon: 5 Fly Me
__ to the Music: 5 Dance 6 Listen, Swayin'
__ to the nines: 7 dressed
to the nth __: 6 degree
__ to the occasion: 4 rise
__ to the People: 5 Power
to the point (French): 7 à propos
__ to the punch: 4 beat
__ to the purple: 4 born
__ to the quick: 3 cut
__ to the rear: 4 step
__ to the Sea: 6 Riders
__ to the teeth: 5 armed
__ to the test: 3 put
__ to the throne: 4 heir
__ to the Trees: 5 I Talk
__ to the wall: 4 push
__ to the West Wind: 3 Ode
__ to the wire: 4 down
__ to the wise...: 5 A word
__ to the World: 3 Joy
To thine own __ be true: 4 self
__ to think of it: 4 come
to this extent in Latin: 8 quoad hoc
Totie: 6 Fields
Totino's: 5 pizza
alternative: 5 Jeno's, Tony's 6 Ellio's 7 Celeste 8 DiGiorno 9 Tombstone 10 Freschetta
Toto: 3 dog
owner: 7 Dorothy
song: Africa (1982)
Hold the Line (1978)
I Won't Hold You Back (1983)
Rosanna (1982)
vocalist: Bobby Kimball
__ to toe: 4 head
toto, in: 3 all 5 fully, quite 6 wholly 8 as a whole, entirely, from A to Z 9 competely 10 altogether, completely, to the limit
__ to Treat a Lady: 5 No Way
__ to trot: 3 hot
__ Tots: 5 Tater
__-totsy: 5 hotsy
totter: 4 limp, reel, rock, roll, slip, sway, trip 5 lurch, quake, shake, waver, weave 6 careen, dodder, falter, linger, quiver, seesaw, shimmy, teeter, topple, wabble, waddle, weaken, wobble 7 blunder, stagger, stumble, tremble, whiffle 8 flounder, hesitate 9 oscillate
__-totter: 6 teeter
Totter: 6 Audrey
tottering: 4 sick 5 shaky 6 unfirm, wabbly, wobbly 7 rickety, unsound 9 doddering 10 ramshackle
toucan: 3 pet 4 bird, toco
feature: 3 neb, nib 4 beak, bill
touch: 3 bit, dab, eat, hit, hug, jot, pat, paw, pet, rub, sip, tag, tap, tie 4 abut, dash, drop, feel, hint, join, kiss, lick, loan, meet, melt, move, peck, snip, tint 5 brush, cover, drink, equal, flair, frisk, graze, grope, knack, nudge, probe, reach, rival, sense, shade, shave, skill, smack, speck, taste, tinge, trace, verge, whiff 6 adjoin, affect, allude, bedaub, border, breath, butt on, caress, cuddle, detail, excite, finger, fondle, handle, impact, little, shadow, smooth, strain, streak, strike, stroke, talent, tickle, trifle 7 ability, concern, contact, discuss, disturb, embrace, examine, faculty, impress, inkling, inspect, inspire, involve, larceny, massage, mastery, mention, modicum, palpate, quicken, refer to, request, soupçon, speak of, texture, verge on, whisper 8 artistry, bear upon, border on, come up to, converge, deftness, facility, interest, neighbor, osculate, spoonful 9 keep close, measure up, partake of, pertain to, scintilla, suspicion, undertone 10 green thumb, intimation, manipulate, smattering, sprinkling, suggestion, virtuosity
and go: 5 hairy, risky 6 tricky, unsafe, unsure, urgent 7 parlous 8 perilous, ticklish 9 dangerous, debatable, hazardous, uncertain 10 precarious
barely ~: 4 kiss 5 graze 6 glance 9 glance off
don't ~: 4 duck, shun, skip 5 avoid, elude, evade, forgo 6 eschew, give up 7 abstain, boycott 8 forswear, renounce, swear off 10 circumvent
down: 4 land 5 light, perch 6 alight, arrive, settle 8 get there
easy ~: 3 pat, tap 4 lick 5 flick, softy 6 caress, pigeon, softie, sucker, victim 8 pushover
ender: 4 back, down, hole, line, tone, wood 5 stone
gentle ~: 3 hug, pat, pet 6 cuddle, stroke 7 embrace, snuggle
get in ~: 5 reply 7 respond 8 reach out
keep in ~: 4 call, meet 5 phone, reach, write 6 roll in, show up 7 check in, contact 9 get hold of, telephone 10 get a hold of
loving ~: 3 hug, pat, pet 6 cuddle, stroke 7 embrace
off: 4 fire 5 begin, spark, start 6 ignite, kindle 7 actuate, trigger 8 detonate, initiate, motivate 9 instigate
on: 4 abut 5 cover, refer, treat 6 go into, review, talk of 7 mention, pertain, refer to, speak of 8 allude to, deal with, point out
out of ~: 4 away 5 apart 6 cut off, lonely, remote 7 distant 8 detached, isolated
put in ~: 5 refer
science of ~: 7 haptics
up: 3 fix 4 edit 5 amend, emend, gloss, paint, patch, renew 6 better, doctor, modify, polish, redact, repair, revamp, revise 7 correct, enhance, improve, perfect, restore 8 renovate 9 refurbish
up against: 4 abut, join, meet 6 adjoin 8 border on, neighbor
upon: 4 note 5 cover, treat 6 advert, allude, go into, review, talk of 7 mention, refer to, speak

of 8 allude to, deal with, point out 9 appertain
touch __: 3 off 4 base, down, upon 5 and go
touch __ with: 4 base
touch-__: 4 tone, type 5 me-not 6 tackle
touch-__ phone: 4 tone
__ touch: 4 soft 5 Midas 6 common
Touch __ the Morning: 4 Me in
touchdown: 4 goal 7 arrival, landing
  make a ~: 5 score
Touché cryer: 6 fencer
touched: 4 daft 5 batty, dotty 6 cuckoo, swayed 7 bonkers, fanatic, grabbed, stirred 8 affected, obsessed, peculiar, softened 9 eccentric, impressed, pixilated
  down: 3 lit 4 alit
Touched by an Angel (CBS fantasy)
  cast: Valerie Bertinelli (Gloria) Roma Downey (Monica) John Dye (Andrew) Della Reese (Tess)
touchiness: 6 spleen, temper 9 surliness
touching: 3 sad 4 near, next 5 sorry 6 moving, tender 7 against, contact, emotive, piteous, pitiful, wistful 8 adjacent, eloquent, pathetic, poignant, stirring 9 affecting, emotional, resting on 10 contiguity, contiguous, expressive, impressive, juxtaposed, pathetical
touch-me-__: 3 not
Touch Me (song)
  artist: Cathy Dennis, Doors, Samantha Fox
Touch Me in the Morning (1973 song)
  artist: Diana Ross
Touch Not the Cat
  author: Mary Stewart
Touch of Class, A (1973 film)
  cast: Glenda Jackson, George Segal
Touch of Evil (1958 film)
  cast: Charlton Heston, Janet Leigh, Orson Welles
  director: Orson Welles
Touch of Grey (1987 song)
  artist: Grateful Dead
__ Touch of Mink: 4 That
Touch of the __, A: 4 Poet
__ Touch of Venus: 3 One
touchstone: 4 norm, test 5 gauge, ideal, model 7 measure, pattern 8 exemplar, paradigm, standard 9 archetype, benchmark, criterion, yardstick
Touch the Wind, song subtitled: 6 Eres Tu
__ Touch This: 5 U Can't
touch-tone: 5 phone 9 telephone
touchy: 3 hot 4 edgy 5 cross, dicey, hairy, huffy, jumpy, moody, risky, testy, wired 6 chancy, cranky, crusty, feisty, fretty, grumpy, ireful, ornery, snappy, tricky, unsafe 7 bearish, bristly, crabbed, fretful, grouchy, huffish, peevish, peppery, prickly 8 choleric, churlish, fretsome, growling, grumpish, liverish, perilous, petulant, snappish, ticklish 9 excitable, fractious, hotheaded, irascible, irritable, querulous, sensitive, splenetic 10 easily hurt, ill-natured, out of sorts, precarious
touchy-feely: 9 sensitive
tough: 3 fit 4 firm, goon, hale, hard, hood, iron, mean, punk, ropy, thug, wiry 5 beefy, bossy, bully, burly, chewy, cruel, hairy, hardy, harsh, heavy, hefty, hunky, husky, lusty, macho, picky, rigid, ropey, rough, rowdy, stern, stiff, stout, tight 6 brawny, feisty, flinty, gritty, gunsel, hearty, knotty, mighty, potent, rascal, robust, rugged, savage, severe, sinewy, steely, sticky, stocky, strict, strong, sturdy, taxing, thorny, trying, uphill, virile 7 adamant, arduous, austere, callous, doughty, durable, fibrous, gristly, hard-set, hard-won, hoodlum, onerous, ruffian, serious, Spartan, staunch, steeled, stringy, vicious, villain 8 athletic, baffling, cohesive, despotic, exacting, forceful, gangster, grievous, grueling, hardened, hard-line, hooligan, indurate, leathery, muscular, obdurate, overdone, powerful, puissant, puzzling, resolute, rigorous, ruthless, seasoned, stalwart, stubborn, tiresome, toilsome, unsavory, vigorous 9 Atlantean, confirmed, demanding, difficult, draconian, hard-nosed, herculean, laborious, merciless, obstinate, resilient, resistant, roughneck, strapping, strenuous, stringent, tenacious, two-fisted, unbending, unsparing, well-built 10 able-bodied, courageous, despotical, exhausting, forbidding, formidable, hard-bitten, hardboiled, headstrong, inflexible, iron-fisted, no-nonsense, oppressive, perplexing, pugnacious, red-blooded, refractory, reinforced, tyrannical, unyielding
  get ~: 5 adapt 6 harden, punish 8 accustom 9 acclimate, condition, crack down, habituate
  guy: 4 goon, thug 5 he-man 6 outlaw, Samson, Tarzan 7 brigand, bruiser, Goliath, ruffian 8 gangster, Heracles, Hercules, hooligan 10 powerhouse
  hang ~: 6 endure, take it 7 persist 8 tolerate 9 persevere, withstand
  hanging ~: 3 set 7 adamant 8 stalwart
  luck: 3 woe 6 mishap 9 adversity 10 hard knocks, misfortune
  not ~: 3 lax 4 easy, soft 5 slack 7 lenient 8 yielding 9 easygoing 10 permissive
  nut to crack: 5 poser 6 enigma 7 mystery, stumper
  situation: 3 fix, jam 4 bind, mess 5 pinch 6 plight 7 dilemma
  street ~: 4 punk
  to outwit: 3 hip, sly 4 foxy, keen, wily, wise 5 acute, canny, quick, ready, savvy, sharp, smart 6 brainy, bright, clever, crafty, shrewd 7 cunning, knowing 8 sensible 9 farseeing, judicious, on the ball, realistic, sagacious 10 discerning, insightful, perceptive, thoughtful
tough __: 4 love, luck 5 break, it out
tough __ to crack: 3 nut
tough __ to hoe: 3 row
__ tough: 3 get 4 hang
Tough!: 5 sue me 6 too bad
__-Tough: 4 Semi
tough as __: 5 nails
toughen: 4 gird, tone 5 build, enure, inure, shore, steel 6 anneal, beef up, harden, prop up, season, temper, tone up 7 bolster, brace up, build up, burgeon, coarsen, develop, empower, enhance, fortify, shore up, stiffen, tighten 8 bourgeon, buttress, energize, indurate, vitalize 9 acclimate, climatize, intensify, reinforce 10 invigorate, strengthen
  up: 5 adapt, build, enure, inure 8 accustom 9 condition, habituate
Tough Guys (1986 film)
  cast: Kirk Douglas, Burt Lancaster
Tough Guys Don't Dance
  author: Norman Mailer
toughie: 5 poser 6 enigma, puzzle, riddle 7 mystery, stinker, stumper
toughness: 3 vim 4 dint, grit, thew 5 brawn, force, might, power, sinew, spunk, thews, vigor 6 energy, muscle 7 fitness, muscles, potence, potency, stamina 8 backbone, hardness, strength, vitality 9 beefiness, endurance, fortitude, puissance, stability 10 brute force, moral fiber
tough nut to __: 5 crack
toujours __: 3 gai 7 perdrix
Toulouse: 4 city, town
  city near ~: 4 Albi
  locale: 6 France
  river: 7 Garonne
Toulouse-Lautrec, Henri de: 6 artist, French 7 painter
__ to understand...: 3 Am I
toupee: 3 rug, wig 4 hair 6 carpet, peruke 9 hairpiece
tour: 2 do 3 hop, job, run 4 term, time, trek, trip, turn, walk 5 drive, hitch, jaunt, shift, spell, stint, stump, swing, visit 6 cruise, junket, outing, ramble, safari, travel, voyage 7 circuit, explore, getaway, holiday, journey, stretch, weekend 8 conquest, go abroad, sightsee, vacation 9 barnstorm, excursion, globe-trot, overnight, round trip 10 expedition, hit the road, knock about
  again: 5 resee
  date: 3 gig 7 booking 10 engagement
  de force: 4 coup, feat 5 stunt 7 classic, exploit, triumph
  go for another ~: 4 reup
  guide: 3 map
  leader: 5 guide 6 docent, escort
  of duty: 5 hitch, spell, stint
  participant: 3 pro 6 bowler, golfer
  planning org.: 3 AAA
  segment: 3 leg 4 stop
  vehicle: 3 bus 5 coach 9 transport
__ tour: 5 Cook's, grand 7 package
Tourane today: 6 Da Nang
Tour de France: 4 race 8 bike race
  participant: 5 biker, racer
tour en __: 4 l'air
touring: 4 away 6 abroad 9 on the road 10 on vacation
tourist: 7 pilgrim, visitor, voyager 8 stranger, traveler, vagabond, wayfarer 9 jet-setter, journeyer, sightseer 10 day-tripper, vacationer
  attraction: 4 cave 5 sight 6 cavern
  magnet: 5 Mecca
  need: 3 map 4 visa 6 camera
  stop: 3 inn, spa 5 B and B, hotel, motel 6 resort 10 motor court, motor lodge
tourist __: 4 trap 5 class, court
tourmaline: 3 gem 7 mineral 8 gemstone 9 rubellite
tournament: 4 game, meet, tilt 5 event, fight, joust, match 7 contest, tourney
  attire: 5 armor
  compete in a ~: 5 joust
  kind of ~: 4 open 5 pro-am
  pass: 3 bye
  round: 5 semis 6 finals
Tourneau: 5 watch 10 wristwatch
  alternative: *see* wristwatch
tour of __: 4 duty
Tour of the Moon, A
  author: Jules Verne
Tours: 4 city, town
  locale: 6 France
  river: 5 Loire
__ to use: 3 put
tousle: 4 muss 6 muss up, ruffle, rumple, tangle 7 snarl up
tousled: 5 messy, mussy 6 blowsy, blowzy, matted, mussed, unneat, untidy 7 blowsed, blowzed, ruffled, rumpled, tangled, unkempt 8 messed up, mussed up, uncombed 10 disheveled, disordered
Toussaint: 9 L'Overture
tout: 4 hype, plug, push 5 boost, extol, shill 6 advise, extoll, herald, hype up, praise, talk up, tip off 7 acclaim, boast of, glorify, lionize, promote, show off, solicit, tipster 8 advocate, ballyhoo 9 advertise, brag about, publicize, recommend 10 make much of
  British ~: 4 spiv
  hangout: 3 OTB 5 track 9 racetrack
  offering: 3 tip 6 hot tip
  talk: 5 spiel
  topic: 4 odds
tout __: 5 à fait, à vous
__ tout: 5 pas du
tout de suite: 3 now, PDQ 4 anon, soon 6 at once, pronto 7 rapidly 8 in a flash, in a jiffy, promptly, right now 9 forthwith, instantly, on the spot, right away 10 here and now, this moment
tout le monde: 3 all 6 French 8 everyone
__ to Utopia: 4 Road
__ tov: 3 yom 5 mazal, mazel
Tovah: 8 Feldshuh
toves
  what the slithy ~ did: 4 gyre
tow: 3 lug, tug 4 drag, draw, haul, pull, yank 5 ferry, flaxy, trail, trawl 6 convey, flaxen, propel 7 wrecker

8 haul away 9 drag along, pull along, transport
ender: 3 age 4 boat, head, line, path 6 headed
ski ~: 4 J-bar, T-bar
tow ___: 3 bar, bug, car 5 truck
tow-___ zone: 4 away
___ tow: 3 ski 4 rope
toward: 4 in re 5 about 6 almost, facing, nearly 7 apropos, vis-à-vis 8 fronting, not quite 9 headed for, regarding 10 concerning
prefix: 4 pros-
Toward Freedom
author: Jawaharlal Nehru
towardly: 6 timely
towards: 3 via 4 in re 5 about 6 almost, facing, nearly 7 apropos, vis-à-vis 8 fronting, not quite 9 as regards, headed for, regarding 10 concerning
move ~: 5 aim at, favor 6 orient 7 head for
___ to Watch Over Me: 7 Someone
tow-away ___: 4 zone
___-to-wear: 5 ready
towel: 3 dry 4 wipe 5 linen
again: 5 redry
fabric: 5 crash, terry
feature: 3 nap 4 fuzz
holder: 3 rod
off: 3 dry, mop 4 wipe
starter: 4 dish
target: 5 spill
throw in the ~: 4 give, quit 5 yield 6 give up, resign 7 concede, succumb 8 say uncle 9 surrender
word: 3 his 4 hers
towel ___: 4 rack
___ towel: 3 tea 4 bath, face 5 guest, paper
___ to Wellville, The: 4 Road
tower: 3 top 4 hulk, keep, loom, mast, rear, rise, soar 5 mount, pylon, spire 6 belfry, castle, column, exceed, pillar, prison, turret 7 citadel, lookout, minaret, obelisk, shelter, steeple, surpass, zikurat 8 dominate, fastness, fortress, high-rise, monolith, monument, pinnacle, surmount, ziggurat, zikkurat 9 campanile, rise above, stand tall 10 lighthouse, skyscraper, stronghold
above: 3 top 5 dwarf, excel 6 exceed 7 eclipse, surpass 8 bestride, dominate, outclass, outshine, outstrip, overhang, overlook 9 transcend 10 outperform, overshadow, put to shame
bell ~: 5 spire 6 belfry 7 steeple 8 pinnacle
ivory ~: 4 lair 5 haven 6 asylum, escape 7 hideout, retreat 8 hideaway 9 sanctuary
of strength: 6 pillar 7 bastion 9 supporter
Old Testament ~: 5 Babel
prehistoric stone ~: 6 chulpa 7 chullpa
ringers: 5 bells 6 chimes
rural ~: 4 silo
starter: 5 watch
TV ~: 4 mast
___ tower: 5 ivory, water 7 conning, control
___ Tower: 4 Coit 5 Ivory, Sears 6 Eiffel
Tower Bridge river: 6 Thames
towering: 4 high, huge, tall, vast 5 giant, great, jumbo, large, lofty, steep, stiff 6 alpine, high up, mighty 7 hulking, immense, mammoth, massive, sizable, soaring, stately, sublime, supreme, titanic 8 colossal, elevated, enormous, gigantic, imposing, king-size, oversize, sizeable, superior, ultimate, uplifted, whapping, whopping 9 Herculean, humongous, monstrous, overlarge, paramount, unequaled 10 cloud-swept, gargantuan, impressive, monumental, preeminent, prodigious, snow-capped, stupendous, surpassing, tremendous
Towering Inferno, The (1974 film)
cast: Fred Astaire, Susan Blakely, Richard Chamberlain, Faye Dunaway, William Holden, Jennifer Jones, Steve McQueen, Paul Newman, Robert Vaughn, Robert Wagner
cat: 4 Elke
director: Irwin Allen
Tower of ___: 5 Babel, Hanoi 6 London
Tower of Ivory
author: Archibald MacLeish
Tower of London, once: 4 gaol
___ Tower of Pisa: 7 Leaning
Tower of Pisa, like the: 5 atilt
Tower of Strength (1961 song)
artist: Gene McDaniels
Towers: 9 Constance
Towers of Trezibond, The
author: Rose Macaulay
___ Tower, The: 4 Dark 5 Ebony 7 Leaning
tow-headed: 4 fair 5 blond, light, sandy 6 blonde
towhee cousin: 5 serin
To whom ___ concern...: 5 it may
town: 4 burg, city, seat 5 place, urban 6 hamlet, Podunk 7 borough, village 9 boondocks, community, municipal 10 metropolis, settlement
ender: 5 house, scape
starter: 4 down, home 5 cross 6 shanty
town ___: 3 car 4 hall 5 clerk, crier, house 7 meeting
___ town: 3 cow, new 4 boom, go to, skip, tank 5 ghost, on the
___-town: 5 out-of, small
___ Town: 3 Our 4 Bean, Boom, Boys, Cape 5 Funky, Magic, On the
Town Beyond the Wall, The
author: Elie Wiesel
Town Car: 3 car 4 auto, Linc 7 Lincoln 10 automobile
Town & Country: 3 car 4 auto 8 Chrysler 10 automobile
Towne: 6 Robert
___-Towners, The: 5 Out-of
townhouse: 4 home 5 condo 9 residence
townie: 5 local 8 resident 10 inhabitant
Town Like Alice, A
author: Nevil Shute
Townsend: 6 Robert
towns ender: 3 man, men 4 folk 5 woman, women 6 people
Townshend, Pete
group: Who, The
song: Let My Love Open the Door (1980)
townsman: 5 local 7 citizen 8 resident
town-square structure: 6 gazebo
Town, The
author: Conrad Richter
___ Town Too: 3 Her
Town Without Pity (1961 film)
cast: Kirk Douglas, E.G. Marshall
composer: Dimitri Tiomkin
theme singer: Gene Pitney
To Wong ___, Thanks...: 3 Foo
___-to-work law: 5 right
___ to worry!: 3 Not
towpath: 5 track, trail
Towson: 4 city, town
locale: 8 Maryland
toxic: 6 malign, poison, septic 7 adverse, baleful, baneful, harmful, hurtful, noxious, ruinous 8 damaging, negative, venomous, virulent 9 dangerous, injurious, poisonous 10 calamitous, disastrous, pernicious
chemical: 3 PCB 5 venom 6 dioxin
condition: 6 sepsis
gas: 5 radon
org. overseeing ~ cleanups: 3 EPA
toxin: 5 ricin, venin, venom 6 curara, curare, poison, venene, venine 7 botulin, hemlock, henbane 8 pathogen 9 wolfsbane 10 belladonna
starter: 4 anti 5 neuro
Toxin
author: Robin Cook
toxiphobe fear: 6 poison
toxophilite: 6 archer, bowman
famous ~: 4 Tell
weapon: 3 bow 5 arrow
toy: 3 top 4 ball, doll, game, hoop, jest, kite, play, sled, yo-yo 5 block, dally, flirt, GI Joe, kazoo, Legos, small, sport, tease, train, truck 6 bauble, cap gun, coquet, fiddle, geegaw, gewgaw, glider, kewpie, lead on, little, popgun, puppet, rattle, Slinky, stilts, tinker, trifle 7 balloon, fribble, Frisbee, trinket 8 Hula Hoop, jump rope, pinwheel, water gun 9 bagatelle, miniature, paper doll, play games, plaything, pogo stick, squirt gun 10 mess around, peashooter, tin soldier, trifle with
'90s ~ disk: 3 pog
ball: 4 Nerf
bathtub ~: 4 boat, duck
beach ~: 4 pail
holder: 3 box 5 chest, trunk
maker: 3 elf 4 Lego, Tomy 5 Ideal 6 Hasbro, Mattel
with: 3 rag, use 5 flirt, tease 6 finger, lead on, trifle
(with): 4 fool 6 fiddle
toy ___: 3 dog 4 line, with 5 chest
toyer: 5 flirt 7 dallier, trifler
Toyland visitor: 4 babe
toy-mouse stuffing: 6 catnip
Toynbee, Arnold: 6 writer 7 English 9 historian
work: A Study of History
Toyota: 3 car 4 auto, city, town 10 automobile
competitor: 5 Mazda 6 Nissan
locale: 5 Japan
model: 3 RAV 4 Echo 5 Camry, Paseo, Supra 6 Avalon, Celica, Matrix, Previa, Sienna, Solara, Spyder, Tercel 7 Corolla, Sequoia 8 Cressida 10 Highlander 11 Landcruiser
Toyota ___4: 3 RAV
___ to you!: 5 Here's
___ to You: 3 Run 4 So in 5 Close, It's Up, I Turn
___ to you, New York...: 5 It's up
To your health!: 5 salud, skoal, toast 6 cheers, prosit
Toys
song: A Lover's Concerto (1965)
Toys ___: 3 R Us
Toys for ___: 4 Tots
Toys in the Attic
author: Lillian Hellman
character: 3 Gus 4 Anna, Lily 5 Prine 6 Carrie, Julian
Toy Soldiers (1989 song)
artist: Martika
Toy Soldiers (1991 film)
cast: Sean Astin
Toy Story (1995 film)
director: John Lasseter
dog: 4 Scud
studio: 5 Pixar
voice cast: Tim Allen, Tom Hanks, Don Rickles, Jim Varney
Toy Symphony
composer: Joseph Haydn
___ to Z: 5 from A
To Zante
author: Edgar Allan Poe
___ to Zanzibar: 4 Road
tpk.: 3 hwy., rte.
tra-___: 4 la-la
Trabert, Tony: 7 netster 9 tennis pro
milieu: 5 court
trace: 3 bit, dab, jot, map, ray 4 atom, clew, clue, copy, dash, draw, drop, find, hint, hunt, iota, lick, mark, seek, sign, spot, step, tint, whit, wisp 5 crumb, grain, infer, pinch, proof, relic, scrap, shade, shred, smell, spark, speck, spoor, stalk, tinge, token, touch, track, trail, whiff 6 breath, deduce, derive, detect, follow, little, nuance, pursue, record, shadow, sketch, strain, streak, trifle 7 glimmer, outline, remains, remnant, run down, smidgen, smidgin, snippet, soupçon, unearth, vestige, whisper 8 chalk out, discover, evidence, fragment, landmark, particle, smell out, smidgeon, tincture 9 adumbrate, attribute, delineate, duplicate, ferret out, footprint, reproduce, scintilla, search for, suspicion, track down, undertone 10 indication, intimation, sprinkling, suggestion
leave no ~ of: 3 end 4 doom, raze, ruin 5 blast, crush, total, wreck 7 despoil, destroy, scourge, scuttle, wipe out 8 bulldoze, clean out, decimate, demolish, lay waste 9 devastate 10 annihilate, obliterate

__ tracer: 4 skip
Tracer: 3 car 4 auto 7 Mercury 10 automobile
tracer, medical: 6 iodine
Tracer of Lost Persons: Mr. Keen
tracery: 3 web 7 lattice, network 8 filigree
traces
kick over the ~: 4 riot 5 rebel 6 mutiny, revolt 7 run amok, run riot
Tracey: 4 Gold 6 Ullman
trachea: 4 tube 8 windpipe
neighbor: 6 larynx
Traci: 5 Lords 7 Bingham
Trac II: 5 razor
alternative: 4 Atra
tracing: 4 copy, line 6 ectype 7 drawing, outline
tracing __: 4 tape 5 paper
track: 3 dog, pan, rut, way 4 hunt, lane, line, mark, path, rail, road, sign, spot, step, tail, wake, walk 5 alley, chase, orbit, rails, route, scent, spoor, stalk, trace, trail, tread 6 artery, course, follow, groove, pursue 7 channel, circuit, heading, imprint, monitor, pathway, railway, recount, towpath 8 bearings, footpath 9 direction, footprint 10 beaten path, footprints, impression, indication, keep tabs on, passageway, trajectory
advisor: 4 tout
alternative: 3 OTB
and field need: 4 shot 6 hammer, hurdle 7 javelin
animal ~: 5 spoor
athlete: 5 miler, racer 6 runner 7 hurdler 10 high jumper
bet: 5 wager 6 exacta 8 perfecta, quinella 9 quiniella
circuit: 3 lap 4 loop 6 course
distance: 4 mile
down: 3 dog, tag 4 find, hunt, seek, tail 5 catch, chase, scour, stalk, trace, trail 6 detect, follow, locate, look up, pursue, search, shadow, turn up 7 bird-dog, capture, go after, run down, scout up, unearth 8 discover, scout out, smell out, sniff out 9 apprehend, ferret out
event: 3 run 4 dash, meet 5 event, relay 6 discus, sprint 7 hurdles, javelin, shot put
figures: 4 odds
framework: 6 gantry
get off the ~: 5 stray 6 derail
hit the ~: 3 jog, run 4 trot 8 exercise
in Spanish: 3 vía
keep ~ of: 5 watch 6 follow 7 monitor, oversee
lose ~ of: 6 mislay 7 misfile 8 misplace
official: 5 timer 7 referee, starter
off the ~: 4 asea, lost 5 at sea 6 afield, astray, errant 8 mistaken 10 digressing, on a tangent
off the beaten ~: 6 afield, lonely 8 isolated, secluded
on ~: 7 correct, working 10 successful
path: 4 lane
patron: 6 better, bettor 7 gambler, wagerer
racer: 3 car 4 auto, cart, kart 5 horse 6 go-cart, go-kart, runner 8 sprinter
shape: 4 oval
side ~: 4 spur
starter: 4 back, race, side 5 sound
surface: 4 turf
tear up the ~: 4 zoom
tire ~: 3 rut
trial: 3 mud 4 heat 8 humidity
unit: 4 yard 5 meter
winnings: 5 purse
word on a ~ ticket: 3 win 4 show 5 place
track __: 4 down, meet, shoe, shot, suit 6 record
__ track: 4 fast 5 laugh, mommy, storm 6 inside
track and __: 5 field
trackball
relative: 5 mouse
__-track betting: 3 off
tracker: 5 loran, NORAD, radar, sonar 6 hunter
Tracker: 3 Geo, SUV 5 Chevy 9 Chevrolet
tracking __: 4 poll
__-track mind: 3 one
__ track of: 4 keep, lose
tracks: 8 railroad
cover another's ~: 4 abet 7 collude
make ~: 3 hie, run 4 bolt, flee, race, rush, tear 5 hurry, scoot, scram, spank 6 depart, hasten 8 fugitate 10 accelerate, get hopping
stop in one's ~: 4 halt 5 pause 6 arrest, freeze, hold up 7 suspend, terrify 8 paralyze, prohibit 10 scare stiff
wrong side of the ~: 4 slum
__ tracks: 3 hen 4 make
Tracks of My Tears, The (song)
artist: Miracles, Johnny Rivers
__-track tape: 5 eight
tract: 3 lot 4 area, belt, land, plat, plot, zone 5 essay, field, patch, space 6 extent, locale, parcel, region, sector, spread 7 booklet, expanse, grounds, leaflet, quarter, section, stretch, terrain, writing 8 brochure, circular, district, freehold, locality, location, pamphlet, property 9 territory 10 exposition, literature
tract __: 5 house
tractable: 4 easy, meek, tame 6 broken, docile, gentle, pliant 7 dutiful, passive, plastic, pliable, subdued, trained, willing 8 amenable, biddable, flexible, gracious, lamblike, obedient, resigned, yielding 9 adaptable, agreeable, compliant, malleable 10 governable, manageable, submissive
traction: 4 drag, grip, pull 8 friction 9 adherence 10 resistance
lose ~: 4 skid, slip 5 coast, skate, slide 7 slither
tractor
adjunct: 5 baler, mower 7 trailer
home: 4 barn, farm
maker: 5 Deere
owner: 5 sower 6 farmer, grower, plower, reaper, tiller 7 planter 9 harvester 10 agronomist, cultivator
tractor __: 4 feed, pull
tractor-trailer: 2 tk. 3 rig 4 semi 5 truck
Tracy: 3 Lee 4 Dick 6 Austin, Morgan, Pollan 7 Chapman, Spencer 8 Caulkins, Lawrence, Scoggins
to Hepburn: 6 costar
Tracy and Hepburn
author: Garson Kanin
Tracy, Dick: 3 cop 9 detective
drawer: 5 Gould
foe: 5 Itchy 7 Flat Top, Mumbles 9 Prune Face
wife: 4 Tess
Tracy, Spencer: 5 actor
film: Adam's Rib (1949)
Bad Day at Black Rock (1955)
Boom Town (1940)
Boys Town (1938, AA)
Broken Lance (1954)
Captains Courageous (1937, AA)
Desk Set (1957)
Dr. Jekyll and Mr. Hyde (1941)
Edison, the Man (1940)
Father of the Bride (1950)
Father's Little Dividend (1951)
Fury (1936)
Guess Who's Coming to Dinner (1967)
Inherit the Wind (1960)
It's a Mad Mad Mad Mad World (1963)
Judgment at Nuremberg (1961)
Keeper of the Flame (1943)
The Last Hurrah (1958)
Northwest Passage (1940)
The Old Man and the Sea (1958)
Pat and Mike (1952)
The Power and the Glory (1933)
San Francisco (1936)
Stanley and Livingstone (1939)
State of the Union (1948)
Test Pilot (1938)
Thirty Seconds Over Tokyo (1944)
Tortilla Flat (1942)
Without Love (1945)
Woman of the Year (1942)
trade: 3 biz, job 4 deal, game, line, sell, shop, swap, swop, wind, work 5 bandy, craft, sales, skill, truck 6 barter, change, deal in, handle, market, métier, peddle, switch 7 calling, traffic 8 business, commerce, dealings, exchange, industry, regulars, vocation 9 carpentry, clientele, customers, newspaper, patronage, situation, traffic in 10 buy and sell, employment, enterprise, line of work, livelihood, merchantry, occupation, profession, quid pro quo
abroad: 4 ship 6 export, import 7 smuggle
agreement: 4 GATT 5 NAFTA
carriage ~: 5 elite
carry on a ~: 3 ply 4 work
ender: 3 off 4 mark 5 craft
horse ~: 4 deal 5 argue 6 barter 7 bargain 8 exchange 9 negotiate 10 compromise, do business
in: 4 deal, sell 5 carry, stock 6 handle, redeem, retail
journal: 5 organ 6 review 8 magazine 10 instrument, periodical
medieval ~ union: 4 club, gild 5 guild
off: 6 rotate 7 mediate 9 take turns 10 compromise
org.: 4 assn. 5 assoc.
place: 3 mkt, OTC 4 AMEX, exch., mart, NYSE 6 market, NASDAQ
regulating org.: 3 ICC
show presentation: 4 demo
suffix: 3 -ery, -ier
union: 5 guild, local 8 sodality 9 coalition 10 federation
with: 9 patronize
trade __: 3 war 4 name, show, wind 5 guild, paper, route, union 6 places, school, secret 7 balance, barrier, council, deficit
trade-__: 3 off
__ trade: 3 rag 4 fair, free 5 horse
__-trade law: 4 fair
trademark: 3 tag 4 logo, mark 5 brand, label 6 emblem, patent, slogan, symbol 7 imprint
trader: 3 arb 4 boat 6 argosy, dealer, seller, vender, vendor 8 merchant, retailer 10 shopkeeper
order: 3 buy 4 sell
__ trader: 5 floor, horse
__-trader: 3 day
Trader __: 3 Vic 4 Horn
tradesperson: 5 plier, plyer 6 worker 8 merchant
__-trade zone: 4 free 7 foreign
Tradiciones Peruanas
author: Ricardo Palma
trading __: 4 card, post 5 stamp
__ trading: 7 insider, program
__-trading: 5 horse
Trading Places (1983 film)
cast: Don Ameche, Dan Aykroyd, Ralph Bellamy, Jamie Lee Curtis, Denholm Elliott, Eddie Murphy
director: John Landis
tradition: 4 form, lore 5 ethic, mores, usage 6 belief, legacy, legend, mythos, ritual 7 culture, customs 8 folkways, habitude, heritage, localism, practice 9 formality, mythology 10 background, convention, observance
__ tradition: 4 oral
traditional: 3 old 4 folk 5 right, stock, typic, usual 6 age-old, common, normal, rooted, spoken, wonted 7 popular, regular, routine, typical 8 apple-pie, everyday, habitual, historic, ordinary, orthodox, standard 9 ancestral, customary, legendary, unwritten 10 accustomed, prevailing
traditionalistic: 5 rigid 7 diehard, old-line 8 orthodox
traditions: 4 lore 8 folklore
of ~: 5 loral
traduce: 4 gibe, jeer, jibe, mock, slam, slur, snub 5 abuse, decry, libel, scorn, smear, spurn, taunt 6 defame, deride, dump on, heckle, impugn, injure, malign, offend, rebuff, slight, vilify 7 affront, asperse, blacken, degrade, disdain, put down, rank out, slander 8 backbite, badmouth,

belittle, denounce, lie about, ridicule, vilipend **9** blaspheme, denigrate, discredit, disparage, humiliate **10** calumniate, disrespect
traducement: **3** dig **4** barb, gibe, jibe, slam, slap, slur, snub **5** abuse, libel, scorn, taunt **6** rebuff, slight **7** affront, calumny, catcall, disdain, mockery, obloquy, offense, put-down, slander **8** contempt, derision, ridicule **9** aspersion, cheap shot, contumely **10** defamation, disrespect, opprobrium
Trafalgar: **4** cape **6** battle, square
locale: **5** Spain **6** London **7** England
traffic: **3** jam **4** deal, sell **5** trade, truck **6** barter, deal in, handle, influx, logjam **7** bargain, bootleg, cartage, freight **8** business, commerce, dealings, gridlock, vehicles **9** move goods, patronage **10** buy and sell, passengers
be rude in ~: **5** cut in **6** cut off
circle: **6** rotary
controller: **4** cone **5** light, pylon
director: **3** cop **5** arrow
in: **5** trade **6** handle **10** buy and sell
jam unit: **3** car, van **4** auto **5** truck **10** automobile
noise: **4** beep, honk, horn **5** blare
reporter's transport: **6** copter
report source: **5** radio
sign: **3** Slo **4** Slow, Stop **5** Merge, Yield
signal: **3** red **5** amber, green, light **6** yellow
sign shape: **5** arrow **7** octagon **8** triangle
slower: **4** bump **9** speed bump
time: **8** rush hour
trouble: **3** jam **4** clog **5** snarl, tie-up **6** logjam **7** squeeze **8** blockage, clogging, crowding, gridlock, overflow **9** profusion **10** bottleneck, congestion
traffic __: **3** cop, jam **4** cone **5** court, light **6** circle, island, signal
__ traffic: **3** air **4** thru
Traffic (1972 film)
cast: Jacques Tati
director: Jacques Tati
Traffic (2000 film)
cast: Don Cheadle, Benicio Del Toro, Michael Douglas, Catherine Zeta-Jones
director: Steven Soderbergh
__-traffic control: **3** air
__ tragacanth: **3** gum
tragedies, like some: **5** Greek
tragedy: **3** lot, woe **4** blow, doom, play **5** drama, genre, shock, story, wreck **6** mishap **7** bad luck, failure, setback **8** accident, calamity, disaster, hardship, reversal **9** adversity, cataclysm, mischance **10** misfortune
Tragedy (song)
artist: Bee Gees, Fleetwoods
Tragedy of Korosko, The
author: Arthur Conan Doyle
Tragedy of Nan, The
author: John Masefield
tragic: **3** sad **4** dire, grim **5** awful, fatal, sorry, woful **6** deadly, woeful **7** adverse, doleful, fateful, forlorn, hapless, painful, pitiful, ruinous, unhappy **8** crushing, dreadful, grievous, hopeless, ill-fated, mournful, pathetic, pitiable, shocking, terrible, wretched **9** anguished, appalling, harrowing, ill-omened, miserable, sorrowful **10** calamitous, deplorable, disastrous, ill-starred, lamentable, pathetical, petrifying
fate: **4** doom, ruin **7** undoing **8** downfall **9** cataclysm, ruination
tragic __: **4** flaw **5** irony
Tragical History of Dr. Faustus, The
author: Christopher Marlowe
Tragic Muse, The
author: Henry James
Tragic Overture
composer: Johannes Brahms
Tragic Symphony
composer: Franz Schubert
tragus site: **3** ear
trail: **3** dog, lag, rut, spy, tag, tow, way **4** drag, draw, flag, haul, hunt, mark, path, plod, pull, road, slog, step, tail, wake, walk **5** byway, chase, dally, delay, droop, ensue, piste, route, scent, smell, spoor, spy on, stalk, tarry, trace, track **6** course, dangle, dawdle, follow, groove, linger, loiter, pursue, ramble, shadow, ski run **7** draggle, footway, go after, nose out, pathway, pugmark, pursuit, shuffle, succeed, towpath **8** drop back, footpath, hang back, hang down, straggle, tag along **9** come after, lag behind, poke along, track down **10** bridle path, drop behind, fall behind, footprints
boat's ~: **4** wake
boss: **6** drover
ender: **4** head, side **6** blazer **7** blazing, breaker
hit the ~: **3** run **4** tour **5** start **6** depart, set off, set out **7** take off **8** campaign, set forth
hound ~: **4** odor **5** scent, spoor, track
leave the ~: **5** stray
like many a ~: **4** cold
mark a ~: **4** lead **5** blaze, guide **7** pioneer
mix: **4** gorp
off: **4** fade **6** lessen **7** fade out **9** fizzle out
off the ~: **4** lost **6** afield, astray
paper ~: **5** proof **6** record
resolutely: **3** bug, dog **4** tail **5** harry, haunt, hound **6** harass, plague, pursue **7** bird-dog
secondary ~: **5** byway **6** bypath
ski ~: **5** piste
the field: **3** lag **4** lose **8** slip away **9** fall short
user: **5** hiker
trail __: **3** mix **4** bike, boss
__ trail: **4** bike **5** audit, paper, vapor **6** nature
__ Trail: **6** Oregon **7** Santa Fe, Tamiami **8** Chisholm, Overland
trailblaze: **4** lead **5** guide **7** go first, pioneer
trailblazer: **7** pioneer **8** explorer, vagabond **10** pathfinder
Trailblazer: **3** SUV **5** Chevy **9** Chevrolet
Trail Blazers: **4** five, team
org.: **3** NBA
rival: *see* NBA team
sport: **10** basketball
Trail Driver, The
author: Zane Grey
trailer: **3** van **4** clip, semi **5** promo
brand of ~: **5** Ryder, U-Haul
trailer __: **4** camp, park **5** court, truck
__ trailer: **5** house **6** tandem, travel
__-trailer: **7** tractor
trailing: **4** last **5** in tow **6** behind, in back, losing **7** lagging **8** rambling
train: **2** el **3** row, toy **4** beam, file, form, hone, mold, rail, rear, tail, tame, wake **5** aim at, coach, drill, enure, equip, focus, groom, guide, inure, level, nurse, point, prime, queue, study, suite, teach, tutor **6** column, convoy, course, direct, escort, ground, harden, school, season, series, string, update, warm up, zero in **7** break in, caravan, cortege, develop, educate, engrain, express, implant, ingrain, limited, nurture, prepare, qualify, railway, retinue, vehicle, work out **8** accustom, drum into, espalier, exercise, indurate, initiate, instruct, limber up, practice, rehearse, sequence **9** catechize, condition, cultivate, draw a bead, enlighten, entourage, habituate, make ready, retainers, transport **10** cannonball, continuity, discipline, evangelize, housebreak, procession, specialize, succession, superliner
Amtrak's bullet ~: **5** Acela
away from: **4** wean
bed on a ~: **5** berth
bullet ~ locale: **5** Japan
ender: **3** man, men **4** band, load **6** bearer
express ~: **3** ltd. **7** limited
freight ~: **6** coaler
fuel: **4** coal
in Spanish: **4** tren
line: **2** RR, ry. **3** rwy. **7** railway **8** railroad
lose one's ~: **6** forget, wander
mail locale: **3** RPO
NYC: **3** BMT, IRT
of thought: **5** logic **9** reasoning
on a ~: **6** aboard **7** en route **8** embarked **9** in transit, traveling
part: **3** car **5** diner **6** bar car, boxcar, engine, smoker **7** caboose **10** locomotive
patron: **5** rider **9** passenger
rush-hour: **3** exp. **7** express
shift a ~: **5** shunt
sound: **4** whoo **8** choo choo
stop: **3** sta., stn. **5** depot **7** station
take the ~: **4** ride **5** board **6** travel **7** commute
wheel sound: **5** clack
__ train: **3** air, sky **4** hop a, milk, mule **5** drive, gravy, local, model, power, wagon **6** bullet **7** express, freight
__-train: **5** cross
__ Train: **4** Love, Mule **5** Crewe, Peace, Wagon
trained: **4** able, deft, tame **5** slick **6** adroit, au fait, broken, docile, expert, nimble, pliant, versed **7** capable, skilled, subdued **8** dextrous, graceful, lamblike, masterly, obedient, seasoned, skillful, well-bred **9** competent, compliant, dexterous, efficient, masterful, qualified, tractable **10** accustomed, manageable, proficient, submissive
get ~: **5** learn
trainee: **4** tiro, tyro **5** newie, pupil **6** greeny, intern, novice **7** interne, learner, recruit **8** beginner, neophyte **9** fledgling **10** first-timer, tenderfoot
trainer: **5** coach, tutor **6** mentor **7** pedagog, teacher **8** educator **9** abecedary, pedagogue **10** instructor
place: **3** gym, spa **9** health spa
training: **5** drill **6** basics, tune-up **7** buildup, culture, tuition, workout **8** coaching, exercise, guidance, learning, pedagogy, practice, teaching, tutelage **9** chalk talk, education, grounding, paedagogy, schooling **10** background, discipline, experience, foundation, groundwork, upbringing
exercise: **6** lesson **8** maneuver
govt. ~ program: **4** CETA
manual ~ system: **5** sloid, slojd, sloyd
room complaint: **4** ache
training __: **3** aid **5** table **6** wheels
__ training: **5** basic **6** manual, spring, weight
Training Day (2001 film)
cast: Tom Berenger, Scott Glenn, Ethan Hawke, Denzel Washington
__ Train Lane: **5** Night
__ Train Robbery, The: **5** Great
Trains and Boats And __: **6** Planes
__ Train to Clarksville: **4** Last
traipse: **4** roam, step, trek, walk **5** range, tramp **6** linger, loiter, ramble, stride, stroll, trudge, wander **7** meander, saunter **9** gallivant **10** knock about
trait: **3** way **4** bent, cast, mark **5** habit, quirk, thing **6** detail, oddity **7** earmark, feature, quality **8** hallmark, property **9** attribute, mannerism
carrier: **3** DNA **4** gene
desirable ~: **4** plus **5** asset **6** virtue **8** resource, strength **9** advantage
heroic ~: **4** grit, guts, will **5** moxie, pluck, valor **6** daring, mettle **7** bravery, courage **8** audacity, backbone, boldness, gumption, strength, tenacity **9** brashness, fortitude, gallantry **10** confidence
traitor: **3** rat **4** fink, nark **5** enemy, Judas, knave, rebel, sneak, viper **6** ratter, snitch **7** ratfink, serpent **8** apostate, betrayer, deceiver, defector, deserter, forsaker, informer, mutineer, quisling, renegade, turncoat, two-timer **9** ill-wisher **10** subversive, tattletale, treasonist

traitorous: 4 base, evil 5 false, snaky 6 untrue 7 lawless, unloyal 8 disloyal, recreant, two-faced 9 dishonest, faithless, insidious, two-timing 10 inconstant, perfidious, rebellious
act ~: 6 betray
traits: 4 ways 6 makeup, nature 9 character 10 ins and outs
good character ~: 5 arete
Trajan: 5 Roman 6 Caesar
see also Latin
trajectile: 4 dart 5 arrow 6 bullet, pellet 7 missile
trajectory: 3 arc 4 line 5 curve, orbit, track 6 course 7 heading 9 direction
in a ~: 5 arced
Tralee: 4 city, town
locale: 4 Eire, Erin 5 Kerry 7 Ireland
tram: 3 car 7 coal car 8 cable car
cargo: 3 ore
ender: 3 car, way 4 line
in America: 9 streetcar
trammel: 3 tie 4 curb, rein, trap 5 deter, tie up 6 fetter, halter, hamper, hinder, hobble, impede, thwart 7 enchain, inhibit 8 hold back, obstacle, obstruct, restrain, restrict 9 constrain, deterrent, hindrance, restraint 10 constraint, impediment, inhibition
Trammell, Alan
sport: 8 baseball
trammels: 5 bonds, gyves 6 chains 7 bilboes, bondage, fetters, slavery 8 manacles, shackles 9 handcuffs, restraint
tramp: 3 bum 4 hike, hobo, plod, roam, rove, slog, trek, walk 5 march, pound, range, stamp, stomp, stump, tread 6 beggar, ramble, rascal, stride, stroll, trapes, trudge, wander 7 drifter, floater, migrant, outcast, traipse, vagrant 8 derelict, long haul, traveler, vagabond, wanderer 9 gallivant, rail rider 10 hitchhiker, knock about, panhandler, ragamuffin
tramp __: 7 steamer
trample: 4 hurt, mall, maul 5 crush, stamp, stomp, tread, tromp, worst 6 defeat, injure, ravage, squash, step on, subdue 7 flatten, oppress, run over 8 infringe, override, overrule, vanquish
on: 5 bully 7 oppress, violate 8 browbeat, domineer, keep down 9 dictate to, tyrannize 10 boss around, intimidate, lord it over
trampoline
like a ~: 4 taut
surface: 3 bed
tramp steamer: 4 boat
__, Tramps & Thieves: 6 Gypsys
__ tramway: 5 cable 6 aerial
trance: 4 coma, daze, muse 5 dream, sleep, spell 6 revery, vision 7 ecstasy, rapture, reverie 8 daydream, hypnosis 10 brown study
come out of a ~: 4 wake 5 awake, waken 6 awaken, come to
__ trance: 3 in a
trance-inducing: 8 hypnotic, mesmeric
Trane
alternative: 5 Rheem 6 Lennox 7 Carrier, Fedders 9 Friedrich
tranquil: 4 calm, cool, easy, even, mild 5 quiet, staid, stoic 6 at ease, gentle, hushed, irenic, low-key, mellow, placid, poised, sedate, serene, smooth 7 amiable, at peace, easeful, equable, halcyon, orderly, pacific, relaxed, restful, stoical, unmoved 8 amicable, carefree, composed, irenical, laid-back, pastoral, peaceful, soothing 9 collected, easy-going, impassive, nerveless, peaceable, quiescent, temperate, unexcited, unruffled, unworried 10 nonchalant, rippleless, unagitated, untroubled
be ~: 4 rest 5 relax
in music: 7 placido
tranquilize: 4 calm, lull 5 quiet, relax, still 6 settle, soothe 7 compose, quieten 8 mitigate, unruffle
__ Tranquillitatis: 4 Mare
tranquillity: 4 calm, ease, hush, lull, rest 5 order, peace, quiet 6 repose, temper 7 concord, harmony 8 calmness, coolness, serenity 9 composure, stillness
__ Tranquillity: 5 Sea of
Trans __ Range: 4 Alai
Trans-__ Pipeline: 6 Alaska
transact: 2 do 3 buy 4 sell 5 close, enact, sew up 6 clinch, finish, handle, manage, settle, wrap up 7 carry on, conduct, execute, operate, perform 8 carry out, practice 9 discharge, negotiate 10 do business, effectuate, take care of
transaction: 4 coup, deal, sale 5 trade 6 affair, matter 7 bargain 8 business, contract, covenant, exchange, purchase 9 agreement, execution
cashless ~: 4 swap, swop 5 trade 6 barter
transactions: 7 traffic
Trans Alai: 5 range 9 mountains
locale: 4 Asia 10 Kyrgyzstan, Tajikistan
Transalpine __: 4 Gaul
Trans Am: 3 car 4 auto 7 Pontiac 10 automobile
rival: 6 Camaro
transatlantic: 7 oversea 8 overseas
transceiver: 3 set 5 radio
button: 3 vol. 4 send 6 volume 7 squelch
user: 4 CBer
transcend: 3 cap 4 lead, pass 5 excel, outdo 6 better, exceed 7 eclipse, surpass 8 go beyond, outrival, outshine, outstrip, outweigh, surmount 9 cut across, rise above 10 overshadow, tower above
transcendent: 5 whole 6 entire, innate 7 eternal, perfect, sublime, supreme 8 absolute, abstract, infinite, platonic, splendid, superior, towering, ultimate 9 boundless, exceeding, masterful, unequaled
transcendental: 6 innate, mystic 7 eternal, perfect, sublime, supreme 8 absolute, infinite, mystical, peerless, superior, ultimate 9 boundless, exceeding, intuitive, matchless, spiritual, unworldly
Transcendental Blues (2000 album)
artist: Steve Earle
transcending prefix: 5 ultra-
transcribe: 4 copy, tape, type 5 write 6 record, render 7 put down 8 take down, write out 9 audiotape, duplicate, reproduce, write down
transcriber: 7 copyist 9 scrivener, secretary 10 amanuensis
transcript: 4 copy, tape, text 6 ectype, record 9 audiotape, duplicate, facsimile, recording
datum: 3 GPA 5 grade
transcription: 6 record 9 rendition
transdermal __: 5 patch
transfer: 3 lug 4 bear, cart, cede, deed, give, haul, mail, move, pass, post, sell, send, ship, taxi, tote 5 bring, carry, ferry, relay, shift 6 assign, change, convey, depute, pass on, remove 7 consign, convert, deliver, forward, removal 8 delegate, delivery, dispatch, hand over, make over, movement, relegate, relocate, sign over, transmit, turn over 10 abdication, assignment, reposition
art: 5 decal, rub-on
illegal goods: 4 push 7 bootleg
transfer __: 3 RNA
__ transfer: 4 wire
transference: 5 shift
thought ~: 9 telepathy
transferred employee benefit: 4 relo
transfigure: 6 change, modify
transfix: 3 awe 4 hold, nail, spit, stun 5 rivet, spike, stick 6 arrest, empale, impale, pierce, skewer, thrust 7 bewitch, enchant, engross, petrify 8 paralyse, paralyze 9 captivate, fascinate, hypnotize, mesmerize, penetrate, spellbind
transfixed: 4 rapt 6 enrapt 10 fascinated
transform: 4 turn, vary 5 act on, alter, morph, renew 6 affect, change, modify, mutate, reform, revamp 7 act upon, commute, convert, process, remodel, reshape, restyle 8 innovate, make over
into: 6 become
transformation: 5 shift 6 change, switch 7 renewal 8 flip-flop, mutation 9 about-face
transformer
part: 4 core
unit: 4 watt
__ transformer: 5 Tesla
Transformers (2007 film)
cast: Megan Fox, Shia LaBeouf
transfuse: 3 mix 5 endue, indue 6 infuse, inject 7 diffuse, instill 8 permeate 9 percolate
transfusion: 7 mixture
liquids: 4 sera
transgress: 3 err, sin 5 break 6 offend 7 infract, violate 9 misbehave 10 contravene
transgression: 3 sin 4 slip, vice 5 crime, error, fault, guilt, lapse, wrong 6 breach 7 misdeed, offense 8 iniquity, trespass 9 violation
transgressor: 4 thug 5 crook, felon, thief 6 bandit, outlaw, sinner 7 brigand, convict, culprit, hoodlum, mobster, villain 8 criminal, evildoer, fugitive, hooligan, murderer, offender, prisoner, scofflaw 9 desperado, miscreant, racketeer, wrongdoer 10 delinquent, lawbreaker, trespasser
transient: 4 hobo 5 brief, guest, rover, short 7 drifter, migrant, passing, ranging, vagrant, visitor 8 fleeting, flitting, fugitive, gadabout, meteoric, runagate, stranger, temporal, vagabond, volatile 9 ephemeral, journeyer, migratory, momentary, short-term, temporary 10 changeable, evanescent, fly-by-night, short-lived, unenduring
transistor
part: 5 diode
predecessor: 4 tube
transistor __: 5 radio
transit: 6 motion, travel 7 osmosis, passage, portage 8 carriage, crossing, movement 10 conveyance, theodolite
in ~: 6 aboard, coming 7 en route 8 embarked, on the way
__ transit: 4 mass 5 rapid
__ transit gloria mundi: 3 sic
transition: 4 flux 5 segue, shift 6 change, growth 7 passage, passing 8 movement, progress, upheaval 9 evolution
logician ~: 4 then, thus 5 hence 9 therefore
make a slow ~: 6 ease in
sudden ~: 4 leap 5 surge 7 upsurge, upswing
transitive __: 4 verb
transitory: 5 brief 7 passing 8 fleeting, flitting, fugitive, temporal, volatile 9 ephemeral, momentary, short-term, temporary 10 pro tempore, short-lived, unenduring
translate: 3 put 4 read 5 alter, gloss 6 change, decode, recast, render, reword 7 clarify, commute, convert, explain 8 construe, decipher, rephrase, simplify, spell out 9 elucidate, explicate, interpret, make clear 10 paraphrase
translating device: 5 coder
translation: 3 key 4 crib 5 gloss 7 reading, version 9 rendering, rendition, rewording
translocation: 5 shift
translucent: 4 thin 5 clear, lucid, sheer 6 glassy, limpid 8 knowable, luminous, pellucid
transmission: 3 fax 6 spread 8 delivery
choice: 3 low 4 gear, park 5 drive, first 6 manual, second 7 reverse 9 automatic
understand a ~: 4 read
transmit: 3 fax 4 beam, mail, pass, pipe, send, ship, take 5 carry, issue, radio, relay, remit, route 6 convey, funnel, hand on, impart, instil, pass on, siphon, spread, syphon 7 channel, conduct, consign, deliver, diffuse, forward, instill, project, radiate 8 bequeath,

TR

dispatch, hand down, televise **9** broadcast, propagate
transmittable: 8 catching **10** contagious, infectious
transmittal: 7 mailing, passage **8** delivery, dispatch, shipment
transmitter: 3 sdr., set **6** sender
neural ~: 4 axon **5** axone
prefix for ~: 5 micro, neuro
transmogrify: 6 change, modify, mutate
transmundane: 6 occult **7** psychic
transmutation: 4 flux **5** shift **6** change **8** make-over **10** alteration, conversion, revolution
transmute: 5 alter **6** change, modify
transoceanic: 7 oversea **8** overseas
transoceanic flight
pioneer: 4 Post **7** Earhart, Markham **9** Lindbergh, Wiley Post
transpacific: 7 oversea **8** overseas
transparent: 4 lacy, open, pure, thin **5** clear, filmy, gauzy, lucid, plain, sheer, white **6** candid, flimsy, glassy, hyalin, limpid, patent, simple **7** artless, crystal, evident, hyaline, obvious **8** apparent, clear-cut, gossamer, knowable, luminous, manifest, peekaboo, pellucid **9** guileless, ingenuous **10** diaphanous, see-through
transpicuous: 5 clear, lucid, sheer **6** limpid **10** see-through
transpire: 2 go **4** pass **5** arise, break, ensue, occur **6** befall, betide, elapse, emerge, happen, result, turn up **7** come out, develop **9** come about, eventuate, take place **10** come to pass
transplant: 4 move **5** graft, plant, repot **6** remove, uproot **8** displace, emigrate, relocate, resettle **9** immigrate
participant: 5 donee, donor
transport: 2 RV **3** ATV, bus, cab, car, jet, lug, run, SST, SUV, tow, van, wow **4** auto, bear, bike, boat, cart, hack, haul, jeep, lift, limo, move, oust, pack, raft, rail, ride, semi, send, ship, stir, take, taxi, tote, tram **5** barge, bring, canoe, carry, charm, exile, ferry, fetch, kayak, liner, lorry, moped, plane, stage, train, trike, truck, umiak, wagon **6** banish, big rig, convey, copter, deport, excite, go-cart, go-kart, jitney, ravish, remove, thrill **7** beatify, bewitch, bicycle, carrier, conduct, delight, deliver, elevate, enthral, forward, inthral, passage, passion, rapture, taxicab, vehicle **8** airplane, carriage, displace, enthrall, entrance, haul away, inthrall, railroad, relegate, rickshaw, shipping, tricycle **9** ambulance, captivate, carry away, electrify, enrapture, fascinate, freighter, limousine, motor home, order to go, spellbind **10** automobile, conveyance, enthusiasm, exaltation, expatriate, exultation, helicopter, stagecoach
transportation: 4 lift, ride **7** traffic
system: 4 line **8** railroad
Transportation Dept. div: 3 FAA
transported: 4 rapt **5** borne **6** enrapt **9** overjoyed **10** spellbound
transporter: 5 dolly **6** bearer **7** carrier, vehicle **8** conveyor **9** consignee
transpose: 3 put **4** move, swap, swop **5** alter, shift **6** change, invert, switch **7** reorder, reverse **8** exchange, flip-flop, relocate **9** rearrange
transposition: 8 exchange
Trans-Siberian Railroad city: 4 Omsk **6** Moscow **7** Irkutsk **11** Vladivostok
transude: 4 ooze, seep
Transvaal resident: 4 Boer
transverse: 4 span **5** cross **6** skewed, zigzag **8** diagonal
to: 6 across
transversely: 4 over **6** across **7** athwart
Transylvania, from: 6 Balkan **8** Romanian, Rumanian
trap: 3 bag, get, gin, nab, net, web, yap **4** bait, door, dupe, fool, grab, hook, land, lure, nail, plot, ploy, ruse, snag, take, wile **5** bazoo, box in, catch, decoy, feint, lasso, mouth, noose, prank, seize, setup, snare, trick **6** ambush, bunker, collar, come-on, corner, corral, device, dupery, enmesh, gambit, gotcha, immesh, inmesh, rope in, suck in, tangle, trip up **7** beguile, capture, deceive, dragnet, ensnare, insnare, mineral, pitfall, springe, trammel **8** accouter, accoutre, artifice, entangle, intrigue, inveigle, maneuver, overtake, quagmire, surprise **9** ambuscade, bushwhack, deception, quicksand, stratagem **10** ambushment, bring to bay, circumvent, conspiracy, enticement, lobster pot, subterfuge, temptation
booby ~: 4 mine, ruse, trap **5** snare **7** pitfall **8** obstacle **9** explosive
elephant ~: 5 kheda **6** keddah, khedah
ender: 5 light **7** shooter **8** shooting
filler: 4 sand
fish ~: 3 net, pot **4** weir **5** seine **6** eelpot
fly ~: 3 web **5** mouth **6** cobweb
fodder: 4 bait **6** cheese
like some ~s: 6 baited
sand ~: 6 bunker, hazard
set a ~: 4 bait, draw, hook, lure **5** decoy, snare, tempt, trick **6** allure, entice, induce, lead on, rope in, suck in **7** attract, capture, ensnare, mislead
shut one's ~: 6 clam up
starter: 3 fly, rat **4** clap, fire **5** mouse **6** rattle
trap __: 4 door
__ trap: 4 lint, sand, set a **5** booby, radar, speed, steel **7** tourist
trap, as ~: 6 adsorb
use ~: 4 cook **5** grill
trapdoor: 4 drop **5** hatch **6** device
locale: 5 floor
Trapeze (1956 film)
cast: Tony Curtis, Burt Lancaster, Gina Lollobrigida
trapeze artist: 7 acrobat
like a ~: 5 agile, gutsy **6** daring **8** fearless, intrepid **9** unfearing
need: 3 net
often: 5 flier, flyer
Trapeze, The
artist: Erté
trapezium: 4 bone **5** shape
locale: 5 wrist
trapezoid: 4 bone **5** shape
locale: 5 wrist
trapped: 5 at bay, stuck **6** in a box, in a fix, in a jam **7** in a mess, up a tree **9** on the spot **10** in hot water, on the ropes
Trapped (2002 film)
cast: Kevin Bacon, Courtney Love, Charlize Theron
trapped like __: 4 a rat
trapper: 6 hunter
bundle: 3 kip
commodity: 4 hide, pelt
Trapper John, M.D. (CBS drama)
cast: Gregory Harrison (Dr. George 'Gonzo' Gates)
Brian Mitchell (Dr. Justin 'Jackpot' Jackson)
Christopher Norris (Nurse Gloria Brancusi)
Pernell Roberts (Dr. John McIntyre)
Charles Siebert (Dr. Stanley Riverside)
trappings: 4 garb, gear **5** dress, getup, goods, robes, stuff **6** attire, finery, livery, outfit, tackle, things **7** apparel, clothes, costume, effects, garment, panoply, raiment, rigging **8** clothing **9** caparison, equipment, ornaments, trimmings **10** adornments, Sunday best
Trappist: 4 monk
home: 5 abbey
Trappist __: 4 monk **6** cheese
traps game: 4 golf **5** skeet
trapshooting: 5 skeet
shout: 4 pull
__ Trap, The: 6 Parent, Tender
trash: 3 sap **4** junk, rout, scum, whip **5** abuse, chaff, drain, dregs, dross, filth, offal, outdo, quash, scorn, scrap, smash, spoil, waste, wreck **6** burn up, debris, deface, defeat, defile, grunge, impugn, litter, ravage, refuse, review, rubble, scraps, shards **7** baloney, deplete, destroy, garbage, profane, residue, rubbish, trounce **8** demolish, fool away, leavings, leftover, mistreat, oddments, sediment, shavings, squander **9** criticize, devastate, dissipate, eradicate, overpower, pick apart, scourings, sweepings, vandalize
collector: 5 sanit. **6** ashman **10** sanitation
collector in Britain: 7 dustman
compactor part: 6 basket
hauler: 4 scow
holder: 4 dump **6** ashcan **8** Dumpster, landfill
ignore the ~ can: 5 strew **6** litter **7** clutter, scatter **9** make a mess
see also baloney
trash __: 3 bin, can
trashing: 6 defeat
trashy: 4 base, junk, punk **5** cheap **6** grungy, shoddy, sleazy **7** raffish **8** unusable **9** worthless
Trask: 3 Cal **4** Adam, Aron
trattoria: 6 eatery **7** Italian **10** ristorante
dessert: 6 gelati, gelato **7** spumoni, tortoni **8** tiramisu
device: 6 grater
drink: 4 vino **7** chianti
order: 4 eels, orzo, vino, ziti **5** pasta, penne, pesce, pollo, squid, zitti, zuppa **7** lasagna, lasagne, pastina, ravioli **8** bucatini, calamari, farfalle, linguine, linguini, macaroni, rigatoni **9** agnolotti, angelhair, cavatelli, manicotti, scungilli, spaghetti **10** cannelloni, fettuccini, tortellini, vermicelli
topping: 5 pesto **8** marinara
Traubel, Helen: 6 singer **7** soprano
specialty: 5 opera
trauma: 4 blow, hurt, jolt, pain **5** agony, shock, upset, wound **6** damage, injury, ordeal, strain, stress **7** anguish, torture **8** collapse, upheaval **9** confusion, suffering
aftermath: 4 scar
site: 2 ER
traumatic: 6 tragic **7** painful **8** chilling, grievous **9** harrowing, torturous **10** disturbing, petrifying, terrifying, tormenting
traumatize: 4 hurt, scar **5** shock, wound **6** stress
traumatophobe fear: 6 injury
travail: 3 ado, woe **4** pain, toil, work **5** agony, grind, labor **6** misery **7** anguish, despair, torment **8** distress, drudgery, exertion, hardship **9** adversity, grunt work, suffering **10** hard knocks, infelicity
Travail
author: Émile Zola
travel: 2 go **3** fly, gad, jet **4** move, ride, roam, rove, sail, tour, trek, trip, waft, walk, wend **5** drive, jaunt, motor, range, swing, visit **6** biking, cruise, flying, junket, motion, ramble, repair, set out, voyage, wander **7** commute, explore, go to see, journey, migrate, passage, proceed, transit, weekend **8** ambulate, go abroad, go places, movement, progress, set forth, sightsee, vacation **9** adventure, circulate, excursion, overnight, range over, round trip, seafaring, take a trip, wayfaring **10** expedition, knock about, locomotion, navigation, wanderlust
abbr.: 3 arr., ETA, ETD
account: 3 log
across: 4 span **5** cover **7** stretch **8** traverse
agent offering: 4 tour **6** cruise **8** vacation
aimlessly: 3 gad **4** roam, rove **6** ramble
bag: 4 grip **5** trunk **8** suitcase
brief ~: 7 sojourn
document: 4 visa **8** passport
fast: 3 fly **4** zoom
guide: 8 Baedeker, handbook, tour book
guide name: 5 Fodor **7** Frommer
in: 2 do
in neutral: 5 coast, glide **6** cruise

mode of ~: 3 bus, cab, car, jet 4 auto, boat, foot, rail, ship 5 liner, plane, train 10 cruise ship
org.: 3 AAA
plan: 5 route 8 schedule 9 itinerary
prepare to ~: 4 pack
reference: 3 map 4 plan 5 atlas, chart, globe
to work: 4 ride 5 drive 7 commute
watchdog: 4 NTSB
travel __: 4 time 5 agent 6 agency 7 trailer
__ travel: 4 time 5 space
traveler: 4 goer, hobo 5 farer, gypsy, nomad, rover, tramp 6 roamer, sailor, vender, vendor 7 drifter, migrant, pilgrim, rambler, tourist, trekker, trouper, vagrant, voyager 8 commuter, explorer, gadabout, seafarer, vagabond, wanderer, wayfarer 9 itinerant, jet-setter, journeyer, navigator, passenger, sightseer 10 adventurer, hitchhiker, vacationer
bane: 4 duty, wait 5 delay 6 jet lag
choice: 3 bus, car, jet 4 auto, boat, ship 5 liner, plane, route, train
fast ~: 7 bad news
need: 3 bag, inn, map 4 visa 5 hotel, motel 7 lodging, luggage 8 passport
world ~: 5 nomad, rover 7 voyager 8 gadabout, vagabond, wanderer, wayfarer 10 adventurer
__ traveler: 6 fellow
Traveler: 3 car 4 auto 6 Hudson 10 automobile
traveler's __: 5 check
Travelers
competitor: *see* insurance company
Travelin' Band (1970 song)
artist: Creedence Clearwater Revival
traveling: 4 gone 6 aboard, abroad, errant, mobile 7 en route, nomadic, on the go 8 embarked, underway 9 itinerant, migratory, on the move, on the road, peregrine, wayfaring 10 locomotion, navigation
group: 4 band 6 convoy, safari 7 caravan, cortege 9 cavalcade 10 expedition, procession
traveling __: 3 bag
Travelin' Man (1961 song)
artist: Ricky Nelson
Traveller: 4 mare 5 horse, steed 6 equine
rider: Robert E. Lee
Travelodge: 5 motel
alternative: *see* motel
travelogue: 5 short
Travels with Charley
author: John Steinbeck
Travels With My __: 4 Aunt
Travers: 2 P.L. 4 Bill, Mary 5 Henry
traversal: 4 xing 6 bridge 8 crossing, junction, overpass 10 cloverleaf
traverse: 4 move, rove, span, walk 5 cover, cross, range 6 bridge, go over 7 explore, viaduct 8 go across, overpass 9 cut across, intersect, negotiate, range over 10 crisscross
traverse __: 3 rod
traversing: 6 across
Travers, P.L.: 6 writer 10 Australian
work: Mary Poppins
travesty: 4 mock, sham 5 farce, roast, spoof 6 parody, satire, send-up 7 burlesk, lampoon, mockery, takeoff 9 burlesque, imitation 10 caricature, distortion
Travis: 4 Bill 5 McGee, Nancy, Randy, Tritt 7 William
Travolta, John: 5 actor
film: Be Cool (2005)
Blow Out (1981)
Broken Arrow (1996)
Carrie (1976)
A Civil Action (1998)
Domestic Disturbance (2001)
Face/Off (1997)
The General's Daughter (1999)
Get Shorty (1995)
Grease (1978)
Hairspray (2007)
Ladder 49 (2004)
Look Who's Talking (1989)
Lucky Numbers (2000)
Michael (1996)
Perfect (1985)
Phenomenon (1996)
Primary Colors (1998)
Pulp Fiction (1994)
Saturday Night Fever (1977)
Swordfish (2001)
The Taking of Pelham 123 (2009)
Urban Cowboy (1980)
Wild Hogs (2007)
song: Let Her In (1976)
Summer Nights (1978)
You're the One That I Want (1978)
spouse: Kelly Preston
TV: Welcome Back, Kotter
trawl: 3 net, tow 4 drag, fish 7 dragnet, fish net
trawl __: 3 net
trawler: 4 boat 6 angler 9 fisherman
equipment: 3 net 5 seine
tray: 3 hod 4 till 5 plate 6 salver, server 7 platter 9 container, lazy Susan
starter: 3 ash
tray __: 5 table
__ tray: 3 bed, tea 6 cheese 7 butler's
Traynor, Pie: 6 Pirate 9 infielder
tre: 5 three 7 Italian
follower: 7 quattro
preceder: 3 due
tre __: 5 corde
Treacher: 6 Arthur
treacherous: 3 icy, sly 4 evil, ugly 5 false, hairy, lying, Punic, risky, slick, snaky 6 chancy, feline, rotten, shifty, tricky, unsafe, untrue, wicked 7 corrupt, crooked, devious, knavish, ominous 8 disloyal, menacing, perilous, slippery, two-faced 9 betraying, dangerous, deceitful, deceptive, faithless, hazardous, insidious, nefarious, two-timing, underhand, unhealthy
one: 5 viper
treachery: 5 fraud, guile 6 deceit, dupery 7 falsity, perfidy, sellout, treason 8 bad faith, betrayal, sabotage 9 deception, desertion, dirty work, duplicity, fourberie, two-timing 10 conspiracy, dishonesty, disloyalty, infidelity, untrueness
treacly: 5 sweet
tread: 3 pad 4 gait, pace, plod, rung, slog, step, walk 5 clomp, crush, march, stamp, track, tramp 6 squash, step on, stride, trudge 7 oppress, stamp on, trample 8 ambulate, footstep
ender: 4 mill
heavily: 5 stomp, tromp
on one's toes: 3 bug, get, irk, try, vex 4 gall, miff, rile 5 anger, annoy, grate, peeve, pique, upset 6 bother, enrage, nettle, offend, ruffle 7 affront, agitate, disturb, incense, inflame, outrage, provoke 8 distress, irritate 9 infuriate 10 antagonize, exasperate
on the heels of: 4 tail 5 trail
riser plus ~: 5 stair
the boards: 3 act 4 play 7 perform
warily: 9 pussyfoot
tread __: 5 water
treadless: 4 bald
treadmill: 3 rut 7 routine 10 monotonous
use a ~: 3 run
tread the __: 6 boards
treas.: 4 exec.
treason: 5 crime 6 felony, mutiny, revolt 7 perfidy 8 betrayal, sedition 9 duplicity, treachery 10 disloyalty, untrueness
commit ~: 6 betray, desert 7 sell out
in French: 11 lèse majesté
__ treason: 4 high
treasonous: 3 bad 7 corrupt 8 disloyal 9 seditious
treasure: 3 gem, pet 4 find, gold, like, love, pile, save 5 adore, angel, cache, catch, go for, guard, hoard, jewel, money, pearl, prize, trove, value 6 esteem, revere, riches, wealth 7 care for, cherish, fortune, idolize, jewelry, paragon, worship 8 enshrine, hold dear, inshrine, remember, richness, valuable 9 care about, nonpareil, reverence 10 appreciate, sweetheart
guarder: 5 gnome
hide ~: 4 bury 5 cache, inter, stash
holder: 4 safe 5 chest 6 coffer
hunter gear: 3 map 5 scuba, sonar
map features: 3 xes 4 exes
trove: 4 mine 7 bonanza
treasure __: 4 hunt 5 chest, house
treasure-__: 5 trove
treasured: 4 dear 5 sweet 7 beloved, darling 8 precious, valuable 9 priceless
Treasure Island: 5 novel
author: Robert Louis Stevenson
character: 3 Jim, Pew 4 Bill 5 Bones, Hands 6 Israel, pirate, Silver 7 Ben Gunn, Hawkins, Livesey 8 Black Dog, Long John, Smollett 9 Bill Bones, Trelawney 10 Jim Hawkins
director: Victor Fleming
prop: 3 map
topic: 6 piracy
Treasure of Love (1956 song)
artist: Clyde McPhatter
Treasure of the Sierra Madre, The (1948 film)
cast: Humphrey Bogart, Walter Huston
composer: Max Steiner
director: John Huston
treasurer: 3 CFO 4 fisc 6 banker, bursar, purser 8 official
treasures: 9 valuables
Treasure State capital: 6 Helena
treasury: 4 bank, fisc, fund, mine, safe, till 5 chest, hoard, purse, store, vault 6 coffer, museum 7 archive 8 exchange, Fort Knox, money box, war chest 9 anthology, exchequer, strongbox 10 collection, compendium, cumulation, depository, repository, storehouse
Treasury
agent: 4 T-man
Dept. agcy.: 3 ATF, IRS
offering: 4 bill, bond, note 5 E bond, T-bill, T-bond, T-note
treat: 4 blow, cure, dose, gift, heal, verb 5 dress, goody, nurse, party, stand, sweet, taffy, toffy 6 buy for, dainty, doctor, employ, go into, goodie, handle, look on, luxury, morsel, pay for, regale, regard, sundae, tidbit, toffee 7 discuss, indulge, operate, process, provide, take out, touch on 8 deal with, delicacy, lollipop, look upon, medicate, minister, play host, pleasure, surprise 9 act toward, amusement, entertain, interpret, prescribe, spring for, touch upon 10 minister to, reckon with, speak about, write about
as inferior: 5 deign, stoop 7 stoop to 10 condescend, look down on, talk down to
badly: 4 snub 5 abuse, cheat, shaft, spurn, wrong 6 demean, deride, ill-use, slight 7 swindle 8 mistreat
ender: 3 ise
glass: 6 temper 7 toughen
tenderly: 4 baby 6 cosset, dote on, pamper 7 cater to, indulge
__ treat: 5 Dutch
__-treat: 3 ill 4 heat
Treat: 8 Williams
treater's phrase: 4 on me
treating, he's: 5 payer
treatise: 5 essay, paper 6 thesis, volume 7 descant, discant, writing 9 discourse, monograph 10 commentary, exposition, literature
Treatise of Human Nature, A
author: David Hume
Treatise on Money
author: John Maynard Keynes
Treat Me Nice (1957 song)
artist: Elvis Presley
treatment: 3 use 4 cure, diet 5 style, usage 6 design, method, remedy 7 conduct, healing, reading, regimen, surgery, therapy 8 analysis, approach, behavior, handling, medicine, practice, strategy 9 attention, doctoring, execution, operation, reception 10 management, medication
bad ~: 4 harm 5 abuse 6 attack, injury, insult, misuse 7 affront, assault, beating, mauling, slander, torment, torture 8 deri-

sion, inequity **9** injustice, invective **10** backbiting, defamation, disrespect, imputation, oppression, revilement, upbraiding
favored ~: 4 bias **9** advantage, privilege, seniority **10** preference
__ treatment: 5 water **6** silent, window
treaty: 4 bond, pact **5** peace, terms, truce **6** accord, cartel, league **7** charter, compact, concord, entente **8** alliance, contract, covenant, protocol **9** agreement, armistice, concordat **10** convention, settlement
1629 ~ city: 5 Nîmes
1814 ~ site: 5 Ghent
1993 ~: 5 NAFTA
initials: 4 SALT **5** SEATO
modern ~ subject: 5 A-test
party to a ~: 4 ally **9** signatory
signer: 5 inker
subject: 6 border **8** boundary, frontier **9** perimeter
__ treaty: 5 peace **7** test-ban
Treaty of __: 5 Ghent, Paris
Treaty of Nanking port: 4 Amoy
Trebek: 4 Alex, host **5** emcee
answer ~: 3 ask **5** query **7** inquire
homeland: 6 Canada
treble: 4 clef, high **6** shrill **8** piercing
clef lines: 5 EGBDF
staff marking: 5 G clef
Tredia: 3 car **4** auto **10** automobile, Mitsubishi
tree: 3 apa, ash, bay, bel, elm, fig, fir, koa, oak, ule, yew **4** acle, agba, akee, bael, baum, cork, hebe, ilex, ipil, itea, kaki, karo, kola, lime, neem, ombu, palm, pear, pich, pili, pine, plum, poon, pulp, shea, sloe, sorb, teak, trap, upas **5** abele, alder, algum, almon, almug, apple, arbre, areca, aspen, athel, babul, balsa, beech, birch, bodhi, boldo, cacao, carob, cedar, ceiba, cirio, ebony, elder, erica, ficus, genip, guava, hakea, hazel, henna, holly, ixora, karri, kauri, kiawe, kukui, larch, lehua, lemon, limba, mahoe, mahua, mahwa, mango, maple, mohwa, mowra, mulga, olive, osier, papal, papaw, peach, pecan, plant, ramon, rowan, shrub, smoke, stimy, stymy, sumac, thuja, thuya, wahoo, yapon, yulan **6** acacia, acajou, alerce, almond, amugis, anatto, annona, antiar, balata, balche, banana, banian, banyan, baobab, bonduc, boojum, calaba, carapa, cashew, cassia, cercis, cherry, citron, cobnut, coffee, cornel, corner, deodar, durian, fatsia, fustet, fustic, gaboon, gingko, ginkgo, hognut, jarrah, jujube, kapuka, kowhai, laurel, lebbek, lichee, linden, litchi, locust, longan, loquat, lungan, mammee, mastic, mayten, medlar, mimosa, mowrah, nutmeg, obeche, orange, padauk, padouk, papaya, pawpaw, pignut, pituri, pomelo, poplar, pumelo, quince, redbud, rubber, sapele, sapota, sorrel, spruce, storax, stymie, sumach, tarata, timber, tupelo, walnut, wandoo, willow, yaupon **7** acerola, almique, ambatch, annatto, apricot, araroba, arbutus, assagai, assegai, avocado, avodire, banksia, boxwood, buckeye, cajeput, camphor, canella, catalpa, champac, cypress, deodara, dogwood, filbert, geebung, genipap, hemlock, hickory, juniper, karanda, leechee, logwood, madrone, mesquit, morello, plumcot, pommelo, pummelo, quassia, redwood, sapling, sequoia, seringa, soursop, syringa, tangelo, wallaba, yohimbe, zelkova **8** alamiqui, albizzia, allspice, andiroba, barbasco, basswood, bauhinia, bayberry, beefwood, bergamot, bluewood, calabash, caragana, carnauba, champaca, chestnut, cinchona, cinnamon, coat rack, cockspur, cocobolo, coolabah, crabwood, divi-divi, gardenia, hardwood, hawthorn, hibiscus, hornbeam, jelutong, landmark, limequat, magnolia, mahogany, mandarin, mangrove, mesquite, milkwood, mulberry, oiticica, oleaster, palmetto, photinia, piassava, rosewood, sandarac, seedling, shaddock, shagbark, softwood, sycamore, tamarack, tamarind, tamarisk **9** ailanthus, bloodwood, buckthorn, butternut, candlenut, hackberry, jacaranda, nectarine, persimmon, pistachio, poinciana, sapodilla, sassafras, tangerine **10** arborvitae, blackthorn, breadfruit, bring to bay, buttonwood, cottonwood, eucalyptus, grapefruit, vegetation
Africa: 4 kola, shea **5** babul, limba **6** balata, baobab, gaboon, obeche, padauk, padouk, sapele **7** almique, ambatch, assagai, assegai, avodire, yohimbe **8** alamiqui, sandarac **9** bloodwood
anchor: 4 root **7** rootage
aromatic ~: 3 fir **4** pine **5** cedar **8** bayberry, rosewood
Asia: 4 toon, upas **5** henna **6** cassia, durian, lichee, litchi, padauk, padouk **7** champac, leechee, zelkova **8** caragana, champaca **9** candlenut, carambola
Australia: 5 hakea, karri, mulga **6** jarrah, pituri, wandoo **7** banksia, cajeput, geebung **8** beefwood, coolabah **10** eucalyptus
banned ~ spray: 4 Alar
barking up the wrong ~: 5 wrong **6** all wet, misled, way off **7** deluded, off-base **8** deceived, mistaken **9** misguided **10** ill-advised
bark up the wrong ~: 3 err **7** blunder
branch: 4 limb, rame
branches: 5 shade **6** canopy **8** overhang
bump: 4 burl, knar, knot, knur **5** gnarl
Canada: 5 maple
China: 5 yulan **6** gingko, ginkgo, lichee, litchi, longan, lungan **7** leechee **14** mandarin. loquat
Christmas ~: 3 fir **4** pine **6** balsam
citrus ~: 3 bel **4** bael, lime **5** lemon **6** orange, pomelo, pumelo **7** pommelo, pummelo, tangelo **8** bergamot, mandarin, shaddock **9** tangerine **10** grapefruit
combining form: 3 dry- **4** dryo- **5** dendr- **6** dendri-, dendro- **7** -dendron
covering: 4 bark
cut down a ~: 3 axe, hew, log, saw **4** fell **5** clear **6** lumber
decorate the ~: 4 trim
end: 5 stump
ender: 3 top **4** nail **6** hopper
Europe: 4 sorb **5** larch, rowan
evergreen ~: 3 yew **4** pine **5** athel, boldo, cacao, erica, hakea, olive, thuja, thuya **6** alerce, laurel, longan, loquat, lungan, spruce **7** arbutus, cypress, juniper **8** gardenia **9** sapodilla **10** arborvitae
fallen ~: 3 log
family ~: 5 roots **8** pedigree **9** forebears
feller: 3 axe, saw **5** axman **6** axeman
graft a ~ branch: 6 inarch
graft site: 4 node
group: 4 mott **5** copse, grove, motte, stand, woods **6** forest **7** coppice, orchard
growth: 4 leaf **5** frond **6** needle **7** foliage
hardwood ~: 3 ash, oak **4** poon, teak **5** ebony, larch, lehua **6** jarrah, locust, wandoo **7** wallaba **8** mahogany
Hawaii: 3 koa **4** ohia **5** kukui, lehua
hybrid ~: 7 plumcot **8** limequat
India: 3 bel **4** bael, pich, poon, teak **5** bodhi, ebony, mahua, mahwa, mohwa, mowra, papal, pipal, rohan **6** banian, banyan, deodar, mowrah, nutmeg, peepul **7** deodara, karanda, soursop **8** cinnamon
Japan: 4 kaki **6** bonsai, loquat
juice: 3 sap
like a summer ~: 6 in leaf
like ground around a ~: 5 rooty
like some ~ barks: 5 mossy
like some ~ trunks: 6 gnarly
locale: 5 woods
malady: 6 dry rot
Mediterranean: 4 cork **5** carob **6** mastic
Mexico: 5 cirio **6** boojum, sapota
New Zealand: 4 hebe, karo, rimu **5** kauri, mapau **6** kapuka, kowhai, tarata
nymph: 5 dryad
ornament: 4 star **5** angel
palm ~: 4 sago **5** areca **8** carnauba, piassava
part: 5 bough, trunk **6** branch
part of a family ~: 3 son **4** aunt **5** niece, uncle **6** cousin, father, mother, nephew **8** daughter
Philippines: 3 tua **4** acle, ipil, pili **5** almon, lauan **6** amugis
product: 4 pulp, wood **5** resin **6** lumber
rings: 6 annuli
science: 8 forestry
shade ~: 3 ash, elm, oak **5** beech, maple **6** linden
shoot: 4 twig
small ~: 5 shrub
South America: 4 ombu **5** boldo, maqui **6** alerce, carapa, mayten, rubber **7** araroba, seringa, wallaba **8** andiroba, carnauba, cinchona, crabwood, oiticica, piassava
Southwest: 5 alamo, piñon
spigot: 5 spile
sprite: 5 nymph
stunted ~: 5 scrub
tissue: 5 xylem **6** phloem
trim a ~: 3 lop **5** prune
tropical ~: 3 apa, fig **4** agba, akee, kola, neem, palm, upas **5** balsa, cacao, ficus, genip, guava, ixora, kiawe, mahoe, mango, ramon **6** anatto, annona, antiar, balata, banana, baobab, bonduc, calaba, cashew, coffee, fustic, jujube, lebbek, mammee, mimosa, obeche, padauk, padouk, papaya, pawpaw **7** acerola, annatto, avocado, genipap, quassia, yohimbe **8** albizzia, allspice, barbasco, bauhinia, calabash, cocobolo, divi-divi, mahogany, mangrove, tamarind, tamarisk **9** jacaranda, poinciana, sapodilla **10** breadfruit, grapefruit
trunk: 4 bole
trunk, in Britain: 4 stam
up a ~: 6 in a fix, in a jam **7** trapped **10** in hot water, on the ropes
West Indies: 4 pich **7** canella **8** milkwood
tree __: 4 farm, toad **5** house, shrew **7** surgeon
tree-__: 6 hugger
__ tree: 3 hat, up a **4** coat **5** fruit, money, shade **6** family **7** clothes
__ Tree: 5 Lemon
Tree at My Window
author: Robert Frost
treed: 5 at bay **7** trapped **8** cornered **10** out on a limb
__ tree falls...: 3 If a
Tree Grows in Brooklyn, A
author: Betty Smith
treehouse support: 4 limb **6** branch
treeless area: 5 llano, marsh, pampa
treelike: 6 sylvan **8** arboreal
tree-lined: 5 shady
road: 4 pkwy. **5** paseo **7** parkway
__ Tree National Park: 6 Joshua
tree of life location: 4 Eden
Tree of Man, The
author: Patrick White
Tree Planters State: 3 Neb. **4** Nebr. **8** Nebraska
trees: 4 wood **5** silva, sylva, woods **6** timber
Trees
author: Joyce Kilmer
Trees, The
author: Conrad Richter
tree-to-be: 4 seed **5** acorn
tref, not: 6 kasher, kosher
__ Treize: 5 Louis

trek: **4** hadj, hike, plod, roam, rove, slog, tour, trip, walk **5** jaunt, march, range, tramp **6** foot it, junket, outing, safari, trapes, travel, trudge, wander **7** journey, migrate, odyssey, passage, traipse **8** ambulate **9** migration **10** emigration, expedition, knock about, pilgrimage
__ Trek: **4** Star
trekker: **5** hiker **8** traveler, vagabond, wayfarer **9** journeyer
trellis: **3** web **5** arbor **7** lattice
ender: **4** work
piece: **4** lath
plant: **3** ivy **5** grape
Tremain: **6** Johnny
Tremayne: **3** Les
tremble: **3** jar **4** lick, rock, stir **5** cower, pulse, quail, quake, shake, throb **6** cringe, dodder, jitter, quaver, quiver, recoil, shiver, teeter, thrill, totter, twitch, wabble, weaken, wobble **7** flutter, pulsate, shudder, vibrate **9** oscillate, palpitate
trembler: **4** bird **5** quake **10** earthquake
trembling: **5** jumpy, quaky, shaky, timid **6** ashake, tremor **7** jittery, vibrant **9** doddering, thrilling, vibration
tremendous: **3** big **4** huge, vast **5** awful, giant, great, hefty, jumbo, large, marvy, massy, super **6** mighty **7** amazing, awesome, fearful, hulking, immense, mammoth, massive, sizable, titanic **8** colossal, enormous, fabulous, gigantic, king-size, oversize, sizeable, terrible, terrific, towering, whapping, whopping **9** boundless, deafening, excellent, fantastic, Herculean, humongous, marvelous, monstrous, overlarge, wonderful **10** formidable, gargantuan, monumental, prodigious, stupendous
tremendousness: **5** range, reach **6** import **7** breadth, expanse **8** enormity, grandeur **9** amplitude, magnitude **10** dimensions, importance
tremor: **4** vibe **5** L wave, quake, seism, shake, shock **6** quaver, quiver, ripple, shiver, wabble, wobble **7** flutter, shudder, tremble **8** upheaval **9** trembling, vibration **10** aftershock, earthquake
Tremor Christ (1994 song)
artist: Pearl Jam
tremorous: **5** shaky
tremula, populus: **5** aspen
tremulous: **4** edgy, wavy **5** jumpy, shaky, timid **6** afraid, ashake, craven, on edge, scared, yellow **7** fearful, jittery, nervous, panicky, quivery, shaking **8** cowardly, shuddery, skittish **9** quivering **10** frightened, shuddering
trench: **3** cut, pit, rut **4** dike, foss, hole, moat **5** canal, ditch, fosse, gouge, gulch, gully **6** dugout, furrow, groove, gullet, gulley, gutter, trough **7** channel, foxhole **9** earthwork **10** depression, excavation
moon ~: **5** rille
ocean ~: **4** deep
trench __: **4** coat **7** warfare
__ Trench: **4** Java **7** Mariana
trenchant: **4** acid, keen, tart **5** blunt, clear, crisp, edged, pithy, sharp, terse **6** biting, gnomic, ireful, strong **7** acerbic, caustic, cutting, driving, graphic, mordant, peppery, piquant, pointed, pungent, salient, telling **8** clear-cut, critical, distinct, emphatic, forceful, incisive, poignant, powerful, sardonic, scathing **9** corrosive, effective, graphical, unsparing **10** razor-sharp, to the point
trencher: **5** plate
ender: **3** man, men
trencherman: **5** diner, eater **7** epicure, glutton **8** consumer, devourer, gourmand
trend: **3** fad, run **4** bent, bias, flow, look, mode, rage, tend, tide, tone, turn **5** craze, drift, style, tenor, thing, vogue **6** course, temper **7** current, fashion, in-thing, leaning **8** movement, tendency **9** direction, gravitate **10** likelihood
ender: **6** setter **7** setting
hot ~: **3** fad **4** rage **5** craze, mania, vogue **7** in thing
starter: **4** down
__ Trend: **5** Motor
trendy: **3** hip, hot, mod, new, now, out **4** chic, posh, tony **5** faddy, fresh, novel, sharp, smart, swank, swish, toney, vogue **6** chichi, latest, modish, snappy, swanky, unique **7** à la mode, current, in style, in vogue, popular, stylish, voguish **8** brand-new, last word, original, up-to-date **9** different, in fashion **10** all the rage, avant-garde, futuristic, innovative
group: **5** elite **6** jet set **7** in-crowd, society **8** well-to-do **9** beau monde **10** upper crust
no longer ~: **3** old **4** worn **5** dated, dusty, hoary, passé, stale, trite **6** old-hat **7** archaic, run-down, worn-out **8** obsolete, out of use, timeworn **9** hackneyed, out-of-date **10** antiquated
Trent: **4** city, Lott, town **5** river **6** Reznor **7** Barbara
city locale: **5** Italy
river: **5** Adige
River locale: **7** England
__ Trent D'Arby: **7** Terence
Trenton: **4** city, town **7** capital
county: **6** Mercer
locale: **8** Michigan **9** New Jersey
river: **8** Delaware
Trento river: **5** Adige
Trent's Last Case
author: E.C. Bentley
trepid: **5** timid **6** afeard, afraid, scared **7** abashed, afeared, alarmed, anxious, chicken, daunted, fearful, nervous, panicky, spooked **8** cowardly, fearsome, hesitant, timorous **9** petrified, terrified **10** frightened
not ~: **4** bold, pert **5** brash, brave, fresh, gutsy, macho, nervy, pushy, saucy **6** brassy, brazen, cheeky, daring, flashy, heroic, plucky, spunky **7** dashing, defiant, forward, gallant, valiant **8** fearless, forceful, immodest, impudent, resolute, spirited, unafraid, valorous **9** audacious, confident, dauntless, shameless, undaunted, unfearing **10** courageous, incautious, unreserved
trepidation: **4** fear **5** alarm, angst, dread, panic, qualm, shock, worry **6** creeps, dismay, fright, horror, stress, terror **7** anxiety, jitters **8** blue funk, cold feet, disquiet **9** cold sweat **10** uneasiness
tres: **5** three **7** Spanish
follower: **6** cuatro
preceder: **3** dos
très: **4** very **6** French
très __: **4** bien
Trés __: **4** Bien
trespass: **3** sin **4** tort **5** crime, error, fault, lapse, poach **6** breach, butt in, horn in, inroad, invade, meddle, nose in, offend **7** break in, impinge, intrude, misdeed, obtrude, offense, pillage, violate **8** encroach, infringe, invasion, muscle in, overstep **9** interlope, intrude on, intrusion, misbehave, obtrusion, penetrate, violation **10** encroach on, infraction, wrongdoing
Trespass (1992 film)
cast: Ice Cube, Ice-T, Bill Paxton
trespasser: **7** invader **8** criminal, intruder **10** interloper
Trespasser, The
author: D.H. Lawrence
trespassing: **6** inroad **7** ingress **9** violation
tress: **4** curl, hair, lock **5** braid, plait **6** strand **7** ringlet
tresses: **3** mop **4** hair **8** coiffure
trestle: **4** beam, rack **6** bridge
Trevayne
author: Robert Ludlum
Trevi Fountain
locale: **4** Rome **5** Italy
money: **4** euro, lira, lire
Trevino, Lee: **6** golfer
Trevor: **4** Nunn **6** Claire, Howard **7** Berbick **9** Griffiths
trews: **5** pants
T-rex: **5** biped **8** dinosaur
trey: **4** card, trio **6** triple **7** low card **9** three-spot
card before ~: **5** deuce
topper: **4** four
Trey: **5** Wingo **6** Parker, Wilson
Tri-__ Pictures: **4** Star
__ Tri: **5** Quang
triacetate fiber: **5** Arnel
triad: **4** trin, trio **5** chord, trine **6** triple, troika
triage site: **2** ER
trial: **3** woe **4** bane, care, case, drag, gage, load, loss, pain, pest, pill, suit, test **5** assay, check, essay, fight, fling, grief, pilot, proof, thorn, worry **6** action, burden, dry run, hassle, misery, ordeal, sorrow, tryout **7** attempt, contest, hearing, lawsuit, process, test run, trouble **8** acid test, analysis, audition, crucible, distress, endeavor, gauntlet, hardship, irritant, nuisance, struggle, tribunal, vexation **9** adversity, nightmare, probation, suffering, tentative **10** affliction, difficulty, experiment, heartbreak, indictment, irritation, litigation, misfortune, visitation
balloon: **4** test **6** feeler **7** enquiry, inquiry
bring to ~: **6** charge, indict **7** arraign **9** prosecute
companion: **5** error
evidence: **3** DNA
figure: **2** DA **5** judge, juror **6** lawyer **7** bailiff **9** barrister
precursor: **3** nab **4** bust, raid **6** arrest, collar **7** capture, hearing **9** detention
ritual: **4** oath, plea
run: **4** test **5** trial, whirl **10** experiment
scene: **5** venue
session: **6** assize
trial __: **3** run **6** docket, lawyer **7** balloon
__ Trial: **6** Monkey, Scopes
trial and __: **5** error
Trial and Error (1997 film)
cast: Jeff Daniels, Michael Richards, Charlize Theron, Rip Torn
__ trial basis: **3** on a
trial by __: **4** fire, jury
Trial by Jury
composer: W.S. Gilbert, Arthur Sullivan
Trial of a Poet
author: Karl Shapiro
Trial Run
author: Dick Francis
trials: **3** woe **10** infelicity
Trial, The
author: Franz Kafka
Triaminic
alternative: see cold remedy
triangle: **4** trio **5** shape, slice **6** triple **10** percussion
in heraldry: **5** gyron
kind of ~: **5** acute, right **6** obtuse **7** scalene **9** isosceles
part: **3** leg **4** base, side
ratio: **4** sine **6** cosine, secant **7** tangent
sound: **4** ting
tip: **4** apex **6** vertex
__ Triangle: **6** Devil's, Golden **7** Bermuda
triangular: **7** deltoid
heraldic charge: **5** gyron
insert: **6** gusset
letter: **5** delta
sail: **3** jib **5** raffe **6** lateen, raffee, raffie
sign: **5** Yield
support: **6** A-frame
wall: **5** gable
triathlete need: **4** bike
triathlon: **4** meet **5** event **7** contest
event: **3** run **4** swim **8** bike race
__ Triathlon: **7** Ironman
tribal: **6** racial
division: **4** clan **6** family
leader: **4** head **5** chief, elder **6** senior **9** matriarch, patriarch
Tribal-Love Rock Musical, The: **4** Hair
tribe: **3** Fox, Han, Kaw, Oto, Ree, Sac, Ute **4** clan, Coos, Cree, Crow, Cuna, Erie, Eyak, Hopi, Inca, Iowa,

Levi, Maya, Otoe, Pima, Pomo, race, Sauk, Seri, Tama, Taos, Tewa, Tiwa, Tupi, Yana, Yuma, Zuni **5** Ahtna, Bantu, Brulé, Caddo, Carib, Creek, Haida, horde, Huron, Inuit, Kansa, Kaska, Kiowa, Lenca, Lipan, Maidu, Makah, Miami, Miwok, Modoc, ocean, Omaha, Osage, Otomi, Piute, Ponca, Sioux, stock, Taino, Teton, Unami, Washo, Wintu, Yaqui **6** Abnaki, Ahtena, Apache, Arawak, Aymara, Cayuga, Cayuse, Dakota, Galibi, Innuit, Inupik, Jivaro, Kechua, Laguna, Lakota, Lengua, Lumbee, Mandan, Micmac, Mohave, Mohawk, Mojave, Munsee, nation, Navaho, Navajo, Nootka, Oglala, Ojibwa, Oneida, Ottawa, Paiute, Papago, Patwin, Pawnee, people, Pequot, Piegan, Plains, Pueblo, Quapaw, Salish, Santee, Seneca, Shasta, Skagit, Tanana, Toltec, Washoe, Wintun, Yahgan, Yakima, Yokuts **7** Abenaki, Arapaho, Arikara, Atakapa, Bannock, Chibcha, Chilcat, Chilkat, Chinook, Choctaw, Chumash, Guarani, Huastec, Kechuan, kindred, Klamath, Koyukon, Kutchin, Kutenai, Lakhota, lineage, Mahican, Mazatec, Miskito, Mohegan, Mohican, Naskapi, Nipmuck, Ojibway, Quechua, Quichua, San Blas, Shawnee, Takelma, Tanaina, Tlingit, Washita, Wichita, Wyandot, Yankton, Yavapai, Yucatec, Zapotec **8** Arapahoe, Cahuilla, Caingang, Cherokee, Cheyenne, Chippewa, Comanche, Delaware, Flathead, Hunkpapa, Illinois, Iroquois, Kickapoo, Kwakiutl, Malecite, Maricopa, Mikasuki, Missouri, Muskogee, Nez Percé, Onondaga, Ouachita, Powhatan, Puyallup, Quechuan, Sahaptin, Seminole, Shoshone, Squamish, Tarascan, Wabanaki, Wahpeton **9** Blackfoot, Chickasaw, Havasupai, Jicarilla, Karankawa, Menominee, Mescalero, Nanticoke, Penobscot, Saulteaux, Suquamish, Tehuelche, Tsimshian, Tuscarora, Wahpekute, Wampanoag, Winnebago, Wyandotte **10** Adirondack, Araucanian, Assiniboin, Athabaskan, Bellabella, Bellacoola, Chiricahua, Gros Ventre, Miniconjou, Potawatomi, Tarahumara
  see also Indian
tribes
  father of twelve ~: 5 Jacob
tribulation: 3 woe **4** care, pain **5** agony, curse, grief, trial, worry **6** burden, hassle, misery, ordeal, sorrow **7** bad luck, bad time, despair, reverse, sadness, trouble **8** distress, hard luck, hardship, hard time, headache, rainy day **9** adversity, heartache, suffering **10** hard knocks, misfortune
tribunal: 4 jury **5** court, forum, trial
Tribune: 5 paper **9** newspaper
  locale: 5 Tampa **7** Chicago, Oakland
Tribune-Review: 5 paper **9** newspaper
  locale: 10 Pittsburgh
tributary: 4 fork **5** creek, river **6** branch, feeder, inflow, stream **8** waterway **9** confluent, secondary, streamlet **10** collateral
tribute: 3 tax **4** geld, hand, kudo, toll **5** award, honor, kudos, salvo, toast **6** bounty, esteem, eulogy, heriot, homage, impost, praise, salute **7** acclaim, mention, ovation, plaudit, respect **8** accolade, applause, citation, encomium, flattery, good word, libation, memorial, monument, offering **9** extolment, laudation, panegyric, reference **10** compliment, exaltation
  pay ~ to: 4 hail **5** exalt, extol, honor **6** extoll, praise, salute **8** eulogize
Tribute: 3 SUV **5** Mazda
trice: 3 sec **4** jiff **5** jiffy **6** moment, second **7** eyewink, instant **9** twinkling
triceps
  locale: 3 arm
triceratops: 8 dinosaur
Tricia's mom: 3 Pat
trick: 2 do **3** art, con, fox, gag, use, way **4** bilk, dupe, fool, game, gull, have, hoax, lark, lure, nick, plot, ploy, rook, ruse, sham, snow, take, trap, verb, wile **5** antic, apery, blind, bluff, caper, catch, cheat, cozen, decoy, dodge, feint, fraud, hocus, knack, lying, phony, prank, put on, quirk, set up, shift, shill, skill, snare, spell, spoof, stunt **6** ambush, befool, deceit, delude, device, dupery, entrap, gambit, humbug, lead on, method, outwit, phoney, racket, rip off, scheme, secret, take in **7** beguile, deceive, defraud, ensnare, evasion, exploit, fake out, finagle, finesse, gimmick, insnare, knavery, know-how, mislead, sleight, snooker, snow job, swindle, tactics, two-time **8** artifice, disguise, flimflam, hang of it, hoodwink, illusion, maneuver, outsmart, pettifog, practice, pretense, sucker in, throw off **9** bamboozle, deception, disinform, expedient, four-flush, imposture, stratagem, technique, victimize **10** ambushment, hocus-pocus, imposition, shenanigan, subterfuge, tomfoolery
  alternative: 5 treat
  dirty ~: 5 cheat **8** mischief **9** duplicity
  do the ~: 4 work **7** satisfy, succeed **10** accomplish
  ender: 4 ster
  not missing a ~: 8 watchful **9** observant
trick __: 4 knee **6** ending
__ trick: 3 hat **4** card **5** do the
__ Trick: 5 Cheap
trickery: 3 art **4** hoax, scam **5** craft, dodge, fraud, guile, spoof, sting **6** deceit, dupery **7** con game, evasion, knavery, snow job **8** artifice, cheating, flimflam, intrigue, jugglery, pretense **9** chicanery, deception, fourberie, imposture, shell game, swindling **10** dishonesty
  get by ~: 4 gull **5** cheat, mulct **6** extort, fleece **7** defraud, swindle
__ trick in the book!, The: 6 oldest
trickle: 3 bit **4** drip, drop, flow, leak, ooze, seep, weep **5** exude, issue **6** filter, murmur, stream **7** distill, dribble **9** percolate
trickle-__ theory: 4 down
Trick of It, The
  author: Michael Frayn
Trick or __!: 5 treat
__-Trick Pony: 3 One
tricks: 5 magic
  bag of ~: 7 arsenal
  bid to take no ~: 5 nullo
  like dirty ~: 6 covert
__ tricks: 5 bag of, dirty
__ tricks?: 4 How's
tricks of the __: 5 trade
trickster: 4 liar **5** cheat, knave, rogue **6** rascal **8** swindler
trick-winning feat: 4 slam
tricky: 3 sly **4** cagy, deep, foxy, wily **5** cagey, dicey, false, lying, risky, rocky, shady, sharp, slick, tight **6** artful, chancy, crafty, knotty, quirky, shifty, shrewd, smooth, sneaky, sticky, subtle, thorny, touchy **7** complex, crooked, cunning, devious, elusive, elusory, evasive, furtive, knavish, prickly **8** delicate, delusive, guileful, involved, scheming, slippery, ticklish **9** deceitful, deceptive, designing, difficult, dishonest, insidious, insincere, intricate, sensitive, strategic, underhand **10** mendacious, misleading, perplexing, precarious, serpentine, touch-and-go, unreliable, untruthful
  problem: 5 poser **7** dilemma
tricolor: 4 flag
tricorne: 3 hat
tricot: 6 fabric **8** material
tricycle: 6 wheels
  user: 3 kid, tot **9** youngster
trident: 5 spear
  like a ~: 5 forky, tined **6** forked
  part: 4 tine
Trident: 10 chewing gum
  alternative: ***see*** chewing gum
tried and true: 4 safe, sure **5** liege, loyal, sound **6** proven, tested, trusty **7** staunch **8** approved, reliable **9** certified, qualified, reputable, steadfast, unfailing, venerable **10** dependable, time-tested
trier: 5 judge **10** prosecutor
Trieste: 4 city, gulf, port, town
  city near ~: 5 Udine
  locale: 5 Italy **6** Istria
trifecta: 3 bet **5** wager **6** gamble
trifle: 3 bit, jot, sou, toy **4** cake, dash, drop, hint, laze, play, snip, whit **5** curio, dally, flirt, pinch, shade, smack, speck, straw, taste, touch, trace **6** bauble, bêtise, coquet, dabble, dawdle, diddly, doodle, frivol, geegaw, gewgaw, lead on, linger, little, misuse, monkey, palter, potter, putter **7** bibelot, dessert, fribble, fritter, modicum, novelty, soupçon, toy with, trinket **8** fraction, lollygag, nicknack, particle, picayune, spoonful, squander **9** bagatelle, bric-a-brac, no big deal, play games, plaything, suspicion **10** dillydally, fool around, knickknack, mess around, play around, suggestion, triviality
  away: 5 drain, waste **8** misspend, squander **9** dissipate
  with: 5 tease **6** lead on
  (with): 3 toy **5** flirt **6** monkey, tinker
trifler: 5 flirt, toyer **7** dawdler
trifles: 6 trivia **8** minutiae
trifling: 3 low **4** lazy, mere, poor, puny, tiny, vain **5** banal, dinky, extra, light, minor, petty, silly, small, sorry, sport, teeny **6** little, measly, minute, paltry, slight, teensy, yeasty **7** nominal, shallow, trivial **8** needless, niggling, nugatory, optional, picayune, piddling, uncostly, unneeded **9** frivolity, frivolous, minuscule, redundant, worthless **10** negligible
  amount: 3 fig **8** pittance
trifocals: 5 specs **6** frames **7** glasses **10** spectacles
trig: 4 math, neat, tidy
  cousin: 3 alg. **7** algebra **8** calculus, geometry
  function: 3 cos, cot., sin, tan **4** cosh, sine, sinh, tanh **5** cosec. **6** arcsin, arctan, cosine, secant **7** tangent **8** cosecant
trigger: 4 spur, stir **5** cause, rouse, spark, start **6** elicit, ignite, incite, prompt, set off **7** inspire, produce, provoke **8** activate, generate, initiate, motivate, touch off **9** stimulate **10** bring about, give rise to, lead the way
  like some ~ fingers: 5 itchy
  mechanism: 5 timer
  pull the ~: 4 fire **5** shell, shoot
  quick on the ~: 5 sharp **6** astute
trigger __: 6 finger
trigger-__: 5 happy
__ trigger: 4 hair
Trigger: 5 horse, steed **6** equine
  rider: Roy Rogers
triglyceride: 5 ester
__ trigonometry: 5 plane
trike: 5 cycle
  part: 5 wheel
  rider: 3 kid, tot **9** youngster
trilby: 3 hat
  material: 4 felt
Trilby
  author: George du Maurier
trill: 4 pipe, roll, sing **5** chirr, churr **6** chirre, quaver, warble **7** chirrup, vibrato
  relative: 7 tremolo
Trillin, Calvin piece: 5 essay
Trilling: 6 Lionel
trillion
  combining form: 4 tera-, treg- **5** trega-
trillions: 4 lots **6** scores **7** legions
trillionth
  combining form: 4 pico-
trillium: 5 plant **6** flower
Trillo: 5 Manny
trilobite: 6 fossil
trilogy: 4 trio **6** triple
  first of a ~: 5 part I
trim: 3 bob, cut, fit, lop, mow, top, wax **4** beat, clip, crop, deck, dock,

drub, edge, edit, form, hale, lace, lean, lick, neat, nice, pare, skin, slim, snip, snug, taut, thin, tidy, whip **5** adorn, array, clean, dress, erase, frame, frill, kempt, level, order, plane, prank, prink, prune, shape, shave, shear, sleek, slick, smart, spank, state, whack **6** barber, bedeck, border, comely, cut off, cut out, dapper, defeat, delete, digest, edging, even up, excise, fettle, fringe, health, kilter, neaten, piping, reduce, repair, spruce, svelte, thrash, wallop **7** abridge, clobber, compact, curtail, cut away, cut back, cut down, dress up, festoon, fitness, garnish, gilding, healthy, lambast, orderly, overrun, scissor, shapely, shorten, slender, smother, spangle, swindle, trounce, whittle, willowy **8** beautify, beribbon, boil down, clean-cut, condense, decorate, downsize, emblazon, graceful, lambaste, neatness, ornament, pare down, pretty up, slice off, spruce up, to rights, trimming, truncate, well-kept **9** adornment, beautiful, condition, cut back on, embellish, embroider, reprehend, scale down, shipshape, situation, smarten up, stabilize, summarize **10** abbreviate, blue-pencil, commission, decoration, fastidious, neat as a pin, statuesque
again: **5** recut, remow
a tree: **5** prune
in fighting ~: **5** tough **6** strong
__ trim: **5** out of
trimaran: **4** boat
__-Trimeton: **5** Chlor
trimmed: **5** level **7** fringed
it's often ~: **4** hair, sail
Trimmed Lamp, The
author: O. Henry
trimmer: **5** edger, razor
trimming: **4** edge, lace, trim **5** frame, frill **6** fringe **7** garnish **8** ornament **9** adornment **10** decoration
trimmings: **7** fixings **9** trappings
trim one's __: **5** sails
trin: **4** trio **5** triad **7** triplet **9** threesome
trine: **4** trio **5** triad **6** triple **7** triplet **9** threefold, threesome
Trini: **5** Lopez **8** Alvarado
Trinidad: **4** isle **6** island
Trinidad and Tobago: **4** isls. **5** isles **6** nation **7** country, islands
money: **4** cent **6** dollar
org.: **3** OAS
writer: **6** Selvon
Trinitron maker: **4** Sony
trinity: **4** trio **6** triple
Trinity: **5** river
author: Leon Uris
city on the ~: **6** Dallas **9** Fort Worth
part: **3** Son **6** Father **9** Holy Ghost **10** Holy Spirit
__ Trinity: **4** Holy
trinket: **3** toy **4** bead, gaud, junk, rock **5** bijou, charm, curio, dodad, glass, jewel, stone **6** bangle, bauble, doodad, gadget, geegaw, gewgaw, trifle **7** bibelot, fribble, jewelry, nothing, novelty, whatnot **8** bracelet, gimcrack, hardware, nicknack, ornament, reminder, sparkler, wristlet **9** bagatelle, objet d'art, plaything **10** decoration, knickknack
trio: **4** Magi, team, trey, trin **5** leash, three, triad, trine **6** triune, troika **7** ternion, trilogy, trinity, triplet **8** ensemble, triangle, triptych **9** threesome **10** triplicate
maybe: **4** band **5** combo
times three: **5** nonet
times two: **6** sextet
__ Triomphe: **5** Arc de
trip: **3** err, hop, run **4** bomb, buck, bust, fall, flop, hadj, hike, lope, lose, miss, play, skip, slip, step, tour, trek **5** drive, error, flunk, foray, jaunt, lapse, lurch, pitch, slide, swing **6** blow it, bungle, canter, cruise, errand, falter, flight, frolic, header, junket, outing, plunge, ramble, slip on, slip up, sprawl, spring, topple, totter, travel, tumble, vision, voyage **7** blunder, confuse, faux pas, founder, go under, go wrong, journey, misstep, mistake, odyssey, passage, stumble, wash out, weekend **8** fall flat, fall over, flounder, lay an egg, long haul, pratfall, throw off, unsettle **9** excursion, false move, false step, overnight, strike out **10** disconcert, expedition, pilgrimage
boat ~: **4** sail **6** cruise, voyage
delayer: **4** flat
ego ~: **5** pride **6** vanity
end a ~: **4** dock, land **6** arrive
ender: **4** wire **6** hammer
head ~: **6** vision **7** reverie
long ~: **4** trek **7** journey, sojourn **10** pilgrimage
motor ~: **4** spin
pleasure ~: **5** jaunt **6** junket, outing
prepare for a ~: **4** pack
record: **3** log **5** diary **7** journal, logbook
round ~: **4** tour **5** jaunt **6** junket, travel **7** circuit, journey **9** excursion
segment: **3** leg
short ~: **4** spin **5** jaunt, whirl **6** dayhop, errand, outing
souvenir: **5** photo **6** magnet, T-shirt
take a ~: **5** motor **6** travel
taker: **7** tourist **8** traveler **10** vacationer
the light fantastic: **4** step **5** dance, party, rumba, tango, waltz **6** cha-cha, rhumba **7** cut a rug
up: **4** trap **6** ascent
(up): **4** foul
__ trip: **3** ego **4** head, road, side **5** field, guilt, power, round, take a **6** return **7** fishing
__-trip: **3** day
tripe
see baloney
triphosphate: **5** ester
triple: **3** hit **4** trey **5** leash, triad, trine **6** triune, troika **7** ternion, trilogy, trinity **8** triangle **9** threesome
triple __: **3** sec **4** axel, jump, play **5** cream, crème **6** threat
__ triple: **3** RBI
Triple __: **5** Crown **7** Entente
Triple Alliance country: Austria-Hungary, Germany, Italy
Triple Crown: **5** award
event: **4** race **5** Derby **7** Belmont **9** Preakness
horse: **5** Omaha **7** Assault **8** Affirmed, Citation **9** Sir Barton, Whirlaway **10** Count Fleet, Gallant Fox, War Admiral **11** Seattle Slew, Secretariat
jockey: **5** Sande **6** Arcaro, Loftus **7** Cauthen, Cruguet, Longden **8** Mehrtens, Saunders, Turcotte **9** Earl Sande **10** Kurtsinger
triple-decker: **4** club **8** sandwich
Triple Fool, The
author: John Donne
triplet: **4** trin, trio **5** trine
triple witching __: **4** hour
triplicate: **4** trio
tripmeter setting: **3** OOO
tripod: **5** easel, stand
part: **3** leg
Tripoli: **4** city, port, town **7** capital
locale: **5** Libya **6** Africa **7** Lebanon, Mideast
native: **6** Libyan **8** Lebanese
old ~ governor: **3** dey
__-tripper: **3** ego
__ Tripper: **3** Day
trippet: **3** cam
Trippin' (1998 song)
artist: Missy Elliott, Total
tripping: **4** foul
Tripplehorn: **6** Jeanne
trip-routing org.: **3** AAA
trip the __ fantastic: **5** light
Triptik org.: **3** AAA
Trip to Bountiful, The (1985 film)
cast: John Heard, Geraldine Page
triptych: **4** trio
image: **5** icons
panel: **5** volet
trireme: **4** boat **6** galley
complement: **4** crew
tool: **3** oar
weapon: **3** ram
Tris: **7** Speaker
Triscuit: **7** cracker
alternative: *see* cracker
trisection part: **5** third
Trish: **9** Van Devere
Trisha: **8** Yearwood
triskaidekaphobe fear: **8** thirteen
Tristan: **6** knight
love: **6** Iseult, Isolde
Mark to: **5** uncle
Tristan da Cunha: **4** isle **6** island
Tristan und Isolde: **5** opera
composer: **6** Wagner
role: **4** Mark **5** Melot **8** Brangäne, King Mark, Kurwenal
setting: **6** France **7** England **8** Brittany, Cornwall
triste: **3** sad **6** French **9** sorrowful **10** melancholy
__ Triste: **5** Valse
__ Tristesse: **7** Bonjour
Tristia
author: Ovid
Tristram: **4** poem **6** Coffin, Shandy
author: Edward Arlington Robinson
Tristram Shandy
author: Laurence Sterne
trite: **3** set **4** dull, flat, worn **5** banal, chain, corny, hokey, musty, passé, silly, stale, stock, tired, vapid **6** common, jejune, old hat, used-up **7** clichéd, drained, fatuous, humdrum, insipid, prosaic, routine, trivial, worn-out **8** bathetic, bromidic, cornball, mildewed, ordinary, outdated, outmoded, overused, shopworn, timeworn, well-worn **9** exhausted, hackneyed, moth-eaten, played-out, prosaical, ready-made **10** dullsville, overworked, pedestrian, threadbare, uninspired, unoriginal, warmed-over
not as ~: **5** newer
remark: **6** cliché, saying **7** bromide **8** chestnut **9** platitude
triton: **4** newt **5** shell **8** seashell
Triton: **3** god **4** moon
daughter: **6** Pallas
parent: **8** Poseidon **10** Amphitrite
planet: **7** Neptune
sister: **5** Rhode
Tritt: **6** Travis
triturate: **5** grind, pound **6** powder **7** crumble **9** granulate, pulverize
triumph: **3** hit, joy, win **4** best, coup, crow, feat, gain, luck, palm, riot, sell, sink **5** cinch, exult, gloat, glory, homer, pride, revel, score, sweep **6** big hit, big win, make it, pan out, shoo-in, splash, subdue, thrive, winner, win out **7** achieve, conquer, delight, elation, jubilee, luck out, make out, prevail, prosper, rejoice, succeed, success, sure bet, swagger, trounce, victory, work out **8** blow away, conquest, dominate, flourish, get ahead, go places, hit it big, jubilate, make good, overcome, pushover, reveling, smash hit, takeover, vanquish, walkover **9** celebrate, checkmate, exultance, festivity, grand slam, jubilance, landslide, merriment, overwhelm, rejoicing, sensation, subjugate, sure thing **10** ascendance, ascendancy, ascendence, ascendency, attainment, clean sweep, exultation, gold record, jubilation, jump for joy
again: **5** rewin
exclamation: **3** aah, aha, hah, oho, olé, yay **4** I win, ta-da **5** hoo-ha, ta-dah, voilà **6** eureka, gotcha, hoo-hah, hoorah, hooray, hurrah, hurray, I did it, yippee **7** whoopee, whoopie
triumphal __: **4** arch
Triumph and Tragedy
author: Winston Churchill
triumphant: **5** happy, lucky, on top, proud **6** elated, joyful, joyous **7** gleeful, winning, winsome **8** boastful, champion, dominant, exultant, glorious, jubilant, out front, unbeaten **9** fortunate, rejoicing, triumphal **10** flying high, victorious

be ~: 4 brag, crow 5 exult, revel 7 rejoice 9 celebrate 10 effervesce, jump for joy
Triumph of the Egg, The
author: Sherwood Anderson
Triumph of the Spirit (1989 film)
cast: Willem Dafoe, Robert Loggia, Edward James Olmos
triumvirate: 4 trio 6 triple
triune: 4 trio 6 triple
trivia: 7 details, trifles 8 factoids, minutiae 10 fine points
bit of ~: 7 factoid
category: 5 music 6 movies, sports 10 television
collection: 3 ana
trivial: 4 idle, mean, puny 5 empty, least, light, minor, petty, small, trite 6 atomic, flimsy, little, meager, minute, paltry, scanty, slight, stupid, yeasty 7 nominal, puerile, shallow 8 atomical, everyday, ill-spent, needless, nugatory, picayune, piddling, skin-deep, trifling, unneeded 9 frivolous, momentary, secondary, senseless, valueless, vanishing, worthless 10 diminutive, evanescent, immaterial, incidental, irrelevant, negligible, nonserious, unprofound
detail: 3 nit 8 nonissue
most ~: 5 least
Trivial Breath
author: Elinor Wylie
trivialites: 7 details 8 minutiae, niceties
triviality: 6 trifle 9 frivolity
Trivial Pursuit: 4 game 9 board game
edition: 5 genus
maker: 6 Hasbro
need: 4 dice 5 cards 6 wedges 9 questions
Trix: 6 cereal
competitor: *see* cereal
-trix cousin: 3 -ess
Trixie: 6 Norton
friend: 5 Alice
trk. agency: 3 ICC
troche: 4 pill 6 pastil, tablet 7 lozenge 8 pastille
trochee: 4 foot
relative: 4 iamb 6 dactyl 7 anapest, pyrrhic, spondee
trodden starter: 4 down
Troggs
song: Love Is All Around (1968) Wild Thing (1966)
troglodyte: 7 recluse 8 anchoret 9 anchorite, barbarian
troglodytic: 6 lonely 8 solitary, unsocial 9 reclusive, withdrawn
trogon: 4 bird
Troi
friend: 4 Worf 5 Riker
Troia: 5 Ilium
troika: 4 sled, trio 5 triad 6 triple
Troilus
brother: 5 Paris 6 Hector
parent: 5 Priam 6 Hecuba 7 Priamus
sister: 9 Cassandra
slayer of ~: 8 Achilles
Troilus and Cressida: 4 play
author: William Shakespeare
role: 4 Ajax 5 Helen, Paris, Priam 6 Aeneas, Hector, Nestor 7 Antenor, Calchas, Helenus, Ulysses 8 Achilles, Diomedes, Menelaus, Pandarus 9 Agamemnon, Cassandra, Deiphobus, Patroclus, Thersites 10 Andromache
setting: 4 Troy
Troilus and Criseyde: 4 poem
author: Chaucer
__ trois: 5 pas de
__ Trois Mousquetaires: 3 Les
Trojan: 5 Paris 6 Dardan
ally: 4 Ares
king: 5 Priam 8 Leomedon
like the ~ horse: 5 false 9 deceitful
opponent: 5 UCLAn
work like a ~: 4 toil 5 slave
Trojan __: 3 War 5 horse
Trojan horse: 4 ruse 10 subterfuge
like the ~: 6 hollow
Trojans: 3 USC 9 Troy State
Trojans, The
composer: Hector Berlioz
Trojan War
cause: 5 Helen
epic: 5 Iliad
hero: 4 Ajax
instigator: 4 Eris
lure: 5 apple
Trojan Women, The
author: Euripides
troll: 4 doll, fish, ogre, pull 5 angle, carol, gnome
concern: 6 bridge
whence the word ~: 5 Norse
__ Troll: 4 Atta
troller: 6 angler 7 trawler 9 fisherman
hook: 5 drail
need: 3 net
trolley
in America: 4 cart
line: 8 railroad
passage: 4 fare
sound: 5 clang
take the ~: 4 ride
trolley __: 3 bus, car 4 line
Trolley Song, The word: 5 clang
Troll Garden, The
author: Willa Cather
Trollope, Anthony: 6 writer 7 British
work: Barchester Towers
The Claverings
Phineas Finn
Phineas Redux
trombone: 4 horn, wind 5 brass 7 sackbut 10 instrument
accessory: 4 mute
effect: 4 wawa
part: 5 slide, valve
__ trombone: 5 slide
trombonist: 3 Ory 6 Dorsey, Kid Ory, Miller 9 Teagarden
tromp: 4 hike, plod 5 stamp 6 stride 7 clobber, shellac 8 shellack
trompe __: 5 l'oeil
Trondheim: 5 fiord, fjord
Troon: 3 spa 4 town
locale: 8 Scotland
troop: 3 mob 4 army, band, body, crew, gang, herd, host, mass, pack, ring, step, team, unit, walk 5 bunch, corps, crowd, drove, flock, force, group, hands, horde, march, party, squad, swarm 6 clique, detail, gather, legion, muster, number, outfit, parade, throng 7 brigade, company, crowd in, numbers, platoon 8 assemble, assembly, regiment, soldiers 9 gathering, multitude, personnel 10 collection, contingent, detachment
deployment: 6 tactic 8 maneuver, movement 9 operation
ender: 4 ship
group: 3 BSA, rgt. 4 regt., unit 5 corps, force, squad 8 division, regiment 9 battalion
lodging: 4 bunk, post 6 billet 8 barracks, quarters
mover: 3 APC, LST 6 amtrac 7 amtrack
stopover: 4 camp 5 étape 7 bivouac
troupe: 3 USO
Troop Beverly Hills (1989 film)
cast: Mary Gross, Shelley Long, Craig T. Nelson, Betty Thomas
trooper: 3 cop 5 horse 6 equine 7 charger, dragoon, officer, soldier 8 war-horse 9 legionary, policeman
bulletin: 3 APB
concern: 3 mph 5 radar 8 speeding
like a ~: 9 earnestly, zealously
starter: 4 para
__ trooper: 5 state
Trooper: 3 SUV 5 Isuzu
troops: 4 army 7 cavalry 8 military, presence 9 personnel
call for ~: 5 rally
disband ~: 5 demob
supply fresh ~ to: 5 reman
supply ~ to: 3 man 6 deploy
__ troops: 5 shock
trop, de: 7 surplus, too much 9 redundant
trope: 5 irony 8 metaphor, metonymy 9 hyperbole 10 synecdoche
__-Tropez: 5 Saint
trophy: 3 cup 4 Emmy, Obie, Tony 5 award, booty, crown, grail, honor, medal, Oscar, prize 6 reward, ribbon, spoils, statue 7 guerdon, laurels, memento 8 citation, gold star, reminder 9 loving cup 10 blue ribbon, decoration
room: 3 den
take home a ~: 3 win
winner: 5 champ 6 victor
trophy __: 4 room
tropical: 3 hot 4 lush, rank, warm 5 balmy, fiery, humid 6 baking, steamy, sticky, sultry, toasty, torrid 7 blazing, boiling, burning, searing, summery 8 broiling, ovenlike, parching, roasting, sizzling, steaming, stifling 9 scorching 10 equatorial, sweltering
fish: 4 mola 5 manta, moray, tetra 6 louvar
fruit: 4 akee 5 guava, mango 6 banana 7 soursop
shrub: 3 bay 5 aalii, ficus, guava, ixora, urena 6 annona, cleome, coffee, mimosa, papaya, pawpaw 7 quassia 8 abutilon, barbasco, bayberry, bignonia, columnea, divi-divi, guaiacum, huisache, mangrove 9 bouvardia, monacillo 10 frangipani
spot: 3 isl. 4 isle, reef 5 atoll 6 island
tree: 3 apa, fig 4 agba, akee, kola, neem, palm, upas 5 balsa, cacao, ficus, genip, guava, ixora, kiawe, mahoe, mango, ramon 6 anatto, annona, antiar, balata, banana, baobab, bonduc, calaba, cashew, coffee, fustic, jujube, lebbek, mammee, mimosa, obeche, padauk, padouk, papaya, pawpaw 7 acerola, annatto, avocado, genipap, quassia, yohimbe 8 albizzia, allspice, barbasco, bauhinia, calabash, cocobolo, divi-divi, mahogany, mangrove, tamarind, tamarisk 9 jacaranda, poinciana, sapodilla 10 breadfruit, grapefruit
tropical __: 4 fish 5 storm
Tropicana product: 2 OJ
tropic of __: 6 Cancer 9 Capricorn
Tropic of Cancer
author: Henry Miller
Tropic of Capricorn
author: Henry Miller
Tropic Thunder (2008 film)
cast: Jack Black, Robert Downey, Jr., Ben Stiller
director: Ben Stiller
troppo: 7 too much
__ troppo: 3 non
trot: 3 hie, jog, pad, run 4 crib, gait, lope, move, pony, ride, step 5 hurry 6 canter 7 scamper 10 cheat sheet
ender: 4 line
hot to ~: 4 avid 5 eager 6 gung ho 7 anxious, excited 10 raring to go
out: 4 show 6 flaunt, parade 7 display, exhibit, present, show off 8 brandish 10 wave around
relative: 4 walk 6 canter, gallop
trot __: 3 out
__ trot: 3 fox, jog 5 hot to 6 turkey
troth: 3 vow 6 pledge, verity 7 loyalty, promise 8 espousal, fidelity 10 engagement
plight one's ~: 3 wed 4 mate 5 marry, unite 10 get hitched, settle down, tie the knot
Trotsky: 3 Red 4 Leon
foe: 5 Lenin
trotter: 4 foot 5 horse, pacer, racer 6 equine
burden: 5 sulky 6 driver
Trottier, Bryan
milieu: 3 ice 4 rink 5 arena
org.: 3 NHL
troubadour: 6 singer
prop: 4 lute
song: 4 alba 6 ballad
trouble: 3 ado, ail, bug, ill, irk, row, vex, woe 4 care, fret, fuss, gall, hurt, loss, mess, pain, spot, to-do, work 5 annoy, beset, curse, eat at, exert, get to, grief, grind, harry, haunt, hitch, mix up, pains, peeve, press, spook, trial, upset, visit, worry 6 bother, burden, crisis, crunch, danger, effort, grieve, harass, hassle, hazard, holdup, malady, matter, mayhem, misery, mishap, ordeal, pester, pickle, plague, plight, pother, prey on, put out, puzzle, sadden, scrape,

sorrow, stir up, strain, stress, strife, tsuris, tumult, unrest 7 afflict, agitate, bad news, concern, dilemma, discord, disturb, illness, perplex, perturb, problem, setback, shake up, torment, tsouris 8 aggrieve, disorder, disquiet, distress, exercise, exertion, friction, hard luck, hardship, headache, hot water, impose on, irritate, jeopardy, mischief, nuisance, pressure, quandary, struggle, unsettle, vexation 9 adversity, annoyance, commotion, complaint, deep water, heartache, incommode, make a fuss, make waves, suffering, take pains, weigh down 10 affliction, difficulty, discomfort, disconcert, hard knocks, infliction, misfortune
  amount of ~: 4 heap, peck
  borrow ~: 5 worry
  ender: 4 shot, some 5 maker, shoot 7 shooter 8 shooting
  exclamation: 4 help, oh-oh, uh-oh, yipe 5 yikes, yipes
  make ~: 4 abet 5 rouse 6 foment, incite, stir up, work up 7 agitate, inflame, provoke 9 instigate, misbehave
  no ~: 4 easy 6 picnic
  partner: 4 toil
  without ~: 6 easily 7 handily 9 hands down 10 swimmingly
trouble __: 4 spot
trouble-__: 7 shooter
__ trouble: 6 borrow
T-R-O-U-B-L-E (1993 song)
  artist: Travis Tritt
troubled: 3 sad 4 blue, down, glum, sore 5 antsy, beset, itchy, jumpy, tense, upset, woful 6 gloomy, in a fix, in a jam, morose, queasy, queazy, somber, uneasy, woeful 7 anxious, doleful, jittery, joyless, keyed up, nervous, restive, unhappy, uptight, worried 8 downcast, obsessed, restless, skittish 9 cheerless, concerned, excitable, heartsick, ill at ease, miserable, sorrowful, woebegone 10 chapfallen, high-strung, melancholy, solicitous, unbalanced
  not ~: 6 at ease 7 content, relaxed 8 carefree, composed, tranquil
troubled __: 6 waters
Trouble in July
  author: Erskine Caldwell
troubleless: 4 easy 6 picnic, simple, smooth 7 no sweat 8 carefree, no bother, pushover 9 no problem 10 child's play, elementary, manageable
troublemaker: 3 imp 4 punk 5 rogue, rowdy, scamp, snake 6 bad egg, gadfly, gossip, heller, menace, rascal, weasel 7 gremlin, hellion 8 agitator, hooligan, nuisance 9 firebrand 10 instigator
troublemakers: 6 bad lot
Trouble Man (1972 song)
  artist: Marvin Gaye
troubles: 5 grief 6 misery, sorrow 7 travail 8 hardship 9 suffering 10 affliction, infelicity
... __ troubles: 5 sea of
troubleshoot: 3 fix 5 debug 7 correct, rectify
troubleshooter: 5 fixer 8 mediator 9 go-between 10 arbitrator
troublesome: 4 hard, ugly 5 heavy, pesky, pesty, rough, spiny, tight, tough 6 feisty, knotty, taxing, thorny, tricky, trying, unruly, uphill 7 arduous, awkward, irksome, onerous, painful, prickly, weighty 8 alarming, annoying, tiresome 9 dangerous, demanding, difficult, laborious, pestilent, upsetting, vexatious, wearisome, worrisome 10 bothersome
Trouble With Harry, The (1955 film)
  cast: John Forsythe, Edmund Gwenn, Shirley MacLaine
  director: Alfred Hitchcock
troubling: 3 bad 8 annoying 9 dangerous 10 bothersome
troublous: 6 stormy 9 turbulent
trou-de-__: 4 loup
trough: 3 cup, hod 4 duct, moat 5 canal, ditch, flume, gully, slump 6 feeder, furrow, gulley, gutter, manger, trench, valley 7 channel 8 low point 10 depression
  contents: 4 feed
  diner: 3 hog, pig 5 horse, swine
trounce: 3 wax, win, zap 4 bash, beat, bury, drub, dust, flog, lick, mall, maul, rout, trim, whip, whup 5 baste, crush, paste, pound, stomp, swamp, total, trash, waste, whomp, worst 6 defeat, hammer, pommel, pummel, thrash, wallop 7 clobber, lambast, put away, triumph 8 lambaste, overcome, walk over 9 checkmate, overpower, overwhelm
trouncing: 4 rout 6 defeat 7 beating, debacle
Troup, Bobby
  spouse: Julie London
troupe: 4 band, bevy, cast, crew, gang, ring, team 5 party, squad 6 muster, outfit 7 company 8 ensemble
trouper: 5 actor 6 player 7 actress, veteran 8 thespian, traveler 9 performer
trousers: 4 slax 5 cords, jeans, Levi's, pants 6 Capris, chinos, denims, khakis, slacks 7 gauchos 8 breeches, britches, flannels, knickers, overalls 9 corduroys, dungarees, plus fours 10 hiphuggers
  like some ~: 4 wide 5 baggy, loose 7 sagging
  material: 5 chino, denim, twill
  measure: 4 lgth. 5 waist 6 inseam, length
  part: 3 leg 4 cuff, knee, loop, seat 6 crease, pocket
  partner: 5 shirt
  tartan ~: 5 trews
  see also pants
trousseau: 8 wardrobe
  collector: 5 bride 7 fiancée
trout: 4 char, fish, pogy 9 cutthroat, namaycush, steelhead
  home: 5 river
__ trout: 3 sea 4 lake 5 brook 7 rainbow
__ Trout: 5 Paris
Trout Quintet
  composer: Franz Schubert
__ trouvé: 5 objet
Trouville-sur-__: 3 Mer
trove: 5 booty, cache, hoard 8 treasure 9 discovery, stockpile 10 collection, storehouse
  treasure ~: 4 mine 7 bonanza
T. Rowe __: 5 Price
trowel: 4 tool 5 scoop
Troy: 4 city, town 5 Ilium 6 Aikman 7 Donahue 8 Shondell
  locale: 4 Ohio 7 Alabama, New York 8 Michigan
  peak of ancient ~: 5 Mt. Ida
  school: 3 RPI, TSU
Troy (2004 film)
  cast: Eric Bana, Orlando Bloom, Brad Pitt
Troyanos, Tatiana: 5 mezzo 6 singer 7 soprano
  specialty: 5 opera
Troyer: 5 Verne
Troy State
  athletes: 7 Trojans
  locale: 7 Alabama
Tru
  star: Robert Morse
  subject: 6 Capote
truancy: 5 hooky 6 no-show 7 absence
truant: 4 AWOL 5 idler 6 loafer 7 at large, runaway, shirker, slacker 8 absentee, layabout, loiterer, sluggard 9 do-nothing, goldbrick, lazybones 10 malingerer
  soldier: 4 AWOL 8 deserter
truant __: 7 officer
truce: 4 halt, lull, rest, stay 5 letup, pause, peace, terms 6 accord, treaty 7 amnesty, détente, respite 8 breather, reprieve 9 agreement, armistice, cease-fire, cessation, white flag 10 cooling off, moratorium, suspension
  flag color: 5 white
Trucial __: 4 Oman 5 Coast 6 States
Trucial States: 3 UAE
truck: 3 GMC, rig, ute, van 4 haul, jeep, Mack, pull, semi, swap, swop, take 5 bring, carry, crate, dolly, lorry, trade, U-Haul 6 camion, convey, dumper, hauler, pickup, wheels 7 deliver, traffic, vehicle 8 leavings 9 transport 10 do business
  agency: 3 ICC
  attachment: 4 plow
  bring by ~: 4 haul, ship 6 cart in
  British ~: 5 lorry
  ender: 3 age 4 load, stop
  filler: 4 load 5 cargo 7 freight
  fuel: 6 diesel 8 gasoline
  group: 5 fleet 6 convoy
  hand ~: 4 cart 5 dolly 6 barrow
  how a ~ goes uphill: 5 in low
  maker: 3 GMC 4 Mack
  military ~: 6 camion
  part: 3 bed, cab 4 axle 7 tractor, trailer
  radio: 2 CB
  rental name: 5 Ryder, U-Haul
  stop: 5 diner 6 eatery 10 restaurant
  stop sign: 3 gas 4 eats, food
  unit: 3 ton
truck __: 4 farm, stop
__ truck: 3 tow 4 dump, fire, hand 5 panel 6 pickup 7 flatbed, trailer
Truckee
  city on the ~: 4 Reno
trucker: 6 hauler
  choice: 4 gear
  often: 4 CBer
truckle: 3 bow, woo 4 bend 5 court, cower, crawl 6 comply, kowtow, stroke, submit 7 adulate, conform, flatter 8 butter up, kowtow to 9 prostrate 10 toe the line
  to: 4 obey 6 submit 8 fawn over
truckler: 5 toady 6 fawner, flunky, minion, yes man 7 flunkey 8 adulator
truckload: 4 gobs, lots, many, tons 5 cargo, goods, heaps, piles, scads 6 oceans, oodles, plenty, stacks 7 freight 8 good deal, shipment 9 multitude
truculent: 4 mean, rude, ugly 5 cross, gruff, harsh, nasty 6 animal, brutal, feisty, fierce, grumpy, ornery, savage, sullen, unkind, wanton 7 abusive, beastly, callous, defiant, hateful, hostile, hurtful, scrappy, vicious 8 barbaric, bullying, fiendish, grumpish, inhumane, militant, pitiless, ruthless, sadistic, scathing, vengeful 9 barbarous, combative, cutthroat, ferocious, merciless, monstrous 10 aggressive, pugnacious, vindictive
Trudeau: 5 Garry 6 Pierre
Trudeau, Garry
  spouse: Jane Pauley
Trudeau, Pierre: 2 P.M. 8 Canadian
  party: 3 Lib. 7 Liberal
  predecessor: 5 Clark 7 Pearson
  successor: 5 Clark 6 Turner
trudge: 3 lag 4 hike, plod, slog, step, trek, wade, walk 5 clomp, clump, march, shlep, stump, tramp, tread 6 linger, lumber, schlep, trapes 7 schlepp, stumble, traipse 9 plug along
  in muck: 5 slosh
  (on): 5 press
true: 3 yes 4 fast, firm, real, sure 5 aline, exact, level, loyal, no lie, plumb, right, sound, valid 6 actual, adjust, ardent, direct, honest, likely, proper, spot on, square, steady, worthy 7 certain, correct, devoted, dutiful, factual, for real, genuine, literal, natural, precise, sincere, staunch, up-front, upright 8 accurate, bona fide, candidly, constant, definite, faithful, knightly, obedient, official, on target, orthodox, regulate, reliable, resolute, rightful, straight, unerring, verified, yeomanly 9 allegiant, authentic, axiomatic, confirmed, dedicated, fraternal, heartfelt, honorable, intrinsic, on the mark, patriotic, realistic, sincerely, steadfast, undoubted, unfailing, unfeigned, veracious, veritable 10 aboveboard, dependable, infallible, inviolable, legitimate, on the level, scrupulous, straighten, unaffected, undeniable, unimagined, unmistaken, unswerving, upstanding, verifiable
  at times: 3 ans. 6 answer
  be ~: 6 adhere, cleave 7 abide by,

stand by **8** hold fast
come ~: 5 ensue, occur **6** betide, happen, pan out, result **7** develop **9** eventuate, take place, transpire
ender: 4 born, love **5** penny
it can't be ~: 4 oh no
name that means ~: 4 Vera
not ~: 4 fake, sham **5** bogus, false, lying, wrong **6** made-up, unreal **7** inexact **8** cooked-up, disloyal, mistaken, specious **9** concocted, deceptive, dishonest, erroneous, imaginary, incorrect, synthetic, trumped-up **10** fabricated, fallacious, fictitious, fraudulent, groundless, inaccurate, mendacious, misleading, perfidious, unfaithful
old-style: 5 sooth
prefix: 4 docu-
regard as ~: 3 buy **4** avow, hold **5** adopt, agree, trust **6** accept, affirm, assent, assume, credit **7** believe, concede, embrace, respect, swallow **10** understand
say is ~: 4 aver, avow **6** affirm, attest
show to be ~: 5 prove
to type: 4 even, firm, like, same **5** level **6** steady **7** equable, logical, regular, uniform **8** coherent, constant, of a piece, rational **9** accordant, agreeable, congenial, congruent, congruous, consonant, unanimous, unfailing, unvarying **10** compatible, concurrent, consistent, dependable, harmonious, homogenous, invariable, legitimate, persistent, reasonable, unchanging
tried and ~: 4 safe, sure **5** liege, loyal, sound **6** proven, tested, trusty **7** staunch **8** approved, reliable **9** certified, qualified, reputable, steadfast, unfailing, venerable **10** dependable, time-tested
up: 4 even **5** align, aline **6** adjust **10** straighten
true-__: 4 blue, life
true-__ test: 5 false
__ true: 4 come, ring
__ true!: 3 How, It's
True __: 4 Blue, Grit, Lies, Love **5** Crime **6** Colors
True Believer (1989 film)
cast: Robert Downey Jr., James Woods
true-blue: 5 loyal, moral **7** devoted, dutiful, sincere, staunch **8** constant, faithful, reliable, virtuous, yeomanly **9** allegiant, dedicated, steadfast **10** inviolable
True Blue (1986 song)
artist: Madonna
True Colors (1986 song)
artist: Cyndi Lauper
True Confessions: 4 film **5** novel
author: John Gregory Dunne
cast: Robert De Niro, Charles Durning, Robert Duvall, Ed Flanders
True Crime (1999 film)
cast: Clint Eastwood, Lisa Gay Hamilton, Denis Leary, Diane Venora
director: Clint Eastwood

true-false __: 4 exam, test
True Grit (1969 film): 5 oater **7** western
cast: Glen Campbell, Kim Darby, John Wayne
Trueheart: 4 Tess
trueheartedness: 5 ardor, faith **7** honesty, loyalty **8** devotion, fidelity **9** integrity, sincerity **10** allegiance, attachment, dedication, resolution
True Lies (1994 film)
cast: Tom Arnold, Jamie Lee Curtis, Arnold Schwarzenegger
dance: 5 tango
director: James Cameron
truelove
see sweetheart
True Love: 4 song **5** waltz
artist: Bing Crosby
composer: Cole Porter
__ True Love: 5 My Own
True Romance (1993 film)
cast: Patricia Arquette, Dennis Hopper, Gary Oldman, Christian Slater
__ True Thing: 3 One
true-to-life: 4 real **6** actual **7** factual, genuine **9** authentic, realistic **10** historical, reallistic
true to one's __: 4 word
__ True to You in My Fashion: 6 Always
__ True What They Say About Dixie?: 4 Is it
Truex: 6 Ernest
Truffaut, François: 5 actor **6** French **8** director
film: The Bride Wore Black (1968) Close Encounters of the Third Kind (1977) Day for Night (1973) Fahrenheit 451 (1967) Jules and Jim (1961) Shoot the Piano Player (1960) Small Change (1976) Stolen Kisses (1968) The Story of Adele H (1975)
truffle: 6 fungus **8** mushroom
spore sac: 5 ascus
truism: 3 saw **4** fact, rule **5** adage, axiom, maxim, moral, motto **6** dictum, gospel, phrase, saying **7** proverb **8** aphorism **9** platitude **10** folk wisdom
truly: 4 amen, just, very **5** quite, right **6** aright, indeed, in fact, it is so, justly, really, so be it, verily **7** at heart, de facto, exactly, frankly, no doubt, validly **8** actually, candidly, honestly, in effect, lawfully, strictly **9** assuredly, certainly, decidedly, factually, in reality, literally, no mistake, sincerely **10** far and away, rightfully, unerringly, verifiably
see also of course
__ truly: 5 yours
Truly (1982 song)
artist: Lionel Richie
Truly __ Deeply: 5 Madly
Truman: 4 Bess **5** Harry **6** Capote **8** Margaret
Truman, Harry S: 9 president
birthplace: 5 Lamar
child: 8 Margaret
home: 8 Missouri
opponent: 5 Dewey **7** Wallace **8** Thurmond

V.P.: 7 Barkley
wife: 4 Bess
Truman Show, The (1998 film)
cast: Jim Carrey, Noah Emmerich, Ed Harris, Laura Linney
director: Peter Weir
dog: 5 Pluto
Trumbull: 7 Douglas
trump: 4 beat, best, suit **5** excel, one-up, outdo **6** better, defeat, outwit **7** surpass **10** outperform
high ~: 3 ace
play a ~ card: 4 ruff
up: 3 rig **4** fake, make **5** hatch **6** cook up, create, devise, invent, scheme **7** concoct **8** conceive, contrive, misquote **9** fabricate
trump __: 4 card
__-trump: 5 one no, two no
Trump: 5 Ivana **6** Donald, Ivanka
rival: 5 Icahn
Trump __: 5 Plaza, Tower **6** Castle
Trump Castle: 6 casino
employee: 6 dealer **7** pit boss **8** croupier
Trump, Donald
spouse: Marla Maples, Melania, Ivana Trump
trumped-up: 5 false **9** imaginary, unfounded **10** fictitious
story: 4 tale **6** canard
trumpery
see baloney
trumpet: 4 horn, hype, roar, wind **5** boast, brass, bugle, sound **6** carnyx, herald, lituus, report **7** buisine, clarion, promote, salpinx **8** announce, proclaim **9** pronounce, publicize **10** instrument, promulgate
accessory: 4 mute
cousin: 4 horn **5** bugle **6** cornet
creeper: 5 plant **6** flower
play a ~: 4 blow
sound: 4 blat, wail, wawa **5** blare, blast, tusch **6** wah-wah **7** fanfare, tantara **8** flourish
__ trumpet: 3 ear
__ Trumpet: 7 Gideon's
trumpeter: 4 bird, swan **5** Davis, James **6** Alpert **7** Nichols **8** Cheatham, Eldridge, Ferguson, Mangione, Marsalis **9** Armstrong, Gillespie **10** Herb Alpert, Miles Davis, Red Nichols **11** Beiderbecke
Trumpeter's Lullaby, A
composer: Leroy Anderson
Trumpet Overture
composer: Felix Mendelssohn
trumpets
Roman ~: 5 tubae
truncate: 3 cut, lop, top **4** chop, clip, crop, pare, trim **5** prune, shear **6** lessen, reduce **7** abridge, curtail, shorten **9** telescope **10** abbreviate
truncated: 5 brief, short **6** little, stubby
truncheon: 3 bat, rod **4** cane, club, cosh, mace **5** baton, billy, flail, staff, stick **6** cudgel, ferule **7** war club **8** bludgeon **9** bastinado, blackjack **10** nightstick, shillelagh
trundle: 3 bed, cot **4** roll **5** wheel **6** lumber

trunk: 3 box, log **4** body, bole, case, main, stem **5** aorta, chest, snout, stalk, torso **6** coffer, locker, thorax **7** baggage, luggage **8** suitcase, wardrobe **9** container, proboscis **10** footlocker, travel case
chambers: 5 atria
combining form: 4 corm- **5** cormo-
feature: 4 bark, knar, knot
fill a ~: 4 pack
in Britain: 4 boot
item: 4 jack, tire **5** spare **9** spare tire
of a ~: 6 aortal, aortic
of the lower ~: 5 iliac
palm ~: 6 caudex
place: 4 tree
tree ~ in Britain: 4 stam
upper ~: 6 thorax
trunks: 6 shorts **8** swimwear
like some tree ~: 6 gnarly
Truro
locale: 7 Cape Cod
truss: 3 tie **4** bind, lash, tape **5** tie up **6** begird, bind up, fasten, wrap up **7** bandage **8** make fast **10** cantilever
up: 4 bind **6** hobble, hogtie **7** shackle **9** constrain, hamstring
trust: 3 let **4** care, lean, lend, loan, rely **5** bet on, faith, stock **6** accept, assume, bank on, belief, cartel, charge, commit, confer, credit, expect, lean on, look to, office, rely on **7** advance, believe, build on, combine, consign, count on, custody, entrust, intrust, keeping, mission, presume, suppose, surmise, swear by **8** covenant, credence, delegate, depend on, gamble on, megacorp, monopoly, optimism, reliance, rely upon, sign over, sureness, wardship **9** believe in, build upon, certitude, confide in, count upon, patronize, syndicate **10** commission, confidence, conviction, dependance, dependence, obligation
brain ~: 5 board, panel **7** cabinet, council **8** advisors **9** syndicate **10** counselors
ender: 6 buster, worthy **7** busting
hold in ~: 6 escrow
in: 7 believe **10** set store by
trust __: 4 fund
__ trust: 5 blind, brain **6** living
trustbuster concern: 6 cartel **8** monopoly
trusted
not to be ~: 3 sly **4** cagy, foxy, wily **5** cagey, false, lying, shady, slick **6** artful, crafty, shifty, shrewd, smooth, sneaky, tricky **7** crooked, cunning, devious, elusive, elusory, evasive, furtive, knavish **8** delusive, guileful, scheming, slippery **9** deceitful, deceptive, designing, dishonest, insidious, insincere **10** mendacious, misleading, serpentine, unreliable, untruthful
to be ~: 4 fair **5** moral **6** honest, square, worthy **7** ethical, genuine, sincere, upright **8** bona fide, credible, reliable, truthful,

virtuous **9** heartfelt, honorable, reputable, righteous, veracious **10** aboveboard, evenhanded, high-minded, law-abiding, legitimate, on the level, reasonable, scrupulous, upstanding
trustee: 5 agent **8** director, executor, guardian, watchdog **9** custodian, executive
watchdog: 8 executor, guardian
trustees: 5 board, panel **7** council **9** committee, syndicate **10** commission, management
trusteeship: 4 care, egis **5** aegis **6** charge **7** custody, keeping **8** auspices **10** protection
trustiness: 7 honesty, loyalty **9** constancy, fixedness
trusting: 4 easy, naif **5** naive **6** simple **7** hopeful **8** gullable, gullible, lamblike, unartful **9** childlike, credulous, ingenuous, unworldly **10** falling for, optimistic
trustworthiness: 5 honor **6** virtue **7** honesty, loyalty, probity **8** fidelity, veracity **9** sincerity
trustworthy: 4 fair, good, just, open, safe, true **5** loyal, moral, solid, sound, tried, valid **6** decent, honest, mature, secure, square **7** ethical, genuine, sincere, staunch, tenable, up-front, upright **8** accurate, constant, credible, harmless, reliable, straight, true-blue, truthful, unerring **9** authentic, honorable, plausible, realistic, reputable, righteous, rock-solid, steadfast, unfailing, veracious
trusty: 4 naif, open **5** loyal, naive, solid **6** honest, mature, square **7** ethical, staunch, up-front, upright **8** accurate, constant, faithful, jailbird, reliable, sensible, straight, truthful **9** authentic, honorable, righteous, rock-solid, steadfast, unfailing, veracious **10** dependable, inviolable, on the level, principled
truth: 3 law **4** fact **5** axiom, facts, maxim, right, scoop, score **6** candor, factum, gospel, verity **7** epigram, lowdown, loyalty, precept, proverb, reality, theorem **8** accuracy, aphorism, validity, veracity **9** actuality, certainty, good faith, integrity, platitude, precision, principle, sincerity **10** exactitude, factuality, honestness, legitimacy, principium
alternative: 4 dare
in ~: 3 nay, yea **5** quite **6** indeed, really **8** actually
moment of ~: 4 test **8** showdown, zero hour
name meaning ~: 4 Vera
old-style: 5 sooth
presumed ~: 5 given
stretch the ~: 3 lie **5** fudge **6** invent
tell the ~: 5 level, own up
twister: 4 liar
twist the ~: 3 con, fib **4** bull, dupe, fake, hoax, sham, snow **5** bluff, fudge, libel, put on **6** delude, invent, malign **7** deceive, distort, falsify, mislead, perjure, slander **8** misguide, misstate **9** disinform, dissemble, misinform **10** equivocate, exaggerate
truth __: 5 serum
__ truth: 5 naked **6** gospel
__-truth: 4 half
Truth: 9 Sojourner
author: Émile Zola
Truth About Cats and Dogs, The (1996 film)
cast: Jamie Foxx, Janeane Garofalo, Uma Thurman
Truth About Charlie, The (2002 film)
cast: Thandie Newton, Tim Robbins, Mark Wahlberg
truthful: 4 open **5** exact, frank, legit, moral, right **6** actual, candid, honest, infelt, square, trusty **7** correct, factual, literal, precise, sincere **8** accurate, out-front, reliable, straight, verified **9** guileless, honorable, ingenuous, outspoken, realistic, unfeigned, veracious **10** aboveboard, forthright, from the hip, on the level, point-blank, scrupulous
Truthful James
creator: Bret Harte
truthfully: 6 as it is **8** like it is **9** sincerely **10** point-blank
truthfulness: 5 honor **7** honesty, loyalty, probity **8** accuracy, veracity **9** sincerity
truth-in-lending
org.: 3 FTC
stat.: 3 APR
Truth or __: 4 Dare
Truth or Consequences: 4 city, town **8** game show
host: Bob Barker
locale: 9 New Mexico
Truth or Dare
artist: Madonna
__ Truth, The: 5 Awful, Naked
truTV
alternative: ***see*** cable channel
try: 2 go **3** aim, bid, irk, pop, tax, vex **4** hear, push, rack, risk, seek, shot, stab, test, tire, turn **5** annoy, check, crack, essay, fling, judge, prove, taste, weary, weigh, whack, whirl **6** aspire, effort, handle, harass, plague, sample, strain, strive, tackle, verify **7** afflict, attempt, compete, examine, go for it, have a go, inspect, referee, torment, venture **8** audition, bear down, check out, distress, drive for, endeavor, evaluate, exercise, go all out, irritate, make a bid, shoot for, struggle **9** challenge, give it a go, have a go at, prosecute, take a shot, take a stab, undertake **10** adjudicate, chip away at, enterprise, experiment
again: 4 redo
ender: 3 out **4** sail
for: 6 pursue **8** aspire to
(for): 3 aim, vie **5** angle, steer
hard: 4 push **5** apply, exert, sweat **6** strain **8** put forth
on: 3 fit **4** test, wear **8** check out
one's patience: 3 irk **4** rile **5** weary **7** provoke
out: 4 test **5** assay, prove **7** inspect **8** audition, evaluate, rehearse **10** experiment
ready to ~: 4 game
to find: 4 seek **5** trace, track, trail **6** gun for, pursue **7** fish for, go after, hunt for, look for, scout up **8** quest for, run after, scout out, sniff out **9** track down
to get answers: 4 pump, quiz **5** grill, query **7** canvass, consult, inquire, request
to learn: 4 cram, quiz, read **5** probe, query, train **6** bone up, digest, go over, take up **7** analyze, dissect, inquire **8** look into, read up on, research **10** experiment
try __: 3 out **6** square
try __ size: 5 on for
__ try: 7 college
Try __ might...: 3 as I
Try __ see: 5 it and
Try Again (2000 song)
artist: Aaliyah
Try a Little Tenderness (1969 song)
artist: Three Dog Night
Trygve: 3 Lie **8** Haavelmo
successor: 3 Dag
trying: 4 hard **5** rough, stiff, tight, tough **6** rugged, severe, taxing, thorny, uphill, vexing **7** arduous, awkward, hard-won, irksome, onerous, painful, prickly **8** annoying, exacting, grueling, no picnic, rigorous, ticklish, tiresome, toilsome, worrying **9** demanding, difficult, fatiguing, laborious, strenuous, stressful, upsetting, vexatious, wearisome **10** bothersome, enervating, formidable, irritating, oppressive, unamenable
time: 4 bind **5** trial **6** crisis, crunch **7** squeeze, trouble **9** adversity, emergency **10** misfortune
Trying to Save Piggy Sneed
author: John Irving
Tryin' to Get the Feeling Again (1976 song)
artist: Barry Manilow
Tryin' to Live My Life Without You (1981 song)
artist: Bob Seger
Tryon: 3 Tom **6** Thomas
try one's __: 4 hand, luck
try on for __: 4 size
Tryon, Thomas: 5 actor **6** writer
work: All That Glitters
Crowned Heads
Harvest Home
In the Fire of Spring
Lady
Nigh of the Moonbow
Night Magic
The Other
The Wings of the Morning
tryout: 4 test **5** essay **7** attempt, hearing **8** audition **9** probation, rehearsal **10** experiment
tryst: 4 date **7** liaison, meeting, vis-à-vis **9** tête-à-tête **10** engagement, rendezvous
Try to Remember: 4 song **5** waltz
T.S.: 5 Eliot
tsade: 6 Hebrew, letter
predecessor: 2 pe **3** peh
successor: 4 koph, qoph
tsar: 4 czar, Ivan, male, Paul, tzar **5** Boris, Fedor, mogul, Peter **6** Alexis, despot, Fyodor, tyrant **7** emperor, kingpin, Mikhail, monarch **8** autocrat, dictator, Nicholas **9** Alexander, oppressor, potentate
see also czar
Tsar's Bride, The
composer: Nikolai Rimsky-Korsakov
__-tse: 3 Lao
tsetse: 3 fly
territory: 6 Africa
Tse-tung: 3 Mao
TSgt. employer: 4 USAF
T-shirt: 3 top
like a: 6 casual
material: 6 cotton
size: 2 lg., XL **3** lge., med., sml. **5** large, small **6** medium
tsimmes: 4 stew **6** uproar
Tsk!: 3 tut **4** alas, pity **5** shame **6** tut-tut **8** for shame
Tsotsi
author: Athol Fugard
tsp.: 3 amt. **4** meas.
tsps., three: 4 tbsp.
T-square: 5 ruler
TSU
locale: 5 Texas **7** Houston
tsunami: 4 wave **9** tidal wave
tsuris: 3 woe **6** hassle **7** trouble
TSX: 3 car **4** auto **5** Acura **10** automobile
TT manufacturer: 4 Audi
t-top: 4 roof
TTU conference: 9 Big Twelve
__ tu: 3 eri
__ Tu: 4 Eres
tub: 3 keg, vat **4** boat, cask **5** basin **6** barrel, firkin, vessel **8** hogshead, puncheon **9** container
hot ~: 3 spa **5** sauna **7** Jacuzzi **9** whirlpool
Japanese ~: 4 furo
old ~: 4 scow
ritual: 4 bath
starter: 4 bath, wash
toy: 4 boat, duck **6** duckie **10** rubber duck
use the ~: 3 wet **4** lave, soak, wash **5** bathe, clean **6** splash
wooden ~ of yore: 3 soe
__ tub: 3 hot
tuba: 4 horn, wind **5** brass **7** helicon, saxhorn **9** euphonium **10** sousaphone
Tubb: 6 Ernest
Tubbs beat: 5 Miami
tubby
see obese
Tubby girlfriend: 4 Lulu
Tubby the Tuba
author: Paul Tripp
illustrator: Henry Cole
tube: 2 IV, TV **4** duct, flue, hose, pipe, vial **5** diode, phial, pipet, stent, straw, telly, TV set **6** subway, teevee, tunnel **7** conduit, pipette, snorkel, trachea **8** cylinder, idiot box, railroad, windpipe **10** television
boob ~: 2 TV **5** TV set **10** television
cathode ray ~: 8 terminal
in America: 6 subway
light in a ~: 4 neon
put on the ~: 3 air **9** broadcast

trophy: 4 Emmy
see also television, TV
tube ___: 3 pan, top 4 foot, sock 7 railway
___ tube: 4 boob, test 5 inner 6 vacuum
tubeless ___: 4 tire
tuber: 3 oca, oka, yam 4 apio, coco, corm, eddo, root, spud, taro 5 ahipa, baddo, tater 6 jicama, manioc, potato, tanier, tannia, turnip, yautia 7 cassava, cocoyam, dasheen, malanga, sunroot, tannier 8 girasole 9 arracacha, arrowhead, arrowroot, yucca root
Andes ~: 3 oca, oka
like a ~: 5 rooty
Polynesian ~: 4 corm, eddo, taro
tubes
down the ~: 4 gone, lost, no-go 5 kaput
go down the ~: 4 fail
tubing: 4 hose, pipe
Tubman: 7 Harriet
Tubular Bells (1974 song)
artist: Mike Oldfield
Tucci: 7 Stanley
Tuchman: 7 Barbara
tuck: 3 hem 4 cram, fold, seam, wrap 5 plait, pleat, shove 6 gather, insert, pucker, ruffle 7 crinkle, swaddle 8 contract, fold over 9 squeeze in
away: 3 eat, sup 4 bury, dine, hide, nosh 5 cache, feast, gorge, munch, stash 6 devour, ingest, inhale, pig out 7 conceal, consume, partake, protect, scarf up, snack on 8 chow down, ensconce, gobble up, take food, withhold, wolf down 9 have a bite, have a meal, polish off, scarf down 10 gormandize, keep secret
nip and ~: 5 close, tight
partner: 3 nip
tuck ___: 4 away
___ tuck: 5 tummy
___ Tuck: 5 Friar
tucked
away: 4 dark 5 blind, perdu, privy 6 covert, hidden, inside, latent, occult, perdue, secret, unseen 7 private, unknown 8 secluded, ulterior 9 concealed, covered up, incognito, invisible, nonpublic, out of view, potential, recondite, underhand, unexposed 10 enshrouded, undercover, underlying, under wraps, undetected, unviewable
in: 4 abed, cosy, cozy, safe, snug, warm 5 comfy, cozey, cozie 6 secure 7 nestled 9 cuddled up, sheltered
it may be ~ in: 5 shirt
tucker
bib and ~: 4 duds, garb, rags, togs 5 getup 6 attire, finery, outfit 7 apparel, clothes, raiment, threads 8 wardrobe 10 Sunday best
out: 4 jade, tire 5 weary 7 exhaust, fatigue, frazzle 9 prostrate
Tucker: 3 car 4 auto 5 Chris, Tanya 6 Sophie 7 Forrest, Michael, Preston, Richard 10 automobile
tuckered out: 4 beat, worn 5 all in, spent, tired, weary 8 fatigued 9 exhausted
___ tuckered out: 5 plumb
Tucker, Forrest: 5 actor
TV: F Troop
Tucker, Michael
spouse: Jill Eikenberry
Tucker, Richard: 5 tenor 6 singer
specialty: 5 opera
Tucker: The Man and His Dream (1988 film)
cast: Joan Allen, Jeff Bridges, Martin Landau
director: Francis Ford Coppola
Tuck Everlasting (2002 film)
cast: Alexis Bledel, William Hurt, Ben Kingsley, Sissy Spacek
Tuck, Friar quaff: 3 ale
Tucson: 4 city, town
athletes: 8 Wildcats
county: 4 Pima
locale: 4 Ariz. 7 Arizona
river: 9 Santa Cruz
Tucson-to-Flagstaff dir.: 3 NNW
Tudor: 4 Mary 5 house 8 Henry VII 9 Henry VIII 10 automobile
Tues.: 3 day
follower: 3 Wed.
Mon., to ~: 4 yest.
preceder: 3 Mon.
Tuesday: 4 Weld
was named for him: 3 Tiu
___ Tuesday: 3 Fat, 'Til 4 Ruby 5 Black, Super 6 Shrove
Tuesdays with Morrie
author: Mitch Albom
___ Tuesday, This Must Be Belgium: 5 If It's
tufa: 4 rock 9 limestone
like ~: 6 porous
Tuff ___: 5 Enuff
tuft: 3 wad 4 floc, knot, wisp 5 clump, shock 6 goatee, tassel 7 cluster, cowlick, plumage, topknot, tussock 8 feathers
starter: 5 candy
tufted: 5 rough 6 comate
tuft-hunter: 4 snob 5 snoot
Tuft of Flowers, The
author: Robert Frost
Tufts: 5 Sonny 10 university
locale: 4 Mass.
Tu Fu
contemporary: 4 Li Po
tug: 3 lug, tow 4 boat, drag, draw, haul, jerk, pull, ship, yank 5 heave, hitch, pluck, wrest 6 pull on, strain, wrench 7 jerk out
at the heart: 4 move 5 touch 6 affect
ender: 4 boat
of war: 4 game 5 fight 6 strife 7 contest 8 conflict
tow: 5 barge
tug ___: 5 of war
Tug: 6 McGraw
Tugboat ___: 5 Annie
tugboat sound: 4 toot
Tuileries, Jardin des: 4 parc
locale: 5 Paris 6 France
tuille: 5 armor 6 tasset 10 protection
tuition: 3 fee 4 cost 5 price 6 charge 7 lessons 8 learning, teaching, training 9 education, schooling
recipient: 6 bursar 9 treasurer 10 controller
Tulane: 6 school 10 university
athletes: 9 Green Wave
locale: 9 Louisiana 10 New Orleans
Tula resident: 6 Toltec
tulip: 4 bulb 5 plant 6 flower
part: 5 tepal
Tull: 6 Jethro
tulle: 4 silk
garment: 4 tutu
Tulle: 4 city, town
locale: 6 France
___ Tully Hall: 5 Alice
Tulsa: 4 city, town
city near ~: 3 Ada 4 Enid
conference: 3 WAC
locale: 4 Okla. 8 Oklahoma
newspaper: 5 World
river: 8 Arkansas
school: 3 ORU
tum: 3 gut 5 belly, tease 6 middle 7 midriff, stomach 10 midsection
tumble: 3 dip, sag 4 dive, drop, fall, flip, flop, roll, slip, trip 5 crash, learn, pitch, slide, slump, smash, spill, upset, whirl 6 jumble, plunge, sprawl, topple 7 descend, descent, give way, plummet, stumble, subvert 8 disorder, overturn 9 cartwheel 10 disarrange, somersault
ender: 3 bug, set 4 weed
out: 4 wake 5 awake, waken 6 awaken
take a ~: 4 fall, trip
tumble-___: 3 dry 4 down
___ Tumble 4 Ya: 3 I'll
Tumblebrutus: 3 cat
tumbledown: 6 flimsy, unfirm 7 rickety, run-down 8 decrepit, untended 9 crumbling 10 ramshackle
structure: 3 hut 5 shack 6 lean-to, shanty
tumbler: 3 cup 5 glass 7 acrobat, gymnast, vaulter
contents: 3 ice 4 soda 5 water
movement: 5 split
pad: 3 mat 7 cushion
place: 3 gym 4 lock
turner: 3 key
Tumbleweed
author: Janwillem van de Wetering
Tumbleweeds cartoonist: 4 Ryan
tumbling: 5 sport 10 gymnastics
Tumbling Dice (1972 song)
artist: Rolling Stones
Tumbling Tumbleweeds (song)
artist: Gene Autry
tumbrel: 4 cart 5 wagon
tumid: 6 turgid 7 bloated, fustian, orotund, pompous, swollen 8 enlarged, inflated, puffed up 9 bombastic, distended, overblown, puffed out 10 rhetorical
tummy: 3 gut 5 belly 6 middle, paunch 7 abdomen, midriff, stomach 10 midsection
butterflies in the ~: 6 nerves
exercise: 5 sit up
noise: 5 growl 6 rumble 7 grumble
soother: 6 bicarb
trouble: 4 ache
tummy ___: 4 tuck
Tums: 7 antacid
alternative: *see* antacid
target: 3 gas 4 acid
tumult: 3 ado, din, row 4 flap, fuss, mess, riot, stew, stir, to-do 5 babel, brawl, chaos, fight, furor, hoo-ha, noise, shout, storm, swirl 6 affray, bedlam, clamor, dither, émeute, flurry, fracas, hassle, hubbub, jangle, lather, mayhem, outcry, pother, racket, rumpus, squall, strife, unrest, uproar 7 anarchy, clangor, ferment, quarrel, rampage, ruction, tempest, trouble, turmoil 8 disarray, disorder, outbreak, paroxysm, seething, upheaval, wildness 9 agitation, commotion, confusion, maelstrom 10 convulsion, excitement, hullabaloo, hurly-burly, turbulence
tumultuous: 4 wild 5 aroar, noisy, rough, rowdy 6 fierce, hectic, raging, stormy, unruly 7 chaotic, rampant, raucous, riotous, violent 8 anarchic 9 clamorous, turbulent 10 anarchical, boisterous, disorderly, in an uproar
tun: 3 vat 4 cask 9 container
tuna: 4 fish 5 tunny 6 bonito, cactus 7 bluefin, Charlie 8 albacore, food fish, skipjack, Star Kist 9 Bumble Bee, yellowfin
anagram: 4 aunt
catcher: 3 net 4 hook 5 seine 7 netting
Hawaiian ~: 3 ahi
holder: 3 can, tin
how ~ is packed: 5 in oil 7 in water
salad ingredient: 4 mayo 6 celery
tuna ___: 4 fish, melt 5 on rye, salad 9 casserole
Tuna ___: 6 Helper
Tuna-Fishing
artist: Salvador Dali
Tunbridge Wells: 3 spa
tundra: 4 moor 5 biome, plain, waste 7 lowland
animal: 3 elk 4 loon, tern 5 raven 6 falcon, musk ox, rabbit 7 caribou, lemming, penguin 8 squirrel 9 polar bear
___ tundra: 6 alpine
tune: 3 air, fix, lay, set 4 aria, dial, lied, lilt, pean, sing, song 5 adapt, carol, chant, ditty, music, paean, piece, price 6 adjust, chorus, jingle, melody, number, outlay, strain 7 ariette, conform, euphony, harmony, refrain 8 modulate, readjust, regulate 9 harmonize, reconcile 10 conformity
ender: 5 smith
in ~: 5 on key, sweet 7 melodic 8 sonorous 9 consonant, melodious 10 euphonious, harmonious
like some ~s: 6 catchy
tune ___: 3 out
___-tune: 4 fine
Tune: 5 Tommy
___ Tune: 6 Elmer's
tuned
in: 3 hep, hip 4 wise 5 aware, savvy 6 versed, wise to, with it 7 knowing, mindful 8 apprised, informed, skillful 9 cognizant, sensitive 10 perceptive
out: 4 cold, numb 6 deaf to, inured 7 blind to, callous 8 hardened,

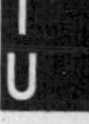

uncaring 9 apathetic, insensate, unfeeling
tuneful: 5 in key, lyric, sweet **6** ariose, arioso, dulcet **7** lyrical, melodic, musical **8** sonorous **9** melodious **10** euphonious, harmonious
tunefulness: 7 harmony
__ tuner: 5 piano
__ Tunes: 6 Looney
Tune, Tommy musical: 4 Nine
tune-up: 8 practice, training
need: 4 plug **5** point **9** condenser, spark plug
Tune Weavers
song: Happy, Happy Birthday Baby (1957)
tung: 3 oil
tunga: 4 flea
tungsten: 5 metal **7** element, wolfram
ore: 9 scheelite
tunic: 3 alb **4** coat, robe **5** cotta, shirt, stola **6** blouse, chiton, jacket
eye ~: 4 uvea
Vietnamese ~: 5 aodai
tunicate, marine: 4 salp **5** salpa
tuning: 10 regulation
tuning __: 4 fork
Tunisia: 6 nation **7** country
capital: 5 Tunis
city: 4 Sfax **5** Susah, Tunis **6** Ariana
desert: 6 Sahara
gulf: 5 Gabès
island off ~: 6 Djerba
it's n. of ~: 5 Medit.
language: 6 Arabic, Berber
money: 5 dinar
mountain range: 5 Atlas
neighbor: 5 Libya **7** Algeria
ruler: 3 bey
tunnel: 3 dig, pit **4** adit, bore, hole, mine, tube **5** gouge, shaft **6** burrow, escape, subway **7** channel, passage **8** catacomb, crawlway, crosscut, excavate **9** penetrate, undermine, underpass **10** passageway
builder: 3 ant **4** mole **5** emmet, miner **6** gopher
make a ~: 3 dig **4** bore, mine, root **6** burrow **8** excavate, scoop out **9** hollow out
tunnel __: 6 vision
__ tunnel: 4 wind
Tunnel of Love (1987 song)
artist: Bruce Springsteen
__ tunnel syndrome: 6 carpal
Tunney, Gene: 5 boxer
milieu: 4 ring
tunny: 4 fish, tuna **7** bluefin **8** albacore
Tupac: 6 Shakur
song: California Love (1996)
Dear Mama (1995)
How Do U Want It (1996)
I Get Around (1993)
Keep Ya Head Up (1993)
Smile (1997)
tupelo: 4 tree
Tupelo: 4 city, town
locale: 4 Miss.
singer from ~: Elvis Presley
Tupolev: 3 SST **5** plane **7** Russian **8** airplane
tuppence: 4 coin **5** money
Tupper: 4 Amos, Earl
Turandot: 5 opera
composer: Giacomo Puccini
librettist: Giuseppe Adami
role: 3 Liù, Tiu **4** Pang, Ping, Pong **5** Calaf, Timur **8** Pu-tin-Pao
setting: 5 China **6** Peking **7** Beijing
tune: 4 aria
turban: 3 hat **8** headgear **9** headdress
material: 6 Madras
poolside ~: 5 towel
wearer: 4 Sikh **5** Hindu, swami, swamy
turbid: 5 mirky, muddy, murky, roily, thick **6** cloudy, opaque **7** clouded, muddied, muddled, unclear **8** darkened
turbine: 5 motor **6** diesel, engine **9** generator
part: 4 vane **5** rotor **6** stator
__ turbine: 3 air, gas **4** wind **5** steam, water
turbo-__ engine: 6 ramjet
turbofan: 6 engine
turbojet: 5 plane **6** engine **8** airplane
turboprop: 5 plane **6** engine **8** airplane
turboshaft: 6 engine
turbot: 4 bret, fish **5** brill
TurboTax company: 6 Intuit
turbulence: 4 fury, rage, stew **5** chaos, noise **6** bedlam, lather, racket, squall, tumult, unrest, uproar **7** anarchy, discord, ferment **8** disarray, disorder **9** commotion, confusion **10** disharmony, storminess
turbulent: 4 wild **5** bumpy, noisy, roily, rough, rowdy, wroth **6** choppy, fierce, hectic, jouncy, raging, stormy, unruly **7** chaotic, foaming, furious, howling, lawless, moiling, rampant, raucous, riotous, roaring, ruffled, untamed, violent **8** agitated, blustery, restless, swirling **9** disturbed, inclement, stirred up, unsettled **10** blustering, boisterous, disordered, disorderly, in an uproar, rebellious, tumultuous, unpeaceful
Turcotte, Ron: 6 jockey
milieu: 5 track
tureen: 4 bowl **5** crock **6** vessel **9** container
accessory: 5 ladle
contents: 4 soup
turf: 3 sod **4** area, home, lawn, soil **5** earth, grass, realm, space, sward **6** domain, ground, locale, region, sphere, swarth **7** habitat, quarter, terrain **8** locality, location, vicinity **9** bailiwick, community, home field, racetrack, territory **10** greensward
add more ~: 5 resod
grabber: 5 cleat
loose ~: 5 divot
material: 4 peat
starter: 5 Astro
surf and ~: 4 meal **6** dinner, entrée
warriors: 4 band, gang, pack
__-turf: 5 surf-'n'
Turgenev, Ivan: 6 writer **7** Russian
birthplace: 4 Orel
character: 5 Elena
work: Fathers and Sons
A Month in the Country
A Sportsman's Sketches
turgid: 5 tumid, windy, wordy **7** pompous, stilted, unterse **8** inflated **9** distended, overblown **10** rhetorical
Turhan: 3 Bey
Turia
city on the ~: 8 Valencia
Turin: 4 city, town **5** Adela
city near ~: 4 Asti
locale: 5 Italy
river: 5 the Po
Shroud of ~: 5 relic
Turing: 4 Alan
__ Turismo Omologato: 4 Gran
Turk: 5 Asian **6** Othman **7** Ottoman, upstart **9** Anatolian
neighbor: 5 Greek, Irani, Iraqi **6** Syrian **8** Georgian **9** Bulgarian
__ Turk: 5 Grand, Young
Turkana: 4 lake
locale: 3 Afr. **5** Kenya **6** Africa
Turkel: 3 Ann
turkey: 3 dud **4** bird, bomb, bust, flop, fowl, loss, meat, play **5** lemon, ninny **6** defeat, fiasco, mishap **7** blunder, debacle, failure, gobbler, misstep, poultry, stumble, washout **8** downfall **9** jellyfish **10** nonsuccess
baster: 4 chef, cook **5** pipet
do the ~: 5 baste, carve, stuff, truss
female ~: 3 hen
go cold ~: 4 quit
like some ~s: 5 plump **6** basted
like some ~ stuffing: 4 sagy
male ~: 3 tom **7** gobbler
meat choice: 3 leg **4** dark **5** thigh, white **6** breast **9** drumstick
relative: ***see*** fowl
roaster: 4 oven
talking ~: 4 open **9** outspoken
topper: 5 gravy
walk like a ~: 5 strut
young ~: 5 poult
see also ninny
turkey __: 4 trot **5** shoot
__ turkey: 4 cold, talk, wild
Turkey: 6 nation **7** country, Stearns
ancient city: 5 Adana **6** Edessa, Sestos
ancient region: 6 Aeolia
bovine: 5 Kurdi
candy: 5 halva **6** halvah **7** halavah
capital: 6 Ankara
cavalryman: 5 spahi **6** spahee
chamber: 3 oda **4** odah
city: 4 Urfa **5** Adana, Brusa, Bursa, Izmir, Konya, Maras **6** Angora, Ankara, Edirne, Elâzig **7** Antalya **8** Istanbul
coffee: 5 mocha
decree: 5 irade
garment: 6 caftan, kaftan
government of old: 5 porte
gulf: 5 Izmir
highest point: 6 Ararat
inn: 5 serai **6** imaret
island near ~: 5 Samos **6** Cyprus, Rhodes, Rhodos
lake: 3 Van
language: 6 Othman **7** Ottoman
liquor: 4 raki **5** rakee
locale: 4 Asia **6** Europe
money: 4 lira **5** asper, kurus **6** sequin **7** piaster, piastre
mountain: 3 Ida **6** Ararat, Pontic, Taurus, Zagros **7** Ala Dagh
mountain dweller: 4 Kurd
neighbor: 4 Irak, Iran, Iraq **5** Syria **6** Greece **7** Armenia, Georgia **8** Bulgaria **10** Azerbaijan
org.: 4 NATO
poet: 6 Hikmet
port: 5 Izmir **6** Smyrna **8** Istanbul
region: 6 Levant
river: 4 Aras, Kura **5** Murat **6** Tigris
robe: 6 dolman
scholars: 5 ulema
sea: 5 Egean **6** Aegean **7** Marmara
soldier: 5 Nizam
staple: 6 sesame
sword: 5 kilij
title: 3 aga, bey **4** agha, amir, emir **5** ameer, emeer, pacha, pasha
topper: 3 fez
weight: 3 oka
Turkey Hill: 8 ice cream
alternative: ***see*** ice cream
Turkey in the __: 5 Straw
turkey trot: 5 dance
Turkic
language: 5 Tatar, Yakut
tent: 4 yurt
Turkish
see Turkey
Turkish __: 3 rug **4** bath **5** taffy, towel **6** coffee
Turkish bath: 5 sauna
like a ~: 3 hot **5** humid **6** steamy
need: 5 towel
Turkish delight: 5 candy
Turkish Letters
author: Mary Wortley Montagu
Turkish Van: 3 cat **5** felid **6** feline
__-Turkish War: 5 Italo
Turkmenistan: 6 nation **7** country
capital: 9 Ashkhabad
desert: 7 Kara Kum
neighbor: 4 Iran **10** Kazakhstan, Uzbekistan
once: 3 SSR
river: 4 Oxus
Turkoman: 3 rug **6** Afghan, carpet **7** Afghani
Turks and Caicos: 4 isls. **5** isles **7** islands
Turk's-head: 4 knot **6** cactus
Turku: 4 city, town
locale: 7 Finland
to a Swede: 3 Åbo
Turman: 5 Glynn
turmeric: 5 spice **9** condiment
turmoil: 3 ado **4** flap, fuss, mess, riot, stew, stir, to-do **5** chaos, furor, hoo-ha, mix-up, storm, swirl, upset, whirl **6** action, bedlam, clamor, flurry, frenzy, hassle, hubbub, lather, mayhem, pother, racket, squall, tumult, unrest, uproar **7** anarchy, anxiety, ferment, mad rush, rampage, rioting **8** disarray, disorder, disquiet, distress, madhouse, upheaval **9** agitation, confusion, maelstrom, mobocracy **10** donnybrook, excitement, hullabaloo
in ~: 6 uneasy
inner ~: 3 woe **5** angst, dread,

worry 7 anxiety, malaise 8 disquiet 10 inquietude, uneasiness
turn: 2 go 3 arc, lap, rat, rot, try, use, yaw 4 bend, bent, curl, deed, eddy, fork, gift, head, hook, lean, loop, mold, move, play, roll, shot, sour, spin, sway, tack, till, tilt, time, tour, veer, vein, walk, wind 5 alter, at bat, crank, curve, cycle, decay, drift, favor, flair, go bad, jaunt, knack, level, orbit, pivot, point, quirk, round, scare, screw, shape, sheer, shift, shunt, snake, spell, spoil, stint, swing, swirl, taint, trend, twirl, twist, whack, wheel, whirl 6 attack, become, circle, curdle, defect, detour, direct, divert, employ, go back, go sour, gyrate, invert, modify, molder, mutate, orient, outing, ramble, recoil, renege, revert, revolt, rotate, spiral, sprain, strain, stroll, swerve, switch, swivel, talent, wrench, zigzag 7 acidify, capsize, convert, deviate, digress, diverge, flexure, incline, meander, retract, reverse, revolve, seizure, service, shy away, subvert, utilize, veer off, winding 8 aptitude, go around, persuade, renounce, resort to, rotation, surprise 9 about-face, alternate, backslide, circulate, decompose, excursion, hang a left, influence, oscillate, pirouette, promenade, sidetrack, sinuosity, transform, transmute, volte-face 10 come around, double back, hang a right, propensity, revolution, right-about, succession
180-degree ~: 3 uey
a blind eye to: 8 overlook
about: 4 slew, slue 6 slough
a deaf ear to: 4 deny 5 scorn 6 refuse, slight
against: 5 rebel 6 betray, revolt 7 sell out
around: 5 rally, shift 6 invert 7 correct, redress, reverse
aside: 4 skew, veer 5 avert, parry, repel, shunt 6 divert, swerve 7 deflect, prevent, ward off 10 discourage
away: 4 shun 5 avert, spurn 6 ignore, rebuff, recoil, refuse 7 repulse 8 alienate
back: 5 repel, spurn 6 rebuff, thwart 7 regress, relapse, repulse 8 stave off
bad: 3 rot 5 spoil
combining form: 4 trop- 5 tropo-
do a ~: 4 solo 7 perform
down: 3 dim, nix 4 deny, mute, shun, veto 5 say no, scorn, spurn, waive 6 bounce, pass on, rebuff, reduce, refuse, reject, resist, soften 7 decline, disdain, dismiss, exclude, ward off 8 disallow, throw out 9 blackball, cast aside, frown upon, repudiate 10 disapprove
ender: 3 key, off, out 4 coat, down, over, pike, sole, spit 5 about, stile, stone, table 6 around, buckle
for the better: 5 rally
full ~: 5 orbit 10 revolution
give a ~: 5 alarm, scare, shake, shock, spook, throw 6 dismay, rattle 7 fluster, startle, unnerve 8 affright, frighten, surprise, unsettle 9 take aback 10 disconcert, intimidate
good ~: 5 favor 8 courtesy, kindness 10 kindliness
green over: 4 envy 5 covet 8 begrudge
half a ~: 3 zag, zig
in: 3 lie, nap 4 flop, rest, sing 5 rat on, sleep, spill 6 betray, expose, finger, fink on, give up, retire, squeal, submit, tell on, tender 7 deliver, go to bed, lie down, sack out, saw logs, sell out 8 give away, hand over, inform on, snitch on, squeal on, tattle on 9 deliver up, go to sleep, hit the hay 10 call it a day, hit the sack, put forward
in ~: 8 one by one
inside out: 4 comb, sack 5 evert, probe, rifle, scour 6 forage, invert, ravage, ravish, search 7 examine, inspect, pillage, ransack, rummage 8 overhaul 9 go through 10 scrutinize
into: 5 end up 6 become, evolve, modify 8 emerge as
left: 3 haw
loose: 5 let go 6 unbind 7 manumit, release
off: 3 vex 4 bore, kill, sour, stop 5 close, douse, dowse, repel 6 offend, revolt, sadden, sicken, unplug 7 disgust, repulse 8 alienate, shut down 9 displease 10 disenchant, extinguish
of phrase: 5 idiom 7 wording 10 expression
on: 4 open, send, spur 5 elate, impel, light, liven, pep up, start 6 arouse, enable, excite, ignite, kindle, please, pump up, thrill, tickle, vivify, work up 7 actuate, animate, delight, enchant, enliven, gladden, inspire, juice up, liven up, power up, start up 8 activate, energize, enspirit, inspirit, interest, vitalize 9 captivate, instigate, stimulate, throw open, titillate 10 invigorate
one's back on: 4 shun 5 avoid, scorn 6 desert, disown, ignore, refuse, reject 7 abandon, forsake, neglect 8 overlook, renounce 9 disregard, repudiate 10 leave alone
one's nose up at: 5 scorn, sneer, spurn 7 disdain 10 look down on
out: 2 ax, go 3 axe, can, rig 4 come, fare, fire, form, make, oust, rise, show, wake 5 arise, eject, end up, enter, equip, evict, exile, expel, get up, occur, pop in, prove, waken, write, yield 6 appear, arrive, attend, betide, blow in, drop in, go well, happen, invent, result, roll in, show up 7 appoint, cashier, dismiss, furnish, produce, release, succeed 8 accouter, accoutre, assemble, breeze in 9 arise from, caparison, eventuate, fabricate
out badly: 3 die, sag 4 bomb, fail, flop, fold, lose, miss, sink 6 fizzle 7 founder, go under, let down 8 backfire, collapse, fall flat, go astray, languish 9 fall short 10 go bankrupt, go downhill
outward: 5 evert, flare
over: 3 tip 4 give, mull, muse, plow, roll, till 5 crank, refer, relay, think, upend, yield 6 assign, commit, fork up, hand in, invert, pass on, ponder, render, rotate, supply, topple 7 capsize, commend, consign, deliver, entrust, intrust, lay down, provide, reverse, revolve 8 consider, delegate, meditate, mull over, relegate, ruminate, transfer 9 reflect on, surrender 10 deliberate, get started, relinquish, think about
over a new leaf: 6 change, reform 7 redress, shape up 10 go straight
partner: 4 toss 5 twist
right: 3 gee
sharp ~: 3 jog, zag, zig 4 jink 6 dogleg
signal: 5 arrow
single ~: 10 revolution
starter: 4 down
suddenly: 4 veer 6 careen
tail: 3 run 4 bolt, flee 6 escape 7 retreat, run away, take off 8 fugitate, run for it 9 cut and run, skedaddle
take a wrong ~: 3 err 5 stray 6 slip up 8 go astray, trespass 9 misbehave 10 transgress
the key: 6 fasten, secure
the other cheek: 5 spare 6 pardon 7 forgive, let it go, let pass 8 bear with, overlook
the tables: 5 shift 6 oppose 7 revenge, reverse 9 retaliate
things around: 5 rally 7 rectify, redress
to: 3 ask, see 7 consult
(to): 5 refer 6 resort
to a ~: 9 perfectly
topsy-turvy: 5 upend, upset 6 invert, jumble, muss up 7 derange 8 disarray, unsettle
toss and ~: 5 brood, worry 7 agonize
toward: 4 face, meet 6 engage 7 eyeball 8 confront
up: 4 come, find, show, spot 5 learn, occur, pop in, reach 6 appear, arrive, attend, blow in, detect, locate, report, reveal 7 hit upon, punch in, uncover, unearth, weigh in 8 discover, get there 9 get to know, track down, transpire 10 come to pass
up one's nose: 5 sneer
upside-down: 4 comb, flip 6 invert 7 ransack, reverse, rummage, shake up 8 overturn

turn ___: 3 off, out, pro 4 away, back, down, over, tail 5 a hair, loose
turn ___ ear: 5 a deaf
turn ___ evidence: 6 state's
turn ___ new leaf: 5 over a
___ turn: 3 to a 4 star 5 out of
Turn ___ Screw, The: 5 of the
___ Turn: 5 It's My, Rose's
___-Turn: 3 No U
turn a ___: 4 hair 6 corner, profit
turn a ___ ear: 4 deaf
turn a ___ eye: 5 blind
turnabout: 6 switch 7 reverse 8 apostasy, flip-flop, reversal 9 inversion, one-eighty
in French: 9 volte-face
turnaround: 6 change 8 flip-flop, upheaval
Turn Around, Look at Me (1968 song)
artist: Vogues
Turn Back the Hands of Time (1970 song)
artist: Tyrone Davis
turncoat: 3 rat 4 fink, nark 5 Judas, rebel, snake, viper 6 ratter 7 ratfink, stoolie, tattler, traitor 8 apostate, betrayer, forsaker, quisling, recreant, renegade, squealer, two-timer
turndown: 2 no 3 nay 4 veto 6 denial, rebuff 7 refusal, regrets 9 rejection 10 nonconsent
emphatic ~: 5 never, no sir, no way
slangy ~: 3 nah 4 nope, uh-uh
turned: 4 rank, sour 5 swung 6 rancid 7 gone bad 8 inedible
back on: 5 relit
be ~ off by: 4 hate 5 abhor 6 detest, loathe
down: 3 low 5 faint, piano, quiet
off: 8 outraged 9 disgusted, squeamish 10 displeased, grossed out
on: 3 lit 4 into 6 enrapt 8 obsessed
up: 4 loud 5 forte, noisy 7 blaring, booming, jarring, pealing, rackety, raucous, reboant, roaring 8 crashing, piercing, plangent, rumbling, sonorous, strident 9 big-voiced, clamorous, deafening 10 boisterous, resounding, stentorian, strepitous, thundering, vociferous
well ~ out: 4 chic, neat, trim 5 dandy, natty, sharp, sleek, smart, swank 6 chichi, classy, dapper, jaunty, snappy, snazzy, spiffy, sporty, spruce, swanky 7 dashing, stylish 8 handsome
turner: 7 gymnast, tumbler
device: 5 lathe
starter: 4 wood
___-turner: 4 page
Turner: 3 Ike, J.M.W., Joe, Nat, Ted 4 John, Lana, Tina 5 Sammy 6 Big Joe, Janine, Odessa, Sherri 8 Kathleen
network: 3 CNN, TBS, TNT
Turner Field
site: 7 Atlanta
Turner & Hooch (1989 film)
cast: Tom Hanks, Craig T. Nelson, Mare Winningham
Turner, Ike and Tina
song: Proud Mary (1971)
Turner, John: 2 P.M. 8 Canadian
predecessor: 7 Trudeau
successor: 8 Mulroney
Turner, Kathleen: 7 actress
film: The Accidental Tourist (1988)
Body Heat (1981)
The Jewel of the Nile (1985)
The Man With Two Brains (1983)
Moonlight and Valentino (1995)

Peggy Sue Got Married (1986)
Prizzi's Honor (1985)
Romancing the Stone (1984)
Serial Mom (1994)
Switching Channels (1988)
The Virgin Suicides (2000)
The War of the Roses (1989)
Turner, Lana: 7 actress
film: The Bad and the Beautiful (1952)
Dr. Jekyll and Mr. Hyde (1941)
Imitation of Life (1959)
Johnny Eager (1941)
Marriage Is a Private Affair (1944)
Peyton Place (1957)
The Postman Always Rings Twice (1946)
Weekend at the Waldorf (1945)
Ziegfeld Girl (1941)
spouse: Lex Barker
Turner, Nat: 5 rebel, slave
__-Turner Overdrive: 7 Bachman
Turner, Ted
spouse: Jane Fonda
Turner, Tina
born: Anna Mae Bullock
song: Better Be Good to Me (1984)
I Don't Wanna Fight (1993)
It's Only Love (1985)
Private Dancer (1985)
Typical Male (1986)
We Don't Need Another Hero (1985)
What's Love Got to Do With It (1984)
spouse: Ike Turner
turning: 6 aswirl, rotary **7** sinuous, winding **8** gyration **9** diversion **10** divergence
point: 3 hub **4** axis, axle, crux **5** hinge, pivot, rally **6** climax, crisis **8** juncture, landmark, zero hour **9** milestone
starter: 4 wood
tool: 5 lathe
tossing and ~: 5 awake **8** restless
turning __: 5 point
Turning Point
author: Jimmy Carter
Turning Point, The (1977 film)
cast: Anne Bancroft, Mikhail Baryshnikov, Leslie Browne, Shirley MacLaine
director: Herbert Ross
Turning to Stone (1985 film)
director: Eric Till
turnip: 4 root **5** tuber **6** veggie **9** vegetable
Scottish ~: 4 neep
Turn It Up (1998 song)
artist: Busta Rhymes
turnkey: 6 gaoler, jailer **10** doorkeeper
domain: 4 jail
Turn Me Loose (1959 song)
artist: Fabian
turnoff: 4 exit
Turn of the Screw, The
author: Henry James
character: 5 Flora, Grose, Miles, Quint
turn-on: 6 thrill **8** pleasure
turn one's __: 4 head
turn one's __ on: 4 back
turn one's __ to: 4 hand
turnout: 3 rig **4** gate **5** crowd, getup, yield **6** output, throng **7** meeting **8** assembly, audience **9** gathering, listeners, multitude **10** attendance, production
turnover: 5 knish, upset **6** change, pastry, resale, samosa **8** movement
turn over __ leaf: 4 a new
turnpike: 4 road **5** route **6** artery **7** highway, thruway **10** expressway
access: 4 ramp
like a ~: 5 laned
maneuver: 5 merge
stop: 5 motel, plaza
tariff: 4 toll
turns: 10 ins and outs
take ~: 4 vary **5** spell **6** rotate, switch **8** exchange, trade off **9** alternate, change off
__ turns out...: 4 As it
turnstile: 4 exit, gate **5** entry **6** entrée, portal **7** ingress **8** entrance, entryway **10** admittance
cheater: 4 slug
drop-in: 5 token
opening: 4 slot
turntable
abbr.: 3 rpm
extension: 3 arm **7** tonearm
topper: 2 LP **5** album **6** record
turn the __: 4 tide **5** trick **6** corner, tables
Turn the Beat Around (1976 song)
artist: Vicki Sue Robinson
turn the other __: 5 cheek
__ Turn to Cry: 5 Judy's
Turn to Stone
artist: ELO
turn toward combining form: 5 -trope
Turn! Turn! Turn! (1965 song)
artist: Byrds
turn up one's __ at: 4 nose
Turn Your Love Around (1981 song)
artist: George Benson
Turow, Scott: 6 writer
work: The Burden of Proof
The Laws of Our Fathers
Limitations
One L
Ordinary Heroes
Personal Injuries
Pleading Guilty
Presumed Innocent
Reversible Errors
turpentine: 5 pitch
source: 4 pine
Turpin: 3 Ben **4** Dick
Turpin, Dick horse: 9 Black Bess
turpitude: 4 evil, vice **5** wrong **10** corruption
turquoise: 3 gem **4** aqua, blue **5** color, green **6** bluish **7** blueish, mineral **8** gemstone, greenish
like ~: 6 bluish **7** blueish
month: 3 Dec. **8** December
relative: ***see*** blue color
turret: 5 spire, tower **7** steeple
Turteltaub: 3 Jon
turtle: 3 pet **4** soup **6** animal, cooter, ridley **7** reptile, snapper **8** stinkpot **9** hawksbill **10** loggerhead
about to turn ~: 5 alist
ender: 4 back, dove, head, neck
genus: 4 emys
group: 4 bale
home: 4 pond **5** shell
plate: 5 scute
plates: 5 scuta
toon ~: 5 ninja
__ turtle: 3 box, mud, sea **4** turn
__ Turtle: 4 Mock
turtledove: 4 bird
see also sweetheart
...__ turtledoves...: 3 two
Turtle Island
author: Gary Snyder
turtleneck: 6 blouse **7** sweater **8** pullover
material: 4 wool
what a ~ hides: 4 nape
Turtles
song: Elenore (1968)
Happy Together (1967)
It Ain't Me Babe (1965)
She'd Rather Be With Me (1967)
You Showed Me (1969)
__ turtle soup: 4 mock
Turturro: 4 Aida, John
Turturro, John: 5 actor
film: Barton Fink (1991)
Clockers (1995)
Five Corners (1988)
Mac (1992)
O Brother, Where Art Thou? (2000)
Quiz Show (1994)
Rounders (1998)
The Taking of Pelham 123 (2009)
__-turvy: 5 topsy
Tuscaloosa: 4 city, town
locale: 3 Ala. **7** Alabama
Tuscan: 5 order, Pisan **8** language
Tuscany
city: 4 Pisa **5** Massa, Prato, Siena **7** Firenze, Leghorn, Livorno **8** Florence
locale: 5 Italy
river: 4 Arno
Tuscarora: 6 Indian **7** Amerind
ally: 6 Cayuga, Mohawk, Oneida, Seneca **8** Onondaga
Tush (1975 song)
artist: ZZ Top
Tushingham: 4 Rita
tusk: 5 ivory, tooth
Tusk (1979 song)
artist: Fleetwood Mac
tusker: 3 hog **4** boar **5** swine **6** walrus
tussah: 3 bug **6** fabric, insect
__ Tussaud's Wax Museum: 3 Mme.
Tussi home: 6 Africa, Rwanda **7** Burundi
tussle: 4 bout, fray, tilt **5** brawl, brush, clash, fight, melee, mix-up, run-in, set-to **6** barney, battle, go at it, hassle **7** grapple, mix it up, scuffle, wrestle **8** conflict, do battle, scramble, skirmish, struggle **9** fistfight, square off **10** donnybrook, free-for-all
tussock: 4 tuft
Tussy: 9 deodorant
alternative: ***see*** deodorant
tut: 3 tsk **6** tsk tsk **8** for shame
__ Tut: 4 King
tutee: 5 pupil **7** learner, student
tutelage: 4 care **7** keeping **8** guidance, training, wardship **9** oversight, schooling **10** protection
tutelary deity: 3 Lar
tutor: 4 guru **5** coach, drill, edify, groom, guide, ready, teach, train **6** direct, ground, master, mentor, school **7** adviser, advisor, educate, lecture, teacher, trainer **8** academic, educator, instruct, lecturer **9** abecedary, governess, preceptor **10** instructor
charge: 5 pupil
Oxford ~: 3 don
tutorial: 6 lesson **7** session **9** pedagogic
Tutsi
foe: 4 Hutu
home: 6 Africa, Rwanda **7** Burundi
Tutte le feste: 4 aria
tutti: 3 all
tutti-frutti: 8 ice cream
alternative: ***see*** ice cream flavor
Tutti-Frutti (1956 song)
artist: Little Richard
Tuttle: 5 Frank **6** Lurene
Tut-tut!: 3 tsk **6** tsk tsk
tutu: 5 skirt **7** costume
event: 6 ballet
fabric: 5 tulle
Tutu, Desmond: 8 Nobelist **11** archibishop
Tuvalu: 6 nation **7** country
city: 8 Funafuti
formerly: 6 Ellice
money: 4 cent **6** dollar
TUV neighbor: 3 JKL, PRS, WXY **4** oper.
tu-whit tu-__: 4 whoo
tuxedo: 4 coat, suit **6** formal, jacket **8** black tie **10** formal wear, monkey suit
accessory: 6 bowtie **10** cummerbund
junction: 4 seam
occasion: 4 prom **7** wedding
wearer: 5 groom
TV: 3 set **4** tube **5** telly **7** console, monitor **8** boob tube, idiot box **9** goggle box
adjunct: 3 VCR **4** dish **5** cable **6** aerial **7** antenna **9** DVD player **10** rabbit ears
band: 3 UHF, VHF
big week in ~: 6 sweeps
cartoon: 6 kidcom
children's ~: 6 kidvid
commercial: 2 ad **4** advt., spot
fare: 4 film, news, soap, talk **5** drama, movie **6** series, sitcom **7** cartoon **8** game show **9** soap opera
feature: 6 stereo
former ~ network: 6 Dumont
free ~ ad: 3 PSA
knob: 3 hor., vol. **4** dial, tint, vert **5** tuner **8** vertical **10** horizontal
listing abbr.: 3 TBA
monitoring device: 5 V-chip
network: 2 CW **3** ABC, BBC, CBC, CBS, Fox, NBC, PBS **4** ESPN
networks: 5 media
news hour: 3 six, ten **5** six p.m., ten p.m. **6** eleven **8** eleven p.m.
not edited for ~: 5 uncut
nuisance: 4 snow
on ~: 6 airing **7** running **8** telecast **9** broadcast

on-the-spot ~ report: 4 nemo
overseer: 3 FCC
part: 3 CRT 4 tube 5 diode, tuner 6 screen
part of ~: 4 tele 6 vision
part of a ~ broadcast: 5 audio, video
pay ~: 5 cable
premiere season: 4 fall
put on ~: 3 air 9 broadcast
record label in ~ ads: 4 K-Tel
remote control: 4 nemo
remote-control button: 4 mute 6 volume 7 channel
reporter: 6 anchor
room: 3 den
show on ~ again: 5 reair
signal receiver: 4 dish
statuette: 4 Emmy
studio need: 4 mike 6 camera 10 microphone
studio sign: 5 on air
summer ~ fare: 5 rerun
tower: 4 mast
tube filler: 5 xenon
watch, as a ~ show: 6 have on
see also television
TV __: 6 dinner
__ TV: 5 cable, Court
__-TV: 3 pay
TV-14: 6 rating
TVA
part of ~: 4 Auth., Tenn. 6 Valley 9 Authority, Tennessee
product: 3 pwr. 4 elec. 5 power 11 electricity
project: 3 dam
TV-G: 6 rating
TV Guide: 3 mag 8 magazine
abbr.: 3 TBA
detail: 7 air time
onetime ~ reviewer: 5 Amory
span: 4 week
TV Land
alternative: *see* cable channel
TV-M: 6 rating
TV-PG: 6 rating
TV-Y: 6 rating
twa: 3 two 8 Scottish
preceder: 3 ane
TWA: 7 airline
airline bought by ~: 5 Ozark
airline that bought ~: 8 American
part of ~: 5 Trans, World 8 Airlines
twaddle
see baloney
twain: 3 duo, two 4 both, pair 6 couple
Twain: 4 Mark 6 Shania
Twain, Mark: 6 writer 8 humorist
work: The Celebrated Jumping Frog of Calaveras County
A Connecticut Yankee in King Arthur's Court
Following the Equator
Huckleberry Finn
The Innocents Abroad
The Prince and the Pauper
Pudd'nhead Wilson
Roughing It
Tom Sawyer
Twain, Shania: 6 singer
born: Eileen Edwards
homeland: Canada
song: From This Moment On (1998)
That Don't Impress Me Much (1999)
You're Still the One (1998)
twang: 5 drawl, pluck, plunk 6 accent 8 localism, nasality
twangy: 5 nasal
__ T. Washington: 6 Booker
'Twas the __ before Christmas...: 5 night
tweak: 3 nip, rag 4 pull, twit 5 annoy, pinch, pluck, tease, twist 6 adjust, modify 7 jerk out 8 fine-tune 10 adjustment
target: 4 nose 7 schnozz 10 schnozzola
tweed: 6 fabric 8 material
like ~: 5 nubby 6 coarse
wearer: 6 preppy 7 preppie
__ tweed: 5 Irish 6 Harris 7 Donegal
Tweed: 4 Boss 5 river 7 Shannon, William
locale: 7 England 8 Scotland
nemesis: 4 Nast
river to the ~: 6 Yarrow
Tweedlee Dee (1955 song)
artist: LaVern Baker, Georgia Gibbs
tweeds: 5 pants
'tween: 5 'twixt 7 amongst 9 youngster
tweet: 4 call, peep, pipe, sing 5 cheep, chirp 7 chitter, twitter 8 bird call
Tweety: 4 bird, toon
home: 4 cage
Twelfth Night
author: William Shakespeare
character: 4 Toby 5 Belch, Feste, Maria, Viola 6 Olivia, Orsino 9 Toby Belch
Twelfth of Never, The (song)
artist: Johnny Mathis, Donny Osmond
twelve: 4 noon 5 dozen 6 midday 8 high noon, meridian, midnight, noontime
combining form: 5 dodec- 6 dodeca-
dozen: 5 gross
every ~ months: 4 yrly. 6 yearly
months: 4 year
one of ~: 5 juror, month
twelve-__ limit: 4 mile
Twelve __: 4 Oaks
Twelve Days of Christmas
gift: 5 birds, lords, maids, rings, swans 6 ladies, pipers 8 drummers, pear tree 9 gold rings, partridge 10 French hens 11 turtledoves 12 calling birds
Twelve Little Preludes
composer: J.S. Bach
Twelve Monkeys (1995 film)
cast: Brad Pitt, Christopher Plummer, Madeleine Stowe, Bruce Willis
twelvemonth: 4 year
Twelve Oaks neighbor: 4 Tara
Twelve O'Clock High
org.: 4 USAF
twelve-string __: 6 guitar
Twelve Thirty (1967 song)
artist: Mamas & the Papas
Twelvetrees: 5 Helen
__ Twenties: 7 Roaring
twenty: 5 score
change for a ~: 4 ones, tens 5 fives
combining form: 4 icos- 5 eicos-, icosa-, icosi- 6 eicosa-
give ~ lashes: 4 cane, drub, whip 5 flail 6 larrup 7 scourge 10 flagellate
twenty-__ seven: 4 four
twenty-first century: 3 new 5 fresh, novel 6 latest, modern, modish, recent, timely, with-it 7 current, topical 8 up-to-date 10 avant-garde, modernized, present-day
twenty-four
carat: 4 pure 7 sincere 8 rightful
one of ~: 4 hour
twenty lashes with __ noodle: 4 a wet
Twenty-Mule __ Borax: 4 Team
twenty-one: 4 game 7 pontoon 8 card game 9 blackjack, vingt-et-un
words: 4 stay 5 hit me
Twenty Questions
category: 6 animal 7 mineral 9 vegetable
reply: 2 no 3 yes
twenty-six
all: 4 A to Z
Twenty Thousand Leagues Under the Sea: 5 novel
author: Jules Verne
character: 3 Ned 4 Land, Nemo 6 Pierre 7 Aronnax, Conseil, Ned Land
twenty-twenty __: 6 vision
Twenty Years After
author: Alexandre Dumas (père)
Twenty Years on Broadway autobiographer: 5 Cohan
't weren't nothin': 6 shucks
twerp: 4 jerk, nerd, pest, punk, twit, wimp 5 creep, dweeb 6 nudnik, squirt 7 nebbish 9 pipsqueak
twi-__ doubleheader: 5 night
Twi: 8 language
twice: 3 bis 5 again 6 doubly
combining form: 2 bi-
halved: 4 once
in music: 3 bis
think ~: 5 pause 7 scruple 8 reassess 10 reconsider
thinking ~: 7 careful, prudent
__ twice: 5 think
Twice in a Lifetime (1985 film)
cast: Ann-Margret, Ellen Burstyn, Gene Hackman
Twice Shy
author: Dick Francis
twice-told: 3 old
Twice-Told Tales
author: Nathaniel Hawthorne
twiddle one's thumbs: 4 idle, laze 5 shirk 6 lounge 7 goof off, sit back 8 malinger, mark time, slack off 9 do nothing
twig: 4 limb, stem, wand 5 shoot, sprig, stick 8 offshoot
broom: 5 besom
willow ~: 5 withe
twiggy: 4 lank, lean, slim, thin, wiry 5 lanky, spare 6 dainty, gangly, skinny, slight, slinky, svelte 7 gracile, scraggy, scrawny, slender, spidery, willowy 8 gangling 9 sylphlike
Twiggy: 5 model 6 Lawson
emulate ~: 3 sit 4 pose 5 model
real name: Lesley Hornby
twiglike
see twiggy
twigs: 4 wood 6 tinder 8 firewood, kindling
twilight: 3 ebb, e'en, end 4 dusk, soft 5 gloam, night 6 sunset 7 decline, evening, sundown 8 eventide, gloaming 9 afterglow, nightfall, nighttime
like ~: 5 dusky
turn to ~: 6 darken
Twilight
artist: 3 ELO
Twilight (1998 film)
cast: Gene Hackman, Paul Newman, Susan Sarandon, Reese Witherspoon
Twilight __: 4 Time, Zone
Twilight __ Gods, The: 5 of the
Twilight Eyes
author: Dean Koontz
Twilight in Italy
author: D.H. Lawrence
Twilight Time (1958 song)
artist: Platters
Twilight Zone (song)
artist: Golden Earring, Manhattan Transfer
Twilight Zone, The (CBS sci-fi)
host: Rod Serling
like ~: 4 eery 5 eerie
twilit: 3 dim 4 dark, gray 5 dusky, murky 7 shadowy 9 unlighted
twill fabric: 5 chino, denim, serge 6 coburg, coutil, oxford 7 Cheviot, estamin, foulard, hickory, nankeen, silesia, Viyella 8 canotier, casimere, casimire, moleskin, prunella, prunelle, prunello, shalloon, Venetian 9 bombazeen, bombazine, cassimere, gabardine, henrietta, paramatta, sharkskin 10 broadcloth
twin: 3 bed 4 dual, mate, same 5 clone, match, sosie 6 double, duplex, ringer, second 7 brother, similar, twofold 8 matching, selfsame 9 duplicate, facsimile, identical, look-alike 10 dead ringer
Biblical ~: 4 Esau 5 Jacob
identical ~: 5 sosie
mythical: 5 Remus 7 Romulus
twin __: 3 bed 4 bill, room 7 killing
twin-__: 4 size
twin-__ camera: 4 lens
twin-__ plane: 6 engine
__ twin: 7 Siamese
Twin
Hall-of-Famer: 5 Carew 7 Puckett 8 Rod Carew 9 Killebrew
Twin __: 5 Peaks 6 Cities
Twin City: 6 St. Paul 11 Minneapolis
suburb: 5 Eagan, Edina
twine: 4 bend, coil, cord, curl, lace, loop, rope, wind, wrap, yarn 5 dance, twist, weave 6 enlace, enmesh, immesh, inlace, inmesh, lacing, strand, string, thread 7 cordage, meander, sinuate, wreathe 8 encircle, entangle, filament, undulate 9 corkscrew, interlace, interwind 10 interweave
material: 4 jute 5 ramee, ramie, sisal
nautical ~: 7 marline
twin-engine: 5 plane 8 airplane
Twin Falls: 4 city, town
locale: 5 Idaho

twinge: 3 tic 4 ache, kink, pain, pang, stab 5 cramp, crick, pinch, prick, qualm, smart, spasm, throb, throe 6 injury, misery, stitch, twitch 7 scruple
twining plant: 4 bine 5 vetch
Twinings: 3 tea
alternative: 6 Lipton, Nestea, Salada, Tetley 7 Bigelow, Red Rose
twinkle: 4 glow, wink 5 blink, flash, gleam, glint, shine 6 glance 7 flicker, glimmer, glisten, glitter, light up, shimmer, sparkle 9 coruscate
it may ~: 3 eye
twinkler: 4 star
twinkle-toed: 4 spry 5 agile 6 nimble
Twinkle, Twinkle, Little __: 4 Star
twinkling: 4 jiff, tick, wink 5 jiffy, trice 6 minute, moment, second 7 instant
in the ~ of an eye: 7 quickly
twin-lens __: 6 camera
Twin Peaks (ABC drama)
character: 4 Dale, Pete 5 Harry, Josie, Laura, Sarah 6 Cooper, Leland, Palmer, Truman 7 Packard
creator: David Lynch
setting: 5 Idaho
twins: 3 duo 4 pair
__ twins: 7 Bobbsey
Twins: 3 ten 4 sign, team 6 Gemini
home: 4 Minn. 9 Minnesota
month: 3 Jun., May 4 June
org.: 3 ALC, MLB
predecessor: 4 Bull
rival: *see* baseball team
sport: 8 baseball
successor: 4 Crab
Twins (1988 film)
cast: Danny DeVito, Kelly Preston, Arnold Schwarzenegger
cat: 6 Julius
director: Ivan Reitman
twin-size __: 3 bed
Twin Sombreros
author: Zane Grey
twiny: 6 clingy 10 meandering
twirl: 4 coil, curl, loop, reel, roll, spin, turn, wave, wind 5 pivot, swing, twist, wheel 6 gyrate, rotate 7 revolve, sinuate 8 gyration 9 pirouette
__ twirler: 5 baton
twirling: 8 gyration, rotation 10 revolution
twirp: 4 jerk, nerd, pest, punk, twit, wimp 5 dweeb 6 nudnik, squirt 7 nebbish 9 pipsqueak
twist: 3 arc, ply 4 bend, bias, coif, coil, curl, hank, jerk, jink, kink, knot, loaf, loop, pull, roll, ruse, skew, spin, turn, veer, warp, wind, wisp, yank, yarn 5 braid, color, curve, dance, gnarl, helix, knead, mix-up, quirk, screw, slant, snake, snarl, tweak, twine, twirl, weave, whirl, wring 6 deform, enlace, garble, hairdo, inlace, oddity, pastry, ramble, rotate, scheme, spiral, sprain, squirm, strain, swivel, tangle, volute, wiggle, wrench, writhe, zigzag 7 contort, distort, entwine, falsify, intwine, meander, revolve, sinuate, torsion, wreathe, wriggle, wrinkle 8 coiffure, curlicue, curlycue, jaundice, misquote, misstate 9 corkscrew, sinuosity, variation 10 intertwine, interweave, wrap around
around one's little finger: 3 use 6 misuse 7 control 10 manipulate
in the wind: 4 hang 6 dangle 7 draggle
of fate: 4 luck 5 fluke, quirk 8 fortuity
one's arm: 4 make 5 force 6 coerce, compel, lean on 8 browbeat, bulldoze, pressure 10 bear down on
relative: 4 frug
the truth: 3 con, fib, lie 4 bull, dupe, fake, hoax, sham, snow 5 bluff, fudge, libel, put on 6 delude, invent, malign 7 deceive, distort, falsify, mislead, perjure, slander 8 misguide, misstate 9 disinform, dissemble, misinform 10 equivocate, exaggerate
violently: 3 pry 5 wrest, wring 6 snatch, wrench
__-twist: 3 arm
Twist: 6 Oliver
__ Twist Again: 4 Let's
Twist and Shout (1964 song)
artist: Beatles
twisted: 3 wry 4 awry, bent, vile, wove 5 askew, bandy, curly, kinky, snaky, wound, wrung 6 gnarly, matted, skewed, zigzag 7 crooked, knotted 8 depraved, tortuous 9 malformed
Twisted (2004 film)
cast: Andy Garcia, Samuel L. Jackson, Ashley Judd
Twisted Thing, The
author: Mickey Spillane
twister: 4 wind 5 storm 7 cyclone, tornado 9 hurricane, whirlwind
__ twister: 3 arm 6 tongue
Twister (1996 film)
cast: Cary Elwes, Helen Hunt, Bill Paxton
director: Jan De Bont
dog: 4 Toby 5 Moose
twisting: 4 wavy 5 snaky 6 aswirl, zigzag 7 crooked, sinuous, winding 8 flexuous, tortuous 10 serpentine
arm ~: 8 coercion, pressure
Twistin' the Night Away (1962 song)
artist: Sam Cooke
twist of __: 4 fate
twist-off __: 3 cap
__ Twist of Faith, A: 6 Simple
Twist of Fate (1983 song)
artist: Olivia Newton-John
Twist, Oliver request: 4 more
twist one's __: 3 arm
twists: 10 ins and outs
Twist, The (1960 song)
artist: Chubby Checker
twit: 3 ass, guy, rag, rib 4 bait, dolt, fool, gibe, hoot, jeer, jibe, mock, razz 5 roast, scorn, sneer, taunt, tease, tweak 6 berate, deride, dimwit, gibe at, needle, nudnik, rebuke 7 burlesk, catcall, censure, contemn, lampoon, upbraid 8 brickbat, reproach, ridicule, satirize 9 birdbrain, burlesque, make fun of, poke fun at, raspberry 10 nincompoop
twitch: 3 tic, wag 4 jerk, jump, kick, pain, pull, yank 5 blink, spasm, start 6 jiggle, quaver, quiver, shiver, squirm, twinge, wiggle 7 flutter, shudder, tremble, wriggle 9 vellicate
twitchy: 4 edgy 5 itchy, jumpy, tense 6 on edge, pacing, uneasy 7 anxious, fidgety, jittery, nervous, ruffled 8 agitated, fluttery, restless 9 excitable, flustered, irritable, tremulous 10 hysterical
Twits, The
author: Roald Dahl
twitter: 4 flap, peep, pipe 5 cheep, chirp 6 lather, tingle 7 shudder 8 bird call
Twittering Machine, The
artist: Paul Klee
Twitty, Conway
born: Harold Jenkins
song: Danny Boy (1959)
It's Only Make Believe (1958)
Lonely Blue Boy (1960)
Twix: 3 bar 5 candy 8 candy bar 9 chocolate
alternative: *see* candy brand
'twixt: 3 'mid 4 amid 5 among, 'tween 6 amidst, mongst 7 amongst, between
partner: 5 'tween
something ~ cup and lip: 4 slip
Twizzlers: 5 candy 8 licorice
two: 3 duo 4 duad, duet, dyad, pair 5 brace, deuce, twain 6 couple, number 7 couplet, doublet, wee hour
bits: 7 quarter
break in ~: 5 halve, sever 6 bisect 8 separate 9 intersect
cents' worth: 3 tip 4 view 6 advice, tipoff 7 comment 9 viewpoint
combining form: 3 bin-, bis-, duo-, dyo-, twi-
cubed: 5 eight
divisible by ~: 4 even
easy ~ points: 5 lay-up
ender: 3 fer 4 some 5 pence, penny
for ~: 4 dual 5 a deux
for ~ musically: 4 a due
halves: 4 buck 5 whole 6 dollar, single 7 one-spot, smacker 8 simoleon
in ~: 5 apart, cleft, split 6 halved 7 asunder, divided 9 separated
in French: 4 deux
in German: 4 zwei
in Italian: 3 due
in Portuguese: 4 dois
in Scottish: 3 twa
in ~ shakes of a lamb's tail: 3 now 4 soon 6 at once, in a sec, pronto 7 hastily, quickly, rapidly, shortly 8 directly, promptly, right now, speedily 9 forthwith, in a minute, in a second, right away 10 this moment
in Spanish: 3 dos
it takes ~: 5 tango
not divisible by ~: 3 odd
number ~: 2 VP 4 aide, veep 6 veepee
of a kind: 4 pair, same 5 alike 9 identical 10 synonymous
of ~ minds: 4 torn 8 wavering 9 undecided 10 ambivalent, indecisive, on the fence
one of ~: 6 either
one or ~: 3 few 4 a few 5 scant 6 meager, paltry 7 handful, limited 9 hardly any
put one's ~ cents in: 3 pry 4 poke 6 butt in, horn in, kibitz, meddle, worm in 7 barge in, break in, chime in, intrude, obtrude 9 interfere
put two and ~ together: 3 add 5 solve 9 figure out, puzzle out
second of ~: 6 latter
song for ~: 4 duet
the ~: 4 both
times: 3 dbl. 5 twice 6 double
to Mohs: 6 gypsum
turn ~ into eight: 4 cube
worth ~ thumbs down: 3 bad 5 gross, lousy 7 beastly, ghastly, ungodly 8 dreadful, horrible, horrific, terrible 9 appalling, atrocious, frightful, revolting 10 abominable, deplorable, disgusting, horrendous
two __: 4 bits, o' cat, pair
two __ kind: 3 of a
two __ of a lamb's tail: 6 shakes
two __ time: 3 at a
two __ worth: 5 cents
two-__: 3 bit, ply 4 a-cat, beat, fold, shot, spot, step, tier, tone 5 color, cycle, edged, faced, phase, sided, track 6 bagger, fisted, handed, master, seater, suiter, timing 7 wheeler
two-__ conversion: 5 point
two-__ general: 4 star
two-__ hit: 4 base
two-__ house: 6 family
two-__ paper towels: 3 ply
two-__ sloth: 4 toed
two-__ street: 3 way
two-__ suit: 5 piece
two-__ system: 5 party
two-__ warning: 6 minute
Two __: 3 Men 5 Ninas, Women 6 Hearts, Lovers 7 Princes, Sisters
Two __ Before the Mast: 5 Years
Two __ for Sister Sara: 5 Mules
Two __ People: 6 Sleepy
Two __ Souls: 4 Lost
Two __, The: 5 Jakes
Two __ the Road: 3 for
Two __ the Seesaw: 3 for
Two-__ Woman: 5 Faced
Two and a Half Men (CBS sitcom)
cast: Jon Cryer (Alan Harper)
Conchata Ferrell (Berta)
Angus T. Jones (Jake Harper)
Charlie Sheen (Charlie Harper)
__ two aspirin...: 4 Take
two at __: 5 a time
two-bagger: 3 dbl. 6 double
two-base __: 3 hit
two-bit: 4 puny 5 cheap, lousy, minor, petty 8 inferior, picayune
__, two, buckle my shoe: 3 One

two-by-four: 4 beam 5 board, plank 6 timber
two-by-twelve: 5 plank
two-by-two
vessel: 3 ark
Two by Two: 7 musical
composer: Richard Rodgers
role: 4 Noah
star: Danny Kaye
two cents __: 5 worth
two-dimensional: 4 flat 5 plane 6 planar
measure: 4 area
not ~: 5 solid
of ~ space: 5 areal
Two Doors Down (1978 song)
artist: Dolly Parton
Two Duchesses
author: Émile Zola
two-face: 9 hypocrite
two-faced: 5 false, lying, snaky 6 rotten, untrue 7 corrupt, unloyal 8 disloyal, recreant 9 deceitful, deceptive, faithless, insincere, underhand, unethical 10 traitorous, unfaithful
Two-Faced Woman (1941 film)
cast: Constance Bennett, Melvyn Douglas, Greta Garbo
director: George Cukor
Two-Face foe: 6 Batman
Two Faces Have I (1963 song)
artist: Lou Christie
two-family __: 5 house
two-finger sign: 3 vee
two-fisted: 5 macho, tough
two fives for __: 4 a ten
twofold: 4 dual, twin 5 binal, duple 6 binary, binate, double, doubly, duplex 9 duplicate
two-footer: 5 biped
Two for the Money (2005 film)
cast: Matthew McConaughey, Al Pacino, Rene Russo
Two Gentlemen of Verona: 4 play 6 comedy
author: William Shakespeare
character: 5 Julia, Speed 6 Launce, Silvia, Thurio 7 Antonio, Lucetta, Proteus 8 Eglamour, Panthino 9 Valentine
dog: 4 Crab
setting: 5 Italy
__ two hats: 4 wear
Two Hearts (1988 song)
artist: Phil Collins
Two hearts that beat __: 5 as one
Two Hundred Motels (1971 film)
director: Frank Zappa
...two if __: 5 by sea
Two Jakes, The (1990 film)
cast: Harvey Keitel, Jack Nicholson, Madeleine Stowe, Meg Tilly
director: Jack Nicholson
two-l ___, The: 5 llama
two left __: 4 feet
two-letter sequence: 6 digram
Two Lovers (2009 film)
cast: Gwyneth Paltrow, Joaquin Phoenix
two-masted vessel: 4 brig, yawl 5 ketch
Two Men
author: Edward Arlington Robinson
two mints in one: 5 Certs
two-minute __: 7 warning
Two Mules for Sister Sara (1970 film): 5 oater
cast: Clint Eastwood, Shirley MacLaine
__ & Two Noughts: 4 A Zed
two of __: 5 a kind
Two Out of Three Ain't Bad (1978 song)
artist: Meat Loaf
Two owls and ___...: 4 a hen
two-page ad: 6 spread
two-pair, high: 6 aces up
two-part: 4 dual 6 binary, double
combining form: 5 dicho-
two-party __: 6 system
twopence: 4 coin
two-percent: 4 milk
alternative: 4 skim
two-person: 4 dual 6 double, paired
two-piece __: 4 suit
two-pointer: 4 hoop 5 score 6 basket
easy ~: 5 tap-in 10 tip-in. lay-up
__-two punch: 3 one
two-quark particle: 4 pion 7 pi meson
two-reeler: 5 short
two-rod: 6 dipole
two-run homer requirement: 5 one on
twoscore: 5 forty
two-seater: 3 car 4 auto 10 automobile
two shakes __ lamb's tail: 3 of a
two-shilling piece: 6 florin
two-shoes
goody ~: 4 prig 7 puritan 9 nice Nelly
two-sided: 4 dual 6 duplex 9 bilateral
Two Sisters
author: Gore Vidal
twosome: 2 pr. 3 duo 4 duad, duet, dyad, pair, span 5 brace 6 adjoin, couple, daters 7 doublet 9 newlyweds
two-spot: 5 deuce
two-star __: 7 general
two-step: 5 dance, music
two-striper: 3 NCO, PFC
Two Thieves, The
author: T.F. Powys
__, Two, Three: 3 One
__, two, three, four: 3 Hup
Two Tickets to Paradise (1978 song)
artist: Eddie Money
two-time: 4 burn, dupe, fool, have, nick, snow, take 5 cheat, cozen, shaft, trick, wrong 6 delude, sucker, take in 7 beguile, cheat on, deceive, mislead 8 hoodwink 9 bamboozle, victimize 10 double-deal
two-timer: 3 cad 7 traitor 8 turncoat 9 hypocrite
two-timing: 5 false, lying 6 deceit 7 knavish, unloyal 8 disloyal, forsworn, recreant 9 dishonest, faithless, treachery, underhand, unethical 10 inconstant, infidelity, perfidious, traitorous, unfaithful
two-toed sloth: 4 unau
Two-ton __ Galento: 4 Tony
two to one: 4 odds 5 ratio
two-track: 6 stereo
Two Treatises on Government
author: John Locke
two-unit: 6 duplex
two-way __: 6 mirror, street
Two Way Stretch (1965 film)
director: Robert Day
Two Weeks Notice (2002 film)
cast: Sandra Bullock, Hugh Grant
two-wheeled vehicle: 4 cart, dray 5 dolly 6 barrow 8 rickshaw
two-wheeler: 4 bike 5 cycle 7 bicycle
Two Women: 4 film 5 novel
author: Albert Moravia
cast: Jean-Paul Belmondo, Sophia Loren
director: Vittorio De Sica
two-year-old: 3 kid, tot 4 tike, tyke
Two Years Before the Mast
author: Richard Henry Dana
Twyla: 5 Tharp
Twyman, Jack
milieu: 5 court
org.: 3 NBA
sport: 10 basketball
TX
see Texas
Ty: 4 Cobb 6 Hardin
contemporary: 4 Babe, Tris
Tycho: 5 Brahe 6 crater
tycoon: 4 boss, king 5 baron, mogul, nabob, nawab 6 fat cat 7 big shot, magnate 8 big wheel, director 9 executive, financier 10 capitalist
home: 5 manor 6 estate 7 mansion
Tycoon
author: Harold Robbins
__ Tycoon, The: 4 Last
Ty-D-__: 3 Bol
tye: 4 rope 5 chain
Tyger, The
author: William Blake
tyke: 3 imp, tad, tot 5 child, wee 'un, youth 6 moppet 7 toddler 9 little boy, youngster
Tylenol: 9 analgesic 10 painkiller
alternative: *see* pain reliever brand
target: 4 ache
unit: 6 caplet, tablet
Tyler: 3 Liv 4 Anne, city, John, Judy, town 6 Bonnie 7 Collins
locale: 5 Texas
Tyler, Anne: 6 writer
work: The Accidental Tourist
The Amateur Marriage
Back When We Were Grownups
Breathing Lessons
Celestial Navigation
The Clock Winder
Digging to America
Dinner at the Homesick Restaurant
Earthly Possessions
If Morning Ever Comes
Ladder of Years
Morgan's Passing
Noah's Compass
Patchwork Planet
Saint Maybe
Searching for Caleb
A Slipping-Down Life
Tin Can Tree
Tyler, Bonnie
homeland: Wales
song: Holding Out for a Hero (1984)
It's a Heartache (1978)
Total Eclipse of the Heart (1983)
Tyler, John: 9 president
home: 8 Virginia
predecessor: 8 Harrison
successor: 4 Polk
wife: 5 Julia 7 Letitia
Tyler, Liv: 7 actress
film: Armageddon (1998)
Cookie's Fortune (1999)
Heavy (1996)
The Lord of the Rings... (2001)
One Night at McCool's (2001)
Stealing Beauty (1996)
that thing you do! (1996)
__ Tyler Moore: 4 Mary
Tylo: 6 Hunter
tympanic __: 4 bone
tympanum: 4 drum
Tynan, Joe
portrayer: Alan Alda
Tyndall: 4 John
Tyndareus
wife: 4 Leda
Tyne: 4 Daly 5 river
ender: 5 mouth
locale: 7 England 8 Scotland
type: 3 ilk, peg 4 cast, copy, font, form, kind, mold, norm, rank, sign, sort 5 brand, breed, class, genre, genus, group, input, likes, model, order, print, stamp, style 6 assort, kidney, letter, manner, nature 7 dash off, epitome, italics, pattern, put down, species, variety 8 category, classify, exemplar, paradigm, printing, specimen 9 character 10 persuasion, pigeonhole, transcribe
assortment: 4 font
ender: 3 set 4 cast, face 5 style, write 6 script, setter, writer
starter: 3 tin 4 logo, tele 6 stereo
style: 4 font 5 agate, roman 6 italic 7 italics 8 boldface
typewriter ~: 4 pica 5 elite 7 courier
widths: 3 ems, ens
__ type: 5 blood, not my 7 movable
__-type: 5 large, touch
typecast: 4 sort, type 10 categorize
Typee
author: Herman Melville
sequel: 4 Omoo
typeface: 4 City, Elan, font, Pica, Saga, Skia, Zeal 5 Abadi, Aldus, Arial, Basel, Bembo, Boton, Dante, Delta, Devin, Didot, Dutch, Elite, Emona, Gamma, Goudy, Imago, Kabel, Kalix, Norma, print, Romic, Sabon, Savoy, Swiss, Weiss, Wilke 6 Aldine, Amasis, Apollo, Auriol, Avenir, Batang, Bodoni, Bulmer, Caslon, Catull, Caxton, Cerigo, Cooper, Corona, Cosmos, Delima, Dialog, Esprit, Fenice, Futura, Gareth, Geneva, Glypha, Gothic, Guardi, Joanna, Legacy, Lucida, Maxima, Melior, Minion, Modern, Monaca, Myriad, Nofret, Odense, Optima, Orator, Praxis, Quorum, Romana, Serifa, Syndor, Syntax, Tahoma, Utopia, Zurich 7 Amerigo, Barmeno, Bauhaus, Bergamo, Berling, Bookman, Calisto, Candida, Centaur, Century, Courier, Cremona, Cushing, Diotima, Electra,

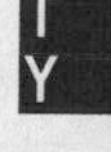

Formata, Korinna, Leawood, Matisse, Memphis, Origami, Pacella, Panache, Peignot, Photina, Plantin, Poetica, Present, Sassoon, Shannon, Spartan, Tiepolo, Tiffany, Univers, Vectora, Verdana, Walbaum **8** Broadway, Caecilia, Cantoria, Carniola, Compacta, Concorde, Fournier, Frutiger, Galliard, Garamond, Giovanni, Hadriano, Meridien, Minister, Novarese, Palatino, Perpetua, Rockwell, Slimbach, Souvenir **9** Helvetica **10** Avant Garde, Times Roman
- **detail: 5** serif **9** sans serif
- **option: 4** bold **6** italic **7** italics **9** underline

typesetter: 10 compositor
- **boo-boos: 6** errata
- **line: 6** em dash, en dash
- **org.: 3** ITU
- **short last line: 5** widow

typewriter
- **accessory: 6** eraser
- **key: 3** Tab **5** Shift **8** Caps Lock
- **name: 5** Smith **6** Corona
- **part: 3** key **5** spool **6** ribbon
- **sound: 5** clack, click
- **symbol: 5** brace, colon, comma, paren., slash **6** equals **7** bracket, percent, virgule **8** asterisk **9** ampersand, pound sign, semicolon **10** equals sign **11** parenthesis
- **type: 4** pica **5** elite

Typewriter, The
- **composer:** Leroy Anderson

Typhoid ___: 4 Mary

typhoon: 4 blow, wind **7** tempest **9** hurricane

Typhoon
- **author:** Joseph Conrad

typic: 7 regular **8** symbolic **10** emblematic, figurative, indicative

typical: 3 avg. **5** ideal, model, stock, usual **6** common, normal, wonted **7** average, classic, general, natural, regular, routine **8** everyday, expected, habitual, ordinary, orthodox, standard **9** customary, essential, prevalent **10** accustomed, emblematic, legitimate, prevailing
- **preceder: 5** proto
- **suffix: 3** -ish

typically: 5 about **6** mainly, mostly **7** as a rule, largely, roughly, usually **8** by nature **9** generally, naturally, on average, primarily, regularly **10** on the whole, ordinarily

Typical Male (1986 song)
- **artist:** Tina Turner

typification: 5 ideal, model **7** epitome, essence, paragon **8** exemplar **9** archetype **10** apotheosis, embodiment

typify: 5 sum up **6** embody, imbody, mirror **7** suggest **8** stand for **9** adumbrate, epitomize, exemplify, personify, represent **10** illustrate

typist: 9 secretary
- **colleague: 5** clerk, steno
- **need: 6** eraser
- **output: 3** wds. **4** memo **5** words
- **stat.: 3** wpm

typo: 4 flaw, slip **5** error **7** erratum, mistake **8** misprint **10** inaccuracy

typographic
- **flourish: 5** serif

typos: 6 errata
- **check for ~: 5** proof
- **make some ~: 3** err

Tyr
- **son: 4** Odin

Tyra: 5 Banks

tyrannical: 4 firm, hard **5** bossy, cruel, picky, rigid, stern, tough **6** severe **7** austere, Spartan **8** absolute, despotic, dogmatic, exacting, hard-line, imperial, rigorous **9** arbitrary, demanding, draconian, imperious, inclement, stringent, unbending, unsparing **10** autocratic, despotical, dogmatical, inflexible, iron-fisted, iron-handed, no-nonsense, oppressive, peremptory

tyrannically: 4 hard

tyrannize: 4 ride **5** bully, grind **6** hector **7** oppress **8** browbeat, dominate, domineer, keep down **9** dictate to, persecute, trample on **10** boss around, intimidate, lord it over, ride herd on

tyranno ending: 4 saur

Tyrannosaurus ___: 3 Rex

tyranny: 7 cruelty, fascism **8** coercion, iron hand, severity **9** autocracy, despotism, oligarchy **10** absolutism, domination, oppression

tyrant: 4 czar, ogre, tsar, tzar **5** bully **6** despot, ramrod **8** autocrat, dictator, martinet **9** oppressor **10** inquisitor
- **get rid of a ~: 4** oust **5** eject **6** depose, unseat **7** boot out, kick out **8** dethrone **9** overthrow

Tyre: 4 city, port, town
- **king of ~: 5** Hiram
- **locale: 7** Lebanon **9** Phoenicia
- **queen of ~: 5** Elise

tyro: 3 cub **4** naif, pleb **5** newie, plebe, pupil **6** newbie, novice, rookie **7** amateur, dabbler, learner, new hand, recruit, trainee **8** beginner, initiate, neophyte, newcomer, putterer **9** fledgling, greenhorn, novitiate **10** apprentice, catechumen, dilettante, tenderfoot
- **like a ~: 3** new **5** green **9** untrained

Tyrol
- **capital: 9** Innsbruck
- **garb: 6** dirndl
- **locale: 4** Alps **7** Austria
- **river: 4** Isar
- **song: 5** yodel, yodle

Tyrone: 5 Davis, Power **7** Guthrie

Tyrrhenian Sea
- **gulf: 5** Gaeta
- **island: 3** Sar. **6** Lipari **8** Sardinia **9** Stromboli
- **locale: 5** Italy
- **port: 6** Naples
- **river to the ~: 8** Volturno

___ Tyrrhenum: 4 Mare

Tyson: 4 Mike **6** Cicely

Tyson, Cicely: 7 actress
- **film:** Sounder (1972)
- **spouse:** Miles Davis

Tyson, Mike: 5 boxer
- **Holyfield, to ~: 5** rival
- **milieu: 4** ring
- **spouse:** Robin Givens

Tyus, Wyomia: 6 runner **8** sprinter

Tzara, Tristan movement: 4 Dada

___-tze: 3 Lao

Tzigane
- **composer:** Maurice Ravel

tzimmes: 4 fuss, stew **6** uproar **9** casserole **10** hullabaloo

___-tzu: 3 Lao

___ Tzu: 4 Shih

u.: **3** sch. **4** coll., inst.
ü
dots: **6** umlaut
U: **4** elem. **5** ritzy, Thant, vowel **6** letter **7** element, uranium
92 for ~: **4** at. no.
followers: **3** VWX **4** VWXY **5** VWXYZ
in phonetic alphabet: **7** Uniform
preceders: **3** RST **4** QRST **5** PQRST
U ___: **2** Nu **4** bolt, Turn **5** Thant
U ___ Touch This: **4** Can't
U ___ uncle: **4** as in
U-___: **4** boat, Haul, turn
___ U: **5** I Hate, Thank
___-U: **3** non
U2
homeland: Ireland
members: Bono, Hewson, Evans, Clayton, Mullen
song: Desire (1988)
Discothéque (1997)
I Still Haven't Found What I'm Looking For (1987)
Mysterious Ways (1991)
One (1992)
Theme From Mission: Impossible (1996)
Where the Streets Have No Names (1987)
With or Without You (1987)
U-235: **7** isotope
device: **5** A-bomb
regulator: **3** AEC, NRC
U-571 (2000 film)
cast: Jon Bon Jovi, Harvey Keitel, Matthew McConaughey, Bill Paxton
UAE
group: **4** OPEC **10** Arab League
honcho: **4** amir, emir, Zaid **5** ameer, emeer, sheik **6** shaikh, sheikh
money: **4** fils **6** dirham
neighbor: **4** Oman
part: **4** Arab **5** Dibai, Dubai **6** United **8** Abu Dhabi, Emirates
see also United Arab Emirates
UAL
destination: **3** JFK, LAX, LGA, ORD, SFO
former ~ rival: **3** TWA
see also United
UAR part: **4** Arab **5** Egypt, Syria **6** United **8** Republic
UAW: **5** union
locale: **6** Motown **7** Detroit **8** Michigan
members: **5** labor
product: **3** car, SUV **4** auto **5** coupe, sedan, truck
UB40
song: Can't Help Falling in Love (1993)
Here I Am (1991)
Red Red Wine (1988)
The Way You Do the Things You Do (1990)
Ubangi: **5** river
feeder: **4** Uele
outlet: **5** Congo
ubi ___: **4** sunt **5** supra
ubiety: **8** presence
___ ubique: **5** hic et
ubiquitous: **4** rife **5** broad **7** all-over, popular **9** pervasive, prevalent, universal, worldwide **10** everywhere
ubiquity: **8** presence **9** existence
U-boat: **3** sub **6** vessel
sinker: **6** ashcan **7** torpedo
U-bolt place: **4** door, hasp **5** latch
U-Boot, danger for a: **3** eis
U Can't Touch This (1990 song)
artist: M.C. Hammer
UCB conference: **6** Pac-Ten
Uccello: **5** Paolo
UCLA: **3** sch.
athlete: **5** Bruin
group: **4** NCAA **6** Pac-Ten
part of ~: **3** Cal., Los **4** Univ. **7** Angeles
rival: **3** USC
stat: **3** GPA
U. Conn: **3** sch. **4** coll.
conference: **7** Big East
locale: **6** Storrs
Udall: **2** Mo **3** Tom **4** Mark **6** Morris **7** Stewart
Udall, Nicholas school: **4** Eton
udder output: **4** milk
___ Ude: **4** Ulan
Ueberroth: **5** Peter
Uecker: **3** Bob
Uele: **5** river
locale: **5** Congo
river to the ~: **4** Bomu **5** Mbomu
Uffizi contents: **3** art **4** arte
UFO: **8** aircraft
dossier: **5** X file
movies: **5** sci-fi
occupant: **2** ET **3** ETI **5** alien **7** Martian
shape: **4** disk **6** saucer
UFT
member: **4** tchr. **7** teacher
rival: **3** NEA
Uganda: **6** nation **7** country
capital: **7** Kampala
city: **4** Gulu **5** Jinja, Mbale **6** Masaka **7** Entebbe, Kampala
exile: **3** Idi **4** Amin
lake: **5** Kioga, Kyoga **6** Albert, Mobuto **8** Victoria
money: **4** cent **8** shilling
mountain: **5** Elgon
neighbor: **5** Congo, Kenya, Sudan **6** Rwanda **8** Tanzania
people: **7** Turkana
river from ~: **4** Nile
Uggams, Leslie: **6** singer **7** actress
TV: Roots, Sing Along With Mitch
Ugh!: **3** ick **4** yuck **5** gross
ugli: **5** fruit **6** citrus **7** tangelo
relative: ***see*** citrus
ugly: **3** low **4** base, dark, dour, evil, fell, foul, glum, mean, vile **5** angry, awful, black, dirty, grave, gross, major, messy, nasty, pesky, pesty, rough, sorry, surly **6** brutal, crabby, filthy, gloomy, grisly, horrid, morose, odious, sordid, sullen, wicked **7** beastly, crabbed, hideous, ignoble, low-down, noisome, ominous, peevish, serious, servile, squalid, vicious, violent **8** depraved, grievous, horrible, menacing, scowling, shocking, sinister, spiteful, terrible, unseemly, wretched **9** appalling, bellicose, dangerous, execrable, frightful, grotesque, loathsome, monstrous, obnoxious, offensive, repellent, repelling, repugnant, repulsive, revolting, saturnine, troublous, truculent, unsightly, vexatious **10** despicable, disgusting, forbidding, formidable, ill-favored, malevolent, pugnacious, scandalous, uninviting, unpleasant
___ Ugly: **6** Coyote
ugly duckling: **4** swan
Ugly Duckling, The
author: Hans Christian Andersen
Ugo: **5** Betti **7** Foscolo **8** Tognazzi
U Got the Look (1987 song)
artist: Prince
___-Ugrian: **5** Finno
uh-___: **3** huh
U-Haul: **3** van **5** truck
rival: **5** Ryder
uh cousin: **2** er, um **4** ahem
UHF part: **4** freq., high **5** ultra **9** frequency
uh-huh
see of course, yes
uhlan: **6** lancer **7** dragoon, soldier
Uhnak: **7** Dorothy
uh-oh: **4** my-my, oh my, oops, yipe **5** yikes, yipes **6** my oh my, oh dear, whoops
uh-uh: **2** no **3** nah, naw, nay, nix, non **4** nein, nope, nyet **5** I won't, ixnay, never, no how, noway **6** no deal, noways, nowise **7** I refuse **8** forget it, I will not, negative, negatory **9** by no means, fat chance, I think not **10** count me out, not a chance, thumbs down
Highlander's ~: **3** nae
Uhuru
author: Robert Ruark
Uinta: **5** range
locale: **4** Utah
mountain: **9** Kings Peak
'U' Is for Undertow
author: Sue Grafton
UK: **7** England
award: **3** GBE, MBE, OBE
carrier of old: **4** BOAC
city: **4** Lond.
clock setting: **3** GMT
defenders: **3** RAF
fast way to the ~: **3** SST
half of the ~: **4** Gr. Br., Gt. Br.
inc. in the ~: **3** ltd.
money, once: **3** LSD, stg.
network: **3** BBC
part of the ~: **3** Eng., Ire. **4** Scot.
party: **3** Lib.
recording company: **3** EMI
religion: **4** Angl.
ruling body: **4** Parl.
S.S. in the ~: **3** HMS
territory: **3** Gib.
title: **3** esq.
VIP: **2** p.m. **4** QE II
see also England, United Kingdom
ukase: **4** fiat, word **5** edict, irade, order **6** decree, ruling **9** directive, ordinance
Ukraine: **6** nation **7** country
city: **4** Kiev, Lvov **5** Lutsk, Odesa, Yalta **6** Odessa **7** Donetsk, Kharkov, Poltava
dance: **5** gopak, hopak **6** trepak
figure skater: **5** Baiul
legislature: **4** Rada
money: **5** ruble **6** rouble
neighbor: **6** Poland, Russia **7** Belarus, Hungary, Moldova, Romania **8** Slovakia
once: **3** SSR
peninsula: **6** Crimea
river: **4** Prut, Seim, Seym **5** Dnepr, Seret, Siret, Tisza **7** Dnieper
Ukrainian: **4** Slav **7** Cossack **8** language
ukulele: **6** string
cousin: **5** banjo **6** guitar
feature: **4** fret, neck
play a ~: **5** pluck, strum, thrum
Ukulele ___: **3** Ike
Ulalume: **4** poem
author: Edgar Allan Poe
like the skies in ~: **5** ashen
monogram: **3** EAP
Ulan ___: **3** Ude **5** Bator
Ulan Bator: **4** city, town **7** capital
formerly: **4** Urga
locale: **8** Mongolia
Ulanov: **4** Igor
Ulanova, Galina: **6** dancer **7** Russian **8** danseuse **9** ballerina
ule: **4** tree **6** caucho, rubber **10** rubber tree
-ule: **3** -kin **4** tiny **5** small, teeny **6** teensy
Ulee's Gold (1997 film)
cast: Jessica Biel, Peter Fonda
Ulf: **7** Nilsson **8** von Euler
___ U Like Me Now: **3** How
Ulla: **9** Jacobsson
Ullman: **4** Norm **6** Tracey
Ullmann, Liv: **7** actress **9** Norwegian
film: Autumn Sonata (1978)
Cries and Whispers (1972)
Faithless (2000)
Gaby-A True Story (1987)
The Passion of Anna (1969)
Persona (1966)
Scenes From a Marriage (1973)
Shame (1968)
Ullsten: **3** Ola
Ulm's river: **6** Danube
ulna: **4** bone
locale: **3** arm **7** forearm
neighbor: **6** radius
ulnar: **5** nerve
ulp: **4** gasp
Ulrich: **4** Lars **5** Skeet
ulster: **4** coat **6** jacket **7** topcoat **8** overcoat **9** outerwear
ulterior: **4** dark **6** buried, covert, future, hidden, secret, unsaid, unseen **7** cryptic, obscure, selfish **8** obscured, personal, shrouded **9** concealed, cryptical, enigmatic, equivocal, invisible, secondary **10** undercover, under wraps, undivulged, unrevealed
motive: **4** plan, wile **6** agenda, design, reason, scheme
ultima ___: **5** Thule
ultimate: **3** end, max, nth **4** best, last, most **5** basic, final, ideal, limit, prime **6** far-out, height, latest,

utmost 7 capping, closing, extreme, highest, maximum, paragon, primary, radical, sublime, supreme 8 absolute, crowning, decisive, empyreal, empyrean, eventual, farthest, furthest, greatest, terminal, towering 9 elemental, paramount, unequaled, unmatched, worthiest 10 concluding, conclusive, consummate, definitive, lattermost, overriding, preeminent, surpassing
objective: 3 aim 4 goal 5 be-all 6 payoff, reason, target 7 mission, outcome, purpose 8 terminus 10 aspiration, conclusion
purpose: 3 aim 4 goal 6 end-all, end use, object, target
ultimately: 3 yet 4 last 6 at last, lastly 7 by and by, finally, for good, someday 8 after all, in future, in the end, sometime 9 basically, hereafter, in due time, presently, somewhere 10 completely, eventually
Ultimate Reality
Buddhist symbol of ~: 5 lotus
ultima Thule: 4 isle 6 island 7 highest 8 farthest, furthest
ultimatum: 6 demand, or else, threat 7 dictate 9 challenge
ending: 4 else
___ Ultimatum, The: 6 Bourne
ultra: 4 very 5 rabid 6 all-out, far-out, too-too 7 extreme, radical, too much 9 excessive, extremist, fanatical 10 immoderate, outlandish
Ultra Brite: 10 toothpaste
alternative: *see* toothpaste
ultraconservative: 4 fogy 5 fogey 7 diehard 8 far right, rightist 9 hidebound
ultraist: 5 rebel 7 fanatic, liberal, radical 8 maverick, nihilist, pacifist, reformer 9 anarchist, extremist, firebrand 10 immoderate, left-winger
ultramarine: 4 blue 5 color
relative: *see* blue color
ultramodern: 3 neo, new 5 novel, style 10 avant-garde
ultrasonic: 4 fast 5 quick, rapid, swift 6 speedy
ultrasound: 4 exam, test
image: 8 sonogram
ultraviolet ___: 3 ray 4 lamp 5 light
ultraviolet-blocking chemical: 4 PABA
ulu: 5 knife
Ulu: 8 Grosbard
ululate: 3 bay 4 bawl, hoot, howl, keen, wail, weep, yell, yowl 6 holler
ululation: 3 bay 4 wail 6 lament
Ulupalakua
locale: 4 Maui 6 Hawaii
Ulyanov: 5 Lenin 8 Vladimir
Ulysses
author: James Joyce
character: 4 Buck 5 Bloom, Molly 7 Dedalus, Leopold, Stephen 8 Mulligan 10 Molly Bloom
dog: 5 Athos
last word of ~: 3 yes
rival: 4 Aias, Ajax
see also Odysseus
___ Ulysses Grant: 5 Hiram
Ulysses S. ___: 5 Grant
um: 2 er 7 stammer, stutter 8 hesitate 9 hem and haw
___-um: 5 no-see
Uma: 7 Thurman
U Mass
location: 6 Boston
umber: 5 brown, color 7 reddish 9 earth tone
relative: *see* brown color
___ umber: 3 raw 5 burnt
Umberto: 3 Eco 6 Nobile
see also Italian
Umberto D (1952 film)
director: Vittorio De Sica
umbilical ___: 4 cord
umbilicus: 5 navel 8 omphalos
umble ___: 3 pie
'umble character: 4 Heep 5 Uriah
umbo: 4 boss, knob
umbra: 4 soul 5 ghost, shade 6 fantom, shadow, spirit 7 phantom
umbrage: 3 ire 4 fury, huff, rage 5 anger, pique, shade, spite, wrath 6 grudge, injury, malice, rancor, shadow 7 chagrin, offense 8 vexation 9 annoyance 10 ill feeling, irritation, resentment
take ~ at: 4 mind 6 object, resent
umbrageous: 5 leafy, shady 6 touchy 9 sensitive
umbrella: 4 egis, gamp, palm, tree 5 aegis 6 brolly, screen 7 overall, parasol, shelter 8 sunshade 9 inclusive 10 protection
in Britain: 6 brolly
of song: 5 smile
picnic ~: 4 tree
-shaped tree: 6 acacia
spoke: 3 rib
umbrella ___: 5 stand
___ umbrella: 4 golf 5 beach
Umbrella, The
author: Guy de Maupassant
umbrette
relative: 5 heron
Umbria
city: 4 Todi 6 Assisi 7 Perugia
locale: 5 Italy
province: 5 Terni
Umbrian: 8 language
___-Umbrian: 4 Osco
Umbriel: 4 moon
planet: 6 Uranus
Umeki, Miyoshi
Oscar: Sayonara
umiak: 4 boat 6 vessel 10 watercraft
builder: 5 Inuit 6 Eskimo, Innuit, Inupik
home: 6 Alaska
kin: 5 canoe, kayak
umlaut, half an: 3 dot
Umm: 7 Kulthum
ump ender: 3 ire 4 teen
umpire: 3 ref 5 judge 7 arbiter, mediate, referee 8 mediator, moderate 9 interpose, moderator, officiate 10 adjudicate, arbitrator, negotiator, peacemaker
call: 3 out 4 balk, fair, foul, safe
need: 4 mask 5 whisk
purview: 4 base 5 plate
ride the ~: 3 boo 4 jeer, razz
umpteen: 4 many 6 a lot of, divers, gobs of, lots of, myriad, tons of, untold 7 a host of, a slew of, copious, heaps of, loads of, no end of, piles of, profuse, scads of 8 a bunch of, abundant, an army of, manifold, numerous, oodles of, scores of 9 a passel of, bountiful, countless, quite a few 10 innumerous, jillions of, zillions of
UMW: 5 union
member: 5 miner
opening: 4 adit
'un
young ~: 4 tike, tyke 6 infant
Un ___ in Maschera: 5 Ballo
Un-___ My Heart: 5 Break
UN
agcy.: 3 FAO, ILO, IMF, WHO 6 UNICEF
arm of the ~: 4 agcy.
Day mo.: 3 Oct.
delegate: 3 amb.
license plate abbr.: 3 DPL
like the ~: 4 intl.
locale: 3 NYC 7 New York 8 East Side 9 Manhattan
member: 3 Alb., Alg., Arg., Col., Den., Eng., Eth., Fin., Ger., Ind., Ire., Isr., Lat., Nor., Pan., Pol., Rom., RSA, Rus., Swe., Syr., Tun., USA 4 Chad, Cuba, Ital., Laos, Mali, Peru, Port., Togo 5 Haiti
name in ~ history: 3 Dag, Lie 4 Kofi 5 Annan 6 Trygve, U Thant
observer grp.: 3 PLO
onetime ~ group: 3 IRO
una ___: 4 voce 5 corda
Una: 6 Merkel 7 O'Connor
unabashed: 4 bold, open 6 at ease, brassy, brazen, daring 7 blatant 8 fearless, impudent 9 barefaced, shameless
unabating: 5 usual 6 inborn 7 abiding, chronic, lasting 8 constant, enduring, habitual 9 ceaseless, chronical, continual, incessant, ingrained, perennial, sustained 10 deep-seated, inveterate, persistent, relentless, unyielding
unabbreviated: 4 full 5 total, whole 6 entire 7 plenary 8 complete, finished, thorough 10 exhaustive
unable: 4 weak 5 inept, unfit 6 clumsy 7 hog-tied, not up to 8 helpless, unfitted 9 incapable, powerless, sidelined, unskilled 10 impuissant, inadequate, unequipped
is ~ to: 4 can't 6 cannot
to say no: 3 lax 5 timid 6 docile 7 lenient, servile, slavish 8 lamblike, yielding 9 spineless 10 obsequious, submissive
unabridged: 4 full 5 total, uncut, whole 6 entire, intact 7 plenary 8 absolute, complete, finished, thorough 10 exhaustive
dictionary: 4 tome
unaccented: 4 weak 6 atonic
unacceptable: 3 bad, out 4 tabu 5 lousy, taboo, wrong 7 damaged 8 below par, improper, rejected, unwanted 9 half-baked, obnoxious, offensive, repugnant, unwelcome
it's ~: 4 no-no, tabu 5 taboo
unaccommodating: 5 loath, rigid, stern 9 unwilling 10 inflexible
unaccompanied: 3 odd 4 lone, sole, solo, stag 5 alone, apart 6 single 8 deserted, detached, isolated, solitary 9 abandoned, a cappella, by oneself, on one's own 10 unescorted
unaccountable: 3 odd 5 weird 6 arcane, mystic 7 strange, unusual 8 baffling, peculiar, puzzling, uncommon, unwonted 9 unheard-of, unnatural
unaccounted for: 3 MIA 4 AWOL, lost 5 short 6 absent 7 at large, left out, mislaid, missing, omitted 9 misplaced
unaccustomed: 3 new 4 rare 5 alien, green, new to, novel 6 exotic, quaint 7 altered, bizarre, foreign, special, strange, unknown, unusual, variant 8 ignorant, imported, singular, uncommon, untaught, unwonted 9 different, eccentric, unskilled, untrained
to: 5 new at
Unaccustomed ___ am...: 3 as I
unacknowledged: 6 secret 7 virtual 8 nameless 9 anonymous
unacquired: 6 inborn, innate, native 7 natural 10 congenital, connatural, indigenous
unactualized: 6 latent 7 dormant
una de ___: 4 gato
unadept: 5 gawky, inept 6 clumsy, gauche 7 awkward, boorish, gawkish, halting, unhandy 8 bumbling, bungling, cloddish, clownish, helpless, inexpert, tactless, unpoised 9 all thumbs, graceless, ham-handed, inelegant, maladroit, stumbling 10 blundering, left-handed, unskillful
unadmired one: 4 nerd, wimp 5 dweeb, loser, schmo
unadorned: 4 bald, bare, mere 5 naked, plain, stark 6 barren, modest, severe, simple 7 austere, factual, Spartan, unfussy 9 bare-bones
unadulterated: 4 mere, pure 5 clean, sheer 6 simple 8 pristine, spotless, straight 9 stainless 10 immaculate
unadvised: 4 rash 5 brash, hasty 6 unwary, unwise 7 foolish, unaware 8 careless, heedless, ignorant, mistaken, reckless, unwarned 9 hot-headed, imprudent, in the dark, unknowing 10 incautious, indiscreet, uninformed
unaffected: 4 calm, cool, homy, naif, true 5 aloof, frank, homey, naive, plain 6 candid, casual, direct, folksy, honest, modest, simple, steady 7 artless, callous, genuine, natural, sincere, unmoved, up-front 8 innocent, laid-back, unartful, unspoilt 9 childlike, easygoing, guileless, impassive, ingenuous, unaltered, unchanged, unexcited, unruffled, unstirred, unstudied, untouched, unworldly 10 impervious, unagitated
unaffectedness: 4 ease 10 simplicity
unaffectionate: 4 cold, cool 5 aloof 6 chilly 7 distant
unaffiliated: 3 ind. 4 neut. 7 neutral

unafraid: **4** bold, game, tame **5** brave, gutsy, nervy **6** awless, daring, gritty, heroic, plucky, spunky **7** aweless, defiant, doughty, gallant, impavid, staunch, valiant **8** fearless, heroical, intrepid, resolute, stalwart, valorous **9** audacious, confident, dauntless, dreadless, undaunted, unfearing **10** courageous, undismayed
unaggressive: **3** lax **4** meek **5** mousy, timid **6** mousey
one: **4** lamb **8** pushover, pussycat
unagi: **3** eel
unagitated: **4** calm, cold, cool, even, mild **5** aloof, quiet, sober, staid, stoic, tepid **6** at ease, casual, frigid, frosty, gentle, low-key, mellow, placid, poised, remote, sedate, serene, steady, stolid **7** amiable, assured, at peace, distant, equable, glacial, neutral, offhand, pacific, relaxed, stoical **8** amicable, carefree, composed, detached, laid-back, lukewarm, moderate, peaceful, pleasant, rational, reserved, together, tranquil **9** apathetic, collected, easygoing, impassive, incurious, nerveless, quiescent, temperate, unexcited, unextreme, unruffled, unstirred, unworried, withdrawn **10** coolheaded, impersonal, nonchalant, phlegmatic, reasonable, restrained, unaffected, untroubled
unaided: **4** solo **5** alone **9** by oneself
unaimed: **6** chance, random **9** haphazard
unal: **6** single **8** singular
unalarmed: **4** calm, cool **5** stoic **6** at ease, sedate **9** undaunted
Unalaska: **4** isle **6** island
resident: **5** Aleut **8** Aleutian
unalert: **6** dozing, unwary **7** napping, nodding **8** sleeping **10** incautious
unaligned: **6** uneven, zigzag **7** crooked, neutral **8** far apart, peaceful **9** irregular **10** achromatic, uninvolved
unalike: **3** odd **4** mixt **5** mixed, other **6** atypic, sundry, unique, varied **7** altered, changed, diverse, offbeat, special, strange, unequal, variant, various **8** aberrant, assorted, atypical, contrary, discrete, distinct, opposite, peculiar, separate **9** deviating, different, disparate, divergent, irregular, multiform, otherwise, unrelated **10** antithetic, at variance, discordant, discrepant, dissimilar, individual, mismatched, poles apart, unfamiliar
unallowed: **4** tabu **5** taboo **7** not done **8** verboten **9** forbidden
unalloyed: **4** pure **5** solid, stark **6** simple, single **7** perfect
unalterable: **4** firm, sure **5** final, fixed, rigid **6** rooted, stable, static **7** binding, settled **8** constant, definite, ironclad **9** obstinate, permanent, tenacious **10** changeless
unaltered: **4** same **6** intact **8** pristine
unambiguity: **7** clarity **8** lucidity **9** certainty, plainness, precision **10** directness, exactitude
unambiguous: **5** clear, lucid, plain, vivid **6** cogent, direct, honest, limpid **7** certain, evident, express, obvious **8** absolute, apparent, clean-cut, definite, distinct, explicit, knowable, manifest, palpable, specific **9** graspable **10** spelled out
unambitious: **4** lazy **8** slothful
one: **3** bum **5** idler, sloth **6** loafer **8** layabout
unamenable: **5** fussy, rigid, stiff **6** feisty, trying **7** prickly **8** exacting **9** demanding, difficult, fractious, obstinate **10** inflexible, refractory
unamicable: **3** icy **4** cold **5** aloof **6** remote **7** distant, hostile **8** reserved **10** unfriendly
unamusing: **5** sober, staid **6** solemn, somber **7** deadpan, serious **9** humorless **10** no-nonsense
unanchored: **6** adrift **8** unmoored
unanimated: **4** calm **5** quiet **6** serene
unanimity: **5** peace, union, unity **6** accord **7** concord, harmony, oneness, rapport **9** agreement, consensus **10** solidarity
unanimous: **5** as one, at one, solid, total **6** common, shared, united **7** unified **8** accepted, agreeing, communal, in unison **9** accordant, concerted, consonant, of one mind, undivided **10** agreed upon, concordant, consensual, consistent, harmonious, like-minded, undisputed
unanimously: **5** as one, at one **6** to a man **8** together
unanswerable: **4** sure, true **5** solid, sound, valid **6** proven, tested **7** certain, factual, genuine, logical, telling **8** official, verified **9** confirmed **10** compelling, conclusive, convincing, documented, unarguable
ask an ~ question: **5** stump **6** baffle, puzzle, stymie **7** confuse, mystify, nonplus, perplex **8** bewilder, confound **9** dumbfound
question: **6** enigma, riddle **7** mystery, paradox, stumper **9** conundrum
Unanswered Question, The
composer: Charles Ives
unanticipated: **3** pop **6** abrupt, sudden **8** surprise
unanxious: **4** calm, safe **6** at ease, secure **8** carefree **9** protected
unappareled: **4** bare, nude **5** naked **6** peeled, unclad **8** disrobed, in the raw, undraped **9** au naturel, in the buff, unclothed, uncovered, undressed **10** stark-naked
unapparent: **6** hidden **9** invisible **10** impalpable, intangible, unviewable
unappeasable: **4** grim, hard, mean **5** harsh, stern, stony **6** savage **7** vicious **8** ruthless **9** ferocious, heartless, merciless, unfeeling **10** implacable, ironfisted, relentless, vindictive
unappetizing: **4** blah, flat, icky **5** grody, gross, nasty, vapid, yucky **6** stinky **7** insipid **8** unsavory **9** savorless, tasteless **10** flavorless
food: **4** glop **5** gruel, swill
unappreciative: **7** selfish **9** forgetful, thankless **10** ungracious, ungrateful
unapproachable: **4** cold, cool, mean **5** aloof, nasty, surly **6** chilly, frigid, ornery, remote **7** distant, glacial, hateful, hostile **8** contrary, hesitant, inimical, reserved, spiteful **9** bellicose, malicious, withdrawn **10** malevolent, pugnacious
unapproached: **5** alone **9** matchless
unapt: **4** dull, slow **5** unfit **6** clumsy, klutzy, oafish, undeft **7** awkward **8** cloddish, fumbling, improper **9** all thumbs, graceless, ill-suited, impolitic, imprudent, inapropos, incapable, lumbering, maladroit **10** inapposite, indecorous, irrelevant, malapropos, nongermane, out of order, out of place, unskillful, unsuitable
unarguable: **3** net **4** last, sure **5** clean, clear, final, valid **6** cogent **7** certain, flat-out, obvious, telling **8** absolute, accurate, critical, deciding, decisive, definite, official, positive, ultimate, verified **9** clinching, effectual, revealing **10** compelling, conclusive, convincing, definitive, undeniable, undoubtful
unarm: **6** defeat **8** overcome **10** neutralize
unarmed: **5** clean **9** powerless **10** barehanded, weaponless
Unarmed Victory
author: Bertrand Russell
unartful: **4** open **5** green, naive **6** candid, simple **7** natural **8** innocent, trusting **9** childlike, guileless, ingenuous, unguarded, unstudied, unworldly **10** unaffected, unreserved, unschooled
unashamed: **4** open **6** brassy, brazen **7** forward **8** immodest
— Unashamed: **4** Cora
unasked-for: **9** causeless, unmerited, voluntary **10** gratuitous, unprovoked
unaspirated: **4** lene
unassailable: **4** safe **6** secure **8** airtight
unassertive: **3** coy, shy **4** mild **5** timid **6** demure, modest **7** bashful, passive **8** resigned, retiring **9** groveling
unassisted: **4** solo **5** alone
unassuming: **3** shy **4** meek, mild, prim **5** lowly, mousy, plain, quiet, timid **6** demure, folksy, humble, modest, mousey, simple **7** bashful **8** reserved, retiring **9** diffident
unassured: **3** shy **5** timid **9** diffident, flinching, tentative
unattached: **4** free, stag **5** alone, loose, stray, unwed **6** adrift, single, untied **7** at large, movable **8** mateless, moveable, separate, wifeless **9** at liberty, separated, unmarried **10** disjointed, friendless, spouseless
unattainable: **5** ideal **7** utopian
unattended: **4** lone **5** alone **6** lonely **7** private **8** solitary **9** abandoned, by oneself
unattested: **9** anonymous
unattired: **4** bare, nude **5** naked **6** unclad **8** disrobed, in the raw, starkers **9** au naturel, in the buff, unclothed, undressed
unattributed: **4** anon **9** anonymous
unau: **5** sloth
unauthentic: **4** sham **5** false **8** spurious **10** fictitious **11** counterfeit
unauthorized: **4** tabu **5** shady, taboo **6** banned **7** crooked, illegal, illicit, pirated, wildcat **8** criminal, improper, outlawed, unlawful, verboten, wrongful **9** felonious, forbidden **10** prohibited
look: **4** peek, peep
unavailability: **4** lack, need, want **6** dearth **7** absence, paucity **8** sparsity **9** privation **10** deficiency
unavailable: **4** busy **5** in use, taken **6** absent **7** engaged **8** occupied
unavailing: **4** idle, null, vain **6** futile, otiose **7** inutile, of no use, useless **8** bootless, hopeless **9** for naught, fruitless, pointless, worthless
Una voce poco fa: **4** aria
unavoidable: **3** set **4** firm, sure **5** fated **7** certain, decided, settled **8** destined, ordained, required **9** impending, necessary, requisite
unaware: **5** blind **6** deaf to, spacey **7** in a daze, mooning, out cold, out of it **8** careless, heedless, ignorant, mindless, nescient, suddenly **9** forgetful, negligent, oblivious, unadvised, unknowing, unmindful, unwitting **10** insensible, out to lunch, unfamiliar, uninformed
unawares: **5** aback, short **8** abruptly, off-guard, suddenly **9** by mistake **10** by accident, by surprise
take ~: **5** catch **6** ambush, pounce **7** startle **8** surprise
unbaked: **3** raw
unbalance: **5** addle **6** madden **7** derange, shake up **8** unsettle **10** disconcert
unbalanced: **4** alop **5** shaky **6** biased, jiggly, uneven, wabbly, wobbly **7** erratic, partial, unequal, unsound **8** lopsided, one-sided, partisan, top-heavy, unstable, unsteady **9** arbitrary, eccentric, unsettled **10** immoderate, prejudiced
at sea: **5** alist
Un Ballo in Maschera
composer: Giuseppe Verdi
unbar: **4** open **5** loose **6** loosen, open up
unbarred: **4** free, open **5** loose
unbearable: **5** awful **6** enough **7** painful, too much, very bad **8** grievous **10** deplorable
Unbearable Bassington, The
author: Saki
Unbearable Lightness of Being, The: **4** film **5** novel
author: Milan Kundera
cast: Juliette Binoche, Daniel Day Lewis, Lena Olin
unbeatable: **5** ideal **9** nonpareil **10** infallible, invincible
unbeaten: **5** on top **7** winning **8** at the top, dominant, flawless, out front **9** in the lead, on a streak **10** flying high, successful, triumphant, victorious
unbecoming: **3** low **5** inapt, inept, rough, tacky **6** clumsy, gauche **7** awkward, lowbred **8** improper,

indecent, shameful, uncomely, unseemly, unsuited, unworthy **9** ill-suited, maladroit, offensive, salacious, tasteless, unfitting, unsightly **10** indelicate
unbefitting: **5** below **7** beneath **8** unseemly, unworthy
'Unbegun' Symphony
composer: PDQ Bach
Un bel di: **4** aria
unbelievable: **4** tall, thin, weak **5** fishy, flaky, kooky, phony, thick **6** flakey, flimsy, kookie, phoney, screwy **7** amazing, awesome, dubious, surreal, suspect, too much, ungodly **8** cockeyed, doubtful, fabulous, reaching, unlikely **9** marvelous, unheard-of **10** incredible
Unbelievable (1991 song)
artist: EMF
Unbelievable!: **3** wow **5** great
unbelievably: **4** oh so, very **8** terribly
unbeliever: **5** pagan **7** atheist, infidel, sceptic, skeptic
unbelieving: **5** pagan **7** cynical **9** atheistic, quizzical, skeptical
unbend: **4** thaw **5** relax **6** unfold, unwind **10** straighten
unbending: **3** set **4** firm, hard, iron **5** aloof, balky, bossy, cruel, dug in, exact, fixed, picky, rigid, stern, stiff, stony, tense, tight, tough **6** dogged, formal, mulish, severe, steely, stoney, strict, strong, wooden **7** adamant, austere, decided, distant, do-or-die, hard-set, piggish, Spartan, uptight **8** despotic, exacting, hardened, hard-line, locked in, obdurate, reserved, resolute, rigorous, stubborn **9** demanding, draconian, impliable, inelastic, iron-jawed, obstinate, pigheaded, steadfast, stringent, tenacious **10** despotical, hard-bitten, implacable, inexorable, inflexible, iron-fisted, no-nonsense, oppressive, relentless, set in stone, tyrannical, unswayable, unyielding
unbent: **6** in a row, linear **8** straight
unbiased: **4** cold, even, fair, just, open **5** aloof, equal, valid **6** honest, square **7** factual, liberal, neutral **8** balanced, detached, straight **9** equitable, impartial, objective, uncolored, unslanted **10** even-handed, open-minded, reasonable
unbidden: **7** unasked **9** uninvited, voluntary
unbigoted: **4** just **7** liberal, neutral **8** catholic **9** impartial, unslanted
unbilled performer: **5** extra
unbind: **4** free, undo **5** loose **6** loosen, redeem **7** release, set free **8** let loose, liberate, set loose **9** disengage, extricate, turn loose
unbleached: **6** greige **7** natural
hue: **3** tan **4** ecru **5** beige, brown
unblemished: **4** pure **5** clean, clear, sound **6** unhurt **7** perfect **8** absolute, flawless, innocent, spotless, unflawed, unmarked, unmarred **9** faultless, snow-white, stainless, undamaged, undefiled, uninjured, unstained, unsullied, untouched
unblended: **4** neat **6** simple, single
unblessed: **5** curst **6** cursed, doomed, jinxed **7** hapless **8** ill-fated, luckless **10** ill-starred
unblock: **4** free, open **5** clear
unblocked: **4** open **8** passable **9** navigable, unstopped **10** accessible
unblurred: **5** clear, lucid **7** crystal
unblushing: **6** brassy, brazen **7** blatant **9** shameless **10** indelicate
unbolt: **4** open **5** loose **6** loosen
unbolted: **4** open **5** loose
unborn: **6** future
of an ~: **5** fetal **6** foetal
unbosoming: **5** story **6** avowal, exposé **9** admission, allowance, assenting, assertion, narration, statement, utterance **10** concession, confession, disclosure, divulgence, profession, recitation, revelation
unbothered: **4** airy, calm **6** at ease, blithe, breezy, cheery, jaunty, jovial **7** buoyant **8** carefree, cheerful, feckless, laid back, reckless **9** easygoing **10** flying high, insouciant, untroubled
unbound: **4** free **5** loose **6** untied
unbounded: **3** big **4** vast **7** endless, immense **8** infinite **9** excessive, limitless, unlimited
unbowed: **6** in a row, linear **8** straight
unbox: **4** open
unbranded cow: **4** calf **5** stray **8** maverick
unbreakable: **4** firm **5** solid, tight, tough **6** rugged, strong **7** durable, lasting **9** resistant, toughened
Un-Break My Heart (1996 song)
artist: Toni Braxton
unbribed: **5** clean **6** honest **10** upstanding
unbridled: **4** rash, wild **5** feral, rabid **6** ferine **7** beastly, rampant **9** ferocious, impetuous, out of hand **10** immoderate
unbroken: **3** one **4** deep, even, fast, wild **5** feral, level, rabid, solid, sound, whole **6** direct, entire, ferine, intact, smooth, steady **7** beastly, endless, nonstop, perfect, regular, running **8** constant, flawless, profound, straight, unwaning **9** ceaseless, continual, faultless, ferocious, incessant, inviolate, perpetual, undivided **10** continuous, immaculate, relentless, successive, unimpaired
horse: **5** bronc **6** bronco
unbuckle: **4** open **5** loose **6** loosen
unbuild: **4** bomb, rase, raze **5** level, wreck **7** destroy, flatten **8** bulldoze, demolish, dynamite, pull down, tear down **9** devastate, knock down
unburden: **3** rid **4** dump, ease, free, lose, open **5** clear, empty **6** reveal, soothe, unload **7** confess, confide, divulge, lay bare, lighten, relieve, tell all, unbosom **8** disclose, get rid of, shake off, throw off **9** disburden, dispose of, untrouble
unburdensome: **4** easy, snap **5** cinch, cushy **6** breeze, picnic, simple **8** duck soup, painless, pushover **10** child's play, effortless, unexacting
unbutton: **4** undo **5** loose **6** loosen
unbuttoned: **5** loose **10** disheveled
uncaged: **4** free, open **5** loose
uncalculable: **4** vast **6** cosmic, untold **7** endless, immense **8** infinite, unending **9** boundless, countless, limitless, unbounded, unlimited **10** bottomless, numberless
uncalled-for: **5** undue, wrong **6** unfair, wanton **7** unasked, uncouth **8** improper, needless, overmuch **9** merciless, misguided **10** groundless
uncancelled: **3** new **4** mint
uncanny: **3** odd **4** eery **5** eerie, queer, scary, weird **6** creepy, secret, spooky **7** ghostly, magical, oddball, strange, unusual **8** singular **9** fantastic, unearthly, unheard-of, unnatural **10** astounding, incredible, miraculous, mysterious, mystifying, prodigious, remarkable, superhuman
uncap: **3** pop **4** open
uncarbonated: **4** flat **5** still
uncared-for: **5** alone **7** run-down **8** untended **9** neglected
uncareful: **4** rash, wild **5** brash, hasty **6** daring, madcap, unwary, unwise **8** feckless, headlong, heedless, pell-mell, reckless **9** audacious, breakneck, daredevil, desperate, foolhardy, imprudent **10** incautious
uncaring: **5** stony **6** stoney, unkind **7** callous **8** hardened, heedless **9** apathetic, heartless, insensate, unfeeling, unpitying **10** neglectful, nonchalant, unmerciful, unthinking
Uncas craft: **5** canoe
unceasing: **7** abiding, endless, eternal, lasting, undying **8** enduring, timeless, unending, untiring, unwaning **9** continual, deathless, incessant, perennial, perpetual **10** continuous, unflagging
unceasingly: **4** ever **5** on end **6** always
uncelebrated: **7** unknown **8** nameless
unceremonious: **4** curt, homy, rude **5** blunt, brusk, crude, frank, gruff, homey, rough, short **6** abrupt, candid, casual, coarse, folksy, vulgar **7** boorish, brusque, cursory, offhand, uncivil **8** churlish, impolite, informal, inurbane, tactless **9** outspoken **10** indelicate
dismissal: **2** ax **3** axe **4** boot, sack **7** heave-ho **9** eighty-six
unceremoniously, leave: **4** drop, dump, jilt **5** chuck, ditch **6** desert **7** abandon, forsake
uncertain: **3** dim **4** asea, hazy, iffy, moot, open, torn, wary **5** at sea, chary, dicey, fluid, hairy, leery, muddy, risky, rocky, shaky, vague **6** casual, chancy, fickle, fitful, queasy, queazy, unsafe, unsure **7** dubious, erratic, guarded, halting, mutable, protean, suspect, unclear, unfixed **8** cautious, doubtful, doubting, hesitant, insecure, lukewarm, nebulous, not final, perilous, possible, shifting, slippery, ticklish, unsteady, variable, wavering **9** ambiguous, debatable, equivocal, faltering, hazardous, irregular, mercurial, on thin ice, reluctant, skeptical, tentative, undecided, unsettled, whimsical **10** ambivalent, bewildered, borderline, changeable, contingent, disputable, improbable, inconstant, indecisive, indefinite, indistinct, inexplicit, irresolute, precarious, suspicious, touch and go, unreliable, unresolved, up for grabs, up in the air, weak-willed, wishy-washy
amount: **3** any, few **4** some
response: **4** shot, stab **5** guess, hunch, maybe **6** notion, theory **7** feeling, opinion, perhaps, surmise, venture **9** suspicion **10** conjecture, hypothesis, prediction, projection
state: **5** limbo
__ uncertain terms: **4** in no
uncertainty: **4** risk **5** doubt, peril, qualm, query, worry **6** hazard, wonder **7** anxiety, concern, dilemma, dubiety, reserve, scruple, trouble **8** disquiet, distrust, mistrust, quandary, question, suspense **9** ambiguity, confusion, dubiosity, guesswork, hesitancy, misgiving, suspicion, vagueness **10** hesitation
show ~: **5** shrug
sound of ~: **2** er, uh, um
state of ~: **5** limbo
UNCF
part of: **4** Coll., Fund **5** Negro **6** United **7** College
unchain: **4** free, save **5** loose **6** loosen, redeem **7** release **8** liberate
unchained: **4** free **5** loose **6** untied
Unchained Melody (song)
artist: Les Baxter and his Orchestra, Roy Hamilton, Al Hibbler, Righteous Brothers
Unchain My Heart (1961 song)
artist: Ray Charles
unchallenged: **5** alone
unchangeable: **4** firm **5** fixed, rigid **6** stable, steady, strong **8** constant, resolute **9** immovable, immutable, permanent, steadfast, unmovable
unchangeableness: **3** rut **6** fixity, tedium **8** dullness, evenness, flatness, monotony, sameness **10** continuity, uniformity
unchanged: **4** as is, same **10** monotonous, unaffected
unchanging: **4** even, firm, same, sure **5** fixed, level, rigid **6** rooted, stable, static, steady **7** abiding, equable, eternal, lasting, regular, settled, stabile, uniform **8** constant, definite, enduring, ironclad, unfading **9** continual, immutable, perennial, permanent, perpetual, unfailing, unvarying **10** consistent, dependable, invariable, true to type

UN

uncharitable: **4** hard, mean **5** harsh **6** stingy, unkind **8** inhumane, spiteful, uncaring **9** heartless, unfeeling
uncharitableness: **5** spite **6** rancor
uncharted: **7** unknown
unchecked: **4** rash, wild **7** rampant **9** out of hand
spread ~: **4** rage
uncinch: **4** open **5** loose **6** loosen
uncircumspect: **4** rash **6** unwary **8** careless **9** unguarded **10** headstrong
uncivil: **4** bold, curt, flip, pert, rude **5** blunt, brash, fresh, gruff, harsh, nervy, rough, sassy, saucy, short, surly **6** abrupt, awless, brazen, cheeky, coarse, snippy **7** aweless, bearish, caddish, ill-bred, uncouth **8** churlish, flippant, growling, impolite, impudent, insolent, inurbane, snippety, tactless **9** barbarian, barbarous, insulting, offensive, out of line, ungallant **10** indecorous
uncivilized: **4** rude, wild **5** crass, crude, feral, gross, pagan, rabid, rough **6** animal, brutal, coarse, ferine, Gothic, rugged, savage, unholy, vulgar, wicked **7** beastly, boorish, brutish, ill-bred, lawless, loutish, uncouth, ungodly **8** barbaric, churlish, impolite **9** barbarian, barbarous, ferocious, primitive, unrefined
one: **5** beast, brute **6** animal
place: **4** wild **6** jungle
unclad: **3** raw **4** bare, nude **5** naked, stark **9** in the buff, in the nude, unattired
unclasp: **4** open **5** loose **6** loosen
Unclay
author: T.F. Powys
uncle: **3** kin, man, rel. **4** male **5** I give, I quit **6** enough **7** I give up, kinsman **8** relative
brother: **3** dad, pop **6** father
Dutch ~: **6** mentor **7** adviser, advisor
everybody's ~: **3** Sam
in Spanish: **3** tio
kid: **3** coz **6** cousin
mom: **4** gram, nana
say ~: **4** quit **5** yield **6** accede, fess up, give up, relent, submit **7** concede **9** acquiesce, surrender
sister: **3** mom **6** mother
starter: **5** grand
wife: **4** aunt **5** aunty **6** auntie
__ uncle: **3** cry, say **5** Dutch
__-uncle: **5** great
Uncle __: **3** Ned, Sam **4** Ben's, Buck **5** Remus, Vanya **6** Fester, Miltie
Uncle __ Cabin: **4** Tom's
Uncle __ Rice: **4** Ben's
U.N.C.L.E. agent: **4** Solo **8** Kuryakin
Uncle Albert/Admiral Halsey (1971 song)
artist: Paul McCartney
unclean: **4** evil, foul, rank, vile **5** black, dirty, dusty, fetid, germy, grimy, messy, muddy, nasty, sooty **6** filthy, foetid, impure, rancid, rotten, sloppy, soiled, sordid **7** corrupt, decayed, defiled, smeared, smudged, spotted, squalid, stained, sullied, tainted, unkempt, unswept **8** befouled, polluted, profaned, shameful, slovenly, stinking, vitiated **9** tarnished **10** bedraggled, besmirched, desecrated, insanitary
uncleaned: **5** dirty, dusty **8** unwashed
uncleanness: **5** filth, taint **8** impurity **9** pollution **10** corruption, defilement
unclear: **3** dim **4** hazy **5** blear, faint, foggy, fuzzy, mirky, misty, muddy, murky, shaky, vague, wooly **6** arcane, bleary, cloudy, opaque, turbid, woolly **7** cryptic, dubious, evasive, obscure, suspect **8** abstruse, darkened, nebulous, puzzling **9** confusing, cryptical, difficult, enigmatic, equivocal, illegible, uncertain, undecided, unfocused, unsettled **10** indefinite, indistinct, perplexing, unexplicit, unreadable
make ~: **3** dim, fog **4** blur, roil, veil **5** bedim, befog **6** darken **7** becloud, confuse, mystify, obscure **8** bewilder, confound **9** obfuscate
Uncle Ben's: **4** rice
alternative: **6** Minute **7** Success **8** Carolina
Uncle Buck (1989 film)
cast: John Candy, Amy Madigan
director: John Hughes
Uncle Fester: **6** Addams
Uncle Miltie: **5** Berle
Uncle Ned
composer: Stephen Foster
Uncle Remus: **10** tale teller
creator: Joel Chandler Harris
epithet: **4** Br'er
Uncle Sam: **10** government
agent: **3** Fed
artist: J.M. Flagg
feature: **3** hat **5** beard
invitation: **6** call-up **8** I Want You
Uncle Tom's Cabin
author: Harriet Beecher Stowe
character: **3** Eva **5** Eliza, Simon, Topsy **6** Legree **9** Little Eva
Uncle Vanya
author: Anton Chekhov
character: **4** Ilia, Ivan **5** Marya, Sonya **6** Astrov, Helena, Marina
uncloak: **6** show up **7** lay bare, undress
uncloaked: **4** open **5** overt **8** knowable
unclog: **4** free, open **5** clear **6** unstop
unclogger, sink: **5** Drano **7** plunger
unclose: **3** ope **4** open, undo
unclosed: **4** open
unclothe: **4** bare, peel **5** strip **6** reveal **7** disrobe, uncover, undress
unclothed: **3** raw **4** bare, nude **5** naked, stark **9** in the buff, unattired
unclouded: **4** fair, pure **5** clear, light, sunny **6** bright **8** sunshiny
uncluttered: **4** neat, open, tidy, trim **5** clean, kempt **6** simple, spruce **7** orderly **8** well-kept **9** shipshape **10** fastidious
uncoerced: **4** free **9** voluntary
uncoil: **6** spread, unfold, unwind **7** untwine **9** spread out **10** straighten
uncollected: **3** due **7** payable
uncolored: **4** fair, just **6** square **8** balanced, unbiased **9** equitable, impartial, objective, unslanted **10** even-handed, impersonal
uncombed: **6** blowsy, blowzy, matted, shaggy, unneat, untidy **7** blowsed, blowzed, knotted, tousled, unkempt
uncomfortability scale: **3** THI
uncomfortable: **4** achy, hard, sore, worn **5** close, rough, stiff, tight, tired, upset, weary **6** aching, in pain, pained, queasy, queazy, thorny, uneasy **7** awkward, chafing, cramped, galling, hurting, nervous, painful, wracked **8** annoying, fatigued, restless, sheepish, smarting, strained, troubled, wretched **9** agonizing, exhausted, ill at ease, miserable, suffering, wearisome
uncommitted: **4** free, open **7** neutral **8** cut loose, floating, lukewarm, wavering **9** undecided, unpledged **10** off the hook, on the fence
uncommon: **3** odd **4** eery, rare **5** alien, eerie, novel, queer, weird **6** arcane, atypic, exotic, freaky, quirky, scanty, scarce, single, unique **7** bizarre, curious, deviant, extreme, notable, oddball, offbeat, special, strange, unusual **8** aberrant, abnormal, atypical, far apart, freakish, original, peculiar, precious, singular, sporadic, superior, unwonted **9** anomalous, different, divergent, eccentric, egregious, fantastic, irregular, recherché, startling, unheard of, wonderful **10** at a premium, hard to find, infrequent, inimitable, noteworthy, occasional, prodigious, remarkable, sporadical, surprising, unfamiliar, unfrequent, unorthodox
in French: **9** recherché
in Latin: **4** rara
sense: **3** ESP **9** intuition, telepathy
uncommonly: **4** very **5** extra, oddly **6** rarely, seldom **8** not often **9** extremely, strangely, unusually **10** especially
uncommunicative: **3** mum, shy **4** cool, curt **5** aloof, close, quiet, short **6** remote, silent **7** distant, evasive, guarded, on the QT **8** hush-hush, reserved, reticent, retiring, taciturn **9** clammed up, secretive, voiceless, withdrawn
uncompanionable: **5** aloof **6** remote **7** distant **8** reserved, solitary **9** withdrawn **10** antisocial, unsociable
uncompassionate: **5** stern, stony **6** stoney **7** callous **9** unfeeling
uncompelled: **4** free **9** voluntary
uncomplaining: **4** calm, meek, mild **5** stoic **6** dogged, gentle, serene, stolid **7** patient, stoical **8** detached, enduring, resigned, tolerant, untiring **9** apathetic, easygoing, forgiving, impassive, unruffled **10** forbearing, unflagging
uncompleted: **7** halfway, partial **10** fractional, in the works
uncomplex: **4** easy **5** basic **6** simple **8** duck soup **10** child's play, elementary
uncompliant: **4** wild **6** mulish, unruly **7** naughty, wayward, willful **8** contrary, perverse, stubborn **9** obstinate **10** delinquent, disorderly, rebellious, refractory, self-willed
uncomplicated: **4** easy **5** basic, clear, plain **6** facile, simple **8** duck soup
uncompounded: **6** simple, single
uncomprehending: **4** dull **5** dense, dopey, silly, thick, vapid **6** obtuse, vacant **7** foolish, vacuous **9** airheaded, half-baked
uncompromising: **4** firm, grim, hard, sure **5** bossy, cruel, picky, rigid, stern, tough **6** severe, strict, strong, wilful **7** adamant, austere, decided, diehard, precise, radical, Spartan, willful **8** despotic, exacting, hard-core, hard-line, ironclad, locked in, obdurate, resolute, rigorous, stubborn **9** brick-wall, demanding, draconian, obstinate, pigheaded, steadfast, stringent, tenacious, unbending **10** despotical, inflexible, iron-fisted, no-nonsense, oppressive, tyrannical
response: **5** never
unconcealed: **4** bare, open **5** clear, naked, overt, plain **6** in view, patent, public **7** exposed, glaring, obvious, visible **8** apparent, clear-cut, explicit, knowable, manifest **9** barefaced **10** observable
unconcentrated: **4** thin **5** loose **6** effuse, strewn **7** diffuse, general **9** dispersed, scattered, spread out **10** discursive
unconcern: **6** laxity **7** neglect **8** lethargy **9** disregard **10** detachment, neutrality
unconcerned: **4** cold, cool, easy, lazy **5** aloof, blasé, blind, staid, stoic, stony **6** at ease, blithe, deaf to, low-key, mellow, placid, sedate, serene, stoney **7** at peace, callous, distant, languid, neutral, offhand, relaxed, stoical, unaware, unmoved **8** carefree, careless, composed, detached, feckless, hardened, heedless, laid-back, lukewarm, reserved, tranquil **9** apathetic, collected, forgetful, impassive, incurious, negligent, oblivious, temperate, unruffled, untouched, unworried, withdrawn **10** nonchalant, regardless
uncondensed: **5** total, whole **6** entire **7** plenary **8** complete, finished, thorough **10** exhaustive
unconditional: **4** flat, full, open **5** clean, total, utter **6** all-out, entire **7** assured, blanket, certain, flat-out, genuine **8** absolute, complete, outright, thorough **9** downright, no-strings, out-and-out, unlimited
unconditionally: **5** fully **6** flatly, in full, purely, wholly **7** cap-a-pie, flat out, totally, utterly **8** entirely, from A to Z **9** all the way, every inch **10** absolutely, completely, positively
unconfident: **3** shy **4** weak **5** timid **6** afraid, unsure **7** fearful, nervous **8** doubtful, hesitant **9** faltering, tentative **10** indecisive

unconfined: **4** free **5** loose **6** untied **7** at large **9** boundless, unlimited **10** on the loose
unconfirmed: **7** rumored **8** baseless **9** tentative, uncertain
uncongealed: **4** soft, thin **5** runny **6** liquid, watery
unconnected: **4** free **5** loose **6** parted **7** severed **8** detached, distinct, separate **9** disjoined, disunited, excursive, unrelated
unconquerable: **4** safe **6** secure **10** impassable, invincible
unconscionable: **5** undue **6** amoral, unfair, unholy, unjust, wanton, wicked **7** extreme, immoral, knavish, ungodly **8** criminal **9** barbarous, dishonest, excessive, unethical
unconscious: **3** out **4** numb **6** asleep, bombed, latent, zonked **7** out cold, stunned, unaware **8** benumbed, comatose, in a faint, lifeless, swooning **9** automatic, entranced, flattened, insensate, passed out, repressed, senseless, stupefied, unknowing, unmindful, unwitting **10** knocked out, suppressed
become ~: **4** doze **5** faint, sleep, swoon **6** go limp, nod off **7** pass out **8** black out, fall over, keel over
render ~: **2** KO **4** drug, kayo, stun **5** floor, punch **7** flatten **8** knock out
unconsenting: **5** balky, loath **6** averse, mulish **7** hostile, opposed **8** contrary, hesitant **9** reluctant
unconsidered: **6** random **9** unadvised, unnoticed
unconstitutional: **7** illegal **8** outlawed **10** prohibited, proscribed
unconstrained: **4** free **5** loose, merry **8** outgoing **9** unlimited, voluntary **10** licentious
unconstraint: **7** liberty, license
unconsumed: **5** extra **6** unused **7** surplus, uneaten **8** leftover, residual **9** remaining
uncontaminated: **4** pure **5** clean **8** pristine, sanitary, spotless **9** stainless **10** immaculate
uncontested: **6** united **7** unified **9** concerted, of one mind, unanimous **10** consensual, undisputed
uncontrived: **5** naïve **6** candid, honest **7** artless, genuine, natural, sincere **8** innocent **9** guileless
uncontrollable: **3** mad **4** amok, wild **5** amuck **6** bratty, fierce, strong, unruly **7** excited, frantic, freaked, furious, lawless, rampant, violent **8** obdurate, stubborn **9** fractious, insurgent, obstinate **10** licentious
circumstance: **4** fate, luck **5** karma
uncontrolled: **3** mad **4** rash, wild **5** blind **7** chaotic, rampant **10** licentious
unconventional: **3** odd **4** beat, eery **5** crazy, dotty, eerie, flaky, fresh, kinky, kooky, novel, outré, queer, weird **6** atypic, clever, far-out, flakey, freaky, kookie, quirky, unique, way-out **7** bizarre, curious, deviant, liberal, oddball, offbeat, raffish, strange, unusual **8** aberrant, atypical, bohemian, creative, freakish, informal, inspired, original, peculiar, uncommon **9** anomalous, divergent, eccentric, fantastic, ingenious, inventive, irregular **10** innovative, unorthodox
unconversant: **8** ignorant
unconvinced: **6** unsure **8** doubtful **9** skeptical
unconvincing: **4** lame, poor, thin, weak **6** flimsy **8** unlikely
uncooked: **3** raw
uncool: **5** nerdy **7** nowhere **8** tiresome **9** loathsome, malicious
one: **4** geek, nerd **5** dweeb
uncooperative: **5** balky, rigid **6** mulish, ornery **7** hostile, piggish **9** pigheaded, unwilling **10** refractory
uncoordinated: **5** gawky, inept **6** clumsy, klutzy, oafish **7** awkward, doltish, gawkish, hulking **8** bumbling, bungling, cloddish **9** all thumbs, graceless, lumbering, maladroit, stumbling
uncork: **3** pop **4** open **6** broach
uncorked: **4** open **9** unstopped
uncorroborated: **8** baseless **9** tentative
uncorrupt: **4** just, pure **8** innocent **9** high-toned
uncorrupted: **4** fair, good, pure, true **5** clean **6** virgin **8** pristine, spotless, virginal **9** stainless **10** immaculate
uncostly: **3** low **6** modest, on sale **7** cut-rate, reduced **8** trifling **10** economical, marked down, reasonable, rock-bottom
uncounted: **4** many **6** myriad, untold **10** unnumbered
uncouple: **4** part **5** sever, split, unpeg **6** cut off, detach, divide **7** disjoin, split up **8** break off, disunite, separate, set apart **9** disengage **10** disconnect
uncourageous: **3** shy **5** timid **6** scared
one: **5** sissy **6** coward **7** chicken, dastard
uncourteous: **3** raw **4** loud, rude **5** crass, crude, nervy, rough **6** coarse **7** bearish, boorish, lowbred, lowbrow, uncouth **8** churlish, inurbane **9** inelegant, tasteless, unrefined
uncourtly: **5** brash, rough **7** forward **8** inurbane **9** ungallant
uncouth: **3** low, raw **4** loud, non-U, rude **5** brash, crass, crude, gawky, gross, rough, tacky **6** clumsy, coarse, gauche, oafish, rustic, unmeet, vulgar **7** awkward, bearish, boorish, caddish, forward, gawkish, ill-bred, loutish, lowbred, raffish, raunchy, strange, uncivil **8** barbaric, clownish, impolite, indecent, ungainly, unseemly **9** backwater, graceless, inelegant, low-minded, tasteless, ungallant, ungenteel, unrefined **10** indecorous, indelicate, outlandish, ungracious, unpolished
one: **3** ape, oaf **4** boor, clod
uncover: **3** ope **4** bare, find, grub, leak, open, show, tell **5** dig up, learn, shuck, strip **6** denude, detect, expose, ferret, locate, open up, reveal, strike, turn up, unfold, unmask, unveil, unwrap **7** display, divulge, exhibit, hit upon, lay bare, lay open, let slip, rout out, unearth **8** disclose, discover, disinter, give away, smell out, unclothe **9** get to know, make known, stumble on **10** make public
uncovered: **3** raw **4** bald, bare, nude, open **5** naked, stark **10** unshielded
uncovering: **6** espial, exposé **8** exposure **9** detection, discovery **10** disclosure
uncreative: **5** bland **6** boring, in a rut
uncredited: **8** nameless **9** anonymous
uncritical: **6** casual **7** cursory, offhand, shallow **8** careless, slipshod **9** credulous, easygoing, imprecise **10** falling for
uncrowded: **4** open, thin **5** broad, roomy **6** sparse **8** far apart, spacious **10** commodious
unction: **4** balm **5** salve **8** liniment, ointment **9** demulcent, emollient
extreme ~: **4** rite **9** sacrament
unctuous: **4** oily **5** slick, suave **6** greasy, smooth **7** fawning, servile **8** slippery **9** adulatory, insincere, lubricous **10** lubricated, lubricious, obsequious
uncultivable: **4** arid, poor **5** waste **6** barren, fallow **7** parched
uncultivated: **4** rude, wild **5** fresh, rough **6** coarse, fallow **7** boorish, lawless, natural, uncouth **8** plebeian
uncultured: **3** raw **4** non-U, rude, wild **5** crude, gross, rough **6** coarse, gauche **7** boorish, loutish **8** churlish, plebeian, unpoised **9** backwater, barbarian, barbarous, graceless, inelegant
one: **3** oaf **4** boor, clod, slob
uncurbed: **4** fast, open, wild **5** loose **6** rakish, wanton **8** depraved **9** dissolute, libertine, salacious **10** libidinous, licentious, lubricious, profligate
uncurl: **6** unfold **9** spread out **10** straighten
uncurled: **8** straight
uncustomary: **3** odd **8** peculiar, uncommon **9** different
uncut: **4** pure **5** rough, total, whole **6** entire, in full, intact **7** plenary **8** complete, finished, thorough **9** undivided **10** exhaustive, full-length, in one piece, in the rough, unabridged
UND
see Notre Dame
undamaged: **2** OK **4** mint, okay, okeh, okey, safe, well **5** sound, whole **6** entire, intact, secure **7** perfect **8** all right, complete, flawless **9** faultless, untouched **10** immaculate, in one piece
__ Undarum: **4** Mare
undaunted: **3** icy **4** bold, game **5** brave, gutsy, nervy, stout **6** awless, daring, gritty, heroic, plucky, spunky, steely **7** aweless, defiant, doughty, gallant, impavid, staunch, valiant **8** fearless, heroical, intrepid, resolute, stalwart, unafraid, valorous **9** audacious, confident, dreadless, steadfast, unalarmed, unfearful, unfearing **10** courageous, fire-eating, mettlesome, undeterred, undismayed
__ und Drang: **5** Sturm
Undead, The (1957 film)
director: Roger Corman
undecaying: **8** enduring **9** immutable, permanent **10** changeless
undeceitful: **6** candid, honest **8** straight
undeceive: **8** disabuse **9** enlighten, unbeguile **10** disenchant
undeceptive: **4** open **6** honest, trusty **7** ethical, genuine, up-front **8** reliable, straight, truthful **9** veracious **10** aboveboard, dependable, on the level
undecided: **4** iffy, moot, open, torn **5** vague **6** unsure **7** dubious, neutral, not sure, pendant, pendent, pending, unclear **8** doubtful, hesitant, lukewarm, waffling, wavering **9** debatable, dithering, equivocal, tentative, uncertain, unsettled **10** ambivalent, borderline, indecisive, indefinite, irresolute, of two minds, on the fence, unfinished, unresolved, up in the air, wishy-washy
be ~: **4** hang, pend **5** waver
perch for the ~: **5** fence
undecipherable: **4** deep **6** knotty, thorny, tricky **7** complex **8** abstruse, involved, mazelike, tortuous **9** Byzantine, Daedalean, difficult, enigmatic, intricate **10** circuitous, convoluted, perplexing
undeclared: **5** tacit **6** unsaid **7** implied
undecorated: **4** bare **6** simple **7** Spartan
undefended: **4** open **8** wide open **9** unguarded **10** vulnerable
undefiled: **4** pure **5** clean **6** chaste, virgin **8** pristine, spotless, unsoiled, virginal **9** stainless **10** immaculate
undefined: **9** limitless, open-ended **10** indefinite
undeliverable letter: **4** nixy **5** nixie
undemanding: **4** easy, meek, snap, soft **5** cinch, cushy, light **6** breeze, picnic, simple **8** duck soup, painless, pushover **10** child's play, effortless
undemocratic rule: **5** junta
undemonstrative: **3** shy **5** aloof, staid, stoic, timid **6** demure **7** distant, languid, stoical **8** listless, reserved, retiring **9** apathetic, withdrawn
undeniability: **7** urgency **9** necessity
undeniable: **4** real, sure, true **5** clear, sound **6** actual, patent, proven, simple **7** certain, evident, for sure, obvious **8** absolute, accurate, decisive, definite, manifest, outright, positive **9** necessary, undoubted **10** conclusive, inevitable, unarguable, undoubtful, unimagined
it's ~: **4** fact **5** given, thing, truth

6 verity 7 reality 9 actuality, certainty
undeniably: 6 easily, indeed 9 hands down 10 definitely, far and away
undependable: 5 loose, shaky 6 fickle, no-good, tricky, unsafe, unsure 7 dubious, erratic, wayward 8 careless, derelict, skittish, unstable, variable 9 uncertain 10 unreliable
one: 4 kook 5 flake 6 maniac 7 lunatic
under: 3 low, sub 4 down 5 below, infra, lower, neath 6 asleep, junior, lesser, nether, pinned 7 beneath, subject 8 downward, governed, held down, included, inferior, sleeping, subsumed 9 covered by, subject to 10 hypnotized, inferior to, insentient, subjugated, subsidiary, supporting, underneath
combining form: 6 infero-
ender: 3 age 4 wear 5 world 6 ground
prefix: 3 sub- 4 hypo-
sail: 4 asea 5 at sea
starter: 4 here 5 there
the covers: 4 abed 8 sleeping
way: 5 afoot, going
under ___: 3 way 4 fire, foot, oath 5 cover, wraps 6 arrest
under ___ and key: 4 lock
under ___ of: 4 pain
___ under: 4 down, fall, plow, snow 7 knuckle
___-under: 4 over
Under ___: 4 Fire 5 Siege
Under ___ Wood: 4 Milk
underachiever: 5 loser 7 also-ran, failure
social ~: 4 nerd
underage: 5 minor, young 6 callow 7 deficit 8 immature, juvenile, youthful 9 shortfall 10 inadequacy
Under a Glass Bell
author: Anaïs Nin
undercarriage: 4 body 5 frame 7 chassis 9 framework
underclassman: 5 pupil 6 rookie 7 student 8 beginner, freshman 9 collegian
undercoat: 6 sealer
undercoating prevents it: 4 rust 5 decay 6 patina 7 tarnish 9 corrosion, iron oxide, oxidation
undercooked: 3 raw, red 4 pink, rare
undercounted: 3 low 5 short
undercover: 6 covert, hidden, masked, secret, spying, unseen, veiled 7 cloaked, furtive, on the QT, private, sub rosa 8 hush-hush, obscured, on the sly, secluded, shrouded, stealthy 9 concealed, disguised, incognito, nonpublic, secretive, unexposed
agent: 3 spy 4 mole 5 plant
Cold War ~ gp.: 3 KGB
cop: 4 narc, nark 5 agent, narco
go ~: 3 spy 4 hide 6 hole up, lay low, lie low 7 sleeper
govt. ~ group: 3 CIA, NSA
officer, at times: 4 bait, lure 5 decoy, shill 6 come-on
operation: 5 sting
recognize, as an ~ cop: 4 make, name 6 finger
Undercover Angel (1977 song)
artist: Alan O'Day
Undercover of the Night (1983 song)
artist: Rolling Stones
undercurrent: 4 aura, eddy, hint, pull, race, tide 5 drift, sense, tenor, tinge, trace, trend, vibes 6 flavor, murmur 7 feeling, riptide 8 overtone, tendency, undertow 9 direction, undertone, whirlpool
undercut: 5 blunt, erode 6 weaken 7 cripple, sandbag, subvert, torpedo 8 sabotage 9 attenuate, bring down, undermine
underdeveloped: 4 puny 5 runty, short 8 immature
underdevelopment: 4 lack, want 7 paucity, poverty 10 meagerness
underdog: 5 loser 8 longshot 9 dark horse
underdone: 3 raw 4 rare
underestimate: 3 err 6 slight 7 mistake, neglect, put down 8 belittle, minimize, misjudge 9 deprecate, disesteem, disparage, sell short, underrate
underestimation: 5 error 7 mistake 8 miscount, omission
underfed: 4 puny 6 meager 7 starved 8 starving 9 emaciated
Under Fire (1983 film)
cast: Joanna Cassidy, Gene Hackman, Nick Nolte
___ Under Fire: 5 Grace 7 Courage
underfoot: 8 in the way
crush ~: 5 crush, stamp, stomp, worst 6 defeat 7 flatten, trample
it may be ~: 3 mat, rug 4 sole
underfunded: 5 short
undergarment: 4 slip 5 stays, teddy 6 corset, girdle 8 lingerie 10 foundation
undergird: 5 brace 6 hold up, prop up 7 shore up, support 8 buttress 9 reinforce 10 strengthen
undergo: 4 bear, feel, have 5 abide, stand, yield 6 endure, suffer 7 receive, sustain, weather 8 meet with, stand for, submit to, tolerate 9 encounter, put up with, withstand 10 experience
undergraduate: 4 soph 5 pupil 6 junior, senior 7 scholar, student 8 freshman 9 sophomore
British ~: 5 sizar, sizer
see also college
underground: 4 deep, tube 5 metro 6 buried, covert, hidden, secret, subway, sunken 7 covered, on the QT, private, radical 8 hush-hush, on the sly 9 concealed, resistant, resistive
chamber: 4 cave, kiva, mine 5 vault 6 bunker, cavern, grotto
dweller of folklore: 5 gnome, troll
event: 5 A-test, H-test, N-test
explorer: 5 caver 9 spelunker
find: 3 oil, ore 7 mineral 9 petroleum
go ~: 4 hide 6 hole up, lay low, lie low
growth: 4 root 5 radix, tuber 7 radicle, rhizome
org.: 3 UMW
passage: 4 mine, pipe 5 drain, sewer 7 conduit, culvert
retreat: 3 pit 6 dugout, trench 7 foxhole 10 excavation
rodent: 4 mole 6 gopher
room: 6 bunker, cellar 8 basement
root: 5 tuber
worker: 5 miner
WWII ~ resistance movement: 3 EAM 4 ELAS 6 Maquis
underground ___: 5 movie
Underground City, The
author: Jules Verne
Underground Man, The
author: Ross Macdonald
undergrowth: 5 brush, gorse, scrub, shrub 6 bushes 7 thicket 9 chaparral, shrubbery
underhand: 3 sly 4 wily 5 shady, sharp 6 crafty, secret, shifty, shrewd, sneaky, tricky, unfair, unjust 7 crooked, cunning, devious, furtive, oblique, on the QT, sub rosa 8 guileful, hush-hush, indirect, scheming, slippery, sneaking, stealthy, two-faced 9 concealed, deceitful, deceptive, dishonest, insidious, secretive, two-timing, unethical 10 fraudulent, undeserved
throw: 3 lob 4 toss 5 pitch
underhanded: 3 sly 4 foul, wily 5 cheap, dirty, false, shady, snaky, undue 6 covert, secret, sneaky, tricky, unfair 7 corrupt, crooked, devious, furtive, knavish 8 delusive, guileful, scheming, sneaking 9 deceitful, dishonest, insincere, unethical 10 mendacious, unreliable, untruthful
one: 5 rogue, sneak 6 con man
underhandedness: 4 hoax, ruse, sham, wile 5 craft, fraud, guile, lying 6 deceit, humbug 7 cunning, falsity, slyness, snow job, swindle 8 artifice, cheating, flimflam, pretense, trickery 9 chicanery, duplicity, imposture, treachery, two-timing 10 craftiness, dishonesty, subterfuge
underivative: 3 new 5 early, first, fresh, novel, prime 7 genuine, radical, seminal 8 creative, original, primeval, singular 9 authentic, demiurgic, formative, ingenious, inspiring, inventive, primitive 10 archetypal, avant-garde, innovative, primordial, refreshing
underline: 4 mark, rule 6 accent, legend, play up, stress 7 bracket, caption, feature, point to, point up 8 indicate 9 emphasize, highlight, italicize, punctuate, reinforce, spotlight 10 accentuate
underling: 4 aide, pawn 6 deputy, flunky, lackey, minion, stooge, yes man 7 flunkey, lacquey
underlining: 6 stress 8 emphasis
under lock and ___: 3 key
underlying: 4 root 5 basal, basic, prime, vital 6 bottom, hidden, latent, veiled 7 crucial, lurking, primary, radical 8 cardinal, critical 9 concealed, elemental, essential, intrinsic, necessary, primitive 10 elementary
sentiment: 5 pulse
___-under-Lyne: 6 Ashton
Under Milk Wood
author: Dylan Thomas
undermine: 3 dig, sag, sap 4 flag, foil, hurt, ruin, tire, undo, wane, wear 5 blunt, erode, wreck 6 damage, debase, impair, poison, reduce, shrink, soften, thwart, tunnel, weaken 7 corrupt, cripple, deplete, disable, eat away, exhaust, fatigue, sandbag, subvert, torpedo, unnerve, vitiate 8 enervate, enfeeble, excavate, sabotage, threaten, undercut 9 attenuate, bring down, frustrate, hollow out 10 debilitate, demoralize, devitalize
underneath: 4 down 5 below, infra, lower, neath, under 6 nether 7 covered
prefix: 5 intra-
undernourished: 4 bony, thin 5 boney 6 ill-fed, skinny 7 scrawny, starved 8 starving
under one's ___: 3 hat 4 belt, nose, wing 5 thumb 6 breath
underpaid one: 4 peon 5 slave 6 drudge
underpass: 6 tunnel 8 crossing 10 cloverleaf
in Britain: 4 tube 5 metro 6 subway
underpin: 4 hold 5 shore 6 prop up 7 shore up
underpinning: 4 base, prop, root, stay 5 basis, brace 7 footing, support 8 buttress
underplay: 5 gloze 8 discount, minimize, palliate, pooh-pooh, shrug off, talk down 9 gloss over, whitewash
___ under pressure: 5 grace
Under Pressure (1981 song)
artist: Queen
underprivileged: 4 poor 5 broke, needy, sorry 6 bad off, hard up, ill off, in need, in want 7 hapless, have-not, pinched 8 badly off, bankrupt, beggarly, deprived, ill-fated, indigent, strapped 9 destitute, insolvent, moneyless, penniless, penurious 10 down and out, pauperized, straitened
underrate: 7 cry down, devalue 8 belittle, minimize, misjudge, play down, write off 9 devaluate, disparage, sell short 10 depreciate
underscore: 6 accent, play up, stress 7 feature, iterate, point up 9 emphasize, highlight, punctuate, spotlight 10 accentuate
underscoring: 6 accent 8 emphasis
undersea measure: 5 depth 6 fathom, league
undershirt: 3 tee 8 lingerie
in Britain: 4 vest 7 singlet
size: 3 med. 5 large, small 6 medium
undershoot: 4 miss
underside: 3 bed 4 base, foot 5 floor 6 bottom, ground 7 reverse, support 10 foundation
on the ~: 5 below, lower 6 nether 7 beneath 8 downward 9 covered by
Under Siege (1992 film)
cast: Gary Busey, Erika Eleniak, Tommy Lee Jones, Steven Seagal
undersize: 3 wee 4 baby, puny, tiny 5 dwarf, elfin, pigmy, pygmy, short,

small, teeny, weeny **6** bantam, lesser, little, midget, minute, peewee, petite, pocket, slight, teensy **7** stunted **9** miniature **10** diminutive, teeny-weeny
underspend: 3 eke **4** save **5** skimp **6** scrape, scrimp **8** conserve, roll back, withhold **9** economize **10** cut corners
understand: 3 dig, get, ken, see **4** grok, hear, know, note, read, tell, wake **5** catch, get it, grasp, infer, learn, savvy, sense, think, waken **6** absorb, accept, assume, decode, deduce, expect, fathom, follow, gather, intuit, master, reckon, take in, take it **7** believe, catch on, cognize, concede, discern, explain, feel for, find out, imagine, make out, presume, realize, suppose, surmise, suspect **8** conceive, conclude, consider, decipher, perceive, register, relate to, tolerate **9** apprehend, figure out, get to know, interpret, penetrate, recognize **10** appreciate, assimilate, comprehend, sympathize
easy to ~: 5 clear, lucid, plain, vivid **6** cogent, simple **7** evident, express, legible, obvious **8** apparent, coherent, distinct, explicit, knowable, luculent, luminous, manifest, palpable, readable **9** graspable **10** explicable, reasonable, spelled out
hard to ~: 4 mazy **5** tough **6** arcane, knotty, opaque, sticky, thorny, tricky **7** complex, labored, obscure, unclear **8** abstruse, baffling, puzzling **9** difficult, intricate **10** formidable, mystifying, perplexing
in sci-fi: 4 grok
slow to ~: 5 dense **6** obtuse
Understand?: 3 see **5** get it, get me
understandable: 5 clear, lucid, plain, vivid **6** cogent, simple **7** evident, express, legible, obvious **8** apparent, coherent, distinct, explicit, knowable, luculent, luminous, manifest, palpable, readable **9** graspable **10** explicable, reasonable, spelled out
make ~: 7 clarify, clear up **9** bring home, elucidate, explicate, get across **10** illuminate, illustrate
understanding: 3 ken, wit **4** deal, grip, idea, kind, nice, pact, pity, tact, view, wise, wits **5** grasp, light, savvy, sense **6** accord, acumen, belief, import, intent, kindly, lenity, notion, reason, sanity, uptake, wisdom **7** ability, compact, concord, empathy, entente, harmony, inkling, insight, knowing, liberal, mastery, meaning, message, opinion, patient, purport, purview, rapport, reading, tactful, thought **8** amicable, contract, decision, generous, judgment, keenness, kindness, lenience, sympathy, tolerant **9** accepting, awareness, forgiving, fraternal, handshake, intellect, intuition, knowledge, observant, sensitive, sharpness, tolerance, viewpoint **10** perception, perceptive, responsive, supportive
come to an ~: 4 jibe **5** agree **6** accord, settle **7** concede, consent, go along, resolve **8** cut a deal, play ball **9** acquiesce, harmonize, negotiate
exclamation of ~: 4 I see, okay **5** got it, right **6** I get it, righto
with the ~: 2 if **8** as long as, assuming, provided **9** given that, providing, subject to, supposing **10** in the event
words of ~: 3 ohs **5** I know **6** I get it
Understanding (song)
artist: Bob Seger, Xscape
Understanding Media
author: Marshall McLuhan
understate: 5 fudge **8** downplay, minimize, play down **9** soft-pedal
understated: 3 low **4** soft **5** faint, piano, quiet **6** low-key, subtle
understatement: 7 litotes
understood: 3 pat **4** on to **5** given, known, roger, tacit **6** unsaid, wise to **7** assumed, down pat, implied **8** accepted, implicit, inferred, presumed, unspoken, unstated, unvoiced, very well, wordless **9** axiomatic, customary, intuitive, unwritten
easily ~: 5 clear, lucid, plain, vivid **6** cogent, simple **7** evident, express, legible, logical, obvious **8** apparent, clear-cut, coherent, distinct, explicit, knowable, luculent, luminous, manifest, palpable, readable, sensible **9** graspable **10** explicable, reasonable, spelled out
not easily ~: 4 deep, mazy **5** tough **6** arcane, hidden, knotty, occult, opaque, secret, sticky, thorny, tricky **7** complex, Delphic, labored, obscure, unclear **8** abstract, abstruse, baffling, esoteric, profound, puzzling **9** difficult, intricate, recondite **10** fathomless, formidable, mysterious, mystifying, perplexing
Understood!: 4 I dig, I see **5** got it, I'm hip, roger **6** I get it
understudy: 3 sub **5** actor **6** backup, player **7** stand-in **9** alternate, attendant **10** substitute
undertake: 3 try **4** wage **5** begin, essay, start **6** assume, embark, go into, hazard, launch, pledge, set out, tackle **7** address, attempt, get into, go about, pitch in, presume, promise, propose, venture **8** approach, commence, contract, endeavor, engage in, have a try, initiate, practice, set about, shoulder **9** answer for, enter upon, guarantee, volunteer **10** bargain for, make a run at
undertaking: 3 act, job **4** deal, duty, move, task, work **5** essay, labor **6** action, affair, effort, matter **7** attempt, mission, project, pursuit, venture **8** activity, business, endeavor, movement, struggle **9** adventure, operation
easy ~: 4 snap **5** cinch **6** breeze, picnic **8** duck soup, kid stuff **9** no trouble **10** child's play
Undertaking, The
author: John Donne
under the __: 3 gun, sun **4** wire **5** radar, table **7** weather
Under the __: 3 Sea
Under the Boardwalk (1964 song)
artist: Drifters
__ under the bridge: 5 water
Under the Bridge (1992 song)
artist: Red Hot Chili Peppers
__ under the collar: 3 hot
under-the-counter: 7 bootleg, crooked, illegal, illicit **8** improper, unlawful **10** not allowed, prohibited, unlicensed
__ Under the Elms: 6 Desire
Under the hawthorne in the __: 4 dale
__ under the haystack...: 3 he's
Under the Mountain Wall
author: Peter Matthiessen
Under the Net
author: Iris Murdoch
Under the Sea-Wind
author: Rachel Carson
__ Under the Sun: 4 Evil
under-the-table: 6 covert, secret **7** furtive, illegal **8** hush-hush
Under the Tonto Rim
author: Zane Grey
Under the Tuscan Sun (2003 film)
cast: Diane Lane
Under the Volcano
author: Malcolm Lowry
under-the-wipers item: 5 flier, flyer **7** leaflet **8** circular **9** broadside
undertone: 3 hum **4** hint **5** rumor, tinge, touch, trace **6** flavor, mumble, murmur, mutter **7** feeling, whisper **10** atmosphere, suggestion
undertow: 4 race, tide **9** whirlpool
Under Two Flags
author: Ouida
undervalue: 5 lower **7** cry down **8** belittle, write off **9** disparage, downgrade **10** depreciate
underwater: 4 sunk **6** sunken **9** submarine, submerged
boat: 3 sub **9** submarine
breathing apparatus: 4 gill **5** scuba
cave dweller: 3 eel
explorer: 5 Beebe **8** Cousteau
go ~: 3 dip **4** dive, sink, swim **5** drown, scuba **6** fall in **7** capsize, founder, immerse **8** submerge **9** scuba-dive, shipwreck
organism: 4 alga, kelp **5** polyp
shelf: 4 reef **5** ledge
tracker: 5 sonar
underway: 5 afoot, astir **6** moving **7** going on, ongoing **8** in motion **9** advancing, happening, occurring, on the move, traveling **10** in progress
get ~: 5 begin, start **6** set off, set out **8** set forth, shove off
underwear: 3 bra **4** BVDs, slip, stay **6** bikini, boxers, briefs, corset, shorts **7** drawers, garment, Jockeys **8** clothing, lingerie, skivvies **9** long johns
brand: 3 BVD **5** Hanes **6** Jockey
__ underwear: 4 long **7** thermal
underweight: 4 bony, lank, lean, puny, thin **5** boney **6** gangly, skinny **7** angular, scrawny, starved **8** angulose, angulous
Under Western Eyes
author: Joseph Conrad
Underwood: 3 Ron **5** Blair
underworld: 3 mob **4** hell **5** abyss, Hades, Mafia, Orcus **6** Erebus, racket **7** inferno **8** riffraff **9** criminals, gangsters, syndicate
Babylonian ~: 5 Aralu **6** Arallu
Biblical ~: 5 Sheol
entrance: 6 Averno
figure: 3 don **5** devil, Satan
god: 3 Dis **5** Orcus, Pluto
lingo: 5 argot
river: 4 Styx **5** Lethe
weapon: 3 gat
woman: 4 moll
Underworld
author: Don DeLillo
underwrite: 3 pay **4** back, fund, seal, sign **5** angel, endow, float, stake **6** assure, cosign, ensure, insure, secure **7** approve, endorse, finance, indorse, promise, sponsor, support, warrant **8** bankroll, sanction **9** guarantee, subscribe, subsidize
a risk: 5 cover **6** ensure, insure, shield **7** protect, warrant **9** guarantee, indemnify
underwriter: 5 angel **6** backer, patron **7** sponsor **9** guarantor, supporter **10** benefactor, grubstaker
govt. bank ~: 4 FDIC **5** FSLIC
undeserved: 4 foul **5** undue **6** shabby, unjust **7** extreme, low-down **8** improper, needless, wrongful **9** excessive, underhand, unmerited **10** gratuitous, inordinate
charge: 5 frame **6** bad rap **7** frameup
undeserving: 3 low **4** base **5** unfit **6** no-good **7** ignoble **8** unworthy, wretched **9** no-account **10** ineligible
undesignated: 8 nameless **9** anonymous
undesigned
see random
undesirable: 4 icky **5** creep **7** dreaded, loathed, outcast, scorned, shunned, useless **8** annoying, disliked, rejected, unsavory, unsought, unwanted **9** defective, loathsome, obnoxious, offensive, repellent, repugnant, unhealthy, unlikable, unpopular, unwelcome
act: 4 no-no, tabu **5** taboo
undesired: 7 unasked **8** needless
undetailed: 7 general, sketchy
undetected: 6 hidden, latent, secret, unseen, veiled **7** lurking **8** shrouded **9** concealed, invisible, unexposed, unnoticed **10** out of sight, tucked away, unobserved
undetermined: 4 open **5** vague **7** pending **9** uncertain, undecided, unsettled
undeterred: 6 dogged, steady **7** devoted, staunch **8** resolute, tireless, untiring **9** dedicated, energetic, tenacious, undaunted, unwearied **10** determined, persist-

ent, relentless, unflagging, unswerving, unwavering
un, deux, __: 5 trois
undeveloped: 4 puny 5 crude, young 6 latent, little 7 ignored 8 backward, immature, inchoate, untaught 9 embryonic, half-baked, incipient, potential, premature, primitive, shapeless, unevolved, untrained
undeviating: 4 even, firm, sure 5 fixed, level 6 direct, linear, rooted, smooth, stable, static, steady 7 literal, regular, settled, uniform 8 constant, definite, directly, ironclad, straight 9 permanent 10 dependable, foursquare
undeviatingly: 5 right 6 wholly 7 exactly, totally, utterly 8 entirely, reliably, squarely 9 honorably, literally, perfectly, precisely 10 absolutely, completely, dependably 12 scrupulously
undexterous: 5 inapt, inept, unapt
undies: 6 briefs, shorts 7 drawers 8 lingerie, skivvies
undifferentiated: 4 like, same, such 5 equal 6 on a par 7 similar, uniform 8 matching, parallel, selfsame 9 identical 10 comparable, consistent, equivalent, tantamount, true to type
undignified: 5 crude, gross 6 coarse, vulgar 8 immodest, improper, indecent, unseemly 9 inelegant 10 in bad taste, indecorous, indelicate, out of place
undiluted: 4 neat, pure 5 sheer 6 strong 8 straight
undiminished: 5 total, whole 6 entire 7 plenary, undying 8 finished, thorough 10 exhaustive
undiplomatic: 5 brash 8 inurbane, tactless 9 maladroit, unguarded
undirected: 7 aimless, erratic 8 headless, unguided
undisciplined: 3 lax, raw 4 wild 7 coltish 10 disorderly
undisclosed: 6 hidden, secret 7 private 8 ulterior 9 potential
undiscounted: 5 at par
undiscovered: 6 unseen 7 unknown 9 unheard-of, unnoticed
undisguised: 4 bald, open 5 clear, naked, overt, plain 6 direct, honest, in view, patent, public 7 exposed, obvious, visible 8 apparent, clear-cut, explicit, knowable, manifest 10 observable
undismayed: 4 bold, game 5 brave, gutsy, nervy, stout 6 daring, gritty, heroic, plucky, spunky 7 doughty, gallant, valiant 8 fearless, intrepid, stalwart, unafraid, valorous 9 audacious, confident, dauntless, undaunted, unfearing 10 chivalrous, courageous, mettlesome
undisputable: 4 sure 5 final 7 assured, certain 8 admitted, positive, unerring 9 undoubted
undisputed: 4 sure 5 final 7 assured, certain 8 admitted, positive, unerring 9 arbitrary, unanimous, undoubted, universal 10 inarguable, undoubtful
Undisputed (2002 film)
cast: Peter Falk, Ving Rhames, Wesley Snipes
undistinguished: 4 blah, so-so 5 bland, plain 6 boring, common, humble, simple 7 average, unknown 8 mediocre, nameless, ordinary 10 pedestrian
group: 4 ruck 8 riffraff
undistorted: 4 real, true 5 right 6 honest 7 correct 8 faithful, straight
undistracted: 4 rapt 8 absorbed 9 engrossed, undivided
undisturbed: 4 calm, cool, even 5 quiet 6 in situ, low-key, mellow, placid, sedate, serene, smooth, virgin 7 amiable, at peace, easeful, equable, pacific, relaxed, stoical 8 amicable, composed, laid-back, peaceful, tranquil, unbroken, virginal 9 collected, easy-going, impassive, quiescent, temperate
undiversified: 4 same 5 alike 7 similar, uniform
undivided: 3 one 4 full, sole 5 solid, total, uncut, whole 6 entire, joined, single, steady, united 7 intense 8 absorbed, combined, complete, integral, thorough, unbroken, vigilant 9 concerted, connected, engrossed, exclusive, unanimous 10 collective, continuous, unflagging, unswerving
undivulged: 6 buried, covert, hidden, secret 7 sub rosa 8 ulterior 10 under wraps, unrevealed
undo: 4 free, open, ruin 5 annul, crimp, erase, loose, quash, queer, smash, spoil, stimy, stymy, untie, unzip, upset, wreck 6 cancel, defeat, injure, loosen, negate, offset, stymie, unbind, unfold, unlock, unwind, unwrap 7 abolish, destroy, nullify, release, restore, reverse, screw up, shatter, subvert, unclose, unravel 8 abrogate, come open, demolish, outsmart, overturn, separate, take down, unbutton, unfasten, unloosen 9 bring down, disengage, dismantle, overreach, overthrow, take apart, undermine 10 counteract, disconnect, impoverish, invalidate, lay waste to, neutralize
undocumented one, perhaps: 5 alien 7 refugee 9 foreigner, immigrant, outlander 10 noncitizen
undoing: 3 end 4 bane, blow, doom, loss, ruin 6 defeat 7 bad luck, failure 8 calamity, collapse, disgrace, downfall, reversal 9 adversity, annulment, mischance, perdition, ruination 10 affliction, misfortune, subversion, visitation
undomesticated: 4 wild 5 feral, rabid 6 ferine, savage 7 beastly 9 ferocious
undone: 5 kaput, loose 6 beaten, broken, doomed, ruined, untied 7 crushed, smashed, wrecked 8 finished, wiped out 9 destroyed, shattered 10 irremedial
come ~: 3 rip 4 fray, open, tear, wear 5 break, burst, crack, shred, split 7 frazzle, give way, rupture 8 fragment, separate 9 disengage, pull apart 10 disconnect
leave ~: 4 omit, wait 5 slack 8 overlook
remain ~: 4 hang, pend, wait 5 await, delay
wish ~: 3 rue 5 mourn 6 bemoan, bewail, grieve, lament, regret 8 repent of
undoubted: 4 true 5 right 9 veritable 10 undeniable, undisputed
undoubtedly
see of course
undoubtful: 3 set 4 sure 5 clear, on ice, valid 7 certain, settled 8 accurate, definite, destined, fail-safe, ironclad, unerring 9 authentic, axiomatic, foolproof, unfailing 10 conclusive, inevitable, infallible, unarguable, undeniable, undisputed, verifiable
undraped: 4 bare, nude 5 naked, stark 9 in the buff, in the nude 10 unshielded
undreamed of: 6 untold
undress: 4 doff, peel, shed 5 strip 6 denude, devest, show up 7 disrobe, slip off, take off, uncloak 8 get out of, unattire, unclothe 9 dismantle, slip out of
undressed: 4 bare, nude 5 naked 9 unattired
undry: 3 wet 4 damp, dank, dewy, oozy 5 humid, juicy, misty, moist, muddy, muggy, rainy, soggy 6 clammy, drippy, oozing, sodden, steamy, sweaty, watery 7 drizzly, sopping 8 dripping 9 drizzling, saturated, succulent
Undset: 6 Sigrid
und so __: 6 weiter
__ und Tabu: 5 Totem
__ und Träume: 5 Nacht
undue: 5 stiff 6 unfair, unjust 7 extreme, too much 8 improper, needless, overmuch, unseemly, untimely 9 exceeding, excessive, overblown, unfitting 10 exorbitant, gratuitous, immoderate, inordinate, undeserved
undulate: 4 beat, curl, roll, sway, wave 5 slink, surge, swell, swing, twine 6 billow, ripple 7 slither
undulating: 4 wavy 6 zigzag 7 sinuous
undulation: 4 beat, wave 5 swell 6 billow 9 arabesque 10 earthquake
unduly: 3 too 4 over, very 6 overly 8 overmuch, to a fault, unfairly, unjustly 9 extremely 10 improperly
undusted: 5 dirty 6 filthy
__ und Verklärung: 3 Tod
undying: 7 abiding, endless, eternal, lasting, unended 8 constant, enduring, immortal, infinite, timeless, unending, unfading 9 ceaseless, incessant, perennial, permanent, perpetual, unceasing 10 continuing, persistent
uneager: 3 shy 4 loth 5 loath 6 afraid, averse 8 hesitant 9 reluctant 10 indisposed, uninclined
unearned __: 3 run 6 income
unearth: 3 dig, get, see 4 find, grub, root 5 delve, dig up, learn, trace 6 dredge, exhume, expose, locate, reveal, strike, turn up, unbury 7 find out, root out, rout out, uncover 8 discover, disinter, dredge up, excavate 9 ascertain, determine, ferret out, stumble on, track down
unearthing: 9 detection, discovery 10 excavation
unearthly: 4 eery 5 eerie, scary, weird 6 absurd, divine, fantom, occult, spooky, unholy 7 ghastly, ghostly, haunted, phantom, uncanny, ungodly 8 ethereal, ghoulish, spectral 9 spiritual 10 immaterial, ridiculous, sepulchral, superhuman
unease: 4 fear 5 alarm, angst, dread, panic, qualm 6 dismay, fright, horror, phobia, terror 7 anxiety, concern, malaise, tension 9 misgiving 10 foreboding, infirmness, solicitude
uneasiness: 4 care 5 angst, qualm, worry 6 nerves, regret 7 fidgets, jitters, malaise, scruple, tension 8 disquiet, hangover 9 tightness 10 discomfort, discontent, impatience
uneasy: 4 edgy 5 antsy, chary, itchy, jumpy, queer, shaky, tense, upset 6 afraid, on edge, pacing, queasy, queazy, shaken 7 alarmed, anxious, awkward, fearful, fidgety, fretful, jittery, keyed up, nervous, restive, uptight, worried 8 agitated, bothered, dismayed, fluttery, fretsome, harassed, insecure, restless, skittish, strained, troubled 9 all nerves, concerned, disturbed, excitable, impatient, in turmoil, perturbed, unsettled 10 disquieted, high-strung, solicitous
feel ~: 4 fret 5 worry 6 jitter, regret
Uneasy Rider (1973 song)
artist: Charlie Daniels
uneaten: 5 scrap 8 leftover 9 remaining, untouched 10 unconsumed
uneconomical: 6 lavish 8 wasteful
uneducated: 6 simple, unread 7 loutish, lowbrow 8 ignorant, untaught 9 benighted, inerudite, unlearned, untutored 10 illiterate, unlettered
uneffusive: 3 shy 4 wary 5 chary, leery, mousy, quiet, timid 6 demure, modest 7 bashful 8 cautious, reserved, reticent, retiring, sheepish 9 diffident, reluctant, withdrawn
unelaborate: 5 plain 6 simple
unelected group: 4 outs 5 junta
unelevated: 3 low 4 flat 5 short 8 knee-high, sea-level
unembellished: 4 bald, bare, real 5 basic, plain, stark 6 barren, common, honest, severe, simple 7 austere, Spartan 8 ordinary 9 bare-bones
unemotional: 3 dry, icy 4 blah, cold, cool, flat 5 aloof, bland, chill, quiet, stoic, stony 6 chilly, frigid, low-key, mellow, placid, remote, sedate, serene, stolid, stoney, wooden 7 amiable, at peace, callous, deadpan, equable, glacial, ice-cold, pacific, relaxed, stoical 8 amicable, composed, laid-back, listless, obdurate, peaceful, reserved, reticent, tranquil 9 apa-

thetic, collected, easy-going, heartless, impassive, nerveless, quiescent, temperate, unfeeling

unemploy: **3** axe, can **4** fire **6** lay off

unemployed: **4** free, idle **5** fired **6** unused **7** jobless, laid off, loafing, resting **8** inactive, leisured, on layoff, workless **9** at liberty, on the dole, out of a job, out of work, unengaged

unemployment: **6** layoff **7** leisure **9** recession

unencouraging word: **3** nah, nay **4** nope

unencumbered: **3** rid **4** free **5** loose

unending: **4** ever, long **6** eterne, steady **7** abiding, abysmal, endless, eternal, lasting, nonstop, undying **8** constant, enduring, immortal, infinite, timeless, unwaning **9** boundless, ceaseless, continual, countless, incessant, limitless, perennial, perpetual, unceasing **10** continuous

unendingly: **4** ever **6** always **7** forever, for good **8** evermore, for keeps **9** eternally **10** at all times, constantly, enduringly

unendurable: **3** bad, sad **4** grim, vile **5** awful, cruel, harsh **6** rotten **7** adverse, beastly, brutish, heinous, hurtful, painful, ruinous **8** criminal, dreadful **9** appalling, atrocious, injurious, miserable, third-rate **10** abominable, detestable, inadequate, pernicious

unenduring: **5** brief, short **7** passing **8** fleeting, flitting **9** ephemeral, momentary, temporary, transient **10** evanescent, transitory

unenergetic: **4** beat, lazy, limp **5** all in, spent, tired, weary **6** done in, drowsy, pooped, sleepy **7** drained, worn out **8** careworn, dog-tired, drooping, fatigued, flagging **9** burned out, exhausted, played out, pooped out, prostrate **10** half-asleep

unengaged: **4** free **7** resting **8** on layoff **9** at liberty, on the dole, out of a job, out of work **10** unemployed

unenlightened: **3** raw **4** dark, naif **5** naive **7** out of it, unaware **8** ignorant, medieval **9** in the dark, mediaeval

unentertaining: **4** arid, blah, drab, dull, flat, limp, tame **5** bland, inane, prosy, trite, vapid **6** boring, jejune **7** humdrum, insipid, tedious **8** tiresome, zestless **9** colorless **10** dullsville, lackluster

unenthusiastic: **4** cold, cool **5** aloof, blasé, stoic, tepid, token **7** languid, stoical **8** lukewarm, negative **9** apathetic, reluctant, unwilling

unequal: **3** odd **5** other **6** spotty, uneven, unlike **7** distant, diverse, unalike, varying **8** lopsided, one-sided **9** different, differing, disparate, divergent, irregular, unmatched **10** dissimilar, ill-matched, mismatched, off-balance, poles apart, unbalanced

unequaled: **4** A-one, best, only, sole, tops **5** alone **6** unique **7** in front, supreme **8** peerless, towering, ultimate **9** matchless, nonpareil, paramount, unmatched, unrivaled **10** inimitable, preeminent, surpassing, unrivalled

unequipped: **5** unfit **6** unable **8** helpless **9** incapable, powerless, unskilled **10** inadequate, ineligible, unskillful, unsuitable

unequivocal: **4** sure **5** clear, exact, plain **6** direct, patent **7** certain, decided, evident, flat-out, obvious, precise **8** absolute, apparent, clear-cut, decisive, definite, distinct, dogmatic, emphatic, explicit, knowable, manifest, outright, palpable, positive, readable, specific, straight **9** downright, out-and-out, outspoken, trenchant **10** dogmatical, foursquare, peremptory, point-blank

response: **2** no **3** nah, naw, nay, nix, non **4** nein, nope, nyet, uh-uh **5** ixnay, never, no how, no way **6** no deal, nowise **7** not ever **8** at no time, forget it, negative, not at all **9** by no means, fat chance **10** count me out, impossible, not a chance, thumbs down

unequivocally: **5** fully **6** easily, surely, wholly **8** for keeps **10** point-blank

unequivocating: **4** open **5** bluff, blunt, frank, plain, vocal **6** candid, direct, honest **7** artless, genuine, sincere, up-front **8** straight, truthful **9** guileless, ingenuous, outspoken, veracious **10** aboveboard, forthright, foursquare, free-spoken, from the hip, point-blank

unerring: **4** sure, true **5** exact, right, valid **7** certain, correct, factual, literal, perfect, precise **8** accurate, dogmatic, fail-safe, flawless, reliable **9** errorless, faultless, foolproof, unfailing **10** dogmatical, impeccable, infallible, undisputed, undoubtful

unerringly: **5** truly **7** exactly **9** literally, precisely **10** faithfully

unescorted: **4** lone, solo, stag **5** alone

unessential: **5** extra, small **6** slight **8** needless **9** redundant **10** gratuitous

unethical: **3** bad, low **5** dirty, fishy, shady, sharp, slick, wrong **6** sneaky, unfair, wicked **7** corrupt, crooked, illegal, immoral, knavish **8** cheating, flimflam, improper, slippery, two-faced, wrongful **9** dishonest, mercenary, two-timing, underhand **10** fly-by-night

one: **5** knave, louse, rogue, scamp, sneak, swine **9** miscreant

uneven: **3** odd **4** alop **5** bumpy, erose, hilly, jerky, lumpy, ridgy, rough **6** broken, craggy, fickle, fitful, hackly, jagged, jiggly, jouncy, knobby, patchy, ragged, rugged, spotty, unfair, wabbly, wobbly **7** cragged, erratic, knurled, mutable, notched, scraggy, serrate, unequal, unlevel **8** lopsided, one-sided, unsmooth, unsteady, variable **9** differing, disparate, irregular, mercurial, spasmodic, unaligned **10** capricious, changeable, ill-matched, inconstant, off-balance, unbalanced

unevenness: **9** disparity, imbalance **10** coarseness, inequality, unjustness

uneventful: **4** blah, dull, slow **5** quiet **6** boring, dreary, normal, smooth **7** humdrum, prosaic, regular, routine, tedious **8** ordinary, standard **9** prosaical

unevolved: **4** wild **5** crude, early **7** ancient **8** primeval **9** primitive, vestigial **10** aboriginal, primordial

unexacting: **3** lax **4** easy, kind, mild, snap, soft **5** cinch, cushy, light, loose **6** breeze, gentle, kindly, picnic, simple **7** clement, ruthful, sparing **8** duck soup, flexible, laid-back, merciful, painless, placable, pushover, tolerant, untaxing **9** assuasive, compliant, easygoing, forgiving, indulgent **10** child's play, effortless, forbearing, permissive

unexaggerated: **4** real, true **5** sober **6** actual, candid **7** literal

unexampled: **4** lone, rare **6** unique **8** peerless, singular **9** matchless, nonpareil, unmatched **10** inimitable, one-of-a-kind, sui generis

unexcelled: **4** A-one, tops **5** alone

unexceptional: **4** so-so **5** typic, usual **6** common, decent, modest **7** average, regular, routine, typical **8** adequate, everyday, familiar, mediocre, middling, moderate, ordinary, standard

unexcessive: **2** OK **3** low **4** mild, sane **5** cheap, sober **6** modest **7** average, low-cost **8** moderate, sensible **9** excusable, low-priced, realistic, temperate, tolerable **10** acceptable, controlled, economical, reasonable, restrained

unexcitable: **4** even **5** quiet, stoic **6** serene, stolid **7** equable, ice-cold

unexcited: **4** calm, cool, even **5** blasé, quiet, sober, staid, stoic **6** at ease, low-key, mellow, placid, sedate, serene, stolid **7** amiable, at peace, equable, pacific, relaxed, stoical **8** amicable, carefree, composed, laid-back, peaceful, tranquil **9** collected, easy-going, impassive, quiescent, temperate, unstirred **10** nonchalant, phlegmatic, unaffected, unagitated

unexciting: **4** blah, dull, flat, tame **5** bland, ho-hum **6** stodgy **7** tedious

work: **5** McJob

unexclusive: **4** open **6** public **8** exoteric

unexpansive: **3** shy **4** meek **5** quiet, timid **6** demure, modest **7** bashful **8** reserved, reticent, retiring **9** diffident, shrinking, withdrawn **10** restrained, unassuming

unexpected: **3** odd **5** fluky, swift **6** abrupt, casual, chance, flukey, ironic, sudden **7** amazing, unusual **8** abnormal, surprise **9** haphazard, impetuous, impulsive, startling, unplanned **10** accidental, contingent

benefit: **5** bonus, gravy, treat

development: **4** snag **5** twist **7** wrinkle

movement: **3** jab **4** dash, dive, jump, leap, poke **5** bound, burst, lunge, lurch, pitch, surge, swing, swipe **6** charge, plunge, pounce, spring, strike, thrust

unexpectedly: **5** short **8** suddenly, unawares

unexplainable: **4** eery **5** eerie, weird

unexplained: **3** odd **4** dark **5** alien **6** hidden, occult, secret **7** obscure, strange, unknown **10** mysterious

sighting: **3** UFO

unexplicit: **4** hazy **5** fuzzy, muzzy, vague **7** evasive, muddled, oblique, unclear **9** ambiguous, equivocal **10** ambivalent, clear as mud, indefinite, left-handed, misleading

unexplored: **5** novel **7** foreign, strange, unknown

unexposed: **6** buried, hidden, latent, masked, unseen, veiled **7** cloaked, covered **8** screened, secluded, shrouded **9** concealed, incognito, out of view **10** tucked away, undercover, under wraps, undetected, unrevealed

unexpressed: **4** mute **5** quiet, tacit **6** latent, silent, unsaid, untold **7** implied **8** implicit, ulterior

unexpressive: **4** cold **5** blank **7** deadpan **8** taciturn

unexpurgated: **3** all **4** full **5** total, uncut, whole **6** entire, intact **7** plenary **8** complete, finished, thorough **9** inviolate **10** definitive, exhaustive, unabridged

unextinguished: **4** live **7** burning

unextreme: **6** normal **9** temperate **10** reasonable, unagitated

unfaceted gem: **4** opal **5** pearl

unfacile: **5** inapt

unfaded: **3** new **5** fresh **6** bright **8** unwilted

unfading: **7** eternal, undying **9** deathless, permanent **10** unchanging

unfailing: **4** same, sure, true **5** loyal, solid **6** trusty **7** certain, endless, eternal, staunch **8** absolute, constant, diligent, faithful, reliable, straight, surefire, unerring, untiring, unwaning **9** assiduous, boundless, ceaseless, continual, counted on, perennial, perpetual, rock-solid, steadfast, unlimited **10** bottomless, consistent, continuous, delivering, dependable, infallible, invariable, persistent, true to type, unchanging, undoubtful, unflagging

unfair: **3** low **4** foul, mean **5** cruel, dirty, petty, undue, wrong **6** biased, rigged, uneven, unjust **7** bigoted, crooked, immoral, partial **8** cheating, criminal, grievous, improper, one-sided, partisan, unlawful, wrongful **9** arbitrary, dishonest, underhand, unethical **10** ill-matched, prejudiced, ungrounded, unsporting

accusation: **6** bad rap **9** cheap shot

be ~ to: **5** wrong **8** misjudge

judgment: **5** frame

unfairly: **5** badly **10** improperly

unfairness: **4** bias **6** racism **7** bigotry **8** inequity, nepotism **9** injustice, prejudice **10** favoritism, inequality
unfaithful: **5** false **6** fickle, shifty, untrue **7** corrupt, unloyal **8** cheating, disloyal, forsworn, recreant, sneaking, two-faced **9** deceitful, insincere, two-timing
Unfaithful (2002 film)
cast: Richard Gere, Diane Lane
director: Adrian Lyne
unfaked: **4** true **6** candid, honest
unfaltering: **3** set **4** firm, sure **5** bound **6** bent on, steady **7** abiding, decided, nonstop **8** enduring, resolute, sedulous, tireless, untiring **9** dead set on, steadfast, tenacious, undaunted, unfailing
unfalteringly: **4** hard
unfamed: **6** no-name, unsung **7** obscure, unknown **8** nameless, ordinary **9** anonymous, unheard-of
unfamiliar: **3** new, odd **5** alien, novel, weird **6** exotic, remote **7** bizarre, curious, foreign, obscure, strange, unalike, unaware, unknown, unusual **8** ignorant, original, peculiar, uncommon, unversed **9** anomalous, different, fantastic, recondite, unheard-of, unknowing, unskilled, unwitting
with: **5** new at, new to
unfar: **4** near, nigh **5** handy **6** at hand **7** close by **8** adjacent **9** alongside, proximate
unfarmed: **6** fallow
unfashionable: **3** old, out **5** dated, dowdy, not in, passé **6** frumpy, old-hat **7** archaic **8** obsolete, outdated, outmoded **9** out-of-date **10** antiquated, out of style
one: **4** geek, nerd, wonk **7** egghead
unfasten: **4** open, undo **5** loose, untie, unzip **6** detach, loosen **7** release, tear off **9** disengage
unfastened: **4** open **5** loose **6** untied
become ~: **5** loose **6** loosen
unfastidious: **5** messy **6** untidy **7** unkempt **8** slovenly
unfathomable: **4** deep, vast **6** arcane, opaque **7** abysmal, complex, eternal, obscure **8** abstruse, baffling, esoteric, profound, puzzling **9** boundless, enigmatic, limitless, soundless, unlimited, unplumbed **10** bottomless
unfavorable: **3** bad, ill **4** poor **5** risky **7** adverse, hostile, ominous, unlucky **8** contrary, inimical, negative, sinister, untimely, untoward **10** detractive, lamentable, thumbs-down
more ~: **5** worse
review: **3** pan
unfavorably: **3** ill
unfavored: **5** curst **6** cursed, jinxed **7** accurst, hapless **8** ill-fated, luckless **10** ill-starred
unfazed: **4** calm, cool, even **6** serene
unfearful: **4** bold, game **5** brave, gutsy, nervy **6** awless, daring, gritty, heroic, plucky, spunky **7** aweless, defiant, doughty, gallant, staunch, valiant **8** heroical, intrepid, resolute, stalwart, valorous **9** audacious, dauntless, dreadless **10** courageous
unfearing: **4** bold, game **5** brave, stout **6** awless, daring, heroic, plucky **7** aweless, doughty, gallant, valiant **8** heroical, intrepid, resolute, spirited, stalwart, unafraid, valorous **9** audacious, confident, dauntless, undaunted **10** courageous, invincible, mettlesome, undismayed
unfeasible: **3** out **4** airy **6** absurd **7** utopian **8** hopeless, quixotic **9** grandiose, ludicrous, visionary **10** idealistic, impossible, unworkable
unfed: **5** empty **6** hungry **7** peckish, starved **8** edacious, esurient, famished, ravenous, starving **9** voracious
unfeeling: **3** icy **4** cold, hard, numb **5** crass, cruel, harsh, rough, stern, stony **6** brutal, severe, stoney, unkind **7** callous, ice-cold, inhuman **8** benumbed, churlish, deadened, exacting, hardened, indurate, obdurate, pitiless, ruthless, tactless, uncaring **9** apathetic, bloodless, heartless, impassive, inanimate, inclement, insensate, merciless, senseless, unpitying **10** insensible, mechanical, nonchalant, regardless, unmerciful
unfeigned: **4** real, true **5** frank **6** candid, hearty, honest, infelt, square **7** earnest, genuine, natural, sincere **8** truthful **9** childlike, heartfelt
unfermented juice: **4** must
unfertile: **3** dry **4** arid, poor, sere
unfetter: **4** free **5** let go, loose **6** redeem **7** manumit, release
unfettered: **4** free, wild **5** loose **6** single, untied **9** unlimited
unfilled: **4** open **5** blank, empty **6** hollow, hungry, vacant **7** untaken
unfilleted: **4** bony **5** boney
unfinished: **3** cut, raw **5** crude, rough **6** ragged **7** lacking, ongoing, partial, reduced, sketchy **8** abridged, cut short, formless, half-done, immature **9** condensed, curtailed, deficient, half-baked, imperfect, roughhewn, shortened, tentative, undecided **10** diminished, expurgated, incomplete
room: **4** loft **5** attic **6** garret **8** basement
work: **7** backlog
Unfinished Business (1984 film)
director: Don Owen
Unfinished Life, An (2005 film)
cast: Morgan Freeman, Jennifer Lopez
Unfinished Life, AN (2005 film)
cast: Robert Redford
Unfinished Symphony
composer: Franz Schubert
unfirm: **5** shaky **6** flimsy, wobbly **7** dubious, rickety, tenuous **8** doubtful, insecure, unstable **9** jellylike, quivering, teetering, tentative, tottering **10** indecisive, jerry-built, precarious, ramshackle, tumbledown
unfit: **4** weak **5** inapt, inept, unapt **6** feeble, flabby, unable **7** amateur, laid low, not up to, untoned **8** below par, decrepit, improper, inexpert, unsuited, unworthy **9** ill-suited, incapable, sedentary, unhealthy, unskilled **10** inadequate, inapposite, ineligible, nongermane, out of place, out of shape, unequipped, unprepared, unskillful, unsuitable
be ~ for: **10** disqualify
for consumption: **4** rank **5** moldy **6** rancid, rotten **8** inedible
for farming: **3** dry **4** arid, sere **5** dusty **6** barren, desert, torrid **7** bone-dry, parched **9** waterless
make ~: **4** lame, maim, ruin **5** lay up, wreck **6** injure **8** sabotage **9** hamstring
unfitness: **9** inability **10** disability, inadequacy
unfitting: **5** inapt, undue **8** improper **9** incorrect **10** unbecoming
unfix: **5** loose **6** detach, loosen **8** separate
unfixable: **5** kaput **9** incurable **10** inveterate, remediless
unfixed: **4** as is **8** floating, variable **9** uncertain **10** indefinite
unflagging: **4** firm **5** fixed, hardy **6** active, dogged, gritty, plucky, spunky, steady **7** dynamic, patient, scrappy, staunch **8** constant, diligent, resolute, sedulous, tireless, untiring, unwaning **9** assiduous, continual, deathless, energetic, laborious, steadfast, tenacious, unceasing, undivided, unfailing, unwearied **10** determined, persistent, relentless, undeterred, unwearying
unflappable: **3** set **4** calm, cool, easy **5** quiet, stoic **6** low-key, mellow, placid, sedate, serene **7** amiable, assured, at peace, equable, pacific, relaxed, stoical **8** amicable, composed, laid-back, peaceful, tranquil **9** collected, easy-going, impassive, quiescent, temperate, unruffled
unflattering: **4** mean **5** ideal, snide **6** unkind **7** hurtful, perfect **8** scornful, sneering, spiteful
unflawed: **5** sound **8** absolute **10** impeccable
unfledged: **4** naif **5** naive, young **7** puerile **8** juvenile **9** premature
hawk: **4** eyas
unflinching: **4** firm, game **5** brave, fixed, gutsy, stoic **6** dogged, gritty, plucky **7** staunch **8** fearless, intrepid, resolute, stalwart, untiring **9** dauntless, obstinate, steadfast, tenacious, undaunted **10** foursquare, relentless
unfluctuating: **4** even, firm **5** level **6** stable, static, steady **7** equable, uniform **8** constant **9** unvarying
unflustered: **4** calm, cool, even **5** stoic **6** serene **10** phlegmatic
unfocused: **4** hazy **5** foggy, fuzzy, muddy, muzzy, vague **6** bleary, blurry, woolly **7** blurred, unclear **10** ill-defined, indistinct
unfold: **3** fan, ope **4** dawn, grow, open, show, undo **5** widen **6** evince, evolve, expand, expose, extend, fan out, loosen, mature, reveal, spread, unbend, uncoil, uncurl, unfurl, unroll, unwind, unwrap **7** blossom, clarify, clear up, develop, display, divulge, dope out, explain, flatten, lay bare, narrate, present, produce, reel out, resolve, stretch, uncover, untwist **8** announce, describe, disclose, discover, manifest, shake out, uncrease **9** bear fruit, elaborate, elucidate, explicate, expound on, make known, spread out **10** illustrate, straighten, stretch out
unfolded: **4** open
unfolding: **6** course **7** ongoing, process **8** progress, showdown **9** evolution, expansion
unforbidden: **4** fine, okay **9** allowable
unforced: **7** natural, willing **8** optional **9** unlabored, voluntary
unforeseeable: **3** odd **5** fluky, lucky **6** chance, flukey, random, sudden **7** aimless, oddball **9** haphazard, hit-or-miss, uncertain, unplanned, unwitting **10** accidental, fortuitous, unexpected, unintended
unforeseen: **5** lucky **6** abrupt, casual, chance, sudden **8** surprise **9** startling **10** accidental, contingent, fortuitous
unforgettable: **8** enduring, haunting **9** memorable, nostalgic, obsessive
Unforgettable (song)
artist: Natalie Cole, Nat King Cole, Dinah Washington
unforgivable: **5** awful **6** odious, unjust **7** heinous, ignoble **8** grievous, horrible, shameful, terrible **9** abhorrent, atrocious **10** deplorable, despicable
Unforgiven (1992 film)
cast: Clint Eastwood, Morgan Freeman, Gene Hackman, Richard Harris
director: Clint Eastwood
unforgiving: **5** stern, stony **6** stoney **8** ruthless, vengeful **9** merciless
unformed: **8** inchoate, nebulous **9** amorphous, shapeless
unforthcoming: **3** mum **6** silent **8** taciturn **9** secretive, withdrawn
unfortunate: **3** bad, ill, sad **5** broke, curst, needy, sorry, woful **6** bad off, cursed, doomed, hard up, ill off, in need, in want, jinxed, tragic, unwise, woeful, wretch **7** accurst, adverse, hapless, pinched, ruinous, unhappy, unlucky **8** accursed, badly off, bankrupt, beggarly, forsaken, hopeless, ill-fated, ill-timed, indigent, luckless, sinister, strapped, stricken, terrible, tragical, troubled, untimely, untoward, wretched **9** destitute, insolvent, moneyless, out of luck, penniless, penurious **10** disastrous, down and out, ill-starred, lamentable, pauperized, straitened
feeling for the ~: **4** pity **6** warmth **7** empathy **8** sympathy **10** compassion, kindliness, tenderness
unfortunately: **8** sad to say **10** sorry to say

Unfortunate Traveller, The
author: Thomas Nashe
unfouled: **4** pure **5** clean **8** unsoiled
unfounded: **4** idle **5** false **6** untrue **7** invalid **8** baseless, mistaken, spurious **9** erroneous, trumped-up **10** bottomless, fabricated, fallacious, gratuitous, groundless
report: **3** lie **4** buzz, dirt, tale, talk, word **5** bruit, rumor **6** canard, earful, gossip, tattle **7** fiction, hearsay, whisper **9** falsehood, grapevine, invention **10** suggestion
unfreeze: **4** melt, thaw **5** deice **6** soften **7** thaw out
unfrequent: **4** rare **6** seldom, spotty **8** far apart, on and off, sporadic, uncommon **9** irregular, scattered, spasmodic **10** occasional, sporadical
unfrequented: **5** quiet **6** lonely, secret **7** private **8** secluded, solitary
unfriendliness: **4** bile **5** chill, spite, venom **6** animus, enmity, grudge, hatred, malice, rancor, spleen **7** ill will **8** acrimony, bad blood **9** animosity, antipathy, harshness, hostility **10** antagonism, resentment
unfriendly: **3** icy, ill **4** cold, cool, sour **5** aloof, chill, crisp, gruff, nasty, surly **6** chilly, unkind **7** against, distant, glacial, hostile, warlike **8** contrary, grudging, inimical, spiteful, vengeful **9** alienated, combative, estranged, jaundiced, malicious **10** antisocial, forbidding, ill-natured, impersonal, insociable, pugnacious, unamicable
one: **3** foe **5** enemy **9** ill-wisher
sound: **3** grr **5** growl, snarl
unfrocking: **7** removal **8** ejection **9** dismissal **10** deposition
unfruitful: **6** meager **7** sterile **9** infertile
unfulfilled: **7** lacking, missing, wanting **8** deprived **10** incomplete
unfun: **4** blah, dull, tame **6** boring, dreary, stodgy, stuffy **7** humdrum, tedious **8** dragging, tiresome **9** wearisome **10** dullsville, lackluster, monotonous, pedestrian
unfurl: **4** open, show **6** spread, unfold **7** display, roll out **9** spread out
unfurled: **4** open
unfurling: **9** expansion
unfurnished: **4** bare **5** empty
unfussy: **5** basic, clean, plain **6** simple **8** informal **9** unadorned
ungainly: **5** gawky, inept, stiff, weedy **6** clumsy, klutzy, oafish, wooden **7** awkward, gawkish, hulking, lumpish, uncouth **8** bumbling, bungling, cloddish, lubberly, unwieldy **9** all thumbs, graceless, lumbering, maladroit, stumbling, unwieldly
ungallant: **4** rude **5** crass, crude, surly **7** boorish, caddish, ill-bred, loutish, uncivil, uncouth **8** impolite, inurbane, tactless **9** insulting, uncourtly **10** indelicate, ungracious, unmannerly
ungenerous: **4** mean, near, sour **5** close, small **6** skimpy, sordid, stingy **7** miserly, selfish **8** ungiving
one: **5** miser
ungenteel
see uncouth
ungentle: **5** rough **8** baseborn
ungentlemanly: **5** rough **7** caddish, ill-bred, lowbred, uncouth **8** inurbane
ungenuine: **4** fake, sham **8** spurious **10** apocryphal **11** counterfeit
Unger, Felix: **7** neatnik
actor: **6** Carney, Lemmon **7** Randall
unginned: **5** seedy
ungiving: **4** mean **5** cheap, close, tight **6** frugal, greedy, stingy **7** chintzy, miserly, selfish, sparing, thrifty **8** churlish, grasping, grudging **9** illiberal, mercenary, pennywise **10** abstemious, avaricious, economical, pinchpenny, skinflinty, ungenerous
one: **5** miser **7** hoarder, Scrooge **8** tightwad **9** skinflint **10** cheapskate, pinchpenny
unglazed clay: **7** biscuit
unglue: **5** break, shake, upset **6** rattle **7** depress, nonplus, unnerve **8** dispirit, psych out, unsettle, unstring **9** discomfit, embarrass **10** demoralize, disconcert, discourage, dishearten
unglued: **4** amok **5** upset **6** addled **7** flipped, frantic, haywire **8** frenetic, frenzied **9** unscrewed **10** disordered, unbalanced
come ~: **4** flip, rage, rail, rant, rave, yell **5** break, go ape, go mad, shout, storm **6** bellow **7** carry on, explode, flare up, give way, go crazy, lash out, run amok, thunder **8** freak out, get angry, harangue **9** come apart, go bananas, raise Cain **10** hit the roof
ungodliness: **3** sin **7** impiety
ungodly: **4** vile **5** awful **6** horrid, unholy, wicked **7** corrupt, impious, profane **8** depraved, dreadful, horrible, shocking, terrible **9** appalling, atrocious, barbarous, frightful, monstrous, unearthly **10** horrendous, irreverent, outrageous, petrifying
ungovernable: **4** wild **6** unruly **7** naughty, rampant, violent, wayward **8** indocile, stubborn **9** obstinate, out of hand
ungoverned: **7** lawless **8** anarchic, headless **9** audacious **10** anarchical
ungraceful: **5** stiff **6** wooden **8** bungling **9** inelegant, maladroit
ungracious: **4** bold, curt, pert, rude **5** blunt, brash, brusk, crude, fresh, gruff, harsh, nervy, rough, sassy, saucy, sharp, short, surly **6** abrupt, brazen, coarse, vulgar **7** bearish, boorish, brusque, forward, loutish, selfish, uncouth **8** churlish, heedless, impolite, impudent, insolent, inurbane, petulant, tactless **9** thankless, ungallant **10** unthinking
be ~: **5** foist **6** demand, impose, insist, meddle **7** intrude, obtrude, presume **9** incommode
ungrateful: **6** klutzy **7** selfish **9** forgetful, thankless
ungroomed: **5** mangy, messy, mussy, rough, seedy **6** ragged, shabby, shoddy, unneat, untidy **7** scruffy, unkempt **8** slovenly, tattered **10** bedraggled, threadbare
ungrounded: **4** wide **5** false, wrong **6** afield, all wet, unfair, unjust, untrue **7** in error, invalid, unsound **8** mistaken, specious **9** erroneous, incorrect **10** fallacious, groundless, ill-advised, inaccurate, mendacious, misleading
ungrudging: **6** giving **7** liberal **8** generous **9** unselfish **10** free-handed, munificent, unstinting
ungrudgingly: **6** freely, gladly, warmly **7** happily, readily **8** cheerily, heartily, joyfully, joyously **9** naturally, willingly **10** cheerfully
ungual: **4** claw **5** talon **6** unguis **7** toenail **10** fingernail
unguarded: **4** naif, open, rash, weak **5** frank, naive **6** candid, unwary, unwise **7** artless, exposed, offhand, sincere, up-front **8** careless, heedless, unartful **9** guileless, impolitic, imprudent, impulsive, ingenuous **10** accessible, incautious, indiscreet, undefended, unthinking, unvigilant, unwatchful, vulnerable
unguent: **4** balm **5** cream, salve **6** hot oil, lotion **8** lenitive, liniment, ointment **9** emollient
apply ~: **3** oil **5** bless **6** anoint, ordain **8** sanctify **9** lubricate **10** consecrate
unguided: **7** aimless **8** headless **10** leaderless, rudderless, undirected
unguis: **4** claw, hoof, nail **5** talon **7** toenail **10** fingernail
ungulate: **5** rhino, tapir **6** hoofed
UNH
locale: **6** Durham
unhackneyed: **3** new **5** fresh, novel **7** offbeat **8** brand-new, creative, original **10** avant-garde, innovative
unhallowed: **8** diabolic, temporal **10** diabolical, irreverent
unhampered: **4** free **5** clear
unhand: **4** free **5** let go, loose **6** acquit **7** release, set free **8** liberate **9** surrender
unhandled: **3** new
unhandy: **5** bulky, inapt, inept **6** clumsy **7** unadept **8** inexpert **9** maladroit **10** cumbersome
unhappily: **4** alas **8** sad to say **10** sorry to say
unhappiness: **3** woe **4** care **5** blues, gloom, grief **6** misery, sorrow **7** sadness, tragedy **8** distress
exclamation of ~: **4** alas **5** alack **8** lackaday
unhappy: **3** low **4** hurt, sour **5** curst, teary **6** booing, cursed, gloomy, in pain, tragic **7** griping, hurting, letdown, pouting, unlucky **8** bleeding, dejected, grieving, ill-fated, luckless, mournful, saddened, scowling, tragical, untoward **9** afflicted, aggrieved, disgusted, long-faced **10** ill-starred, in the dumps, out of joint, unpleasant
see also gloomy
unhardened: **4** easy, kind, mild, soft **5** sweet **6** gentle, kindly, mellow, tender **7** lenient, pliable **8** flexible, moderate, tolerant, yielding **9** easygoing, indulgent, sensitive **10** permissive
unharmed: **4** safe **5** sound, whole **6** intact, secure **7** perfect **8** unmarked **9** inviolate, unscathed, untouched
unharmonious: **5** noisy **7** raucous
unhasty: **4** poky, slow **9** leisurely
unhat: **4** doff
unhatched fish: **3** egg, roe
unhazardous: **4** safe **6** secure **8** harmless, riskless
UNHCR predecessor: **3** IRO
unhealthful: **3** bad **5** toxic **7** noisome, unclean **9** unhealthy
atmosphere: **4** smog **9** pollution
unhealthiness: **7** illness, malaise **8** debility, sickness **9** infirmity **10** feebleness
unhealthy: **3** bad, ill **4** sick, weak **5** frail, pasty, risky, unfit **6** ailing, feeble, infirm, nocent, peaked, rancid, rotten, sallow, sickly, unwell **7** baneful, harmful, invalid, laid low, noisome, noxious, parlous, unsound **8** below par, delicate, negative, perilous, perverse, virulent **9** dangerous, degrading, hazardous, injurious, nefarious, poisonous **10** corruptive, germridden, jeopardous, out of shape, unsanitary
unheard: **3** mum **4** mute **6** silent
unheard-of: **3** new, odd **4** rare **5** alien, novel **6** unique, unsung **7** obscure, offbeat, strange, uncanny, unfamed, unknown, unusual **8** nameless, shocking, singular, uncommon, unlikely **9** different, wonderful **10** outlandish, phenomenal, unfamiliar, unrenowned
unhearing: **4** deaf, rash **8** heedless, reckless **10** regardless
unheavy: **4** easy **5** light **8** untaxing
unheedful: **3** lax **4** deaf **5** loose, slack **7** cursory, offhand **8** careless, mindless, reckless, slapdash, slipshod **9** forgetful, negligent **10** behindhand, headstrong, neglectful, nonchalant, unthinking
unhelped: **4** solo **5** alone
unhelpful: **7** of no use
unhesitating: **4** firm **6** all-out, prompt **7** assured, decided **8** emphatic, forceful, hellbent, resolute **10** conclusive
unhesitatingly: **6** openly **7** readily **8** promptly **10** forcefully
unhidden: **4** open **5** clear, overt, plain **6** in view, patent, public **7** exposed, obvious, visible **8** apparent, clear-cut, explicit, knowable, manifest **10** observable
unhindered: **3** rid **4** free, open, safe **5** clear **7** set free
unhinge: **5** addle, freak, upset **6** flurry, madden, sicken **7** agitate, confuse, derange, fluster, unnerve **8** confound, disquiet, frighten, unsettle **9** dislocate **10** discompose

unhip: **5** geeky, nerdy **6** square, uncool **7** out of it
one: **4** geek, nerd **5** dweeb
unhitch: **5** loose **6** detach, loosen
unholy: **4** base, evil, vile **5** awful **6** guilty, wicked **7** corrupt, heinous, immoral, impious, profane, ungodly **8** blameful, culpable, depraved, dreadful, shocking **9** appalling, barbarous, dishonest, unearthly, unnatural **10** horrendous, iniquitous, irreverent, outrageous, virtueless
mess: **5** havoc **7** debacle **8** collapse, disaster **9** cataclysm
Unholy Loves
author: Joyce Carol Oates
unhook: **5** loose **6** loosen **8** liberate
unhooked: **5** loose
unhopeful: **6** gloomy **8** dejected, downbeat, negative **9** cheerless, defeatist **10** dispirited
unhorse: **5** throw **6** topple, unseat
unhot: **5** tepid **8** lukewarm
unhumorous: **5** sober, staid **6** solemn, somber **7** deadpan **10** no-nonsense
unh-unh
see nah
unhurried: **4** easy, lazy, poky, slow **6** draggy, otiose, torpid **7** gradual, halting, impeded, lagging, languid **8** crawling, creeping, dawdling, dilatory, dragging, drawn-out, hesitant, plodding, slothful, sluggish, toddling **9** easygoing, leisurely, lethargic, prolonged, slow-going, snaillike **10** deliberate, protracted
unhurriedly: **6** calmly, lazily, slowly **8** bit by bit, casually **9** by degrees, gradually, languidly, leisurely, piecemeal **10** composedly, inch by inch, indolently, step by step
unhurt: **2** OK **4** okay, safe **5** sound, whole **6** intact **8** unmarked **9** inviolate, unscathed, untouched
unhygienic: **5** dirty **6** filthy **7** unclean
uni-: **3** mon-, one **4** mono-
relative: **3** mon- **4** mono-
Uni-Ball: **3** pen
alternative: **3** Bic **5** Pilot **7** Sharpie **9** PaperMate
unicellular creature: **6** amoeba
unicorn: **5** money **6** animal, equine
feature: **4** horn, mane
unicorn fish: **4** unie
Unicorn, The
author: Iris Murdoch
Unicorn, The (1968 song)
artist: Irish Rovers
unicycle part: **5** pedal, wheel **7** ratchet
unidealistic: **9** pragmatic, realistic
unidentified: **6** secret **7** unknown, unnamed **8** nameless, unmarked **9** anonymous
plane: **5** bogey, bogie
unidentified __ object: **6** flying
unification: **5** union, unity **6** fusion, hookup, merger **7** linkage, melding **8** alliance **9** coalition, synthesis
unified: **3** one **5** as one **6** allied, united **7** grouped **8** cohesive, hooked up **9** unanimous **10** collective, integrated
group: **4** core **5** cadre, force, staff **9** personnel
unified __ theory: **5** field
uniform: **4** even, garb, like, same, suit **5** alike, dress, equal, fixed, habit, khaki, level, paced, plane **6** attire, livery, smooth, stable, static, steady **7** costume, equable, orderly, regalia, regular, similar, stripes **8** balanced, constant, of a piece, selfsame **9** analogous, consonant, identical, olive drab, unvarying **10** consistent, dependable, invariable, monolithic, monotonous, true to type, unchanging
Army ~: **3** ODs **5** drabs **6** khakis
make ~: **4** even, sand **5** level, plane **6** smooth
material: **5** chino, khaki
part: **4** sash **5** braid, medal, shirt, tunic **6** lacing **7** epaulet
(prefix): **3** iso-
WWII lady in ~: **3** WAC **4** WAAC
uniformed group: **4** army, navy, team **7** marines **8** air force
uniformity: **5** order **6** parity **8** likeness, monotony, sameness **9** constancy, fixedness
uniformly: **4** even, such **5** alike **6** evenly **7** equally **9** unvarying **10** the same way
unify: **4** fuse, join, meld **5** blend, marry, merge, unite **6** center, link up **7** combine **8** coalesce, federate **9** commingle, integrate **10** amalgamate, synthesize
unilateral: **6** one-way
Unilever
brand: **4** Ragú
unilluminated: **3** dim **4** dark **5** dusky, mirky, murky **6** gloomy, somber **7** darkish, shadowy, subdued **9** tenebrous
unimaginable: **4** rare **6** unique, untold **8** doubtful, singular, uncommon, unlikely **9** fantastic, ineffable, marvelous, unheard-of
unimaginative: **3** dry **4** arid, dull, flat, tame **5** banal, corny, ho-hum, hokey, passé, prosy, stale, trite, usual, vapid **6** barren, common, jejune, old hat, square, stodgy **7** clichéd, fatuous, humdrum, insipid, prosaic, routine, tedious, vanilla **8** bromidic, lifeless, ordinary, outdated, outmoded, well-worn **9** hackneyed, prosaical **10** dullsville
unimagined: **4** live, real, true **5** right **6** actual, living **7** certain, correct, de facto, genuine, literal, sincere **8** concrete, definite, existent, existing, material, physical, tangible, verified **9** authentic, confirmed, veritable **10** definitive, historical, undeniable, unmistaken
unimpaired: **5** clean, sound, whole **6** intact **7** healthy, perfect **8** unbroken
unimpassioned: **4** calm, cool **5** sober, staid, stoic **6** sedate, severe, somber **7** ascetic, austere, stoical, subdued **8** composed **9** collected, pragmatic **10** controlled, restrained
unimpeachable: **4** sure **7** genuine, upright **8** innocent, spotless **9** guiltless
unimpeded: **4** free, open, wild **5** clear **6** untied
unimportant: **4** idle, mere **5** extra, least, light, minor, petty, small, sorry **6** frothy, humble, little, minute, paltry, slight, yeasty **7** trivial, useless **8** needless, nugatory, optional, picayune, piddling, trifling **9** frivolous, redundant, senseless, valueless, worthless
unimpressed: **4** cold **7** unmoved
unimproved: **4** as is
uninclined: **5** loath **6** averse **7** uneager **8** hesitant **9** reluctant **10** indisposed
unindustrious
see lazy
uninfected: **5** clean **7** sterile **8** sanitary
uninformed: **4** naif **5** naive **7** out of it, unaware **8** ignorant **9** in the dark, unadvised
uninhabited: **4** wild **5** bleak, empty **6** barren, lonely, vacant **8** deserted, desolate, lifeless
uninhibited: **4** bold, free, open **5** frank, loose **6** amoral, candid, earthy **7** natural, relaxed **8** cut loose, informal, uncurbed **9** audacious, expansive, fancy-free, footloose, liberated, unbridled, unchecked
uninhibitedness: **4** élan **5** verve **7** abandon, freedom, license **8** wildness **10** exuberance
uninitiate: **7** amateur, dabbler **9** greenhorn, half-baked, unskilled **10** dilettante, half-cocked, tenderfoot
uninitiated: **4** naif **5** naive **8** ignorant
uninjured: **4** safe **5** sound, whole **6** intact **8** unmarked **9** unscathed, untouched
uninspired: **4** arid, drab, dull, flat, so-so, tame **5** banal, corny, hokey, passé, stale, stock, trite, vapid **6** common, jejune, old hat **7** clichéd, fatuous, humdrum, prosaic, sterile **8** bromidic, everyday, mediocre, ordinary, outdated, outmoded **9** hackneyed, ponderous, prosaical **10** dullsville
uninsulated: **6** chilly, drafty
unintelligent: **4** dull, slow **5** dense, silly, thick **6** obtuse, simple **7** shallow, vacuous, witless **8** mindless **9** brainless, dim-witted, senseless **10** dull-witted
one: **3** ass **4** clod, dolt **5** ninny **7** dullard
unintelligible: **6** opaque **7** garbled, jumbled, muddled, slurred, unclear **9** illegible, uncertain **10** incoherent
unintended: **6** chance, random **7** aimless **9** haphazard, undevised, unplanned, unwitting **10** accidental, fortuitous
unintentional: **5** fluky **6** casual, chance, flukey, random **7** aimless **9** haphazard, undevised, unplanned, unwitting **10** accidental, fortuitous, unexpected
unintentionally: **8** by chance, unawares
uninterested: **4** cool **5** aloof, blasé, bored, jaded **6** remote **7** distant, languid, offhand **8** detached, listless, lukewarm, negative, unbiased **9** apathetic, impassive, incurious, turned off, withdrawn
uninteresting: **3** dry **4** arid, blah, drab, dull, flat, tame **5** banal, bland, dusty, ho-hum, plain, prosy, stale, tired, trite, vapid **6** boring, common, dismal, dreary, jejune, stodgy **7** humdrum, insipid, prosaic, tedious **8** bromidic, tiresome **9** fatiguing, prosaical, soporific, tasteless, wearisome **10** dullsville
uninterrupted: **5** clean, level, solid **6** direct, smooth, steady **7** endless, nonstop **8** constant, enduring, straight, unbroken, unending **9** ceaseless, continual, incessant, perennial, perpetual, sustained, unceasing
continue ~: **3** yak, yap **4** talk **5** run on **6** rattle **7** maunder
uninterruptedly: **5** on end
uninvited: **7** unasked **8** unbidden, unsought **9** unwelcome **10** gratuitous, unprompted
guest: **6** drop-in **7** crasher
Uninvited (1998 song)
artist: Alanis Morissette
uninviting: **4** icky, ugly **5** gross, yucky **9** repellent, revolting
uninvolved: **6** simple **7** neutral **8** innocent **9** unaligned
union: **3** mix **4** bloc, bond, gild, weld **5** blend, guild, labor, local, match, state **6** accord, fusion, league, merger, nation **7** amalgam, concord, joining, melding, mixture, society, wedding **8** alliance, assembly, compound, congress, junction, juncture, marriage, sodality **9** coalition, composite, employees, matrimony, symbiosis, syndicate, synthesis, unanimity **10** confluence, connection, consortium, federation, fraternity, government, Solidarity
actors' ~: **3** SAG **5** AFTRA
bane: **4** scab
branch: **5** local
combining form: **3** gam- **4** gamo-, -gamy **6** -gamous
Detroit ~: **3** UAW
dockworkers' ~: **3** ILA
educ. ~: **3** AFT, NEA, UFT
form a ~: **3** wed **4** bond, join, yoke **5** marry, merge, unite **7** combine, make one **9** integrate **10** tie the knot
issue: **3** bid **4** call, need, plea **5** claim, order, price **6** appeal, demand **7** inquiry, proviso, request **8** petition **9** provision, ultimatum **10** injunction
largest U.S. ~: **3** NEA
letters: **6** AFL-CIO
levy: **4** dues **7** charges **10** assessment
medieval trade ~: **5** guild
orch. ~: **3** AFM
regulating agcy.: **4** NLRB
supporters: **5** labor **7** hard hat **9** work force **10** blue collar
to Greeks and Cypriots: **6** enosis
trade ~: **5** guild, local, union **8** sodality **9** coalition **10** federation
Western Union ~: **3** ITU

wirers' ~: 4 IBEW
Wobblies' ~: 3 IWW
union __: 3 rep 4 card, jack, shop, suit 5 label, scale
__ union: 5 craft, labor, trade 6 credit
Union: 4 city, town 6 sta. stn. 8 The North
member: 5 state
opp.: 3 CSA
Union __: 3 Day 4 Jack 7 Carbide, Pacific, Station
__ Union: 6 Soviet 7 Western
unionize: 4 ally 5 unite 9 affiliate
Union Jack: 4 flag
holder: 4 mast
Union Label grp.: 5 ILGWU
Union of __ Africa: 5 South
Union of the Snake (1983 song)
artist: Duran Duran
Union Pacific: 8 railroad
terminus: 5 Omaha
Union Pacific (1939 film)
cast: Joel McCrea, Robert Preston, Barbara Stanwyck
director: Cecil B. DeMille
Union Station client: 6 Amtrak
Union-Tribune: 5 paper 9 newspaper
locale: 8 San Diego
unique: 3 new, odd, one 4 best, lone, only, rare, sole, solo 5 alone, novel, primo 6 far-out, single 7 oddball, offbeat, onliest, special, strange, unalike, unusual 8 distinct, isolated, peculiar, peerless, separate, singular, solitary, specific, standout, uncommon 9 anomalous, different, exclusive, matchless, nonpareil, recherché, unequaled, unheard-of, unmatched, unrivaled 10 individual, inimitable, one and only, one-of-a-kind, particular, phenomenal, refreshing, remarkable, sui generis, unexampled, unrivalled
in Latin: 10 sui generis
thing: 4 oner
uniquely: 4 only 9 specially 10 especially
uniqueness: 7 novelty 8 identity 9 freshness 11 originality
unisex garb: 5 jeans, pants 6 slacks, T-shirt 8 trousers
Unisom: 8 sleep aid
alternative: 5 Nytol 6 Compoz 7 Sominex
unison: 6 accord 7 concert, concord, harmony 8 sameness 9 agreement
be in ~: 4 sync 5 agree 9 harmonize
in ~: 5 as one 6 at once, in sync 7 en masse 8 as a group, combined, together 9 all at once, in concert, unanimous 10 conjointly
speak in ~: 6 chorus
Unisys
competitor: 3 IBM
unit: 3 arm, one 4 gram, item, limb, link, part, team, wing 5 block, bunch, corps, digit, group, party, piece, pound, squad, troop, whole 6 degree, detail, entity, league, length, member, module, outfit, sample, square, system 7 article, brigade, chapter, element, integer, platoon, portion, section, segment 8 assembly, division, fraction, molecule, specimen, squadron, work crew 9 apartment, appliance, battalion, component 10 assemblage, complement, department, detachment, stand-alone
combining form: 4 -plex
unit __: 4 rule
__ unit: 4 wall 6 mobile
unitary: 6 single
Unitas, Johnny: 2 QB
sport: 8 football
unit-cost word: 3 per 4 each 6 apiece
unite: 3 mix, tie, wed 4 ally, band, bond, fuse, join, knit, knot, link, lock, meet, pool, weld, yoke 5 blend, focus, marry, merge, money, rally, stick, unify 6 adjoin, attach, cement, cleave, club up, cohere, concur, couple, embody, gather, hook up, imbody, league, link up, mingle, pair up, relate, splice, team up 7 combine, conjoin, connect, hitch on, match up, partner 8 assemble, coalesce, converge, solidify, unionize 9 affiliate, associate, commingle, cooperate, integrate, interlink 10 amalgamate, close ranks, go partners, hook up with, intertwine, join forces, synthesize
united: 3 one 4 mixt 5 as one, at one, joint, mixed, solid 6 agreed, allied, banded, joined, linked, pooled, tied in 7 federal, unified 8 combined, in accord, in league, joined up 9 assembled, concerted, corporate, in cahoots, of one mind, plugged in, unanimous, undivided 10 affiliated, agreed upon, associated, collective, concordant, integrated, like-minded
be ~: 4 jell, join 5 agree, merge 6 cleave, cohere 7 conform
group: 4 bloc, bund, ring 5 junta, party 6 cartel, clique, league 7 combine, council, entente, faction 8 alliance 9 anschluss, coalition, syndicate 10 federation
(prefix): 3 syn-
united __: 5 front
United: 5 mover 7 airline, van line
alternative: *see* airline, U.S.
former ~ rival: 3 TWA 5 Pan Am, USAir 7 Braniff, Eastern 8 National
rival: 6 Allied
United __: 3 Way 7 Nations
United __ College Fund: 5 Negro
United __ Day: 7 Nations
United __ Emirates: 4 Arab
United __ International: 5 Press
United __ of America: 6 States
United __ of Brazil: 6 States
United __ of Indonesia: 6 States
United __ Republic: 4 Arab
United __ Service: 6 Parcel
United __ States: 4 Arab
United Arab Emirates: 6 nation 7 country
capital: 8 Abu Dhabi
group: 4 OPEC 10 Arab League
honcho: 4 amir, emir, Zaid 5 ameer, emeer, sheik 6 shaikh, sheikh
money: 4 fils 6 dirham
neighbor: 4 Oman
part: 4 Arab 5 Dibai, Dubai 6 United 8 Abu Dhabi, Emirates
United Artists offering: 4 film 5 movie
United Federation of Planets
member: 5 Earth 6 Vulcan
United Kingdom: 6 nation 7 country
capital: 6 London
city: 3 Ayr 4 Bath, Rhyl, Ryde, York 5 Blyth, Crewe, Derby, Dover, Egham, Leeds, Luton, Neath, Newry, Poole, Rugby 6 Antrim, Batley, Bolton, Bootle, Dudley, Dundee, Eccles, Exeter, Havant, Irvine, Jarrow, Kendal, London, Lurgan, Oldham, Ossett, Oxford, Seaham, Slough, Stroud, Widnes, Wishaw, Yeovil 7 Airdrie, Banbury, Belfast, Berwick, Bexhill, Bristol, Burnley, Cannock, Cardiff, Crawley, Falkirk, Glasgow, Ipswich, Lisburn, Margate, Newport, Norwich, Paisley, Reading, Renfrew, Staines, Sunbury, Swansea, Swindon, Telford, Walsall, Watford 8 Aberdeen, Bearsden, Bradford, Brighton, Coventry, Dumfries, Greenock, Hastings, Hereford, Plymouth, Stirling 9 Cambridge, Edinburgh, Leicester, Liverpool, Rotherham, Sheffield, Stockport, Worcester 10 Birmingham, Chelmsford, Colchester, Eastbourne, Gloucester, Manchester, Nottingham, Sunderland 11 Bournemouth
money: 4 quid 5 penny, pound 8 new pence, new penny, shilling 9 sovereign
native: 4 Brit 6 Briton
org.: 4 NATO
see also England, Great Britain
United Nations
see UN
United States: 6 nation 7 country
money: 4 cent, dime 5 eagle, penny 6 dollar, nickel 7 quarter
neighbor: 6 Canada, Mexico
org.: 3 OAS 4 NATO
see also U.S.
United States of __: 6 Brazil 7 America
United Way request: 4 give
unit investment __: 5 trust
unit of __: 7 measure
units, __, hundreds: 4 tens
unity: 5 amity, peace, whole 6 accord, esprit, fusion 7 concord, harmony, oneness, rapport 8 alliance, good will, sameness, sympathy, totality 9 agreement, coherence, communion, consensus, integrity, synthesis, unanimity, wholeness 10 congruence, consonance, friendship, singleness, solidarity
Unity of India, The
author: Jawaharlal Nehru
__ Unit Zappa: 4 Moon
univ.: 3 sch. 4 coll., inst.
degree: 3 BLS, LHD, LL.B. 4 B.Lit.
discourse: 4 lect.
employee: 2 TA 4 prof. 5 instr.
grant source: 3 NSF
hotshot: 4 BMOC
major: 3 Eng., lit., mus. 4 biol., chem., hist., phys. 6 phys. ed.
offering: 2 BA, BS 3 deg.
requirement: 3 GED
senior's hurdle: 3 GRE 4 GMAT, MCAT
sports org.: 4 NCAA
see also school
see also college, school, university
UNIVAC preceder: 5 Eniac
univalve: 5 shell 8 seashell
universal: 3 big 4 rife, wide 5 broad, total 6 common, cosmic, entire, global, public 7 all-over, diffuse, general, natural, stellar 8 accepted, catholic, cosmical, sweeping 9 customary, extensive, pervasive, prevalent, unlimited, worldwide 10 ecumenical, prevailing, ubiquitous, undisputed, widespread
be ~: 4 rule
donor: 5 type O
philosopher's ~: 3 Tao
prefix: 4 omni-
principle: 3 law 5 axiom
wish: 5 amity, order, peace 6 accord 7 harmony 10 friendship
universal __: 5 donor, joint
Universal: 6 studio
competitor: *see* movie studio
creation: 4 film 5 movie
former owner: 3 MCA
workplace: 3 lot 10 soundstage
Universal __ Code: 7 Product
universally acknowledged: 5 given 7 evident, granted, obvious 8 manifest 9 axiomatic 10 understood
universe: 5 world 6 cosmos, nature 8 creation 9 macrocosm 10 everything
be part of the ~: 4 last, live 5 abide, exist 6 endure, remain 7 breathe, subsist, survive 8 continue
Buddhist symbol of the ~: 5 lotus
combining form: 4 cosm-
of the ~: 6 cosmic 8 cosmical
preceder: 5 chaos
Universe, like Mr.: 5 macho, manly
université preceder: 5 lycée 6 lyceum
university: 6 campus, school 7 college 9 alma mater
award: 6 degree 7 diploma, master's 9 doctorate, sheepskin
degree: 2 AB, BA, MA, MS 3 MBA, Ph.D.
feature: 4 dorm, quad 5 court 6 campus 9 courtyard, dormitory
head: 4 prex, prez 5 prexy 9 president
keepsake: 2 yb. 8 yearbook
major: 3 art, bio., eco., Eng., geo., mus. 4 econ., hist., math 5 drama, music 6 phys. ed., speech 7 biology, English, geology, history, physics, theater 9 chemistry, economics, sociology 10 philosophy
offering: 4 term 5 class 6 course 7 program, regimen, seminar

sports org.: 4 NCAA
staffer: 4 dean 6 bursar, docent, lector 8 lecturer 9 professor, registrar 10 instructor
woman: 4 coed
see also college, school
__ university: 4 free 5 state
University __: 4 Wits
__ University: 4 Open
University of Akron athletes: 4 Zips
University of Alabama
athletes: 7 Blazers
locale: 10 Birmingham, Tuscaloosa
University of Arizona
athletes: 8 Wildcats
locale: 6 Tucson
University of Arkansas athletes: 10 Razorbacks
University of California
athletes: 6 Bruins
locale: 8 Berkeley 10 Los Angeles
University of Central Florida
locale: 7 Orlando
University of Cincinnati athletes: 8 Bearcats
University of Colorado
athletes: 9 Buffaloes
locale: 7 Boulder
University of Connecticut
athletes: 7 Huskies
locale: 6 Storrs
University of Delaware
athletes: 8 Blue Hens
locale: 6 Newark
University of Florida athletes: 6 Gators
University of Georgia
athletes: 8 Bulldogs
locale: 6 Athens
University of Hawaii
athletes: 8 Warriors
locale: 8 Honolulu
University of Houston athletes: 7 Cougars
University of Idaho
athletes: 7 Vandals
locale: 6 Moscow
University of Illinois
athletes: 6 Illini
locale: 9 Champaign
University of Iowa athletes: 8 Hawkeyes
University of Kansas
athletes: 8 Jayhawks
locale: 8 Lawrence
University of Kentucky
athletes: 8 Wildcats
locale: 9 Lexington
University of Louisville athletes: 9 Cardinals
University of Maine
athletes: 10 Black Bears
locale: 5 Orono
University of Maryland
athletes: 5 Terps 9 Terrapins
University of Massachusetts
athletes: 9 Minutemen
locale: 7 Amherst
University of Memphis athletes: 6 Tigers
University of Miami athletes: 5 Canes 10 Hurricanes
University of Michigan
athletes: 10 Wolverines
locale: 8 Ann Arbor
University of Mississippi
athletes: 6 Rebels 7 Ole Miss
locale: 6 Oxford
University of Missouri
athletes: 6 Tigers
locale: 8 Columbia
University of Montana
athletes: 9 Grizzlies
locale: 8 Missoula
University of Nebraska
athlete: 6 Husker 10 Cornhusker
locale: 7 Lincoln
University of Nevada
athletes: 6 Rebels 8 Wolf Pack
locale: 4 Reno 8 Las Vegas
University of New Hampshire
athletes: 8 Wildcats
locale: 6 Durham
University of New Mexico athletes: 5 Lobos
University of North Carolina
athletes: 8 Tar Heels
locale: 10 Chapel Hill
University of Oklahoma
athletes: 7 Sooners
locale: 6 Norman
University of Oregon
athletes: 5 Ducks
locale: 6 Eugene
University of Pennsylvania athletes: 7 Quakers
University of Pittsburgh athletes: 8 Panthers
University of Rhode Island
athletes: 4 Rams
locale: 8 Kingston
University of South Carolina
athletes: 9 Gamecocks
locale: 8 Columbia
University of Tennessee
athletes: 4 Vols 10 Volunteers
locale: 9 Knoxville
University of Texas
athletes: 6 Miners 9 Longhorns
locale: 6 Austin, El Paso
University of Toledo athletes: 7 Rockets
University of Utah athletes: 4 Utes
University of Vermont
athletes: 10 Catamounts
locale: 10 Burlington
University of Virginia athletes: 9 Cavaliers
University of Washington
athletes: 7 Huskies
locale: 7 Seattle
University of Wisconsin
athletes: 7 Badgers
locale: 7 Madison
University of Wyoming
athletes: 7 Cowboys
locale: 7 Laramie
University Park school: 3 PSU 9 Penn State
unjaded: 4 naif 5 fresh, naive 8 innocent, wide-eyed 9 ingenuous
unjam: 4 free 6 unclog
unjust: 4 foul, hard 5 undue, wrong 6 biased, shabby, unfair 7 low-down, partial 8 improper, one-sided, partisan, wrongful 9 arbitrary, injurious, underhand, unmerited 10 oppressive, prejudiced, undeserved, ungrounded
criticism: 6 bad rap 9 cheap shot
verdict: 5 frame
unjustified: 5 undue 6 unjust, wanton 8 baseless 10 groundless
unjustness: 9 prejudice 10 inequality, unevenness, unfairness
unkempt: 4 wild 5 crude, dirty, dowdy, messy, mussy, ratty, seamy, seedy 6 blowsy, blowzy, coarse, frowsy, frowzy, frumpy, grubby, grungy, ragged, shabby, shaggy, sloppy, unneat, untidy 7 blowsed, blowzed, rumpled, scruffy, squalid, tousled, unclean 8 mussed up, slipshod, slovenly, uncombed 9 neglected, ungroomed 10 bedraggled, disheveled, disorderly, unpolished
one: 4 slob 5 sight
unkeyed: 6 atonal
unkind: 4 curt, evil, hard, mean 5 catty, cruel, harsh, nasty, snide, stern 6 animal, brutal, fierce, savage, shabby, wanton 7 beastly, callous, hateful, hurtful, inhuman, vicious 8 barbaric, fiendish, inhumane, pitiless, ruthless, sadistic, spiteful, tactless, uncaring, unsubtle, vengeful 9 barbarous, bloodless, cutthroat, ferocious, heartless, inclement, malicious, merciless, monstrous, truculent, unfeeling 10 ill-natured, unfriendly, vindictive
unkindness: 4 fury 5 anger, spite, venom, wrath 6 enmity, hatred, malice, rancor, spleen 7 ill will, sarcasm 8 acerbity, acrimony, asperity, rudeness 9 animosity, antipathy, harshness 10 disservice, irritation, resentment
unknowable: 4 dark, deep, vast 6 arcane, mystic, occult 7 abysmal, obscure 8 esoteric, mystical, oracular, profound 9 recondite, unsounded 10 fathomless, mysterious
unknowing: 4 naif 5 blind, naive 7 out of it, unaware 8 ignorant 9 in the dark, unadvised, unwitting 10 unfamiliar
unknowingly: 8 unawares
unknowledgeable: 3 raw 5 green, naive 6 gauche, simple 8 ignorant, innocent, untaught 9 untrained
unknown: 3 new 4 dark 5 alien, novel 6 exotic, far-off, hidden, humble, occult, remote, secret, unsung, untold 7 distant, faraway, foreign, obscure, strange, unfamed, unnamed, unnoted 8 desolate, nameless, stranger 9 anonymous, concealed, incognito, uncharted, unheard-of 10 indefinite, mysterious, unexplored, unfamiliar, unrevealed
author: 4 anon. 9 anonymous
hitherto ~: 5 fresh 7 offbeat 8 original 9 different 10 innovative, newfangled
legal ~: 3 Doe, Roe
parts ~: 5 about 6 around 9 scattered, somewhere
Unknown Soldier and his Wife, The
author: Peter Ustinov
unlabored: 6 innate, simple 7 natural 8 unforced
unlace: 4 open 5 loose 6 loosen
unlade: 4 dump 6 remove, unload 7 lighten, off-load 9 discharge
unladylike: 7 ill-bred, lowbred 8 inurbane
unlash: 5 loose 6 loosen
unlatch: 3 ope 4 open 5 loose 6 loosen
unlatched: 4 open 5 loose
unlaundered: 5 dirty 6 soiled
unlawful: 4 tabu 5 taboo, wrong 6 banned, unfair 7 bootleg, crooked, illegal, illicit 8 criminal, improper, verboten, wrongful 9 felonious, forbidden, nefarious 10 actionable, disorderly, flagitious, indictable, iniquitous, not allowed, prohibited, unlicensed
act: 4 tort 5 bribe, crime, heist, theft, wrong 6 felony, holdup, murder 7 larceny, misdeed, offense, treason 8 atrocity, burglary, delictum, thievery, trespass 9 violation 10 infraction
Unlawful Entry (1992 film)
cast: Ray Liotta, Kurt Russell, Madeleine Stowe
unleaded: 3 gas 8 gasoline
unlearned: 6 innate, unread 8 ignorant 9 backwater, inerudite 10 illiterate, uneducated, unschooled
unleash: 4 free, vent 5 loose, wreak 6 loosen 7 release 9 force upon
one's anger: 4 rage, rant, rave, yell 5 erupt, freak, storm 6 blow up, rail at, scream 7 bluster, bristle, explode, rampage 8 boil over, have a fit, run amuck 9 blow a fuse, fulminate, go berserk 10 hit the roof, kick up a row
upon: 5 let at
unleashed: 5 loose 6 untied
unleavened bread: 5 matzo 6 matzah, matzoh
unled: 4 free 5 alone 9 on one's own
unless: 3 but 4 nisi, save 6 and yet, except 7 barring
in law: 4 nisi
Unless __ my guess...: 5 I miss
unlessened: 5 whole 6 entire 8 complete
unlet: 6 vacant 7 for rent 9 available
unlettered: 9 untutored 10 illiterate, uneducated, unschooled
unlevel: 5 bumpy, rocky, rough 6 craggy, jagged, ridged, rugged, uneven 7 serrate 8 unsmooth
unlicensed: 7 illegal, illicit 8 unlawful
unlighted: 3 dim 4 dark, ebon, inky 5 black, dusky, mirky, murky 6 dismal, dreary, gloomy 7 shadowy, sunless 8 jetblack 9 tenebrous 10 pitch-black
unlike: 3 new 5 other 6 motley 7 distant, diverse, offbeat, unequal, variant, various 8 clashing, contrary, discrete, distinct, opposite, separate 9 different, disparate, dissonant, divergent, unrelated 10 atypical of, contrasted, discordant, dissimilar, mismatched, poles apart, strange for
be ~: 4 vary 5 range 6 change, depart, differ, modify, mutate 7 deviate, diverge 8 contrast 9 transform
unlikely: 4 rare, slim 5 faint 6 absurd, remote, slight 7 dubious, outside, suspect 8 doubtful 9 unheard-of 10 improbable, incredible, infeasible

unlikeness: **9** disparity, diversity **10** difference, divergence
unlimber: **5** stiff
unlimited: **3** big **4** full, vast **5** clear, great, total **6** all-out, entire, untold **7** endless, full-out, immense, no end of, no end to **8** absolute, complete, infinite, wide open **9** boundless, countless, extensive, full-blown, full-scale, no-strings, sovereign, unbounded, unfailing, universal **10** indefinite, innumerous, numberless, unconfined, unfathomed, unfettered, unnumbered
__ Unlimited Orchestra: **4** Love
unlink: **4** part **5** sever, split **6** cut off, detach, divide **7** disjoin, split up **8** break off, disunite, separate, set apart, uncouple **10** disconnect
unlit: **4** dark **5** black **6** gloomy **9** in the dark, lightless, tenebrous **10** blacked out, pitch black
buoy: **3** nun
unlived in: **5** empty **6** vacant
unlively: **4** dull, flat, tame **6** dreary **7** insipid, prosaic **9** bloodless, colorless **10** dullsville, lackluster, monotonous
unload: **3** rid, tip **4** drop, dump, sell, vend **5** clear, drain, empty, use up **6** divest, peddle, remove, unlade **7** drop off, exhaust, let go of, lighten, pour out, recount, relieve **8** evacuate, get rid of, jettison, unburden **9** discharge, dispose of, liquidate, move goods **10** auction off
unloading: **8** emptying **9** clearance, discharge
unlock: **3** ope **4** open, undo **5** loose, solve **6** decode, loosen
unlocked: **4** open **5** loose
unloose: **4** undo **5** eject **6** rescue **7** release
unloved: **5** hated **7** loathed **8** abhorred, despised, detested, disliked, forsaken **9** unpopular
unlovely: **9** tasteless **10** unpleasant
unloyal: **5** false **6** fickle, untrue **8** cheating, forsworn, two-faced **9** deceitful, faithless, insincere, two-timing **10** capricious, changeable, inconstant, traitorous, unfaithful, unreliable
unlucky: **5** black, curst, sorry **6** cursed, doomed, jinxed **7** hapless, ominous, unhappy **8** ill-fated, luckless, sinister, untimely, untoward **9** ill-omened, out of luck **10** calamitous, disastrous, ill-starred, out of joint
UNLV: **3** sch. **4** coll.
org.: **4** NCAA
part of ~: **3** Las, Nev. **5** Vegas **6** Nevada
unmalleable: **3** set **4** hard **5** rigid, stern **6** flinty, mulish, steely **7** adamant, dead set, diehard **8** hard-line, locked in, obdurate, resolute, stubborn **9** hidebound, immovable, obstinate, pig-headed, steadfast, unbending **10** bull-headed, determined, implacable, inflexible, unamenable, unswerving, unyielding
unman: **8** dispirit, frighten **10** dishearten
unmanageable: **4** wild **5** balky, bulky **6** ornery, unruly **7** defiant, naughty, problem, wayward **8** contrary, obdurate, stubborn, unwieldy **9** difficult, obstinate, out of hand, unwieldly **10** disorderly, rebellious
unmannerly
see rude
unmarked: **4** safe **5** blank, sound, whole **6** intact, unhurt **8** unharmed **9** uninjured, unscarred, unscathed, untouched
unmarred: **4** mint, pure **5** clean, whole **6** virgin **7** perfect **8** flawless, pristine, virginal **9** faultless, inviolate, untouched **10** immaculate
unmarried: **4** sole **5** unwed **6** single **7** widowed **8** bachelor, divorced, eligible, unwedded, wifeless **10** spouseless, unattached
one: **4** maid, miss **6** single **8** bachelor
Unmarried Woman, An (1978 film)
cast: Alan Bates, Jill Clayburgh
director: Paul Mazursky
role: **5** Erica
unmask: **4** bare, leak, show **6** detect, expose, reveal, show up **7** display, divulge, exhibit, lay bare, let slip, uncover **8** disclose, smell out **9** make known **10** make public
unmasking: **6** baring, espial, exposé **8** exposure **9** detection **10** revelation
unmatched: **3** odd **5** alone **6** unique **7** supreme, unequal **8** peerless, ultimate, unpaired **9** nonpareil, unequaled, unrivaled **10** inimitable, unexampled, unrivalled
unmechanized: **6** by hand, manual
unmediated: **5** blunt **6** candid, direct, head-on **7** express **8** outright, straight **9** downright, firsthand **10** face-to-face, forthright, point-blank, to the point
unmeet: **5** bawdy, crass, crude, gross, inapt, rough **6** coarse, common, ribald, risqué, vulgar **7** uncouth **8** improper, indecent, unseemly **10** indecorous, indelicate
unmelodic: **6** atonal **7** raucous
unmemorable: **4** dull, so-so **5** stock, trite, usual **6** common, normal, wonted **7** average, generic, humdrum, insipid, mundane, prosaic, routine, vanilla **8** everyday, familiar, mediocre, middling, ordinary, plebeian, standard, workaday **9** quotidian **10** pedestrian, second-rate, uneventful, uninspired
unmentionable: **4** tabu **5** taboo **8** anathema **9** off-limits
unmentionables: **6** undies **7** drawers **8** lingerie, skivvies **9** underwear
unmerciful: **4** hard **5** cruel, stern, stony **6** brutal, flinty, stoney **7** bestial, hurtful **8** inhumane, pitiless, ruthless, uncaring, vengeful **9** ferocious, heartless, inclement, monstrous, unfeeling, unpitying, unsparing
unmerited: **6** unjust **8** unworthy **10** gratuitous, unasked-for, undeserved
unmetamorphosed animal: **5** larva
unmethodical: **5** messy **6** patchy, random, spotty **7** chaotic, erratic, jumbled, mixed up, muddled **8** anarchic, confused, pell-mell, sporadic **9** cluttered, desultory, haphazard, irregular, piecemeal, scrambled, spasmodic **10** all mixed-up, disorderly, out-of-order, topsy-turvy, upside down
unmeticulous: **6** sloppy **8** slipshod
unmew: **7** release **8** liberate
unmindful: **3** lax **5** blind, hasty **6** remiss, sloppy **7** napping, out of it, unaware **8** careless, derelict, heedless, ignorant, sleeping, slipshod, snoozing **9** forgetful, imprudent, in the dark, negligent, oblivious **10** incautious, neglectful, nonchalant, regardless, unthinking
unmindfulness: **5** sleep **6** apathy, laxity, phlegm, stupor, torpor **7** boredom, languor, neglect **8** dullness, hebetude, lethargy **9** disregard, lassitude, unconcern **10** drowsiness, remissness, sleepiness
unmistakable: **4** sure **5** clear, naked, plain, vivid **6** cogent, patent, simple, strong **7** certain, decided, evident, express, glaring, obvious, visible **8** apparent, definite, distinct, emphatic, explicit, knowable, manifest, palpable, positive, readable **9** graspable, prominent **10** spelled out
unmistakably: **4** just **5** truly **6** indeed, in fact, really, surely, verily **7** de facto, exactly, for real, in truth, utterly **8** for a fact **9** assuredly, certainly, genuinely, in reality, precisely **10** absolutely, admittedly, definitely, positively
unmistaken: **2** OK, so **4** okay, okeh, okey, true **5** exact, right, sound **6** actual, dead-on **7** correct, factual, precise **8** accurate, official, on target **9** on the beam, veracious **10** unimagined
unmitigated: **4** pure, rank **5** sheer, stark, total, utter, whole **6** arrant, simple **7** blatant, chronic, perfect **8** absolute, clear-cut, complete, outright, positive **9** chronical, downright, out-and-out
unmitigated __: **4** gall
unmix: **4** cull, sift **6** filter, screen, strain **8** separate
unmixed: **4** neat, pure **5** sheer, solid **6** simple, single, strong **8** straight
unmoist: **3** dry **4** arid
unmoored: **6** adrift **8** castaway **10** unanchored
unmotivated: **4** idle, lazy **5** bored **6** otiose **8** indolent **9** apathetic, shiftless
unmovable: **5** fixed **9** steadfast **10** inexorable, motionless, unyielding
unmoved: **4** cool **5** blasé, quiet, stoic **6** in situ, low-key, mellow, placid, sedate, serene **7** amiable, at peace, equable, pacific, relaxed, stoical **8** amicable, composed, laid-back, peaceful, tranquil **9** apathetic, collected, easy-going, impassive, quiescent, temperate, unstirred, untouched **10** motionless, spiritless, unaffected
remain ~: **5** sit by
unmoving: **4** firm **5** inert, still **6** at rest, halted, static **8** stagnant **9** quiescent **10** motionless, stationary, stock-still
unmusical: **5** harsh **6** off-key, shrill **7** grating, jarring, raucous **8** jangling, strident **9** dissonant, out of tune **10** cacophonic, discordant, inharmonic
Unnamable, The
author: Samuel Beckett
unnatural: **3** odd **4** eery **5** false, phony, put-on, queer, stagy, stiff, weird **6** atypic, ersatz, forced, freaky, la-de-da, la-di-da, made-up, morbid, off-key, phoney, pseudo, staged, stagey, unholy **7** assumed, bizarre, feigned, labored, mincing, stilted, strange, studied, uncanny, unusual **8** aberrant, abnormal, affected, atypical, freakish, lah-di-dah, mannered, perverse, strained **9** anomalous, contrived, divergent, eccentric, grotesque, imitation, insincere, irregular, monstrous, synthetic **10** artificial, fabricated, factitious, far-fetched, outlandish, outrageous, theatrical
unneat
see messy
unnecessary: **5** extra, undue **6** excess **7** nominal, surplus, useless **8** needless, optional, unneeded **9** avoidable, causeless, extrinsic, pointless, redundant **10** extraneous, gratuitous
make ~: **7** obviate
unneeded: **5** extra, minor, spare **7** trivial **8** optional, picayune, trifling **9** redundant
unnerve: **3** cow, sap **4** faze, ride **5** alarm, appal, chill, daunt, floor, get to, panic, shake, spook, throw, upset **6** appall, disarm, dismay, needle, rattle, unglue, weaken **7** agitate, buffalo, disturb, fluster, perturb, shake up, unhinge **8** bewilder, bowl over, confound, dispirit, distract, enervate, enfeeble, frighten, psych out, throw off, unsettle, unstring **9** give a turn, give pause, undermine **10** demoralize, disconcert, discourage, dishearten, intimidate
unnerved: **5** tense, timid **6** jangly **8** fluttery **9** unsettled **10** hysterical
unnerving: **4** eery **5** eerie, scary **8** terrible **9** appalling **10** petrifying
unnotable: **4** fair, so-so **6** not bad **7** average **8** adequate, mediocre, middling, ordinary, passable **9** tolerable
unnoticed: **5** perdu **6** hidden, perdue, secret, unseen **7** ignored, unheard **8** passed by, unheeded, winked at **9** neglected **10** overlooked, undetected, unobserved, unremarked
unnumbered: **4** vast **6** myriad, untold **7** endless **8** infinite, manifold **9** boundless, countless, limitless, uncounted, unlimited

uno: 6 numero 7 Italian, Spanish 8 card game
follower: 3 dos, due
minus uno: 4 cero, nada
numero ~: 4 boss 5 first 8 champion 10 celebrated
numero ~ place: 5 first, on top
unobjectionable: 4 safe 8 harmless, nontoxic 9 innocuous
unobliging: 5 loath 6 forced 7 evasive 8 grudging, hesitant 9 reluctant, unwilling, unwishful 10 begrudging
unobscure: 5 clear, lucid, naked 8 knowable, luminous, manifest, pellucid
unobscured: 4 open 5 light, overt
unobservant: 3 lax 5 blind, loose, slack 6 remiss 7 cursory 8 careless, heedless, mindless, reckless, slapdash, slipshod 9 incurious, negligent, oblivious 10 neglectful
unobserved: 6 unseen 8 secretly 9 unnoticed 10 undetected
unobstruct: 4 free, open 5 clear
unobstructed: 4 free, open 5 clear
unobtrusive: 4 meek 5 quiet 6 casual, humble, low-key, modest, unseen 7 subdued 8 reserved, retiring, tasteful 9 unnoticed
unobtrusiveness: 7 modesty
unoccupied: 4 free, idle, open 5 empty, spare 6 vacant 7 untaken 8 deserted, desolate, inactive 9 abandoned, available 10 up for grabs
be ~: 4 laze, loaf, loll, rest 5 relax 6 dawdle, loiter, lounge, piddle 7 hang out 8 kill time, malinger, slack off, vegetate 9 bum around, goldbrick, sit around, waste time 10 fool around, knock about, take it easy
uno, dos, __: 4 tres
uno, due, __: 3 tre
unofficial: 7 private 8 informal 9 irregular
Unofficial Rose, An
author: Iris Murdoch
unona: 5 shrub
unoppressive: 3 lax 4 easy, mild, soft 5 light, loose, quiet 6 benign, casual, docile, gentle 7 amiable, clement, lenient, no sweat, relaxed 8 amenable, carefree, flexible, informal, merciful, no bother, obliging, outgoing, painless, peaceful, pleasant, tolerant, yielding 9 compliant, forgiving, indulgent, no problem, tractable 10 child's play, effortless, forbearing, manageable, permissive, submissive, unexacting
unordained: 3 lay 4 laic 6 laical
unordinary: 4 rare 8 singular
unoriginal: 3 old 4 dull 5 corny, hokey, passé, stale, trite, vapid 6 common, jejune, old hat 7 clichéd, fatuous, humdrum, prosaic 8 bromidic, outdated, outmoded 9 hackneyed, imitative, prosaical 10 derivative
be ~: 3 ape 4 copy, echo 5 mimic 6 do like, mirror, repeat 7 emulate, imitate 8 make like, parallel, simulate 9 duplicate, reiterate, reproduce
one: 3 ape 5 mimic 6 copier
unornamented: 4 bare 5 plain 6 modest, simple 7 Spartan
unorthodox: 3 odd 4 eery 5 eerie, weird 6 atypic, errant, far-out, freaky, quirky 7 beatnik, bizarre, deviant, lawless, liberal, offbeat, strange 8 aberrant, abnormal, atypical, bohemian, freakish, peculiar 9 anomalous, different, dissident, divergent, eccentric, fantastic, heretical, irregular
opinion: 6 heresy 7 dissent 9 blasphemy, sacrilege
unostentatious: 5 plain 6 humble, modest, simple
unostentatiousness: 7 modesty
unpackaged: 5 loose
unpaid: 3 due 4 free 5 owing 6 mature 7 donated, overdue, past due, payable 8 honorary 9 in arrears, unsettled, voluntary, volunteer 10 delinquent, gratuitous, on the house, unsalaried
bill: 4 debt 6 arrear, red ink 7 arrears, deficit 9 liability, shortfall 10 obligation
labor: 6 corvée
worker: 4 serf 5 helot, slave 6 vassal 7 bondman, chattel, villein
unpaired: 3 odd 8 mateless 9 unmatched
unpalatable: 4 blah, vile 6 bitter 7 insipid 8 unsavory 9 tasteless 10 flavorless
unparalleled: 3 ten 4 best, lone, only, rare, sole, tops 5 alone, first, prime 6 unique, utmost 7 all-time, leading, stellar, supreme, unusual 8 champion, foremost, greatest, peerless, renowned, singular, splendid, superior, towering, ultimate, uncommon 9 matchless, nonpareil, number one, paramount, solid gold, unequaled, unmatched, unrivaled 10 consummate, preeminent, unrivalled
unpardonable: 4 vile 6 odious 7 heinous, ignoble 8 horrible, shameful, terrible 9 abhorrent 10 abominable
unpartnered: 4 lone, solo, stag 5 alone 6 single 8 deserted 9 by oneself, on one's own, separated
unpasteurized: 3 raw
unpatriotic: 8 disloyal, renegade 9 seditious 10 rebellious, subversive, traitorous
unpeaceful: 5 rowdy 6 fierce 7 chaotic, lawless, violent, warlike 8 mutinous 9 insurgent, turbulent 10 anarchical, disorderly, rebellious
unpeg: 4 open 6 detach, loosen 8 separate, uncouple 9 disengage 10 disconnect
unpen: 6 let out 7 release, set free 8 let loose
unperceived: 6 unseen 7 unknown 9 unnoticed
unperceptive: 8 tactless
unpermissable: 4 tabu 5 taboo
unpersevering: 4 lazy 6 otiose
unpersuasive: 4 lame, weak
unperturbed: 4 calm, cool 5 quiet, staid, stoic 6 low-key, mellow, placid, poised, sedate, serene 7 amiable, at peace, equable, pacific, relaxed, stoical 8 amicable, composed, laid-back, peaceful, tranquil 9 collected, easy-going, impassive, quiescent, temperate
unphysical: 4 airy 7 ghostly 8 bodiless, ethereal, rarefied 9 spiritual 10 immaterial, intangible
unpigmented: 6 albino
unpin: 4 free, open 5 loose 6 detach, loosen 8 let loose
unpinned: 4 free, open 5 loose
unpitying: 4 grim, hard, mean 5 cruel, harsh, stern, stony 6 brutal, fierce, flinty, savage 7 bestial, callous 8 inhumane, ruthless, uncaring, vengeful 9 barbarous, cutthroat, dog-eat-dog, ferocious, heartless, inclement, merciless, monstrous, unfeeling, unsparing 10 implacable, inexorable, ironfisted, relentless, unmerciful, unyielding
unplanned: 5 ad-lib, fluky, loose 6 casual, chance, flukey, random 7 aimless 8 rambling 9 impetuous, unwitting 10 accidental, fortuitous, unexpected, unintended
unplanted: 6 fallow 8 untilled
unpleasant: 3 bad 4 foul, grim, hard, icky, rude, sore, sour, ugly 5 awful, gross, harsh, lousy, nasty, rough, seamy, yucky 6 Augean, bitter, horrid, odious, rotten, severe, sticky 7 bad news, grating, hellish, hideous, irksome, painful, unhappy 8 abrasive, annoying, brackish, churlish, horrible, no picnic, terrible, unlovely, unsavory, wretched 9 appalling, frightful, loathsome, monstrous, murderous, obnoxious, offensive, repellant, repulsive, revolting, thankless, unlikable, unsightly, unwelcome 10 forbidding, ill-natured
combining form: 3 cac- 4 caco-
incident: 4 drag, mess 5 run-in 6 bummer, downer
most ~: 5 worst
one: 3 nag 4 pest, pill 6 noodge
task: 4 duty, onus 6 burden 9 millstone
unpleasantry: 3 cut, dig 4 barb, slam, slap, slur, snub 5 crack, sneer, taunt 6 insult, rebuff, slight 7 affront, put-down 8 rudeness 9 aspersion, cheap shot, insolence
unpliable: 4 hard 5 fixed, rigid, rusty, stiff 6 frozen 7 brittle 8 hardened, ossified 9 petrified 10 inflexible
unplowed: 6 fallow 8 untilled
unplug: 3 tap 7 turn off 10 disconnect
__ Unplugged: 3 MTV 6 Alanis
unpointed: 4 dull
unpoised: 6 clumsy, gauche 7 awkward, boorish, ill-bred, unadept 8 inurbane 9 graceless, unrefined 10 uncultured, unpolished
unpolished: 3 raw 4 wild 5 blunt, crude, green, rough 6 coarse, gauche, rustic, vulgar 7 awkward, boorish, loutish, lowbred, uncouth, unkempt 8 homespun, tactless, unpoised, unsubtle 9 backwater, inelegant, makeshift, primitive, tasteless 10 amateurish
unpolluted: 4 pure, safe 5 clean 8 pristine, sanitary, spotless 9 stainless 10 antiseptic, immaculate
unpopular: 3 out 5 hated, lousy, nerdy, wimpy 7 avoided, scorned, shunned, unloved, wimpish 8 despised, detested, disliked, rejected, unvalued, unwanted 9 disdained, obnoxious, unwelcome 10 ostracized, out of favor, unaccepted
one: 4 geek, nerd 5 twerp, twirp
play: 4 bomb, flop 6 turkey
unpopulated: 5 bleak 8 desolate
unpowdered: 5 shiny
unpracticed: 5 fresh, green, rusty, young 8 inexpert
unprecedented: 3 new 5 first, novel 6 signal, unique 8 original, singular, uncommon 9 unheard-of, unrivaled 10 phenomenal, unrivalled
unpredictable: 4 iffy 5 dicey, fluky, wacky 6 chance, chancy, fickle, fitful, flukey, random, touchy, tricky, whacky 7 erratic, wayward 8 doubtful, slippery, unstable, unsteady 9 mercurial, uncertain, whimsical
unpredictably: 8 by chance, randomly
move ~: 3 zag, zig
unprejudiced: 4 even, fair, just, open 5 equal 6 honest, square 7 liberal, neutral 8 balanced, catholic, detached, tolerant, unbiased 9 equitable, impartial, objective, unbigoted, uncolored 10 reasonable
unpremeditated: 5 ad-lib 6 random, snappy 7 offhand 9 unguarded
unprepared: 5 ad-lib, rough, unfit 6 unwary 7 offhand 9 impromptu 10 flat-footed, improvised
catch ~: 3 jar 4 numb, rock, stun 5 abash, floor, shock 6 appall, dismay 7 astound, horrify, shake up, stagger, stupefy 8 astonish, bowl over, paralyze, surprise, unsettle 9 electrify, galvanize, overwhelm 10 scare stiff
unprescribed: 6 chosen 8 optional, unbidden 9 voluntary, volunteer 10 unprompted, volitional
unpresuming: 3 shy 4 meek, nice 5 quiet, timid 6 demure, humble, modest 7 bashful 8 reserved, retiring 9 diffident 10 unaffected
unpresumptuous: 4 nice 6 kindly, modest, polite 7 genteel, refined 8 delicate, gracious, ladylike, obliging, pleasant, well-bred 9 agreeable, courteous
unpretended: 4 real, true 6 candid, modest 7 sincere 9 heartfelt, unfeigned
unpretentious: 4 easy, homy, meek, real 5 homey, lowly, naïve, plain, quiet, small, sober 6 casual, demure, folksy, honest, humble, modest, simple 7 artless, genuine, natural, sincere, up-front 8 discreet, down home, innocent, laid-back, ordinary, reserved, retiring 9 diffident, easygoing, guileless, uncomplex, unspoiled

unpretentiously: **6** freely, simply **7** frankly, plainly, readily **8** casually, directly, honestly, modestly **9** naturally, sincerely **10** informally
unpretentiousness: **7** modesty, reserve **8** delicacy, humility, meekness **9** reticence **10** diffidence, simplicity
Unpretty (1999 song)
artist: TLC
unpreventable: **4** sure **5** fated **7** certain **10** inevitable, in the cards
unprincipled: **3** sly **4** bent, evil **5** shady, venal **6** amoral, shifty, tricky, unfair, wanton, wicked **7** corrupt, crooked, devious, immoral, knavish **8** cheating, two-faced **9** cutthroat, deceitful, dishonest, dissolute, mercenary, miscreant, reprobate, shameless, two-timing, unethical **10** licentious
one: **3** cad, cur **4** boor, toad **5** knave, rogue, scamp, swine **6** rascal **9** miscreant, scoundrel **10** blackguard
unprocessed: **3** raw **5** crude, rough **6** coarse **7** natural **9** inelegant, makeshift, primitive **10** amateurish
unproductive: **4** arid, idle, lean, null, poor, sere, slow, vain **6** barren, desert, effete, fallow, futile **7** inutile, sterile, useless **8** bootless **9** for naught, fruitless, pointless, to no avail, valueless, worthless
unprofessional: **3** lax **7** amateur **8** improper **9** negligent, nonexpert, unethical, unfitting, untrained
unproficient: **5** inapt, inept **6** clumsy, gauche **7** awkward, labored, unadept **8** bumbling, bungling, fumbling, inexpert **9** all thumbs, unskilled **10** amateurish, unskillful
unprofitable: **4** vain **6** barren, futile **7** sterile, useless **8** bootless **9** pointless, thankless, valueless, worthless
unprofound: **5** empty, inane, silly **7** foolish, shallow, trivial **8** skin-deep **9** frivolous, senseless
unprogressive: **4** lazy, slow **5** slack **6** leaden, remiss **7** halting, lagging **8** backward, dawdling, dilatory, plodding, slothful, sluggish **9** backwater, ponderous, prolonged **10** protracted
unprohibited: **2** OK **5** legal, legit, licit **6** kosher, lawful **8** all right **9** allowable **10** acceptable, legitimate
unprolific: **4** idle, slow, vain **6** barren, hollow **7** sterile, useless **8** plodding **9** fruitless **10** unavailing
unpromising: **3** dim **4** dire **5** bleak **6** gloomy **7** ominous
unprompted: **6** wilful **7** offhand, unasked, willful **9** impulsive, uninvited, voluntary
unpronounced: **4** mute **6** silent
unpropitious: **7** adverse, ominous **8** sinister, untimely, untoward
unprosperous: **4** poor **5** broke, needy **8** beggarly, dirt poor, indigent **9** dead broke, destitute, on welfare, penniless, penurious **10** down-and-out, down at heel, straitened
unprotected: **4** bare, open **5** naked **7** exposed **8** helpless, insecure **9** in the open, unguarded **10** barehanded, vulnerable
unprotesting: **4** meek **5** stoic **6** docile **7** passive, patient, stoical, subdued **8** amenable, biddable, obedient, resigned, yielding **9** agreeable, compliant, peaceable, tractable **10** reconciled, submissive
unprovoked: **6** wanton **10** gratuitous, groundless, unasked-for
unpublished: **6** covert, secret **8** hush-hush **10** classified, privileged, restricted, under wraps, unrevealed
unpunctual: **4** late, slow **5** tardy **7** belated **8** detained **9** irregular
unqualified: **4** firm, flat, open, pure, rank, weak **5** gross, sheer, total, unfit, utter **6** simple, unable **7** flat-out, not up to, perfect, plenary **8** absolute, complete, outright, positive, straight, thorough, unfitted **9** downright, incapable, out-and-out, unalloyed, unlimited, unskilled **10** consummate
unquenchable: **6** greedy **8** ravening **9** voracious **10** gluttonous, insatiable
desire: **4** ache, pang **6** regret
unquestionable: **4** sure, true **5** clear **6** actual, patent, proven **7** certain, evident, factual, genuine, obvious **8** absolute, accurate, bona fide, decisive, definite, flawless, manifest **9** authentic, axiomatic, faultless, undoubted, veritable **10** undeniable
unquestionably
see of course
unquestioned: **4** sure **5** clear **9** unanimous
unquestioning: **4** naif **5** naive **6** steady **9** steadfast
unravel: **3** run **4** fray, undo **5** clear, plumb, solve **6** decode, loosen **7** clear up, comb out, dope out, resolve, unweave, work out **8** decipher, separate, untangle **9** figure out, penetrate, puzzle out
unravelling: **6** answer **8** solution
unreactive: **4** logy, slow **5** inert, quiet **6** latent, stolid, torpid **7** passive **8** listless, sluggish **9** impassive, inanimate, lethargic, quiescent **10** insentient, motionless
unread: **8** ignorant, untaught **9** unlearned, untutored **10** illiterate, uneducated
unreadable: **6** in code **7** obscure, scrawly, unclear **8** scrawled **9** illegible **10** indistinct
unready: **4** lazy **5** slack, tardy **7** laggard, lagging **8** dallying, dilatory, feckless **10** flat-footed
unreal: **4** eery, fake, mock, sham **5** bogus, eerie, false, phony, put-on **6** ersatz, fabled, forged, made-up, phoney, pseudo **7** assumed, feigned **8** abstract, chimeric, delusive, fanciful, illusive, illusory, imagined, invented, mistaken, mythical, notional, spurious **9** dreamlike, imaginary, imitation, insincere, legendary, pretended, simulated, storybook, synthetic, visionary, wonderful **10** artificial, chimerical, fabricated, fictitious, fraudulent, intangible, misleading
see also wonderful
unrealistic: **4** wild **5** crazy, silly **6** absurd **7** asinine, blue-sky, foolish, utopian **8** fanciful, illusive, illusory, quixotic, romantic **9** half-baked, illogical, visionary **10** chimerical, idealistic, improbable, quixotical, starry-eyed
unreality: **7** fantasy **8** ideality, illusion **9** dreamland, fairyland
unrealized: **6** future, latent **7** budding, dormant **8** inactive, sleeping **9** potential **10** in abeyance, smoldering
unreasonable: **3** mad **4** dear, wild **5** pricy, silly, steep, undue **6** absurd, all wet, biased, far-out, lavish, pricey, stupid, too-too, unfair, unholy, unjust **7** extreme, foolish, invalid, ungodly **8** improper, overmuch, stubborn **9** arbitrary, excessive, illogical, misguided, senseless, unearthly **10** exorbitant, far-fetched
unreasoned: **7** invalid **9** illogical **10** fallacious, ill-founded, irrational
unrecalled: **9** forgotten, repressed **10** suppressed
unrecognized: **7** unknown **9** anonymous, thankless, unnoticed
unreconstructed: **4** firm **5** rigid **7** diehard, fogyish, old-line **8** loyalist, mossback, orthodox, partisan **9** immovable **10** inflexible
unreduced: **5** total, whole **6** entire **7** plenary **8** complete, finished, thorough **10** exhaustive
unreel: **6** unwind **7** untwine
unrefined: **3** raw **4** rude, wild **5** crass, crude, gross, rough, wooly **6** coarse, earthy, grainy, impure, risqué, vulgar, woolly **7** boorish, loutish, natural, raffish, uncouth **8** impolite, plebeian, unpoised, unseemly **9** backwater, inelegant, makeshift, primitive, tasteless **10** amateurish, indecorous
unregulated: **4** free
unrehearsed: **5** ad-lib **7** offhand **9** extempore, impromptu **10** improvised, off-the-cuff
unrelated: **5** other **6** unlike **7** strange, unalike **8** discrete, distinct, separate **9** different, inapropos **10** dissimilar, extraneous, irrelevant
unrelaxed: **4** taut **5** antsy, jumpy **7** nervous **8** strained **9** ill at ease
unrelenting: **3** set **4** grim, hard **5** cruel, harsh, rigid, stern, stiff, stony, tough **6** mortal, savage, severe, steady, stoney **7** adamant, dead set, endless **8** constant, diligent, pitiless, ruthless, sedulous, unabated, unbroken **9** ceaseless, continual, incessant, merciless, perpetual, tenacious, unbending, unfailing, unsparing
unreliable: **3** bad **4** fake, weak **5** false, flaky, lying, risky, shaky **6** errant, fickle, flakey, hollow, shifty, sneaky, tricky, unsafe, unsure **7** dubious, erratic, furtive, unloyal, unsound **8** delusive, derelict, fallible, mistaken, skittish, slippery, unstable, wavering **9** deceitful, deceptive, erroneous, faithless, incorrect, irregular, makeshift, shiftless, uncertain **10** capricious, changeable, fly-by-night, inaccurate, precarious
source: **4** liar **5** rumor
unreligious: **4** laic **6** laical **7** secular **8** temporal **9** atheistic
unremarkable: **4** so-so **5** usual **6** normal **8** middling, ordinary, standard
unremembered: **4** lost, past **6** bygone **7** faraway, ignored **8** passed by **9** forgotten, neglected, unnoticed **10** overlooked
unremitting: **4** hard **5** stern **6** all-out, steady **7** endless, lasting, nonstop **8** constant, enduring, sedulous, unbroken, unending, untiring **9** ceaseless, incessant, perennial, perpetual
unremunerative: **8** bootless **9** for naught, worthless **10** profitless
unrenowned: **6** unsung **7** obscure **8** nameless, ordinary **9** unheard-of
unrepeatable: **4** lone, rare, sole **6** unique **7** curious, oddball, special, strange, uncanny, unusual **8** atypical, peculiar, singular, unwonted **9** exclusive, marvelous, unheard-of **10** phenomenal, prodigious
unrepentant: **3** bad, set **4** evil, mean **5** cruel, rigid, stony **6** flinty, no good, sinful, steely, wicked **7** baleful, corrupt, crooked, hateful, immoral, lawless, satanic, vicious **8** depraved, devilish, diabolic, fiendish, hardened, indurate, infamous, obdurate, stubborn **9** execrable, malicious, monstrous, nefarious, obstinate, rancorous **10** adamantine, iniquitous, malevolent, perfidious, villainous
unrequired: **7** useless **8** needless, optional **10** expendable
unrequited love, avenger of: **7** Anteros, Anterus
unreserved: **4** bold, free, open **5** blunt, frank **6** candid, direct, hearty, simple **7** gushing, up-front **8** effusive, outgoing, unartful **9** expansive, ingenuous, outspoken **10** forthright, free-spoken, from the hip, unreticent
unreservedness: **4** ease
unresisting: **4** meek **7** passive, servile **8** lamblike, resigned, yielding
unresolved: **4** iffy, moot, open **6** chancy **7** pending **8** doubtful, hesitant, lukewarm, unsolved, waffling **9** ambiguous, insoluble, uncertain, undecided, unsettled **10** ambivalent, indefinite, up for grabs, up in the air
unrespectable: **3** low **4** base **5** shady **6** shifty, shoddy, tricky **7** corrupt, crooked, devious, dubious, suspect **8** shameful, slippery, unsavory **9** dishonest, notorious, underhand, unethical **10** fly-by-night, scandalous, suspicious
unresponsive: **3** shy **4** cold, cool, slow **5** aloof, inert, stony **6** stoney **7** ice-cold **8** lukewarm, sluggish

unrest: **3** war **4** flux, fuss, mess, riot, to-do **5** chaos, swirl **6** bedlam, crisis, mayhem, strife, tumult, uproar **7** anarchy, anxiety, discord, ferment, fidgets, protest, tension, trouble, turmoil **8** disarray, disorder, disquiet, movement, sedition, upheaval **9** agitation, confusion, rebellion **10** discontent, dissension, inquietude, turbulence
unrestrained: **4** free, rash, wild **5** loose **6** adrift, all-out, hearty, lavish, savage, wanton **7** gushing, lawless, rampant, violent **8** effusive, informal, outgoing **9** unlimited
unrestraint: **5** haste **6** excess **7** abandon, freedom, license
unrestricted: **4** free, open **5** clean, loose **6** freely, public **8** absolute **9** boundless, limitless, open-ended, universal, unlimited
unrestrictedness: **4** play, span **5** range, reach, scope, space **6** leeway, margin **7** breadth, compass, freedom, liberty, license **8** free hand, latitude **9** elbow room
unreticent: **4** free, open **5** bluff, blunt, frank, vocal **6** candid, direct **7** up-front **9** outspoken **10** forthright, point-blank, unreserved
unrevealed: **6** hidden, occult, secret **7** unknown **8** ulterior **9** out of view, unexposed **10** undivulged
unrewarding: **3** off **6** barren **9** thankless
unrig: **9** dismantle, take apart **10** disconnect
unrighteous: **4** evil **5** wrong **6** unjust
unrigorous: **5** loose
unrinsed: **5** foamy, soapy, sudsy **7** lathery
unrip: **6** reveal **8** disclose, tear open **9** take apart
unripe: **4** sour **6** latent **8** immature, juvenile **9** premature
unrivaled: **4** best, only, rare **5** alone **6** deluxe, expert, select, single, unique **7** exalted, in front, leading, premium, supreme, vintage **8** dominant, peerless **9** a cut above, matchless, nonpareil, unequaled, unmatched **10** consummate, inimitable, preeminent, surpassing, world-class
see also wonderful
unrobed: **4** bare, nude **5** naked
unroll: **4** open **6** spread, unfold, unwind **7** display, stretch
unromantic: **6** earthy **8** sensible **9** practical, pragmatic, realistic **10** hard-bitten, hard-boiled
unruffled: **4** calm, cool, even **5** quiet, sober, staid, stoic **6** at ease, low-key, mellow, placid, poised, sedate, serene, smooth, stolid **7** amiable, at peace, easeful, equable, pacific, patient, relaxed, stoical **8** amicable, carefree, composed, laid-back, peaceful, tranquil **9** collected, easy-going, impassive, quiescent, temperate, unstirred, unworried **10** nonchalant, phlegmatic, unaffected, unagitated, untroubled
unruliness: **5** chaos **7** license **8** disorder **9** mobocracy
unruly: **3** bad **4** wild **5** balky, rowdy **6** bratty, feisty, hoiden, hoyden, ornery, wilful **7** coltish, defiant, forward, lawless, naughty, playful, problem, rampant, raucous, restive, wayward, willful **8** contrary, factious, heedless, indocile, mutinous, perverse, stubborn **9** fractious, out of hand, out of line, turbulent **10** boisterous, disorderly, headstrong, ill-behaved, licentious, rebellious, refractory, tumultuous
unsafe: **3** mad **4** weak **5** hairy, risky, shaky **6** chancy, touchy **7** harmful, parlous, unsound **8** alarming, fearsome, insecure, perilous, slippery, ticklish, unstable **9** dangerous, explosive, hazardous, on thin ice, uncertain **10** precarious, ramshackle, touch and go, unreliable, vulnerable
Unsafe at Any Speed
author: Ralph Nader
unsafety: **4** risk **5** peril **6** danger, hazard **8** jeopardy **10** insecurity
unsaid: **5** tacit **6** silent **7** implied **8** implicit, inferred, ulterior, unspoken, unstated, unvoiced, wordless **9** intimated, unuttered, unwritten **10** undeclared, understood
unsalaried: **6** unpaid **8** honorary **9** volunteer
unsalted: **4** blah, flat **5** bland, plain **9** tasteless **10** flavorless
unsanctioned: **4** null, void **7** invalid, negated **9** cancelled, rescinded **10** unratified
unsanitary: **5** dirty, grimy, sooty **6** filthy, fouled, grubby, grungy, soiled **7** smudged, stained, tainted **8** befouled, begrimed, maculate, polluted, slovenly **9** blackened, tarnished, unhealthy **10** besmirched, germ-ridden
unsatisfactorily: **3** ill **5** badly **9** adversely
unsatisfactory: **3** bad, off **4** lame, poor, thin, weak **5** amiss, inept **6** futile, no good, rotten **7** lacking, limited **8** below par, mediocre, schlocky, unworthy **9** deficient **10** inadequate, lamentable
most ~: **5** worst
unsatisfied: **3** due **5** eager, empty, itchy, owing **6** greedy, hungry, unpaid **7** longing, overdue, payable, starved, thirsty, wishful **8** covetous, desirous, edacious, esurient, famished, ravenous, starving, unfilled **9** hankering, in arrears, insatiate, unsettled, voracious
unsatisfying: **4** blah, lame, poor, thin **6** faulty **10** inadequate
unsavory: **4** dull, foul, icky, rank, sour **5** bland, gross, nasty, seamy, shady, tough **6** rancid **7** insipid, odorous **8** stinking **9** offensive, repugnant, tasteless **10** bad-tasting, flavorless, unpleasant
sort: **5** rogue **6** bad egg **9** scoundrel
unsay: **6** recall, recant **7** retract **8** take back, withdraw **9** backpedal
unscathed: **4** safe **5** sound, whole **6** intact, unhurt **8** unharmed, unmarked **9** uninjured, unscarred, untouched **10** in one piece
unscheduled: **3** TBA **4** open
unschooled: **3** raw **4** naif **5** naive **6** simple **8** ignorant, inexpert, unartful **9** inerudite, ingenuous **10** illiterate, unlettered
unscientific: **6** untrue **7** invalid, unsound **9** illogical, unfounded **10** unreasoned
unscramble: **6** decode **8** decipher, simplify, untangle **9** puzzle out
unscrew: **4** open **5** loose **6** loosen
unscripted: **5** ad-lib **9** extempore, impromptu, tossed-off, whipped up **10** improvised, off-the-cuff
unscrupulous: **3** sly **4** base, foul **5** dirty, false, shady, sharp, venal **6** amoral, crafty, shifty, sneaky, unfair **7** corrupt, crooked, devious, illegal, immoral, knavish, low-down, selfish **8** degraded, ruthless, scheming, slippery, two-faced, wrongful **9** deceitful, degrading, dishonest, mercenary, shameless, underhand, unethical
one: **4** vamp **6** con man
plan: **3** con **4** scam
unseal: **3** ope **4** open
unsealed: **4** open **9** unstopped
unseasoned: **3** new, raw **4** naif **5** green, naive, plain, young **7** strange **8** immature, inexpert **9** tasteless
unseat: **4** buck, oust **5** throw **6** depose, remove, topple **7** dismiss, kick out, subvert, unhorse **8** dethrone, supplant **9** overthrow
unsecured: **5** loose
unseeded: **6** fallow **8** untilled
unseemly: **4** rude, ugly **5** crude, gross, inapt, nasty, spicy, undue **6** coarse, spicey, unmeet, vulgar **7** lowbred, raffish, uncouth **8** immodest, improper, indecent, untimely, untoward **9** inelegant, low-minded, tasteless, unrefined **10** in bad taste, indecorous, indelicate, malapropos, out of place, suggestive, unbecoming, unsuitable
unseen: **4** dark **6** hidden, latent, masked, occult, secret, veiled **7** cloaked, furtive, lurking, obscure, private **8** hush-hush, imagined, obscured, secluded, shrouded, ulterior **9** concealed, disguised, invisible, out of view, unexposed, unnoticed **10** out of sight, tucked away, undercover, under wraps, undetected, unobserved, unviewable
___ **unseen:** **5** sight
Unseld, Wes
milieu: **5** court
org.: 3 NBA
sport: **10** basketball
unselfish: **4** kind **5** noble, sweet **6** giving, humane, kindly, loving, polite **7** devoted, gallant, heedful, helpful, liberal, mindful, tactful **8** generous, gracious, obliging **9** sensitive **10** altruistic, benevolent, charitable, chivalrous, free-handed, humanistic, open-handed, thoughtful, ungrudging
unsentimental: **5** stony **6** stoney **9** pragmatic, realistic **10** hard-bitten
unseparated: **3** one **5** fused, whole **6** joined, merged, united
Unser: **2** Al **5** Bobby, racer **8** car racer **9** auto racer
milieu: **5** track
rival: **4** Foyt
unset: **5** runny **9** tentative **10** up in the air
unsettle: **4** faze, trip **5** get to, shake, shock, spook, throw, upset, worry **6** bother, flurry, jumble, rattle, ruffle, sicken, unglue **7** agitate, confuse, derange, disrupt, disturb, fluster, perturb, shake up, trouble, unhinge, unnerve **8** befuddle, confound, convulse, disarray, disorder, displace, disquiet, psych out, surprise, throw off, unstring **9** discomfit, give a turn, unbalance **10** demoralize, disarrange, discommode, discompose, disconcert
unsettled: **3** due **4** edgy, iffy, live, moot, open **5** antsy, fluid, owing, shaky, tense, upset **6** chancy, cloudy, mobile, on edge, shaken, thrown, uneasy, unpaid **7** anxious, dubious, fidgety, hanging, migrant, mutable, overdue, payable, pending, rattled, restive, shook up, unclear, unquiet **8** agitated, changing, confused, darkened, doubtful, floating, fluttery, immature, insecure, restless, shifting, unnerved, unstable, variable, volatile, waffling, wavering, wobbling **9** ambiguous, debatable, delirious, disturbed, explosive, flustered, ill at ease, in arrears, itinerant, migratory, perturbed, squeamish, tentative, turbulent, uncertain, undecided **10** borderline, changeable, disordered, disorderly, inconstant, indecisive, indefinite, irresolute, on the fence, unbalanced, unresolved, up for grabs, up in the air
unsettling: **5** eerie **6** creepy **8** involved, puzzling **9** confusing, difficult, obscuring, upsetting **10** disruptive, disturbing, embroiling, misleading, perplexing
unshackle: **4** free, save **6** loosen **7** deliver, manumit, release **8** liberate **9** discharge **10** emancipate
unshackled: **4** free, wild **5** loose **6** untied
unshakable: **4** firm, sure **5** solid **7** adamant **8** implicit, resolute, stubborn **9** immovable, tenacious **10** hard-bitten
unshaken: **4** sure **6** steady **8** resolute **10** determined, unwavering
unshaped: **8** inchoate **9** amorphous
unshared: **4** sole **6** single **9** exclusive
unsharpened: **4** dull **5** blunt **8** edgeless
unshaven: **5** hairy, rough **7** bearded, bristly, hirsute, unshorn
unsheltered: **4** open **7** exposed **9** in the open **10** vulnerable
unshielded: **4** bare, nude, open **5** naked **7** exposed **8** undraped **9** in the open, uncovered **10** vulnerable
unshod: **8** barefoot, shoeless

unshorn: **5** bushy, furry, fuzzy, hairy **6** shaggy **7** bearded, bristly, hirsute **8** unshaven **9** whiskered **10** long-haired
unshortened: **3** all **4** A to Z, full **5** uncut, whole **6** entire, intact **8** complete **10** exhaustive, unabridged
unshrinking: **4** bold, game **5** brash, brave, crass, gutsy, nervy, pushy, stout **6** brassy, brazen, cheeky, daring, heroic, plucky, spunky, steely **7** doughty, forward, gallant, staunch, valiant **8** fearless, intrepid, resolute, stalwart, unafraid **9** audacious, dauntless, steadfast, tenacious, unalarmed, undaunted, unfearing **10** courageous, fire-eating, mettlesome, undeterred, undismayed
unshrouded: **4** open **5** clear, overt, plain **6** in view, patent, public **7** obvious, visible **8** apparent, clear-cut, explicit, manifest **10** observable
unshut: **4** open **9** unstopped
unshy: **5** brash **6** brassy **7** forward
unsightly: **4** ugly **5** awful, gross, plain **6** horrid **7** hideous **8** terrible, wretched **9** appalling, frightful, loathsome, monstrous, offensive, repellant, revolting **10** lackluster, unbecoming, unpleasant
unsimilar: **9** different, disparate, divergent **10** dissimilar
unsimulated: **6** honest **7** artless, genuine, sincere **9** guileless, heartfelt, ingenuous, unfeigned
Unsinkable Molly Brown, The (1964 film)
cast: Harve Presnell, Debbie Reynolds
unskilled: **3** new, raw **5** fresh, gawky, inapt, inept, unfit **6** clumsy, klutzy, oafish, unable **7** awkward, gawkish **8** bumbling, bungling, inexpert **9** all thumbs, graceless, incapable, lumbering, maladroit, stumbling **10** dilettante, unequipped, unfamiliar, uninitiate
in: **5** bad at
one: **3** cub **4** tyro **6** novice **7** amateur, learner, recruit, trainee **8** beginner, freshman, initiate, neophyte, newcomer **9** fledgling, greenhorn **10** apprentice, tenderfoot
sailor: **6** lubber **10** landlubber
worker: **4** peon **5** prole **7** laborer
writer: **4** hack **6** drudge
unskillful: **5** crude, green, inept, unapt, unfit **6** clumsy, gauche, klutzy, oafish **7** awkward, unadept **8** bumbling, bungling, cloddish, fumbling, inexpert **9** all thumbs, incapable, maladroit **10** amateurish, unequipped
Unskinny Bop (1990 song)
artist: Poison
unslanted: **4** fair, just **5** sober **6** candid, honest, square **7** neutral **8** detached, moderate, rational, unbiased **9** equitable, impartial, objective, unbigoted, uncolored **10** evenhanded, fair-minded, impersonal, open-minded
unsleeping: **5** alert, awake, aware **7** wakeful **8** vigilant, watchful
unsmiling: **4** dour **5** grave, stony **6** severe, stoney **7** serious **8** lowering
unsmooth: **5** bumpy, lumpy **6** jagged, uneven **7** unlevel
unsmudged: **5** clean **8** unsoiled
unsnap: **4** open **5** loose **6** loosen
unsociable: **3** shy **4** cold, cool **5** aloof, timid **6** crabby, silent, sullen **7** distant, hostile, recluse **8** brooding, reserved, retiring, solitary **9** reclusive, secretive, withdrawn **10** antisocial
unsoiled: **4** pure **5** clean, fresh, snowy, white **6** chaste, washed **8** dirtless, germfree, hygienic, innocent, pristine, sanitary, spotless, unfouled **9** blameless, guiltless, honorable, laundered, lily-white, sparkling, stainless, undefiled, unsmudged, unspotted, unstained, unsullied, untainted, untouched **10** immaculate, impeccable
unsolicited: **4** free **6** gratis **7** offered **8** unsought **9** undesired, uninvited, unwelcome, voluntary **10** gratuitous
manuscripts: **5** slush
Unsolved Mysteries (NBC/CBS)
host: Robert Stack
unsophisticate: **4** babe, lamb **5** yokel
unsophisticated: **4** hick, homy, naif, pure **5** corny, crass, crude, green, homey, naive, rough, rural **6** callow, earthy, folksy, gauche, honest, rustic, simple **7** artless, genuine, natural, sincere **8** homespun, innocent, lamblike, wide-eyed **9** backwater, childlike, guileless, ingenuous, unworldly **10** unaffected
unsound: **3** bad, ill **4** daft, idle, sick, weak **5** false, frail, inane, risky, shaky, silly, wacky, wrong **6** absurd, ailing, broken, faulty, flawed, flimsy, infirm, laid up, marred, screwy, sickly, unsafe, untrue, unwell, unwise, whacky **7** damaged, fatuous, fragile, in error, inexact, invalid, parlous, rickety, shallow **8** cockeyed, decrepit, delicate, fallible, ill-spent, impaired, insecure, mistaken, perilous, specious, unbacked, unhinged, unstable, unsteady **9** afflicted, bedridden, breakable, dangerous, defective, erroneous, frangible, hazardous, illogical, imperfect, incorrect, senseless, sophistic, tottering, unhealthy **10** fallacious, groundless, ill-founded, inaccurate, indisposed, irrational, jerry-built, unbalanced, ungrounded, unreliable
unsounded: **4** mute **5** tacit **10** bottomless, fathomless, unknowable
unsparing: **4** firm, free, hard **5** ample, bossy, cruel, harsh, picky, rigid, stern, tough **6** lavish, severe **7** austere, copious, liberal, profuse, Spartan **8** abundant, despotic, exacting, generous, handsome, hard-line, rigorous **9** bountiful, demanding, draconian, merciless, plentiful, stringent, trenchant, unpitying **10** altruistic, charitable, despotical, inflexible, iron-fisted, munificent, no-nonsense, oppressive, tyrannical, unmerciful
unspeakable: **4** dire **5** awful **6** horrid, odious **7** beastly, fearful, heinous **8** dreadful, horrible, nameless, shocking **9** appalling, atrocious, execrable, frightful, ineffable, loathsome, monstrous, obnoxious, offensive, repellent, repugnant, repulsive, revolting
unspeaking: **3** mum **4** mute **5** close, muted, quiet **6** silent **7** muzzled, quieted, stilled **8** hushed up **9** clammed up, secretive, voiceless **10** buttoned up, restrained, speechless, tongue-tied
unspecific: **4** hazy **5** broad, fuzzy, loose, vague **7** diffuse, general, inexact **8** nebulous, sweeping **9** ambiguous, imprecise **10** indefinite, undetailed
unspecified: **4** hazy **5** fuzzy, loose, muddy, murky, vague **6** unsure **7** general, obscure, sketchy, unclear **8** nebulous **9** enigmatic, imprecise, uncertain, undecided **10** ill-defined, indefinite
amount: **3** any, few **4** some
individual: **3** one **6** anyone **7** someone
unspiritual: **3** lay **4** laic **6** laical **7** earthly, mundane, profane, secular, terrene, worldly **8** material, temporal
unspoiled: **3** new **4** good **5** fresh **6** virgin **7** like new, perfect **8** pristine, spotless, virginal **9** good as new, stainless **10** immaculate
unspoken: **5** tacit **6** silent, unsaid **7** assumed, implied **8** implicit, unvoiced **9** intimated **10** understood
unspontaneous: **5** phony **6** forced, phoney **7** labored **8** affected, overdone, strained **9** contrived, rehearsed, unnatural **10** artificial
unsportsmanlike: **5** dirty **6** unfair
conduct: **7** low blow **9** cheap shot **10** defamation
unspotted: **5** clean **6** chaste **8** unsoiled **9** blameless, faultless
unstable: **4** weak **5** dizzy, fluid, giddy, shaky, tippy **6** fickle, fitful, jiggly, mobile, unfirm, unsafe, wabbly, wiggly, wobbly **7** dubious, erratic, mutable, parlous, protean, rickety, tottery, unsound, weaving **8** doubtful, insecure, shifting, slippery, ticklish, unsteady, variable, volatile, wavering **9** dangerous, mercurial, sensitive, teetering, uncertain, unsettled, vagarious **10** borderline, capricious, changeable, inconstant, irrational, precarious, unbalanced, unreliable
socially ~: **6** anomic
unstained: **5** clean **6** chaste **8** pristine, spotless, unsoiled **9** untouched
unstamped enclosure: **3** env., SAE
unstated: **5** tacit **6** unsaid **8** unvoiced **9** intimated **10** understood
unsteady: **4** wavy **5** dizzy, rocky, shaky, slack, tippy, tipsy **6** fickle, fitful, infirm, jiggly, uneven, wabbly, wobbly **7** erratic, halting, mutable, rickety, unsound, weaving **8** lopsided, slippery, ticklish, unstable, variable, volatile, wavering **9** irregular, mercurial, teetering, uncertain **10** capricious, changeable, inconstant, nonuniform, precarious, ramshackle, unbalanced
unstick: **4** open **5** loose **6** loosen
unstinting: **6** lavish **7** liberal, profuse **8** generous, princely **10** altruistic, charitable, free-handed, ungrudging
unstirred: **4** calm, cool **5** aloof **7** callous, unmoved **9** impassive, unexcited, unruffled **10** impervious, unaffected, unagitated, untroubled
unstop: **3** ope **4** open **5** clear **6** unclog
unstopped: **4** open **6** unshut **8** draining, uncorked, unsealed **9** unblocked, unclogged
unstrap: **4** open **5** loose **6** loosen
unstressed: **4** weak **6** at ease, atonic
unstrict: **3** lax **4** easy, soft **5** broad, loose, slack **6** casual **7** lenient **8** tolerant, yielding **9** easygoing **10** permissive
unstring: **4** jolt, rock **5** alarm, daunt, shake, upset, worry **6** dismay, rattle, unglue **7** agitate, disturb, horrify, perturb, stagger, unnerve **8** disquiet, distress, frighten, unsettle **9** discomfit **10** demoralize, discompose, disconcert, intimidate
unstructured: **6** blobby **8** formless, inchoate, nebulous, unformed, unshaped **9** amorphous, shapeless
unstrung: **5** fazed, upset **6** shaken **7** nervous **8** agitated **9** flustered **10** confounded
unstudied: **6** simple **7** natural, offhand **8** unartful **9** guileless, ingenuous **10** improvised, unaffected
unstylish: **3** out **5** dowdy, tacky **6** frumpy **8** outmoded
unsubstantial: **4** aery, less, limp, null, thin **5** empty, frail, light, wrong **6** dreamy, flimsy **7** fragile, rickety, unsound **8** delicate, ethereal **9** breakable, frangible
unsubstantiated: **4** idle **5** false **6** flimsy, untrue **7** invalid **8** baseless, fanciful, mistaken, spurious **9** erroneous, trumped-up, unfounded **10** fabricated, fallacious, gratuitous, groundless
unsubtle: **5** blunt, gross, overt, plain **6** gauche, patent **7** blatant, glaring, obvious **8** explicit, flagrant, tactless **9** barefaced **10** in-your-face
unsuccessful: **4** vain **6** futile, in vain **7** failing, unlucky, useless **9** fruitless
be ~: **4** fail, lose **8** fall flat
venture: **3** dog, dud **4** bomb, bust, flop **5** lemon, loser **6** fiasco, fizzle **7** debacle, failure, washout **8** disaster
unsuccinct: **4** long **5** gabby, windy, wordy **6** chatty, prolix, turgid **7** gushing, lengthy, unterse,

UN

verbose, voluble **8** babbling, inflated, rambling **9** bombastic, garrulous, jabbering, talkative **10** bigmouthed, blathering, discursive, long-winded, loquacious, rhetorical

unsuitable: 4 lame **5** inapt, tacky, unapt, unfit, wrong **8** improper, unseemly, untimely **9** incorrect **10** ineligible, irrelevant, unequipped

unsuitably: 4 awry **5** amiss **7** wrongly **10** improperly

unsuited: 5 unfit **10** inapposite, unbecoming

unsullied: 4 pure **5** clean **6** chaste, virgin **8** flawless, innocent, pristine, sanitary, spotless, unsoiled, virginal, virtuous **9** blameless, faultless, guiltless, stainless **10** immaculate

unsung: 7 obscure, unfamed, unknown **8** nameless **9** anonymous, unheard-of **10** unrenowned

unsupported: 5 shaky **8** baseless **10** groundless

unsuppressed: 4 wild **6** wanton

unsure: 4 asea, iffy, lost, torn, wary, weak **5** at sea, chary, leery, shaky, vague, wimpy **6** chancy **7** dubious, guarded, suspect, wimpish **8** cautious, doubtful, doubting, hesitant, untrusty, wavering **9** ambiguous, faltering, skeptical, tentative, unassured, uncertain, undecided **10** indecisive, indefinite, irresolute, precarious, suspicious, touch and go, unreliable, up for grabs, up in the air

response: 5 maybe **6** I guess **7** it may be, perhaps **9** it could be

unsurpassable: 5 ideal, prime **6** superb **7** leading, perfect, sublime, supreme **8** crowning, foremost, greatest, peerless, ultimate **9** excellent, first-rate, matchless, nonpareil, paramount, sovereign, unequaled, unmatched **10** consummate, inimitable, preeminent

unsurpassed: 4 A-one, best, tops **5** alone, first, prime **6** finest **7** all-time, highest, supreme **8** greatest, peerless, splendid **9** matchless, nonpareil, unequaled **10** preeminent

unsusceptible: 6 immune

unsuspecting: 4 easy, naif **5** naive **6** unwary **7** taken in, unaware **8** gullable, gullible, innocent, off-guard, trustful, trusting **9** confiding, credulous, ingenuous, unadvised, unwitting

one: 4 babe, lamb, naif **9** greenhorn

unsuspicious: 4 naif **5** naive **6** unwary

unsustained: 5 brief, short **7** cursory **8** fleeting **9** ephemeral, momentary **10** short-lived, transitory

unswayable: 4 firm, iron **7** adamant **9** unbending **10** inflexible

unswept: 4 foul **5** dirty, dusty, grimy, messy **6** filthy, grubby, grungy, untidy **7** unclean **8** begrimed, slovenly

unswerving: 4 firm, true **5** loyal, rigid **6** all-out, direct, in a row, linear, steady **7** adamant **8** directly, emphatic, forceful, resolute, straight, untiring **9** religious, steadfast, tenacious, undivided **10** conclusive, undeterred

unswervingly: 4 hard **8** candidly, directly, honestly, promptly, straight **9** precisely

unsymmetrical: 4 alop **6** uneven **8** lopsided, one-sided **10** off-balance

unsympathetic: 3 icy **4** cold, cool, hard **5** aloof, harsh, nasty, stony **6** flinty, frigid, stoney, unkind **7** callous, unmoved **8** lukewarm, tactless **9** apathetic, heartless, merciless, repellent, unfeeling, unpitying **10** hard-boiled, unfriendly

unsystematic: 5 messy **6** random, spotty **7** aimless, chaotic, jumbled, mixed up, muddled **8** confused, slipshod **9** haphazard, illogical **10** disordered, disorderly, in disarray

untactful: 5 brash **6** clumsy **7** forward **8** unsubtle **9** maladroit **10** indelicate, unthinking

untainted: 4 good, pure **5** clean, fresh **6** chaste **7** sinless **8** innocent, pristine, unsoiled, virtuous **9** guiltless

untaken: 4 free, open **5** empty, to let **6** unused, vacant **8** unfilled **9** available **10** unoccupied

untamed: 4 wild **5** feral, rabid **6** animal, ferine, fierce, savage **7** beastly, coltish, lawless **9** ferocious, primitive, turbulent

untangle: 4 comb **5** ravel, solve **6** decode, unwind **7** clear up, explain, unravel, unsnarl, untwine, untwist, unweave **8** decipher **9** extricate **10** disembroil, unscramble

untanned: 4 pale **5** white **6** pallid

untapped: 3 new **6** latent, virgin **8** virginal

untarnished: 4 pure **5** clean **6** bright, chaste **7** perfect, shining, sinless **8** absolute, flawless, innocent, pristine, spotless, virtuous **9** faultless, guiltless, stainless **10** immaculate

untaught: 4 naif **5** crude, naive **6** unread **8** ignorant **10** uneducated, unschooled

untaxing: 4 easy, soft **5** cushy, light **6** casual, frothy, gentle, simple, smooth **7** unheavy **8** carefree **10** effortless, manageable, unexacting

untempered: 6 wanton **7** extreme, too much **8** a bit much **9** excessive **10** immoderate, inordinate

untenable: 4 thin, weak **5** inane, silly, wacky **6** absurd, faulty, flawed, screwy, whacky **7** fatuous **8** baseless, cockeyed, specious **9** illogical, senseless **10** groundless, incredible

untended: 5 seedy **6** grungy, shabby, shoddy **7** rickety, rundown, scruffy, squalid **8** decrepit, derelict, forsaken, tattered **9** abandoned, crumbling, neglected **10** in bad shape, ramshackle, tumbledown, uncared-for

Untermeyer, Louis: 6 writer

work: Burning Bush

Modern American Poetry

unter opposite: 4 über

unterse: 4 long **5** gabby, windy, wordy **6** chatty, prolix, turgid **7** gushing, lengthy, verbose, voluble **8** babbling, inflated, rambling **9** bombastic, garrulous, jabbering, talkative **10** bigmouthed, blathering, discursive, long-winded, loquacious, rhetorical, unsuccinct

Unterseeboot: 3 sub **5** U-boat

untested: 3 new, raw **5** green **6** callow **8** immature

unthinkable: 6 absurd **8** hopeless **10** infeasible, out of reach

unthinking: 3 lax **4** rash, rude **5** brash, hasty, nervy **6** blithe, remiss, sloppy, stupid, unwise, vacant **7** boorish, foolish, selfish, shallow, witless **8** careless, feckless, heedless, impolite, knee-jerk, mindless, off-guard, slapdash, slipshod, tactless, uncaring **9** automatic, haphazard, impetuous, imprudent, impulsive, negligent, oblivious, senseless, unguarded, unheedful, unheeding, unmindful, untactful, unwitting **10** incautious, irrational, nonchalant

unthinkingly, say: 5 blurt **8** blurt out

unthorough: 6 remiss, sloppy **7** botched **8** careless, slapdash, slipshod **9** haphazard, hit-or-miss, negligent **10** jerry-built

unthought-of: 3 new **5** novel **8** original

unthreatened: 2 OK **4** safe **6** secure **8** home-free **9** protected **10** impervious

unthreatening: 4 meek, mild, tame, weak **6** docile, gentle **8** biddable, harmless, lamblike, obedient **9** compliant, tractable **10** spiritless, submissive

unthrifty: 6 lavish **7** liberal **8** prodigal, wasteful **10** immoderate, profligate

untidiness: 4 mess, muss **6** litter **7** clutter **8** disarray, disorder **9** confusion

untidy: 4 wild **5** a mess, dirty, dowdy, messy, mussy **6** blowsy, blowzy, frowsy, frowzy, sloppy, unneat **7** blowsed, blowzed, chaotic, jumbled, rumpled, scruffy, tousled, unkempt, unswept **8** littered, slapdash, slipshod, slovenly, uncombed **9** cluttered, ungroomed **10** bedraggled, disarrange, disarrayed, disheveled, disordered, disorderly, in disorder, topsy-turvy

make ~: 4 muss **6** jumble, mess up, ruffle, rumple, tangle, tousle **7** clutter, crumple, disturb, rummage, wrinkle **8** dishevel **10** disarrange

one: 4 slob

untie: 4 free, open, undo **5** let go, loose **6** loosen **7** disjoin, release, set free **8** disunite, let loose, liberate, separate, set loose **9** disengage, extricate **10** disconnect

the knot: 4 free, part **5** sever **6** loosen **7** break up, divorce, split up **10** put asunder

untied: 4 free **5** let go, loose **6** undone **7** at large, rescued, unbound **8** cut loose, detached, let loose, released, set loose **9** at liberty, unchained, unimpeded, unleashed **10** disengaged, on the loose, unattached, unconfined, unfastened, unfettered, unshackled

untighten: 4 ease, open **5** loose, relax, unzip **6** loosen

until: 4 as of, till, up to **6** before, down to **7** as far as, pending, prior to **9** meanwhile

now: 3 yet **5** since, so far

__ Until Dark: 4 Wait

Until It Sleeps (1996 song)

artist: Metallica

untilled: 4 idle **6** fallow, unused **8** unplowed, unseeded **9** unplanted

untimely: 5 inapt, undue **7** awkward, too late, unlucky **8** improper, mistimed, oversoon, too early, unseemly, untoward **9** ill-suited, premature **10** irrelevant, malapropos, unsuitable

untiring: 5 perky **6** dogged, steady, strong **7** devoted, patient, staunch **8** constant, resolute, sedulous, tireless, unwaning **9** ceaseless, continual, continued, dedicated, energetic, tenacious, unceasing, unfailing, unstinted, unwearied **10** continuing, determined, persistent, relentless, undeterred, unflagging, unswerving, unwavering, unwearying

untiringly: 4 hard

untitled: 6 common **7** lowborn **8** baseborn, nameless

__ unto Caesar...: 6 render

__ unto itself: 4 a law

untold: 4 many, vast **6** a lot of, divers, gobs of, hidden, lots of, myriad, umteen **7** a host of, a slew of, copious, endless, heaping, heaps of, no end of, piles of, private, profuse, scads of, umpteen, unknown **8** a bunch of, abundant, an army of, infinite, manifold, numerous, oodles of, scores of, umpsteen, very many **9** a passel of, boundless, bountiful, countless, limitless, quite a few, uncounted, unlimited **10** innumerous, numberless, staggering, suppressed, unnumbered, zillions of

years: 3 eon **4** aeon

untoned: 4 soft **5** slack, unfit **6** flabby **7** flaccid **10** out of shape

unto starter: 4 here **5** there, where

Unto The Sons

author: Gay Talese

untouchable: 4 tabu **6** sacred **7** outcast **9** inviolate, sacred cow **10** sacrosanct

Untouchable: 4 Ness, T-man

untouchables: 4 rank **5** caste **6** status

Untouchables, The (1987 film)

cast: Sean Connery, Kevin Costner, Robert De Niro, Andy García

director: Brian De Palma

Untouchables, The (ABC drama)
cast: Robert Stack (Eliot Ness)
narrator: Walter Winchell
untouched: 3 new **4** pure **5** blank, fresh, sound, whole **6** entire, intact, secure, unhurt, virgin **7** perfect, uneaten, unmoved **8** flawless, leftover, sanitary, spotless, unharmed, unmarked, unmarred, unsoiled, virginal **9** apathetic, incorrupt, undamaged, uninjured, unscathed, unstained **10** immaculate, unaffected
Unto us __ is given: 4 a son
untoward: 7 adverse, unhappy, unlucky **8** contrary, improper, perverse, stubborn, unseemly, untimely **10** disastrous, disturbing, out of place
Untraceable (2008 film)
cast: Colin Hanks, Diane Lane
untraditional, musically: 6 atonal
untrained: 3 new, raw **4** soft, weak **5** crude, fresh, green, messy, rough **6** callow **7** amateur **8** ignorant, inexpert **10** disorderly
untried: 3 new **5** fresh, green, young **6** virgin **7** strange **8** original, virginal
untrodden: 3 new **5** fresh
untrouble: 4 ease, lull **5** allay, cheer, salve **6** pacify, solace, soothe, stroke **7** appease, assuage, compose, console, mollify, placate, relieve **8** calm down, unburden **9** alleviate, pour oil on **10** conciliate, smooth over
untroubled: 4 calm, cool, easy **5** clear, quiet, staid, still, stoic **6** at ease, blithe, hushed, low-key, mellow, placid, sedate, serene, smooth, steady **7** amiable, at peace, easeful, equable, halcyon, pacific, relaxed, stoical **8** amicable, carefree, composed, laid-back, peaceful, tranquil **9** collected, easy-going, impassive, quiescent, temperate, unruffled, unstirred, unworried **10** insouciant, nonchalant, unagitated, unbothered
untroublesome: 4 easy **5** light **6** facile, simple **9** no problem
untrue: 3 not, off **4** sham **5** false, lying, not so, wrong **6** faulty, hollow, made-up **7** in error, inexact, invalid, unloyal, unsound **8** delusive, disloyal, forsworn, libelous, mistaken, perjured, recreant, specious, spurious, two-faced **9** deceptive, dishonest, distorted, erroneous, faithless, imprecise, incorrect, insincere, out of line, unfounded **10** apocryphal, fallacious, fictitious, inaccurate, inconstant, mendacious, misleading, perfidious, traitorous, unfaithful, ungrounded
declare ~: 4 deny **5** rebut **6** negate, recant, reject **7** disavow, dispute, gainsay **8** disclaim **9** repudiate **10** contradict
untrueness: 7 perfidy, treason **9** perfidity, treachery **10** disloyalty, infidelity
untrustworthy: 5 false, shady, sharp, snaky **6** fickle, rotten, shifty, sneaky, tricky, unsafe, unsure, untrue **7** corrupt, crooked, devious, dubious **8** derelict, disloyal, fallible, guileful, slippery, two-faced, unsteady, untrusty **9** conniving, deceitful, dishonest, faithless, two-timing, unassured
sort: 4 liar **5** rogue, scamp, sneak
untruth: 3 fib, lie **4** tale **5** story **6** canard, dupery **7** calumny, fallacy, falsity, fiction **9** deception, falsehood, invention, mendacity **10** imputation, inveracity
untruthful: 5 false, lying **6** shifty, tricky **7** crooked, devious, fibbing **8** delusive, guileful **9** deceitful, dishonest, faithless, insincere **10** mendacious
be ~: 3 con, fib, lie **4** dupe, fake, hoax, snow **5** bluff, couch, fudge **6** delude, invent, take in **7** concoct, deceive, distort, falsify, mislead, perjure **8** misguide, misquote, misstate, simulate, soft-soap **9** disinform, dissemble, four-flush, misinform **10** equivocate, exaggerate
be ~ with: 5 lie to **7** deceive
one: 4 liar **5** cheat, phony **6** fibber **7** deluder **8** deceiver, perjurer **9** con artist, falsifier, trickster **10** fabricator
unturned, leave no stone: 4 seek **5** scour **6** search, strive **7** persist, ransack, rummage **9** persevere
untutored: 3 raw **5** rough **6** unread **8** inexpert, untaught **10** illiterate, uneducated, unlettered, unschooled
untwine: 4 free **5** loose, ravel **6** uncoil, unreel, unwind **7** untwist **8** untangle
untwist: 5 ravel **6** spread, unfold, unwind **7** untwine **8** untangle **10** straighten
a rope, nautically: 5 feaze, feeze
untypical: 7 strange **8** isolated **9** anomalous, divergent
unum: 3 one **5** Latin
unusable: 4 junk **5** passé, sorry **6** crummy, no-good, trashy **7** inutile **8** bootless, obsolete, outmoded, pathetic, wretched **9** no-account, worthless **10** antiquated, superseded
become ~: 3 rot **4** mold, rust, sour, turn **5** decay, go bad, spoil, taint **6** molder **7** corrode, crumble **9** break down
unused: 3 new **4** free, idle, mint, over **5** blank, extra, fresh, spare **6** fallow, vacant, virgin **7** sitting, surplus, untaken **8** leftover, pristine, residual, untilled, virginal **10** on the shelf, unconsumed, unemployed
go ~: 3 sit **5** lie by **6** remain
unusual: 3 new, odd **4** eery, rare **5** alien, eerie, freak, fresh, funny, novel, outré, queer, weird **6** atypic, clever, exotic, freaky, quaint, quirky, scarce, unique, way-out **7** amazing, awesome, bizarre, curious, deviant, oddball, offbeat, special, strange, uncanny **8** aberrant, abnormal, atypical, creative, far apart, freakish, inspired, isolated, original, peculiar, singular, striking, uncommon, unwonted **9** anomalous, arresting, different, divergent, eccentric, fantastic, ingenious, inventive, irregular, laughable, marvelous, memorable, recherché, unheard-of, unnatural **10** individual, infrequent, innovative, noteworthy, occasional, outlandish, phenomenal, prodigious, remarkable, surprising, suspicious, unexpected, unfamiliar
article: 5 curio, relic **7** bibelot, whatnot **9** objet d'art **10** knick-knack
combining form: 4 anom- **5** anomo-
in Latin: 4 rara
person: 4 oner
unusually: 4 very **5** extra, oddly **6** mighty, rarely **7** awfully **8** terribly **9** curiously, extremely, strangely **10** especially, peculiarly, remarkably, uncommonly
unuttered: 5 quiet, tacit **6** unsaid **7** implied **8** implicit, unvoiced
unvaried: 4 same **6** boring **7** one-note **9** wearisome **10** monotonous
unvarnished: 3 raw **4** bare, open, pure, real **5** frank, naked, plain, stark **6** candid, honest, simple **7** genuine, literal **9** unadorned
unvarnished __: 5 truth
unvarying: 4 even, same, sure **5** rigid **6** smooth, stable, static, steady **7** equable, regular, routine, uniform **8** constant **9** continual, uniformly **10** consistent, homogenous, monotonous, true to type, unchanging
unveil: 3 ope **4** bare, leak, open, show, tell **6** expose, reveal **7** display, divulge, exhibit, lay bare, lay open, let slip, uncover **8** disclose, discover **9** make known **10** make public
unveiled: 4 open **5** clear, naked, overt, plain, shown **6** in view, patent, public **7** obvious, visible **8** apparent, clear-cut, explicit, knowable, manifest **10** observable
unveiling: 6 exposé **10** appearance, disclosure, revelation
cry of ~: 4 ta-da **5** ta-dah
unventilated: 4 shut **5** close, stale, thick **6** stuffy **8** confined **9** sealed off **10** oppressive
unveracious: 5 false, lying **7** devious **8** two-faced **9** deceitful, dishonest, insincere **10** mendacious, perfidious, untruthful
unverified: 8 spurious **9** equivocal **10** apocryphal
unversed: 3 raw **4** naif **5** fresh, green, naive, young **10** unfamiliar
one: 4 lamb, naif **6** rookie
unviewable: 5 perdu **6** covert, hidden, latent, minute, unseen **8** obscured **9** concealed, invisible **10** intangible, not in sight, out of sight, tucked away, unapparent
unvigilant: 6 unwary **7** napping **8** sleeping **9** unguarded **10** incautious
unvoiced: 4 mute **5** tacit **6** silent, unsaid **7** implied **8** implicit, inferred, unspoken, wordless **9** intimated, unuttered **10** understood
unwaning: 6 steady **7** chronic, endless, eternal, lasting, regular **8** constant, enduring, frequent, habitual, unbroken, unending, untiring **9** ceaseless, chronical, continual, incessant, perennial, permanent, perpetual, recurrent, unceasing, unfailing **10** persistent, persisting, relentless, repetitive, unflagging
unwanted: 5 spare **7** unasked **8** leftover, loveless, needless **9** unpopular, unwelcome
give ~ advice: 6 butt in, meddle
guest: 3 ant, bug, fly, nag **4** bore, drag, drip, flea, gnat, pain, pest, pill **5** creep, mouse **6** insect **7** termite **8** headache, housefly, mosquito, nuisance **9** cockroach
layer: 4 dust
plant: 4 weed
pounds: 4 flab
unwarranted: 5 unapt, undue, wrong **6** unfair, unjust **8** baseless, improper, mistaken **9** misguided, unfounded **10** bottomless, groundless
unwary: 4 naif, rash **5** brash, hasty, naive **7** unalert **8** careless, heedless, off-guard, reckless, sleeping **9** credulous, impetuous, imprudent, unadvised, uncareful, unguarded **10** falling for, ill-advised, incautious, indiscreet, unprepared, unvigilant, unwatchful
unwashed: 4 foul **5** dirty, dusty, grimy, muddy **6** filthy, grubby, grungy, smutty, soiled **7** smudged **8** begrimed **9** uncleaned **10** insanitary
great ~: 5 plebs **6** masses, people **8** riffraff **9** hoi polloi
unwasteful: 6 frugal **7** sparing, thrifty **10** economical
unwatchful: 3 lax **6** unwary **7** napping **9** unguarded **10** incautious
unwavering: 3 set **4** even, fast, firm, sure **5** fixed, loyal, solid, stony **6** all-out, stable, steady, stoney **7** abiding, dead set, decided, intense, staunch **8** constant, emphatic, enduring, faithful, forceful, hellbent, ironclad, resolute, unshaken, untiring **9** dedicated, immovable, iron-jawed, steadfast **10** conclusive, determined, foursquare, invariable, undeterred, unswerving
unwaxed: 4 dull, flat **10** lusterless
unwearied: 5 fresh **8** tireless, untiring **10** undeterred, unflagging
unwearying: 5 hyper **8** diligent, resolute, tireless, untiring **9** energetic **10** persistent, unflagging
unweave: 5 ravel **7** unravel **8** untangle **9** come apart
unwed: 5 alone **6** single **8** bachelor, divorced, eligible, solitary, wifeless **9** by oneself, on one's own, unmarried **10** spouseless, unattached
unwelcome: 5 lousy, pesky, pesty **7** shut out, unasked **8** excluded,

rejected, unsought, unwanted **9** obnoxious, thankless, uninvited, unpopular **10** ill-favored, unpleasant
unwelcoming: 3 icy **4** cold, cool **6** chilly **10** unfriendly
unwell: 3 bad, ill, low **4** sick, weak **6** ailing, infirm, laid up, poorly, queasy, queazy, sickly **7** unsound **8** diseased **9** afflicted, bedridden, unhealthy **10** indisposed, out of sorts
unwellness: 6 malady **7** ailment, disease, illness, malaise **8** debility, disorder, sickness **9** complaint, fragility, frailness, infirmity **10** affliction
unwet: 3 dry **4** arid, sere **7** drained, parched, thirsty **8** rainless **9** anhydrous, shriveled, waterless **10** dehydrated, desiccated
unwheeled vehicle: 4 sled **6** glider, sleigh **8** toboggan
unwholesome: 4 gamy, sour **5** gamey **6** impure, morbid, sickly **7** noisome **8** virulent **9** unhealthy
unwieldy: 5 bulky, gross, heavy, hefty **6** clumsy, clunky **7** awkward, hulking, massive, weighty **8** ungainly **9** lumbering, ponderous **10** burdensome, cumbersome
unwilling: 3 coy, shy **4** loth **5** loath **6** afraid, averse, forced **7** evasive, opposed **8** grudging, hesitant, negative **9** compelled, demurring, reluctant, resistant, shrinking, unwishful **10** begrudging, indisposed, intolerant, unobliging
  be ~: 4 balk **5** demur, hedge, tarry, waver **6** boggle, object, recoil, refuse, regret, resist, seesaw, shrink, waffle **7** decline, hold off, protest, scruple, shy away **8** complain, disagree, hang back, hesitate, hold back, pull back, question **9** hem and haw, make a fuss, pussyfoot, vacillate **10** disapprove, equivocate, think twice
  be ~ to: 4 hate **5** abhor, scorn **6** detest, loathe **7** despise, disdain, dislike **9** abominate **10** flinch from, recoil from
  to move: 4 iron **5** rigid **6** flinty, intent **7** adamant, diehard **8** hardened, hard-line, hellbent, obdurate, resolute, stubborn **9** immovable, immutable, obstinate, steadfast **10** inflexible
unwillingness: 7 refusal **8** aversion **10** hesitation
  to work: 5 sloth **7** languor **8** idleness, laziness, lethargy, otiosity **9** fainéance, indolence, passivity, slackness **10** torpidness
unwilted: 4 dewy **5** crisp, fresh, green **7** unfaded, verdant
unwind: 4 free, reel, rest, undo **5** loose, ravel, relax, spool **6** loosen, spread, unbend, uncoil, unfold, unreel, unroll, unwrap **7** cool off, ease off, recline, sit back, slacken, untwine, untwist **8** calm down, loosen up, recreate, separate, slow down, untangle, wind down **9** quiet down **10** take a break, take it easy
unwise: 4 naif, rash **5** inane, inept, naive, silly **7** foolish, unsound **8** childish, immature, reckless **9** foolhardy, impolitic, imprudent, misguided, senseless, unadvised, uncareful, unguarded **10** ill-advised, indiscreet, irrational, unthinking
  act: 4 no-no, tabu **5** taboo
  in an ~ way: 4 illy
unwished-for: 8 rejected, unsought, unwanted **9** thankless, uninvited, unpopular, unwelcome **10** unpleasant
unwitting: 6 chance **7** unaware, unmeant **8** innocent **9** forgetful, unknowing, unplanned **10** accidental, unfamiliar, unintended, unthinking
  victim: 4 pawn **5** patsy
unwittingly: 8 by chance, casually, unawares **9** by mistake **10** by accident
unwonted: 4 rare **7** unusual **8** singular, uncommon
unworkable: 7 of no use, useless, utopian **9** idealized, visionary **10** impossible, unfeasible
unworldly: 4 naif **5** green, naive **6** astral, dreamy **7** artless, corn-fed **8** ethereal, innocent, lamblike, trusting, unartful, wide-eyed **9** celestial, ingenuous, spiritual, visionary **10** idealistic, unaffected
unworried: 4 calm, cool, easy **6** placid, serene **8** carefree, composed, tranquil **9** unruffled **10** insouciant, nonchalant, unagitated, untroubled
unworthy: 3 low **4** base, vile **5** unfit **6** no-good, shabby **7** ignoble **8** shameful, wretched **9** degrading, no-account, unmerited, valueless **10** ineligible, inglorious, out of place, unbecoming
  of: 5 below **7** beneath **10** inferior to, too good for
unwrap: 3 ope **4** open, undo **6** unfold, unwind **7** uncover
unwrinkle: 4 iron **5** press **6** smooth
unwritten: 4 oral **5** tacit, vocal **6** spoken, unsaid, verbal **8** accepted, narrated **9** customary **10** understood, unrecorded
  on: 5 blank, clean, empty **8** unmarked
  rule: 4 wont **5** usage **6** custom, policy **7** folkway **8** practice **9** etiquette, precedent, tradition **10** convention, observance
unwrought: 5 crude, rough
unyielding: 3 set **4** deaf, firm, grim, hard, iron, taut **5** fixed, rigid, rocky, solid, stern, stiff, tight, tough **6** flinty, mulish, steely, strong, wilful **7** adamant, chronic, decided, granite, hard-set, staunch, willful **8** hard-core, hard-line, locked in, obdurate, resolute, ruthless, stubborn **9** chronical, dead set on, difficult, hard-nosed, immovable, impliable, insistent, iron-jawed, merciless, obstinate, pigheaded, steadfast, tenacious, unbending, unmovable, unpitying **10** foursquare, headstrong, implacable, inexorable, inflexible, invincible
  one: 4 mule **7** diehard, holdout
unzip: 4 ease, open, undo **6** loosen **7** disjoin **8** unfasten **9** disengage, untighten
Unzipped (1995 film)
  director: Douglas Keeve
up: 4 hike, lift, over **5** alert, aloft, astir, at bat, awake, aware, boost, happy, light, on end, raise, risen **6** arisen, awoken, elated, uphill **8** cheerful, increase, vigilant, watchful **9** attentive, conscious
  neither ~ nor down: 4 even
  prefix: 3 ano-
up __: 5 a tree, quark, to now, to par **6** in arms **7** against
up __ air: 5 in the
up __ elbows: 5 to the
up __ good: 4 to no
up __ grabs: 3 for
up __ hilt: 5 to the
up __ point: 3 to a
up __ the wall: 7 against
up-__: 5 close, front, tempo **6** to-date
up-__-minute: 5 to-the
__ up: 3 act, add, ate, buy, cry, cut, dig, dry, eat, fed, fix, gas, get, gum, het, ice, jam, key, lap, lay, let, mix, mop, one, own, pay, pep, pin, pop, put, rev, run, set, sew, sit, sop, sum, tee, tie, tog, use **4** a leg, ante, back, ball, bang, bear, beef, blow, bone, buck, bulk, burn, call, chat, chin, clam, come, cook, crop, curl, doll, draw, drum, ease, fair, fess, fill, fold, foul, free, gear, give, goof, grow, hang, hard, haul, heat, hoke, hold, hole, hook, jack, jazz, keep, kick, lace, lash, line, look, make, mark, mess, move, muck, open, pass, pent, perk, pick, pile, pipe, play, pony, prop, pull, pump, rack, rake, ramp, rile, ring, roll, root, send, show, shut, sign, size, slip, slow, snap, soak, soup, step, stir, suit, take, talk, tank, team, tear, tidy, tied, tone, tool, trip, tune, turn, warm, wash, whip, wind, wise, work, wrap **5** brace, break, bring, brush, buddy, build, catch, chalk, choke, clean, clear, climb, cough, cover, crack, crank, cross, dream, dress, duked, dummy, fetch, flare, goose, gussy, ham it, hurry, juice, light, liven, louse, match, mix it, patch, phony, piled, rough, round, scare, scarf, screw, scrub, shake, shape, shoot, shore, sober, speak, speed, spiff, split, stack, stand, start, stick, think, touch, trump, write **6** buckle, butter, button, cooped, double, follow, freeze, geared, gummed, loosen, messed, polish, rustle, spruce, square, strike, thumbs, washed **7** measure, ponying, ratchet, wrought
__ up!: 3 Get **4** Shut **5** Heads, Put 'em, Surf's
__-up: 3 fly, jam, lay, nip, one, pop, put, sit, tie **4** bang, beat, chin, foul, hang, high, made, mock, pile, pull, push, send, slip, tune, warm, wrap **5** close, heads, hyped, smash, start, stuck, write **6** backer, bottom, change, follow, higher, runner, washed
Up (2009 film)
  voice cast: Edward Asner, Christopher Plummer
Up __ & Personal: 5 Close
Up __ Roof: 5 on the
Up __ We Belong: 5 Where
U.P.: 2 RR
up a __: 4 tree **5** stump
__ up against: 4 come
up against the __: 4 wall
up and __: 5 about **6** around
up-and-__: 4 down **5** comer **6** coming
Up and __!: 4 at 'em
up and around: 5 about **8** stirring
up-and-coming: 3 apt **4** able **6** bright, gifted, likely, odds-on **7** budding **8** talented **9** ambitious, promising
  one: 4 doer **6** dynamo **7** hustler **8** achiever, go-getter, live wire, operator
up-and-down: 8 vertical, volatile, whole hog **9** irregular, mercurial **10** capricious, thoroughly, throughout
__ Up and Dream: 4 Wake
__-up-and-go: 3 get
up-and-up
  on the ~: 4 fair **5** legit, licit **6** kosher
Upanishads studier: 5 Hindu **6** Hindoo
Up Around the Bend (1970 song)
  artist: Creedence Clearwater Revival
upbeat: 4 glad, rosy **5** alive, arsis, happy, light, merry **6** blithe, cheery, genial, jovial, joyful, joyous **7** buoyant, gleeful, hopeful, pleased, tickled **8** blissful, cheerful, ecstatic, euphoric, exultant, jubilant, mirthful, positive, sanguine, thrilled **9** confident, delighted, overjoyed, promising, rejoicing, vivacious **10** flying high, heartening, optimistic
upbraid: 3 jaw, nag, rag **4** lash, rail, rate, twit **5** abuse, blame, chide, scold **6** berate, rebuke **7** bawl out, censure, chew out, condemn, lambast, reprove, tell off **8** admonish, chastise, denounce, lambaste, reproach **9** castigate, criticize, dress down, excoriate, fulminate, reprehend, reprimand **10** denunciate, tongue-lash, vituperate
upbraiding: 5 abuse **6** earful, rebuke, tirade **7** lecture, reproof **8** berating, hard time, scolding **9** going-over, reprimand, talking-to **10** admonition, bawling-out, chewing-out, correction, impugnment
upbringing: 7 history **8** training **9** education, framework, grounding, schooling **10** background, experience
__-up call: 4 wake
upclimb: 4 rise
Up Close & Personal (1996 film)
  cast: Michelle Pfeiffer, Robert Redford
upcoming: 6 future **7** by and by, looming, nearing **8** eventual,

expected, imminent, oncoming 9 impending, onrushing, potential 10 subsequent
upcountry: 6 inland
Up Country
  author: Nelson DeMille
UPC, part of: 3 Bar 4 Code 9 Universal
  site: 4 mdse.
update: 4 post, redo 5 amend, brief, emend, renew, reset, train 6 inform, revise 7 freshen, improve, refresh, restore 8 renovate, revision 9 modernize, refurbish 10 rejuvenate
updated: 3 new 5 added, fresh, newer 6 modern 7 current 8 brand-new, improved 9 au courant 10 redesigned
__-up demand: 4 pent
Updike, John: 6 writer
  work: Bech Is Back
    Pigeon Feathers
    Rabbit at Rest
    Rabbit Is Rich
    Rabbit Redux
    Rabbit, Run
    Terrorist
    Too Far to Go
    The Widows of Eastwick
updo: 4 coif 9 hairstyle
__ Up, Doc?: 5 What's
updraft: 7 thermal
upend: 3 tip 5 raise 6 defeat, invert, topple 7 capsize, reverse, tip over 8 flip over, overturn, turn over
upended: 7 upright 8 inverted, vertical 9 inside-out 10 topsy-turvy
up for __: 5 grabs
__ up for: 4 make 5 stand, stick
up-front: 4 open, true 5 frank 6 candid, honest, trusty 7 genuine, natural, sincere, upright 9 ingenuous, outspoken, unguarded, veracious 10 aboveboard, forthright, from the hip, point-blank, unaffected, unreserved, unreticent
  be ~: 5 level 9 come clean
upgo: 4 rise 6 ascend, ascent
upgrade: 4 bump, hill, lift, rise 5 boost, emend, raise 6 ascent, better, enrich, glacis, polish, reform 7 advance, elevate, enhance, improve, promote, sharpen 8 increase, progress 9 acclivity, meliorate, refurbish 10 ameliorate
upgrading: 9 elevation 10 betterment, exaltation
upgrowth: 4 rise 5 surge
upheaval: 4 mess, riot 5 chaos, quake, storm, throe 6 bedlam, blowup, mayhem, trauma, tremor, tumult, unrest, uproar 7 anarchy, ferment, new deal, temblor, tempest, turmoil 8 disarray, disaster, eruption, outburst, shakeout, uprising 9 agitation, cataclysm, confusion, explosion, tidal wave 10 disruption, earthquake, hurly-burly, revolution, transition, turnaround
  primeval ~: 5 chaos
upheave: 4 lift, rear 5 hoist, raise 7 elevate 9 bear aloft
uphill: 4 hard 5 rough, tough 6 rising, taxing, thorny, trying 7 arduous, hard-won, labored, onerous, operose, skyward, sloping 8 climbing, grueling, toilsome 9 acclivous, ascending, demanding, difficult, effortful, laborious, punishing, strenuous 10 enervating, exhausting, formidable, oppressive
uphold: 3 aid 4 back, bear, help, lift, obey, prop 5 boost, brace, carry, hoist, honor, prove, raise, shore, vouch 6 affirm, assist, attest, defend, ratify, second 7 approve, bolster, confirm, elevate, endorse, indorse, justify, promote, respect, stand by, stick by, support, sustain 8 advocate, buttress, champion, maintain, preserve, side with 9 encourage, recommend, stabilize, vindicate 10 strengthen
upholder: 8 believer, mainstay 9 proponent, supporter
upholding: 9 consoling, succoring 10 comforting, reassuring, sustaining
upholster: 3 pad
upholstery
  fabric: 5 frise, vinyl 6 damask, velour 7 tabaret, velours 8 moquette 9 horsehair, Naugahyde
  lace for ~: 5 orris
  tool: 3 awl
UPI: 4 wire 8 news wire
  former ~ equipment: 3 TTY
  part of ~: 4 Intl. 5 Press 6 United
up in __: 4 arms 5 smoke
Up in Smoke (1978 film)
  cast: Tommy Chong, Cheech Marin
up in the __: 3 air
__-up job: 4 bang
upkeep: 5 costs, price 6 budget, outlay 7 repairs, support 8 expenses, overhead 10 sustenance
upland: 4 hill 5 ridge, table 7 plateau
  plain: 4 moor, wold
uplay: 5 stock, store
uplift: 4 buoy 5 cheer, edify, exalt, hoist, raise 6 reform, uphold 7 advance, elevate 10 exhilarate, regenerate
  seismic ~: 5 horst
uplifted: 4 tall 5 lofty 7 soaring 8 towering
uplifting: 7 refined 8 artistic, cultural 9 enriching, nurturing 10 artistical, broadening, civilizing, exaltation
__ Up Little Susie: 4 Wake
__-upmanship: 3 one
UPN
  successor: 5 The CW
Upolu: 4 isle 6 island
  locale: 5 Samoa
  port: 4 Apia
upon: 2 on 4 atop, onto 7 on top of
  in French: 3 sur
  prefix: 3 epi-, sur-
  starter: 4 here 5 there, where
__ upon: 3 hit, put, set, sit 4 call, come, fall, look 5 build, count, enter, foist, pitch, smile, touch 6 chance, happen
__ up on: 4 bone, gang, keep, pick, read 5 brush, check
__-upon: 3 put
__ upon a time: 4 once
up one's __: 5 alley 6 sleeve
__ up one's act: 5 clean
__ up one's hands: 5 throw
__ up one's heels: 4 kick
__ up one's sleeve: 4 card 5 laugh
upon my __: 4 word
Up on the Roof (1962 song)
  artist: Drifters
__-upon-Trent: 6 Burton
__-upon-Tweed: 7 Berwick
__ up or shut up: 3 put
upper: 3 top 4 high 5 above, berth, elite 6 higher 7 eminent, loftier, topmost 8 overhead, superior
  atmosphere: 3 sky 5 ether 6 aether
  boot ~: 4 vamp
  case: 7 capital
  chamber: 4 loft 5 attic 6 dormer, garret, Senate
  crust: 4 rich 5 elite 6 gentry, jet set 7 society 8 nobility 9 exclusive, gentility 10 haute monde
  ender: 3 cut 4 case, most
  garment: 4 vest 6 jerkin 9 waistcoat
  get the ~ hand: 4 beat, bury, drub, rout, stun 5 cream, crush, drown, quell, smash, total, trash, upset, waste 6 defeat, subdue 7 clobber, conquer, oppress, put away, stagger, take out, torpedo, trounce 8 bear down, blow away, bulldoze, overcome, roll over, shellack, suppress, vanquish 9 overpower, overthrow, subjugate 10 take care of
  hand: 4 edge 7 control, victory 9 advantage, authority, dominance
  have the ~ hand: 4 boss, head, lead, rule 5 reign 6 direct, govern, manage 7 command, control, dictate, prevail, shellac, triumph 8 dominate, overrule 9 subjugate, tyrannize 10 monopolize, run the show
  keep a stiff ~ lip: 4 cope 6 bear up, hang in, manage 8 face up to
  limit: 3 cap, lid, max, top 7 ceiling, maximum 8 pinnacle
  part: 3 cap, lid, tip, top 4 apex, peak, roof 5 cover, crest, crown, spire 6 finial, summit, vertex 7 ceiling 8 pinnacle
  prefix: 3 ano-
  trunk: 5 chest 6 thorax
upper __: 3 air, arm 4 case, deck, hand 5 berth, class, crust, house
__-upper: 5 fixer 6 pepper, picker, warmer 7 cheerer
Upper __: 5 Volta
Upper __ Side: 4 East, West
upper-class: 4 posh 5 elite, noble 6 aristo 7 moneyed 8 affluent, highborn 9 important, patrician
upperclassman: 2 sr. 3 snr. 6 senior
upper-crust: 6 aristo 8 literati, well-bred 9 exclusive, highbrows, patrician 10 haute monde, illuminati
uppercut: 3 hit, jab 4 bash, belt, biff, blow, clip, jolt, slam, slug, sock 5 clout, punch, smack, smash, swipe, whack, whomp 6 thwack, wallop 8 haymaker 10 roundhouse
  target: 4 chin
Upper Egypt: 4 Cush, Kush
upper house member: 3 sen. 7 senator
__ upper lip: 5 stiff
uppermost: 3 top 4 main 5 chief, prime 6 apical 7 highest, leading, primary, supreme 8 dominant, greatest, loftiest 9 paramount, principal 10 overriding, preeminent
upper right in heraldry: 6 canton
uppers
  on one's: *see* needy
uppity: 6 remote 8 snobbish, superior 10 hoity-toity
  act ~: 4 snap 5 deign
  one: 4 snip, snob 5 snoot
Uppsala: 4 city, town
  locale: 6 Sweden
upraise: 4 lift 5 boost, cheer, erect, hoist 7 console, elevate, lighten 8 heighten
upraised: 4 high 5 above, aloft 8 elevated
uprear: 4 lift 5 erect, hoist
upright: 3 leg 4 fair, good, jamb, just, pier, pile, post, prim, pure, true, vert. 5 clean, erect, frank, jambe, legit, moral, noble, on end, piano, plumb, proud, pylon, shaft, sheer, solid, sound 6 candid, column, decent, honest, picket, pillar, raised, square, trusty, worthy 7 endways, ethical, factual, upended 8 baluster, credible, innocent, keyboard, reliable, standing, straight, vertical, virtuous 9 blameless, exemplary, honorable, reputable, righteous, veracious 10 aboveboard, evenhanded, forthright, high-minded, inculcable, law-abiding, on the level, principled, scrupulous, vertically
  relative: 5 grand 6 spinet
uprightly: 9 honorably
uprightness: 5 honor 6 virtue 7 honesty, loyalty, probity 8 morality, nobility, veracity 10 principles
uprise: 5 rebel, swell 7 elevate
uprising: 4 riot 6 émeute, mutiny, revolt 7 ferment 8 civil war, outbreak, upheaval 9 rebellion 10 insurgence, insurgency, revolution
upriver: 6 inland
uproar: 3 ado, cry, din, row 4 flap, fuss, mess, rage, riot, stir, to-do 5 babel, brawl, chaos, furor, hoo-ha, mania, melee, mix-up, noise, stink, storm 6 babble, bedlam, bustle, clamor, fracas, furore, hassle, hoo-hah, hubbub, jangle, mayhem, outcry, pother, racket, ruckus, rumpus, strife, tumult, unrest 7 anarchy, clangor, clatter, dispute, ferment, rampage, ruction, tempest, turmoil 8 big scene, brouhaha, disarray, disorder, hangover, madhouse, violence 9 commotion, confusion, hue and cry, maelstrom, mobocracy 10 donnybrook, hubba-hubba, hullabaloo, hurly-burly, turbulence
  in an ~: 4 busy, wild 6 heated,

hectic, woolly 7 chaotic, excited, frantic, furious, hurried 8 confused, exciting, feverish, frenetic, frenzied 9 turbulent 10 boisterous, disordered, tumultuous
uproarious: 4 loud, wild 5 a riot, forte, funny, merry, noisy 7 blaring, booming, jarring, pealing, rackety, raucous, reboant 8 crashing, piercing, plangent, rumbling, sonorous, strident, turned up 9 big-voiced, clamorous, deafening, hilarious 10 boisterous, gut-busting, hysterical, resounding, stentorian, strepitous, thundering, vociferous
uproariousness: 3 din 5 noise
uproot: 3 rid 4 grub, move, pull, weed 5 exile, pluck, purge 6 remove, rip out 7 destroy, extract, jerk out, tear out, weed out, wipe out 8 demolish, dislodge, displace 9 eliminate, eradicate, extirpate 10 annihilate, do away with, transplant
uprooting: 7 pulling, removal 9 taking out 10 extraction
__-ups: 3 lay, mix 4 mock, send 5 close, cover, grown 6 higher
UPS
competitor: 3 DHL 5 FedEx
delivery: 3 ctn., pak., pkg.
part: 4 Serv. 6 Parcel, United 7 Service
units: 3 lbs.
upsa-__: 5 daisy
ups and __: 5 downs
upscale: 4 nice, posh, rich, tony 5 ritzy, swank, toney 6 swanky 7 moneyed, wealthy 8 affluent 9 expensive, luxurious
upset: 3 ail, bug, get, ire, irk, mad, tip, vex, win 4 beat, gall, hurt, jolt, miff, pain, rile, rout, sick, sore, tilt, undo 5 agita, alarm, angry, annoy, cross, fazed, floor, get to, harry, huffy, jumpy, key up, livid, messy, mix up, peeve, pique, psych, riled, scare, shake, shock, spill, spilt, spoil, spook, steam, teary, throw, tizzy, vexed, worry 6 affect, bother, defeat, dismay, enrage, excite, flurry, fuming, grieve, harass, hassle, heated, in a pet, invert, jumble, madden, mess up, muddle, nettle, offend, peeved, pick on, piqued, pother, put out, queasy, queazy, raging, rankle, rattle, raving, ruffle, shaken, sicken, sorrow, stir up, sullen, tackle, tee off, thrown, thwart, topple, trauma, tumble, uneasy, unglue, work up 7 agitate, annoyed, beat out, capsize, chagrin, conquer, depress, derange, disrupt, disturb, excited, fluster, frantic, furious, illness, in a huff, in a snit, jittery, licking, make ill, muddled, nervous, nettled, outplay, peevish, perturb, pouting, provoke, ranting, rattled, reverse, ruffled, rummage, screw-up, shake up, shatter, shocked, shook up, spilled, steamed, stewing, subvert, tearful, teed off, tick off, tip over, toppled, trouble, turmoil, unglued, unhinge, unnerve, victory, worried 8 agitated, bothered, bowl over, burned up, capsized, confound, confused, convulse, dismayed, disorder, disquiet, distract, distress, embitter, exercise, freak out, fretting, imbitter, in a tizzy, incensed, irritate, outraged, overcome, override, overrule, overturn, provoked, snappish, steaming, surprise, troubled, unsettle, unstring, unstrung, worked up 9 aggravate, agitation, bellicose, bristling, bummed-out, concerned, discomfit, dislocate, displease, disturbed, indignant, indispose, knock over, make waves, overpower, overthrow, overwhelm, perturbed, seeing red, sniveling, sorrowful, squeamish, throw over, ticked off, unsettled 10 demoralize, disarrange, discomfort, discompose, disconcert, disgruntle, disheveled, disordered, displeased, disquieted, disruption, distraught, distressed, exasperate, freaked out, hysterical, in disarray, infuriated, make a scene, overturned, psyched out, queasiness, revolution, run afoul of, tipped over, upside-down
be ~ about: 3 rue 4 care, moan, mope 5 worry 6 bemoan, bewail, lament, regret, repent, repine 7 cry over, deplore, scruple 8 look back, weep over 9 apologize 10 be sorry for, disapprove
get ~: 4 burn, pout, stew 6 blow up, seethe, simmer 7 bristle, smolder
political ~: 4 coup 5 purge 6 revolt, stroke 10 revolution
state: 3 pet 4 huff, snit, stew 5 pique 6 temper
with: 5 mad at
upsetting: 3 sad 5 tight 6 trying 7 hurtful 8 grievous 9 confusing, saddening 10 depressing, disruptive, lamentable, unsettling
Upshaw: 4 Dawn, Gene
Upshaw, Dawn: 6 singer 7 soprano
specialty: 5 opera
upshot: 3 end 4 core, gist, meat, pith 5 issue, sense 6 burden, effect, ending, payoff, result, thrust 7 meaning, outcome, product, purport 8 key point 9 aftermath, outgrowth, substance 10 conclusion, denouement, resolution
upside-__ cake: 4 down
upside-down: 4 cake 5 upset 7 haywire, in chaos, jumbled, mixed-up 8 backward, bottom up, confused, inverted, reversed 10 disorderly
sleeper: 5 sloth
smile: 5 frown, scowl
turn ~: 4 comb, flip 6 invert 7 ransack, reverse, rummage, shake up 8 overturn
Upside Down (1980 song)
artist: Diana Ross
__ up sides: 6 choose
upsilon: 5 Greek 6 letter
follower: 3 phi
preceder: 3 tau
upslope: 4 rise
upstager: 3 ham
upstairs: 4 over 5 above 10 management
kick ~: 4 bump 5 boost, favor, raise 6 better, move up 7 advance, elevate, endorse, further, promote
Upstairs, Downstairs
role: 4 maid
__ up stakes: 4 pull
upstanding: 4 good, just, true 5 clean, erect, moral, solid 6 decent, honest 7 ethical, upright 8 elevated 9 honorable 10 law-abiding, scrupulous
upstart: 4 snob, Turk 5 yahoo 6 nobody 7 parvenu, wannabe 9 arriviste, latecomer, nonentity, pretender, vulgarian, young Turk 10 jackanapes
__-up-sticks: 4 pick
upsurge: 4 boom, jump, leap, rise, wave 6 expand 7 enlarge 8 increase 9 crescendo
upsweep: 3 bun 4 coif, puff 6 hairdo 7 beehive, chignon 8 coiffure 9 pompadour
upswing: 4 boom, leap, rise 5 boost, rally, surge 8 increase
__ upswing: 4 on an
upsy-__: 5 daisy
uptake
quick on the ~: 3 apt 4 keen 5 alert, quick, sharp, smart 6 adroit, astute, bright 9 astucious, receptive
slow on the ~: 3 dim 5 dense 6 obtuse
__-up terminal: 4 dial
up the __: 4 ante, wall 5 creek, river
Up the __ Staircase: 4 Down
__ Up the Band: 6 Strike
__ up the curtain: 4 ring
Up the Down Staircase (1967 film)
cast: Sandy Dennis, Eileen Heckart
Up the Ladder to the Roof (1970 song)
artist: Supremes
__ up the pieces: 4 pick
__ up the rear: 5 bring
__ up the road: 4 burn
__ up the works: 3 gum
__ up the wrong tree: 4 bark
uptick: 4 gain, rise 8 increase
uptight: 4 edgy, prim 5 antsy, itchy, jumpy, stiff, tense, testy 6 jangly, on edge, strict, sullen, uneasy 7 anxious, fearful, jittery, nervous, prudish, restive, worried 8 agitated, choleric, fluttery, restless, skittish, strained, troubled 9 concerned, excitable, ill at ease, irascible, querulous, unbending, withdrawn 10 distressed, frightened, high-strung, restrained, suspicious
Uptight (Everything's Alright) (1966 song)
artist: Stevie Wonder
up to __: 3 now, par 4 date 5 snuff, speed 7 scratch
__ up to: 3 add, own, put 4 face, feel, lead, live, look, play 5 stand
up-to-date: 2 in 3 hot, mod, new, now 4 chic 5 faddy, fresh, in use, today 6 extant, latest, modern, modish, newest, recent, red-hot, timely, trendy, with it 7 abreast, à la mode, current, faddish, in-thing, in vogue, popular, present, stylish, voguish 8 advanced, brand-new, neoteric 9 au courant, in fashion 10 all the rage, avant-garde, newfangled
in French: 9 au courant
make ~: 3 fix 5 fix up, refit, renew 6 extend, resume 7 freshen, furbish, remodel, restore 8 overhaul, renovate 9 modernize, refurbish 10 revitalize
__ Up to Make Up: 5 Break
Upton: 8 Sinclair
up to no __: 4 good
up to one's __: 4 ears, neck 6 elbows
up to one's __ tricks: 3 old
up to the __: 4 hilt 6 elbows
up-to-the-__: 6 minute
__ up to the bar: 4 step
up-to-the-minute: 3 hip, hot, mod, new 4 chic 5 vogue 6 modern, modish, snappy, timely, trendy 7 in style, in vogue, stylish
uptown: 4 posh, rich 5 ritzy, swank 6 swanky 7 moneyed, stylish, worldly
Uptown Girl (1983 song)
artist: Billy Joel
Uptown Hoedown
composer: PDQ Bach
Uptown New York (1932 film)
cast: Jack Oakie
U.P. Trail, The
author: Zane Grey
uptrend: 4 rise
upturn: 3 tip 4 boom, jump, rise 5 boost, rally, surge 6 invert 8 increase
brief ~: 3 pip 4 blip 5 spike
market ~: 5 rally 6 uptick 8 recovery 10 turnaround
upturned: 5 on end
Up Up and Away
composer: Jimmy Webb
Up, Up and Away (1967 song)
artist: Fifth Dimension
__-up visor: 4 flip
upward: 4 atop, over 5 above, aloft 7 hanging 8 in the sky, overhead, vertical
combining form: 3 ano- 6 sursum-
extension: 4 rise
move ~: 4 lift, rise 5 arise, climb, hoist, raise, surge 6 ascend 7 surface
movement: 4 rise 6 ascent
prefix: 3 ana-, ano-
shove: 4 lift, push 5 boost, heave, hoist 6 assist, thrust
slope: 4 bank, hill, rise 5 grade 6 ascent, glacis 7 hillock, incline 8 gradient, hillside 9 acclivity, elevation
slope ~: 4 rise 5 climb 6 ascend
upwardly mobile professional, young: 4 suit 5 yuppy 6 yuppie
upwards of: 4 over 5 above 6 nearly 8 more than
upwelling: 4 gush, rise 5 surge, swell 6 influx, onrush
Up Where We Belong (1982 song): 4 duet
artist: Joe Cocker, Jennifer Warnes

__ up with: 3 put 4 come, take
__ up with the Joneses: 4 keep
__ Up Your Overcoat: 6 Button
__ Up Your Shakespeare: 5 Brush
Ur: 4 city, town
  locale: 4 Irak, Iraq 5 Sumer
uraeus: 3 asp 5 snake 7 reptile
Ural: 5 range, river
  city on the ~: 4 Orsk 6 Guryev
  locale: 6 Russia
Urals: 4 mtns. 5 range 9 mountains
  area east of the ~: 4 Asia
  area west of the ~: 3 Eur. 6 Europe
  locale: 6 Russia
  metropolis: 3 Ufa
Urania: 4 Muse
  lover: 6 Apollo
  parent: 4 Zeus 9 Mnemosyne
  sister: 4 Clio 5 Erato 6 Thalia 7 Euterpe 8 Calliope 9 Melpomene 10 Polyhymnia 11 Terpsichore
uranium: 5 metal 7 element
  mineral: 6 curite
uranium __: 5 oxide 6 dating 7 dioxide
uranology: 9 astronomy
Uranus: 3 orb 6 planet
  child: 5 Titan
  daughter: 4 Rhea, Thea, Thia 5 Aetna 6 Phoebe, Tethys, Themis 9 Mnemosyne
  moon: 4 Puck 5 Ariel 6 Bianca, Juliet, Oberon, Portia 7 Belinda, Caliban, Miranda, Ophelia, Sycorax, Titania, Umbriel 8 Cordelia, Cressida, Rosalind 9 Desdemona
  mother: 4 Gaea
  son: 4 Anax 6 Cronos, Cronus 7 Iapetus, Oceanus 8 Hyperion
  wife: 4 Gaea
urb: 4 city 8 downtown 9 inner city
urban: 3 mun. 4 city, town 5 civic, metro 6 public 7 built-up, central, village 8 citified, downtown, nonrural 9 inner-city, municipal
  area: 4 park, slum, ward 5 block 6 ghetto
  blight: 4 slum, smog 5 smaze 6 litter
  combining form: 5 metro-
  dwelling: 4 flat, loft 5 condo 6 duplex 9 apartment
  employee: 8 commuter
  executive: 5 mayor
  greenery: 4 lawn, park 6 common, square 7 reserve 8 preserve
  noise: 4 beep, honk, toot 5 blare, blast, siren
  oasis: 4 park 6 common 8 preserve 10 playground
  opposite: 5 rural 6 rustic, sylvan 7 bucolic 8 agrarian, Arcadian, pastoral 9 backwoods 10 provincial
  planner, at times: 5 zoner
  porch: 5 stoop
  professional: 5 yuppy 6 yuppie
  route: 2 av., st. 3 ave. 4 blvd. 6 avenue, street 9 boulevard
  tawdrily ~: 4 neon
  threat: 3 mob 4 gang, pack, ring
  transport: 3 bus, cab, els 4 hack, taxi, tram 5 moped
  walker: 3 ped. 10 pedestrian
urban __: 4 myth 6 blight, legend, sprawl 7 renewal
Urban: 4 pope 7 pontiff
Urban __: 6 Cowboy
Urbana: 4 city, town
  locale: 8 Illinois
  team: 6 Illini
Urban Cowboy (1980 film)
  cast: John Travolta, Debra Winger
urbane: 4 chic 5 bland, civil, ritzy, slick, suave 6 poised, polite, smooth 7 affable, courtly, elegant, gallant, genteel, politic, refined, tactful, worldly 8 cultured, debonair, finished, gracious, mannerly, obliging, pleasant, polished, well-bred 9 civilized, courteous, debonaire, high-toned 10 cultivated, debonnaire
Urban Horrors
  author: Ray Bradbury
urbanity: 4 tact 5 charm, class, couth, grace, style 6 polish 7 culture, finesse, manners 8 breeding, civility, courtesy 9 gallantry 10 refinement
urbanize: 6 citify
Urban Prospect, The
  author: Lewis Mumford
urbia: 6 cities
urbi et __: 4 orbi
__ urbis conditae: 4 anno
urchin: 3 imp, pup 4 brat, waif 5 gamin, scamp 6 gamine 9 young punk 10 holy terror, ragamuffin
  sea ~: 7 echinus
  sea ~ feature: 5 spine
  street ~: 3 imp 4 waif 5 gamin, stray 6 orphan 9 foundling 10 ragamuffin
__ urchin: 3 sea 6 street
Urdu: 5 Indic 8 language
  poet: 6 Ghalib
Ure: 4 Mary 6 Andrew
Urea: 5 nymph
  father: 8 Poseidon
  lover: 6 Apollo
uredo: 5 hives
urethane: 5 ester
Urey, Harold: 7 chemist 8 Nobelist
Urfa: 4 city, town
  locale: 6 Turkey
  once: 6 Edessa
urge: 2 id 3 ask, beg, egg, get, yen 4 coax, goad, itch, lust, move, pray, prod, push, spur, warn, whim, will, wish 5 drive, egg on, fancy, impel, lobby, plead, press, rally, tempt 6 adjure, advise, cajole, charge, demand, desire, enjoin, exhort, incite, induce, insist, prompt, propel, reason, whip up, work on 7 beseech, cheer on, counsel, craving, entreat, impetus, implore, impulse, inspire, longing, passion, promote, propose, push for, put up to, quicken, request, solicit, wanting, wheedle 8 advocate, appeal to, appetite, argue for, insist on, instinct, maneuver, motivate, persuade, petition, press for, pressure, stimulus, weakness, yearning 9 encourage, hankering, importune, influence, instigate, recommend, stimulate 10 compulsion, incitement, inducement, motivation, persuasion, sweet tooth, temptation
  have an ~ for: 4 ache, itch, long, lust, miss, pine, seek, want, wish 5 covet, crave, fancy, yearn 6 demand, desire, hanker, hunger, thirst 8 feel like
  not to: 4 warn 5 deter 7 caution 8 dissuade 9 talk out of 10 discourage
  on: 3 egg 4 abet, goad, move, poke, prod, push, spur 5 drive, impel, press, shove 6 compel, incite, induce, prompt, propel, thrust, turn on 7 inspire, quicken 8 mobilize, motivate, persuade, pressure, railroad 9 instigate
urgency: 4 need, rush, zeal 5 haste, hurry, press, speed 6 crisis, stress 7 gravity 8 exigence, exigency, pressure, priority 9 immediacy, necessity
  without ~: 4 idly 6 slowly
urgent: 4 dire, rush 5 acute, grave, vital 6 crying 7 burning, crucial, driving, earnest, exigent, hurry-up, instant, intense, primary, serious, weighty 8 critical, exigeant, foremost, pressing, required 9 called-for, demanding, desperate, essential, immediate, impelling, important, insistent, momentous, necessary, paramount 10 compelling, imperative, passionate, touch and go
  appeal: 4 plea, suit 6 demand, orison, prayer 8 entreaty, petition
  letters: 3 PDQ, SOS 4 ASAP
  situation: 4 emer. 9 emergency
Urgent (1981 song)
  artist: Foreigner
urgently: 4 hard 5 madly 6 keenly 7 acutely 8 intently, severely, strongly 9 earnestly, intensely, seriously
urger: 6 patron 7 apostle, booster 8 advocate, espouser, exponent, lobbyist 9 apologist, proponent, supporter
urging: 6 behest 7 coaxing 8 advocacy 9 wheedling 10 insistence
Uri: 6 canton, Geller
Uriah: 4 Heep 7 Hittite
Urich, Robert: 5 actor
  TV: Soap, Spenser: For Hire, Vega$
Uriel: 5 angel
Urim and __: 7 Thummim
Uris, Leon: 6 writer
  character: 3 Ari
  work: Armageddon
    Battle Cry
    Exodus
    A God in Ruins
    The Haj
    Mila 18
    Mitla Pass
    O'Hara's Choice
    QB VII
    Redemption
    Topaz
    Trinity
URL: 7 address 10 Web address
  ender: 3 com, edu, gov, net, org
  part: 3 dot, www
  starter: 4 http
urn: 4 bowl, vase 6 brewer, holder, vessel 7 amphora, samovar 9 container 10 jardiniere
  homophone for ~: 3 ern 4 earn, erne
  protuberance: 3 ear
urne contents: 4 café
Urquhart: 6 Thomas
Ursae __: 7 Majoris, Minoris
Ursa Major: 4 bear
  constellation near ~: 5 Draco
  star in ~: 5 Mizar
Ursa Minor: 4 bear
ursid: 4 bear 6 Kodiak 7 grizzly
  noise: 5 growl
Ursula: 5 saint 6 Le Guin 7 Andress
Uru.
  locale: 5 S. Amer.
  neighbor: 3 Arg. 4 Braz.
  org.: 3 OAS
Uruguay: 6 nation 7 country
  capital: 10 Montevideo
  city: 4 Melo 5 Salto 10 Montevideo
  money: 4 peso 9 centesimo
  neighbor: 6 Brazil 9 Argentina
  org.: 3 OAS
  writer: 6 Reyles 7 Sánchez 9 Benedetti
  see also Spanish
__-Urundi: 6 Ruanda
us: 4 pron. 7 pronoun
  according to Pogo: 5 enemy
  belonging to ~: 3 our
  between ~: 7 sub rosa 8 secretly 9 entre nous, privately
  how others see ~: 5 image 9 depiction 10 appearance, conception, impression, perception, projection
  in German: 3 uns
  in Spanish: 3 nos
  not ~: 4 rest, them 6 others
  them or ~: 4 side
  them, to ~: 3 foe 5 enemy
  with ~: 4 here, left 5 alive 6 extant, living, on hand 7 current, on board, ongoing, present 9 attending, remaining, surviving
Us: 3 mag 8 magazine
__ Us: 5 One of, Toys R
U.S.: 7 America 9 the States
  alliance: 3 OAS 4 NATO
  ally: 3 Eng. 5 the U.K.
  business competitor: 3 Jpn.
  citizen: 4 Amer.
  coin word: 4 unum 5 trust
  financial capital: 3 NYC
  former capital: 3 NYC
  language: 7 English
  leader: 4 pres. 9 president
  money: 3 dol. 4 buck, cent, dime, half 5 penny 6 dollar, nickel 7 quarter 10 half dollar
  national flower: 4 rose
  neighbor: 3 Mex. 6 Canada, Mexico
  of the ~: 4 Amer., natl.
  region: 4 N. Eng.
  soldier: 4 Yank
  southernmost ~ city: 4 Hilo
  state: 3 Ala., Ark., Cal., Del., Fla., Ida., Kan., Ken., Neb., Nev., Ore., Tex., Wis., W. Va., Wyo. 4 Ariz., Colo., Conn., Mass., Mich., Minn., Miss., Mont., N. Car., N. Dak., Nebr., N. Mex., Ohio, Okla., Penn., S. Car., S. Dak., Tenn., Utah, Wash., Wisc.

5 Calif., Idaho, Maine, Penna., Texas 6 Alaska, Hawaii, Kansas, Nevada, Oregon 7 Alabama, Arizona, Florida, Georgia, Montana, New York, Vermont, Wyoming 8 Arkansas, Colorado, Delaware, Kentucky, Maryland, Michigan, Missouri, Nebraska, Oklahoma 9 Louisiana, Minnesota, New Jersey, New Mexico, Tennessee, Wisconsin 10 California, Washington 11 Connecticut, Mississippi, North Dakota, Rhode Island, South Dakota 12 New Hampshire, Pennsylvania, West Virginia 13 Massachusetts, North Carolina, South Carolina
territory: 4 Guam
trading partner: 3 EEC
U.S. __: 4 Army, Navy, Open
U.S. __ Corps: 6 Marine
U.S. __ Force: 3 Air
U.S. __ Guard: 5 Coast
U.S. __ Service: 6 Postal, Secret 7 Customs
USA: 4 army, serv., svce. 7 channel, network 9 the States
alternative: *see* cable channel
see also army, U.S.
USA __: 5 Today
U.S.A.
author: John Dos Passos
__ U.S.A.: 6 Inside, Surfin'
usable: 3 fit 4 open 5 ready, utile 6 at hand, liquid 7 helpful, in order, running, working 8 valuable, workable 9 adaptable, available, operative, practical 10 accessible, applicable, employable, functional, utilizable
make ~: 3 fit 5 adapt, alter 6 adjust, change, modify, revise, tailor 7 remodel 8 regulate
make ~ again: 5 refit, renew 9 refurbish
__ us a child...: 4 Unto
USAF: 3 svc. 4 serv., svce.
decoration: 3 DFC
part: 3 Air, SAC 5 Force
plane: 4 VTOL
rank: 2 lt. 3 amn., gen. 4 capt., genl., Ssgt., TSgt.
weapon: 3 ABM
see also Air Force
USAFA: 3 sch. 4 acad., coll. 7 academy
grad: 2 lt. 5 lieut.
home: 4 Colo.
USA for Africa
song: We Are the World (1985)
usage: 3 way 4 form, mode, rule, wont, word 5 habit 6 custom, manner, method, praxis 7 diction, fashion, formula, lexicon, routine, wording 8 currency, habitude, handling, phrasing, practice 9 operation, procedure, tradition, treatment 10 acceptance, convention, employment, management
fee: 3 tax 4 duty, levy, toll 6 charge, impost, tariff, towage 10 assessment
informal ~: 4 cant 5 argot, lingo, slang 6 jargon, patois, pidgin 7 dialect 10 street talk, vernacular
US Airways
former ~ rival: 3 TWA 5 Pan Am 7 Braniff, Eastern 8 National
rival: 3 UAL 5 Delta 6 United 7 Jet Blue 8 American 9 Southwest 11 America West, Continental
USAR, part of: 3 Air, Res. 7 Reserve
__ us a son is given: 4 unto
__ U.S. Bonds: 4 Gary
USC: 3 sch. 6 school
group: 6 Pac-Ten
locale: 2 L.A. 3 Cal.
rival: 3 Cal. 4 UCLA
student's rival: 5 UCLAn
U.S. Capitol architect: 7 Latrobe 8 Bulfinch
USCG
part of ~: 5 Coast, Guard
rank: 3 ens. 4 capt. 5 lt com.
signal: 3 SOS
USCGA
locale: 4 Conn. 9 New London
U.S. Coast __: 5 Guard
USDA
part of ~: 3 Agr. 4 Dept. 10 Department
rating: 5 Prime 6 Choice
use: 3 end, ply, run, tap 4 good, help, milk, need, take, turn, wear 5 adopt, apply, avail, eat up, enjoy, point, put in, sense, spend, trick, usage, value, waste, wield, worth 6 accept, behoof, custom, do with, draw on, employ, engage, expend, handle, invoke, manage, milage, moment, occupy, play on, praxis, profit, reason, resort, rip off 7 benefit, break in, consume, control, deplete, exhaust, exploit, harness, meaning, mileage, operate, purpose, service, toy with, utility, utilize 8 call upon, exercise, function, gobble up, handling, occasion, practice, put forth, work with 9 advantage, implement, occupancy, operation, partake of, patronize, put to work, relevance, treatment, usability, victimize 10 administer, capitalize, employment, fall back on, make do with, manipulate, run through, usefulness
a Nautilus: 5 train 7 work out 8 exercise
be of ~: 3 aid 4 help 5 avail, serve 6 assist, profit, wait on 7 benefit, suffice
deny ~: 3 ban, bar 5 debar, expel 6 censor, forbid, outlaw 7 boycott, exclude, rule out 8 disallow, prohibit 9 blackball, ostracize, proscribe
don't ~: 4 shun 5 avoid, forgo 6 eschew, give up 7 abstain, boycott, refrain 8 renounce, swear off
easy to ~: 5 handy 6 nearby, wieldy 7 close by 8 portable 10 accessible, convenient, timesaving
effectively: 5 wield
entirely: 5 eat up 7 exhaust 9 polish off
for a while: 6 borrow
hard to ~: 7 awkward 8 affected, unwieldy 9 ponderous 10 cumbersome
have ~ for: 4 need 7 require
have no ~ for: 4 hate 5 abhor 6 detest, loathe 7 despise
in ~: 4 busy 5 taken 6 extant, living, modern 7 current, engaged, present 8 employed, occupied, up-to-date 9 prevalent, spoken for
let ~: 4 lend, loan, pool 5 allot, share 6 assign, oblige
make ~ of: 5 apply, avail, exert, wield 6 employ, look to, resort 7 utilize 10 fall back on, profit from
make ready for ~ again: 5 refit
no ~: 6 futile 8 hopeless 9 pointless
no longer in ~: 3 out 4 gone 5 dated, dusty, moldy, musty, passé, stale 6 old-hat 7 archaic, outworn 8 obsolete, outdated, outmoded, timeworn 9 discarded, moth-eaten, out-of-date 10 antiquated, superseded
not in ~: 4 free, idle 6 fallow, vacant 7 untaken 8 untilled
of ~: 5 handy 6 useful 7 helpful 8 valuable 9 practical 10 beneficial, convenient, worthwhile
of no ~: 4 vain 6 futile, hollow, otiose 7 inutile, useless, worn-out 8 bootless, hopeless, pathetic 9 pointless, worthless 10 profitless, unavailing, unworkable
one's hands: 4 mime, wave 6 beckon, signal 9 pantomime
one's head: 6 reason 8 cogitate 9 cerebrate
one's noodle: 6 ideate, reason 7 analyze 8 cogitate 9 cerebrate, figure out
out of ~: 3 old 5 dated, fusty, hoary, passé 6 bygone 7 archaic, outworn 8 obsolete, timeworn 9 forgotten, moss-grown 10 antiquated, superseded
pay for the ~ of: 4 hire, rent 5 lease 6 engage 7 charter 8 sublease
ready for ~: 9 available 10 disposable
save for future ~: 5 set by 7 lay away
show ~: 4 fade, fray, wear 5 decay, erode, scuff 6 abrade, weaken 7 corrode, crumble, wear out, weather 8 wear down
skillfully: 3 ply 5 wield
sparingly: 3 eke 4 keep, save 5 hoard, lay by, lay up, skimp, stash, stint 6 ration, scrimp 7 cut back, protect, store up 8 conserve, maintain, preserve, scrimp on, sock away 9 cut back on, economize, preserves, safeguard
temporarily: 4 loan 6 borrow
unnecessarily: 5 drain, waste 6 burn up 7 fribble, splurge 8 squander 9 dissipate, overspend, throw away 10 gamble away, run through, trifle away
up: 3 eat 4 blow, lose 5 drain, empty, put in, spend, waste 6 expend, finish, run out 7 consume, deplete, exhaust, play out, wipe out 8 run out of, squander 9 dissipate, finish off, go through, polish off 10 fail to keep, run through
use __ as directed: 4 only
__ use: 5 put to
__-use: 3 ill
Use __ My Girl: 4 Ta Be
used: 3 old 4 worn 5 spent, tired 7 worn-out 8 pre-owned, recycled 9 hackneyed, moth-eaten 10 hand-me-down, secondhand, threadbare
get ~ to: 6 grow on 7 break in 8 accustom, grow upon 9 acclimate, reconcile
get ~ (to): 5 adapt, enure, inure 6 attune 9 habituate
much ~: 4 flat 5 banal, corny, stale, stock, tired, trite 6 common, jejune 7 clichéd, insipid, worn-out 8 bathetic, bromidic, cornball, ordinary, shopworn, timeworn, well-worn 9 hackneyed, moth-eaten, played out 10 pedestrian, uninspired, unoriginal, warmed-over
never ~ , in coin-collecting: 3 unc.
no longer ~: 3 obs., old, out 5 dated, passé 6 bygone, old hat, square 7 archaic, outworn 8 obsolete, outdated, outmoded, timeworn 10 antiquated, out of style
one: 4 dupe, mark, pawn, tool 5 patsy 6 flunky, lackey, minion, pigeon, puppet, stooge, sucker, victim 7 cat's-paw, flunkey 8 creature, henchman 10 instrument
seldom ~: 5 dusty
to: 3 did 5 would 6 at home 10 accustomed
(to): 4 wont 5 prone
to be: 3 was 4 were
up: 3 out 4 bare, gone, shot, worn 5 spent, trite 6 barren, vacant 7 run-down, worn-out 10 threadbare
useful: 3 fit 4 good 5 handy, utile 6 aidful, benign 7 gainful, helpful, working 8 fruitful, positive, remedial, salutary, suitable, valuable 9 covetable, desirable, effective, effectual, efficient, expedient, favorable, of service, practical, pragmatic 10 all-purpose, applicable, beneficial, convenient, functional, mechanical, productive, profitable, worthwhile
be ~: 2 do 3 pay 5 serve 6 assist
item: 3 aid 5 asset
more ~: 6 better 8 improved, superior 10 preferable
prove ~: 3 aid 4 help 5 avail
usefulness: 4 good, wear 5 avail, value, worth 7 service, utility 9 handiness 10 importance
useless: 4 idle, null, vain, weak, worn 5 inept, no-win, scrap 6 barren, futile, hollow, no good, otiose 7 inutile, worn-out 8 abortive, bootless, feckless, hopeless, needless, pathetic 9 desperate, for naught, fruitless,

pointless, thankless, valueless, worthless **10** expendable, for nothing, impossible, pathetical, profitless, unavailing, unrequired, unworkable
become ~: **3** rot **4** ruin, sour, turn **5** decay, go bad, spoil, taint **6** mildew, molder **7** crumble **9** decompose
uselessly: **6** vainly **8** futilely **9** to no avail **10** for nothing
Use Me (1972 song)
artist: Bill Withers
Usenet protocol: **4** http
Use No __: **5** Hooks
user: **5** buyer, eater **6** client, hacker, patron **7** habitué, shopper **8** consumer, customer, operator **9** purchaser
annoyance: **4** spam **8** down time
user __: **3** fee **5** group
__ user: **3** end
user-friendly: **5** handy **6** simple **9** foolproof, practical
feature: **4** icon
username, enter one's: **5** log in
Use Ta Be My Girl (1978 song)
artist: O'Jays
USGA
part of ~: **4** Golf **5** Assoc.
ush: **4** seat **6** escort
u-shaped bend: **5** oxbow
usher: **3** see, sit **4** lead, page, seat, take **5** bring, guide, see in, steer **6** convoy, escort, herald, launch, lead in, show in **7** bring in, conduct, go first, marshal, precede, preface, show out **9** accompany, attendant, introduce **10** doorkeeper, gatekeeper, inaugurate, pave the way, show around
ender: **4** ette
in: **5** begin, greet, set up, start **6** herald, launch **7** receive, welcome **8** antecede, initiate **9** institute, introduce, originate **10** inaugurate, lead the way
(in): **3** see **4** ring, show
offering: **3** arm **4** wing
route: **5** aisle
USIA div.: **3** VOA
__ Us If You Can: **5** Catch
using: **3** via **7** by way of, through **9** by means of **10** by virtue of
refrain from ~: **5** avoid, spurn **6** eschew **7** boycott
USLTA
part of ~: **4** Lawn **5** Assoc. **6** Tennis
USMA
see Army, West Point
USMA grad: **2** lt. **5** lieut.
U.S. Marine __: **5** Corps
U.S. Marshals (1998 film)
cast: Robert Downey Jr., Tommy Lee Jones, Kate Nelligan, Wesley Snipes
USMC: **4** serv., svce.
part of ~: **5** Corps **6** Marine
rank: **3** maj., PFC
rookie: **3** pvt., rct.
vessel: **3** LST
see also Marines, military
USN: **3** svc. **4** Navy, serv., svce.
branch: **3** ONI
cops: **2** SP
member: **3** CNO
offense: **4** AWOL
outpost: **3** NAS
rank: **2** lt. **3** adm., cdr., CPO, CWO, ens., yeo. **4** capt., RAdm, VAdm. **5** comdr.
rookie: **3** rct.
see also military, Navy
USNA: **3** sch. **4** coll. **13** Annapolis, Navy
freshman: **4** pleb **5** plebe
part of ~: **3** Nav. **4** Acad. **5** Naval **7** Academy
student: **3** mid **5** middy
__ Us Now Praise Famous Men: **3** Let
USO
attendee: **2** GI **3** NCO, PFC
show introducer: **2** MC **5** emcee
stalwart: **4** Hope **7** Bob Hope
U.S. Open
org.: **3** PGA
stadium: **4** Ashe
U.S. Open golf champs:
2009 - Lucas Glover
2008 - Tiger Woods
2007 - Angel Cabrera
2006 - Geoff Ogilvy
2005 - Michael Campbell
2004 - Retief Goosen
2003 - Jim Furyk
2002 - Tiger Woods
2001 - Retief Goosen
2000 - Tiger Woods
1999 - Payne Stewart
1998 - Lee Janzen
1997 - Ernie Els
1996 - Steve Jones
1995 - Corey Pavin
1994 - Ernie Els
1993 - Lee Janzen
1992 - Tom Kite
1991 - Payne Stewart
1990 - Hale Irwin
1989 - Curtis Strange
1988 - Curtis Strange
1987 - Scott Simpson
1986 - Ray Floyd
1985 - Andy North
1984 - Fuzzy Zoeller
1983 - Larry Nelson
1982 - Tom Watson
1981 - David Graham
1980 - Jack Nicklaus
1979 - Hale Irwin
1978 - Andy North
1977 - Hubert Green
1976 - Jerry Pate
1975 - Lou Graham
1974 - Hale Irwin
1973 - Johnny Miller
1972 - Jack Nicklaus
1971 - Lee Trevino
1970 - Tony Jacklin
1969 - Orville Moody
1968 - Lee Trevino
1967 - Jack Nicklaus
1966 - Billy Casper
1965 - Gary Player
1964 - Ken Venturi
1963 - Julius Boros
1962 - Jack Nicklaus
1961 - Gene Littler
1960 - Arnold Palmer
1959 - Billy Casper
1958 - Tommy Bolt
1957 - Dick Mayer
1956 - Cary Middlecoff
1955 - Jack Fleck
1954 - Ed Furgol
1953 - Ben Hogan
1952 - Julius Boros
1951 - Ben Hogan
1950 - Ben Hogan
1949 - Cary Middlecoff
1948 - Ben Hogan
1947 - Lew Worsham
1946 - Lloyd Mangrum
1942-45 - no tournament
1941 - Craig Wood
1940 - Lawson Little
1939 - Byron Nelson
1938 - Ralph Guldahl
1937 - Ralph Guldahl
1936 - Tony Manero
1935 - Sam Parks Jr
1934 - Olin Dutra
1933 - Johnny Goodman
1932 - Gene Sarazen
1931 - Billy Burke
1930 - Bobby Jones
1929 - Bobby Jones
1928 - Johnny Farrell
1927 - Tommy Armour
1926 - Bobby Jones
1925 - Willie Macfarlane
1924 - Cyril Walker
1923 - Bobby Jones
1922 - Gene Sarazen
1921 - Jim Barnes
1920 - Ted Ray
1919 - Walter Hagen
1917-18 - no tournament
1916 - Chick Evans
1915 - John Travers
1914 - Walter Hagen
1913 - Francis Ouimet
1912 - John McDermott
1911 - John McDermott
1910 - Alex Smith
1909 - George Sargent
1908 - Fred McLeod
1907 - Alec Ross
1906 - Alex Smith
1905 - Willie Anderson
1904 - Willie Anderson
1903 - Willie Anderson
1902 - Laurie Auchterlonie
1901 - Willie Anderson
1900 - Harry Vardon
1899 - Willie Smith
1898 - Fred Herd
1897 - Joe Lloyd
1896 - James Foulis
1895 - Horace Rawlins
U.S. Open tennis champs:
2009 - Juan Martin del Potro, Kim Clijsters
2008 - Roger Federer, Serena Williams
2007 - Roger Federer, Justine Henin
2006 - Roger Federer, Maria Sharapova
2005 - Roger Federer, Kim Clijsters
2004 - Roger Federer, Svetlana Kuznetsova
2003 - Andy Roddick, Justine Henin
2002 - Pete Sampras, Serena Williams
2001 - Lleyton Hewitt, Venus Williams
2000 - Marat Safin, Venus Williams
1999 - Andre Agassi, Serena Williams
1998 - Patrick Rafter, Lindsay Davenport
1997 - Patrick Rafter, Martina Hingis
1996 - Pete Sampras, Steffi Graf
1995 - Pete Sampras, Steffi Graf
1994 - Andre Agassi, Arantxa Sanchez Vicario
1993 - Pete Sampras, Steffi Graf
1992 - Stefan Edberg, Monica Seles
1991 - Stefan Edberg, Monica Seles
1990 - Pete Sampras, Gabriela Sabatini
1989 - Boris Becker, Steffi Graf
1988 - Mats Wilander, Steffi Graf
1987 - Ivan Lendl, Martina Navratilova
1986 - Ivan Lendl, Martina Navratilova
1985 - Ivan Lendl, Hana Mandlikova
1984 - John McEnroe, Martina Navratilova
1983 - Jimmy Connors, Martina Navratilova
1982 - Jimmy Connors, Chris Evert Lloyd
1981 - John McEnroe, Tracy Austin
1980 - John McEnroe, Chris Evert Lloyd
1979 - John McEnroe, Tracy Austin
1978 - Jimmy Connors, Chris Evert
1977 - Guillermo Vilas, Chris Evert
1976 - Jimmy Connors, Chris Evert
1975 - Manuel Orantes, Chris Evert
1974 - Jimmy Connors, Billie Jean King
1973 - John Newcombe, Margaret Court
1972 - Ilie Nastase, Billie Jean King
1971 - Stan Smith, Billie Jean King
1970 - Ken Rosewall, Margaret Court
1969 - Rod Laver, Margaret Court
1968 - Arthur Ashe, Virginia Wade
1967 - John Newcombe, Billie Jean King
1966 - Fred Stolle, Maria Bueno
1965 - Manuel Santana, Margaret Smith
1964 - Roy Emerson, Maria Bueno
1963 - Rafael Osuna, Maria Bueno
1962 - Rod Laver, Margaret Smith
1961 - Roy Emerson, Darlene Hard
1960 - Neale Fraser, Darlene Hard
1959 - Neale Fraser, Maria Bueno
1958 - Ashley Cooper, Althea Gibson
1957 - Mal Anderson, Althea Gibson
1956 - Ken Rosewall, Shirley Fry
1955 - Tony Trabert, Doris Hart
1954 - Vic Seixas, Doris Hart
1953 - Tony Trabert, Maureen Connolly
1952 - Frank Sedgman, Maureen Connolly

1951 - Frank Sedgman, Maureen Connolly
1950 - Art Larsen, Margaret duPont
1949 - Pancho Gonzales, Margaret duPont
1948 - Pancho Gonzales, Margaret duPont
1947 - Jack Kramer, Louise Brough
1946 - Jack Kramer, Pauline Betz
1945 - Frank Parker, Sarah Cooke
1944 - Frank Parker, Pauline Betz
1943 - Joe Hunt, Pauline Betz
1942 - Fred Schroeder, Pauline Betz
1941 - Bobby Riggs, Sarah Cooke
1940 - Don McNeill, Alice Marble
1939 - Bobby Riggs, Alice Marble
1938 - Don Budge, Alice Marble
1937 - Don Budge, Anita Lizana
1936 - Fred Perry, Alice Marble
1935 - Wilmer Allison, Helen Jacobs
1934 - Fred Perry, Helen Jacobs
1933 - Fred Perry, Helen Jacobs
1932 - Ellsworth Vines, Helen Jacobs
1931 - Ellsworth Vines, Helen Moody
1930 - John Doeg, Betty Nuthall
1929 - Bill Tilden, Helen Wills
1928 - Henri Cochet, Helen Wills
1927 - Rene Lacoste, Helen Wills
1926 - Rene Lacoste, Molla Mallory
1925 - Bill Tilden, Helen Wills
1924 - Bill Tilden, Helen Wills
1923 - Bill Tilden, Helen Wills
1922 - Bill Tilden, Molla Mallory
1921 - Bill Tilden, Molla Mallory
1920 - Bill Tilden, Molla Mallory
1919 - William Johnston, Hazel Wightman
1918 - R.L. Murray, Molla Bjurstedt
1917 - R.L. Murray, Molla Bjurstedt
1916 - Dick Williams, Molla Bjurstedt
1915 - William Johnston, Molla Bjurstedt
1914 - Richard Williams, Mary Browne
1913 - Maurice McLoughlin, Mary Browne
1912 - Maurice McLoughlin, Mary Browne
1911 - Bill Larned, Hazel Hotchkiss
1910 - Bill Larned, Hazel Hotchkiss
1909 - Bill Larned, Hazel Hotchkiss
1908 - Bill Larned, Maud Wallach
1907 - Bill Larned, Evelyn Sears
1906 - William Clothier, Helen Homans
1905 - Beals Wright, Elisabeth Moore
1904 - Holcombe Ward, May Sutton
1903 - Laurie Doherty, Elisabeth Moore
1902 - Bill Larned, Marion Jones
1901 - Bill Larned, Elisabeth Moore
1900 - Malcolm Whitman, Myrtle McAteer
1899 - Malcolm Whitman, Marion Jones
1898 - Malcolm Whitman, Juliette Atkinson
1897 - Robert Wrenn, Juliette Atkinson
1896 - Robert Wrenn, Elisabeth Moore
1895 - Fred Hovey, Juliette Atkinson
1894 - Robert Wrenn, Helen Hellwig
1893 - Robert Wrenn, Aline Terry
1892 - Oliver Campbell, Mabel Cahill
1891 - Oliver Campbell, Mabel Cahill
1890 - Oliver Campbell, Ellen Roosevelt
1889 - Henry Slocum Jr., Bertha Townsend
1888 - Henry Slocum Jr., Bertha Townsend
1887 - Richard Sears, Ellen Hansell
1886 - Richard Sears
1885 - Richard Sears
1884 - Richard Sears
1883 - Richard Sears
1882 - Richard Sears
1881 - Richard Sears

__ U.S. Patent Off.: 3 Reg.
__ U.S. Pat. Off.: 3 Reg.
__ us pray: 3 Let
USPS
alternative: 3 fax **5** e-mail
circuit: 3 rte.
item: 3 ltr. **4** mail **6** stamps
letters: 3 RFD
limbo: 3 DLO
part of ~: 3 Svc. **4** Svce. **6** Postal **7** Service
units: 3 lbs., ozs.
VIP: 3 PMG
see also mail, post office
USS Enterprise officer: 3 cdr.
USSR
aircraft: 3 MiG
neighbor: 3 Afg.
part of ~: 3 Rus., Sov., Ukr.
secret police: 3 KGB **4** NKVD, OGPU
successor: 3 CIS
see also Russia
USTA
see tennis
Ustinov, Peter: 3 Sir **5** actor **7** British
film: Beau Brummel (1954)
Billy Budd (1962)
Lorenzo's Oil (1992)
Quo Vadis? (1951)
Romanoff and Juliet (1961)
Spartacus (1960, AA)
Topkapi (1964, AA)
work: The Love of Four Colonels
Romanoff and Juliet
The Unknown Soldier and His Wife
USU
see Utah State
usual: 3 par, set, typ. **4** norm **5** fixed, grind, plain, stock, typic **6** common, normal, proper, wonted **7** average, chronic, current, general, generic, natural, regular, routine, typical **8** accepted, constant, everyday, expected, familiar, frequent, habitual, ordinary, orthodox, standard, workaday **9** chronical, customary, generical, prevalent, quotidian **10** accustomed, legitimate, mainstream,

prevailing, white-bread, widespread
as ~: 8 normally
combining form: 5 normo-
procedure: 4 wont **5** habit, usage **6** custom, policy, system **7** routine **8** practice **9** tradition **10** observance
usually: 3 oft **5** often **6** mainly, mostly **7** as a rule **8** commonly, normally **9** generally, in general, in the main, most often, regularly, routinely, sometimes **10** by and large, frequently, habitually, on the whole, ordinarily
Usual Suspects, The (1995 film)
cast: Stephen Baldwin, Gabriel Byrne, Chazz Palminteri, Kevin Pollak, Kevin Spacey
usurer: 5 shark **6** lender **7** Shylock **8** creditor **9** loan shark
interest, to a ~: 3 vig **8** vigorish
usurp: 4 grab **5** annex, co-opt, seize, wrest **6** assume, borrow, cut out, hijack, pirate **7** preempt **8** arrogate, displace, highjack, move in on, muscle in, supplant, take over **9** lay hold of **10** commandeer, dispossess, encroach on, infringe on, plagiarize
usurpation: 4 coup, grab **7** seizure **8** takeover **10** arrogation, assumption
U.S. Virgin Islands: 3 ter. **4** terr.
USX product: 5 steel
UT
see Utah
Uta: 5 Hagen **6** Pippig
Utah: 5 state
canyon: 5 Bryce
city: 3 Roy **4** Alta, Lehi, Moab, Orem **5** Kanab, Logan, Magna, Ogden, Provo, Sandy **6** Draper, Kearns, Layton, Murray, Tooele **7** Midvale **8** Riverton, St. George **9** Bountiful, Cedar City, Kaysville, Millcreek **10** Clearfield, West Jordan
county: 4 Juab **5** Piute **6** Tooele, Uintah **8** Salt Lake
grp.: 3 LDS
Indian: 3 Ute **5** Piute **6** Paiute
inst.: 3 BYU
lake: 9 Great Salt
mountain: 5 Lasal, Uinta **7** Wasatch **9** Kings Peak
national forest: 5 Uinta
national park: 4 Zion **6** Arches
neighbor: 5 Idaho **6** Nevada **7** Arizona, Wyoming **8** Colorado **9** New Mexico
once: 7 Deseret
pro team: 4 Jazz
resort: 4 Alta
state animal: 3 elk
state bird: 7 sea gull
state cooking pot: 9 Dutch oven
state fish: 5 trout
state flower: 4 sego **8** sego lily
state fossil: 10 allosaurus
state fruit: 6 cherry
state gem: 5 topaz
state insect: 8 honeybee
state mineral: 6 copper
state rock: 4 coal
state tree: 10 blue spruce
Utah State
athletes: 6 Aggies
locale: 5 Logan
ute: 7 vehicle
cousin: 3 ATV
__-ute: 5 sport
Ute: 5 tribe **6** Indian, Siouan **7** Amerind **8** language, Shoshone
language family: 5 Numic
utensil: 3 pan **4** fork, tool **5** knife, ladle, scoop, spoon **6** device, gadget, vessel **7** cutlery **9** implement, tableware **10** instrument, silverware
coating: 5 glaze **6** enamel
eating ~: 4 fork **5** knife, spoon, spork
kitchen ~: 3 pan, pot, wok **5** knife, ladle, parer, ricer, sieve **6** baster, boiler, cooker
kitchen ~ brand: 3 Oxo **4** Ekco
maker: 6 cutler
point: 4 tine
utensils: 3 kit **4** gear **7** cutlery **9** equipment
UTEP
athlete: 5 Miner
conference: 3 WAC
part of ~: 4 Paso **5** Texas
rival: 3 BYU
Utica: 4 city, town
locale: 7 New York
util: 3 tel. **4** elec.
utile: 5 handy **6** usable, useful **7** helpful, useable **8** availing, feasible **9** practical **10** applicable, beneficial, functional
utilitarian: 6 useful **7** helpful **8** sensible **9** efficient, practical, pragmatic, realistic
utility: 3 gas, use **4** help, wear **5** avail, power, value, water, worth **6** profit **7** benefit, fitness, purpose, service **8** adequacy, efficacy, function **9** relevance **10** expediency, usefulness
bill abbr.: 3 kwh
building: 4 shed **6** lean-to
device: 5 gauge, meter **9** indicator
regulating agcy.: 3 PSC
vehicle: 3 rig, van **4** jeep, semi **5** dolly, lorry, truck, U-Haul **6** pickup
utility __: 3 man **4** pole, room **6** closet
utility room
feature: 5 drier, dryer **6** washer
__-utility vehicle: 5 sport
utilization: 8 exercise **10** employment
utilize: 3 ply, tap, use **4** take, turn **5** apply, exert, put in, wield **6** draw on, employ, handle, occupy, resort **7** consume, exploit, harness **8** exercise, profit by, put to use, resort to **9** make use of
Utley: 5 Chase **7** Garrick
utmost: 3 nth, top, ult. **4** full, last, main **5** chief, final, first, ideal, limit, major, prime **6** all-out **7** capital, extreme, highest, leading, maximal, maximum, supreme **8** absolute, cardinal, farthest, greatest, ultimate **9** nth degree, paramount, sovereign **10** preeminent

do one's ~: **3** aim, try, vie **4** moil, push, toil **5** essay, fight, labor, sweat **6** strain, strive, tackle, take on **7** attempt, compete, contend **8** bear down, endeavor, go all out, scramble, shoot for, struggle **10** go for broke, go the limit

Uto-__: **7** Aztecan

utopia: **4** Eden **5** bliss **6** Avalon, heaven **7** Arcadia, Erewhon **8** paradise **9** happiness, Shangri-la

Utopia: **5** essay
author: Thomas More

Utopia, Ltd.: **8** operetta
composer: W.S. Gilbert, Arthur Sullivan

utopian: **4** airy **5** dream, ideal, lofty **6** dreamy, edenic **7** perfect **8** idealist, platonic, quixotic, romantic **9** grandiose, idealized, just right, visionary **10** idealistic, impossible, optimistic, quixotical, unfeasible, unworkable

Utrecht: **4** city, town
city near ~: **3** Ede **5** Zeist **6** Arnhem
locale: **7** Holland **11** Netherlands

Utrillo, Maurice: **6** artist, French **7** painter
contemporary: **5** Monet

__ ut supra: **4** vide

Uttar Pradesh
city: **4** Agra **6** Jhansi, Kanpur
locale: **5** India

utter: **3** air, cry, jaw, put, say **4** chin, give, main, mere, pure, rank, talk, tell, vent **5** blurt, chant, couch, gross, mouth, right, sheer, shout, speak, stark, state, thoro, total, voice, whole **6** affirm, all-out, arrant, assert, entire, intone, mumble, mutter, recite, reveal, strict **7** breathe, chime in, declaim, declare, deliver, dictate, divulge, exclaim, express, extreme, flat-out, glaring, perfect, whisper **8** absolute, announce, bring out, complete, disclose, flagrant, outright, proclaim, profound, shocking, thorough, throw out, vocalize **9** downright, egregious, ejaculate, enunciate, make known, out-and-out, pronounce, verbalize, wholesale **10** articulate, asseverate, consummate
ender: **4** most
loudly: **3** baa, cry **4** blat, bray, honk, hoot, wail, yell **5** bleat, neigh **6** bellow, holler, scream, whinny
sharply: **3** rap **4** bark, snap
softly: **3** hum **4** sigh **5** drone **6** mumble, murmur, mutter **7** whisper
suddenly: **4** blab **5** blurt **7** exclaim, let slip **8** blurt out

utterance: **4** rant, talk, word **5** parol, reply, spiel, voice, words **6** phrase, remark, saying, speech **7** opinion, oration **8** delivery, language, response, sentence, speaking **9** assertion, discourse, elocution, statement **10** confession, expression, peroration, recitation, revelation, vocalizing

uttered: **4** oral **5** spake, spoke, vocal **6** spoken **9** vocalized

utterly: **3** all **4** just, only **5** fully, quite, right, stark **6** purely, simply, wholly **7** totally **8** entirely **9** every inch, extremely, perfectly, to the core **10** absolutely, altogether, completely, thoroughly, to the limit

uttermost: **4** last, most **5** first, major, prime **7** capital, highest, maximum **8** cardinal, farthest, furthest, greatest

U-turn: **8** flip-flop, reversal **9** about-face, one-eighty

U Turn (1997 film)
cast: Powers Boothe, Jennifer Lopez, Nick Nolte, Sean Penn
director: Oliver Stone

UV __: **4** rays **6** filter

Uwe: **7** Johnson

Uxmal resident: **5** Mayan

uxor: **4** wife **5** Latin
husband: **3** vir

Uzbekistan: **6** nation **7** country
capital: **8** Tashkent
desert: **8** Kyzyl Kum
neighbor: **10** Kazakhstan, Kyrgyzstan, Tajikistan
once: **3** SSR
river: **4** Oxus

Uzi: **3** gun **7** firearm, Israeli **9** automatic

V

V: 4 elem., five 6 letter 7 element 8 vanadium
23 for ~: 4 at. no.
followers: 3 WXY 4 WXYZ
inverted ~: 5 caret
preceders: 3 STU 4 RSTU 5 QRSTU
V __: 4 neck, sign
V __ Victor: 4 as in
V-__: 4 chip
V-__ engine: 3 six 5 eight
V.: 5 novel
author: Thomas Pynchon
V8 juice: 4 beet 6 carrot, celery, tomato 7 lettuce, parsley, spinach 10 watercress
V-8 unit: 3 cyl. 8 cylinder
Va.
neighbor: 3 Ken., W. Va. 4 N. Car.
training base: 5 Ft. Lee
see also Virginia
__-Vac: 4 Mini, Ray-o
vaca catcher: 5 reata 6 gaucho
vacancy: 3 gap 4 post, room, slot, void 5 house, space 6 rental 7 absence, opening 8 position 9 apartment, emptiness, situation 10 job opening
sign: 5 to let 9 available
vacant: 4 bare, free, open, void 5 blank, clear, empty, inane, to let, unlet, vapid 6 absent, barren, dreamy, glassy, hollow, unused, used up, wooden 7 deadpan, drained, untaken, vacuous 8 depleted, deserted, desolate, dreaming, listless, unfilled 9 abandoned, available, evacuated, exhausted, unlived in 10 abstracted, glassy-eyed, tenantless, unoccupied, unthinking
hour: 6 recess 7 leisure 8 free time 9 idle hours, spare time 10 recreation, relaxation
vacate: 2 go 4 exit, quit 5 clear, empty, leave 6 depart, give up, go away, resign 7 abandon, abolish, move out, nullify, retreat 8 abdicate, abrogate, evacuate, part with, withdraw 9 disappear, discharge, move out of 10 relinquish
vacated: 4 bare, left, open, went 5 empty 6 barren 9 available
vacation: 4 rest, stay, tour 5 break, leave, R and R, visit 6 cruise, outing, recess, travel 7 holiday, leisure, liberty, respite, sojourn, time off 8 furlough, go abroad 10 recreation, sabbatical
ender: 4 land
home: 2 RV 5 cabin, lodge, motel, villa 6 A-frame, camper 8 bungalow
military ~: 5 leave 8 furlough
month: 3 Aug., Jul. 4 July 6 August
on ~: 3 far, off, out 4 away, gone 6 absent 9 elsewhere
option: 4 tour, trip 5 jaunt 6 cruise, flight, junket, safari, voyage 9 excursion 10 expedition
prepare for a ~: 4 load, pack 8 get ready
souvenir: 5 photo 6 T-shirt 8 postcard 10 photograph
spot: 4 cape, lake 5 shore 6 resort
time: 6 summer 7 dog days
vehicle: 2 RV 9 Winnebago 10 mobile home
Vacation (song)
artist: Connie Francis, Go-Go's
vacationer: 5 guest 6 lodger, renter, roomer 7 tourist, visitor, voyager 8 traveler, wayfarer 9 sightseer, sojourner 10 day-tripper
goal: 3 tan 4 rest 5 break, peace, quiet 6 suntan 7 holiday, respite 8 breather, calmness, downtime, quietude 10 inactivity, recreation, relaxation
winter ~: 5 skier
vacationing: 4 away 6 abroad, faroff 9 elsewhere, not at home
Vacaville: 4 city, town
locale: 10 California
Vaccaro: 6 Brenda
vaccinate: 6 inject 7 protect 8 immunize 9 inoculate
vaccine: 4 hypo, oral, shot 5 serum 8 medicine 9 antitoxin 10 medication
container: 4 vial 5 ampul, phial 6 ampule 7 ampoule
place to get a ~: 3 arm
polio ~ developer: 4 Salk 5 Sabin
__ vaccine: 4 oral, Salk 5 Sabin
Vachel: 7 Lindsay
vacillate: 3 wag 4 halt, lick, sway, yo-yo 5 hedge, hover, pause, shift, swing, waver 6 change, dither, falter, linger, seesaw, teeter, wabble, waffle, wobble 7 stagger, whiffle 8 fence-sit, hesitate, straddle 9 alternate, fluctuate, hem and haw, oscillate, pussyfoot
vacillating: 4 torn, weak 5 shaky, timid 6 fickle, infirm, unsure 7 halting 8 hesitant, unstable, unsteady, variable 9 uncertain, undecided, unsettled 10 ambivalent, capricious, indecisive, irresolute, of two minds, on the fence, weak-willed, wishy-washy
vacillation: 4 bend, rock, sway, tilt 5 delay, doubt, pause, qualm, swing 6 teeter, totter 8 wavering 10 averseness, hesitation, indecision, reluctance
Václav: 5 Havel
V.A. concern: 3 POW
vacuity: 3 gap 4 gulf, hole, void 5 abyss, space 6 cavity, hollow, torpor 7 absence, languor, opening 8 lethargy, nihility 9 blankness, emptiness, inanition
vacuole former: 6 amoeba
vacuous: 4 bare, dull, idle, null, void 5 blank, clear, empty, inane, silly, vapid 6 absent, stupid, vacant 7 drained, foolish, shallow 9 airheaded, half-baked 10 weakminded
vacuum: 3 gap 4 void 5 clean, space, sweep 8 nihility 9 emptiness 10 outer space
brand: 5 Kirby, Oreck 6 Hoover 10 Electrolux
like a ~: 5 blank, empty 6 barren, hollow 7 airless 8 deserted, desolate, lifeless
part: 3 bag 4 hose, wand 5 brush
target: 4 crud, dirt, gunk, soil 5 grime
tube gas: 5 argon
tube type: 5 diode
use a ~: 4 suck
vacuum __: 3 pan 4 pump, tube 5 gauge 6 bottle 7 cleaner, sweeper
vacuum-__: 4 pack 6 packed
vacuuming: 5 chore 9 housework
vacuum-tube part: 6 dynode
vade mecum: 5 bible, guide 8 handbook
Vader, Darth: 7 villain
foe: 4 Leia, Luke, Solo
like ~: 4 evil
Vadim, Roger: 6 French 8 director
spouse: Brigitte Bardot, Jane Fonda
__ Vadis?: 3 Quo
VAdm. employer: 3 USN
Vaduz: 4 city, town 7 capital
locale: Liechtenstein
vagabond: 3 bum 4 hobo, idle, roam 5 farer, gypsy, nomad, rover, tramp 6 beggar, errant, roamer, roving 7 aimless, drifter, migrant, nomadic, outcast, rambler, roaming, tourist, trekker 8 derelict, drifting, explorer, gadabout, homeless, prodigal, rambling, rootless, traveler, wanderer, wayfarer 9 footloose, itinerant, itinerate, journeyer, transient, wandering, wayfaring 10 hitchhiker, journeying, pathfinder, ragamuffin
Vagabond King, The
composer: Rudolf Friml
Vagabond Lover, The: 6 Vallee
vagarious: 6 chancy, fickle, quirky, spotty 7 erratic, flighty 8 careless, fanciful, rambling, unstable, variable 9 arbitrary, eccentric, fluctuant, haphazard, impulsive, irregular, mercurial, wandering, whimsical 10 capricious
vagary: 4 whim 5 fancy, quirk 6 notion, whimsy 7 caprice, impulse, whimsey 8 crotchet
vagrant: 3 bum 4 hobo 5 stray, tramp 6 beggar 7 drifter, floater, nomadic, outcast, sinuous 8 derelict, homeless, traveler, wanderer 9 itinerant, transient, wayfaring 10 ragamuffin
vague: 3 dim, lax 4 dark, hazy 5 exact, faint, foggy, fuzzy, loose, mirky, misty, muddy, murky, rough, shady 6 arcane, bleary, cloudy, dreamy, unsure 7 blurred, cryptic, dubious, evasive, general, obscure, shadowy, sketchy, unclear 8 abstruse, doubtful, nebulous, oracular, puzzling 9 ambiguous, amorphous, confusing, cryptical, dreamlike, enigmatic, equivocal, hard to see, imprecise, shapeless, tenebrous, uncertain, undecided, unfocused 10 clear as mud, ill-defined, indefinite, indistinct, inexplicit, perplexing, unexplicit, unspecific
amount: 4 some
form: 4 blob, glob, lump, mass, spot 5 smear 6 smudge 7 splotch
idea: 4 clew, clue 6 notion
make ~: 3 fog 4 blur, daze, mist 5 befog, blear, cloud, muddy, smear 6 smudge 7 becloud, obscure
Vague: 4 Vera
vagueness: 4 haze 9 ambiguity, fogginess, fuzziness, ignorance
Vail: 4 city, town
conveyor: 3 tow 4 T-bar
enjoy ~: 3 ski 4 skee
like ~ in winter: 5 snowy, white
locale: 8 Colorado
vain: 4 idle, null, puny, smug 5 cocky, empty, no-win, petty, proud 6 barren, futile, hollow 7 fustian, haughty, inutile, pompous, shallow, sterile, stuck-up, useless 8 abortive, arrogant, boastful, bootless, cocksure, egoistic, hopeless, inflated, nugatory, puffed up, snobbish, specious, trifling 9 bigheaded, conceited, desperate, for naught, frivolous, fruitless, hubristic, pointless, senseless, thankless, to no avail, worthless 10 big-talking, egocentric, egoistical, for nothing, profitless, swaggering, unavailing
be in ~: 3 die 4 bust, fail, flop, lose 7 founder 9 fall short
claim: 5 boast
ender: 5 glory 8 glorious
in ~: 6 futile 9 fruitless, to no avail
male: 3 fop 4 dude 5 dandy 9 pretty boy
walk: 5 mince, strut 6 prance, sashay 7 flounce, peacock, swagger
vainglorious: 4 smug 5 proud 7 fustian, haughty, pompous 8 arrogant, boastful 9 conceited
vainglory: 4 pomp 5 pride 7 conceit 10 narcissism, pretension
vainly: 8 futilely 9 to no avail, uselessly 10 for nothing
act ~: 5 groom, preen, primp 7 deck out, dress up, spiff up
vair: 3 fur 7 minever, miniver
Val: 5 Avery, Guest 6 Kilmer
Val __: 4 lace 6 d'Isère
Valachi Papers, The
author: Peter Maas
Valais, capital of: 4 Sion
Val d'__: 4 Arno
Valdai Hills
river that starts in the ~: 5 Volga
Valdez: 4 city, Juan, Luis, town
locale: 6 Alaska
product: 3 oil
__ Valdez: 5 Exxon
Valdosta: 4 city, town
locale: 7 Georgia
vale: 4 glen 6 hollow
Vale: 5 Jerry, Vicki
valediction: 5 leave 7 goodbye, parting, sendoff 8 farewell 9 departure 10 separation
Valediction, A
author: John Donne
valedictorian's pride: 3 GPA
valedictory: 6 speech 7 goodbye, parting 8 farewell 9 departing

valence
atom with a ~ of one: 5 monad
Valencia: 4 city, port, town
locale: 5 Spain
river: 5 Turia
Valenciennes: 4 lace
Valene: 5 Ewing
Valens, Ritchie
song: Donna (1958)
La Bamba (1959)
valentine
color: 3 red
decor: 5 Cupid, heart 6 cherub
message: 6 be mine
month: 3 Feb. 8 February
purchase: 4 rose 9 chocolate
words: 5 I love 7 love you 8 I love you
words on a Spanish ~: 5 te amo
see also sweetheart
Valentine: 4 pope 5 Karen, saint 7 pontiff
author: George Sand
__ Valentine: 4 Be my
Valentine, A
author: Edgar Allan Poe
__ Valentine's Day: 5 Saint
Valentine's Day figure: 4 Amor, Eros 5 Cupid 8 Dan Cupid
Valentino, Rudolph: 5 actor
costar: 5 Banky, Naldi
film: The Sheik (1921)
Son of the Sheik (1926)
__ vale of tears: 4 this
__ Valera: 7 Eamon De
Valeria: 6 Golino
Valerie: 6 Harper, Hobson 7 Perrine, Simpson 10 Bertinelli
Valerie (1987 song)
artist: Steve Winwood
Valery: 7 Bryusov
Valéry __ D'Estaing: 7 Giscard
valet: 6 butler, flunky, Jeeves 7 flunkey, footman, man's man, servant 9 launderer 10 manservant
valet __: 7 parking
valet de __: 7 chambre
Valhalla: 4 Eden, hall 6 heaven 7 Elysium, Nirvana, rapture 8 paradise 9 Shangri-la
dweller: 4 Odin, Thor 5 Othin
locale: 6 Asgard
valiance: 4 grit, guts 5 nerve 7 bravery, heroism 9 fortitude, gallantry
valiant: 4 bold, game 5 brave, gutsy, nervy, noble, stout 6 awless, daring, gritty, heroic, plucky, spunky 7 aweless, defiant, doughty, gallant, impavid, staunch 8 fearless, heroical, intrepid, resolute, stalwart, unafraid 9 audacious, confident, dauntless, dreadless, herculean, undaunted, unfearful, unfearing 10 chivalrous, courageous, mettlesome, undismayed
Valiant
see Prince Valiant
valid: 2 OK 4 good, okay, real, sure, true 5 exact, jural, legal, legit, licit, right, solid, sound 6 cogent, kasher, kosher, lawful, proven, tested 7 binding, certain, correct, factual, genuine, in force, logical, precise, telling 8 accurate, attested, bona fide, credible, flawless, in effect, official, original, rightful, unbiased, unerring, verified 9 authentic, certified, confirmed, effective, errorless, pertinent, veracious, veritable 10 acceptable, accredited, applicable, compelling, conclusive, convincing, defendable, defensible, documented, legitimate, meaningful, on the level, reasonable, sanctioned, unarguable, undoubtful
be ~: 4 deem, have, hold, keep 5 allow, apply, claim, favor, judge, stand 6 accept, defend, embody, endure, permit 7 condone, signify, support, sustain 8 indicate, maintain, sanction, stand for, underpin 9 approve of, epitomize, put up with, represent, symbolize, withstand 10 illustrate
reasoning: 5 logic, sense 6 reason, sanity 7 thought 9 coherence, deduction, good sense, induction, inference, rationale, reasoning, syllogism
validate: 2 OK 3 vet 4 okay, seal, test 5 prove 6 affirm, attest, ratify, verify 7 approve, bear out, certify, confirm, endorse, indorse, justify, sustain 8 legalize, sanction, vouch for 9 authorize, establish, sign off on 10 constitute, legitimize
validation: 2 OK 4 okay 5 proof 9 collation 10 comparison
__-validation: 5 cross
validity: 5 force, punch, right, truth 6 weight 7 cogency, grounds, reality 8 efficacy, legality, strength 9 authority, soundness, substance 10 foundation, lawfulness, legitimacy
valise: 3 bag 4 case, grip 7 carry-on, luggage 8 suitcase 9 briefcase
Valkyrie (2008 film)
cast: Kenneth Branagh, Tom Cruise
Valkyries
lord: 4 Odin 5 Othin
mother: 4 Erda
__ Vallarta: 6 Puerto
Valle __: 6 d'Aosta
Vallee: 4 Rudy
Vallejo: 4 city
city near ~: 4 Napa
locale: 10 California
Valleri (1968 song)
artist: Monkees
Valletta: 4 city 5 Amber 7 capital
locale: 5 Malta
valley: 4 dale, dell, glen 5 basin, cañon, gorge, notch, plain, swale 6 arroyo, bottom, canyon, coulee, dingle, hollow, ravine, trough 7 channel, lowland 10 depression
ancient Greek ~: 5 Nemea
broad ~: 4 glen, lawn, park 5 field, green, plaza 6 common, meadow, valley
Canadian ~: 5 droke
European river ~: 4 Saar
German ~: 4 Ruhr 5 Mosel
Golden State ~: 4 Napa
lily of the ~: 5 plant 6 flower
lunar ~: 4 rill 5 rille
narrow ~: 5 combe, coomb 6 coombe
Peloponnesian ~: 5 Nemea
side of a ~: 6 coteau
wine ~: 4 Napa 5 Loire, Rhine
__ valley: 4 rift
Valley __: 4 Girl, Song 5 Forge
Valley __ Dolls: 5 of the
__ Valley: 5 Bekaa 7 Silicon
__ Valley, CA: 4 Napa, Simi 5 Death, Squaw
__ Valley Days: 5 Death
Valley Forge: 4 city, town
author: Maxwell Anderson
locale: 4 Penn.
Valley Girl
exclamation: 4 as if 5 oh wow 7 fer shur 8 whatever
word: 3 tre 4 like 6 gnarly 7 totally
Valley Girl (1982 song)
artist: Frank Zappa
Valley Girl (1983 film)
cast: Nicolas Cage, Colleen Camp, Frederic Forrest
__ Valley, ID: 3 Sun
Valley Island: 4 Maui
Valley of Fear, The
author: Arthur Conan Doyle
Valley of Horses, The
author: Jean Auel
Valley of Tears (1957 song)
artist: Fats Domino
Valley of the __: 3 Sun 5 Kings
Valley of the Dolls (1968 song)
artist: Dionne Warwick
Valley of the Dolls character: 5 Neely
Valley of the Kings
locale: 5 Egypt
town near the ~: 5 Luxor
Valley of the Moon, The
author: Jack London
Valley of Unrest, The
author: Edgar Allan Poe
Valley of Wild Horses
author: Zane Grey
__ Valley, OH: 4 Enon
__ Valley P.T.A.: 6 Harper
__ Valley Ranch: 6 Hidden
Valley Road, The (1988 song)
artist: Bruce Hornsby and the Range
__ Valley Serenade: 3 Sun
Valley Song
author: Athol Fugard
__ Valley, The: 3 Big
Valli: 4 June 5 Alida 7 Frankie
Valli, Frankie
song: Can't Take My Eyes... (1967)
Grease (1978)
My Eyes Adored You (1975)
Our Day Will Come (1975)
Swearin' to God (1975)
Vallone: 3 Raf
Valo, Elmer
sport: 8 baseball
valor: 4 grit, guts, sand 5 fight, heart, moxie, nerve, pluck, spunk 6 daring, mettle, spirit, starch 7 bravery, courage, heroism, prowess, stomach 8 audacity, backbone, boldness, firmness 9 derring-do, fortitude, gallantry, hardihood, hardiness 10 knighthood, resolution
valorous: 4 bold, game 5 brave, gutsy, nervy, stout 6 awless, daring, gritty, heroic, plucky, spunky 7 aweless, defiant, doughty, gallant, impavid, staunch 8 fearless, heroical, intrepid, resolute, stalwart, unafraid 9 audacious, dauntless, dreadless, undaunted, unfearful, unfearing 10 chivalrous, courageous, undismayed
valorousness: 4 grit 7 heroism, prowess
Valotte (1984 song)
artist: Julian Lennon
Valova: 5 Elena
Valparaiso: 4 city, port, town
locale: 5 Chile 7 Indiana
see also Spanish
valse: 5 dance, waltz 6 French
Valse __: 6 Triste
valuable: 3 gem, hot 4 dear, gold, plum, rich 5 asset, jewel, of use 6 costly, golden, nugget, prized, scarce, silver, usable, useful, worthy 7 antique, helpful, useable 8 esteemed, heirloom, held dear, in demand, precious, relevant, salutary, treasure 9 cherished, commodity, expensive, important, priceless, rewarding, treasured 10 beneficial, high-priced, invaluable, productive, profitable, worthwhile
extra: 4 perk 5 bonus, gravy, lucre 6 reward 8 dividend
least ~ part: 4 lees 5 chaff, dregs, trash, waste 6 refuse 7 garbage, residue 8 sediment 9 remainder
more ~: 5 finer 6 better 7 greater 8 souped up, stronger, superior, worthier 9 healthier, improving, sharpened 10 preferable
pass as ~: 5 foist 6 fob off, impose 9 insinuate
valuables: 4 swag 7 jewelry 8 treasure
place for ~: 4 safe 5 vault 6 coffer
valuate: 6 assess, survey 8 appraise
valuation: 3 est. 5 price, worth 6 rating 8 estimate 9 appraisal 10 assessment, estimation, evaluation
value: 3 buy, sum, use 4 cost, rate 5 asset, gauge, merit, price, prize, sense, worth 6 amount, assess, beauty, esteem, import, moment, profit, regard, repute, revere, virtue, weight 7 bargain, benefit, caliber, care for, cherish, content, expense, meaning, premium, quality, respect, service, stature, utility 8 appraise, estimate, hold dear, standard, treasure 9 appraisal, care about, recommend, reverence, substance 10 assessment, excellence, importance, set store by, usefulness
add ~ to: 6 better, enrich 7 build up, elevate, enhance, fortify 8 decorate 9 embellish 10 supplement
be of ~: 5 count, weigh 6 cut ice, matter, regard 8 interest 10 have weight
for face ~: 5 at par
get extra ~ from: 5 reuse
having practical ~: 5 handy, utile 6 usable, useful
high ~: 7 premium

VA

highly: **4** love, rate **5** award, honor, prize **6** admire, esteem, regard, revere **7** cherish, idolize, premium **8** accolade, hold dear, hold high, look up to, treasure, venerate **9** care about, recommend **10** appreciate
item of ~: **5** asset **6** virtue **8** resource, strength **9** commodity
judgment: **4** idea, view **5** slant, stand **6** belief, notion **7** concept, feeling, opinion, outlook, thought **8** attitude, position **9** sentiment, viewpoint **10** assessment, conception, conviction, impression, persuasion, philosophy, standpoint
lacking ~: **9** worthless
lacking face ~: **5** no par
lessen the ~ of: **5** abase **6** derate
lose ~: **4** sink **5** lower **6** reduce **7** decline, deflate **8** decrease **10** depreciate
making no ~ judgments: **6** amoral
of little ~: **6** crumby, crummy, paltry
put a ~ on: **3** tag **4** deem, rank, rate **5** gauge, grade, guess, judge, quote, scale, weigh **6** assess, charge, esteem, figure, regard, size up, survey **7** measure **8** appraise, classify, estimate **9** determine
reduced in ~: **7** debased **8** degraded **9** worthless
system: **5** ethic **6** morals **9** principle
take at face ~: **4** rely **5** bet on, trust **6** accept, assume, bank on, commit, credit, expect, lean on, look to **7** believe, consign, count on, entrust, presume, suppose, swear by **8** depend on, rely upon
too highly: **6** exceed **8** misjudge, overrate **9** overprize **10** exaggerate, overassess, overesteem, overpraise
value-__ tax: **5** added
__ value: **3** par **4** book, cash, face **5** added **6** market, resale
Value __: **4** Line
valued: **4** dear **7** beloved, darling **8** esteemed, precious **9** priceless
valueless: **3** nil **4** idle, null **5** empty, petty **6** futile **7** trivial, useless **8** ill-spent, unworthy **9** worthless
values: **5** ethic, ethos, mores **6** ethics, ideals, morals **7** culture **8** folkways **9** standards **10** principles
lack of ~: **5** anomy **6** anomie
__ values: **6** family
valuing: **4** fond, love **5** honor **6** caring, doting, esteem, liking, loving, regard **7** adoring, concern, devoted, fervent, opinion, prizing, respect, worship **8** admiring, approval, devotion, enamored, fondness, interest **9** affection, deference, reverence **10** admiration, cherishing, estimation, observance, passionate, respecting, veneration
valve: **3** tap **4** cock, flap, gate **6** faucet, spigot **7** hydrant, shutoff
air ~: **6** intake
butterfly ~: **6** damper
device with a ~: **4** pump **5** heart
exhaust ~: **6** cutout
Fleming ~: **5** diode
nautical ~: **7** seacock
part: **4** stem
safety ~: **4** duct, vent **5** spout **6** nozzle, outlet **7** channel
__ valve: **3** PCV **5** check **6** aortic, intake, mitral, relief, safety **7** bleeder
valveless
instrument: **4** horn **5** bugle **7** trumpet
vamoose: **2** go **3** fly, git, lam, run **4** flee, scat, shoo **5** leave, leg it, scram **6** beat it, begone, decamp, get out **7** abscond, get lost, go south, head out, make off, take off **8** hightail, shove off **9** bundle off, disappear **10** hightail it
vamp: **3** fix **4** Bara, mend, minx, riff **5** ad-lib, charm, fix up, flirt, intro, patch, siren **6** repair **7** beguile, enticer, Jezebel, patch up **8** beguiler, coquette **9** captivate, hypnotize, improvise, temptress
vamped: **5** ad-lib **6** casual **9** extempore, impromptu **10** improvised, off-the-cuff, unscripted
__ Vamp From East Broadway: **3** I'm a
vampire: **7** Dracula **9** Nosferatu
bane: **5** cross, stake **6** garlic
craving: **4** bite **5** blood
female ~: **5** lamia
like ~ movies: **4** gory **5** lurid **6** bloody
portrayer: **6** Cruise, Lugosi
time: **5** night
trademark: **4** fang
vampire __: **3** bat
Vampire Armand, The
author: Anne Rice
Vampire Chronicles, The
author: Anne Rice
Vampire Lestat, The
author: Anne Rice
van: **5** front, truck, U-Haul **7** fourgon, trailer, vehicle **9** forefront
ender: **4** load, pool **5** guard
in the ~: **5** ahead, first **7** leading
line: **5** fleet, mover
starter: **4** mini
van __: **4** pool
van __ Waals forces: **3** der
__ van: **5** motor **6** moving
Van: **4** lake **5** Bobby, McCoy **6** Heflin **7** Cliburn, Johnson **8** Morrison
locale: **6** Turkey
Van __: **4** Dine, Gogh **5** Halen **6** Heusen
Van __ belt: **5** Allen
Van __, CA: **4** Nuys
Van __ Mungo: **6** Lingle
Van __ Parks: **4** Dyke
Van __'s Land: **6** Diemen
vanadium: **5** metal, steel **7** element
ore: **10** vanadinite
Van Allen: **5** James
Van Allen __: **4** belt
Van Ark: **4** Joan
van Beethoven: **6** Ludwig
Van Brocklin: **4** Norm
Van Buren: **6** Martin **7** Abigail
sister: **7** Landers
Van Buren, Martin: **9** president
former occupation: **6** lawyer
home: **7** New York **10** Kinderhook
opponent: **5** White **7** Webster **8** Harrison
V.P.: **7** Johnson
wife: **6** Hannah
Vance: **5** Cyrus, Dazzy, Philo **6** Colvig, Palmer, Vivian **7** Packard
Vance AFB, home of: **4** Enid, Okla.
Vance, Dazzy: **6** Dodger **7** pitcher
Van Cleef: **3** Lee
Vancouver: **4** city, isle, peak, port, town **5** mount **6** George, island **8** mountain
locale: **6** Canada **10** Washington
newspaper: **3** Sun **8** Province
pro team: **7** Canucks
vandal: **3** Hun **5** rowdy, thief **6** looter, pirate **7** brigand, defacer, hoodlum, invader, ravager **8** pillager **9** barbarian, despoiler, destroyer, plunderer
vandalism: **4** evil, harm **5** prank **6** damage **7** knavery, roguery, trouble **8** mischief, sabotage **9** high jinks, rascality, treachery **10** demolition, dirty trick, impishness, misconduct, wrongdoing
vandalize: **3** mar **4** harm **5** trash, wreck **6** damage, deface **7** despoil **8** sabotage
Van Damme: **10** Jean-Claude
Van de __ generator: **6** Graaff
Vandenberg AFB, city near: **6** Lompoc
van der __ forces: **5** Waals
Van Der Beek: **5** James
Vanderbilt: **3** Amy **6** Gloria **9** Cornelius
athletes: **10** Commodores
conference: **3** SEC
locale: **9** Nashville, Tennessee
Vanderbilt, Gloria: **8** designer
logo: **4** swan
son: Anderson Cooper
spouse: Sidney Lumet
Vander Meer: **6** hurler, Johnny **7** pitcher
van der Meer, Simon: **5** Dutch **8** Nobelist **9** physicist
Van der Post, Laurens: **6** writer **12** South African
work: The Dark Eye in Africa
A Far-Off Place
The Heart of the Hunter
The Lost World of the Kalahari
Venture to the Interior
Vander Pyl: **4** Jean
__ van der Rohe: **4** Mies
van der Waals: **8** Johannes
Van Devere, Trish: **5** actor **7** actress
spouse: George C. Scott
Vandeweghe: **4** Kiki
van de Wetering, Janwillem: **5** Dutch **6** writer
work: The Blond Baboon
The Japanese Corpse
The Mind Murders
Outsider in Amsterdam
Tumbleweed
Van Diemen's Land
today: **8** Tasmania
Van Dien: **6** Caspar
Van Dine, S.S.: **5** alias
Van Doren: **4** Carl, Mark **5** Mamie **7** Charles
Van Doren, Mark: **4** poet
Vandross, Luther
song: The Best Things in Life... (1992)
Don't Want to Be a Fool (1991)
Endless Love (1994)
Here and Now (1990)
Power of Love/Love Power (1991)
Van Duyn, Mona: **4** poet
van Dyck, Anthony: **6** artist **7** painter
home: **8** Flanders
Vandyke __: **5** beard **6** collar
Van Dyke: **2** W.S. **4** Dick **5** Jerry, Leroy, Parks
Van Dyke, Dick: **5** actor
film: Bye Bye Birdie (1963)
Cold Turkey (1971)
Divorce American Style (1967)
Mary Poppins (1964)
Night at the Museum (2006)
TV: Diagnosis Murder, The Dick Van Dyke Show
Van Dyken: **3** Amy
Vandyke site: **4** chin
vane
direction: **4** east, west **5** north, south
part: **4** cock **5** arrow **7** rooster
starter: **7** weather
support: **6** cupola
turner: **4** wind
__ vane: **4** wind **7** weather
Vanessa: **5** Angel **6** Marcil **8** Huxtable, Redgrave, Williams
composer: Samuel Barber
sister: **4** Lynn
van Eyck, Jan: **6** artist **7** painter
homeland: **8** Flanders
Van Fleet: **2** Jo
Vangelis
homeland: Greece
song: Chariots of Fire (1982)
Van Gogh in __: **5** Arles
van Gogh, Vincent: **6** artist **7** painter
biography: Lust For Life
brother: **4** Theo
homeland: **7** Holland
locale: **5** Arles
medium: **3** oil
painting: **6** Irises **10** Sunflowers
vanguard: **4** head **5** front, scout **7** new wave **9** forefront, precursor **10** avant-garde
Van Halen: **4** Alex **5** Eddie
members: **4** Roth **5** Hagar **7** Anthony
song: Dance the Night Away (1979)
Finish What Ya Started (1988)
I'll Wait (1984)
Jump (1984)
Panama (1984)
When It's Love (1988)
Why Can't This Be Love (1986)
Van Helsing (2004 film)
cast: Kate Beckinsale, Hugh Jackman
Van Heusen, James: **8** composer
collaborator: Sammy Cahn
song: All the Way
Call Me Irresponsible
High Hopes
Love and Marriage
Moonlight Becomes You
My Kind of Town

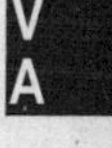

Personality
Pocketful of Miracles
The Road to Morocco
The Second Time Around
Swinging on a Star
The Tender Trap
Thoroughly Modern Millie

vanilla: **4** bean, mild **5** plain, plant **6** flavor, flower **7** prosaic **8** ice cream, mediocre, ordinary, standard **9** prosaical, tasteless **10** lackluster
alternative: ***see*** ice cream flavor
vanilla ___: **4** bean **5** fudge **7** extract
___ vanilla: **5** plain
Vanilla ___: **3** Ice, Sky
vanilla bean: **5** spice **6** legume
Vanilla Fudge
song: You Keep Me Hangin' On (1968)
Vanilla Ice
song: Ice Ice Baby (1990)
Play That Funky Music (1990)
vanilla-like bean: **5** tonka
Vanilla Sky (2001 film)
cast: Tom Cruise, Penélope Cruz, Cameron Diaz, Kurt Russell
director: Cameron Crowe
___ Vanilli: **5** Milli
vanish: **2** go **3** die **4** fade, lift, melt **5** leave **6** die out, escape, go away, perish **7** abscond **8** dissolve, evanesce, fade away, vaporize **9** disappear, dissipate, evaporate
make ~: **6** dispel
vanish ___ thin air: **4** into
vanished: **4** gone, lost **6** absent, bygone **7** extinct, missing **9** elsewhere
Vanished
author: Danielle Steel
Vanished Diamond, The
author: Jules Verne
___ Vanishes, The: **4** Lady
vanishing: **3** off **7** trivial **9** momentary
sound: **4** poof
vanishing ___: **5** cream, point
Vanishing Prairie, The (1954 film)
director: James Algar
vanity: **3** ego **4** airs, show **5** pride **6** egoism, hubris, hybris **7** conceit, egotism, ego trip, hauteur **8** self-love, smugness **9** arrogance, vainglory **10** narcissism, pretension
verbalize ~: **4** brag, crow **5** boast **6** flaunt, parade **7** lay it on, show off, talk big **10** grandstand
vanity ___: **3** bag, box **4** case
Vanity Fair
author: William Makepeace Thackeray
character: **4** Pitt, Smee, Wirt **5** Becky, Sharp **6** Amelia, Dobbin, George, Rawdon, Sedley, Steyne **7** Crawley, Osborne, William
Vanity Fare
song: Hitchin' a Ride (1970)
van Leeuwenhoek: **5** Anton
Van Lingle: **5** Mungo
Van Lustbader: **4** Eric
Vanna: **4** host **5** White
boss: **4** Merv
cohost: **3** Pat
turnover: **3** an a, an e, an i, an o
Vannelli: **4** Gino
Van Nuys: **4** city, town
locale: **10** California
town near ~: **6** Encino
Vanocur: **6** Sander
Van Patten: **4** Dick, Nels **5** Joyce
Van Peebles: **5** Mario **6** Melvin
vanquish: **3** zap **4** beat, best, lick, rout, sink, slay **5** break, crush, quell, repel, smash, worst **6** defeat, humble, reduce, subdue, wallop **7** conquer, put down, repress, subvert, trample, triumph **8** overcome, overturn, surmount **9** checkmate, overpower, overthrow, overwhelm, subjugate
Vanquish: **9** analgesic **10** painkiller
alternative: ***see*** pain reliever brand
vanquisher: **6** victor, winner **9** conqueror
vanquishment: **6** defeat **7** beating, debacle, triumph **8** conquest
Van Sant: **3** Gus
Van Shelton: **5** Ricky
Van Slyke: **4** Andy **5** Helen
Van Susteren: **5** Greta
vantage point: **5** light, perch, venue **8** landmark, position
Vantage Point (2008 film)
cast: Dennis Quaid, Forest Whitaker
van Tilburg Clark: **6** Walter
Vanua ___: **4** Levu
Vanuatu: **4** isls. **5** isles **6** nation **7** islands
capital: **8** Port-Vila
formerly: **4** N. Heb.
volcano: **4** Gaua **5** Yasur **6** Ambrym, Lopevi
Van Valkenburgh: **7** Deborah
Van Winkle: **3** Rip
emulate ~: **3** nap **5** sleep
___ Vanya: **5** Uncle
Vanya in English: **6** Johnny
Vanya on 42nd Street (1994 film)
cast: Julianne Moore, Wallace Shawn
director: Louis Malle
Van Zant: **6** Ronnie
Vanzetti
colleague: **5** Sacco
vapid: **4** arid, blah, drab, dull, flat, limp, mild, tame, weak **5** bland, corny, empty, hokey, inane, passé, prosy, stale, trite **6** barren, boring, common, jejune, old hat, vacant **7** clichéd, fatuous, humdrum, insipid, mundane, prosaic, puerile, tedious, vacuous **8** bromidic, lifeless, outdated, outmoded, tiresome, zestless **9** colorless, driveling, hackneyed, pointless, prosaical, tasteless, wearisome **10** dullsville, flavorless, lackluster, spiritless, uninspired, unoriginal, wishy-washy
vapor: **3** dew, fog, gas **4** fume, haze, mist, smog **5** fumes, miasm, smoke, steam **6** breath, miasma **8** dampness, moisture **9** effluvium, sogginess **10** exhalation
assimilate ~: **6** adsorb
combining form: **3** atm- **4** atmo-, mano- **5** atmid- **6** atmido-
ender: **4** ware
mine ~: **4** damp
vapor ___: **4** lock **5** trail
___ vapor: **5** water
vaporize: **6** aerify, finish, gasify, vanish **7** distill **8** evanesce **9** disappear
vaporizer: **4** mist **5** spray **6** shower, spritz, squirt **7** aerosol **8** atomizer, droplets **9** sprinkler **10** sprinkling
vaporous: **4** fumy **5** gassy, misty, smoky **6** asteam **8** volatile
VapoRub maker: **5** Vicks
___ Vaporum: **4** Mare
vaquero: **6** cowboy, gaucho **7** cowpoke **8** wrangler
gear: **4** bola **5** reata, riata
var.: **4** misc.
Varanasi today: **7** Benares
Vardalos: **3** Nia
Vardar: **5** river
locale: **6** Greece **9** Macedonia
___ Varden trout: **5** Dolly
Vardon Trophy awarder: **3** PGA
Varens: **5** Adele
Varèse, Edgard: **6** French **8** composer
___ Vargas Llosa: **5** Mario
variable: **4** iffy **5** fluid **6** fickle, fitful, myriad, patchy, uneven **7** erratic, mutable, protean, wayward **8** changing, floating, shifting, slippery, ticklish, unstable, unsteady, volatile, wavering **9** irregular, mercurial, parameter, spasmodic, uncertain, unsettled, vagarious **10** capricious, changeable, inconstant
star: **4** Mira, nova
variable-___ mortgage: **4** rate
___ variable: **6** random
variable-interest loan: **3** ARM
variance: **5** clash **6** breach, change, permit, rancor, strife, switch **7** discord, dispute, dissent **8** argument, conflict, disunity, division, flip-flop **9** about-face, departure, deviation, disaccord, diversity **10** alteration, difference, dissension, dissidence, divergence
at ~: **7** unalike **9** different, disparate, dissonant **10** discrepant
variant: **5** other **6** byform, unlike **7** deviant, diverse, spinoff, unalike, version **8** discrete, distinct, modified, separate **9** different, differing, divergent, exception
variation: **5** range, shade, shift, twist **6** change **8** contrast, mutation **9** departure, deviation, disparity, diversion, diversity, exception, gradation **10** aberration, adaptation, alteration, difference, digression, divergence, inequality, inflection, innovation
cause of hereditary ~: **6** allele
color ~: **3** hue **4** tint, tone **5** blend, shade, tinct, tinge
molecular ~: **6** isomer
rug color ~: **6** abrash
___ Variations: **6** Enigma
varicolored: **4** pied **6** motley **7** brindle, dappled, mottled, piebald **8** brindled, speckled **9** multihued **10** variegated
flower: **4** glad, rose **5** canna, pansy, phlox, stock, viola **6** azalea, dahlia, oxalis, zinnia **7** anemone, comfrey, lobelia, petunia, verbena **8** clematis, gladiola, gloxinia, hibiscus, rain lily, sweet pea **9** carnation, cineraria, fairy lily, gladiolus, impatiens, portulaca, pyrethrum **10** floribunda, frangipani, snapdragon, zephyr lily
varied: **3** odd **4** many, misc., mixt **5** mixed **6** divers, motley, sundry **7** diverse, unalike **8** assorted, discrete, manifold, multiple, separate **9** different, disparate **13** miscellaneous
variegated: **4** pied **6** dapple, motley **7** dappled, diverse **8** brindled, speckled **9** checkered, different
stone: **5** agate
variegation: **5** prism **7** rainbow
variety: **3** ilk, mix **4** form, kind, make, sort, type **5** array, brand, breed, class, combo, genre, genus, grade, order, range, stock **6** change, kidney, manner, medley, strain, stripe **7** mélange, mixture, pattern, quality, species **8** category, mishmash, mixed bag, quantity, specimen **9** diversity, potpourri **10** assortment, collection, cumulation, difference, divergency, miscellany
variety ___: **4** meat, show **5** store
___-variety: **6** garden
variety show segment: **3** act **4** skit
Varig stop: **3** Rio
various: **3** odd **4** many, mixt **5** mixed **6** divers, legion, motley, sundry, unlike **7** certain, diverse, several, unalike **8** assorted, discrete, distinct, manifold, multiple, numerous, separate **9** different, disparate, divergent **10** dissimilar, individual
at ~ times: **6** cyclic **8** cyclical, frequent, periodic, repeated, seasonal, sporadic **9** recurrent, recurring, spasmodic **10** occasional
combining form: **5** parti-
varlet: **3** cad **5** knave, rogue **6** rascal **7** so-and-so **9** reprobate, scoundrel
varmint: **5** beast, rogue **6** animal, rascal **9** scoundrel
Varner: **4** Eula
Varney, Jim persona: **6** Ernest **7** Worrell
varnish: **4** coat, gild **5** adorn, cover, glaze, gloss, japan, paint, stain **6** enamel, finish, luster, polish, smooth **7** coating, encrust, incrust, lacquer, shellac **8** decorate, palliate, shellack **9** embellish
apply, as ~: **5** apply, lay on
ingredient: **3** lac **5** elemi, resin, rosin
oil: **4** tung
resin: **5** anime, copal, damar, elemi, kauri **6** dammar, guaiac, mastic
Varrick: **7** Charley
Varsi: **5** Diane
varsity: **4** team **5** A-team
award: **6** letter
___ varsity: **6** junior, senior
Varsity ___, The: **4** Drag
vary: **3** run **4** yo-yo **5** alter, range, shift, swing, waver **6** assort, change, depart, differ, modify, mutate, swerve **7** deviate, digress, dissent, diverge, inflect, qualify

8 contrast, disagree, displace, modulate, separate 9 alternate, change off, diversify, fluctuate, hem and haw, oscillate, permutate, take turns, transform
__ Vary: 7 Karlovy
varying: 6 patchy 7 diverse, mutable, unequal, variant
Vasco: 6 da Gama
Vasco __ de Balboa: 5 Núñez
vascular channel: 4 vein
vase: 3 jar, urn 6 bowpot, holder 8 boughpot 9 container 10 jardiniere, receptacle
  occupant: 3 bud, mum 4 posy 7 bouquet, nosegay
  Roman ~ stone: 5 murra 6 murrha
__ vase: 4 Ming
__ Vashem: 3 Yad
Vasily: 7 Rozanov, Smyslov 8 Aksyonov 9 Kandinsky, Zhukovsky
  see also Russian
Vaslav: 8 Nijinsky
vassal: 4 leud, serf 5 liege, slave 7 subject, villein
  of a ~: 6 feudal
  place: 4 fief 5 manor
  shogun ~: 6 daimio, daimyo
vassalage: 7 slavery 9 captivity, servitude
Vassar: 6 school 7 college
  most ~ grads: 5 women
vast: 3 big 4 huge, tidy, wide 5 ample, broad, enorm, giant, great, jumbo, large 6 cosmic, gaping, mighty, untold 7 endless, eternal, hulking, immense, mammoth, massive, sizable, titanic 8 colossal, cosmical, detailed, enormous, expanded, far-flung, gigantic, infinite, king-size, oversize, sizeable, spacious, sweeping, towering, whapping, whopping 9 boundless, capacious, cavernous, expansive, extensive, Herculean, humongous, limitless, monstrous, overlarge, prolonged, spread-out, unbounded, unlimited 10 fathomless, gargantuan, large-scale, monumental, prodigious, staggering, stupendous, tremendous, unknowable, unnumbered, voluminous, widespread
  amount: 3 sea 4 lots, slew, tons 5 array, ocean
  holdings: 5 realm 6 empire 7 kingdom 8 dominion 9 territory
vastly: 3 far 4 a lot, lots, many, much, tons, very 5 amply, loads, no end, quite, scads, truly 6 a bunch, deeply, highly, hugely, plenty, rather, really 7 acutely, aplenty, greatly, largely, notably 8 famously, markedly, very many, very much 9 copiously, decidedly, extremely, glaringly, immensely, in a big way, intensely, like crazy, supremely 10 abundantly, enormously, especially, incredibly, profoundly, remarkably, strikingly, thoroughly, uncommonly
vastness: 4 room, size 7 breadth 8 enormity 9 amplitude, immensity, largeness, magnitude 10 infinitude
  symbol of ~: 3 sea 5 ocean
vat: 3 tub, tun 4 cask, keir, kier, tank 6 barrel, kettle, vessel 7 caldron, cistern 8 cauldron 9 container 10 receptacle
  worker: 4 dyer
__ Vat: 6 Angkor
vat-dye ingredient: 6 isatin
vatic: 8 Delphian, divining, oracular 9 prophetic 10 portending
Vatican City
  head: 4 pope 7 pontiff 10 Holy Father
  money: 4 euro
  name: 3 Leo 4 John, Paul, Pius 5 Urban 6 Adrian, Sixtus, Victor 7 Clement, Gregory, Stephen 8 Benedict, Boniface, Innocent, John Paul 9 Alexander, Celestine
  neighbor: 4 Rome 5 Italy
  of ~: 5 papal
  ruling body: 5 curia
  staffer: 6 legate
  treasure: 5 Pietà
  wear: 5 orale
vaticinal: 8 Delphian, oracular, sibyllic 9 prescient, prophetic 10 prognostic
vaticinate: 7 predict, presage 8 foreshow, prophesy
vaticinator: 4 seer 5 augur, sibyl 6 medium, oracle 7 diviner, palmist, prophet, psychic 9 Cassandra, predictor, visionary 10 forecaster, foreteller, mind reader, palm reader, soothsayer
VAT, part of: 3 tax 5 added, value
vaudeville: 4 show 7 burlesk 9 bawdy show, burlesque 10 lampoonery
  routine: 3 act 4 olio, skit, solo
  show: 4 perf. 5 revue 6 review
vaudevillian: 5 comic 6 dancer, hoofer
  prop: 4 cane 8 straw hat
Vaughan: 4 Arky 5 Billy, Sarah
Vaughan, Sarah
  nickname: 5 Sassy 9 Divine One
  song: Broken-Hearted Melody (1959)
    C'est la Vie (1955)
    Make Yourself Comfortable (1954)
    Mr. Wonderful (1956)
    Whatever Lola Wants (1955)
Vaughan Williams: 5 Ralph
Vaughn: 5 Billy, Hippo, Vince 6 Monroe, Robert
Vaughn, Robert: 5 actor
  role: 4 Solo 8 Napoleon
  TV: The Man From U.N.C.L.E.
Vaughn, Vince: 5 actor
  film: Be Cool (2005)
    The Break-Up (2006)
    The Cell (2000)
    Clay Pigeons (1998)
    A Cool, Dry Place (1999)
    Domestic Disturbance (2001)
    Fred Claus (2007)
    Made (2001)
    Return to Paradise (1998)
    Wedding Crashers (2005)
vault: 3 pit 4 arch, dome, jump, leap, room, safe, soar, span, till, tomb 5 bound, clear, crypt, mount, store 6 bounce, cavern, hurdle, prance, spring 7 dungeon, lockbox 8 catacomb, jump over, leapfrog, overleap, surmount, treasury 9 negotiate, strongbox 10 depository, repository
  architectural ~ feature: 5 groin
  cracker: 4 yegg 5 thief 7 burglar
  of heaven: 3 sky 8 empyrean
  rib: 5 ogive 6 lierne
__ vault: 4 pole
vaulted alcove: 4 apse 6 recess
vaulter: 7 acrobat, gymnast, tumbler 9 aerialist
vaunt: 4 brag, crow 5 boast, pride 6 parade 7 big talk, boast of, talk big 8 flourish 9 brag about, crow about
vav: 6 Hebrew, letter
  predecessor: 2 he 3 heh
  successor: 5 zayin
Va-va-__!: 4 voom
vaw: 6 Hebrew, letter
  predecessor: 2 he 3 heh
  successor: 5 zayin
Vaya con __: 4 Dios
vb.
  form: 3 inf. 5 infin.
  modifier: 3 adv.
  tense: 3 fut. 4 pres., pret. 6 imperf.
  type: 3 int., irr. 4 intr. 5 irreg., trans.
vbs., like some: 5 irreg.
VCR: 3 VHS 4 Beta 7 Betamax
  accessory: 3 mic
  button: 3 fwd., rec, rew 4 play, stop 5 eject, pause, reset
  descendant: 4 TiVo
  feature: 5 timer
  function: 5 erase 6 delete
  input: 4 tape 9 videotape
  maker: 3 JVC, RCA 5 Sanyo 9 Panasonic
  need: 2 TV 5 TV set 6 remote 10 television
  part: 5 video 8 cassette, recorder
  place for a ~: 3 den 6 TV room
  sound adjuster: 3 AVC
  speed setting: 3 SLP
__ V. Debs: 6 Eugene
VDT: 6 screen 8 terminal
V-E __: 3 Day
veal: 4 meat 6 course, entree
  in French: 4 veau
  serving: 4 chop 6 cutlet 7 piccata
  source: 4 calf
veal cordon __: 4 bleu
__ Vecchio: 5 Ponte
Vecellio: 6 Titian
Vector
  author: Robin Cook
Vectra: 3 car 4 auto, Opel 10 automobile
Ved: 5 Mehta
Veda believer: 5 Hindu 6 Hindoo
Veda language: 3 Skr., Skt. 4 Skrt. 8 Sanskrit
V-E Day
  conflict: 4 WWII
  month: 3 May
Vedder: 5 Eddie, Elihu
Vedic
  god: 4 Agni, Kama, Siva, Soma, Yama 5 Indra, Shiva, Surya 6 Brahma, Varuna, Vishnu 7 Ganesha, Hanuman, Krishna
  goddess: 4 Devi, Kali, Usha 5 Durga, Ushas 7 Lakshmi, Parvati 9 Sarasvati
Vee, Bobby
  song: Come Back When You Grow Up (1967)
    Devil or Angel (1960)
    The Night Has a Thousand Eyes (1962)
    Rubber Ball (1960)
    Run to Him (1961)
    Take Good Care of My Baby (1961)
Veeck: 4 Bill, Mike
veejay
  cousin: 4 host 5 emcee
  employer: 3 MTV
veep: 4 exec 9 number two
  boss: 4 prex, prez 5 prexy
veer: 3 yaw, zag, zig 4 bend, lean, skew, skid, slew, slue, tack, turn 5 avert, curve, dodge, drift, pivot, shift, slant, slide, swing, twist, wheel 6 careen, change, divert, slough, swerve, switch, swivel, wander 7 deflect, deviate 8 angle off, sheer off, sideslip 9 turn aside
veering: 5 dodge, shift, swing 6 change, swerve, switch 8 maneuver, movement, straying, variance 9 avoidance, departure, deviation, diversion, variation 10 aberration, alteration, deflection, digression, divergence, separation
veery: 4 bird 6 thrush
vee starter: 3 jay
veg: 3 bum 4 laze 5 idler 6 loafer 7 goof-off, slacker 8 indolent, sluggard 9 do nothing, goldbrick, lazybones 10 ne'er-do-well
Vega: 3 car 4 auto, star 5 Chevy 7 Suzanne 9 Chevrolet 10 automobile
  constellation: 4 Lyra
Vega$ (ABC drama)
  cast: Bart Braverman (Binzer)
    Tony Curtis (Philip Roth)
    Robert Urich (Dan Tanna)
Vega, Lope de: 4 poet 7 Spanish 10 playwright
vegan taboo: 4 meat
Vegas
  action: 3 bet 4 ante, play 5 wager
  alternative: 4 Reno 5 Tahoe
  area: 5 strip
  cube: 3 die
  cubes: 4 dice
  game: 4 faro, keno 5 craps, poker, slots 8 baccarat, roulette 9 blackjack, twenty-one
  headliner: 4 Anka 6 Newton
  lighting: 4 neon
  natural: 5 seven 6 eleven
  posting: 4 odds
  worker: 6 dealer 7 pit boss 8 croupier
  see also Las Vegas
__ Vegas: 3 Las
vegetable: 3 cos, pea, yam 4 bean, beet, Bibb, cole, corn, cuke, herb, kail, kale, leek, lime, ocra, okra, okro, pepo, root, soup, taro 5 chard, chive, cress, cubeb, gourd, green, olive, onion, plant, pulse, savoy, tater 6 carrot, celery, cushaw, edible, endive, greens, jicama, legume, lentil, peanut,

pepper, pickle, potato, radish, russet, squash, tomato, turnip **7** arugula, avocado, bok choy, cabbage, cardoon, gherkin, haricot, lettuce, parsley, parsnip, produce, pumpkin, salsify, shallot, spinach, wax bean **8** broccoli, celeriac, chickpea, collards, cucumber, earthnut, eggplant, kohlrabi, scallion, soya bean, tamarind, zucchini **9** artichoke, asparagus, aubergine, broad bean, crookneck, green bean, groundnut, red pepper, sweetcorn, tomatillo **10** bell pepper, cos lettuce, kidney bean, red cabbage, runner bean, string bean, Swiss chard, watercress
cooker: **3** wok
Creole ~: **4** ocra, okra, okro
green ~: **3** pea **7** cabbage, lettuce
holder: **3** can, tin **7** package **9** container
Japanese ~: **3** udo
leafy ~: **4** kail, kale **5** chard **7** lettuce
matter: **4** pulp **9** cellulose
processor: **5** dicer, ricer **6** slicer
starchy ~: **3** yam **5** tuber **6** potato
tray item: **3** dip **5** olive **6** carrot, celery
vegetable __: **3** oil
__ vegetable: **5** green
vegetable-oil ingredient: **5** olein **6** oleine
__, vegetable, or mineral: **6** animal
vegetables: **4** crop **5** yield **7** harvest, produce
big name in ~: **5** Libby **6** Libby's **8** Birdseye, Del Monte **10** Green Giant
like some ~: **5** green, leafy **7** verdant
old-style: **5** pease
prepare ~: **4** dice **5** cream, slice, steam **7** stir-fry
preserve ~: **3** can **6** freeze **9** freeze-dry
__-vegetarian: **3** ovo
vegetarian no-no: **4** meat
vegetate: **3** bud **4** grow, idle, loaf **5** bloom **6** sprout **7** blossom, burgeon, go to pot **8** bourgeon, go to seed, languish, pass time, stagnate **9** germinate
vegetation: **4** tree **5** flora, grass, plant, scrub **6** plants, shrubs **7** foliage, herbage **9** shrubbery
lacking ~: **3** dry **4** arid **6** barren, fallow **7** parched, sterile **8** deserted, desolate, infecund, lifeless **9** fruitless
rife with ~: **4** lush, rich, wild **5** dense, green **6** lavish **7** fertile, teeming, verdant **8** abundant, tropical **9** plentiful, succulent
veggie
see vegetable
vehemence: **4** fury, heat, rage, zeal **5** anger, furor **6** frenzy **7** emotion, passion **8** strength, wildness **9** eagerness, fieriness, intensity **10** enthusiasm, impatience
with ~: **4** hard **5** hotly **6** loudly, wildly **7** angrily, like mad **8** fiercely **9** furiously, violently **10** vigorously
vehement: **3** hot, mad **4** ired, loud, warm **5** angry, eager, fiery, hyper, rabid **6** ablaze, ardent, fervid, fierce, hearty, heated, stormy, strong **7** burning, earnest, fervent, frantic, furious, intense, rampant, violent, zealous **8** emphatic, forceful, hopped up, inflamed **9** desperate, ferocious **10** hysterical, passionate, pronounced, vociferant, vociferous
vehicle: **3** bus, cab, car, LST, SUV, ute, van, way **4** auto, bike, boat, cart, dray, hack, jeep, limo, pram, raft, shay, ship, sled, tank, taxi, tool **5** agent, buggy, canoe, coach, craft, crate, liner, means, moped, organ, plane, train, trike, truck, U-Haul, wagon **6** agency, hansom, jalopy, medium, wheels **7** bicycle, carrier, channel, chariot, machine, phaeton **8** tricycle **9** expedient, implement, machinery, mechanism, transport **10** automobile, conveyance, instrument, motorcycle
all-purpose ~: **3** ute
all-terrain ~: **3** SUV **4** jeep
British ~: **4** pram **5** lorry
city ~: **3** bus, cab **4** hack, taxi
commuter ~: **3** bus **5** train
construction-site ~: **5** dozer
defective ~: **3** dud **4** heap **5** crate, lemon, wreck **6** jalopy, junker **7** clunker **10** hunk of junk
emergency ~: **4** raft **9** ambulance
family ~: **3** car, van **4** auto **5** sedan
gravity-powered ~: **4** luge, pung, sled **6** sleigh **8** toboggan
horse-pulled ~: **4** cart, dray **5** buggy, wagon **8** carriage
kid's ~: **5** trike, wagon
moving ~: **3** van **5** truck, U-Haul
off-road ~: **3** ATV **4** jeep **6** Hummer, Humvee
one-wheeled ~: **6** barrow
recreational ~: **3** ATV **5** canoe
replacement ~: **6** loaner
rescue ~: **6** copter **7** chopper
sticker: **5** decal
suffix: **6** -mobile
two-wheeled ~: **4** cart **5** dolly **6** barrow **8** rickshaw
utility ~: **3** rig, van **4** jeep, semi **5** dolly, lorry, truck, U-Haul **6** pickup
vacation ~: **2** RV **6** camper **9** Winnebago **10** mobile home
WWII ~: **3** LCT, LST **4** jeep
__ vehicle: **5** motor **7** off-road
vehicles: **7** traffic
Veidt: **6** Conrad
veil: **3** dim **4** film, hide, mask, pall, wrap **5** cache, cloak, cloud, couch, cover, drape, guise, purda, shade **6** enfold, infold, mantle, pardah, purdah, screen, shadow, shield, shroud **7** becloud, blanket, conceal, cover up, curtain, eclipse, enclose, envelop, inclose, obscure, pretext, protect, secrete, shut off, shut out, yashmac, yashmak **8** disguise, enshroud, mantilla, pretense **9** adumbrate, semblance **10** camouflage, keep secret
fabric: **3** net **5** tulle **6** barege
__ veil: **6** bridal **7** humeral
veiled: **4** dark **6** covert, hidden, latent, occult, secret, unseen **7** furtive, private **8** hush-hush **9** innermost, unexposed **10** mysterious, undercover, underlying, under wraps, undetected
__ Veil Falls: **6** Bridal
Veil of __: **4** Isis
__ Veil, The: **4** Blue **7** Seventh
vein: **3** rib, way **4** bent, duct, line, lode, mine, mode, mood, note, seam, tone, turn **5** humor, layer, metal, stria, style, tenor **6** manner, nature, pocket, spirit, strain, streak, stripe, temper, thread **7** fashion, stratum **8** attitude, vena cava **9** capillary, character, striation **10** complexion, mother lode
combining form: **3** ven- **4** veni-, veno- **5** phleb- **6** phlebo-
leaf ~: **3** rib
material: **3** ore **4** gold, lode
opposite: **6** artery
place: **4** mine **8** gold mine
__ vein: **5** renal **7** jugular
vel.: **3** spd.
measure: **3** MPH
velar: **3** low **5** gruff, husky **6** hoarse **7** grating, rasping, throaty **8** gravelly, guttural
Velázquez, Diego: **6** artist **7** painter
homeland: **5** Spain
Velcro: **4** hook **8** fastener **10** attachment
alternative: **4** band, cord, lace, rope, snap **5** strap **6** string, thread **8** fastener, shoelace
emulate ~: **5** cling, stick **6** adhere, cleave
Velcro Fly (1986 song)
artist: ZZ Top
veldt: **3** lea, sod **5** campo, field, green, llano **6** meadow, pampas **7** pasture, savanna **8** savannah **9** grassland
beast: **3** gnu **4** lion **5** eland, hyena, oribi **6** hyaena, impala
Velez: **4** Lupe **6** Lauren
VelJohnson: **8** Reginald
velleity: **4** bent, will, wish **6** desire, liking **7** leaning, passion **8** affinity, penchant, soft spot, tendency **10** attraction, favoritism, partiality
vellicate: **3** pet **6** caress, stroke, tickle, tingle **8** convulse **9** stimulate, titillate
vellum: **5** paper
velocipede: **4** bike **5** trike **7** bicycle, vehicle **8** tricycle
need: **4** gear, tire
velociraptor: **8** dinosaur
velocity: **3** spd. **4** pace, rate **5** haste, hurry, speed, tempo **8** alacrity, celerity, dispatch, movement, rapidity **9** fleetness, quickness, swiftness **10** expedition, promptness
abbr.: **3** mph
cockpit ~ reading: **3** IAS
decrease the ~ of: **4** slow **5** brake **6** retard, slow up **8** slow down **10** decelerate
__ velocity: **6** escape
velour: **6** fabric **8** material
velouté: **5** sauce
velum: **6** palate
__ Velva: **4** Aqua
Velveeta maker: **5** Kraft
velvet: **5** panne **6** fabric **7** jobbery
ender: **3** een **4** leaf
hat: **5** toque
velvet __: **5** glove
__ velvet: **7** crushed
__ Velvet: **4** Blue **5** Black
Velvet Fog, The: Mel Tormé
velvetlike fabric: **6** velour **7** mockado, velours **8** moquette
velvety: **4** soft **5** downy, furry, nappy, plush, silky **6** creamy, fleecy, flossy, fluffy, smooth **7** squishy **8** cushiony
surface: **3** nap **4** down **6** fleece
Venable: **6** Evelyn
vena cava: **4** vein **9** capillary
counterpart: **5** aorta
venal: **6** sordid **7** corrupt **8** bribable, hireling **9** mercenary, on the take, rapacious
venality: **4** vice **5** graft, greed **6** payoff, payola **7** bribery, jobbery **8** baseness **9** extortion, looseness, shadiness **10** corruption, dishonesty, immorality
vend: **4** hawk, sell **6** market, peddle, retail, unload **7** publish **9** dispose of, liquidate **10** auction off
vended: **3** sld. **4** sold
vendee: **5** buyer **6** emptor, patron **8** consumer, customer
vendetta: **4** feud **7** quarrel, rivalry
undertake a ~: **6** avenge **7** revenge
__ Vendetta: **4** V for
vendible: **4** ware **7** salable **9** commodity **10** marketable
vendibles: **4** line **5** goods, wares
vending machine
buy: **4** Coke, nosh, soda **5** candy, Pepsi, snack **6** coffee **8** candy bar **9** chocolate
fooler: **4** slug
part: **4** slot **7** plunger **10** coin return
vendition: **4** sale **7** auction
vendor: **5** crier **6** dealer, grocer, hawker, pedlar, pedler, seller, trader **7** peddler, pitcher **8** huckster, merchant
area: **4** cart **5** booth, kiosk
street ~ offering: **4** nosh, pita **5** frank, snack **6** hot dog **7** pretzel **8** ice cream
veneer: **4** coat, face, mask **5** cloak, cover, front, gloss, inlay, layer, paint, sheet, shell **6** enamel, facade, facing, finish, lamina **7** coating, encrust, incrust, lacquer, outside, overlay, surface **8** covering, exterior, laminate, pretense **9** semblance **10** appearance
cover with ~: **4** coat **5** layer **7** overlay **8** laminate
venerable: **3** old **4** aged, sage, wise **5** hoary, noble **6** age-old, august, sacred, solemn **7** ancient, elderly, honored, revered, stately, vintage **8** esteemed, glorious **9** dignified, estimable, graybeard, honorable, respected **10** gray-haired
one: **5** elder **6** senior **8** superior **9** matriarch, patriarch
Venerable __: **4** Bede
venerate: **4** laud, love **5** adore, deify, honor **6** admire, esteem, hallow,

revere 7 beatify, cherish, glorify, idolize, observe, respect, worship 8 look up to
venerated: 7 beloved 8 esteemed
veneration: 3 awe 5 honor, piety 6 esteem, regard 7 respect, worship 9 adoration, deference, reverence 10 admiration, estimation
object of ~: 4 icon, idol, ikon 5 eikon
Venetian: 6 fabric 7 Italian
see also Venice
Venetian Alps city: 5 Udine
venetian blind
component: 4 slat
wood: 4 teak
__ Veneto: 3 Via
Venez.
locale: 5 S. Amer.
Venezia: 4 city, town
locale: 5 Italy 6 Italia
see also Venice
Venezuela: 6 nation 7 country
capital: 7 Caracas
city: 6 Cumana 7 Cabimas, Caracas 8 La Guaira 9 Maracaibo
dance: 6 joropo
falls: 5 Angel
gulf: 5 Paria 9 Maracaibo
Indian: 5 Carib
island near ~: 5 Aruba 6 Tobago 7 Curaçao 8 Trinidad
lake: 9 Maracaibo
money: 7 centimo
neighbor: 6 Brazil, Guyana 8 Colombia
org.: 3 OAS 4 OPEC
river: 3 Aro 5 Apure
writer: 5 Bello 8 Gallegos
see also Spanish
vengeance: 5 spite 6 rancor 7 payback, redress, revenge 8 reprisal, requital 9 repayment, tit for tat
obtain, as ~: 5 exact, force, wreak 6 demand, direct 7 call for, command, inflict
take ~: 3 fix, get 6 avenge 7 get even 9 retaliate
with a ~: 6 wildly 7 like mad 8 fiercely 9 furiously, violently
__ vengeance: 5 with a
Vengeance is ___: 4 mine
vengeful: 4 mean 5 cruel, harsh, nasty 6 animal, brutal, fierce, savage, unkind, wanton 7 beastly, callous, hurtful, vicious 8 barbaric, fiendish, inhumane, pitiless, punitive, ruthless, sadistic, spiteful 9 cutthroat, ferocious, malicious, merciless, monstrous, rancorous, splenetic, truculent, unpitying 10 implacable, malevolent, unfriendly, unmerciful, vindictive
vengefulness: 5 spite 6 malice, rancor, spleen
veni: 5 I came, Latin
follower: 4 vidi
venial: 9 allowable, excusable, tolerable 10 forgivable, pardonable
veniality: 3 sin 4 evil, vice 5 crime, error 7 misdeed, offense 8 atrocity, iniquity, trespass 9 blasphemy, evildoing, sacrilege, violation 10 immorality, infraction, misconduct, peccadillo, transgress, wickedness, wrongdoing
Venice: 4 city, gulf, port, town
beach: 4 Lido
city near ~: 5 Padua, Udine
explorer: 4 Polo
feature: 5 canal
locale: 5 Italy
money: 6 sequin
old ruler of ~: 4 doge
symbol of ~: 4 lion
transporter: 5 poler 7 gondola
villain of ~: 4 Iago
Venice of Japan, The: 5 Osaka
venire __: 6 facias
veniremen: 4 jury 5 panel
venison: 4 deer, game, meat
cut: 4 rump, side 5 flank, thigh 6 haunch
like ~: 4 gamy 5 gamey
veni, vidi, __: 4 vici
Venner: 5 Elsie
venom: 4 bile, gall, hate 5 anger, spite, toxin 6 enmity, grudge, hatred, malice, poison, rancor, spleen 7 cruelty, ill will 8 acrimony, bad blood 9 animosity, hostility, nastiness 10 bitterness, grumpiness, resentment, unkindness
conveyor: 4 fang
extract ~ from: 4 milk
with ~: 6 acidly 10 spitefully
venomous: 4 mean 5 catty, snaky, toxic 6 aspish, deadly, fierce, ireful, lethal 7 baleful, baneful, hateful, hostile, vicious, waspish 8 spiteful, viperous, virulent 9 malicious, poisonous, rancorous, splenetic 10 malevolent, pernicious, vindictive
snake: 3 asp 5 krait, mamba
Venora: 5 Diane
vent: 3 air, gap 4 duct, emit, exit, flue, hole, open, pipe, slit, snap, talk 5 drain, eject, empty, erupt, expel, issue, spout, state, utter, voice, wreak 6 air out, airway, crater, let out, louver, louvre, outgas, outlet, window 7 air duct, air hole, chimney, express, fissure, opening, orifice, pour out, release, relieve, unleash 8 aperture, blowhole, fumarole, proclaim, vocalize 9 cast forth, discharge, force upon, ventilate
dermal ~: 4 pore 5 stoma 10 sweat gland
fireplace ~: 4 flue, vent 6 airway 7 chimney 10 smokeshaft
like a clogged dryer ~: 5 fuzzy, linty
one's spleen: 4 boil, fume, rage, rant, rave, yell 5 erupt, steam, wrath 6 blow up, rail at, scream, seethe 7 explode, rampage, run riot, run wild 8 boil over, have a fit, outburst, run amuck 9 blow a fuse, fulminate, go berserk 10 hit the roof, kick up a row
with frenzy: 5 wreak 7 unleash
__-vent: 5 vol-au
vented, not: 6 pent-up
ventilate: 3 air 6 aerate, air out 7 freshen 9 circulate
ventilated: 4 airy, open 5 windy 6 breezy
poorly ~: 5 heavy, muggy, musty, stale, thick 6 stuffy, sultry 7 airless, clogged 8 stagnant, stifling 10 oppressive, sweltering
ventilation: 3 air 4 puff, vent, wind 5 draft 6 breeze, oxygen 10 exhalation
channel: 4 duct, pipe
system: 4 flue 6 airway
ventilator: 3 fan 6 blower 7 air-cool 9 propeller
Ventimiglia: 4 Milo
venting: 5 vocal 8 emission, harangue
Ventnor: 3 ave. 6 avenue
vent one's __: 6 spleen
ventre à __: 5 terre
ventricle neighbor: 5 aorta 6 atrium
ventriloquist dummy's home: 5 trunk
Ventura: 3 Ace, car 4 auto 5 Jesse, Robin 7 Pontiac 10 automobile
Ventura Highway (1972 song)
artist: America
Ventura, Robin
sport: 8 baseball
venture: 3 bet, bid, job, try 4 dare, risk, shot, sink, spec, stab 5 assay, brave, essay, fling, foray, guess, put up, stake, wager 6 chance, effort, gamble, hazard, plunge, take on 7 attempt, daresay, presume, project, pursuit, surmise 8 activity, endeavor 9 adventure, speculate, take a risk, undertake, volunteer 10 enterprise, experiment, investment, pet project, take a flyer
a thought: 3 say 5 guess, opine 7 comment, suppose, surmise
ender: 4 some
(forth): 5 sally
joint ~: 4 co-op
like ~ capital investments: 5 dicey, risky 6 chancy, daring, unsafe 9 uncertain 10 precarious
speculative ~: 5 flier, flyer
unsuccessful ~: 3 dog, dud 4 bomb, bust, flop 5 lemon, loser 6 fiasco, fizzle 7 debacle, failure, washout 8 disaster
venture __: 7 capital
__ venture: 5 joint
Venture: 3 van 5 Chevy 9 Chevrolet
Ventures
song: Hawaii Five-O (1969) Walk-Don't Run (1960)
venturesome: 4 bold, game, rash 5 brave, gutsy, nervy, risky, stout 6 awless, daring, gritty, heroic, plucky, spunky, sturdy 7 aweless, defiant, doughty, gallant, staunch, valiant 8 fearless, heroical, intrepid, overbold, reckless, resolute, spirited, stalwart, unafraid, valorous 9 audacious, daredevil, dauntless, dreadless, foolhardy, undaunted, unfearful 10 courageous
one: 5 darer
Venture to the Interior
author: Laurens Van der Post
Venturi, Ken: 6 golfer
venturous: 5 brave 6 daring 8 reckless 9 foolhardy 10 courageous
venue: 4 site 5 locus, place, scene 6 ground, locale 7 setting 8 locality, location 9 nightclub
Venus: 3 dea, orb 6 beauty, planet, sphere 8 Williams
artist: Erté
equivalent: 9 Aphrodite
father: 7 Jupiter
part of ~ atmosphere: 4 neon
sister: 6 Serena
son: 4 Amor, Eros 5 Cupid
where ~ was found: 4 Milo 5 Melos, Milos
Venus (song)
artist: Frankie Avalon, Bananarama, Shocking Blue
Venus __: 6 de Milo 7 flytrap
Venus Among the Fishes
author: Scott O'Dell
Venus and Adonis
painter: Peter Paul Rubens
Venus d'__: 5 Arles
Venus de Milo: 6 statue
lack: 4 arms
site: 6 Louvre
Venus flytrap: 5 plant 6 flower
feature: 5 hinge
Venusian: 2 ET 5 alien
Venus of __: 5 Melos
Venus of the Counting House
author: Émile Zola
Venus of Urbino: 4 nude
Venus's-hair: 4 fern
Vep: 4 Irma
__ Ver.: 3 Com., Rev. 4 Auth.
__ vera: 4 aloe 5 cutis
Vera: 4 Lynn 5 Billy, Miles, Vague 6 Panova, Zorina 7 Caspary 8 Brittain
Vera __: 4 Cruz
Vera-__: 5 Ellen
veracious: 4 just, open, real, true 5 exact, frank, legit, right, valid 6 honest, square, trusty 7 correct, ethical, factual, genuine, up-front, upright 8 accurate, credible, like it is, reliable, straight, truthful, verified 9 righteous 10 aboveboard, dependable, forthright, on the level, scrupulous
veracity: 5 honor, right, truth 6 candor 7 honesty, probity 8 accuracy, like it is, openness 9 exactness, frankness, integrity, precision, rectitude, sincerity 10 exactitude, factuality, honestness
Veracruz: 4 city, port, town 5 state
ancient ~ Indian: 5 Olmec
capital of ~: 6 Jalapa
locale: 6 Mexico
see also Spanish
Vera Cruz Indian
ancient ~: 5 Olmec
veranda: 5 lanai, porch 6 piazza 7 balcony
verb
ender: 3 ose
poetic ~: 3 ope
suffix: 3 -ate, -eth, -ify, -ize 4 -esce
tense: 3 fut. 4 past, pres. 6 future 7 perfect, present 8 preterit
type: 3 int., irr., reg. 7 regular 9 irregular 10 transitive

verbal: **4** oral, said, told **5** parol, vocal **6** spoken, stated **7** lingual **8** narrated **9** expressed, unwritten, vocalized
attack: **3** rap **4** bash, belt, flak, lash, slam, slur **5** abuse, flack, salvo, smear **6** insult, outcry **7** barrage, potshot, slander **8** outburst, reproach **9** criticism **10** defamation
departure: **5** aside **10** digression
exchange: **4** quip, talk **6** banter **7** jesting, joshing, kidding, ribbing, teasing **8** chitchat, repartee **9** small talk, table talk
fanfare: **4** ta-da **5** ta-dah
fight: **4** spat **5** fight, set-to **6** debate **7** dispute, polemic, quarrel, rhubarb **8** argument, polemics, squabble **9** bickering, encounter **10** war of words
give a ~ account: **4** tell **6** recite
noun: **6** gerund
sigh: **4** alas
significance: **6** action
stumble: **2** er, uh, um
verbal __: **4** noun
verbalization: **6** speech **8** language **9** statement, utterance
verbalize: **3** say **4** talk **5** speak, state, utter, voice **6** mumble, murmur, phrase, relate **7** dictate, express, recount **8** set forth, vocalize **9** pronounce **10** articulate
verbalized: **4** oral **5** vocal
verbally: **5** aloud, parol **8** viva voce
fight ~: **5** argue, claim, plead **6** appeal, bicker, debate, dicker, haggle, oppose, reason **7** contend, dispute, dissent, protest, quarrel, quibble, wrangle **8** disagree, hash over, squabble **9** lock horns **10** controvert, deliberate
verbatim: **3** sic **5** exact **7** exactly, literal **8** directly **9** literally, precisely **10** accurately
repeat ~: **4** cite **5** quote **6** parrot, recite, repeat, retell **7** excerpt, extract
verbena: **5** plant **6** flower
tree: **4** teak
verbiage: **4** talk **7** diction, wording **8** parlance, phrasing, pleonasm **9** elocution, floridity, loquacity, prolixity, tautology, verbosity, wordiness **10** redundancy, vocabulary
verbose: **4** glib, long **5** gabby, talky, windy, wordy **6** prolix **7** diffuse, flowery, fustian, gushing, lengthy, tedious, unterse, voluble **8** inflated, involved, rambling, tortuous **9** bombastic, garrulous, overblown, ponderous, redundant, talkative **10** bigmouthed, discursive, longwinded, loquacious, palaverous, pleonastic, repetitive, rhetorical
verbosity: **4** wind **8** rhetoric, verbiage **9** garrulity, loquacity, wordiness
verboten: **4** tabu **5** taboo **6** banned **7** illegal, illicit **8** criminal, improper, outlawed, unlawful, wrongful **9** felonious, forbidden **10** prohibited
item: **4** nono, tabu **5** taboo
Verdana: **4** font **8** typeface
verdant: **4** lush **5** fresh, green, leafy, virid **6** floral, grassy **8** blooming, unwilted
relative: ***see*** green color
__ verde: **4** palo
__ Verde: **4** Cape, Mesa
verdict: **6** answer, decree, guilty, ruling **7** finding, opinion **8** decision, judgment, sentence **10** conclusion, conviction, resolution
follower: **6** appeal
giver: **4** jury **5** juror, panel, peers **8** tribunal **9** veniremen
unjust ~: **5** frame **6** bum rap
Verdict, The (1982 film)
cast: James Mason, Paul Newman, Milo O'Shea, Charlotte Rampling, Jack Warden
director: Sidney Lumet
Verdi, Giuseppe: **7** Italian **8** composer
aria: **5** eri tu
baritone: **4** Iago
highlight: **4** aria
milieu: **5** opera
work: Aïda
Alzira
Araldo
Attila
Don Carlos
Ernani
Falstaff
Il Trovatore
La Forza del Destino
La Traviata
Luisa Miller
Macbeth
Nabucco
Oberto
Otello
Rigoletto
Un Ballo in Maschera
Verdon, Gwen: **6** dancer **7** actress
role: **4** Lola
spouse: Bob Fosse
Verdugo: **5** Elena
Verdun: **4** city, town **6** battle
fighter: **5** poilu
locale: **6** Canada, France, Québec
river: **4** Maas **5** Meuse
village near ~: **5** Ornes
see also French
verdure: **3** lea, ley **5** grass **6** meadow **7** foliage, herbage, pasture **8** greenery **9** grassland, greenness, pasturage
Vere, Aubrey Thomas De: **4** poet
Vereen: **3** Ben
verge: **3** eve, hem, lip, rim **4** abut, brim, edge, join, line, side, tend **5** brink, limit, skirt, touch **6** adjoin, border, bounds, fringe, limits, margin **7** extreme, incline, selvage **8** approach, boundary, come near, neighbor, selvedge, surround **9** extremity, juxtapose, perimeter, periphery, threshold **10** lean toward
on: **4** near, tend **5** touch
on the ~ of: **4** near **6** at hand, likely
upon: **4** meet, near **5** reach, verge **6** come at, gain on **7** advance **8** approach **9** catch up to, close in on **10** draw near to, move toward
Vergil: **4** poet **5** Roman
contemporary: **6** Horace
work: **6** Aeneid
Verhoeven, Paul: **8** director
film: Basic Instinct (1992)
RoboCop (1987)
Total Recall (1990)
veridical: **4** just, true **6** honest **7** correct
verifiable: **4** real, true **7** certain **8** tangible **10** historical, legitimate, undoubtful
verification: **4** test **5** audit, check, proof **8** acid test **9** collation
verified: **4** real, true **5** legit, valid **6** actual, proven **7** certain, factual, genuine **8** accurate, bona fide, definite, official, positive, truthful **9** authentic, confirmed, pertinent **10** conclusive, defendable, definitive, documented, legitimate, sanctioned, unarguable, unimagined
verify: **3** peg, try, vet **4** test **5** audit, check, probe, prove, vouch **6** attest, hold up, settle, size up **7** bear out, certify, collate, confirm, eyeball, find out, stand up, support, sustain **8** check out, document, make sure, validate, vouch for **9** ascertain, check up on, determine, establish, recognize
verily: **4** amen **5** truly **6** indeed, it is so, really **8** in effect
old-style: **5** pardi, pardy **6** pardie, perdie
Verily!: **3** yea **4** amen
verisimilar: **4** true **6** liable, likely **8** apparent, credible, probable, rational **9** doubtless, inferable, plausible **10** believable, imaginable, presumable, prima facie, reasonable, supposable
verisimilitude: **4** show **7** realism, reality **8** likeness **9** semblance
veritable: **4** real, true **5** legit, right, valid **6** actual, kasher, kosher **7** factual, genuine **8** bona fide, verified **9** authentic, undoubted **10** unimagined
__ vérité: **5** video **6** cinéma
verity: **4** fact **5** troth, truth **6** gospel **7** reality **8** accuracy **9** actuality
Verizon
ancestor: **5** NYNEX
competitor: **6** Sprint **7** T-Mobile **8** MetroPCS
employee: **5** wirer **8** operator
Vermeer, Jan: **6** artist **7** painter
contemporary: **5** Steen
homeland: **7** Holland **11** Netherlands
vermeil: **3** red **5** color
relative: ***see*** red color
vermicelli: **5** pasta **7** noodles **9** spaghetti
alternative: ***see*** pasta
vermilion: **3** red **5** color
relative: ***see*** red color
Vermillion sch.: **3** USD
vermin: **3** bug, rat **4** flea, scum **5** mouse **6** insect
Vermont: **5** state
capital: **10** Montpelier
city: **5** Barre **7** Rutland **10** Burlington, Montpelier
harvest: **3** sap
lake: **9** Champlain
mountains: **5** Green
neighbor: **6** Canada, Quebec **7** New York
product: **5** sirup, syrup
ski area: **5** Okemo, Stowe
state bird: **6** thrush
state butterfly: **7** monarch
state cold water fish: **10** brook trout
state insect: **8** honeybee
state mineral: **4** talc **6** garnet
state tree: **10** sugar maple
state warm water fish: **7** walleye
tree: **5** maple
vermouth: **4** wine **5** booze, drink, white **6** liquor **7** alcohol, potable **8** beverage, cocktail, libation
ingredient: **7** martini
Verna: **5** Bloom
vernacular: **4** cant **5** argot, idiom, lingo, slang **6** jargon, patois, patter, speech, tongue, vulgar **7** demotic, dialect **8** jive talk, language, parlance **9** idiomatic **10** colloquial
vernal: **5** fresh, young **6** tender **8** juvenile, youthful **10** springlike
season: **6** spring
vernal __: **7** equinox
Verne: **5** Jules, Larry **6** Troyer
Verne, Jules: **6** French, writer
captain: **4** Nemo
character: Phileas Fogg
work: 800 Leagues on the Amazon
Among the Cannibals
Around the World in Eighty Days
The Blockade Runners
Caesar Cascabel
The Castaways of the Flag
The Castle of the Carpathians
The Chase of the Golden Meteor
The Desert of Ice
The English at the North Pole
Facing the Flag
The Field of Ice
Five Weeks in a Balloon
A Floating City
From the Earth to the Moon
Giant Raft
The Green Ray
Hector Servadac
In Search of the Castaways
Invasion of the Sea
Journey to the Center of the Earth
Magellania
The Master of the World
Michael Strogoff
The Mighty Orinoco
The Mysterious Island
Off on a Comet
Paris in the Twentieth Century
Robur the Conqueror
A Tour of the Moon
Twenty Thousand Leagues...
The Underground City
The Vanished Diamond
A Voyage to the Center of the Earth
Vernon: **4** Duke, John **5** Smith **6** Castle
Vero Beach: **4** city, town
locale: **7** Florida
Verona: **4** city, town
locale: **5** Italy
river: **5** Adige
Veronese: **5** Paolo

Veronica: **4** Lake, pase **5** Hamel, saint **10** Cartwright
rival: **5** Betty
Veronica's Closet (NBC sitcom)
cast: Kirstie Alley (Ronnie Chase)
dog: **5** Buddy
Verrazano-__ Bridge: **7** Narrows
verruca: **4** wart
verrucose: **5** warty
vers __: **5** libre
__ versa: **4** vice
Versace: **6** Gianni
Versailles: **3** car **4** auto **7** Lincoln
attraction: **6** palace, palais
see also French
versant: **4** able, deft **5** adept, aware, crack, handy, privy **6** adroit, artful, expert, wise to **7** abreast, capable, knowing, learned, trained **8** familiar, informed, seasoned, skillful, talented **9** cognizant, competent, efficient, masterful, practiced, qualified **10** proficient
versatile: **4** able **5** handy **6** adroit, gifted, mobile **7** protean, skilled **8** flexible, talented **9** adaptable, all-around, many-sided **10** adjustable, all-purpose, changeable
transport: **3** ATV, ute
worker: **5** do-all **8** handyman
versatility: **4** sway **5** array, gamut, range, reach, scale, scope, sweep, width **6** extent, leeway, sphere **7** breadth, expanse, purview, variety **8** latitude, spectrum **9** diversity **10** assortment, parameters
verse: **3** lay, ode **4** epic, idyl, poem, rime, rune, song, text **5** canto, epode, haiku, idyll, lyric, poesy, psalm, rhyme, stave, stich **6** ballad, jingle, poetry, school, sonnet, stanza **7** couplet, passage, refrain, sestina, triolet **8** clerihew, doggerel, limerick, quatrain, rondelet
alternative: **5** prose
analyze ~: **4** scan
ancient Greek ~ form: **4** epos
chapter and ~: **6** detail
honorer in ~: **4** poet **5** odist
Japanese ~: **5** haiku
part: **4** line **5** stave, stich **6** stanza
quote chapter and ~: **4** list, tell **6** detail, relate, report **7** account, analyze, itemize, narrate, recount, specify **8** describe **9** elaborate, enumerate, expound on, make clear
reciter: **4** bard, poet **8** poetizer **9** sonneteer, versifier
short syllable, in ~: **4** mora
syllable: **4** foot, iamb **6** dactyl **7** spondee, trochee
title starter: **5** ode to
writer: **4** bard, poet **5** odist **6** author, rhymer **9** balladist
see also poet, poetry
__ verse: **4** free **5** blank, light **6** heroic
versed: **3** hep, hip **4** up on, wise **5** savvy **6** au fait, expert, posted, up to it, wise to, with it **7** abreast, knowing, learned, mindful, skilled, trained, tuned in **8** apprised, educated, familiar, informed, literate, polished, schooled, skillful, well-read **9** abreast of, au courant, cognizant, competent, in the know, plugged in, practiced, qualified **10** acquainted, proficient
become ~: **3** see **5** grasp, learn **6** absorb, master, pick up, soak up, take in **7** find out **8** discover **9** catch on to **10** apprentice, get down pat
be ~ in: **3** get **4** know **5** grasp, sense **6** fathom **7** realize **10** comprehend, understand
versifier: **4** bard, poet **5** rimer
versify: **4** rime **5** rhyme
version: **4** side, tale **5** model, story **6** report, sketch **7** account, edition, reading, summary, variant **9** chronicle, narrative, portrayal, rendering, rendition, rewording **10** adaptation, paraphrase
abbreviated ~: **4** mini **6** digest
first ~: **4** plan, plot **5** draft **6** design, layout, sketch **7** outline **9** blueprint
new ~: **6** change, update **7** redraft, rewrite **8** overhaul, revision **9** amendment, redaction **10** adjustment, alteration, correction, emendation
verso: **4** leaf, page **5** folio, recto, sheet **7** reverse
opposite: **5** recto
versus: **6** contra **7** against, athwart **8** opposing **9** counter to, opposed to **10** contrary to
__ Versus the Volcano: **3** Joe
vert: **5** color, green **6** French
vert.
not ~: **3** hor.
vertebra: **4** bone **5** spine **6** lumbar, sacrum **8** backbone
head-supporting ~: **5** atlas
neighbor: **4** disc, disk
vertex: **3** cap, tip, top **4** acme, apex, head, node, peak **5** crest, crown, spire **6** apogee, corner, height, summit, tipoff, zenith **8** pinnacle
vertical: **5** apeak, erect, on end, plumb, sheer, steep **6** upward **7** upended, upright, upwards **8** baluster, straight **9** up-and-down **10** lengthways, lengthwise, straight-up
at sea: **5** apeak, apeek
be ~: **5** stand
face: **4** crag, hill **5** bluff, cliff **8** mountain **9** precipice
line: **5** y-axis
lineup: **4** heap, mass, pile **5** mound, stack
make ~: **5** plumb
nearly ~: **5** erect, steep **8** towering
passageway: **3** rod **4** axis, beam, pole, post **5** pylon, shaft, stalk **6** column, pillar
post: **4** beam, jamb **5** jambe **8** doorpost **9** doorframe
vertical __: **4** file
vertically: **5** on end **7** upright **8** vertical
vertiginous: **5** dizzy, faint **7** rolling **8** gyrating, spinning, whirling
Vertigo (1958 film)
cast: Barbara Bel Geddes, Kim Novak, James Stewart
composer: Bernard Herrmann
director: Alfred Hitchcock
verve: **2** go **3** pep, vim, zip **4** brio, dash, élan, fire, kick, life, snap, zeal, zest, zing **5** ardor, flair, gusto, moxie, oomph, punch, savor, spark, vigor **6** bounce, energy, esprit, fervor, pizazz, spirit **7** abandon, panache, pizzazz **8** flourish, vitality, vivacity **9** animation **10** enthusiasm, exuberance, liveliness
sans ~: **4** blah, drab, dull, flat **5** banal, bland, ho-hum, vapid **6** boring, jejune **7** humdrum, languid **8** lifeless **9** apathetic, lethargic, wearisome **10** dullsville, flavorless, lackluster, monotonous, pedestrian, spiritless
very: **3** far, too **4** mere, most, much, oh so, such **5** amply, mucho, quite, right, truly, ultra **6** actual, adverb, damned, danged, darned, deeply, ever so, highly, hugely, rather, really, sorely, unduly, vastly **7** acutely, awfully, but good, greatly, largely, only too, rabidly **8** selfsame, terribly **9** certainly, decidedly, downright, extremely, seriously, supremely, unusually, zealously **10** absolutely, enormously, especially, incredibly, profoundly, remarkably, sure-enough, thoroughly, uncommonly
in Dutch: **4** zeer
in French: **4** très
in German: **4** sehr
in Italian: **5** molto
in music: **5** assai, molto
in Spanish: **3** muy
very __!, The: **4** idea
very __ yours: **5** truly
Very __ Array: **5** Large
Very __ for May: **4** Warm
very foolish fond old man, Shakespeare's: **4** Lear
Very funny!: **4** ha-ha **6** ha ha ha
Very Hungry Caterpillar, The
author: Eric Carle
__ very least: **5** at the
Very Private Eye, A
author: Barbara Pym
Very Thought __, The: **5** of You
Very Warm for May: **7** musical
composer: Oscar Hammerstein, Jerome Kern
Very well: **6** so be it
vesicle: **3** sac **4** cyst **5** bursa, pouch **7** blister
__ vesicle: **4** otic
Vesle
city on the ~: **5** Reims **6** Rheims
vespa: **4** wasp
Vespasian: **5** Roman **6** Caesar
son: **5** Titus
vespers: **4** hour **7** worship **8** evensong
preceder: **5** nones
vespertilian: **3** bat **6** mammal
vespiary: **4** hive, nest **6** apiary
animal: **4** wasp
Vespucci: **7** Amerigo
vessel: **3** ark, can, dau, dow, jar, jug, LCT, LST, mug, pan, pot, tub, urn, vat, wok **4** bark, boat, bowl, brig, dhow, dory, ewer, pail, ship, vase, yawl **5** barge, basin, canoe, craft, crock, cruet, ferry, flask, ketch, laker, liner, oiler, shell, skiff, sloop, stein, U-boat, umiak, yacht **6** barque, bateau, beaker, bireme, bottle, bucket, caique, dinghy, kettle, tanker, wherry **7** amphora, galleon, pitcher, rowboat, samovar, steamer, trireme, tumbler, utensil **8** crucible, decanter, sailboat, test tube **9** catamaran, container, freighter, hydrofoil, outrigger, tube. kayak **10** cruise ship, hydroplane, icebreaker, ocean liner, receptacle
anatomical ~: **3** vas
Arab ~: **3** dau, dow **4** dhow
beaked ~: **5** cruet **6** beaker, carafe **7** alembic
blood ~: **4** vein **5** aorta **6** artery
combining form: **3** vas- **4** vaso- **5** angio-
cook's ~: **3** pan, pot, wok **6** kettle, teapot, vessel **7** dishpan, roaster, skillet **8** saucepan
dispatch ~: **5** aviso
doctor's ~: **5** ampul **6** ampule **7** ampoule
drinking ~: **3** cup, mug **5** flask, glass **6** goblet **7** tumbler
earthenware ~: **3** jug, pot **4** ewer **6** bottle, carafe
expensive ~: **5** yacht
glass ~: **5** ampul **6** ampule **7** ampoule
harbor ~: **3** tow **4** boat **5** barge, ferry
heating ~: **4** etna
lab ~: **5** ampul, flask **6** ampule, beaker, retort **7** ampoule **8** test tube
large ~: **3** vat
Mediterranean ~: **4** saic **6** caique
ocean ~: **4** boat, ship **5** liner
pear-shaped ~: **6** aludel
river ~: **4** boat **5** canoe, craft, kayak **6** vessel **7** rowboat **9** outrigger
Roman ~: **6** bireme **7** trireme
sailing ~: **4** boat, ship, yawl **5** craft, sloop **6** barque
small ~: **4** boat **5** canoe, kayak, skiff **6** dinghy **8** sailboat **9** catamaran
spouted ~: **3** jug **4** ewer **7** pitcher
stout ~: **3** mug **4** toby **5** stein
two-masted ~: **4** boat, brig **5** ketch, yacht **8** sailboat
wrecked ~: **4** hulk
WWI ~: **5** U-boat
WWII ~: **3** LCT, LST **5** E-boat
see also boat, ship
__ vessel: **5** blood
vest: **4** robe **5** array, dicky, endow **6** belong, bestow, confer, dickey, dickie, jerkin, weskit **7** apparel, deck out, empower, entrust, garment, intrust **9** authorize, waistcoat **10** flak jacket
fitted ~: **6** bodice
in America: **10** undershirt
vest-__: **6** pocket
__ vest: **4** flak, life
vesta: **5** match **7** lighter
Vesta: **8** asteroid
brother: **5** Pluto **7** Jupiter, Neptune
equivalent: **6** Hestia
parent: **3** Ops **6** Saturn
sister: **4** Juno **5** Ceres

vestal: **6** chaste, virgin **8** virginal **9** religious
vested: **3** due **5** legal, privy **6** lawful, proper, select **7** decreed, favored **8** eligible, enjoined, entitled, licensed, official, rightful **9** empowered, legalized, statutory **10** admissible, authorized, privileged
be ~ in: **6** relate **8** belong to
vestibule: **4** hall **5** entry, foyer, lobby **7** hallway, ingress, passage **8** anteroom, corridor, entrance, entryway **10** passageway
vestige: **3** ash **4** dreg, hint, sign **5** relic, scrap, shred, spark, token, trace **6** shadow **7** glimmer, memento, remains, remnant **8** landmark, souvenir **9** suspicion **10** indication
leave no ~ of: **4** doom, raze, ruin, sack **5** crush, level, total, wreck **6** blow up, ravage **7** destroy, flatten, pillage, wipe out **8** bankrupt, bulldoze, clean out, decimate, demolish **9** bring down, devastate **10** annihilate, obliterate
vestigial: **3** old **5** basic **6** simple **7** ancient, austere, natural, surplus **8** earliest, enduring, leftover, residual **9** lingering, primitive, remaining, unevolved **10** aboriginal, elementary, indigenous
Vesti la giubba: **4** aria
singer: **5** Canio
vestment: **4** garb, robe **5** dress, habit **6** attire
church ~: **3** alb **4** cope **5** amice, fanon, orale
synagogue ~: **5** ephod
vest-pocket: **3** wee **4** baby, puny, tiny **5** bitty, small, teeny **6** bantam, little, minute, peewee, petite, pocket, teensy **9** itsy-bitsy, itty-bitty, miniature, pint-sized **10** diminutive, teeny-weeny
Vesuvius: **7** volcano
city near ~: **6** Naples
locale: **5** Italy **6** Europe
output: **4** lava
vet: **3** doc, DVM **4** ex-GI **7** examine, inspect, old hand **8** check out, evaluate, old-timer, skillful, validate
case for a ~: **4** lice
do a ~ job: **4** spay **6** declaw, deflea, neuter
patient: **3** cat, cow, dog, ewe, hog, kid, pet, pup, ram, sow **4** calf, goat, lamb, mare, mule **5** horse, kitty, puppy **6** canine, equine, feline, kitten
theater: **3** Nam **7** Vietnam
see also veteran
vetch: **3** ers **4** crop, tare **5** ervil, plant **6** axseed, flower, forage
veteran: **2** GI **3** old, pro **5** adept **6** expert, old pro **7** old hand, soldier, trouper, warrior **8** long-time, old guard, old-timer, seasoned, skillful, warhorse **9** exercised, practiced, qualified, shellback **10** specialist
abbreviation for a ~: **3** ret.
benefit: **6** GI Bill
not a ~: **3** neo **4** tiro, tyro **6** rookie **8** beginner, newcomer **9** greenhorn **10** tenderfoot
org.: **3** DAV, VFW
Veterans Day mo.: **3** Nov.
veterinary medicine: **7** science
study: **7** animals
veto: **2** no **3** ban, bar, nay, nix **4** deny, kill, nyet, shun, stop, tabu **5** debar, quash, spurn **6** abjure, bounce, defeat, denial, forbid, negate, outlaw, pass on, rebuff, reject **7** decline, disdain, dismiss, embargo, exclude, put down, refusal, rule out **8** disallow, negation, override, overrule, preclude, prohibit, throw out, turn down, vote down **9** blackball, cast aside, frown upon, interdict, proscribe, rejection, repudiate, shoot down **10** disapprove, nonconsent, thumbs down
vetoed: **4** tabu **9** forbidden **10** prohibited
vets, theater for some: **3** Nam
'Vette
alternative: **3** Jag **5** T-bird
vex: **3** bug, get, ire, irk, nag, try **4** faze, fret, gall, hurt, miff, pain, ride, rile, roil, tire, wear **5** anger, annoy, chafe, chivy, eat at, grate, harry, haunt, hound, peeve, pique, press, spite, stump, taunt, tease, upset, weary, worry **6** badger, bother, chivvy, fester, harass, hassle, hector, madden, needle, nettle, noodge, offend, pester, plague, pother, put out, rankle, ruffle **7** afflict, agitate, bedevil, disturb, enflame, grate on, inflame, perturb, provoke, tick off, torment, trouble, turn off **8** aggrieve, confound, disquiet, distress, exercise, irritate **9** aggravate, displease, embarrass **10** antagonize, discompose, exasperate
vexation: **4** care, pain, pest **5** anger, grief, pique, trial, upset, worry, wrath **6** bother, hassle **7** affront, trouble, umbrage **8** headache, irritant, nuisance **9** abashment, annoyance **10** irritation, resentment
exclamation of ~: **3** tch, tsk
vexatious: **4** mean, ugly **5** pesky, pesty **6** thorny, trying **7** irksome, nagging, onerous, painful, teasing **8** annoying, tiresome, worrying **9** worrisome **10** bothersome, disturbing, in one's hair, irritating
vexed: **3** mad **4** ired, sore **5** angry, cross, fed up, huffy, irate, upset **6** galled, ireful, peeved **7** furious, in a snit **9** irritated **10** hopping mad, up in the air
be ~: **4** mind **6** resent, see red **7** dislike **8** object to
vexer: **5** poser **6** enigma, puzzle, riddle, teaser **7** mystery, problem, stumper, toughie **9** conundrum **10** puzzlement
vexing: **6** trying **7** galling, irksome **8** tiresome, worrying **9** annoyance, difficult **10** bothersome, irritating
__ vez: **4** otra
Vezina Trophy org.: **3** NHL
V for Vendetta (2006 film)
cast: Natalie Portman
VFW
celebration: **7** Flag Day
hall subj.: **4** WWII
member: **3** vet **4** ex-GI
VH-1: **7** network
alternative: **3** MTV
viewing: **5** video
VHF part: **4** freq., high, very **9** frequency
VHS: **3** VCR **4** tape **9** videotape
alternative: **4** Beta **7** Betamax
VI: **3** six
__ VI: **5** Henry
via: **3** per **4** thru **5** along, using **7** by way of, through, towards **9** by means of **10** by virtue of
ender: **4** duct
Via __: **5** Appia **6** Lactea, Veneto
Via __ Corso: **3** del
Via Appia terminus: **4** Rome
viability: **4** life
viable: **5** alive **6** doable, likely **7** tenable, working **8** credible, feasible, possible, workable **9** plausible, potential, practical **10** achievable, applicable, attainable, imaginable, reasonable
Viadent: **10** toothpaste
alternative: ***see*** toothpaste
viaduct: **4** link, road, span **6** bridge **8** crossing, overpass, traverse **10** connection
vial: **5** ampul, flask **6** ampule, bottle **7** ampoule **8** test tube **9** container
Via Lactea: **8** Milky Way
units: **5** astra
viand: **4** dish, food **8** delicacy
viands: **4** diet, food **7** aliment, edibles **8** eatables, victuals **9** foodstuff, nutriment, provender **10** delicacies, provisions, sustenance
vibe: **4** aura **6** tremor **9** intuition, resonance, sensation
Vibe: **3** car **4** auto **7** Pontiac
vibes: **4** aura **5** karma **7** portent **8** reaction, response **9** sensation **10** instrument, percussion
bad ~: **4** omen **5** doubt, qualm, smell **6** augury, signal, threat **7** warning **8** distrust, mistrust, wariness **9** chariness, harbinger, misgiving, suspicion **10** foreboding, gut feeling, indication, prediction
get ~: **4** feel, know, mind, read **5** grasp, sense, smell **6** absorb, divine, intuit, notice, pick up, reason, take in **7** believe, catch on, discern, observe, realize **8** perceive **9** apprehend **10** anticipate, have a hunch, understand
good ~: **4** bond **5** unity **6** accord **7** concord, empathy, harmony, rapport **8** affinity **9** agreement, communion **10** friendship
have ~: **5** react, sense **6** intuit
__ vibes: **3** bad **4** good
vibraharp: **10** instrument, percussion
vibrant: **4** rich **5** alive, peppy, sound, vital, vivid, zesty, zippy **6** lively, virile **7** aquiver, dynamic, glowing, pulsing, ringing **8** animated, colorful, resonant, sonorous, spirited, vigorous **9** brilliant, energetic, pulsating, sparkling, throbbing, trembling, vivacious **10** responsive, shimmering
vibraphone: **10** instrument, percussion
vibraphonist: **5** Norvo **7** Hampton
vibrate: **3** hum **4** beat, echo, lick, ring, rock, sway, whir **5** pulse, quake, shake, sound, swing, throb, whirr **6** judder, quiver, rattle, ripple, shimmy, shiver, thrill **7** flutter, pulsate, resound, tremble **8** resonate **9** fluctuate, oscillate
vibrating: **4** wavy **5** snaky **7** rippled, shaking, sinuous **8** rippling **10** serpentine, undulating
vibration: **4** beat **5** drone, pulse, quake, seism, sound, throb **6** quiver, tremor **7** shaking **9** pulsation, quivering, resonance, throbbing, trembling
__ Vibrations: **4** Good
vibrations, good: **7** rapport
vibrato: **5** trill **7** tremolo
Vic: **4** Dana **6** Damone, Morrow **7** Tayback
__ Vic: **3** Old
Vic and Sade: **9** radio show
vicar: **5** envoy, proxy **6** cleric, deputy, pastor **8** delegate, minister, preacher **9** churchman, clergyman, surrogate **10** substitute
assistant: **6** curate
residence: **5** manse **7** rectory **9** parsonage
__ vicar: **3** lay
vicarious: **7** by proxy, deputed, done for **8** imagined, indirect **9** delegated, pretended, secondary, surrogate **10** empathetic, on behalf of, secondhand
Vicar of Wakefield, The: **5** novel
author: Oliver Goldsmith
character: **4** Livy **5** Sophy **6** George, Olivia, Sophia, Wilmot **7** Charles, Deborah **8** Arabella, Burchell, Primrose **9** Thornhill
vice: **3** sin **4** evil, flaw, lust **5** crime, fault, wrong **6** defect, deputy, foible **7** cussing, devilry, failing, frailty **8** bad habit, deviltry, drinking, gambling, iniquity, swearing, venality, weakness **9** depravity, evildoing, looseness, lubricity, turpitude, veniality, weak point **10** corruption, immorality, profligacy, wickedness
squad: **5** bunco
versa: **9** about-face, in reverse, inversely **10** conversely, oppositely
vice __: **4** pres. **5** squad, versa
vice-__: **6** consul, regent **7** admiral
__ Vice: **5** Miami
__ Vicente, Brazil: **3** Sao
vice president: **4** veep
first ~: **5** Adams
viceroy: **3** bug **4** king **5** chief, royal, ruler **6** gerent, insect, leader **7** emperor, monarch **8** overlord **9** sovereign
vice squad action: **4** raid
vichy __: **5** water
Vichy: **3** spa **4** city, town
locale: **6** France
river: **6** Allier
vichyssoise: **4** soup
ingredient: **4** leek
vici
preceder: **4** vidi
vicinage: **4** area **8** purlieus

vicinity: 4 area, hood, turf 5 place, range 6 locale, region, sector 7 section 8 ballpark, district, environs, locality, nearness, precinct, premises, purlieus 9 immediacy, local area, outskirts, proximity, territory
- **covering the ~:** 5 areal
- **immediate ~:** 5 midst 8 nearness, presence 9 closeness, proximity
- **in the ~:** 4 near 5 about, anear, close 6 around 7 close by

vicious: 3 bad 4 evil, foul, mean, ugly, vile, wild 5 catty, cruel, feral, harsh, lousy, nasty, rough, surly, tough 6 animal, brutal, fierce, horrid, malign, rotten, savage, sordid, sullen, unkind, wanton, wicked 7 beastly, callous, hateful, heinous, hellish, hurtful, immoral, inhuman, intense, parlous, violent 8 barbaric, churlish, depraved, diabolic, fiendish, infamous, inhumane, perverse, pitiless, ruthless, sadistic, spiteful, vengeful, venomous, virulent 9 abhorrent, atrocious, barbarian, barbarous, cutthroat, dangerous, ferocious, frightful, malicious, merciless, miscreant, monstrous, nefarious, poisonous, truculent 10 backbiting, defamatory, diabolical, ill-humored, ill-natured, malevolent, profligate, slanderous, villainous, vindictive, virtueless
- **in a ~ circle:** 4 vain 5 inane 6 absurd, futile, stupid 7 insipid 9 for naught, frivolous, pointless, worthless 10 ridiculous

vicious __: 6 circle

Vicious: 3 Sid

viciously: 4 hard 5 madly 7 cruelly, harshly, sternly 8 ardently, bitterly, brutally, doggedly, fiercely, intently, savagely, severely, strongly, terribly 9 callously, furiously, intensely, zealously 10 gruelingly, pitilessly, ruthlessly, vehemently, vigorously

viciousness: 4 evil 6 malice 7 cruelty 8 enormity, ferocity

vicissitude: 5 trial 6 change, switch 7 reverse 8 flip-flop, mutation, obstacle, reversal 9 about-face

vicissitudes: 4 life

Vickers: 3 Ann, Jon 6 Martha

Vickers, Jon: 5 tenor 6 singer
- **specialty:** 5 opera

Vicki: 4 Baum, Vale 8 Lawrence

Vicki __ Robinson: 3 Sue

Vickrey: 7 William

Vicksburg: 4 city, town 6 battle
- **event:** 5 siege
- **locale:** 4 Miss. 11 Mississippi

Vicky Cristina Barcelona (2008 film)
- **cast:** Javier Bardem, Penélope Cruz, Scarlett Johansson
- **director:** Woody Allen

victim: 4 butt, dupe, gull, mark, pawn, prey, tool 5 clown, patsy, slave 6 hunted, pigeon, puppet, quarry, stooge, sucker, target, wretch 8 casualty, easy mark, fatality, innocent, pushover, sufferer 9 sacrifice, scapegoat, soft touch

victimize: 3 con, use 4 burn, clip, dupe, fool, gull, have, hoax, nick, snow 5 abuse, cheat, cozen, gouge, set up, stiff, sting, trick 6 chisel, fleece, pick on, prey on, rope in, sucker 7 deceive, defraud, exploit, mislead, swindle, two-time 8 flimflam, hoodwink, prey upon 9 bamboozle, persecute

Victim of the Aurora
- **author:** Thomas Keneally

Victims of Duty
- **author:** Eugène Ionesco

Victim, The
- **author:** Saul Bellow

__ victis: 3 vae

victor: 4 hero, king 5 champ, first, queen 6 master, winner 8 champion, defeater, medalist 9 conqueror 10 subjugator, vanquisher
- **prize:** 5 medal 6 laurel, spoils
- **shout:** 4 I win, I won 5 we win, we won

Victor: 4 Hess, Hugo, Jory, Kiam, pope 5 Borge, Buono, Lasky, Moore, Young 6 French, Mature 7 Fleming, Herbert, pontiff, Saville, Sen Yung 8 Grignard, McLaglen, Seastrom

__ Victor: 3 RCA

Victoria: 3 car, cat, sta. 4 auto, city, Ford, Holt, isle, lake, town 5 Falls, queen, ruler, state 6 desert, island 7 Beckham, capital, Jackson, station, Tennant 9 Principal, waterfall 10 automobile
- **capital:** 9 Melbourne
- **city:** 7 Geelong 9 Melbourne
- **granddaughter:** 3 Ena
- **Lake ~ locale:** 6 Africa
- **locale:** 5 Kenya, Texas 6 Canada, Mexico, Uganda 8 Hong Kong, Tanzania 9 Australia 10 Seychelles, Tamaulipas
- **prime minister:** 4 Peel
- **to Albert:** 6 cousin
- **to William IV:** 5 niece

Victoria __: 3 Day 4 Land 5 Cross, Falls

Victoria __ Angeles: 5 de los

__ Victoria: 5 Crown

Victoria Cross: 5 medal

Victorian: 3 Age, Era 4 prig, prim 5 prude, style 6 prissy, quaint, stuffy 7 prudish 8 bluenose 9 bourgeois
- **garden feature:** 4 maze
- **garment:** 6 bustle, corset, girdle
- **like ~ houses:** 6 gaslit

Victorian __: 3 Era

Victoria's Secret purchase: 3 bra 5 teddy, thong 7 nightie 8 negligee

Victorien: 6 Sardou

victorious: 5 on top 7 arrived, winning, winsome 8 unbeaten 9 fortunate 10 successful, triumphant
- **be ~:** 3 win 4 beat, best, lick, stun 5 outdo, upset 6 defeat 7 conquer, prevail, succeed, triumph 8 overcome 9 overpower, overwhelm, rise above
- **be ~ again:** 5 rewin

__ Victorious: 6 Purlie

Victor/Victoria (1982 film)
- **cast:** Julie Andrews, James Garner, Alex Karras, Robert Preston, Lesley Ann Warren
- **composer:** Henry Mancini
- **director:** Blake Edwards

Victorville: 4 city, town
- **locale:** 10 California

victory: 3 hit, win 4 feat, luck, palm 5 upset 6 big hit, winner 7 laurels, success, triumph 8 conquest, dominion 9 checkmate, grand slam, supremacy, upper hand 10 ascendance, ascendancy, ascendence, ascendency
- **complete ~:** 5 sweep 7 triumph 9 landslide 10 clean sweep
- **easy ~:** 4 rout 5 waltz 7 debacle, pasting, shutout, washout 8 conquest, disaster, drubbing, stampede, walkover 9 landslide, thrashing, trouncing
- **emblem of ~:** 5 title 6 laurel, wreath 10 blue ribbon
- **gain a ~:** 3 win 4 beat, earn, sway, take 5 score, upset 6 defeat 7 achieve, conquer, edge out, prevail, realize, succeed, triumph, trounce 8 overcome 9 overwhelm
- **goddess of ~:** 4 Nike
- **insure a ~:** 5 sew up 6 clinch
- **margin of ~:** 4 neck, nose
- **opposite:** 4 loss 6 defeat, losing, mishap 7 failure
- **overly relish ~:** 4 brag, crow 5 gloat 7 rub it in, swagger 9 whoop it up
- **shout:** 4 hoot, howl, yell 5 bingo, cheer, whoop 6 holler, hurrah, scream
- **sign:** 3 vee
- **sure ~:** 4 lock 5 cinch 9 certainty

victory __: 3 lap 6 garden

__ victory: 7 Cadmean, Pyrrhic

__ victory!: 4 On to

Victory
- **author:** Joseph Conrad

Victory (song)
- **artist:** Kool and the Gang, Notorious B.I.G., Puff Daddy

Victory __: 4 ship 5 at Sea

__ Victory: 4 Dark 6 Bright, Winged

Victrola: 10 phonograph
- **descendant:** 4 hi-fi, iPod 6 stereo 7 boombox 8 CD player
- **maker:** 3 RCA
- **part:** 4 horn 5 crank 6 needle, stylus

victual: 4 chow, fare, feed, food, grub, meat 6 supply 7 aliment, edibles 9 foodstuff, nutriment 10 comestible, provisions, sustenance

victuals: 4 chow, diet, eats, fare, food, grub, meal 5 board, table 6 repast, viands 7 aliment, edibles, rations 8 eatables 9 foodstuff, nutriment, provender 10 provisions, sustenance

vicuña: 4 wool 6 animal, fabric, mammal
- **home:** 5 Andes
- **relative:** 5 camel, llama 6 alpaca 7 guanaco 8 Bactrian 9 dromedary

__-vid: 3 kid

Vida: 4 Blue

Vidal: 4 Gore 7 Sassoon 9 Christina

Vidal, Gore: 6 writer
- **pseudonym:** Edgar Box
- **work:** The Best Man, Burr, Empire, An Evening with Richard Nixon, Kalki, Myra Breckinridge, Rocking the Boat, Two Sisters, Visit to a Small Planet

Vidalia __: 5 onion

videlicet: 5 to wit 6 namely

video: 4 clip, film, tape 6 record 8 news clip
- **arcade patron:** 5 gamer
- **award:** 3 Ava
- **companion:** 5 audio
- **display:** 6 screen 7 monitor 8 terminal
- **ender:** 4 disc, disk, tape, text 5 phone 6 taping 8 cassette 10 conference
- **make a ~:** 4 tape 6 record
- **room:** 3 den
- **screen dot:** 5 pixel
- **what ~ means:** 4 I see

video __: 3 art 4 game 5 drama 6 camera, jockey, screen, vérité

__ video: 4 home 5 music 7 reverse

__ Video: 7 Captain

videocassette
- **contents:** 4 film, show, tape 5 flick, movie 7 picture

video game: 4 Myst, Pong 6 Pacman, Tetris 10 Donkey Kong
- **center:** 6 arcade
- **game maker:** 3 NES 4 Sega 5 Atari
- **hero:** 5 Mario, Sonic
- **Microsoft ~ console:** 4 Xbox

Video Killed the Radio Star (1979 song)
- **artist:** Buggles

videos
- **network with ~:** 3 MTV

video-store
- **section:** 4 kids 5 sci-fi 6 family

video-store section: 5 drama 6 action, comedy, horror 7 mystery

videotape: 4 tape 5 movie 6 record
- **borrow a ~:** 4 rent
- **material:** 5 Mylar
- **speed meas.:** 3 ips

vidi: 4 I saw 5 Latin
- **follower:** 4 vici
- **preceder:** 4 veni

Vidor: 4 King 7 Charles

vie: 3 pit 4 play 5 fight, match, rival 6 oppose, strive, take on 7 compete, contend, contest 8 scramble, struggle 9 challenge
- **(for):** 2 go 3 try 5 fight
- **for office:** 3 run
- **with:** 5 rival 6 take on

__ vie: 5 eau de

Vieira: 8 Meredith

viejo: 3 old 7 Spanish
- **opposite:** 5 nuevo

Vieni __ Mar: 3 Sul

Vienna: 4 city, town, Wien 7 capital
- **dance:** 5 waltz
- **locale:** 3 Aus. 4 Aust. 7 Austria 8 Virginia
- **river:** 5 Donau 6 Danube
- *see also* Austrian, German

Vienna __: 7 Fingers, sausage

Vienna __ Choir: 4 Boys

Vienna Fingers
- **alternative:** *see* cookie brand

Vienne
city on the ~: **7** Limoges
Viennese __: **5** table
Vientiane: **4** city, town **7** capital
locale: **4** Laos
vier: **4** four **5** rival **9** combatant, contender **10** competitor, contestant
doubled: **4** acht
follower: **4** fünf
preceder: **4** drei
Viet __: **3** Nam **4** Cong, Minh
Vietcong grp.: **3** NLF
Viet Journal
author: James Jones
Vietnam: **6** nation **7** country
Buddhism of ~: **8** Mahayana
capital: **5** Hanoi
city: **3** Hue **5** Hanoi, My Lai **6** Can Tho, Da Nang **7** Bien Hoa, Qui Nhon **8** Haiphong, Nha Trang
ender: **3** ese
farming area: **5** paddy
festival: **3** Tet
former president: **4** Diem
language: **5** Hmong
money: **2** xu **3** hao **4** dong
neighbor: **4** Laos **5** China **8** Cambodia
Nobelist in Peace: **3** Tho
people: **4** Miao
region: **4** Anam **5** Annam
sea: **10** South China
tunic: **5** aodai
Vietnam __: **3** War
__ Vietnam: **5** North, South
Vietnamese: **5** Asian **8** language
Vietnam Veterans Memorial architect: Maya Lin
Vieux __: **5** Carré
view: **3** eye, see, spy **4** deem, espy, gaze, hold, idea, look, mark, mind, read, scan, show, side, spot **5** audit, judge, scape, scene, scope, sight, slant, stand, stare, tenet, vista, watch **6** advert, aspect, behold, belief, eyeful, gander, gape at, glance, look at, notice, notion, peek at, peer at, reckon, regard, squint, survey, take in, thesis, vision **7** believe, close-up, concept, discern, examine, explore, eyeball, eyeshot, feeling, glimpse, inspect, lookout, look-see, observe, opening, opinion, outlook, picture, scenery, tableau, thought, witness **8** analysis, attitude, check out, consider, judgment, look upon, overlook, panorama, perceive, position, prospect, seascape, theorize **9** check over, cityscape, landscape, lay eyes on, sentiment, spectacle, viewpoint **10** appearance, assessment, conception, conjecture, contention, conviction, eyewitness, get a load of, impression, inspection, persuasion, philosophy, reflection, rubberneck, scrutinize, standpoint, think about
a computer file: **6** access
aerial ~ provider: **5** blimp **7** airship, balloon **8** aircraft, zeppelin **9** dirigible
again: **5** resee
combining form: **5** -scape
come into ~: **4** loom, rise **5** heave **6** appear, emerge
command a ~: **4** face, look, view **6** survey **7** lookout **8** overlook, prospect **9** look out on
dim ~: **5** gloom **7** despair **8** cynicism, dark side, glumness **9** dejection, pessimism **10** depression, gloominess, melancholy
ender: **4** data **5** point **6** finder
express a ~: **5** opine
follower: **5** point
grand ~: **5** sight, sweep, vista **7** horizon, scenery **8** panorama, prospect **9** landscape
have in ~: **3** aim **4** plan **6** aspire, design, expect, intend **7** resolve **10** have in mind
hold another ~: **6** differ **7** dissent **8** disagree
hold in ~: **3** eye, spy **4** espy, spot **5** watch **7** discern **8** perceive **10** get a load of
in ~: **4** open **5** clear, plain **6** patent, public **7** exposed, obvious, visible **8** apparent, clear-cut, explicit, imminent, manifest, unhidden, unveiled **10** observable, unshrouded
in full ~: **4** open, seen **6** openly
in ~ of: **6** herein **7** because
mind's-eye ~: **5** image **7** concept **10** appearance, envisaging, impression, perception, projection
out of ~: **6** buried, hidden, latent, unseen **7** cloaked, covered, obscure, on the QT **8** abstruse, eclipsed, secluded, shrouded **9** concealed, disguised, incognito, innermost, in the dark, unexposed **10** cloistered, tucked away, unrevealed
point of ~: **4** mind, side, view **5** angle, light, slant **6** aspect, vision **7** feeling, opinion, outlook, posture
put on ~: **3** air **4** bare, show **6** expose, flaunt, lay out, parade, reveal **7** display, exhibit, present, show off, trot out **8** showcase **10** illustrate
quick ~: **3** see **4** gaze, look, peek **6** gander, glance **7** eyeshot, glimpse, look-see
range of ~: **3** ken **6** vision **8** eyesight
screen from ~: **4** hide **6** enisle **7** conceal, confine, isolate, seclude **8** cloister, separate **9** keep apart, segregate, sequester **10** quarantine
share a ~: **5** agree, match **6** accord, concur **7** conform **9** harmonize **10** go together
side ~: **7** contour, profile **10** silhouette
starter: **5** world
suffix: **5** -scape
take a dim ~ of: **5** knock, scorn **7** censure, deplore, put down, run down **8** bad-mouth, belittle, derogate, disfavor **9** deprecate, disesteem, disparage, poormouth **10** disapprove
with alarm: **4** fear **5** dread, panic **6** dismay **10** foreboding
within ~: **4** near, nigh **5** close, handy **6** around, nearby **7** close by, close to, looming **8** imminent, next door, proximal **9** alongside, bordering **10** accessible, near-at-hand
View __ Kill, A: **3** to a
View __ the Bridge, A: **4** From
viewable: **7** in sight, visible
viewer: **4** eyer, seer **7** witness **8** attendee, beholder, observer, onlooker, playgoer, showgoer **9** moviegoer, spectator **10** eyewitness
gem ~: **5** loupe
viewers: **8** assembly, audience
View from the Bridge, A
author: Arthur Miller
View from the Fortieth Floor, The
author: Theodore H. White
View From the Top (2003 film)
cast: Christina Applegate, Candice Bergen, Gwyneth Paltrow, Mark Ruffalo
viewing: **4** look **5** sight
combining form: **5** -scopy **6** -scopic
viewpoint: **4** idea, side **5** angle, light, slant, stand **6** aspect, stance **7** horizon, opinion, outlook, posture, vantage **8** attitude, position, two cents **9** direction **10** estimation, philosophy
views, old-style: **5** seest
View, The (ABC talk)
cast: Joy Behar, Whoopi Goldberg, Elisabeth Hasselbeck, Sherri Shepherd, Barbara Walters
View to a Kill, A: **4** film, song **5** novel
artist: Duran Duran
author: Ian Fleming
cast: Grace Jones, Roger Moore, Tanya Roberts, Christopher Walken
director: John Glen
Viggo: **9** Mortensen
vigil: **4** wake **5** watch **7** lookout **8** eagle eye, sharp eye, stakeout **10** weather eye
light: **5** taper **6** candle, shames **7** shammes **9** luminaria
vigilance: **4** care, heed **5** watch **6** acuity **7** caution, lookout **9** alertness, attention **10** discretion
vigilant: **2** up **4** keen, live, wary **5** acute, alert, awake, aware, sharp **6** prompt **7** all ears, careful, guarded, heads-up, heedful, mindful, on alert, on guard, prudent, wakeful **8** cautious, keen-eyed, on the job, open-eyed, watchful **9** attentive, conscious, observant, on the ball, provident, receptive, undivided, wide-awake **10** on one's toes, perceptive, protective, unsleeping
be ~: **5** watch
one: **5** guard **6** heeder, sentry
Vigilius: **4** pope **7** pontiff
vignette: **6** sketch **7** profile **8** portrait
Vigny, Alfred Victor de: **4** poet **6** French, writer **10** playwright
Vigoda: **3** Abe
vigor: **3** pep, vim, zip **4** brio, dash, dint, élan, fire, kick, life, push, snap, thew, zeal, zing **5** brawn, drive, force, juice, might, moxie, oomph, power, prime, punch, sinew, spark, steam, teeth, thews, verve **6** action, bounce, energy, esprit, fervor, health, muscle, spirit, starch **7** fitness, muscles, pizzazz, potence, potency, prowess, stamina **8** ambition, dynamism, industry, strength, vitality **9** animation, beefiness, briskness, diligence, endurance, fortitude, freshness, hardiness, huskiness, intensity, lustiness, puissance, soundness, stoutness, toughness, well-being **10** brawniness, brute force, enterprise, enthusiasm, exuberance, get up and go, heartiness, initiative, liveliness, mightiness, robustness, sturdiness
ending: **3** ous
full of ~: **4** hale **5** alert, lusty, peppy, perky, zippy **6** active, bubbly, feisty, lively, potent, robust, strong, sturdy, virile **7** dashing, dynamic, healthy, vibrant, zestful **8** animated, muscular, powerful, spirited **9** energetic, sprightly, strenuous, vivacious
in music: **4** brio
lacking ~: **4** weak, worn **6** effete, feeble **7** worn-out
lack of ~: **6** anemia, anergy **7** anaemia
lose ~: **4** fade, fail, wilt **5** droop
name meaning ~: **6** Ernest
with fresh ~: **4** anew **5** newly **6** afresh **7** freshly
__ vigor: **6** hybrid
Vigor: **3** car **4** auto **5** Acura **10** automobile
vigorish: **3** fee **5** usury **8** interest
collector: **4** bank **6** bookie, lender, usurer **8** creditor **9** bookmaker, loan shark **10** pawnbroker
vigorlessness: **6** anemia **7** anaemia **10** enervation, exhaustion, feebleness
vigorous: **3** fit **4** hale, hard, iron, live, racy, spry, well, wiry **5** alive, beefy, brisk, burly, fresh, hardy, hefty, hunky, husky, lusty, nervy, peppy, pithy, sharp, smart, sound, stiff, stout, tough, vital, zippy **6** active, ardent, brawny, hearty, lively, living, mighty, potent, robust, rugged, sinewy, steely, stocky, strong, sturdy, virile **7** bracing, doughty, driving, dynamic, healthy, intense, rousing, vibrant, zestful **8** athletic, bouncing, emphatic, forceful, indurate, muscular, powerful, puissant, spirited, stalwart, tireless, youthful **9** Atlantean, energetic, exuberant, Herculean, in the pink, strapping, strenuous, well-built **10** able-bodied, fortifying, red-blooded
activity: **4** push **7** workout **8** exercise
vigorously: **4** hard **5** amain **7** like mad **8** mightily, up a storm **9** seriously **10** vehemently
VII: **5** seven **6** septet

VIII: **4** octo **5** eight, octet
Vijay: **5** Singh **8** Amritraj
Viking: **5** probe **7** brigand, corsair **8** Norseman **9** buccaneer **10** freebooter
headgear: **6** helmet
maybe: **4** fair **5** blond, light **6** blonde, golden **10** fair-haired
poet: **5** scald, skald
reading: **4** edda
touchdown site: **4** Mars
weapon: **3** axe
Vikings: **4** team **5** Norse **6** eleven
home: **9** Minnesota
org.: **3** NFC, NFL
rival: *see* NFL team
sport: **8** football
__-Vikings: **4** Dell
Vikings at Helgeland
author: Henrik Ibsen
Vikki: **4** Carr
Vila: **3** Bob **4** city, town **7** capital
locale: **6** Vanatu
Vilas, Guillermo: **6** netman **7** netster **9** tennis pro
milieu: **5** court
vile: **3** low **4** base, dark, evil, mean **5** dirty, slimy, sorry **6** abased, coarse, filthy, grungy, impure, sleazy, sordid, vulgar **7** bestial, corrupt, debased, demonic, ignoble, immoral, noisome, noxious, pitiful, satanic, twisted, unclean, vicious **8** daemonic, degraded, depraved, diabolic, indecent, infamous, sinister, unworthy **9** dastardly, demonical, nefarious, obnoxious, repugnant, repulsive, satanical, worthless **10** diabolical, flagitious, indecorous, indelicate, inexpiable, iniquitous, loathesome, malodorous, petrifying, villainous, virtueless
remark: **5** rumor **6** canard **7** untruth
see also awful
Vile Bodies
author: Evelyn Waugh
vileness: **4** evil **8** enormity **9** indecency
Vilhelm: **6** Moberg **8** Bjerknes
vilification: **3** dig **4** barb, gibe, jibe, slam, slap, slur, snub **5** abuse, libel, scorn, taunt **6** attack, insult, rebuff, slight **7** affront, calumny, catcall, disdain, mockery, obloquy, offense, put-down, slander **8** contempt, derision, ridicule **9** aspersion, cheap shot, contumely **10** defamation, disrespect, opprobrium
vilifier: **6** censor, critic **7** defamer, reviler **8** asperser, attacker, impugner, maligner **9** belittler, derogater, detractor, muckraker **10** denigrator, deprecator, disparager
vilify: **3** dis, pan, rap **4** cuss, damn, gibe, jeer, jibe, mock, slam, slur, snub **5** abuse, curse, decry, knock, libel, rip up, roast, scorn, smear, spurn, sully, taunt **6** assail, attack, berate, debase, defame, deride, dump on, heckle, impugn, injure, insult, malign, offend, rebuff, revile, scorch, slight **7** affront, asperse, blacken, blister, censure, degrade, disdain, put down, rank out, rip into, run down, slander, traduce **8** backbite, bad-mouth, belittle, call down, denounce, mudsling, ridicule, tear down, tear into, throw mud **9** blaspheme, denigrate, discredit, disparage, dress down, excoriate, fulminate, humiliate, skin alive **10** blackguard, calumniate, disrespect, speak ill of, villainize, vituperate
vilifying: **8** libelous **9** invidious **10** defamatory, derogatory
vilipend: **4** gibe, jeer, jibe, mock, slam, slur, snub **5** abuse, decry, libel, scorn, spurn, taunt **6** defame, deride, dump on, heckle, impugn, malign, offend, rebuff, slight **7** affront, asperse, degrade, disdain, put down, rank out, slander, traduce **8** belittle, denounce, ridicule **9** denigrate, discredit, disparage, disregard, humiliate **10** calumniate, disrespect
villa: **4** casa, home **5** lodge **6** estate **7** mansion **9** residence
boundary: **4** wall
features: **5** atria
Russian ~: **5** dacha **6** datcha
Villa: **6** Pancho
Villa __, GA: **4** Rica
__ Villa!: **4** Viva
Villa d' __: **4** Este
village: **2** tp. **3** twp. **4** burg, dorp, town **5** exurb, place, thorp, urban **6** center, hamlet, suburb, thorpe **8** township **10** crossroads
center: **5** green
green: **4** park **5** plaza **6** common, square
Hindu ~ chief: **5** patel
Japanese ~: **4** mura
medieval ~: **5** bourg
not chartered, as a ~ (abbr.): **5** uninc.
oldest continuously inhabited US ~: **5** Acoma
Russian ~: **3** mir
South African ~: **5** craal, kraal
__ village: **6** global
Village __: **4** Tale **5** Voice **6** People
Village Blacksmith, The
author: Henry Wadsworth Longfellow
Village of the Damned, The
author: John Wyndham
Village People
song: In the Navy (1979)
Macho Man (1978)
Y.M.C.A. (1978)
Villager: **3** car, van **4** auto **5** Edsel **7** Mercury **10** automobile
Village, The (2004 film)
cast: Adrien Brody, William Hurt, Joaquin Phoenix
Village Voice award: **4** Obie
Village Wedding
artist: Jan Steen
villain: **3** cad, cur **4** heel, ogre, part **5** baddy, brute, creep, demon, devil, enemy, fiend, heavy, rogue, tough **6** baddie, bad egg, bad guy, bad man, daemon, daimon, rascal, wretch **7** caitiff, lowlife, menacer, monster **8** antihero, criminal, evildoer, offender **9** archfiend, ill-wisher, libertine, miscreant, reprobate, scoundrel **10** blackguard, malefactor, profligate
fairy tale ~: **4** ogre **5** giant, troll **7** monster
foe: **4** hero
greeting for the ~: **3** boo **4** hiss, siss
greet the ~: **3** boo **4** jeer **8** sibilate
heroine's answer to a ~: **5** never
lament: **6** curses, foiled
laugh: **3** hah, heh
opera ~ often: **4** alto, bass **5** basso
thwart the ~: **4** foil **6** thwart
visage: **4** leer **5** scoff, smirk, sneer
villainize: **4** slam, slur **5** decry, libel, smear, sully, taint **6** accuse, assail, defame, insult, malign, revile, vilify **7** rip into, slander **8** badmouth, besmirch, mudsling **9** denigrate, deprecate, disparage **10** speak ill of
villainous: **3** bad **4** base, evil, foul, vile **5** black, nasty **6** rotten, sinful, wicked **7** heinous, ignoble, immoral, knavish, satanic, vicious **8** depraved, devilish, diabolic, grievous, infamous, shameful, sinister **9** atrocious, dishonest, miscreant, monstrous, nefarious, notorious, satanical **10** diabolical, iniquitous, maleficent, virtueless
expression: **4** leer **5** scowl, smirk, sneer **7** snicker
sort: **4** ogre **5** meany **6** meanie
stare: **3** eye **4** leer, ogle **5** sneer
villains: **6** bad lot
villainy: **4** evil **5** wrong **6** infamy **7** knavery, misdeed **10** wickedness
Villanova: **6** school **10** university
athletes: **8** Wildcats
conference: **7** Big East
locale: **4** Penn.
Villa, Pancho: **6** bandit **7** Mexican
emulate ~: **4** raid
see also Spanish
Villechaize: **5** Hervé
villein: **4** serf **5** helot, slave **6** vassal, worker **7** chattel, servant, subject
Villella, Edward: **6** dancer **7** danseur
specialty: **6** ballet
Villette
author: Charlotte Brontë
Vilma: **5** Banky
Vilnius: **4** city, town **7** capital
locale: **9** Lithuania
vim: **3** pep, zip **4** brio, dash, dint, élan, thew, zeal, zest, zing **5** brawn, force, gusto, might, oomph, power, spark, steam, thews, verve, vigor **6** action, bounce, energy, esprit, muscle, pizazz, spirit **7** fitness, muscles, pizzazz, potence, potency, sparkle, stamina **8** strength, vitality **9** animation, beefiness, endurance, fortitude, hardiness, huskiness, puissance, stoutness, toughness **10** brawniness, brute force, enthusiasm, get up and go, liveliness, mightiness, robustness, sturdiness
full of ~: **5** alert, brisk, peppy, perky, vital, zesty, zingy, zippy **6** active, bright, bubbly, feisty, frisky, lively **7** dashing, dynamic, piquant, vibrant, zestful **8** animated, skittish, spirited, vigorous **9** energetic, sparkling, sprightly, vivacious
vim and __: **5** vigor
vin: **4** wine **5** blanc, Médoc, pinot, rouge **7** Chablis **8** Bordeaux, Burgundy **9** champagne, Sauternes **10** Beaujolais, Chardonnay
__ vin: **5** coq au
Vin: **6** Diesel, Scully
vinaigrette: **5** sauce **8** dressing
Vince: **4** Gill, Neil **6** Vaughn **7** Edwards **8** DiMaggio, Guaraldi, Lombardi
Vince Lombardi Trophy awarder: **3** NFL
Vincent: **4** Gene **5** Canby, d'Indy, Perez, Price, Spano **6** Hamlin **7** Sherman, van Gogh, Youmans **8** Bugliosi, D'Onofrio, Gardenia, McEveety **10** Jan-Michael
brother: **4** Theo
in Italian: **8** Vincenzo
successor: **5** Selig
Vincent (1972 song)
artist: Don McLean
Vincent & __: **4** Theo
Vincent __: **6** de Paul
__ Vincent Benét: **7** Stephen
Vincent de Paul: **5** saint
Vincente: **6** Ibañez **8** Minnelli
daughter: **4** Liza
wife: **4** Judy
__ Vincent Peale: **6** Norman
Vincent & Theo (1990 film)
cast: Paul Rhys, Tim Roth
director: Robert Altman
Vincenzo: **7** Bellini
vincible: **5** prone **6** liable **8** beatable, in danger **9** sensitive **10** assailable, attackable, penetrable, vulnerable
vincit __ veritas: **5** omnia
__ vincit amor: **5** omnia
__ vincit omnia: **4** amor
vinculum: **3** tie **4** bond, link, lock, seam, yoke **5** annex, joint, nexus, tag on **6** bridge, hookup, joiner **7** coupler **8** ligament **9** fastening **10** attachment, connection, connective
vin de __: **4** pays
vindicable: **6** proper, venial **7** tenable **9** excusable **10** condonable, defensible, pardonable
vindicate: **5** clear, right **6** acquit, avenge, defend, excuse, refute, uphold **7** absolve, justify, redress, revenge, support **8** champion, disprove, maintain, plead for **9** challenge, do justice, exculpate, exonerate, whitewash **10** disculpate, speak up for
vindicated: **4** free **6** exempt **7** cleared **9** acquitted **10** exonerated, off the hook
vindication: **4** plea **6** pardon, reason
vindictive: **4** mean **5** cruel, harsh, nasty **6** animal, bitter, brutal, fierce, savage, unkind, wanton **7** beastly, callous, hateful, hurtful, vicious **8** avenging, barbaric, fiendish, grudging, inhumane, pitiless, puni-

tive, ruthless, sadistic, spiteful, vengeful, venomous, virulent **9** cutthroat, ferocious, malicious, merciless, monstrous, rancorous, resentful, splenetic, truculent **10** implacable
feeling: **3** ire **4** bile, fury, hate, rage **5** anger, wrath **6** rancor, spleen **7** outrage, umbrage **8** acrimony, vexation
vindictiveness: **5** spite **6** malice, rancor, spleen **9** vengeance
vine: **3** ivy **5** haoma, kudzu, liana, liane, plant, vetch **6** briony, bryony **7** creeper, jasmine **8** clematis, wistaria, wisteria **9** jessamine
combining form: **4** viti-
die on the ~: **3** ebb, rot, sag **4** fade, wilt **5** decay, lapse **6** go soft, worsen **7** decline, dwindle **8** languish, vegetate **9** fizzle out, waste away **10** degenerate, retrogress
emulate a ~: **5** climb
ender: **4** yard **7** dresser
Hawaiian: **5** maile
like a ~: **5** twiny
place for a ~: **5** arbor
product: **5** berry, grape, melon
starter: **5** grape
wax ~: **4** hoya
vine-covered: **5** ivied
vinegar: **4** acid **6** acetum **10** acetic acid
combining form: **4** acet- **5** aceto-
flavorer: **6** balsam
full of ~: **4** flip, pert **5** sassy
holder: **3** jar, jug **5** cruet, flask **6** bottle, carafe **8** decanter
like ~: **4** sour **6** acidic **7** acerbic
malt ~: **6** alegar
partner: **3** oil
radical: **6** acetyl
source: **4** wine **5** cider
__ vinegar: **4** rice, wine, wood **5** cider
vinegary: **4** acid, sour, tart **5** acerb, sharp **6** acetal, acetic, acidic, bitter, crusty **7** gone bad, pungent **9** crotchety
Vineland: **4** city, town
locale: **9** New Jersey
__ Vines Have Tender Grapes: **3** Our
vineyard: **5** field **8** cropland
French ~: **3** cru **5** Médoc
pick of the ~: **5** grape
valley: **4** Napa
__ Vineyard: **7** Martha's
Ving: **6** Rhames
Vingt ans après character: **5** Athos
vingt-et-un: **4** game **8** card game
alias: **7** pontoon **9** blackjack, twenty-one
Vinick
portrayer: **4** Alda
Vinny: **10** Testaverde
vino: **4** wine **6** blanco **7** Chianti
like ~ tinto: **4** rojo
region: **4** Asti
variety: **5** soave
vinous: **4** winy **5** winey
vins, like some: **5** blanc, rouge
Vinson Massif: **4** peak **5** mount
locale: **10** Antarctica
vintage: **3** era, old **4** best, crop, rare, wine, year **5** epoch, prime **6** choice, mature, select **7** classic **8** outdated, outmoded, superior **9** excellent, out-of-date, unrivaled, venerable **10** back-number, unrivalled
vintage __: **4** wine, year
vintner: **9** winemaker
need: **3** vat **7** cistern **8** cauldron
prefix: **3** oen- **4** oeno-
Vinton, Bobby
nickname: Polish Prince
song: Blue on Blue (1963)
Blue Velvet (1963)
I Love How You Love Me (1968)
Mr. Lonely (1964)
My Heart Belongs to Only You (1964)
My Melody of Love (1974)
Please Love Me Forever (1967)
Rose Are Red (1962)
There! I've Said It Again (1963)
vinyl: **2** EP, LP **6** fabric, record **8** material
fabric: **9** Naugahyde
viol: **6** string **7** quinton **10** instrument
feature: **4** fret
__ viol: **4** bass
viola: **5** plant **6** flower, string
cousin: **4** bass **5** cello
viola __: **6** d'amore
viola da __: **5** gamba
Viola's love: **6** Orsino
violate: **4** defy **5** abuse, break, flout, force, rebel **6** breach, ignore, invade, oppose, resist, revolt **7** assault, disobey, disrupt, infract, profane, sell out **8** encroach, infringe, trespass **9** desecrate, disregard, trample on **10** contravene, transgress
violation: **3** sin **4** foul **5** abuse, break, crime, lapse, wrong **6** breach **7** assault, misdeed, offense **8** dishonor, invasion, trespass **9** blasphemy, injustice, sacrilege, veniality **10** defilement, disloyalty, illegality, infraction
__ violation: **6** moving
violence: **4** fury, heat, rage, riot **5** might, power, storm **6** attack, duress, émeute, mayhem, rumble, uproar **7** assault, battery, cruelty, passion, rampage **8** coercion, disorder, ferocity, fighting, foul play, savagery, severity, struggle, wildness **9** brutality, harshness, intensity, onslaught, roughness, terrorism **10** brute force, compulsion, fierceness, inhumanity, revolution, storminess, wrongdoing
wanton ~: **4** fury **5** abuse, anger, crime, wrath **7** offense, outrage **9** barbarism, evildoing
violent: **3** hot, mad **4** gory, ugly, wild **5** acute, cruel, fiery, irate, lurid, rabid, rough, sharp, wroth **6** brutal, fierce, heated, mighty, potent, raging, savage, severe, stormy, strong **7** aroused, berserk, enraged, furious, intense, lawless, radical, rampant, vicious **8** coercive, demoniac, forceful, forcible, inflamed, maddened, maniacal, powerful, terrible, vehement, volcanic, wild-eyed **9** ferocious, gale-force, hotheaded, turbulent **10** immoderate, infuriated, passionate, tumultuous, unpeaceful
downfall: **4** ruin **5** wrack
episode: **4** rant **5** quake, seism **10** earthquake
struggle: **3** fit **5** agony, spasm, throe **7** seizure **8** paroxysm
weather: **4** gale, gust, hail, snow **5** blast, sleet, storm **6** precip, squall **7** cyclone, monsoon, tempest, thunder, tornado, twister **8** blizzard, downpour **9** hurricane, windstorm **10** cloudburst
Violent Bear It Away, The
author: Flannery O'Connor
violently: **4** bang, hard **5** madly, rough **7** like mad **8** insanely **9** extremely **10** vehemently
aggressive type: **5** Rambo
angry one: **5** rager
force ~: **6** wrench
issue ~: **5** eruct
shake ~: **5** upset **6** quiver **7** agitate, disturb **8** convulse, unsettle **10** discompose
twist ~: **3** pry **5** wrest, wring **6** snatch, wrench
violet: **4** blue **5** color, grape, mauve, plant **6** dahlia, flower, purple
like a shrinking ~: **3** coy, shy **5** timid **6** demure, modest **7** bashful **8** blushing, reserved
mineral: **6** iolite
relative: *see* blue color
-scented compound: **5** irone
starter: **5** ultra
sweet ~: **5** parma
violin: **4** lira **5** ko-kiu **6** fiddle, lirica, string
ancestor: **5** rebec **6** rebeck
attachment: **4** mute
bow part: **4** frog
cousin: **4** bass **5** cello
ender: **5** maker **6** making
fine ~: **5** Amati, Strad
maker: **5** Amati **10** Stradivari
material: **6** catgut
part: **3** peg **4** neck **5** f hole, waist
relative: **5** rebab, viola
stroke: **5** upbow
Violin
author: Anne Rice
violinist: **4** Auer, Bull, Hahn **5** Elman, Fodor, Stern, Tatum, Ysaye **6** Enesco, Midori, Morini, Mutter **7** Heifetz, Joachim, Kubelik, Menuhin, Ole Bull, Perlman, Szigeti **8** Kreisler, Milstein, Oistrakh, Zukerman **9** Zimbalist **10** Isaac Stern, Mischa Auer
Austrian ~: **8** Kreisler
Belgian ~: **5** Ysaye
Czech ~: **7** Kubelik
direction: **4** arco
German ~: **6** Mutter
Hungarian ~: **4** Auer **7** Joachim, Szigeti
Israeli ~: **7** Perlman **8** Zukerman
Japanese ~: **6** Midori
jazz ~: **5** Tatum
need: **3** bow **5** resin, rosin
Norwegian ~: **4** Bull
Romanian ~: **6** Enesco
Russian ~: **5** Elman **8** Milstein, Oistrakh **9** Zimbalist
Viorst: **6** Judith
VIP: **4** BMOC, exec., lion **5** biggy, celeb, mogul, mover, Mr. Big, nabob **6** biggie, bigwig, cheese, honcho, kahuna, shaker **7** big shot, hotshot, magnate, notable **8** luminary, somebody, superior **9** big cheese, celebrity, dignitary, key player, muck-a-muck, personage
part of ~: **4** very **6** person **9** important
viper: **3** asp **5** adder, cobra, snake **6** animal, gaboon **7** reptile, serpent, traitor **8** betrayer, quisling, turncoat **9** no-goodnik, puff adder, scoundrel **10** blackguard, fer-de-lance
ender: **4** fish
group: **4** nest
like a ~: **6** hooded
relative: *see* snake
weapon: **4** fang **5** venom
__ viper: **3** pit
Viper: **3** car **4** auto **5** Dodge **10** automobile
viperous: **6** aspish **7** hostile **8** venomous **9** poisonous
Vipers' Tangle
author: François Mauriac
V.I.P.s, The (1963 film)
cast: Richard Burton, Louis Jourdan, Elizabeth Taylor
vir: **3** man **5** Latin
wife: **4** uxor
virago: **3** nag **5** harpy, scold, shrew **6** beldam, chider, noodge **7** beldame, needler **8** fishwife, harridan, spitfire **9** henpecker, termagant, Xanthippe
viral: **8** catching, virulent **9** spreading **10** contagious, infectious
vireo: **4** bird
Virgil: **4** Earp, poet **5** Roman, Tibbs **7** Thomson
brother: **5** Wyatt **6** Morgan
described its eruption: **4** Etna **5** Aetna
genre: **4** epos, idyl **5** idyll
see also Latin
virgin: **3** new **4** mint, pure **5** first, fresh **6** intact, unused, vestal **7** initial, untried **8** brand-new, innocent, original, primeval, pristine, spotless, unmarred, untapped **9** primaeval, unspoiled, unsullied, untouched **10** immaculate
virgin __: **4** wool
Virgin: **4** sign **5** Virgo **6** August **9** September
predecessor: **4** Lion
successor: **6** Scales **7** Balance
the ~: **4** sign
Virgin __: **4** Mary **5** Queen **7** Islands
__ Virgin: **5** Like a **7** Blessed
virginal: **3** new **4** pure **5** first, fresh, piano **6** intact, modest, unused, vestal **7** initial, untried **8** brand-new, innocent, keyboard, original, primeval, pristine, spotless, unmarred, untapped **9** lily-white, primaeval, unspoiled, unsullied, untouched **10** immaculate
Virginia: **4** Dare, Grey, Mayo, Wade **5** Apgar, Bruce, state, Woolf **6** Madsen **7** McKenna
bay: **10** Chesapeake
capital: **8** Richmond
caverns: **5** Luray
city: **5** Burke, Salem **6** Oakton,

Reston, Vienna **7** Fairfax, Hampton, Herndon, MacLean, Norfolk, Roanoke, Suffolk **8** Dale City, Danville, Groveton, Hopewell, Leesburg, Manassas, Quantico, Richmond, Staunton, Tuckahoe **9** Annandale, Arlington, Chantilly, Franconia, Jefferson, Lake Ridge, Lynchburg, Newington **10** Alexandria, Appomattox, Blacksburg, Cave Spring, Chesapeake, Petersburg, Portsmouth, Waynesboro, Winchester, Woodbridge
conference: 3 ACC
explorer: 7 Raleigh
famous family of ~: 4 Lees
mountain: 6 Rogers **8** Catoctin
national park: 10 Shenandoah
neighbor: 8 Kentucky, Maryland **9** Tennessee
once: 6 colony **10** settlement
school: 3 ODU, VMI
state beverage: 4 milk
state bird: 8 cardinal
state dog: 8 foxhound
state fish: 10 brook trout
state flower: 7 dogwood
state shell: 6 oyster
state tree: 7 dogwood
Virginia __: 3 ham **4** reel
__, Virginia,...: 3 Yes
Virginia City neighbor: 4 Reno
Virginia ham: 4 meat
Virginian-Pilot: 5 paper **9** newspaper
locale: 7 Norfolk
Virginians, The
author: William Makepeace Thackeray
Virginian, The (NBC western)
cast: Lee J. Cobb (Judge Henry Garth)
Janes Drury (The Virginian)
Doug McClure (Trampas)
Virginia reel: 5 dance
Virginia Tech: 3 VPI
athletes: 6 Hokies **8** Gobblers
conference: 7 Big East
locale: 10 Blacksburg
...Virginia Woolf
author: Edward Albee
Virgin in a Tree
artist: Paul Klee
Virgin Islander, certain: 6 Cruzan
Virgin Islands
clock setting: 3 AST
island: 7 St.Croix **8** St. Thomas
urbanite: 6 Cruzan
__ Virgin Islands: 6 Danish **7** British
__-virgin olive oil: 5 extra
Virgin Suicides, The (2000 film)
cast: Kirsten Dunst, Kathleen Turner, James Woods
director: Sofia Coppola
Virgin with the Monkey
artist: Albrecht Dürer
Virgo: 4 sign **6** Virgin
constellation near ~: 5 Libra **6** Corvus
follower: 5 Libra
month: 3 Aug. **4** Sept. **6** August **9** September
preceder: 3 Leo
star in ~: 5 Spica
virgule: 5 slash **8** diagonal
virid: 4 jade, lime **5** green **7** emerald
relative: ***see*** green color
virile: 4 bold, hale, iron, male, sexy, wiry **5** beefy, burly, hardy, hefty, hunky, husky, lusty, macho, manly, stout, tough, vital **6** brawny, hearty, mighty, potent, robust, rugged, sinewy, steely, stocky, strong, sturdy **7** doughty, healthy, vibrant **8** athletic, forceful, indurate, muscular, powerful, puissant, stalwart, vigorous **9** Atlantean, energetic, Herculean, masculine, masterful, strapping, well-built **10** able-bodied, red-blooded
type: 4 hunk **5** Atlas, he-man, Rambo **6** Samson, Tarzan **7** Goliath **8** Heracles, Hercules, macho man, tough guy
virility
deprive of ~: 5 unman
Virna: 4 Lisi
virtu: 6 curios **10** objets d'art
virtual: 5 quasi, tacit **7** implied **8** implicit, indirect
virtual __: 6 memory **7** reality, storage
virtually: 4 nigh **6** almost, nearly **8** as good as, in effect **9** basically, in essence
virtue: 4 boon, good, hope, love, plus **5** asset, faith, honor, merit, power, right, value, worth **6** ethics, purity **7** benefit, charity, dignity, feature, honesty, justice, modesty, probity, quality, stature **8** chastity, fineness, goodness, kindness, morality, nobility, prudence, strength **9** advantage, character, fortitude, good point, innocence, integrity, rectitude **10** excellence, generosity, honestness, temperance, worthiness
Buddhist ~: 8 paramita
by ~ of: 3 via **5** due to, using **7** because, owing to, through **8** thanks to
cardinal ~: 4 hope **5** faith **7** charity, justice **8** prudence **9** fortitude **10** temperance
cite the ~ of: 4 laud **5** exalt, extol **6** esteem, extoll, praise **7** acclaim, commend, worship **8** eulogize **9** brag about **10** compliment
model of ~: 5 saint
religious ~: 4 zeal **5** faith, piety **8** devotion **9** reverence **10** devoutness, veneration
symbol of ~: 4 halo
Virtue is __ own reward: 3 its
virtueless: 3 bad, low **4** evil, vile **5** cruel **6** no good, unholy **7** corrupt, crooked, heinous, immoral, vicious **8** depraved, diabolic, ignominy, sinister **9** execrable, loathsome, malicious, monstrous, nefarious, repugnant, revolting **10** malevolent, villainous
Virtue of Selfishness, The
author: Ayn Rand
Virtues of Aging, The
author: Jimmy Carter
virtuosity: 3 art **5** craft, skill, touch **7** mastery, prowess **8** artistry, wizardry **9** expertise **10** brilliance
virtuoso: 3 ace **4** star, whiz **5** adept, brain, maven, mavin **6** artist, expert, genius, master, player, wizard **7** artiste, egghead, hotshot, old hand, prodigy, thinker **8** Einstein, highbrow, musician **9** performer, superstar **10** mastermind, specialist
performance: 5 éclat
virtuous: 4 good, just, nice, pure **5** clean, moral, noble, pious, right, sound **6** chaste, decent, honest, worthy **7** ethical, saintly, upright **8** celibate, elevated, faithful, innocent, spotless, straight, true-blue **9** blameless, exemplary, guiltless, honorable, righteous, unsullied, untainted, wholesome **10** goody-goody, high-minded, immaculate, inculpable, inviolable, moralistic, principled
one: 5 angel, model, saint
path of ~ conduct: 3 Tao
virtuousness: 5 grace, honor, merit **6** esteem, renown **7** decency, dignity, honesty, loyalty, probity **8** eminence, fairness, goodness, morality, nobility, veracity **9** adoration, character, gallantry, greatness, integrity, rectitude, reverence, sincerity **10** admiration
virtute et __: 5 armis
virulence: 6 rancor **8** acrimony **9** animosity, hostility **10** bitterness
virulent: 5 fatal, sharp, toxic, viral **6** bitter, deadly, ireful, lethal, malign, septic **7** baneful, cutting, harmful, hateful, hostile, vicious **8** scathing, spiteful, venomous **9** corrosive, infective, injurious, malicious, poisonous, rancorous, resentful, splenetic, unhealthy, vitriolic **10** infectious, malevolent, pernicious, vindictive
__ virumque cano: 4 Arma
virus: 3 bug **4** germ **6** grippe **7** illness, microbe **9** infection, influenza
antibacterial ~: 5 phage
computer ~: 4 worm
starter: 4 echo
target: 2 PC **3** CPU **8** computer
__ virus: 3 DNA, RNA
visa: 4 pass **6** papers, permit **7** passage
Visa: 10 credit card
charge: 4 debt **7** arrears **9** arrearage, liability
rival: 8 Discover **10** Diner's Club, MasterCard
use ~: 3 buy **6** charge **8** purchase
visage: 3 mug **4** cast, face, look, puss **6** aspect **8** features **10** expression
villain ~: 4 leer **5** scoff, smirk, sneer
Visalia: 4 city, town
locale: 10 California
vis-à-vis: 4 sofa **5** tryst **6** direct, toward **7** against, towards **8** opposite **10** compared to, face-to-face
Visayan Islands, one of the: 5 Samar
viscera: 4 guts **5** heart **7** innards
visceral: 3 gut **5** inner **8** physical **9** emotional, innermost, intuitive
viscid: 4 icky, ropy **5** gluey, gooey, gummy, ropey, thick **9** glutinous
substance: 3 goo **4** ooze **5** slime
Visconti: 7 Luchino
viscount: 4 lord, peer, rank **5** noble, title **8** nobleman
superior: 4 earl
viscountess: 4 lady, peer, rank **5** noble, title
viscous: 4 ropy **5** gluey, gooey, goopy, gummy, ropey, slimy, thick **6** clammy, glairy, liquid, sirupy, sticky, syrupy, viscid **8** adhesive **9** glutinous, jellylike **10** gelatinous
liquid: 3 oil **4** lard **5** pitch **6** grease **9** lubricant, petroleum
substance: 3 tar **4** goop **5** slime
Viscuso: 3 Sal
vise: 4 grip, hold, tool **5** clamp, press **6** C-clamp **7** gripper
part: 3 jaw
Vishnu: 6 avatar **9** Preserver
avatar of ~: 4 Rama
companion: 4 Siva **5** Shiva **6** Brahma
worshiper: 5 Hindu **6** Hindoo
visibility: 4 look, show **5** scene, sight **6** glance, seeing **7** display, exhibit, eyeshot, glimpse, observe, viewing **9** spectacle **10** appearance, exhibition, perception
improve ~: 5 defog, deice
problem: 3 fog **4** haze, mist, smog **5** smaze
visible: 4 bold, open, seen **5** clear, overt, plain **6** in view, marked, patent, public **7** evident, exposed, glaring, in sight, obvious, outward **8** apparent, clear-cut, definite, explicit, external, manifest, palpable, revealed, striking, tangible, unhidden, unveiled, viewable **9** big as life, obtrusive **10** detectable, noticeable, observable, pronounced, unshrouded
barely ~: 3 dim **4** dull, hazy, pale **5** faded, faint, fuzzy, vague, woozy **6** subtle **7** obscure, unclear
be ~: 3 see **4** come, show, view **5** pop up, shine **6** appear, arrive, attend, expose, flaunt, lay out, mirror, parade, report, reveal, show up, turn up, unfold, unfurl, unveil **7** exhibit, trot out, turn out, uncover **8** bring out, discover, indicate, manifest, stick out **9** make known, spectacle
become ~: 4 loom **6** appear, emerge
make ~: 5 flare, flash, light, shine **6** ignite, illume, kindle, turn on **7** inflame, lighten **8** brighten, enkindle, illumine **9** highlight, set fire to, set on fire, spotlight **10** illuminate
Visigoth
foe: 3 Hun
king: 6 Alaric
vision: 3 eye **4** idea, trip, view **5** angel, dream, ideal, image, scope, sight **6** beauty, eyeful, fantom, looker, mirage, optics, oracle, seeing, spirit, trance **7** concept, dazzler, fantasy, insight, outlook, phantom, realize, stunner **8** daydream, eyesight, head trip, illusion, keenness, knockout, prophecy **9** foresight, intuition, nightmare, pipe dream

10 appearance, astuteness, conception, envisaging, perception, prescience, revelation, standpoint
beatific ~: 8 afflatus
combining form: 4 -opia, opto- 5 -opsia
field of ~: 3 ken 4 view 5 range, reach, scope, sight, vista 7 compass, horizon, purview
frightening ~: 8 bad dream 9 nightmare
good ~: 6 acuity 8 keenness
of ~: 5 optic 6 visual
starter: 4 Pana, tele 5 cable
vision ___: 5 quest
___ vision: 4 X-ray 6 double, tunnel
visionary: 3 fey 4 airy, seer 5 lofty 6 dreamy, mystic, unreal, zealot 7 utopian 8 creative, delusory, fanciful, illusive, illusory, mystical, mythical, quixotic, romantic, theorist 9 ambitious, idealized, imaginary, prophetic, stargazer, unworldly 10 Don Quixote, idealistic, impossible, quixotical, starry-eyed, unfeasible, unworkable
of old: 4 aery
Vision of Love (1990 song)
artist: Mariah Carey
Vision of Sir Launfal, The
author: James Russell Lowell
visions, having: 6 adream
Visions of Cody
author: Jack Kerouac
Vision, The
author: Dean Koontz
visit: 2 do 3 see 4 call, chat, come, go to, stay, stop, talk, tour 5 go see, haunt, pop by, pop in, run in, smite, tarry, wreak 6 arrive, attend, befall, call on, come by, come to, drop by, drop in, look up, remain, show up, stop by, stop in, take in, travel 7 afflict, go to see, holiday, inflict, sit in on, sojourn, stop off, swing by, trouble 8 call upon, converse, drop over, frequent, look in on, pay a call, stay with, stopover, vacation 9 force upon, get around, hang out at, interview, touch base 10 come around, pay a call on, social call
anew: 5 resee
hotel ~: 4 rest, stay 7 holiday, respite, sojourn 8 stopover, vacation
nautical ~: 3 gam
often: 5 haunt 7 hang out 8 frequent 9 hang out at 10 hang around
___ visit: 5 state
Visit ___ Small Planet: 3 to a
visitation: 5 trial 6 mishap, ordeal 7 undoing
Visit From St. Nicholas, A: 4 poem
opener: 4 'twas
writer: 5 Moore
visiting: 4 here 6 in town
visiting ___: 4 card 5 hours, nurse
visitor: 5 guest 6 caller, drop-in 7 company, habitué, invitee, tourist 8 stranger 9 foreigner, sightseer, transient 10 vacationer
annual ~: 5 Santa
from space: 2 ET 5 alien, comet
receive a ~: 3 see 4 host, mark, view 5 greet, lodge, pop in, put up 6 attend, behold 7 receive 9 entertain, recognize 10 anticipate
room: 5 salon 6 parlor 7 gallery
Visitor: 4 Nana
visitors: 4 team 5 party 7 company, society 8 assembly 9 gathering
accepting ~: 6 at home
Visit to a Small Planet
author: Gore Vidal
cat: 10 Clementine
dog: 3 Red
visor: 4 bill, brim, mask 8 eyeshade, sunshade
___ visor: 3 sun 6 flip-up
visored headgear: 4 kepi 5 armet
Vissi d'arte: 4 aria
opera: 5 Tosca
vista: 4 view 5 scape, scene, sight, sweep 7 horizon, outlook, scenery 8 panorama, prospect 9 landscape
___ Vista: 4 Alta 5 Buena, Chula
VISTA part: 4 Amer., Serv. 7 America, Service 10 Volunteers
Vistula: 5 river
city on the ~: 6 Cracow, Krakow, Warsaw
locale: 6 Poland
river to the ~: 3 Bug, San
visual: 4 seen 5 optic 6 beheld, imaged, ocular 7 graphic, optical, seeable, sensory 8 viewable 9 graphical, sensorial
aid: 3 map 4 grid, plan, plot 5 chart, graph, table 6 sketch 7 diagram 9 blueprint, floor plan
enhancers: 5 specs 7 glasses 8 contacts
examination: 4 gaze, look, peek, scan 5 sight, study 6 gander, glance, review, survey 7 glimpse, look-see, viewing 8 once-over, scrutiny 10 inspection
signal: 3 bat 4 wink 5 blink, flick 6 squint 7 flutter, twinkle 8 high sign
starter: 5 audio
visual ___: 3 aid 4 arts 5 field, range
___-visual: 5 audio
visualization: 7 imagery 9 imagining, picturing
visualize: 3 see 5 fancy, think 6 call up 7 dream up, imagine, picture, project, realize, think up 8 envisage, envision 9 conjure up 10 anticipate, call to mind, conceive of
visually, examine: 4 look
vita: 6 résumé 7 profile 9 biography
___ vita: 5 dolce
vitae
aqua ~: 5 booze, drink, sauce 6 liquor 7 alcohol, liqueur, potable, spirits, whiskey 9 firewater, inebriant, moonshine 10 intoxicant
curriculum ~: 3 bio 6 digest, précis, record, résumé 7 outline, summary 8 synopsis
lignum ~: 4 tree
starter: 5 arbor
___ vitae: 4 aqua 5 arbor
vital: 3 key, nec., req. 4 live, main, must 5 acute, alive, basic, fresh, lusty, major, peppy, sound 6 lively, living, needed, urgent, virile 7 central, crucial, dynamic, organic, pivotal, primary, radical, vibrant, zestful 8 cardinal, critical, decisive, integral, pressing, required, spirited, vigorous 9 energetic, essential, important, mandatory, momentous, necessary, paramount, requisite, right-hand, strategic, vivacious 10 bottom-line, imperative, meaningful, portentous, underlined, underlying
élan ~: 4 life, soul 6 psyche, spirit
fluid: 3 sap 5 blood, serum
force: 4 soul 5 anima, being 6 energy, psyche 8 vivacity
moment: 4 D-day 5 H-hour 6 crisis 8 juncture, zero hour 9 crossroad, emergency
part: 3 cog 9 essential, necessity
remove ~ parts: 3 gut 4 sack 5 rifle 6 ravage 7 destroy, pillage, plunder, ransack 8 clean out, decimate
sign: 5 pulse
something ~: 4 must, need 5 vital 9 essential, necessity, requisite 10 imperative, obligation, sine qua non
spark: 3 vim, zip 4 brio, dash, élan, fire, life, soul, zest, zing 5 being, gusto, heart, nerve, oomph, pluck, verve, vigor 6 animus, bounce, energy, esprit, psyche, spirit 7 essence, passion 9 animation, life force 10 enthusiasm, excitement, exuberance, get-up-and-go, liveliness
stat: 3 age, DOB 6 height, weight
stats: 3 bio 5 story 6 résumé 7 profile
vital ___: 5 force, signs
___ vital: 4 élan
Vitale: 4 Dick
vitality: 2 go 3 pep, vim, zip 4 dint, élan, guts, kick, life, push, snap, soul, thew, zest, zing 5 ardor, brawn, drive, force, juice, might, oomph, power, prime, punch, spark, spunk, steam, thews, verve, vigor 6 action, bounce, energy, fervor, muscle, pizazz, spirit, starch 7 fitness, muscles, pizzazz, potence, potency, sparkle, stamina 8 presence, strength, vivacity 9 animation, beefiness, endurance, fortitude, hardiness, huskiness, lustiness, puissance, stoutness, toughness 10 brawniness, brute force, ebullience, exuberance, get up and go, liveliness, mightiness, robustness, sturdiness
have ~: 4 live 5 exist 7 breathe, prosper 8 flourish
lack of ~: 6 anemia, anergy 7 anaemia
vitalize: 4 gird, tone 5 build, liven, pep up, shore, steel 6 anneal, arouse, beef up, harden, prop up, pump up, temper, tone up, turn on, vivify 7 animate, bolster, brace up, build up, burgeon, develop, empower, enhance, enliven, fortify, juice up, liven up, quicken, shore up, stiffen, toughen 8 activate, bourgeon, buttress, energize, enspirit, indurate, inspirit 9 impassion, intensify, reinforce, stimulate 10 invigorate, rejuvenate
Vitallium: 5 alloy
component: 6 cobalt 8 chromium 10 molybdenum
Vital Parts
author: Thomas Berger
vitals: 6 inside, organs 7 filling, innards 8 contents
Vital Signs
author: Robin Cook
vitamin
A source: 4 kail, kale 6 carrot
B ~: 6 biotin, folate, niacin
C: 4 acid
chain: 3 GNC
C source: 3 ade 4 lime 6 citrus, orange
D source: 4 milk
monitor: 3 FDA
P: 5 rutin
quantity: 2 IU 3 RDA 4 dose, pill 5 bolus 6 pellet, tablet 7 capsule
starter: 4 mega 5 multi
vitamin B ___: 7 complex
___ vitamins: 7 One-a-Day
vitamins, add: 6 enrich
like ~: 3 OTC
Vitara: 3 SUV 6 Suzuki
Vitas: 10 Gerulaitis
vitiate: 3 mar, sap 4 harm, hurt, jade, thin, tire 5 abase, quash, spoil, taint, weary 6 damage, debase, defile, dilute, impair, infect, injure, negate, weaken 7 abolish, corrupt, degrade, deprave, exhaust, fatigue, pollute, subvert, tire out, wear out 8 abrogate, enervate, enfeeble 9 attenuate, undermine, water down 10 adulterate, debilitate, devitalize, emasculate, invalidate
vitiated: 6 coarse, filthy, impure, soiled 7 corrupt, dirtied, stained, sullied, tainted, unclean 8 maculate, polluted, unchaste 9 tarnished, unrefined 10 unsanitary
vitiation: 8 baseness 9 annulment, depravity 10 corruption, debasement, degeneracy
Viti Levu: 4 isle 6 island
locale: 4 Fiji
Vito: 6 Scotti 8 Corleone
vitreous: 5 clear, lucid 6 glassy 7 crystal 10 reflective
vitreous ___: 5 humor
vitrify: 4 jell 6 anneal, harden 7 calcify, congeal 8 indurate, solidify
vitriol: 4 acid, bile
___ vitriol: 5 oil of
vitriolic: 4 acid 5 acrid, sharp 6 bitter 7 hostile, mocking 8 derisive, scathing, scornful, stinging, virulent 10 disdainful
vittles: 4 chow, eats, fare, feed, food, grub 7 aliment, edibles 9 provender 10 provisions
have ~: 3 eat 4 dine, nosh 5 feast, gorge, graze, munch, scarf, snack 6 devour, ingest, nibble, pig out, take in 7 consume, put away, scarf up 8 chow down, gobble up, take food, wolf down 9 have a bite, have a meal, polish off, scarf down 10 break bread

Vittorio: **6** De Seta, De Sica **7** Alfieri, Gassman
Vittorio the Vampire
author: Anne Rice
vituperate: **3** jaw **4** lash, rail, slur **5** abuse, blame, curse, growl, scold **6** accuse, bark at, berate, defame, injure, insult, malign, revile, vilify, yell at **7** bawl out, censure, chew out, condemn, lambast, rip into, run down, upbraid **8** denounce, lace into, lambaste, tear into **9** blaspheme, castigate, find fault, fulminate **10** blackguard
vituperation: **5** abuse **6** insult, tirade **7** censure **8** diatribe, scolding
vituperator: **3** nag **5** scold, shrew **6** chider, grouch, kvetch, virago, whiner **7** caviler, rebuker, reviler **8** grumbler **9** henpecker, termagant, Xanthippe **10** castigator, complainer
Vitus: **5** saint **6** Bering
__ & Viv: **3** Tom
viva: **5** huzza **6** hoorah, hooray, hurrah, hurray, huzzah **8** long live
voce: **4** oral **5** aloud, vocal **6** loudly, orally **7** out loud **8** verbally
viva __: **4** voce
Viva: **10** paper towel
alternative: **5** Scott **6** Bounty, Brawny
Viva __!: **5** Villa **6** Zapata
Viva __ Vegas: **3** Las
ViVa
author: e.e. cummings
vivace: **5** speed, tempo **8** velocity
vivacious: **3** gay **4** pert, spry **5** alert, alive, brash, brisk, happy, jazzy, jolly, merry, peppy, perky, vital, zesty **6** active, bouncy, breezy, bright, hearty, jaunty, lively, upbeat **7** animate, dashing, jumping, playful, rocking, vibrant, zestful **8** animated, bubbling, cheerful, spirited, sportive, swinging **9** convivial, ebullient, energetic, exuberant, sparkling, sprightly **10** frolicsome, full of life
vivacity: **2** go **3** pep, vim, zip **4** brio, dash, élan, fire, jazz, life, snap, soul, zest **5** flair, oomph, spark, spunk, verve, vigor **6** action, bounce, energy, esprit, gaiety, gayety, pizazz, spirit **7** abandon, panache, pizzazz, sparkle **8** flourish, keenness, vitality **9** animation **10** ebullience, enthusiasm, exuberance, get up and go, liveliness, vital force
Viva Las Vegas (1964 film)
cast: Ann-Margret, Elvis Presley
Vivaldi, Antonio: **7** Italian **8** composer
work: The Four Seasons
__ vivant: **3** bon
vivant, bon: **7** gourmet **8** hedonist, sybarite **9** epicurean **10** voluptuary
Vivarin
alternative: **5** No-Doz
Viva Zapata! (1952 film)
cast: Marlon Brando, Arnold Moss, Anthony Quinn
director: Elia Kazan
vive: **5** huzza **6** hoorah, hooray, hurrah, hurray, huzzah
on the qui ~: **4** wary **5** alert **6** uneasy **7** heads-up, heedful, wakeful **8** keen-eyed, vigilant, watchful
__ vive: **3** qui
Vive __!: **5** le roi
Viveca: **8** Lindfors
__ vivendi: **5** modus
Vivian: **5** Vance **6** Blaine
Vivica A. __: **3** Fox
vivid: **3** gay **4** bold, live, loud, rich **5** clear, gaudy, juicy, light, lucid, lurid, plain, sharp, showy **6** bright, cogent, lively, strong **7** evident, express, glowing, graphic, intense, obvious, shining, vibrant **8** animated, apparent, colorful, definite, distinct, dramatic, eloquent, explicit, luminous, manifest, palpable, powerful, striking **9** brilliant, graphical, graspable, memorable **10** expressive, flamboyant, spelled out
display: **4** riot
quality: **5** color **10** brightness
Vivid: **6** bleach
alternative: **5** Purex, Snowy **6** Clorox **8** Borateem
Vivien: **5** Leigh **8** Merchant
vivify: **5** hop up, liven, pep up, rouse **6** bestir, pump up, turn on **7** animate, enliven, inspire, juice up, liven up, quicken, refresh **8** activate, energize, enspirit, inspirit, vitalize **9** stimulate **10** invigorate
Vivitar: **6** camera
alternative: *see* camera
__-vivre: **6** savoir
vixen: **3** fox **5** flirt, harpy, shrew, siren **6** animal, chider **8** spitfire **9** termagant, Xanthippe
home: **3** den
offspring: **3** kit
Vixen: **8** reindeer
colleague: *see* reindeer
viz.: **2** i.e. **5** id est, to wit **6** namely **10** for example
vizier superior: **3** aga **4** agha
Vizquel: **4** Omar
Vizsla: **3** dog **5** canid **6** canine
V-J Day ended it: **4** WWII
VJ employer: **3** MTV
Vladimir: **5** Lenin, Putin, saint **6** Prelog **7** Kramnik, Nabokov **8** Horowitz, Sloukhin, Zworykin **9** Ashkenazy **10** Mayakovsky
see also Russian
Vladivostok: **4** city, port, town
locale: **6** Russia **7** Siberia
Vlasic ad animal: **5** stork
__ Vleck: **7** John van
V-Letter and Other Poems
author: Karl Shapiro
VMD
see vet
VMI: **3** sch. **4** coll.
locale: **8** Virginia **9** Lexington
student: **5** cadet **6** Keydet **7** soldier
V-neck: **5** shirt **6** blouse **7** sweater
vo-__: **4** tech
VO5
rival: **4** Pert **5** Prell
VOA agcy.: **4** USIA
__ vobiscum: **3** pax **4** deus
vocab.: **3** lex., wds.
vocabulary: **4** cant, list **5** lexis, lingo, words **6** jargon **7** lexicon **8** glossary, language, verbiage **9** thesaurus **10** dictionary
special ~: **5** argot, idiom, lingo, slang **6** jargon, patois
unit: **4** word **5** idiom, sound **6** lexeme, phrase **8** morpheme **9** utterance
vocal: **4** glib, loud, oral, said, song, sung **5** blunt, frank, lyric, noisy **6** choral, facile, fluent, phonic, spoken, verbal, voiced **7** out loud, uttered, venting **8** eloquent, narrated, operatic, phonetic, strident, viva voce **9** clamorous, expressed, intonated, outspoken, talkative, unwritten **10** articulate, bigmouthed, expressive, forthright, free-spoken, pronounced, stentorian, unreticent
composition: **4** aria **5** motet **6** arioso
effect: **5** trill **7** vibrato
ender: **3** ist
expression: **6** speech
fanfare: **4** ta-da **5** ta-dah
gaffe: **4** flub, gaff, goof, slip **5** error, gaffe, lapse **7** blooper, misstep
group: **4** trio **5** choir, octet **6** chorus **7** octette **8** ensemble
of a ~ sound: **5** tonal
preceder: **4** vamp **5** intro
range: **4** alto, bass **5** tenor **7** soprano
space between ~ cords: **7** glottis
vocal __: **5** cords
vocalist: **4** alto, bass, diva **5** mezzo, tenor **6** canary, singer **7** caroler, chanter, crooner, soprano, warbler **8** baritone, barytone, choir boy, musician **9** chanteuse, choir girl, chorister, contralto **10** coloratura, prima donna
vocalists: **5** choir **6** chorus **7** chorale **8** ensemble, glee club
vocalization: **6** speech **8** language **9** statement, utterance
vocalize: **3** rap, say **4** moan, sing, talk, vent **5** argue, chant, chirp, croon, groan, shout, speak, utter, voice, yodel, yodle **6** convey, impart, intone, mumble, murmur, warble **7** belt out, discuss, express, inflect **8** set forth, sound off **9** enunciate, pronounce, verbalize
displeasure: **3** boo **4** jeer **5** scoff, whoop **6** deride **7** catcall **8** ridicule
vocalized: **4** oral, said **6** spoken, verbal, voiced **7** sounded, uttered **8** narrated, viva voce **9** recounted
pause: **2** er, uh, um
vocalizing: **4** talk **5** pitch, spiel **6** homily, sermon, speech, tirade **7** bombast, lecture, oration, oratory, prattle **8** dialogue, diatribe, harangue, rhetoric **9** discourse, elocution, monologue, utterance **10** expressing, filibuster, recitation
vocally: **5** aloud **7** out loud **8** viva voce
vocation: **3** job **4** game, line, post, walk, work **5** craft, field, niche, thing, trade **6** career, métier, office, racket **7** calling, mission, pursuit **8** business, lifework, practice **9** specialty **10** department, employment, livelihood, nine-to-five, occupation, profession, walk of life
voce
sotto ~: **6** softly
sotto ~ remark: **5** aside
viva ~: **4** oral **5** aloud, vocal **6** loudly, orally **7** out loud **8** verbally
__ voce: **3** sub, una **4** viva **5** mezza, sotto
vociferant: **4** loud, wild **5** brash, noisy, rowdy, vocal **6** brassy, flashy, strong, unruly **7** blaring, booming, intense, raucous, riotous, roaring **8** emphatic, piercing, strident, vehement **9** clamorous, deafening **10** boisterous, disorderly, loud-voiced, resounding, stentorian, tumultuous, uproarious
vociferate: **3** cry **4** bawl, call, hoot, howl, roar, wail, yell **5** shout, whoop **6** bellow, holler, scream, shriek **7** screech, ululate **8** shout out
vociferation: **3** din **5** shout **6** racket **9** utterance
vociferous: **4** loud **5** forte, noisy **6** shrill **7** blaring, blatant, booming, jarring, pealing, rackety, ranting, raucous, reboant, roaring **8** crashing, piercing, plangent, rumbling, shouting, sonorous, strident, turned up, vehement **9** big-voiced, clamorous, deafening, insistent **10** boisterous, resounding, stentorian, strepitous, thundering, uproarious
vodka: **5** drink **8** beverage
brand: **4** Skyy **5** Popov, Stoli **7** Absolut, Smirnov **9** Grey Goose
cousin: **3** gin
drink: **6** gimlet **8** salty dog **10** bloody Mary, Moscow mule **11** screwdriver
vodun: **3** hex **5** magic, spell **6** voodoo **7** sorcery **10** witchcraft
__ Vogler: **3** Abt
vogue: **3** fad, mod, now, ton **4** chic, mode, rage **5** craze, dance, favor, style, trend **6** custom, latest, modish, trendy, with it **7** fashion, in thing, popular **8** last word **9** nattiness **10** acceptance, dernier cri, modishness, popularity
in ~: **3** hip, hot, now **4** chic **5** faddy **6** classy, latest, modish, trendy **7** current, popular, stylish **8** accepted, up-to-date **10** newfangled
no longer in ~: **3** out **5** dated, passé
Vogue (1990 song)
artist: Madonna
Vogues
song: Five O'Clock World (1965) My Special Angel (1968) Turn Around, Look at Me (1968) You're the One (1965)
voguish: **3** hip, mod **4** chic, tony **5** haute, natty, nifty, sharp, smart, swank, swell, toney **6** chi-chi,

classy, dapper, dressy, flossy, modish, snappy, trendy **7** à la mode, current, dashing, elegant, in style, popular, stylish **8** up-to-date **9** high-class, in fashion **10** all the rage
Voi __ sapete: **3** che
voice: **3** air, cry, put, say **4** alto, bass, call, part, roar, talk, tell, tone, vent, vote, yell **5** opine, organ, say-so, shout, sound, speak, state, tenor, utter, words **6** active, assert, choice, intone, mumble, murmur, mutter, option, phrase, speech, tongue **7** declare, divulge, express, mention, opinion, passive, present, recount, soprano **8** announce, baritone, barytone, decision, language, proclaim, put forth, set forth, sound off, suffrage, vocalize **9** comment on, contralto, elocution, emphasize, enunciate, make known, pronounce, statement, utterance, verbalize, vox populi **10** articulate, coloratura, inflection, intonation, preference
  an objection: **5** argue, demur, groan
  box: **6** larynx
  combining form: **4** phon- **5** phono-
  ender: **4** over **5** print
  give ~ to: **5** speak, utter
  gravelly ~: **4** rasp **5** grate **7** scratch
  in full ~: **5** aroar
  inner ~: **8** scruples, superego **10** conscience, principles
  let one's ~ be heard: **6** assert, insist **7** declare, speak up **8** sound off, speak out **10** stand up for
  lift up one's ~: **4** sing **5** chant, croon **6** intone, warble **7** belt out, perform **8** melodize, vocalize **10** carry a tune
  low ~: **3** hum **4** deep **6** breath, mumble, murmur, mutter **7** whisper
  of ~ pitch: **5** tonal
  quality: **4** tone **5** twang **6** accent
  raise one's ~: **4** roar, yell **5** shout **6** bellow, holler, scream
  range: **4** alto, bass **5** mezzo, tenor **7** soprano **8** baritone
  singing ~: **5** pipes
  small ~: **4** soul **8** scruples, superego **10** conscience, moral sense
  transmitter: **4** mike **9** megaphone
  vote: **3** aye, nay, yea
  with one ~: **5** as one, whole **6** in sync, united **7** en masse, jointly, unified **8** as a group, combined, communal, in unison, mutually, together, unitedly **9** accordant, all at once, in concert, unanimous **10** agreed upon, conjointly, harmonious, like-minded
voice __: **3** box **4** coil, mail, part, vote
voice-__ analyzer: **6** stress
Voice __ Turtle, The: **5** of the
voice box
  combining form: **6** laryng- **7** laryngo-
voiced: **4** oral **5** aloud, vocal **6** spoken **9** vocalized
__-voiced: **4** deep **5** rough
voiceless: **3** mum **4** hush, mute **5** quiet, still **6** silent **9** noiseless **10** speechless, tongue-tied
  consonant: **4** surd
voicemail, check: **6** call in
Voice of America org.: **4** USIA
Voice of Israel
  author: Abba Eban
Voice of the Night, The
  author: Dean Koontz
voiceover: **6** review **7** remarks **8** analysis, exegesis **9** discourse, narration **10** commentary, exposition, expression
  do a ~: **3** dub **4** tape **6** record
  edit a ~: **5** redub
voices
  eight ~: **5** octet **7** octette
  five ~: **7** quintet
  for ~: **5** lyric, vocal **6** choral **7** lyrical, musical
  four ~: **7** quartet
  six ~: **6** sextet **8** sextette
  three ~: **4** trio
Voices of the Night
  author: Henry Wadsworth Longfellow
Voice, The (1981 song)
  artist: Moody Blues
void: **3** gap, nix **4** bare, dump, emit, gulf, hole, lack, null, zero **5** abysm, abyss, annul, blank, clear, drain, eject, empty, quash, space, waste **6** barren, cancel, cavity, glassy, hollow, negate, recant, repeal, revoke, vacant, vacuum **7** abolish, absence, deflate, deplete, drained, emptied, invalid, negated, nullify, opening, rescind, reverse, vacancy, vacuity, vacuous **8** abrogate, dissolve, evacuate, nihility, overturn, throw out **9** blankness, cancelled, discharge, emptiness, repudiate **10** blue-pencil, invalidate, unratified
  become ~: **3** end **5** cease, lapse **6** breach, expire, weaken **7** default, misstep, regress, relapse **9** terminate
  declare ~: **5** quash **6** repeal, revoke **7** rescind **8** override, overrule **9** discharge, repudiate
  partner: **4** null
voided serve: **3** let
Voight, Jon: **5** actor
  daughter: Angelina Jolie
  film: Ali (2001)
    Catch-22 (1970)
    Coming Home (1978, AA)
    Conrack (1974)
    Deliverance (1972)
    Desert Bloom (1986)
    Enemy of the State (1998)
    Glory Road (2006)
    Heat (1995)
    Lara Croft: Tomb Raider (2001)
    Midnight Cowboy (1969)
    Mission: Impossible (1996)
    The Odessa File (1974)
    Pearl Harbor (2001)
    The Rainmaker (1997)
    Runaway Train (1985)
    Table for Five (1983)
voilà: **4** ta-da **5** ta-dah, there **6** behold, presto
voile: **5** ninon **6** fabric **7** chiffon
Voina i __: **3** mir
voir __: **4** dire
Voit
  competitor: **3** AMF **6** Wilson **8** Rawlings, Spalding **9** Brunswick
vol.: **2** bk.
  measure: **2** cc., ml. **4** cu. ft., cu. in, cu. yd.
Vol: **10** Tennessean
Volans
  neighbor: **5** Mensa
volant: **6** aerial, flying **8** airborne, in the air
Volare: **3** car **4** auto **8** Plymouth
Volare (song)
  artist: Dean Martin, Bobby Rydell
  word: **3** blu, nel **7** dipinto
volary: **6** aviary **8** birdcage, dovecote **9** birdhouse
volatile: **4** fumy **5** gassy, irate, saucy **6** fickle **7** erratic, flighty, nervous **8** fugitive, skittish, ticklish, unstable, unsteady, variable **9** ephemeral, excitable, explosive, fugacious, hotheaded, mercurial, momentary, transient, unsettled, up-and-down, whimsical **10** capricious, changeable, inconstant, short-lived, transitory
  liquid: **5** nitro
volatility: **5** folly **6** whimsy **8** dallying, zaniness **9** flippancy, frivolity, giddiness, lightness, sauciness, silliness
  measure, on Wall Street: **4** beta
volcanic: **5** angry, irate **6** fuming, heated, ireful, raging, red-hot **7** enraged, igneous, steamed, violent **8** inflamed, volatile, wrathful **10** hysterical
  crater: **4** maar **7** caldera
  emission: **3** ash **4** fume **6** ejecta
  formation: **4** cone
  in appearance: **5** conic **7** conical
  rock: **4** lava, slag, tuff **5** magma **6** basalt, pumice **8** obsidian
volcanic __: **3** ash **4** cone, tuff
volcano: **3** Aso, Oku, Usu **4** Akan, cone, Etna, Fogo, Fuji, Gaua, Nasu, peak, Póas, Popo, Ruiz, Taal **5** Alaid, Asama, Azuma, Fuego, Hekla, Irazú, Kelut, Manam, Mayon, mound, Pelee, Raung, Tacan, Unzen, Yasur **6** Ambrym, Arenal, Bagana, Bandai, Chokai, Colima, Dukono, Erebus, Krafla, Láscar, Lassen, Lopevi, Masaya, Merapi, Ontake, Oshima, Pacaya, Pavlof, Puracé, Rabaul, Sangay, Semeru, Slamet, Tiatia, Toluca, Ulawun **7** Adatara, Bulusan, Canlaon, El Misti, Erta-Ale, Galeras, Gareloi, Iliamna, Kerinci, Kilauea, Langila, Orizaba, Redoubt, Ruapehu **8** Cotopaxi, Gamalama, Karthala, Karymsky, Mauna Loa, mountain, Pinatubo, St. Helens, Vesuvius, Wrangell **9** Momotombo, Santorini, Stromboli, Tolbachik **10** Nyiragongo
  Africa: **3** Oku **4** Fogo **7** Erta-Ale **8** Karthala **10** Nyiragongo
  Alaska: **6** Katmai, Pavlof **7** Gareloi, Iliamna, Redoubt **8** Wrangell
  Antarctic: **6** Erebus
  Asia: **3** Aso, Usu **4** Akan, Fuji, Gaua, Nasu, Taal **5** Alaid, Asama, Azuma, Kelut, Manam, Mayon, Raung, Unzen, Yasur **6** Ambrym, Bagana, Bandai, Chokai, Dukono, Lopevi, Merapi, Ontake, Oshima, Rabaul, Semeru, Slamet, Tiatia, Ulawun **7** Adatara, Bulusan, Canlaon, Kerinci, Langila **8** Gamalama, Karymsky, Pinatubo **9** Tolbachik
  California: **6** Lassen
  Cameroon: **3** Oku
  Cape Verde Islands: **4** Fogo
  Caribbean: **5** Pelee
  cavity: **3** pit **6** crater
  Central America: **4** Póas **5** Fuego, Irazú, Tacan **6** Arenal, Masaya, Pacaya **9** Momotombo
  Chile: **6** Láscar
  Colombia: **4** Ruiz **5** Huila, Pasto **6** Puracé **7** Galeras
  Comoros: **8** Karthala
  Congo: **10** Nyiragongo
  Costa Rica ~: **4** Póas **5** Irazu **6** Arenal
  crack: **4** vent
  Ecuador: **6** Sangay **8** Cotopaxi
  emulate a ~: **4** blow, spew, spue **5** erupt
  Ethiopia: **7** Erta-Ale
  Europe: **4** Etna **8** Vesuvius **9** Santorini, Stromboli
  extinct Caucasus ~: **6** Kazbek
  goddess: **4** Pele
  Greece: **9** Santorini
  Guatemala: **5** Fuego, Tacan **6** Pacaya
  Hawaii: **7** Kilauea **8** Mauna Loa
  Hokkaido: **3** Usu **4** Akan **6** Oshima
  Honshu: **5** Azuma **6** Bandai, Chokai, Ontake **7** Adatara
  Iceland: **5** Hekla **6** Krafla
  Indonesia: **5** Kelut, Raung **6** Dukono, Merapi, Semeru, Slamet **7** Kerinci **8** Gamalama
  Italy: **4** Etna **8** Vesuvius **9** Stromboli
  Japan: **3** Aso, Usu **4** Akan, Fuji, Nasu **5** Asama, Azuma, Oyama, Unzen **6** Asosan, Bandai, Chokai, Ontake, Oshima **7** Adatara
  Java: **5** Kelut, Raung **6** Merapi, Semeru, Slamet
  Kyushu: **5** Unzen
  Luzon: **4** Taal **5** Mayon **7** Bulusan **8** Pinatubo
  Martinique: **5** Pelee
  Mexico: **4** Popo **6** Colima, Toluca **7** Orizaba
  mud ~: **5** salse
  New Zealand: **7** Ruapehu
  Nicaragua: **6** Masaya **9** Momotombo
  opening: **5** Mauna
  output: **3** ash **4** lava
  Papua New Guinea: **5** Manam **6** Bagana, Rabaul, Ulawun **7** Langila
  Peru: **7** El Misti
  Philippines: **3** Apo **4** Taal **5** Mayon **7** Bulusan, Canlaon **8** Pinatubo
  Philippines ~: **3** Apo
  residue: **3** ash **5** ember **6** cinder

Russia: **5** Alaid **6** Tiatia **8** Karymsky **9** Tolbachik
shape: **4** cone
Sicily: **4** Etna **5** Aetna
South America: **4** Ruiz **6** Láscar, Puracé, Sangay **7** El Misti, Galeras **8** Cotopaxi
Sumatra: **7** Kerinci
Vanuatu: **4** Gaua **5** Yasur **6** Ambrym, Lopevi
Washington: **8** St. Helens
Volcano (1997 film)
cast: Anne Heche, Tommy Lee Jones
dog: **3** Max
Volcano Island: **7** Iwo Jima
vole: **5** mouse **6** animal, mammal, rodent **10** field mouse
relative: *see* rodent
__ volens: **6** nolens
__ volente: **3** deo
Volga: **5** river
city on the ~: **5** Gorki
denizen: **5** Tatar
locale: **6** Russia
river to the ~: **3** Oka **4** Kama
Volga Boatman
ingredient: **5** vodka
Volgograd: **4** city, town
locale: **6** Russia
volitate: **3** fly **4** flit **5** drift, glide, hover **7** flutter
volitation: **4** flit, trip **5** glide **6** aviate, flight, voyage **7** flutter, getaway, journey **8** aviation, hovering **9** departure
volition: **4** will, wish **6** choice, desire, intent, option **8** free will **9** intention **10** discretion, preference, resolution
do on one's own ~: **5** offer **6** enlist, sign up **7** pitch in, proffer, recruit, stand up, venture **9** undertake, volunteer **10** put forward
volitional: **5** meant **6** wilful **7** planned, willful **8** intended **9** voluntary **10** preplanned, purposeful
Volkswagen: **3** car **4** auto **10** automobile
model: **3** Bug, Fox, GTI **4** Golf **5** Jetta **6** Beetle, Cabrio, Passat, Rabbit **7** Eurovan **8** Scirocco
rival: **4** Audi, Opel
volley: **4** fire, rain **5** blast, burst, salvo, storm **6** attack **7** barrage, battery **8** enfilade, outbreak, shelling **9** broadside, cannonade, discharge, fusillade
ender: **4** ball
volleyball: **4** game **5** sport
need: **3** net
position: **6** digger, hitter, libero, passer, setter **7** blocker **8** attacker
shot: **4** dink, kill **5** spike
where ~ was first played: **4** YMCA
__ volleyball: **5** beach
volplane: **3** fly **4** soar **5** coast, float, glide
Volpone: **4** play **6** comedy
author: Ben Jonson
character: **5** Celia, Mosca **7** Bonario, Corvino, Voltore
Volstead Act
opponent: **3** Wet
supporter: **3** Dry

Volsunga Saga king: **4** Atli
Volta: **10** Alessandro
__ Volta: **5** Upper
voltage: **5** force, power **6** energy, muscle **7** stamina **8** dynamism, momentum, strength **9** magnetism, supremacy
jump: **5** surge
measure: **3** EMF
reduction: **6** dim out
regulator: **5** zener
voltaic: **8** electric **10** electrical
voltaic cell part: **5** anode
Voltaire: **6** French, writer **11** philosopher
love: **6** Émilie
real name: **6** Arouet
work: Candide
volte-face: **4** turn **7** reverse **9** turnabout
volt ender: **3** age **5** meter **7** ammeter
volubility: **8** glibness **9** eloquence, garrulity, gift of gab, readiness
voluble: **4** glib, long **5** gabby, talky, windy, wordy **6** prolix **7** diffuse, lengthy, unterse, verbose **8** rambling **9** bombastic, garrulous, talkative **10** bigmouthed, discursive, long-winded, loquacious, palaverous, rhetorical
volume: **4** book, bulk, mass, much, room, size, tome **5** album, space, total **6** amount, cubage, degree, extent, number **7** edition, writing **8** capacity, contents, loudness, quantity, strength, treatise **9** amplitude, dimension, intensity, largeness, magnitude
control: **4** knob **5** fader
decrease the ~: **3** gag **4** calm, hush, lull, mute **5** quiet, shush **6** deaden, muffle, muzzle, shut up, stifle, subdue **7** be quiet, silence **8** pipe down, suppress **9** quiet down **10** extinguish, keep it down
increase the ~: **3** amp **5** amp up, blare
lacking ~: **4** bony, lank, lean, puny, slim, thin, trim **5** gaunt, lanky, reedy, wispy **6** flimsy, meager, skimpy, skinny, slight, slinky, sparse, wasted **7** haggard, scrawny, slender **8** skeletal, twiglike, wisplike **9** emaciated, paper-thin, wafer-thin
setting: **3** low **4** bass, high
unit: **2** cc **3** cup **4** cu. ft., cu. in., cu. yd., gill, peck, sone **5** liter, minim, quart, stere **6** bushel, gallon **8** hogshead **9** board foot, cubic foot, cubic yard **10** cubic meter, fluid ounce
volumes: **4** a lot, much **6** plenty
voluminous: **3** big **4** full, much, vast, wide **5** ample, broad, bulky, great, large, roomy **6** legion **7** copious, massive, sizable **8** abundant, sizeable, spacious **9** billowing, capacious, cavernous, expansive, extensive
voluminousness: **7** bigness, fulness **8** hugeness, wideness **9** abundance, amplitude, broadness, immensity, largeness, magnitude, plenitude
voluntarily: **5** unbid **6** freely **8** by choice **9** on one's own, willingly
voluntary: **4** free **5** meant, unbid **6** chosen, freely, unpaid, wilful, willed, wished **7** elected, planned, unasked, willful, witting **8** intended, optional, unbidden, unforced **10** autonomous, considered, deliberate, gratuitous, purposeful, unprompted, volitional
volunteer: **4** bite **5** enrol, offer **6** chip in, enlist, enroll, helper, sign up, tender, unpaid **7** advance, pitch in, proffer, recruit, soldier, stand up, suggest, venture **9** undertake **10** put forward, unsalaried
firefighter: **4** vamp
literacy ~: **5** coach, tutor **6** master, mentor **7** teacher **8** educator, lecturer **9** professor **10** instructor
words: **4** I can **5** I will **7** I'll do it
Volunteers (1985 film)
cast: John Candy, Tom Hanks, Rita Wilson
Volunteers?: **6** Anyone
Volunteer State: **4** Tenn. **9** Tennessee
Volupta
daughter: **6** Psyche
father: **4** Eros
voluptuary: **4** roué **7** playboy **8** hedonist, sybarite **9** bon vivant, libertine
volute: **4** coil **5** helix, shell, twist, whorl **6** spiral **8** seashell **9** corkscrew
imperial ~: **5** shell **8** seashell
Volvo: **3** car **4** auto **10** automobile
competitor: **4** Saab
like a ~: **7** Swedish
__ vomica: **3** nux
Von __ Express: **5** Ryan's
von Baeyer, Adolf: **7** chemist **8** Nobelist
von Behring, Emil: **8** Nobelist
von Bismarck: **4** Otto
von Braun: **7** Wernher **9** rocketeer
contemporary: **3** Ley
von Bülow: **4** Hans **5** Claus, Sunny
portrayer: **5** Close, Irons
von Clausewitz: **4** Carl
Vonda: **7** Shepard **8** McIntyre
von Euler, Ulf: **8** Nobelist
von Frisch, Karl: **8** Nobelist
von Fürstenberg: **4** Egon **5** Diane
von Hindenburg: **4** Paul
von Karajan, Herbert: **8** Austrian **9** conductor
Von Kempelen and His Discovery
author: Edgar Allan Poe
von Laue, Max: **8** Nobelist **9** physicist
von Leibnitz: **7** Wilhelm
Vonnegut Jr., Kurt: **6** writer
work: Bluebeard
Breakfast of Champions
Cat's Cradle
Deadeye Dick
Galápagos
Happy Birthday, Wanda June
Hocus Pocus
Jailbird
Mother Night
Player Piano
The Sirens of Titan
Slapstick
Slaughterhouse-Five

von Richthofen: **3** ace **5** baron **6** German **7** Manfred **8** Red Baron
Von Ryan's Express (1965 film)
cast: Trevor Howard, Frank Sinatra
von Schiller: **9** Friedrich
von Stade: **9** Frederica
von Stroheim: **5** Erich
von Suttner, Bertha: **8** Nobelist
von Sydow: **3** Max
von Trapp: **5** Maria
von Weber: **4** Carl **5** Maria
von Webern: **5** Anton
Von Zell: **5** Harry
Von Zeppelin: **9** Ferdinand
voodoo: **3** hex, obi **5** magic, obeah, spell, vodun **7** sorcery **10** witchcraft
amulet: **4** mojo
country: **5** Haiti
__-voom!: **4** Va-va
voracious: **4** avid **5** eager, piggy, unfed **6** greedy, hungry, piggie **7** gorging, lustful, peckish, piggish, starved **8** edacious, esurient, famished, grasping, ravening, ravenous, starving **9** devouring, dog-hungry, ferocious, insatiate, predatory, rapacious, vulturous **10** gluttonous, insatiable, omnivorous, prodigious
voracity: **5** greed **6** desire, hunger **7** edacity **8** appetite, cupidity, gluttony, yearning **9** eagerness
Vorobyeva: **5** Irina
vortex: **4** eddy, gyre, tide, wind **9** maelstrom, whirlpool
Vosges: **5** range
capital: **6** Épinal
region: **6** Alsace
__ vos jeux: **6** faites
Vos Savant: **7** Marilyn
__ vostra salute!: **4** Alla
votary: **3** fan **4** buff **6** adorer, backer, patron **7** admirer, booster, devotee **8** adherent, advocate, defender, follower, partisan **9** proponent, religious, supporter **10** enthusiast
vote: **2** ay, no **3** aye, nay, opt, yea, yes **4** poll **5** elect, enact, voice **6** ballot, choice, choose, decide **8** decide on, majority, suffrage **9** determine, franchise **10** plebiscite, referendum, settle upon
against: **2** no **3** con, nay **4** veto
for: **2** ay **3** aye, yea, yes **5** elect **6** assent, choose
in: **4** pass, pick **5** elect
one too young to ~: **4** baby **5** child, minor, youth **6** infant, junior **8** juvenile, underage **9** schoolboy, youngster **10** adolescent, schoolgirl
right to ~: **6** ballot **9** franchise
seeker: **3** pol **9** candidate
solicit a ~: **4** urge **5** lobby **8** campaign
stockholder's ~: **5** proxy
straw ~: **4** poll **6** survey
__ vote: **5** straw, voice **7** popular, protest, write-in
voted: **3** x'ed
voter: **6** native **7** citizen, denizen, elector **8** resident, taxpayer **10** inhabitant

no ~: **8** opponent
type of ~: **3** Dem., Ind., Lib., Rep. **7** Liberal **8** Democrat **10** Republican
__ voter law: 5 motor
voters: 6 public **7** country **8** citizens, populace **9** citizenry **10** electorate
voting: 4 poll **5** count, tally **6** ballot, option, sample, survey **7** canvass **8** choosing, election **9** balloting, franchise **10** referendum
age: 8 majority **9** adulthood
booth closer: 3 bar **5** lever
district: 4 ward **8** precinct
group: 4 bloc **5** party **7** council, faction **8** alliance **9** coalition **10** federation
power: 5 agent, proxy **8** delegate
voting __: 5 booth
votive __: 4 Mass
__ votre permission: 4 avec
...votre santé: 5 toast **6** French
vouch: 4 avow, back **5** swear **6** affirm, assert, assure, attest, pledge, uphold, verify **7** certify, confirm, declare, profess, promise, swear to, testify, warrant, witness **8** attest to, maintain **9** guarantee **10** asseverate
ender: 4 safe
for: 6 affirm, assure, attest, depone, verify **7** certify, confirm, endorse, indorse, sponsor, testify, warrant, witness **8** accredit, attest to, sanction, validate **9** guarantee, recommend, testify to
voucher: 3 tag **4** chit, rcpt. **5** alibi, paper **6** coupon, credit, ticket **7** receipt **9** indenture
vouchsafe: 4 give **5** deign, grant **6** accord, bestow **10** condescend
vous __: 4 etes
__-vous français?: 6 Parlez
__ vous plaît: 3 s'il
vow: 4 aver, oath, word **5** swear, troth **6** affirm, assert, assure, pledge, plight **7** declare, promise, warrant **8** affiance, covenant **9** assurance, guarantee **10** commitment, engagement
giver: 4 mate, monk **5** bride, groom
marriage ~: 3 I do
take a ~: 3 wed **5** marry **10** get hitched
venue: 5 altar **6** chapel
vowel: 6 letter
disappearance: 7 aphesis
French ~ sound: 5 nasal
Greek ~: 3 eta **4** iota **5** alpha, omega **7** epsilon, omicron
group: 5 AEIOU
mark: 5 breve **6** macron, umlaut
sometime ~: 3 wye
sound: 4 shwa **5** schwa
vox __: 3 Dei, pop. **6** humana, populi
Vox Pop: 9 radio show
voyage: 4 sail, tour, trip **5** jaunt, quest **6** cruise, flight, junket, travel **7** journey, passage **8** crossing, navigate **10** expedition
on a ~: 4 asea **5** at sea
__ voyage: 3 bon **6** maiden
__ Voyage Home, The: 4 Long
voyager: 5 farer, rover **7** tourist **8** traveler, wanderer, wayfarer **9** journeyer, passenger **10** adventurer, vacationer
Voyager: 3 car, van **4** auto **5** probe **7** Mercury **8** Plymouth **10** spacecraft
__, Voyager: 3 Now
Voyager org.: 4 NASA
Voyage to the Bottom of the Sea (ABC sci-fi)
cast: Richard Basehart (Adm. Harriman Nelson)
David Hedison (Capt. Lee Crane)
producer: Irwin Allen
Voyage to the Center of the Earth, A
author: Jules Verne
Voyageurs: 4 park
locale: 9 Minnesota
voyaging: 4 asea **5** at sea **9** wayfaring **10** navigation
Voyna i __: 3 mir
V.P.
'70s ~: 3 GRF, NAR, STA
part of: 4 vice **9** president
Vries, Hugo De: 5 Dutch **8** botanist
Vronsky girl: 4 Anna
vroom maker: 5 motor **6** engine **7** turbine
vs.: 3 opp. **7** against **8** opposite
V.S.: 7 Naipaul **9** Pritchett
Vsevolod: 6 Ivanov
v-shaped: 7 angular, notched **8** angulose, angulous
__ vs. the Red Baron: 6 Snoopy
__ vs. Wade: 3 Roe
Vt.
clock setting: 3 EDT, EST
neighbor: 3 Que. **4** Mass.
region: 4 N. Eng.
see also Vermont
VTOL: 5 plane
user: 4 USAF
__ vu: 4 déjà
Vue: 3 SUV **6** Saturn
Vulcan: 3 god **5** Sarek, Spock
equivalent: 10 Hephaestus
forge: 4 Etna **5** Aetna
mother: 4 Juno
wife: 4 Maia
vulcanize: 6 harden **8** indurate **10** strengthen
vulcanized __: 6 rubber
vulcanologist concern: 4 lava, rock **5** magma
vulgar: 3 bad, low, raw **4** base, blue, foul, lewd, loud, racy, rude, vile **5** bawdy, cheap, crass, crude, dirty, gaudy, gross, nasty, rough, spicy, tacky **6** brassy, coarse, common, filthy, flashy, garish, little, native, public, ribald, risqué, smutty, sordid, spicey, tawdry, unmeet, X-rated **7** bearish, beastly, boorish, ignoble, loutish, lowbred, naughty, obscene, profane, raffish, uncouth **8** barbaric, baseborn, degraded, everyday, familiar, improper, impudent, indecent, off-color, ordinary, plebeian, shameful, tactless, unseemly **9** barbarian, barbarous, idiomatic, inelegant, low-minded, lubricous, offensive, tasteless, unrefined **10** colloquial, disgusting, indecorous, indelicate, scurrilous, ungracious, unmannerly, unpolished, vernacular
vulgarian: 3 cad, cur **4** boor, heel, lout, worm **5** brute, churl, knave, rogue, scamp **6** rascal **7** parvenu, peasant, upstart **9** arriviste, miscreant, reprobate, scoundrel **10** blackguard
vulgarity: 5 filth **7** crudity **8** lewdness **9** barbarity, grossness, indecency **10** coarseness, corruption, smuttiness
Vulgate: 5 Bible
vulnerability: 5 peril **8** jeopardy, weakness **9** liability
vulnerable: 4 open, puny, weak **5** frail, naked, wimpy **6** anemic, atonic, effete, feeble, flabby, flimsy, liable, tender, unsafe **7** anaemic, exposed, fragile, parlous, subject, wimpish **8** delicate, helpless, pervious, pithless, vincible, wide open **9** dangerous, dependant, dependent, faltering, on the spot, powerless, sensitive, unguarded **10** barehanded, undefended, unshielded
vulpine: 3 sly **4** foxy **6** crafty **8** guileful
vulture: 4 bird **6** condor **7** buzzard **9** ossifrage
vulturous: 8 ravaging **9** ferocious, on the hunt, pillaging, predatory, rapacious, voracious **10** plundering, predacious
v.v. part: 4 vice **5** versa
VW: 3 Bug, GTI **4** Golf **5** Jetta **6** Beetle, Cabrio, Passat, Rabbit **7** Eurovan **8** Scirocco
follower: 3 XYZ
preceder: 3 STU **4** RSTU **5** QRSTU
__ v. Wade: 3 Roe

W

W: 3 dir., mag 4 elem., west 6 letter 7 wolfram 8 magazine, tungsten 9 direction
74 for ~: 4 at. no.
follower: 3 XYZ
in phonetic alphabet: 7 Whiskey
preceder: 3 TUV 4 STUV 5 RSTUV
sometimes: 5 vowel
W (2008 film)
cast: Elizabeth Banks, Josh Brolin, Ellen Burstyn, James Cromwell
director: Oliver Stone
W __ wall: 4 as in
W. __ Maugham: 8 Somerset
__ W: 4 C and
W-2: 4 form
ID: 3 SSN
WA
clock setting: 3 PDT, PST
see also Washington
WAAC part: 3 Aux. 5 Corps
__ Waart: 5 Edo de
Wabash: 5 river 6 avenue
locale: 3 Ill., Ind. 4 Ohio 7 Chicago, Indiana 8 Illinois
river to the ~: 10 Tippecanoe
Wabasha: 4 city, town
locale: 9 Minnesota
Wabash Cannonball: 5 train
WAC: 2 GI 6 GI Jane 10 conference
colleague: 3 WAF 4 Wave
school: 3 BYU, SMU 4 Rice, UTEP 5 Tulsa 6 Hawaii, Nevada 10 Boise State 11 Fresno State
Wace: 4 poet 6 Norman
work: Roman de Brut
Wachovia: 4 bank
Wackiest Ship in the Army, The (1960 film)
cast: Jack Lemmon, Ricky Nelson
wacky: 3 odd 4 bats, daft, loco, wild, zany 5 balmy, daffy, flaky, goofy, inane, nutty, silly 6 absurd, flakey, screwy 7 comical, erratic, fatuous, foolish, unsound 8 cockeyed, peculiar, specious 9 eccentric, illogical, off-center, senseless, untenable 10 groundless, irrational, off-the-wall, ridiculous
Waco: 4 city, town
athletes: 5 Bears
locale: 5 Texas
river: 6 Brazos
school: 6 Baylor
wad: 3 gob, pad 4 ball, chaw, chew, glob, heap, hunk, lump, mass, mint, pile, plug, ream, roll, slew, tuft 5 bunch, chunk, clump, money, stuff 6 boodle, bundle, moolah, packet 7 fortune, tobacco 8 bankroll, compress
starter: 5 tight
unit: 3 fin, one, ten 4 five 5 C-note, fiver 7 sawbuck
up: 5 crush 7 crumple
Waddell, Rube: 6 hurler 7 pitcher
wadding: 3 pad 4 fill 7 filling, padding
waddle: 4 limp, plod, roll, sway 6 lumber, toddle, totter, wabble, wobble 7 shuffle
wade: 4 ford, plod, slog, toil 5 bathe, labor, slosh 6 drudge, paddle, splash, tackle, trudge 9 light into
in: 5 begin, start
through: 4 read, slog 5 learn, study 6 peruse 8 pore over
wade __: 4 into
Wade: 4 Adam, peak 5 Boggs, mount 8 mountain, Virginia
locale: 10 Antarctica
opponent: 3 Roe
__ Wade: 4 Roe v. 5 Roe vs.
wader: 4 boot, ibis, rail, shoe 5 crane, egret, heron, snipe, stilt, stork 6 avocet, jacana, plover 8 footwear, overshoe 9 shorebird
Wade, Virginia: 7 netster 9 tennis pro
milieu: 5 court
wadi: 5 gulch, gully 6 arroyo, gulley, ravine
wading __: 4 bird, pool
wading bird: 4 ibis, rail 5 crane, egret, heron, snipe, stilt, stork 6 avocet, jacana, plover 9 shorebird
Wadkins, Lanny: 6 golfer
wads: 4 lots 5 scads 6 oodles, scores
__ Wadsworth Longfellow: 5 Henry
WAF: 5 flier, flyer
wafer: 4 disc, disk 5 cooky, snack 6 cookie 7 biscuit
wafer-__: 4 thin
waferlike: 4 thin 6 narrow 7 slender
__ Wafers: 5 Nilla
waffle: 4 cake, Eggo, sway 5 bread, hedge, shift, waver 6 weasel 7 quibble 8 hesitate 9 hem and haw, vacillate 10 equivocate
topper: 4 oleo 5 sirup, syrup 6 butter
waffle __: 4 iron
waffling: 9 undecided, unsettled 10 indecisive, unresolved
waft: 4 bear, blow, gust, puff, ride 5 carry, drift, float, glide, whiff 6 convey
wag: 3 bob, nod, wit 4 card, flap, lash, rock, sway, wave, zany 5 clown, comic, cutup, joker, shake, swing 6 gossip, jester, kidder, quiver, switch, twitch, wiggle 7 buffoon, farceur, flutter, punster, wise guy 8 banterer, comedian, fish-tail, humorist, jokester, kibitzer, quipster 9 oscillate, pendulate, prankster, vacillate
ender: 4 tail
remark: 3 gag, pun 4 barb, joke, quip 6 zinger
starter: 3 wig
wage: 2 do 3 cut, fee, pay 4 make 5 bacon, bread, money, share 6 income, pursue, return, reward, salary 7 carry on, conduct, payment, stipend 8 earnings, engage in, receipts, take-home 9 emolument, prosecute, undertake 10 recompense
earner: 5 prole 6 worker 7 employe 8 employee
earner cry: 4 TGIF
ender: 6 worker
war: 5 fight 6 battle
wage __: 3 war 5 scale, slave 6 earner
__ wage: 4 base 5 basic 6 annual, living
wager: 3 bet, lay, pot 4 ante, game, play, risk 5 flyer, hedge, put up, stake 6 chance, exacta, gamble, hazard, parlay, pledge, plunge 7 quinela, venture 8 long shot, make book, perfecta, quinella, quiniela, trifecta 9 challenge, speculate
maker: 6 bettor 7 gambler
minimum ~: 4 chip
spot for a ~: 3 OTB 5 track
__ wager: 4 lay a
wages: 3 cut, fee, pay 5 bacon, bread, price, share 6 income, return, reward, salary 7 payment, revenue, stipend 8 earnings, receipts, take-home 9 emolument 10 recompense
collect ~: 4 earn
like some ~: 6 hourly
old-style: 4 meed
slave ~: 7 peanuts 8 pittance
withhold ~: 4 dock
wages of ___, The: 5 sin is
Wages of Sin
author: Andrew Greeley
Wagga Wagga resident: 6 Aussie
wagger: 4 tail
waggery: 4 jape 8 drollery, jocosity, wordplay, zaniness 10 jocularity
waggish: 4 arch 5 droll, funny, silly, witty 6 impish, jocose 7 amusing, comical, jesting, jocular, knavish, playful 8 farcical, humorous 9 facetious, whimsical
waggle: 4 wave 5 shake, swing 9 oscillate
waggling: 5 snaky 6 zigzag 7 crooked, erratic 8 tortuous
Waggoner: 4 Lyle
Wagnalls: 4 Adam
Wagner: 4 Jack 5 Honus 6 Robert 7 Lindsay, Richard
Wagner Act org.: 4 NLRB
Wägner, Elin: 6 writer 7 Swedish
Wagner, Honus: 6 Pirate 9 shortstop
like a ~ baseball card: 4 rare
Wagner, Lindsay: 7 actress
TV: The Bionic Woman
Wagner, Richard
cycle: 4 Ring
father-in-law: 5 Liszt
genre: 5 opera
role: 3 Eva 4 Elsa, Erda, Norn 5 Senta
wife: 5 Minna
work: Die Meistersinger
Die Walküre
The Flying Dutchman
Götterdämmerung
Lohengrin
Parsifal
Rienzi
Siegfried
Tannhaüser
Tristan and Isolde
Wagner, Robert: 5 actor
spouse: Jill St. John, Natalie Wood
TV: Hart to Hart, It Takes a Thief, Switch
TV role: 4 Hart
wagon: 4 cart, dray, wain 5 buggy 7 teacart, tumbrel, tumbril, vehicle 8 carriage, pushcart 10 Radio Flyer
chuck ~: 7 canteen
ender: 4 load
fall off the ~: 5 drink, lapse 6 revert 7 regress, relapse 9 backslide
farm ~: 4 dray, wain
fix one's ~: 6 avenge 7 get back, revenge
go on the ~: 4 quit 7 abstain, refrain
horse and ~: 3 rig
load: 3 hay
on the ~: 5 sober
part: 4 axle, neap 5 sprag
starter: 4 band 6 battle
station ~: 3 car 4 auto 10 automobile
wheels: 5 pasta 8 macaroni
wagon __: 5 train
wagon-__: 3 lit
__ wagon: 3 sag, tea 5 chuck, paddy 7 covered, station
__ Wagon: 7 Welcome
Wagoneer: 3 SUV 4 Jeep
Wagoner: 6 Porter
wagonload: 5 cargo, goods 6 weight 7 freight 8 shipment
__ Wagon, The: 3 War 4 Band, Last
wagon train
direction: 4 west
puller: 4 mule, team
Wagon Train (NBC/ABC western)
cast: Ward Bond (Seth Adams) Robert Horton (Flint McCullough)
Wag the Dog (1997 film)
cast: Robert De Niro, Anne Heche, Dustin Hoffman, Denis Leary
director: Barry Levinson
Wah __, The: 6 Watusi
__ Wah Diddy: 3 Doo
wahine: 4 girl, lady 5 woman 8 Hawaiian
dance: 4 hula
feast: 4 luau
instrument: 3 uke
welcome: 3 lei 5 aloha
Wahl: 3 Ken
Wahlberg: 4 Mark 6 Donnie
Wahlberg, Mark: 5 actor
film: The Big Hit (1998)
Boogie Nights (1997)
Four Brothers (2005)
The Happening (2008)
The Italian Job (2003)
Max Payne (2008)
The Perfect Storm (2000)
Planet of the Apes (2001)
Rock Star (2001)
Shooter (2007)
Three Kings (1999)
We Own the Night (2007)
wahoo: 3 cry 4 fish, peto, tree, yell 6 yippee 8 mackerel
__ wahr: 5 nicht
Wah Watusi, The (1962 song)
artist: Orlons
waif: 3 kid 4 calf, dogy 5 dogey, dogie, gamin, stray 6 orphan, urchin 9 foundling 10 ragamuffin, street Arab
Waikiki
feast: 4 luau
locale: 4 Oahu 6 Hawaii 8 Honolulu

music maker: 3 uke
ride: 4 wave
welcome: 3 lei 5 aloha
wail: 3 bay, cry, sob 4 bawl, bray, fuss, howl, keen, kick, mewl, moan, pule, weep, yell, yowl 5 mourn, whine 6 bellow, bemoan, bewail, boohoo, grieve, holler, lament, repine, scream, shriek, snivel, squall, squeal 7 blubber, carry on, deplore, ululate, whimper 8 complain 9 caterwaul, make a fuss, shed tears, ululation 10 vociferate
wailer: 5 siren 7 banshee
wailing: 5 noisy, tears 6 lament 8 mourning 9 querulous 10 waterworks
wain: 4 cart 5 wagon
ender: 4 scot 6 wright
Wain: 3 Bea 4 John
Wain, John: 4 poet 6 writer 7 British
work: Hurry on Down
wainscot: 5 panel
Wainwright: 5 James, Rufus 6 Loudon
battleground: 6 Bataan
waist: 6 bodice, middle 8 beltline 10 midsection
ender: 4 band, coat, line 5 cloth
pincher: 6 corset
size: 4 girt 5 girth
starter: 5 shirt
waist-__: 4 deep, high
__ waist: 4 wasp
waistband: 4 belt, sash 6 girdle
waistcoat: 4 vest
waistline reducer: 4 diet 6 corset
wait: 3 sit 4 bide, halt, hang, lurk, rest, stay 5 abide, await, dally, delay, hover, pause, poise, stall, tarry, watch 6 cool it, expect, hold on, holdup, hole up, lie low, linger, loiter, remain 7 interim, look for, stand by, sweat it 8 downtime, hesitate, interval, mark time, sit tight, sweat out 9 interlude 10 anticipate, hang around, standstill
after a ~: 6 at last 7 finally
around: 4 loll, stay 5 abide, hover, tarry 6 dawdle, linger, loiter, remain 7 hang out, sojourn
don't ~: 3 act 5 cut in
ender: 5 staff 6 people, person
for: 6 expect, plan on 7 count on 10 anticipate
in line: 5 stand
lie in ~: 4 lurk 5 sculk, skulk 6 waylay 8 surprise
on: 4 help, tend 5 nurse, serve 6 assist, attend, tend to 7 care for, cater to, deliver, service 8 attend to, minister 10 minister to
on the phone: 4 hold
out: 5 abide 6 endure, suffer 7 stomach, survive 8 stand for 9 withstand
partner: 3 see
wait __: 6 tables
__ wait: 5 lie in
Wait __ the Sun Shines, Nellie: 3 'Til
__ Wait: 3 I'll 5 I Can't
wait a __: 3 bit, sec 6 minute, moment
Wait a minute!: 3 hey 4 stop
wait and __: 3 see
Waite: 4 Hoyt, John 5 Ralph
waiter: 4 mozo 6 carhop, garçon, server
aide: 6 busboy
at times: 5 adder
burden: 4 tray 5 order, plate
help a ~: 3 bus
inattentive ~ reward: 5 no tip
injunction: 5 enjoy
offering: 4 menu
one way to call a ~: 4 ahem
reward: 3 tip
starter: 4 dumb, head
waiting: 5 on tap, ready 6 in line 7 abeyant 8 abeyance 9 expectant
area: 5 depot, lobby, queue 6 lounge 7 ingress
in the wings: 5 ready 9 available
waiting __: 4 game, list, room 6 period
__ waiting: 4 call
Waiting for Godot: 4 play
author: Samuel Beckett
cast: Bert Lahr, Tom Ewell
character: 4 Didi, Gogo 5 Pozzo 8 Estragon, Vladimir
Waiting for Lefty: 4 play 8 one-acter
author: Clifford Odets
Waiting for the Robert __: 4 E. Lee
Waiting for Tonight (1999 song)
artist: Jennifer Lopez
Waiting on a Friend (1981 song)
artist: Rolling Stones
waiting room
cry: 4 next
reading: 3 mag 8 magazine
Waiting, The (1981 song)
artist: Tom Petty and the Heartbreakers
Waiting to Exhale (1995 film)
cast: Angela Bassett, Whitney Houston, Lela Rochon
waitperson
see waiter
Waits: 3 Tom
waits for no one, it: 4 time
Wait Until Dark (1967 film)
cast: Alan Arkin, Richard Crenna, Audrey Hepburn
composer: Henry Mancini
Waitz, Grete: 6 runner 9 Norwegian 10 marathoner
waive: 4 cede, stay 5 defer, delay, forgo, grant, let go, remit, table, yield 6 forego, give up, hold up, pass up, put off, resign, shelve 7 abandon, decline, suspend 8 disclaim, hand over, overlook, postpone, prorogue, renounce, set aside, sign away, turn down 9 disregard, surrender 10 relinquish
waiver: 7 release 9 dismissal 10 abdication, disclaimer
Wajda: 7 Andrzej
wake: 3 see 4 call, prod, rise, stir, wash 5 arise, get up, liven, nudge, pep up, rally, renew, rouse, shake, track, trail, train, vigil, waves 6 arouse, bestir, come to, excite, fire up, kindle, revive, stir up 7 enliven, freshen, quicken, ripples, roll out, turn out 8 backwash 9 aftermath, galvanize, obsequies, stimulate, tumble out 10 understand
in the ~ of: 5 after, due to 6 astern 7 owing to 9 following
one up: 8 disabuse, set right
Wake __: 6 Forest, Island
Wake __ Dream: 5 Up and
Wakefield: 4 city, town
cleric: 5 vicar
locale: 7 England 9 Yorkshire
Wake Forest: 10 university
conference: 3 ACC
wakeful: 4 wary 5 alert, alive, astir 7 careful, heedful, on guard 8 open-eyed, restless, vigilant, watchful, wide-eyed 9 attentive, insomniac, observant, sleepless, wide-awake 10 on the alert, unsleeping
Wake Me Up Before You Go-Go (1984 song)
artist: George Michael
waken: 3 see 4 call, prod, rise, stir 5 arise, get up, liven, nudge, pep up, rally, renew, rouse, roust, shake 6 arouse, bestir, come to, excite, fire up, kindle, recall, revive, stir up, wake up 7 enliven, freshen, provoke, quicken, roll out, turn out 9 galvanize, recollect, stimulate, tumble out 10 understand
__ wake of: 5 in the
waker-upper: 4 java 5 alarm, latte 6 coffee
wake-up
call: 5 alarm
time: 2 a.m. 7 morning
Wake Up Everybody (1975 song)
artist: Harold Melvin and the Blue Notes
Wake Up Little Susie (1957 song)
artist: Everly Brothers
Waking __ Devine: 3 Ned
waking dream, a: 4 hope
Waking, The
author: Theodore Roethke
Waking the Dead (2000 film)
cast: Jennifer Connelly, Billy Crudup, Hal Holbrook
waking up: 5 astir
Waksman, Selman: 8 Nobelist
Walbrook: 5 Anton
Walburga: 5 saint
Walcott: 3 Joe 5 boxer, Derek 9 Jersey Joe
Walcott, Jersey Joe: 5 boxer
milieu: 4 ring
opponent: 7 Charles
Wald: 5 Jerry 6 George
Walden: 4 pond 6 Robert
author: Henry David Thoreau
Waldheim: 4 Kurt
Waldo: 5 Janet
uncle: 5 Magoo 6 Quincy
__ Waldo?: 6 Where's
__ Waldo Emerson: 5 Ralph
__ Waldo Pepper, The: 5 Great
Waldorf: 5 salad
ingredient: 4 mayo, nuts 5 apple 6 celery
Waldorf-Astoria: 5 hotel
Waldstein Sonata
composer: Ludwig van Beethoven
wale: 3 rib 4 welt 5 ridge 8 swelling
Wales
bay: 8 Cardigan
capital: 7 Cardiff
cheese: 10 caerphilly
city: 4 Rhyl 5 Neath 7 Cardiff, Newport, Swansea 8 Holyhead, Llanelly
dog: 5 corgi
golfer: 7 Woosnam
historian: 7 Nennius
John, in ~: 4 Evan
land west of ~: 4 Eire
language: 6 Celtic
meter: 6 cywydd
natives: 5 Cymry, Kymry
poet: 7 Herbert
product: 4 coal
river: 3 Dee, Usk, Wye
saint: 5 David
symbol: 4 leek
waterfall: 7 Rhaiadr
writer: 3 Map 4 Abse 6 Thomas 7 Nennius 8 Williams
Walesa, Lech: 4 Pole 8 Nobelist
Walgreen
rival: 3 CVS 7 Rite-Aid
walk: 3 pad, way 4 file, gait, hike, lane, mall, move, pace, path, pier, plod, road, roam, rove, slog, step, tour, trek, turn, wend, work 5 aisle, alley, amble, byway, court, dance, field, jaunt, leg it, march, mosey, paseo, scuff, slink, stalk, strut, stump, track, trail, tramp, tread, troop 6 by-path, canter, career, escort, foot it, go free, hoof it, junket, lumber, parade, patrol, prance, ramble, region, stride, stroll, toddle, trapes, travel, trudge, wander 7 advance, calling, circuit, gangway, meander, passage, pathway, saunter, schlepp, shamble, shuffle, swagger, traipse 8 ambulate, carriage, cloister, crossing, exercise, footpath, pavement, platform, traverse, vocation 9 esplanade, promenade, territory 10 beat the rap, discipline, hit the road, knock about, profession
a beat: 5 guard 6 patrol
all over: 5 abuse 6 berate, dump on 7 rough up 8 belittle, ill-treat, mistreat 9 deprecate, disparage, victimize 10 disrespect
a tightrope: 4 dare
destination: 5 first
down the aisle: 3 wed 5 marry 10 tie the knot
ender: 3 out, way 4 away, over 5 about
heavily: 4 plod, slog 5 clomp, clump, pound, stomp, tramp, tromp 6 lumber
in: 5 enter 6 arrive
in Spanish: 4 anda
in water: 4 wade 5 slosh
like a duck: 6 waddle
off with: 5 filch, steal 6 pilfer, thieve
of life: 4 turf, work 5 field, orbit, realm 6 career, métier, milieu, sphere 7 calling, purview, station 8 province, vocation 9 bailiwick 10 occupation, profession
on air: 5 exult
on eggs: 6 tiptoe 9 pussyfoot
on tiptoe: 5 creep, sneak
out: 4 exit, quit 5 leave, split 6 picket, resign, strike
out on: 4 quit 6 desert 7 abandon, forsake 8 forswear 9 foreswear, throw over
over: 7 trounce 10 kick around

ready to ~: 5 fed up
sidewise: 4 crab
starter: 3 cat, jay, sky 4 cake, moon, rope, side 5 board, cross, sleep
take a ~: 2 go 4 quit 5 leave
the line: 4 heed, obey 6 listen, submit
through: 8 practice, rehearse
tiredly: 4 plod, slog 6 lumber, trudge
unsteadily: 4 limp, reel 6 teeter, totter 7 stagger
walk __: 3 out 4 over 5 on air, out on 6 on eggs, shorts 7 through
walk __ from: 4 away
walk __ on: 3 out
walk __ with: 3 off
__ walk: 4 bird 5 take a 6 Castle, nature, random, widow's 7 Lambeth
__-walk: 4 duck, hand, race
Walk __: 4 On By
Walk __ a Man: 4 Like
Walk __ In: 5 Right
Walk __ in My Shoes: 5 a Mile
Walk __ Man: 5 Like a
Walk __ Moon, A: 5 on the
Walk __ Renee: 4 Away
Walk __ way: 4 this
Walk __ Wild Side: 5 on the
Walk, __ Run: 4 Don't
__ Walk: 4 Don't
Walk a Mile in My Shoes (1970 song)
artist: Joe South
walk away __: 4 from
Walk Away Renee (1966 song)
artist: Left Banke
Walk, Don't Run (1966 film)
cast: Samantha Eggar, Cary Grant, Jim Hutton
setting: 5 Japan
Walk-Don't Run (1960 song)
artist: Ventures
__ Walked In: 4 Love
__ Walked Into My Life: 4 If He
Walken, Christopher: 5 actor
film: The Addiction (1995)
At Close Range (1986)
Batman Returns (1992)
Biloxi Blues (1988)
Blast From the Past (1999)
Brainstorm (1983)
Catch Me If You Can (2002)
Click (2006)
The Dead Zone (1983)
The Deer Hunter (1978, AA)
The Dogs of War (1980)
Man on Fire (2004)
Pennies From Heaven (1981)
Scotland, Pa. (2002)
Suicide Kings (1998)
A View to a Kill (1985)
walker: 3 ped. 10 pedestrian
starter: 3 jay 4 wire 5 floor, track
Walker: 3 Hal 4 Ally, Doak, John, Mort, town 5 Alice, Clint, Evans, Larry, Marcy, Nancy, Percy, T-Bone 6 Jimmie, Junior, Robert 8 Herschel, Margaret
Walker __: 3 Cup
Walker, Alice: 6 writer
work: The Color Purple
Meridian
Walker, Clint: 5 actor
TV: Cheyenne
Walker, John: 7 chemist 8 Nobelist
Walker, Larry
sport: 8 baseball
Walker, Margaret: 6 writer
work: Jubilee
Walker, Robert: 5 actor
Walker, Texas Ranger (CBS western)
cast: Clarence Gilyard (Jimmy Trivette)
Chuck Norris (Cord Walker)
Noble Willingham (C.D. Parker)
Sheree J. Wilson (Alex Cahill)
Walker Through Walls, The
author: Marcel Aymé
Walk Hand in Hand (1956 song)
artist: Tony Martin
__ Walk Home, The: 4 Long
walkie-talkie: 5 radio
word: 4 over 5 roger
walk-in __: 6 closet
Walkin' After Midnight (1957 song)
artist: Patsy Cline
walking
combining form: 5 -grade
in heraldry: 7 passant
leaf: 3 bug 4 fern 6 insect
manner of ~: 4 gait, pace, step
on air: 4 glad, high 5 happy, merry 6 blithe, cheery, elated, jovial, joyful, joyous, upbeat 7 gleeful, pleased, tickled 8 blissful, cheerful, ecstatic, euphoric, exultant, jubilant, mirthful, thrilled 9 delighted, overjoyed, rapturous, rejoicing, rhapsodic
on eggs: 8 cautious
papers: 5 the ax 8 pink slip
shoe: 4 flat
starter: 3 jay 5 sleep
stealthily: 4 atip
stick: 3 bug 4 cane 5 staff 6 insect
walking __: 4 bass, beam, fern, fish, leaf, line, tall 5 horse, on air, stick 6 papers, shorts
walking-__ money: 6 around
Walking __ Orleans: 5 to New
Walking Man, The: Eddie Yost
walking on __: 3 air 4 eggs
walking-on-air feeling: 3 joy 5 bliss 7 ecstasy, elation, rapture 8 euphoria, gladness 9 happiness
Walking on a Thin Line (1984 song)
artist: Huey Lewis and the News
Walking on Broken Glass (1992 song)
artist: Annie Lennox
Walking on Sunshine (1985 song)
artist: Katrina and the Waves
Walking on Thin Ice (1981 song)
artist: Yoko Ono
Walking to New Orleans (1960 song)
artist: Fats Domino
Walkin' in the Rain... (1972 song)
artist: Love Unlimited
Walk in the Clouds, A (1995 film)
cast: Anthony Quinn, Keanu Reeves
director: Alfonso Arau
Walkin' the Floor Over You (song)
artist: Ernest Tubb
Walk Like a Man (1963 song)
artist: Four Seasons
Walk Like an Egyptian (1986 song)
artist: Bangles
Walkman: 4 Sony 5 radio 6 stereo
successor: 4 iPod
walk of __: 4 life
walk off __: 4 with
Walk of Fame embedment: 4 star
Walk of Life (1985 song)
artist: Dire Straits
walk on __: 3 air 4 eggs
walk-on: 4 part, role, supe 5 cameo, extra 6 player 7 bit part
Walk On By (song)
artist: Dionne Warwick, Leroy Van Dyke
Walk on the Moon, A (1999 film)
cast: Diane Lane, Viggo Mortensen, Anna Paquin, Liev Schreiber
Walk on the Wild Side (1973 song)
artist: Lou Reed
Walk on the Wild Side, A
author: Nelson Algren
Walk on Water (1988 song)
artist: Eddie Money
walkout: 6 strike 8 stoppage 9 departure, job action
walkover: 4 rout, snap 6 picnic, simple 7 success, triumph
Walk Right Back (1961 song)
artist: Everly Brothers
Walk Right In (1963 song)
artist: Rooftop Singers
__ walks in beauty...: 3 She
walk the __: 4 line 5 plank
walk the dog toy: 4 yo-yo
Walk the Line (2005 film)
cast: Joaquin Phoenix, Reese Witherspoon
Walk This Way (song)
artist: Aerosmith, Run-D.M.C.
walk-through: 9 rehearsal
Walk to Remember, A (2002 film)
cast: Peter Coyote, Daryl Hannah, Mandy Moore
walk-up: 3 apt 4 flat 9 apartment
__ Walküre: 3 Die
walkway: 4 hall, lane, path, ramp 5 aisle, alley 7 ingress 8 footpath 9 esplanade
covered ~: 4 stoa 6 arcade
wall: 3 dam 4 dike, side 5 fence, hem in, levee, panel 6 escarp, facade, screen, septum 7 barrier, bastion, bulwark, defense, divider, enclose, inclose, parapet, rampart, surface 8 bulkhead, membrane, obstacle, palisade, paneling, retainer, stockade 9 barricade, hindrance, partition, roadblock 10 battlement, embankment, impediment
Biblical ~ word: 4 mene 5 tekel
classroom ~ hanging: 3 map
climber: 4 vine
column: 4 anta
covering: 4 tile 5 paint, panel 6 stucco
decoration: 4 dado 5 arras 7 drapery
defensive ~: 6 bailey 7 ballium 9 barricade
display: 3 art 5 arras, mural, op art 7 picture 8 painting
dividing ~: 6 septum
drive up the ~: 3 bug, irk, nag 4 rile 5 annoy, peeve 6 enrage, harass, pester 7 torment, trouble
ender: 3 eye 4 eyed, less 5 board, paper 6 flower 8 papering
fixture: 4 rack, safe
hanging: 3 art 5 arras, litho, photo, pin-up, shelf, tapis 6 cobweb, sconce 7 diploma, picture 8 painting
in: 6 immure 7 enclose, inclose
in jai alai: 6 rebote
like some ~s: 4 viny 5 ivied
off: 4 shut 6 screen, seal up 7 confine 8 imprison 9 partition
off the ~: 5 daffy, hyper, weird 7 strange
recess: 5 niche 6 alcove
sea ~: 4 dike 5 levee 10 breakwater
starter: 3 dry, sea 4 fire, foot, side 5 flood, stone
to wall: 9 extensive
triangular ~: 5 gable
up against the ~: 7 trapped
writing on the ~: 4 omen, sign 7 portent, warning 8 graffiti
wall __: 3 box, rue 4 fern, plug, rock, tent, unit 5 plate 6 socket
__ wall: 3 dry, sea 4 cell, fire, pack, rock 5 blank, flood, gable, party, up the
Wall: 2 St. 3 Art 6 Street
__ Wall: 4 High 6 Berlin 7 Chinese, Mending, Western
wallaby: 3 'roo 6 animal, mammal 9 marsupial
female: 4 jill
male: 4 jack
relative: *see* marsupial
young: 4 joey
Wallace: 3 Dee, Lew 4 Ford, Mike 5 Beery, Edgar, Jerry, Shawn 6 Dewitt, George, Irving, Marcia 7 Langham, Richard, Stegner, Stevens, William 9 Carothers
colleague: 5 Kroft, Safer, Stahl 6 Rooney 7 Bradley
specialty: 4 list
Wallace, Dee: 7 actress
film: Cujo (1983)
E.T. The Extra-Terrestrial (1982)
The Howling (1981)
Wallace, Edgar: 6 writer
work: King Kong
The Terror
Wallace, Jerry
song: Primrose Lane (1959)
Wallace, Lew: 6 writer
work: Ben-Hur
Wallach: Eli: 5 actor
spouse: Anne Jackson
Wallach, Otto: 7 chemist 8 Nobelist
wallaroo: 4 euro 6 animal, mammal 9 marsupial
relative: *see* marsupial
Walla Walla: 4 city, town
locale: 10 Washington
__ Wallbanger: 6 Harvey
Wallenda: 4 Karl 7 aerobat 9 aerialist
walkway: 4 wire 8 high wire
Waller, Edmund: 4 poet 7 British
work: Go, Lovely Rose
Waller, Fats: 7 pianist 8 composer
genre: 4 jazz
real first name: 6 Thomas
wallet: 8 billfold
item: 2 ID 3 one, ten 4 bill, five 6 dollar
lifter: 3 dip 10 pickpocket
Walley: 7 Deborah
walleye: 4 dory, fish, pike 7 pollock 8 John Dory

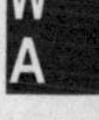

wallflower: 4 herb 5 loner, plant 9 introvert
like a ~: 3 shy 5 timid 8 reticent, retiring, unsocial 9 withdrawn 10 unsociable
not a ~: 5 mixer
Wallflowers
member: Jakob Dylan
song: One Headlight (1997)
Wallis: 3 Hal 5 Shani 7 Simpson 8 Warfield
Wallis and __ Islands: 6 Futuna
__ Wall of China: 5 Great
wallop: 3 bam, bop, hit, jar, tan, zap 4 bang, bash, beat, belt, best, blow, boff, clip, deck, drub, jolt, kick, lick, pelt, rout, slam, slap, slog, slug, sock, swat, trim, wham, whip 5 baste, blast, clout, crush, knock, paste, pound, punch, shock, smack, smash, smite, spank, swipe, thump, whack, whang, whomp 6 attack, batter, buffet, defeat, hammer, impact, pommel, pummel, strike, thrash, thwack 7 clobber, lambast, shellac, take out, trounce 8 haymaker, lambaste, shellack, vanquish
packing a ~: 5 harsh 6 potent 8 powerful
walloping: 3 big 4 huge 7 massive
wallow: 4 bask, loll, roll, slop 5 enjoy, glory, lie in, lurch, pitch, revel 6 relish, roll in, splash 7 delight, immerse 8 flounder 9 luxuriate
in: 4 brag, crow, teem 5 gloat 6 abound 7 swagger
wallpaper
put up ~: 4 hang 5 paste
unit: 4 bolt, roll
wall rue: 4 fern
__ Walls: 4 Four 5 Hello
walls have __, the: 4 ears
Wall St. Lays __: 5 an Egg
Wall Street: 6 market
arena: 4 AMEX, NYSE
asset: 3 stk. 4 bond 5 stock
concern: 3 yld. 5 yield 6 growth
decline: 3 dip 5 slide 7 falloff
dread: 5 crash, panic
good news on ~: 5 rally, runup
initials: 3 IPO, LBO, OTC 4 DJIA
locale: 3 NYC 7 New York 9 Manhattan
membership: 4 seat
name: 3 Dow, Dun
optimist: 4 bull
option: 3 put 4 call
order: 3 buy 4 sell
pessimist: 4 bear
phrase: 5 at par, no par
publication: 6 Forbes 7 Barron's, Fortune
unit: 3 shr. 5 share
volatility measure: 4 beta
watchdog: 3 SEC
worker: 3 arb, MBA 6 broker 7 analyst
Wall Street (1987 film)
cast: Michael Douglas, Daryl Hannah, Hal Holbrook, Charlie Sheen, Martin Sheen
director: Oliver Stone
theme: 5 greed
Wall, The
author: John Hersey
wall-to-wall: 6 carpet, loaded, packed 7 crowded 9 extensive, inclusive
Wally: 3 Cox 4 Amos 7 Cleaver, Schirra 8 Westmore
Walmart
rival: 5 Kohl's, Sears 6 Penney
Walmsley: 3 Jon
walnut: 4 tree, wood 5 brown 7 hickory, reddish
innards: 4 meat
relative: *see* brown color
__ walnut: 5 maple
Walnut Creek: 4 city, town
locale: 10 California
Walpole: 4 earl, Hugh 6 Horace, Robert
Walpole, Horace: 6 writer 7 British 9 historian
work: The Castle of Otranto
Walpole, Hugh: 3 Sir 6 writer 7 British
work: Mr. Perrin and Mr. Traill
Walpurgis __: 5 Night
walrus: 6 animal, mammal
feature: 4 musk, tusk
female: 3 cow
kin: 4 seal 7 sea lion
male: 4 bull
young: 3 pup
Walsh: 2 Ed, J.T. 3 Joe, Kay 4 Bill, peak 5 mount, Raoul 8 mountain
locale: 5 Yukon 6 Canada
Walston, Ray: 5 actor
film: Damn Yankees (1958)
Kiss Me, Stupid (1964)
Paint Your Wagon (1969)
Popeye (1980)
South Pacific (1958)
TV: My Favorite Martian, Picket Fences
__-walsy: 5 palsy
Walt: 4 Kuhn 5 Kelly 6 Disney 7 Bellamy, Frazier, Whitman
Walt __ World: 6 Disney
Walter: 3 Map 4 Abel, Camp, Egan, Hess, Hill, Hunt, Kerr, Kohn, Lang, Reed 5 Bruno, Hagen, Lantz, Mitty, Pater, Scott 6 Alston, Carlos, Farley, Huston, Koenig, Murphy, Payton, Piston, Slezak, Wanger 7 Brennan, Catlett, Gilbert, Gropius, Haworth, Jessica, Johnson, Matthau, Mirisch, Mondale, Pidgeon, Raleigh 8 Brattain, Chrysler, Connolly, Cronkite, Damrosch, Lippmann, Winchell 9 Annenberg
successor: 3 Dan
Walter __ Army Medical Center: 4 Reed
Walter __ Disney: 5 Elias
Walter __ Mare: 4 de la
Walter, Bruno: 7 maestro 9 conductor
Walter, Jessica
spouse: Ron Leibman
Walters: 5 Bucky, Julie 7 Barbara, Charles
Walters, Barbara: 4 host 6 anchor 8 reporter 10 journalist
network: 3 ABC
Walters, Julie: 7 actress
film: Billy Elliot (2000)
Car Trouble (1985)
Educating Rita (1983)
The Wedding Gift (1993)
Waltham: 4 city, town
locale: 4 Mass.
Walther: 5 Bothe 6 Nernst
Walton: 3 Sam 4 Bill 5 Izaak 6 Ernest
Walton, Bill: 5 cager
milieu: 5 court
org.: 3 NBA
sport: 10 basketball
Walton, Ernest: 8 Nobelist 9 physicist
Walton, Izaak: 6 writer 7 British 9 fisherman
need: 3 rod
work: The Compleat Angler
Waltons, The (CBS drama)
cast: Joe Conley (Ike Godsey)
Ellen Corby (Esther Walton)
Will Geer (Zeb Walton)
David W. Harper (Jim Bob Walton)
Kami Kotler (Elizabeth Walton)
Michael Learned (Olivia Walton)
Mary McDonough (Erin Walton)
Judy Norton-Taylor (Mary Ellen Walton)
Eric Scott (Ben Walton)
Richard Thomas (John Boy Walton)
Ralph Waite (John Walton)
Jon Walmsley (Jason Walton)
dog: 8 Reckless
narrator: Earl Hamner Jr.
waltz: 5 dance, glide, music, valse 6 prance
predecessor: 7 ländler
through: 3 ace
variation: 6 Boston
waltz __: 4 time
__ Waltz: 6 Devil's, Minute 7 Emperor
Waltz, Christoph: 5 actor
film: Inglourious Basterds (2009, AA)
Waltzing Cat, The
composer: Leroy Anderson
Wambaugh, Joseph: 5 ex-cop 6 writer
work: The Blooding
The Delta Star
Echoes in the Darkness
Finnegan's Week
Floaters
Fugitive Nights
The Glitter Dome
The Golden Orange
Lines and Shadows
The New Centurions
The Onion Field
WAM, composer taught by: 3 LvB
wammus: 4 coat 6 jacket
wampum: 4 peag 5 beads
see also moolah
WaMu: 4 bank
wan: 4 ashy, pale, thin, weak, worn 5 ashen, faint, livid, pasty, waxen, white 6 anemic, blanch, chalky, feeble, pallid, peaked, sallow, sickly 7 anaemic, bilious, ghastly, haggard, languid 8 bleached, liverish 9 albescent, bloodless, colorless, ghostlike, lily-white, washed-out, whey-faced 10 pasty-faced
Wanamaker: 3 Sam, Zöe 4 John
contemporary: 4 Macy
wand: 3 rod 4 twig 5 baton, sprig, staff, stick 7 scepter, sceptre 8 caduceus
magic ~ owner: 5 fairy 6 wizard 8 magician, sorcerer
__ wand: 5 fairy, magic
Wanda: 5 Sykes 9 Landowska
wander: 3 err, gad, sin 4 hike, mill, rave, roam, rove, trek, veer, walk 5 amble, drift, float, jaunt, mosey, prowl, range, stray, tramp 6 cruise, ramble, stroll, trapes, travel 7 deviate, digress, diverge, get lost, journey, maunder, meander, migrate, saunter, traipse 8 go astray, straggle 9 bat around, circulate, expatiate, gallivant, globetrot, hopscotch
let one's mind ~: 3 nod 4 miss 8 daydream
wanderer: 3 bum, gad 4 hobo, waif 5 gipsy, gypsy, nomad, stray, tramp 6 estray 7 pilgrim, vagrant, voyager 8 explorer, gadabout, stranger, vagabond, wayfarer 9 itinerant 10 adventurer
Wanderer, The (song)
artist: Dion, Donna Summer
__ Wanderer, The: 5 Happy
wandering: 4 lost 6 astray, errant 7 aimless, erratic, journey, migrant, nomadic 8 vagabond 9 delirious, departure, excursion, excursive, itinerant, migratory, peregrine, wayfaring 10 aberration, digression, discursion, incoherent
Wandering __: 3 Jew
wanderlust
indulge ~: 4 roam, rove 5 range 6 travel
wane: 3 die, dim, ebb, lag, sag, sap 4 fade, fail, fall, flag, lull, sink, tire 5 abate, blunt, decay, let up, slack 6 go down, impair, lessen, recede, reduce, relent, shrink, soften, weaken, wither 7 decline, deplete, die away, drop off, dwindle, ease off, exhaust, fatigue, slacken, subside, tail off, thin out 8 blow over, contract, decrease, diminish, enervate, enfeeble, fade away, moderate, peter out, slack off, taper off, wind down 9 attenuate, disappear, undermine, waste away 10 debilitate, devitalize, falling off
__ wane: 5 on the
Waner, Lloyd: 6 Pirate 10 outfielder
Waner, Paul: 6 Pirate 10 outfielder
Wang: 3 Wei 4 Lung, Vera 5 Chung, Wayne 7 Garrett
Wanger, Walter: 8 producer
wangle: 3 fix, get 4 coax, plot 5 swing 6 manage, obtain 7 acquire, arrange, connive, finagle, finesse, procure, pull off 8 bring off, conspire, maneuver 9 machinate
Wang Lung: 6 farmer
wife: 4 O-Lan
Wang, Wayne: 8 director
film: The Center of the World (2001)
Chan Is Missing (1982)
Dim Sum... (1984)
Eat a Bowl of Tea (1989)
The Joy Luck Club (1993)
Smoke (1995)
Wang Wei: 4 poet 7 Chinese
waning: 3 ebb 7 decline 8 decrease 9 abatement, remission
Wankel: 6 engine

engine part: 5 rotor
___-Wan Kenobi: 3 Obi
wannabe: 5 yahoo **7** aspirer, parvenu, upstart **8** emulator **9** arriviste, pretender, soi-disant, vulgarian **10** self-styled
Wannabe (1997 song)
artist: Spice Girls
Wanna bet?: 6 oh yeah
Wanna buy ___?: 5 a duck
___ Wanna Cry: 5 I Don't
___ Wanna Do: 4 All I
Wanna make ___?: 4 a bet
wanness: 6 anemia, pallor **7** anaemia
want: 3 aim, yen **4** ache, lack, like, long, lust, miss, need, pine, seek, will, wish **5** covet, crave, fancy, yearn **6** aspire, choose, dearth, demand, desire, famine, hanker, hunger, misery, penury, please, prefer, thirst **7** absence, burn for, call for, craving, hope for, itch for, longing, paucity, poverty, require, sigh for, wish for **8** exigence, exigency, feel like, scarcity, shortage, sparsity, spoil for, yearn for, yearning **9** appetence, go without, hanker for, hankering, indigence, neediness, privation, starve for **10** deficiency, desiderate, have need of, meagerness, scantiness, skimpiness
ad abbr.: 3 EEO
answer a ~ ad: 5 apply
be in ~: 4 need
in ~: 4 poor **5** broke, needy **6** bad off, hard up, ill off **7** pinched **8** badly off, bankrupt, beggarly, indigent, strapped **9** destitute, insolvent, moneyless, penniless, penurious **10** down and out, pauperized, straitened
want ___: 3 ads **4** list
wanted: 7 at large, welcome **10** on the loose
one: 7 escapee, runaway
poster word: 5 alias, alive, armed **6** reward
Wanted (2008 film)
cast: Morgan Freeman, Angelina Jolie, James McAvoy
Wanted Dead or Alive (1987 song)
artist: Bon Jovi
Wanted: Dead or Alive (CBS western)
cast: Steve McQueen (Josh Randall)
___ wanted list: 4 most
___ want for Christmas...: 4 All I
wanting: 4 less, slim **5** minus, scant, short, shy of **6** absent, devoid, faulty, in need, meager, scanty, skimpy **7** lacking, missing, slender **8** deprived, inferior **9** defective, deficient, destitute, half-baked, imperfect **10** inadequate, incomplete
___ want is a room somewhere: 4 All I
want-it-all type: 3 hog, pig **7** glutton
___ Want Me: 5 Do You
wanton: 4 lewd, mean, rake, rash, wild **5** cruel, harsh, loose, nasty, undue **6** animal, brutal, fierce, lavish, rakish, savage, unkind, wicked, wilful **7** beastly, callous, drastic, extreme, hurtful, lustful, naughty, rampant, vicious, wayward, willful **8** barbaric, careless, depraved, fiendish, heedless, inhumane, mindless, needless, perverse, pitiless, prodigal, reckless, ruthless, sadistic, vengeful, wasteful **9** cutthroat, dissolute, egregious, excessive, fanatical, ferocious, libertine, lubricous, luxuriate, malicious, merciless, monstrous, senseless, shameless, truculent, unbridled **10** deliberate, groundless, immoderate, inordinate, malevolent, motiveless, outrageous, profligate, unprovoked, vindictive
wantonness: 4 evil **7** abandon, license **8** lewdness
___ Want to Be Right: 5 I Don't
___ Want to Dance?: 5 Do You
___ Want to Know a Secret?: 5 Do You
___ Want to Set the World on Fire: 5 I Don't
___ Want to Walk Without You: 5 I Don't
wapiti: 3 elk **4** deer **6** animal, mammal
relative: *see* deer
Wapner, Joseph: 5 judge
Wapshot Chronicle, The
author: John Cheever
war: 4 game **5** fight, jehad, jihad **6** attack, battle, combat, enmity, strife **7** contend, crusade, quarrel **8** card game, conflict, fighting, struggle **9** bloodshed, hostility **10** contention, take up arms
1850s ~ zone: 6 Crimea
1960s ~ zone: 3 Nam
advocate: 4 hawk
at ~: 8 battling, fighting
cause of an 1840s ~: 5 opium
chest: 4 fund **6** coffer **8** treasury **9** exchequer
civil ~: 6 revolt **7** anarchy **8** sedition, uprising **9** rebellion **10** revolution
club: 4 mace **6** cudgel **9** truncheon
cry: 5 alarm, motto, whoop **6** slogan
ender: 4 fare, head, lock, lord, path, time, V-day **5** horse, plane, ships, truce **6** monger
games: 4 test **5** drill **9** maneuvers
god: 4 Ares, Mars, Odin **5** Othin
goddess: 4 Enyo **6** Athena, Athene
hero: 3 ace **5** flier, flyer, pilot **7** aviator
of words: 6 debate **8** argument
partner: 4 ally
prepare for ~: 3 arm **5** rearm **8** embattle
reward: 5 booty **6** spoils
wage ~: 5 fight **6** invade **9** prosecute
war ___: 3 cry, hat **4** game, hawk, nose, room, zone **5** bride, chest, cloud, dance, games, paint, party, story, whoop **6** bonnet, hammer, powers, vessel **7** surplus
___ war: 3 air, hot **4** cold, holy, wage **5** act of, price, trade, tug of, world **7** declare
War: 9 rock group
song: The Cisco Kid (1973)
Gypsy Man (1973)
Low Rider (1975)
Spill the Wine (1970)
Summer (1976)
Why Can't We Be Friends? (1975)
The World Is a Ghetto (1972)
War (song)
artist: Bruce Springsteen, Edwin Starr
War ___: 7 Requiem
War ___ Peace: 3 and
War ___ Roses, The: 5 of the
War ___, The: 4 Game, Lord, Room **5** Wagon
War ___ Worlds, The: 5 of the
___ War: 3 Tek **4** Boer, Cold, Gulf, Man o' **5** Creek, Great, Hart's, Opium, Sioux **6** Balkan, Korean, Pequot, Six-Day, Social, Trojan **7** Crimean, Gordon's, Mexican, Murphy's, Vietnam
War and Peace: 4 epic **5** novel
author: Leo Tolstoy
character: 4 Berg, Ilya, Vera **5** Boris, Julie, Marya, Sonya **6** Hélène, Rostov
game: 4 faro
War Between the ___, The: 5 Tates **6** States
War Between the Tates, The
author: Alison Lurie
warble: 4 call, pipe, sing **5** croon, trill, yodel, yodle **6** intone, strain **8** vocalize
warbler: 4 bird, lark, wren **6** singer **8** vocalist
Warbucks, Daddy
like ~: 4 rich
underling: 3 Asp **6** Asp, The, Punjab
ward: 5 Annie
Warburg, Otto: 8 Nobelist
ward: 4 area, zone **5** child, minor **6** canton, charge, orphan, parish, region **7** adoptee, lookout, protege, quarter **8** district, division, godchild, precinct **9** dependent, foundling, pensioner, territory **10** department, protection
ender: 4 robe, room
heeler: 3 pol **10** politician
off: 4 fend, foil, halt, stay, stop **5** avert, avoid, block, check, deter, guard, parry, rebut, repel, stimy, stymy **6** defend, divert, rebuff, shield, stymie, thwart **7** deflect, obviate, prevent, repulse, rule out **8** preclude, turn down **9** forestall, frustrate, keep at bay, turn aside, withstand
starter: 3 lee, man, sea, sky, sun, way **4** east, home, land, left, side, west, wind **5** coast, front, north, right, river, shore, south, space, stern **6** heaven, hither **7** thither **9** northeast, northwest, southeast, southwest
ward ___: 3 off **6** heeler
Ward: 3 Jay **4** Bond, Burt, Fred, Sela **5** Anita, Baker, Simon **6** Rachel **7** Artemus, Cleaver **10** Montgomery
June, to ~: 4 wife
to the Beaver: 3 Dad
Ward, Anita
song: Ring My Bell (1979)
Ward, Artemus: 6 writer
birthplace: 5 Maine
___ Ward Beecher: 5 Henry
ward eight: 5 drink **8** beverage, cocktail
ingredient: 4 soda **7** whiskey **9** grenadine **10** lemon juice
warden: 5 guard **6** deacon, jailer, keeper, ranger **7** manager, officer **8** governor, overseer, watchdog **9** caretaker, custodian **10** doorkeeper, gamekeeper
African game ~: 6 askari
starter: 6 church
___ warden: 4 fish, game **7** air-raid
Warden: 4 Jack
___ Ward Howe: 5 Julia
wardrobe: 4 duds, rags, togs **5** dress, suits, trunk **6** attire, closet, locker, outfit **7** apparel, armoire, clothes, outfits, threads **8** clothing, costumes, cupboard, garments **9** ensembles, furniture, trousseau, vestments **10** chiffonier, Sunday best
wardship: 4 care **5** trust **7** custody, keeping **8** auspices, tutelage
wards starter: 3 man, sea, sky, sun **4** east, home, land, side, west **5** coast, front, north, river, shore, south, stern **6** heaven, hither
ware: 4 delf **5** delft, goods **7** article, pottery, product **8** ceramics, vendible **9** commodity
ender: 4 room **5** house
starter: 3 bar, sea **4** cook, dish, firm, flat, gift, hard, iron, oven, slip, soft, stem **5** brass, china, glass, stone, table, vapor **6** copper, course, dinner, enamel, hollow, jasper, luster, silver, willow, wooden **7** crackle, earthen, granite, kitchen
___ ware: 5 cameo, delft, Imari, Mocha **6** bamboo, Fiesta, jasper, Jesuit, Parian, queen's, Samian, Sèvres **7** Belleek, biscuit, Dresden, lacquer, Limoges, Nanking, Satsuma
warehouse: 4 stow **5** depot, étape, store **6** bodega **8** magazine **9** stockpile, stockroom **10** depository, repository
charge: 4 stor. **7** storage
Chinese ~: 4 hong **6** godown
renovated ~ space: 4 loft
stamp: 4 recd.
unit: 3 bin, box, ton **4** skid **5** crate
wares: 4 line, mdse. **5** goods, stock, store **7** produce **8** articles, material, products **9** vendibles
warfare: 6 battle, combat, strife **7** discord **8** campaign, conflict, fighting, struggle **10** opposition
combining form: 5 -machy
___ warfare: 5 class **6** trench
Warfield: 4 Paul **6** Marsha, Wallis
WarGames (1983 film)
cast: Matthew Broderick, Dabney Coleman, Ally Sheedy
dog: 4 Beau
org.: 5 NORAD
warhead
carrier: 4 ICBM
remove the ~: 6 disarm
Warhol, Andy: 6 artist **9** pop artist
film: 5 Trash

subject: 3 can, Mao 6 Monroe 7 Marilyn, soup can
war-horse: 5 steed 7 charger, palfrey, trooper, veteran 8 destrier
War in a Time of Peace
author: David Halberstam
wariness: 5 doubt, qualm 8 distrust, mistrust 9 chariness, leeriness, misgiving, suspicion 10 insecurity, precaution, skepticism
Waring: 4 Fred 7 blender
competitor: 5 Oster
War is __: 4 hell
War Is Kind
author: Stephen Crane
Warks: 6 county
locale: 7 England
warlike: 7 hawkish, hostile, lawless, martial 8 fighting, inimical, militant, military, ructious 9 bellicose, combative, soldierly 10 aggressive, pugnacious, unfriendly
name meaning ~: 6 Marcia, Marsha
warlock: 4 male 5 witch 6 wizard 8 magician, sorcerer
circle: 5 coven
warm: 3 hot 4 bake, cook, cosy, cozy, fond, heat, homy, kind, melt, mild, nice, rich, snug, thaw 5 aglow, angry, balmy, chafe, close, cozey, cozie, happy, homey, human, riled, sunny, tepid, toast 6 ardent, fervid, genial, gung-ho, hearty, heated, heat up, kindly, living, loving, simmer, sweaty, tender, toasty 7 affable, amiable, amorous, clement, cordial, earnest, excited, fervent, flushed, glowing, intense, melting, prepare, sincere, summery, thermal 8 animated, cheerful, effusive, friendly, gracious, intimate, maternal, moderate, outgoing, parental, pleasant, roasting, sizzling, sociable, sweating, tropical, tucked in, vehement 9 congenial, emotional, heartfelt, microwave, scorching, temperate, unextreme 10 empathetic, hospitable, passionate, personable, perspiring, responsive, sweltering
getting ~: 4 near 5 close 7 close by
hello: 3 hug 4 kiss 7 embrace
in the pocket: 4 rich 5 flush 6 loaded 7 wealthy 8 well-to-do
sensation: 4 glow
spot: 5 ingle 6 hearth 9 fireplace
spring: 3 spa 4 bath
springs: 7 thermae
up: 4 heat, melt, thaw 5 ready, train 7 prepare 8 practice, rehearse, unfreeze
warm __: 4 spot, tone 5 front
warm-__: 7 blooded, hearted
warmed-over: 4 flat 5 banal, tired, trite
warmer
bench ~: 3 sub 5 scrub 9 alternate 10 substitute
starter: 3 leg
winter ~: 3 tea 4 coat, muff 5 cocoa, glove, quilt, scarf, toddy 6 hot tea 8 hot toddy
warmer-__: 5 upper
__ warmer: 3 leg 4 foot 5 bench, chair
__ Warm for May: 4 Very
warmhearted: 4 kind 6 decent, genial, gentle, humane, kindly, loving, tender 7 clement, lenient, sparing 8 gracious, merciful 10 altruistic, benevolent
warmheartedness: 6 regard 7 empathy 8 kindness, sympathy 10 compassion
warming __: 3 pan
__ warming: 6 global
warming starter: 5 heart, house
warmness: 4 heat 8 calidity 9 torridity 10 caloricity
warmonger: 4 hawk 7 soldier 9 guerrilla, mercenary
Warm Springs: 3 spa 6 resort
locale: 7 Georgia
warmth: 4 heat, pity, zeal 5 ardor, heart 6 fervor, spirit 7 emotion, passion 8 lyricism, radiance, radiancy, sympathy 9 geniality, sincerity 10 cordiality, friendship, kindliness, liveliness
source: 3 sun 4 oven 5 stove 6 burner, heater 9 fireplace
without ~: 3 icy 4 cold 5 icily, stony 6 coldly, stoney 7 stonily
warm the __: 5 bench
warm-up: 4 prep 5 drill 7 workout 9 rehearsal
gear: 6 sweats
warn: 3 tip 4 hint, post, tell, urge 5 alert, guide, order 6 advise, clue in, enjoin, exhort, fill in, forbid, inform, notify, prompt, remind, signal, tip off 7 apprise, apprize, caution, counsel, cry wolf, forearm, predict, prepare, presage, reprove, suggest 8 acquaint, admonish, dissuade, foreshow, foretell, forewarn, prophesy, threaten 9 adumbrate 10 give notice
of: 4 bode 5 augur 6 herald 7 bespeak, portend 8 forebode, prophesy 10 foreshadow
Warner: 3 Abe, Pop, Rex 4 Jack, John, Saem, Seth 5 David, Harry, Julie, Oland 6 Baxter, Sylvia
Warner Bros.: 3 Abe, Sam 4 Jack 5 Harry 6 studio
competitor: ***see*** movie studio
creation: 4 film 5 movie
toon: 3 Taz 4 Bugs, Fudd, Pepe 5 Daffy, Elmer, Porky, Wile E. 6 Coyote 8 Porky Pig 9 Bugs Bunny, Daffy Duck, Elmer Fudd, Pepe Le Pew, Sylvester 10 Road Runner
Warner, John
spouse: Elizabeth Taylor
Warner, Rex: 6 writer 7 British
Warner, Sylvia: 4 poet 6 writer 7 British
work: The Corner That Held Them
Lolly Willowes
Warnes, Jennifer
song: Right Time of the Night (1977)
The Time of My Life (1987)
Up Where We Belong (1982)
warning: 3 SOS, tip 4 hint, omen, sign 5 alarm, alert, siren, token 6 advice, alarum, augury, beacon, beware, caveat, lesson, Mayday, notice, signal, threat, tipoff, tocsin 7 caution, example, heads up, ominous, pointer, portent, presage, red flag, symptom 8 guidance, reminder 9 foretaste, foretoken, indicator 10 admonition, admonitory, cautionary, foreboding, indication, injunction, intimation, prediction, suggestion
canine ~: 3 grr 4 gnar 5 gnarl, gnarr, growl, snarl
device: 4 horn 5 alarm, flare, fusee, fuzee, siren 6 beacon, claxon, klaxon 7 monitor
early ~ system: 5 NORAD 7 DEW line
exclamation: 2 no 3 grr, nix, shh 4 ahem, fore, no no, oh-oh, uh-oh 6 beware 7 gangway
without ~: 5 short 7 swiftly 8 suddenly, unawares
word of ~: 4 don't 6 beware, danger
warning __: 4 shot 5 track
__ warning: 5 early, flood, storm
war of __: 6 nerves 9 attrition
War of 1812
battle site: 4 Erie
hero: 7 Jackson
issue: 6 Canada
treaty site: 5 Ghent
War of the __: 5 Roses 6 Worlds
War of the Roses, The (1989 film)
cast: Danny DeVito, Michael Douglas, Kathleen Turner
director: Danny DeVito
War of the Saints, The
author: Jorge Amado
War of the Worlds
author: H.G. Wells
foe: 4 Mars
name: 5 Orson 6 Welles
War of the Worlds (2005 film)
cast: Tom Cruise, Dakota Fanning, Tim Robbins
director: Steven Spielberg
warp: 3 mar 4 bend, bias 5 color, curve, screw, slant, twist 6 buckle, change, debase, deform, garble, poison, wrench 7 contort, corrupt, deflect, deprave, distort, texture 8 jaundice, misquote, misshape 9 brutalize 10 aberration
count: 4 sley
opposite: 4 weft, woof
work with ~: 5 weave
warp __: 5 speed
__ warp: 4 time
warpath
be on the ~: 4 fume, rage, stew 5 storm 6 see red, seethe 7 flame up
on the ~: 5 irate 6 raging 7 furious 8 incensed, wrathful
warped: 4 bent 6 skewed 7 crooked 8 lopsided 9 malformed
warplane: 3 MiG 6 bomber
warrant: 3 let, vow 4 back, bail, earn, word, writ 5 basis, merit, paper, proof, prove, swear, vouch 6 assert, assure, attest, depone, ensure, excuse, permit, pledge, reason 7 bear out, call for, certify, declare, deserve, empower, endorse, entitle, go-ahead, indorse, intitle, justify, license, mandate, passage, promise, summons, testify 8 attest to, guaranty, occasion, sanction, security, subpoena, vouch for 9 authorize, guarantee, indemnify, indemnity 10 green light, permission, underwrite
officer: 4 bo's'n, rank 5 bosun
__ warrant: 5 bench 6 arrest, search
warrantable: 6 lawful 7 tenable 9 allowable
warranted: 5 legal, licit 6 lawful 10 admissible, guaranteed, legitimate
warranty: 4 bail, bond 6 pledge, surety 7 promise 8 contract, covenant, guaranty 9 assurance, guarantee
without a ~: 4 as is
word: 6 defect
Warren: 4 Earl, Moon, Sapp 5 Giles, Harry, Oates, Spahn, Zevon 6 Beatty, Burger 7 Buffett, Harding, Leonard, Michael, William 8 Jennifer
veep: 3 Cal 6 Calvin
warren dweller: 6 rabbit
Warren, Harry: 8 composer
song: About a Quarter to Nine
Boulevard of Broken Dreams
Chattanooga Choo Choo
Cheerful Little Earful
Forty-Second Street
Go Into Your Dance
I Only Have Eyes for You
I've Got a Gal in Kalamazoo
Jeepers Creepers
Lullaby of Broadway
Lulu's Back in Town
The More I See You
Shuffle Off to Buffalo
That's Amore
We're in the Money
You'll Never Know
You Must Have Been a Beautiful Baby
You're Getting to Be a Habit With Me
Warren, Leonard: 6 singer 8 baritone, barytone
specialty: 5 opera
Warren, Lesley Ann
spouse: Jon Peters
Warren, Mrs. creator: George Bernard Shaw
Warren, Robert Penn: 4 poet 6 writer
work: All the King's Men
At Heaven's Gate
World Enough and Time
__ Warren's Profession: 3 Mrs.
War Requiem
composer: Benjamin Britten
Warrick: 4 Ruth
warrior: 2 GI 4 hero 5 ninja 6 archer, bowman, knight 7 fighter, samurai, soldier, veteran 9 combatant, conscript, legionary, mercenary 10 campaigner, contestant
Japan ~: 7 samurai
Old West ~: 5 brave 6 Apache
__ warrior: 4 cold, road 5 happy 6 Indian 7 weekend
__ Warrior: 4 Road
__: Warrior Princess: 4 Xena
Warriors: 4 five, team
org.: 3 NBA
rival: ***see*** NBA team
sport: 10 basketball
Warrior's Barrow, The
author: Henrik Ibsen

Warrior, The (1984 song)
artist: Patty Smyth
war-room fixture: 3 map 5 radar 7 hot line
__ Wars: 4 Star 5 Punic 6 Gallic
Warsaw: 4 city, pact, town 7 capital
city near ~: 4 Lodz
locale: 6 Poland
river: 7 Vistula
Warsaw Pact
member: 3 GDR 4 USSR 6 Poland, Russia 7 Hungary, Romania 8 Bulgaria 11 East Germany
opposite: 4 NATO
War Scenes
composer: Ned Rorem
warship: 4 boat 5 razee 6 PT boat 7 flattop, frigate, galleon, gunboat, monitor 8 corvette, ironclad, man-of-war 9 destroyer, minelayer 10 patrol boat
initials: 3 USS
warships: 5 fleet 6 armada
Wars of the __: 5 Roses
Warszawa instrumentalist: 3 Eno
wart: 4 flaw 5 fault 6 defect 7 blemish, failing, verruca
ender: 3 hog
starter: 5 worry
__ War, The: 4 Holy 5 Art of
warthog: 5 beast 6 animal, mammal 7 critter
tooth: 4 tusk
warts and all: 4 as is 6 openly 7 frankly, plainly 8 candidly, honestly
warty: 5 bumpy 6 knobby 9 verrucose
critter: 4 frog, toad
War Wagon, The (1967 film): 5 oater 7 western
cast: Kirk Douglas, Howard Keel, John Wayne
Warwick, Dionne
cousin: Whitney Houston
song: Alfie (1967)
Anyone Who Had a Heart (1964)
Don't Make Me Over (1963)
Do You Know the Way to San José (1968)
Heartbreaker (1982)
I'll Never Fall in Love Again (1970)
I'll Never Love This Way Again (1979)
I Say a Little Prayer (1967)
Love Power (1987)
Message to Michael (1966)
That's What Friends Are For (1985)
Then Came You (1974)
This Girl's in Love With You (1969)
Valley of the Dolls (1968)
Walk On By (1964)
Warwickshire: 6 county
locale: 7 England
river: 4 Avon
town: 5 Rugby
War With the Newts, The
author: Karel Capek
wary: 3 shy 4 cagy, safe, wise 5 alert, cagey, canny, chary, leery 6 unsure 7 careful, dubious, guarded, heads-up, heedful, mindful, on guard, prudent, sparing, wakeful 8 cautious, discreet, doubtful, doubting, hesitant, keen-eyed, vigilant, watchful 9 attentive, defensive, eagle-eyed, reluctant, sharp-eyed, skeptical, uncertain, wide-awake 10 on one's toes, suspicious
be ~: 4 mind 5 doubt, watch 7 look out, suspect 8 distrust, mistrust 10 disbelieve
was: 4 verb 5 lived 7 existed, had been
at: 6 went to 8 attended
not what it ~: 5 rusty 9 neglected 10 out of shape
__ was: 4 time
__ was a crooked man...: 5 There
__ was a cunning hunter: 4 Esau
__ was a lad...: 5 When I
__ Was a Lady: 5 Eadie, Nelly 7 DuBarry
__ was a man!: 4 This
__ Was a Rolling Stone: 4 Papa
Wasatch: 5 range
locale: 4 Utah 5 Idaho
ski resort: 4 Alta
Was blind but now __: 4 I see
__ was going to St. Ives: 3 As I
wash: 3 dip, lap, mop, wet 4 bath, coat, eddy, film, flow, gush, lave, lick, soak, soap, swab, swob, tint, wipe 5 bathe, clean, douse, dowse, float, flush, groom, heave, paint, rinse, scour, scrub, slosh, spirt, spurt, surge, swamp, swell, swirl, swish, tinge 6 drench, lather, lotion, murmur, neaten, purify, ravine, shower, sponge 7 cleanse, coating, deterge, dunking, freshen, immerse, launder, laundry, moisten, overlay, scrub up, shampoo 8 ablution, hose down, irrigate, lavation, prove out, spruce up 9 deodorize, disinfect, freshen up, hold water, take a bath 10 ebb and flow
against: 3 lap 4 lick 5 lap at
away: 4 wear 5 erode, leach, purge
cycle: 4 soak, spin 5 rinse
down: 4 hose 7 swallow
ender: 3 day, out, rag, tub 4 able, bowl, room 5 basin, board, cloth, stand, woman, women
get ruined in the ~: 3 run
off: 5 clean, rinse
one's hands of: 6 disown 7 abandon, bail out, disavow, forsake 8 forswear, renounce 9 foreswear, repudiate
out: 4 bomb, bust, fade, fail, lose, slip, trip 5 elute, erode, flunk 6 bleach, blow it, falter 7 blunder, founder, go under, go wrong, misstep, stumble 8 backfire, etiolate, fall flat, flounder, lay an egg
starter: 3 eye, hog 4 back 5 black, brain, mouth, stone, white
wash __: 3 out 4 down
__ wash: 3 car, dry
__-wash: 4 hand
Wash __: 4 'n Dri
Wash.
airport: 4 Natl.
neighbor: 3 Can., Ida., Ore. 4 Oreg.
Sq. campus: 3 NYU
see also Washington
wash-and-wear material: 5 nylon 6 Dacron 9 synthetic
washbasin user: 5 laver
washboard __: 3 abs
washboard, use a: 5 scrub
Washbourne: 4 Mona
washbowl: 4 sink 5 basin 6 lavabo
washcloth: 5 linen
in Britain: 7 flannel
washday
brand: 3 All, Biz, Era, Fab, Yes 4 Bold, Dash, Gain, Surf, Tide, Wisk 5 Cheer, Dreft, Purex 6 Calgon, Clorox, Dynamo, Oxydol 7 Octagon 9 Ivory Snow
challenge: 3 tar 4 soil 5 paint, stain 6 collar 7 splotch
washed: 4 neat, pure, tidy 5 clean, snowy, sweet, white 6 bathed, bright, decent, spruce 7 refined, shining 8 dirtless, germfree, hygienic, pristine, purified, sanitary, spotless, unfouled, unsoiled 9 laundered, sparkling, stainless, unsmudged, unspotted, unstained 10 immaculate, impeccable
__-washed: 4 acid
washed-out: 3 wan 4 drab, dull, pale 5 faded 8 bleached, fatigued 9 colorless, enervated, etiolated, exhausted 10 lackluster
washed-up: 4 shot, sunk 5 kaput, spent 7 done for, through 8 finished
__ was here: 6 Kilroy
washer starter: 4 dish
washing: 6 lavabo, lavage 7 laundry 8 ablution 9 housework
washing __: 4 soda
washing machine: 6 Bendix, Maytag 9 appliance, Whirlpool
companion: 5 drier, dryer
contents: 4 load, suds 6 bundle 7 laundry
phase: 4 soak, spin 5 cycle, rinse
Washington: 3 mtn., Ned 4 lake, peak 5 Dinah, Mount, state 6 Denzel, George, Irving, Martha 8 mountain 10 government
Washington (state)
airport: 6 Sea-Tac
cape: 5 Alava
capital: 7 Olympia
city: 4 Kent 5 Lacey, Pasco 6 Auburn, Burien, Renton, Tacoma, Yakima 7 Bothell, Cascade, Edmonds, Everett, Olympia, Pullman, Redmond, Seattle, Spokane 8 Bellevue, East Hill, Fairwood, Finn Hill, Kirkland, Lakewood, Longview, Lynnwood, Meridian, Parkland, Puyallup, Richland, Spanaway 9 Bremerton, Des Moines, Fort Lewis, Inglewood, Kennewick, Oak Harbor, Sammamish, Shoreline, South Hill, Vancouver, Wenatchee 10 Bellingham, Federal Way, Marysville, North Creek, Paine Field, Silver Firs, Walla Walla
conference: 6 Pac-Ten
Indian: 5 Makah 6 Nootka, Yakima 8 Puyallup, Sahaptin 9 Suquamish
motto: 4 Al-ki
mountain: 5 Adams 7 Rainier 8 St. Helens
national park: 7 Olympic
neighbor: 5 Idaho 6 Canada, Oregon
pro team: 8 Mariners, Seahawks 11 SuperSonics
school: 7 Gonzaga
state bird: 9 goldfinch
state fish: 5 trout
state fossil: 7 mammoth
state fruit: 5 apple
state insect: 9 dragonfly
state tree: 7 hemlock
volcano: 8 St. Helens
waterfall: 8 Sluiskin
waterway: 5 Puget
Washington __ here: 5 slept
Washington and __: 3 Lee
Washington, D.C.: 4 city, town 7 capital
airport: 6 Dulles, Reagan 8 National
athletes: 5 Bison, Hoyas
ballplayer: 3 Nat 8 National
bank: 5 Riggs
court in ~: 5 lobby
helper: 4 aide, page
hostess: 5 Mesta
hundred: 6 Senate
newspaper: 4 Post 5 Times
onetime ~ ballplayer: 7 Senator
river: 7 Potomac 9 Anacostia
school: 6 Howard 10 Georgetown
stadium: 3 RFK
suburb: 5 Olney 8 Bethesda 9 Arlington
subway: 5 Metro
team: 7 Wizards 8 Capitals, Redskins
Washington, Denzel: 5 actor
film: American Gangster (2007)
Antwone Fisher (2003)
The Bone Collector (1999)
Courage Under Fire (1996)
Crimson Tide (1995)
Cry Freedom (1987)
Déjà Vu (2006)
Devil in a Blue Dress (1995)
Glory (1989, AA)
The Great Debaters (2007)
He Got Game (1998)
The Hurricane (1999)
Inside Man (2006)
John Q (2002)
Malcolm X (1992)
The Manchurian Candidate (2004)
Mo' Better Blues (1990)
Much Ado About Nothing (1993)
The Pelican Brief (1993)
Philadelphia (1993)
The Preacher's Wife (1996)
Remember the Titans (2000)
The Siege (1998)
The Taking of Pelham 123 (2009)
Training Day (2001, AA)
TV: St. Elsewhere
Washington, Dinah
song: Baby (You've Got What It Takes) (1960)
A Rockin' Good Way (1970)
Unforgettable (1959)
What a Diff'rence a Day Makes (1959)

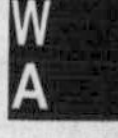

Washington, George: 7 general **9** president
bill: 3 one
former occupation: 7 soldier **8** surveyor
home: 8 Virginia
no-no: 3 lie
opponent: 4 Howe **8** Burgoyne **10** Cornwallis
portraitist: 5 Peale **6** Stuart
signature part: 3 Geo.
successor: 5 Adams
V.P.: 5 Adams
wife: 6 Martha
Washington Jr., Grover
song: Just the Two of Us (1981)
Washington Post, The
composer: John Philip Sousa
Washington Square
author: Henry James
Washington State
athletes: 7 Cougars
conference: 6 Pac-Ten
locale: 7 Pullman
Wash 'n __: 3 Dri
wash one's __ of: 5 hands
washout: 3 dud **4** bust, flop, loss, rout **6** defeat, fiasco, mishap, turkey **7** blunder, debacle, failure, letdown, misstep, stumble **8** disaster, downfall
washroom: 2 W.C. **3** lav, loo **4** bath **8** lavatory
washstand item: 4 ewer **5** basin
Wash tributary: 4 Ouse
__-washy: 5 wishy
Wasilla: 4 city, town
locale: 6 Alaska
__ was in the beginning...: 4 as it
__ was I to know?: 3 How
__ was no lady...: 4 That
wasn't it: 3 hid
__ Was One-and-Twenty: 5 When I
__ was only a bird...: 3 She
wasp: 3 bug **4** pest **6** hornet, insect
colony: 4 nest
genus: 5 vespa
like a ~: 6 winged
prey: 3 ant
wasp __: 5 waist
__ wasp: 3 fig, mud, sea
waspish: 4 mean, sour **5** cross, huffy, testy **6** crabby, cranky, crusty, feisty, grumpy, ornery **7** grouchy, huffish, peevish, prickly **8** grumpish, petulant, snappish, venomous **9** crotchety, fractious, irascible, irritable, querulous, splenetic **10** ill-humored, malevolent, out of sorts
waspishness: 5 spite **6** enmity, rancor, spleen **8** acrimony, ill humor **9** hostility, petulance
Wass: 3 Ted
wassail: 5 drink, toast
ingredient: 4 wine **5** clove
wassailer: 7 reveler **9** bacchanal **10** merrymaker
quaff: 3 nog **4** grog **6** eggnog
song: 4 noel **5** carol
__ was saying...: 3 As I
wasser: 5 water **6** German
frozen: 3 eis
Wassermann, Jakob: 6 writer **8** Austrian
work: The World's Illusion
Wasserstein, Wendy: 10 playwright
work: An American Daughter
The Heidi Chronicles
The Sisters Rosensweig
Wassily: 8 Leontief **9** Kandinsky
Wasson: 5 Craig
waste: 3 eat, sap, use **4** blow, fade, junk, kill, lose, loss, moor, orts, rase, raze, ruin, sack, scum, sink, slay, slop, void, wilt **5** chaff, decay, drain, dregs, dross, havoc, level, offal, scrap, spend, spoil, swamp, swill, trash, use up, wilds **6** barren, burn up, debris, desert, excess, lavish, litter, misuse, murder, ravage, refuse, rubble, scraps, shrink, tundra, wither **7** aridity, atrophy, deplete, despoil, destroy, eat away, fribble, garbage, pillage, play out, rubbish, rummage, splurge, trounce **8** badlands, dust bowl, enfeeble, languish, leavings, lifeless, misapply, misspend, quagmire, sediment, spoliate, squander, throw out **9** devastate, dissipate, leftovers, marshland, misemploy, overpower, overspend, ruination, sweepings, throw away, while away **10** gamble away, run through, trifle away, wilderness, wreak havoc
allowance: 4 tret
as time: 4 kill
away: 4 melt, wane **6** shrink, wither **8** emaciate, languish
don't ~: 5 reuse
ender: 4 land **5** paper, water **6** basket
holder: 6 ashcan **8** Dumpster, landfill, trash can
lay ~ to: 3 aid **4** ruin, sack, undo **5** harry, smash, smite, wreck **6** ravage **7** consume, destroy, pillage, plunder, ransack **8** desolate, freeboot **9** depredate
maker: 5 haste
matter: 5 dross, trash **6** refuse **7** garbage
no time: 3 hie, run **4** dash, race **5** speed
time: 3 lag **4** futz, idle, laze, loaf, moon, mope **5** amble, dally, mosey, stall, tarry **6** dawdle, diddle, linger, loiter, lounge, trifle **7** saunter **8** lollygag, straggle **10** dillydally, fool around
waste __: 4 pipe
__ waste: 3 lay **4** go to
wastebasket: 3 can **8** trash can **10** receptacle
wasted: 4 lean, lost, thin **5** spent, tired **8** fatigued, misspent
Wasted Days and Wasted Nights (1975 song)
artist: Freddy Fender
Wasted on the Way (1982 song)
artist: Crosby, Stills & Nash
wasteful: 4 wild **6** lavish, wanton **7** liberal, ruinous **8** careless, cavalier, overdone, prodigal **9** unthrifty **10** immoderate, inordinate, profligate, thriftless
be ~: 5 use up **6** frivol, lavish, misuse **7** deplete **8** misspend, squander **9** dissipate, throw away **10** run through
wasteland: 4 moor, wild **5** heath, waste **6** desert, jungle
like a ~: 4 arid **5** bleak, stark **6** barren **8** desolate
Waste Lands, The
author: Stephen King
Waste Land, The: 4 poem
author: T.S. Eliot
subject: 3 Apr. **5** April **6** lilacs
Waste not, want not: 3 saw **5** adage, maxim **6** saying
waste one's __: 4 time **6** breath
__ was the sky so deep a hue: 4 ne'er
wastrel: 5 knave, rogue **6** loafer, rascal **7** spender **8** prodigal **10** ne'er-do-well, profligate
no ~: 5 saver
__ Wat: 6 Angkor
Watanabe: 3 Ken
watch: 3 eye, see, spy **4** case, duty, Ebel, espy, gaze, heed, look, mark, mind, note, peer, Rado, scan, tend, view, wait **5** Casio, clock, Elgin, guard, Lorus, Omega, Rolex, scout, Seiko, spy on, stare, timer, Timex, vigil **6** advert, attend, Bulova, follow, Fossil, gape at, gaze at, gaze on, listen, look at, Movado, notice, patrol, picket, police, Pulsar, regard, sentry, shadow, Swatch, ticker **7** baby-sit, care for, Citizen, glimpse, look for, lookout, monitor, observe, oversee, protect, spy upon, stare at, witness **8** chaperon, eagle eye, glance at, Longines, look in on, scope out, scrutiny, see after, sentinel, spectate, stake out, Tag Heuer, take heed, Tourneau **9** chaperone, look after, oversight, safeguard, supervise, timepiece, vigilance **10** eyewitness, get a load of, keep tabs on, monitoring, rubberneck, scrutinize, stand guard, take care of, take notice, timekeeper, weather eye
brand: 4 Ebel, Rado **5** Casio, Elgin, Lorus, Omega, Rolex, Seiko, Timex **6** Bulova, Fossil, Movado, Piaget, Pulsar, Swatch **7** Citizen **8** Longines, Tag Heuer, Tourneau
display: 3 LCD, LED
ender: 3 dog, eye, man, men **4** band, case, word **5** maker, tower
feature: 5 alarm, timer
for: 5 await **6** expect **7** count on **8** reckon on **9** count upon **10** anticipate
holder: 3 fob **4** band **5** chain, wrist
intently: 3 eye **4** gawk, gaze, ogle **5** stare **6** take in **7** eyeball
keep ~: 4 look **6** patrol
numeral: 3 III, VII, XII **4** VIII
one's step: 6 behave, beware **7** look out **8** watch out **10** toe the line
out: 6 beware **7** heads up
out for: 4 heed, mind **8** beware of
over: 3 sit **4** keep, mind, tend **5** cover **6** cradle, defend, manage **7** protect, shelter, sit with **8** chaperon, shepherd **9** chaperone, safeguard **10** take care of
part: 4 band, case, dial, face, hand, stem **5** bezel, crown, jewel **6** detent **7** crystal **8** movement
pocket: 3 fob
secretly ~: 3 spy **4** tail **5** spy on
something to ~: 4 step **5** mouth
sound: 4 beep, tick **5** alarm
starter: 3 dog **4** stop **5** wrist
tend to a ~: 3 set **4** wind **5** reset
watch __: 3 cap, fob, out **4** fire, list, over **5** chain, guard, night **6** pocket **7** meeting
__ watch: 5 clock, night, storm, Swiss, wrist **6** analog, quartz **7** digital
Watch __ back!: 4 your
Watch __ Rhine: 5 on the
Watch __ step!: 4 your
watchband: 5 strap
watchdog: 5 super **6** keeper, warden **7** curator, janitor, manager, monitor, steward **8** executor, guardian, overseer **9** attendant, bodyguard, caretaker, concierge, custodian, protector **10** baby sitter, doorkeeper, supervisor
breed: 5 Akita, boxer **8** doberman, shepherd **10** Rottweiler
watcher: 3 fan, spy **4** eyer, nana **5** guard, nanny, spier **6** nannie **7** lookout, witness **8** beholder, onlooker **9** governess, spectator **10** eyewitness
weight ~ bane: 4 nosh **5** snack, sweet **7** munchie
weight ~ concern: 3 fat **8** calories
__ watcher: 4 bird, poll **5** clock
Watchers
author: Dean Koontz
__ Watchers: 6 Weight
watchful: 4 keen, wary **5** alert, awake, aware, canny, chary, glued, ready **6** intent, prompt **7** all ears, careful, guarded, heads-up, heedful, mindful, on guard, wakeful **8** cautious, keen-eyed, on the job, open-eyed, parental, prepared, vigilant **9** attentive, conscious, defensive, expectant, farseeing, observant, on the ball, regardful, wide-awake **10** longheaded, on one's toes, protective, suspicious, unsleeping
eye: 5 vigil **7** lookout **8** guidance, tutelage, wardship **9** oversight
watchfulness: 4 care, heed **7** caution **9** vigilance
watching
closely: 7 all eyes
one's step: 4 wary **5** canny, chary, leery **7** careful, guarded, heedful, prudent **8** cautious, vigilant, watchful **9** judicious **10** deliberate, scrupulous
Watching Scotty Grow (1971 song)
artist: Bobby Goldsboro
Watching the Wheels (1981 song)
artist: John Lennon
Watch it!: 3 hey **7** look out **9** be careful
watchkeeper: 3 spy **5** guard, scout **6** patrol, picket, ranger, sentry, warden **7** curator, flagger, lookout, spotter **8** observer, sentinel **9** caretaker, custodian, detective, signaller
watchmaker: 7 jeweler **10** horologist
art: 5 horol. **8** horology
length unit: 5 ligne

lens: 5 loupe
watchman: 5 guard 8 defender, sentinel 9 bodyguard, protector
__ watchman: 5 night
Watch Mr. Wizard (NBC) host: Don Herbert
watch one's __ Q's: 5 P's and
Watch on the Rhine
author: Lillian Hellman
watch the __: 6 birdie
watchtower: 4 beam 6 beacon 7 lookout 10 lighthouse
watchword: 5 motto 6 phrase, slogan
watch your __: 4 step
water: 3 dew, wet 4 aqua, hose, need, rain, soak, spit, tear, thin 5 douse, dowse, drink, drool, fluid, oxide, souse, spray 6 dampen, dilute, drench, liquid, weaken 7 logical, moisten, utility 8 Adam's ale, beverage, inundate, irrigate, moisture, saturate, sprinkle
add ~ to: 4 thin 6 dilute, weaken
away from ~: 6 inland
barrier: 3 dam 4 dike, weir 5 levee 10 embankment
beach ~: 4 surf
bird: 4 coot, ibis 5 egret, heron
blow out of the ~: 4 beat, best, rout, stun 5 cream, crush, outdo 6 dazzle, defeat, thrash 7 astound, conquer, overrun, stagger, stupefy, trounce 8 astonish, bowl over, vanquish 9 devastate, dumbfound, overpower, overwhelm
boatman: 3 bug 6 insect
body of ~: 3 sea 4 lake, pond, pool, tarn 5 creek, ocean, river, sound 6 lagoon, strait, stream
border: 4 bank 5 beach, coast, shore 7 seaside 8 littoral, seaboard, seashore 9 shoreline
bottled ~: 4 Naya 5 Evian 7 Perrier 8 Aquafina 9 Arrowhead
bounce on ~: 3 dap
cannon target: 3 mob 5 crowd
carrier: 3 rut 4 duct, hose, line, pail, pipe, race 5 canal, ditch, drain, flume, gulch, gully 6 arroyo, furrow, gulley, gutter, outlet, siphon, strait, syphon, trench, trough 7 channel, conduit, culvert, passage 8 aqueduct
chestnut: 5 tuber
closet: 2 WC 3 lav, loo 7 latrine 8 bathroom, lavatory
collector: 4 sump
color: 4 aqua
combining form: 4 aqua-, aqui-, hydr- 5 hydat-, hydro- 6 hydato-
company: 4 util. 7 utility
container: 3 cup, pan, pot, urn, vat 4 ewer, olla, pail, tank, vase 5 glass 6 goglet, guglet 7 cistern, gurglet 9 reservoir
container of India: 4 lota 5 lotah
containing ~: 7 hydrous
convey over ~: 5 ferry
cook in ~: 4 boil
cooler: 3 ice
covered with ~: 5 awash, soggy, soppy 6 soaked, sodden 7 sopping 8 drenched, dripping 9 saturated
craft: 3 dau, dow 4 boat, dhow, ship 5 canoe, liner, shell, sloop 6 jetski
deep ~: 3 fix, jam 4 bind, mess 5 pinch 6 crisis, pickle, plight, scrape, strait 7 dilemma, problem, trouble 8 quandary 9 adversity 10 difficulty
dog: 3 gob, tar 6 sailor
down: 3 cut, wet 4 thin 5 blunt 6 dilute, rarefy, rarify, soften, weaken 7 vitiate 10 adulterate
draw ~: 4 pump
droplets: 3 dew 4 mist 5 vapor 8 dampness, moisture
empty of ~: 4 bail
ender: 3 bed, bus, log, man, men, way 4 buck, fall, fowl, leaf, mark, shed, side, weed 5 borne, color, craft, cress, front, melon, power, proof, scape, spout, tight, works 6 course, finder, logged, marked 8 colorist, proofing
fish out of ~: 6 misfit 7 oddball 8 maverick
flounder in ~: 5 slosh 6 splash
form: 3 ice 5 steam, vapor
free from ~: 5 wring
frozen ~: 3 ice 6 icicle
get ~ from a well: 4 draw
glide on ~: 3 ski 4 skee
go by ~: 4 sail
heater: 6 boiler
hold ~: 4 wash 6 cohere 9 make sense
holder: 3 cup, pan, pot 4 ewer, olla, pail, tube, vase 5 basin, glass 6 bottle 7 canteen
holding ~: 4 sane 5 sound 7 logical
hole: 4 pond, well
hot ~: 3 fix 4 bind 6 pickle 7 problem, trouble 9 deep water 10 difficulty
in French: 3 eau
in hot ~: 7 trapped
in Latin: 4 aqua
in Spanish: 4 agua
it doesn't hold ~: 3 net 5 sieve 8 colander
jet: 5 spirt, spurt
keep one's head above ~: 5 tread
leave the ~: 6 emerge 7 surface
let the ~ out: 3 tap 4 vent 5 drain 6 siphon 7 draw off
low ~: 3 ebb
main: 4 line, pipe
make soda ~: 6 aerate
moccasin: 5 snake 7 serpent
moisten with ~: 4 soak, wash 5 bathe, douse, flush 6 drench, shower 7 immerse
mover: 3 oar
of flowing ~: 5 lotic
of still ~: 6 lentic 7 lenitic
on the ~: 4 asea 5 at sea 6 afloat
organism: 4 alga
out of the ~: 6 ashore, on land
pipe: 4 main 5 hooka 6 hookah
pistol: 3 toy
pitcher: 4 ewer
plant: 4 alga
platform by the ~: 4 dock, pier, quay, slip 5 berth, jetty, wharf
play in the ~: 4 swim, wade 5 slosh
power: 5 hydro
power org.: 3 TVA
prefix: 4 aqua- 5 hydro-
rat: 6 animal, mammal, rodent
receptacle: 4 sink 5 basin
regulator: 3 tap 5 valve 6 faucet, spigot 7 hydrant
remove ~: 4 bail, pump 5 wring
ring of ~: 4 moat
running, as ~: 5 aflow
salt ~: 3 bay, sea 5 brine, ocean
science of ~: 9 hydrology
search in ~: 6 dredge
seek ~: 5 dowse 6 divine
slide: 5 chute, flume
soapy ~: 4 suds 6 lather
softener: 5 borax
sound: 6 babble, gurgle, murmur, ripple, splash
source: 3 tap 4 well 6 faucet 7 aquifer
spend like ~: 5 waste 6 lavish 8 squander
sport: 4 polo 6 diving 8 swimming
sprite: 4 nixy 5 kelpy, nixie, nymph 6 kelpie
starter: 3 cut, sea 4 back, dish, fair, fire, head, jerk, lime, rain, salt, tide 5 break, flood, fresh, shear, under, waste, White 6 ground
stay above ~: 5 float
step through ~: 4 wade
surround with ~: 6 enisle
take on ~: 4 leak
tester: 3 toe
test the ~: 4 poll 5 query 6 survey 7 canvass
thoroughly: 4 soak 6 drench 8 saturate
throw cold ~ on: 5 deter 6 sadden 8 dispirit
throw ~ on: 5 douse, dowse 6 drench, splash 8 saturate 10 extinguish
toilet ~: 5 scent 7 cologne, perfume 9 fragrance
tonic ~: 4 fizz 5 mixer
tread ~: 4 swim
treat sea ~: 6 desalt 10 desalinate, desalinize
wheel: 5 noria
white ~: 6 rapids
without ~: 3 dry 4 arid, neat, sere
water __: 3 boy, bug, dog, gap, gun, rat, ski 4 down, hole, lily, line, main, mill, pipe, polo, sign, taxi 5 meter, nymph, power, slide, table, tower, vapor, wings 6 ballet, cannon, closet, cooler, heater, pistol, sprite, supply 7 buffalo, carrier, spaniel
water __ the bridge: 5 under
water-__: 3 bus 4 fast 7 soluble
__ water: 3 hot, ice, low, tap 4 bath, cold, hard, high, hold, holy, rose, salt, soda, soft 5 above, bilge, first, fresh, heavy, in hot, still, tonic, tread, vichy, white 6 branch, ground, static, toilet 7 mineral, quinine, seltzer
__-water: 4 blue, deep
Water __: 3 Rat 5 Music 6 Bearer
Water-__: 3 Pik
__ Water: 3 Hot 5 Afton, Black, Muddy
water-balloon sound: 5 splat
Water Bearer: 4 sign 8 Aquarius
month: 3 Feb., Jan. 7 January 8 February
predecessor: 4 Goat
successor: 4 Fish
waterborne: 4 asea 5 at sea 6 afloat
__-water bottle: 3 hot
Waterboy, The (1998 film)
cast: Fairuza Balk, Kathy Bates, Adam Sandler, Henry Winkler
water buffalo: 4 arni 5 arnee
Waterbury: 4 city, town
locale: 4 Conn.
water clover: 4 fern 5 plant
watercolor: 3 art 5 paint 6 canvas, fresco, medium 7 picture 8 painting
watercolorist: 6 artist 7 painter
watercourse: 4 duct 5 canal, creek, drain, gully, river 6 gulley, gutter, stream 7 channel, conduit, culvert
dry ~: 4 wadi, wady
watercraft: 3 dau, dow 4 boat, dhow, ship 5 canoe, liner, shell, sloop 6 jetski
watercress: 6 veggie 9 vegetable
unit: 5 sprig
Waterdance, The (1992 film)
cast: Helen Hunt, Wesley Snipes, Eric Stoltz
watered-down: 3 cut 4 tame, thin, weak 9 tasteless
ideas: 3 pap
waterfall: 5 chute, sault, spout 7 cascade, torrent
Africa ~: 8 Victoria
Alberta ~: 7 Panther
Argentina ~: 6 Iguaçu 7 Iguassú
Australia ~: 5 Tully
Austria ~: 7 Gastein 8 Krimmler
Brazil ~: 6 Iguaçu 7 Iguassú
British Columbia ~: 5 Della
California ~: 7 Feather
Canada ~: 5 Della 7 Niagara, Panther
effect: 5 spray
Ethiopia ~: 6 Fincha
France ~: 8 Gavarnie
Guyana ~: 8 Kaieteur
Hawaii ~: 5 Akaka
Idaho ~: 8 Shoshone
Italy ~: 4 Toce
Japan ~: 5 Kegon
Nevada ~: 6 Ribbon
New York ~: 7 Niagara
New Zealand ~: 6 Helena
Ontario ~: 7 Niagara
Scottish ~: 3 lin 4 linn
South Africa ~: 6 Tugela
Sweden ~: 6 Handol, Skykje
Switzerland ~: 6 Simmen
U.S. ~: 5 Akaka 6 Ribbon 7 Feather, Niagara 8 Shoshone, Sluiskin
Venezuela ~: 5 Angel
Wales ~: 7 Rhaiadr
Washington ~: 8 Sluiskin
Zambia ~: 8 Victoria
Zimbabwe ~: 8 Victoria
__ Waterfall: 3 By a, To a
Waterfalls (1995 song)
artist: TLC
__-water flat: 4 cold
Waterford: 4 city, port, town
locale: 7 Ireland
worker: 6 etcher
Waterford __: 5 glass 7 crystal
waterfowl: 4 duck
__ Waterfowl: 3 To a

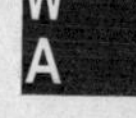

waterfront: 4 dock, port 5 beach, shore
city with a ~: 4 port
inn: 5 botel 6 boatel
org.: 3 ILA
sight: 4 pier, quay 5 wharf 6 marina
__ Waterfront: 5 On the
Watergate: 5 hotel
acronym: 5 CREEP
record: 4 tape
witness: 4 Dean
__ Waterhouse: 5 Price
watering
can alternative: 4 hose
hole: 3 bar, pub 4 pond, well 5 haunt, oasis 6 bar car, bistro, lounge, saloon, tavern
place: 4 well 5 river 6 spring
watering __: 3 can 4 hole, spot
__-watering: 5 mouth
water-insoluble substance: 5 lipid, olein 6 lipide, oleine
waterless: 3 dry 4 arid, sere 7 parched, thirsty 8 droughty 10 dehydrated
Water Lilies
painter: Claude Monet
waterlog: 4 soak 5 souse, steep, swamp 7 moisten 8 saturate
waterlogged: 3 wet 5 soggy 6 sodden
Waterloo: 4 city, ruin, town 6 battle, defeat 8 downfall
commander: 3 Ney
locale: 4 Iowa 6 Canada 7 Belgium, Ontario
Waterloo (1974 song)
artist: ABBA
Waterloo __: 6 Bridge 7 Station
Waterloo Bridge
painter: Claude Monet
Waterman
filler: 3 ink
invention: 3 pen
one end of a ~: 3 nib
__-water mark: 3 low 4 high
Watermark (1988 album)
artist: Enya
watermelon: 4 pepo 5 fruit
covering: 4 rind
like ~: 5 seedy
shape: 4 oval
Water-Method Man, The
author: John Irving
Water Music
composer: George Frideric Handel
Water of Kronos, The
author: Conrad Richter
water park feature: 5 flume, slide
water polo: 5 sport
waterproof: 4 seal 5 caulk, tight 10 impervious
coat: 5 loden
fabric: 5 loden 7 Gore-Tex, oilskin 8 oilcloth
waterproofing: 5 grout
Water Runs Dry (1995 song)
artist: Boyz II Men
Waters: 4 John, Matt 5 Alice, Ethel, Muddy 7 Crystal
Waters, Ethel: 6 singer 7 actress
song: 5 Dinah
TV: Beulah
waters, healing: 3 spa
watershed: 5 basin 8 landmark
dividing line: 5 ridge
Watership Down: 5 novel
author: Richard Adams
waterside: 5 shore
accommodations: 5 botel 6 boatel
Waters, John: 8 director
film: Cry-Baby (1990)
Hairspray (1988)
Serial Mom (1994)
water skiing: 5 sport
gear: 6 handle 7 tow rope
Waterston, Sam: 5 actor
film: Hopscotch (1980)
The Killing Fields (1984)
The Man in the Moon (1991)
Rancho Deluxe (1975)
Serial Mom (1994)
TV: I'll Fly Away, Law & Order
__ water taffy: 4 salt
watertight: 5 right, tight 10 impervious
make ~: 4 calk 5 caulk 6 batten
water-to-wine town: 4 Cana
water under the __: 6 bridge
waterway: 5 canal, river 6 stream
waterways, like some: 6 inland
waterwheel: 5 noria, sakia
waterwitch: 5 dowse
waterworks: 5 tears 6 crying 7 sobbing, wailing, weeping
turn on the ~: 3 cry, sob 7 blubber
Waterworks, The
author: E.L. Doctorow
Waterworld (1995 film)
cast: Kevin Costner, Dennis Hopper, Jeanne Tripplehorn
role: 5 Enola
watery: 3 wet 4 damp, pale, thin, weak 5 fluid, moist, runny, soggy, soupy, stale 6 dilute, liquid, marshy, sodden 7 aqueous, diluted, hydrous, wettish 9 tasteless 10 flavorless
expanse: 3 sea 5 ocean
sound: 4 glug 5 swash
Watkins: 5 Peter
Watkins __, NY: 4 Glen
Watley, Jody
hometown: Chicago
song: Don't You Want Me (1987)
Everything (1989)
Friends (1989)
Looking for a New Love (1987)
Real Love (1989)
Some Kind of Lover (1988)
This Is for the Lover in You (1996)
Watson: 2 MD 3 Bob, Tom 4 John 5 Bubba, James 6 Lucile
colleague: 4 Bell 5 Crick 6 Holmes
Watson, James: 8 Nobelist 10 geneticist
concern: 3 DNA
Watson, Tom: 6 golfer
WATS, part of: 3 Tel. 4 Area, Serv., Wide 7 Service 9 Telephone
watt: 4 unit 7 measure
ender: 3 age 5 meter
measure: 5 power
relative: 3 amp, ohm 6 ampere
starter: 4 kilo, mega
Watt: 5 James
author: Samuel Beckett
Watterson: 4 Bill
wattle: 4 jowl 6 dewlap, lappet
wattlebird: 3 iao
Watts: 5 André, Isaac, Naomi 7 Charlie, Rolonda
Watts, André: 7 pianist
Watts, Charlie: 7 drummer
genre: 4 rock
Watts, Isaac: 6 writer 7 British
work: Horae Lyricae
Watusi: 5 dance
home: 6 Africa, Rwanda 7 Burundi
__ Watusi, The: 3 Wah
Waugh: 4 Alec 6 Evelyn 7 Auberon, Hillary
Waugh, Auberon: 6 writer 7 British
work: A Bed of Flowers
Consider the Lilies
The Foxglove Saga
Path of Dalliance
Waugh, Evelyn: 6 writer 7 British
work: Black Mischief
Brideshead Revisited
Decline and Fall
The End of the Battle
A Handful of Dust
A Little Order
The Loved One
Men at Arms
Officers and Gentlemen
The Ordeal of Gilbert Pinfold
Scoop
Vile Bodies
Waugh, Hillary
work: 30 Manhattan East
Last Seen Wearing
Madman at My Door
Waukegan: 4 city, town
locale: 8 Illinois
native: Jack Benny
Waukesha: 4 city, town
locale: 9 Wisconsin
Wausau: 4 city, town
locale: 9 Wisconsin
Wauwatosa: 4 city, town
locale: 9 Wisconsin
wave: 3 set, wag 4 curl, flap, foam, perm, rash, sign, surf, sway, tide 5 crest, crimp, heave, pulse, shake, surge, swell, swing, swirl, twirl 6 beckon, billow, comber, dangle, hairdo, influx, motion, onrush, ripple, roller, ruffle, salute, signal, waggle, wigwag 7 breaker, flutter, gesture, pulsate, shudder, tsunami, upsurge 8 brandish, flourish, indicate, outbreak, undulate, whitecap 9 oscillate 10 inundation, outpouring
amplifier: 5 laser, maser
a red flag: 6 enrage 7 caution 8 forewarn
around: 4 show 6 flaunt, parade 7 display, exhibit, show off, trot out 8 brandish
away: 4 shoo
barrier: 4 mole 5 jetty, levee, wharf 7 sea wall 10 breakwater
big ~: 3 sea
combining form: 3 cym-, kym- 4 cymo-, kymo-
cutter: 4 prow
destination: 5 beach, coast, shore
down: 4 flag, hail 6 call to, signal, yell to 7 yell for
ender: 4 band, form 6 length
heraldic ~: 4 undé 5 undée
in Spanish: 3 ola
new ~: 5 novel 6 exotic, modern 8 vanguard 9 inventive 10 avant-garde, innovative
part: 5 crest, spume 6 billow
phenomenon: 4 chop
rise on a ~: 5 scend
starter: 3 air 5 micro, short
tidal ~: 6 tumult 7 tempest, tsunami, turmoil 8 disaster, upheaval 9 cataclysm
to: 4 hail 5 greet 7 welcome 9 recognize
wave __ future: 5 of the
__ wave: 3 new 4 beta, cold, heat, long, sine 5 alpha, brain, crime, delta, radio, shock, sound, tidal, water 7 carrier
__ Wave: 4 Heat
WAVE counterpart: 3 WAF 4 WAAC
wavelength
be on the same ~: 5 agree, click 8 hit it off
on the same ~: 5 alike 6 in sync
waveless: 4 calm
wavelike pattern: 5 moiré
wave of the __: 6 future
waver: 4 halt, lick, reel, sway, vary, yo-yo 5 hedge, pause 6 boggle, change, dither, falter, palter, recoil, seesaw, swerve, teeter, totter, wabble, waffle, wobble 7 flicker, flutter, stagger, stumble, whiffle 8 flip-flop, flounder, hesitate 9 fluctuate, hem and haw, oscillate, pussyfoot, vacillate 10 deliberate, dillydally, equivocate
flag ~: 4 gale, wind 7 patriot
wavering: 4 torn, weak 5 fluid, shaky, timid 6 fickle, unsure 7 erratic, halting, mutable, protean 8 hesitant, shifting, unstable, unsteady, variable 9 faltering, mercurial, uncertain, undecided, unsettled 10 ambivalent, changeable, hesitation, indecisive, irresolute, of two minds, unreliable, weak-willed, wishy-washy
Waverley
author: Walter Scott
waves: 3 sea 4 surf, wake
braving the ~: 4 asea 5 at sea 6 afloat 7 sailing
don't make ~: 4 obey 6 accept, comply
make ~: 4 stir 5 rebel, shake, upset 6 revolt 7 trouble 9 instigate 10 complicate, exasperate
rise in ~: 5 heave, pitch, surge, swell 6 billow
sound of ~: 4 roar
starter: 3 air
Waves: 10 Pepperdine
__ waves of grain: 5 amber
Waves, The
author: Virginia Woolf
wavy: 5 curly, curvy, snaky 6 curvey, gyrose, permed 7 curling, curving, rippled, sinuous, winding 8 rippling, squiggly, tortuous, twisting 9 tremulous, vibrating 10 serpentine, undulating
in heraldry: 4 onde, undé 5 undée
make ~: 4 curl 5 crimp, frizz, swirl
waw: 6 Hebrew, letter
predecessor: 2 he 3 heh
successor: 5 zayin
__ Wawa: 4 Baba
wawa device: 4 mute
wax: 4 grow, rise, trim 5 build, lipid,

mount, sheen, shine, swell, widen **6** dilate, expand, finish, gather, lipide, lipoid, polish, record, spread, thrive **7** amplify, augment, broaden, build up, cerumen, develop, enlarge, fill out, magnify, Simoniz, trounce **8** heighten, increase, lipoidal, paraffin **9** lubricant, lubricate **10** strengthen

apply ~ to: **4** seal

car ~: **7** Simoniz

cleaner: **4** Q-tip

closure: **4** seal

combining form: **3** cer- **4** cero-

ender: **4** bill, wing, work **5** berry

insert: **4** wick

maker: **3** bee, ear

opposite: **4** wane

pencil: **6** crayon

product: **4** seal **6** candle

starter: **3** ear **4** bees

target: **3** car **4** auto **5** floor, table **9** furniture

vine: **4** hoya

whole ball of ~: **3** all **5** total **8** entirety, sum total **9** aggregate **10** everything

wrap in ~: **4** cere

wax ___: **4** bean **5** paper, wroth **6** museum

___ wax: **7** sealing

Waxahachie: **4** city, town

locale: **5** Texas

waxed

cheese: **4** Edam **5** Gouda

it's often ~: **5** floor, floss

waxed ___: **5** paper

waxen: **3** wan **4** pale **5** livid, pasty, white **6** pallid **7** pliable **8** lustrous **9** colorless

waxing: **6** growth **8** blooming, increase

Waxman: **2** Al **5** Franz

waxwing: **4** bird

waxy: **4** oily **5** slick **6** sallow **8** lustrous, slippery **9** ceraceous, lubricous

way: **4** gate, lane, line, mode, path, plan, plot, road, room, vein, walk **5** alley, entry, habit, knack, means, orbit, route, space, steps, style, track, trail, trait, trick, usage **6** access, artery, avenue, course, custom, living, manner, method, nature, policy, scheme, street, system **7** bearing, channel, conduct, fashion, ingress, passage, process, routine, stretch, vehicle **8** approach, behavior, distance, entrance, practice, tendency **9** boulevard, direction, elbowroom, mannerism, procedure, technique **10** instrument

about one: **3** air **5** style **6** aspect, manner **7** bearing **8** carriage, demeanor, presence **9** character, mannerism **10** appearance, deportment

across the ~ from: **3** opp. **8** opposite

all the ~: **5** fully **6** wholly **9** to the hilt **10** completely, to the limit

a long ~: **3** far **4** afar **6** far cry

any old ~: **5** about **6** remiss **8** reckless **9** haphazard **10** incautious

back when: **4** once, past, yore **8** formerly

be on your ~: **2** go **3** run **4** exit **5** leave

by ~ of: **3** via **4** thro, thru **7** through

by the ~: **9** in passing

combining form: **3** -ode

covered ~: **4** stoa **6** arcade **7** gallery, portico **9** colonnade

down: **3** bad, low **4** base, deep **5** woful **6** gloomy, nether, sunken, woeful **7** forlorn **9** depressed, in the pits **10** dispirited, rock-bottom

ender: **3** lay **4** bill, laid, side, ward, worn **5** farer, point **6** faring

every which ~: **5** messy, mussy **6** hectic, untidy **7** chaotic, haywire, jumbled, lawless, riotous, tangled **8** anarchic, confused, pell-mell **10** anarchical, disjointed, disordered, disorderly, topsy-turvy, tumultuous

feel one's ~: **5** grope **6** fumble **8** flounder **9** cast about

find a ~: **4** cope, lead **6** manage

from ~ back: **5** of old **6** age-old **7** veteran

get in the ~ of: **4** clog **5** deter **6** hamper, hinder, impair, impede, impose **8** handicap, obstruct

get out of the ~: **4** duck **5** dodge, evade **8** sidestep

get the hard ~: **3** pry **5** wrest, wring **6** extort, wrench

get the old-fashioned ~: **4** earn

get under ~: **4** sail, send **5** begin, speed, start **7** proceed **9** strike out

give ~: **3** sag **4** fall, move, snap **5** budge, burst, split, yield **6** buckle, cave in, relent, retire, tumble, weaken **7** crumble, crumple, succumb **8** collapse, fall down, withdraw

give ~ (to): **5** defer

go all the ~: **4** last **6** endure, hold on, linger **7** carry on, persist, survive **8** continue, plug away **9** hang tough, keep going, persevere, stand firm **10** tough it out

go out of one's ~: **6** bother

having a ~ with words: **8** eloquent

in: **4** door, gate **5** entry **6** entrée, portal **8** entrance

in a ~: **5** kinda, sorta **6** kind of, sort of **7** somehow **8** as it were, possibly

in a bad ~: **3** ill **4** illy, sick

in a big ~: **4** a lot, lots, much, tons **5** loads, no end **6** galore, highly, hugely, oodles **7** aplenty, grandly, greatly, largely **8** beaucoup, lavishly, terribly **9** copiously, extremely, immensely, liberally, profusely **10** abundantly, a great deal, enormously, prodigally

in any ~: **5** at all

in Italian: **3** via

in Latin: **4** iter

in one ~ or another: **7** somehow

in Spanish: **3** vía

in such a ~: **4** as if, so as, thus

in that ~: **4** ergo, then, thus

in the same ~: **3** too **4** also **6** as well **8** likewise **9** similarly

in the worst ~: **3** bad **5** badly

in this ~: **4** thus **6** hereby

in what ~: **3** how **5** how so

lead the ~: **5** guide **7** conduct, pioneer, trigger, usher in **8** initiate **9** instigate

long ~ around: **6** bypass, detour

look the other ~: **6** ignore **7** neglect **8** overlook

lose one's ~: **3** err **5** drift, stray **6** ramble **7** digress, diverge, meander **9** wander off

make one's ~: **4** wend **6** stroll, travel

no ~: **3** nah, naw, nay, nix, non **4** nein, nope, nyet, uh-uh **5** I won't, ixnay, my eye, never **7** I refuse **8** forget it, I will not, negative, negatory **9** fat chance, I think not, rejection **10** count me out, impossible, not a chance, thumbs down

not in any ~: **5** nohow

numbered: **3** rte. **5** route **10** interstate

off: **3** far, yon **4** afar, ramp **8** mistaken **9** incorrect **10** inaccurate

on: **4** ramp **6** access

one ~ or another: **7** somehow

on the ~: **3** off **6** coming **7** en route **8** imminent **9** in the wind

on the ~ out: **5** dated, hoary, passé, stale **6** old hat **9** hackneyed

other ~ around: **9** vice versa

out: **4** door, exit, gate **5** weird **6** egress, escape, outlet, refuge **7** bizarre, radical **8** creative, loophole, recourse

out of harm's ~: **4** alee, safe **6** secure

out of the ~: **3** far **4** awry **6** afield, astray

paper deliverer's ~: **5** route

partner: **4** will

pave the ~: **4** ease **5** ready, usher **6** smooth **9** introduce

point the ~: **4** lead **5** spark, steer, teach, train, tutor, usher **6** direct, orient **7** conduct **8** instruct **9** spearhead

put another ~: **5** resay **8** rephrase

right of ~: **8** priority

rubbing the wrong ~: **5** nasty **7** caustic **10** unpleasant

rub the wrong ~: **3** get, ire, irk, vex **4** miff, rile, roil **5** annoy, chafe, grate, peeve **6** abrade, offend

set on its ~: **4** send **6** convey, propel **8** dispatch

show the ~: **4** lead **5** guide, point **6** direct, lead in, lead on **7** pioneer

since ~ back when: **6** in ages **9** for a while

smooth the ~: **4** ease **5** set up **6** loosen **7** further, lighten, prepare **8** expedite, mitigate, moderate, simplify

stand in the ~: **3** bar **6** hinder, impede **9** foreclose

starter: **3** air, any, fly, key, lee, mid, run, sea, sky, sub **4** arch, area, belt, bike, door, fair, folk, foot, free, gang, gate, half, hall, head, high, park, path, race, rail, road, roll, ship, side, slip, some, taxi, thru, tide, tram, walk **5** alley, cable, cause, cross, drive, entry, green, hatch, motor, speed, spill, stair, stern, water **6** breeze, sluice

that ~: **4** thus **6** like so, thusly

the ~: **3** how

the same ~: **5** alike **9** similarly, uniformly **10** comparably

things are: **6** status

to go: **5** huzza, route **6** hoorah, hooray, hurrah, hurray, huzzah

to put it another ~: **5** I mean

under ~: **8** in motion **9** on the move **10** in progress

up: **4** rise **5** slope, stair **6** ascent **7** incline

up the slope: **3** tow **4** T-bar

with words: **4** tact **9** diplomacy

wrong ~: **8** backward **9** backwards **10** upside-down

way ___ world: **5** of the

way-___: **3** out

___ way: **3** in a **4** atta, give, make **5** by the, harm's, in the, on the, under

Way ___ Flesh, The: **5** of All

Way ___ Look Tonight, The: **3** You

Way ___, The: **4** It Is, West **5** Ahead

Way ___ West: **3** Out

Way ___ Yonder in New Orleans: **4** Down

___ Way: **5** Milky **6** Appian, United

Wayans: **3** Kim **5** Damon **6** Keenen

___-way bulb: **5** three

___-way chili: **4** five

Way cool!: **3** rad

___ Way Corrigan: **5** Wrong

Way Down (1977 song)

artist: Elvis Presley

Way Down Yonder in New Orleans (1959 song)

artist: Freddy Cannon

wayfarer: **5** nomad, rover **6** roamer **7** pilgrim, tourist, trekker, voyager **8** gadabout, traveler, vagabond, wanderer **9** journeyer, meanderer, passenger **10** adventurer

refuge: **3** inn **5** hotel, lodge, motel **6** hostel **9** roadhouse

Wayfarer: **3** car **4** auto **5** Dodge

wayfaring: **6** roving, travel **7** journey, nomadic, on the go, roaming, vagrant, walking **8** drifting, gadabout, rambling, vagabond, voyaging **9** itinerant, itinerate, on the move, traveling, wandering **10** jetsetting, journeying

Way It Is, The (1986 song)

artist: Bruce Hornsby and the Range

Way I Want to Touch You, The (1975 song)

artist: Captain & Tennille

Wayland: **7** Flowers

waylay: **4** jump, lurk **5** prowl **6** accost, ambush, assail, attack, hold up, kidnap, lay for **7** set upon **8** pounce on, surprise **9** bushwhack, intercept

Waylon: **8** Jennings

Wayne: **4** Dyer, John, Wang **5** Bruce, David, Morse **6** Knight, Morris, Newton, Rogers **7** Anthony, Gretzky, Millner

Wayne, Bruce: **6** Batman

dog: **3** Ace

home: **5** manor

__ Wayne, IN: 4 Fort
Wayne, John: 5 actor
birthplace: 4 Iowa
film: The Alamo (1960)
Angel and the Badman (1947)
Back to Bataan (1945)
The Big Trail (1930)
The Comancheros (1961)
Dark Command (1940)
Donovan's Reef (1963)
El Dorado (1967)
The Fighting Seabees (1944)
The Flying Leathernecks (1951)
Flying Tigers (1942)
Fort Apache (1948)
Hatari! (1962)
The High and the Mighty (1954)
Hondo (1953)
How the West Was Won (1962)
The Longest Day (1962)
The Long Voyage Home (1940)
The Man Who Shot Liberty Valance (1962)
McLintock! (1963)
McQ (1974)
North to Alaska (1960)
Operation Pacific (1951)
The Quiet Man (1952)
Reap the Wild Wind (1942)
Red River (1948)
Rio Bravo (1959)
Rio Grande (1950)
Rio Lobo (1970)
Rooster Cogburn (1975)
Sands of Iwo Jima (1949)
The Searchers (1956)
She Wore a Yellow Ribbon (1949)
The Shootist (1976)
The Sons of Katie Elder (1965)
Stagecoach (1939)
Tall in the Saddle (1944)
They Were Expendable (1945)
True Grit (1969, AA)
The War Wagon (1967)
nickname: 4 Duke
real name: Marion Morrison
Waynesboro: 4 city, town
locale: 8 Virginia
Wayne's World (1992 film)
cast: Lara Flynn Boyle, Tia Carrere, Dana Carvey, Rob Lowe, Mike Myers
catchword: 3 not
setting: 6 Aurora 9 Illinois
Way of All Flesh, The
author: Samuel Butler
way of a man with __, the: 5 a maid
Way of Love, The (1972 song)
artist: Cher
way of the __: 5 cross, world
way of the gods, literally: 6 Shinto
__ way or the other: 3 one
way-out: 3 odd 5 weird 6 freaky 7 bizarre, offbeat, strange, unusual 8 aberrant, abnormal, freakish, peculiar 9 irregular 10 off-the-wall
waypost: 6 marker 8 landmark 9 milestone
ways: 6 habits, traits 7 customs 8 patterns 10 ins and outs
and means: 7 capital, revenue 9 resources
change one's ~: 4 mend 6 reform 7 shape up 10 make amends
go different ~: 4 part 5 split 8 separate
see the error of one's ~: 6 repent
set in one's ~: 4 firm, iron 5 balky, fixed, rigid, stern, stiff, stony 6 dogged, mulish, ornery 7 adamant, piggish, willful 8 contrary, indurate, obdurate, perverse, resolute, stubborn 9 fractious, hard-nosed, immovable, obstinate, pigheaded, tenacious, unbending 10 bullheaded, hard-bitten, hardheaded, headstrong, inflexible, refractory, unshakable, unyielding
starter: 4 side
__ Ways: 4 Evil
__ ways about it: 5 no two
ways and __: 5 means
__-way street: 3 one, two
Way That You Love Me, The (1989 song)
artist: Paula Abdul
__ Way, The: 4 Hard 5 Milky 6 Family
way to __ heart..., The: 5 a man's
__ way to go!: 4 Atta
__ Way to Go!: 5 What a
Way to Natural Beauty, The
author: Cheryl Tiegs
__ Way to Pay Old Debts: 4 A New
Way Upstream
author: Alan Ayckbourn
wayward: 4 lost, wild 6 errant, feisty, fickle, mulish, ornery, unruly, wanton, wicked, wilful 7 aimless, defiant, deviant, erratic, flighty, impious, naughty, willful 8 contrary, factious, obdurate, perverse, stubborn, variable 9 dissolute, obstinate, whimsical 10 capricious, changeable, delinquent, disorderly, headstrong, inconstant, rebellious, refractory, self-willed
Wayward Bus, The
author: John Steinbeck
waywardness: 8 mischief 10 misconduct
Wayward Wind, The (1956 song)
artist: Gogi Grant
Way West, The: 4 film 5 novel
author: A.B. Guthrie
Way West, The (1967 film)
cast: Jack Elam, Kirk Douglas, Lola Albright, Richard Widmark, Robert Mitchum, Sally Field, Stubby Kaye
Way We Were, The: 4 film, song
artist: Barbra Streisand
cast: Robert Redford, Barbra Streisand
director: Sydney Pollack
Way You Do the Things You Do, The (1964 song)
artist: Temptations
Way You Look Tonight, The
composer: Dorothy Fields, Jerome Kern
Way You Look Tonight, The (1961 song)
artist: Lettermen
Way You Make Me Feel, The (1987 song)
artist: Michael Jackson
__ way you slice it: 3 any
WB
mascot: 4 frog
successor: 5 The CW
WBA
area: 4 ring 5 arena
athlete: 3 pug 5 boxer
part: 4 Assn. 5 Assoc., World 6 Boxing
result: 2 KO 3 TKO
WBC
area: 4 ring 5 arena
athlete: 3 pug 5 boxer
part: 5 World 6 Boxing
__ W. Bush: 6 George
W.C.: 3 lav, loo 4 bath, john 5 Handy 6 Fields 8 bathroom, lavatory
WCTU
member: 3 Dry
target: 3 alc., wet 6 saloon
wd.
component: 3 ltr., syl. 4 syll.
connecting ~: 4 conj.
descriptive ~: 3 adj., adv.
ender: 4 suff.
group: 3 phr.
shortened ~: 4 abbr.
source: 4 etym. 5 deriv.
starter: 4 pref.
stock: 5 vocab.
see also word
WD40: 9 lubricant
we
not: 4 they
__ we: 5 royal
__ we?: 5 Shall
We __ Family: 3 Are
We __ Harder: 3 Try
We __ Kings of Orient Are: 5 Three
We __ Little Christmas: 5 Need a
We __ Love: 3 Got 5 Are in
We __ Not Alone: 3 Are
We __ not amused: 3 are
We __ Overcome: 5 Shall
We __ please: 5 aim to
We __ robbed!: 3 was, wuz
We __ Start the Fire: 5 Didn't
We __ the Champions: 3 Are
We __ the World: 3 Are
We __ Work It Out: 3 Can
__ We?: 5 Didn't
We Accuse!
author: Stewart Alsop
weak: 3 dim, low, wan 4 lame, limp, meek, mild, pale, poor, puny, sick, slim, soft, tame, thin 5 faded, faint, frail, inept, light, lousy, reedy, runny, rusty, shaky, slack, spent, stale, timid, unfit, vapid, wimpy 6 ailing, anemic, atonic, craven, dilute, effete, fading, faulty, feeble, flabby, flimsy, infirm, mortal, sickly, skimpy, slight, tender, unable, unsafe, unsure, unwell, wabbly, watery, wobbly, yellow 7 anaemic, diluted, failing, flaccid, fragile, insipid, lacking, languid, limited, maudlin, muffled, nervous, puerile, rickety, run-down, shallow, slender, spindly, stifled, tenuous, unsound, useless, wimpish, worn out 8 cowardly, decrepit, delicate, flagging, helpless, hesitant, immature, insecure, pathetic, sluggish, timorous, unstable, wavering 9 deficient, dependant, dependent, enervated, exhausted, faltering, frangible, inaudible, nerveless, powerless, prostrate, spineless, tasteless, unguarded, unhealthy, untenable, untrained, whispered 10 improbable, inadequate, indecisive, irresolute, pathetical, unaccented, unreliable, unstressed, vulnerable, wishy-washy
combining form: 4 lept- 5 lepto-
ender: 4 ling
in phonetics: 5 lenis
in the knees: 5 dazed, dizzy, faint, giddy, shaky, woozy 6 wobbly 7 reeling 8 unsteady
knees: 4 fear 8 cold feet, timidity 9 cowardice 10 faint heart
one: 4 prey 6 victim
point: 4 vice 5 minus 6 defect, foible
weak-__: 5 kneed 6 headed, minded, willed
Weak (1993 song)
artist: SWV
weaken: 3 cut, sap, tax 4 fade, fail, flag, jade, sink, thin, tire, wane, wear, wilt 5 abate, blunt, break, decay, droop, erode, faint, lapse, lower, mince, relax, shake, water, weary 6 damage, debase, defuse, defuze, dilute, ease up, enerve, falter, impair, lessen, reduce, relent, soften, strain, temper, totter 7 break up, crumble, decline, degrade, deplete, dwindle, exhaust, fatigue, give way, qualify, relapse, tail off, tire out, tremble, unnerve, vitiate, wear out 8 decrease, diminish, enervate, enfeeble, languish, minimize, mitigate, moderate, paralyse, paralyze, peter out, slow down 9 attenuate, indispose, undermine, water down 10 adulterate, debilitate, devitalize, dishearten, emasculate
weakened: 5 spent 6 feeble 7 haggard, injured, starved 8 starving
weakening: 7 decline 9 abatement, attrition 10 diminution
Weakest Link, The: 8 game show
host: Anne Robinson
weak-kneed: 6 craven 7 fearful, wimpish 9 spineless 10 indecisive, irresolute, wishy-washy
weakling: 3 sap 4 baby, wimp, wuss 5 sissy, softy 6 coward, softie 7 chicken, crybaby, quitter 8 mama's boy, pushover 9 cream puff, jellyfish
like a ~: 4 puny
no ~: 5 he-man
weak-minded: 4 daft 5 daffy, dizzy, dopey, goofy, inane, sappy, silly 6 absurd 7 asinine, doltish, fatuous, foolish, vacuous, witless 9 dim-witted, half-baked, senseless 10 addlepated, boneheaded, cockamamie, half-witted, ill-advised
weakness: 3 gap 4 flaw, need, urge, vice 5 fault, lapse, minus, taste 6 anemia, defect, foible, hurdle, liking 7 anaemia, barrier, blemish, failing, fatigue, frailty, languor, malaise, passion 8 appetite, debility, delicacy, drawback, fondness, handicap, obstacle, penchant, shortage, soft spot, tendency 9 blind spot, detriment, fragility, frailness, hindrance, infirmity, lassitude, liability, proneness, sore point, specialty 10 deficiency, fee-

bleness, impairment, impediment, inadequacy, incapacity, indecision, insecurity, insipidity, invalidity, partiality, proclivity, propensity
cause: **6** anemia **7** anaemia
minor ~: **4** vice **6** foible
muscle ~: **5** atony **6** atonia
weak-willed: **6** fickle **8** hesitant, wavering **9** faltering, spineless, uncertain **10** ambivalent, irresolute, wishy-washy
one: **3** sop
weal: **4** luck, welt **9** happiness, well-being **10** prosperity
__ weal: **6** common
weald: **4** wood **5** woods
__ We All?: **5** Aren't
wealth: **5** means, store **6** assets, bounty, clover, estate, luxury, moolah, plenty, riches **7** capital, fortune, revenue **8** holdings, opulence, opulency, property, richness, security **9** abundance, affluence, plenitude, profusion, resources, substance **10** belongings, cornucopia, luxuriance, prosperity
combining form: **4** plut-
ill-gotten ~: **4** pelf **5** booty, lucre
starter: **6** common
see also moolah
Wealth of Nations, The
author: Adam Smith
wealthy: **4** rich **5** flush **6** loaded, monied **7** booming, moneyed, opulent, upscale, well-off **8** affluent, in clover, thriving, well-to-do **9** fortunate, pecunious, well-fixed **10** in the dough, in the money, privileged, propertied, prosperous, successful, well-heeled
become ~: **6** do well, make it, thrive **7** make out, prosper, succeed **8** fare well, flourish, go places, grow rich, hit it big, make good **9** make money
make ~: **6** enrich
one: **4** have **5** nabob, nawab **6** fat cat
wean: **6** cut off **8** break off, separate **9** ablactate, break away, disengage
weapon: **3** arm, bow, gat, gun, rod **4** bomb, épée, mine **5** arrow, lance, spear, sword **6** cudgel **7** firearm, grenade, missile **8** catapult
cop ~: **5** baton, taser **9** billy club
__ Weapon: **6** Lethal
weaponless: **5** clean **7** unarmed **10** barehanded
weaponry: **4** arms, guns **6** rifles, sabers, swords **7** cannons, pistols **8** bayonets, bazookas, matériel, ordnance, shotguns **9** artillery, firepower, munitions
weapons: **4** arms **7** battery **8** materiel, ordnance **9** artillery, munitions
cross ~ with: **4** face **6** attack, battle, engage, take on
depot: **6** armory
equip with ~: **3** arm **5** enarm **7** fortify **8** embattle
strip of ~: **5** unarm **6** disarm
wear: **3** don, irk, rub, tax, use, vex **4** fade, fray, gall, garb, gear, jade, last, tire **5** chafe, decay, erode, get on, graze, grind, model, put on, scuff, sport, try on **6** abrade, attire, fit out, have on, hold up, milage, pester, scrape, slip on, suit up, weaken **7** apparel, clothes, corrode, crumble, display, dress in, erosion, exhaust, exhibit, fatigue, inroads, mileage, overuse, service, show off, stand up, utility, weather **8** abrasion, clothing, friction, garments, stand for, wash away **9** attrition, corrosion, undermine **10** exasperate, impairment, usefulness
starter: **3** day, eye, ski **4** foot, head, knit, mens, neck, play, rain, skee, swim **5** beach, dance, inner, night, outer, sleep **6** formal, lounge, sports **7** evening, leather, leisure
wear __: **3** off, out **4** down, thin
wear __ hats: **3** two
wear __ one's welcome: **3** out
__ wear: **4** men's **6** active, women's **7** wash and
wear and __: **4** tear
__ Wear Daily: **6** Women's
We are __ amused: **3** not
We Are Family (1979 song)
artist: Sister Sledge
We Are the Champions (1977 song)
artist: Queen
We Are the World (1985 song)
artist: USA for Africa
wearied: **4** beat, limp **5** spent **6** dished **9** prostrate
weariness: **5** ennui **6** tedium **7** boredom, fatigue, languor **8** lethargy **9** lassitude **10** enervation, exhaustion
exclamation: **5** ho-hum **7** heigh-ho
wearing: **4** hard **6** clad in, taxing **7** erosion, erosive **8** tiresome **9** laborious **10** enervating
wearisome: **4** arid, blah, dull, tame **5** bland, heavy, ho-hum, vapid **6** boring, dreary, taxing, trying **7** humdrum, insipid, lengthy, tedious **8** dragging, tiresome, unvaried **9** difficult, laborious **10** cumbersome, enervating, monotonous
become ~: **4** cloy, jade, pall
task: **5** chore, grind **6** burden
wearisomeness: **3** rut **5** ennui **6** tedium **7** boredom **8** banality, monotony
wear the __: **5** pants
wear two __: **4** hats
weary: **3** irk, sag, sap, tax, try, vex **4** beat, bore, cloy, fade, flag, glut, jade, lazy, pall, sick, tire, worn **5** all in, annoy, blasé, bored, drain, fed up, had it, jaded, spent, taxed, tired **6** burden, bushed, done in, drowsy, harass, pooped, punchy, sicken, sleepy, weaken, zonked **7** depress, disgust, drained, exhaust, fatigue, languid, oppress, overtax, run-down, tire out, vitiate, worn out **8** careworn, dog-tired, drooping, enervate, enfeeble, fatigued, flagging, listless, out of gas, overwork, peter out, wiped out, worn-down **9** bone-tired, burned out, dead-tired, disgusted, enervated, exhausted, grow tired, impatient, lethargic, overtired, played out, prostrate, tucker out **10** debilitate, devitalize, dishearten, exasperate, knocked out, overworked
grow ~: **3** sag **4** fade, flag, jade, tire **7** fatigue, tire out **8** peter out **9** tucker out
looking ~: **5** drawn
make ~: **4** bore
sound: **4** sigh
__-weary: **3** war **5** world
wearying
see wearisome
weasel: **4** fink, mink **5** fitch, otter, pekan, ratel, sable, skunk, sneak, stoat, tayra **6** animal, badger, ermine, ferret, marten, waffle **7** foumart, polecat **8** carcajou, foulmart, kolinsky, muishond **9** pussyfoot, scoundrel, wolverine **10** equivocate
Africa: **5** ratel **8** muishond
Asia: **5** ratel **8** kolinsky
cousin: **4** mink **5** otter, pekan, sable, skunk
Europe: **5** fitch, sable **6** ermine **7** foumart, polecat **8** foulmart
North America: **4** mink **5** skunk **6** badger, marten **7** polecat **8** carcajou **9** wolverine
out: **6** recant, renege **9** disengage
out of: **4** duck **5** avoid, dodge, evade, get by, shirk **7** disavow **8** go back on **9** get around
South America: **5** tayra **6** grison
use ~ words: **5** dodge, evade, fudge, hedge, skirt, waver **6** waffle **8** flip-flop, sidestep **9** hem and haw, pussyfoot, stonewall, vacillate **10** equivocate
word: **3** pop **5** maybe
weasel __: **3** out **4** word **5** out of
Weasley: **3** Ron
weather: **3** dry **4** last, take, wear **5** brave, clime, stand, stick **6** bear up, endure, expose, make it, resist, season **7** climate, ride out, survive, undergo **8** elements, overcome, stand for, surmount **9** rise above, withstand **10** get through, stick it out
away from the ~: **4** alee
bad ~: **4** gale, hail, rain, snow **5** sleet, storm **7** tornado **8** blizzard **9** hurricane
cause of extreme ~: **6** El Niño
combining form: **6** meteor-
device: **4** vane **9** barometer, rain gauge
ender: **4** cast, cock, vane, worn **5** board, glass, proof **6** caster
eye: **5** vigil, watch **7** lookout **8** scrutiny
factor: **5** chill
feel under the ~: **3** ail
forecast: **3** dry, hot, wet **4** cold, cool, damp, fair, gale, hail, mild, rain, snow, warm **5** clear, crisp, foggy, gusty, humid, muggy, sleet, storm, sunny **6** cloudy, frigid, stormy **7** drizzle
hot ~: **6** dog day
info: **4** rept. **6** report
line: **5** front
permitting: **5** maybe
phenomenon: **4** haze **5** storm **6** fogdog **7** rainbow
probe: **5** sonde
satellite: **4** ESSA **5** Tiros
science of ~: **11** meteorology
stat.: **3** THI, WCF
system: **3** low **4** high **5** front
under the ~: **3** ill **4** achy, sick **6** ailing, infirm, laid up, peaked, queasy, queazy, sickly, unwell **7** run-down, unsound **8** diseased **9** afflicted, bedridden **10** indisposed, out of sorts
wet ~: **4** rain, snow **5** sleet **7** drizzle
winter ~: **4** snow **5** sleet **8** blizzard
with a ~ eye open: **8** vigilant
weather __: **3** eye, map **4** deck, ship, tide, vane **5** gauge, strip **6** report **7** balloon, station
weather-__: **4** wise **5** bound **6** beaten
__-weather: **3** all
Weather __: **6** Bureau
__ Weather: **6** Stormy
weather-beaten: **3** old **4** aged, worn **5** erose **6** rugged, shabby **7** rickety, run-down **8** decrepit, timeworn **10** bedraggled, ramshackle, tumbledown
weathercock: **4** vane
weathered: **5** hardy, hoary **6** brawny, robust, rugged, shabby, strong, sturdy **7** run-down **8** decrepit, timeworn **9** crumbling, well-built **10** able-bodied, broken-down, ramshackle, threadbare
__ weather eye open: **5** keep a
__-weather friend: **4** fair
weather-map feature: **5** ridge **6** isobar, isohel
Weathers: **4** Carl
weather the __: **5** storm
weathervane holder: **4** roof **6** cupola
Weatherwax: **3** Ken **4** Rudd
weatherworn: **5** erose **6** beaten
weave: **4** join, knit, reel, spin, sway, wind **5** blend, braid, lurch, plait, snake, twine, twist **6** careen, dodder, splice, teeter, totter, zigzag **7** entwine, intwine, meander, texture **8** contrive **9** fabricate, interfold, interlace **10** crisscross, intertwine
a chair seat: **4** cane
fabric ~: **3** net **5** satin, twill **6** Madras
having an open ~: **5** meshy
mate: **3** bob
starter: **4** hair
__ weave: **6** basket
weaver
device: **4** loom **5** frame
ender: **4** bird
frame: **4** sley
hitch: **4** knot
Weaver: **4** Earl **5** Fritz **6** Dennis **7** Charley **9** Sigourney
__ Weaver: **5** Dream
weaverbird: **6** bishop, whidah, whydah
Weaver, Dennis: **5** actor
colleague: Amanda Blake, James Arness
TV: Gentle Ben, Gunsmoke, McCloud
Weaver, Sigourney: **7** actress
film: Alien (1979)

Aliens (1986)
Copycat (1995)
Dave (1993)
Death and the Maiden (1994)
Galaxy Quest (1999)
Ghostbusters (1984)
Ghostbusters II (1989)
Gorillas in the Mist (1988)
Heartbreakers (2001)
The Ice Storm (1997)
A Map of the World (1999)
Working Girl (1988)
The Year of Living Dangerously (1983)

weaving: **4** mesh **5** craft **8** unstable, unsteady
term: **4** weft
web: **3** net **4** maze, mesh, trap **5** snare, snarl, toils **6** morass, tangle, tissue **7** complex, lattice, netting, network, pitfall, trellis **8** filagree, filigree, gossamer, membrane **9** fillagree, labyrinth **10** wickerwork
ender: **4** feet, foot, worm
like a ~: **4** lacy **5** filmy, wispy
make a ~: **4** spin **5** weave
starter: **3** cob, orb
victim: **3** fly
web __: **4** foot
web-__: **4** toed **6** footed
__ web: **4** food **6** spider
Web: **8** Internet **10** cyberspace
access the ~: **5** log on
ad: **6** banner
address: **3** URL
address start: **4** http
address suffix: **3** com, edu, gov, net
auction site: **4** eBay
communiqué: **2** IM
company: **6** dot-com
connector: **5** modem
ender: **4** cast
explore the ~: **4** surf
language: **4** html, Java
leave the ~: **6** log off
locale: **3** URL **7** address
page access: **4** link
service: **3** AOL **5** Yahoo!
site info: **3** FAQ
software: **6** applet **7** browser
worker: **5** sysop
see also Internet
Web __: **4** page, site **6** portal
W.E.B.: **6** Du Bois
Web and the Rock, The
author: Thomas Wolfe
Webb: **4** Jack, Spud **5** Chick, Chloe, Jimmy **6** Karrie, Pierce **7** Clifton **8** Beatrice
Webb, Chick: **7** drummer
genre: **4** jazz
Webber: **6** Robert
__ Webber: **5** Lloyd, Paine
Webb, Jack: **5** actor
spouse: Julie London
Webb, Karrie: **6** golfer
__ We Be Friends?: **4** Can't
We Belong (1984 song)
artist: Pat Benatar
Weber: **3** Max **4** Dick, Joan, Pete **6** Steven
opera: **6** Oberon
Weber, Dick: **3** PBA **6** bowler
milieu: **4** lane **5** alley
Weber, Joan
song: Let Me Go Lover (1954)
Weber, Steven: **5** actor
TV: Wings
web-footed
bird: **3** auk **4** duck, loon, nene, swan **5** goose, solan
mammal: **4** mink **5** coypu, otter **6** beaver
weblike: **4** lacy **5** meshy
Webster: **4** John, Noah **6** Daniel **8** Nicholas
Webster (ABC sitcom)
cast: Susan Clark (Katherine Papadapolis)
Alex Karras (George Papadapolis)
Emmanuel Lewis (Webster Long)
Webster, Daniel: **6** orator
Webster Groves: **4** city, town
locale: **8** Missouri
Webster, John: **7** British **10** playwright
work: The Duchess of Malfi
The White Devil
Webster, Noah: **6** writer **13** lexicographer
alma mater: **4** Yale
__ Web, The: **5** Glass
We Built This City (1985 song)
artist: Starship
webzine: **4** e-mag
We Can Work It Out (song)
artist: Beatles, Stevie Wonder
wed: **3** tie **4** bind, bond, fuse, join, link, mate, tied, yoke **5** blend, bound, elope, fused, marry, mated, merge, unite, yoked **6** allied, couple, eloped, joined, linked, merged, splice, united **7** blended, combine, conjoin, connect, coupled, espouse, married, spliced **8** coalesce, combined, espoused **9** coalesced, commingle, conjoined, connected, dedicated, integrate **10** commingled, get hitched, got hitched, integrated, tie the knot
ender: **4** lock
pledge to ~: **5** troth **10** engagement
starter: **5** newly
Wed.: **3** day
follower: **3** Thu. **4** Thur. **5** Thurs.
preceder: **3** Tue. **4** Tues.
to Thurs.: **4** yest.
__ We Dance: **5** Shall
wedded: **5** joint **7** marital, nuptial, spousal **8** conjugal **9** connubial
Weddell: **3** sea
locale: **10** Antarctica
wedding: **5** union **6** bridal **8** espousal, marriage, nuptials **9** matrimony
announcement word: **3** née
avoid a big ~: **5** elope
band: **4** ring
cake feature: **4** tier
conveyance: **4** limo **9** limousine
dessert: **4** cake
gift: **5** dowry **6** dowery
keepsake: **5** album
official: **2** JP **5** rabbi **8** minister
old-fashioned ~ word: **4** obey
party member: **3** kin **5** bride, groom, in-law, niece, usher **7** best man
party members: **6** family **7** kinfolk
ring holder: **6** bearer
route: **5** aisle
site: **5** altar **6** chapel
throw: **6** garter **7** bouquet
tradition: **5** toast
wear: **3** tux **4** gown, lace, tuck, veil **5** dress, satin, tiara **6** tuxedo
words: **3** I do, vow
worker: **2** DJ **6** deejay
wedding __: **3** day **4** band, cake, ring **5** chest, march
__ wedding: **4** June **6** golden, silver
Wedding __, The: **4** Gift **5** March **6** Singer **7** Planner
__ Wedding: **5** Delta, Royal **6** Betsy's, Double, Polish, Silver **7** Muriel's, Waikiki
wedding anniversaries:
1st - Paper
2nd - Cotton
3rd - Leather
4th - Linen, Silk
5th - Wood
6th - Iron
7th - Wool, Copper
8th - Bronze
9th - Pottery, China
10th - Tin, Aluminum
11th - Steel
12th - Silk
13th - Lace
14th - Ivory
15th - Crystal
20th - China
25th - Silver
30th - Pearl
35th - Coral, Jade
40th - Ruby
45th - Sapphire
50th - Gold
55th - Emerald
60th - Diamond
Wedding Bell Blues (1969 song)
artist: Fifth Dimension
composer: Laura Nyro
Wedding Crashers (2005 film)
cast: Vince Vaughn, Owen Wilson
Wedding Date (2005 film)
cast: Debra Messing, Dermot Mulroney
Wedding Gift, The (1993 film)
cast: Jim Broadbent, Thora Hird, Julie Walters
Wedding Night, The (1935 film)
cast: Anna Sten
Wedding Planner, The (2001 film)
cast: Jennifer Lopez, Matthew McConaughey
Wedding Singer, The (1998 film)
cast: Drew Barrymore, Adam Sandler
Wedding Song (1971 song)
artist: Paul Stookey
Wedding, The
author: Danielle Steel
Wedekind, Frank: **6** German, writer
wedel: **4** turn
perform a ~: **3** ski **4** skee
__ we devils?: **5** Aren't
wedge: **3** ram **4** club, cram, cusp, hunk, iron, lump, pack, plug, push, shim, slab **5** block, chock, chunk, cleat, coign, jam in, quoin, slice, stick, stuff **6** coigne, cotter **7** segment, squeeze, stuff in **8** doorstop, golf club, keystone
in: **3** jam **5** block **6** hinder, impede, squash, squish **7** squeeze **8** obstruct **9** insinuate, interpose **10** infiltrate
machinist's ~: **3** gib
shaped: **6** cuneal
splitting ~: **4** froe, frow
use a ~: **4** golf, loft
wooden ~: **4** shim
wedged, become: **5** lodge
Wedgeworth: **3** Ann
wedgie: **4** shoe **8** footwear
Wedgwood: **4** blue **5** china **6** Josiah
competitor: **5** Lenox **6** Mikasa
style: **6** jasper
We Didn't Start the Fire (1989 song)
artist: Billy Joel
wedlock: **8** marriage **9** matrimony
Wednesday: **6** Addams
__ Wednesday: **3** Any, Ash
We Don't Need Another Hero (1985 song)
artist: Tina Turner
We Don't Talk Anymore (1979 song)
artist: Cliff Richard
We Do Our Part org.: **3** NRA
wee: **3** sma **4** baby, itsy, puny, tiny **5** bitsy, bitty, early, light, pigmy, pygmy, short, small, teeny, weeny **6** atomic, bantam, little, minute, peewee, petite, pocket, teensy **8** atomical, atomlike **9** itsy-bitsy, itty-bitty, miniature, minuscule, pint-sized, undersize **10** diminutive, teeny-weeny, vest-pocket
bit: **4** dram, iota
enter the ~ hours: **5** laten
hour: **3** one, two **4** four **5** one a.m., three, two a.m. **6** four a.m. **7** three a.m.
hours: **4** late **5** night **7** morning
one: **3** tot **4** tike, tyke **6** infant, sprite **10** homunculus
Wee __ Hours: **5** Small
Wee __ Winkie: **6** Willie
Weeb: **6** Ewbank
weed: **4** pest, pull, rake, tare **5** plant **6** arnica, garden, henbit, jimson, joe-pye, nettle, uproot **7** burdock, pussley, thistle **8** plantain, purslane, toadflax **9** crab grass, dandelion, dog fennel, groundsel **10** goatsbeard, nightshade, pennycress, quack grass
Biblical ~: **4** tare
out: **4** cull, thin **6** select, uproot, winnow **7** extract **9** eradicate
rooter: **3** hoe **6** harrow
starter: **3** hog, may, pig, pin, rag, sea, tar **4** bind, blue, duck, fire, gout, gulf, hawk, iron, knap, knot, loco, milk, poke, pond, rich, rock, silk **5** skunk, stink **6** tumble
weed __: **3** out
__ weed: **4** loco **6** jimson
Weed-__: **4** B-Gon
__-Weed Factor, The: **3** Sot
weedy: **5** lanky, rangy **7** scrawny, spindly **8** ungainly **9** overgrown
__-wee Herman: **3** Pee
week: **4** time **6** period **8** hebdomad
component: **3** day
ender: **3** day, end **5** night
seven times a ~: **5** daily **7** diurnal
starter: **3** mid **4** work
Week __ Glance: **3** at a

__ Week: 3 One 4 Holy, Whit 5 Great 7 Passion
weekday abbr.: 3 Fri., Mon., Thu., Tue., Wed. 4 Thur., Tues. 5 Thurs.
weekend __: 3 bag 7 warrior
__ Weekend: 3 USA
Weekend Edition (NPR news)
  host: Liane Hansen, Scott Simon
Weekend in New England (1976 song) artist: Barry Manilow
__ Weekend, The: 4 Lost
Weekend Update show: 3 SNL
__ Wee King: 3 Pee
weekly: 5 paper 8 magazine, periodic 9 newspaper 10 periodical
  starter: 4 news
weeks, 52: 4 year
Weems: 3 Ted 5 Mason 6 Parson
weenie: 5 frank 6 hot dog 7 sausage
  holder: 3 bun
__-weenie: 5 eenie 6 teenie
__-weensie: 6 eensie 7 teensie
__-weensy: 5 eensy 6 teensy
__-weentsy: 6 eentsy 7 teentsy
weeny: 4 nerd, tiny 5 frank, sissy, small, teeny 6 hot dog, little, teensy 9 itty-bitty, pipsqueak, undersize
  no ~: 5 he-man
__-weeny: 5 teeny
weep: 3 cry, sob 4 bawl, drip, howl, keen, mewl, moan, ooze, pule, seep, tear, wail, yell, yowl 5 let go, mourn 6 bemoan, bewail, boohoo, grieve, lament, regret, snivel, squall 7 blubber, deplore, trickle, ululate, whimper 8 complain 9 break down, make a fuss, percolate, shed tears
  for: 4 pity 6 bemoan, lament
  (for): 4 feel
  over: 6 bewail, regret, repent
  ready to ~: 5 misty
...__ weepers: 6 losers
__ Weep for Me: 6 Willow
weeping: 5 tears 6 lament, sorrow 7 in tears, tearful 8 mourning 9 sniveling 10 waterworks
weeping __: 6 willow
Weep No More, My Lady
  author: Mary Higgins Clark
weepy: 5 mushy, teary 6 crying 7 maudlin, sobbing, tearful, wet-eyed 9 sniveling, teary-eyed 10 blubbering, lachrymose
__ Wee Reese: 3 Pee
weevil: 3 bug 4 pest 6 insect
  food: 4 boll 6 cotton
__ weevil: 4 boll
__ we forget: 4 lest
weft: 4 woof 7 filling
  having warp and ~: 5 woven
Wegener: 6 Alfred
We Got a Love Thing (1992 song)
  artist: CeCe Peniston
__ We Got Fun: 4 Ain't
We Got Love (1959 song)
  artist: Bobby Rydell
We Got the Beat (1982 song)
  artist: Go-Go's
We have met the enemy and he __: 4 is us 6 is ours
__! We Have No Bananas: 3 Yes
__ we having fun yet?: 3 Are
We hold __ truths...: 5 these
Weidman, Jerome: 6 writer 10 playwright
  work: Counselors-at-Law
    A Family Fortune
    Fiorello!
    I Can Get It for You Wholesale
    Other People's Money
    Praying for Rain
    The Temple
    What's In It for Me?
weigh: 3 see, try 4 heft, mull, muse, rate, tell 5 gauge, study, think 6 assess, burden, cumber, lumber, matter, muse on, ponder, rehash, review 7 analyze, balance, compare, examine, measure, reflect, signify, sort out 8 appraise, consider, estimate, evaluate, factor in, militate, mull over, ruminate 9 speculate, sweat over, think over 10 deliberate, meditate on, scrutinize
  anchor: 4 sail 7 cast off 8 shove off 9 cast loose
  down: 3 tax 4 load 5 press, worry 6 burden, cumber, hamper, sadden, saddle, strain 7 depress, oppress, overtax, trouble 8 encumber, obstruct, overload 10 overburden
  in: 5 opine 6 arrive, report, show up, turn up 8 register
  on: 3 tax 5 haunt 7 oppress 8 distress
  (upon): 4 bear
weigh __: 4 down
weighed down: 4 full 5 heavy, laden 7 replete
weigh-station stopper: 3 van 4 semi 5 truck
weight: 4 bulk, heft, load, mass, onus, pull 5 clout, power, slant, value, worth 6 accent, burden, import, lading, moment, sinker, strain, stress 7 ballast, density, G-factor, gravity, tonnage, tunnage 8 emphasis, leverage, plumb bob, poundage, pressure, prestige, strength, validity 9 authority, heaviness, heftiness, influence, magnitude, millstone 10 difficulty, importance, prominence
  allowance: 4 tare, tret
  Asian ~: 4 tael 5 catty, liang, picul
  attach ~ to: 6 accept 7 believe, presume
  carry ~: 4 tell 5 count 6 matter 7 signify
  check the ~: 4 heft, lift 5 hoist
  dead ~: 4 load, onus 10 impediment
  ender: 6 lifter 7 lifting
  extra ~: 4 flab
  fabric ~ unit: 6 denier
  freight ~: 3 ton
  gain ~: 4 grow 5 put on, swell, widen 6 expand, spread 7 broaden, enlarge, fill out, thicken
  Greek ~: 5 oboli 6 obolus
  Indian ~: 3 ser 4 tola
  lose ~: 4 diet, slim 6 reduce
  metric ~: 3 ton 4 gram 5 tonne
  Mideast ~: 4 rotl 5 artal
  packing some ~: 5 heavy, hefty, laden
  pharmacist's ~: 4 dram, gram
  plan: 4 diet 7 regimen
  starter: 3 fly 4 make, over 5 heavy, light, paper, penny 6 bantam, middle, welter 7 cruiser, feather, hundred
  system: 4 Troy
  take off ~: 4 diet, slim, thin 6 reduce, shrink 7 lighten 8 slim down
  throw one's ~ around: 5 bully 7 oppress 8 browbeat, domineer 9 tyrannize 10 intimidate, lord it over
  unit: 2 kg., lb. 3 cwt, keg, mol, ton 4 dram, gram, kilo, pint 5 carat, grain, ounce, point, pound 6 denier 7 megaton 8 kilogram 9 centigram, metric ton, milligram
__ weight: 4 dead, lose, troy 5 gross, put on 6 atomic
weight-and-fortune cost, once: 4 cent 5 penny
weighted __: 7 average
weightiness: 4 heft 6 moment 9 heaviness, magnitude
weightless: 5 light, wispy 6 dainty, slight 7 wispish 8 feathery
weightlifter
  bane: 3 fat 4 flab
  pride: 3 abs, bod 5 torso 6 biceps 7 muscles 8 physique
  routine: 4 curl, jerk, reps 5 squat
  sound: 5 grunt
  unit: 3 rep
weightlifting: 5 sport
weights and measures agcy.: 3 NBS
weighty: 3 big 4 deep 5 bulky, dense, grave, gross, heavy, hefty, major, meaty, obese, staid, stout 6 cogent, fleshy, leaden, portly, severe, solemn, somber, strong, taxing, urgent 7 big-deal, crucial, earnest, hulking, massive, onerous, porcine, salient, serious 8 critical, crushing, exacting, grievous, powerful, profound, unwieldy 9 difficult, important, momentous, ponderous, unwieldly 10 burdensome, cumbersome, meaningful, oppressive, persuasive, portentous
Weill: 4 Kurt 5 Sandy 7 Sanford
Weill, Kurt: 8 composer
  collaborator: 6 Brecht
  musical: Knickerbocker Holiday
    Lady in the Dark
    Lost in the Stars
    One Touch of Venus
    The Threepenny Opera
  spouse: Lotte Lenya
Weil, Simone: 6 French, mystic, writer
Weimar
  see German
Weimaraner: 3 dog 5 canid 6 canine
Weinberger: 6 Caspar
weir: 3 dam 4 dike 5 levee 7 barrier 9 barricade 10 embankment
Weir: 3 Bob 4 Mike 5 Peter
weird: 3 odd 4 camp, eery, zany 5 awful, crazy, dippy, eerie, flaky, funky, funny, kooky, outré 6 atypic, creepy, far-out, flakey, freaky, kookie, occult, quirky, spooky, way-out 7 bizarre, curious, deviant, erratic, fearful, ghastly, ghostly, macaber, macabre, magical, nerdish, oddball, offbeat, strange, surreal, uncanny, unusual 8 aberrant, abnormal, atypical, eldritch, freakish, haunting, horrific, peculiar, uncommon 9 anomalous, divergent, eccentric, fantastic, grotesque, irregular, unearthly, unnatural 10 Kafkaesque, mysterious, off the wall, outlandish, unorthodox
Weird Al: 8 Yankovic
weirdo: 4 geek, kook, zany 7 oddball 8 original 9 character, eccentric
Weird Science (1985 film)
  cast: Anthony Michael Hall, Kelly LeBrock, Ilan Mitchell-Smith, Bill Paxton
  director: John Hughes
Weir, Mike: 6 golfer
Weis: 2 Al 3 Don
Weiss: 4 font 5 Peter 8 typeface
Weisshorn: 3 alp
Weissmuller, Johnny: 5 actor
  film: Tarzan and His Mate (1934)
    Tarzan Escapes (1936)
    Tarzan Finds a Son! (1939)
    Tarzan, the Ape Man (1932)
    Tarzan Triumphs (1943)
Weiss, Peter: 6 German, writer
  work: Marat/Sade
Weisz: 6 Rachel
Weisz, Rachel: 7 actress
  film: The Brothers Bloom (2009)
    The Constant Gardener (2005, AA)
    Enemy at the Gates (2001)
    The Mummy (1999)
Weizman: 4 Ezer
Welby: 2 dr., GP, MD 6 doctor, Marcus
  org.: 3 AMA
Welch: 3 Bob 5 Lenny 6 Raquel, Tahnee
Welch, Raquel: 7 actress
  daughter: 6 Tahnee
  film: Bandolero! (1968)
    Fantastic Voyage (1966)
    Fathom (1967)
    The Four Musketeers (1975)
    The Last of Sheila (1973)
    Mother, Jugs & Speed (1976)
    Myra Breckinridge (1970)
    One Million Years B.C. (1966)
    The Three Musketeers (1974)
Welch's: 5 jelly
  alternative: 5 Kraft 6 Knott's 7 Polaner 8 Smucker's
welcome: 3 ave, hug 4 good, hail, meet, nice, okay, take 5 admit, adopt, allow, ask in, go for, greet, hello, howdy, let in, see in 6 accept, assent, comply, entrée, invite, lead in, listen, ring in, salute, show in, wanted 7 desired, embrace, honored, include, invited, ovation, receive, usher in 8 accepted, befriend, greeting, pleasant, pleasing, stand for 9 agreeable, cherished, desirable, enjoyable, entertain, favorable, handshake, put up with, reception, recognize, red carpet, sign off on 10 appreciate, concur with, give the nod, gratifying, refreshing, salutation, satisfying
  make ~: 5 ask in, greet, put up 7 receive
  uncivilly: 3 boo 4 hiss, jeer
  warm ~: 3 hug 4 kiss 7 embrace

welcome __: 3 mat
__ welcome: 5 hero's
Welcome __: 3 Ode 4 Back 5 Wagon
Welcome!: 2 Hi 5 Enter, Hello, Howdy 6 Come in 9 Greetings
Welcome Back (1976 song)
artist: John Sebastian
Welcome Back, Kotter (ABC sitcom)
cast: Robert Hegyes (Juan Epstein)
Lawrence-Hilton Jacobs (Freddie 'Boom Boom' Washington)
Gabe Kaplan (Gabe Kotter)
Ron Palillo (Arnold Horshack)
Marcia Strassman (Julie Kotter)
John Travolta (Vinnie Barbarino)
Welcome Ode
composer: Benjamin Britten
Welcome to Hard Times
author: E.L. Doctorow
Welcome to Mooseport (2004 film)
cast: Gene Hackman, Ray Romano
Welcome to Our City
author: Thomas Wolfe
Welcome to the Jungle (1988 song)
artist: Guns N' Roses
welcoming: 4 open 7 cordial 8 friendly 9 favorable, receptive 10 hospitable
weld: 3 arc, fix 4 bind, bond, fuse, join, link 5 braze, stick, unite 6 cement, fasten, solder 8 junction, juncture
Weld: 7 Tuesday, William
welded: 4 firm
__ welding: 3 arc 4 skip, spot 5 flash, forge
Weldon: 3 Fay
__ Weldon Johnson: 5 James
Weld, Tuesday: 7 actress
spouse: Dudley Moore, Pinchas Zukerman
TV: The Many Loves of Dobie Gillis
welfare: 3 aid 4 dole, good, sake 5 state 6 health, profit 7 benefit, success 8 interest 9 happiness 10 prosperity
on ~: 4 poor 5 needy 8 indigent 9 destitute, penurious 10 down-and-out, down at heel, straitened
welfare __: 5 state
__ welfare: 5 child 6 social
Welk, Lawrence: 10 bandleader
intro: 4 A one
song: Calcutta (1960)
well: 3 fit, pit, spa 4 ably, bore, fine, good, hale, hole, ooze, pool, root, sane, sump, to a T 5 abyss, amply, fount, fully, happy, hardy, husky, lucky, quite, right, shaft, sound, store, whole 6 aright, easily, hearty, highly, nicely, origin, proper, rather, really, robust, source, spring, strong, wholly 7 adeptly, capably, chipper, clearly, closely, fitting, greatly, happily, healthy, rightly, soundly, up to par 8 blooming, entirely, expertly, famously, flow over, fountain, heartily, laudably, properly, smoothly, strongly, suitably, thriving, very much, vigorous, worthily 9 admirably, advisable, carefully, correctly, extremely, favorably, fittingly, fortunate, inside out, in the pink, perfectly, reservoir, undamaged, water hole 10 able-bodied, abundantly, accurately, adequately, becomingly, completely, intimately, pleasantly, profoundly, skillfully, splendidly, swimmingly, thoroughly
act ~: 6 behave
as ~: 3 too, yet 4 also, more 5 along 6 either, to boot 7 besides 8 likewise, moreover 10 in addition
as ~ as: 3 and 6 beyond 9 including
contents: 3 ink, oil 5 water
do ~: 3 ace 5 excel, shine 6 make it, thrive 7 prosper 8 flourish, make good
do ~ enough: 4 cope 6 manage 7 make out
doing ~: 4 rich 7 booming 8 affluent, thriving 10 prospering, prosperous, successful
done: 10 impressive
ender: 4 away, born, head 6 spring
enough: 9 tolerably 10 acceptably, adequately
feed too ~: 4 cloy, glut, sate 5 gorge, stuff 7 surfeit 8 overfill
functioning ~: 5 sound
get ~: 4 heal, mend 5 rally 6 recoup 7 rebound, recover 10 recuperate
go ~: 6 pan out 7 succeed, work out
go together ~: 4 mesh 5 blend, click
less ~: 5 worse
look ~ on: 4 suit 6 become 7 enhance, flatter
make ~: 4 cure, heal 6 recoup
mechanism: 4 pump
not ~ done: 5 messy 6 shabby, shoddy, sloppy, untidy 7 unkempt 8 careless, fouled-up, slapdash, slipshod 9 haphazard, hit-or-miss, neglected
not sit ~: 3 irk, vex 4 gall, rile 5 anger, annoy, chafe, grate 6 bother, nettle, pester, rankle 8 irritate 10 exasperate
oil ~: 6 gusher
over: 4 brim, gush 5 spill
partner: 4 good 5 alive
put: 3 apt 6 cogent, timely 8 relevant, suitable 10 to the point
speak ~ of: 4 laud 6 esteem, praise 7 commend 9 recommend 10 compliment
starter: 3 dry, ink 4 fare 5 speed, stair
think ~ of: 5 favor 6 admire, esteem 8 look up to
thought-out: 4 sane
turned out: 4 chic, neat, trim 5 dandy, natty, sharp, sleek, smart, swank 6 chichi, classy, dapper, jaunty, snappy, snazzy, spiffy, sporty, spruce, swanky 7 dashing, stylish 8 handsome
up: 4 rise 5 heave, surge, swell 6 billow 8 escalate
wear ~: 4 last 6 endure
well: 4 my my, oh my 5 golly
work ~: 5 click
well-__: 3 fed, off, put 4 bred, done, kept, made, nigh, paid, read, to-do, worn 5 aimed, armed, aware, being, built, known, liked, timed 6 chosen, earned, heeled, rested, served, spoken, suited, versed, wisher 7 advised, behaved, defined, dressed, founded, groomed, meaning, rounded, trained, treated, written
__ well: 3 dry, oil 7 wishing
__ well!: 4 All's, Very 5 All is, Sleep
Well!: 6 I never
Well, __!: 5 I'll be
Well, __ You Evah!: 3 Did
Wella: 7 shampoo
alternative: 4 Flex, Pert 5 Prell, Suave 7 Finesse, Pantene
well-adapted: 8 apposite
well-adjusted: 4 sane 5 sound 6 stable 8 composed, rational, sensible, together 10 reasonable
well-advised: 5 sound 7 prudent 8 rational 10 reasonable
We'll always have __: 5 Paris
Welland: 4 city, port, town 5 canal
locale: 6 Canada 7 Ontario
Welland Canal terminus: 4 Erie
well-appointed: 4 lush, posh 5 fancy, grand, plush, ritzy, swank 6 deluxe, lavish, ornate, swanky 7 elegant, opulent, stately 8 imposing, palatial, splendid 9 elaborate, luxurious, sumptuous
Wellaway!: 4 alas 5 alack
modern ~: 6 oh dear
well-balanced: 4 calm, cool, even, fair, just, trim 6 serene, smooth, stable, steady 7 equable, uniform 8 composed, peaceful, tranquil 9 equitable, impartial, temperate, unruffled 10 consistent, unagitated, unwavering
well-balanced __: 4 diet
well-behaved: 4 good, ruly 6 polite 7 orderly 8 decorous, mannerly
kid: 4 doll 5 angel
well-being: 4 ease, good, sake 5 vigor 6 health, luxury, profit 7 benefit, comfort, rapture, success 8 felicity, interest 9 affluence, happiness 10 prosperity
We'll Be Together (1987 song)
artist: Sting
wellborn: 5 noble 6 titled 8 ladylike 9 patrician
people: 5 elite 6 gentry 7 society 8 nobility 10 upper crust
well-bred: 4 nice 5 civil, noble, suave 6 gentle, polite, taught, urbane 7 courtly, gallant, genteel, refined, trained 8 cultured, ladylike, mannerly, polished 9 courteous, patrician 10 cultivated, thoughtful, upper-crust
well-built: 3 big 4 hale, iron, wiry 5 beefy, burly, hardy, hefty, hunky, husky, lusty, solid, sound, stout, tough 6 brawny, hearty, mighty, potent, robust, rugged, sinewy, stable, steely, stocky, strong, sturdy, virile 7 doughty 8 athletic, forceful, indurate, muscular, powerful, puissant, stalwart, vigorous 9 Atlantean, Herculean, strapping 10 able-bodied, red-blooded
__-well card: 3 get
WellCare: 3 HMO
well-cared-for: 4 tidy 5 sleek 6 smooth 8 polished
well-chosen: 6 wilful 7 advised, express, reputed, willful 8 moderate 9 designful, judicious, voluntary 10 considered, deliberate, felicitous, thought-out
well-considered: 4 sane 5 lucid, sober, sound 7 careful, planned, serious, studied 8 rational, sensible 9 conscious, practical, pragmatic, provident, realistic 10 calculated, deliberate, purposeful, reasonable, thoughtful
well-constructed: 5 sound
well-coordinated: 4 deft, spry 5 agile 6 limber, nimble 8 athletic, graceful 9 dexterous
well-defined: 5 clear, plain, sharp, vivid 6 cogent 7 evident, express, obvious, precise, salient 8 apparent, clean-cut, clear-cut, definite, distinct, explicit, manifest, palpable 9 graspable, trenchant, unblurred 10 spelled out
well-deserved: 4 fair, just, meet 5 right 6 lawful, proper 7 condign, fitting 8 rightful, suitable
well-designed: 4 neat
Well, Did You Evah!
composer: Cole Porter
well-disposed: 7 willing 8 amenable 9 agreeable, favorable, receptive, tractable 10 hospitable, open-minded
__ well done: 4 a job
Well done!: 4 nice 5 bravo
well-done, not: 4 pink, rare 6 medium
well-dressed: 5 natty, sleek, smart, swank 6 dapper, jaunty, rakish, snazzy, spiffy, sporty, swanky 8 handsome
well-educated: 5 smart 6 brainy 7 erudite, learned 8 literate 9 scholarly
__ well enough alone: 5 leave
Weller: 5 Peter 6 Thomas
Wellesley: 4 city, town
grad: 5 woman 6 alumna
locale: 4 Mass.
student: 4 coed
Welles, Orson: 5 actor 8 director
film: Butterfly (1981)
Casino Royale (1967)
Catch-22 (1970)
Chimes at Midnight (1967)
Citizen Kane (1941)
Compulsion (1959)
Crack in the Mirror (1960)
Follow the Boys (1944)
I'll Never Forget What's 'is Name (1967)
Jane Eyre (1944)
Journey Into Fear (1942)
The Lady From Shanghai (1948)
Macbeth (1948)
The Magnificent Ambersons (1942)
A Man for All Seasons (1966)
Othello (1952)
The Stranger (1946)
The Third Man (1949)
Tomorrow Is Forever (1946)
Touch of Evil (1958)
The Trial (1962)

role: 4 Kane, Lime
spouse: Rita Hayworth
Wellesz: 4 Egon
well-expressed: 4 glib 5 vivid 6 moving 8 eloquent, stirring, touching 10 articulate, persuasive
well-favored: 5 bonny 6 comely, lovely, pretty 8 charming, fetching, handsome 9 appealing, beautiful 10 attractive
well-fixed: 5 flush 6 loaded, monied 7 moneyed, wealthy 8 affluent, in clover 10 in the dough, in the money, privileged, propertied, prosperous
well-flavored: 5 sharp, spicy, tangy, tasty, zesty 6 savory 7 peppery, piquant, pungent
well-formed: 6 comely 8 gorgeous, handsome, pleasing, splendid, striking, stunning 9 appealing, beautiful, exquisite 10 attractive
well-founded: 4 good, just, sane 5 solid, sound, valid 6 secure, stable, strong 8 luculent
We'll go to __, and eat bologna...: 5 Coney
well-groomed: 4 neat, tidy, trim 5 clean, crisp, kempt, natty, sleek, smart, swank 6 combed, dapper, jaunty, rakish, snazzy, spiffy, sporty, spruce, swanky 7 duded up 8 clean-cut 9 spruced up 10 fastidious
well-grounded: 4 just 5 sober, sound, valid 6 cogent, versed 7 learned
well-handled: 4 deft 5 adept, slick 6 adroit, clever, facile, nimble 7 skilled 8 masterly, skillful 9 dexterous, ingenious, masterful, practiced
wellhead: 4 font 8 fountain
well-heeled: 4 rich 5 flush 6 loaded, monied 7 moneyed, opulent, wealthy 8 affluent, in clover, thriving 10 in the dough, in the money, privileged, propertied, prosperous
Well, I __!: 5 never
Well, I'll be!: 3 gee 4 gosh 5 golly
well-informed: 4 up on, wise 6 at home, versed 7 knowing, learned 8 educated
Wellington: 4 boot, city, shoe, town 7 capital 8 footwear
alma mater: 4 Eton
horse: 10 Copenhagen
locale: 7 Florida 10 New Zealand
to Napoleon: 3 foe 5 enemy
Wellington __: 4 boot
__ Wellington: 4 beef 6 Duke of
Wellington's Victory
composer: Ludwig van Beethoven
well-intentioned: 4 kind 6 do-good
__ well it were done quickly: 5 'Twere
well-kept: 4 neat, tidy, trim 5 clean 6 spruce 7 orderly 9 shipshape 10 fastidious
well-known: 3 big, VIP 4 star 5 known, large, noted 6 common, famous, public 7 eminent, leading, notable, popular, splashy, storied 8 familiar, glorious, historic, infamous, renowned 9 acclaimed, important, legendary, notorious, prominent, reputable, superstar 10 celebrated, proverbial, recognized
become ~: 6 emerge
well-liked: 7 popular
well-lit: 5 shiny, sunny 6 bright, lucent 7 shining 11 illuminated
well-made: 5 solid, sound 6 rugged, strong, sturdy
well-maintained: 4 neat
Wellman: 7 William
well-mannered: 4 good, nice 5 couth 6 polite, urbane 7 orderly, refined 8 gracious, mannerly, pleasing
behavior: 4 tact 7 decorum 8 breeding, civility, courtesy, protocol, urbanity 9 etiquette, gallantry, gentility 10 politeness, refinement
well-marked: 5 plain, sharp 7 express, obvious, precise 8 definite, distinct, explicit
well-meaning: 4 kind
We'll Meet Again
author: Mary Higgins Clark
wellness: 6 fettle, health 7 fitness 9 salubrity
grp.: 3 HMO, NIH, PPO
We'll Never Have to Say Goodbye Again (1978 song)
artist: England Dan and John Ford Coley
well-nigh: 4 most 5 about 6 almost
well-off: 4 rich 5 flush, lucky 6 loaded, monied 7 moneyed, opulent, wealthy 8 affluent, in clover, thriving 9 fortunate 10 in the dough, in the money, privileged, propertied, prosperous, successful
well-ordered: 4 neat, tidy 6 spruce
well-organized: 4 neat, tidy 5 sound 6 cogent 7 logical, tenable 8 analytic, coherent, methodic, rational, sensible, together 9 pragmatic 10 analytical, consistent
well-outlined: 4 neat, trim 5 clear, crisp 7 regular 8 clean-cut, distinct
well-padded
see obese
well-paying: 7 gainful 9 lucrative 10 profitable
well-planned: 4 neat 6 clever, superb 7 orderly 8 methodic, skillful, terrific 9 dexterous, effective, efficient, excellent, exemplary 10 methodical
well-pleased: 5 cocky, proud 7 haughty, pompous, stuck-up 8 arrogant, egoistic, puffed up 9 conceited 10 hoity-toity
well-practiced: 5 adept
well-prepared: 4 ripe 5 ready 7 careful, prudent 8 seasoned 9 provident 10 farsighted, thoughtful
well-proportioned: 3 fit 4 trim 5 sleek 6 comely 9 beautiful
well-protected: 4 safe 6 secure 7 guarded
well-provided: 4 rife 5 laden 6 jammed, lavish, loaded, packed 7 crammed, crowded, fraught, glutted, replete, teeming 8 abundant, brimming, swarming 9 abounding, chock-full, jam-packed, plenteous, plentiful
well-put: 3 apt 6 clever 7 apropos, germane 8 apposite, skillful
well-read: 4 wise 5 smart 6 versed 7 erudite, learned 8 literary, studious 9 scholarly
well-reasoned: 4 sage, sane, wise 5 lucid, smart, sober, solid, sound 6 astute, shrewd 7 logical, politic, prudent, sapient 8 balanced, rational, sensible 9 judicious, practical, pragmatic, realistic, sagacious 10 reasonable, thoughtful
well-received: 7 in favor, likable, popular, voguish 8 accepted, approved 10 celebrated
well-recognized: 5 known 6 famous 7 popular 10 celebrated
well-regulated: 4 neat 7 careful, ordered, orderly, precise 8 methodic 9 by the book, efficient, organized 10 meticulous, scrupulous, structured, systematic
well-rehearsed: 3 set 5 ready 6 all set, primed 8 geared up, prepared
well-rounded: 4 sage 5 plump 6 versed 7 learned 8 cultured, educated
Wells: 2 H.G. 3 Ida 4 Dawn, Mary 5 Kitty
Wells __: 5 Fargo
well-schooled: 5 canny, smart 6 brainy 7 erudite, learned 8 masterly, skillful
Wells Fargo transport: 5 stage
Wells, H.G.: 6 writer 7 British
race: 4 Eloi 8 Morlocks
work: Experiment in Autobiography
The History of Mr. Polly
The Invisible Man
The Island of Dr. Moreau
Mankind in the Making
Men Like Gods
Mind at the End of Its Tether
A Modern Utopia
The New Machiavelli
The Open Conspiracy
Outline of History
A Short History of the World
The Time Machine
The War of the Worlds
The World of William Clissold
We'll Sing in the Sunshine (1964 song)
artist: Gale Garnett
Wells, Mary
song: My Guy (1974)
The One Who Really Loves You (1962)
Two Lovers (1962)
You Beat Me to the Punch (1962)
well-spent: 8 fruitful 9 rewarding 10 beneficial, worthwhile
well-spoken: 5 slick 6 fluent 8 ladylike 9 courteous 10 articulate
wellspring: 4 font, mine 5 fount 6 origin, source 8 fountain 10 derivation
well-stocked: 4 full, rife 5 laden 6 filled, jammed, loaded, packed 7 crammed, crowded, replete, stuffed, teeming 8 brimming
well-stuffed: 4 full 5 beefy, burly, obese, plump, pudgy, pursy, stout, tubby 6 chubby, chunky, fleshy, portly, rotund, stocky 9 corpulent 10 abdominous
well-suited: 3 fit 8 apposite 9 congenial
well-supplied: 4 rich 6 lavish 8 abundant, affluent 9 abounding, bounteous, bountiful, luxurious, plentiful, sumptuous
be ~: 4 teem 5 swarm 6 abound 8 overflow
We'll tak __ o' kindness yet: 4 a cup
Well-Tempered Clavier, The
composer: J.S. Bach
__ Well That...: 4 All's
well-thought-of: 6 prized, valued 7 admired, exalted, honored, revered 8 esteemed 9 acclaimed, honorable, reputable, respected, venerable, venerated
well-thought-out: 4 sane 5 sound 8 sensible
well-timed: 5 happy 6 timely 7 apropos, hopeful 9 favorable, opportune 10 auspicious, felicitous, propitious
well-to-do: 4 rich 5 flush 6 jet set, loaded, monied 7 moneyed, opulent, wealthy, well-off 8 affluent, in clover, thriving 9 fortunate 10 in the dough, in the money, privileged, propertied, prosperous
well-trained: 6 versed 7 skilled 8 educated, polished, skillful 9 competent, practiced
one: 3 ace 5 adept 6 expert, master, wizard 10 specialist
well-tuned: 7 lyrical, melodic 10 euphonious, harmonious
well-turned: 6 comely 7 shapely 9 beautiful
well-used: 3 old 5 dated, hoary, passé, stale 8 decrepit, outdated, outmoded, time-worn 9 hackneyed 10 threadbare, unoriginal
well-versed: 4 ripe 5 adept 6 at home, au fait, expert, fluent 8 lettered, skillful 9 practiced
in French: 6 au fait
well-wisher: 3 pal 4 ally, chum 5 amigo, buddy, crony 6 backer, cohort, friend, patron 7 comrade 8 sidekick 9 associate, colleague, confidant, supporter 10 benefactor, compatriot
gesture: 5 toast
well-worn: 5 stale, trite 10 threadbare
well-written: 5 clear 7 flowing, legible 8 coherent, eloquent, readable
Welsh: 3 pig 5 swine 6 Cymric, Kymric 8 language
rabbit ingredient: 6 cheese
Welsh __: 5 corgi 6 rabbit 7 rarebit
Welshman: 4 Celt
welt: 4 blow, scar, seam, wale, weal 5 mouse, ridge, smash, spank, wheal, wound 6 bruise, injury, streak, stripe 8 swelling 9 contusion
welter: 5 parch, pitch 7 shrivel 9 dehydrate, desiccate
ender: 6 weight
welterweight: 5 boxer 7 fighter
weapon: 4 fist
Welty, Eudora: 6 writer
work: A Curtain of Green
Delta Wedding
The Golden Apples
The Optimist's Daughter

The Ponder Heart
The Wide Net
Welu, Billy: 3 PBA 6 bowler
milieu: 4 lane 5 alley
___ We Meet Again: 4 Till
___ we met?: 6 Haven't
wen: 3 sac 4 bleb, bump, cyst 7 blister
___ Wences: 5 Señor
Wenceslas Square
locale: 6 Prague
Wenceslaus: 5 saint
wend: 4 walk 6 travel 7 proceed
Wendell: 5 Berry, Corey 7 Stanley, Willkie
___ Wendell Holmes: 6 Oliver
Wenders: 3 Wim
Wendie: 6 Malick
Wendie Jo: 7 Sperber
Wendt, George: 5 actor
TV: Cheers
Wendy: 6 Barrie, Carlos, Hiller 8 Williams
Wendy's
rival: *see* restaurant chain
Wendy's, go to: 3 eat 6 eat out
Wenner, Jann: 9 publisher
Wensleydale: 6 cheese
went: 5 split 7 buckled, took off 8 departed, sashayed, traveled, withdrew 9 collapsed, shoved off 10 hit the road
after: 5 set at
down: 4 fell
for: 3 bit, OK'd 4 OK'ed 6 okayed
up: 4 rose 5 arose
___ Went Over the Mountain, The: 4 Bear
___ went thataway!: 4 They
___! Went the Strings of My Heart: 4 Zing
___ Went to Haiti: 5 Katie
were: 7 existed, had been
as it ~: 6 in a way 7 so to say 9 so to speak 10 in some sort
ender: 4 wolf
if it ~ not for: 6 except 7 besides, without 8 omitting 9 apart from, aside from, excluding
___ were: 4 as it 5 as you
Were ___ That Special Face: 5 Thine
We're ___ Dressing: 3 Not
We're ___ Money: 5 in the
We're ___ See the Wizard: 5 Off to
We're ___ we're out of the money: 4 in or
___ Were a Bell: 3 If I
___ Were a Carpenter: 3 If I
We're All Alone (1977 song)
artist: Rita Coolidge
We're an American Band (1973 song)
artist: Grand Funk
___ Were a Rich Man: 3 If I
___ Were Expendable: 4 They
We're having ___ wave: 5 a heat
We're in the Money
composer: Al Dubin, Harry Warren
___ Were King of the Forest: 3 If I
___ Were Never Lovelier: 3 You
We're number ___!: 3 one
We're Off to See the Wizard
composer: Harold Arlen, Yip Harburg
We're Ready (1986 song)
artist: Boston
___ Were, The: 5 Way We
___ Were the Days: 5 Those
werewolf: 7 monster
feature: 4 fang, hair
Werewolves of London (1978 song)
artist: Warren Zevon
___ were you...: 3 If I
Werfel, Franz: 6 writer 8 Austrian
work: Goat Song
The Song of Bernadette
Werner: 5 Arber, Oskar, Peter 6 Alfred, Erhard, Herzog 9 Forssmann, Klemperer 10 Heisenberg
see also German
___ Werner Fassbinder: 6 Rainer
Wernher: 8 von Braun
Werther
composer: Jules Massenet
Wertmuller: 4 Lina
Wes: 6 Craven, Unseld 9 Covington 10 Montgomery
Wes Craven's New Nightmare (1994 film)
cast: Robert Englund, Heather Langenkamp
Weser: 5 river
city on the ~: 6 Bremen
locale: 7 Germany
Wesker, Arnold: 7 British 10 playwright
weskit: 4 vest
Wesley: 4 John 6 Snipes 7 Charles, Ruggles
...___ we speak: 6 even as
Wesson: 3 oil
alternative: 6 Crisco, Mazola 7 Puritan
partner: 5 Smith
west: 2 pt. 3 way 5 point 6 course 7 bearing, heading 9 direction
ender: 3 ern 4 ward 5 bound, wards
on a map: 4 left
sink in the ~: 3 set
starter: 3 mid 5 north, south
way ~: 5 trail
wind: 8 favonian
West: 3 key, Mae 4 Adam 5 Jerry 6 Dottie, Morris 7 Anthony, Rebecca 8 Benjamin, Jessamyn, Occident 9 Nathanael
from the ~: 3 occ. 10 occidental
the ~ had one: 4 code
West ___: 3 End 4 Bank, Goth, Side 5 Coast, Haven, Point, Saxon 6 Africa, Bengal, Berlin, Indies, Sussex
West ___ Beach: 4 Palm
West ___, CT: 5 Haven
West ___ Story: 4 Side
West, ___ and You, The: 5 a Nest
___ West: 3 Far, Key, Old 4 Wild 6 Middle
West, Adam
role: 6 Batman
West Allis: 4 city, town
locale: 9 Wisconsin
West Bank
city: 6 Hebron
grp.: 3 PLO
Westbrook: 6 Pegler
West Coast
airport: 3 LAX, SEA, SFO
campus: 3 USC 4 UCLA
clock setting: 3 PDT, PST
st.: 3 Cal., Ore. 4 Oreg., Wash. 5 Calif.
West Covina: 4 city, town
locale: 10 California
West End Girls (1986 song)
artist: Pet Shop Boys
westerly: 4 wind
starter: 5 north, south
Westerly: 4 town
locale: Rhode Island
western ___: 6 omelet
Western: 4 tale 5 novel, oater
alliance: 3 OAS 4 NATO
Athletic Conference player: 3 Ute
author: Bret Harte, Louis L'Amour, Zane Grey
backdrop: 4 mesa 5 butte, cañon 6 canyon
beast: 5 bison
capital: 5 Boise, Salem 6 Denver, Helena 7 Olympia, Phoenix 10 Sacramento
character: 6 cowboy, outlaw 7 marshal, sheriff
exclamation: 5 wahoo
half a ~ city: 5 Walla
hero: 4 Earp
horse: 10 Indian pony
howler: 6 coyote
Indian: 3 Ute 4 Crow, Hopi 5 Piute 6 Apache, Navaho, Navajo, Paiute 8 Shoshone
lizard: 3 uta
painter: 9 Remington
plot element: 6 ambush
reptile: 3 uta
sch.: 3 USC 4 UCLA
setting: 4 fort
show: 5 oater, rodeo
state: 3 Ida., Ore. 4 Ariz., Colo., Mont., Oreg., Utah, Wash. 5 Idaho 6 Oregon 7 Arizona, Montana 8 Colorado 10 California, Washington
tie: 4 bola, bolo
wear: 4 boot, spur, vest
Western ___: 4 Wall 5 Samoa, Slavs, Union 6 saddle, Sahara
Western Athletic Conference
school: 3 SMU 4 Rice, UTEP 5 Tulsa 6 Hawaii, Nevada 10 Boise State 11 Fresno State
Western Australia capital: 5 Perth
Western Hemisphere: 4 Amer. 8 Americas
former alliance: 3 PAU
pact: 3 OAS 5 NAFTA
Western Michigan
athletes: 7 Broncos
conference: 3 MAC
locale: 9 Kalamazoo
western omelet
ingredient: 3 egg, ham 5 onion
___ Western Reserve: 4 Case
Western Sahara
neighbor: 7 Algeria, Morocco 10 Mauritania
Western Samoa: 4 isls. 5 isles 6 nation 7 country, islands
capital: 4 Apia
island: 5 Upolu
money: 4 sene, tala
Western Star
poet: Stephen Vincent Benét
Western Union
message: 4 wire 5 cable, teleg., telex 8 telegram
union: 3 ITU
Western Union (1967 song)
artist: Five Americans
wester starter: 3 nor, sou 5 north, south
___ West, FL: 3 Key
West Flanders city: 5 Ypres
West Haven: 4 city, town
locale: 4 Conn.
Westheimer: 4 Ruth 6 Dr. Ruth
Westin: 5 hotel
alternative: *see* hotel
___ West India Company: 5 Dutch
West Indies: 5 isles 7 islands
bird: 4 tody
city: 6 Havana
dance: 5 limbo
explorer: 7 Hawkins 8 Columbus
fish: 6 bigeye
fruit: 5 mamey 6 annona 7 acerola
Indian: 5 Carib, Taino
island: 3 cay, key 4 Cuba, Saba 5 Aruba, Haiti 6 Tobago 7 Bahamas, Jamaica 8 Antilles, Barbados, Trinidad, Windward 10 Hispaniola, Martinique, Puerto Rico
magic: 3 obi 5 obeah 6 voodoo
music: 3 ska
native: 5 Carib, Cuban 6 Aruban, Creole 7 Haitian 8 Bahamian, Jamaican 9 Barbadian
Nobelist in Literature: 7 Walcott
republic: 5 Haiti
rodent: 6 agouti
sea: 8 Sargasso 9 Caribbean
shrub: 4 anil, pich
stew: 5 blaff 9 pepper pot
tree: 4 pich 7 canella
witchcraft: 3 obi 5 obeah 6 voodoo
writer: 7 Naipaul, Walcott
Westinghouse: 6 George 9 appliance
alternative: *see* appliance brand
West, Jerry: 5 cager
milieu: 5 court
org.: 3 NBA
sport: 10 basketball
West Lafayette: 4 city, town
locale: 7 Indiana
school: 6 Purdue
Westlake: 6 Donald
West Linn: 4 city, town
locale: 6 Oregon
West, Mae: 7 actress
feathers: 3 boa
film: Belle of the Nineties (1934)
Every Day's A Holiday (1937)
Goin' to Town (1935)
Go West, Young Man (1936)
I'm No Angel (1933)
Klondike Annie (1936)
My Little Chickadee (1940)
Myra Breckinridge (1970)
She Done Him Wrong (1933)
role: 3 Lil
Westminster: 4 city, town 5 abbey
district: 4 Soho
locale: 8 Colorado 10 California
Westmore: 3 Bud, Ern 4 Perc 5 Frank, Monty, Wally 6 George
Westmoreland: 7 general, William
Westmorland: 6 county
locale: 7 England
West, Morris: 6 writer 10 Australian
work: The Devil's Advocate
The Shoes of the Fisherman

West, Nathanael: 6 writer
work: A Cool Million
The Day of the Locust
Miss Lonelyhearts
West of the Pecos
author: Zane Grey
Weston: 4 city, Jack, town **5** Celia
locale: 7 Florida
West Orange: 4 city, town
locale: 9 New Jersey
Westover: 4 Russ
Westphalia
city: 5 Essen **6** Bochum
locale: 7 Germany
once: 5 duchy
Westphalian __: 3 ham
West Point: 4 Army, USMA
byword: 4 duty **5** honor **7** country
freshman: 4 pleb **5** plebe
grad: 2 lt. **5** lieut. **10** lieutenant
mascot: 4 mule
meal: 4 mess
student: 5 cadet
subject: 3 war
Westport: 4 city, town
locale: 4 Conn.
West, Rebecca: 4 Dame **5** alias **6** writer **7** British
work: The Bird Falls Down
The Fountain Overflows
Henry James
The Judge
St. Augustine
The Thinking Reed
__-West relations: 4 East
__ West show: 4 Wild
West Side Story (1961 film): 7 musical
cast: Richard Beymer, George Chakiris, Rita Moreno, Russ Tamblyn, Natalie Wood
character: 3 Doc **4** A-rab, Luis, Pepe, Riff, Tony, Toro **5** Anita, Chino, Indio, Juano, Maria, Moose, Nardo, Tiger, Velma **6** Action, Diesel, Gee-Tar, Krupke, Minnie **7** Anxious, Big Deal, Clarice, Estella, Nibbles, Pauline, Rosalia, Schrank, Snowboy **8** Baby John, Bernardo, Consuelo, Glad Hand, Teresita **9** Francisca, Graziella, Margarita **10** Mouthpiece
composer: Leonard Bernstein, Stephen Sondheim
director: Jerome Robbins, Robert Wise
dustup: 6 rumble
gang: 4 Jets **6** Sharks
song: 5 Maria **7** Tonight
__ West, The: 3 Way
West Virginia: 5 state
capital: 10 Charleston
city: 7 Weirton **8** Fairmont, Wheeling **10** Charleston, Huntington, Morgantown
conference: 7 Big East
neighbor: 4 Ohio **8** Kentucky, Maryland, Virginia
resource: 4 coal
state animal: 9 black bear
state bird: 8 cardinal
state butterfly: 7 monarch
state fish: 10 brook trout
state fruit: 5 apple
state state fossil: 5 coral
state tree: 10 sugar maple
West Virginia University
locale: 10 Morgantown
West Wing, The (NBC drama)
cast: Alan Alda (Arnold Vinick)
Stockard Channing (Abigail Bartlet)
Dulé Hill (Charlie Young)
Allison Janney (C.J. Cregg)
Rob Lowe (Sam Seaborn)
Janel Moloney (Donna Moss)
Richard Schiff (Toby Ziegler)
Martin Sheen (Josiah 'Jed' Bartlet)
Jimmy Smits (Matt Santos)
John Spencer (Leo McGarry)
Bradley Whitford (Josh Lyman)
West With the Night
author: Beryl Markham
Westworld (1973 film)
cast: Richard Benjamin, James Brolin, Yul Brynner
director: Michael Crichton
wet: 3 dip, sop **4** damp, dank, dewy, lick, soak, wash **5** bathe, bedew, douse, dowse, drown, foggy, humid, juicy, misty, moist, muggy, rainy, rinse, slimy, snowy, soggy, soppy, souse, spray, teary, water **6** clammy, dampen, drench, liquid, slushy, soaked, sodden, soused, splash, steamy, stormy, sweaty, watery **7** aqueous, drizzle, moisten, pouring, raining, showery, soaking, sopping, spatter, squishy, teeming **8** dampness, drenched, dripping, hose down, irrigate, moisture, saturate, slippery, sprinkle **9** drizzling, saturated, water down
all ~: 5 wrong **7** in error, off-base **8** cockeyed, mistaken **9** erroneous **10** inaccurate
and spongy: 5 boggy, muddy **6** swampy
behind the ears: 3 new **4** naif **5** green, naive, young **6** callow, tender **8** immature
blanket: 4 bore, drag, drip **9** pessimist, worrywart
combining form: 5 hygro-
down: 4 hose, soak **5** douse, dowse, rinse, spray, water **6** dampen **7** moisten **8** irrigate, saturate, sprinkle **10** besprinkle
ender: 4 land **5** lands
expanse: 3 sea **5** ocean
get one's feet ~: 4 wade **5** begin **6** splash
one's whistle: 4 swig **5** drink **6** imbibe, tipple **7** swallow
very ~: 5 adrip, soggy, soppy **10** bedraggled
weather: 4 rain **5** storm **6** shower
wet __: 3 bar, mop **4** suit **7** blanket
__ wet: 3 all **7** soaking, sopping
__ we talk?: 3 Can
wet-eyed: 5 teary, weepy **7** tearful **9** sniveling
We the Living
author: Ayn Rand
We, the People
author: Elmer Rice
__ we there yet?: 3 Are
wetland: 3 bog, fen **5** marsh, swamp **7** lowland
vegetation: 5 sedge
wetness: 8 dampness, humidity, moisture **9** sogginess
exemplar of ~: 3 mop
wet-noodle stroke: 4 lash
wet one's __: 7 whistle
__ We Trust: 5 In God
We try harder company: 4 Avis
wet-suit
material: 5 latex
wearer: 5 diver
Wettig, Patricia: 7 actress
spouse: Ken Olin
TV: thirtysomething
wettish: 4 damp, dank, dewy, oozy **5** humid, misty, moist, muddy, muggy, soggy **6** clammy, drippy, liquid, sodden, steamy, sweaty, watery **7** drizzly, sopping **9** saturated
__, we various passions find: 5 In men
We've Got Tonight (1983 song)
artist: Kenny Rogers, Sheena Easton
We've Got Tonite (1978 song)
artist: Bob Seger
We've Only Just Begun (1970 song)
artist: Carpenters
We want __!: 4 a hit
We Were Soldiers (2002 film)
cast: Sam Elliott, Mel Gibson, Greg Kinnear, Madeleine Stowe
__ We Were, The: 3 Way
We will __ undersold!: 5 not be
Weymouth: 4 city, port, Tina, town
locale: 4 Mass.
WFU
see Wake Forest
wgt., small: 2 mg., oz. **3** mcg.
W.H.: 5 Auden **6** Hudson
whack: 2 go **3** bat, box, hit, pop, pow, rap, try **4** bang, bash, beat, belt, biff, blow, clip, club, cuff, ding, flog, hurt, nail, shot, slam, slap, slug, sock, stab, swat, trim, turn, wham **5** clout, crack, fling, knock, pound, smack, smash, smite, spank, thump, whang, whirl **6** buffet, defeat, hammer, strike, thrash, wallop **7** attempt, clobber, lambast **8** lambaste **9** fisticuff
out of ~: 4 awry **5** atilt **7** damaged, haywire **10** broken-down
starter: 4 bush
take a ~: 3 try **5** swing
throw out of ~: 4 skew **7** distort
__ whack: 5 out of
__ whack at: 5 have a, take a
whacker, weed: 3 hoe
whale: 3 sei **4** lash, whip **5** giant, minke, titan **6** animal, beluga, mammal **7** finback, monster, Monstro, scourge **8** cetacean, colossus, humpback, Moby Dick, narwhale **9** leviathan
combining form: 3 cet- **4** ceto-
constellation: 5 Cetus
ender: 4 back, boat, bone
female: 3 cow
food: 4 brit **5** krill
group: 3 gam, pod
have a baby ~: 5 calve
home: 3 sea **5** ocean **8** high seas
hunter of fiction: 4 Ahab
killer ~: 3 orc **4** orca **7** grampus
male: 4 bull
on a ~ watch, perhaps: 4 asea **5** at sea
relative: *see* cetacean
tail: 5 fluke
the tar out of: 3 tan **4** rout **5** cream **6** defeat, ravage **9** overpower
young: 4 calf
whale __: 3 oil **5** shark
__ whale: 4 blue **5** sperm
whalebone: 6 baleen
garment: 6 corset
Whale: James: 8 director
whalelike: 3 big **5** bulky **7** hulking, immense, massive **8** enormous, gigantic, whopping
whaler: 4 boat, ship
does a ~ job: 6 flench, flense
sunk by a whale: 5 Essex
word: 4 thar **5** blows
Whales of August, The (1987 film)
cast: Bette Davis, Lillian Gish, Vincent Price, Ann Sothern
Whalley, Joanne
spouse: Val Kilmer
wham: 3 hit, pow **4** bang, boom, slam, slap, slug, sock **5** blast, crash, kapow, noise, smack, smash, sound, whack **6** larrup, wallop **8** abruptly
whammy: 3 hex **4** jinx **5** curse, shock, spell **8** surprise
put the ~ on: 3 hex **4** damn, jinx **5** curse **7** bedevil, bewitch, condemn **9** imprecate
whang: 3 hit **4** bash, beat, belt, drub, flog, sock, swat **5** knock, noise, pound, punch, smack, thump, whack **6** batter, buffet, larrup, strike, thrash, thwack, wallop **7** clobber
wharf: 4 dock, pier, port, quay, slip **5** berth, jetty, levee **6** harbor, marina **7** harbour, landing **9** anchorage **10** breakwater
workers' org.: 3 ILA
wharf __: 3 rat
Wharton: 6 school
degree: 3 MBA
locale: 4 Penn.
subj.: 4 econ. **7** finance
Wharton, Edith: 6 writer
work: The Age of Innocence
A Backward Glance
Ethan Frome
The House of Mirth
Old New York
what: 3 huh, yes
at ~ time: 4 when
come ~ may: 6 surely **7** somehow **10** in any event
do ~ one can: 3 try **6** strive **7** attempt, have a go, venture **9** have a go at, have a shot, have a stab **10** have a whack
ender: 3 not **4** ever **6** soever
for: 3 why **9** reprimand
give ~ for: 3 rag **4** rail **5** chide, scold **6** berate, rail at, rebuke, vilify **7** bawl out, censure, chasten, chew out, lecture, reprove, tell off, upbraid **8** admonish, chastise, denounce, lace into, lambaste, reproach, sail into, tear into **9** castigate, criticize, dress down, light into, reprehend, reprimand **10** denunciate, tongue-lash
have I done: 4 oh no

have we here: 3 oho
in ~ place: 5 where
in ~ way: 3 how 5 how so
it takes: 5 knack, savvy, skill 6 talent 7 ability, faculty, know-how, prowess 8 aptitude, capacity, facility 9 expertise, potential 10 capability, right stuff
no matter ~: 6 anyhow, anyway 9 at any rate 10 in any event, regardless
not ~ it was: 5 rusty 9 neglected 10 out of shape
say ~: 3 ask 7 inquire
starter: 4 some
they say: 4 buzz, talk 5 rumor 6 gossip 9 grapevine
what's ~: 5 truth 7 reality 10 bottom line, brass tacks
what __: 3 for
what __ you: 4 have
what-__: 3 not
__ what?: 3 Now, Say 4 Know 5 Guess
What __!: 4 a gas 5 a deal, a drag, a dump
What __?: 3 now 4 is it, of it, to do
What __, a mind reader?: 3 am I
What __ Believes: 5 a Fool
What __ Beneath: 4 Lies
What __ bid?: 3 am I
What __ Bob?: 5 About
What __ boy am I!: 5 a good
What __ can I say?: 4 else, more
What __, chopped liver?: 3 am I
What __ do for you?: 4 can I
What __ doing here?: 3 am I
What __ done?: 5 have I
What __ for Love: 4 I Did
What __ Glory?: 5 Price
What __ God wrought?: 4 hath
What __ Happened to Baby Jane?: 4 Ever
What __ mind reader?: 4 am I a
What __ mood I'm in: 5 a rare
What __ My Love: 3 Now
What __ of baloney!: 4 a lot
What __ of Fool Am I: 4 Kind
What __ rare...?: 4 is so
What __ Sammy Run?: 5 Makes
What __ say?: 4 can I
What __ Scared Of?: 4 Was I
What __ to Go!: 4 a Way
What __ Want: 3 You 5 Women
What __ Wants: 5 a Girl
What __ Woman Knows: 5 Every
What __ wrong?: 4 went
What a __!: 4 dump 5 world
What About Bob? (1991 film)
cast: Richard Dreyfuss, Julie Hagerty, Bill Murray
What About Us? (2002 song)
artist: Brandy
What About Your Friends (1992 song) artist: TLC
What a Diff'rence a Day Makes (1959 song)
artist: Dinah Washington
What a Fool Believes (1970 song)
artist: Doobie Brothers
What a Girl Wants (1999 song)
artist: Christina Aguilera
What a Girl Wants (2003 film)
cast: Amanda Bynes, Colin Firth
What a good boy __!: 3 am I
What am __?: 4 I bid
What a piece of work __: 5 is man
What a pity!: 4 alas 5 alack 6 too bad
What a rare mood __: 4 I'm in
What a relief __: 4 it is
What a relief!: 4 phew, whew
What a Wonderful World (1988 song) artist: Louis Armstrong
What Becomes of the Brokenhearted (1977 song)
artist: Jimmy Ruffin
Whatcha Gonna Do? (1977 song)
artist: Pablo Cruise
whatchamacallit: 4 tool 5 dodad, gismo, gizmo, thing 6 doodad, gadget, widget
Whatcha See Is Whatcha Get (1971 song)
artist: Dramatics
What color is an __?: 6 orange
__ What Comes Natur'lly: 4 Doin'
...what course __ may take...: 6 others
What did I tell you?: 3 see
What'd I Say (song)
artist: Elvis Presley, Ray Charles
What Dreams May Come (1998 film)
cast: Cuba Gooding Jr., Annabella Sciorra, Max von Sydow, Robin Williams
dog: 6 Ginger
What else?: 3 and
whatever: 3 any 8 anything
anything ~: 5 aught, ought
in ~ place: 8 anywhere
person: 5 whoso
Whatever Gets You Thru the Night (1974 song)
artist: John Lennon
What Ever Happened to Baby Jane? (1962 film)
cast: Victor Buono, Joan Crawford, Bette Davis
Whatever Happened to Jacy Farrow?
author: Larry McMurtry
Whatever Lola Wants: 4 song 5 tango
artist: Dinah Shore, Sarah Vaughan
composer: Jerry Ross, Richard Adler
Whatever Works (2009 film)
cast: Henry Cavill, Larry David, Evan Rachel Wood
director: Woody Allen
Whatever you want!: 4 okay 6 name it
What Every Woman Knows
author: James M. Barrie
whatfor: 6 reason 9 rationale
__ what friends are for: 5 That's
What happened __...: 3 was
What happened __?: 4 next, then
What Happens in Vegas (2008 film)
cast: Cameron Diaz, Ashton Kutcher
What has four wheels and __?: 5 flies
What hath God wrought sender: 5 Morse
what have __: 3 you
What have I done!: 4 oh no
What Have I Done to Deserve This? (1987 song)
artist: Dusty Springfield, Pet Shop Boys
What have we here?: 3 aha, oho 5 hello
What have you been __?: 4 up to
What Have You Done for Me Lately (1986 song)
artist: Janet Jackson
What I Am (1989 song)
artist: Edie Brickell and the New Bohemians
what-if feeling: 6 regret
What in __ Hill...?: 3 Sam
What Is Life (1971 song)
artist: George Harrison
What is so __...: 4 rare
What Is This Thing Called Love
composer: Cole Porter
what it __: 5 takes
__ what it's worth: 3 for
What It Takes (1990 song)
artist: Aerosmith
What Kind of Fool (song)
artist: Barbra Streisand, Tams
What Kind of Fool Am I (1962 song) artist: Sammy Davis Jr.
What Kind of Man Would I Be? (1989 song)
artist: Chicago
What Lies Beneath (2000 film)
cast: Harrison Ford, Miranda Otto, Michelle Pfeiffer, Diana Scarwid
What'll __?: 3 I do 4 it be
What'll I Do
composer: Irving Berlin
What Maisie Knew
author: Henry James
What Makes Sammy Run?
author: Budd Schulberg
__ what may: 4 come
What, me worry? mag: 3 Mad
whatnot: 5 curio, stand 7 étagère, trinket 8 nicknack 10 knickknack
What Planet Are You From? (2000 film)
cast: Annette Bening, Ben Kingsley, Greg Kinnear, Garry Shandling
director: Mike Nichols
What Price Glory?
author: Maxwell Anderson
what's-__-name: 3 her, his
What's __?: 2 up 3 new
What's __ for me?: 4 in It
What's __ Got to Do With It: 4 Love
What's __ like?: 5 not to
What's __ name?: 3 in a
What's __ on?: 5 going
What's __ pleasure?: 4 your
What's __ Pussycat?: 3 New
What's __ you?: 6 eating
What's Going On (song)
artist: Cyndi Lauper, Marvin Gaye
What's Hecuba to him __ to Hecuba: 4 or he
what's-his-name: 6 whosis
What's in __?: 5 a name
What's in it __?: 5 for me
What's in It for Me?
author: Jerome Weidman
whatsis: 5 do-dad, gismo, gizmo 6 doodad, gadget
What's it all about, __?: 5 Alfie
What's It All About?
author: Michael Caine
What's It Gonna Be (song)
artist: Busta Rhymes, Janet Jackson
What's Love Got to Do With It: 4 film, song
artist: Tina Turner
cast: Angela Bassett, Laurence Fishburne
What's Missing?
artist: Paul Klee
what's more: 3 and 4 also 7 besides
What's My Line?: 8 game show
group: 5 panel
host: 4 Daly 6 Blyden, Bruner
regular: 4 Cerf 6 Arlene 7 Bennett, Dorothy, Francis 9 Kilgallen
What's My Name? (1993 song)
artist: Snoop Doggy Dogg
What's New Pussycat? (1965 song)
artist: Tom Jones
What's O'Clock
author: Amy Lowell
whatsoever: 5 at all
What's the __?: 3 dif, use 4 rush
What's the __ of Wond'rin'?: 3 Use
What's the __ word?: 4 good
What's the big idea?: 3 hey
What's the Frequency, Kenneth? (1994 song)
artist: R.E.M.
What's the Worst That Could Happen? (2001 film)
cast: Danny DeVito, Glenne Headly, Martin Lawrence, John Leguizamo
__ What's Up: 5 U Know
What's Up, Doc? (1972 film)
cast: Madeline Kahn, Ryan O'Neal, Barbra Streisand
What's up, Doc? voice: 5 Blanc
What's Up, Tiger Lily? (1966 film)
director: Woody Allen
What's your __?: 4 name, sign 7 problem
What's Your Name (song)
artist: Don & Juan, Lynyrd Skynyrd
Whatta Man (1994 song)
artist: En Vogue, Salt-n-Pepa
what the __: 3 hey 4 heck, hell
What the Butler Saw
author: Joe Orton
What the hey: 6 oh well
What the World Needs Now Is Love (1965 song)
artist: Jackie DeShannon
What this country __...: 5 needs
What thou __, write: 5 seest
What time __?: 4 is it
What was __ do?: 3 I to
What Was I Scared Of?
author: Dr. Seuss
What will __ think of next?: 4 they
What Will Mary Say (1963 song)
artist: Johnny Mathis
What Women Want (2000 film)
cast: Mel Gibson, Helen Hunt, Marisa Tomei
__ What You Did: 4 I Saw
What You Don't Know (1989 song)
artist: Exposé
What You Need (1986 song)
artist: INXS
__ what you think!: 5 That's
What You Want (1998 song)
artist: Mase, Total
wheat: 5 durum, emmer, grain, spelt 6 bulgur, cereal, golden 8 semolina
alternative: *see* brown color
bundle: 5 sheaf
cracked ~: 6 bulgur, groats
ender: 3 ear 4 worm
feature: 3 awn 4 bran, germ

5 spica, stalk
grow ~: 4 farm
like ~: 5 awned
product: 5 bread, flour, pasta 6 farina
protein: 6 gluten
rust: 6 fungus
starter: 4 buck
wheat __: 4 germ 5 bread
__ wheat: 5 durum
__-wheat: 5 whole
Wheat: 4 Zack
Wheat __: 4 Chex 5 Thins
Wheat Chex: 6 cereal
competitor: *see* cereal
wheat flakes: 6 cereal
Wheaties: 6 cereal
competitor: *see* cereal
Wheatley, Phillis: 4 poet
Wheaton: 3 Wil 4 city, town
locale: 8 Illinois, Maryland
Wheat Thins: 7 cracker
alternative: *see* cracker
Wheat, Zack: 6 Dodger 10 outfielder
whee: 5 oh boy
wheedle: 3 con, get, oil, ply 4 coax, prod, snow, urge, worm 5 charm, court, kotow 6 cajole, entice, induce, kowtow, work on 7 beguile, finagle, flatter, lay it on 8 blandish, butter up, freeload, inveigle, persuade, play up to, scrounge, soft-soap 9 sweet-talk 10 spread it on
wheedling: 4 oily 5 charm, guile 6 urging 7 blarney, coaxing 8 cajolery, entreaty, flattery, humoring, jollying, soft soap, stroking 9 sweet talk 10 persuasion
wheel: 4 bike, disk, drum, gyre, helm, hoop, limb, reel, ring, roll, spin, tire, turn, veer 5 cycle, mogul, orbit, pivot, round, swing, twirl, whirl 6 caster, circle, gyrate, honcho, pulley, roller, rotate, swivel 7 bicycle, big shot, circuit, ratchet, revolve, trundle 8 auto part, tricycle 9 pirouette 10 velocipede
alignment measure: 5 toe in 6 camber
around: 4 spin, turn 5 pivot
big ~: 4 head, king, name 5 chief, mogul, nabob 6 top dog, tycoon 7 notable 9 executive
cover: 3 mag 6 fender, hubcap
ender: 3 man, men 4 base, work 5 chair, house, works 6 barrow, wright
fifth ~: 5 spare
furniture ~: 6 caster
hub: 4 nave
of fortune: 4 fate 5 karma
part: 3 hub, rim 4 gear 5 spoke 6 flange
partner: 4 deal
play the ~: 3 bet 5 wager 6 gamble
projection: 3 cam
rim: 6 flange
rod: 4 axle 5 spoke
shaft ~: 3 cam
sharp-toothed ~: 5 rowel
ship's ~: 4 helm 6 tiller
starter: 3 cog, fly, pin 4 cart, free, gear
take the ~: 4 helm 5 drive, pilot, steer 8 navigate
toothed ~: 4 gear, pawl
tooth on a ~: 3 cog
train ~ sound: 5 clack
water ~: 5 noria
__ wheel: 3 big, mag 4 wire 5 at the, brake, color, daisy, fifth 6 Ferris, paddle, prayer 7 potter's
__-wheel: 4 side 5 stern
wheel and __: 4 axle, deal
wheel-back: 5 chair
wheelbarrow: 4 cart
wheelbarrow __: 4 race
__-wheel drive: 3 all 4 four 5 front
wheeler-__: 6 dealer
__ wheeler: 6 paddle
__-wheeler: 3 six, two 4 side 5 three 8 eighteen
Wheeler: 4 Anne, Bert
wheeler-dealer: 4 doer 5 Mr. Big
__ Wheeler Wilcox: 4 Ella
wheeling: 4 roll, spin 5 swirl, twirl, whirl 8 rotation
Wheeling: 4 city, town
locale: 3 W. Va. 8 Illinois
river: 4 Ohio
Wheelock: 7 Eleazar
wheel of __: 4 life 7 fortune
Wheel of Fortune: 8 game show
buy: 3 an A, an E, an I, an O 5 vowel
category: 5 event, place, thing, title 6 phrase
host: 5 Sajak, White 7 Woolery 8 Stafford
prize: 3 car 4 cash, trip
turn: 4 spin
Wheel of Fortune, The (1952 song)
artist: Kay Starr
wheels: 3 car 4 auto 5 crate, truck 7 vehicle 10 automobile
adjust the ~: 5 align, aline
expensive ~: 3 BMW 4 limo 5 Caddy, Rolls
grease the ~: 4 ease 6 assist
home on ~: 2 RV 6 camper 9 motor home
kid's ~: 4 bike 5 trike, wagon
off-road ~: 3 ATV
on ~: 6 mobile 7 movable 8 moveable, portable
one on two ~: 5 biker 7 cyclist
spinning one's ~: 5 stuck 6 in a rut
temporary ~: 6 loaner
wagon ~: 8 macaroni
see also automobile, car
__ wheels: 3 mag
__ Wheels: 3 Hot 5 Helen
wheeze: 4 gasp, hiss, pant, puff, rasp, sigh 5 cough, snore 6 breath, sizzle 7 breathe, whistle
cause: 6 asthma
Whelan: 3 Tim 4 Jill
Whelchel: 4 Lisa
whelk: 5 shell 8 seashell
whelm: 6 engulf, ingulf 8 overcome
whelp: 3 dog, pup 4 seal 5 puppy, youth
when: 4 then 5 while 6 during, just as, whilst
back ~: 4 once, past, yore 8 formerly 9 at one time 10 previously
ender: 4 ever 6 soever
from way back ~: 6 age-old
in Spanish: 6 cuando
since way back ~: 6 in ages 9 for a while
when __ comes to shove: 4 push
__ when: 3 say 5 if and
__ when?: 5 Since
When __ a lad,...: 4 I was
When __ Be Loved: 5 Will I
When __ Collide: 6 Worlds
When __ Comes Marching Home: 6 Johnny
When __ door not...: 3 is a
When __ eat?: 4 do we
When __ Eyes Are Smiling: 5 Irish
When __ Fears: 5 I Have
When __ in Love: 5 I Fall
When __ Married: 5 We Get
When __ Marries: 5 a Girl
When __ Met Sally ...: 5 Harry
When __ One-and-Twenty: 4 I Was
When __ said and done...: 5 all is
When __ See You Again: 5 Will I
When __ seventeen...: 4 I was
When __ Sleepy Time Down South: 3 It's
When __ Smiling: 5 You're
When __ to Old to Dream: 5 I Grow
When __ Up: 5 I Grow
When __ Wish Upon a Star: 3 You
When __ You: 5 I Lost, I Need
When!: 4 stop 6 enough, no more
When a Girl Marries: 9 radio show
When a Man Loves a Woman (1994 film)
cast: Ellen Burstyn, Andy Garcia, Meg Ryan
When a Man Loves a Woman (song)
artist: Michael Bolton, Percy Sledge
whence: 9 therefore
When donkeys fly!: 5 never, no how, no way 8 forget it 9 fat chance 10 impossible, not a chance
When Doves Cry (1984 song)
artist: Prince
whenever: 6 at will
Whenever I Call You Friend (1978 song) artist: Kenny Loggins
When Harry Met Sally... (1989 film)
cast: Billy Crystal, Carrie Fisher, Meg Ryan
director: Rob Reiner
When I __ my lips...: 3 ope
When I Fall in Love (1961 song)
artist: Lettermen
When I Grow Too __ Dream: 5 Old to
When I Grow Up (1964 song)
artist: Beach Boys
When I Have Fears
author: John Keats
__ When I Laugh: 4 Only
When I Looked at Him (1989 song)
artist: Exposé
When I Lost You
composer: Irving Berlin
When I'm Back on My Feet Again (1990 song)
artist: Michael Bolton
When I Need You (1977 song)
artist: Leo Sayer
When in Rome, __...: 4 do as
When in the course of human __...: 6 events
When Irish Eyes are Smiling: 5 waltz
When I Take My Sugar __: 5 to Tea
When I Think of You (1986 song)
artist: Janet Jackson
When It's Love (1988 song)
artist: Van Halen
When I Wanted You (1980 song)
artist: Barry Manilow
When I was a __...: 3 lad
When I Was One-and-Twenty
author: A.E. Housman
When Lilacs Last...
author: Walt Whitman
When My Baby Smiles __: 4 at Me
When My Blue Moon... (1956 song)
artist: Elvis Presley
when one's __ comes in: 4 ship
When pigs fly!: 5 never, nohow, no way 8 forget it 9 fat chance 10 impossible, not a chance
when push __ to shove: 5 comes
When She Was Good
author: Philip Roth
when the __ are down: 5 chips
When the Bough Breaks
author: Jonathan Kellerman
When the Boy in Your Arms (1961 song) artist: Connie Francis
When the Frost Is on the Punkin
author: James Whitcomb Riley
When the Going Gets Tough... (1985 song)
artist: Billy Ocean
When the moon __ the seventh house: 4 is in
When the moon hits your eye: 5 amore
When there's __...: 5 a will
When We Dead Awaken
author: Henrik Ibsen
When We Get Married (1961 song)
artist: Dreamlovers
When We Were Kings subject: 3 Ali
When We Were Very Young
author: A.A. Milne
When Will __ Loved: 3 I Be
When Will I Be Loved (song)
artist: Everly Brothers, Linda Ronstadt
When Will I See You Again (1974 song) artist: Three Degrees
When Worlds Collide: 5 novel
author: Edwin Balmer, Philip Wylie
planet: 4 Zyra
When You're Hot... (1971 song)
artist: Jerry Reed
When You're in Love... (1979 song)
artist: Dr. Hook
When You Wish Upon __: 5 a Star
where: 4 site, spot 5 place, point 7 whither 8 location, position
ender: 4 fore, from, into, unto, upon, with 6 soever, withal
starter: 3 any 4 else, ever, some 5 every
where __: 5 it's at
Where __?: 3 am I 4 was I
Where __ All the Flowers Gone: 4 Have
Where __ Dare: 6 Eagles
Where __ I?: 3 was
Where __ Life ...: 6 There's
Where __ Love: 5 Is the
Where __ Our Love Go: 3 Did
Where __ smoke...: 6 there's
whereabouts: 4 loca, loci 5 place 6 locale 8 bearings, location, position, presence 9 situation
forget the ~: 4 lose 6 mislay 7 misfile 8 misplace
Where America's day begins: 4 Guam

Where Are the Children?
author: Mary Higgins Clark
whereas: 3 for 5 since, while 6 though, whilst 7 because 10 seeing that
Where did __ wrong?: 3 I go
Where Did Our Love Go (1964 song)
artist: Supremes
Where Do __?: 3 I Go
Where Do Broken Hearts Go (1988 song)
artist: Whitney Houston
Where Does My Heart Beat Now (1991 song)
artist: Celine Dion
Where Eagles Dare (1969 film)
cast: Richard Burton, Clint Eastwood, Mary Ure
gun: 4 Sten
wherefore: 6 motive, reason 7 grounds, purpose 9 rationale
partner: 3 why
Wherefore art thou __?: 5 Romeo
Where Have All the Cowboys Gone? (1997 song)
artist: Paula Cole
Where I Live
author: Tennessee Williams
Where Is Love? musical: 6 Oliver!
Where Is the Life That Late __?: 4 I Led
Where Is the Love (1972 song)
artist: Donny Hathaway, Roberta Flack
Where Love Has Gone
author: Harold Robbins
Where or When: 4 song
composer: Lorenz Hart, Richard Rodgers
__ where prohibited: 4 void
Where's __?: 5 Daddy, Poppa, Waldo 7 Charley
Where's Charley? (1952 film): 7 musical
cast: Ray Bolger
composer: Frank Loesser
role: 3 Amy
Where's Daddy?
author: William Inge
Where's Poppa? (1970 film)
cast: George Segal, Ruth Gordon
Where's the __?: 4 beef, fire
Where's the Rest __?: 4 of Me
Where the __ meet to eat: 5 elite
Where the Boys Are (1961 song)
artist: Connie Francis
...where the buffalo __: 4 roam
__ where the heart...: 6 Home is
Where there's __...: 4 life 5 a will
wherever: 4 site, spot 5 place 6 locale 7 whither 8 anyplace, locality, position
you are: 4 here
Wherever He __: 4 Ain't
wherewithal: 6 assets, moolah 7 ability, capital 9 potential, resources
has the ~: 3 can
having the ~: 4 able
lacks the ~: 6 cannot
see also moolah
wherry: 4 boat 5 craft 6 vessel
implement: 3 oar 6 paddle
whet: 4 edge, file, hone, stir 5 grind, pique, raise, rally, rouse, strop, tempt 6 arouse, awaken, excite, kindle 7 quicken, sharpen 8 increase, motivate 9 acuminate, appetizer, intensify, stimulant, stimulate
ender: 5 stone
whether __: 4 or no 5 or not
Whether __ nobler...: 3 'tis
whetstone: 4 hone
use a ~: 5 grind 7 sharpen
whetted: 4 keen 5 sharp 6 pointy 9 acuminate
Whew!: 6 I'm beat
feeling: 6 relief
whey: 4 sera 5 dairy, serum
partner: 4 curd
whey-faced: 3 wan 4 ashy 5 ashen
which
at ~ time: 4 when
besides ~: 3 and 4 also, plus 8 moreover
ender: 4 ever 6 soever
every ~ way: 5 about, messy, mussy 6 hectic, remiss, untidy 7 chaotic, haywire, jumbled, lawless, riotous, tangled 8 anarchic, confused, pell-mell, reckless 10 anarchical, disjointed, disordered, disorderly, topsy-turvy, tumultuous
in ~ case: 4 then
person: 3 who 4 whom
person's: 5 whose
which __ the wind blows: 3 way
Which came first?
choice: 3 egg 7 chicken
whichever: 3 any 6 either
Which nobody can __: 4 deny
__ which way: 3 any 5 every
__ Which Way But Loose: 5 Every
which way the __ blows: 4 wind
__ Which Way You Can: 3 Any
Which Way You Goin' Billy? (1970 song)
artist: Poppy Family
__ which will live in infamy: 5 a date
whiff: 3 air, fan 4 dash, gust, hint, lick, odor, puff, waft 5 aroma, scent, smell, sniff, snort, touch, trace 6 breath, inhale 7 draught, soupçon, whisper 9 strike out, suspicion
Whiffenpoof: 3 Eli 5 Yalie 7 Bulldog
word: 3 baa
whiffle: 4 yo-yo 5 hedge, waver 6 dither, seesaw, teeter, totter 8 fence-sit, flip-flop, hesitate 9 hem and haw, pussyfoot, vacillate 10 dillydally, equivocate
Whigs: 5 party
while: 4 laze, pass, time, when 5 altho, space, spell 6 during, moment, much as, period, though 7 interim, stretch, whereas 8 although, as long as, meantime 10 even though
a ~ ago: 4 once 6 before 7 earlier 9 at one time, in the past 10 beforehand, previously
all the ~: 6 during 10 throughout
a short ~ ago: 6 lately, of late 8 recently 9 yesterday
away: 3 use 5 spend, use up, waste 6 expend, misuse 7 deplete, fritter 8 squander 9 dissipate
away hours: 4 idle, laze, loaf, loll 5 dally 6 dawdle, loiter 8 kill time, malinger, slack off 9 bum around, goldbrick, sit around, waste time 10 dillydally, fool around, knock about, take it easy
in a ~: 3 yet 4 anon, soon, then 5 after, later 7 by and by, later on, shortly, someday 8 directly, sometime 9 afterward, hereafter 10 before long, eventually
long ~: 4 ages, days, eons 5 years
once in a ~: 3 occ. 6 rarely, seldom 7 at times 8 scarcely 9 sometimes 10 hardly ever
prefix for ~: 4 erst
short ~: 3 bit 4 jiff 5 jiffy 7 instant
starter: 3 ere 4 erst, mean 5 worth
stay a ~: 5 abide, dwell 6 hold on, linger, remain 7 sojourn 8 continue
stop for a ~: 4 rest 5 break, pause 7 breathe, suspend
use for a ~: 6 borrow
__ while: 3 in a
While My Pretty One Sleeps
author: Mary Higgins Clark
__ while the iron is hot: 6 strike
While the Sun Shines
author: Terrence Rattigan
While You See a Chance (1981 song)
artist: Steve Winwood
while-you-wait: 4 fast 5 quick, rapid 6 prompt, snappy 7 instant 9 immediate, on-the-spot
While You Were Sleeping (1995 film)
cast: Peter Boyle, Sandra Bullock, Peter Gallagher, Bill Pullman
__ While You Work: 7 Whistle
whillikers: 3 gee 4 gosh 5 golly
whilom: 4 erst, once 6 former 7 one-time, quondam
whim: 4 lark, urge, wish 5 fancy, quirk 6 desire, notion, vagary 7 caprice, impulse 8 crotchet
__ whim: 3 on a
whimbrel: 4 bird
whimper: 3 cry, sob 4 bawl, fuss, mewl, moan, pule, wail, weep 5 bleat, whine 6 boohoo, snivel 7 blubber 8 complain 9 make a fuss, shed tears
alternative: 4 bang
go out with a ~: 6 fizzle
whimpering: 5 tears 7 tearful 9 querulous, sniveling
whimsical: 3 fey, odd 5 droll, funny, light, silly, witty 6 dreamy, fickle, jocose, quaint 7 amusing, comical, curious, erratic, jocular, playful, waggish, wayward 8 fanciful, farcical, humorous, peculiar, skittish, volatile 9 arbitrary, eccentric, facetious, fantastic, frivolous, grotesque, imaginary, quizzical, uncertain 10 capricious, changeable, outlandish
whimsy: 5 humor, quirk 6 vagary 9 frivolity
whine: 3 cry, sob 4 carp, fuss, howl, kick, mewl, moan, pule, sigh, sing, wail, yowl 5 bleat, cavil, drone, gripe, groan, sound 6 grouch, grouse, kvetch, murmur, repine, snivel, squawk, squeak, yammer 7 grumble, nitpick, quibble, whimper 8 complain 9 bellyache, complaint, criticism, criticize, make a fuss
whiner: 5 grump, shrew 6 grouch, kvetch, moaner 7 crybaby
whinny: 4 bray 5 bleat, neigh
companion: 5 snort
whiny: 6 cranky 7 fretful, peevish 8 fretsome, petulant 9 querulous
whip: 3 mix, rod, tan, tar, top 4 beat, belt, best, cane, crop, drub, flay, flog, hide, hurt, jerk, lash, lick, race, rout, stir, trim 5 birch, blend, knout, mop up, shake, spank, strap, thong, trash, whale, whisk, whomp, worst 6 berate, defeat, ferule, hammer, larrup, lather, punish, switch, thrash, wallop 7 bawl out, chew out, clobber, conquer, lambast, lay into, overrun, rawhide, scamper, scourge, shellac, trounce 8 bludgeon, chastise, give it to, lambaste, shellack 9 castigate, dress down, horsewhip, overwhelm 10 discipline, tongue-lash
ender: 3 saw 4 cord, lash, tail, worm 5 sawed, stall 6 stitch
into shape: 4 tidy 5 train 7 arrange 8 organize 9 supervise
mark: 4 weal, welt
riding ~: 4 crop 5 quirt
sound: 5 crack
starter: 4 bull 5 horse
together: 3 mix 4 meld, stir 5 blend, merge 7 combine 8 intermix 9 integrate 10 amalgamate
up: 3 fix, set 4 brew, goad, make, prod, spur, stir, urge 5 drive, hatch, prick, start 6 arouse, create, devise, excite, foment, incite, kindle 7 agitate, disturb, enflame, inflame, provoke 8 contrive, generate 9 fabricate, instigate
whip __: 3 off 4 hand
whip __ shape: 4 into
__ Whip: 4 Cool 7 Miracle
Whip Hand
author: Dick Francis
Whip It
artist: Devo
Whiplash, Snidely, like: 4 evil
whipped-cream portion: 4 glob 6 dollop
whipped-up: 5 ad-lib 7 offhand 9 extempore, impromptu, tossed-off 10 improvised, off-the-cuff, unscripted
whippersnapper: 3 boy, lad, pup 4 brat, punk 5 minor, whelp, youth 6 urchin 9 stripling
whippet: 3 dog 5 pooch 6 canine
whipping __: 3 boy 5 cream
whipping boy: 3 sap 4 dupe, fool, goat, lamb 5 chump, patsy 6 pigeon, sucker, victim 7 cat's-paw, doormat 8 pushover 9 scapegoat
whippoorwill: 4 bird
relative: 9 nighthawk
whir
see whirr
whirl: 2 go 3 try 4 daze, eddy, reel, ride, roll, rush, shot, spin, stab, to-do, turn, zoom 5 crack, fling, pivot,

round, swing, swirl, twirl, twist, whack, wheel **6** circle, flurry, gyrate, hassle, hubbub, rotate, swivel, tumble **7** attempt, revolve, turmoil **8** gyration, trial run **9** pirouette **10** hullabaloo, spin around
ender: **4** pool, wind
give it a ~: **3** try **6** tackle **7** attempt
__ whirl: **3** in a
__-Whirl: **5** Tilt-a
whirling: **5** aspin, dizzy **6** rotary **8** gyration
whirling __: **7** dervish
whirlpool: **3** spa **4** eddy, tide **5** swirl **6** hot tub, vortex **8** undertow **9** maelstrom
whirlpool __: **4** bath
Whirlpool: **9** appliance
alternative: ***see*** appliance brand
whirlwind: **2** oe **4** rash, wind **5** hasty, quick, rapid, storm, swift **6** speedy, vortex **7** cyclone, tornado, twister **8** headlong **9** breakneck, dust devil, impetuous, impulsive **10** waterspout
Whirlwind
author: James Clavell
whirlybird: **4** giro **6** copter **7** chopper **8** autogiro **10** helicopter
blade: **5** rotor
Whirly Girl (1983 song)
artist: OXO
whirr: **3** hum **4** birr, buzz, roll, whiz **5** churr, drone, noise, skirr **6** bustle **7** vibrate
whish: **5** sound, zip by
whisk: **3** fly, zip **4** dart, dash, flit, race, rush, stir, tear, whip, whiz **5** broom, brush, flick, hurry, mixer, shoot, speed, sweep, swish **6** beater, hasten, scurry **8** brush off
user: **3** ump **6** umpire
whisk __: **5** broom
Whiskas: **7** cat food
alternative: ***see*** pet food brand
whisker: **3** awn **6** barbel **7** bristle
by a ~: **6** barely **8** narrowly
__ whisker: **3** by a, cat **4** cat's
whiskered: **5** hairy **7** bearded, bristly, hirsute
whiskers: **4** fuzz, hair **5** beard **6** goatee
creature with ~: **3** cat **6** walrus
like ~: **5** bushy
where ~ grow: **4** chin, face, neck **5** cheek
whiskey: **3** rye **5** booze, drink, hooch, sauce **6** chaser, hootch, liquor, redeye, rotgut, Scotch **7** alcohol, bourbon, spirits **8** beverage **9** firewater, hard stuff, moonshine
a way to drink ~: **4** neat **10** on the rocks
bottle: **4** pint **5** fifth
holder: **4** cask **5** flask
measure: **4** dram, shot **5** proof **6** jigger
source: **3** rye **4** corn, mash
whiskey __: **4** jack, sour
__ whiskey: **3** rye **4** corn, malt **5** Irish **6** bonded, Scotch **7** blended, bourbon
Whiskey Rebellion suppressor: **3** Lee
whiskey sour: **5** drink **8** beverage, cocktail
ingredient: **10** lemon juice
whisper: **3** hum, pst, tip **4** buzz, hint, hiss, psst, sigh, tell, wind, word **5** rumor, sound, speak, tinge, touch, trace, utter, whiff **6** breath, gossip, intone, mumble, murmur, mutter, report, rustle, shadow, sizzle, tipoff **7** breathe, confide, soupçon **8** innuendo, intimate, sibilate **9** insinuate, suspicion, susurrate, undertone **10** suggestion
__ whisper: **5** stage
whispered: **3** low **4** soft, weak **5** bated, faint, muted, piano, quiet **6** hushed **7** muffled, subdued **8** dampened, deadened **9** toned down **10** turned down
whisperer's request: **6** closer
__ Whisperer, The: **5** Horse
whispering: **5** rumor **6** canard, gossip, report **7** hearsay **9** grapevine
Whispering Bells (1957 song)
artist: Dell-Vikings
Whispers
author: Dean Koontz
whist: **4** game **8** card game
relative: **6** bridge, écarté
variety: **6** Boston
whistle: **4** blow, hiss, pipe, sign **5** blast, siren **6** signal, wheeze
after the ~: **4** late
blow the ~: **4** sing, tell **6** accuse, inform
blow the ~ on: **4** halt **5** blame **6** betray, charge, expose, give up, turn in **7** sell out
for: **7** solicit
sound: **4** toot
starter: **5** penny
stop: **4** town
time: **4** noon
wet one's ~: **4** swig **5** drink **6** imbibe, tipple **7** swallow
whistle __: **4** stop **5** Dixie
whistle-__: **4** stop **6** blower
__ whistle: **5** organ, penny
Whistle __ You Work: **5** While
whistle-blower: **4** fink **7** tattler, traitor **10** tattletale
Whistle Blower, The (1986 film)
cast: Michael Caine
whistle in the __: **4** dark
whistler: **4** bird, wolf **9** thickhead
Whistler, James McNeill: **6** artist **7** painter
Whistler's mother's wear: **5** shawl
whistle-stop: **4** tour
whistles, with all the bells and: **6** deluxe
Whistle While You Work
singer: **3** Doc **5** dwarf, Happy **6** Grumpy, Sleepy, Sneezy **7** Bashful
whistling __: **4** buoy, duck, swan
whit: **3** bit, fig, jot **4** atom, dash, drop, iota, mite, mote **5** crumb, grain, pinch, scrap, shred, speck, trace **6** little, trifle **7** minimum, modicum, smidgen, smidgin, tiny bit **8** fragment, least bit, particle, smidgeon **9** scintilla
not a ~: **3** nil, zip **4** nada, none, zero **5** zilch **6** naught, nought **7** nothing
Whit: **7** Bissell
Whitaker: **4** Jack **6** Forest **7** Johnnie
Whitaker, Forest: **5** actor
film: Bird (1988)
The Crying Game (1992)
Diary of a Hitman (1992)
Good Morning, Vietnam (1987)
The Great Debaters (2007)
Hope Floats (1998)
The Last King of Scotland (2006, AA)
Light It Up (1999)
Panic Room (2002)
Phenomenon (1996)
Platoon (1986)
Species (1995)
Vantage Point (2008)
Waiting to Exhale (1995)
Oscar role: **4** Amin
Whitcomb: **3** Ian
__ Whitcomb Riley: **5** James
white: **3** wan **4** fair, pale, pure, wine **5** Anglo, ashen, bread, clean, clear, color, hoary, ivory, light, Mâcon, milky, pasty, Pinot, snowy, soave, Tokay, waxen, Yquem **6** Arneis, chalky, creamy, pallid, peaked, pearly, silver, washed **7** aligoté, cabinet, Catawba, Chablis, frosted, heurige, Madeira, Moselle, neutral, niveous, Orvieto, silvery, Vouvray **8** Albariño, blanched, bleached, Frascati, Muscadet, Riesling, Sancerre, Sauterne, Sylvaner, vermouth **9** alabaster, albescent, bloodless, Caucasian, colombard, colorless, Meursault **10** achromatic, Chardonnay, immaculate, Montrachet
alternative: **3** rye **5** wheat
and yellow flower: **7** calypso **8** camomile **9** calla lily, chamomile
as a sheet: **3** wan **4** ashy, pale **5** ashen
black plus ~: **4** gray, grey
black, to ~: **3** opp. **8** opposite
cliffs locale: **5** Dover
cloud: **3** pet **4** fish
collar: **6** worker
color: **4** bone, milk, snow **5** cream, ivory, milky **6** argent, oyster, silver **8** eggshell **9** alabaster
combining form: **3** alb- **4** albo-, leuc-, leuk- **5** leuco-, leuko-
complement: **4** yolk
egg ~: **5** glair **6** glaire
ender: **3** cap, fly, out **4** bait, face, fish, tail, wash, wood **5** print, smith **6** throat, washed **7** washing
flag: **5** truce **9** surrender
flower: **3** mum **4** flag, iris, lily **5** calla, camas, daisy, lilac, lotus, peony, poppy, tulip, yucca **6** camass, crocus, lupine, mallow, maypop, myrtle, spirea, thrift, violet, yarrow **7** aconite, arbutus, catalpa, dog rose, dogwood, freesia, hogweed, jasmine, jonquil, rambler, saguaro, spiraea **8** aconitum, ageratum, arum lily, asphodel, boltonia, camellia, erigeron, gardenia, hawthorn, hepatica, hyacinth, larkspur, magnolia, oleander, rockrose, snowball, snowdrop, tamarisk, trillium, tuberose, viburnum, wistaria, wisteria **9** arrowhead, bloodroot, calla lily, candytuft, colicroot, edelweiss, horehound, hydrangea, jessamine, mayflower, narcissus, pussytoes, water lily **10** bluebottle, buttonbush, cornflower, delphinium, Easter lily, fleur-de-lis, goatsbeard, Indian pipe, marguerite, mock orange, poinsettia, ranunculus, spider lily
gem: **4** opal **5** pearl
grayish ~: **6** oyster, silver
in black and ~: **5** clear, plain **8** explicit
in heraldry: **6** argent
lie: **3** fib **4** tale **5** story
lightning: **5** booze, hooch **6** hootch
mineral: **5** chalk
name meaning ~: **6** Bianca **7** Blanche
out: **5** erase, scrub **6** delete, efface, remove **7** expunge
pages: **8** listings **9** directory
paper: **3** rpt. **6** report
sale buy: **5** linen, sheet, towel
starter: **3** bob **4** lint
stuff: **4** snow
turn ~: **4** pale **6** blanch **8** etiolate
water: **6** rapids
wine: **3** kir **5** Mâcon, Mosel, pinot, Rhine, soave, Tokay, Yquem **7** Catawba, Chablis, Madeira, Moselle, Orvieto, Vouvray **8** Albariño, Frascati, Muscadet, Riesling, Sancerre, Sauterne, Sylvaner **10** Chardonnay, Montrachet
with shock: **3** wan **4** ashy, pale **5** ashen
woman in ~: **5** bride, nurse
yellowish ~: **4** bone **5** cream, ivory **8** eggshell
white __: **3** ant, hat, lie, oak, rat, tie **4** belt, flag, heat, meat, sale, wine **5** bread, bucks, cloud, dwarf, goods, horse, light, magic, noise, pages, paper, sauce, space, water **6** knight, matter, pepper
white __ cell: **5** blood
white __ ghost: **3** as a
white __ sheet: **3** as a
white-__: **3** hot **5** faced, glove **6** collar
white-__ deer: **6** tailed
__ white: **3** egg **6** pearly
__-white: **3** off, tin **4** milk, snow **5** ivory
White: **2** E.B., T.H. **3** sea **5** Barry, Betty, Byron, David, Karyn, Perry, range, river, Vanna **6** Jaleel **7** Patrick **8** Stanford
river: **4** Nile
river locale: **8** Arkansas
sea locale: **6** Russia
White __: **3** Sea, Sox **4** Fang, Heat, Nile **5** House, Sands **6** Castle, Nights, Rabbit
White __ Can't Jump: **3** Men
White __, NM: **5** Sands
White __ of Dover: **6** Cliffs
__ White: **4** Snow
White Album, The
author: Joan Didion

White April
poet: Lizette Reese
white as ___: 5 chalk 6 a ghost, a sheet
white as a ___: 5 ghost, sheet
White, Barry
song: Can't Get Enough... (1974)
I'm Gonna Love You... (1973)
It's Ecstasy... (1977)
Never, Never Gonna Give Ya Up (1973)
Practice What You Preach (1994)
What Am I Going to Do With You (1975)
You're the First... (1974)
White, Betty
spouse: Allen Ludden
whiteboard need: 6 eraser, marker
white-bread: 4 tame 5 usual 8 ordinary
white buck
singer with ~ shoes: Pat Boone
white bucks: 4 shoe 8 footwear
white cabbage: 6 veggie 9 vegetable
whitecap: 4 foam, wave 6 billow
White Christmas: 4 film, song
artist: Bing Crosby
cast: Rosemary Clooney, Bing Crosby, Danny Kaye, Vera-Ellen
composer: Irving Berlin
record label: 5 Decca
White Cloud: 10 paper towel
alternative: 5 Scott 6 Marcal 7 Charmin 8 Northern, Soft Weve 10 Cottonelle
white-collar ___: 5 crime 6 worker
white-collar worker: 5 clerk, yuppy 6 yuppie 7 cashier, employe 8 employee 10 amanuensis, bookkeeper
White Company, The
author: Arthur Conan Doyle
White Devil, The
author: John Webster
White, E.B.: 6 writer
work: Charlotte's Web
The Elements of Style
Stuart Little
whiteface
one in ~: 4 mime 5 mimer
white-faced: 3 wan 4 ashy, pale 5 ashen
White Fang: 4 film 5 novel
author: Jack London
cast: Klaus Maria Brandauer, Ethan Hawke
White Fang creator: Soupy Sales
whitefish: 4 chub 5 cisco 6 pollan
White Goddess, The
author: Robert Graves
white gold: 5 alloy
white hat wearer: 2 RN 4 chef, hero 5 nurse
Whitehead, Alfred North: 7 British 11 philosopher
work: Principia Mathematica
Science and the Modern World
Whitehead, William: 4 poet
White Heat (1949 film)
cast: James Cagney, Virginia Mayo, Edmond O'Brien
composer: Max Steiner
___ White Hope, The: 5 Great
Whitehorse: 4 city, town
locale: 5 Yukon 6 Canada
river: 5 Yukon
white-hot: 3 mad 5 angry, fiery, irate, livid, rabid, riled, wroth 6 crazed, fuming, ireful, raging, raving, torrid 7 boiling, burning, enraged, frantic, furious, ranting 8 frenzied, in a tizzy, incensed, inflamed, sizzling, wrathful 10 blistering, infuriated
White House
'70s ~ daughter: 3 Amy 5 Susan
architect: 5 Hoban
area: 4 lawn
dog: 3 Her, Him 4 Fala 5 Buddy
dweller: 4 prez 9 first lady, president
French ~: 6 Élysée
group: 3 NSC, OMB 7 cabinet
initials: 3 DDE, FDR, HST, JFK, LBJ, RMN
nickname: 3 Abe, Cal, Ike 4 Bill
room: 4 East
section: 4 wing
staffer: 4 aide
turndown: 4 veto
Web site suffix: 3 gov
see also president
White Hunter, Black Heart (1990 film)
cast: Clint Eastwood, Jeff Fahey
director: Clint Eastwood
white-knuckled: 4 taut 5 jumpy, tense 6 on edge 7 anxious, excited, fretful, jittery, keyed up, nervous, restive, uptight, worried 9 strung out 10 distressed
Whitelaw: 4 Reid
___ White Lies: 6 Little
Whiteman: 4 Paul
White Men Can't Jump (1992 film)
cast: Woody Harrelson, Rosie Perez, Wesley Snipes
White Mischief (1988 film)
cast: John Hurt, Sarah Miles, Greta Scacchi
whiten: 4 fade, pale 5 chalk, frost 6 blanch, bleach, blench, silver 7 decolor, grizzle, lighten 8 etiolate 9 whitewash 10 decolorize
White Nile people: 4 Nuer
White Noise
author: Don DeLillo
White Oleander (2002 film)
cast: Robin Wright Penn, Michelle Pfeiffer, Noah Wyle, Renée Zellweger
White Palace (1990 film)
cast: Susan Sarandon, James Spader
White, Patrick: 6 writer 8 Nobelist 10 Australian
work: The Tree of Man
White Peacock, The
author: D.H. Lawrence
White, Perry: 4 boss 6 editor
White Plains: 4 city, town
locale: 7 New York
White Rabbit
associate: 5 Alice
like the ~: 4 late
White Rabbit (1967 song)
artist: Jefferson Airplane
White Room (1968 song)
artist: Cream
Whiter Shade of Pale, A (1967 song)
artist: Procol Harum
___ whites: 6 pearly
White Sands (1992 film)
cast: Willem Dafoe, Samuel L. Jackson, Mary Elizabeth Mastrantonio, Mickey Rourke
White Sands county: 5 Otero
White Sea
bay: 5 Dvina, Onega
river to the ~: 5 Dvina
___ White Season: 4 A Dry
___ white shark: 5 great
White Silver Sands (song)
artist: Bill Black Combo, Don Rondo
White Smoke
author: Andrew Greeley
White Sox: 3 ten 4 team
Hall-of-Famer: 7 Appling
home: 7 Chicago
org.: 3 ALC, MLB
rival: *see* baseball team
sport: 8 baseball
White Sport Coat, A (1957 song)
artist: Marty Robbins
White Squall (1996 film)
cast: Jeff Bridges, Caroline Goodall
director: Ridley Scott
White, Stanford: 9 architect
whitetail: 4 deer
White, T.H.: 6 writer 7 British
work: The Age of Scandal
The Book of Merlyn
The Candle in the Wind
The Ill-Made Knight
The Once and Future King
The Sword in the Stone
White, Theodore H.: 6 writer 10 journalist
work: Breach of Faith
Fire in the Ashes
The Making of the President
Thunder Out of China
The View from the Fortieth Floor
white tornado cleaner: 4 Ajax
White, Vanna: 4 host
colleague: Pat Sajak
whitewall: 4 tire, tyre 5 wheel
whitewash: 4 coat, hide 5 chalk, gloss, mince, paint 6 deceit, dupery, excuse, whiten 7 absolve, conceal, cover up, encrust, incrust, justify, pretend 8 downplay, minimize, overlook, palliate, play down 9 collusion, deception, dissemble, exonerate, gloss over, soft-pedal, sugarcoat, vindicate
ingredient: 4 lime
white water: 6 rapids
craft: 4 raft 5 canoe
site: 5 cañon 6 canyon
white-water rafting: 5 sport
___ White Way: 5 Great
White Wedding (1982 song)
artist: Billy Idol
Whitey: 4 Ford 6 Herzog
whither: 5 where 8 wherever
ender: 6 soever
Whither thou ___...: 5 goest
whiting: 4 fish, hake
Whiting: 4 John 7 Richard 8 Margaret
Whiting, Richard: 8 composer
song: Ain't We Got Fun
Beyond the Blue Horizon
Hooray for Hollywood
On the Good Ship Lollipop
Sleepy Time Gal
Too Marvelous for Words
whitish: 4 ashy, pale 5 ashen, milky 6 chalky, pearly 7 opaline 8 blanched 10 opalescent
color: 6 silver
stone: 4 opal
Whitley: 8 Strieber
whitlow: 6 agnail
Whitman: 3 Mae 4 Mayo, poet, Slim, Walt 6 Stuart
Whitman, Walt: 4 poet
work: Crossing Brooklyn Ferry
I Hear America Singing
I Sing the Body Electic
Leaves of Grass
O Captain! My Captain!
Out of the Cradle Endlessly Rocking
Song of Myself
Song of the Open Road
When Lilacs Last in the Dooryard Bloom'd
Whitmore: 5 James
role: 6 Truman
Whitney: 3 Eli 4 peak 5 Blake, mount 7 Houston 8 mountain
invention: 3 gin
locale: 10 California
partner: 5 Pratt
___ Whitney Payson: 4 Joan
Whittaker: 5 Roger 8 Chambers
Whittier: 4 city, John, poet, town
locale: 10 California
Whittier, John Greenleaf: 4 poet
work: Barbara Frietchie
The Barefoot Boy
Ichabod
Maud Muller
Snow-Bound
whittle: 4 chip, mold, pare, trim 5 carve, model, shape, shave, slash 6 lessen, reduce, sculpt 7 curtail 8 decrease, diminish, wear away 9 sculpture
down: 4 pare, trim 5 erode 9 undermine
whittling material: 4 pine, wood 5 balsa
Whitty, May: 4 Dame
Whitworth, Kathy: 6 golfer
whiz: 3 ace, fly, hum, pro, run, zip 4 buzz, dart, flit, hiss, race, rush, whir, zoom 5 adept, brain, hurry, maven, mavin, smart, speed, swish, whirr, whisk, woosh 6 artist, expert, genius, hurtle, marvel, master, sizzle, sprint, whoosh 7 egghead, hotshot, old hand, prodigy, thinker 8 Einstein, highbrow, skillful, virtuoso 10 mastermind
at: 5 adept 6 adroit 7 skilled 8 skillful, talented 9 dexterous 10 proficient
gee ~: 4 gosh 5 golly
kid: 5 brain 6 dynamo, wizard 7 prodigy
no ~ kid: 5 dunce
whiz ___: 3 kid
whiz-___: 4 bang
___ whiz!: 3 Gee
___ Whiz: 5 Cheez
who: 7 pronoun
ender: 4 ever 6 soever
one ~ (suffix): 3 -ist
sayer: 3 owl
who's ~: 5 elite 7 society 8 register 9 directory

___ who?: 3 Sez 4 Says 5 Guess
Who
  composer: Jerome Kern
Who ___?: 4 is it 5 Cares
Who ___ it?: 5 needs
Who ___ I Turn To: 3 Can
Who ___ kidding?: 3 am I
Who ___ my purse...: 6 steals
Who ___ Roger Rabbit: 6 Framed
Who ___ that masked man?: 3 was
Who ___ the Bomp: 3 Put
Who ___ there?: 4 goes
Who ___ to say?: 3 am I
Who ___ Trust?: 5 Do You
Who ___ Turn To: 4 Can I
Who ___ You: 3 Are 5 Loves, Needs
Whoa!: 4 halt, stop
Whoa, ___!: 6 Nellie
Who am ___ say?: 3 I to
___ Who Came In..., The: 3 Spy
___ Who Came to Dinner, The: 3 Man
Who Can It Be Now? (1982 song)
  artist: Men at Work
Who Can I Turn To (1964 song)
  artist: Tony Bennett
Who cares!: 6 so what 7 big deal
Who Cares
  composer: George Gershwin, Ira Gershwin
Who Dat (1999 song)
  artist: JT Money, Solé
Who Do You Trust?: 8 game show
  host: Johnny Carson
whodunit: 4 book, tale 5 genre, novel, prose, story 7 mystery 9 narrative
  award: 5 Edgar
  board game: 4 Clue
  character: 4 heir 6 butler
  item: 4 body, clew, clue, plot 5 alibi, crime, twist 6 murder
  name: 3 Rex 4 Erle 5 Queen, Stout 6 Agatha, Ellery 7 Gardner 8 Christie
whoever: 6 anyone, person 8 somebody
___ Who Fell to Earth, The: 3 Man
Who Framed Roger Rabbit (1988 film)
  cast: Joanna Cassidy, Charles Fleischer, Bob Hoskins, Stubby Kaye, Christopher Lloyd
  director: Robert Zemeckis
Who goes there?
  asker: 5 guard 6 sentry
  preceder: 4 halt
___! Who goes there?: 4 Halt
___ Who Had a Heart: 6 Anyone
Who Is Killing the Great Chefs of Europe? (1978 film)
  cast: Jacqueline Bisset, Robert Morley, George Segal
Who Killed ___ Robin?: 4 Cock
___ Who Knew Too Much, The: 3 Man
Who knows what ___...: 4 evil
whole: 3 all, lot, one, sum 4 A to Z, bulk, full, hale, mint, unit, well 5 every, gross, round, sound, total, uncut, unity, utter 6 corpus, entire, entity, intact, unhurt 7 healthy, jackpot, oneness, perfect, plenary 8 absolute, assembly, complete, entirety, finished, fullness, integral, livelong, organism, sum total, thorough, together, totality, unbroken, unharmed, unmarred 9 aggregate, inviolate, recovered, undamaged, undivided, uninjured, unreduced, unscathed, untouched 10 able-bodied, big picture, collective, everything, exhaustive, in one piece, opera omnia, unabridged, unimpaired, unlessened
  alternative: 4 skim
  as a ~: 6 en bloc, in full, in toto 7 en masse 9 in general 10 altogether
  ball of wax: 3 all 5 total 8 entirety, sum total 9 aggregate 10 everything
  bunch: 3 lot, ton 4 bevy, lots, many, raft, scad, slew 6 legion, myriad, oodles, umteen, untold 7 umpteen 8 umpsteen 9 countless
  combining form: 3 hol-, pan- 4 holo-, pano-, pant-, toti- 5 panta-, panto-
  ender: 4 sale, some 7 hearted
  hog: 4 full 5 fully 7 flat out, in depth, totally 8 complete, entirely, from A to Z, in detail, thorough 9 extensive, inside out, up-and-down 10 completely, exhaustive, meticulous
  make ~: 4 cure, heal, mend 5 right, treat 6 remedy, repair 7 correct, relieve, restore 8 medicate
  nine yards: 4 A to Z 5 whole 8 entirety
  on the ~: 5 in all 6 mainly, mostly 7 as a rule, at large, overall, usually 9 generally, in general, primarily 10 altogether, by and large
  part of the ~: 4 item, unit 5 piece 6 member, sample 7 portion, section, segment 8 fraction
whole ___: 3 hog 4 milk, note, rest, step 5 blood
whole ___ ball game: 3 new
whole ___ yards, the: 4 nine
whole-___: 3 hog 4 time 5 grain, wheat
___ whole: 3 as a 5 on the
Whole ___ Loving: 5 Lotta
Whole ___ World, A: 3 New
___ whole cloth: 5 out of
whole-grain: 5 bread
  feature: 5 fiber
wholehearted: 4 real, true, warm 5 total 6 all-out, ardent, steady 7 devoted, earnest, fervent, genuine, serious, sincere 8 implicit 9 committed, dedicated, heartfelt, steadfast, undivided, unfeigned
wholeheartedness: 6 candor 7 honesty, probity 8 openness 9 frankness, integrity, sincerity
Whole Lot of Shakin' Going On (1957 song)
  artist: Jerry Lee Lewis
Whole Lotta Love (1969 song)
  artist: Led Zeppelin
Whole Lotta Loving (1958 song)
  artist: Fats Domino
wholeness: 5 unity 8 entirety 9 integrity 10 perfection
whole new ___ game: 4 ball
Whole New World, A (1993 song)
  artist: Peabo Bryson, Regina Belle
Whole Nine Yards, The (2000 film)
  cast: Rosanna Arquette, Michael Clarke Duncan, Natasha Henstridge, Matthew Perry, Bruce Willis
wholesale: 4 mass, sell 5 broad, price, total, utter 6 at cost, in bulk, market 7 overall 8 complete, outright, sweeping 9 extensive 10 commercial, in quantity, large-scale, widespread
  quantity: 5 crate, gross 6 job lot
wholesaler: 6 dealer, jobber 8 merchant
wholesome: 3 fit 4 good, pure, safe 5 clean, moral, sound, sweet 6 chaste, decent, edible 7 ethical, healthy 8 clean-cut, edifying, hygienic, innocent, salutary, sanitary, virtuous 9 exemplary, favorable, healthful, righteous 10 beneficial, nourishing, nutritious, salubrious
Whole Ten Yards, The (2004 film)
  cast: Amanda Peet, Matthew Perry, Bruce Willis
Who let the ___ out?: 4 dogs
whole-wheat: 5 bread
...who lived in ___: 5 a shoe
Who'll Stop the Rain (1978 film)
  cast: Michael Moriarty, Nick Nolte, Tuesday Weld
wholly: 3 all 4 only, well 5 fully, quite, right 6 bodily, flatly, in full, in toto, purely, simply, solely 7 cap-a-pie, en masse, totally, utterly 8 entirely, from A to Z 9 all the way, downright, every inch, expressly, like a book, out-and-out, perfectly, plenarily, to the hilt 10 absolutely, altogether, completely, positively, thoroughly, to the limit
Who Lost an American?
  author: Nelson Algren
___ Who Loved Cat Dancing, The: 3 Man
___ Who Loved Me, The: 3 Spy
Who loves ya, ___?: 4 baby
Who Loves You (1975 song)
  artist: Four Seasons
whom: 7 pronoun
  ender: 4 ever 6 soever
Who, me?: 3 moi
whomp: 3 hit 4 blow, drub, flog, rout, thud, whip 5 baste, pound, punch, smite, worst 6 defeat, hammer, larrup, thwack, wallop 7 trounce
___ Whom the Bell Tolls: 3 For
Who Needs You (1957 song)
  artist: Four Lads
whoop: 3 boo, cry 4 hoot, howl, jeer, yell 5 cheer, laugh, shout, yahoo 6 bellow, cry out, holler, hoorah, hooray, hurrah, hurray, outcry, scream, shriek, squawk, war cry 7 exclaim 9 battle cry 10 vociferate
  it up: 4 riot, romp 5 caper, gloat, party, revel 6 frolic, gambol 7 carouse
whoop-___: 4 de-do 5 de-doo
___ whoop: 3 war
whoop-de-do: 3 ado 5 furor 7 revelry
whoopee: 3 yay 5 oh boy, wahoo 6 hooray, hot dog
  make ~: 4 romp 5 revel 6 frolic, gambol 7 carouse
whoopee ___: 7 cushion
Whoopee! (1930 film)
  cast: Eddie Cantor
___ Whoopee: 5 Makin'
whooper: 4 swan 5 crane
Whoopi: 8 Goldberg
  disguise: 3 nun
whooping ___: 5 crane
whooping it up: 4 wild 5 noisy 7 raucous, riotous 9 clamorous 10 boisterous, disorderly, tumultuous, uproarious
Whoops!: 4 uh-oh, yipe 5 yikes, yipes 6 pardon 8 excuse me, pardon me
whoosh: 3 run 4 dart, rush, whiz 5 swish 6 hurtle 8 rustling
whop: 5 punch, thump 6 strike
whopper: 3 lie 4 lulu, tale 6 canard 8 tall tale 9 falsehood, humdinger, mendacity
  teller: 4 liar 6 fibber 7 deluder 8 deceiver
Whopper: 9 hamburger
  part: 3 bun 4 mayo 5 patty, sauce 6 burger, pattie, pickle, tomato 7 ketchup, lettuce
  rival: 6 Big Mac
whopping: 3 big 4 huge, vast 5 giant, great, hefty, jumbo, large 6 mighty 7 hulking, immense, mammoth, massive, sizable, titanic 8 colossal, enormous, gigantic, king-size, oversize, sizeable, towering 9 Herculean, humongous, monstrous, overlarge, whalelike 10 gargantuan, monumental, prodigious, stupendous, tremendous
Who Put the Bomp (1961 song)
  artist: Barry Mann
whorl: 4 coil, curl, eddy, loop 5 curve, helix, swirl 6 spiral 7 sinuate 9 corkscrew, sinuosity
whorled: 6 spiral 7 helical, sinuate 8 circular
Who's ___ eating my porridge?: 4 been
Who's ___ Girl: 4 That
Who's ___ Now: 5 Sorry
Who's ___ of Virginia Woolf?: 6 Afraid
Who's ___ the Mint?: 7 Minding
Who's ___ Who: 6 Zoomin'
Who's Afraid of Virginia Woolf?: 4 film, play
  author: Edward Albee
  cast: Richard Burton, Sandy Dennis, George Segal, Elizabeth Taylor
  director: Mike Nichols
___ Who's Coming to Dinner: 5 Guess
Whose ___ Is It Anyway?: 4 Life, Line
Whose Body?
  author: Dorothy Sayers
Whose Life Is It Anyway? (1981 film)
  cast: John Cassavetes, Richard Dreyfuss, Christine Lahti
Whose Line Is It Anyway? (ABC comedy) host: Drew Carey
whosever: 7 anyone's 8 anybody's
Whose woods these ___ think I know: 4 are I
Who's Holding Donna Now (1985 song)
  artist: DeBarge
Who Shot J.R.? series: 6 Dallas

whosis: 5 do-dad, gismo, gizmo 6 doodad, gadget
Who's Johnny (1986 song)
artist: DeBarge
Who Slew Auntie __?: 3 Roo
Who's minding the __?: 5 store
whoso: 6 anyone 7 anybody
whosoever: 6 anyone 7 anybody
Who's on __?: 5 first
Who's Sorry Now (1958 song)
artist: Connie Francis
__ Who's Talking: 4 Look
Who's That Girl (1987 song)
artist: Madonna
Who's That Knocking at My Door? (1968 film)
cast: Zina Bethune, Harvey Keitel
director: Martin Scorsese
Who's the Boss? (ABC sitcom)
cast: Tony Danza (Tony Micelli)
Katherine Helmond (Mona Robinson)
Judith Light (Angela Bower)
Alyssa Milano (Samantha Micelli)
Danny Pintauro (Jonathan Bower)
Who's there? reply: 5 It's me
who's who: 5 elite 7 society 8 register 9 directory
Who's Who entry: 3 bio
Who's Zoomin' Who (1985 song)
artist: Aretha Franklin
Who, The
members: Daltrey, Townshend, Entwistle, Moon
rock opera: Tommy, Quadrophenia
song: Happy Jack (1967)
I Can See for Miles (1967)
I'm Free (1969)
Magic Bus (1968)
Pinball Wizard (1969)
See Me, Feel Me (1970)
Squeeze Box (1976)
Who Are You (1978)
Won't Get Fooled Again (1971)
You Better You Bet (1981)
Who Wants to Be a Millionaire (ABC quiz)
host: Meredith Vieira, Regis Philbin
Who was that __ man?: 6 masked
Who Will You Run To (1987 song)
artist: Heart
whse. contents: 3 gds. 4 ctns., mdse.
box: 3 ctn.
whup: 4 beat, flog, lick 5 paste, spank 7 trounce
why: 5 query 6 motive, reason 7 grounds, purpose 9 rationale
cousin: 3 how, who 4 what, when 5 where
Why (song)
artist: Donny Osmond, Frankie Avalon
Why __ fall in love...: 5 can't I
Why __ Love You?: 3 Do I
Why __ thou forsaken me?: 4 hast
Why __ We Be Friends?: 4 Can't
Why __ woman be more like a man?: 5 can't a
Why Baby Why (1957 song)
artist: Pat Boone
Why Can't I Touch You (1970 song)
artist: Ronnie Dyson
Why Can't This Be Love (1986 song)
artist: Van Halen
Why Can't We Be Friends? (1975 song)
artist: War
Why Do Fools Fall in Love (song)
artist: Diana Ross, Frankie Lymon and the Teenagers, Gale Storm
Why Do I Love You?
composer: Jerome Kern
Why England Slept
author: John F. Kenndy
whyfor: 6 motive, reason 9 rationale
Why Is There Air? comic: 5 Cosby
Why not?: 3 yes 4 let's, okay, sure
Why Not the Best?
author: Jimmy Carter
why, oh, why __?: 5 can't I
__ Why the Caged Bird Sings: 5 I Know
Why, the very __!: 4 idea
WI
see Wisconsin
Wian: 5 Casey
wicca: 5 magic 7 sorcery 10 white magic, witchcraft
Wichita: 4 city, town 5 tribe 6 Indian 7 Amerind
athletes: 8 Shockers
county: 8 Sedgwick
locale: 3 Kan. 6 Kansas
school: 3 WSU
town near ~: 4 Iola
Wichita Falls: 4 city, town
locale: 5 Texas
town near ~: 5 Olney
Wichita Lineman (1968 song)
artist: Glen Campbell
composer: Jimmy Webb
Wichita State
athletes: 8 Shockers
locale: 6 Kansas
wick: 4 cord, fuse 7 draw off 8 draw away
surroundings: 3 wax 5 taper 6 candle 8 paraffin
wicked: 3 bad, ill 4 base, blue, dark, evil, foul, mean, ugly, vile 5 awful, cruel, nasty, spicy, wrong 6 amoral, guilty, impish, little, malign, rotten, severe, spicey, unholy, wanton 7 corrupt, debased, demonic, heinous, hellish, immoral, low-down, naughty, parlous, profane, satanic, ungodly, vicious, wayward 8 daemonic, depraved, devilish, diabolic, dreadful, fiendish, indecent, infamous, infernal, perilous, shameful, spiteful, terrible, wrongful 9 abandoned, atrocious, dangerous, demonical, dissolute, egregious, hazardous, heartless, laborious, malicious, miscreant, nefarious, satanical, shameless, unethical, wonderful 10 abominable, diabolical, indelicate, inexpiable, iniquitous, maleficent, malevolent, outrageous, pernicious, profligate, scandalous, villainous
one: 5 beast, brute, demon, devil, fiend, knave 6 savage, sinner 7 dastard 9 barbarian
thing: 3 sin 4 evil, vice 5 crime 7 misdeed, offense 8 atrocity, iniquity, trespass 9 sacrilege 10 misconduct
see also wonderful
Wicked __ of the West: 5 Witch
Wicked Day, The
author: Mary Stewart
Wicked Game (1991 song)
artist: Chris Isaak
wickedness: 3 ill, sin 4 evil, vice 5 wrong 6 infamy 7 devilry, impiety, perfidy 8 atrocity, deviltry, ignominy, iniquity, villainy 9 depravity 10 corruption
Wicked Wasp of Twickenham: 4 Pope
wicker: 4 twig 5 osier 6 willow
ender: 4 work
expert: 5 caner
like ~: 4 wove 5 woven
product: 3 web 5 creel
Wicker: 3 Tom
Wicker Man, The (1973 film)
cast: Britt Ekland, Christopher Lee
wicket: 4 gate, hoop 7 ingress
cricket ~: 3 end
croquet ~: 4 hoop
ender: 6 keeper
material: 4 wire
topper: 4 bail
__ wicket: 6 sticky
Wickford Point
author: J.P. Marquand
wickiup: 3 hut 4 tipi 5 tepee 6 teepee, wigwam
wide: 3 big 4 full, open, vast 5 ample, baggy, beamy, broad, hippy, large, loose, roomy, squat, thick, wrong 6 astray, gaping 7 dilated, general 8 catholic, extended, far-flung, spacious, sweeping, tolerant 9 boundless, capacious, cavernous, expansive, extensive, inclusive, off-course, outspread, spread-out, universal 10 commodious, inaccurate, indefinite, large-scale, off the mark, voluminous
all wool and a yard ~: 4 real, true 6 trusty 7 genuine, sincere 8 constant, faithful, true-blue
berth: 4 room 6 leeway 7 license
divergence: 3 gap 4 gulf 5 abyss
ender: 6 spread
far and ~: 6 afield 7 broadly, largely 10 everywhere
give a ~ berth: 4 shun 5 avoid, scorn 6 eschew 10 shrink from
look far and ~: 4 hunt 5 scour
make half as ~: 4 fold
of the mark: 3 off 5 amiss, wrong 6 faulty 7 in error, inexact 8 mistaken 9 erroneous, imprecise, off-target 10 inaccurate
open: 5 agape 6 gaping 9 unlimited 10 undefended, vulnerable
open ~: 4 gape, yawn
partner: 3 far
shoe: 2 EE 3 EEE 4 EEEE, six E, ten E 5 five E, nine E 6 eight E, seven E 7 eleven E, twelve E
starter: 4 city 5 state, store, world 6 county, double, nation, single 7 country 8 district
street: 3 ave. 4 blvd. 6 avenue 9 boulevard
wide __: 5 awake, world
wide __ mark: 5 of the
wide __ spaces: 4 open
wide-__: 4 eyed, open 5 awake 6 screen 7 ranging
wide-__ lens: 5 angle
wide-__ plane: 4 body
wide-awake: 4 wary 5 alert, aware 6 prompt 7 heads-up, wakeful 8 keen-eyed, on the job, vigilant, watchful 9 attentive, observant, on the ball 10 on one's toes
__ wide berth to: 5 give a
wide-eyed: 4 agog, naif 5 agape, alert, naive 7 wakeful 9 unworldly
remark: 3 gee, wow 5 golly
widen: 3 wax 4 grow, ream 5 add to, bloat, flare, swell 6 beef up, dilate, expand, extend, let out, open up, spread, unfold 7 augment, broaden, burgeon, develop, distend, enlarge, inflate, open out, ream out, stretch, thicken 8 bourgeon, escalate, heighten, increase, lengthen 9 branch out, spread out 10 liberalize
a hole: 4 ream
widened at the top: 5 evase
wideness: 5 scope 7 breadth 9 amplitude
__ wide net: 5 cast a
Wide Net, The
author: Eudora Welty
widening: 6 growth, spread 8 increase 9 extension
wide of the __: 4 mark
wide-open: 5 agape, naked, risky 7 yawning 9 limitless
wide-ranging: 3 big 5 broad 7 blanket 8 far-flung
Wide Sargasso Sea
author: Jean Rhys
__ Wide Shut: 4 Eyes
widespread: 3 big 4 rife, vast 5 broad, roomy, usual 6 common, public, ruling 7 current, diffuse, general, generic, popular, rampant, routine 8 epidemic, everyday, far-flung, frequent, ordinary, pandemic, spacious, sweeping 9 boundless, capacious, expansive, extensive, generical, pervasive, prevalent, universal, wholesale 10 epidemical
be ~: 5 reign 6 abound 7 prevail 8 dominate
__ wide swath: 4 cut a
wide vertical band in heraldry: 4 pale
__ Wide Web: 5 World
Wide World of Sports host: 5 McKay
widgeon: 4 bird, duck, fowl
relative: ***see*** duck
widget: 5 do-dad, gismo, gizmo, thing 6 device, dingus, doodad, gadget 7 machine 9 doohickey
Widmark: 7 Richard
__ widow: 4 golf 5 black
Widowers' Houses
author: George Bernard Shaw
Widow for One Year, A
author: John Irving
widow's __: 4 mite, peak, walk
__ Widow, The: 5 Merry 7 College
width: 2 AA, EE 3 AAA, EEE 4 EEEE, girt, size, span 5 girth, range, reach, scope 6 extent, length, spread 7 breadth, compass, expanse, measure 8 diameter, distance, latitude 9 amplitude, broadness, dimen-

WH

sion, immensity, largeness, squatness, thickness **10** wiggle room
ender: **4** wise
having no ~: **4** one-D
length and ~: **4** area, size **5** scope, space **6** extent
length times ~: **4** area
shoe ~: **2** AA, EE **3** AAA, EEE **4** AAAA, EEEE
starter: **4** band
typesetter: **2** em, en
wie __: **5** geht's
Wie: **8** Michelle
org.: **4** LPGA
Wiebe, Rudy: **6** writer **8** Canadian
work: The Mad Trapper
__ Wiedersehen: **3** auf
Wiedersehen, auf: **3** bye **4** ciao, ta ta **5** adios, later **7** goodbye **8** farewell
wield: **3** ply, use **4** have, hold, work **5** apply, exert **6** employ, handle **7** control, operate, possess, utilize **8** brandish, exercise, flourish, put to use **9** make use of **10** manipulate
wieldy: **5** handy, utile **6** useful **9** easy to use, practical **10** convenient, functional
Wien: **4** city, town **6** Vienna **7** Wilhelm
locale: **7** Austria
see also German, Vienna
wiener: **4** meat **5** frank **6** hot dog
ender: **5** wurst
roast: **6** picnic **7** cookout **8** barbecue
topping: **5** kraut **10** sauerkraut
unit: **4** link
wrapping: **4** skin **6** casing
Wiener schnitzel base: **4** veal
Wienerwald: **3** mts. **4** Alps, mtns. **5** range
locale: **7** Austria
Wiesbaden: **3** spa **4** city, town
locale: **5** Hesse **7** Germany
Wieschaus, Eric: **8** Nobelist
Wiesel, Elie: **6** writer **8** Nobelist
work: The Accident
The Fifth Son
The Gates fo the Forest
Legends of Our Time
Night
One Generation After
Souls on Fire
The Testament
The Town Beyond the Wall
Wiesel, Torsten: **8** Nobelist
Wiesenthal: **5** Simon
Wiest, Dianne: **7** actress
film: the Birdcage (1995)
Bullets Over Broadway (1994, AA)
Cookie (1989)
Edward Scissorhands (1990)
Footloose (1984)
Hannah and Her Sisters (1986, AA)
The Horse Whisperer (1998)
I Am Sam (2001)
Little Man Tate (1991)
Parenthood (1989)
The Purple Rose of Cairo (1985)
wife: **4** lady, mate **5** bride, woman **6** matron, missis, missus, spouse, the Mrs. **7** consort, partner **8** helpmate, helpmeet **9** companion, other half **10** better half, monogamist
former: **2** ex **8** divorcée
partner: **4** mate **5** hubby **7** husband
starter: **3** ale **4** fish, good **5** house
wear: **4** ring
__ wife had seven sacks...: **4** Each
wifeless: **5** unwed **6** single **8** eligible, unwedded **9** unmarried **10** unattached
Wife of __: **4** Bath
wife-to-be: **7** fiancée **9** betrothed
Wifey
author: Judy Blume
wig: **3** rug **4** hair **6** peruke, toupee **9** hairpiece, headpiece
cousin: **4** fall
ender: **3** wag
flip one's ~: **4** rage **5** freak **8** freak out
starter: **3** big, ear **4** peri
wearer: **5** clown **9** barrister
__ wig: **4** buzz **6** fright
__ Wiggily: **5** Uncle
wiggle: **3** wag **4** jerk, push, worm **5** slink, twist **6** jiggle, shimmy, squirm, twitch, writhe, zigzag
room: **4** play **5** space, width **6** leeway **7** freedom **8** latitude
wiggle __: **4** room
Wigglesworth, Michael: **6** writer
work: The Day of Doom
wiggly: **6** fickle **7** mutable **8** slippery, unstable, unsteady, wavering **9** mercurial
__ Wiggs of the Cabbage Patch: **3** Mrs.
wiggy: **3** odd **5** flaky **8** crackers **9** eccentric
wight: **5** being, human **10** human being
Wight: **4** isle **6** island
resort: **5** Cowes
wigwag: **4** wave **6** signal
wigwam: **4** tent **7** shelter
cousin: **4** tipi **5** tepee **6** teepee
like a ~: **5** conic **7** conical
Wil: **7** Shriner, Wheaton
Wilander: **4** Mats **5** Swede **7** netster **9** tennis pro
milieu: **5** court
Wilbert: **8** Harrison, Robinson
Wilbur: **4** Post **6** Wright **7** Richard
horse: **4** Mr. Ed
Wilbur, Richard: **4** poet
work: Things of This World
__ wilco: **5** roger
Wilcox: **4** Fred **5** Larry **7** Herbert
Wilcoxon: **5** Henry
wild: **3** mad, rad **4** avid, camp, free, lush, nuts, rank, rash, rude, zany **5** crazy, eager, feral, giddy, manic, messy, noisy, rabid, rough, rowdy, wacky, windy **6** animal, choppy, crazed, far-out, fierce, hectic, hoiden, hoyden, lavish, madcap, native, raging, rakish, raving, remote, rugged, savage, stormy, unruly, untidy, wanton, whacky **7** berserk, bizarre, brutish, chaotic, coltish, escaped, flighty, foolish, frantic, furious, howling, intense, lawless, natural, overrun, raffish, rampant, riotous, runaway, unkempt, untamed, vicious, violent, wayward **8** barbaric, blustery, deserted, desolate, ecstatic, freakish, frenzied, in a furor, maniacal, reckless, romantic, rowdyish, sporting, sportive, unbroken, uncurbed, unhinged, wasteful **9** barbarian, barbarous, delirious, dissolute, disturbed, fanatical, ferocious, foolhardy, grotesque, hotheaded, impetuous, imprudent, in a dither, inclement, last-ditch, luxuriant, neglected, overgrown, primitive, thrilling, turbulent, unbridled, unchecked, unimpeded, unrefined, wasteland, wrought-up **10** blustering, boisterous, disheveled, disordered, disorderly, distracted, hysterical, immoderate, incautious, indigenous, irrational, outlandish, outrageous, passionate, profligate, rebellious, self-willed, tumultuous, uncultured, unfettered, unpolished, unshackled, uproarious
about: **4** into **5** hot on **7** taken by
be ~ for: **4** like, love **5** adore **6** admire, revere **7** cherish, idolize, worship **8** hold dear, treasure
blue yonder: **3** sky **5** ether **6** aether
bunch: **3** mob **4** pack **5** horde
canine: **3** fox **4** wolf **5** dhole, dingo **6** coyote, jackal
card: **5** deuce, joker
cat: **4** eyra, lion, lynx, puma **5** civet, tiger **6** cougar, jaguar, ocelot **7** panther
combining form: **5** agrio-
ender: **3** cat **4** fire, fowl, life, wood **6** flower
equine: **3** ass **5** bronc, kiang **6** bronco, brumby, ladino **7** broncho
go ~: **4** flip **7** run amok **8** run amuck
make less ~: **4** tame **5** break **6** soften **7** harness **8** tone down
one: **4** brat **5** beast, raver, yahoo **6** animal
on the ~ side: **4** lewd, racy **5** bawdy, lurid **6** risqué, vulgar **8** immodest, off-color **10** indelicate
party: **5** blast **6** bustup **7** blowout
run ~: **4** rage, riot **7** rampage **8** cut loose **9** go berserk
running ~: **4** amok **5** amuck **7** haywire
sheep: **4** dall **5** argal, urial **6** argali
sow ~ oats: **3** sin **5** act up **7** carry on **9** misbehave
time: **4** toot **5** binge, spree **6** bender
wild __: **4** boar, card, oats, rice, rose **5** goose, guess, pitch **6** cherry, turkey
wild-__: **4** eyed **6** headed
wild-__ chase: **5** goose
__ wild: **3** run **6** deuces **7** running
__-wild: **3** hog
Wild: **4** Earl
home: **9** Minnesota
org.: **3** NHL
rival: ***see*** hockey team
sport: **6** hockey
Wild __: **3** One **4** Hunt, West **5** Night, River, Thing, World **7** Kingdom
Wild __ at Coole, The: **5** Swans
Wild __ Hickok: **4** Bill
Wild __ show: **4** West
Wild __, The: **3** One **4** Boys, Duck, Seed **5** Bunch
wild-and-__: **6** woolly
Wild Animals I Have Known
author: E.T. Seton
Wild Bill: **6** Hickok
wild blue yonder org.: **4** USAF
wild boar, name meaning: **6** Wilbur
Wild Boys, The (1984 song)
artist: Duran Duran
Wild Bunch, The (1969 film)
cast: Ernest Borgnine, William Holden, Warren Oates, Edmond O'Brien, Robert Ryan
director: Sam Peckinpah
wildcat: **4** eyra, lynx **6** animal, ocelot **7** illegal **9** speculate **10** prohibited
concern: **3** oil **4** well
wildcat __: **6** strike
Wildcat: **3** car **4** auto **5** Buick
Wildcats: **3** KSU **9** Villanova
Wildcats (1986 film)
cast: Goldie Hawn, Swoosie Kurtz, Nipsey Russell
Wild Cherry
song: Play That Funky Music (1976)
Wild Duck, The
author: Henrik Ibsen
Wilde: **3** Kim, Ted **5** Oscar **6** Cornel
Wild, Earl: **7** pianist
wildebeest: **3** gnu **6** animal **8** antelope
hunter: **4** lion
relative: ***see*** antelope
Wilde, Oscar: **3** wit **5** Irish **6** writer **10** playwright
work: The Ballad of Reading Gaol
De Profundis
The Happy Prince and Other Tales
An Ideal Husband
The Importance of Being Earnest
Lady Windermere's Fan
The Picture of Dorian Gray
Salomé
A Woman of No Importance
Wilder: **4** Alec, Gene **5** Billy **6** Robert **7** Matthew **8** Thornton
Wilder, Billy: **8** director
film: The Apartment (1960, AA)
Avanti! (1972)
Buddy Buddy (1981)
Double Indemnity (1944)
A Foreign Affair (1948)
The Fortune Cookie (1966)
The Front Page (1974)
Irma la Douce (1963)
Kiss Me, Stupid (1964)
The Lost Weekend (1945, AA)
Love in the Afternoon (1957)
The Major and the Minor (1942)
One, Two, Three (1961)
Sabrina (1954)
The Seven Year Itch (1955)
Some Like It Hot (1959)
The Spirit of St. Louis (1957)
Stalag 17 (1953)
Sunset Blvd. (1950)
Witness for the Prosecution (1957)
Wilder, Gene: **5** actor
film: Blazing Saddles (1974)
The Frisco Kid (1979)
The Producers (1968)

Quackser Fortune... (1970)
Silver Streak (1976)
Stir Crazy (1980)
Willy Wonka... (1971)
The Woman in Red (1984)
Young Frankenstein (1974)
spouse: Gilda Radner
wilderness: **4** bush **5** waste, woods **6** desert, forest, jungle, sticks **7** barrens, outback **8** badlands **9** boondocks, confusion
home: **4** camp
outing: **4** hike, trek
path: **5** trace, trail
wilderness __: **4** area
Wilderness Road blazer: **5** Boone
Wilderness were Paradise __!: **4** enow
Wilder, Thornton: **6** writer **10** playwright
work: The Bridge of San Luis Rey
The Eighth Day
The Ides of March
The Matchmaker
Our Town
The Skin of Our Teeth
Theophilus North
wild-eyed: **3** mad **4** avid, keen **5** eager, manic, rabid **6** ardent, crazed, fervid, gung-ho, raging **7** devoted, fervent, intense, violent, zealous **8** frenetic, frenzied, maniacal, spirited **9** ambitious, delirious, fanatical **10** hysterical, infuriated, passionate
wildfire: **5** blaze **6** flames
like ~: **3** PDQ **4** fast **5** apace **6** presto **7** fleetly, hastily, quickly, rapidly, swiftly **8** in a flash, in a jiffy, in no time, pell-mell, speedily **9** forthwith, hurriedly, instantly, posthaste
Wildfire
author: Zane Grey
Wildfire (1975 song)
artist: Michael Murphey
wildflower: **5** bluet, daisy **6** lupine
site: **3** lea, ley **6** meadow
Wildflowers (1999 film)
cast: Tomas Arana, Clea DuVall, Daryl Hannah, Eric Roberts
Wild Geese, The
author: Mori Ōgai
wild-goose __: **5** chase
Wild Hearts Can't Be Broken (1991 film)
cast: Gabrielle Anwar, Cliff Robertson
Wild Hogs (2007 film)
cast: Tim Allen, Martin Lawrence, William H. Macy, John Travolta
Wild Horse Mesa
author: Zane Grey
Wild Horses
author: Dick Francis
Wild Horses (1971 song)
artist: Rolling Stones
Wilding, Michael
spouse: Elizabeth Taylor
Wild Kingdom (NBC) host: Marlin Perkins
wildlife: **5** fauna **6** beasts **7** animals
home: **4** nest **9** sanctuary
wildly: **4** amok **5** amuck, madly **7** like mad **8** insanely **9** fervently, like crazy
wildness: **6** tumult **7** abandon, license **8** ferocity, violence **9** looseness, vehemence
consequence of ~: **4** walk
Wild Night (song)
artist: John Cougar Mellencamp, Van Morrison
__ wild oats: **3** sow
Wild One (1960 song)
artist: Bobby Rydell
Wild One, The (1954 film)
cast: Marlon Brando
__ Wild Rose: **3** To a
Wild Rovers (1971 film)
cast: William Holden, Karl Malden, Ryan O'Neal
wilds: **4** bush **5** waste **6** desert, forest, jungle, sticks **7** barrens, outback **8** badlands **9** backwater, boondocks **10** hinterland
Wildside (1991 song)
artist: Marky Mark and the Funky Bunch
Wildspitze's region: **5** Tirol, Tyrol
Wild Swans at Coole, The
author: William Butler Yeats
wild-tasting: **4** gamy **5** gamey
__ Wild, The: **5** River **6** Joker's
Wild Thing (song)
artist: Tone Loc, Troggs
Wild Things (1998 film)
cast: Kevin Bacon, Neve Campbell, Matt Dillon, Theresa Russell
Wild West show: **5** rodeo
Wild Wild West (1999 film)
cast: Kenneth Branagh, Salma Hayek, Kevin Kline, Will Smith
Wild Wild West, The (CBS western)
cast: Robert Conrad (James West)
Michael Dunn (Miguelito Loveless)
Ross Martin (Artemus Gordon)
wildwood: **6** forest **10** timberland
wile: **3** art **4** coax, lure, ploy, ruse, trap **5** dodge, feint, shift, trick **6** cajole, deceit, device, dupery, entice, gambit **7** beguile, finesse, gimmick **8** artifice, intrigue, maneuver, pretense **9** chicanery, deception, duplicity, imposture, stratagem **10** subterfuge
Wile E. __: **6** Coyote
wiles: **3** art **5** craft, guile **7** cunning, knavery, slyness **8** foxiness **9** chicanery **10** artfulness, shrewdness
Wiley: **4** Post **6** Harvey
Wilford: **7** Brimley
Wilfred: **4** Owen **7** Jackson
Wilfrid: **5** Blunt, Sheed **9** Hyde-White, Pelletier
Wilhelm: **4** Hoyt, Wien **5** Grimm, Raabe, Wundt **6** Heinse **7** Ostwald, Röntgen, Von Opel **8** Leibnitz, Roentgen
in English: **7** William
Wilhelm __: **4** Tell
Wilhelm, Hoyt: **6** hurler **7** pitcher
Wilhelm Tell
author: Friedrich von Schiller
wiliness: **3** art **5** craft, guile
Wilke: **4** font **8** typeface
Wilkens, Lenny
milieu: **5** court
org.: **3** NBA
sport: **10** basketball
Wilkes-Barre: **4** city, town
locale: **4** Penn.
__ Wilkes Booth: **4** John
Wilkie: **7** Collins
Wilkins: **3** Roy **7** Maurice **8** Micawber
will: **3** aim, opt **4** give, urge, want, wish, word **5** crave, drive, endow, fancy, heart, leave, moxie, nerve, paper, pluck, shall **6** animus, choose, decree, demand, desire, intend, intent, legacy, liking, ordain, pass on, please, spirit **7** bequest, craving, longing, passion, probate, purpose, resolve **8** ambition, appetite, backbone, bequeath, bestowal, decision, firmness, hand down, pleasure, volition, yearning **9** endurance, hankering, hardiness, intention, testament **10** discipline, insistence, preference, resolution
against one's ~: **8** forcibly
at ~: **6** freely **7** anytime **8** whenever
bend to one's ~: **8** dominate, override, overrule
combining form: **5** -bulia
create good ~: **6** endear
divine ~: **4** fate **5** karma **6** kismet
ender: **5** power
exert one's ~: **3** opt **6** choose, select
free ~: **6** choice, option **8** volition
good ~: **5** asset, unity **7** harmony **8** kindness **9** readiness, tolerance **10** friendship
ill ~: **4** hate **5** odium, spite, venom **6** animus, enmity, grudge, hatred, malice, rancor **8** acrimony, aversion, bad blood **9** animosity, antipathy, hostility **10** antagonism, resentment
I ~ not: **3** nah, naw, nay, nix, non **4** nein, nope, nyet, uh-uh **5** ixnay, never, no how, no way **6** no deal, noways, nowise **8** forget it, negative, negatory **9** by no means, fat chance **10** count me out, thumbs down
partner: **3** way
power: **5** force, spine **6** desire **8** decision
starter: **4** free, good
subject: **4** heir **6** estate, legacy **7** bequest
(to): **5** leave **8** bequeath
to win: **6** fervor **8** ambition **9** obsession
will-__-wisp: **4** o'-the
__ will: **3** ill **4** free
__-will: **4** poor, self
Will: **4** Geer, Hays, Weng **5** Cuppy, Smith **6** Durant, George, Patton, Rogers, Shortz **7** Ferrell, Kellogg, Sampson **8** Hutchins
wife: **4** Anne
Will __ Love Me Tomorrow: **3** You
Willa: **6** Cather
Willamette: **5** river
city on the ~: **5** Salem **6** Eugene **8** Portland
locale: **6** Oregon
University site: **5** Salem
Willard: **3** rat **4** Emma, Espy, Jess **5** Libby, Scott **6** Motley **7** Frances
sequel: **3** Ben
Willard, Jess: **3** pug **5** boxer
milieu: **4** ring
__ Will Be: **4** This
__ will be done: **3** thy
will be in Spanish: **4** será
__ will dwell...: **4** and I
__-willed: **4** weak **6** strong
Willem: **5** Dafoe **7** Barents **8** de Sitter **9** de Kooning, Einthoven
Willemstad: **4** port
locale: **7** Curaçao
__ Will Find a Way: **4** Love
willful: **5** meant **6** dogged, mulish, ornery, unruly, wanton **7** adamant, froward, naughty, piggish, planned, studied, wayward, witting **8** indocile, intended, obdurate, perverse, stubborn **9** arbitrary, conscious, fractious, hard-nosed, obstinate, pigheaded, voluntary **10** bullheaded, considered, deliberate, determined, headstrong, inflexible, persistent, preplanned, purposeful, refractory, unprompted, unyielding, volitional
willfulness: **4** grit, guts **5** moxie, pluck, spunk **7** courage, resolve **8** tenacity **9** assiduity, endurance **10** confidence, doggedness
Will & Grace (NBC sitcom)
cast: Sean Hayes (Jack McFarland)
Eric McCormack (Will Truman)
Debra Messing (Grace Adler)
Megan Mullally (Karen Walker)
__ Will Hunting: **4** Good
__ william: **5** sweet
William: **4** Boyd, Hurt, Inge, Katt, Kidd, Mayo, Penn, Pitt, Roth, Tell **5** Beebe, Blake, Bligh, Bragg, Casey, Clark, Eythe, Hanna, James, Marcy, Paley, Parry, saint, Simms, Stein, Wyler, Yeats **6** Baffin, Bendix, Boeing, Bolcom, Castle, Caxton, Conrad, Cowper, Cremer, Devane, Dunbar, Empson, Farnum, Fowler, Gaddis, Gaines, Gargan, Gibson, Halsey, Harris, Harvey, Henley, Hickey, Holden, Hopper, Jenney, Kapell, Kelvin, Levitt, Morris, Morton, Murphy, Perkin, Plomer, Powell, Ramsay, Rowley, Safire, Sansom, Seward, Sharpe, Shirer, Styron, Talman, Warren **7** Baldwin, Brennan, Buckley, Cobbett, Collins, Crookes, Dampier, Daniels, Douglas, Frawley, Giauque, Golding, Goldman, Hazlitt, Hewlett, Hogarth, Huggins, Kennedy, Lederer, Painter, Saroyan, Shatner, Sherman, Thomson, Vickrey, Wellman, Wrigley **8** Atherton, Bradford, Brewster, Carleton, Congreve, Demarest, DeVaughn, Dieterle, Faulkner, Friedkin, Herschel, Keighley, Kunstler, Lipscomb, McKinley, Phillips, Proxmire, Ragsdale, Shockley, Stafford, Steinitz **9** Gladstone, Rehnquist, Steinberg, Thackeray, Whitehead, Wycherley **10** Blackstone, Manchester, Wordsworth
of Orange foe: **6** De Witt
sweet ~: **4** pink **5** plant **6** flower
to Charles: **3** son
William __: **4** Tell **5** H. Macy **6** Wilson
William __ Benét: **4** Rose
William __ Blatty: **5** Peter
William __ Bryan: **8** Jennings

William __ Bryant: 6 Cullen
William __ Garrison: 5 Lloyd
William __ Gladstone: 5 Ewart
William __ Harrison: 5 Henry
William __ Hearst: 8 Randolph
William __ Howells: 4 Dean
William __ Sherman: 8 Tecumseh
William __ Taft: 6 Howard
William __ Thackeray: 9 Makepeace
William __ Williams: 6 Carlos
William __ Yeats: 6 Butler
__ William: 5 sweet
William and __: 4 Mary
William Butler __: 5 Yeats
William Carlos __: 8 Williams
William Cullen __: 6 Bryant
William Dean __: 7 Howells
William F. __: 4 Cody
William F. __ Jr.: 7 Buckley
William H. __: 4 Gass, Macy
William Henry __: 8 Harrison
William Howard __: 4 Taft
William III: 4 king
house: 6 Orange
successor: 4 Anne
William IV, to Victoria: 5 uncle
William Jennings __: 5 Bryan
William L. __: 6 Shirer
William Lloyd __: 8 Garrison
William Makepeace __: 9 Thackeray
William O. __: 7 Douglas
William of __: 4 Sens **5** Occam **6** Ockham, Orange **10** Malmesbury
William of Baskerville creator: Umberto Eco
William of Malmesbury: 6 writer **7** British
work: Chronicles of the Kings of England
William Peter __: 6 Blatty
William Randolph __: 6 Hearst
William Ratcliff
composer: César Cui
William Rose __: 5 Benét
Williams: 3 Don, Guy, Hal, Joe, Ted **4** Amir, Andy, Cara, Hank, Jody, John, Otis, Paul, Remo **5** Anson, Barry, Betty, Billy, Brian, Cindy, Cynda, Danny, Emlyn, Grant, Kelli, Mason, Robin, Roger, Treat, Venus **6** Ashley, Bernie, Cootie, Esther, JoBeth, Montel, Serena **7** Charles, Deniece, Maurice, Vanessa **8** Kimberly, Michelle **9** Tennessee
ender: 4 burg, port
__ Williams: 4 Remo **7** Carbine
__-Williams: 7 Sherwin
William S. __: 4 Hart **7** Gilbert, Knowles **9** Burroughs
Williams and the Zodiacs, Maurice
song: Stay (1960)
Williams, Andy
song: Are You Sincere (1958)
Butterfly (1957)
Canadian Sunset (1956)
Can't Get Used to Losing You (1963)
Days of Wine and Roses (1963)
Dear Heart (1964)
The Hawaiian Wedding Song (1959)
I Like Your Kind of Love (1956)
Lonely Street (1959)
Love Story (1971)
On the Street Where You Live (1964)
The Village of St. Bernadette (1959)
Williams, Bernie
sport: 8 baseball
Williams, Billy: 3 Cub **10** outfielder
Williams, Billy Dee: 5 actor
film: The Bingo Long Traveling All-Stars & Motor Kings (1976)
The Empire Strikes Back (1980)
Lady Sings the Blues (1972)
Nighthawks (1981)
Return of the Jedi (1983)
The Visit (2000)
Williams, Charles: 6 writer **7** British
work: All Hallows' Eve
Descent into Hell
Williams, Cindy: 7 actress
film: American Graffiti (1973)
TV: Laverne & Shirley
Williams, Deniece
song: It's Gonna Take a Miracle (1982)
Let's Hear It for the Boy (1984)
Too Much, Too Little, Too Late (1978)
Williams, Emlyn: 5 Welsh **6** writer
work: The Corn Is Green
Williams, Esther: 7 actress, swimmer
film: Bathing Beauty (1944)
Dangerous When Wet (1953)
Easy to Love (1953)
Easy to Wed (1946)
Jupiter's Darling (1955)
Million Dollar Mermaid (1952)
Neptune's Daughter (1949)
On an Island With You (1948)
This Time for Keeps (1947)
spouse: Fernando Lamas
__ Williams III: 8 Clarence
Williams, John: 6 writer **8** composer **9** conductor
film score: The Accidental Tourist
Amistad
Born on the Fourth of July
Catch Me If You Can
Close Encounters of the Third Kind
The Empire Strikes Back
E.T. The Extra-Terrestrial
Harry Potter and the Sorcerer's Stone
Home Alone
Indiana Jones and the Kingdom of the Crystal Skull
Jaws
Jurassic Park
Munich
Raiders of the Lost Ark
Return of the Jedi
Saving Private Ryan
Schindler's List
Star Wars
Superman
War of the Worlds
The Witches of Eastwick
Williams, Mason
song: Classical Gas (1968)
Williams, Michelle: 7 actress
TV: Dawson's Creek
Williamson: 4 Jack, peak **5** Kevin, mount, Nicol **8** mountain
locale: 10 California
__ William Sound: 6 Prince
Williamsport: 4 city, town
locale: 4 Penn. **5** Penna.
Williams, Robin: 5 actor **8** comedian
film: Awakenings (1990)
The Best of Times (1986)
Bicentennial Man (1999)
The Birdcage (1995)
Cadillac Man (1990)
Dead Poets Society (1989)
Death to Smoochy (2002)
The Fisher King (1991)
Good Morning, Vietnam (1987)
Good Will Hunting (1997, AA)
Hook (1991)
Insomnia (2002)
Jack (1996)
Jakob the Liar (1999)
Jumanji (1995)
License to Wed (2007)
Man of the Year (2006)
Moscow on the Hudson (1984)
Mrs. Doubtfire (1993)
Night at the Museum (2006)
One Hour Photo (2002)
Patch Adams (1998)
Popeye (1980)
Seize the Day (1986)
Toys (1992)
What Dreams May Come (1998)
The World According to Garp (1982)
World's Greatest Dad (2009)
film voice: Aladdin (1992)
forte: 5 ad-lib
role: 5 genie
TV: Mork & Mindy
Williams, Roger: 7 pianist
song: Autumn Leaves (1955)
Born Free (1966)
Near You (1958)
Williams, Serena: 7 netster **9** tennis pro
milieu: 5 court
sister: 5 Venus
Williams, Ted: 6 Red Sox **10** outfielder
Williams, Tennessee: 10 playwright
work: Battle of Angels
Camino Real
Cat on a Hot Tin Roof
Clothes for a Summer Hotel
The Eccentricities of a Nightingale
Eight Mortal Ladies Possessed
The Glass Menagerie
Hard Candy
In the Bar of a Tokyo Hotel
The Knightly Quest
A Lovely Day for Creve Coeur
The Milk Train Doesn't Stop Here Anymore
The Night of the Iguana
Orpheus Descending
Period of Adjustment
The Roman Spring of Mrs. Stone
The Rose Tattoo
The Seven Descents of Myrtle
Small Craft Warnings
Something Unspoken
A Streetcar Named Desire
Suddenly Last Summer
Summer and Smoke
Sweet Bird of Youth
Where I Live
Williams, Vanessa: 6 singer
song: Colors of the Wind (1995)
Dreamin' (1989)
Love Is (1993)
Save the Best for Last (1992)
Williams, Venus: 7 netster **9** tennis pro
milieu: 5 court
sister: 6 Serena
__ William's War: 4 King
Williams, William Carlos: 4 poet
work: Between Walls
Paterson
Queen-Anne's-Lace
The Red Wheelbarrow
Smell!
This Is Just to Say
To a Poor Old Woman
Young Sycamore
William Tecumseh __: 7 Sherman
William Tell: 5 opera
composer: Gioacchino Rossini
song: 4 aria
William the Conqueror: 4 king **6** Norman
daughter: 5 Adela
son: 6 Henry I
William Wilson
author: Edgar Allan Poe
__ Will I Be Loved: 4 When
Willie: 2 GI **3** Pep **4** Mays **5** Aames, McGee, Stark **6** Keeler, Lanier, Morris, Nelson, Sutton **7** McCovey **8** Stargell **9** Shoemaker
willies: 4 fear **6** shakes **7** anxiety, fidgets, jitters, shivers
__ Willie Winkie: 3 Wee
__ Will I Know: 3 How
willing: 4 game, glad, life **5** can-do, eager, prone, ready **6** prompt **7** content, dutiful, pleased **8** amenable, cheerful, desirous, disposed, gracious, inclined, obedient, prepared, reliable, unforced, yielding **9** agreeable, compliant, energetic, in the mood, tractable **10** consenting, submissive
is ~ to: 5 would
more than ~: 4 avid, keen **5** eager
one: 5 taker
partner: 4 able **5** ready
to listen: 4 fair, open **8** amenable, flexible **9** receptive
__ willing, and able: 5 ready
Willingham: 5 Noble **6** Calder
Willingham, Calder: 6 writer
work: Eternal Fire
willingly: 3 yes **4** lief **5** lieve **6** gladly, openly, rather **7** happily, readily **8** by choice **9** agreeably, favorably
Willis: 4 Bill, Lamb, Reed **5** Bruce, Chuck
Willis, Bruce: 5 actor
film: Armageddon (1998)
Bandits (2001)
Billy Bathgate (1991)
The Bonfire of the Vanities (1990)
Death Becomes Her (1992)
Die Hard (1988)
Die Hard 2 (1990)
Die Hard With a Vengeance (1995)
The Fifth Element (1997)
Hart's War (2002)
In Country (1989)
The Jackal (1997)
The Last Boy Scout (1991)
Live Free or Die Hard (2007)
Mercury Rising (1998)
Nobody's Fool (1994)

The Siege (1998)
Sin City (2005)
The Sixth Sense (1999)
Sunset (1988)
Twelve Monkeys (1995)
The Whole Nine Yards (2000)
The Whole Ten Yards (2004)
spouse: Demi Moore
TV: Moonlighting
Willis, Chuck
song: C.C. Rider (1957)
What Am I Living For (1958)
Will It Go Round in Circles (1973 song)
artist: Billy Preston
Will it play in __?: 6 Peoria
williwaw: 4 wind
Willkie: 7 Wendell
will-o'-the-wisp: 5 plant
locale: 3 fen **5** marsh, swamp
willow: 4 itea, tree **5** osier, shrub
flower: 5 ament **6** catkin
tree: 4 itea **5** osier **6** poplar
twig: 5 withe
__ willow: 5 pussy **7** weeping
Willow (1988 film)
cast: Val Kilmer, Joanne Whalley
director: Ron Howard
Willow __ for Me: 4 Weep
__ Willowes: 5 Lolly
Willow Tree
artist: Erté
willowy: 4 lank, lean, slim, tall, thin, trim, wiry **5** lanky, leggy, lithe, spare **6** dainty, gangly, limber, lissom, skinny, slight, slinky, supple, svelte, twiggy **7** gracile, lissome, scraggy, scrawny, slender, spidery, sylphic **8** gangling, graceful **9** lithesome, sylphlike **10** long-legged
willpower: 4 grit **5** drive, spine **6** spirit **7** resolve **8** backbone, firmness, strength **10** discipline, resolution
Will Rogers Follies prop: 5 lasso **6** lariat
Wills: 3 Bob **4** Mark **5** Chill, Helen, Maury
__ Will Say We're in Love: 6 People
__ Wills Moody: 5 Helen
Willson, Meredith: 8 composer
score: The Music Man, The Unsinkable Molly Brown
Will Success Spoil Rock Hunter? (1957 film)
cast: Jayne Mansfield, Tony Randall
Will, The
author: James M. Barrie
willy-__: 5 nilly
Willy: 4 orca **5** Loman, whale, Wonka **6** Brandt
son: 4 Biff
__ Willy: 4 Free **6** Little
willy-nilly: 6 random **7** aimless, erratic, offhand **8** pell-mell, reckless, slapdash, slipshod **9** arbitrary, desultory, haphazard, hit-or-miss, irregular
Will You Be There (1993 song)
artist: Michael Jackson
Will You Love Me Tomorrow (1960 song) artist: Shirelles
Will You Still Love Me? (1986 song)
artist: Chicago

Willys: 3 car **4** auto **10** automobile
model: 3 Ace **4** Aero **6** Knight **7** Bermuda **8** Aero-Lark, Americar, Overland **10** Aero-Falcon
Willys-Knight contemporary: 3 Reo
Willy Wonka... (1971 film)
cast: Jack Albertson, Gene Wilder
Wilma: 7 Rudolph **10** Flintstone
daughter: 7 Pebbles
husband: 4 Fred
Wilmette: 4 city, town
locale: 8 Illinois
Wilmington: 4 city, town
locale: 8 Delaware
Wilmut: 3 Ian
Wilshire 5000: 5 index
Wilson: 2 Al **3** Ann, Don **4** Bill, Carl, city, Earl, Flip, Hack, Hugh, Luke, Mara, Mary, Owen, peak, Peta, Pete, Rita, town, Trey **5** Angus, Brian, Cindy, Colin, Debra, Ethel, Gahan, Larry, Marie, mount, Nancy, Rainn, Scott, Sloan **6** August, Demond, Dennis, Dooley, Edmund, Harold, Harris, Jackie, Mizner, Mookie, Robert **7** Charles, Kenneth, Lanford, Pickett, Woodrow **8** mountain
competitor: 3 AMF **4** Voit **8** Rawlings, Spalding **9** Brunswick
locale: 7 Rockies **8** Colorado **10** California
Wilson, Angus: 6 writer **7** British
work: The Mulberry Bush
Wilson, Ann
lead singer of: Heart
song: Almost Paradise... (1984)
Surrender to Me (1989)
Wilson, Charles: 8 Nobelist **9** physicist
Wilson, Colin: 6 critic, writer **7** British
work: Anti-Sartre
Existential Essays
The Occult
The Outsider
Wilson, Edmund: 6 writer
cat: 4 Lulu
work: Axel's Castle
Patriotic Gore
A Piece of My Mind
The Wound and the Bow
Wilson, Ethel: 6 writer **8** Canadian
Wilson, Hack: 3 Cub **7** slugger **10** outfielder
Wilson, Harold
predecessor: 5 Heath **11** Douglas-Home
successor: 5 Heath **9** Callaghan
Wilson, Jackie
lead singer of: Dominoes
song: Alone at Last (1960)
Baby Workout (1963)
Higher and Higher (1967)
Lonely Teardrops (1958)
My Empty Arms (1961)
Night (1960)
Wilson, Lanford: 10 playwright
work: The Hot l Baltimore
Talley's Folly
Wilson, Marie
role: 4 Irma
Wilson, Owen: 5 actor
film: Behind Enemy Lines (2001)
The Darjeeling Limited (2007)
Drillbit Taylor (2008)

I Spy (2002)
Marley & Me (2008)
The Minus Man (1999)
Permanent Midnight (1998)
Shanghai Noon (2000)
Starsky & Hutch (2004)
Wedding Crashers (2005)
Zoolander (2001)
Wilson Phillips: 4 trio
members: Carnie Wilson, Wendy Wilson, Chynna Phillips
song: The Dream Is Still Alive (1991)
Hold On (1990)
Impulsive (1990)
Release Me (1990)
You're in Love (1991)
Wilson, Rita
spouse: Tom Hanks
Wilson, Sloan: 6 writer
work: All the Best People
Ice Brothers
The Man in the Gray Flannel Suit
Small Town
A Summer Place
Wilson, Woodrow: 8 Nobelist **9** president
alma mater: 9 Princeton
birthplace: 8 Staunton, Virginia
film portrayer: 4 Knox
former occupation: 7 teacher
home: 9 New Jersey
opponent: 4 Debs, Taft **6** Hughes **9** Roosevelt
predecessor: 4 Taft
real first name: 6 Thomas
successor: 7 Harding
V.P.: 8 Marshall
wife: 5 Edith, Ellen
wilt: 3 ebb, sag **4** drop, fade, fail, flag, sink, tire **5** droop, dry up, faint, slump, sweat, waste, wizen **6** cave in, dry out, go limp, slouch, weaken, wither **7** decline, dwindle, give out, shrivel, succumb, swelter **8** collapse, languish **9** break down
wilted: 4 limp **6** droopy **8** flagging
Wilton: 4 city, town
locale: 4 Conn.
Wilton __: 3 rug **6** carpet
Wilts: 6 county
locale: 7 England
Wiltshire: 6 cheese, county **10** sheep breed
city: 7 Swindon
locale: 7 England
Wilt the __: 5 Stilt
wily: 3 sly **4** arch, cagy, foxy **5** cagey, canny, sharp, slick **6** artful, astute, clever, crafty, feline, shifty, shrewd, smooth, sneaky, tricky **7** crooked, cunning, devious, furtive, knavish, knowing **8** guileful, scheming, slippery, stealthy **9** astucious, deceitful, deceptive, designing, insidious, underhand **10** contriving, intriguing, serpentine
in a ~ way: 5 slyly
Wim: 7 Wenders
Wimbledon
call: 3 let, out **5** deuce, fault
division: 4 men's **6** women's **7** doubles
game: 6 tennis
need: 3 net
rating: 4 seed
shot: 3 ace, lob **5** serve, smash

surface: 4 lawn **5** grass
Wimbledon winners:
2009 - Roger Federer, Serena Williams
2008 - Rafael Nadal, Venus Williams
2007 - Roger Federer, Venus Williams
2006 - Roger Federer, Amelie Mauresmo
2005 - Roger Federer, Venus Williams
2004 - Roger Federer, Maria Sharapova
2003 - Roger Federer, Serena Williams
2002 - Lleyton Hewitt, Serena Williams
2001 - Goran Ivanisevic, Venus Williams
2000 - Pete Sampras, Venus Williams
1999 - Pete Sampras, Lindsay Davenport
1998 - Pete Sampras, Jana Novotna
1997 - Pete Sampras, Martina Hingis
1996 - Richard Krajicek, Steffi Graf
1995 - Pete Sampras, Steffi Graf
1994 - Pete Sampras, Conchita Martinez
1993 - Pete Sampras, Steffi Graf
1992 - Andre Agassi, Steffi Graf
1991 - Michael Stich, Steffi Graf
1990 - Stefan Edberg, Martina Navratilova
1989 - Boris Becker, Steffi Graf
1988 - Stefan Edberg, Steffi Graf
1987 - Pat Cash, Martina Navratilova
1986 - Boris Becker, Martina Navratilova
1985 - Boris Becker, Martina Navratilova
1984 - John McEnroe, Martina Navratilova
1983 - John McEnroe, Martina Navratilova
1982 - Jimmy Connors, Martina Navratilova
1981 - John McEnroe, Chris Evert Lloyd
1980 - Bjorn Borg, Evonne Cawley
1979 - Bjorn Borg, Martina Navratilova
1978 - Bjorn Borg, Martina Navratilova
1977 - Bjorn Borg, Virginia Wade
1976 - Bjorn Borg, Chris Evert
1975 - Arthur Ashe, Billie Jean King
1974 - Jimmy Connors, Chris Evert
1973 - Jan Kodes, Billie Jean King
1972 - Stan Smith, Billie Jean King
1971 - John Newcombe, Evonne Goolagong
1970 - John Newcombe, Margaret Court
1969 - Rod Laver, Ann Jones
1968 - Rod Laver, Billie Jean King
1967 - John Newcombe, Billie Jean King
1966 - Manuel Santana, Billie Jean King
1965 - Roy Emerson, Margaret Smith
1964 - Roy Emerson, Maria Bueno

1963 - Chuck McKinley, Margaret Smith
1962 - Rod Laver, Karen Susman
1961 - Rod Laver, Angela Mortimer
1960 - Neale Fraser, Maria Bueno
1959 - Alex Olmedo, Maria Bueno
1958 - Ashley Cooper, Althea Gibson
1957 - Lew Hoad, Althea Gibson
1956 - Lew Hoad, Shirley Fry
1955 - Tony Trabert, Louise Brough
1954 - Jaroslav Drobny, Maureen Connolly
1953 - Vic Seixas, Maureen Connolly
1952 - Frank Sedgman, Maureen Connolly
1951 - Dick Savitt, Doris Hart
1950 - Budge Patty, Louise Brough
1949 - Ted Schroeder, Louise Brough
1948 - Bob Falkenburg, Louise Brough
1947 - Jack Kramer, Margaret Osborne
1946 - Yvon Petra, Pauline Betz
1940-45 - no tournament
1939 - Bobby Riggs, Alice Marble
1938 - Don Budge, Helen Wills Moody
1937 - Don Budge, Dorothy Round
1936 - Fred Perry, Helen Jacobs
1935 - Fred Perry, Helen Moody
1934 - Fred Perry, Dorothy Round
1933 - Jack Crawford, Helen Moody
1932 - Ellsworth Vines, Helen Moody
1931 - Sidney Wood, Cilly Aussem
1930 - Bill Tilden, Helen Moody
1929 - Henri Cochet, Helen Wills
1928 - Rene Lacoste, Helen Wills
1927 - Henri Cochet, Helen Wills
1926 - Jean Borotra, Kathleen Godfree
1925 - Rene Lacoste, Suzanne Lenglen
1924 - Jean Borotra, Kathleen McKane
1923 - Bill Johnston, Suzanne Lenglen
1922 - Gerald Patterson, Suzanne Lenglen
1921 - Bill Tilden, Suzanne Lenglen
1920 - Bill Tilden, Suzanne Lenglen

Wimmer: **2** Al **5** Brian
wimp: **4** nerd, wuss **5** dweeb, loser, sissy, softy, twerp, twirp **6** coward, craven, moaner, nobody, softie **7** chicken, crybaby, dastard, milksop, quitter **8** mama's boy, poltroon, pushover, weakling **9** cream puff, fraidy cat, jellyfish, nonentity
  no ~: **4** hunk **5** he-man **6** Samson **7** bruiser **8** Heracles, Hercules, tough guy **10** powerhouse
  (out): **7** chicken
  word: **4** can't
wimpish: **5** timid **6** craven, scared, yellow **7** chicken, fearful, gutless, servile **8** cowardly, recreant, timorous **9** dastardly, fraidy-cat, weak-kneed **10** scaredy-cat
wimple: **5** scarf **6** gorget
  wearer: **3** nun **6** sister **8** prioress
wimpy: **4** mild, puny, weak **5** frail, nerdy **6** anemic, atonic, craven, effete, feeble, flabby, flimsy, unsure **7** anaemic, fragile, languid **8** delicate, helpless, pithless **9** faltering, lethargic, powerless, unpopular **10** vulnerable
Wimpy's payback time: **3** Tue. **4** Tues. **7** Tuesday
Wimsey, Peter: **4** lord
  alma mater: **4** Eton
  work for ~: **4** case
win: **3** bag, get, hit **4** beat, earn, gain, land, lead, luck, reap, sway, take **5** carry, reach, score, upset **6** attain, better, big hit, come by, disarm, gammon, garner, make it, master, obtain, pan out, pick up, rack up, secure, snatch, thrive **7** achieve, acquire, capture, conquer, convert, edge out, luck out, make out, prevail, procure, prosper, pull off, realize, receive, shut out, succeed, success, triumph, trounce, victory, work out **8** come into, conquest, convince, flourish, get ahead, go places, make good, outscore, overcome, persuade **9** checkmate, landslide, overwhelm **10** accomplish
  against: **4** beat, best, drub, rout **5** crush, outdo, upset, worst **6** better, defeat, outrun, outwit, subdue, thrash **7** conquer, nose out, outplay, trounce **8** knock out, outscore, outshine **9** overpower, overwhelm
  back: **6** recoup, redeem, regain **7** recover, restore **8** retrieve
  barely: **4** edge **7** edge out, nose out
  don't ~: **4** fail, fall, lose
  ender: **4** some
  every game: **5** sweep
  lopsided ~: **4** romp, rout **7** laugher
  over: **3** get, wow **4** draw, hook, sell, sway **5** carry, charm **6** allure, defeat, disarm, endear, induce, reason **7** convert, recruit, satisfy **8** convince, persuade, talk into **9** argue into, influence, prevail on, reconcile **10** conciliate
  seek to ~: **3** woo **5** chase, court, spark **6** pursue **10** bill and coo
  surprise ~: **5** upset
  will to ~: **6** desire, fervor **8** ambition **9** obsession
win __: **3** out
Win, __ or Draw: **4** Lose
__ Win: **5** Eat to
Winans: **4** CeCe
Win Ben Stein's Money: **8** game show
win by __: **5** a neck, a nose
wince: **3** shy **4** duck, jump **5** cower, dodge, quail, start **6** blanch, blench, cringe, flinch, recoil, shrink, swerve, writhe **7** back off, grimace **8** draw back **9** make a face
Wincer: **5** Simon
winch: **5** crank **6** lifter **8** windlass
Winchell: **4** Paul **6** Walter
Winchester: **5** rifle
Winchester Cathedral (1966 song)
  artist: New Vaudeville Band
wind: **3** air, jug **4** berg, bise, blow, bora, coil, curl, fife, furl, gale, gust, hint, loop, oboe, pipe, puff, puna, reel, roll, tuba, turn, urua, waft, wrap, zobo **5** aulos, blast, bugle, bumpa, crook, curve, draft, flute, foehn, gazoo, hooey, kazoo, rumor, screw, shawm, snake, spool, storm, titzu, trade, twine, twirl, twist, weave, zonda **6** alboka, arctic, biniou, boreal, boreas, breath, breeze, carnyx, coil up, cornet, encoil, fujara, ghibli, lituus, notice, ramble, samiel, shofar, simoom, solano, spiral, squall, squirm, swerve, syrinx, vortex, zephyr, zigzag **7** arghool, austral, bagpipe, baloney, bassoon, boloney, buisine, chinook, clarion, current, cyclone, draught, entwine, hautboy, helicon, hogwash, inkling, intwine, khamsin, lyricon, meander, mistral, monsoon, musette, norther, ocarina, onshore, pampero, panpipe, piccolo, sackbut, salpinx, saxhorn, saxtuba, shiwaya, shophar, sinuate, sirocco, slither, talinka, tempest, tonette, tornado, trumpet, twister, typhoon, whisper, wreathe **8** altohorn, anabatic, boasting, claptrap, clarinet, encircle, favonian, hornpipe, levanter, mirliton, nonsense, offshore, post horn, recorder, Santa Ana, scirocco, trombone, westerly, williwaw **9** alpenhorn, corkscrew, dust devil, dust storm, empty talk, euphonium, gibberish, harmattan, harmonica, hurricane, jet stream, nor'easter, northerly, nor'wester, sandstorm, saxophone, sou'easter, southerly, sou'wester **10** balderdash, contrabass, cor Anglais, flugelhorn, instrument, intimation, sousaphone, suggestion
  250 mph ~: **9** jet stream
  about: **4** coil, furl, gird, loop, ring, turn **5** curve, twine **6** circle, engird **7** envelop **8** go around, surround **9** encompass
  Africa: **4** berg **6** ghibli, samiel **9** harmattan
  Aleutians: **8** williwaw
  Alps: **4** bise
  ancient ~ instrument: **5** aulos
  Argentina: **7** pampero
  away from the ~: **4** alee
  be in the ~: **4** loom **6** impend
  burst of ~: **4** gust
  California: **8** Santa Ana
  catcher: **4** sail
  cold ~: **4** bise, bora, puna **7** mistral, pampero **8** williwaw
  combining form: **4** anem- **5** anemo-, venti-, vento-
  cyclonic storm ~: **9** hurricane
  danger: **5** shear
  deprive of ~: **5** stall **6** becalm
  dir.: **3** ENE, ESE, NNE, NNW, SSE, SSW, WNW, WSW
  down: **4** slow, wane **5** close, relax **6** lessen, reduce **7** thin out **8** slack off, surcease, taper off **9** terminate
  dry ~: **4** berg, bise **5** foehn **6** samiel, simoom **7** chinook, mistral **8** Santa Ana
  dusty ~: **9** harmattan
  east ~: **6** solano **8** levanter
  Egypt: **7** khamsin
  ender: **3** age, bag, row **4** burn, fall, flaw, lass, mill, pipe, sock, surf, ward **5** blast, blown, break, burnt, shake, storm, swept **6** burned, flower, jammer, screen, shield, sucker **7** sailing, surfing
  equipped with a ~ indicator: **5** vaned
  Europe: **4** bise, bora, fohn **5** foehn
  France: **7** mistral
  gentle westerly ~: **6** zephyr
  get a second ~: **5** rally **8** come back
  get ~ of: **4** hear **5** scent, smell **8** discover
  god: **5** Eurus, Njord
  goddess: **4** Aura
  go like the ~: **3** fly, hie, run **4** dash, race, whiz **5** speed **6** hurtle
  Hawaii: **4** kona
  hot ~: **6** ghibli, samiel, simoom, solano **7** khamsin, sirocco **8** Santa Ana
  humid ~: **5** zonda
  Indian Ocean: **7** monsoon
  indicator: **4** sock, vane
  instrument: **3** sax **4** horn, oboe, tuba **5** flute **6** cornet **7** ocarina, trumpet **8** trombone
  in the ~: **4** near, nigh **6** coming **7** brewing, looming, pending **8** imminent, on the way **9** impending, proximate
  Mediterranean: **6** solano **7** sirocco **8** levanter
  mountain ~: **9** katabatic
  mountainside ~: **5** foehn
  move like the ~: **4** blow
  night ~: **9** katabatic
  north ~: **4** bora **6** arctic, boreal, boreas
  off the ocean ~: **9** sea breeze
  of the ~: **5** eolic
  Peru: **4** puna
  rainy ~ direction: **4** east
  resistance: **4** drag
  ride the ~: **3** fly **4** luff, scud, soar **5** glide
  rising ~: **8** anabatic
  Rocky Mountains: **7** chinook
  run before the ~: **4** gybe, jibe
  Sahara: **6** simoom
  seasonal ~: **7** monsoon
  solar ~ phenomenon: **6** aurora
  south ~: **7** austral
  South America: **5** zonda
  starter: **4** down, head, tail, wood **5** cross, whirl
  stiff ~: **5** noser, storm **6** squall **7** cyclone, tempest
  straw in the ~: **4** omen, sign **5** token **6** augury, herald, signal **7** portent, presage, warning **9** foretoken, harbinger, indicator **10** indication
  take the ~ out of: **6** defeat, hamper, hinder, hogtie, hold up, impede, stymie, thwart **8** obstruct **9** frustrate, hamstring, undermine
  toward the ~: **8** aweather
  toward the equator: **5** trade

twist in the ~: 4 hang 6 dangle 7 draggle
up: 3 end 4 halt, land, quit, stop 5 cease, crank 6 finish, run out, settle, wrap up 7 achieve, adjourn, break up, play out 8 complete, conclude, finalize, pack it in, surcease 9 close down, culminate, terminate 10 call it a day, completion, consummate, put through
up at: 4 go to 5 get to, reach 6 come to, land on 8 amount to 9 set foot in
violent ~: 6 squall
warm ~: 4 berg 5 foehn, zonda 7 chinook
west ~: 8 favonian
wind __: 3 gap, tee 4 down, vane 5 chill, gauge, power, shear 6 chimes, energy, sprint, tunnel 7 erosion, turbine
wind __ factor: 5 chill
wind-__: 4 bell 5 borne, swept 6 screen, shaken
__ wind: 3 ill 4 head, tail 5 bag of, cross, in the, solar, trade 6 second
Wind __ National Park: 4 Cave
Wind __ Willows, The: 5 in the
__ Wind: 6 Second, Summer
__, Wind and Fire: 5 Earth
Windaus, Adolf: 7 chemist 8 Nobelist
windbag: 4 bore 6 magpie 8 prattler 9 loudmouth
like a ~: 5 gassy
words: 3 gas 5 boast 6 hot air
Wind Beneath My Wings (1989 song)
artist: Bette Midler
windborne: 5 eolic 6 eolian
Windbreaker: 4 coat, wrap 5 shell 6 anorak, jacket 7 slicker 9 outerwear
close a ~: 5 zip up 6 zipper
Wind Cave: 4 park
locale: 4 S. Dak.
windcheater: 4 coat 6 jacket
wind chill __: 6 factor
winded: 9 exhausted 10 breathless
be ~: 4 huff, pant, puff
become ~: 4 drop, fade, tire 5 droop, weary 6 weaken 7 fatigue, give out, poop out, wear out 8 peter out, wear down 9 grow weary
__-winded: 4 long 5 short
__-winder: 4 stem
__ Windermere's Fan: 4 Lady
winder starter: 4 side
Windex
alternative: 9 Glass Plus
windfall: 4 boon, luck, plum 5 manna, melon, prize 7 bonanza, godsend, jackpot 8 blessing
windflower: 7 anemone
Windhoek: 4 city, town
locale: 6 Africa 7 Namibia
windigo: 5 giant
winding: 4 bent, mazy, turn, wavy 5 bowed, curly, curvy, snaky 6 curvey, spiral, zigzag 7 angular, bending, crooked, curving, sinuous, turning 8 angulose, angulous, cockeyed, tortuous, twisting 9 spiraling 10 circuitous, convoluted, meandering, roundabout, serpentine
device: 4 stem
shape: 3 ess
__-winding: 4 self
Winding: 3 Kai
Winding Stair, The
author: William Butler Yeats
Wind in the Willows, The
author: Kenneth Grahame
character: 4 Mole, Toad 5 Otter 6 Badger 8 Sea-Farer, Water Rat
windjammer: 4 boat 6 vessel 8 sailboat
windlass: 3 gin 4 crab 5 crank, winch 6 grouch, lifter 7 capstan
windless: 4 calm
windmill blade: 4 vane
Windmills of the Gods
author: Sidney Sheldon
Windmills of Your __, The: 4 Mind
__ wind of: 3 get 5 catch
window: 5 light, oriel 6 lancet 7 opening 8 casement, fenestra, porthole
$2 ~ action: 3 bet 5 wager 6 exacta 8 perfecta, quinella, trifecta 9 quiniella
attic ~: 6 dormer
bay ~: 5 belly, oriel 6 paunch
covering: 5 blind, drape, glass, grill, shade 6 grille, screen 7 curtain, drapery
dressing: 4 mask 5 front 6 facade, veneer
ender: 4 pane, sill
install a ~: 5 glaze
installer: 7 glazier
it may have a ~: 3 env. 8 envelope
opening: 6 louver, louvre
out the ~: 4 away, gone, lost 6 missed, ruined, wasted 8 departed, vanished
part: 4 jamb, pane, sash 5 frame, jambe, ledge 6 casing, lintel
shopper: 4 eyer 7 browser
small ~: 4 vent 5 oxeye
sticker: 5 decal
window __: 3 box 4 seat, sill 5 shade
window-__: 4 shop
__ window: 3 bay 5 storm 6 dormer, French, launch 7 picture
__ Window: 3 At a 4 Rear
windowpane adhesive: 5 putty
Windows
owner: 4 user
precursor: 3 DOS 5 MS-DOS
runner: 2 PC 8 computer
window-shop: 3 gad 4 roam 6 browse 7 saunter
windpipe: 4 tube 6 airway 7 trachea
combining form: 7 tracheo-
Wind River __: 5 Range
__ winds: 5 trade
Wind, Sand and Stars
author: Antoine de Saint-Exupéry
windshield
adjunct: 4 tint 5 visor, vizor
annoyance: 3 ice 5 frost, sleet
attachment: 5 decal
clear a ~: 4 wipe 5 defog, deice 7 defrost
material: 5 glass
Winds of War, The
author: Herman Wouk
Windsor: 3 car 4 auto, city, town 8 Chrysler 10 automobile
locale: 3 Ont. 6 Canada 7 Ontario 10 California
merry ones: 5 wives
racetrack near ~: 5 Ascot
Windsor __: 3 tie 4 knot 5 bench, chair 6 Castle
Windsor Beauties, The
painter: Peter Lely
Windsor Castle
river near ~: 6 Thames
school near ~: 4 Eton
Windsor Forest
poet: Alexander Pope
Windstar: 3 SUV, van 4 Ford
windstorm: 4 gale 6 squall 7 cyclone, tempest, tornado
windsurfer mecca: 4 Maui 6 Hawaii
windsurfing: 5 sport
__ Wind, The: 7 Wayward
windup: 3 end 4 wrap 5 close, finis 6 ending, finale, finish 7 last act, outcome 8 curtains, terminus 10 completion, conclusion, denouement, resolution
Windward Island: 7 Grenada, St. Lucia 8 Dominica 9 St. George's 10 Grenadines
windward, not: 4 alee
wind-worn: 5 erose 6 eroded
windy: 3 raw 4 airy, wild 5 brisk, fresh, gusty, sharp, wordy 6 breezy, drafty, prolix, stormy, turgid 7 blowing, gusting, lengthy, pompous, verbose, voluble 8 blustery, boastful, inflated, rambling 9 bombastic, garrulous, overblown, redundant, talkative, windswept 10 bigmouthed, blustering, long-winded, loquacious, meandering, palaverous, rhetorical
Windy (1967 song)
artist: Association, The
Windy City: 3 Chi. 7 Chicago
el train initials: 3 CTA
windy-day
hobbyist: 5 kiter
wear: 5 parka
wine: 3 kir, red, zin 4 Cava, hock, port, rosé, sake, saki, Sekt 5 blush, color, corvo, drink, Gamay, Mâcon, Médoc, Pinot, Rhine, Rioja, soave, Tavel, Tokay, Yquem 6 Arneis, Barolo, claret, Graves, Malaga, purple 7 aligoté, Amarone, Auslese, Barbera, cabinet, Catawba, Chablis, Chianti, Concord, heurige, Madeira, malmsey, Marsala, Moselle, Musigny, Orvieto, Pommard, retsina, vintage, Vouvray 8 Albariño, beverage, Bordeaux, burgundy, Cabernet, cold duck, Dolcetto, Dubonnet, Frascati, Montilla, Muscadet, muscatel, Riesling, Sancerre, Sauterne, spumante, Sylvaner, vermouth 9 Bardolino, champagne, colombard, dandelion, lambrusco, Meursault, Zinfandel 10 Beaujolais, Chambertin, Chardonnay, Hochheimer, Montrachet
additive: 4 stum
and dine: 3 woo 4 feed, fete 5 treat 9 entertain
Austria: 7 heurige
bouquet: 4 nose 5 aroma, scent 9 fragrance
byproduct: 5 argal, argol
California ~ valley: 4 Napa
color kin: 4 rose, ruby, rust 5 brick, coral, grape, poppy, rusty, sandy 6 cerise, cherry, claret, garnet, maroon 7 carmine, crimson, fuchsia, magenta, pimento, scarlet, sultana, vermeil 8 amaranth, cardinal, dubonnet, geranium, rubicund 9 carnation, cranberry, vermilion 10 strawberry
combining form: 2 en- 3 eno-, oen-, vin- 4 oeno-, vini-, vino-
container: 3 tun, vat 4 cask, skin 6 barrel, foudre
cooler base: 3 ade
designation: 3 cru, dry, red, sec 4 aged, brut, rosé, seco, year 5 blush, sweet, white 7 vintage
drink: 5 negus 6 bishop 7 sangria
dry ~: 5 gamay, soave
ender: 4 skin 5 glass, maker, press 6 bibber, grower, making 7 tasting
France: 4 Moët 5 Gamay, Mâcon, Médoc, tavel, Yquem 6 claret, Graves 7 aligoté, Chablis, Musigny, Pommard, Vouvray 8 Bordeaux, Cabernet, Muscadet, Sancerre 9 Bourdeaux, champagne, Meursault 10 Beaujolais, Chambertin, Montrachet
France ~ region: 5 Loire, Médoc, Rhone
Germany: 4 hock, Sekt 7 Auslese, cabinet, Moselle 8 cold duck 10 Hochheimer
Germany ~ region: 5 Mainz, Rhine
good ~ quality: 4 body
Greece: 7 malmsey, retsina
Greek ~ pitcher: 4 olpe
holder: 6 bottle, carafe, flagon 8 decanter
honey: 7 oenomel
hot spiced ~: 5 glogg, negus
Hungary: 5 Tokay
Hungary ~ city: 4 Eger
Iberian ~ center: 5 Porto
improve, as ~: 3 age
impurity: 6 ketone
inferior ~ in Britain: 5 plonk
In Portuguese: 5 vinho
Italy: 5 corvo, soave 6 Arneis, Barolo 7 Amarone, Barbera, Chianti, Marsala, Orvieto 8 Dolcetto, Frascati, spumante 9 Bardolino, lambrusco
Italy ~ measure: 4 orna
Italy ~ region: 4 Asti
Japan: 4 sake, saki
like ~: 6 fruity
make hot spiced ~: 4 mull
name: 4 Remy 5 Gallo
new ~: 4 must
of ~: 5 vinic
off-tasting, as ~: 5 corky
partner: 4 dine 6 cheese
place: 6 cellar
Portugal: 4 port 7 Madeira, malmsey
prepare grapes for ~: 5 stomp
product: 6 brandy
purchase: 3 jug 6 bottle, carafe
quality: 4 nose
red ~: 4 port 5 gamay, Médoc,

pinot, tavel **6** barolo, claret
Rhine ~: 4 hock
rice ~: 4 sake, saki
Roman ~ pitcher: 4 olpe
sediment: 4 lees **5** dregs **7** residue **9** settlings
serve ~: 4 pour **6** decant
shop: 6 bodega
Sicily: 5 corvo **7** Marsala
source: 5 elder, grape
Spain: 4 Cava **5** rioja, tinto **6** Malaga **8** Albariño, Montilla
sparkling ~: 4 Asti
stopper: 4 cork
white ~: 3 kir **5** Mosel, pinot, Rhine, soave **7** Chablis
wine __: 3 bag, bar **4** list **5** press **6** cellar, cooler **7** steward
__ wine: 3 jug, May, red **4** rice **5** blush, Rhine, Rhone, table, white **7** dessert, vintage
wine and __: 4 dine **6** cheese
wine-colored: 6 vinous
wineglass: 5 flute **6** goblet
feature: 4 stem
__ wine in old bottles: 3 new
winemaking device: 5 press
winery: 7 château
Winesap: 5 apple
relative: *see* apple
Winesburg, Ohio
author: Sherwood Anderson
wineskin: 4 bota
Winfield: 4 Dave, Paul **5** Scott
Winfield, Dave: 10 outfielder
Winfrey: 5 Oprah
company: 5 Harpo
wing: 3 ala, arm, ell, fly **4** limb, sect, unit **5** add-on, annex, graze, organ, pinna, sweep **6** branch, member, pinion **7** aileron, airfoil, chapter, faction, section **8** addition, division, forelimb **9** appendage, extension **10** finger food, take flight
build a ~: 3 add **5** add on, annex **6** adjoin, append, tack on
building ~: 3 ell **5** annex **6** alette
combining form: 4 pter- **5** ptero-
ender: 3 bow, man, men, tip **4** back, ding, over, span **5** chair **6** spread
in America: 6 fender
it: 3 fly **4** soar, vamp **5** ad-lib **6** make up **9** improvise
left ~: 7 liberal
of a ~: 4 alar **5** alary, alate **6** alated
one on the ~: 4 bird **5** flier, flyer
on the ~: 5 aloft **6** flying **7** soaring **8** in flight
political ~: 4 left **5** right
shape: 5 delta
spurious ~: 5 alula
starter: 3 lap, red, wax **4** bite, gull, lace **5** clear, swept
take ~: 3 fly **4** soar **6** aviate
take under one's ~: 4 help **6** shield **7** protect
under one's ~: 4 safe **5** in tow
wing __: 3 nut, tip **5** chair
wing-__: 4 ding
__ wing: 4 take **5** delta, on the
__-wing: 4 left **5** right
wing-ding: 4 bash, fete, gala **5** party, spree **7** jubilee, rampage **8** jamboree **9** festivity
winged: 4 alar **5** alary, alate, quick, rapid, swift **6** alated, speedy **9** impromptu
child: 4 Amor, Eros **5** Cupid **6** cherub
combining form: 7 -pterous
nuisance: 3 fly **4** gnat, wasp **5** midge
one: 5 angel **6** cherub
walker: 3 emu **4** emeu
woman: 3 WAF
Winged __: 5 Horse **7** Victory
Winged Victory: 4 Nike
Winger, Debra: 7 actress
film: Big Bad Love (2002)
Black Widow (1987)
Cannery Row (1982)
Forget Paris (1995)
Leap of Faith (1992)
Legal Eagles (1986)
An Officer and a Gentleman (1982)
Shadowlands (1993)
Terms of Endearment (1983)
Urban Cowboy (1980)
spouse: Arliss Howard, Timothy Hutton
wingless stage: 5 larva
winglike: 4 alar **5** alary, alate **6** alated
Wingrave: 4 Owen
wings
beat, as ~: 4 bate, flap **7** flutter
clear the ~: 5 deice
earn one's ~: 4 pass **5** cut it, train **6** make it **7** qualify **9** measure up **10** pass muster
in Latin: 4 alae
waiting in the ~: 5 on tap, ready **9** available
__ wings: 5 in the, water **7** buffalo
Wings: 6 Hauser
author: Danielle Steel
Wings (1927 film)
cast: Richard Arlen, Clara Bow, Buddy Rogers
Wings (NBC sitcom)
cast: Crystal Bernard (Helen Chappel)
Timothy Daly (Joe Hackett)
Steven Weber (Brian Hackett)
Wings of the Dove, The
author: Henry James
Wings of the Morning, The
author: Thomas Tryon
wingspread: 4 span
__ Wing, The: 4 West
wingtip: 4 shoe **8** footgear, footwear
Winifred: 5 saint
win in __: 5 a rout, a walk
wink: 3 bat **4** jiff, sign, tick **5** blink, flash, flick, flirt, gleam, jiffy, shake **6** minute, moment, second, signal, squint **7** flicker, flutter, gesture, glad eye, glimmer, glitter, instant, nictate, signify, sparkle, squinch, twinkle **8** high sign **9** nictitate, twinkling
at: 6 excuse, ignore, permit **7** absolve, condone, forgive, let pass, let ride **8** let slide, overlook, shrug off, tolerate **9** disregard, put up with
catch a ~: 3 nod **4** doze **5** sleep **6** nod off
double ~: 5 blink
in a ~: 4 anon, soon **7** quickly
like a ~: 3 coy
of the eye: 4 jiff **5** jiffy, trice **6** moment **7** instant
starter: 3 eye **4** hood
wink __: 3 out
Wink: 10 Martindale
winker: 6 eyelid
Winkler: 5 Henry, Irwin
Winkler, Henry: 5 actor
film: The Lords of Flatbush (1974)
Memories of Me (1988)
Night Shift (1982)
The Waterboy (1998)
TV: Happy Days
winks, forty: 3 nap **4** doze, rest **5** sleep **6** catnap, snooze **7** slumber
taking forty ~: 5 adoze **6** asleep
Winky Dink and You dog: 6 Woofer
Win, Lose or Draw: 8 game show
host: Vicki Lawrence, Bert Convy
Winn-__: 5 Dixie
Winnebago: 2 RV **4** lake **5** tribe **6** camper, Indian **7** Amerind **8** language
locale: 9 Wisconsin
winner: 3 hit **4** hero **5** champ, smash **6** big hit, select, top dog, victor **7** triumph, victory **8** champion, medalist **9** conqueror, number one **10** subjugator, vanquisher
Derby ~ flower: 4 rose
starter: 5 bread, prize
winner __ all: 4 take
Winner: 7 Michael
winner's __: 6 circle
Winner Takes It All, The (1980 song)
artist: ABBA
Winnie: 7 Mandela
Winnie __: 3 Mae
Winnie __ Pu: 4 Ille
Winnie the Pooh: 4 book
author: A.A. Milne
character: 3 owl, Roo **5** Kanga **6** Eeyore
winning: 4 cute, nice **5** ahead, on top, sweet **6** lovely, taking **7** likable, lovable **8** adorable, alluring, charming, engaging, fetching, inviting, loveable, pleasing **9** disarming, endearing **10** attractive, bewitching, enchanting, personable, successful, triumphant, victorious
barely ~: 5 one up, up one
gesture: 5 V sign
margin: 4 neck, nose **5** a neck, a nose
streak: 3 run
winning __: 5 smile **6** streak
Winning __ everything!: 4 isn't
Winninger: 7 Charles
Winningham: 4 Mare
winnings: 3 pot **4** gain, loot **5** prize, purse **6** profit
in horse racing: 5 purse
Winnipeg: 4 city, lake, town
hockey player: 3 Jet
locale: 6 Canada **8** Manitoba
newspaper: 9 Free Press
Winnipesaukee: 4 lake
winnow: 4 cull, pick, sift, sort **5** glean **6** choose, filter, screen **7** examine, sort out, weed out **8** separate
wino: 3 sot **4** lush **5** souse, toper **7** tippler, tosspot
affliction: 3 D.T.'s
Winona: 4 city, town **5** Ryder
locale: 9 Minnesota
Win one for the __: 6 Gipper
Winooski, city on the: 10 Montpelier
win, place or __: 4 show
Winslet, Kate: 7 actress
film: Enigma (2001)
Eternal Sunshine of the Spotless Mind (2004)
Finding Neverland (2004)
Iris (2001)
Quills (2000)
The Reader (2008, AA)
Revolutionary Road (2008)
Sense and Sensibility (1995)
Titanic (1997)
spouse: Sam Mendes
Winslow: 3 Ola **4** city, town **5** Homer
locale: 4 Ariz. **7** Arizona
Winslow Boy, The
author: Terrence Rattigan
Winslow Boy, The (1999 film)
cast: Nigel Hawthorne, Gemma Jones, Jeremy Northam, Rebecca Pidgeon
director: David Mamet
winsome: 4 cute, nice **5** bonny, sweet **6** bonnie, comely, lovely, pretty, taking **7** darling, likable, lovable **8** adorable, alluring, charming, engaging, fetching, gorgeous, handsome, inviting, loveable, pleasing, striking, stunning **9** beautiful, disarming, endearing, ravishing **10** attractive, bewitching, delightful, enchanting, triumphant, victorious
winsomeness: 5 charm **6** allure, appeal, beauty, glamor **7** glamour **8** elegance, radiance **9** good looks **10** attraction
Winsor: 5 McCay **8** Kathleen
heroine: 5 Amber
Winston: 3 Ron **5** Smith **9** Churchill
Winston-__, NC: 5 Salem
Winston Cup
entry: 3 car **4** auto **5** racer
Winstone: 3 Ray
Winston-Salem: 4 city, town
locale: 4 N. Car.
school: 3 WFU **10** Wake Forest
winter: 4 cold **6** season **9** Jack Frost
aid: 4 plow **6** deicer
ailment: 3 flu **4** ague, cold **5** strep
air: 4 noel **5** carol
coating: 3 ice **4** hoar, snow
do ~ airport work: 5 deice
ender: 4 time **5** berry, green
enjoy a ~ sport: 3 ski **4** skee, sled **5** skate
exclamation ~: 3 brr
festival: 4 yule
follower: 3 spr. **6** spring
forecast: 3 icy **4** cold, snow **5** frost, nippy, sleet, snowy **6** chilly **8** blizzard
month: 3 Dec., Feb., Jan., Mar. **5** March **7** January **8** December, February
month, in Spanish: 5 enero, marzo **7** febrero **9** diciembre
prefix: 3 mid
quarters: 3 den
runner: 3 ski **4** skee **5** skate
sight: 6 breath
sign: 6 Pisces **8** Aquarius **9** Capricorn
sign of ~: 3 ice **4** snow **5** sleet, slush **6** icicle

sound: 5 achoo 6 ahchoo, hachoo 7 kerchoo
transportation: 3 tow 4 luge, sled, T-bar 8 toboggan
vacationer: 5 skier
warmer: 3 fur, nog 4 coat, grog 5 cocoa, quilt, toddy 6 eggnog, hot tea 8 hot toddy 9 comforter
wear: 4 coat, muff 5 glove, loden, parka, scarf 6 anorak 8 earmuffs
weather: 4 snow 5 sleet 8 blizzard
woe: 3 flu 4 ague
winter __: 5 break
__ winter: 6 old man
Winter: 4 Alex 5 Edgar 6 Johnny
Winter __: 4 Moon 5 Games 6 Palace
Winter __ Discontent, The: 5 of Our
Winter __, FL: 5 Haven
Winter __ too long in country towns...: 4 lies
__ Winterbourne: 3 Mrs.
Winter Games org.: 3 IOC
wintergreen: 5 fruit
fruit: 8 teaberry
__ wintergreen: 5 oil of
Wintergreen for President
composer: George Gershwin, Ira Gershwin
__ Winter Group: 5 Edgar
Winterhalter, Hugo
song: Canadian Sunset (1956)
Winter Haven: 4 city, town
locale: 7 Florida
Winter Moon
author: Dean Koontz
Winter of Artifice
author: Anaïs Nin
Winter of Our Discontent, The
author: John Steinbeck
character: 4 Joey 5 Alfio, Allen, Ellen, Ethan
Winter Olympics
see Olympics
Winter on Majorca, A
author: George Sand
Winter Palace
resident: 4 czar, tsar, tzar
river: 4 Neva
Winters: 4 Yvor 7 Shelley 8 Jonathan
Winterset
author: Maxwell Anderson
character: 3 Mio 4 Carr, Piny 5 Garth, Lucia, Trock 6 Esdras
Winters, Shelley: 7 actress
film: Alfie (1966)
The Diary of Anne Frank (1959, AA)
Harper (1966)
I Am a Camera (1955)
Let No Man Write My Epitaph (1960)
Lolita (1962)
Next Stop, Greenwich Village (1976)
The Night of the Hunter (1955)
Odds Against Tomorrow (1959)
A Patch of Blue (1965, AA)
A Place in the Sun (1951)
The Poseidon Adventure (1972)
spouse: Tony Franciosa, Vittorio Gassman
Winter's Tale, A
author: Jean Stafford
Winter's Tales
author: Isak Dinesen
Winter's Tale, The
author: William Shakespeare
Winters, Yvor: 4 poet
win the __: 3 day
Winthrop: 4 desk, John
wintry: 3 icy, raw 4 cold, cool 5 bleak, chill, crisp, gelid, harsh, nippy, polar, snowy 6 arctic, biting, brumal, chilly, frigid, frosty, frozen, hiemal 7 glacial, ice-cold, numbing, shivery 8 freezing, hibernal 9 inclement
see also winter
Wintu: 6 Indian 7 Amerind
Winwood: 7 Estelle
Winwood, Steve
group: Spencer Davis Group, Blind Faith, Traffic
song: Back in the High Life Again (1987)
Don't You Know What the Night Can Do? (1988)
The Finer Things (1987)
Higher Love (1986)
Holding On (1988)
Roll With It (1988)
Valerie (1987)
While You See a Chance (1981)
__ Wip: 5 Reddi
wipe: 3 dab, dry, mop, rub 4 buff, dust, swab, swob, wash 5 brush, clean, clear, erase, towel 6 dry off, remove, rub off, sponge 8 take away 10 obliterate
off the books: 5 annul, erase 6 cancel 7 rescind, scratch 8 dissolve 10 invalidate
off the map: 4 rase, raze, ruin, sack, undo 5 blast, crush, level, smash, total, trash, waste, wreck 6 defeat, ravage, uproot 7 despoil, destroy, flatten, shatter, torpedo 8 bulldoze, decimate, demolish, desolate, spoliate 9 depredate, devastate, eradicate, extirpate, overwhelm, pulverize, take apart 10 annihilate, obliterate
out: 4 bomb, rase, raze, rout, ruin, slay 5 erase, purge, use up 6 cancel, defeat, delete, efface, finish, remove, rub off, uproot 7 abolish, destroy, expunge, pluck up, trounce 8 decimate, get rid of 9 eliminate, eradicate, extirpate, liquidate 10 annihilate, extinguish, obliterate
the slate clean: 6 pardon 7 absolve, forgive, release 8 overlook
wipe __: 3 off, out
wipe __ the map: 3 off
wiped: 5 tired 8 dog-tired, tired out 9 exhausted
not ~ out: 5 alive 6 extant, living 9 surviving
out: 4 lost, worn 5 all in, kaput, weary 6 undone 7 drained 8 deprived 9 destitute, insolvent 10 straitened
Wipe Out (1963 song)
artist: Surfaris
wiper: 3 rag 6 eraser 8 squeegee
foot ~: 3 mat
__-Wipes: 5 Handi
wipe the __ with: 5 floor
wire: 4 line, send 5 cable, teleg., telex 6 report 7 message 8 telegram 9 electrify, telegraph 10 finish line
bacteriologist's ~: 4 oese
bender: 6 pliers
chicken ~: 4 mesh
electrical ~: 4 cord
enclosure: 4 cage
ender: 3 man, men, tap 4 draw, hair, work, worm 5 drawn, grass 6 haired, puller, tapper, walker 7 pulling, tapping
feature: 6 ground
high-tension ~ support: 5 pylon
inside ~: 3 tip 6 tipoff
live ~: 4 doer, grig 6 dynamo 7 busy bee, hustler 8 fireball, go-getter 9 workhorse 10 powerhouse
measure: 3 mil
mesh: 5 sieve
problem: 5 short
sender of old: 3 TTY 8 teletype
service: 3 UPI
services: 5 media
starter: 3 hay 4 hard, news, trip
wire __: 5 brush, cloth, gauze, house 6 cutter 7 service
wire-__ terrier: 6 haired
__ wire: 4 high, live 5 piano 6 barbed 7 chicken
__-wire: 3 hot
__-wire act: 4 high
wired: 4 edgy 5 eager, hyper, jumpy, manic, ready, tense 6 aflame, touchy 7 anxious, excited, fired up, frantic, nervous 8 fluttery, frenetic, frenzied, juiced up, prepared, strained 10 distressed, high-strung
__-wired: 4 hard
wirehair of film: 4 Asta
wireless: 5 radio
wirer: 7 lineman
wire-rims: 5 specs 7 glasses 10 spectacles
wirers' union: 4 IBEW
wiretap: 3 bug, pry 9 eavesdrop
wiry: 4 hale, iron, lank, lean, slim, spry, thin 5 agile, beefy, burly, hardy, hefty, hunky, husky, kinky, lanky, light, lusty, rangy, spare, stiff, stout, tough 6 brawny, dainty, gangly, hearty, limber, lissom, mighty, potent, robust, rugged, sinewy, skinny, slight, slinky, steely, stocky, strong, sturdy, supple, svelte, twiggy, virile 7 bristly, doughty, gracile, lissome, scraggy, scrawny, slender, spidery, stringy, willowy 8 athletic, forceful, gangling, indurate, muscular, powerful, puissant, stalwart, vigorous 9 Atlantean, Herculean, strapping, sylphlike, well-built 10 able-bodied, red-blooded
Wisc. neighbor: 3 Ill. 4 Iowa, Mich., Minn.
Wisconsin: 5 river, state
athlete: 6 Badger
bay: 5 Green
capital: 7 Madison
city: 5 Ripon 6 Beloit, De Pere, Mequon, Neenah, Racine, Wausau 7 Kenosha, Madison, Muskego, Oshkosh 8 Franklin, Green Bay, La Crosse, Oak Creek, Superior, Waukesha, West Bend 9 Caledonia, Eau Claire, Fitchburg, Fond du Lac, Manitowoc, Milwaukee, New Berlin, Sheboygan, Watertown, Wauwatosa, West Allis 10 Brookfield, Greenfield, Janesville, Sun Prairie
conference: 6 Big Ten
Indian: 9 Menominee, Winnebago 10 Potawatomi
lake: 9 Winnebago
motto: 7 Forward
native language: 3 Fox, Sac 4 Sauk 9 Winnebago
neighbor: 4 Iowa 8 Illinois, Michigan 9 Minnesota
product: 6 cheese
school: 5 Ripon 6 Beloit 9 Marquette
state animal: 6 badger
state beverage: 4 milk
state bird: 5 robin
state dance: 5 polka
state domestic animal: 8 dairy cow
state flower: 6 violet
state fossil: 9 trilobite
state grain: 4 corn
state insect: 8 honeybee
state mineral: 6 galena
state stone: 7 granite
state tree: 10 sugar maple
wisdom: 3 wit 4 info, mind, wits 5 depth, savvy, sense 6 acumen, brains, genius, reason, sanity 7 balance, insight, know-how 8 judgment, keenness, learning, maturity, prudence, sagacity, sageness, sapience 9 erudition, foresight, knowledge, stability 10 astuteness, experience, horse sense, philosophy, profundity, shrewdness
combining form: 5 -sophy
Egyptian god of ~: 5 Thoth
folk ~: 3 saw 5 adage, gnome, maxim, moral 6 byword, dictum, saying, slogan, truism 7 epigram, proverb 8 aphorism, apothegm 9 platitude
Greek goddess of ~: 6 Athena, Athene
lacking ~: 4 naif 5 naive
morsel of ~: 5 pearl
tooth: 5 molar
words of ~: 3 saw 5 adage, motto
wisdom __: 5 tooth
Wisdom: 6 Norman
Wisdom of __: 5 Jesus 7 Solomon
Wisdom of Eve, The
author: Mary Orr
wise: 3 hep, hip 4 just, mode, onto, sage, sane, wary 5 alert, aware, canny, fresh, nervy, privy, right, savvy, sharp, slick, smart, sound 6 astute, clever, manner, method, shrewd, sophic, taught, versed, with it 7 careful, erudite, knowing, logical, mindful, owllike, politic, process, prudent, sapient, tactful, tuned in 8 apprised, discreet, educated, impudent, informed, insolent, oracular, profound, rational, sensible, well-read 9 advisable, astucious, cognizant, farseeing, in the know, intuitive, judicious, pansophic, plugged in, provident, sagacious, scholarly, Solomonic,

venerable **10** all-knowing, diplomatic, discerning, farsighted, insightful, longheaded, omniscient, perceptive, reasonable, reflective, thoughtful
about: 4 on to **5** hep to
become ~: 6 evolve, grow up, mature, mellow **8** maturate
bird: 3 owl
crack ~: 4 jeer, jest, joke
ender: 4 acre **5** crack **7** cracker
get ~: 9 smarten up
goddess: 6 Athena, Athene
guy: 3 wag **4** guru, mage, sage **5** magus **6** oracle **9** know-it-all **10** jackanapes
men: 4 Magi
starter: 3 any, end, man **4** crab, edge, flat, like, long, side, step **5** clock, coast, cross, least, other, penny, slant, width **6** corner, length, street **7** breadth
to: 3 hep, hip **4** in on, up on **5** aware, privy, savvy **6** versed, with it **7** knowing, mindful, tuned in **8** familiar, informed, sensible **9** au courant, cognizant, conscious, in the know, observant, on the beam, plugged in, sensitive **10** acquainted, conversant, perceptive, understood
up: 5 edify, ready **6** get hep **9** enlighten
wise __: 3 guy
wise __ owl: 4 as an
__ wise: 3 get **5** crack
__-wise: 5 penny **7** weather, worldly
wiseacre: 5 joker **6** smarty **7** smartie **9** know-it-all **10** jackanapes, smart aleck
Wise Blood
author: Flannery O'Connor
__ wise child...: 4 It's a
wisecrack: 3 dig, gag, mot, pun **4** gibe, jape, jest, joke, quip **5** humor, reply, spoof **6** gasser, remark **7** comment, observe, sarcasm **8** reaction, response **9** rejoinder, witticism
wisecracker: 3 wag, wit **4** zany **5** clown, comic, joker **8** comedian
wisecracking: 5 humor **6** comedy, joking, send-up **7** jesting, takeoff **8** drollery
__ wise guy, eh?: 3 Oh a
Wiseman: 5 Adele **6** Joseph
Wise Men gift: 4 gold **5** myrrh **12** frankincense
wisent: 5 bison
wiser, maybe: 5 older
Wise, Robert: 8 director
film: Blood on the Moon (1948)
The Body Snatcher (1945)
Born to Kill (1947)
Curse of the Cat People (1944)
The Day the Earth Stood Still (1951)
The Desert Rats (1953)
Executive Suite (1954)
The Haunting (1963)
I Want to Live! (1958)
Odds Against Tomorrow (1959)
Run Silent, Run Deep (1958)
The Sand Pebbles (1966)
The Set-Up (1949)
So Big (1953)
Somebody Up There Likes Me (1956)
The Sound of Music (1965, AA)
Star! (1968)
Star Trek -The Motion Picture (1979)
Three Secrets (1950)
Tribute to a Bad Man (1956)
Two for the Seesaw (1962)
West Side Story (1961, AA)
wish: 3 aim, bid, yen **4** envy, hope, itch, long, miss, pine, pray, urge, want, whim, will **5** covet, crave, dream, fancy, order, yearn **6** aspire, desire, hanker, hunger, intent, please, thirst **7** command, longing, require **8** ambition, daydream, pleasure, volition, yearning **9** appetence, hankering, intention **10** aspiration, desiderate
ender: 4 bone
for: 4 need, want **5** covet, fancy **6** desire
(for): 4 hope, long, pant, pine, sigh **5** spoil, yearn
granter: 5 genie
joy to: 4 fete **5** bless, honor, toast **10** compliment, felicitate
something to ~ on: 4 star **5** a star
(to): 6 aspire
undone: 3 rue **6** bemoan, regret
universal ~: 5 peace
wish __: 4 list
wish __ were here: 3 you
Wish __, wish...: 4 I may
__ Wish: 5 Death
Wish-Bone: 8 dressing
alternative: 9 Seven Seas **11** Good Seasons
__-wisher: 3 ill **4** well
wishes
as one ~: 6 at will
best ~: 7 regards **8** blessing, respects
last ~: 4 will **9** testament
Wishin' and Hopin' (1964 song)
artist: Dusty Springfield
wishing: 4 avid **5** eager, itchy **6** hungry **7** athirst, hopeful, jealous, longing, thirsty, wistful **8** aspiring, covetous, desirous, grasping, yearning **9** ambitious
wishing __: 4 well
Wishing Well (1988 song)
artist: Terence Trent D'Arby
...wishing will make __: 4 it so
Wishing You Were Here (1974 song)
artist: Chicago
Wish me __!: 4 luck
wishy-__: 5 washy
Wish you were __: 4 here
wishy-washy: 4 weak **5** vapid **6** fickle, jejune **7** insipid **8** hesitant, lukewarm, wavering **9** faltering, uncertain, undecided, weak-kneed **10** ambivalent, indecisive, irresolute, weak-willed
reply: 5 maybe **7** perhaps **8** possibly **9** it could be, it might be, perchance
Wisk: 9 detergent
alternative: *see* detergent
wisp: 3 bit **4** hint, puff, tuft **5** shock, shred, trace, twist **6** bundle, strand, streak, thread **7** smidgen, smidgin, snippet **8** fragment, smidgeon
wispy: 4 thin **5** faint, filmy **6** dainty, skinny, slight **7** slender **8** feathery **10** weightless
wistaria
see wisteria
Wister: 4 Owen
wisteria: 4 vine **5** plant, shrub **6** flower
wistful: 3 sad **6** dreamy, musing **7** forlorn, longing, pensive, wishful **8** desirous, mournful, touching, yearning **9** nostalgic, plaintive **10** meditative, melancholy, reflective, thoughtful
exclamation: 4 ah me, alas **5** oh gee
one: 4 ruer **5** piner
sound: 4 sigh
wit: 3 wag **4** card, mind **5** comic, grasp, humor, irony, joker, sally, sense **6** acuity, acumen, banter, brains, esprit, jester, levity, reason, sanity, satire, wisdom **7** farceur, insight, marbles, punster, sparkle **8** badinage, comedian, drollery, humorist, jocosity, jokester, judgment, keenness, lucidity, quipster, raillery, repartee, sagacity, saneness, sapience, wordplay **9** acuteness, awareness, ingenuity, jokesmith, mentality **10** astuteness, braininess, brainpower, brilliance, cleverness, jocularity, perception, pleasantry, shrewdness
bit of ~: 3 gag, pun **4** jest, joke, quip **5** crack **6** bon mot, zinger **7** epigram **8** one-liner **9** wisecrack
lacking ~: 4 dull **5** prosy, vapid **7** humdrum, prosaic, tedious
like some ~: 3 dry **4** acid **5** sharp **6** biting
starter: 3 dim, nit
to ~: 3 viz. **4** scil. **6** namely, such as **9** videlicet **10** explicitly, for example
__ wit: 5 attic
__-wit: 4 half
witch: 3 hag **5** crone **6** beldam **7** beldame, warlock **8** conjurer, sorcerer **9** sorceress
conveyance: 5 broom
creation: 3 hex **4** brew **5** curse
ender: 5 craft
familiar: 3 cat **9** grimalkin
feature: 4 wart
group: 5 coven, esbat
home: 5 Endor
hunt: 5 purge **6** search
hunt locale: 5 Salem
laugh: 6 cackle
repellent: 6 amulet
witch __: 4 hunt **5** hazel **6** doctor
witchcraft: 5 magic, obeah, spell, wicca **6** hoodoo, occult, voodoo **7** sorcery **8** black art, wizardry **9** conjuring **10** black magic
Witchcraft (1958 song)
artist: Frank Sinatra
Witch Doctor (1958 song)
artist: David Seville and the Chipmunks
witches' brew need: 4 frog, newt
Witches of Eastwick, The (1987 film)
cast: Cher, Jack Nicholson, Michelle Pfeiffer, Susan Sarandon
composer: John Williams
witching __: 4 hour
Witching Hour, The
author: Anne Rice
Witch of __: 5 Endor
Witch of Coos, The
author: Robert Frost
Witch of the Low Tide, The
author: John Dickson Carr
__ Witch of the West: 6 Wicked
__ Witch Project, The: 5 Blair
witch's __: 4 brew
Witchy Woman (1972 song)
artist: Eagles
with: 5 among **6** dating, mongst, near to, next to **7** amongst, through **9** alongside, escorting, including **10** attached to, supporting
ender: 3 out **4** draw, drew, held, hold **5** drawn, stand, stood
in French: 4 avec
in German: 3 mit
in music: 3 con
in Spanish: 3 con
it: 3 hep, hip **4** chic
prefix: 3 col-, com-, con-, sym-, syn-
starter: 4 here **5** forth, there, where
with __: 5 child **6** reason
with __ and main: 5 might
with __ arms: 4 open
with __ breath: 5 bated
with __ colors: 6 flying
with __ gloves: 3 kid
with __ grace: 3 bad **4** good
with __ on: 5 bells
with __ to: 5 an eye **6** regard
with __ voice: 3 one
__ with: 3 toy **4** deal, go in, hold, live, make, over, part, side **5** alive, go out, plead, put up, taken **6** reckon
...with __ bodkin: 5 a bare
...with __-foot pole!: 4 a ten
With __ Born Again: 5 You I'm
With __ in My Heart: 5 a Song
With __ My Heart Is Laden: 3 Rue
With __ of thousands!: 5 a cast
With __ ring...: 4 this
With __ toward none...: 6 malice
With __ You Get Eggroll: 3 Six
with a __: 5 nod to
with a __ of salt: 5 grain
...with a __ on my knee: 5 banjo
With a __ in My Heart: 4 Song
...with a cherry __: 5 on top
__ with a grain of salt: 4 take
__ With a Kiss: 6 Sealed
withal: 3 yet **7** however **8** likewise
starter: 5 there, where
With a Little Bit of Luck
composer: Alan Jay Lerner, Frederick Loewe
With a Little Luck (1978 song)
artist: Paul McCartney
with all one's __: 5 heart
with an __ to: 3 eye
With a Song in My Heart: 4 song
composer: Lorenz Hart, Richard Rodgers
__ With a View: 5 A Room
__ With a Z: 4 Liza
__ With Bob Costas: 5 Later
__ with care: 6 handle
__ With Charley: 7 Travels
__ With Dick and Jane: 3 Fun
__ With Dirty Faces: 6 Angels

withdraw: **2** go **3** ebb **4** exit, flee, move, part, quit **5** demit, leave, steal, unsay **6** abjure, bow out, depart, flinch, get out, recall, recant, recede, recoil, refuse, remove, renege, repeal, retire, revoke, secede, shrink, vacate **7** abandon, back off, back out, bail out, disavow, drop out, ease out, get away, get lost, give way, make off, pull out, retract, retreat, scratch, seclude, take off **8** abdicate, check out, disclaim, fall back, forswear, phase out, pull back, take away, take back **9** back-pedal, disappear, disengage, foreswear, sequester, stand down, take a hike **10** give ground
from: **4** wean **5** avoid
withdrawal: **3** ebb **4** exit **5** leave **6** egress, exodus, recall **7** leaving, parting, pullout, regress, removal, retreat **8** apostasy, reaction, solitude **9** abolition, deduction, defection, departure, desertion, secession, seclusion, sundering **10** alienation, evacuation, extraction, retraction, revocation
withdrawn: **3** shy **4** cold, cool, gone **5** aloof, timid **6** chilly, lonely, modest, remote, silent **7** bashful, distant, glacial, private, recluse, removed, retired, uptight **8** departed, detached, isolated, reserved, reticent, retiring, secluded, shielded, solitary, taciturn **9** diffident, flinching, inhibited, reclusive, retreated, secretive, shrinking **10** antisocial, cloistered, restrained, unagitated, unsociable
__ with envy: **5** green
wither: **3** dry, rot **4** fade, rust, sear, wane, wilt **5** decay, droop, dry up, parch, waste **6** blight, scorch, shrink **7** atrophy, shrivel **8** decrease, emaciate, languish **9** desiccate
withered: **3** dry **4** sere **7** parched, wizened
withering: **3** rot **4** wane **5** decay **6** biting, fading **7** atrophy, decline **8** decrease **9** crumbling
witherite, metal in: **6** barium
Withers, Bill
song: Ain't No Sunshine (1971)
Just the Two of Us (1981)
Lean on Me (1972)
Use Me (1972)
Witherspoon: **4** Cora **5** Reese
Witherspoon, Reese: **7** actress
film: Best Laid Plans (1999)
Election (1999)
A Far Off Place (1993)
Freeway (1996)
Just Like Heaven (2005)
Legally Blonde (2001)
Rendition (2007)
Sweet Home Alabama (2002)
Twilight (1998)
Vanity Fair (2004)
Walk the Line (2005, AA)
spouse: Ryan Phillippe
With Every Beat of My Heart (1989 song) artist: Taylor Dayne
__ with faint praise: **4** damn
__ With Father: **4** Life
__ with fire: **4** play
__ With Flowers: **5** Say It
with flying __: **6** colors
with full authority in Latin: **9** pleno jure
__ with gas: **7** cooking
__ With Harry, The: **7** Trouble
withhold: **4** deny, hide, keep, save **5** check, sit on, skimp, stint **6** bridle, clam up, deduct, refuse, retain **7** abstain, conceal, forbear, refrain, reserve **8** decrease, diminish, hold back, keep back, subtract
withholding: **6** rebuff, rebuke **7** refusal **8** defiance
withholding __: **3** tax
within: **4** amid **7** between, through
combining form: **3** end-, ent- **4** endo-, ento-
prefix: **5** infra-, inter-, intra-, intro-
within __: **4** hail **5** reach **6** reason
within an __ of: **3** ace **4** inch
Within the Gates
author: Sean O'Casey
within the walls in Latin: **10** intra muros
with-it: **3** hip **5** faddy, swank, swish **6** modern, modish, slangy, swanky
__ with it!: **3** Get **4** Deal **5** Get on
__ With Judy: **5** A Date
with kid __: **6** gloves
__ with kindness: **4** kill
__ With Love: **5** To Sir
With malice toward __...: **4** none
__ With Me: **4** Come, Here, Stay **5** Abide, Dance
__ With Me Henry: **5** Dance
with might and __: **4** main
__ With Music: **5** Say It
...__ with Nineveh and Tyre: **5** is one
__ With No Name, A: **5** Horse
With no sugar __: **5** added
with one __: **5** voice
with one's __ closed: **4** eyes
with one's __ down: **5** pants
with one's eyes __: **4** open **6** closed
__ with one's feet: **4** vote
with open __: **4** arms
without: **3** bar, out **4** less, sans **5** minus, outer **6** absent, beyond, devoid, except **7** lacking, outside **8** devoid of, outdoors
delay: **4** ASAP, stat **5** apace
in French: **4** sans
in Latin: **4** sine
in music: **5** senza
suffix: **4** -less
without __: **4** a fee, a sou, fail **5** a cent, a clue, merit **6** number
without __ ado: **7** further
without __ a hair: **7** turning
without __ to stand on: **4** a leg
Without __: **3** You **4** Love **5** a Song **6** Limits
without a __: **3** sou **5** doubt, hitch **6** stitch
without a __ stand on: **5** leg to
__ Without a Cause: **5** Rebel
Without a doubt!: **3** yes
__ without a net: **4** work
__ without end: **5** world
without further __: **3** ado
__ without leave: **6** absent
Without Limits (1998 film)
cast: Billy Crudup, Monica Potter, Jeremy Sisto, Donald Sutherland
Without Love (1970 song)
artist: Tom Jones
without missing __: **5** a beat
__ Without Pity: **4** Time, Town
without turning __: **5** a hair
Without You (song)
artist: Johnny Tillotson, Mariah Carey, Mötley Crüe, Nilsson
__ with pride: **5** swell
With Reagan: The Inside Story
author: Edwin Meese
with respect to, in math: **6** modulo
With Rue My Heart Is Laden
author: A.E. Housman
With silver __ and cockle...: **5** bells
withstand: **4** bear, buck, cope, defy, face, lump, stem, take **5** abide, brace, brave, brook, enure, inure, repel, stick **6** combat, endure, oppose, resist, suffer, take it, win out **7** hold out, ride out, survive, sustain, undergo, wait out, ward off, weather **8** confront, stand for, tolerate **9** go through, hang tough, stand up to
__ With the Blue Dress On: **5** Devil
__ With the Golden Arm, The: **3** Man
__ With the Golden Gun, The: **3** Man
...with the greatest of __: **4** ease
With the jawbone of __: **5** an ass
__ With the Light Brown Hair: **6** Jeanie
__ With the Moon: **6** Racing
__ with the punches: **4** roll
__ with the same brush: **3** tar
with the stroke of __: **4** a pen
__ With the Wind: **4** Gone
With this ring, __ wed: **5** I thee
With This Ring (1967 song)
artist: Platters
__ With Wolves: **6** Dances
__ With You: **4** Rock **5** Being, Stuck **6** When I'm
With You I'm Born Again (1980 song)
artist: Billy Preston
witigo: **5** giant
witless: **4** daft, dopy, dull, soft **5** dense, dopey, inane, silly **6** obtuse, simple, stupid **7** doltish, fatuous, foolish **8** headless, mindless **9** half-baked, insensate **10** unthinking, weak-minded
witness: **3** see **4** espy, eyer, mark, note, seer, sign, view **5** proof, prove, vouch, watch **6** attend, attest, behold, depone, depose, looker, look on, record, regard, signer, viewer **7** bear out, certify, confirm, endorse, eyeball, indorse, observe, testify, watcher **8** attest to, beholder, evidence, looker-on, look upon, observer, onlooker, vouch for **9** bystander, signatory, spectator, testimony **10** get a load of
bear ~: **4** aver **5** swear, vouch **6** attest, depose **7** testify **8** attest to
bear false ~: **3** lie **5** libel **7** perjure **9** dissemble
starter: **3** eye
statement: **3** I do **4** oath **9** testimony
witness __: **5** stand
__ witness: **4** star **6** expert
Witness (1985 film)
cast: Harrison Ford, Lukas Haas, Kelly McGillis
director: Peter Weir
group: **5** Amish
witnesses: **7** gallery **8** assembly, audience **10** attendance
Witness for the Prosecution: **4** film, play
author: Agatha Christie
cast: Marlene Dietrich, Elsa Lanchester, Charles Laughton, Tyrone Power
director: Billy Wilder
wits: **4** mind **5** grasp, sense **6** acumen, brains, reason, sanity, wisdom **7** balance, insight, marbles **8** judgment, keenness, lucidity, presence, prudence, sagacity, sageness, saneness, sapience **9** acuteness, awareness, ingenuity, intellect, mentality, smartness, soundness **10** astuteness, brainpower, cleverness, perception, shrewdness
wits' end, at: **7** frantic **8** frenetic, frenzied
Witt: **6** Alicia **8** Katarina
__-witted: **3** fat **4** dull, slow **5** quick, ready, sharp, thick
__ Witter: **4** Dean
witticism: **3** gag, mot, pun **4** jest, joke, quip **5** crack, humor **6** bon mot, retort, ripost, zinger **7** epigram, riposte **8** drollery, one-liner, repartee, wordplay **9** wisecrack **10** pleasantry
witticisms, exchange: **6** banter
witting: **6** wilful **7** willful **9** voluntary **10** deliberate
wittingly: **9** knowingly, on purpose, purposely, willfully **10** designedly
Witt, Katarina: **6** German, skater
witty: **3** gay **4** keen, racy **5** campy, droll, funny, light, salty **6** bright, clever, jocose, lively **7** amusing, comical, jesting, jocular, waggish **8** humorous, original, piercing **9** brilliant, diverting, facetious, laughable, sparkling, whimsical
one: **3** wag **4** card
remark: **3** mot **5** sally, squib **6** banter, bon mot
__ Wives Club, The: **5** First
__ Wives of Windsor, The: **5** Merry
__ wives' tale: **3** old
wives' tale, old: **4** lore, myth **6** legend
wiz
see wizard
wizard: **3** ace, pro **4** mage, seer, tops **5** adept, magus, shark **6** expert, genius, master, pundit, shaman **7** charmer, diviner, hotshot, old hand, prodigy, prophet, warlock **8** conjurer, conjuror, magician, sorcerer, virtuoso **9** authority, enchanter **10** soothsayer
assistant: **7** famulus
weapon: **3** hex **5** curse, spell
Wizard
alternative: **5** Glade **7** Airwick, Renuzit **8** Stick-Ups
Wizard __, The: **4** of Id, of Oz
Wizard, Mr. subject: **3** sci. **7** science
Wizard of __ Park: **5** Menlo

Wizard of Oz, The (1939 film)
cast: Ray Bolger, Billie Burke, Judy Garland, Jack Haley, Margaret Hamilton, Bert Lahr, Frank Morgan
character: **4** Gale, Lion, Zeke **5** Henry, Witch **6** Aunt Em, Glinda, Marvel, Tin Man **7** Dorothy, Hickory **8** Munchkin **9** Scarecrow
director: Victor Fleming
dog: **4** Toto
flower: **5** poppy
last word of ~: **4** home
music: **5** Arlen **7** Harburg
producer: **5** Leroy
prop: **3** axe **5** broom **6** oilcan
setting: **3** Kan. **6** Kansas
studio: **3** MGM
tint: **5** sepia
wizardry: **5** magic **7** sorcery **10** virtuosity, witchcraft
Wizards: **4** five, team
home: **10** Washington
org.: **3** NBA
rival: *see* NBA team
sport: **10** basketball
wizen: **3** dry **4** wilt **5** dry up **6** shrink **7** shrivel **9** desiccate
wizened: **3** dry, old **4** aged, sere, thin, worn **5** aging **6** ageing, little, shrunk **7** ancient, dried up, elderly **8** grizzled, shrunken, withered, wrinkled **9** geriatric, getting on, senescent, shriveled, up in years
Wiz, The (1978 film)
cast: Lena Horne, Michael Jackson, Mabel King, Richard Pryor, Diana Ross, Ted Ross, Nipsey Russell
composer: Charlie Smalls
director: Sidney Lumet
song: **4** Home **7** Be a Lion **10** Ease on Down
WJM staffer: **3** Lou, Ted **4** Mary **5** Grant **6** Baxter, Murray, Sue Ann
wk., day of the: **3** Fri., Mon., Sat., Sun., Thu., Tue., Wed. **4** Thur., Tues. **5** Thurs.
WKRP in Cincinnati (CBS sitcom)
cast: Loni Anderson (Jennifer Marlowe)
Frank Bonner (Herb Tarlek)
Howard Hesseman (Johnny Fever)
Gordon Jump (Arthur Carlson)
Tim Reid (Gordon Sims/Venus Flytrap)
Richard Sanders (Les Nessman)
Gary Sandy (Andy Travis)
Jan Smithers (Bailey Quarters)
medium: **5** radio
producer: MTM
sign: **5** on air
wks., many: **2** mo. **3** mos.
WNBA
player: **5** woman
team: **3** Sun **4** Lynx **5** Fever, Shock, Sting, Storm **6** Comets, Sparks **7** Liberty, Mercury, Mystics, Rockers **8** Monarchs
WNW: **3** dir. **9** direction
opposite: **3** ESE
Wo-__: **3** Fat
woad: **3** dye **5** stain **7** pigment **8** colorant, tincture
wobble: **3** bob **4** reel, rock, sway **5** lurch, quake, shake, swing, waver **6** careen, falter, quaver, shimmy, teeter, totter, tremor, waddle **7** stagger, stammer, stumble, tremble **9** oscillate, vacillate
Wobblies' union: **3** IWW
wobbly: **4** sick, weak **5** dizzy, loose, rocky, shaky, tippy **6** flimsy, infirm, uneven **7** rickety **8** insecure, unstable, unsteady **9** irregular, teetering, tentative, tottering, unsettled **10** precarious, unbalanced
Wobegon: **4** lake
Wodehouse, P.G.: **6** writer **7** British **8** humorist
character: **6** Bertie, Jeeves **7** Wooster
work: The Code of the Woosters
French Leave
Jeeves
The Plot That Thickened
woe: **4** care, pain **5** agony, angst, blues, dolor, gloom, grief, trial, worry **6** blight, misery, regret, sorrow, trials, tsuris **7** anguish, anxiety, despair, problem, sadness, tragedy, travail, trouble, tsouris **8** calamity, disaster, distress, hardship, mourning, the blues **9** adversity, dejection, heartache, suffering **10** affliction, depression, desolation, difficulty, heartbreak, infelicity, melancholy, misfortune
ender: **6** begone
Woe __!: **4** is me
woebegone: **3** low, sad **4** blue, down, glum, grim, mopy **5** bleak, mopey **6** broody, dismal, dreary, gloomy, morose, somber **7** doleful, forlorn, hangdog, joyless, unhappy **8** dejected, dolorous, downcast, mournful, troubled, wretched **9** bummed-out, cheerless, depressed, heartsick, long-faced, miserable, plaintive, sorrowful **10** chapfallen, despondent, dispirited, lugubrious, melancholy
woeful: **3** low, sad **4** blue, down, glum **5** awful, sorry **6** bitter, feeble, gloomy, morose, racked, somber **7** hapless, joyless, piteous, pitiful, tearful, unhappy **8** agonized, dejected, dolorous, downcast, God-awful, grieving, hopeless, luckless, mournful, pathetic, pitiable, poignant, sinister, tortured, troubled **9** afflicted, aggrieved, anguished, bummed out, cheerless, heartsick, plaintive, sniveling, sorrowful **10** calamitous, chapfallen, dispirited, distressed, inadequate, lachrymose, lamentable, melancholy, pathetical
comment: **4** ah me, alas **6** lament
see also awful
woefulness: **4** funk **5** blahs, blues, dolor, gloom, grief **6** misery, sorrow **7** despair, malaise, sadness **8** distress, doldrums **9** bleakness, dejection, hard times, heartache, pessimism **10** abjectness, affliction, depression, desolation, discontent, gloominess, heartbreak, low spirits, melancholy
Woe is me!: **4** alas, oh no **5** alack **6** oh dear
Wohl: **3** Ira
wok: **3** pan **6** cooker, frypan **7** steamer **9** frying pan
concoction: **6** lo mein **8** chow mein **9** fried rice
use a ~: **7** stir-fry
Wole: **7** Soyinka
wolf: **3** eat, fur **4** bolt, cram, gulp, lobo, roué **5** bayer, canid, dig in, gorge, ogler **6** animal, canine, devour, gobble, guzzle **7** consume, engorge, swallow **8** gobble up, lothario, whistler **9** libertine, polish off
cry ~: **4** warn
down: **3** eat **4** bolt, gulp **5** scarf **6** devour, englut, gobble, guzzle, inhale **7** put away
ender: **5** berry, hound
group: **4** pack
in sheep's clothing: **4** fake **5** knave, viper **7** traitor
keep the ~ from the door: **4** toil, work **7** peg away **9** grind away
Kipling ~: **5** Akela
pack member: **5** U-boat
relative: *see* canine
sea ~: **6** pirate **7** brigand, corsair **9** buccaneer
sound: **4** howl
starter: **4** were
tooth: **4** fang
young: **3** cub, pup
wolf __: **3** cub, dog **4** call, down, note, pack
wolf __ the door, The: **4** is at
__ wolf: **3** cry, sea **4** lone **6** timber
Wolf: **5** Peter, Scott **7** Blitzer
constellation: **5** Lupus
Wolf (1994 film)
cast: Jack Nicholson, Michelle Pfeiffer, James Spader
director: Mike Nichols
Wolf __: **3** Gal **6** number, Solent
__ Wolf: **4** Teen **6** Howlin'
Wolfe: **3** Ian, Tom **4** Nero **5** James **6** Thomas
Wolfen (1981 film)
cast: Albert Finney, Edward James Olmos, Diane Venora
Wolfe, Nero, like: **5** obese
Wolfert: **3** Ira
Wolfe, Thomas: **6** writer
work: From Death to Morning
The Hills Beyond
Look Homeward, Angel
Mannerhouse
Of Time and the River
A Portrait of Bascom Hawke
The Return of Buck Gavin
The Story of a Novel
The Third Night
The Web and the Rock
Welcome to Our City
You Can't Go Home Again
Wolfe, Tom: **6** writer
work: The Bonfire of the Vanities
The Electric Kool-Aid Acid Test
From Bauhaus to Our House
I Am Charlotte Simmons
In Our Time
A Man in Full
Mauve Gloves & Madmen...
The Pump House Gang
The Purple Decades
Radical Chic
The Right Stuff
Wolfgang: **4** Paul, Puck **5** Pauli **6** Mozart **8** Borchert, Ketterle, Petersen **10** Reitherman
see also German
Wolfgang __ Mozart: **7** Amadeus
__ Wolfgang Korngold: **5** Erich
__ Wolfgang von Goethe: **6** Johann
wolfhound: **3** dog **5** canid **6** canine
Russian ~: **6** borzoi
__ wolfhound: **5** Irish **7** Russian
wolfhound, Russian: **6** borzoi
wolf in __ clothing: **6** sheep's
Wolf in Sheep's Clothing, The
source: **4** Esop **5** Aesop
wolflike: **6** lupine, savage **7** lustful **8** ravenous **9** ferocious, predatory
Wolfman Jack records: **3** LPs
Wolf Man, The (1941 film)
cast: Lon Chaney Jr., Claude Rains
__ Wolf McQuade: **4** Lone
Wolf, Peter group: J. Geils Band
wolfram: **7** element **8** tungsten
wolfsbane: **5** plant, toxin **6** flower, poison
Wolf Solent
author: J.C. Powys
__ Wolf, The: **3** Sea
__ Wolf Too: **4** Teen
Wolfville school: **6** Acadia
Wolitzer: **3** Meg
Wolsey: **6** Thomas
successor: **4** More
wolverine: **6** animal, weasel
relative: *see* weasel
Wolverine state: **4** Mich. **8** Michigan
Wolverton Mountain (1962 song)
artist: Claude King
Wolves
see Timberwolves
Womack: **5** Bobby **6** Lee Ann
woman: **3** gal, her, Mrs., she **4** aunt, Dame, girl, lady, lass, maid, miss, wife **5** adult, bride, human, madam, niece, queen **6** Amazon, damsel, female, lassie, madame, maiden, matron, mortal, mother, person, spouse **7** colleen, dowager, duchess, fiancée, grown-up **8** aviatrix, countess, daughter, ladylove, princess **9** earthling, great-aunt **10** demoiselle, girlfriend, handmaiden, individual
bio word: **3** née
combining form: **3** gyn- **4** gyne-, gyno-, -gyny **5** gynec- **6** gyneco-, -gynous
ender: **4** kind **5** power
garment of ancient Greece: **6** peplos, peplus
hat: **5** toque **6** Breton, cloche
Muslim ~ garment: **4** izar **5** burqa, burka **6** burkha, chadar, chador **7** bourkha, chaddar, chuddar
robe of old: **5** simar
starter: **3** lay, mad **4** bond, char, club, door, farm, Manx, news, oars, wash, work **5** chair, clans, dairy, Dutch, freed, horse, Irish, lines, marks, noble, sales, Scots, scrub, stunt, towns **6** anchor, camera, church, clergy, crafts, drafts, French, gentle, patrol, police, repair, select, spokes, sports, states, tribes, vestry, washer, yachts

7 Cornish, council, counter, country, English, service, working
that ~: 3 her, she
title: 3 Mrs. 4 dame, lady 5 queen 7 czarina, empress 8 countess, princess
wear: 4 slip 5 dress, skirt, teddy 6 blouse, camise, halter 8 camisole
__ woman: 3 to a 5 point, stunt 6 career
Woman (song)
artist: John Lennon, Peter and Gordon
Woman __ Importance, A: 4 of No
Woman __ Seven: 5 Times
Woman __ Sometime Thing, A: 3 Is a
Woman __ Year: 5 of the
__ Woman: 3 I Am, I'm a 4 Evil 5 Born a, Cobra, Devil, Gypsy, She's a, Smart 6 Little, Marked, Modern, Police, Pretty, Witchy, Wonder
woman about __: 4 town
womanhood: 8 majority, maturity 9 adulthood
Woman in __, The: 3 Red 5 Green
Woman in Love (1980 song)
artist: Barbra Streisand
Woman in Mind
author: Alan Ayckbourn
Woman in Red, The (1984 film)
cast: Kelly LeBrock, Gilda Radner, Gene Wilder
director: Gene Wilder
Woman in the Dunes, The
author: Kobo Abe
Woman in White
author: Wilkie Collins
Woman Is a Sometime Thing, A
composer: DuBose Heyward, George Gershwin, Ira Gershwin
womanly: 6 female 8 feminine, ladylike
__ woman never yields: 5 A wise
woman of __: 7 letters
Woman of No Importance, A
author: Oscar Wilde
woman of the __: 5 house, world
Woman of the Inner Sea
author: Thomas Keneally
Woman of the Pharisees, A
author: François Mauriac
Woman of the Year (1942 film)
cast: Katharine Hepburn, Spencer Tracy
Woman's __: 3 Day 5 World
__-woman show: 3 one
__ Woman, The: 5 Other 6 Bionic, Spider 7 Miracle
Woman Times Seven (1967 film)
cast: Rossano Brazzi, Shirley MacLaine, Peter Sellers
director: Vittorio De Sica
Woman, Woman (1967 song)
artist: Gary Puckett and the Union Gap
wombat: 6 animal, mammal 9 marsupial
female: 4 jill
male: 4 jack
relative: *see* marsupial
young: 4 joey
women
ender: 4 folk, kind
for men and ~: 4 coed 6 unisex
magazine for ~: 4 Elle, Self 5 Cosmo 6 Allure
org. for ~: 3 DAR, NOW
org. for ~ golfers: 4 LPGA
__ Women: 3 Two 5 Jake's, Smart 6 Little
...Women __ From Venus: 3 Are
Women and Love
author: Shere Hite
Women Drying Their Hair
artist: John Sloan
Women in Love: 4 film 5 novel
author: D.H. Lawrence
cast: Alan Bates, Glenda Jackson, Oliver Reed
Women Ironing
artist: Edgar Degas
Women of __, The: 5 Arles
women's __: 4 wear
Women's __: 3 Lib
Women's __ Daily: 4 Wear
Women, The: 4 film, play
author: Clare Boothe Luce
cast: Joan Crawford, Rosalind Russell, Norma Shearer
director: George Cukor
writer: Clare Boothe Luce
Women, The (2008 film)
cast: Annette Bening, Eva Mendes, Debra Messing, Jada Pinkett Smith
director: Meg Ryan
Women Who Run With the Wolves
author: Clarissa Pinkola Estés
won: 5 money
as good as ~: 5 on ice 7 assured 8 in the bag 10 guaranteed
homophone: 3 one
to be ~: 9 on the line
won __ soup: 3 ton
wonder: 3 awe 5 doubt, query, stare, think 6 boggle, marvel, ponder, puzzle, rarity 7 enquire, inquire, miracle, portent, prodigy, reflect, suspect 8 mistrust, question, rara avis, surprise, theorize 9 amazement, curiosity, reverence, sensation, spectacle, speculate 10 admiration, conjecture, disbelieve, phenomenon, puzzlement, skepticism
about: 4 mull 5 doubt 7 suspect 8 consider, distrust, meditate, mistrust, mull over, question, turn over 9 reflect on 10 deliberate
aloud: 3 ask 7 request
cause ~: 3 awe 5 amaze 8 surprise
combining form: 8 thaumato-
ender: 4 land, work
exclamation: 3 boy, gee, wow 4 gosh 5 golly, hello 6 jiminy, whizzo 7 jeepers, jimminy
showing ~: 5 agape, in awe
suffix: 4 -ment
word of ~: 3 gee, ooh, wow
wonder __: 3 boy 4 drug 5 child
__ wonder: 3 boy 4 girl 5 small 6 one-hit
Wonder (1996 song)
artist: Natalie Merchant
Wonder __: 5 Woman
Wonder __, The: 5 of You, Years
Wonder Boys (2000 film)
cast: Michael Douglas, Robert Downey Jr., Tobey Maguire, Frances McDormand
wonderful: 3 aah, ace, def, fab, ooh, rad 4 aces, A-one, boss, braw, cool, dece, fine, gear, good, keen, neat, nice, okay, phat, tuff 5 dandy, ducky, grand, great, legit, marvy, moral, neato, nobby, noble, prime, slick, super, swell 6 bang on, bang-up, bonzer, bosker, choice, divine, dreamy, far-out, gnarly, groovy, lovely, peachy, proper, slap-up, spot on, superb, terrif, tiptop, unreal, whizzo, wicked 7 amazing, awesome, capital, corking, ethical, perfect, ripping, skookum, stellar, strange, sublime 8 all right, dazzling, dynamite, especial, eximious, fabulous, five-star, four-star, frabjous, glorious, heavenly, jim-dandy, laudable, pleasant, pleasing, slam-bang, smashing, splendid, standout, sterling, stick-out, striking, superior, terrific, top-level, topnotch, uncommon, very good 9 admirable, agreeable, beautiful, bodacious, brilliant, Endsville, excellent, exemplary, exquisite, fantastic, first-rate, high-grade, hunky-dory, marvelous, reputable, sollicker, startling, top-flight, unheard-of 10 acceptable, astounding, beneficial, creditable, first-class, hotsy-totsy, incredible, jack-a-dandy, miraculous, out of sight, peachy-keen, phenomenal, prodigious, remarkable, staggering, stupendous, super-duper, surprising, tremendous
time: 4 idyl 5 blast, idyll
Wonderful __ of Oz, The: 6 Wizard
Wonderful Adventures of Nils, The
author: Selma Lagerlöf
Wonderful Guy, A
composer: Oscar Hammerstein, Richard Rodgers
Wonderful Ice Cream Suit, The (1999 film)
cast: Joe Mantegna, Esai Morales, Edward James Olmos
__ Wonderful Life: 4 It's a
Wonderful One-Hoss Shay, The
author: Oliver Wendell Holmes
Wonderful Time Up There, A (1958 song)
artist: Pat Boone
Wonderful Wizard of Oz, The
author: L. Frank Baum
Wonderful! Wonderful! (song)
artist: Johnny Mathis, Tymes
Wonderful World (song)
artist: Herman's Hermits
__ Wonderful World: 4 It's a 5 What a
Wondering (1957 song)
artist: Patti Page
Wonderland
cake phrase: 5 eat me
character: 4 dodo, hare
drink: 3 tea
girl: 5 Alice
__ Wonderland: 6 Alex in, Boogie, Winter 7 Alice in
Wonderland by Night (1960 song)
artist: Bert Kaempfert, Louis Prima and Keely Smith
Wonder Like You, A (1961 song)
artist: Ricky Nelson
Wonder Man (1945 film)
cast: Danny Kaye, Virginia Mayo, Vera-Ellen
wonderment: 3 awe 8 surprise 9 amazement 10 admiration
Wonder of You, The (1970 song)
artist: Elvis Presley
__ Wonders of the World: 5 Seven
Wonder, Stevie
hometown: Saginaw
instrument: 5 piano 9 harmonica
song: Blowin' in the Wind (1966)
Boogie On Reggae Woman (1974)
Do I Do (1982)
Ebony and Ivory (1982)
For Once in My Life (1968)
Go Home (1985)
Heaven Help Us All (1970)
Higher Ground (1973)
I Ain't Gonna Stand for It (1981)
If You Really Love Me (1971)
I Just Called to Say I Love You (1984)
I'm Wondering (1967)
I Was Made to Love Her (1967)
I Wish (1976)
Living for the City (1973)
Master Blaster (Jammin') (1980)
My Cherie Amour (1969)
Part-Time Lover (1985)
A Place in the Sun (1966)
Send One Your Love (1979)
Shoo-Be-Doo-Be-Doo-Da-Day (1968)
Signed, Sealed, Delivered I'm Yours (1970)
Sir Duke (1977)
Supersition (1972)
That Girl (1982)
That's What Friends Are For (1985)
Uptight (Everything's Alright) (1966)
We Can Work It Out (1971)
Yester-Me, Yester-You, Yesterday (1969)
You Are the Sunshine of My Life (1973)
You Haven't Done Nothin' (1974)
__ wonder what you are: 4 How I
Wonder Woman (ABC/CBS adventure)
cast: Lynda Carter (Diana Prince/Wonder Woman)
Lyle Waggoner (Maj. Steve Trevor)
role: 4 Etta
Wonder Years, The (ABC sitcom)
cast: Olivia d'Abo (Karen Arnold)
Jason Hervey (Wayne Arnold)
Dan Lauria (Jack Arnold)
Alley Mills (Norma Arnold)
Fred Savage (Kevin Arnold)
wondrous: 8 striking 9 marvelous, thrilling 10 miraculous, phenomenal
Wong: 2 B.D. 7 Anna May
wonk: 4 geek, grub, nerd 5 brain, dweeb, grind 7 egghead 8 bookworm
__ wonk: 6 policy
Wonka, Willy
creator: Roald Dahl
portrayer: Gene Wilder, Johnny Depp
wont: 4 rule 5 habit, usage 6 custom,

likely, manner, praxis **7** routine **8** habitude, inclined, penchant, practice, tendency **10** accustomed, consuetude, convention, observance, proclivity
(to): **4** used
won't: **5** shan't **7** refuses
I ~: **2** no **3** nah, naw, nay, nix, non **4** nein, nope, nyet, uh-uh **5** ixnay, never, no how, no way **6** no deal, noways, nowise **8** forget it, negative, negatory **9** by no means, fat chance **10** count me out, not a chance, thumbs down
wonted: **5** typic, usual **6** common, normal **7** regular, routine, typical **8** everyday, habitual, ordinary, orthodox, standard **9** customary, prevalent **10** prevailing
Won't Get Fooled Again (1971 song)
artist: Who, The
__ Won the War: **4** How I
won ton: **4** soup **8** dumpling
Won't you __ neighbor?: **4** be my
woo: **3** beg **4** date, love, rush **5** charm, chase, court, spark, spoon, tempt **6** caress, pursue **7** address, entreat, propose, romance, solicit, step out **8** butter up, fawn over, go steady, persuade, run after, serenade **9** cultivate, importune, shine up to **10** bill and coo, chase after, curry favor
pitch ~: **4** neck **5** spoon
__ woo: **5** pitch
Woo: **4** John
wood: **3** log, oak **4** aloe, club, pine, teak **5** balsa, birch, cedar, copse, ebony, grove, maple, spoon, trees, weald **6** brassy, cherry, driver, forest, lumber, timber, walnut **7** brassey, brassie, coppice, thicket **8** golf club, kindling, mahogany **10** timberland
black ~: **5** ebony
color: **5** stain
combining form: **3** hyl-, xyl- **4** hylo-, lign-, xylo- **5** ligni-, ligno-
component: **6** lignin
cut ~: **3** axe, hew, saw
durable ~: **4** teak **5** cedar, larch
ender: **3** bin, cut, lot, man, men **4** bine, chat, cock, land, lark, note, pile, ruff, shed, wind, work, worm **5** block, borer, chuck, craft, print, waxen **6** carver, cutter, lander, pecker, turner, worker
feature: **5** grain
flaw: **4** knar, knot **8** knothole
fragrant ~: **4** aloe **5** cedar
furniture ~: **3** oak **4** acle, pine, teak **5** alder, ebony, maple **6** cherry, gaboon
hard ~: **3** ash, oak **4** teak **5** cedar, maple
holder: **4** nail **5** screw
join ~: **4** nail **6** hammer
joint: **5** tenon **7** mortise
knotty ~: **4** pine
light ~: **5** balsa
like some ~: **4** aged
louse: **6** isopod
made of ~: **5** treen
mahoganylike ~: **4** agba
measure: **4** cord
piece: **4** chip, lath, slab, slat **5** board **6** billet
problem: **6** dry rot
processor: **3** saw **4** mill **7** sawmill
product: **3** tar **4** slat **5** board, plank, table **6** bureau, timber **7** cabinet
rat: **6** animal, mammal, rodent
residue: **3** ash
saw ~: **5** sleep, snore
smooth ~: **4** sand **5** plane
sorrel: **3** oca, oka **6** oxalis
splitter: **4** mall, maul
stack of ~: **4** rick
starter: **3** bog, box, dog, dye, fat, gum, log, red, sap **4** bass, beef, bent, cord, cork, dead, fire, hard, iron, king, pine, pulp, rose, sass, soft, sour, teak, wild, worm **5** briar, brush, devil, drift, fruit, green, heart, lance, light, match, moose, olive, satin, stink, torch, touch, tulip, white, zebra **6** button, candle, cotton, grease, marble, orange, pepper, poison, sandal, spring, summer, yellow
tissue: **5** xylem **6** phloem
tool: **3** adz, axe, saw **4** adze, vise **5** bevel, gouge, lathe, plane **6** chisel
tropical ~: **4** teak **5** balsa, ebony
twist in ~: **4** warp
white ~: **5** birch
wood __: **4** pulp
__ wood: **5** knock **6** gopher
Wood: **2** Ed **3** Ron, Sam **4** Lana **5** Craig, Grant, Peggy **6** Elijah, Evelyn, Lauren **7** Brenton, Natalie
__ Wood: **7** Belleau, Plastic
Woodard, Alfre: **7** actress
film: Bopha! (1993)
Crooklyn (1994)
Down in the Delta (1998)
Heart and Souls (1993)
Love and Basketball (2000)
Mumford (1999)
Passion Fish (1992)
Primal Fear (1996)
film (voice): Dinosaur (2000)
wood ash product: **3** lye
woodborer: **3** bug **6** insect
woodcarving: **5** craft
woodchopper: **5** axman **6** axeman
woodchuck: **6** animal, mammal, rodent **9** groundhog
look-alike: **5** hyrax **6** dassie
relative: *see* rodent
...__ woodchuck could chuck wood?: **3** if a
woodcock: **4** bird, fowl
relative: *see* fowl
Woodcraft
author: William Simms
Wood, Craig: **6** golfer
woodcut: **5** plate **9** engraving
woodcutter
in a children's story: **3** Ali
woodcutting: **7** logging
wooded: **5** leafy, treed **6** silvan, sylvan **9** arboreous
country, old-style: **5** weald
wooden: **4** dull **5** gawky, rigid, stiff **6** clumsy, gauche, stolid, vacant **7** awkward, deadpan, gawkish, stilted **8** bumbling, lifeless, ligneous, ungainly **9** clapboard, impassive, maladroit, ponderous, unbending **10** glassy-eyed, inflexible, poker-faced, ungraceful
boat: **5** canoe, umiak
clog: **4** geta
container: **3** box **4** case **5** crate
ender: **4** head, ware
frame: **4** rack
pin: **3** peg **4** nogg **5** dowel
post: **3** rod **5** stake **6** picket, timber
stake: **5** spile
strip: **4** lath
travel on ~ runners: **3** ski **4** skee
tub of yore: **3** soe
wedge: **4** shim
yoke: **6** cangue
wooden __: **4** shoe **6** Indian
Wooden Horse, The (1950 film)
director: Jack Lee
Wooden, John: **5** coach
milieu: **5** court
org.: **4** NCAA
sport: **10** basketball
wooden shoe: **4** clog **5** sabot
sailor: **3** Nod **6** Wynken **7** Blynken
sound: **4** clop
Wood, Grant: **6** artist **7** painter
home: **4** Iowa
Woodhouse, Emma: **10** matchmaker
woodland: **4** bush, park, wood **5** silva, sylva, woods **6** forest, timber
creature: **4** deer
deity: **4** faun **5** satyr
plant: **4** moss, tree
Woodlanders, The
author: Thomas Hardy
Woodlawn: **5** Holly
Woodman Spare That __: **4** Tree
Wood, Natalie: **7** actress
film: Bob & Carol & Ted & Alice (1969)
Brainstorm (1983)
The Great Race (1965)
Gypsy (1962)
Inside Daisy Clover (1965)
Kings Go Forth (1958)
Love With the Proper Stranger (1963)
Marjorie Morningstar (1958)
Miracle on 34th Street (1947)
Rebel Without a Cause (1955)
Sex and the Single Girl (1964)
Splendor in the Grass (1961)
The Star (1952)
West Side Story (1961)
sister: **4** Lana
spouse: Robert Wagner
woodpecker: **4** bird
relative: **7** wryneck
tool: **3** neb
__ Woodpecker: **5** Woody
Wood, Peggy
TV role: **4** Mama
wood-pulp product: **5** rayon
Woodrow: **6** Wilson
woods: **4** park **5** copse, grove, trees, weald **6** forest, lumber, timber **7** coppice, thicket **8** outdoors **9** backwater **10** timberland
babe in the ~: **4** fawn, lamb, naif **6** victim **9** unworldly
be out of the ~: **4** mend **5** rally **7** get well, rebound, recover **8** snap back **9** get better **10** bounce back, come around, convalesce, recuperate
carrier: **5** caddy **6** caddie
dweller: **4** deer **7** raccoon
element: **4** tree
ender: **3** man, men
home in the ~: **4** nest
like a babe in the ~: **4** naif **5** naive
like some ~: **4** piny **5** piney
neck of the ~: **4** area **6** locale, region, sphere **7** quarter **8** locality, location, purlieus, vicinity **9** territory
out of the ~: **4** safe **6** better, secure **8** home free **10** in the clear
small ~: **5** copse, grove **7** coppice
starter: **4** back, king
Woods: **3** Ren **4** Elle **5** James, Tiger
__ Woods, CA: **4** Muir
__ Woods Conference: **7** Bretton
woodsia: **4** fern
Woods, James: **5** actor
film: Another Day in Paradise (1998)
Any Given Sunday (1999)
Casino (1995)
Contact (1997)
Ghosts of Mississippi (1996)
Immediate Family (1989)
John Q (2002)
Nixon (1995)
Once Upon a Time in America (1984)
The Onion Field (1979)
The Specialist (1994)
True Believer (1989)
The Virgin Suicides (2000)
TV: Shark
woodsman's leaving: **5** stump
wood-splitter head: **5** wedge
__ woods these are...: **5** Whose
Woods, Tiger: **6** golfer
daughter: **3** Sam
real first name: **7** Eldrick
wife: **4** Elin
Woodstock
attendee: **5** hippy **6** hippie
setting: **4** farm **6** Bethel **7** New York
Woodstock (1970 song)
artist: Crosby, Stills & Nash
wood-stove receptacle: **6** ashpan
woodsy: **5** bosky **6** silvan, sylvan
area: **5** glade
home: **4** camp
Woodward: **3** Bob **6** Edward, Joanne, Robert
Woodward, Joanne: **7** actress
film: A Big Hand for the Little Lady (1966)
A Fine Madness (1966)
From the Terrace (1960)
The Glass Menagerie (1987)
The Long Hot Summer (1958)
Mr. & Mrs. Bridge (1990)
No Down Payment (1957)
Paris Blues (1961)
Rachel, Rachel (1968)
Summer Wishes, Winter Dreams (1973)
They Might Be Giants (1971)
The Three Faces of Eve (1957, AA)
Winning (1969)
WUSA (1970)
role: **3** Eve
spouse: Paul Newman

woodwind: 3 sax 4 oboe, reed
of old: 5 shawm
woodworker: 6 joiner 9 carpenter
woodworm: 3 bug 6 insect
woody: 5 bosky 6 silvan, sylvan
fiber: 4 bast
Woody: 5 Allen, Hayes 6 Herman, Strode 7 Guthrie 9 Harrelson 10 Woodpecker
frequent costar: 3 Mia
son: 4 Arlo
Woody Herman's Thundering __: 4 Herd
Woody Woodpecker: 4 toon
creator: Walter Lantz
wooer: 4 beau 5 flame, lover, swain 6 steady, suitor 7 admirer, gallant, tempter 8 loverboy, paramour 9 boyfriend, inamorato
word: 5 honey
woof: 3 arf 4 bark, weft 6 bowwow 7 texture
crosser: 4 warp
work with ~: 5 weave
woof-woof: 5 doggy 6 doggie
__-woogie: 6 boogie
Woo-Hah!!... (1996 song)
artist: Busta Rhymes
wooing: 4 suit 6 dating 7 pursuit, romance 9 courtship 10 engagement
Woo, John: 8 director
film: Broken Arrow (1996)
A Bullet in the Head (1990)
Face/Off (1997)
Mission: Impossible II (2000)
wool: 3 fur 4 pelt 5 cloth 6 alpaca, angora, fabric, fleece 7 kashmir 8 cashmere
all ~ and a yard wide: 4 real, true 6 trusty 7 genuine, sincere 8 constant, faithful, true-blue
coarse ~: 3 aba 4 abba 5 tweed
coil of ~: 5 skein
combining form: 3 lan- 4 erio-, lani-, lano-
ender: 4 sack, skin 6 gather, grower 7 growing 8 gatherer 9 gathering
fabric: 3 rep 4 felt, repp 5 baize, Kasha, khaki, loden, plush, serge, tweed, voile 6 alpaca, Angora, armure, chally, damask, gloria, jersey, kersey, merino, mohair, moreen, poplin, saxony, stamin, tartan, tricot, vicuña, wadmal 7 bunting, challie, challis, Cheviot, drugget, duvetyn, flannel, grogram, paisley, tabinet, Viyella, worsted 8 algerine, homespun, marocain, shalloon, tabbinet, Venetian, whipcord 9 astrakhan, calamanco, grenadine, henrietta, paramatta 10 Irish tweed
fine ~: 6 alpaca, angora 7 kashmir 8 cashmere
foreign particle in ~: 4 moit, mote
garment: 5 shawl 7 sweater 8 mackinaw
grease: 5 suint
harvest ~: 5 shear
knot: 4 burl
like ~: 4 warm 6 fleecy, toasty
low-grade ~: 5 mungo
outerwear: 5 ruana
pull the ~ over: 5 trick 6 take in 7 mislead
raw ~: 6 fleece
source: 3 ewe, ram 5 llama, sheep 6 alpaca
spun ~: 4 yarn
substitute: 5 Orlon
tease ~: 3 tum
type of ~: 4 ragg
water-repellent ~: 5 loden
weight unit: 3 tod
wool __: 3 fat 4 clip 6 sponge 7 stapler
__ wool: 5 lamb's, steel 6 Angora, virgin
__ wool and a yard wide: 3 all
woolens: 4 hose 5 socks 7 hosiery
Woolery, Chuck
spouse: Jo Ann Pflug
Wooley, Sheb
song: The Purple People Eater (1958)
Woolf, Virginia: 6 writer 7 British
work: Between the Acts
Jacob's Room
Mrs. Dalloway
Orlando
A Room of One's Own
To the Lighthouse
The Waves
woolgather: 4 hope, moon 5 fancy 7 imagine, picture 8 daydream, space out 9 fantasize
woolgathering: 6 revery, trance 7 reverie
Woolite: 8 cleanser 9 detergent
Woollcott, Alexander: 3 wit 6 writer
Woolley: 5 Monty 7 Charles
wool-like fabric: 7 satinet 9 satinette
woolly: 5 downy, fuzzy, rough, rowdy 6 fleecy, hectic, lanate, lanose, rugged 7 chaotic, muddled, sweater, unclear 8 confused 9 rough-hewn, unrefined
bear: 3 bug 6 insect
woolly __: 4 bear, worm 5 aphid 6 monkey 7 mammoth
__-woolsey: 6 linsey
Woolsey: 5 James 6 Robert
Woolsey, James former org.: 3 CIA
Woolworth: 2 F.W. 5 Frank
Woolworth Building architect: 7 Gilbert
wooly
see woolly
Wooly Bully (1965 song)
artist: Sam the Sham and the Pharaohs
Woonsocket: 4 city, town
locale: Rhode Island
Woosnam, Ian: 6 golfer
Wooster: 6 Bertie
__-wootsy: 6 tootsy
woozy: 5 dizzy, faint, tipsy 7 muddled
__-wop: 3 doo
Wopat: 3 Tom
Worcester: 4 city, town
athletes: 9 Crusaders
ender: 5 shire
locale: 7 England 8 Hereford
school: 9 Holy Cross
Worcester __: 5 china
__ Worcester: 5 Royal
Worcestershire: 5 sauce 6 county
locale: 7 England
Worcs: 6 county
locale: 7 England
word: 3 put, saw, tip, vow 4 chat, name, news, oath, talk, term, will 5 couch, edict, idiom, order, rumor, say-so, sound, ukase, usage 6 adverb, advice, behest, byword, confab, decree, dictum, gossip, notice, parole, phrase, pledge, plight, remark, report, rumble, saying, signal, slogan, speech, tipoff 7 account, article, bidding, command, comment, concept, dictate, go-ahead, hearsay, mandate, message, missive, promise, proverb, tidings, warrant, whisper 8 bulletin, chitchat, colloquy, dispatch, language, locution, morpheme 9 adjective, assurance, directive, discourse, guarantee, statement, tête-à-tête, utterance 10 commitment, communiqué, discussion, expression, green light, injunction, intimation
combining form: 3 log- 4 logo-, -onym 5 gloss- 6 glosso-, glotto-
ender: 3 age 4 book, less, play 5 smith 6 monger
in French: 3 mot
in Spanish: 7 palabra
starter: 3 key, mis 4 buzz, fore, head, loan, pass 5 after, backs, catch, cross, guide, swear, watch 6 broads, double
word __: 4 game
word __ word: 3 for
__ word: 3 at a, in a, key 4 code, form, full, good, last, loan 5 dirty, empty, entry, ghost, guide, nonce, smear, vogue 6 weasel
wordbook: 3 lex. 4 dict., thes. 7 lexicon 9 thesaurus 10 dictionary
word-for-word: 5 exact 6 verbal 7 literal, precise 8 faithful, verbatim
wordiness: 3 gas 8 rhetoric, verbiage 9 garrulity, loquacity, prolixity, verbosity
wording: 4 text 5 style, usage 6 phrase 7 diction 8 language, locution, parlance, verbiage
wordless: 3 mum 4 mute 5 tacit 6 silent, unsaid 8 unvoiced 9 noiseless 10 speechless, tongue-tied, understood
word of __: 5 honor, mouth
Word of Honor
author: Nelson DeMille
word-of-mouth: 4 oral 6 verbal 9 unwritten
WordPerfect
headquarters: 4 Orem
wordplay: 3 pun, wit 6 banter, bon mot, ripost 7 riposte, waggery 8 badinage, drollery, repartee 9 equivoque, witticism 10 persiflage, spoonerism
given to ~: 5 punny
word processor: 7 program 8 software
alternative: 3 pen
command: 3 cut 4 edit, quit, save, sort 5 paste 6 delete
feature: 6 tab set
words: 3 row 4 talk, text, tiff 5 set-to, vocab., voice 6 strife 7 wording 8 squabble 9 utterance 10 vocabulary
at a loss for ~: 5 blank, dazed 7 shocked, stunned 8 overcome 9 awestruck 10 bowled over, nonplussed, speechless
bandy ~: 3 rap 4 chat, spar 5 argue
choice ~: 5 and/or, or not
contest of ~: 3 bee
eat one's ~: 6 recant 7 retract 9 back-pedal
empty ~: 3 rot 4 bunk, wind 5 prate, stuff, tripe 6 bunkum, humbug 7 blarney, bombast, fustian, hogwash, malarky, palaver 8 buncombe, claptrap, malarkey, nonsense 9 gibberish, moonshine 10 mumbo jumbo
four-letter ~: 5 oaths 7 cursing, cussing 8 swearing 9 blasphemy, profanity 10 expletives
give ~ to: 3 say 5 speak, utter, voice 6 assert 7 express 8 proclaim 9 enunciate, verbalize 10 articulate
good with ~: 4 glib 5 suave 6 facile, fluent 8 eloquent 10 articulate, loquacious
have ~: 4 spat 5 scrap 7 quarrel, wrangle 8 squabble
in other ~: 5 id est 6 namely, that is
like a play on ~: 5 punny
not mincing ~: 5 blunt, frank 6 candid 10 forthright, free-spoken, from the hip, unreserved
of few ~: 4 curt 5 brief, crisp, pithy, short, terse 6 snappy 7 brusque, clipped, concise, laconic 8 succinct 10 aphoristic, to the point
opening ~: 5 intro 6 prolog 7 prelude 8 foreword, preamble, prologue
parting ~: 5 I quit, see ya 6 so long 8 au revoir
play on ~: 3 pun 9 equivoque
put into ~: 3 say 4 limn, talk 5 speak, state, utter, vocal, voice 6 phrase, relate, spoken 7 express 8 vocalize
run ~ together: 4 slur 6 garble, mumble
stock of ~: 5 lexis 7 lexicon
to live by: 5 adage, credo, creed, motto
use four-letter ~: 4 cuss 5 curse, swear 9 blaspheme
use weasel ~: 5 dodge, evade, fudge, skirt, waver 6 waffle 8 flip-flop, sidestep 9 hem and haw, pussyfoot, stonewall, vacillate 10 equivocate
war of ~: 6 debate 8 argument
way with ~: 4 tact 9 diplomacy
__ words: 5 mince, of few, war of
Words (1967 song)
artist: Monkees
Words for the Wind
author: Theodore Roethke
Words Get in the Way (1986 song)
artist: Gloria Estefan
wordsmith: 6 author, editor, scribe, writer 8 essayist, novelist, reporter 9 columnist 10 journalist, librettist, playwright
Words of Love (1966 song)
artist: Mamas & the Papas
Words, The
author: Jean-Paul Sartre

__ words were never spoken: 5 truer
Wordsworth, William: 7 British
colleague: 5 Byron, Keats 7 Shelley
piece: 3 ode 4 poem
work: Elegaic Stanzas
I Wandered Lonely as a Cloud
Lines Composed a Few Miles Above Tintern Abbey
Lucy Gray
Lyrical Ballads
Michael
My Heart Leaps Up
Ode: Intimations of Immortality
Ode to Duty
She Was a Phantom of Delight
The Solitary Reaper
Tintern Abbey
The World Is Too Much With Us
__ word with: 5 have a
wordy: 4 long 5 gabby, talky, windy 6 chatty, prolix, turgid 7 diffuse, gushing, lengthy, tedious, unterse, verbose, voluble 8 babbling, inflated, rambling 9 bombastic, garrulous, jabbering, redundant, talkative 10 bigmouthed, blathering, discursive, long-winded, loquacious, palaverous, pleonastic, rhetorical, roundabout, unsuccinct
wore: 5 had on 7 sported
__ Wore a Yellow Ribbon: 3 She
Worf: 5 alien 7 Klingon
portrayer: Michael Dorn
work: 2 do, go 3 dig, gig, job, ply, run 4 book, deed, duty, farm, line, moil, opus, play, push, slog, slot, task, till, toil, walk 5 chore, craft, drama, grind, knead, labor, serve, shape, skill, slave, solve, stint, sweat, thing, trade, wield, wreak 6 behave, career, create, drudge, effort, employ, handle, hustle, living, métier, muscle, oeuvre, office, output, racket, strain, strive 7 achieve, calling, carry on, come off, control, exploit, fashion, mission, operate, peg away, product, project, pursuit, scratch, service, slavery, succeed, swindle, travail, trouble, writing 8 activity, business, contract, creation, drudgery, exercise, exertion, function, industry, lifework, maneuver, painting, plug away, position, practice, progress, struggle, toil away, vocation 9 cultivate, freelance, grind away, handiwork, moonlight, salt mines, sculpture, servitude, specialty 10 accomplish, assignment, buckle down, commission, commitment, concoction, daily grind, effectuate, employment, engagement, handicraft, livelihood, magnum opus, manipulate, nine-to-five, occupation, production, profession, take effect
alone: 4 solo
around: 4 duck, shun 5 avoid, elude, evade, skirt 6 bypass, eschew, ignore 8 sidestep 10 circumvent
assignment: 4 task 5 chore, stint 6 errand 7 project 8 activity
at ~: 4 busy 5 astir 6 active, on duty 7 dynamic, engaged, in force 8 bustling, employed, in action, on the job 9 assiduous, on the move 10 in progress
averse to ~: 4 idle, lazy 6 otiose, torpid 7 laggard, languid, passive 8 indolent, slothful 9 do-nothing, lethargic, sedentary, shiftless 10 languorous
avoid ~: 4 idle, laze, loaf 5 dog it, shirk, slack 6 dawdle 7 goof off 8 lollygag, malinger, slack off 9 bum around, pussyfoot 10 featherbed, mess around
away: 3 peg, ply
back from ~: 4 home
body of ~: 5 canon 6 corpus, oeuvre
cease ~: 4 quit 5 leave 6 bow out, resign, retire 8 hang it up, step down 10 give notice
combining form: 4 -ergy, -urgy
comprehensive ~: 5 summa
creative ~: 6 design 9 blueprint, invention
crew: 4 team, unit 5 corps, labor, staff 9 personnel
detail: 4 spec
dirty ~: 5 fraud 6 deceit, dupery 7 falsity, perfidy 9 chicanery, deception, duplicity, hypocrisy, treachery 10 dishonesty
ender: 3 day, man, men, out 4 boat, book, fare, flow, folk, load, room, shop, week 5 bench, force, horse, house, place, sheet, space, table, woman, women 6 people 7 station
Euclid ~: 8 Elements
evade ~ in Britain: 5 sculk, skulk
evader: 5 idler 6 loafer, truant 7 goof-off, shirker, slacker 8 fainéant 9 do-nothing, goldbrick, lazybones 10 ne'er-do-well
for: 4 earn, help 5 serve 6 assist 7 benefit, cater to, promote
free: 4 undo 5 loose, untie 6 loosen, unbind 7 release, unhitch, unloose 9 disengage
get to ~: 5 begin, start 6 set off, set out 7 lead off, proceed 8 commence, set about, set forth
give ~ to: 4 hire 6 employ, engage, sign on, take on 10 give a job to
great ~: 4 opus, tome 10 magnum opus
hard: 4 moil, plod, slog, toil 5 labor, slave 6 drudge, hustle, strain 8 struggle 9 persevere
hard ~: 4 moil, toil 5 grind, sweat 7 travail 8 drudgery, exertion, industry 10 punishment
hater: 5 drone, idler 6 loafer, rascal, truant 7 dawdler, laggard, shirker, slacker 8 parasite 9 do-nothing, goldbrick, lazybones 10 ne'er-do-well
history: 4 vita 6 résumé
house ~: 5 chore
in: 3 mix 9 interpose, introduce 10 specialize
in the ~ cited: 5 op. cit.
in unison: 4 sync
life's ~: 5 trade 6 career 7 calling
not ~ out: 4 fail, flop
not ~ very hard: 5 coast 7 goof off
of art: 7 drawing 8 painting, pastiche
off from ~: 4 free, idle 7 dormant, loafing, resting 8 inactive 9 loitering
on: 3 bug, nag 4 coax, urge 5 press 6 attend, cajole, pester, tackle 7 wheedle 8 pressure 9 importune
out: 2 do 3 fix, jog, win 4 plan 5 crack, educe, solve, sweat, swing, train 6 devise, evolve, figure, finish, get fit, go well, handle, happen, make it, reason, result, settle, thrive, tone up 7 achieve, arrange, develop, prevail, program, prosper, resolve, satisfy, succeed, triumph, unravel 8 bring off, conclude, contrive, exercise, finalize, flourish, get ahead, go places, make good, rehearse 9 calculate, construct, determine, elaborate, formulate, negotiate 10 accomplish, aerobicize, compromise
out of ~: 4 free, idle 7 jobless 9 at liberty 10 unemployed
over: 4 mall, maul, redo 6 bang up, thrash
overwhelm with ~: 4 snow 6 deluge 9 snow under
period: 4 week
place: 4 cube, desk 6 office 7 cubicle
prepare for ~: 5 dress, shave
provider: 5 hirer 8 employer
put to ~: 3 use 4 hire 5 apply 6 employ, engage
quickly (through): 6 breeze
reason for a ~ break: 5 lunch 6 coffee
refuse to ~: 6 strike
safety agcy.: 4 OSHA
shift: 4 days 5 stint 6 nights
slowly: 4 drag, plod, slog 5 crawl 6 trudge
starter: 3 art, cut, leg, net, pin, tin, wax 4 bead, body, busy, case, duct, fire, flat, foot, form, fret, hack, hand, head, heel, home, iron, life, mesh, mill, open, over, road, rock, scut, seat, slop, stud, team, time, wire, wood 5 after, brain, brick, brush, clock, craft, earth, fancy, field, frame, frost, glass, grill, guess, house, metal, paper, patch, piece, press, quill, spade, steel, stone, wheel 6 breast, bridge, bright, crewel, donkey, drudge, ground, master, needle, rubble, school, silver, stucco, timber, wicker
stop ~: 4 halt, quit 5 relax 6 retire 8 knock off 10 call it a day
things out: 4 cope 6 manage
(through): 4 wade
to do: 6 agenda
together: 3 fit, nod 4 gybe, jibe 5 agree, unite, yield 6 accede, accord, assent, club up, concur, league 7 approve, comport, consent 8 coincide 9 acquiesce, cooperate 10 join forces
(together): 4 band
toward: 6 pursue 7 go after 8 quest for 9 cultivate, strive for
travel to ~: 4 ride 5 drive 7 commute
unexciting ~: 5 McJob
unfinished ~: 7 backlog
unit: 3 erg, job 4 task 5 joule 9 foot-pound
unwillingness to ~: 5 sloth 7 languor 8 laziness, lethargy, otiosity 9 fainéance, indolence, passivity 10 torpidness
up: 3 irk 4 move, rile, spur, stir 5 hatch, peeve, rouse, shape, upset 6 arouse, enrage, excite, foment, incite, kindle, turn on 7 agitate, develop, enflame, enthuse, ferment, fluster, improve, inflame, inspire, produce, provoke 8 generate 9 instigate, stimulate
up to: 8 grow into
well: 4 mesh, tick 5 click
with: 3 use 5 apply, wield 6 employ, engage, handle 7 operate 10 manipulate
work __: 3 off, out 4 camp, farm, into, load, over, song 5 ethic, force, of art, order, rules, sheet, train
work __ a net: 7 without
work __ charm: 5 like a
work __ sweat: 3 up a
work __ team: 3 as a
work-__: 4 hour 5 study 7 release
__ work: 3 dog 4 case, desk, mill, scut 5 dirty, grunt, out of 6 social
__-work: 4 book, make
__ Work: 5 Men at
workable: 4 easy, snap 5 cinch 6 breeze, doable, likely, simple, usable, viable 7 no sweat, plastic, useable 8 credible, duck soup, feasible, possible 9 malleable, operative, plausible, potential, practical 10 achievable, applicable, attainable, imaginable
workaday: 5 usual 6 common 7 mundane, prosaic, routine 8 ordinary 9 practical, prosaical
workaholic: 5 type A
work as __: 5 a team
work behind __: 5 a desk
workbench item: 3 nut 4 adze, nail, tool 5 clamp 6 pliers
workbook: 4 text 5 guide 6 manual
worked
get ~ up: 3 irk 4 rave, rile 5 anger, peeve, upset
up: 3 mad 4 agog 5 angry, irate, tense, upset 7 frantic, furious 8 frenetic, frenzied
worker: 3 ant, bee 4 doer, hand, help, serf 5 labor, prole, slave, stiff 6 earner, jobber, toiler 7 artisan, employe, laborer, peasant 8 employee 9 hired hand, operative 10 blue collar, wage earner
cry: 4 TGIF
ID: 3 SSN
office ~: 4 asst. 5 clerk 9 assistant, secretary
perk: 4 ESOP 5 bonus
protection org.: 4 EEOC, NLRB, OSHA
starter: 4 auto, dock, head, iron, mine, time, wage, wood 5 field, house, metal, piece, steel, stone 6 wonder 7 leather
worldwide ~ grp.: 3 ILO
worker __: 3 ant, bee

__ worker: 4 case, fast, mine 5 guest 6 social 7 migrant
__-worker: 6 wonder 7 counter
workers: 4 crew, help, team 5 staff 9 personnel
group: 5 union
supply with ~: 3 man 5 staff
workers' __: 4 comp
Workers of the world __!: 5 unite
__ Worker, The: 7 Miracle
workhorse: 5 slave 6 dynamo 8 live wire
__ Work if You Can Get It: 4 Nice
working: 4 at it, busy, live, spry 5 alive, astir, going, perky 6 active, in gear, lively, usable, useful, viable 7 dynamic, engaged, in force, on track, running, useable 8 animated, bustling, employed, laboring, occupied, on the job, operable 9 assiduous, effective, energetic, in process, on the move, operation, operative, practical, reckoning, sprightly
again: 5 fixed 7 rebuilt
good ~ condition: 6 kilter
no longer ~: 3 ret. 4 retd. 7 retired
one ~ hard: 5 plier, plyer
or not: 4 as is
people: 5 labor, staff 9 personnel
person: 5 prole 7 laborer
starter: 4 lamp, wood
stop ~: 4 fail, rest 6 retire 9 break down
time: 5 shift, stint
together: 6 in sync
working __: 3 day, dog 4 face, girl, hour, rail 5 asset, class, fluid, order, stiff, title 6 papers 7 capital, drawing, storage
Working Girl (1988 film)
cast: Alec Baldwin, Joan Cusack, Harrison Ford, Melanie Griffith, Sigourney Weaver
character: 4 Tess
director: Mike Nichols
Working My Way Back to You (song)
artist: Four Seasons, Spinners
workings: 4 core 5 gears 7 innards 9 apparatus, machinery, mechanism 10 components
working without __: 4 a net
__ Work It Out: 5 We Can
work like __: 4 a dog 6 a charm
workman ender: 4 like, ship
workmanship: 3 art 5 craft, flair, skill, style 7 mastery 8 artistry 9 expertise
workmate: 4 ally 7 partner 9 associate, colleague 10 compatriot
workmen's __: 4 comp
work of __: 3 art
work on __: 4 spec
work-order detail: 4 spec
workout: 5 drill 6 warm-up 7 routine, session 8 aerobics, exercise, practice, training 9 rehearsal 10 gymnastics, isometrics
aftermath: 4 ache 5 cramp 8 soreness
attire: 6 sweats 7 leotard
facility: 3 gym, spa 4 YMCA, YWCA
routine: 4 curl 5 press, squat
target: 3 abs 4 flab, pecs 5 delts, quads 6 biceps 7 triceps
workplace: 4 desk, shop 5 store 6 office
workroom: 4 shop 6 studio 7 atelier
works: 4 goes, mill 5 opera, plant 7 insides 9 machinery, mechanism
complete ~: 5 canon 6 corpus, oeuvre 10 collection, opera omnia
gum up the ~: 3 err, jam 4 flub, mess, muff, slip 5 botch, fluff 6 boggle, bumble, bungle, fumble 7 blunder, stumble 9 mishandle, mismanage
in the ~: 5 afoot 7 pending 8 imminent 9 impending
starter: 3 gas 4 iron, salt 5 skunk, steel, water, wheel
the ~: 3 all, sum 5 total 6 entire 10 everything
__ works: 5 in the, skunk 6 public
__ Works Administration: 6 Public
__ Works Hard for the Money: 3 She
workshop: 6 clinic, studio 7 atelier
hardware: 3 nut 4 nail 5 screw
tool: 3 saw 4 file, rasp, vise 5 drill, gouge, lathe, plane 6 chisel, hammer
Works of Love, The
author: Wright Morris
workstations, connected: 3 LAN
worktable: 5 bench
workweek
part: 3 Fri., Mon., Thu., Tue., Wed. 4 Thur., Tues. 5 Thurs. 6 Friday, Monday 7 Tuesday 8 Thursday 9 Wednesday
start of a French ~: 5 lundi
work without __: 4 a net
world: 3 orb 4 life 5 Earth, field, globe, realm 6 cosmos, domain, global, milieu, nature, planet, region, sphere 7 mankind, society 8 creation, everyone, humanity, province, universe 9 biosphere, everybody, humankind, human race, macrocosm, microcosm
book: 5 atlas
bring into the ~: 4 bear, have 5 beget
combining form: 4 cosm- 5 cosmo-
come up in the ~: 4 rise 5 go far 8 get ahead
ender: 4 ling, view, wide
in a perfect ~: 7 ideally
in one's own ~: 5 spacy 6 spacey
it makes the ~ go round: 4 love
most of the ~: 3 sea 5 ocean, water
natural ~: 8 creation, universe
nether ~: 4 hell 5 Hades 7 inferno
next ~: 8 paradise 9 hereafter
not of this ~: 4 eery 5 eerie 8 eldritch 9 unearthly
on top of the ~: 4 glad 5 happy, merry 6 blithe, cheery, elated, jovial, joyful, joyous, upbeat 7 gleeful, pleased, tickled 8 blissful, cheerful, ecstatic, euphoric, exultant, jubilant, mirthful, thrilled 9 delighted, overjoyed, rejoicing
out of this ~: *see* alien 9 wonderful
real ~: 9 actuality, existence
show the ~: 3 air 4 bare 6 reveal
starter: 5 after, other, under 6 nether
supporter: 5 Atlas
think the ~ of: 4 love 5 adore 6 admire, esteem
traveler: 5 nomad, rover 7 voyager 8 gadabout, vagabond, wanderer, wayfarer 10 adventurer
trip around the ~: 5 orbit
world-__: 4 view 5 class, weary 6 famous, shaker
__ world: 4 free, real, wide 5 dream, lower, small 6 nether
World: 5 paper 9 newspaper
locale: 5 Tulsa
World __: 3 Cup 4 Bank, War I 5 Court, War II 6 Series
World __ Much With Us, The: 5 Is Too
World __ Web: 4 Wide
__ World: 3 New, Old 4 Cool, Wild 5 Ghost, Night, Small, Third, Young 6 Wayne's, Woman's 7 Another, Perfect
World According to Garp, The: 4 film 5 novel
author: John Irving
cast: Glenn Close, Mary Beth Hurt, John Lithgow, Robin Williams
director: George Roy Hill
dog: 7 Bonkers
World According to Me, The
star: Jackie Mason
world-class: 4 A-one, best, fine 5 elite, great, prime, super 6 select 7 capital 8 champion, peerless 9 excellent
WorldCom
competitor: 3 GTE
WorldCom partner: 3 MCI
World Cup
game: 6 soccer
objective: 4 goal 5 score
org.: 4 FIFA
ploy: 4 punt
World Enough and Time
author: Robert Penn Warren
World Factbook compiler: 3 CIA
World-Herald: 5 paper 9 newspaper
locale: 5 Omaha
World Is a Ghetto, The (1972 song)
artist: War
World Is a Wedding, The
author: Delmore Schwartz
World Is Not Enough, The
author: Zoé Oldenbourg
World Is Not Enough, The (1999 film)
cast: Pierce Brosnan, Judi Dench, Sophie Marceau, Denise Richards
World Is Too Much With Us, The
author: William Wordsworth
worldly: 5 blasé, suave 6 uptown, urbane 7 earthly, knowing, mundane, profane, secular, selfish 8 material, physical, temporal 9 practical
starter: 5 other
worldly-__: 4 wise
worldly-wise: 3 hep, hip 4 cool 5 canny 6 urbane, with it 7 knowing 9 au courant
World of Henry Orient, The (1964 film)
cast: Tom Bosley, Angela Lansbury, Paula Prentiss, Peter Sellers
World of Tomorrow, The (1984 film)
director: Lance Bird
World of William Clissold, The
author: H.G. Wells
__ world order: 3 new
World's __: 3 End 4 Fair
__ Worlds Collide: 4 When
World's End
author: Upton Sinclair
World Series: 5 event
month: 3 Oct. 7 October
prelude: 4 ALCS, NLCS
sport: 8 baseball
World Series of Golf site: 5 Akron
__ World Service: 3 BBC
World's Fair: 4 expo 5 novel
1893 site: 3 USA 7 Chicago 8 Illinois
1904 site: 3 USA 7 St. Louis 8 Missouri
1933 site: 3 USA 7 Chicago 8 Illinois
1939 site: 3 USA 6 Queens 7 New York
1958 site: 7 Belgium 8 Brussels
1962 site: 3 USA 7 Seattle 10 Washington
1964 site: 3 USA 6 Queens 7 New York
1967 site: 6 Canada 8 Montreal
1970 site: 5 Japan, Osaka
1992 site: 5 Spain 7 Seville
2000 site: 7 Germany, Hanover
2005 site: 5 Aichi, Japan
2008 site: 5 Spain 8 Zaragoza
2010 site: 5 China 8 Shanghai
author: E.L. Doctorow
World's Greatest Dad (2009 film)
cast: Daryl Sabara, Robin Williams
World's Illusion, The
author: Jakob Wassermann
world's mine __, The: 6 oyster
__ World Symphony: 3 New
__ World, The: 4 Lost 6 Silent
World Trade Center (2006 film)
cast: Maria Bello, Nicolas Cage, Maggie Gyllenhaal
director: Oliver Stone
__ World Turns: 5 As the
World War I
see WWI
World War II
see WWII
world-weary: 5 blasé, bored, jaded, sated 6 cloyed 8 satiated 9 apathetic, surfeited
feeling: 5 ennui 6 apathy, tedium 7 boredom, languor 9 lassitude
sound: 4 sigh
worldwide: 3 big, int. 4 intl. 6 common, cosmic, global 7 general 8 catholic, cosmical, pandemic 9 extensive, planetary, universal 10 ecumenical, prevailing, ubiquitous
World Wide Web: 3 Net 8 Internet
World Wildlife Fund symbol: 5 panda
...world will __ path...: 5 beat a
world without __: 3 end
World Without End, __: 4 Amen
World Without Love, A (1964 song)
artist: Peter and Gordon
World Without Sun (1964 film)
director: Jacques-Yves Cousteau

Worley: 6 Jo Anne
worm: 3 cur 4 bait, heel, naid, nema, push, toad 5 churl, crawl, knave, leech, rogue, scamp, sneak 6 rascal, squirm, teredo, wiggle 7 annelid, wheedle, wriggle 8 fish bait 9 insinuate, miscreant, reprobate, scoundrel, slitherer, vulgarian 10 blackguard
catcher: 4 beak, bird 5 robin
combining form: 5 vermi-
ender: 4 hole, seed, wood 5 grass
in: 5 enter 6 meddle 9 insinuate, interpose
into: 5 enter 9 penetrate 10 infiltrate
like a ~: 4 slow 6 apodal 7 apodous
measuring ~: 3 bug 6 insect
out: 6 recant, renege 8 withdraw
product: 4 silk
starter: 4 book, flat, glow, inch, silk, tape 5 blood, earth
__-Worm: 4 Glow
worm's-__ view: 3 eye
worms, can of: 7 problem 9 adversity
Worms' river: 5 Rhine
wormwood
flower: 9 santonica
gall and ~: 7 dudgeon 10 bitterness, resentment
worn: 3 old, wan 4 beat, gone, shot, used 5 all in, drawn, had it, jaded, kaput, put on, ratty, seedy, spent, stale, tatty, tired, trite, weary 6 beat-up, bushed, effete, eroded, frayed, pooped, ragged, rugged, ruined, shabby, used up 7 clichéd, damaged, decayed, drained, haggard, pinched, raggedy, rundown, useless, wizened 8 decrepit, dog-eared, dog-tired, fatigued, frazzled, out of gas, overused, tattered, timeworn, tired out, wiped out, wrung out 9 burned out, exhausted, hackneyed, motheaten, overtired, played out, pooped out 10 overworked, secondhand, threadbare
become ~: 4 fray, wear 5 decay, erode 7 corrode, weather
irregularly ~: 5 erose
starter: 3 way 4 care, shop, time 7 weather
to a frazzle: 4 beat 5 all in, tense, tired 6 bushed
what's ~: 4 duds, garb, gear 5 array, dress, getup 6 attire, outfit 7 apparel, clothes, costume, raiment, threads, toggery 8 clothing, garments, wardrobe
worn-out: 3 old 4 beat, dull, gone, limp, shot, used, weak 5 bored, drawn, had it, jaded, kaput, spent, stale, stock, tired, trite, weary 6 bushed, dished, effete, frayed, pooped, ragged, ruined, shabby, used up 7 clichéd, drained, haggard, pinched, run-down, useless 8 depleted, fatigued, overused, tattered 9 enervated, exhausted, hackneyed, prostrate 10 dullsville, overworked, threadbare
phrase: 6 cliché 7 bromide 8 chestnut 9 platitude

Worrell: 6 Ernest
worried: 5 tense, upset 6 afraid, hung up, on edge, pacing, uneasy 7 anxious, fearful, fretful, nervous, uptight 8 bothered, fluttery, fretsome, restless, troubled 9 concerned, disturbed, ill-at-ease, perturbed, tormented 10 distracted, distraught, distressed, frightened, solicitous
act ~: 4 pace
worrier: 9 pessimist
risk: 5 ulcer
worrisome: 5 tight 8 annoying 9 vexatious
worry: 3 ail, bug, dog, eat, nag, vex, woe 4 bait, care, fear, fret, fuss, goad, pain, pest, stew, tire 5 angst, annoy, beset, brood, chafe, doubt, eat at, grief, harry, press, shake, sweat, tease, trial, upset 6 bother, excite, gnaw at, harass, hassle, hector, matter, misery, needle, pester, plague, pother, prey on, regret, sorrow, stress, take on 7 afflict, agonize, anguish, anxiety, anxious, bad news, bedevil, concern, depress, disturb, oppress, perturb, problem, tension, torment, trouble 8 aggrieve, disquiet, distress, exercise, headache, irritate, sweat out, unsettle, vexation 9 annoyance, beleaguer, heartache, importune, misgiving, persecute, tantalize, tightness, weigh down 10 infliction, irritation, perplexity, solicitude, uneasiness
about: 4 fret 5 dread, sweat
cause: 4 risk 5 peril
ender: 4 wart
perhaps: 4 ager
words of ~: 4 oh-oh, uh-oh
worry __: 5 beads
__ worry: 5 not to
__ Worry Be Happy: 4 Don't
worrying: 5 pesky 6 knotty, thorny, trying, vexing 7 galling, grating, irksome 8 annoying, nettling 9 vexatious 10 bothersome, irritating, nettlesome
stop ~: 5 relax 6 unwind 7 cool off, lay back 8 calm down, loosen up 9 hang loose 10 settle down, simmer down
worrywart: 7 killjoy, skeptic 8 sourpuss 9 gloomy Gus, pessimist 10 wet blanket
worse: 8 inferior
for wear: 4 worn 6 ragged 7 wornout
worsen: 4 sink 6 impair 7 decline, fall off, relapse 8 compound, diminish 9 aggravate 10 degenerate, exacerbate, go downhill, retrogress
worsening: 3 dip, sag 4 dive 5 lapse, slide, slump 7 decline, failing 8 downturn, nosedive, slowdown 9 downslide, downswing
__ worse than...: 5 a fate
worship: 3 awe 4 laud, like, love, pray 5 adore, chant, deify, exalt, extol, go for, honor, lauds 6 admire, chapel, dote on, esteem, extoll, homage, matins, praise, prayer, pray to, regard, revere 7 adulate, care for, cherish, glorify, idolize, lionize, liturgy, magnify, respect, service, vespers 8 canonize, devotion, dote upon, hold dear, look up to, offering, sanctify, treasure, venerate 9 adoration, adulation, bow down to, care about, celebrate, genuflect, reverence 10 admiration, invocation, veneration
combining form: 5 -latry
house of ~: 4 shul 5 abbey, schul 6 bethel, chapel, church, mosque, temple 9 cathedral, synagogue 10 tabernacle
object of ~: 3 god 4 icon, idol, ikon 5 deity, eikon
supreme ~: 6 latria
__ worship: 4 hero, idol 6 nature
worshiped: 7 beloved
one: 4 hero, icon, idol, star 7 beloved, darling, pop star 8 favorite, folk hero, luminary 9 celebrity, superstar
worshiper: 3 fan 7 devotee 8 adherent, disciple, follower 10 aficionado
worshipers: 5 flock, laity 6 parish
worship from __: 4 afar
worshipful: 5 pious 6 devout, loving
Worsley, Gump
milieu: 3 ice 4 rink 5 arena 6 hockey
org.: 3 NHL
worst: 4 beat, best, do in, drub, lick, rout, whip 5 crush, nadir, whomp 6 defeat, outwit, subdue, thrash 7 clobber, conquer, overrun, shellac, succeed, the pits, trample, trounce 8 outsmart, overcome, shellack, vanquish 9 faultiest, polish off 10 rock bottom
in the ~ way: 3 bad 5 badly
think the ~ of: 4 hate 5 abhor 6 detest, loathe 7 despise, dislike 8 execrate 9 abominate
worst-__ scenario: 4 case
Worst __ in London, The: 4 Pies
worsted: 4 yarn 5 cloth 6 fabric 8 material
be ~: 4 fail, lose
fabric: 5 serge 6 wadmal 7 estamin, etamine 8 casimere, casimire, sanglier, Venetian 9 cassimere, gabardine, sharkskin
Worst That Could Happen (1969 song)
artist: Brooklyn Bridge
__ worst way: 5 in the
wort: 4 mash
worth: 3 use, val. 4 cost, note 5 avail, merit, price, ratal, sense, value 6 assets, beauty, credit, import, moment, riches, virtue, weight 7 account, benefit, caliber, dignity, meaning, quality, stature, utility 8 goodness, property 9 substance, valuation 10 estimation, excellence, expediency, importance, perfection, usefulness, worthiness
be ~: 4 cost, rate 5 price, quote, value 6 charge, come to 7 sell for 8 amount to
determine ~: 4 rate 5 assay 6 assess, size up 7 valuate 8 appraise, evaluate
ender: 5 while
net ~: 6 estate
not ~ mentioning: 5 lousy, minor, petty 7 trivial 8 trifling 9 smalltime 10 incidental
of ~: 5 utile
two cents' ~: 3 tip 4 view 6 advice, tipoff 7 comment 9 viewpoint
worth __: 4 a try 5 doing
__ worth: 3 net
__-worth: 4 self
Worth: 4 Mary 5 Irene
worthier: 6 better
worthiest: 3 top 4 best 5 prime 7 leading, optimal, supreme 8 foremost, ultimate 9 nonpareil 10 preeminent
worthily: 4 ably, fine, to a T, well 6 aright, nicely 7 adeptly, capably 8 expertly, laudably, properly, smoothly, suitably 9 admirably, inside out, perfectly 10 adequately, skillfully, splendidly, thoroughly
worthiness: 5 merit, worth 6 virtue 7 dignity 8 morality 9 greatness
worthless: 4 idle, junk, null, poor, puny, vain, vile 5 cheap, empty, inane, junky, sorry 6 abject, crumby, crummy, drossy, futile, hollow, no-good, paltry, trashy 7 inutile, invalid, pitiful, trivial, useless 8 bootless, degraded, feckless, pathetic, piddling, trifling, unusable, wretched 9 for naught, miserable, no-account, pointless 10 despicable, pathetical, profitless, unavailing
amount: 3 sou 6 diddly
matter: 4 slag 5 chaff, dregs 6 debris, refuse 7 rubbish
talk: *see* baloney
worth one's __: 4 salt
__ Worth, TX: 4 Fort
worthwhile: 4 good 5 of use 6 aidful, benign, paying, useful 7 gainful, helpful, livable 8 fruitful, liveable, positive, readable, remedial, salutary, valuable 9 covetable, desirable, effectual, expedient, favorable, important, lucrative, rewarding, well-spent 10 beneficial, meaningful, productive, profitable
be ~: 3 pay
consider ~: 5 prize, value 6 esteem 8 hold dear 9 recommend
worthy: 3 fit 4 good, true 5 moral, noble, solid 6 choice, decent, figure, honest 7 upright 8 eligible, laudable, luminary, reliable, topnotch, valuable, virtuous 9 admirable, blameless, deserving, estimable, excellent, exemplary, first-rate, honorable, incorrupt, personage, praisable, reputable, righteous, top-drawer 10 creditable, dependable, first-class, invaluable, satisfying
be ~ of: 4 earn, rate 5 merit 6 beseem 7 deserve, warrant
of: 3 due 7 condign, merited 8 rightful, suitable
starter: 3 air, sea 4 news, note, road 5 blame, crash, thank, trust 6 credit, flight, praise
suffix: 4 -able, -ible
Wotan: 4 Odin 5 Othin

Wot's It to Ya (1987 song)
artist: Robbie Nevil
Wouk, Herman: 6 writer
work: Aurora Dawn
The Caine Mutiny
City Boy
Don't Stop the Carnival
The Glory
The Hope
Inside, Outside
Marjorie Morningstar
This Is My God
War and Remembrance
The Winds of War
Youngblood Hawke
would: 6 used to
possibly ~: 5 might
rather: 6 prefer 10 like better
Would __ to you?: 4 I lie
would-be: 5 quasi 8 aspiring 9 potential 10 self-styled
Would I Lie to You? (1985 song)
artist: Eurythmics
Wouldn't It Be Loverly
composer: Alan Jay Lerner, Frederick Loewe
Wouldn't It Be Nice (1966 song)
artist: Beach Boys
Wouldn't Take Nothing...
author: Maya Angelou
Would thou hadst __ been born: 4 ne'er
Would you like to swing on __?: 5 a star
wound: 3 cut, hit 4 bump, burn, clip, gash, harm, hurt, maim, nick, pain, scar, stab, welt 5 pique, prick, slash, slice, sting 6 boo-boo, bruise, coiled, damage, grieve, injure, injury, insult, lesion, mangle, offend, open up, pierce, scrape, trauma 7 anguish, contuse, scratch, torment, twisted 8 abrasion, distress, lacerate, mistreat 9 contusion, meandered 10 laceration, traumatize
cover: 4 scab 5 gauze 7 bandage
rub salt in the ~: 3 vex 5 harry 6 harass, pester, pick on, plague 7 afflict, agonize, anguish, bedevil, oppress, torment, torture 8 distress, irritate 9 persecute
slightly: 4 wing 5 prick
up: 4 taut 5 tense 7 through 8 fluttery 9 engrossed
__ wound: 5 flesh
Wound and the Bow, The
author: Edmund Wilson
wounded: 4 hurt 5 burnt 6 burned 7 injured 9 miserable
be ~: 6 suffer
cry from the ~: 5 medic
Wounded __, SD: 4 Knee
wove: 8 entwined, worked in 9 zigzagged
woven: 9 contrived 10 interlaced
material: 4 knit, mesh, wool 5 linen 6 fabric 8 barathea
starter: 4 hand
together: 4 mixt 5 mixed 6 melded, merged, united 7 blended 8 combined
wow: 3 awe, gee, man, ooh 4 gosh, stun 5 amaze, golly, oh boy, shock, smash, zowie 6 far out, jiminy, oh baby, oo-la-la, please, thrill 7 astound, attract, beguile, delight, enchant, jeepers, jimminy, omigosh, stagger, win over 8 bowl over, entrance, knock out 9 dumbfound, overwhelm, sensation, transport
starter: 3 bow
__-wow: 3 bow
Wozniak: 5 Steve
company: 5 Apple
partner: 4 Jobs
Wozzeck: 5 opera
composer: Alban Berg
W.P.: 8 Kinsella
WPA
creator: 3 FDR
project: 4 road
wpm: 4 stat.
part of ~: 3 min., per, wds. 5 words 6 minute
__-wracking: 5 nerve
wrack up: 4 ruin 5 crash, total, wreck 7 destroy, rear-end, shatter
wrack-up: 8 accident
wraith: 5 ghost, shade, spook 6 fantom, spirit 7 phantom, specter 8 presence 10 apparition
wraithlike: 7 ghostly 9 invisible 10 immaterial
wrangle: 3 row 4 earn, feud, flap, herd, spar, spat, tiff 5 argue, brawl, clash, fight, scene, scrap, set-to 6 barney, bicker, fracas, haggle, hassle, racket, ruckus, rumble, rumpus, scheme 7 connive, contest, dispute, fall out, quarrel, quibble, round up, ruction, scuffle 8 argument, brouhaha, disagree, exchange, have at it, squabble, struggle 9 brannigan, bump heads, have words, lock horns 10 contention, falling-out, tangle with
wrangler: 6 cowboy, drover, gaucho 7 cowpoke, rancher, vaquero 8 buckaroo, stockman
need: 6 lariat
Wrangler: 3 SUV 4 Jeep
Wranglers: 5 jeans, pants 9 dungarees
wrangling: 5 fight 6 strife 7 discord 8 friction, polemics 9 bellicose 10 contention, discussion
wrap: 3 boa, fur, lap 4 bind, cape, coat, do up, fold, hide, mask, pack, roll, tape, tuck, veil, wind 5 capot, cloak, cover, drape, scarf, shawl, stole, tie up, twine 6 bundle, capote, dolman, encase, enfold, ermine, finish, incase, infold, jacket, mantle, muffle, roll up, sarong, shroud, swathe 7 bandage, blanket, car coat, enclose, envelop, inclose, package, protect, sheathe, swaddle, sweater 8 bundle up, covering, encircle, enshroud, fur piece, muffle up, surround
around: 4 coil 5 twine, twist
around one's little finger: 3 use 6 misuse 7 control 10 manipulate
ender: 6 around
evening ~: 3 boa, fur 4 mink, muff 5 stole
food ~: 4 foil, Glad 5 cello, Saran 6 Baggie 7 plastic 10 cellophane
gift ~: 5 paper
Indian ~: 4 sari 5 saree
in wax: 4 cere
nautically: 4 frap
Spanish ~: 5 manta 6 sarape, serape
up: 2 do 3 cap, end 4 fold, furl, halt, quit, stop, tape 5 cease, close, enrol, truss 6 enfold, enroll, finish, infold 7 adjourn, envelop, play out 8 complete, conclude, finalize, pack it in, transact 9 terminate 10 call it a day, consummate
__ wrap: 3 ear 4 gift, word 6 bubble 7 plastic
__-wrap: 4 gift 5 plain 6 shrink
__ Wrap: 5 Saran
wrapped: 4 done
homophone: 4 rapt
in red tape: 5 sat on
up: 6 intent 7 engaged, through 8 absorbed, immersed, obsessed 9 engrossed
wrapped __: 4 up in
Wrapped Around Your Finger (1984 song)
artist: Police
wrapper: 4 robe 6 casing 8 covering, envelope
still in the ~: 3 new 6 unused 8 brand-new 9 untouched
wrapping
material: 5 twine
paper: 5 kraft
wiener ~: 6 casing
wraps
keep under ~: 5 sit on 6 hush up 7 secrete
take the ~ off: 4 bare, open 6 expose, reveal, unmask 7 lay bare, uncover
under ~: 6 covert, hidden, masked, secret, unseen, veiled 7 cloaked, furtive, private 8 hush-hush, obscured, secluded, shrouded, stealthy, ulterior 9 concealed, disguised 10 tucked away
__ wraps: 5 under
wrap-up: 3 end 5 recap 6 ending, epilog, finale, finish 7 summary 8 terminus 9 summation 10 conclusion, denouement, resolution
wrath: 3 ire, sin 4 bile, fury, hate, rage 5 anger 6 choler, dander, rancor, spleen, temper 7 dudgeon, offense, outrage, passion, umbrage 8 acrimony, asperity, vexation 10 irritation, resentment
wrathful: 3 hot, mad 4 ired, sore 5 angry, cross, huffy, irate, livid, riled, wroth 6 fuming, heated, ireful, peeved, raging, raving, red-hot, stormy 7 enraged, furious, ranting 8 choleric, incensed, inflamed, maddened, outraged, storming 9 indignant, irritated, resentful, splenetic 10 displeased, freaked out, infuriated
Wray: 3 Fay 4 Link
role: Ann Darrow
wreak: 4 vent, work 5 visit, wreck 6 incite 7 inflict, unleash 8 carry out 9 force upon, knock down, retaliate 10 bring about, perpetrate
havoc on: 4 loot, raid, ruin, sack 5 rifle, spoil, strip, waste, wreck 6 harrow, maraud, ravage 7 despoil, destroy, pillage, plunder, ransack 9 depredate, desecrate, devastate, vandalize
vengeance: 3 fix, get 9 retaliate
wreath: 3 lei 4 haku, loop, ring 5 crown 6 anadem, diadem, laurel 7 chaplet, circlet, coronet, festoon, garland
bridal ~: 5 plant 6 flower
heraldic ~: 5 torse
laurel ~ alternative: 5 medal
ornamental: 4 cone
place for a ~: 4 brow
Wreath and a Curse, A
author: Robert Anderson
wreathe: 4 coil, curl, wind 5 twine, twist 7 sinuate 10 interweave
with laurels: 5 honor
wreck: 3 mar, sap 4 bash, dash, harm, heap, hulk, hurt, mess, rase, raze, ruin, sink, undo 5 beach, blast, botch, break, crack, crash, crate, crush, level, relic, shock, smash, spoil, total, trash 6 bang up, batter, blight, damage, debris, derail, impair, jalopy, junker, mangle, pile-up, quench, ravage, topple 7 butcher, capsize, crack up, debacle, despoil, destroy, disable, failure, flatten, founder, louse up, scuttle, shatter, smash-up, subvert, torpedo, tragedy, wrack up 8 accident, bulldoze, demolish, derelict, lay waste, pull down, sabotage, spoliate, take down, tear down 9 collision, devastate, dismantle, knock down, overwhelm, pulverize, rear-ender, take apart, undermine, vandalize 10 demolition, rattletrap, run aground
ender: 3 age
starter: 4 ship
__-Wreck: 5 Rent-a
wreckage: 4 loss, ruin 5 havoc, ruins 6 debris 7 flotsam
wrecked: 4 lost 5 kaput 6 undone 8 finished, stranded
vessel: 4 hulk
wrecker: 3 tow 8 tow truck
need: 5 crane, hoist
wrecker's __: 4 ball
wrecking __: 3 bar, car 4 crew 5 crane
Wreck of the Edmund Fitzgerald, The (1976 song)
artist: Gordon Lightfoot
Wreck of the Hesperus, The
author: Henry Wadsworth Longfellow
Wreck of the Mary __, The: 5 Deare
wren: 4 bird 7 warbler 8 songbird
__ wren: 3 emu
wrench: 3 rip, tug 4 jerk, pang, pull, rack, tear, tool, turn, warp, yank 5 exact, force, screw, seize, twist, wrest, wring 6 extort, snatch, sprain, strain 7 contort, distort, spanner, squeeze 9 dislocate
monkey ~: 4 snag 5 block, crimp, hitch, snarl 7 barrier, problem, setback 8 handicap, obstacle 10 impediment
open: 4 rive
part: 3 jaw
throw a monkey ~ into: 5 block

6 hamper, hinder 7 disrupt 8 obstruct, sabotage 9 frustrate, undermine
__ wrench: 3 lug 4 pipe 5 Allen 6 monkey, socket
__-wrenching: 3 gut
Wren, Christopher: 3 Sir 7 British 9 architect
wrest: 3 pry, tug 4 levy, pull, tear, yank 5 exact, seize, usurp, wring 6 extort, ravage, snatch, wrench 7 deprive, distort, extract 9 force away
out: 5 pluck 9 extirpate
wrestle: 4 cope 5 fight 6 battle, strive, tussle 7 contend, grapple, scuffle 8 struggle
Wrestle ender: 5 mania
wrestlers, like: 5 beefy 6 brawny
wrestling: 5 sport
defeat again, in ~: 5 repin
Japanese: 4 sumo
locale: 5 arena
maneuver: 3 pin 4 hold, lock, slam 6 nelson 7 armlock 8 headlock, scissors
match: 4 bout 5 fight, round 6 tussle 7 contest 9 encounter
official: 3 ref 5 timer 7 referee
pro ~ org.: 3 WWF
result: 3 pin 4 draw
round: 4 fall
surface: 3 mat 6 canvas
__ wrestling: 3 arm, mud 4 sumo 5 wrist 6 Indian
wretch: 3 cur 4 toad 5 sneak 6 misfit, pariah, rascal, victim 7 outcast, sad case, sad sack, villain 8 sufferer 9 miscreant, poor devil, reprobate, scoundrel 10 blackguard
wretched: 3 low, sad 4 base, mean, vile 5 awful, ratty, sorry 6 abject, broody, bummed, dreary, flimsy, gloomy, grotty, grungy, humble, paltry, shabby, sordid 7 crushed, forlorn, hapless, hurting, ignoble, in a funk, low-down, piteous, pitiful, squalid, unhappy 8 beggarly, dejected, desolate, dolorous, downcast, God-awful, hopeless, luckless, pathetic, pitiable, unworthy 9 afflicted, cheerless, depressed, desperate, in the pits, sorrowful, thankless, woebegone, worthless 10 despairing, despondent, distressed, down-and-out, melancholy, pathetical
feel ~: 3 ail 6 suffer
see also awful
wretchedness: 3 woe 4 pain 5 grief 6 misery, sorrow 7 despair, squalor
wriggle: 4 worm 5 crawl, creep, snake, twist 6 jiggle, squirm, thrash, twitch, wiggle, writhe
wriggler: 3 eel 5 larva
wriggly: 4 eely 7 squirmy
wright: 5 maker
starter: 4 mill, play, ship, wain 5 wheel
Wright: 3 Amy 4 Gary, town 5 Betty, Chely, James, Robin 6 Judith, Mickey, Morris, Teresa, Wilbur 7 Charles, Orville, Richard
Wright, Frank Lloyd: 9 architect
Wright, Mickey: 6 golfer
Wright-Patterson: 3 AFB
__ Wright Penn: 5 Robin
Wright, Richard: 6 writer
work: Native Son
Wright, Robin: 7 actress
film: Forrest Gump (1994)
Message in a Bottle (1999)
The Pledge (2001)
The Princess Bride (1987)
State of Grace (1990)
spouse: Sean Penn
Wrigley: 4 Bill, Phil 6 Philip 7 William
product: 3 gum 10 chewing gum
Wrigley Field: 5 arena 8 ballpark
home: 3 Chi. 7 Chicago
like ~ walls: 4 viny 5 ivied
player: 3 Cub
wring: 3 dry, pry 4 levy, milk, rack 5 choke, exact, force, screw, twist, wrest 6 coerce, dry out, extort, wrench 7 contort, extract, squeeze 8 compress, strangle, throttle
wringer
hand ~: 4 ruer
put through the ~: 5 grill 7 torment 8 question 9 challenge
wringing wet: 5 soggy, soppy 10 bedraggled
wrinkle: 4 fold, line, muss, ruck 5 crimp, crush, purse, ridge, twist 6 crease, furrow, method, pucker, ruffle, rumple, shrink 7 crinkle, crumple, scrunch, shrivel 8 compress 9 corrugate, crow's-foot
anatomical ~: 4 ruga
new ~: 4 rage 5 trend 9 departure
wrinkled: 5 seamy 6 rugged 7 wizened 8 leathery 9 roughened 10 corrugated, disheveled
wrinkle-resistant fabric: 5 Orlon 6 Dacron
wrinkles
remove ~: 4 iron 5 press 8 facelift
wrist: 5 joint
bone: 6 carpal, carpus, hamate
combining form: 5 carpo-
coverer: 6 sleeve
ender: 4 band, lock 5 watch
jewelry: 5 chain 6 bangle 8 bracelet
movement: 5 flick
neighbor: 4 hand 7 forearm
nerve: 5 ulnar
slap on the ~: 5 chide, scold 6 punish, rebuke 7 lecture, reprove, upbraid 8 admonish, reproach 9 reprehend, reprimand
wristband: 4 cuff
wristlet: 6 bangle, gewgaw 7 jewelry, trinket 8 ornament
wristwatch: 4 Rado 5 Casio, Elgin, Lorus, Omega, Rolex, Seiko, Timex 6 Bulova, Fossil, Movado, Pulsar, Swatch 7 Citizen 8 Longines, Tag Heuer, Tourneau 9 timepiece
writ: 3 law 4 mise 5 paper 6 decree, elegit 7 command, mandate, process, refusal, summons, warrant 8 document, replevin, sanction, subpoena 9 prescript 10 court order, injunction
writ __: 5 large
__ Writ: 4 Holy 6 Sacred
write: 3 ink, jot, pen 4 copy, sign 5 draft, ghost, print 6 author, draw up, indite, notify, pencil, record, scrawl, scribe 7 bang out, compose, dash off, engross, jot down, produce, publish, put down, set down, turn out 8 inscribe, knock off, knock out, mark down, note down, scribble, set forth, take down 9 autograph, drop a line, formulate, lucubrate 10 correspond, journalize, put on paper, transcribe
able to read and ~: 8 literate
a check: 4 draw
anew: 5 repen
at length: 6 ramble 7 expound 9 expatiate 10 dissertate
back: 5 reply 6 answer 9 respond to
down: 4 list, note 6 record 7 devalue 8 register 9 devaluate 10 transcribe
hastily: 3 jot 4 dash 6 scrawl
nothing to ~ home about: 4 fair, so-so 7 average 8 mediocre, middling, ordinary, passable 9 tolerable
off: 4 drop 5 amort., lower 6 cancel, deduct, forget, pardon 7 devalue, discard 8 amortize, give up on 9 devaluate, downgrade, underrate 10 undervalue
one's name: 4 sign 9 autograph
on metal: 4 etch
on the front: 6 enface
plans for: 4 spec 7 spec out
software: 6 encode 7 program
starter: 4 type 5 ghost
to: 5 reach 7 contact 8 approach 9 check with, touch base 10 get a hold of
up: 5 cover 8 describe 9 expound on, publicize
without credit: 5 ghost
write __: 3 off, out 4 down
write-in __: 4 vote
write-off: 9 abatement, deduction
writer: 3 Ade, Bly, Day, Lee, Nin, Poe, Tan 4 Agee, Asch, Auel, Bate, Baum, Buck, Bull, Cain, Cobb, Cook, Dana, Dick, Dove, Edel, Fast, Gale, Gass, Grau, Grey, Hall, Hart, Inge, Jong, King, Koch, Loos, Luce, Mead, Muir, Nash, poet, Pohl, Puzo, Rand, Reed, Rice, Riis, Roth, Saki, Shaw, Tate, Uris, Ward, West, Wouk 5 Adams, Aiken, Albee, Alger, Barry, Barth, Beard, Benet, Berry, Blish, Bloom, Blume, Bogan, Boyle, Brown, Busch, Cable, Chase, Child, Clark, Corso, Crane, Dodge, Drury, Dunne, Elkin, Fromm, Frost, Glück, Green, Greer, Guare, Haley, Harte, Hayne, Hearn, Hecht, Henry, Herne, Hicks, Himes, Hurst, James, Jones, Kesey, Kopit, Kumin, Levin, Lewis, Lurie, Mamet, Oates, O'Hara, Paley, Percy, Plath, Potok, Price, Purdy, Riley, Royce, Selby, Seton, Seuss, Sheed, Simms, Smith, Steel, Stein, Stone, Stout, Stowe, Tryon, Turow, Twain, Tyler, Vidal, Waugh, Welty, White, Wolfe, Wylie, Yerby 6 Alcott, Algren, Asimov, Auster, author, Baraka, Barlow, Barnes, Barzun, Bellow, Berger, Bester, Bidart, Bierce, Bowles, Brooks, Bryant, Butler, Capote, Carson, Carver, Cather, Catton, Chopin, Ciardi, Cooper, Coover, critic, Cullen, De Voto, Dickey, Didion, Dobyns, Dunbar, Duncan, Durant, Dwight, Ferber, Fisher, Forché, French, Fuller, Gaddis, Gaines, Gelber, Gibson, Gilman, Godwin, Harper, Harris, Hawkes, Hayden, Heller, Henley, Hersey, Hobson, Hoffer, Holmes, Horgan, Howard, Hughes, Hunter, Irving, Judson, Keller, Knebel, Knight, Koontz, Krantz, London, Lowell, Ludlum, Mailer, Merton, Millay, Miller, Morley, Morris, Motley, Nevins, Norris, Norton, O'Neill, Parker, Peirce, Porter, Rogers, Rosten, Runyon, Sandoz, scribe, Shirer, Snyder, Sontag, Sparks, Styron, Updike, Walker, Warner, Warren, Wiesel, Wilder, Wilson, Wright 7 Angelou, Ashbery, Baldwin, Bambara, Beattie, Beecher, Bennett, Biggers, Brodkey, Bullins, Burgess, Carruth, Cheever, Clavell, Costain, Cozzens, Creeley, DeLillo, DeMille, De Vries, Diderot, Dillard, Dreiser, Ellison, Ellmann, Emerson, Erdrich, Farrell, Friedan, Gardner, Garland, Gaskell, Glasgow, Grafton, Greeley, Gregory, Gunther, Guthrie, Hammett, Hellman, Herbert, Heyward, Howells, Hurston, Ignatow, Jackson, Jansson, Jarrell, Jeffers, Johnson, Kaufman, Kennedy, Kerouac, Kinnell, La Farge, Lardner, Lazarus, Malamud, Marcuse, Marquis, Masters, McKenny, Mencken, Merrill, Mitford, Mumford, Niebuhr, O'Connor, Parkman, Pynchon, Richter, Robbins, Roberts, Rölvaag, Sanders, Saroyan, Sheldon, Skinner, Stegner, Stevens, Tarbell, Theroux, Thoreau, Thurber, Wallace, Webster, Weidman, Wescott, Wharton, Winters 8 Anderson, Bartlett, Benchley, Berenson, Berryman, Billings, Bontemps, Bradbury, Bukowski, Buntline, Caldwell, Calisher, Chandler, Clampitt, Connelly, Crichton, cummings, DeForest, Doctorow, Eberhart, essayist, Faulkner, Friedman, Ginsberg, Glaspell, Gurganus, Hoagland, Kinsella, Koestler, Kosinski, MacLeish, Marquand, McCarthy, McMurtry, Melville, Michener, Mitchell, Morrison, Nordhoff, novelist, O'Donnell, Perelman, Phillips, Pulitzer, Rawlings, reporter, Rinehart, Salinger, Sandburg, Sinclair, Southern, Spillane, Spingarn, Stafford, Steffens, Sullivan, Vonnegut, Williams, Zukofsky 9 Barthelme, Bemelmans, Bodenheim, Burroughs, Buscaglia, Chayefsky, Childress, columnist, Dos Passos, dramatist, Gernsback, Hansberry, Hawthorne, Hemingway, Highsmith, Kellerman, Lindbergh, Macdonald, McCullers, Podhoretz, Roosevelt, Santayana, Schulberg, scribbler, Steinbeck, Woollcott, wordsmith, Yourcenar

10 biographer, Bradstreet, Fitzgerald, freelancer, Halberstam, journalist, Kingsolver, librettist, playwright, Tarkington, Untermeyer, Willingham **11** Auchincloss, Matthiessen, Schlesinger, Schoolcraft, Stratemeyer, Thackeray, Whitehead, Wodehouse **10** Bainbridge, Chesterton, Galsworthy, Muggeridge, Richardson

Algerian ~: 6 Djebar
Argentine ~: 6 Borges, Gálvez, Sábato **8** Cortázar **9** Güiraldes, Sarmiento **11** Bioy Casares
Australian ~: 4 Stow, West **5** Stead, White **6** Furphy, Jolley, Palmer, Porter **7** Herbert, Manning, Travers **8** Franklin, Keneally **9** Moorehead **10** McCullough
Austrian ~: 5 Broch, Freud, Kafka, Kraus, Musil, Zweig **6** Handke, Lorenz, Werfel **7** Stifter **8** Bernhard **9** Aichinger **10** Wassermann
Belgian ~: 10 Conscience
Bosnian ~: 6 Andric
Brazilian ~: 5 Amado, Ramos **7** Alencar, Queiròs
British ~: 3 Pym **4** Amis, Cary, Dahl, Ford, Glyn, Hall, Lamb, Lear, More, Rhys, Ryle, Snow, Wain, West **5** Arlen, Auden, Bates, Blunt, Bowen, Byatt, Defoe, Doyle, Eliot, Frayn, Green, Hardy, James, Lewis, Locke, Mason, Menen, Milne, Moore, Murry, Noyes, Orczy, Paine, Pater, Pepys, Powys, Reade, Rolfe, Shute, Watts, Waugh, Wells, White, Woolf, Young **6** Aldiss, Ambler, Austen, Barnes, Binyon, Braine, Brontë, Brophy, Browne, Bryher, Bunyan, Burney, Butler, Clarke, Conrad, Evelyn, Fowles, Fraser, Gibbon, Graves, Greene, Hallam, Hilton, Hudson, Huxley, Milton, Morgan, Morris, Orwell, Petrie, Popper, Potter, Powell, Ruskin, Sansom, Sayers, Sterne, Storey, Symons, Walton, Warner, Warton, Wilson **7** Bennett, Bentley, Blunden, Burgess, Carroll, Chatwin, Collins, Corelli, Dickens, Douglas, Drabble, Durrell, Firbank, Fleming, Forster, Francis, Gissing, Golding, Grahame, Haggard, Hartley, Hazlitt, Johnson, Kipling, le Carré, Marryat, Marston, Maugham, Meynell, Mitford, Montagu, Painter, Peacock, Renault, Russell, Shelley, Sitwell, Spencer, Stephen, Stewart, Surtees, Tolkien, Toynbee, Ustinov, Walpole **8** Beerbohm, Brookner, Christie, Connelly, Fielding, Forester, Jhabvala, Lawrence, Macaulay, Matineau, Meredith, Mortimer, Quennell, Runciman, Sillitoe, Smollett, Strachey, Trollope, Williams **9** Blackwood, Churchill, du Maurier, Goldsmith, Isherwood, Masefield, Massinger, Mitchison, Partridge, Priestley, Pritchett, Radcliffe, Stapledon,
Bulgarian-born ~: 7 Canetti
Cameroonian ~: 4 Beti
Canadian ~: 3 Roy **5** Blais, Engel, Moore, Mowat, Munro, Wiebe **6** Atwood, Davies, Moodie, Nowlan, Parker, Wilson **7** Findley, Gallant, McLuhan, Richter **9** Callaghan **10** Haliburton, Montgomery
Chilean ~: 5 Rojas **6** Bombal, Donoso **7** Allende, Barrios, Dorfman, Edwards **9** Blest Gana
Chinese ~: 6 Lao She, Lao-tzu, Pa Chin
Colombian ~: 6 Rivera **7** Márquez
Cuban ~: 5 Martí **6** Arenas, Barnet **10** Carpentier
Czech ~: 5 Capek, Hasek, Klíma **6** Hrabal **7** Jirásek, Kundera **9** Skvorecky
Danish ~: 4 Bang, Nexö **6** Jensen **7** Dinesen, Holberg **8** Andersen, Jacobsen **9** Gjellerup
deg.: 3 BFA, MFA **4** Lit.B., Lit.M.
Dutch ~: 7 Erasmus, Spinoza **8** Couperus
Ecuadoran ~: 5 Adoum **8** Montalvo
Egyptian ~: 9 el Saadawi
Finnish ~: 4 Kivi **5** Canth **8** Haavikko **9** Sillanpää
French ~: 3 Sue **4** Aymé, Gary, Gide, Hugo, Loti, Sade, Sand, Weil, Zola **5** Butor, Camus, Dumas, Duras, Giono, Green, Hémon, Renan, Sagan, Simon, Taine, Verne **6** Aragon, Balzac, Barrès, Belloc, Boulle, Céline, Cixous, Daudet, France, Guitry, Lesage, Marcel, Pascal, Proust, Sartre **7** Aubigné, Bergson, Bourget, Claudel, Cocteau, Colette, Duhamel, Mauriac, Maurois, Mérimée, Prévost, Queneau, Rolland, Romains, Scudéry, Simenon **8** Bataille, Beauvoir, Bernanos, Cendrars, Flaubert, Goncourt, Gringore, Huysmans, Maritain, Perrault, Proudhon, Rabelais, Rousseau, Sarraute, Stendhal, Voltaire **9** Giraudoux, Montaigne **10** La Fontaine, Maupassant, Oldenbourg **11** Montesquieu, Sainte-Beuve
German ~: 4 Benn, Böll, Mann, Marx **5** Arnim, Grass, Grimm, Hesse, Heyse, Raabe, Zweig **6** Döblin, Goethe, Heinse, Jünger, Kleist, Luther, Walser **7** Fontane, Freytag, Gutzkow, Hoffman, Johnson, Novalis, Richter, Wieland **8** Borchert, Remarque, Spengler, Wedekind **10** Schliemann
Ghanaian ~: 5 Aidoo, Armah **7** Awoonor
Greek ~: 5 Plato **6** Zoilus **8** Plotinus, Plutarch, Xenophon **11** Kazantzakis
Guadeloupean ~: 5 Condé
Guatemalan ~: 8 Asturias
Guyanese ~: 6 Harris
Hebrew ~: 5 Agnon
Hungarian ~: 6 Molnár
ID: 6 byline
Indian ~: 3 Rao **5** Anand, Desai, Mehta **6** Hosain, Tagore **7** Narayan, Rushdie **9** Premchand **10** Markandaya
Irish ~: 5 Behan, Joyce, Moore **6** Binchy, Crofts, Heaney, O'Brien **7** Beckett, Maturin, Murdoch, O'Connor **8** Carleton, Donleavy, O'Faolain **9** Edgeworth, O'Flaherty
Israeli ~: 2 Oz **7** Amichai **9** Appelfeld
Italian ~: 3 Eco **5** Svevo **6** Basile, Silone **7** Alberti, Alfieri, Aretino, Bassani, Calvino, Capuana, Cassola, Collodi, Deledda, Foscolo, Manzoni, Morante, Moravia, Rovetta **8** Ginzburg **18** Pico della Mirandola
Jamaican ~: 7 Brodber
Japanese ~: 2 Oe **7** Abe Kobo, Mishima **8** Kawabata, Mori Ōgai **9** Nagai Kafu **10** Dazai Osamu **11** Endo Shusaku
jingle ~: 5 adman
Lebanese ~: 6 Gibran
Martinican ~: 8 Glissant
Mexican ~: 5 Rulfo, Yañez **6** Azuela, Guzmán **7** Fuentes
Moroccan ~: 10 Ben Jelloun
name meaning ~: 9 Schreiber
need: 3 pad, pen **5** paper **6** editor, eraser, pencil
New Zealand ~: 5 Frame, Marsh **8** Ihimaera, Sargeson **9** Mansfield
Nigerian ~: 5 Aluko, Amadi, Nwapa **6** Achebe **7** Ekwensi, Equiano, Munonye
Norwegian ~: 4 Duun **5** Bojer **6** Hamsun, Sandel **10** Falkberget
Old English ~: 7 Aelfric
org.: 3 BMI, PEN **5** ASCAP
Peruvian ~: 5 Palma **7** Alegría **8** Arguedas
Philippine ~: 5 Rizal
Polish ~: 6 Milosz, Mrozek **8** Borowski, Konwicki **10** Gombrowicz **11** Sienkiewicz
Puerto Rican ~: 5 Ferré
Roman ~: 4 Livy **5** Pliny **7** Martial, Sallust, Tacitus **9** Suetonius
Russian ~: 4 Grin **5** Babel, Gogol, Gorky **6** Daniel, Ivanov, Krylov, Kuprin, Olesha, Panova, Yashin **7** Aksakov, Amalrik, Bryusov, Fadayev, Gladkov, Katayev, Nabokov, Pushkin, Rozanov, Sologub, Tolstoy **8** Aksyonov, Andreyev, Bulgakov, Karamzin, Nekrasov, Saltykov, Sloukhin, Turgenev, Zamyatin **9** Goncharov, Sholokhov, Sinyavsky **10** Zoshchenko **11** Aleshkovsky, Dostoyevsky **12** Solzhenitsyn
Salvadoran ~: 7 Alegría
Scottish ~: 3 Tey **5** Scott, Smith, Spark **6** Buchan, Cronin **7** Boswell, Carlyle **8** Mitchell **9** Stevenson
South African ~: 4 Head **5** Paton **6** Cloete, Fugard, Plomer **7** Coetzee **8** Abrahams, Gordimer, Jacobson **9** Schreiner **10** Van der Post
Spanish ~: 3 Aub **4** Cela **5** Benet **6** Alemán, Chacel, Marías, Matute, Sender **7** Alarcón, Arrabal, Unamuno **8** Marquina **9** Cervantes, Gironella **11** Pérez Galdós
starter: 3 sky **4** copy, song, type **5** ghost, speed, story **6** screen, script, speech, sports
Swedish ~: 5 Weiss **6** Bremer, Moberg, Myrdal, Wägner, Wahlöö **7** Bergman, Johnson, Sjöwall **8** Almqvist, Lagerlöf, Matinson **9** Söderberg **10** Lagerkvist, Swedenborg
Swiss ~: 5 Meyer, Ramuz, Spyri **6** Frisch, Piaget
Trinidadian ~: 6 Selvon
unskilled ~: 4 hack
Uruguayan ~: 6 Reyles **9** Benedetti
Venezuelan ~: 8 Gallegos
Welsh ~: 3 Map **4** Abse **6** Thomas **7** Nennius **8** Williams
West Indian ~: 7 Naipaul, Walcott
Yiddish ~: 6 Singer **8** Aleichem

__ writer: 5 ghost
writer's __: 5 block, cramp
write-up: 4 puff **5** story **6** report, review **7** article **9** publicity
writhe: 4 jerk **5** crawl, creep, flail, twist, wince **6** recoil, squirm, suffer, thrash, thresh, wiggle **7** agonize, contort, wriggle **8** struggle **10** twist about
writhing: 5 snaky **7** sinuous **10** serpentine
writing: 3 ode **4** book, opus, play, poem, tome, work **5** diary, essay, novel, paper, piece, print, prose, story, theme, tract **6** column, letter, medium, record, review, scrawl, script, thesis, volume **7** article, caption, journal, letters **8** document, libretto, longhand, pamphlet, scribble, treatise **9** autograph, cuneiform, discourse, editorial, reference, shorthand, signature, term paper **10** journalism, literature, manuscript, penmanship
bad ~: 4 slop **5** tripe **8** hack work
brief ~: 5 squib
collection: 4 anth. **7** omnibus **9** anthology
combining form: 6 grapho-, -graphy
comprised of quotes: 5 cento
dull, as ~: 5 prosy
manner: 4 vein
metrical ~: 3 ode **4** poem **5** verse
need: 3 ink, pen **6** marker, pencil, stylus
on the wall: 4 omen, sign **7** portent, warning **8** graffiti
piece of ~: 3 ode **4** book, memo, note, play, poem, text **5** essay, music, novel, prose, story, theme, verse **6** thesis **7** article **8** material **10** literature
put in ~: 3 log, pen **4** mark **5** enter **6** record **7** catalog, jot down, set down **8** mark down, take down **10** transcribe
secret ~: 4 code **6** cipher
starter: 3 sky **4** hand, type **5** spee[d] **6** screen, script, speech

style: 5 genre
table: 4 desk 7 rolltop 9 secretary
writing ___: 4 desk 5 paper
writing ___ wall: 5 on the
Writing on the Wall, The (1961 song)
artist: Adam Wade
written
articles may be ~ on it: 4 spec 5 paper
communication: 4 line 6 letter 7 missive
history: 6 annals, record
___ Written in a Country Churchyard: 5 Elegy
Written in the Stars (1999 song)
artist: LeAnn Rimes
Written on the Wind (1956 film)
cast: Lauren Bacall, Rock Hudson, Robert Stack
Wroclaw: 4 city, town
locale: 6 Poland
river: 4 Oder, Odra
wrong: 3 bad, ill, sin 4 awry, base, evil, goof, harm, hurt, tort, vice, wide 5 abuse, amiss, askew, badly, cheat, crime, error, false, fault, funny, guilt, inapt, libel, lying, shady, spite 6 adrift, afield, all wet, amoral, astray, damage, defame, errant, erring, faulty, felony, gauche, guilty, injure, injury, insult, liable, malign, offend, rotten, slight, unfair, unjust, untrue, way off, wicked 7 affront, at fault, awkward, blunder, crooked, cruelty, erratic, faux pas, foolish, illegal, illicit, immoral, in error, inexact, invalid, inverse, misdeed, naughty, not done, off-base, offense, oppress, outrage, reverse, slander, to blame, two-time, unsound 8 aggrieve, blamable, criminal, culpable, dishonor, foul play, ill-treat, improper, indecent, inequity, iniquity, maltreat, misdoing, mistaken, mistreat, perverse, shameful, specious, unfairly, unjustly, unlawful, villainy 9 blameable, discredit, erroneous, felonious, grievance, harmfully, ill-suited, imprudent, incorrect, injustice, misguided, off-target, out of line, persecute, turpitude, unethical, violation 10 censurable, despicable, detestable, fallacious, groundless, ill-advised, immorality, impose upon, inaccurate, inapposite, infraction, malapropos, mendacious, misfigured, mishandled, misleading, mistakenly, oppression, out of order, out of place, ungrounded, unsuitable, wickedness
application: 6 misuse
back the ~ horse: 4 lose
be ~: 3 err 7 blunder, mistake 8 misjudge
be rubbed the ~ way: 4 mind 6 resent 8 object to
do ~: 3 err, sin 5 stray 9 misbehave
ender: 4 doer 5 doing
give the ~ idea: 4 dupe, fool, hoax, scam 5 bluff, cheat, put on, trick 6 delude, lead on, rope in, suck in, take in 7 confuse, deceive, defraud, mislead 8 hoodwink, inveigle, misguide, throw off 9 misinform 10 lead astray
go ~: 3 err 4 bomb, bust, fail, flop, lose, slip, trip 5 flunk, misdo, stray 6 blow it, falter 7 blunder, founder, misstep, stumble, wash out 8 fall flat, flounder, lay an egg 9 misbehave, strike out
have something ~: 3 ail 4 hurt 6 suffer
ignorant of right and ~: 6 amoral
in the ~: 6 guilty, liable 7 at fault, to blame 8 blamable, culpable 9 blameable
legal ~: 4 tort
marked ~: 3 x'ed
morally ~: 3 bad 4 evil 6 horrid, sinful, wicked 7 baneful, corrupt, heinous, immoral 8 depraved 9 nefarious 10 villainous
prefix: 3 mal-, mis-
prove ~: 5 parry, rebut 6 negate, oppugn, refute 7 confute, explode 8 disprove, overturn 10 contradict, controvert, invalidate
right a ~: 6 avenge 7 get even, pay back, redress, requite 9 retaliate, retribute
rubbing the ~ way: 5 nasty 7 caustic 8 abrasive 10 unpleasant
rub the ~ way: 3 get, ire, irk, vex 4 miff, rile, roil 5 anger, annoy, chafe, grate, peeve 6 abrade, offend
way: 8 backward 9 backwards 10 upside-down
Wrong ___ Corrigan: 3 Way
wrongdoer: 4 perp 8 criminal 9 miscreant 10 delinquent
wrongdoing: 3 sin 4 evil 5 abuse, fault 7 knavery, misdeed, offense, outrage, scandal 8 iniquity, mischief, trespass 9 improbity, injustice
aid in ~: 4 abet 7 collude
lure into ~: 5 snare, tempt, trick 6 entrap, lead on, suck in 7 beguile, ensnare 8 entangle, inveigle
___ wrong foot: 5 on the
wrongful: 4 evil, tabu 5 taboo 6 banned, unfair, unjust, wicked 7 illegal, illicit, immoral, lawless 8 criminal, improper, outlawed, unlawful, verboten 9 dishonest, felonious, forbidden, injurious, unethical 10 prohibited
act, in law: 4 tort
combining form: 3 mal-
wrong-headed: 6 unwise 9 impolitic, imprudent, misguided 10 ill-advised
Wrong Man, The (1957 film)
cast: Henry Fonda, Vera Miles
director: Alfred Hitchcock
___, Wrong Number: 5 Sorry
wrong way
be rubbed the ~: 4 mind 6 resent 8 object to
Wrong Way ___: 8 Corrigan
wroth: 3 hot, mad 4 ired, sore 5 angry, cross, huffy, irate, livid, riled 6 fuming, ireful, peeved, raging, raving, red-hot, stormy 7 boiling, enraged, furious, ranting, steamed, violent 8 choleric, incensed, inflamed, maddened, outraged, seething, white-hot, wrathful 9 indignant, irritated, resentful, splenetic, turbulent 10 freaked out, infuriated
wrought: 4 done 6 worked 8 executed, rendered 9 performed
highly ~: 5 gaudy, showy 6 ornate 7 opulent 9 elaborate, luxurious 10 ornamented
wrought ___: 4 iron
wrought-up: 4 wild 5 angry, huffy, irate, manic, rabid 6 crazed, raving, roused 7 excited, furious 8 frenzied, incensed 9 indignant 10 flipped out, freaked out
WRX: 3 car 4 auto 6 Subaru
wry: 3 dry 4 awry, bent 5 askew, droll 6 aslant, ironic, rueful, skewed 7 crooked, cynical, mocking, twisted 8 lopsided, perverse, sardonic 9 contorted, distorted, sarcastic
look: 4 moue
___ W's: 4 five
W.S.: 6 Merwin 7 Gilbert, Van Dyke
W. Somerset ___: 7 Maugham
W's, one of the five: 3 who, why 4 what, when 5 where
WSU
conference: 6 Pac-Ten
team: 7 Cougars
WSW: 3 dir.
opposite: 3 ENE
wt.: 2 cg., ct., gm., gr., kg., kt., lb., mg., oz. 4 avdp. 5 avoir.
wts. and meas. agency: 3 NBS
Wuhl, Robert: 5 actor
TV: Arli$$
wunderbar: 4 fine, neat 5 dandy, grand, great, super 6 superb 7 awesome, stellar 8 fabulous, five-star, glorious, smashing, splendid, terrific, topnotch 9 excellent, fantastic, first-rate, marvelous 10 first-class, phenomenal
Wunderbar
composer: Cole Porter
wunderkind: 5 comer 7 prodigy, whiz kid
wurst: 4 meat 7 sausage
starter: 4 brat 5 knack, knock, liver 6 wiener
___-Württemberg: 5 Baden
WUSA (1970 film)
cast: Paul Newman, Anthony Perkins, Joanne Woodward
wuss: 4 nerd 5 dweeb 8 weakling 11 milquetoast
Wuthering Heights: 4 film 5 novel
author: Emily Brontë
cast: David Niven, Merle Oberon, Laurence Olivier
cat: 9 Grimalkin
character: 4 Dean 5 Cathy, Edgar, Nelly 6 Linton 7 Hareton, Hindley 8 Earnshaw, Isabella 9 Catherine 10 Heathcliff
director: William Wyler
dog: 4 Juno, Wolf 7 Gnasher, Skulker
like ~: 6 Gothic
setting: 4 moor
___-Wuzzy: 5 Fuzzy
W. Va.
neighbor: 3 Ken. 4 Ohio, Penn.
setting: 3 EDT, EST
see also West Virginia
WWI
airplane: 4 Spad
battle: 4 Yser 5 Marne, Somme, Ypres
leader: 4 Foch, Spee 6 Kaiser 8 Pershing
soldier: 5 Anzac, poilu 8 doughboy
soldiers: 3 AEF, RAF
venue: 3 Eur.
WWII
address: 3 APO
agcy.: 3 OPA, OSS, OWI
aircraft carrier: 6 Hornet
arena: 3 ETO
auxiliary: 4 WAAC, WAAF
battle site: 4 Caen, St. Lô 5 Anzio 6 Bataan
bomber: 5 Stuka
Brit. group: 3 RAF 4 WAAF
celebration: 5 VE Day, VJ Day
code machine: 6 Enigma
conference site: 5 Cairo, Yalta 6 Tehran 7 Potsdam
craft: 3 LCI, LCT, LST 5 E-boat, U-boat 6 amtrac, PT boat 7 amtrack
fare: 4 Spam
female: 3 WAC 4 WAAC, Wasp, Wave
fliers: 3 AAF, RAF, WAF
general: 3 DDE
gun: 4 Bren, Sten 6 ack ack, garand
journalist: 4 Pyle
nickname: 3 Hap, Ike
one-third of a ~ film title: 4 Tora
Pope: 4 Pius
side: 4 Axis 6 Allies
soldier: 2 GI 5 Amvet, GI Joe
sub detector: 5 asdic, sonar
supply base: 3 Lae
turning point: 4 D-Day
underground: 3 EAM 4 EDES, ELAS 6 Maquis
vehicle: 4 jeep, tank
weapon: 5 A-bomb
WWW: 3 Net 8 Internet
address: 3 URL
address source: 3 ISP
address starter: 4 http
connector: 5 modem
part of ~: 3 Web 4 Wide 5 World
periodical: 5 e-zine
see also Internet, Web
www.army.___: 3 mil
www.harvard.___: 3 edu
www.unicef.___: 3 org
WXY on a telephone: 4 nine
WY
see Wyoming
Wyandot: 5 Huron, tribe 6 Indian 7 Amerind 8 language
cousin: 4 Erie
Wyandotte: 4 cave, city, town
locale: 8 Michigan
Wyatt: 4 Earp, Jane 6 Thomas
colleague: 3 Doc 6 Morgan, Virgil
Wyatt Earp (1994 film)
cast: Kevin Costner, Jeff Fahey, Gene Hackman, Dennis Quaid
Wyatt, Jane: 7 actress
film: Lost Horizon (1937)
TV: Father Knows Best

Wycherley, William: 7 British
10 playwright
work: The Country Wife
The Plain Dealer
Wyclef: 4 Jean
Wycliffe: 4 John
Wyden: 3 Ron
wye: 4 pipe **6** letter
follower: 3 zed, zee
preceder: 2 ex
Wyeth: 2 N.C. **5** Jamie **6** Andrew, artist **7** painter
subject: 5 Helga
Wyle: 4 Noah
Wyler: 7 William
Wylie: 4 Paul **6** Elinor, Philip
Wylie, Elinor: 4 poet **6** writer
work: Black Armour
Jennifer Lorn
Nets to Catch the Wind
Trivial Breath
Wyman: 4 Bill, Jane
Wyman, Jane: 7 actress
film: All That Heaven Allows (1955)
Johnny Belinda (1948, AA)
Larceny, Inc. (1942)
The Lost Weekend (1945)
Magnificent Obsession (1954)
Pollyanna (1960)
So Big (1953)
The Yearling (1946)
spouse: Ronald Reagan
TV: Falcon Crest
Wyndham: 4 John **5** hotel, Lewis
alternative: *see* hotel
Wyndham, John: 6 writer **7** British
genre: 5 sci-fi
work: The Day of the Triffids
Out of the Deeps
The Village of the Damned
Wynette, Tammy
song: Stand By Your Man (1968)
spouse: George Jones
Wynken, Blynken and Nod: 4 trio
writer: 5 Field
Wynn: 2 Ed **3** Bob **5** Early, Steve **6** Keenan
Wynn, Early: 6 hurler, Indian **7** pitcher
Wynonna: 4 Judd
mother: 5 Naomi
sister: 6 Ashley
Wynter: 4 Dana
Wynton: 8 Marsalis
dad: 5 Ellis
Wyo.
neighbor: 3 Ida., Neb. **4** Colo., Mont., Nebr., S. Dak., Utah
see also Wyoming
Wyomia: 4 Tyus
Wyoming: 4 city, town **5** state
author: Zane Grey
capital: 8 Cheyenne
city: 4 Cody **6** Casper **7** Laramie **8** Cheyenne
Indian: 7 Arapaho **8** Arapahoe **10** Miniconjou
locale: 8 Michigan
mountain: 6 Tetons **7** Bighorn, Laramie
national park: 10 Grand Teton
neighbor: 4 Utah **5** Idaho **7** Montana **8** Colorado, Nebraska
state bird: 10 meadowlark
state gemstone: 4 jade
state mammal: 7 buffalo
state tree: 10 cottonwood
WYSIWYG, part of: 3 Get, See, You **4** What
Wystan Hugh __: 5 Auden
Wythe: 6 George

x-__: 3 ray 4 axis
X: 3 chi, unk., var. 4 axis, mark, spot, tick 6 delete, letter 7 mark off, unknown 8 check off, variable 10 chromosome
  file: 7 dossier
  in phonetic alphabet: 4 X-ray
  mark with an ~: 4 sign
  out: 5 erase 6 cancel, delete, excise, strike 7 expunge 8 cross off 9 eliminate 10 obliterate
  perhaps: 3 tac, tic, toe
  preceder: 3 UVW 4 TUVW 5 STUVW
  rated ~: 4 lewd, racy 5 spicy 6 erotic, risqué, sultry, torrid
X __ the spot: 5 marks
X __ xylophone: 4 as in
X-__: 3 Men 5 rated
X-__, The: 5 Files
X-__ vision: 3 ray
__ X: 3 Gen 5 Brand 7 Malcolm
X2 (2003 film)
  cast: Hugh Jackman, Famke Janssen, Ian McKellen, Patrick Stewart
Xanadu: 6 estate
  owner: 4 Kane
  river: 4 Alph
Xanadu (1980 song)
  artist: ELO, Olivia Newton-John
...Xanadu did __ Khan...: 5 Kubla
Xander: 8 Berkeley
xanthic: 6 yellow
  relative: *see* yellow color
Xanthippe: 3 nag 5 harpy, scold, shrew, vixen 6 chider, noodge, virago 8 fishwife 9 henpecker, termagant
  husband: 8 Socrates
Xanthippus
  son: 8 Pericles
xanthous: 5 flaxy 6 flaxen
Xavier: 5 Cugat 7 Francis, Herbert 8 McDaniel
  athletes: 10 Musketeers
  ex: 4 Abbe 5 Charo
  locale: 4 Ohio 10 Cincinnati
X-axis, like the: 3 hor. 10 horizontal
__ X. Bushman: 7 Francis
Xe: 4 elem. 5 xenon 7 element
  54 for ~: 4 at. no.
x'ed: 5 voted 6 erased, marked 7 deleted 9 marked off, struck out, ticked off 10 crossed out, eliminated
Xena (TV adventure)
  cast: Lucy Lawless (Xena)
  Renee O'Connor (Gabrielle)
  Ted Raimi (Joxer)
  Kevin Smith (Ares)
  horse: 4 Argo
Xenia: 4 city, town
  locale: 4 Ohio
xenon: 3 gas 7 element 8 noble gas
  discoverer: William Ramsay
  like ~: 5 inert 8 inactive
xenophobe
  fear: 6 aliens 9 strangers 10 foreigners
Xenophon: 5 Greek 6 writer
  work: Anabasis
__-Xer: 3 Gen
Xeres product: 6 sherry
xerography powder: 5 toner
xerophyte: 5 plant 6 cactus
Xerox: 4 copy, same 5 clone, ditto 6 double, ectype 7 replica 8 knockoff, likeness 9 duplicate, imitation, photocopy, reproduce
  competitor: 4 Mita 5 Canon, Ricoh 7 Brother
  precursor: 5 ditto, mimeo
Xerxes: 4 king 7 Persian
  composer: George Frideric Handel
  parent: 6 Atossa, Darius
  wife: 6 Esther
X-Files, The (Fox sci-fi)
  cast: Gillian Anderson (Dana Scully)
  David Duchovny (Fox Mulder)
  Annabeth Gish (Monica Reyes)
  creator: Chris Carter
  dog: 8 Queequeg
  employer: FBI
  like ~: 4 eery 5 eerie
  topic: 3 ETs, UFO 5 alien
X-Games telecaster: 4 ESPN
xi: 5 Greek 6 letter 8 particle
  follower: 7 omicron
  preceder: 2 nu 4 mu nu
Xiaoping: 4 Deng
__-Xing: 3 Ped
X-ing a Paragrab
  author: Edgar Allan Poe
Xingú: 5 river
  locale: 6 Brazil
  the ~ flows into it: 6 Amazon
XJS: 3 car 4 auto 6 Jaguar
XKE: 3 car, Jag 4 auto 6 Jaguar
XKR: 3 car 4 auto 6 Jaguar
XL: 4 size 5 forty
  it's smaller than ~: 2 lg. 3 lge., med.
XLI Poems
  author: e.e. cummings
X marks the __: 4 spot
Xmas: 4 Noel, yule 8 yuletide
  mo.: 3 Dec.
  see also Christmas
X-Men (2000 film)
  cast: Halle Berry, Hugh Jackman, Famke Janssen, Ian McKellen, Anna Paquin, Rebecca Romijn-Stamos, Patrick Stewart
  director: Bryan Singer
XOXOX: 4 hugs 6 kisses
X-rated: 4 lewd 5 adult, spicy 6 erotic, risqué, smutty, spicey, sultry, vulgar
  perhaps: 5 uncut
x-ray: 7 analyze 9 skiagraph 10 photograph, radiograph
  blocker: 4 lead
  descendant: 3 MRI, NMR
  dose: 3 rad, rem 8 roentgen
  machine: 6 imager
Xscape
  members: Scott, Burruss, Cottle
  song: The Arms of the One...(1998)
  Just Kickin' It (1993)
  Keep On, Keepin' On (1996)
  My Little Secret (1998)
  Understanding (1994)
  Who Can I Run To? (1995)
XT: 2 PC 3 IBM 8 computer
Xterra: 3 SUV 6 Nissan
XXX
  drink: 3 ale
  opposite: 3 OOO
  part: 3 tac, tic, toe
XXX (2002 film)
  cast: Vin Diesel, Samuel L. Jackson
xylem: 6 tissue
  source: 4 tree, wood
xylographer: 6 etcher 8 engraver
xylophone: 7 balafon 8 amadinda
y
  letter like an inverted ~: 6 lambda
-y
  comparative of: 3 -ier
  equivalent: 3 -ish
  plural of: 3 -ies
Y: 4 axis, elem. 6 letter 7 element, yttrium
  39 for ~: 4 at. no.
  having a ~ chromosome: 4 male 9 masculine
  in phonetic alphabet: 6 Yankee
  preceders: 3 VWX 4 UVWX 5 TUVWX
  sometimes: 5 vowel
  wearer: 3 Eli 5 Yalie 7 Bulldog
Y __ yellow: 4 as in
Ya __ have heart: 5 gotta
Y.A.: 6 Tittle
Yabba __ doo!: 5 dabba
yacht: 4 boat, ship, yawl 5 craft, ketch, racer, sloop 6 vessel 7 cruiser 8 sailboat
  device: 5 loran, radar
  flag: 6 burgee
  heading: 4 tack
  jib: 5 Genoa
  like a ~: 4 chic, lush, posh, tony 5 fancy, plush, ritzy, swank 6 chichi, classy, deluxe, flashy, lavish, snazzy, swanky 7 elegant, refined 8 palatial, princely 9 expensive, high-class, luxurious, sumptuous
  shelter: 5 basin
  squad: 4 crew 5 hands
  stopover: 5 botel 6 boatel
  yon ~: 3 her, she
yacht __: 4 club
yachter: 6 boater, sailor 7 mariner
yachtie
  see yachter
yachting: 4 asea 5 at sea, naval, sport 8 nautical 10 navigation
yack
  see yak
yackety-__: 3 yak 4 yack
yackety-yak: 3 gab, gas, rap 4 blab, chat, chin 5 prate
Yada yada yada...: 3 etc.
yager: 6 hunter
yahoo: 3 rah 4 boor, lout, rube 5 brute, cheer, churl, clown, rowdy, schmo, yokel 6 lummox, schmoe 7 bounder, lowbrow, lowlife, parvenu, peasant, ruffian, upstart, whoopee, whoopie 9 arriviste 10 Philistine
Yahoo: 7 Serious
Yahoo!: 3 ISP
  competitor: 3 AOL
Yahtzee: 4 game
  need: 4 dice 8 score pad
Yahweh: 4 Lord 6 Adonai
yak: 2 ox 3 cow, gab, gas, jaw, rap, say, yap 4 blab, bull, buzz, chat, chin, gush, talk 5 bovid, clack, noise, prate, run on, speak, spout 6 animal, babble, bovine, gabble, gibber, gossip, jabber, mammal, natter, parley, patter, rattle, yammer 7 blather, blether, chatter, maunder, palaver, prattle, twaddle 8 converse, ramble on, spout off 9 go on and on, quadruped, touch base 10 chew the fat, chew the rag
  habitat: 4 Asia 5 Tibet 6 Xizang 7 Sitsang
  relative: *see* bovine
  young: 4 calf
__-yak: 6 yakety, yakity 7 yackety
Yakety __: 3 Sax, Yak
Yakety Sax (1963 song)
  artist: Boots Randolph
Yakety Yak (1958 song)
  artist: Coasters
Yakima: 4 city, town 5 river, tribe 6 Indian 7 Amerind
  locale: 10 Washington
yakity-__: 3 yak
yakker: 6 gossip, magpie 8 prattler 10 chatterbox
yakkety-yak
  see yak
yakking: 7 chatter, palaver 8 babbling, chitchat 9 loquacity 10 loquacious
Yakov: 8 Smirnoff
yaks: 4 oxen 6 cattle
Yakutsk: 4 city, port, town
  river: 4 Lena
Yale: 4 Lary, peak 5 Elihu, Linus, mount 8 mountain
  athletes: 4 Elis 8 Bulldogs
  cheer: 5 boola
  Harvard, to ~: 5 rival
  league: 3 Ivy
  locale: 4 Conn. 7 Rockies, Sawatch 8 Colorado, New Haven
  product: 4 lock
Yalie: 3 Eli 7 Bulldog 10 Ivy Leaguer
  rival: 6 Cantab
y'all: 8 everyone 9 everybody
Yalow, Rosalyn: 8 Nobelist 9 physicist
Yalta: 4 city, port, town
  locale: 6 Crimea 7 Ukraine
Yalu: 5 river
  River locale: 9 Manchuria 10 North Korea
yam: 5 tuber 6 veggie 9 vegetable
__ yam: 7 candied
Yamaguchi, Kristi: 6 skater
Yamaha
  rival: 6 Harley 8 Kawasaki
yammer: 3 gab, gas, jaw, rap, yak, yap 4 beef, blab, chat, chin, moan, roar 5 gripe, groan, prate, shout, speak, whine 6 cry out, kvetch, snivel, squawk 7 grumble 8 complain 9 bellyache, make a fuss

Yamoussoukro: **4** city, town **7** capital
locale: **10** Ivory Coast
Yamuna: **5** river
city on the ~: **4** Agra **5** Delhi
locale: **5** India
Yan: **4** cook **6** Martin
pan: **3** wok
Yanan region: **6** Shensi
Yañez, Augustín: **6** writer **7** Mexican
work: The Edge of the Storm
yang
of the ~: **9** masculine
partner: **3** yin
Yangon: **4** city, town **7** capital
locale: **4** Asia **5** Burma **7** Myanmar
Yangtze: **5** river
city on the ~: **5** Wuhan **6** Anqing
river to the ~: **3** Han
yank: **3** lug, rip, tow, tug **4** draw, jerk, pull, snap, tear **5** hitch, pluck, twist, wrest **6** evulse, snatch, twitch, wrench **7** extract, jerk out
Yank: **5** GI Joe **7** soldier **8** American, doughboy **10** Northerner
ally: **4** Brit **5** poilu, Tommy
foe: **3** Reb
Yank at __, A: **4** Eton **6** Oxford
Yankee: **4** ALer
Hall-of-Famer: **4** Ford, Ruth **5** Berra, Combs, Gomez **6** Dickey, Gehrig, Mantle **7** Lazzeri, Rizzuto, Ruffing **8** Babe Ruth, DiMaggio **9** Lou Gehrig, Yogi Berra **10** Bill Dickey, Earle Combs, Lefty Gomez, Whitey Ford
manager: **4** Dent, Houk, King, Neun **5** Berra, Chase, Green, Lemon, Torre **6** Chance, Dickey, Harris, Howser, Martin, McGraw, Virdon **7** Donovan, Girardi, Huggins, Merrill, Michael, Shawkey, Stengel **8** Fletcher, Griffith, McCarthy, Piniella, Robinson **9** Elberfeld, Showalter, Stallings
nickname: **4** A-Rod, Babe, Yogi **5** DiMag **7** Bambino, Scooter
Yankee __: **4** bond **6** dollar, Doodle
Yankee __ Dandy: **6** Doodle
Yankee __ soup: **4** bean
Yankee Clipper: **5** DiMag **8** DiMaggio
brother: **3** Dom **5** Vince
Yankee Doodle
mount: **4** pony
Yankee Doodle Boy, The
composer: George M. Cohan
__ Yankee Doodle dandy: **3** I'm a
Yankee Doodle Dandy (1942 film)
cast: James Cagney, Walter Huston, Joan Leslie
Yankees: **3** ten **4** team
home: **3** NYC **5** Bronx **7** New York
org.: **3** ALE, MLB
rival: ***see*** baseball team
sport: **8** baseball
__ Yankees: **4** Damn
Yankee Stadium
surface: **5** grass

Yankovic, Weird Al: **8** parodist
song: Eat It (1984)
Yanks
see Yankee
Yanks (1979 film)
cast: William Devane, Lisa Eichhorn, Richard Gere, Vanessa Redgrave
Yao: **4** Ming
Yaoundé: **4** city, town **7** capital
locale: **8** Cameroon
yap: **3** gab, jaw, yak **4** bark, chat, puss, trap, yell, yelp **5** clack, mouth, prate, run on, shout **6** babble, gossip, holler, jabber, kisser, squawk, yammer **7** blather, blether, chatter, kyoodle, prattle **8** idle talk, mouth off
Yaphet: **5** Kotto
yar: **6** lively **10** responsive
__ Yar: **4** Babi
Yarborough, Cale: **9** auto racer
Yarbrough, Glenn group: Limeliters
yard: **3** lot **4** lawn **5** close, court, depot, grass, patio, plant **6** corral, garden **7** terrace **8** backyard, barnyard, clearing, outdoors **9** courtyard, enclosure **10** playground, quadrangle
1000 ~s: **4** one K
bought at a ~ sale: **4** worn **10** hand-me-down, secondhand
covering: **4** lawn **5** grass
do ~ work: **3** mow, sod **4** rake **5** resod
enclosure: **5** fence, hedge
ender: **3** age, arm, man, men **5** stick **6** master
European ~: **5** meter, metre
fraction: **4** foot, inch
goods: **5** cloth, stuff **6** fabric **8** material, textiles
like some ~s: **5** weedy
pest: **4** mole **6** gopher
sale staple: **3** LPs **4** toys **9** bric-a-brac, glassware
starter: **4** back, barn, deer, dock, door, farm, junk, ship, tilt, vine **5** brick, court, steel, stock **6** church, lumber, school, switch
tool: **4** rake **5** mower
whole nine ~s: **4** a to z **8** entirety
yard __: **4** sale **5** goods, of ale
__ yard: **4** back, navy **6** square
Yard: **5** Molly
yardage
first-down ~: **3** ten
gain ground ~: **4** rush
yardbird: **3** con **5** felon **6** inmate **7** convict **8** internee, prisoner
Yardbirds
members: Clapton, Beck, Page
song: For Your Love (1965)
Heart Full of Soul (1965)
I'm a Man (1965)
Shapes of Things (1966)
yard-long: **6** legume
__ Yards: **6** Camden
yardstick: **4** norm, test **5** gauge, ruler, scale **7** measure **8** standard **9** benchmark, criterion **10** touchstone
org.: **4** ANSI
__ Yard, The: **7** Longest
yare: **5** agile **6** lively **10** responsive

yarmulke: **3** cap, hat **6** beanie
yarn: **3** lie **4** saga, tale **5** alibi, fable, fiber, story, twine **6** crewel, strand, string, thread **7** fiction, worsted **8** anecdote, tall tale **9** adventure, fairy tale, fish story, invention, narration, narrative, tall story
ball of ~: **4** clew, hank **5** skein
difficulty: **4** knot **6** tangle
flaw: **4** slub
holder: **5** spool
looped ~: **6** boucle
low-grade ~: **3** abb
make ~: **4** spin **5** weave
material: **4** ragg, wool **6** angora
measure: **6** denier
metallic ~: **5** lurex
silk ~: **4** poil
spin a ~: **3** fib, lie **6** relate
unit: **3** ply **4** hank **5** skein
Yarra: **5** river
city on the: **9** Melbourne
locale: **8** Victoria **9** Australia
Yarrow, Peter: **6** singer **10** folk singer
colleague: Mary Travers, Paul Stookey
Yasbeck: **3** Amy
Yashica: **6** camera
alternative: ***see*** camera
yashmak: **4** veil
Yasmin
mother: **4** Rita
Yasmine: **6** Bleeth
Yasodhara: **3** nun **8** princess
husband: **6** Buddha
son: **6** Rahula
Yasser: **6** Arafat
Yastrzemski sport: **8** baseball
Yates: **5** Peter
Yat-sen: **3** Sun
yaw: **4** bend, keel, roll, tack, tilt, turn, veer **5** drift, lurch, pitch **6** swerve **7** deviate **9** deviation
yawl: **4** boat, ship **5** yacht **8** sailboat **9** jolly boat
look-alike: **5** ketch
pole: **4** boom, mast, spar
yawn: **3** gap, nap **4** doze, gape, part, tire **5** sleep **6** drowse, snooze **8** oscitate, tiresome **10** catch flies
inducer: **4** bore **5** ennui **6** tedium **7** boredom **8** monotony
yawning: **4** open **5** agape **6** gaping, sleepy **7** abysmal **8** profound **9** cavernous **10** bottomless
hole: **5** abyss, chasm
yawny: **4** dull **6** boring **7** tedious **8** tiresome **9** heavy-eyed, somnolent
yawp: **4** bawl **6** bellow
yay: **3** cry, olé, rah **6** goodie **7** whoopee
Yay __!: **4** team
Yazoo: **5** river
locale: **4** Miss. **9** Vicksburg
Yb: **4** elem. **9** ytterbium
70 for ~: **4** at. no.
Ybor City: **4** city, town
locale: **7** Florida
neighbor: **5** Tampa
yclept: **5** named **6** called
yds.: **4** lgth., meas.
Ye __ Tea Shoppe: **4** Olde
yea: **2** ay **3** aye, yes **4** vote **5** goody, truly **6** assent, goodie, hoorah, hooray, hot dog, hurrah, indeed, it is so **7** in truth **8** thumbs up
opposite: **3** nay
Yeager, Chuck: **3** ace **5** flier, flyer, pilot **7** aviator
milestone: **5** Mach 1
yeah
opposite: **3** nah **4** nope
see also of course
Yeah, right!: **4** as if, I bet, sure **6** I'll bet, I'm sure, oh sure
yeanling: **4** lamb
year: **4** time **5** grade **6** junior, length, senior **7** vintage **8** freshman **9** sophomore
ender: **3** end **4** book, long
hold back a ~: **5** flunk
once a ~: **6** annual **8** annually, per annum, periodic **9** perennial, regularly
part: **3** day **4** week **5** month **7** quarter
solar-lunar ~ discrepancy: **5** epact
symbolically: **6** candle
year __ day, A: **4** and a
year-__: **3** end **5** round
__ year: **3** new, off **4** leap **5** lunar, once a, solar **6** fiscal, school
__-year: **3** all, man **5** light, woman **6** person
Year __ Cat: **5** of the
__ Year 2525: **5** In the
yearbook: **6** annual
photo: **2** sr. **3** snr. **6** senior
Yeardley: **5** Smith
year-end
drink: **3** nog **6** eggnog
helper: **3** elf
month: **3** Dec. **8** December
reward: **5** bonus
tune: **4** Noel **5** carol
Year in Provence, A
author: Peter Mayle
__ Year Itch, The: **5** Seven
yearling: **4** deer, fawn, lamb **5** sheep
Yearling, The: **5** novel
author: Marjorie Kinnan Rawlings
character: **3** Lem, Ora **4** Buck, Ezra, Flag, Jody **5** Hutto, Twink **6** Baxter, Oliver **9** Forrester, Weatherby
yearly: **6** annual **8** annually, per annum, periodic **9** perennial, regularly
yearn: **4** ache, burn, hope, itch, long, lust, moon, mope, pant, pine, sigh, wish **5** chafe, dream **6** hanker, hunger, thirst **8** languish
for: **4** envy, miss, need, seek, want **5** covet, crave, fancy **7** welcome
(to): **6** aspire, desire
yearning: **3** yen **4** ache, hope, itch, love, urge, want, will, wish **5** eager, fancy, itchy **6** desire, hunger, thirst **7** avidity, longing, thirsty, wishful, wistful **8** ambition, appetite, desirous, voracity **9** appetence, eagerness, hankering **10** aspiration
sound: **4** sigh
year of __: **5** grace
Year of Living Dangerously, The (1983 film)
cast: Mel Gibson, Linda Hunt,

Sigourney Weaver
director: Peter Weir
Year of the __: 3 Gun 5 Comet, Tiger 6 Dragon
Year of the Cat (1977 song)
artist: Al Stewart
Year of the Intern, The
author: Robin Cook
__-Year Plan: 4 Five
years: 3 age 4 ages 6 dotage 7 oldness 8 agedness, caducity, coon's age, lifespan, lifetime, long time 10 generation, senescence
ago: 4 once, past, then
formative ~: 5 teens, youth 7 boyhood 8 girlhood 9 childhood 10 immaturity, pubescence
from ~ past: 3 old 5 olden 6 bygone 7 archaic 8 outmoded
hundred ~: 7 century 9 centenary
in French: 3 ans
many ~: 3 eon 4 aeon, ages
ten ~: 5 decad 6 decade
up in ~: 3 old 4 aged 5 aging 6 ageing 7 ancient, elderly, wizened 8 grizzled 9 geriatric, getting on, senescent
years __: 3 ago
__ years: 3 dog 6 golden 7 donkey's
__ Years After: 6 Twenty
__ Years Before the Mast: 3 Two
__ Year's Day: 3 New
__ Year's Eve: 3 New
__ Year's Kisses: 4 This
__ Years of Our Lives, The: 4 Best
__ Years, The: 5 Happy 6 Living, Wonder
__ Years' War: 3 Ten 5 Seven 6 Thirty 7 Hundred
Yearwood, Trisha
song: How Do I Live
yeas and __: 4 nays
yeasayer: 5 toady 6 flunky, lackey, minion, stooge 7 flunkey 8 kowtower, servitor 9 sycophant 10 bootlicker, conformist
yeast: 4 koji 6 fungal, fungus, lather, leaven 7 ferment
brewers' ~: 4 barm
use ~: 6 leaven
work, as ~: 4 rise
__ yeast: 7 brewer's
yeasty: 5 barmy, foamy, petty 6 bouncy, frothy, paltry 7 buoyant, fired up, trivial 8 agitated, animated, exciting, piddling, trifling, youthful 9 ebullient, energetic, exuberant, frivolous
Yeats, William Butler: 4 poet 5 Irish 6 writer 8 Nobelist 10 playwright
colleague: John Synge, T.S. Eliot
work: Byzantium
The Countess Cathleen
Down by the Salley Gardens
The Fiddler of Dooney
The Herne's Egg
The Hour Glass
The Lake Isle of Innisfree
Leda and the Swan
Long-Legged Fly
Purgatory
Sailing to Byzantium
The Second Coming
The Wild Swans at Coole
The Winding Stair
yecch: 3 ick, ugh 5 gross
yegg: 5 thief 7 burglar, peteman 8 peterman, picklock 11 safecracker
activity: 5 crime, heist, theft 7 break-in
target: 4 safe 5 vault 9 strongbox
ye, hear: 4 oyes, oyez
Yehudi: 7 Menuhin
yell: 3 cry, rah, yap, yip 4 bark, bawl, call, hoot, howl, rage, rant, roar, snap, wail, weep, yelp, yowl 5 cheer, hallo, hillo, hullo, huzza, shout, spout, voice, wahoo, whoop 6 bellow, cry out, halloa, halloo, hallow, hilloa, holler, hoorah, hooray, hulloo, hurrah, hurray, huzzah, lament, outcry, scream, shriek, shrill, squawk, squeal 7 belt out, call out, exclaim, screech, sing out, thunder, ululate 8 complain, let loose, speak out 9 caterwaul, make a fuss, throw a fit 10 vociferate
at: 5 abuse, curse, scold 6 berate, malign, revile, vilify 7 bawl out, censure, chew out, condemn, rip into, upbraid 8 denounce, lace into, lambaste, tear into 9 castigate 10 vituperate
for: 4 hail 5 cheer 6 praise, salute 7 applaud, approve, commend, welcome 10 compliment
__ yell: 5 rebel
__ Yeller: 3 Old
yelling: 3 din 5 noise, noisy 6 ruckus, tumult
__ Yello: 5 Mello
yellow: 3 low 4 bisk, buff, gold, sand, weak, yolk 5 amber, blond, cream, flaxy, ivory, lemon, maize, straw, tawny, timid 6 afeard, afraid, bisque, blonde, craven, fallow, flaxen, golden, scared 7 afeared, chicken, fearful, gutless, saffron, wimpish 8 cowardly, liverish, recreant 9 spineless, tremulous 10 frightened
belly: 4 wimp 5 sissy 6 coward, craven 7 chicken, dastard 8 weakling 9 fraidy cat, jellyfish
blue and ~: 5 green
brownish ~: 4 buff, sand 7 nankeen
color: 4 bisk, buff, corn, gold, lime, rust, sand 5 amber, blond, brass, coral, cream, flaxy, lemon, maize, ocher, ochre, peach, rusty, straw, tawny 6 banana, bisque, blonde, canary, chammy, citron, crocus, flaxen, shammy, shamoy 7 apricot, chamois, citrine, jasmine, mustard, nankeen, old gold, saffron, xanthic 8 daffodil, primrose 9 buttercup, champagne, goldenrod, jessamine
combining form: 4 flav- 5 chrys-, flavo-, luteo-, xanth- 6 chryso-, xantho-
compound: 5 aloin
dark ~: 5 ocher, ochre
dye: 6 kamala
ender: 4 bird, cake, legs, tail, weed, wood 5 belly 6 hammer, throat
flower: 3 mum 4 flag, iris, lily 5 broom, tulip 6 acacia, arnica, cosmos, crocus, mullen, orchid, violet, yarrow 7 berseem, cowslip, day lily, freesia, jonquil, mullein, ragwort, tea rose 8 asphodel, daffodil, hyacinth, laburnum, marigold, primrose, rockrose, tidytips 9 buttercup, calendula, celandine, colicroot, corydalis, dandelion, forsythia, goldenrod, groundsel, horsemint, narcissus 10 goatsbeard, marguerite, nasturtium, ranunculus, wallflower
grayish ~: 3 dun 6 chammy, citron, shammy, shamoy 7 chamois
greenish ~: 4 lime 6 acacia, citron 7 luteous 9 champagne
jacket: 4 pest, wasp 6 insect
jacket cousin: 6 hornet
ocher: 3 sil
orangish ~: 5 ocher, ochre 6 crocus 7 saffron
pinkish ~: 5 coral, peach 7 apricot
red and ~: 6 orange
reddish ~: 4 rust, sand 5 brass, coral, ocher, ochre, rusty
vehicle: 3 cab 4 taxi
white and ~ flower: 7 calypso 8 camomile 9 calla lily, chamomile
word on a ~ sign: 5 merge
yellow __: 3 dog, pad 5 alert, fever, light, pages 6 jacket
yellow-__: 7 bellied
yellow-__ contract: 3 dog
yellow-__ sapsucker: 7 bellied
__ yellow: 5 lemon
Yellow __: 3 Cab, Sea, Sky 4 Bird, Hats
Yellow __ of Texas, The: 4 Rose
Yellow __ Road: 5 Brick
Yellow __, The: 3 Kid
__ Yellow: 5 Crome 6 Mellow
Yellowbeard (1983 film)
cast: Peter Boyle, Graham Chapman, Tommy Chong, Marty Feldman, Cheech Marin
yellow-bellied: 4 weak 5 timid 6 craven, scared 9 nerveless, spineless
yellowbelly: 6 coward 8 poltroon
Yellow Bird (1961 song)
artist: Arthur Lyman Group
Yellow Brick Road
flower: 5 poppy
__ Yellow Brick Road: 7 Goodbye
yellowcake: 3 ore
yellow-fever carrier: 5 aedes 8 mosquito
yellowfin: 3 ahi 4 fish, tuna
yellow-haired: 5 blond 6 blonde, flaxen
yellowhammer: 4 bird
Yellowhammer State: 3 Ala. 7 Alabama
yellowish: 3 tan 4 eggy 5 amber, flaxy, sandy 6 flaxen, sallow
brown: 5 amber, khaki, tawny, umber
color: 3 tan 4 bone, drab, fawn, foxy, jade, nude, rust 5 amber, camel, cocoa, coral, cream, ivory, khaki, olive, putty, rusty, sandy, tawny 6 auburn, bister, bistre, ginger, russet, salmon, sienna, suntan 7 apricot, caramel, dogwood 8 cinnamon 9 alabaster 10 chartreuse
pink: 5 peach
red: 5 coral, sandy
white: 5 cream
yellow jacket: 3 bug 4 wasp 6 insect
genus: 5 vespa
Yellowknife: 4 city, town
locale: 3 NWT 6 Canada
Yellow Newtown: 5 apple
relative: *see* apple
Yellow Pages entries: 3 ads, cos.
yellow-rayed flower: 9 coreopsis, owl's claws, rudbeckia, sunflower 10 coneflower, gaillardia
yellow-red dye: 6 anatto
__ Yellow Ribbon...: 4 Tie a
Yellow River
joiner: 3 Wei
locale: 5 China, Korea
port: 5 Jinan
Yellow Room, The
author: Mary Roberts Rinehart
Yellow Rose of Texas, The (1955 song)
artist: Johnny Desmond, Mitch Miller
Yellow Sea
arm: 5 Bohai, Pohai
locale: 5 Korea
port: 6 Lüshun
river to the ~: 4 Yalu
Yellowstone: 4 lake, park 5 falls, river
gateway: 4 Cody
locale: 5 Idaho 7 Montana, Wyoming
mgr.: 3 NPS
river: 5 Lewis, Snake
river to the ~: 7 Bighorn
sight: 3 elk 4 bear 5 bison, moose 6 geyser
visitor: 6 camper 7 tourist
Yellow Submarine (1966 song)
artist: Beatles
__ Yellow Taxi: 3 Big
Yellow Transparent: 5 apple
relative: *see* apple
yelp: 3 yap, yip 4 bark, howl, yell, yowl 6 bellow, holler, squawk, squeak, squeal 7 kyoodle, screech
Yeltsin: 5 Boris, Naina
aide: 5 Lebed
see also Russian
Yemana, Nick portrayer: 3 Soo
Yemen: 6 nation 7 country
capital: 4 San`a 5 Sanaa
city: 3 Ibb 4 Aden, Taiz 5 Mocha, Mukha, Taizz
group: 10 Arab League
gulf near ~: 4 Aden
locale: 6 Arabia 7 Mideast
money: 4 rial 10 dinar. riyal
neighbor: 4 Oman
of old: 5 Sheba
port: 4 Aden
Yemeni: 4 Arab
neighbor: 5 Omani, Saudi
port dweller: 5 Adeni
yen: 4 ache, coin, itch, lust, need, pine, urge, want, wish 5 fancy, money 6 desire, hunger, thirst 7 craving, impulse, itching, longing, passion 8 appetite, yearning 9 hankering 10 compulsion

for: 4 ache, long, want, wish 5 yearn 6 desire, hanker 7 dream of
fraction: 3 sen
have a ~ for: 4 long, want 5 crave, fancy, yearn
Yenan region: 6 Shensi
Yenisei: 5 river
city on the ~: 6 Abakan
locale: 6 Russia
yenta: 5 snoop 6 gossip 7 meddler 8 busybody, quidnunc
Yentl (1983 film)
cast: Amy Irving, Mandy Patinkin, Barbra Streisand
director: Barbra Streisand
Yeobright: 4 Clym
yeo. employer: 3 USN
Yeoh: 8 Michelle
Ye Olde ___: 6 Shoppe
yeoman: 4 rank 6 sailor
place: 4 navy
yeomanly: 4 true 5 loyal 7 devoted 8 faithful, true-blue 9 allegiant, dedicated
Yeoman of the Guard, The
composer: Arthur Sullivan, W.S. Gilbert
role: 4 Jack, Kate 5 Elsie 6 Meryll, Phoebe 7 Fairfax, Leonard, Wilfred
yeoman's ___: 4 work 7 service
yep
opposite: 3 nah 4 nope
see also of course
yerba ___: 4 maté 5 buena
Yerby, Frank: 6 writer
work: Devilseed
The Foxes of Harrow
Goat Song
Judas, My Brother
Mackenzie's Hundred
An Odor of Sanctity
Yer darn ___!: 6 tootin'
Yerevan: 4 city, town 7 capital
locale: 7 Armenia
Yerma
author: Frederico García Lorca
Yertle the Turtle
creator: Dr. Seuss
home: 4 pond
yes
alternative to ~: 5 maybe 7 perhaps 8 possibly, probably 9 it could be, it might be, perchance
follower: 3 sir 4 ma'am 5 siree 6 sirree
in French: 3 oui
in Japanese: 3 hai
in Scottish: 2 ay 3 aye
man: 5 sheep, toady 6 flunky, jackal, lackey, minion 7 Babbitt, flunkey, lacquey, spaniel 8 assenter, emulator, truckler 9 sycophant, underling 10 conformist, handshaker
say ~: 2 OK 3 nod 4 okay 5 agree, yield 6 accede, accept, assent, permit 7 approve, consent, go along
silent ~: 3 nod
vote: 2 ay 3 aff., aye, yea
see also of course
yes ___: 3 man 5 and no
yes-___ answer: 4 or-no
Yes: 9 detergent
alternative: ***see*** detergent
Yes ___?: 4 or no
Yes, ___: 4 Dear, I Can
Yes, ___!: 3 sir 4 ma'am 5 siree 6 sirree
Yes, ___, That's My Baby: 3 Sir
Yes, Dear (CBS sitcom)
cast: Anthony Clark (Greg Warner)
Jean Louisa Kelly (Kim Warner)
Mike O'Malley (Jimmy Hughes)
Liza Snyder (Christine Hughes)
yeshiva: 6 school
student: 3 Jew
teacher: 5 rabbi, rebbe
Yes, I ___: 3 Can
Yes, I'm Ready (song)
artist: Barbara Mason, KC and the Sunshine Band, Teri DeSario
yes-man: 5 toady 6 echoer, fawner, flunky, lackey 7 flunkey, lacquey 8 adulator, kowtower 9 flatterer
Yes Man (2008 film)
cast: Jim Carrey, Zooey Deschanel
Yes Sir, That's My Baby: 4 song
artist: Eddie Cantor
composer: Gus Kahn
yesterday: 4 past 8 recently 10 not long ago, recent past
born ~: 3 raw 4 naif 5 naive
not born ~: 5 sharp 6 astute 7 veteran
Yesterday (1965 song)
artist: Beatles
___ Yesterday: 4 Born, Only
Yesterday Once More (1973 song)
artist: Carpenters
Yesterday's Songs (1981 song)
artist: Neil Diamond
Yester Lover (1968 song)
artist: Miracles
Yester-Me... (1969 song)
artist: Stevie Wonder
yesteryear: 3 eld 4 past, yore 9 olden days
Yes We Can Can (1973 song)
artist: Pointer Sisters
Yes, Yes, ___: 6 Yvette
yet: 3 but, now, too 4 also, even, more, till 5 along, altho, as yet, by now, so far, still, to now 6 as well, even so, hereto, in time, one day, though, to boot, to date, withal 7 besides, despite, earlier, finally, further, howbeit, however, prior to, someday, thus far, up to now 8 after all, although, hitherto, likewise, moreover, sometime, until now 9 at any rate, in spite of 10 all the same, beyond this, even though, eventually, in addition, ultimately, up until now
and ~: 3 but 6 unless
as ~: 3 now, yet 5 so far, still 6 erenow, hereto, to date 7 thus far, till now 8 right now, until now 10 heretofore, up until now
didn't ~: 5 hasn't
to a poet: 3 e'en
to be decided: 4 open 9 ambiguous, debatable 10 in question, unresolved, up in the air
___ yet: 3 but, not 4 as of
yeti: 5 biped 6 legend 7 snowman, Tibetan
cousin: 7 Bigfoot
___ yet to be, The: 6 best is
Yevtushenko, Yevgeny: 4 poet 7 Russian
yew: 4 tree 5 taxus 9 evergreen
Yggdrasil: 4 tree
Yiddish: 8 language
humorist: 8 Aleichem
interjection: 2 oy 5 oy vey
writer: 6 Singer 8 Aleichem
yield: 3 bow, buy, net, pay, sag 4 bear, bend, cede, crop, drop, dump, earn, fail, fall, flex, fold, give, hand, lose, melt, quit, shed, take 5 agree, allow, break, bring, budge, chuck, defer, ditch, fit in, forgo, grant, let go, offer, relax, say OK, share, total, waive 6 accede, accept, accrue, afford, assent, buckle, cave in, comply, concur, desist, fess up, fold up, forego, fork up, give in, give up, income, output, permit, profit, relent, render, resign, return, say yes, soften, submit, suffer, supply, tender 7 abandon, blossom, bring in, concede, consent, crumple, forfeit, forsake, furnish, give off, give way, harvest, produce, proffer, prosper, provide, radiate, release, revenue, sell for, succumb, takings, turnout, undergo 8 abdicate, back down, collapse, earnings, forswear, generate, get rid of, give over, hand over, jettison, part with, proceeds, say uncle, throw out, turn over 9 acquiesce, cast aside, deliver up, discharge, dispose of, foreswear, reconcile, send forth, surrender, throw away 10 bring forth, capitulate, come around, condescend, relinquish, toe the line, toe the mark
bank ~: 3 int. 8 interest
don't ~: 5 force, press 6 be firm, insist, pester 7 persist, protest, speak up 8 speak out 9 importune, stand firm
quarry ~: 3 gem, ore 4 rock 5 jewel 6 gravel 7 crystal, mineral
to: 5 act on 6 accept 7 act upon, indulge
Yield: 4 sign 8 road sign 10 street sign
yielding: 3 lax 4 easy, limp, meek, soft 5 mushy, shaky 6 docile, humble, pliant, spongy, supple, tender 7 dutiful, elastic, lenient, passive, plastic, pliable, springy, squishy, willing 8 amenable, biddable, flexible, gracious, obedient, resigned, tractile, unstrict 9 agreeable, compliant, malleable, resilient, tractable 10 abdication, concession, submission, submissive
not ~: 3 set 4 firm, hard, iron, taut 5 fixed, harsh, rigid, stern, stiff, tight 6 flinty, mulish, severe, steely, strict, wooden 7 adamant, dead set, diehard, precise 8 exacting, hard-line, immobile, indurate, ironclad, obdurate, resolute, stubborn 9 demanding, difficult, immovable, inelastic, obstinate, pigheaded, steadfast, stringent, unbending 10 bullheaded, determined, implacable, inexorable, inflexible, invariable, relentless, unchanging, unswerving
Yikes!: 3 eek 4 egad, oh no, oh oh, uh-oh 5 egads
yin
of the ~: 8 feminine
partner: 4 yang
yip: 3 arf, cry 4 bark, yell, yelp, yowl 6 squeal
Yip: 7 Harburg
yipe: 2 ow 3 eek, yow 4 egad, ouch, yeow 5 egads 7 holy cow
Yipes!: 3 eek 4 egad, oh no, oh oh, uh-oh 5 egads
yippee: 3 yay 5 huzza, wahoo 6 hoorah, hooray, hot dog, hurrah, hurray, huzzah
yipper: 3 pup 5 puppy, whelp
___ Yisrael: 5 Eretz
Yitzhak: 5 Rabin 6 Shamir
Y Kant Tori Read
artist: Tori Amos
y, letter like an inverted: 6 lambda
YM: 3 mag 8 magazine
Yma: 5 Sumac
YMCA
activity: 4 swim 7 workout
class: 3 CPR
member: 3 boy, man
part of ~: 4 assn., Men's 5 Young 9 Christian
Y.M.C.A. (1978 song)
artist: Village People
Ymir: 5 giant
yo-___-ho: 5 heave
Yo!: 3 hey 4 ahoy 6 hey you
Yo, ___!: 6 Adrian
Yoakam: 6 Dwight
yod: 6 Hebrew, letter
follower: 4 caph, kaph
preceder: 3 tet 4 teth
yodel: 4 sing 6 warble 8 vocalize
place to ~: 4 Alps 5 Tirol, Tyrol 7 Austria
yodh: 6 Hebrew, letter
follower: 4 caph, kaph
preceder: 3 tet 4 teth
Yoelson: 3 Asa 6 Jolson
yoga
point: 6 chakra
position: 5 asana, lotus
practice: 4 anga
practitioner: 5 Hindu 6 Hindoo
principle: 5 prana
type: 5 hatha
Yogi: 4 Bear 5 Berra 7 catcher
team: 5 Yanks 7 Yankees
yogurt: 5 dairy 7 dessert
base: 4 milk 7 culture
brand: 4 TCBY 6 Dannon 7 Yoplait
like some ~: 5 no fat 6 low-fat
variety: 5 plain 6 banana 7 vanilla
___ yogurt: 6 frozen
yogurtlike drink: 5 kefir
___ Yo Hands: 4 Clap
Yo-ho-ho, and a bottle of ___: 3 rum
yoke: 3 tie, wed 4 bind, bond, join, link, pair, tack, team 5 chain,

hitch, marry, nexus, strap, unite **6** attach, burden, cohere, collar, couple, fasten, hook on, hook up, inspan, secure, splice **7** bondage, bracket, combine, conjoin, connect, coupler, harness, helotry, hitch on, peonage, serfdom, shackle, slavery **8** coupling, crossbar, ligature, vinculum **9** associate, restraint, servitude **10** oppression
combining form: 3 zyg- **4** zygo-
lace ~: 6 guimpe
locale: 4 neck
part: 5 oxbow
sharers: 4 team
together: 3 mix, tie, wed **4** ally, bind, link, yoke **5** hitch, unite **6** append, couple, league, team up **7** combine, conjoin, connect **8** coalesce, federate **9** associate, integrate
wooden ~: 6 cangue
yokel: 3 oaf **4** boor, clod, hick, rube **5** yahoo **6** lummox, rustic **7** bumpkin, hayseed, peasant, plowboy **9** hillbilly **10** clodhopper, provincial
Yoko: 3 Ono
son: 4 Sean
Yokohama: 4 city, port, town
locale: 5 Japan
Yokum: 5 Abner, Mammy, Pansy, Pappy **7** Lucifer
creator: Al Capp
home: 8 Dogpatch
yolk: 6 yellow
companion: 5 white
yolk __: 3 sac
yom __: 3 tov
Yom Kippur: 6 Jewish **7** holiday
instrument: 6 shofar **8** ram's horn
observe ~: 4 fast **5** atone
yon: 5 there **6** way off, yonder
opposite: 6 hither
Yond' Cassius has ___: 5 a lean
yonder: 3 far, yon **4** afar, away **5** there **6** beyond, far off, remote **7** distant, faraway, farther, further
folks: 4 them, they
over ~: 4 thar **5** there
things: 5 those
wild blue ~: 3 sky **5** ether **6** aether
Yonkers: 4 city, town
locale: 7 New York
Yoo-hoo!: 3 hey **4** psst **5** hello **7** hello-o-o **8** over here
Yoplait
competitor: 4 TCBY **6** Dannon
Yorba Linda: 4 city, town
locale: 10 California
yore: 3 eld **4** past **5** of old **7** ages ago, long ago **9** antiquity, olden days **10** yesteryear
of ~: 3 old **6** bygone, gone by
Yorick
lament for ~: 4 alas
York: 3 sgt. **4** cape, city, Dick, town **5** Alvin, House **7** Michael **8** Susannah
ender: 4 town **5** shire
House of ~ symbol: 9 white rose
locale: 7 England
__ York City: 3 New
Yorkie: 3 dog **6** lap dog
York Imperial: 5 apple
relative: *see* apple
Yorkin: 3 Bud
Yorks: 6 county
locale: 7 England
Yorkshire: 3 pig **5** swine **6** county
city: 5 Leeds, Otley **6** Batley, Ossett **8** Bradford **9** Rotherham, Sheffield
locale: 7 England
river: 3 Ure **4** Aire, Ouse
Yorkshire __: 7 pudding, terrier
Yorktown: 6 battle
locale 8 Virginia
York University
location: 6 Canada **7** Ontario, Toronto
Yosemite: 4 park **5** falls
feature: 8 Half Dome
locale: 10 California
mgr.: 3 NPS
peak: 4 Kuna **9** El Capitan
river: 6 Merced **8** Tuolumne
Yosemite __: 3 Sam **5** Falls
Yost: 3 Ned
Yost, Eddie
sport: 8 baseball
Yo te __: 3 amo
Yothers: 4 Tina
you: 4 self, thee, thou **7** pronoun
away with ~: 2 go **4** exit, move **5** be off, leave, scram **6** beat it, depart, get out, move it, vanish **7** amscray, buzz off, get away, get lost, move off, move out, push off, take off, vamoose **8** clear out, run along, shove off **9** move along, take a hike **10** get a move on, hit the road, shuffle off
before ~ know it: 4 anon, soon
between ~ and me: 7 sub rosa **8** in secret, secretly **9** entre nous, privately
how do ~ do: 2 hi **4** ciao, hail **5** aloha, hello, howdy **7** bon jour, welcome **8** greeting
I caught ~: 3 aha
in French: 4 vous
in German: 3 sie
in Spanish: 5 usted
I told ~ so: 3 see
May I help ~ ?: 3 yes
see ~ later: 3 bye **4** ciao, ta-ta **5** adios **7** goodbye **8** sayonara
you __ say that again: 3 can
you-__: 3 all, uns
__ you!: 3 Sez **4** Says **5** After, I dare
You __!: 3 bet **6** betcha
You __?: 4 rang
You __ a mouthful: 4 said
You __ Beautiful: 5 Are So
You __ Be in Pictures: 6 Oughta
You __ be joking!: 4 must
You __ Be Right: 3 May
You __ be there!: 5 had to
You __ bother!: 6 needn't
You __ Can Tell: 5 Never
You __ Change That: 4 Can't
You __ Cheat an Honest Man: 4 Can't
You __ Count on Me: 3 Can
You __ Destiny: 5 Are My
You __ for It: 5 Asked
You __ Get a Man With a Gun: 4 Can't
You __ Go Home Again: 4 Can't
You __ Have Everything: 4 Can't
You __ Have to Be So Nice: 5 Didn't
You __ have worried!: 6 needn't
You __ heard nothin' yet!: 4 ain't
You __ here: 3 are
You __ Hurry Love: 4 Can't
You __ it!: 3 did, got **4** said
You __ It Well: 4 Wear
You __ kidding!: 5 aren't
You __ Know: 6 Oughta
You __ Know Me: 4 Don't
You __ Live Once: 4 Only
You __ Live Twice: 4 Only
You __ Love: 3 Are **5** Are My
You __ Lucky Star: 5 Are My
You __ Me: 4 Send **6** Needed, Showed
You __ Me, Al: 4 Know
You __ Meant for Me: 4 Were
You __ Me Hangin' On: 4 Keep
You __ Me Love You: 4 Made
You __ Mouthful: 5 Said a
You __ My Breath Away: 4 Take
You __ my day!: 4 made
You __ My Destiny: 3 Are
You __ My Lucky Star: 3 Are
You __ My Sunshine: 3 Are
You __ Own Me: 4 Don't
You __ rat!: 5 dirty
You __ Right: 5 May Be
You __ Say: 4 Don't
You __ See Me: 4 Won't
You __ seen nothin' yet!: 4 ain't
You __ serious?: 5 aren't
You __ Sixteen: 3 Are
You __ So Beautiful: 3 Are
You __ Sunshine: 5 Are My
You __ Take It With You: 4 Can't
You __ There: 3 Are
You __ the Sunshine of My Life: 3 Are
You __ to Me: 6 Belong
You __ Too Much: 4 Talk
You __ Up My Life: 5 Light
You __ What It Takes: 3 Got
You __ what you eat: 3 are
You __ worry!: 6 needn't
__ You: 3 For **4** I Got, I'm in, Miss, Near, Only, Over **5** All of, Bless, I Miss, I Need, I Want, Lovin', Run to
You ain't __ nothin' yet: 4 seen **5** heard
___ You Ain't Ma Baby?: 4 or Is
You Ain't Woman Enough (1966 song)
artist: Loretta Lynn
You and I (1982 song)
artist: Crystal Gayle, Eddie Rabbitt
__ you and me: 7 between
You and Me (1977 song)
artist: Alice Cooper
You and Me Against the World (1974 song)
artist: Helen Reddy
__ you any wool?: 4 Have
You Are (1983 song)
artist: Lionel Richie
You Are __: 4 Here, Love **5** There
You Are Everything (1971 song)
artist: Stylistics
You Are Love
composer: Jerome Kern, Oscar Hammerstein
You Are My __ Star: 5 Lucky
You Are My Destiny (1958 song)
artist: Paul Anka
You Are My Love (1955 song)
artist: Joni James
You Are My Sunshine (1962 song)
artist: Ray Charles
You Are Not Alone (1995 song)
artist: Michael Jackson
You Are So Beautiful (1975 song)
artist: Joe Cocker
You Are There (CBS drama)
host: Walter Cronkite
You Are the Sunshine of My Life (1973 song)
artist: Stevie Wonder
You Are the Woman (1976 song)
artist: Firefall
__ you asked...: 5 Since
You Asked __ It: 3 For
__ you asleep?: 3 Are
__ You Babe: 4 I Got
You Beat Me to the Punch (1962 song)
artist: Mary Wells
__ You Being Served?: 3 Are
You Belong to Me
author: Mary Higgins Clark
You Belong to Me (song)
artist: Carly Simon, Duprees
__ You Belong to Me: 7 Tonight
You Belong to the City (1985 song)
artist: Glenn Frey
__ you be my neighbor?: 4 Won't
You bet!: 3 yep, yes, yup **4** okay, sure, yeah **6** and how **7** for sure *see* of course
You Bet __ Life: 4 Your
You Better Sit Down Kids (1967 song)
artist: Cher
You Bet Your Life (game show)
host: Groucho Marx
You bet your sweet __!: 5 bippy
you can __ that again: 3 say
You can __ horse...: 5 lead a
You can __ man from Harvard...: 5 tell a
You can bank on it!: 6 I'm sure
You can bet __!: 4 on it
You Can Call Me Al (1986 song)
artist: Paul Simon
You Can Count on Me (2000 film)
cast: Matthew Broderick, Rory Culkin, Laura Linney, Mark Ruffalo
You Can Depend on Me (1961 song)
artist: Brenda Lee
You Can Do Magic (1982 song)
artist: America
You can fool __ of the people...: 4 some
You can say that again!: 4 amen
You Can't __ Everything: 4 Have
You Can't Change That (1979 song)
artist: Ray Parker Jr.
You Can't Deny It (1990 song)
artist: Lisa Stansfield
You Can't Get a Man With a Gun
composer: Irving Berlin
singer: Annie Oakley
You Can't Get There From Here
author: Ogden Nash

You Can't Go Home Again
author: Thomas Wolfe
character: 4 Else **6** Esther, McHarg, Webber
You Can't Hurry Love (1966 song)
artist: Supremes
You can't judge ___...: 5 a book
You can't make ___ purse...: 5 a silk
You Can't Sit Down (1963 song)
artist: Dovells
You Can't Take It With You: 4 play
author: George S. Kaufman, Moss Hart
You can't teach ___ dog...: 5 an old
___-you card: 5 thank
___ You Come Again: 4 Here
You Couldn't Be ___: 5 Cuter
You da ___!: 3 man
You'd Be So Nice...
composer: Cole Porter
You'd Be Surprised
composer: Irving Berlin
You Decorated My Life (1979 song)
artist: Kenny Rogers
You Didn't Have to ___ Nice: 4 Be So
___ you didn't know!: 4 As if
You dirty ___!: 3 rat
___ you do: 5 how do
You Don't ___ Me: 3 Own **4** Know
You Don't Bring Me Flowers (1978 song): 4 duet
artist: Barbra Streisand, Neil Diamond
You Don't Have to Be a Baby to Cry (1963 song)
artist: Caravelles
You Don't Have to Say You Love Me (song)
artist: Dusty Springfield, Elvis Presley
You Don't Know ___: 4 Jack **5** Paree
You Don't Know How It Feels (1994 song) artist: Tom Petty
You Don't Know Me (song)
artist: Jerry Vale, Ray Charles
You Don't Mess Around With Jim (1972 song)
artist: Jim Croce
You Don't Mess With the Zohan (2008 film)
cast: Adam Sandler, John Turturro
You Don't Owe Me a Thing (1957 song)
artist: Johnnie Ray
You Don't Own Me (1964 song)
artist: Lesley Gore
You don't say!: 4 gosh **6** indeed, my word, really
You Don't Say (game show) host: Tom Kennedy
You Do Something to Me
composer: Cole Porter
(You Drive Me) Crazy (1999 song)
artist: Britney Spears
___ you for real?: 3 Are
You Give Good Love (1985 song)
artist: Whitney Houston
You Give Love a Bad Name (1986 song)
artist: Bon Jovi
___ You Glad You're You?: 5 Aren't

___ you go: 5 pay as, there
You go, ___!: 4 girl
You Go ___ Head: 4 to My
You Got It (song)
artist: Bonnie Raitt, New Kids on the Block, Roy Orbison
You Got It All (1987 song)
artist: Jets
You Got Lucky (1982 song)
artist: Tom Petty and the Heartbreakers
You Gotta Be (1994 song)
artist: Des'ree
You Gotta Be a Football ___: 4 Hero
You got that right!: 6 I'll say
You Got What It Takes (1967 song)
artist: Dave Clark Five
You Haven't Done Nothin (1974 song)
artist: Stevie Wonder
___ you heard?: 4 Have
___ You in September: 3 See
___, You Is My Woman: 4 Bess
___ you jest!: 6 Surely
You Keep Me Hangin' On (song)
artist: Kim Wilde, Supremes, Vanilla Fudge
___ you kidding?: 3 Are
___ You Kind of Glad We Did?: 5 Aren't
___ You Knocking: 5 I Hear
you-know-___: 3 who
___ you know!: 4 A lot
___ You Know: 3 Now **4** Don't
You Know I Can't Hear You...
author: Robert Anderson
You Know Me, Al
author: Ring Lardner
You know the ___!: 5 drill
___ you later!: 3 See
You Learn (1996 song)
artist: Alanis Morissette
You Light Up My Life (1977 film)
cast: Didi Conn
You Light Up My Life (1977 song)
artist: Debby Boone
You'll Accomp'ny Me (1980 song)
artist: Bob Seger
You'll Lose a Good Thing (1962 song)
artist: Barbara Lynn
You'll Never Find... (1976 song)
artist: Lou Rawls
You'll Never Know
composer: Harry Warren, Mack Gordon
You'll Never Never Know (1956 song)
artist: Platters
You'll Never Walk Alone
composer: Oscar Hammerstein, Richard Rodgers
You'll See (1995 song)
artist: Madonna
___ You Lonesome Tonight?: 3 Are
___ You Look Tonight, The: 3 Way
___ you loud and clear!: 5 I read
___ You Love: 5 I Wish
you love in Latin: 4 amas
___ You Love Me Tomorrow: 4 Will
Youma
author: Lafcadio Hearn
___-you-ma'am: 5 thank
You Make Loving Fun (1977 song)
artist: Fleetwood Mac

You Make Me Feel Brand New (1974 song)
artist: Stylistics
You Make Me Feel Like Dancing (1976 song)
artist: Leo Sayer
___ You Make Me Feel, The: 3 Way
You Make My Dreams (1981 song)
artist: Hall and Oates
Youmans: 7 Vincent
You May Be Right (1980 song)
artist: Billy Joel
You, Me and Dupree (2006 film)
cast: Matt Dillon, Michael Douglas, Kate Hudson, Owen Wilson
You Mean the World to Me (1994 song)
artist: Toni Braxton
You Might Think (1984 song)
artist: Cars
You Must Have Been a Beautiful Baby
composer: Harry Warren, Johnny Mercer
You Must Love Me
show: 5 Evita
You Must Love Me (1996 song)
artist: Madonna
You Must Remember This
author: Joyce Carol Oates
You Needed Me (1978 song)
artist: Anne Murray
___ You Need Is Love: 3 All
You Never Can Tell
author: George Bernard Shaw
You never had ___ good!: 4 it so
young: 3 new, raw **4** baby, kids **5** brood, early, fresh, green, issue, small **6** babies, boyish, callow, calves, family, infant, junior, litter, little, modern, recent, tender, vernal **7** boylike, budding, girlish, growing, infants, kittens, newborn, progeny, puerile, teenage, untried **8** blooming, childish, girllike, ignorant, immature, juvenile, preadult, teenaged, underage, unversed, youthful **9** childlike, fledgling, half-grown, offspring, unfledged **10** adolescent, blossoming, burgeoning, developing, little ones, sophomoric, tenderfoot, unseasoned
ender: 4 ster **5** berry
young ___: 3 man, one **4** lady **5** adult, blood, thing
young-___: 3 uns **4** eyed
Young: 2 Cy, MC **3** Gig **4** Alan, Burt, Chic, Neil, Paul, Sean **5** Angus, Barry, Faron, Kathy, Steve **6** Andrew, Edward, Lester, Robert, Roland, Thomas **7** Brigham, Loretta, Malcolm, Terence
partner: 5 Ernst
Young ___: 4 Turk
Young ___ Brown: 6 Widder
Young ___, The: 5 Lions, Miner **7** Doctors, Savages
Young ___ With a Horn: 3 Man
___ Young: 3 Too **7** Forever
___ & Young: 5 Ernst
Young, Alan: 5 actor
TV: Mister Ed
Young and the Restless, The: 4 soap

Youngblood: 4 Jack **5** Hawke
Young Blood (1957 song)
artist: Coasters
Youngbloods
song: Get Together (1969)
Young, Brigham territory: 4 Utah
___ Young Cannibals: 4 Fine
Young, Cy: 6 hurler **7** pitcher
Young Dr. Malone: 9 radio show
Young Emotions (1959 song)
artist: Ricky Nelson
younger: 5 minor **6** junior
Younger: 3 Bob, Jim **4** Cole, John
Younger ___: 4 Edda
Younger Than Springtime
composer: Oscar Hammerstein, Richard Rodgers
Young, Faron
song: Hello Walls (1961)
Young Frankenstein (1974 film)
cast: Peter Boyle, Marty Feldman, Teri Garr, Madeline Kahn, Cloris Leachman, Kenneth Mars, Gene Wilder
director: Mel Brooks
role: 4 Igor, Inga
___ Young, Gifted and Black: 4 To Be
Young, Gig: 5 actor
spouse: Elizabeth Montgomery
Young Girl (1968 song)
artist: Gary Puckett and the Union Gap
Young Goodman Brown
author: Nathaniel Hawthorne
Young Guns (1988 film)
cast: Emilio Estevez, Lou Diamond Phillips, Charlie Sheen, Kiefer Sutherland
Young-Holt Unlimited
song: Soulful Strut (1968)
Young, John Paul
song: Love Is in the Air (1978)
Young, Lester: 11 saxophonist
genre: 4 jazz
nickname: 4 Pres
youngling: 3 pup **5** youth
Young Lions, The: 4 film **5** novel
Young Lions, The (1958 film)
cast: Marlon Brando, Montgomery Clift, Dean Martin
Young Lions, The (novel)
author: Irwin Shaw
Young Love (1957 song)
artist: Sonny James, Tab Hunter
Young Lovers (1963 song)
artist: Paul and Paula
___, Young Lovers: 5 Hello
___ young man: 5 angry
Youngman: 5 Henny
repertoire: 4 gags **5** jokes **9** one-liners
Young Man From Atlanta, The
author: Horton Foote
Young Man With a Horn (1950 film)
cast: Lauren Bacall, Doris Day, Kirk Douglas
Young MC
song: Bust a Move (1989)
Young Miner, The
author: Horatio Alger
Young Mr. Lincoln (1939 film)
cast: Alice Brady, Henry Fonda
director: John Ford
Young, Neil
song: Heart of Gold (1972)

Young, Robert: 5 actor
TV: Father Knows Best, Marcus Welby, M.D.
Young, Sean: 7 actress
film: Ace Ventura: Pet Detective (1994)
Blade Runner (1982)
Cousins (1989)
Hold Me, Thrill Me, Kiss Me (1992)
No Way Out (1987)
Once Upon a Crime (1992)
Stripes (1981)
youngster: 3 boy, cub, kid, lad, pup, tad, tot 4 baby, brat, girl, lass, teen, tike, tyke 5 chick, child, kiddy, laddy, minor, pupil, sprig, 'tween, whelp, youth 6 junior, lassie, moppet 7 sapling, student 8 half-pint, juvenile, teenager 9 fledgling, stripling 10 adolescent
in Spanish: 4 niña, niño
naughty ~: 4 brat 6 urchin
query: 3 why
ride: 4 pony
Youngstown: 4 city
city near ~: 6 Girard
locale: 4 Ohio
Young Sycamore
author: William Carlos Williams
Young Tom Edison (1940 film)
cast: Mickey Rooney
Young Turk: 5 comer
Young Turks (1981 song)
artist: Rod Stewart
Young Widder Brown: 9 radio show
Young World (1962 song)
artist: Ricky Nelson
__ you not!: 4 I kid
__ You Now: 5 I Need
Yount, Robin: 6 Brewer 9 shortstop
__ you one!: 4 I owe
You Only Live Twice: 4 film 5 novel
You Only Live Twice (1967 film)
cast: Sean Connery, Donald Pleasance
scriptwriter: Roald Dahl
You Only Live Twice (novel)
author: Ian Fleming
You Oughta Know (1995 song)
artist: Alanis Morissette
You Ought to Be With Me (1972 song) artist: Al Green
your: 3 thy
ender: 4 self 6 selves
like ~: 4 poss. 10 possessive
not on ~ life: 3 nay 5 never
to ~ health: 5 salud, salut, skoal, toast 6 cheers, prosit 7 l'chayim 9 happy days
your __ serv.: 4 obdt.
Your __ Don't Dance: 4 Mama
Your __ Heart: 7 Cheatin'
Your __ Parade: 3 Hit
Your __ Too Big: 5 Feet's
__ your battle stations: 3 Man
__ your best shot!: 4 take
__ Your Blessings: 5 Count
__ Your Booty: 5 Shake
__ your disposal!: 4 I'm at
__ Your Dog: 4 Curb
...you're __ the old ball game: 5 out at
You're __: 7 Sixteen
You're __ and don't know it: 5 a poet
You're __ Hear from Me: 5 Gonna
You're __ Need to Get By: 4 All I
You're __ Old Once!: 4 Only
You're __ talk!: 5 one to
You're __ the One: 5 Still
You're a __, Alice!: 4 riot
__ you ready yet?: 5 Aren't
You're a fine __ talk!: 5 one to
You're a Grand Old Flag
composer: George M. Cohan
You're all __!: 3 wet
You're All I Need to Get By (1968 song)
artist: Marvin Gaye, Tammi Terrell
You Really Got Me (1964 song)
artist: Kinks
__ You're a Rich Man: 4 Baby
You're Getting to Be a Habit With Me
composer: Al Dubin, Harry Warren
You're in Love (1991 song)
artist: Wilson Phillips
You're in My Heart (1977 song)
artist: Rod Stewart
__, you're it!: 3 Tag
You're Makin' Me High (1996 song)
artist: Toni Braxton
You Remind Me of Something (1995 song)
artist: R. Kelly
You're My Best Friend (1976 song)
artist: Queen
You're My Everything (1967 song)
artist: Temptations
You're My World (1977 song)
artist: Helen Reddy
You're No Good (1975 song)
artist: Linda Ronstadt
You're Not Alone (1989 song)
artist: Chicago
__! You're on Candid Camera!: 5 Smile
You're Only Human (1985 song)
artist: Billy Joel
You're Only Old Once!
author: Dr. Seuss
You're pulling my __!: 3 leg
You're putting __!: 4 me on
Your Erroneous Zones
author: Wayne Dyer
__ you're satisfied!: 5 I hope
You're Sixteen (song)
artist: Johnny Burnette, Ringo Starr
__ You're Smiling: 4 When
You're So Vain (1972 song)
artist: Carly Simon
You're Still the One (1998 song)
artist: Shania Twain
You're the First... (1974 song)
artist: Barry White
You're the flower of my __: 5 heart
You're the Inspiration (1984 song)
artist: Chicago
You're the One (song)
artist: SWV, Vogues
You're the One That I Want (1978 song)
artist: John Travolta, Olivia Newton-John
film: 6 Grease
You're the Top
composer: Cole Porter
You're welcome: 6 de nada
Your excellency: 4 Sire
__ Your Eyes Only: 3 For
__ your fingers: 4 snap 5 cross
__ Your Girl: 7 Forever
Your Good Thing (1969 song)
artist: Lou Rawls
__ Your Hand in the Hand: 3 Put
Your Hit Parade: 9 radio show
__ your life!: 5 Not on
Your lights __: 5 are on
__ Your Love: 3 For, It's 5 I Want, Prove, Shake
__ Your Love Tonight: 5 I Need
__ Your Lucky Stars: 5 Thank
Your Majesty: 4 Ma'am, Sire
Your Mama Don't Dance (song)
artist: Loggins & Messina, Poison
Your mileage may __: 4 vary
__ Your Name: 4 Sign 5 What's
__ your old man!: 3 So's
__ your pardon!: 4 I beg
Your Precious Love (1967 song)
artist: Marvin Gaye, Tammi Terrell
yours: 5 thine
and mine: 3 our 4 ours
like ~: 4 poss. 10 possessive
not ~: 3 his 4 hers, mine 6 theirs
yours __: 5 truly
__ your seat belt: 6 fasten
__-yourself: 4 do-it
__ Yourself: 5 Enjoy 7 Express, Respect
yourself, by: 4 solo 5 alone
__ Yourself Go: 3 Let
__ Yourself Up: 4 Pick
Your Show of Shows (NBC variety)
cast: Sid Caesar
Imogene Coca
Howard Morris
Carl Reiner
writer: Woody Allen, Mel Brooks, Larry Gelbart, Neil Simon
Yours, Mine and Ours (1968 film)
cast: Lucille Ball, Henry Fonda, Van Johnson
Your Song (1970 song)
artist: Elton John
__ Your Wagon: 5 Paint
Your Wildest Dreams (1986 song)
artist: Moody Blues
You said it!: 3 yes 4 amen 6 and how, I agree, so true
__ you satisfied?: 3 Are
You say __...: 6 potato
You Send Me (1957 song)
artist: Sam Cooke, Teresa Brewer
__ you serious?: 3 Are
You Shook Me All Night Long (1980 song)
artist: AC/DC
You Should Be Dancing (1976 song)
artist: Bee Gees
You Should Be Mine (song)
artist: Brian McKnight & Mase, Jeffrey Osborne
You Showed Me (1969 song)
artist: Turtles
__, You Sinners: 4 Sing
Youskevitch, Igor: 6 dancer 7 danseur
specialty: 6 ballet
__ you so!: 5 I told
Yousuf: 5 Karsh
__ you sure?: 3 Are
You Take My Breath Away (1979 song)
artist: Rex Smith
You Talk Too Much (1960 song)
artist: Joe Jones
youth: 3 boy, cub, kid, lad, pup, tad, tot 4 baby, brat, girl, lass, male, teen, tike, tyke 5 bloom, chick, child, laddy, minor, prime, pupil, puppy, sprig, 'tween, whelp 6 junior, lassie, maiden, moppet, nonage, shaver 7 boyhood, sapling, student 8 girlhood, half-pint, juvenile, minority, small fry, teenager 9 childhood, fledgling, freshness, greenness, ignorance, innocence, puerility, salad days, schoolboy, stripling, youngster 10 adolescent, boyishness, immaturity, pubescence, schoolgirl
club for rural ~: 5 Four-H
magazine: 4 Teen
org.: 3 BSA 4 YMHA, YWCA, YWHA 5 GSUSA
stopover: 6 hostel
subculture: 6 hip-hop
uncool ~: 4 nerd
youth __: 5 group 6 hostel
Youth
Fountain of ~ site: 6 Bimini
__ you the clever one!: 5 Aren't
You there!: 3 hey 4 ahoy
youthful: 3 new 5 fresh, green, young 6 active, boyish, callow, infant, tender, vernal, yeasty 7 budding, buoyant, girlish, puerile 8 childish, immature, juvenile, underage, vigorous 9 childlike 10 adolescent, bright-eyed, full of life, sophomoric, starry-eyed
youthfulness: 5 prime, youth 9 greenness 10 immaturity
__ you think you are?: 5 Who do
__ You Top This?: 3 Can
__ You to Want Me: 5 I Want
__ You Truly: 5 I Love
__ You Trust?: 5 Who Do
YouTube
clip: 5 video
You Turn Me On (1975 song)
artist: Ian Whitcomb
You used to come __...: 5 at ten
__ You Use Me?: 5 Could
You've __ a Friend: 3 Got
You've __ Mail: 3 Got
__ You've Gone: 5 After
You've got __!: 5 a deal
You've Got a Friend (1971 song)
artist: James Taylor
You've Got a Friend __: 4 in Me
You've Got Mail (1998 film)
cast: Dabney Coleman, Tom Hanks, Greg Kinnear, Parker Posey, Meg Ryan
director: Nora Ephron
You've got mail co.: 3 AOL
(You've Got) The Magic Touch (1956 song)
artist: Platters
You've Got Your Troubles (1965 song)
artist: Fortunes
You've Made __ Very Happy: 4 Me So
You've Really Got __ On Me: 5 a Hold

You Want This (1994 song)
artist: Janet Jackson
You Wear It Well (1972 song)
artist: Rod Stewart
__ You Went Away: 5 Since
__ You Were Here: 4 Wish 7 Wishing
You Were Meant for Me (1996 song)
artist: Jewel
You Were Never Lovelier (1942 film)
cast: Fred Astaire, Rita Hayworth
music: Jerome Kern
You Were on My Mind (1965 song)
artist: We Five
__ You Were Sleeping: 5 While
__ You Wish Upon a Star: 4 When
You Won't See Me (1974 song)
artist: Anne Murray
You wouldn't __!: 4 dare
You, You, You (1953 song)
artist: Ames Brothers
Yow, Kay: 5 coach
milieu: 5 court
org.: 3 NBA
sport: 10 basketball
yowl: 3 bay, cry, yip 4 bawl, howl, long, mewl, wail, weep, yell, yelp 5 whine 6 holler, scream, squall, squeal 7 protest, screech, ululate 9 caterwaul
yowzah
see of course, yes
yo-yo: 3 oaf, toy 4 dolt, jerk, sway, vary 5 dunce, waver 6 nitwit 7 dingbat, whiffle 9 fluctuate, mercurial, vacillate 10 nincompoop
brand: 6 Duncan
part: 5 spool 6 string
Yo-Yo: 2 Ma
Yo-Yo (1971 song)
artist: Osmonds
__ y Plata: 3 Oro
Ypsilanti: 4 city, town
athletes: 6 Eagles
locale: 8 Michigan
river: 5 Huron
school: 3 EMU
yr.
100 ~: 3 cen.
by the ~: 5 per an.
opener: 3 Jan.
part: 2 mo. 3 spr. 4 quar.
part of an academic ~: 3 sem.
prior to ~ 1: 3 BCE
Ysaye, Eugene: 7 Belgian 9 violinist
Yser: 5 river
River locale: 6 France 7 Belgium
__ Ysidro, CA: 3 San
YSL fragrance: 5 Opium
ytterbium: 5 metal 7 element 9 rare earth
yttrium: 5 metal 7 element 9 rare earth
Yuan: 3 Lee
Yüang-chang: 3 Chu
Yuba City: 4 city, town
locale: 10 California
Yuban: 6 coffee
alternative: 5 Sanka 7 Folgers, Melitta, Nescafé, Savarin 9 Hills Bros.
Yucatán: 5 state 7 Mexican
city: 4 Muná, Peto, Umán 5 Motul, Tekax, Ticul 6 Cancún, Mérida
Indian: 4 Maya 5 Mayan
see also Spanish
yucca: 4 palm 5 plant 6 flower 10 Joshua tree
cousin: 4 aloe 5 agave, sotol 6 cactus
fiber: 5 istle, ixtle
root: 5 amole
yuck: 3 ick, ugh 4 joke 5 gross, laugh 7 chuckle 8 laughter
yucky: 4 icky, vile 5 gross, nasty, slimy 6 grungy, horrid 8 inedible 9 repugnant 10 disgusting, uninviting, unpleasant
stuff: 3 goo 4 goop, gunk
Yugoslavia: 6 nation 7 country
bovine: 4 Busa
capital: 8 Belgrade
city: 3 Nis 5 Vrsac 7 Novi Sad 8 Belgrade
former leader: 4 Tito
former ~ republic: 6 Bosnia
gulf: 8 Quarnero
lake: 7 Scutari
money: 4 para 5 dinar
neighbor: 7 Albania, Croatia, Hungary, Romania 8 Bulgaria 9 Macedonia
Nobelist in Chemistry: 6 Prelog
Nobelist in Literature: 6 Andric
port: 6 Rijeka 9 Dubrovnik
region: 5 Banat
river: 4 Sava 5 Tisza
tennis pro: 5 Seles
writer: 6 Adamic
yuk: 4 joke 5 laugh 7 chuckle
yukky: 5 slimy
see also yucky
Yukon: 3 GMC, SUV, ter. 4 city, terr., town 5 river 9 territory
area E. of the ~: 3 NWT
city: 4 Faro, Mayo 7 Old Crow 8 Carcross, Keno City 10 Dawson City, Mount Lorne, Whitehorse
discovery: 4 gold
dog: 5 husky
dweller: 6 Eskimo
home: 4 iglu 5 igloo
locale: 6 Canada
mountain: 4 King 5 Logan, Walsh 6 Steele 7 Lucania
native: 3 Esk. 5 Kaska 6 Eskimo
neighbor: 6 Alaska
river: 5 Liard
river to the ~: 6 Tanana 8 Klondike
vehicle: 4 sled
wear: 5 parka
Yul: 7 Brynner
yule: 4 Noel 9 Christmas
yule __: 3 log
yuletide: 4 Noel, Xmas 9 Christmas
aroma: 5 myrrh
beginning of ~: 6 Advent
burner: 3 log
buy: 4 tree
décor: 5 holly
display: 6 crèche
drink: 3 nog 6 eggnog
figure: 5 Santa
mo.: 3 Dec.
song: 4 Noel 5 carol
sound: 4 ho ho
tree: 3 fir
trio: 4 Magi
see also Christmas
Yulin: 6 Harris
yum: 5 goody 6 goodie 9 delicious
__ Yum: 6 Bubble
Yuma: 4 city, town 5 tribe 6 Indian 7 Amerind 8 language
locale: 7 Arizona
yummy: 4 good 5 sapid, tasty 6 edible, savory, toothy 8 heavenly, luscious, noshable, tempting 9 delicious, flavorful, good to eat, nectarous, palatable, succulent, toothsome 10 appetizing, delectable
Yummy Yummy Yummy (1968 song)
artist: Ohio Express
Yum-Yum
sash: 3 obi
yup
opposite: 3 nah
see also of course, yes
Yupik: 6 Eskimo
yuppie: 4 suit 10 button-down
abode: 4 loft 5 condo
auto: 4 Audi 6 Beamer, Beemer
couple, maybe: 4 dink
farewell: 4 ciao
Yuri: 7 Gagarin, Zhivago 8 Andropov
in English: 6 George
love: 4 Lara
portrayer: 4 Omar
see also Russian
yurt: 4 tent 7 shelter
Yury: 6 Olesha
Yves: 5 Klein, Leroy 6 Tanguy 7 Montand 9 St. Laurent
see also French
__-Yves Cousteau: 7 Jacques
Yvette: 7 Mimieux
see also French
Yvonne: 5 Craig 7 De Carlo, Elliman, Sherman 8 Mitchell
Yvor: 7 Winters
YWCA part: 4 Assn. 5 Assoc., Young 6 Women's 9 Christian
Yzerman: 5 Steve
Z: 3 zed, zee 4 axis, zeta 6 izzard, letter
Anglo-Saxon ~: 4 yogh
A to ~: 5 gamut, whole 6 entire 9 full-dress 10 completely, exhaustive, to the limit
from A to ~: 5 fully, gamut 6 in toto, wholly 7 in depth 8 thorough, whole hog 9 full-range, like a book 10 soup to nuts, thoroughly
in comics: 5 sleep, snore
in phonetic alphabet: 4 Zulu
Z (1969 film)
cast: Yves Montand, Irene Papas
director: Costa-Gavras
Z __ zebra: 4 as in
__ Z: 3 A to
'Z' __ Zero: 5 Is for
0
degrees longitude setting: 3 GST
figure above ~: 5 paren.
on a telephone: 4 oper.
see also zero
007: 3 spy
foe: 3 KGB
school: 4 Eton
watch: 5 Rolex
0600: 5 six a.m.
Z-28: 3 car 4 auto 6 Camaro 10 automobile
zabaglione: 7 dessert
ingredient: 3 egg 4 wine, yolk 5 sugar
zabuton: 3 mat, pad 7 cushion
Zac: 5 Efron
Zach: 5 Braff 8 Galligan
Zachariah
daughter: 3 Abi
Zachary: 5 Scott 6 Quinto, Taylor
Zacherle, John
song: Dinner With Drac (1958)
Zack: 5 Wheat
Zadora: 3 Pia
zaftig: 5 beefy, buxom, fubsy, heavy, obese, plump, pudgy, pursy, stout 6 chubby, fleshy, portly, pyknic, rotund, stocky 7 adipose, paunchy 8 roly-poly 9 corpulent 10 overweight
zafu: 7 cushion
shape: 5 round
stuffing: 5 kapok
zag: 4 turn, veer 6 swerve
starter: 3 zig
Zager and Evans
song: In the Year 2525 (1969)
Zagnut: 3 bar 5 candy 8 candy bar
alternative: *see* candy brand
ingredient: 7 coconut
__ Zagora, Bulgaria: 5 Stara
Zagreb: 4 city, town 7 capital
city near ~: 5 Fiume, Sisak, Sisek
locale: 6 Europe 7 Croatia
river: 4 Sava
Zaharias, Babe Didrikson: 6 golfer 7 Mildred
Zahn: 5 Paula, Steve
Zaire: 5 Congo, river 6 nation 7 country
city in ~: 4 Boma 6 Matadi
lake: 4 Kivu 5 Mweru 6 Albert, Mobuto 10 Tanganyika
language: 4 Luba
money: 5 zaire 6 likuta, makuta
people of ~: 4 Luba 5 Mongo
river: 4 Uele
Zale, Tony: 5 boxer
milieu: 4 ring
Zal, Roxana: 7 actress
Zambezi: 5 river
basin people: 4 Lozi
locale: 6 Angola, Zambia 8 Zimbabwe
river to the ~: 5 Kafue
town on the ~: 4 Sena
Zambia: 6 nation 7 country
capital: 6 Lusaka
city: 5 Kabwe, Kitwe, Ndola 6 Lusaka
lake: 5 Mweru 6 Kariba 9 Bangweulu
language: 4 Lozi
money: 5 ngwee 6 kwacha
neighbor: 5 Congo 6 Angola, Malawi 7 Namibia 8 Tanzania, Zimbabwe 10 Mozambique
people: 4 Cewa, Lozi 5 Bemba, Chewa, Lunda, Ngoni, Nguni
waterfall: 8 Victoria
Zamboni: 7 machine
creation: 3 ice
where to see a ~: 4 rink
Zandalee (1991 film)
cast: Judge Reinhold, Marisa Tomei, Nicolas Cage

Zander: 5 Robin
Zane: 4 Grey, Lisa 5 Billy, Lasky
Zanesville: 4 city, town
 author from ~: 4 Grey
 locale: 4 Ohio
Zanetto
 composer: Pietro Mascagni
Zaniah: 4 star
zaniness: 6 joking, levity 7 foolery, inanity, jesting, waggery 8 clowning, drollery 9 frivolity 10 buffoonery
Zanoni
 author: Edward Bulwer-Lytton
Zantac: 7 antacid
 alternative: *see* antacid
Zanuck: 6 Darryl 7 Richard
zany: 3 nut, wag 4 card, fool, kook, loon, luny, wack, wild 5 balmy, batty, campy, clown, comic, crazy, cutup, daffy, dizzy, flake, flaky, funny, goofy, joker, kooky, loony, nutty, sappy, silly, wacky, weird 6 flakey, jester, kookie, looney, madcap, screwy, weirdo, whacko, whacky 7 buffoon, comical, farceur, flighty, foolish, half-wit, show-off 8 clownish, comedian, humorist, humorous 9 eccentric, harlequin, ludicrous, prankster, screwball, simpleton, slapstick 10 off-the-wall, outlandish
Zanzibar: 4 city, isle, port, town 6 island
 island north of ~: 5 Pemba
 locale: 8 Tanzania
zap: 4 beat, drub, jolt, nuke, rout, ruin, slay, swat, zest 5 crush, shoot, smite 6 cancel, charge, defeat, energy, finish, impugn, lay out, pommel, pummel, rebuke, rub out, thrash, wallop 7 abolish, bombard, conquer, expunge, sparkle, trounce 8 dispatch, get rid of, knock off, vanquish 9 overthrow
 channel surfers ~ them: 3 ads
Zapata: 8 Emiliano 9 guerrilla
 see also Spanish
__ Zapata!: 4 Viva
Zappa: 5 Frank 7 Dweezil 8 Moon Unit
Zappa, Frank
 song: Valley Girl (1982)
zapper
 victim: 3 bee, bug, fly 4 gnat, moth, pest 5 aphid, aphis 6 hornet, insect 8 mosquito
__ zapper: 3 bug
zappy: 4 spry 5 agile, brisk, peppy, perky, zingy, zippy 6 active, blithe, bouncy, breezy, chirpy, jaunty, nimble, snappy 7 animate, chipper, playful 8 animated, cheerful 9 energetic, exuberant, sprightly, vivacious 10 frolicsome, rollicking
Zara
 composer: Thomas Arne
Zaragoza: 4 city, town
 locale: 5 Spain 6 Aragón, Mexico 8 Coahuila
 river: 4 Ebro
zarf: 3 cup 6 finjan
Zarkov
 friend: 6 Gordon
ZaSu: 5 Pitts
Zátopek: 4 Emil 5 Czech 6 runner 10 marathoner
Zayak: 6 Elaine
zayin: 6 Hebrew, letter
 predecessor: 3 vav, vaw, waw
 successor: 4 heth 5 cheth
Zaza
 composer: Ruggiero Leoncavallo
Zazie
 author: Raymond Queneau
Zbigniew: 7 Herbert 10 Brzezinski
zeal: 3 vim 4 fire, push, zest 5 ardor, drive, flame, gusto, mania, oomph, piety, verve, vigor 6 energy, fervor, relish, spirit, warmth 7 emotion, loyalty, passion, urgency 8 alacrity, delirium, devotion, dispatch, fervency, industry, keenness 9 animation, assiduity, diligence, eagerness, godliness, intensity, monomania, readiness, sincerity, vehemence 10 enterprise, enthusiasm, fanaticism, fierceness, initiative, intentness, liveliness
 with great ~: 5 hotly
__ Zealand: 3 New
Zealander: 4 Dane
zealot: 3 nut 5 bigot, crank, fiend, freak 6 addict 7 diehard, fanatic 8 crusader, reformer 9 extremist, sectarian, visionary 10 enthusiast
zealous: 3 hot, mad 4 avid, keen 5 afire, antsy, eager, fired, itchy, pushy, rabid, ready 6 ablaze, active, ardent, devout, fervid, gung-ho, hearty, loving, red-hot 7 burning, devoted, earnest, fanatic, fervent, flaming, glowing, intense 8 fireball, frenetic, obsessed, partisan, spirited, vehement, wild-eyed 9 ambitious, dedicated, emotional, fanatical, possessed, strenuous 10 inspirited, passionate, solicitous
zealously: 4 hard, very 6 keenly 8 heartily 9 seriously, viciously
zebra: 3 ref 6 animal, equine 7 referee
 ender: 4 wood
 female: 4 mare
 group: 4 herd
 home: 6 Africa
 like a ~: 5 maned 7 striped
 male: 8 stallion
 predator: 4 lion
 relative: *see* equine
 young: 4 colt, foal
zebu: 5 bovid 6 animal, bovine
 feature: 4 hump
 relative: *see* bovine
Zebulon: 4 Pike
 son: 4 Elon
Zebulun
 parent: 4 Leah 5 Jacob
 sibling: 3 Dan, Gad 4 Levi 5 Asher, Dinah, Judah 6 Joseph, Reuben, Simeon 8 Benjamin, Issachar, Naphtali
Zechariah
 follower: 7 Malachi
 preceder: 6 Haggai
zed: 3 zee 6 izzard
Zedillo: 7 Ernesto
Zedong: 3 Mao
zee: 3 zed
 preceder: 3 wye
__ Zee: 6 Tappan, Zuider
Zeena
 creator: Edith Wharton
 spouse: 5 Ethan
Zeffirelli, Franco: 8 director
 film: Hamlet (1990)
  La Traviata (1982)
  Otello (1986)
  Romeo and Juliet (1968)
  The Taming of the Shrew (1967)
Zelazny, Roger: 6 writer
 genre: 5 sci-fi
Zelda: 6 Gilroy 10 Fitzgerald
Zelda __ Fitzgerald: 5 Sayre
Zelig (1983 film)
 cast: Woody Allen, Mia Farrow
 director: Woody Allen
Zell: 3 Sam
Zellweger, Renée: 7 actress
 film: Bridget Jones's Diary (2001)
  Chicago (2002)
  Cinderella Man (2005)
  Cold Mountain (2003, AA)
  Jerry Maguire (1996)
  Leatherheads (2008)
  Me, Myself & Irene (2000)
  Miss Potter (2006)
  Nurse Betty (2000)
  One True Thing (1998)
  Price Above Rubies (1998)
Zemeckis, Robert: 8 director
 film: Back to the Future (1985)
  Back to the Future Part II (1989)
  Back to the Future Part III (1990)
  Beowulf (2007)
  Cast Away (2000)
  Contact (1997)
  Death Becomes Her (1992)
  Forrest Gump (1994, AA)
  I Wanna Hold Your Hand (1978)
  The Polar Express (2004)
  Romancing the Stone (1984)
  Used Cars (1980)
  What Lies Beneath (2000)
  Who Framed Roger Rabbit (1988)
Zen
 enlightenment: 6 satori
 greeting: 6 gassho
 head cook: 5 tenzo
 interview: 7 dokusan
 master: 4 monk
 master's poem: 5 haiku
 meditation: 5 zazen
 meditation hall: 4 dojo 5 zendo
 origin: 5 Japan
 poem: 4 waka 5 haiku
 retreat: 7 sesshin
 school: 4 Soto 6 Rinzai
 sitting posture: 5 seiza
 teaching: 5 sutra
 temple room: 5 zendo
 term: 4 hara, koan 5 mondo
__ Zen: 4 Soto 6 Rinzai
zenana: 5 haram, harem, harim 6 hareem
 room: 3 oda 4 odah
zendo: 4 dojo, hall
Zener __: 5 cards
zenith: 3 cap, top 4 acme, apex, peak, roof 5 crest, crown, prime 6 apogee, climax, height, heyday, heydey, summit, tiptop, vertex 7 maximum 8 capstone, eminence, high noon, high spot, meridian, pinnacle 9 crescendo, elevation, high point
 at the ~: 4 atop
 opposite: 5 nadir 6 bottom 7 the pits 10 rock bottom
Zenith: 2 TV 5 TV set 10 television
 alternative: *see* electronics company
 product: 3 VCR 6 remote
Zeno: 5 Greek
 follower of ~: 5 Stoic
 where ~ taught: 4 stoa
Zenobia: 5 queen
 husband: 5 Ethan
 land: 7 Palmyra
Zeno of __: 4 Elea 6 Citium
Zeno's __: 7 paradox
Zephaniah
 follower: 6 Haggai
 preceder: 8 Habakkuk
Zepho
 grandfather: 4 Esau
zephyr: 4 wind 6 breeze
 like a ~: 4 mild, soft 5 balmy, light 6 gentle 7 pacific, subdued 8 moderate, pleasant, tranquil 9 temperate
 lily: 5 plant 6 flower
Zephyr: 3 car 4 auto 7 Lincoln, Mercury
 mother: 3 Eos
zeppelin: 5 blimp, craft 7 balloon 8 aircraft 9 dirigible
 like a ~: 3 LTA 5 rigid
__ Zeppelin: 3 Led 4 Graf
Zeppo: 4 Marx
 brother: 5 Chico, Gummo, Harpo 7 Groucho
Zerah
 grandfather: 4 Esau
Zerbe: 7 Anthony
Zeresh
 husband: 5 Haman
Zermat: 6 resort
Zermatt
 locale: 4 Alps
zero: 3 nil, nix, zip 4 love, meek, nada, nary, none, null, void 5 aught, blank, nadir, ought, zilch 6 bubkes, bupkis, cipher, naught, nobody, nought, number 7 nothing, nullity, scratch, shutout 8 goose egg, lifeless, nihility 9 nonentity 10 lackluster, rock bottom
 below ~: 4 cold 6 frigid
 chance: 3 nah 4 nope, uh-uh 5 never, no how 8 forget it
 ground ~: 4 goal 5 focus 6 target 8 bull's-eye 9 objective
 hour: 4 D-day 6 crisis 7 due date 8 deadline, exigence, exigency, juncture 9 countdown, crossroad, emergency
 in: 3 aim, set 5 focus, point, train 6 fixate
 in on: 5 level 6 locate 7 pin down 8 pinpoint
 in tennis: 4 love
 less than ~: 3 neg. 8 negative
 letters above ~: 4 oper
 like ~: 4 oval 5 ovate, ovoid, round 7 rounded 8 elliptic 9 egg-shaped 10 elliptical
 longitude setting: 3 GMT
 more than ~: 3 pos. 8 positive
 put back to ~: 5 reset
 through nine: 5 digit

visibility ~: 3 fog 4 haze, mist, smog
zero __: 4 hour, in on
zero-__ bond: 6 coupon
zero-__ budgeting: 4 base
zero-__ game: 3 sum
__ zero: 6 ground 7 ceiling
__-zero: 3 sub
Zero: 5 plane 6 Mostel 8 airplane
zero-dimensional object: 5 point
Zero Effect (1998 film)
cast: Ryan O'Neal, Bill Pullman, Ben Stiller
zero-star: 3 bad 4 poor 5 awful
movie: 3 dud 4 bomb, flop 6 turkey
zest: 3 pep, vim, zap, zip 4 bite, body, brio, élan, jazz, kick, life, peel, salt, snap, tang, zeal, zing 5 ardor, charm, cheer, gusto, liven, moxie, oomph, punch, savor, spark, spice, taste, verve 6 bounce, energy, fervor, flavor, ginger, pizazz, relish, spirit 7 delight, elation, passion 8 appetite, interest, keenness, piquancy, pleasure, pungency, vitality 9 animation, eagerness, enjoyment, flavoring, seasoning, tanginess 10 ebullience, enthusiasm, exuberance, get-up-and-go, heartiness, liveliness
add ~ to: 5 liven, pep up 6 excite, perk up, spur on, stir up, vivify 7 animate 8 energize, vitalize 10 exhilarate, invigorate
source: 4 peel, rind 6 citrus
Zest: 4 soap
alternative: *see* soap
Zesta: 7 cracker, saltine
alternative: *see* cracker
Zest for Life author: Émile Zola
zestful: 4 racy 5 alive, eager, jazzy, kicky, peppy, spicy, tasty, vital 6 feisty, frisky, lively, spicey 7 peppery, piquant, pungent 8 animated, exciting, vigorous 9 ebullient, energetic, exuberant, vivacious 10 inspirited
zestless: 5 stale, vapid 6 boring
zesty: 3 hot 5 jazzy, peppy, spicy, tangy, tasty 6 frisky, red-hot, spicey 7 piquant, pungent, vibrant 8 spirited 9 energetic, flavorful, vivacious, with a kick
zeta: 5 Greek 6 letter
follower: 3 eta
preceder: 7 epsilon
Zeta-Jones, Catherine: 7 actress
film: America's Sweethearts (2001)
Chicago (2002, AA)
Entrapment (1999)
Intolerable Cruelty (2003)
The Legend of Zorro (2005)
The Mask of Zorro (1998)
The Terminal (2004)
Traffic (2000)
spouse: Michael Douglas
Zetterling, Mai: 7 actress
Zeus: 3 god 8 Olympian
attendant of ~: 3 Bia
brother: 5 Hades 8 Poseidon
changed her into a spring: 4 Aura
daughter: 3 Ate 4 Clio, Eris, Hebe, Muse 5 Erato, Grace, Helen, Irene 6 Athena, Athene, Pandia, Thalia, Urania 7 Artemis, Astraea, Euterpe 8 Calliope, Harmonia 9 Aphrodite, Melpomene 10 Persephone, Polyhymnia 11 Terpsichore
daughter-in-law: 5 Niobe
equivalent: 4 Jove 7 Jupiter
mount where ~ was worshiped: 3 Ida
Norse ~: 4 Odin 5 Othin
parent: 4 Rhea 6 Cronos, Cronus, Kronos
shield: 4 egis 5 aegis
sister: 4 Hera 6 Hestia 7 Demeter
son: 3 Pan 4 Ares 5 Argus, Minos 6 Apollo, Castor, Hermes, Pollux 7 Bacchus, Perseus 8 Dionysus, Heracles, Myrmidon, Tantalus
Temple of ~ locale: 5 Nemea
wife: 4 Hera
Zevon: 6 Warren
Zez: 7 Confrey
Zheng He
landed here in 1416: 4 Aden
Zhivago: 4 Yuri 6 doctor
love: 4 Lara
__ Z. Hobson: 5 Laura
Zhou __: 5 En-lai
Zia
author: Scott O'Dell
Ziegfeld: 3 Flo 7 Florenz
Ziegfeld __: 4 Girl 7 Follies
Ziegfeld, Flo
spouse: Billie Burke, Anna Held
Ziegfeld Follies: 5 revue 6 review
designer: Erté
__ Ziegfeld, The: 5 Great
Ziegler: 3 Ron 4 Karl
Ziering: 3 Ian 5 Nikki
zig: 4 dart, turn, veer 5 angle 6 swerve 8 sidestep
ender: 3 zag
Zigeunerliebe
composer: Franz Lehár
ziggurat: 5 tower
Ziggy: 4 toon 5 comic, Elman 6 Marley
cat: 3 Sid
creator: Tom Wilson
dog: 4 Fuzz
duck: 4 Wack
fish: 6 Goldie
parrot: 4 Josh
zigzag: 4 awry, bent, tack, turn, wind 5 askew, bowed, forky, snaky, twist, weave 6 forked, jagged, ramble, wiggle 7 angular, crooked, devious, erratic, meander, oblique, sinuous, snaking, stagger, twisted, winding 8 angulose, angulous, cockeyed, diagonal, indirect, rambling, serrated, tortuous, twisting, waggling 9 interlace, irregular, unaligned 10 meandering, nonuniform, transverse, undulating
cut in a ~: 4 pink
zilch: 3 nil, nix, zip 4 nada, none, zero 5 squat, zippo 6 cipher, cypher, naught, nought 7 nothing 8 goose egg
in Spanish: 4 nada
in tennis: 4 love
zillions: 4 a lot, many 5 scads 6 oceans
of: 6 divers, myriad, umteen, untold 7 copious, profuse, umpteen 8 abundant, manifold, numerous, umpsteen 9 bountiful, countless, quite a few
Zilpah
son: 3 Gad 5 Asher
Zima brewer: 5 Coors
Zimbabwe: 6 nation 7 country
bovine: 4 Tuli 7 Mashona
capital: 6 Harare
city: 5 Gweru 6 Harare, Kadoma, Kwekwe, Mutare
grassland: 4 veld 5 veldt
lake: 6 Kariba
language: 7 Ndebele
money: 4 cent 6 dollar
neighbor: 6 Zambia 8 Botswana 10 Mozambique
once: 4 Rhod. 8 Rhodesia
people: 5 Shona 7 Mashona, Ndebele 8 Matabele
waterfall: 8 Victoria
Zimbalist, Efrem: 5 actor 7 Russian 9 violinist
spouse: Alma Gluck
teacher: 4 Auer
Zimbalist Jr., Efrem: 5 actor
daughter: 9 Stephanie
TV: 77 Sunset Strip, The FBI
Zimmer: 3 Don
Zina: 7 Bethune
zinc: 5 metal 7 element 9 galvanize
alloy: 5 brass 6 oreide, ormolu, oroide 8 calamine, gunmetal
ore: 6 blende 7 zincite 9 willemite 10 sphalerite
zine: 3 mag 4 E-mag
zinfandel: 3 red 4 wine 5 grape 6 claret
like ~: 3 dry
relative: *see* wine
zing: 3 pep, vim, zip 4 brio, dash, élan, fire, hurt, kick, life, slur, zest 5 abuse, ardor, gusto, oomph, spark, taste, verve, vigor 6 energy, esprit, flavor, impugn, insult, offend 7 lambast, potence, potency, put down 8 lambaste, vitality 9 animation, criticize, eagerness, excoriate 10 enthusiasm, exuberance, get-up-and-go
add ~ to: 5 spice 6 flavor, pepper
zinger: 3 mot 4 barb, quip, slur 6 ripost 7 offense, riposte 9 witticism
zingy: 4 cool, tart 8 animated, spirited 9 exuberant, sprightly 10 full of life
Zinnemann, Fred: 8 director
zinnia: 5 plant 6 annual, flower
Zion: 4 city, park, town 6 Israel 8 Holy Land
locale: 4 Utah 8 Illinois
Zion National Park
location: 4 Utah
sight: 5 cañon 6 canyon
zip: 2 go 3 fly, hie, nil, pep, rip, run, vim 4 bite, brio, dart, dash, élan, fire, flit, life, nada, none, race, rush, tang, tear, whiz, zero, zest, zing, zoom 5 drive, flair, gusto, hurry, oomph, punch, scoot, spank, speed, spice, squat, taste, verve, vigor, whisk, zilch 6 barrel, bounce, bustle, cipher, energy, fasten, gallop, hasten, hustle, move it, naught, nought, pizazz, relish, rocket, scurry, spirit 7 floor it, hop to it, nothing, pizzazz, potence, potency, quicken, scamper, sparkle, stamina 8 goose egg, hightail, step on it, strength, vitality, vivacity 9 animation, hotfoot it, make haste, shake a leg, skedaddle 10 ebullience, enthusiasm, exuberance, get a move on, get hopping, get up and go, hightail it, liveliness
add ~ to: 5 liven 6 flavor 7 enliven
by: 2 go 3 fly 4 tear 5 whish
over the surface: 4 skim 5 skate
through: 8 look over
(through): 6 breeze
up: 5 close 6 fasten
zip __: 3 gun 4 code
Zip-__-Doo-Dah: 4 a-Dee
ZIP+4 org.: 4 USPS
Zip Drive maker: 6 Iomega
Zip it!: 5 quiet, shush 6 shut up
Ziploc: 3 bag
alternative: 4 Glad 5 Hefty 8 Reynolds 9 Saran Wrap
zipper: 3 tie 8 fastener
cover: 3 fly
zippo: 3 nil 4 nada 5 zilch 6 bubkes, bupkis 7 nothing 8 goose egg
Zippo, part of a: 4 wick
Zipporah
husband: 5 Moses
son: 7 Eliezer, Gershom
zippy: 4 go-go, spry 5 brisk, jazzy, peppy, spicy, tangy 6 frisky, lively, spicey 7 dynamic, hyped-up, vibrant 8 animated, spirited, vigorous 9 ebullient, energetic, exuberant, sprightly
zircon: 3 gem 6 ligure 7 mineral 8 gemstone
__ zirconia: 5 cubic
zirconium: 5 metal 7 element
zit: 6 pimple 7 blemish
zither: 4 ch'in, koto, mvet, vina 5 fidla, qanun, veena 6 chakay, string, valiha 8 autoharp, dulcimer, psaltery, yang chin 10 instrument
forerunner: 4 asor
geisha's ~: 4 koto
play the ~: 5 strum
ziti: 5 pasta 7 noodles 8 macaroni
alternative: *see* pasta
__ ziti: 5 baked
zloty: 4 coin 5 money 8 currency
fraction: 5 grosz
locale: 6 Poland
Zmed: 6 Adrian
Zn: 4 elem., zinc 7 element
30 for ~: 4 at. no.
Zobeide
sculptor: Erté
zodiac: 4 belt 5 chart
animal: 3 ram 4 bull, crab, fish, goat, lion 8 scorpion
boundary: 4 cusp
Chinese ~ animal: 2 ox 3 dog, pig, rat 4 goat, hare 5 horse, sheep, snake, tiger 6 dragon, monkey, rabbit 7 rooster
division: 5 house
zodiac signs:
Aquarius - Water Bearer (Jan.-Feb.)
Aries - Ram (Mar.-Apr.)

Cancer - Crab (Jun.-Jul.)
Capricorn - Goat (Dec.-Jan.)
Gemini - Twins (May-Jun.)
Leo - Lion (Jul.-Aug.)
Libra - Scales (Sep.-Oct.)
Pisces - Fish (Feb.-Mar.)
Sagittarius - Archer (Nov.-Dec.)
Scorpio - Scorpion (Oct.-Nov.)
Taurus - Bull (Apr.-May)
Virgo - Maiden (Aug.-Sep.)
Zoe: **7** Saldana **8** Caldwell
Zoë: **5** Akins
zoea: **5** larva
Zoeller, Fuzzy: **6** golfer
Zola: **4** Budd **5** Émile
Zola, Émile: **6** French, writer
portraitist: Édouard Manet
portrayer: Paul Muni
work: Albine
Argent
Assommoir
Belly of Pairs
Debacle
Doctor Pascal
The Dram Shop
Dream
Earth
The Experimental Novel
Germinal
Hélène
The Human Beast
J'Accuse
Joie de Vivre
La Bête Humaine
Labor
La Confession de Claude
La Curée
The Ladies' Delight
La Fortune des Rougons
The Land of Darkness
Les Rougon-Macquart
Les Trois Villes
Lourdes
Madeleine Férat
Money
Mysteries of Marseilles
Nana
Pot Luck
Quatre Evangiles
Rêve
Savage Paris
Sin of Father Mouret
Soirées de Médan
Terre
Thérèse Raquin
Travail
Truth
Two Dutchesses
Venus of the Counting House
Zest for Life
Zoltán: **5** Korda **6** Kodály
zombie: **5** booze, drink **6** liquor **7** alcohol, machine, potable **8** beverage, cocktail, libation, potation **9** automaton **10** intoxicant
ingredient: **3** rum **10** fruit juice
like a ~: **6** undead
Zombie
author: Joyce Carol Oates
Zombies
song: She's Not There (1964)
Tell Her No (1965)
Time of the Season (1969)
Zona: **4** Gale
zone: **4** area, band, belt, ward **5** bourn, level, place, realm, space, tract **6** ground, locale, region, sector, sphere **7** circuit, quarter, section, segment **8** district, locality, precinct, province **9** territory
combat ~: **5** arena, front
demilitarized ~: **5** limbo **6** buffer **10** no man's land
time ~ abbr.: **3** AST, CDT, CST, EDT, EST, GMT, MDT, MST, PDT, PST
__ zone: **3** end, war **4** drop, free, rift, time **5** fault, in the, no-fly **6** buffer, combat, strike **7** comfort, neutral, tow-away
__ Zone: **3** End **4** Love **5** Canal **6** Arctic, Danger, Frigid, Torrid
zoning unit: **4** acre
zonk: **7** stupefy **8** knock out
out: **3** nod **4** doze **5** crash, sleep **6** drowse, nod off, snooze, turn in **7** drop off **9** hit the hay **10** hit the sack
zonked: **5** weary **9** insensate **10** insentient, knocked out
out: **6** asleep, dozing **7** napping **8** sleeping, snoozing **9** somnolent **10** slumbering
zoo: **9** mare's nest, menagerie **10** animal park, safari park
barrier: **4** moat
enclosure: **4** cage **6** aviary
petting ~ beast: **4** deer, goat **5** sheep
resident: *see* animal
staffer: **3** DVM, vet **6** keeper
Zooey: **9** Deschanel
Zoo in Budapest (1933 film)
director: Rowland V. Lee
Zoolander (2001 film)
cast: Ben Stiller, Christine Taylor, Owen Wilson
director: Ben Stiller
zoology: **7** science
band of color, in ~: **5** vitta
branch of ~: **9** zoography **10** entomology **11** herpetology, ichthyology, ornithology
classification: **6** family
foot: **3** pes
stripe: **5** vitta
study: **5** fauna **7** animals
suffix: **4** -acea **5** -oidea
zoom: **3** fly, hie, hum, jet, rip, run, zip **4** buzz, dart, dash, dive, flit, lens, race, rush, tear, whiz **5** flash, mount, scoot, shoot, spank, speed, surge, sweep, whirl **6** barrel, gallop, hasten, hurtle, hustle, move it, rocket, scurry, streak **7** floor it, hop to it, quicken, scamper, shoot up **8** hightail, outstrip, pour it on, step on it **9** hotfoot it, shake a leg, skedaddle, skyrocket **10** get a move on, go pell-mell, hightail it
in: **3** pan **5** focus
zoom __: **4** lens
zoophilist org.: **4** SPCA
zoophobe fear: **7** animals
Zoo Story, The: **4** play
author: Edward Albee
zoot __: **4** suit
Zoot: **4** Sims
Zora __ Hurston: **5** Neale
Zorba the Greek: **4** film **5** novel
setting: **5** Crete
Zorba the Greek (1964 film)
cast: Alan Bates, Lila Kedrova, Irene Papas, Anthony Quinn
Zorba the Greek (novel)
author: Nikos Kazantzakis
zorilla: **7** polecat
Zorina: **4** Vera
Zorn's __: **5** lemma
Zoroastrian: **5** Parsi **6** Parsee
Bible: **4** Zend **6** Avesta
king: **4** Yima
Zorro
portrayer: **8** Banderas, Hamilton, Williams
wear: **4** cape, mask
see also Spanish
zounds: **4** egad, oath **5** egads **6** my word **8** gadzooks
zowie: **3** wow **5** oh boy **6** hot dog
zoysia: **5** grass
Zr: **4** elem. **7** element **9** zirconium
40 for ~: **4** at. no.
z's: **3** nap **5** sleep **6** catnap, snooze
grab some ~: **3** nap **4** doze, rest **5** sleep, snore **6** catnap, drowse, nod off, snooze, turn in **7** drop off, slumber
Zsa Zsa: **5** Gabor
mother: **5** Jolie
real name: **4** Sari
secret: **3** age
sister: **3** Eva **5** Magda
Zubin: **5** Mehta
zucchetto: **3** cap
zucchini: **6** veggie **9** vegetable
Zucker: **5** David, Jerry
Zuckerman Bound
author: Philip Roth
Zuckerman Unbound
author: Philip Roth
Zuckmayer, Carl: **6** German **10** playwright
work: The Devil's General
Zuider Zee: **4** lake
locale: **7** Holland **11** Netherlands
sight: **4** dike
Zukerman, Pinchas: **7** Israeli **9** violinist
spouse: Tuesday Weld
Zukor: **6** Adolph
Zulu: **5** Bantu **8** language
council: **6** indaba
ender: **4** land
home: **5** Natal
Zumwalt: **4** Elmo **7** admiral
Zuni: **5** tribe **6** Indian **7** Amerind **8** language
Zuniga: **6** Daphne
zuppa __: **7** di pesce, inglese
Zurer: **6** Ayelet
Zurich: **4** city, font, lake, town **8** typeface
banker: **5** gnome
city SW of ~: **4** Bern **5** Berne
locale: **11** Switzerland
peak: **3** alp
river: **4** Sihl **6** Limmat
zwei: **3** two **6** German
cubed: **4** acht
follower: **4** drei
preceder: **4** eins
squared: **4** vier
Zweig: **6** Arnold, Stefan
Zwick: **4** Joel **6** Edward
zwieback: **4** rusk **5** bread **7** biscuit
Zworykin: **8** Vladimir
zygoma: **4** bone
locale: **5** skull **7** cranium **9** braincase
zygomatic: **4** bone **5** malar
locale: **5** skull **7** cranium **9** braincase
zygote component: **6** gamete
zymology: **7** science
study: **7** enzymes
ZZ Top
members: Gibbons, Hill, Beard
song: Legs (1984)
Sleeping Bag (1985)
Tush (1975)
Velcro Fly (1986)
zzz: **5** sleep, snore **6** snooze